City Profiles USA

A Traveler's Guide to Major U.S. and Canadian Cities

2000-2001

Fifth Edition

Providing Telephone Numbers, Fax and Toll-Free Numbers, Location or Mailing Addresses, World Wide Web and E-Mail Addresses, and Other Important Contact Data for 250 U.S. and Canadian Cities, Including

- Airports, Airlines, Car Rental, and Other Transportation Services
- Attractions
- Banks
- Business Services
- Chambers of Commerce
- City Government Offices
- Colleges & Universities
- Convention Centers
- Convention & Visitor Bureaus
- County Seats
- Events
- Hospitals
- Hotels
- Libraries
- Newspapers & Magazines
- On-Line Resources
- Restaurants
- Shopping
- Sports Teams and Facilities
- Television & Radio Stations

***Edited By* Dawn Bokenkamp Toth**

Omnigraphics

615 Griswold Street • Detroit, Michigan 48226

ISBN 0-7808-0347-7
ISSN 1082-9938

Printed in the United States of America

Omnigraphics, Inc.
615 Griswold Street • Detroit, MI 48226
Phone: 800-234-1340 • Fax: 800-875-1340
www.omnigraphics.com

Contents

State-by-State Contents

City-by-City Contents

Introduction

City Profiles USA provides important contact information for travel-related services and facilities in 250 major cities throughout the United States and Canada. This fifth edition contains **more than 64,500 individual listings**—an increase of about 10,000 listings since last edition.

Information contained in *City Profiles USA* is obtained through original research, including direct contact with convention and visitor bureaus, chambers of commerce, and other local organizations. All data obtained from these organizations, or from other information resources, are independently verified to assure the highest level of accuracy possible.

The number of listings in *City Profiles USA* that contain electronic contact data has continued to increase, with **more than 18,000 World Wide Web addresses** included here—nearly 5,500 more than last edition.

38 New Cities in This Edition

- Abilene, TX
- Alexandria, VA
- Bar Harbor, ME
- Bloomington, IN
- Brownsville, TX
- Champaign, IL
- Columbia, MO
- Daytona Beach, FL
- Dubuque, IA
- Duluth, MN
- Fort Collins, CO
- Gettysburg, PA
- Halifax, NS
- Hattiesburg, MS
- Hilton Head Island, SC
- Independence, MO
- Jackson, WY
- Johnson City, TN
- Key West, FL
- Lafayette, LA
- Las Cruces, NM
- Macon, GA
- Monterey, CA
- Myrtle Beach, SC
- Naples, FL
- Ocean City, MD
- Palm Springs, CA
- Pensacola, FL
- Peoria, IL
- Plano, TX
- Rehoboth Beach, DE
- Saint Augustine, FL
- Scottsdale, AZ
- Tupelo, MS
- Tuscaloosa, AL
- Vancouver, WA
- Williamsburg, VA
- Youngstown, OH

Scope and Arrangement

City Profiles USA includes:

- the largest U.S. and Canadian cities, by population;
- the capital city in each of the 50 U.S. states; and
- other important U.S. travel destinations.

The focus throughout is on individual cities rather than metropolitan areas, but information about important facilities or services located in suburban and other outlying areas is included where appropriate.

The U.S. cities are organized by *states*, with individual city profiles grouped alphabetically within each state section. (A limited amount of general contact information is given for each of the 50 states as well.) Profiles of Canadian cities follow the U.S. listings and are presented alphabetically by *city* name.

Content of Listings

Listings in *City Profiles USA* include, at a minimum, the name of a facility or service and its telephone number; most listings also include location information or a full mailing address (including zip code). To the extent that the information is available to us, listings also include fax numbers, toll-free telephone numbers, World Wide Web addresses, and e-mail addresses.

Each city's profile begins with a brief description of the city, followed by a list of "city facts" denoting the city's population, land and water areas, latitude and longitude, county in which the city is located, time zone, and principal area code(s). Information for each city is then grouped according to the following categories:

1. **Temperature and Precipitation.** Average monthly high and low temperatures as well as the average monthly precipitation for the area are presented in a table format.
2. **Important Phone Numbers.** Included here are local or toll-free numbers for AAA, American Express Travel, Emergency, HotelDocs, Poison Control, Time/Temp, Weather, and, in some cases, Medical and/or Dental Referral, Events lines, and Road Conditions.

3. **Information Sources.** The city's main library and, if applicable, Freenet program; convention and visitor bureau, visitor center, or similar organization; convention center; city hall and mayor's office; chamber of commerce; county seat; economic development board; and similar information resources are listed here. Included within this group is a subcategory for **On-Line Resources** that contains listings for city-specific World Wide Web sites.

4. **Transportation Services.** Telephone numbers are given here for airports, airport transportation, scheduled airlines, charter airlines, car rental agencies, limo/taxi services, mass transit, and rail and bus stations. Other useful information, such as the distance and cab fare from the airport to the city's downtown area, is also included.

5. **Accommodations.** Two subcategories of information are included here: hotel reservation services and hotels, motels, resorts. Listings for hotel reservation services include bed and breakfasts.

6. **Restaurants.** Listings include a notation on the type of cuisine offered.

7. **Goods and Services.** Types of facilities listed here include major malls and shopping centers; banks; and business services such as postal/packaging services and secretarial/temporary employment services.

8. **Media.** Listing data are provided for local newspapers, magazines, and business journals; television stations; and radio stations. Television station listings note the network affiliation; and radio station listings include the format. (A chart explaining the codes used to describe radio formats and television network affiliations is presented at the back of the book, on the inside back cover.)

9. **Colleges/Universities.** Institutions of higher learning located in or near the city are listed here.

10. **Hospitals.** Contact information is provided for hospitals and medical centers located in the city profiled and, in some cases, in the surrounding metropolitan and suburban areas.

11. **Attractions.** Two subgroups are included in this category: Sports Teams and Facilities and Attractions. Under Sports Teams and Facilities, contact data are provided for sports teams as well as for similar facilities, such as race tracks, stadiums, and arenas. The Attractions subgroup provides listing data for museums, historic homes and buildings, art galleries, symphonies, theaters, parks and other recreational areas, and similar sites.

12. **Events.** Listings include the name of each event, the related phone number, and the month in which the event is scheduled to take place.

Supplemental Fax Data

Area codes are provided throughout this directory for every telephone number listed, whether local or toll-free. However, since the area codes for fax numbers are nearly always the same as the area code given for the phone number, this information is *not* repeated with the fax number. In those instances where the fax area code *is* different from the telephone area code, an asterisk is inserted to the right of the fax number and the area code appears below the name/address information:

Hot Rooms
1 E Erie St Suite 225............................Chicago IL 60611 773-468-7666 649-0559*
*Fax Area Code: 312

An asterisk to the right of the fax number may also indicate that the number given is not the organization's direct fax line. In this case, a brief explanatory note is given below the name/address information (e.g., *Fax:* Sales).

Special Features

In addition to the city-by-city listings that make up the main body of this publication, a number of useful quick-lookup features are conveniently located at the front of the book. These include:

- A list of major **airline companies**, with full contact data as available.
- A table of **airport codes** presented alphabetically, in code order, together with the airport name.
- A cumulated list of **airports** included for the cities profiled, with contact data for each.
- Detailed **area code** tables, organized both numerically (by area code) and geographically. Accompanying these tables is information concerning recent and upcoming area code changes, including the dates such changes are scheduled to take effect and the permissive dialing period that will precede the changes.
- Contact information for major national **car rental agencies**
- A cumulated, alphabetical list of the **convention centers** included in the city profiles, with contact data provided for each center.
- A consolidated list of the **convention and visitor bureaus** (and similar organizations, such as visitor centers) included among the city profiles, with full contact data for each.
- Major national **credit card companies**, with contact information.
- Lists of **hotel reservation services** and **hotel chains** that appear in the city profiles, cumulated here as individual alphabetical lists with full contact information as available.

- A **mileage** table illustrating the distance (by air and by car) between major U.S. cities.
- A list of web sites for **on-line travel services**.
- A table of **weather information** phone numbers for each of the cities listed in this directory; and a table of **on-line weather services** that provides listings for weather-related world wide web sites.

In addition, a table of the **abbreviations used in this directory** is provided just inside the front cover of the book; and a **radio and television format** chart that explains the format and/or network abbreviations that appear in listings for individual radio and television stations within the city profiles is given just inside the back cover.

U.S. and **Canadian time zone maps** featuring the cities covered in this directory precede the city listings in the main body of the book.

Calendar of Events

The events calendar consolidates the annual events held in each of the 250 cities profiled into a single quick-lookup section. The calendar is organized by states, and then by cities within each state grouping. Events for each city are then presented chronologically by month within this state/city framework. Events in Canadian cities follow the events listings for the United States and are organized city by city, with each city's events presented in chronological order.

Individual events listings include the name of the event, the related telephone number, a web address (if available), and additional information about the general time frame in which the event is scheduled to take place.

Comments Welcome

As noted at the beginning of this Introduction, much of the information contained in *City Profiles USA* was compiled with assistance from representatives of local organizations throughout the United States, and the editors are sincerely grateful for their cooperation and assistance. Our efforts to expand upon this work in future editions, while continuing to maintain the highest degree of accuracy, will be ongoing.

Comments concerning this publication, including suggestions for additions or improvements, are welcome. Please send to:

Editor, *City Profiles USA*
Omnigraphics, Inc.
901 E. Las Olas Blvd., Suite 201
Fort Lauderdale, FL 33301
Phone: 954-524-3511
Fax: 954-524-7041
E-mail: editorial@omnigraphics.com

Special Features

1. Area Code Changes (Recent and Upcoming)

Special Features

- Area code 424 was introduced in **California** on July 17, 1999, as a general purpose overlay, within the same geographic area where the 310 area code is in effect.
- Area code 628 was introduced in **California** on October 21, 1999, as a general purpose overlay, within the same geographic area where the 415 area code is in effect.
- Area code 657 will take effect in **California** on October 7, 2000, as a general purpose overlay, within the same geographic area where the 714 area code is in effect.
- Area code 669 was introduced in **California** on January 1, 2000, as a general purpose overlay, within the same geographic area where the 408 area code is in effect.
- Area code 752 will take effect in **California** on February 12, 2000, as a general purpose overlay, within the same geographic area where the 909 area code is in effect.
- Area code 764 was introduced in **California** on September 18, 1999, as a general purpose overlay, within the same geographic area where the 650 area code is in effect.
- Area code 935 will take effect in **California** on June 10, 2000, as a result of the split of the 619 area code. Permissive dialing will allow callers to continue using 619 until December 9, 2000.
- Area code 951 will take effect in **California** on February 12, 2000, as a result of the split of the 909 area code. Permissive dialing will allow callers to continue using 909 until September 9, 2000.
- Area code 321 was introduced in **Florida** on April 1, 1999. In the first phase, the new area code was used as a general purpose overlay within five counties where the 407 area code was in effect. In the second phase, which began on November 1, 1999, the 321 area code was introduced as a result of the split of the 407 area code along the Atlantic coast. Permissive dialing will allow callers to continue using 407 in this area until October 1, 2000.
- Area code 863 was introduced in **Florida** on September 20, 1999, as a result of the split of the 941 area code. Permissive dialing will allow callers to continue using 941 until May 22, 2000.
- Area code 337 was introduced in **Louisiana** on October 11, 1999, as a result of the split of the 318 area code. Permissive dialing will allow callers to continue using 318 until July 10, 2000.
- Area code 586 will take effect in **Michigan** on February 5, 2000, as a general purpose overlay, within the same geographic area where the 810 area code is in effect.
- Area code 347 was introduced in **New York** on October 1, 1999, as a general purpose overlay, within the same geographic area where the 718 area code is in effect.
- Area code 631 was introduced in **New York** on November 1, 1999, as a result of the split of the 516 area code. Permissive dialing will allow callers to continue using 516 until April 1, 2000.
- Area code 646 was introduced in **New York** on July 1, 1999, as a general purpose overlay, within the same geographic area where the 212 area code is in effect.
- Area code 971 was introduced in **Oregon** on July 11, 1999, as a general purpose overlay, within the same geographic area where the 503 area code is in effect.
- Area code 267 was introduced in **Pennsylvania** on July 1, 1999, as a general purpose overlay, within the same geographic area where the 215 area code is in effect.
- Area code 484 was introduced in **Pennsylvania** on July 1, 1999, as a general purpose overlay, within the same geographic area where the 610 area code is in effect.
- Area code 865 was introduced in **Tennessee** on November 1, 1999, as a result of the split of the 423 area code. Permissive dialing will allow callers to continue using 423 until April 24, 2000.
- Area code 469 was introduced in **Texas** on July 1, 1999, as a general purpose overlay, within the same geographic area where the 214 and 972 area codes are in effect.
- Area code 571 will take effect in **Virginia** on April 1, 2000, as a general purpose overlay, within the same geographic area where the 703 area code is in effect.
- Area code 564 will take effect in **Washington** on February 5, 2000, as a general purpose overlay, within the same geographic area where the 360 area code is in effect.
- Area code 262 was introduced in **Wisconsin** on September 25, 1999, as a result of the split of the 414 area code. Permissive dialing will allow callers to continue using 414 until March 4, 2000.

2. Area Codes in Geographic Order

Alabama
205 Birmingham and Tuscaloosa
256 north and east central
334 south
Alaska
907 all locations
Arizona
480 east of Phoenix including Tempe and Scottsdale
520 outside Phoenix
602 Phoenix
623 west of Phoenix including Glendale
Arkansas
501 Little Rock and northwest
870 east and south
California
209 central
213 Los Angeles
310 Long Beach/west
323 Los Angeles
408* west central
415 San Francisco
424 Long Beach/west
510 Oakland
530 north
559 central
562 Long Beach/east
619* San Diego and surrounding area (except north)
626 Pasadena/east
650 south of San Francisco
661 Bakersfield and northern LA county
669 west central
707 northwest
714* northern Orange County
760 southeast except San Diego area
805 south
818 Burbank and Glendale area
831 west central
858 San Diego/north
909* San Bernardino
916 Sacramento and surrounding area
925 east of Oakland
949 southern Orange County
Canada
204 all locations in Manitoba
250 outside Vancouver area including Vancouver Island
306 all locations in Saskatchewan
403 southern Alberta
416 Toronto
418 eastern Quebec
450 outside Montreal metro area
506 all locations in New Brunswick
514 Montreal metro area
519 southern Ontario
604 Vancouver area
613 northeast of Toronto
705 eastern Ontario
709 all locations in Newfoundland
780 central and northern Alberta
807 western Ontario
819 western Quebec
867 all locations in Yukon & Northwest Territories
902 all locations in Nova Scotia & Prince Edward Island
905 north of Toronto
Caribbean, Bahamas & Bermuda
242 Bahamas
246 Barbados
264 Anguilla
268 Antigua & Barbuda
284 British Virgin Islands
345 Cayman Islands
441 Bermuda
473 Grenada
649 Turks and Caicos
664 Montserrat
758 Saint Lucia
767 Dominica
784 Saint Vincent & Grenadines
787 Puerto Rico
809 Caribbean
868 Trinidad and Tobago
869 Saint Kitts and Nevis
876 Jamaica
Colorado
303 Denver
719 south and east
720 Denver
970 west and north
Connecticut
203 southwest
860 except southwest
Delaware
302 all locations
District of Columbia
202 all locations
Florida
305 southeast
321 central and east central
352 Gainesville area
407 central
561 east
727 Saint Petersburg/ Clearwater
786 southeast
813 Tampa
850 northwest
904 northeast
941 central and southwest
954 Fort Lauderdale and surrounding area
Georgia
404 Atlanta
678 Atlanta area
706 north except Atlanta area
770 Atlanta suburbs
912 south
Guam
671 all locations
Hawaii
808 all locations
Idaho
208 all locations
Illinois
217 central
224 suburban Chicago
309 west
312 Chicago
618 south
630 northeast
708 northeast
773 Chicago (outside central commercial area)
815 north
847 suburban Chicago
Indiana
219 north
317 Indianapolis metro area
765 central except Indianapolis metro area
812 south
Iowa
319 east
515 central
712 west
Kansas
316 south
785 north except Kansas City
913 Kansas City
Kentucky
270 west
502 north including Louisville
606 east
Louisiana
225 east central
318 north and west
504 southeast
Maine
207 all locations
Maryland
240 west
301 west
410 east
443 east
Massachusetts
413 west
508 southeast
617 Boston metro area
781 outside metro Boston
978 northeast except Boston
Michigan
231 northwest
248 east (Oakland County)
313 Detroit and inner suburbs
517 central
616 southwest
734 west of Detroit
810* east (except Oakland County)
906 north
Minnesota
218 north
320 central except Minneapolis/Saint Paul metro area
507 south
612 Minneapolis
651 Saint Paul and east central
Mississippi
228 Gulfport/Biloxi and surrounding area
601 south except Gulfport/ Biloxi and surrounding area
662 north
Missouri
314 Saint Louis
417 southwest
573 east except Saint Louis metro area
636 east (outside Saint Louis)
660 north except Kansas City and Saint Joseph
816 Kansas City and Saint Joseph
Montana
406 all locations
Nebraska
308 west
402 east
Nevada
702 Las Vegas area
775 all locations except Las Vegas
New Hampshire
603 all locations
New Jersey
201 northeast
609 southeast
732 east central
856 southwest
908 west central
973 northwest
New Mexico
505 all locations
New York
212 New York City
315 north central
347 New York City
516 Long Island
518 northeast
607 south central
646 New York City
716 west
718 New York City
914 southeast
917 New York City
North Carolina
252 east
336 Greensboro and Winston-Salem areas
704 southwest
828 west
910 south central
919 north central
North Dakota
701 all locations
Ohio
216 Cleveland metro area
330 northeast except Cleveland
419 northwest
440 north central except Cleveland metro area
513 southwest
614 east and central except Columbus area
740 Columbus area
937 southwest except Cincinnati area
Oklahoma
405 central
580 south and west
918 northeast
Oregon
503 Portland area
541 outside Portland area
Pennsylvania
215 Philadelphia
267 Philadelphia
412 Pittsburgh metro area
484 southeast
570 northeast
610 southeast
717 southeast
724 outside Pittsburgh metro area
814 west
Rhode Island
401 all locations
South Carolina
803 central
843 east
864 northwest
South Dakota
605 all locations
Tennessee
423 east
615 north central
901 west
931 Nashville and north central
Texas
210 San Antonio metro area
214 Dallas
254 north central
281 Houston
361 Corpus Christi and surrounding area
409 southeast
469 Dallas
512 Austin and surrounding area
713 Houston
806 northwest
817 Fort Worth metro area and Arlington
830 south central
832 Houston
903 northeast
915 west
940 north
956 south
972 Dallas
Toll calls: from Canada and the Caribbean
880
881
Toll-free; all states
800
877
888
Utah
435 all locations except Salt Lake City/Ogden/Provo metro areas
801 Salt Lake City/Ogden/ Provo metro areas
Vermont
802 all locations
Virginia
540 west and north
703* northeast
757 Norfolk and surrounding area
804 east
Washington
206 Seattle area
253 Tacoma area
360* west except Seattle, Tacoma and Everett areas
425 east of Seattle between Everett and Kent
509 east
West Virginia
304 all locations
Wisconsin
262 southeast except Milwaukee
414 Milwaukee
608 southwest
715 north
920 southeast except Milwaukee and surrounding area (south)
Wyoming
307 all locations

*Area codes affected by upcoming changes. Please refer to the table on page 12, Area Code Changes (Recent and Upcoming). Information there is organized by state name, with the state name presented in bold.

3. Area Codes in Numerical Order

201 ... New Jersey
202 ... District of Columbia
203 ... Connecticut
204 ... Manitoba
205 ... Alabama
206 ... Washington
207 ... Maine
208 ... Idaho
209 ... California
210 ... Texas
212 ... New York
213 ... California
214 ... Texas
215 ... Pennsylvania
216 ... Ohio
217 ... Illinois
218 ... Minnesota
219 ... Indiana
224 ... Illinois
225 ... Louisiana
228 ... Mississippi
231 ... Michigan
240 ... Maryland
242 ... Bahamas
246 ... Barbados
248 ... Michigan
250 ... British Columbia
252 ... North Carolina
253 ... Washington
254 ... Texas
256 ... Alabama
262 ... Wisconsin
264 ... Anguilla
267 ... Pennsylvania
268 ... Antigua and Barbuda
270 ... Kentucky
281 ... Texas
284 ... British Virgin Islands
301 ... Maryland
302 ... Delaware
303 ... Colorado
304 ... West Virginia
305 ... Florida
306 ... Saskatchewan
307 ... Wyoming
308 ... Nebraska
309 ... Illinois
310 ... California
312 ... Illinois
313 ... Michigan
314 ... Missouri
315 ... New York
316 ... Kansas
317 ... Indiana
318 ... Louisiana
319 ... Iowa
320 ... Minnesota
321 ... Florida
323 ... California
330 ... Ohio
334 ... Alabama
336 ... North Carolina
345 ... Cayman Islands
347 ... New York
352 ... Florida
360* ... Washington
361 ... Texas
401 ... Rhode Island
402 ... Nebraska
403 ... Alberta
404 ... Georgia
405 ... Oklahoma
406 ... Montana
407 ... Florida
408* ... California
409 ... Texas
410 ... Maryland
412 ... Pennsylvania
413 ... Massachusetts
414 ... Wisconsin
415 ... California
416 ... Ontario
417 ... Missouri
418 ... Quebec
419 ... Ohio
423 ... Tennessee
424 ... California
425 ... Washington
435 ... Utah
440 ... Ohio
441 ... Bermuda
443 ... Maryland
450 ... Quebec
469 ... Texas
473 ... Grenada
480 ... Arizona
484 ... Pennyslvania
501 ... Arkansas
502 ... Kentucky
503 ... Oregon
504 ... Louisiana
505 ... New Mexico
506 ... New Brunswick
507 ... Minnesota
508 ... Massachusetts
509 ... Washington
510 ... California
512 ... Texas
513 ... Ohio
514 ... Quebec
515 ... Iowa
516 ... New York
517 ... Michigan
518 ... New York
519 ... Ontario
520 ... Arizona
530 ... California
540 ... Virginia
541 ... Oregon
559 ... California
561 ... Florida
562 ... California
570 ... Pennsylvania
573 ... Missouri
580 ... Oklahoma
601 ... Mississippi
602 ... Arizona
603 ... New Hampshire
604 ... British Columbia
605 ... South Dakota
606 ... Kentucky
607 ... New York
608 ... Wisconsin
609 ... New Jersey
610 ... Pennsylvania
612 ... Minnesota
613 ... Ontario
614 ... Ohio
615 ... Tennessee
616 ... Michigan
617 ... Massachusetts
618 ... Illinois
619* ... California
623 ... Arizona
626 ... California
630 ... Illinois
636 ... Missouri
646 ... New York
649 ... Turks and Caicos
650 ... California
651 ... Minnesota
660 ... Missouri
661 ... California
662 ... Mississippi
664 ... Montserrat
669 ... California
671 ... Guam
678 ... Georgia
701 ... North Dakota
702 ... Nevada
703* ... Virginia
704 ... North Carolina
705 ... Ontario
706 ... Georgia
707 ... California
708 ... Illinois
709 ... Newfoundland
712 ... Iowa
713 ... Texas
714* ... California
715 ... Wisconsin
716 ... New York
717 ... Pennsylvania
718 ... New York
719 ... Colorado
720 ... Colorado
724 ... Pennsylvania
727 ... Florida
732 ... New Jersey
734 ... Michigan
740 ... Ohio
757 ... Virginia
758 ... Saint Lucia
760 ... California
765 ... Indiana
767 ... Dominica
770 ... Georgia
773 ... Illinois
775 ... Nevada
780 ... Alberta
781 ... Massachusetts
784 ... Saint Vincent & the Grenadines
785 ... Kansas
786 ... Florida
787 ... Puerto Rico
800 ... Toll-free; all states
801 ... Utah
802 ... Vermont
803 ... South Carolina
804 ... Virginia
805 ... California
806 ... Texas
807 ... Ontario
808 ... Hawaii
809 ... Caribbean
810* ... Michigan
812 ... Indiana
813 ... Florida
814 ... Pennsylvania
815 ... Illinois
816 ... Missouri
817 ... Texas
818 ... California
819 ... Quebec
828 ... North Carolina
830 ... Texas
831 ... California
832 ... Texas
843 ... South Carolina
847 ... Illinois
850 ... Florida
856 ... New Jersey
858 ... California
860 ... Connecticut
864 ... South Carolina
867 ... Northwest Territories
868 ... Trinidad and Tobago
869 ... Saint Kitts and Nevis
870 ... Arkansas
876 ... Jamaica
877 ... Toll-free; all states
888 ... Toll-free; all states
901 ... Tennessee
902 ... Nova Scotia
903 ... Texas
904 ... Florida
905 ... Ontario
906 ... Michigan
907 ... Alaska
908 ... New Jersey
909* ... California
910 ... North Carolina
912 ... Georgia
913 ... Kansas
914 ... New York
915 ... Texas
916 ... California
917 ... New York
918 ... Oklahoma
919 ... North Carolina
920 ... Wisconsin
925 ... California
931 ... Tennessee
937 ... Ohio
940 ... Texas
941 ... Florida
949 ... California
954 ... Florida
956 ... Texas
970 ... Colorado
972 ... Texas
973 ... New Jersey
978 ... Massachusetts

*Area codes affected by upcoming changes. Please refer to the table on page 12, Area Code Changes (Recent and Upcoming). Information there is organized by state name, with the state name presented in bold.

4. Airports

Airport	City	State	Phone
Abilene Regional Airport (ABI)	Abilene	TX	915-676-6367
Akron-Canton Regional Airport (CAK)	North Canton	OH	330-896-2385
Albany International Airport (ALB)	Albany	NY	518-242-2200
Albuquerque International Airport (ABQ)	Albuquerque	NM	505-842-4366
Alpena County Regional Airport (APN)	Alpena	MI	517-354-2907
Amarillo International Airport (AMA)	Amarillo	TX	806-335-1671
Anchorage International Airport (ANC)	Anchorage	AK	907-266-2525
Ann Arbor Airport (ARB)	Ann Arbor	MI	734-994-2841
Asheville Regional Airport (AVL)	Fletcher	NC	828-684-2226
Atlantic City International Airport (ACY)	Pleasantville	NJ	609-645-7895
Augusta State Airport (AUG)	Augusta	ME	207-626-2306
Austin Straubel International Airport (GRB)	Green Bay	WI	920-498-4800
Baltimore-Washington International Airport (BWI)	Baltimore	MD	410-859-7111
Bangor International Airport (BGR)	Bangor	ME	207-947-0384
Baton Rouge Metropolitan Airport (BTR)	Baton Rouge	LA	225-355-0333
Billings Logan International Airport (BIL)	Billings	MT	406-657-8495
Birmingham International Airport (BHM)	Birmingham	AL	205-595-0533
Bishop International Airport (FNT)	Flint	MI	810-235-6560
Bismarck Municipal Airport (BIS)	Bismarck	ND	701-222-6502
Blue Grass Airport (LEX)	Lexington	KY	606-425-3114
Boise Air Terminal (BOI)	Boise	ID	208-383-3110
Bradley International Airport (BDL)	Windsor Locks	CT	860-292-2000
Brownsville-South Padre Island International Airport (BRO)	Brownsville	TX	956-542-4373
Buffalo Niagara International Airport (BUF)	Cheektowaga	NY	716-630-6000
Burbank-Glendale-Pasadena Airport (BUR)	Los Angeles	CA	818-840-8840
Burlington International Airport (BTV)	Burlington	VT	802-863-2874
Bush Field (AGS)	Augusta	GA	706-798-2656
Bush Intercontinental Airport (IAH)	Houston	TX	281-233-3000
Calgary International Airport (YYC)	Calgary	AB	403-735-1200
Capital Airport (SPI)	Springfield	IL	217-788-1063
Capital City Airport (LAN)	Lansing	MI	517-321-6121
Charleston International Airport (CHS)	Charleston	SC	843-767-1100
Charlotte/Douglas International Airport (CLT)	Charlotte	NC	704-359-4000
Chattanooga Metropolitan Airport (CHA)	Chattanooga	TN	423-855-2200
Cheyenne Municipal Airport (CYS)	Cheyenne	WY	307-634-7071
Chicago Midway Airport (MDW)	Chicago	IL	773-838-0600
Chicago O'Hare International Airport (ORD)	Chicago	IL	773-686-2200
Cincinnati-Northern Kentucky International Airport (CVG)	Cincinnati	OH	606-767-3151
Cleveland Hopkins International Airport (CLE)	Cleveland	OH	216-265-6000
Colorado Springs Municipal Airport (COS)	Colorado Springs	CO	719-550-1900
Columbia Metropolitan Airport (CAE)	Columbia	SC	803-822-5010
Columbia Regional Airport (COU)	Columbia	MO	573-442-9770
Columbus Metropolitan Airport (CSG)	Columbus	GA	706-324-2449
Corpus Christi International Airport (CRP)	Corpus Christi	TX	361-289-0171
Dallas Love Field (DAL)	Dallas	TX	214-670-6080
Dallas-Fort Worth International Airport (DFW)	Dallas	TX	972-574-8888
Dane County Regional Airport (MSN)	Madison	WI	608-246-3380
Dayton International Airport (DAY)	Vandalia	OH	937-454-8200
Daytona Beach International Airport (DAB)	Daytona Beach	FL	904-248-8069
Denver International Airport (DEN)	Denver	CO	303-342-2000
Des Moines International Airport (DSM)	Des Moines	IA	515-256-5050
Detroit City Airport (DET)	Detroit	MI	313-852-6400
Detroit Metropolitan Airport (DTW)	Detroit	MI	734-942-3685
Dubuque Regional Airport (DBQ)	Dubuque	IA	319-589-4127
Duluth International Airport (DLH)	Duluth	MN	218-727-2968
Eastern Iowa Airport (CID)	Cedar Rapids	IA	319-362-3131
Edmonton International Airport (YEG)	Edmonton	AB	780-890-8900
El Paso International Airport (ELP)	El Paso	TX	915-772-4271
Eppley Airfield (OMA)	Omaha	NE	402-422-6800
Erie International Airport (ERI)	Erie	PA	814-833-4258
Eugene Airport (EUG)	Eugene	OR	541-682-5430
Evansville Regional Airport (EVV)	Evansville	IN	812-421-4401
Fairbanks International Airport (FAI)	Fairbanks	AK	907-474-2500
Flagstaff Pulliam Airport (FLG)	Flagstaff	AZ	520-556-1234
Forbes Field (FOE)	Topeka	KS	785-862-2362
Fort Collins/Loveland Municipal Airport (FNL)	Loveland	CO	970-962-2850
Fort Lauderdale Executive Airport (FXE)	Fort Lauderdale	FL	954-938-4966
Fort Lauderdale/Hollywood International Airport (FLL)	Fort Lauderdale	FL	954-359-6100
Fort Smith Municipal Airport (FSM)	Fort Smith	AR	501-646-1693
Fort Wayne International Airport (FWA)	Fort Wayne	IN	219-747-4146
Fresno Air Terminal (FAT)	Fresno	CA	559-498-4095
General Mitchell International Airport (MKE)	Milwaukee	WI	414-747-5300
Grand Forks International Airport (GFK)	Grand Forks	ND	701-795-6981
Great Falls International Airport (GTF)	Great Falls	MT	406-727-3404
Greater Peoria Regional Airport (PIA)	Peoria	IL	309-697-8272
Greater Pittsburgh International Airport (PIT)	Pittsburgh	PA	412-472-3525
Greater Rochester International Airport (ROC)	Rochester	NY	716-464-6000
Greater Rockford Airport (RFD)	Rockford	IL	815-965-8639
Greenville-Spartanburg Airport (GSP)	Greer	SC	864-877-7426
Gulfport/Biloxi Regional Airport (GPT)	Gulfport	MS	228-863-5951
Halifax International Airport (YHZ)	Elmsdale	NS	902-873-1234
Hancock County Airport (BHB)	Ellsworth	ME	207-667-7329
Harrisburg International Airport (MDT)	Middletown	PA	717-948-3987
Hartsfield Atlanta International Airport (ATL)	Atlanta	GA	404-530-6600
Hattiesburg-Laurel Regional Airport (PIB)	Moselle	MS	601-649-2444
Hector International Airport (FAR)	Fargo	ND	701-241-1501
Helena Regional Airport (HLN)	Helena	MT	406-442-2821
Hilton Head Island Airport (HXD)	Hilton Head Island	SC	843-689-5400
Honolulu International Airport (HNL)	Honolulu	HI	808-836-6413
Hot Springs Memorial Field (HOT)	Hot Springs	AR	501-624-3306
Huntsville International Airport (HSV)	Huntsville	AL	256-772-9395
Indianapolis International Airport (IND)	Indianapolis	IN	317-487-9594
Jackson Hole Airport (JAC)	Jackson	WY	307-733-7682
Jackson International Airport (JAN)	Jackson	MS	601-939-5631
Jacksonville International Airport (JAX)	Jacksonville	FL	904-741-4902
Jean-Lesage International Airport (YQB)	Sainte-Foy	QC	418-640-2600
John F Kennedy International Airport (JFK)	Jamaica	NY	718-244-4444
John Wayne Airport/Orange County (SNA)	Santa Ana	CA	949-252-5200
Juneau International Airport (JNU)	Juneau	AK	907-789-7821
Kahului Airport (OGG)	Maui	HI	808-872-3830
Kansas City International Airport (MCI)	Kansas City	MO	816-243-5237
Kent County International Airport (GRR)	Grand Rapids	MI	616-336-4500
Key West International Airport (EYW)	Key West	FL	305-296-5439
Kona International Airport (KOA)	Kailua-Kona	HI	808-329-2484
Lafayette Regional Airport (LFT)	Lafayette	LA	337-266-4400
LaGuardia Airport (LGA)	Flushing	NY	718-476-5000
Lambert Saint Louis International Airport (STL)	Saint Louis	MO	314-426-8000
Las Cruces International Airport (LRU)	Las Cruces	NM	505-524-2762
Lehigh Valley International Airport (ABE)	Allentown	PA	610-266-6000
Lester B Pearson International Airport (YYZ)	Toronto	ON	416-247-7678
Lincoln Municipal Airport (LNK)	Lincoln	NE	402-474-2770
Little Rock National Airport/Adams Field (LIT)	Little Rock	AR	501-372-3439
Logan International Airport (BOS)	Boston	MA	617-561-1818
Long Beach Municipal Airport (LGB)	Long Beach	CA	562-570-2600
Long Island MacArthur Airport (ISP)	Ronkonkoma	NY	631-467-3210
Los Angeles International Airport (LAX)	Los Angeles	CA	310-646-5252
Louisville International Airport (SDF)	Louisville	KY	502-368-6524
Lubbock International Airport (LBB)	Lubbock	TX	806-775-2035
Luis Munoz Marin International Airport (SJU)	San Juan	PR	787-791-4670
Manchester Municipal Airport (MHT)	Manchester	NH	603-624-6556
McCarran International Airport (LAS)	Las Vegas	NV	702-261-5743
McGhee Tyson Airport (TYS)	Alcoa	TN	865-970-2773
Meadows Field Airport (BFL)	Bakersfield	CA	661-393-7990
Memphis International Airport (MEM)	Memphis	TN	901-922-8000
Miami International Airport (MIA)	Miami	FL	305-876-7515
Michiana Regional Airport (SBN)	South Bend	IN	219-233-2185
Midcontinent Airport (ICT)	Wichita	KS	316-946-4700
Middle Georgia Regional Airport (MCN)	Macon	GA	912-788-3760
Midland International Airport (MAF)	Midland	TX	915-560-2200
Minneapolis-Saint Paul International Airport (MSP)	Minneapolis	MN	612-726-5500
Mobile Regional Airport (MOB)	Mobile	AL	334-633-0313
Modesto City Airport (MOD)	Modesto	CA	209-577-5318
Monterey Peninsula Airport (MRY)	Monterey	CA	831-648-7000
Montgomery Regional Airport (MGM)	Montgomery	AL	334-281-5040
Montréal International Airport Dorval (YUL)	Montréal	QC	514-394-7377
Montréal International Airport Mirabel (YMX)	Mirabel	QC	514-394-7377
Morgantown Municipal Airport (MGW)	Morgantown	WV	304-291-7461
Myrtle Beach International Airport (MYR)	Myrtle Beach	SC	843-448-1589
Naples Municipal Airport (APF)	Naples	FL	941-643-1415
Nashville International Airport (BNA)	Nashville	TN	615-275-1600
Natrona County International Airport (CPR)	Casper	WY	307-472-6688
New Orleans International Airport (MSY)	Kenner	LA	504-464-0831
Newark International Airport (EWR)	Newark	NJ	973-961-6000
Newport News/Williamsburg International Airport (PHF)	Newport News	VA	757-877-0221
Norfolk International Airport (ORF)	Norfolk	VA	757-857-3351
Oakland International Airport (OAK)	Oakland	CA	510-577-4000
Ogden-Hinckley Airport (OGD)	Ogden	UT	801-629-8251
Ontario International Airport (ONT)	Ontario	CA	909-937-2700
Orlando International Airport (MCO)	Orlando	FL	407-825-2001
Ottawa Macdonald-Cartier International Airport (YOW)	Gloucester	ON	613-248-2125
Palm Beach International Airport (PBI)	West Palm Beach	FL	561-471-7412
Palm Springs Municipal Airport (PSP)	Palm Springs	CA	760-323-8161
Palo Alto Airport (PAO)	Palo Alto	CA	650-856-7833
Pensacola Regional Airport (PNS)	Pensacola	FL	850-435-1746
Philadelphia International Airport (PHL)	Philadelphia	PA	215-937-6937
Phoenix Sky Harbor International Airport (PHX)	Phoenix	AZ	602-273-3300
Piedmont Triad International Airport (GSO)	Greensboro	NC	336-665-5600
Pierre Municipal Airport (PIR)	Pierre	SD	605-773-7447
Pocatello Regional Airport (PIH)	Pocatello	ID	208-234-6154
Port Columbus International Airport (CMH)	Columbus	OH	614-239-4000
Portland International Airport (PDX)	Portland	OR	503-460-4040
Portland International Jetport (PWM)	Portland	ME	207-774-7301
Raleigh-Durham International Airport (RDU)	Raleigh	NC	919-840-2100
Rapid City Regional Airport (RAP)	Rapid City	SD	605-394-4195
Reno-Tahoe International Airport (RNO)	Reno	NV	775-328-6400
Richmond International Airport (RIC)	Richmond	VA	804-226-3052
Roanoke Regional Airport (ROA)	Roanoke	VA	540-362-1999
Robert Mueller Municipal Airport (AUS)	Austin	TX	512-472-5439
Rochester Municipal Airport (RST)	Rochester	MN	507-282-2328
Ronald Reagan Washington National Airport (DCA)	Washington	DC	703-417-8000
Sacramento Metropolitan Airport (SMF)	Sacramento	CA	916-929-5411
Saint Petersburg-Clearwater International Airport (PIE)	Clearwater	FL	727-531-1451

4. AIRPORTS

Airport	City	State	Phone
Salisbury-Wicomico County Regional Airport (SBY)	Salisbury	MD	410-548-4827
Salt Lake City International Airport (SLC)	Salt Lake City	UT	801-575-2400
San Antonio International Airport (SAT)	San Antonio	TX	210-207-3411
San Diego International Airport - Lindbergh Field (SAN)	San Diego	CA	619-231-2100
San Francisco International Airport (SFO)	San Francisco	CA	650-761-0800
San Jose International Airport (SJC)	San Jose	CA	408-501-7600
Santa Fe Municipal Airport (SAF)	Santa Fe	NM	505-473-7243
Sarasota-Bradenton International Airport (SRQ)	Sarasota	FL	941-359-5200
Savannah International Airport (SAV)	Savannah	GA	912-964-0514
Seattle-Tacoma International Airport (SEA)	Seattle	WA	206-431-4444
Shreveport Regional Airport (SHV)	Shreveport	LA	318-673-5370
Sikorsky Memorial Airport (BDR)	Stratford	CT	203-576-8162
Sioux Falls Regional Airport (FSD)	Sioux Falls	SD	605-336-0762
Smith Reynolds Airport (INT)	Winston-Salem	NC	336-767-6361
Southwest Florida International Airport (RSW)	Fort Myers	FL	941-768-4321
Spokane International Airport (GEG)	Spokane	WA	509-624-3218
Springfield-Branson Regional Airport (SGF)	Springfield	MO	417-869-0300
Syracuse Hancock International Airport (SYR)	Syracuse	NY	315-454-4330
Tallahassee Regional Airport (TLH)	Tallahassee	FL	850-891-7800
Tampa International Airport (TPA)	Tampa	FL	813-870-8700
Theodore Francis Green State Airport (PVD)	Warwick	RI	401-737-4000
Toledo Express Airport (TOL)	Swanton	OH	419-865-2351
Tri-Cities Regional Airport (TRI)	Blountville	TN	423-325-6000
Tucson International Airport (TUS)	Tucson	AZ	520-573-8000
Tulsa International Airport (TUL)	Tulsa	OK	918-838-5000
Tupelo Regional Airport (TUP)	Tupelo	MS	662-841-6570
Tweed-New Haven Regional Airport (HVN)	New Haven	CT	203-466-8833
University of Illinois Willard Airport (CMI)	Savoy	IL	217-244-8600
Vancouver International Airport (YVR)	Vancouver	BC	604-276-6101
Ventura County Airport (OXR)	Oxnard	CA	805-388-4274
Washington Dulles International Airport (IAD)	Washington	DC	703-572-2730
Westchester County Airport (HPN)	White Plains	NY	914-285-4860
Wheeling-Ohio County Airport (HLG)	Wheeling	WV	304-234-3865
Wilkes-Barre/Scranton International Airport (AVP)	Avoca	PA	570-346-0672
Will Rogers World Airport (OKC)	Oklahoma City	OK	405-680-3200
William P Hobby Airport (HOU)	Houston	TX	713-640-3000
Winnipeg International Airport (YWG)	Winnipeg	MB	204-987-9400
Worcester Regional Airport (ORH)	Worcester	MA	508-799-1741
Yeager Airport (CRW)	Charleston	WV	304-345-0661
Youngstown-Warren Regional Airport (YNG)	Vienna	OH	330-856-1537

5. Airport Codes

A

ABE ALLENTOWN, PA
ABI ABILENE, TX
ABQ ALBUQUERQUE, NM
ACY ATLANTIC CITY, NJ
AGS AUGUSTA, GA
ALB ALBANY, NY
AMA AMARILLO, TX
ANC ANCHORAGE, AK
APF NAPLES, FL
ARB ANN ARBOR, MI
ATL ATLANTA, GA
AUG AUGUSTA, ME
AUS AUSTIN, TX
AVL ASHEVILLE, NC
AVP WILKES-BARRE/SCRANTON, PA

B

BDL HARTFORD, CT
BDR BRIDGEPORT, CT
BFL BAKERSFIELD, CA
BGR BANGOR, ME
BHB BAR HARBOR, ME
BHM BIRMINGHAM, AL
BIL BILLINGS, MT
BIS BISMARCK, ND
BNA NASHVILLE, TN
BOI BOISE, ID
BOS BOSTON, MA
BRO BROWNSVILLE, TX
BTR BATON ROUGE, LA
BTV BURLINGTON, VT
BUF BUFFALO, NY
BUR LOS ANGELES, CA (BURBANK)
BWI BALTIMORE, MD

C

CAE COLUMBIA, SC
CAK AKRON/CANTON, OH
CHA CHATTANOOGA, TN
CHS CHARLESTON, SC
CID CEDAR RAPIDS, IA
CLE CLEVELAND, OH
CLT CHARLOTTE, NC
CMH COLUMBUS, OH
CMI CHAMPAIGN, IL
COS COLORADO SPRINGS, CO
COU JEFFERSON CITY, MO
CPR CASPER, WY
CRP CORPUS CHRISTI, TX
CRW CHARLESTON, WV
CSG COLUMBUS, GA
CVG CINCINNATI, OH
CYS CHEYENNE, WY

D

DAB DAYTONA BEACH, FL
DAL DALLAS, TX (LOVE FIELD)
DBQ DUBUQUE, IA
DAY DAYTON, OH
DCA WASHINGTON, DC (NATIONAL)
DEN DENVER, CO
DET DETROIT, MI (CITY)
DFW DALLAS/FT WORTH, TX
DLH DULUTH, MN
DSM DES MOINES, IA
DTW DETROIT, MI (METRO)

E

ELP EL PASO, TX
ERI ERIE, PA
EUG EUGENE, OR
EVV EVANSVILLE, IN
EWR NEW YORK, NY/NEWARK, NJ (NEWARK)
EYW KEY WEST, FL

F

FAI FAIRBANKS, AK
FAR FARGO, ND
FAT FRESNO, CA
FLG FLAGSTAFF, AZ
FLL FORT LAUDERDALE/HOLLYWOOD, FL
FNT FLINT, MI
FOE TOPEKA, KS
FSD SIOUX FALLS, SD
FSM FORT SMITH, AR
FWA FORT WAYNE, IN

G

GEG SPOKANE, WA
GFK GRAND FORKS, ND
GPT GULFPORT/BILOXI, MS
GRB GREEN BAY, WI
GRR GRAND RAPIDS, MI
GSO GREENSBORO, NC
GSP GREENVILLE-SPARTANBURG, SC
GTF GREAT FALLS, MT

H

HLG WHEELING, OH
HLN HELENA, MT
HNL HONOLULU, HI
HOT HOT SPRINGS, AR
HOU HOUSTON, TX (HOBBY)
HPN STAMFORD, CT
HSV HUNTSVILLE, AL
HVN NEW HAVEN, CT
HXD HILTON HEAD ISLAND, SC

I

IAD WASHINGTON, DC (DULLES)
IAH HOUSTON, TX (INTERCONTINENTAL)
ICT WICHITA, KS
IND INDIANAPOLIS, IN
INT WINSTON-SALEM, NC

J

JAC JACKSON, WY
JAN JACKSON, MS
JAX JACKSONVILLE, FL
JFK NEW YORK, NY/NEWARK, NJ (KENNEDY)
JNU JUNEAU, AK

L

LAN LANSING, MI
LAS LAS VEGAS, NV
LAX LOS ANGELES, CA (INTL)
LBB LUBBOCK, TX
LEX LEXINGTON, KY
LFT LAFAYETTE, LA
LGA NEW YORK, NY/NEWARK, NJ (LA GUARDIA)
LGB LONG BEACH, CA
LIT LITTLE ROCK, AR
LNK LINCOLN, NE
LRU LAS CRUCES, NM

M

MCI KANSAS CITY, MO
MCN MACON, GA
MCO ORLANDO, FL
MDT HARRISBURG, PA
MDW CHICAGO, IL (MIDWAY)
MEM MEMPHIS, TN
MGM MONTGOMERY, AL
MGW MORGANTOWN, WV
MHT MANCHESTER, NH
MIA MIAMI, FL
MKE MILWAUKEE, WI
MOB MOBILE, AL
MOD MODESTO, CA
MRY MONTEREY, CA
MSN MADISON, WI
MSP MINNEAPOLIS/SAINT PAUL, MN
MSY NEW ORLEANS, LA
MYR MYRTLE BEACH, SC

O

OAK OAKLAND/SAN FRANCISCO, CA (OAKLAND)
OGD OGDEN, UT
OKC OKLAHOMA CITY, OK
OMA OMAHA, NE
ONT ONTARIO, CA
ORD CHICAGO, IL (O'HARE)
ORF NORFOLK, VA
ORH WORCESTER, MA
OXR VENTURA COUNTY, CA (OXNARD)

P

PBI WEST PALM BEACH, FL
PDX PORTLAND, OR
PHF NEWPORT NEWS/WILLIAMSBURG, VA
PHL PHILADELPHIA, PA/ WILMINGTON, DE
PHX PHOENIX, AZ
PIA PEORIA, IL
PIB HATTIESBURG, MS
PIE SAINT PETERSBURG, FL
PIH POCATELLO, ID
PIR PIERRE, SD
PIT PITTSBURGH, PA
PNS PENSACOLA, FL
PSP PALM SPRINGS, CA
PVD PROVIDENCE, RI
PWM PORTLAND, ME

R

RAP RAPID CITY, SD
RDU RALEIGH/DURHAM, NC
RFD ROCKFORD, IL
RIC RICHMOND, VA
RNO RENO, NV
ROA ROANOKE, VA
ROC ROCHESTER, NY
RST ROCHESTER, MN
RSW FORT MYERS, FL

S

SAF SANTA FE, NM
SAN SAN DIEGO, CA
SAT SAN ANTONIO, TX
SAV SAVANNAH, GA
SBN SOUTH BEND, IN
SBY SALISBURY, MD
SDF LOUISVILLE, KY
SEA SEATTLE/TACOMA, WA
SFO SAN FRANCISCO/OAKLAND, CA (INTL)
SGF SPRINGFIELD, MO
SHV SHREVEPORT, LA
SJC SAN JOSE, CA
SLC SALT LAKE CITY, UT
SMF SACRAMENTO, CA
SNA ORANGE COUNTY, CA (SANTA ANA)
SPI SPRINGFIELD, IL
STL SAINT LOUIS, MO
SYR SYRACUSE, NY

T

TLH TALLAHASSEE, FL
TOL TOLEDO, OH
TPA TAMPA/SAINT PETERSBURG, FL
TRI JOHNSON CITY, TN
TUL TULSA, OK
TUP TUPELO, MS
TUS TUCSON, AZ
TYS KNOXVILLE, TN

Y

YEG EDMONTON, AB
YHZ HALIFAX, NS
YMX MONTREAL (MIRABEL), QC
YNG YOUNGSTOWN, OH
YOW OTTAWA, ON
YQB QUEBEC, QC
YUL MONTREAL (DORVAL), QC
YVR VANCOUVER, BC
YWG WINNIPEG, MB
YYC CALGARY, AB
YYZ TORONTO, ON

6. Airline Companies

Phone | Fax

Aer Lingus 538 Broad Hollow Rd .... Melville NY 11747 631-577-5700 752-2043
TF: 800-474-7424 ■ *Web:* www.aerlingus.ie

Aeroflot Russian International Airlines
1411 4th Ave Suite 420 .... Seattle WA 98101 206-464-1005 464-0452
TF: 888-686-4949 ■ *Web:* www.aeroflot.com

Aerolineas Argentinas 630 5th Ave Suite 1661 .... New York NY 10111 212-698-2080 698-2069
TF: 800-333-0276 ■ *Web:* www.aeroargentinas.com

AeroMexico 13405 Northwest Fwy Suite 140 .... Houston TX 77040 713-744-8400 460-3334
TF: 800-237-6639 ■ *Web:* www.aeromexico.com

Air Afrique 1350 Ave of the Americas 6th Fl .... New York NY 10019 212-586-5908 541-7539
TF: 800-456-9192 ■ *Web:* www.travelfile.com/get/aafrica.html

Air ALM 1150 NW 72nd Ave Suite 530 .... Miami FL 33126 305-592-7646 594-1030
TF: 800-327-7230

Air Aruba 760 NW 107th Ave Suite 214 .... Miami FL 33172 305-551-2400 551-3192
TF: 800-882-7822 ■ *Web:* www.interknowledge.com/air-aruba

Air Canada 1133 Ave of the Americas 16th Fl .... New York NY 10036 212-869-8840 930-8355*
**Fax:* Hum Res ■ *TF:* 800-776-3000
■ *Web:* www.aircanada.ca

Air Canada PO Box 14000 .... Dorval QC H4Y1H4 514-422-5000 422-5055*
**Fax:* Sales ■ *TF:* 800-776-3000 ■ *Web:* www.aircanada.ca

Air China 45 E 49th St .... New York NY 10017 212-371-9898 935-7951
TF: 800-982-8802
■ *Web:* www.airchina.com.cn/english/index.htm

Air France 120 W 56th St .... New York NY 10019 212-830-4000 830-4431
TF: 800-237-2747 ■ *Web:* www.airfrance.com

Air India 570 Lexington Ave 15th Fl .... New York NY 10022 212-407-1300 838-9533
TF: 800-223-7776 ■ *Web:* www.airindia.com

Air Jamaica 95-25 Queens Blvd 7th Fl .... Rego Park NY 11374 718-830-0622 275-8717
TF: 800-523-5585

Air Lanka 16250 Ventura Blvd Suite 115 .... Encino CA 91436 818-990-9712 501-2098
TF: 800-247-5265 ■ *Web:* www.airlanka.com

Air Midwest Inc PO Box 7724 .... Wichita KS 67277 316-942-8137 945-0947
TF: 800-428-4322 ■ *Web:* www.usair.com

Air New Zealand Ltd
1960 E Grand Ave Suite 900 .... El Segundo CA 90245 310-648-7000 648-7017
TF: 800-262-1234 ■ *Web:* www.airnz.com

Air Wisconsin Airlines Corp
W6390 Challenger Dr Suite 203 .... Appleton WI 54914 920-739-5123 749-4158
TF: 800-241-6522 ■ *Web:* www.airwis.com

AirTran Airways 9955 AirTran Blvd .... Orlando FL 32827 407-251-5600 251-5567
TF: 800-247-8726 ■ *Web:* www.airtran.com

Alaska Airlines Inc PO Box 68900 .... Seattle WA 98168 206-433-3200 433-3366*
**Fax:* Mktg ■ *TF:* 800-426-0333 ■ *Web:* www.alaskaair.com

Alitalia Airlines 666 5th Ave 6th Fl .... New York NY 10103 212-903-3300 903-3541*
**Fax:* Mktg ■ *TF:* 800-223-5730
■ *Web:* www.alitalia.it/english

All Nippon Airways Co Ltd
1251 Ave of the Americas 8th Fl .... New York NY 10020 212-840-3700 840-3704*
**Fax:* Hum Res ■ *TF:* 800-235-9262
■ *Web:* www.ana.co.jp/eng/index.html

Allegheny Airlines Inc 1000 Rosedale Ave .... Middletown PA 17057 717-944-8720 948-5406

Aloha Airlines Inc PO Box 30028 .... Honolulu HI 96820 808-484-1111 484-3200
TF: 800-367-5250 ■ *Web:* www.alohaair.com

America West Airlines Inc
4000 E Sky Harbor Blvd .... Phoenix AZ 85034 480-693-0800 693-5546*
**Fax:* Mail Rm ■ *TF:* 800-235-9292
■ *Web:* www.americawest.com

American Airlines Inc PO Box 619616 .... DFW Airport TX 75261 817-963-1234 963-1933*
**Fax:* Mail Rm ■ *TF:* 800-433-7300 ■ *Web:* www.aa.com

American Trans Air Inc
7337 W Washington St .... Indianapolis IN 46231 317-247-4000 243-4169*
**Fax:* Hum Res ■ *TF:* 800-225-2995 ■ *Web:* www.ata.com

Ansett Australia Airlines
c/o Air New Zealand 1960 E Grand Ave
Suite 900 .... El Segundo CA 90245 310-648-7000 648-7017
TF: 888-426-7388 ■ *Web:* www.ansett.com.au/home_fm.htm

Asiana Airlines Inc
3530 Wilshire Blvd Suite 145 .... Los Angeles CA 90010 213-365-4500 365-9630
TF: 800-227-4262 ■ *Web:* www.asiana.co.kr/english/

Atlantic Coast Airlines 515 Shaw Rd .... Dulles VA 20166 703-925-6000 925-6299
Web: www.atlanticcoast.com

Atlantic Southeast Airlines Inc
100 Hartsfield Ctr Pkwy Suite 800 .... Atlanta GA 30354 404-766-1400 209-0162
TF: 800-282-3424

Austrian Airlines 17-20 Whitestone Expy 5th Fl .... Whitestone NY 11357 718-670-8600 670-8619
TF: 800-843-0002 ■ *Web:* www.aua.com/aua

Avianca Airlines 8125 NW 53rd St Suite 111 .... Miami FL 33166 305-599-7200 477-0597
TF: 800-284-2622

Aviateca
1758 NW 68th Ave Miami International
Airport Bldg 706 .... Miami FL 33122 305-223-0312 223-1731
TF: 800-327-9832 ■ *Web:* www.grupotaca.com

Phone | Fax

Bahamasair Holdings Ltd 3024 NW 79th Ave .... Miami FL 33122 305-526-2003 871-4580
TF: 800-222-4262 ■ *Web:* www.bahamasair.com

Bering Air PO Box 1650 .... Nome AK 99762 907-443-5422 443-5919
TF: 800-478-5422

Big Sky Airlines 1601 Aviation Pl .... Billings MT 59105 406-245-9449 259-8750
TF: 800-237-7788 ■ *Web:* www.bigskyair.com

British Airways 75-20 Astoria Blvd .... Jackson Heights NY 11370 718-397-4000 397-4364
TF: 800-247-9297 ■ *Web:* www.british-airways.com

Business Express Airlines Inc
55 Washington St Suite 300 .... Dover NH 03820 603-740-3000 740-3050
TF: 800-345-3400 ■ *Web:* www.flybex.com

BWIA International Airways
330 Biscayne Blvd Suite 310 .... Miami FL 33132 305-371-2942 381-8743
TF: 800-538-2942

Canadian Airlines International Ltd
700 2nd St SW Suite 2800 .... Calgary AB T2P2W2 403-294-2000 294-6142
TF: 800-426-7000 ■ *Web:* www.cdnair.ca

Cape Air 660 Barnstable Rd .... Hyannis MA 02601 508-771-6944 775-8815
TF: 800-352-0714

Cape Smythe Air Service Inc PO Box 549 .... Barrow AK 99723 907-852-8333 852-2509
TF: 800-478-8333

Cathay Pacific Airways
300 Continental Blvd Suite 500 .... El Segundo CA 90245 310-615-1113 615-0042
TF: 800-233-2742 ■ *Web:* www.cathay-usa.com

Cayman Airways Ltd
6100 Blue Lagoon Dr Suite 130 .... Miami FL 33126 305-266-6760 267-2930
TF: 800-422-9626 ■ *Web:* www.caymanairways.com

Chautauqua Airlines Inc
2500 S High School Rd Suite 160 .... Indianapolis IN 46241 317-484-6000 484-6040
TF: 800-428-4322 ■ *Web:* www.flychautauqua.com

China Airlines Ltd
6053 W Century Blvd Suite 800 .... Los Angeles CA 90045 310-641-8888 641-0864
TF: 800-227-5118 ■ *Web:* www.china-airlines.com

Comair Inc PO Box 75352 .... Cincinnati OH 45275 606-525-2550 767-2960*
**Fax:* Cust Svc ■ *Web:* www.comair.com

Continental Airlines Inc 1600 Smith St .... Houston TX 77002 713-324-5000 324-5940*
**Fax:* Hum Res ■ *TF:* 800-525-0280
■ *Web:* www.continental.com

Continental Express PO Box 4607 Dept HQSCE .... Houston TX 77210 713-324-5000 324-4915
TF: 877-324-2639 ■ *Web:* www.continental.com/express

Corsair 5757 W Century Blvd Suite 650 .... Los Angeles CA 90045 310-670-7318 670-7707
TF: 800-677-0720 ■ *Web:* www.corsair-int.com

Czech Airlines
1350 Ave of the Americas Suite 601 .... New York NY 10019 212-765-6545 765-6588
TF: 800-223-2365 ■ *Web:* www.csa.cz

Delta Air Lines Inc
PO Box 20706 Hartsfield Atlanta
International Airport .... Atlanta GA 30320 404-715-2600 715-5494
TF: 800-221-1212 ■ *Web:* www.delta-air.com

Delta Connection 444 S River Rd .... Saint George UT 84790 435-634-3000 634-3305
TF: 800-453-9417

Eagle Scenic Aviation Group
2705 Airport Dr .... North Las Vegas NV 89032 702-739-1900 895-7824
TF: 800-634-6801 ■ *Web:* www.scenic.com

EgyptAir 720 5th Ave 11th Fl .... New York NY 10019 212-581-5600 586-6599
TF: 800-334-6787

El Al Israel Airlines Ltd 120 W 45th St 18th Fl .... New York NY 10036 212-852-0600 768-9440
TF: 800-223-6700 ■ *Web:* www.elal.com

Era Aviation Inc 6160 Carl Brady Dr .... Anchorage AK 99502 907-243-6633 266-8383
TF: 800-866-8394

Ethiopian Airlines 405 Lexington Ave Suite 520 .... New York NY 10174 212-867-0095 692-9589
TF: 800-445-2733

EVA Air 12440 E Imperial Hwy Suite 250 .... Norwalk CA 90650 562-565-6000 565-6120
TF: 800-695-1188
■ *Web:* www.evaair.com.tw/english/eindex.htm

Finnair 228 E 45th St .... New York NY 10017 212-499-9000 499-9037
TF: 800-950-5000 ■ *Web:* www.finnair.fi

Frontier Airlines Inc PO Box 39177 .... Denver CO 80239 303-371-7000
TF: 800-432-1359 ■ *Web:* www.frontierairlines.com

Garuda Indonesian Airways
9841 Airport Blvd Suite 300 .... Los Angeles CA 90045 310-348-9577 215-3517*
**Fax:* Acctg ■ *TF:* 800-342-7832

Great Lakes Aviation Ltd 1965 330th St .... Spencer IA 51301 712-262-1000 262-1001
TF: 800-241-6522 ■ *Web:* www.greatlakesav.com

Grupo Taca 8370 W Flagler St Suite 210A .... Miami FL 33144 305-871-1587 871-5066
TF: 800-327-9832 ■ *Web:* www.grupotaca.com

Gulf Air Co 3555 Timmons Ln Suite 1000 .... Houston TX 77027 713-621-2771 960-8687
TF: 888-359-4853 ■ *Web:* www.gulfairco.com

Gulfstream International Airlines
1815 Griffin Rd Suite 400 .... Dania Beach FL 33004 954-266-3000 266-3030
TF: 800-457-4853

6. AIRLINE COMPANIES

Company / Address	City	State	Zip	Phone	Fax
Hawaiian Airlines Inc 3375 Koapaka St Suite G350	Honolulu	HI	96819	808-835-3700	838-6746
TF: 800-367-5320 ■ *Web:* www.hawaiianair.com					
Horizon Air Industries Inc 19521 International Blvd	Seattle	WA	98188	206-241-6757	431-4696
TF: 800-547-9308 ■ *Web:* www.horizonair.com					
Iberia Airlines of Spain 6100 Blue Lagoon Dr Suite 200	Miami	FL	33126	305-267-7747	262-8763
TF: 800-772-4642 ■ *Web:* www.iberia.com					
Icelandair 5950 Symphony Woods Rd Suite 410	Columbia	MD	21044	410-715-1600	715-3547
TF: 800-223-5500 ■ *Web:* www.icelandair.is					
Island Express 750 SW 34th St	Fort Lauderdale	FL	33315	954-359-0383	359-7944
Japan Airlines 655 5th Ave 4th Fl	New York	NY	10022	212-838-4400	310-1430
TF: 800-525-3663 ■ *Web:* www.japanair.com					
Kenmore Air Harbor Inc 6321 NE 175th St	Kenmore	WA	98028	425-486-1257	485-4774
TF: 800-543-9595 ■ *Web:* www.kenmoreair.com					
KLM Royal Dutch Airlines 565 Taxter Rd	Elmsford	NY	10523	914-784-2000	784-2103
TF: 800-374-7747 ■ *Web:* www.klm.nl					
Korean Air 6101 W Imperial Hwy	Los Angeles	CA	90045	310-417-5200	417-3051
TF: 800-438-5000 ■ *Web:* www.koreanair.com					
Kuwait Airways 350 Park Ave 24th Fl	New York	NY	10022	212-659-4200	659-4291
TF: 800-458-9248					
LAB Flying Service Inc PO Box 272	Haines	AK	99827	907-766-2222	766-2734
TF: 800-426-0543 ■ *Web:* www.goworldnet.com/hailabf.htm					
LACSA 3600 Wilshire Blvd Suite 1100	Los Angeles	CA	90010	213-385-9424	385-5880
TF Sales: 800-225-2272*					
Laker Airways 6261 NW 6th Way Suite 201	Fort Lauderdale	FL	33309	954-202-0444	359-7698
TF: 888-525-3711 ■ *Web:* www.totallyflorida.com/flights/laker					
LanChile Airlines 9700 S Dixie Hwy 11th Fl	Miami	FL	33156	305-670-1961	670-9553
TF: 800-735-5526 ■ *Web:* www.lanchile.com					
LanPeru Airlines 9700 S Dixie Hwy 11th Fl	Miami	FL	33156	305-670-1961	670-9553
TF: 800-735-5526					
Lauda Air 701 Lincoln Rd Suite 106	Miami Beach	FL	33139	305-538-8701	538-5701
TF: 800-588-8399					
Lloyd Aéreo Boliviano 4000 W Flagler St	Miami	FL	33134	305-374-4600	476-7987
TF: 800-327-7407 ■ *Web:* www.labairlines.com					
LOT Polish Airlines 500 5th Ave Suite 408	New York	NY	10110	212-869-1074	302-0191
TF: 800-223-0593 ■ *Web:* www.lot.com					
LTU International Airways 100 N Biscayne Blvd Suite 500	Miami	FL	33132	305-530-2208	358-3770*
**Fax:* Sales ■ *TF:* 800-888-0200 ■ *Web:* www.ltu.com					
Lufthansa USA 1640 Hempstead Tpke	East Meadow	NY	11554	516-296-9200	296-9490
TF: 800-645-3880 ■ *Web:* www.lufthansa-usa.com					
Malaysia Airlines 100 N Sepulveda Blvd Suite 400	El Segundo	CA	90245	310-535-9288	535-9085
TF: 800-552-9264 ■ *Web:* www.malaysiaairlines.com					
Malev-Hungarian Airlines 630 5th Ave Suite 1900	New York	NY	10111	212-757-6480	459-0675
TF: 800-223-6884 ■ *Web:* www.malev.hu/ew/angol					
Martinair 5550 Glades Rd Suite 600	Boca Raton	FL	33431	561-391-6165	391-2188
TF: 800-627-8462 ■ *Web:* www.martinairusa.com					
Mesa Air Group Inc 410 N 44th St Suite 700	Phoenix	AZ	85008	602-685-4000	685-4350
TF: 800-637-2247 ■ *Web:* www.mesa-air.com					
Mesaba Airlines Inc 7501 26th Ave S	Minneapolis	MN	55450	612-726-5151	725-4901
TF: 800-225-2525 ■ *Web:* www.mesaba.com					
MetroJet 2345 Crystal Dr	Arlington	VA	22227	888-638-7653	
Web: www.flymetrojet.com					
Mexicana Airlines 6151 W Century Blvd Suite 1124	Los Angeles	CA	90045	310-646-0401	216-5714
TF: 800-531-7921 ■ *Web:* www.mexicana.com					
Midway Airlines 2801 Slater Rd Suite 200	Morrisville	NC	27560	919-595-6000	595-6482*
**Fax:* Mktg ■ *TF:* 800-446-4392 ■ *Web:* www.midwayair.com					
Midwest Express Airlines Inc 6744 S Howell Ave	Oak Creek	WI	53154	414-570-4000	570-0077
TF: 800-452-2022 ■ *Web:* www.midwestexpress.com					
National Airlines 6020 Spencer St	Las Vegas	NV	89119	702-944-2800	944-2855*
**Fax:* Hum Res ■ *TF:* 888-757-5387 ■ *Web:* www.nationalairlines.com					
New England Airlines Inc 56 Airport Rd	Westerly	RI	02891	401-596-2460	596-7366
TF: 800-243-2460 ■ *Web:* www.block-island.com/nea					
Northwest Airlines Inc 5101 Northwest Dr	Saint Paul	MN	55111	612-726-2111	726-3942
TF: 800-225-2525 ■ *Web:* www.nwa.com					
Olympic Airways 645 5th Ave	New York	NY	10022	212-735-0200	735-0215
TF: 800-223-1226 ■ *Web:* www.olympicair.com					
Pacific Wings PO Box 19	Paia	HI	96779	808-873-0877	873-9720
Pakistan International Airlines Corp 521 5th Ave 14th Fl	New York	NY	10175	212-370-9150	808-4695
TF: 800-221-2552 ■ *Web:* www.piac.com					
Peninsula Airways Inc 6100 Boeing Ave	Anchorage	AK	99502	907-243-2485	243-6848
TF: 800-448-4226					
Philippine Airlines Inc 447 Sutter St 2nd Fl	San Francisco	CA	94108	415-391-0270	433-6733
TF: 800-435-9725 ■ *Web:* www.philippineair.com					
Piedmont Airlines Inc 5443 Airport Terminal Rd	Salisbury	MD	21804	410-742-2996	742-3968
TF: 800-428-4322					
PSA Airlines Inc 3400 Terminal Dr	Vandalia	OH	45377	937-454-1116	454-5828
TF: 800-235-0986					
Qantas Airways Ltd 841 Apollo St Suite 400	El Segundo	CA	90245	310-726-1400	726-1401
TF: 800-227-4500 ■ *Web:* www.qantas.com					
Reeve Aleutian Airways Inc 4700 W International Airport Rd	Anchorage	AK	99502	907-243-1112	249-2276
TF: 800-544-2248 ■ *Web:* www.reeveair.com					
Reno Air Inc PO Box 30059	Reno	NV	89520	800-736-6247	829-5754
Web: www.renoair.com					
Royal Air Maroc 55 E 59th St Suite 17B	New York	NY	10022	212-750-5115	754-4215
TF: 800-344-6726 ■ *Web:* www.kingdomofmorocco.com					
Royal Jordanian Airlines 6 E 43rd St 27th Fl	New York	NY	10017	212-949-0060	949-0488
TF: 800-223-0470					
Sabena-Belgian World Airlines 1155 Northern Blvd	Manhasset	NY	11030	516-562-9200	562-9390
TF: 800-955-2000 ■ *Web:* www.sabena.com					
Saeta Airlines 242 NW Lajeune Rd 2nd Fl	Miami	FL	33126	305-442-4484	477-3945
TF: 800-827-2382					
Saudi Arabian Airlines 12555 N Burrough Dr	Houston	TX	77067	281-873-1000	873-1068
TF: 800-472-8342 ■ *Web:* www.saudiairlines.com					
Scandinavian Airlines System North America 9 Polito Ave	Lyndhurst	NJ	07071	201-896-3600	896-3725
TF: 800-221-2350 ■ *Web:* www.flysas.com					
Shuttle by United PO Box 66100	Chicago	IL	60666	800-748-8853	700-2214
Singapore Airlines Ltd 5670 Wilshire Blvd 18th Fl	Los Angeles	CA	90036	323-934-8833	934-4482
TF: 800-742-3333 ■ *Web:* www.singaporeair.com					
SkyWest Airlines 444 S River Rd	Saint George	UT	84790	435-634-3000	634-3305
TF: 800-453-9417 ■ *Web:* www.skywest.com					
South African Airways 515 E Las Olas Blvd	Fort Lauderdale	FL	33301	954-769-5000	769-5079
TF: 800-722-9675 ■ *Web:* www.saairways.com.au					
Southwest Airlines Co PO Box 36611	Dallas	TX	75235	214-792-4000	792-5015*
**Fax:* Hum Res ■ *TF:* 800-435-9792 ■ *Web:* www.southwest.com					
Spirit Airlines Inc 1400 Lee Wagener Blvd	Fort Lauderdale	FL	33315	954-447-7965	447-7979
TF: 800-772-7117 ■ *Web:* www.spiritair.com					
Surinam Airways Ltd 5775 Blue Lagoon Dr Suite 190	Miami	FL	33126	305-262-9922	261-0884
TF: 800-327-6864					
SwissAir Transport Co Ltd 41 Pinelawn Rd	Melville	NY	11747	631-844-4500	844-4565
TF: 800-221-4750 ■ *Web:* www.swissair.com					
TACA International Airlines 6824 Veterans Blvd Suite 100	Metairie	LA	70003	504-887-7671	888-3746
TF: 800-535-8780 ■ *Web:* www.grupotaca.com					
TAP Air Portugal 399 Market St	Newark	NJ	07105	973-344-4490	344-7344
TF: 800-221-7370 ■ *Web:* www.tap-airportugal.pt/en/					
TAROM Romanian Air Transport 342 Madison Ave 16th Fl	New York	NY	10173	212-687-6243	661-6056
Web: tarom.digiro.net					
Thai Airways International Ltd 720 Olive Way	Seattle	WA	98101	206-467-9898	467-8461*
**Fax:* Sales ■ *TF:* 800-426-5204 ■ *Web:* www.thaiair.com					
Tower Air Inc JFK International Airport Hangar 17	Jamaica	NY	11430	718-553-4300	553-4312
TF: 800-348-6937 ■ *Web:* www.towerair.com					
Trans World Airlines Inc 515 N 6th St 1 City Ctr	Saint Louis	MO	63101	314-589-3000	589-3129
TF: 800-221-2000 ■ *Web:* www.twa.com					
TransBrasil Airlines Inc 5757 Blue Lagoon Dr Suite 400	Miami	FL	33126	305-591-8322	262-9972
TF: 800-872-3153 ■ *Web:* www.transbrasil.com.br					
Turkish Airlines 437 Madison Ave	New York	NY	10022	212-339-9662	339-9680
TF: 800-874-8875 ■ *Web:* www.turkishairlines.com					
United Airlines Inc PO Box 66100	Chicago	IL	60666	847-700-4000	700-2214
TF: 800-241-6522 ■ *Web:* www.ual.com					
United Express 1200 E Algonquin Rd	Elk Grove Township	IL	60007	847-700-4000	
TF: 800-241-6522					
US Airways Express 2345 Crystal Dr Crystal Park	Arlington	VA	22227	703-872-7000	872-7410*
**Fax:* Hum Res ■ *TF:* 800-428-4322					
US Airways Inc 2345 Crystal Dr Crystal Pk 4	Arlington	VA	22227	703-872-7000	294-5097*
**Fax:* Acctg ■ *TF:* 800-428-4322 ■ *Web:* www.usairways.com					
US Airways Shuttle Inc PO Box 710616 La Guardia Airport	Flushing	NY	11371	718-397-6200	397-6040
Vanguard Airlines 7000 Squibb Rd 3rd Fl	Mission	KS	66202	913-789-1388	789-1779
TF: 800-826-4827 ■ *Web:* www.flyvanguard.com					
Varig Brazilian Airlines 380 Madison Ave 17th Fl	New York	NY	10017	212-850-8200	850-8201
TF: 800-468-2744 ■ *Web:* www.varig.com.br					
VASP Brazilian Airlines 4000 W Flagler St	Miami	FL	33134	305-442-1140	448-8840
TF: 800-732-8277 ■ *Web:* www.vasp.com.br/iindex.htm					
Virgin Atlantic Airways Ltd 747 Belden Ave	Norwalk	CT	06850	203-750-2000	750-6400
TF: 800-862-8621 ■ *Web:* www.fly.virgin.com					
Wings West Aviation Services 835 Airport Dr	San Luis Obispo	CA	93401	805-541-1010	541-1756
TF: 800-433-7300					
Yute Air Alaska Inc PO Box 190169	Anchorage	AK	99519	907-243-1011	243-2811

7. Car Rental Agencies

Company	City	State	Zip	Phone	Fax	Toll Free
Alamo Rent A Car Inc PO Box 22776 **Fax:* Cust Svc ■ *Web:* www.goalamo.com	Fort Lauderdale	FL	33335	954-522-0000	954-468-2108*	800-327-9633
Avis Rent A Car Inc 900 Old Country Rd *Web:* www.avis.com	Garden City	NY	11530	516-222-3000	516-222-4796	800-331-1084
Budget Rent A Car Corp 4225 Naperville Rd *Web:* www.budgetrentacar.com	Lisle	IL	60532	630-955-1900	630-955-7799	800-527-0700
Dollar Rent A Car Systems Inc 5330 E 31st St **Fax:* Sales ■ *Web:* www.dollarcar.com	Tulsa	OK	74135	918-669-3000	918-669-3007*	800-800-4000
Enterprise Rent-A-Car Co 600 Corporate Pk Dr *Web:* www.pickenterprise.com	Saint Louis	MO	63105	314-512-5000	314-512-4286	800-325-8007
Hertz Corp 225 Brae Blvd *Web:* www.hertz.com	Park Ridge	NJ	07656	201-307-2000	201-307-2644	800-654-3131
National Car Rental 7700 France Ave S **Fax:* Cust Svc ■ *Web:* www.nationalcar.com	Minneapolis	MN	55435	612-830-2121	612-830-2936*	800-627-7777
Payless Car Rental System Inc 2350 N 34th St N *Web:* www.paylesscar.com	Saint Petersburg	FL	33713	727-321-6352	727-323-3529	800-729-5377
Rent-A-Wreck of America Inc 11460 Cronridge Dr Suite 120 *Web:* www.rent-a-wreck.com	Owings Mills	MD	21117	410-581-5755	410-581-1566	800-535-1391
Thrifty Rent-A-Car System Inc 5310 E 31st St **Fax:* Hum Res ■ *Web:* www.thrifty.com	Tulsa	OK	74135	918-665-3930	918-669-2228*	800-367-2277
U-Save Auto Rental of America Inc 4780 I-55 Suite 300 *Web:* www.usaveautorental.com	Jackson	MS	39211	601-713-4333	601-713-4317	800-438-2300

8. Credit Card Companies

Company	City	State	Zip	Phone	Fax	Toll Free
American Express Co Inc 200 Vesey St 3 World Financial Ctr American Express Tower C **Fax:* Mail Rm ■ **TF:* Cust Svc ■ *Web:* www.americanexpress.com	New York	NY	10285	212-640-2000	212-619-9802*	800-528-4800*
Carte Blanche 183 Inverness Dr W **Fax:* Cust Svc	Englewood	CO	80112	303-799-9000	303-649-2891*	800-234-6377
Diners Club International 8430 W Bryn Mawr Ave *Web:* www.citibank.com/dinersus	Chicago	IL	60631	773-380-5100	773-380-5532	800-234-6377
Discover Financial Services Inc 2500 Lake Cook Rd **TF:* Cust Svc ■ *Web:* www.discovercard.com	Riverwoods	IL	60015	847-405-0900	847-405-2009	800-347-2683*
First Card Services 2500 Westfield Dr **Fax:* Hum Res ■ **TF:* Cust Svc ■ *Web:* www.firstcard.com	Elgin	IL	60123	847-888-6000	847-888-6578*	800-888-5640*
MasterCard International Inc 2000 Purchase St **Fax:* Hum Res ■ *Web:* www.mastercard.com	Purchase	NY	10577	914-249-2000	914-249-4135*	800-247-4623
Visa International PO Box 8999 **Fax:* Hum Res ■ *Web:* www.visa.com	San Francisco	CA	94128	650-432-3200	650-432-3273*	800-847-2911

9. Mileage Between Major United States Cities

	Atlanta	Baltimore	Boston	Charlotte	Chicago	Cleveland	Dallas	Denver	Detroit	Houston	Indianapolis	Jacksonville	Kansas City	Los Angeles	Memphis	Miami	Milwaukee	Minneapolis	New Orleans	New York	Philadelphia	Phoenix	Pittsburgh	Portland	Saint Louis	San Antonio	San Diego	San Francisco	Seattle	Washington DC
Atlanta		**654**	**1110**	**240**	**710**	**728**	**820**	**1430**	**732**	**790**	**527**	**313**	**822**	**2190**	**382**	**665**	**799**	**1121**	**480**	**855**	**748**	**1827**	**683**	**2664**	**565**	**995**	**2146**	**2485**	**2625**	**620**
Baltimore	577		**427**	**418**	**717**	**358**	**1357**	**1643**	**514**	**1404**	**569**	**751**	**1070**	**2647**	**911**	**1094**	**790**	**1113**	**1135**	**199**	**102**	**2312**	**245**	**2797**	**828**	**1632**	**2681**	**2823**	**2708**	**45**
Boston	945	360		**848**	**1005**	**657**	**1755**	**2000**	**799**	**1830**	**929**	**1162**	**1435**	**3015**	**1341**	**1520**	**1091**	**1390**	**1507**	**210**	**315**	**2670**	**574**	**3144**	**1207**	**2018**	**2984**	**3130**	**3016**	**450**
Charlotte	227	365	721		**737**	**516**	**1058**	**1580**	**630**	**1029**	**551**	**390**	**974**	**2412**	**630**	**740**	**827**	**1151**	**722**	**618**	**512**	**2034**	**495**	**2779**	**731**	**1239**	**2407**	**2721**	**2739**	**382**
Chicago	590	606	855	587		**348**	**920**	**1020**	**279**	**1090**	**185**	**1007**	**542**	**2050**	**537**	**1395**	**90**	**410**	**919**	**810**	**785**	**1742**	**476**	**2117**	**289**	**1209**	**2093**	**2173**	**2052**	**710**
Cleveland	554	308	551	435	308		**1189**	**1362**	**172**	**1306**	**318**	**909**	**819**	**2382**	**732**	**1252**	**435**	**758**	**1055**	**471**	**428**	**2032**	**129**	**2432**	**579**	**1453**	**2385**	**2483**	**2391**	**360**
Dallas	730	1212	1550	930	800	1025		**785**	**1156**	**245**	**892**	**1039**	**505**	**1400**	**454**	**1345**	**1015**	**949**	**517**	**1560**	**1443**	**1002**	**1208**	**2043**	**655**	**270**	**1348**	**1750**	**2131**	**1305**
Denver	1210	1510	1765	1358	900	1227	655		**1283**	**1035**	**1063**	**1743**	**606**	**1030**	**1043**	**2105**	**1038**	**920**	**1277**	**1795**	**1739**	**813**	**1427**	**1261**	**863**	**946**	**1095**	**1255**	**1341**	**1615**
Detroit	596	397	613	504	238	90	999	1156		**1276**	**284**	**1045**	**769**	**2288**	**719**	**1385**	**360**	**685**	**1070**	**649**	**609**	**2008**	**296**	**2384**	**534**	**1445**	**2368**	**2399**	**2327**	**516**
Houston	695	1251	1595	927	940	1114	215	865	1105		**995**	**887**	**743**	**1540**	**574**	**1190**	**1179**	**1183**	**352**	**1610**	**1511**	**1164**	**1365**	**2243**	**839**	**199**	**1490**	**1910**	**2369**	**1365**
Indianapolis	426	511	807	428	165	263	763	1000	240	865		**840**	**501**	**2063**	**474**	**1186**	**270**	**593**	**802**	**731**	**659**	**1725**	**364**	**2237**	**246**	**1191**	**2078**	**2289**	**2245**	**575**
Jacksonville	285	681	1017	341	863	770	908	1467	831	821	699		**1135**	**2353**	**694**	**348**	**1112**	**1456**	**557**	**951**	**845**	**2002**	**829**	**2961**	**882**	**1082**	**2355**	**2747**	**2972**	**715**
Kansas City	676	963	1251	803	414	700	451	558	645	644	453	950		**1577**	**482**	**1481**	**564**	**443**	**839**	**1233**	**1170**	**1235**	**870**	**1820**	**256**	**784**	**1588**	**1861**	**1858**	**1042**
Los Angeles	1935	2320	2595	2119	1745	2049	1240	850	1983	1375	1809	2147	1356		**1807**	**2715**	**2069**	**1857**	**1858**	**2795**	**2703**	**376**	**2430**	**962**	**1836**	**1387**	**124**	**385**	**1134**	**2645**
Memphis	337	793	1137	521	482	630	420	879	623	484	384	590	369	1603		**997**	**622**	**914**	**414**	**1102**	**1007**	**1465**	**759**	**2308**	**283**	**725**	**1805**	**2116**	**2317**	**854**
Miami	605	954	1255	652	1190	1087	1110	1715	1152	970	1024	326	1241	2340	872		**1458**	**1769**	**860**	**1334**	**1230**	**2348**	**1180**	**3257**	**1226**	**1385**	**2678**	**3093**	**3303**	**1055**
Milwaukee	668	642	857	658	81	335	857	914	252	1005	243	942	443	1744	556	1267		**337**	**1033**	**894**	**872**	**1771**	**564**	**2023**	**376**	**1287**	**2132**	**2172**	**1979**	**811**
Minneapolis	907	939	1123	939	355	630	862	700	543	1056	511	1191	413	1524	699	1511	299		**1346**	**1217**	**1195**	**1677**	**887**	**1724**	**630**	**1245**	**2001**	**1979**	**1653**	**1090**
New Orleans	424	999	1359	649	833	924	443	1082	939	318	712	504	680	1673	358	669	910	1051		**1335**	**1229**	**1496**	**1138**	**2536**	**698**	**547**	**1840**	**2278**	**2590**	**1099**
New York	760	172	190	533	740	405	1375	1640	482	1420	646	838	1097	2465	957	1090	733	1018	1171		**101**	**2445**	**379**	**2914**	**976**	**1820**	**2803**	**2930**	**2841**	**235**
Philadelphia	666	90	271	451	666	360	1299	1579	443	1341	585	758	1038	2394	881	1019	694	985	1089	83		**2374**	**308**	**2859**	**904**	**1737**	**2773**	**2902**	**2816**	**143**
Phoenix	1592	2005	2300	1783	1453	1749	887	586	1690	1017	1499	1794	1049	357	1263	1982	1464	1280	1316	2145	2083		**2087**	**1268**	**1481**	**1002**	**353**	**762**	**1465**	**2300**
Pittsburgh	521	197	483	362	410	115	1070	1320	205	1137	330	703	781	2136	660	1010	446	743	919	317	259	1828		**2549**	**609**	**1476**	**2440**	**2609**	**2521**	**259**
Portland	2172	2361	2540	2290	1758	2055	1633	982	1969	1836	1885	2439	1497	825	1849	2708	1719	1427	2063	2445	2412	1005	2165		**2057**	**2095**	**1086**	**637**	**174**	**2784**
Saint Louis	467	733	1038	568	262	492	547	796	455	679	231	751	238	1589	240	1061	327	466	598	875	811	1272	559	1723		**952**	**1833**	**2118**	**2135**	**862**
San Antonio	882	1418	1766	1105	1051	1256	252	802	1238	189	999	1011	702	1204	631	1148	1107	1110	507	1584	1507	849	1291	1720	792		**1297**	**1740**	**2180**	**1587**
San Diego	1891	2296	2584	2081	1734	2034	1184	834	1971	1304	1788	2092	1336	112	1561	2272	1738	1532	1609	2433	2373	299	2117	931	1564	1129		**514**	**1258**	**2602**
San Francisco	2135	2457	2699	2301	1860	2166	1470	955	2091	1645	1949	2374	1506	345	1802	2595	1842	1584	1926	2570	2523	653	2264	534	1744	1490	458		**810**	**2845**
Seattle	2182	2334	2493	2285	1737	2026	1681	1021	1938	1891	1872	2455	1506	959	1867	2734	1692	1395	2101	2408	2380	1114	2138	145	1724	1787	1063	678		**2721**
Washington DC	545	35	395	330	595	306	1185	1465	396	1220	494	647	945	2280	765	925	637	934	966	215	123	1983	192	2354	712	1388	2276	2435	2329	

Road mileage: bold
Air mileage: light

10. Convention Centers

Name / Address	City	State	ZIP	Phone	Fax
Abilene Civic Center 1100 N 6th St	Abilene	TX	79601	915-676-6211	676-6343
Aksarben Coliseum/Event Center 6800 Mercy Rd Suite 100 *TF:* 800-228-6001	Omaha	NE	68106	402-561-7000	561-7012
Alamodome 100 Montana St *TF:* 800-884-3663 ■ *Web:* www.alamodome.com	San Antonio	TX	78203	210-207-3663	207-3646
Albuquerque Convention Center PO Box 1293	Albuquerque	NM	87103	505-768-4575	768-3239
Allen County War Memorial Coliseum 4000 Parnell Ave *Web:* www.memorialcoliseum.com	Fort Wayne	IN	46805	219-482-9502	484-1637
Amarillo Civic Center 401 S Buchanan St *Web:* www.civicamarillo.com	Amarillo	TX	79101	806-378-4297	378-4234
AmericasMart 240 Peachtree St NW Suite 2200 *Web:* www.americasmart.com	Atlanta	GA	30303	404-220-2659	220-2650
Anaheim Convention Center 800 W Katella Ave	Anaheim	CA	92802	714-999-8950	999-8965
Arlington Convention Center 1200 Ballpark Way *Web:* www.ci.arlington.tx.us/aconvctr/	Arlington	TX	76011	817-459-5000	459-5091
Asheville Civic Center 87 Haywood St	Asheville	NC	28801	828-259-5736	259-5777
Atlanta Civic Center 395 Piedmont Ave NE	Atlanta	GA	30308	404-523-6275	525-4634
Atlantic City Convention Center 2001 Kirkman Blvd *Web:* www.atlanticcitynj.com/conventi/convnew.html	Atlantic City	NJ	08401	609-449-2000	449-2090
Auditorium at Equitable Center 787 7th Ave	New York	NY	10019	212-314-4004	314-4001
Augusta Civic Center Community Dr	Augusta	ME	04330	207-626-2405	626-5968
Augusta-Richmond County Civic Center 601 7th St *Web:* www.augustaciviccenter.com	Augusta	GA	30901	706-722-3521	724-7545
Austin Convention Center 500 E Cesar Chavez St *Web:* www.convention.ci.austin.tx.us	Austin	TX	78701	512-476-5461	404-4416
Bakersfield Convention Center 1001 Truxtun Ave *Web:* www.centennialgarden.com	Bakersfield	CA	93301	661-852-7300	861-9904
Baltimore Convention Center 1 W Pratt St *TF:* 800-207-1175	Baltimore	MD	21201	410-649-7000	649-7008
Bangor Civic Center 100 Dutton St *Web:* www.maineguide.com/bangor/basspark/	Bangor	ME	04401	207-942-9000	947-5105
Bayfront Center/Mahaffey Theater 400 1st St S *TF:* 800-874-9015	Saint Petersburg	FL	33701	727-892-5798	892-5858
Bayfront Plaza Convention Center 1901 N Shoreline Blvd	Corpus Christi	TX	78401	361-883-8543	883-0788
Bayside Expo Center 200 Mt Vernon St *Web:* www.baysideexpo.com	Boston	MA	02125	617-474-6000	265-8434
Benton Convention Center 301 W 5th St	Winston-Salem	NC	27102	336-727-2976	727-2879
Birmingham-Jefferson Civic Center 1 Civic Ctr Plaza **Fax:* Sales ■ *TF:* 800-535-7146 ■ *Web:* www.bjcc.org	Birmingham	AL	35203	205-458-8400	458-8437*
Bismarck Civic Center 601 E Sweet Ave	Bismarck	ND	58504	701-222-6487	222-6599
Blaisdell Neal S Center 777 Ward Ave	Honolulu	HI	96814	808-527-5400	527-5499
Bloomington Convention Center 302 S College Ave *Web:* www.kiva.net/~downtown	Bloomington	IN	47403	812-336-3681	349-2981
Blue Cross Arena at the War Memorial 1 War Memoriail Sq *Web:* www.bluecrossarena.com	Rochester	NY	14614	716-758-5300	758-5327
Boise Centre on the Grove 850 W Front St *Web:* www.boise.org/tour/bcg.html	Boise	ID	83702	208-336-8900	336-8803
Boutwell Municipal Auditorium 1930 8th Ave N	Birmingham	AL	35203	205-254-2820	254-2921
Brown County Expo Centre 1901 S Oneida St	Green Bay	WI	54304	920-494-3401	494-6868
Brown George R Convention Center 1001 Avenida de Las Americas *TF:* 800-427-4697	Houston	TX	77010	713-853-8001	853-8090
Buffalo Convention Center Convention Center Plaza *TF:* 800-995-7570	Buffalo	NY	14202	716-855-5555	855-3158
Burlington Memorial Auditorium 250 Main St	Burlington	VT	05401	802-864-6044	863-4322
Bushnell Memorial Hall 166 Capitol Ave	Hartford	CT	06106	860-987-6000	987-6070
Calgary Convention Centre 120 9th Ave SE	Calgary	AB	T2G0P3	403-261-8500	261-8510
CaliforniaMart 110 E 9th St Suite A727	Los Angeles	CA	90079	213-630-3631	630-3707
Carlson Center 2010 2nd Ave *Web:* www.carlson-center.com	Fairbanks	AK	99701	907-451-7800	451-1195
Carson City Community Center 851 E Williams St *Web:* www.carson-city.nv.us/recreation/ccrooms.htm	Carson City	NV	89701	775-887-2290	887-2256
Casper Events Center 1 Events Dr *TF:* 800-442-2256	Casper	WY	82601	307-235-8441	235-8445
Centennial Hall Convention Center 101 Egan Dr	Juneau	AK	99801	907-586-5283	586-1135
Century Center 120 S Saint Joseph St *Web:* centurycenter.org/	South Bend	IN	46601	219-235-9711	235-9185
Century II Convention & Cultural Center 225 W Douglas Ave	Wichita	KS	67202	316-264-9121	268-9268
Cervantes Convention Center at America's Center 701 Convention Plaza	Saint Louis	MO	63101	314-342-5036	342-5040
Charleston Civic Center & Coliseum 200 Civic Center Dr	Charleston	WV	25301	304-345-1500	357-7432
Charlotte Convention Center 501 S College St *TF:* 800-432-7488 ■ *Web:* www.charlotteconventionctr.com	Charlotte	NC	28202	704-339-6000	339-6111
Charlotte Merchandise Mart 2500 E Independence Blvd *Web:* www.charlottemerchmart.com	Charlotte	NC	28205	704-333-7709	375-9410
Chattanooga/Hamilton County Convention & Trade Center 1 Carter Plaza *TF:* 800-962-5213 ■ *Web:* www.chattconvention.org	Chattanooga	TN	37402	423-756-0001	267-5291
Cheyenne Civic Center 2101 O'Neil Ave	Cheyenne	WY	82001	307-637-6363	637-6365
Cincinnati Gardens 2250 Seymour Ave	Cincinnati	OH	45212	513-631-7793	631-2666
Civic Auditorium 615 1st Ave N	Grand Forks	ND	58203	701-746-2601	746-2532
Civic Center Complex 1 NW ML King Blvd **Fax:* Hum Res	Evansville	IN	47708	812-435-5000	425-1105*
Cleveland Convention Center 500 Lakeside Ave *TF:* 800-543-2489	Cleveland	OH	44114	216-348-2200	348-2262
Cobb Galleria Centre 2 Galleria Pkwy *Web:* www.cobbgalleria.com	Atlanta	GA	30339	770-955-8000	955-7719
Cobo Conference & Exhibition Center 1 Washington Blvd *Web:* www.cobocenter.com	Detroit	MI	48226	313-877-8777	877-8577
Coconut Grove Convention Center 2700 S Bayshore Dr	Miami	FL	33133	305-579-3310	579-3393
Colorado Convention Center 700 14th St *Web:* denverconvention.com	Denver	CO	80202	303-228-8000	228-8104
Colorado Springs City Auditorium 221 E Kiowa St	Colorado Springs	CO	80903	719-578-6652	635-7806
Columbia Expo Center 2200 I-70 Dr SW	Columbia	MO	65203	573-446-3976	446-1159
Columbus Civic Center 400 4th St *TF:* 800-711-3986 ■ *Web:* www.columbusga.com/civiccenter	Columbus	GA	31901	706-653-4472	653-4481
Columbus Ironworks Convention & Trade Center 801 Front Ave	Columbus	GA	31901	706-327-4522	327-0162
Commonwealth Convention Center 221 4th St *TF:* 800-701-5831	Louisville	KY	40202	502-595-4381	584-9711
Concourse Exhibition Center at Showplace Square 8th & Brannan Sts *TF:* 800-877-8522 ■ *Web:* www.sfdesigncenter.com	San Francisco	CA	94103	415-864-1500	490-5885
Constitution Hall 1776 D St NW	Washington	DC	20006	202-628-4780	628-2570
Cumberland County Civic Center 1 Civic Ctr Sq *Web:* www.theciviccenter.com	Portland	ME	04101	207-775-3481	828-8344
Dallas Convention Center 650 S Griffin St *TF:* 877-850-2100	Dallas	TX	75202	214-939-2700	939-2795
Dallas Market Center 2100 Stemmons Fwy Suite MS160 *Web:* www.dallasmarketcenter.com	Dallas	TX	75207	800-325-6587	655-6130
Dane County Exposition Center 1919 Expo Way	Madison	WI	53713	608-267-3976	267-0146
Dayton Convention Center 22 E 5th St *TF:* 800-822-3498	Dayton	OH	45402	937-333-4700	333-4711
Dubuque Five Flags Center 405 Main St	Dubuque	IA	52001	319-589-4254	589-4351
Duluth Entertainment Convention Center 350 Harbor Dr *TF:* 800-628-8385 ■ *Web:* www.decc.org	Duluth	MN	55802	218-722-5573	722-4247
East Ridge Convention Center 1417 N Mack Smith Rd	Chattanooga	TN	37412	423-899-6370	899-5849
Eastwood Expo Center PO Box 2186 2445 Belmont Ave	Youngstown	OH	44504	330-743-1654	743-2902
Eccles David Conference Center 2415 Washington Blvd *TF:* 800-237-2690 ■ *Web:* www.oecenter.com	Ogden	UT	84401	801-395-3200	395-3201
Egan William A Civic & Convention Center 555 W 5th Ave *Web:* www.egancenter.com	Anchorage	AK	99501	907-263-2800	263-2858
El Paso Convention & Performing Arts Center 1 Civic Center Plaza *TF:* 800-351-6024	El Paso	TX	79901	915-534-0600	534-0686
Empire State Plaza Convention Center Concourse Level Base of EGG *Web:* www.albany.org/arenas/empire3.html	Albany	NY	12242	518-474-4759	473-2190
Ernest N Morial Convention Center 900 Convention Center Blvd	New Orleans	LA	70130	504-582-3023	582-3088
Euro-Canadian Cultural Centre 3127 Bowwood Dr NW	Calgary	AB	T3B2E7	403-288-2255	286-8457
Exchange The Conference Center 212 Northern Ave Boston Fish Pier	Boston	MA	02210	617-790-1900	790-1910
Expo Center of Taylor County 1700 Hwy 36	Abilene	TX	79602	915-677-4376	677-0709
Expo Square PO Box 4735	Tulsa	OK	74159	918-744-1113	744-8725

Name / Address	City	State	ZIP	Phone	Fax
Exposition Gardens 1601 W Northmoor Rd	Peoria	IL	61614	309-691-6332	691-2372
Web: www.eventcenter.org					
Fair Park PO Box 159090	Dallas	TX	75315	214-670-8400	670-8907
Fargo Civic Memorial Auditorium & Centennial Hall 207 N 4th St	Fargo	ND	58102	701-241-1480	241-1483
Farm Show Complex 2301 N Cameron St	Harrisburg	PA	17110	717-787-5373	783-8710
Farnham Dudgeon Civic Center 405 Mero St	Frankfort	KY	40601	502-564-5335	564-3310
First Union Spectrum 3601 S Broad St	Philadelphia	PA	19148	215-336-3600	389-9506
Web: www.comcast-spectacor.com					
Five Seasons Center 370 1st Ave NE	Cedar Rapids	IA	52401	319-398-5211	362-2102
Web: www.5seasons.com					
FleetCenter 1 Fleet Ctr	Boston	MA	02114	617-624-1050	624-1818
Web: www.fleetcenter.com					
Fort Smith Civic Center 55 S 7th St	Fort Smith	AR	72901	501-785-2495	784-2366
Fort Worth/Tarrant County Convention Center 1111 Houston St	Fort Worth	TX	76102	817-884-2222	212-2756
Web: www.fortworth.com/fwtccc.htm					
Four Seasons Arena 400 3rd St NW	Great Falls	MT	59404	406-727-8900	452-8955
Web: www.city-of-great-falls.com/events/expopark/four_seasons.htm					
Franklin County Veterans Memorial 300 W Broad St	Columbus	OH	43215	614-221-4341	221-8422
Freedom Hall Civic Center Liberty Bell Blvd	Johnson City	TN	37604	423-461-4855	461-4867
Web: www.freedomhall-tn.com					
Fresno Convention Center 700 M St	Fresno	CA	93721	559-498-1511	488-4634
Web: www.ci.fresno.ca.us/convention					
Gaillard Municipal Auditorium 77 Calhoun St	Charleston	SC	29403	843-577-7400	724-7389
Georgia World Congress Center 285 International Blvd NW	Atlanta	GA	30313	404-223-4200	223-4211
Web: www.gwcc.com					
Giftcenter 888 Brannan St Suite 609	San Francisco	CA	94103	415-861-7733	431-2710
Glendale Civic Auditorium 1401 N Verdugo Rd	Glendale	CA	91208	818-548-2147	543-0793
Web: www.ci.glendale.ca.us/civicaud/index.html					
Golden Spike Arena Events Center 1000 N 1200 West	Ogden	UT	84404	801-399-8544	392-1995
TF: 800-442-7362					
Gonzalez Henry B Convention Center 200 E Market St	San Antonio	TX	78205	210-207-8500	223-1495
Web: www.ci.sat.tx.us/convfac/					
Graham Bill Civic Auditorium 99 Grove St	San Francisco	CA	94102	415-974-4000	974-4084
Grand Center 245 Monroe Ave NW	Grand Rapids	MI	49503	616-742-6600	742-6590
Web: www.grandcenter.com/grand.htm					
Grand Wayne Center 120 W Jefferson Blvd	Fort Wayne	IN	46802	219-426-4100	420-9080
Great Falls Convention Center & Theatre 2 Park Dr S	Great Falls	MT	59401	406-454-3915	454-3468
Greater Columbus Convention Center 400 N High St	Columbus	OH	43215	614-645-5000	221-7239
TF: 800-626-0241 ■ *Web:* www.columbusconventions.com					
Greater Fort Lauderdale/Broward County Convention Center 1950 Eisenhower Blvd	Fort Lauderdale	FL	33316	954-765-5900	763-9551
Web: www.co.broward.fl.us/convention-center.htm					
Greensboro Coliseum Complex 1921 W Lee St	Greensboro	NC	27403	336-373-7400	373-2170
Hartford Civic Center 1 Civic Center Plaza	Hartford	CT	06103	860-249-6333	241-4226
Web: www.hartfordciviccenter.com					
Hawaii Convention Center 1801 Kalakua Ave	Honolulu	HI	96815	808-943-3500	943-3599
Helena Civic Center 340 Neill Ave	Helena	MT	59601	406-447-8481	447-8480
Hot Springs Convention Auditorium 134 Convention Blvd PO Box K	Hot Springs	AR	71902	501-321-1705	321-2136
Hynes John B Veterans Memorial Convention Center 900 Boylston St	Boston	MA	02115	617-954-2000	954-2125
TF: 800-845-8800 ■ *Web:* www.mccahome.com					
IMA Sports & Convention Complex 3501 Lapeer Rd	Flint	MI	48503	810-744-0580	744-2906
Independence Arena/Ovens Auditorium 2700 E Independence Blvd	Charlotte	NC	28205	704-372-3600	335-3118
Indiana Convention Center & RCA Dome 100 S Capitol Ave	Indianapolis	IN	46225	317-262-3410	262-3685
Web: www.iccrd.com					
INFOMART 1950 Stemmons Fwy Suite 6038	Dallas	TX	75207	214-800-8000	800-8100
Web: www.infomartusa.com					
International Convention Center 4434 E 14th St	Brownsville	TX	78521	956-546-8878	
International Exposition Center 6200 Riverside Dr	Cleveland	OH	44135	216-265-7000	267-7876
Jacob Brown Civic Center 600 International Blvd	Brownsville	TX	78520	956-982-1820	982-1358
Javits Jacob K Convention Center 655 W 34th St	New York	NY	10001	212-216-2000	216-2588
Web: www.javitscenter.com					
Kaiser Henry J Convention Center 10 10th St	Oakland	CA	94607	510-238-7765	238-7767
Kansas City Convention Center 301 W 13th St	Kansas City	MO	64105	816-871-3700	871-3710
TF: 800-821-7060 ■ *Web:* www.kcconvention.com					
Kansas City Market Center 1775 Universal Ave Suite 1700	Kansas City	MO	64120	816-241-6200	483-4338
Kansas Expocentre 1 Expocentre Dr	Topeka	KS	66612	785-235-1986	235-2967
King Street Palace 1000 King St	Charleston	SC	29403	843-723-1075	538-6641
Knoxville Civic Auditorium/Coliseum 500 E Church Ave	Knoxville	TN	37915	865-544-5399	544-5386
Knoxville Convention Exhibition Center PO Box 2603	Knoxville	TN	37901	865-544-5371	544-5376
Lane County Fair & Convention Center 796 W 13th Ave	Eugene	OR	97402	541-682-4292	682-3614
Lansing Center 333 E Michigan Ave	Lansing	MI	48933	517-483-7400	483-7439
Las Vegas Convention Center 3150 Paradise Rd	Las Vegas	NV	89109	702-892-0711	892-2824*
**Fax:* Mktg ■ *TF:* 800-332-5333					
Lawrence David L Convention Center 1001 Penn Ave	Pittsburgh	PA	15222	412-565-6000	565-6008
TF: 800-222-5200 ■ *Web:* www.pgh-conventionctr.com					
Lawrence Joel Veterans Memorial Coliseum Complex 2825 University Pkwy	Winston-Salem	NC	27105	336-725-5635	727-2922
Web: www.ljvm.com					
Lexington Convention Center 430 W Vine St	Lexington	KY	40507	606-233-4567	253-2718
Long Beach Convention & Entertainment Center 300 E Ocean Blvd	Long Beach	CA	90802	562-436-3636	436-9491
Web: www.longbeachcc.com					
Los Angeles Convention & Exhibition Center 1201 S Figueroa St	Los Angeles	CA	90015	213-741-1151	765-4266
TF: 800-448-7775 ■ *Web:* www.lacclink.com					
Lubbock Memorial Civic Center 1501 6th St	Lubbock	TX	79401	806-775-2243	775-3240
Web: interoz.com/lubbock/cc.htm					
Macon City Auditorium 200 Coliseum Dr	Macon	GA	31217	912-751-9152	751-9154
Madison Civic Center 211 State St	Madison	WI	53703	608-266-6550	266-4864
Web: www.madcivic.org					
Manhattan Center Studios 311 W 34th St	New York	NY	10001	212-279-7740	465-2367
Mayo Civic Center 30 Civic Center Dr SE	Rochester	MN	55904	507-281-6184	281-6277
TF: 800-422-2199 ■ *Web:* www.ci.rochester.mn.us/mcc					
McCormick Place 2301 S Lake Shore Dr	Chicago	IL	60616	312-791-7000	791-6227*
**Fax:* Mktg ■ *Web:* www.mccormickplace.com					
Mellon Arena 66 Mario Lemieux Pl	Pittsburgh	PA	15219	412-642-1800	642-1925
Web: www.civicarena.com					
Memorial Coliseum PO Box 9277 402 S Shoreline Dr	Corpus Christi	TX	78469	361-884-8227	884-1440
Memphis Cook Convention Center 255 N Main St	Memphis	TN	38103	901-576-1200	576-1212
TF: 800-726-0915 ■ *Web:* www.memphisconvention.com					
Merchandise Mart The 470 Merchandise Mart	Chicago	IL	60654	312-527-7630	527-7998
Web: www.merchandisemart.com					
Mesa Community & Conference Center 201 N Center	Mesa	AZ	85201	480-644-2178	644-2617
MetraPark 308 6th Ave N	Billings	MT	59101	406-256-2400	256-2479
TF: 800-366-8538 ■ *Web:* www.metrapark.com					
Metro Hall 55 John St	Toronto	ON	M5V3C6	416-392-8000	
Web: www.metrotor.on.ca					
Metro Toronto Convention Centre 255 Front St W	Toronto	ON	M5V2W6	416-585-8000	585-8198*
**Fax:* Sales ■ *Web:* www.mtccc.com					
Metrolina Expo Center PO Box 26652 7100 Statesville Rd	Charlotte	NC	28221	704-596-4643	598-8786
Web: www.metrolinaexpo.com					
Miami Convention Center 400 SE 2nd Ave	Miami	FL	33131	305-579-6341	372-2919
Miami-Dade County Auditorium 2901 W Flagler St	Miami	FL	33135	305-547-5414	541-7782
Web: www.metro-dade.com/parks/dca.htm					
Midwest Express Center 400 W Wisconsin Ave	Milwaukee	WI	53203	414-908-6000	908-6010
Web: www.wcd.org/site/home/fac/mid_exp_cen/main.html					
Minneapolis Convention Center 1301 2nd Ave S	Minneapolis	MN	55403	612-335-6000	335-6757
Web: www.mplsconvctr.org					
Mississippi Trade Mart 1200 E Mississippi St	Jackson	MS	39205	601-354-7051	
Mobile Civic Center 401 Civic Center Dr	Mobile	AL	36602	334-434-7261	434-7551
Mobile Convention Center 1 S Water St	Mobile	AL	36602	334-415-2100	415-2150
TF: 800-566-2453					
Modesto Centre Plaza 10th & K St	Modesto	CA	95354	209-577-6444	544-6729
Web: www.centreplaza.com					
Monona Terrace Community & Convention Center 1 John Nolan Dr	Madison	WI	53703	608-261-4000	261-4049
Web: mononaterrace.visitmadison.com					
Monterey Conference Center 1 Portola Plaza	Monterey	CA	93940	831-646-3770	646-3777
TF: 800-742-8091 ■ *Web:* www.monterey.org/mcc/index.html					
Montgomery Civic Center PO Box 4037	Montgomery	AL	36101	334-241-2100	241-2117
Web: www.civic-center.ci.montgomery.al.us					
Montgomery County Memorial Hall 125 E First St	Dayton	OH	45402	937-225-5898	225-4922
Web: www.memorialhalldayton.com					
Morris Civic Auditorium 211 N Michigan St	South Bend	IN	46601	219-235-9198	235-5945
Moscone Center 747 Howard St	San Francisco	CA	94103	415-974-4000	974-4073

Phone *Fax*

Myriad Convention Center
1 Myriad Gardens .... Oklahoma City OK 73102 405-232-8871 297-1683
TF: 800-654-3676 ■ *Web:* www.myriadevents.com
Myrtle Beach Convention Center
2101 N Oak St .... Myrtle Beach SC 29577 843-918-1225 444-6408
TF: 800-537-1690 ■ *Web:* www.myrtlebeachconvcntr.com
Nashville Convention Center 601 Commerce St... Nashville TN 37203 615-742-2000 742-2014*
**Fax:* Mktg
Nashville Municipal Auditorium 417 4th Ave N... Nashville TN 37201 615-862-6390 862-6394
Web: www.nashville.org/ma
Navy Pier 600 E Grand Ave .... Chicago IL 60611 312-595-5000 595-5050
New Haven Veterans Memorial Coliseum
275 S Orange St .... New Haven CT 06510 203-772-4200 495-7745
Newport Marina & Event Center
4 Commercial Wharf .... Newport RI 02840 401-846-1600 847-7754
Nob Hill Masonic Center
1111 California St .... San Francisco CA 94108 415-776-4702 776-3945
Norfolk Scope Cultural & Convention Center
201 E Brambleton Ave .... Norfolk VA 23501 757-664-6464 664-6990
Web: www.norfolkscope.com
Northrop Memorial Auditorium
84 Church St SE .... Minneapolis MN 55455 612-625-6600 626-1750
Web: www.cee.umn.edu/northrop
Oakland Convention Center 550 10th St .... Oakland CA 94607 510-451-4000
TF: 800-262-5526
Ocean Center Arena 101 N Atlantic Ave ...... Daytona Beach FL 32118 904-254-4500 254-4512
TF: 800-858-6444 ■ *Web:* www.oceancenter.com
Ocean City Convention Center
4001 Coastal Hwy .... Ocean City MD 21842 410-289-8311 289-0058
TF: 800-626-2326 ■ *Web:* www.ocean-city.com/convention/
Ogden Eccles Conference Center
2415 Washington Blvd .... Ogden UT 84401 801-395-3200 395-3201
TF: 800-337-2690
Omaha Civic Auditorium PO Box 719 .... Omaha NE 68101 402-444-4750 444-4739
Oncenter Complex 800 S State St .... Syracuse NY 13202 315-435-8000 435-8112
Web: www.oncenter.org
Orange County Convention Center
9800 International Dr .... Orlando FL 32819 407-345-9800 345-9876*
**Fax:* Mktg ■ *Web:* www.orlandoconvention.com
Oregon Convention Center
777 NE ML King Jr Blvd .... Portland OR 97232 503-235-7575 235-7417
TF: 800-791-2250 ■ *Web:* www.oregoncc.org
Oregon State Fair & Expo Center
2330 17th St NE .... Salem OR 97303 503-378-3247 373-1788
Orlando Centroplex & Expo Center
500 W Livingston St .... Orlando FL 32801 407-849-2000 423-3482
Web: www.orlandocentroplex.com
Osborn Prime F Convention Center
1000 Water St .... Jacksonville FL 32204 904-630-4000 630-4029
Web: www.jaxevents.com/osborn.html
Ottawa Congress Centre 55 Colonel By Dr .... Ottawa ON K1N9J2 613-563-1984 563-7646
TF: 800-450-0077
Palm Springs Convention Center
277 N Avenida Caballeros .... Palm Springs CA 92262 760-325-6611 322-6921*
**Fax:* Sales ■ *TF:* 800-333-7535
■ *Web:* www.palmspringscc.com
Palmer Auditorium & City Coliseum 400 S 1st St.... Austin TX 78704 512-472-5111 320-4405
Web: www.austinconventioncenter.com
Palmetto Exposition Center PO Box 5823 .... Greenville SC 29606 864-233-2562 233-0619
Web: www.palmettoexpo.com
Pennsylvania Convention Center
1101 Arch St .... Philadelphia PA 19107 215-418-4700 418-4747
TF: 800-428-9000 ■ *Web:* www.paconvention.com
Pensacola Civic Center 201 E Gregory St .... Pensacola FL 32501 850-432-0800 432-1707
Web: www.pensacolaciviccenter.com
Peoria Civic Center 201 SW Jefferson St .... Peoria IL 61602 309-673-8900 673-9223
Web: www.peoriaciviccenter.com
Pershing Auditorium 226 Centennial Mall S .... Lincoln NE 68508 402-441-8744 441-7913
Web: www.pershingauditorium.com
Phoenix Civic Plaza Convention Center
225 E Adams St .... Phoenix AZ 85004 602-262-7272 495-3642
TF: 800-282-4842
Pikes Peak Center 190 S Cascade Ave .... Colorado Springs CO 80903 719-520-7453 520-7462
Web: www.pikespeakcenter.org
Plano Centre 2000 E Springcreek Pkwy .... Plano TX 75074 972-422-0296 424-0002
Web: www.planocentre.com
Polk County Convention Complex
501 Grand Ave .... Des Moines IA 50309 515-242-2500 242-2530
Portland Metropolitan Exposition Center
2060 N Marine Dr .... Portland OR 97217 503-736-5200 736-5201
Web: www.expocenter.org
Prairie Capital Convention Center
1 Convention Ctr Plaza .... Springfield IL 62701 217-788-8800 788-0811
Web: www.springfield-pccc.com
Providence Civic Center 1 LaSalle Sq .... Providence RI 02903 401-331-0700 751-6792
Web: www.provcc.com

Phone *Fax*

Pyramid The 1 Auction Ave .... Memphis TN 38105 901-521-9675 528-0153
Raleigh Convention & Conference Center
500 Fayetteville Street Mall .... Raleigh NC 27601 919-831-6011 831-6013
Reardon Civic Center 500 Minnesota Ave .... Kansas City KS 66101 913-371-1610 342-6160
Reno-Sparks Convention Center 4590 S Virginia St... Reno NV 89502 775-827-7600 827-7713
Rhode Island Convention Center 1 Sabin St ..... Providence RI 02903 401-458-6000 458-6500
Web: www.guidetori.com
Richmond Center 400 E Marshall St .... Richmond VA 23219 804-783-7300 225-0508
Richmond Coliseum 601 E Leigh St .... Richmond VA 23219 804-780-4970 780-4606
Web: www.richmondcoliseum.org
RiverCentre 175 W Kellogg Blvd .... Saint Paul MN 55102 651-265-4800 265-4899
Web: www.rivercentre.org
RiverCentre Convention Center 920 W Sioux Ave..... Pierre SD 57501 605-224-6877 224-1042
Web: www.rivercentre.org
Riverside Centroplex 275 S River Rd .... Baton Rouge LA 70802 225-389-3030 389-4954
Riverside Convention Center 3443 Orange St...... Riverside CA 92501 909-787-7950 222-4706
Riverside Municipal Auditorium
3485 Mission Inn Ave .... Riverside CA 92501 909-787-7678 682-8464
Roanoke Civic Center 710 Williamson Rd .... Roanoke VA 24016 540-981-1201 853-6583
Web: www.roanokeciviccenter.com/
Robinson Center Markham &
Broadway Sts 7 Statehouse Plaza .... Little Rock AR 72201 501-376-4781 374-2255
Web: www.littlerock.com/facilities/robinson.html
Robson Square Conference Centre
800 Robson St .... Vancouver BC V6Z2C5 604-660-2830 685-9407
Web: www.robsonsquare.com
Rochester Auditorium Center 875 E Main St....... Rochester NY 14605 716-271-3250 423-9539
Rochester Riverside Convention Center
123 E Main St .... Rochester NY 14604 716-232-7200 232-1510
Rose Quarter Facilities 1 Center Ct Suite 200 ...... Portland OR 97227 503-235-8771 234-4503
Rushmore Plaza Civic Center
444 Mount Rushmore Rd N .... Rapid City SD 57701 605-394-4115 394-4119
Web: www.gotmine.com
Sabin Albert B Cincinnati Convention Center
525 Elm St .... Cincinnati OH 45202 513-352-3750 352-6226
Web: www.cincycenter.com
Sacramento Convention Center 1400 J St .... Sacramento CA 95814 916-264-5291 264-7687
Web: www.sacto.org/cvsd/convctr/
Salt Palace Convention Center
100 S West Temple .... Salt Lake City UT 84101 801-534-4777 534-6383
Web: www.saltpalace.com
San Antonio Municipal Auditorium
100 Auditorium Cir .... San Antonio TX 78205 210-207-8511 207-4263
San Diego Concourse 202 C St .... San Diego CA 92101 619-615-4100 615-4115
San Diego Convention Center
111 W Harbor Dr .... San Diego CA 92101 619-525-5000 525-5005
Web: www.sandiegocc.org
San Francisco Civic Auditorium
99 Grove St .... San Francisco CA 94102 415-974-4000 974-4084
San Jose Convention & Cultural Facilities
408 S Almaden Blvd .... San Jose CA 95110 408-277-5277 277-3535
TF: 800-533-2345 ■ *Web:* www.sjcc.com
San Jose McEnery Convention Center
150 W San Carlos St .... San Jose CA 95113 408-277-3900 277-3535*
**Fax:* Mktg ■ *TF:* 800-533-2345 ■ *Web:* www.sjcc.com/sjmcc
Sands Expo & Convention Center
201 E Sands Ave .... Las Vegas NV 89109 702-733-5556 733-5353
Savannah Civic Center
Liberty & Montgomery Sts .... Savannah GA 31401 912-651-6550 651-6552
Scranton Cultural Center
420 N Washington Ave .... Scranton PA 18503 570-346-7369 346-7365
SeaGate Convention Centre 401 Jefferson Ave........ Toledo OH 43604 419-255-3300 255-7731
TF: 800-243-4667 ■ *Web:* www.toledo-seagate.com
Seattle Center 305 Harrison St .... Seattle WA 98109 206-684-7200 684-7342
Web: www.seattlecenter.com
Shaw Conference Centre 9797 Jasper Ave......... Edmonton AB T5J1N9 780-421-9797 425-5121
Shreveport Civic Center Complex
400 Clyde Fant Pkwy .... Shreveport LA 71101 318-673-5100 673-5105
Shrine Auditorium & Exposition Center
665 W Jefferson Blvd .... Los Angeles CA 90007 213-748-5116 742-9922
Sioux Falls Arena 1201 West Ave N .... Sioux Falls SD 57104 605-367-7288 338-1463
Soldiers & Sailors Memorial Auditorium
399 McCallie Ave .... Chattanooga TN 37402 423-757-5156 757-5326
Spokane Center W 334 Spokane Falls Blvd .... Spokane WA 99201 509-353-6500 353-6511
Web: www.spokane-areacvb.org/spokanecenter
Springfield Civic Center 1277 Main St .... Springfield MA 01103 413-787-6600 787-6645
TF: 800-639-8602 ■ *Web:* www.civic-center.com
Stambaugh Henry H Auditorium
1000 5th Ave .... Youngstown OH 44504 330-747-5175 747-1981
Statehouse Convention Center
Markham & Main Sts 1 Statehouse Plaza ..... Little Rock AR 72201 501-376-4781 376-7833
TF: 800-844-4781 ■ *Web:* www.littlerock.com/facilities/
statehouse_convention.html

10. CONVENTION CENTERS

Name / Address	City	State	Zip	Phone	Fax
Stockton Memorial Civic Auditorium 525 N Center St	Stockton	CA	95202	209-941-8223	941-8262
Sweeney Convention Center 201 W Marcy St *TF:* 800-777-2489 ■ *Web:* www.santafe.org/destination/sweeney.html	Santa Fe	NM	87501	505-984-6760	984-6679
Tacoma Convention Center 1320 Broadway Plaza	Tacoma	WA	98402	253-572-3200	591-4105
Tacoma Dome Arena & Exhibition Hall 2727 E D St **Fax:* Mktg ■ *Web:* www.ci.tacoma.wa.us/tdome	Tacoma	WA	98421	253-272-3663	593-7620*
Tallahassee-Leon County Civic Center 505 W Pensacola St *TF:* 800-322-3602 ■ *Web:* www.tlccc.org	Tallahassee	FL	32301	850-487-1691	222-6947
Tampa Convention Center 333 S Franklin St *TF:* 800-426-5630	Tampa	FL	33602	813-274-8511	274-7430
Topeka Civic Theatre 3028 SW 8th Ave *Web:* www.topekacivictheatre.com	Topeka	KS	66606	785-357-5211	357-0719
Township The 1703 Taylor St	Columbia	SC	29201	803-252-2032	779-2208
Travis County Exposition Center 7311 Decker Ln	Austin	TX	78724	512-473-9200	928-9953
Tucson Convention Center 260 S Church St	Tucson	AZ	85701	520-791-4101	791-5572
Tullio Louis J Convention Center 809 French St *Web:* www.erieciviccenter.com/arena.htm	Erie	PA	16501	814-452-4857	455-9931
Tulsa Convention Center 100 Civic Ctr *TF:* 800-678-7177 ■ *Web:* www.tulsaconvention.com	Tulsa	OK	74103	918-596-7177	596-7155
Tupperware Convention Center 14901 S Orange Blossom Trail	Orlando	FL	32837	407-826-4475	847-1813
Turnbull Conference Center FSU Ctr for Professional Development *Web:* www.cpd.fsu.edu/facilities/index.htm	Tallahassee	FL	32306	850-644-3801	644-2589
Union Station 2501 Wall Ave	Ogden	UT	84401	801-629-8444	629-8555
University Plaza Trade Center 625 Saint Louis St	Springfield	MO	65806	417-864-7744	831-5893
Vancouver Trade & Convention Centre 999 Canada Pl *Web:* www.vtcc.com	Vancouver	BC	V6C3C1	604-641-1987	641-1436
Vanderburgh Auditorium Convention Center 715 Locust St	Evansville	IN	47708	812-435-5770	435-5610
Veterans Memorial Auditorium 833 5th Ave	Des Moines	IA	50309	515-323-5400	323-5401
Veterans Memorial Auditorium 83 Park St	Providence	RI	02903	401-222-1467	222-1466
Veterans Memorial Coliseum 1145 E Adams St *Web:* www.jaxevents.com/veterans.html	Jacksonville	FL	32202	904-630-3905	630-3913
Veterans Memorial Coliseum 50 2nd Ave Bridge	Cedar Rapids	IA	52401	319-286-5038	286-5130
Villita Assembly Building 401 Villita St	San Antonio	TX	78205	210-978-2795	978-4634
Von Braun Civic Center 700 Monroe St *Web:* www.vbcc.com	Huntsville	AL	35801	256-533-1953	551-2203
War Memorial Auditorium 800 NE 8th St	Fort Lauderdale	FL	33304	954-761-5380	761-5361
Washington Convention Center 900 9th St NW **Fax:* Mktg ■ *TF:* 800-368-9000 ■ *Web:* www.dcconvention.com	Washington	DC	20001	202-789-1600	789-8365*
Washington State Convention & Trade Center 800 Convention Pl *Web:* www.wsctc.com	Seattle	WA	98101	206-694-5000	694-5399
Wheeling Civic Center 2 14th St *Web:* www.wheelingciviccenter.com	Wheeling	WV	26003	304-233-7000	233-7001
Whiting Auditorium 1241 E Kearsley St *TF:* 888-823-6837	Flint	MI	48503	810-237-7337	237-7335
Wilson Edgar H Convention Centre 200 Coliseum Dr *Web:* www.maconcentreplex.com	Macon	GA	31217	912-751-9152	751-9154
Winnipeg Convention Centre 375 York Ave *Web:* www.wpgconvctr.mb.ca	Winnipeg	MB	R3C3J3	204-956-1720	943-0310
Worcester's Centrum Centre 50 Foster St *Web:* www.centrumcentre.com	Worcester	MA	01608	508-755-6800	929-0111

11. Convention and Visitor Information

Name / Address	City	State	Zip	Phone	Fax
Abilene Convention & Visitors Bureau 1101 N 1st St *TF:* 800-727-7704 ■ *Web:* www.abilene.com/visitors	Abilene	TX	79601	915-676-2556	676-1630
Akron/Summit County Convention & Visitors Bureau 77 E Mill St *TF:* 800-245-4254 ■ *Web:* www.visitakron-summit.org	Akron	OH	44308	330-374-7560	374-7626
Alabama Convention & Visitor Development PO Box 79 *TF:* 800-240-9452 ■ *Web:* www.montgomery.al.us	Montgomery	AL	36109	334-261-1100	261-1111
Albany County Convention & Visitors Bureau 25 Quackenbush Sq *TF:* 800-258-3582 ■ *Web:* www.albany.org	Albany	NY	12207	518-434-1217	434-0887
Albuquerque Convention & Visitors Bureau 20 First Plaza Suite 601 *TF:* 800-284-2282 ■ *Web:* www.abqcvb.org	Albuquerque	NM	87102	505-842-9918	247-9101
Alexandria Convention & Visitors Bureau 221 King St *TF:* 800-388-9119 ■ *Web:* www.funside.com	Alexandria	VA	22314	703-838-4200	838-4683
Amarillo Convention & Visitor Council PO Box 9480 *TF:* 800-692-1338 ■ *Web:* www.amarillo-cvb.org	Amarillo	TX	79105	806-374-1497	373-3909
Anaheim/Orange County Visitor & Convention Bureau 800 W Katella Ave *Web:* www.anaheimoc.org	Anaheim	CA	92802	714-999-8999	991-8963
Anchorage Convention & Visitors Bureau 524 W 4th Ave *TF:* 800-446-5352 ■ *Web:* www.anchorage.net	Anchorage	AK	99501	907-276-4118	278-5559
Ann Arbor Area Convention & Visitors Bureau 120 W Huron St *TF:* 800-888-9487 ■ *Web:* www.annarbor.org	Ann Arbor	MI	48104	734-995-7281	995-7283
Annapolis & Anne Arundel County Conference & Visitors Bureau 26 West St *Web:* visit-annapolis.org	Annapolis	MD	21401	410-268-8687	263-9591
Arlington Convention & Visitors Bureau 1905 E Randol Mill Rd Suite 650 *TF:* 800-433-5374 ■ *Web:* www.acvb.org	Arlington	TX	76011	817-265-7721	265-5640
Arlington Convention & Visitors Service 2100 Clarendon Blvd *Web:* www.co.arlington.va.us/acvs	Arlington	VA	22201	703-228-3988	228-3667
Asheville Area Convention & Visitors Bureau PO Box 1010 *TF:* 800-257-1300 ■ *Web:* www.ashevillechamber.org/cvb_top.htm	Asheville	NC	28802	828-258-6102	254-6054
Atlanta Convention & Visitors Bureau 233 Peachtree St NE Suite 100 **Fax:* Sales ■ *TF:* 800-285-2682 ■ *Web:* www.acvb.com/	Atlanta	GA	30303	404-521-6600	577-3293*
Atlantic City Convention & Visitors Authority 2314 Pacific Ave *TF:* 800-262-7395 ■ *Web:* www.atlanticcitynj.com	Atlantic City	NJ	08401	609-449-7130	345-2200
Augusta Metropolitan Convention & Visitors Bureau 1450 Greene St Suite 110 *TF:* 800-726-0243 ■ *Web:* www.augustaga.org	Augusta	GA	30901	706-823-6600	823-6609
Austin Convention & Visitors Bureau 201 E 2nd St *TF:* 800-926-2282 ■ *Web:* www.austin360.com/acvb	Austin	TX	78701	512-474-5171	404-4383
Baltimore Area Convention & Visitors Assn 100 Light St 12th Fl *TF:* 800-343-3468 ■ *Web:* www.baltconvstr.com	Baltimore	MD	21202	410-659-7300	727-2308
Bangor Convention & Visitors Bureau 519 Main St *TF:* 800-916-6673 ■ *Web:* www.bangorcvb.org	Bangor	ME	04401	207-947-5205	990-1427
Baton Rouge Area Convention & Visitors Commission 730 North Blvd *TF:* 800-527-6843 ■ *Web:* www.bracvb.com	Baton Rouge	LA	70802	225-383-1825	346-1253
Billings Convention & Visitors Bureau PO Box 31177 *TF:* 800-735-2635	Billings	MT	59107	406-245-4111	245-7333
Bismarck-Mandan Convention & Visitors Bureau PO Box 2274 *TF:* 800-767-3555 ■ *Web:* www.bismarck-mandancvb.org	Bismarck	ND	58502	701-222-4308	222-0647
Bloomington/Monroe County Convention & Visitors Bureau 2855 N Walnut St *TF:* 800-800-0037 ■ *Web:* www.visitbloomington.com	Bloomington	IN	47404	812-334-8900	334-2344
Boise Convention & Visitors Bureau 168 N 9th St Suite 200 *TF:* 800-635-5240 ■ *Web:* www.boise.org/bcvb/index.html	Boise	ID	83702	208-344-7777	344-6236
Boulder Convention & Visitors Bureau 2440 Pearl St *TF:* 800-444-0447 ■ *Web:* visitor.boulder.net/	Boulder	CO	80302	303-442-2911	938-8837
Branson/Lakes Area Convention & Visitors Bureau PO Box 1897 *TF:* 800-214-3661 ■ *Web:* www.bransoncvb.com	Branson	MO	65615	417-334-4080	334-4139

Organization	Address	City	State	ZIP	Phone	Fax	Notes
Brownsville Convention & Visitors Bureau	PO Box 4697	Brownsville	TX	78523	956-546-3721	546-3972	*TF:* 800-626-2639 ■ *Web:* www.brownsville.org
Burlington Convention & Visitors Bureau	60 Main St Suite 100	Burlington	VT	05401	802-863-3489	863-1538	*Web:* www.vermont.org
Calgary Convention & Visitors Bureau	237 8th Ave SE Suite 200	Calgary	AB	T2G0K8	403-263-8510	262-3809	*TF:* 800-661-1678 ■ *Web:* www.visitor.calgary.ab.ca
Carson City Convention & Visitors Bureau	1900 S Carson St Suite 200	Carson City	NV	89701	775-687-7410	687-7416	*TF:* 800-638-2321 ■ *Web:* www.carson-city.org
Casper Area Convention & Visitors Bureau	PO Box 399	Casper	WY	82602	307-234-5362	265-2643	*TF:* 800-852-1889 ■ *Web:* www.trib.com/ADS/CASPER/
Cedar Rapids Area Convention & Visitors Bureau	PO Box 5339	Cedar Rapids	IA	52406	319-398-5009	398-5089	*TF:* 800-735-5557 ■ *Web:* www.fyiowa.com/iowa/cvb/
Central Illinois Tourism Development Office	700 E Adams St	Springfield	IL	62701	217-525-7980	525-8004	
Champaign-Urbana Convention & Visitors Bureau	1817 S Neil St Suite 201	Champaign	IL	61820	217-351-4133	351-0906	*TF:* 800-369-6151 ■ *Web:* www.cupartnership.org/cvb
Charleston Area Convention & Visitors Bureau	PO Box 975	Charleston	SC	29402	843-853-8000	853-0444	*TF:* 800-868-8118 ■ *Web:* www.charlestoncvb.com
Charleston Convention & Visitors Bureau	200 Civic Center Dr	Charleston	WV	25301	304-344-5075	344-1241	*TF:* 800-733-5469 ■ *Web:* www.charlestonwv.com
Charlotte Convention & Visitors Bureau	122 E Stonewall St	Charlotte	NC	28202	704-334-2282	342-3972	*TF:* 800-722-1994 ■ *Web:* charlottecvb.org
Chattanooga Area Convention & Visitors Bureau	2 Broad St	Chattanooga	TN	37402	423-756-8687	265-1630	*TF:* 800-322-3344 ■ *Web:* www.chattanooga.net/cvb
Chesapeake Public Communications Dept	306 Cedar Rd	Chesapeake	VA	23322	757-382-6241	382-8530	*Web:* www.chesapeake.va.us
Cheyenne Area Convention & Visitors Bureau	309 W Lincolnway	Cheyenne	WY	82003	307-778-3133	778-3190	*TF:* 800-426-5009 ■ *Web:* www.cheyenne.org
Chicago Convention & Tourism Bureau	2301 S Lake Shore Dr	Chicago	IL	60616	312-567-8500	567-8533	*Web:* www.chicago.il.org
Chicago Office of Tourism	78 E Washington St	Chicago	IL	60602	312-744-2400	744-2359	*Web:* www.ci.chi.il.us/Tourism
Cobb County Convention & Visitors Bureau	1 Galleria Pkwy	Atlanta	GA	30339	678-303-2622	303-2625	*TF:* 800-451-3480 ■ *Web:* www.cobbcvb.com
Colorado Springs Convention & Visitors Bureau	104 S Cascade Ave Suite 104	Colorado Springs	CO	80903	719-635-7506	635-4968	*TF:* 800-368-4748 ■ *Web:* www.coloradosprings-travel.com
Columbia Convention & Visitors Bureau	300 S Providence Rd	Columbia	MO	65203	573-875-1231	443-3986	*Web:* www.ammultimedia.com/visitcolumbiamo.com/
Columbia Metropolitan Convention & Visitors Bureau	PO Box 15	Columbia	SC	29202	803-254-0479	799-6529	*TF:* 800-264-4884 ■ *Web:* www.columbiasc.net
Columbus Convention & Visitors Bureau	1000 Bay Ave	Columbus	GA	31901	706-322-1613	322-0701	*TF:* 800-999-1613
Convention & Visitors Assn of Lane County Oregon	PO Box 10286	Eugene	OR	97440	541-484-5307	343-6335	*TF:* 800-547-5445 ■ *Web:* www.cvalco.org
Convention & Visitors Bureau of Greater Cleveland	50 Public Sq Tower City Ctr Suite 3100	Cleveland	OH	44113	216-621-4110	621-5967	*TF:* 800-321-1001 ■ *Web:* www.travelcleveland.com/
Convention & Visitors Bureau of Greater Kansas City	1100 Main St Suite 2550	Kansas City	MO	64105	816-221-5242	691-3805	*TF:* 800-767-7700 ■ *Web:* www.visitkc.com
Convention & Visitors Bureau of Greater Portland	305 Commercial St	Portland	ME	04101	207-772-5800	874-9043	*Web:* www.visitportland.com
Corpus Christi Convention & Visitors Bureau	1201 N Shoreline Blvd	Corpus Christi	TX	78401	361-881-1888	887-9023	*TF:* 800-766-2322 ■ *Web:* www.corpuschristi-tx-cvb.org
Dallas Convention & Visitors Bureau	1201 Elm St Suite 2000	Dallas	TX	75270	214-571-1000	571-1008	*TF:* 800-232-5527 ■ *Web:* www.dallascvb.com
Dayton/Montgomery County Convention & Visitors Bureau	1 Chamber Plaza Suite A	Dayton	OH	45402	937-226-8248	226-8294	*TF:* 800-221-8235 ■ *Web:* www.daytoncvb.com
Daytona Beach Area Convention & Visitors Bureau	126 E Orange Ave	Daytona Beach	FL	32114	904-255-0415	255-5478	*TF:* 800-544-0415 ■ *Web:* www.daytonabeach.com
Denver Metro Convention & Visitors Bureau	1555 California St Suite 300	Denver	CO	80202	303-892-1112	892-1636	*TF:* 800-645-3446 ■ *Web:* www.denver.org
Dubuque Convention & Visitors Bureau	770 Town Clock Plaza	Dubuque	IA	52001	319-557-9200	557-1591	*TF:* 800-798-4748 ■ *Web:* www.dubuque.org
Duluth Convention & Visitors Bureau	100 Lake Place Dr	Duluth	MN	55802	218-722-4011	722-1322	*TF:* 800-438-5884 ■ *Web:* www.visitduluth.com
Durham Convention & Visitors Bureau	101 E Morgan St	Durham	NC	27701	919-687-0288	683-9555	*TF:* 800-446-8604 ■ *Web:* dcvb.durham.nc.us/
Edmonton Tourism	9797 Jasper Ave NW	Edmonton	AB	T5J1N9	780-496-8400	496-8413	*TF:* 800-463-4667 ■ *Web:* www.tourism.ede.org
El Paso Convention & Visitors Bureau	1 Civic Center Plaza	El Paso	TX	79901	915-534-0696	534-0687	*TF:* 800-351-6024 ■ *Web:* www.elpasocvb.com
Erie Area Convention & Visitors Bureau	101 Boston Store Pl	Erie	PA	16501	814-454-7191	459-0241	*Web:* www.erie.net/~chamber/tourist.html
Evansville Convention & Visitors Bureau	401 SE Riverside Dr	Evansville	IN	47713	812-425-5402	421-2207	*TF:* 800-433-3025 ■ *Web:* www.evansvillecvb.org/
Fairbanks Convention & Visitors Bureau	550 1st Ave	Fairbanks	AK	99701	907-456-5774	452-2867	*TF:* 800-327-5774 ■ *Web:* fairbanks.polarnet.com
Fargo-Moorhead Convention & Visitors Bureau	2001 44th St SW	Fargo	ND	58103	701-282-3653	282-4366	*TF:* 800-235-7654 ■ *Web:* www.fargomoorhead.org
Flagstaff Convention & Visitors Bureau	211 W Aspen Ave	Flagstaff	AZ	86001	520-779-7611	556-1305	*TF:* 800-217-2367 ■ *Web:* www.flagstaff.az.us/convention.html
Flint Area Convention & Visitors Bureau	519 S Saginaw St	Flint	MI	48502	810-232-8900	232-1515	*TF Sales:* 800-253-5468* ■ *Web:* flint.org
Fort Collins Convention & Visitors Bureau	429 S Howes St Suite 101	Fort Collins	CO	80521	970-482-5821	493-8061	*TF:* 800-274-3678 ■ *Web:* www.ftcollins.com
Fort Smith Convention & Visitors Bureau	2 N 'B' St	Fort Smith	AR	72901	501-783-8888	784-2421	*TF:* 800-637-1477 ■ *Web:* www.fortsmith.org
Fort Wayne/Allen County Convention & Visitors Bureau	1021 S Calhoun St	Fort Wayne	IN	46802	219-424-3700	424-3914	*TF:* 800-767-7752 ■ *Web:* www.fwcvb.org
Fort Worth Convention & Visitors Bureau	415 Throckmorton St	Fort Worth	TX	76102	817-336-8791	336-3282	*TF:* 800-433-5747 ■ *Web:* www.fortworth.com
Frankfort/Franklin County Tourist & Convention Commission	100 Capital Ave	Frankfort	KY	40601	502-875-8687	227-2604	*TF:* 800-960-7200 ■ *Web:* www.frankfortky.org
Fresno Convention & Visitors Bureau	808 M St	Fresno	CA	93721	559-233-0836	445-0122	*TF:* 800-788-0836 ■ *Web:* www.fresnocvb.org
Garden Grove Visitors Bureau	12866 Main St Suite 102	Garden Grove	CA	92840	714-638-7950	636-6672	
Garland Convention & Visitors Bureau	200 N 4th St	Garland	TX	75046	972-205-2749	205-2504	
Gettysburg Convention & Visitors Bureau	35 Carlisle St	Gettysburg	PA	17325	717-334-6274	334-1166	*Web:* www.gettysburg.com
Grand Rapids/Kent County Convention & Visitors Bureau	140 Monroe Ctr Suite 300	Grand Rapids	MI	49503	616-459-8287	459-7291	*TF:* 800-678-9859 ■ *Web:* www.grcvb.org
Greater Bakersfield Convention & Visitors Bureau	1033 Truxtun Ave	Bakersfield	CA	93301	661-325-5051	325-7074	*TF:* 800-325-6001 ■ *Web:* www.visitbfield.com
Greater Birmingham Convention & Visitors Bureau	2200 9th Ave N	Birmingham	AL	35203	205-458-8000	458-8086	*TF:* 800-458-8085 ■ *Web:* www.bcvb.org
Greater Boston Convention & Visitors Bureau	2 Copley Pl Suite 105	Boston	MA	02116	617-536-4100	424-7664	*TF:* 888-433-2673 ■ *Web:* www.bostonusa.com
Greater Buffalo Convention & Visitors Bureau	617 Main St Suite 400	Buffalo	NY	14203	716-852-0511	852-0131	*TF:* 800-283-3256 ■ *Web:* www.buffalocvb.org
Greater Cincinnati Convention & Visitors Bureau	300 W 6th St	Cincinnati	OH	45202	513-621-2142	621-5020	*TF:* 800-246-2987 ■ *Web:* www.cincyusa.com
Greater Columbus Convention & Visitors Bureau	90 N High St	Columbus	OH	43215	614-221-6623	221-5618	*TF:* 800-354-2657 ■ *Web:* www.columbuscvb.org
Greater Des Moines Convention & Visitors Bureau	601 Locust St Suite 222	Des Moines	IA	50309	515-286-4960	244-9757	*TF:* 800-451-2625 ■ *Web:* www.desmoinesia.com

Phone Fax

Greater Fort Lauderdale Convention & Visitors Bureau 1850 Eller Dr Suite 303... Fort Lauderdale FL 33316 954-765-4466 765-4467
TF: 800-356-1662 ■ *Web:* www.co.broward.fl.us/sunny.htm

Greater Grand Forks Convention & Visitors Bureau 4251 Gateway Dr .... Grand Forks ND 58203 701-746-0444 746-0775
TF: 800-866-4566 ■ *Web:* www.grandforkscvb.org/

Greater Greenville Convention & Visitors Bureau 206 S Main St .... Greenville SC 29601 864-421-0000 421-0005
TF: 800-717-0023 ■ *Web:* www.greatergreenville.com

Greater Hartford Convention & Visitors Bureau
1 Civic Center Plaza .... Hartford CT 06103 860-728-6789 293-2365
TF: 800-446-7811 ■ *Web:* www.grhartfordcvb.com

Greater Houston Convention & Visitors Bureau
901 Bagby St.. Houston TX 77002 713-437-5200 227-6336
TF: 800-446-8786 ■ *Web:* www.houston-guide.com/

Greater Lansing Convention & Visitors Bureau
1223 Turner St .... Lansing MI 48906 517-487-6800 487-5151
TF: 800-648-6630 ■ *Web:* www.lansing.org

Greater Madison Convention & Visitors Bureau
615 E Washington Ave .... Madison WI 53703 608-255-2537 258-4950
TF: 800-373-6376 ■ *Web:* www.visitmadison.com

Greater Miami Convention & Visitors Bureau
701 Brickell Ave Suite 2700.................................. Miami FL 33131 305-539-3000 539-3113
TF: 800-933-8448 ■ *Web:* www.miamiandbeaches.com

Greater Milwaukee Convention & Visitors Bureau 510 W Kilbourn Ave .... Milwaukee WI 53203 414-273-3950 273-5596
TF: 800-231-0903 ■ *Web:* www.milwaukee.org

Greater Minneapolis Convention & Visitors Assn 33 S 6th St Multifoods Tower Suite 4000.. Minneapolis MN 55402 612-661-4700 335-5839
TF: 800-445-7412 ■ *Web:* www.minneapolis.org

Greater Morgantown Convention & Visitors Bureau 709 Beechurst Ave .... Morgantown WV 26505 304-292-5081 291-1354
TF: 800-458-7373 ■ *Web:* www.mgtn.com

Greater New Haven Convention & Visitors Bureau 59 Elm St .... New Haven CT 06510 203-777-8550 782-7755
TF: 800-332-7829 ■ *Web:* www.newhavencvb.org/

Greater Omaha Convention & Visitors Bureau
6800 Mercy Rd Suite 202 .... Omaha NE 68106 402-444-4660 444-4511
TF: 800-332-1819 ■ *Web:* www.visitomaha.com

Greater Oxnard & Harbors Tourism Bureau
200 W 7th St .... Oxnard CA 93030 805-385-7545 385-7571
TF: 800-269-6273 ■ *Web:* www.oxnardtourism.com

Greater Phoenix Convention & Visitors Bureau
400 E Van Buren St 1 Arizona Ctr Suite 600.......... Phoenix AZ 85004 602-254-6500 253-4415
TF: 877-266-5749 ■ *Web:* www.arizonaguide.com/phxcvb

Greater Pittsburgh Convention & Visitors Bureau 425 6th Ave 30th Fl .... Pittsburgh PA 15219 412-281-7711 644-5512
TF: 800-359-0758 ■ *Web:* www.pittsburgh-cvb.org

Greater Raleigh Convention & Visitors Bureau
421 Fayetteville St Mall Suite 1505....................... Raleigh NC 27601 919-834-5900 831-2887
TF: 800-849-8499 ■ *Web:* www.raleighcvb.org

Greater Rochester Visitors Assn
126 Andrews St...Rochester NY 14604 716-546-3070 232-4822
TF: 800-677-7282 ■ *Web:* www.visitrochester.com

Greater Springfield Convention & Visitors Bureau 1441 Main St .... Springfield MA 01103 413-787-1548 781-4607
TF: 800-723-1548 ■ *Web:* www.valleyvisitor.com

Greater Toledo Convention & Visitors Bureau
401 Jefferson Ave.. Toledo OH 43604 419-321-6404 255-7731
TF: 800-243-4667 ■ *Web:* www.toledocvb.com/

Greater Vancouver Convention & Visitors Bureau 200 Burrard St Suite 210 .... Vancouver BC V6C3L6 604-683-2000 682-6839
TF: 800-663-6000 ■ *Web:* www.tourism-vancouver.org

Greater Vancouver Convention & Visitors Bureau 200 Burrard St Suite 210 .... Vancouver BC V6C3L6 604-683-2000 682-6839
TF: 800-663-6000 ■ *Web:* www.tourism-vancouver.org

Greater Wilmington Convention & Visitors Bureau 100 W 10th St Suite 20 .... Wilmington DE 19801 302-652-4088 652-4726
Web: www.wilmcvb.org/

Green Bay Area Visitor & Convention Bureau
PO Box 10596 .... Green Bay WI 54307 920-494-9507 494-9229
TF: 800-236-3976 ■ *Web:* www.greenbaywi.com

Greensboro Area Convention & Visitors Bureau 317 S Greene St .... Greensboro NC 27401 336-274-2282 230-1183
TF: 800-344-2282 ■ *Web:* www.greensboronc.org

Harrisburg-Hershey-Carlisle Tourism & Convention Bureau 25 N Front St.................... Harrisburg PA 17101 717-231-7788 231-7790
TF: 800-995-0969 ■ *Web:* www.visithhc.com/

Hawaii Visitors & Convention Bureau
2270 Kalakaua Ave Suite 801 .... Honolulu HI 96815 808-923-1811 924-0290
TF: 800-464-2924 ■ *Web:* www.visit.hawaii.org

Hilton Head Island Visitors & Convention Bureau PO Box 5647......... Hilton Head Island SC 29938 843-785-3673 785-7110
TF: 800-523-3373 ■ *Web:* www.hiltonheadisland.org

Phone Fax

Hot Springs Convention & Visitors Bureau
PO Box K .... Hot Springs AR 71902 501-321-2277 321-2136
TF: 800-772-2489 ■ *Web:* www.hotsprings.org

Huntington Beach Conference & Visitors Bureau 101 Main St Suite 2A .. Huntington Beach CA 92648 714-969-3492 969-5592
Web: www.hbvisit.com/

Huntsville/Madison County Convention & Visitor's Bureau 700 Monroe St...................... Huntsville AL 35801 256-551-2230 551-2324
TF: 800-772-2348 ■ *Web:* www.huntsville.org

Indianapolis Convention & Visitors Assn
200 S Capitol Ave 1 RCA Dome Suite 100 ..... Indianapolis IN 46225 317-639-4282 639-5273
TF: 800-323-4639 ■ *Web:* www.indy.org

Irving Convention & Visitors Bureau
3333 N MacArthur Blvd Suite 200 .... Irving TX 75062 972-252-7476 257-3153
TF: 800-247-8464 ■ *Web:* www.irvingtexas.com

Jacksonville Convention & Visitors Bureau
201 E Adams St... Jacksonville FL 32202 904-798-9111 798-9103
TF: 800-733-2668 ■ *Web:* www.jaxcvb.com

Jefferson City Convention & Visitors Bureau
213 Adams St.. Jefferson City MO 65102 573-634-3616 634-3805
TF: 800-769-4183 ■ *Web:* www.jcchamber.org/cvb

Johnson City Convention & Visitors Bureau
603 E Market St... Johnson City TN 37601 423-461-8000 926-7360
TF: 800-852-3392

Juneau Convention & Visitors Bureau
369 S Franklin St Suite 203 .... Juneau AK 99801 907-586-1737 586-1449
TF: 888-581-2201 ■ *Web:* www.traveljuneau.com/

Kansas City Kansas/Wyandotte County Convention & Visitors Bureau 727 Minnesota Ave.. Kansas City KS 66117 913-321-5800 371-3732
TF: 800-264-1563

Kent County/Dover Convention & Visitors Bureau
9 E Loockerman St Suite 203 .... Dover DE 19901 302-734-1736 734-0167
TF: 800-233-5368 ■ *Web:* www.visitdover.com

Key West Visitors Center 402 Wall St.................... Key West FL 33040 305-294-2587 294-7806
TF: 800-648-6269 ■ *Web:* www.fla-keys.com/keywest/index.htm

Knoxville Convention & Visitors Bureau
601 W Summit Hill Dr Suite 200B...................... Knoxville TN 37902 865-523-7263 673-4400
TF: 800-727-8045 ■ *Web:* www.knoxville.org

Lafayette Convention & Visitors Commission
PO Box 52066 .... Lafayette LA 70505 337-232-3737 232-0161
TF: 800-346-1958 ■ *Web:* www.lafayettetravel.com

Las Cruces Convention & Visitors Bureau
211 N Water St.. Las Cruces NM 88001 505-541-2444 541-2164
TF: 800-343-7827 ■ *Web:* www.lascrucescvb.org

Las Vegas Convention & Visitors Authority
3150 Paradise Rd.. Las Vegas NV 89109 702-892-0711 892-2824
TF: 800-332-5333 ■ *Web:* www.lasvegas24hours.com

Lexington Convention & Visitors Bureau
301 E Vine St... Lexington KY 40507 606-233-7299 254-4555
TF: 800-845-3959 ■ *Web:* www.visitlex.com/

Lincoln Convention & Visitors Bureau
1135 M St Suite 200... Lincoln NE 68508 402-434-5335 436-2360
TF: 800-423-8212 ■ *Web:* www.lincoln.org/cvb/

Little Rock Convention & Visitors Bureau
PO Box 3232 .... Little Rock AR 72203 501-376-4781 374-2255
TF: 800-844-4781 ■ *Web:* www.littlerock.com/lrcvb/

Long Beach Convention & Visitors Bureau
1 World Trade Ctr Suite 300 .... Long Beach CA 90831 562-436-3645 435-5653
TF: 800-452-7829 ■ *Web:* www.golongbeach.org

Los Angeles Convention & Visitors Bureau
633 W 5th St Suite 6000.................................. Los Angeles CA 90071 213-624-7300 624-9746
TF: 800-228-2452 ■ *Web:* www.lacvb.com

Louisville & Jefferson County Convention & Visitors Bureau 400 S 1st St.............................. Louisville KY 40202 502-582-3732 584-6697
TF: 800-792-5595 ■ *Web:* www.louisville-visitors.com

Lubbock Convention & Tourism Bureau
PO Box 561 .... Lubbock TX 79408 806-747-5232 747-1419
TF: 800-692-4035 ■ *Web:* www.lubbocklegends.com/

Macon-Bibb County Convention/Visitors Bureau
PO Box 6354 .... Macon GA 31208 912-743-3401 745-2022
TF: 800-768-3401 ■ *Web:* www.maconga.org

Maine Tourism Assn State House Stn 59.............Augusta ME 04333 207-287-5711 287-8070
TF: 888-624-6345 ■ *Web:* www.visitmaine.com

Memphis Convention & Visitors Bureau
47 Union Ave... Memphis TN 38103 901-543-5300 543-5350
TF: 800-873-6282 ■ *Web:* www.memphistravel.com

Mesa Convention & Visitors Bureau 120 N Center St... Mesa AZ 85201 480-827-4700 827-0727
TF: 800-283-6372 ■ *Web:* www.arizonaguide.com/mesa

Metro Jackson Convention & Visitors Bureau
921 N President St .... Jackson MS 39202 601-960-1891 960-1827
TF: 800-354-7695 ■ *Web:* www.visitjackson.com

Metropolitan Detroit Convention & Visitors Bureau
211 W Fort St Suite 1000 .... Detroit MI 48226 313-202-1800 202-1808
TF: 800-225-5389 ■ *Web:* www.visitdetroit.com

Name / Address	City	State	ZIP	Phone	Fax
Metropolitan Richmond Convention & Visitors Bureau 550 E Marshall St *TF:* 800-370-9004	Richmond	VA	23219	804-782-2777	780-2577
Metropolitan Toronto Convention & Visitors Assn 207 Queen's Quay W *TF:* 800-363-1990 ■ *Web:* www.tourism-toronto.com	Toronto	ON	M5J1A7	416-203-2600	203-6753
Metropolitan Tucson Convention & Visitors Bureau 130 S Scott Ave *TF:* 800-638-8350 ■ *Web:* www.arizonaguide.com/visittucson/	Tucson	AZ	85701	520-624-1817	884-7804
Missoula Convention & Visitors Bureau PO Box 7577 *TF:* 800-526-3465 ■ *Web:* www.missoulachamber.com	Missoula	MT	59807	406-543-6623	543-6625
Mobile Convention & Visitors Corp 1 S Water St *TF:* 800-566-2453 ■ *Web:* www.mobile.org	Mobile	AL	36602	334-208-2000	208-2060
Mobile Dept of Tourism 1 S Water St	Mobile	AL	33602	334-415-2003	415-2426
Modesto Convention & Visitors Bureau 1114 J St *TF:* 800-266-4282 ■ *Web:* www.modestocvb.org/	Modesto	CA	95353	209-571-6480	571-6486
Monroe County Tourist Development Council 1201 White St Suite 102 *TF:* 800-352-5397 ■ *Web:* www.fla-keys.com	Key West	FL	33040	305-296-1552	296-0788
Monterey Peninsula Visitors & Convention Bureau PO Box 1770 *Web:* www.monterey.com	Monterey	CA	93942	831-649-1770	648-5373
Montgomery Area Chamber of Commerce Convention & Visitor Development PO Box 79 *TF:* 800-240-9452 ■ *Web:* www.montgomerychamber.org	Montgomery	AL	36101	334-261-1100	261-1111
Myrtle Beach Area Convention Bureau 1200 N Oak St *TF:* 800-488-8998 ■ *Web:* www.myrtlebeach-info.com	Myrtle Beach	SC	29577	843-626-7444	448-3010
Nashville Convention & Visitors Bureau 161 4th Ave N *TF:* 800-657-6910 ■ *Web:* www.nashvillecvb.com	Nashville	TN	37219	615-259-4730	244-6278
New Hampshire Office of Travel & Tourism PO Box 1856 *TF:* 800-386-4664 ■ *Web:* www.visitnh.gov	Concord	NH	03302	603-271-2343	271-6784
New Orleans Metropolitan Convention & Visitors Bureau 1520 Sugar Bowl Dr *TF:* 800-672-6124 ■ *Web:* www.neworleanscvb.com	New Orleans	LA	70112	504-566-5011	566-5046
New York Convention & Visitors Bureau 810 7th Ave 3rd Fl *TF:* 800-692-8474 ■ *Web:* www.nycvisit.com	New York	NY	10019	212-484-1200	484-1222
Newport County Convention & Visitors Bureau 23 America's Cup Ave *TF:* 800-326-6030 ■ *Web:* www.gonewport.com	Newport	RI	02840	401-849-8048	849-0291
Newport News Tourism Development Office 2400 Washington Ave 7th Fl *TF:* 888-493-7386 ■ *Web:* www.newport-news.org	Newport News	VA	23607	757-926-3561	926-6901
Norfolk Convention & Visitors Bureau 232 E Main St *TF:* 800-368-3097 ■ *Web:* www.vgnet.com	Norfolk	VA	23510	757-664-6620	622-3663
Ocean City Convention & Visitors Bureau 4001 Coastal Hwy *TF:* 800-626-2326 ■ *Web:* www.ocean-city.com	Ocean City	MD	21842	410-289-8181	723-8655
Ogden/Weber Convention & Visitors Bureau 2501 Wall Ave Union Stn *TF:* 800-255-8824 ■ *Web:* www.ogdencvb.org/	Ogden	UT	84401	801-627-8288	399-0783
Oklahoma City Convention & Visitors Bureau 189 W Sheridan St *TF:* 800-225-5652 ■ *Web:* www.okccvb.org	Oklahoma City	OK	73102	405-297-8910	297-8888
Orlando/Orange County Convention & Visitors Bureau 6700 Forum Dr Suite 100 *TF:* 800-643-9492 ■ *Web:* www.go2orlando.com	Orlando	FL	32821	407-363-5871	370-5022
Ottawa Tourism & Convention Authority 130 Albert St Suite 1800 *TF:* 800-363-4465 ■ *Web:* www.tourottawa.org	Ottawa	ON	K1P5G4	613-237-5150	237-7339
Palm Beach County Convention & Visitors Bureau 1555 Palm Beach Lakes Blvd Suite 204 *Web:* www.palmbeachfl.com	West Palm Beach	FL	33401	561-471-3995	471-3990
Pennsylvania's Northeast Territory Convention & Visitors Bureau 300 Penn Ave *TF:* 800-229-3526 ■ *Web:* www.visitnepa.org	Scranton	PA	18503	570-963-6363	963-6852
Pensacola Convention & Visitors Bureau 1401 E Gregory St *TF:* 800-874-1234 ■ *Web:* www.visitpensacola.com	Pensacola	FL	32501	850-434-1234	432-8211
Peoria Area Convention & Visitors Bureau 403 NE Jefferson St *TF:* 800-747-0302 ■ *Web:* www.peoria.org	Peoria	IL	61603	309-676-0303	676-8470
Philadelphia Convention & Visitors Bureau 1515 Market St Suite 2020 *TF:* 800-537-7676 ■ *Web:* www.libertynet.org/phila-visitor	Philadelphia	PA	19102	215-636-3300	636-3327
Pierre Convention & Visitors Bureau PO Box 548 *TF:* 800-962-2034 ■ *Web:* www.pierre.org/cvb.htm	Pierre	SD	57501	605-224-7361	224-6485
Plano Convention & Visitors Bureau 2000 E Spring Creek Pkwy *TF:* 800-817-5266 ■ *Web:* www.planocvb.com	Plano	TX	75074	972-422-0296	424-0002
Portland Oregon Visitors Assn 26 SW Salmon St 3 World Trade Ctr *TF:* 800-962-3700 ■ *Web:* www.pova.com	Portland	OR	97204	503-275-9750	275-9774
Providence Warwick Convention & Visitors Bureau 1 W Exchange St *TF:* 800-233-1636 ■ *Web:* www.providencecvb.com/	Providence	RI	02903	401-274-1636	351-2090
Puerto Rico Convention Bureau 1730 Rhode Island Ave NW Suite 601 *TF:* 800-875-4765 ■ *Web:* www.meetpuertorico.com	Washington	DC	20036	202-457-9262	331-0824
Rapid City Convention & Visitors Bureau PO Box 747 *TF:* 800-487-3223 ■ *Web:* www.rapidcitycvb.com/	Rapid City	SD	57709	605-343-1744	348-9217
Rehoboth Beach Convention Center 229 Rehoboth Ave	Rehoboth Beach	DE	19971	302-227-4641	227-4643
Reno-Sparks Convention & Visitors Authority 4590 S Virginia St *TF:* 800-443-1482 ■ *Web:* www.playreno.com	Reno	NV	89502	775-827-7600	827-7686
Riverside Convention & Visitors Bureau 3737 6th St *Web:* www.riversidecb.com	Riverside	CA	92501	909-222-4700	222-4712
Riverside Visitors Center 3660 Mission Inn *Web:* www.riverside-chamber.com/visi.htm	Riverside	CA	92501	909-684-4636	321-3581
Roanoke Valley Convention & Visitors Bureau 114 Market St *TF:* 800-635-5535 ■ *Web:* www.visitroanokeva.com/	Roanoke	VA	24011	540-342-6025	342-7119
Rochester Convention & Visitors Bureau 150 S Broadway Suite A *TF:* 800-634-8277 ■ *Web:* www.rochestercvb.org	Rochester	MN	55904	507-288-4331	288-9144
Rockford Area Convention & Visitors Bureau 211 N Main St *TF:* 800-521-0849 ■ *Web:* www.gorockford.com	Rockford	IL	61101	815-963-8111	963-4298
Sacramento Convention & Visitors Bureau 1303 J St Suite 600 *TF:* 800-272-2334 ■ *Web:* www.sacramentocvb.org	Sacramento	CA	95814	916-264-7777	264-7788
Saint Johns County Convention & Visitors Bureau 88 Riberia St Suite 400 *TF:* 800-653-2489 ■ *Web:* www.oldcity.com/vcb	Saint Augustine	FL	32084	904-829-1711	829-6149
Saint Louis Convention & Visitors Commission 1 Metropolitan Sq Suite 1100 *TF:* 800-325-7962 ■ *Web:* www.st-louis-cvc.com	Saint Louis	MO	63102	314-421-1023	421-0039
Saint Paul Convention & Visitors Bureau 175 W Kellogg Blvd RiverCentre Suite 502 *TF:* 800-627-6101 ■ *Web:* www.stpaulcvb.org	Saint Paul	MN	55102	651-265-4900	265-4999
Salem Convention & Visitors Assn 1313 Mill St SE *TF:* 800-874-7012 ■ *Web:* www.scva.org	Salem	OR	97301	503-581-4325	581-4540
Salt Lake Convention & Visitors Bureau 90 S West Temple *TF:* 800-541-4955 ■ *Web:* www.visitsaltlake.com	Salt Lake City	UT	84101	801-521-2822	534-4927
San Antonio Convention & Visitors Bureau PO Box 2277 *TF:* 800-447-3372 ■ *Web:* www.sanantoniocvb.com/	San Antonio	TX	78298	210-207-6700	207-6782
San Bernardino Convention & Visitors Bureau 201 N 'E' St Suite 103 *TF:* 800-867-8366 ■ *Web:* san-bernardino.org	San Bernardino	CA	92401	909-889-3980	888-5998
San Diego Convention & Visitors Bureau 401 B St Suite 1400 *Web:* www.sandiego.org	San Diego	CA	92101	619-232-3101	696-9371
San Francisco Convention & Visitors Bureau 201 3rd St Suite 900 *Web:* www.sfvisitor.org	San Francisco	CA	94103	415-974-6900	227-2602
San Jose Convention & Visitors Bureau 333 W San Carlos St Suite 1000 *TF:* 800-726-5673	San Jose	CA	95110	408-295-9600	295-3937
Santa Fe Convention & Visitors Bureau PO Box 909 *TF:* 800-777-2489 ■ *Web:* www.santafe.org	Santa Fe	NM	87504	505-984-6760	984-6679
Savannah Area Convention & Visitors Bureau PO Box 1628 *TF:* 800-444-2427 ■ *Web:* www.savcvb.com	Savannah	GA	31402	912-644-6401	944-0468
Scottsdale Convention & Visitor's Bureau 7343 Scottsdale Mall *TF:* 800-877-1117 ■ *Web:* www.arizonaguide.com/cities/scottsdale/index.html	Scottsdale	AZ	85251	480-945-8481	947-4523
Seattle-King County Convention & Visitors Bureau 520 Pike St Suite 1300 *TF:* 800-535-7071 ■ *Web:* www.seeseattle.org/home/skccvb.htm	Seattle	WA	98101	206-461-5840	461-5855
Shreveport-Bossier Convention & Tourist Bureau PO Box 1761 *TF:* 800-551-8682 ■ *Web:* www.shreveport-bossier.org/	Shreveport	LA	71166	318-222-9391	222-0056
Sioux Falls Convention & Visitors Bureau 200 N Phillips Ave Suite 102 *TF:* 800-333-2072 ■ *Web:* www.siouxfalls.org/	Sioux Falls	SD	57104	605-336-1620	336-6499

11. CONVENTION AND VISITOR INFORMATION

				Phone	Fax
South Bend/Mishawaka Convention & Visitors Bureau PO Box 1677	South Bend	IN	46634	219-234-0051	289-0358
TF: 800-828-7881 ■ *Web:* www.cdiguide.com/IN/219/b_com/southben.html					
Spokane Convention & Visitors Bureau 801 W Riverside Ave Suite 301	Spokane	WA	99201	509-624-1341	623-1297
TF: 800-248-3230 ■ *Web:* www.spokane-areacvb.org					
Springfield Convention & Visitors Bureau 109 N 7th St	Springfield	IL	62701	217-789-2360	544-8711
TF: 800-545-7300 ■ *Web:* www.springfield.il.us/visit/					
Springfield Missouri Convention & Visitors Bureau 3315 E Battlefield Rd	Springfield	MO	65804	417-881-5300	881-2231
TF: 800-678-8767 ■ *Web:* www.springfieldmo.org					
Stockton/San Joaquin Convention & Visitors Bureau 46 W Fremont St	Stockton	CA	95202	209-943-1987	943-6235
TF: 800-350-1987 ■ *Web:* www.ssjcvb.org					
Syracuse Convention & Visitors Bureau 572 S Salina St	Syracuse	NY	13202	315-470-1910	471-8545
TF: 800-234-4797 ■ *Web:* www.syracusecvb.org					
Tacoma-Pierce County Visitor & Convention Bureau 1001 Pacific Ave Suite 400	Tacoma	WA	98402	253-627-2836	627-8783
TF: 800-272-2662 ■ *Web:* www.tpctourism.org					
Tallahassee Area Convention & Visitors Bureau 106 E Jefferson St	Tallahassee	FL	32301	850-413-9200	487-4621
TF: 800-628-2866 ■ *Web:* www.co.leon.fl.us/visitors/index.htm					
Tampa/Hillsborough Convention & Visitors Assn 400 N Tampa St Suite 1010	Tampa	FL	33602	813-223-1111	229-6616
TF: 800-826-8358 ■ *Web:* www.thcva.com					
Tempe Convention & Visitors Bureau 51 W 3rd St Suite 105	Tempe	AZ	85281	480-894-8158	968-8004
TF: 800-283-6734 ■ *Web:* www.arizonaguide.com/cities/tempe/index.html					
Topeka Convention & Visitors Bureau 1275 SW Topeka Blvd	Topeka	KS	66612	785-234-1030	234-8282
TF: 800-235-1030 ■ *Web:* www.topekacvb.org/					
Tourism Winnipeg 279 Portage Ave	Winnipeg	MB	R3B2B4	204-943-1970	942-4043
TF: 800-665-0204 ■ *Web:* www.tourism.winnipeg.mb.ca					
Travel Industry Assn of Kansas 700 SW Jackson St Suite 702	Topeka	KS	66603	785-233-9465	357-6629
Web: www.tiak.org					
Trenton Convention & Visitors Bureau Lafayette & Barrack Sts	Trenton	NJ	08608	609-777-1770	292-3771
Web: www.trentonnj.com					
Tulsa Convention & Visitors Bureau 616 S Boston Ave Suite 100	Tulsa	OK	74119	918-585-1201	592-6244
TF: 800-558-3311 ■ *Web:* www.tulsachamber.com/cvb.htm					
Tupelo Convention & Visitors Bureau 399 E Main St	Tupelo	MS	38801	662-841-6521	841-6558
TF: 800-533-0611 ■ *Web:* tupelo.net					
Tuscaloosa Convention & Visitors Bureau PO Box 3167	Tuscaloosa	AL	35403	205-391-9200	391-2125
TF: 800-538-8696 ■ *Web:* www.tcvb.org					
Utah County Convention & Visitors Bureau 51 S University Ave Suite 111	Provo	UT	84601	801-370-8393	370-8050
TF: 800-222-8824					
Virginia Beach Convention And Visitor Bureau 2101 Parks Ave Suite 500	Virginia Beach	VA	23451	757-437-4700	437-4747
TF: 800-700-7702 ■ *Web:* www.vbfun.com					
Visitor Marketing City of Oakland 250 Frank Ogawa Plaza Suite 3330	Oakland	CA	94612	510-238-2935	839-5924
Web: www.ocva.com					
Washington DC Convention & Visitors Assn 1212 New York Ave NW Suite 600	Washington	DC	20005	202-789-7000	789-7037
Web: www.washington.org					
Wheeling Convention & Visitors Bureau 1401 Main St	Wheeling	WV	26003	304-233-7709	233-1470
TF: 800-828-3097 ■ *Web:* www.wheelingcvb.com					
Wichita Convention & Visitors Bureau 100 S Main St Suite 100	Wichita	KS	67202	316-265-2800	265-0162
TF: 800-288-9424 ■ *Web:* www.wichita-cvb.org					
Williamsburg Area Convention & Visitors Bureau 201 Penniman Rd	Williamsburg	VA	23185	757-253-0192	229-2047
TF: 800-368-6511 ■ *Web:* www.visitwilliamsburg.com					
Winston-Salem Convention & Visitors Bureau PO Box 1409	Winston-Salem	NC	27102	336-728-4200	728-4220
TF: 800-331-7018 ■ *Web:* www.wscvb.com					
Worcester County Convention & Visitors Bureau 33 Waldo St	Worcester	MA	01608	508-753-2920	754-2703
TF: 800-231-7557 ■ *Web:* www.worcester.org					
Youngstown/Mahoning County Convention & Visitors Bureau 100 Federal Plaza E Suite 101	Youngstown	OH	44503	330-747-8200	747-2331
TF: 800-447-8201 ■ *Web:* www.youngstowncvb.com					

12. Hotel Chains

				Phone	Fax
Adam's Mark Hotels & Resorts 11330 Olive St Rd PO Box 419039	Saint Louis	MO	63141	314-567-9000	567-0602
TF: 800-444-2326 ■ *Web:* www.adamsmark.com					
Admiral Benbow Inns 2160 Kingston Ct Suite N	Marietta	GA	30067	770-952-9145	952-3318
TF: 800-451-1986 ■ *Web:* www.admiralbenbow.com					
AmericInn International Inc 18202 Minnetonka Blvd	Deephaven	MN	55391	612-476-9020	476-7601
TF: 800-634-3444 ■ *Web:* www.americinn.com					
Bass Hotels & Resorts Inc 3 Ravinia Dr Suite 2900	Atlanta	GA	30346	770-604-2000	604-5403
Web: www2.basshotels.com					
Baymont Inns & Suites Inc 250 E Wisconsin Ave	Milwaukee	WI	53202	414-905-2000	905-2957*
**Fax:* Mktg ■ *TF:* 800-301-0200 ■ *Web:* www.baymontinns.com					
Best Inns & Suites 13 Corporate Sq Suite 250	Atlanta	GA	30329	404-321-4045	321-4482
TF: 800-237-8466 ■ *Web:* www.bestinns.com					
Best Western International Inc 6201 N 24th Pkwy	Phoenix	AZ	85016	602-957-4200	957-5942*
**Fax:* Mktg ■ *TF:* 800-528-1234 ■ *Web:* www.bestwestern.com					
Best Western Kings Row Inns 4200 N State Line Ave	Texarkana	AR	71854	870-774-3851	772-8440
TF: 800-643-5464					
Budget Host International PO Box 14341	Arlington	TX	76094	817-861-6088	861-6089
TF: 800-283-4678 ■ *Web:* www.budgethost.com					
Chalet Susse International Inc PO Box 657	Wilton	NH	03086	603-654-2000	654-2664
TF: 800-524-2538 ■ *Web:* www.sussechalet.com					
Choice Hotels International Inc 10750 Columbia Pike	Silver Spring	MD	20901	301-592-5000	592-6157
TF: 800-547-0007 ■ *Web:* www.hotelchoice.com					
Clarion Hotels & Resorts 10750 Columbia Pike	Silver Spring	MD	20901	301-592-5000	592-6177*
**Fax:* PR ■ *TF:* 800-424-6423 ■ *Web:* www.hotelchoice.com					
Club Hotels by Doubletree 755 Crossover Ln	Memphis	TN	38117	901-374-5000	374-6015*
**Fax:* Mktg ■ *TF:* 800-222-8733 ■ *Web:* www.clubhotels.com					
Comfort Inns & Suites 10750 Columbia Pike	Silver Spring	MD	20901	301-592-5000	592-6177*
**Fax:* PR ■ *TF:* 800-228-5150 ■ *Web:* www.comfortinns.com					
Concorde Hotels International 1 Penn Pl Suite 2127	New York	NY	10119	212-935-1045	752-8916
TF: 800-888-4747 ■ *Web:* www.concorde-hotels.com					
Country Hearth Inns 217 S Elm St	Prospect	OH	43342	740-494-4311	494-2442
TF: 800-848-5767 ■ *Web:* www.countryhearth.com					
Country Inns & Suites by Carlson PO Box 59159	Minneapolis	MN	55459	612-449-2525	449-1338
Web: www.countryinns.com					
Courtyard by Marriott 1 Marriott Dr	Washington	DC	20058	301-380-3000	897-9014*
**Fax:* PR ■ *TF:* 800-321-2211 ■ *Web:* www.courtyard.com					
Cross Country Inns Inc 6077 Frantz Rd Suite 203	Dublin	OH	43017	614-766-0037	766-6953
TF: 800-621-1429					
Crossland Economy Studios 450 E Las Olas Blvd Suite 1100	Fort Lauderdale	FL	33301	954-713-1600	713-1665
TF: 800-398-7829 ■ *Web:* www.crosslandstudios.com					
Crowne Plaza Hotels & Resorts 3 Ravinia Dr Suite 2900	Atlanta	GA	30346	770-604-2000	604-5403
TF: 800-227-6963 ■ *Web:* www2.basshotels.com/crowneplaza					
Days Inns of America Inc 1 Sylvan Way	Parsippany	NJ	07054	973-428-9700	496-6057
TF: 800-329-7466 ■ *Web:* www.daysinn.com					
Drury Inns Inc 10801 Pear Tree Ln	Saint Louis	MO	63074	314-429-2255	429-2255*
**Fax:* Sales ■ *TF:* 800-378-7946 ■ *Web:* www.drury-inn.com					
Econo Lodges 10750 Columbia Pike	Silver Spring	MD	20901	301-592-5000	592-6157
TF: 800-228-5150 ■ *Web:* www.hotelchoice.com					

Phone Fax

Embassy Suites Inc 755 Crossover Ln..................Memphis TN 38117 901-374-5000 374-5760
TF: 800-426-7866 ■ *Web:* www.embassy-suites.com

Exel Inns of America 4706 E Washington Ave......Madison WI 53704 608-241-5271 241-3224
TF: 800-356-8013 ■ *Web:* www.exelinns.com

Extended StayAmerica Inc
450 E Las Olas Blvd Suite 1100.............Fort Lauderdale FL 33301 954-713-1600 713-1665
TF: 800-398-7829 ■ *Web:* www.extstay.com

Family Inns of America Inc PO Box 10.........Pigeon Forge TN 37868 865-453-4988 453-0220
TF: 800-251-9752

Fiesta Americana Hotels 5950 Berkshire Ln 9th Fl...Dallas TX 75225 214-891-3150 891-3158*
**Fax:* PR ■ *TF:* 800-343-7821 ■ *Web:* www.fiestamexico.com

Four Seasons Hotels & Resorts 1165 Leslie St.....Toronto ON M3C2K8 416-449-1750 441-4374
TF: 800-332-3442 ■ *Web:* www.fourseasons.com

Hampton Inns Div Promus Hotel Corp
755 Crossover Ln Suite 101.............................Memphis TN 38117 901-374-5000 374-5051
TF: 800-426-7866 ■ *Web:* www.hampton-inn.com

Harley Hotels Inc PO Box 818020.......................Cleveland OH 44181 440-891-3600 234-1537
TF: 800-321-2323 ■ *Web:* harleyhotels.com

Hawthorn Suites 13 Corporate Sq Suite 250...........Atlanta GA 30329 404-321-4045 321-4482
TF: 800-527-1133 ■ *Web:* www.hawthorn.com

Hilton Hotels Corp 9336 Civic Ctr Dr...............Beverly Hills CA 90210 310-278-4321 205-4613
TF: 800-445-8667 ■ *Web:* www.hilton.com

Homestead Village Inc
2100 RiverEdge Pkwy 9th Fl...............................Atlanta GA 30328 770-303-2200 303-0079

Homewood Suites Div Promus Hotel Corp
755 Crossover Ln...Memphis TN 38117 901-374-5000 374-5760*
**Fax:* Cust Serv ■ *Web:* www.homewood-suites.com

Howard Johnson International Inc
1 Sylvan Way...Parsippany NJ 07054 973-428-9700 496-6057
TF: 800-446-4656 ■ *Web:* www.hojo.com

Hyatt Hotels & Resorts 200 W Madison St............Chicago IL 60606 312-750-1234 750-8041
TF: 800-233-1234 ■ *Web:* www.hyatt.com

Inns of America 755 Raintree Dr Suite 200...........Carlsbad CA 92009 760-438-6661 431-9212
TF: 800-826-0778 ■ *Web:* www.innsamerica.com

Inter-Continental Hotels Corp
100 Chopin Plaza 5th Fl.......................................Miami FL 33131 305-381-8140 381-8250
TF: 800-327-0200 ■ *Web:* www.interconti.com

Kelly Inns Ltd 2600 N Louise Ave......................Sioux Falls SD 57107 605-334-2371 334-8480
Web: www.kellyinns.com

La Quinta Inns Inc 112 E Pecan St..................San Antonio TX 78205 210-302-6000 302-6008*
**Fax:* PR ■ *TF:* 800-687-6667 ■ *Web:* www.laquinta.com

Lexington Hotel Suites & Inns
2120 Walnut Hill Ln Suite 106..............................Irving TX 75038 972-714-0585 355-4891
TF: 800-537-8483 ■ *Web:* www.lexres.com

Marriott International Inc 10400 Fernwood Rd....Bethesda MD 20817 301-380-3000 380-7752*
**Fax:* Mail Rm ■ *TF:* 800-228-9290
■ *Web:* www.marriott.com

Masters Economy Inns PO Box 13069................Savannah GA 31416 912-352-4493 352-0314
TF: 800-633-3434 ■ *Web:* www.masters-inns.com

Phone Fax

Motel 6 Inc 14651 Dallas Pkwy Suite 500.................Dallas TX 75240 972-386-6161 702-5947*
**Fax:* Mktg ■ *TF:* 800-466-8356 ■ *Web:* www.motel6.com

Omni Hotels 420 Decker Dr Suite 200.......................Irving TX 75062 972-730-6664 887-9240
TF: 800-843-6664 ■ *Web:* www.omnihotels.com

Quality Inns 10750 Columbia Pike...................Silver Spring MD 20901 301-592-5000 592-6177*
**Fax:* PR ■ *TF:* 800-228-5151 ■ *Web:* www.hotelchoice.com

Radisson Hotels Worldwide PO Box 59159....Minneapolis MN 55459 612-212-5526 212-3400
TF: 800-333-3333 ■ *Web:* www.radisson.com

Ramada Franchise Systems Inc
339 Jefferson Rd...Parsippany NJ 07054 973-428-9700 428-6057
Web: ramada.com

Red Carpet Inns 1726 Montreal Cir...........................Tucker GA 30084 770-270-1180 270-1077
TF: 800-251-1962 ■ *Web:* www.reservahost.com

Red Roof Inns Inc 4355 Davidson Rd......................Hilliard OH 43026 614-876-3200 771-7838
TF: 800-843-7663 ■ *Web:* www.redroof.com

Residence Inn by Marriott Inc 1 Marriott Dr....Washington DC 20058 301-380-9000 380-5197
TF: 800-331-3131 ■ *Web:* www.residenceinn.com

Ritz-Carlton Hotel Co LLC
3414 Peachtree Rd NE Suite 300.........................Atlanta GA 30326 404-237-5500 365-9643*
**Fax:* Sales ■ *TF:* 800-241-3333 ■ *Web:* www.ritzcarlton.com

Rodeway Inns 10750 Columbia Pike...............Silver Spring MD 20901 301-592-5000 592-6176
TF: 800-228-2000 ■ *Web:* www.hotelchoice.com

Sheraton Hotels & Resorts
777 Westchester Ave..................................White Plains NY 10604 914-640-8100 640-8310
TF: 800-325-3535 ■ *Web:* www.sheraton.com

ShoLodge Inc 130 Maple Dr N.....................Hendersonville TN 37075 615-264-8000 264-3670
TF: 800-222-2222 ■ *Web:* www.shoneysinn.com

Sleep Inns 10750 Columbia Pike.....................Silver Spring MD 20901 301-592-5000 592-6177*
**Fax:* PR ■ *TF:* 800-627-5337 ■ *Web:* www.hotelchoice.com

StudioPLUS 3575 Tates Creek Rd........................Lexington KY 40517 606-271-6160 245-8936
TF: 800-646-8000 ■ *Web:* www.studioplus.com

Super 8 Motels Inc PO Box 4090.........................Aberdeen SD 57402 605-225-2272 229-8903
TF: 800-800-8000 ■ *Web:* www.super8.com

Travelers Inns 1800 E Imperial Hwy Suite 120...........Brea CA 92821 714-256-2070 256-2165
TF: 800-633-8300

Vagabond Inns Inc
2361 Rosecrans Ave Suite 375.....................El Segundo CA 90245 310-297-9600 297-9610
TF: 800-522-1555 ■ *Web:* www.vagabondinns.com

Wellesley Inn & Suites 700 Rt 46E........................Fairfield NJ 07004 973-882-1010 882-7619
TF: 800-444-8888 ■ *Web:* www.wellesleyinnandsuites.com

Westin Hotels & Resorts
777 Westchester Ave..................................White Plains NY 10604 914-640-8100 640-8310
TF: 877-443-4585 ■ *Web:* www.westin.com

Wyndham Hotels & Resorts
1950 Stemmons Fwy Suite 6001..........................Dallas TX 75207 214-863-1000 863-1510*
**Fax:* Hum Res ■ *TF:* 800-996-3426
■ *Web:* www.wyndham.com

13. Hotel Reservation Services

Phone Fax

AAA Reservation Services
1740 Jackson Ave.......................................New Orleans LA 70113 504-522-1785 566-0405
TF: 888-840-2331

ABC: Accommodations of Boston & Cambridge
335 Pearl St..Cambridge MA 02139 617-491-0274 547-5478
TF: 800-253-5542

Accommodation Finder PO Box 808....................Key West FL 33041 305-292-2688 292-8586
TF: 888-453-9937 ■ *Web:* www.keystravel.com

Accommodations Express
801 Asbury Ave 6th Fl...................................Ocean City NJ 08226 609-391-2100 525-0111
TF: 800-444-7666 ■ *Web:* www.accommodationsxpress.com

Accommodations Plus
JFK Airport Terminal 4 Bldg 51..........................Jamaica NY 11430 718-995-4444 995-6824
TF: 800-733-7666 ■ *Web:* www.accommodationsplus.com

Accommodations USA 1327 E Vine St..............Kissimmee FL 34744 407-931-0003 931-1003

Advance Reservations Inn Arizona PO Box 950.......Tempe AZ 85280 480-990-0682 990-3390
TF: 800-456-0682 ■ *Web:* tucson.com/inn

Adventure Alaska Bed & Breakfast
Reservations 6740 Lawlor Cir........................Anchorage AK 99502 907-243-0265 243-2557
Web: www.alaska.net/~alaskabb/

Adventures Bed & Breakfast Reservation Service
15 E Main St..Le Roy NY 14482 716-768-2699 768-9386
TF: 800-724-1932 ■ *Web:* www.3z.com/bandbres

Alaska Sourdough Bed & Breakfast Assn
889 Cardigan Cir...Anchorage AK 99503 907-563-6244 563-6073
Web: www.alaskan.com/aksourdoughbba/

Phone Fax

Alberta Gem B&B & Reservation Agency
11216 48th Ave...Edmonton AB T6H0C7 780-434-6098 434-6098
Web: www.bbcanada.com/1301html

Alexandria & Arlington Bed & Breakfast Network
512 S 25th St...Arlington VA 22202 703-549-3415 549-3411
TF: 888-549-3415 ■ *Web:* www.aabbn.com

All Islands Bed & Breakfast 463 Iliwahi Loop...........Kailua HI 96734 808-263-2342 263-0308
TF: 800-542-0344 ■ *Web:* home.hawaii.rr.com/allislands

All Keys Reservation Service 4 Hunts Lane........Key West FL 33040 305-296-0048 296-7951
TF: 800-255-5397

American International Travel
100 2nd Ave S Suite 1010....................Saint Petersburg FL 33701 800-782-9872 897-4007
TF: 800-681-3965

American Wolfe International
1890 Palmer Ave Suite 202...........................Larchmont NY 10538 914-833-3303 833-3308
TF: 800-223-5695

AmeriRoom-Philadelphia Hotel
Reservation Bureau 22 Empire Dr.....West Atlantic City NJ 08232 800-888-5825 645-1147
Web: www.ameriroom.com

Anchorage Adventures & Accommodations
200 W 34th St Suite 342.................................Anchorage AK 99503 907-344-4676 274-4671
TF: 888-655-4723 ■ *Web:* www.see-alaska.com

Annapolis Accommodations 66 Maryland Ave.....Annapolis MD 21401 410-280-0900 263-1703
TF: 800-715-1000

Association of Bed & Breakfasts in
Philadelphia PO Box 562...........................Valley Forge PA 19481 610-783-7838 783-7787
TF: 800-344-0123

13. HOTEL RESERVATION SERVICES

Phone Fax

Atlantic City Toll-Free Reservations
PO Box 665 .... Northfield NJ 08225 609-646-7070 646-8655
TF: 800-833-7070 ■ *Web:* www.actollfree.com

B & B Agency of Boston 47 Commercial Wharf....... Boston MA 02110 617-720-3540 523-5761
TF: 800-248-9262 ■ *Web:* www.boston-bnbagency.com

Bed & Breakfast & Beyond Reservation Service 3115 Napoleon Ave....... New Orleans LA 70125 504-896-9977 896-2482
TF: 800-886-3709 ■ *Web:* www.nolabandb.com

Bed & Breakfast Accommodations
PO Box 12011 .... Washington DC 20005 202-328-3510 332-3885
Web: www.bnbaccom.com

Bed & Breakfast Assn of Downtown Toronto
PO Box 190 Stn B .... Toronto ON M5T2W1 416-368-1420 368-1653
TF: 888-559-5515 ■ *Web:* www.bnbinfo.com

Bed & Breakfast Assoc Bay Colony Ltd
PO Box 57166 .... Boston MA 02457 888-486-6018 449-5958
Web: www.bnbboston.com/

Bed & Breakfast Association of Seattle
PO Box 31772 .... Seattle WA 98103 206-547-1020
TF: 800-348-5630 ■ *Web:* www.seattlebandbs.com

Bed & Breakfast Atlanta Reservation Services
1608 Briarcliff Rd Suite 5....... Atlanta GA 30306 404-875-0525 875-8198
TF: 800-967-3224 ■ *Web:* www.bedandbreakfastatlanta.com

Bed & Breakfast Directory for San Diego
PO Box 3292 .... San Diego CA 92163 619-297-3130
TF: 800-619-7666 ■ *Web:* www.sandiegobandb.com

Bed & Breakfast Homes of Toronto Assn
PO Box 46093 .... College Park ON M5B2L8 416-363-6362
Web: www.bbcanada.com/toronto2.html

Bed & Breakfast Honolulu 3242 Kaohinani Dr...... Honolulu HI 96817 808-595-7533 595-2030
TF: 800-288-4666 ■ *Web:* www.hawaiibnb.com

Bed & Breakfast Inc-A Reservation Service
PO Box 52257 .... New Orleans LA 70152 504-488-4640 488-4639
TF: 800-729-4640 ■ *Web:* www.historiclodging.com

Bed & Breakfast Newport Ltd 33 Russell Ave....... Newport RI 02840 401-846-5408 846-1828
TF: 800-800-8765 ■ *Web:* www.bbnewport.com

Bed & Breakfast of Hawaii PO Box 449....... Kapaa HI 96746 808-822-7771 822-2723
TF: 800-733-1632 ■ *Web:* www.bandb-hawaii.com/

Bed & Breakfast of Philadelphia PO Box 21....... Devon PA 19333 610-687-3565 995-9524
TF: 800-448-3619 ■ *Web:* www.bnbphiladelphia.com/

Bed & Breakfast Reservation Service
8211 Goodwood Blvd Suite F....... Baton Rouge LA 70806 225-923-2337 923-2374
TF: 800-926-4320 ■ *Web:* www.bnbtravel.com

Bed & Breakfast Reservations
PO Box 600035 .... Newtonville MA 02460 617-964-1606 332-8572
TF: 800-832-2632 ■ *Web:* www.bbreserve.com/

Bed & Breakfast San Francisco
PO Box 420009 .... San Francisco CA 94142 415-899-0060 899-9923
TF: 800-452-8249 ■ *Web:* www.bbsf.com

Bed & Breakfast-Cambridge & Greater Boston
PO Box 1344 .... Cambridge MA 02238 617-262-1155 227-0021
TF: 800-888-0178

Bed & Breakfasts in Québec CP 1000 Succ M ..... Montréal QC H1V3R2 514-252-3138 252-3173
Web: www.agricotours.qc.ca

Best Canadian Bed & Breakfast Network
1064 Balfour Ave .... Vancouver BC V6H1X1 604-738-7207 732-4998
Web: www.corpinfohub.com/best_can/

Big Easy/Gulf Coast Reservation Service
233 Cottonwood Dr .... Gretna LA 70056 504-433-2563 391-1903
TF: 800-368-4876 ■ *Web:* www.crescentcity.com/fql/

Boston & New England Reservation Service
61 South St .... Northborough MA 01532 508-393-7470 393-9199
TF: 800-754-7470

Branson Nights Reservations
109 N Business 65 .... Branson MO 65616 417-335-6971 335-6025
TF: 800-329-9999 ■ *Web:* www.branson-nights.com

Branson Vacation Reservations
1316 W Hwy 76 Suite 155....... Branson MO 65616 417-335-8747 335-2254
TF: 800-221-5692 ■ *Web:* www.bransonvacation.com

Branson's Best Reservations
3150 Green Mountain Dr....... Branson MO 65616 417-339-2204 339-4051
TF: 800-800-2019 ■ *Web:* www.bransonbest.com

Branson/Lakes Area Lodging Assn PO Box 430.... Branson MO 65615 417-332-1400 239-1400
TF: 888-238-6782

California Reservations
165 8th St Suite 201....... San Francisco CA 94103 415-252-1107 252-1483
TF: 800-576-0003 ■ *Web:* www.cal-res.com

California Suites Reservations
9940 Buisness Pk Dr Suite 135....... Sacramento CA 95827 916-363-9700 363-9465
TF: 800-363-9779 ■ *Web:* www.calsuites.com

Capitol Reservations
1730 Rhode Island Ave NW Suite 1210....... Washington DC 20036 202-452-1270 452-0537
TF: 800-847-4832 ■ *Web:* www.visitdc.com

Cayman Island Hotel Reservations Service
6100 Blue Lagoon Dr Suite 150....... Miami FL 33126 305-266-6742 267-2931
TF: 800-327-8777

Phone Fax

Central Reservation Service
220 Lookout Pl Suite 200 .... Maitland FL 32751 407-740-6442 740-8222
TF: 800-548-3311 ■ *Web:* www.reservation-services.com

Chicago Bed & Breakfast Reservations
PO Box 14088 .... Chicago IL 60614 773-248-0005 248-7090
TF: 800-375-7084

Citywide Reservation Services 839 Beacon St....... Boston MA 02215 617-267-7424 267-9408
TF: 800-468-3593 ■ *Web:* www.cityres.com

Colonial Williamsburg Reservation Center
PO Box 1776 .... Williamsburg VA 23187 757-253-2277 565-8797
TF: 800-447-8679 ■ *Web:* www.history.org

Colours Destinations 255 W 24th St....... Miami Beach FL 33140 305-532-9341 534-0362
TF: 800-277-4825 ■ *Web:* www.colours.net

Corporate Lodging Service 2310 Kansas Ave....... Kenner LA 70062 504-828-0380 467-3037
TF: 800-995-0137

Downtown Accommodations
1415 W Georgia St 1403....... Vancouver BC V6G3C8 604-454-8179 682-5634
Web: www.dtaccomm.com

Eugene Area Bed & Breakfast Assn
2013 Charnelton St....... Eugene OR 97405 541-343-3553 343-0383
TF: 800-507-1354 ■ *Web:* www.pond.net/~bnbassoc/

Executive Accommodations
291 E 2nd Ave Suite 200 .... Vancouver BC V5T1B8 604-875-6674 875-6684
TF: 800-557-8483 ■ *Web:* www.travelsuites.com

Executive Inn Express 300 10th Ave....... Seattle WA 98122 206-223-9300 233-0241
TF: 800-906-6226

Executive Residence Inc
2601 Elliott Ave Suite 3181....... Seattle WA 98121 206-329-8000 382-0511
TF: 800-428-3867 ■ *Web:* www.halcyon.com/execres/execres

Express Hotel Reservations 3825 Iris Ave....... Boulder CO 80301 303-440-8481 440-0166
TF: 800-356-1123 ■ *Web:* www.express-res.com

Florida Hotel Network
300 71st St Suite 301 .... Miami Beach FL 33141 305-538-3616 538-5858
TF: 800-538-3616

Florida SunBreak 111 Alton Rd....... Miami Beach FL 33139 305-532-1516 532-0564
TF: 800-786-2732 ■ *Web:* www.lvacation.com/p6802.htm

Global Reservations Inc
15721 N Greenway Hayden Loop Suite 101... Scottsdale AZ 85260 480-596-5156 707-6223

Globe Corporate Stay International
6204 Daimler Way Suite 103 .... Raleigh NC 27607 919-851-1511 859-0725
TF: 800-533-2370

Good Earth Travel Adventures Reservations
PO Box 8510 Suite 202....... Canmore AB T1W2V2 403-678-9358 678-9384
TF: 888-979-9797 ■ *Web:* www.goodearthtravel.com

Grand Canyon National Park Lodges
PO Box 699 .... Grand Canyon AZ 86023 520-638-2631 638-9247*
**Fax:* Mail Rm

Greater Miami & the Beaches Hotel Assn
407 Lincoln Rd Suite 10G....... Miami Beach FL 33139 305-531-3553 531-8954
TF: 800-531-3553 ■ *Web:* www.gmbha.org

Greater New Orleans Hotel-Motel Assn
321 St Charles Ave Suite 610....... New Orleans LA 70130 800-695-2264 525-9327

Greater Tacoma Bed & Breakfast Reservation Service 3312 N Union Ave....... Tacoma WA 98407 253-752-8175 759-4025
TF: 800-406-4088 ■ *Web:* www.tacoma-inns.org

Greek Hotel & Cruise Reservation Center
17220 Newhope St Suite 227 .... Fountain Valley CA 92708 714-641-3502 641-0303
TF: 800-736-5717 ■ *Web:* www.cruiseair.com

Greenville Area Central Reservations
PO Box 10527 .... Greenville SC 29603 864-233-0461 421-0005
TF: 800-351-7180

Gulf Coast Hotel Reservations PO Box 116 .... Biloxi MS 39533 228-875-1006 875-7641
TF: 888-388-1006 ■ *Web:* www.biloxi-ms.com

HATA USA 811 Hammockwood Ct....... Sarasota FL 34232 941-379-8031 722-5124
TF: 800-356-8392

Hawaii's Best Bed & Breakfasts PO Box 563 .... Kamuela HI 96743 808-885-4550 885-0559
TF: 800-262-9912 ■ *Web:* www.bestbnb.com/

Historic Charleston Bed & Breakfast Reservations Service 57 Broad St .... Charleston SC 29401 800-743-3583 722-9589
TF: 800-743-3583 ■ *Web:* www.charleston.net/com/bed&breakfast

Hospitalité Canada 12 rue Sainte-Anne .... Québec QC G1R3X2 418-694-1602 393-8942

Hot Rooms 1 E Erie St Suite 225....... Chicago IL 60611 773-468-7666 649-0559
TF: 800-468-3500 ■ *Web:* www.hotrooms.com

Hotel Reservations Network Inc
8140 Walnut Hill Ln Suite 800....... Dallas TX 75231 214-361-7311 361-7299
TF Sales: 800-964-6835* ■ *Web:* www.hoteldiscount.com

IDP Reservations 921 W 46th St .... Miami Beach FL 33140 305-538-2151 538-1701
TF: 800-436-8611 ■ *Web:* www.idpreservations.com

Jackson Hole Central Reservations
PO Box 2618 .... Jackson WY 83001 307-733-4005 733-1286
TF: 800-443-6931 ■ *Web:* www.jacksonholeresort.com

Jackson Hole Resort Reservations LLC
PO Box 12739 .... Jackson WY 83002 307-733-6331 733-4728
TF: 800-329-9205 ■ *Web:* www.jacksonholeres.com

				Phone	Fax
Key West Key 726 Passover Ln *TF:* 800-881-7321 ■ *Web:* www.keywestkey.com	Key West	FL	33040	305-294-4357	294-2974
Know Before You Go Reservations 4720 W Irlo Bronson Memorial Hwy *TF:* 800-749-1993 ■ *Web:* www.1travel.com/knowbeforeyougo	Kissimmee	FL	34746	407-352-9813	352-9814
Las Vegas Holidays 1830 E Sahara Ave Suite 109 *TF:* 800-926-6836 ■ *Web:* www.lvholidays.com	Las Vegas	NV	89104	702-697-8800	697-8847
Las Vegas Hotel Reservation Services 1820 E Desert Inn Rd 2nd Fl *TF:* 800-728-4106 ■ *Web:* www.lasvegasreservations.com/	Las Vegas	NV	89109	702-794-2061	
Lexington Services 2120 Walnut Hill Ln Suite 100 *TF:* 800-537-8483 ■ *Web:* www.lexres.com	Irving	TX	75038	972-714-0585	255-3163
Myrtle Beach Reservation Service 1551 21st Ave N Suite 20 *TF:* 800-626-7477 ■ *Web:* www.mbhospitality.com	Myrtle Beach	SC	29577	843-626-7477	
National Reservation Bureau 1820 E Desert Inn Rd Suite 200 *TF:* 800-831-2754	Las Vegas	NV	89109	702-794-2820	794-3515
New Mexico Central Reservations 20 1st Plaza Galleria NW Suite 603 *TF:* 800-466-7829 ■ *Web:* www.nmtravel.com	Albuquerque	NM	87102	505-766-9770	247-8200
New Orleans Accommodations Bed & Breakfast Service 671 Rosa Ave Suite 208 *TF:* 888-340-0070 ■ *Web:* www.neworleansbandb.com/	Metairie	LA	70005	504-838-0071	838-0140
New Otani North America Reservation Center 120 S Los Angeles St *TF:* 800-421-8795	Los Angeles	CA	90012	213-629-1114	620-9808
New World Bed & Breakfast 150 5th Ave Suite 711 *TF:* 800-443-3800	New York	NY	10011	212-675-5600	675-6366
Newport Reservations 174 Bellevue Ave Suite 203 *TF:* 800-842-0102 ■ *Web:* www.aqua.net/lodging/newportres/newportres.html	Newport	RI	02840	401-842-0102	842-0104
Oakwood Corporate Housing 2222 Corinth Ave *TF:* 800-888-0808 ■ *Web:* www.oakwood.com	Los Angeles	CA	90064	310-478-1021	444-2210
Oakwood Corporate Housing 3035 Prospect Park Dr Suite 120 *TF:* 800-483-1335	Rancho Cordova	CA	95670	916-631-3777	631-3773
Oakwood Corporate Housing 1500 Edwards Ave Suite I *TF:* 800-259-2086 ■ *Web:* www.oakwood.com	New Orleans	LA	70123	504-733-7033	733-8393
Ocean City Hotel-Motel-Restaurant Assn PO Box 340 *TF:* 800-626-2326 ■ *Web:* www.ocean-city.com/ochmra.htm	Ocean City	MD	21842	410-289-6733	289-5645
Pacific Reservation Service PO Box 46894 *TF:* 800-684-2932 ■ *Web:* www.seattlebedandbreakfast.com/	Seattle	WA	98146	206-439-7677	431-0932
Phoenix Scottsdale Hotel Reservations 2415 E Camelback Rd Suite 700 *TF:* 800-728-3227	Phoenix	AZ	85016	602-954-1425	627-9405
Premier Lodging Reservations PO Box 601 *TF:* 800-322-5766 ■ *Web:* www.jhlodging.com	Teton Village	WY	83025	307-733-0353	733-3487
Private Lodging Service PO Box 18557	Cleveland	OH	44118	216-321-3213	321-8707
Quikbook 381 Park Ave S 3rd Fl *TF:* 800-789-9887 ■ *Web:* www.quikbook.com	New York	NY	10016	212-532-1660	532-1556
Reservations Center PO Box 680368 *TF:* 800-255-6451 ■ *Web:* www.rescenter.com	Park City	UT	84068	435-649-1592	649-1593
Reservations USA PO Box 1410 *TF:* 800-251-4444 ■ *Web:* www.reservationsusa.com	Pigeon Forge	TN	37868	865-453-1000	453-7484
RMC Travel Centre 424 Madison Ave Suite 705 *TF:* 800-782-2674	New York	NY	10017	212-754-6560	754-6571
Room Exchange 450 7th Ave *TF:* 800-846-7000 ■ *Web:* www.hotelrooms.com	New York	NY	10123	212-760-1000	760-1013
Room Finders USA 1112 N Rampart St *TF:* 800-473-7829 ■ *Web:* www.roomsusa.com	New Orleans	LA	70116	504-522-9373	529-1948
San Diego Hotel Reservations 7380 Clairemont Mesa Blvd Suite 218 *TF:* 800-728-3227	San Diego	CA	92111	858-627-9300	627-9405
San Francisco Reservations 22 2nd St 4th Fl *TF:* 800-677-1550 ■ *Web:* www.hotelres.com	San Francisco	CA	94105	415-227-1500	227-1520
Santa Fe Central Reservations/Taos Valley Resort Assn 320 Artist Rd Suite 10 *Web:* www.taoswebb.com/NMResv	Santa Fe	NM	87501	800-776-7669	984-8682
Scottsdale Resort Accommodations 7025 E Greenway Pkwy Suite 250 *TF:* 888-868-4378 ■ *Web:* www.arizonaguide.com/sra/	Scottsdale	AZ	85254	480-515-2300	515-2700
Seattle Super Saver 520 Pike St Suite 1300 *TF:* 800-535-7071 ■ *Web:* www.seeseattle.org/hotels/superhm.htm	Seattle	WA	98101	206-461-5800	461-5855
Selective Hotel Reservations Inc 44 Pond St *TF:* 800-223-6764	Nahant	MA	01908	781-581-0844	581-3714
Show Me Hospitality B&B Reservations 163 Fountain *TF:* 800-348-5210	Branson	MO	65616	417-335-4063	336-6772
Southern Arizona Innkeepers Assn 4725 E Sunrise Dr Suite 139	Tucson	AZ	85718	520-299-6787	299-6431
Southwest Florida Reservations 12290 Treeline Ave *TF:* 800-733-7935	Fort Myers	FL	33913	941-768-3633	768-9792
Squaw Valley Central Reservations PO Box 2007 *TF:* 800-545-4350 ■ *Web:* www.squaw.com	Olympic Valley	CA	96146	530-583-6985	581-7106
Taylor-Made Reservations 39 Touro St *TF:* 800-848-8848 ■ *Web:* www.enjoy-newport.com	Newport	RI	02840	401-848-0300	848-0301
Travel Discounts PO Box 3396 *Web:* www.traveldiscounts.com	Carmel By-The-Sea	CA	93921	831-626-1212	626-1252
Travel Now 100 16th St Suite 5 *TF:* 800-681-1993 ■ *Web:* www.travel-now.com	Miami Beach	FL	33139	305-532-7273	532-7638
USA Hotels 1831 Weeksville Rd *TF:* 800-872-4683 ■ *Web:* www.1800usahotels.com	Elizabeth City	NC	27909	252-331-1555	331-2021
Utell International Resorts 360 Lexington Ave *TF:* 800-223-6510	New York	NY	10017	212-220-8701	220-9010
Vacation Co 42 New Orleans Rd *TF:* 800-845-7018 ■ *Web:* www.vacationcompany.com/	Hilton Head Island	SC	29928	843-686-6100	686-3255
Vacations on Hilton Head Plaza at Shelter Cove Suite N *TF:* 800-732-7671 ■ *Web:* www.800beachme.com	Hilton Head Island	SC	29928	843-686-3500	686-3701
Washington DC Accommodations 2201 Wisconsin Ave NW Suite C-110 *TF:* 800-554-2220 ■ *Web:* www.dcaccommodations.com	Washington	DC	20007	202-289-2220	338-4517
Western Canada Bed & Breakfast Innkeepers Assn 2803 W 4th Ave *Web:* www.wcbbia.com	Vancouver	BC	V6K4P3	604-255-9199	
Winter Park Resort Travel Services PO Box 36 *TF:* 800-525-3538 ■ *Web:* www.digitalfrontier.com/wpmj/	Winter Park	CO	80482	970-726-5587	726-5993

14. On-Line Travel Services

1-800-Fly-Cheap ... www.1800flycheap.com
1travel.com Inc ... www.1travel.com
Accommodation Search Engine ... www.ase.net
All Hotels on the Web ... www.all-hotels.com
Arthur Frommer's BudgetTravel Online ... www.frommers.com
Atevo Inc ... www.atevo.com
Best Fares USA Inc ... www.bestfares.com
Best in the World Travel Directory ... www.thebestintheworld.com
Biztravel.com Inc ... www.biztravel.com
Breezenet's Guide to Airport Rental Cars ... www.bnm.com
ByeByeNOW.com ... www.byebyenow.com
CheapFares.com ... www.cheapfares.com
CheapTickets Inc ... www.cheaptickets.com
City Central ... www.enn2.com/citycentral.htm
City Insights ... cityinsights.com
CityNet.com ... www.citynet.com
ClickCity ... www.clickcity.com
CNN Interactive Travel Guide ... www.cnn.com/TRAVEL
Digital City Inc ... www.digitalcities.com
DigitalCity ... www.digitalcity.com
Ecotravel Center ... www.ecotour.org
EventsWorldWide ... www.eventsworldwide.com
Excite City.Net ... www.city.net
Expedia Inc ... www.expedia.com
Fodor's Travel Online Inc ... www.fodors.com
Freetime Guide to Events & Attractions ... www.ftguide.com
Frommer's 200 Places ... www.frommers.com/destinations
Funtastik Travel Hotel Reservation Service ... www.funtastik.com
GetThere.com Inc ... www.getthere.com
Global Online Travel ... www.got.com
Great Outdoors ... www.greatoutdoors.com
History Channel Traveler ... www.historytravel.com
HotelBook ... www.hotelbook.com
HotelGuide Network ... hotelguide.net
HotelNetDiscount Directory ... www.aladv.com/hotelnet
Hotels & Travel on the Net ... www.hotelstravel.com
InfoHub Specialty Travel Guide ... www.infohub.com
Inns & Outs-The Bed & Breakfast Source ... www.innsandouts.com
International Home Exchange Network ... www.homexchange.com
Internet Guide to Bed & Breakfast Inns ... www.traveldata.com
Internet The Guide to Hostels ... www.hostels.com
Internet Travel Network ... www.itn.net
INUSA Tour Guide ... www.inusa.com/tour/index.htm
InYourTown.com ... www.inyourtown.com
Lanier's Travel Guides Online ... www.travelguides.com
LastMinuteTravel.com Inc ... www.lastminutetravel.com
LeisurePlanet.com ... www.leisureplanet.com
Lonely Planet Publications ... www.lonelyplanet.com
Lycos City Guide ... cityguide.lycos.com
MainTour ... www.maintour.com
MapQuest.com Inc ... www.mapquest.com
Maps On Us ... www.mapsonus.com
National Hotel Directory ... www.evmedia.com/cities.html
Net Cruise Travel ... www.netcruise.com
NITC Travelbase ... www.travelbase.com
OAG Online ... www.oag.com
Online CityGuide ... www.olcg.com
Places To Stay ... www.placestostay.com/index.html
Preview Travel Inc ... www.previewtravel.com
Rand McNally Online ... www.randmcnally.com
Real-Time Flight Tracking ... www.thetrip.com/usertools/flighttracking
Resorts OnLine ... www.resortsonline.com
Rezworks Corp ... www.rezworks.com
Roadside America ... www.roadsideamerica.com
Rough Guide Travel ... travel.roughguides.com
SkiResorts.com ... www.skiresorts.com
Speedtrap Registry Inc ... www.speedtrap.com
TerraQuest ... www.terraquest.com
Tourist Guide ... www.touristguide.com
Tourist.com ... www.tourist.com/
TRAVEL.org ... www.travel.org/na.html
TravelASSIST ... travelassist.com
Traveler's Net ... www.travelersnet.com
TravelFacts ... www.travelfacts.com
TravelFile ... www.travelfile.com
TravelHub Inc ... www.travelhub.com
TravelNow.com Inc ... www.travelnow.com
TravelnStore.com Inc ... www.travelnstore.com
Travelocity.com ... www.travelocity.com
Travelscape.com Inc ... www.travelscape.com
TravelSource ... www.travelsource.com
TravelSphere.com ... www.travelsphere.com
TravelWeb ... www.travelweb.com
Travelzoo.com Corp ... www.travelzoo.com
Trip.com Inc ... www.trip.com
TripSpot ... www.tripspot.com
Uniglobe Travel Online Inc ... www.uniglobe.com
US National/State Parks ... usparks.about.com
USA CityLink ... usacitylink.com
VacationSpot.com ... vacationspot.com
Virtual Relocation.com Inc ... www.virtualrelocation.com
WebFlyer ... www.webflyer.com
Weekend Guide ... www.weekendguide.com
Western Cybertourist ... cybertourist.com
What's Going On ... whatsgoingon.com
World Travel Guide ... www.wtg-online.com
WWW Virtual Tours ... www.dreamscape.com/frankvad/tours.html
Yahoo! Travel ... travel.yahoo.com

15. On-Line Weather Services

AccuWeather Inc ... www.accuweather.com
American Weather Concepts ... www.weatherconcepts.com
American Weather Enterprises ... www.americanweather.com
CNN Weather ... www.cnn.com/weather/
EarthWatch Weather On-Demand ... www.earthwatch.com
How the Weather Works ... www.weatherworks.com
Intellicast USA Weather ... www.intellicast.com
National Weather Service ... iwin.nws.noaa.gov
Rain or Shine Weather ... www.rainorshine.com
USA Today Weather ... www.usatoday.com/weather/wfront.htm
Weather 24 ... www.weather24.com
Weather Channel ... www.weather.com
Weather Underground ... www.wunderground.com
WeatherCast.com ... www.tvweather.com
WeatherLabs ... www.weatherlabs.com
WeatherOffice.com ... www.weatheroffice.com
weatherOnline! ... weatheronline.com
Weatherplanner ... www.weatherplanner.com
WeatherPost ... www.weatherpost.com
WOAI Weather Center ... www.woai.com/weather.htm
World Climate ... www.worldclimate.com
WSI Intellicast ... www.intellicast.com
Yahoo! Weather ... weather.yahoo.com

16. Weather Information

Birmingham, AL 205-945-7000
Huntsville, AL 256-533-1990
Mobile, AL 334-478-6666
Montgomery, AL 205-945-7000
Tuscaloosa, AL 205-979-1300
Anchorage, AK 907-936-2525
Fairbanks, AK 907-452-3553
Juneau, AK 907-586-3997
Flagstaff, AZ 520-774-3301
Glendale, AZ 602-265-5550
Mesa, AZ 602-265-5550
Phoenix, AZ 602-265-5550
Scottsdale, AZ 602-265-5550
Tempe, AZ 602-265-5550
Tucson, AZ 520-881-3333
Fort Smith, AR 501-785-9000
Hot Springs, AR 501-525-0011
Little Rock, AR 501-371-7777
Anaheim, CA 858-675-8706
Bakersfield, CA 661-833-8888
Chula Vista, CA 858-289-1212
Fresno, CA 559-442-1212
Garden Grove, CA ... 858-675-8706
Glendale, CA 213-554-1212
Huntington Beach, CA 714-550-4636
Long Beach, CA 213-554-1212
Los Angeles, CA 213-554-1212
Modesto, CA 209-982-1793
Monterey, CA 831-656-1725
Oakland, CA 510-562-8573
Oxnard, CA 805-988-6610
Palm Springs, CA ... 760-345-3711
Riverside, CA 213-554-1212
Sacramento, CA 916-646-2000
San Diego, CA 858-289-1212
San Francisco, CA ... 650-364-7974
San Jose, CA 650-364-7974
Santa Ana, CA 858-675-8706
Stockton, CA 209-982-1793
Aurora, CO 303-337-2500
Boulder, CO 303-337-2500
Colorado Springs, CO 719-573-6846
Denver, CO 303-871-1492
Fort Collins, CO 970-484-8920
Bridgeport, CT 203-366-4242
Hartford, CT 203-366-4242
Stamford, CT 203-366-4242
Dover, DE 302-674-9262
Rehoboth Beach, DE . 302-855-9262
Wilmington, DE 302-429-9000
Washington, DC 202-936-1212
Daytona Beach, FL ... 904-252-8000
Fort Lauderdale, FL .. 954-748-4444
Hialeah, FL 305-229-4522
Jacksonville, FL 904-741-4311
Key West, FL 305-292-5000
Miami, FL 305-229-4522
Naples, FL 941-594-1234
Orlando, FL 321-255-2900
Saint Petersburg, FL . 813-645-2506
Tallahassee, FL 850-422-1212
Tampa, FL 813-645-2506
Atlanta, GA 770-603-3333
Augusta, GA 706-724-0056
Savannah, GA 912-964-1700
Honolulu, HI 808-973-5286
Boise, ID 208-342-8303
Champaign, IL 217-351-2900
Chicago, IL 815-834-0675
Peoria, IL 309-697-8620
Rockford, IL 815-963-5913
Springfield, IL 217-753-3000
Evansville, IN 812-425-5549
Fort Wayne, IN 219-424-5050
Indianapolis, IN 317-635-5959
South Bend, IN 219-232-1121
Cedar Rapids, IA 319-393-0500
Des Moines, IA 515-270-2614
Dubuque, IA 319-583-9955
Kansas City, KS 913-384-5555
Topeka, KS 785-271-7575
Wichita, KS 316-681-1371
Lexington, KY 606-253-4444
Louisville, KY 502-585-1212
Metairie, LA 504-828-4000
New Orleans, LA 504-828-4000
Shreveport, LA 318-635-7575
Bangor, ME 207-942-2026
Portland, ME 207-688-3216
Annapolis, MD 410-936-1212
Baltimore, MD 410-936-1212
Ocean City, MD 410-742-8400
Boston, MA 617-936-1234
Springfield, MA 413-499-2627
Worcester, MA 508-792-9600
Ann Arbor, MI 734-973-2929
Detroit, MI 313-961-8686
Flint, MI 810-232-3333
Grand Rapids, MI ... 616-776-1234
Lansing, MI 517-321-7576
Duluth, MN 218-729-6697
Minneapolis, MN 612-512-1111
Rochester, MN 507-281-8888
Gulfport/Biloxi, MS .. 601-693-5311
Jackson, MS 601-936-2189
Tupelo, MS 662-842-8422
Branson, MO 417-866-1010
Columbia, MO 573-442-5171
Jefferson City, MO ... 573-442-2222
Kansas City, MO 913-384-5555
Saint Louis, MO 314-321-2222
Springfield, MO 417-866-1010
Billings, MT 406-652-1916
Great Falls, MT 406-453-5469
Helena, MT 406-443-5151
Lincoln, NE 402-475-6100
Omaha, NE 402-392-1111
Las Vegas, NV 702-248-4800
Reno, NV 775-793-1300
Concord, NH 603-225-5191
Manchester, NH 603-225-5191
Paterson, NJ 973-267-1093
Trenton, NJ 609-261-6600
Albuquerque, NM 505-821-1111
Santa Fe, NM 505-988-5151
Albany, NY 518-476-1111
Buffalo, NY 716-844-4444
New York, NY 631-924-0517
Rochester, NY 716-334-0013
Syracuse, NY 315-786-9969
Asheville, NC 828-251-6435
Charlotte, NC 704-570-9288
Durham, NC 919 515 8225
Greensboro, NC 336-370-9369
Raleigh, NC 919-515-8225
Bismarck, ND 701-223-3700
Fargo, ND 701-235-2600
Grand Forks, ND 701-775-7777
Akron, OH 330-869-8686
Cincinnati, OH 513-241-1010
Cleveland, OH 216-931-1212
Columbus, OH 614-469-1010
Dayton, OH 937-258-2000
Toledo, OH 419-936-1212
Youngstown, OH 216-265-2370
Oklahoma City, OK .. 405-478-3377
Tulsa, OK 918-743-3311
Eugene, OR 541-484-1200
Portland, OR 503-243-7575
Salem, OR 503-363-4131
Erie, PA 216-265-2370
Gettysburg, PA 717-264-1144
Philadelphia, PA 610-936-1212
Pittsburgh, PA 412-936-1212
Newport, RI 401-848-0028
Providence, RI 401-277-7777
Providence, RI 401-224-1010
Charleston, SC 843-744-3207
Columbia, SC 803-822-8135
Greenville, SC 864-233-3000
Hilton Head Island, SC 843-686-6397
Myrtle Beach, SC 843-293-6600
Rapid City, SD 605-341-7531
Sioux Falls, SD 605-330-4444
Johnson City, TN 423-586-3771
Knoxville, TN 865-521-6300
Memphis, TN 901-544-0399
Nashville, TN 615-244-9393
Amarillo, TX 806-358-7755
Arlington, TX 817-787-1111
Austin, TX 512-451-2424
Brownsville, TX 956-546-5378
Corpus Christi, TX ... 361-289-1861
Dallas, TX 214-787-1111
El Paso, TX 915-562-4040
Fort Worth, TX 214-787-1111
Garland, TX 214-787-1111
Houston, TX 713-529-4444
Irving, TX 214-787-1111
Lubbock, TX 806-745-1058
Plano, TX 214-787-1111
San Antonio, TX 210-225-0404
Provo, UT 801-975-4499
Salt Lake City, UT ... 801-975-4499
Burlington, VT 802-862-2475
Montpelier, VT 802-655-2322
Alexandria, VA 202-936-1212
Chesapeake, VA 757-666-1212
Newport News, VA .. 757-877-1221
Norfolk, VA 757-666-1212
Richmond, VA 804-348-9382
Roanoke, VA 540-982-2303
Virginia Beach, VA ... 757-666-1212
Williamsburg, VA 757-877-1221
Olympia, WA 360-357-6453
Seattle, WA 206-464-2000
Spokane, WA 509-624-8905
Tacoma, WA 206-464-2000
Charleston, WV 304-345-2121
Morgantown, WV 304-296-1212
Green Bay, WI 920-494-2363
Madison, WI 608-936-1212
Milwaukee, WI 414-936-1212
Casper, WY 307-234-4804
Cheyenne, WY 307-635-9901
Edmonton, AB 780-468-4940
Halifax, NS 902-426-9090
Montreal, QC 514-283-4006
Ottawa, ON 613-998-3439
Quebec, QC 418-235-4771
Toronto, ON 416-661-0123
Vancouver, BC 604-664-9010
Winnipeg, MB 204-983-2050

Calendar of Events

This calendar covers events held in 250 US and Canadian cities. This calendar is organized first by US states and then by cities within each state grouping, with events for each city presented chronologically by month. Events in Canadian cities follow the US listings. General telephone numbers are provided for each event.

ALABAMA

Birmingham

February
World of Wheels Custom Auto Show (mid-February) 205-655-4950

March
Alabama Jubilee Rodeo (mid-March) 205-458-8400
Cottontail's Arts & Crafts Show (early March) 205-836-7178
Home & Garden Show (mid-March) 205-680-0234
Powerman Alabama Duathlon (late March) 205-320-1121
Sakura Festival (late March) 205-879-1227
Tannehill Spring Craft Show (mid-March) 205-477-5711
Tannehill Trade Days (late March-November) 205-477-5711

April
American Indian Dance Festival & Pow Wow (early April) 256-378-7252
Birmingham Amateur Radio HamFest (mid-April) 205-458-8400
Birmingham Festival of Arts Salute (mid-April) 205-252-7652
Bluegrass at Horsepens 40 (late April-early May) 256-570-0002
Bruno's Memorial Golf Classic (late April-early May) 205-967-4745
www.brunosmemorialclassic.com
Garden Fiesta Plant Sale (early April) 205-879-1227
NASCAR Talladega DieHard 500 (mid-April) 256-362-9064
Spring Folklore Festival (mid-April) 205-477-5711
Tannehill Trade Days (late March-November) 205-477-5711
Tannehill Trout Tournament (late April) 205-477-5711

May
Bluegrass at Horsepens 40 (late April-early May) 256-570-0002
Bruno's Memorial Golf Classic (late April-early May) 205-967-4745
www.brunosmemorialclassic.com
Do Dah Day Festival (mid-May) 205-595-7281
Eddleman Pro Tennis Classic (early May) 205-980-1000
Imagination Festival (late May) 205-595-6306
Southern Appalachian Dulcimer Festival (early May) 205-477-5711
Tannehill Civil War Reenactment (late May) 205-477-5711
Tannehill Trade Days (late March-November) 205-477-5711
Whistle Stop Festival & 5K Run (mid-May) 205-956-5962

June
Cahaba Riverfest (early June) 205-322-5326
City Stages-A Birmingham Festival (mid-June) 205-251-1272
www.citystages.org
Tannehill Trade Days (late March-November) 205-477-5711

July
Crape Myrtle Festival (late July) 205-254-2472
Function at Tuxedo Junction Jazz Festival (late July) 205-788-3672
Summerfest (late July-early August) 205-324-2426
Tannehill Trade Days (late March-November) 205-477-5711

August
Birmingham Heritage Festival (early August) 205-324-3333
www.bham.net/heritage
Great Southern Kudzu Festival (late August) 205-324-1911
Summerfest (late July-early August) 205-324-2426
Tannehill Trade Days (late March-November) 205-477-5711

September
Birmingham Fall Home Show (mid-September) 205-680-0234
Dixie Classic & Heartland Cruisers Open Car Show (late September) 205-477-5711
Oktoberfest (mid-September) 205-923-6564
Septemberfest (late September) 256-378-7252
Southern Women's Show (late September-early October) 800-849-0248
Tannehill Labor Day Celebration (early September) 205-477-5711
Tannehill Trade Days (late March-November) 205-477-5711

October
Alabama State Fair (late October) 205-458-8001
Birmingham Jam (early October) 205-323-0569
Bluff Park Art Show (early October) 205-822-0078
Magic City Classic Parade & Football Game (late October) 205-254-2391
NASCAR Winston 500 (early October) 256-362-9064
Southern Women's Show (late September-early October) 800-849-0248
Tannehill Trade Days (late March-November) 205-477-5711
Taste of Birmingham (mid-October) 205-987-0757

November
Christmas Light Show (November-December) 256-378-7252
Festival of Trees (late November-late December) 205-939-9671
Tannehill Trade Days (late March-November) 205-477-5711
Viva Health Vulcan Run Weekend (early November) 205-879-5344
www.run42k.com
Zoolight Safari (late November-December) 205-879-0458
www.birminghamzoo.com

December
Christmas at Arlington (December) 205-780-5656
Christmas at the Alabama (late December) 205-252-2262
Christmas Heritage Tour (December) 205-426-1628
Christmas Light Show (November-December) 256-378-7252
Festival of Trees (late November-late December) 205-939-9671
Tannehill Village Christmas (mid-December) 205-477-5711
Zoolight Safari (late November-December) 205-879-0458
www.birminghamzoo.com

Huntsville

January
Galaxy of Lights (late November-early January) 256-830-4447

April
Huntsville Pilgrimage (mid-April) 256-533-5723
Panoply-Huntsville's Festival of the Arts (late April) 256-519-2787
www.panoply.org/

May
Cotton Row Run (late May) 256-533-5723
Down Home Blues Festival (late May) 256-551-1020

June
Black Arts Festival (late June) 256-837-9387
Living History Weekends (June-August) 256-536-2882

July
Living History Weekends (June-August) 256-536-2882

August
Living History Weekends (June-August) 256-536-2882

September
Big Spring Jam (late September) 256-533-5723
www.bigspringjam.org/
Northeast Alabama State Fair (early September) 256-533-5723
Old Fashioned Trade Day (early September) 256-536-0097
State Fiddling Bluegrass Convention (mid-September) 256-859-4470

October
Cornucopia (mid-October) 256-830-4447
Indian Heritage Festival (mid-October) 256-536-2882

November
Civil War Living History Weekend (early November) 256-536-2882
Galaxy of Lights (late November-early January) 256-830-4447
Sorghum & Harvest Festival (early November) 256-536-2882
Under the Christmas Tree (early November) 256-881-1701

December
Galaxy of Lights (late November-early January) 256-830-4447
Rocket City Marathon (mid-December) 256-828-6207

Mobile

January
Delchamps Senior Bowl (mid-January) 334-438-2276
Senior Bowl (January) 334-470-7730

February
Mardi Gras (February-March) 334-470-7730

March
A Taste of the Colony (mid-March) 334-861-6992
Africatown Folk Festival (March) 334-470-7730
Azalea Trail Run & Festival (late March) 334-473-7223
Mardi Gras (February-March) 334-470-7730
Mobile Historic Homes Tours (mid-March) 334-470-7730
Providence Festival of Flowers (mid-March) 334-639-2050

April
Dauphin Island Regatta (late April) 334-470-7730
Mobile Jazz Festival (mid-April) 334-470-7730
Taste of Mobile (April) 334-415-2000

May
Blessing of the Fleet at Bayou la Batre (May) 334-824-2415
Dauphin Island Spring Festival (early May) 334-861-5525
Thunder on the Bay (mid-May) 334-861-6992

July
Alabama Deep Sea Fishing Rodeo (mid-July) 334-470-7730
Mobile Fourth of July Celebration (July 4) 334-470-7730

August
Labor Day Invitational Billfish Tournament (late August-early September) 334-343-1619

September
Labor Day Invitational Billfish Tournament (late August-early September) 334-343-1619
September Celebration (September) 334-470-7730

October
Bayfest Music Festival (early October) 334-470-7730
Colonial Isle Dauphine (early October) 334-861-6992
Greater Gulf State Fair (mid-late October) 334-470-7730
www.mobilefair.com/
National Shrimp Festival (October) 334-968-6904

November
Christmas Jubilee (late November) 334-415-2000
Craft Bugs Holiday Fantasy (late November) 334-343-5533
Deep South Dulcimer Festival (early November) 334-452-8496
International Carnival (mid-November) 334-470-7730
Junior League Christmas Jubilee (mid-November) 334-471-3348
Mobile International Festival (mid-November) 334-470-7730
Renaissance Festival (mid-November) 334-861-6992
Women's Encampment (early November) 334-861-6992

December
Candlelight Christmas at Oakleigh (early December) 334-415-2000
Christmas at Fort Gaines (early December) 334-861-6992
Christmas in Mobile Festival Arts & Crafts Show (late December) 334-415-2100
First Night Mobile (December 31) 334-470-7730

Montgomery

March
Blue-Gray Intercollegiate Tennis Championship (mid-March) 334-271-7001
World Championship Rodeo (mid-March) 334-265-1867

April
Calico Fort Arts & Crafts Fair (early April) 334-227-3250

May
Flimp Festival (early May) 334-244-5700
Greek Festival (early May) 334-263-1366
Jubilee CityFest (late May) 334-834-7220
NCAA Division II National Baseball Championship (late May) 334-241-2300

July
Montgomery State Farmers Market Day (mid-July) 334-242-5350

August
Broadway Under the Stars (late August) 334-240-4004

September
Alabama Highland Games (late September) 334-361-4571

October
Festival in the Park (early October) 334-241-2300
Oktoberfest (early October) 334-272-6527
South Alabama State Fair (early October) 334-272-6831

November
Taste of Montgomery (November) 334-277-1840
Turkey Day Classic Parade (late November) 334-229-4100

December
Blue-Gray All Star Football Classic (December) 334-265-1266
Christmas on the River Parade (early December) 800-252-2262

Tuscaloosa

March
Sakura Festival (March) 800-538-8696
Tannehill Trade Days (late March-November) 205-477-5711

April
Heritage Week (mid-April) 800-538-8696
Moundville Easter Pageant (mid-April) 800-538-8696
Tannehill Trade Days (late March-November) 205-477-5711

May
Tannehill Dulcimer Festival (early May) 205-477-5711
Tannehill Trade Days (late March-November) 205-477-5711

June
Tannehill Trade Days (late March-November) 205-477-5711

July
Tannehill Trade Days (late March-November) 205-477-5711

August
International CityFest & Weindorf (late August) 205-553-9009
www.cityfest.org
Tannehill Trade Days (late March-November) 205-477-5711

ALABAMA — Tuscaloosa (Cont'd)

September
Bryant Namesake Reunion (early September) 800-538-8696
Moundville Native American Festival
(late September-early October) 800-538-8696
Tannehill Trade Days (late March-November) 205-477-5711

October
Kentuck Festival of the Arts (mid-late October) 205-758-1257
www.dbtech.net/kentuck
Moundville Native American Festival
(late September-early October) 800-538-8696
Tannehill Trade Days (late March-November) 205-477-5711

November
Tannehill Trade Days (late March-November) 205-477-5711

December
Dickens Downtown (early December) 800-538-8696
Hilaritas (early December) 800-538-8696
Tuscaloosa Christmas Afloat (mid-December) 800-538-8696
West Alabama Christmas Parade (early December) 800-538-8696

ALASKA

Anchorage

January
Alyeska Ski Resort Winter Fest (early January) 907-754-1111
Anchorage Folk Festival (mid-January) 907-566-2334
Northern Lights (September-March) 907-276-4118
Polar Bear Jump Off Festival (mid-January) 907-224-5230
Sled Dog Races (January-February) 907-562-2235

February
Fur Rendezvous Winter Carnival (mid-February) 907-277-8615
www.alaska.net/~furrondy/
Iditasport (mid-February) 907-345-4505
Northern Lights (September-March) 907-276-4118
Sled Dog Races (January-February) 907-562-2235

March
Iditarod Trail Sled Dog Race (early March) 907-376-5155
International Ice Carving Competition (early March) 907-279-5650
Northern Lights (September-March) 907-276-4118
Tour of Anchorage Cross-Country Ski Race (March) 907-276-4118

April
Native Youth Olympics (late April-early May) 907-265-5900
Spring Carnival (mid-April) 907-754-2265

May
Native Youth Olympics (late April-early May) 907-265-5900
Saturday Market (May-September) 907-272-5634

June
Anchorage Festival of Music (mid-June) 907-276-2465
www.alaska.net/~anchfest/
Irish Music & Cultural Festival of Alaska (early June) 907-566-2028
Juneteenth Festival (mid-June) 907-278-1778
Mayor's Midnight Sun Marathon (mid-June) 907-343-4474
Saturday Market (May-September) 907-272-5634
Ship Creek King Salmon Derby (early-mid-June) 907-276-6472
Summer Solstice Celebration (late June) 907-276-4118
Summer Solstice Festival (mid-June) 907-279-9581
Taste of Anchorage (early June) 907-562-9911
Three Barons Fair (early-mid-June) 907-272-2873

July
Bear Paw Festival (early July) 907-694-4702
Freedom Days Festival (July 4) 907-276-4118
Girdwood Forest Fair (early July) 907-783-2931
Mount Marathon Race (July 4) 907-224-8051
Saturday Market (May-September) 907-272-5634

August
Alaska State Fair (late August-early September) 907-276-4118
www.alaska.net/~design/fair/
Saturday Market (May-September) 907-272-5634
Seward Silver Salmon Derby (mid-late August) 907-224-3046

September
Alaska State Fair (late August-early September) 907-276-4118
www.alaska.net/~design/fair/
Northern Lights (September-March) 907-276-4118
Saturday Market (May-September) 907-272-5634

October
Northern Lights (September-March) 907-276-4118
Quyana Alaska (mid-October) 907-274-3611

November
Carrs Great Alaska Shootout (late November) 907-786-1230
Great Alaska Shootout (late November) 907-786-1230
Holiday Food & Gift Show (early November) 907-277-7469
Northern Lights (September-March) 907-276-4118

December
Northern Lights (September-March) 907-276-4118
Northern Lights Invitational Basketball Tournament
(late December) 907-786-1230
Swedish Christmas Celebration (early December) 907-274-2336
Torchlight Ski Parade (December 31) 907-754-1111
Tree Lighting Ceremony (early December) 907-276-5015

Fairbanks

February
Nenana Ice Classic (early February-early April) 907-832-5446
Yukon Quest International Sled Dog Race (February) 907-452-7954

March
Chatanika Days (mid-March) 907-389-2164
Fairbanks Winter Carnival (mid-March) 907-452-1105
Festival of Alaska Native Arts (early March) 907-474-7181
Ice Art Competition (early March) 907-451-8250
www.icealaska.com
Limited North American Sled Dog Race (early March) 907-456-5774
Nenana Ice Classic (early February-early April) 907-832-5446
North Pole Winter Carnival (mid-March) 907-488-2242
Open North American Championship Sled Dog Race
(mid-March) 907-488-9685

April
Arctic Man Ski & Sno Go Classic (April) 907-456-6867
Nenana Ice Classic (early February-early April) 907-832-5446

June
Midnight Sun Run (late June) 907-452-7211
Nenana River Daze (early June) 907-456-5774
North Pole Summer Festival (mid-June) 907-488-2242
Yukon 800 Marathon Boat Race (June) 800-327-5774

July
Deltana Fair (late July) 907-895-3247
Fairbanks Preservation Society 4th of July Celebration
(July 4) 907-456-8848
Fairbanks Summer Arts Festival (late July-early August) 907-474-8869
Golden Days (mid-July) 907-452-1105
World Eskimo-Indian Olympics (mid-July) 907-456-5774

August
Fairbanks Summer Arts Festival (late July-early August) 907-474-8869
Tanana Valley State Fair (August) 907-452-3750

September
Equinox Marathon (mid-September) 907-479-6908

November
Athabascan Fiddling Festival (mid-November) 907-452-1825
Winter Solstice Celebration
(late November-mid-December) 907-452-8671

December
Candle Lighting Festival (early December) 907-488-2242
Winter Solstice Celebration
(late November-mid-December) 907-452-8671

Juneau

February
Gold Medal Basketball Tournament
(late February-early March) 907-586-1737

March
Gold Medal Basketball Tournament
(late February-early March) 907-586-1737

April
Alaska Folk Festival (early April) 907-586-1737

May
Juneau Jazz & Classics Festival (late May) 907-463-3378

August
Golden North Salmon Derby (August) 907-586-1737

December
Gallery Walk (early December) 907-586-1737

ARIZONA

Flagstaff

February
Flagstaff Winterfest (February) 800-842-7293

June
Pine Country Rodeo (mid-June) 520-774-9541

July
Festival of Arts & Crafts Extraordinaire (early July) 520-779-1227
Independence Day Festival (July 4) 520-774-6272

August
Flagstaff Chili Cook-off (late August) 520-526-4314
Flagstaff Summerfest (early August) 520-774-9541

September
Coconino County Fair (Labor Day Weekend) 520-774-5130
Flagstaff Festival of Science
(late September-early October) 800-842-7293

October
Flagstaff Festival of Science
(late September-early October) 800-842-7293

November
Worldfest International Film Festival
(early-mid-November) 800-501-0111

December
Christmas Herb & Craft Sale (early December) 520-774-1442

Glendale

January
Annual Quilt Show (mid-January-mid-March) 623-939-5782

February
Annual Quilt Show (mid-January-mid-March) 623-939-5782

March
Annual Quilt Show (mid-January-mid-March) 623-939-5782

April
A Family A Fair (early April) 623-930-2820
Glendale Jazz Festival (late-April) 623-930-2960
Juried Fine Arts Competition (early April) 623-939-5782
Performances in the Park (late April) 623-937-4754

June
Community Bank Concerts (June-July) 623-930-2820

July
Community Bank Concerts (June-July) 623-930-2820
Fourth of July Celebration (July 4) 623-937-4754

September
Front Porch Festival (late-September) 623-435-0556

November
Hot Air Balloon Race & Thunderbird Balloon Classic
(early November) 480-312-6802
Sahuaro Ranch Days (early November) 623-939-5782

Mesa

February
Arizona Scottish Highland Games (late February) 602-431-0095
Blues Blast (late February) 602-644-2242
Territorial Days (mid-February) 602-644-2351
Valley of the Sun Polka Festival (mid-February) 602-237-4024

March
Acorn's Spring Antique Show & Sale (late March) 400-030-2660
Air Show Spectacular (mid-March) 480-988-1013
Mesa Day (early March) 602-644-2351

April
Country Thunder USA (late April) 480-966-9920

May
Cinco de Mayo Celebrations (early May) 602-644-2230
Mesa Southwest Antique Guild Show & Sale (mid-May) 602-943-1766
Peach Festival (mid-May) 480-987-3333
Queen Creek Potato Festival (late May) 480-987-3333

July
Independence Day Celebrations (July 4) 602-644-2011

October
Native American Pow Wow (mid-October) 602-644-2169

November
Arizona Woodcarvers Show (late November) 480-895-7036
Dia de los Muertos Festival (early November) 480-833-5875
Fountain Festival of the Arts & Crafts (early November) 480-837-1654
Gilbert Days (mid-late November) 480-380-8399
M-Car Grand Prix (early November) 480-969-1307

Phoenix

January
Arizona Stock Show & Rodeo
(late December-early January) 602-258-8568
www.anls.org/
Copper World Classic Auto Racing
(late January-early February) 602-252-3833
Fiesta Bowl (early January) 480-350-0900
Phoenix Open Golf Tournament (late January) 602-870-0163

February
Arizona Renaissance Festival
(early February-late March) 520-463-2700
www.opus1.com/emol/azrenfest/index.html
ARR Desert Classic Marathon (mid-February) 623-933-2425
Copper World Classic Auto Racing
(late January-early February) 602-252-3833
Fountain Hills Great Fair (late February) 480-837-1654
Lost Dutchman Days (late February) 480-982-3141

March
Arizona Renaissance Festival
(early February-late March) 520-463-2700
www.opus1.com/emol/azrenfest/index.html
Arizona's Cactus League Spring Training (March) 480-969-1307
Chandler Ostrich Festival (mid-March) 480-963-4571
Indy Racing League Phoenix 200 (late March) 602-252-2227
Scottsdale Arts Festival (mid-March) 480-994-2787
scottsdalearts.org/saf/
Scottsdale Desert Festival of Fine Art (late March) 480-837-5637

April
Easter Pageant (April) 480-964-7164
Maricopa County Fair (late April-early May) 602-252-0717

ARIZONA — Phoenix (Cont'd)

Music by Moonlight Thursday Night Concert Series (mid-April-mid-September) ... 480-488-1072
Southwest Salsa Challenge (late April) ... 602-955-3947

May
Cinco de Mayo Festival (early May) ... 602-279-4669
Maricopa County Fair (late April-early May) ... 602-252-0717
Music by Moonlight Thursday Night Concert Series (mid-April-mid-September) ... 480-488-1072

June
Music by Moonlight Thursday Night Concert Series (mid-April-mid-September) ... 480-488-1072

July
July 4th Festivities (July 4) ... 602-256-4125
Music by Moonlight Thursday Night Concert Series (mid-April-mid-September) ... 480-488-1072

August
Music by Moonlight Thursday Night Concert Series (mid-April-mid-September) ... 480-488-1072

September
Music by Moonlight Thursday Night Concert Series (mid-April-mid-September) ... 480-488-1072

October
Arizona State Fair (early-late October) ... 602-252-6771
www.azstatefair.com
Coors Light World Finals Drag Boat Racing (late October) ... 602-268-0200
Cowboy Artists of America Exhibition (late October-late November) ... 602-257-1880
www.phxart.org/index_events.html

November
Cowboy Artists of America Exhibition (late October-late November) ... 602-257-1880
www.phxart.org/index_events.html
Fountain Hills Festival of Arts & Crafts (mid-November) .. 480-837-1654
French Week in Arizona (mid-November) ... 602-954-6573
Holiday Out West Arts & Crafts Festival (late November) ... 480-488-2014
Hot Air Balloon Race & Thunderbird Balloon Classic (early November) ... 480-312-6802

December
Arizona Stock Show & Rodeo (late December-early January) ... 602-258-8568
www.anls.org/
Fiesta of Lights (mid-December) ... 602-261-8604
Indian Market (mid-December) ... 602-495-0901
Pueblo Grande Indian Market (mid-December) ... 602-495-0901
Tumbleweed Christmas Tree Lighting Ceremony (December) ... 480-786-2727

Scottsdale

January
Borgata Farmers Market (October-April) ... 480-998-1822
Fiesta Bowl (early January) ... 480-350-0900
Ollie the Trolley's City Tours (October-April) ... 480-970-8130
Scottsdale Celebration of Fine Art (mid-January-late March) ... 480-443-7695

February
Borgata Farmers Market (October-April) ... 480-998-1822
Equine Spectacular (mid-February) ... 480-502-5600
Ollie the Trolley's City Tours (October-April) ... 480-970-8130
Scottsdale Arabian Horse Show (mid-late February) ... 480-312-6802
Scottsdale Celebration of Fine Art (mid-January-late March) ... 480-443-7695

March
Borgata Farmers Market (October-April) ... 480-998-1822
Jump into Spring Hunter Jumper Horse Show (late March) ... 480-312-6802
Ollie the Trolley's City Tours (October-April) ... 480-970-8130
Scottsdale Arts Festival (mid-March) ... 480-994-2787
scottsdalearts.org/saf/
Scottsdale Celebration of Fine Art (mid-January-late March) ... 480-443-7695
Scottsdale Desert Festival of Fine Art (late March) ... 480-837-5637

April
Arizona Quarter Horse Amateur Horse Show (early April) ... 480-443-8800
Borgata Farmers Market (October-April) ... 480-998-1822
Merry-Go-Round Horse Show (early April) ... 480-312-6802
Music by Moonlight Thursday Night Concert Series (mid-April-mid-September) ... 480-488-1072
Ollie the Trolley's City Tours (October-April) ... 480-970-8130
PRCA Pro Rodeo Series (mid-April) ... 480-502-5600
www.rawhide.com
Region 7 All-Arabian Championship Horse Show (late April-early May) ... 480-312-6802
Scottsdale Culinary Festival (mid-April) ... 480-945-7193
Scottsdale Spring Festival (mid-April) ... 480-312-6802

May
Knix Spring Rodeo Connection at Rawhide (early May-late June) ... 480-502-5600
Music by Moonlight Thursday Night Concert Series (mid-April-mid-September) ... 480-488-1072
Region 7 All-Arabian Championship Horse Show (late April-early May) ... 480-312-6802

June
Knix Spring Rodeo Connection at Rawhide (early May-late June) ... 480-502-5600
Music by Moonlight Thursday Night Concert Series (mid-April-mid-September) ... 480-488-1072
WestWorld Summer Rodeo Series (June-mid-September) ... 480-312-6802

July
Music by Moonlight Thursday Night Concert Series (mid-April-mid-September) ... 480-488-1072
WestWorld Summer Rodeo Series (June-mid-September) ... 480-312-6802

August
Music by Moonlight Thursday Night Concert Series (mid-April-mid-September) ... 480-488-1072
WestWorld Summer Rodeo Series (June-mid-September) ... 480-312-6802

September
Music by Moonlight Thursday Night Concert Series (mid-April-mid-September) ... 480-488-1072
National Truck Rodeo (early September) ... 480-312-6802
WestWorld Summer Rodeo Series (June-mid-September) ... 480-312-6802

October
Borgata Farmers Market (October-April) ... 480-998-1822
Greek Festival (late October) ... 480-312-6802
Ollie the Trolley's City Tours (October-April) ... 480-970-8130

November
Borgata Farmers Market (October-April) ... 480-998-1822
Hot Air Balloon Race & Thunderbird Balloon Classic (early November) ... 480-312-6802
Ollie the Trolley's City Tours (October-April) ... 480-970-8130

December
Borgata Farmers Market (October-April) ... 480-998-1822
Ollie the Trolley's City Tours (October-April) ... 480-970-8130
Rawhide's Rollickin' New Year's Eve (December 31) ... 480-502-5600

Tempe

January
Fiesta Bowl (early January) ... 480-350-0900
Fiesta Bowl Parade (early January) ... 480-350-0900
Tempe's Fantasy of Lights (late November-early January) ... 480-894-8158

March
Spring Festival of the Arts (late March-early April) ... 480-967-4877

April
Spring Festival of the Arts (late March-early April) ... 480-967-4877
Spring POW WOW Competition (mid-April) ... 480-965-5224

May
Arizona Special Olympics Summer Games (early May) ... 602-230-1200

June
Grand Canyon State Games (late June) ... 480-517-9700

July
Fourth of July Celebration (July 4) ... 480-967-7891

October
Fiesta Bowl Duck Race (October) ... 480-350-0900
Mill Avenue Masquerade (October 31) ... 480-967-4877

November
Tempe's Fantasy of Lights (late November-early January) ... 480-894-8158
Tempe's Thanksgiving Soccer Tournament (late November) ... 480-966-4053

December
Fall Festival of the Arts (early December) ... 480-967-4877
New Year's Eve Block Party (December 31) ... 480-894-8158
Tempe's Fantasy of Lights (late November-early January) ... 480-894-8158

Tucson

January
Indian America (early January) ... 520-622-4900
Square & Round Dance & Clogging Festival (mid-January) ... 520-885-5032

February
La Fiesta de los Vaqueros Rodeo (late February) ... 520-624-1817
Nortel Open (mid-February) ... 800-882-7660
Tucson Gem & Mineral Show (mid-February) ... 520-322-5773
Tucson Rodeo (late February) ... 520-741-2233

March
4th Avenue Street Fair (late March & early December) ... 520-624-5004

April
Big Boys Toy Show (early April) ... 520-762-3247
International Mariachi Conference (late April) ... 520-884-9920
Pima County Fair (mid-April) ... 520-762-9100
Spring Fling (early April) ... 520-621-5610
Wildflower Festival (early April) ... 520-742-6455

May
Cinco de Mayo (early May) ... 520-791-4873
Music Under the Stars (early May-mid-June) ... 520-791-4873
Wyatt Earp Days (late May) ... 800-457-3423

June
Juneteenth Festival (mid-June) ... 520-791-4355
Music Under the Stars (early May-mid-June) ... 520-791-4873
Shakespeare in the Park (late June) ... 520-791-4079
Summerset Suite (June-July) ... 520-743-3399

July
Independence Day (July 4) ... 520-791-4860
Summerset Suite (June-July) ... 520-743-3399

August
Vigilante Days (early August) ... 800-457-3423

October
Desert Thunder Pro Rodeo (mid-October) ... 520-721-1621
Fall Festival (mid-October) ... 520-394-0060
Fiesta de los Chiles (late October) ... 520-326-9255
Tucson Heritage Experience Festival (early October) ... 520-621-3701

November
El Tour de Tucson (late November) ... 520-745-2033
Holiday Craft Market (late November) ... 520-624-2333
Western Music Festival (early November) ... 520-743-9794

December
4th Avenue Street Fair (late March & early December) ... 520-624-5004
Balloon Glo (early December) ... 520-621-9034
Fiesta de Guadalupe (December) ... 520-624-1817
Insight.com Bowl (late December) ... 520-624-1817
Luminaria Nights (early December) ... 520-326-9255
Tucson Marathon (early December) ... 520-320-0667
www.tucsonmarathon.com

ARKANSAS

Fort Smith

May
Old Fort Days Barrel Race Futurity Derby (mid-May) ... 501-783-6176
Old Fort Days Rodeo (late May-early June) ... 501-783-6176

June
Old Fort Days Rodeo (late May-early June) ... 501-783-6176
Old Fort River Festival (early June) ... 501-783-6363

July
Freedomfest-Greenwood (July) ... 501-996-6357
Mayor's July 4th Celebration (July 4) ... 501-782-2041

September
Arkansas-Oklahoma State Fair (late-September) ... 501-783-6176
Fort Smith Blues Festival (early September) ... 501-783-6353
Fort Smith Riverfront Blues Festival (mid-September) ... 501-785-1201
biz.ipa.net/blues/
Hanging Dice Nationals Street Custom Car Show (early September) ... 501-783-6176

October
Valley of the Arkansas Gathering (late October) ... 501-783-8888

November
Holiday Market (mid-November) ... 501-784-2365

December
Fort Smith Christmas Parade (early December) ... 501-782-2041

Hot Springs

January
Holiday in the Park (late December-early January) ... 800-543-2284

April
Racing Festival of the South (mid-April) ... 501-623-4411

June
BrickFest (late June) ... 501-332-2721

October
Arkansas Oktoberfest (mid-October) ... 800-772-2489
Arts & Crafts Fair (early October) ... 501-623-6841
Hot Springs Documentary Film Festival (mid-October) ... 501-321-4747
www.docufilminst.org
Oktoberfest Fur Kinder (early October) ... 501-321-1700

November
Historic Downtown District Open House (late November) .. 501-623-2849

December
Courthouse Lighting Ceremony (early December) ... 501-623-6841
Holiday in the Park (late December-early January) ... 800-543-2284
Holiday Luminaries (early December) ... 501-624-5555
Osborne Family Holiday Lighting (mid-late December) ... 501-624-5333

Little Rock

January
Arkansas Marine Expo (mid-January) ... 501-455-1001
Eagle Watch Barge Tours (mid-January) ... 501-868-5806
Great Southern Gun Show (late-January) ... 888-325-4482

ARKANSAS — Little Rock (Cont'd)

Martin Luther King Jr Holiday Celebration (mid-January) 501-324-9333

February
Arkansas Flower & Garden Show (mid-February) 501-821-4000
Depression Glass Show & Sale (late February-early March) 501-375-0435
Eagle Awareness Days (early February) 501-727-5441
Greater Little Rock Flower & Garden Show (late February) 501-376-4781

March
Decorative Arts Forum (mid-March) 501-372-4000
Depression Glass Show & Sale (late February-early March) 501-375-0435
Toughman Contest (early March) 501-376-4781

May
Arkansas Territorial Restoration Arts & Crafts Festival (early May) 501-376-4781
Quapaw Quarter Spring Tour of Homes (early May) 501-376-4781
Riverfest (late May) 501-376-4781
Toadsuck Daze (early May) 501-376-4781
Wildwood Festival of Music & the Arts (late May-late June) 501-821-7275

June
Juneteenth Celebration (mid-June) 501-376-4781
Wildwood Festival of Music & the Arts (late May-late June) 501-821-7275
Wildwood Jazz Festival (early June) 501-821-7275

July
Pops On The River (July 4) 501-376-4781

August
Summer Shakespeare Festival (mid-late August) 501-376-4781
Zoo Days (mid-late August) 501-666-2406

September
Arkansas River Blues Festival (mid-September) 501-376-4781
Burns Park Arts & Crafts Fair (mid-September) 800-844-4781
Summerset (early September) 501-758-1424

October
Arkansas State Fair (early October) 501-372-8341
Timberfest (early October) 870-942-3021
Wildwood International Children's Festival (mid-October) 501-376-4781

November
Arkansas Holiday Light Up & Laser Show (late November-late December) 800-844-4781
Holiday House (mid-November) 501-666-0658

December
Arkansas Holiday Light Up & Laser Show (late November-late December) 800-844-4781
Christmas Showcase Arkansas (early December) 501-376-4781
Festival of Trees (early December) 501-664-8573
Zoo Lights (early December) 501-666-2406

CALIFORNIA

Anaheim

January
Christmas Fantasy Parade (late November-early January) 714-781-4560

February
Flying U Rodeo (early February) 714-704-2400

May
Cinco de Mayo Celebration (early May) 714-765-5274
Gogh Van Orange Art & Music Festival (early May) 714-538-3581
Orange County Art & Jazz Festival (mid-May) 714-541-2787

June
Fantasy in the Sky (June-September) 714-781-4560

July
Fantasy in the Sky (June-September) 714-781-4560
Orange County Fair (mid-July) 714-708-3247
www.ocfair.com

August
Fantasy in the Sky (June-September) 714-781-4560
Southern California Home & Garden Show (mid-late August) 714-978-8888

September
Fantasy in the Sky (June-September) 714-781-4560
Oktoberfest (mid-September-early November) 714-563-4166

October
Anaheim Harvest Festivals (late October) 707-778-6300
www.harvestfestival.com
Harvest Festival (late October) 714-999-8900
Oktoberfest (mid-September-early November) 714-563-4166

November
Christmas Fantasy Parade (late November-early January) 714-781-4560
Oktoberfest (mid-September-early November) 714-563-4166

December
Christmas Fantasy Parade (late November-early January) 714-781-4560

Bakersfield

March
Appaloosa Horse Show (late March) 661-833-4900
Saint Patrick's Day Parade (mid-March) 661-325-5892

April
Horseless Carriage Auto Expo (mid-April) 661-833-4917
Kern River Fesitval (mid-April) 760-376-2629
Pacific Coast Junior National Livestock Show (early April) 661-833-4934
Quarter Horse Show (late April) 661-833-4917
Village Artisans Spring Fair (late April) 661-328-1943

May
5th of May Festivity (May 5) 661-323-9334
Bakersfield Jazz Festival (mid-May) 661-664-3093
Downtown Street Faires (late May-late August) 661-325-5892
Lilac Festival (mid-May) 661-242-4663
Stampede Day's Rodeo (early May) 661-325-8476
Vintage Sailplane Regatta & Blue Feather Fly In (late May) 661-822-5267
Western Street Rod Nationals (late May) 661-833-4917

June
Downtown Street Faires (late May-late August) 661-325-5892
One Act Festival (mid-late June) 661-831-8114
Springtyme Faire (mid-June) 661-822-6062

July
Country Faire (early July) 661-245-1212
Downtown Street Faires (late May-late August) 661-325-5892

August
Downtown Street Faires (late May-late August) 661-325-5892
Mountain Festival Art Show (mid-August) 661-245-3358

September
Apple Harvest Fair (mid-September) 661-822-4180
Fall Festival (early September) 661-245-1212
Great Kern County Fair (mid September-early October) 661-833-4900
www.kerncountyfair.com

October
Great Kern County Fair (mid September-early October) 661-833-4900
www.kerncountyfair.com
Oktoberfest (mid-October) 661-327-2424

December
Bakersfield Christmas Parade (early December) 661-325-3410
McFarland Christmas Festival (mid-December) 661-725-2518

Chula Vista

April
Taste of the Arts (mid-April) 619-585-5627

May
Cinco de Mayo Celebration (early May) 619-422-1982

June
Concerts in the Park (early June-mid-August) 619-585-5627
Lemon Festival (early June) 619-422-1982

July
Concerts in the Park (early June-mid-August) 619-585-5627

August
Concerts in the Park (early June-mid-August) 619-585-5627
Downtown Third Avenue Lemon Festival (early August) 619-422-1982

September
Bonitafest (late September) 619-472-8520
Harbor Day & Tall Ship Festival (mid-September) 858-268-1250
Soap Box Derby (mid-September) 619-585-1405

October
Arturo Barrios Invitational 10K/5K (late October) 619-450-6510

December
Holiday Festival (early December) 619-691-5071
Starlight Yule Parade (early December) 619-422-1982

Fremont

May
Fremont Family Carnival (mid-May) 510-490-2848
Niles Wildflower & Art Festival (early May) 510-742-9868

June
Charlie Chaplin Days (early June) 510-742-9868
Mission Days (mid-June) 510-657-1797

July
Festival of the Arts (late July) 510-795-2244
Newark's Music at the Grove Summer Concert Series (early July-mid-August) 510-745-1124
Summer Evening Concerts (mid-July-late August) 510-791-4340

August
Newark's Music at the Grove Summer Concert Series (early July-mid-August) 510-745-1124
Niles Antique Faire (late August) 510-742-9868
Summer Evening Concerts (mid-July-late August) 510-791-4340

November
Niles Holiday Open House & Tree Lighting Ceremony (late November-late December) 510-742-9868

December
Niles Holiday Open House & Tree Lighting Ceremony (late November-late December) 510-742-9868

Fresno

January
Hmong National New Year (late December-early January) 559-233-4622
Kwanzaa Festival (late December-early January) 559-268-7102

February
Carnival (late February) 559-485-4810
Fresno County Blossom Trail (late February-early March) 559-233-0836

March
Fresno County Blossom Trail (late February-early March) 559-233-0836
Mariachi Festival (early March) 559-455-5761
Sanger Blossom Days Festival (early March) 559-875-4575

April
Clovis Rodeo (late April) 559-299-8838
William Saroyan Festival (late April) 559-221-1441

May
Easton May Day Celebration (early May) 559-233-0836
Raisin Bowl Regatta (early May) 559-822-2332
Sudz in the City (mid-May) 559-266-9982
Tower Arts Festival (mid-May) 559-498-8560

June
Kingsburg Gun Shoot (late June) 559-897-2925
Kingsburg Summer Band Concerts Under the Stars (late June-late July) 559-897-2925
Miss California Pageant (mid-June) 559-233-0836
Shaver Lake Fishing Derby (mid-June) 559-841-3350

July
High Sierra Regatta (July) 559-822-2666
Kingsburg Summer Band Concerts Under the Stars (late June-late July) 559-897-2925
Obon Odori Festival (mid-July) 559-442-4054

September
Sanger Grape Bowl Festival (mid-September) 559-875-4575

October
Civil War Revisited (early October) 559-441-0862
Fresno Fair (mid-October) 559-453-3247
Renaissance Festival (late October) 559-436-3434

December
Hmong National New Year (late December-early January) 559-233-4622
Kwanzaa Festival (late December-early January) 559-268-7102

Garden Grove

February
Tet Festival (early February) 714-775-6820

March
Crystal Cathedral Glory of Easter (late March-April) 714-544-5679

April
Crystal Cathedral Glory of Easter (late March-April) 714-544-5679

May
Garden Grove Strawberry Festival (late May) 714-638-0981
Gogh Van Orange Art & Music Festival (early May) 714-538-3581

June
Fantasy in the Sky (June-September) 714-781-4560

July
Fantasy in the Sky (June-September) 714-781-4560
Orange County Fair (mid-July) 714-708-3247
www.ocfair.com

August
Fantasy in the Sky (June-September) 714-781-4560

September
Fantasy in the Sky (June-September) 714-781-4560

October
Halloween Carnival (late October) 714-741-5200
Korean Festival (early-October) 714-741-3310
Orange County Wine Festival (early October) 714-530-0430

November
Crystal Cathedral Glory of Christmas (late November-December) 714-544-5679

December
Crystal Cathedral Glory of Christmas (late November-December) 714-544-5679
Songs of Christmas (early December) 714-741-5200

Glendale

January
Tournament of Roses Parade (January 1) ... 626-795-9311

June
Valley Fair (mid-June) ... 818-557-1600

October
Days of Verdugo Festival (mid-October) ... 818-240-2464

Huntington Beach

January
Pacific Shoreline Marathon (late January) ... 949-661-6062

February
Taste of Huntington Beach (early February) ... 714-842-4481

March
Tern Island Clean-Up (late March) ... 714-840-1575

May
Duck-A-Thon (mid-May) ... 714-374-1951

June
Concours d'Elegance (early June) ... 714-842-4481

July
G-Shock US Open of Surfing (late July) ... 949-366-4584
Independence Day Parade (July 4) ... 714-536-5486
Orange County Fair (mid-July) ... 714-708-3247
www.ocfair.com
Surf City Festival (late July) ... 714-536-8888

August
Distance Derby (mid-August) ... 714-536-5486
Summer Horse Classic (early August) ... 714-536-5258

September
Civil War Reenactment (Labor Day weekend) ... 714-962-5777
Huntington Beach Summer Surf Contest (early September) ... 714-536-5486
Old World Village Oktoberfest (late September-late October) ... 714-895-8020

October
Old World Village Oktoberfest (late September-late October) ... 714-895-8020
Rose Show & Sale (late October) ... 714-897-2533

December
Cruise of Lights (mid-late December) ... 714-840-7542
Huntington Harbour Cruise of Lights (mid-December) ... 714-840-7542

Long Beach

January
Martin Luther King Celebration & Parade (mid-January) ... 562-570-6816
Whale Watching (January-March) ... 562-436-3645

February
Bob Marley Reggae Festival (mid-February) ... 562-436-3661
Queen Mary Scottish Festival (mid-February) ... 562-435-3511
Whale Watching (January-March) ... 562-436-3645

March
Whale Watching (January-March) ... 562-436-3645

April
Grand Prix of Long Beach (early April) ... 562-436-9953
Kaleidoscope Festival (late April) ... 562-985-2288

May
Beach Charities BeachFest (early May) ... 949-376-6942
Long Beach Lesbian & Gay Pride Festival (mid-May) ... 800-354-7743

June
Aloha Concert Jam (late June) ... 562-436-3645

July
Cajun & Zydeco Festival (late July) ... 562-427-3713
Orange County Fair (mid-July) ... 714-708-3247
www.ocfair.com

August
International Sea Festival (August) ... 562-570-3100
Long Beach Jazz Festival (early August) ... 562-436-7794
Long Beach Renaissance Arts Festival (late August) ... 562-570-5333
Long Beach Sea Festival (August) ... 562-570-3100

September
Belmont Shore Car Show (mid-September) ... 562-434-3066
Grecian Festival (early September) ... 562-494-8929
Harvest Festival (early September) ... 562-436-3661
KLON Blues Festival (Labor Day weekend) ... 562-985-1686
Long Beach Blues Festival (early September) ... 562-985-5566

October
Anaheim Street International Festival (early October) ... 562-436-3645

December
Belmont Shore Christmas Parade (early December) ... 562-434-3066
New Year's Eve Blues & Reggae Cruise & Fireworks (December 31) ... 562-799-7000
New Year's Eve Gala on Queen Mary (December 31) ... 562-435-3511
www.queenmary.com
New Year's Eve on Pine Square (December 31) ... 562-436-4259
Parade of a Thousand Lights (late December) ... 562-435-4093

Los Angeles

January
Martin Luther King Celebration & Parade (mid-January) ... 562-570-6816
Rose Bowl Game (early January) ... 626-449-4100
Tournament of Roses Parade & Rose Bowl (January 1) ... 626-449-4100

February
Chinese New Year's Parade in Chinatown (February) ... 213-617-0396
Golden Dragon Parade (mid-February) ... 213-617-0396
Grammy Awards (February-March) ... 310-392-3777
www.grammy.com

March
Academy Awards (late March) ... 310-247-3000
City of Los Angeles Marathon (early March) ... 310-444-5544
www.lamarathon.com
Crystal Cathedral Glory of Easter (late March-April) ... 714-544-5679
Grammy Awards (February-March) ... 310-392-3777
www.grammy.com
Los Angeles Bach Festival (mid-March) ... 213-385-1345
Spring Festival of Flowers (late March-mid-April) ... 818-952-4400

April
Crystal Cathedral Glory of Easter (late March-April) ... 714-544-5679
Earth Day Heal the Bay (mid-April) ... 310-581-4188
Fiesta Broadway Cinco de Mayo Celebration (late April) ... 310-914-0015
Israeli Festival (late April-early May) ... 818-757-0123
LA Fiesta Broadway (late April) ... 310-914-8308
Renaissance Pleasure Faire (April-June) ... 800-523-2473
members.aol.com/piranhant2/RPFS97Picts.html
Spring Festival of Flowers (late March-mid-April) ... 818-952-4400
Thai New Year Festival (mid-April) ... 213-624-7300

May
Cinco de Mayo Celebrations (early May) ... 213-628-1274
Fiesta de las Artes (late May) ... 310-376-0951
Israeli Festival (late April-early May) ... 818-757-0123
Old Pasadena Summer Fest (late May) ... 626-797-6803
Renaissance Pleasure Faire (April-June) ... 800-523-2473
members.aol.com/piranhant2/RPFS97Picts.html
Spring Fest (mid-May) ... 626-282-5767
UCLA Jazz & Reggae Festival (late May) ... 310-825-9912
UCLA Pow Wow (early May) ... 310-206-7513
Venice Art Walk (mid-May) ... 310-392-9255

June
California Plaza's Moonlight Concerts (June-October) ... 213-687-2159
Concours on Rodeo (late June) ... 310-858-6100
Great American Irish Fair & Music Festival (mid-June) ... 818-503-2511
Los Angeles Gay & Lesbian Pride Celebration (late June) ... 323-686-0950
Mariachi USA Festival (late June) ... 323-848-7717
Playboy Jazz Festival (mid-June) ... 310-449-4070
Renaissance Pleasure Faire (April-June) ... 800-523-2473
members.aol.com/piranhant2/RPFS97Picts.html
Sawdust Festival (late June-late August) ... 949-494-3030
Summer Nights at the Ford (mid-June-early September) ... 213-974-1396

July
California Plaza's Moonlight Concerts (June-October) ... 213-687-2159
Lotus Festival (early July) ... 213-624-7300
Malibu Art Festival (late July) ... 310-456-9025
Old Pasadena Jazz Fest (early July) ... 213-624-7300
Outfest-Los Angeles Gay & Lesbian Film Festival (mid-July) ... 323-960-9200
Page Museum's Fossil Excavation at La Brea Tar Pits (mid-July-mid-September) ... 323-934-7243
Pageant of the Masters/Festival of the Arts (early July-late August) ... 949-494-1145
Sawdust Festival (late June-late August) ... 949-494-3030
Summer Nights at the Ford (mid-June-early September) ... 213-974-1396

August
African Marketplace & Cultural Faire (late August-early September) ... 323-734-1164
California Plaza's Moonlight Concerts (June-October) ... 213-687-2159
Nisei Week Japanese Festival (mid-August) ... 213-687-7193
Page Museum's Fossil Excavation at La Brea Tar Pits (mid-July-mid-September) ... 323-934-7243
Pageant of the Masters/Festival of the Arts (early July-late August) ... 949-494-1145
Sawdust Festival (late June-late August) ... 949-494-3030
Summer Nights at the Ford (mid-June-early September) ... 213-974-1396

September
African Marketplace & Cultural Faire (late August-early September) ... 323-734-1164
Alpine Village Oktoberfest (early September-October) ... 310-327-4384
California Plaza's Moonlight Concerts (June-October) ... 213-687-2159
Festival of Philippine Arts & Culture (mid-September) ... 213-389-3050
Los Angeles City's Birthday Celebration (early September) ... 213-680-2821
Los Angeles County Fair (early September-early October) ... 909-623-3111
Page Museum's Fossil Excavation at La Brea Tar Pits (mid-July-mid-September) ... 323-934-7243
Summer Nights at the Ford (mid-June-early September) ... 213-974-1396
Thai Cultural Day (mid-late September) ... 310-827-2910

October
Alpine Village Oktoberfest (early September-October) ... 310-327-4384
California Plaza's Moonlight Concerts (June-October) ... 213-687-2159
Los Angeles County Fair (early September-early October) ... 909-623-3111
Los Angeles International Film Festival (late October) ... 323-856-7707
www.afifest.com
Scandinavian Festival (early October) ... 323-661-4273
South Bay Greek Festival (early October) ... 310-540-2434

November
Hollywood Christmas Parade (late November) ... 323-469-8311
Intertribal Marketplace (early November) ... 323-221-2164

December
Christmas Boat Parade (mid-December) ... 800-831-7678
Griffith Park Light Festival (December) ... 323-913-4688
Las Posadas Candlelight Procession (mid-December) ... 213-628-1274
Los Angeles Music Week (early December) ... 310-670-6898

Modesto

January
Modesto A's Swap Meet (late January) ... 209-874-5414

February
Antiques & Collectibles Show & Sale (mid-February & late November) ... 209-571-6480
Ripon Almond Blossom Festival (late February) ... 209-571-6480

March
Saint Patrick's Jazz Bash (mid-March) ... 209-869-3280

April
Knight's Ferry Peddler's Fair (mid April-mid May) ... 209-881-3217

May
Central Valley Renaissance Festival (mid-May) ... 209-571-6480
Cinco de Mayo Celebration (early May) ... 209-571-6480
Knight's Ferry Peddler's Fair (mid April-mid May) ... 209-881-3217
Modesto Farmers Market (late May-late November) ... 209-632-9322
Oakdale Chocolate Festival (mid-May) ... 209-847-2244
Spring Art Show (mid-May) ... 209-529-3369

June
1st Annual American Graffiti Car Show (mid-June) ... 888-746-9763
Modesto Farmers Market (late May-late November) ... 209-632-9322
Scottish Games & Gathering of the Clans (early June) ... 209-538-0821

July
July 4th Parade & Festival (July 4) ... 209-571-6480
Modesto Farmers Market (late May-late November) ... 209-632-9322

August
Delicato Vineyards Grape Stomp (late August) ... 209-239-1215
Modesto Farmers Market (late May-late November) ... 209-632-9322
Tracy Dry Bean Festival (early August) ... 209-835-2131

September
Greek Food Festival (mid-September) ... 209-522-7694
International Festival (late September-early October) ... 209-521-3852
Modesto Farmers Market (late May-late November) ... 209-632-9322
Modesto Home Show (mid-September) ... 209-571-2755
Oktoberfest (late September) ... 209-577-5757
Scandi Fest (late September) ... 209-667-1452
Turlock Poultry & Dairy Festival (mid-September) ... 209-571-6480

October
International Festival (late September-early October) ... 209-521-3852
Manteca Pumpkin Festival (early October) ... 209-823-6121
Modesto Farmers Market (late May-late November) ... 209-632-9322
Riverbank Cheese & Wine Exposition (mid-October) ... 209-869-4541

November
Antiques & Collectibles Show & Sale (mid-February & late November) ... 209-571-6480
Modesto Farmers Market (late May-late November) ... 209-632-9322

December
Modesto Christmas Parade (early December) ... 209-571-6480

Monterey

January
AT&T Pebble Beach National Pro-Am (late January-early February) ... 831-649-1533
www.attpbgolf.com
Whalefest (mid-late January) ... 831-644-7588

February
AT&T Pebble Beach National Pro-Am (late January-early February) ... 831-649-1533
www.attpbgolf.com

March
Dixieland Monterey (early March) ... 888-349-6879
www.dixiejazz.com/monterey.html
Pebble Beach Spring Horse Show (late March-early April) ... 831-624-2756
www.ridepebblebeach.com
SRAM Sea Otter Classic (mid-March) ... 650-306-1414
www.seaotter.org

April
Big Sur International Marathon (late April) ... 831-625-6226
www.bsim.org
Monterey Bay Arts & Crafts Fair (late April) ... 831-622-0700
www.pacrep.org
Monterey Wine Festival (early April) ... 800-656-4282
www.montereywine.com
Old Monterey Seafood & Music Festival (mid-April) ... 831-655-2607
Pebble Beach Spring Horse Show (late March-early April) ... 831-624-2756
www.ridepebblebeach.com
Wildflower Show (mid-April) ... 831-648-3116

CALIFORNIA — Monterey (Cont'd)

May
Great Monterey Squid Festival (late May) 831-372-2259
www.montereysquid.com

June
California Chocolate Abalone Dive (June) 831-375-1933
Downtown Celebration (late June) 831-655-8070
Great Cannery Row Sardine Festival (mid-June) 831-372-2259
Old Monterey Sidewalk Fine Arts Festival (mid-June) 831-655-2607

July
Brewmasters Classic (early July) 831-375-7275
Carmel Beach Bach Festival (mid-July-early August) 831-624-2046
www.bachfestival.org
Carmel Shakespeare Festival (late July-mid-October) 831-622-0100
www.pacrep.org
Pacific Grove Feast of Lanterns (late July) 831-372-7625
Pebble Beach Equestrian Classics
(late July-early August) 831-624-2756
www.ridepebblebeach.com
TheatreFest (early July & early November) 831-622-0700

August
Carmel Beach Bach Festival (mid-July-early August) 831-624-2046
www.bachfestival.org
Carmel Shakespeare Festival (late July-mid-October) 831-622-0100
www.pacrep.org
Monterey County Fair (mid-August) 831-372-5863
www.montereycountyfair.com
Monterey Historic Automobile Races (late August) 800-327-7322
www.laguna-seca.com
Northern California Golf Assn Amateur Championship
(late August) 831-625-4653
Pebble Beach Concours d'Elegance (late August) 831-659-0663
Pebble Beach Equestrian Classics
(late July-early August) 831-624-2756
www.ridepebblebeach.com
Steinbeck Festival (early August) 831-796-3833
www.steinbeck.org

September
Carmel Shakespeare Festival (late July-mid-October) 831-622-0100
www.pacrep.org
Cherry's Jubilee (late September) 831-759-1836
Festa Italia (mid-September) 831-649-6544
Greek Festival (early September) 831-424-4434
Honda Grand Prix of Monterey (mid-September) 800-327-7322
www.laguna-seca.com
Monterey Jazz Festival (mid-September) 800-309-3378
www.montereyjazzfestival.org
TomatoFest (September) 831-624-1581

October
California International Airshow (early October) 888-845-7469
www.ca-airshow.com
Carmel Performing Arts Festival (early-mid-October) 831-644-8383
www.carmelfest.org
Carmel Shakespeare Festival (late July-mid-October) 831-622-0100
www.pacrep.org
Monterey Antique & Collectibles Show (early October) 831-655-0264
Monterey Bay Bird Festival (early October) 831-728-3890
www.elkhornslough.org/birdfes2.htm
Old Monterey Historic Faire & Festival (early October) 831-655-2607

November
Cannery Row Christmas Tree Lighting (November 25) 831-372-2259
www.canneryrow.com
Great Wine Escape Weekend (mid-November) 831-375-9400
www.wines.com/monterey
TheatreFest (early July & early November) 831-622-0700
Twelve Days of Christmas
(late November-late December) 831-624-1581

December
Christmas in the Adobes (mid-December) 831-647-6226
www.mbay.net/~mshp/
Downtown Celebration Sidewalk Sale (early December) 831-655-2607
First Night Monterey (December 31) 831-373-4778
First Night Monterey (December31) 831-655-2607
Stillwell's Snow in the Park (mid-December) 831-373-3304
Twelve Days of Christmas
(late November-late December) 831-624-1581

Oakland

January
Grand National Roadster Show (mid-January) 415-490-5800

March
Potomac Public Cruise (mid-March-mid-November) 510-839-7533
Stitches Fair & Market (late March) 800-237-7099

April
Pacific Power Expo (mid-April) 510-452-6262
Pacific Sail Expo (late April) 800-817-7245
www.sailexpo.com/
Potomac Public Cruise (mid-March-mid-November) 510-839-7533
Spring Boat Show (mid-April) 510-452-6262

May
Carijama Oakland Carnival (late May) 510-535-2450
www.carnaval.com
Cinco de Mayo (early May) 510-536-4477
Festival of Greece (mid-May) 510-531-3400
Home & Garden Show (early May) 800-222-9351
Potomac Public Cruise (mid-March-mid-November) 510-839-7533

June
Juneteenth Celebration (mid-June) 510-632-9525
Potomac Public Cruise (mid-March-mid-November) 510-839-7533
Silver Star Pow Wow & Indian Market (mid-June) 415-554-0525

July
Oakland Fourth of July Celebration (July 4) 510-814-6000
Potomac Public Cruise (mid-March-mid-November) 510-839-7533
Scottish Highland Games (early July) 510-615-5555

August
Chinatown StreetFest (late August) 510-893-8979
Potomac Public Cruise (mid-March-mid-November) 510-839-7533

September
Italian Fiesta (mid-September) 510-814-6000
Potomac Public Cruise (mid-March-mid-November) 510-839-7533

October
Black Cowboys Parade & Heritage Festival
(early October) 510-238-7275
Halloween on the Square (late October) 510-814-6000
Potomac Public Cruise (mid-March-mid-November) 510-839-7533

November
Oakland Tree Lighting Ceremony (late November) 510-814-6000
Potomac Public Cruise (mid-March-mid-November) 510-839-7533

December
Christmas at Dunsmuir (December) 510-615-5555
Lighted Yacht Parade & Santa Parade (early December) .. 510-208-4646

Oxnard

February
Celebration of the Whales (mid-February-mid-March) 805-985-4852
Oasis del Espiritu Santo Convention
(late February-early March) 805-486-2424

March
Celebration of the Whales (mid-February-mid-March) 805-985-4852
Oasis del Espiritu Santo Convention
(late February-early March) 805-486-2424

April
Point Mugu Air Show (late April) 805-989-8548
Strawberry Classic Golf Tournament (late April) 805-983-4653

May
California Strawberry Festival (mid-May) 805-385-7545
Cinco de Mayo (early May) 805-486-0266
Mariachi Festival (early May) 800-269-6273

June
Heritage Square Summer Concert Series
(late June-late August) 805-483-7960
Seabee Days Celebration (late June) 805-982-4493

July
Channel Islands Harbor Boat Show
(late July-early August) 805-985-4852
Heritage Square Summer Concert Series
(late June-late August) 805-483-7960
Obon Festival (mid-July) 805-483-5948
Ventura County Boat Show (late July) 805-985-4852

August
Channel Islands Harbor Boat Show
(late July-early August) 805-985-4852
Heritage Square Summer Concert Series
(late June-late August) 805-483-7960
Ventura County Fair (early-mid-August) 805-648-3376

September
Fiestas Patrias (mid-September) 805-486-0266
Grey Whale Migration (September-December) 805-985-4852

October
Celtic Lands Faire (early October) 805-486-2424
Grey Whale Migration (September-December) 805-985-4852
Multi-Cultural Festival (late October) 805-385-7434
Port Hueneme Harbor Days (early October) 800-269-6273
Taste of Ventura County Food & Wine Festival
(October) 805-985-4852

November
Galaxy of Gems Show (late November) 805-525-5415
Grey Whale Migration (September-December) 805-985-4852

December
Grey Whale Migration (September-December) 805-985-4852
Oxnard's HomeTown Christmas Parade
(early December) 805-385-7545
Parade of Lights (early December) 800-269-6273
Ship Model Expo & Sale (December) 805-984-6260

Palm Springs

January
Desert Arts Festival (late January & late November) 760-323-7973
Indio Desert Circuit Horse Shows
(late January-mid-March) 760-775-7731
www.palmsprings.com/active/horseshow/
NORTEL Palm Springs International Film Festival
(mid-late January) 760-778-8979
www.psfilmfest.org
Wildlights at the Living Desert
(late November-early January) 760-346-5694

February
Black History Festival & Parade (late February) 760-416-5715
Desert AIDS Walk (mid-February) 760-323-2118
Frank Sinatra Celebrity Invitational (mid-February) 760-202-4422
Indio Desert Circuit Horse Shows
(late January-mid-March) 760-775-7731
www.palmsprings.com/active/horseshow/
Italian Festival (early February) 760-329-4879
Tour de Palm Springs (early February) 760-770-4626
www.tourdepalmsprings.com

March
Cabazon Band of Mission Indians Anual Pow Wow
(March) 800-827-2946
Crossroads Renaissance Festival (late March) 800-320-4736
Indio Desert Circuit Horse Shows
(late January-mid-March) 760-775-7731
www.palmsprings.com/active/horseshow/
Indio Pow Wow Spring Celebration Festival
(late March) 760-342-2593
La Quinta Arts Festival (mid-March) 760-564-1244
Nabisco Dinah Shore Golf Tournament (late March) 760-324-4546
www.palm-springs.com/golf/nabisco.html
Village Arts Festival (early March) 760-325-9116

April
City of Palm Springs Clogging Festival (late April) 760-323-8272
Palm Springs Car Classic (early April) 760-323-1057
www.palmspringscarclassic.com

June
Nabisco Mission Hills Desert Junior Golf Tournament
(late June) 760-324-4546

August
Palm Springs International Short Film Festival
(early August) 760-778-8979
www.psfilmfest.org

October
Halloween Carnival (late October) 760-416-5715
Palm Springs Bike Weekend (mid-October) 760-323-4141
www.palmsprings-bikewknd.com
Palm Springs Exotic Car Show & Auction (late October) 760-320-3290

November
Desert Arts Festival (late January & late November) 760-323-7973
Gay Pride Celebration (early November) 760-416-0711
Indio Pow Wow Thanksgiving Celebration
(late November) 760-342-2593
Palm Desert Golf Cart Parade (early November) 760-346-0611
Skins Game (late November) 760-776-6688
Wildlights at the Living Desert
(late November-early January) 760-346-5694

December
Christmas Craft Show (early December) 760-323-8272
Festival of Lights Parade (early December) 760-325-5749
Palm Springs Gay & Lesbian Film Festival
(early December) 760-770-2042
Wildlights at the Living Desert
(late November-early January) 760-346-5694

Riverside

February
Riverside County Fair & National Date Festival
(mid-late February) 760-863-8247
www.palmsprings.com/active/festival/
Riverside Dickens Festival (early February) 909-781-3168

April
Apple Blossom Festival Weekend (April) 909-797-6833
Riverside Orange Blossom Festival (late April) 909-715-3400
www.orangeblossomfestival.org

May
Cinco de Mayo (early May) 909-340-5906

June
Cherry Valley Cherry Festival (early June) 909-845-8466

July
Concerts in the Park (July-August) 909-780-6222
Independence Day Celebration (July 4) 909-683-7100

August
Concerts in the Park (July-August) 909-780-6222

September
Harvest Festival (mid-September) 707-778-6300

October
Family Village Festival (late October) 909-782-5273

November
Christmas on Main Street (mid-November) 909-781-7335
Festival of Lights (November) 909-781-7335
Festival of Trees (late November) 909-875-8756
Mission Inn 5K/10K Run (mid-November) 909-781-8241

Sacramento

January
Martin Luther King Community Celebration
(mid-January) 916-395-1895

CALIFORNIA — Sacramento (Cont'd)

February
Autorama (early February) 503-236-0632
Chinese New Year Celebration (late February) 916-777-5880
Mardi Gras Parade (early February) 916-443-6223
Sacramento Home & Garden Show (late February) 916-924-9934
Sacramento Sports Boat & RV Show (mid-February) 916-452-6403

March
LPGA Longs Drugs Challenge (late March-early April) 916-434-2224
Sacramento Boat Show (mid-March) 916-263-3218
Sacramento Camellia Show (early March) 916-264-5181
Saint Patrick's Day Parade (mid-March) 916-264-7031

April
Bockbierfest (early April) 916-442-7360
Chalk it Up to Sacramento! (late April) 916-484-5710
Festival of the Arts (mid-April) 916-278-6156
Highland Scottish Games (late April) 916-557-0764
LPGA Longs Drugs Challenge (late March-early April) 916-434-2224
Pioneer Traders' & Crafts Faire (late April) 916-445-4422
Spring Collectors' Fair (mid-April) 916-264-7031
Sutter Street Antique Market (mid-April & mid-September) 916-985-7452

May
Cinco de Mayo Celebrations (early May) 916-263-3021
Downtown Concert Series (early May-late August) 916-442-8575
Elk Grove Western Festival (early May) 916-685-3911
Fair Oaks Fiesta (early May) 916-967-2903
Friday Night Concerts (early May-mid-July) 916-442-8575
Pacific Coast Rowing Championship (mid-May) 916-985-7239
Pacific Rim Street Fest (mid-May) 916-264-7031
Sacramento County Fair (early May) 916-263-2975
Sacramento Jazz Jubilee (late May) 916-372-5277
www.sacjazz.com
Sutter Street Arts & Crafts Fair (early May) 916-985-2698
Thursday Night Market (May-September) 916-442-8575
Waterfront Art Fest (early May) 916-442-7644
Wednesday Farmers' Market (May-November) 916-442-8575

June
Crawdad Festival (mid-June) 916-777-5880
Downtown Concert Series (early May-late August) 916-442-8575
Fair Oaks Renaissance Tudor Fayre (late June) 916-966-1036
Friday Night Concerts (early May-mid-July) 916-442-8575
Pony Express Reride (mid-June) 916-264-7031
Sacramento Heritage Festival (early June) 916-481-2583
Shakespeare Lite (mid-June-mid-July) 916-442-8575
Starlight Movie Series (June-August) 916-264-7031
Thursday Night Market (May-September) 916-442-8575
US Pro Water Ski & Pro Wake Board Tournament (late June) 800-334-6541
Water Festival (early June) 916-985-2698
Wednesday Farmers' Market (May-November) 916-442-8575

July
Downtown Concert Series (early May-late August) 916-442-8575
Folsom Championship Rodeo (early July) 916-985-2698
Friday Night Concerts (early May-mid-July) 916-442-8575
Sacramento Shakespeare Festival (July) 916-558-2228
Shakespeare Lite (mid-June-mid-July) 916-442-8575
Starlight Movie Series (June-August) 916-264-7031
Strauss Festival (late July) 916-685-3911
Thursday Night Market (May-September) 916-442-8575
Wednesday Farmers' Market (May-November) 916-442-8575

August
California State Fair (mid-August-early September) 916-263-3093
www.calexpo.org
Downtown Concert Series (early May-late August) 916-442-8575
Festa Italiana (mid-August) 916-482-5900
Japanese Cultural Bazaar (early August) 916-446-0121
Starlight Movie Series (June-August) 916-264-7031
Thursday Night Market (May-September) 916-442-8575
Wednesday Farmers' Market (May-November) 916-442-8575

September
California State Fair (mid-August-early September) 916-263-3093
www.calexpo.org
Fall Collectors' Faire (mid-September) 916-558-3912
Festival of Cinema (mid-late September) 916-442-5189
Greek Food Festival (early September) 916-443-2033
Old Sacramento Oktoberfest (mid-September) 916-558-3912
Sacramento International Festival of Cinema (mid-late September) 916-442-7378
Sutter Street Antique Market (mid-April & mid-September) 916-985-7452
Thursday Night Market (May-September) 916-442-8575
US National Handcar Races (mid-September) 916-445-1018
Wednesday Farmers' Market (May-November) 916-442-8575

October
Oktoberfest (early October) 916-442-7360
Renaissance Faire & Tournament (mid-October) 916-355-7285
Wednesday Farmers' Market (May-November) 916-442-8575

November
Gift & Gourmet Show (mid-November) 916-483-9173
International Railfair (early-mid-November) 916-991-4343
Native American Arts & Crafts Show (late November) 916-324-0971
Wednesday Farmers' Market (May-November) 916-442-8575

December
California International Marathon (early December) 916-983-4622
Christmas Craft Faire (early December) 916-985-7452
Christmas Memories Celebration (December) 916-323-3047

San Bernardino

March
Miss San Bernardino Pageant (mid-March) 909-889-3980
Western Art Show & Sale (late March) 909-270-5632

April
Renaissance Pleasure Faire (April-June) 800-523-2473
members.aol.com/piranhant2/RPFS97Picts.html

May
California 500 (early May) 909-429-5000
National Orange Show (late May) 909-888-6788
www.nationalorangeshow.com
Renaissance Pleasure Faire (April-June) 800-523-2473
members.aol.com/piranhant2/RPFS97Picts.html
San Bernardino County Fair (mid-May) 760-951-2200
Soap Box Derby (mid-May) 909-888-6788
Village Classic & Vintage Car Show (late May) 909-337-2533

June
Cherry Festival (early June) 909-845-9541
Four Moons Pow Wow (early June) 909-823-6150
Renaissance Pleasure Faire (April-June) 800-523-2473
members.aol.com/piranhant2/RPFS97Picts.html

July
Fourth of July Celebration (July 4) 909-384-5031
Grapes & Gourmet Wine & Food Festival (early July) 909-384-5426

August
Shakespeare on the Square (August) 909-381-5037
Western Little League Tournament (mid-August) 909-887-6444

September
Route 66 Rendezvous (mid-September) 909-889-3980
route-66.org/

October
Red Ribbon Week & Downtown Parade (late October) 909-885-0509

November
Harvest Fair (early-mid-November) 909-384-5426

December
Christmas Parade (early December) 909-885-3268
Christmas Tree Lighting & Holiday Kick-off (early December) 909-381-5037
Parks & Recreation Holiday Craft Fair (early December) 909-381-5037

San Diego

January
Nations of San Diego International Dance Festival (mid-January) 619-239-9255
San Diego Boat Show (early January) 858-274-9924
San Diego Marathon (mid-January) 858-792-2900
www.sdmarathon.com/

February
San Diego Film Festival (February-May) 858-534-0497
San Diego New Year Celebration (February) 619-234-4447

March
Ocean Beach Kite Festival (early March) 619-236-1212
San Diego Crew Classic (late March) 619-236-1212
San Diego Film Festival (February-May) 858-534-0497

April
Art Alive (late April) 619-232-7931
Del Mar National Horse Show (late April-early May) 858-792-4288
Lakeside Western Days & Rodeo (mid-April) 619-236-1212
Rosarito-Ensenada 50 Mile Fun Bicycle Ride (late September & mid-April) 619-583-3001
San Diego Film Festival (February-May) 858-534-0497

May
Del Mar National Horse Show (late April-early May) 858-792-4288
Fiesta Cinco de Mayo (early May) 619-236-1212
Mainly Mozart Festival (late May-early June) 619-239-0100
www.mainlymozart.org/
Ramona Rodeo (mid-May) 619-236-1212
San Diego American Indian Cultural Days (mid-May) 619-281-5964
San Diego Film Festival (February-May) 858-534-0497

June
Del Mar Fair (mid-June-early July) 858-755-1161
La Jolla Festival of the Arts & Food Faire (mid-June) 619-236-1212
Mainly Mozart Festival (late May-early June) 619-239-0100
www.mainlymozart.org/
Port of San Diego International Triathlon (late-June) 619-236-1212
San Diego Polo Matches (June-October) 858-481-9217
Summer Organ Festival (June-August) 619-226-0819

July
Coronado Independence Day Celebration (July 4) 619-437-8788
Del Mar Fair (mid-June-early July) 858-755-1161
Hot Air Balloon Classic (July 4) 858-481-6800
MCAS Miramar Air Show (late July-early August) 619-236-1212
San Diego Polo Matches (June-October) 858-481-9217
US Open Sandcastle Competition (mid-July) 619-424-6663
World Championship Over-the-Line Tournament (mid-July) 619-236-1212

August
MCAS Miramar Air Show (late July-early August) 619-236-1212
San Diego Polo Matches (June-October) 858-481-9217
Summer Organ Festival (June-August) 619-226-0819
World Body Surfing Championships (mid-August) 760-966-4535

September
Adams Avenue Street Fair (late September) 619-282-7329
www.gothere.com/AdamsAve/index.htm
Cabrillo Festival (late September) 619-557-5450
California American Indian Days Celebration (late September) 619-281-5964
Harvest Festival (late September) 619-615-4100
Oceanside Harbor Days (late September) 760-722-1534
Rosarito-Ensenada 50 Mile Fun Bicycle Ride (late September & mid-April) 619-583-3001
San Diego Polo Matches (June-October) 858-481-9217
San Diego Street Scene (mid-September) 619-557-8490
World Series of Powerboats Racing (mid-September) 619-236-1212

October
Borrego Springs Desert Festival (late October) 760-767-5555
Rancho Bernardo Fall Art & Wine Festival (mid-October) 858-487-1767
San Diego Polo Matches (June-October) 858-481-9217

November
Fall Village Faire (early November) 760-434-8887
Poway Street Fair (November) 858-748-0022
San Diego Dixieland Jazz Festival (late November) 619-297-5277
Score Baja 1000 Race (early November) 619-236-1212

December
Christmas on the Prado (early December) 619-239-0512
Culligan Holiday Bowl (late December) 619-236-1212
First Night San Diego (December 31) 619-280-5838
Holiday Bowl (late December) 619-283-5808
Poinsettia Festival (early December) 760-943-1950
San Diego Harbor Parade of Lights (mid-late December) 619-232-3101
Vista Holiday Parade (early December) 760-726-1122

San Francisco

January
Chinese New Year Celebration (late January) 650-484-1200
Sports & Boat Show (mid-January) 415-469-6065
www.sfboatshow.com

February
Arts of the Pacific Asian Show (mid-February) 310-455-2886
Pacific Orchid Exposition (late February) 415-546-9608

March
Bouquets to Art (mid-late March) 415-750-3504
Contemporary Crafts Market (mid-March & early November) 415-995-4925
International Asian Film Festival (early-mid-March) 415-863-0814
Macy's Flower Show (late March-early April) 415-393-3724
Saint Patrick's Day Parade (mid-March) 415-661-2700
San Francisco Garden Show (mid-March) 800-829-9751
www.gardenshow.com/sf/index.html

April
Cherry Blossom Festival (mid-April) 415-974-6900
Macy's Flower Show (late March-early April) 415-393-3724
San Francisco International Film Festival (late April-early May) 415-931-3456

May
Carnaval (late May) 415-826-1401
www.carnaval.com/sf/
Cinco de Mayo Celebrations (early May) 415-826-1401
Norway Day Festival (early May) 925-676-4708
San Francisco Examiner Bay to Breakers (mid-May) 415-777-7770
www.baytobreakers.com
San Francisco International Film Festival (late April-early May) 415-931-3456
Traditional Music & Dance Festival (mid-May) 415-771-3112

June
Ethnic Dance Festival (mid-late June) 415-392-4400
North Beach Festival (mid-June) 415-989-6426
San Francisco International Lesbian & Gay Film Festival (mid-late June) 415-703-8663
Stern Grove Midsummer Music Festival (mid-June-mid-August) 415-252-6252
www.sterngrove.org/
Street Performers Festival (early June) 415-705-5500

July
Fillmore Street Festival (early July) 415-249-4625
Fourth of July Waterfront Festival (July 4) 415-777-7120
Jazz & Wine Festival at Embarcadero Center (late July) 800-733-6318
Jazz and All That Art (early July) 415-249-4625
San Francisco Shakespeare Festival (July-early October) 415-422-2222
www.sfshakes.org
Stern Grove Midsummer Music Festival (mid-June-mid-August) 415-252-6252
www.sterngrove.org/

August
A la Carte A la Park (late August-early September) 415-383-9378
Nihonmachi Street Fair (early August) 415-771-9861
San Francisco Shakespeare Festival (July-early October) 415-422-2222
www.sfshakes.org
Stern Grove Midsummer Music Festival (mid-June-mid-August) 415-252-6252
www.sterngrove.org/

September
A la Carte A la Park (late August-early September) 415-383-9378
Festival of the Culinary Arts (mid-September) 800-229-2433
www.baychef.com

CALIFORNIA — San Francisco (Cont'd)

Ghirardelli Square Chocolate Festival (early-mid-September) 415-775-5500
Las Americas (mid-September) 415-705-5500
San Francisco Blues Festival (mid-September) 415-979-5588
www.sfblues.com/
San Francisco Fringe Theater Festival (mid-September) ... 415-673-3847
www.sffringe.org
San Francisco Shakespeare Festival (July-early October) 415-422-2222
www.sfshakes.org

October
Fleet Week (mid-October) 415-705-5500
Great Halloween & Pumpkin Festival (mid-October) 415-249-4625
San Francisco Jazz Festival (late October-early November) 800-627-5277
San Francisco Shakespeare Festival (July-early October) 415-422-2222
www.sfshakes.org

November
Contemporary Crafts Market (mid-March & early November) 415-995-4925
San Francisco Jazz Festival (late October-early November) 800-627-5277

San Jose

January
San Jose International Auto Show (January) 408-277-3900

February
CineQuest-San Jose Film Festival (late February-early March) 408-995-5033
Clam Chowder Cook-Off (early February) 831-423-5590
Hoi Tet Festival (mid-February) 408-295-9210

March
Arts & Crafts & Music Festival (late March & mid-May) ... 408-842-9316
CineQuest-San Jose Film Festival (late February-early March) 408-995-5033
Irish Week Celebration (mid-March) 408-279-6002
www.theduke.com/irishweek/

May
Arts & Crafts & Music Festival (late March & mid-May) ... 408-842-9316
Cinco de Mayo Festival (early May) 408-258-0663
Fiestas Patrias (early May) 408-258-0663
Metro Fountain Blues Festival (early May) 408-924-6262
as.sjsu.edu/upcoming.html
San Jose Historical Museum Walking Tours (May-October) 408-287-2290
Wine & Arts Prune Festival (late May) 408-378-6252

June
Gay Pride Parade & Festival (mid-June) 408-278-5563
Juneteenth Festival (mid-June) 408-292-3157
Mountain Winery Summer Series (June-September) 408-741-0763
San Jose Historical Museum Walking Tours (May-October) 408-287-2290
Strawberry Festival (early June) 408-379-3790

July
Chinese Summer Festival (mid-July) 408-287-2290
Mariachi Conference & Festival (mid-July) 408-292-5197
Mountain Winery Summer Series (June-September) 408-741-0763
Obon Festival (mid-July) 408-293-9292
San Jose America Festival (early July) 408-298-6861
San Jose Historical Museum Walking Tours (May-October) 408-287-2290
Santa Clara County Fair (late July-early August) 408-494-3247

August
Harvest Festival (late August-December) 800-321-1213
www.harvestfestival.com
Mountain Winery Summer Series (June-September) 408-741-0763
San Jose Historical Museum Walking Tours (May-October) 408-287-2290
San Jose Jazz Festival (mid-August) 408-288-7557
Santa Clara County Fair (late July-early August) 408-494-3247

September
Almaden Art & Wine Festival (late September) 408-268-1133
Harvest Festival (late August-December) 800-321-1213
www.harvestfestival.com
Mountain Winery Summer Series (June-September) 408-741-0763
San Jose Historical Museum Walking Tours (May-October) 408-287-2290
SoFa Street Fair (mid-September) 408-295-2265

October
Harvest Festival (late August-December) 800-321-1213
www.harvestfestival.com
Italian American Cultural Festival (early October) 408-293-7122
Oktoberfest (mid-October) 408-453-1110
San Jose Historical Museum Walking Tours (May-October) 408-287-2290
San Pedro Square Brew Ha Ha (early October) 408-279-1775

November
Harvest Festival (late August-December) 800-321-1213
www.harvestfestival.com
Santa Cruz Christmas Craft & Gift Festival (late November) 831-423-5590

December
Harvest Festival (late August-December) 800-321-1213
www.harvestfestival.com
Los Posadas (mid-December) 408-467-9890
San Jose Holiday Parade (December) 408-995-6635

Santa Ana

April
Floral Park Home & Garden Tour (late April) 714-543-3218
www.floralpark.com

May
Cinco de Mayo Celebration (early May) 714-571-4200

June
Fantasy in the Sky (June-September) 714-781-4560

July
Fantasy in the Sky (June-September) 714-781-4560
Orange County Fair (mid-July) 714-708-3247
www.ocfair.com

August
Antique Car Parade (August) 714-571-4200
Fantasy in the Sky (June-September) 714-781-4560

September
Fantasy in the Sky (June-September) 714-781-4560
Mexican Independence Festival (mid-September) 714-571-4200

December
Star of Bethlehem (December) 714-547-7000

Santa Barbara

April
Earth Day (April 22) 805-963-0583

Stockton

January
Stockton Ag Expo (late January) 209-547-2960

March
Dixieland Jazz Festival (early March) 888-474-7407
Lodi Spring Wine Show (late March) 209-369-2771

April
Cherry Blossom Festival (mid-April) 209-953-8800
Lockeford Street Fairs (April) 209-727-3142
Stockton Asparagus Festival (late April) 209-943-1987
www.asparagusfest.com/

May
Lodi Street Faires (early May & early October) 209-367-7840
Wine Tasting Event (May) 209-466-0331

June
Festa Italiana (early June) 209-368-3077
San Joaquin County Fair (mid-late June) 209-466-5041
Tower Park Poker Run (late June) 209-369-1041

July
All-American WaterFest (July 4) 209-943-1987
Eberhardt Bob Memorial Pro-Am Heart Invitational (late July) 209-477-2683
Stockton Obon Festival (late July) 209-466-6701

August
California Dry Bean Festival (early August) 209-835-2131
Delicata Grape Stomp (late August) 209-239-1215

September
Big Dog Poker Run (early September) 209-369-1041
Lodi Grape Festival & National Wine Show (mid-September) 209-369-2771
Wine on the Waterfront (early September) 209-464-7644

October
Countywide Art Tour (mid-October) 209-465-6092
Lodi Street Faires (early May & early October) 209-367-7840
Oktoberfest (mid-October) 209-369-2771
Wine Stroll (early October) 209-831-4170

COLORADO

Aurora

July
Kids Spree (late-July) 303-739-7546

August
Men's Masters Slow Pitch-ASA National Championship Tournament (late August) 303-695-7201

September
Gateway to the Rockies Festival (mid-September) 303-361-6169

October
Pumpkin Fest (late October) 303-361-2936

Boulder

January
Boulder Bach Festival (late January) 303-494-3159
www.aescon.com/music/bbf/index.htm
Colorado Mahler Festival (mid-January) 303-447-0513
www.aescon.com/music/mahler/index.htm

May
Bolder Boulder 10K (late May) 303-444-7223
www.bolderboulder.com
Boulder Creek Festival (late May) 303-449-3825
Kinetic Conveyance Sculpture Challenge (early May) 303-444-5600

June
Colorado Music Festival (late June-early August) 303-449-1397
www.aescon.com/music/cmf/
Colorado Shakespeare Festival (late June-early August) ... 303-492-0554
www.coloradoshakes.org

July
Boulder Art Fair (mid-July) 303-449-3774
Christmas in July (mid-July) 303-770-0057
Colorado Dance Festival (early July-early August) 303-442-7666
Colorado Music Festival (late June-early August) 303-449-1397
www.aescon.com/music/cmf/
Colorado Shakespeare Festival (late June-early August) ... 303-492-0554
www.coloradoshakes.org
Lyric Theatre Festival (July) 303-492-8008

August
Colorado Dance Festival (early July-early August) 303-442-7666
Colorado Music Festival (late June-early August) 303-449-1397
www.aescon.com/music/cmf/
Colorado Shakespeare Festival (late June-early August) ... 303-492-0554
www.coloradoshakes.org

September
Boulder Fall Festival (late September) 303-449-3774

December
Boulder Artwalk (early December) 303-444-9106
Lights of December Parade (early December) 303-449-3774

Colorado Springs

January
Great Fruitcake Toss (early January) 719-685-5089
Kwanzaa Cultural Celebration (late December-early January) 719-473-6566

February
Carnivale & Gumbo Cook-off (early February) 719-685-5089
Food-A-Rama (early February) 719-576-4228

March
Saint Patrick's Day Parade (mid-March) 719-635-8803

May
Cavalcade of Music (early May) 719-520-7469
Cinco de Mayo Celebration (early May) 719-578-6120
Territory Days (late May) 719-475-0955

June
Clayfest & Mud Ball (mid-June) 719-685-5795
Donkey Derby Days (late June) 719-689-3315
Pikes Peak Invitational Soccer Tournament (late June-early July) 719-590-9977
Zebulon! A Festival of Arts (mid-June-mid-July) 719-475-2465

July
Colorado Championship Chili Cook-off (mid-July) 719-593-2700
Colorado Springs Opera Festival (late July-early August) .. 719-520-7469
El Paso County Fair (late July) 719-575-8690
Fabulous Fourth (July 4) 719-633-4611
Farmers' Market (July-September) 719-598-4215
Lone Feather Indian Council Pow Wow (mid-July) 719-495-0798
National Little Britches Finals Rodeo (late July) 719-520-6711
Pikes Peak Auto Hill Climb (early July) 719-685-4400
www.ppihc.com/
Pikes Peak Highland Games & Celtic Festival (mid-July) 719-481-4597
Pikes Peak Invitational Soccer Tournament (late June-early July) 719-590-9977
Race to the Clouds (July 4) 719-685-4400
Ute Pass Stampede (mid-July) 719-687-6606
Zebulon! A Festival of Arts (mid-June-mid-July) 719-475-2465

August
Colorado Springs Opera Festival (late July-early August) .. 719-520-7469
Farmers' Market (July-September) 719-598-4215
Labor Day Arts & Crafts Festival (late August-early September) 719-685-1008
Mountain Arts Festival (early August) 719-687-7956
Pikes Peak or Bust Rodeo (early August) 719-635-3548

September
Balloon Classic (early September) 719-471-4833
www.balloonclassic.com
Family Day & Antique Car Show (late September) 719-488-0880
Farmers' Market (July-September) 719-598-4215
Labor Day Arts & Crafts Festival (late August-early September) 719-685-1008

October
Great Pikes Peak Cowboy Poetry Gathering (early October) 719-531-6333
Oktoberfest (early October) 719-635-7506
Pikes Peak Bluegrass Festival (mid-October) 719-447-9797

COLORADO — Colorado Springs (Cont'd)

November
In Their Honor Parade & Air Show (early November) 719-635-8803
Madrigal Christmas Celebration (late November-mid-December) 719-594-2237

December
First Night Pikes Peak (December 31) 719-471-9790
Gallery of Trees & Lights (December) 719-635-7506
Kwanzaa Cultural Celebration (late December-early January) 719-473-6566
Madrigal Christmas Celebration (late November-mid-December) 719-594-2237

Denver

January
Blossoms of Lights (early December-early January) 303-331-4000
Colorado Indian Market & Western Art Roundup (early January & mid-July) 806-355-1610
Denver Boat Show (early January) 303-228-8000
National Western Stock Show & Rodeo (early-mid-January) 303-297-1166
Winterfest Weekends (late November-early January) 303-534-2367

February
Buffalo Bill's Birthday Celebration (late February) 303-526-0744
Denver Auto Show (early February) 303-831-1691

March
Denver March Pow Wow (mid-late March) 303-295-4444
Saint Patrick's Day Parade (mid-March) 303-399-9226

June
Capitol Hill People's Fair (early June) 303-830-1651
Greek Festival (late June) 303-388-9314
Greek Marketplace (mid-June) 303-388-9314
International Buskerfest (late June) 303-534-6161
Juneteenth Festival (mid-June) 303-399-7138
Lodo Beer Wine & Food Festival (mid-June) 303-458-6685
Renaissance Festival (early June-early August) 303-688-6010
Summer Nights (late June-late August) 303-534-2367

July
Cherry Blossom Festival (mid-July) 303-295-1844
Cherry Creek Arts Festival (July 4) 303-355-2787
Colorado Indian Market & Western Art Roundup (early January & mid-July) 806-355-1610
Independence Day Celebration (July 4) 303-399-1859
Renaissance Festival (early June-early August) 303-688-6010
Summer Nights (late June-late August) 303-534-2367
Theater in the Park (late-July-early August) 303-770-2106
Winter Park Jazz Festival (mid-July) 970-726-4118

August
Colorado State Fair (late August-early September) 800-876-4567
Renaissance Festival (early June-early August) 303-688-6010
Summer Nights (late June-late August) 303-534-2367
Theater in the Park (late-July-early August) 303-770-2106

September
Colorado State Fair (late August-early September) 800-876-4567
Festival of Mountain & Plain: A Taste of Colorado (early September) 303-534-6161
Oktoberfest (mid-September) 303-534-2367

October
Boo at the Zoo (late October) 303-376-4846
Colorado Performing Arts Festival (early October) 720-913-8206
Denver International Film Festival (mid-October) 303-321-3456
Great American Beer Festival (early October) 303-447-0816
Spirits of the Past (late October) 303-399-1859

November
Rocky Mountain Book Festival (early November) 303-839-8320
Rocky Mountain Children's Book Festival (mid-November) 303-839-8320
Winterfest Weekends (late November-early January) 303-534-2367
World's Largest Christmas Lighting Display (late November-December) 303-892-1112

December
Blossoms of Lights (early December-early January) 303-331-4000
First Night Colorado (December 31) 303-399-9005
Parade of Lights (early December) 303-534-6161
Wild Lights (December) 303-331-4110
Winterfest Weekends (late November-early January) 303-534-2367
World's Largest Christmas Lighting Display (late November-December) 303-892-1112

Fort Collins

March
Boat Show (mid-March) 970-407-1866
Gem & Mineral Show (late March) 970-484-6752
Home & Garden Show (early March) 970-407-1866
Saint Patrick's Day Parade (mid-March) 970-484-6500

April
Grateful Disc Spring Frisbee Festival (late April) 970-484-6932
Northern Colorado Artists Association Annual Juried Art Show (mid-April-late May) 970-223-6450

May
Cinco de Mayo Celebration (early May) 970-484-6500
Northern Colorado Artists Association Annual Juried Art Show (mid-April-late May) 970-223-6450
WineFest (late May) 970-482-2700

June
1882 Fort Collins Waterworks Open House (mid-June) 970-221-0533
Annual Garden Tour (late June) 970-224-0430
Colorado Brewers' Festival (late June) 970-484-6500
www.downtownfortcollins.com/3.htm
Concert Under the Stars (June-August) 970-484-6500
Taste of Fort Collins (mid-June) 303-777-6887

July
Concert Under the Stars (June-August) 970-484-6500
Fourth of July Celebration (July 4) 970-221-6790
Rendezvous & Skookum Day (mid-July) 970-221-6738

August
Concert Under the Stars (June-August) 970-484-6500
NewWestFest (late August) 970-484-6500
www.downtownfortcollins.com/4.htm

September
Colorado International Invitational Poster Exhibition (mid-September-late October) 970-491-7634
Historic Homes Tour (mid-September) 970-221-0533
Magic in the Rockies International Magic Show (early September) 970-484-7014

October
Anheuser-Busch Pumpkin Carving Contest (late October) 970-490-4691
Colorado International Invitational Poster Exhibition (mid-September-late October) 970-491-7634

November
Great Christmas Hall Artisans Fair (mid-November) 970-221-6735
Great Christmas Hall of Trees (mid-November) 970-221-6735
Thanksgiving Day Run (late November) 970-224-2582

December
First Night Fort Collins (December 31) 970-484-6500
www.downtownfortcollins.com/5.htm
Victorian Christmas Open House (early December) 970-221-0533
www.fortnet.org/plf/XMAS.HTM

CONNECTICUT

Bridgeport

March
Model Railroad Show (late March) 203-259-9592

May
Fairfield Dogwood Festival (early-May) 203-259-5596
Westport Handcrafts Show (late May) 203-227-7844

June
Barnum Festival (June-early July) 203-367-8495
Stratford Day (mid-June) 203-377-0771

July
Barnum Festival (June-early July) 203-367-8495
Festival Italiano (early July) 203-227-6279
Fourth of July Celebration & Fireworks (July 4) 203-367-8495

August
Greatest Bluefish Tournament on Earth (late August) 203-366-2583
WICC Greatest Bluefish Tournament on Earth (August) 203-366-6000

September
SoundFest (early September) 203-335-1433

November
Westport Creative Arts Festival (early November) 203-222-1388

Hartford

January
Festival of Light (late November-early January) 860-728-6789

February
Hartford Flower Show (mid-February) 860-529-2123

March
Annual Daffodil Festival (late March) 860-236-5621
Hebron Maple Festival (mid-March) 860-244-8181

May
Big Bass Tournaments (late May-early September) 860-713-3131

June
Big Bass Tournaments (late May-early September) 860-713-3131
Greater Hartford Open (late June-early July) 860-246-4446
Music Under the Stars Concert Series (early June-late September) 860-713-3131
Taste of Hartford (mid-June) 860-728-3089

July
Big Bass Tournaments (late May-early September) 860-713-3131
Festival of Jazz (early-mid-July) 800-332-7829
Greater Hartford Open (late June-early July) 860-246-4446
Music Under the Stars Concert Series (early June-late September) 860-713-3131
Nutmeg State Games (mid-July) 860-528-4588
Riverfest (early July) 860-293-0131

August
Big Bass Tournaments (late May-early September) 860-713-3131
Connecticut Family Folk Festival (early August) 860-632-7547
Family Day Festival (late August) 860-722-6567
Music Under the Stars Concert Series (early June-late September) 860-713-3131
Podunk Blue Grass Music Festival (mid-August) 860-742-2430

September
Big Bass Tournaments (late May-early September) 860-713-3131
Farmington Antique Weekend (early September) 800-793-4480
Music Under the Stars Concert Series (early June-late September) 860-713-3131
Riverfront Recapture Rowing Regatta (late September) 860-713-3131

October
Greater Hartford Marathon (early October) 860-525-3435
www.hartfordmarathon.com/

November
Festival of Light (late November-early January) 860-728-6789

December
Festival of Light (late November-early January) 860-728-6789
First Night (December 31) 860-728-3089

New Haven

January
Rolling Thunder Monster Truck Tour (early January) 203-772-4200
UI Fantasy of Lights (mid-November-early January) 203-777-2000

February
Winterfest (early February) 203-378-2700

April
Film Fest New Haven (early April) 203-481-6789
www.filmfest.org/
Goldenbells Festival (mid-late April) 203-281-4768
Wooster Square Cherry Blossom Festival (mid-April) 203-865-5842

May
Freddie Fixer Parade & Festival (early-mid-May) 203-389-1119
Kite Fly & Spring Festival (early May) 203-230-5226
Meet the Artists & Artisans (mid-May & early October) 203-874-5672

June
Blessing of the Fleet (early June) 203-777-8550
Fair on the Green (early June) 203-874-1982
Gem & Mineral Show (mid-June) 203-929-3404
International Festival of Arts & Ideas (mid June-early July) 203-498-1212
www.icomm.ca/ifoa/
Saint Andrew's Italian Festival (late June) 203-865-9846
Saint Anthony's Feast (mid-June) 203-624-1418
Saint Francis Strawberry Festival (mid-June) 203-294-1112

July
Celebrate New Haven Fourth (early July) 203-946-7821
International Festival of Arts & Ideas (mid June-early July) 203-498-1212
www.icomm.ca/ifoa/
New England Arts and Crafts Festival (mid-July) 203-878-6647
Savin Rock Festival (late July) 203-937-3511

August
Pilot Pen International Tennis Tournament (late August) 203-776-7331
SNET Jazz Festival (August) 203-946-7821

September
Cider and Donuts Festival (mid-September) 203-777-8550
Fall Festival & Chili Cookoff (mid-September) 203-387-7700
North Haven Agricultural Fair (early-mid-September) 203-239-3700
Saint Barbara Greek Festival (early September) 203-795-1347
www.saintbarbara.org

October
Meet the Artists & Artisans (mid-May & early October) 203-874-5672

November
Celebration of American Crafts (early November-late December) 203-562-4927
UI Fantasy of Lights (mid-November-early January) 203-777-2000

December
Celebration of American Crafts (early November-late December) 203-562-4927
UI Fantasy of Lights (mid-November-early January) 203-777-2000

Stamford

January
Winterfest (late January) 203-322-1646

February
Winterbloom (late February) 203-322-6971

March
Norwalk Seaport's Festival of Crafts (mid-March) 203-838-9444

April
Spring Challenge Rowing Regatta (April) 203-840-0770

May
Bruce Museum Outdoor Art Festival (mid-October & late May) 203-869-0376

CONNECTICUT — Stamford (Cont'd)

Outdoor Antiques Fair (May) 203-838-2115
Spring on the Farm (late May) 203-322-1646

June
Afternoon of Jazz Festival (late June) 212-290-8600
Ox Ridge Summershow (mid-June) 203-655-2559
www.oxridge.com/soe.html

July
Fourth of July Celebration & Fireworks (July 4) 203-977-4150
Round Hill Highland Scottish Games (early July) 203-854-7806
Victorian Ice Cream Social (mid-July) 203-838-9799

August
Cannon Grange Fair (late August) 203-972-0207
SoNo Arts Celebration Weekend (early August) 203-855-8823

September
Antiques Alfresco (mid-September) 203-655-9233
Harvest Fair (mid-September) 203-322-1646
Norwalk International In-Water Boat Show (late September) 212-922-1212
Norwalk Oyster Festival (early September) 203-838-9444
Stamford Historical Society Quilt Show (late September) .. 203-329-1183

October
Bruce Museum Outdoor Art Festival (mid-October & late May) 203-869-0376
Norwalk Aquarium Society Show (early October) 203-227-7253

November
American Craftsmanship Show (mid-November) 203-762-7257
Gem & Mineral Show (early November) 203-322-4670
Holiday Parade (late November) 203-348-5285

December
Antiquarius Christmas Antiques Show (mid-December) 203-869-6899
Victorian Christmas Celebration (mid-December) 203-838-9799

DELAWARE

Dover

March
Easter Egg Hunt (late March) 302-739-5656

May
Old Dover Days (early May) 302-734-1736
Summer Performing Arts Series (May-September) 302-736-7050

June
African American Festival (late June) 302-736-0101
Dover Music Festival (late June) 302-736-7050
Summer Performing Arts Series (May-September) 302-736-7050

July
Delaware State Fair (mid-late July) 302-398-3269
www.delawarestatefair.com
July 4th Celebration (July 4) 302-734-7513
Summer Performing Arts Series (May-September) 302-736-7050

August
Summer Performing Arts Series (May-September) 302-736-7050

September
SplitFire Spark Plug 200 & 500 (September) 302-734-7223
Summer Performing Arts Series (May-September) 302-736-7050

October
Governor's Fall Festival (early October) 302-739-5656
Governor's Haunted House (October 31) 302-739-5656

December
First Night Dover (December 31) 302-674-8581
Governor's Christmas Open House (mid-December) 302-739-5656

Rehoboth Beach

January
Avenue of Lights (late November-early January) 302-227-2233

March
Chocolate Festival (mid-March) 302-227-8259

April
Easter Promenade (late April) 302-227-2233
Fun Fly (early April) 302-227-6996
Greater Delaware Kite Festival (early April) 302-227-6996

May
Annual Sidewalk Sales (mid-May & early October) 302-227-2233

June
Best of the Beach Art Auction (mid-June) 302-644-2900

July
July 4th Fireworks (July 4) 302-227-2772
Milford Sun Fun Fest (early July) 302-422-3344

September
Dewey Beach Sprint Triathalon (late September) 302-226-0510
Make-A-Wish Two Million Dollar Golf Tournament (mid-September) 302-658-9474

October
Annual Christmas Shop (early October) 302-227-7202
Annual Sidewalk Sales (mid-May & early October) 302-227-2233
Autumn Jazz Festival (mid-late October) 302-226-2166
www.atbeach.com/announce/jazzfestival.html
Coast Day (early October) 302-831-8083
Sea Witch Halloween & Fiddler's Festival (late October) 302-227-2233
www.beach-fun.com/seawitch.html

November
Autumn Faire (mid-November) 302-945-3627
Avenue of Lights (late November-early January) 302-227-2233
Christmas Tree Lighting (late November) 302-227-2233
Rehoboth Beach Independent Film Festival (mid-November) 302-645-9095
www.rehobothfilm.com
Thanksgiving Ball (mid-November) 302-644-2900

December
Avenue of Lights (late November-early January) 302-227-2233
Hometown Christmas Parade (mid-December) 302-227-8950

Wilmington

January
A Christmas Display (mid-November-early January) 610-388-6741
Yuletide at Winterthur (mid-November-early January) 800-448-3883

March
Saint Patrick's Day Parade (March) 302-652-2970
Saint Patrick's Day Tea (mid-March) 302-761-4340

April
Hagley's Storybook Garden Party (late April) 302-658-2400

May
A Day in Old New Castle (mid-late May) 302-322-8411
Civil War Reenactment (late May) 305-655-5704
Festival of Fountains (May) 610-388-1000
Wilmington Flower Market (early May) 302-995-5699
Wilmington Garden Day (early May) 302-428-6172

June
Clifford Brown Jazz Festival (early June) 302-571-4205
Greek Festival (early June) 302-654-4447
Saint Anthony's Italian Festival (mid-June) 302-421-3790

July
African Festival (early-mid-July) 302-657-2108
Ice Cream Festival (mid-July) 302-761-4340

August
Cool Blues & Micro Brew (early-mid-August) 302-571-4100
Garrison Days (mid-August) 302-834-7941

September
DuPont Riverfest (late September) 302-658-1870
Jazz Fest (early September) 610-388-6221
Taste of Wilmington Festival (late September) 302-888-2929

October
Hagley's Craft Fair (mid-October) 302-658-2400
Rehoboth Jazz Festival (mid-October) 800-296-8742

November
A Christmas Display (mid-November-early January) 610-388-6741
Chrysanthemum Festival (early-late November) 610-388-1000
Yuletide at Winterthur (mid-November-early January) 800-448-3883

December
A Christmas Display (mid-November-early January) 610-388-6741
First Night Wilmington (December 31) 302-658-9327
Yuletide at Winterthur (mid-November-early January) 800-448-3883

DISTRICT OF COLUMBIA

Washington

January
Christmas on 'S' Street (December-early January) 202-387-4062
Martin Luther King Jr Birthday Observance (mid-January) 202-619-7222

February
Chinese New Year Parade (mid-February) 202-357-2700
Washington Boat Show (mid-February) 202-789-1600

March
DC Spring Antiques Fair (early March) 301-924-5002
Harambee Carnival (early March) 301-530-3697
National Cherry Blossom Festival (late March-early April) 202-728-1137
www.gwjapan.com/cherry/
Patuxent Wildlife Art Show & Sale (late March) 301-292-8331
Saint Patrick's Day Parade (mid-March) 301-879-1717
Smithsonian Kite Festival (late March) 202-357-3030
Washington Flower & Garden Show (early March) 202-789-1600
Washington International Flower & Garden Show (early March) 703-823-7960

April
Dulles International Antiques Show & Sale (mid-April) 703-802-0066
Garden Fair & Plant Sale (mid-April) 202-544-8733
National Cherry Blossom Festival (late March-early April) 202-728-1137
www.gwjapan.com/cherry/
National Cherry Blossom Parade (early April) 202-728-1137
Smithsonian's Craft Show (mid-April) 202-357-2700
Washington International Filmfest (late April-early May) ... 202-724-5613
White House Easter Egg Roll (mid-April) 202-456-2200
White House Spring Garden Tours (mid-April) 202-456-2200

May
Candlelight Vigil (mid-May) 202-737-3400
Goodwill Embassy Tour (early May) 202-636-4225
Memorial Day Ceremonies at Arlington National Cemetery (late May) 202-685-2892
Washington International Filmfest (late April-early May) ... 202-724-5613
Washington National Cathedral Flower Mart (early May) .. 202-537-6200

June
Festival of American Folklife (late June-early July) 202-357-2700
Jazz Art Festival (late June-early August) 202-723-7500

July
Festival of American Folklife (late June-early July) 202-357-2700
Founder's Day Water Lily Festival (late July) 202-426-6905
Independence Day Parade (July 4) 202-619-7222
www.july4thparade.com
Jazz Art Festival (late June-early August) 202-723-7500
Washington Theatre Festival (early July-early August) 202-628-6161

August
Jazz Art Festival (late June-early August) 202-723-7500
Washington Theatre Festival (early July-early August) 202-628-6161

October
Marine Corps Marathon (late October) 202-789-7000
Taste of DC (early October) 202-724-4093

November
Washington Craft Show (mid-November) 203-254-0486

December
Capital Area Auto Show (late December) 202-789-1600
Christmas on 'S' Street (December-early January) 202-387-4062
DC Winter Antiques Fair (early December) 301-924-5002
Holiday Concert: Bethesdoy Chamber Singers (early December) 202-785-2040
National Christmas Tree Lighting/Pageant of Peace (December) 202-619-7222
White House Christmas Tours (late December) 202-456-7041

FLORIDA

Daytona Beach

January
Antique Show & Sale (mid-January) 904-255-0285
Daytona Beach Doll Show (mid-January) 904-672-2341
Gem & Mineral Show & Sale (mid-January) 904-255-9478
Miss Daytona Beach & Miss Volusia County Pageant (mid-January) 904-677-4589
Orange City/Blue Spring Manatee Festival (late January) .. 904-775-9224
Rolex 24 hours of Daytona Race (late January) 904-253-7223
www.daytona24hr.com
Speedweeks (late January-mid-February) 904-253-7223
www.daytonausa.com

February
Art Fiesta (late February) 904-424-2175
Black Heritage Festival (early February) 904-428-6225
Daytona 500 NASCAR Winston Cup Series Race (mid-February) 904-253-7223
www.daytonausa.com
Daytona Bike Week (late February-early March) 904-252-2453
www.officialbikeweek.com
Gatorade 125-Mile Qualifying Races for the Daytona 500 (mid-February) 904-253-7223
www.daytonausa.com
NAPA Auto Parts 300 NASCAR Busch Series Race (mid-February) 904-253-7223
www.daytonausa.com
Speedweeks (late January-mid-February) 904-253-7223
www.daytonausa.com
World Series of Asphalt Stock Car Racing (early-mid-February) 904-427-4129

March
Central Florida Balloon Rally (late March) 904-736-1010
Daytona Beach Garden Show (mid-March) 904-252-1511
Daytona Bike Week (late February-early March) 904-252-2453
www.officialbikeweek.com
IMAGES-A Festival of the Arts (mid-March) 904-423-4733
Motorcycle Swap Meet (early March) 904-257-2269
Speedway Spectacular Car Show & Swap Meet (late March) 904-255-7355

April
Native American Festival (mid-April) 904-676-3216
Very Special Arts Festival (late April) 904-255-6475

May
Art in the Park (early May) 904-676-3257
Greater Daytona Beach Striking Fish Tournament (late May) 904-756-7058

July
Boardwalk Pier Fireworks (July 4) 904-255-0415

September
Oktoberfest (mid-September) 904-677-0676

October
Daytona Beach Biketoberfest (late October) 800-854-1234
daytonainfo.com/bikeweek/

FLORIDA — Daytona Beach (Cont'd)

November
- **Daytona Turkey Run Car Show & Swap Meet** (late November) 904-255-7355

December
- **Home for the Holidays Parade** (mid-December) 904-676-3257
- **World Karting Association Racing** (late December) 904-253-7223
  www.daytonausa.com

Fort Lauderdale

January
- **Florida Renaissance Festival** (late January-early March) 954-776-1642
  www.ren-fest.com/fla1.html
- **Micron PC Bowl** (early January) 954-564-5000
- **Riverwalk Winter Arts & Crafts Show** (mid-January) 954-761-5363

February
- **Canadafest** (early February) 954-921-3404
- **Fiesta Tropical Mardi Gras Carnival** (late February) 954-922-9959
- **Florida Renaissance Festival** (late January-early March) 954-776-1642
  www.ren-fest.com/fla1.html
- **Greek Festival** (February) 954-467-1515
- **Seminole Tribal Festival** (mid-February) 954-967-3706
- **Sistrunk Historical Festival** (early February) 954-357-7514
- **Taste of Fort Lauderdale** (late February) 954-485-3481

March
- **Florida Renaissance Festival** (late January-early March) 954-776-1642
  www.ren-fest.com/fla1.html
- **Fort Lauderdale International Auto Show** (March) 954-765-5933
- **Hollywood Jazz Festival** (mid-March) 954-921-3404
- **Irish Fest** (mid-March) 954-946-1093
- **Las Olas Art Festival** (early March) 954-525-5500
- **Saint Patrick's Day Parade & Festival** (mid-March) 954-921-3404

April
- **Fort Lauderdale Billfish Tournament** (late April) 954-563-0385
- **Fort Lauderdale Seafood Festival** (early April) 954-463-4431
- **Fort Lauderdale Spring Boat Show** (mid-late April) 954-764-7642
- **New Riverfest** (April) 954-765-4466
- **Pompano Beach Seafood Festival** (late April) 954-941-2940

May
- **Air & Sea Show** (early May) 954-765-4466
  www.airseashow.com/
- **Cajun Zydeco Crawfish Festival** (early May) 954-489-3255

June
- **NationsBank Starlight Musicals** (mid-June-late August) 954-627-6500

July
- **Beethoven by the Beach** (early July) 800-226-1812
- **NationsBank Starlight Musicals** (mid-June-late August) 954-627-6500
- **Pompano Beach Rainbow Festival** (late July) 954-786-4111

August
- **Hollywood Beach Latinfest** (mid-August) 954-921-3460
- **NationsBank Starlight Musicals** (mid-June-late August) 954-627-6500

September
- **Las Olas Art Fair** (early September) 954-472-3755

October
- **Art a la Carte** (October) 954-525-5500
- **Fort Lauderdale International Boat Show** (late October-early November) 954-764-7642
- **Fort Lauderdale International Film Festival** (late October-mid-November) 954-760-9898
  ftlaudfilmfest.com
- **Promenade in the Park** (October) 954-525-5500
- **Viva Broward** (early October) 954-527-0627

November
- **Broward County Fair** (late November) 954-963-3247
- **Fort Lauderdale International Boat Show** (late October-early November) 954-764-7642
- **Fort Lauderdale International Film Festival** (late October-mid-November) 954-760-9898
  ftlaudfilmfest.com
- **Riverwalk Blues Festival** (early November) 954-761-5934

December
- **Chris Evert Pro-Celebrity Tennis Classic** (early December) 561-394-2400
- **Christmas on Las Olas** (early December) 954-765-4466
- **Light Up Fort Lauderdale** (December 31) 954-765-4466
- **New River Boat Parade** (mid-late December) 954-791-0202
- **Winterfest Boat Parade** (mid-December) 954-767-0686

Hialeah

January
- **Hialeah Spring Festival** (late January-mid-February) 305-828-9898

February
- **Hialeah Spring Festival** (late January-mid-February) 305-828-9898

March
- **Widener Handicap** (late March) 305-885-8000

April
- **Flamingo Stakes** (early April) 305-885-8000

October
- **Hispanic Heritage Month** (October) 305-687-2671

November
- **Holiday Country Craft Show** (late-November) 305-821-1130

Jacksonville

January
- **Gator Bowl** (early January) 904-798-9111

February
- **Jacksonville Boat-A-Rama** (early February) 904-724-3003
- **Jacksonville Scottish Highland Games** (late February) 904-641-1119
- **Jacksonville Wine Experience** (mid-February) 904-358-6336

March
- **Gate River Run** (early March) 904-739-1917
- **Jacksonville Spring Fair** (late March-early April) 904-358-6336
- **Mayport/Fort George Seafood Festival** (mid-March) 904-249-9336
- **Tournament Player's Championship** (late March) 904-285-7888

April
- **Historic Homes & Gardens Tour** (late April) 904-389-2449
- **Jacksonville Spring Fair** (late March-early April) 904-358-6336
- **King Neptune Seafood Festival** (mid-April) 904-249-3972
- **Springing the Blues Festival** (early April) 904-249-3972
  www.springingtheblues.com/

May
- **American Music Festival** (late May) 904-354-5479
- **Kuumba Festival** (late May) 904-353-2270
- **Mug Race** (early May) 904-264-4094
- **World of Nations** (early May) 904-630-0837

July
- **Greater Jacksonville Kingfish Tournament** (mid-July) 904-798-9111
- **Jacksonville Pro Rodeo** (July) 904-630-3900
- **July Fourth Celebration** (July 4) 904-630-3520

September
- **Riverside Arts & Music Festival** (early September) 904-389-2449

October
- **Greater Jacksonville Agricultural Fair** (mid-late October) 904-353-0535

November
- **Caribbean Carnival** (early November) 904-798-9111
- **Jacksonville Jazz Festival** (mid-November) 904-353-7770
- **Jacksonville Light Parade** (late November) 904-798-9111

December
- **Jacksonville Downtown Countdown** (December 31) 904-630-3520

Key West

January
- **Hog's Breath Ska King Mackerel Tournament** (late January-early February) 305-296-0364
- **Key West Crafts Show** (late January) 305-294-2587
- **Key West Literary Seminar** (mid-January) 888-293-9291

February
- **Hog's Breath Ska King Mackerel Tournament** (late January-early February) 305-296-0364
- **Monroe County Festival of the Seas** (early February) 305-296-2454
- **Old Island Days Art Festival** (mid-late February) 305-294-1241

March
- **Civil War Days** (early March) 305-292-6713
- **Conch Shell Blowing Contest** (mid-late March) 305-294-9501

April
- **Conch Republic Independence Celebration** (mid-late April) 305-296-0213
- **Key West & Lower Keys Fishing Tournament** (mid-late April) 305-745-3332
- **Key West Garden Club Flower Show** (early April) 305-294-3210
- **Red Ribbon Bed Race** (late April) 305-296-7511
- **Seven Mile Bridge Run** (mid-April) 305-743-8513
- **Taste of Key West** (mid-April) 305-296-6196
- **Turtle Kraals 5K Trot** (early April) 305-296-7182

May
- **Key West Songwriters Festival** (early-mid-May) 305-294-5015
- **Super Boat Races** (late May) 305-296-8963

June
- **Big Pine & Lower Keys Dolphin Tournament** (mid-June) 305-872-2411
- **Key West Gator Club Dolphin Tournament** (mid-late June) 305-296-7511

July
- **Hemingway Days Festival** (mid-late July) 305-294-4440
  www.hemingwaydays.com
- **Sport Divers Mini Lobster Season** (late July) 305-289-2320
- **Underwater Music Festival** (early-mid-July) 305-872-2411

September
- **Mercury Outboards' SLAM Tournament** (mid-September) 305-664-2002
- **Womenfest Key West** (mid-September) 305-296-4238

October
- **Fantasy Fest** (late October) 305-296-1817
- **Goombay** (mid-late October) 305-293-8898
- **Key West Theatre Festival** (early-mid-October) 305-292-3725
- **Oktoberfest** (early October) 305-872-2411

November
- **Corvettes in Paradise Show** (early November) 305-872-9641
- **Cuban American Heritage Festival** (early November) 305-294-7618
  www.keywestcubanclub.com
- **Historic Seaport Music Festival** (late November) 305-296-7182
- **Hog's Breath 5K Run** (late November) 305-296-7182
- **Key West World Championship Race** (early-mid-November) 305-296-6166
- **Lower Keys Golf Tournament** (mid-late November) 305-872-2411
- **Pirates in Paradise Festival** (late November) 305-743-4386
- **Reef Relief's Cayo Carnival** (mid-November) 305-294-3100
  www.reefrelief.org

December
- **City Christmas Parade** (mid-December) 305-292-8100
- **Island Art Fair** (mid-late December) 305-872-2411

Miami

January
- **Art Deco Weekend Festival** (mid-January) 305-672-2014
- **Art Expo** (early January) 305-558-1758
- **Beaux Arts Festival of the Arts** (mid-January) 305-284-3535
  www.pinecrest.com/beaux-arts/
- **Freddick Bratcher Florida Dance Festival** (late January) 305-448-2021
- **Key Biscayne Art Festival** (late January) 305-361-0049
- **Kwanzaa Celebration** (late December-early January) 305-936-5805
- **La Settimana del Cinema Italiano** (mid-January) 305-861-2000
- **Metropolitan South Florida Fishing Tournament** (December-mid-May) 305-569-0066
- **Miccosukee Tribe's Indian Arts Festival** (early January) 305-223-8380
- **National Children's Theatre Festival** (mid-January) 305-444-9293
- **Ocean Drive Street Festival** (mid-January) 305-672-2014
- **Orange Bowl** (early January) 305-643-7100
- **Original Miami Beach Antique Show** (late January-early February) 305-754-4931
- **Redlands Natural Arts Festival** (mid-January) 305-247-5727
- **Santa's Enchanted Forest** (late November-early January) 305-893-0090
- **Taste of the Grove** (late January) 305-444-7270

February
- **Bob Marley Festival** (mid-February) 305-358-7550
- **Coconut Grove Arts Festival** (mid-February) 305-447-0401
- **Dade Radio Tropical Hamboree Show** (early February) 305-223-7060
- **Doral-Ryder Open** (late February-early March) 305-477-4653
- **February Home Show** (early February) 305-666-5944
- **Homestead Championship Rodeo** (early February) 305-247-3515
  www.homesteadrodeo.com
- **Metropolitan South Florida Fishing Tournament** (December-mid-May) 305-569-0066
- **Miami Beach Festival of the Arts** (early February) 305-672-1272
- **Miami Film Festival** (early February) 305-377-3456
  www.filmsocietyofmiami.com
- **Miami International Boat Show** (mid-February) 305-531-8410
- **Miami International Map Fair** (early February) 305-375-1492
- **Original Miami Beach Antique Show** (late January-early February) 305-754-4931
- **Outdoor Festival of the Arts** (early February) 305-673-7730
- **Saint Stephen's Arts & Crafts Show** (mid-February) 305-558-1758

March
- **Calle Ocho Festival** (early March) 305-644-8888
- **Carnaval Miami** (early March) 305-644-8888
- **Dade County Fair & Exposition** (mid-March-early April) 305-223-7060
- **Doral-Ryder Open** (late February-early March) 305-477-4653
- **Ericsson Open** (late March-early April) 305-442-3367
  www.ericsson-open.com
- **Florida Derby** (mid-March) 305-931-7223
- **Grand Prix of Miami** (mid-March) 305-539-3000
- **Italian Renaissance Festival** (mid-March) 305-250-9133
- **Metropolitan South Florida Fishing Tournament** (December-mid-May) 305-569-0066
- **Miami International Orchid Show** (early March) 305-444-8484
- **Subtropics Music Festival** (mid-March-mid-May) 305-758-6676

April
- **Dade County Fair & Exposition** (mid-March-early April) 305-223-7060
- **Dade Heritage Days** (early April-mid-May) 305-358-9572
- **Ericsson Open** (late March-early April) 305-442-3367
  www.ericsson-open.com
- **Fairchild Tropical Garden Caribbean Festival** (late April) 305-667-1651
- **Metropolitan South Florida Fishing Tournament** (December-mid-May) 305-569-0066
- **Miami Billfish Tournament** (early April) 305-598-2525
- **South Beach Film Festival** (mid-late April) 305-532-1233
  members.aol.com/sobefilm
- **Subtropics Music Festival** (mid-March-mid-May) 305-758-6676
- **Taste of the Beach** (mid-April) 305-672-1270

May
- **Arabian Nights Festival** (early May) 305-688-4611
- **Coconut Grove Bed Race** (mid-May) 305-444-7270
- **Dade Heritage Days** (early April-mid-May) 305-358-9572
- **Great Sunrise Balloon Race & Festival** (late May) 305-596-9040
- **Metropolitan South Florida Fishing Tournament** (December-mid-May) 305-569-0066
- **Roots & Culture Festival** (mid-May) 305-751-4222
- **Springtime Harvest Festival** (early May) 954-987-4275
- **Subtropics Music Festival** (mid-March-mid-May) 305-758-6676

June
- **Florida Dance Festival** (mid-late June) 800-252-0808
- **Miami/Bahamas Goombay Festival** (early June) 305-372-9966

July
- **4th of July at Bayfront Park** (July 4) 305-358-7550
- **Colombian Festival** (mid-July) 305-448-5558
- **International Mango Festival** (mid-July) 305-667-1651
- **Key Biscayne 4th of July Parade & Fireworks** (July 4) 305-365-8901
- **Tropical Agricultural Fiesta** (mid-July) 305-248-3311

August
- **Miami Reggae Festival** (early August) 305-891-2944

September
- **Festival Miami** (mid-September-mid-October) 305-284-4940

October
- **Caribbean Festival** (mid-October) 305-653-1877
- **Columbus Day Regatta** (mid-October) 305-539-3000

FLORIDA — Miami (Cont'd)

Festival Miami (mid-September-mid-October) 305-284-4940
Greater Miami Race for the Cure (mid-October) 305-666-7223
Hispanic Heritage Festival (October) 305-541-5023
West Indian Carnival Extravaganza (mid-October) 305-435-4845

November
Banyan Arts & Crafts Festival (mid-November) 305-444-7270
Miami Book Fair International (mid-November) 305-237-3258
Puerto Rican Festival (late November) 305-448-5145
Santa's Enchanted Forest (late November-early January) ... 305-893-0090
South Florida International Auto Show (early-mid-November) 305-947-5950
www.sfliautoshow.com
South Miami Art Festival (early November) 305-661-1621

December
Big Orange New Year's Eve Celebration (December 31) ... 305-358-7550
King Mango Strut (late December) 305-444-7270
King Orange Jamboree Parade (late December) 305-371-4600
Kwanzaa Celebration (late December-early January) 305-936-5805
Metropolitan South Florida Fishing Tournament (December-mid-May) 305-569-0066
Santa's Enchanted Forest (late November-early January) ... 305-893-0090

Naples

January
Art in the Park (November-May) 941-262-6517
Collier County Fair (mid-January) 941-455-1444
Naples Invitational Art Fest (late January) 941-263-1667

February
Art Encounter (February) 941-262-6517
Art in the Park (November-May) 941-262-6517
Naples National Art Festival (late February) 941-262-6517

March
Art in the Park (November-May) 941-262-6517
Classic Swamp Buggy Races (early March & mid-late May & late October) 941-774-2701
www.swampbuggy.com
Naples St Patrick's Day Parade (mid-March) 941-774-6086
Naples/Fort Myers Bluegrass Jam (mid-March) 941-992-2184
National Art Association Founders Exhibit (March) 941-262-6517

April
Art in the Park (November-May) 941-262-6517
Lunar Festival (mid-April) 941-992-2184

May
Art in the Park (November-May) 941-262-6517
Classic Swamp Buggy Races (early March & mid-late May & late October) 941-774-2701
www.swampbuggy.com
Millenium Lifestyle & Business Expo (early-mid-May) 941-435-3742
Summerjazz on the Gulf (May-September) 941-261-2222

June
Summerjazz on the Gulf (May-September) 941-261-2222

July
Fourth of July Festival (July 4) 941-434-4717
Summerjazz on the Gulf (May-September) 941-261-2222

August
Summerjazz on the Gulf (May-September) 941-261-2222

September
American Street Craft Show (early September) 941-435-3742
Summerjazz on the Gulf (May-September) 941-261-2222

October
Classic Swamp Buggy Races (early March & mid-late May & late October) 941-774-2701
www.swampbuggy.com
Octoberfest & Sidewalk Sale (late October) 941-435-3742
Swamp Buggy Parade (mid-late October) 941-774-2701
World Orchid Symposium (late October) 941-261-2222

November
Art in the Park (November-May) 941-262-6517
Thanksgiving Weekend Festival (late November) 941-435-3742

December
Art in the Park (November-May) 941-262-6517
Christmas Walk & Festival of Lights (early December) 941-435-3742
Grand Millenium Parade (early December) 941-435-3742

Orlando

January
Florida Citrus Bowl (January 1) 407-423-2476
www.orlandocentroplex.com
Orlando Scottish Highland Games (mid-January) 407-699-4510
Orlando-UCF Shakespeare Festival (October-May) 407-245-0985
Surf Expo (early January) 407-345-9800
Walt Disney World Marathon (early January) 407-939-7810

February
Bach Music Festival (late February) 407-646-2182
Central Florida Fair (late February-early March) 407-295-3247
Orlando-UCF Shakespeare Festival (October-May) 407-245-0985
Silver Spurs Rodeo (mid-February & early October) 800-847-4052

March
Central Florida Fair (late February-early March) 407-295-3247
Orlando-UCF Shakespeare Festival (October-May) 407-245-0985
Winter Park Sidewalk Arts Festival (mid-March) 407-644-8281
www.wpsaf.org/

April
Epcot International Flower & Garden Show (mid April-late May) 407-824-4321
Maitland Arts & Fine Crafts Festival (mid-April) 407-644-0741
Orlando-UCF Shakespeare Festival (October-May) 407-245-0985

May
Epcot International Flower & Garden Show (mid April-late May) 407-824-4321
Orlando-UCF Shakespeare Festival (October-May) 407-245-0985

June
Florida Film Festival (mid-late June) 407-629-1088
www.floridafilmfestival.org

July
Summer Festival (mid-July) 407-943-7992
Walt Disney World Fourth of July Celebration (July 4) 407-824-2222

October
Epcot International Food & Wine Festival (late October-late November) 407-824-4321
Halloween Horror Nights (October) 800-447-0675
International Orchid Fair (late October) 407-396-1887
Orlando Craft Fair (early October) 407-860-0092
Orlando-UCF Shakespeare Festival (October-May) 407-245-0985
Silver Spurs Rodeo (mid-February & early October) 800-847-4052
Walt Disney World National Car Rental Golf Classic (late October) 407-824-2250

November
Epcot International Food & Wine Festival (late October-late November) 407-824-4321
Festival of the Masters (mid-November) 407-824-4321
Fiesta in the Park (early November) 407-649-3152
Orlando-UCF Shakespeare Festival (October-May) 407-245-0985

December
Orlando's Singing Christmas Trees (mid-December) 407-425-2555
Orlando-UCF Shakespeare Festival (October-May) 407-245-0985

Pensacola

January
Pensacola Mardi Gras (early January-early March) 850-473-8858
www.boogieinc.com/margra.htm

February
Pensacola Mardi Gras (early January-early March) 850-473-8858
www.boogieinc.com/margra.htm

March
Pensacola Mardi Gras (early January-early March) 850-473-8858
www.boogieinc.com/margra.htm

April
Pensacola JazzFest (mid-April) 850-433-8382
artsnwfl.org/jazz/fest.htm

May
Fiesta Of Five Flags Regional Pistol Match (early May) ... 850-433-6512
Fiesta Spring Antique Show (early May) 850-433-6512
Pensacola Crawfish Creole Fiesta (early May) 850-433-6512
www.fiestafiveflags.org/crawfish.html
Penwheels/Fiesta Fishing Rodeo (early May) 850-433-6512
SpringFest (mid-May) 850-469-1069
www.springfest.net

June
Fiesta of Five Flags (early-mid-June) 850-433-6512
www.fiestafiveflags.org
Fiesta Of Five Flags Golf Tournament (mid-June) 850-433-6512

August
Jubilee's Bushwacker & Music Festival (early August) 850-932-1500

September
Fiesta Fall Antique Show (mid-September) 850-433-6512
Jubilee's Lobster Fest (early September) 850-932-1500
Pensacola Seafood Festival (mid-September) 850-433-6512
www.fiestafiveflags.org/seafood.html
Pensacola Seafood Festival 5k Run/Walk (late September) 850-433-6512
www.fiestafiveflags.org/5k_run.html

October
Pensacola Interstate Fair (late October) 850-944-4500
www.pensacolafair.com/flash.htm

November
Great Gulf Coast Arts Festival (early November) 850-432-9906
www.greatgulfcoastart.org

December
First Night Pensacola (December 31) 850-932-0095

Saint Augustine

January
Confederate Encampment (late January) 904-829-6506
Matanzas 5K & Fun Run (late January) 904-739-1917
Nights of Lights Festival (late November-late January) 904-829-5681
Winter Dance Festival (mid-January) 904-829-1617

February
Flight to Freedom (late February) 904-461-2035
Menendez Day (February 15) 904-825-1010
Menendez Festival (mid-late February) 904-825-5088
Native American Pow Wow (late February) 904-829-2201

March
Blessing of the Fleet (late March) 904-825-1010
Legends of Golf Tournament (mid-March) 904-940-0321
Lighthouse Festival & 5K Run (mid-March) 904-829-0745
Passion Play (mid-late March-early April) 904-797-5675
Saint Johns County Fair (mid March) 904-829-5681
Serales' Raid (mid-late March) 904-824-9823
Spring Arts & Crafts Festival (late March) 904-829-1711
Union Encampment (mid-March) 904-829-6506

April
Cabbage & Potato Festival (late April) 904-692-1420
Earth Day Celebration (late April) 904-808-7009
Easter Parade (early April) 904-829-2992
Easter Sunday Promenade (early April) 904-829-2992
EPIC Celebration of Spring (mid-April) 904-829-3295
Gamble Rogers Folk Festival (late April-early May) 904-794-0222
Historic Inns & Garden Tour (mid-April) 904-829-3295
Passion Play (mid-late March-early April) 904-797-5675
Saint Augustine Beach Run (mid-April) 904-471-4816
Saint Augustine Flower, Garden & Art Show (mid-April) ... 904-829-3295
Seafood Festival (early April) 904-824-1978
Taste of Saint Augustine (mid-April) 904-829-3295
Torch Light Tour (early Feb-early April) 904-829-6506
Victorian Spring (late April) 904-825-5033

May
Antique Car Show (late May) 904-471-0341
Blue Water Tournament (late May) 904-829-5676
Cannon Firing Season (late May-early September) 904-829-6506
Celebrate Ponte Vedra (May) 904-280-0614
Celebration of Centuries (mid-May-mid-June) 800-653-2489
Fine Art & Jazz Show (early May) 888-352-9463
Gamble Rogers Folk Festival (late April-early May) 904-794-0222
Hot Times in the Old Town (early May) 904-829-1711
Memorial Weekend Cathedral Festival (late May) 904-797-1563
Mother's Day Arts & Crafts Show (early May) 904-471-7731
Nature Photo Contest (early May-mid-July) 904-824-3337
Vilano Bridge Run (early May) 904-824-1761

June
Beach Bash (early June) 904-461-2000
Cannon Firing Season (late May-early September) 904-829-6506
Celebration of Centuries (mid-May-mid-June) 800-653-2489
Drake's Raid (early June) 904-829-1711
Greek Landing Day Festival (late June) 904-829-8205
Kingbuster Fishing Tournament (mid-June) 904-992-9600
Nature Photo Contest (early May-mid-July) 904-824-3337
Spanish Night Watch (mid-June) 904-797-7217
Voices of the Past (mid-June) 904-824-2056

July
Ancient City King Fish Tournament (early-mid-July) 904-471-2730
Atlantic Shakespeare Festival (late July-mid-August) 904-471-1965
Cannon Firing Season (late May-early September) 904-829-6506
Fourth of July Celebration (July 4) 800-653-2489
Nature Photo Contest (early May-mid-July) 904-824-3337

August
Atlantic Shakespeare Festival (late July-mid-August) 904-471-1965
Cannon Firing Season (late May-early September) 904-829-6506
Conch House Challenge (late August) 888-463-4742

September
Cannon Firing Season (late May-early September) 904-829-6506
Days In Spain (early September) 904-825-1010
Founder's Day (early September) 904-825-1010

October
Halloween Nights (late October) 904-471-9010

November
Fall Arts & Crafts Festival (late November) 904-829-1711
Great Chowder Debate (early November) 904-829-8646
Lincolnville Festival (early November) 904-829-8379
Nights of Lights Festival (late November-late January) 904-829-5681

December
18th Century Christmas Caroling (mid-December) 904-829-1711
British Night Watch (early December) 904-829-1711
Carols by Candlelight (early December) 904-461-2000
Christmas Tour of Homes (early December) 904-829-1711
Grand Illumination (early December) 904-794-7682
La Fiesta de Navidad (mid-December) 904-829-1711
Las Posadas Celebration (mid-December) 904-826-0209
Luminaries in the Plaza (early-mid-December) 904-797-3908
Nights of Lights Festival (late November-late January) 904-829-5681
Regatta of Lights (mid-December) 800-653-2489
Saint Augustine Christmas Parade (early December) 904-829-5681

Saint Petersburg

January
Largo Folk Festival (late January) 727-582-2123

February
Mid-Winter Regatta (late February) 727-822-3873

March
Festival of States (late March-early April) 727-898-3654
International Folk Fair (mid-March) 727-551-3365

FLORIDA — Saint Petersburg (Cont'd)

Pinellas County Fair (late March) 727-541-6941
Renaissance Festival (early March-mid-April) 727-586-5423
Spring Boat Show (March) 727-892-5767
Thistle Mid-Winter Sailboat Races (early March) 727-822-3873

April
American Stage in the Park (mid-April-mid-May) 727-822-8814
Festival of States (late March-early April) 727-898-3654
Mainsail Arts Festival (mid-April) 727-892-5885
Renaissance Festival (early March-mid-April) 727-586-5423
Saint Petersburg-Isla Mujeras Regatta (late April) 727-822-3873

May
American Stage in the Park (mid-April-mid-May) 727-822-8814
Taste of Pinellas (late May-early June) 727-893-7734

June
Taste of Pinellas (late May-early June) 727-893-7734

July
4th of July Celebration (July 4) 727-821-6164
July 4th Celebration (July 4) 727-893-7494

November
Holiday Show of Fine Arts & Crafts (November) 727-822-7872
Ribfest (mid-November) 727-896-2727
Sail Expo Saint Petersburg (early November) 727-464-7200
Saint Petersburg Fall Boat Show (November) 727-892-5767

December
First Night Saint Petersburg (December 31) 727-823-8906
Holiday Lighted Boat Parade (early December) 727-893-7329
Santa Parade (early December) 727-893-8581
Snowfest (early December) 727-898-3654

Tallahassee

January
Hernando Desoto Winter Encampment (early January) 850-922-6007
Tallahassee Marathon (mid-January) 850-893-9739

March
Havana Music Fest (early March) 850-539-8114
Jazz & Blues Festival (mid-March) 850-576-1636
Natural Bridge Battle Reenactment (March) 850-925-6216
Springtime Tallahassee (late March-early April) 850-224-5012

April
Rose Festival (late April) 800-704-2350
Spring Farm Days (April) 850-575-8684
Springtime Tallahassee (late March-early April) 850-224-5012

May
Humanatee Festival (mid-May) 850-922-6007
Southern Shakespeare Festival (early May) 850-513-3087
www.southernshakespeare.org

June
Watermelon Festival (late June) 850-997-5552

July
Celebrate America (July 4) 850-891-3866
Summer Swamp Stomp (mid-July) 850-575-8684

August
Caribbean Carnival (late August) 850-878-2198

September
Native American Heritage Festival (September) 850-576-8684

October
Halloween Howl (late October) 850-575-8684
Zoobilee (early October) 850-575-8684

November
December on the Farm (early November) 850-576-1636
North Florida Fair (early November) 850-878-3247

December
Knott House Candlelight Tour (early December) 850-922-2459
Market Days (early December) 850-575-8684
Winter Festival (mid-late December) 850-413-9200

Tampa

January
Country Folk Art Show (early January & mid-October) 800-345-3247
Outback Bowl (January 1) 813-874-2695
Winter Equestrian Festival (late January-early April) 813-623-5801

February
Fiesta Day (mid-February) 813-248-3712
Florida State Fair (February) 813-621-7821
www.fl-ag.com/statefair
Gasparilla Distance Classic (mid-February) 813-229-7866
Gasparilla Pirate Fest (early February) 813-223-1111
GTE Classic (mid-February) 813-948-4653
Illuminated Night Parade (mid-February) 813-248-3712
Krewe of the Knights of Sant' Yago Illuminated Night Parade (mid-February) 813-248-3712
Old Hyde Park Village Art Festival (early October & late February) 813-251-3500
Winter Equestrian Festival (late January-early April) 813-623-5801

March
Florida Strawberry Festival (mid-March) 813-752-9194
Gasparilla Festival of the Arts (early March) 813-876-1747
President's Cup Regatta (early March) 813-253-6241
Winter Equestrian Festival (late January-early April) 813-623-5801

April
All Makes Auto Swap Meet (early April) 419-478-5292
Brandon Balloon Classic (late April) 813-689-1221
Sun 'n Fun EAA Fly-In (mid-April) 863-644-2431
Winter Equestrian Festival (late January-early April) 813-623-5801

May
Old Hyde Park Village Live Music Series (May-October) 813-251-3500

June
Old Hyde Park Village Live Music Series (May-October) 813-251-3500

July
Celebrate America (early July) 727-562-4800
Freedom Fest (early July) 813-223-1111
Old Hyde Park Village Live Music Series (May-October) 813-251-3500

August
Old Hyde Park Village Live Music Series (May-October) 813-251-3500

September
Greek Festival (mid-September) 419-243-9189
Old Hyde Park Village Live Music Series (May-October) 813-251-3500

October
Country Folk Art Show (early January & mid-October) 800-345-3247
Guavaweeen (late October) 813-248-3712
Hillsborough County Fair (late October-early November) 813-223-1111
Old Hyde Park Village Art Festival (early October & late February) 813-251-3500
Old Hyde Park Village Live Music Series (May-October) 813-251-3500
Taste of Florida (early October) 813-259-7376

November
Hillsborough County Fair (late October-early November) 813-223-1111
Ruskin Seafood & Arts Festival (early November) 813-645-3808
Tampa Recreation's International Festival (mid-November) 813-931-2106

December
First Night Tampa (late December) 813-223-1111

West Palm Beach

January
$25,000 He's My Man Royal Palm Classic (late January) 561-683-2222
Challenge Cup Polo Tournament (early-mid-January) 561-793-1440
Florida Winter Equestrian Festival (January-March) 561-793-5867
FOTOFusion (late January) 561-276-9797
Oshogatsu Japanese New Year Celebration (early January) 561-495-0233
Palm Beach International Art & Antiques Fair (late January-early February) 561-659-8007
South Florida Fair (mid-January-early February) 561-793-0333
www.gopbi.com/southfloridafair
Sterling Cup Polo Tournament (late January-mid-February) 561-793-1440

February
$25,000 James W Paul 3/8th Mile Derby (late February) 561-683-2222
Antiques Show & Sale (mid-February) 561-243-0223
Artigras (mid-February) 561-694-2300
Boca Raton Outdoor Art Festival (late February) 561-392-2500
Downtown Delray Craft Festival (late February-early March) 954-472-3755
Fiesta of Arts (early February) 561-393-7806
Florida Winter Equestrian Festival (January-March) 561-793-5867
Hatsume Fair (late February) 561-495-0233
Indian River Native American Festival (late February) 561-978-4500
Old-time Street Celebration (early February) 561-393-7806
Palm Beach International Art & Antiques Fair (late January-early February) 561-659-8007
Palm Beach International Food & Wine Festival (late February-early March) 561-220-2690
Palm Beach Renaissance Festival (early-mid-February) 800-676-7333
Palm Beach Seafood Festival (early February) 561-832-6397
Palm Beach Tropical Flower Show (late February) 561-655-5522
South Florida Fair (mid-January-early February) 561-793-0333
www.gopbi.com/southfloridafair
Sterling Cup Polo Tournament (late January-mid-February) 561-793-1440
Winter Festival (late February) 561-451-4485

March
$25,000 Arthur J Rooney Sr-St Patrick's Invitational (mid-March) 561-683-2222
$25,000 Palm Beach Invitational (late March) 561-683-2222
Boynton Beach's GALA (late March) 561-375-6236
Downtown Delray Craft Festival (late February-early March) 954-472-3755
Florida Winter Equestrian Festival (January-March) 561-793-5867
Gold Cup of the Americas (early-mid March) 561-793-1440
Palm Beach Boat Show (late March) 800-940-7642
Palm Beach International Food & Wine Festival (late February-early March) 561-220-2690
Spring Fling (late March) 561-393-7806
US Open Polo Championship (mid-March-early April) 561-793-1440

April
$25,000 Bob Balfe/Molyneux Cup Puppy Stakes (late April) 561-683-2222
Delray Affair (early April) 561-278-0424
www.delrayaffair.com
PGA Seniors' Championship (mid-April) 561-627-1800
SunFest of Palm Beach County (late April-early May) 561-659-5980
www.gopbi.com/sunfest
US Open Polo Championship (mid-March-early April) 561-793-1440
West Palm Beach Italian Festival (early April) 561-832-6397

May
All Florida Exhibit (late May-mid-July) 561-392-2500
Jet Car Nationals (mid-May) 561-622-1400
Pioneer Days Festival (late May) 561-793-0333
SunFest of Palm Beach County (late April-early May) 561-659-5980
www.gopbi.com/sunfest

June
All Florida Exhibit (late May-mid-July) 561-392-2500
Tropical Fruit Festival (late June) 561-233-1759

July
All Florida Exhibit (late May-mid-July) 561-392-2500
Fourth on Flagler (July 4) 561-659-8004
Wine & All That Jazz (late July) 561-395-4433

August
Boca Festival Days (August) 561-395-4433
Bon Festival (August) 561-495-0233

September
Moroso Chrysler Classic Show (mid-September) 561-622-1400
US Croquet National Championship (late September & early October) 561-753-9141

October
$25,000 Fall Futurity (late October) 561-683-2222
All Ford Show (early October) 561-622-1400
Oktoberfest (mid-late October) 561-967-6464
Seafare (October) 561-747-6639
US Croquet National Championship (late September & early October) 561-753-9141

November
Fine Arts Festival (late November) 561-746-3101
Harvest Fest (mid-November) 561-278-0424

December
Chris Evert Pro-Celebrity Tennis Classic (early December) 561-394-2400
Festival of Trees (December) 561-243-7356
Holiday Street Parade (early December) 561-393-7806
Winter Fantasy on the Waterway (mid-December) 561-395-4433

GEORGIA

Atlanta

January
Atlanta Boat Show (early January) 770-951-2500
Atlanta Garden & Patio Show (late January) 770-998-9800
National King Week (January) 404-524-1956
Super Bowl XXXIV (late January) 404-223-9200

February
Southeastern Flower Show (mid-February) 404-888-5638

March
Atlanta Home Show (late March) 770-998-9800
Saint Patrick's Day Celebration (mid-March) 404-523-2311

April
Atlanta Dogwood Festival (early April) 404-329-0501
www.dogwood.org/
Atlanta Renaissance Festival (late April-early June) 770-964-8575
Atlanta Steeplechase (early April) 404-222-6688
Down to Earth Day Celebration (April 22) 404-873-3173
www.efg.org
Georgia Renaissance Festival (late April-early June) 770-964-8575
www.garenfest.com
Inman Park Spring Festival & Tour of Homes (late April) 770-242-4895
PGA BellSouth Classic (late Maech-early April) 770-951-8777

May
Atlanta Caribbean Folk Festival (late May) 404-753-3497
Atlanta Film & Video Festival (mid-May) 404-352-4254
www.imagefv.org/afvf/home.html
Atlanta Jazz Festival (late May) 404-817-6851
Atlanta Renaissance Festival (late April-early June) 770-964-8575
Georgia Renaissance Festival (late April-early June) 770-964-8575
www.garenfest.com
Rose Show & Sale (early May) 404-876-5859
Springfest Festival (early May) 770-498-5702

June
Atlanta Renaissance Festival (late April-early June) 770-964-8575
Georgia Renaissance Festival (late April-early June) 770-964-8575
www.garenfest.com
Georgia Shakespeare Festival (early June-late December) 404-264-0020
www.gashakespeare.org
Stone Mountain Village Arts & Crafts Festival (mid-June) 770-498-2097

July
Georgia Shakespeare Festival (early June-late December) 404-264-0020
www.gashakespeare.org
National Black Arts Festival (late July-early August) 404-730-7315
Salute 2 America Parade (July 4) 404-521-6600
Thunder over Atlanta Fireworks (July 4) 404-523-2311

GEORGIA — Atlanta (Cont'd)

August
Georgia Shakespeare Festival (early June-late December) 404-264-0020
www.gashakespeare.org
National Black Arts Festival (late July-early August) 404-730-7315

September
Atlanta Greek Festival (late September) 404-633-5870
Georgia Shakespeare Festival (early June-late December) 404-264-0020
www.gashakespeare.org
Labor Day Weekend Festival (early September) 404-523-2311
Montreaux Atlanta International Jazz Festival (early September) 404-521-6600
Roswell Arts Festival (late September) 770-640-3253
Yellow Daisy Festival (early September) 770-498-5702

October
Fright Fest (October) 770-948-9290
Georgia Shakespeare Festival (early June-late December) 404-264-0020
www.gashakespeare.org
Scottish Festival & Highland Games (mid-October) 770-498-5702
Tour of Southern Ghosts (mid-late October) 770-469-1105
Vinings Fall Festival (early October) 770-438-8080

November
Art of the Season (late November-early December) 404-220-2659
Atlanta Marathon (late November) 404-231-9064
Georgia Shakespeare Festival (early June-late December) 404-264-0020
www.gashakespeare.org
Holiday Celebration (late November-late December) 770-498-5600
Peachtree International Film Festival (early-mid-November) 770-729-8487
www.peachtreefilm.org/festival

December
Art of the Season (late November-early December) 404-220-2659
CNN Center Tuba Christmas (mid-December) 770-887-5856
Festival of Trees (early December) 404-325-6635
First Night Atlanta (December 31) 404-881-0400
Georgia Shakespeare Festival (early June-late December) 404-264-0020
www.gashakespeare.org
Holiday Celebration (late November-late December) 770-498-5600
New Year's Eve Peach Drop (December 31) 404-523-2311
Peach Bowl (December 31) 404-586-8500

Augusta

January
Augusta Cutting Horse Futurity & Festival (late January) 706-724-4067

March
Gem & Mineral Show (mid-March) 706-796-5025
Regatta Fest (late March) 706-724-4439
Sacred Heart Garden & Flower Show (late March) 706-826-4700
Saint Patrick's Day Celebration (mid-March) 706-821-1754
Springtime Made in The South (early March) 706-722-3521

April
Craft Festival (mid-April) 706-541-0321
Masters Tournament (April) 706-667-6000

May
Garden City Folk Festival (early May) 706-826-4702
June Jazz Candlelight Concert Series (May) 706-821-1754
Riverwalk Bluegrass Festival (late May) 706-821-1754

June
West Paint Party (early June & mid-October) 706-826-4702

July
Augusta Southern National Drag Boat Races (mid-July) 706-724-2452
Riverwalk Fourth Celebration (July 4) 706-821-1754

August
River Race Augusta (mid-August) 706-724-4148

September
Arts in the Heart of Augusta (mid-September) 706-826-4702
Boshears' Memorial Fly In (late September) 706-733-1647
Historic Augusta Antique Show & Sale (mid-September) 706-724-0436
Taste of Augusta (late September) 706-868-7683

October
Fall Fest (early October) 803-278-5404
Grecian Festival (early October) 706-821-1755
Hispanic Festival (mid-October) 706-821-1754
Oktoberfest (early October) 706-860-0935
West Paint Party (early June & mid-October) 706-826-4702

November
Christmas Made in The South (mid-November) 706-722-3521
Festival of Lights (late November) 706-821-1754

Columbus

March
Spring Celebration (late March-mid-April) 706-663-2281

April
Riverfest Weekend (late April) 706-322-0756
Spring Celebration (late March-mid-April) 706-663-2281

May
Chill Out Columbus Style Jazz Festival (early May) 706-323-3687

June
Miss Georgia Pageant (late June) 706-322-2315

September
Columbus-Fort Benning Shrine Circus (September) 706-561-5448

October
Autumn Adventure (October) 706-663-2281
Buick Challenge PGA Golf Tournament (early October) 706-663-2281
Columbus Day Uptown Jam (early October) 706-596-0111

November
Fantasy in Lights (late November-late December) 706-663-2281
Steeplechase at Callaway Gardens (early November) 706-324-6252

December
Bi-City Christmas Parade (mid-December) 334-291-4719
Christmas Parade (early December) 706-322-1613
Fantasy in Lights (late November-late December) 706-663-2281

Macon

March
Cherry Blossom Festival (mid-March) 912-751-7429

May
Tubman Museum Pan African Festival (early May) 912-743-8544

July
Midsummer Macon (early-late July) 912-477-1110

September
Georgia Music Festival (mid-September) 912-743-3401
Ocmulgee Indian Celebration (mid-September) 912-743-3401

October
Arrowhead Arts & Crafts Festival (late October) 912-474-8770
Georgia State Fair (late October) 912-746-7184

December
Christmas in Macon (late Novemer-late December) 912-743-3401
First Night Macon (late December) 912-741-8000

Savannah

February
Georgia Heritage Celebration (early February) 912-651-2128
Savannah Irish Festival (mid-February) 912-927-0331
www.savannahdigital.com/savirish

March
Saint Patrick's Day Celebration on the River (mid-March) 912-234-0295
Savannah Onstage International Arts Festival (early March) 912-236-5745
www.savannahonstage.org/
Savannah Tour of Homes & Gardens (late March) 912-234-8054
Southern Home Show (early March) 912-354-6193

April
Hidden Gardens (mid-late April) 912-238-0248
Nogs Tour of Hidden Gardens (mid-April) 912-644-6401
Siege & Reduction Weekend (mid-April) 912-786-5787
Spring Fling (mid-April) 912-232-4903

May
Arts-on-the-River Weekend (mid-May) 912-651-6417
Scottish Games & Highland Gathering (mid-May) 912-644-6401
Seafood Festival (early May) 912-234-0295
www.savriverstreet.com/schedule.htm

June
City Market Blues Festival (early June) 912-232-4903

July
4th of July Celebration (July 4) 912-234-0295

August
Savannah Maritime Festival (late August) 912-238-4434

September
Jazz Festival (late September) 912-232-2222
Savannah Jazz Festival (late September) 912-232-2222

October
Oktoberfest on the River (early October) 912-234-0295
www.savriverstreet.com/schedule.htm
Savannah Greek Festival (mid-October) 912-236-8256
Telfair Art Fair (early-mid-October) 912-232-1177
www.telfair.org/news.html#calendar

December
Christmas on the River (early December) 912-234-0295
Christmas Tour of Homes (mid-December) 800-627-5030
New Years Eve at City Market (December 31) 912-232-4903

HAWAII

Honolulu

January
Hula Bowl (late January) 808-947-4141
Narcissus Festival (January-February) 808-923-1811
Narcissus Festival/Night in Chinatown (late January) 808-533-3181
Royal Hawaiian Rowing Challenge (late December-early January) 604-272-1060

February
Hawaii Mardi Gras Celebration (late February) 808-923-1811
Narcissus Festival (January-February) 808-923-1811
NFL Pro Bowl (early February) 808-486-9500

March
Cherry Blossom Festival Culture & Craft Fair (early March) 808-949-2255
www.calendar.gohawaii.com
Honolulu Festival (mid-March) 808-922-0254
Saint Patrick's Day Parade (March 17) 808-923-1811

April
Honolulu International Bed Race (late April) 808-923-1811
Merrie Monarch Festival (early April) 808-935-9168

May
Downtown Faire (early May) 808-521-8941
Lei Day Celebration (early May) 808-266-7654
Outrigger Hotels Hawaiian Oceanfest (late May-early June) 808-521-4322
Warrior Society Pow Wow (early May) 808-947-3206

June
Fancy Fair (mid-June) 808-531-0481
King Kamehameha Celebration Floral Parade (mid-June) 808-586-0333
King Kamehameha Day Celebration (mid-June) 808-935-9338
Matsuri in Hawaii Festival (mid-June) 808-926-0647
Outrigger Hotels Hawaiian Oceanfest (late May-early June) 808-521-4322

July
Bud Light Tin Man Triathalon (mid-July) 808-923-1811
Hawaii International Jazz Festival (mid-July) 808-941-9974

August
Bank of Hawaii Ki Ho Alu Festival (mid-August) 808-537-8615

September
Aloha Festivals (September-late October) 808-589-1771
Bankoh Nawahineokekai Championship Long Distance Canoe Races (September-October) 808-537-8658

October
Aloha Festivals (September-late October) 808-589-1771
Bankoh Nawahineokekai Championship Long Distance Canoe Races (September-October) 808-537-8658
Ironman Triathlon (October) 808-329-0063

November
Hawaii International Film Festival (November) 808-528-3456
www.hiff.org
Triple Crown of Surfing (mid-November-mid-December) 808-637-4558
World Invitational Hula Festival (early November) 808-486-3185

December
Aloha Bowl (December 25) 808-947-4141
Honolulu Marathon (mid-December) 808-734-7200
www.honolulumarathon.org/
Rainbow Classic (late December) 808-956-6501
Royal Hawaiian Rowing Challenge (late December-early January) 604-272-1060
Triple Crown of Surfing (mid-November-mid-December) 808-637-4558

IDAHO

Boise

January
Idaho Business Expo (late January) 208-323-4464

April
Race to Robie Creek (mid-April) 208-368-9990

May
Idaho Great Potato Marathon (early May) 208-344-5501

June
Boise River Festival (late June) 208-338-8887
Boise Tour Train & Trolley (June-October) 208-342-4796
Hewlett-Packard LaserJet Women's Challenge (early June) 208-345-7223
Idaho City Arts & Crafts Festival (early June) 208-392-4553
Idaho Shakespeare Festival (mid-June-September) 208-323-9700
www.idahoshakespeare.org
National Oldtime Fiddlers' Contest (mid-June) 208-549-0452

July
Boise Tour Train & Trolley (June-October) 208-342-4796
Idaho Shakespeare Festival (mid-June-September) 208-323-9700
www.idahoshakespeare.org
Snake River Stampede (mid-July) 208-466-8497

August
Boise Tour Train & Trolley (June-October) 208-342-4796
Idaho Shakespeare Festival (mid-June-September) 208-323-9700
www.idahoshakespeare.org
Western Idaho Fair (mid-August) 208-376-3247

September
Art in the Park (early September) 208-345-8330
Boise Tour Train & Trolley (June-October) 208-342-4796

IDAHO — Boise (Cont'd)

Idaho Shakespeare Festival (mid-June-September) 208-323-9700
www.idahoshakespeare.org
Nike Open Golf Tournament (mid-September) 208-939-6028
Womens Fitness Celebration (late September) 208-331-2221
www.celebrateall.org

October
Boise Tour Train & Trolley (June-October) 208-342-4796

November
Festival of Trees (late November-early December) 208-367-2797

December
Festival of Trees (late November-early December) 208-367-2797

Pocatello

January
Eastern Idaho Agriculture Show (mid-January) 208-233-1525

March
Dodge National Circuit Finals Rodeo (mid-March) 208-233-1525
Spring Fair (March) 208-233-1525

May
Iris Festival (late May-early June) 208-233-1525
Pocatello Stock Car Racing (late May-early September) 208-233-1525

June
Black Powder Shoot & Trapper Rendezvous (mid-June) 208-233-1525
Duck Race & Riverfest (mid-June) 208-233-1525
Idaho State High School Rodeo (mid-June) 208-233-1525
Iris Festival (late May-early June) 208-233-1525
Pocatello Stock Car Racing (late May-early September) 208-233-1525

July
Pocatello Stock Car Racing (late May-early September) 208-233-1525
Wild West Nationals Moto Cross (mid-July) 208-237-1340

August
Bannock County Fair & Rodeo (August) 208-237-1340
Greek Festival (mid- August) 208-232-5519
Health Line Classic (early August) 208-239-1818
Pocatello Stock Car Racing (late May-early September) 208-233-1525
Shoshone-Bannock Indian Festival (August) 208-238-3700

September
Eastern Idaho State Fair (early September) 208-785-0510
Pocatello Stock Car Racing (late May-early September) 208-233-1525

November
Christmas in Nightime Skies (late November) 208-233-1525
Festival of Trees (late November) 208-233-1525
Night Lights of Christmas Parade (late November) 208-232-7545

ILLINOIS

Champaign

January
Land of Lincoln Hunting & Fishing Show (January) 217-893-1613

March
Champaign-Urbana Home Show (March) 217-333-5000
Model Railroad Show & Swap Session (late March) 217-367-4092

May
Annual Duck Race (early May) 217-352-4229
British Car Festival (late May) 217-367-4092
Champaign County Town & Country Amateur Art Show
(mid-late May) 217-398-2376
Dinosaur Day (early May) 217-384-4062
Hit the Streets Festival (early May) 217-351-4070
Market at the Square (late May-October) 217-367-4092

June
Market at the Square (late May-October) 217-367-4092
Midwest Regional Firefighters Combat Challenge
(June) 217-351-4133
Strawberry Moon Shine Social (June) 217-384-4062
Taste of Champaign-Urbana (June) 217-351-4133

July
Champaign County Fair (July) 217-351-4133
Drum Corps International (July) 217-351-4133
Fourth of July Celebrations (July 4) 217-351-4133
Market at the Square (late May-October) 217-367-4092
Sounds of Summer Concerts (July) 217-367-1536

August
Market at the Square (late May-October) 217-367-4092
Sweetcorn Festival (August) 217-351-4133
US National Hot Air Balloon Championships (August) 217-351-4133

September
Market at the Square (late May-October) 217-367-4092
Mayor's Race Duathlon (September) 217-351-4133

October
Fall Arts & Crafts Bazaar (October) 217-351-4133
Halloween Fun Fest (late October) 217-356-2700
Market at the Square (late May-October) 217-367-4092

November
Chris Cringle Craft Show & Sale (November) 217-333-5000
Christmas Past (November) 217-586-2612
Turkey Trot (late November) 217-367-1536

December
Candles over the Prairie Grove (December) 217-367-1536
Carol Concerts (December) 217-333-6280

Chicago

February
Chicago Auto Show (mid-February) 312-744-3315
chicago-autoshow.com/
Chinese New Year Parade (late February) 312-225-0303
Medinah Shrine Circus (late February-mid-March) 312-266-5050
WinterBreak (February) 312-744-3315

March
Chicago Flower & Garden Show (mid-March) 312-321-0077
Chicago Park District Spring Flower Show
(late March-early May) 312-742-7737
Maple Syrup Festival (late March) 847-824-8360
Medinah Shrine Circus (late February-mid-March) 312-266-5050
Saint Patrick's Day Celebration & Fireworks
(mid-March) 312-942-9188
South Side Irish St Patrick's Day Parade (mid-March) 773-239-7755

April
Chicago Earth Day (April 22) 773-549-0606
Chicago Park District Spring Flower Show
(late March-early May) 312-742-7737

May
Chicago Park District Spring Flower Show
(late March-early May) 312-742-7737

June
Belmont Street Fair (early June) 773-868-3010
Celebrate on State Street (mid-June) 312-782-9160
Chicago Blues Festival (early June) 312-744-3370
Chicago Country Music Festival (late June) 312-744-3315
Chicago Gospel Festival (mid-June) 312-744-3315
Grant Park Music Festival (mid-June-mid-August) 312-742-7638
www.grantparkmusicfestival.com
Old Town Art Fair (mid-June) 312-337-1938
Printers Row Book Fair (early June) 312-987-1980
Taste of Chicago (late June-early July) 312-744-3370
Wells Street Art Festival (mid-June) 312-951-6106

July
Fiesta de Hemingway (mid-July) 708-848-2222
Grant Park Music Festival (mid-June-mid-August) 312-742-7638
www.grantparkmusicfestival.com
National Sporting Goods Assn World Sports Expo
(early-mid-July) 847-439-4000
Oz Festival (late July-early August) 312-744-3315
Taste of Chicago (late June-early July) 312-744-3370
Taste of Lincoln Avenue (late July) 773-975-1022
Venetian Night (late July) 312-744-3315

August
Chicago Air & Water Show (late August) 312-744-3370
Chicago Underground Film Festival (mid-August) 773-327-3456
www.cuff.org/
Gold Coast Art Fair (early August) 312-787-2677
Grant Park Music Festival (mid-June-mid-August) 312-742-7638
www.grantparkmusicfestival.com
Latin Music Festival (late August) 312-744-3370
Oz Festival (late July-early August) 312-744-3315

September
Berghoff Oktoberfest (mid-September) 312-427-3170
Celtic Fest (mid-September) 312-744-3315
Chicago Jazz Festival (early September) 312-744-3370
Taste of Polonia Festival (early September) 773-777-8898

October
Chicago International Film Festival (mid-October) 312-425-9400
www.chicago.ddbn.com/filmfest
LaSalle Banks Chicago Marathon (mid-October) 312-243-0003
www.chicagomarathon.com/

November
Magnificent Mile Lights Festival (mid-November) 312-642-3570
SOFA-Sculpture Objects & Fundamental Art
(early November) 312-654-0870

Peoria

June
Metro Centre Fine Arts Fair (mid-June) 309-692-6690
Steamboat Festival (mid-June) 309-681-0696
www.mtco.com/~pace/sb.html
Tremont Turkey Festival (mid-June) 309-925-4331

July
Antique Car Show (late July) 309-927-3345
Rib Fest (mid-July) 309-681-0696
www.mtco.com/~pace/rf.html

August
Chillifest & Corn Boil (early August) 309-274-4556
Italian American Summer Fiesta (mid-August) 309-681-8665
Taste of Peoria (mid-August) 309-681-0696
www.mtco.com/~pace/tp.html

September
Central Illinois Black Expo (mid-September) 309-673-8900
Greater Peoria Open (late September) 309-673-7161
Home Living Show (late September) 309-673-8900
Pekin Marigold Festival (early September) 309-346-2106

October
Fall Family Riverfest (late October) 309-685-9312
Gospel Jubilee (late October) 309-681-0696
www.mtco.com/~pace/gj.html
Hall-zoo-een (late October) 309-681-0696
www.mtco.com/~pace/hz.html
Mid-America Waterfowl Expo (early October) 309-673-8900
Peoria Jaycees Annual Haunted House
(mid-late October) 309-676-5292

November
East Peoria Festival Of Lights
(late November-late December) 800-365-3743
www.epcc.org/festival_of_lights.htm
Greater Peoria Farm Show
(late November-early December) 309-673-8900
Julep's Closet (early November) 309-685-9312
Santa Parade (late November) 309-681-0696
www.mtco.com/~pace/sp.html#santa
Yule Like Peoria (late November) 309-681-0696
www.mtco.com/~pace/sp.html#yule

December
East Peoria Festival Of Lights
(late November-late December) 800-365-3743
www.epcc.org/festival_of_lights.htm
Greater Peoria Farm Show
(late November-early December) 309-673-8900

Rockford

January
Northern Illinois Farm Show (early January) 815-968-5600

February
Boat Vacation & Fishing Show (late February) 815-877-8043
Rockford Home Show (late February-early March) 815-877-8043

March
Rockford Home Show (late February-early March) 815-877-8043
Saint Patrick's Day Celebration (mid-March) 815-624-6694
Spring Folk Craft & Art Expo (mid-March) 815-968-5600

May
Young at Heart Festival (late May) 815-633-3999

June
Civil War Days (late June) 815-397-9112

August
Winnebago County Fair (mid-August) 815-239-1641

September
On the Waterfront Festival (early September) 815-963-8111
onthewaterfront.com/

December
First Night (December 31) 815-963-6765
Splendor & Majesty Christmas Musical
(early December) 815-963-8111

Springfield

January
Capital City Farm Show (mid-January) 217-498-9404
Keepsake Country Craft Show (late January & mid-July) 217-787-8560

February
Maple Syrup Time (late February) 217-529-1111
Motorcycle Show & Swap Meet (late February) 217-788-8800
Springfield All Sports Show (late February-early March) 217-629-7077

March
Springfield All Sports Show (late February-early March) 217-629-7077

May
Old Capitol Art Fair (late May) 800-545-7300
Springfield Scottish Highland Games & Celtic Festival
(mid-May) 217-546-5802

June
International Carillon Festival (early June) 217-753-6219
Theatre in the Park (June) 217-632-4000

July
Keepsake Country Craft Show (late January & mid-July) 217-787-8560
Summer Festival (mid-July) 217-632-4000

August
Illinois State Fair (mid-August) 800-545-7300
www.state.il.us/fair/
Springfield Air Rendezvous (mid-August) 800-545-7300
www.springfield-il.com/airshow/

September
Bluegrass Festival (early September) 217-632-4000
Brinkerhoff Fall Fair (early September) 217-789-2360
Central Illinois Blues Fest (early September) 217-546-8881
Edwards Place Fine Crafts Fair (late September) 217-523-2631
Ethnic Festival (early September) 217-529-8189
International Ethnic Festival (early September) 217-529-8189
Traditional Music Festival (early September) 217-632-4000

ILLINOIS — Springfield (Cont'd)

October
Central Illinois Polka Festival (late October)........ 800-545-7300
Indian Summer Festival (mid-October)........ 217-529-1111

November
Chrysanthemum Festival (mid-late November)........ 217-753-6228
Festival of Trees (late November)........ 217-788-3293
Harvest Feast at New Salem (early November)........ 217-632-4000
Holiday Market (mid-late November)........ 217-529-1111

December
Christmas Parade (early December)........ 217-528-8669
Christmas Walk (early December)........ 217-544-1723
Dana-Thomas House Christmas (mid-late December)........ 217-782-6776
First Night Springfield (December 31)........ 800-545-7300
Holiday Lights at the Zoo (mid-late December)........ 217-753-6217

INDIANA

Bloomington

February
Chocolate Fest (early February)........ 812-334-8900

March
Antique Show (late March)........ 812-332-5233
Coin Show (early-mid-March)........ 812-332-3432
Indiana Heritage Quilt Show (early March)........ 812-334-8900
Mini-Play Festival (early March)........ 812-332-4401

April
Easter Egg Hunt (early April)........ 812-336-3681
Hometown Cinema Film Festival (early-mid-April)........ 812-337-1091

May
Bloomington Early Music Festival (late May)........ 812-334-8900
Gold Wing Road Riders Convention (late May)........ 812-334-8900

June
Art Fair on the Square (mid-late June)........ 812-334-8900
Fair for the Arts (June-August)........ 812-349-3737
SummerFest (mid-June)........ 812-349-2800
Taste of Bloomington (mid-late June)........ 812-334-8900

July
Fair for the Arts (June-August)........ 812-349-3737

August
Fair for the Arts (June-August)........ 812-349-3737

Evansville

January
Collector's Carnival
(late January & late April & late October)........ 812-471-9419
Mid-States Arts Exhibition (early December-late January).. 812-425-2406

March
Sugarbush Festival (early March)........ 812-479-0771

April
Collector's Carnival
(late January & late April & late October)........ 812-471-9419
Heritage Week (late April)........ 812-682-4488
Kite Day (late April)........ 812-853-3956

May
Pioneer Days Festival (early May)........ 812-479-0771

June
Thunder Festival (mid-June-early July)........ 812-464-9576

July
Thunder Festival (mid-June-early July)........ 812-464-9576

August
Germania Mannerchor Volksfest (early August)........ 812-422-1915

September
Arts & Crafts Show (late September)........ 812-867-4935
Native American Days (late September)........ 812-853-3956

October
Big Rivers Arts & Crafts Festival (early October)........ 270-926-4433
Boo at the Zoo (mid-October)........ 812-428-0715
Collector's Carnival
(late January & late April & late October)........ 812-471-9419
Golden Harvest Arts & Crafts Show (early October)........ 812-422-5600
Haunted Hay Rides (late October)........ 812-479-0771
West Side Nut Club Fall Festival (early October)........ 812-464-5993

November
Christmas Main Street Parade (mid-November)........ 812-424-2986
Fantasy of Lights (late November-late December)........ 812-474-2348
Victorian Christmas (November-December)........ 812-426-1871
Winter Carnival (late November)........ 812-867-6217

December
Fantasy of Lights (late November-late December)........ 812-474-2348
First Night (December 31)........ 812-422-2111
Mid-States Arts Exhibition (early December-late January).. 812-425-2406
Victorian Christmas (November-December)........ 812-426-1871

Fort Wayne

May
National Print Exhibition (late May-early July)........ 219-424-7195

June
Fort Wayne Hoosier Marathon (early-June)........ 219-749-7288
members.aol.com/VernC3/marathon.htm
Germanfest (mid-June)........ 219-436-4064
Greek Fest (late June)........ 219-426-9706
Indiana Black Expo (early June)........ 219-422-6486
National Print Exhibition (late May-early July)........ 219-424-7195
New Haven Canal Days (early June)........ 219-749-2972

July
Allen County Fair (late July)........ 219-637-5818
Berne Swiss Days (late July)........ 219-589-3632
Gathering of the People (late July)........ 219-244-7702
Indiana Highland Games (late July)........ 219-486-9543
National Print Exhibition (late May-early July)........ 219-424-7195
Three Rivers Festival (mid-July)........ 219-745-5556

August
Irish Fest (mid-August)........ 219-423-3343

September
Auburn Cord-Duesenberg Festival (early September)........ 219-925-1444
Hispanic American Festival (early-mid-September)........ 219-744-5129
Johnny Appleseed Festival (mid-September)........ 219-424-3700

November
Festival of Gingerbread (late November-mid-December)........ 219-426-2882
Festival of Trees (late November-early December)........ 219-424-6287

December
Festival of Gingerbread (late November-mid-December)........ 219-426-2882
Festival of Trees (late November-early December)........ 219-424-6287

Indianapolis

January
Circle City Grand National Rodeo (early January)........ 317-639-6411
Indiana Motorcycle & Watercraft Expo (late January)........ 317-540-4344
Indianapolis Home Show (late January-early February)........ 317-927-7500
Winterland Holiday Light Display
(late November-early January)........ 765-664-3918

February
Carquest World of Wheels (early February)........ 317-236-6515
Indianapolis Boat Sport & Travel Show (late February)........ 317-543-4344
Indianapolis Home Show (late January-early February)........ 317-927-7500
Maple Fair (late February-early March)........ 765-569-3430

March
Indiana Flower & Patio Show (mid-March)........ 317-576-9933
Maple Fair (late February-early March)........ 765-569-3430
Saint Patrick's Day Parade (mid-March)........ 317-236-6515

April
Earth Day Indiana Festival (April 22)........ 317-767-3672
ideanet.doe.state.in.us/earthdayind/
Hoosier Horse Fair & Expo (mid-April)........ 317-927-7500

May
500 Festival (May)........ 800-638-4296
Broad Ripple Art Fair (early May)........ 317-255-2464
Indianapolis 500 (late May)........ 317-481-8500
Indy Festival (May)........ 317-237-3400

June
Indian Market (late June)........ 317-636-9378
Italian Festival (mid-June)........ 317-636-4478
Middle Eastern Festival (mid-June)........ 317-547-9356
Strawberry Festival (mid-June)........ 317-636-4577
Talbott Street Art Fair (mid-June)........ 800-323-4639

July
4th Fest (July 4)........ 317-633-6363
Circlefest (late July)........ 317-237-2222
Indiana Black Expo (mid-July)........ 317-925-2702

August
Africafest (mid-August)........ 317-923-1331
Animals & All that Jazz (August)........ 317-630-2001
Brickyard 400 (early August)........ 317-481-8500
Indiana Avenue Jazz Festival (mid-August)........ 317-236-2099
Indiana State Fair (mid-August)........ 317-927-7500
www.state.in.us/statefair
RCA Championships (mid-August)........ 317-632-4100
www.rcatennis.com

September
Greek Festival (mid-September)........ 317-283-3816
Hoosier Storytelling Festival (late September)........ 317-255-7628
Oktoberfest (early-mid-September)........ 317-888-6940
Penrod Arts Fair (mid-September)........ 317-252-9895

October
Circle City Classic (early October)........ 317-237-5222
Fall Home Show (late October)........ 317-927-7500
Halloween ZooBoo (late October)........ 317-630-2001
Heartland Film Festival (late October)........ 317-464-9405
www.heartlandfilmfest.org

November
Celebration of Lights (late November)........ 317-237-2222
Winterland Holiday Light Display
(late November-early January)........ 765-664-3918

December
Harrison Victorian Christmas (December)........ 317-631-1898
Hoosier Classic (late December)........ 317-917-2727
IU Basketball Classic (early December)........ 317-262-3410
Merry Prairie Days (December)........ 317-773-0666
Winterland Holiday Light Display
(late November-early January)........ 765-664-3918

South Bend

March
Saint Patrick's Day Celebration (mid-March)........ 219-235-9951

May
Junior Irish Memorial Day Soccer Tournament
(late May)........ 219-273-1209
Studebaker Swap (early May)........ 219-287-3381
Swap Meet & Car Show (late May)........ 219-289-2292

June
Ethnic Festival (mid-June)........ 219-235-9952
Mishawaka Summerfest (late June)........ 219-258-1664

August
Amish Acres Arts & Crafts Festival (mid-August)........ 800-800-4942
Firefly Festival (early August)........ 219-288-3472
www.nd.edu/~crosenbe/firefly.html
Midwest RV Super Show (mid-August)........ 317-247-6258
Saint Joseph County 4-H Fair (early August)........ 219-291-4870

October
ZooBoo Halloween (late October)........ 219-288-4639

November
Zooltide-Light Up a Heart
(late November-late December)........ 219-288-4639

December
Downtown for the Holidays (early December)........ 219-235-9951
Zooltide-Light Up a Heart
(late November-late December)........ 219-288-4639

IOWA

Cedar Rapids

January
Fantasy of Lights (late November-early January)........ 319-398-5009
Greater Iowa Boat & Sports Show (mid-January)........ 319-377-7660

February
Springfest Arts & Crafts Sale
(late February-early March)........ 319-377-7660
Winterfest (early February)........ 319-398-5009
World's Toughest Rodeo (mid-February)........ 319-363-1888

March
Maple Syrup Festival (early March)........ 319-362-0664
Saint Patrick's Day Parade (mid-March)........ 319-390-3501
Springfest Arts & Crafts Sale
(late February-early March)........ 319-377-7660

April
Cedar Rapids Antique Show & Collectors Fair
(early April & early October)........ 319-362-1729

May
Art on the Fence (mid-May)........ 319-363-4942
Cedar Rapids Ethnic Fest (late May)........ 319-362-1302
Marion Arts Festival (mid-May)........ 319-377-6316
www.fyiowa.com/iowa/tour/marion/festive.htm
Olde World Faire (early May)........ 319-895-6862

June
Cedar Rapids BBQ Round Up (late June)........ 319-398-5211
Cedar Rapids Freedom Festival (late June-early July)........ 319-398-5009
www.fyiowa.com/freedom/
Celebration of the Arts (late June)........ 319-398-5322
Grant Wood Art Festival (mid-June)........ 319-462-4267
Hiawatha Hog Wild Days (mid-June)........ 319-393-3668

July
All Iowa Fair (mid-July)........ 319-365-8656
Bluegrass Festival-Amana (mid-July)........ 800-245-5465
Cedar Rapids Freedom Festival (late June-early July)........ 319-398-5009
www.fyiowa.com/freedom/
Heritage Days Celebration (early July)........ 319-895-8214
Ushers Ferry Civil War Reenactment (mid-July)........ 319-286-5763

August
Old Time Country Fair (late August)........ 319-286-5763
Tanager Place Hot Air Balloon Festival (early August)........ 319-365-9164
Wild West Weekend (mid-August)........ 319-286-5763

September
Swamp Fox Festival Heritage Celebration
(early September)........ 319-377-6316
Taste of Iowa (early September)........ 319-398-5009
www.tasteofiowa.org/

IOWA — Cedar Rapids (Cont'd)

October
Cedar Rapids Antique Show & Collectors Fair (early April & early October) 319-362-1729

November
Art & Craft Show Weekend (late November) 319-364-1641
Autumnfest Arts & Craft Show (early November) 319-365-8656
Christmas on the River Arts & Crafts Sale (late November) 319-362-8070
Fantasy of Lights (late November-early January) 319-398-5009
Festival of Trees (mid-November) 319-369-8733

December
Fantasy of Lights (late November-early January) 319-398-5009
Firstar Eve (December 31) 319-368-4444

Davenport

July
Mississippi Valley Blues Festival (early July) 319-322-1706

Des Moines

January
Craft Festival (late January) 515-276-8551
Des Moines Boat Tackle & Sports Show (mid-January) 515-262-3111
Festival of Lanterns (mid-January-early February) 515-242-2934
Iowa Pork Congress (late January) 515-323-5444
Monster Jam (early January) 515-323-5444
World of Wheels (late January) 515-323-5444

February
Bass Masters Fishermen's Swap Meet & Boat Show (late February) 515-262-3111
Des Moines Home & Garden Show (late February) 515-323-5444
Festival of Lanterns (mid-January-early February) 515-242-2934
Fox Family Fair (early February) 515-323-5444
Iowa Winter Beef Expo (mid-February) 515-262-3111
Skywalk Open Golf Tournament (early February) 515-243-6625

March
Iowa Sports & Vacation Show (early March) 515-323-5444
Kids Fest (mid-March) 515-288-1981
Potpourri Painters Craft Show (late March) 515-262-3111
Spring into the Past (late March) 515-281-6412
World's Toughest Rodeo (late March) 515-323-5444

April
Block & Bridle Horse Show (late April) 515-262-3111
Drake Relays Week (late April) 515-271-3711
Governor & First Lady Easter Egg Hunt (late April) 515-281-7205
Iowa Horse Fair (mid-April) 515-262-3111
Mayor's Annual Ride for Trails (mid-April) 515-283-4500

May
Annual Herb Sale (early May) 515-242-2934

June
Fall Antique Jamboree (mid-June & mid-August) 515-222-3642
World Pork Expo (mid-June) 515-286-4960

August
Fall Antique Jamboree (mid-June & mid-August) 515-222-3642
Iowa State Fair (early-mid-August) 515-262-3111
www.iowastatefair.com
National Balloon Classic (early August) 515-961-8415

September
Appaloosa Horse Show (mid-September) 515-262-3111
Fall Festival (late September) 515-628-2409
Iowa Renaissance Festival (mid-September) 515-262-3111
Latinos Unidos Fiesta (mid-September) 515-242-2934
Pufferbilly Days (mid-September) 800-266-6312
Valley Arts Festival (late September) 515-225-6009
Wings Wheels & Water Festival (late September) 515-964-0685

October
Autumn Festival & Craft Show (late October) 515-323-5444
Covered Bridge Festival (mid-October) 515-462-1185
Fall Classic Horse Show (early October) 515-262-3111
Happily Haunted Halloween Treasure Trail (mid-late October) 515-242-2934

November
Christmas Walk (mid-November-late December) 515-628-2409
Festival of Trees & Lights (late November) 515-241-6494
Two Rivers Art Expo (mid-November) 515-277-1511

December
Christmas Walk (mid-November-late December) 515-628-2409
Firstar Eve (December 31) 515-245-6100
Holiday Lights & Holiday Wonderland (December) 515-242-2934

Dubuque

March
Arts & Crafts Fair (mid-March) 319-556-1994
Arts & Crafts Show (mid-late March) 319-589-4254
BestFest (late March) 319-583-3755
Home Show (mid-March) 319-589-4254
Saint Patrick's Day Parade & Gaelic Gallop (mid-March) 319-875-2311

April
Arbor Day Celebration (late April) 319-556-2100
City Expo (mid-late April) 319-589-4116

May
Dubuquefest (mid-May) 319-557-9200
Dubuquefest House Tour (mid-May) 319-557-2556
Farmer's Market (early May-late October) 319-588-4400
Historic Old Main Event (late May) 319-588-4400

June
Catfish Festival (late June) 319-583-8535
Farmer's Market (early May-late October) 319-588-4400
High School Alumni Basketball Tournament (June) 319-589-4263
Jazz Fest (mid-June) 319-557-1677
Rose Festival (mid-June) 319-556-2100
Senior Fair (mid-June) 319-556-1994

July
Dubuque County Fair (late July-early August) 319-588-1406
Dyersville Independence Day Celebration (July 3) 319-875-2311
Farmer's Market (early May-late October) 319-588-4400
Fireworks Spectacular (July 3) 319-588-5700
Racing Collectibles Show (early-mid-July) 319-875-2727

August
Arts & Crafts Festival (early August) 319-582-9269
Dubuque County Fair (late July-early August) 319-588-1406
Farmer's Market (early May-late October) 319-588-4400
Four Mounds Blues Fest (early-mid-August) 319-557-7292
Summerfest (mid-August) 319-582-8804
Taste of Dubuque: A County Celebration (early August) 800-226-3369

September
Dragon Boat Festival (mid-September) 319-557-1429
Farmer's Market (early May-late October) 319-588-4400
Home Show & Arts & Crafts Fair (late September) 319-556-1994

October
Farmer's Market (early May-late October) 319-588-4400
Heartland Creative Arts & Crafts Fair (mid-October) 319-556-1994

November
Christmas Candlewalk (late November) 319-582-3320

KANSAS

Kansas City

February
National Wildlife Art Show (mid-February) 913-888-6927

May
Blue Devil Barbecue Cookoff (early May) 913-321-5800
Polski Day (early May) 913-321-5800

June
Highland Games & Scottish Festival (early June) 913-432-6823

July
Farm Heritage Days (mid-July) 913-721-1075
Wyandotte County Fair (late July-early August) 913-788-7898

August
Tiblow Days (late August) 913-321-5800
Wyandotte County Fair (late July-early August) 913-788-7898

September
Central Avenue Parade (late September) 913-371-4511
Grinter Applefest (late September) 913-299-0373
Renaissance Festival (early September-mid-October) 800-373-0357
www.kcrenfest.com

October
Renaissance Festival (early September-mid-October) 800-373-0357
www.kcrenfest.com
Silver City Celebration (early October) 913-321-5800
Turner Days (mid-October) 913-287-7500
Wyandotte Days (mid-October) 913-321-5800

November
Avenue Area Christmas Lighting Ceremony (mid-November) 913-371-0065
Kansas Day at the American Royal (early-November) 816-221-9800

December
Santa's Express (mid-December) 913-721-1075

Topeka

January
Topeka Boat & Outdoor Show (late January) 785-235-1986
Topeka Farm Show (early January) 785-235-1986

April
Combat Air Museum & Pancake Feed & Fall Fling (late April) 785-862-3303

June
KSHSAA Rodeo (mid-June) 785-235-1986
Mountain Plains Art Fair (early June) 785-231-1010
Sunflower Music Festival (June) 785-231-1010

July
Fiesta Mexicana (mid-July) 785-232-5088
Kansas River Valley Art Fair (late July) 785-295-3888
KBHA Quarter Horse Show (late July) 785-235-1986

August
Topeka Railroad Days (late August-early September) 785-232-5533

September
Cider Days (late September) 785-235-1986
Huff N' Puff Balloon Rally (mid-September) 785-234-1030
NHRA Parts America Nationals (late September-early October) 800-437-2237
Topeka Railroad Days (late August-early September) 785-232-5533

October
Apple Festival (early October) 785-295-3888
Fall Parade of Homes (early-mid-October) 785-273-1260
Festival of Beers (early October) 785-862-3303
Gem & Mineral Show (mid-October) 785-235-1986
NHRA Parts America Nationals (late September-early October) 800-437-2237

November
Miracle on Kansas Avenue Parade (late November) 785-234-9336

December
Festival of Trees (early December) 785-233-2566
Holiday Happenings (early December) 785-368-3888

Wichita

January
Kansas Day Celebration (late January) 316-265-3933
US Hot Rod Thunder Nationals (mid-January) 316-755-1243

February
Equi-Fest of Kansas (late February) 316-755-1243
National BMX Tournament (mid-February) 316-755-1243
Wichita Home Show (early February) 316-265-4226

March
Midian Shrine Circus (mid-March) 316-264-7551
Saint Patrick's Day Parade (mid-March) 316-946-1322
Wichita Lawn Flower & Garden Show (early March) 316-721-8740

April
Great Plains Motorcycle Show (early April) 316-722-4201
Great Plains Wood Carvers' Show & Sale (early April) 316-941-0653
Newman Renaissance Faire (late April) 800-736-7585
Sand Creek Folklife Festival (late April) 316-283-7925
Tulip Festival (mid-April) 316-264-0448
Wichita Gem & Mineral Show (late April) 316-943-1785
Wichita Indian Art Market & Exhibition (mid-April) 316-262-5221
Wichita Jazz Festival (late April) 316-684-1100
www.southwind.net/wichita-jazz/

May
Cinco De Mayo Festival (early May) 800-288-9424
Park City Bluegrass Festival (early May) 316-744-2026
Polkatennial (early May) 316-722-4201
Wichita River Festival (early-mid-May) 316-267-2817
www.southwind.net/river-fest/

June
McConnell Air Show (mid-June) 316-652-6172

July
Celebrate (early July) 316-943-4221
Chisholm Trail Festival (early July) 316-282-0640
Christmas in July (early July) 316-265-2020
Mid-America All-Indian Center Pow Wow (late July) 316-524-1210
Prairie Port Festival (late July) 316-321-3150

September
Fall Festival Arts & Crafts Show (late September) 316-773-9300
Mexican Independence Weekend (mid-September) 316-265-2800
Wichita Black Arts Festival (early September) 316-691-1499

October
Asian Festival (late October) 316-689-8729
Old Sedgwick County Fair (early October) 316-264-0671

November
Holiday Wreath Festival (mid-November) 316-264-3386

December
An Old Fashioned Christmas (early December) 316-264-0671
Holidays at the Wichita Art Museum (early December) 316-268-4921
Pioneer Christmas Arts & Crafts Expo (early December) 316-722-5016
Wichita Winter Fest (early December) 316-946-1323

KENTUCKY

Frankfort

May
Deafestival (late May) 800-372-2907
Governor's Derby Breakfast (early May) 502-564-2611

June
Capital Expo Festival (early June) 502-875-8687
Kentucky Herb Festival (mid-June) 502-695-8431

July
Franklin County Fair & Horse Show (late July) 502-695-9035

September
Capital City Bass Classic (late September) 502-223-8261
Kentucky Folklife Festival (mid-September) 502-564-3016
Switzer Covered Bridge Day (late September) 502-875-8687

KENTUCKY — Frankfort (Cont'd)

October
- **Great Pumpkin Festival** (mid-October) ... 502-223-2261

November
- **Candlelight Tour & Christmas 'Round the Fountain** (late November) ... 502-223-2261
- **Kentucky Book Fair** (late November) ... 502-227-4556

December
- **Christmas Arts & Crafts Expo** (early December) ... 502-695-9179
- **Kentucky's Capital Christmas** (early December) ... 502-875-8687

Lexington

January
- **Bluegrass State Games** (mid-January & mid-late July) ... 606-255-0336

March
- **Boy's Sweet Sixteen Tournament** (early March) ... 606-233-3535
- **Champagne Run Hunter/Jumper Show** (late March) ... 606-263-4638
- **Lexington Lions Club Bluegrass Fair** (early March) ... 606-233-1465
- **Saint Patrick's Day Parade** (mid-March) ... 606-278-7349

April
- **Kentucky Arabian Horse Association Annual Show** (early April) ... 502-241-5244
- **Rolex Kentucky Three Day Event** (late April) ... 606-254-8123
  www.rk3de.org

May
- **High Hope Steeplechase** (mid-May) ... 606-255-5727
- **Kentucky Guild of Artists & Craftsmen Spring Fair** (mid-May & early October) ... 606-986-3192
- **Kentucky High School Rodeo Assn Annual Rodeo** (late May) ... 270-395-4889
- **Mayfest** (early May) ... 606-231-7335
- **Memorial Stakes Day Chili Cook-off** (late May) ... 606-255-0752

June
- **Festival of the Bluegrass** (mid-June) ... 606-846-4995
  www.musicliveshere.com/fbg.htm
- **Great American Brass Band Festival** (mid-June) ... 800-755-0076
- **Lexington Egyptian Event** (mid-June) ... 606-231-0771
- **Mid-South Regional Pony Club Rally** (late June) ... 502-244-1797
- **Paso Fino Festival of the Bluegrass** (mid-June) ... 513-724-3220
- **Polo at the Park** (June-September) ... 606-233-4303

July
- **Bluegrass State Games** (mid-January & mid-late July) ... 606-255-0336
- **Breyerfest** (late July) ... 606-233-4303
- **July 4th Festival** (early July) ... 606-258-3123
- **Lexington Shakespeare Festival** (July) ... 606-266-4423
- **Mid-America Miniature Horse Association Julep Cup** (mid-July) ... 800-848-1224
- **Polo at the Park** (June-September) ... 606-233-4303

August
- **Bluegrass Festival Hunter/Jumper Show** (mid-late August) ... 606-266-6937
- **Kentucky Hunter/Jumper Assn Show** (late August) ... 606-266-6937
- **Polo at the Park** (June-September) ... 606-233-4303
- **Woodland Art Fair** (mid-August) ... 606-254-7024

September
- **All-Arabian Combined Classic I & II** (early September) ... 606-233-4303
- **Bluegrass Classic Dog Show** (early September) ... 606-527-3865
- **Festival of the Horse** (mid-September) ... 502-863-2547
- **Harvest Festival** (late September) ... 606-257-3221
- **Kentucky National Hunter/Jumper Show** (late September) ... 606-233-4303
- **Polo at the Park** (June-September) ... 606-233-4303
- **Red Mile Harness Racing Grand Circuit Meet** (late September-early October) ... 606-255-0752
- **Roots & Heritage Festival** (mid-September) ... 606-231-2611

October
- **Kentucky Guild of Artists & Craftsmen Spring Fair** (mid-May & early October) ... 606-986-3192
- **Red Mile Harness Racing Grand Circuit Meet** (late September-early October) ... 606-255-0752

November
- **Sheiks & Shreiks Arabian Fun Show** (early November) ... 606-988-0805
- **Southern Lights Holiday Festival** (mid-November-late December) ... 606-255-5727

December
- **Lexington Christmas Parade** (early December) ... 606-231-7335
- **Southern Lights Holiday Festival** (mid-November-late December) ... 606-255-5727

Louisville

January
- **DinnerWorks** (mid-January-mid-February) ... 502-896-2146
- **Kentucky Golf Show** (mid-January) ... 502-367-5000
- **Sport Boat & Vacation Show** (late January-early February) ... 502-367-5000

February
- **DinnerWorks** (mid-January-mid-February) ... 502-896-2146
- **Humana Festival of New American Plays** (late February-late March) ... 502-584-1265
- **National Farm Machinery Show & Tractor Pull** (mid-February) ... 502-367-5000
- **National Gun Days** (early February & early June) ... 502-367-5000
- **Sport Boat & Vacation Show** (late January-early February) ... 502-367-5000

March
- **Humana Festival of New American Plays** (late February-late March) ... 502-584-1265
- **Kentucky Derby Festival** (late March-early May) ... 800-928-3378
  www.kdf.org
- **Mid-America Trucking Show** (late March) ... 502-367-5000
  www.truckingshow.com/

April
- **Cherokee Triangle Art Fair** (late April) ... 502-451-3534
- **Derby Festival Great Balloon Glow** (late April) ... 502-584-6383
- **Derby Festival Great Balloon Race** (late April) ... 502-584-6383
- **Derby Festival Great Steamboat Race** (late April) ... 502-584-6383
- **Derby Festival KyDzFest** (late April) ... 502-584-6383
- **Derby Festival Pegasus Parade** (late April) ... 502-584-6383
- **Derby Festival Planes of Thunder** (mid-April) ... 502-584-6383
- **Kentucky Derby Festival** (late March-early May) ... 800-928-3378
  www.kdf.org
- **Revolutionary War Encampment** (mid-April) ... 502-896-2433
- **Thunder over Louisville** (mid-April) ... 502-584-6383

May
- **Derby City Square Dance Festival** (mid-May) ... 502-367-5000
- **Kentucky Derby** (early May) ... 502-582-3732
  www.kentuckyderby.com
- **Kentucky Derby Festival** (late March-early May) ... 800-928-3378
  www.kdf.org
- **Kentucky Oaks** (early May) ... 502-636-4400
- **Kentucky Reggae Festival** (late May) ... 502-583-0333

June
- **Kentucky Shakespeare Festival** (mid-June-mid-July) ... 502-583-8738
  www.kyshakes.org
- **National Gun Days** (early February & early June) ... 502-367-5000

July
- **Kentucky Shakespeare Festival** (mid-June-mid-July) ... 502-583-8738
  www.kyshakes.org
- **National City Music Weekend** (late July) ... 502-348-5237
- **Strassenfest** (early July) ... 502-561-3440
- **Waterside Art & Blues Festival** (early July) ... 502-896-2146

August
- **Kentucky State Fair** (late August) ... 502-582-3732

September
- **Corn Island Storytelling Festival** (mid-September) ... 502-582-3732
- **Strictly Bluegrass Festival** (mid-September) ... 502-582-3732

October
- **Autumn Fest** (early October) ... 502-583-3577
- **Saint James Art Fair** (early October) ... 502-635-1842

November
- **Dickens on Main Street** (late November) ... 502-574-3333
- **Light Up Louisville International Festival** (late November) ... 502-584-2121

LOUISIANA

Baton Rouge

January
- **Creole Christmas at Magnolia Mound** (mid-December-early January) ... 225-343-4955

February
- **Baton Rouge BREC Rodeo** (mid-February) ... 225-769-7805
- **Junior Livestock Show** (mid-February) ... 225-388-2255
- **Krewe Mystic Mardi Gras Parade** (early February) ... 225-383-1825
- **PRCA Rodeo** (mid-February) ... 225-388-2255
- **Spring Junior Livestock Show** (mid-February) ... 225-383-1825

March
- **Audubon Pilgrimage** (mid-March) ... 225-383-1825
- **FestForAll** (early March) ... 225-383-1825
- **Jackson Assembly Antique Festival** (late March) ... 225-383-1825
- **Zippity Zoo Day** (late March) ... 225-775-3877

April
- **Baton Rouge Earth Day Festival** (mid-April) ... 225-383-1825
- **Magnolia Mound Market Days Festival** (early April) ... 225-383-1825

May
- **Breaux Bridge Crawfish Festival** (early May) ... 225-383-1825

June
- **Big Easy Charity Horse Show** (mid-June) ... 225-388-2255
- **June Quarter Horse Show** (early June) ... 225-388-2255

July
- **July 4th Celebration** (July 4) ... 225-383-1825
- **State Horse Show** (mid-July) ... 225-388-2255

October
- **Boo at the Zoo** (late October) ... 225-775-3877
- **Greater Baton Rouge State Fair** (late October) ... 225-383-1825

November
- **Dixie Jubilee Horse Show** (early November) ... 225-388-2255

December
- **Christmas on the River** (December) ... 225-383-1825
- **Creole Christmas at Magnolia Mound** (mid-December-early January) ... 225-343-4955
- **Victorian Holiday** (mid-December) ... 602-262-5029

Lafayette

January
- **Kwanzaa Celebration** (early January) ... 337-233-4758

February
- **Carencro Boudin & Cracklin Festival** (mid-late February) ... 337-896-3378
- **Children's Carnival** (late February) ... 337-845-4217
- **Children's Mardi Gras Parade** (mid-February) ... 337-232-3808
- **King's Court** (mid-February) ... 337-291-5566
- **King's Parade** (mid-February) ... 337-232-3808
- **Le Festival de Mardi Gras à Lafayette** (mid-February) ... 337-265-3904
- **Mardi Gras Association Parade** (mid-February) ... 337-232-3808

March
- **Cajun Fun Fest** (mid-March) ... 337-365-1540
- **Festival du Courtableau** (mid-late March) ... 337-826-3627
- **Saint Ignatius Rainbeau Festival** (mid-late March) ... 337-662-3325

April
- **Downtown Alive!** (April-June & September-November) ... 337-291-5566
- **Festival International de Louisiane** (late April) ... 337-232-8086
  fil.net-connect.net
- **Herb Fest** (mid-April) ... 337-232-3737
  www.herbfest.com
- **La Fete de Vermilionville** (mid-April) ... 337-233-4077
- **Tour d'Acadiana** (mid-April) ... 337-232-3808

May
- **Cajun Heatland State Fair** (late May-early June) ... 337-265-2100
- **Downtown Alive!** (April-June & September-November) ... 337-291-5566
- **Zydeco Extravaganza** (late May) ... 337-234-9695

June
- **Cajun Heatland State Fair** (late May-early June) ... 337-265-2100
- **Downtown Alive!** (April-June & September-November) ... 337-291-5566

July
- **Fourth Futurity Festival** (early July) ... 337-896-7223

August
- **Le Cajun Music Awards Festival** (mid-August) ... 337-232-3808
  www.cajunfrenchmusic.org

September
- **Downtown Alive!** (April-June & September-November) ... 337-291-5566
- **Festivals Acadiens** (mid-late September) ... 337-232-3808

October
- **Downtown Alive!** (April-June & September-November) ... 337-291-5566

November
- **Acadiana Culinary Classic** (early November) ... 337-265-2100
- **Downtown Alive!** (April-June & September-November) ... 337-291-5566

December
- **Cajun & Creole Christmas** (December) ... 337-232-3808
- **Christmas at Vermilionville** (December) ... 337-233-4077
- **Christmas Renaissance 'Festival of Light'** (early December) ... 337-232-1267
- **Christmas Under the Lamppost** (early December) ... 337-828-3817
- **Lafayette Christmas Parade** (early December) ... 337-232-3808

Metairie

January
- **Chinese New Year Festival** (late January) ... 504-482-6682

March
- **Mensaje's Spanish Festival** (late March-early April) ... 504-468-7527

April
- **Mensaje's Spanish Festival** (late March-early April) ... 504-468-7527

July
- **Christmas in July** (late July) ... 504-465-9985

September
- **Collector's Festival** (late September) ... 504-363-1580
- **Pet Fest** (late September) ... 504-734-7590
- **Westwego Festival** (mid-September) ... 504-436-0812

October
- **Family Day** (early October) ... 504-468-7293
- **Gretna Heritage Festival** (early October) ... 504-363-1580
- **Gumbo Festival** (mid-October) ... 504-436-4712
- **Jeff Fest** (late October) ... 504-888-2900
  www.jfest.com

November
- **Christmas Village** (late November-mid-December) ... 504-468-7293
- **Louisiana Railroad Festival** (mid-November) ... 504-363-1580
- **Veteran's Day Program** (November 11) ... 504-363-1580

December
- **Christmas Tree Lighting** (early December) ... 504-363-1580
- **Christmas Village** (late November-mid-December) ... 504-468-7293
- **Holly Jolly Christmas Bonfires** (mid-December) ... 504-468-7293

New Orleans

January
Celebration in the Oaks (late November-early January) 504-488-2896
Sugar Bowl (January) 504-525-8573

February
Lundi Gras (mid-February) 504-566-5005
Mardi Gras (late February) 504-566-5011
New Orleans Boat & Sportsfishing Show (early February) 504-846-4446
Nokia Sugar Bowl Mardi Gras Marathon (early February) 504-525-8573
Sweet Arts & Beaux Arts Ball (mid-February) 504-528-3805
Winn-Dixie Showdown (late February) 504-587-3663

March
Compaq Classic of New Orleans (late March-early April) 504-831-4653
Los Islenos Festival (late March) 504-682-2713
Louisiana Black Heritage Festival (mid-March) 504-827-0112
Saint Joseph's Day Festivities (mid-March) 504-522-7294
Saint Patrick's Day Parade (mid-March) 504-525-5169
www.neworleansweb.org/stpat.html
Spring Fiesta (mid-March) 504-566-5011
Tennessee Wiliams/New Orleans Literary Festival (late March) 504-286-6680
www.gnofn.org/~twfest/

April
Compaq Classic of New Orleans (late March-early April) 504-831-4653
Crescent City Classic (early April) 504-861-8686
French Quarter Festival (mid-April) 504-522-5730
New Orleans Jazz & Heritage Festival (late April-early May) 504-522-4786
www.insideneworleans.com/entertainment/nojazzfest

May
Greek Festival (late May) 504-282-0259
Louisiana Crawfish Festival (early May) 337-332-6655
New Orleans Jazz & Heritage Festival (late April-early May) 504-522-4786
www.insideneworleans.com/entertainment/nojazzfest

June
Great French Market Tomato Festival (early June) 504-522-2621
Reggae Riddums International Arts Festival (mid-June) 504-367-1313
www.reggaeriddums.org

July
Go 4th on the River (July 4) 504-528-9994
New Orleans Wine & Food Experience (mid-July) 504-529-9463
www.nowfe.com/

October
Boo at the Zoo (late October) 504-861-2537
Celtic Nations Heritage Festival of Louisiana (late October) 504-486-1113
Gumbo Festival (mid-October) 504-436-4712
Halloween in New Orleans (late October) 800-672-6124
Jeff Fest (late October) 504-888-2900
www.jfest.com
New Orleans Film & Video Festival (early-mid-October) 504-523-3818
www.neworleansfilmfest.com/
Oktoberfest (October) 504-566-5011
Swamp Festival (early-mid-October) 504-861-2537

November
Bayou Classic Football Game (late November) 504-587-3663
Celebration in the Oaks (late November-early January) 504-488-2896
Destrehan Plantation Fall Festival (mid-November) 504-764-9315

December
Celebration in the Oaks (late November-early January) 504-488-2896
New Orleans Christmas (December) 504-522-5730
New Years Eve Countdown (December 31) 504-566-5011

Shreveport

January
Christmas in Roseland (late November-early January) 318-938-5402

February
Mardi Gras in the Ark-La-Tex (late February-early March) 318-746-0252

March
Mardi Gras in the Ark-La-Tex (late February-early March) 318-746-0252
Redbud Festival (mid-March) 318-226-8884

April
First Bloom Festival (late April) 318-938-5402
Holiday in Dixie (early-mid-April) 318-865-5555
Nike Shreveport Open Golf Tournament (mid-April) 318-798-6463

May
Artbreak (early May) 318-673-6500
Jazz & Gumbo Music Festival (mid-May) 318-226-4552
Mudbug Madness (late May) 318-222-7403
www.mudbugmadness.com

June
Champion Lake Pro Classic (mid-June) 318-222-7442
Downtown Neon Saturday Nights (June-September) 318-673-6500
Let the Good Times Roll Festival (mid-June) 318-222-7403

July
Downtown Neon Saturday Nights (June-September) 318-673-6500
Fourth of July Celebration (July 4) 318-459-3515

August
Downtown Neon Saturday Nights (June-September) 318-673-6500

September
Downtown Neon Saturday Nights (June-September) 318-673-6500
Pioneer Days (late September) 318-938-7289

October
Louisiana State Fair (late October-early November) 318-635-1361
Red River Rally (early October) 318-222-9391
www.softdisk.com/sites/rumble/
Red River Revel (early October) 318-424-4000
www.redriverrevel.com

November
Christmas in Roseland (late November-early January) 318-938-5402
December on the Red (late November-late December) 318-222-9391
Louisiana State Fair (late October-early November) 318-635-1361
Rackets Over the Red (late November-late December) 318-222-7403

December
Christmas in Roseland (late November-early January) 318-938-5402
December on the Red (late November-late December) 318-222-9391
Rackets Over the Red (late November-late December) 318-222-7403
Sanford Independence Bowl (late December) 318-221-0712

MAINE

Augusta

June
Whatever Week Festival (mid-June-early July) 207-623-4559

July
Mile of Art (late July) 207-623-4559
Whatever Week Festival (mid-June-early July) 207-623-4559

August
Windsor Fair (mid-late August) 207-623-4559

Bangor

March
Bangor Boating and Marine Exposition (late March) 207-947-5555
YWCA Spring Fair (mid-March) 207-947-5555

April
Bangor Garden Show (early April) 207-947-5555
Bangor Home and Better Living Show (mid-April) 207-947-5555
Kenduskeag Canoe Race (mid-April) 207-947-5205

May
Shrine Circus (early May) 207-947-5555

June
World's Largest Garage Sale (mid-June) 207-942-9000

July
Bangor State Fair (late July-early August) 207-947-5205
Fourth of July Celebration (July 4) 207-947-5205
Shakespeare Festival (late July) 207-947-5205

August
Bangor State Fair (late July-early August) 207-947-5205
Sidewalk Art Festival (early August) 207-947-5205

October
Living History Days (early October) 207-581-2871
United Maine Craftsman Show (mid-October) 207-942-9000

November
Downtown Christmas Parade (late November) 207-947-5205

Bar Harbor

February
Acadia Crossing Cross Country Ski Race (early February) 207-288-3511

May
Mount Desert Island Tour de Cure (May) 207-623-2232

June
Bar Harbor Days & Chowder Cookoff (mid-June) 207-288-5103
Blessing of the Boats & Seaman's Memorial Day (mid-June) 207-288-5571
Spring 5K Race & 1 Mile Fun Run (mid-June) 207-288-3511

July
Arcady Music Festival (mid-July-late August) 207-288-2141
Art & Photography Show (late July) 207-288-5103
Bar Harbor Music Festival (early July-early August) 212-222-1026
Downeast Church Fair (mid-July) 207-288-5103
Downeast Dulcimer & Folk Harp Festival (early-mid-July) 207-288-5653
Fireworks Over Frenchman Bay (early July) 207-288-5103
July 4th Festivities Seafood Festival (early July) 207-288-5103
July 4th Independence Day Parade (early July) 207-288-5103
Native American Festival (mid-July) 207-288-3519
Penobscot Valley Craft Show (late July) 207-794-3543
Step Back in Time (early July-October) 207-288-9605

August
Annual Book Fair (late August) 207-288-4245
Arcady Music Festival (mid-July-late August) 207-288-2141
Bar Harbor Music Festival (early July-early August) 212-222-1026
Island Arts Association Summer Fair in the Park (early August) 207-288-5008
Step Back in Time (early July-October) 207-288-9605

September
Bar Harbor Film Festival (early-mid-September) 207-288-3686
www.barharborfilmfest.com
Step Back in Time (early July-October) 207-288-9605

October
Acadia Triathalon (early October) 207-288-3511
Bar Harbor Half Marathon (October) 207-288-3511
Maine War Canoe & Sea Kayak Championship (early-mid-October) 207-288-3519
Step Back in Time (early July-October) 207-288-9605
Walktoberfest (early October) 207-623-2232

November
Early Bird Sale (mid-late November) 207-288-5103

December
Bar Harbor Village Holidays (December) 207-288-5103
Children's Christmas Bazaar (mid-December) 207-288-5008
Christmas Village Holiday B&B & Inn Tour (early-mid-December) 207-288-5103
Island Arts Association Holiday Fair (early December) 207-288-5008

Portland

March
Maine Boat Builders Show (mid-March) 207-774-1067

June
Greek Heritage Festival (late June) 207-774-0281
Old Port Festival (early June) 207-772-6828

July
Family Fun Day (late July) 207-772-2811
Yarmouth Clam Festival (mid-July) 207-846-3984

August
Art in the Park (mid-August) 207-767-7660
Italian Street Festival (mid-August) 207-773-0748
Maine Festival (early August) 207-772-9012
Portland Chamber Music Festival (late August) 800-320-0257
www.lsiweb.com/festival/
Sidewalk Art Show (mid-August) 207-828-6666

September
Bluegrass Festival (early September) 207-725-6009
Cumberland Fair (late September) 207-287-3221

October
Maine Marathon (early October) 207-741-2084

December
New Year's Eve Portland (December 31) 207-772-9012

MARYLAND

Annapolis

January
Annapolis Heritage Antique Show (late January) 410-222-1919
Christmas in Annapolis (late November-early January) 410-268-8687

June
Annapolis Waterfront Festival (mid-June) 410-268-8828
Mid-Atlantic Wine Festival (mid-June) 410-280-3306

July
Fourth of July Celebration (July 4) 410-263-1183

August
Annapolis Rotary Crab Feast (early August) 410-841-2841
www.annapolisrotary.com
Kunta Kinte Heritage Festival (mid-August) 410-349-0338
Maryland Renaissance Festival (August-October) 410-266-7304
www.rennfest.com

September
Anne Arundel County Fair (mid-September) 410-923-3400
Anne Arundel County Fair Rodeo (mid-September) 410-923-3400
Maryland Renaissance Festival (August-October) 410-266-7304
www.rennfest.com
Maryland Seafood Festival (early September) 410-268-7682

October
Anne Arundel Scottish Highland Games (early October) 410-849-2849
Fall Craft Show (early October) 410-255-5632
Maryland Renaissance Festival (August-October) 410-266-7304
www.rennfest.com
US Powerboat Show (mid-October) 410-268-8828
US Sailboat Show (early October) 410-268-8828

November
Christmas in Annapolis (late November-early January) 410-268-8687

December
Candlelight Pub Crawl (early-mid-December) 410-263-5401
Christmas in Annapolis (late November-early January) 410-268-8687
First Night Annapolis (December 31) 410-268-8553
www.fstngt.org

Baltimore

January
Baltimore on Ice (January-March) 800-282-6632
Orioles Winter Carnival (mid-January) 410-685-9800
PJI National ArenaCross (late January) 410-347-2010
Zoo Lights (late November-early January) 410-396-7102

February
ACC Craft Fair (late February) 800-836-3470
Baltimore on Ice (January-March) 800-282-6632

March
Baltimore on Ice (January-March) 800-282-6632

May
Preakness Celebration Week (early May) 410-837-3030

July
Artscape (late July) 410-396-4575
www.artscape.org

August
Maryland State Fair (late August-early September) 410-252-0200

September
Maryland State Fair (late August-early September) 410-252-0200
Rhythm Festival (mid-September) 410-664-6322
www.syntropo.com/birds/

October
Maryland Million Day (mid-October) 410-252-2100
Portfest (early October) 410-752-8632

November
Kennedy Krieger Institute Festival of Trees (late November) 410-502-9460
Zoo Lights (late November-early January) 410-396-7102

December
Baltimore Holiday Tree Lighting (early December) 410-837-4636
Baltimore's New Year's Eve Extravaganza (December 31) 410-837-4636
Christmas at Harborplace (December) 410-332-4191
Christmas Music at Lexington Marketplace (December) 410-685-6169
Lighted Boat Parade (early December) 410-837-4636
Zoo Lights (late November-early January) 410 396 7102

Ocean City

January
Nautical & Wildlife Art Festival (mid-January) 410-524-9177
North American Craft Show (mid-January) 410-524-9177
Ocean City Hot Rod & Custom Car Show (early January) 800-626-2326
Victorian Christmas (early-late January) 800-523-2888
Winterfest of Lights (mid-late November-late January) 410-289-2800
World of Wheels (early January) 410-798-6304

February
Seaside Boat Show (mid-February) 410-641-6301

March
International Auto Show of the Eastern Shore (mid-March) 800-345-1487
Quota Club Antique Show (mid-March) 410-289-8311
Saint Patrick's Day Parade & Festival (mid-March) 410-289-6156

April
Maryland International Kite Festival (late April) 410-289-7855
Spring Amateur Golf Classic (mid-April) 410-798-6304
Ward World Championship Wildfowl Carving Competition (late April) 410-742-4988

May
Cruisin' Ocean City (late May) 410-798-6304
Springfest (early May) 410-289-2800
Springfest Boat Show (early May) 800-322-3065
White Marlin Parade (early May) 410-289-1413

June
Arts Atlantica (early June) 800-626-2326
Slovenian Festival & Polka Beach Party (late June) 410-524-6440

July
Fireworks Jubilee (July 4) 800-626-2326
Jamboree in the Park (July 4) 410-250-0125
Jesus at the Beach Music & Ministry Festival (late July) 410-289-1296
Ocean City Tuna Tournament (mid-July) 800-322-3065

August
Antiques by the Sea (mid-August) 410-289-3453
White Marlin Open Fishing Tournament (early August) 410-289-9229

September
Labor Day Weekend Arts & Crafts Festival (early September) 410-352-5851
Sunfest (late September) 410-289-2800
Sunfest Boat Show (late September) 800-322-3065
Sunfest Kite Festival (late September) 410-289-7855

October
Barbershop Singers Annual Jamboree (early October) 800-626-2326
Christmas Craft Expo (late October) 410-524-9177
Endless Summer Cruisin' (mid-October) 410-798-6304
Fall Fest of Fine Art (late October) 410-524-9177
Mid-Atlantic Surf Fishing Tournament (early October) 410-213-2042
Oktoberfest (mid-October) 800-626-2326

Winefest on the Beach (early October) 800-626-2326
www.winefest.com

November
Holiday Shopper's Fair (late November) 410-289-8311
Winterfest of Lights (mid-late November-late January) 410-289-2800

December
Winterfest of Lights (mid-late November-late January) 410-289-2800

MASSACHUSETTS

Boston

January
Auto Zone World of Wheels (early January) 617-367-3555
Boston Wine Festival (January-April) 617-330-9355
Regattabar Jazz Festival (late January-late May) 617-536-4100
World of Wheels (mid-January) 617-474-6000

February
Boston Wine Expo (early February) 617-385-5015
Boston Wine Festival (January-April) 617-330-9355
New England Home Show (late February) 617-385-5000
Regattabar Jazz Festival (late January-late May) 617-536-4100
Skating on Frog Pond (late February-mid-March) 617-635-4505

March
Boston Wine Festival (January-April) 617-330-9355
Concerts on the Hatch Shell (late March-early November) 617-727-9547
New England Spring Flower Show (early March) 617-536-9280
Regattabar Jazz Festival (late January-late May) 617-536-4100
Saint Patrick's Day Celebration (mid-March) 617-536-4100
Skating on Frog Pond (late February-mid-March) 617-635-4505

April
Boston Marathon (mid-April) 617-236-1652
www.bostonmarathon.org
Boston Wine Festival (January-April) 617-330-9355
Concerts on the Hatch Shell (late March-early November) 617-727-9547
Regattabar Jazz Festival (late January-late May) 617-536-4100

May
Concerts on the Hatch Shell (late March-early November) 617-727-9547
Regattabar Jazz Festival (late January-late May) 617-536-4100

June
Boston Globe Jazz Festival (mid-June) 617-929-2649
Boston Harborfest (late June-early July) 617-227-1528
www.bostonharborfest.com
Central Square World's Fair (early June) 617-876-1655
Concerts on the Hatch Shell (late March-early November) 617-727-9547

July
Boston Antique & Classic Boat Festival (mid-July) 617-666-8530
Boston Harborfest (late June-early July) 617-227-1528
www.bostonharborfest.com
Concerts on the Hatch Shell (late March-early November) 617-727-9547
Fourth of July on the Esplanade (July 4) 617-267-2400
www.july4th.org/index.htm

August
Caribbean Carnival (mid-late August) 781-380-7559
Celebrate Seaport (early August) 617-385-4200
Concerts on the Hatch Shell (late March-early November) 617-727-9547

September
Art Festival Newbury Street (early-mid-September) 617-267-2224
Boston Film Festival (mid-September) 781-925-1373
Cambridge River Festival (early September) 617-349-4380
Concerts on the Hatch Shell (late March-early November) 617-727-9547
Newburyport Waterfront Festival (early September) 978-462-6680

October
Boston International Festival (late October) 781-861-9729
Concerts on the Hatch Shell (late March-early November) 617-727-9547
Halloween on the Harbor (late October) 617-727-7676
Halloween Prowl (late October) 781-784-5691
Harvard Square Oktoberfest (mid-October) 617-491-3434
Head of the Charles Regatta (mid-October) 617-782-8889
Honey Harvest (mid-October) 617-333-0690

November
Christmas Craft Show (late November) 617-367-3555
Christmas Festival (mid-November) 617-742-3973
Concerts on the Hatch Shell (late March-early November) 617-727-9547
New England International Auto Show (early November) 617-474-6000

December
Boston Common Tree Lighting (early December) 617-635-4505
Boston Tea Party Reenactment (mid-December) 617-338-1773
Crafts at the Castle (early December) 617-523-6400
First Night Boston (December 31) 617-542-1399
www.firstnight.org
Tree Lighting & Carol Festival (early December) 617-236-3744

Springfield

January
Antique-A-Rama (January) 413-737-2443
Bright Nights at Forest Park (November-January) 413-733-3800

March
Holyoke Saint Patrick's Parade (mid-March) 413-536-1646

May
Westfest (May) 413-568-2904

June
ACC Craft Fair (mid-June) 413-737-2443
Peter Pan Taste of Springfield (mid-June) 413-733-3800

July
Puerto Rican Cultural Festival (late July) 413-737-7450
Star Spangled Springfield (July 4) 413-733-3800

September
Glendi Festival (mid-September) 413-737-1496
Old Sturbridge Agricultural Fair (late September) 508-347-3362
www.osv.org/pages/cofe.htm
The Big E-New England Great State Fair (September) 413-737-2443
www.thebige.com/

October
Columbus Day Parade (early October) 413-732-7449

November
Bright Nights at Forest Park (November-January) 413-733-3800
Parade of the Big Balloons (late November) 413-733-3800
Peachbasket Festival & Hall of Fame Tip-Off Classic (late November) 413-781-6500

December
Bright Nights at Forest Park (November-January) 413-733-3800
Holiday Gala (early December) 413-263-6800

Worcester

January
Worcester Music Festival (October-April) 508-754-3231

February
Worcester Music Festival (October-April) 508-754-3231

March
Worcester Music Festival (October-April) 508-754-3231

April
Worcester Music Festival (October-April) 508-754-3231

May
New England Rowing Championships (early May) 508-753-2920

July
Longsjo Bike Race (early July) 978-464-2300
New England Summer Nationals (early July) 508-987-3375

August
A Celebration of Craftmanship (mid-August) 508-347-3362
Taste of Massachusetts (August) 978-779-5521

September
Brimfield Outdoor Antique Shows (early September) 800-628-8379
Harvest Festival (September) 978-779-5521
Spencer Fair (September) 508-753-2920

October
AppleFest (October) 978-464-2300
Worcester Music Festival (October-April) 508-754-3231

November
Worcester Music Festival (October-April) 508-754-3231

December
Beginning of a New England Christmas The (early-mid-December) 508-347-3362
First Night Worcester (December 31) 508-799-1400
Worcester Music Festival (October-April) 508-754-3231

MICHIGAN

Ann Arbor

January
Ann Arbor Folk Music Festival (late January) 734-763-5750

February
Winter Carnival (mid-February) 734-994-2780

March
Ann Arbor Film Festival (early March) 734-668-8397
aafilmfest.org
Pow Wow (early-mid-March) 734-764-9044

April
Ann Arbor Antiques Market (April-November) 734-995-7281

May
Ann Arbor Antiques Market (April-November) 734-995-7281

June
Ann Arbor Antiques Market (April-November) 734-995-7281
Ann Arbor Summer Festival (late June-mid-July) 734-647-2278
www.mlive.com/aasf

MICHIGAN — Ann Arbor (Cont'd)

Frog Island Festival (late June) 734-761-1800
www.a2ark.org
Summer Symphony (June-August) 734-677-4831

July
Ann Arbor Antiques Market (April-November) 734-995-7281
Ann Arbor Art Fair Extravaganza (mid-late July) 734-995-7281
Ann Arbor Street Art Fair (mid-July) 734-995-7281
Ann Arbor Summer Festival (late June-mid-July) 734-647-2278
www.mlive.com/aasf
Summer Symphony (June-August) 734-677-4831

August
Ann Arbor Antiques Market (April-November) 734-995-7281
Heritage Festival (mid-August) 734-327-2051
Summer Symphony (June-August) 734-677-4831

September
Ann Arbor Antiques Market (April-November) 734-995-7281
Ann Arbor Blues & Jazz Festival (early September) 734-747-9955
a2.blues.jazzfest.org
Big Ten Run (late September) 734-973-6730

October
Ann Arbor Antiques Market (April-November) 734-995-7281
Ann Arbor Winter Art Fair (late October) 734-995-7281

November
Ann Arbor Antiques Market (April-November) 734-995-7281

December
Festival of Lights (December 31) 734-483-4444
New Year Jubilee (December 31) 734-483-4444

Detroit

January
Christmas Flower Show & Open House
(December-mid-January) 313-852-4064
Detroit Boat Show (late January-early February) 734-261-0123
North American International Auto Show (mid-January) 248-643-0250
Plymouth International Ice Sculpture Spectacular
(mid-January) 734-459-6969
Traditions of the Season (December-early January) 313-271-1620

February
Detroit Boat Show (late January-early February) 734-261-0123

March
Builders Home & Detroit Flower Show (mid-March) 248-737-4477
Detroit Autorama (mid-March) 248-650-5560

May
Detroit Riverfront Festivals (May-September) 313-202-1800
Eastern Market Flower Day (mid-May) 313-833-1560
Greektown Art Fair (mid-May) 734-662-3382

June
Art on the Pointe (mid-June) 313-884-4222
Detroit Riverfront Festivals (May-September) 313-202-1800
International Freedom Festival (late June-early July) 313-923-7400
Meadow Brook Music Festival (June-August) 248-377-0100
Mexicantown Mercado (mid-June-early September) 313-842-0450
Tenneco Automotive Grand Prix of Detroit (early June) 313-393-7749

July
APBA Gold Cup Thunderfest Races (early July) 313-331-7770
Detroit Riverfront Festivals (May-September) 313-202-1800
International Freedom Festival (late June-early July) 313-923-7400
Meadow Brook Music Festival (June-August) 248-377-0100
Mexicantown Mercado (mid-June-early September) 313-842-0450
Michigan All-Morgan Horse Show (early July) 810-793-4583
Michigan Tastefest (early July) 313-872-0188
Spirit of Detroit Thunderfest (mid-July) 313-331-7770

August
African World Festival (mid-August) 313-494-5800
Detroit Riverfront Festivals (May-September) 313-202-1800
Meadow Brook Music Festival (June-August) 248-377-0100
Mexicantown Mercado (mid-June-early September) 313-842-0450
Michigan State Fair (late August-early September) 313-369-8250

September
Art & Apples Craft Show (mid-September) 248-651-4110
Detroit Festival of the Arts (mid-September) 313-577-5088
Detroit Riverfront Festivals (May-September) 313-202-1800
Mexicantown Mercado (mid-June-early September) 313-842-0450
Michigan State Fair (late August-early September) 313-369-8250
Montreux Detroit Jazz Festival (early September) 313-963-7622
www.montreuxdetroitjazz.com/
Old Car Festival (mid-September) 313-271-1620

October
Fall Chrysanthemum Show (mid-October-late November) 313-852-4064
Fall Harvest Days (early-mid-October) 313-271-1620
Original Old World Market (mid-October) 313-871-8600
Zoo Boo-The Nighttime Zoo (late October) 248-541-5835

November
America's Thanksgiving Day Parade (late November) 313-923-7400
Detroit Aglow (mid-November) 313-961-1403
Fall Chrysanthemum Show (mid-October-late November) 313-852-4064
Festival of Trees (late November-early December) 313-745-0178
www.metroguide.com/fot
Ford House Holiday Tours (November-December) 313-884-4222

December
Christmas Flower Show & Open House
(December-mid-January) 313-852-4064
Festival of Trees (late November-early December) 313-745-0178
www.metroguide.com/fot
Ford Fleet Festival (early December) 313-852-4051
Ford House Holiday Tours (November-December) 313-884-4222
Traditions of the Season (December-early January) 313-271-1620

Flint

May
Mott Community College Student Art Show (May) 810-762-0474

June
Civil War Weekend (late June) 800-648-7275
Country Music Fest (mid-June) 810-732-2040
Flint Art Fair (early-June) 810-234-1695
Flint's Juneteenth Festival (mid-June) 810-766-7144
Saint John Festival of Flags (late June) 810-653-2377
Summer Antique Auto Fair (late June) 810-760-1169

July
Fourth of July Festival (early July) 810-766-7463
Honoring the Eagle Pow Wow (mid-July) 810-736-7100

August
Antique Machine Show (early August) 800-648-7275
Crim Festival of Races (late August) 810-235-3396
www.doitsports.com/crim/
Flint Jazz Festival (mid-August) 810-736-7017
Genesee County Fair (mid-late August) 810-687-0953
Michigan Renaissance Festival
(mid-August-late September) 800-601-4848
Railfans Weekend (mid-August) 800-648-7275

September
Michigan Renaissance Festival
(mid-August-late September) 800-601-4848
Septemberfest (mid-September) 810-686-9861

October
Huckleberry Ghost Train (October) 810-736-7100

Grand Rapids

January
Victorian Christmas at Voigt House
(mid-November-early January) 616-456-4600

February
Grand Center Boat Show (February) 616-530-1919

March
Saint Patrick's Day Parade (mid-March) 616-247-5127
Saladin Shrine Circus (mid-late March) 616-957-4100
West Michigan Home & Garden Show (mid-March) 616-530-1919

April
East Rotary Antique Fair & Sale (mid-April) 616-243-5333

May
Parade of Homes (late May-early June) 616-281-2021
Tulip Time (early-mid-May) 800-822-2770

June
Buffalo Days (mid-June) 616-784-4853
Festival of the Arts (June) 616-459-2787
Grand Valley Artist Reeds Lake Art Festival (late June) 616-458-0315
Parade of Homes (late May-early June) 616-281-2021
Summer in the City (mid-June-late August) 616-774-7124
Three Fires Indian Pow Wow (mid-June) 616-458-8759

July
African American Festival (mid-July) 616-245-5756
Grand Rapids Jazz & Blues Festival (late July) 616-774-7124
Grand Regatta (mid-July) 616-364-5150
Polish Harvest Festival (late July) 616-452-3363
Summer in the City (mid-June-late August) 616-774-7124

August
Festa Italiana (early August) 616-456-3178
Riverside Arts & Craft Fair (mid-August) 616-454-7900
Summer in the City (mid-June-late August) 616-774-7124
Thunder on the Grand Championship Drag Boat Race
(late August) 616-795-0065
West Michigan Grand Prix (late August) 616-222-4000
www.westmichigangrandprix.com/

September
Celebration on the Grand (mid-September) 616-456-3696
Foremost Insurance Championship (early September) 616-235-0943
Germanfest (early September) 616-364-0456
Grand Valley Indian Pow Wow (early September) 616-364-4697
Hispanic Festival (mid-September) 616-742-0200
Kent Harvest Trails (late September-mid-October) 616-452-4647
Klein Rodeo (early September) 616-887-9945
Labor Day Parade and Rally (early September) 616-241-6555
Meijer Food Fair (mid-September) 616-791-3257

October
Downtown Discovery Days (mid-October) 616-774-7124
Kent Harvest Trails (late September-mid-October) 616-452-4647
Pulaski Days Celebration (early October) 616-459-8287
Zoo Goes Boo (late October) 616-336-4300

November
Christmas Around the World
(late November-late December) 616-957-1580
Victorian Christmas at Voigt House
(mid-November-early January) 616-456-4600

December
Christmas Around the World
(late November-late December) 616-957-1580
Victorian Christmas at Voigt House
(mid-November-early January) 616-456-4600

Lansing

January
Central Michigan Boat Show (late January) 517-485-2309

March
Home & Garden Show (mid-March) 517-686-0660

May
Lansing Art Festival (late May) 517-337-1731
Mexican Fiesta (Memorial Day Weekend) 517-394-4639
Michigan Parades Into the 21st Century (mid-May) 517-323-2000

July
Ingham County Fair (late July-early August) 517-676-2428

August
Bluegrass Music Festival (late August) 517-589-8097
Car/Capital Celebration (late August) 517-372-0529
Ingham County Fair (late July-early August) 517-676-2428
Island Art Fair (early August) 517-627-9843
Lansing Jazzfest (early August) 517-371-4600
LPGA Tournament (late August) 517-372-4653
National Folk Festival (mid-August) 517-355-2370

September
Riverfest (early September) 517-483-4499

October
Old Town Lansing Art & Octoberfest (mid-October) 517-487-3322

November
Festival of Trees (late November) 517-483-7400
Wonderland of Lights (late November-late December) 517-371-3926

December
Festeve (late December) 517-487-3322
Wonderland of Lights (late November-late December) 517-371-3926

MINNESOTA

Duluth

January
Duluth Winter Festival (early-late January) 218-722-4011
Festival of Lights (late November-early January) 218-722-4011
Martin Luther King Day Gathering (mid-January) 218-722-5573
Memorial Park Winter Carnival (late January) 218-723-3567
Mid-Winter Blues Fest (late January) 218-727-8981
Semester Day Snow Festival (late January) 218-724-9832

February
John Beargrease Sled Dog Marathon (early February) 218-722-7631
www.beargrease.com
Polar Bear Picnic (late February-early March) 218-723-3748
President's Day Snow Festival (mid-February) 218-724-9832
Red Flannel Days (early-mid-February) 218-722-4651

March
Fun Fair (early March) 218-722-5573
Gingerbread Craft Show (late March) 218-722-5573
Polar Bear Picnic (late February-early March) 218-723-3748

April
Annual Volunteer Get-Together (early-mid-April) 218-723-3724
Duluth Yesterdays (late April-early May) 218-722-4011
Easter Egg Hunt (early April) 218-723-3748
Taste of the Nation (early April) 218-722-8826

May
Duluth Yesterdays (late April-early May) 218-722-4011
Heritage Preservation Fair (mid-May) 218-722-8826
Mayflower Festival (late May) 218-724-9832
Memorial Day Parade (May 31) 218-624-5518
Mother's Day at the Zoo (early May) 218-723-3748
YWCA Mother's Day Walk/Run (early May) 218-722-7425

June
Father's Day at the Zoo (mid-late June) 218-723-3748
Grandma's Marathon (mid-June) 218-727-0947
www.grandmasmarathon.com
Lake Superior Paper Industries Tours
(early June-early September) 218-628-5100
Park Point Art Fair (late June) 715-398-5970

July
4th of July Pike Lake Boat Parade (July 4) 218-722-4011
Feast with the Beasts Food Festival (late July) 218-723-3748
FourthFest (July 4) 218-722-4011
Hermantown Summerfest (mid-July) 218-727-7667
Lake Superior Paper Industries Tours
(early June-early September) 218-628-5100
Two Harbors Folk Festival (mid-July) 218-834-2600

August
Bayfront Blues Festival (mid-August) 715-394-6831
www.bayfrontblues.com/bayfront/index.html

MINNESOTA — Duluth (Cont'd)

Duluth International Folk Festival (early August) 218-733-7543
Glensheen Festival of Fine Art & Craft (late August) 218-726-8910
Lake Superior Paper Industries Tours (early June-early September) 218-628-5100
North Saint Louis County Fair (early August) 800-372-6437

September
Duluth Lions Club Apple Harvest Festival (late September) 218-722-4011
Fallfest (mid-late September) 218-724-9832
Grandparent's Day at the Zoo (mid-September) 218-723-3748
Lake Superior Paper Industries Tours (early June-early September) 218-628-5100
Northshore Inline Marathon (mid-September) 218-723-1503
www.northshoreinline.com
Octoberfest (late September) 218-723-3748
Ragtime Music Festival (mid-September) 218-724-7696

October
Boo at the Zoo (late October) 218-723-3748
Scandanavian Festival (early October) 715-392-2773
Ship of Ghouls (late October) 218-722-7876
www.decc.org/attractions/ghouls.htm

November
Christmas at Glensheen (late November-late December) 218-726-8910
Duluth National Snocross (late November) 218-722-4011
Festival of Lights (late November-early January) 218-722-4011

December
Christmas at Glensheen (late November-late December) 218-726-8910
Festival of Lights (late November-early January) 218-722-4011
Zoo Year's Eve (December 31) 218-723-3748

Minneapolis

March
Dayton's Bachman's Flower Show (mid-late March) 612-375-3018
Northwest Sports Show (early-mid-March) 612-827-5833

April
Easter Egg-Stravaganza (mid-April) 612-883-8600
International Film Fest (late April-early May) 202-724-5613
Spring Festival Arts & Crafts Affair (early April) 612-445-7223

May
Eagle Creek Rendezvous (late May) 612-445-6900
Farmers Market on Nicollet Mall (May-October) 612-338-3807
International Film Fest (late April-early May) 202-724-5613
Main Street Days (mid-May) 612-931-0132
Mayday Parade & Festival (early May) 612-721-2535
Summit Avenue Walking Tours (May-September) 651-297-2555
Warehouse District Art Walk (mid-May) 612-344-1700

June
Alive After Five Concerts (June) 612-338-3807
Civil War Weekend (mid-June) 612-726-1171
Farmers Market on Nicollet Mall (May-October) 612-338-3807
Juneteenth Festival (mid-June) 612-375-7622
Midsommar Celebration & Scandinavian Art Fair (mid-June) 612-871-4907
Stone Arch Festival of the Arts (mid-June) 612-378-1226
Summit Avenue Walking Tours (May-September) 651-297-2555
Twin Cities Juneteenth Celebration (mid-June) 612-529-5553

July
Farmers Market on Nicollet Mall (May-October) 612-338-3807
Minneapolis Aquatennial (mid-late July) 612-661-4700
Minnesota Fringe Theater Festival (late July-early August) 612-823-6005
members.aol.com/mnfringe/
Sommerfest (early July) 612-661-4700
Summit Avenue Walking Tours (May-September) 651-297-2555
Twin Cities Ribfest (late July) 612-338-3807
Viennese Sommerfest (July) 612-371-5656

August
Bloomington Jazz Festival (mid-August) 612-948-8877
Cedarfest (mid-August) 612-673-0401
Farmers Market on Nicollet Mall (May-October) 612-338-3807
Minnesota Fringe Theater Festival (late July-early August) 612-823-6005
members.aol.com/mnfringe/
Minnesota Renaissance Festival (mid-August-late September) 612-445-7361
Minnesota State Fair (late August-early September) 651-642-2200
www.statefair.gen.mn.us
Oyster & Guinness Festival (late August) 612-904-1000
Summit Avenue Walking Tours (May-September) 651-297-2555
Uptown Art Fair (early August) 612-661-4700

September
Country Folk Art Show (late September) 651-642-2200
Farmers Market on Nicollet Mall (May-October) 612-338-3807
Minnesota 4-H Horse Show (mid-September) 651-642-2200
Minnesota Renaissance Festival (mid-August-late September) 612-445-7361
Minnesota State Fair (late August-early September) 651-642-2200
www.statefair.gen.mn.us
Semstone Truck Rodeo (mid-September) 651-642-2200
Summit Avenue Walking Tours (May-September) 651-297-2555
Western Saddle Club Horse Show (late September) 651-642-2200

October
Fall Home & Garden Show (early October) 612-335-6000
Farmers Market on Nicollet Mall (May-October) 612-338-3807
Midwest Fall Antique Auto Show (early October) 651-642-2200
Twin Cities Marathon (early October) 612-673-0778

November
Hollidazzle Parades (late November-December) 612-338-3807
Ski Snowmobile & Winter Sports Show (mid-November) 612-335-6000

December
Holidays at the Zoo (December) 612-431-9298
Hollidazzle Parades (late November-December) 612-338-3807
New Year's Eve Fireworks Celebration (December 31) 612-673-5123

Rochester

May
Gold Rush of Olmsted County (early May-late September) 507-288-0320

June
Gold Rush of Olmsted County (early May-late September) 507-288-0320
Mantorville Melodramas (mid-June-late August) 507-635-5420
Old Tyme Days (late June) 507-635-5420
Rochesterfest (mid-late June) 507-285-8769

July
Gold Rush of Olmsted County (early May-late September) 507-288-0320
Mantorville Melodramas (mid-June-late August) 507-635-5420

August
Berne Swissfest (early August) 507-635-5420
Gold Rush of Olmsted County (early May-late September) 507-288-0320
Mantorville Melodramas (mid-June-late August) 507-635-5420

September
Fall Harvest Festival (mid-September) 507-281-6114
Gold Rush of Olmsted County (early May-late September) 507-288-0320
Marigold Days (early September) 507-635-5420
Three Rivers Rendezvous (late September) 507-282-9447

November
Festival of Trees (late November) 507-287-2222
Mayowood Holiday Tours (early November) 507-282-9447
Polka Party (mid-November) 800-533-1655

December
Yule-Fest (early December) 507-285-8076

Saint Paul

January
Capital City Lights (November-February) 651-297-6985
Gaslight Tours (late January-early February) 651-297-2555
Saint Paul Winter Carnival (late January-early February) 651-223-4710
www.winter-carnival.com/
Winter on the Hill (late January-early February) 651-297-2555

February
Capital City Lights (November-February) 651-297-6985
Gaslight Tours (late January-early February) 651-297-2555
Saint Paul Winter Carnival (late January-early February) 651-223-4710
www.winter-carnival.com/
Scottish Ramble & Highland Dance Competition (mid-February) 651-292-3276
Winter on the Hill (late January-early February) 651-297-2555

March
An Irish Celebration (mid-March) 651-292-3225

April
American Craft Council Craft Expo (mid-April) 651-224-7361
Saint Paul Art Crawl (early October & mid-April) 651-292-4373
www.stpaul-artcrawl.org/
Spring Babies (early-mid-April) 612-431-9213

May
Cinco de Mayo Mexican Fiesta (early May) 651-222-6347
Festival of Nations (early May) 651-647-0191

June
Bavarian Sommerfest (late June) 651-439-7128
Classic Cars on Wabasha (June-mid-October) 651-266-8989
Twin Cities Juneteenth Celebration (mid-June) 612-529-5553

July
Classic Cars on Wabasha (June-mid-October) 651-266-8989
Rondo Days Festival (mid-July) 651-646-6597
Taste of Minnesota (early July) 651-772-9980
Thursday Night Live Outdoor Concerts (July) 651-774-5422

August
Classic Cars on Wabasha (June-mid-October) 651-266-8989
Fur Trade Weekend 1827 (late August) 612-725-2413
Minnesota State Fair (late August-early September) 651-642-2200
www.statefair.gen.mn.us

September
Classic Cars on Wabasha (June-mid-October) 651-266-8989
Minnesota State Fair (late August-early September) 651-642-2200
www.statefair.gen.mn.us
Oktoberfest (mid-late September) 651-439-7128

October
Classic Cars on Wabasha (June-mid-October) 651-266-8989
Fall Colors Art Festival (early October) 651-439-4001
Saint Paul Art Crawl (early October & mid-April) 651-292-4373
www.stpaul-artcrawl.org/
Twin Cities Marathon (early October) 612-673-0778

November
Capital City Lights (November-February) 651-297-6985

December
Capital City Lights (November-February) 651-297-6985
Capital New Year (December 31) 612-920-9054
Grand Meander (early December) 651-699-0029
www.grandave.com/
Hill House Holidays (mid-late December) 651-297-2555
Holiday Bazaar (early December) 651-292-3230
Holidays at the Zoo (December) 612-431-9298
Saint Paul Ice Fishing & Winter Sports Show (early December) 651-297-6985

MISSISSIPPI

Gulfport/Biloxi

February
Mardi Gras (February) 800-237-9493

March
Biloxi Oyster Festival (mid-March) 228-374-2330
Gulf Coast Spring Pilgrimage (mid-late March) 228-863-0550
Saint Patrick's Day Parade (mid-March) 228-864-2551

April
Country Cajun Crawfish Festival (mid-April) 228-594-3700

May
Biloxi Blessing of the Fleet (early May) 228-435-5578
Biloxi Shrimp Festival (early May) 228-435-5578
Great Biloxi Schooner Races (early May) 228-435-6320

June
Juneteenth Celebration (mid-June) 228-388-4038
Mississippi Gulf Coast Fair & Expo (June) 228-594-3700

July
Crab Festival (early July) 228-467-6509
July 4th Celebration (July 4) 228-374-3105
Mississippi Deep Sea Fishing Rodeo (early July) 228-863-2713

August
Mississippi Coast Pro Rodeo (mid-August) 228-594-3700

September
Biloxi Seafood Festival (mid-September) 228-374-2717
Bull Bash (mid-September) 228-832-0080
Mississippi Gulf Coast Blues Festival (early September) 228-497-5615
Oktoberfest (late September-early October) 228-436-4878
Sun Herald Sand Sculpture Contest (mid-September) 228-896-2434

October
Crusin' the Coast (mid-October) 228-896-6699
Fall Muster (late October) 228-388-1313
George Ohr's Fall Festival of Arts (late October) 228-435-6308
Oktoberfest (late September-early October) 228-436-4878
Scottish Games & Celtic Festival (early October) 228-864-8055

November
Biloxi Christmas City USA (mid-November) 228-896-9336
Peter Anderson Art Festival (early November) 228-875-4424

December
Christmas on the Water (early December) 228-374-3105
Christmas on the Water Boat Parade (early December) 228-374-3611
Victorian Christmas (mid-December) 228-388-9074

Hattiesburg

March
Children's Book Festival (mid-late March) 601-266-4186

May
A Day in the Park (early May) 601-649-1206
Hub City Hustle Triathalon (late May) 601-268-5010
Okatoma Festival (early May) 601-765-6012
Old Time Festival (early May) 601-296-7500

July
Fireworks Spectacular (early July) 601-426-6320
Paul B Johnson Fireworks (July 4) 601-582-7721

August
Pinebelt Expo (mid August) 601-296-7500
Taste of the Pinebelt (mid-August) 601-296-7500

September
Mississippi Pecan Festival (late September) 601-525-3792

October
Hub Fest (mid-October) 601-296-7500
Zoo Boo (late October) 601-545-4576

November
Holiday Fantasy (mid-late November) 601-296-7500

December
Hattiesburg Historic Downtown Holiday (mid-December) 601-545-4503
Holiday Lights Safari (mid-December) 601-545-4576
Victorian Candelit Christmas (mid-December) 601-583-8723

Jackson

February
Dixie National Livestock Show & Rodeo (early-mid-February) 601-961-4000
Gem & Mineral Show (late February) 601-961-4000

March
Mal's Saint Paddy's Day Parade (March) 601-984-1109
Spring Festival at Mynelle Garden (late March) 601-960-1894

April
Zoo Blues (mid-April) 601-960-1891

May
International Crawfish Festival (early May) 601-354-6113
Jubilee Jam (mid-May) 601-960-2008
www.jubileejam.com
Mississippi Heritage Festival (late May) 601-960-1891

June
Hog Wild In June (late June) 601-354-6113

July
Hot Air Balloon Race (early July) 601-859-1307
Old Fashion Independence Day (July 4) 601-354-6113

August
Scottish Highland Games (mid-August) 601-960-1891
Sky Parade (late August-early September) 601-982-8088

September
Celtic Fest (early September) 601-960-1891
Farish Street Festival (late September) 601-960-2384
Sky Parade (late August-early September) 601-982-8088
WellsFest (late September) 601-353-0658

October
Jackson County Fair (early October) 601-948-7575
Mississippi State Fair (early October) 601-961-4000
Natives & Pioneers Heritage Fair (early October) 601-856-7546
Pioneer & Indian Festival (late October) 601-856-7546

November
Capital City Football Classic (mid-November) 601-960-1891
Harvest Festival (November) 601-354-6113
Mistletoe Marketplace (early November) 601-960-1891

December
Chimneyville Crafts Festival (early December) 601-981-0019
Christmas at the New Capitol (December) 601-359-3114
Festival of Christmas Trees (December) 601-960-1457
Holiday Jubilee (early December) 601-960-1891

Tupelo

April
Oxford Conference for the Book (early April) 662-232-5993

May
Calhoun City Arts And Crafts Festival (late May) 662-628-6990
Gum Tree Arts Festival (early May) 662-841-6521

June
Heritage Day Festival (early June) 662-423-9571
Oleput Mardi Gras Festival (June) 662-841-6521

August
Bodock Festival (late August) 662-489-5042
Elvis Presley Festival (early August) 662-841-1245
Hancock Fabric Show (late August-early September) 662-844-1473

September
Hancock Fabric Show (late August-early September) 662-844-1473
North Mississippi Fair (mid-September) 662-566-5600

MISSOURI

Branson

February
Buddy Bass Tournament (mid-February) 417-546-2741

March
Branson Fest (late March) 417-334-4136
White Bass Round Up (mid-March) 417-546-2741

April
Band Choral & Orchestra Festival (late April-early May) 417-335-3554
National Church Choir Festival (late April) 417-335-3554
World-Fest (mid-April-mid-May) 800-952-6626

May
Band Choral & Orchestra Festival (late April-early May) 417-335-3554
Great American Music Festival (mid-May-early June) 800-952-6626
Plumb Nellie Festival & Craft Show (late May) 417-334-1548
World-Fest (mid-April-mid-May) 800-952-6626

June
Christian Family Week (mid-June) 417-334-4191
Great American Music Festival (mid-May-early June) 800-952-6626
Lawrence Welk Polka Fest (early June) 800-505-9355
National Children's Festival (mid-June-late August) 800-952-6626

July
Independence Day Celebration & Fireworks Display (July 4) 417-334-3050
National Children's Festival (mid-June-late August) 800-952-6626
Spirit of '76 Independence Day Celebration (early July) 417-337-8387
Taney County Fair (mid-late July) 417-546-2741

August
Crusin' Branson Lights Automobile Festival (mid-August) 417-334-4136
Farm Family Week (August) 417-334-4084
National Children's Festival (mid-June-late August) 800-952-6626
Old Time Fiddle Contest (mid-August) 417-334-1548
White River Valley Arts & Crafts Fair (early August) 417-546-2741

September
Autumn Daze Craft Festival (mid-September) 417-334-1548
Fall Harvest Festival (early September-late October) 417-334-4191
National Festival of Craftsmen (early September-late October) 800-952-6626
Ozark Mountain Country Fall Foliage Drive (late September-early November) 800-519-1600
State of the Ozarks Fiddlers Convention (mid-September) 417-338-2911

October
Fall Harvest Festival (early September-late October) 417-334-4191
Harvest Moon Festival (early October) 417-546-2741
National Festival of Craftsmen (early September-late October) 800-952-6626
Ozark Mountain Country Fall Foliage Drive (late September-early November) 800-519-1600

November
Branson Area Festival of Lights (early November-late December) 417-334-4136
Central Pro-Am Bass Tournament (early November) 417-881-2158
Old Time Country Christmas (early November-late December) 800-952-6626
Ozark Mountain Christmas (November-late December) 800-214-3661
Ozark Mountain Country Fall Foliage Drive (late September-early November) 800-519-1600
Veterans Homecoming (early-mid-November) 417-334-4136

December
Adoration Parade & Lighting Ceremony (early December) 417-334-4136
Branson Area Festival of Lights (early November-late December) 417-334-4136
Candlelight Christmas Open House (early December) 417-334-1548
Old Time Country Christmas (early November-late December) 800-952-6626
Ozark Mountain Christmas (November-late December) 800-214-3661

Columbia

January
Columbia Values Diversity Celebration (mid-January) 573-874-7488

February
Home & Garden Show (late February) 573-882-2056

March
Annual Business Expo (late March) 573-874-1132
Spring Craft Show (mid-late March) 573-882-2056

April
Earth Day (April 22) 573-875-0539

May
Memorial Day Weekend Celebration (late May) 573-443-2651
Salute to Veterans Airshow (late May) 573-443-2651
Salute to Veterans Parade (late May) 573-443-2651

June
Art in the Park (early June) 573-443-8838
JW Boone Ragtime Festival (early June) 573-875-1231
Thursdays Downtown Twilight Festivals (June & September) 573-442-6816

July
Boone County Fair (late July) 573-474-9435
Fire in the Sky Fireworks Extravaganza (July 4) 573-449-0917
International Buckskin Horse World Championship Show (late July) 573-445-8338
Show-Me State Games (mid-late July) 573-882-2101

August
US Cellular Balloon Classic (late August) 573-814-4000

September
Boone County Heritage Festival (mid-September) 573-875-1231
Columbia Festival of the Arts (late September) 573-874-1132
Lions Antique Show (early September) 573-882-2056
Thursdays Downtown Twilight Festivals (June & September) 573-442-6816

November
Fall Craft Show (early November) 573-882-2056
Holiday Parade (late November) 573-442-6816

December
Christmas Candlelight Tour (early December) 573-875-1231
Downtown Holiday Festival (early December) 573-442-6816
First Night Celebration (December 31) 573-817-2781

Independence

March
Bingham-Waggoner Fashion Show (mid-March) 816-461-3491
Vaile Tea Party (late March) 816-461-5135

April
Farm & Flower Festival (late April) 816-252-0608

May
Farmer's Market Saturdays (early May-late October) 816-252-0608
Flint Knap-In (mid-May & mid-September) 816-795-8200
Historic Site Trolley Tours (early May) 816-325-7111
Presidential Wreath Laying (May 8) 816-833-1400
Truman Birthday Celebration (May 8) 816-252-0608
Truman Health Walk (early May) 816-833-2088
Truman Walking Tours (late May-early September) 816-254-7199

June
Children's Day at Missouri Town 1855 (early June) 816-795-8200
Farmer's Market Saturdays (early May-late October) 816-252-0608
Strawberry Festival (early June) 816-252-9098
Truman Walking Tours (late May-early September) 816-254-7199

July
Bingham-Waggoner Antique & Craft Fair (mid-July) 816-461-3491
Farmer's Market Saturdays (early May-late October) 816-252-0608
Independence Day at Fort Osage National Historic Landmark (July 4) 816-795-8200
Independence Day at Missouri Town 1855 (July 4) 816-795-8200
Truman Walking Tours (late May-early September) 816-254-7199

August
Children's Day at Fort Osage National Historic Landmark (early August) 816-795-8200
Dawg Days Animal Fair Craft Show & Flea Market (early August) 816-252-0608
Farmer's Market Saturdays (early May-late October) 816-252-0608
Harry S Truman Appreciation Ceremony (early August) 816-833-1400
Truman Walking Tours (late May-early September) 816-254-7199

September
Bingham-Waggoner Quilt Show (September) 816-461-3491
Farmer's Market Saturdays (early May-late October) 816-252-0608
Flint Knap-In (mid-May & mid-September) 816-795-8200
Fort Osage Rendezvous (mid-September) 816-795-8200
Santa-Cali-Gon Days Festival (early September) 816-252-4745
Santa-Cali-Gon Quilt Show (early September) 816-325-7370
Truman Walking Tours (late May-early September) 816-254-7199

October
Enchanted Forest (late October) 816-257-4654
Farmer's Market Saturdays (early May-late October) 816-252-0608
Fort Osage Militia Muster (mid-October) 816-795-8200
Frontier Fright Night (late October) 816-795-8200
Missouri Town Fall Festival (early October) 816-795-8200
Spirits of the Past (late October) 816-795-8200
Trick 'n Treat & Halloween Parade (late October) 816-252-4745

November
Best Little Arts & Crafts Show in Independence (mid-late November) 816-325-7370
Holiday Open House (early November) 816-252-0608
Lighting of Jackson County Courthouse & Queen City Christmas Tree (early November) 816-252-0608
Spirit of Christmas Past Homes Tour (late November-late December) 816-461-3491

December
Frontier Christmas (early December) 816-795-8200
Missouri Town Christmas Celebration (mid-December) 816-795-8200
Spirit of Christmas Past Homes Tour (late November-late December) 816-461-3491
Windows on the Past (mid-December) 816-795-8200

Jefferson City

March
Luck of the Irish 5K Run & Walk (mid-March) 573-761-9000

May
Old Car Roundup & Show (late May) 573-636-6666
State High School Track Championships (mid-late May) 573-445-4443
Super Cruise Car Show (late May) 573-634-3616

July
Cole County Fair (late July-early August) 573-634-3616
Independence Day Celebration (July 4) 573-634-3616
Missouri Shakespeare Festival (early July) 573-634-6482
webcom.com/~bkirk/studio/park.html
Show-Me State Games (mid-late July) 573-882-2101

August
Cole County Fair (late July-early August) 573-634-3616

September
Capital Jazz Fest (early September) 573-681-5000
Fall Festival & Crafts Fair (early September) 573-634-2824

October
Hartsburg Pumpkin Festival (early October) 573-657-4556

December
Christmas Parade (early December) 573-634-3616
Old Fashioned Christmas Celebration (early December) 573-634-7267
Washington Park Winter Skating Recital (mid-December) 573-634-6482

Kansas City

March
Greater Kansas City Auto Show (early March) 816-871-3700
Kansas City St Patrick's Day Parade (March 17) 816-931-7373

April
Brookside Art Annual (late April-early May) 816-523-0091
Kansas City Home Show (mid-April-early May) 816-942-8800
Shrimp Festival (late April-early May) 904-277-0717

May
Brookside Art Annual (late April-early May) 816-523-0091
Cinco de Mayo Celebration (early May) 816-221-4747
Kansas City Home Show (mid-April-early May) 816-942-8800
Shrimp Festival (late April-early May) 904-277-0717

June
Heartland of America Shakespeare Festival (late June-mid-July) 816-531-7728
Highland Games & Scottish Festival (early June) 913-432-6823
Juneteenth Celebrations (mid-June) 816-483-1300
Kansas City River Valley Festival (late June) 816-960-0800
Kiki's Crawfish Fiesta (early June) 816-842-1271
Settlers' Day (early June) 816-792-2655

July
Heartland of America Shakespeare Festival (late June-mid-July) 816-531-7728
Kansas City Blues & Jazz Festival (late July) 800-530-5266
Kansas City Jaycees Rodeo (early July) 816-761-5055

August
Abdallah Shrine Rodeo (mid-August) 913-362-5300
Ethnic Enrichment Festival (late August) 816-842-7530

September
Fiesta Hispana (late September) 816-765-1992
Greek Festival (September) 816-942-9100
Plaza Fine Arts Fair (late September) 816-753-0100
Renaissance Festival (early September-mid-October) 800-373-0357
www.kcrenfest.com
Spirit Festival (Labor Day weekend) 816-221-4444

October
American Royal Barbecue Contest (early October) 816-221-9800
American Royal Livestock Horse Show & Rodeo (late October-early November) 800-821-5857
www.americanroyal.com/
Excelsior Springs Waterfest (October) 816-792-7691
Renaissance Festival (early September-mid-October) 800-373-0357
www.kcrenfest.com

November
American Royal Livestock Horse Show & Rodeo (late October-early November) 800-821-5857
www.americanroyal.com/
Plaza Lighting Ceremony (late November) 816-753-0100

Saint Louis

January
Elvis Birthday Celebration (early January) 314-727-0880
Great Saint Louis Golf Show (mid-January) 800-221-1280
Greater Saint Louis Auto Show (late January-early February) 314-342-5000
Way of Lights (late November-early January) 314-241-3400
Winter Wonderland (late November-early January) 314-615-7275

February
Greater Saint Louis Auto Show (late January-early February) 314-342-5000
Missouri WineFest (mid-February) 314-576-7100
Saint Louis Boat & Sports Show (early February) 314-567-0020
Soulard Mardi Gras (early-mid February) 314-421-1023
Spring Home & Garden Show (late February) 314-994-7700

March
Saint Patrick's Day Parade & Run (mid-March) 314-421-1800

April
Grand South Grand House Tour (mid-April) 314-773-4844
Great Saint Louis Kite Festival (mid-April) 636-938-4800
Missouri Spring Festival of Art (early April) 314-889-0433
Taste of the Nation Food Festival (late April) 314-863-5500
World War II Weekend (late April) 314-544-5714

May
African Arts Festival (late May) 314-935-5645
Annie Malone Parade (mid-May) 314-531-0120
Art & Soul (late May) 314-436-6500
Circus Flora (early-mid-May) 314-531-6273
Laumeier Contemporary Art Fair (early May) 314-821-1209
Lewis & Clark Rendezvous (mid-May) 636-946-7776
Memorial Day Festival (late May) 314-241-5875
Saint Louis Alive Music Festival (late May-early June) 314-995-4963
Saint Louis Antiques Show (early May) 314-968-7340
Saint Louis Storytelling Festival (early May) 314-516-5036
Six Flags Music Festival (mid-May) 636-938-4800
Tilles Spring Arts & Crafts Fair (mid-May) 636-391-0922
Valley of Flower Festival (early May) 314-837-0033

June
An Art Affair (mid-June) 314-576-7100
Grand Festival of Nations (mid-June) 314-773-7733
Jazz Festivals (June) 314-577-5100
Lafayette Square Victorian Art Festival (early June) 314-772-5724
Saint Louis Alive Music Festival (late May-early June) 314-995-4963
Saint Louis Earth Day Community Festival (early June) 314-776-4442
Taste of Westport Food Festival (early June) 314-576-7100
Whitaker Jazz Festival (early June) 314-577-5100

July
Fair Saint Louis (early July) 314-434-3434
Miller Music Blast (early July) 314-241-5875
Soulard Bastille Day Celebration (mid-July) 314-773-6767

August
Greek Festival (late August-early September) 314-361-6924
Moonlight Ramble (mid-August) 314-644-4660
Saint Louis Blues Heritage Festival (mid-August) 314-644-1551
Saint Louis Strassenfest (early August) 314-849-6322

September
American Indian Society Pow Wow (mid-September) 314-544-5714
Art Happening (early September) 314-889-0433
Big Muddy Roots & Blues Music Festival (early September) 314-241-5875
Goldenrod Ragtime (early September) 636-946-2020
Great Apple Jubilee (early September) 314-233-0513
Great Forest Park Balloon Race (mid September) 314-993-2468
Greek Festival (late August-early September) 314-361-6924
Greentree Festival (early-mid-September) 314-822-5855
Japanese Festival (Labor Day weekend) 314-577-5100
Laclede's Landing Big Muddy Blues Festival (early September) 314-241-5875
Polish Festival (early September) 314-921-1192
Saint Louis Art Fair (early September) 314-863-0278
Saint Louis County Fair & Air Show (early September) 636-530-9386
Saint Louis National Charity Horse Show (mid-late September) 636-458-7994
Tilles Fall Arts & Crafts Fair (mid-September) 636-391-0922

October
Best of Missouri Market (early October) 800-642-8842
Greater Saint Louis Beer Festival (early October) 314-576-7100
Historic Shaw Art Fair (early October) 314-771-3101
International Folkfest (mid-October) 314-773-9090
Loop in Motion Arts Festival (early October) 314-725-4466
Saint Louis International Film Festival (late October-early November) 314-454-0042

November
Festival of the Trees (late November) 314-849-4440
Holiday Festival of Lights (mid-November) 314-577-7049
Holiday Flower Show (late November) 314-577-5100
Saint Louis International Film Festival (late October-early November) 314-454-0042
Way of Lights (late November-early January) 314-241-3400
Winter Wonderland (late November-early January) 314-615-7275

December
Kwanzaa Holiday Expo (mid-December) 314-367-3440
Way of Lights (late November-early January) 314-241-3400
Winter Wonderland (late November-early January) 314-615-7275

Springfield

April
Frisco Days (mid-April) 417-864-7015

May
Artsfest (early May) 417-869-8380

June
Sheep & Wool Days (early June) 417-881-1659
SMSU Summer Tent Theater (late June-early August) 417-836-5979
Watercolor USA (early June-early August) 417-837-5700

July
Firefall (early July) 417-864-1049
Hall of Fame All-Star Game (early July) 417-889-3100
Ozark Empire Fair (late July-early August) 417-833-2660
SMSU Summer Tent Theater (late June-early August) 417-836-5979
Watercolor USA (early June-early August) 417-837-5700

August
Fall Hunting Classic (late August) 417-873-5111
Nike Ozarks Open (mid-August) 417-886-0408
Ozark Empire Fair (late July-early August) 417-833-2660
SMSU Summer Tent Theater (late June-early August) 417-836-5979
Watercolor USA (early June-early August) 417-837-5700

September
1860 Lifestyle Exposition (mid-September) 417-862-6293
Balloonfest (mid-September) 417-269-5437

October
Halloween Spooktacular (late October) 417-833-1570

November
Ozark Mountain Christmas Festival of Lights (early November-late December) 417-881-5300

December
First Night Springfield (December 31) 417-869-8380
Ozark Mountain Christmas Festival of Lights (early November-late December) 417-881-5300

MONTANA

Billings

February
Billings Home & Garden Show (mid-February) 406-245-0404
Northern Rodeo Association Finals (early February) 406-256-2422

April
Antique & Collectible Extravaganza (late April & late September) 308-436-8355

June
Custer's Last Stand Re-enactment (late June) 406-665-1672

July
Big Sky State Games (late July) 406-254-7426
Mexican Fiesta (late July-early August) 406-252-0191
Summerfair (mid-July) 406-256-6804

August
Crow Fair (mid-August) 406-638-2601
Mexican Fiesta (late July-early August) 406-252-0191
MontanaFair (mid-August) 406-256-2400

September
Antique & Collectible Extravaganza (late April & late September) 308-436-8355
Laurel Herbstfest (late September) 406-628-8105

October
Northern International Livestock Expo Pro Rodeo (mid-October) 406-256-2495
Northern International Livestock Expo Stock Show & Sale (early October) 406-256-2495

November
Festival of Trees (early November) 406-256-2422
Holiday Parade (late November) 406-259-5454

December
Chase Hawks Memorial Rough Stock Invitational Rodeo (mid-December) 406-248-9295
Fantasy of Lights (mid-late December) 406-252-9600
Holiday Festival (mid-December) 406-248-2212
New Year's Pow Wow (late December) 406-638-2601

Great Falls

January
Montana Agricultural & Industrial Exhibit (mid-January) 406-761-7600
Montana Pro Rodeo Finals (mid-January) 406-761-4434

March
CM Russell Auction of Original Western Art (mid-March) 406-761-6453

April
Ice Breaker Fun Run (late April) 406-771-1265

June
Lewis & Clark Festival (late June) 406-761-4434

July
Luminaria Walk on the River Edge Trail (July 16th) 406-761-4434
Montana State Fair (late July-early August) 406-727-1481

August
Montana State Fair (late July-early August) 406-727-1481

September
Cottonwood Festival (early September) 406-452-3462

December
Christmas Stroll (early December) 406-761-4434

Helena

February
Race to the Sky (early February) 406-442-4008

March
Spring Art & Craft Show (mid-March) 406-449-4790

April
Helena Railroad Fair (late April) 406-442-4120

June
Governor's Cup Art & Craft Show (early June) 406-449-4790
Governor's Cup Marathon (early June) 406-444-8261
Governor's Cup Race (early June) 406-447-3414
www.govcup.bcbsmt.com/index.html
Montana Traditional Jazz Festival (late June) 406-449-7969

July
Last Chance Stampede & Rodeo (late July) 406-442-1098

August
Kaleidoscope Summer Festival (early August) 406-442-0400

October
Autumn Art & Craft Show (late October) 406-449-4790
Oktoberfest/Bullfest (mid-October) 406-442-6449

November
Bald Eagle Migration (November-December) 406-442-4120
Downtown Helena Fall Art Walk (late November) 406-447-1535
Holiday Craft Fair (late November) 406-443-2242

December
Bald Eagle Migration (November-December) 406-442-4120
Festival of Trees (early December) 406-442-7920

NEBRASKA

Lincoln

February
- **Boat Sport & Travel Show** (early February) 402-466-8102
- **Nebraska Builders Home & Garden Show** (mid-February) 402-423-4225

March
- **Gem & Mineral Show** (late March) 402-472-7564
- **Home Garden & Leisure Show** (mid-March) 402-474-5371
- **Midwest Invitational Tournament** (mid-March) 402-434-9217
- **Shrine Circus** (mid-late March) 402-474-6890

April
- **Spring Affair** (late April) 402-472-2679
- **Taste of Nebraska** (mid-April) 402-483-2630

May
- **Annual Square and Round Dance Festival** (early May) 402-434-5335
- **Downtown Performance Series** (May-September) 402-434-6900
- **Haymarket Farmers Market** (May-October) 402-434-6906
- **Lincoln Marathon & Half Marathon** (early May) 402-434-5335 www.lincolnrun.org/marathon

June
- **Downtown Performance Series** (May-September) 402-434-6900
- **Haymarket Farmers Market** (May-October) 402-434-6906
- **Haymarket Heydays** (mid-June) 402-434-6906
- **Jazz in June** (June) 402-472-2540

July
- **Downtown Performance Series** (May-September) 402-434-6900
- **Haymarket Farmers Market** (May-October) 402-434-6906
- **July Jamm** (late July) 402-434-6900
- **Lancaster County Fair & Rodeo** (late July-early August) 402-441-6545

August
- **Downtown Performance Series** (May-September) 402-434-6900
- **Haymarket Farmers Market** (May-October) 402-434-6906
- **Lancaster County Fair & Rodeo** (late July-early August) 402-441-6545
- **Nebraska State Fair** (late August-early September) 402-474-5371

September
- **Downtown Performance Series** (May-September) 402-434-6900
- **Haymarket Farmers Market** (May-October) 402-434-6906
- **Nebraska State Fair** (late August-early September) 402-474-5371

October
- **Boo at the Zoo** (late October) 402-475-6741
- **Haymarket Farmers Market** (May-October) 402-434-6906

November
- **Arts in General** (mid-November) 402-481-5117
- **Holidays in the Haymarket** (mid-November-mid-December) 402-434-6900
- **Winter Lights** (late November) 402-475-6741

December
- **Holidays in the Haymarket** (mid-November-mid-December) 402-434-6900
- **Star City Holiday Parade Weekend Festival** (early December) 402-441-7391
- **Victorian Holidays Past** (December) 402-471-4764

Omaha

January
- **Cathedral Flower Festival** (late January) 402-558-3100

February
- **Omaha Boat Sport & Travel Show** (late February) 402-393-3339

April
- **Spring Festival-An Arts & Crafts Affair** (early April) 402-331-2889

June
- **NCAA World Series** (mid-June) 402-422-1212
- **Nebraska Shakespeare Festival** (mid-June-early July) 402-280-2391
- **Renaissance Faire of the Midlands** (early June) 402-345-5401
- **Shakespeare on the Green** (late June-early July) 402-444-4660
- **Summer Arts Festival** (late June) 402-896-5976

July
- **Jazz on the Green** (early July-August) 402-342-3300
- **Nebraska Shakespeare Festival** (mid-June-early July) 402-280-2391
- **Shakespeare on the Green** (late June-early July) 402-444-4660
- **Westfair!** (mid-July) 712-323-7722

August
- **Jazz on the Green** (early July-August) 402-342-3300
- **Omaha Classic** (early August) 402-399-1800

September
- **River City Roundup** (late September) 402-554-9602
- **Septemberfest** (early September) 402-346-4800

NEVADA

Carson City

January
- **Winter Wine & All That Jazz** (mid-January) 775-687-7410

March
- **Cowboy Jubilee & Poetry** (early March) 775-883-1532
- **Mother Earth Awakening Pow Wow** (mid-March) 775-882-6929

April
- **Eagle Valley Muzzleloaders Spring Rendevous** (late April) 775-887-1221
- **Multi-Cultural Festival** (mid-April) 775-887-3060
- **Rsvp Spring Fun Fair** (late April-early May) 775-687-4680

May
- **Cinco de Mayo Chili Cook Off** (early May) 775-847-0311
- **Comstock Historic Preservation Week** (mid-May) 775-847-0311
- **Kit Carson Trail Walk** (late May-late October) 775-687-7410
- **Robert's House Antique Sale** (May-early October) 775-882-1805
- **Rsvp Spring Fun Fair** (late April-early May) 775-687-4680

June
- **A Taste of Downtown** (late June) 775-883-7654
- **Carson City Rendezvous** (early June) 775-687-7410
- **Carson Valley Days** (early June) 775-782-8144
- **Farmers Market** (June-August) 775-687-7410
- **Father's Day Pow Wow/Arts & Crafts Show** (mid-June) 775-882-6929
- **July 4th Celebration Week** (late June-early July) 775-687-4680
- **Kit Carson Rendezvous & Wagon Train** (mid-June) 775-884-3633
- **Kit Carson Trail Historic Home Tour** (mid-June) 775-687-7410
- **Kit Carson Trail Walk** (late May-late October) 775-687-7410
- **Pony Express Re-ride** (mid-June) 775-882-1283
- **Pops Party Concert** (mid-June) 775-882-1565
- **Robert's House Antique Sale** (May-early October) 775-882-1805
- **Run What You Brung Classic Car Show** (late June) 775-882-0829
- **Stewart Indian School Museum Arts & Crafts Festival & Pow Wow** (mid-June) 775-882-6929

July
- **Carson City IRPA Rodeo** (early July) 775-577-9427
- **Farmers Market** (June-August) 775-687-7410
- **July 4th Celebration Week** (late June-early July) 775-687-4680
- **Kit Carson Trail Walk** (late May-late October) 775-687-7410
- **Lake Tahoe Shakespeare Festival** (late July-late August) 800-747-4697 www.laketahoeshakespeare.com
- **Nevada State Railroad Museum's Transportation Fair** (early July) 775-687-6953
- **Outdoor Movie Film Festival** (July-August) 775-687-6953
- **Robert's House Antique Sale** (May-early October) 775-882-1805
- **Silver Dollar Car Classic** (late July-early August) 775-687-7410
- **Virginia City Rodeo** (late July) 775-847-0311
- **Wa She Shudeh Pow Wow** (late July) 775-265-4191

August
- **Farmers Market** (June-August) 775-687-7410
- **Kit Carson Trail Walk** (late May-late October) 775-687-7410
- **Lake Tahoe Shakespeare Festival** (late July-late August) 800-747-4697 www.laketahoeshakespeare.com
- **Outdoor Movie Film Festival** (July-August) 775-687-6953
- **Robert's House Antique Sale** (May-early October) 775-882-1805
- **Silver Dollar Car Classic** (late July-early August) 775-687-7410

September
- **Carson City Mint/Nevada State Museum Coin Show** (mid-September) 775-687-6953
- **Carson Valley Street Celebration** (mid-September) 775-782-8144
- **Kit Carson Trail Walk** (late May-late October) 775-687-7410
- **Robert's House Antique Sale** (May-early October) 775-882-1805

October
- **High Desert Jazz Festival** (mid-October) 775-883-1976
- **Kit Carson Trail Ghost Walk** (late October) 775-687-7410
- **Kit Carson Trail Walk** (late May-late October) 775-687-7410
- **La Ka L'el Be Pow Wow** (late October) 775-265-4191
- **Nevada Day Celebration** (late October) 775-882-2600
- **Robert's House Antique Sale** (May-early October) 775-882-1805

November
- **Beer Tasting & Auction** (early November) 775-883-1976
- **Silver & Snowflake Festival of Lights** (November) 775-882-1565

December
- **Christmas on the Comstock** (December) 775-847-0311
- **Christmas Tree Lighting** (early December) 775-882-1565
- **Victorian Christmas Home Tour** (mid-December) 775-882-1805

Las Vegas

February
- **Las Vegas International Marathon & Half-Marathon** (February) 702-876-3870 www.lvmarathon.com
- **Las Vegas Mardi Gras** (mid-February) 702-678-5777

March
- **Winston Cup Race** (early March) 702-644-4444

April
- **Big League Weekends** (early April) 702-386-7200
- **Las Vegas Senior Classic** (late April) 702-242-3000
- **Native American Arts Festival** (early April) 702-455-7955
- **World Series of Poker** (late April-mid-May) 702-366-7397

May
- **International Food Festival** (May) 702-258-8961
- **Las Vegas Invitational PGA Golf Tournament** (mid-May) 702-242-3000
- **World Series of Poker** (late April-mid-May) 702-366-7397

September
- **International Mariachi Festival** (mid-September) 800-637-1006

October
- **Columbus Day Parade** (mid-October) 702-892-0711
- **Las Vegas Jaycees State Fair** (early October) 702-457-8832

November
- **Comdex Computer Show** (mid-November) 781-449-6600
- **Fremont Street Holiday Festival** (late November) 800-249-3559 www.vegasexperience.com

December
- **Las Vegas Bowl** (late December) 702-895-3900
- **National Finals Rodeo** (early-mid-December) 702-895-3900
- **Parade of Lights** (early December) 702-293-2034

Reno

June
- **Celebrate the River** (early June) 775-827-7600
- **Far West Regional Wheelchair Tennis Championship** (mid-June) 775-852-7077
- **Hometown Farmers Market** (mid-June-late August) 775-353-2291
- **Reno Rodeo** (mid-June) 775-329-3877 www.renorodeo.org/

July
- **Big Easy** (mid-July) 775-332-3333 www.nevadanet.com/bigeasy/
- **Hometown Farmers Market** (mid-June-late August) 775-353-2291
- **Reno Basque Festival** (late July) 775-329-1476
- **Reno Summer Arts Festival** (July) 775-329-1324 www.artown.org/
- **Skyfire** (July 4) 775-332-3333
- **Uptown Downtown Artown Festival** (July) 775-334-2536

August
- **Best in the West Rib Cook-off** (late August-early September) 775-356-3300
- **Hometown Farmers Market** (mid-June-late August) 775-353-2291
- **Hot August Nights** (early August) 775-356-1956 www.nevadanet.com/hotaugustnights/
- **Nevada State Fair** (late August) 775-688-5767
- **Shakespeare at Sand Harbor** (August) 775-831-0494
- **Silver State Marathon** (late August) 775-849-0419

September
- **Best in the West Rib Cook-off** (late August-early September) 775-356-3300
- **Great Reno Balloon Race** (early September) 775-826-1181 www.nevadanet.com/grbr/
- **National Championship Air Races** (mid-September) 775-972-6663 www.nevadanet.com/airraces/
- **Street Vibrations** (late September) 775-329-7469
- **Virginia City Camel Races** (mid-September) 775-847-0311

October
- **Celtic New Year Celebration** (mid-October) 775-323-3138 www.renoceltic.org/
- **Great Italian Festival** (mid-October) 775-786-5700
- **Lake Tahoe Marathon** (mid-October) 530-544-7095 www.laketahoemarathon.com/
- **Nevada Day Parade** (October 31) 800-367-7366

November
- **National Senior Pro Rodeo Finals** (early-mid-November) 775-323-8842

December
- **Festival of Trees** (early-late December) 775-827-7600
- **Sparks Hometown Christmas** (early December) 775-353-2291

NEW HAMPSHIRE

Concord

June
- **Motorcycle Week-End Show** (mid-June) 603-366-2000
- **Nevers' 2nd Regiment Band Concerts** (late June-mid-July) 603-228-3901
- **Strawberry Moon Festival** (June) 603-224-2508

July
- **Canterbury Country Fair** (late July) 603-783-9955
- **Nevers' 2nd Regiment Band Concerts** (late June-mid-July) 603-228-3901
- **Race Fever Street Festival** (early July) 603-224-2508
- **Summer Market Days** (July) 603-224-2508

August
- **Craftsmen's Fair** (early August) 603-224-1471
- **Hopkinton State Fair** (late August-early September) 603-746-4191
- **Old Time Fiddling Championship** (late August) 603-225-5512
- **Peanut Carnival** (early August) 603-225-8690

September
- **Hopkinton State Fair** (late August-early September) 603-746-4191

October
- **Harvest Moon Festival** (October) 603-456-2600

Manchester

July
- **Downtown Syncopation Summer Concert Series** (early July-late August) 603-645-6285

August
- **Downtown Syncopation Summer Concert Series** (early July-late August) 603-645-6285

September
- **Riverfest** (mid-September) 603-666-6600

November
- **Winter Craft Festival** (late November) 603-224-3375

NEW JERSEY

Atlantic City

January
Grand Christmas Exhibition (November-January) 800-998-4552
Sail Expo (late January) 609-449-2000

February
Atlantic City Classic Car Auction (mid-February) 856-768-6900
Atlantic City International Power Boat Show (early February) 609-449-2000
Winter Crafts Show (late February) 609-965-2111

March
Atlantique City Spring Festival (late March) 609-926-1800
Saint Patrick's Day Parade (mid-March) 609-347-5427

April
Atlantic City Archery Classic (late April) 609-343-5043
Easter Weekend Festival & Parade (mid-April) 609-344-7855

May
American Indian Arts Festival (late May-early October) 609-261-4747

June
American Indian Arts Festival (late May-early October) 609-261-4747
Beachfest (mid-June) 609-484-9020
Boardwalk Festival of the Arts Show (mid-June) 609-344-7855
New Jersey Fresh Seafood Festival (early June) 609-348-7100
Red White & Blueberry Festival (late June) 609-561-9080

July
American Indian Arts Festival (late May-early October) 609-261-4747
Fourth of July Celebration (July 4) 609-347-5427
Kentucky Avenue Festival (mid-July) 609-348-7100
Mount Carmel Festival (mid-July) 609-561-0180

August
American Indian Arts Festival (late May-early October) 609-261-4747
Fall Harvest Grape Stomping Festival (early August-early October) 609-965-2111
Ocean Life Festival (early August) 609-449-7130

September
American Indian Arts Festival (late May-early October) 609-261-4747
Boardwalk Indian Summer Craft Show (mid-September) ... 609-347-5837
Fall Harvest Grape Stomping Festival (early August-early October) 609-965-2111
Latino Festival (early September) 609-345-2772
Miss America Pageant (mid-September) 609-345-7571
www.missamerica.org

October
American Indian Arts Festival (late May-early October) 609-261-4747
Atlantic City Marathon Festival (mid-October) 609-601-1786
www.virtualac.com/marathon
Atlantique City Fall Festival (mid-October) 609-926-1800
East Coast International Auto Show (early October) 609-883-5056
Fall Harvest Grape Stomping Festival (early August-early October) 609-965-2111
Oktoberfest (early October) 609-348-7100
Wheaton Village Craft Show (early October) 800-998-4552

November
Grand Christmas Exhibition (November-January) 800-998-4552
Ocean City Doll Show (late November) 609-525-9300

December
Grand Christmas Exhibition (November-January) 800-998-4552

Jersey City

March
Cathedral Arts Festival (mid-March) 201-659-2211

May
Communipaw Commemoratives (mid-May & mid-September) 201-915-3401

June
Cultural Arts Festival (mid-June) 201-547-5522

September
Communipaw Commemoratives (mid-May & mid-September) 201-915-3401
Egyptian Festival (mid-September) 201-547-5522
Greek Festival (early September) 201-547-5522
Irish Festival (late September) 201-547-5522
Italian Festival (mid-September) 201-547-5522
Korean Festival (late September) 201-547-5522
New Jersey Ethnic & Diversity Festival (late September) .. 609-777-0999

October
Artists' Studio Tour (early October) 201-547-6969

Newark

February
Flower & Garden Show (late February-early March) 732-469-4000

March
Flower & Garden Show (late February-early March) 732-469-4000

June
Newark Black Film Festival (late June-early August) 973-596-6550

July
Newark Black Film Festival (late June-early August) 973-596-6550

August
Newark Black Film Festival (late June-early August) 973-596-6550

September
Newark Festival of People (early September) 973-733-8004

November
Junior Museum Festival (late November) 973-596-6550

December
Newark Jazz Connection (early December) 973-733-6454

Paterson

June
Wayne Days (mid-June) 973-628-9183

July
Jazz It Up Festival (late July) 973-523-9201
Peruvian Festival & Parade (late July) 973-523-9201

August
Puerto Rican Festival & Parade (late August) 973-523-9201

September
Great Falls Festival (Labor Day weekend) 973-523-9201

Trenton

January
Super Science Weekend (January) 609-984-0676

June
First Union Classic The (early June) 609-777-1770
Heritage Days (June) 609-777-1770

August
Trenton Jazz Festival (late August) 609-777-1770
www.trentonnj.com/trentonjazz/index.html

December
Crossing The (December 25) 215-493-4076

NEW MEXICO

Albuquerque

January
Crossroads Winter Championship Series (mid-late January) 505-632-2287

March
Fiery Food Show (early March) 505-298-3835
www.fiery-foods.com/ffshow/
Indian Festival of Living Arts (late March) 505-843-7270
Rio Grande Arts & Crafts Festival (mid-March) 505-292-7457
www.riograndefestivals.com

April
American Indian Week (late April) 505-843-7270
Children's Fair (late April) 505-767-6700
Gathering of Nations Pow Wow (late April) 505-836-2810
www.gatheringofnations.com

May
Herb & Wildflower Festival (mid-May) 505-344-7240
Magnifico! Albuquerque Festival of the Arts (mid-May) 505-842-9918
Run for the Zoo (early May) 505-764-6200

June
Father's Day Multi-Cultural Festival (late June) 505-843-7270
Festival Flamenco Internacional (early-mid-June) 505-344-8695
New Mexico Arts & Crafts Fair (late June) 505-884-9043

August
Las Fiestas de San Lorenzo (mid-August) 505-867-3311
Summer Festival & Frontier Market (early August) 505-471-2261

September
Bernalillo Wine Festival (early September) 505-867-3311
Duke City Marathon (late September) 505-768-3483
New Mexico State Fair (mid-late September) 505-265-1791
www.nmstatefair.com

October
Albuquerque International Balloon Fiesta (early-mid-October) 800-284-2282
www.aibf.org/
Grecian Festival (early October) 505-247-9411
International Arabian Horse Show (late October) 800-733-9918

San Felipe Pueblo Arts & Crafts Show (early October) 505-842-9918
Santa Fe Furniture Expo (early October) 800-299-9886

November
Holiday Ole (mid-November) 505-881-0199
Southwest Arts Festival (mid-November) 505-875-1748
Weems Artfest (mid-November) 505-293-6133
Ye Merry Olde Christmas Faire (late November) 505-856-1970
Zia Arts & Crafts Festival (late November) 505-842-9918

December
Holiday Parade (early December) 505-768-3483
Indian Pueblo Christmas Celebrations (late December) 505-843-7270

Las Cruces

January
Dearholt Desert Trail Run (mid-January) 505-524-7824

March
Nostalgia Club Antique & Collectible Show (mid-September & mid-March) 505-526-8624
Run Old Mesilla (late March) 505-524-7824

April
Frontier Days (mid-late April) 505-526-8911
Gus Macker 3-on-3 Basketball Tournament (April) 505-525-2796
MVTC Triathalon (mid-April) 505-524-7824

May
Cinco de Mayo Fiesta (early May) 505-524-3262
New Mexico Wine & Chile War Festival (late May) 505-646-4543
Picacho Street Antique & Collectible Flea Market (late May) 505-526-8624

June
Juneteenth Celebration (mid-late June) 505-524-2906
San Juan Fiesta (late June) 505-526-8171
Serra Club Antique & Collectible Show (early June) 505-526-8624

July
Burn Lake Triathalon (mid-July) 505-541-2554
Christmas in July (mid-July) 505-528-3276
Fourth of July Celebration (July 4) 505-528-3149
Independence Day Run (July 4) 505-541-2554

August
Great American People Race (late August) 505-544-0469

September
Arts Hop (mid-September) 505-523-6403
Diez y Sies de Septembre Fiesta (mid-September) 505-524-3262
Harvest of Fun (mid-September) 505-528-3276
Nostalgia Club Antique & Collectible Show (mid-September & mid-March) 505-526-8624
Oktoberfest (late September) 505-524-8032
Southern New Mexico State Fair (late September) 505-524-8612

October
Fort Selden Riverwalk (late October) 505-524-8032
La Viña Wine Festival (early October) 505-882-7632
Whole Enchilada Fiesta (early October) 505-647-1228

November
Baylor Pass Mountain Trail Run (mid-November) 505-524-7824
Las Cruces International Mariachi Conference (mid-November) 505-523-2681
Nutcracker Suite (early November) 505-524-8032
Renaissance Craftfaire (early November) 505-523-6403
Saint Genevieve's Antique & Craft Show (late November) 505-526-8624
Turkey Trot (late November) 505-524-7824

December
Christmas Carols & Luminaries on the Plaza (December 24) 505-524-3262
Christmas Lights Guided Night Walk (mid-December) 505-524-8032
Old Fashion Christmas (mid-December) 505-528-3276

Santa Fe

January
San Ildefonso Feast Day Celebration (late January) 505-455-2273
Winter Fiesta (late January-early February) 505-983-5615

February
Winter Fiesta (late January-early February) 505-983-5615

March
Pro Musica Holy Week Baroque Festival (late March-early April) 505-988-4640

April
Pro Musica Holy Week Baroque Festival (late March-early April) 505-988-4640

May
Santa Fe Bicycle Trek (mid-May) 505-982-1282
Santa Fe Century Bike Ride (mid-May) 505-982-1282
Taste of Santa Fe (early May) 505-984-6760

June
San Juan Feast Day Celebration (late June) 505-852-4400
Santa Fe Air Show (early-mid-June) 505-471-5111
www.santafeairshow.com
Spring Festival (June) 505-471-2261

NEW MEXICO — Santa Fe (Cont'd)

July
- **Behind Adobe Walls House Tours** (late July-mid-August) 505-982-9301
- **Eight Northern Indian Pueblos Artists & Craftsmen Show** (mid-July) 505-852-4265
- **High Country Arts & Crafts Festival** (early July) 505-587-2519
- **Rodeo de Santa Fe** (mid-July) 505-471-4300
- **Santa Fe Chamber Music Festival** (mid-July-mid-August) 505-983-2075 www.santafechambermusic.org
- **Santa Fe Wine Festival** (early July) 505-471-2261
- **Traditional Spanish Market** (late July) 505-983-4038

August
- **Antique Ethnographic Show** (mid-August) 505-992-8929
- **Antique Indian Art Show & Sale** (mid-August) 505-992-8929
- **Behind Adobe Walls House Tours** (late July-mid-August) 505-982-9301
- **Buffalo Roast** (mid-August) 505-827-6474
- **Mountain Man Trade Fair** (mid-August) 505-476-5100
- **Old West Show & Sale** (mid-August) 505-992-8929
- **Picuris Feast Day Celebration** (mid-August) 505-984-6760
- **Santa Clara Feast Day Celebration** (early August) 505-753-7326
- **Santa Fe Bluegrass & Old Time Music Festival** (late August) 505-984-6760
- **Santa Fe Chamber Music Festival** (mid-July-mid-August) 505-983-2075 www.santafechambermusic.org
- **Santa Fe Indian Market** (late August) 505-983-5220 www.swaia.org/imarket.htm

September
- **Festival de Santa Fe** (early September) 505-988-7575
- **Santa Fe Trail** (September) 505-438-1464
- **Santa Fe Wine & Chile Fiesta** (late September) 505-982-8686
- **Taos Feast Day Celebration** (late September) 505-984-6760

October
- **Nambe Feast Day Celebration** (early October) 505-455-2036

November
- **Tesque Feast Day Celebration** (early November) 505-983-2667

December
- **Pojoaque Feast Day Celebration** (early December) 505-455-2278

NEW YORK

Albany

January
- **Grand Union Food Show** (mid-January) 518-473-0559
- **Mid-Winter Blues Festival** (mid-late January) 518-473-1845
- **Winterfest** (late January) 518-584-3255

February
- **Albany American Wine Festival** (early February) 518-452-0707
- **Great Northeast Home Show** (early February) 518-383-6183
- **New York in Bloom** (mid-February) 518-434-1217

March
- **Capital District Garden & Flower Show** (mid-March) 518-434-1217
- **Great American International Auto Show** (early March) 518-452-0584
- **New York State Chocolate Festival** (late March) 518-434-1217
- **Northeast Great Outdoors Show** (late March) 518-383-6183

April
- **Capital Springfest** (April-May) 800-258-3582

May
- **Capital Springfest** (April-May) 800-258-3582
- **Tulip Festival** (early May) 518-434-2032
- **Waterford/RiverSpark Canalfest** (early May) 518-237-7999

June
- **Alive at Five Concert Series** (early June-early July) 518-434-1217
- **House & Garden Tour** (mid-June) 518-436-9826
- **Old Songs Festival of Traditional Music & Dance** (late June) 518-765-2815
- **Riverfront Arts Festival** (mid-June) 518-273-0552

July
- **Alive at Five Concert Series** (early June-early July) 518-434-1217
- **Fabulous Fourth Festivities** (July 4) 518-473-0559
- **Fleet Blues Fest** (mid-July) 518-434-1217
- **Independence Day Celebration** (July 4) 518-473-0559

August
- **Altamont Fair** (mid-August) 518-861-6671
- **Empire State African American Cultural Festival** (early August) 518-473-0559
- **International Food Festival** (mid-late August) 518-434-1217
- **Italian Festival** (early August) 518-456-0292

September
- **Capital District Scottish Games** (early September) 518-438-4297 techage.com/cdsg/
- **Lark Street Festival** (mid-September) 518-482-2203
- **Shaker Heritage Society Craft & Harvest Festival** (late September) 518-456-7890

October
- **Victorian Spring Ball** (late October) 518-583-7224

November
- **Capital Holiday** (late November-late December) 800-258-3582
- **Festival of Trees** (late November-early December) 518-463-4478
- **Great New York State Snow & Travel Expo** (early November) 518-383-6183

December
- **Capital Holiday** (late November-late December) 800-258-3582
- **Festival of Trees** (late November-early December) 518-463-4478
- **First Night Albany** (December 31) 518-434-1217

Buffalo

January
- **Festival of Lights** (early November-January) 800-421-5223

February
- **Ice Castle Extravaganza/Winter Festival** (mid-February) 716-357-4569

March
- **Saint Patrick's Day Parade** (mid-March) 716-825-9535

April
- **Dingus Day** (early April) 716-852-0511

May
- **Antique World Expo** (late May & late August) 716-759-8483
- **Buffalo Marathon** (early May) 716-837-7223
- **Hellenic Festival** (mid-May) 800-283-3256

June
- **Allentown Art Festival** (mid-June) 716-881-4269
- **Friendship Festival** (late June-early July) 716-852-0511
- **Juneteenth** (mid-June) 716-691-8106
- **Shakespeare in Delaware Park** (late June-August) 716-876-7430 www.thebard.org

July
- **Art & Music Festival** (late July) 716-924-5848
- **Blues Festival** (late July) 716-855-8800
- **Canal Fest of the Tonawandas** (late July) 716-692-3292 www.canalfest.org
- **Friendship Festival** (late June-early July) 716-852-0511
- **Italian Festival** (mid-July) 716-874-6133
- **Italian Heritage & Food Festival** (mid-July) 716-851-4144
- **Quaker Days** (mid-July) 716-662-3366
- **Shakespeare in Delaware Park** (late June-August) 716-876-7430 www.thebard.org
- **Taste of Buffalo** (mid-July) 716-831-9376
- **Waterfront Festival Summer Concert Series** (July-August) 716-884-8865

August
- **Antique World Expo** (late May & late August) 716-759-8483
- **Caribbean Festival** (mid-August) 716-881-3266
- **Erie County Fair & Expo** (mid-August) 716-649-3900 www.ecfair.org
- **Hawk Creek Wildlife Weekend** (early August) 716-652-8646
- **Polish American Arts Festival** (mid-August) 716-686-3930
- **Shakespeare in Delaware Park** (late June-August) 716-876-7430 www.thebard.org
- **Traditional German-American Festival** (late August) 716-684-4745
- **Waterfront Festival Summer Concert Series** (July-August) 716-884-8865

October
- **Shocktober** (late October) 716-852-0511
- **World Pumpkin Weigh-off** (early October) 716-759-2260

November
- **Festival of Lights** (early November-January) 800-421-5223
- **Friendship Tree Lighting** (late November) 716-852-0511

December
- **Festival of Lights** (early November-January) 800-421-5223
- **First Night Buffalo** (December 31) 716-852-0511
- **Victorian Christmas Festival** (early December) 607-587-9441

New York

January
- **Big Apple Circus** (late October-mid-January) 212-268-2500
- **Empire State Building Holiday Lights** (December-early January) 212-736-3100
- **Lincoln Center Family Art Show** (mid-December-early January) 212-875-5151
- **National Black Fine Art Show** (late January) 212-777-5218
- **New York National Boat Show** (early-mid-January) 212-984-7070
- **Outsider Art Fair** (late January) 212-777-5218
- **Radio City Christmas Spectacular** (November-January) 212-247-4777
- **Seafest** (September-June) 212-245-0072
- **Winter Wildlife Holiday Lights** (late November-early January) 718-367-1010

February
- **Chinese New Year Celebrations** (early-mid-February) 212-431-9740
- **New York Restaurant & Foodservice Show** (late February) 212-216-2000
- **Passports to Off Broadway Theatres** (February-April) 212-768-1818
- **Seafest** (September-June) 212-245-0072

March
- **Art Expo New York** (early March & mid-September) 212-216-2000
- **New York Underground Film Festival** (mid-March) 212-925-3440 www.nyuff.com
- **Passports to Off Broadway Theatres** (February-April) 212-768-1818
- **Saint Patrick's Day Parade** (mid-March) 212-484-1222
- **Seafest** (September-June) 212-245-0072

April
- **African Film Festival** (mid-late April) 718-638-5000
- **Crafts on Columbus** (late April-early May) 212-866-2239
- **Earth Day New York** (April 22) 212-922-0048 home.dti.net/earthday/events99.html
- **Gen Art Film Festival** (late April-early May) 212-290-0312 www.genart.org/
- **Passports to Off Broadway Theatres** (February-April) 212-768-1818
- **Seafest** (September-June) 212-245-0072

May
- **9th Avenue International Food Festival** (mid-May) 212-581-7217
- **Brooklyn Botanical Garden Center Flower Sale** (early May) 718-622-4433
- **Crafts on Columbus** (late April-early May) 212-866-2239
- **Gen Art Film Festival** (late April-early May) 212-290-0312 www.genart.org/
- **Seafest** (September-June) 212-245-0072

June
- **American Crafts Festival** (mid-June) 212-875-5000
- **Bell Atlantic Jazz Festival** (early-mid-June) 212-219-3006
- **Belmont Stakes** (early June) 718-641-4700
- **Bryant Park Summer Film Festival** (mid-June-August) 212-512-5700
- **JVC Jazz Festival** (mid-late June) 212-501-1390
- **New York Lesbian & Gay Film Festival** (early-mid-June) 212-254-7228
- **Queens Day Festival** (mid-June) 718-886-5069
- **Seafest** (September-June) 212-245-0072
- **Shakespeare in the Park** (late June-late August) 212-539-8500
- **SummerStage** (mid-June-early August) 212-360-2777
- **Welcome Back to Brooklyn Festival** (mid-June) 718-855-7882

July
- **4th of July Concert in Battery Park** (July 4) 212-835-2789
- **Bryant Park Summer Film Festival** (mid-June-August) 212-512-5700
- **Celebrate Brooklyn Festival** (July-late August) 718-855-7882
- **Great July 4th Festival** (July 4) 212-809-4900
- **Lincoln Center Festival** (early-late July) 212-875-5000 www.lincolncenter.org/festival/
- **Macy's Fireworks Celebration** (July 4) 212-695-4400
- **Mostly Mozart Festival** (late July-mid-August) 212-875-5030
- **Shakespeare in the Park** (late June-late August) 212-539-8500
- **SummerStage** (mid-June-early August) 212-360-2777
- **Washington Square Music Festival** (July) 212-431-1088

August
- **Bryant Park Summer Film Festival** (mid-June-August) 212-512-5700
- **Celebrate Brooklyn Festival** (July-late August) 718-855-7882
- **Mostly Mozart Festival** (late July-mid-August) 212-875-5030
- **Shakespeare in the Park** (late June-late August) 212-539-8500
- **SummerStage** (mid-June-early August) 212-360-2777
- **US Open Tennis Championships** (late August-mid-September) 718-760-6200 www.usopen.org

September
- **Art Expo New York** (early March & mid-September) 212-216-2000
- **New York Film Festival** (late September-mid-October) 212-875-5610 www.filmlinc.com/nyff/nyff.htm
- **Seafest** (September-June) 212-245-0072
- **US Open Tennis Championships** (late August-mid-September) 718-760-6200 www.usopen.org

October
- **5th Avenue Art & Antiques Show** (mid-October) 212-249-4865
- **Big Apple Circus** (late October-mid-January) 212-268-2500
- **Chrysanthemum & Bonsai Festival** (mid-October) 718-817-8700
- **Greenwich Village Halloween Parade** (late October) 914-758-5519
- **New York Film Festival** (late September-mid-October) 212-875-5610 www.filmlinc.com/nyff/nyff.htm
- **Seafest** (September-June) 212-245-0072

November
- **Big Apple Circus** (late October-mid-January) 212-268-2500
- **Macy's Thanksgiving Day Parade** (late November) 212-494-5432
- **New York Marathon** (early November) 212-860-4455 www.nyrrc.org
- **Radio City Christmas Spectacular** (November-January) 212-247-4777
- **Seafest** (September-June) 212-245-0072
- **Winter Wildlife Holiday Lights** (late November-early January) 718-367-1010

December
- **Big Apple Circus** (late October-mid-January) 212-268-2500
- **Empire State Building Holiday Lights** (December-early January) 212-736-3100
- **First Night New York** (December 31) 212-818-1777
- **Lincoln Center Family Art Show** (mid-December-early January) 212-875-5151
- **New Year's Eve Celebration & Ball Drop in Times Square** (December 31) 212-768-1560
- **Paul Winter's Winter Solstice Celebration** (mid-December) 212-662-2133
- **Radio City Christmas Spectacular** (November-January) 212-247-4777
- **Rockefeller Center Christmas Tree Lighting** (early December) 212-332-6500
- **Seafest** (September-June) 212-245-0072
- **Winter Wildlife Holiday Lights** (late November-early January) 718-367-1010

Rochester

January
- **Festival of Lights** (mid-November-early January) 716-394-4922

May
- **Flower City Market Days** (mid-May-mid-June) 716-428-6907
- **Lilac Festival** (mid-late May) 716-546-3070 www.roch.com/lilacfestival/

June
- **Flower City Market Days** (mid-May-mid-June) 716-428-6907
- **Harbor Festival** (late June) 716-428-6690

NEW YORK — Rochester (Cont'd)

Maplewood Rose Festival (mid-June) ... 716-428-6690
Rochester HarborFest (late June) ... 716-865-3320
Rochester International LPGA Tournament (early-mid-June) ... 716-427-7040

July
Corn Hill Arts Festival (mid-July) ... 716-262-3142
Historic Hill Cumorah Pageant (early & mid-July) ... 315-597-6808
Monroe County Fair (late July-early August) ... 716-334-4000
Park Avenue Festival (late July-early August) ... 716-428-6690
Time Warner MusicFest (mid-July) ... 716-428-6690

August
Monroe County Fair (late July-early August) ... 716-334-4000
Park Avenue Festival (late July-early August) ... 716-428-6690
Rochester Air Show (late August) ... 716-256-4960

September
Clothesline Art Festival (mid-September) ... 716-473-7720

October
Celebrate Your Roots at the Market (early October) ... 716-428-6907
Ghost Walk (mid-late October) ... 716-546-7029
Hilton Apple Fest (early October) ... 716-392-7773
Rochester River Romance (early October) ... 716-428-6690

November
Dickens Old Fashioned Christmas Festival (mid-November-late December) ... 716-392-3456
Festival of Lights (mid-November-early January) ... 716-394-4922

December
Dickens Old Fashioned Christmas Festival (mid-November-late December) ... 716-392-3456
Festival of Lights (mid-November-early January) ... 716-394-4922
Yuletide in the Country (early-mid-December) ... 716-538-6822

Syracuse

January
Lights on the Lake (late November-early January) ... 315-451-7275

February
Winterfest (mid-February) ... 315-470-1900

March
International Auto Show Expo (mid-March) ... 315-487-7711
Saint Patrick's Day Parade (mid-March) ... 315-448-8044

June
Downtown Farmer's Market (mid-June-October) ... 315-422-8284
Hot Air Balloon Festival (mid-June) ... 315-451-7275
Syracuse International Horse Show (late June) ... 315-487-7711
Syracuse Jazz Fest (late June) ... 315-422-8284
www.syracusejazzfest.com
Thornden Rose Festival (mid-June) ... 315-473-4330

July
Arabian Horse Championship (mid-July) ... 315-487-7711
Downtown Farmer's Market (mid-June-October) ... 315-422-8284
Festival of Centuries (late July) ... 315-453-6767
Great American Antiquefest (mid-July) ... 315-451-7275
New York State Rhythm & Blues Fest (mid-July) ... 315-470-1910
Pops in the Park (July) ... 315-473-4330
Summerfame (mid-July-mid-August) ... 315-963-4249
Syracuse Arts and Crafts Festival (mid-July) ... 315-422-8284
Taste of Syracuse (early July) ... 315-484-1123

August
Downtown Farmer's Market (mid-June-October) ... 315-422-8284
Empire Appaloosa Show (early August) ... 315-487-7711
Great New York State Fair (late August-early September) ... 315-487-7711
www.nysfair.org
Summerfame (mid-July-mid-August) ... 315-963-4249

September
Autumn in New York Horse Show (late September-early October) ... 315-487-7711
Downtown Farmer's Market (mid-June-October) ... 315-422-8284
Golden Harvest Festival (mid-September) ... 315-638-2519
Great New York State Fair (late August-early September) ... 315-487-7711
www.nysfair.org
Harvest Happenings (mid-September) ... 315-435-8511
New York Morgan Horse Show (mid-September) ... 315-487-7711
Oktoberfest (mid-September) ... 315-451-7275

October
Autumn in New York Horse Show (late September-early October) ... 315-487-7711
Downtown Farmer's Market (mid-June-October) ... 315-422-8284
Zoo Boo (late October) ... 315-435-8511

November
Lights on the Lake (late November-early January) ... 315-451-7275

December
Holiday Festival of Trees (early December) ... 315-474-6064
Lights on the Lake (late November-early January) ... 315-451-7275

Yonkers

May
Westchester County Fair (late May-early June) ... 914-968-4200

June
Westchester County Fair (late May-early June) ... 914-968-4200

July
Untermyer Performing Arts Festival (early July-mid-August) ... 914-377-6442

August
Untermyer Performing Arts Festival (early July-mid-August) ... 914-377-6442

September
Yonkers Hudson Riverfest (mid-September) ... 914-377-3378

NORTH CAROLINA

Asheville

January
Candlelight Christmas Evenings (early November-early January) ... 800-543-2961
Christmas at Biltmore Estate (late November-early January) ... 800-543-2961
www.biltmore.com

February
Arts & Crafts Antique Conference (mid-February) ... 800-257-1300
Hands On Asheville (early February-late March) ... 800-280-0005
Winter Pastimes: The Arts in America's Largest Home (early February-early May) ... 800-543-2961

March
Biltmore Estate's Easter Egg Hunt (late March) ... 800-543-2961
www.biltmore.com
Comedy Classic Weekend (early March) ... 828-252-2711
Hands On Asheville (early February-late March) ... 800-280-0005
Winter Pastimes: The Arts in America's Largest Home (early February-early May) ... 800-543-2961

April
Biltmore Estate's Festival of Flowers (early April-early May) ... 800-543-2961
www.biltmore.com
Winter Pastimes: The Arts in America's Largest Home (early February-early May) ... 800-543-2961

May
Biltmore Estate's Festival of Flowers (early April-early May) ... 800-543-2961
www.biltmore.com
Black Mountain Music Festival (late May & mid-October) ... 828-281-3382
Days in the Gardens (early May) ... 828-252-5190
Great Smoky Mountain Trout Festival (late May) ... 828-456-3575
Lake Eden Arts Festival (late May) ... 828-686-8742
www.theleaf.com
Spring Herb Festival (early May) ... 828-689-5974
Spring Wildflower & Bird Pilgrimage (early May) ... 828-251-6444
Very Special Arts Festival (early May) ... 828-298-7484
Winery Al Fresco Jazz Celebration (late May) ... 800-543-2961
Winter Pastimes: The Arts in America's Largest Home (early February-early May) ... 800-543-2961

June
Happy Trails Week (mid-June) ... 828-877-3130

July
Bele Chere Festival (late July) ... 828-258-6111
Craft Fair of the Southern Highlands (mid-July) ... 828-298-7928
Fourth of July Celebration (July 4) ... 828-259-5800
Red White & Blues at the Winery (early July) ... 800-543-2961

August
Big Band Dance Weekend (late August) ... 800-438-5800
Goombay Festival (late August) ... 828-252-4614
Mountain Dance & Folk Festival (early August) ... 828-258-6101
Village Art & Craft Fair (early August) ... 828-274-2831

September
Jazz Weekends at the Winery (late September-late October) ... 800-543-2961
Michaelmas Fair (late September-late October) ... 800-543-2961
OctoberFest (late September) ... 800-438-5800
Wonderful Winery Weekend (early September) ... 800-543-2961

October
Asheville Greek Festival (early October) ... 828-299-7244
Black Mountain Music Festival (late May & mid-October) ... 828-281-3382
Forest Festival Day (early October) ... 828-877-3130
Jazz Weekends at the Winery (late September-late October) ... 800-543-2961
Michaelmas Fair (late September-late October) ... 800-543-2961
Thomas Wolfe Festival (early October) ... 828-253-8304

November
Asheville Christmas Parade (late November) ... 828-251-4117
Candlelight Christmas Evenings (early November-early January) ... 800-543-2961
Christmas at Biltmore Estate (late November-early January) ... 800-543-2961
www.biltmore.com
Christmas Parade (late November) ... 828-259-5800
High Country Christmas Art & Craft Show (late November) ... 828-254-0072
Light Up Your Holidays (late November-late December) ... 828-259-5800

December
Candlelight Christmas Evenings (early November-early January) ... 800-543-2961
Christmas at Biltmore Estate (late November-early January) ... 800-543-2961
www.biltmore.com
First Night Asheville (December 31) ... 828-259-5800
Light Up Your Holidays (late November-late December) ... 828-259-5800

Charlotte

January
Festival of Lights (late November-early January) ... 704-331-2701
www.lattaplantation.org

February
Mid-Atlantic Boat Show (early February) ... 704-339-6000
Southern Farm Show (early February) ... 704-376-6594
Southern Spring Show (late February-early March) ... 704-376-6594

March
Charlotte Festival-New Plays in America Series (early March) ... 704-372-1000
Southern Spring Show (late February-early March) ... 704-376-6594

April
AutoFair 1 (early April) ... 704-455-3200
www.charlottemotorspeedway.com
Center CityFest Outdoor Festival (late April) ... 704-483-6266
Charlotte Observer Marathon (early April) ... 704-358-5425
Charlotte Steeplechase Races (late April) ... 704-423-3400
Great American Antique & Collectible Spectacular (early April & early November) ... 704-596-4643
Home Depot Invitational (late April) ... 704-846-4699
Loch Norman Highland Games (mid-April) ... 704-875-3113
Mint Museum Home & Garden Tour (mid-April) ... 704-337-2000
Southern Ideal Home Show (early April) ... 704-376-6594

May
Blooming Arts Festival (early May) ... 704-283-2784
Charlotte Film & Video Festival (early-mid-May) ... 704-337-2000
Coca-Cola 600 (late May) ... 704-455-3200
Lake Norman Festival (mid-May) ... 704-664-3898
Nascar Parade & Speed Street Festival (late May) ... 704-455-6814
www.600festival.com
Qualifying Races for Winston No Bull Twin 25s (late May) ... 704-455-3200
www.charlottemotorspeedway.com
Winston ARCA Race (late May) ... 704-455-3200
www.charlottemotorspeedway.com

June
Antiques Spectacular (early June & early November) ... 704-596-4643
Legends Summer Shootout Auto Racing Series (June-August) ... 704-455-3200
www.charlottemotorspeedway.com

July
Grandfather Mountain Highland Games (mid-July) ... 828-733-1333
July 4th Fireworks (July 4) ... 704-334-2282
Legends Summer Shootout Auto Racing Series (June-August) ... 704-455-3200
www.charlottemotorspeedway.com
WBT Skyshow (July 4) ... 704-374-3500

August
Legends Summer Shootout Auto Racing Series (June-August) ... 704-455-3200
www.charlottemotorspeedway.com

September
Christian Music Festival (late September) ... 704-588-2600
Festival in the Park (mid-September) ... 704-331-2700
International Festival (late September) ... 704-547-2407
LakeFest (mid-September) ... 704-892-1922
National Balloon Rally & Hot Air Balloon Festival (mid-September) ... 704-873-2893
Southeastern Origami Festival (late September) ... 704-375-3692

October
Carolina Renaissance Festival (early October-mid-November) ... 704-896-5555
Good Guys Southeastern Rod & Custom Car Show (late October) ... 704-455-3200
www.charlottemotorspeedway.com
North American Karting Championships (mid-October) ... 704-455-3200
www.charlottemotorspeedway.com

November
Antiques Spectacular (early June & early November) ... 704-596-4643
Carolina Renaissance Festival (early October-mid-November) ... 704-896-5555
Carolina's Carrousel Parade (late November) ... 800-231-4636
Charlotte International Auto Show (mid-November) ... 704-364-1078
Country Christmas Classic Craft and Gift Show (late November) ... 704-596-4643
Festival of Lights (late November-early January) ... 704-331-2701
www.lattaplantation.org
Great American Antique & Collectible Spectacular (early April & early November) ... 704-596-4643
Latta Plantation Holiday Festival (late November) ... 704-875-2312
www.lattaplantation.org
Southern Christmas Show (mid-late November) ... 704-376-6594

NORTH CAROLINA — Charlotte (Cont'd)

December
4th Ward Christmas Tour (early December) 704-372-0282
Festival of Lights (late November-early January) 704-331-2701
www.lattaplantation.org
Holiday Skylights Tree Lighting Ceremony (early December) 704-378-1335
Shrine Bowl of the Carolinas (mid-December) 704-547-1414

Durham

January
KwanzaaFest (early January) 919-560-2729
North Carolina International Jazz Festival (late January-late April) 919-660-3300

February
Native American Pow Wow (mid-February) 919-286-3366
North Carolina International Jazz Festival (late January-late April) 919-660-3300

March
CROP Walk (late March) 919-688-3843
North Carolina International Jazz Festival (late January-late April) 919-660-3300

April
Double Take Film Festival (early April) 919-660-3699
North Carolina International Jazz Festival (late January-late April) 919-660-3300

May
Air Expo (early May) 919-840-2100
Bimbe Festival (late May) 919-560-4355
Pine Cone's Old Time Bluegrass Music Festival (early May) 919-990-1900
Summer Festival of Creative Arts (late May-mid-August) 919-684-4741

June
American Dance Festival (mid-June-late July) 919-684-6402
americandancefestival.org
Brightleaf Music Workshop & Finale (late June-early August) 919-493-0385
Edible Arts Festival of Food & Art (early June) 919-560-2787
Summer Festival of Creative Arts (late May-mid-August) 919-684-4741

July
American Dance Festival (mid-June-late July) 919-684-6402
americandancefestival.org
Brightleaf Music Workshop & Finale (late June-early August) 919-493-0385
Festival for the Eno (early July) 919-477-4549
Summer Festival of Creative Arts (late May-mid-August) 919-684-4741

August
Brightleaf Music Workshop & Finale (late June-early August) 919-493-0385
Summer Festival of Creative Arts (late May-mid-August) 919-684-4741

September
Bull Durham Blues Festival (mid-September) 919-683-1709
Centerfest (mid-September) 919-560-2722
Triangle Triumph Road Race (late September) 919-990-7938

Greensboro

January
African-American Arts Festival (mid-January-mid-March) 336-373-7523
Artists Hang-Up & Put-Down (mid-late January) 336-333-7460
Holiday of Lights (early January) 919-839-2443
US Hot Rod Monster Jam (late January) 336-373-7400

February
African-American Arts Festival (mid-January-mid-March) 336-373-7523
Seafest (mid-February) 336-288-3769

March
African-American Arts Festival (mid-January-mid-March) 336-373-7523
Eastern Music Festival Wine Tasting (late March) 336-333-7450
Re-Enactment of the Battle of Guilford Courthouse (mid-March) 336-545-5315

April
Greater Greensboro Chrysler Classic (mid-April) 336-379-1570
Home & Garden Tour (mid-April) 336-292-0057
Oak Ridge Easter Horse Show (mid-April) 336-643-4151
Serendipity Weekend (mid-April) 336-316-2301
Street Rod Safari (mid-April) 800-488-0444
Tulip Days at Chinqua-Penn Plantation (April) 336-349-4576

May
Carolina Blues Festival (mid-May) 336-274-2282
GYC Carnival (early May) 336-373-2173

June
African American Heritage Festival (early June) 336-449-4846
Charlotte Hawkins Brown Gravesite Ceremonies (early June) 336-449-4846
Eastern Music Festival (mid-June-late July) 336-333-7450
www.greensboro.com/emf/
State Games of North Carolina (late June) 800-277-8763

July
Eastern Music Festival (mid-June-late July) 336-333-7450
www.greensboro.com/emf/
Fun Fourth Festival (early July) 336-274-2282
www.greensboro.com/festival/
Ice Cream Festival (mid-July) 336-379-8748
Revolutionary War Encampment (early July) 336-545-5315

August
Gatsby Weekend (late August) 336-349-4576
Greensboro Gun Show (late August) 336-674-9287
Pony Baseball Palomino World Series (mid-August) 336-852-8488
Rock Festival (mid-August) 336-288-3769

September
Chili Championship & Rubber Duck Regatta (mid-September) 800-443-4093
Greensboro Agricultural Fair (mid-late September) 336-373-7400
Native American Pow Wow (mid-September) 336-273-8686
Tannenbaum Park Colonial Fair (early September) 336-545-5315

October
Boo at the Zoo (late October) 800-488-0444
City Stage Street Festival (early October) 336-274-2282
Stewfest Weekend (early October) 336-349-4576

Raleigh

January
Bass & Saltwater Fishing Expo (early January) 336-855-0208
Raleigh Antiques Extravaganza (mid-January) 336-924-8337

February
Carolian Power & Sailboat Show (mid-February) 336-855-0208
Home & Garden Show (mid-February) 919-831-6011
International Auto Show (late February) 919-831-6011
Run for the Roses (mid-February) 919-231-0714

March
Greater Raleigh Antique Show (early March & mid-November) 919-782-5782
Saint Patrick's Day Parade (mid-March) 919-846-9739

April
Civil War Living History (mid-April) 919-733-4994
Southern Ideal Home Show (mid-April & late September) 919-851-2911

May
Artsplosure Jazz & Arts Festival (mid-May) 919-832-8699
www.artsplosure.org/
Brookhill Steeplechase (early May) 919-510-7915
Celebration of the Outdoors (early May) 919-552-1410
Great Raleigh Road Race (early May) 919-831-6011
Nike Carolina Classic (early May) 919-380-0011
North Carolina Special Olympics Summer Games (mid-May) 800-843-6276

June
Tarheel Regatta (early June) 919-662-5704

July
Capitol's July 4th Celebration (early July) 919-733-4994
Farmers Market Festival (early July) 919-733-7417
North Carolina State Farmers Market Festival (early July) 919-733-7417

August
Lazy Daze Festival (late August) 919-469-4061

September
Carolina Fall Boat Show (early September) 336-855-0208
Grecian Festival (mid-September) 919-781-4548
Oktoberfest (late September) 919-834-5900
Southern Ideal Home Show (mid-April & late September) 919-851-2911

October
Brightleaf Festival (early October) 919-365-6318
International Festival (early October) 919-834-5900
Natural History Halloween (late October) 919-733-7450
North Carolina State Fair (mid-October) 919-733-2145
www.ncstatefair.org

November
Carolina Christmas Show (mid-late November) 919-831-6011
Greater Raleigh Antique Show (early March & mid-November) 919-782-5782
Native American Celebration (early November) 919-733-7450
Old Reliable Run (mid-November) 919-829-4843
Raleigh Christmas Parade (late November) 919-420-0120

December
Christmas Celebration on the Mall (early December) 919-733-4994
First Night Raleigh (December 31) 919-832-8699
Living Christmas Tree (mid-December) 919-832-2257

Winston-Salem

January
Tanglewood Festival of Lights (mid-November-mid-January) 336-778-6300

May
Greek Festival (early May) 336-765-7145

June
Crosby Celebrity Golf Tournament (early June) 336-721-2246
Music at Sunset (late June) 336-725-1035
Taste of the Triad (mid-June) 336-727-7393

August
National Black Theater Festival (early August) 336-723-2266
www.nbtf.org

September
Carolina Craftsmen Labor Day Classic (mid-September) 336-274-5550
Fiddle & Bow Festival (September) 336-727-1038

October
Dixie Classic Fair (early October) 336-727-2236
www.dcfair.com
Vantage Championship Seniors Golf Tournament (early-mid October) 336-721-2246

November
Christmas Parade (late November) 336-777-3796
Piedmont Crafts Fair (late November) 336-725-1516
Tanglewood Festival of Lights (mid-November-mid-January) 336-778-6300
Winston-Salem Crafts Guild Craft Show (mid-November) 252-727-2976

December
Candle Tea Christmas Festival (early December) 336-722-6171
First Night Piedmont (December 31) 336-722-9002
Old Salem Christmas (mid-December) 800-441-5305
Salem Christmas (late December) 336-721-7300
Tanglewood Festival of Lights (mid-November-mid-January) 336-778-6300

NORTH DAKOTA

Bismarck

January
Bismarck Mandan Winter Daze (late January through late February) 701-222-4308
U-Mary Jazz Festival (late January) 701-255-7500

February
Agri-International (mid-February) 701-222-4308
Bismarck Mandan Winter Daze (late January through late February) 701-222-4308

June
Fort Lincoln's Players Theatre (mid-June-late August) 701-663-4758
Frontier Army Days (late June) 701-663-9571
Missouri River Expo (early June) 701-222-6487

July
Block Party (early July) 701-223-1958
Capitol Curling Summer Bonspiel (mid-July) 701-222-6455
Crazy Days (late July) 701-223-1958
Fort Lincoln's Players Theatre (mid-June-late August) 701-663-4758
Mandan Rodeo Days (early July) 701-663-1136

August
Capitol A'Fair (early August) 701-223-5986
Fort Lincoln's Players Theatre (mid-June-late August) 701-663-4758
Fur Traders' Rendezvous (mid-August) 701-663-4758
Great Plains Jazz Festival (mid-August) 701-221-9588
Nu'Eta Corn & Buffalo Festival (August) 701-663-9571

September
Bismarck Marathon (early September) 701-255-1525
Folkfest (mid-September) 701-223-1958
Great American Folkfest (September) 701-223-5660
International Indian Arts Exposition (early September) 701-255-3285
United Tribes International Pow-Wow (early September) 701-255-3285

October
Fall Craft Show (mid-October) 701-667-3285
Flickertail Woodcarvers Show (mid-October) 701-222-4308
Polkafest (October) 701-222-4308
PRCA Edge of the West (mid-October) 701-222-6489

November
Festival of Trees (early November) 701-223-5986

December
Custer Christmas (mid-December) 701-663-4758
Fantasy of Lights Parade (early December) 701-223-1958

Fargo

January
Boat & Marine Show (late January) 701-241-9100
Fargo Farm Show (mid-January) 701-241-9100

February
Winter Festival (mid-February) 701-241-1350

March
Red River Valley Home & Garden Show (early March) 701-241-9100
Red River Valley Sportsmen Show (early March) 701-241-9100

April
Renaissance Festival (mid-April) 701-241-9100

June
Red River Valley Fair (mid-June) 701-282-2200
Rib Fest & More (mid-June) 701-241-9100
Scandinavian Hjemkomst Festival (late June) 218-233-8484
Trollwood Park Weekends (early June-late August) 701-241-8160

July
Downtown Fargo Street Fair (mid-July) 701-241-1570
Trollwood Park Weekends (early June-late August) 701-241-8160

NORTH DAKOTA — Fargo (Cont'd)

August
Christmas Bazaar (late August) 701-241-8160
Pioneer Days at Bonanzaville (mid-August) 701-282-2822
Riverfront Days (late August) 701-235-2895
Trollwood Park Weekends (early June-late August) 701-241-8160
We Fest (early August) 218-847-1681

September
Big Iron Agricultural Expo (mid-September) 701-282-2200
Valley Fest (early September) 701-282-3653

November
Holiday Community Parade (late November) 701-241-1570
Merry Prairie Christmas (late November-late December) ... 800-235-7654
Santa's Village at Rheault Farm (late November-late December) 701-241-8160

December
Light Up the Night (December 31) 701-241-8160
Merry Prairie Christmas (late November-late December) ... 800-235-7654
Santa's Village at Rheault Farm (late November-late December) 701-241-8160
Skyway Bazaar (early December) 701-241-1570

Grand Forks

March
University of North Dakota Writers' Conference (late March) 701-777-3321

April
Time Out Wacippi (early April) 701-746-0444
Wacipi/Time Out (mid-April) 701-777-4291

June
Summerthing (late June & July) 800-866-4566

July
Forx Fest (late July) 800-866-4566
GGF Fair & Exhibition (mid-July) 800-866-4566
Red River Duck Race & Fireworks Display (early July) 800-866-4566
Summerthing (late June & July) 800-866-4566

August
Catfish Days (mid-August) 800-866-4566
Heritage Days (mid-August) 800-866-4566

September
Potato Bowl (mid-September) 800-866-4566

October
Arts & Crafts Show (early October) 800-866-4566

December
First Night Greater Grand Forks (December 31) 701-746-0444

OHIO

Akron

February
Maple Sugaring Days (late February-mid-March) 330-666-3711
Witan's Annual French Market (late February) 330-928-7179

March
Maple Sugaring Days (late February-mid-March) 330-666-3711
Stitchery Showcase (late March) 330-836-5533

April
Peninsula Jazz Festival (early April) 330-657-2665

May
Cherry Blossom Festival (mid-May) 330-745-3733
May Garden Mart (mid-May) 330-836-5533

June
Antique & Classic Car Show (mid-June) 330-836-5533
Boston Mills Art Festival (late June-early July) 330-657-2334
Jazz Festival (mid-June) 330-657-2291

July
Akron Arts Expo (late July) 330-375-2804
Akron Rib & Music Festival (early July) 330-375-2804
All-American Soap Box Derby (late July) 330-733-8723
www.aasbd.org
Boston Mills Art Festival (late June-early July) 330-657-2334
Crooked River Fine Arts Festival (late July-early August) .. 330-971-8137
Music in the Valley Festival (early July) 330-666-3711
Shakespeare at Stan Hywet Hall (mid-July) 330-836-5533
Summit County Fair (late July) 330-633-6200

August
Civil War Reenactment (mid-August) 330-666-3711
Crooked River Fine Arts Festival (late July-early August) .. 330-971-8137
NEC Invitational (August) 330-644-2299
Pro Football Hall of Fame Week (early August) 330-456-8207
Twinsburg Twins Days Festival (early August) 330-425-3652
www.twinsdays.org

September
Chickenfest (mid-September) 330-753-8471
Labor of Love Run (early September) 330-688-9078
Mum Festival (late September) 330-745-3141
Yankee Peddler Festival (mid-late September) 800-535-5634

October
Boo at the Zoo (late October) 330-375-2550
Harvest Festival (early October) 330-666-3711
Wonderful World of Ohio Mart (early October) 330-836-5533

November
Holiday Tree Festival (late November) 330-379-8424

December
Christmas Craft Show (early-mid-December) 330-972-7570
First Night Akron (December 31) 330-762-9550
Holiday Lights Celebration (December) 330-375-2550
Home for the Holidays (December) 330-836-5533
Victorian Holiday Tour (December) 330-972-6909

Cincinnati

January
Festival of Lights (late November-early January) 513-281-4700

February
Cincinnati Auto Expo (mid-February) 513-281-0022

March
Cincinnati Heart Mini-Marathon (late March) 513-281-4048
Cincinnati St Patrick Parade (mid-March) 513-251-2222
GalleryFurniture.Com Stakes Horseracing (March) 800-733-0200
Spring Floral Show (mid-March-late April) 513-352-4080

April
Cincinnati Flower Show (late April) 513-872-5194
www.cincyflowershow.com/
Spring Floral Show (mid-March-late April) 513-352-4080

May
Appalachian Festival (early May) 513-232-8230
Cincinnati May Festival (mid-May) 513-621-1919
Jammin' on Main (early May) 513-621-6994
May Festival (late May) 513-381-3300
Summerfair (early May) 513-531-0050
Taste of Cincinnati (late May) 513-579-3199

June
Kids Fest (early June) 513-621-2142
Oldiesfest (mid-late June) 513-321-8900

July
All-American Birthday Party (early July) 513-621-2142
Coors Light Festival (mid-July) 513-871-3900
Riverfront Stadium Festival (mid-July) 513-871-3900

August
Gold Star Chili Fest (early August) 513-579-3191
Hamilton County Fair (early-mid-August) 513-761-4224

September
Celtic Music & Cultural Festival (early September) 513-533-4822
Harvest Festival (late September) 513-281-4700
Oktoberfest Zinzinnati (mid-September) 513-579-3199
www.gccc.com/oktfest.htm
Riverfest (early September) 513-621-6994

October
Boofest (October) 513-287-7000
Tall Stacks (mid-October) 513-744-8820
Taste of Findlay Market (late October) 513-241-0464

November
Festival of Lights (late November-early January) 513-281-4700
Holiday in Lights (late November-late December) 513-287-7103

December
Festival of Lights (late November-early January) 513-281-4700
Holiday in Lights (late November-late December) 513-287-7103

Cleveland

January
Mid America Sail & Power Boat Show (mid-late January) 216-676-6000

February
Auto Rama (early February) 216-348-2200
Cleveland Home & Garden Show (mid-February) 800-600-0307
Greater Cleveland Auto Show (late February-early March) 216-676-6000
National Home & Garden Show (mid-February) 216-676-6000

March
American & Canadian Sport Travel & Outdoor Show (mid-March) 216-529-1300
Cleveland International Film Festival (late March) 216-621-1374
www.clevefilmfest.org/
Greater Cleveland Auto Show (late February-early March) 216-676-6000
Saint Patrick's Day Parade (mid-March) 216-621-4110

April
EarthFest (April 22) 216-281-6468
www.earthdaycoalition.org/earthfest.html
Jazzfest (mid-April) 216-987-4400
Tri-C JazzFest (mid-April) 216-987-4400

May
CVS-Cleveland Marathon (early May) 800-467-3826

June
American Indian Pow Wow (June 19-20) 216-281-8480

July
Cain Park Arts Festival (early July) 216-371-3000
Cleveland Grand Prix (mid-July) 216-781-3500

August
Cleveland National Air Show (late August-early September) 216-781-0747
Cuyahoga County Fair (mid-August) 800-321-1001

September
Cleveland National Air Show (late August-early September) 216-781-0747
Johnny Appleseed Festival (mid-September) 440-834-4012

October
Boo at the Zoo (late October) 216-661-6500
Hale Farm Harvest Festival (mid-October) 800-589-9703
Haunted Hayrides (mid-October) 800-366-3276
Ohio Arts & Crafts Christmas Festival (late October) 440-243-0090
Shaker Apple Festival Weekend (early October) 216-921-1201

November
American Legion Holiday Parade (late November) 216-432-4046
Cleveland Christmas Connection (mid-November) 440-835-9627
Ski Skate & Snowboard Show (early November) 216-676-6000

December
500,000 Country Lights (December) 800-366-3276
Holiday Lights Festival (early-mid-December) 216-661-6500

Columbus

January
Wildlight Wonderland (late November-early January) 614-645-3550

March
Saint Patrick's Day Parade (mid-March) 614-645-4375

April
Central Ohio Daffodil Society Show (mid-April) 614-645-8733
Equine Affaire-The Great American Horse Exposition (early April) 740-845-0085

May
Asian Festival (late May) 614-292-0613
PGA Memorial Tournament at Muirfield (late May-early June) 614-889-6700
Rhythm & Food: A Taste of Columbus (late May) 614-221-6623

June
Columbus Arts Festival (early June) 614-224-2606
www.gcac.org/
June Teenth Festival (mid-June) 614-299-4488
PGA Memorial Tournament at Muirfield (late May-early June) 614-889-6700
Rose Festival (mid-June) 614-645-3379

July
Crusin' on the Riverfront (late July-early August) 614-258-1983
Ohio State Fair Horse Show (late July-late August) 614-644-4035
Red White & Boom (early July) 614-263-4444

August
Crusin' on the Riverfront (late July-early August) 614-258-1983
Ohio State Fair (early-late August) 614-644-3247
www.ohiostatefair.com
Ohio State Fair Horse Show (late July-late August) 614-644-4035

September
Fall Festival of Roses (late September) 614-645-8733
Oktoberfest (early September) 614-224-4300

October
All American Quarter Horse Congress (mid-October) 740-943-2346
Columbus International Film & Video Festival (mid-October) 614-841-1666
www.infinet.com/~chrisawd/

November
Columbus International Festival (early November) 614-228-4010
Columbus Marathon (early November) 614-794-1566
www.columbusmarathon.com/
Wildlight Wonderland (late November-early January) 614-645-3550

December
Capital Holiday Lights (December) 800-345-4386
First Night Columbus (December 31) 614-481-0020
Wildlight Wonderland (late November-early January) 614-645-3550
Winterfair (early December) 614-486-7119

Dayton

January
Dayton Sports Fishing Travel & Outdoor Show (mid-January) 937-443-4700
Miami Valley Boat Show (mid-January) 937-278-4776

February
Country Peddler Shows (late February & early June) 937-278-4776

March
Dayton Auto Show (mid-March) 937-443-4700
Dayton Home & Garden Show (late March) 937-443-4700

OHIO — Dayton (Cont'd)

April
Easter Eggstravaganza (early April) ... 937-226-8248

May
A World A'Fair (mid-May) ... 937-233-0050
Art in the Park (late May) ... 937-278-0655
International Festival (late May-early June) ... 937-443-4700
Ohio Folk Festival (mid-May) ... 937-293-2841

June
City Folk Festival (mid-June) ... 937-223-3655
Country Peddler Shows (late February & early June) ... 937-278-4776
Fiesta Latino Americano (mid-June) ... 937-296-3300
International Festival (late May-early June) ... 937-443-4700
Women in Jazz Festival (late June) ... 937-461-5300

July
Dayton Black Cultural Festival (early July) ... 937-224-7100
Dayton Horse Show (late July-early August) ... 937-461-4740
Family Fourth of July (July 4) ... 937-224-1518
Go 4th Celebration (July 4) ... 937-296-3281
SummerFest (late July) ... 937-268-8199
US Air & Trade Show (late July) ... 937-898-5901
www.usats.org/

August
Dayton Horse Show (late July-early August) ... 937-461-4740
Fly City Music Festival (late August) ... 937-222-9768
Grand American World Trapshooting Tournament (mid-August) ... 937-898-1945
Jazz at the Bend Jazz Festival (late August) ... 937-233-2489

September
Greek Festival (early September) ... 937-224-0601
Montgomery County Fair (early September) ... 937-224-1619
Oktoberfest (late September) ... 937-223-5277
US Air Force Marathon (mid-September) ... 937-255-3334
World Reggae Festival (early September) ... 937-225-2333

October
Dayton Art Institute Oktoberfest (early October) ... 937-223-5277
Dayton Industrial Expo (late October) ... 937-443-4700
MetroParks RiverFest (early October) ... 937-278-8231

Toledo

March
Irish Heritage Festival (mid-March) ... 419-321-6404
Rod & Custom Auto-Rama (early March) ... 419-474-1006

May
Rallies by the River (early May-late August) ... 419-243-8024
Rock Rhythm n' Blues (late May) ... 419-243-8024

June
Crosby Festival of the Arts (late June) ... 419-936-2986
Jamie Farr LPGA Tournament (late June-early July) ... 419-882-7153
Old West End Historic Festival Home Tours (early June) .. 419-243-1100
Old West End Spring Festival (early June) ... 419-321-6404
Rallies by the River (early May-late August) ... 419-243-8024

July
Art on the Mall (mid-July) ... 419-530-2586
Jamie Farr LPGA Tournament (late June-early July) ... 419-882-7153
Kroger Freedom Celebration (early July) ... 419-243-8024
Lagrange Street Polish Festival (mid-July) ... 419-255-8406
Lucas County Fair (late July) ... 419-893-2127
Rallies by the River (early May-late August) ... 419-243-8024
Toledo Area Artists Exhibition (early July-early August) ... 419-255-8000
Warren-Sherman Festival (late July-early August) ... 419-242-6479

August
German-American Festival (late August) ... 419-321-6404
Northwest Ohio Rib-Off (early August) ... 419-242-9587
Rallies by the River (early May-late August) ... 419-243-8024
Toledo Area Artists Exhibition (early July-early August) ... 419-255-8000
Warren-Sherman Festival (late July-early August) ... 419-242-6479

September
RiverFest (early September) ... 419-243-8024

October
Sunshine Bazaar & Quilt Auction (mid-October) ... 419-865-0251

November
Lights Before Christmas (early November-late December) ... 419-385-5721

December
First Night Toledo (December 31) ... 419-241-3777
Homespun Holidays (early-mid-December) ... 419-535-3050
Lights Before Christmas (early November-late December) ... 419-385-5721

Youngstown

January
Birthday Bash (late January) ... 330-792-7620
Festival of Lights (late November-early January) ... 330-533-3773
Summer Concerts in the Park (June-February) ... 330-755-7275

February
Summer Concerts in the Park (June-February) ... 330-755-7275

March
Maple Syrup Festival (mid-late March) ... 330-726-8105

April
Celtic Festival (early April) ... 330-727-8663
Easter Egg Hunt (April) ... 330-726-8105

May
Austintown Log Cabin Tours (May-August) ... 330-792-1129
Memorial Day Ceremony & Parade (late May) ... 330-792-1129
Mother's Day Tea Party (mid-May) ... 330-743-5934
Strock Stone House Tours (May-August) ... 330-792-1129
Walk on Wick Arts & Music Festival (May) ... 330-747-8200
YWCA Women Artists: A Celebration Art Exhibit (mid-May) ... 330-746-6361

June
Austintown Log Cabin Tours (May-August) ... 330-792-1129
Easter Seals Drive for Dough Carnival (early June) ... 330-743-1168
Spring into Summer Festival (late June) ... 330-654-4989
Strock Stone House Tours (May-August) ... 330-792-1129
Summer Concerts in the Park (June-February) ... 330-755-7275
Thursday Night Music in the Park (June-August) ... 330-726-8105
Tuesday Concerts in the Park (mid-June-late August) ... 330-792-1129

July
Austintown Log Cabin Tours (May-August) ... 330-792-1129
Austintown's 4th of July (July 4) ... 330-792-1129
City Fest (July) ... 330-747-8200
Greater Youngstown Italian Festival (early-mid-July) ... 330-549-0130
Log Cabin Day Arts & Crafts Show (late July) ... 330-792-1129
Mahoning Valley Rib Cook-Off (late July) ... 330-792-7620
Market Day at the Fairgrounds (July) ... 330-533-4026
National Midyear Show (early July-late August) ... 330-743-1711
Strock Stone House Tours (May-August) ... 330-792-1129
Summer Concerts in the Park (June-February) ... 330-755-7275
Sunfest (late July-early August) ... 330-740-7106
Thursday Night Music in the Park (June-August) ... 330-726-8105
Tuesday Concerts in the Park (mid-June-late August) ... 330-792-1129
Twin Oaks Pioneer Festival (mid-July & late September) .. 330-538-3097
Wednesday Night Hay Rides & Bonfire (July-August) ... 330-726-8105
YSU Summer Festival of the Arts (early-mid-July) ... 330-742-2307

August
Austintown Log Cabin Tours (May-August) ... 330-792-1129
Mahoning Valley Kennel Club-Steel Valley Cluster-Dog Show (early August) ... 330-652-9622
Mahoning Valley Parent Magazine-Family Fun Day (early August) ... 330-792-7620
National Midyear Show (early July-late August) ... 330-743-1711
Shaker Woods Festival (mid-late August) ... 330-482-0214
www.shakerwoods.com
Strock Stone House Tours (May-August) ... 330-792-1129
Summer Concerts in the Park (June-February) ... 330-755-7275
Sunfest (late July-early August) ... 330-740-7106
Thursday Night Music in the Park (June-August) ... 330-726-8105
Tuesday Concerts in the Park (mid-June-late August) ... 330-792-1129
Twin Oaks Pioneer Festival (mid-July & late September) .. 330-538-3097
Wednesday Night Hay Rides & Bonfire (July-August) ... 330-726-8105

September
Antiques in the Woods (mid-September) ... 330-457-7202
Canfield Fair (early September) ... 800-447-8201
Harvest Festival (mid-September) ... 330-533-4161
Octoberfest (late September-early October) ... 330-726-8105
Summer Concerts in the Park (June-February) ... 330-755-7275
Twin Oaks Pioneer Festival (mid-July & late September) .. 330-538-3097

October
Arts & Crafts Show (late October) ... 330-747-8200
Christmas in the Woods (early-mid-October) ... 724-728-7084
Ghost Lights of Halloween (October) ... 330-533-3773
Haunted Hayrides (mid-late October) ... 330-726-8105
Haunted House & Hayrides (October) ... 330-792-7620
Octoberfest (late September-early October) ... 330-726-8105
Pumpkin Carve-Out (mid-late October) ... 330-726-8105
Summer Concerts in the Park (June-February) ... 330-755-7275
Trick or Treat Town (mid-late October) ... 330-792-7620

November
Christmas in the Mill (late November) ... 330-740-7115
Community Christmas Tree Lighting Ceremony (late November) ... 330-792-1129
Festival of Lights (late November-early January) ... 330-533-3773
Summer Concerts in the Park (June-February) ... 330-755-7275

December
American Holiday Fine Arts & Antique Show & Sale (early December) ... 330-743-1711
Festival of Lights (late November-early January) ... 330-533-3773
Holiday of Lights (December) ... 330-792-7620
Summer Concerts in the Park (June-February) ... 330-755-7275

OKLAHOMA

Oklahoma City

January
Holiday Treefest (late November-early January) ... 405-602-6664
International Finals Rodeo (mid-January) ... 405-235-6540

February
An Affair of the Heart Craft Show (early February & late October) ... 405-948-6704
Bullnanza (early February) ... 800-234-3393
Celebration of African-American Heritage (early February) ... 405-951-0000
Oklahoma City Home & Garden Show (mid-February & late March) ... 405-948-6704
Sportsfest (early February) ... 405-235-4222
WinterTales Storytelling Festival (mid-February) ... 405-270-4848

March
Oklahoma City Home & Garden Show (mid-February & late March) ... 405-948-6704
Spring Fair & Livestock Exposition (late March) ... 405-948-6704
www.agcenter.net/springfair/default.htm
Timed Event Championship of the World (mid-March) ... 800-595-7433

April
89ers Days PRCA Rodeo (late April) ... 800-595-7433
Centennial Horse Show (mid-late April) ... 405-557-9400
Festival of the Arts (late April) ... 405-297-8910
Lazy E Spring Barrel Futurity (early April) ... 800-595-7433
Oklahoma Farm Show (mid-April) ... 405-948-6704
Spring Festival of the Arts (late April) ... 405-270-4848

May
Big 12 Baseball Tournament (mid-May) ... 800-225-5652
Cowboy Chuck Wagon Gathering (late May) ... 405-478-2250
National Reining Horse Derby (mid-May) ... 405-297-8938
Paseo Arts Festival (late May) ... 405-525-2688

June
Aerospace America International Air Show (early June) ... 405-685-9546
National Appaloosa Horse Show (late June-mid-July) ... 405-297-8938
Prix De West Invitational Exhibition & Sale (mid-June) ... 405-478-2250
Red Earth Native American Cultural Festival (mid-June) .. 405-427-5228
Sooner State Summer Games (June) ... 405-235-4222
Sunday Twilight Concert Series (June-late August) ... 405-270-4848
www.artscouncilokc.com

July
Fourth of July Festival (July 4) ... 800-225-5652
International Arabian Horse Show (late July) ... 405-948-6700
National Appaloosa Horse Show (late June-mid-July) ... 405-297-8938
Southwest Street Rod Nationals (mid-July) ... 405-948-6700
Sunday Twilight Concert Series (June-late August) ... 405-270-4848
www.artscouncilokc.com

August
Balloon Fest (mid-August) ... 405-794-4000
Sunday Twilight Concert Series (June-late August) ... 405-270-4848
www.artscouncilokc.com

September
Arts Festival Oklahoma (Labor Day weekend) ... 405-682-7536
Oklahoma State Fair (September-early October) ... 800-225-5652
www.oklafair.org/

October
An Affair of the Heart Craft Show (early February & late October) ... 405-948-6704
Grand National Morgan Horse Show (early October) ... 800-225-5652
Heritage Hills Historic Homes Tour (mid-October) ... 405-528-8485
National Finals Steer Roping (late October) ... 800-595-7433
Oklahoma State Fair (September-early October) ... 800-225-5652
www.oklafair.org/

November
Crystal Lights Holiday Display (late November-late December) ... 405-297-3995
Holiday Treefest (late November-early January) ... 405-602-6664
Prairie Circuit Finals Rodeo (mid-November) ... 800-595-7433
World Championship Quarter Horse Show (mid-November) ... 800-225-5652

December
All-College Basketball Tournament (late December) ... 800-225-5652
Crystal Lights Holiday Display (late November-late December) ... 405-297-3995
Holiday Treefest (late November-early January) ... 405-602-6664
World Championship Barrel Racing Futurity (mid-December) ... 405-948-6704

Tulsa

January
Chili Bowl Midget Nationals (early January) ... 918-838-3777
www.chilibowl.com
Longhorn Rodeo (late January) ... 918-596-7177
Tulsa Boat Sport & Travel Show (January) ... 918-744-1113
Tulsa Nationals Wrestling Tournament (mid-January) ... 918-366-4411

February
Akdar Shrine Circus (late February-early March) ... 918-587-6658
National Rod & Custom Car Show (late February) ... 918-257-8073
Tulsa Women's Show (early February) ... 800-225-4342

March
Akdar Shrine Circus (late February-early March) ... 918-587-6658
Greater Tulsa Antiques Show (mid-March) ... 918-682-7420
Greater Tulsa Home & Garden Show (mid-March) ... 918-663-5820
International Auto Show (mid-March) ... 918-742-2626
Tulsa Indian Art Festival (mid-March) ... 918-583-2253

April
Tulsa Charity Horse Show (late April) ... 918-742-5556
Tulsa Easter Pageant (early April) ... 918-596-5990

May
Mayfest (mid-May) ... 918-582-6435
tulsadowntown.org/mayfest.htm
Tulsa Championship Rodeo (early May) ... 918-744-1113

OKLAHOMA — Tulsa (Cont'd)

June
Juneteenth on Greenwood Heritage Festival (mid-June)... 918-582-1741
Reggaefest/World Peace Festival (late June)..................... 918-596-2001
TulsaFest (late June)... 918-595-7776

July
Gatesway International Balloon Festival (late July-early August).. 918-251-2676
Summer in the City (mid-July)... 918-583-2617
Tulsa Boom River Celebration & Great American Duck Drop (July 4).. 918-596-2001
Tulsa County Free Fair (late July)..................................... 918-746-3709

August
Bok Williams Jazz on Greenwood (early August & mid-August)...................................... 918-584-3378
Gatesway International Balloon Festival (late July-early August).. 918-251-2676
Tulsa Morgan Horse Extravaganza (early August)............. 918-744-1113

September
Chili Cookoff & Bluegrass Festival (early-mid- September).. 918-583-2617
Oklahoma Scottish Games & Gathering (mid-September).. 918-560-0228
Tulsa State Fair (late September-early October)................ 918-744-1113
www.tulsastatefair.com

October
Oktoberfest (mid-October)... 918-596-2001
www.tulsaoktoberfest.org
Tulsa State Fair (late September-early October)................ 918-744-1113
www.tulsastatefair.com

December
Christmas Parade of Lights (early December)..................... 918-583-2617
Zoolightful (December).. 918-560-0228

OREGON

Eugene

January
Mid-Winter Square Dance Festival (late January)............. 541-942-7539
Whale Watching (November-March)...................................... 800-547-5445

February
Oregon Asian Celebration (mid-February).......................... 541-687-9600
Whale Watching (November-March)...................................... 800-547-5445

March
Daffodil Drive Day (mid-March)... 800-547-5445
Oregon Dunes Mushers Mail Run (early March)............... 541-269-1269
Whale Watching (November-March)...................................... 800-547-5445

April
Saturday Market (April-November).. 541-686-8885
www.efn.org/~smarket/

May
Rhododendron Festival & Parade (mid-May)..................... 541-997-3128
Saturday Market (April-November).. 541-686-8885
www.efn.org/~smarket/
Spring Garden Tours (May).. 800-726-3657
Wildflower Festival (mid-May).. 541-747-3817

June
Oregon Bach Festival (late June-early July)........................ 541-346-5669
bachfest.uoregon.edu
Saturday Market (April-November).. 541-686-8885
www.efn.org/~smarket/

July
Bohemia Mining Days (late July).. 541-942-8985
www.efn.org/~bohemia
Coburg Golden Years (mid-July)... 541-484-5307
Cottage Grove Amateur Rodeo (early July)......................... 541-942-2411
Creswell's Old Fashioned July 4th (July 4)......................... 541-895-5161
Oregon Bach Festival (late June-early July)........................ 541-346-5669
bachfest.uoregon.edu
Oregon Country Fair (mid-July)... 541-343-4298
www.efn.org/~ocf/
Saturday Market (April-November).. 541-686-8885
www.efn.org/~smarket/

August
Applegate Trail Days (early August).................................... 541-935-1068
Coburg Classic Car Show (early August)............................. 541-344-8081
Lane County Fair (mid-August)... 541-687-4292
Oregon Festival of American Music (early-mid-August)..... 541-687-6526
www.ofam.org
Saturday Market (April-November).. 541-686-8885
www.efn.org/~smarket/
Scandinavian Festival (August).. 541-998-6154
Ukrainian Celebration (early August)................................... 541-726-7309

September
Asian Kite Festival (mid-September).................................... 541-687-9600
Centennial Bank Eugene Celebration (mid-September)...... 541-681-4108
Coburg Antique Fair (early September)............................... 541-688-1181
Saturday Market (April-November).. 541-686-8885
www.efn.org/~smarket/

October
Saturday Market (April-November).. 541-686-8885
www.efn.org/~smarket/

November
Saturday Market (April-November).. 541-686-8885
www.efn.org/~smarket/
Whale Watching (November-March)...................................... 800-547-5445

December
Christmas Light Parade & Yule Fest (mid-December)....... 541-998-6154
Christmas Light Up the Valley (December)........................... 541-896-3330
Festival of Lights (December)... 800-547-5445
Whale Watching (November-March)...................................... 800-547-5445

Portland

January
Seven Up Winter Wonderland Celebration of Lights (late November-early January)..................................... 503-232-3000

February
International Film Festival (mid-February-early March)..... 503-221-1156
Seafood & Wine Festival (late February)............................ 800-262-7844

March
International Film Festival (mid-February-early March)..... 503-221-1156

April
Tulip Festival (late April).. 503-228-5108

May
Cinco de Mayo Celebration (early May).............................. 503-222-9807

June
Evening Concerts at the Zoo (mid-June-mid-August)......... 503-226-1561
Portland Rose Festival (early June)..................................... 503-227-2681
www.rosefestival.org
Rose Festival Airshow (late June).. 503-227-2681
Starlight Parade (early June).. 503-227-2681

July
Evening Concerts at the Zoo (mid-June-mid-August)......... 503-226-1561
Oregon Brewers Festival (late July)..................................... 503-778-5917
www.oregonbrewfest.com
Portland Scottish Highland Games (mid-July).................... 503-293-8501
Waterfront Blues Festival (early July).................................. 503-973-3378
www.waterfrontbluesfest.com

August
Bite-A Taste of Portland (mid-August)................................. 503-248-0600
Clark County Fair (early-mid-August).................................. 360-737-6180
www.clarkcofair.com
Evening Concerts at the Zoo (mid-June-mid-August)......... 503-226-1561
Festa Italiana (late August).. 503-771-0310
Homowo Festival of African Arts (mid-August).................. 503-288-3025
Mount Hood Jazz Festival (early August)............................ 503-232-3000
Oregon State Fair (late August-early September)............... 503-378-3247
Washington County Fair & Rodeo (early August)............... 503-648-1416

September
Oregon State Fair (late August-early September)............... 503-378-3247
Portland Creative Conference (mid-September).................. 503-234-1641
Portland Marathon (late September)................................... 503-226-1111
www.portlandmarathon.org

October
Greek Festival (early October)... 503-234-0468

November
America's Largest Christmas Bazaar (late November-early December)...................................... 503-736-5200
Christmas at the Pittock Mansion (late November-late December)...................................... 503-823-3624
Festival of Lights at the Grotto (late November-late December)...................................... 503-254-7371
Seven Up Winter Wonderland Celebration of Lights (late November-early January)..................................... 503-232-3000

December
America's Largest Christmas Bazaar (late November-early December)...................................... 503-736-5200
Christmas at the Pittock Mansion (late November-late December)...................................... 503-823-3624
Festival of Lights at the Grotto (late November-late December)...................................... 503-254-7371
Seven Up Winter Wonderland Celebration of Lights (late November-early January)..................................... 503-232-3000
Zoolights (December)... 503-226-1561

Salem

January
Salem Collectors' Market (September-July)........................ 503-393-1261

February
Celebrate Oregon Wine & Food Festival (mid-February)... 503-581-0540
Salem Collectors' Market (September-July)........................ 503-393-1261

March
Salem Collectors' Market (September-July)........................ 503-393-1261

April
Oregon AG Fest (late April)... 503-581-4325
Salem Collectors' Market (September-July)........................ 503-393-1261

May
Keizer Iris Festival (early May)... 503-393-9111
Salem Collectors' Market (September-July)........................ 503-393-1261
Salem Rodeo Days (mid-May).. 503-371-6040

June
Salem Collectors' Market (September-July)........................ 503-393-1261
Sheep to Shawl (early June).. 503-581-4325

July
Bite of Salem (late July).. 503-581-4325
Civil War Reenactment (early July)...................................... 503-393-1172
Destruction Derby & Fireworks (early July)........................ 503-581-4325
Marion County Fair (early-mid-July)..................................... 503-581-1466
Salem Art Fair & Festival (mid-July)................................... 503-581-2228
www.oregonlink.com/art/art_festival.html
Salem Collectors' Market (September-July)........................ 503-393-1261
Summer in the City Festival (late July)............................... 503-581-4325
West Salem Waterfront Parade (late July)........................... 503-581-4325

August
Oregon State Fair (late August-early September)............... 503-378-3247
Salem Belly Dance Festival (early August)......................... 503-378-7875
Salem Music on the Green (August).................................... 503-581-4325

September
Mission Mill Museum Classic Car Show (late September)... 503-585-7012
Oregon State Fair (late August-early September)............... 503-378-3247
Salem Collectors' Market (September-July)........................ 503-393-1261

October
Great Northwest Train Show (early October)....................... 503-378-3247
Quilt Show & Hand Weavers Sale (early October).............. 503-581-4325
Salem Collectors' Market (September-July)........................ 503-393-1261

November
Salem Collectors' Market (September-July)........................ 503-393-1261

December
Festival of Lights Parade (mid-December)........................... 800-874-7012
Holidays at the Capitol (December)..................................... 503-581-4325
Salem Collectors' Market (September-July)........................ 503-393-1261

PENNSYLVANIA

Allentown

January
Elvis Birthday Bash (mid-January).. 610-252-3132
Lights in the Parkway (late November-mid-January).......... 610-437-7616

March
Spring Corn Festival (early March)...................................... 610-797-2121

May
Mayfair Festival of the Arts (late May)............................... 610-437-6900
mayfairfestival.org/

June
Cement Belt Free Fair (mid-June).. 610-262-9750
German Festival (late June-early July)................................ 800-963-8824
Pennsylvania Shakespeare Festival (mid-June-mid-July).. 610-282-3192
www4.allencol.edu/~psf/

July
German Festival (late June-early July)................................ 800-963-8824
Pennsylvania Shakespeare Festival (mid-June-mid-July).. 610-282-3192
www4.allencol.edu/~psf/

August
Das Awkscht Fescht (early August)...................................... 610-967-2317
Great Allentown Fair (late August-early September).......... 610-433-7541
www.allentownfairpa.org
Musikfest (mid-August)... 610-861-0678
www.musikfest.org/
Wheels of Time Rod & Custom Jamboree (mid-August)... 610-865-4114

September
Celtic Classic Highland Games & Festival (late September)... 610-868-9599
www.celticfest.org/
Great Allentown Fair (late August-early September).......... 610-433-7541
www.allentownfairpa.org
Riverside Art Festival (mid-September)............................... 610-250-6710

October
Antique Show (late October).. 610-433-7541
Apparitions of Allentown: A Walk of Historic Haunts (late October)... 610-435-4664
Boo at the Zoo (late October).. 610-799-4171
Fall Foliage Festival (October)... 610-799-4171
Harvest Festival (mid-October)... 610-868-5044
Lehigh Valley Air Show (mid-October)................................. 610-231-5229
Mule & Viking Art & Craft Show (early October)................ 610-821-3305

November
Allentown Tree Lighting Ceremony (late November).......... 610-776-7117
Christkindlmarkt (late November-mid-December)................ 610-861-0678
Lights in the Parkway (late November-mid-January).......... 610-437-7616
Time of Thanksgiving (mid-November)................................. 610-797-2121

December
Bach Choir of Bethlehem Christmas Concert (early December).. 610-866-4382
Christkindlmarkt (late November-mid-December)................ 610-861-0678
Lights in the Parkway (late November-mid-January).......... 610-437-7616

Erie

March
- **Maple Syrup Festival** (mid-March) ... 814-835-5356
- **Professional Bowlers Tour** (late March-early April) ... 814-899-9855
- **Saint Patrick's Day Parade** (mid-March) ... 814-454-7191

April
- **Professional Bowlers Tour** (late March-early April) ... 814-899-9855

May
- **Erie Zoo Parade** (mid-May) ... 814-864-4091
- **Spring Highland Festival** (early May) ... 814-836-1955

June
- **American Folkways Festival** (late June & early September) ... 814-385-6040
- **Erie Summer Festival of the Arts** (late June) ... 814-871-7493
- **Wild Rib Cookoff & Music Festival** (early June) ... 814-833-7343

July
- **4th of July Fireworks** (July 4) ... 814-838-3591
- **Cherry Festival** (early July) ... 814-725-4262
- **Greek Festival** (mid-July) ... 814-838-8808
- **Harborfest** (mid-July) ... 814-899-9173

August
- **Erie County Fair** (late August-early September) ... 814-739-2232
- **We Love Erie Days** (mid-August) ... 814-454-7191

September
- **American Folkways Festival** (late June & early September) ... 814-385-6040
- **Erie County Fair** (late August-early September) ... 814-739-2232
- **Heritage Wine Fest** (late September) ... 814-725-8015
- **Wine Country Harvest Festival** (late September) ... 814-725-4262

October
- **ZooBoo** (mid-late October) ... 814-864-4091

December
- **First Night Erie** (December 31) ... 814-877-7097
- **ZooLumination** (mid-late December) ... 814-864-4091

Gettysburg

April
- **History Meets the Arts** (mid-late April) ... 717-334-8151

May
- **Apple Blossom Festival** (early May) ... 717-334-6274
- **Gettysburg Spring Bluegrass Festival** (mid-May) ... 717-642-8749
- **Gettysburg Spring Outdoor Antique Show** (early-mid-May) ... 717-334-6274
- **Gettysburg Square-Dance Round-Up** (late May) ... 717-528-4442
- **Memorial Day Parade & Ceremonies** (late May) ... 717-334-6274

June
- **Adams County Historic Properties Tour** (mid-June) ... 717-334-8188
- **Gettysburg Brass Band Festival** (mid-late June) ... 717-334-6274
- **Gettysburg Civil War Book Fair** (late June) ... 717-334-6274
- **Gettysburg Civil War Collectors Show** (late June) ... 717-334-6274
- **Gettysburg Civil War Heritage Days** (late June-early July) ... 717-334-6274
- **Mason-Dixon Civil War Collector's Show** (late June) ... 717-334-6274
- **New Oxford Flea Market & Antique Show** (mid-late June) ... 717-334-6274
- **Sunday in the Park Concert Series** (early June-mid-late August) ... 717-334-2028

July
- **Civil War Battle Reenactments** (early July & late September) ... 717-338-1525
- **Gettysburg Civil War Heritage Days** (late June-early July) ... 717-334-6274
- **Gettysburg Firemen's Festival** (early July) ... 717-334-6274
- **Sunday in the Park Concert Series** (early June-mid-late August) ... 717-334-2028

August
- **Gettysburg Fall Bluegrass Festival** (late August-early September) ... 717-642-8749
- **Littlestown Good Ole Days Festival** (mid-late August) ... 717-334-6274
- **South Mountain Fair** (late August) ... 717-334-6274
- **Sunday in the Park Concert Series** (early June-mid-late August) ... 717-334-2028

September
- **Adams County Heritage Festival** (late September) ... 717-334-0752
- **Civil War Battle Reenactments** (early July & late September) ... 717-338-1525
- **East Berlin Colonial Day** (mid-September) ... 717-259-0822
- **Eisenhower World War II Weekend** (mid-late September) ... 717-338-9114
- **Fairfield Pippenfest** (late September) ... 717-642-5640
- **Gettysburg Fall Bluegrass Festival** (late August-early September) ... 717-642-8749
- **Gettysburg Fall Outdoor Antique Show** (late September) ... 717-334-6274

October
- **National Apple Harvest Festival** (early October) ... 717-677-9413

November
- **Anniversary of Lincoln's Gettysburg Address** (November 19) ... 717-334-6274
- **Gettysburg Yuletide Festival** (late November-mid-December) ... 717-334-6274
- **International Gift Festival** (mid-November) ... 717-334-6274
- **Remembrance Day** (mid-November) ... 717-334-6274

December
- **Gettysburg Yuletide Festival** (late November-mid-December) ... 717-334-6274

Harrisburg

March
- **Pennsylvania National Arts & Crafts Show** (late March) ... 717-796-0531

April
- **Zembo Shrine Circus** (early April) ... 717-238-8107

May
- **Harrisburg Arts Festival** (late May) ... 717-238-5180

June
- **Susquehanna River Celebration** (early June) ... 717-255-3020

July
- **Harrisburg Independence Weekend Festival** (early July) ... 717-255-3020

September
- **City Island Flower & Craft Festival** (mid-September) ... 717-234-6500
- **Kipona Festival** (early September) ... 717-255-3020

November
- **Harrisburg Holiday Parade** (mid-November) ... 717-255-3020

Philadelphia

January
- **Bach Festival of Philadelphia** (September-March) ... 215-247-2224 www.libertynet.org/bach/
- **Mummers Parade** (January 1) ... 215-686-3622
- **Philadelphia Boat Show** (mid-January) ... 610-449-9910

February
- **Bach Festival of Philadelphia** (September-March) ... 215-247-2224 www.libertynet.org/bach/
- **Black Writer's Festival** (mid-February) ... 215-732-5207
- **Chocolate Festival** (mid-February) ... 215-925-7465
- **Junior Jazz Weekend** (mid-February) ... 215-963-0667
- **Mardi Gras JAMboree** (late February) ... 215-925-7465
- **PECO Energy Jazz Festival** (mid-February) ... 215-636-1666
- **Renninger Antique** (late February) ... 610-337-4000
- **US Hot Rod Grand Slam Monster Jam** (mid-February) ... 215-336-3600

March
- **Bach Festival of Philadelphia** (September-March) ... 215-247-2224 www.libertynet.org/bach/
- **Book & Cook Fair** (mid-March) ... 215-636-1666
- **Maple Syrup Festival** (late March) ... 215-922-2317
- **Philadelphia Flower Show** (early March) ... 215-418-4700
- **Purim Festival** (early March) ... 215-923-3811

April
- **Chestnut Hill Garden Festival Blooms** (late April-early May) ... 215-248-8504
- **Historic Houses in Flower** (late April) ... 215-763-8100
- **Penn Relays** (mid-April) ... 215-898-6128
- **Philadelphia Festival of World Cinema** (late April-early May) ... 215-569-9700 www.libertynet.org/pfwc/
- **Philadelphia Open House Tours** (late April-mid-May) ... 215-928-1188
- **Springside School Antiques Show** (mid-April) ... 215-247-7200

May
- **Chestnut Hill Garden Festival Blooms** (late April-early May) ... 215-248-8504
- **Devon Horse Show & Country Fair** (late May-early June) ... 610-964-0550
- **Festival of Fountains** (late May-early September) ... 610-388-1000
- **Flower & Garden Festival** (early May) ... 215-794-4000
- **Jam Festival** (late May) ... 215-629-3237
- **Jam on the River** (late May) ... 215-636-1666
- **Pennsylvania Fair** (mid-May) ... 215-639-9000
- **Philadelphia Festival of World Cinema** (late April-early May) ... 215-569-9700 www.libertynet.org/pfwc/
- **Philadelphia Open House Tours** (late April-mid-May) ... 215-928-1188

June
- **Devon Horse Show & Country Fair** (late May-early June) ... 610-964-0550
- **Festival of Fountains** (late May-early September) ... 610-388-1000
- **First Union US Pro Championship The** (mid-June) ... 215-973-3580
- **Manayunk Arts Fest** (late June) ... 215-482-9565
- **Midsommarfest** (early June) ... 215-389-1776
- **Odunde African Street Festival & Marketplace** (mid-June) ... 215-732-8508
- **Rittenhouse Square Fine Arts Annual** (early June) ... 877-689-4112
- **Welcome America** (late June-early July) ... 215-636-1666

July
- **Festival of Fountains** (late May-early September) ... 610-388-1000
- **Philadelphia International Film Festival** (mid-late July) ... 215-879-8209
- **Welcome America** (late June-early July) ... 215-636-1666

August
- **Festival of Fountains** (late May-early September) ... 610-388-1000

September
- **Bach Festival of Philadelphia** (September-March) ... 215-247-2224 www.libertynet.org/bach/
- **Festival of Fountains** (late May-early September) ... 610-388-1000
- **Yo Philadelphia Festival** (early September) ... 215-636-1666

October
- **Bach Festival of Philadelphia** (September-March) ... 215-247-2224 www.libertynet.org/bach/
- **Philadelphia Museum of Art Craft Show** (late October-early November) ... 215-684-7930 www.libertynet.org/pmacraft/

November
- **Advanta Tennis Championships for Women** (mid-November) ... 610-828-5777
- **Bach Festival of Philadelphia** (September-March) ... 215-247-2224 www.libertynet.org/bach/
- **Philadelphia Museum of Art Craft Show** (late October-early November) ... 215-684-7930 www.libertynet.org/pmacraft/

December
- **Bach Festival of Philadelphia** (September-March) ... 215-247-2224 www.libertynet.org/bach/
- **Market Street East Holiday Festival** (late December) ... 215-625-4962

Pittsburgh

January
- **Celebration of Lights-Hartwood** (November-January) ... 800-366-0093
- **Pittsburgh Zoo Holiday Lights Festival** (December-early January) ... 412-665-3639
- **Sparkle Season** (late November-early January) ... 412-566-4190
- **Winter Flower Show** (late November-early January) ... 412-622-6915

February
- **Winterfest** (early February) ... 814-352-7777

March
- **Maple Sugar Fest** (late March) ... 412-422-6558
- **Saint Patrick's Day Parade** (mid-March) ... 412-621-0600
- **Science & Engineering Fair** (mid-March) ... 412-237-1821
- **Spring Flower Show** (late March-mid-April) ... 412-622-6915

April
- **Spring Flower Show** (late March-mid-April) ... 412-622-6915

May
- **Pittsburgh Children's Festival** (mid-May) ... 412-321-5520
- **Pittsburgh Folk Festival** (late May) ... 800-366-0093
- **UPMC Pittsburgh City Marathon** (early May) ... 412-647-7866

June
- **Greater Pittsburgh Renaissance Festival** (late June) ... 412-281-7711
- **Juneteenth Celebration** (mid-June) ... 412-281-7711
- **Mellon Jazz Festival** (mid-late June) ... 800-366-0093
- **Station Square Festival** (early June) ... 412-621-7223
- **Three Rivers Arts Festival** (early-mid-June) ... 412-281-8723 www.artsfestival.net
- **US Beer & Music Festival** (late June) ... 412-562-9900
- **WTAE-TV4 Summerfest** (late June) ... 412-462-6666

July
- **Pittsburgh Vintage Grand Prix** (mid-July) ... 800-366-0093
- **Southside Summer Street Spectacular** (mid-July) ... 412-481-0651
- **Westmoreland Arts & Heritage Festival** (early July) ... 724-834-7474

August
- **Pittsburgh Three Rivers Regatta** (early August) ... 412-338-8765
- **Shadyside Summer Arts & Jazz Festival** (early August) ... 412-681-2809
- **Summerfest** (mid-August) ... 412-562-9900

September
- **Penn's Colony Festival & Marketplace** (mid-late September) ... 412-487-6922
- **Pittsburgh Irish Festival** (mid-September) ... 412-661-1221

October
- **Head of the Ohio Regatta** (early October) ... 412-232-7506
- **Pittsburgh International Lesbian & Gay Film Festival** (mid-October) ... 412-232-3277 www.pilgff.com

November
- **Celebration of Lights-Hartwood** (November-January) ... 800-366-0093
- **Sparkle Season** (late November-early January) ... 412-566-4190
- **Three Rivers Film Festival** (early-mid-November) ... 412-681-5449 cinema.pgh.pa.us/FilmFest
- **Winter Flower Show** (late November-early January) ... 412-622-6915

December
- **Celebration of Lights-Hartwood** (November-January) ... 800-366-0093
- **First Night Pittsburgh** (December 31) ... 888-744-3378
- **Pittsburgh Zoo Holiday Lights Festival** (December-early January) ... 412-665-3639
- **Sparkle Season** (late November-early January) ... 412-566-4190
- **Winter Flower Show** (late November-early January) ... 412-622-6915

Scranton

March
- **Pennsylvania National Arts & Crafts Show** (mid-March) ... 717-796-0531
- **Saint Patrick's Day Parade** (mid-March) ... 570-348-3412
- **Spring Carnival** (mid-March) ... 570-679-2611

May
- **Armed Forces Airshow** (early May) ... 570-824-1879
- **Jazz Fest at Cherry Blossom Time** (early May) ... 570-823-3165

August
- **Moscow Country Fair** (mid-August) ... 570-842-7252

September
- **La Festa Italiana** (early September) ... 800-229-3526
- **Wings Over Montage** (early September) ... 570-969-7669

PENNSYLVANIA — Scranton (Cont'd)

November
Artisan's Marketplace (late November) 570-586-8191

RHODE ISLAND

Newport

February
Newport Winter Festival (mid-late February) 401-847-7666

March
Newport Irish Heritage Month (March) 401-845-9123

June
Great Chowder Cook-off (early-mid-June) 401-846-1600
Newport International Polo Series (early June-mid-September) 401-847-7090
Secret Garden Tour (mid-June) 401-847-0514

July
Black Ships Festival (mid-July) 401-846-2720
July 3rd Clambake (July 3) 401-847-1441
Newport Flower Show (mid-July) 401-847-1000
Newport International Polo Series (early June-mid-September) 401-847-7090
Newport Music Festival (early July) 401-846-1133
www.newportmusic.org
Small Boat Regatta (mid-July) 401-847-1018

August
Ben & Jerry's Newport Folk Festival (early August) 401-847-3700
newportfolk.com
Newport International Polo Series (early June-mid-September) 401-847-7090
Newport Jazz Festival (early August) 401-847-3700
www.festivalproductions.net/jvc/newport/index.shtml

September
Classic Yacht Regatta (early September) 401-847-1018
Newport International Boat Show (mid September) 401-846-1115
Newport International Polo Series (early June-mid-September) 401-847-7090
Taste of Rhode Island (late September) 401-846-1600
We Rose for Rose Regatta (mid-September) 401-847-4242

October
Bowen's Wharf Waterfront Seafood Festival (mid-October) 401-849-2243
Fiesta Italiana (early October) 401-849-8048
Harvest Fair (early October) 401-846-2577
Home for the Holidays Craft & Gift Expo (mid-October) 401-846-1600
Octoberfest (early October) 401-846-1600

November
Craft Fair (late November) 401-847-3213
Taste of Newport (mid-November) 401-849-2300

December
Christmas in Newport (December) 401-849-6454
Christmas Tree Lighting (early December) 401-849-2243
Victorian Christmas Feast (mid-December) 401-846-3772

Providence

January
Providence Auto Show (mid-January) 401-274-1636
Providence Boat Show (late January) 401-458-6000

February
Rhode Island Spring Flower & Garden Show (mid-February) 401-458-6000

May
Gaspee Days Arts & Crafts Festival (late May) 401-461-9068
Water Fire Providence (mid-May-late December) 401-331-3624

June
Festival of Historic Houses (mid-June) 401-831-7440
Water Fire Providence (mid-May-late December) 401-331-3624

July
Providence Walking Tours (early July-late September) 401-831-7440
Water Fire Providence (mid-May-late December) 401-331-3624

August
Providence Walking Tours (early July-late September) 401-831-7440
Water Fire Providence (mid-May-late December) 401-331-3624

September
Heritage Day Festival (mid-September) 401-222-2669
Providence Walking Tours (early July-late September) 401-831-7440
Providence Waterfront Festival (mid-September) 401-785-9450
users.ids.net/~festival/
Water Fire Providence (mid-May-late December) 401-331-3624

October
Water Fire Providence (mid-May-late December) 401-331-3624

November
Water Fire Providence (mid-May-late December) 401-331-3624

December
First Night Providence (December 31) 401-521-1166
Holiday Tours in Historic Providence (mid-December) 401-831-8587
Latin Christmas Carol Celebration (early December) 401-863-2123
Water Fire Providence (mid-May-late December) 401-331-3624

SOUTH CAROLINA

Charleston

January
Holiday Festival of Lights (mid-November-early January) 843-853-8000
Low Country Oyster Festival (mid-January) 843-577-4030

February
Blues Festival (early-mid February) 843-762-9125
LowCountry Blues Bash (early-mid-February) 800-868-8118
Southeastern Wildlife Exposition (February) 800-221-5273
Visitor Value Days (late November-February) 800-868-8118

March
Festival of Houses & Gardens (March-April) 843-723-1623
Flowertown Festival (late March) 843-871-9622

April
Charleston Maritime Harborfest (mid-April) 843-577-8878
Festival of Houses & Gardens (March-April) 843-723-1623
Low Country Cajun Festival (early-mid-April) 843-762-2172
World Grits Festival (mid-April) 843-563-2150

May
Spoleto Festival USA (late May-early June) 843-722-2764
www.spoletofestivalusa.com/

June
Carolina Day (late June) 843-883-3123
Charleston Antiques Show (mid-June) 843-849-1949
Spoleto Festival USA (late May-early June) 843-722-2764
www.spoletofestivalusa.com/
This Magic Moment (late June) 843-853-8000

July
Festival on the Fourth (July 4) 843-556-5660
Summer Classic Horse Show (July) 843-768-2500

August
Folly River Float Frenzy & Fish Fry (mid-August) 843-588-6663

September
Big Kahuna Tournament (September) 843-588-3474
Fall Candlelight Tours of Homes & Gardens (late September-early October) 843-722-4630
Moja Arts Festival (late September-early October) 843-724-7305
Scottish Games & Highland Gathering (September) 843-884-4371

October
Charleston Garden Festival (early October) 843-722-7526
Fall Candlelight Tours of Homes & Gardens (late September-early October) 843-722-4630
Moja Arts Festival (late September-early October) 843-724-7305
Taste of Charleston (October) 843-577-4030

November
Battle of Secessionville (early November) 843-795-3049
Charleston Cup (early November) 843-766-6208
Holiday Festival of Lights (mid-November-early January) 843-853-8000
Plantation Days (November) 843-556-6020
Visitor Value Days (late November-February) 800-868-8118

December
Christmas in Charleston (December) 843-853-8000
Holiday Festival of Lights (mid-November-early January) 843-853-8000
Plantation Christmas at Middleton Place (December) 843-556-6020

Columbia

February
Carolina Marathon (late February) 803-929-1996
www.carolinamarathon.org/

March
Carolina Classic Home & Garden Show (mid-March) 803-256-6238
Greek Bake Sale (early March) 803-252-6758
Saint Patrick's Day Festival (mid-March) 803-738-1499
South Carolina Oyster Festival (mid-March) 803-695-0676
Spring Things Art & Craft Show (mid-March) 803-772-3336

April
Columbia International Festival (early April) 803-799-3452
NatureFest (late April) 803-776-4396
Riverfest Celebration (mid-April) 803-254-0479
Vista After Five Spring Concerts (early April-late May) 803-256-7501

May
Main Street Jazz (late May) 803-254-0479
Mayfest (early May) 803-254-0479
Vista After Five Spring Concerts (early April-late May) 803-256-7501

July
Lexinton County Peach Festival (early July) 803-254-0479

August
Jubilee Festival of Heritage (mid-August) 803-252-7742

September
Congaree Western Weekend Festival & Rodeo (mid-September) 803-755-2512
Greek Festival (late September) 803-252-6758
Labor Day Festival (early September) 803-345-1100

October
South Carolina State Fair (early October) 803-254-0479

November
Vista Lights (mid-November) 803-254-0479

December
Christmas Candlelight Tours (early December) 803-252-7742
Christmas Traditions (early December) 803-779-8717
Lights Before Christmas at the Zoo (December) 803-779-8717

Greenville

February
Boat RV & Sport Show (early February) 864-233-2562

April
Main Street Jazz (early April-early-October) 864-467-5780
Thursday Night Downtown Alive (April-September) 864-467-8089

May
Freedom Weekend Aloft Balloon Race (Memorial Day weekend) 864-232-3700
Main Street Jazz (early April-early-October) 864-467-5780
River Place Festival (early May) 864-467-5780
Thursday Night Downtown Alive (April-September) 864-467-8089

June
Main Street Jazz (early April-early-October) 864-467-5780
Music on the Mountain (June-August) 864-288-6470
Thursday Night Downtown Alive (April-September) 864-467-8089

July
Country Corn Festival (mid-July) 864-834-0704
Main Street Jazz (early April-early-October) 864-467-5780
Music on the Mountain (June-August) 864-288-6470
Thursday Night Downtown Alive (April-September) 864-467-8089

August
Antiques Extravaganza (mid-August) 864-233-2562
Main Street Jazz (early April-early-October) 864-467-5780
Music on the Mountain (June-August) 864-288-6470
Thursday Night Downtown Alive (April-September) 864-467-8089

September
Art in the Park (mid-September) 864-467-6627
Main Street Jazz (early April-early-October) 864-467-5780
Thursday Night Downtown Alive (April-September) 864-467-8089

October
Aunt Het Festival (early October) 864-862-2586
Back to Nature Festival (mid-October) 864-288-6470
Boo in the Zoo Festival (late October) 864-467-4300
Fall for Greenville-A Taste of Our Town (mid-October) 864-370-1795
Halloween Spooktacular (late October) 864-288-6470
Main Street Jazz (early April-early-October) 864-467-5780
Michelin Cycling Classic (mid-October) 864-467-6627

November
Christmas Light Show (late November-late December) 864-421-0000

December
Christmas Light Show (late November-late December) 864-421-0000
First Night Greenville (December 31) 864-467-5780
Holiday Fair & Crafts Show (early December) 864-233-2562

Hilton Head Island

January
Hilton Head Playhouse Series (September-May) 843-686-3945

February
Hilton Head Playhouse Series (September-May) 843-686-3945

March
Hilton Head Playhouse Series (September-May) 843-686-3945

April
Art & Flower Show (late April) 843-785-3673
Golf Fair (mid-April) 843-785-1136
Hilton Head Playhouse Series (September-May) 843-686-3945
MCI Classic (mid-April) 800-234-1107

May
Arts & Crafts Show (late May & mid-October) 843-686-3090
Hilton Head Playhouse Series (September-May) 843-686-3945

June
Antique Show (late June & early November) 843-686-3090
HarbourFest (mid-June-late August) 843-785-1106
Week of Champions (early-mid-June) 843-757-2150

July
Banana Open Mixed Doubles (mid-July) 843-785-6613
HarbourFest (mid-June-late August) 843-785-1106
July 4th Celebration (July 4) 843-785-3673

August
Banana Open Singles (mid-August) 843-785-6613
HarbourFest (mid-June-late August) 843-785-1106

September
Hilton Head Island Celebrity Golf Tournament (early September) 843-842-7711
Hilton Head Playhouse Series (September-May) 843-686-3945

SOUTH CAROLINA — Hilton Head Island (Cont'd)

October
Arts & Crafts Show (late May & mid-October) 843-686-3090
Chili Cook-off (early October) 843-785-7738
Ghost Stories (late October) 843-363-4530
Hilton Head Playhouse Series (September-May) 843-686-3945

November
Antique Show (late June & early November) 843-686-3090
Hilton Head Playhouse Series (September-May) 843-686-3945
Taste of the Season (mid-November) 843-785-3673
Thanksgiving Hayride (late November) 843-363-4530

December
Hilton Head Playhouse Series (September-May) 843-686-3945

Myrtle Beach

January
Holiday Celebration (early November-late January) 843-626-7444
Treasures by the Sea (early November-mid-February) 800-356-3016

February
Myrtle Beach Marathon (late February) 843-293-7223
www.coastal.edu/mbmarathon
Treasures by the Sea (early November-mid-February) 800-356-3016

March
Canadian American Days Festival (mid-late March) 843-626-7444
www.mbchamber.com/canamhomepage.html
Carolina Women's Show (mid-March) 800-610-7469
Doll Show & Sale (mid-March) 843-248-5643
Georgetown Plantation Tours (late March) 843-546-4358
Grand Strand Passion Play (late March) 843-448-3155
Saint Patrick's Day Festival (mid-March) 843-361-0038
Spring Arts & Crafts Show (mid-March) 843-448-2513

April
Grand Strand Fishing Rodeo (early April-late October) 843-626-7444
www.mbchamber.com/fishrodeo.html
SOS Spring Safari (mid-late April) 888-767-3113
Spring Games Kite Festival (early-mid-April) 843-448-7261
Taste of Broadway Spring Festival (early-mid-April) 843-444-3200

May
Art in the Park (early May) 843-249-4937
Blessing of the Inlet (early May) 843-651-5099
Blue Crab Arts & Crafts Festival (mid-May) 843-249-6604
Frantic Atlantic Spring King Classic
(mid-late May & mid-late September) 843-249-7881
Grand Strand Fishing Rodeo (early April-late October) 843-626-7444
www.mbchamber.com/fishrodeo.html
Harley Davidson Biker Rally (mid-May) 843-651-5555
Rivertown Music Festival (early May) 843-444-5614

June
Grand Strand Fishing Rodeo (early April-late October) 843-626-7444
www.mbchamber.com/fishrodeo.html
Pier King Mackerel Tournament
(early June & mid-September) 843-626-7444
Sun Fun Festival (early June) 843-626-7444
www.mbchamber.com/sunfun.html

July
Grand Strand Fishing Rodeo (early April-late October) 843-626-7444
www.mbchamber.com/fishrodeo.html
Murrells Inlet Fourth of July Boat Parade (July 4) 843-651-5675

August
Carolina Craftsman Summer Classic (early August) 843-918-1225
DuPont World Amateur Handicap
(late August-early September) 843-477-8833
Grand Strand Fishing Rodeo (early April-late October) 843-626-7444
www.mbchamber.com/fishrodeo.html

September
DuPont World Amateur Handicap
(late August-early September) 843-477-8833
Frantic Atlantic Spring King Classic
(mid-late May & mid-late September) 843-249-7881
Grand Strand Fishing Rodeo (early April-late October) 843-626-7444
www.mbchamber.com/fishrodeo.html
Mark Sloan Golf Tournament (early September) 843-626-3638
Myrtle Beach Greek Festival (late September) 843-448-3773
Pier King Mackerel Tournament
(early June & mid-September) 843-626-7444

October
Frantic Atlantic Big Bucks Bonanza (early-mid-October) 843-249-7881
Grand Strand Fishing Rodeo (early April-late October) 843-626-7444
www.mbchamber.com/fishrodeo.html
Great American Shootout Soccer Tournament
(mid-late October) 843-449-9622
Home Improvement Expo (early-mid-October) 843-347-7311
Oktoberfest (early October) 843-918-1242
Taste of the Town (late October-early November) 843-448-6062

November
Dickens Christmas Show & Festival (mid-November) 843-448-9483
Holiday Celebration (early November-late January) 843-626-7444
Intracoastal Christmas Regatta (late November) 843-280-6354
South Carolina State Bluegrass Festival
(late November) 843-918-1226
Taste of the Town (late October-early November) 843-448-6062
Treasures by the Sea (early November-mid-February) 800-356-3016

December
Holiday Celebration (early November-late January) 843-626-7444
Treasures by the Sea (early November-mid-February) 800-356-3016

SOUTH DAKOTA

Pierre

February
Gun Show (February) 605-224-1371

March
Farm Home & Sports Show (mid-March) 605-224-1240

April
Fort Pierre Horse Races (mid April-early May) 605-223-2178

May
Fort Pierre Horse Races (mid April-early May) 605-223-2178

June
Casey Tibbs Match of Champions Bronc Riding Event
(early June) 605-223-2449
Dakota Blast (mid-June) 605-223-3154
Infisherman's Pro/AM Walleye Tournament (late June) 605-224-7361
Shrine Circus (mid-June) 605-224-7361
Volksmarch at Crazy Horse (early June) 605-673-4681

July
Downtown Pierre Crazy Days (late July) 605-224-7825
Fourth of July Rodeo (July 4) 605-224-7361

August
August Jamboree & Old West Shoot-out (late August) 605-223-3154
South Dakota State Fair (late August-early September) 605-353-7340
Sturgis Motorcycle Rally & Races (mid-August) 605-347-6570

September
Fall Arts & Crafts Show (late September) 605-224-7754
Goosefest (late September) 605-224-7361
South Dakota State Fair (late August-early September) 605-353-7340

November
Capital Christmas Trees Display
(late November-late December) 605-773-3765

December
Capital Christmas Trees Display
(late November-late December) 605-773-3765

Rapid City

January
Black Hills Stock Show & Rodeo
(late January-early February) 605-355-3861

February
Black Hills Stock Show & Rodeo
(late January-early February) 605-355-3861

March
Home & Industry Show (late March) 800-487-3223

June
Black Hills Heritage Festival (late June-early July) 605-341-5714
Black Hills Passion Play (early June-early September) 800-487-3223
Blue Grass Festival (late June) 605-394-4101

July
Black Hills Heritage Festival (late June-early July) 605-341-5714
Black Hills Jazz & Blues Festival (late July) 605-394-4101
Black Hills Passion Play (early June-early September) 800-487-3223
Days of '76 (late July-early August) 800-999-1876
Spearfish Festival in the Park (July) 800-487-3223

August
Black Hills Passion Play (early June-early September) 800-487-3223
Central States Fair (mid-late August) 605-355-3861
Days of '76 (late July-early August) 800-999-1876

September
Black Hills Passion Play (early June-early September) 800-487-3223

October
Badlands Circuit Finals Rodeo (late October) 605-394-4115
Black Hills Pow Wow (early October) 605-341-0925
Custer State Park Buffalo Roundup (early October) 605-255-4515
Mount Rushmore International Marathon (mid-October) 605-348-7866

Sioux Falls

January
Sioux Empire Farm Show (late January) 605-373-2016
Winter Fest (late January) 605-338-4009

February
Artists of the Plains Art Show & Sale (mid-February) 605-336-4007

March
Augustana Jazz Festival (early March) 605-336-4049

April
Almost Forgotten Crafts (late April) 605-367-4210
Festival of Choirs (early April) 605-367-7957

June
Northern Prairie Storytelling Festival (early June) 605-331-6622

August
Sioux Empire Fair (early-mid-August) 605-367-7178

September
Northern Plains Tribal Art Show & Market
(late September) 605-334-4060
Sidewalk Arts Festival (early September) 605-336-1167

October
University of Sioux Falls Cougar Days (early October) 605-331-5000
Viking Days (early October) 605-336-5521

TENNESSEE

Chattanooga

January
Enchanted Garden of Lights
(mid-November-early January) 423-756-8687

February
Houston Museum's Antiques Show & Sale
(late February) 423-267-7176
Taste of Chattanooga (early February) 423-265-4397

March
Longhorn World Championship Rodeo (early March) 423-266-6627

April
Dixieland Excursions (April-November) 423-894-8028
Wildflower Festival (early April) 423-821-1160

May
Chattanooga Traditional Jazz Festival (early May) 423-266-0944
Dixieland Excursions (April-November) 423-894-8028
Downtown Partnership Nightfall Concerts
(late May-late September) 423-265-0771
Pat Boone Celebrity Spectacular (mid-May) 423-842-5757
Praters Mill Country Fair (May & October) 423-756-8687
River Roast (mid-May) 423-266-7070

June
Dixieland Excursions (April-November) 423-894-8028
Riverbend Festival (late June) 423-265-4112

July
Dixieland Excursions (April-November) 423-894-8028

August
Dixieland Excursions (April-November) 423-894-8028

September
Dixieland Excursions (April-November) 423-894-8028
Downtown Partnership Nightfall Concerts
(late May-late September) 423-265-0771
Hamilton County Fair (late September) 423-756-8687

October
Dixieland Excursions (April-November) 423-894-8028
Fall Color Cruise & Folk Festival (late October) 423-892-0223
Praters Mill Country Fair (May & October) 423-756-8687

November
Dixieland Excursions (April-November) 423-894-8028
Enchanted Garden of Lights
(mid-November-early January) 423-756-8687

December
Enchanted Garden of Lights
(mid-November-early January) 423-756-8687

Johnson City

January
Fantasy in Lights (mid-November-early January) 423-764-1161

April
Spring Garden Fair (late April) 423-288-6071

July
Canjoe Festival (late July-early August) 800-606-4833
Farm Fest (mid-late July) 423-288-6071
Fireworks in the Park (July 4) 423-727-5800
Folklife Festival (mid-July) 423-239-6786
Fourth of July Fireworks (July 4) 423-245-2856
Fun Fest (mid-late July) 423-392-8809
www.kingsportchamber.org/funfest
Pepsi Independence Day Celebration (July 4) 423-928-9211
Roan Mountain State Park's Independence Day Activities
(early July) 423-772-0190

August
Appalachian Fair (late August) 423-477-3211
www.appalachianfair.com
Bristol Racefest (late August) 423-989-4850
Canjoe Festival (late July-early August) 800-606-4833
Davy Crockett Celebration (mid-August) 423-257-4655
Old Butler Days (mid-August) 423-768-2432
Quiltfest (early August) 423-753-1010
Unity Day Festival (early August) 423-461-8830

Calendar of Events

TENNESSEE — Johnson City (Cont'd)

September
Archie Campbell Homecoming Day (early September) 423-235-5216
Downtown Kingsport Arts & Crafts Festival (September 11 & 12) 423-246-6550
Fall Folks Arts Festival (late September) 423-288-6071
Fort Watauga Knap-In (mid-September) 423-543-5808
Old Time Fiddlers & Bluegrass Festival (mid-September) 423-247-9181
Overmountain Victory Trail March & Celebration (late September) 423-543-5808
Riverfront Festival (September) 423-345-2213
Roan Mountain Fall Naturalists Rally (early-mid-September) 423-772-0190
Roan Mountain State Park's Fall Festival (mid-September) 423-772-0190
Times of the Tiptons (mid-September) 423-926-3631

October
Cranberry Festival (early October) 423-739-5455
Halloween Haunts & Happenings (late October) 423-753-1550
Harvest Hoedown (early October) 423-323-5686
Heritage Days (mid-October) 423-272-1961
Jericho Shrine Circus (late October) 423-323-1982
Mountainfest Arts & Crafts Show (late October) 423-652-2674
National Storytelling Festival (early October) 423-753-2171
Spirits of the Harvest (mid-October) 888-538-1791
Spooktacular Halloween Party (late October) 423-434-4263
Stories From the Pumpkin Patch (late October) 423-926-3631
Unicoi County Apple Festival (early October) 423-743-3000
www.valleybeautiful.org/evntappl.htm
Witches Wynd (late October) 423-288-6071

November
Christmas Craft Show & Sale (late November) 423-753-1010
Christmas Crafts Show (mid-November) 423-543-5808
Fantasy in Lights (mid-November-early January) 423-764-1161
Thanksgiving Garrison at Fort Watauga (late November) 423-543-5808

December
Candlelight Tour (early December) 423-538-7396
Children's Christmas Event (mid-December) 423-753-1010
Christmas at President Andrew Johnson Homestead (mid-December) 423-638-3551
Christmas at the Carter Mansion (mid-December) 423-543-5808
Christmas Garrison at Fort Watauga (mid-late December) 423-543-5808
Christmas in the Country Craft Show & Sale (early December) 423-288-6071
Fantasy in Lights (mid-November-early January) 423-764-1161
Visions of Christmas Candlelight Tour (mid-December) 423-926-3631
Yule Log Ceremony (early December) 423-288-6071

Knoxville

February
Smoky Mountain Marathon (late February) 865-588-7465

March
Knoxville Boat Show (early March) 865-588-1233

April
Dogwood Arts Festival (early-mid-April) 865-637-4561
Knoxville Western Film Caravan (late April) 865-522-2600

May
International Jubilee Festival (late May) 865-522-5851
Ragin' Cajun Cookout (late May) 865-558-9040

June
Statehood Day Celebration (early June) 865-525-2375

July
Fourth of July Celebration & Anvil Shoot (early July) 865-494-7680
Kuumba Festival (early July) 865-525-0961

September
Artfest (early September-late October) 865-523-7543
Boomsday (early September) 865-693-1020
Tennessee Valley Fair (mid-September) 865-637-5840

October
Artfest (early September-late October) 865-523-7543
Tennessee Fall Homecoming (early October) 865-494-7680

November
Christmas in the City (late November-late December) 865-215-4248
Fantasy of Trees (late November) 865-541-8385
Foothills Craft Guild Fall Show & Sale (mid-November) 865-483-6400

December
Christmas in the City (late November-late December) 865-215-4248

Memphis

January
Christmas at Graceland (late November-early January) 800-238-2000
Dr Martin Luther King Jr Celebration/March (January) 901-525-2458
Memphis Boat Show (mid-January) 901-684-6211

February
Zydeco Festival (mid-February) 901-526-0110

April
Africa in April Cultural Awareness Festival (mid-April) 901-947-2133
Information Open House (early April) 901-383-4116
Spring Festival (mid-April) 901-526-0110
Spring Music Festival (mid-April) 901-526-0110
Spring's Best Plant Sale (mid-April) 901-685-1566

May
Beale Street Music Festival (early May) 901-525-4611
www.memphisinmay.org/beale/index.html
Memphis Cotton Makers Jubilee (early May) 901-774-1118
Memphis in May International Festival (May) 901-525-4611
www.memphisinmay.org

June
Carnival Memphis (early-mid-June) 901-278-0243
Ducks Unlimited Great Outdoors Festival (early June) 901-523-8463
Germantown Charity Horse Show (early June) 901-754-7443
Juneteenth Freedom Festival (mid-June) 901-385-4943
Memphis Italian Festival (early June) 901-767-6949

August
Choctaw Indian Cultural Festival (early August) 901-785-3160
Elvis Presley International Tribute Week (early-mid-August) 901-332-3322

September
Memphis Music & Heritage Festival (early September) 901-525-3655
Mid-South Fair (late September-early October) 901-274-8800
www.midsouthfair.com
Southern Heritage Classic (early September) 901-398-6655

October
Arts in the Park (mid-October) 901-761-1278
Mid-South Fair (late September-early October) 901-274-8800
www.midsouthfair.com
Native American Days (late October) 901-785-3160
Pink Palace Crafts Fair (early October) 901-320-6320

November
Christmas at Graceland (late November-early January) 800-238-2000

December
Beale Street New Year's Eve Celebration (December 31) 901-526-0110
Christmas at Graceland (late November-early January) 800-238-2000
First Tennessee Memphis Marathon (early December) 800-893-7223
Liberty Bowl (late December) 901-795-7700
Memphis Christmas Parade (early December) 901-575-0540
New Year's Eve Festival (December 31) 901-526-0110

Nashville

January
Nashville Boat & Sport Show (early January) 615-742-2000

February
Antiques & Garden Show of Nashville (mid-February) 615-352-1282
Heart of Country Antiques Show (mid-February) 615-883-2211

March
Nashville Lawn & Garden Show (early March) 615-352-3863

April
Main Street Festival (late April) 615-791-9924
Southern Gospel Music Fest (mid-late April) 888-326-3378
Tin Pan South (mid-April) 615-251-3472
Wildflower Fair (early April) 615-353-2148

May
Colonial Fair Day (early May) 615-859-7979
Dancin' in the District (early May-late July) 615-256-9596
Historic Edgefield Tour of Homes (mid-May) 615-226-3340
Iroquois Steeplechase (early May) 615-322-7450
Tennessee Crafts Fair (early May) 615-665-0502
Tennessee Renaissance Festival (May) 615-259-4747

June
American Artisan Festival (mid-June) 615-298-4691
Balloon Classic (mid-June) 615-329-7807
Chet Atkins' Musician Days (late June) 615-256-9596
Dancin' in the District (early May-late July) 615-256-9596
Fan Fair (mid-June) 615-862-8980
International Country Music Fan Fair (mid-June) 615-889-7503

July
Dancin' in the District (early May-late July) 615-256-9596
Independence Day Celebration (July 4) 615-862-8400

August
Americana Sampler Craft Folk Art & Antique Show (early August) 615-227-2080
Tennessee Walking Horse National Celebration (late August-early September) 931-684-5915

September
African Street Festival (mid-September) 615-299-0412
Belle Meade Fall Fest (mid-September) 615-356-0501
Franklin Jazz Festival (early September) 615-790-7094
Italian Street Fair (early September) 615-255-5600
TACA Fall Crafts Fair (late September) 615-665-0502
Tennessee State Fair (early-mid-September) 615-862-8980
Tennessee Walking Horse National Celebration (late August-early September) 931-684-5915

October
Boo at the Zoo (mid-late October) 615-371-8462
Grand Ole Opry Birthday Celebration (mid-October) 615-889-6611
Music City Hog Jam (early October) 615-259-4700
NAIA Pow Wow (mid-October) 615-726-0806
Oktoberfest (early October) 615-256-2729

November
A Country Christmas (early November-late December) 615-871-6169
Longhorn World Championship Rodeo (mid-November) 800-357-6336
Nashville's Country Holidays (early November-late December) 615-259-4700

December
A Country Christmas (early November-late December) 615-871-6169
Nashville's Country Holidays (early November-late December) 615-259-4700

TEXAS

Abilene

January
Abilene Kennel Club All-Breed Dog Show (late January) 915-676-2556
Big Country Cat Fanciers Show (late January) 915-676-6211
Celebration Park Display (mid-November-early January) 915-691-1034
Texas Gun & Knife Show (mid-January & mid-May) 915-676-6211

February
Crossroads Gun & Knife Show (late February & late July & early December) 915-676-6211

March
Celebrate Abilene (late March-mid-April) 915-676-3775

April
Big Country Quarter Horse Assn Spring Show (late April) 915-677-4376
Celebrate Abilene (late March-mid-April) 915-676-3775
Central Texas Gem & Mineral Show (mid-April) 915-676-6211
Texas Amateur Quarter Horse Assn State Championship Show (late April) 915-677-4376
Western Heritage Classic Fashion Show (early April) 915-672-3051
World's Largest Barbecue (mid-April) 915-677-7241

May
Big Country Cutting Horse Assn Show (late May) 915-677-4376
Coors Original Team Roping (early May) 915-677-4376
Cowboys Heritage Texas Team Roping (late May) 915-677-4376
KEAN Big Bass Bonanza (mid-late May) 915-676-7711
Key City Amateur Radio Ham Fest (early May) 915-672-8889
Stars Over Abilene Quilt Show (late May) 915-676-6211
Sunburn Grand Prix (late May) 915-698-2176
Texas Gun & Knife Show (mid-January & mid-May) 915-676-6211
Western Heritage Classic (early May) 915-677-4376
Western Heritage Classic Parade (early May) 915-677-4376

June
Arts & Crafts Festival (mid-June) 915-676-6211
Fort Griffin Fandangle (mid-late June) 915-762-3838
Police Athletic Federation Annual Games (late June) 915-676-6523
Supercar Show (mid-June) 915-676-6211
Travis Boat Show (late June) 915-676-6211

July
American Country Peddler Arts & Crafts Show (late July-early August) 915-676-6211
Crossroads Gun & Knife Show (late February & late July & early December) 915-676-6211
Texas Firefighters Olympics (mid-late July) 915-676-6433
Texas State 4-H Horse Show (mid-late July) 915-677-4376

August
American Country Peddler Arts & Crafts Show (late July-early August) 915-676-6211
Big Country Appreciation Day (August-November) 915-696-5609
Biggest Little Arts & Crafts Show (mid-August & late September)) 915-676-6211
KTXS Festival of Fun (late August) 915-677-2281

September
Altrusa Antique Show (mid-September) 915-676-6211
Big Country Appreciation Day (August-November) 915-696-5609
Biggest Little Arts & Crafts Show (mid-August & late September)) 915-676-6211
Chili Super Bowl (early September) 915-675-8412
Hot Air Balloon Festival (late September) 915-675-8041
West Texas Fair & Rodeo (mid-September) 915-677-4376

October
Abilene Shoot-out (early October) 915-698-2176
Big Country Appreciation Day (August-November) 915-696-5609
Southwest Regional Fly-In (mid-October) 915-676-2556
West Texas Renaissance Faire (early October) 915-672-3010
camalott.com/~renfaire

November
Big Country Appreciation Day (August-November) 915-696-5609
Celebration Park Display (mid-November-early January) 915-691-1034
Christmas Carousel (early November) 915-676-6211
Christmas in November (mid-November) 915-676-6211
City Sidewalks Tree Lighting (late November) 915-676-6211
KTXS Parade of Lights (late November-early December) 915-677-2281

December
Celebration Park Display (mid-November-early January) 915-691-1034
Cowboy Christmas Ball (mid-December) 915-823-3259
Crossroads Gun & Knife Show (late February & late July & early December) 915-676-6211
KTXS Parade of Lights (late November-early December) 915-677-2281

Amarillo

January
Mel Phillips' Outdoor World Sportsman's Show (late January) ... 806-378-4297
www.searchtexas.com/melphillips/outdoorworld/
Super Bull Tour (late January) ... 806-378-3096

February
Circus Gatti (late February) ... 806-378-4297
Panhandle Boat Sport & Travel Show (early February) ... 806-383-4408
www.searchtexas.com/boatshow/

March
Best of Texas Festival (late March) ... 806-374-0802

May
FunFest (late May) ... 806-374-0802

June
Coors Ranch Rodeo (early-mid June) ... 806-376-7767
Texas Musical Drama (early June-late August) ... 806-655-2181

July
Range Riders Rodeo (early July) ... 806-355-2212
Texas Musical Drama (early June-late August) ... 806-655-2181

August
Texas Musical Drama (early June-late August) ... 806-655-2181

September
Boys Ranch Rodeo (Labor Day weekend) ... 806-372-2341
Octoberfest (early September) ... 806-373-7800
Tri-State Fair (mid-September) ... 806-376-7767

October
High Plains Book Festival (early October) ... 806-651-2231
bookfestival.arn.net/

November
WRCA World Championship Ranch Rodeo (mid-November) ... 806-374-9722

December
Amarillo Farm & Ranch Show (early December) ... 806-378-4297

Arlington

February
Neil Sperry's All Garden Show (late February-early March) ... 817-459-5000

March
International Week (late March-early April) ... 817-272-2355
Neil Sperry's All Garden Show (late February-early March) ... 817-459-5000
Texas Indian Market (late March) ... 817-459-5000

April
Cardboard Boat Regatta (mid-April) ... 817-860-6752
International Week (late March-early April) ... 817-272-2355
Semana de Cultura (early April) ... 817-272-2099

May
Yacht Club Regatta (early May) ... 817-275-8074

June
Auto Swap Meet (early June) ... 972-647-2331
Texas Scottish Festival & Games (early June) ... 817-654-2293
www.cyberramp.net/~ceilidh/

July
Fourth of July Celebration (July 4) ... 817-459-6100

August
Country at Heart Art & Craft Show (early August) ... 817-459-5000

September
National Championship Indian Pow Wow (early September) ... 972-647-2331
Taste of Arlington (mid-September) ... 817-459-5000

November
Young Country Christmas Fireworks to Music (late November) ... 214-855-1881

December
Celebration of Lights (early-December) ... 817-459-6122

Austin

January
Austin Boat & Fishing Show (mid-January) ... 512-494-1128
www.austinboatshow.net
Austin Home & Garden Show (mid-January) ... 512-476-5461
FronteraFest (late January) ... 512-499-8497

March
Austin Founders Trail Ride (early-mid-March) ... 512-477-4711
Austin/Travis County Livestock Show & Rodeo (mid-March) ... 512-467-9811
Jerry Jeff Walker's Birthday Celebration (late March) ... 512-477-0036
South By Southwest Music Festival (mid-March) ... 512-467-7979
sxsw.kdi.com/music/index.shtml
Texas Independence Day Celebration (early March) ... 512-477-1836
Travis County Livestock Show & PRCA Rodeo (mid-March) ... 512-467-9811
Wildflower Days Festival (late March & late May) ... 512-292-4200
Zilker Kite Festival (early March) ... 512-478-0098

April
Austin International Poetry Festival (early April) ... 512-346-8717
Austin Rugby Tournament (early April) ... 512-926-9017
www.austinrugby.com/
Austin Theatre Week (mid-April) ... 512-499-8388
Bob Marley Festival (early April) ... 512-312-0435
Louisiana Swamp Romp (late April) ... 512-441-9015

May
Cinco de Mayo Celebration (May 5) ... 512-499-6720
Fiesta Laguna Gloria (mid-May) ... 512-458-6073
www.amoa.org
Heritage Homes Tour (early May) ... 512-474-5198
Old Pecan Street Festival (early May & late September) ... 512-441-9015
Spamarama (early May) ... 512-834-1960
Wildflower Days Festival (late March & late May) ... 512-292-4200
Wooden Boat Show (late May) ... 512-288-5359
Zilker Garden Festival (early May) ... 512-477-8672

June
Austin Collectors Exposition (late June) ... 512-454-9882
Juneteenth Freedom Festival (mid-June) ... 512-472-6838
New Texas Festival (early June) ... 512-476-5775
Women in Jazz Concert Series (early June) ... 512-258-6947

July
Freedom Festival & Fireworks (July 4) ... 800-926-2282
Frontier Days (mid-July) ... 512-255-5805
Western Days (late July) ... 512-285-4515

August
Austin Chronicle Hot Sauce Festival (late August) ... 512-454-5766

September
Austin Jazz & Arts Festival (early September) ... 512-477-9438
Canterbury Faire (late September) ... 512-327-7622
Diez y Seis de Septiembre (September 16) ... 512-476-3868
Old Pecan Street Festival (early May & late September) ... 512-441-9015
Pioneer Farm Fall Festival (mid-September) ... 512-837-1215
Republic of Texas Chilympiad (late September) ... 512-478-0098
Volunteer Firemen's BBQ Extravaganza (mid-September) ... 512-282-3600
Zilker Fall Jazz Festival (early September) ... 512-440-1414

October
Austin Heart of Film Festival (October) ... 512-478-4795
Ben Hur Shrine Circus (early October) ... 512-327-3810
Halloween on Sixth Street (October 31) ... 512-476-8876
Oktoberfest (mid-October) ... 512-479-0598
Texas Wildlife Exposition (early October) ... 512-389-4472

November
Pow Wow & American Indian Heritage Festival (early November) ... 512-414-3849
Victorian Christmas on Sixth Street (late November) ... 512-441-9015

December
Armadillo Christmas Bazaar (mid-late December) ... 512-447-1605
www.armadillobazaar.com

Brownsville

January
Fly-Ins (October-March) ... 956-748-2112

February
Charro Days Festival (late February) ... 956-542-4245
Fly-Ins (October-March) ... 956-748-2112
Sombrero Festival (late February) ... 956-542-4341
Spring Faculty Art Exhibition (early February-early March) ... 956-544-8247

March
Brownsville Art League International Art Show (early March) ... 956-542-0941
Confederate Air Force Fiesta (early March) ... 956-541-8585
Fly-Ins (October-March) ... 956-748-2112
Semana Santa (Holy Week) (late March-early April) ... 956-761-6433
Spring Faculty Art Exhibition (early February-early March) ... 956-544-8247

April
Brownsville Art League International Student Art Show (late April-early May) ... 956-542-0941
Semana Santa (Holy Week) (late March-early April) ... 956-761-6433
South Padre Island Easter Egg Hunt (early April) ... 956-761-6433

May
Birdathon (mid-May) ... 956-541-8034
Brownsville Art League International Student Art Show (late April-early May) ... 956-542-0941
Feast with the Beast (mid-May) ... 956-546-7187
Friday Night Fireworks Over the Bay (late May-early September) ... 956-761-3000
Memorial Day Fireworks over the Bay (late May) ... 956-761-3000
Shrimp on the Barbie Cook-Off (May) ... 956-761-2831

June
CineSol Latino Film Festival (early June) ... 956-428-8983
Friday Night Fireworks Over the Bay (late May-early September) ... 956-761-3000

July
Beachcomber's Art Show (late July) ... 956-423-6707
Friday Night Fireworks Over the Bay (late May-early September) ... 956-761-3000
South Padre Island Fireworks Extravaganza (July 4) ... 956-761-3000

August
Friday Night Fireworks Over the Bay (late May-early September) ... 956-761-3000

September
Brownsville Appreciation Day at the Zoo (mid-September) ... 956-546-7187
Friday Night Fireworks Over the Bay (late May-early September) ... 956-761-3000

October
Boo at the Zoo (late October) ... 956-546-7187
Fall Faculty Art Exhibition (October-November) ... 956-544-8247
Fly-Ins (October-March) ... 956-748-2112
South Padre Island Bikefest (mid-October) ... 956-761-3000
Zoofari Fundraiser (early October) ... 956-546-7187

November
Christmas Tree Lighting Ceremony (late November) ... 956-546-3721
Fall Faculty Art Exhibition (October-November) ... 956-544-8247
Fly-Ins (October-March) ... 956-748-2112
Rio Grande Valley Arts & Crafts Expo (early November) ... 956-542-0941

December
Christmas Parade (early December) ... 956-542-4341
Fly-Ins (October-March) ... 956-748-2112

Corpus Christi

February
South Texas Ranching Heritage Festival (February) ... 361-595-3712

March
Oysterfest (early March) ... 361-729-2388

April
Artfest (mid-April) ... 361-884-6406
Buccaneer Days & Rodeo (mid-April-early May) ... 361-882-3242

May
Beach to Bay Marathon (mid-May) ... 361-225-3338
Buccaneer Days & Rodeo (mid-April-early May) ... 361-882-3242
Corpus Christi Maritime Festival (May) ... 361-883-5011
US Open Windsurfing Regatta (late May) ... 361-985-1555

July
Deep Sea Roundup (early July) ... 361-749-5919
Rockport Art Festival (early July) ... 361-729-6445

August
La Feria De Las Flores (early August) ... 361-883-8543

September
Bayfest (mid-September) ... 361-887-0868
Shrimporee (September) ... 361-758-2750

October
Rockport Seafair (mid-October) ... 361-729-3312
Texas Jazz Festival (mid-October) ... 361-883-4500

December
Annual Christmas Tree Forest (December) ... 361-980-3500
Harbor Lights (December) ... 361-985-1555

Dallas

January
Cotton Bowl (January 1) ... 214-634-7525
www.swbellcottonbowl.com
Dallas Boat Show (late January-early February) ... 972-714-0177
Kidfilm Festival (mid-January) ... 214-821-3456

February
Dallas Boat Show (late January-early February) ... 972-714-0177
Golden Gloves Tournament (mid-February) ... 214-670-8400

March
Dallas Blooms (March-early April) ... 214-327-8263
Dallas Home & Garden Show (early March) ... 800-654-1480
Dallas Video Festival (late March) ... 214-999-8999
www.videofest.org/2000
North Texas Irish Festival (early March) ... 214-821-4174
Saint Patrick's Day Parade (mid-March) ... 972-991-6677

April
Dallas Blooms (March-early April) ... 214-327-8263
Mesquite Rodeo (April-September) ... 972-285-8777
USA Film Festival (late April) ... 214-821-6300
Waxahachie Scarborough Renaissance Fair (April-June) ... 972-938-1888

May
Dallas Artfest (late May) ... 214-361-2011
www.500inc.org
Mesquite Rodeo (April-September) ... 972-285-8777
Waxahachie Scarborough Renaissance Fair (April-June) ... 972-938-1888

June
Dallas Summer Musicals (June-October) ... 214-421-0662
www.dallassummermusicals.org/
Mesquite Rodeo (April-September) ... 972-285-8777
Shakespeare Festival of Dallas (mid-June-late July) ... 214-559-2778
Waxahachie Scarborough Renaissance Fair (April-June) ... 972-938-1888

July
Dallas Summer Musicals (June-October) ... 214-421-0662
www.dallassummermusicals.org/
Mesquite Rodeo (April-September) ... 972-285-8777

TEXAS — Dallas (Cont'd)

Oasis Fireworks to Music (early July) 214-855-1881
Shakespeare Festival of Dallas (mid-June-late July) 214-559-2778
Taste of Dallas (mid-July) 214-741-7180

August
Dallas Morning News Dance Festival (late August-early September) 214-953-1977
Dallas Summer Musicals (June-October) 214-421-0662
www.dallassummermusicals.org/
Mesquite Rodeo (April-September) 972-285-8777

September
American Indian Art Festival & Market (September-November) 214-891-9640
Dallas Air Show (mid-September) 214-350-1651
Dallas Morning News Dance Festival (late August-early September) 214-953-1977
Dallas Summer Musicals (June-October) 214-421-0662
www.dallassummermusicals.org/
Greek Food Festival (late September) 972-991-1166
Mesquite Rodeo (April-September) 972-285-8777
Montage (mid-September) 214-361-2011
www.500inc.org
Plano Balloon Festival (mid-September) 972-867-7566
State Fair of Texas (late September-mid-October) 214-565-9931
www.texfair.com

October
American Indian Art Festival & Market (September-November) 214-891-9640
Dallas Summer Musicals (June-October) 214-421-0662
www.dallassummermusicals.org/
State Fair of Texas (late September-mid-October) 214-565-9931
www.texfair.com

November
American Indian Art Festival & Market (September-November) 214-891-9640

December
White Rock Marathon (early December) 214-528-2962

El Paso

January
El Paso Chamber Music Festival (early January) 915-833-9400

February
Southwestern International Livestock Show & Rodeo (early-mid-February) 915-534-4229

March
Siglo de Oro Drama Festival (early March) 915-532-7273

April
First Thanksgiving Festival (late April) 915-534-0677

May
International Balloon Festival (Memorial Day weekend) 915-886-2222

June
International Mariachi Festival (late June) 915-566-4066
Viva El Paso! (June-August) 915-565-6900

July
Viva El Paso! (June-August) 915-565-6900

August
Viva El Paso! (June-August) 915-565-6900

September
Fiesta de las Flores (Labor Day weekend) 915-542-3464
Shakespeare on the Rocks Festival (early September) 915-565-6900

October
Amigo Airsho (mid-October) 915-545-2865
Border Folk Festival (mid-October) 915-532-7273
Kermezaar Arts & Crafts Show (mid-October) 915-584-5685

November
A Christmas Fair (mid-November) 915-584-3511

December
Sun Carnival Football Classic (late December) 915-533-4416
Tour of Lights (mid-late December) 915-544-0062

Fort Worth

January
Southwestern Exposition & Livestock Show (late January-early February) 817-877-2400

February
Last Great Gunfight (early February) 800-433-5747
Southwestern Exposition & Livestock Show (late January-early February) 817-877-2400

March
Cowtown Goes Green (mid-March) 800-433-5747

April
Main Street Fort Worth Arts Festival (mid-April) 817-336-2787
Mayfest (late April-early May) 800-433-5747

May
Mayfest (late April-early May) 800-433-5747

June
Fort Worth Chisholm Trail Round-Up (mid-June) 817-625-7005
Juneteenth Celebration (mid-June) 800-433-5747
Shakespeare In the Park (June-July) 800-433-5747

July
Fort Worth Fourth (July 4) 800-433-5747
Oasis Fireworks to Music (early July) 214-855-1881
Shakespeare In the Park (June-July) 800-433-5747

August
Stockyards Championship Rodeo (early August-late November) 800-433-5747

September
Fort Worth RetroFest (mid-September-mid-November) 817-924-0492
Pioneer Days (mid-September) 800-433-5747
Stockyards Championship Rodeo (early August-late November) 800-433-5747

October
Fort Worth International Air Show (early October) 817-870-1515
Fort Worth RetroFest (mid-September-mid-November) 817-924-0492
Oktoberfest (early October) 800-433-5747
Red Steagall Cowboy Gathering (late October) 800-433-5747
Stockyards Championship Rodeo (early August-late November) 800-433-5747

November
Fort Worth RetroFest (mid-September-mid-November) 817-924-0492
Parade of Lights (late November-late December) 800-433-5747
Stockyards Championship Rodeo (early August-late November) 800-433-5747

December
Parade of Lights (late November-late December) 800-433-5747

Garland

June
Garland Summer Musicals (June-July) 972-205-2790

July
Garland Summer Musicals (June-July) 972-205-2790
Star Spangled 4th (July 4) 972-205-2749

August
Labor Day Jubilee (late August-early September) 972-276-9366

September
Labor Day Jubilee (late August-early September) 972-276-9366
State Fair of Texas (late September-mid-October) 214-565-9931
www.texfair.com

October
Autumn Fest (late October) 972-205-2749
It's a Gas Vintage Car Show (mid-October) 972-205-2749
State Fair of Texas (late September-mid-October) 214-565-9931
www.texfair.com
Trick or Treat Trot (late October) 972-205-2749

December
Christmas Tree Lighting (December) 972-205-2749

Houston

January
Houston International Boat Sport & Travel Show (mid-January) 713-526-6361
Houston Methodist Hospital Marathon (mid-January) 713-957-3453
www.houstonmarathon.com

February
Houston Livestock Show & Rodeo (mid-February-early March) 713-791-9000
www.hlsr.com
World Championship Bar-B-Que Contest (mid-February) 713-791-9000

March
Bayou City Art Festival (late March & mid-October) 713-521-0133
Fotofest (early March-early April) 713-529-9140
www.fotofest.org
Houston Livestock Show & Rodeo (mid-February-early March) 713-791-9000
www.hlsr.com

April
Fotofest (early March-early April) 713-529-9140
www.fotofest.org
Houston International Festival (late April) 713-654-8808
Worldfest Houston International Film Festival (early-mid-April) 713-965-9955
www.worldfest.org

May
Cinco de Mayo Festival (May 5) 713-437-5200
Moody Gardens Red White & Boom/Palm Beach (late May) 409-744-4673
Texas Crawfish Festival (mid-late May) 281-353-9310

June
Juneteenth Celebration (mid-June) 713-437-5200

July
Freedom Festival (July 4) 713-621-8600

August
Hot Air Balloon Festival (late August) 281-488-7676
Houston International Jazz Festival (early August) 713-839-7000

October
Asian-American Festival (mid-October) 713-861-8270
Bayou City Art Festival (late March & mid-October) 713-521-0133
Festa Italiana (mid-October) 713-524-4222
Greek Festival (early October) 713-526-5377
International Quilt Festival (late October-early November) 713-781-6864
Oktoberfest (early October) 281-890-5500
Texas Renaissance Festival (early October-mid-November) 800-458-3435
Texian Market Days (late October) 281-343-0218
www.georgeranch.org
Wings Over Houston Airshow (mid-October) 713-644-1018
www.wingsoverhouston.com

November
Fall Motor Fest (early November) 281-890-5500
International Quilt Festival (late October-early November) 713-781-6864
Texas Renaissance Festival (early October-mid-November) 800-458-3435
Thanksgiving Day Parade (late November) 713-654-8808
Uptown Tree Lighting Ceremony (late November) 713-621-2011

December
Christmas Candlelight Tours (early December) 713-655-1912

Irving

April
Motocross (April) 972-438-7676

May
Cinco de Mayo Festival (early May) 972-721-2501

June
Canalfest & Boat Parade (early June) 972-556-0625
Irving Heritage Festival (mid-June) 972-721-2424

July
Fourth of July Pops Concert & Fireworks (July 4) 972-831-8818
Independence Day Parade & Old-Fashioned Picnic (July 4) 972-721-2501
Irving Open Tennis Tournament (late July-early August) 972-252-7476

August
Irving Open Tennis Tournament (late July-early August) 972-252-7476
Taste of Irving (early August) 972-579-4390

September
Bedford Blues Festival & Arts Fair (early September) 214-855-1881
Las Colinas Horse Trials (late September) 972-869-0600

October
A Ghostly Affair (late October) 972-790-8505
Annual Main Event (late October) 972-259-1249
Las Colinas Fall Horse Show (early October) 972-869-0600
North Texas Hunter/Jumper Show (October) 972-869-0600

December
Christmas Parade & Santa in the Park (mid-December) 972-259-7881

Lubbock

March
West Texas Native American Association Pow Wow (late March) 806-792-0757

April
ABC Rodeo (early April) 806-747-5232
Cork & Fork Affair (early-April) 806-749-2212
Lubbock Arts Festival (mid-April) 806-744-2787

June
High Noon Concert Series (June-August) 806-747-5232

July
4th on Broadway (July 4) 806-747-5232
www.broadwayfestivals.com/
High Noon Concert Series (June-August) 806-747-5232

August
Grape Crush (August) 806-745-2258
High Noon Concert Series (June-August) 806-747-5232

September
Buddy Holly Music Festival (early September) 806-749-2929
www.broadwayfestivals.com/buddy/
Fiesta del Llano (mid-September) 806-762-5059
Garden & Arts Fiesta (mid-September) 806-767-3724
National Cowboy Symposium & Celebration (early September) 806-795-2455
Panhandle South Plains Fair (late September-early October) 806-763-2833
Performing Arts Festival (mid-September) 806-792-5251

TEXAS — Lubbock (Cont'd)

October
Farmer Stockman Show (early October) 806-747-7134
Panhandle South Plains Fair (late September-early October) 806-763-2833
Texas Tech Intercollegiate Rodeo (mid-October) 806-742-3351

December
Lights on Broadway (early-December) 806-747-5232
www.broadwayfestivals.com/

Plano

January
Back to Grandma's Attic Craft Show (January-April) 800-783-4526
City of Plano Martin Luther King Celebration (mid-January) 972-422-0296
Martin Luther King Jr Celebration & Parade (mid-January) 972-941-7174

February
Back to Grandma's Attic Craft Show (January-April) 800-783-4526
Taste of Plano (late February) 972-519-8262
Very Special Arts Festival (late February) 972-941-7272

March
Back to Grandma's Attic Craft Show (January-April) 800-783-4526
Collin County Community College Jazz Festival (late March) 972-881-5790
Country at Heart Craft Show (March-December) 800-783-4526
Dallas Video Festival (late March) 214-999-8999
www.videofest.org/2000
North Texas Irish Festival (early March) 214-821-4174

April
Back to Grandma's Attic Craft Show (January-April) 800-783-4526
Country at Heart Craft Show (March-December) 800-783-4526
Mesquite Rodeo (April-September) 972-285-8777
Scarborough Faire Renaissance Festival (mid-April-early June) 972-938-3247
Waxahachie Scarborough Renaissance Fair (April-June) 972-938-1888

May
Cottonwood Art Festival (early October & early May) 972-231-4798
Country at Heart Craft Show (March-December) 800-783-4526
Mesquite Rodeo (April-September) 972-285-8777
Scarborough Faire Renaissance Festival (mid-April-early June) 972-938-3247
Waxahachie Scarborough Renaissance Fair (April-June) 972-938-1888

June
Country at Heart Craft Show (March-December) 800-783-4526
Mesquite Rodeo (April-September) 972-285-8777
Scarborough Faire Renaissance Festival (mid-April-early June) 972-938-3247
Waxahachie Scarborough Renaissance Fair (April-June) 972-938-1888

July
Country at Heart Craft Show (March-December) 800-783-4526
Mesquite Rodeo (April-September) 972-285-8777

August
Country at Heart Craft Show (March-December) 800-783-4526
Mesquite Rodeo (April-September) 972-285-8777

September
Country at Heart Craft Show (March-December) 800-783-4526
Greek Food Festival (late September) 972-991-1166
HarvestFest (late September) 888-649-8499
Mesquite Rodeo (April-September) 972-285-8777
Plano Balloon Festival (mid-September) 972-867-7566
State Fair of Texas (late September-mid-October) 214-565-9931
www.texfair.com

October
Boo at the Zoo (late October) 214-670-5656
Columbus Day Weekend Sidewalk Sale (mid-October) 972-578-1591
Cotton Jubilee (mid-October) 903-455-1510
www.greenville-chamber.org/jubilee.htm
Cottonwood Art Festival (early October & early May) 972-231-4798
Country at Heart Craft Show (March-December) 800-783-4526
Halloween at the Wax Museum (early-late October) 972-263-2391
State Fair of Texas (late September-mid-October) 214-565-9931
www.texfair.com

November
Christmas Crafts Fair (late November) 972-941-7250
Country at Heart Craft Show (March-December) 800-783-4526
Dickens of a Christmas (November) 888-649-8499

December
Christmas in Old Downtown Plano (early December) 972-941-7250
Country at Heart Craft Show (March-December) 800-783-4526
Data Music Festival (mid-December) 214-987-3282

San Antonio

January
Great Country River Festival (mid-January) 210-227-4262
Lighting Ceremony & Riverwalk Holiday Parade (late November-early January) 210-227-4262
River Walk Mud Festival & Mud Parade (mid-January) 210-227-4262

February
Carnaval del Rio (early February) 210-227-4262
Home & Garden Show (February & September) 210-207-3663
San Antonio Stock Show & Rodeo (early-mid-February) 210-225-5851

March
Alamo Irish Festival (mid-March) 210-344-4317
Remembering the Alamo Living History Weekend (early March) 210-650-3343
Saint Patrick's River Dyeing (mid-March) 210-497-8435
Saint Patrick's Street Parade (mid-March) 210-497-8435
Spring Break Out Extreme (mid-March) 210-697-5050
Tejano Music Awards Fanfair & Festival (early March) 210-222-8862

April
Festival de Animales (late April) 210-734-7184
Fiesta Arts Fair (mid-April) 210-224-1848
Fiesta del Mercado (mid-late April) 210-207-8600
Fiesta Gardenfest (late April) 210-222-1521
Fiesta Mariachi Festival (late April) 210-227-4262
Fiesta San Antonio (mid-April) 210-227-5191
Lowrider Custom Car & Truck Festival (early April) 210-432-1896
Mission San Jose Spring Festival (mid-April) 210-922-0543
Starving Artists Show (early April) 210-226-3593
Taste of New Orleans (mid-April) 210-637-8328
Viva Botanica (mid-April) 210-207-3255

May
Clogger's Showcase (early May) 210-492-8700
Festival of the Armed Forces Air Show (late May) 210-207-6700
National Skeet Shooting Association Showcase (mid-May) 210-688-3371
Return of the Chili Queens (late May) 210-207-8600
Tejano Conjunto Festival (mid-May) 210-271-3151

June
Encanto en la Mision (mid-June-late July) 210-822-2453
Juneteenth Festival (mid-June) 210-533-4383
Latino Laugh Festival (early June) 800-447-3372
Musica San Antonio: A Festival Celebration (early June) 210-434-6711
San Antonio CineFestival (early June) 210-271-3151

July
Encanto en la Mision (mid-June-late July) 210-822-2453
Freedom Fest (early July) 210-207-8600
San Antonio Conjunto Shootout (mid-July) 210-246-9626

August
Texas Folklife Festival (early August) 210-458-2300

September
Fiestas Patrias (mid-September) 210-207-8600
Home & Garden Show (February & September) 210-207-3663
JazzsAlive (late September) 210-207-8480
National Sporting Clays Championship (mid-September) 210-688-3371
Westin Texas Open at La Cantera (late September) 210-341-0823

October
Haymarket Festival (early October) 210-207-8600
Oktoberfest San Antonio (early-mid-October) 210-222-1521
Wurstfest (late October-early November) 800-221-4369
Zoo Boo (October 31) 210-734-7184

November
Artesanos del Pueblo (mid-November) 210-922-3218
Lighting Ceremony & Riverwalk Holiday Parade (late November-early January) 210-227-4262
River Walk Holiday Festival (late November-late December) 210-227-4262
San Antonio Marathon (early November) 210-732-1332
samarathon.org/
Wurstfest (late October-early November) 800-221-4369

December
Alamo Bowl (December 30) 210-226-2695
www.alamobowl.com
Celebrate San Antonio (December 31) 210-207-8480
Fiesta De Las Luminarias (December) 210-227-4262
Floating Christmas Pageant (early-mid-December) 210-225-0000
Lighting Ceremony & Riverwalk Holiday Parade (late November-early January) 210-227-4262
River Walk Arts & Crafts Fair (mid-December) 210-229-2104
River Walk Holiday Festival (late November-late December) 210-227-4262

UTAH

Ogden

March
Gem & Mineral Show (mid-March) 801-629-8444

April
Jazz Concert (early April) 801-626-8500

June
A Taste of Ogden (early June) 801-394-6634
Solstice Celebration (mid-June) 801-621-7595

July
Ogden Heritage Street Festival (mid-July) 801-629-8242
Ogden Pioneer Days Rodeo & Celebration (July) 801-629-8214
Weber County Fair (late July-August) 801-399-8711

August
Festival of the American West (early August) 435-797-1143
Weber County Fair (late July-August) 801-399-8711

September
Ogden Greek Festival (late September) 801-399-2231
Wildwoods Bash (mid-September) 801-621-7595

November
Ogden Christmas Parade (late November) 801-629-8242
Storytelling Festival (mid-November) 801-626-8500

December
Christmas Village (December) 801-629-8284
First Night Ogden (December 31) 801-394-6634

Provo

January
Sundance Institute Film Festival (late January) 801-328-3456
www.sundance.org/festival/index.htm

June
America's Freedom Festival (mid-June-early July) 801-370-8019
Lehi Roundup (late June) 801-370-8393
Springville Art City Days (mid-June) 801-370-8393

July
America's Freedom Festival (mid-June-early July) 801-370-8019
Pioneer Day Celebrations (mid-July) 800-541-4955
Santaquin Cherry Days (late July-early August) 801-370-8393
Spanish Fork Fiesta Days (late July) 801-370-8393
World Dance & Music Folkfest (early July) 801-489-2726

August
Alpine Days (mid-August) 801-756-6347
Highland Fling (early August) 801-370-8393
Park City Art Festival (early August) 435-649-8882
Santaquin Cherry Days (late July-early August) 801-370-8393
Swiss Days (late August) 435-654-3666

December
Torchlight Parade (late December) 435-649-8111

Salt Lake City

January
Festival of Lights (early November-early January) 801-264-2241
Sundance Institute Film Festival (late January) 801-328-3456
www.sundance.org/festival/index.htm
Utah Auto Show (late January) 801-534-4777

February
Utah Boat & Fishing Show (mid-February) 801-534-4777

March
Home & Garden Show (early-mid-March) 801-534-4777
US Freestyle Championships (early March) 801-742-2222

May
Cinco de Mayo (early May) 801-355-2521
Living Traditions Festival (mid-May) 801-596-5000
Madeleine Festival of Arts & Humanities (late May) 801-328-8941
Memorial Day & Spring Celebration (late May) 801-584-8391

June
Mormon Miracle Pageant (late June) 435-835-3000
Utah Arts Festival (late June) 801-322-2428
www.uaf.org/

July
Days of '47 Celebration (mid-late July) 801-521-2822
Days of '47 Pioneer Parade (late July) 801-521-2822
Days of '47 World Championship Rodeo (mid-late July) 801-521-2822
Deseret News Marathon (late July) 801-468-2560
Festival of the American West (late July-early August) 800-225-3378
Utah's Days of '47 (mid-late July) 801-538-1050

August
Festival of the American West (late July-early August) 800-225-3378
Railroader's Festival (early August) 435-471-2209

September
Hispanic Dance (mid-September) 801-534-4777
Peach Days (early September) 435-723-3931
Utah State Fair (mid-September) 801-538-8440
www.utah-state-fair.com

October
Bison Roundup (late October) 801-773-2941
Oktoberfest (early October) 801-532-0459
Scottish Celebration & Blessing of the Clans (late October) 801-363-3889

November
Christmas Lights at Temple Square (late November-late December) 801-240-1000
Dickens Festival (late November-early December) 801-538-8440
Festival of Lights (early November-early January) 801-264-2241
Nouveau Beaujolais Festival (late November) 435-645-6640

December
Candlelight Christmas (mid-December) 801-584-8391
Christmas Lights at Temple Square (late November-late December) 801-240-1000
Dickens Festival (late November-early December) 801-538-8440
Festival of Lights (early November-early January) 801-264-2241
Festival of Trees (early December) 801-588-3677
First Night New Years Eve Celebration (December 31) 801-359-5118
Snowbird's Winterfest (early December) 801-742-2222

VERMONT

Burlington

January
Stowe Winter Carnival (late January-early February) 802-253-7321

February
Burlington Winter Festival (mid-February) 802-864-0123
Stowe Winter Carnival (late January-early February) 802-253-7321

May
Vermont City Marathon & Marathon Relay (late May) 802-863-8412

June
Discover Jazz Festival (mid-June) 802-863-7992

July
Stoweflake Hot Air Balloon Festival (mid-July) 802-253-7321
www.stoweinfo.com
Vermont Brewers Festival (mid-July) 802-244-6828
www.tastebeer.together.com
Vermont Mozart Festival (mid-July-mid-August) 802-862-7352

August
Champlain Valley Fair (late August-early September) 802-878-5545
www.cvfair.com
Champlain Valley Folk Festival (early August) 800-769-9176
www.cvfest.together.com
Latino Festival (early August) 802-864-0123
Vermont Mozart Festival (mid-July-mid-August) 802-862-7352

September
Champlain Valley Fair (late August-early September) 802-878-5545
www.cvfair.com
Fall Harvest Festival (mid-September) 802-879-5226
Marketfest (mid-September) 802-863-1648

October
Essex Fall Craft Show (late October) 802-878-4786
Vermont International Film Festival (late October) 802-660-2600

November
Church Street Marketplace Holiday Season (late November-late December) 802-863-1648
Green Mountain Festival of Trees (late November) 802-656-5100

December
Church Street Marketplace Holiday Season (late November-late December) 802-863-1648
Colchester Holiday Show (early December) 802-878-7559
First Night Burlington (December 31) 802-863-6005
www-1stnight.together.com
International Craft Fair & Cultural Expo (early December) 802-863-6713

Montpelier

January
Vermont Farm Show (late January) 802-828-2433

September
Barre Art Show (late September) 802-476-7513
Barre Tones Barber Shop Musical (late September) 802-229-7623
Lawn Fest (mid-September & early October) 802-244-8089
Old Time Fiddler's Contest (late September) 802-476-0256

October
Lawn Fest (mid-September & early October) 802-244-8089
New England Bach Festival (early-mid-October) 802-257-4523
www.sover.net/~musicctr

VIRGINIA

Alexandria

January
Lee Birthday Celebrations (mid-January) 703-548-8454

February
George Washington Birthday Celebration Weekend (mid-February) 703-549-7662
George Washington Birthday Night Ball (February) 703-838-4242
George Washington Celebration Parade (mid-February) 703-549-7662

March
Annual Needlework Exhibition (March) 703-780-4000
Antiques in Alexandria (mid-March) 703-549-5922
Saint Patrick's Day Celebration & Parade (early March) 703-549-4535

April
18th Century Grand Ball (mid-April) 703-838-4242
Braddock Day (early April) 703-549-2997
Earth Day (April 22) 703-838-4844
Historic Garden Tour of Alexandria (mid-late April) 804-644-7776
www.vagardenweek.org
History Walking Tours (April-October) 703-838-4200

May
Civil War Symposium (mid-May) 703-838-4848
Deutche Marque Concours d'Elegance Car Exhibition (early May) 703-780-4000
History Walking Tours (April-October) 703-838-4200
Memorial Day Jazz Festival (late May) 703-838-4844
Mount Vernon's Wine Tasting & Sunset Tour (mid-May) 703-799-8604

June
Alexandria Red Cross Waterfront Festival (mid-June) 703-549-8300
Civil War Reunion Day (mid-June) 703-838-4848
History Walking Tours (April-October) 703-838-4200
Juneteenth Commemoration (mid-late June) 703-838-4356

July
African-American Festival (late July) 703-838-4844
History Walking Tours (April-October) 703-838-4200
Independence Day Celebration (July 4) 703-780-2000
USA & Alexandria Birthday Celebration (early-mid-July) 703-838-4343
Virginia Scottish Games & Festival (late July) 703-912-1943

August
Carlyle Housewarming (early August) 703-549-2997
Friendship Fire House Festival (early August) 703-838-4399
History Walking Tours (April-October) 703-838-4200
Irish Festival (mid-August) 703-838-4844
Native American Indian Festival (late August) 703-838-4844
Tavern Day (early August) 703-838-4242

September
Annual Tour of Historic Alexandria Homes (late September) 800-388-9119
Crafts Fair (mid-September) 703-780-2000
Hard Times Chili Cook-Off (late September) 800-388-9119
History Walking Tours (April-October) 703-838-4200
Italian Festival (mid-September) 703-838-4844

October
18th Century Masquerade Ball (October) 703-838-4242
Alexandria Archaeology Super Weekend (early October) 703-838-4399
Alexandria Arts Safari (early October) 800-388-9119
Full Harvest Family Days (late October) 703-780-2000
Historic Alexandria Hauntings Family-Friendly Trick or Treat (late October) 703-838-4242
History Walking Tours (April-October) 703-838-4200
Scottish Heritage Festival (early October) 703-838-4844

November
Alexandria Holiday Tree Lighting Ceremony (late November) 800-388-9119
Christmas with the Presidents (late November-late December) 703-780-4000
Historic Alexandria Antiques Show & Sale (late November) 800-388-9119

December
Campagna Center's Designer Tour of Homes (early December) 703-549-0111
Campagna Center's Scottish Christmas Walk Weekend (early December) 703-549-0111
Christmas in Camp Open House (mid-December) 703-838-4848
Christmas with the Presidents (late November-late December) 703-780-4000
First Night Alexandria (December 31) 800-388-9119
Historic Alexandria Candlelight Tours (mid-December) 703-838-4242
Mount Vernon by Candlelight Weekends (late november-mid-December) 703-780-2000

Arlington

January
Joy To The World Holiday/Grand Illumination (late November-early January) 703-528-3527

March
Saint Patricks Day Celebration (March 17) 703-557-0613

April
Arlington Farmers Market (mid-April-mid-December) 703-228-6400

May
Arlington Farmers Market (mid-April-mid-December) 703-228-6400
Crystal City Water Park (late May-late September) 703-413-0789
Marine Corps Sunset Parades (late May-mid-August) 202-433-4173
Taste of Arlington (mid-May) 703-486-0626
Wolf Trap Summer Season (late May-mid-September) 703-255-1868

June
Arlington Farmers Market (mid-April-mid-December) 703-228-6400
Crystal City Water Park (late May-late September) 703-413-0789
Fairfax Fair (mid-June) 703-324-3247
General & Mrs Lee's Wedding Anniversary (June 30) 703-557-0613
Herndon Festival (early June) 703-435-6868
Marine Corps Sunset Parades (late May-mid-August) 202-433-4173
Wolf Trap Summer Season (late May-mid-September) 703-255-1868

July
Arlington Farmers Market (mid-April-mid-December) 703-228-6400
Crossroads Village Antique Car Show (late July) 810-736-7100
Crystal City Water Park (late May-late September) 703-413-0789
Marine Corps Sunset Parades (late May-mid-August) 202-433-4173
Wolf Trap Summer Season (late May-mid-September) 703-255-1868

August
Arlington County Fair (mid-August) 703-228-6400
www.capaccess.org/com/arlcty/fair
Arlington Farmers Market (mid-April-mid-December) 703-228-6400
Crystal City Water Park (late May-late September) 703-413-0789
Marine Corps Sunset Parades (late May-mid-August) 202-433-4173
Wolf Trap Summer Season (late May-mid-September) 703-255-1868

September
Arlington Farmers Market (mid-April-mid-December) 703-228-6400
Crystal City Water Park (late May-late September) 703-413-0789
International Children's Festival (mid-September) 703-642-0862
Labor Day Jazz Celebration (early September) 703-435-6868
Rosslyn Jazz Festival (mid-September) 703-522-6628
Wolf Trap Summer Season (late May-mid-September) 703-255-1868

October
Arlington Farmers Market (mid-April-mid-December) 703-228-6400
Theodore Roosevelt's Birthday Celebration (late October) 703-289-2553

November
Arlington Farmers Market (mid-April-mid-December) 703-228-6400
Joy To The World Holiday/Grand Illumination (late November-early January) 703-528-3527
Light Up Rosslyn (late November-early December) 703-522-6628
Northern Virginia Christmas Market (mid-November) 757-486-0220
Veterans Day Ceremonies (November 11) 202-619-7222

December
Arlington Farmers Market (mid-April-mid-December) 703-228-6400
Bringing in Christmas (December) 703-557-0613
Candlelight Tours & Concerts (mid-December) 703-437-1794
Joy To The World Holiday/Grand Illumination (late November-early January) 703-528-3527
Light Up Rosslyn (late November-early December) 703-522-6628

Chesapeake

March
Chesapeake Eggstravaganza (late March) 757-382-8466

April
Sheep to Shawl (mid-April) 757-382-6591

May
Chesapeake Jubilee (mid-May) 757-482-4848
Stardust Ball (late May) 757-382-2330

June
Hampton Roads Highland Games (late June) 757-481-2165
Harborfest (early June) 757-441-2345
www.festeventsva.org/haborfest.html
Scottish Festival (late June) 757-481-2165

July
Annual 4th In the Park (July) 757-543-5721

September
Beef Fest (mid-September) 757-487-6122
Civil War Days (early September) 757-382-6591
Labor Day Celebration (early September) 757-382-6411

October
Bark in the Park (mid-October) 757-382-6411
Great American Food Fest (early October) 757-382-6159

November
Chesapeake Holiday Wonderland (late November-early December) 757-482-6241
Indian River Craft Show (mid-November) 757-382-8464

December
Battle of Great Bridge Reenactment (early December) 757-382-6411
Chesapeake Holiday Wonderland (late November-early December) 757-482-6241
Holiday Tree Lighting (early December) 757-382-6241
Kwanzaa Celebrations (late December) 757-382-6411

Newport News

January
Artful Giving & Home for the Holidays (mid-November-early January) 757-596-8175
Celebration in Lights (late November-early January) 757-926-8451
Star of Wonder (late November-early January) 757-595-1900
Wildlife Arts Festival (late January) 757-595-1900

April
Annual Civil War Re-enactment (late April) 757-887-1862
Ella Fitzgerald Music Festival (late April) 757-594-8752

June
Jubilee on the James (mid-June) 757-926-8451

July
Stars in the Sky (July 4) 757-926-8451

August
King-Lincoln Music Festival (late August) 757-926-8451
Peninsula Fine Arts Center Juried Exhibition (late August-early November) 757-596-8175

September
Hampton Bay Days Festival (mid-September) 757-727-6122
Peninsula Fine Arts Center Juried Exhibition (late August-early November) 757-596-8175

October
Fall Festival (early October) 888-493-7386
October Oyster Roast (mid-October) 888-493-7386
Peninsula Fine Arts Center Juried Exhibition (late August-early November) 757-596-8175

November
Artful Giving & Home for the Holidays (mid-November-early January) 757-596-8175
Celebration in Lights (late November-early January) 757-926-8451
Peninsula Fine Arts Center Juried Exhibition (late August-early November) 757-596-8175
Star of Wonder (late November-early January) 757-595-1900

VIRGINIA — Newport News (Cont'd)

December
A Newsome House Christmas (December) 757-247-2360
Artful Giving & Home for the Holidays (mid-November-early January) 757-596-8175
Celebration in Lights (late November-early January) 757-926-8451
Christmas in the Field Civil War Re-enactment (mid-December) 757-887-1862
Star of Wonder (late November-early January) 757-595-1900
Yuletides at the Mariners Museum (late December) 757-596-2222

Norfolk

January
Garden of Lights Holiday Festival (late November-early January) 757-441-5830

March
Crawford Bay Crew Classic (late March) 757-393-9933

April
Downtown Doo Dah Parade (early April) 757-441-2345
International Azalea Festival-Norfolk (mid-April) 757-622-2312

May
AFR'AM Fest (late May) 757-456-1743
www.aframfest.com
Art Explosure (early May) 757-622-4262
Concerts at the Point (May-June) 757-441-2345
www.festeventsva.org/concert.html
Elizabeth River Run (early May) 757-421-2602
Greek Festival (early May) 757-440-0500
Ocean View Beach Festival (mid-May) 757-583-0000
Stockley Gardens Art Festival (mid-May) 757-625-6161
Town Point Jazz & Blues Festival (mid-May) 757-441-2345
www.festeventsva.org/jazznblues.html

June
Bayou Boogaloo & Cajun Food Festival (late June) 757-441-2345
www.festeventsva.org/bayoo.html
Cock Island Race (late June-early July) 757-393-9933
Concerts at the Point (May-June) 757-441-2345
www.festeventsva.org/concert.html
Harborfest (early June) 757-441-2345
www.festeventsva.org/haborfest.html
Seawall Festival (early June) 757-393-5327

July
Cock Island Race (late June-early July) 757-393-9933
Great American Picnic (July 4) 757-441-2345
Town Point Air Show & 4th of July Celebration-Norfolk (early July) 757-441-2345

August
A Fare for the Arts (late August) 757-393-5327

September
Reggae on the River (mid-September) 757-441-2345
www.festeventsva.org/reggae.html
Virginia Children's Festival (mid-September) 757-441-2345
www.festeventsva.org/childrensfest.html

October
Peanut Festival (mid-October) 757-539-6751
Town Point Virginia Wine Festival (mid-October) 757-441-2345
www.festeventsva.org/winefest.html

November
Garden of Lights Holiday Festival (late November-early January) 757-441-5830
Holidays in the City (late November-late December) 757-441-2345
Holly Festival (mid-late November) 757-668-7098

December
First Night Norfolk (December 31) 757-441-2345
www.festeventsva.org/firstnight.html
Garden of Lights Holiday Festival (late November-early January) 757-441-5830
Holidays in the City (late November-late December) 757-441-2345

Richmond

April
Azalea Festival Parade (mid-April) 804-233-2093
Easter on Parade (late April) 804-643-2826
Historic Garden Week (mid-late April) 804-644-7776
Strawberry Hill Races (early-mid-April) 804-228-3200

May
Arts in the Park (early May) 804-353-8198
Camptown Races (early May) 804-752-6678
James River Wine Festival (early May) 804-359-4645

June
Dogwood Dell Festival of the Arts (mid-June-mid-August) 804-780-6091
Ykrop's Target Family Jubilee (early June) 804-782-2777

July
Dogwood Dell Festival of the Arts (mid-June-mid-August) 804-780-6091
The Big Gig (mid-July) 804-643-2826

August
Agribusiness Food Festival (early August) 804-228-3200
Dogwood Dell Festival of the Arts (mid-June-mid-August) 804-780-6091

September
Rainbow of Arts (September) 804-748-1130
State Fair of Virginia (late September-early October) 804-228-3200

October
2nd Street Festival (early October) 804-643-2826
Festival 1893 (mid-October) 804-358-7166
Harvest Festival at Meadow Farm (mid-October) 804-501-5523
Second Street Festival (early October) 804-782-2777
State Fair of Virginia (late September-early October) 804-228-3200

November
Crestar Richmond Marathon (mid-November) 804-285-9495
Great Southern Weapons Fair (late November) 804-228-3200
James River Parade of Lights (November) 804-748-1567

December
Capital City Kwanzaa Festival (late December) 804-782-2777
Gardenfest of Lights (early-late December) 804-782-2777

Roanoke

March
Saint Patrick's Day Parade (mid-March) 800-635-5535

April
Local Colors (mid-April) 800-635-5535
Strawberry Festival (late April-early May) 800-635-5535
Vinton Dogwood Festival (late April) 800-635-5535

May
Railfair & Model Mania (early May) 540-342-5670
Roanoke Festival in the Park (late May-early June) 540-342-6025
Strawberry Festival (late April-early May) 800-635-5535
Virginia State Championship Chili Cookoff (early May) 540-342-2028

June
Roanoke Festival in the Park (late May-early June) 540-342-6025

July
Commonwealth Games of Virginia (mid-July) 800-635-5535
Salem Fair & Exposition (early July) 540-342-6025

August
Vinton Old-Time Bluegrass Festival (mid-August) 540-345-8548
Virginia Mountain Peach Festival (early August) 540-342-2028

September
Henry Street Heritage Festival (mid-late September) 800-635-5535
Olde Salem Days (mid-September) 540-772-8871
Roanoke Jazz & Blues Festival (mid-September) 540-981-2889

October
Life on Wagon Road (mid-October) 540-427-1800
Native American Heritage Festival & PowWow (early October) 540-342-6025
Zoo Boo (late October) 540-343-3241

November
Greening of the Market (late November) 540-342-2028

December
Dickens of a Christmas (early-mid-December) 540-342-2028
Festival of Lights Parade (early December) 540-981-2889
First Night Roanoke (December 31) 540-342-2640
Roanoke Christmas Parade (early December) 540-853-2889

Virginia Beach

January
Holiday Lights at the Beach (late November-early January) 757-491-7866
Whale Watching (late December-early March) 757-437-4949

February
Mid-Atlantic Sports & Boat Show (mid-February) 757-934-7504
Whale Watching (late December-early March) 757-437-4949

March
Mid-Atlantic Wildfowl Festival (early March) 757-437-8432
Shamrock Sportsfest Marathon (mid-March) 757-481-5090
Whale Watching (late December-early March) 757-437-4949

April
Virginia International Waterfront Arts Festival (early April-early May) 757-664-6492

May
Beach Music Weekend (mid-May) 757-491-7866
Big Band Weekend (late May) 757-491-7866
Cinco de Mayo (early May) 757-491-7866
Cinco de Mayo Celebration (early May) 757-491-7866
Pungo Strawberry Festival (late May) 757-721-6001
Virginia International Waterfront Arts Festival (early April-early May) 757-664-6492

June
Bayou Boogaloo & Cajun Food Festival (late June) 757-441-2345
www.festeventsva.org/bayoo.html
Boardwalk Art Show (mid-June) 757-425-0000
Elvis is Everywhere Festival (early June) 800-446-8038

August
Men's Pro-Am Volleyball Tournament (mid-August) 757-437-4882
Virginia Beach East Coast Surfing Championships (late August) 800-861-7873

September
American Music Festival (early September) 757-437-4800
Blues at the Beach (early September) 757-491-7866
Neptune Festival & Air Show (late September) 757-498-0215
ShowDeo (early September) 757-427-6020

October
Boardwalk Exotic Auto Expo (mid-October) 757-491-7866
October Brewfest (late October) 757-463-1940

November
Holiday Lights at the Beach (late November-early January) 757-491-7866

December
Holiday Lights at the Beach (late November-early January) 757-491-7866
Whale Watching (late December-early March) 757-437-4949

Williamsburg

March
Annual Garden Symposium (late March) 800-603-0948
President Tyler's Birthday Celebration (March 29) 804-829-5377

April
Fife Fiddle & Fun (late April) 757-253-4838
Historic Garden Week (mid-late April) 804-644-7776
Revolutionary War Weekend (late April) 757-898-3400
Williamsburg Folk Art Show (mid-April) 717-337-3060

May
Civil War Weekend (late May) 757-898-3400
Jamestown Founding Weekend (mid-May) 757-898-3400
Jamestown Landing Day (May 13) 757-253-4838

July
Civil War Encampment (late July-early August) 804-829-5075
First Assembly Day (late July) 757-898-3400
Independence Day Celebration (July 4) 757-890-3300
Williamsburg Independence Day (July 4) 800-447-8678

August
Civil War Encampment (late July-early August) 804-829-5075

October
Feast & the Fury Living History Weekend (mid-October) 804-829-5121
Michelob Championship at Kingsmill (early October) 757-253-3985
Yorktown Day Celebration (mid-late October) 757-890-3300
Yorktown Victory Celebration (late October) 757-253-4838

November
A Colonial Christmas (late November-late December) 757-253-4838
Virginia's First Thanksgiving Festival (early November) 804-829-6018

December
A Colonial Christmas (late November-late December) 757-253-4838
Berkeley Plantation's Colonial Christmas (mid-December) 804-829-6018
Grand Illuminaton The (early December) 800-447-8679
Lighted Boat Parade (early December) 757-898-5060
Williamsburg Area Christmas Parade (early December) 757-229-6511
Williamsburg's First Night Celebration (December 31) 757-258-0015
Winter & Wine Festival (early December) 757-229-0999
Yorktown Holiday Tree Lighting (early December) 757-890-3300

WASHINGTON

Olympia

March
Capital Food & Wine Festival (late March) 360-438-4366

May
Shakespeare Festival (late May-August) 360-943-9492
Wooden Boat Festival (mid-May) 360-943-5404

June
Shakespeare Festival (late May-August) 360-943-9492
Super Saturday (June) 360-866-6000

July
Capital Lakefair (mid-July) 360-586-3460
Greater Olympia Dixieland Jazz Festival (early July) 360-754-8129
Music in the Park (July-August) 360-357-8948
Oregon Trail Days (late July) 360-264-5075
Shakespeare Festival (late May-August) 360-943-9492
Thurston County Fair (late July-early August) 360-786-5453
Yelm Prairie Days (mid-July) 360-458-3492

August
Music in the Park (July-August) 360-357-8948
Shakespeare Festival (late May-August) 360-943-9492
Thurston County Fair (late July-early August) 360-786-5453

September
Harbor Days (September) 360-352-4557

October
Olympia Film Festival (mid-late October) 360-754-6670
www.olywa.net/ofs/festival/

WASHINGTON — Olympia (Cont'd)

December
Parade of Lighted Ships (early December) 360-357-6767
Winterfest in Historic Tenino (early December) 360-264-5855

Seattle

January
Chinese New Year's Celebration (January) 206-382-1197
Seattle International Boat Show (mid-January) 206-634-0911
www.seattle-boatshow.com/
Winterfest (late November-early January) 206-684-7200

February
Festival Sundiata (mid-February) 206-684-7200
Northwest Flower & Garden Show (early February) 800-229-6311

March
Seattle Fringe Festival (mid-March) 206-526-1959

April
Cherry Blossom & Japanese Cultural Festival (mid-April) 206-684-7200
www.bizshop.com/sakura.htm
Imagination Celebration (early April) 206-684-7200

May
Cinco de Mayo Celebration (early May) 206-706-7776
Northwest Folklife Festival (late May) 206-684-7300
www.nwfolklife.org/folklife
Seattle International Film Festival (mid-May-early June) 206-464-5830
University District Street Fair (mid-May) 206-632-9084

June
AT & T Summer Nights at the Pier (late June-late August) 206-281-8111
www.summernights.org
Pioneer Square Fire Festival (early June) 206-622-6235
Seattle International Film Festival (mid-May-early June) 206-464-5830

July
AT & T Summer Nights at the Pier (late June-late August) 206-281-8111
www.summernights.org
Bite of Seattle (July) 206-232-2982
Eatonville Arts Festival (late July-early August) 360-832-4000
Family Fourth at Lake Union (July 4) 206-281-8111
Fourth of Jul-Ivars at the Waterfront (July 4) 206-587-6500
www.keepclam.com
Indian Pow Wow (late July) 206-285-4425
Seafair Summer Festival (early July-early August) 206-728-0123
www.seafair.com/

August
AT & T Summer Nights at the Pier (late June-late August) 206-281-8111
www.summernights.org
Bubble Festival (mid-August) 206-443-2001
Eatonville Arts Festival (late July-early August) 360-832-4000
Seafair Summer Festival (early July-early August) 206-728-0123
www.seafair.com/

September
Bumbershoot Festival (early September) 206-684-7200
www.bumbershoot.org/
Fiesta Patrias (mid-September) 206-706-7776

October
Salmon Days Festival (October) 425-392-0661

November
Hmong New Year's Celebration (early November) 206-684-7284
Seattle Marathon (late November) 253-552-1702
www.seattlemarathon.org/
Winterfest (late November-early January) 206-684-7200

December
Holiday Parade of Boats Cruise (December) 206-674-3500
Winterfest (late November-early January) 206-684-7200

Spokane

January
Cathedral & the Arts Music Series (October-March) 509-838-4277
Northwest Bach Festival (late January-early February) 509-326-4942
www.spokane.net/nwbachfest

February
Cathedral & the Arts Music Series (October-March) 509-838-4277
Northwest Bach Festival (late January-early February) 509-326-4942
www.spokane.net/nwbachfest

March
Cathedral & the Arts Music Series (October-March) 509-838-4277
Saint Patricks Day Parade (mid-March) 509-747-3230
Shrine Circus (late March) 509-624-1341

May
Bloomsday Race (early May) 509-838-1579
Bloomsday Trade Show (early May) 509-838-1579
Spokane Lilac Festival (mid-May) 509-747-3230
www.spolilacfest.com/

June
ArtFest (early June) 509-456-3931
Spokane Hoop Fest (late June) 509-747-3230
www.hoopfest.org/

July
AHRA World Finals Drag Racing (late July) 509-244-3663
Cherry Pickers Trot & Pit Spit (mid-July) 509-238-6970
Mozart on a Summer's Eve (late July) 509-326-4942

September
Green Bluff Apple Festival (late September-late October) 509-238-4709
Pig-Out in the Park (early September) 509-921-2205
Spokane Interstate Fair (early-mid-September) 509-747-3230

October
Cathedral & the Arts Music Series (October-March) 509-838-4277
Green Bluff Apple Festival (late September-late October) 509-238-4709
Homefest (mid-October) 509-838-8755
Inland Craft Warnings (early October) 509-328-7240

November
Arts & Crafts Christmas Show & Sale (mid-November) 509-924-0588
Cathedral & the Arts Music Series (October-March) 509-838-4277
Christmas Arts & Crafts Sale (mid-November) 509-924-0588
Christmas Tree Elegance (late November-early December) 509-326-3136

December
Cathedral & the Arts Music Series (October-March) 509-838-4277
Christmas Candlelight Concert (mid-December) 800-325-7328
Christmas Tree Elegance (late November-early December) 509-326-3136

Tacoma

January
Fantasylights (late November-early January) 253-627-2836
Tacoma Third Thursday Artwalk (early January-late December) 253-591-5341
Zoolights (late December-early January) 253-591-5337

February
Mardi Gras at Freighthouse Square (early February) 253-305-0678
Wintergrass Bluegrass Festival (late February) 253-926-4164

April
Daffodil Festival Grand Floral Parade (mid-April) 253-627-6176
Floral Daffodil Marine Regatta (mid-April) 253-752-3555
Isia Spring Fever Skating Competition (mid-April) 253-798-4000
Junior Daffodil Parade (mid-April) 253-756-9020
Puyallup Spring Fair (mid-April) 253-841-5045

May
Civil War Encampment & Battle Demonstration (late May) 800-260-5997
Norwegian Heritage Festival (mid-May) 206-242-5289
WIAA Spring Fest (late May) 425-746-7102

June
Gardens of Tacoma Tour (late June) 253-474-0400
Gig Harbor Peninsula on Parade (early June) 253-851-6865
Meeker Days Hoedown & Blue Grass Festival (mid-June) 253-840-2631
Tacoma Farmers Market (June-September) 253-272-7077

July
Art a La Carte (early July) 253-627-2836
Art Ala Carte-Tacoma (early July) 253-305-1036
Ethnic Fest (late July) 253-798-7590
Freedom Fair (early July) 253-761-9433
Seafirst Freedom Fair & Fireworks Spectacular (July 4) 253-761-9433
Sprint PCS Taste of Tacoma (early July) 206-232-2982
Tacoma Farmers Market (June-September) 253-272-7077
Tacoma Old Town Blues Festival (mid-July) 253-627-1290
Thursday Night Concerts in the Park (early July-late August) 253-581-1076

August
Fort Nisqually Brigade Encampment (early August) 253-591-5339
Tacoma Farmers Market (June-September) 253-272-7077
Thursday Night Concerts in the Park (early July-late August) 253-581-1076

September
Maritime Fest (mid-September) 253-383-2429
Tacoma Farmers Market (June-September) 253-272-7077
Western Washington Fair (early September) 253-841-5045
www.thefair.com

October
Scandinavian Days Festival (early October) 253-845-5446

November
Fantasylights (late November-early January) 253-627-2836

December
Fantasylights (late November-early January) 253-627-2836
Festival of Trees (early December) 253-552-1368
First Night Tacoma (December 31) 253-798-7205
Holiday Parade & Tree Lighting (early December) 253-627-2175
Tacoma Third Thursday Artwalk (early January-late December) 253-591-5341
Zoolights (late December-early January) 253-591-5337

Vancouver

March
Spring Castles Programs (early March-early June) 360-992-1821

April
Earth Action Day (mid-April) 360-696-8478
Home & Garden Idea Fair (late April) 360-992-3231
International Discovery Walk Festival (late April) 360-892-6758
www.ava.org/vanciml
Spring Castles Programs (early March-early June) 360-992-1821
Vancouver Farmers Market Saturdays (April-October) 360-737-8298

May
Fort James Health & Safety Fair (early May) 360-834-3021
Hazel Dell Parade of Bands (mid-May) 360-576-1195
Herb Festival (mid-May) 360-686-3537
Queen Victoria's Birthday (late May) 360-696-7655
Spring Castles Programs (early March-early June) 360-992-1821
Spring Dance (late May) 360-694-7026
Sturgeon Festival (late May) 360-696-8478
Vancouver Farmers Market Saturdays (April-October) 360-737-8298

June
Rose Show (late June) 360-693-6822
Spring Castles Programs (early March-early June) 360-992-1821
Vancouver Farmers Market Saturdays (April-October) 360-737-8298

July
Amboy Territorial Days Celebration (early-mid-July) 360-686-3383
An Olde-Fashioned Fourth (early July) 360-686-3537
Antique Aircraft Fly-In (early July) 360-694-7026
Camas Days (late July) 360-834-2472
Clark County Rural Heritage Fair (mid-July) 360-687-4554
Fort Vancouver Brigade Encampment (mid-July) 360-696-7655
Fort Vancouver Days Celebration (early-mid-July) 360-696-8171
Fort Vancouver Fourth of July Celebration (July 4) 360-693-5481
Harvest Days Celebration (mid-July) 360-687-1510
LaCenter Summer Our Days Festival (late July) 360-263-7168
Mount Tum Tum Native American Indian Encampment (early July) 360-247-5235
Our Days Festival (late July) 360-263-8850
River Rhythms & Chili Cook-Off (early-mid-July) 360-696-8171
Seafarer's International Festival (late July) 360-694-9300
www.teleport.com/~vancsea/festival.html
Vancouver Farmers Market Saturdays (April-October) 360-737-8298

August
Founders Day (late August) 360-696-7655
Vancouver Farmers Market Saturdays (April-October) 360-737-8298

September
Candlelight Tour (mid-September) 360-696-7655
Vancouver Farmers Market Saturdays (April-October) 360-737-8298

October
Vancouver Farmers Market Saturdays (April-October) 360-737-8298

December
Christmas at Fort Vancouver (mid-December) 360-696-7655

WEST VIRGINIA

Charleston

May
Native American PowWow (mid-May) 800-238-9488
Vandalia Gathering (late May) 304-558-0220
West Virginia Dance Festival (late May) 304-558-0220
West Virginia International Film Festival (early May) 304-342-7100
www.wviff.org

June
Black Bear 40k Bicycle Race (late June) 304-558-3500
Mountain Heritage Arts & Crafts Festival (mid-June & late September) 304-725-2055
www.jeffersoncounty.com/mha&cf/
Rhododendron Art & Craft Show (early June) 304-744-4323
West Virginia Day Celebration (mid-June) 304-345-1738

August
Multifest (early August) 304-342-4600
Sternwheel Regatta (late August) 304-348-6419

September
Kanawha County Majorette Festival (mid-September) 304-348-6169
Mound Arts & Crafts Festival (mid-September) 800-238-9488
Mountain Heritage Arts & Crafts Festival (mid-June & late September) 304-725-2055
www.jeffersoncounty.com/mha&cf/

October
A Taste of Charleston (mid-October) 843-577-4030
Octoberfest (mid-October) 800-238-9488

November
Capital City Arts & Crafts Show (mid-November) 304-345-1500
Winter Wonderland (November-December) 304-348-6419

December
Winter Wonderland (November-December) 304-348-6419

Morgantown

May
- **Traditional Appalachian Mountain Music** (late May) — 304-363-3030

June
- **18th Century Rendezvous** (mid-June & late October) — 304-363-3030
- **Concerts in the Park** (June-late August) — 304-296-8356
- **Courthouse Square Noontime Concerts** (June-October) — 304-291-7257
- **Three Centuries of American Farm Life Exhibit** (early June-early July) — 304-363-3030

July
- **4th of July Celebration & Parade** (July 4) — 304-292-0062
- **Concerts in the Park** (June-late August) — 304-296-8356
- **Courthouse Square Noontime Concerts** (June-October) — 304-291-7257
- **Old Fashioned Brass Band Concert** (July 4) — 304-363-3030
- **Three Centuries of American Farm Life Exhibit** (early June-early July) — 304-363-3030

August
- **Concerts in the Park** (June-late August) — 304-296-8356
- **Courthouse Square Noontime Concerts** (June-October) — 304-291-7257
- **Dunkard Valley Frontier Festival** (late August) — 304-879-5500
- **Monongalia County Fair** (early-mid-August) — 304-291-7201

September
- **Black Heritage Festival** (early September) — 304-622-4256
- **Courthouse Square Noontime Concerts** (June-October) — 304-291-7257
- **Fall Home Show** (mid-September) — 304-983-6255
- **Mason-Dixon Festival** (mid-September) — 304-594-1104
- **Mill Day** (late September) — 304-599-1575
- **Wine & Jazz Festival** (late September) — 304-292-5081

October
- **18th Century Rendezvous** (mid-June & late October) — 304-363-3030
- **Courthouse Square Noontime Concerts** (June-October) — 304-291-7257
- **Fall Eighteenth Century Rendezvous** (late October) — 304-292-5081
- **Fall Frolic** (mid-October) — 800-524-4043
- **Haunted Hayride** (October) — 304-296-0150
- **Mountaineer Balloon Festival** (early October) — 304-296-8356

November
- **Christmas at Picketts Fort** (late November-early December) — 304-363-3030
- **Grand National Championship** (mid-November) — 800-848-2263
- **Holiday Open House** (mid-November) — 304-296-7825
- **Mountaineer Week** (early November) — 304-293-2702
- **Mountaineer Week Craft Show** (mid-November) — 304-293-2702

December
- **Christmas at Picketts Fort** (late November-early December) — 304-363-3030
- **Gospel Music Concert** (early December) — 304-363-3030

Wheeling

January
- **City of Lights** (early November-mid-January) — 304-233-2575
- **Winter Festival of Lights** (early November-early January) — 304-233-7709

March
- **Wheeling Celtic Celebration** (early March) — 304-232-3087

May
- **Big Boy Classic 20K Run** (late May) — 304-242-7322

June
- **African-American Jubilee** (late June) — 304-233-7709
- **West Virginia Day Celebration** (late June) — 304-233-7709

July
- **Independence Day Symphony & Fireworks** (July 4) — 304-233-7709
- **Jamboree in the Hills** (mid-July) — 800-624-5456
- **Upper Ohio Valley Italian Festival** (July) — 304-233-1090

August
- **American Heritage Glass & Craft Festival** (early August) — 304-233-7709
- **Car Show & Swap Meet** (late August) — 888-645-3229

September
- **Fall Horse Show** (mid-September) — 304-243-4042

October
- **Dungeon of Horrors** (mid-late October) — 304-843-1993
- **Oglebayfest** (early October) — 304-243-4000

November
- **City of Lights** (early November-mid-January) — 304-233-2575
- **Fantasy in Lights Parade** (mid-November) — 304-233-2575
- **Winter Festival of Lights** (early November-early January) — 304-233-7709

December
- **City of Lights** (early November-mid-January) — 304-233-2575
- **New Years Eve Celebration** (December 31) — 304-232-5050
- **Winter Festival of Lights** (early November-early January) — 304-233-7709

WISCONSIN

Green Bay

February
- **Arti Gras** (early February) — 920-494-9507

May
- **De Pere Celebration** (late May) — 920-433-7767

June
- **Bayfest** (June) — 920-465-2145

July
- **Brown County Fair** (late July) — 920-336-6123
- **Celebrate Americafest** (July 4) — 920-494-9507
- **Garden Walk** (mid-July) — 920-490-9457
- **Oneida Indian Pow Wow & Festival of Performing Arts** (July) — 920-869-1600
- **Pulaski Polka Days** (late July) — 920-822-3869

August
- **Artstreet** (late August) — 920-435-2787

November
- **Holiday Parade** (late November) — 920-494-9507

Madison

January
- **Holiday Fantasy of Lights** (late November-early January) — 608-222-7630
- **Winter Concerts in the Gardens** (January-March) — 608-246-4551

February
- **Garden Expo** (mid-February) — 608-262-5255
- **Winter Concerts in the Gardens** (January-March) — 608-246-4551
- **Zor Shrine Circus** (mid-February) — 608-274-2260

March
- **International Children's Film Festival** (March) — 608-266-9055
- **Spring Flower Show** (mid-March) — 608-246-4550
- **Winter Concerts in the Gardens** (January-March) — 608-246-4551

April
- **Capital City Jazz Festival** (late April) — 608-877-4171
- **Crazy Legs Run** (late April) — 608-263-7894
- **Dane County Farmers' Market** (late April-early November) — 920-563-5037 — www.madfarmmkt.org/
- **Executive Residence Public Tours** (April-August) — 608-266-3554
- **Midwest Horse Fair** (mid-April) — 608-267-3976

May
- **Audubon Art Fair** (early May) — 608-255-2473
- **Dane County Farmers' Market** (late April-early November) — 920-563-5037 — www.madfarmmkt.org/
- **Executive Residence Public Tours** (April-August) — 608-266-3554
- **Heroes Madison Marathon** (late May) — 608-256-9922 — www.madison-marathon.com
- **Madison Folk Music Festival** (early May) — 608-836-8422
- **Wednesday Farmers' Market** (May-late October) — 920-563-5037

June
- **Badger State Summer Games** (mid-late June) — 608-226-4780
- **Concerts in the Gardens** (June-August) — 608-246-4551
- **Concerts on the Square** (late June-late July) — 608-257-0638
- **Cows on the Concourse** (early June) — 608-221-8698
- **Dane County Farmers' Market** (late April-early November) — 920-563-5037 — www.madfarmmkt.org/
- **Executive Residence Public Tours** (April-August) — 608-266-3554
- **Hometown USA Festival** (mid-June) — 608-831-5696
- **June Jam** (early June) — 608-276-6606
- **Rhapsody in Bloom** (mid-June) — 608-246-4550
- **Summer Concerts in the Gardens** (early June-mid-August) — 608-246-4551
- **Tuesday Noon Concerts** (June-September) — 608-266-0382
- **Wednesday Farmers' Market** (May-late October) — 920-563-5037

July
- **Art Fair off the Square** (mid-July) — 608-798-4811
- **Concerts in the Gardens** (June-August) — 608-246-4551
- **Concerts on the Square** (late June-late July) — 608-257-0638
- **Dane County Fair** (mid-July) — 608-224-6455
- **Dane County Farmers' Market** (late April-early November) — 920-563-5037 — www.madfarmmkt.org/
- **Executive Residence Public Tours** (April-August) — 608-266-3554
- **Maxwell Street Days** (mid-July) — 608-266-6033
- **Mount Horeb Art Fair** (mid-July) — 608-437-5914
- **Paddle & Portage** (late July) — 608-255-1008
- **Rhythm & Booms** (early July) — 800-951-2264 — www.rhythmandbooms.com
- **Summer Concerts in the Gardens** (early June-mid-August) — 608-246-4551
- **Tuesday Noon Concerts** (June-September) — 608-266-0382
- **Umbrella Daze** (mid-July) — 608-423-3780
- **Wednesday Farmers' Market** (May-late October) — 920-563-5037

August
- **Concerts in the Gardens** (June-August) — 608-246-4551
- **Dane County Farmers' Market** (late April-early November) — 920-563-5037 — www.madfarmmkt.org/
- **Executive Residence Public Tours** (April-August) — 608-266-3554
- **National Mustard Day** (early August) — 608-437-3986
- **Summer Concerts in the Gardens** (early June-mid-August) — 608-246-4551
- **Triangle Ethnic Fest** (mid-August) — 800-373-6376
- **Tuesday Noon Concerts** (June-September) — 608-266-0382
- **Wednesday Farmers' Market** (May-late October) — 920-563-5037
- **Wisconsin Quarter Horse Show** (mid-late August) — 608-267-3976

September
- **Dane County Farmers' Market** (late April-early November) — 920-563-5037 — www.madfarmmkt.org/
- **Taste of Madison** (early September) — 800-373-6376
- **Tuesday Noon Concerts** (June-September) — 608-266-0382
- **Wednesday Farmers' Market** (May-late October) — 920-563-5037
- **Willy Street Fair** (mid-September) — 608-256-3527
- **World Dairy Expo** (late September-early October) — 608-224-6455

October
- **Dane County Farmers' Market** (late April-early November) — 920-563-5037 — www.madfarmmkt.org/
- **Fall Festival** (mid-October) — 608-437-5914
- **Halloween at the Zoo** (late October) — 608-266-4732
- **Isthmus Jazz Festival** (early October) — 608-266-6550
- **Wednesday Farmers' Market** (May-late October) — 920-563-5037
- **World Dairy Expo** (late September-early October) — 608-224-6455

November
- **Dane County Farmers' Market** (late April-early November) — 920-563-5037 — www.madfarmmkt.org/
- **Holiday Art Fair** (late November) — 608-257-0158
- **Holiday Fantasy of Lights** (late November-early January) — 608-222-7630
- **International Holiday Festival** (mid-November) — 608-266-6550
- **Kwanzaa Holiday Marketplace** (late November) — 608-255-9600
- **Winter Art Festival** (mid-November) — 608-798-4811

December
- **Capitol Christmas Pageant** (early December) — 608-849-9529
- **Executive Residence Christmas Tours** (December) — 608-266-3554
- **Firstar Eve** (December 31) — 608-255-2537
- **Holiday Fantasy of Lights** (late November-early January) — 608-222-7630
- **Holiday Flower & Train Show** (December) — 608-246-4718
- **Jingle Bell Run** (mid-December) — 608-221-9800

Milwaukee

January
- **US International Snow Sculpting Competition** (late January) — 414-476-5573

February
- **Greater Milwaukee Auto Show** (late February-early March) — 414-908-6000
- **International Arts Festival** (February) — 414-273-3950
- **Milwaukee Boat Show** (mid-February) — 414-908-6000

March
- **Greater Milwaukee Auto Show** (late February-early March) — 414-908-6000
- **Spring Craft & Gift Show** (early March) — 414-321-2100

May
- **Cinco de Mayo Festival** (early May) — 414-671-5700
- **Grape Lakes Food & Wine Festival** (mid-May) — 414-224-3850

June
- **Bavarian Volksfest** (late June) — 414-462-9147
- **Jazz in the Park** (early June-late August) — 414-271-1416
- **Juneteenth Day** (mid-June) — 414-372-3770
- **Lakefront Festival of the Arts** (mid-June) — 414-224-3283
- **Milwaukee Highland Games** (early June) — 262-796-0807
- **Milwaukee Journal Sentinel Rose Festival** (mid-June) — 414-273-3950
- **Polish Fest** (late June) — 414-529-2140 — www.execpc.com/~polshfst/
- **Rainbow Summer** (early June-late August) — 414-273-7206
- **RiverSplash** (early June) — 414-286-8436
- **Senior Fest** (early June) — 414-647-6040
- **Shermanfest-Milwaukee's Premier Blues Festival** (mid-June) — 414-444-9813 — www.bluesaccess.com
- **Strawberry Festival** (late June) — 800-827-8020
- **Summerfest** (late June-early July) — 800-837-3378 — www.summerfest.com/

July
- **Bastille Days** (mid-July) — 414-271-1416
- **Festa Italiana** (mid-July) — 920-232-2192
- **German Fest** (late July) — 414-464-9444 — www.germanfest.com/
- **Great Circus Parade Week** (mid-July) — 414-273-7877
- **Greater Milwaukee Open** (early-mid-July) — 414-365-4466
- **Jazz in the Park** (early June-late August) — 414-271-1416
- **Rainbow Summer** (early June-late August) — 414-273-7206
- **South Shore Water Frolics** (mid-July) — 414-224-2753
- **Summerfest** (late June-early July) — 800-837-3378 — www.summerfest.com/

August
- **African World Festival** (early August) — 414-372-4567
- **Gen Con Game Fair** (early August) — 800-529-3976
- **Irish Feast** (mid-August) — 414-476-3378
- **Jazz in the Park** (early June-late August) — 414-271-1416
- **Mexican Fiesta** (mid-late August) — 414-383-7066
- **Milwaukee a la Carte** (mid-August) — 414-771-3040
- **Rainbow Summer** (early June-late August) — 414-273-7206
- **Wisconsin State Fair** (early August) — 800-231-0903 — www.wsfp.state.wi.us/

September
- **Harvest Fair** (late September) — 414-266-7000
- **Indian Summer Festival** (mid-September) — 414-774-7119 — indiansummer.org/
- **Oktoberfest** (September) — 414-964-4221
- **TosaFest** (mid-September) — 414-476-5300

November
- **Holiday Craft & Gift Show** (late November) — 414-321-2100 — www.craftfairusa.com
- **Holiday Folk Fair** (mid-November) — 414-225-6225
- **Milwaukee Christmas Parade** (mid-November) — 414-273-3950

December
- **Christmas in the Country** (early December) — 262-377-9620
- **Christmas in the Ward** (early December) — 414-273-1173
- **Firstar Eve Celebration** (December 31) — 414-765-6500

WYOMING

Casper

February
Cowboy State Games Winter Sports Festival (early February) 307-577-1125

March
Central Wyoming Home & Garden Show (late March) 307-577-3030

April
Wyoming Outdoors Sports Show (early April) 307-577-3030

June
Classicfest (late June-early July) 307-235-8441
Cowboy State Summer Games (early-June) 307-577-1125
Mountain Man Rendezvous & Primitive Skills Contest (late June) 307-235-8462

July
Bear Trap Summer Festival (late July) 307-235-9325
Central Wyoming Fair & Rodeo (mid-July) 800-852-1889
Classicfest (late June-early July) 307-235-8441
PRCA Night Rodeo (mid-July) 307-235-5775

August
Platte Bridge Cavalry Encampment (early August) 307-235-8462

October
PRCA Season Finale Rodeo (late October-early November) 307-235-8441

November
Christmas Parade (late November) 800-852-1889
PRCA Season Finale Rodeo (late October-early November) 307-235-8441
Wyoming Ski & Winter Sports Show (mid-November) 307-235-8441

December
Christmas with the Frontier Soldiers (early December) 307-235-8462
Cowboy Shootout (late December) 307-235-8441

Cheyenne

May
Cheyenne Street Railway (mid-May-September) 307-778-3133

June
Cheyenne Gunslinger Gunfights (early June-late July) 307-778-3133
Cheyenne Motorsports Shootout (late June) 307-778-3133
Cheyenne Street Railway (mid-May-September) 307-778-3133
Superday (late June) 307-637-6423
Tumbleweed Buckle Series Rodeo (June-August) 307-634-4171

July
Cheyenne Frontier Days (late July) 307-778-7200
Cheyenne Frontier Days Western Art Show & Sale (late July) 307-778-7290
Cheyenne Gunslinger Gunfights (early June-late July) 307-778-3133
Cheyenne Street Railway (mid-May-September) 307-778-3133
Old Fashioned Melodrama (early July-mid-August) 307-638-6543
Tumbleweed Buckle Series Rodeo (June-August) 307-634-4171
Wyoming Open Golf Tournament (mid-July) 307-637-6418

August
Cheyenne Farmer's Market (early August-early October) 307-635-9291
Cheyenne Street Railway (mid-May-September) 307-778-3133
Laramie County Fair (early August) 307-778-3133
Old Fashioned Melodrama (early July-mid-August) 307-638-6543
Outdoor Arts & Crafts Festival (early August) 307-777-7022
Tumbleweed Buckle Series Rodeo (June-August) 307-634-4171

September
Cheyenne Farmer's Market (early August-early October) 307-635-9291
Cheyenne Street Railway (mid-May-September) 307-778-3133
Cheyenne Western Film Festival (mid-September) 307-635-4646

October
Cheyenne Farmer's Market (early August-early October) 307-635-9291

November
Cheyenne Christmas Parade Craft Show & Concert (Thanksgiving weekend) 307-638-0151
Silver Bells in the City (late November) 517-372-4636

Jackson

January
International Rocky Mountain Stage Stop Sled Dog Race (late January-mid-February) 307-734-1163
www.wyomingstagestop.org

February
International Rocky Mountain Stage Stop Sled Dog Race (late January-mid-February) 307-734-1163
www.wyomingstagestop.org
Jackson Hole Alliance Silent Art & Antique Auction (mid-February-early March) 307-733-9417
Sean Nurse Memorial Ski Race (February) 307-733-6433
Shriner's All-American Cutter Races (mid-February) 307-733-8853

March
Anheuser-Busch Spring Snow Carnival (mid-late March) 800-827-4433
Celebrity Winter Extravaganza (early March) 307-734-2878
Jackson Hole Alliance Silent Art & Antique Auction (mid-February-early March) 307-733-9417
Ski School Kids Carnival (mid-late March) 307-733-4826
Town Downhill (early March) 307-733-6433
World Championship Snowmobile Hillclimb (late March) 307-734-9653

May
Don MacLeod Cookout (mid-May) 307-733-9605
Old West Days (late May) 307-733-3316
www.jacksonholechamber.com/owd.shtml
Town Square Shoot-Out (late May-early September) 307-733-3316

June
Grand Teton Music Festival Season (late June-late August) 307-733-1128
www.gtmf.org
Town Square Shoot-Out (late May-early September) 307-733-3316

July
4th of July Celebration (July 4) 307-733-3316
Grand Teton Music Festival Family Picnic & Concert (July 4) 307-733-1128
Grand Teton Music Festival Season (late June-late August) 307-733-1128
www.gtmf.org
Mangy Moose Micro-Brew Festival (mid-July) 307-733-4913
Mountain Artists' Rendezvous Art Show (mid-July & late August) 307-733-8792
Rockin the Tetons Festival (mid-July) 800-827-4433
Teton County Fair (late July-early August) 307-733-5289
Teton Valley Balloon Festival (early July) 208-354-2500
Town Square Shoot-Out (late May-early September) 307-733-3316

August
Grand Teton Music Festival Season (late June-late August) 307-733-1128
www.gtmf.org
Mountain Artists' Rendezvous Art Show (mid-July & late August) 307-733-8792
Targhee Bluegrass Festival (mid-August) 800-827-4433
Teton County Fair (late July-early August) 307-733-5289
Town Square Shoot-Out (late May-early September) 307-733-3316

September
Jackson Hole Fall Arts Festival (mid-September) 307-733-3316
www.jacksonholechamber.com/fallarts.shtml
Jackson Hole Wildlife Film Festival (late September) 307-733-7016
Town Square Shoot-Out (late May-early September) 307-733-3316

CANADA

Calgary

January
Alberta Bobsleigh Cup (mid-January) 403-286-2632
Canada Luge Championships (early January) 403-247-5452
www.coda.ab.ca
HomeExpo (mid-January) 403-261-0101
Playrites Festival (late January-early March) 403-294-7402

February
Alberta Luge Cup (early February) 403-247-9884
Calgary Boat & Sportsmen's Show (mid-February) 403-261-0101
Calgary Winter Festival (mid-February) 403-543-5480
www.calgarywinterfest.com
Chinese New Year's Carnival (mid-February) 403-262-5071
Cowboy Festival (early February) 403-261-8500
Playrites Festival (late January-early March) 403-294-7402
Provincial Bobsleigh Championships (mid-late February) 403-286-2632
Spring Home & Garden Show (late February) 403-261-0101

March
International Auto Show (mid-March) 403-261-0101
Playrites Festival (late January-early March) 403-294-7402
Rodeo Royal (mid-March) 403-261-0101
Spring Craft Show (late March-early April) 403-261-0101

April
Aggie Days (mid-April) 403-261-0114
Blue Mountain Spring Antique Show (mid-April) 800-755-4081
Dairy Classic (late April) 403-261-0101
Easter Promenade (early April) 403-245-1703
Spring Craft Show (late March-early April) 403-261-0101

May
4th Street Lilac Festival (late May) 403-229-0902
Bloom Fest (late May) 403-232-9300
Calgary International Children's Festival (mid-late May) 403-294-7414

June
4-H on Parade (early June) 403-261-0162
Calgary International Jazz Festival (late June-early July) 403-249-1119
Calgary Summer Antique Show (late June) 403-247-5452
Carifest Caribbean Festival (early-mid-June) 403-292-0310
National The Horse Jumping at Spruce Meadows (early June) 403-974-4200
www.sprucemeadows.com
Native Awareness Week (mid-late June) 403-261-3022

July
Alberta Dragon Boat Races (late July-early August) 403-246-5757
Calgary Folk Music Festival (late July) 403-233-0904
www.canuck.com/folkfest/
Calgary International Jazz Festival (late June-early July) 403-249-1119
Calgary Stampede (early-mid-July) 403-261-0101
Historic Calgary Week (late July-early August) 403-261-3662
Jazzoo (early July-late August) 403-232-9300
North American Show Jumping at Spruce Meadows (early July) 403-974-4200
www.sprucemeadows.com

August
Alberta Dragon Boat Races (late July-early August) 403-246-5757
Calgary International Organ Festival (late August-early September) 403-543-5115
www.ciof.com
Historic Calgary Week (late July-early August) 403-261-3662
Jazzoo (early July-late August) 403-232-9300

September
Artwalk (mid-September) 403-255-2729
Blue Mountain Fall Antique Show (mid-September) 800-755-4081
Calgary International Organ Festival (late August-early September) 403-543-5115
www.ciof.com
Calgary Philharmonic Orchestra's BBQ on the Bow (early September) 403-271-2494
Canadian Country Music Week (early September) 403-716-2105
www.ccma.org
Chalk Walk (mid-September) 403-245-1703
Fall Home Show (mid-September) 403-261-0101
Heritage Park Old Time Fall Fair (early September) 403-259-1950

October
Artist Direct Christmas Show (mid-October) 403-253-1966
Boo at the Zoo (late October) 403-232-9383
Cody Snyder's Canadian Classic BullBustin (early October) 403-938-5255
Taste of Banff and Lake Louise (early October) 403-762-8421

November
Banff Festival of Mountain Films (early November) 403-762-6675
www.banffcentre.ab.ca/CMC/
Esther Honens Calgary International Piano Competition & Festival (mid-late November) 403-299-0130
www.culturenet.ca/esther-honens/

December
Wildlights New Year's Eve Party (December 31) 403-232-9300

Edmonton

March
Edmonton Boat & Sportsmen's Show (early March) 780-245-9008
Edmonton Home & Garden Show (mid-March) 780-471-7210
Edmonton Women's Show (mid-March & mid-October) 780-490-0215
Local Heroes International Screen Festival (early-mid-March) 780-421-4084
Northlands Farm & Ranch Show (late March) 780-471-7210

April
Edmonton Kiwanis Music Festival (late April-early May) 780-488-3498

May
Edmonton Kiwanis Music Festival (late April-early May) 780-488-3498
Kinsmen Rainmaker Rodeo (late May) 780-459-1724
Medieval Days (late May-early June) 780-464-0249
Northern Alberta International Children's Festival (late May-early June) 780-459-1542

June
Jazz City International Music Festival (late June-early July) 780-432-7166
Medieval Days (late May-early June) 780-464-0249
Northern Alberta International Children's Festival (late May-early June) 780-459-1542
Works The: A Visual Arts Celebration (late June-early July) 780-426-2122

July
Edmonton Canada Day (July 1) 780-488-6213
Edmonton International Street Performers Festival (mid-late July) 780-425-5162
Edmonton's Klondike Days (mid-late July) 780-423-2822
Jazz City International Music Festival (late June-early July) 780-432-7166
Works The: A Visual Arts Celebration (late June-early July) 780-426-2122

August
Cariwest: Edmonton's Caribbean Carnival (mid-August) 780-421-7800
Edmonton Folk Music Festival (early August) 780-429-1899
www.efmf.ab.ca
Edmonton Heritage Festival (early August) 780-488-3378
Edmonton's International Fringe Theatre Event (mid-late August) 780-448-9000
www.fringe.alberta.com/fta

September
Edmonton Home Show (mid-September) 780-424-0515
Symphony Under the Sky Festival (early September) 780-428-1414

October
Edmonton New Music Festival (early October) 800-563-5081
Edmonton Women's Show (mid-March & mid-October) 780-490-0215

November
Canadian Finals Rodeo (early-mid-November) 780-471-7210
Farmfair International (early-mid-November) 780-471-7210

December
First Night Edmonton (December 31) 780-448-9200

Halifax

February
- **Halifax Carnival** (mid-February) — 902-423-3740
- **Halifax International Boat Show** (mid-February) — 888-454-7469
- **Halifax Winterfest** (late February) — 902-423-3740

April
- **Easter Egg Hunt** (early April) — 902-424-7353
- **Nova Scotia Ideal Home Show** (mid-April & late September) — 902-468-4999
- **Springtime at the Forum** (late April-early May) — 902-425-5656

May
- **On the Waterfront Festival** (mid-May) — 902-463-7529
- **Scotia Festival of Music** (late May-early June) — 902-429-9467 — www3.ns.sympatico.ca/scotia.festival/
- **Springtime at the Forum** (late April-early May) — 902-425-5656

June
- **Alexander Keith's Magical History Tour** (June-September) — 902-422-2069
- **Fort Nites in the Hill** (June-July) — 902-425-9500
- **Greek Fest** (mid-June) — 902-479-1271 — www.greekfest.org/home.html
- **Nova Scotia International Tattoo Festival** (late June-early July) — 902-420-1114 — www.nstattoo.ca
- **Nova Scotia Multicultural Festival** (mid-June) — 902-423-6534
- **Scotia Festival of Music** (late May-early June) — 902-429-9467 — www3.ns.sympatico.ca/scotia.festival/

July
- **Alexander Keith's Magical History Tour** (June-September) — 902-422-2069
- **DuMaurier Atlantic Jazz Festival** (mid-late July) — 902-492-2225 — jazzfest.ns.sympatico.ca
- **Fisherman's Cove Canada Day Gala** (July 1) — 902-465-6093
- **Fort Nites in the Hill** (June-July) — 902-425-9500
- **Great Nova Scotia Mussel Festival** (mid-July) — 902-857-9555
- **Halifax Dragon Boat Festival** (late July) — 902-425-5454 — www.dragonboat.halifax.ns.ca
- **Halifax Highland Games** (early July) — 902-425-2445
- **Halifax-Dartmouth Canada Day** (July 1) — 902-490-4729
- **Halifax-Dartmouth Natal Day** (late July-early August) — 902-490-4729
- **Lebanese Summer Festival** (mid-July) — 902-473-2720
- **Maritime Old Time Jamboree** (mid-July) — 902-434-5466
- **Nova Scotia International Tattoo Festival** (late June-early July) — 902-420-1114 — www.nstattoo.ca
- **Provincial Rose Show** (mid-July) — 902-453-6801
- **Sharkarama at Fisherman's Cove** (late July) — 902-465-6093
- **Three Day Flea Market Extravaganza** (mid-July) — 902-429-0375

August
- **Alexander Keith's Magical History Tour** (June-September) — 902-422-2069
- **Halifax County Exhibition** (mid-August) — 902-384-3008 — www.nova-scotia.com/halifaxcounty/
- **Halifax Flower Show** (late August) — 902-453-6801
- **Halifax International Busker Festival** (early-mid-August) — 902-429-3910 — buskers.ns.sympatico.ca
- **Halifax-Dartmouth Natal Day** (late July-early August) — 902-490-4729
- **Nova Scotia Designer Craft Council Summer Craft Festival** (mid-August) — 902-423-3837

September
- **Alexander Keith's Magical History Tour** (June-September) — 902-422-2069
- **Atlantic Film Festival** (mid-late September) — 902-422-3456 — www.atlanticfilm.com
- **Atlantic Fringe Festival** (early September) — 902-435-4837
- **Nova Scotia Ideal Home Show** (mid-April & late September) — 902-468-4999
- **Nova Scotia International Air Show** (mid-September) — 902-465-2725 — www3.ns.sympatico.ca/nsias/
- **Terry Fox Run** (mid-September) — 902-423-8131

October
- **Atlantic Winter Fair** (early-mid-October) — 902-876-8222 — www.nova-scotia.com/atlanticwinterfair/
- **Halloween at the Cove** (late October) — 902-465-6093

November
- **Christmas at the Forum** (early November) — 902-425-5656
- **Festival of the Arts** (mid-November) — 902-423-3837
- **Holiday Parade of Lights** (late November) — 902-423-3740
- **Open Waters Festival** (mid-November) — 902-494-3820
- **Santa Claus Parade** (late November) — 902-477-7665

December
- **Christmas at the Cove** (December) — 902-465-6093
- **Christmas Tree Lighting Ceremony** (early December) — 902-423-3740
- **Halifax Regional Municipality New Years Eve Celebration** (December 31) — 902-490-4729
- **New Year's Eve Public Concert & Balls** (December 31) — 902-423-3740

Montreal

January
- **Christmas at the Fort** (mid-December-early January) — 514-861-6701
- **Christmas at the Garden** (mid-November-early January) — 514-872-1400
- **Santa Claus Village** (early December-early January) — 514-281-0170

March
- **Montréal Sportsmen's Show** (late March) — 514-397-2222
- **Montréal Spring Gift Show** (early March) — 514-397-2222

May
- **Festival de Theatre des Ameriques** (late May-early June) — 514-842-0704
- **International Interior Design Show** (mid-late May) — 514-397-2222
- **Montréal Air Show** (mid-May) — 800-678-5440

June
- **Artists Promenade** (June-August) — 514-496-7678
- **Beer Mundial** (mid-late June) — 514-722-9640 — www.festivalmondialbiere.qc.ca
- **Festival de Theatre des Ameriques** (late May-early June) — 514-842-0704
- **Festival International de Jazz de Montréal** (late June-early July) — 514-523-3378 — www.montrealjazzfest.com
- **Montréal Fringe Festival** (mid-late June) — 514-849-3378
- **National Bank Duck Race** (late June) — 514-496-7678
- **Players Grand Prix of Canada** (mid-June) — 514-350-0000 — www.grandprix.ca
- **Saint Jean-Baptiste Day Celebration** (June 24) — 514-872-4058
- **Tropicalissimo Latin Extravaganza** (June-August) — 514-496-7678
- **Worldwide Kite Rendez-Vous** (late June) — 514-765-7213

July
- **African & Creole Arts Festival** (mid-late July) — 514-499-9239
- **Artists Promenade** (June-August) — 514-496-7678
- **Canada Day** (July 1) — 514-873-2015
- **Canada Day Celebrations** (July 1) — 514-283-7363
- **Canada's International Men's Tennis Championships** (late July-early August) — 514-273-1515 — www.tenniscanada.com
- **Classical Music Festival** (July) — 450-759-7636
- **Festival International de Jazz de Montréal** (late June-early July) — 514-523-3378 — www.montrealjazzfest.com
- **Francofolies of Montréal** (late July-mid-August) — 514-871-1881 — www.francofolies.com
- **Just for Laughs Festival** (mid-late July) — 514-845-2322 — www.hahaha.com
- **Lachine International Folklore Festival** (early July) — 514-634-7526
- **Nights of Africa International Festival** (early-late July) — 514-499-9239
- **Tropicalissimo Latin Extravaganza** (June-August) — 514-496-7678

August
- **Artists Promenade** (June-August) — 514-496-7678
- **Canada's International Men's Tennis Championships** (late July-early August) — 514-273-1515 — www.tenniscanada.com
- **Francofolies of Montréal** (late July-mid-August) — 514-871-1881 — www.francofolies.com
- **International Food Festival** (early-mid-August) — 514-861-8241
- **Montréal World Film Festival** (late August-early September) — 514-848-3883
- **Tropicalissimo Latin Extravaganza** (June-August) — 514-496-7678

September
- **Chinese Lantern Festival** (mid-late September) — 514-872-1400
- **Montréal World Film Festival** (late August-early September) — 514-848-3883

October
- **Black & Blue Festival** (mid-October) — 514-875-7026
- **Great Pumpkin Ball** (mid-October-early November) — 514-872-1400
- **International Festival of New Cinema & New Media** (mid-late October) — 514-847-9272 — www.fcmm.com
- **International Orchid Show** (mid-October) — 514-934-0680
- **International Tourism and Travel Show** (late October-early November) — 514-397-2222

November
- **Christmas at the Garden** (mid-November-early January) — 514-872-1400
- **Great Pumpkin Ball** (mid-October-early November) — 514-872-1400
- **International Tourism and Travel Show** (late October-early November) — 514-397-2222

December
- **Christmas at the Fort** (mid-December-early January) — 514-861-6701
- **Christmas at the Garden** (mid-November-early January) — 514-872-1400
- **Santa Claus Village** (early December-early January) — 514-281-0170

Ottawa

January
- **Christmas Lights Across Canada** (early December-early January) — 613-239-5000
- **Deck the Halls at Parliament Hill** (late December-early January) — 613-239-5000

February
- **Keskinada Loppet Cross-Country Skiing Event** (mid-February) — 819-827-4641 — www.impacttraining.com/keski/
- **Winterlude** (February) — 613-239-5000

March
- **Ottawa Spring Home Show** (late March) — 613-241-2888

May
- **Canadian Tulip Festival** (early-mid-May) — 613-567-4447 — www.tulipfestival.ca
- **National Capital Air Show** (late May) — 613-526-1030 — ncas.ottawa.com
- **National Capital Marathon Race Weekend** (early May) — 613-234-2221 — www.ncm.ca
- **Odawa Pow Wow** (late May) — 613-722-3811
- **Reflections of Canada-A Symphony of Sound & Light** (mid-May-early September) — 613-239-5100

June
- **Canadian Sunset Ceremony** (mid-June) — 613-239-5000
- **Children's Festival de la Jeunesse** (mid-June) — 613-728-5863 — www.childfest.ca
- **Festival Franco-ontarien** (late June) — 613-741-1225
- **Governor General's Garden Party** (June) — 613-998-7113 — www.gg.ca
- **Italian Week Festival** (early-mid-June) — 613-726-0920
- **National Capital Dragon Boat Race Festival** (late June) — 613-238-7711 — www.dragonboat.net
- **Ottawa Fringe Festival** (late June) — 613-232-6162
- **Parliament Hill Changing the Guard Ceremony** (late June-late August) — 613-239-5000
- **Reflections of Canada-A Symphony of Sound & Light** (mid-May-early September) — 613-239-5100
- **Strawberry Moon: A Midsummer Festival** (mid-June) — 613-236-5330

July
- **Canada Day at Parliament Hill** (July 1) — 613-239-5000
- **Casino Sound of Light** (late July-mid-August) — 819-771-3389
- **HOPE Beach Volleyball Tournament** (mid-July) — 613-237-1433 — www.hopeottawa.on.ca
- **Ottawa Blues Festival** (early July) — 613-233-8798 — www.ottawa-bluesfest.ca
- **Ottawa Chamber Music Festival** (late July-early August) — 613-234-8008 — www.chamberfest.com
- **Ottawa International Jazz Festival** (mid-late July) — 613-241-2633
- **Parliament Hill Carillon Concerts** (July-August) — 613-239-5000
- **Parliament Hill Changing the Guard Ceremony** (late June-late August) — 613-239-5000
- **Pride Festival** (mid-late July) — 613-237-9872 — www.gaycanada.com/ottawa-pride/
- **Reflections of Canada-A Symphony of Sound & Light** (mid-May-early September) — 613-239-5100

August
- **Casino Sound of Light** (late July-mid-August) — 819-771-3389
- **Central Canada Exhibition** (mid-late August) — 613-237-7222 — www.the-ex.com
- **CKCU Ottawa Folk Festival** (late August) — 613-230-8234 — ottawafolk.org
- **Ottawa Chamber Music Festival** (late July-early August) — 613-234-8008 — www.chamberfest.com
- **Parliament Hill Carillon Concerts** (July-August) — 613-239-5000
- **Parliament Hill Changing the Guard Ceremony** (late June-late August) — 613-239-5000
- **Reflections of Canada-A Symphony of Sound & Light** (mid-May-early September) — 613-239-5100

September
- **Fall Rhapsody** (mid-September-early October) — 613-239-5000
- **Ottawa Fall Home Show** (late September) — 613-241-2888
- **Reflections of Canada-A Symphony of Sound & Light** (mid-May-early September) — 613-239-5100

October
- **Fall Rhapsody** (mid-September-early October) — 613-239-5000
- **Oktoberfest** (mid-October) — 613-564-1485
- **Ottawa International Animation Festival** (late October) — 613-232-8769 — www.awn.com/ottawa/

November
- **Contemporary Showcase Festival** (late November) — 613-829-4402
- **Harvestfest** (late November) — 613-833-3059
- **Lebanorama** (mid-November) — 613-742-6952
- **Signatures Craft Show & Sale** (early November & mid-December) — 416-465-2379

December
- **Christmas Lights Across Canada** (early December-early January) — 613-239-5000
- **Deck the Halls at Parliament Hill** (late December-early January) — 613-239-5000
- **Ottawa Christmas Craft Show** (mid-late December) — 613-564-1485
- **Signatures Craft Show & Sale** (early November & mid-December) — 416-465-2379

Quebec

January
- **Noël à Québec** (early December-early January) — 418-692-2613
- **Québec City International Bonspiel** (late January) — 418-683-4431
- **Québec Winter Carnival** (late January-mid-February) — 418-626-3716 — www.carnaval.qc.ca

February
- **NAYA Cup** (early-mid-February) — 418-827-4561
- **Québec International Pee-Wee Hockey Tournament** (mid-late February) — 418-524-3311
- **Québec Winter Carnival** (late January-mid-February) — 418-626-3716 — www.carnaval.qc.ca

March
- **Mont-Sainte-Anne Loppet** (early March) — 418-827-4561

April
- **Easter in Québec** (mid-April) — 418-649-2608
- **Snow Festival** (early April) — 418-848-2411

June
- **International Children's Folklore Festival** (late June-early July) — 418-666-2153
- **International Jazz & Blues Festival** (late June-early July) — 888-515-0505
- **Sainte-Jean-Baptiste Day** (June 24) — 418-640-0799
- **Summer Activities at Place-Royale** (late June-late August) — 418-643-6631

CANADA — Quebec (Cont'd)

July

- **Canada Day Festivities** (July 1) 418-649-2608
- **DuMaurier Québec City Summer Festival** (early-mid-July) 418-692-4540
- **International Children's Folklore Festival** (late June-early July) 418-666-2153
- **International Jazz & Blues Festival** (late June-early July) 888-515-0505
- **International Summer Festival** (early-mid-July) 418-692-5200 www.festival-ete-quebec.qc.ca
- **Québec Horse Show** (early July) 418-647-2727
- **Saint Ann's Day Celebrations** (July 26) 418-827-3781
- **Summer Activities at Place-Royale** (late June-late August) 418-643-6631

August

- **Antique Car Show** (late August) 418-681-4307
- **Expo-Québec** (late August) 418-691-7110
- **Festival of Early Music** (late August-late September) 418-681-3010
- **Linseed Festival** (late August) 418-337-6416
- **Potato Festival** (early August) 418-277-2415
- **Québec International Film Festival** (late August-early September) 514-848-3883
- **Summer Activities at Place-Royale** (late June-late August) 418-643-6631

September

- **Autumn Festival** (mid-September-mid-October) 418-827-4561
- **Festival of Early Music** (late August-late September) 418-681-3010
- **Québec International Film Festival** (late August-early September) 514-848-3883

October

- **Autumn Festival** (mid-September-mid-October) 418-827-4561
- **Greater Snow Geese Festival** (early-mid-October) 418-827-3776
- **Hunter's Show** (late October) 418-323-2994
- **International Traditional Art Festival** (mid-October) 418-647-1598
- **Québec Wine & Food Show** (late October) 418-683-4150
- **Québec's International Festival of Traditional Arts** (mid-October) 418-647-1598

December

- **Arts & Crafts Show** (mid-December) 418-644-4000
- **Gründig Snowboard World Cup** (late December) 418-827-1122
- **Noël à Québec** (early December-early January) 418-692-2613
- **Snowboard World Cup** (mid-December) 418-827-4561
- **Surf World Cup at Mont-Sainte-Anne** (mid-December) 418-827-4561

Toronto

January

- **Cavalcade of Lights** (late November-early January) 416-392-7341
- **Stages Celebration** (January-March) 416-203-2500
- **Toronto Home Show** (late January) 416-674-8425
- **Trees Around the World** (late November-mid-January) 416-392-7341
- **Victorian Christmas Flower Show** (early December-early January) 416-392-7288

February

- **Stages Celebration** (January-March) 416-203-2500
- **Winter Fest** (mid-February) 416-395-7300

March

- **Canada Blooms Flower Show** (mid-March) 416-512-1305
- **Stages Celebration** (January-March) 416-203-2500
- **Toronto Sportsman's Show** (mid-late March) 416-674-8425
- **Toronto St Patrick's Parade** (mid-March) 416-487-1566 www.icomm.ca/parade98/

April

- **Images Festival of Independent Film and Video** (late April-early May) 416-971-8405 www.interlog.com/~images

May

- **Big City Hoedown 8** (late May) 416-927-7151
- **Images Festival of Independent Film and Video** (late April-early May) 416-971-8405 www.interlog.com/~images
- **MILK International Children's Festival** (mid-May) 416-973-3000
- **Toronto Jewish Film Festival** (May) 416-324-8600 www.web-sights.com/tjff

June

- **Benson & Hedges Symphony of Fire Fireworks Competition** (late June-early July) 416-314-9900 www.ontarioplace.com/bhi.html
- **Farmer's Market Sounds in the City Concert Series** (early June-early October) 416-392-0458
- **Gay Pride Week** (June) 416-927-7433
- **International Dragon Boat Race Festival** (late June) 416-364-0693
- **International Marketplace** (June-September) 416-973-3000
- **Italian Celebration** (late June-early July) 416-531-2672
- **Medieval Renaissance Festival** (mid-late June) 416-487-3294
- **Metro International Caravan** (mid-late June) 416-977-0466
- **North by Northeast Music Festival** (mid-June) 416-863-6963 www.virtualnoise.com/nxne
- **Toronto Downtown Jazz Festival** (late June-early July) 416-973-3000 www.tojazz.com
- **Toronto Lion Dance Festival** (early June) 416-392-0335 www.liondancefest.com

July

- **Beaches International Jazz Festival** (late July) 416-698-2152 www.beachesjazz.com
- **Benson & Hedges Symphony of Fire Fireworks Competition** (late June-early July) 416-314-9900 www.ontarioplace.com/bhi.html
- **Caribana Festival** (mid-July-early August) 416-465-4884
- **CHIN Picnic International & Shopping Bazar** (early July) 416-531-9991
- **Farmer's Market Sounds in the City Concert Series** (early June-early October) 416-392-0458
- **Fringe of Toronto Festival** (early-mid-July) 416-966-1062 www.fringetoronto.com
- **International Marketplace** (June-September) 416-973-3000
- **Italian Celebration** (late June-early July) 416-531-2672
- **Outdoor Art Exhibition** (mid-July) 416-408-2754
- **Scream In High Park-One of Canada's Largest Outdoor Literary Festivals** (mid-July) 416-532-6948 scream.interlog.com
- **Toronto Downtown Jazz Festival** (late June-early July) 416-973-3000 www.tojazz.com
- **Toronto Fall Gift Show** (late July) 416-263-3000
- **Toronto Harbour Parade of Lights** (July 1) 416-941-1041 www.paradeoflights.org
- **Toronto Molson Indy** (mid-July) 416-872-4639 www.molson.com/motorsport/toronto/

August

- **Canadian National Exhibition** (late August-early September) 416-393-6000 www.theex.com
- **Caribana Festival** (mid-July-early August) 416-465-4884
- **Farmer's Market Sounds in the City Concert Series** (early June-early October) 416-392-0458
- **Great Canadian Bug Show** (mid-August) 905-642-2886 www3.sympatico.ca/bugshow
- **Hot & Spicy Food Festival** (mid-August) 416-973-4000
- **International Marketplace** (June-September) 416-973-3000
- **Taste of the Danforth** (early August) 416-469-5634

September

- **Bell Canadian Open** (early-mid-September) 416-581-6863 www.bell.ca/cdnopen/
- **Canadian International Air Show** (early September) 416-393-6061 www.cias.org
- **Canadian National Exhibition** (late August-early September) 416-393-6000 www.theex.com
- **Country Harvest Festival** (September) 416-487-3294
- **Farmer's Market Sounds in the City Concert Series** (early June-early October) 416-392-0458
- **International Marketplace** (June-September) 416-973-3000
- **Ontario Place Offshore Challenge** (mid-September) 416-314-9900 www.ontarioplace.com/opoffshore.html
- **Toronto Fall Home Show** (late September-early October) 416-263-3000
- **Toronto International Film Festival** (early-mid-September) 416-968-3456
- **Vegetarian Food Fair** (mid-September) 416-973-3000

October

- **Canadian International Marathon** (mid-October) 416-972-1062
- **Creative Sewing & Needlework Festival** (late October) 905-709-0100
- **Creative Sewing & Needlework Festival** (early-mid-October) 416-973-3000
- **Fall Classic Collector Car Auction & Swap Meet** (late October) 416-674-8425
- **Farmer's Market Sounds in the City Concert Series** (early June-early October) 416-392-0458
- **HarvestFest** (mid-October) 416-973-3000
- **International Festival of Authors** (late October) 416-973-3000
- **Toronto Fall Home Show** (late September-early October) 416-263-3000

November

- **Cavalcade of Lights** (late November-early January) 416-392-7341
- **Christmas in the Village** (mid-November-late December) 416-736-1733
- **Country Christmas at Gibson House Museum** (mid-November-late December) 416-395-7432
- **Mennonite Christmas Festival** (late November) 416-973-3000
- **One of a Kind Christmas Canadian Craft Show & Sale** (late November-early December) 416-393-6000
- **Royal Agricultural Winter Fair** (early-mid-November) 416-872-7777
- **Santa Claus Parade** (late November) 416-249-7833
- **Trees Around the World** (late November-mid-January) 416-392-7341

December

- **Cavalcade of Lights** (late November-early January) 416-392-7341
- **Christmas in the Village** (mid-November-late December) 416-736-1733
- **Country Christmas at Gibson House Museum** (mid-November-late December) 416-395-7432
- **First Night Toronto** (December 31) 416-362-3692
- **International Christmas Fair & Marketplace** (early December) 416-213-1035
- **One of a Kind Christmas Canadian Craft Show & Sale** (late November-early December) 416-393-6000
- **Toronto Christmas Story** (early-mid-December) 416-598-8979
- **Trees Around the World** (late November-mid-January) 416-392-7341
- **Victorian Christmas Flower Show** (early December-early January) 416-392-7288

Vancouver

January

- **Chinese New Year** (late January-mid-February) 604-662-3207

February

- **Chinese New Year** (late January-mid-February) 604-662-3207

March

- **Vancouver Playhouse International Wine Festival** (late March-early April) 604-872-6622 www.winefest.bc.sympatico.ca

April

- **Vancouver Playhouse International Wine Festival** (late March-early April) 604-872-6622 www.winefest.bc.sympatico.ca

May

- **Hycroft House & Garden Fair** (early May) 604-731-4661
- **Music West Festival** (mid-May) 604-683-2000 www.musicwest.com
- **Vancouver International Marathon** (early May) 604-872-2928 www.vanmarathon.bc.ca

June

- **Bard on the Beach Shakespeare Festival** (mid-June-early September) 604-737-0625 www.faximum.com/bard
- **Canadian International Dragon Boat Festival** (mid-June) 604-688-2382
- **DuMaurier International Jazz Festival** (late June) 604-872-5200 www.jazzfest.bc.sympatico.ca
- **Enchanted Evenings Musical Performances** (mid-June-August) 604-662-3207
- **Vandusen Flower & Garden Show** (early June) 604-878-9274

July

- **Bard on the Beach Shakespeare Festival** (mid-June-early September) 604-737-0625 www.faximum.com/bard
- **Benson & Hedges Symphony of Fire** (late July-early August) 604-738-4304
- **Best of the West Antique Expo** (early July) 604-857-1263
- **Canada Day Celebrations** (July 1) 604-666-8477
- **Dancing on the Edge** (early-mid-July) 604-689-0691
- **Enchanted Evenings Musical Performances** (mid-June-August) 604-662-3207
- **Vancouver Folk Music Festival** (mid-July) 604-681-0041 www.thefestival.bc.ca
- **Vancouver International Comedy Festival** (late July-early August) 604-683-0883

August

- **Abbotsford International Air Show** (early August) 604-852-8511
- **Air Canada Championship** (late August) 604-899-4641
- **Bard on the Beach Shakespeare Festival** (mid-June-early September) 604-737-0625 www.faximum.com/bard
- **Benson & Hedges Symphony of Fire** (late July-early August) 604-738-4304
- **Enchanted Evenings Musical Performances** (mid-June-August) 604-662-3207
- **Pacific National Exhibition** (late August-early September) 604-253-2311 www.pne.bc.ca
- **Vancouver Chamber Music Festival** (early August) 604-602-0363 www.interchg.ubc.ca/vrs
- **Vancouver International Comedy Festival** (late July-early August) 604-683-0883

September

- **Bard on the Beach Shakespeare Festival** (mid-June-early September) 604-737-0625 www.faximum.com/bard
- **Mid-Autumn Moon Festival** (mid-September) 604-662-3207
- **Molson Indy Vancouver** (early September) 604-684-4639
- **Pacific National Exhibition** (late August-early September) 604-253-2311 www.pne.bc.ca
- **Vancouver Fringe Festival** (early September) 604-257-0350

October

- **BC Home Show** (mid-October) 604-433-5121 www.southex.com/bchomeshow/
- **Vancouver International Writers Festival** (late October) 604-681-6330
- **Vancouver Ski & Snowboard Show** (late October) 604-878-0557
- **Vancouver Waterfront Antique Show** (late October) 800-667-0619

November

- **Christmas at Hycroft House** (mid-November) 604-731-4661

December

- **Celebration of Lights** (early-late December) 604-666-8477
- **Christmas Carolship Parade** (December) 604-878-9988 www.carolships.org

Winnipeg

January

- **Lights of the Wild** (mid-December-early January) 204-986-6921

February

- **Festival du Voyageur** (mid-late February) 204-237-7692 www.festivalvoyageur.mb.ca

June

- **Red River Exhibition** (late June) 204-888-6990
- **Scottish Heritage Festival** (late June) 204-888-9380
- **Winnipeg International Airshow** (early June) 204-257-8400
- **Winnipeg International Children's Festival** (early June) 204-958-4730
- **Winnipeg Jazz Festival** (mid-late June) 204-989-4656

July

- **Winnipeg Folk Festival** (mid-July) 204-231-0096 www.wpgfolkfest.mb.ca
- **Winnipeg Fringe Festival** (late July) 204-956-1340 www.uwinnipeg.ca/academic/as/theatre/thefring.htm

August

- **Folklorama** (early-mid-August) 204-982-6210 www.folklorama.ca

September

- **Oktoberfest** (mid-September) 204-956-1720

December

- **Lights of the Wild** (mid-December-early January) 204-986-6921
- **Santa Claus Parade** (early December) 204-782-2247

City Profiles USA

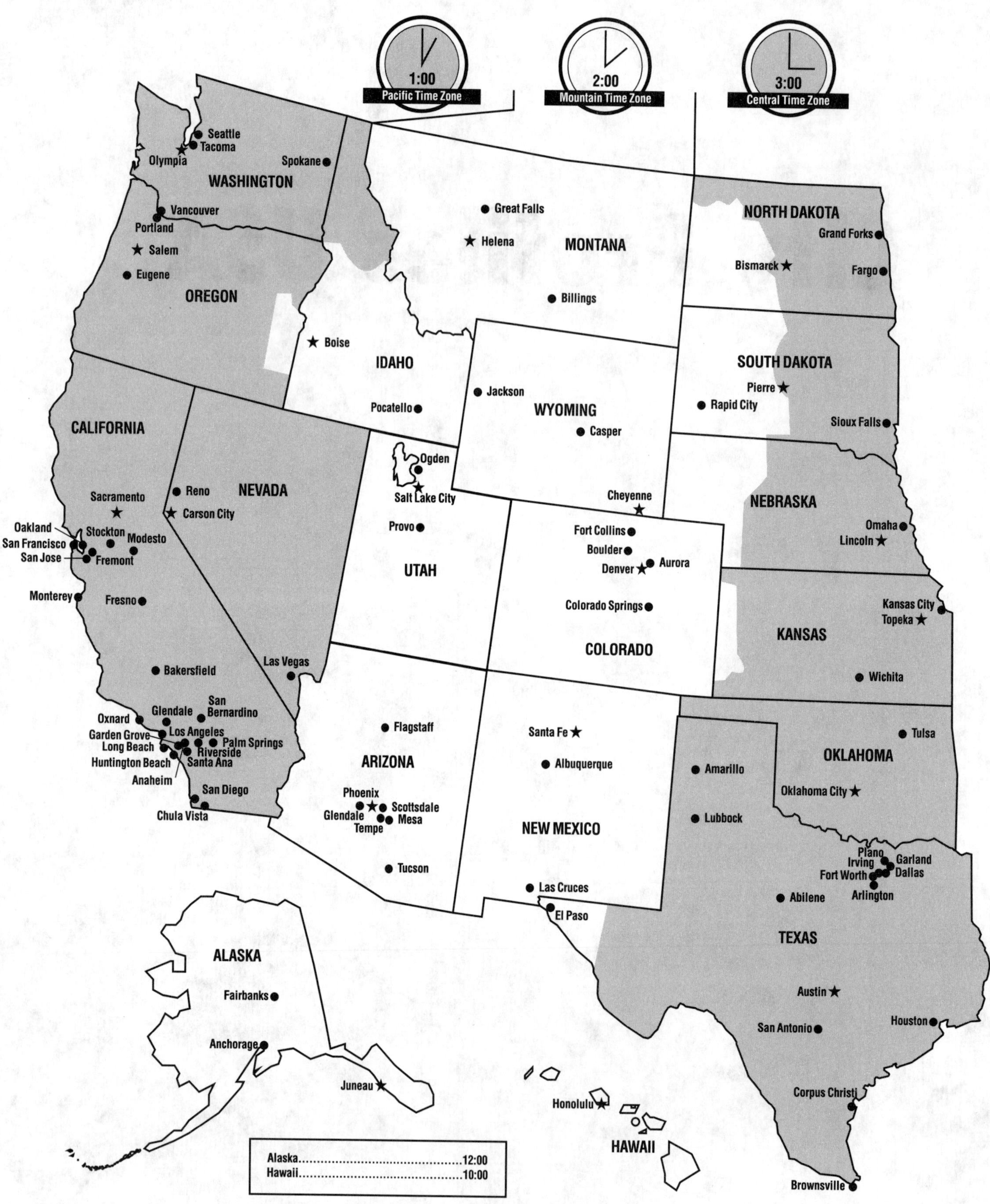
1:00
Pacific Time Zone
2:00
Mountain Time Zone
3:00
Central Time Zone
WASHINGTON
Seattle
Tacoma
Olympia
Spokane
Vancouver
Portland
Salem
Eugene
OREGON
IDAHO
Boise
Pocatello
MONTANA
Great Falls
Helena
Billings
NORTH DAKOTA
Grand Forks
Bismarck
Fargo
SOUTH DAKOTA
Pierre
Rapid City
Sioux Falls
WYOMING
Jackson
Casper
Cheyenne
CALIFORNIA
Sacramento
Oakland
San Francisco
San Jose
Stockton
Modesto
Fremont
Monterey
Fresno
Bakersfield
Oxnard
Glendale
San Bernardino
Garden Grove
Los Angeles
Long Beach
Palm Springs
Riverside
Huntington Beach
Santa Ana
Anaheim
San Diego
Chula Vista
NEVADA
Reno
Carson City
Las Vegas
UTAH
Ogden
Salt Lake City
Provo
COLORADO
Fort Collins
Boulder
Denver
Aurora
Colorado Springs
NEBRASKA
Omaha
Lincoln
KANSAS
Kansas City
Topeka
Wichita
ARIZONA
Flagstaff
Phoenix
Scottsdale
Glendale
Mesa
Tempe
Tucson
NEW MEXICO
Santa Fe
Albuquerque
Las Cruces
El Paso
OKLAHOMA
Tulsa
Oklahoma City
TEXAS
Amarillo
Lubbock
Plano
Irving
Garland
Fort Worth
Dallas
Arlington
Abilene
Austin
San Antonio
Houston
Corpus Christi
Brownsville
ALASKA
Fairbanks
Anchorage
Juneau
HAWAII
Honolulu
Alaska.....................................12:00
Hawaii.....................................10:00

3:00
Central Time Zone
4:00
Eastern Time Zone
MAINE
VERMONT
Burlington
Bangor
Bar Harbor
Augusta
Montpelier
Portland
Concord
NEW HAMPSHIRE
Manchester
NEW YORK
Boston
Worcester
Syracuse
Albany
Springfield
MASSACHUSETTS
Rochester
Providence
Buffalo
Hartford
Newport
RHODE ISLAND
Yonkers
New Haven
CONNECTICUT
Bridgeport
Scranton
Paterson
Stamford
Erie
PENNSYLVANIA
Newark
New York City
Allentown
Jersey City
Philadelphia
NEW JERSEY
Harrisburg
Trenton
Pittsburgh
Gettysburg
Wilmington
Atlantic City
Baltimore
Dover
DELAWARE
Morgantown
Rehoboth Beach
Arlington
Ocean City
MARYLAND
Alexandria
Annapolis
Washington D.C.
Richmond
Williamsburg
Newport News
Virginia Beach
Norfolk
Chesapeake
Roanoke
VIRGINIA
WEST VIRGINIA
Charleston
MINNESOTA
Duluth
St. Paul
Minneapolis
WISCONSIN
Green Bay
Rochester
MICHIGAN
Grand Rapids
Lansing
Flint
Milwaukee
Madison
Ann Arbor
Detroit
IOWA
Dubuque
Cedar Rapids
Rockford
Chicago
Des Moines
South Bend
Fort Wayne
Toledo
Cleveland
Akron
Youngstown
OHIO
Wheeling
INDIANA
Columbus
Dayton
Indianapolis
Cincinnati
Peoria
Champaign
Springfield
MISSOURI
Kansas City
Independence
Columbia
Jefferson City
St. Louis
ILLINOIS
Bloomington
Evansville
Louisville
Frankfort
Lexington
KENTUCKY
Springfield
Branson
Johnson City
Knoxville
Nashville
TENNESSEE
Chattanooga
Memphis
Fort Smith
ARKANSAS
Little Rock
Hot Springs
Greensboro
Winston-Salem
Durham
Raleigh
NORTH CAROLINA
Asheville
Charlotte
Greenville
SOUTH CAROLINA
Columbia
Myrtle Beach
Charleston
Huntsville
Tupelo
Birmingham
Tuscaloosa
MISSISSIPPI
Atlanta
Augusta
GEORGIA
Macon
Montgomery
Columbus
Savannah
Hilton Head Island
Shreveport
Jackson
ALABAMA
LOUISIANA
Hattiesburg
Baton Rouge
Lafayette
Biloxi
Gulfport
Pensacola
Mobile
Metairie
New Orleans
Tallahassee
Jacksonville
St. Augustine
Daytona Beach
Orlando
Tampa
St. Petersburg
FLORIDA
West Palm Beach
Fort Lauderdale
Miami
Naples
Hialeah
Key West

Alabama

Population (1999): 4,369,862 **Area (sq mi): 52,423**

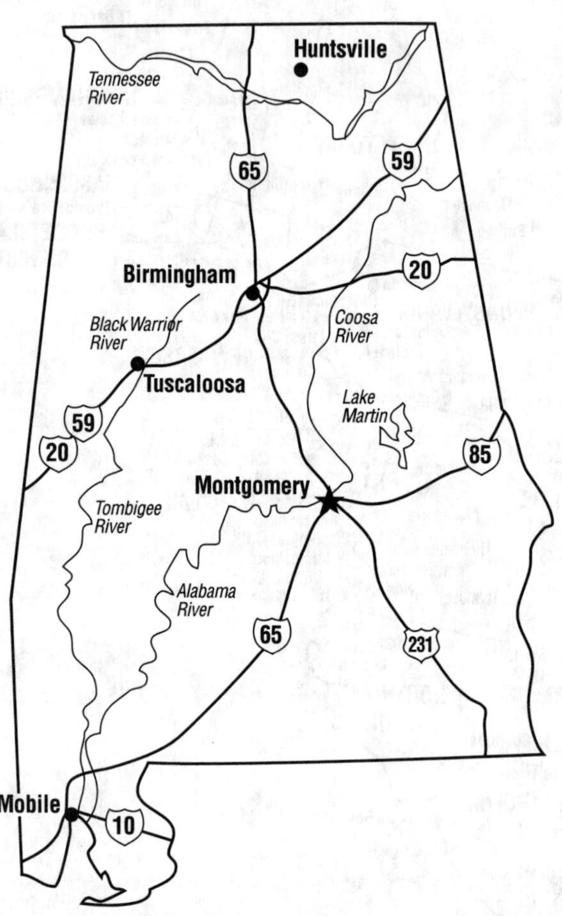

— State Information Sources —

				Phone	Fax
Alabama Business Council PO Box 76 ..... Montgomery	AL	36101		334-834-6000	262-7371
Web: www.bcatoday.org					
Alabama Economic & Community Affairs Dept PO Box 5690 ..... Montgomery	AL	36103		334-242-5100	242-5099
Web: www.adeca.state.al.us					
Alabama Public Library Service 6030 Monticello Dr ..... Montgomery	AL	36130		334-213-3900	213-3993
Web: www.apls.state.al.us ■ *E-mail:* webstaff@apls.state.al.us					
Alabama State Government Information				334-242-8000	
Web: www.state.al.us					
Alabama State Parks Div 64 N Union St ..... Montgomery	AL	36130		334-242-3334	353-8629
TF: 800-252-7275 ■ *Web:* www.dcnr.state.al.us/Parks/state_parks_index_1a.html					
Alabama Tourism & Travel Bureau PO Box 4927 ..... Montgomery	AL	36103		334-242-4169	242-4554
TF: 800-252-2262 ■ *Web:* www.touralabama.org ■ *E-mail:* info@touralabama.org					

ON-LINE RESOURCES

Alabama Cities ..... dir.yahoo.com/Regional/U_S__States/Alabama/Cities
Alabama Counties & Regions ..... dir.yahoo.com/Regional/U_S__States/Alabama/Counties_and_Regions
Alabama Information Directory ..... www.alabamainfo.com
Alabama Information Network ..... ain.state.al.us
Alabama Mountain Lakes Assn ..... www.almtlakes.org
Alabama Scenario ..... scenariousa.dstylus.com/al/indexf.htm
Alabama Travel & Tourism Guide ..... www.travel-library.com/north_america/usa/alabama/index.html
AlaWeb ..... alaweb.asc.edu
Everything Alabama ..... isl-garnet.uah.edu/ALABAMA/alabama.html
InAlabama.com ..... www.inalabama.com
Rough Guide Travel Alabama travel.roughguides.com/content/769/index.htm
Travel.org-Alabama ..... travel.org/alabama.html
Yahoo! Get Local Alabama ..... dir.yahoo.com/Regional/U_S__States/Alabama

— Cities Profiled —

Birmingham

Nicknamed the "Pittsburgh of the South," Birmingham's steel industry roots can be seen at Sloss Furnaces National Historic Landmark, an ironworks plant that utilized ore dug from the Birmingham area hills between 1882 and 1971. The memorabilia of such state greats as Paul "Bear" Bryant, Jesse Owens, and Joe Louis are on display at the Alabama Sports Hall of Fame in Birmingham; exhibits at the Alabama Jazz Hall of Fame include the memorabilia of city native Erskine Hawkins, who wrote "Tuxedo Junction." Five Points South entertainment district has varied clubs, shopping, and restaurants. A short drive from Birmingham is DeSoto Caverns, where tours of the stalagmite and stalactite formations culminate in a sound, water, and laser light show. The University of Alabama at Birmingham is the city's largest employer.

Population	252,997	**Longitude**	86-80-25 W
Area (Land)	144.4 sq mi	**County**	Jefferson
Area (Water)	1.2 sq mi	**Time Zone**	CST
Elevation	600 ft	**Area Code/s**	205
Latitude	33-52-06 N		

— Average Temperatures and Precipitation —

TEMPERATURES

	Jan	Feb	Mar	Apr	May	Jun	Jul	Aug	Sep	Oct	Nov	Dec
High	52	57	66	75	81	87	90	89	84	75	65	56
Low	31	35	42	49	58	65	70	69	63	50	42	35

PRECIPITATION

	Jan	Feb	Mar	Apr	May	Jun	Jul	Aug	Sep	Oct	Nov	Dec
Inches	5.1	4.7	6.2	5.0	4.9	3.7	5.3	3.6	3.9	2.8	4.3	5.1

— Important Phone Numbers —

	Phone		Phone
AAA	205-978-7000	**Poison Control Center**	205-933-4050
American Express Travel	800-528-4800	**Time/Temp**	205-979-8463
Emergency	911	**Travelers Aid**	205-322-5426
HotelDocs	800-468-3537	**Weather**	205-945-7000
Medical Referral	205-581-9800		

— Information Sources —

				Phone	Fax
Better Business Bureau Serving Central Alabama & the Wiregrass Area PO Box 55268	Birmingham	AL	35255	205-558-2222	558-2239
Web: www.birmingham-al.bbb.org					
Birmingham Area Chamber of Commerce 2027 1st Ave N.	Birmingham	AL	35203	205-323-5461	250-7669
Web: www.birminghamchamber.com					
Birmingham City Hall 710 N 20th St.	Birmingham	AL	35203	205-254-2000	254-2115
Web: www.ci.bham.al.us					
Birmingham Economic Development Dept 710 N 20th St 3rd Fl.	Birmingham	AL	35203	205-254-2799	254-7741
Web: www.ci.bham.al.us/OED/default.htm					
Birmingham-Jefferson Civic Center 1 Civic Center Plaza	Birmingham	AL	35203	205-458-8400	458-8437*
**Fax:* Sales ■ *TF:* 800-535-7146 ■ *Web:* www.bjcc.org ■ *E-mail:* info@bjcc.org					
Birmingham Mayor 710 N 20th St	Birmingham	AL	35203	205-254-2277	254-2926
Web: www.ci.bham.al.us/office.htm					
Birmingham Public Library 2100 Park Pl.	Birmingham	AL	35203	205-226-3600	226-3743
Web: www.bham.lib.al.us					
Greater Birmingham Convention & Visitors Bureau 2200 9th Ave N.	Birmingham	AL	35203	205-458-8000	458-8086
TF: 800-458-8085 ■ *Web:* www.bcvb.org					
Jefferson County 716 N 21st St Rm A690	Birmingham	AL	35263	205-325-5555	325-4860

On-Line Resources

4Birmingham.com	www.4birmingham.com
About.com Guide to Birmingham	birminghamal.about.com
Area Guide Birmingham	birmingham.areaguides.net
Birmingham Information Connection	www.bhaminfo.com
Birmingham Net	www.bham.net
City Knowledge Birmingham	www.cityknowledge.com/al_birmingham.htm
Excite.com Birmingham City Guide	www.excite.com/travel/countries/united_states/alabama/birmingham
NITC Travelbase City Guide Birmingham	www.travelbase.com/auto/guides/birmingham-area-al.html
Online CityGuide Birmingham	www.onlinecityguide.com/al/birmingham

— Transportation Services —

AIRPORTS

■ **Birmingham International Airport (BHM)**

	Phone
5 miles NE of downtown (approx 10 minutes)	205-595-0533
Web: www.bhamintlairport.com	

Airport Transportation

	Phone
Birmingham Door To Door $12 fare to downtown	205-591-5550
Radio Cab $7-10 fare to downtown	205-833-8294

Commercial Airlines

	Phone		Phone
AirTran	800-247-8726	**Southwest**	800-435-9792
American	800-433-7300	**TWA**	800-221-2000
Comair	800-354-9822	**United**	800-241-6522
Delta	800-221-1212	**US Airways**	800-428-4322
Northwest	800-225-2525	**US Airways Express**	800-428-4322

Charter Airlines

	Phone		Phone
Alliance Executive Charter Services	800-232-5387	**Signature Flight Support**	205-849-3834
Flying M Aviation Inc.	800-359-0357	**United Beechcraft**	205-591-6830

CAR RENTALS

	Phone		Phone
Alamo	205-592-2200	**Enterprise**	205-323-4446
Avis	205-592-8901	**Hertz**	205-591-6090
Budget	205-322-3596	**National**	205-592-7259

LIMO/TAXI

	Phone		Phone
A & B Taxi Service	205-799-0797	**Cliff's Limousine**	205-942-3771
Alabama Limousine	205-591-7555	**Homewood Cab**	205-871-4684
Bushelon Limousine Service	205-781-4423	**Yellow Cab**	205-252-1131
Carey Limousine	205-591-5959		

MASS TRANSIT

	Phone
Metro Area Express $1 Base fare	205-521-0101

RAIL/BUS

				Phone
Amtrak Station 1819 Morris Ave	Birmingham	AL	35203	800-872-7245
TF: 800-872-7245				
Greyhound Bus Station 618 N 19th St	Birmingham	AL	35203	205-251-3210
TF: 800-231-2222				

— Accommodations —

HOTELS, MOTELS, RESORTS

				Phone	Fax
Adams Inn 300 10th St N	Birmingham	AL	35203	205-328-8560	328-8598

Birmingham — Hotels, Motels, Resorts (Cont'd)

	City	State	ZIP	Phone	Fax
Baymont Inns 513 Cahaba Park Cir *TF:* 800-301-0200	Birmingham	AL	35243	205-995-9990	995-0563
Best Suites of America 140 State Farm Pkwy *TF:* 800-237-8466	Birmingham	AL	35209	205-940-9990	940-9930
Best Western Civic Center 2230 Civic Center Blvd *TF:* 800-636-4669	Birmingham	AL	35203	205-328-6320	328-6681
Best Western Hotel-Medical Center 800 11th St S. *TF:* 800-528-1234	Birmingham	AL	35205	205-933-1900	933-8476
Clarion Hotel 5216 Airport Hwy *TF:* 800-252-7466	Birmingham	AL	35212	205-591-7900	592-6476
Comfort Inn 1485 Montgomery Hwy *TF:* 800-228-5150	Birmingham	AL	35216	205-823-4300	823-6535
Comfort Inn Oxmoor 195 Oxmoor Rd *TF:* 800-221-2222	Birmingham	AL	35209	205-941-0990	941-1527
Comfort Inn Vestavia 1485 Montgomery Hwy *TF:* 800-228-5150	Birmingham	AL	35216	205-823-4300	823-6585
Courtyard by Marriott 500 Shades Creek Pkwy. *TF:* 800-321-2211 ■ *Web:* courtyard.com/BHMHW	Homewood	AL	35209	205-879-0400	879-6324
Courtyard by Marriott Hoover 1824 Montgomery Hwy *TF:* 800-321-2211 ■ *Web:* courtyard.com/BHMHO	Hoover	AL	35244	205-988-5000	988-4659
Days Inn Airport 5101 Airport Hwy *TF:* 800-329-7466	Birmingham	AL	35212	205-592-6110	591-5623
Embassy Suites 2300 Woodcrest Pl *TF:* 800-362-2779	Birmingham	AL	35209	205-879-7400	870-4523
Fairfield Inn by Marriott 155 Vulcan Rd *TF:* 800-228-2800 ■ *Web:* fairfieldinn.com/BHMFH	Birmingham	AL	35209	205-945-9600	945-9600
Hampton Inn Mountain Brook 2731 US Hwy 280. *TF:* 800-426-7866	Birmingham	AL	35223	205-870-7822	871-7610
Hampton Inn South 1466 Montgomery Hwy *TF:* 800-426-7866	Birmingham	AL	35216	205-822-2224	822-9421
Holiday Inn Airport 5000 10th Ave N. *TF:* 800-465-4329	Birmingham	AL	35212	205-591-6900	591-2093
Holiday Inn East 7941 Crestwood Blvd *TF:* 800-465-4329	Birmingham	AL	35210	205-956-8211	956-1234
Holiday Inn Express 4627 Hwy 280 S *TF:* 800-465-4329	Birmingham	AL	35242	205-991-9977	995-0570
Holiday Inn Homewood 260 Oxmoor Rd *TF:* 800-465-4329	Birmingham	AL	35209	205-942-2041	290-9309
Holiday Inn South On-The-Lake 1548 Montgomery Hwy *TF:* 800-465-4329 ■ *Web:* www.basshotels.com/holiday-inn/?_franchisee=BHMSO	Birmingham	AL	35216	205-822-4350	822-0350
Howard Johnson 275 Oxmoor Rd *TF:* 800-446-4656	Birmingham	AL	35209	205-942-0919	942-1678
Inn Towne Lodge 400 Beacon Pkwy W *TF:* 800-347-2031	Birmingham	AL	35209	205-942-2031	942-2031
La Quinta Motor Inn 905 11th Ct W *TF:* 800-531-5900	Birmingham	AL	35204	205-324-4510	252-7972
Microtel 251 Summit Pkwy	Birmingham	AL	35209	205-945-5550	945-8823
Motel Birmingham 7905 Crestwood Blvd. *TF:* 800-338-9275	Birmingham	AL	35210	205-956-4440	956-3011
Mountain Brook Inn 2800 Hwy 280 W. *TF:* 800-523-7771	Birmingham	AL	35223	205-870-3100	414-1738
National 9 Inn 2224 5th Ave N.	Birmingham	AL	35203	205-324-6107	324-0633
Pickwick Hotel 1023 20th St S. *TF:* 800-255-7304	Birmingham	AL	35205	205-933-9555	933-6918
Quality Inn Hotel & Suites 260 Goodwin Crest Dr. *TF:* 800-290-8099	Birmingham	AL	35209	205-290-8000	290-8001
Radisson Hotel Birmingham 808 S 20th St. *TF:* 800-333-3333	Birmingham	AL	35205	205-933-9000	933-0920
Ramada Inn & Suites 420 S 20th St. *TF:* 800-272-6232	Birmingham	AL	35233	205-322-7000	322-3046
Red Roof Inn 151 Vulcan Rd *TF:* 800-843-7663	Birmingham	AL	35209	205-942-9414	942-9499
Redmont Hotel 2101 5th Ave N	Birmingham	AL	35203	205-324-2101	324-0610
Residence Inn by Marriott 3 Greenhill Pkwy. *TF:* 800-331-3131 ■ *Web:* www.residenceinn.com/BHMOX	Birmingham	AL	35242	205-991-8686	991-8729
Rime Garden Suites 5320 Beacon Dr *TF:* 800-772-7463	Birmingham	AL	35210	205-951-1200	951-1692
Riverchase Inn Galleria 1800 Riverchase Dr. *TF:* 800-239-2401 ■ *E-mail:* rchaseinn@aol.com	Birmingham	AL	35244	205-985-7500	733-8122
Roebuck Parkway Inn 9225 Parkway E *TF:* 800-545-1734	Birmingham	AL	35206	205-836-5400	
Sheraton Birmingham Hotel 2101 Civic Center Blvd *TF:* 800-325-3535	Birmingham	AL	35203	205-324-5000	307-3045
Sheraton Perimeter Park South Hotel 8 Perimeter Dr *TF:* 800-325-3535	Birmingham	AL	35243	205-967-2700	972-8603
Shoney's Inn 226 Summit Pk. *TF:* 800-222-2222 ■ *Web:* www.shoneysinn.com/al1.htm	Homewood	AL	35209	205-916-0464	916-0298
StudioPLUS 101 Cahaba Park Cir *TF:* 800-646-8000	Birmingham	AL	35242	205-408-0107	408-6072
StudioPLUS 40 State Farm Pkwy. *TF:* 800-646-8000	Birmingham	AL	35209	205-290-0102	912-2092
Super 8 East 1813 Crestwood Blvd *TF:* 800-800-8000	Birmingham	AL	35210	205-956-3650	956-3650
Super 8 Motel 140 Vulcan Rd *TF:* 800-800-8000	Birmingham	AL	35209	205-945-9888	945-9928
Travelodge 1098 9th Ave SW. *TF:* 800-528-1234	Bessemer	AL	35020	205-424-0880	424-2345
Tutwiler Hotel 2021 Park Pl N *TF:* 800-845-1787	Birmingham	AL	35203	205-322-2100	325-1183
Villager Lodge 1313 3rd Ave N	Birmingham	AL	35203	205-323-8806	323-5591
Wynfrey Hotel Riverchase 1000 Riverchase Galleria *TF:* 800-476-7006	Birmingham	AL	35244	205-987-1600	988-4597

— Restaurants —

	City	State	ZIP	Phone
Alabama Steaks (Steak) 4500 Montevallo Rd	Birmingham	AL	35210	205-951-3955
Ali Baba (Persian) 110 Centre at Riverchase *Web:* www.alibabarst.com/	Birmingham	AL	35216	205-823-2222
Anthony's (Italian) 2131 7th Ave S.	Birmingham	AL	35233	205-324-1215
Arman's (Italian) 2117 Cahaba Rd	Birmingham	AL	35223	205-871-5551
Bombay Cafe (Continental) 2839 7th Ave S	Birmingham	AL	35233	205-322-1930
Bottega (Italian) 2240 Highland Ave.	Birmingham	AL	35205	205-939-1000
Bright Star (Greek) 304 19th St N	Bessemer	AL	35020	205-426-1861
Cafe de France (French) 2612 Lane Park Rd.	Birmingham	AL	35223	205-871-1000
Cobb Lane (American) 1 Cobb Ln	Birmingham	AL	35205	205-933-0462
Costa's Famous Barbecue (Barbecue) 613 Old Springville Rd	Birmingham	AL	35215	205-853-9933
Dugan's (English) 2011 Highland Ave.	Birmingham	AL	35205	205-933-9020
Fish Market Restaurant (Seafood) 1681 Montgomery Hwy	Hoover	AL	35216	205-823-3474
Full Moon Barbecue (Barbecue) 525 25th St S.	Birmingham	AL	35233	205-324-1007
Great Wall Chinese Restaurant (Chinese) 706 W Valley Ave.	Birmingham	AL	35209	205-945-1465
Highlands Bar & Grill (Southern) 2011 11th Ave S	Birmingham	AL	35205	205-939-1400
Hosie Barbecue & Fish (Barbecue) 321 17th St N.	Birmingham	AL	35203	205-326-3495
Hot & Hot Fish Club (Continental) 2180 11th Ct S.	Birmingham	AL	35205	205-933-5474
Irondale Cafe (Southern) 1906 1st Ave N	Irondale	AL	35210	205-956-5258
John's Restaurant (Seafood) 112 21st St N	Birmingham	AL	35203	205-322-6014
Johnny Ray's (Barbecue) 316 Valley Ave	Birmingham	AL	35209	205-945-7437
Julian's American Bistro (American) 2101 5th Ave N	Birmingham	AL	35203	205-324-2101
Justin's (Seafood) 4500 Valleydale Rd	Birmingham	AL	35242	205-991-7447
La Cocina (Mexican) 2111 7th Ave S.	Birmingham	AL	35233	205-252-7626
La Paree (American) 2013 5th Ave N.	Birmingham	AL	35203	205-251-5936
La Paz (Mexican) 99 Euclid Ave.	Birmingham	AL	35213	205-879-2225
Magic City Brewery (American) 420 21st St S	Birmingham	AL	35205	205-328-2739
Mandarin Inn (Chinese) 64 Church St	Birmingham	AL	35213	205-871-4531
Meadowlark Restaurant (Continental) 534 Industrial Rd.	Alabaster	AL	35007	205-663-3141
Merritt House (Continental) 2220 Highland Ave S	Birmingham	AL	35205	205-933-1200
Mill The (American) 1035 20th St S.	Birmingham	AL	35205	205-939-3001
Rib It Up (Barbecue) 830 1st Ave N.	Birmingham	AL	35206	205-328-7427
Rossi's (Italian) 2737 Hwy 280 E.	Mountain Brook	AL	35223	205-879-2111
Salvatore's (Italian) 720 Old Towne Rd	Birmingham	AL	35216	205-822-7310
Surin West (Thai) 1918 11th Ave.	Birmingham	AL	35205	205-324-1928
Top That Grille (American) 1308 1st Ave N	Birmingham	AL	35203	205-324-8950
Winston's (American) 1000 Riverchase Galleria	Birmingham	AL	35244	205-987-1600
Zydeco (Cajun) 2001 15th Ave S	Birmingham	AL	35215	205-933-1032

— Goods and Services —

SHOPPING

	City	State	ZIP	Phone	Fax
Brookwood Village 623 Brookwood Village	Birmingham	AL	35209	205-871-0406	870-7990
Century Plaza 241 Century Plaza US 78 & Oporto Rd	Birmingham	AL	35210	205-591-2451	591-2462
Eastwood Mall 7703 Crestwood Blvd.	Birmingham	AL	35210	205-591-8077	591-8074

Birmingham — Shopping (Cont'd)

	City	State	ZIP	Phone	Fax
Riverchase Galleria 3000 Galleria Mall *Web:* www.thegalleria.com ■ *E-mail:* info@thegalleria.com	Birmingham	AL	35244	205-985-3039	985-3040
Western Hills Mall PO Box 28286	Birmingham	AL	35228	205-923-2525	923-7952

BANKS

	City	State	ZIP	Phone	Fax
AmSouth Bank of Alabama 1900 5th Ave N *TF:* 800-284-4100 ■ *Web:* www.amsouth.com	Birmingham	AL	35203	205-326-5164	320-5185
BancorpSouth Bank 1910 3rd Ave N	Birmingham	AL	35203	205-323-7181	251-2320
Colonial Bank Birmingham 1928 1st Ave N *TF:* 800-388-1477 ■ *Web:* www.colonialbank.com	Birmingham	AL	35203	205-325-1649	325-1825
Compass Bank 701 20th St S *TF:* 800-239-2265 ■ *Web:* www.compassweb.com ■ *E-mail:* feedback@compassbnk.com	Birmingham	AL	35296	205-933-3000	933-3043
First Commercial Bank 300 21st St N	Birmingham	AL	35203	205-868-4850	868-4854
National Bank of Commerce of Birmingham 1927 1st Ave N	Birmingham	AL	35203	205-583-3600	583-3292
Regions Bank 417 N 20th St **Fax:* Hum Res	Birmingham	AL	35202	205-326-7100	326-7756*
SouthTrust Bank of Alabama NA 420 20th St N *TF:* 800-239-2300	Birmingham	AL	35203	205-254-5000	254-3200

BUSINESS SERVICES

	Phone		Phone
Alabama Messenger	205-252-3672	**Kinko's**	205-252-2509
Alabama Temps	205-836-8181	**Manpower Temporary Services**	205-408-2706
Courier Express	205-941-1880	**Post Office**	205-521-0302
Federal Express	800-238-5355	**Systematic Services Inc**	205-870-3500
Interim Personnel Services	205-879-5027	**UPS**	800-742-5877
Kelly Services	205-871-7082	**Yellow Cab Delivery Service**	205-252-1131

— Media —

PUBLICATIONS

	City	State	ZIP	Phone	Fax
Birmingham Business Journal 2101 Magnolia Ave S Suite 400	Birmingham	AL	35205	205-322-0000	322-0040
Birmingham Magazine PO Box 10127	Birmingham	AL	35202	205-323-5461	226-8850
Birmingham News‡ 2200 4th Ave N *Web:* www.al.com/birmingham ■ *E-mail:* feedback@al.com	Birmingham	AL	35203	205-325-2222	325-2283
Birmingham Post-Herald‡ 2200 4th Ave N *Web:* www.postherald.com ■ *E-mail:* postherald@aol.com	Birmingham	AL	35203	205-325-2343	325-2410
Birmingham Times 115 3rd Ave W	Birmingham	AL	35204	205-251-5158	323-2294
Over The Mountain Journal 2016 Columbiana Rd **Fax:* News Rm	Birmingham	AL	35216	205-823-9646	824-1246*
Southern Accents 2100 Lakeshore Dr *TF:* 800-366-4712	Birmingham	AL	35209	205-877-6000	877-6990

‡Daily newspapers

TELEVISION

	City	State	ZIP	Phone	Fax
WABM-TV Ch 68 (UPN) 651 Beacon Pkwy W Suite 105	Birmingham	AL	35209	205-943-2168	290-2115
WBIQ-TV Ch 10 (PBS) 2112 11th Ave S Suite 400 *TF:* 800-239-5233	Birmingham	AL	35205	205-328-8756	251-2192
WBRC-TV Ch 6 (Fox) PO Box 6 *Web:* www.wbrc.com ■ *E-mail:* info@wbrc.com	Birmingham	AL	35201	205-322-6666	583-4356
WCFT-TV Ch 33 (ABC) 800 Concourse Pkwy Suite 200 *Web:* www.abc3340.com ■ *E-mail:* info@www.abc3340.com	Birmingham	AL	35244	205-403-3340	982-3942
WIAT-TV Ch 42 (CBS) PO Box 59496	Birmingham	AL	35259	205-322-4200	320-2713
WPXH-TV Ch 44 (PAX) 2085 Golden Crust Dr *Web:* www.pax.net/WPXH	Birmingham	AL	35209	205-870-4404	870-0744
WTTO-TV Ch 21 (WB) 651 Beacon Pkwy W Suite 105	Birmingham	AL	35209	205-943-2168	290-2115
WVTM-TV Ch 13 (NBC) 1732 Valley View Dr *Web:* www.nbc13.com	Birmingham	AL	35209	205-933-1313	323-3314

RADIO

	City	State	ZIP	Phone	Fax
WAPI-AM 1070 kHz (N/T) 244 Goodwin Crest Dr Suite 200	Birmingham	AL	35209	205-945-4646	942-8959
WATV-AM 900 kHz (Oldies) 3025 Ensley Ave	Birmingham	AL	35208	205-741-9288	780-4034
WBHM-FM 90.3 MHz (NPR) 650 11th St S *Web:* www.wbhm.org ■ *E-mail:* patrick@wbhm.uab.edu	Birmingham	AL	35294	205-934-2606	934-5075
WDJC-FM 93.7 MHz (Rel) 2727 19th Pl S **Fax Area Code:* 800	Birmingham	AL	35209	205-879-3324	802-4555*
WERC-AM 960 kHz (N/T) 530 Beacon Pkwy W Suite 600 *Web:* www.werc960am.com	Birmingham	AL	35209	205-439-9600	439-8390
WJOX-AM 690 kHz (Sports) 244 Goodwin Crest Dr *Web:* www.wjox690.com ■ *E-mail:* wjox@quicklink.net	Birmingham	AL	35209	205-945-4646	942-8959
WMJJ-FM 96.5 MHz (AC) 530 Beacon Pkwy W Suite 600 *Web:* www.magic96fm.com	Birmingham	AL	35209	205-439-9600	439-8390
WODL-FM 106.9 MHz (Oldies) 301 Beacon Pkwy W Suite 200 *Web:* www.wodl.com	Birmingham	AL	35209	205-916-1100	916-1145
WOWC-FM 102.5 MHz (Ctry) 530 Beacon Pkwy W Suite 600 *Web:* www.wowc.com	Birmingham	AL	35209	205-439-9600	439-8390
WYSF-FM 94.5 MHz (AC) 244 Goodwin Crest Dr	Birmingham	AL	35209	205-945-4646	933-6708
WZRR-FM 99.5 MHz (CR) 244 Goodwin Crest Dr Suite 300	Birmingham	AL	35209	205-945-4646	942-8959
WZZK-FM 104.7 MHz (Ctry) 301 Beacon Pkwy W Suite 200 *Web:* www.wzzk.com ■ *E-mail:* wzzk@bhm.tis.net	Birmingham	AL	35209	205-916-1100	916-1150

— Colleges/Universities —

	City	State	ZIP	Phone	Fax
Bessemer State Technical College PO Box 308	Bessemer	AL	35021	205-428-6391	424-5119
Birmingham-Southern College 900 Arkadelphia Rd *TF:* 800-523-5793 ■ *Web:* www.bsc.edu	Birmingham	AL	35254	205-226-4600	226-3074
Herzing Institute 280 W Valley Ave *Web:* www.herzing.edu ■ *E-mail:* herzing@scott.net	Homewood	AL	35209	205-916-2800	916-2807
Jefferson State Community College 2601 Carson Rd *TF Admissions:* 800-239-5900 ■ *Web:* www.jscc.cc.al.us	Birmingham	AL	35215	205-853-1200	815-8499
Lawson State Community College 3060 Wilson Rd SW *Web:* www.ls.cc.al.us	Birmingham	AL	35221	205-925-2515	929-6316
Miles College 50500 Myron Massey Blvd *TF Admissions:* 800-445-0708	Fairfield	AL	35064	205-929-1000	929-1668
Samford University 800 Lakeshore Dr *Web:* www.samford.edu	Birmingham	AL	35229	205-870-2011	870-2654
University of Alabama Birmingham 1619 S 19th St *TF:* 888-309-8435 ■ *Web:* www.uab.edu	Birmingham	AL	35200	205-934-4011	934-4779
Virginia College 65 Bagby Dr Suite 100 *Web:* www.vc.edu	Homewood	AL	35209	205-802-1200	802-7045

— Hospitals —

	City	State	ZIP	Phone	Fax
Bessemer Carraway Medical Center PO Box 847	Bessemer	AL	35021	205-481-7000	481-7595
Birmingham Baptist Medical Center-Montclair Campus 800 Montclair Rd	Birmingham	AL	35213	205-592-1000	592-5653
Birmingham Baptist Medical Center-Princeton Campus 701 Princeton Ave SW	Birmingham	AL	35211	205-783-3000	783-3758
Brookwood Medical Center 2010 Brookwood Medical Center Dr **Fax:* Hum Res	Birmingham	AL	35209	205-877-1000	877-2279*
Carraway Methodist Medical Center 1600 Carraway Blvd	Birmingham	AL	35234	205-502-6000	226-5280
Children's Hospital of Alabama 1600 7th Ave S	Birmingham	AL	35233	205-939-9100	939-9929
Cooper Green Hospital of Alabama 1515 6th Ave S	Birmingham	AL	35233	205-930-3200	930-3497
HealthSouth Medical Center 1201 11th Ave S	Birmingham	AL	35205	205-930-7000	930-7606

Birmingham — Hospitals (Cont'd)

	City	State	ZIP	Phone	Fax
Lloyd Noland Hospital & Health System 701 Lloyd Noland Pkwy	Fairfield	AL	35064	205-783-5121	783-5158
Medical Center East 50 Medical Park East Dr	Birmingham	AL	35235	205-838-3000	838-3227
Saint Vincent's Hospital 810 St Vincent's Dr *Web:* www.stv.org	Birmingham	AL	35205	205-939-7000	930-2168
University of Alabama Hospital 619 S 19th St *Web:* www.health.uab.edu	Birmingham	AL	35249	205-934-4011	934-6321
Veterans Affairs Medical Center 700 S 19th St	Birmingham	AL	35233	205-933-8101	933-4497

— Attractions —

	City	State	ZIP	Phone	Fax
16th Street Baptist Church 1530 6th Ave N *Web:* www.16thstreet.org ■ *E-mail:* chamlin@16thstreet.org	Birmingham	AL	35203	205-251-9402	251-9811
Alabama Jazz Hall of Fame 1631 4th Ave N *Web:* www.jazzhall.com/jazz	Birmingham	AL	35203	205-254-2731	254-2785
Alabama Sports Hall of Fame 2150 Civic Ctr Blvd *Web:* www.tech-comm.com/ashof	Birmingham	AL	35203	205-323-6665	252-2212
Alabama Symphonic Assn PO Box 2125 *Web:* www.nbc13.com/aso ■ *E-mail:* orchestra@nbc13.com	Birmingham	AL	35201	205-251-6929	251-6840
Alabama Theatre 1817 3rd Ave N *Web:* www.alabamatheatre.com	Birmingham	AL	35203	205-252-2262	251-3155
Arlington Antebellum Home & Gardens 331 Cotton Ave SW	Birmingham	AL	35211	205-780-5656	788-0585
Ballet South 2726 1st Ave S *Web:* www.alabamaballet.org	Birmingham	AL	35233	205-322-4300	322-4444
Barber Vintage Motorsports Museum 2721 5th Ave S *Web:* www.barbermuseum.org	Birmingham	AL	35233	205-252-8377	252-8079
Bessemer Flea Market 813 8th Ave N	Bessemer	AL	35020	205-425-8510	
Bessemer Hall of History 1905 Alabama Ave *Web:* www.bham.net/bessemercc/exhibits.html	Bessemer	AL	35020	205-426-1633	
Birmingham Botanical Gardens 2612 Lane Park Rd *Web:* www.bbgardens.org	Birmingham	AL	35223	205-414-3900	879-3751
Birmingham Broadway Series 2027 1st Ave N 18 Commerce Ctr	Birmingham	AL	35203	205-328-8222	254-6068
Birmingham Chamber Music Society Samford University Reid Chapel	Birmingham	AL	35229	205-879-4902	879-8421
Birmingham Children's Theater 3 Civic Center Plaza *Web:* www.bham.net/bct	Birmingham	AL	35201	205-458-8181	458-8895
Birmingham Civil Rights Institute 520 16th St N *Web:* www.bham.net/bcri	Birmingham	AL	35203	205-328-9696	323-5219
Birmingham Fairgrounds Flea Market 2331 Bessemer Rd *TF:* 800-362-7538	Birmingham	AL	35208	205-822-3348	
Birmingham Festival Theater 1901 1/2 11th Ave S	Birmingham	AL	35205	205-933-2383	
Birmingham Museum of Art 2000 8th Ave N *Web:* www.artsbma.org	Birmingham	AL	35203	205-254-2566	254-2714
Birmingham Opera Theater 1817 3rd Ave N	Birmingham	AL	35203	205-322-6737	
Birmingham Zoo 2630 Cahaba Rd *Web:* www.bhm.tis.net/zoo ■ *E-mail:* wreeder@traveller.com	Birmingham	AL	35223	205-879-0409	879-9426
Children's Dance Foundation 2830 19th St S	Birmingham	AL	35209	205-870-0073	870-1301
DeSoto Caverns 5181 DeSoto Caverns Pkwy	Childersburg	AL	35044	256-378-7252	378-3678
Environmental Center 900 Arkadelphia Rd Birmingham Southern College *TF:* 800-523-5793	Birmingham	AL	35254	205-226-4934	226-3046
Five Points Music Hall 1016 20th St S	Birmingham	AL	35205	205-322-2263	
Five Points South 20th St S & 11th Ave S	Birmingham	AL	35233	205-458-8000	
Hoover Library Theatre 200 Municipal Dr *Web:* www.hoover.lib.al.us/theatre	Hoover	AL	35216	205-444-7888	444-7894
International Motor Sports Hall of Fame & Museum 3198 Speedway Blvd *Web:* www.bham.net/sports/sports.html	Talladega	AL	35160	256-362-5002	362-5002
McWane Center Science Museum 200 19th St N *Web:* www.mcwane.org	Birmingham	AL	35203	205-714-8300	714-8400
Meyer Robert R Planetarium 900 Arkadelphia Rd Birmingham Southern College	Birmingham	AL	35254	205-226-4770	
Oak Mountain State Park S I-65 & Exit 246 *Web:* www.bham.net/oakmtn	Birmingham	AL	35124	205-620-2520	620-2531
Ruffner Mountain Nature Center 1214 81st St S *Web:* www.bham.net/ruffner	Birmingham	AL	35206	205-833-8112	836-3960
Sloss Furnaces National Historic Landmark 20 32nd St N	Birmingham	AL	35222	205-324-1911	324-6758
Southern Danceworks 2830 19th St S Suite C	Birmingham	AL	35209	205-870-0073	870-1301
Southern Museum of Flight 4343 73rd St N *Web:* www.bham.net/flight/museum.html ■ *E-mail:* pamip01@aol.com	Birmingham	AL	35206	205-833-8226	836-2439
Southern Research Institute 2000 9th Ave S *TF:* 800-967-6774 ■ *Web:* www.sri.org/ ■ *E-mail:* southern@sri.org	Birmingham	AL	35205	205-581-2000	581-2726
Tannehill Ironworks Historical State Park 12632 Confederate Pkwy *Web:* www.tannehill.org/	McCalla	AL	35111	205-477-5711	477-9400
Terrific New Theatre 2821 2nd Ave S	Birmingham	AL	35233	205-328-0868	
VisionLand Amusement Park 5051 Prince St *Web:* www.visionlandpark.com ■ *E-mail:* administration@visionlandpark.com	Bessemer	AL	35022	205-481-4750	481-4758
Vulcan Park 20th St & Valley Ave *Web:* www.ci.bham.al.us/parks/vulcan.htm	Birmingham	AL	35209	205-328-2863	
Ward George Park 16th Ave & 14th St S	Birmingham	AL	35204	205-254-2391	
Woods John H Imax Dome Theater 200 19th St N *Web:* www.mcwane.org/IMAX_Theater.htm	Birmingham	AL	35203	205-714-8300	714-8400

SPORTS TEAMS & FACILITIES

	City	State	ZIP	Phone	Fax
Alabama Angels (soccer) 3408 Westbury Pl	Birmingham	AL	35223	205-967-5854	822-6321
Alabama Saints (soccer) 3408 Westbury Pl *E-mail:* ronbuff@bham.mindspring.com	Birmingham	AL	35223	205-967-5854	967-6321
Birmingham Barons (baseball) 100 Ben Chapman Dr *Web:* www.barons.com ■ *E-mail:* barons@barons.com	Birmingham	AL	35244	205-988-3200	988-9698
Birmingham Bulls (hockey) PO Box 1506 *Web:* www.birminghambulls.com	Birmingham	AL	35201	205-458-8833	458-8489
Birmingham Race Course PO Box 101748 *TF:* 800-998-8238 ■ *Web:* www.bhamdogs.com	Birmingham	AL	35210	205-838-7500	838-7407
Talladega Super Speedway 3366 Speedway Blvd *Web:* www.daytonausa.com/ts	Talladega	AL	35160	256-362-2261	761-4777

— Events —

	Phone
Alabama Jubilee Rodeo (mid-March)	205-458-8400
Alabama State Fair (late October)	205-458-8001
American Indian Dance Festival & Pow Wow (early April)	256-378-7252
Birmingham Amateur Radio HamFest (mid-April)	205-458-8400
Birmingham Fall Home Show (mid-September)	205-680-0234
Birmingham Festival of Arts Salute (mid-April)	205-252-7652
Birmingham Heritage Festival (early August)	205-324-3333
Birmingham Jam (early October)	205-323-0569
Bluegrass at Horsepens 40 (late April-early May)	256-570-0002
Bluff Park Art Show (early October)	205-822-0078
Bruno's Memorial Golf Classic (late April-early May)	205-967-4745
Cahaba Riverfest (early June)	205-322-5326
Christmas at Arlington (December)	205-780-5656
Christmas at the Alabama (late December)	205-252-2262
Christmas Heritage Tour (December)	205-426-1628
Christmas Light Show (November-December)	256-378-7252
City Stages-A Birmingham Festival (mid-June)	205-251-1272
Cottontail's Arts & Crafts Show (early March)	205-836-7178
Crape Myrtle Festival (late July)	205-254-2472
Dixie Classic & Heartland Cruisers Open Car Show (late September)	205-477-5711
Do Dah Day Festival (mid-May)	205-595-7281
Eddleman Pro Tennis Classic (early May)	205-980-1000
Festival of Trees (late November-late December)	205-939-9671
Function at Tuxedo Junction Jazz Festival (late July)	205-788-3672
Garden Fiesta Plant Sale (early April)	205-879-1227

Birmingham — Events (Cont'd)

	Phone
Great Southern Kudzu Festival (late August)	205-324-1911
Home & Garden Show (mid-March)	205-680-0234
Imagination Festival (late May)	205-595-6306
Magic City Classic Parade & Football Game (late October)	205-254-2391
NASCAR Talladega DieHard 500 (mid-April)	256-362-9064
NASCAR Winston 500 (early October)	256-362-9064
Oktoberfest (mid-September)	205-923-6564
Powerman Alabama Duathlon (late March)	205-320-1121
Sakura Festival (late March)	205-879-1227
Septemberfest (late September)	256-378-7252
Southern Appalachian Dulcimer Festival (early May)	205-477-5711
Southern Women's Show (late September-early October)	800-849-0248
Spring Folklore Festival (mid-Aprill)	205-477-5711
Summerfest (late July-early August)	205-324-2426
Tannehill Civil War Reenactment (late May)	205-477-5711
Tannehill Labor Day Celebration (early September)	205-477-5711
Tannehill Spring Craft Show (mid-March)	205-477-5711
Tannehill Trade Days (late March-November)	205-477-5711
Tannehill Trout Tournament (late April)	205-477-5711
Tannehill Village Christmas (mid-December)	205-477-5711
Taste of Birmingham (mid-October)	205-987-0757
Viva Health Vulcan Run Weekend (early November)	205-879-5344
Whistle Stop Festival & 5K Run (mid-May)	205-956-5962
World of Wheels Custom Auto Show (mid-February)	205-655-4950
Zoolight Safari (late November-December)	205-879-0458

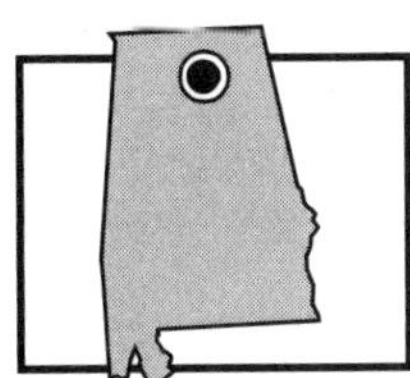

Huntsville

Huntsville's past as a cotton processing center and seat of government is preserved in the Twickenham Historic District, Huntsville Depot Museum, and Alabama's Constitution Village, a living history museum. Since 1950, however, the city has been known as a center for space technology. The U.S. Space and Rocket Center, the world's largest space attraction, offers hands-on astronaut training exhibits, as well as displays of many NASA spacecraft. The Center includes the Space Museum, Rocket and Shuttle parks, the Spacedome Theater, the U.S. Space Camp and Academy, and a bus tour of NASA's George C. Marshall Space Flight Center.

Population	175,979	**Longitude**	86-56-82 W
Area (Land)	145.4 sq mi	**County**	Madison
Area (Water)	0.3 sq mi	**Time Zone**	CST
Elevation	641 ft	**Area Code/s**	256
Latitude	34-71-88 N		

— Average Temperatures and Precipitation —

TEMPERATURES

	Jan	Feb	Mar	Apr	May	Jun	Jul	Aug	Sep	Oct	Nov	Dec
High	48	54	63	73	79	87	89	89	83	73	62	53
Low	29	33	41	49	57	65	69	68	62	49	41	33

PRECIPITATION

	Jan	Feb	Mar	Apr	May	Jun	Jul	Aug	Sep	Oct	Nov	Dec
Inches	5.2	4.9	6.6	4.9	5.1	4.1	4.9	3.5	4.1	3.3	4.9	5.9

— Important Phone Numbers —

	Phone		Phone
AAA	256-539-7493	**Poison Control Center**	800-462-0800
American Express Travel	256-539-0671	**Time/Temp**	256-721-0034
Emergency	911	**Weather**	256-533-1990

— Information Sources —

					Phone	Fax
Better Business Bureau Serving Northern Alabama PO Box 383	Huntsville	AL	35804	256-533-1640	533-1177
Web: www.northalabama.bbb.org ■ *E-mail:* info@northalabama.bbb.org					
Chamber of Commerce of Huntsville/Madison County PO Box 408	Huntsville	AL	35804	256-535-2000	535-2015
Web: www.hsvchamber.org ■ *E-mail:* hcc@hsvchamber.org					
Huntsville City Hall PO Box 308	Huntsville	AL	35804	256-532-7304	
Web: www.ci.huntsville.al.us					
Huntsville-Madison County Public Library PO Box 443	Huntsville	AL	35804	256-532-5940	532-5997
Web: www.hpl.lib.al.us/					
Huntsville Mayor PO Box 308	Huntsville	AL	35804	256-532-7304	532-7525
Web: ci.huntsville.al.us/mayor					
Huntsville Urban Development Dept PO Box 308	Huntsville	AL	35804	256-532-7353	535-4236
Huntsville/Madison County Convention & Visitor's Bureau 700 Monroe St	Huntsville	AL	35801	256-551-2230	551-2324
TF: 800-772-2348 ■ *Web:* www.huntsville.org ■ *E-mail:* cvb@iquest.com					
Madison County 100 Northside Sq	Huntsville	AL	35801	256-532-3327	532-3768
Von Braun Civic Center 700 Monroe St	Huntsville	AL	35801	256-533-1953	551-2203
Web: www.vbcc.com ■ *E-mail:* marketing@vbcc.com					

On-Line Resources

Area Guide Huntsville	huntsville.areaguides.net
City Knowledge Huntsville	www.cityknowledge.com/al_huntsville.htm
Excite.com Huntsville City Guide	www.excite.com/travel/countries/united_states/alabama/huntsville
Huntsville Virtual Times	hsv.com
NITC Travelbase City Guide Huntsville	www.travelbase.com/auto/guides/huntsville-al.html
RocketCity.com	www.rocketcity.com/

— Transportation Services —

AIRPORTS

■ **Huntsville International Airport (HSV)**

	Phone
12 miles W of downtown (approx 20 minutes)	256-772-9395

Web: www.hsvairport.org/airport.html

Airport Transportation

	Phone
Executive Connection $20 fare to downtown	256-772-0186
Huntsville Cab $17 fare to downtown	256-539-8288

Commercial Airlines

	Phone		Phone
AirTran	800-247-8726	**Northwest**	800-225-2525
American	800-433-7300	**United Express**	800-241-6522
Atlantic Southeast	800-282-3424	**US Airways**	800-428-4322
Delta	800-221-1212		

Charter Airlines

	Phone		Phone
Huntsville Aviation Corp	256-772-8092	**Signature Flight Support**	256-772-9341

CAR RENTALS

	Phone		Phone
Americar	256-772-3176	**Hertz**	256-772-9331
Avis	256-772-9301	**National**	256-772-9336
Budget	256-534-6464	**Thrifty**	256-880-0597

LIMO/TAXI

	Phone		Phone
A1 United Deluxe Cab	256-534-9213	**Jetport Taxi Cab**	256-534-4141
AAA Cab	256-539-9444	**Rocket City Cab**	256-534-4524
Executive Connection	256-772-0186	**VIP Limousine**	256-551-8745
Huntsville Cab	256-539-8288		

MASS TRANSIT

	Phone
Huntsville Public Transit $1 Base fare	256-532-7433

Huntsville (Cont'd)

RAIL/BUS

				Phone
Greyhound Bus Station 601 Monroe St NW *TF:* 800-231-2222	Huntsville	AL	35801	256-534-1681

— Accommodations —

HOTELS, MOTELS, RESORTS

				Phone	Fax
Baymont Inns & Suites 4890 University Dr *TF:* 800-301-0200	Huntsville	AL	35816	256-830-8999	837-5720
Comfort Inn 3788 University Dr. *TF:* 800-228-5150	Huntsville	AL	35816	256-533-3291	536-7389
Country Inn & Suites 4880 University Dr *TF:* 800-456-4000	Huntsville	AL	35816	256-837-4070	837-4535
Courtyard by Marriott Huntsville 4804 University Dr *TF:* 800-321-2211 ■ *Web:* courtyard.com/HSVCH	Huntsville	AL	35816	256-837-1400	837-3582
Days Inn 102 Arlington Dr *TF:* 800-329-7466	Madison	AL	35758	256-772-9550	772-9550
Days Inn 810 6th Ave NE *TF:* 800-329-7466	Decatur	AL	35602	256-355-3520	355-7213
Econo Lodge University 3772 University Dr *TF:* 800-553-2666	Huntsville	AL	35816	256-534-7061	534-7061
Executive Lodge Suite Hotel 1535 Sparkman Dr *TF:* 800-248-4722	Huntsville	AL	35816	256-830-8600	830-8899
Extended StayAmerica 4751 Governor's House Dr. *TF:* 800-398-7829	Huntsville	AL	35805	256-830-9110	830-4935
Federal Square Suites 8781 Hwy 20 W. *TF:* 800-458-1639	Huntsville	AL	35758	256-772-8470	772-0620
Four Points By Sheraton 1000 Glenn Hearn Blvd *TF:* 800-241-7873	Huntsville	AL	35824	256-772-9661	464-9116
GuestHouse Suites 4020 Independence Dr.	Huntsville	AL	35816	256-837-8907	837-5435
Hampton Inn Huntsville 4815 University Dr NW *TF:* 800-426-7866	Huntsville	AL	35816	256-830-9400	830-0978
Holiday Inn Express 3808 University Dr. *TF:* 800-345-7720	Huntsville	AL	35816	256-721-1000	722-2016
Holiday Inn Huntsville Airport 9035 Hwy 20 W *TF:* 800-465-4329	Madison	AL	35758	256-772-7170	464-0762
Holiday Inn Research Park 5903 University Dr *TF:* 800-845-7275	Huntsville	AL	35806	256-830-0600	830-9576
Holiday Inn Space Center 3810 University Dr *TF:* 800-345-7720	Huntsville	AL	35816	256-837-7171	837-9257
Huntsville Hilton Hotel 401 Williams Ave SW *TF:* 800-445-8667	Huntsville	AL	35801	256-533-1400	534-7787
Joe Wheeler Resort PO Box K *TF:* 800-544-5639	Rogersville	AL	35652	256-247-5461	247-5471
Kings Inn 11245 S Memorial Pkwy *TF:* 800-824-3513	Huntsville	AL	35803	256-881-1250	881-1250
Knights Inn 4404 University Dr NW. *TF:* 800-843-5644	Huntsville	AL	35816	256-864-0388	864-0388
La Quinta Motor Inn Research Park 4870 University Dr NW *TF:* 800-531-5900	Huntsville	AL	35816	256-830-2070	830-4412
La Quinta Motor Inn Space Center 3141 University Dr NW *TF:* 800-531-5900	Huntsville	AL	35816	256-533-0756	539-5414
Lake Guntersville Lodge & Convention Center 1155 Lodge Dr. *TF:* 800-548-4553	Guntersville	AL	35976	256-571-5440	571-5459
Madison Inn 4430 University Dr	Huntsville	AL	35816	256-890-0700	890-0407
Marriott Space Center 5 Tranquility Base. *TF:* 800-228-9290 ■ *Web:* marriotthotels.com/HSVAL	Huntsville	AL	35805	256-830-2222	895-0904
Quality Inn 1412 Glen Blvd. *TF:* 800-228-5151	Fort Payne	AL	35968	256-845-4013	845-2344
Radisson Inn 8721 Madison Blvd *TF:* 800-333-3333	Madison	AL	35758	256-772-8855	464-0783
Radisson Suite Hotel 6000 S Memorial Pkwy *TF:* 800-333-3333	Huntsville	AL	35802	256-882-9400	882-9684
Ramada Inn 3502 Memorial Pkwy SW. *TF:* 800-272-6232	Huntsville	AL	35801	256-881-6120	881-6120
Ramada Inn Airport 8716 Hwy 20 W. *TF:* 800-272-6232	Madison	AL	35758	256-772-0701	772-8900
Villager Lodge 3100 University Dr *TF:* 800-328-7829	Huntsville	AL	35816	256-533-0610	533-9849

— Restaurants —

				Phone
Beauregard's (Southern) 511 Jordan Ln NW	Huntsville	AL	35805	256-837-2433
BJ's Bar-B-Que (Barbecue) 12009 Hwy 231/431 N.	Meridianville	AL	35759	256-828-1976
Bombay Cuisine (Indian) 420 Jordan Ln NW.	Huntsville	AL	35805	256-536-3360
Bubba's (American) 109 Washington St	Huntsville	AL	35801	256-534-3133
Cafe 302 (American) 2700 Winchester Rd.	Huntsville	AL	35811	256-852-3442
Cafe Berlin (German) 505 Airport Rd SW	Huntsville	AL	35802	256-880-9920
Camino Real (Mexican) 4116 University Dr NW	Huntsville	AL	35816	256-830-1188
Dragon Garden (Chinese) 6125 University Dr NW	Huntsville	AL	35806	256-922-0810
El Mejicano Restaurant (Mexican) 2713 Patton Rd SW	Huntsville	AL	35805	256-534-2371
End Zone (Steak) 1909 University Dr NW	Huntsville	AL	35816	256-536-2234
Five Points Restaurant (American) 816 Wellman Ave NE	Huntsville	AL	35801	256-536-7356
Fogcutter (Steak/Seafood) 3805 University Dr NW.	Huntsville	AL	35816	256-539-2121
Fratelli's Ristorante Italiano (Italian) 501 Jordan Ln	Huntsville	AL	35805	256-830-1660
Green Bottle Grille (American) 975 Airport Rd	Huntsville	AL	35802	256-882-0459
Green Hills Grille (American) 5100 Sanderson Rd.	Huntsville	AL	35805	256-837-8282
Herrington's Restaurant (American) 1401 Weatherly Rd SE	Huntsville	AL	35812	256-880-6066
House of Mandarin (Chinese) 3810 University Dr	Huntsville	AL	35816	256-837-3877
Korea House Restaurant (Korean) 405 Jordan Ln NW	Huntsville	AL	35805	256-837-9207
La Alameda (Mexican) 3807 University Dr NW	Huntsville	AL	35816	256-539-6244
Lofton's Restaurant (American) 401 Williams Ave SW	Huntsville	AL	35801	256-533-1400
Mikato Japanese Steak House (Japanese) 4061 Independence Dr NW	Huntsville	AL	35816	256-830-1700
Mill Bakery & Eatery (American) 2003-B Whitesburg Dr	Huntsville	AL	35801	256-534-4455
Miwon Restaurant (Japanese/Korean) 404 Jordan Ln NW	Huntsville	AL	35805	256-533-7771
Ol' Heidelberg (German) 6125 University Dr NW Suite E-14	Huntsville	AL	35806	256-922-0556
Oriental Chef (Korean) 2701 Patton Rd SW	Huntsville	AL	35805	256-539-8100
Peanut Factory Bar & Grill (American) 903 Memorial Pkwy NW	Huntsville	AL	35801	256-534-7092
Rosie's Mexican Cantina (Mexican) 6125 University Dr NW	Huntsville	AL	35816	256-922-1001
Santa Fe Grill (Southwest) 964 Airport Rd SW	Huntsville	AL	35802	256-880-2010
Shogun Japanese Steak & Seafood House (Japanese) 3780 University Dr	Huntsville	AL	35816	256-534-3000
Tai Pan Palace (Chinese) 2012 S Memorial Pkwy	Huntsville	AL	35801	256-539-5797
Tortellini Inc (Italian) 7500 S Memorial Pkwy	Huntsville	AL	35802	256-881-5798

— Goods and Services —

SHOPPING

				Phone	Fax
Madison Square Mall 5901 University Dr	Huntsville	AL	35806	256-830-5407	
Market Square Mall 721 Clinton Ave W.	Huntsville	AL	35804	256-533-3414	533-3454
Parkway City Mall 2801 Memorial Pkwy S. **Fax:* Cust Svc	Huntsville	AL	35801	256-533-0700	533-9349*

BANKS

				Phone	Fax
Colonial Bank 101 Governors Dr. **Fax:* Cust Svc ■ *TF:* 800-533-0655	Huntsville	AL	35801	256-551-4700	551-4856*
Compass Bank 114 Governors Dr **Fax:* Cust Svc ■ *TF:* 800-239-1166	Huntsville	AL	35801	256-532-6273	532-6277*
Regions Bank 216 West Side Sq. **Fax:* Cust Svc ■ *TF:* 800-734-4667	Huntsville	AL	35801	256-535-0100	535-0338*
SouthTrust Bank of Huntsville NA 409 Madison St SE	Huntsville	AL	35801	256-533-3600	551-4061

BUSINESS SERVICES

	Phone
Federal Express	800-238-5355
Kelly Services	256-536-5315
Kinko's	256-830-4959
Manpower Temporary Services	256-539-0676
Olsten Staffing Services	256-533-4724
Post Office	256-461-6602
Professional Carriers of Alabama	256-851-7241
UPS	800-742-5877

— Media —

PUBLICATIONS

				Phone	Fax
Huntsville Times‡ 2317 S Memorial Pkwy *TF:* 800-239-5271 ■ *Web:* www.al.com/hsvtimes/hsv.html	Huntsville	AL	35801	256-532-4000	532-4420

‡Daily newspapers

Huntsville (Cont'd)

TELEVISION

				Phone	Fax
WAAY-TV Ch 31 (ABC) 1000 Monte Sano Blvd SE **Fax:* News Rm ■ *Web:* www.waaytv.com	Huntsville	AL	35801	256-533-3131	533-5191*
WAFF-TV Ch 48 (NBC) 1414 Memorial Pkwy N *Web:* www.waff.com	Huntsville	AL	35801	256-533-4848	534-4101
WHIQ-TV Ch 25 (PBS) 2112 11th Ave S Suite 400 *Web:* www.aptv.org	Birmingham	AL	35205	205-328-8756	251-2192
WHNT-TV Ch 19 (CBS) PO Box 19 *Web:* www.whnt19.com	Huntsville	AL	35804	256-533-1919	536-9468
WZDX-TV CH 54 (Fox) 1309 N Memorial Pkwy *Web:* www.fox54.com	Huntsville	AL	35801	256-533-5454	533-5315

RADIO

				Phone	Fax
WAHR-FM 99.1 MHz (AC) 2714 Lawrence Ave SW *Web:* www.wahr.com ■ *E-mail:* wahr@hiwaay.net	Huntsville	AL	35805	256-536-1568	536-4416
WDJL-AM 1000 kHz (Oldies) 6420 Stringfield Rd	Huntsville	AL	35806	256-852-1223	852-1900
WEUP-AM 1600 kHz (Urban) 2609 Jordan Ln NW	Huntsville	AL	35816	256-837-9387	837-9404
WEUP-FM 92.1 MHz (Urban) 2609 Jordan Ln NW	Huntsville	AL	35816	256-837-9387	837-9404
WJAB-FM 90.9 MHz (NPR) PO Box 1687 *E-mail:* mburns@asnaam.aamu.edu	Normal	AL	35762	256-851-5795	851-5907
WLOR-AM 1550 kHz (Urban) 2523 Bronco Cir NW	Huntsville	AL	35814	256-721-0035	722-0318
WLRH-FM 89.3 MHz (NPR) South Loop Rd University of Alabama-Huntsville *Web:* www.wlrh.org	Huntsville	AL	35899	256-895-9574	830-4577
WNDA-FM 95.1 MHz (Rel) 2407 9th Ave SW *Web:* www.wnda.com ■ *E-mail:* wnda@juno.com	Huntsville	AL	35805	256-534-2433	533-6265
WOCG-FM 90.1 MHz (Rel) 7000 Adventist Blvd *Web:* www.oakwood.edu/wocg ■ *E-mail:* wocg@oakwood.edu	Huntsville	AL	35896	256-726-7418	
WTAK-FM 106.1 MHz (CR) 200 Lime Quarry Rd *Web:* www.wtak.com	Madison	AL	35758	256-772-9825	464-3291
WTKI-AM 1450 kHz (N/T) 2305 Holmes Ave *Web:* www.wtki1450.com	Huntsville	AL	35816	256-533-1450	536-4349

— Colleges/Universities —

				Phone	Fax
Alabama A & M University 4900 Meridian St **Fax:* PR ■ *Web:* www.aamu.edu	Normal	AL	35762	256-851-5000	851-5654*
Calhoun Community College 6250 Hwy 31 N *TF:* 800-626-3628 ■ *Web:* www.calhoun.cc.al.us	Decatur	AL	35601	256-306-2500	306-2885
JF Drake State Technical College 3421 Meridian St N	Huntsville	AL	35811	256-539-8161	539-6439
Oakwood College 7000 Adventist Blvd *TF:* 800-824-5312 ■ *Web:* www.oakwood.edu	Huntsville	AL	35896	256-726-7000	726-7154
Southeastern Institute of Technology PO Box 1485	Huntsville	AL	35807	256-837-9726	726-3434
University of Alabama Huntsville 301 Sparkman Dr *TF:* 800-824-2255 ■ *Web:* www.uah.edu	Huntsville	AL	35899	256-890-6120	890-6073

— Hospitals —

				Phone	Fax
Athens-Limestone Hospital 700 W Market St *Web:* www.alhosp.com ■ *E-mail:* info@alhosp.com	Athens	AL	35611	256-233-9292	233-9277
Crestwood Medical Center 1 Hospital Dr *Web:* crestwoodmedcenter.com	Huntsville	AL	35801	256-882-3100	880-4246
Decatur General Hospital 1201 7th St SE	Decatur	AL	35601	256-341-2000	341-2648
Huntsville Hospital System 101 Sivley Rd SW *Web:* www.hhsys.org ■ *E-mail:* burri@mktg-pr.hhsys.org	Huntsville	AL	35801	256-533-8020	517-8416
Parkway Medical Center Hospital 1874 Beltline Rd **Fax:* Admissions ■ *Web:* www.parkway-pavilion.com	Decatur	AL	35601	256-301-2211	301-8415*

— Attractions —

				Phone	Fax
Alabama Constitution Village 109 Gates Ave *TF:* 800-678-1819	Huntsville	AL	35801	256-564-8100	564-8151
Burritt Museum & Park 3101 Burritt Dr *E-mail:* bm-recep@ci.huntsville.al.us	Huntsville	AL	35801	256-536-2882	532-1784
Harrison Brothers Hardware Store 124 Southside Sq	Huntsville	AL	35801	256-536-3631	
Huntsville Art League 2801 S Memorial Pkwy Gallery	Huntsville	AL	35801	256-534-3860	
Huntsville Depot Museum 320 Church St *Web:* www.earlyworks.com	Huntsville	AL	35801	256-564-8100	
Huntsville Museum of Art 300 Church St S *Web:* www.hsv.tis.net/hma	Huntsville	AL	35801	256-535-4350	532-1743
Huntsville Opera Theater 700 Monroe St Von Braun Center Playhouse *Web:* fly.hiwaay.net/~mbeutjer/hot.html	Huntsville	AL	35802	256-881-4796	
Huntsville Symphony Orchestra PO Box 2400 *Web:* www.hso.org ■ *E-mail:* hso@ro.com	Huntsville	AL	35804	256-539-4818	539-4819
Huntsville/Madison County Botanical Garden 4747 Bob Wallace Ave *Web:* www.hsvbg.org/ ■ *E-mail:* vmhurst@traveller.com	Huntsville	AL	35805	256-830-4447	830-5314
Limestone Zoological Park & Exotic Wildlife Refuge 30193 Nick Davis Rd *Web:* www.garply.com/~wildside/ ■ *E-mail:* wildside@garply.com	Harvest	AL	35749	256-230-0330	230-0990
Little River Canyon National Preserve PO Box 45 *Web:* www.nps.gov/liri/	Fort Payne	AL	35967	256-997-9239	997-9153
Madison County Nature Trail 5000 S Shawdee Rd	Huntsville	AL	35803	256-883-9501	
Maple Hill Cemetery 203 Maple Hill Dr	Huntsville	AL	35801	256-535-6485	535-6489
Monte Sano State Park 5105 Nolen Ave	Huntsville	AL	35801	256-534-3757	539-7069
Russell Cave National Monument 3729 County Rd 98 *Web:* www.nps.gov/ruca/	Bridgeport	AL	35740	256-495-2672	495-9220
Twickenham Historic District Downtown Huntsville	Huntsville	AL	35801	256-551-2230	
US Space & Rocket Center 1 Tranquility Base *TF:* 800-637-7223 ■ *Web:* www.ussrc.com/ ■ *E-mail:* joeb@spacecamp.com	Huntsville	AL	35805	256-837-3400	837-6137
Weeden House Museum 300 Gates Ave SE	Huntsville	AL	35801	256-536-7718	

SPORTS TEAMS & FACILITIES

				Phone	Fax
Huntsville Channel Cats (hockey) 700 Monroe St *Web:* www.channelcats.net	Huntsville	AL	35801	256-551-2383	551-2382
Huntsville Speedway 357 Hegia Burrow Rd *Web:* www.huntsvillespeedway.com ■ *E-mail:* dstewart@traveller.com	Huntsville	AL	35803	256-882-9191	882-9131
Huntsville Stars (baseball) 3125 Leeman Ferry Rd Joe Davis Stadium *Web:* www.huntsvillestars.com	Huntsville	AL	35801	256-882-2562	880-0801

— Events —

	Phone
Big Spring Jam (late September)	256-533-5723
Black Arts Festival (late June)	256-837-9387
Civil War Living History Weekend (early November)	256-536-2882
Cornucopia (mid-October)	256-830-4447
Cotton Row Run (late May)	256-533-5723
Down Home Blues Festival (late May)	256-551-1020
Galaxy of Lights (late November-early January)	256-830-4447
Huntsville Pilgrimage (mid-April)	256-533-5723
Indian Heritage Festival (mid-October)	256-536-2882
Living History Weekends (June-August)	256-536-2882
Northeast Alabama State Fair (early September)	256-533-5723
Old Fashioned Trade Day (early September)	256-536-0097
Panoply-Huntsville's Festival of the Arts (late April)	256-519-2787
Rocket City Marathon (mid-December)	256-828-6207
Sorghum & Harvest Festival (early November)	256-536-2882

Huntsville — Events (Cont'd)

	Phone
State Fiddling Bluegrass Convention (mid-September)	256-859-4470
Under the Christmas Tree (early November)	256-881-1701

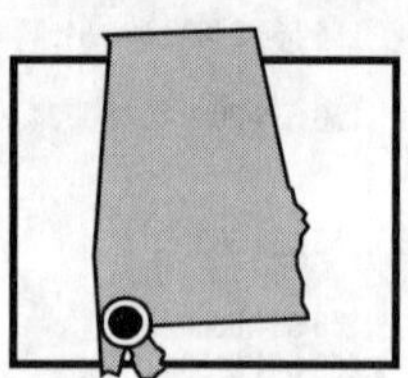

Mobile

Mobile's beautiful azaleas are featured each year at the city's Azalea Trail Festival. Depending on when blooms peak, every March or April visitors can view a 27-mile long trail of the city's most colorful floral displays. Azaleas are also featured at the Bellingrath Gardens and Home, along with 65 acres of various other flowers that bloom during all four seasons. The estate is the former home of Coca-Cola bottling pioneer Walter D. Bellingrath and contains one of the finest antiques collections in the Southeast. Mobile Bay is the site of the USS Alabama Battleship Memorial Park, which includes the USS Alabama (WWII battleship), USS Drum (WWII submarine), and the B-52 bomber, "Calamity Jane." Mobile Bay was also the site where, in 1864, Confederate torpedoes sank the ironclad Tecumseh, on which Admiral David Farragut said, "Damn the torpedoes! Full speed ahead!" South of Mobile, across the bay, are the white sand beaches and resort hotels of Gulf Shores.

Population	202,181	**Longitude**	88-04-31 W
Area (Land)	118.0 sq mi	**County**	Mobile
Area (Water)	38.6 sq mi	**Time Zone**	CST
Elevation	16 ft	**Area Code/s**	334
Latitude	30-69-42 N		

— Average Temperatures and Precipitation —

TEMPERATURES

	Jan	Feb	Mar	Apr	May	Jun	Jul	Aug	Sep	Oct	Nov	Dec
High	60	64	71	79	85	90	91	91	87	80	70	63
Low	40	43	50	57	64	71	73	73	69	57	49	43

PRECIPITATION

	Jan	Feb	Mar	Apr	May	Jun	Jul	Aug	Sep	Oct	Nov	Dec
Inches	4.8	5.5	6.4	4.5	5.7	5.0	6.9	7.0	5.9	2.9	4.1	5.3

— Important Phone Numbers —

	Phone		Phone
AAA	334-265-1237	**Poison Control Center**	800-462-0800
American Express Travel	334-476-5095	**Time/Temp**	334-660-0044
Emergency	911	**Weather**	334-478-6666

— Information Sources —

				Phone	Fax
Better Business Bureau Serving Southern Alabama PO Box 2008 *Web:* www.mobile.bbb.org	Mobile	AL	36602	334-433-5494	438-3191
Mobile Area Chamber of Commerce PO Box 2187 *Web:* www.mobcham.org ■ *E-mail:* info@mobcham.org	Mobile	AL	36652	334-433-6951	432-1143
Mobile City Hall PO Box 1827 *Web:* www.ci.mobile.al.us	Mobile	AL	36633	334-208-7411	208-7482
Mobile Convention & Visitors Corp 1 S Water St *TF:* 800-566-2453 ■ *Web:* www.mobile.org ■ *E-mail:* info@mobile.org	Mobile	AL	36602	334-208-2000	208-2060
Mobile Convention Center 1 S Water St *TF:* 800-566-2453	Mobile	AL	36602	334-415-2100	415-2150
Mobile County 205 Government St *Web:* www.acan.net/government/local/county	Mobile	AL	36644	334-690-8700	690-5079
Mobile Dept of Tourism 1 S Water St	Mobile	AL	33602	334-415-2003	415-2426
Mobile Mayor PO Box 1827	Mobile	AL	36633	334-208-7395	208-7548
Mobile Public Library 701 Government St *Web:* www2.acan.net/~mplhp	Mobile	AL	36602	334-434-7073	434-5865
Mobile Urban Development Dept PO Box 1827 *Web:* www.ci.mobile.al.us/html/urban/index.html	Mobile	AL	36633	334-208-7198	208-7896

On-Line Resources

About.com Guide to Mobile	mobile.about.com
Area Guide Mobile	mobile.areaguides.net
Excite.com Mobile City Guide	www.excite.com/travel/countries/united_states/alabama/mobile
Harbinger The	entropy.me.usouthal.edu/harbinger
InMobile.com	www.inmobile.com
Mobile Free-Net	www.maf.mobile.al.us
Mobile Home Page	cityshowcase.com/mobile/
Mobile Today	www.wimi.com/mobile
Mobile.TheLinks.com	mobile.thelinks.com
NITC Travelbase City Guide Mobile	www.travelbase.com/auto/guides/mobile-area-al.html

— Transportation Services —

AIRPORTS

■ **Mobile Regional Airport (MOB)**	Phone
14 miles W of downtown (approx 30 minutes)	334-633-0313

Airport Transportation

	Phone
Airport Limousine $19 fare to downtown	334-633-5693
Mobile Bay Transportation $19 fare to downtown	334-633-5693

Commercial Airlines

	Phone		Phone
American	800-433-7300	**Northwest**	800-225-2525
Delta	800-221-1212	**US Airways**	800-428-4322

Charter Airlines

	Phone		Phone
Alliance Executive Charter Services	800-232-5387	**Charter Services Inc**	334-633-6090
		Mobile Air Center	334-633-5000

CAR RENTALS

	Phone		Phone
Alamo	800-327-9633	**Hertz**	334-633-4000
Avis	334-633-4743	**National**	334-633-4003
Budget	334-633-0660	**Thrifty**	800-367-2277
Enterprise	334-639-9609		

LIMO/TAXI

	Phone		Phone
Mike Cab Co	334-457-9448	**Southern Comfort Limousine**	334-661-5466
Quality Limousine	334-476-2046	**Yellow Cab**	334-476-7711

MASS TRANSIT

	Phone
Mobile Transit Authority $1.25 Base fare	334-344-5656

RAIL/BUS

				Phone
Amtrak Station 11 Government St *TF:* 800-872-7245	Mobile	AL	36602	334-432-4052
Greyhound Bus Station 2545 Government Blvd *TF:* 800-231-2222	Mobile	AL	36602	334-478-6089

Mobile (Cont'd)

— Accommodations —

HOTEL RESERVATION SERVICES

	Phone	Fax
Reservations USA	865-453-1000	453-7484

TF: 800-251-4444 ■ *Web:* www.reservationsusa.com ■ *E-mail:* reserve@lodging4u.com

HOTELS, MOTELS, RESORTS

Name / Address	City	State	Zip	Phone	Fax
Adam's Mark Hotel 64 S Water St — *TF:* 800-444-2326 ■ *Web:* www.adamsmark.com/mobil.htm	Mobile	AL	36602	334-438-4000	415-0123
Best Suites of America 150 Beltline Hwy S — *TF:* 800-237-8466	Mobile	AL	36608	334-343-4949	
Best Western Battleship Inn 2701 Battleship Pkwy	Mobile	AL	36601	334-432-2703	432-6111
Best Western Bradbury Inn 180 S Beltline Hwy — *TF:* 800-528-1234	Mobile	AL	36608	334-343-9345	342-5366
Budget Inn 555 Government St	Mobile	AL	36602	334-433-0590	434-0048
Clarion Hotel Mobile 3101 Airport Blvd — *TF:* 800-982-9822	Mobile	AL	36606	334-476-6400	476-9360
Comfort Inn 5650 Tillmans Corner Pkwy — *TF:* 800-228-5150	Mobile	AL	36619	334-666-6604	666-0710
Comfort Suites 70 Springdale Blvd — *TF:* 800-221-2222	Mobile	AL	36606	334-471-1515	478-0477
Courtyard by Marriott 1000 S Beltline Hwy — *TF:* 800-321-2211 ■ *Web:* courtyard.com/MOBCY	Mobile	AL	36609	334-344-5200	341-0300
Days Inn Airport 3650 Airport Blvd — *TF:* 800-329-7466	Mobile	AL	36608	334-344-3410	344-8790
Days Inn Tillman's Corner 5480 Inn Rd — *TF:* 800-329-7466	Mobile	AL	33619	334-661-8181	660-0194
Drury Inn Hotel 824 S Beltline Hwy — *TF:* 800-378-7946	Mobile	AL	36609	334-344-7700	344-7700
Econo Lodge Midtown 1 South Beltline Hwy — *TF:* 800-553-2666	Mobile	AL	36606	334-479-5333	471-4937
Extended StayAmerica 508 Springhill Plaza Ct — *TF:* 800-398-7829	Mobile	AL	36608	334-344-2514	344-9683
Family Inns Of America 900 S Beltline Hwy — *TF:* 800-251-9752	Mobile	AL	36609	334-344-5500	342-4744
GuestHouse Inn 3132 Government Blvd	Mobile	AL	36606	334-471-2402	471-9912
Gulf State Park Resort 21250 E Beach Blvd — *TF:* 800-544-4853	Gulf Shores	AL	36542	334-948-4853	948-5998
Hampton Inn 930 S Beltline Hwy — *TF:* 800-426-7866	Mobile	AL	36609	334-344-4942	341-4520
Holiday Inn 5465 Hwy 90 W — *TF:* 800-465-4329	Mobile	AL	36619	334-666-5600	666-2773
Holiday Inn Express 255 Church St — *TF:* 800-465-4329	Mobile	AL	36602	334-433-6923	433-8869
Holiday Inn Historic District 301 Government St — *TF:* 800-465-4329 ■ *Web:* www.basshotels.com/holiday-inn/?_franchisee=MOBDW ■ *E-mail:* historic@iar.net	Mobile	AL	36602	334-694-0100	694-0160
Holiday Inn Mobile 850 S Beltline Hwy — *TF:* 800-465-4329	Mobile	AL	36609	334-342-3220	342-8919
La Quinta Inn 816 S Beltline Hwy — *TF:* 800-687-6667	Mobile	AL	36609	334-343-4051	343-2897
Malaga Inn 359 Church St — *TF:* 800-235-1586	Mobile	AL	36602	334-438-4701	438-4701
Marriott's Grand Hotel 1 Grand Blvd — *TF:* 800-544-9933 ■ *Web:* marriotthotels.com/PTLAL	Point Clear	AL	36564	334-928-9201	928-1149
Motel 6 5488 Inn Dr — *TF:* 800-466-8356	Mobile	AL	36619	334-660-1483	660-7832
Motel 6 Airport 400 S Beltline Hwy — *TF:* 800-466-8356	Mobile	AL	36608	334-343-8448	343-7502
Radisson Admiral Semmes Hotel 251 Government St — *TF:* 800-333-3333	Mobile	AL	36602	334-432-8000	405-5942
Ramada Bay Resort 1525 Battleship Pkwy — *TF:* 800-272-6232	Mobile	AL	35627	334-626-7200	
Ramada Plaza Hotel 600 S Beltline Hwy — *TF:* 800-272-6232	Mobile	AL	36608	334-344-8030	344-8055
Red Roof Inn 33 S Beltline Hwy — *TF:* 800-843-7663	Mobile	AL	36606	334-476-2004	476-2054
Residence Inn 950 S Beltline Hwy — *TF:* 800-331-3131 ■ *Web:* www.residenceinn.com/residenceinn/MOBRI	Mobile	AL	36609	334-304-0570	304-0580
Rest Inn 3651 Government Blvd	Mobile	AL	36693	334-666-7751	666-7751
Rodeway Inn 1724 Michigan Ave — *TF:* 800-228-2000	Mobile	AL	36605	334-471-1115	471-1165
Shoney's Inn 162 S Beltline Hwy — *TF:* 800-222-2222 ■ *Web:* www.shoneysinn.com/al2.htm	Mobile	AL	36608	334-344-2121	344-5855
Super 8 Motel 5676 Tillmans Corner Pkwy — *TF:* 800-800-8000	Mobile	AL	36619	334-666-0003	661-0800
Warren Inn 6501 Airport Blvd	Mobile	AL	36608	334-342-0100	344-6713

— Restaurants —

Name / Address	City	State	Zip	Phone
Azalea City Grill (American) 1000 Gaillard Dr	Mobile	AL	36608	334-344-7353
Banana Docks Cafe (Seafood) 36 Hillcrest Rd	Mobile	AL	36608	334-342-2775
Brandi's Restaurant (Soul) 1610 St Stephens Rd	Mobile	AL	36603	334-438-3201
Captain's Table (American) 2701 Battleship Pkwy	Mobile	AL	36601	334-433-3790
Catalina Seafood Restaurant (Seafood) 450 Azalea Rd	Mobile	AL	36609	334-342-1501
China Doll Restaurant (Chinese) 233 Dauphin St	Mobile	AL	36602	334-433-7511
Cock of the Walk (Seafood) 4815 Halls Mill Rd	Mobile	AL	36602	334-666-1875
Delhi Palace (Indian) 3674 Airport Blvd	Mobile	AL	36608	334-341-6171
Eats Of Eden Cafe (Vegetarian) 3952 Airport Blvd	Mobile	AL	36608	334-380-9388
El Chico Restaurant (Mexican) 830 S Beltline Hwy	Mobile	AL	36609	334-344-0134
For Pete's Sake (American) 4610 Springhill Ave	Mobile	AL	36608	334-344-8286
Golden China Restaurant (Chinese) 309 Bel Air Blvd	Mobile	AL	36606	334-478-8465
Gus's Azalea Manor Courtyard (Continental) 751 Dauphin St	Mobile	AL	36602	334-433-4877
Hall's Catfish & Seafood (Seafood) 3951 Government Blvd	Mobile	AL	36602	334-666-9248
Japanese Imperial Steak House (Japanese) 3686 Airport Blvd	Mobile	AL	36608	334-343-8100
Joe's Crab Shack (Seafood) 3716 Airport Blvd	Mobile	AL	36608	334-414-2727
Justine's Courtyard & Carriageway (Continental) 80 Saint Michael St	Mobile	AL	36602	334-438-4535
La Louisiana (Continental) 2400 Airport Blvd	Mobile	AL	36602	334-476-8130
Lakeside Lodge (American) 650 S Cody Rd	Mobile	AL	36602	334-343-2211
Lighthouse (Steak/Seafood) 2522 Government Blvd	Mobile	AL	36602	334-471-2000
Loretta's (Continental) 19 S Conception St	Mobile	AL	36602	334-432-2200
Mayme's (Cajun) 359 Church St	Mobile	AL	36602	334-438-4701
Michael's Midtown Cafe (Continental) 153 S Florida St	Mobile	AL	36606	334-473-5908
Nan Seas (Seafood) 4170 Bay Front Rd	Mobile	AL	36605	334-479-9132
O'Charley's (Steak) 3649 Airport Blvd	Mobile	AL	36608	334-344-0200
Oliver's (American) 251 Government St	Mobile	AL	36609	334-432-8000
Papageorge's Supper Club (Steak/Seafood) 2600 Government Blvd	Mobile	AL	36606	334-478-9099
Peking Seafood Restaurant (Chinese) 2662 Government Blvd	Mobile	AL	36606	334-471-6511
Picklefish The (American) 251 Dauphin St	Mobile	AL	36602	334-434-0000
Pier 4 (Steak/Seafood) 1420 Battleship Pkwy	Spanish Fort	AL	36527	334-626-6710
Pillars (Continental) 1757 Government St	Mobile	AL	36604	334-478-6341
Port City Brewery (American) 225 Dauphin St	Mobile	AL	36602	334-438-2739
Quatorze (French) 54 S Conception St	Mobile	AL	36602	334-690-7770
Revere's (Steak/Seafood) 3346 Cottage Hill Rd	Mobile	AL	36606	334-478-3700
Riverview Cafe & Grill (American) 64 S Water St	Mobile	AL	36602	334-438-4000
Roussos (Seafood) 166 S Royal St	Mobile	AL	36602	334-433-3322
Saucy-q Bar B Que (Barbecue) 1252 Government St	Mobile	AL	36604	334-433-7427
Solomons Restaurant (American) 5753 Old Shell Rd	Mobile	AL	36608	334-344-0380
TP Crockmier's (American) 170 S Florida St	Mobile	AL	36606	334-476-1890

— Goods and Services —

SHOPPING

Name / Address	City	State	Zip	Phone	Fax
Bel Air Mall 3299 Bel Air Mall	Mobile	AL	36606	334-473-8623	476-5722
Cotton City Antique Mall 2012 Airport Blvd	Mobile	AL	36606	334-479-9747	
Mobile Festival Centre 3725 Airport Blvd	Mobile	AL	36608	334-341-0500	343-0829
Springdale Mall 3250 Airport Blvd	Mobile	AL	36606	334-471-1945	479-1374

BANKS

Name / Address	City	State	Zip	Phone	Fax
AmSouth Bank 7860 Airport Blvd — *TF:* 800-267-6884	Mobile	AL	36608	334-434-3270	434-3274
Regions Bank 106 Saint Francis St	Mobile	AL	36602	334-690-1212	690-1030
South Alabama Bank 100 Saint Joseph St — *Web:* www.southalabamabank.com ■ *E-mail:* southalabama@southalabamabank.com	Mobile	AL	36602	334-431-7800	431-7851
SouthTrust Bank of Alabama NA 61 Saint Joseph St	Mobile	AL	36602	334-431-9200	431-9256

Mobile (Cont'd)

BUSINESS SERVICES

	Phone		Phone
Airborne Express	800-247-2676	**Mail Boxes Etc**	800-789-4623
BAX Global	800-225-5229	**Manpower Temporary Services**	334-344-8900
DHL Worldwide Express	800-225-5345	**Norrell Staffing Services**	334-476-9995
Federal Express	800-238-5355	**Post Office**	800-275-8777
Kelly Services	334-342-6991	**Snelling Temporaries**	334-473-4445
Kinko's	334-344-1122	**UPS**	800-742-5877

— Media —

PUBLICATIONS

Name / Address	City	State	Zip	Phone	Fax
Mobile Register‡ PO Box 2488	Mobile	AL	36652	334-433-1551	434-8662
TF: 800-239-1340 ■ *Web:* www.mobileregister.com/ ■ *E-mail:* register@dibbs.net					

‡*Daily newspapers*

TELEVISION

Name / Address	City	State	Zip	Phone	Fax
WALA-TV Ch 10 (Fox) 210 Government St.	Mobile	AL	36602	334-434-1010	434-1073
WEAR-TV Ch 3 (ABC) 4990 Mobile Hwy	Pensacola	FL	32506	850-456-3333	455-0159
Web: www.wear.pensacola.com ■ *E-mail:* news@weartv.com					
WEIQ-TV Ch 42 (PBS) 2112 11th Ave S.	Birmingham	AL	35205	205-328-8756	
WJTC-TV Ch 44 (UPN) 661 Azalea Rd	Mobile	AL	36609	334-602-1544	602-1547
Web: www.wjtc.com					
WKRG-TV Ch 5 (CBS) 555 Broadcast Dr	Mobile	AL	36606	334-479-5555	473-8130
TF: 800-957-4885 ■ *Web:* www.wkrg.com ■ *E-mail:* tv5@wkrg.com					
WPMI-TV Ch 15 (NBC) 661 Azalea Rd	Mobile	AL	36609	334-602-1500	602-1550
Web: www.wpmi.com ■ *E-mail:* nbc15@wpmi.com					

RADIO

Name / Address	City	State	Zip	Phone	Fax
WABB-FM 97.5 MHz (CHR) 1551 Springhill Ave	Mobile	AL	36604	334-432-5572	438-4044
Web: www.wabb.com					
WBHY-FM 88.5 MHz (Rel) PO Box 1328	Mobile	AL	36633	334-473-8488	473-8854
Web: www.goforth.org					
WBLX-FM 92.9 MHz (Urban) 1204 Dauphin St.	Mobile	AL	36604	334-432-7609	432-2054
Web: www.93blx.com					
WGOK-AM 900 kHz (Rel) 1 Office Pk Suite 215	Mobile	AL	36609	334-432-8661	432-1921
WHIL-FM 91.3 MHz (NPR) PO Box 8509	Mobile	AL	36689	334-380-4685	460-2189
Web: www.whil.org					
WKSJ-FM 94.9 MHz (Ctry) 555 Broadcast Dr 3rd Fl	Mobile	AL	36606	334-450-0100	473-6662
WRKH-FM 96.1 MHz (CR) 555 Broadcast Dr 3rd Fl	Mobile	AL	36606	334-450-0100	473-6662
Web: www.961therocket.com					

— Colleges/Universities —

Name / Address	City	State	Zip	Phone	Fax
Bishop State Community College 351 N Broad St.	Mobile	AL	36603	334-690-6412	438-2463
Web: www.bscc.cc.al.us ■ *E-mail:* info@bscc.cc.al.us					
Bishop State Community College Southwest Campus 925 Dauphin Island Pkwy	Mobile	AL	36605	334-479-7476	473-2049
Web: www.bscc.cc.al.us/sw_camp.htm ■ *E-mail:* info@bscc.cc.al.us					
Spring Hill College 4000 Dauphin St.	Mobile	AL	36608	334-380-4000	460-2186
TF: 800-742-6704 ■ *Web:* www.shc.edu					
University of Mobile 5735 College Pkwy	Mobile	AL	36613	334-675-5990	675-6329
TF: 800-946-7267 ■ *Web:* www.umobile.edu ■ *E-mail:* adminfo@maf.mobile.al.us					
University of South Alabama 307 University Blvd	Mobile	AL	36688	334-460-6101	460-7023
TF Admissions: 800-872-5247 ■ *Web:* www.usouthal.edu					

— Hospitals —

Name / Address	City	State	Zip	Phone	Fax
Mercy Medical Center 101 Villa Dr	Daphne	AL	36526	334-626-2694	621-4331
Mobile Infirmary Medical Center PO Box 2144	Mobile	AL	36652	334-431-2400	435-2543
Providence Hospital 6801 Airport Blvd	Mobile	AL	36608	334-633-1000	633-1529*
*Fax: Admitting ■ *Web:* www.providencehospital.org ■ *E-mail:* info@providencehospital.org					
Springhill Memorial Hospital 3719 Dauphin St	Mobile	AL	36608	334-344-9630	460-5298*
*Fax: Admitting ■ *Web:* www.springhillmemorial.com					
University of South Alabama Doctors Hospital 1700 Center St	Mobile	AL	36604	334-415-1000	415-1001
Web: www.southalabama.edu/usacwh					
University of South Alabama Medical Center 2451 Fillingim St.	Mobile	AL	36617	334-471-7000	470-1672

— Attractions —

Name / Address	City	State	Zip	Phone	Fax
Bellingrath Gardens & Home 12401 Bellingrath Garden Rd	Theodore	AL	36582	334-973-2217	973-0540
Web: www.zebra.net/~wlee/bellingrath.html ■ *E-mail:* bellingrath@juno.com					
Big Zion African Methodist Episcopal Church 112 S Bayou St	Mobile	AL	36602	334-433-8431	
Bragg-Mitchell Mansion 1906 Spring Hill Ave	Mobile	AL	36607	334-471-6364	
Carlen House 54 S Carlen St	Mobile	AL	36606	334-470-7768	470-7768
Cathedral of the Immaculate Conception 2 S Claiborne St	Mobile	AL	36602	334-434-1565	
Chickasabogue Park 760 Aldock Rd	Mobile	AL	36613	334-452-8496	457-0541
Conde-Charlotte House 104 Theatre St	Mobile	AL	36602	334-432-4722	
Dauphin Island S end of Hwy 193	Dauphin Island	AL	36528	334-861-5524	861-2154
Dauphin Island Sea Lab Estuarium 101 Bienville Blvd	Dauphin Island	AL	36528	334-861-2141	861-4646
Exploreum Imax Theater 65 Government St.	Mobile	AL	36602	334-208-6883	208-6889
Exploreum Museum of Science 65 Government St.	Mobile	AL	36602	334-208-6883	208-6889
TF: 877-625-4386 ■ *Web:* www.exploreum.com					
Fleamarket Mobile 401 Schillinger Rd N	Mobile	AL	36608	334-633-7533	639-0570
Fort Conde 150 S Royal St.	Mobile	AL	36602	334-434-7304	434-7659
Fort Gaines Historic Site E end of Dauphin Island	Dauphin Island	AL	36528	334-861-6992	
Government Street Presbyterian Church 300 Government St.	Mobile	AL	36602	334-432-1749	434-9324
Grand Oak Wildlife Preservation Park PO Box 545	Saraland	AL	36571	334-679-5757	679-5758
Historic Blakeley Park 33707 Hwy 225	Spanish Fort	AL	36527	334-580-0005	580-0005
Web: www.siteone.com/tourist/blakeley/index.html ■ *E-mail:* blakeley@siteone.com					
Mobile Ballet 4351 Dowtowner Loop N	Mobile	AL	36609	334-342-2241	344-5421
Web: olympus.asms.net/ballet					
Mobile Botanical Gardens 5151 Museum Dr Langan Pk	Mobile	AL	36602	334-342-0555	
Mobile Medical Museum 1504 Springhill Ave	Mobile	AL	36604	334-434-5055	434-5080
Mobile Museum of Art PO Box 8426	Mobile	AL	36689	334-343-2667	343-2680
Mobile Museum of Art Downtown Gallery 300 Dauphin St.	Mobile	AL	36602	334-694-0533	
Web: www.mobilemuseumofart.com					
Mobile Opera Inc PO Box 66633	Mobile	AL	36660	334-476-7372	476-7373
Web: www.mobileopera.org					
Mobile Theatre Guild 14 N Lafayette St.	Mobile	AL	36604	334-433-7513	
Museum of the City of Mobile 355 Government St.	Mobile	AL	36602	334-434-7569	208-7686
National African-American Archives & Museum 564 ML King Ave	Mobile	AL	36603	334-433-8511	433-4265
Oakleigh Period House Museum 350 Oakleigh Pl	Mobile	AL	366042	334-432-1281	432-8843
Phoenix Fire Museum 203 S Claiborne St	Mobile	AL	36602	334-434-7554	434-7686
Playhouse in the Park Mobile Municipal Park	Mobile	AL	36608	334-344-1537	
Richards-DAR House 256 N Joachim St	Mobile	AL	36602	334-434-7320	
Saenger Theatre 6 Joachim St S	Mobile	AL	36602	334-433-2787	433-2087
Southern Belle/Alabama Cruises 12402 Bellingrath Gardens Rd	Theodore	AL	36582	334-973-1244	973-1255
USS Alabama Battleship Memorial Park 2703 Battleship Pkwy	Mobile	AL	36602	334-432-5951	
Web: www.ussalabama.com					
Waterville USA 906 Gulf Shores Pkwy	Gulf Shores	AL	36542	334-948-2106	948-7918
Web: www.watervilleusa.com ■ *E-mail:* wville@gulftel.com					

SPORTS TEAMS & FACILITIES

Name / Address	City	State	Zip	Phone	Fax
Ladd-Peebles Stadium 1621 Virginia St	Mobile	AL	36604	334-208-2500	208-2514
Mobile BayBears (baseball) 755 Bolling Brothers Blvd Hank Aaron Stadium	Mobile	AL	36606	334-479-2327	476-1147
Web: www.mobilebaybears.com ■ *E-mail:* baybears@mobilebaybears.com					

Mobile — Sports Teams & Facilities (Cont'd)

				Phone	Fax
Mobile Greyhound Park 7101 Old Pascagoula Rd	Theodore	AL	36582	334-653-5000	653-9185
Web: www.mobilegreyhoundpark.com ■ *E-mail:* mgp7101@bellsouth.net					
Mobile International Speedway 7800 Park Blvd	Irvington	AL	36544	334-957-2026	957-2063
Web: www.mobilespeedway.com/					
Mobile Mysticks (hockey) 401 Civic Center Dr	Mobile	AL	36602	334-208-7825	208-7931
Web: www.mysticks.com ■ *E-mail:* mysticks@mysticks.com					

— Events —

	Phone
A Taste of the Colony (mid-March)	334-861-6992
Africatown Folk Festival (March)	334-470-7730
Alabama Deep Sea Fishing Rodeo (mid-July)	334-470-7730
Azalea Trail Run & Festival (late March)	334-473-7223
Bayfest Music Festival (early October)	334-470-7730
Blessing of the Fleet at Bayou la Batre (May)	334-824-2415
Candlelight Christmas at Oakleigh (early December)	334-415-2000
Christmas at Fort Gaines (early December)	334-861-6992
Christmas in Mobile Festival Arts & Crafts Show (late December)	334-415-2100
Christmas Jubilee (late November)	334-415-2000
Colonial Isle Dauphine (early October)	334-861-6992
Craft Bugs Holiday Fantasy (late November)	334-343-5533
Dauphin Island Regatta (late April)	334-470-7730
Dauphin Island Spring Festival (early May)	334-861-5525
Deep South Dulcimer Festival (early November)	334-452-8496
Delchamps Senior Bowl (mid-January)	334-438-2276
First Night Mobile (December 31)	334-470-7730
Greater Gulf State Fair (mid-late October)	334-470-7730
International Carnival (mid-November)	334-470-7730
Junior League Christmas Jubilee (mid-November)	334-471-3348
Labor Day Invitational Billfish Tournament (late August early September)	334-343-1619
Mardi Gras (February-March)	334-470-7730
Mobile Fourth of July Celebration (July 4)	334-470-7730
Mobile Historic Homes Tours (mid-March)	334-470-7730
Mobile International Festival (mid-November)	334-470-7730
Mobile Jazz Festival (mid-April)	334-470-7730
National Shrimp Festival (October)	334-968-6904
Providence Festival of Flowers (mid-March)	334-639-2050
Renaissance Festival (mid-November)	334-861-6992
Senior Bowl (January)	334-470-7730
September Celebration (September)	334-470-7730
Taste of Mobile (April)	334-415-2000
Thunder on the Bay (mid-May)	334-861-6992
Women's Encampment (early November)	334-861-6992

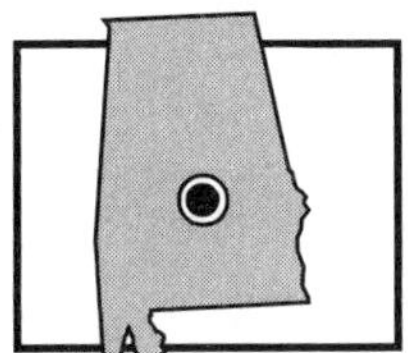

Montgomery

Montgomery is the birthplace of the Civil War, and of the the modern Civil Rights Movement. In 1861 Montgomery was the city where Jefferson Davis was sworn in as president of the Confederate States of America. Nearly 100 years later, Rosa Parks refused to give up her seat on a city bus in Montgomery, and four years later Dr. Martin Luther King, Jr. ended the Civil Rights March from Selma on the steps of the capital in Montgomery. A Civil Rights Memorial at the Southern Poverty Law Center in Montgomery chronicles key events and lists the names of 40 people who died in the struggle for racial equality between 1955 and 1968. (The Memorial was designed by Maya Lin, the artist who designed the Vietnam Veterans Memorial in Washington, DC.) Another reminder of this era is the Dexter Avenue King Memorial Baptist Church, the first pulpit of Dr. King and the center of the Montgomery bus boycott. Other attractions in Montgomery include the final resting place, as well as a life-size statue, of country music singer Hank Williams; and the one-time home of F. Scott Fitzgerald and his wife Zelda, a Montgomery native. North of the city is the Jasmine Hill Gardens and Outdoor Museum, which features a 17-acre garden and an extensive collection of fountains, pools, and Greek statuary, as well as an 1830s cottage.

Population	197,014	**Longitude**	86-30-00 W
Area (Land)	135.0 sq mi	**County**	Montgomery
Area (Water)	0.8 sq mi	**Time Zone**	CST
Elevation	250 ft	**Area Code/s**	334
Latitude	32-36-67 N		

— Average Temperatures and Precipitation —

TEMPERATURES

	Jan	Feb	Mar	Apr	May	Jun	Jul	Aug	Sep	Oct	Nov	Dec
High	56	61	69	76	83	89	91	90	87	78	69	60
Low	36	39	46	53	61	68	72	71	66	53	45	39

PRECIPITATION

	Jan	Feb	Mar	Apr	May	Jun	Jul	Aug	Sep	Oct	Nov	Dec
Inches	4.7	5.5	6.3	4.5	3.9	3.9	5.2	3.7	4.1	2.5	4.1	5.2

— Important Phone Numbers —

	Phone		Phone
AAA	334-265-1237	**Poison Control Center**	800-462-0800
Emergency	911	**Time/Temp**	334-262-8871
HotelDocs	800-468-3537	**Travelers Aid**	334-269-0488
Medical Referral	334-286-3463	**Weather**	205-945-7000

— Information Sources —

				Phone	Fax
Better Business Bureau Serving Central Alabama & the Wiregrass Area PO Box 55268	Birmingham	AL	35255	205-558-2222	558-2239
Web: www.birmingham-al.bbb.org					
Montgomery Area Chamber of Commerce PO Box 79	Montgomery	AL	36101	334-834-5200	265-4745
Web: www.montgomerychamber.org					
Montgomery City-County Public Library 245 High St	Montgomery	AL	36104	334-240-4999	240-4980
Web: mccpl.lib.al.us ■ *E-mail:* mdevore@mccpl.lib.al.us					
Montgomery City Hall 103 N Perry St	Montgomery	AL	36104	334-241-4400	241-2266
Web: ns1.montgomery.al.us/city					
Montgomery Civic Center PO Box 4037	Montgomery	AL	36101	334-241-2100	241-2117
Web: www.civic-center.ci.montgomery.al.us					
Montgomery Community Development Dept PO Box 1111	Montgomery	AL	36101	334-241-2996	241-4432
Montgomery County PO Box 1667	Montgomery	AL	36102	334-832-4950	832-2533
Montgomery Mayor PO Box 1111	Montgomery	AL	36101	334-241-2000	241-2600
Montgomery Visitors Center 300-A Water St Union Station	Montgomery	AL	36104	334-262-0013	261-1111

On-Line Resources

About.com Guide to Montgomery	montgomery.about.com
Area Guide Montgomery	montgomery.areaguides.net
City Knowledge Montgomery	www.cityknowledge.com/al_montgomery.htm
Excite.com Montgomery City Guide	www.excite.com/travel/countries/united_states/alabama/montgomery
Mainstreet USA Montgomery	www.mainstreetusa.com/al/montgomery/
Montgomery Area Information Site	www.bwsolutions.com/montgomery/
Montgomery Home Page	www.montgomery-al.com
NITC Travelbase City Guide Montgomery	www.travelbase.com/auto/guides/montgomery-al.html
OnLine Montgomery	www.onlinemontgomery.com

— Transportation Services —

AIRPORTS

■ **Montgomery Regional Airport (MGM)**

	Phone
7 miles SW of downtown (approx 15 minutes)	334-281-5040

Web: www.montgomeryairport.org ■ *E-mail:* executive-director@montgomeryairport.org

Montgomery (Cont'd)

Airport Transportation

	Phone
Airport Shuttle $13 fare to downtown	334-313-2868
Yellow Cab $14 fare to downtown	334-262-5225

Commercial Airlines

	Phone		Phone
American Eagle	800-433-7300	**Northwest**	800-225-2525
Delta	800-221-1212	**US Airways Express**	800-428-4322

Charter Airlines

	Phone		Phone
KC Aviation	334-288-6081	**Southstar Aviation**	334-281-9005
Montgomery Aviation	334-288-7334		

CAR RENTALS

	Phone		Phone
Avis	334-284-0211	**Hertz**	334-284-1560
Budget	334-288-6621	**National**	334-284-1910
Enterprise	334-277-4300		

LIMO/TAXI

	Phone		Phone
Checker Cab	334-263-2512	**Yellow Cab**	334-262-5225
Original Queen Cab	334-263-7137	**Young's Limo**	334-262-1634
Prestigious Limo	334-834-9009		

MASS TRANSIT

	Phone
Montgomery Area Transit System $1.50 Base fare	334-262-7321

RAIL/BUS

				Phone
Greyhound/Trailways Bus Station 950 W South Blvd	Montgomery	AL	36105	334-286-0120

— Accommodations —

HOTELS, MOTELS, RESORTS

				Phone	Fax
American Host Motel 3131 Mobile Hwy	Montgomery	AL	36108	334-834-0222	834-0222
Baymont Inns & Suites 5225 Carmichael Rd *TF:* 800-301-0200	Montgomery	AL	36106	334-277-6000	279-8207
Best Suites of America 5155 Carmichael Rd *TF:* 800-237-8466	Montgomery	AL	36106	334-270-3223	270-1423
Best Western Montgomery Lodge 977 W South Blvd. *TF:* 800-528-1234	Montgomery	AL	36105	334-288-5740	286-0042
Comfort Suites 5924 Monticello Dr *TF:* 800-228-5150	Montgomery	AL	36117	334-272-1013	260-0425
Courtyard by Marriott 5555 Carmichael Rd *TF:* 800-321-2211 ■ *Web:* courtyard.com/MGMCH	Montgomery	AL	36117	334-272-5533	279-0853
Days Inn 2625 Zelda Rd. *TF:* 800-329-7466	Montgomery	AL	36107	334-269-9611	263-7393
Days Inn Airport 1150 W South Blvd. *TF:* 800-329-7466	Montgomery	AL	36105	334-281-8000	284-6540
Diplomat Inn 3951 Norman Bridge Rd.	Montgomery	AL	36105	334-288-1120	288-3639
Econo Lodge 4135 Troy Hwy *TF:* 800-553-2666	Montgomery	AL	36116	334-284-3400	284-3400
Econo Lodge 1040 W South Blvd *TF:* 800-553-2666	Montgomery	AL	36105	334-286-6100	286-6100
Embassy Suites 300 Tallapoosa St	Montgomery	AL	36104	334-269-5055	269-0360
Extended StayAmerica 2491 Eastern Blvd. *TF:* 800-398-7829	Montgomery	AL	36117	334-279-1204	279-1076
Fairfield Inn by Marriott 5601 Carmichael Rd *TF:* 800-228-2800 ■ *Web:* fairfieldinn.com/MGMFI	Montgomery	AL	36117	334-270-0007	270-0007
Governors House Hotel & Convention Center 2705 E South Blvd *TF:* 800-334-8459 ■ *E-mail:* govhousehotl@earthlink.com	Montgomery	AL	36116	334-288-2800	288-6472
Hampton Inn East 1401 Eastern Bypass Blvd *TF:* 800-426-7866	Montgomery	AL	36117	334-277-2400	277-6546
Holiday Inn Hwy 80 W. *TF:* 800-465-4329	Selma	AL	36701	334-872-0461	872-0461
Holiday Inn Airport 1100 W South Blvd. *TF:* 800-465-4329	Montgomery	AL	36105	334-281-1660	281-1660
Holiday Inn East Holidome 1185 Eastern Bypass Blvd *TF:* 800-465-4329	Montgomery	AL	36117	334-272-0370	270-0339
Holiday Inn Hotel & Suites 120 Madison Ave *TF:* 800-465-4329	Montgomery	AL	36104	334-264-2231	263-3179
Knights Inn 995 W South Blvd *TF:* 800-843-5644	Montgomery	AL	36105	334-284-4004	284-3539
La Quinta Motor Inn 1280 Eastern Blvd. *TF:* 800-687-6667	Montgomery	AL	36117	334-271-1620	244-7919
Motel 6 1051 Eastern Blvd *TF:* 800-466-8356	Montgomery	AL	36117	334-277-6748	277-9195
Quality Inn 5175 Carmichael Rd *TF:* 800-228-5151	Montgomery	AL	36106	334-277-1919	279-6624
Ramada Inn East 1355 Eastern Bypass Blvd *TF:* 800-272-6232	Montgomery	AL	36117	334-277-2200	270-3338
Regency Inn 1771 Congressman Dickinson Dr *TF:* 888-301-2992	Montgomery	AL	36109	334-260-0444	
Relax Inn 4130 Birmingham Hwy	Montgomery	AL	36108	334-263-6911	
Residence Inn by Marriott 1200 Hilmar Ct *TF:* 800-331-3131 ■ *Web:* www.residenceinn.com/MGMRI	Montgomery	AL	36117	334-270-3300	260-0907
Springhill Suites by Marriott 5041 Carmichael Rd *TF:* 800-228-2800 ■ *Web:* www.springhillsuites.com/MGMSH	Montgomery	AL	36106	334-409-9999	409-0061
Statehouse Inn 924 Madison Ave *TF:* 800-552-7099	Montgomery	AL	36104	334-265-0741	834-6126
Stillwaters Resort & Conference Center 1816 Stillwaters Dr *TF:* 800-633-4954 ■ *Web:* www.stillwaters.com	Dadeville	AL	36853	256-825-7021	825-4147
StudioPLUS 5115 Carmichael Rd *TF:* 800-646-8000	Montgomery	AL	36106	334-273-0075	273-1092
Super 8 Motel 1288 W South Blvd	Montgomery	AL	36105	334-284-1900	288-0610
Town Plaza Motor Hotel 743 Madison Ave	Montgomery	AL	36104	334-269-1561	
Travel Inn 970 W South Blvd	Montgomery	AL	36105	334-288-2600	
Travelodge 4231 Mobile Hwy *TF:* 800-578-7878	Montgomery	AL	36108	334-288-0610	288-0610
Villager Lodge 2750 Chestnut St *TF:* 800-328-7829	Montgomery	AL	36107	334-834-4055	263-6703
Wynfield Inn 1110 Eastern Blvd	Montgomery	AL	36117	334-272-8880	272-8880

— Restaurants —

				Phone
Buffalo's American Grille (American) 843 Taylor Rd	Montgomery	AL	36117	334-284-9464
Capitol Oyster Bar (Seafood) 115 E South Blvd.	Montgomery	AL	36105	334-288-4217
Darryl's 1885 Restaurant & Pub (American) 2701 Eastern Blvd	Montgomery	AL	36117	334-277-1885
Dell'Amalia Ristorante (Italian) 3007-H McGehee Rd.	Montgomery	AL	36111	334-286-4825
Eastbrook Cafe (Southern) 520 Coliseum Blvd.	Montgomery	AL	36109	334-272-2438
Ellis Seafood (Seafood) 840 W Fairview Ave.	Montgomery	AL	36108	334-262-6602
Green Lantern (Steak) 5725 Troy Hwy	Montgomery	AL	36116	334-288-3665
Hickory House Restaurant (American) 4100 Norman Bridge Rd	Montgomery	AL	36105	334-281-7117
Jade Palace (Chinese) 6050 Atlanta Hwy	Montgomery	AL	36117	334-270-3288
Jalapenos (Mexican) 4019 Eastern Blvd	Montgomery	AL	36116	334-288-1221
Jubilee Seafood Co (Seafood) 1057 Woodley Rd.	Montgomery	AL	36106	334-262-6224
Lek's Taste of Thailand (Thai) 5421 Atlanta Hwy.	Montgomery	AL	36109	334-244-8994
Magnolia Cafe (Steak/Seafood) 7839 Vaughn Rd.	Montgomery	AL	36116	334-272-3366
Martha's Place (Southern) 458 Sayre St.	Montgomery	AL	36104	334-263-9135
Mings Garden (Chinese) 1741 Eastern Bypass.	Montgomery	AL	36117	334-277-8188
New China (Chinese) 3848 Harrison Rd	Montgomery	AL	36109	334-244-4020
Ryan's Family Steakhouse (Steak) 4135 Atlanta Hwy.	Montgomery	AL	36109	334-271-4340
Sahara Restaurant (Steak/Seafood) 511 E Edgemont Ave	Montgomery	AL	36111	334-262-1215
San Marcos (Mexican) 61 N Burbank Dr.	Montgomery	AL	36117	334-279-6680
Sassafras Tea Room (American) 532 Clay St	Montgomery	AL	36104	334-265-7277
Shogun Japanese Steak & Seafood House (Japanese) 5215 Carmichael Rd	Montgomery	AL	36106	334-271-6999
Sinclair's (American) 1051 E Fairview Ave	Montgomery	AL	36106	334-834-7462
TP Crockmiers (Steak/Seafood) 5620 Calmar Dr	Montgomery	AL	36116	334-277-1840
Vineyard & Corner Cafe (Mediterranean) 2960A Zelda Rd	Montgomery	AL	36106	334-271-4441
Vintage Year (American) 407 Cloverdale Rd	Montgomery	AL	36106	334-264-8463
Vittorio's (Italian) 5338 Atlanta Hwy.	Montgomery	AL	36109	334-270-8888

Montgomery — Restaurants (Cont'd)

				Phone
Young House (Southern) 231 N Hull St	Montgomery	AL	36104	334-262-0409

— Goods and Services —

SHOPPING

				Phone	Fax
Eastdale Mall 5501 Atlanta Hwy	Montgomery	AL	36117	334-277-7359	277-1386
Montgomery Mall Southern Blvd & McGehee Rd	Montgomery	AL	36116	334-284-1533	281-4618

BANKS

				Phone	Fax
Aliant Bank PO Box 135	Montgomery	AL	36101	334-270-3000	270-3013
TF: 800-949-5666					
Amsouth Bank 201 Monroe St	Montgomery	AL	36104	334-834-9500	240-1397
TF: 800-333-7485					
Colonial Bank 1 Commerce St	Montgomery	AL	36104	334-240-5000	954-1155*
**Fax:* Hum Res ■ *Web:* www.hsv.tis.net/colonial					
Compass Bank 3480 Eastern Blvd	Montgomery	AL	36116	334-409-7453	409-7312
First Tuskegee Bank 100 Commerce St	Montgomery	AL	36104	334-262-0800	262-4333
Regions Bank 8 Commerce St	Montgomery	AL	36104	800-734-4667	832-8913*
**Fax Area Code:* 334					
Southtrust Bank 210 Water St Union Station	Montgomery	AL	36104	334-270-2340	270-2345
TF Cust Svc: 800-239-2300*					
Sterling Bank 4121 Carmichael Rd Suite 100	Montgomery	AL	36106	334-279-7800	244-4429*
**Fax:* Cust Svc ■ *Web:* www.sterlingmontgomery.com ■ *E-mail:* info@sterlingmontgomery.com					

BUSINESS SERVICES

	Phone
Airborne Express	800-247-2676
BAX Global	800-225-5229
DHL Worldwide Express	800-225-5345
Federal Express	800-238-5355
Interim Personnel	334-260-0788
Kelly Services	334-272-6522
Kinko's	334-277-1477
Mail Boxes Etc	800-789-4623
Manpower Temporary Services	334-281-4441
Montgomery Air Freight	334-281-9157
Post Office	800-275-8777
Snelling Personnel Services	334-270-0100
UPS	800-742-5877

— Media —

PUBLICATIONS

				Phone	Fax
Montgomery Advertiser‡ PO Box 1000	Montgomery	AL	36101	334-262-1611	261-1505
Web: www.accessmontgomery.com					
Montgomery Independent 1810 W 5th St	Montgomery	AL	36106	334-265-7323	265-7320
Web: www.the-independent.com					

‡Daily newspapers

TELEVISION

				Phone	Fax
WAIQ-TV Ch 26 (PBS) 1255 Madison Ave	Montgomery	AL	36107	334-264-9900	264-7045
Web: www.aptv.org					
WAKA-TV Ch 8 (CBS) 3020 East Blvd	Montgomery	AL	36116	334-279-8787	272-6444
Web: www.waka.com ■ *E-mail:* waka@mindspring.com					
WCOV-TV Ch 20 (Fox) PO Box 250045	Montgomery	AL	36125	334-288-7020	288-5414
Web: www.wcov.com ■ *E-mail:* wcovtv20@mont.mindspring.com					
WHOA-TV Ch 32 (ABC) 3251 Harrison Rd	Montgomery	AL	36109	334-270-3200	271-6348
Web: www.whoa32.com					
WSFA-TV Ch 12 (NBC) PO Box 251200	Montgomery	AL	36125	334-288-1212	613-8303
Web: www.wsfa.com ■ *E-mail:* wsfanews12@aol.com					

RADIO

				Phone	Fax
WACV-AM 1170 kHz (N/T) PO Box 210723	Montgomery	AL	36121	334-244-1170	244-1176
WBAM-FM 98.9 MHz (CHR) PO Box 210519	Montgomery	AL	36121	334-213-0598	279-9563
Web: www.star989.com					
WHHY-FM 101.9 MHz (CHR) 3435 Norman Bridge Rd	Montgomery	AL	36105	334-264-2288	834-9102
WLBF-FM 89.1 MHz (Rel) PO Box 210789	Montgomery	AL	36121	334-271-8900	260-8962
E-mail: spaceradio@mindsprung.com					
WLWI-FM 92.3 MHz (Ctry) PO Box 4999	Montgomery	AL	36103	334-240-9274	240-9219
Web: www.wlwi.com					
WMSP-AM 740 kHz (Sports) 1 Commerce St Suite 300	Montgomery	AL	36104	334-240-9274	240-9219
Web: www.sportsradio740.com					
WNZZ-AM 950 kHz (B/EZ) 1 Commerce St Suite 300	Montgomery	AL	36104	334-240-9274	240-9219
WRWO-FM 96.1 MHz (AC) PO Box 210723	Montgomery	AL	36121	334-244-0961	279-9563
WVAS-FM 90.7 MHz (NPR) 915 S Jackson St	Montgomery	AL	36101	334-229-4287	269-4995
WXFX-FM 95.1 MHz (Rock) PO Box 250210	Montgomery	AL	36125	334-264-2288	834-9102

— Colleges/Universities —

				Phone	Fax
Alabama State University 915 S Jackson St	Montgomery	AL	36101	334-229-4100	229-4984
TF: 800-253-5037 ■ *Web:* www.alasu.edu					
Auburn University Montgomery 7300 University Dr	Montgomery	AL	36117	334-244-3000	244-3762
TF Admissions: 800-227-2649 ■ *Web:* www.aum.edu					
Faulkner University 5345 Atlanta Hwy	Montgomery	AL	36109	334-272-5820	260-6137
TF: 800-879-9816 ■ *Web:* www.faulkner.edu					
Huntingdon College 1500 E Fairview Ave	Montgomery	AL	36106	334-833-4497	833-4347
TF Admissions: 800-763-0313 ■ *Web:* www.huntingdon.edu					
Patterson John M State Technical College 3920 Troy Hwy	Montgomery	AL	36116	334-288-1080	284-9357
Web: www.jptech.cc.al.us ■ *E-mail:* jptech@montgomerymindstring.com					
South College 122 Commerce St	Montgomery	AL	36104	334-263-1013	262-7326
Web: www.southcollege.edu/campus_mont.htm					
Southern Christian University 1200 Taylor Rd	Montgomery	AL	36117	334-277-2277	387-3878
Web: www.southernchristian.edu ■ *E-mail:* scuniversity@mindspring.com					
Trenholm State Technical College 1225 Air Base Blvd	Montgomery	AL	36108	334-832-9000	832-9777
Web: www.tstc.cc.al.us					
Troy State University University Ave	Troy	AL	36082	334-670-3100	670-3733
Web: www.troyst.edu					

— Hospitals —

				Phone	Fax
Baptist Medical Center South 2105 E South Blvd	Montgomery	AL	36116	334-288-2100	286-5602*
**Fax:* Hum Res					
Jackson Hospital 1725 Pine St	Montgomery	AL	36106	334-293-8000	293-8934*
**Fax:* Hum Res ■ *Web:* www.jackson.org					

— Attractions —

				Phone	Fax
Alabama Artists Gallery 201 Monroe St Suite 110	Montgomery	AL	36104	334-242-4076	240-3269
Alabama Dance Theatre 1018 Madison Ave	Montgomery	AL	36104	334-241-2590	241-2504
Web: www.freenet.tlh.fl.us/ADT/					
Alabama Dept of Archives & History Public Services Div 624 Washington Ave	Montgomery	AL	36130	334-242-4363	240-3433
Alabama Shakespeare Festival Wynton M Blount Cultural Pk	Montgomery	AL	36117	334-271-5353	271-5348
TF: 800-841-4273 ■ *Web:* www.asf.net ■ *E-mail:* pr4bard@wsnet.com					
Alabama State Capitol 600 Dexter Ave	Montgomery	AL	36130	334-242-3750	242-2788
Alabama War Memorial 120 N Jackson St	Montgomery	AL	36104	334-262-6638	262-9694
TF: 800-234-5544					
Civil Rights Memorial 400 Washington Ave	Montgomery	AL	36104	334-264-0286	

Montgomery — Attractions (Cont'd)

				Phone	Fax
Davis Theatre for the Performing Arts 251 Montgomery St *Web:* www.tsum.edu/davis	Montgomery	AL	36104	334-241-9567	241-9756
Dexter Avenue King Memorial Baptist Church 454 Dexter Ave	Montgomery	AL	36104	334-263-3970	263-3970
Eufaula National Wildlife Refuge 509 Old State Hwy 165	Eufaula	AL	36027	334-687-4065	687-5906
Executive Mansion 1142 S Perry St	Montgomery	AL	36104	334-834-3022	240-3466
Faulkner University Dinner Theatre 5345 Atlanta Hwy	Montgomery	AL	36109	334-260-6190	
First White House of the Confederacy 644 Washington Ave	Montgomery	AL	36104	334-242-1861	
Fitzgerald F Scott & Zelda Museum 919 Felder Ave	Montgomery	AL	36106	334-264-4222	
Folmar Anita P Youth Art Gallery 1018 Madison Ave	Montgomery	AL	36104	334-241-2787	241-2504
Gayle WA Planetarium 1010 Forest Ave *Web:* www.tsum.edu/planet	Montgomery	AL	36106	334-241-4799	240-4309
Horseshoe Bend National Military Park 11288 Horseshoe Bend Rd. *Web:* www.nps.gov/hobe/	Daviston	AL	36256	256-234-7111	329-9905
Jasmine Hill Gardens & Outdoor Museum 3001 Jasmine Hill Rd *Web:* www.jasminehill.org ■ *E-mail:* jasminehill@jasminehill.com	Wetumpka	AL	36092	334-567-6463	567-6466
Loard Leon Gallery of Fine Arts 2781 Zelda Rd	Montgomery	AL	36106	334-270-9010	270-0150
Maxwell Air Force Base Air Base Blvd & Day St *Web:* www.maxwell.af.mil	Montgomery	AL	36112	334-953-2014	953-3379
Montgomery Ballet 6009 E Shirley Ln	Montgomery	AL	36117	334-409-0522	409-2311
Montgomery Museum of Fine Arts 1 Museum Dr *Web:* www.fineartsmuseum.com ■ *E-mail:* mmfa@wsnet.com	Montgomery	AL	36117	334-244-5700	244-5774
Montgomery State Farmers Market 1655 Federal Dr *TF:* 800-243-4769	Montgomery	AL	36107	334-242-5350	240-3275
Montgomery Symphony Orchestra 250 Montgomery St Davis Theatre	Montgomery	AL	36104	334-240-4004	240-4034
Montgomery Zoo 2301 Coliseum Pkwy *Web:* www.mindspring.com/~zoonet/montgome/montgome.html	Montgomery	AL	36110	334-240-4900	240-4916
Old Alabama Town 301 Columbus St *TF:* 888-240-1850 ■ *Web:* www.mindspring.com/~olaltown/	Montgomery	AL	36104	334-240-4500	240-4519
Tuskegee Institute National Historic Site 1212 Old Montgomery Rd *Web:* www.nps.gov/tuin/	Tuskegee Institute	AL	36088	334-727-3200	727-4597
World Heritage Museum 119 W Jeff Davis Ave	Montgomery	AL	36104	334-263-7229	

SPORTS TEAMS & FACILITIES

				Phone	Fax
Crampton Bowl Stadium 1022 Madison Ave	Montgomery	AL	36104	334-240-4200	241-2301
Garrett Coliseum 1555 Federal Dr. *Web:* agencies.state.al.us/garrett/	Montgomery	AL	36107	334-242-5597	240-3242
Montgomery Motorsports Park 2600 N Belt Dr	Montgomery	AL	36110	334-260-9660	260-9320
VictoryLand Greyhound Racing Exit 22 off I-85 *Web:* www.victoryland.com ■ *E-mail:* victoryland@worldaccess.com	Shorter	AL	36075	334-269-6087	727-0737

— Events —

	Phone
Alabama Highland Games (late September)	334-361-4571
Blue-Gray All Star Football Classic (December)	334-265-1266
Blue-Gray Intercollegiate Tennis Championship (mid-March)	334-271-7001
Broadway Under the Stars (late August)	334-240-4004
Calico Fort Arts & Crafts Fair (early April)	334-227-3250
Christmas on the River Parade (early December)	800-252-2262
Festival in the Park (early October)	334-241-2300
Flimp Festival (early May)	334-244-5700
Greek Festival (early May)	334-263-1366
Jubilee CityFest (late May)	334-834-7220
Montgomery State Farmers Market Day (mid-July)	334-242-5350
NCAA Division II National Baseball Championship (late May)	334-241-2300
Oktoberfest (early October)	334-272-6527
South Alabama State Fair (early October)	334-272-6831
Taste of Montgomery (November)	334-277-1840
Turkey Day Classic Parade (late November)	334-229-4100
World Championship Rodeo (mid-March)	334-265-1867

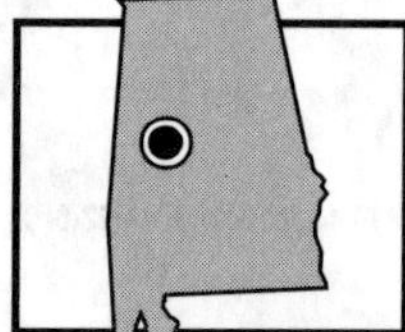

Tuscaloosa

Discovered by Hernando DeSoto in 1540, Tuscaloosa is named after the Choctaw Indian Chief Tushkauloosa. (Literally translated, Tushkauloosa means Black Warrior; the Black Warrior River is the most important river in the area and the largest inland waterway system of any state in the U.S.) Tuscaloosa was the capitol of Alabama from 1826 until 1847, when it was moved to Montgomery. Area architecture features a variety of styles, reflecting the varied influences in home building, including Italianate, French, Greek and Roman Revival, Frontier, Gothic, and Victorian. No other structure in northern Alabama illustrates the French influences on early Alabama architecture as well as The Old Tavern, built in 1827. Its style is similar to buildings in Mobile and New Orleans. The Jemison-Van de Graaff Mansion, an 1863 antebellum mansion, is one of the few remaining examples of Italianate architecture in the South. The McGuire-Strickland House, a raised Creole cottage in Greek Revival style, was built in 1820 and is believed to be the oldest wood-frame structure in Tuscaloosa County. The oldest operating theatre in Tuscaloosa is the Bama Theater. Two of the colleges in Tuscaloosa are The University of Alabama, home to the Crimson Tide football team as well as the Paul W. Bryant Museum (Paul "Bear" Bryant was the team's long-time coach); and Stillman College, which was founded in 1876 to train black ministers. Today, Stillman is a private college, and the renowned Stillman College Choir performs regularly in the area and around the U.S. Popular events in Tuscaloosa include the Kentuck Arts Festival in October, the International Cityfest in August, and the Sakura Festival in March.

Population	83,376	**Longitude**	87-32-27 W
Area (Land)	47.1 sq mi	**County**	Tuscaloosa
Area (Water)	10.1 sq mi	**Time Zone**	CST
Elevation	227 ft	**Area Code/s**	205
Latitude	33-14-15 N		

— Average Temperatures and Precipitation —

TEMPERATURES

	Jan	Feb	Mar	Apr	May	Jun	Jul	Aug	Sep	Oct	Nov	Dec
High	53	58	68	76	83	89	91	91	86	77	66	57
Low	32	36	44	51	59	67	71	70	64	51	42	36

PRECIPITATION

	Jan	Feb	Mar	Apr	May	Jun	Jul	Aug	Sep	Oct	Nov	Dec
Inches	5.5	5.3	6.6	5.5	4.3	3.8	5.0	3.5	3.3	3.4	4.1	5.2

— Important Phone Numbers —

	Phone		Phone
AAA	205-759-1202	**Poison Control Center**	800-462-0800
Emergency	911	**Weather**	205-979-1300
Medical Referral	205-759-7742		

— Information Sources —

				Phone	Fax
Better Business Bureau Serving Central Alabama & the Wiregrass Area PO Box 55268 *Web:* www.birmingham-al.bbb.org	Birmingham	AL	35255	205-558-2222	558-2239
Chamber of Commerce of West Alabama PO Box 020410 *Web:* www.tuscaloosachamber.com ■ *E-mail:* chamber@dbtech.net	Tuscaloosa	AL	35402	205-758-7588	391-0565

Tuscaloosa — Information Sources (Cont'd)

				Phone	Fax
Tuscaloosa City Hall 2201 University Blvd	Tuscaloosa	AL	35401	205-349-2010	349-0214*
**Fax:* Hum Res ■ *Web:* www.ci.tuscaloosa.al.us					
Tuscaloosa Convention & Visitors Bureau PO Box 3167	Tuscaloosa	AL	35403	205-391-9200	391-2125
TF: 800-538-8696 ■ *Web:* www.tcvb.org ■ *E-mail:* tuscacvb@dbtech.net					
Tuscaloosa County PO Box 20113	Tuscaloosa	AL	35402	205-349-3870	
Tuscaloosa Mayor 2201 University Blvd City Hall	Tuscaloosa	AL	35401	205-349-0200	
Tuscaloosa Public Library 1801 River Rd	Tuscaloosa	AL	35401	205-345-5820	752-8300
Web: tuscaloosa-library.org					
West Alabama Planning & Development Council 4200 Hwy 69 N Suite 1	Northport	AL	35473	205-333-2990	333-2713
Web: www.uronramp.net/~wapdc ■ *E-mail:* wapdc@coa.state.al.us					

On-Line Resources

4Tuscaloosa.com	www.4tuscaloosa.com
Area Guide Tuscaloosa	tuscaloosa.areaguides.net
City Knowledge Tuscaloosa	www.cityknowledge.com/al_tuscaloosa.htm
Excite.com Tuscaloosa City Guide	www.excite.com/travel/countries/united_states/alabama/tuscaloosa
NITC Travelbase City Guide Tuscaloosa	www.travelbase.com/auto/guides/tuscaloosa-al.html
Online City Guide to Tuscaloosa	www.olcg.com/al/tcl/main.html
Tuscaloosa Online	www.dbtech.net/tuscaloosa
Tuscaloosa Weather Underground	www.wunderground.com/forecasts/TCL.html
Tuscaloosa Web Directory	www.tuscaloosaweb.com

— Transportation Services —

AIRPORTS

	Phone
■ **Birmingham International Airport (BHM)**	
75 miles NE of downtown Tuscaloosa (approx 65 minutes)	205-595-0533

Airport Transportation

	Phone
Birmingham Door to Door $35-45 fare to downtown Tuscaloosa	205-591-5550
Radio Cab $60-65 fare to downtown Tuscaloosa	205-758-2831

Commercial Airlines

	Phone		Phone
AirTran	800-247-8726	**Southwest**	800-435-9792
American	800-433-7300	**TWA**	800-221-2000
Comair	800-354-9822	**United**	800-241-6522
Delta	800-221-1212	**US Airways**	800-428-4322
Northwest	800-225-2525	**US Airways Express**	800-428-4322

Charter Airlines

	Phone		Phone
Alliance Executive Charter Services	800-232-5387	**Flying M Aviation Inc.**	800-359-0357
Bama Air Inc.	205-349-3991	**Signature Flight Support**	205-849-3834
		United Beechcraft	205-591-6830

CAR RENTALS

	Phone		Phone
Alamo-Birmingham	205-592-2200	**Enterprise**	205-349-4446
Avis	205-345-3333	**Enterprise-Birmingham**	205-323-4446
Avis-Birmingham	205-592-8901	**Hertz-Birmingham**	205-591-6090
Budget-Birmingham	205-322-3596	**National-Birmingham**	205-592-7259

LIMO/TAXI

	Phone		Phone
Stardust Limousine	205-349-5466	**Tuscaloosa Radio Cab**	205-349-3669

MASS TRANSIT

	Phone
Tuscaloosa Transit $.80 Base fare	205-556-3876

RAIL/BUS

				Phone
Amtrak Station 2105 Greensboro Ave	Tuscaloosa	AL	35401	800-872-7245
Greyhound Bus Station 2520 Stillman Blvd	Tuscaloosa	AL	35401	205-758-6651
TF: 800-231-2222				

— Accommodations —

HOTEL RESERVATION SERVICES

	Phone	Fax
American International Travel	800-782-9872	897-4007*
**Fax Area Code:* 727 ■ *TF:* 800-681-3965		

HOTELS, MOTELS, RESORTS

				Phone	Fax
Bel-Aire Motel 3715 University Blvd E	Tuscaloosa	AL	35404	205-553-3560	
Best Western Catalina Inn 2015 McFarland Blvd	Northport	AL	35476	205-339-5200	330-1335
TF: 800-528-1234					
Best Western Park Plaza 3801 McFarland Blvd E	Tuscaloosa	AL	35406	205-556-9690	556-9690
TF: 800-235-7282					
Comfort Inn 4501 McFarland Blvd E	Tuscaloosa	AL	35401	205-345-1434	345-1434
TF: 800-228-5150					
Country Inn & Suites 4801 McFarland Blvd	Tuscaloosa	AL	35401	205-345-9999	
Courtyard by Marriott 4115 Courtney Dr	Tuscaloosa	AL	35405	205-750-8384	750-8389
TF: 800-321-2211					
Crimson Inn 1509 University Blvd	Tuscaloosa	AL	35401	205-758-3483	
Days Inn Suites 1201 Skyland Blvd	Tuscaloosa	AL	35401	205-759-5000	759-9864
TF: 800-329-7466					
Econo Lodge & Suites 1930 McFarland Blvd	Northport	AL	35476	205-330-0345	330-0345
TF: 800-553-2666					
Fairfield Inn 4101 Courtney Dr	Tuscaloosa	AL	35401	205-366-0900	366-0900
TF: 800-228-2800					
Four Points by Sheraton 320 Bryant Dr	Tuscaloosa	AL	35401	205-752-3200	343-1136
TF: 800-477-2262					
Hampton Inn 6400 Interstate Dr	Cottondale	AL	35453	205-562-9000	562-9859
TF: 800-426-7866					
Hampton Inn University 600 Harper Lee Dr	Tuscaloosa	AL	35404	205-553-9800	553-0082
TF: 800-426-7866					
Jameson Inn 5021 Oscar Baxter Rd	Tuscaloosa	AL	35405	205-345-5018	345-5828
TF: 800-526-3766					
Key West Inn 4700 Doris Pate Dr	Tuscaloosa	AL	35405	205-556-3232	556-7797
TF: 800-311-3811					
Knights Inn 4810 Skyland Blvd	Tuscaloosa	AL	35405	205-556-1330	556-1330
TF: 800-843-5644					
La Quinta Inn 4122 McFarland Blvd E	Tuscaloosa	AL	35405	205-349-3270	758-0440
TF: 800-531-5900					
Masters Economy Inn 3600 McFarland Blvd	Tuscaloosa	AL	35405	205-556-2010	556-8522
TF: 800-633-3434					
Microtel Inn 6331 Interstate Dr	Tuscaloosa	AL	35401	205-556-1555	556-9722
TF: 888-771-7171					
Moon Winx Lodge 3410 University Blvd E	Tuscaloosa	AL	35404	205-553-1520	
Motel 6 4700 McFarland Blvd	Tuscaloosa	AL	35405	205-759-4942	759-1093
TF: 800-466-8356					
Ole English Inn 3100 University Dr E	Tuscaloosa	AL	35404	205-553-3640	
Quality Inn 4541 Jug Factory Rd	Tuscaloosa	AL	35401	205-759-9878	759-9878
Ramada Inn 631 Skyland Blvd E	Tuscaloosa	AL	35405	205-759-4431	758-9655
TF: 800-272-6232					
Shoney's Inn 3501 McFarland Blvd E	Tuscaloosa	AL	35405	205-556-7950	556-5119
TF: 800-222-2222					
Sleep Inn 4300 Skyland Blvd	Tuscaloosa	AL	35405	205-556-5696	556-5696
Super 8 Motel 4125 McFarland Blvd	Tuscaloosa	AL	35405	205-758-8878	752-8331
TF: 800-800-8000					
Travelodge 3920 E McFarland Blvd	Tuscaloosa	AL	35405	205-553-1550	553-1550
TF: 800-578-7878					

— Restaurants —

				Phone
Alabama Grill (American) 514 Greensboro Ave	Tuscaloosa	AL	35401	205-345-0846
C & B Restaurant (American) 3380 McFarland Blvd N	Tuscaloosa	AL	35401	205-333-8150
Cancun Restaurant (Mexican) 2200 McFarland Blvd E	Tuscaloosa	AL	35404	205-758-0875
Catfish Heaven (Seafood) 2502 21st St	Tuscaloosa	AL	35401	205-752-7222
Champs Sports Grille (American) 320 Bryant Dr Sheraton Hotel	Tuscaloosa	AL	35401	205-752-3200
City Cafe (American) 408 Main Ave	Northport	AL	35476	205-758-9171
Cocopelli's Cafe (Continental) 1410 University Blvd Suite 2	Tuscaloosa	AL	35401	205-349-4033

Tuscaloosa — Restaurants (Cont'd)

				Phone
Country Hic Cafe (Barbecue) 4215 Greensboro Ave	Tuscaloosa	AL	35405	205-345-6114
Country Kitchen (Homestyle) 4416 Skyland Blvd E.	Tuscaloosa	AL	35405	205-553-4710
Crimson Cafe (American) 1301 University Blvd	Tuscaloosa	AL	35401	205-750-0203
DePalma's (Italian) 2300 University Blvd	Tuscaloosa	AL	35401	205-759-1879
Web: www.depalmascafe.com ■ *E-mail:* info@depalmascafe.com				
Evangeline's (Continental) 1653 McFarland Blvd N	Tuscaloosa	AL	35406	205-752-0830
Ezell's Catfish Cabin (American) 3520 McFarland Blvd E	Tuscaloosa	AL	35405	205-553-0881
Foxfire (Barbecue) 13242 Hwy 69 S.	Tuscaloosa	AL	35405	205-752-5000
Globe The (American) 430 Main Ave	Northport	AL	35476	205-391-0949
Golden Crown (Chinese) 502 15th St	Tuscaloosa	AL	35401	205-758-1234
Harvey's (American) 4710 McFarland Blvd E.	Tuscaloosa	AL	35405	205-553-8466
Hickory Pit (Barbecue) 2417 Skyland Blvd E	Tuscaloosa	AL	35401	205-556-8454
Horne's (Barbecue) 101 15th St.	Tuscaloosa	AL	35401	205-752-1913
Jack's (American) 1200 Hackberry Ln	Tuscaloosa	AL	35401	205-758-6520
Johnny Ray's (Barbecue) 415 15th St	Tuscaloosa	AL	35401	205-349-1600
Logan's Roadhouse (American) 1511 Skyland Blvd	Tuscaloosa	AL	35401	205-349-3554
Mezzanine The (Continental) 508 Greensboro Ave	Tuscaloosa	AL	35401	205-752-0020
Moma Jewels (Homestyle) 5600 McFarland Blvd E	Tuscaloosa	AL	35405	205-752-7580
New Millenium (American) 1753 Eutaw Hwy.	Tuscaloosa	AL	35401	205-758-2583
O'Charley's (Continental) 3799 McFarland Blvd	Tuscaloosa	AL	35405	205-556-5143
Pepito's (Mexican) 1301 McFarland Blvd N.	Tuscaloosa	AL	35406	205-391-4861
Rama Jama's (American) 1000 Paul Bryant Dr	Tuscaloosa	AL	35401	205-750-0901
Steamers (Seafood) 500 15th St	Tuscaloosa	AL	35401	205-752-5522
Thai House (Thai) 1306 University Blvd Suite D.	Tuscaloosa	AL	35401	205-758-7426
Thomas Bar-B-Que (Barbecue) 1406 Crescent Ridge Rd NE.	Tuscaloosa	AL	35404	205-553-3942
Trey Yuen (Chinese) 4200 McFarland Blvd E.	Tuscaloosa	AL	35405	205-752-0088
Uncle Abe's (American) 900 Skyland Blvd E	Tuscaloosa	AL	35405	205-759-2238
Waysider The (American) 1512 Greensboro Ave	Tuscaloosa	AL	35401	205-345-8239
Wing's Sports Grille (American) 500 Harper Lee Dr.	Tuscaloosa	AL	35401	205-556-5658
Woodrow's Bar-B-Que (Barbecue) 9711 Hwy 43 N	Tuscaloosa	AL	35401	205-333-1033
Wright's Restaurant (American) 927 26th Ave E	Tuscaloosa	AL	35404	205-553-0694

— Goods and Services —

SHOPPING

				Phone	Fax
McFarland Mall 900 Skyland Blvd E	Tuscaloosa	AL	35405	205-759-4794	759-5163
Spiller Antique Mall 2420 7th St	Tuscaloosa	AL	35401	205-391-0308	391-0329
University Mall 1701 McFarland Blvd E.	Tuscaloosa	AL	35401	205-553-8414	554-0993

BANKS

				Phone	Fax
AmSouth Bank 719 Skyland Blvd E.	Tuscaloosa	AL	35405	205-391-5765	758-9402
Bank of Tuscaloosa 2735 University Blvd E	Tuscaloosa	AL	35404	205-391-1085	391-1089
Compass Bank 2350 McFarland Blvd E	Tuscaloosa	AL	35404	205-391-2565	391-2554
TF: 800-239-5175					
First Federal Bank FSB 2315 9th St Suite 1	Tuscaloosa	AL	35401	205-391-6700	391-6714
TF: 800-239-6929					
National Bank of Commerce 1101 Greensboro Ave	Tuscaloosa	AL	35401	205-345-5870	759-1102
Regions Bank 2222 9th St	Tuscaloosa	AL	35401	205-345-4610	750-2692
Security Federal Bank 2301 University Blvd	Tuscaloosa	AL	35401	205-345-8800	758-5616
Southtrust Bank 4239 University Blvd E	Tuscaloosa	AL	35404	205-391-0252	391-0254
West Alabama Bank & Trust 1501 Skyland Blvd E Suite E	Tuscaloosa	AL	35405	205-759-8480	759-2180

BUSINESS SERVICES

	Phone		Phone
Kelly Services	205-759-4451	**Post Office**	205-344-6000
Kwik Kopy Printing	205-507-1112	**Printing One**	205-391-9211
Mail Boxes Etc	205-345-5345	**UPS**	800-742-5877

— Media —

PUBLICATIONS

				Phone	Fax
Tuscaloosa News‡ PO Box 20587	Tuscaloosa	AL	35402	205-345-0505	349-0802

‡*Daily newspapers*

TELEVISION

				Phone	Fax
WABM-TV Ch 68 (UPN) 651 Beacon Pkwy W Suite 105	Birmingham	AL	35209	205-943-2168	290-2115
WBRC-TV Ch 6 (Fox) PO Box 6	Birmingham	AL	35201	205-322-6666	583-4356
Web: www.wbrc.com ■ *E-mail:* info@wbrc.com					
WCFT-TV Ch 33 (ABC) 800 Concourse Pkwy Suite 200	Birmingham	AL	35244	205-403-3340	982-3942
Web: www.abc3340.com ■ *E-mail:* info@www.abc3340.com					
WIAT-TV Ch 42 (CBS) PO Box 59496	Birmingham	AL	35259	205-322-4200	320-2713
WJRD-TV Ch 49 (PAX) 5455 Jug Factory Rd	Tuscaloosa	AL	35405	205-349-4902	349-4369
TF: 888-557-4949 ■ *Web:* www.newschannel49.com ■ *E-mail:* sky49@dbtech.net					
WTTO-TV Ch 21 (WB) 651 Beacon Pkwy W Suite 105	Birmingham	AL	35209	205-943-2168	290-2115
WVTM-TV Ch 13 (NBC) 1732 Valley View Dr	Birmingham	AL	35209	205-933-1313	323-3314
Web: www.nbc13.com					

RADIO

				Phone	Fax
WACT-AM 1420 kHz (Rel) 3900 11th Ave S.	Tuscaloosa	AL	35401	205-333-9800	333-8834*
**Fax:* Sales					
WLXY-FM 100.7 MHz (CR) 142 Skyland Blvd	Tuscaloosa	AL	35405	205-345-7200	349-1715
Web: www.wlxy.com					
WOWC-FM 102.5 MHz (Ctry) 530 Beacon Pkwy W Suite 600	Birmingham	AL	35209	205-439-9600	439-8390
Web: www.wowc.com					
WQZZ-FM 104.3 MHz (Urban) 601 Greensboro Ave Suite 507	Tuscaloosa	AL	35401	205-345-4787	345-4790
WRTR-FM 105.5 MHz (Rock) 3900 11th Ave S.	Tuscaloosa	AL	35401	205-333-9800	333-8834*
**Fax:* Sales					
WTBC-AM 1230 kHz (N/T) 2110 McFarland Blvd E Suite C.	Tuscaloosa	AL	35404	205-758-5523	752-9696
Web: www.wtbc1230.com ■ *E-mail:* wtbc@dbtech.net					
WTID-FM 101.7 MHz (AC) 142 Skyland Blvd	Tuscaloosa	AL	35405	205-345-7200	349-1715
WTSK-AM 790 kHz (Rel) 142 Skyland Blvd	Tuscaloosa	AL	35405	205-345-7200	349-1715
WTUG-FM 92.9 MHz (AC) 142 Skyland Blvd	Tuscaloosa	AL	35405	205-345-7200	349-1715
Web: www.wtug.com ■ *E-mail:* wtug@dbtech.net					
WTXT-FM 98.1 MHz (Ctry) 3900 11th Ave S.	Tuscaloosa	AL	35401	205-333-9800	333-8834*
**Fax:* Sales ■ *Web:* wtxt.com ■ *E-mail:* wtxt@tusc.net					
WUAL-FM 91.5 MHz (NPR) University of Alabama Phifer Hall Suite 297	Tuscaloosa	AL	35487	205-348-6644	348-6648
Web: www.wual.ua.edu					
WWPG-AM 1280 kHz (Rel) 601 Greensboro Ave Suite 507	Tuscaloosa	AL	35401	205-345-4787	345-4790
WZBQ-FM 94.1 MHz (CHR) 3900 11th Ave S.	Tuscaloosa	AL	35402	205-333-9800	333-8834*
**Fax:* Sales					

— Colleges/Universities —

Name	City	State	Zip	Phone	Fax
Shelton State Community College 950 Old Greensboro Rd	Tuscaloosa	AL	35405	205-759-1541	391-3910
Web: www.shelton.cc.al.us/					
Stillman College PO Box 1430	Tuscaloosa	AL	35403	205-349-4240	366-8996
TF: 800-841-5722 ■ *Web:* www.stillman.edu					
University of Alabama PO Box 870132	Tuscaloosa	AL	35487	205-348-6010	348-9046
TF Admissions: 800-933-2262 ■ *Web:* www.ua.edu					

— Hospitals —

Name	City	State	Zip	Phone	Fax
DCH Regional Medical Center 809 University Blvd E	Tuscaloosa	AL	35401	205-759-7111	759-6168
Web: www.dchhealthcare.com ■ *E-mail:* info@dchhealthcare.com					

— Attractions —

Name	City	State	Zip	Phone	Fax
Alabama Museum of Natural History 6th Ave Smith Hall University of Alabama	Tuscaloosa	AL	35487	205-348-7550	348-9292

Tuscaloosa — Attractions (Cont'd)

				Phone	Fax
Arts Council of Tuscaloosa 600 Greensboro Ave	Tuscaloosa	AL	35401	205-758-8083	345-2787
TF: 800-239-1611					
Bama Theatre 600 Greensboro Ave	Tuscaloosa	AL	35401	205-758-5195	
Battle-Friedman House 1010 Greensboro Ave	Tuscaloosa	AL	35401	205-758-6138	
Children's Hands-On Museum 2213 University Blvd	Tuscaloosa	AL	35401	205-349-4235	349-4276
E-mail: chom@dbtech.net					
First Thursday Art Nights 503 Main Ave	Tuscaloosa	AL	35401	205-758-1257	
Gorgas House Capstone Dr University of Alabama Campus	Tuscaloosa	AL	35401	205-348-5906	
Jemison-Van de Graaff Mansion 1305 Greensboro Ave	Tuscaloosa	AL	35401	205-391-9200	
Kentuck Art Center 503 Main Ave	Northport	AL	35476	205-758-1257	
Kentuck Gallery 503 Main Ave	Northport	AL	35476	205-758-1257	
Kentuck Museum & Annex 503 Main Ave	Northport	AL	35476	205-758-1257	
Lake Lurleen State Park Hwy 82 W	Coker	AL	25452	205-391-9200	
McGuire-Strickland House 2828 6th St	Tuscaloosa	AL	35401	205-758-2238	
Mercedes-Benz Visitor Center 1 Mercedes Dr	Vance	AL	35490	205-507-2252	507-2255
TF: 888-286-8762					
Mildred Warner House 1925 8th St	Tuscaloosa	AL	35401	205-553-6200	
Moody Sarah Gallery of Art 103 Garland Hall University of Alabama Campus	Tuscaloosa	AL	35401	205-348-1890	
Mound State Monument Hwy 69	Moundville	AL	35474	205-348-7550	
Moundville State Archaeological Park 1 Mound Pkwy	Moundville	AL	35474	205-371-2572	371-4180
Web: www.ua.edu/mndville.htm					
Murphy Will J African American Museum 2601 Bryant Dr Murphy-Collins Home	Tuscaloosa	AL	35401	205-758-2861	
Old Tavern Museum 500 28th Ave	Tuscaloosa	AL	35401	205-758-2238	758-8163
Oliver Lock & Dam 3955 3rd St S	Northport	AL	35476		
Paul W Bryant (Bear) Museum 300 Paul W Bryant Dr	Tuscaloosa	AL	35487	205-348-4668	348-8883
Web: www.ua.edu/pwbryant.htm					
Renaissance Art Gallery 431 Main Ave	Northport	AL	35476	205-752-4422	752-4422
Tannehill Ironworks Historical State Park 12632 Confederate Pkwy	McCalla	AL	35111	205-477-5711	477-9400
Web: www.tannehill.org/					
Theatre Tuscaloosa 9500 Old Greensboro Rd Box 135	Tuscaloosa	AL	35405	205-391-2277	
Tuscaloosa Capitol 2800 6th St Capitol Pk	Tuscaloosa	AL	35401	205-752-2575	
Tuscaloosa Children's Theatre PO Box 0020496	Tuscaloosa	AL	35401	205-553-8102	
Tuscaloosa County Preservation Society 500 28th Ave	Tuscaloosa	AL	35401	205-758-2238	
Tuscaloosa Symphony Orchestra 614 Greensboro Ave	Tuscaloosa	AL	35401	205-752-5515	345-2787
University of Alabama Arboretum Pelham Loop Rd	Tuscaloosa	AL	35401	205-553-3278	553-3278
University of Alabama Moody Music Building 810 2nd Ave	Tuscaloosa	AL	35401	205-348-7110	348-1473

SPORTS TEAMS & FACILITIES

				Phone
Greenetrack Greyhound Park I-59 at Exit 45 Union Rd	Eutaw	AL	35462	205-372-9318

— Events —

	Phone
Bryant Namesake Reunion (early September)	800-538-8696
Dickens Downtown (early December)	800-538-8696
Heritage Week (mid-April)	800-538-8696
Hilaritas (early December)	800-538-8696
International CityFest & Weindorf (late August)	205-553-9009
Kentuck Festival of the Arts (mid-late October)	205-758-1257
Moundville Easter Pageant (mid-April)	800-538-8696
Moundville Native American Festival (late September-early October)	800-538-8696
Sakura Festival (March)	800-538-8696
Tannehill Dulcimer Festival (early May)	205-477-5711
Tannehill Trade Days (late March-November)	205-477-5711
Tuscaloosa Christmas Afloat (mid-December)	800-538-8696
West Alabama Christmas Parade (early December)	800-538-8696

Alaska

Population (1999): 619,500 **Area (sq mi): 656,424**

— State Information Sources —

				Phone	Fax
Alaska Commerce & Economic Development Dept					
333 Willoughby Ave 9th Fl	Juneau	AK	99811	907-465-2500	465-5442
Web: www.commerce.state.ak.us					
Alaska Parks & Outdoor Recreation Div					
3601 C St Suite 1200	Anchorage	AK	99503	907-269-8700	269-8907
Web: www.dnr.state.ak.us/parks/ ■ *E-mail:* tic@dnr.state.ak.us					
Alaska State Chamber of Commerce					
217 2nd St Suite 201	Juneau	AK	99801	907-586-2323	463-5515
Web: www.alaskachamber.com/ ■ *E-mail:* asccjuno@ptialaska.net					
Alaska State Government Information				907-465-2111	
Web: www.state.ak.us					
Alaska State Library PO Box 110571	Juneau	AK	99811	907-465-2910	465-2151
Web: sled.alaska.edu					
Alaska Tourism Div PO Box 99801	Juneau	AK	99811	907-465-2012	465-2287
Web: www.commerce.state.ak.us/tourism/homenew.htm					

ON-LINE RESOURCES

Alaska Cities . . . . dir.yahoo.com/Regional/U_S__States/Alaska/Cities
Alaska Cities By Borough . . . dir.yahoo.com/Regional/U_S__States/Alaska/Boroughs__Census_Areas__and_Regions
Alaska Guide . . . . www.alaskaguide.com
Alaska Information Cache . . . . www.akcache.com/akhome.html
Alaska Internet Travel Guide . . . . www.alaskaone.com/travel
Alaska Online Highways . . . . www.akohwy.com
Alaska Scenario . . . . scenariousa.dstylus.com/ak/indexf.htm
Alaska State Guide & Vacation Planner . . . . www.travelalaska.com
Alaska Travel & Tourism Guide . . . . www.travel-library.com/north_america/usa/alaska/index.html
Alaska's Inside Passage . . . . www.alaskainfo.org
Alaskan.com . . . . www.alaskan.com
Allure of Alaska . . . . www.allurealaska.com
North to Alaska . . . . www.north-to-alaska.com
Rough Guide Travel Alaska travel.roughguides.com/content/1587/index.htm
Tour Alaska . . . . www.alaskanet.com/Tourism
Travel.org-Alaska . . . . travel.org/alaska.html
Yahoo! Get Local Alaska . . . . dir.yahoo.com/Regional/U_S__States/Alaska

— Cities Profiled —

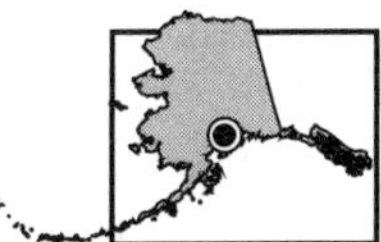

Anchorage

Located as far west as Honolulu and as far north as Helsinki, Finland, Anchorage is home to 40 percent of Alaska's population. Its location on Cook Inlet keeps mid-winter high temperatures in the 20s, allowing year-round outdoor activities. The area's national parks and forests are home to bears, moose, wolves, lynx, Dall sheep, mountain goats, and bald eagles. Mount McKinley, America's highest peak, is in Denali National Park, 122 miles north of Anchorage. Alaska's official sport, dog mushing, is showcased every spring in the 1,049-mile Iditarod Sled Dog Race from Anchorage to Nome.

Population	254,982	**Longitude**	149-90-03 W
Area (Land)	1697.6 sq mi	**County**	Anchorage Borough
Area (Water)	263.9 sq mi	**Time Zone**	Alaska
Elevation	101 ft	**Area Code/s**	907
Latitude	61-21-81 N		

— Average Temperatures and Precipitation —

TEMPERATURES

	Jan	Feb	Mar	Apr	May	Jun	Jul	Aug	Sep	Oct	Nov	Dec
High	21	26	33	43	54	62	65	63	55	41	27	23
Low	8	12	18	29	39	47	52	50	42	29	15	10

PRECIPITATION

	Jan	Feb	Mar	Apr	May	Jun	Jul	Aug	Sep	Oct	Nov	Dec
Inches	0.8	0.8	0.7	0.7	0.7	1.1	1.7	2.4	2.7	2.0	1.1	1.1

— Important Phone Numbers —

	Phone		Phone
AAA	907-344-4310	**Medical Referral**	907-562-1567
American Express Travel	907-266-6600	**Poison Control Center**	907-261-3193
Dental Referral	907-279-9144	**Road Conditions**	907-273-6037
Emergency	911	**Time/Temp**	844
Events Line	907-276-3200	**Weather**	907-936-2525
HotelDocs	800-468-3537		

— Information Sources —

				Phone	Fax
Anchorage Chamber of Commerce 441 W 5th Ave Suite 300 *Web:* www.anchoragechamber.org	Anchorage	AK	99501	907-272-2401	272-4117
Anchorage City Hall PO Box 196650 *Web:* www.ci.anchorage.ak.us	Anchorage	AK	99519	907-343-4311	
Anchorage Community Planning & Development Dept PO Box 196650 *Web:* www.ci.anchorage.ak.us/Services/Departments/Com ■ *E-mail:* wwcpd@ci.anchorage.ak.us	Anchorage	AK	99519	907-343-4309	343-4220
Anchorage Convention & Visitors Bureau 524 W 4th Ave *TF:* 800-446-5352 ■ *Web:* www.anchorage.net ■ *E-mail:* info@anchorage.net	Anchorage	AK	99501	907-276-4118	278-5559
Anchorage Mayor PO Box 196650 *Web:* www.ci.anchorage.ak.us/Mayor ■ *E-mail:* cityhall@ci.anchorage.ak.us	Anchorage	AK	99519	907-343-4431	343-4499
Anchorage Municipality PO Box 196650 *Web:* www.ci.anchorage.ak.us/Services	Anchorage	AK	99519	907-343-4311	343-4313
Better Business Bureau Serving Alaska 2805 Bering St Suite 5 *Web:* www.alaska.bbb.org ■ *E-mail:* info@anchorage.bbb.org	Anchorage	AK	99503	907-562-0704	562-4061
Loussac ZJ Library 3600 Denali St *Web:* www.ci.anchorage.ak.us/Services/Departments/Culture/Library/hour.html#loussac	Anchorage	AK	99503	907-343-2975	562-1244
William A Egan Civic & Convention Center 555 W 5th Ave *Web:* www.egancenter.com ■ *E-mail:* egan@egancenter.com	Anchorage	AK	99501	907-263-2800	263-2858

On-Line Resources

4Anchorage.com	www.4anchorage.com
Alaska's Best	alaskasbest.com
Anchorage CityLink	www.usacitylink.com/anchor
Anchorage Home Page	www.alaskaone.com/anchorage
Anchorage Online	www.alaskanet.com/Anchorage
Anchorage Points of Interest	www.alaska-online.com
Anchorage Restaurant Guide	www.akdining.com
Area Guide Anchorage	anchorage.areaguides.net
Bell's Alaska Travel Guide Anchorage	www.alaskan.com/bells/anchorage.html
City Knowledge Anchorage	www.cityknowledge.com/ak_anchorage.htm
Excite.com Anchorage City Guide	www.excite.com/travel/countries/united_states/alaska/anchorage
Interactive Anchorage Walking Tour	www.alaskadirect.com/walktour.html
Onroute Destinations Anchorage	www.onroute.com/destinations/alaska/anchorage.html

— Transportation Services —

AIRPORTS

■ **Anchorage International Airport (ANC)**

	Phone
5 miles SW of downtown (approx 15 minutes) Web: www.dot.state.ak.us/external/aias/aia/aiawlcm.htm	907-266-2525

Airport Transportation

	Phone
Yellow Cab $12-14 fare to downtown	907-272-2422

Commercial Airlines

	Phone		Phone
Alaska	907-266-7200	**ERA Aviation**	800-866-8394
Continental	800-525-0280	**Korean Air**	907-243-3329
Delta	800-221-1212	**Northwest**	800-225-2525

Charter Airlines

	Phone		Phone
Alaska Bush Carrier Inc	907-243-3127	**Ketchum Air Service Inc**	907-243-5525
Birchwood Air Service	907-276-0402	**Regal Air**	907-243-8535
Evergreen Helicopters of Alaska Inc	907-276-2454	**Rust's Flying Service Inc**	907-243-1595
FS Air Service Inc	907-248-9595	**Security Aviation Inc**	907-248-2677
Jayhawk Air	907-276-4404	**Spernak Airways Inc**	907-272-9475

CAR RENTALS

	Phone		Phone
Affordable	907-243-3370	**Hertz**	907-243-4118
Alamo	907-248-0017	**National**	907-243-3406
Avis	907-243-2377	**Thrifty**	907-276-2855
Budget	907-243-0150	**U-Save Auto**	907-272-8728
Dollar	907-248-5338		

LIMO/TAXI

	Phone		Phone
A Touch of Class Limousine	907-562-2498	**Luxury Limousine**	907-562-6274
Alaska Cab	907-563-5353	**My Chauffeur Limousine**	907-562-5466
Anchorage Taxi	907-278-8000	**Prestige Limousine**	907-243-6669
Checker Cab	907-276-1234	**Yellow Cab**	907-272-2422

MASS TRANSIT

	Phone
People Mover $1 Base fare	907-343-6543

RAIL/BUS

				Phone
Alaska Railroad Station 411 W 1st Ave	Anchorage	AK	99501	907-265-2494

Anchorage (Cont'd)

— Accommodations —

HOTEL RESERVATION SERVICES

	Phone	Fax
Adventure Alaska Bed & Breakfast Reservations	907-243-0265	243-2557
Web: www.alaska.net/~alaskabb/ ■ *E-mail:* alaskabb@alaska.net		
Alaska Sourdough Bed & Breakfast Assn	907-563-6244	563-6073
Web: www.alaskan.com/aksourdoughbba/ ■ *E-mail:* aksbba@alaska.net		
Anchorage Adventures & Accommodations	907-344-4676	274-4671
TF: 888-655-4723		

HOTELS, MOTELS, RESORTS

Name / Address	City	State	ZIP	Phone	Fax
8th Avenue Hotel 630 W 8th Ave	Anchorage	AK	99501	907-274-6213	272-6308
TF: 800-478-4837					
Alaska Wilderness Plantation 2910 W 31st Ave	Anchorage	AK	99517	907-243-3519	243-1059
TF: 800-478-9657 ■ *Web:* www.jakesalaska.com/					
Anchorage Eagle Nest Hotel 4110 Spenard Rd	Anchorage	AK	99517	907-243-3433	248-9258
TF: 800-848-7852					
Anchorage Hotel 330 'E' St	Anchorage	AK	99501	907-272-4553	277-4483
TF: 800-544-0988					
Anchorage Suite Lodge 441 E 15th Ave	Anchorage	AK	99501	907-276-3114	279-9861
TF: 888-598-3114					
Anchorage Uptown Suites 234 E 2nd Ave	Anchorage	AK	99501	907-279-4232	279-4231
TF: 800-478-4232 ■ *Web:* www.alaskan.com/anchorageuptownsuites/					
Best Western Barratt Inn 4616 Spenard Rd	Anchorage	AK	99517	907-243-3131	249-4917
TF: 800-221-7550 ■ *Web:* www.barrattinn.com					
Best Western Golden Lion Hotel 1000 E 36th Ave	Anchorage	AK	99508	907-561-1522	561-1522
TF: 800-528-1234					
Best Western Kodiak 236 W Rezanof Dr	Kodiak	AK	99615	907-486-5712	486-3430
TF: 888-563-4254					
Captain Cook Hotel 939 W 5th Ave	Anchorage	AK	99501	907-276-6000	343-2298
TF: 800-843-1950					
Chelsea Inn 3836 Spenard Rd	Anchorage	AK	99517	907-276-5002	277-7642
TF: 800-770-5002					
Comfort Inn 111 W Ship Creek Ave	Anchorage	AK	99501	907-277-6887	274-9830
TF: 800-362-6887					
Courtyard by Marriott 4901 Spenard Rd	Anchorage	AK	99517	907-245-0322	248-1886
TF: 800-321-2211 ■ *Web:* courtyard.com/ANCCY					
Days Inn Downtown 321 E 5th Ave	Anchorage	AK	99501	907-276-7226	265-5145
TF: 800-329-7466					
Econo Lodge 642 E 5th Ave	Anchorage	AK	99501	907-274-1515	272-1516
TF: 800-553-2666					
Executive Suite Hotel 4360 Spenard Rd	Anchorage	AK	99517	907-243-6366	248-2161
TF: 800-770-6366 ■ *Web:* www.executivesuitehotel.com ■ *E-mail:* suites@alaska.net					
Hilton Hotel 500 W 3rd Ave	Anchorage	AK	99501	907-272-7411	265-7140
TF: 800-245-2527 ■ *Web:* www.hilton.com/hotels/ANCAHHH					
Holiday Inn Downtown Anchorage 239 W 4th Ave	Anchorage	AK	99501	907-279-8671	258-4733
TF: 800-465-4329 ■ *Web:* www.basshotels.com/holiday-inn/?_franchisee=ANCAK ■ *E-mail:* gmanc@lodgian.com					
Homestead Inn 4215 Spenard Rd	Anchorage	AK	99517	907-248-6048	
Web: www.corecom.net/~homeinn/					
Inlet Tower Suites 1200 L St	Anchorage	AK	99501	907-276-0110	258-4914
TF: 800-544-0786					
Long House Alaskan Hotel 4335 Wisconsin St	Anchorage	AK	99517	907-243-2133	243-6060
TF: 800-243-2133					
Merrill Field Motel 420 Sitka St	Anchorage	AK	99501	907-276-4547	276-5064
TF: 800-898-4547					
Mush Inn Motel 333 Concrete St	Anchorage	AK	99501	907-277-4554	277-5721
TF: 800-478-4554					
Nelchina Point Suites 1601 Nelchina St	Anchorage	AK	99501	907-279-1601	272-0657
TF: 800-720-1601					
Northern Lights Hotel 598 W Northern Lights Blvd	Anchorage	AK	99503	907-561-5200	563-8217
TF: 800-235-6546					
Northwoods Guest House 2300 W Tudor Rd	Anchorage	AK	99517	907-243-3249	248-4709
Parkwood Inn 4455 Juneau St	Anchorage	AK	99503	907-563-3590	563-5560
TF: 800-478-3590					
Puffin Inn 4400 Spenard Rd	Anchorage	AK	99517	907-243-4044	248-6853
TF: 800-478-3346 ■ *Web:* www.puffininn.net					
Puffin Place Studios & Suites 1058 W 27th Ave	Anchorage	AK	99503	907-279-1058	276-4922
TF: 800-478-3346					
Ramada Limited 207 Muldoon Rd	Anchorage	AK	99504	907-338-3000	929-7070
TF: 800-272-6232					
Regal Alaskan Hotel 4800 Spenard Rd	Anchorage	AK	99517	907-243-2300	243-8815
TF: 800-544-0553					
Rodeway Inn 1104 E 5th Ave	Anchorage	AK	99501	907-274-1650	279-9351
TF: 800-228-2000					
Royal Suite Lodge 3811 Minnesota Dr	Anchorage	AK	99503	907-563-3114	563-4296
TF: 800-282-3114					
Shepherd's Inn 2224 D St	Anchorage	AK	99503	907-279-3437	279-3438
Sheraton Anchorage 401 E 6th Ave	Anchorage	AK	99501	907-276-8700	276-7561
TF: 800-325-3535					
Ship Creek Hotel 505 W 2nd Ave	Anchorage	AK	99501	907-278-5050	276-2929
TF: 800-844-0242					
Snowshoe Inn 826 K St	Anchorage	AK	99501	907-258-7669	258-7463
Sourdough Visitors Lodge Motel 801 Erickson St	Anchorage	AK	99501	907-279-4148	258-3623
TF: 800-777-3716					
Super 8 Motel of Anchorage 3501 Minnesota Dr	Anchorage	AK	99503	907-276-8884	279-8194
TF: 800-800-8000					
Voyager Hotel 501 K St	Anchorage	AK	99501	907-277-9501	274-0333
TF: 800-247-9070					
WestCoast International Inn 3333 W International Airport Rd	Anchorage	AK	99502	907-243-2233	248-3796
TF: 800-544-0986 ■ *Web:* www.westcoasthotels.com/international					
Westin Alyeska Prince Hotel & Ski Resort 1000 Arlberg Ave	Girdwood	AK	99587	907-754-1111	754-2290
TF: 800-880-3880					
Westmark Anchorage Hotel 720 W 5th Ave	Anchorage	AK	99501	907-276-7676	276-3615
TF: 800-544-0970 ■ *Web:* www.westmarkhotels.com/locations/anchorage/westmark_anchorage.html					
Westmark Inn Third Ave 115 E 3rd Ave	Anchorage	AK	99501	907-272-7561	272-3879
TF: 800-544-0970 ■ *Web:* www.westmarkhotels.com/locations/anchorage/westmark_inn_anchorage.html					

— Restaurants —

Name / Address	City	State	ZIP	Phone
Alaska Glacier Brewhouse (American) 737 W 5th Ave	Anchorage	AK	99501	907-274-2739
Alaska Salmon Chower House (Seafood) 443 W 4th Ave	Anchorage	AK	99501	907-278-6901
Arctic Roadrunner (American) 5300 Old Seward Hwy	Anchorage	AK	99518	907-561-1245
Bistro 401 (Seafood) 401 E 6th Ave	Anchorage	AK	99501	907-276-8700
Blondie's Cafe (American) 333 W 4th Ave	Anchorage	AK	99501	907-279-0698
Bootlegger's Cove Restaurant (American) 1200 L St	Anchorage	AK	99501	907-276-0110
Chair 5 Restaurant (American) Linblad St	Girdwood	AK	99587	907-783-2500
China Express (Chinese) 425 W 5th Ave	Anchorage	AK	99501	907-276-8989
Club Paris (Steak) 417 W 5th Ave	Anchorage	AK	99501	907-277-6332
Coach House Restaurant (American) 115 E 3rd Ave	Anchorage	AK	99501	907-272-7561
Corsair (American) 944 W 5th Ave	Anchorage	AK	99501	907-278-4502
Crow's Nest (American) 939 W 5th Ave	Anchorage	AK	99501	907-276-6000
Cusack's Brew Pub (American) 598 W Northern Lights Blvd	Anchorage	AK	99503	907-561-5200
Daruma (Japanese) 550 W Tudor Rd	Anchorage	AK	99503	907-561-6622
Elevation 92 (Seafood) 1007 W 3rd Ave	Anchorage	AK	99501	907-279-1578
Fiori D'Italia (Italian) 2502 McRae Rd	Anchorage	AK	99503	907-243-9990
Flying Machine Restaurant (Seafood) 4800 Spenard Rd	Anchorage	AK	99517	907-243-2300
Gesine's at Four Corners Restaurant (International) 6700 Jewel Lake Rd	Anchorage	AK	99502	907-243-0507
Ginza Restaurant (Japanese) 712 W 4th Ave	Anchorage	AK	99501	907-274-4120
Greek Corner (Greek) 302 Fireweed Ln	Anchorage	AK	99503	907-276-2820
Gweenie's Old Alaska Restaurant (American) 4333 Spenard Rd	Anchorage	AK	99517	907-243-2090
Harry's Restaurant & Bar (American) 101 W Benson Blvd	Anchorage	AK	99503	907-562-5994
Hogg Brothers Cafe (American) 1049 W Northern Lights Blvd	Anchorage	AK	99503	907-276-9649
Hong Kong Restaurant (Asian) 2412 Spenard Rd	Anchorage	AK	99503	907-274-6141
How How Restaurant (Asian) 207 Muldoon Rd	Anchorage	AK	99504	907-337-2116
Humpy's Great Alaskan Alehouse (American) 610 W 6th Ave	Anchorage	AK	99501	907-276-2337
Imperial Palace (Chinese) 400 Sitka St	Anchorage	AK	99501	907-274-9167
Jen's Restaurant (Steak/Seafood) 701 W 36th Ave	Anchorage	AK	99503	907-561-5367
Josephines (Polynesian) 401 E 6th Ave 16th Fl	Anchorage	AK	99501	907-276-8700
Kaze Japanese Restaurant (Japanese) 930 W 5th Ave	Anchorage	AK	99501	907-276-2215
Kodiak Kafe (Steak/Seafood) 225 E 5th Ave	Anchorage	AK	99501	907-258-5233
Korea House (Korean) 3337 Fairbanks St	Anchorage	AK	99503	907-276-5188
La Mex (Mexican) 2550 Spenard Rd	Anchorage	AK	99501	907-274-7511
Lucero's Restaurant (Italian) 612 F St	Anchorage	AK	99501	907-258-9794
Lucky Wishbone (American) 1033 E 5th Ave	Anchorage	AK	99501	907-272-3454
Marx Brothers Cafe (New American) 627 W 3rd Ave	Anchorage	AK	99501	907-278-2133
Mesa Grill Restaurant (American) 720 W 5th Ave	Anchorage	AK	99501	907-278-3433
Mexico in Alaska Restaurant (Mexican) 7305 Old Seward Hwy	Anchorage	AK	99518	907-349-1528

Anchorage — Restaurants (Cont'd)

Name / Address	City	State	ZIP	Phone
Noodle House (Korean) 3301 Spenard Rd	Anchorage	AK	99503	907-563-9880
O'Malley's on the Green (American) 3651 O'Malley Rd	Anchorage	AK	99516	907-522-3322
Phyllis's Cafe & Salmon Bake (Seafood) 436 D St	Anchorage	AK	99508	907-274-6576
Sacks Cafe (American) 625 W 5th Ave	Anchorage	AK	99501	907-276-3546
Sawaddi Thai Restaurant (Thai) 219 E Diamond Blvd	Anchorage	AK	99515	907-522-3663
Sea Galley (Seafood) 4101 Credit Union Dr	Anchorage	AK	99503	907-563-3520
Simmering Pot (American) 239 W 4th Ave	Anchorage	AK	99501	907-279-8671
Simon & Sefort's Saloon & Grill (Steak/Seafood) 420 L St	Anchorage	AK	99501	907-274-3502
Snow Goose Restaurant (Steak/Seafood) 717 W 3rd Ave	Anchorage	AK	99501	907-277-7727
Sorrento's Restaurant (Italian) 610 E Fireweed Ln	Anchorage	AK	99503	907-278-3439
Sourdough Mining Co (American) 5200 Juneau St	Anchorage	AK	99518	907-563-2272
Southside Bistro (American) 1320 Huffman Park Dr	Anchorage	AK	99515	907-348-0088
Tempura Kitchen (Japanese) 3826 Spenard Rd	Anchorage	AK	99517	907-277-2741
Thai Cuisine Too (Thai) 328 G St	Anchorage	AK	99501	907-277-8424
Turnagain House (Steak/Seafood) 103 Seward Hwy	Indian	AK	99540	907-653-7500
Villa Nova Restaurant (Continental) 5121 Arctic Blvd Suite I	Anchorage	AK	99503	907-561-1660

— Goods and Services —

SHOPPING

Name / Address	City	State	ZIP	Phone	Fax
Anchorage 5th Avenue Mall 320 W 5th Ave	Anchorage	AK	99501	907-258-5535	279-3765
Diamond Center 800 E Diamond Blvd	Anchorage	AK	99515	907-344-2501	349-2411
Mall at Sears 600 E Northern Lights Blvd	Anchorage	AK	99508	907-264-6600	264-6600
Nordstrom 603 D St	Anchorage	AK	99501	907-279-7622	
Northway Mall 3101 Penland Pkwy	Anchorage	AK	99508	907-276-5520	279-7192
Pia's Scandinavian Woolens Factory Outlet 345 'E' St	Anchorage	AK	99501	907-277-7964	
University Center 3901 Old Seward Hwy Suite 9E	Anchorage	AK	99503	907-562-0347	561-1963

BANKS

Name / Address	City	State	ZIP	Phone	Fax
First Interstate Bank 716 W 4th Ave Suite 102 *TF:* 800-688-2660 ■ *Web:* www.fibank.com	Anchorage	AK	99501	907-277-2166	274-7343
First National Bank of Anchorage PO Box 100720	Anchorage	AK	99510	907-276-6300	777-3528
KeyBank NA Alaska District PO Box 100420 *TF:* 800-478-6363	Anchorage	AK	99510	907-562-6100	564-0387
National Bank of Alaska PO Box 100600 *Web:* www.nationalbankofalaska.com	Anchorage	AK	99510	907-276-1132	265-2068
Northrim Bank 3111 C St *TF:* 800-478-3311 ■ *Web:* www.arctic.net/northrim/	Anchorage	AK	99503	907-562-0062	261-3388

BUSINESS SERVICES

	Phone
Alaska Temp Service	907-561-5405
Anchorage Express	907-561-1009
Anchorage Messenger Service	907-278-2736
ASAP Printing	907-562-9240
DHL Worldwide Express	907-243-1503
Elite Employment Service	907-276-8367
Express Delivery Service	907-562-7333
Federal Express	800-238-5355
Kelly Services	907-561-5070
Kinko's	907-344-0056
Mail Boxes Etc	907-276-7888
Manpower Temporary Services	907-562-1440
Mila Inc	907-562-6452
Olsten Staffing Services	907-563-0090
Post Office	800-275-8777
UPS	800-742-5877
Western Parcel Express	907-243-3839

— Media —

PUBLICATIONS

Name / Address	City	State	ZIP	Phone	Fax
Alaska Business Monthly PO Box 241288 *TF:* 800-770-4373 ■ *Web:* www.akbizmag.com ■ *E-mail:* info@akbizmag.com	Anchorage	AK	99524	907-276-4373	279-2900
Alaska Journal of Commerce 4220 B St Suite 210	Anchorage	AK	99503	907-561-4772	563-4744
Alaska Magazine 619 E Ship Creek Ave Suite 329 *Web:* www.alaskamagazine.com ■ *E-mail:* lac@groupz.net	Anchorage	AK	99501	907-272-6070	258-5360
Anchorage Daily News‡ PO Box 149001 *Web:* www.adn.com	Anchorage	AK	99514	907-257-4200	258-2157

‡Daily newspapers

TELEVISION

Name / Address	City	State	ZIP	Phone	Fax
KAKM-TV Ch 7 (PBS) 3877 University Dr *E-mail:* kakm-tv@kakm.pbs.org	Anchorage	AK	99508	907-563-7070	273-9192
KIMO-TV Ch 13 (ABC) 2700 E Tudor Rd *Web:* www.aksupersite.com	Anchorage	AK	99507	907-561-1313	561-8934
KTBY-TV Ch 4 (Fox) 1840 S Bragaw St	Anchorage	AK	99508	907-274-0404	264-5180
KTUU-TV Ch 2 (NBC) 701 E Tudor Rd Suite 220 *Web:* www.ktuu.com ■ *E-mail:* ktuu@ktuu.com	Anchorage	AK	99503	907-762-9202	561-0882
KTVA-TV Ch 11 (CBS) 1007 W 32nd Ave	Anchorage	AK	99503	907-273-3170	273-3189
KYES-TV Ch 5 (UPN) 3700 Woodland Dr Suite 800	Anchorage	AK	99517	907-248-5937	243-0709

RADIO

Name / Address	City	State	ZIP	Phone	Fax
KASH-FM 107.5 MHz (Ctry) 800 E Diamond Blvd Suite 3-370	Anchorage	AK	99515	907-522-1515	349-6801
KBFX-FM 100.5 MHz (CR) 800 E Diamond Blvd Suite 3-370	Anchorage	AK	99515	907-522-1515	522-0672
KBRJ-FM 104.1 MHz (Ctry) 11259 Tower Rd	Anchorage	AK	99515	907-344-2200	349-3299
KBYR-AM 700 kHz (N/T) 1007 W 32nd Ave	Anchorage	AK	99503	907-273-3170	273-4189
KEAG-FM 97.3 MHz (Oldies) 11259 Tower Rd	Anchorage	AK	99515	907-344-2200	349-3299
KGOT-FM 101.3 MHz (CHR) 800 E Diamond Blvd Suite 3-370 *Web:* www.alaskanet.com/kgot/ ■ *E-mail:* kgot@alaskanet.com	Anchorage	AK	99515	907-272-5945	522-0672
KHAR-AM 590 kHz (Nost) 11259 Tower Rd	Anchorage	AK	99515	907-344-2200	349-3299
KKRO-FM 102.1 MHz (Rock) 11259 Tower Rd	Anchorage	AK	99515	907-344-2200	349-3299
KLEF-FM 98.1 MHz (Clas) 3601 C St Suite 290 *Web:* www.klef.com ■ *E-mail:* klef@klef.com	Anchorage	AK	99503	907-561-5556	562-4219
KNBA-FM 90.3 MHz (NPR) 818 E 9th Ave	Anchorage	AK	99501	907-279-5622	258-8803
KNIK-FM 105.3 MHz (NAC) 1007 W 32nd Ave	Anchorage	AK	99503	907-273-3171	273-3189
KSKA-FM 91.1 MHz (NPR) 3877 University Dr	Anchorage	AK	99508	907-563-7070	273-9435

— Colleges/Universities —

Name / Address	City	State	ZIP	Phone	Fax
Alaska Pacific University 4101 University Dr *TF Admissions:* 800-252-7528 ■ *Web:* www.alaskapacific.edu ■ *E-mail:* apu@corcom.com	Anchorage	AK	99508	907-561-1266	564-8317
University of Alaska Anchorage 3211 Providence Dr *Web:* www.uaa.alaska.edu ■ *E-mail:* ayenrol@uaa.alaska.edu	Anchorage	AK	99508	907-786-1800	786-4888
Wayland Baptist University Anchorage 5530 E Northern Lights Suite 24 *Web:* www.wbu.edu/ak/index.html ■ *E-mail:* wbualctr@alaska.net	Anchorage	AK	99504	907-333-2277	337-8122

— Hospitals —

Name / Address	City	State	ZIP	Phone	Fax
Columbia Alaska Regional Hospital 2801 DeBarr Rd	Anchorage	AK	99508	907-276-1131	264-1143
Providence Alaska Medical Center PO Box 196604	Anchorage	AK	99519	907-562-2211	261-3048

— Attractions —

Name / Address	City	State	ZIP	Phone	Fax
4th Avenue Theatre 630 W 4th Ave	Anchorage	AK	99501	907-257-5600	257-5633
Alagnak Wild River PO Box 7 *Web:* www.nps.gov/alag/	King Salmon	AK	99613	907-246-3305	246-4286

Anchorage — Attractions (Cont'd)

	City	State	ZIP	Phone	Fax
Alaska Aviation Heritage Museum 4721 Aircraft Dr *Web:* www.airmodels.com ■ *E-mail:* museum@airmodels.com	Anchorage	AK	99502	907-248-5325	248-6391
Alaska Botanical Gardens Campbell Airstrip Rd	Anchorage	AK	99501	907-770-3692	265-3180
Alaska Center for the Performing Arts 621 W 6th Ave *E-mail:* acpa@customcpu.com	Anchorage	AK	99501	907-263-2900	263-2927
Alaska Experience Center 705 W 6th Ave	Anchorage	AK	99501	907-276-3730	
Alaska Experience Theatre 705 W 6th Ave *Web:* www.alaska.net/~alaskaxp	Anchorage	AK	99501	907-272-9076	272-5716
Alaska Museum of Natural History 11723 Old Glenn Hwy *Web:* www.alaska.net/~nathist/	Eagle River	AK	99577	907-694-0819	694-0919
Alaska Native Heritage Center 8800 Heritage Center Dr *Web:* www.alaskanative.net	Anchorage	AK	99506	907-330-8000	330-8030
Alaska Zoo 4731 O'Malley Rd *Web:* www.goworldnet.com/akzoo.htm	Anchorage	AK	99516	907-346-3242	346-2673
Anchorage Museum of History & Art 121 W 7th Ave *Web:* www.ci.anchorage.ak.us/Services/Departments/Culture/Museum/index.html ■ *E-mail:* museum@ci.anchorage.ak.us	Anchorage	AK	99501	907-343-4326	343-6149
Anchorage Opera 1507 Spar Ave *Web:* www.anchorage.com/opera/	Anchorage	AK	99501	907-279-2557	279-7798
Anchorage Symphony Orchestra 400 D St Suite 230	Anchorage	AK	99501	907-274-8668	272-7916
Aniakchak National Monument & Preserve PO Box 7 *Web:* www.nps.gov/ania/	King Salmon	AK	99613	907-246-3305	246-4286
Artique Ltd 314 G St	Anchorage	AK	99501	907-277-1663	272-2024
Big Game Alaska Wildlife Park Milepost 79 Seward Hwy	Portage Glacier	AK	99587	907-783-2025	783-2370
Chugach State Park Milepost 115.3 Seward Hwy	Indian	AK	99540	907-345-5014	
Dance Spectrum 1300 E 68th Ave	Anchorage	AK	99518	907-344-9545	
Denali National Park & Preserve PO Box 9 *Web:* www.nps.gov/dena/	Denali Park	AK	99755	907-683-2294	683-9617
Eagle River Nature Center 32750 Eagle River Rd	Eagle River	AK	99577	907-694-2108	
Eklutna Historical Park 16515 Centerfield Dr *Web:* www.alaskaone.com/eklutna/	Eagle River	AK	99577	907-696-2828	696-2845
Elmendorf Air Force Base Wildlife Museum 8481 19th ST	Elmendorf AFB	AK	99506	907-552-2282	
Elmendorf State Hatchery 941 N Reeves Blvd	Anchorage	AK	99501	907-274-0065	
Fraternal Order of Alaska State Troopers Museum 320 W 5th Ave *Web:* www.alaska.net/~foast/	Anchorage	AK	99501	907-279-5050	279-5054
Heritage Library Museum 301 W Northern Lights Blvd	Anchorage	AK	99503	907-265-2834	265-2002
Hilltop Ski Area 7015 Abbott Rd	Anchorage	AK	99516	907-346-1446	346-3391
Imaginarium Science Discovery Center 737 W 5th Ave *Web:* www.imaginarium.org ■ *E-mail:* imagine@alaska.net	Anchorage	AK	99501	907-276-3179	258-4306
Indian Valley Mine 6470 Village Pkwy	Anchorage	AK	99504	907-337-7749	
Katmai National Park & Preserve PO Box 7 *Web:* www.nps.gov/katm/	King Salmon	AK	99613	907-246-3305	246-4286
Kenai Fjords National Park PO Box 1727 *Web:* www.nps.gov/kefj/	Seward	AK	99664	907-224-3874	224-2144
Kincaid Park Raspberry Rd	Anchorage	AK	99518	907-343-6397	
Lake Clark National Park & Preserve 4230 University Dr Suite 311 *Web:* www.nps.gov/lacl/	Anchorage	AK	99508	907-271-3751	271-3707
Leiser Mann Memorial Greenhouses 5200 DeBarr Rd Russian Jack Springs Pk	Anchorage	AK	99508	907-343-4717	
Midnight Sons Barbershop Chorus PO Box 100495	Anchorage	AK	99510	907-275-3776	
Mike Alex Cabin Eklutna Village Rd	Eklutna	AK	99664	907-688-3824	688-6021
Mush a Dog Team Gold Rush Park 17620 S Birchwood Loop Rd	Chugiak	AK	99567	907-688-1391	688-7731
Oscar Anderson House Museum 420 M St Elderberry Pk	Anchorage	AK	99501	907-274-2336	274-3600
Port of Anchorage 2000 Anchorage Port Rd	Anchorage	AK	99501	907-343-6200	277-5636
Russian Jack Springs Park DeBarr & Boniface Rds	Anchorage	AK	99504	907-333-8338	
Wolf Song of Alaska 6th Ave & C St	Anchorage	AK	99511	907-346-3073	346-1221
Wrangell-Saint Elias National Park & Preserve PO Box 439 *Web:* www.nps.gov/wrst/	Copper Center	AK	99573	907-822-5235	822-7216

SPORTS TEAMS & FACILITIES

	City	State	ZIP	Phone	Fax
Alaska Arctic Ice (hockey) PO Box 212366 *E-mail:* jkknuejr@alaska.net	Anchorage	AK	99521	907-333-8353	249-6836
Alaska Sinbad Sailors (hockey) 3101 Penland Pkwy Suite K26 *E-mail:* kelsey@sinbad.net	Anchorage	AK	99503	907-274-6223	274-9444
Anchorage Aces (hockey) 1600 Gambell St Sullivan Arena *Web:* www.anchorageaces.com/	Anchorage	AK	99501	907-258-2237	278-4297
Anchorage Bucs (baseball) 16th St Mulcahy Stadium *Web:* www.alaska.net/~enigma/bucs/ ■ *E-mail:* bucs@alaska.net	Anchorage	AK	99501	907-561-2827	561-2920
Anchorage Glacier Pilots (baseball) 16th Ave & Cordova St Mulcahy Stadium	Anchorage	AK	99503	907-274-3627	274-3628
George M Sullivan Sports Arena 1600 Gambell St	Anchorage	AK	99501	907-279-0618	274-0676

— Events —

	Phone
Alaska State Fair (late August-early September)	907-276-4118
Alyeska Ski Resort Winter Fest (early January)	907-754-1111
Anchorage Festival of Music (mid-June)	907-276-2465
Anchorage Folk Festival (mid-January)	907-566-2334
Bear Paw Festival (early July)	907-694-4702
Carrs Great Alaska Shootout (late November)	907-786-1230
Freedom Days Festival (July 4)	907-276-4118
Fur Rendezvous Winter Carnival (mid-February)	907-277-8615
Girdwood Forest Fair (early July)	907-783-2931
Great Alaska Shootout (late November)	907-786-1230
Holiday Food & Gift Show (early November)	907-277-7469
Iditarod Trail Sled Dog Race (early March)	907-376-5155
Iditasport (mid-February)	907-345-4505
International Ice Carving Competition (early March)	907-279-5650
Irish Music & Cultural Festival of Alaska (early June)	907-566-2028
Juneteenth Festival (mid-June)	907-278-1778
Mayor's Midnight Sun Marathon (mid-June)	907-343-4474
Mount Marathon Race (July 4)	907-224-8051
Native Youth Olympics (late April-early May)	907-265-5900
Northern Lights (September-March)	907-276-4118
Northern Lights Invitational Basketball Tournament (late December)	907-786-1230
Polar Bear Jump Off Festival (mid-January)	907-224-5230
Quyana Alaska (mid-October)	907-274-3611
Saturday Market (May-September)	907-272-5634
Seward Silver Salmon Derby (mid-late August)	907-224-3046
Ship Creek King Salmon Derby (early-mid-June)	907-276-6472
Sled Dog Races (January-February)	907-562-2235
Spring Carnival (mid-April)	907-754-2265
Summer Solstice Celebration (late June)	907-276-4118
Summer Solstice Festival (mid-June)	907-279-9581
Swedish Christmas Celebration (early December)	907-274-2336
Taste of Anchorage (early June)	907-562-9911
Three Barons Fair (early-mid-June)	907-272-2873
Torchlight Ski Parade (December 31)	907-754-1111
Tour of Anchorage Cross-Country Ski Race (March)	907-276-4118
Tree Lighting Ceremony (early December)	907-276-5015

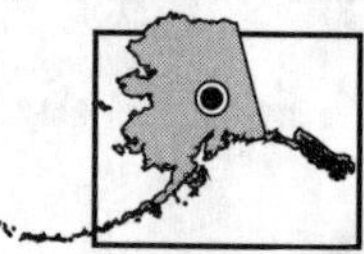

Fairbanks

Founded in the early 1900s by E.T. Barnette, Fairbanks is named for Charles W. Fairbanks, a senator from Indiana who later became Vice President of the United States under Theodore Roosevelt. The city is located in the heart of Alaska's interior and is a good starting point for trips to the Arctic National Wildlife Refuge, Gates of the Arctic National Park and Preserve, or the North Slope. Denali National Park and Mt. McKinley are just over 100 miles southwest of the city, and the Arctic Circle is only 200 miles away. During summer, the midnight sun provides almost 24 hours of light in Fairbanks, and the long sunny days are ideal for a trip to Denali Park to see moose, caribou, bear, fox, wolves, and other wildlife. In spring and fall,

Fairbanks (Cont'd)

Creamers Field Bird Sanctuary is an excellent place to see wild swans, geese, ducks, and cranes. The winter months offer an opportunity to see the Aurora Borealis (Northern Lights) and to enjoy winter sports, including skiing and dog sledding.

Population 33,295
Area (Land) .... 31.3 sq mi
Area (Water) .... 0.8 sq mi
Elevation .... 440 ft
Latitude .... 64-84-87 N
Longitude .... 147-72-23 W
County .... Fairbanks North Star Borough
Time Zone .... Alaska
Area Code/s 907

— Average Temperatures and Precipitation —

TEMPERATURES

	Jan	Feb	Mar	Apr	May	Jun	Jul	Aug	Sep	Oct	Nov	Dec
High	-1	7	24	41	59	70	72	66	55	32	11	2
Low	-19	-14	-2	20	38	50	53	47	36	18	-6	-15

PRECIPITATION

	Jan	Feb	Mar	Apr	May	Jun	Jul	Aug	Sep	Oct	Nov	Dec
Inches	0.5	0.4	0.4	0.3	0.6	1.4	1.9	2.0	1.0	0.9	0.8	0.9

— Important Phone Numbers —

	Phone
American Express Travel	907-452-7636
Dental Referral	907-563-3003
Emergency	911
Events Line	907-456-4636
Poison Control Center	907-456-7182
Time/Temp	907-488-1111
Weather	907-452-3553

— Information Sources —

				Phone	Fax
Better Business Bureau Serving Alaska					
Fairbanks Branch PO Box 74675	Fairbanks	AK	99707	907-451-0222	451-0228
Web: www.alaska.bbb.org ■ *E-mail:* info@anchorage.bbb.org					
Carlson Center 2010 2nd Ave	Fairbanks	AK	99701	907-451-7800	451-1195
Web: www.carlson-center.com ■ *E-mail:* carlson@polarnet.com					
Fairbanks Chamber of Commerce 250 Cushman St Suite 2D	Fairbanks	AK	99701	907-452-1105	456-6968
Web: www.fairbankschamber.org					
Fairbanks City Hall 800 Cushman St.	Fairbanks	AK	99701	907-459-6881	459-6710*
**Fax:* City Clerk ■ *Web:* www.touralaska.org/fairbanks/					
Fairbanks Convention & Visitors Bureau 550 1st Ave	Fairbanks	AK	99701	907-456-5774	452-2867
TF: 800-327-5774 ■ *Web:* fairbanks.polarnet.com ■ *E-mail:* info4fbk@polarnet.com					
Fairbanks Mayor 800 Cushman St	Fairbanks	AK	99701	907-459-6793	459-6710
Web: www.touralaska.org/fairbanks/citymayr.htm					
Fairbanks North Star Borough PO Box 71267	Fairbanks	AK	99707	907-459-1000	459-1224
Fairbanks North Star Borough Public Library & Regional Center 1215 Cowles St	Fairbanks	AK	99701	907-459-1020	459-1024
Log Cabin Visitors Center 550 1st Ave	Fairbanks	AK	99701	907-456-5774	452-2867

On-Line Resources

About.com Guide to Fairbanks .... fairbanks.about.com
Area Guide Fairbanks .... fairbanks.areaguides.net
Bell's Alaska Travel Guide Fairbanks .... www.alaskan.com/bells/fairbanks.html
City Knowledge Fairbanks .... www.cityknowledge.com/ak_fairbanks.htm
Excite.com Fairbanks City Guide .... www.excite.com/travel/countries/united_states/alaska/fairbanks
Fairbanks Community Network .... www.fairnet.org
Fairbanks Home Page .... www.alaskaone.com/fairbanks
Fairbanks Visitors Guide .... www.newsminer.com/visitor/fairbanks/index.html
Welcome to Fairbanks .... www.mosquitonet.com/~ranchmotel/

— Transportation Services —

AIRPORTS

	Phone
■ **Fairbanks International Airport (FAI)** 4 miles SW of downtown (approx 15 minutes)	907-474-2500

Airport Transportation

	Phone
Fairbanks Taxi $12 fare to downtown	907-456-3333
GO Shuttle Service $7 fare to downtown	907-474-3847

Commercial Airlines

	Phone
40-Mile Air Ltd	907-883-5191
Air North	800-764-0407
Alaska	907-474-0481
American	800-433-7300
Delta	800-221-1212
Frontier Flying Service	907-474-0014

Charter Airlines

	Phone
Arctic Circle Air Service Inc	907-474-0112
Larry's Flying Service Inc	907-474-9169
Tanana Air Service	907-474-0301
Tundra Copters	907-474-0394
Warbelow's Air Ventures	907-474-0518
Wright Air Service Inc	907-474-0502

CAR RENTALS

	Phone
Affordable	907-452-7341
Avis	907-474-0900
Budget	907-474-0855
Hertz	907-452-4444
Rent-A-Wreck	907-452-1606
U-Save Auto	907-479-7060

LIMO/TAXI

	Phone
Diamond Cab	907-455-7777
Eagle Yellow Cab	907-457-5555
Fairbanks Taxi	907-456-3333
King Cab	907-452-5464
Limousines by Tiffany	907-456-3916
Tundra Cab	907-452-3375
Yellow Cab	907-451-0000

MASS TRANSIT

	Phone
MACS Transit $1.50 Base fare	907-459-1011

RAIL/BUS

				Phone
Alaska Railroad Station 280 N Cushman St	Fairbanks	AK	99701	907-265-2494
Gray Line Bus Lines 1980 S Cushman St	Fairbanks	AK	99701	907-456-7741

— Accommodations —

HOTELS, MOTELS, RESORTS

				Phone	Fax
AAAA Care Bed & Breakfast 557 Fairbanks St.	Fairbanks	AK	99709	907-479-2447	479-2484
TF: 800-478-2705 ■ *Web:* www.alaskan.com/aaaacare ■ *E-mail:* aaaacare@ptialaska.net					
Alaska Motel 1546 Cushman St	Fairbanks	AK	99701	907-456-6393	452-4833
Alaskan Motor Inn 419 Lacey St.	Fairbanks	AK	99701	907-452-4800	451-0107
Ambassador Inn 415 5th Ave	Fairbanks	AK	99701	907-451-9555	451-9556
Bridgewater Hotel 723 1st Ave.	Fairbanks	AK	99701	907-452-6661	452-6126
TF: 800-528-4916 ■ *Web:* www.fountainheadhotels.com/bridge.html ■ *E-mail:* info@fountainheadhotels.com					
Captain Bartlett Inn 1411 Airport Way	Fairbanks	AK	99701	907-452-1888	452-7674
TF: 800-544-7528					
Chena Hot Springs Resort 206 Driveway St.	Fairbanks	AK	99701	907-452-7867	456-3122
TF: 800-478-4681 ■ *Web:* www.alaskaone.com/chena ■ *E-mail:* chenahs@polarnet.com					
College Inn 700 Fairbanks St	Fairbanks	AK	99709	907-474-3666	474-3668
TF: 800-770-2177 ■ *Web:* www.mosquitonet.com/~akhotel ■ *E-mail:* akhotel@mosquitonet.com					
Comfort Inn Chena River 1908 Chena Landings Loop	Fairbanks	AK	99701	907-479-8080	479-8063
TF: 800-228-5150					
Fairbanks Golden Nugget Hotel 900 Noble St	Fairbanks	AK	99701	907-452-5141	452-5458
Fairbanks Hotel 517 3rd Ave	Fairbanks	AK	99701	907-456-6411	456-1792
TF: 888-329-4685 ■ *Web:* www.alaska.net/~fbxhotl ■ *E-mail:* fbxhotl@alaska.net					

Fairbanks — Hotels, Motels, Resorts (Cont'd)

	City	State	ZIP	Phone	Fax
Fairbanks Princess Hotel 4477 Pikes Landing Rd *TF:* 800-426-0500	Fairbanks	AK	99709	907-455-4477	455-4476
Fairbanks Super 8 Motel 1909 Airport Way *TF:* 800-800-8000	Fairbanks	AK	99701	907-451-8888	451-6690
Golden North Motel 4888 Old Airport Way *TF:* 800-447-1910 ■ *Web:* www.akpub.com/goldennorth ■ *E-mail:* akttt@akpub.com	Fairbanks	AK	99709	907-479-6201	479-5766
Northern Light Hotel 427 1st Ave *TF:* 800-235-6546	Fairbanks	AK	99701	907-452-4456	456-2696
Regency Fairbanks Hotel 95 10th Ave. *TF:* 800-348-1340 ■ *Web:* www.regencyfairbankshotel.com ■ *E-mail:* reservations@regencyfairbankshotel.com	Fairbanks	AK	99701	907-452-3200	452-6505
River's Edge Resort Cottages 4200 Boat St. *TF:* 800-770-3343 ■ *Web:* www.riversedge.net ■ *E-mail:* reresort@alaska.net	Fairbanks	AK	99709	907-474-0286	474-3695
Sophie Station Hotel 1717 University Ave *TF:* 800-528-4916	Fairbanks	AK	99709	907-479-3650	479-7951
Tamarac Inn Motel 252 Minnie St.	Fairbanks	AK	99701	907-456-6406	456-7238
Villages The 205 Palace Cir *TF:* 800-770-7612	Fairbanks	AK	99701	907-456-7612	456-8358
Wedgewood Resort Hotel 212 Wedgewood Dr. *TF:* 800-528-4916 ■ *Web:* www.fountainheadhotels.com/wedge.html ■ *E-mail:* info@fountainheadhotels.com	Fairbanks	AK	99701	907-452-1442	451-8184
Westmark Hotel 813 Noble St *TF:* 800-544-0970 ■ *Web:* www.westmarkhotels.com/locations/fairbanks/westmark_fairbanks_hotel.html	Fairbanks	AK	99701	907-456-7722	451-7478
Westmark Inn 1521 S Cushman St *TF:* 800-544-0970 ■ *Web:* www.westmarkhotels.com/locations/fairbanks/westmark_fairbanks_inn.html	Fairbanks	AK	99701	907-456-6602	452-2724

— Restaurants —

	City	State	ZIP	Phone
Ah Sa Wan (Chinese) 600 Old Steese Hwy	Fairbanks	AK	99701	907-451-7788
Alaska Salmon Bake In Alaskaland (Seafood) Airport Way & Peger Rd	Fairbanks	AK	99709	907-452-7274
Campbell House (Steak/Seafood) 11 Mile Old Steese Hwy	Fairbanks	AK	99712	907-457-7462
Castle The (Steak/Seafood) 4510 Airport Way	Fairbanks	AK	99709	907-474-2165
Chatanika Lodge (American) 5760 Steese Hwy	Fairbanks	AK	99712	907-389-2164
Dog House Pub (American) 3400 College Rd.	Fairbanks	AK	99709	907-474-4004
Dog House Restaurant (American) 3412 College Rd	Fairbanks	AK	99709	907-479-0099
Edgewater on the River (Continental) 4477 Pikes Landing Rd	Fairbanks	AK	99709	907-455-4477
Ester Gold Camp (Seafood) Main St.	Ester	AK	99725	907-479-2500
Fox Roadhouse (Barbecue) 2195 Old Steese Hwy	Fairbanks	AK	99707	907-457-7461
Gambardella's Pasta Bella (Italian) 706 2nd Ave	Fairbanks	AK	99701	907-456-3417
Golden Shanghai (Chinese) 1900 Airport Way	Fairbanks	AK	99701	907-451-1100
Oriental House (Chinese) 1101 Noble St.	Fairbanks	AK	99701	907-456-1172
Pikes Landing (American) 4438 Airport Way	Fairbanks	AK	99706	907-479-7113
Pump House The (American) 796 Chena Pump Rd *Web:* www.ptialaska.net/~pumphse/	Fairbanks	AK	99709	907-479-8452
Riverview Seafood Cookout (Seafood) 1316 Badger Rd	Fairbanks	AK	99707	907-488-5880
Royal Fork Buffet (American) 414 3rd St	Fairbanks	AK	99701	907-452-5655
Slough Foot Sue's (American) 1411 Airport Way	Fairbanks	AK	99701	907-452-1888
Soapy Smith's Pioneer Restaurant (Homestyle) 543 2nd Ave	Fairbanks	AK	99701	907-451-8380
Souvlaki (Greek) 310 1st Ave	Fairbanks	AK	99701	907-452-5393
Turtle Club (Steak/Seafood) 10 Mile Old Steese Hwy	Fairbanks	AK	99712	907-457-3883
Two Rivers Lodge (American) 4968 Chena Hot Springs Rd *Web:* www.alaskaone.com/2rvslodge	Fairbanks	AK	99712	907-488-6815
Vallata (Italian) 2190 Goldstream Rd	Fairbanks	AK	99709	907-455-6600

— Goods and Services —

SHOPPING

	City	State	ZIP	Phone	Fax
Alaska Rag Co 552 2nd Ave.	Fairbanks	AK	99701	907-451-4401	451-4401
Great Alaskan Bowl Co 4630 Old Airport Rd	Fairbanks	AK	99709	907-474-9663	474-9669
Shoppers Forum Mall 1255 Airport Rd	Fairbanks	AK	99701	907-452-6422	

BANKS

	City	State	ZIP	Phone	Fax
Denali State Bank 119 N Cushman St. **Fax:* Mktg ■ *TF:* 888-458-4291	Fairbanks	AK	99701	907-456-1400	451-1954*
First National Bank of Anchorage 800 Noble St *TF:* 800-856-4362	Fairbanks	AK	99701	907-452-1871	451-7140
KeyBank NA 100 Cushman St. *TF:* 800-539-2968	Fairbanks	AK	99701	907-452-2146	451-7578
Mount McKinley Mutual Savings Bank 530 4th Ave *TF:* 888-515-1774	Fairbanks	AK	99701	907-452-1751	456-5982
National Bank of Alaska 613 Cushman St	Fairbanks	AK	99701	907-459-4318	459-4346

BUSINESS SERVICES

	Phone		Phone
Airborne Express	800-247-2676	**Mail Boxes Etc**	800-789-4623
BAX Global	800-225-5229	**Manpower Temporary Services**	907-474-8875
DHL Worldwide Express	800-225-5345	**Post Office**	800-275-8777
Federal Express	800-238-5355	**UPS**	800-742-5877
Kinko's	907-456-7348		

— Media —

PUBLICATIONS

	City	State	ZIP	Phone	Fax
Fairbanks Daily News-Miner‡ PO Box 70710 *Web:* www.newsminer.com ■ *E-mail:* web@newsminer.com	Fairbanks	AK	99707	907-456-6661	452-7917

‡Daily newspapers

TELEVISION

	City	State	ZIP	Phone	Fax
KATN-TV Ch 2 (ABC) 516 2nd Ave Suite 400 *Web:* www.aksupersite.com ■ *E-mail:* comments@aksupersite.com	Fairbanks	AK	99701	907-452-2125	456-8225
KFXF-TV Ch 7 (Fox) 3650 Bradock St *Web:* www.tvtv.com	Fairbanks	AK	99701	907-452-3697	456-3428
KTVF-TV Ch 11 (NBC) 3528 International Way	Fairbanks	AK	99701	907-452-5121	452-5120
KUAC-TV Ch 9 (PBS) PO Box 755620 University of Alaska *Web:* zorba.uafadm.alaska.edu/kuac/tvpage.html	Fairbanks	AK	99775	907-474-7491	474-5064
KXD-TV Ch 13 (CBS) 3650 Bradock St Suite 2	Fairbanks	AK	99701	907-452-3697	456-3428

RADIO

	City	State	ZIP	Phone	Fax
KCBF-AM 820 kHz (Ctry) 1060 Aspen St	Fairbanks	AK	99709	907-451-5910	451-5999
KFAR-AM 660 kHz (N/T) 1060 Aspen St *Web:* akradio.com/kfar ■ *E-mail:* kfar@akradio.com	Fairbanks	AK	99709	907-451-5910	451-5999
KIAK-AM 970 kHz (N/T) 546 9th Ave Suite 200 *Web:* www.am970.com	Fairbanks	AK	99707	907-457-1921	457-2128
KIAK-FM 102.5 MHz (Ctry) PO Box 73410 *Web:* www.kiak.com	Fairbanks	AK	99707	907-457-1921	457-2128
KUAC-FM 89.9 MHz (NPR) PO Box 755620 *Web:* www.uaf.edu/KUAC ■ *E-mail:* fnssd@aurora.alaska.edu	Fairbanks	AK	99775	907-474-7491	474-5064
KWLF-FM 98.1 MHz (AC) 1060 Aspen St. *Web:* akradio.com/kwlf	Fairbanks	AK	99709	907-451-5910	451-5999
KXLR-FM 95.9 MHz (CR) 1060 Aspen St.	Fairbanks	AK	99709	907-451-5910	451-5999

— Colleges/Universities —

	City	State	ZIP	Phone	Fax
University of Alaska Fairbanks PO Box 757480 *TF:* 800-478-1823 ■ *Web:* www.uaf.alaska.edu ■ *E-mail:* fnaws@aurora.alaska.edu	Fairbanks	AK	99775	907-474-7500	474-5379

— Hospitals —

	City	State	ZIP	Phone	Fax
Fairbanks Memorial Hospital 1650 Cowles St	Fairbanks	AK	99701	907-452-8181	458-5324

Fairbanks (Cont'd)

— Attractions —

				Phone	Fax
Alaskaland Fairbanks North Star Borough Airport Way & Peger Rd	Fairbanks	AK	99701	907-459-1087	459-1199
Alaskaland Pioneer Air Museum 2300 Airport Way	Fairbanks	AK	99701	907-452-5609	
Web: www.akpub.com/akttt/aviat.html					
Alyeska Trans-Alaska Pipeline Visitor Center Steese Hwy & Mile Marker 8	Fairbanks	AK	99701	907-456-3301	459-5894
Bering Land Bridge National Preserve PO Box 220	Nome	AK	99762	907-443-2522	443-6139
Web: www.nps.gov/bela/					
Cape Krusenstern National Monument PO Box 1029	Kotzebue	AK	99752	907-442-3890	442-8316
Web: www.nps.gov/noaa/					
Creamers Field Bird Sanctuary 1300 College Rd	Fairbanks	AK	99701	907-451-7059	452-6410
Web: www.alaskabird.org					
Davis Charles W Concert Hall Fine Arts Building University of Alaska	Fairbanks	AK	99775	907-474-7555	474-6420
E-mail: fymusic@aurora.alaska.edu					
Denali National Park & Preserve PO Box 9	Denali Park	AK	99755	907-683-2294	683-9617
Web: www.nps.gov/dena/					
Ester Gold Camp PO Box 109-B	Ester	AK	99725	907-479-2500	474-1780
Fairbanks Arts Association 2300 Airport Way Alaskaland Civic Ctr.	Fairbanks	AK	99707	907-456-6485	456-4112
Fairbanks Light Opera Theatre PO Box 72787	Fairbanks	AK	99707	907-456-3568	
Web: www.alaskasbest.com/flot.htm					
Fairbanks Shakespeare Theatre 288 Bias Rd	Fairbanks	AK	99712	907-457-7638	457-1114
Web: www.fairbanks-shakespeare.org ■ *E-mail:* fst@mosquitonet.com					
Fairbanks Symphony Orchestra PO Box 82104	Fairbanks	AK	99708	907-479-3407	474-6420
E-mail: fnjs@aurora.alaska.edu					
Gates of the Arctic National Park & Preserve 201 1st Ave Doyon Bldg	Fairbanks	AK	99701	907-456-0281	456-0590
Web: www.nps.gov/gaar/					
Georgeson Botanical Garden W Tanana Dr University of Alaska Fairbanks Campus	Fairbanks	AK	99775	907-474-1944	474-1841
Web: bonanza.lter.uaf.edu/~salrm/GBG_WWW/GBG.html ■ *E-mail:* ffpsh@aurora.alaska.edu					
Gold Dredge Number Eight Nine Mile Old Steese Hwy	Fairbanks	AK	99708	907-457-6058	
Ice Alaska 500 2nd Ave	Fairbanks	AK	99701	907-451-8250	456-1951
Web: www.alaska.net/~iceart/ ■ *E-mail:* iceart@alaska.net					
JoAnn & Monte's Alaska Show 401 E 6th Ave Sheraton Anchorage Hotel	Anchorage	AK	99501	907-278-8313	
Little El Dorado Gold Camp 1975 Discovery Dr	Fairbanks	AK	99709	907-479-7613	
Web: www.eldoradogoldmine.com ■ *E-mail:* reservations@eldoradogoldmine.com					
Moose Mountain Ski Resort Moose Mountain Rd	Fairbanks	AK	99708	907-455-8362	455-8362
Palace Theatre & Saloon Airport Way & Peger Rd	Fairbanks	AK	99709	907-452-7274	456-6997
Pioneer Memorial Park Museum Airport Way & Peger Rd	Fairbanks	AK	99707	907-456-8579	
Riverboat Discovery 1975 Discovery Dr.	Fairbanks	AK	99709	907-479-6673	479-4613
Web: www.riverboatdiscovery.com ■ *E-mail:* reservations@riverboatdiscovery.com					
SS Nenana Alaskaland Park	Fairbanks	AK	99707	907-456-8858	
Tanana Valley Farmer's Market Aurora & College Drs Tanana Valley Fairgrounds	Fairbanks	AK	99708	907-456-3276	
University of Alaska Museum 907 Yukon Dr.	Fairbanks	AK	99775	907-474-7505	474-5469
Web: www.uaf.edu/museum ■ *E-mail:* ffaj@aurora.alaska.edu					
Wickersham House Museum Airport Way & Peger Rd	Fairbanks	AK	99707	907-459-1087	
Yukon-Charley Rivers National Preserve 201 1st Ave	Fairbanks	AK	99701	907-456-0593	456-0590
Web: www.nps.gov/yuch/					

— Events —

	Phone
Arctic Man Ski & Sno Go Classic (April)	907-456-6867
Athabascan Fiddling Festival (mid-November)	907-452-1825
Candle Lighting Festival (early December)	907-488-2242
Chatanika Days (mid-March)	907-389-2164
Deltana Fair (late July)	907-895-3247
Equinox Marathon (mid-September)	907-479-6908
Fairbanks Preservation Society 4th of July Celebration (July 4)	907-456-8848
Fairbanks Summer Arts Festival (late July-early August)	907-474-8869
Fairbanks Winter Carnival (mid-March)	907-452-1105
Festival of Alaska Native Arts (early March)	907-474-7181
Golden Days (mid-July)	907-452-1105
Ice Art Competition (early March)	907-451-8250
Limited North American Sled Dog Race (early March)	907-456-5774
Midnight Sun Run (late June)	907-452-7211
Nenana Ice Classic (early February-early April)	907-832-5446
Nenana River Daze (early June)	907-456-5774
North Pole Summer Festival (mid-June)	907-488-2242
North Pole Winter Carnival (mid-March)	907-488-2242
Open North American Championship Sled Dog Race (mid-March)	907-488-9685
Tanana Valley State Fair (August)	907-452-3750
Winter Solstice Celebration (late November-mid-December)	907-452-8671
World Eskimo-Indian Olympics (mid-July)	907-456-5774
Yukon 800 Marathon Boat Race (June)	800-327-5774
Yukon Quest International Sled Dog Race (February)	907-452-7954

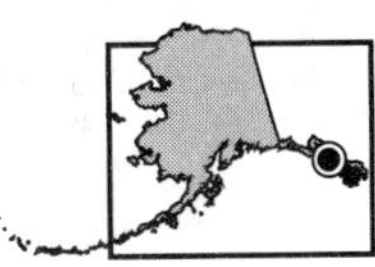

Juneau

Juneau began as a gold rush town in 1880, and the Alaska State Museum near the city's waterfront includes gold rush memorabilia as well as exhibits of Eskimo and Native American artifacts. Activities and trips available in Juneau include gold panning, rafting, sea kayaking, skiing (Douglas Island's Eaglecrest ski area is across Gastineau Channel from Juneau), and glacier sightseeing. The 3.3-million-acre Glacier Bay National Park and Preserve is just 50 miles west of Juneau and is accessible by sea or by air. Glacier Bay features 16 glaciers and a variety of wildlife, including whales, seals, porpoises, mountain goats, and birds. Admiralty Island and Pack Creek Bear Preserve can also be reached by boat or plane - Admiralty Island has the highest concentration of brown bears in the world, and visitors with a permit may view the bears at Pack Creek.

Population	29,756	**Longitude**	134-45-35 W
Area (Land)	2593.6 sq mi	**County**	Juneau Borough
Area (Water)	487.6 sq mi	**Time Zone**	Alaska
Elevation	50 ft	**Area Code/s**	907
Latitude	58-32-24 N		

— Average Temperatures and Precipitation —

TEMPERATURES

	Jan	Feb	Mar	Apr	May	Jun	Jul	Aug	Sep	Oct	Nov	Dec
High	29	34	39	47	55	61	64	63	56	47	37	32
Low	19	23	27	32	39	45	48	47	43	37	27	23

PRECIPITATION

	Jan	Feb	Mar	Apr	May	Jun	Jul	Aug	Sep	Oct	Nov	Dec
Inches	4.5	3.8	3.3	2.8	3.4	3.2	4.2	5.3	6.7	7.8	4.9	4.4

— Important Phone Numbers —

	Phone		Phone
AAA	888-460-4222	**Poison Control Center**	907-261-3193
Emergency	911	**Time/Temp**	907-586-3185
Events Line	907-586-5866	**Weather**	907-586-3997
Medical Referral	907-586-2611		

Juneau (Cont'd)

— Information Sources —

	City	State	Zip	Phone	Fax
Alaskan Convention & Tourist Services 206 Behrends Ave	Juneau	AK	99801	907-586-1462	586-2682
Centennial Hall Convention Center 101 Egan Dr	Juneau	AK	99801	907-586-5283	586-1135
Davis Log Cabin Visitor Information Center 134 3rd St *E-mail:* JuneauInfo@aol.com	Juneau	AK	99801	907-586-2201	586-6304
Juneau Borough 155 S Seward St	Juneau	AK	99801	907-586-5278	586-5385
Juneau Chamber of Commerce 3100 Channel Dr Suite 300 *E-mail:* jchcom@ptialaska.net	Juneau	AK	99801	907-463-3488	463-3489
Juneau City Hall 155 S Seward St **Fax:* City Clerk ■ *Web:* www.juneau.lib.ak.us	Juneau	AK	99801	907-586-5278	586-2536*
Juneau Convention & Visitors Bureau 369 S Franklin St Suite 203 *TF:* 888-581-2201 ■ *Web:* www.traveljuneau.com/ ■ *E-mail:* jcvb@ptialaska.net	Juneau	AK	99801	907-586-1737	586-1449
Juneau Economic Development Council 612 W Willoughby Ave Suite A *Web:* www.ptialaska.net/~jedc/	Juneau	AK	99801	907-463-3662	463-3929
Juneau Mayor 155 S Seward St *Web:* www.juneau.lib.ak.us/cbj/assembly/assemb.htm	Juneau	AK	99801	907-586-5257	586-5385
Juneau Planning Dept 155 S Seward St	Juneau	AK	99801	907-586-5230	586-3365
Juneau Public Library 292 Marine Way *Web:* www.juneau.lib.ak.us/library/jpl.htm	Juneau	AK	99801	907-586-5324	586-5383

On-Line Resources

Best Read Guide Juneau	bestreadguide.com/juneau
City Knowledge Juneau	www.cityknowledge.com/ak_juneau.htm
Excite.com Juneau City Guide	www.excite.com/travel/countries/united_states/alaska/juneau
Juneau Alaska-The Capital City Home Page	www.juneau.lib.ak.us/juneau.htm
Juneau CityLink	www.usacitylink.com/citylink/juneau
Juneau Home Page	www.juneau.com
Non Profit Public Information	www.record.org
Travel Connection	www.alaska4you.com
Virtual Juneau	www.alaska.net/~dpharris/

— Transportation Services —

AIRPORTS

■ **Juneau International Airport (JNU)**

	Phone
8 miles N of downtown (approx 20 minutes)	907-789-7821

Airport Transportation

	Phone
Alaska Taxi $16-18 fare to downtown	907-780-6400
Capital Cab $17 fare to downtown	907-586-2772
Taku Glacier Cab $16 fare to downtown	907-586-2121

Commercial Airlines

	Phone		Phone
Delta	800-221-1212	**LAB Flying Service**	800-426-0543

Charter Airlines

	Phone		Phone
Air North Charter	907-789-2007	**Haines Airways**	907-766-2646
Alaska Coastal Airlines Inc	907-789-7818	**Ward Air Inc**	907-789-9150
Alaska Seaplanes	907-789-3331	**Wings of Alaska**	907-789-0790
Coastal Helicopters Inc	907-789-5600		

CAR RENTALS

	Phone		Phone
Allstar/Practical	907-790-2414	**National**	907-789-9814
Hertz	907-789-9494	**Rent-A-Wreck**	907-789-4111

LIMO/TAXI

	Phone		Phone
Alaska Taxi	907-780-6400	**Juneau Limousine**	907-463-5466
Capital Cab	907-586-2772	**Taku Glacier Cab**	907-586-2121

MASS TRANSIT

	Phone
Capital Transit $1.25 Base fare	907-789-6901

— Accommodations —

HOTELS, MOTELS, RESORTS

	City	State	Zip	Phone	Fax
Adlersheim Lodge 34 Mile Glacier Hwy	Juneau	AK	99801	907-723-4447	
Alaskan Hotel 167 S Franklin St *TF:* 800-327-9347	Juneau	AK	99801	907-586-1000	463-3775
Bergman Hotel 434 3rd St	Juneau	AK	99801	907-586-1690	463-2678
Best Western Country Lane Inn 9300 Glacier Hwy *TF:* 800-528-1234	Juneau	AK	99801	907-789-5005	789-2818
Best Western Landing 3434 Tongass Ave *TF:* 800-428-8304	Ketchikan	AK	99901	907-225-5166	225-6900
Blueberry Lodge 9436 N Douglas Hwy *Web:* www.alaska.net/~jayjudy/ ■ *E-mail:* jayjudy@alaska.net	Juneau	AK	99801	907-463-5886	463-5886
Breakwater Inn 1711 Glacier Ave *TF:* 800-544-2250 ■ *Web:* www.alaskaone.com/breakwater/ ■ *E-mail:* breakwtr@ptialaska.net	Juneau	AK	99801	907-586-6303	463-4820
Driftwood Lodge 435 Willoughby Ave *TF:* 800-544-2239	Juneau	AK	99801	907-586-2280	586-1034
Glacier Bay Country Inn Mile 1 Tong Rd *TF:* 800-628-0912 ■ *Web:* www.glacierbayalaska.com ■ *E-mail:* info@glacierbayalaska.com	Gustavus	AK	99826	907-697-2288	697-2289
Goldbelt Hotel 51 W Egan Dr *TF:* 800-478-6909	Juneau	AK	99801	907-586-6900	463-3567
Gustavus Inn at Glacier Bay Mile 1 Gustavus Rd *TF:* 800-649-5220	Gustavus	AK	99826	907-697-2254	697-2255
Imperial Hotel 241 Front St	Juneau	AK	99801	907-463-3340	
Inn at the Waterfront 455 S Franklin St	Juneau	AK	99801	907-586-2050	586-2999
Mount Juneau Inn 1801 Glacier Hwy *Web:* www.mtjuneauinn.com	Juneau	AK	99801	907-463-5855	463-5423
Pearson's Pond Luxury Inn 4541 Sawa Cir	Juneau	AK	99801	907-789-3772	789-6722
Prospector Hotel 375 Whittier St *TF:* 800-331-2711 ■ *Web:* www.prospectorhotel.com	Juneau	AK	99801	907-586-3737	586-1204
Pybus Point Lodge 1873 Shell Simmons Rd	Juneau	AK	99801	907-790-4866	
Super 8 Motel 2295 Trout St *TF:* 800-800-8000	Juneau	AK	99801	907-789-4858	789-5819
Travelodge Juneau Airport 9200 Glacier Hwy *TF:* 800-578-7878	Juneau	AK	99801	907-789-9700	789-1969
Westmark Baranof Hotel 127 N Franklin St *TF:* 800-544-0970 ■ *Web:* www.westmarkhotels.com/locations/juneau/juneau.html	Juneau	AK	99801	907-586-2660	586-8315
Whaler's Cove Lodge Mile 1 Killisnoo Rd	Angoon	AK	99820	907-788-3123	788-3104

— Restaurants —

	City	State	Zip	Phone
Armadillo Tex-Mex Cafe (Mexican) 431 S Franklin St	Juneau	AK	99801	907-586-1880
Atrium Cafe (American) 8800 Glacier Hwy	Juneau	AK	99801	907-789-2020
Breakwater Restaurant (Seafood) 1711 Glacier Ave	Juneau	AK	99801	907-586-6303
Canton House (Chinese) 8585 Old Daily Rd	Juneau	AK	99801	907-789-5075
Capital Cafe (American) 127 N Franklin St	Juneau	AK	99801	907-586-2660
Chan's Thai Kitchen (Thai) 11806 Glacier Hwy	Juneau	AK	99801	907-789-9777
Chinooks Restaurant (Continental) 51 W Eagan Dr	Juneau	AK	99801	907-586-6900
Cookhouse The (American) 200 Admiral Way	Juneau	AK	99801	907-463-3658
Donna's Restaurant (American) 9131 Glacier Hwy	Juneau	AK	99801	907-789-1470
El Sombrero (Mexican) 157 S Franklin St	Juneau	AK	99801	907-586-6770
Fernando's Restaurant (Mexican) 116 N Franklin St	Juneau	AK	99801	907-463-3992
Fiddlehead Restaurant (Continental) 429 W Willoughby Ave *Web:* www.alaska.net/~fiddle/	Juneau	AK	99801	907-586-3150
Glacier Restaurant (American) 1873 Shell Simmons Dr	Juneau	AK	99801	907-789-9538
Gold Creek Salmon Bake (American) 1061 Salmon Creek Ln	Juneau	AK	99801	907-789-0052
Gold Dining Room (Steak/Seafood) 127 N Franklin St	Juneau	AK	99801	907-586-2660
Grandma's Feather Bed (Steak/Seafood) 2348 Mendenhall Loop Rd	Juneau	AK	99801	907-789-5566
Hangar On The Wharf (Seafood) 2 Marine Way Suite 106	Juneau	AK	99801	907-586-5018
Jovany's (Italian) 9121 Glacier Hwy	Juneau	AK	99801	907-789-2339
Mi Casa (Mexican) 9200 Glacier Hwy	Juneau	AK	99801	907-789-3636

Juneau — Restaurants (Cont'd)

				Phone
Mike's Place (Continental) 1102 2nd St	Juneau	AK	99824	907-364-3271
Olivia's de Mexico (Mexican) 222 Seward St	Juneau	AK	99801	907-586-6870
Oriental Express (Chinese) 210 Seward St	Juneau	AK	99801	907-586-6990
Rick's Cafe (American) 702 Willoughby Ave	Juneau	AK	99801	907-463-5111
Second Course (Asian) 214 Front St	Juneau	AK	99801	907-463-5533
Summit Restaurant (Seafood) 455 S Franklin St	Juneau	AK	99801	907-586-2050
TK Maguire's (Steak/Seafood) 375 Whittier St	Juneau	AK	99801	907-586-3737
Valley Restaurant (American) 9320 Glacier Hwy	Juneau	AK	99801	907-789-1422
Vintage Fare Cafe (American) 8745 Glacier Hwy	Juneau	AK	99801	907-789-1865

— Goods and Services —

SHOPPING

				Phone	Fax
Mendenhall Mall 9109 Mendenhall Mall Rd	Juneau	AK	99801	907-789-0090	789-0019
Merchant's Wharf Mall 2 Marine Way	Juneau	AK	99801	907-463-4847	586-1476
Mount Juneau Artists 211 Front St Miners Mercantile Mall	Juneau	AK	99801	907-586-2108	
Mount Juneau Trading Post 151 S Franklin St	Juneau	AK	99801	907-586-3426	
Senate Shopping Mall 175 S Franklin St	Juneau	AK	99801	907-463-4163	463-4122

BANKS

				Phone	Fax
Alaska Federal Savings Bank 2094 Jordan Ave	Juneau	AK	99801	907-789-4844	790-5110
First Bank 1 SeaAlaska Plaza	Juneau	AK	99801	907-586-8001	586-8004
First National Bank of Anchorage 238 Front St	Juneau	AK	99801	907-586-2550	586-5426
KeyBank NA 234 Seward St	Juneau	AK	99801	907-586-6800	463-4983
National Bank of Alaska 123 Seward St	Juneau	AK	99801	907-586-3324	463-3997

BUSINESS SERVICES

	Phone		Phone
Airborne Express	800-247-2676	**Mail Boxes Etc**	800-789-4623
BAX Global	800-225-5229	**Post Office**	907-586-7987
DHL Worldwide Express	907-747-3063	**UPS**	800-742-5877
Federal Express	800-238-5355	**Western Parcel Express**	907-789-5161

— Media —

PUBLICATIONS

				Phone	Fax
Capital City Weekly 1910 Alex Holden Way	Juneau	AK	99801	907-789-4144	789-0987
Web: www.capweek.com ■ *E-mail:* capweek@ptialaska.net					

TELEVISION

				Phone	Fax
KATH-TV Ch 5 (NBC) 1107 W 8th St	Juneau	AK	99801	907-586-8384	586-8394
KIRO-TV Ch 7 (CBS) 2807 3rd Ave	Seattle	WA	98121	206-728-7777	441-4840
Web: www.kirotv.com ■ *E-mail:* kironews7@kiro-tv.com					
KJUD-TV Ch 8 (ABC) 175 S Franklin St Suite 320	Juneau	AK	99801	907-586-3145	463-3041
Web: www.aksupersite.com					
KTOO-TV Ch 3 (PBS) 360 Egan Dr	Juneau	AK	99801	907-586-1670	586-3612
Web: www.juneau.com/ktoo/ ■ *E-mail:* ktoo@juneau.com					

RADIO

				Phone	Fax
KCAW-FM 104.7 MHz (NPR) 2B Lincoln St	Sitka	AK	99835	907-747-5877	747-5977
E-mail: kcaw@ptialaska.net					
KINY-AM 800 kHz (AC) 1107 W 8th St Suite 2	Juneau	AK	99801	907-586-6037	586-3266
Web: www.ptialaska.net/~kiny ■ *E-mail:* kiny@ptialaska.net					
KJNO-AM 630 kHz (N/T) 3161 Channel Dr 2nd Fl	Juneau	AK	99801	907-586-3630	463-3685
KSUP-FM 106.3 MHz (Rock) 1107 W 8th St Suite 2	Juneau	AK	99801	907-586-6037	586-3266
Web: www.ptialaska.net/~ksup ■ *E-mail:* ksup@ptialaska.net					
KTKU-FM 105.1 MHz (Ctry) 3161 Channel Dr Suite 2	Juneau	AK	99801	907-586-3630	463-3685
KTOO-FM 104.3 MHz (NPR) 360 Egan Dr	Juneau	AK	99801	907-586-1670	586-3612
Web: www.juneau.com/ktoo/radio ■ *E-mail:* ktoo@juneau.com					

— Colleges/Universities —

				Phone	Fax
University of Alaska Southeast Juneau Campus 11120 Glacier Hwy	Juneau	AK	99801	907-465-6457	465-6365
TF Admissions: 877-465-4827 ■ *Web:* www.jun.alaska.edu					

— Hospitals —

				Phone	Fax
Bartlett Memorial Hospital 3260 Hospital Dr	Juneau	AK	99801	907-586-2611	
Web: www.bartletthospital.org					
Juneau Medical Clinic 9309 Glacier Hwy Suite B301	Juneau	AK	99801	907-789-6766	789-6703

— Attractions —

				Phone	Fax
Admiralty Island & Pack Creek Bear Preserve 101 Egan Dr	Juneau	AK	99801	907-586-8751	
Alaska State Capitol 4th & Seward Sts	Juneau	AK	99801	907-465-2479	465-3234
Alaska State Museum 395 Whittier St	Juneau	AK	99801	907-465-2901	465-2976
Web: www.educ.state.ak.us/lam/museum/asmhome.html					
Alaskan Brewing Co 5429 Shaune Dr	Juneau	AK	99801	907-780-5866	
Web: www.alaskanbeer.com					
Auk Nu Glacier Bay Tours 76 Egan Dr 1st Fl	Juneau	AK	99801	907-463-5510	586-1337
Eaglecrest Ski Area 155 S Seward St	Juneau	AK	99801	907-586-5284	586-5677
Web: www.juneau.lib.ak.us/eaglecrest/eaglcrst.htm					
Glacier Bay National Park & Preserve PO Box 140	Gustavus	AK	99826	907-697-2230	697-2654
Web: www.nps.gov/glba/					
House of Wickersham 213 7th St	Juneau	AK	99801	907-586-9001	789-3118
Juneau Arts & Humanities Council 206 N Franklin St	Juneau	AK	99801	907-586-2787	586-2148
E-mail: jahc@alaska.net					
Juneau Douglas City Museum 114 4th St	Juneau	AK	99801	907-586-3572	586-3203
Web: www.juneau.lib.ak.us/parksrec/museum/museum.htm					
Juneau Symphony Juneau Douglas High School Auditorium	Juneau	AK	99802	907-586-4676	586-4676
Juneau Trail System 400 Willoughby Ave	Juneau	AK	99801	907-465-4563	
Klondike Gold Rush National Historical Park 2nd St & Broadway	Skagway	AK	99840	907-983-2921	983-9249
Web: www.nps.gov/klgo/klgo_vvc.htm ■ *E-mail:* klgo_ranger_activities@nps.gov					
Mendenhall Glacier 13 miles W of downtown	Juneau	AK	99801	907-586-8800	
Mount Roberts Tramway 490 S Franklin St	Juneau	AK	99801	907-463-3412	463-5095
Web: www.alaska.net/~junotram/ ■ *E-mail:* junotram@alaska.net					
Oliver Inlet State Marine Park 400 Willoughby Ave	Juneau	AK	99801	907-465-4563	465-5330
Perseverance Theatre 914 3rd St	Douglas	AK	99824	907-364-2421	364-2603
Saint James Bay State Marine Park 40 miles N of Juneau	Juneau	AK	99801	907-465-4563	
Saint Nicholas Russian Orthodox Church 326 5th St	Juneau	AK	99801	907-586-1023	
Shelter Island State Marine Park 25 miles N of Juneau Shelter Island	Juneau	AK	99801	907-465-4563	
Sitka National Historical Park 106 Metlakatla	Sitka	AK	99835	907-747-6281	747-5938
Web: www.nps.gov/sitk/					

— Events —

	Phone
Alaska Folk Festival (early April)	907-586-1737
Gallery Walk (early December)	907-586-1737
Gold Medal Basketball Tournament (late February-early March)	907-586-1737
Golden North Salmon Derby (August)	907-586-1737
Juneau Jazz & Classics Festival (late May)	907-463-3378

Arizona

Population (1999): 4,778,332 **Area (sq mi): 114,006**

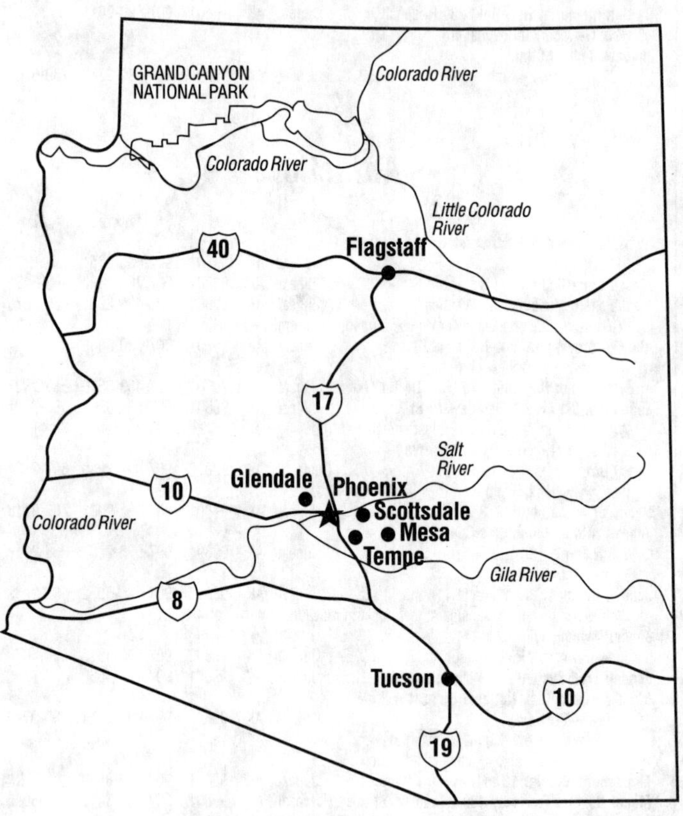

— State Information Sources —

				Phone	Fax
Arizona Chamber of Commerce					
1221 E Osborn Rd Suite 100	Phoenix	AZ	85014	602-248-9172	265-1262
Web: www.azchamber.com					
Arizona Commerce Dept					
3800 N Central Ave Suite 1500	Phoenix	AZ	85012	602-280-1300	280-1305
Web: www.commerce.state.az.us/					
Arizona Library Archives & Public Records Dept					
1700 W Washington St Rm 200	Phoenix	AZ	85007	602-542-4035	542-4972
Web: www.dlapr.lib.az.us ■ *E-mail:* archive@dlapr.lib.az.us					
Arizona State Government Information				602-542-4900	
Web: www.state.az.us/					
Arizona State Parks 1300 W Washington St.	Phoenix	AZ	85007	602-542-4174	542-4180
Web: www.pr.state.az.us					
Arizona Tourism Office					
2702 N 3rd St Suite 4015	Phoenix	AZ	85004	602-230-7733	240-5475
TF: 888-520-3434 ■ *Web:* www.arizonaguide.com					

ON-LINE RESOURCES

AccessArizona.com . . . . . www.accessarizona.com
American Southwest Arizona Guide . . . . . www.americansouthwest.net/arizona
Arizona Cities . . . . . dir.yahoo.com/Regional/U_S__States/Arizona/Cities
Arizona Counties & Regions . . . . dir.yahoo.com/Regional/U_S__States/Arizona/Counties_and_Regions
Arizona Destinations . . . . . amdest.com
Arizona Information Center . . . . . www.azinfo.com
Arizona Online Highways . . . . . www.azohwy.com
Arizona Scenario . . . . . scenariousa.dstylus.com/az/indexf.htm
Arizona Travel & Tourism Guide . . . . . www.travel-library.com/north_america/usa/arizona/index.html
Arizona Vacation Guide . . . . . www.arizonatourism.com/index.html
Arizona's WebHub . . . . . azwebhub.com
C Arizona . . . . . www.carizona.com
Cybertourist Arizona . . . . . www.cybertourist.com/arizona.shtml
Rough Guide Travel Arizona travel.roughguides.com/content/1186/index.htm
Travel.org-Arizona . . . . . travel.org/arizona.html
Yahoo! Get Local Arizona . . . . . dir.yahoo.com/Regional/U_S__States/Arizona

— Cities Profiled —

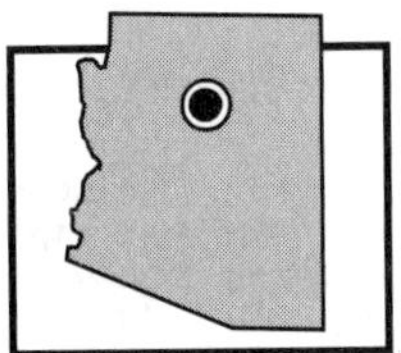

Flagstaff

Located in the northern part of Arizona, Flagstaff sits at the base of the San Francisco Peaks, the state's highest point at 12,633 feet. The combination of the city's altitude (7,000 feet), low humidity, and terrain create a mild climate year-round, though the area does experience a four-season year. The top attraction for visitors to the Flagstaff area is the Grand Canyon National Park, and rafting trips down the Colorado River or air trips in the Canyon can be arranged from Flagstaff. Tours of the Hopi, Navajo, Zuni, and White Mountain Apache areas of Arizona also are available. Other nearby attractions include the dormant volcanoes at Sunset Crater National Monument. Lowell Observatory, from which the planet Pluto was first observed, is located on Mars Hill in Flagstaff. The Observatory is open to the public and features both historic and modern telescopes. Native American displays can be seen at the Museum of Northern Arizona in Flagstaff.

Population 56,657
Area (Land) .... 63.2 sq mi
Area (Water) .... 0 sq mi
Elevation .... 6910 ft
Latitude .... 35-16-46 N
Longitude .... 111-66-30 W
County .... Coconino
Time Zone .... MST
Area Code/s 520

— Average Temperatures and Precipitation —

TEMPERATURES

	Jan	Feb	Mar	Apr	May	Jun	Jul	Aug	Sep	Oct	Nov	Dec
High	42	45	49	58	67	78	82	79	73	63	51	43
Low	15	18	21	27	33	41	51	49	41	31	22	16

PRECIPITATION

	Jan	Feb	Mar	Apr	May	Jun	Jul	Aug	Sep	Oct	Nov	Dec
Inches	2.0	2.1	2.6	1.5	0.7	0.4	2.8	2.8	2.0	1.6	2.0	2.4

— Important Phone Numbers —

	Phone
AAA	800-222-4357
Emergency	911
HotelDocs	800-468-3537
Medical Referral	520-779-3366
Poison Control Center	800-362-0101
Weather	520-774-3301

— Information Sources —

				Phone	Fax
Better Business Bureau Serving Central Northeast Northwest & Southwest Arizona 4428 N 12th St	Phoenix	AZ	85014	602-264-1721	263-0997
Web: www.phoenix.bbb.org					
Coconino County 219 E Cherry Ave	Flagstaff	AZ	86001	520-779-6800	779-6687
Web: co.coconino.az.us					
Flagstaff Chamber of Commerce 101 W Rt 66	Flagstaff	AZ	86001	520-774-4505	779-1209
Web: www.flagstaff.az.us/chamber.htm ■ *E-mail:* chamber@flagstaff.az.us					
Flagstaff City-Coconino County Public Library System 300 W Aspen Ave	Flagstaff	AZ	86001	520-779-7670	774-9573
Flagstaff City Hall 211 W Aspen Ave.	Flagstaff	AZ	86001	520-774-5281	779-7696
Web: www.flagstaff.az.us					
Flagstaff Community Development Dept 211 W Aspen Ave	Flagstaff	AZ	86001	520-779-7685	779-7696
Flagstaff Convention & Visitors Bureau 211 W Aspen Ave	Flagstaff	AZ	86001	520-779-7611	556-1305
TF: 800-217-2367 ■ *Web:* www.flagstaff.az.us/convention.html					
Flagstaff Mayor 211 W Aspen Ave	Flagstaff	AZ	86001	520-779-7600	776-7696
Flagstaff Visitor Center 1 E Rt 66	Flagstaff	AZ	86001	520-774-9541	556-1308
TF: 800-842-7293					

On-Line Resources

Area Guide Flagstaff .... www.areaguide.net/flagstaff
City Knowledge Flagstaff .... www.cityknowledge.com/az_flagstaff.htm
Excite.com Flagstaff City Guide .... www.excite.com/travel/countries/united_states/arizona/flagstaff
Flagstaff Arizona .... flagstaff-arizona.com
Flagstaff CityLink .... www.usacitylink.com/citylink/flagstaf/
Flagstaff Guide .... www.flagguide.com
Flagstaff Link .... www.flaglink.com/home.asp
NITC Travelbase City Guide Flagstaff .... www.travelbase.com/auto/guides/flagstaff-az.html

— Transportation Services —

AIRPORTS

	Phone
■ **Flagstaff Pulliam Airport (FLG)**	
3 miles S of downtown (approx 10 minutes)	520-556-1234

Airport Transportation

	Phone
Sun Taxi $10 fare to downtown	520-774-7400

Commercial Airlines

	Phone
America West	800-235-9292

CAR RENTALS

	Phone
Avis	520-774-8421
Budget	520-779-5255
Enterprise	520-836-9050
Hertz	520-774-4452
National	520-779-1975

LIMO/TAXI

	Phone
A Friendly Cab	520-774-4444
Arizona Taxi & Tours	520-779-1111
Harper's Limo	520-779-1234

MASS TRANSIT

	Phone
Pine County Transit $.75 Base fare	520-779-6624

RAIL/BUS

				Phone
Amtrak Station 1 E Rt 66	Flagstaff	AZ	86001	520-774-8679
TF: 800-872-7245				
Greyhound Bus Station 399 S Malpias Ln	Flagstaff	AZ	86001	520-774-4573
TF: 800-231-2222				

— Accommodations —

HOTEL RESERVATION SERVICES

	Phone	Fax
Advance Reservations Inn Arizona	480-990-0682	990-3390
TF: 800-456-0682 ■ *Web:* tucson.com/inn ■ *E-mail:* micasa@primenet.com		
Grand Canyon National Park Lodges	520-638-2631	638-9247*
**Fax:* Mail Rm		

HOTELS, MOTELS, RESORTS

				Phone	Fax
AmeriSuites Hotel 2455 S Beulah Blvd	Flagstaff	AZ	86001	520-774-8042	774-5524
TF: 800-833-1516					
Autolodge Flagstaff 1313 S Milton Rd.	Flagstaff	AZ	86001	520-774-6621	
Best Western Grand Canyon Squire Inn PO Box 130	Grand Canyon	AZ	86023	520-638-2681	638-2782
TF: 800-622-6966 ■ *Web:* www.grandcanyonsquire.com					
Best Western Pony Soldier Motel 3030 E Rt 66	Flagstaff	AZ	86004	520-526-2388	527-8329
TF: 800-356-4143					

Flagstaff — Hotels, Motels, Resorts (Cont'd)

				Phone	Fax
Bright Angel Lodge 1 Main St	Grand Canyon	AZ	86023	520-638-2631	638-2876
Budget Host Saga Motel 820 W Hwy 66	Flagstaff	AZ	86001	520-779-3631	
TF: 800-283-4678 ■ *Web:* www.budgethost.com/text/Arizona.html#Arizona ■ *E-mail:* mail@budgethost.com					
Chalet Lodge 1990 E Route 66	Flagstaff	AZ	86004	520-774-2779	
Comfort Inn 914 S Milton Rd	Flagstaff	AZ	86001	520-774-7326	774-7328
TF: 800-228-5150					
Days Inn 1000 W Rt 66	Flagstaff	AZ	86001	520-774-5221	774-4977
TF: 800-329-7466					
Days Inn 2735 S Woodlands Village Blvd	Flagstaff	AZ	86001	520-779-1575	779-0044
TF: 800-329-7466					
Days Inn 3601 E Lockett Rd	Flagstaff	AZ	86004	520-527-1477	527-0228
TF: 800-329-7466					
Econo Lodge 2355 S Beulah Blvd	Flagstaff	AZ	86001	520-774-2225	774-2225
TF: 800-490-6562					
Econo Lodge Lucky Lane 2480 E Lucky Ln	Flagstaff	AZ	86001	520-774-7701	774-7855
TF: 800-553-2666					
Economy Inn 224 Mikes Pike	Flagstaff	AZ	86001	520-774-8888	
El Tovar Hotel PO Box 699	Grand Canyon	AZ	86023	520-638-2631	638-2855
Embassy Suites Flagstaff 706 S Milton Rd	Flagstaff	AZ	86001	520-774-4333	774-0216
TF: 800-362-2779 ■ *Web:* www.thecanyon.com/embassyflagstaff/ ■ *E-mail:* embassyflagstaff@thecanyon.com					
Fairfield Inn by Marriott 2005 S Milton Rd	Flagstaff	AZ	86001	520-773-1300	773-1462
TF: 800-574-6395 ■ *Web:* fairfieldinn.com/FLGFI					
Family Inn 121 S Milton Rd	Flagstaff	AZ	86001	520-774-8820	774-1044
Flagstaff Travelodge 2610 E Rt 66	Flagstaff	AZ	86004	520-526-1399	527-8626
Hampton Inn 3501 E Lockett Rd	Flagstaff	AZ	86004	520-526-1885	526-9885
TF: 888-222-2052					
Hassayampa Inn 122 E Gurley St	Prescott	AZ	86301	520-778-9434	445-8590
TF: 800-322-1927 ■ *Web:* www.hassayampainn.com ■ *E-mail:* inn@primenet.com					
Highland Country Inn 223 S Milton Rd	Flagstaff	AZ	86001	520-774-5041	774-5651
Holiday Inn 2320 E Lucky Ln	Flagstaff	AZ	86004	520-526-1150	779-2610
TF: 800-465-4329					
Howard Johnson Hotel 2200 E Butler Ave	Flagstaff	AZ	86004	520-779-6944	774-3990
TF: 800-446-4656					
Howard Johnson Inn 3300 E Rt 66	Flagstaff	AZ	86004	520-526-1826	527-1872
TF: 800-437-7137					
Inn Suites Hotel Flagstaff/Grand Canyon 1008 E Rt 66	Flagstaff	AZ	86001	520-774-7356	556-0130
TF: 800-898-9124 ■ *Web:* www.innsuites.com/hotelflagstaff.htm					
L'Auberge de Sedona 301 L'Auberge Ln	Sedona	AZ	86336	520-282-7131	282-1064
TF: 800-272-6777 ■ *Web:* www.lauberge.com					
La Quinta Inn 2015 S Beulah Blvd	Flagstaff	AZ	86001	520-556-8666	214-9140
TF: 800-687-6667					
Little America Hotel 2515 E Butler Ave	Flagstaff	AZ	86004	520-779-2741	779-7983
TF: 800-352-4386					
Monte Vista Hotel 100 N San Francisco St	Flagstaff	AZ	86001	520-779-6971	779-2904
TF: 800-545-3068 ■ *Web:* www.hotelmontevista.com ■ *E-mail:* montev@infomagic.com					
Motel 6 2745 S Woodlands Village Blvd	Flagstaff	AZ	86001	520-779-3757	779-3757
TF: 800-466-8356					
Poco Diablo Resort PO Box 1709	Sedona	AZ	86339	520-282-7333	282-2090
TF: 800-528-4275					
Quality Inn 2000 S Milton Rd	Flagstaff	AZ	86001	520-774-8771	773-9382
TF: 800-228-5151					
Radisson Woodlands Plaza Hotel 1175 W Rt 66	Flagstaff	AZ	86001	520-773-8888	773-0597
TF: 800-333-3333					
Ramada Limited 2350 E Lucky Ln	Flagstaff	AZ	86004	520-779-3614	774-5834
TF: 800-272-6232					
Ramada Limited 2755 Woodlands Village Blvd	Flagstaff	AZ	86001	520-773-1111	774-1449
TF: 800-272-6232					
Red Roof Inn 2520 E Lucky Ln	Flagstaff	AZ	86004	520-779-5121	774-3809
TF: 800-545-5525					
Relax Inn 1500 E Route 66	Flagstaff	AZ	86001	520-779-4469	
Residence Inn by Marriott 3440 N Country Club Rd & I-40	Flagstaff	AZ	86004	520-526-5555	527-0328
TF: 800-331-3131 ■ *Web:* www.residenceinn.com/FLGRI					
Rodeway Inn 913 S Milton Rd	Flagstaff	AZ	86001	520-774-5038	774-8232
TF: 800-228-2000					
Sleep Inn 2765 Woodlands Village Blvd	Flagstaff	AZ	86001	520-556-3000	774-1901
TF: 800-753-3746					
Super 8 Motel 3725 Kasper Ave	Flagstaff	AZ	86004	520-526-0818	526-8786
TF: 888-324-9131					
Travelodge Flagstaff University 801 W Hwy 66	Flagstaff	AZ	86001	520-774-3381	774-1648
TF: 800-578-7878					
Weatherford Hotel 23 N Leroux St	Flagstaff	AZ	86001	520-774-2731	773-8951

— Restaurants —

				Phone
August Moon Chinese Restaurant (Chinese) 1300 S Milton Rd	Flagstaff	AZ	86001	520-774-5280
Beaver Street Brewery (American) 11 S Beaver St	Flagstaff	AZ	86001	520-779-0079
Buster's Restaurant & Bar (American) 1800 S Milton Rd	Flagstaff	AZ	86001	520-774-5155
Cafe Espress (Gourmet) 16 N San Francisco St	Flagstaff	AZ	86001	520-774-0541
Charly's Pub & Grill (Southwest) 23 N Leroux St	Flagstaff	AZ	86001	520-779-1919
Chez Marc Bistro (French) 503 Humphreys St	Flagstaff	AZ	86001	520-774-1343
Collins Irish Pub (Irish) 2 E Rt 66	Flagstaff	AZ	86001	520-214-7363
Cottage Place (Continental) 126 W Cottage Ave	Flagstaff	AZ	86001	520-774-8431
Crown Railroad Cafe (American) 2700 S Woodlands Village Blvd	Flagstaff	AZ	86001	520-774-6775
Dara Thai (Thai) 14 S San Francisco	Flagstaff	AZ	86001	520-774-0047
Dehli Palace Cuisine of India (Indian) 2700 S Woodlands Village Blvd	Flagstaff	AZ	86001	520-556-0019
El Charro Cafe (Mexican) 409 S San Francisco St	Flagstaff	AZ	86001	520-779-0552
Fiddlers (Steak) 702 S Milton Rd	Flagstaff	AZ	86001	520-774-6689
Grand Canyon Cafe (Chinese) 110 E Hwy 66	Flagstaff	AZ	86001	520-774-2252
Hassib's (Lebanese) 211 S San Francisco St	Flagstaff	AZ	86001	520-774-1037
Mad Italian (Italian) 101 S San Francisco St	Flagstaff	AZ	86001	520-779-1820
Pasto (Italian) 19 E Aspen Ave	Flagstaff	AZ	86001	520-779-1937
Sakura (Japanese) 1175 W Rt 66	Flagstaff	AZ	86001	520-773-9118
Salsa Brava (Mexican) 1800 S Milton Rd	Flagstaff	AZ	86001	520-774-1083
Tamale Pot (Mexican) 1924 E Arrowhead Ave	Flagstaff	AZ	86004	520-773-1515
Village Inn (American) 1111 S Milton Rd	Flagstaff	AZ	86001	520-774-8754
Wienerschnitzel (American) 1302 E Santa Fe Ave	Flagstaff	AZ	86001	520-774-3211
Woodlands Cafe (Southwestern) 1175 W Rt 66	Flagstaff	AZ	86001	520-773-9118

— Goods and Services —

SHOPPING

				Phone	Fax
Flagstaff Mall 4650 N Hwy 89	Flagstaff	AZ	86004	520-526-4827	527-8196
Web: www.westcor.com/flg ■ *E-mail:* flg@westcor.com					
Historic Downtown Flagstaff 323 W Aspen Ave	Flagstaff	AZ	86002	520-774-1330	774-1397

BANKS

				Phone	Fax
Bank of America 4550 N Hwy 89	Flagstaff	AZ	86004	520-526-2574	526-8691
TF Cust Svc: 800-284-8491*					
Bank One Arizona NA 100 W Birch Ave	Flagstaff	AZ	86001	520-779-7411	779-7402
National Bank of Arizona 123 N Leroux St	Flagstaff	AZ	86001	520-779-9000	779-0333
TF: 888-244-6622					
Norwest Bank NA 211 N Leroux	Flagstaff	AZ	86001	520-214-2480	214-2484
TF Cust Svc: 800-326-6000*					

BUSINESS SERVICES

	Phone		Phone
Airborne Express	800-247-2676	**Kinko's**	520-779-5159
BAX Global	800-225-5229	**Mail Boxes Etc**	800-789-4623
DHL Worldwide Express	800-225-5345	**Post Office**	520-527-2440
Federal Express	800-238-5355	**UPS**	800-742-5877

— Media —

PUBLICATIONS

				Phone	Fax
Arizona Daily Sun‡ PO Box 1849	Flagstaff	AZ	86002	520-774-4545	774-4790

‡Daily newspapers

TELEVISION

				Phone	Fax
KAET-TV Ch 8 (PBS) PO Box 871405	Tempe	AZ	85287	480-965-3506	965-1000
Web: www.kaet.asu.edu ■ *E-mail:* kaet@asu.edu					
KBPX-TV Ch 13 (PAX) 2158 N 4th St	Flagstaff	AZ	86004	520-527-1300	527-1394
Web: www.pax.net/KBPX					
KNAZ-TV Ch 2 (NBC) 2201 N Vicky St	Flagstaff	AZ	86004	520-526-2232	526-8110
KNXV-TV Ch 15 (ABC) 515 N 44th St	Phoenix	AZ	85008	602-273-1500	685-3000
Web: www.knxv.com ■ *E-mail:* news15@primenet.com					
KPHO-TV Ch 5 (CBS) 4016 N Black Canyon Hwy	Phoenix	AZ	85017	602-264-1000	650-0761
Web: www.kpho.com					
KPNX-TV Ch 12 (NBC) 1101 N Central Ave	Phoenix	AZ	85004	602-257-1212	257-6619
KSAZ-TV Ch 10 (Fox) 511 W Adams St	Phoenix	AZ	85003	602-257-1234	262-0177

Flagstaff (Cont'd)

RADIO

				Phone	Fax
KAFF-AM 930 kHz (Ctry) PO Box 1930	Flagstaff	AZ	86002	520-774-5231	779-2988
Web: www.kaff.com					
KAFF-FM 93.0 MHz (Ctry) PO Box 1930	Flagstaff	AZ	86002	520-774-5231	779-2988
Web: www.kaff.com					
KFLX-FM 105.1 MHz (AAA) 112 E Rt 66 Suite 105	Flagstaff	AZ	86001	520-779-1177	774-5179
Web: www.kflx.com					
KMGN-FM 93.9 MHz (CR) PO Box 1930	Flagstaff	AZ	86001	520-774-5231	779-2988
Web: www.kmgn.com					
KNAU-FM 88.7 MHz (NPR) PO Box 5764	Flagstaff	AZ	86011	520-523-5628	523-7647
Web: www.knau.org ■ *E-mail:* knau@nau.edu					
KVNA-AM 600 kHz (N/T) 2690 E Huntington Dr	Flagstaff	AZ	86004	520-526-2700	774-5852
KVNA-FM 97.5 MHz (AC) 2690 E Huntington Dr	Flagstaff	AZ	86004	520-526-2700	774-5852
KZGL-FM 95.9 MHz (Rock) 2690 E Huntington Dr	Flagstaff	AZ	86004	520-526-2700	774-5852
Web: www.kzgl.com					

— Colleges/Universities —

				Phone	Fax
Northern Arizona University PO Box 4084	Flagstaff	AZ	86011	520-523-9011	523-6023
Web: www.nau.edu ■ *E-mail:* Undergraduate.Admissions@nau.edu					
Southwest School Missions Independent Bible Institute 2918 N Aris Ave	Flagstaff	AZ	86004	520-774-3890	774-2655

— Hospitals —

				Phone	Fax
Flagstaff Medical Center 1200 N Beaver St	Flagstaff	AZ	86001	520-779-3366	773-2315

— Attractions —

				Phone	Fax
Arboretum at Flagstaff 4001 S Woody Mountain Rd	Flagstaff	AZ	86001	520-774-1442	774-1441
Web: www.flagguide.com/arboretum/					
Arizona Historical Society Pioneer Museum 2340 N Fort Valley Rd	Flagstaff	AZ	86001	520-774-6272	774-1596
Arizona Snowbowl PO Box 40	Flagstaff	AZ	86002	520-779-1951	779-3019
Web: www.azsnowbowl.com/					
Canyon De Chelly National Monument Rt 7 - 3 mi E of Hwy 191	Chinle	AZ	86503	520-674-5500	674-5507
Web: www.nps.gov/cach/					
Coconino National Forest 2323 E Greenlaw Ln	Flagstaff	AZ	86004	520-527-3600	527-3620
Web: www.fs.fed.us/r3/coconino					
Flagstaff Symphony Orchestra PO Box 5658	Flagstaff	AZ	86011	520-523-5661	523-8994
TF: 888-520-7214 ■ *Web:* www.flagguide.com/symphony ■ *E-mail:* symphony@flagstaff.az.us					
Glen Canyon National Recreation Area PO Box 1507	Page	AZ	86040	520-608-6200	608-6259
Web: www.nps.gov/glca/					
Grand Canyon IMAX Theatre Hwy 64 & US 180 S Entrance	Grand Canyon	AZ	86023	520-638-2203	638-2807
Web: www.imaxtheatre.com/grandcanyon/ ■ *E-mail:* imax@thecanyon.com					
Grand Canyon National Park PO Box 129	Grand Canyon	AZ	86023	520-638-7888	
Web: www.thecanyon.com/nps ■ *E-mail:* info@thecanyon.com					
Grand Canyon National Park Museum Collection Grand Canyon National Park PO Box 129	Grand Canyon	AZ	86023	520-638-7769	638-7797
Hubbell Trading Post National Historic Site Navajo Indian Reservation	Ganado	AZ	86505	520-755-3475	755-3405
Web: www.nps.gov/hutr/					
Lowell Observatory 1400 W Mars Hill Rd	Flagstaff	AZ	86001	520-774-3358	774-6296
Web: www.lowell.edu/					
Meteor Crater & Museum of Astrogeology Exit 233 off I-40	Winslow	AZ	86047	520-289-2362	289-2598
TF: 800-289-5898 ■ *Web:* www.meteorcrater.com					
Montezuma Castle National Monument 2800 Montezuma Castle Hwy	Camp Verde	AZ	86322	520-567-5276	567-3597
Web: www.nps.gov/moca/					
Museum of Northern Arizona 3101 N Fort Valley Rd	Flagstaff	AZ	86001	520-774-5211	779-1527
TF: 800-423-1069 ■ *Web:* www.musnaz.org/					
Navajo National Monument HC 71 Box 3	Tonalea	AZ	86044	520-672-2366	672-2345
Web: www.nps.gov/nava/					
Northern Arizona University Art Museum & Galleries Old Main Bldg North Campus	Flagstaff	AZ	86011	520-523-3471	523-1424
Rainbow Bridge National Monument PO Box 1507	Page	AZ	86040	520-608-6200	608-6283
Web: www.nps.gov/rabr/					
Red Rock State Park 4050 Lower Red Rock Loop Rd	Sedona	AZ	86336	520-282-6907	282-5972
Web: www.pr.state.az.us/parkhtml/redrock.html					
Riordan Mansion State Historic Park 1300 Riordan Ranch St	Flagstaff	AZ	86001	520-779-4395	556-0253
Slide Rock State Park Hwy 89A 7 mi N of Sedona	Sedona	AZ	86339	520-282-3034	282-0245
Web: www.pr.state.az.us/parkhtml/sliderock.html					
Sunset Crater National Monument RR 3 Box 149	Flagstaff	AZ	86004	520-556-7042	714-0565
Web: www.nps.gov/sucr/					
Tuzigoot National Monument PO Box 219	Camp Verde	AZ	86322	520-634-5564	567-3597
Web: www.nps.gov/tuzi/					
Walnut Canyon National Monument Walnut Canyon Rd	Flagstaff	AZ	86004	520-526-3367	527-0246
Web: www.nps.gov/waca/					
Wupatki National Monument HC 33 Box 444A	Flagstaff	AZ	86004	520-556-7040	679-2349
Web: www.nps.gov/wupa/					

— Events —

	Phone
Christmas Herb & Craft Sale (early December)	520-774-1442
Coconino County Fair (Labor Day Weekend)	520-774-5130
Festival of Arts & Crafts Extraordinaire (early July)	520-779-1227
Flagstaff Chili Cook-off (late August)	520-526-4314
Flagstaff Festival of Science (late September-early October)	800-842-7293
Flagstaff Summerfest (early August)	520-774-9541
Flagstaff Winterfest (February)	800-842-7293
Independence Day Festival (July 4)	520-774-6272
Pine Country Rodeo (mid-June)	520-774-9541
Worldfest International Film Festival (early-mid-November)	800-501-0111

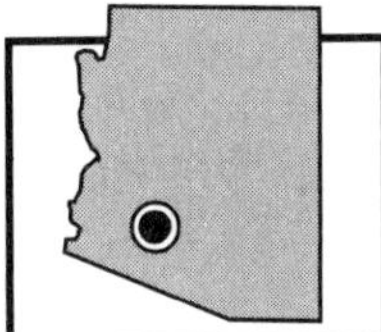

Glendale

Glendale, the business and financial center of Phoenix's Northwest metropolitan area, is home to the world's largest jet fighter training base, Luke Air Force Base. Known locally as the "Antique Shopping Capital of Arizona," Glendale boasts two attractions that are listed on the National Register of Historic Places"Catlin Court Historic District and Sahuaro Ranch Park. Catlin Court features renovated turn-of-the-century bungalows that house antique and other specialty shops, galleries, and restaurants along gaslight-lined streets. Sahuaro Ranch Park is noted both for its turn-of-the-century buildings and for its natural beauty, featuring peacocks, citrus groves, and a rose garden. Downtown Glendale is home to the Cerreta Candy Company, which makes candy for famous theme parks such as Disneyland and Knott's Berry Farm. Factory tours are available to visitors.

Population	193,482	**Longitude**	112-12-05 W
Area (Land)	52.2 sq mi	**County**	Maricopa
Area (Water)	0.1 sq mi	**Time Zone**	MST
Elevation	1,150 ft	**Area Code/s**	623
Latitude	33-35-02 N		

Glendale (Cont'd)

— Average Temperatures and Precipitation —

TEMPERATURES

	Jan	Feb	Mar	Apr	May	Jun	Jul	Aug	Sep	Oct	Nov	Dec
High	67	72	76	85	94	103	105	103	98	88	75	67
Low	38	42	46	52	60	69	77	75	68	56	45	38

PRECIPITATION

	Jan	Feb	Mar	Apr	May	Jun	Jul	Aug	Sep	Oct	Nov	Dec
Inches	0.9	0.9	1.0	0.3	0.1	0.1	0.8	1.3	0.9	0.7	0.7	1.2

— Important Phone Numbers —

	Phone		Phone
AAA	623-979-3700	**Medical Referral**	602-252-2015
American Express Travel	623-933-8256	**Poison Control Center**	602-253-3334
Dental Referral	602-957-4864	**Time/Temp**	602-265-5550
Emergency	911	**Weather**	602-265-5550
HotelDocs	800-468-3537		

— Information Sources —

				Phone	Fax
Better Business Bureau Serving Central Northeast Northwest & Southwest Arizona 4428 N 12th St	Phoenix	AZ	85014	602-264-1721	263-0997
Web: www.phoenix.bbb.org					
Glendale Chamber of Commerce PO Box 249	Glendale	AZ	85311	623-937-4754	937-3333
TF: 800-437-8669 ■ *Web:* www.glendaleazchamber.org ■ *E-mail:* info@glendaleazchamber.org					
Glendale City Hall 5850 W Glendale Ave	Glendale	AZ	85301	623-930-2000	915-2690
Web: www.ci.glendale.az.us					
Glendale Economic Development Dept 5850 W Glendale Ave	Glendale	AZ	85301	623-930-2988	931-5730
Web: www.ci.glendale.az.us/localgov/economic_dev					
Glendale Mayor 5850 W Glendale Ave.	Glendale	AZ	85301	623-930-2260	937-2764
Glendale Public Library 5959 W Brown St	Glendale	AZ	85302	623-930-3530	842-4209
Web: www.ci.glendale.az.us/localgov/library/library.htm					
Maricopa County 301 W Jefferson St 10th Fl	Phoenix	AZ	85003	602-506-3415	506-5997
Web: www.maricopa.gov					

On-Line Resources

Arizona Guide to Glendale .... www.arizonaguide.com/clients/glendale/
Glendale City Net .... www.excite.com/travel/countries/united_states/arizona/glendale

— Transportation Services —

AIRPORTS

■ **Phoenix Sky Harbor International Airport (PHX)**

	Phone
13 mi SE of downtown Glendale (approx 30 minutes)	602-273-3300
Web: www.phxskyharbor.com/skyharbr	

Airport Transportation

	Phone
Phoenix Transit System $1.25 fare to downtown Glendale	602-253-5000
SuperShuttle $15 fare to downtown Glendale	602-244-9000

Commercial Airlines

	Phone		Phone
America West	800-235-9292	**SkyWest**	800-453-9417
American	800-433-7300	**Southwest**	602-273-1221
Continental	800-525-0280	**TWA**	800-221-2000
Northwest	800-225-2525	**United**	800-241-6522
Shuttle by United	800-748-8853	**US Airways**	800-428-4322

Charter Airlines

	Phone		Phone
Corporate Jets Inc	480-948-2400	**Grand Aire Express Inc**	800-704-7263
Cutter Aviation Inc	602-273-1237	**Southwest Aircraft Charter**	480-969-2715
Global Group Inc	623-877-9350	**West Coast Charters Inc**	800-352-6153

CAR RENTALS

	Phone		Phone
Alamo	602-244-0897	**Enterprise**	623-931-9275
Budget	800-227-3678	**Hertz**	602-267-8822
Dollar	602-275-7588	**Thrifty**	623-412-1004

LIMO/TAXI

	Phone		Phone
Aries Limousine	623-930-8139	**Westown Taxi**	623-937-4238
TLC Cab	623-937-3158		

MASS TRANSIT

	Phone
Phoenix Transit System $1.25 Base fare	602-253-5000

RAIL/BUS

				Phone
Amtrak Station 401 W Harrison St	Phoenix	AZ	85003	602-253-0121
TF: 800-872-7245				
Greyhound/Trailways Bus Station 2115 E Buckeye Rd	Phoenix	AZ	85034	602-389-4200
TF: 800-231-2222				

— Accommodations —

HOTELS, MOTELS, RESORTS

				Phone	Fax
Best Western Inn 11201 Grand Ave	Youngtown	AZ	85363	623-933-8211	933-5062
TF: 800-528-1234					
Best Western Sage Inn 5940 NW Grand Ave	Glendale	AZ	85301	623-939-9431	937-3137
TF: 800-528-1234					
Crystal Motel 6352 NW Grand Ave	Glendale	AZ	85301	623-937-4166	
Econo Lodge 1520 N 84th Dr	Tolleson	AZ	85353	623-936-4667	936-3173
TF: 800-553-2666					
El Rancho Inn 4332 NW Grand Ave.	Glendale	AZ	85301	623-937-4721	
Holiday Inn Express 7885 W Arrowhead Towne Center Dr	Glendale	AZ	85308	623-412-2000	412-5522
TF: 800-465-4329					
Merv Griffin's Wickenburg Inn & Dude Ranch 34801 N Hwy 89	Wickenburg	AZ	85390	520-684-7811	684-2981
TF: 800-942-5362 ■ *Web:* www.merv.com/wickenburg/home.html ■ *E-mail:* wickenburg@merv.com					
Motel 6 11133 Grand Ave	Youngtown	AZ	85363	623-977-1318	977-7749
TF: 800-466-8356					
Ramada Plaza Hotel Metrocenter 12027 N 28th Dr.	Phoenix	AZ	85029	602-866-7000	942-7572
TF: 800-566-8535					
Rancho de los Caballeros 1551 S Vulture Mine Rd	Wickenburg	AZ	85390	520-684-5484	684-2267
Rock Haven Motel 5120 NW Grand Ave	Glendale	AZ	85301	623-937-0071	
Sheraton Crescent Hotel 2620 W Dunlap Ave	Phoenix	AZ	85021	602-943-8200	371-2857
TF: 800-423-4126					
Sierra Suites Hotels 9455 N Black Canyon Hwy	Phoenix	AZ	85021	602-395-0900	395-1900
TF: 800-474-3772					
Springhill Suites by Marriott 7810 W Bell Rd	Glendale	AZ	85308	623-878-6666	878-6611
TF: 888-227-9400					
Two Palms Motel 6924 NW Grand Ave	Glendale	AZ	85301	623-931-4449	
Wyndham Metrocenter Hotel 10220 N Metro Pkwy E	Phoenix	AZ	85051	602-997-5900	943-6156
TF: 800-996-3426					

— Restaurants —

				Phone
Ah-so Restaurant (Japanese) 6033 W Bell Rd	Glendale	AZ	85308	602-978-1177
Cajun Grill (Cajun) 7700 W Arrowhead Towne Ctr	Glendale	AZ	85308	623-486-9887
Caramba (Mexican) 5421 W Glendale Ave.	Glendale	AZ	85301	623-934-8888
Dragon Inn (Chinese) 5840 W Bell Rd	Glendale	AZ	85308	602-843-4330
El Paso Barbeque (American) 4303 W Peoria	Glendale	AZ	85302	623-931-2438
Erawan Restaurant (Thai) 15615 N 59th Ave.	Glendale	AZ	85306	602-978-1641

Glendale — Restaurants (Cont'd)

				Phone
Far East Restaurant (Chinese) 5131 W Glendale Ave	Glendale	AZ	85301	623-934-9951
Glendale Cafe (American) 5910 NW Grand Ave	Glendale	AZ	85301	623-435-2405
Golden Dragon Restaurant (Chinese) 6002 N 67th Ave	Glendale	AZ	85301	623-842-1896
Habachi-san (Japanese) 7700 W Arrowhead Towne Center Dr	Glendale	AZ	85308	623-412-8622
Iron Works Restaurant (American) 17233 N 45th Ave	Glendale	AZ	85308	602-843-0909
Island Teriyaki (Japanese) 5932 W Bell Rd	Glendale	AZ	85308	602-439-8315
Kiss the Cook Restaurant (American) 4915 W Glendale Ave	Glendale	AZ	85301	623-939-4663
La Palma (Mexican) 6028 N 43rd Ave	Glendale	AZ	85301	623-934-5306
La Perla Cafe (Mexican) 5912 W Glendale Ave	Glendale	AZ	85301	623-939-7561
Manuel's Fine Mexican Food (Mexican) 5670 W Peoria Ave	Glendale	AZ	85302	623-979-3500
Paesano Ristorante (Italian) 4356 W Thunderbird Rd	Glendale	AZ	85306	602-978-0771
Portofino Ristorante (Italian) 6020 W Bell Rd	Glendale	AZ	85308	602-938-1902
Rosario Ristorante (Italian) 9250 N 43rd Ave	Glendale	AZ	85302	623-931-1810
Shish Kebab House (Middle Eastern) 5023 W Olive Ave	Glendale	AZ	85302	623-937-8757
Village Inn (American) 5959 W Thunderbird Rd	Glendale	AZ	85306	602-843-1594

— Goods and Services —

SHOPPING

Name	City	State	Zip	Phone	Fax
Arrowhead Towne Center 7700 W Arrowhead Towne Ctr	Glendale	AZ	85308	623-979-7777	979-4447
Old Towne Shopping District 58th & Glendale Aves	Glendale	AZ	85301	623-435-0556	

BANKS

Name	City	State	Zip	Phone	Fax
Bank of America 5800 W Glenn Dr	Glendale	AZ	85301	602-915-6705	934-5182
Bank One 7003 N 57th Dr *TF:* 800-366-2265	Glendale	AZ	85301	602-589-3300	589-4204
Community Bank 4482 W Peoria Ave **Fax:* Cust Svc	Glendale	AZ	85302	623-939-3200	931-2997*
First Arizona Savings 4961 W Bell Rd Suite 10	Glendale	AZ	85308	602-547-1010	439-5474
M & I Thunderbird Bank 5704 W Glenn Dr **Fax Area Code:* 623	Glendale	AZ	85301	602-336-3863	435-1224*
Norwest Bank 6702 W Camelback Rd	Glendale	AZ	85303	623-873-2707	873-7447
Wells Fargo Bank 5732 W Glenn Dr **Fax Area Code:* 623 ■ *TF:* 800-869-3557	Glendale	AZ	85301	602-528-7301	939-7062*

BUSINESS SERVICES

	Phone		Phone
Allied Forces Temporary Service	623-435-8665	**Olsten Staffing Services**	623-930-7151
DHL Worldwide Express	800-225-5345	**Post Office**	800-275-8777
Federal Express	800-238-5355	**UPS**	800-742-5877
Kinko's	602-978-5050		

— Media —

PUBLICATIONS

Name	City	State	Zip	Phone	Fax
Arizona Republic‡ PO Box 1950 *TF:* 800-331-9303 ■ *Web:* www.azcentral.com	Phoenix	AZ	85001	602-444-8000	444-8044

‡*Daily newspapers*

TELEVISION

Name	City	State	Zip	Phone	Fax
KAET-TV Ch 8 (PBS) PO Box 871405 *Web:* www.kaet.asu.edu ■ *E-mail:* kaet@asu.edu	Tempe	AZ	85287	480-965-3506	965-1000
KNXV-TV Ch 15 (ABC) 515 N 44th St *Web:* www.knxv.com ■ *E-mail:* news15@primenet.com	Phoenix	AZ	85008	602-273-1500	685-3000
KPHO-TV Ch 5 (CBS) 4016 N Black Canyon Hwy *Web:* www.kpho.com	Phoenix	AZ	85017	602-264-1000	650-0761
KPNX-TV Ch 12 (NBC) 1101 N Central Ave	Phoenix	AZ	85004	602-257-1212	257-6619
KSAZ-TV Ch 10 (Fox) 511 W Adams St	Phoenix	AZ	85003	602-257-1234	262-0177
KTVK-TV Ch 3 (Ind) 5555 N 7th Ave *E-mail:* feedback@azfamily.com	Phoenix	AZ	85013	602-207-3333	207-3477
KUTP-TV Ch 45 (UPN) 4630 S 33rd St *Web:* www.kutp.com	Phoenix	AZ	85040	602-268-4500	276-4082

RADIO

Name	City	State	Zip	Phone	Fax
KHEP-AM 1280 kHz (Rel) 100 W Clarendon Ave Suite 720	Phoenix	AZ	85013	602-234-1280	234-1586
KKLT-FM 98.7 MHz (AC) 5300 N Central Ave	Phoenix	AZ	85012	602-274-6200	266-3858
KMXP-FM 96.9 MHz (AC) 645 E Missouri Ave Suite 360	Phoenix	AZ	85012	602-279-5577	230-2781
KOOL-FM 94.5 MHz (Oldies) 4745 N 7th St Suite 210 *Web:* www.koolradio.com	Phoenix	AZ	85014	602-956-9696	285-1450
KTAR-AM 620 kHz (N/T) 5300 N Central Ave	Phoenix	AZ	85013	602-274-6200	266-3858
KYOT-FM 95.5 MHz (Nost) 840 N Central Ave *Web:* www.kyot.com	Phoenix	AZ	85004	602-258-8181	440-6530

— Colleges/Universities —

Name	City	State	Zip	Phone	Fax
Arizona State University West Campus PO Box 37100 *Web:* www.west.asu.edu	Phoenix	AZ	85069	602-543-5500	543-8312
Glendale Community College 6000 W Olive Ave *Web:* www.gc.maricopa.edu ■ *E-mail:* info@gc.maricopa.edu	Glendale	AZ	85302	623-845-3000	845-3303
Sweetwater Bible College PO Box 5640	Glendale	AZ	85312	602-978-5511	588-3586

— Hospitals —

Name	City	State	Zip	Phone	Fax
Arrowhead Community Hospital 18701 N 67th Ave *Web:* www.baptisthealth.com/family/in_services/arrowhead.html	Glendale	AZ	85308	623-561-1000	561-7142
Glendale Family Health Center 5141 W Lamar Rd	Glendale	AZ	85301	623-931-9361	344-6701
Phoenix Baptist Hospital & Medical Center 2000 W Bethany Home Rd **Fax:* Admitting ■ *Web:* www.baptisthealth.com/family/in_services/pbh.html	Phoenix	AZ	85015	602-249-0212	279-5979*
Walter O Boswell Memorial Hospital 10401 Thunderbird Blvd	Sun City	AZ	85351	623-977-7211	933-3225

— Attractions —

Name	City	State	Zip	Phone	Fax
Barn Comedy Dinner Theatre 6508 W Bell Rd	Glendale	AZ	85308	623-979-5811	
Catlin Court Historic District 7141 N 58th Ave	Glendale	AZ	85301	623-937-4754	
Cerreta Candy Co 5345 W Glendale Ave *Web:* www.cerreta.com	Glendale	AZ	85301	623-930-9000	930-9085
Max's Dinner Theater 6727 N 47th Ave	Glendale	AZ	85301	623-937-1671	
PlayHouse Theatre for Children 7402 W Alexandria Way *Web:* members.aol.com/ptcaz/Main.html ■ *E-mail:* ptcaz@aol.com	Peoria	AZ	85381	623-487-9434	487-9476
Sahuaro Ranch Park 5850 W Glendale Ave	Glendale	AZ	85301	623-930-2820	931-9651
Sundome Center for the Performing Arts 19403 RH Johnson Blvd	Sun City West	AZ	85375	623-584-3118	584-7947

SPORTS TEAMS & FACILITIES

Name	City	State	Zip	Phone	Fax
Arizona Sahuaros (soccer) 16101 N 83rd Ave Peoria Sports Complex *Web:* www.azsahuaros.com ■ *E-mail:* mark@sahuaros.com	Peoria	AZ	85382	602-256-6356	492-0602

— Events —

	Phone
A Family A Fair (early April)	623-930-2820
Annual Quilt Show (mid-January-mid-March)	623-939-5782
Community Bank Concerts (June-July)	623-930-2820
Fourth of July Celebration (July 4)	623-937-4754

Glendale — Events (Cont'd)

	Phone
Front Porch Festival (late-September)	623-435-0556
Glendale Jazz Festival (late-April)	623-930-2960
Hot Air Balloon Race & Thunderbird Balloon Classic (early November)	480-312-6802
Juried Fine Arts Competition (early April)	623-939-5782
Performances in the Park (late April)	623-937-4754
Sahuaro Ranch Days (early November)	623-939-5782

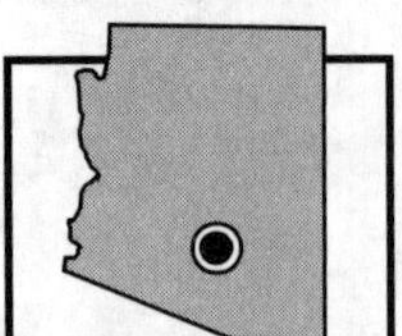

Mesa

Founded in 1878 by Mormon pioneers, Mesa, which means "tabletop" in Spanish, was given its name because of the fact that it is situated on a plateau overlooking the Salt River and the Valley of the Sun. Arizona's third largest city, Mesa has transformed itself from an agricultural community into a top business center, with seven of the top 500 manufacturers listed in Fortune magazine located there. Visitor attractions in Mesa include the Mesa Southwest Museum, the Arizona Museum for Youth, and the Champlin Fighter Aircraft Museum. A wide variety of outdoor recreational activities, from hot-air ballooning to white water rafting, are available throughout the area. Mesa is also the spring training home of the Chicago Cubs.

Population	360,076	**Longitude**	111-44-25 W
Area (Land)	108.61 sq mi	**County**	Maricopa
Area (Water)	0.2 sq mi	**Time Zone**	MST
Elevation	1,234 ft	**Area Code/s**	602
Latitude	33-25-03 N		

— Average Temperatures and Precipitation —

TEMPERATURES

	Jan	Feb	Mar	Apr	May	Jun	Jul	Aug	Sep	Oct	Nov	Dec
High	66	71	76	84	93	103	106	103	98	88	75	67
Low	40	43	47	53	60	68	77	76	69	58	47	40

PRECIPITATION

	Jan	Feb	Mar	Apr	May	Jun	Jul	Aug	Sep	Oct	Nov	Dec
Inches	0.8	0.8	0.9	0.3	0.2	0.1	0.9	1.1	0.9	0.7	0.8	1.1

— Important Phone Numbers —

	Phone		Phone
AAA	480-834-8296	**Medical Referral**	602-252-2844
American Express Travel	480-981-2102	**Poison Control Center**	602-253-3334
Dental Referral	602-957-4864	**Time/Temp**	602-265-5550
Emergency	911	**Weather**	602-265-5550

— Information Sources —

				Phone	Fax
Better Business Bureau Serving Central Northeast Northwest & Southwest Arizona 4428 N 12th St. *Web:* www.phoenix.bbb.org	Phoenix	AZ	85014	602-264-1721	263-0997
Maricopa County 301 W Jefferson St 10th Fl *Web:* www.maricopa.gov	Phoenix	AZ	85003	602-506-3415	506-5997
Mesa Chamber of Commerce 120 N Center St. *Web:* www.arizonaguide.com/cities/mesa/index.html	Mesa	AZ	85201	480-969-1307	827-0727
Mesa City Hall 55 N Center St *Web:* www.ci.mesa.az.us	Mesa	AZ	85201	480-644-2011	644-2418
Mesa Community & Conference Center 201 N Center	Mesa	AZ	85201	480-644-2178	644-2617
Mesa Community Development Office PO Box 1466 *Web:* www.ci.mesa.az.us/mega ■ *E-mail:* richard_mulligan@ci.mesa.az.us	Mesa	AZ	85211	480-644-2387	644-2757
Mesa Convention & Visitors Bureau 120 N Center St *TF:* 800-283-6372 ■ *Web:* www.arizonaguide.com/mesa ■ *E-mail:* mesacvb@getnet.com	Mesa	AZ	85201	480-827-4700	827-0727
Mesa Mayor PO Box 1466 *Web:* www.ci.mesa.az.us/citymgt/welcome.htm	Mesa	AZ	85211	480-644-2388	644-2175
Mesa Public Library 64 E 1st St. *Web:* www.ci.mesa.az.us/library	Mesa	AZ	85201	480-644-2702	644-3490

On-Line Resources

Anthill City Guide Mesa	www.anthill.com/city.asp?city=mesa
City Knowledge Mesa	www.cityknowledge.com/az_mesa.htm
Excite.com Mesa City Guide	www.excite.com/travel/countries/united_states/arizona/mesa
Mesa Link	www.axtek.com/mesalink/
NITC Travelbase City Guide Mesa	www.travelbase.com/auto/guides/mesa-az.html

— Transportation Services —

AIRPORTS

■ **Phoenix Sky Harbor International Airport (PHX)**

	Phone
13 mi W of downtown Mesa (approx 45 minutes) Web: www.phxskyharbor.com/skyharbr	602-273-3300

Airport Transportation

	Phone
Phoenix Transit System $1.25 fare to downtown Mesa	602-253-5000
SuperShuttle $14 fare to downtown Mesa	602-244-9000

Commercial Airlines

	Phone		Phone
Aero California	800-237-6225	**Northwest**	800-225-2525
AeroMexico	800-237-6639	**Shuttle by United**	800-748-8853
America West	800-235-9292	**SkyWest**	800-453-9417
American	800-433-7300	**Southwest**	602-273-1221
British Airways	800-247-9297	**TWA**	800-221-2000
Continental	800-525-0280	**United**	800-241-6522
Great Lakes	800-241-6522	**US Airways**	800-428-4322
Mesa	800-637-2247		

Charter Airlines

	Phone		Phone
Air West Inc	480-396-0688	**SAS Executive Aviation Ltd**	480-832-0704
Corporate Jets Inc	480-948-2400	**Southwest Aircraft Charter**	480-969-2715
Cutter Aviation Inc.	602-273-1237	**West Coast Charters Inc.**	800-352-6153
Grand Aire Express Inc	800-704-7263	**Westec Air Inc**	602-830-5300

CAR RENTALS

	Phone		Phone
Alamo	602-244-0897	**Enterprise**	480-898-8977
Avis	480-649-0399	**Hertz**	602-267-8822
Budget	602-267-1717	**Thrifty**	602-244-0311
Dollar	602-275-7588		

LIMO/TAXI

	Phone		Phone
AAA Cab	602-437-4000	**Roger's Limousine Service**	480-921-3878
Advanced Limousine Service	602-942-5700	**Taxi Taxi**	480-921-7777
Classic Limousine	602-252-5466	**Yellow Cab**	602-252-5071
Neal's Cab	480-835-0555		

MASS TRANSIT

	Phone
Phoenix Transit System $1.25 Base fare	602-253-5000
Valley Metro $1.25 Base fare	602-253-5000

Mesa (Cont'd)

RAIL/BUS

Name / Address	City	State	ZIP	Phone
Greyhound Bus Station 1423 S Country Club Rd *TF:* 800-231-2222	Mesa	AZ	85210	480-834-3360

— Accommodations —

HOTELS, MOTELS, RESORTS

Name / Address	City	State	ZIP	Phone	Fax
Arizona Golf Resort & Conference Center 425 S Power Rd *TF:* 800-528-8282 ■ *Web:* www.arizonaguide.com/arizona.golf/	Mesa	AZ	85206	480-832-3202	981-0151
Best Western Dobson Ranch Inn & Resort 1666 S Dobson Rd *TF:* 800-528-1356	Mesa	AZ	85202	480-831-7000	831-7000
Best Western Mesa Inn 1625 E Main St *TF:* 800-528-1234	Mesa	AZ	85203	480-964-8000	835-1272
Best Western Mezona Inn 250 W Main St *TF:* 800-528-8299	Mesa	AZ	85201	480-834-9233	844-7920
Best Western Papago Inn & Resort 7017 E McDowell Rd *TF:* 800-528-1234	Scottsdale	AZ	85257	480-947-7335	994-0692
Best Western Superstition Springs 1342 S Power Rd *TF:* 800-528-1234	Mesa	AZ	85206	480-641-1164	641-7253
Budget Suites Motel 537 S Country Club Dr	Mesa	AZ	85210	480-969-5248	833-1159
Camelback Resort & Spa 6302 E Camelback Rd *TF:* 800-891-8585	Scottsdale	AZ	85251	480-947-3300	994-0594
Colonade Motel Suites 5440 E Main St *TF:* 800-645-3702	Mesa	AZ	85205	480-981-8888	924-7218
Country Inn & Suites by Carlson 6650 E Superstition Springs Blvd *TF:* 800-456-4000	Mesa	AZ	85206	480-641-8000	641-9600
Courtyard by Marriott 1221 S Westwood St *TF:* 800-321-2211 ■ *Web:* courtyard.com/PHXME	Mesa	AZ	85210	480-461-3000	461-0179
Days Inn 333 W Juanita Ave *TF:* 800-329-7466	Mesa	AZ	85210	480-844-8900	844-0973
Days Inn East 5531 E Main St *TF:* 800-325-2525	Mesa	AZ	85205	480-981-8111	396-8027
Doubletree La Posada Resort 4949 E Lincoln Dr *TF:* 800-222-8733 ■ *Web:* www.doubletreehotels.com/DoubleT/Hotel141/160/160Main.htm	Scottsdale	AZ	85253	602-952-0420	840-8576
Extended StayAmerica 455 W Baseline Rd *TF:* 800-398-7829	Mesa	AZ	85210	480-632-0201	632-0195
Fairfield Inn by Marriott 1405 S Westwood Ave *TF:* 800-228-2800 ■ *Web:* fairfieldinn.com/PHXFM	Mesa	AZ	85210	480-668-8000	668-7313
Hampton Inn 1563 S Gilbert Rd *TF:* 800-426-7866	Mesa	AZ	85204	480-926-3600	926-4892
Hilton Pavillion 1011 W Holmes Ave *TF:* 800-445-8667 ■ *Web:* www.hilton.com/hotels/MESHPHF	Mesa	AZ	85210	480-833-5555	649-1380
Holiday Inn 1600 S Country Club Dr *TF:* 800-465-4329	Mesa	AZ	85210	480-964-7000	833-6419
Holiday Inn Express 5750 E Main *TF:* 800-888-3561	Mesa	AZ	85205	480-985-3600	832-1230
Holiday Inn Hotel & Conference Center 7353 E Indian School Rd *TF:* 800-695-6995	Scottsdale	AZ	85251	480-994-9203	941-2567
Holiday Inn SunSpree Resort 7601 E Indian Bend Rd *TF:* 800-852-5205 ■ *Web:* www.basshotels.com/holiday-inn/?_franchisee=PHXSS ■ *E-mail:* sunspree@getnet.com	Scottsdale	AZ	85250	480-991-2400	998-2261
Homestead Village 1920 W Isabella Ave *TF:* 888-782-9473	Mesa	AZ	85202	480-752-2266	752-7865
Hospitality Suites Resort 409 N Scottsdale Rd *TF:* 800-445-5115 ■ *Web:* www.amdest.com/az/scottsdale/hospitality.html	Scottsdale	AZ	85257	480-949-5115	941-8014
La Quinta Inn & Suites Mesa 902 W Grove Ave *TF:* 800-687-6667	Mesa	AZ	85210	480-844-8747	844-8850
La Quinta Inn & Suites Superstition Springs 6530 E Superstition Springs Blvd *TF:* 800-687-6667	Mesa	AZ	85206	480-654-1970	654-1973
Lost Dutchman Motel 560 S Country Club Dr **Fax Area Code:* 602	Mesa	AZ	85210	480-969-3581	835-7023*
Motel 6 336 W Hampton *TF:* 800-466-8356	Mesa	AZ	85210	480-844-8899	969-6749
Motel 6 630 W Main St *TF:* 800-466-8356	Mesa	AZ	85201	480-969-8111	655-0747
Quality Inn Royal Mesa 951 W Main St *TF:* 800-333-5501	Mesa	AZ	85201	480-833-1231	833-1231
Radisson Resort 7171 N Scottsdale Rd *TF:* 800-333-3333 ■ *Web:* www.arizonaguide.com/radissonscottsdale/	Scottsdale	AZ	85253	480-991-3800	948-1381
Ramada Limited 1750 E Main St *TF:* 800-653-1111	Mesa	AZ	85203	480-969-3600	649-2646
Ramada Suites 1410 S Country Club Dr *TF:* 800-272-6232	Mesa	AZ	85210	480-964-2897	461-0801
Ramada Valley Ho Resort 6850 E Main St *TF:* 800-321-4952 ■ *Web:* www.arizonaguide.com/valleyho/	Scottsdale	AZ	85251	480-945-6321	947-5270
Reflections at Red Mountain 2601 E McKellips Rd	Mesa	AZ	85213	480-844-8064	844-8508
Regal McCormick Ranch Resort 7401 N Scottsdale Rd *TF:* 800-222-8888 ■ *Web:* www.regal-hotels.com/scottsdale ■ *E-mail:* regal@getnet.com	Scottsdale	AZ	85253	480-948-5050	991-5572
Renaissance Cottonwoods Resort 6160 N Scottsdale Rd *TF:* 800-468-3571	Scottsdale	AZ	85253	480-991-1414	948-2205
Saguaro Lake Ranch 13020 Bush Hwy	Mesa	AZ	85215	480-984-2194	380-1490
Scottsdale Conference Resort 7700 E McCormick Pkwy *TF:* 800-528-0293	Scottsdale	AZ	85258	480-991-9000	596-7420
Scottsdale Embassy Suites 5001 N Scottsdale Rd *TF:* 800-528-1456 ■ *Web:* www.arizonaguide.com/embassyscottsdale/	Scottsdale	AZ	85250	480-949-1414	947-2675
Scottsdale Hilton Resort & Villas 6333 N Scottsdale Rd *TF:* 800-528-3119	Scottsdale	AZ	85250	480-948-7750	948-2232
Scottsdale Plaza Resort 7200 N Scottsdale Rd *TF:* 800-832-2025	Scottsdale	AZ	85253	480-948-5000	998-5971
Select Suites Peppertree 1318 S Vineyard St *TF:* 800-354-0893 ■ *Web:* www.selectsuites.com/smesa_main.html	Mesa	AZ	85210	480-833-2959	833-1643
Select Suites Sierra Madre 900 N Country Club Dr *TF:* 800-821-8005 ■ *Web:* www.selectsuites.com/nmesa_main.html	Mesa	AZ	85201	480-962-7940	649-3838
Select Suites Southern Gardens 960 W Southern Ave *TF:* 800-633-5972 ■ *Web:* www.selectsuites.com/fiesta_main.html	Mesa	AZ	85210	480-962-8343	898-3165
Sheraton Mesa 200 N Centennial Way *TF:* 800-456-6372	Mesa	AZ	85201	480-898-8300	964-9279
Shorebird Suites 1362 S Vineyard *TF:* 800-255-8021	Mesa	AZ	85210	480-833-5522	833-5598
Sleep Inn 6347 E Southern Ave *TF:* 888-275-3374	Mesa	AZ	85206	480-807-7760	807-2646
SunBurst Resort 4925 N Scottsdale Rd *TF:* 800-528-7867 ■ *Web:* www.sunburstresort.com	Scottsdale	AZ	85251	480-945-7666	946-4056
Super 8 Motel 6733 E Main St *TF:* 800-800-8000	Mesa	AZ	85205	480-981-6181	981-6181
Super 8 Town Center 3 E Main St *TF:* 800-800-8000	Mesa	AZ	85201	480-834-6060	834-6060
Trails West Motel 6502 E Apache Trail	Mesa	AZ	85205	480-985-9988	
Travelodge 22 S Country Club *TF:* 800-578-7878	Mesa	AZ	85210	480-964-5694	964-5697
Travelodge Suites 4244 E Main St *TF:* 800-578-7878	Mesa	AZ	85205	480-832-5961	830-9274

— Restaurants —

Name / Address	City	State	ZIP	Phone
Aloha Kitchen (Hawaiian) 2950 S Alma School Rd Suite 12	Mesa	AZ	85210	480-897-2451
Annabelle's (New American) 425 S Power Rd	Mesa	AZ	85206	480-832-3202
Bavarian Point (German) 4815 E Main St	Mesa	AZ	85205	480-830-0999
Bill Johnson's Big Apple (Barbecue) 950 E Main St	Mesa	AZ	85203	480-969-6504
Brunello of Mesa (Italian) 1954 S Dobson Rd	Mesa	AZ	85206	480-897-0140
Chevy's (Tex Mex) 1335 S Alma School Rd	Mesa	AZ	85210	480-833-1300
China Gate (Chinese) 2050 W Guadalupe	Mesa	AZ	85202	480-897-0607
D's Thai Food (Thai) 2431 E McKellips St	Mesa	AZ	85213	480-969-0087
Dos Lobos Cantina (Mexican) 200 N Centennial Way	Mesa	AZ	85201	480-898-8300
Ichi Ban (Japanese) 2015 S Alma School Rd	Mesa	AZ	85210	480-777-8433
Jade Empress (Chinese) 1840 W Broadway	Mesa	AZ	85202	480-833-3577
Kwan's Sampan (Chinese) 1927 N Gilbert Rd	Mesa	AZ	85203	480-969-6958
Landmark Restaurant (American) 809 W Main St	Mesa	AZ	85201	480-962-4652
Landry's Seafood (Seafood) 1320 W Southern Ave	Mesa	AZ	85202	480-969-4600
Macayo's (Mexican) 1920 S Dobson Rd	Mesa	AZ	85202	480-820-0237
Matta's (Mexican) 932 E Main St	Mesa	AZ	85203	480-964-7881
Mimi's Cafe (American) 1250 S Alma School Rd	Mesa	AZ	85210	480-833-4646
Monti's at the Ranch (Steak) 1644 S Dobson Rd	Mesa	AZ	85202	480-831-8877
Phuong Hoang Restaurant (Vietnamese) 1116 S Dobson Rd	Mesa	AZ	85202	480-649-1473
Pier de Orleans (Seafood) 61 E University	Mesa	AZ	85201	480-844-0666
Pink Pepper (Thai) 1941 W Guadalupe Rd	Mesa	AZ	85202	480-839-9009
Quail Run Restaurant (American) 200 N Centennial Way	Mesa	AZ	85201	480-464-5038

Mesa — Restaurants (Cont'd)

Name / Address	City	State	ZIP	Phone
Rockin' R Ranch (American) 6136 E Baseline Rd.	Mesa	AZ	85206	480-832-1539
Romeo's Euro Cafe (Mediterranean) 1111 S Longmore	Mesa	AZ	85202	480-962-4224
Seafood Market & Restaurant (Seafood) 1318 W Southern Ave Suite 11	Mesa	AZ	85202	480-890-0435
Steve's Stones (American) 161 N Centennial Way	Mesa	AZ	85201	480-844-8448
Weather Vane (American) 7303 E Main St	Mesa	AZ	85207	480-830-2721
Zuni Grill (Southwest) 1011 W Holmes Ave	Mesa	AZ	85210	480-833-5555
Zur-Kate (German) 4815 E Main St	Mesa	AZ	85205	480-830-4244

— Goods and Services —

SHOPPING

Name / Address	City	State	ZIP	Phone	Fax
Dillard's 1435 W Southern Ave.	Mesa	AZ	85202	480-833-7777	833-4311
Factory Stores of America 2050 S Roslyn Pl	Mesa	AZ	85208	480-984-0697	
TF: 800-772-8336 ■ *Web:* www.factorystores.com/					
Fiesta Mall 2104 Fiesta Mall	Mesa	AZ	85202	480-833-4121	834-8462
Macy's Fiesta Mall 4000 Fiesta Mall	Mesa	AZ	85202	480-835-2100	
Superstition Springs Center 6555 E Southern Ave.	Mesa	AZ	85206	480-396-2570	830-7693
Web: www.westcor.com/ssc ■ *E-mail:* ssc@westcor.com					

BANKS

Name / Address	City	State	ZIP	Phone	Fax
Bank of America Arizona 63 W Main St	Mesa	AZ	85201	480-827-6810	898-7069
Bank One Arizona NA 61 N Country Club Dr	Mesa	AZ	85201	480-890-5008	890-5025
TF Cust Svc: 800-366-2265*					
Fifth Third Bank 1510 W Southern Ave	Mesa	AZ	85202	480-898-7150	898-0045
First International Bank & Trust 6263 E Main St.	Mesa	AZ	85205	480-396-9928	985-6155
Mesa Bank 63 E Main St Suite 100	Mesa	AZ	85201	480-649-5100	649-5111
National Bank of Arizona 1322 S Gilbert Rd	Mesa	AZ	85204	480-892-7300	892-2786
Norwest Bank Arizona NA 305 E Main St Suite 100	Mesa	AZ	85201	480-644-8320	644-8329
Pacific Century Bank 1839 S Alma School Rd Suite 150	Mesa	AZ	85210	480-752-8000	752-8009
Washington Federal Savings & Loan Assn 6835 E Baseline Rd Suite 101	Mesa	AZ	85208	480-924-8077	924-8790
Wells Fargo Bank 4 E Main St	Mesa	AZ	85201	480-827-2300	827-2302

BUSINESS SERVICES

	Phone		Phone
Accountemps	480-820-4616	**Mail Boxes Etc**	480-964-1001
DHL Worldwide Express	800-225-5345	**Manpower Temporary Services**	480-926-3788
Encore Personnel Service	480-839-2888	**Post Office**	800-275-8777
Federal Express	800-238-5355	**Tri City Delivery Service**	480-731-9690
Kinko's	480-833-0036	**UPS**	800-742-5877

— Media —

PUBLICATIONS

Name / Address	City	State	ZIP	Phone	Fax
Tribune‡ 120 W 1st Ave	Mesa	AZ	85210	480-898-6500	898-6463
TF: 800-272-2460					

‡*Daily newspapers*

TELEVISION

Name / Address	City	State	ZIP	Phone	Fax
KAET-TV Ch 8 (PBS) PO Box 871405	Tempe	AZ	85287	480-965-3506	965-1000
Web: www.kaet.asu.edu ■ *E-mail:* kaet@asu.edu					
KNXV-TV Ch 15 (ABC) 515 N 44th St	Phoenix	AZ	85008	602-273-1500	685-3000
Web: www.knxv.com ■ *E-mail:* news15@primenet.com					
KPHO-TV Ch 5 (CBS) 4016 N Black Canyon Hwy	Phoenix	AZ	85017	602-264-1000	650-0761
Web: www.kpho.com					
KPNX-TV Ch 12 (NBC) 1101 N Central Ave.	Phoenix	AZ	85004	602-257-1212	257-6619
KSAZ-TV Ch 10 (Fox) 511 W Adams St.	Phoenix	AZ	85003	602-257-1234	262-0177
KTVK-TV Ch 3 (Ind) 5555 N 7th Ave	Phoenix	AZ	85013	602-207-3333	207-3477
E-mail: feedback@azfamily.com					
KUTP-TV Ch 45 (UPN) 4630 S 33rd St	Phoenix	AZ	85040	602-268-4500	276-4082
Web: www.kutp.com					

RADIO

Name / Address	City	State	ZIP	Phone	Fax
KBAQ-FM 89.5 MHz (NPR) 1435 S Dobson St	Mesa	AZ	85202	480-834-5627	835-5925
KDKB-FM 93.3 MHz (Rock) 1167 W Javelina Ave	Mesa	AZ	85210	480-897-9300	897-1964*
**Fax:* Sales ■ *Web:* www.kdkb.com ■ *E-mail:* rock@kdkb.com					
KHEP-AM 1280 kHz (Rel) 100 W Clarendon Ave Suite 720	Phoenix	AZ	85013	602-234-1280	234-1586
KJZZ-FM 91.5 MHz (NPR) 1435 S Dobson Rd	Mesa	AZ	85202	480-834-5627	835-5925
KKLT-FM 98.7 MHz (AC) 5300 N Central Ave	Phoenix	AZ	85012	602-274-6200	266-3858
KMXP-FM 96.9 MHz (AC) 645 E Missouri Ave Suite 360	Phoenix	AZ	85012	602-279-5577	230-2781
KOOL-FM 94.5 MHz (Oldies) 4745 N 7th St Suite 210	Phoenix	AZ	85014	602-956-9696	285-1450
Web: www.koolradio.com					
KTAR-AM 620 kHz (N/T) 5300 N Central Ave	Phoenix	AZ	85013	602-274-6200	266-3858
KYOT-FM 95.5 MHz (Nost) 840 N Central Ave	Phoenix	AZ	85004	602-258-8181	440-6530
Web: www.kyot.com					
KZZP-FM 104.7 MHz (CHR) 645 E Missouri Ave Suite 360	Phoenix	AZ	85012	602-279-5577	230-2781
Web: www.kzzp.com					

— Colleges/Universities —

Name / Address	City	State	ZIP	Phone	Fax
Mesa Community College 1833 W Southern Ave	Mesa	AZ	85202	480-461-7000	461-7804
Web: www.mc.maricopa.edu					

— Hospitals —

Name / Address	City	State	ZIP	Phone	Fax
Charter Desert Vista Hospital 570 W Brown Rd	Mesa	AZ	85201	480-962-3900	827-0412
Desert Samaritan Medical Center 1400 S Dobson Rd	Mesa	AZ	85202	480-835-3000	835-8711
Web: www.samaritanaz.com/centers/desert_sam.html					
Mesa General Hospital Medical Center 515 N Mesa Dr	Mesa	AZ	85201	480-969-9111	969-0095
Mesa Lutheran Hospital 525 W Brown Rd	Mesa	AZ	85201	480-834-1211	461-2915*
**Fax:* Admitting					
Valley Lutheran Hospital 6644 Baywood Ave	Mesa	AZ	85206	480-981-2000	981-4198

— Attractions —

Name / Address	City	State	ZIP	Phone	Fax
Arizona Museum for Youth 35 N Robson St.	Mesa	AZ	85201	602-644-2468	644-2466
Arizona Performing Arts Theatre 623 W Southern	Mesa	AZ	85210	480-844-8520	844-0358
Web: www.murderink.com ■ *E-mail:* murderink@thewebdepot.com					
Arizona Temple Visitors Center 525 E Main St.	Mesa	AZ	85203	480-964-7164	964-7789
Champlin Fighter Aircraft Museum 4636 E Fighter Aces Dr	Mesa	AZ	85215	480-830-4540	830-4543
Web: www.ci.mesa.az.us/airport/museum.htm					
Confederate Air Force Museum 2017 N Greenfield Rd Falcon Field	Mesa	AZ	85215	480-924-1940	
Goldfield Ghost Town & Mine Hwy 88 E.	Apache Junction	AZ	85219	480-983-0333	
Golfland/SunSplash 155 W Hampton Ave	Mesa	AZ	85210	480-834-8318	461-3496
Web: www.golfland-sunsplash.com					
Hohokam Pima National Monument 1100 Ruins Dr Casa Grande Ruins National Monument	Coolidge	AZ	85228	520-723-3172	723-7209
Mesa Arts Center 155 N Center	Mesa	AZ	85211	602-644-2056	644-2901
Mesa Historical Museum 2345 N Horne	Mesa	AZ	85203	480-835-7358	
Mesa Southwest Museum 53 N MacDonald St.	Mesa	AZ	85201	602-644-2169	644-3424
Mesa Symphony Orchestra 201 N Centre St Mesa Ampitheatre	Mesa	AZ	85201	480-897-2121	897-2121
Mesa Youtheatre 155 N Center Mesa Arts Center	Mesa	AZ	85211	480-644-2681	644-2901
Out of Africa Wildlife Park 9736 N Fort McDowell Rd	Scottsdale	AZ	85264	480-837-7779	837-7379
Web: www.outofafricapark.com					
Park of the Canals 1710 N Horne	Mesa	AZ	85201	480-827-4700	
Sirrine House 160 N Center St.	Mesa	AZ	85201	602-644-2760	

Mesa (Cont'd)

SPORTS TEAMS & FACILITIES

				Phone	Fax
Apache Greyhound Park 2551 W Apache Trail	Apache Junction	AZ	85220	480-982-2371	983-0013
Chicago Cubs Spring Training (baseball) 1235 N Center St	Mesa	AZ	85201	480-964-4467	
Firebird International Raceway Park Maricopa Rd & I-10	Chandler	AZ	85226	602-268-0200	796-0531*

Fax Area Code: 520 ■ *Web:* www.firebirdraceway.com ■ *E-mail:* info@firebirdraceway.com

— Events —

	Phone
Acorn's Spring Antique Show & Sale (late March)	480-830-2660
Air Show Spectacular (mid-March)	480-988-1013
Arizona Scottish Highland Games (late February)	602-431-0095
Arizona Woodcarvers Show (late November)	480-895-7036
Blues Blast (late February)	602-644-2242
Cinco de Mayo Celebrations (early May)	602-644-2230
Country Thunder USA (late April)	480-966-9920
Dia de los Muertos Festival (early November)	480-833-5875
Fountain Festival of the Arts & Crafts (early November)	480-837-1654
Gilbert Days (mid-late November)	480-380-8399
Independence Day Celebrations (July 4)	602-644-2011
M-Car Grand Prix (early November)	480-969-1307
Mesa Day (early March)	602-644-2351
Mesa Southwest Antique Guild Show & Sale (mid-May)	602-943-1766
Native American Pow Wow (mid-October)	602-644-2169
Peach Festival (mid-May)	480-987-3333
Queen Creek Potato Festival (late May)	480-987-3333
Territorial Days (mid-February)	602-644-2351
Valley of the Sun Polka Festival (mid-February)	602-237-4024

Phoenix

Founded in 1860 on the banks of the Salt River, Phoenix was named by an early settler who predicted that, like the bird of legend, the city would rise from the ashes of ancient Hohokam Indian ruins. Today, Phoenix is not only a top vacation destination, but more than 2.3 million people make their home in the Valley of the Sun. Part of the reason for this is the weather in the area - Phoenix has more than 300 sunny days a year - but the area boasts many other fine attractions as well. Camelback Mountain, the most prominent landmark in Phoenix, and the Echo Canyon Recreation Area feature sheer red cliffs, the Praying Monk rock formation, and the famous camel's silhouette. Pueblo Grande Museum and Cultural Park is the site of ancient Hohokam ruins, with permanent exhibits that feature material excavated from the site. The Heard Museum has an extensive collection of both primitive and modern Native American art. The city's 16,500-acre South Mountain Park is the largest municipal park in the world, with more than 300 specimens of plant life; and the Desert Botanical Garden has an extensive collection of desert plants. Air tours of the scenic areas near the Valley of the Sun, including trips to the Grand Canyon, can be chartered from Phoenix.

Population	1,198,064	**Longitude**	112-07-33 W
Area (Land)	419.9 sq mi	**County**	Maricopa
Area (Water)	0.2 sq mi	**Time Zone**	MST
Elevation	1090 ft	**Area Code/s**	602
Latitude	33-44-83 N		

— Average Temperatures and Precipitation —

TEMPERATURES

	Jan	Feb	Mar	Apr	May	Jun	Jul	Aug	Sep	Oct	Nov	Dec
High	66	71	76	85	94	104	106	104	98	88	75	66
Low	41	45	49	55	64	73	81	79	73	61	49	42

PRECIPITATION

	Jan	Feb	Mar	Apr	May	Jun	Jul	Aug	Sep	Oct	Nov	Dec
Inches	0.7	0.7	0.9	0.2	0.1	0.1	0.8	1.0	0.9	0.7	0.7	1.0

— Important Phone Numbers —

	Phone		Phone
AAA	602-274-1116	**Medical Referral**	602-252-2015
American Express Travel	480-949-7000	**Poison Control Center**	602-253-3334
Dental Referral	602-957-4864	**Time/Temp**	602-265-5550
Emergency	911	**Visitor Hotline**	602-252-5588
HotelDocs	800-468-3537	**Weather**	602-265-5550

— Information Sources —

				Phone	Fax
Better Business Bureau Serving Central Northeast Northwest & Southwest Arizona 4428 N 12th St	Phoenix	AZ	85014	602-264-1721	263-0997
Web: www.phoenix.bbb.org					
Greater Phoenix Chamber of Commerce 201 N Central Ave Suite 2700	Phoenix	AZ	85073	602-254-5521	495-8913
Web: www.phoenixchamber.com					
Greater Phoenix Convention & Visitors Bureau 400 E Van Buren St 1 Arizona Ctr Suite 600	Phoenix	AZ	85004	602-254-6500	253-4415
TF: 877-266-5749 ■ *Web:* www.arizonaguide.com/phxcvb					
Maricopa County 301 W Jefferson St 10th Fl	Phoenix	AZ	85003	602-506-3415	506-5997
Web: www.maricopa.gov					
Phoenix City Hall 200 W Washington St	Phoenix	AZ	85003	602-262-6659	
Web: www.ci.phoenix.az.us					
Phoenix Civic Plaza Convention Center 225 E Adams St	Phoenix	AZ	85004	602-262-7272	495-3642
TF: 800-282-4842					
Phoenix Community & Economic Development Dept 200 W Washington St 20th Fl	Phoenix	AZ	85003	602-262-5040	495-5097
Web: www.ci.phoenix.az.us/ecdevidx.html					
Phoenix Mayor 200 W Washington St 11th Fl	Phoenix	AZ	85003	602-262-7111	495-5583
Web: www.ci.phoenix.az.us/CITYGOV/mayoridx.html					
Phoenix Public Library 1221 N Central Ave	Phoenix	AZ	85004	602-262-4636	261-8836
Web: www.ci.phoenix.az.us/LIBRARY/pplidx.html					

On-Line Resources

4Phoenix.com	www.4phoenix.com
About.com Guide to Phoenix	phoenix.about.com/local/southwestus/phoenix
Anthill City Guide Phoenix	www.anthill.com/city.asp?city=phoenix
Area Guide Phoenix	phoenix.areaguides.net
Boulevards Phoenix	www.boulevards.com/cities/phoenix.html
City Knowledge Phoenix	www.cityknowledge.com/az_phoenix.htm
CitySearch Phoenix	phoenix.citysearch.com
DigitalCity Phoenix	home.digitalcity.com/phoenix
Excite.com Phoenix City Guide	www.excite.com/travel/countries/united_states/arizona/phoenix
HotelGuide Phoenix	hotelguide.net/phoenix/
Insiders' Guide to Phoenix	www.insiders.com/phoenix/
Metrowise Phoenix	www.metrowise.com
Phoenix-Best.com	www.phoenix-best.com
Phoenix Guide	www.phoenixaz.com
Phoenix New Times	www.phoenixnewtimes.com
Phoenix Online	www.phoenixonline.com/
Phoenix Traveller	www.thetraveller.com
Phoenix.TheLinks.com	phoenix.thelinks.com/
Rough Guide Travel Phoenix	travel.roughguides.com/content/1197/
Savvy Diner Guide to Phoenix-Scottsdale Restaurants	www.savvydiner.com/phoenix/
Virtual City Entertainment Magazine On-line	www.opus1.com/emol/phoenix/phoenix.html
Virtual Voyages Phoenix	www.virtualvoyages.com/usa/az/phoenix/phoenix.sht
WeekendEvents.com Phoenix	www.weekendevents.com/misccity/phoenix/phoenix.htm

Phoenix (Cont'd)

— Transportation Services —

AIRPORTS

■ **Phoenix Sky Harbor International Airport (PHX)** — Phone

3 miles SE of downtown (approx 15 minutes) 602-273-3300
Web: www.phxskyharbor.com/skyharbr

Airport Transportation

	Phone
AAA Full Transportation System $12 fare to downtown	602-437-4000
SuperShuttle $7 fare to downtown	602-244-9000
Valley Metro $1.25 fare to downtown	602-253-5000
Yellow Cab $10 fare to downtown	602-252-5252

Commercial Airlines

	Phone		Phone
Aero California	800-237-6225	**Shuttle by United**	800-748-8853
AeroMexico	602-954-4750	**SkyWest**	800-453-9417
America West	800-235-9292	**Southwest**	602-273-1221
American	800-433-7300	**TWA**	800-221-2000
British Airways	800-247-9297	**United**	800-241-6522
Continental	800-525-0280	**US Airways**	800-428-4322
Northwest	800-225-2525	**Vanguard**	800-826-4827

Charter Airlines

	Phone		Phone
Corporate Jets Inc	480-948-2400	**Southwest Aircraft Charter**	480-969-2715
Cutter Aviation Inc	602-273-1237	**West Coast Charters Inc**	800-352-6153
Grand Aire Express Inc	800-704-7263	**Westwind Aviation**	623-869-0866
Sawyer Aviation	602-273-3770		

CAR RENTALS

	Phone		Phone
Alamo	602-244-0897	**Hertz**	602-267-8822
Avis	602-273-3222	**National**	602-275-4771
Budget	602-267-4000	**Thrifty**	602-244-0311
Dollar	602-275-7588		

LIMO/TAXI

	Phone		Phone
Arizona Limousines	602-267-7097	**Scottsdale Express**	480-994-1616
Carey Limousine	602-996-1955	**Sky Mountain Limousines**	480-830-3944
Continental Carriage	602-494-2783	**Valley Limousines**	602-254-1955
Courier Cab	602-232-2222	**Yellow Cab**	602-252-5252

MASS TRANSIT

	Phone
DASH Shuttle $.30 Base fare	602-253-5000
Phoenix Transit System $1.25 Base fare	602-253-5000

RAIL/BUS

				Phone
Amtrak Station 401 W Harrison St TF: 800-872-7245	Phoenix	AZ	85003	602-253-0121
Greyhound/Trailways Bus Station 2115 E Buckeye Rd TF: 800-231-2222	Phoenix	AZ	85034	602-389-4200

— Accommodations —

HOTEL RESERVATION SERVICES

	Phone	Fax
Advance Reservations Inn Arizona *TF:* 800-456-0682 ■ *Web:* tucson.com/inn ■ *E-mail:* micasa@primenet.com	480-990-0682	990-3390
Hotel Reservations Network Inc *TF Sales:* 800-964-6835 ■ *Web:* www.hoteldiscount.com	214-361-7311	361-7299
Phoenix Scottsdale Hotel Reservations **Fax Area Code:* 858 ■ *TF:* 800-728-3227	602-954-1425	627-9405*
RMC Travel Centre *TF:* 800-782-2674	212-754-6560	754-6571

HOTELS, MOTELS, RESORTS

				Phone	Fax
Arizona Biltmore Resort 24th St & Missouri *TF:* 800-950-0086 ■ *Web:* www.arizonabiltmore.com ■ *E-mail:* reservations@arizonabiltmore.com	Phoenix	AZ	85016	602-955-6600	381-7600
Best Western Executive Park Hotel 1100 N Central Ave *TF:* 800-528-1234 ■ *Web:* www.westcoasthotels.com/executivepark	Phoenix	AZ	85004	602-252-2100	340-1989
Boulders Resort & Club 34631 N Tom Darlington Dr *TF:* 800-553-1717	Carefree	AZ	85377	480-488-9009	488-4118
Country Suites Westside 3210 Grand Ave *TF:* 800-456-4000	Phoenix	AZ	85017	602-279-3211	230-2145
Courtyard by Marriott 1221 S Westwood St *TF:* 800-321-2211 ■ *Web:* courtyard.com/PHXME	Mesa	AZ	85210	480-461-3000	461-0179
Crowne Plaza 2532 W Peoria Ave *TF:* 800-465-4329	Phoenix	AZ	85029	602-943-2341	371-8470
Crowne Plaza Hotel Phoenix 100 N 1st St *TF:* 800-359-7253	Phoenix	AZ	85004	602-333-0000	333-5181
Days Inn Coliseum 2420 W Thomas Rd *TF:* 800-329-7466	Phoenix	AZ	85015	602-257-0801	258-5336
Doubletree Suites at the Phoenix Gateway Center 320 N 44th St *TF:* 800-222-8733 ■ *Web:* www.doubletreehotels.com/DoubleT/Hotel/01/01Main.htm	Phoenix	AZ	85008	602-225-0500	225-0957
Embassy Suites 2630 E Camelback Rd *TF:* 800-362-2779	Phoenix	AZ	85016	602-955-3992	955-6479
Embassy Suites 2577 W Greenway Rd *TF:* 800-362-2779	Phoenix	AZ	85023	602-375-1777	375-4012
Embassy Suites Camelhead 1515 N 44th St *TF:* 800-447-8483	Phoenix	AZ	85008	602-244-8800	244-8114
Embassy Suites Thomas Road 2333 E Thomas Rd *TF:* 800-362-2779	Phoenix	AZ	85016	602-957-1910	955-2861
Extended StayAmerica 3421 E Elwood St *TF:* 800-398-7829	Phoenix	AZ	85040	602-438-2900	438-2887
Fairfield Inn 17017 N Black Canyon Hwy *TF:* 800-228-2800 ■ *Web:* fairfieldinn.com/PHXBR	Phoenix	AZ	85023	602-548-8888	548-9553
Fairfield Inn by Marriott Phoenix Airport 4702 E University Dr *TF:* 800-228-2800 ■ *Web:* fairfieldinn.com/PHXFA	Phoenix	AZ	85034	480-829-0700	829-8068
Grace Inn at Ahwatukee 10831 S 51st St *TF:* 800-843-6010	Phoenix	AZ	85044	480-893-3000	496-8303
Hampton Inn 1563 S Gilbert Rd *TF:* 800-426-7866	Mesa	AZ	85204	480-926-3600	926-4892
Hilton Pavillion 1011 W Holmes Ave *TF:* 800-445-8667 ■ *Web:* www.hilton.com/hotels/MESHPHF	Mesa	AZ	85210	480-833-5555	649-1380
Hilton Phoenix Airport 2435 S 47th St *TF:* 800-445-8667 ■ *Web:* www.hilton.com/hotels/PHXAHHF	Phoenix	AZ	85034	480-894-1600	921-7844
Holiday Inn Airport East 4300 E Washington St *TF:* 800-465-4329	Phoenix	AZ	85034	602-273-7778	275-5616
Holiday Inn Express Hotel & Suites 620 N 6th St *TF:* 800-465-4329	Phoenix	AZ	85004	602-452-2020	252-2909
Holiday Inn North Central 4321 N Central Ave *TF:* 800-465-4329 ■ *Web:* www.basshotels.com/holiday-inn/?_franchisee=PHXSF ■ *E-mail:* phxsf@aol.com	Phoenix	AZ	85012	602-200-8888	200-8800
Hyatt Regency Phoenix 122 N 2nd St *TF:* 800-233-1234 ■ *Web:* www.hyatt.com/usa/phoenix/hotels/hotel_phxrp.html	Phoenix	AZ	85004	602-252-1234	254-9472
Hyatt Regency Scottsdale at Gainey Ranch 7500 E Doubletree Ranch Rd *TF:* 800-233-1234 ■ *Web:* www.hyatt.com/usa/scottsdale/hotels/hotel_scott.html	Scottsdale	AZ	85258	480-991-3388	483-5550
InnSuites Hotel Phoenix Park 1615 E Northern Ave *TF:* 800-752-2204	Phoenix	AZ	85020	602-997-6285	943-1407
Knights Inn 3541 E Van Buren St *TF:* 800-843-5644	Phoenix	AZ	85008	602-273-7121	231-0973
La Quinta Hotel North 2510 W Greenway Rd *TF:* 800-531-5900	Phoenix	AZ	85023	602-993-0800	789-9172
La Quinta Inn Coliseum 2725 N Black Canyon Fwy *TF:* 800-687-6667	Phoenix	AZ	85009	602-258-6271	340-9255
Le Jardin Hotel & Suites 401 W Clarendon Ave *TF:* 800-448-8355	Phoenix	AZ	85013	602-234-2464	277-2602
Lexington Hotel & City Square Sports Club 100 W Clarendon Ave *TF:* 800-537-8483	Phoenix	AZ	85013	602-279-9811	285-2932
Los Olivos Hotel & Suites 202 E McDowell Rd *TF:* 800-776-5560	Phoenix	AZ	85004	602-528-9100	258-7259
Marriott Courtyard 17010 N Scottsdale Rd *TF:* 800-321-2211 ■ *Web:* courtyard.com/PHXCN	Scottsdale	AZ	85255	480-922-8400	948-3481

Phoenix — Hotels, Motels, Resorts (Cont'd)

				Phone	Fax
Marriott's Camelback Inn Resort Golf Club & Spa 5402 E Lincoln Dr	Scottsdale	AZ	85253	480-948-1700	951-8469
TF: 800-242-2635 ■ *Web:* www.camelbackinn.com ■ *E-mail:* reservations@camelbackinn.com					
Marriott's Mountain Shadows Resort 5641 E Lincoln Dr	Scottsdale	AZ	85253	480-948-7111	951-5430
TF: 800-782-2123 ■ *Web:* www.marriott.com/marriott/phxms/default.asp					
Phoenician The 6000 E Camelback Rd	Scottsdale	AZ	85251	480-941-8200	947-4311
TF: 800-888-8234 ■ *Web:* www.thephoenician.com					
Phoenix Inn 2310 E Highland Ave	Phoenix	AZ	85016	602-956-5221	468-7220
TF: 800-956-5221					
Pointe Hilton at Squaw Peak Resort 7677 N 16th St	Phoenix	AZ	85020	602-997-2626	997-2391
TF: 800-876-4683 ■ *Web:* www.hilton.com/hotels/PHXSPPR					
Pointe Hilton Resort at Tapatio Cliffs 11111 N 7th St	Phoenix	AZ	85020	602-866-7500	993-0276
TF: 800-876-4683 ■ *Web:* www.hilton.com/hotels/PHXTCPR					
Pointe Hilton Resort on South Mountain 7777 S Pointe Pkwy	Phoenix	AZ	85044	602-438-9000	431-6535
TF: 800-876-4683 ■ *Web:* www.hilton.com/hotels/PHXSMPR					
Premier Inn 10402 N Black Canyon Hwy	Phoenix	AZ	85051	602-943-2371	943-5847
TF: 800-786-6835					
Pyramid Inn Airport 3307 E Van Buren St	Phoenix	AZ	85008	602-275-3691	267-0448
Quality Hotel & Resort 3600 N 2nd Ave	Phoenix	AZ	85013	602-248-0222	265-6331
TF: 800-221-2222					
Quality Inn Royal Mesa 951 W Main St	Mesa	AZ	85201	480-833-1231	833-1231
TF: 800-333-5501					
Quality Suites 3101 N 32nd St	Phoenix	AZ	85018	602-956-4900	957-6122
Ramada Hotel Camelback 502 W Camelback Rd	Phoenix	AZ	85013	602-264-9290	264-3068
TF: 800-688-2021					
Ramada Inn Downtown 401 N 1st St	Phoenix	AZ	85004	602-258-3411	258-3171
TF: 800-272-6232					
Ramada Limited Airport 4120 E Van Buren St	Phoenix	AZ	85008	602-275-5746	275-9488
TF: 800-272-6232					
Ramada Limited Suites 3211 E Pinchot Ave	Phoenix	AZ	85018	602-957-1350	508-0572
TF: 800-272-6232					
Ramada Plaza Hotel Metrocenter 12027 N 28th Dr	Phoenix	AZ	85029	602-866-7000	942-7572
TF: 800-566-8535					
Ramada Suites 1410 S Country Club Dr	Mesa	AZ	85210	480-964-2897	461-0801
TF: 800-272-6232					
Residence Inn by Marriott 8242 N Black Canyon Fwy	Phoenix	AZ	85051	602-864-1900	995-8251
TF: 800-331-3131 ■ *Web:* www.residenceinn.com/PHXRI					
Ritz-Carlton Phoenix 2401 E Camelback Rd	Phoenix	AZ	85016	602-468-0700	468-0793
TF: 800-241-3333 ■ *Web:* www.ritzcarlton.com/location/NorthAmerica/Phoenix/main.htm					
Royal Palms 5200 E Camelback Rd	Phoenix	AZ	85018	602-840-3610	840-6927
TF: 800-672-6011 ■ *Web:* www.royalpalmshotel.com					
Royal Suites 10421 N 33rd Ave	Phoenix	AZ	85051	602-942-1000	993-2965
TF: 800-647-5786					
San Carlos Hotel 202 N Central Ave	Phoenix	AZ	85004	602-253-4121	253-6668
TF: 800-678-8946					
Scottsdale Embassy Suites 5001 N Scottsdale Rd	Scottsdale	AZ	85250	480-949-1414	947-2675
TF: 800-528-1456 ■ *Web:* www.arizonaguide.com/embassyscottsdale/					
Scottsdale Princess 7575 E Princess Dr	Scottsdale	AZ	85255	480-585-4848	585-0091
TF: 800-344-4758 ■ *Web:* www.scottsdaleprincess.com					
Select Suites Airport Center 4221 E McDowell Rd	Phoenix	AZ	85008	602-267-7917	244-1470
TF: 800-845-3020 ■ *Web:* www.selectsuites.com/air_main.html					
Select Suites Biltmore Center 4341 N 24th St	Phoenix	AZ	85016	602-954-8049	954-0604
TF: 800-827-8704 ■ *Web:* www.selectsuites.com/bilt_main.html					
Sheraton Crescent Hotel 2620 W Dunlap Ave	Phoenix	AZ	85021	602-943-8200	371-2857
TF: 800-423-4126					
Sheraton Mesa 200 N Centennial Way	Mesa	AZ	85201	480-898-8300	964-9279
TF: 800-456-6372					
Sierra Suites Hotels 9455 N Black Canyon Hwy	Phoenix	AZ	85021	602-395-0900	395-1900
TF: 800-474-3772					
Sleep Inn Sky Harbor Airport 2621 S 47th Pl	Phoenix	AZ	85034	480-967-7100	921-7400
TF: 800-753-3746					
Travelodge 1624 N Black Canyon Fwy	Phoenix	AZ	85009	602-269-6281	278-3715
TF: 800-578-7878					
Wigwam Resort & Country Club 300 E Wigwam Blvd	Litchfield Park	AZ	85340	623-935-3811	935-3737
TF: 800-327-0396					
Wyndham Garden Hotel Phoenix Airport 427 N 44th St	Phoenix	AZ	85008	602-220-4400	231-8703
TF: 800-996-3426					
Wyndham Metrocenter Hotel 10220 N Metro Pkwy E	Phoenix	AZ	85051	602-997-5900	943-6156
TF: 800-996-3426					

— Restaurants —

				Phone
Alexi's Grill (Continental) 3550 N Central Ave	Phoenix	AZ	85012	602-279-0982
Another Point in Tyme (American) 7777 S Pointe Pkwy	Phoenix	AZ	85044	602-431-6472
Arriva Mexican Grill (Mexican) 1812 E Camelback Rd	Phoenix	AZ	85016	602-265-9112
Aunt Chilada's (Mexican) 7330 N Dreamy Draw Dr	Phoenix	AZ	85020	602-944-1286
Avanti's (Italian) 2728 E Thomas Rd	Phoenix	AZ	85016	602-956-0900
Baby Kay's Cajun Kitchen (Cajun) 2119 E Camelback Rd	Phoenix	AZ	85016	602-955-0011
Beef Eaters Restaurant (American) 300 W Camelback Rd	Phoenix	AZ	85013	602-264-3838
Bistro 24 (French) 2401 E Camelback Rd	Phoenix	AZ	85016	602-468-0700
Chaparral Room (Continental) 5402 E Lincoln Dr	Scottsdale	AZ	85253	480-948-1700
China Gate (Asian) 3033 W Peoria Ave	Phoenix	AZ	85029	602-944-1982
Compass Restaurant (Continental) 122 N 2nd St	Phoenix	AZ	85004	602-440-3166
Coyote Springs Brewing Co (American) 122 E Washington St	Phoenix	AZ	85004	602-256-6645
Different Point of View (American) 11111 N 7th St	Phoenix	AZ	85020	602-863-0912
Durant's Restaurant (American) 2611 N Central Ave	Phoenix	AZ	85004	602-264-5967
Eddie Matney Bistro (New American) 2398 E Camelback Rd	Phoenix	AZ	85016	602-957-3214
Fish Market Restaurant (Seafood) 1720 E Camelback Rd	Phoenix	AZ	85016	602-277-3474
Web: www.thefishmarket.com				
Focaccia Fiorentina (Italian) 123 N Central Ave	Phoenix	AZ	85004	602-252-0007
Golden Greek (Greek) 7126 N 35th Ave	Phoenix	AZ	85051	602-841-7849
Golden Swan (Southwest) 7500 E Doubletree Ranch Rd	Scottsdale	AZ	85258	480-483-5572
Greekfest (Greek) 1940 E Camelback Rd	Phoenix	AZ	85016	602-265-2990
Hard Rock Cafe (American) 2621 E Camelback Rd	Phoenix	AZ	85016	602-956-3669
Honey Bear's BBQ (Barbecue) 5012 E Van Buren St	Phoenix	AZ	85008	602-273-9148
Hunter Steakhouse (Steak) 10237 N Metro Pkwy	Phoenix	AZ	85051	602-371-0240
La Fontanella (Italian) 4231 E Indian School Rd	Phoenix	AZ	85018	602-955-1213
LaHacienda (Mexican) 7575 E Princess Dr	Scottsdale	AZ	85255	480-585-4848
Landry's Seafood (Seafood) 1320 W Southern Ave	Mesa	AZ	85202	480-969-4600
Little Saigon Vietnamese Restaurant (Vietnamese) 1588 W Montebello Ave	Phoenix	AZ	85015	602-864-7582
Mandarin Delight Chinese Restaurant (Chinese) 645 E Missouri Ave Suite 175	Phoenix	AZ	85014	602-274-5204
Mary Elaine's (New American) 6000 E Camelback Rd	Scottsdale	AZ	85251	480-941-8200
Matador Restaurant (Mexican) 125 E Adams St	Phoenix	AZ	85004	602-254-7563
Matta's (Mexican) 932 E Main St	Mesa	AZ	85203	480-964-7881
Maycayo's (Mexican) 4001 N Central Ave	Phoenix	AZ	85012	602-264-6141
Pink Pepper Cuisine of Thailand (Thai) 245 E Bell Rd	Phoenix	AZ	85022	602-548-1333
Pointe in Tyme (Steak/Seafood) 11111 N 7th St	Phoenix	AZ	85020	602-866-7500
Raffele Italian Restaurant (Italian) 2999 N 44th St	Phoenix	AZ	85018	602-952-0063
Rockin' R Ranch (American) 6136 E Baseline Rd	Mesa	AZ	85206	480-832-1539
RoxSand (Continental) 2594 E Camelback Rd	Phoenix	AZ	85016	602-381-0444
Ruth's Chris Steak House (Steak) 2201 E Camelback Rd	Phoenix	AZ	85016	602-957-9600
Sam's Cafe (Southwest) 2566 E Camelback Rd	Phoenix	AZ	85016	602-954-7100
Shogun Japanese Restaurant & Sushi Bar (Japanese) 12615 N Tatum Blvd	Phoenix	AZ	85032	602-953-3264
Sing High Chop Suey House (Chinese) 27 W Madison St	Phoenix	AZ	85003	602-253-7848
Slickers (American) 1515 N 44th St	Phoenix	AZ	85008	602-244-8800
Steamed Blues (Seafood) 4843 N 8th Pl	Phoenix	AZ	85014	480-966-2722
Steve's Stones (American) 161 N Centennial Way	Mesa	AZ	85201	480-844-8448
Stockyards The (Steak) 5001 E Washington St	Phoenix	AZ	85034	602-273-7378
T-Bone Steak House (Steak) 10037 S 19th Ave	Phoenix	AZ	85041	602-276-0945
Tarbell's (New American) 3213 E Camelback Rd	Phoenix	AZ	85018	602-955-8100
Web: www.tarbells.com/				
Tom's Tavern (American) 2 N Central Ave	Phoenix	AZ	85004	602-257-1688
Trails-end Chuckwagon (Steak) 35th Ave & Greenway Rd	Phoenix	AZ	85053	602-843-5883
Vincent Guerithault on Camelback (Southwest) 3930 E Camelback Rd	Phoenix	AZ	85018	602-224-0225
Windows on the Green (Southwest) 6000 E Camelback Rd	Scottsdale	AZ	85251	480-941-8200
Wrights (Asian) 24th St & Missouri Ave	Phoenix	AZ	85016	602-954-2507

— Goods and Services —

SHOPPING

				Phone	Fax
Biltmore Fashion Park 24th St & Camelback Rd	Phoenix	AZ	85016	602-955-8400	
Borgata of Scottsdale 6166 N Scottsdale Rd	Scottsdale	AZ	85253	480-998-1822	
Dillard's 7621 W Thomas Rd	Phoenix	AZ	85033	623-849-0100	
el Pedregal 34505 N Scottsdale Rd	Scottsdale	AZ	85262	480-488-1072	488-5915

Phoenix — Shopping (Cont'd)

Name / Address	City	State	ZIP	Phone	Fax
Fifth Avenue Area Shops 7087 E 5th Ave	Scottsdale	AZ	85251	480-945-0962	
Indoor SwapMart 5115 N 27th Ave	Phoenix	AZ	85017	602-246-9600	
Los Arcos Mall 1315 N Scottsdale Rd	Scottsdale	AZ	85257	480-945-6376	946-9105
Macy's Fiesta Mall 4000 Fiesta Mall	Mesa	AZ	85202	480-835-2100	
Metrocenter 9617 Metro Pkwy W Suite 1001	Phoenix	AZ	85051	602-997-2641	870-9983
Web: www.westcor.com/met ■ *E-mail:* metro@westcor.com					
Park Central Mall 3121 N 3rd Ave	Phoenix	AZ	85013	602-264-5575	
Phoenix Mercado 7th & Van Buren Sts	Phoenix	AZ	85004	602-256-6322	253-4343
Prime Outlet at New River 4250 W Anthem Way	Phoenix	AZ	85027	623-465-9500	465-9516
Saks Fifth Avenue 2446 E Camelback Rd	Phoenix	AZ	85016	602-955-8000	468-0189
Scottsdale Fashion Square 7014 E Camelback Rd	Scottsdale	AZ	85251	480-990-7800	423-1455
Shops at Arizona Center 400 E Van Buren St Suite 550	Phoenix	AZ	85004	602-271-4000	
Wigwam Outlet Stores I-10 & Litchfield Rd	Phoenix	AZ	85338	623-935-9733	935-9588

BANKS

Name / Address	City	State	ZIP	Phone	Fax
Bank of America NT & SA 101 N 1st Ave	Phoenix	AZ	85003	602-594-2371	594-4376
TF: 800-284-8491 ■ *Web:* www.bofa.com					
Bank One Arizona NA 241 N Central Ave	Phoenix	AZ	85004	602-221-4724	221-1576*
**Fax:* Mktg ■ *TF:* 800-877-0608					
Northern Trust Bank of Arizona NA 2398 E Camelback Rd Suite 400	Phoenix	AZ	85016	602-468-1650	912-8665
Norwest Bank 3300 N Central Ave	Phoenix	AZ	85012	602-248-2223	248-1292
Wells Fargo Bank Arizona NA 100 W Washington St	Phoenix	AZ	85003	602-378-4690	528-1088
TF Cust Svc: 800-869-3557*					

BUSINESS SERVICES

	Phone		Phone
Accountemps	602-264-6488	**Kinko's**	602-241-9440
Corporate Express Delivery Systems	602-286-5620	**Moody's Quick**	602-861-2121
Courier Express	602-254-3237	**Olsten Staffing Services**	602-266-6930
Federal Express	800-463-3339	**Post Office**	800-275-8777
Hawkins & Campbell	602-254-6147	**Stivers Temporary Personnel**	602-264-4580
Kelly Services	602-264-0717	**TRC Staffing Services**	602-840-1333
		UPS	800-742-5877

— Media —

PUBLICATIONS

Name / Address	City	State	ZIP	Phone	Fax
Ahwatukee Foothills News 10631 S 51st St	Phoenix	AZ	85044	480-496-0665	893-1684*
**Fax:* News Rm ■ *Web:* www.ahwatukee.com/afn ■ *E-mail:* afn@netzone.com					
Arizona Business Gazette PO Box 194	Phoenix	AZ	85001	602-444-7300	444-7363
Web: www.azcentral.com					
Arizona Republic‡ PO Box 1950	Phoenix	AZ	85001	602-444-8000	444-8044
TF: 800-331-9303 ■ *Web:* www.azcentral.com					
Business Journal 3030 N Central Ave Suite 1500	Phoenix	AZ	85012	602-230-8400	230-0955
Web: www.amcity.com/phoenix					
Phoenix Magazine 4041 N Central Ave Suite 530	Phoenix	AZ	85012	602-234-0840	604-0166
TF: 800-888-5621					
Tribune‡ 120 W 1st Ave	Mesa	AZ	85210	480-898-6500	898-6463
TF: 800-272-2460					

‡Daily newspapers

TELEVISION

Name / Address	City	State	ZIP	Phone	Fax
KAET-TV Ch 8 (PBS) PO Box 871405	Tempe	AZ	85287	480-965-3506	965-1000
Web: www.kaet.asu.edu ■ *E-mail:* kaet@asu.edu					
KASW-TV Ch 61 (WB) 5555 N 7th Ave	Phoenix	AZ	85013	480-661-6161	207-3277
KDRX-TV Ch 64 (Tele) 4001 E Broadway Suite 11	Phoenix	AZ	85040	602-470-0507	470-0810
KNXV-TV Ch 15 (ABC) 515 N 44th St	Phoenix	AZ	85008	602-273-1500	685-3000
Web: www.knxv.com ■ *E-mail:* news15@primenet.com					
KPHO-TV Ch 5 (CBS) 4016 N Black Canyon Hwy	Phoenix	AZ	85017	602-264-1000	650-0761
Web: www.kpho.com					
KPNX-TV Ch 12 (NBC) 1101 N Central Ave	Phoenix	AZ	85004	602-257-1212	257-6619
KSAZ-TV Ch 10 (Fox) 511 W Adams St	Phoenix	AZ	85003	602-257-1234	262-0177
KTVK-TV Ch 3 (Ind) 5555 N 7th Ave	Phoenix	AZ	85013	602-207-3333	207-3477
E-mail: feedback@azfamily.com					
KTVW-TV Ch 33 (Uni) 3019 E Southern Ave	Phoenix	AZ	85040	602-243-3333	276-8658
Web: www.univision.net/stations/ktvw.htm					
KUSK-TV Ch 7 (Ind) 3211 Tower Rd	Prescott	AZ	86305	520-778-6770	445-5210
Web: www.kusk.com ■ *E-mail:* sauro@kusk.com					
KUTP-TV Ch 45 (UPN) 4630 S 33rd St	Phoenix	AZ	85040	602-268-4500	276-4082
Web: www.kutp.com					

RADIO

Name / Address	City	State	ZIP	Phone	Fax
KDDJ-FM 100.3 MHz (Alt) 4745 N 7th St Suite 410	Phoenix	AZ	85014	602-266-1360	263-4844
KEDJ-FM 106.3 MHz (Alt) 4745 N 7th St Suite 410	Phoenix	AZ	85014	602-266-1360	263-4844
Web: www.accessarizona.com/partners/kedj/home.html					
KESZ-FM 99.9 MHz (AC) 5555 N 7th Ave Suite B300	Phoenix	AZ	85013	602-207-9999	207-3177
KFYI-AM 910 kHz (N/T) 631 N 1st Ave	Phoenix	AZ	85003	602-258-6161	817-1199
Web: www.accessarizona.com/partners/kfyi/					
KHEP-AM 1280 kHz (Rel) 100 W Clarendon Ave Suite 720	Phoenix	AZ	85013	602-234-1280	234-1586
KHOT-FM 105.9 MHz (Urban) 4745 N 7th St Suite 410	Phoenix	AZ	85014	602-266-1360	263-4844
KJZZ-FM 91.5 MHz (NPR) 1435 S Dobson Rd	Mesa	AZ	85202	480-834-5627	835-5925
KKFR-FM 92.3 MHz (CHR) 631 N First Ave	Phoenix	AZ	85003	602-258-6161	817-1199
Web: www.accessarizona.com/partners/power92fm					
KKLT-FM 98.7 MHz (AC) 5300 N Central Ave	Phoenix	AZ	85012	602-274-6200	266-3858
KMLE-FM 107.9 MHz (Ctry) 645 E Missouri Ave Suite 244	Phoenix	AZ	85012	602-264-0108	230-2116
Web: www.kmle108.com					
KMVP-AM 860 kHz (Sports) 5300 N Central Ave	Phoenix	AZ	85012	602-274-6200	241-6810
KMXP-FM 96.9 MHz (AC) 645 E Missouri Ave Suite 360	Phoenix	AZ	85012	602-279-5577	230-2781
KNIX-FM 102.5 MHz (Ctry) 600 E Gilbert Dr	Tempe	AZ	85281	480-966-6236	921-6365
KOOL-FM 94.5 MHz (Oldies) 4745 N 7th St Suite 210	Phoenix	AZ	85014	602-956-9696	285-1450
Web: www.koolradio.com					
KOY-AM 550 kHz (B/EZ) 840 N Central Ave	Phoenix	AZ	85004	602-258-8181	420-9916
KPTY-FM 103.9 MHz (CHR) 7434 E Stetson Dr	Scottsdale	AZ	85251	480-423-9255	423-9382
KSLX-AM 1440 kHz (CR) 4343 E Camelback Rd Suite 200	Phoenix	AZ	85018	480-941-1007	808-2288*
**Fax:* Sales					
KSLX-FM 100.7 MHz (CR) 4343 E Camelback Rd Suite 200	Phoenix	AZ	85018	480-941-1007	808-2288*
**Fax:* Sales ■ *Web:* www.kslx.com					
KTAR-AM 620 kHz (N/T) 5300 N Central Ave	Phoenix	AZ	85013	602-274-6200	266-3858
KUPD-FM 97.9 MHz (Rock) 1900 W Carmen St	Tempe	AZ	85283	480-838-0400	820-8469
Web: www.98kupd.com ■ *E-mail:* kupd@netzone.com					
KVVA-FM 107.1 MHz (Span) 1641 E Osborn Rd Suite 8	Phoenix	AZ	85016	602-266-2005	279-2921
KWCY-FM 103.5 MHz (Ctry) 5555 N 7th Ave 3rd Fl	Phoenix	AZ	85013	602-207-9999	207-3177
KYOT-FM 95.5 MHz (Nost) 840 N Central Ave	Phoenix	AZ	85004	602-258-8181	440-6530
Web: www.kyot.com					
KZON-FM 101.5 MHz (AAA) 840 N Central Ave	Phoenix	AZ	85004	602-258-8181	440-6530
Web: www.kzon.com					

— Colleges/Universities —

Name / Address	City	State	ZIP	Phone	Fax
American Indian College of the Assemblies of God 10020 N 15th Ave	Phoenix	AZ	85021	602-944-3335	943-8299
TF: 800-933-3828					
Arizona State University	Tempe	AZ	85287	480-965-9011	965-3610
Web: www.asu.edu ■ *E-mail:* ugradadm@asuvm.inre.asu.edu					
DeVRY Institute of Technology 2149 W Dunlap Ave	Phoenix	AZ	85021	602-870-9222	331-1494
TF Cust Svc: 800-528-0250 ■ *Web:* www.devry-phx.edu					
GateWay Community College 108 N 40th St	Phoenix	AZ	85034	602-392-5000	392-5329
Web: www.gwc.maricopa.edu					
Glendale Community College 6000 W Olive Ave	Glendale	AZ	85302	623-845-3000	845-3303
Web: www.gc.maricopa.edu ■ *E-mail:* info@gc.maricopa.edu					
Grand Canyon University 3300 W Camelback Rd	Phoenix	AZ	85017	602-249-3300	589-2580
TF Admissions: 800-800-9776 ■ *Web:* www.grand-canyon.edu					
ITT Technical Institute 4837 E McDowell Rd	Phoenix	AZ	85008	602-231-0871	267-8727
TF: 800-879-4881 ■ *Web:* www.itt-tech.edu					

Phoenix — Colleges/Universities (Cont'd)

				Phone	Fax
Lamson Junior College 1126 N Scottsdale Rd *TF:* 800-898-7017	Tempe	AZ	85281	480-898-7000	967-6645
Mesa Community College 1833 W Southern Ave *Web:* www.mc.maricopa.edu	Mesa	AZ	85202	480-461-7000	461-7804
Ottawa University 2340 W Mission Ln. *TF:* 800-235-9586 ■ *Web:* www.ottawa.edu/phoenix/index.html	Phoenix	AZ	85021	602-371-1188	371-0035
Paradise Valley Community College 18401 N 32nd St *Web:* www.pvc.maricopa.edu	Phoenix	AZ	85032	602-787-6500	787-7025
Phoenix College 1202 W Thomas Rd *Web:* www.pc.maricopa.edu	Phoenix	AZ	85013	602-264-2492	285-7813
Scottsdale Community College 9000 E Chaparral Rd *Web:* www.sc.maricopa.edu	Scottsdale	AZ	85256	480-423-6000	423-6200
South Mountain Community College 7050 S 24th St *Web:* www.smc.maricopa.edu ■ *E-mail:* montano@smc.maricopa.edu	Phoenix	AZ	85040	602-243-8000	243-8199
Southwestern College 2625 E Cactus Rd *TF Admissions:* 800-247-2697 ■ *E-mail:* swc@netwrx.net	Phoenix	AZ	85032	602-992-6101	404-2159
Sweetwater Bible College PO Box 5640	Glendale	AZ	85312	602-978-5511	588-3586
University of Phoenix 4605 E Elwood St *Web:* www.uophx.edu	Phoenix	AZ	85040	480-966-7400	303-5874
Western International University 9215 N Black Canyon Hwy *Web:* www.wintu.edu	Phoenix	AZ	85021	602-943-2311	371-8637

— Hospitals —

				Phone	Fax
Carl T Hayden Veterans Affairs Medical Center 650 E Indian School Rd	Phoenix	AZ	85012	602-277-5551	222-6435
Columbia Medical Center-Phoenix 1947 E Thomas Rd	Phoenix	AZ	85016	602-650-7600	650-7495
Del E Webb Memorial Hospital 14502 W Meeker Blvd	Sun City West	AZ	85375	623-214-4000	214-4105
Good Samaritan Regional Medical Center PO Box 2989	Phoenix	AZ	85062	602-239-2000	239-3749
John C Lincoln Hospital North Mountain 250 E Dunlap Ave **Fax:* Admitting	Phoenix	AZ	85020	602-943-2381	997-8972*
Maricopa Medical Center 2601 E Roosevelt St *Web:* www.maricopa.gov/medcenter/mmc.html	Phoenix	AZ	85008	602-344-5011	344-5190
Maryvale Hospital Medical Center 5102 W Campbell Ave	Phoenix	AZ	85031	623-848-5000	848-5553
Mesa General Hospital Medical Center 515 N Mesa Dr	Mesa	AZ	85201	480-969-9111	969-0095
Paradise Valley Hospital 3929 E Bell Rd	Phoenix	AZ	85032	602-867-1881	867-5657
Phoenix Baptist Hospital & Medical Center 2000 W Bethany Home Rd **Fax:* Admitting ■ *Web:* www.baptisthealth.com/family/in_services/pbh.html	Phoenix	AZ	85015	602-249-0212	279-5979*
Phoenix Children's Hospital 1300 N 12th St Suite 404 *Web:* www.phxchildrens.com	Phoenix	AZ	85006	602-239-5920	239-3522
Phoenix Memorial Hospital 1201 S 7th Ave **Fax:* Admitting	Phoenix	AZ	85007	602-258-5111	824-3012*
Saint Joseph's Hospital & Medical Center 350 W Thomas Rd **Fax:* Admitting	Phoenix	AZ	85013	602-406-3000	406-6143*
Saint Luke's Medical Center 1800 E Van Buren St **Fax:* Admitting	Phoenix	AZ	85006	602-251-8100	251-8487*
Scottsdale Healthcare Osborn 7400 E Osborn Rd **Fax:* Admitting	Scottsdale	AZ	85251	480-675-4000	675-4072*
Scottsdale Memorial Hospital-North 9003 E Shea Blvd	Scottsdale	AZ	85260	480-860-3000	860-3510
Tempe Saint Luke's Hospital 1500 S Mill Ave	Tempe	AZ	85281	480-968-9411	784-5630
Thunderbird Samaritan Medical Center 5555 W Thunderbird Rd **Fax:* Admitting ■ *Web:* www.samaritanaz.com/centers/thunderbird_sam.html	Glendale	AZ	85306	602-588-5555	588-5498*
US Public Health Service Phoenix Indian Medical Center 4212 N 16th St **Fax:* Admitting ■ *TF:* 877-733-7462	Phoenix	AZ	85016	602-263-1200	263-1648*
Valley Lutheran Hospital 6644 Baywood Ave	Mesa	AZ	85206	480-981-2000	981-4198
Walter O Boswell Memorial Hospital 10401 Thunderbird Blvd	Sun City	AZ	85351	623-977-7211	933-3225

— Attractions —

				Phone	Fax
Arizona Hall of Fame Museum 1101 W Washington St *Web:* www.dlapr.lib.az.us/ADA/fameindut.htm	Phoenix	AZ	85007	602-255-2110	255-3314
Arizona Mining & Mineral Museum 1502 W Washington St	Phoenix	AZ	85007	602-255-3791	255-3777
Arizona Museum for Youth 35 N Robson St	Mesa	AZ	85201	602-644-2468	644-2466
Arizona Science Center 600 E Washington St *Web:* www.azscience.org/	Phoenix	AZ	85004	602-716-2000	716-2099
Arizona State Capitol Museum 1700 W Washington St *Web:* www.dlapr.lib.az.us/museum/capitol.htm ■ *E-mail:* campus@dlapr.lib.az.us	Phoenix	AZ	85007	602-542-4675	542-4690
Arizona State University's Kerr Cultural Center 6110 N Scottsdale Rd *Web:* www.asukerr.com	Scottsdale	AZ	85253	480-965-5377	483-9646
Arizona Theatre Co 502 W Roosevelt St	Phoenix	AZ	85003	602-256-6899	256-7399
Ballet Arizona 3645 E Indian School Rd *Web:* www.balletarizona.citysearch.com	Phoenix	AZ	85018	602-381-0184	381-0189
Biosphere 2 32540 S Biosphere Rd *Web:* www.bio2.edu	Oracle	AZ	85623	520-896-6200	896-6471
Buffalo Museum of America 10261 N Scottsdale Rd	Scottsdale	AZ	85253	480-951-1022	991-6162
Camelback Mountain & Echo Canyon Recreation Area 5700 N Echo Canyon Pkwy	Phoenix	AZ	85018	602-256-3220	
Champlin Fighter Aircraft Museum 4636 E Fighter Aces Dr *Web:* www.ci.mesa.az.us/airport/museum.htm	Mesa	AZ	85215	480-830-4540	830-4543
Chandler Center for the Arts 250 N Arizona Ave	Chandler	AZ	85224	480-782-2680	782-2684
Deer Valley Rock Art Center 3711 W Deer Valley Rd	Phoenix	AZ	85308	623-582-8007	582-8831
Desert Botanical Garden 1201 N Galvin Pkwy **Fax Area Code:* 623 ■ *Web:* www.dbg.org ■ *E-mail:* dbgadmin@dbg.org	Phoenix	AZ	85008	480-941-1225	754-8124*
Encanto Park 2605 N 15th Ave	Phoenix	AZ	85007	602-262-6412	
Enchanted Island Amusement Park 1202 W Encanto Blvd Encanto Pk *Web:* www.enchantedisland.com ■ *E-mail:* enchantedisland@uswest.net	Phoenix	AZ	85007	602-254-2020	254-1264
Fleischer Museum 17207 N Perimeter Dr *TF:* 800-528-1179 ■ *Web:* www.fleischer.org	Scottsdale	AZ	85255	480-585-3108	585-2225
Frank Lloyd Wright Home-Taliesin 12621 N Frank Lloyd Wright Blvd *Web:* www.arizonaguide.com/taliesinwest	Scottsdale	AZ	85259	480-860-2700	860-8472
Grand Canyon IMAX Theatre Hwy 64 & US 180 S Entrance *Web:* www.imaxtheatre.com/grandcanyon/ ■ *E-mail:* imax@thecanyon.com	Grand Canyon	AZ	86023	520-638-2203	638-2807
Grand Canyon National Park PO Box 129 *Web:* www.thecanyon.com/nps ■ *E-mail:* info@thecanyon.com	Grand Canyon	AZ	86023	520-638-7888	
Hall of Flame Museum of Firefighting 6101 E Van Buren St *Web:* www.hallofflame.org	Phoenix	AZ	85008	602-275-3473	275-0896
Heard Museum 2301 N Central Ave *Web:* www.heard.org	Phoenix	AZ	85004	602-252-8840	252-9757
Herberger Theater Center 222 E Monroe St *Web:* www.herbergertheater.org ■ *E-mail:* herberger@nonline.com	Phoenix	AZ	85004	602-254-7399	258-9521
Historic Heritage Square 7th St & Monroe	Phoenix	AZ	85004	602-261-8948	534-1786
Hoo-hoogam Ki Museum 10005 E Osborn Rd Salt River Indian Reservation	Scottsdale	AZ	85256	480-850-8190	890-8961
Mesa Southwest Museum 53 N MacDonald St	Mesa	AZ	85201	602-644-2169	644-3424
Mystery Castle 800 E Mineral Rd	Phoenix	AZ	85040	602-268-1581	
Orpheum Theatre 203 W Adams St	Phoenix	AZ	85003	602-252-9678	252-1223
Papago Park 625 N Galvin Pkwy	Phoenix	AZ	85032	602-256-3220	
Phoenix Art Museum 1625 N Central Ave *Web:* www.azcentral.com/community/phxart/home.html ■ *E-mail:* info@phxart.org	Phoenix	AZ	85004	602-257-1880	253-8662
Phoenix Civic Plaza 225 E Adams St *TF:* 800-282-4842 ■ *Web:* www.ci.phoenix.az.us/civplaza.html	Phoenix	AZ	85004	602-262-6225	495-3642
Phoenix Heritage Square 115 N 6th St	Phoenix	AZ	85004	602-262-5071	
Phoenix Mountains Preserve 17642 N 40th St	Phoenix	AZ	85032	602-262-6696	
Phoenix Museum of History 105 N 5th St	Phoenix	AZ	85004	602-253-2734	253-2348
Phoenix Symphony Orchestra 455 N 3rd St Suite 390 *TF:* 800-776-9080 ■ *Web:* www.phoenixsymphony.com ■ *E-mail:* info@phoenixsymphony.com	Phoenix	AZ	85004	602-495-1117	253-1772
Phoenix Zoo 455 N Galvin Pkwy *Web:* www.phoenixzoo.org ■ *E-mail:* zooqna@thephxzoo.com	Phoenix	AZ	85008	602-273-1341	273-7078

Phoenix — Attractions (Cont'd)

				Phone	Fax
Pioneer Arizona Living History Museum 3901 W Pioneer Rd	Phoenix	AZ	85027	623-465-1052	465-1029
Web: www.pioneer-arizona.com					
Pueblo Grande Museum & Cultural Park 4619 E Washington St	Phoenix	AZ	85034	602-495-0901	495-5645
Web: www.arizonaguide.com/pueblogrande					
Shemer Arts Center & Museum 5005 E Camelback Rd	Phoenix	AZ	85018	602-262-4727	262-1605
South Mountain Park 10919 S Central Ave	Phoenix	AZ	85040	602-495-0222	495-0212
South Mountain Park/Preserve 10919 S Central Ave	Phoenix	AZ	85040	602-261-8457	
Squaw Peak Recreation Area 2701 E Squaw Peak Dr	Phoenix	AZ	85032	602-262-7901	262-4763
Thompson Boyce Southwestern Arboretum 37615 Hwy 60	Superior	AZ	85273	520-689-2632	689-5858
Web: ag.arizona.edu/BTA					
Tonto National Monument Hwy 88	Roosevelt	AZ	85545	520-467-2241	467-2225
Web: www.nps.gov/tont/					
WestWorld Equestrian Center 16601 N Pima Rd	Scottsdale	AZ	85260	480-312-6802	58-7927
Wrigley Mansion 2501 E Telawa Trail	Phoenix	AZ	85016	602-955-4079	956-8439

SPORTS TEAMS & FACILITIES

				Phone	Fax
America West Arena 201 E Jefferson St	Phoenix	AZ	85004	602-379-2000	379-2002
Web: www.americawestarena.com					
Arizona Cardinals 8701 S Hardy Dr	Tempe	AZ	85284	602-379-0101	379-1819
Web: www.nfl.com/cardinals					
Arizona Diamondbacks 401 E Jefferson St	Phoenix	AZ	85004	602-462-6500	462-6600
Web: www.azdiamondbacks.com					
Arizona Rattlers (football) 201 E Jefferson America West Arena	Phoenix	AZ	85004	602-379-7878	514-8303
Web: www.azrattlers.com					
Arizona Sahuaros (soccer) 16101 N 83rd Ave Peoria Sports Complex	Peoria	AZ	85382	602-256-6356	492-0602
Web: www.azsahuaros.com ■ *E-mail:* mark@sahuaros.com					
Arizona Veterans Memorial Coliseum & Exposition Center 1826 W McDowell Rd Suite 100	Phoenix	AZ	85007	602-252-6771	251-0528
Bank One Ballpark 401 E Jefferson St	Phoenix	AZ	85004	602-462-6500	462-6600
Web: www.azdiamondbacks.com/bob/index.html					
Harlem Globetrotters 400 E Van Buren St Suite 300	Phoenix	AZ	85004	602-258-0000	258-5925
TF: 800-641-4667 ■ *Web:* www.harlemglobetrotters.com					
Manzanita Speedway 3417 W Broadway Rd	Phoenix	AZ	85041	602-276-9401	276-3174
Milwaukee Brewers Spring Training (baseball) 3600 N 51st Ave	Phoenix	AZ	85031	623-245-5555	
Phoenix Coyotes 9375 E Bell Rd	Scottsdale	AZ	85260	480-473-5600	473-5699
Web: www.nhlcoyotes.com/home.shtml					
Phoenix Greyhound Park 3801 E Washington	Phoenix	AZ	85034	602-273-7181	273-6176
Web: www.phxgp.com					
Phoenix International Raceway 1313 N 2nd St Suite 1300	Phoenix	AZ	85004	602-252-3833	254-4622
Phoenix Mercury (basketball) America West Arena 201 E Jefferson	Phoenix	AZ	85004	602-514-8364	
Web: www.wnba.com/mercury					
Phoenix Suns 201 E Jefferson St America West Arena	Phoenix	AZ	85001	602-379-7800	379-7922
Web: www.nba.com/suns					
Arizona Thunder (soccer) 1826 W McDowell Rd Arizona Veterans Memorial Coliseum	Phoenix	AZ	85007	602-263-5425	263-7730
Web: www.arizonathunder.com					
Turf Paradise Racetrack 1501 W Bell Rd	Phoenix	AZ	85023	602-942-1101	588-2002
Web: www.turfparadise.com					

— Events —

	Phone
Arizona Renaissance Festival (early February-late March)	520-463-2700
Arizona State Fair (early-late October)	602-252-6771
Arizona Stock Show & Rodeo (late December-early January)	602-258-8568
Arizona's Cactus League Spring Training (March)	480-969-1307
ARR Desert Classic Marathon (mid-February)	623-933-2425
Chandler Ostrich Festival (mid-March)	480-963-4571
Cinco de Mayo Festival (early May)	602-279-4669
Coors Light World Finals Drag Boat Racing (late October)	602-268-0200
Copper World Classic Auto Racing (late January-early February)	602-252-3833
Cowboy Artists of America Exhibition (late October-late November)	602-257-1880
Easter Pageant (April)	480-964-7164
Fiesta Bowl (early January)	480-350-0900
Fiesta of Lights (mid-December)	602-261-8604
Fountain Hills Festival of Arts & Crafts (mid-November)	480-837-1654
Fountain Hills Great Fair (late February)	480-837-1654
French Week in Arizona (mid-November)	602-954-6573
Holiday Out West Arts & Crafts Festival (late November)	480-488-2014
Hot Air Balloon Race & Thunderbird Balloon Classic (early November)	480-312-6802
Indian Market (mid-December)	602-495-0901
Indy Racing League Phoenix 200 (late March)	602-252-2227
July 4th Festivities (July 4)	602-256-4125
Lost Dutchman Days (late February)	480-982-3141
Maricopa County Fair (late April-early May)	602-252-0717
Music by Moonlight Thursday Night Concert Series (mid-April-mid-September)	480-488-1072
Phoenix Open Golf Tournament (late January)	602-870-0163
Pueblo Grande Indian Market (mid-December)	602-495-0901
Scottsdale Arts Festival (mid-March)	480-994-2787
Scottsdale Desert Festival of Fine Art (late March)	480-837-5637
Southwest Salsa Challenge (late April)	602-955-3947
Tumbleweed Christmas Tree Lighting Ceremony (December)	480-786-2727

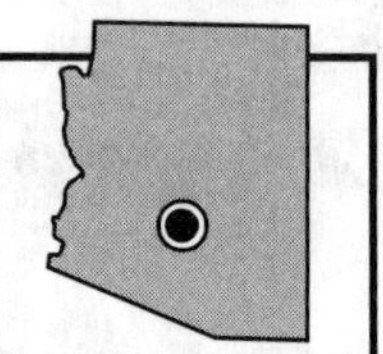

Scottsdale

Scottsdale is located in the Sonoran desert, under the McDowell Mountains, and many of its attractions focus on the Old West. Visitors to the area can re-live the days of the Old West at Rawhide 1880s Western Town, a life-sized replica of a frontier town that is Arizona's largest Western attraction. Rawhide's Main Street is lined with more than 20 specialty stores, including a general store, a working blacksmith, and a Native American Marketplace. Other attractions there include cowboy shootouts and stunt shows, stagecoach rides, gold panning, and the Old West Museum. Each March Rawhide holds its annual U.S. West National Festival of the West, four days celebrating western music, movies, cowboy poetry, chuck wagon cookin', and anything else "Western". Scottsdale is also home to the Buffalo Museum of America, which displays Native American and buffalo history and has a Buffalo Bill room that houses some of the legendary hunter's personal possessions. The Heard Museum contains a collection of Native American art and artifacts. "Native Peoples of the Southwest" is the museum's award-winning exhibit, filled with thousands of pieces of jewelry, basketry, pottery, and textiles. Scottsdale has more than 120 galleries, studios, and museums altogether, as well as several performing arts venues. Located there also is Frank Lloyd Wright's masterpiece, Taliesin West, a National Historic Landmark set amidst 600-acres of the Sonoran Desert. Created entirely from native materials, the complex was originally constructed as Wright's personal residence and architectural school and is still used today as an educational facility.

Population	195,394	**Longitude**	111-52-14 W
Area (Land)	184.5 sq mi	**County**	Maricopa
Area (Water)	0.2 sq mi	**Time Zone**	MST
Elevation	1248 ft	**Area Code/s**	480
Latitude	33-41-10 N		

— Average Temperatures and Precipitation —

TEMPERATURES

	Jan	Feb	Mar	Apr	May	Jun	Jul	Aug	Sep	Oct	Nov	Dec
High	66	71	76	85	94	104	106	104	98	88	75	66
Low	41	45	49	55	64	73	81	79	73	61	49	42

PRECIPITATION

	Jan	Feb	Mar	Apr	May	Jun	Jul	Aug	Sep	Oct	Nov	Dec
Inches	0.7	0.7	0.9	0.2	0.1	0.1	0.8	1.0	0.9	0.7	0.7	1.0

Scottsdale (Cont'd)

— Important Phone Numbers —

	Phone		Phone
AAA	602-274-1116	Medical Referral	602-252-2015
American Express Travel	480-949-7000	Poison Control Center	602-253-3334
Dental Referral	602-957-4864	Time/Temp	602-265-5550
Emergency	911	Weather	602-265-5550
HotelDocs	800-468-3537		

— Information Sources —

				Phone	Fax
Better Business Bureau Serving Central Northeast Northwest & Southwest Arizona 4428 N 12th St.	Phoenix	AZ	85014	602-264-1721	263-0997
Web: www.phoenix.bbb.org					
Maricopa County 301 W Jefferson St 10th Fl.	Phoenix	AZ	85003	602-506-3415	506-5997
Web: www.maricopa.gov					
Scottsdale Chamber of Commerce 7343 Scottsdale Mall	Scottsdale	AZ	85251	480-945-8481	947-4523
TF: 800-877-1117 ■ *Web:* www.scottsdalechamber.com					
Scottsdale City Hall 3939 Civic Center Blvd	Scottsdale	AZ	85251	480-312-2414	312-2738
Web: www.ci.scottsdale.az.us					
Scottsdale Convention & Visitor's Bureau 7343 Scottsdale Mall	Scottsdale	AZ	85251	480-945-8481	947-4523
TF: 800-877-1117 ■ *Web:* www.arizonaguide.com/cities/scottsdale/index.html					
Scottsdale Economic Development Dept 7447 E Indian School Rd	Scottsdale	AZ	85251	480-312-7601	312-2672
Web: www.ci.scottsdale.az.us/economic					
Scottsdale Mayor 3939 Civic Center Blvd.	Scottsdale	AZ	85251	480-312-2433	312-2738
Web: www.ci.scottsdale.az.us/welcome/mayor.asp					
Scottsdale Public Library System 3839 Civic Center Blvd	Scottsdale	AZ	85251	480-312-2474	312-7993
Web: library.ci.scottsdale.az.us					

On-Line Resources

City Knowledge Scottsdale	www.cityknowledge.com/az_scottsdale.htm
Phoenix-Best.com	www.phoenix-best.com
Savvy Diner Guide to Phoenix-Scottsdale Restaurants	www.savvydiner.com/phoenix/
Scottsdale Arizona	scottsdale-arizona.com
Scottsdale Directory	www.scottsdaledirectory.com
Scottsdale Golf Guide	scottsdale-golf.com

— Transportation Services —

AIRPORTS

■ Phoenix Sky Harbor International Airport (PHX)

	Phone
10 miles SW of downtown Scottsdale (approx 20 minutes)	602-273-3300

Web: www.phxskyharbor.com/skyharbr

Airport Transportation

	Phone
Camelback Cab $20 fare to downtown Scottsdale	480-947-1166
Continental Limousines $45 fare to downtown Scottsdale	480-941-9340

Commercial Airlines

	Phone		Phone
Aero California	800-237-6225	Shuttle by United	800-748-8853
AeroMexico	602-954-4750	SkyWest	800-453-9417
America West	800-235-9292	Southwest	602-273-1221
American	800-433-7300	TWA	800-221-2000
British Airways	800-247-9297	United	800-241-6522
Continental	800-525-0280	US Airways	800-428-4322
Northwest	800-225-2525	Vanguard	800-826-4827

Charter Airlines

	Phone		Phone
Aero Jet Services	480-922-7441	Grand Aire Express Inc	800-704-7263
Alliance Executive Charter Services	800-232-5387	Sawyer Aviation	602-273-3770
Corporate Jets Inc	480-948-2400	Southwest Aircraft Charter	480-969-2715
Cutter Aviation Inc	602-273-1237	Southwest Jet Aviation Ltd	480-991-7076
D & D Aviation	602-483-4644	Wayfarer Aviation	914-949-3661
Executive Aircraft Services	480-991-0900	West Coast Charters Inc	800-352-6153
		Westcor Aviation Inc	480-991-6558

CAR RENTALS

	Phone		Phone
Alamo	602-244-0897	Hertz	602-267-8822
Avis	602-273-3222	National	602-275-4771
Budget	602-267-4000	Premier	480-946-2500
Dollar	602-275-7588	Thrifty	602-244-0311

LIMO/TAXI

	Phone		Phone
Camelback Cab	480-947-1166	Scottsdale Express	480-994-1616
Continental Carriage	602-494-2783	Scottsdale Limousines	480-946-8446
Continental Limousines	480-941-9340	Sonoran Sunset Limousines	480-502-0570
Driver Provider Limousines	480-998-7517		

MASS TRANSIT

	Phone
Scottsdale Roundup Downtown Trolley Free	480-970-8130
Valley Metro $1.25 Base fare	602-253-5000

RAIL/BUS

				Phone
Amtrak Station 401 W Harrison St	Phoenix	AZ	85003	602-253-0121
TF: 800-872-7245				
Greyhound/Trailways Bus Station 2115 E Buckeye Rd	Phoenix	AZ	85034	602-389-4200
TF: 800-231-2222				

— Accommodations —

HOTEL RESERVATION SERVICES

	Phone	Fax
Advance Reservations Inn Arizona	480-990-0682	990-3390
TF: 800-456-0682 ■ *Web:* tucson.com/inn ■ *E-mail:* micasa@primenet.com		
Phoenix Scottsdale Hotel Reservations	602-954-1425	627-9405*
**Fax Area Code:* 858 ■ *TF:* 800-728-3227		
Scottsdale Resort Accommodations	480-515-2300	515-2700
TF: 888-868-4378 ■ *Web:* www.arizonaguide.com/sra/		

HOTELS, MOTELS, RESORTS

				Phone	Fax
Best Western Papago Inn & Resort 7017 E McDowell Rd	Scottsdale	AZ	85257	480-947-7335	994-0692
TF: 800-528-1234					
Camelback Resort & Spa 6302 E Camelback Rd	Scottsdale	AZ	85251	480-947-3300	994-0594
TF: 800-891-8585					
Comfort Inn Scottsdale 7350 E Gold Dust Rd	Scottsdale	AZ	85258	480-596-6559	596-0554
TF: 800-228-5150 ■ *Web:* www.arizonaguide.com/comfortinnscottsdale/					
Comfort Suites 3275 Civic Center Blvd	Scottsdale	AZ	85251	480-946-1111	874-1641
TF: 800-228-5150					
Country Inn & Suites by Carlson 10801 N 89th Pl	Scottsdale	AZ	85260	480-314-1200	314-7367*
**Fax Area Code:* 602 ■ *TF:* 800-456-4000 ■ *Web:* www.arizonaguide.com/countryinnscotts					
Courtyard by Marriott Scottsdale Mayo Clinic 13444 E Shea Blvd	Scottsdale	AZ	85259	480-860-4000	860-4308
TF: 800-321-2211					
Days Inn Resort at Fashion Square Mall 4710 N Scottsdale Rd	Scottsdale	AZ	85251	480-947-5411	946-1324
TF: 800-325-2525 ■ *Web:* www.arizonaguide.com/daysinnscottsdale/					
DoubleTree Paradise Valley Resort 5401 N Scottsdale Rd	Scottsdale	AZ	85250	480-947-5400	946-1524
TF: 800-222-8733					
Fairfield Inn Downtown Scottsdale 5101 N Scottsdale Rd	Scottsdale	AZ	85250	480-945-4392	947-3044
TF: 800-228-2800					

Scottsdale — Hotels, Motels, Resorts (Cont'd)

				Phone	Fax
Four Seasons Resort Scottsdale at Troon North 10600 E Crescent Moon Dr	Scottsdale	AZ	85255	480-515-5700	
Hampton Inn 10101 N Scottsdale Rd *TF:* 800-426-7866 ■ *Web:* www.arizonaguide.com/hamptoninnscottsdale/	Scottsdale	AZ	85253	480-443-3233	443-9149
Hampton Inn & Suites 16620 N Scottsdale Rd *TF:* 800-426-7866 ■ *Web:* www.arizonaguide.com/hamptonsuitesscottsdale/	Scottsdale	AZ	85254	480-348-9280	348-9281
Hampton Inn Old Town Scottsdale 4415 N Civic Center Plaza *TF:* 800-426-7866	Scottsdale	AZ	85251	480-941-9400	675-5240
Holiday Inn Hotel & Conference Center 7353 E Indian School Rd *TF:* 800-695-6995	Scottsdale	AZ	85251	480-994-9203	941-2567
Holiday Inn Hotel & Suites 7515 E Butherus Dr *TF:* 800-334-1977	Scottsdale	AZ	85260	480-951-4000	483-9046
Holiday Inn SunSpree Resort 7601 E Indian Bend Rd *TF:* 800-852-5205 ■ *Web:* www.basshotels.com/holiday-inn/?_franchisee=PHXSS ■ *E-mail:* sunspree@getnet.com	Scottsdale	AZ	85250	480-991-2400	998-2261
Homestead Guest Studios 3560 N Marshall Way *TF:* 888-782-9473	Scottsdale	AZ	85251	480-994-0297	994-9036
Homewood Suites Hotel 9880 N Scottsdale Rd *TF:* 800-225-5466	Scottsdale	AZ	85253	480-368-8705	368-8725
Hospitality Suites Resort 409 N Scottsdale Rd *TF:* 800-445-5115 ■ *Web:* www.amdest.com/az/scottsdale/hospitality.html	Scottsdale	AZ	85257	480-949-5115	941-8014
Hyatt Regency Scottsdale at Gainey Ranch 7500 E Doubletree Ranch Rd *TF:* 800-233-1234 ■ *Web:* www.hyatt.com/usa/scottsdale/hotels/hotel_scott.html	Scottsdale	AZ	85258	480-991-3388	483-5550
InnSuites Scottsdale El Dorado Park 7707 E McDowell Rd *TF:* 800-238-8851 ■ *Web:* www.innsuites.com/hotelscottsdale.htm	Scottsdale	AZ	85257	480-941-1202	990-7873
Marriott Courtyard 17010 N Scottsdale Rd *TF:* 800-321-2211 ■ *Web:* courtyard.com/PHXCN	Scottsdale	AZ	85255	480-922-8400	948-3481
Marriott's Camelback Inn Resort Golf Club & Spa 5402 E Lincoln Dr *TF:* 800-242-2635 ■ *Web:* www.camelbackinn.com ■ *E-mail:* reservations@camelbackinn.com	Scottsdale	AZ	85253	480-948-1700	951-8469
Orange Tree Golf & Conference Resort 10601 N 56th St *TF:* 800-228-0386 ■ *Web:* www.arizonaguide.com/orangetree/	Scottsdale	AZ	85254	480-948-6100	483-6074
Phoenician The 6000 E Camelback Rd *TF:* 800-888-8234 ■ *Web:* www.thephoenician.com	Scottsdale	AZ	85251	480-941-8200	947-4311
Radisson Resort 7171 N Scottsdale Rd *TF:* 800-333-3333 ■ *Web:* www.arizonaguide.com/radissonscottsdale/	Scottsdale	AZ	85253	480-991-3800	948-1381
Ramada Valley Ho Resort 6850 E Main St *TF:* 800-321-4952 ■ *Web:* www.arizonaguide.com/valleyho/	Scottsdale	AZ	85251	480-945-6321	947-5270
Regal McCormick Ranch Resort 7401 N Scottsdale Rd *TF:* 800-222-8888 ■ *Web:* www.regal-hotels.com/scottsdale ■ *E-mail:* regal@getnet.com	Scottsdale	AZ	85253	480-948-5050	991-5572
Renaissance Cottonwoods Resort 6160 N Scottsdale Rd *TF:* 800-468-3571	Scottsdale	AZ	85253	480-991-1414	948-2205
Resort Suites of Scottsdale 7677 E Princess Blvd *TF:* 800-541-5203	Scottsdale	AZ	85255	480-585-1234	585-1457
Rodeway Inn Scottsdale 7110 E Indian School Rd *TF:* 800-228-2000 ■ *Web:* www.arizonaguide.com/rodewayinnscottsdale/	Scottsdale	AZ	85251	480-946-3456	874-0492
Scottsdale Conference Resort 7700 E McCormick Pkwy *TF:* 800-528-0293	Scottsdale	AZ	85258	480-991-9000	596-7420
Scottsdale Embassy Suites 5001 N Scottsdale Rd *TF:* 800-528-1456 ■ *Web:* www.arizonaguide.com/embassyscottsdale/	Scottsdale	AZ	85250	480-949-1414	947-2675
Scottsdale Hilton Resort & Villas 6333 N Scottsdale Rd *TF:* 800-528-3119	Scottsdale	AZ	85250	480-948-7750	948-2232
Scottsdale Marriott Suites 7325 E 3rd Ave *TF:* 800-228-9290	Scottsdale	AZ	85251	480-945-1550	945-2005
Scottsdale Pima Inn & Suites 7330 N Pima Rd *TF:* 800-344-0262 ■ *Web:* www.arizonaguide.com/pimasuites/	Scottsdale	AZ	85258	480-948-3800	443-3374
Scottsdale Plaza Resort 7200 N Scottsdale Rd *TF:* 800-832-2025	Scottsdale	AZ	85253	480-948-5000	998-5971
Scottsdale Princess 7575 E Princess Dr *TF:* 800-344-4758 ■ *Web:* www.scottsdaleprincess.com	Scottsdale	AZ	85255	480-585-4848	585-0091
SunBurst Resort 4925 N Scottsdale Rd *TF:* 800-528-7867 ■ *Web:* www.sunburstresort.com	Scottsdale	AZ	85251	480-945-7666	946-4056

— Restaurants —

				Phone
Avanti of Scottsdale (Italian) 3102 N Scottsdale Rd *Web:* www.arizonaguide.com/avanti/	Scottsdale	AZ	85251	480-949-8333
Baby Kay's Cajun Kitchen (Cajun) 7216 E Shoeman Ln	Scottsdale	AZ	85251	480-990-9080
Bandera Scottsdale (American) 3821 N Scottsdale Rd	Scottsdale	AZ	85251	480-994-3524
Bravo Bistro (Mediterranean/Italian) 4327 N Scottsdale Rd *Web:* www.bravobistro.com ■ *E-mail:* tony@bravobistro.com	Scottsdale	AZ	85251	480-481-7614
Buster's Restaurant Bar & Grill (American) 8320 N Hayden Rd	Scottsdale	AZ	85258	480-951-5850
Cafe Terra Cotta (Southwest) 6166 N Scottsdale Rd Suite 100 *Web:* www.cafeterracotta.com	Scottsdale	AZ	85253	480-948-8100
Capers Restaurant & Bar (American) 10601 N 56th St Orange Tree Resort	Scottsdale	AZ	85254	480-443-2119
Caribbean Café & Grill (Caribbean) 9719 N Hayden St	Scottsdale	AZ	85258	480-368-9779
Carlsbad Tavern (Southwest) 3313 N Hayden Rd	Scottsdale	AZ	85251	480-970-8164
Carver's (Steak/Seafood) 10825 N Scottsdale Rd	Scottsdale	AZ	85254	480-998-8777
Chart House Restaurant (Steak/Seafood) 7255 McCormick Pkwy	Scottsdale	AZ	85258	480-951-2550
Coco Pazzo (Italian) 4720 N Scottsdale Rd	Scottsdale	AZ	85251	480-946-9777
Don & Charlie's (Barbecue) 7501 E Camelback Rd	Scottsdale	AZ	85251	480-990-0900
El Chorro Lodge (Continental) 5550 E Lincoln Dr *Web:* www.elchorro.com ■ *E-mail:* elchorro@aol.com	Scottsdale	AZ	85253	480-948-5170
Hearty Hen Cafe (American) 10830 N Scottsdale Rd	Scottsdale	AZ	85254	480-951-1151
Julio G's (Mexican) 7633 E Indian School Rd	Scottsdale	AZ	85251	480-423-1600
Kyoto (Japanese) 7170 E Stetson Dr	Scottsdale	AZ	85251	480-990-9374
Los Olivos Mexican Patio (Mexican) 7328 2nd St	Scottsdale	AZ	85251	480-946-2256
Mancuso's Restaurant (Italian) 6166 N Scottsale Rd Suite 500	Scottsdale	AZ	85253	480-948-9988
Mary Elaine's (French) 6000 E Camelback Rd *Web:* www.thephoenician.com/dining/dine_marymenu.html	Scottsdale	AZ	85251	480-423-2410
Mimi's Cafe (American) 8980 E Shea Blvd	Scottsdale	AZ	85260	480-451-6763
Old Town Tortilla Factory (Southwest) 6910 E Main St	Scottsdale	AZ	85251	480-945-4567
Other Place The (American) 7101 E Lincoln Dr	Scottsdale	AZ	85253	480-948-7910
Palm Court The (Continental) 7700 E McCormick Pkwy	Scottsdale	AZ	85258	480-991-3400
Peaks at Pinnacle Peak (American) 8711 E Pinnacle Peak Rd	Scottsdale	AZ	85255	480-998-2222
Pepin (Spanish) 7363 Scottsdale Mall *Web:* www.arizonaguide.com/pepin/	Scottsdale	AZ	85251	480-990-9026
PF Chang's China Bistro (Chinese) 7014 E Camelback Rd	Scottsdale	AZ	85251	480-949-2610
Piñon Grill (Southwest) 7401 N Scottsdale Rd	Scottsdale	AZ	85253	480-948-5050
Ra (Japanese) 3815 N Scottsdale Rd	Scottsdale	AZ	85251	480-990-9256
Roaring Fork (American) 7243 E Camelback Rd *Web:* www.roaringfork.com	Scottsdale	AZ	85251	480-947-0795
Ruth's Chris Steak House (Steak/Seafood) 7001 N Scottsdale Rd Suite 290	Scottsdale	AZ	85253	480-991-5988

— Goods and Services —

SHOPPING

				Phone	Fax
Borgata of Scottsdale 6166 N Scottsdale Rd	Scottsdale	AZ	85253	480-998-1822	
el Pedregal 34505 N Scottsdale Rd	Scottsdale	AZ	85262	480-488-1072	488-5915
Hilton Village 6166 N Scottsdale Rd	Scottsdale	AZ	85253	480-998-1822	998-7581
Los Arcos Mall 1315 N Scottsdale Rd	Scottsdale	AZ	85257	480-945-6376	946-9105
Pinnacle of Scottsdale 23733 N Scottsdale Rd	Scottsdale	AZ	85255	480-585-8869	585-4545
Scottsdale Fashion Square 7014 E Camelback Rd	Scottsdale	AZ	85251	480-990-7800	423-1455
Scottsdale Seville NE Corner of Scottsdale Rd & Indian Bend	Scottsdale	AZ	85253	480-905-8110	905-8120
Shops at Rawhide 23023 N Scottsdale Rd *TF:* 800-527-1880	Scottsdale	AZ	85255	480-502-1880	502-1301

BANKS

				Phone	Fax
Bank of America 3123 N Scottsdale Rd	Scottsdale	AZ	85251	480-429-4741	941-2168

Scottsdale — Banks (Cont'd)

Name / Address	City	State	Zip	Phone	Fax
Bank One 4031 N Scottsdale Rd	Scottsdale	AZ	85251	480-970-7014	
First International Bank & Trust 6840 E Indian School Rd	Scottsdale	AZ	85251	480-946-2967	946-2739
Norwest Bank Arizona NA 9719 N Hayden Rd	Scottsdale	AZ	85258	480-991-2265	
Valley First Community Bank 7501 E McCormick Pkwy Suite 105	Scottsdale	AZ	85258	480-596-0883	596-0885
Western Security Bank 7401 E Camelback Rd	Scottsdale	AZ	85251	480-947-9888	990-0443

BUSINESS SERVICES

	Phone		Phone
AAA Affordable Courier	480-892-9083	**Kinko's**	480-946-0500
Adecco Employment Personnel Services	480-874-1015	**Kwik-Kopy Printing**	480-947-5291
Airborne Express	800-247-2676	**Mail Boxes Etc**	480-951-9070
Copy Max	480-949-1653	**Olsten Staffing Services**	480-922-3113
DHL Worldwide Express	800-225-5345	**Post Office**	480-949-8893
Federal Express	800-463-3339	**Stivers Temporary Personnel**	480-948-2225
Kelly Services	480-998-0571	**UPS**	800-742-5877
		UPS	800-742-5877

— Media —

PUBLICATIONS

Name / Address	City	State	Zip	Phone	Fax
Arizona Republic‡ PO Box 1950 *TF:* 800-331-9303 ■ *Web:* www.azcentral.com	Phoenix	AZ	85001	602-444-8000	444-8044
Scottsdale Progress Tribune‡ 7525 E Camelback Rd	Scottsdale	AZ	85252	480-941-2300	970-2360
Where Scottsdale Magazine 4383 N 75th St	Scottsdale	AZ	85251	480-481-9981	481-9979

‡Daily newspapers

TELEVISION

Name / Address	City	State	Zip	Phone	Fax
KAET-TV Ch 8 (PBS) PO Box 871405 *Web:* www.kaet.asu.edu ■ *E-mail:* kaet@asu.edu	Tempe	AZ	85287	480-965-3506	965-1000
KASW-TV Ch 61 (WB) 5555 N 7th Ave	Phoenix	AZ	85013	480-661-6161	207-3277
KDRX-TV Ch 64 (Tele) 4001 E Broadway Suite 11	Phoenix	AZ	85040	602-470-0507	470-0810
KNXV-TV Ch 15 (ABC) 515 N 44th St *Web:* www.knxv.com ■ *E-mail:* news15@primenet.com	Phoenix	AZ	85008	602-273-1500	685-3000
KPHO-TV Ch 5 (CBS) 4016 N Black Canyon Hwy *Web:* www.kpho.com	Phoenix	AZ	85017	602-264-1000	650-0761
KPNX-TV Ch 12 (NBC) 1101 N Central Ave	Phoenix	AZ	85004	602-257-1212	257-6619
KSAZ-TV Ch 10 (Fox) 511 W Adams St	Phoenix	AZ	85003	602-257-1234	262-0177
KTVW-TV Ch 33 (Uni) 3019 E Southern Ave *Web:* www.univision.net/stations/ktvw.htm	Phoenix	AZ	85040	602-243-3333	276-8658
KUTP-TV Ch 45 (UPN) 4630 S 33rd St *Web:* www.kutp.com	Phoenix	AZ	85040	602-268-4500	276-4082

— Colleges/Universities —

Name / Address	City	State	Zip	Phone	Fax
Ottawa University 13402 N Scottsdale Rd Suite B170 **Fax Area Code:* 602 ■ *Web:* www.ottawa.edu/phoenix	Scottsdale	AZ	85254	480-998-2297	371-0035*
Rainstar College 4130 N Goldwater Blvd *Web:* www.rainstargroup.com	Scottsdale	AZ	85251	480-423-0375	945-9824
Scottsdale Community College 9000 E Chaparral Rd *Web:* www.sc.maricopa.edu	Scottsdale	AZ	85256	480-423-6000	423-6200
Southwest Institute of Arts 1402 N Miller Rd	Scottsdale	AZ	85257	480-994-9244	994-3228

— Hospitals —

Name / Address	City	State	Zip	Phone	Fax
Charter Desert Vista Hospital 570 W Brown Rd	Mesa	AZ	85201	480-962-3900	827-0412
Maricopa Medical Center 2601 E Roosevelt St *Web:* www.maricopa.gov/medcenter/mmc.html	Phoenix	AZ	85008	602-344-5011	344-5190
Mesa General Hospital Medical Center 515 N Mesa Dr	Mesa	AZ	85201	480-969-9111	969-0095
Phoenix Children's Hospital 1300 N 12th St Suite 404 *Web:* www.phxchildrens.com	Phoenix	AZ	85006	602-239-5920	239-3522
Piper Kenneth M Health Center 9007 E Shea Blvd	Scottsdale	AZ	85260	480-860-3950	860-3572
Scottsdale Healthcare Osborn 7400 E Osborn Rd **Fax:* Admitting	Scottsdale	AZ	85251	480-675-4000	675-4072*
Scottsdale Memorial Hospital-North 9003 E Shea Blvd	Scottsdale	AZ	85260	480-860-3000	860-3510
Tempe Saint Luke's Hospital 1500 S Mill Ave	Tempe	AZ	85281	480-968-9411	784-5630

— Attractions —

Name / Address	City	State	Zip	Phone	Fax
Arizona State University's Kerr Cultural Center 6110 N Scottsdale Rd *Web:* www.asukerr.com	Scottsdale	AZ	85253	480-965-5377	483-9646
Buffalo Museum of America 10261 N Scottsdale Rd	Scottsdale	AZ	85253	480-951-1022	991-6162
CrackerJax Family Fun & Sports Park 16001 N Scottsdale Rd	Scottsdale	AZ	85254	480-998-2800	998-8544
Desert Botanical Garden 1201 N Galvin Pkwy **Fax Area Code:* 623 ■ *Web:* www.dbg.org ■ *E-mail:* dbgadmin@dbg.org	Phoenix	AZ	85008	480-941-1225	754-8124*
Fiddlesticks Family Fun Park & Atlantis Laser Odyssey 8800 E Indian Bend Rd	Scottsdale	AZ	85250	480-951-6060	951-4065
Fleischer Museum 17207 N Perimeter Dr *TF:* 800-528-1179 ■ *Web:* www.fleischer.org	Scottsdale	AZ	85255	480-585-3108	585-2225
Fort McDowell Casino PO Box 18359 **Fax:* Mktg ■ *Web:* www.fortmcdowellcasino.com	Fountain Hills	AZ	85269	480-837-1424	837-4756*
Frank Lloyd Wright Home-Taliesin 12621 N Frank Lloyd Wright Blvd *Web:* www.arizonaguide.com/taliesinwest	Scottsdale	AZ	85259	480-860-2700	860-8472
Hall of Flame Museum of Firefighting 6101 E Van Buren St *Web:* www.hallofflame.org	Phoenix	AZ	85008	602-275-3473	275-0896
Heard Museum 2301 N Central Ave *Web:* www.heard.org	Phoenix	AZ	85004	602-252-8840	252-9757
IMAX Theatre Scottsdale 4343 N Scottsdale Rd Suite 2501	Scottsdale	AZ	85251	480-949-3100	949-3110
MacDonald's Ranch 26540 N Scottsdale Rd	Scottsdale	AZ	85255	480-585-0239	585-1519
McCormick-Stillman Railroad Park 7301 E Indian Bend Rd *Web:* www.ci.scottsdale.az.us/mccormickpark/	Scottsdale	AZ	85250	480-312-2312	994-7001
Out of Africa Wildlife Park 9736 N Fort McDowell Rd *Web:* www.outofafricapark.com	Scottsdale	AZ	85264	480-837-7779	837-7379
Paolo Soleri Windbells Historic Site 6433 Doubletree Ranch Rd *TF:* 800-752-3187	Scottsdale	AZ	85253	480-948-6145	998-4312
Phoenix Art Museum 1625 N Central Ave *Web:* www.azcentral.com/community/phxart/home.html ■ *E-mail:* info@phxart.org	Phoenix	AZ	85004	602-257-1880	253-8662
Phoenix Zoo 455 N Galvin Pkwy *Web:* www.phoenixzoo.org ■ *E-mail:* zooqna@thephxzoo.com	Phoenix	AZ	85008	602-273-1341	273-7078
Pioneer Arizona Living History Museum 3901 W Pioneer Rd *Web:* www.pioneer-arizona.com	Phoenix	AZ	85027	623-465-1052	465-1029
Pueblo Grande Museum & Cultural Park 4619 E Washington St *Web:* www.arizonaguide.com/pueblogrande	Phoenix	AZ	85034	602-495-0901	495-5645
Rancho Verde - Big Birds of Arizona 15419 E Rio Verde Dr	Scottsdale	AZ	85255	480-471-3802	471-3802
Rawhide 1880s Western Town 23023 N Scottsdale Rd *Web:* www.rawhide.com	Scottsdale	AZ	85255	480-502-5600	502-1301
Rawhide Saloon 23023 N Scottsdale Rd *Web:* www.rawhide.com	Scottsdale	AZ	85255	480-502-5600	502-1301
Scottsdale Center for the Arts 7380 E 2nd St *Web:* scottsdalearts.org/sca/ ■ *E-mail:* info@sccarts.org	Scottsdale	AZ	85251	480-994-2787	874-4699
Scottsdale Historical Museum 7333 E Civic Center Mall	Scottsdale	AZ	85251	480-945-4499	970-3251
Scottsdale Museum of Contemporary Art 7380 E 2nd St *Web:* scottsdalearts.org/smoca/ ■ *E-mail:* info@sccarts.org	Scottsdale	AZ	85251	480-874-4644	874-4699

Scottsdale — Attractions (Cont'd)

				Phone	Fax
Scottsdale Symphony Orchestra 3817 N Brown Ave	Scottsdale	AZ	85251	480-945-8071	946-8770
Web: www.scotsymph.org ■ *E-mail:* sso@scotsymph.org					
Scottsdale Thursday Night Art Walk Main St	Scottsdale	AZ	85251	480-990-3939	
Web: www.scottsdalegalleries.com					
Stagebrush Theatre 7020 E 2nd St	Scottsdale	AZ	85251	480-990-7405	990-2182
WestWorld Equestrian Center 16601 N Pima Rd	Scottsdale	AZ	85260	480-312-6802	58-7927

SPORTS TEAMS & FACILITIES

				Phone	Fax
Phoenix Greyhound Park 3801 E Washington	Phoenix	AZ	85034	602-273-7181	273-6176
Web: www.phxgp.com					
San Francisco Giants Spring Training (baseball) 7408 E Osborn Rd	Scottsdale	AZ	85251	480-990-7972	
Scottsdale Scorpions (baseball) 7402 E Osborn Rd Scottsdale Stadium	Scottsdale	AZ	85251	480-496-6700	496-6384
Scottsdale Stadium 7408 East Osborn Rd	Scottsdale	AZ	85251	480-312-2580	
Turf Paradise Racetrack 1501 W Bell Rd	Phoenix	AZ	85023	602-942-1101	588-2002
Web: www.turfparadise.com					

— Events —

	Phone
Arizona Quarter Horse Amateur Horse Show (early April)	480-443-8800
Borgata Farmers Market (October-April)	480-998-1822
Equine Spectacular (mid-February)	480-502-5600
Fiesta Bowl (early January)	480-350-0900
Greek Festival (late October)	480-312-6802
Hot Air Balloon Race & Thunderbird Balloon Classic (early November)	480-312-6802
Jump into Spring Hunter Jumper Horse Show (late March)	480-312-6802
Knix Spring Rodeo Connection at Rawhide (early May-late June)	480-502-5600
Merry-Go-Round Horse Show (early April)	480-312-6802
Music by Moonlight Thursday Night Concert Series (mid-April-mid-September)	480-488-1072
National Truck Rodeo (early September)	480-312-6802
Ollie the Trolley's City Tours (October-April)	480-970-8130
PRCA Pro Rodeo Series (mid-April)	480-502-5600
Rawhide's Rollickin' New Year's Eve (December 31)	480-502-5600
Region 7 All-Arabian Championship Horse Show (late April-early May)	480-312-6802
Scottsdale Arabian Horse Show (mid-late February)	480-312-6802
Scottsdale Arts Festival (mid-March)	480-994-2787
Scottsdale Celebration of Fine Art (mid-January-late March)	480-443-7695
Scottsdale Culinary Festival (mid-April)	480-945-7193
Scottsdale Desert Festival of Fine Art (late March)	480-837-5637
Scottsdale Spring Festival (mid-April)	480-312-6802
WestWorld Summer Rodeo Series (June-mid-September)	480-312-6802

Tempe

Originally called Hayden's Ferry by its founder, Charles Trumbell Hayden, the city was renamed Tempe when an English traveler compared the beauty of the area and its twin buttes to Greece's Mount Olympus and Vale of Tempe. Arizona's first institution of higher education, the Arizona Territorial Normal School, opened in Tempe in 1886. The school is now Arizona State University, the fifth largest university in the U.S. The New York Times named Tempe one of the top 10 college towns in the country. Tempe is host to the annual Fiesta Bowl and is also home to the NFL's Arizona Cardinals and the spring training home of the Anaheim Angels. According to USA Today, Tempe's New Year's Eve Fiesta Bowl Block Party makes it one of the best places in the country to spend New Year's Eve.

Population	167,622	**Longitude**	111-55-50 W
Area (Land)	39.5 sq mi	**County**	Maricopa
Area (Water)	0.1 sq mi	**Time Zone**	MST
Elevation	1,160 ft	**Area Code/s**	480
Latitude	33-23-18 N		

— Average Temperatures and Precipitation —

TEMPERATURES

	Jan	Feb	Mar	Apr	May	Jun	Jul	Aug	Sep	Oct	Nov	Dec
High	67	73	78	87	95	104	107	105	100	90	77	68
Low	38	40	45	50	57	65	74	73	66	55	44	38

PRECIPITATION

	Jan	Feb	Mar	Apr	May	Jun	Jul	Aug	Sep	Oct	Nov	Dec
Inches	0.8	0.8	1.0	0.9	0.9	0.1	0.8	1.2	1.0	0.7	0.7	1.2

— Important Phone Numbers —

	Phone		Phone
AAA	480-949-7993	**Medical Referral**	602-252-2015
American Express Travel	480-949-7000	**Poison Control Center**	602-253-3334
Dental Referral	602-957-4864	**Time/Temp**	602-265-5550
Emergency	911	**Weather**	602-265-5550

— Information Sources —

				Phone	Fax
Better Business Bureau Serving Central Northeast Northwest & Southwest Arizona 4428 N 12th St	Phoenix	AZ	85014	602-264-1721	263-0997
Web: www.phoenix.bbb.org					
Maricopa County 301 W Jefferson St 10th Fl	Phoenix	AZ	85003	602-506-3415	506-5997
Web: www.maricopa.gov					
Tempe Chamber of Commerce PO Box 28500	Tempe	AZ	85285	480-967-7891	966-5365
Web: www.tempechamber.org ■ *E-mail:* info@TempeChamber.org					
Tempe City Hall PO Box 5002	Tempe	AZ	85280	480-967-2001	350-8996
Web: www.tempe.gov					
Tempe Convention & Visitors Bureau 51 W 3rd St Suite 105	Tempe	AZ	85281	480-894-8158	968-8004
TF: 800-283-6734 ■ *Web:* www.arizonaguide.com/cities/tempe/index.html					
Tempe Development Services Dept PO Box 5002	Tempe	AZ	85280	480-350-8340	
Web: www.tempe.gov/tdsi					
Tempe Mayor PO Box 5002	Tempe	AZ	85280	480-350-8865	350-8996
Web: www.tempe.gov/manager/mayor.htm					
Tempe Public Library 3500 S Rural Rd	Tempe	AZ	85282	480-350-5500	350-5544
Web: www.tempe.gov/library					

On-Line Resources

City Knowledge Tempe	www.cityknowledge.com/az_tempe.htm
City News	www.tempe.gov/events.htm
Excite.com Tempe City Guide	www.excite.com/travel/countries/united_states/arizona/tempe
NITC Travelbase City Guide Tempe	www.travelbase.com/auto/guides/tempe-az.html
Tempe in Touch	www.tempe.gov
Tempe Net	www.tempe.net
Ultimate Arizona Vacation Guide	www.webcreationsetc.com/Azguide/Phoenix/

— Transportation Services —

AIRPORTS

■ **Phoenix Sky Harbor International Airport (PHX)**	Phone
4 miles NW of downtown Tempe (approx 10 minutes)	602-273-3300
Web: www.phxskyharbor.com/skyharbr	

Airport Transportation

	Phone
Phoenix Transit System $1.25 fare to downtown Tempe	602-253-5000
Starlite Limousines $25 fare to downtown Tempe	480-905-1234

Commercial Airlines

	Phone		Phone
America West	800-235-9292	**SkyWest**	800-453-9417
American	800-433-7300	**Southwest**	602-273-1221
Continental	800-525-0280	**TWA**	800-221-2000
Mesa	800-637-2247	**United**	800-241-6522
Northwest	800-225-2525	**US Airways**	800-428-4322
Shuttle by United	800-748-8853		

Tempe (Cont'd)

Charter Airlines

	Phone		Phone
Corporate Jets Inc	480-948-2400	**Southwest Aircraft Charter**	480-969-2715
Cutter Aviation Inc	602-273-1237	**West Coast Charters Inc**	800-352-6153
Grand Aire Express Inc	800-704-7263		

CAR RENTALS

	Phone		Phone
Alamo	602-244-0897	**Hertz**	602-267-8822
Budget	800-227-3678	**Thrifty**	602-244-0311
Dollar	480-829-1523	**U-Save Auto**	480-968-0960
Enterprise	480-784-5995		

LIMO/TAXI

	Phone		Phone
AAA Limousine Service Valleywide	480-966-8000	**Starlite Limousines**	480-905-1234
Mirage Limousines Valleywide	480-820-7235	**Transtyle Limousine Services**	480-966-1200

MASS TRANSIT

	Phone
Phoenix Transit System $1.25 Base fare	602-253-5000

RAIL/BUS

	City	State	Zip	Phone
Amtrak Station 401 W Harrison St *TF:* 800-872-7245	Phoenix	AZ	85003	602-253-0121
Greyhound Bus Station 502 S College Ave *TF:* 800-231-2222	Tempe	AZ	85281	480-967-4030

— Accommodations —

HOTEL RESERVATION SERVICES

	Phone	Fax
Advance Reservations Inn Arizona *TF:* 800-456-0682 ■ *Web:* tucson.com/inn ■ *E-mail:* micasa@primenet.com	480-990-0682	990-3390

HOTELS, MOTELS, RESORTS

	City	State	Zip	Phone	Fax
Apache Rivers Inn 2090 E Apache Blvd	Tempe	AZ	85281	480-929-0413	929-0413
Best Western Inn Tempe 670 N Scottsdale Rd *TF:* 800-528-1234	Tempe	AZ	85282	480-784-2233	784-2299
Best Western Suites 665 Via Del Cielo *TF:* 800-528-1234	Casa Grande	AZ	85222	520-836-1600	836-7242
Buttes The 2000 Westcourt Way *TF:* 800-843-1986	Tempe	AZ	85282	602-225-9000	438-8622
Country Inn & Suites by Carlson 808 Scottsdale Rd *TF:* 800-456-4000	Tempe	AZ	85281	480-858-9898	784-2246
Country Suites by Carlson 1660 W Elliot Rd *TF:* 800-456-4000	Tempe	AZ	85283	480-345-8585	345-7461
Courtyard by Marriott 601 S Ash Ave *Web:* courtyard.com/PHXTE	Tempe	AZ	85281	480-966-2800	829-8446
Days Inn Tempe ASU 1221 E Apache Blvd	Tempe	AZ	85281	480-968-7793	966-4450
Desert Rest Motel 2164 E Apache Blvd	Tempe	AZ	85281	480-968-5292	
Econo Lodge 2101 E Apache Blvd *TF:* 800-553-2666	Tempe	AZ	85281	480-966-5832	966-5832
Embassy Suites Hotel Tempe 4400 S Rural Rd *TF:* 800-362-2779	Tempe	AZ	85282	480-897-7444	897-6112
Fiesta Inn 2100 S Priest Dr *TF:* 800-528-6481	Tempe	AZ	85282	480-967-1441	967-0224
Holiday Inn Express 5300 S Priest Dr *TF:* 800-465-4329 ■ *Web:* www.basshotels.com/hiexpress/?_franchisee=PHXTP ■ *E-mail:* tempehi@aol.com	Tempe	AZ	85283	480-820-7500	730-6626
Holiday Inn Phoenix-Tempe/ASU 915 E Apache Blvd *TF:* 800-553-1826	Tempe	AZ	85281	480-968-3451	968-6262
Homestead Village 4909 S Wendler Dr *TF:* 888-782-9473	Tempe	AZ	85282	602-414-4470	414-4466
Innsuites Tempe/Phoenix Airport 1651 W Baseline Rd *TF:* 800-841-4242 ■ *Web:* www.innsuites.com/hoteltempe.htm	Tempe	AZ	85283	480-897-7900	491-1008
La Quinta Inn 911 S 48th St *TF:* 800-687-6667	Tempe	AZ	85281	480-967-4465	921-9172
Lazy 8 Motel 2158 E Apache Blvd	Tempe	AZ	85281	480-894-9306	
Motel 6 1720 S Priest Dr *TF:* 800-466-8356	Tempe	AZ	85281	480-968-4401	929-0810
Motel 6 1612 N Scottsdale Rd *TF:* 800-466-8356	Tempe	AZ	85281	480-945-9506	970-4763
Ramada Plaza/Phoenix Airport 1600 S 52nd St *TF:* 800-346-3049	Tempe	AZ	85281	480-967-6600	829-9427
Ramada Suites 1635 N Scottsdale Rd *TF:* 800-678-8466	Tempe	AZ	85281	480-947-3711	949-7902
Red Roof Inn 1701 W Baseline Rd *TF:* 800-843-7663	Tempe	AZ	85283	480-413-1188	413-1266
Residence Inn 5075 S Priest Dr *TF:* 800-331-3131 ■ *Web:* www.residenceinn.com/residenceinn/PHXRT	Tempe	AZ	85282	480-756-2122	345-2802
Rodeway Inn Phoenix Airport East 1550 S 52nd St *TF:* 800-228-2000	Tempe	AZ	85281	480-967-3000	966-9568
Sheraton San Marcos Golf Resort & Conference Center 1 San Marcos Pl *TF:* 800-528-8071	Chandler	AZ	85224	480-963-6655	963-6777
Sumner Suites 1413 W Rio Salado Pkwy *TF:* 800-743-8483	Tempe	AZ	85281	480-804-9544	804-9548
Tempe Mission Palms Hotel 60 E 5th St *TF:* 800-547-8705 ■ *Web:* www.missionpalms.com	Tempe	AZ	85281	480-894-1400	968-7677
Tempe Super 8 Motel 1020 E Apache Blvd *TF:* 800-800-8000	Tempe	AZ	85281	480-967-8891	968-7868
Tempe/University Travelodge 1005 E Apache Blvd *TF:* 800-578-7878	Tempe	AZ	85281	480-968-7871	968-3991
Twin Palms Hotel 225 E Apache Blvd *TF:* 800-367-0835	Tempe	AZ	85281	480-967-9431	968-1877
Western Lodge Motel 2174 E Apache Blvd	Tempe	AZ	85281	480-894-6759	894-6759

— Restaurants —

	City	State	Zip	Phone
Adriatic Italian Cuisine (Italian) 1402 S Priest Dr	Tempe	AZ	85281	480-303-0773
Alcatraz Brewing Co (American) 5000 S Arizona Mills Cir	Tempe	AZ	85282	480-491-0000
Arizona Roadhouse & Brewery (American) 1120 E Apache Blvd	Tempe	AZ	85281	480-929-9940
Balboa Cafe (American) 404 S Mill Ave	Tempe	AZ	85281	480-966-1300
Broadway Grill (American) 1600 S 52nd St	Tempe	AZ	85281	480-967-6600
Byblos Restaurant (Mediterranean) 3332 S Mill Ave *Web:* www.amdest.com/az/tempe/br/byblos.html	Tempe	AZ	85282	480-894-1945
Cafe Istanbul (Middle Eastern) 903 S Rural Rd	Tempe	AZ	85281	480-731-9499
Casey Moore's Oyster House (Seafood) 850 S Ash Ave	Tempe	AZ	85281	480-968-9935
Char's Thai Restaurant (Thai) 127 E University Dr	Tempe	AZ	85281	480-967-6013
Crocodile Cafe (California) 525 S Mill Ave	Tempe	AZ	85281	480-966-5883
Dale Anderson's The Other Place (American) 2100 S Priest Dr	Tempe	AZ	85282	480-967-8721
Delhi Palace (Indian) 933 E University Dr	Tempe	AZ	85281	480-921-2200
Duck's Restaurant (American) 915 E Apache Blvd	Tempe	AZ	85281	480-968-3451
El Chilito (Mexican) 914 E Baseline Rd	Tempe	AZ	85283	480-839-5899
Firehouse Restaurant (Steak/Seafood) 1639 E Apache Blvd	Tempe	AZ	85281	480-966-4531
Haji Baba (Middle Eastern) 1513 E Apache Blvd	Tempe	AZ	85281	480-894-1905
Harvey's Lakeside Cafe (Seafood) 5350 S Lakeshore Dr	Tempe	AZ	85283	480-756-0508
House of Tricks (American) 114 E 7th St	Tempe	AZ	85281	480-968-1114
Hunter Steakhouse (Steak) 4455 S Rural Rd	Tempe	AZ	85282	480-838-8388
John Henry's Fine Dining (Italian) 909 E Elliot Rd	Tempe	AZ	85283	480-730-9009
Korean Garden (Korean) 1324 S Rural Rd	Tempe	AZ	85281	480-967-1133
Kyoto Bowl (Japanese) 3101 S Mill Ave	Tempe	AZ	85282	480-731-9888
Longhitano's Restaurant (Italian) 1835 E Elliot Rd	Tempe	AZ	85234	480-820-2786
Los Sombreros Mexican Restaurant (Mexican) 1849 N Scottsdale Rd	Tempe	AZ	85281	480-994-1799
Macayo's Depot Cantina (Mexican) 300 S Ash Ave	Tempe	AZ	85281	480-966-6677
Manuel's (Mexican) 1123 W Broadway Blvd	Tempe	AZ	85282	480-968-4437
Mill Landing (Steak/Seafood) 398 S Mill Ave *Web:* www.amdest.com/az/tempe/milllanding.html	Tempe	AZ	85281	480-966-1700
Mill Steak House (Steak) 3300 S Price Rd	Tempe	AZ	85282	480-756-2480
Mission Grill The (American) 60 E 5th St	Tempe	AZ	85281	480-894-1400
Montego Jamaican Cafe (Caribbean) 5004 S Price Rd	Tempe	AZ	85282	480-413-0267
Monti's La Casa Vieja (Steak) 1 W Rio Salado Pkwy *Web:* www.montis.com ■ *E-mail:* montis@primenet.com	Tempe	AZ	85281	480-967-7594
Palapa Taqueria (Mexican) 640 S Mill Ave Suite 105	Tempe	AZ	85281	480-921-8011
Rainforest Cafe (American) 5000 S Arizona Mills Cir Suite 573 *Web:* www.rainforestcafe.com	Tempe	AZ	85283	480-752-9100
Riazzi's Italian Garden (Italian) 2700 S Mill Ave	Tempe	AZ	85282	480-731-9464
Rusty Pelican (Steak/Seafood) 1606 W Baseline Rd	Tempe	AZ	85283	480-345-0972
Siamese Cat (Thai) 5034 S Price Rd	Tempe	AZ	85282	480-820-0406
Some Burros Mexican Food (Mexican) 101 E Baseline Rd	Tempe	AZ	85283	480-839-8226
Spaghetti Bowl (Italian) 1867 E Baseline Rd	Tempe	AZ	85283	480-831-7361
Top of the Rock (American) 2000 Westcourt Way	Tempe	AZ	85282	602-225-9000

Tempe (Cont'd)

— Goods and Services —

SHOPPING

				Phone	Fax
Arizona Mills 5000 Arizona Mills Cir	Tempe	AZ	85282	480-491-7300	491-7400
Web: www.arizonamillsmall.com					
Centerpoint Mill Ave & University Dr	Tempe	AZ	85281	602-244-0500	244-0569
Downtown Tempe 398 S Mill Ave Suite 210	Tempe	AZ	85281	480-921-2300	
Mervyn's 800 E Southern Rd	Tempe	AZ	85282	480-894-9281	894-9281

BANKS

				Phone	Fax
Arizona Bank 7605 S McClintock Dr	Tempe	AZ	85284	480-783-6835	783-6839
Heritage Bank 1333 W Broadway Rd	Tempe	AZ	85282	480-894-2900	921-8166
M & I Thunderbird Bank 2077 S Priest Dr	Tempe	AZ	85282	602-336-3895	921-2539*
**Fax Area Code:* 480					
National Bank of Arizona 1400 E Southern Ave	Tempe	AZ	85282	480-345-8800	730-0425
Wells Fargo Bank 526 S Mill Ave	Tempe	AZ	85281	480-350-2513	966-8098

BUSINESS SERVICES

	Phone
Adecco Employment Personnel Services	480-831-1131
DHL Worldwide Express	800-225-5345
Federal Express	800-238-5355
Initial Staffing Services	480-966-9169
Kinko's	480-894-1797
Mail Boxes Etc	480-967-1414
Post Office	800-275-8777
Stivers Temporary Personnel	480-966-1100
UPS	800-742-5877

— Media —

TELEVISION

				Phone	Fax
KAET-TV Ch 8 (PBS) PO Box 871405	Tempe	AZ	85287	480-965-3506	965-1000
Web: www.kaet.asu.edu ■ *E-mail:* kaet@asu.edu					
KNXV-TV Ch 15 (ABC) 515 N 44th St	Phoenix	AZ	85008	602-273-1500	685-3000
Web: www.knxv.com ■ *E-mail:* news15@primenet.com					
KPHO-TV Ch 5 (CBS) 4016 N Black Canyon Hwy	Phoenix	AZ	85017	602-264-1000	650-0761
Web: www.kpho.com					
KPNX-TV Ch 12 (NBC) 1101 N Central Ave	Phoenix	AZ	85004	602-257-1212	257-6619
KSAZ-TV Ch 10 (Fox) 511 W Adams St	Phoenix	AZ	85003	602-257-1234	262-0177
KTVK-TV Ch 3 (Ind) 5555 N 7th Ave	Phoenix	AZ	85013	602-207-3333	207-3477
E-mail: feedback@azfamily.com					
KUTP-TV Ch 45 (UPN) 4630 S 33rd St	Phoenix	AZ	85040	602-268-4500	276-4082
Web: www.kutp.com					

RADIO

				Phone	Fax
KHEP-AM 1280 kHz (Rel) 100 W Clarendon Ave Suite 720	Phoenix	AZ	85013	602-234-1280	234-1586
KKLT-FM 98.7 MHz (AC) 5300 N Central Ave	Phoenix	AZ	85012	602-274-6200	266-3858
KMXP-FM 96.9 MHz (AC) 645 E Missouri Ave Suite 360	Phoenix	AZ	85012	602-279-5577	230-2781
KNIX-FM 102.5 MHz (Ctry) 600 E Gilbert Dr	Tempe	AZ	85281	480-966-6236	921-6365
KOOL-FM 94.5 MHz (Oldies) 4745 N 7th St Suite 210	Phoenix	AZ	85014	602-956-9696	285-1450
Web: www.koolradio.com					
KTAR-AM 620 kHz (N/T) 5300 N Central Ave	Phoenix	AZ	85013	602-274-6200	266-3858
KUPD-FM 97.9 MHz (Rock) 1900 W Carmen St	Tempe	AZ	85283	480-838-0400	820-8469
Web: www.98kupd.com ■ *E-mail:* kupd@netzone.com					
KYOT-FM 95.5 MHz (Nost) 840 N Central Ave	Phoenix	AZ	85004	602-258-8181	440-6530
Web: www.kyot.com					

— Colleges/Universities —

				Phone	Fax
Arizona State University	Tempe	AZ	85287	480-965-9011	965-3610
Web: www.asu.edu ■ *E-mail:* ugradadm@asuvm.inre.asu.edu					
International Baptist College 2150 E Southern Ave	Tempe	AZ	85282	480-838-7070	838-5432
TF: 800-422-4858					
Lamson Junior College 1126 N Scottsdale Rd	Tempe	AZ	85281	480-898-7000	967-6645
TF: 800-898-7017					
Ottawa University 4545 S Wendler Dr Suite 105	Tempe	AZ	85282	602-438-4468	438-4571
TF: 800-235-9586 ■ *Web:* www.ottawa.edu					
Rio Salado Community College 2323 W 14th St	Tempe	AZ	85281	480-517-8000	517-8199
Web: www.rio.maricopa.edu					

— Hospitals —

				Phone	Fax
Chandler Regional Hospital 475 S Dobson Rd	Chandler	AZ	85224	480-963-4561	899-5548
Web: elmo.netnation.com/~evrhs/crh/crhhome.htm					
Charter Desert Vista Hospital 570 W Brown Rd	Mesa	AZ	85201	480-962-3900	827-0412
Mesa General Hospital Medical Center 515 N Mesa Dr	Mesa	AZ	85201	480-969-9111	969-0095
Scottsdale Healthcare Osborn 7400 E Osborn Rd	Scottsdale	AZ	85251	480-675-4000	675-4072*
**Fax:* Admitting					
Tempe Saint Luke's Hospital 1500 S Mill Ave	Tempe	AZ	85281	480-968-9411	784-5630

— Attractions —

				Phone	Fax
Arizona Historical Society Museum 1300 N College Ave	Tempe	AZ	85281	480-929-0292	967-5450
Web: www.tempe.gov/ahs ■ *E-mail:* ahs@ahs.lib.az.us					
Arizona State University Art Museum 10th St & Mill Ave Nelson Fine Arts Ctr Arizona State University	Tempe	AZ	85287	480-965-2787	965-5254
Web: asuam.fa.asu.edu					
Arizona State University Gallery of Design Architecture & Environmental Design South Bldg PO Box 871905	Tempe	AZ	85287	480-965-8169	965-1594
Arizona State University Life Sciences Center University Dr Life Sciences Bldg C	Tempe	AZ	85287	480-965-3571	965-2519
Arizona State University Meteorite Collection Center for Meteorite Studies Physical Science Bldg Suite C151 MS 872504	Tempe	AZ	85287	480-965-3576	
Arizona State University Museum of Anthropology Anthropology Bldg	Tempe	AZ	85287	480-965-6213	965-7671
Arizona State University Museum of Geology Dept of Geology Physical Sciences Bldg F	Tempe	AZ	85287	480-965-5081	965-8102
Arizona State University Planetarium	Tempe	AZ	85287	480-965-6891	965-7331
Big Surf 1500 N McClintock Rd	Tempe	AZ	85281	480-947-2477	423-9737
Casa Grande Ruins National Monument 1100 Ruins Dr	Coolidge	AZ	85228	520-723-3172	723-7209
Web: www.nps.gov/cagr/					
Centerpoint Mill Ave & University Dr	Tempe	AZ	85281	602-244-0500	244-0569
Childsplay 132 E 6th St Suite 106	Tempe	AZ	85281	480-350-8101	350-8584
Web: www.tempe.gov/childsplay ■ *E-mail:* childsplayaz@juno.com					
Computing Commons Gallery Palm Walk & Orange Mall Computing Commons Rm 140	Tempe	AZ	85287	480-965-3609	965-8698
Fiddlesticks-Family Fun Park 1155 W Elliott Rd	Tempe	AZ	85284	480-961-0800	
Gammage Auditorium Mill Rd & Apache Blvd Arizona State University	Tempe	AZ	85287	480-965-4050	965-2243
Grady Gammage Memorial Auditorium Mill Ave & Apache Blvd	Tempe	AZ	85287	480-965-3434	965-3583
Web: www.asugammage.com					
Hackett House 95 W 4th St	Tempe	AZ	85281	480-350-8181	
Mat Corner The 1020 S Mill Ave	Tempe	AZ	85281	480-966-2055	
Northlight Gallery Tyler & Forest Malls Arizona State University	Tempe	AZ	85287	480-965-6517	965-8338
Petersen House Museum 1414 W Southern Ave	Tempe	AZ	85282	480-350-5100	350-5150
Red River Music Hall 730 N Mill Ave	Tempe	AZ	85281	480-829-0607	829-1552
TF: 800-466-6779 ■ *Web:* www.redrivermusichall.com ■ *E-mail:* info@redrivermusichall.com					
Tempe Historical Museum 809 E Southern Ave	Tempe	AZ	85282	480-350-5100	350-5150
Web: www.tempe.gov/museum/archives.htm					
Tempe Little Theatre 132 E 6th St	Tempe	AZ	85281	480-350-8388	350-8584
Tempe Performing Arts Center 132 E 6th St	Tempe	AZ	85281	480-350-8101	350-8584

Tempe (Cont'd)

SPORTS TEAMS & FACILITIES

				Phone	Fax
Anaheim Angels Spring Training (baseball) Alameda Dr & 48th St	Tempe	AZ	85282	480-350-5265	350-5059
Arizona Cardinals 8701 S Hardy Dr *Web:* www.nfl.com/cardinals	Tempe	AZ	85284	602-379-0101	379-1819
Sun Devil Stadium Stadium Dr & 6th St Arizona State University *Web:* www.thesundevils.com	Tempe	AZ	85287	480-965-5062	965-7663

— Events —

	Phone
Arizona Special Olympics Summer Games (early May)	602-230-1200
Fall Festival of the Arts (early December)	480-967-4877
Fiesta Bowl (early January)	480-350-0900
Fiesta Bowl Duck Race (October)	480-350-0900
Fiesta Bowl Parade (early January)	480-350-0900
Fourth of July Celebration (July 4)	480-967-7891
Grand Canyon State Games (late June)	480-517-9700
Mill Avenue Masquerade (October 31)	480-967-4877
New Year's Eve Block Party (December 31)	480-894-8158
Spring Festival of the Arts (late March-early April)	480-967-4877
Spring POW WOW Competition (mid-April)	480-965-5224
Tempe's Fantasy of Lights (late November-early January)	480-894-8158
Tempe's Thanksgiving Soccer Tournament (late November)	480-966-4053

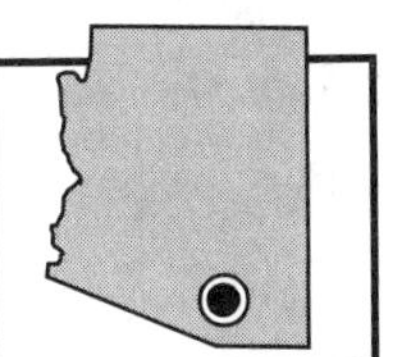

Tucson

The Arizona-Sonora Desert Museum in Tucson features more than 300 species of live animals and some 1,300 species of plants indigenous to the Sonoran Desert. The Sonoran Desert is the only place in the world where saguaro cactus grow, and the largest concentration of this cactus is found at Saguaro National Park just outside Tucson (both east and west of the city). Saguaro-rib ceilings are featured in two rooms of Old Town Artisans, an artisans' marketplace in downtown Tucson. The downtown area is known as the Tucson Arts District due to the city's efforts to use arts as a unifying force for the area. Fine artwork can also be seen at the San Xavier del Bac Mission, located southwest of the city on the Tohono O'odham Indian Reservation; the Mission has been called the "Sistine Chapel of North America." Kitt Peak National Observatory, which houses the world's largest collection of astronomical telescopes, is also located just outside Tucson; and the Santa Catalina Mountains are only a 30-minute drive from the city. Other area attractions include Biosphere 2, a 3.15-acre closed system with seven ecosystems; Coronado National Forest; and the town of Tombstone, featuring the infamous OK Corral and Boot Hill cemetery.

Population	460,466	**Longitude**	110-92-58 W
Area (Land)	156.3 sq mi	**County**	Pima
Area (Water)	0.4 sq mi	**Time Zone**	MST
Elevation	2386 ft	**Area Code/s**	520
Latitude	32-22-17 N		

— Average Temperatures and Precipitation —

TEMPERATURES

	Jan	Feb	Mar	Apr	May	Jun	Jul	Aug	Sep	Oct	Nov	Dec
High	63	68	73	81	90	100	99	97	93	84	73	64
Low	39	41	45	50	58	68	74	72	68	57	46	40

PRECIPITATION

	Jan	Feb	Mar	Apr	May	Jun	Jul	Aug	Sep	Oct	Nov	Dec
Inches	0.9	0.7	0.7	0.3	0.2	0.2	2.4	2.2	1.7	1.1	0.7	1.1

— Important Phone Numbers —

	Phone		Phone
AAA	520-296-7461	**Medical Referral**	520-694-8888
American Express Travel	520-795-8400	**Poison Control Center**	520-626-6016
Dental Referral	602-957-4777	**Road Conditions**	520-573-7623
Emergency	911	**Travelers Aid**	520-622-8900
HotelDocs	800-468-3537	**Weather**	520-881-3333

— Information Sources —

				Phone	Fax
Better Business Bureau Serving the Tucson Area 3620 N 1st Ave Suite 136 *Web:* www.tucson.bbb.org ■ *E-mail:* tucsonaz@gte.net	Tucson	AZ	85719	520-888-5353	888-6262
Metropolitan Tucson Convention & Visitors Bureau 130 S Scott Ave *TF:* 800-638-8350 ■ *Web:* www.arizonaguide.com/visittucson/ ■ *E-mail:* tucson@arizonaguide.com	Tucson	AZ	85701	520-624-1817	884-7804
Pima County 130 W Congress St 10th Fl *Web:* www.co.pima.az.us	Tucson	AZ	85701	520-740-8661	740-8171
Tucson City Hall PO Box 27210 *Web:* www.ci.tucson.az.us/ ■ *E-mail:* web@ci.tucson.az.us	Tucson	AZ	85726	520-791-4204	791-5198
Tucson Convention Center 260 S Church St	Tucson	AZ	85701	520-791-4101	791-5572
Tucson Economic Development Office PO Box 27210	Tucson	AZ	85726	520-791-5093	791-5413
Tucson Mayor PO Box 27210 *Web:* www.ci.tucson.az.us/mcc.html	Tucson	AZ	85726	520-791-4201	791-5348
Tucson Metropolitan Chamber of Commerce 465 W St Mary's Rd *Web:* www.tucsonchamber.org	Tucson	AZ	85701	520-792-2250	882-5704
Tucson Public Library PO Box 27470 *Web:* www.lib.ci.tucson.az.us	Tucson	AZ	85726	520-791-4393	791-3213

On-Line Resources

4Tucson.com	www.4tucson.com
Anthill City Guide Tucson	www.anthill.com/city.asp?city=tucson
Area Guide Tucson	tucson.areaguides.net
Boulevards Tucson	www.boulevards.com/cities/tucson.html
City Knowledge Tucson	www.cityknowledge.com/az_tucson.htm
EMOL Tucson	www.opus1.com/emol/tucson/tucindex.html
Excite.com Tucson City Guide	www.excite.com/travel/countries/united_states/arizona/tucson
Insiders' Guide to Tucson	www.insiders.com/tucson/
InsideTucson.com	www.insidetucson.com
Internet Tucson	www.itucson.com
NITC Travelbase City Guide Tucson	www.travelbase.com/auto/guides/tucson-area-az.html
Rough Guide Travel Tucson	travel.roughguides.com/content/1187/
Tucson CityWomen	www.citywomen.com/tcwomen.htm
Tucson Community Pages	www.tucsonet.com/tucsonet/
Tucson DesertNet	desert.net
Tucson Home Page	tucson.com/tucson
Tucson Online	www.pima.com
Tucson Territory	www.tucsonterritory.com/
Tucson Weekly Observer	bonzo.com/observer/
Tucson's Community Web Project	tucson.com/project
Ultimate Arizona Vacation Guide	www.webcreationsetc.com/Azguide/Tucson/
Virtual Voyages Tucson	www.virtualvoyages.com/usa/az/tucson/tucson.sht

— Transportation Services —

AIRPORTS

■ **Tucson International Airport (TUS)**

	Phone
12 miles S of downtown (approx 15 minutes) Web: www.tucsonairport.org/	520-573-8000

Airport Transportation

	Phone
Suntran $.85 fare to downtown	520-792-9222
Taxi $15-18 fare to downtown	520-624-6611

Tucson (Cont'd)

Commercial Airlines

	Phone		Phone
Aero California	800-237-6225	**Great Lakes**	800-241-6522
America West	800-235-9292	**Northwest**	800-225-2525
American	800-433-7300	**Southwest**	800-435-9792
British Airways	800-247-9297	**TWA**	800-221-2000
Continental	800-525-0280	**United**	800-241-6522
Delta	800-221-1212	**US Airways**	800-428-4322

Charter Airlines

	Phone		Phone
Double Eagle Aviation	520-294-8214	**Ratliff Aviation**	520-746-1411
Jet Arizona	520-295-3500	**Southwest Helicopters Inc**	520-294-4500

CAR RENTALS

	Phone		Phone
Alamo	520-573-4740	**Enterprise**	520-747-9700
Avis	520-294-1494	**Hertz**	520-294-7616
Budget	520-889-8800	**National**	520-573-8050
Dollar	520-573-1100		

LIMO/TAXI

	Phone		Phone
A & A Limousine	520-622-6441	**Foothills Luxury Sedan**	520-750-0365
Caddy Cab	520-887-8744	**Sir Lancelot Limousines**	520-888-3030
Catalina Limousine Service	520-624-5466	**Yellow Cab**	520-624-6611

MASS TRANSIT

	Phone
Old Pueblo Trolley $1 Base fare	520-792-1802
Suntran $.85 Base fare	520-792-9222

RAIL/BUS

				Phone
Amtrak Station 400 E Toole Ave	Tucson	AZ	85701	520-623-4442
Greyhound Bus Station 2 S 4th Ave *TF:* 800-231-2222	Tucson	AZ	85701	520-792-3475

— Accommodations —

HOTEL RESERVATION SERVICES

	Phone	Fax
Advance Reservations Inn Arizona *TF:* 800-456-0682 ■ *Web:* tucson.com/inn ■ *E-mail:* micasa@primenet.com	480-990-0682	990-3390
Southern Arizona Innkeepers Assn	520-299-6787	299-6431

HOTELS, MOTELS, RESORTS

				Phone	Fax
Arizona Inn 2200 E Elm St *TF:* 800-933-1093	Tucson	AZ	85719	520-325-1541	881-5830
Best Western Executive Inn 333 W Drachman St *TF:* 800-528-1234	Tucson	AZ	85705	520-791-7551	623-7803
Best Western Inn Airport 7060 S Tucson Blvd *TF:* 800-772-3847	Tucson	AZ	85706	520-746-0271	889-7391
Best Western Royal Sun Inn & Suites 1015 N Stone Ave *TF:* 800-528-1234	Tucson	AZ	85705	520-622-8871	623-2267
Canyon Ranch Health & Fitness Resort 8600 E Rockcliff Rd *TF:* 800-742-9000 ■ *Web:* www.canyonranch.com	Tucson	AZ	85750	520-749-9000	749-1646
Clarion Hotel Airport 6801 S Tucson Blvd *TF:* 800-526-0550	Tucson	AZ	85706	520-746-3932	889-9934
Clarion Hotel Randolph Park 102 N Alvernon Way *TF:* 800-227-6086	Tucson	AZ	85711	520-795-0330	326-2111
Clarion Santa Rita Hotel & Suites 88 E Broadway Blvd *TF:* 800-252-7466	Tucson	AZ	85701	520-622-4000	620-0376
Country Suites by Carlson 7411 N Oracle Rd *TF:* 800-456-4000	Tucson	AZ	85704	520-575-9255	575-8671
Courtyard by Marriott Airport 2505 E Executive Dr *TF:* 800-321-2211 ■ *Web:* courtyard.com/TUSCA	Tucson	AZ	85706	520-573-0000	573-0470
Courtyard by Marriott Williams Centre 201 S Williams Blvd *TF:* 800-321-2211 ■ *Web:* courtyard.com/TUSCE	Tucson	AZ	85711	520-745-6000	745-2393
Days Inn 222 S Freeway *TF:* 800-329-7466	Tucson	AZ	85745	520-791-7511	622-3481
Doubletree Guest Suites 6555 E Speedway Blvd *TF:* 800-222-8733 ■ *Web:* www.doubletreehotels.com/DoubleT/Hotel121/129/129Main.htm	Tucson	AZ	85710	520-721-7100	721-1991
Doubletree Hotel at Reid Park 445 S Alvernon Way *TF:* 800-222-8733 ■ *Web:* www.doubletreehotels.com/DoubleT/Hotel/03/03Main.htm	Tucson	AZ	85711	520-881-4200	323-5225
Elkhorn Ranch HC 1 Box 97 *Web:* www.guestranches.com/elkhorn	Tucson	AZ	85736	520-822-1040	
Embassy Suites 5335 E Broadway Blvd *TF:* 800-362-2779	Tucson	AZ	85711	520-745-2700	790-9232
Embassy Suites Hotel & Conference Center 7051 S Tucson Blvd *TF:* 800-362-2779	Tucson	AZ	85706	520-573-0700	741-9657
Extended StayAmerica 5050 E Grant Rd *TF:* 800-398-7829	Tucson	AZ	85712	520-795-9510	795-9504
Flying V Ranch 6810 Flying V Ranch Rd	Tucson	AZ	85750	520-299-0702	
Four Points Hotel by Sheraton 350 South Fwy *TF:* 800-325-3535	Tucson	AZ	85745	520-622-6611	622-8143
Hampton Inn Airport 6971 S Tucson Blvd *TF:* 800-426-7866	Tucson	AZ	85706	520-889-5789	889-4002
Hawthorn Suites Hotel 7007 E Tanque Verde Rd *TF:* 800-527-1133	Tucson	AZ	85715	520-298-2300	298-6756
Holiday Inn Broadway 181 W Broadway Blvd *TF:* 800-465-4329	Tucson	AZ	85701	520-624-8711	623-8121
Holiday Inn Express 750 W Starr Pass Blvd *TF:* 800-465-4329	Tucson	AZ	85713	520-624-4455	624-3172
Holiday Inn Tucson Airport 4550 S Palo Verde Rd *TF:* 800-465-4329	Tucson	AZ	85714	520-746-1161	741-1170
Inn Suites Hotel 475 N Granada Ave *TF:* 800-446-6589	Tucson	AZ	85701	520-622-3000	882-0893
InnSuites Tucson Best Western 6201 N Oracle Rd *TF:* 800-842-4242 ■ *Web:* www.innsuites.com/hoteltucson.htm ■ *E-mail:* tucsonoracle@innsuites.com	Tucson	AZ	85704	520-297-8111	297-2935
Lazy K Bar Guest Ranch 8401 N Scenic Dr *TF:* 800-321-7018 ■ *Web:* www.lazykbar.com ■ *E-mail:* lazyk@theriver.com	Tucson	AZ	85743	520-744-3050	744-7628
Loews Ventana Canyon Resort 7000 N Resort Dr *TF:* 800-234-5117 ■ *Web:* www.loewsventanacanyon.com	Tucson	AZ	85750	520-299-2020	299-6832
Omni Tucson National Golf Resort & Spa 2727 W Club Dr *TF:* 800-528-4856 ■ *Web:* www.tucsonnational.com	Tucson	AZ	85742	520-297-2271	742-2452
Plaza Hotel 1900 E Speedway Blvd *TF:* 800-843-8052	Tucson	AZ	85719	520-327-7341	327-0276
Ramada Inn 1601 N Oracle Rd *TF:* 800-777-2999	Tucson	AZ	85705	520-623-6666	884-7422
Residence Inn by Marriott 6477 E Speedway Blvd *TF:* 800-331-3131 ■ *Web:* www.residenceinn.com/TUSAZ	Tucson	AZ	85710	520-721-0991	290-8323
Rodeway Inn 1365 W Grant Rd *TF:* 800-228-2000	Tucson	AZ	85745	520-622-7791	629-0201
Sheraton El Conquistador Resort & Country Club 10000 N Oracle Rd *TF:* 800-325-7832	Tucson	AZ	85737	520-544-5000	544-1228
Sheraton Tucson 5151 E Grant Rd *TF:* 800-257-7275	Tucson	AZ	85712	520-323-6262	325-2989
Smugglers Inn 6350 E Speedway Blvd *TF:* 800-525-8852 ■ *Web:* www.arizonaguide.com/smuggler	Tucson	AZ	85710	520-296-3292	722-3713
Tanque Verde Guest Ranch 14301 E Speedway Blvd *TF:* 800-234-3833 ■ *Web:* www.tvgr.com ■ *E-mail:* dude@tvgr.com	Tucson	AZ	85748	520-296-6275	721-9426
Tucson East Hilton & Towers 7600 E Broadway Blvd	Tucson	AZ	85710	520-721-5600	721-5696
Viscount Suites Hotel 4855 E Broadway Blvd *TF:* 800-527-9666 ■ *Web:* www.viscountsuite.com	Tucson	AZ	85711	520-745-6500	790-5114
Westin La Paloma Hotel Resort 3800 E Sunrise Dr *TF:* 800-228-3000	Tucson	AZ	85718	520-742-6000	577-5878
Westward Look Resort 245 E Ina Rd *TF:* 800-722-2500	Tucson	AZ	85704	520-297-1151	297-9023
White Stallion Ranch 9251 W Twin Peaks Rd *TF:* 888-977-2624 ■ *Web:* www.wsranch.com ■ *E-mail:* wsranch@flash.net	Tucson	AZ	85743	520-297-0252	744-2786

Tucson (Cont'd)

— Restaurants —

				Phone
Anthony's in the Catalinas (Continental) 6440 N Campbell Ave	Tucson	AZ	85718	520-299-1771
Arizona Inn (Continental) 2200 E Elm St	Tucson	AZ	85719	520-325-1541
Breckenridge Brewery & Pub (American) 1980 E River Rd	Tucson	AZ	85718	520-577-0800
Cafe Poca Cosa (Mexican) 88 E Broadway	Tucson	AZ	85701	520-622-6400
Cafe Terra Cotta (Southwest) 4310 N Campbell Ave	Tucson	AZ	85718	520-577-8100
Web: www.cafeterracotta.com ■ *E-mail:* feedback@cafeterracotta.com				
Capriccio (Italian) 4825 N 1st Ave	Tucson	AZ	85718	520-887-2333
Charles (Continental) 6400 E El Dorado Cir	Tucson	AZ	85715	520-296-7173
City Grill (American) 6464 E Tanque Verde Rd	Tucson	AZ	85715	520-733-1111
Cottonwood Cafe (Southwest) 60 N Alvernon Way	Tucson	AZ	85711	520-326-6000
Cuisine of India (Indian) 6751 E Broadway Blvd	Tucson	AZ	85710	520-296-8585
Daniel's Restaurant (Italian) 4340 N Campbell Ave Suite 107	Tucson	AZ	85718	520-742-3200
Delectables Restaurant (American) 533 N 4th Ave	Tucson	AZ	85705	520-884-9289
Dragon View (Chinese) 400 N Bonita Ave	Tucson	AZ	85745	520-792-3811
El Charro (Mexican) 311 N Court Ave	Tucson	AZ	85701	520-622-5465
Web: www.arizonaguide.com/elcharro/				
El Mariachi Restaurant (Mexican) 106 W Drachman	Tucson	AZ	85705	520-791-7793
Frog & Firkin (American) 874 E University Blvd	Tucson	AZ	85719	520-623-7507
Fuego Bar & Grill (Seafood) 6958 E Tanque Verde Rd	Tucson	AZ	85715	520-886-1745
Ghini's Cafe (French) 1803 E Prince Rd	Tucson	AZ	85719	520-326-9095
Gold Room (Southwest) 245 E Ina Rd	Tucson	AZ	85704	520-297-1151
Great Wall of China (Chinese) 2445 S Craycroft Rd	Tucson	AZ	85711	520-747-4049
Jack's Original Barbeque (Barbecue) 5250 E 22nd St	Tucson	AZ	85711	520-750-1280
Janos (Southwest) 3770 E Sunrise Dr	Tucson	AZ	85718	520-615-6100
Web: www.janos.com				
Kingfisher Bar & Grill (Seafood) 2564 E Grant Rd	Tucson	AZ	85716	520-323-7739
La Parrilla Suiza (Mexican) 5602 E Speedway Blvd	Tucson	AZ	85712	520-747-4838
Landmark Cafe (Gourmet) 7117 N Oracle Rd	Tucson	AZ	85704	520-575-9277
Le Bistro (Continental) 2574 N Campbell Ave	Tucson	AZ	85719	520-327-3086
Le Rendez-Vous (French) 3844 Fort Lowell Rd	Tucson	AZ	85716	520-323-7373
Lotus Garden (Chinese) 5975 E Speedway Blvd	Tucson	AZ	85712	520-299-6916
Maine Course (Seafood) 5851 N Oracle Rd	Tucson	AZ	85704	520-887-5518
Mi Nidito Cafe (Mexican) 1813 S 4th Ave	Tucson	AZ	85713	520-622-5081
Mountain View (German) 1220 E Prince Rd	Tucson	AZ	85719	520-293-0375
Olive Tree (Greek) 7000 E Tanque Verde Rd	Tucson	AZ	85715	520-298-1845
Oriental Garden (Japanese/Korean) 15 N Alvernon Way	Tucson	AZ	85711	520-326-4700
Penelope's (French) 3071 N Swan Rd	Tucson	AZ	85712	520-325-5080
Web: www.desert.net/penelopes/				
Pinnacle Peak Steakhouse (Steak) 6541 E Tanque Verde Rd	Tucson	AZ	85715	520-296-0911
Presidio Grill (American) 3352 E Speedway Blvd	Tucson	AZ	85716	520-327-4667
Rancher's Club of Arizona (Steak) 5151 E Grant Rd	Tucson	AZ	85712	520-321-7621
Sachiko Sushi (Japanese) 1101 N Wilmot Rd	Tucson	AZ	85712	520-886-7000
Saguaro Corners (American) 3750 S Old Spanish Trail	Tucson	AZ	85730	520-886-5424
Scordato's (Italian) 4405 W Speedway Blvd	Tucson	AZ	85745	520-792-3055
Seri Melaka (Chinese) 6133 E Broadway Blvd	Tucson	AZ	85711	520-747-7811
Tack Room (Southwest) 2800 N Sabino Canyon Rd	Tucson	AZ	85715	520-722-2800
Web: emol.org/emol/thetackroom/				
Ventana Room (Continental) 7000 N Resort Dr	Tucson	AZ	85750	520-299-2020
Vivace (Italian) 4811 E Grant Rd	Tucson	AZ	85702	520-795-7221

— Goods and Services —

SHOPPING

				Phone	Fax
Antique Mall 3130 E Grant Rd	Tucson	AZ	85716	520-326-3070	
Dillard's 4550 N Oracle Rd	Tucson	AZ	85705	520-293-4550	
El Con Mall 3601 E Broadway Blvd Suite 5B	Tucson	AZ	85716	520-795-9958	323-1856
Foothills Mall 7401 N La Cholla Blvd	Tucson	AZ	85741	520-742-7191	797-0936
Fourth Avenue Historic District 4th Ave	Tucson	AZ	85705	520-624-5004	624-5933
Indoor Swap Meet 3750 E Irvington Rd	Tucson	AZ	85714	520-745-5000	571-9163
Macys Park Mall 5850 E Broadway Blvd	Tucson	AZ	85711	520-322-2100	
Marketplace USA 3750 E Irvington Rd	Tucson	AZ	85714	520-745-5000	571-9163
Old Town Artisans 186 N Meyer Ave	Tucson	AZ	85701	520-623-6024	
Park Mall 5870 E Broadway Blvd	Tucson	AZ	85711	520-747-7575	571-7652
Web: www.park-mall.com					
Plaza Palomino 2970 N Swan Rd	Tucson	AZ	85712	520-795-1177	795-7872
River Center 5605 E River Rd	Tucson	AZ	85715	520-577-7272	
Tucson Mall 4500 N Oracle Rd	Tucson	AZ	85705	520-293-7330	293-0543

BANKS

				Phone	Fax
Arizona Bank 120 N Stone Ave	Tucson	AZ	85701	520-792-2400	620-3244
TF: 800-279-0181					
Bank of America 33 N Stone Ave	Tucson	AZ	85701	520-792-7818	792-7994
TF Cust Svc: 800-944-0404*					
National Bank of Arizona 335 N Wilmot Rd	Tucson	AZ	85711	520-571-1500	513-0134*
**Fax:* Cust Svc					
Wells Fargo Bank 150 N Stone Ave	Tucson	AZ	85701	520-792-5414	792-5312
Wells Fargo Bank 1 S Church Ave	Tucson	AZ	85701	520-620-3413	620-3410

BUSINESS SERVICES

	Phone
A & M Personnel Services	520-323-8778
Arizona Messenger	520-325-1234
Barrett Business Services	520-512-8984
E-Z Messenger Attorney Service	520-623-8436
Federal Express	800-238-5355
Kelly Services	520-748-2681
Kinko's	520-795-7796
Olsten Staffing Services	520-748-9041
Post Office	800-275-8777
Staffing Solutions	520-881-3200
UPS	800-742-5877

— Media —

PUBLICATIONS

				Phone	Fax
Arizona Daily Star‡ PO Box 26807	Tucson	AZ	85726	520-573-4220	573-4107
Web: www.azstarnet.com ■ *E-mail:* wnett@azstarnet.com					
Tucson Citizen‡ PO Box 26767	Tucson	AZ	85726	520-573-4560	573-4569
Web: www.tucsoncitizen.com ■ *E-mail:* citizen@tucsoncitizen.com					
Tucson Lifestyle Magazine 7000 E Tanque Verde Rd Suite 11	Tucson	AZ	85715	520-721-2929	721-8665

‡*Daily newspapers*

TELEVISION

				Phone	Fax
KGUN-TV Ch 9 (ABC) 7280 E Rosewood St	Tucson	AZ	85710	520-722-5486	733-7050
Web: www.kgun9.com					
KHRR-TV Ch 40 (Tele) 2919 E Broadway	Tucson	AZ	85716	520-322-6888	881-7926
KMSB-TV Ch 11 (Fox) 1855 N 6th Ave	Tucson	AZ	85705	520-770-1123	629-7185
KOLD-TV Ch 13 (CBS) 7831 N Business Pk Dr	Tucson	AZ	85743	520-744-1313	744-5235
Web: www.kold-tv.com ■ *E-mail:* admin@kold-tv.com					
KTTU-TV Ch 18 (UPN) 1855 N 6th Ave	Tucson	AZ	85705	520-624-0180	629-7185
KUAT-TV Ch 6 (PBS) University of Arizona PO Box 210067	Tucson	AZ	85721	520-621-5828	621-4122
Web: w3.arizona.edu/~kuat/tv/index.html					
KUVE-TV Ch 52 (Uni) 2301 N Forbes Blvd Suite 108	Tucson	AZ	85745	520-622-0984	620-0046
KVOA-TV Ch 4 (NBC) PO Box 5188	Tucson	AZ	85703	520-792-2270	620-1309
Web: www.kvoa.com					

RADIO

				Phone	Fax
KCEE-AM 790 kHz (Oldies) PO Box 5886	Tucson	AZ	85703	520-623-7556	792-1019
KCUB-AM 1290 kHz (Ctry) 575 W Roger Rd	Tucson	AZ	85705	520-887-1000	887-6397
KFFN-AM 1490 kHz (Sports) 3438 N Country Club Rd	Tucson	AZ	85716	520-795-1490	327-2260
Web: www.theriver.com/thefan ■ *E-mail:* thefan@theriver.com					
KIIM-FM 99.5 MHz (Ctry) 575 W Roger Rd	Tucson	AZ	85705	520-887-1000	887-6397
Web: www.kiimfm.com					
KKLD-FM 94.9 MHz (AC) 3438 N Country Club Rd	Tucson	AZ	85716	520-795-1490	327-2260
Web: www.theriver.com/mixfm ■ *E-mail:* mixfm@theriver.com					
KLPX-FM 96.1 MHz (Rock) 1920 W Copper Dr	Tucson	AZ	85745	520-622-6711	624-3226
KNST-AM 940 kHz (N/T) 4400 E Broadway Blvd Suite 200	Tucson	AZ	85711	520-323-9400	327-9384
KRQQ-FM 93.7 MHz (CHR) 4400 E Broadway Blvd Suite 200	Tucson	AZ	85711	520-323-9400	327-9384
KTKT-AM 990 kHz (N/T) 1920 W Copper Pl	Tucson	AZ	85745	520-622-6711	624-3226
KUAT-AM 1550 kHz (Nost/NPR) PO Box 210067	Tucson	AZ	85721	520-621-7548	621-3360
KUAZ-FM 89.1 MHz (NPR) PO Box 210067	Tucson	AZ	85721	520-621-7548	621-9105
E-mail: kuat@arizona.edu					
KWFM-FM 92.9 MHz (Oldies) 3202 N Oracle Rd	Tucson	AZ	85705	520-623-7556	628-2122
Web: www.theriver.com/cool-fm/ ■ *E-mail:* cool-fm@theriver.com					

— Colleges/Universities —

				Phone	Fax
Chaparral Career College 4585 E Speedway Blvd Suite 204	Tucson	AZ	85712	520-327-6866	325-0108
Web: chap-col.edu					

Tucson — Colleges/Universities (Cont'd)

Phone *Fax*

ITT Technical Institute 1840 E Benson Hwy — Tucson AZ 85714 520-294-2944 889-9528
TF: 800-950-2944 ■ *Web:* www.itt-tech.edu

Pima Community College
4905 E Broadway Blvd — Tucson AZ 85709 520-206-4500 206-4790
Web: www.pima.edu/ ■ *E-mail:* pimaInfo@pimacc.pima.edu

University of Arizona — Tucson AZ 85721 520-621-2211 621-9799
Web: www.arizona.edu ■ *E-mail:* uainfo-team@listserv.arizona.edu

— Hospitals —

Phone *Fax*

Carondelet Saint Joseph's Hospital
350 N Wilmot Rd — Tucson AZ 85711 520-296-3211 721-3921

Carondelet Saint Mary's Hospital
1601 W St Mary's Rd — Tucson AZ 85745 520-622-5833 792-2962

El Dorado Hospital & Medical Center
1400 N Wilmot Rd — Tucson AZ 85712 520-886-6361 885-1507

Kino Community Hospital 2800 E Ajo Way — Tucson AZ 85713 520-294-4471 741-4042
TF: 800-388-5501

Northwest Medical Center
6200 N La Cholla Blvd — Tucson AZ 85741 520-742-9000 469-8101

Southern Arizona Veterans Healthcare System
3601 S 6th Ave. — Tucson AZ 85723 520-792-1450 629-1802*
**Fax:* Hum Res

Tucson Medical Center 5301 E Grant Rd. — Tucson AZ 85712 520-327-5461 324-5277*
**Fax:* Hum Res ■ *TF:* 800-526-5353

University Medical Center
1501 N Campbell Ave — Tucson AZ 85724 520-694-0111 694-4085
Web: www.ahsc.arizona.edu/~umc

— Attractions —

Phone *Fax*

390th Memorial Museum 6000 E Valencia Rd — Tucson AZ 85706 520-574-0287 574-3030

Arizona Historical Society 949 E 2nd St — Tucson AZ 85719 520-628-5774 629-8966
Web: www.tempe.gov/ahs

Arizona Opera Co 3501 N Mountain Ave — Tucson AZ 85719 520-293-4336 293-5097
Web: www.azopera.com

Arizona-Sonora Desert Museum
2021 N Kinney Rd. — Tucson AZ 85743 520-883-1380 883-2500
Web: www.desertmuseum.org

Arizona State Museum
1013 E University Blvd University of Arizona — Tucson AZ 85721 520-621-6302 621-2976
Web: w3fp.arizona.edu/asm

Arizona Theatre Co 40 E 14th St Brady Court — Tucson AZ 85701 520-884-8210 628-9129

Biosphere 2 32540 S Biosphere Rd. — Oracle AZ 85623 520-896-6200 896-6471
Web: www.bio2.edu

Casino of the Sun 7406 S Camino de Oeste — Tucson AZ 85746 520-883-1700 883-0983
TF: 800-344-9435

Center for Creative Photography
1030 N Olive Rd University of Arizona — Tucson AZ 85721 520-621-7968 621-9444
Web: www.ccp.arizona.edu/ccp.html
■ *E-mail:* oncenter@ccp.arizona.edu

Chiricahua National Monument
HCR 2 Box 6500 — Willcox AZ 85643 520-824-3560 824-3421
Web: www.nps.gov/chir/

Civic Orchestra of Tucson PO Box 42764 — Tucson AZ 85733 520-791-9246

Cocoraque Ranch Cattle Drives
6255 N Diamond Hills Ln. — Tucson AZ 85743 520-682-8594

Colossal Cave Mountain Park
16711 E Colossal Cave Rd — Vail AZ 85641 520-647-7275 647-3299
Web: mmm.arizonaguide.com/colossal-cave/

Coronado National Forest
5700 Sabino Canyon Rd — Tucson AZ 85750 520-749-8700

Coronado National Memorial
4101 E Montezuma Canyon Rd. — Hereford AZ 85615 520-366-5515 366-5707
Web: www.nps.gov/coro/

DeGrazia Art Museum 6300 N Swan Rd — Tucson AZ 85718 520-299-9191 299-1381
TF: 800-545-2185

Desert Diamond Casino
7350 S Old Nogales Hwy — Tucson AZ 85706 520-294-7777 295-2771

Flandrau Science Center & Planetarium
University of Arizona — Tucson AZ 85721 520-621-4515 621-8451
Web: www.flandrau.org

Fort Bowie National Historic Site PO Box 158 — Bowie AZ 85605 520-847-2500 847-2221
Web: www.nps.gov/fobo/

Phone *Fax*

Fort Huachuca Museum
Fort Huachuca Army Post — Sierra Vista AZ 85636 520-533-5736

Fort Lowell Museum 2900 N Craycroft Rd — Tucson AZ 85712 520-885-3832

Fourth Avenue Historic District 4th Ave. — Tucson AZ 85705 520-624-5004 624-5933

Franklin Museum 3420 N Vine St — Tucson AZ 85719 520-326-8038

International Wildlife Museum
4800 W Gates Pass Rd — Tucson AZ 85745 520-629-0100 622-1205
Web: www.arizonaguide.com/iwm/

Invisible Theatre 1400 N 1st Ave — Tucson AZ 85719 520-882-9721 884-5410

Kennedy John F Regional Park
3700 S Mission Rd — Tucson AZ 85706 520-791-4873

Kitt Peak National Observatory
950 N Cherry Ave — Tucson AZ 85719 520-318-8600 318-8724
Web: www.noao.edu/kpno/kpno.html ■ *E-mail:* kpno@noao.edu

OK Corral 308 Allen St. — Tombstone AZ 85638 520-457-3456
Web: www.ok-corral.com ■ *E-mail:* okcorral@ok-corral.com

Old Pueblo Archaeology Center
1000 E Fort Lowell Rd — Tucson AZ 85717 520-798-1201 798-1966

Old Town Artisans 186 N Meyer Ave — Tucson AZ 85701 520-623-6024

Old Tucson Studios 201 S Kinney Rd — Tucson AZ 85735 520-883-0100 578-1269*
**Fax:* Mail Rm
■ *Web:* www.emol.org/emol/tucson/oldtucson/otindex.html

Organ Pipe Cactus National Monument
Route 1 Box 100 — Ajo AZ 85321 520-387-6849 387-7144
Web: www.nps.gov/orpi/

Pima Air & Space Museum
6000 E Valencia Rd — Tucson AZ 85706 520-574-0462 574-9238
Web: www.pimaair.org/ ■ *E-mail:* pimaair@azstarnet.com

Red Rock State Park
4050 Lower Red Rock Loop Rd — Sedona AZ 86336 520-282-6907 282-5972
Web: www.pr.state.az.us/parkhtml/redrock.html

Reid Gene C Regional Park
900 S Randolph Way City of Tucson Parks & Recreation Dept. — Tucson AZ 85716 520-791-4873

Reid Park Zoo 1100 S Randolph Way — Tucson AZ 85716 520-791-3204 791-5378
Web: tucson.com/outback/public/reidpark

Rialto The 318 E Congress St — Tucson AZ 85701 520-740-0126

RW Webb Winery/Dark Mountain Brewery
13605 E Benson Hwy — Vail AZ 85641 520-762-5777 762-5898

Sabino Canyon 5900 N Sabino Canyon Rd. — Tucson AZ 85750 520-749-2327 749-9679
Web: mmm.arizonaguide.com/sabino.canyon.tours/

Saguaro National Park
3693 S Old Spanish Trail — Tucson AZ 85730 520-733-5100 733-5183
Web: www.nps.gov/sagu/

San Xavier Del Bac Mission
1950 W San Xavier Rd — Tucson AZ 85746 520-294-2624

Scottish Rite Cathedral 160 S Scott Ave — Tucson AZ 85701 520-622-8364 622-8660

Sosa-Carrillo-Fremont House Museum
151 S Granada Ave — Tucson AZ 85701 520-622-0956 628-5695

Temple of Music & Art 330 S Scott Ave — Tucson AZ 85701 520-884-8210 628-9129

Tohono Chul Park 7366 N Paseo del Norte — Tucson AZ 85704 520-575-8468 797-1213
Web: mmm.arizonaguide.com/tohonochul/

Triple C Chuckwagon Suppers
8900 W Bopp Rd — Tucson AZ 85735 520-883-2333
TF: 800-446-1798

Tucson Arts District downtown — Tucson AZ 85702 520-624-9977 624-4994
Web: tucson.com/TAD/TADHome.HTML
■ *E-mail:* artdist@azstarnet.com

Tucson Botanical Gardens
2150 N Alvernon Way — Tucson AZ 85712 520-326-9255 324-0166

Tucson Children's Museum 200 S 6th Ave — Tucson AZ 85701 520-884-7511 792-0639
Web: www.azstarnet.com/~tuchimu/

Tucson Mountain Park Ajo Way & Kinney Rd. — Tucson AZ 85713 520-740-2690

Tucson Museum of Art & Historic Block
140 N Main Ave — Tucson AZ 85701 520-624-2333 624-7202
Web: www.azstarnet.com/~tmaedu/

Tucson Symphony Orchestra 2175 N 6th Ave. — Tucson AZ 85705 520-882-8585
Web: www.tucsym.org ■ *E-mail:* info@tucsym.org

Tumacacori National Monument
PO Box 67 — Tumacacori AZ 85640 520-398-2341 398-9271
Web: www.nps.gov/tuma/

UApresents 1020 E University Blvd — Tucson AZ 85721 520-621-3341
Web: uapresents.arizona.edu ■ *E-mail:* presents@u.arizona.edu

University of Arizona Museum of Art
Park Ave & Speedway Blvd University of Arizona — Tucson AZ 85721 520-621-7567 621-8770
Web: artmuseum.arizona.edu/art.html

Yozeum The 2900 N Country Club — Tucson AZ 85716 520-322-0100 325-1614
Web: www.playmaxx.com

SPORTS TEAMS & FACILITIES

Phone

Arizona Diamondbacks Spring Training (baseball) 3400 E Camino Campestre Hi Corbett Field — Tucson AZ 85716 520-434-1000

Arizona Stadium 1401 E University of Arizona — Tucson AZ 85721 520-621-2211

Tucson — Sports Teams & Facilities (Cont'd)

				Phone	Fax
Chicago White Sox Spring Training (baseball) 2500 E Ajo Way	Tucson	AZ	85713	520-434-1111	
Colorado Rockies Spring Training (baseball) 3400 E Camino Campestre Hi Corbett Field	Tucson	AZ	85716	520-327-9467	327-5910
TF: 800-388-7625					
Hi Corbett Field 3400 E Camino Campestre	Tucson	AZ	85716	520-327-9700	327-2370
Tucson Greyhound Park 2601 S 3rd Ave	Tucson	AZ	85713	520-884-7576	624-9389
Web: www.tucdogtrak.com					
Tucson Raceway Park 12500 S Houghton Rd	Tucson	AZ	85747	520-762-9200	
Tucson Sidewinders (baseball) 205 E Ajo Way Tucson Electrical Pk	Tucson	AZ	85713	520-434-1021	889-9477
Web: www.tucsonsidewinders.com					

— Events —

	Phone
4th Avenue Street Fair (late March & early December)	520-624-5004
Balloon Glo (early December)	520-621-9034
Big Boys Toy Show (early April)	520-762-3247
Cinco de Mayo (early May)	520-791-4873
Desert Thunder Pro Rodeo (mid-October)	520-721-1621
El Tour de Tucson (late November)	520-745-2033
Fall Festival (mid-October)	520-394-0060
Fiesta de Guadalupe (December)	520-624-1817
Fiesta de los Chiles (late October)	520-326-9255
Holiday Craft Market (late November)	520-624-2333
Independence Day (July 4)	520-791-4860
Indian America (early January)	520-622-4900
Insight.com Bowl (late December)	520-624-1817
International Mariachi Conference (late April)	520-884-9920
Juneteenth Festival (mid-June)	520-791-4355
La Fiesta de los Vaqueros Rodeo (late February)	520-624-1817
Luminaria Nights (early December)	520-326-9255
Music Under the Stars (early May-mid-June)	520-791-4873
Nortel Open (mid-February)	800-882-7660
Pima County Fair (mid-April)	520-762-9100
Shakespeare in the Park (late June)	520-791-4079
Spring Fling (early April)	520-621-5610
Square & Round Dance & Clogging Festival (mid-January)	520-885-5032
Summerset Suite (June-July)	520-743-3399
Tucson Gem & Mineral Show (mid-February)	520-322-5773
Tucson Heritage Experience Festival (early October)	520-621-3701
Tucson Marathon (early December)	520-320-0667
Tucson Rodeo (late February)	520-741-2233
Vigilante Days (early August)	800-457-3423
Western Music Festival (early November)	520-743-9794
Wildflower Festival (early April)	520-742-6455
Wyatt Earp Days (late May)	800-457-3423

Arkansas

Population (1999): 2,551,373 **Area (sq mi): 53,182**

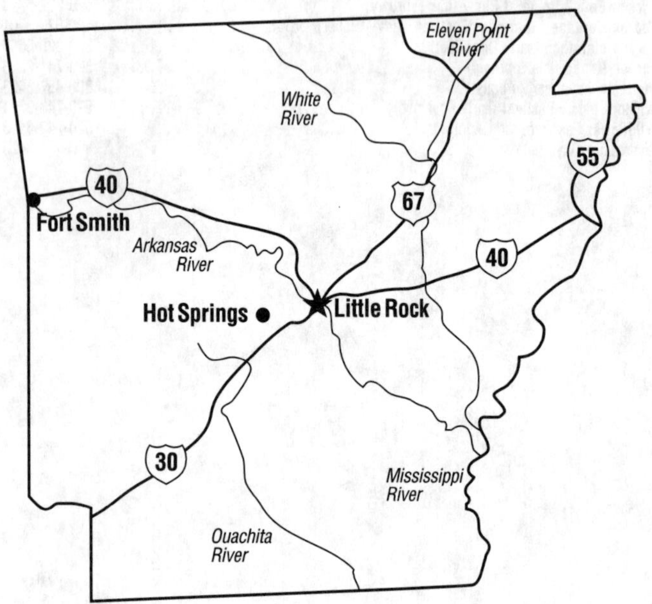

— State Information Sources —

				Phone	Fax
Arkansas Economic Development Commission 1 Capitol Mall Suite 4C-300	Little Rock	AR	72201	501-682-1121	682-7341
TF: 800-275-2672 ■ *Web:* www.aedc.state.ar.us					
Arkansas Parks & Tourism Dept 1 Capitol Mall	Little Rock	AR	72201	501-682-7777	682-1364
TF: 800-628-8725 ■ *Web:* www.arkansas.com/					
Arkansas State Chamber of Commerce PO Box 3645	Little Rock	AR	72203	501-374-9225	372-2722
Web: www.aiea.ualr.edu/dina/statcham					
Arkansas State Government Information				501-682-3000	
Web: www.state.ar.us					
Arkansas State Library 1 Capitol Mall 5th Fl	Little Rock	AR	72201	501-682-1527	682-1529
Web: www.asl.lib.ar.us ■ *E-mail:* dfitts@asl.lib.ar.us					

ON-LINE RESOURCES

Arkansas Cities . . . . dir.yahoo.com/Regional/U_S__States/Arkansas/Cities
Arkansas Counties & Regions . . . . dir.yahoo.com/Regional/U_S__States/Arkansas/Counties_and_Regions
Arkansas Direct . . . . www.arkdirect.com
Arkansas Scenario . . . . scenariousa.dstylus.com/ar/indexf.htm
Arkansas Travel & Tourism Guide . . . www.travel-library.com/north_america/usa/arkansas/index.html
Arkansas USA . . . . arkansasusa.com
Heart of Arkansas . . . . www.heartofarkansas.com
InArkansas.com . . . . www.inarkansas.com
Ozark Connections . . . . www.yournet.com
Ozark Mountains . . . . www.ozarkmtns.com
Rough Guide Travel Arkansas travel.roughguides.com/content/805/index.htm
Travel.org-Arkansas . . . . travel.org/arkansas.html
Yahoo! Get Local Arkansas . . . . dir.yahoo.com/Regional/U_S__States/Arkansas

— Cities Profiled —

Page

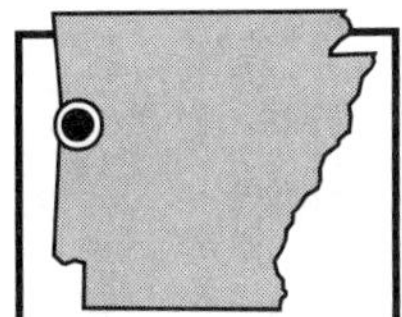

Fort Smith

Fort Smith was one of the first U.S. military posts in the Louisiana Territory, serving as a base of operations for enforcing federal Indian policy from 1817 to 1896. The Fort Smith National Historic Site includes the remains of the two frontier military forts that were the first and second "Fort Smith." Located at the Site also is the restored courtroom of "hanging" Judge Isaac Parker, as well as the "Hell on the Border" jail and a reconstruction of a gallows capable of hanging a dozen men at a time. Among the historic homes open to the public in Fort Smith are the boyhood home of General William O. Darby, founder of "Darby's Rangers;" and "Miss Laura's," a restored Victorian house that is the only former bordello listed on the National Register of Historic Places.

Population	75,637	**Longitude**	94-41-34 W
Area (Land)	46.7 sq mi	**County**	Sebastian
Area (Water)	2.6 sq mi	**Time Zone**	CST
Elevation	450 ft	**Area Code/s**	501
Latitude	35-36-69 N		

— Average Temperatures and Precipitation —

TEMPERATURES

	Jan	Feb	Mar	Apr	May	Jun	Jul	Aug	Sep	Oct	Nov	Dec
High	48	54	64	74	81	88	93	92	85	76	63	51
Low	26	30	39	49	58	66	70	69	62	49	38	29

PRECIPITATION

	Jan	Feb	Mar	Apr	May	Jun	Jul	Aug	Sep	Oct	Nov	Dec
Inches	1.9	2.6	4.0	4.0	5.2	3.4	3.0	2.9	3.2	3.7	4.0	3.0

— Important Phone Numbers —

	Phone		Phone
AAA	501-782-0315	**Time/Temp**	501-785-4441
Emergency	911	**Weather**	501-785-9000
Poison Control Center	501-441-5016		

— Information Sources —

				Phone	Fax
Better Business Bureau Serving Arkansas 1415 S University Ave	Little Rock	AR	72204	501-664-7274	664-0024
Web: www.arkansas.bbb.org					
Fort Smith Chamber of Commerce PO Box 1668	Fort Smith	AR	72902	501-783-6118	783-6110
Web: www.fschamber.com					
Fort Smith City Hall PO Box 1908	Fort Smith	AR	72902	501-784-2208	784-2430
Fort Smith Civic Center 55 S 7th St	Fort Smith	AR	72901	501-785-2495	784-2366
Fort Smith Community Development Office PO Box 1908	Fort Smith	AR	72902	501-784-2209	784-2462
Fort Smith Convention & Visitors Bureau 2 N 'B' St.	Fort Smith	AR	72901	501-783-8888	784-2421
TF: 800-637-1477 ■ *Web:* www.fortsmith.org ■ *E-mail:* tourism@fortsmith.org					
Fort Smith Mayor PO Box 1908	Fort Smith	AR	72902	501-784-2437	784-2494
Fort Smith Public Library 61 S 8th St.	Fort Smith	AR	72901	501-783-0229	782-8571
Web: www.fspl.lib.ar.us/					
Sebastian County 35 S 6th St	Fort Smith	AR	72901	501-783-6139	784-1550

On-Line Resources

Anthill City Guide Fort Smith	www.anthill.com/city.asp?city=fortsmith
Area Guide Fort Smith	fortsmith.areaguides.net
City Knowledge Fort Smith	www.cityknowledge.com/ar_fort_smith.htm
Excite.com Fort Smith City Guide	www.excite.com/travel/countries/united_states/arkansas/fort_smith
Fortsmith.net	www.fortsmith.net

— Transportation Services —

AIRPORTS

	Phone
■ **Fort Smith Municipal Airport (FSM)**	
5 miles SE of downtown (approx 15 minutes)	501-646-1693
Web: www.fortsmithairport.com	

Airport Transportation

	Phone
Razorback Cab $5 fare to downtown	501-783-1118

Commercial Airlines

	Phone		Phone
American	800-433-7300	**Northwest**	800-225-2525
American Eagle	800-433-7300	**United**	800-241-6522
Atlantic Southeast	800-282-3424		

Charter Airlines

	Phone		Phone
Alliance Executive Charter Services	800-232-5387	**TAC Air**	501-646-1611

CAR RENTALS

	Phone		Phone
Avis	501-646-5588	**Hertz**	501-646-7823
Budget	501-648-9101	**National**	501-646-3471
Enterprise	501-648-1117		

LIMO/TAXI

	Phone		Phone
Limousine Services	501-782-5699	**Razorback Cab**	501-783 1118

RAIL/BUS

				Phone
Greyhound Bus Station 116 N 6th St	Fort Smith	AR	72901	501-783-1181
TF: 800-231-2222				

— Accommodations —

HOTELS, MOTELS, RESORTS

				Phone	Fax
Aspen Hotel & Suites 2900 S 68th St.	Fort Smith	AR	72903	501-452-9000	484-0551
TF: 800-627-9417					
Baymont Inns & Suites 2123 Burnham Rd.	Fort Smith	AR	72903	501-484-5770	484-0579
TF: 800-301-0200					
Beland Manor Inn 1320 S Albert Pike	Fort Smith	AR	72903	501-782-3300	782-7674
TF: 800-334-5052 ■ *E-mail:* belandbnb@ipa.net					
Best Western 101 N 11th St.	Fort Smith	AR	72901	501-785-4121	785-0316
TF: 888-765-9467					
Comfort Inn 2120 Burnham Rd	Fort Smith	AR	72903	501-484-0227	484-5885
TF: 800-228-5150					
Days Inn 1021 Garrison Ave.	Fort Smith	AR	72901	501-783-0548	783-0836
TF: 800-329-7466					
Fifth Season Inn 2219 S Waldron Rd	Fort Smith	AR	72903	501-452-4880	452-8653
TF: 800-643-4567					
Hampton Inn 6201-D Rogers Ave	Fort Smith	AR	72903	501-452-2000	452-6668
TF: 800-426-7866					
Holiday Inn City Center 700 Rogers Ave	Fort Smith	AR	72901	501-783-1000	783-0312
TF: 800-453-1895					
Inn Towne Lodge 301 N 11th St.	Fort Smith	AR	72901	501-783-0271	783-0271
TF: 800-440-7829					
Kings Row Inn 5801 Rogers Ave.	Fort Smith	AR	72903	501-452-4200	452-0201
TF: 800-531-5464					
Motel 6 6001 Rogers Ave	Fort Smith	AR	72903	501-484-0576	484-9054
TF: 800-466-8356					
Points Inn 5711 Rogers Ave.	Fort Smith	AR	72903	501-452-4110	452-4891
TF: 800-356-7046					
Quality Inn 2301 Towson Ave.	Fort Smith	AR	72901	501-785-1401	785-2810
TF: 800-228-5151					
Ramada Inn Airport 5103 Towson Ave	Fort Smith	AR	72901	501-646-2931	648-9085
TF: 800-272-6232					
Regency Inn Ltd 1215 S 'W' St	Fort Smith	AR	72901	501-785-4025	
Super 8 Motel 3810 Towson Ave	Fort Smith	AR	72901	501-646-3411	
TF: 800-800-8000					
Thomas Quinn Guest House 815 N 'B' St	Fort Smith	AR	72901	501-782-0499	
Westark Inn 5515 Towson Ave.	Fort Smith	AR	72901	501-646-3491	646-3491

Fort Smith (Cont'd)

— Restaurants —

				Phone
Bangkok Restaurant (Thai) 1517 N 11th St	Fort Smith	AR	72901	501-785-3937
Bella Italia (Italian) 407 N 8th St	Fort Smith	AR	72901	501-785-1550
Calico County (Southern) 2401 S 56th St	Fort Smith	AR	72903	501-452-3299
California Grill (American) 8909 Rogers Ave.	Fort Smith	AR	72903	501-452-5956
Dixie Cafe (Southern) 5428 Ellsworth Rd	Fort Smith	AR	72903	501-452-9300
Emmy's (German) 602 N 16th St	Fort Smith	AR	72901	501-783-0012
Folie A'Deux (International) 2909 Old Greenwood Rd	Fort Smith	AR	72903	501-648-0041
Hong Kong Restaurant (Chinese) 500 N Greenwood Ave	Fort Smith	AR	72901	501-783-7824
Jerry Neel's Bar-B-Que (Barbecue) 1823 Phoenix	Fort Smith	AR	72901	501-646-8085
Juan's (Mexican) 3121 Towson Ave	Fort Smith	AR	72901	501-782-6287
Juanita Bollin's Dining Emporium (American) 407 Garrison Ave	Fort Smith	AR	72901	501-783-1888
Light House Inn (Seafood) 6201 Midland Blvd	Fort Smith	AR	72904	501-783-9420
Ming Garden Chinese Restaurant (Chinese) 3802 Towson Ave	Fort Smith	AR	72901	501-646-3617
Puebla Restaurant (Mexican) 4020 1/2 Midland Blvd	Fort Smith	AR	72904	501-783-3755
Red Barn Steak House (Steak) 3716 Newlon Rd	Fort Smith	AR	72904	501-783-4075
Taliano's Restaurant (Italian) 201 N 14th St	Fort Smith	AR	72901	501-785-2292
Thai Food (Thai) 1900 Midland Blvd	Fort Smith	AR	72904	501-782-7509
Tommy's Seafood & Steakhouse (Steak/Seafood) 2428 Midland Blvd	Fort Smith	AR	72904	501-783-9523
Varsity Sports Grill (American) 318 Garrison Ave	Fort Smith	AR	72901	501-494-7173
Vincent's (Chinese) 1119 East End	Fort Smith	AR	72956	501-471-8543

— Goods and Services —

SHOPPING

Name	City	State	Zip	Phone	Fax
Central Mall 5111 Rogers Ave	Fort Smith	AR	72903	501-452-4706	452-9324
Downtown Fort Smith 623 Garrison Ave	Fort Smith	AR	72901	501-783-8888	
Green Pointe Shopping Center 4300 Rogers Ave	Fort Smith	AR	72903		
May Branch Shopping Center 2909 Old Greenwood Rd	Fort Smith	AR	72903		
Phoenix Village Mall 127 Phoenix Village	Fort Smith	AR	72901	501-646-7889	646-7880

BANKS

Name	City	State	Zip	Phone	Fax
City National Bank PO Box 47	Fort Smith	AR	72902	501-785-2811	785-1040
First National Bank PO Box 7	Fort Smith	AR	72902	501-782-2041	788-4601
Superior Federal Bank FSB 5000 Rogers Ave *TF:* 800-488-6556	Fort Smith	AR	72917	501-452-8900	484-8574

BUSINESS SERVICES

	Phone
Airborne Express	800-247-2676
BAX Global	800-225-5229
DHL Worldwide Express	800-225-5345
Federal Express	800-238-5355
Kelly Services	501-646-6569
Kinko's	501-785-2679
Mail Boxes Etc	800-789-4623
Manpower Temporary Services	501-785-2583
Post Office	501-484-6410
Staffmark Office Staffing	501-452-5100
UPS	800-742-5877

— Media —

PUBLICATIONS

Name	City	State	Zip	Phone	Fax
Southwest Times Record‡ PO Box 1359 *TF:* 888-274-4051 ■ *Web:* www.swtimes.com	Fort Smith	AR	72902	501-785-7700	784-0413

‡*Daily newspapers*

TELEVISION

Name	City	State	Zip	Phone	Fax
KAFT-TV Ch 13 (PBS) 350 S Donaghey Ave	Conway	AR	72032	501-682-2386	682-4122
KFDF-TV Ch 32 (UPN) PO Box 573 *Web:* www.pharis.com/UPN32.htm	Fort Smith	AR	72901	501-288-0040	785-4844
KFSM-TV Ch 5 (CBS) PO Box 369 *Web:* www.kfsm.com	Fort Smith	AR	72902	501-783-3131	
KHBS-TV Ch 40 (ABC) 2415 N Albert Pike *Web:* www.khbs-khog.com	Fort Smith	AR	72904	501-783-4040	785-5375
KPBI-TV Ch 46 (Fox) 523 Garrison Ave Suite 201 *Web:* www.pharis.com/Fox46.htm ■ *E-mail:* fox46@ipa.net	Fort Smith	AR	72902	501-785-4600	785-4844
KPOM-TV Ch 24 (NBC) 4624 Kelley Hwy	Fort Smith	AR	72904	501-785-2400	785-3169

RADIO

Name	City	State	Zip	Phone	Fax
KFDF-AM 1580 kHz (N/T) PO Box 573 *E-mail:* 102404.2602@compuserve.com	Fort Smith	AR	72902	501-288-0040	785-4844
KFPW-AM 1230 kHz (B/EZ) PO Box 303	Fort Smith	AR	72901	501-783-5379	785-2638
KLSZ-FM 102.7 MHz (AC) PO Box 3471	Fort Smith	AR	72913	501-474-3422	474-2649
KMAG-FM 99.1 MHz (Ctry) 423 Garrison Ave	Fort Smith	AR	72901	501-782-8888	785-5946
KTCS-FM 99.9 MHz (Ctry) 5304 Hwy 45 E	Fort Smith	AR	72916	501-646-6151	646-3509
KWHN-AM 1320 kHz (N/T) 423 Garrison Ave	Fort Smith	AR	72902	501-782-8888	785-5946
KZBB-FM 97.9 MHz (CHR) 423 Garrison Ave	Fort Smith	AR	72901	501-782-8888	782-0366
KZKZ-FM 106.3 MHz (Rel) PO Box 6210	Fort Smith	AR	72906	501-646-6700	646-1373

— Colleges/Universities —

Name	City	State	Zip	Phone	Fax
Westark College 5210 Grand Ave *Web:* www.westark.com	Fort Smith	AR	72913	501-788-7000	788-7016

— Hospitals —

Name	City	State	Zip	Phone	Fax
Saint Edward Mercy Medical Center PO Box 17000 **Fax:* Admitting	Fort Smith	AR	72917	501-484-6000	452-3782*
Sparks Regional Medical Center 1311 S 'I' St **Fax:* Admitting ■ *Web:* www.sparks.org ■ *E-mail:* info@sparks.org	Fort Smith	AR	72901	501-441-4000	441-4815*

— Attractions —

Name	City	State	Zip	Phone	Fax
Belle Grove Historic District betw N 5th & N 8th Sts	Fort Smith	AR	72901	501-783-8888	
Clayton House 514 N 6th St	Fort Smith	AR	72901	501-783-3000	
Crawford County Art Center 104 N 13th St	Van Buren	AR	72956	501-474-7767	
Darby House 311 General Darby St	Fort Smith	AR	72901	501-782-3388	783-7590
Downtown Fort Smith 623 Garrison Ave	Fort Smith	AR	72901	501-783-8888	
Fort Smith Art Center 423 N 6th St	Fort Smith	AR	72901	501-784-2787	784-9071
Fort Smith Little Theatre 401 N 6th St	Fort Smith	AR	72901	501-783-2966	
Fort Smith National Historic Site Rogers Ave betw 2nd & 3rd Sts *Web:* www.nps.gov/fosm/	Fort Smith	AR	72902	501-783-3961	783-5307
Fort Smith Symphony Orchestra PO Box 3151 *E-mail:* fssymphony@aol.com	Fort Smith	AR	72913	501-452-7575	452-8985
Fort Smith Trolley Museum 100 S 4th St *Web:* www.fstm.org ■ *E-mail:* info@fstm.org	Fort Smith	AR	72901	501-783-0205	782-0649
Frontier Belle Riverboat Main St	Van Buren	AR	72956	501-471-5441	471-5344
Miss Laura's House 2 N 'B' St	Fort Smith	AR	72901	501-783-8888	784-2421
Old Fort Museum 320 Rogers Ave	Fort Smith	AR	72901	501-783-7841	783-3244
Patent Model Museum 400 N 8th St	Fort Smith	AR	72901	501-782-9014	
Pea Ridge National Military Park PO Box 700 *Web:* www.nps.gov/peri/ ■ *E-mail:* PERI_InterpRanger@nps.gov	Pea Ridge	AR	72751	501-451-8122	451-0219
Scenic Ozark Railway 813 Main St Old Frisco Depot	Van Buren	AR	72956	501-751-8600	751-2225
US National Cemetery 522 Garland Ave	Fort Smith	AR	72901	501-783-5345	785-4189
Weidman's Brewery 422 N 3rd St	Fort Smith	AR	72901	501-782-9898	783-9006

SPORTS TEAMS & FACILITIES

Name	City	State	Zip	Phone	Fax
Blue Ribbon Downs 3700 W Cherokee	Sallisaw	OK	74955	918-775-7771	775-5805
Harper's Stadium Kay Rodgers Park 4317 N 50th St	Fort Smith	AR	72014	501-783-2393	782-9944

Fort Smith (Cont'd)

— Events —

	Phone
Arkansas-Oklahoma State Fair (late-September)	501-783-6176
Fort Smith Blues Festival (early September)	501-783-6353
Fort Smith Christmas Parade (early December)	501-782-2041
Fort Smith Riverfront Blues Festival (mid-September)	501-785-1201
Freedomfest-Greenwood (July)	501-996-6357
Hanging Dice Nationals Street Custom Car Show (early September)	501-783-6176
Holiday Market (mid-November)	501-784-2365
Mayor's July 4th Celebration (July 4)	501-782-2041
Old Fort Days Barrel Race Futurity Derby (mid-May)	501-783-6176
Old Fort Days Rodeo (late May-early June)	501-783-6176
Old Fort River Festival (early June)	501-783-6363
Valley of the Arkansas Gathering (late October)	501-783-8888

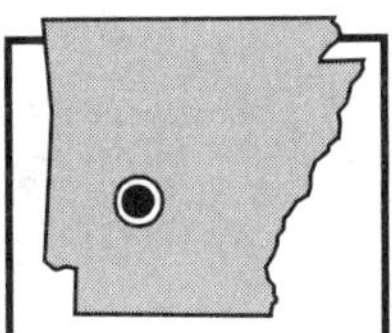

Hot Springs

Hot Springs is a resort city situated in a national park known for its restorative thermal waters. The Hot Springs National Park area includes historic bathhouses, Victorian buildings, art and sculpture galleries, and museums, as well as the natural springs. The five-county area in which the "Spa City" is located is known as the Diamond Lakes Region. The lakes are spread among the Ouachita Mountains, providing for a range of outdoor recreational activities throughout the area. Two of the five lakes, Ouachita and Hamilton, are at Hot Springs; Lake Catherine is near Malvern, Lake Greeson between Glenwood and Murfreesboro, and DeGray Lake is at Arkadelphia. Near Murfreesboro also is Crater of Diamonds State Park, where visitors can hunt for diamonds and keep any they find.

Population	37,961	**Longitude**	93-02-87 W
Area (Land)	29.6 sq mi	**County**	Garland
Area (Water)	0.01 sq mi	**Time Zone**	CST
Elevation	632 ft	**Area Code/s**	501
Latitude	34-50-22 N		

— Average Temperatures and Precipitation —

TEMPERATURES

	Jan	Feb	Mar	Apr	May	Jun	Jul	Aug	Sep	Oct	Nov	Dec
High	50	55	65	74	81	89	93	92	86	76	63	53
Low	29	32	41	50	58	66	70	68	62	51	41	32

PRECIPITATION

	Jan	Feb	Mar	Apr	May	Jun	Jul	Aug	Sep	Oct	Nov	Dec
Inches	3.3	3.9	5.4	5.5	6.4	4.7	5.0	3.5	4.0	4.3	5.6	5.0

— Important Phone Numbers —

	Phone		Phone
AAA	800-632-6808	**Time/Temp**	501-996-6000
Emergency	911	**Weather**	501-525-0011
Poison Control Center	800-376-4766		

— Information Sources —

				Phone	Fax
Better Business Bureau Serving Arkansas 1415 S University Ave	Little Rock	AR	72204	501-664-7274	664-0024
Web: www.arkansas.bbb.org					
Garland County 501 Ouachita Ave	Hot Springs	AR	71901	501-622-3610	624-0665
Greater Hot Springs Chamber of Commerce PO Box 6090	Hot Springs	AR	71902	501-321-1700	321-3551
TF: 800-467-4636 ■ *Web:* hotsprings.dina.org					
Hot Springs City Hall PO Box 700	Hot Springs	AR	71902	501-321-6800	321-6809
Web: www.ci.hot-springs.ar.us ■ *E-mail:* info@ci.hot-springs.ar.us					
Hot Springs Convention & Visitors Bureau PO Box K	Hot Springs	AR	71902	501-321-2277	321-2136
TF: 800-772-2489 ■ *Web:* www.hotsprings.org ■ *E-mail:* hscvb@hotsprings.org					
Hot Springs Mayor PO Box 700	Hot Springs	AR	71902	501-321-6810	321-6814
Tri-Lakes Regional Library 1427 Malvern Ave Rm 144	Hot Springs	AR	71901	501-623-3943	623-6356

On-Line Resources

Area Guide Hot Springs	hotsprings.areaguides.net
Arkansas' Diamond Lakes	www.aiea.ualr.edu/dina/diamond/default.html
City Knowledge Hot Springs	www.cityknowledge.com/ar_hotsprings.htm
Excite.com Hot Springs City Guide	www.excite.com/travel/countries/united_states/arkansas/hot_springs
Hot Springs Internet Newspaper	www.hsnp.com/newspaper
Hot Springs National Park Home Page	www.hsnp.com
Hot Springs Promenade	www.hotspringsar.com
NITC Travelbase City Guide Hot Springs	www.travelbase.com/auto/guides/hot_springs-ar.html

— Transportation Services —

AIRPORTS

	Phone
■ **Hot Springs Memorial Field (HOT)**	
3 miles SW of downtown (approx 10 minutes)	501-624-3306

Airport Transportation

	Phone
Airport Taxi $5 fare to downtown	501-623-2525
Yellow Checker Cab $5 fare to downtown	501-624-1221

Commercial Airlines

	Phone
Aspen Mountain Air Inc	972-641-7337

Charter Airlines

	Phone		Phone
Airborne Flying Services Inc	501-624-4545	**James Flying Service**	800-556-4221

	Phone
■ **Little Rock National Airport/Adams Field (LIT)**	
55 miles NE of downtown Hot Springs (approx 50 minutes)	501-372-3439

Airport Transportation

	Phone
Airport Shuttle $22 fare to downtown	800-643-1505

Commercial Airlines

	Phone		Phone
Delta	800-221-1212	**Southwest**	800-435-9792
Northwest	800-225-2525	**US Airways**	800-428-4322

Charter Airlines

	Phone		Phone
Central Flying Service Inc	501-375-3245	**Omni Air Charter**	501-227-6141
Corporate America Aviation Inc	800-521-8585		

CAR RENTALS

	Phone		Phone
Avis	501-376-9151	**National**	501-376-7221
Budget	501-375-5521	**Thrifty**	501-376-2277
Hertz	501-623-7591		

Hot Springs (Cont'd)

LIMO/TAXI

	Phone
AJS Limousine	501-623-3929
Hot Springs Limousine	501-525-4970
Service Cab	501-624-5656
Yellow Cab	501-623-1616
Yellow Checker Cab	501-624-1221

MASS TRANSIT

	Phone
Hot Springs Intracity Transit $1 Base fare	501-321-2020

RAIL/BUS

				Phone
Greyhound Bus Station 229 W Grand Ave *TF:* 800-231-2222	Hot Springs	AR	71901	501-623-5574

— Accommodations —

HOTELS, MOTELS, RESORTS

				Phone	Fax
Arlington Resort Hotel & Spa 239 Central Ave *TF:* 800-643-1502 ■ *Web:* www.arlingtonhotel.com	Hot Springs	AR	71901	501-623-7771	623-6191
Avanelle Motor Lodge 1204 Central Ave *TF:* 800-225-1360	Hot Springs	AR	71901	501-321-1332	321-1332
Best Western Stagecoach Inn 2520 Central Ave *TF:* 800-643-8722	Hot Springs	AR	71913	501-624-2531	623-0169
Buena Vista Resort 201 Aberina St *TF:* 800-255-9030	Hot Springs	AR	71913	501-525-1321	525-8293
Clarion Resort 4813 Central Ave *TF:* 800-465-4329	Hot Springs	AR	71913	501-525-1391	525-0813
Country Inn Lake Resort 1332 Airport Rd *TF:* 800-822-7402	Hot Springs	AR	71913	501-767-3535	
Cozy Acres Resort 1100 Cozy Acres Rd *Web:* www.cozy-acres.com	Mountain Pine	AR	71956	501-767-5023	
Days Inn 106 Lookout Point *TF:* 800-945-9559	Hot Springs	AR	71913	501-525-5666	525-5666
Downtowner Hotel & Spa 135 Central Ave *TF:* 800-251-1962	Hot Springs	AR	71901	501-624-5521	624-4635
Econo Lodge 4319 Central Ave *TF:* 800-745-6160	Hot Springs	AR	71913	501-525-1660	525-7260
Edgewater Resort 200 Edgewater Cir *TF:* 800-234-3687 ■ *E-mail:* ewresort@hsnp.com	Hot Springs	AR	71913	501-767-3311	760-5359
Hamilton Harbor Resort 203 Sterns Point	Hot Springs	AR	71913	501-767-8300	525-4413
Hideaway Resort 200 Long Island Dr	Hot Springs	AR	71913	501-525-8386	
Hilton Hotel Hot Springs Park 305 Malvern Ave *TF:* 800-844-7275 ■ *Web:* www.hilton.com/hotels/HOTHHHF	Hot Springs	AR	71901	501-623-6600	624-7160
Hot Springs Resort 1871 E Grand Ave *TF:* 800-238-4891	Hot Springs	AR	71901	501-624-4436	624-5199
Hot Springs Vacation Rentals 5380 Central Ave	Hot Springs	AR	71913	501-525-3500	
Knollwood Lodge 130 Knollwood Lodge Rd	Hot Springs	AR	71913	501-767-9231	
Lake Hamilton Resort 2803 Albert Pike Rd *TF:* 800-426-3184	Hot Springs	AR	71913	501-767-5511	767-8576
Long Island Lake Resort 320 Long Island Dr *TF:* 800-467-1598	Hot Springs	AR	71913	501-525-3600	
Majestic Resort & Spa 101 Park Ave *TF:* 800-643-1504	Hot Springs	AR	71901	501-623-5511	624-4737
Mountain Spring Inn 1127 Central Ave *TF:* 888-298-3200	Hot Springs	AR	71901	501-624-7131	624-3965
Paradise Point Resort 326 Paradise Point Rd	Hot Springs	AR	71913	501-760-2738	760-1089
Park Hotel 211 Fountain St *TF:* 800-895-7275	Hot Springs	AR	71901	501-624-5323	623-0052
Patton's Lake Resort 100 San Carlos Point	Hot Springs	AR	71913	501-525-1678	
Quality Inn 1125 E Grand Ave *TF:* 800-221-2222	Hot Springs	AR	71901	501-624-3321	624-5814
Ramada Inn Tower 218 Park Ave *TF:* 888-624-3311 ■ *E-mail:* ramadahot@worldnet.att.net	Hot Springs	AR	71901	501-623-3311	623-8871
Royale Vista Inn 2204 Central Ave *TF:* 800-643-1127	Hot Springs	AR	71901	501-624-5551	624-5703
Sands Central Motel 1525 Central Ave	Hot Springs	AR	71901	501-624-1258	624-2800
Shorecrest Resort 360 Lakeland Dr *TF:* 800-447-9914	Hot Springs	AR	71913	501-525-8113	
South Shore Lake Resort 201 Hamilton Oaks Dr	Hot Springs	AR	71913	501-525-8200	525-4413
Summit Lake Resort 350 Lakeland Dr *TF:* 800-959-5253	Hot Springs	AR	71913	501-525-1162	
Sun Bay Resort 4810 Central Ave *TF:* 800-468-0055 ■ *Web:* www.sunbaypoa.com/	Hot Springs	AR	71913	501-525-4691	520-3020
Super 8 Motel 4726 Central Ave *TF:* 800-800-8000	Hot Springs	AR	71913	501-525-0188	525-7449
Travelier Inn 1045 E Grand Ave	Hot Springs	AR	71901	501-624-4681	624-4684
Vagabond Motel 4708 Central Ave	Hot Springs	AR	71913	501-525-2769	525-4205
Willow Beach Resort 260 Lake Hamilton Dr *TF:* 800-874-1385	Hot Springs	AR	71913	501-525-1362	525-9290

— Restaurants —

				Phone
Acapulco's (Mexican) 320 Ouchita Ave	Hot Springs	AR	71901	501-623-8030
Avanelle Sirloin Room (Steak) 1204 Central Ave	Hot Springs	AR	71901	501-321-1332
Belli Arti Ristorante (Italian) 719 Central Ave	Hot Springs	AR	71901	501-624-7474
Bohemia Restaurant (European) 417 Park Ave	Hot Springs	AR	71901	501-623-9661
Cafe Santa Clare (Southwest) 323 Whittington Ave	Hot Springs	AR	71901	501-624-0166
California Cafe (American) 1000 Shady Grove Rd	Hot Springs	AR	71901	501-262-4667
Don Juan Authentic Mexican (Mexican) 3000 Central Ave	Hot Springs	AR	71913	501-318-0711
Facci's (Italian) 2910 Central Ave	Hot Springs	AR	71913	501-623-9049
Faded Rose (Cajun) 210 Central Ave	Hot Springs	AR	71901	501-624-3200
Grady's Grill (American) 101 Park Ave	Hot Springs	AR	71902	501-623-5511
Hamilton House (Steak/Seafood) 130 Van Lyell Dr	Hot Springs	AR	71913	501-525-2727
Island Bistro (European) 4810 Central Ave	Hot Springs	AR	71913	501-525-1055
J D's Bar-b-que (Barbecue) 5771 Central Ave	Hot Springs	AR	71913	501-525-6364
Lotus Restaurant (Thai/Vietnamese) 711 Central Ave	Hot Springs	AR	71901	501-623-3555
Magnolia Grill (Steak/Seafood) 305 Malvern Ave	Hot Springs	AR	71901	501-623-6600
Schapiro's on Central (American) 510 Central Ave	Hot Springs	AR	71901	501-624-5500
Shanghai Restaurant (Chinese) 608 E Grand Ave	Hot Springs	AR	71901	501-321-1688
Simply Prime Restaurant (Steak) 3812 Central Ave	Hot Springs	AR	71913	501-525-4145
Yanni's (Greek) 211 Fountain St	Hot Springs	AR	71901	501-624-5323

— Goods and Services —

SHOPPING

				Phone	Fax
Hot Springs Mall 4501 Central Ave Suite 100	Hot Springs	AR	71913	501-525-3254	525-0930

BANKS

				Phone	Fax
Alliance Bank of Hot Springs 515 W Grand Ave	Hot Springs	AR	71901	501-318-1017	
Bank of America 528 Central Ave **Fax:* Cust Svc	Hot Springs National Park	AR	71901	501-321-8000	321-8007*
Mercantile Bank 1234 Central Ave	Hot Springs	AR	71901	501-624-5501	321-5033
MNB Bank 548 W Grand Ave	Hot Springs	AR	71901	501-622-6600	622-6620
Regions Bank PO Box 29000 *TF:* 800-272-2083	Hot Springs National Park	AR	71903	501-624-4611	624-4619
Superior Federal Bank 400 Ouachita Ave	Hot Springs	AR	71901	501-623-9284	

BUSINESS SERVICES

	Phone
Airborne Express	800-247-2676
BAX Global	800-225-5229
DHL Worldwide Express	800-225-5345
Federal Express	800-238-5355
Mail Boxes Etc	800-789-4623
Mail Room	501-525-5853
Personnel Resources	501-525-4646
Post Office	501-525-0558
Professional Copy & Mail	501-624-2303
Staffmark	501-525-4443
UPS	800-742-5877

— Media —

PUBLICATIONS

				Phone	Fax
Sentinel-Record‡ 300 Spring St *Web:* www.hotsr.com ■ *E-mail:* hotsr@direclynx.com	Hot Springs	AR	71901	501-623-7711	623-2984

‡*Daily newspapers*

Hot Springs (Cont'd)

TELEVISION

				Phone	Fax
KARK-TV Ch 4 (NBC) 201 W 3rd St	Little Rock	AR	72201	501-340-4444	375-1961
Web: www.kark.com ■ *E-mail:* news4@kark.com					
KATV-TV Ch 7 (ABC) 401 S Main St PO Box 77	Little Rock	AR	72201	501-372-7777	324-7852*
**Fax:* News Rm ■ *Web:* www.katv.com ■ *E-mail:* tv7@katv.com					
KETG-TV Ch 9 (PBS) 350 S Donaghey Ave	Conway	AR	72032	501-682-2386	682-4122
TF: 800-662-2386 ■ *Web:* www.aetn.org					
KLRT-TV Ch 16 (Fox) 11711 W Markham St	Little Rock	AR	72211	501-225-0016	225-0428
Web: www.klrt.com					
KTHV-TV Ch 11 (CBS) PO Box 269	Little Rock	AR	72203	501-376-1111	376-1645

RADIO

				Phone	Fax
KLAZ-FM 105.9 MHz (CHR) PO Box 1739	Hot Springs	AR	71902	501-525-1301	525-4344
TF: 877-525-1059 ■ *Web:* www.klaz.com					
KQUS-FM 97.5 MHz (Ctry) 125 Corporate Terr	Hot Springs	AR	71913	501-525-9700	525-9739
KSBC-FM 90.1 MHz (Rel) 600 Garland Ave	Hot Springs	AR	71913	501-624-4455	624-7870
KXOW-AM 1420 kHz (Nost) PO Box 1739	Hot Springs	AR	71902	501-525-1301	525-4344
TF: 877-525-1059					
KZNG-AM 1340 kHz (N/T) 125 Corporate Terr	Hot Springs	AR	71913	501-525-9700	525-9739
Web: www.amfm.net/kzng					

— Colleges/Universities —

				Phone	Fax
Garland County Community College 101 College Dr	Hot Springs	AR	71913	501-760-4222	760-4100
Web: www.gccc.cc.ar.us					
Henderson State University 1100 Henderson St	Arkadelphia	AR	71999	870-230-5000	230-5066
TF: 800-228-7333 ■ *Web:* www.hsu.edu					
Hendrix College 1600 Washington Ave	Conway	AR	72032	501-329-6811	450-1200
TF Admissions: 800-277-9017 ■ *Web:* www.hendrix.edu ■ *E-mail:* adm@hendrix.edu					
Ouachita Baptist University 410 Ouachita St	Arkadelphia	AR	71998	870-245-5000	245-5500
TF: 800-342-5628 ■ *Web:* www.obu.edu					

— Hospitals —

				Phone	Fax
Levi Hospital 300 Prospect Ave	Hot Springs	AR	71901	501-624-1281	622-3500
TF: 800-264-5384					
National Park Medical Center 1910 Malvern Ave	Hot Springs National Park	AR	71901	501-321-1000	321-2922
Web: www.tenethealth.com/NationalPark					
Saint Joseph's Regional Health Center 300 Werner St	Hot Springs	AR	71913	501-622-1000	622-2035*
**Fax:* Admitting ■ *TF:* 800-345-6621 ■ *Web:* www.saintjosephs.com ■ *E-mail:* info@saintjosephs.com					

— Attractions —

				Phone	Fax
Ar-Scenic Spring 103 Mount Ida St	Hot Springs	AR	71901	501-623-1722	
Arkansas Alligator Farm & Petting Zoo 847 Whittington Ave	Hot Springs	AR	71901	501-623-6172	
Arkansas House of Reptiles 420 Central Ave	Hot Springs	AR	71901	501-623-8516	
Bath House Show 701 Central Ave	Hot Springs	AR	71901	501-623-1415	
Belle of Hot Springs Cruises 5200 Central Ave	Hot Springs	AR	71913	501-525-4438	525-3919
Web: www.direclynx.net/~bellehs					
Buckstaff Bath House 509 Central Ave	Hot Springs	AR	71901	501-623-2308	
Web: www.direclynx.net/~buckstaf ■ *E-mail:* buckstaf@direclynx.net					
Central Country Music Theater 1008 Central Ave	Hot Springs	AR	71901	501-624-2268	
Crater of Diamonds State Park RR 1 Box 364	Murfreesboro	AR	71958	870-285-3113	285-4169
Dryden Potteries 341 Whittington Ave	Hot Springs	AR	71901	501-623-4201	
Hot Springs Health Spa 500 Reserve St	Hot Springs	AR	71901	501-321-1997	321-0368
Hot Springs Mountain Tower 401 Hot Springs Mountain Dr	Hot Springs	AR	71902	501-623-6035	623-4557
Hot Springs National Park Fordyce Bathhouse Visitor Ctr	Hot Springs	AR	71902	501-623-1433	624-1536
Web: www.nps.gov/hosp					
Lake Catherine State Park 1200 Catherine Park Rd	Hot Springs	AR	71913	501-844-4176	844-4244
TF: 800-264-2422 ■ *Web:* www.gorp.com/gorp/location/ar/parks/cath.htm					
Mid-America Science Museum 500 Mid-America Blvd	Hot Springs	AR	71913	501-767-3461	767-1170
Web: www.direclynx.net/~masm ■ *E-mail:* masm@direclynx.net					
Mountain Valley Spring Co PO Box 1610	Hot Springs	AR	71902	501-623-6671	623-5135
TF: 800-643-1501 ■ *Web:* www.hotspringsar.com/mvswc/mvsch2o.htm					
Music Mountain Jamboree 2720 Albert Pike	Hot Springs	AR	71913	501-767-3841	760-2288
National Park Aquarium 209 Central Ave	Hot Springs	AR	71901	501-624-3474	
TF: 800-735-3074					
Panther Valley Ranch 1942 Millcreek Rd	Hot Springs	AR	71901	501-623-5556	
Short-Dodson House 755 Park Ave	Hot Springs	AR	71901	501-624-9555	
Tussaud Josephine Wax Museum 250 Central Ave	Hot Springs	AR	71901	501-623-5836	

SPORTS TEAMS & FACILITIES

				Phone	Fax
Oaklawn Jockey Club 2705 Central Ave	Hot Springs	AR	71901	501-623-4411	623-4088
TF: 800-625-5296 ■ *Web:* www.oaklawn.com/ ■ *E-mail:* winning@oaklawn.com					

— Events —

	Phone
Arkansas Oktoberfest (mid-October)	800-772-2489
Arts & Crafts Fair (early October)	501-623-6841
BrickFest (late June)	501-332-2721
Courthouse Lighting Ceremony (early December)	501-623-6841
Historic Downtown District Open House (late November)	501-623-2849
Holiday in the Park (late December-early January)	800-543-2284
Holiday Luminaries (early December)	501-624-5555
Hot Springs Documentary Film Festival (mid-October)	501-321-4747
Oktoberfest Fur Kinder (early October)	501-321-1700
Osborne Family Holiday Lighting (mid-late December)	501-624-5333
Racing Festival of the South (mid-April)	501-623-4411

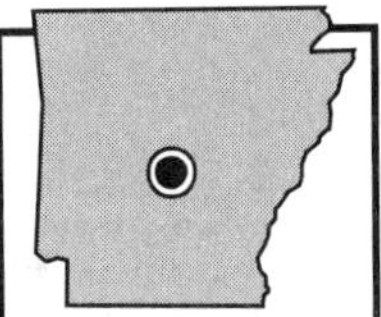

Little Rock

Arkansas' capital city of Little Rock was given its name by French settlers who called the city "La Petite Roche" in order to distinguish it from larger rock outcroppings along the Arkansas River. Little Rock's history, from the 1820s to today, is alive in the Quapaw Quarter. Named for the Arkansas native Quapaw Indians, the Quarter contains some of the city's oldest structures, including some that date from before the Civil War. Across the Arkansas River is North Little Rock, where visitors can see the Old Mill that was used in the opening scene of "Gone With the Wind." Little Rock is also the former home of President Bill Clinton.

Population	175,303	**Longitude**	92-28-94 W
Area (Land)	102.9 sq mi	**County**	Pulaski
Area (Water)	0.3 sq mi	**Time Zone**	CST
Elevation	291 ft	**Area Code/s**	501
Latitude	34-74-64 N		

Little Rock (Cont'd)

— Average Temperatures and Precipitation —

TEMPERATURES

	Jan	Feb	Mar	Apr	May	Jun	Jul	Aug	Sep	Oct	Nov	Dec
High	49	54	64	73	81	89	92	91	85	75	63	53
Low	29	33	42	51	59	67	72	70	64	51	42	33

PRECIPITATION

	Jan	Feb	Mar	Apr	May	Jun	Jul	Aug	Sep	Oct	Nov	Dec
Inches	3.4	3.6	4.9	5.5	5.2	3.6	3.6	3.3	4.1	3.8	5.2	4.8

— Important Phone Numbers —

	Phone
AAA	501-223-9222
Dental Referral	501-771-7650
Emergency	911
HotelDocs	800-468-3537
Medical Referral	501-227-8478
State Highway Road Conditions	501-569-2374
Telefun Events	501-372-3399
Time/Temp	501-376-8111
Weather	501-371-7777

— Information Sources —

				Phone	Fax
Better Business Bureau Serving Arkansas 1415 S University Ave	Little Rock	AR	72204	501-664-7274	664-0024

Web: www.arkansas.bbb.org

				Phone	Fax
Greater Little Rock Chamber of Commerce 101 S Spring St Suite 200	Little Rock	AR	72201	501-374-4871	374-6018

Web: www.littlerockchamber.com

Little Rock City Hall 500 W Markham St. . . . . Little Rock AR 72201 501-371-4500
Web: www.littlerock.org/government/default.html
■ *E-mail:* littlerock@dina.org

Little Rock Convention & Visitors Bureau
PO Box 3232 . . . . . Little Rock AR 72203 501-376-4781 374-2255
TF: 800-844-4781 ■ *Web:* www.littlerock.com/lrcvb/
■ *E-mail:* lrcvbpr@littlerock.com

Little Rock Mayor
500 W Markham St Rm 203 . . . . . Little Rock AR 72201 501-371-4791 371-4498
Web: www.littlerock.org/government/officials/mayor
■ *E-mail:* mayor@littlerock.org

Little Rock Planning & Development Dept
723 W Markham St. . . . . Little Rock AR 72201 501-371-4790 371-6863
Web: www.littlerock.org/government/departments/planning/default.html

Little Rock Public Library 100 Rock St. . . . . Little Rock AR 72201 501-918-3000 375-7451
Web: vera.cals.lib.ar.us

Pulaski County
401 W Markham St Suite 102 . . . . . Little Rock AR 72201 501-340-8431 340-8420

Statehouse Convention Center
Markham & Main Sts 1
Statehouse Plaza. . . . . Little Rock AR 72201 501-376-4781 376-7833
TF: 800-844-4781
■ *Web:* www.littlerock.com/facilities/statehouse_convention.html

On-Line Resources

4LittleRock.com	www.4littlerock.com
Anthill City Guide Little Rock	www.anthill.com/city.asp?city=littlerock
Area Guide Little Rock	littlerock.areaguides.net
Arkansas Times	www.arktimes.com
City Knowledge Little Rock	www.cityknowledge.com/ar_littlerock.htm
Excite.com Little Rock City Guide	www.excite.com/travel/countries/united_states/arkansas/little_rock
Little Rock CityLink	www.usacitylink.com/citylink/lit-rock
Little Rock Free Press	www.aristotle.net/FREEP
Little Rock Info	www.littlerockinfo.com
NITC Travelbase City Guide Little Rock	www.travelbase.com/auto/guides/little_rock-area-ar.html

— Transportation Services —

AIRPORTS

■ **Little Rock National Airport/Adams Field (LIT)**

	Phone
3 miles E of downtown (approx 12-15 minutes)	501-372-3439

Web: lrairport2.dina.org/dina/cities/airport/default.shtml

Airport Transportation

	Phone
Black & White/Yellow Cab $11-13 fare to downtown	501-374-0333
Taxi $8-10 fare to downtown	501-568-0462

Commercial Airlines

	Phone
Delta	800-221-1212
Northwest	800-225-2525
Southwest	800-435-9792
TWA	800-221-2000
United	800-241-6522
United Express	800-241-6522
US Airways	800-428-4322

Charter Airlines

	Phone
Central Flying Service Inc	501-375-3245
Corporate America Aviation Inc	800-521-8585
Omni Air Charter	501-227-6141

CAR RENTALS

	Phone
Avis	501-376-9151
Budget	501-375-5521
Hertz	501-375-7307
National	501-376-7221
Thrifty	501-376-2277

LIMO/TAXI

	Phone
Black & White/Yellow Cab	501-374-0333
Capitol Cab	501-568-0462
Little Rock Limousine	501-224-5466

MASS TRANSIT

	Phone
Central Arkansas Transit $.90 Base fare	501-375-1163

RAIL/BUS

Amtrak Station 1400 Markham St. . . . . Little Rock AR 72201 501-372-6841
TF: 800-872-7245

Greyhound/Trailways Bus Station
118 E Washington St . . . . . North Little Rock AR 72114 501-372-3007
TF: 800-231-2222

— Accommodations —

HOTELS, MOTELS, RESORTS

AmeriSuites Hotel
10920 Financial Center Pkwy . . . . . Little Rock AR 72211 501-225-1075 225-2209
TF: 800-833-1516

Baptist Health Plaza Hotel
1120 Medical Center Dr. . . . . Little Rock AR 72205 501-202-9606 202-9606

Baymont Inns & Suites
1010 Breckenridge St . . . . . Little Rock AR 72205 501-225-7007 225-2631
TF: 800-301-0200

Baymont Inns North Little Rock
4311 Warden Rd. . . . . North Little Rock AR 72116 501-758-8888 758-5055
TF: 800-301-0200

Best Western Governor's Inn
1501 Merrill Dr. . . . . Little Rock AR 72211 501-224-8051 224-8051
TF: 800-422-8051

Best Western Inntowne Hotel 600 I-30 . . . . . Little Rock AR 72202 501-375-2100 374-9045
TF: 800-528-1234

Capital Hotel 111 W Markham St . . . . . Little Rock AR 72201 501-374-7474 370-7091
TF: 800-766-7666 ■ *Web:* www.capitalhotel-lr.com
■ *E-mail:* hospitality@capitalhotel-lr.com

City Center Plaza Hotel
617 S Broadway St. . . . . Little Rock AR 72201 501-376-2071 376-7733

Courtyard by Marriott
10900 Financial Centre Pkwy . . . . . Little Rock AR 72211 501-227-6000 227-6912
TF: 800-321-2211 ■ *Web:* courtyard.com/LITCH

Days Inn 3200 Bankhead Dr. . . . . Little Rock AR 72206 501-490-2010 490-2229
TF: 800-329-7466

Days Inn North 5800 Pritchard Dr. . . . . North Little Rock AR 72117 501-945-4100 945-4100
TF: 800-329-7466

Days Inn South 2600 W 65th St. . . . . Little Rock AR 72209 501-562-1122 562-1122
TF: 800-329-7466

Doubletree Hotel Little Rock
424 W Markham St. . . . . Little Rock AR 72201 501-372-4371 372-0518
TF: 800-937-2789
■ *Web:* www.doubletreehotels.com/DoubleT/Hotel/04/04Main.htm
■ *E-mail:* doubletreelr@aristotle.net

Little Rock — Hotels, Motels, Resorts (Cont'd)

Name / Address	City	State	ZIP	Phone	Fax
Economy Inn 4000 W Markham St	Little Rock	AR	72205	501-664-0950	666-6659
Embassy Suites 11301 Financial Center Pkwy	Little Rock	AR	72211	501-312-9000	312-9455
TF: 800-362-2779					
Empress of Little Rock 2120 S Louisiana	Little Rock	AR	72206	501-374-7966	375-4537
Excelsior Hotel Little Rock 3 Statehouse Plaza	Little Rock	AR	72201	501-375-5000	375-4721
TF: 800-527-1745 ■ *Web:* www.arkexcelsior.com ■ *E-mail:* hotel@arkexcelsior.com					
Extended StayAmerica 600 Hardin Rd	Little Rock	AR	72211	501-954-9199	954-9268
TF: 800-398-7829					
Hampton Inn 6100 Mitchell Dr	Little Rock	AR	72209	501-562-6667	568-6832
TF: 800-426-7866					
Hampton Inn North 500 W 29th St	North Little Rock	AR	72114	501-771-2090	771-0410
TF: 800-426-7866					
Holiday Inn Airport 3201 Bankhead Dr	Little Rock	AR	72206	501-490-1000	490-2029
TF: 800-465-4329					
Holiday Inn Express 3121 Bankhead Dr	Little Rock	AR	72206	501-490-4000	490-0423
TF: 800-465-4329					
Holiday Inn Select 201 S Shackleford Rd	Little Rock	AR	72211	501-223-3000	223-2833
TF: 800-465-4329					
Howard Johnson 111 W Pershing Blvd	North Little Rock	AR	72114	501-758-1440	758-2094
TF: 800-446-4656					
Knights Inn 9709 I-30	Little Rock	AR	72209	501-568-6800	568-6800
TF: 800-843-5644					
La Quinta Hotel & Conference Center 11701 I-30	Little Rock	AR	72209	501-455-2300	455-5876
TF: 800-687-6667					
LaQuinta Fair Park 901 Fairpark Blvd	Little Rock	AR	72204	501-664-7000	
LaQuinta North 4100 E McCain Blvd	North Little Rock	AR	72117	501-945-0808	945-0393
TF: 800-687-6667					
LaQuinta South 2401 W 65th St	Little Rock	AR	72209	501-568-1030	568-5713
TF: 800-687-6667					
Legacy Hotel 625 W Capitol Ave	Little Rock	AR	72201	501-374-0100	374-3067
Little Rock Hilton Inn 925 S University Ave	Little Rock	AR	72204	501-664-5020	664-3104
TF: 800-445-8667 ■ *Web:* www.hilton.com/hotels/LITHIHF/index.html					
Premier Suites 315 N Bowman Rd	Little Rock	AR	72211	501-221-7378	219-1920
Ramada Inn 815 E Oak	Conway	AR	72033	501-329-8392	329-0430
TF: 800-272-6232					
Ramada Inn North 120 W Pershing Blvd	North Little Rock	AR	72114	501-758-1851	758-5616
TF: 800-272-6232					
Red Roof Inn 7900 Scott Hamilton Dr	Little Rock	AR	72209	501-562-2694	562-1723
TF: 800-843-7663					
Riverfront Hilton 2 Riverfront Pl	North Little Rock	AR	72114	501-371-9000	371-9000
TF: 800-345-6565 ■ *Web:* www.hilton.com/hotels/LITRHHF					
StudioPLUS 10800 Kanis Rd	Little Rock	AR	72211	501-227-8689	227-4084
TF: 800-646-8000					
Wilson Inn & Suites 4301 Roosevelt Rd	Little Rock	AR	72206	501-376-2466	376-0253
TF: 800-945-7667 ■ *Web:* www.travelbase.com/destinations/little-rock/wilson-inn/ ■ *E-mail:* wilsoninn@travelbase.com					

— Restaurants —

Name / Address	City	State	ZIP	Phone
Alouette's (French) 11401 N Rodney Parham Rd	Little Rock	AR	72212	501-225-4152
Web: www.alouettes.com/				
Andre's Hillcrest (Continental) 605 N Beechwood St	Little Rock	AR	72205	501-666-9191
Ashley's (Continental) 111 W Markham St	Little Rock	AR	72201	501-374-7474
Brave New Restaurant (Continental) 3701 Old Cantrell Rd	Little Rock	AR	72202	501-663-2677
Browning's (American) 5805 Kavanaugh Blvd	Little Rock	AR	72207	501-663-9956
Bruno's Little Italy (Italian) 315 N Bowman Rd	Little Rock	AR	72211	501-224-4700
Buffalo Grill (American) 1611 Rebsamen Park Rd	Little Rock	AR	72202	501-663-2158
Butcher Shop (Steak) 10825 Hermitage Rd	Little Rock	AR	72211	501-312-2748
Cafe Saint Moritz (Continental) 225 E Markham St	Little Rock	AR	72201	501-372-0411
Catfish Young's (Seafood) 1100 E Roosevelt Rd	Little Rock	AR	72206	501-372-7441
China Cafe (Chinese) 418 W 7th St	Little Rock	AR	72201	501-374-8100
Ciao's (Italian) 405 W 7th St	Little Rock	AR	72201	501-372-0238
Dixie Cafe (Homestyle) 1221 Rebsamen Park Rd	Little Rock	AR	72202	501-664-4100
Doe's Eat Place (American) 1023 W Marckham St	Little Rock	AR	72201	501-376-1195
Faded Rose (Steak) 400 N Bowman Rd	Little Rock	AR	72211	501-224-3377
Fu Lin Chinese Restaurant (Chinese) 200 N Bowman Rd	Little Rock	AR	72211	501-225-8989
Josephine's (Continental) 3 Statehouse Plaza	Little Rock	AR	72201	501-375-5000
Juanita's (Mexican) 1300 S Main St	Little Rock	AR	72202	501-372-1228
Julie's (American) 110 S Shackleford Rd	Little Rock	AR	72211	501-224-4501
La Scala (Italian) 2721 Kavanaugh Blvd	Little Rock	AR	72205	501-663-1196
Lam Garden (Chinese) 612 S Center	Little Rock	AR	72201	501-376-7742
Landry's at the Wharf (Seafood) 2400 Cantrell Rd	Little Rock	AR	72202	501-375-5351
Leo's Greek Castle (Greek) 2925 Kavanaugh Blvd	Little Rock	AR	72205	501-666-7414
Loca Luna (Southern) 3519 Old Cantrell Rd	Little Rock	AR	72203	501-663-4666
Oyster Bar (Seafood) 3003 W Markham St	Little Rock	AR	72205	501-666-7100
Restaurant 1620 (American) 1620 Market St.	West Little Rock	AR	72212	501-221-1620
Slick Willy's (American) 1400 W Markham St.	Little Rock	AR	72201	501-372-5505
Star of India (Indian) 301 N Shackleford Rd	West Little Rock	AR	72211	501-227-9900
Town Pump (American) 1321 Rebsamen Park Rd	Little Rock	AR	72202	501-663-9802
Trio's (American) 8201 Cantrell Rd	Little Rock	AR	72227	501-221-3330

— Goods and Services —

SHOPPING

Name / Address	City	State	ZIP	Phone	Fax
Dillard's 1600 Cantrella Rd	Little Rock	AR	72201	501-376-5200	
McCain Mall US 67 & McCain Blvd.	Little Rock	AR	72216	501-758-6340	758-0131
Park Plaza Mall 6000 W Markham St	Little Rock	AR	72205	501-664-4956	666-2115
Web: www.parkplazamall.com					
River Market 400 E Markham St.	Little Rock	AR	72201	501-375-2552	375-5559
University Mall 300 S University Ave	Little Rock	AR	72205	501-664-3724	

BANKS

Name / Address	City	State	ZIP	Phone	Fax
Metropolitan National Bank 111 Center St.	Little Rock	AR	72201	501-377-7600	377-7640
Web: www.metbank.com					
NationsBank 200 W Capitol Ave	Little Rock	AR	72201	501-378-1000	378-1204*
**Fax:* Mktg					
One National Bank 300 W Capitol Ave.	Little Rock	AR	72201	501-370-4400	370-4505
Pulaski Bank & Trust Co 5800 R St	Little Rock	AR	72207	501-661-7700	661-7380*
**Fax:* Mktg					
Regions Bank 400 W Capitol Ave	Little Rock	AR	72201	501-371-7000	371-7413
TF: 800-482-8430					

BUSINESS SERVICES

	Phone
Corporate Express Delivery Systems	501-372-1178
Federal Express	800-463-3339
Interim Personnel Services	501-664-9585
Kelly Services	501-224-0090
Kinko's	501-372-0775
Olsten Staffing Services	501-954-7000
Post Office	501-375-1712
Snelling Personnel Services	501-223-3753
UPS	800-742-5877

— Media —

PUBLICATIONS

Name / Address	City	State	ZIP	Phone	Fax
Arkansas Business Journal PO Box 3686	Little Rock	AR	72203	501-372-1443	375-0933
Web: www.abnews.com/					
Arkansas Democrat-Gazette‡ PO Box 2221	Little Rock	AR	72203	501-378-3400	372-3908*
**Fax:* News Rm ■ *TF Cust Svc:* 800-482-1121 ■ *Web:* www.ardemgaz.com ■ *E-mail:* news@arkdg.com					

‡Daily newspapers

TELEVISION

Name / Address	City	State	ZIP	Phone	Fax
KARK-TV Ch 4 (NBC) 201 W 3rd St	Little Rock	AR	72201	501-340-4444	375-1961
Web: www.kark.com ■ *E-mail:* news4@kark.com					
KATV-TV Ch 7 (ABC) 401 S Main St PO Box 77	Little Rock	AR	72201	501-372-7777	324-7852*
**Fax:* News Rm ■ *Web:* www.katv.com ■ *E-mail:* tv7@katv.com					
KETS-TV Ch 2 (PBS) 350 S Donaghey St.	Conway	AR	72032	501-682-2386	
KLRT-TV Ch 16 (Fox) 11711 W Markham St	Little Rock	AR	72211	501-225-0016	225-0428
Web: www.klrt.com					
KTHV-TV Ch 11 (CBS) PO Box 269	Little Rock	AR	72203	501-376-1111	376-1645

RADIO

Name / Address	City	State	ZIP	Phone	Fax
KABF-FM 88.3 MHz (Misc) 2101 S Main St	Little Rock	AR	72206	501-372-6119	376-3952
KARN-AM 920 kHz (N/T) 4021 W 8th St	Little Rock	AR	72204	501-661-7500	661-7519*
**Fax:* News Rm ■ *E-mail:* newsradio@karn.com					
KDDK-FM 106.7 MHz (Ctry) 8114 Cantrell Rd 3rd Fl	Little Rock	AR	72227	501-227-9696	228-9547

Little Rock — Radio (Cont'd)

	City	State	Zip	Phone	Fax
KDRE-FM 101.1 MHz (B/EZ) 1 Shackleford Dr Suite 400	Little Rock	AR	72211	501-219-2400	221-3955
KHTE-FM 106.3 MHz (CHR) 1 Shackleford Dr Suite 400	Little Rock	AR	72211	501-219-2400	221-3955
KIPR-FM 92.3 MHz (Urban) 415 N McKinley Suite 920	Little Rock	AR	72205	501-663-0092	664-9201
KITA-AM 1440 kHz (Rel) 723 W 14th St	Little Rock	AR	72202	501-375-1440	375-0947
KKPT-FM 94.1 MHz (CR) 2400 Cottondale Ln	Little Rock	AR	72202	501-664-9410	664-5871
Web: www.kkpt.com					
KLAL-FM 107.7 MHz (Alt) 415 N McKinley Suite 920	Little Rock	AR	72202	501-663-0092	664-6524
KLEC-FM 96.5 MHz (AC) 1 Shackleford Dr Suite 400	Little Rock	AR	72211	501-219-2400	221-3955
KLIH-AM 1250 kHz (Rel) 1429 Merrill Dr	Little Rock	AR	72211	501-221-0100	221-1293
KOKY-FM 94.9 MHz (Urban) 415 N McKinley Suite 920	Little Rock	AR	72205	501-663-0092	664-9201
KOLL-FM 94.9 MHz (Oldies) 8114 Cantrell Rd 3rd Fl	Little Rock	AR	72227	501-227-9696	228-9547
KSSN-FM 95.7 MHz (Ctry) 8114 Cantrell Rd	Little Rock	AR	72227	501-227-9696	228-9547
Web: www.kssn.com/					
KSYG-FM 103.7 MHz (N/T) 2400 Cottondale Ln	Little Rock	AR	72202	501-661-1037	664-5871
Web: www.ksyg.com					
KUAR-FM 89.1 MHz (NPR) 2801 S University Ave	Little Rock	AR	72204	501-569-8485	569-8488
Web: www.ualr.edu/~kuar/ ■ *E-mail:* kuar@ualr.edu					
KURB-FM 98.5 MHz (AC) 1429 Merrill Dr	Little Rock	AR	72211	501-221-0100	221-1293
Web: www.b98.com					
KVLO-FM 102.9 MHz (AC) 1429 Merrill Dr	Little Rock	AR	72211	501-221-0100	221-1293
Web: www.k-love.com					
KYFX-FM 99.5 MHz (Urban) 415 N McKinley St Suite 610	Little Rock	AR	72205	501-666-9499	666-9699

— Colleges/Universities —

	City	State	Zip	Phone	Fax
Arkansas Baptist College 1600 Bishop St	Little Rock	AR	72202	501-374-7856	372-0321
Philander Smith College 812 W 13th St	Little Rock	AR	72202	501-375-9845	370-5225
TF: 800-446-6772 ■ *Web:* www.philander.edu					
Shorter College 604 N Locust St	North Little Rock	AR	72114	501-374-6305	374-9333
University of Arkansas Little Rock 2801 S University Ave	Little Rock	AR	72204	501-569-3000	569-8956
Web: www.ualr.edu					
University of Central Arkansas 201 Donaghey Ave	Conway	AR	72035	501-450-5000	450-5228
TF: 800-243-8245 ■ *Web:* www.uca.edu ■ *E-mail:* admission@ecom.uca.edu					

— Hospitals —

	City	State	Zip	Phone	Fax
Arkansas Children's Hospital 800 Marshall St	Little Rock	AR	72202	501-320-1100	320-4777
Web: www.ach.uams.edu					
Baptist Medical Center 9601 I-630 Exit 7	Little Rock	AR	72205	501-202-2000	202-1159
Baptist Memorial Medical Center 1 Pershing Cir	North Little Rock	AR	72114	501-202-3000	202-3489
Saint Vincent Doctors Hospital 6101 St Vincent Cir	Little Rock	AR	72205	501-661-4000	661-3959
TF: 800-265-8624					
Saint Vincent Health Systems 2 St Vincent Cir	Little Rock	AR	72205	501-660-3000	660-2329
Southwest Hospital 11401 I-30	Little Rock	AR	72209	501-455-7100	455-7286
University of Arkansas for Medical Sciences 4301 W Markham St	Little Rock	AR	72205	501-686-7000	686-8365
Web: www.uams.edu					
Veterans Affairs Medical Center 4300 W 7th St	Little Rock	AR	72205	501-257-1000	257-5404

— Attractions —

	City	State	Zip	Phone	Fax
Arkansas Arts Center 501 E 9th St	Little Rock	AR	72202	501-372-4000	375-8053
Arkansas Museum of Discovery 500 E Markham St Suite 150	Little Rock	AR	72201	501-396-7050	396-7054
Web: www.amod.org ■ *E-mail:* mod@aristotle.net					
Arkansas Repertory Theater 601 Main	Little Rock	AR	72203	501-378-0405	378-0012
Arkansas State Capitol Capitol Ave & Woodlane Dr	Little Rock	AR	72201	501-682-5080	
Arkansas Symphony Orchestra PO Box 7328	Little Rock	AR	72217	501-666-1761	666-3193
Arkansas Territorial Restoration 200 E 3rd St	Little Rock	AR	72201	501-324-9351	324-9345
Web: www.heritage.state.ar.us/atr/her_atr.html ■ *E-mail:* info@dah.state.ar.us					
Ballet Arkansas PO Box 7574	Little Rock	AR	72217	501-664-0833	
Breckling Julius Riverfront Park Cumberland & LaHarpe Sts	Little Rock	AR	72201	501-371-4770	
Central High Museum Visitor Center 2125 W 14th St	Little Rock	AR	72202	501-374-1957	376-4728
Children's Museum of Arkansas 1400 W Markham St Suite 200	Little Rock	AR	72201	501-374-6655	374-4746
Web: www.aristotle.net/kidsonline/					
Community Theater of Little Rock 13401 Chenal Pkwy Capital Keyboard Theatre	Little Rock	AR	72211	501-663-9494	
Decorative Arts Museum 411 E 7th St	Little Rock	AR	72202	501-396-0357	
Hillcrest Historic District Kavanaugh & Beechwood Sts	Little Rock	AR	72201	501-376-4781	
Web: www.hillcrest-lr.org/					
IMAX Theater 3301 E Roosevelt Rd	Little Rock	AR	72206	501-376-4629	244-4906
Web: www.aerospaced.org					
Julius Breckling Park Laharpe/Cantrell & Markham St	Little Rock	AR	72201	501-375-2552	
Little Rock Zoo 1 Jonesboro Dr	Little Rock	AR	72205	501-666-2406	666-7040
Web: www.littlerockzoo.com					
MacArthur Park 9th St & Commerce	Little Rock	AR	72202	501-371-4770	
Old Mill Lakeshore Dr & Fairway Ave	North Little Rock	AR	72216	501-791-8537	
Old State House 300 W Markham St	Little Rock	AR	72201	501-324-9685	324-9688
Web: www.heritage.state.ar.us/acc/index.html					
Opera Theatre at Wildwood 20919 Denny Rd	Little Rock	AR	72223	501-821-7275	821-7280
TF: 888-278-7727 ■ *Web:* www.wildwoodpark.org ■ *E-mail:* parkinfo@wildwoodpark.org					
Pinnacle Mountain State Park 11901 Pinnacle Valley Rd	Roland	AR	72135	501-868-5806	868-5018
Quapaw Quarter 1315 S Scott St	Little Rock	AR	72202	501-371-0075	374-8142
Riverfront Park Riverfront Dr	North Little Rock	AR	72114	501-758-1424	
Robinson Center Markham & Broadway Sts 7 Statehouse Plaza	Little Rock	AR	72201	501-376-4781	374-2255
Web: www.littlerock.com/facilities/robinson.html					
Spirit Riverboat Excursions PO Box 579	North Little Rock	AR	72114	501-376-4150	
Toltec Mounds State Park 490 Toltec Mounds Rd	Scott	AR	72142	501-961-9442	
University of Arkansas at Little Rock Planetarium 2801 S University Ave	Little Rock	AR	72204	501-569-3259	569-3314
Web: www.planetarium.ualr.edu					
University of Arkansas Little Rock Gallery 2801 S University Ave	Little Rock	AR	72204	501-569-3183	569-8775
Villa Marre 1321 S Scott St	Little Rock	AR	72202	501-371-0075	374-8142
War Memorial Park Markham Rd & Fair Pk	Little Rock	AR	72201	501-371-4770	
Wild River Country Water Park 6820 Crystal Hill Rd	North Little Rock	AR	72118	501-753-8600	753-0277
Wildwood Park for the Performing Arts 20919 Denny Rd	Little Rock	AR	72223	501-821-7275	821-7280
TF: 888-278-7727 ■ *Web:* www.wildwoodpark.org ■ *E-mail:* parkinfo@wildwoodpark.org					

SPORTS TEAMS & FACILITIES

	City	State	Zip	Phone	Fax
Arkansas Travelers (baseball) War Memorial Pk Ray Winder Field	Little Rock	AR	72205	501-664-1555	664-1834
Web: www.travs.com ■ *E-mail:* travs@travs.com					
Barton Coliseum 2600 Roosevelt Rd	Little Rock	AR	72216	501-372-8341	372-4197
Web: www.arkfairgrounds.com ■ *E-mail:* arkfair@alltell.net					
War Memorial Stadium Markham & Fair Park	Little Rock	AR	72205	501-663-6385	663-6387

— Events —

	Phone
Arkansas Flower & Garden Show (mid-February)	501-821-4000
Arkansas Holiday Light Up & Laser Show (late November-late December)	800-844-4781
Arkansas Marine Expo (mid-January)	501-455-1001
Arkansas River Blues Festival (mid-September)	501-376-4781
Arkansas State Fair (early October)	501-372-8341

Little Rock — Events (Cont'd)

	Phone
Arkansas Territorial Restoration Arts & Crafts Festival (early May)	501-376-4781
Burns Park Arts & Crafts Fair (mid-September)	800-844-4781
Christmas Showcase Arkansas (early December)	501-376-4781
Decorative Arts Forum (mid-March)	501-372-4000
Depression Glass Show & Sale (late February-early March)	501-375-0435
Eagle Awareness Days (early February)	501-727-5441
Eagle Watch Barge Tours (mid-January)	501-868-5806
Festival of Trees (early December)	501-664-8573
Great Southern Gun Show (late-January)	888-325-4482
Greater Little Rock Flower & Garden Show (late February)	501-376-4781
Holiday House (mid-November)	501-666-0658
Juneteenth Celebration (mid-June)	501-376-4781
King Holiday Celebration (mid-January)	501-324-9333
Pops On The River (July 4)	501-376-4781
Quapaw Quarter Spring Tour of Homes (early May)	501-376-4781
Riverfest (late May)	501-376-4781
Summer Shakespeare Festival (mid-late August)	501-376-4781
Summerset (early September)	501-758-1424
Timberfest (early October)	870-942-3021
Toadsuck Daze (early May)	501-376-4781
Toughman Contest (early March)	501-376-4781
Wildwood Festival of Music & the Arts (late May-late June)	501-821-7275
Wildwood International Children's Festival (mid-October)	501-376-4781
Wildwood Jazz Festival (early June)	501-821-7275
Zoo Days (mid-late August)	501-666-2406
Zoo Lights (early December)	501-666-2406

California

Population (1999): 33,145,121 **Area (sq mi): 163,707**

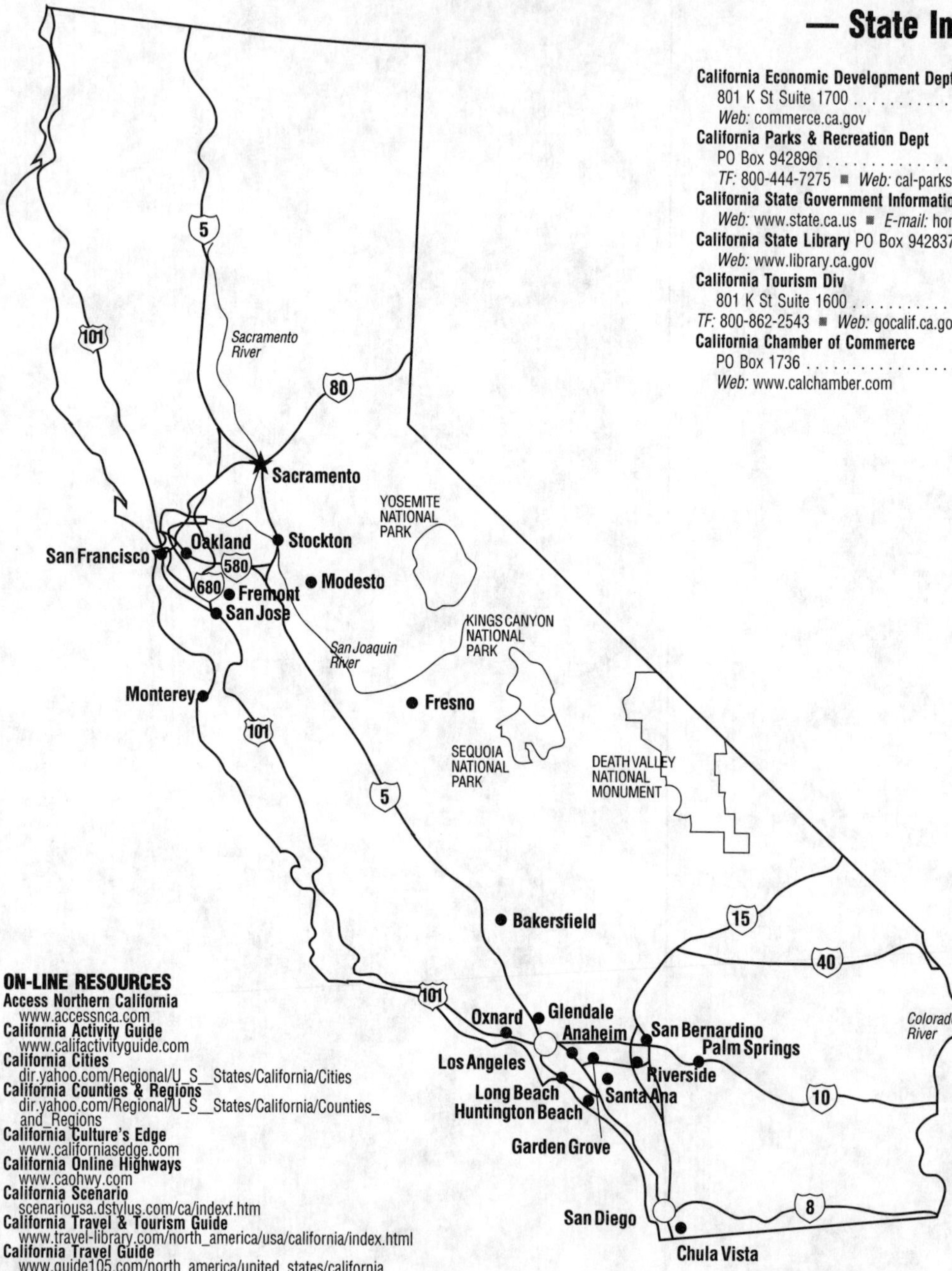

— State Information Sources —

				Phone	Fax
California Economic Development Dept					
801 K St Suite 1700	Sacramento	CA	95814	916-322-1394	322-3524
Web: commerce.ca.gov					
California Parks & Recreation Dept					
PO Box 942896	Sacramento	CA	94296	916-653-1570	657-3903
TF: 800-444-7275 ■ *Web:* cal-parks.ca.gov					
California State Government Information				916-657-9900	
Web: www.state.ca.us ■ *E-mail:* hometeam@library.ca.gov					
California State Library PO Box 942837	Sacramento	CA	94237	916-654-0261	654-0241
Web: www.library.ca.gov					
California Tourism Div					
801 K St Suite 1600	Sacramento	CA	95814	916-322-2881	322-3402
TF: 800-862-2543 ■ *Web:* gocalif.ca.gov ■ *E-mail:* caltour@commerce.ca.gov					
California Chamber of Commerce					
PO Box 1736	Sacramento	CA	95812	916-444-6670	444-6685
Web: www.calchamber.com					

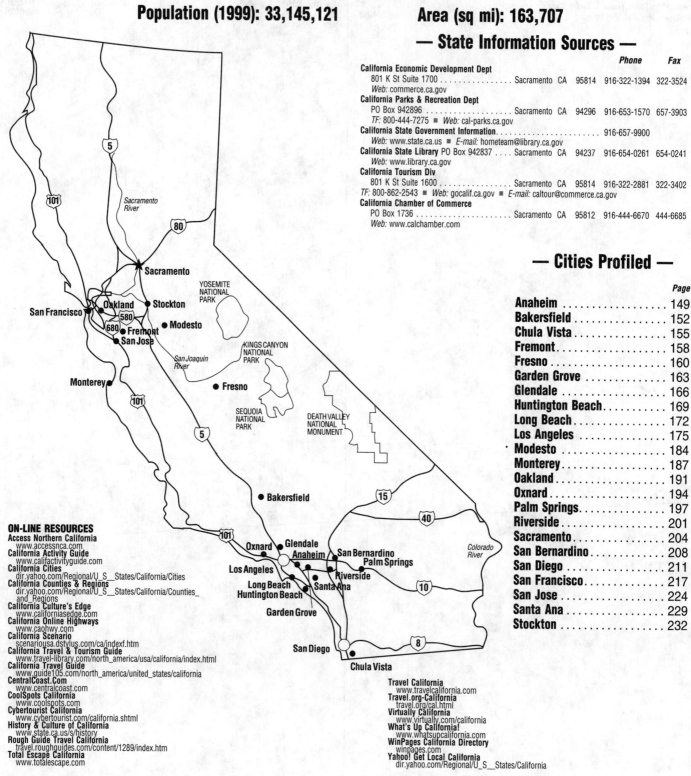

— Cities Profiled —

ON-LINE RESOURCES

Access Northern California
www.accessnca.com
California Activity Guide
www.califactivityguide.com
California Cities
dir.yahoo.com/Regional/U_S__States/California/Cities
California Counties & Regions
dir.yahoo.com/Regional/U_S__States/California/Counties_and_Regions
California Culture's Edge
www.californiasedge.com
California Online Highways
www.caohwy.com
California Scenario
scenariousa.dstylus.com/ca/indexf.htm
California Travel & Tourism Guide
www.travel-library.com/north_america/usa/california/index.html
California Travel Guide
www.guide105.com/north_america/united_states/california
CentralCoast.Com
www.centralcoast.com
CoolSpots California
www.coolspots.com
Cybertourist California
www.cybertourist.com/california.shtml
History & Culture of California
www.state.ca.us/s/history
Rough Guide Travel California
travel.roughguides.com/content/1289/index.htm
Total Escape California
www.totalescape.com
Travel California
www.travelcalifornia.com
Travel.org-California
travel.org/cal.html
Virtually California
www.virtually.com/california
What's Up California!
www.whatsupcalifornia.com
WinPages California Directory
winpages.com
Yahoo! Get Local California
dir.yahoo.com/Regional/U_S__States/California

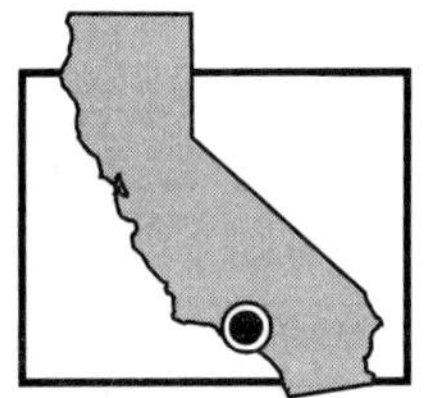

Anaheim

The oldest city in Orange County, Anaheim, which means "home by the river," was named by the city's early German settlers because of its proximity to the Santa Ana River. The city was originally an agricultural community, and was the original home of the Southern California Fruit Exchange, which later became known as SunKist. Anaheim's economic focus shifted from agriculture to tourism in 1955 when Walt Disney opened his Magic Kingdom theme park, which was later renamed Disneyland. Today, Anaheim is not only a top tourist destination, but it's also a top convention destination. The city hosts nearly one million convention delegates each year at the Anaheim Convention Center, the largest convention center on the West Coast. Anaheim is also home to the Anaheim Angels baseball team and the Anaheim Mighty Ducks pro hockey team.

Population	295,153	**Longitude**	117-52-20 W
Area (Land)	44.3 sq mi	**County**	Orange
Area (Water)	1.5 sq mi	**Time Zone**	PST
Elevation	160 ft	**Area Code/s**	714
Latitude	33-50-20 N		

— Average Temperatures and Precipitation —

TEMPERATURES

	Jan	Feb	Mar	Apr	May	Jun	Jul	Aug	Sep	Oct	Nov	Dec
High	69	70	70	73	74	78	83	84	83	80	74	69
Low	46	47	49	51	56	59	63	64	62	58	50	45

PRECIPITATION

	Jan	Feb	Mar	Apr	May	Jun	Jul	Aug	Sep	Oct	Nov	Dec
Inches	2.5	2.3	2.2	0.8	0.2	0.1	0.0	0.1	0.4	0.3	1.7	1.8

— Important Phone Numbers —

	Phone		*Phone*
AAA	714-921-2850	**Medical Referral**	800-318-4953
Emergency	911	**Poison Control Center**	800-876-4766
HotelDocs	800-468-3537	**Weather**	858-675-8706

— Information Sources —

				Phone	*Fax*
Anaheim Chamber of Commerce 100 S Anaheim Blvd Suite 300	Anaheim	CA	92805	714-758-0222	758-0468
Anaheim City Hall 200 S Anaheim Blvd *Web:* www.anaheim.net	Anaheim	CA	92805	714-765-5247	765-5164
Anaheim Convention Center 800 W Katella Ave	Anaheim	CA	92802	714-999-8950	999-8965
Anaheim Mayor 200 S Anaheim Blvd 7th Fl	Anaheim	CA	92805	714-765-5247	765-5164
Anaheim Planning Dept 200 S Anaheim Blvd Suite 162 *Web:* www.anaheim.net/depts_servc/planning	Anaheim	CA	92805	714-765-5139	765-5280
Anaheim Public Library 500 W Broadway *Web:* www.anaheim.net/comm_svc/apl	Anaheim	CA	92805	714-765-1880	765-1730
Anaheim/Orange County Visitor & Convention Bureau 800 W Katella Ave *Web:* www.anaheimoc.org ■ *E-mail:* mail@anaheimoc.org	Anaheim	CA	92802	714-999-8999	991-8963
Better Business Bureau Serving Placentia 550 W Orangethorpe Ave *Web:* www.la.bbb.org	Placentia	CA	92870	714-985-8900	985-8920
Orange County 12 Civic Center Plaza *Web:* www.oc.ca.gov	Santa Ana	CA	92701	714-834-2500	834-2675

On-Line Resources

4OrangeCounty.com	www.4orangecounty.com
Anaheim CityLink	www.usacitylink.com/citylink/anaheim
Annual Guide for the Arts	www.guide4arts.com/oc/
Anthill City Guide Anaheim	www.anthill.com/city.asp?city=anaheim
Area Guide Anaheim	anaheim.areaguides.net
City Knowledge Anaheim	www.cityknowledge.com/ca_anaheim.htm
Excite.com Anaheim City Guide	www.excite.com/travel/countries/united_states/california/anaheim
Focus: Orange County	www.focusoc.com
HotelGuide Anaheim	hotelguide.net/anaheim/

— Transportation Services —

AIRPORTS

■ **John Wayne Airport/Orange County (SNA)** — *Phone*

12 miles S of downtown Anaheim (approx 25 minutes) .949-252-5200
Web: www.ocair.com

Airport Transportation

	Phone
Airport Bus $10 fare to downtown Anaheim	714-938-8900
Express Airport Shuttle $10 fare to downtown Anaheim	800-606-7433
LAXpress Airport Shuttle $20 fare to downtown Anaheim	800-427-7483
SuperShuttle $10 fare to downtown Anaheim	714-517-6600

Commercial Airlines

	Phone		*Phone*
Alaska	800-426-0333	**Northwest**	800-225-2525
America West	800-235-9292	**SkyWest**	800-453-9417
American	800-433-7300	**Southwest**	800-435-9792
American Eagle	800-433-7300	**TWA**	800-221-2000
Continental	800-525-0280	**United Express**	800-241-6522
Delta	800-221-1212	**US Airways**	800-428-4322
Delta Connection	800-221-1212	**US Airways Express**	800-428-4322

Charter Airlines

	Phone		*Phone*
Alliance Executive Charter Services	800-232-5387	**Lenair Aviation Inc**	949-756-8546
Ari Worldwide Aircraft Charters	800-426-9110	**Regency Air LLC**	714-541-3932
Avjet Corp	800-342-8538	**Schubach Aviation**	800-214-8215
Clay Lacy Aviation Inc	800-423-2904	**Signature Flight Support**	949-263-5800
Combs Executive Charter	800-627-8465	**Sunbird Aviation LLC**	800-434-5150
Corporate America Aviation Inc	800-521-8585	**TWC Aviation**	888-892-0035
Helistream	714-662-3163	**West Coast Charter**	949-852-8340

■ **Los Angeles International Airport (LAX)** — *Phone*

40 miles W of downtown Anaheim (approx 50 minutes) .310-646-5252
Web: www.lax2015.org

Airport Transportation

	Phone
Airport Bus $14 fare to downtown Anaheim	714-938-8900
Express Airport Shuttle $12 fare to downtown Anaheim	800-606-7433
LAXpress Airport Shuttle $30 fare to downtown Anaheim	800-427-7483
Prime Time $12 fare to downtown Anaheim	800-262-7433

Commercial Airlines

	Phone		*Phone*
AccessAir	877-462-2237	**Korean Air**	800-438-5000
Aerolineas Argentinas	800-333-0276	**LACSA**	213-385-9424
Air Canada	800-776-3000	**LTU International**	800-888-0200
Air Jamaica	800-523-5585	**Lufthansa**	800-645-3880
Air New Zealand	310-615-1111	**Malaysia Airlines**	800-552-9264
Alitalia	800-223-5730	**Mexicana**	800-531-7923
All Nippon Airways	310-782-3000	**Midwest Express**	800-452-2022
America West	800-235-9292	**National**	888-757-5387
American	800-433-7300	**Northwest**	800-225-2525
American Eagle	800-433-7300	**Pan Am**	800-359-7262
Avianca	800-284-2622	**Philippine**	800-435-9725
British Airways	800-247-9297	**Qantas**	800-227-4500
China Airlines	310-641-8888	**Scandinavian**	800-221-2350
China Eastern	626-583-1500	**Shuttle by United**	800-748-8853
Continental	800-525-0280	**SkyWest**	800-453-9417
Delta	213-386-5510	**Southwest**	800-435-9792
El Al	800-223-6700	**TACA International**	800-535-8780
Hawaiian	310-215-1866	**TWA**	800-221-2000
Iberia	800-772-4642	**United**	800-241-6522
Island Express	562-436-2012	**United Express**	800-241-6522
Japan	800-525-3663	**Varig Brazilian**	310-646-2190
KLM	800-374-7747	**Virgin Atlantic**	800-862-8621

Anaheim (Cont'd)

Charter Airlines

	Phone		Phone
Universal Jet	310-399-7371	**West Coast Charter**	949-852-8340

CAR RENTALS

	Phone		Phone
Alamo	800-327-9633	**Enterprise**	714-991-7195
Avis	714-774-3455	**Hertz**	714-772-0425
Budget	800-221-1203	**Select**	714-740-2212
Dollar	714-750-2886		

LIMO/TAXI

	Phone		Phone
A Taxi Cab	714-547-8000	**Service**	949-496-6332
Best Transportation	714-557-2274	**VIP Coastal Transportation**	800-735-7535
Fox Limousine	800-274-4369	**Yellow Cab**	714-535-2211
Midnight Express/Limousine & Messenger			

MASS TRANSIT

	Phone
Metrolink $3.75 Base fare	714-808-5465
MTA Bus $1.35 Base fare	213-626-4455
OCTA Bus $1 Base fare	714-636-7433

RAIL/BUS

				Phone
Amtrak Station 2150 E Katella Ave *TF:* 800-872-7245	Anaheim	CA	92806	714-385-1448
Greyhound Bus Station 100 W Winston Rd *TF:* 800-231-2222	Anaheim	CA	92805	714-999-1256

— Accommodations —

HOTEL RESERVATION SERVICES

	Phone	Fax
Hotel Reservations Network Inc *TF Sales:* 800-964-6835 ■ *Web:* www.hoteldiscount.com	214-361-7311	361-7299
National Reservation Bureau *TF:* 800-831-2754 ■ *E-mail:* hotelrez@nrbinc.com	702-794-2820	794-3515
USA Hotels *TF:* 800-872-4683 ■ *Web:* www.1800usahotels.com ■ *E-mail:* info@1800usahotels.com	252-331-1555	331-2021

HOTELS, MOTELS, RESORTS

				Phone	Fax
Anaheim Carriage Inn 2125 S Harbor Blvd *TF:* 800-345-2131	Anaheim	CA	92802	714-740-1440	971-5330
Anaheim Desert Palm Inn & Suites 631 W Katella Ave. *TF:* 800-635-5423	Anaheim	CA	92802	714-535-1133	491-7409
Anaheim Hilton & Towers 777 W Convention Way *TF:* 800-222-9923	Anaheim	CA	92802	714-750-4321	740-4460
Anaheim Marriott Hotel 700 W Convention Way *TF:* 800-228-9290	Anaheim	CA	92802	714-750-8000	750-9100
Anaheim Plaza Hotel 1700 S Harbor Blvd *TF:* 800-228-1357	Anaheim	CA	92802	714-772-5900	772-8386
Best Western Anaheim Inn 1630 S Harbor Blvd. *TF:* 800-854-8175	Anaheim	CA	92802	714-774-1050	776-6305
Best Western Courtesy Inn 1200 S West St. *TF:* 800-233-8062	Anaheim	CA	92802	714-772-2470	774-3425
Best Western Park Place Inn 1544 S Harbor Blvd. *TF:* 800-854-8175	Anaheim	CA	92802	714-776-4800	758-1396
Best Western Raffles Inn & Suites 2040 S Harbor Blvd. *TF:* 800-654-0196	Anaheim	CA	92802	714-750-6100	740-0639
Best Western Stovall's Inn 1110 W Katella Ave. *TF:* 800-854-8175	Anaheim	CA	92802	714-778-1880	778-3805
Carousel Inn & Suites 1530 S Harbor Blvd *TF:* 800-854-6767	Anaheim	CA	92802	714-758-0444	772-9960
Castle Inn & Suites 1734 S Harbor Blvd *TF:* 800-521-5653	Anaheim	CA	92802	714-774-8111	956-4736
Comfort Inn & Suites 300 E Katella Way *TF:* 800-228-5150	Anaheim	CA	92802	714-772-8713	778-1235
Comfort Inn Maingate 2200 S Harbor Blvd *TF:* 800-479-5210	Anaheim	CA	92802	714-750-5211	750-2226
Comfort Park Suites 2141 S Harbor Blvd. *TF:* 800-526-9444	Anaheim	CA	92802	714-971-3553	971-4609
Conestoga Hotel 1240 S Walnut St. *TF:* 800-504-7687	Anaheim	CA	92802	714-535-0300	491-8953
Days Inn Maingate 1604 S Harbor Blvd. *TF:* 800-624-3940	Anaheim	CA	92802	714-635-3630	520-3290
Disneyland Hotel 1150 W Cerritos Ave *Web:* disney.go.com/Disneyland/plan/resort_hotels/disneyland_hotel.html	Anaheim	CA	92802	714-778-6600	956-6597
Disneyland Pacific Hotel 1717 S West St *TF:* 800-821-8976 ■ *Web:* disney.go.com/Disneyland/plan/resort_hotels/disneyland_pacific_hotel.html	Anaheim	CA	92802	714-999-0990	776-5763
Embassy Suites 3100 E Frontera St *TF:* 800-362-2779	Anaheim	CA	92806	714-632-1221	632-9963
Fairfield Inn 1460 S Harbor Blvd *Web:* fairfieldinn.com/LAXOC	Anaheim	CA	92802	714-772-6777	999-1727
Four Points Sheraton 1500 S Raymond Ave. *TF:* 800-325-3535	Fullerton	CA	92831	714-635-9000	520-5831
Hanford Hotel 201 N Via Cortez *TF:* 800-324-9909	Anaheim	CA	92807	714-921-1100	637-8790
Hawthorn Suites Hotel 1752 S Clementine St *TF:* 800-992-4884	Anaheim	CA	92802	714-535-7773	776-9073
Holiday Inn Anaheim at the Park 1221 S Harbor Blvd. *TF:* 800-545-7275 ■ *Web:* www.basshotels.com/holiday-inn/?_franchisee=LAXAE ■ *E-mail:* laxae@aol.com	Anaheim	CA	92805	714-758-0900	533-1804
Holiday Inn Express Anaheim 435 W Katella Ave. *TF:* 800-833-7888	Anaheim	CA	92802	714-772-7755	772-2727
Howard Johnson Hotel 1380 S Harbor Blvd *TF:* 800-422-4228	Anaheim	CA	92802	714-776-6120	533-3578
Jolly Roger Hotel 640 W Katella Ave. *TF:* 800-446-1555	Anaheim	CA	92802	714-772-7621	635-2262
Knotts Buena Park Hotel 7675 Crescent Ave **Fax:* Resv ■ *TF:* 800-422-4444	Buena Park	CA	90620	714-995-1111	828-8590*
Park Inn International 1520 S Harbor Blvd *TF:* 800-828-4898	Anaheim	CA	92802	714-635-7275	635-7276
Peacock Suites Hotel 1745 S Anaheim Blvd. *TF:* 800-522-6401	Anaheim	CA	92805	714-535-8255	535-8914
Quality Hotel Maingate 616 Convention Way *TF:* 800-231-6215	Anaheim	CA	92802	714-750-3131	750-9027
Radisson Hotel 1850 S Harbor Blvd *TF:* 800-333-3333	Anaheim	CA	92802	714-750-2801	971-4754
Ramada Limited 921 S Harbor Blvd *TF:* 800-235-3399	Anaheim	CA	92805	714-999-0684	956-8839
Ramada Maingate Saga Inn 1650 S Harbor Blvd. *TF:* 800-854-6097	Anaheim	CA	92802	714-772-0440	991-8219
Residence Inn by Marriott Anaheim 1700 S Clementine St *TF:* 800-331-3131 ■ *Web:* www.residenceinn.com/SNAAH	Anaheim	CA	92802	714-533-3555	535-7626
Rodeway Inn Anaheim 1030 W Ball Rd. *TF:* 800-331-0055	Anaheim	CA	92802	714-520-0101	758-9406
Sheraton Anaheim Hotel 1015 W Ball Rd *TF:* 800-331-7251	Anaheim	CA	92802	714-778-1700	535-3889
Super 8 Anaheim Park Motor Inn 915 S West St *TF:* 800-248-4400	Anaheim	CA	92802	714-778-0350	778-3878
Travelodge 7039 Orangethorpe Ave. *TF:* 800-578-7878	Buena Park	CA	90620	714-521-9220	521-6706
Travelodge International Inn & Suites 2060 S Harbor Blvd. *TF:* 800-251-2345	Anaheim	CA	92802	714-971-9393	971-2706
Tropicana Inn 1540 S Harbor Blvd *TF:* 800-828-4898	Anaheim	CA	92802	714-635-4082	635-1535
Westcoast Anaheim 1855 S Harbor Blvd *TF:* 800-426-0670	Anaheim	CA	92802	714-750-1811	971-3626
Whittier Hilton 7320 Greenleaf Ave *TF:* 800-667-4400	Whittier	CA	90602	562-945-8511	945-6018

— Restaurants —

				Phone
Acapulco Mexican Restaurant (Mexican) 1410 S Harbor Blvd	Anaheim	CA	92802	714-956-7380
Anaheim Grill & Sushi Bar (Japanese) 5115 W Katella St	Anaheim	CA	92802	714-971-5112
Ashoka the Great Cuisine of India (Indian) 2632 W La Palma Ave	Anaheim	CA	92801	714-229-8501

Anaheim — Restaurants (Cont'd)

				Phone
Buccaneer Dining Room (American) 640 W Katella Ave	Anaheim	CA	92802	714-772-7621
Cafe Oasis (American) 777 W Convention Way	Anaheim	CA	92802	714-740-4412
Catch The (Seafood) 1929 S State College Blvd	Anaheim	CA	92806	714-634-1829
Cattleman's Wharf (Steak/Seafood) 1160 W Ball Rd	Anaheim	CA	92802	714-535-1622
Charley Brown's (American) 1751 S State College Blvd	Anaheim	CA	92806	714-634-2211
El Torito Restaurant (Mexican) 1801 E Katella Ave	Anaheim	CA	92805	714-634-1888
Foxfire (Continental) 5717 E Santa Ana Canyon Rd	Anaheim	CA	92807	714-974-5400
Granville's Steakhouse (Steak) 1150 W Cerritos Ave	Anaheim	CA	92802	714-956-6402
Gustav's Jaegerhaus (German) 2525 E Ball Rd	Anaheim	CA	92806	714-520-9500
Hansa House Smorgasbord (Scandinavian) 1840 S Harbor Blvd	Anaheim	CA	92802	714-750-2411
Hasting's Grill (California) 777 Convention Way	Anaheim	CA	92802	714-740-4422
Hooks Point (Steak/Seafood) 1150 W Cerritos Ave	Anaheim	CA	92802	714-956-6404
Hungry Hunter Restaurant (Steak/Seafood) 2438 E Katella Ave	Anaheim	CA	92806	714-978-0985
JW's Steakhouse (Steak) 700 W Convention Way	Anaheim	CA	92802	714-750-8000
Keyaki (Japanese) 1717 S West St	Anaheim	CA	92802	714-999-0990
La Casa Garcia (Mexican) 531 W Chapman Ave	Anaheim	CA	92802	714-740-1108
Loreley Restaurant (German) 1340 Sanderson Ave	Anaheim	CA	92806	714-563-4164
Luigi's D'Italia (Italian) 801 S State College Blvd	Anaheim	CA	92806	714-490-0990
Mama Cozza's (Italian) 2170 W Ball Rd	Anaheim	CA	92804	714-635-0063
Mr Stox (Continental) 1105 E Katella	Anaheim	CA	92805	714-634-2994
Overland Stage (American) 1855 S Harbor Blvd	Anaheim	CA	92802	714-750-1811
Pavia (Italian) 777 Convention Way	Anaheim	CA	92802	714-740-4419
PCH Grill (California) 1717 S West St	Anaheim	CA	92802	714-999-0990
Poppy's Cafe (California) 1221 S Harbor Blvd	Anaheim	CA	92805	714-758-0900
Rufino's Ristorante (Italian) 938 S Euclid	Anaheim	CA	92802	714-491-0880
Sushi Bar The (Japanese) 777 Convention Way	Anaheim	CA	92802	714-750-4321
Thee White House (Italian) 887 S Anaheim Blvd	Anaheim	CA	92805	714-772-1381
Wah Sing Chinese Restaurant (Chinese) 575 W Chapman Ave	Anaheim	CA	92802	714-740-1888
Yamabuki (Japanese) 1717 S West St	Anaheim	CA	92802	714-999-0990

— Goods and Services —

SHOPPING

				Phone	Fax
Anaheim Festival 8020 E Santa Ana Canyon Rd	Anaheim	CA	92808	714-283-3535	283-0525
Anaheim Indoor Marketplace 1440 S Anaheim Blvd	Anaheim	CA	92805	714-999-0888	999-0885
Anaheim Plaza 530 N Euclid St	Anaheim	CA	92801	714-635-3431	758-1374
Block at Orange 20 City Blvd W *Web:* www.theblockatorange.com	Orange	CA	92868	714-769-4000	769-4011
Buena Park Mall 8308 On The Mall	Buena Park	CA	90620	714-828-7722	761-0748
Fullerton Metro Center 1301-1577 S Harbor & 104-276 W Orangethorpe	Fullerton	CA	92632	714-427-5977	427-5922
MainPlace Santa Ana 2800 N Main St	Santa Ana	CA	92705	714-547-7000	547-2643
Mall of Orange 2298 N Orange Mall	Orange	CA	92865	714-998-0440	998-6378

BANKS

				Phone	Fax
Bank of America 1701 E Katella Ave	Anaheim	CA	92805	714-778-7207	778-7601
California Federal Bank 610 N Euclid St *Fax Area Code: 714	Anaheim	CA	92801	800-843-2265	776-9627*
California State Bank 721 N Euclid St	Anaheim	CA	92801	714-778-2265	491-0438
California United Bank 100 W Lincoln Ave	Anaheim	CA	92805	714-491-3488	491-3718
Community Bank 1750 S State College Rd	Anaheim	CA	92806	714-634-2265	978-1607
Sanwa Bank California 4501 E La Palma Ave	Anaheim	CA	92807	714-777-9620	777-9562
Southern California Bank 3800 E La Palma Ave	Anaheim	CA	92807	714-630-4500	630-2493
Washington Mutual Bank 910 S Brookhurst St	Anaheim	CA	92804	714-956-4130	956-4135
Wells Fargo Bank 222 S Harbor Blvd	Anaheim	CA	92805	800-869-3557	

BUSINESS SERVICES

	Phone
Adecco Employment Personnel Services	714-935-1991
DHL Worldwide Express	800-225-5345
Federal Express	800-238-5355
Kinko's	714-970-0722
Mail Boxes Etc	714-635-0724
Manpower Temporary Services	714-970-9100
Pacific Couriers Inc	714-278-6151
Post Office	800-275-8777
UPS	800-742-5877

— Media —

PUBLICATIONS

				Phone	Fax
Anaheim Bulletin 1771 S Lewis St *Fax: News Rm	Anaheim	CA	92805	714-634-1567	704-3714*
Fullerton News-Tribune 1771 S Lewis St *Fax: News Rm	Anaheim	CA	92805	714-634-1567	704-3714*
Orange City News 1771 S Lewis St *Fax: News Rm	Anaheim	CA	92805	714-634-1567	704-3714*
Orange County Business Journal 4590 MacArthur Blvd Suite 100	Newport Beach	CA	92660	949-833-8373	833-8751
Orange County Register‡ 625 N Grand Ave *Web:* www.ocregister.com	Santa Ana	CA	92701	714-835-1234	565-3681
Yorba Linda Star 1771 S Lewis St	Anaheim	CA	92805	714-634-1567	704-3714

‡*Daily newspapers*

TELEVISION

				Phone	Fax
KABC-TV Ch 7 (ABC) 4151 Prospect Ave *Web:* abcnews.go.com/local/kabc ■ *E-mail:* abc7@abc.com	Los Angeles	CA	90027	310-557-3200	557-3360
KCBS-TV Ch 2 (CBS) 6121 Sunset Blvd *Web:* www.kcbs2.com	Los Angeles	CA	90028	323-460-3000	460-3733
KCET-TV Ch 28 (PBS) 4401 Sunset Blvd *Web:* www.kcet.org	Los Angeles	CA	90027	323-666-6500	953-5523
KNBC-TV Ch 4 (NBC) 3000 W Alameda Ave *Web:* www.knbc4la.com	Burbank	CA	91523	818-840-4444	840-3535
KTTV-TV Ch 11 (Fox) 1999 S Bundy Dr *Web:* www.fox11la.com ■ *E-mail:* talkback@fox11la.com	West Los Angeles	CA	90025	310-584-2000	584-2023

RADIO

				Phone	Fax
KABC-AM 790 kHz (N/T) 3321 S La Cienega Blvd *Web:* www.kabc.com	Los Angeles	CA	90016	310-840-4900	838-5222
KBIG-FM 104.3 MHz (AC) 330 N Brand Blvd Suite 800 *Fax: Sales ■ *Web:* www.kbig104.com	Glendale	CA	91203	818-546-1043	637-2267*
KCBS-FM 93.1 MHz (CR) 6121 Sunset Blvd *Web:* www.arrowfm.com	Los Angeles	CA	90028	323-460-3000	460-3733
KEZY-FM 95.9 MHz (AC) 1190 E Ball Rd	Anaheim	CA	92805	714-776-1190	774-1631
KFWB-AM 980 kHz (N/T) 6230 Yucca St *Web:* www.kfwb.com ■ *E-mail:* quake@kfwb.groupw.wec.com	Hollywood	CA	90028	323-462-5392	871-4670
KHWY-FM 98.9 MHz (AC) 1611 E Main St	Barstow	CA	92311	760-256-0326	256-9507
KIIS-FM 102.7 MHz (CHR) 3400 Riverside Dr Suite 800 *Web:* www.kiisfm.com	Burbank	CA	91505	818-845-1027	295-6466
KLAX-FM 97.9 MHz (Span) 10281 W Pico Blvd *Fax: Sales	Los Angeles	CA	90064	310-203-0900	203-8989*
KLOS-FM 95.5 MHz (Rock) 3321 S La Cienega Blvd *Web:* www.955klos.com	Los Angeles	CA	90016	310-840-4900	558-7685
KNX-AM 1070 kHz (N/T) 6121 Sunset Blvd *Web:* www.knx1070.com	Los Angeles	CA	90028	323-460-3000	460-3275
KORG-AM 1190 kHz (N/T) 1190 E Ball Rd	Anaheim	CA	92805	714-776-1190	774-1631
KOST-FM 103.5 MHz (AC) 610 S Ardmore Ave *TF:* 800-929-5678	Los Angeles	CA	90005	213-427-1035	385-0281
KPWR-FM 105.9 MHz (CHR) 2600 W Olive Ave Suite 850	Burbank	CA	91505	818-953-4200	848-0961
KRTH-FM 101.1 MHz (Oldies) 5901 Venice Blvd	Los Angeles	CA	90034	323-937-5230	936-3427
KYSR-FM 98.7 MHz (AC) 3500 W Olive Ave Suite 250 *Web:* www.star987.com	Burbank	CA	91505	818-955-7000	955-6436

— Colleges/Universities —

				Phone	Fax
Azusa Pacific University 1915 W Orangewood Ave	Orange	CA	92868	714-935-9697	935-0356
California State University Fullerton 800 N State College Blvd *Web:* www.fullerton.edu	Fullerton	CA	92831	714-278-2011	278-3990
Chapman University 333 N Glassell St *TF:* 800-282-7759 ■ *Web:* www.chapman.edu ■ *E-mail:* low@chapman.edu	Orange	CA	92866	714-997-6815	997-6713

Anaheim — Colleges/Universities (Cont'd)

				Phone	Fax
ITT Technical Institute 525 N Muller Ave. *Web:* www.itt-tech.edu	Anaheim	CA	92801	714-535-3700	535-1802
Keimyung Baylo University 1126 Norris Brookhurst St	Anaheim	CA	92801	714-533-1495	533-6040
National University 765 The City Dr *TF:* 800-628-8648 ■ *Web:* www.nu.edu	Orange	CA	92868	714-429-5300	429-5307

— Hospitals —

				Phone	Fax
Anaheim Memorial Hospital 1111 W La Palma Ave	Anaheim	CA	92801	714-774-1450	999-6122
Kaiser Permanente Hospital 441 N Lakeview Ave *TF:* 800-464-4000	Anaheim	CA	92807	714-279-4000	279-5590
Martin Luther Hospital 1830 W Romneya Dr	Anaheim	CA	92801	714-491-5200	491-5310
West Anaheim Medical Center 3033 W Orange Ave	Anaheim	CA	92804	714-827-3000	229-6813
Western Medical Center Anaheim 1025 S Anaheim Blvd	Anaheim	CA	92805	714-533-6220	563-2839

— Attractions —

				Phone	Fax
Adventure City 1238 S Beach Blvd	Anaheim	CA	92804	714-236-9300	827-2992
Air Combat USA 230 N Dale Pl. *TF:* 800-522-7590 ■ *Web:* www.aircombatusa.com	Fullerton	CA	92833	714-522-7590	522-7592
Anaheim Museum 241 S Anaheim Blvd.	Anaheim	CA	92805	714-778-3301	778-6740
Block at Orange 20 City Blvd W *Web:* www.theblockatorange.com	Orange	CA	92868	714-769-4000	769-4011
Disneyland PO Box 3232 *Web:* disney.go.com/Disneyland	Anaheim	CA	92803	714-781-4565	
Hobby City Doll & Toy Museum 1238 S Beach Blvd	Anaheim	CA	92804	714-527-2323	236-9762
Knott's Berry Farm 8039 Beach Blvd. *Web:* www.knotts.com	Buena Park	CA	90620	714-827-1776	220-5200
Medieval Times Dinner & Tournament 7662 Beach Blvd. *TF:* 800-899-6600 ■ *Web:* www.medievaltimes.com/CA_realm.htm ■ *E-mail:* buenapark@medievaltimes.com	Buena Park	CA	90620	714-521-4740	670-2721
Movieland Wax Museum 7711 Beach Blvd *Web:* www.movielandwaxmuseum.com ■ *E-mail:* sales@waxmuseum.com	Buena Park	CA	90620	714-522-1155	739-9668
Orange County Performing Arts Center 600 Town Ctr Dr. *Web:* www.ocpac.org	Costa Mesa	CA	92626	714-556-2121	556-0156
Plaza Garibaldi Dinner Theater 1490 S Anaheim Blvd	Anaheim	CA	92805	714-758-9014	
Ripley's Believe It or Not! Museum 7850 Beach Blvd. *Web:* www.movielandwaxmuseum.com/rip.html	Buena Park	CA	90620	714-522-1152	739-9668
Wild Bill's Wild West 7600 Beach Blvd. *TF:* 800-883-1546	Buena Park	CA	90620	714-522-6414	521-1176
Yorba Regional Park 7600 E La Palma	Anaheim	CA	92807	714-970-1460	

SPORTS TEAMS & FACILITIES

				Phone	Fax
Anaheim Angels 2000 Gene Autry Way Edison International Field *Web:* www.angelsbaseball.com	Anaheim	CA	92806	714-940-2000	940-2001
Anaheim Bullfrogs (roller hockey) 2695 E Katella Ave Arrowhead Pond *Web:* www.bullfrogs.com ■ *E-mail:* info@bullfrogs.com	Anaheim	CA	92806	626-732-2290	732-3574
Arrowhead Pond of Anaheim 2695 E Katella Ave *Web:* www.arrowheadpond.com	Anaheim	CA	92806	714-704-2400	704-2443
Edison International Field 2000 Gene Autry Way *Web:* www.angelsbaseball.com/edisonfield	Anaheim	CA	92806	714-940-2000	940-2001
Los Alamitos Race Course 4961 Katella Ave. *Web:* www.webworldinc.com/larace/laqhr	Los Alamitos	CA	90720	714-236-4400	
Mighty Ducks of Anaheim 2695 E Katella Ave Arrowhead Pond of Anaheim. *Web:* www.mightyducks.com	Anaheim	CA	92806	714-704-2700	704-2753
Orange County Zodiac (soccer) 602 N Flower St Eddie West Field *Web:* www.oczodiac.com ■ *E-mail:* comments@oczodiac.com	Santa Ana	CA	92701	949-348-4880	348-4601

— Events —

	Phone
Anaheim Harvest Festivals (late October)	707-778-6300
Christmas Fantasy Parade (late November-early January)	714-781-4560
Cinco de Mayo Celebration (early May)	714-765-5274
Fantasy in the Sky (June-September)	714-781-4560
Flying U Rodeo (early February)	714-704-2400
Gogh Van Orange Art & Music Festival (early May)	714-538-3581
Harvest Festival (late October)	714-999-8900
Oktoberfest (mid-September-early November)	714-563-4166
Orange County Art & Jazz Festival (mid-May)	714-541-2787
Orange County Fair (mid-July)	714-708-3247
Southern California Home & Garden Show (mid-late August)	714-978-8888

Bakersfield

The history of Bakersfield dates back to the mid-1800's when the city's founder, Colonel Thomas Baker, planted alfalfa on a parcel of his land for weary travelers to rest and let their animals graze. The discovery of gold in 1851 and oil in 1865 sparked the development of Bakersfield. These discoveries attracted settlers from many different cultures, including French, Basques, Chinese, Italians, Greeks, and Portuguese, all of whom contributed to the development of the city. Agriculture and oil remain the area's largest industries today. The California Living Museum (CALM) in Bakersfield has been described as a combination zoo-botanical garden-natural history museum, offering visitors the opportunity to learn about plants and animals native to California through its exhibits, which include an aviary and a coyote grotto, and educational programs. Recreational opportunities in Bakersfield include whitewater rafting and kayaking on the Kern River and water skiing, windsurfing, and sailing on Ming Lake.

Population	210,284	**Longitude**	119-00-16 W
Area (Land)	91.8 sq mi	**County**	Kern
Area (Water)	1.3 sq mi	**Time Zone**	PST
Elevation	408 ft	**Area Code/s**	661
Latitude	35-21-27 N		

— Average Temperatures and Precipitation —

TEMPERATURES

	Jan	Feb	Mar	Apr	May	Jun	Jul	Aug	Sep	Oct	Nov	Dec
High	57	64	69	76	85	92	99	97	90	81	67	57
Low	39	43	46	50	57	64	70	69	64	55	45	38

PRECIPITATION

	Jan	Feb	Mar	Apr	May	Jun	Jul	Aug	Sep	Oct	Nov	Dec
Inches	0.9	1.1	1.0	0.6	0.2	0.1	0.0	0.1	0.1	0.3	0.7	0.6

— Important Phone Numbers —

	Phone		Phone
AAA	661-327-4661	**HotelDocs**	800-468-3537
American Express Travel	800-528-4800	**Medical Referral**	661-325-9025
Dental Referral	800-336-8478	**Poison Control Center**	800-876-4766
Emergency	911	**Weather**	661-833-8888

Bakersfield (Cont'd)

— Information Sources —

				Phone	Fax
Bakersfield City Hall 1501 Truxtun Ave	Bakersfield	CA	93301	661-326-3751	324-1850
Web: www.ci.bakersfield.ca.us					
Bakersfield Community & Economic Development Dept 515 Truxtun Ave	Bakersfield	CA	93301	661-326-3765	328-1548
E-mail: edcd@ci.bakersfield.ca.us					
Bakersfield Convention Center 1001 Truxtun Ave	Bakersfield	CA	93301	661-852-7300	861-9904
Web: www.centennialgarden.com					
Bakersfield Mayor 1501 Truxtun Ave.	Bakersfield	CA	93301	661-326-3770	326-3779
Web: www.ci.bakersfield.ca.us/administration/index.htm ■ *E-mail:* mayor@ci.bakersfield.ca.us					
Beale Memorial Library 701 Truxtun Ave	Bakersfield	CA	93301	661-868-0701	868-0799
Web: chiba.netxn.com/~kclib/beale.html					
Better Business Bureau Serving the Bakersfield Area 705 18th St.	Bakersfield	CA	93301	661-322-2074	322-8318
Web: www.bakersfield.bbb.org					
Greater Bakersfield Chamber of Commerce 1033 Truxtun Ave	Bakersfield	CA	93301	661-327-4421	327-8751
Web: www.bakersfield.org/chamber ■ *E-mail:* chamber@bakersfield.org					
Greater Bakersfield Convention & Visitors Bureau 1033 Truxtun Ave	Bakersfield	CA	93301	661-325-5051	325-7074
TF: 800-325-6001 ■ *Web:* www.visitbfield.com ■ *E-mail:* gbcvb@visitbfield.com					
Kern County 1115 Truxtun Ave 5th Fl	Bakersfield	CA	93301	661-868-3198	868-3190

On-Line Resources

4Bakersfield.com	www 4bakersfield.com
Anthill City Guide Bakersfield	www.anthill.com/city.asp?city=bakersfield
Area Guide Bakersfield	bakersfield.areaguides.net
Bakersfield Arts & Entertainment Guide	www.aeguide.com
Bakersfield Gateway.com	www.bakersfieldgateway.com
City Knowledge Bakersfield	www.cityknowledge.com/ca_bakersfield.htm
Excite.com Bakersfield City Guide	www.excite.com/travel/countries/united_states/california/bakersfield/
Kern Online	www.kernonline.com

— Transportation Services —

AIRPORTS

■ Meadows Field Airport (BFL)

	Phone
3 miles NW of downtown (approx 12 minutes)	661-393-7990
Web: www.meadowsfield.com	

Airport Transportation

	Phone
Black & White/Yellow Cab $10-11 fare to downtown	661-327-3535
Checker Cab $11 fare to downtown	661-327-5777
Yellow Cab $13 fare to downtown	661-325-5041

Commercial Airlines

	Phone		Phone
American	800-433-7300	**SkyWest**	800-453-9417
American Eagle	800-433-7300	**United Express**	800-241-6522

Charter Airlines

	Phone		Phone
Bakersfield Air Charter	661-393-0937	**Lloyds Aircraft Service**	661-393-1334

CAR RENTALS

	Phone		Phone
Avis	661-392-4160	**Enterprise**	661-833-9483
Budget	661-399-2367	**Hertz**	661-393-2044

LIMO/TAXI

	Phone		Phone
Bakersfield Limousine Service/ETS	661-861-1663	**Latino Cab**	661-323-9114
Black & White/Yellow Cab	661-327-3535	**Limousine Scene**	661-831-7955
Checker Cab	661-327-5777	**National Taxi Cab**	661-327-4006
Cobra's Cab Co	661-325-8294	**Taxi Chicano Cab**	661-323-8555
Jalisco Taxis	661-325-9494	**Taxi Extra Cab Co**	661-323-1815
		Yellow Cab	661-325-5041

MASS TRANSIT

	Phone
GET Bus $.75 Base fare	661-327-7686

RAIL/BUS

				Phone
Amtrak Station 1501 F St	Bakersfield	CA	93301	661-395-3175
TF: 800-972-7245				
Greyhound Bus Station 1820 18th St	Bakersfield	CA	93301	661-327-5617
TF: 800-231-2222				

— Accommodations —

HOTELS, MOTELS, RESORTS

				Phone	Fax
Apple Farm Inn 2015 Monterey St	San Luis Obispo	CA	93401	805-544-2040	546-9495
TF: 800-374-3705					
Best Western Hill House 700 Truxtun Ave.	Bakersfield	CA	93301	661-327-4064	327-1247
TF: 800-528-1234					
Best Western Inn 2620 Pierce Rd	Bakersfield	CA	93308	661-327-9651	334-1820
TF: 800-424-4900					
Best Western Shore Cliff Lodge 2555 Price St	Pismo Beach	CA	93449	805-773-4671	773-2341
TF: 800-441-8885					
California Inn 3400 Chester Ln	Bakersfield	CA	93309	661-328-1100	328-0433
TF: 800-707-8000					
Comfort Inn 2514 White Ln	Bakersfield	CA	93304	661-833-8000	833-3861
TF: 800-228-5150					
Courtyard by Marriott 3601 Marriott Dr	Bakersfield	CA	93308	661-324-6660	324-1185
TF: 800-321-2211 ■ *Web:* courtyard.com/BFLCH					
Days Inn 3540 Rosedale Hwy	Bakersfield	CA	93308	661-326-1111	326-1513
TF: 800-329-7466					
Doubletree Hotel Bakersfield 3100 Camino Del Rio Ct	Bakersfield	CA	93308	661-323-7111	323-0331
TF: 800-222-8733 ■ *Web:* www.doubletreehotels.com/DoubleT/Hotel141/154/154Main.htm					
Downtowner Inn Motel 1301 Chester Ave	Bakersfield	CA	93301	661-327-7122	327-8350
Extended StayAmerica 3318 California Ave	Bakersfield	CA	93304	661-322-6888	322-3969
TF: 800-398-7829					
Garden Suites Inn 2310 Wible Rd	Bakersfield	CA	93304	661-833-6066	397-5464
Hampton Inn Bakersfield 1017 Oak St.	Bakersfield	CA	93304	661-633-0333	633-0669
TF: 800-426-7866					
Holiday Inn Express 4400 Hughes Ln	Bakersfield	CA	93304	661-833-3000	833-3736
TF: 800-636-1626 ■ *Web:* www.holidayinnexpressbak.com					
Holiday Inn Select 801 Truxtun Ave	Bakersfield	CA	93301	661-323-1900	323-2844
TF: 800-465-4329					
Inns of America North 6100 Knudsen Dr	Bakersfield	CA	93308	661-392-1800	392-1612
TF: 800-826-0778					
Inns of America South 6501 Colony St	Bakersfield	CA	93307	661-831-9200	831-0214
TF: 800-826-0778					
La Quinta Inn 3232 Riverside Dr.	Bakersfield	CA	93308	661-325-7400	324-6032
TF: 800-531-5900					
Motel 6 Olive Tree 5241 Olive Tree Ct	Bakersfield	CA	93308	661-392-9700	392-0223
TF: 800-466-8356					
Motel 6 White Lane 2727 White Ln	Bakersfield	CA	93304	661-834-2828	834-3923
TF: 800-466-8356					
Oxford Inn 4500 Buck Owens Blvd	Bakersfield	CA	93308	661-324-5555	325-0106
TF: 800-822-3050					
Parkway Inn 3535 Rosedale Hwy	Bakersfield	CA	93308	661-327-0681	324-1648
TF: 800-803-1335 ■ *E-mail:* parkwayinn@aol.com					
Quality Inn 1011 Oak St.	Bakersfield	CA	93304	661-325-0772	325-4646
TF: 800-228-5151					
Radisson Suites Inn 828 Real Rd	Bakersfield	CA	93309	661-322-9988	322-3668
TF: 800-333-3333					
Residence Inn by Marriott 4241 Chester Ln	Bakersfield	CA	93309	661-321-9800	321-0721
TF: 800-331-3131 ■ *Web:* www.residenceinn.com/BFLRI					
Rio Bravo Resort 11200 Lake Ming Rd	Bakersfield	CA	93306	661-872-5000	871-8998
TF: 888-517-5500 ■ *Web:* www.riobravoresort.com ■ *E-mail:* relax@riobravoresort.com					
Sheraton Inn 5101 California Ave	Bakersfield	CA	93309	661-325-9700	323-3508
TF: 800-325-3535					
Skyway Inn 1305 Skyway Dr	Bakersfield	CA	93308	661-399-9321	399-2615

Bakersfield — Hotels, Motels, Resorts (Cont'd)

				Phone	Fax
Super 8 Motel 901 Real Rd *TF:* 800-800-8000	Bakersfield	CA	93309	661-322-1012	322-7636
Travelodge Hotel 818 Real Rd *TF:* 800-578-7878	Bakersfield	CA	93309	661-324-6666	324-6670

— Restaurants —

				Phone
Akira's (Japanese) 4154 California Ave	Bakersfield	CA	93309	661-326-1860
Arizona Cafe (Mexican) 809 Baker St	Bakersfield	CA	93305	661-324-3866
Barbecue Factory (Barbecue) 3401 Chester Ave	Bakersfield	CA	93301	661-325-3700
Bill Lee's Bamboo Chopsticks (Chinese) 1203 18th St.	Bakersfield	CA	93301	661-324-9441
Bistro The (Continental) 5105 California Ave	Bakersfield	CA	93309	661-323-3905
Bit Of Germany (German) 1901 Flower St.	Bakersfield	CA	93305	661-325-8874
Britannia Restaurant & Pub (English) 5123 Ming Ave	Bakersfield	CA	93309	661-832-8980
Chateau Basque (French) Union Ave & 1st St *Web:* www.chateaubasque.com	Bakersfield	CA	93307	661-325-1316
China Palace (Chinese) 4142 California Ave	Bakersfield	CA	93309	661-326-8202
Chuy's Mesquite Broiler (Mexican) 2500 New Stine Rd	Bakersfield	CA	93309	661-833-3469
Frugatti's (Italian) 600 Coffee Rd	Bakersfield	CA	93309	661-836-2000
Golden Bell Restaurant (Chinese/Vietnamese) 10818 Rosedale Hwy	Bakersfield	CA	93312	661-589-7441
Hungry Hunter (Steak) 3580 Rosedale Hwy	Bakersfield	CA	93308	661-328-0580
Korea Restaurant (Korean) 6401 White Ln	Bakersfield	CA	93309	661-837-0100
Maitia's Basque Cafe(French) 4420 Coffee Rd	Bakersfield	CA	93308	661-587-9055
Mama Tosca's (Italian) 6631 Ming Ave	Bakersfield	CA	93309	661-831-1242
Maxwells (California) 5600 Auburn St	Bakersfield	CA	93306	661-872-5171
Milano's (Mediterranean) 1229 Skyway Dr	Bakersfield	CA	93308	661-399-3300
Mr Tibbs Ribs (Barbecue) 3508 New Stine Rd.	Bakersfield	CA	93309	661-397-4030
Red Pepper (Mexican) 2641 Oswell Ave	Bakersfield	CA	93306	661-871-5787
Rosa's (Italian) 2400 Columbus St.	Bakersfield	CA	93306	661-872-1606
Saigon Restaurant (Vietnamese) 3113 Chester Ln.	Bakersfield	CA	93304	661-327-8810
Shimura's (Japanese) 5141 Ming Ave	Bakersfield	CA	93309	661-831-1529
Sinaloa (Mexican) 910 20th St	Bakersfield	CA	93301	661-327-5231
Stuart Anderson's Black Angus (Steak/Seafood) 3601 Rosedale Hwy	Bakersfield	CA	93308	661-324-0814
Taj Mahal (Indian) 5416 California Ave	Bakersfield	CA	93309	661-633-2222
Tavern by the Green (Steak/Seafood) 6218 Sundale Ave	Bakersfield	CA	93309	661-831-5225
Thai Orchid (Thai) 13001 Stockdale Hwy Suite D-2	Bakersfield	CA	93311	661-588-3419
Uricchio's Trattoria (Italian) 1400 17th St	Bakersfield	CA	93301	661-326-8870
Wool Growers (French) 620 E 19th St	Bakersfield	CA	93305	661-327-9584

— Goods and Services —

SHOPPING

				Phone	Fax
Antique District H St betw Brundage Ln & California Ave	Bakersfield	CA	93309		
East Hills Mall 3000 Mall View Rd Suite 1178	Bakersfield	CA	93306	661-872-7990	872-4046
Valley Plaza Mall 2701 Ming Ave	Bakersfield	CA	93304	661-832-2436	832-4312

BANKS

				Phone	Fax
Bank of America 1440 Truxtun Ave *TF:* 800-338-5202	Bakersfield	CA	93301	661-395-2313	395-2301
Bank of Stockdale 5151 Stockdale Hwy	Bakersfield	CA	93309	661-833-9292	833-9469
California Federal Bank 5554 California Ave Suite 110 **Fax Area Code:* 661	Bakersfield	CA	93309	800-843-2265	323-3513*
San Joaquin Bank 1301 17th St *TF:* 800-281-0315 ■ *Web:* www.sjbank.com	Bakersfield	CA	93301	661-395-1610	395-1098
Sanwa Bank California 5201 California Ave Suite 100 *TF:* 800-237-2692	Bakersfield	CA	93309	661-327-5345	322-3696
Union Bank of California 5400 Stockdale Hwy *TF:* 800-238-4486	Bakersfield	CA	93309	661-322-5035	322-2624
Washington Mutual Bank 4040 California Ave	Bakersfield	CA	93309	661-322-4053	633-1392
Wells Fargo Bank 1300 22nd St. *TF:* 800-869-3557	Bakersfield	CA	93301	661-861-9971	322-0634
Westamerica Bank 1810 Chester Ave *TF:* 800-848-1088	Bakersfield	CA	93301	661-864-4900	633-0451

BUSINESS SERVICES

	Phone		Phone
Automated Temporary Services	661-832-1900	**Manpower Temporary Services**	661-834-9703
DHL Worldwide Express	800-225-5345	**Pitney Bowes**	800-322-8000
Employers Training Resource	661-324-9675	**Post Office**	661-392-6158
Federal Express	800-238-5355	**UPS**	800-742-5877
Kelly Services	661-395-1991	**Work Force Staffing**	661-327-5019
Kinko's	661-837-1451		

— Media —

PUBLICATIONS

				Phone	Fax
Bakersfield Business Journal 304 18th St.	Bakersfield	CA	93301	661-861-8512	861-1631
Bakersfield Californian‡ PO Box 440 *Web:* www.bakersfield.com	Bakersfield	CA	93302	661-395-7500	395-7519
Bakersfield News Observer 1219 20th St	Bakersfield	CA	93301	661-324-9466	

‡Daily newspapers

TELEVISION

				Phone	Fax
KABE-TV Ch 39 (Uni) 3223 Sillect Ave.	Bakersfield	CA	93308	661-325-3939	325-3971
KBAK-TV Ch 29 (CBS) 1901 Westwind Dr	Bakersfield	CA	93301	661-327-7955	327-5603
KERO-TV Ch 23 (ABC) 321 21st St	Bakersfield	CA	93301	661-637-2323	323-5538
KGET-TV Ch 17 (NBC) 2120 L St *Web:* www.kget.com	Bakersfield	CA	93301	661-283-1700	327-1994
KPXF-TV Ch 61 (PAX) 4910 E Clinton Ave Suite 107 *Web:* www.pax.net/KPXF	Fresno	CA	93727	559-255-1161	255-1061
KUVI-TV Ch 45 (UPN) 3223 N Sillect Ave.	Bakersfield	CA	93308	661-326-1011	328-7576

RADIO

				Phone	Fax
KBID-AM 1350 kHz (Nost) 1400 Easton Dr Suite 144	Bakersfield	CA	93309	661-861-1350	861-0334
KERI-AM 1180 kHz (N/T) 110 S Montclair St Suite 205	Bakersfield	CA	93309	661-832-3100	832-3164
KERN-AM 1410 kHz (N/T) 1400 Easton Dr Suite 144	Bakersfield	CA	93309	661-328-1410	328-0873
KGEO-AM 1230 kHz (N/T) 1400 Easton Dr Suite 144	Bakersfield	CA	93309	661-328-1410	328-0873
KISS-FM 94.1 MHz (Urban) 1400 Easton Dr Suite 144	Bakersfield	CA	93309	661-328-1410	328-0873
KKXX-FM 96.5 MHz (CHR) 1100 Mohawk St Suite 280 *Web:* www.kkxx.com ■ *E-mail:* kkxx@lightspeed.net	Bakersfield	CA	93309	661-322-9929	322-9239
KLLY-FM 95.3 MHz (AC) 3651 Pegasus Dr Suite 107	Bakersfield	CA	93308	661-393-1900	393-1915
KRAB-FM 1061 MHz (Rock) 1100 Mohawk St Suite 280 *E-mail:* krab@lightspeed.net	Bakersfield	CA	93309	661-322-9929	322-9239
KUZZ-FM 107.9 MHz (Ctry) 3223 Sillect Ave	Bakersfield	CA	93308	661-326-1011	328-7503

— Colleges/Universities —

				Phone	Fax
Bakersfield College 1801 Panorama Dr. *Web:* www.bc.cc.ca.us	Bakersfield	CA	93305	661-395-4011	395-4241
California State University Bakersfield 9001 Stockdale Hwy *TF:* 800-788-2782 ■ *Web:* www.csubak.edu	Bakersfield	CA	93311	661-664-2011	664-3389

— Hospitals —

				Phone	Fax
Bakersfield Memorial Hospital 420 34th St	Bakersfield	CA	93301	661-327-1792	326-0706
Good Samaritan Hospital 901 Olive Dr	Bakersfield	CA	93308	661-399-4461	399-4224
Kern Medical Center 1830 Flower St.	Bakersfield	CA	93305	661-326-2000	326-2969
Mercy Hospital 2215 Truxtun Ave.	Bakersfield	CA	93301	661-632-5000	327-2592
Mercy Southwest Hospital 400 Old River Rd	Bakersfield	CA	93311	661-663-6000	327-2592
San Joaquin Community Hospital 2615 Eye St	Bakersfield	CA	93301	661-395-3000	321-3749

Bakersfield (Cont'd)

— Attractions —

				Phone	Fax
Adobe Krow Archives 430 18th St	Bakersfield	CA	93301	661-633-2736	833-9074
Bakersfield Community Theater 2400 S Chester Ave	Bakersfield	CA	93304	661-831-8114	
Bakersfield Museum of Art 1930 R St	Bakersfield	CA	93301	661-323-7219	323-7266
Bakersfield Music Theatre 1931 Chester Ave *Web:* www.bmtshowtiks.com	Bakersfield	CA	93301	661-325-6100	325-6354
Bakersfield Symphony Orchestra 1401 19th St Suite 130	Bakersfield	CA	93301	661-323-7928	323-7331
Buck Owens Production Co Inc 3223 Sillect Ave	Bakersfield	CA	93308	661-326-1011	328-7503
Buena Vista Museum of Natural History 1201 20th St *Web:* www.sharktoothhill.com ■ *E-mail:* bvmnh@datacourse.com	Bakersfield	CA	93301	661-324-6350	324-7522
California Living Museum 10500 Alfred Harrell Hwy *Web:* bizweb.lightspeed.net/calm ■ *E-mail:* calm@lightspeed.net	Bakersfield	CA	93306	661-872-2256	872-2205
Camelot Park Family Entertainment Center 1251 Oak St	Bakersfield	CA	93304	661-325-5453	325-4158
Fort Tejon State Historic Park I-5 & 4201 Fort Tejon Rd	Lebec	CA	93243	661-248-6692	
Fox Theater 2001 H St	Bakersfield	CA	93301	661-324-1369	324-1854
Golden West Casino 1001 S Union Ave	Bakersfield	CA	93307	661-324-6936	324-6977
Kern County Museum 3801 Chester Ave *Web:* www.kruznet.com/kcmuseum ■ *E-mail:* kcmuseum@lightspeed.net	Bakersfield	CA	93301	661-861-2132	322-6415
Kern National Wildlife Refuge PO Box 670	Delano	CA	93216	661-725-2767	725-6041
Kern Valley Museum 49 Big Blue Rd	Kernville	CA	93238	760-376-6683	
Lori Brock Children's Museum 3801 Chester Ave *Web:* www.kcmuseum.org	Bakersfield	CA	93301	661-852-5000	322-6415
Melodrama Music Theater 206 China Grade Loop *Web:* www.melodrama.com	Bakersfield	CA	93308	661-393-7886	393-8717
Minter Field Air Museum Lerdo Hwy & Fwy 99 Shafter Airport *TF:* 800-393-6323	Shafter	CA	93263	661-393-0291	
Shafter Depot Museum 150 Central Valley Hwy	Shafter	CA	93263	661-746-1557	
Slikker Farms 10854 Redbank Rd	Bakersfield	CA	93307	661-366-4200	366-0288

SPORTS TEAMS & FACILITIES

				Phone	Fax
Bakersfield Blaze (basketball) 4009 Chester Ave *Web:* www.bakersfieldblaze.com ■ *E-mail:* blaze1@lightspeed.net	Bakersfield	CA	93301	661-322-1363	322-6199
Bakersfield Condors (hockey) 1001 Truxton Ave *Web:* www.bakersfieldcondors.com ■ *E-mail:* fog@lightspeed.net	Bakersfield	CA	93301	661-324-7825	324-6929
Bakersfield Speedway 5001 N Chester Ave Ext	Bakersfield	CA	93308	661-393-3373	393-7085
Mesa Marin Raceway 11000 Kern Canyon Rd *Web:* www.mesamarin.com	Bakersfield	CA	93306	661-366-5711	366-5123

— Events —

	Phone
5th of May Festivity (May 5)	661-323-9334
Appaloosa Horse Show (late March)	661-833-4900
Apple Harvest Fair (mid-September)	661-822-4180
Bakersfield Christmas Parade (early December)	661-325-3410
Bakersfield Jazz Festival (mid-May)	661-664-3093
Country Faire (early July)	661-245-1212
Downtown Street Faires (late May-late August)	661-325-5892
Fall Festival (early September)	661-245-1212
Great Kern County Fair (mid September-early October)	661-833-4900
Horseless Carriage Auto Expo (mid-April)	661-833-4917
Kern River Fesitval (mid-April)	760-376-2629
Lilac Festival (mid-May)	661-242-4663
McFarland Christmas Festival (mid-December)	661-725-2518
Mountain Festival Art Show (mid-August)	661-245-3358
Oktoberfest (mid-October)	661-327-2424
One Act Festival (mid-late June)	661-831-8114
Pacific Coast Junior National Livestock Show (early April)	661-833-4934
Quarter Horse Show (late April)	661-833-4917
Saint Patrick's Day Parade (mid-March)	661-325-5892
Springtyme Faire (mid-June)	661-822-6062
Stampede Day's Rodeo (early May)	661-325-8476
Village Artisans Spring Fair (late April)	661-328-1943
Vintage Sailplane Regatta & Blue Feather Fly In (late May)	661-822-5267
Western Street Rod Nationals (late May)	661-833-4917

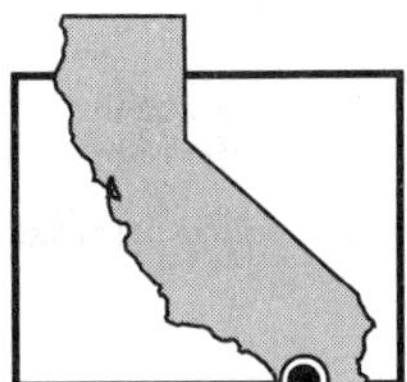

Chula Vista

Situated adjacent to the Pacific Ocean, San Diego Bay, and the foothills of Mount Saint Miguel, the city of Chula Vista offers spectacular views of the natural beauty of California and of Mexico, located just seven miles to the south. In fact, the name Chula Vista comes from the Spanish phrase meaning "beautiful view." Chula Vista Nature Center teaches the natural history and ecology of Southern California's coastal wetlands, providing visitors with the opportunity to observe more than 215 species of birds from the Center's observation tower and a wide variety of marine life in its 4,500 gallon salt water tank. The city is also home to the ARCO Olympic Training Center, the nation's first year-round, warm weather Olympic training facility.

Population	160,553	**Longitude**	117-02-41 W
Area (Land)	29.0 sq mi	**County**	San Diego
Area (Water)	1.8 sq mi	**Time Zone**	PST
Elevation	75 ft	**Area Code/s**	619
Latitude	32-37-42 N		

— Average Temperatures and Precipitation —

TEMPERATURES

	Jan	Feb	Mar	Apr	May	Jun	Jul	Aug	Sep	Oct	Nov	Dec
High	65	66	65	67	67	69	73	75	76	73	69	65
Low	46	47	49	52	56	59	63	65	63	57	50	46

PRECIPITATION

	Jan	Feb	Mar	Apr	May	Jun	Jul	Aug	Sep	Oct	Nov	Dec
Inches	1.6	1.4	1.8	0.8	0.2	0.1	0.0	0.1	0.2	0.4	1.6	1.4

— Important Phone Numbers —

	Phone		Phone
AAA	619-421-0410	**Medical Referral**	800-827-4277
American Express Travel	619-297-8101	**Poison Control Center**	800-876-4766
Dental Referral	619-283-5644	**Time**	760-853-1212
Emergency	911	**Weather**	858-289-1212

— Information Sources —

				Phone	Fax
Better Business Bureau Serving San Diego & Imperial Counties 5050 Murphy Canyon Rd Suite 110 *Web:* www.sandiego.bbb.org	San Diego	CA	92123	858-496-2131	496-2141
Chula Vista Chamber of Commerce 233 4th Ave *Web:* www.chulavistachamber.org ■ *E-mail:* cvcc@pacbell.net	Chula Vista	CA	91910	619-420-6602	420-1269
Chula Vista City Hall 276 4th Ave *Web:* www.ci.chula-vista.ca.us	Chula Vista	CA	91910	619-691-5044	476-5939
Chula Vista Community Development Dept 276 4th Ave *Web:* www.ci.chula-vista.ca.us/comdev.htm	Chula Vista	CA	91910	619-691-5047	476-5310

Chula Vista — Information Sources (Cont'd)

Name / Address	City	State	Zip	Phone	Fax
Chula Vista Mayor 276 4th Ave	Chula Vista	CA	91910	619-691-5044	476-5379
Chula Vista Public Library 365 F St	Chula Vista	CA	91910	619-691-5069	427-4246
Web: www.infopeople.org/chulavista/library					
San Diego County 1600 Pacific Hwy	San Diego	CA	92101	619-531-5507	557-4056
Web: www.co.san-diego.ca.us					

On-Line Resources

Chula Vista California	chula-vista.com
ChulaVista.com	www.chulavista.com
Excite.com Chula Vista City Guide	www.excite.com/travel/countries/united_states/california/chula_vista

— Transportation Services —

AIRPORTS

■ San Diego International Airport - Lindbergh Field (SAN)

	Phone
11 miles NW of downtown Chula Vista (approx 25 minutes)	619-231-2100

Airport Transportation

	Phone
Cloud Nine Shuttle $20 fare to downtown Chula Vista	858-278-8877
Public Shuttle $15 fare to downtown Chula Vista	800-900-7433
Taxi $24 fare to downtown Chula Vista	619-234-6161

Commercial Airlines

	Phone		Phone
AeroMexico	800-237-6639	**Northwest**	800-225-2525
America West	800-235-9292	**SkyWest**	800-453-9417
American	800-433-7300	**Southwest**	800-435-9792
American Eagle	800-433-7300	**TWA**	800-221-2000
British Airways	800-247-9297	**United**	800-241-6522
Delta	800-221-1212	**US Airways**	800-428-4322
LTU International	800-888-0200		

Charter Airlines

	Phone		Phone
Corporate Helicopters of San Diego	619-291-4356	**Lundy Air Charter**	858-505-5660
Jimsair Aviation Services	619-298-7704	**Renown Aviation Inc**	805-937-8484
		Tag Aviation	800-252-6972

CAR RENTALS

	Phone		Phone
Budget	619-498-1144	**Hertz**	619-220-5222
Dollar	619-234-3388	**National**	619-231-7100
Enterprise	619-691-1191	**Thrifty**	619-429-5000

LIMO/TAXI

	Phone		Phone
American Cab	858-292-1111	**Yellow Cab**	619-234-6161
Silver Cab	619-280-5555		

MASS TRANSIT

	Phone
Chula Vista Transit $1.50 base fare	619-233-3004

RAIL/BUS

Name / Address	City	State	Zip	Phone
Greyhound/Trailways Bus Station 120 W Broadway	San Diego	CA	92101	619-239-8082
TF: 800-231-2222				
San Diego Amtrak Station 1050 Kettner Blvd	San Diego	CA	92101	619-239-9021

— Accommodations —

HOTELS, MOTELS, RESORTS

Name / Address	City	State	Zip	Phone	Fax
American Inn & Suites 815 W San Ysidro Blvd	San Ysidro	CA	92173	619-428-5521	428-0693
TF: 800-553-3933					
Best Western Inn 275 Orange Ave	Coronado	CA	92118	619-437-1666	437-0188
TF: 800-528-1234					
Best Western Inn 710 E St	Chula Vista	CA	91910	619-420-5183	420-6254
TF: 800-528-1234					
Big 7 Motel 333 Broadway	Chula Vista	CA	91910	619-422-9278	422-8413
Days Inn 699 E St	Chula Vista	CA	91910	619-585-1999	427-3748
TF: 800-873-4667					
Days Inn 1640 E Plaza Blvd	National City	CA	91950	619-474-9202	477-0568
TF: 800-329-7466					
Good Nite Inn 225 Bay Blvd	Chula Vista	CA	91910	619-425-8200	426-7411
TF: 800-648-3466					
Grand Plaza Inn 1125 E Plaza Blvd	National City	CA	91950	619-474-8115	474-2648
Harbor View Motel 1089 Broadway	Chula Vista	CA	91911	619-422-2967	
Holiday Inn 700 National City Blvd	National City	CA	91950	619-474-2800	474-1689
TF: 800-465-4329					
Holiday Inn Express 4450 Otay Valley Rd	Chula Vista	CA	91911	619-422-2600	425-4605
TF: 800-628-2611					
Hotel Buena Vista Beach Resort 130 27th St	Chula Vista	CA	91911	619-429-8079	429-7924
TF: 800-752-3555					
La Quinta Inn 150 Bonita Rd	Chula Vista	CA	91910	619-691-1211	427-0135
TF: 800-531-5900					
Motel 6 745 E St	Chula Vista	CA	91910	619-422-4200	585-8944
TF: 800-466-8356					
Radisson Suites 801 National City Blvd	National City	CA	91950	619-336-1100	336-1628
Ramada Inn 91 Bonita Rd	Chula Vista	CA	91910	619-425-9999	425-8934
TF: 800-272-6232					
Rodeway Inn 778 Broadway	Chula Vista	CA	91910	619-476-9555	
TF: 800-228-2000					
Royal Vista Inn 632 E St	Chula Vista	CA	91910	619-426-2500	476-8635
Sunshine Inn 946 Broadway	Chula Vista	CA	91911	619-691-6868	420-6975
Travel Inn 394 Broadway	Chula Vista	CA	91910	619-420-6600	420-5556
TF: 800-578-7878					
Traveler Motel Suites 235 Woodlawn Ave	Chula Vista	CA	91910	619-427-9170	427-5247
TF: 800-748-6998					
Vagabond Inn 230 Broadway	Chula Vista	CA	91910	619-422-8305	425-3645
TF: 800-522-1555					

— Restaurants —

Name / Address	City	State	Zip	Phone
Anthony's Fish Grotto (Seafood) 215 W Bay Blvd	Chula Vista	CA	91910	619-425-4200
Arizona Restaurant (Chinese) 2650 Main St	Chula Vista	CA	91911	619-575-1513
Baja Lobster (Seafood) 730 H St	Chula Vista	CA	91910	619-427-8690
Bob's Fish Market (Seafood) 570 Marina Pkwy	Chula Vista	CA	91910	619-476-0400
Butcher Shop (American) 556 Broadway	Chula Vista	CA	91910	619-420-9440
Cafe Ole (Mexican) 833 Broadway	Chula Vista	CA	91911	619-426-0323
Cafe Palacio De Oro (Chinese) 560 Broadway	Chula Vista	CA	91910	619-420-8910
Center Cut Restaurant (Steak/Seafood) 534 Broadway	Chula Vista	CA	91910	619-476-1144
Chez Loma (French) 1132 Loma Ave	Coronado	CA	92118	619-435-0661
China China (Chinese) 386 E H St	Chula Vista	CA	91910	619-585-1111
CoCo's (American) 303 W Broadway	Chula Vista	CA	91910	619-420-9944
Dynasty (Chinese) 945 Otay Lakes Rd	Chula Vista	CA	91913	619-656-8080
El Norteno (Mexican) 1266 3rd Ave	Chula Vista	CA	91911	619-585-1177
Flamingo Cafe (American) 396 Broadway	Chula Vista	CA	91910	619-691-1076
Galley at the Marina (American) 550 Marina Pkwy	Chula Vista	CA	91910	619-422-5714
House of Munich (German) 230 3rd Ave	Chula Vista	CA	91910	619-426-5172
Jade House (Chinese) 569 H St	Chula Vista	CA	91910	619-426-5951
Jimmy's Family Restaurant (American) 1198 3rd Ave	Chula Vista	CA	91910	619-427-7161
Kanpai (Japanese) 301 Palomar St	Chula Vista	CA	91911	619-426-1200
Kim's Korean Restaurant (Korean) 1467 E Plaza Blvd	National City	CA	91950	619-474-0601
Koto Japanese Restaurant (Japanese) 651 Palomar St	Chula Vista	CA	91911	619-691-1418
La Bella's Pizza (Italian) 373 3rd Ave	Chula Vista	CA	91910	619-426-8820
La Costa Azul (Mexican) 1037 Broadway	Chula Vista	CA	91911	619-691-9812
Lai Wah (Chinese) 310 3rd Ave	Chula Vista	CA	91910	619-425-8442
Linlee's III (Chinese) 398 C St	Chula Vista	CA	91910	619-585-8333
Loreto's Mexican Food (Mexican) 200 Broadway	Chula Vista	CA	91910	619-420-5601
Love's Wood Pit BBQ (Barbecue) 89 Bonita Rd	Chula Vista	CA	91910	619-426-8323
Parisi's (Italian) 323 Broadway	Chula Vista	CA	91910	619-420-4490
Poor Gourmet (Italian) 388 F St	Chula Vista	CA	91910	619-691-9646
Rubio's Restaurant (Mexican) 481 Broadway	Chula Vista	CA	91911	619-427-3811
Tamaki Japanese Restaurant (Japanese) 1090 3rd Ave	Chula Vista	CA	91911	619-425-5110
Utage Japanese Restaurant (Japanese) 1200 3rd Ave	Chula Vista	CA	91911	619-425-8980
Zorba'a Family Restaurant (Greek) 100 Broadway	Chula Vista	CA	91910	619-422-8853

— Goods and Services —

SHOPPING

Name / Address	City	State	Zip	Phone	Fax
Chula Vista Center 555 Broadway	Chula Vista	CA	91910	619-422-7500	476-0455*
**Fax:* Cust Svc					

Chula Vista — Shopping (Cont'd)

	City	State	Zip	Phone	Fax
Ferry Landing Marketplace 1201 1st St Suite K-6	Coronado	CA	92118	619-435-8895	
Plaza Bonita I-805 & Sweetwater Rd	National City	CA	91950	619-267-2850	472-5652
San Diego Factory Outlet Center 4498 Camino De La Plaza	San Ysidro	CA	92173	619-690-2999	
Terra Nova Center 374 E 'H' St	Chula Vista	CA	91910	619-425-7990	

BANKS

	City	State	Zip	Phone	Fax
California Commerce Bank 555 Broadway Suite 110	Chula Vista	CA	91910	619-498-8282	498-8277
California Federal Bank 352 H St	Chula Vista	CA	91910	619-427-3111	585-3102
First International Bank 318 4th Ave	Chula Vista	CA	91910	619-425-5000	476-3288
San Diego National Bank 398 H St	Chula Vista	CA	91910	619-585-7651	585-7652
Scripps Bank 1196 3rd Ave	Chula Vista	CA	91911	619-422-2265	425-9107
Union Bank 410 'H' St	Chula Vista	CA	91910	619-426-5330	425-4376

BUSINESS SERVICES

	Phone		Phone
DHL Worldwide Express	800-225-5345	**Mail Boxes Etc**	619-482-0123
Express Secretarial Services	619-482-0682	**Post Office**	800-275-8777
Federal Express	800-238-5355	**Remedy Intelligent Staffing**	619-425-7730
In & Out Mail Center	619-425-4711	**UPS**	800-742-5877
Kinko's	619-426-1811		

— Media —

PUBLICATIONS

	City	State	Zip	Phone	Fax
San Diego Union-Tribune‡ PO Box 120191	San Diego	CA	92112	619-299-3131	293-1896
TF: 800-244-6397 ■ *Web:* www.uniontrib.com ■ *E-mail:* letters@uniontrib.com					
Star-News 279 3rd Ave	Chula Vista	CA	91910	619-427-3000	426-6346*
**Fax:* News Rm					

‡*Daily newspapers*

TELEVISION

	City	State	Zip	Phone	Fax
KFMB-TV Ch 8 (CBS) 7677 Engineer Rd	San Diego	CA	92111	858-571-8888	560-0627
Web: www.kfmb.com ■ *E-mail:* news8@kfmb.com					
KGTV-TV Ch 10 (ABC) PO Box 85347	San Diego	CA	92186	619-237-1010	527-0369
Web: www.sandiegoinsider.com/partners/kgtv					
KNSD-TV Ch 7/39 (NBC) 8330 Engineer Rd	San Diego	CA	92171	858-279-3939	279-1076
Web: www.knsd.com ■ *E-mail:* hinczsd@tvsknsd.nbc.com					
KPBS-TV Ch 15 (PBS) 5200 Campanile Dr	San Diego	CA	92182	619-594-1515	265-6417
Web: www.kpbs.org ■ *E-mail:* letters@kpbs.org					
KSWB-TV Ch 69 (WB) 7191 Engineer Rd	San Diego	CA	92111	858-492-9269	268-0401
XETV-TV Ch 6 (Fox) 8253 Ronson Rd	San Diego	CA	92111	858-279-6666	268-9388
Web: www.fox6.com					

RADIO

	City	State	Zip	Phone	Fax
KFMB-FM 100.7 MHz (AC) 7677 Engineer Rd	San Diego	CA	92111	858-292-7600	279-3380
Web: www.histar.com					
KFSD-FM 92.1 MHz (Clas) 550 Laguna Dr	Carlsbad	CA	92008	760-729-5946	434-2367
KGB-FM 101.5 MHz (CR) 5745 Kearny Villa Rd Suite M	San Diego	CA	92123	858-565-6006	277-1015
Web: www.101kgb.com					
KOGO-AM 600 kHz (N/T) 5050 Murphy Canyon Rd	San Diego	CA	92123	858-278-1130	285-4364*
**Fax Area Code:* 619					
KPBS-FM 89.5 MHz (NPR) 5200 Campanile Dr San Diego State University	San Diego	CA	92182	619-594-8100	265-6478
Web: www.kpbs.org ■ *E-mail:* letters@kpbs.org					
KPLN-FM 103.7 MHz (CR) 8033 Linda Vista Rd	San Diego	CA	92111	858-560-1037	571-0326
Web: www.planetfm.com					
KPOP-AM 1360 kHz (Nost) 5050 Murphy Canyon Rd	San Diego	CA	92123	858-278-1130	285-4372*
**Fax Area Code:* 619					
KSDO-AM 1130 kHz (N/T) 5050 Murphy Canyon Rd	San Diego	CA	92123	858-278-1130	285-4303*
**Fax Area Code:* 619 ■ *Web:* www.ksdoradio.com					
KSON-AM 1240 kHz (Misc) 1615 Murray Canyon Rd Suite 710	San Diego	CA	92108	619-291-9797	543-1353
XHKY-FM 99.3 MHz (Span) 1229 3rd Ave Suite C	Chula Vista	CA	91911	619-585-9090	426-3690
XHTZ-FM 90.3 MHz (Urban) 1229 3rd Ave Suite C	Chula Vista	CA	91911	619-585-9090	426-3690
Web: www.z90.com ■ *E-mail:* bhcomm@electriciti.com					

— Colleges/Universities —

	City	State	Zip	Phone	Fax
National University 660 Bay Blvd	Chula Vista	CA	91910	619-563-7415	563-7414
Web: www.nu.edu					
Southwestern College 900 Otay Lakes Rd	Chula Vista	CA	91910	619-421-6700	482-6489
Web: swc.cc.ca.us					

— Hospitals —

	City	State	Zip	Phone	Fax
Scripps Memorial Hospital-Chula Vista 435 H St	Chula Vista	CA	91910	619-691-7000	691-7523*
**Fax:* Mail Rm ■ *Web:* www.scrippshealth.org/hospitals/chula.html					
Sharp Chula Vista Medical Center 751 Medical Center Ct	Chula Vista	CA	91911	619-482-5800	482-3604*
**Fax:* Admitting					

— Attractions —

	City	State	Zip	Phone	Fax
ARCO Olympic Training Center 1750 Wueste Rd	Chula Vista	CA	91915	619-656-1500	482-6200
Balboa Park 1549 El Prado	San Diego	CA	92101	619-239-0512	
Bonita Historical Museum 4035 Bonita Rd	Bonita	CA	91902	619-267-5141	
Chula Vista Heritage Museum 360 3rd Ave	Chula Vista	CA	91910	619-476-5373	
Chula Vista Nature Center 1000 Gunpowder Point Dr	Chula Vista	CA	91910	619-422-2481	422-2964
Coronado Beach Museum 1126 Loma Ave	Coronado	CA	92118	619-435-7242	
Granger Music Hall 1615 E 4th St	National City	CA	91950	619-477-3451	
Heritage-Americas Museum 2952 Jamacha Rd	El Cajon	CA	92019	619-670-5194	
Old Town State Historic Park 4002 Wallace St	San Diego	CA	92110	619-220-5422	220-5421
San Diego Zoo 2920 Zoo Dr	San Diego	CA	92103	619-231-1515	557-3970
Web: www.sandiegozoo.org					
Sea World of California 500 Sea World Dr	San Diego	CA	92109	619-226-3901	226-3996
Web: www.seaworld.com/seaworld/sw_california/swcframe.html					
US Olympic ARCO Training Center 1750 Wueste Rd	Chula Vista	CA	91915	619-656-1500	482-6200

SPORTS TEAMS & FACILITIES

	City	State	Zip	Phone	Fax
San Diego Chargers 9449 Friars Rd Qualcomm Stadium	San Diego	CA	92108	619-280-2121	280-5107
Web: www.chargers.com					
San Diego Gulls (hockey) 3500 Sports Arena Blvd	San Diego	CA	92110	619-224-4625	224-3010
Web: www.sandiegoarena.com/gulls/gulls.htm					
San Diego Padres 9449 Friars Rd Qualcomm Stadium	San Diego	CA	92108	619-881-6500	497-5339
Web: www.padres.com/ ■ *E-mail:* comments@padres.com					

— Events —

	Phone
Arturo Barrios Invitational 10K/5K (late October)	619-450-6510
Bonitafest (late September)	619-472-8520
Concerts in the Park (early June-mid-August)	619-585-5627
Downtown Third Avenue Lemon Festival (early June)	619-422-1982
Harbor Day & Tall Ship Festival (mid-September)	858-268-1250
Holiday Festival (early December)	619-691-5071
Lemon Festival (early June)	619-422-1982
Soap Box Derby (mid-September)	619-585-1405
Starlight Yule Parade (early December)	619-422-1982
Taste of the Arts (mid-April)	619-585-5627

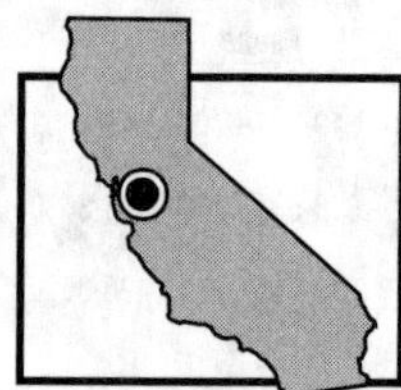

Fremont

Located in the southeastern San Francisco Bay area, Fremont was originally settled by the Spanish in the 1800's with the establishment of Mission San Jose, which remains open to visitors today. Although the area has been settled for nearly 200 years, Fremont was not incorporated as a city until 1956 and therefore is considered to be a "young" city. As part of the Silicon Valley, Fremont is home to many high-tech companies, including Lam Research LSI, Logic/Micronics Computers, and Logitech. The city is also home to the New United Motor Manufacturing Plant (NUMMI), a joint venture between General Motors and Toyota.

Population	204,298	**Longitude**	121-59-49 W
Area (Land)	77.0 sq mi	**County**	Alameda
Area (Water)	10.4 sq mi	**Time Zone**	PST
Elevation	53 ft	**Area Code/s**	510
Latitude	37-31-42 N		

— Average Temperatures and Precipitation —

TEMPERATURES

	Jan	Feb	Mar	Apr	May	Jun	Jul	Aug	Sep	Oct	Nov	Dec
High	58	63	65	70	75	80	82	82	81	75	64	58
Low	41	44	45	47	51	55	57	57	56	52	46	41

PRECIPITATION

	Jan	Feb	Mar	Apr	May	Jun	Jul	Aug	Sep	Oct	Nov	Dec
Inches	2.8	2.2	2.6	1.2	0.3	0.1	0.1	0.1	0.2	0.9	2.1	2.0

— Important Phone Numbers —

	Phone		Phone
AAA	510-770-9280	**Poison Control Center**	800-876-4766
American Express Travel	510-797-7911	**Time**	925-767-8900
Dental Referral	800-422-8338	**Travelers Aid of Alameda County**	510-444-6834
Emergency	911		

— Information Sources —

				Phone	Fax
Alameda County 1221 Oak St.	Oakland	CA	94612	510-272-6984	272-3784
Web: www.co.alameda.ca.us ■ *E-mail:* dpd@co.alameda.ca.us					
Better Business Bureau Serving Oakland/San Francisco Area & Northwest Coastal California 510 16th St Suite 550	Oakland	CA	94612	510-238-1000	238-1018
Web: www.oakland.bbb.org					
Fremont Chamber of Commerce 39488 Stevenson Pl Suite 100	Fremont	CA	94539	510-795-2244	795-2240
Web: www.fremontbusiness.com ■ *E-mail:* fmtcc@infolane.com					
Fremont City Hall PO Box 5006	Fremont	CA	94537	510-494-4800	494-4257
Web: www.ci.fremont.ca.us ■ *E-mail:* cof@ci.fremont.ca.us					
Fremont Economic Development Office PO Box 5006	Fremont	CA	94537	510-494-4833	494-4257
Fremont Main Library 2400 Stevenson Blvd.	Fremont	CA	94538	510-745-1400	793-2987
Web: www.aclibrary.org/branches/frm.html					
Fremont Mayor PO Box 5006	Fremont	CA	94537	510-494-4811	494-4257

On-Line Resources

Excite.com Fremont City Guide .... www.excite.com/travel/countries/united_states/california/fremont
InfoLane's Southern Alameda County Directory .... www.infolane.com/directory/

— Transportation Services —

AIRPORTS

■ **San Jose International Airport (SJC)**

	Phone
14 miles S of downtown Fremont (approx 15 minutes)	408-501-7600
Web: www.sjc.org/	

Airport Transportation

	Phone
Airport Commuter $65 fare to downtown Fremont	888-990-5466
VIP Airport Shuttle $26 fare to downtown Fremont	408-885-1800

Commercial Airlines

	Phone		Phone
America West	800-235-9292	**SkyWest**	800-453-9417
Continental	800-525-0280	**Southwest**	800-435-9792
Delta	800-221-1212	**TWA**	800-221-2000
Mexicana	800-531-7923	**United**	800-241-6522
Northwest	800-225-2525		

Charter Airlines

	Phone		Phone
ACM Aviation Inc.	408-286-3832	**Jet Aviation Business Jets Inc**	818-843-8400
Aris Helicopters LTD	408-998-3266	**Jet Center**	408-297-7552
Centurion Flight Services	650-494-7812	**Silicon Valley Express**	408-292-0677
Executive Jet Management	877-356-5387	**Tag Aviation**	800-252-6972

CAR RENTALS

	Phone		Phone
Able	510-656-6656	**Dollar**	408-808-3655
Avis	510-796-1308	**Hertz**	510-797-9900
Budget	510-487-3324	**Thrifty**	510-651-0333

LIMO/TAXI

	Phone		Phone
Executive Limousine	510-796-4505	**Fremont Taxi**	510-490-2020
Fremont City Cab	510-487-1212	**Veterans Cab**	510-537-3131
Fremont Classic Yellow Cab	510-656-1234	**Yellow Cab of Fremont**	510-490-4321
Fremont Limousine	510-794-1476		

MASS TRANSIT

	Phone
AC Bus $1.25 Base fare	510-817-1717
BART Rail $1.10 Base fare	510-441-2278

RAIL/BUS

				Phone
Amtrak Centerville Station Fremont & Peralta Blvds.	Fremont	CA	94536	800-872-7245

— Accommodations —

HOTELS, MOTELS, RESORTS

				Phone	Fax
Best Western Inn 31140 Alvarado Niles Rd	Union City	CA	94587	510-475-0600	475-0910
TF: 800-528-1234					
Best Western Thunderbird Inn 5400 Mowry Ave.	Fremont	CA	94538	510-792-4300	792-2643
TF: 800-541-4909					
Comfort Inn Hayward 24997 Mission Blvd	Hayward	CA	94544	510-538-4466	581-8029
TF: 800-228-5150					
Courtyard by Marriott 47000 Lakeview Blvd	Fremont	CA	94538	510-656-1800	656-2441
Web: courtyard.com/SJCFE					
Econo Lodge Fremont 46101 Warm Springs Blvd	Fremont	CA	94539	510-656-2800	659-0352
Fremont Islander Motel 4101 Mowry Ave	Fremont	CA	94538	510-796-8200	
Good-Nite Inn 4135 Cushing Pkwy	Fremont	CA	94538	510-226-6483	656-9131
TF: 800-648-3466					
Hilton Newark-Fremont 39900 Balentine Dr	Newark	CA	94560	510-490-8390	651-7828
TF: 800-445-8667 ■ *Web:* www.hilton.com/hotels/NWKNHHF					
Holiday Inn 5977 Mowry Ave N	Newark	CA	94560	510-795-7995	795-0295
Hotel Irvington Studios 3630 Washington Blvd.	Fremont	CA	94538	510-656-9563	
Lord Bradley's Inn 43344 Mission Blvd	Fremont	CA	94539	510-490-0520	
Mission Peak Lodge 43643 Mission Blvd.	Fremont	CA	94539	510-656-2366	438-0868

Fremont — Hotels, Motels, Resorts (Cont'd)

Name / Address	City	State	ZIP	Phone	Fax
Motel 6 34047 Fremont Blvd *TF:* 800-466-8356	Fremont	CA	94555	510-793-4848	791-8172
Quality Inn 47031 Kato Rd	Fremont	CA	94539	510-490-2900	659-8353
Radisson Hotel 32083 Alvarado Niles Rd *TF:* 800-333-3333	Union City	CA	94587	510-489-2200	489-7642
Residence Inn by Marriott 5400 Farwell Pl *TF:* 800-331-3131 ■ *Web:* www.residenceinn.com/SJCBF	Fremont	CA	94536	510-794-5900	793-6587
Woodfin Suites 39150 Cedar Blvd *TF:* 800-237-8811	Newark	CA	94560	510-795-1200	795-8874

— Restaurants —

Name / Address	City	State	ZIP	Phone
369 Shanghai Cafe (Chinese) 46831 Warm Springs Blvd	Fremont	CA	94539	510-668-0369
Barcelona Madrid Restaurant (Spanish) 31014 Union City Blvd	Union City	CA	94587	510-489-7999
Carmen & Family Bar-b-q (Barbecue) 41986 Fremont Blvd.	Fremont	CA	94538	510-657-5464
China Chili (Chinese) 39116 State St	Fremont	CA	95438	510-791-1688
Daily's Grill & Bar (American) 5035 Mowry Ave	Fremont	CA	94538	510-791-0545
El Patio Restaurant (Mexican) 37311 Fremont Blvd	Fremont	CA	94536	510-796-1733
Fremont Market Broiler (Seafood) 39195 Farwell Dr	Fremont	CA	94538	510-791-8675
Helen's Vietnamese Restaurant (Vietnamese) 39150 Argonaut Way	Fremont	CA	94538	510-713-9789
Hobee Restaurant (American) 39222 Fremont Blvd	Fremont	CA	94538	510-797-1244
Kabob House (Afghan) 37405 Fremont Blvd	Fremont	CA	94536	510-745-9599
Korean Kitchen (Korean) 4185 Cushing Pkwy	Fremont	CA	94538	510-226-0333
Lyon's (American) 39350 Paseo Padre Pkwy	Fremont	CA	94538	510-790-9090
Mi Pueblo Restaurant (Mexican) 41025 Fremont Blvd	Fremont	CA	94538	510-656-8177
Mission Jarrito Mexican Restaurant (Mexican) 1530 Washington Blvd	Fremont	CA	94539	510-770-9661
My Thai Restaurant (Thai) 34265 Fremont Blvd.	Fremont	CA	94555	510-797-8980
New Ocean (Seafood) 34420 Fremont Blvd	Fremont	CA	94555	510-794-2813
Nijo Castle (Japanese) 39888 Balentine Dr	Newark	CA	94560	510-657-6456
North China (Chinese) 39144 Paseo Padre Pkwy	Fremont	CA	94538	510-794-4884
Ohlone Yen Ching Restaurant (Chinese) 1616 Washington Blvd	Fremont	CA	94539	510-490-8381
Original Hickory Pit (Barbecue) 39410 Fremont Blvd	Fremont	CA	94538	510-790-1992
Papillon Restaurant (Continental) 37296 Mission Blvd. *Web:* www.papillonrestaurant.com	Fremont	CA	94536	510-793-6331
Ristorante Il Porcino (Italian) 3339 Walnut Ave.	Fremont	CA	94538	510-791-7383
Sei-Sho Japanese Restaurant (Japanese) 40645 Fremont Blvd	Fremont	CA	94538	510-656-8708
Spin a Yarn (Greek/Italian) 45915 Warm Springs Blvd.	Fremont	CA	94539	510-656-9141
Taste Of India (Indian) 5144 Mowry Ave.	Fremont	CA	94538	510-791-1316
Uncle Chong (Chinese) 36659 Fremont Blvd	Fremont	CA	94536	510-792-1668
Vincenza's Italian Kitchen (Italian) 35760 Fremont Blvd.	Fremont	CA	94536	510-797-0102
Willy's Smoke House & BBQ (Barbecue) 36601 Newark Blvd.	Newark	CA	94560	510-794-7236
Yuri Japanese Restaurant (Japanese) 3810 Mowry Ave.	Fremont	CA	94538	510-795-6701

— Goods and Services —

SHOPPING

Name / Address	City	State	ZIP	Phone	Fax
Fremont Hub 39261 Fremont Hub	Fremont	CA	94538	510-792-1720	792-2785
Newpark Mall 2086 Newpark Mall	Newark	CA	94560	510-794-5522	796-7968

BANKS

Name / Address	City	State	ZIP	Phone	Fax
Bank of the West 5120 Mowry Ave *TF:* 800-488-2265	Fremont	CA	94538	510-791-0763	794-6754
Bay View Bank 39390 Fremont Blvd	Fremont	CA	94538	510-793-7111	795-6739
California Bank & Trust 39315 Fremont Blvd *TF:* 800-254-2265	Fremont	CA	94538	510-797-5200	790-3124
Fremont Bank 39150 Fremont Blvd *Web:* www.fremontbank.com ■ *E-mail:* bankinfo@fremontbank.com	Fremont	CA	94538	510-792-2300	795-5758
Sanwa Bank 39533 Paseo Padre Pkwy *TF:* 888-467-2692	Fremont	CA	94538	510-793-2600	651-6458
Union Bank 39305 Paseo Padre Pkwy *TF:* 800-238-4486	Fremont	CA	94538	510-792-9200	792-6513
US Bank 39510 Paseo Padre Pkwy *TF:* 800-872-2657	Fremont	CA	94538	510-794-7700	796-8270
Washington Mutual Bank 38980 Fremont Blvd	Fremont	CA	94536	510-793-3695	713-8082

BUSINESS SERVICES

	Phone		Phone
Adecco Employment Personnel Services	510-790-2066	**Kelly Services**	510-796-7915
DHL Worldwide Express	800-225-5345	**Mail Boxes Etc**	510-791-1122
Federal Express	800-238-5355	**Manpower Temporary Services**	510-440-9040
Interim Personnel Services	510-790-7100	**Post Office**	510-792-8654
		UPS	800-742-5877

— Media —

PUBLICATIONS

Name / Address	City	State	ZIP	Phone	Fax
Argus The‡ PO Box 5050 *TF:* 800-595-9595 ■ *Web:* www.newschoice.com/WebNews/Index/AngArFpg2i.asp	Hayward	CA	94540	510-661-2600	353-7029

‡*Daily newspapers*

TELEVISION

Name / Address	City	State	ZIP	Phone	Fax
KNTV-TV Ch 11 (ABC) 645 Park Ave *Web:* www.kntv.com	San Jose	CA	95110	408-286-1111	286-1530
KRON-TV Ch 4 (NBC) 1001 Van Ness Ave. *Web:* www.kron.com	San Francisco	CA	94109	415-441-4444	561-8136
KTEH-TV Ch 54 (PBS) 1585 Schallenberger Rd. *Web:* www.kteh.org/	San Jose	CA	95130	408-795-5400	995-5446
KTVU-TV Ch 2 (Fox) 2 Jack London Sq *Web:* www.bayinsider.com/partners/ktvu/index.html ■ *E-mail:* ktvu@team.insider.com	Oakland	CA	94607	510-834-1212	272-9957

RADIO

Name / Address	City	State	ZIP	Phone	Fax
KBAY-FM 94.5 MHz (AC) 190 Park Ctr Plaza Suite 200 *Web:* www.kbay.com	San Jose	CA	95113	408-287-5775	293-3341
KFAX-AM 1100 kHz (N/T) PO Box 8125	Fremont	CA	94537	510-713-1100	505-1448
KFFG-FM 97.7 MHz (AAA) 55 Hawthorne St Suite 1100	San Francisco	CA	94105	415-543-1045	995-6867
KGO-AM 810 kHz (N/T) 900 Front St. *Web:* www.kgoam810.com	San Francisco	CA	94111	415-954-8100	362-5827
KOHL-FM 89.3 MHz (CHR) 43600 Mission Blvd.	Fremont	CA	94539	510-659-6221	659-6001

— Colleges/Universities —

Name / Address	City	State	ZIP	Phone	Fax
Devry Institute of Technology 6600 Dumbarton Cir *TF:* 888-201-9941 ■ *Web:* www.fre.devry.edu ■ *E-mail:* eharrell@ifn.net	Fremont	CA	94555	510-574-1200	742-0866
Ohlone College 43600 Mission Blvd *Web:* www.ohlone.cc.ca.us	Fremont	CA	94539	510-659-6000	659-5003
Queen of the Holy Rosary College 43326 Mission Blvd.	Fremont	CA	94539	510-657-2468	657-1734

— Hospitals —

Name / Address	City	State	ZIP	Phone	Fax
Laurel Grove Hospital 19933 Lake Chabot Rd	Castro Valley	CA	94546	510-727-2755	727-2778
Saint Rose Hospital 27200 Calaroga Ave.	Hayward	CA	94545	510-264-4000	887-7421
Washington Hospital 2000 Mowry Ave	Fremont	CA	94538	510-797-1111	791-3496

— Attractions —

Name / Address	City	State	ZIP	Phone
Ardenwood Historic Farm 34600 Ardenwood Blvd *Web:* www.stanford.edu/~wellis/ardenwd	Fremont	CA	94555	510-796-0663

Fremont — Attractions (Cont'd)

				Phone	Fax
Fremont Symphony Orchestra 43600 Mission Blvd Ohlone College Smith Ctr for the Performing Arts	Fremont	CA	94539	510-794-1652	794-1658
Web: www.infolane.com/fmt-symph/ ■ *E-mail:* acutter@aol.com					
Mission San Jose 43300 Mission Blvd	Fremont	CA	94539	510-657-1797	651-8332
Museum of Local History 190 Anza St	Fremont	CA	94539	510-623-7907	
Niles Canyon Railway Museum 5550 Niles Canyon Rd	Sunol	CA	94586	925-862-9063	
Web: www.ncry.org					
Niles Depot 36997 Mission Blvd	Fremont	CA	94536	510-797-4449	
Niles Historic District Niles & Mission Blvds & 'E' St	Fremont	CA	94536	510-742-9868	

SPORTS TEAMS & FACILITIES

				Phone	Fax
Silicon Valley Ambassadors (soccer) 236 Stanford Shopping Ctr Suite 302	Palo Alto	CA	94304	650-618-1523	618-1523
Web: www.goambassadors.com ■ *E-mail:* soccer@goambassadors.com					

— Events —

	Phone
Charlie Chaplin Days (early June)	510-742-9868
Festival of the Arts (late July)	510-795-2244
Fremont Family Carnival (mid-May)	510-490-2848
Mission Days (mid-June)	510-657-1797
Newark's Music at the Grove Summer Concert Series (early July-mid-August)	510-745-1124
Niles Antique Faire (late August)	510-742-9868
Niles Holiday Open House & Tree Lighting Ceremony (late November-late December)	510-742-9868
Niles Wildflower & Art Festival (early May)	510-742-9868
Summer Evening Concerts (mid-July-late August)	510-791-4340

Fresno

Set in the central San Joaquin Valley, Fresno takes its name from the ash trees native to the area (Fresno is the Spanish word for "ash tree'). Originally a dry, desert area, Fresno County was transformed into a fertile farming area through the development of canals called "church ditches" for Morris Church, who dug the first of these canals. Fresno County is now a leading agricultural area, producing $3 billion in more than 250 commercial crops each year. Fresno's Blossom Trail includes more than 65 miles of orchards, vineyards, and citrus groves, as well as historical points of interest. Fresno is also located near three national parks: Yosemite National Park, which includes the highest falls in North America; Sequoia National Park, home of the Giant Sequoia trees; and Kings Canyon National Park, which features giant canyons, lakes, falls, and mountain meadows. Kings River, which flows through Kings Canyon, offers opportunities for whitewater rafting.

Population	398,133	**Longitude**	119-79-86 W
Area (Land)	99.1 sq mi	**County**	Fresno
Area (Water)	0.3 sq mi	**Time Zone**	PST
Elevation	296 ft	**Area Code/s**	559
Latitude	36-84-09 N		

— Average Temperatures and Precipitation —

TEMPERATURES

	Jan	Feb	Mar	Apr	May	Jun	Jul	Aug	Sep	Oct	Nov	Dec
High	54	62	67	75	84	93	99	97	90	80	65	54
Low	27	41	43	47	54	60	65	64	59	51	43	37

PRECIPITATION

	Jan	Feb	Mar	Apr	May	Jun	Jul	Aug	Sep	Oct	Nov	Dec
Inches	2.0	1.8	1.9	1.0	0.3	0.1	0.0	0.0	0.2	0.5	1.4	1.4

— Important Phone Numbers —

	Phone		Phone
AAA	800-222-4357	**Poison Control Center**	800-876-4766
Dental Referral	800-336-8478	**Road Conditions**	800-427-7623
Emergency	911	**Ski Report**	559-233-3330
FUN2DAY	559-222-8222	**Time/Temp**	559-592-8181
Medical Referral	559-449-2000	**Weather**	559-442-1212

— Information Sources —

				Phone	Fax
Better Business Bureau Serving Central California 2519 W Shaw Suite 106	Fresno	CA	93711	559-222-8111	228-6518
Web: www.cencal.bbb.org					
Fresno Chamber of Commerce 1649 Van Ness Ave Suite 103	Fresno	CA	93721	559-495-4800	495-4811
Web: fresno-online.com/chamber/					
Fresno City Hall 2600 Fresno St	Fresno	CA	93721	559-498-4591	488-1015
Web: www.ci.fresno.ca.us					
Fresno Convention & Visitors Bureau 808 M St	Fresno	CA	93721	559-233-0836	445-0122
TF: 800-788-0836 ■ *Web:* www.fresno-online.com/CVB ■ *E-mail:* tourfresno@aol.com					
Fresno Convention Center 700 M St	Fresno	CA	93721	559-498-1511	488-4634
Web: www.ci.fresno.ca.us/convention					
Fresno County 2281 Tulare St Rm 304 Hall of Records	Fresno	CA	93721	559-488-1710	488-1830
Fresno County Free Library 2420 Mariposa St	Fresno	CA	93721	559-488-3184	488-1971
Web: nc.sjvls.lib.ca.us/fresno ■ *E-mail:* libfres1@cybergate.com					
Fresno Development Dept 2600 Fresno St	Fresno	CA	93721	559-498-1591	498-1012
Web: www.ci.fresno.ca.us/development ■ *E-mail:* development@ci.fresno.ca.us					
Fresno Mayor 2600 Fresno St	Fresno	CA	93721	559-498-1561	488-1015
Web: www.ci.fresno.ca.us/city_officials/mayor/index.html ■ *E-mail:* mayor@ci.fresno.ca.us					

On-Line Resources

4Fresno.com	www.4fresno.com
Anthill City Guide Fresno	www.anthill.com/city.asp?city=fresno
Area Guide Fresno	fresno.areaguides.net
Central Valley Internet Project	www.fresno.com/
Central Valley Online	www.fresno.com/cvonline/index.html
City Knowledge Fresno	www.cityknowledge.com/ca_fresno.htm
Excite.com Fresno City Guide	www.excite.com/travel/countries/united_states/california/fresno
Fresno Online	fresno-online.com
Hello Fresno	www.psnw.com/~deb/index.html
HomeFresno.com	www.homefresno.com
Tower 2000	www.tower2000.com/

— Transportation Services —

AIRPORTS

	Phone
■ **Fresno Air Terminal (FAT)**	
5 miles NE of downtown (approx 10 minutes)	559-498-4095
Web: www.fresno.com/flyfresno	

Airport Transportation

	Phone
Fresno Transit $.75 fare to downtown	559-488-1122
Taxi $13 fare to downtown	559-275-1295

Fresno (Cont'd)

Commercial Airlines

	Phone		Phone
American	800-433-7300	United	800-241-6522
American Eagle	800-433-7300	United Express	800-241-6522
Delta	800-221-1212	US Airways	800-428-4322
SkyWest	800-453-9417		

Charter Airlines

	Phone		Phone
Allegiant Air	559-454-7730	Federico Helicopters	559-454-7680
Central California Aviation	559-252-2926	Rogers Helicopters Inc	559-299-4903
Elrod & Assoc Aviation Inc	559-252-8055	Wofford Aviation Inc	559-454-7530

CAR RENTALS

	Phone		Phone
Avis	559-454-5029	Enterprise	559-456-9690
Budget	559-251-5515	U-Save Auto	559-255-4545
Dollar	559-252-4000		

LIMO/TAXI

	Phone		Phone
Aztec Cab	559-266-6961	Limo For You	559-266-0925
Classic Limo	559-441-8111	Yellow Cab	559-275-1234
Independent Cabs	559-264-0211		

MASS TRANSIT

	Phone
Fresno Area Express $.75 Base fare	559-488-1122

RAIL/BUS

				Phone
Amtrak Station 2650 Tulare St Bldg B *TF:* 800-872-7245	Fresno	CA	93721	559-486-7651
Greyhound/Trailways Bus Station 1033 Broadway St *TF:* 800-231-2222	Fresno	CA	93721	209-268-1829

— Accommodations —

HOTELS, MOTELS, RESORTS

				Phone	Fax
Best Western Garden Court Inn 2141 N Parkway Dr *TF:* 800-437-3766	Fresno	CA	93705	559-237-1881	237-9719
Best Western Village Inn 3110 N Blackstone Ave *TF:* 800-722-8878	Fresno	CA	93703	559-226-2110	226-0539
Best Western Water Tree Inn 4141 N Blackstone Ave *TF:* 800-762-9071	Fresno	CA	93726	559-222-4445	226-4589
Chateau Inn 5113 E McKinley Ave *TF:* 800-445-2428 ■ *Web:* www.piccadilly-inn.com/chateau.html	Fresno	CA	93727	559-456-1418	456-4643
Courtyard by Marriott 140 E Shaw Ave *TF:* 800-321-2211 ■ *Web:* courtyard.com/FATCH	Fresno	CA	93710	559-221-6000	221-0368
Courtyard by Marriott 1551 N Peach Ave *TF:* 800-321-2211 ■ *Web:* courtyard.com/FATCY	Fresno	CA	93727	559-251-5200	454-0552
Days Inn 4061 N Blackstone Ave *TF:* 800-329-7466	Fresno	CA	93726	559-222-5641	225-0144
Doubletree Hotel 1055 Van Ness Ave *TF:* 800-222-8733	Fresno	CA	93721	559-485-9000	485-3210
Econo Lodge 445 N Parkway Dr *TF:* 800-553-2666	Fresno	CA	93706	559-485-5012	495-4567
Extended StayAmerica 7135 N Fresno St *TF:* 800-398-7829	Fresno	CA	93720	559-438-7105	438-7203
Fairfield Inn 6065 N Thesta *TF:* 800-228-2800 ■ *Web:* fairfieldinn.com/FATFI	Fresno	CA	93710	559-435-5838	435-6439
Holiday Inn Airport 5090 E Clinton Way *TF:* 800-465-4329	Fresno	CA	93727	559-252-3611	456-8243
Holiday Inn Express 6051 N Thesta *TF:* 800-435-9746	Fresno	CA	93710	559-435-6593	435-8694
Hyatt Lodge 4290 N Blackstone Ave *TF:* 800-233-1234	Fresno	CA	93726	559-227-4015	225-0535
La Quinta Inn 2926 Tulare St *TF:* 800-531-5900	Fresno	CA	93721	559-442-1110	237-0415
Piccadilly Inn Airport 5115 E McKinley Ave *TF:* 800-468-3587	Fresno	CA	93727	559-251-6000	251-6956
Piccadilly Inn Shaw 2305 W Shaw Ave *TF:* 800-468-3587	Fresno	CA	93711	559-226-3850	226-2448
Piccadilly Inn University 4961 N Cedar Ave *TF:* 800-468-3587	Fresno	CA	93726	559-224-4200	227-2382
Radisson Hotel 2233 Ventura St *TF:* 800-333-3333	Fresno	CA	93721	559-268-1000	486-6625
Ramada Inn 324 E Shaw Ave *TF:* 800-272-6232	Fresno	CA	93710	559-224-4040	222-4017
Red Roof Inn 6730 N Blackstone Ave *TF:* 800-843-7663	Fresno	CA	93710	559-431-3557	439-7824
Red Roof Inn 5021 N Barcus *TF:* 800-843-7663	Fresno	CA	93722	559-276-1910	276-2974
Residence Inn by Marriott 5322 N Diana Ave *TF:* 800-331-3131 ■ *Web:* www.residenceinn.com/FATRI	Fresno	CA	93710	559-222-8900	222-9089
San Joaquin Suites Hotel 1309 W Shaw Ave *TF:* 800-775-1309	Fresno	CA	93711	559-225-1309	225-6021
Sheraton Four Points Hotel 3737 N Blackstone Ave *TF:* 800-742-1911	Fresno	CA	93726	559-226-2200	222-7147

— Restaurants —

				Phone
Bacio Ristorante Italiano (Italian) 936 E Olive Ave	Fresno	CA	93728	559-485-2222
Brix Cantina (Continental) 1153 N Fulton Ave	Fresno	CA	93728	559-237-4226
Brix (American) 6763 N Palm Ave	Fresno	CA	93704	559-435-5441
Butterfield's Brewing Co (American) 777 E Olive St	Fresno	CA	93728	559-264-5521
Cedar Lanes (American) 3131 N Cedar Ave	Fresno	CA	93703	559-222-4424
Central Fish Co (Japanese) 1535 Kern St	Fresno	CA	93706	559-237-2049
Daily Planet (California) 1211 N Wishon Ave *Web:* www.tower2000.com/dailyplanet/	Fresno	CA	93728	559-266-4259
Di Cicco's (Italian) 144 N Blackstone Ave	Fresno	CA	93701	559-237-7054
El Torito (Mexican) 2840 E Tulare St	Fresno	CA	93721	559-485-1171
Elbow Room (American) 731 W San Jose	Fresno	CA	93704	559-227-1234
Fresno Cafe (Mexican) 2146 Ventura Ave	Fresno	CA	93727	559-268-2146
George's Shish Kebab (Armenian) 2405 Capitol St	Fresno	CA	93721	559-264-9433
Il Vesuvio (Italian) 7089 N Marks Ave	Fresno	CA	93711	559-446-1443
Imperial Garden (Chinese) 6640 N Blackstone Ave	Fresno	CA	93710	559-435-4406
La Rocca's Ristorante (Italian) 6735 N 1st St	Fresno	CA	93710	559-431-1278
La Vita's (Mexican) 3280 E Tulare St	Fresno	CA	93702	559-739-8646
Livingstone's Restaurant & Pub (American) 831 E Fern Ave	Fresno	CA	93728	559-485-5198
Lotus Garden (Chinese) 7089 N Marks Ave	Fresno	CA	93711	559-431-1829
Miyako (Japanese) 132 W Nees Ave	Fresno	CA	93711	559-431-8121
Oka Sushi (Japanese) 2040 W Bullard Ave	Fresno	CA	93711	559-432-1475
Pacific Seafood (Seafood) 1055 E Herndon Ave	Fresno	CA	93720	559-439-2778
Peppermill Restaurant (American) 5123 N Blackstone Ave	Fresno	CA	93710	559-224-9411
Peppino's (Italian) 5088 N Blackstone Ave	Fresno	CA	93710	559-225-4394
Richard's (American) 1609 E Belmont Ave	Fresno	CA	93701	559-266-4077
Ripe Tomato (French) 5064 N Palm Ave	Fresno	CA	93704	559-225-1850
Santa Fe (American) 935 Santa Fe Ave	Fresno	CA	93721	559-266-2170
Silver Dollar Hofbrau (German) 333 E Shaw Ave	Fresno	CA	93710	559-227-6000
Smuggler's Restaurant (American) 3787 N Blackstone Ave	Fresno	CA	93726	559-222-5681
Veni Vidi Vici (California) 1116 N Fulton	Fresno	CA	93728	559-266-5510
Vintage Press (Continental) 216 N Willis St	Visalia	CA	93291	559-733-3033
Yoshino Restaurant (Japanese) 6226 N Blackstone Ave	Fresno	CA	93710	559-431-2205

— Goods and Services —

SHOPPING

				Phone	Fax
Fashion Fair Shopping Mall 645 E Shaw Ave	Fresno	CA	93726	559-224-1591	224-1040
Fig Garden Village 5082 N Palm Ave Suite A	Fresno	CA	93704	559-226-4084	226-7960
Fulton's Folly Antique Mall 920 E Olive Ave	Fresno	CA	93728	559-268-3856	
Macy's 4888 N Fresno St Fashion Sq Mall	Fresno	CA	93726	559-228-3333	
Manchester Center 1901 E Shields Ave Suite 243	Fresno	CA	93726	559-227-1901	227-1602

BANKS

				Phone	Fax
Bank of America National Trust & Savings Assn 2611 S Cedar Ave	Fresno	CA	93725	559-486-2251	445-7395
Bank of the West 515 E Shaw Ave	Fresno	CA	93710	559-221-4300	221-6060
California Federal Bank 3141 N Cedar Ave **Fax Area Code:* 559	Fresno	CA	93703	800-843-2265	228-0934*
Regency Bank 7060 N Fresno St	Fresno	CA	93720	559-438-2600	438-2699
Sanwa Bank California 2035 Fresno St *TF:* 888-467-2692	Fresno	CA	93721	559-487-2101	487-2118
United Security Bank NA 2151 W Shaw Ave	Fresno	CA	93711	559-225-0101	248-4929
Wells Fargo Bank 1206 Van Ness Ave	Fresno	CA	93721	559-442-6222	233-3790
Westamerica Bank 1172 E Shaw Ave *TF:* 800-848-1088	Fresno	CA	93710	559-221-2300	221-2232

Fresno (Cont'd)

BUSINESS SERVICES

	Phone		Phone
Adecco Employment Personnel Services	559-224-0751	Kelly Services	559-248-0991
Airborne Express	800-247-2676	Kinko's	559-225-0513
Denham Personnel Services	559-222-5284	Olsten Staffing Services	559-226-0823
Federal Express	800-238-5355	Post Office	800-275-8777
Fresno Courier Service	559-275-8855	United Couriers	559-497-9557
		UPS	800-742-5877

— Media —

PUBLICATIONS

				Phone	Fax
Fresno Bee‡ 1626 'E' St	Fresno	CA	93786	559-441-6111	441-6436*
Fax: News Rm ■ *TF:* 800-877-7300 ■ *Web:* www.fresnobee.com ■ *E-mail:* letters@fresnobee.com					

‡Daily newspapers

TELEVISION

				Phone	Fax
KFSN-TV Ch 30 (ABC) 1777 G St	Fresno	CA	93706	559-442-1170	266-5024
KFTV-TV Ch 21 (Uni) 3239 W Ashlan Ave	Fresno	CA	93722	559-222-2121	222-2890
KGMC-TV Ch 43 (Ind) 706 W Herndon Ave	Fresno	CA	93650	559-435-7000	435-3201
Web: www.cocolatv.com ■ *E-mail:* cocolatv@psnw.com					
KJEO-TV Ch 47 (CBS) 4880 N 1st St	Fresno	CA	93726	559-222-2411	225-5305*
Fax: News Rm ■ *Web:* www.kjeo.com					
KMPH-TV Ch 26 (Fox) 5111 E McKinley Ave	Fresno	CA	93727	559-453-8850	255-9626
KMSG-TV Ch 59 (Tele) 706 W Herndon Ave	Fresno	CA	93650	559-435-5900	435-1448
KNXT-TV Ch 49 (Ind) 1550 N Fresno St	Fresno	CA	93703	559-488-7440	488-7444
KPXF-TV Ch 61 (PAX) 4910 E Clinton Ave Suite 107	Fresno	CA	93727	559-255-1161	255-1061
Web: www.pax.net/KPXF					
KSEE-TV Ch 24 (NBC) 5035 E McKinley Ave	Fresno	CA	93727	559-454-2424	454-2485
Web: www.ksee24.com					
KVPT-TV Ch 18 (PBS) 1544 Van Ness Ave	Fresno	CA	93721	559-266-1800	650-1880
Web: www.kvpt.org					

RADIO

				Phone	Fax
KALZ-FM 102.7 MHz (AC) 4991 E McKinley Ave Suite 124	Fresno	CA	93727	559-251-8614	251-3347
KBOS-FM 94.9 MHz (CHR) 1066 E Shaw Ave	Fresno	CA	93710	559-243-4300	243-4301
Web: www.kbos.com					
KCBL-AM 1340 kHz (Sports) 1066 E Shaw Ave	Fresno	CA	93710	559-243-4300	243-4301
KFSO-FM 92.9 MHz (Oldies) 4991 E McKinley Ave Suite 124	Fresno	CA	93727	559-251-8614	251-3347
KMEG-FM 97.9 MHz (Oldies) 1071 W Shaw Ave	Fresno	CA	93711	559-490-9800	490-4199
KMJ-AM 580 kHz (N/T) 1071 W Shaw Ave	Fresno	CA	93711	559-266-5800	266-3714
Web: www.kmj58.com					
KRNC-FM 105.9 MHz (Span) 107 W Shaw Ave	Fresno	CA	93711	559-490-0106	490-5888
KVPR-FM 89.3 MHz (NPR) 3437 W Shaw Ave	Fresno	CA	93711	559-275-0764	275-2202
KYNO-AM 1300 kHz (Sports) 1981 N Gateway Blvd Suite 101	Fresno	CA	93727	559-255-1041	456-8077

— Colleges/Universities —

				Phone	Fax
California Christian College 4881 E University Ave	Fresno	CA	93703	559-251-4215	251-4231
Web: www.calchristiancollege.org ■ *E-mail:* cccfresno@aol.com					
California State University Fresno 5241 N Maple Ave	Fresno	CA	93740	559-278-4240	278-4812*
Fax: Admissions ■ *Web:* www.csufresno.edu					
Fresno City College 1101 E University Ave	Fresno	CA	93741	559-442-4600	237-4232
Web: www.fcc.cc.ca.us					
Fresno Pacific University 1717 S Chestnut Ave	Fresno	CA	93702	559-453-2000	453-5502
TF Admissions: 800-660-6089 ■ *Web:* www.fresno.edu					
Heald Business College 255 W Bullard Ave	Fresno	CA	93704	559-438-4222	438-6368
TF: 800-284-0844					
State Center Community College District 1525 E Weldon Ave	Fresno	CA	93704	559-226-0720	229-7039
Web: www.scccd.cc.ca.us					

— Hospitals —

				Phone	Fax
Clovis Community Medical Center 2755 E Herndon Ave	Clovis	CA	93611	559-323-4000	323-4098
Fresno Community Hospital & Medical Center PO Box 1232	Fresno	CA	93715	559-459-6000	459-2450
Saint Agnes Medical Center 1303 E Herndon Ave	Fresno	CA	93720	559-449-3000	449-3990
University Medical Center 445 S Cedar Ave	Fresno	CA	93702	559-453-4000	459-4787
Valley Children's Hospital 9300 Valley Children's Pl	Madera	CA	93836	559-225-3000	353-5161*
Fax: Admitting ■ *Web:* www.valleychildrens.org					
Veterans Affairs Medical Center 2615 E Clinton Ave	Fresno	CA	93703	559-225-6100	228-6911

— Attractions —

				Phone	Fax
African American Historical & Cultural Museum 1857 Fulton Ave	Fresno	CA	93721	559-268-7102	268-7135
American Historical Society of Germans from Russia 3233 N West Ave	Fresno	CA	93705	559-229-8287	229-6078
Web: www.ahsgr.org ■ *E-mail:* ahsgr@aol.com					
Artes Americas 1630 Van Ness Ave	Fresno	CA	93704	559-266-2623	
Boyden Caverns Hwy 180 Kings Canyon National Pk	Sequoia National Forest	CA	93633	209-736-2708	
Chaffee Zoological Gardens of Fresno 894 W Belmont Ave	Fresno	CA	93728	559-498-2671	498-4859
Web: www.chaffeezoo.org ■ *E-mail:* toucan@chaffeezoo.org					
Club One Casino 1033 Van Ness Ave	Fresno	CA	93721	559-497-3000	237-2582
Discovery Center 1944 N Winery Ave	Fresno	CA	93703	559-251-5533	251-5531
E-mail: discoverycenter2@juno.com					
Duncan Water Gardens 6901 E McKenzie Ave	Fresno	CA	93727	559-252-1657	
Forestiere Underground Gardens 5021 W Shaw Ave	Fresno	CA	93722	559-271-0734	
Fresno Arts Museum 2233 N 1st St	Fresno	CA	93703	559-441-4220	441-4227
Fresno Ballet 1432 Fulton St	Fresno	CA	93721	559-233-2623	233-2670
Fresno Betsuin Buddhist Temple 1340 Kern St	Fresno	CA	93706	559-442-4054	442-1978
Fresno Metropolitan Museum of Art History & Science 1515 Van Ness Ave	Fresno	CA	93721	559-441-1444	441-8607
Web: www.fresnomet.org					
Fresno Philharmonic Orchestra 2601 W Shaw Ave Suite 103	Fresno	CA	93711	559-261-0600	261-0700
Web: www.fresnophil.org/					
Fresno Storyland 890 W Belmont Ave Roeding Pk	Fresno	CA	93728	559-264-2235	495-1594
Good Co Players Second Space Theater 1105 N Wishon Ave	Fresno	CA	93728	559-266-0211	266-1342
Web: www.tower2000.com/rockas-gcp/index2.html ■ *E-mail:* gcplayers@lightspeed.net					
Kearney Mansion Museum 7160 W Kearney Blvd	Fresno	CA	93706	559-441-0862	441-1372
Web: www.valleyhistory.org					
Kearney Park Kearney Blvd	Fresno	CA	93706	559-488-3004	
Kings Canyon National Park	Three Rivers	CA	93271	559-565-3341	565-3730*
Fax: Mail Rm ■ *Web:* www.nps.gov/seki					
Legion of Valor Museum 2425 Fresno St Veterans Memorial Auditorium	Fresno	CA	93721	559-498-0510	498-3773
Meux Home Museum 1007 R St	Fresno	CA	93721	559-233-8007	
Mexican Cultural Institute of Central California 830 Van Ness Ave	Fresno	CA	93721	559-445-2615	495-0535
Nonini Winery 2640 N Dickenson	Fresno	CA	93722	559-275-1936	
Rocka's Roger Dinner Theater 1226 N Wishon Ave	Fresno	CA	93728	559-266-9494	
Web: www.tower2000.com/rockas-gcp/					
Roeding Park 890 W Belmont Ave	Fresno	CA	93728	559-498-1551	
San Joaquin Gardens 5555 N Fresno St	Fresno	CA	93710	559-439-4770	439-2457
Sanger Depot Museum 1770 7th St	Sanger	CA	93657	559-875-5505	
Sequoia National Park	Three Rivers	CA	93271	559-565-3341	565-3730
Web: www.nps.gov/seki/					
Shin-Zen Japanese Friendship Gardens 7775 N Friant Rd	Fresno	CA	93710	559-498-1551	498-1588
Sierra National Forest 1600 Tollhouse Rd	Clovis	CA	93611	559-297-0706	294-4809
Web: www.yosemite.com/forest/sierra/sierra.htm					
Simonian Farms 2629 S Clovis Ave	Fresno	CA	93725	559-237-2294	441-1198
Web: www.fresno-online.com/simonian ■ *E-mail:* simonian@fresno-online.com					
Spectrum Gallery 1306 N Wishon Ave Tower District	Fresno	CA	93728	559-266-0691	

Fresno — Attractions (Cont'd)

				Phone	Fax
Table Mountain Rancheria Casino & Bingo 8184 Table Mountain Rd	Friant	CA	93626	559-822-2485	822-2084
Theatre Three 1544 Fulton St.	Fresno	CA	93721	559-486-3333	486-3333
Tower Theatre for the Performing Arts 815 E Olive Ave	Fresno	CA	93728	559-485-9050	485-3941
Web: www.tower2000.com/boxoffice/ ■ *E-mail:* tower@tower2000.com					
Warnors Theatre 1400 Fulton St.	Fresno	CA	93720	559-264-6863	264-5643
Wild Water Adventures 11413 E Shaw Ave	Clovis	CA	93611	559-297-6540	297-6549
Woodward Park 7775 Friant Rd	Fresno	CA	93710	559-498-1551	
Yosemite Mountain Sugar Pine Railroad 56001 Hwy 41	Fish Camp	CA	93623	559-683-7273	
Yosemite National Park PO Box 577	Yosemite National Park	CA	95389	209-372-0200	
Web: www.yosemitepark.com					

SPORTS TEAMS & FACILITIES

				Phone	Fax
Fresno Bandits (football) PO Box 72.	Fresno	CA	93707	559-264-9249	264-9246
Fresno Falcons (hockey) 700 M St Fresno Selland Arena	Fresno	CA	93701	559-264-7644	
Fresno's Fighting Falcons (hockey) 2300 Tulare St Suite 150	Fresno	CA	93721	559-650-4000	497-6077
Web: www.fresnofalcons.com					
Selland Arena 700 M St Fresno Convention Ctr.	Fresno	CA	93721	559-498-1511	488-4634

— Events —

	Phone
Carnival (late February)	559-485-4810
Civil War Revisited (early October)	559-441-0862
Clovis Rodeo (late April)	559-299-8838
Easton May Day Celebration (early May)	559-233-0836
Fresno County Blossom Trail (late February-early March)	559-233-0836
Fresno Fair (mid-October)	559-453-3247
High Sierra Regatta (July)	559-822-2666
Hmong National New Year (late December-early January)	559-233-4622
Kingsburg Gun Shoot (late June)	559-897-2925
Kingsburg Summer Band Concerts Under the Stars (late June-late July)	559-897-2925
Kwanzaa Festival (late December-early January)	559-268-7102
Mariachi Festival (early March)	559-455-5761
Miss California Pageant (mid-June)	559-233-0836
Obon Odori Festival (mid-July)	559-442-4054
Raisin Bowl Regatta (early May)	559-822-2332
Renaissance Festival (late October)	559-436-3434
Sanger Blossom Days Festival (early March)	559-875-4575
Sanger Grape Bowl Festival (mid-September)	559-875-4575
Shaver Lake Fishing Derby (mid-June)	559-841-3350
Sudz in the City (mid-May)	559-266-9982
Tower Arts Festival (mid-May)	559-498-8560
William Saroyan Festival (late April)	559-221-1441

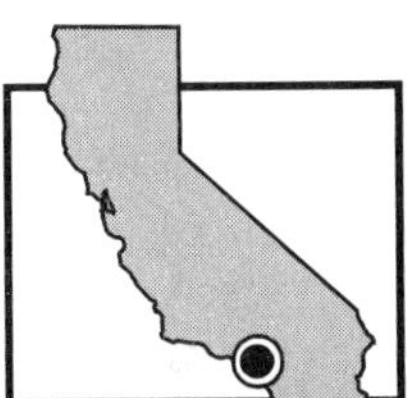

Garden Grove

Located in the heart of Orange County, Garden Grove is easily accessible to businesses and attractions in Los Angeles, Long Beach, and San Diego via the Garden Grove Freeway. The most spectacular attraction in Garden Grove is the $18 million Crystal Cathedral. Built in 1980, the cathedral is an all-glass church designed to resemble a four-pointed crystal star. Tours are available throughout the year, and Sunday services are televised worldwide. The city's Village Green Cultural Arts Complex features a theater, an amphitheater, a meeting center, and a greenbelt for outdoor entertainment. The greenbelt is the site of Garden Grove's most popular event, the annual Strawberry Festival, which draws nearly half a million visitors each year. Other annual events in Garden Grove include the Korean Festival and the Tet Festival, which celebrates the cultural traditions of the Vietnamese community.

Population	151,264	**Longitude**	117-57-33 W
Area (Land)	17.9 sq mi	**County**	Orange
Area (Water)	0.0 sq mi	**Time Zone**	PST
Elevation	90 ft	**Area Code/s**	714
Latitude	33-46-43 N		

— Average Temperatures and Precipitation —

TEMPERATURES

	Jan	Feb	Mar	Apr	May	Jun	Jul	Aug	Sep	Oct	Nov	Dec
High	69	70	70	73	74	78	83	84	83	80	74	69
Low	46	47	49	51	56	59	63	64	62	58	50	45

PRECIPITATION

	Jan	Feb	Mar	Apr	May	Jun	Jul	Aug	Sep	Oct	Nov	Dec
Inches	2.5	2.3	2.2	0.8	0.2	0.1	0.0	0.1	0.4	0.3	1.7	1.8

— Important Phone Numbers —

	Phone		Phone
AAA	714-848-2227	**Medical Referral**	714-741-3311
American Express Travel	714-671-6967	**Poison Control Center**	800-876-4766
Dental Referral	714-634-8944	**Weather**	858-675-8706
Emergency	911		

— Information Sources —

				Phone	Fax
Better Business Bureau Serving Placentia 550 W Orangethorpe Ave.	Placentia	CA	92870	714-985-8900	985-8920
Web: www.la.bbb.org					
Garden Grove Chamber of Commerce 12866 Main St Suite 102	Garden Grove	CA	92840	714-638-7950	636-6672
Web: www.gardengrovechamber.org					
Garden Grove City Hall 11222 Acacia Pkwy	Garden Grove	CA	92842	714-741-5000	741-5205
Web: www.ci.garden-grove.ca.us					
Garden Grove Community Development Dept 11222 Acacia Pkwy	Garden Grove	CA	92840	714-741-5120	741-5136
Web: www.ci.garden-grove.ca.us/internet/commdev.html					
Garden Grove Mayor 11222 Acacia Pkwy	Garden Grove	CA	92840	714-741-5100	741-5044
Garden Grove Regional Library 11200 Stanford Ave.	Garden Grove	CA	92840	714-530-0711	530-0961
Garden Grove Visitors Bureau 12866 Main St Suite 102	Garden Grove	CA	92840	714-638-7950	636-6672
Orange County 12 Civic Center Plaza	Santa Ana	CA	92701	714-834-2500	834-2675
Web: www.oc.ca.gov					

On-Line Resources

Annual Guide for the Arts	www.guide4arts.com/oc/
City Knowledge Garden Grove	www.cityknowledge.com/ca_garden_grove.htm
Excite.com Garden Grove City Guide	www.excite.com/travel/countries/united_states/california/garden_grove/
Garden Grove Online	www.gardengrove.com/
Orange County's Premier Website	www.ocpremier.com

Garden Grove (Cont'd)

— Transportation Services —

AIRPORTS

■ Long Beach Municipal Airport (LGB)

	Phone
8 miles W of downtown Garden Grove (approx 15 minutes)	562-570-2600

Airport Transportation

	Phone
Express Shuttle $31 fare to downtown Garden Grove	800-606-7433
LAXpress Airport Shuttle $31 fare to downtown Garden Grove	800-427-7483
Prime Time Shuttle $41 fare to downtown Garden Grove	800-262-7433
Yellow Cab $43 fare to downtown Garden Grove	562-435-6111

Commercial Airlines

	Phone		Phone
American	800-433-7300	**United**	800-241-6522
American Eagle	800-433-7300	**United Express**	800-241-6522
Island Express	562-436-2012	**US Airways**	800-428-4322
TWA	800-221-2000		

Charter Airlines

	Phone		Phone
Aeroplex Aviation	562-426-5500	**Long Beach Air Charter**	562-425-3774
Air Palm Springs	760-322-1104	**Rainbow Air**	562-424-0119
Ari Worldwide Aircraft Charters	800-426-9110	**US Helicopters**	562-497-0390
Island Express Helicopter Service	310-510-2525	**Valley Executive Charter**	562-989-4321
Jet Connection	310-378-1411	**West Coast Charter**	949-852-8340

■ John Wayne Airport/Orange County (SNA)

	Phone
12 miles SE of downtown Garden Grove (approx 20 minutes)	949-252-5200

Airport Transportation

	Phone
Express Shuttle $20 fare to downtown Garden Grove	800-606-7433
LAXpress Airport Shuttle $21 fare to downtown Garden Grove	800-427-7483
Prime Time Shuttle $26 fare to downtown Garden Grove	800-262-7433
Yellow Cab $31 fare to downtown Garden Grove	714-535-2211

Commercial Airlines

	Phone		Phone
America West	800-235-9292	**Malaysia Airlines**	800-552-9264
American	800-433-7300	**SkyWest**	800-453-9417
Continental	800-525-0280	**United**	800-241-6522
Delta	714-534-8468	**United Express**	800-241-6522

Charter Airlines

	Phone		Phone
Alliance Executive Charter Services	800-232-5387	**Lenair Aviation Inc**	949-756-8546
Ari Worldwide Aircraft Charters	800-426-9110	**Regency Air LLC**	714-541-3932
Avjet Corp	800-342-8538	**Schubach Aviation**	800-214-8215
Clay Lacy Aviation Inc	800-423-2904	**Signature Flight Support**	949-263-5800
Combs Executive Charter	800-627-8465	**Sunbird Aviation LLC**	800-434-5150
Corporate America Aviation Inc	800-521-8585	**TWC Aviation**	888-892-0035
Helistream	714-662-3163	**West Coast Charter**	949-852-8340

■ Los Angeles International Airport (LAX)

	Phone
29 miles NW of downtown Garden Grove (approx 60 minutes)	310-646-5252

Web: www.lax2015.org

Airport Transportation

	Phone
Express Shuttle $30 fare to downtown Garden Grove	800-606-7433
LAXpress Airport Shuttle $31 fare to downtown Garden Grove	800-427-7483
Prime Time Shuttle $39 fare to downtown Garden Grove	800-262-7433
Yellow Cab $65 fare to downtown Garden Grove	323-221-1234

Commercial Airlines

	Phone		Phone
AccessAir	877-462-2237	**Korean Air**	800-438-5000
Aerolineas Argentinas	800-333-0276	**LACSA**	213-385-9424
Air Canada	800-776-3000	**LTU International**	800-888-0200
Air Jamaica	800-523-5585	**Lufthansa**	800-645-3880
Air New Zealand	310-615-1111	**Mexicana**	800-531-7923
Alitalia	800-223-5730	**Midwest Express**	800-452-2022
All Nippon Airways	310-782-3000	**National**	888-757-5387
America West	800-235-9292	**Northwest**	800-225-2525
American	800-433-7300	**Pan Am**	800-359-7262
American Eagle	800-433-7300	**Philippine**	800-435-9725
Avianca	800-284-2622	**Qantas**	800-227-4500
British Airways	800-247-9297	**Scandinavian**	800-221-2350
China Airlines	310-641-8888	**Shuttle by United**	800-748-8853
China Eastern	626-583-1500	**SkyWest**	800-453-9417
Continental	800-525-0280	**Southwest**	800-435-9792
Delta	213-386-5510	**TACA International**	800-535-8780
El Al	800-223-6700	**TWA**	800-221-2000
Hawaiian	310-215-1866	**United**	800-241-6522
Iberia	800-772-4642	**United Express**	800-241-6522
Island Express	562-436-2012	**US Airways**	800-428-4322
Japan	800-525-3663	**Varig Brazilian**	310-646-2190
KLM	800-374-7747	**Virgin Atlantic**	800-862-8621

Charter Airlines

	Phone		Phone
Universal Jet	310-399-7371	**West Coast Charter**	949-852-8340

CAR RENTALS

	Phone		Phone
Alamo	800-327-9633	**Enterprise**	714-539-1161
Avis	714-774-3455	**Hertz**	714-772-0425
Budget	800-221-1203	**Thrifty**	714-778-6550
Dollar	800-800-4000	**Thrifty**	310-645-1880

LIMO/TAXI

	Phone		Phone
Fox Limousine	800-274-4369	**VIP Coastal Transportation**	800-735-7535
Harbour Transportation	714-636-0151	**West Coast Taxi**	714-547-8000
Limousine Services	800-465-4667		

MASS TRANSIT

	Phone
OCTA Bus $1 Base fare	714-636-7433

RAIL/BUS

				Phone
Amtrak Station 2150 E Katella Ave *TF:* 800-872-7245	Anaheim	CA	92806	714-385-1448
Greyhound/Trailways Bus Station 1000 E Santa Ana Blvd *TF:* 800-231-2222	Santa Ana	CA	92701	714-542-3927

— Accommodations —

HOTELS, MOTELS, RESORTS

				Phone	Fax
Best Western Inn 1176 W Katella Ave *TF:* 800-528-1234	Anaheim	CA	92802	714-776-0140	776-5801
Best Western Plaza International Inn 7912 Garden Grove Blvd *TF:* 800-528-1234	Garden Grove	CA	92861	714-894-7568	894-6308
Harbor Motel 12812 Palm St	Garden Grove	CA	92840	714-537-8008	
Hollandease Motel 13571 Harbor Blvd	Garden Grove	CA	92843	714-537-2710	638-9096
Hospitality Inn Garden Grove 7900 Garden Grove Blvd	Garden Grove	CA	92841	714-898-1306	894-6308
Howard Johnson 11632 Beach Blvd *TF:* 800-446-4656	Stanton	CA	90680	714-891-7688	
Hyatt Regency Alicante 100 Plaza Alicante *TF:* 800-233-1234	Garden Grove	CA	92840	714-750-1234	740-0465
Inncal Hotel 8062 Garden Grove Blvd *TF:* 800-550-0055	Garden Grove	CA	92644	714-898-3500	898-3500
InnSuites Buena Park Suite Hotel & Resort 7555 Beach Blvd *TF:* 888-522-5885 ■ *Web:* www.innsuites.com/hotelbuenapark.htm	Buena Park	CA	90620	714-522-7360	523-2883
Legacy Suites 12550 Lampson Ave	Garden Grove	CA	92840	714-748-8990	750-1149
National Inn 9797 Garden Grove Blvd	Garden Grove	CA	92644	714-636-5110	

Garden Grove — Hotels, Motels, Resorts (Cont'd)

				Phone	Fax
Ramada Inn Disneyland					
10022 Garden Grove Blvd	Garden Grove	CA	92844	714-534-1818	539-9930
TF: 800-917-5555					
Sandman Motel 12091 Trask Ave	Garden Grove	CA	92843	714-539-2500	539-4303
Travelodge 13659 Beach Blvd	Westminster	CA	92683	714-373-3200	895-5801
TF: 800-432-6343					
Tropic Lodge 8791 Garden Grove Blvd	Garden Grove	CA	92841	714-537-6752	
West Garden Inn 14052 Brookhurst St	Garden Grove	CA	92843	714-636-4890	530-8712

— Restaurants —

				Phone
Anh Hong (Vietnamese) 10195 Westminster Ave	Garden Grove	CA	92843	714-537-5230
Apollo Burgers (American) 12012 Chapman Ave	Garden Grove	CA	92840	714-971-0825
Azteca (Mexican) 12911 Main St	Garden Grove	CA	92840	714-638-3790
BC Seafood (Seafood) 12158 Brookhurst St	Garden Grove	CA	92840	714-537-6402
Black Angus (Steak) 12900 Euclid St	Garden Grove	CA	92840	714-638-9981
Calvin's Place (American) 12563 Harbor Blvd	Garden Grove	CA	92840	714-539-8174
Coco's (American) 12032 Harbor Blvd	Garden Grove	CA	92840	714-750-7477
Demiceli Italian Restaurant (Italian)				
12172 Brookhurst St	Garden Grove	CA	92640	714-530-4440
Four Seasons (Seafood) 14390 Brookhurst St	Garden Grove	CA	92843	714-531-4965
Furiwa Seafood (Chinese) 13826 Brookhurst St	Garden Grove	CA	92843	714-534-3996
Haus of Pizza (Italian) 12912 Harbor Blvd	Garden Grove	CA	92840	714-636-0591
HomeTown Buffet (American) 9635 Chapman Ave	Garden Grove	CA	92841	714-636-7550
In Chon Won Restaurant (Korean)				
13321 Brookhurst St	Garden Grove	CA	92843	714-539-8989
Jaimes Restaurant (Mexican) 11915 Euclid St	Garden Grove	CA	92840	714-537-8785
Korea House Barbecue (Korean)				
12118 Brookhurst St	Garden Grove	CA	92840	714-636-1700
La Fayette (French) 12532 Garden Grove Blvd	Garden Grove	CA	92843	714-537-5011
Leilani's Best Cuisine (Filipino) 9522 Chapman Ave	Garden Grove	CA	92641	714-530-7444
Loffler's (American) 12455 Haster St	Garden Grove	CA	92840	714-971-2311
Manta's Burgers (American) 12401 Haster St	Garden Grove	CA	92640	714-971-5704
Maxwell's (Continental) 12752 Valley View Ave	Garden Grove	CA	92645	714-898-0081
Mimi's Cafe (American) 7955 Garden Grove Blvd	Garden Grove	CA	92841	714-898-5042
Moen (Korean) 8335 Garden Grove Blvd	Garden Grove	CA	92844	714-636-5161
New Peking Restaurant (Chinese) 12801 Harbor Blvd	Garden Grove	CA	92840	714-530-8833
Odondo Seafood Restaurant (Seafood)				
8315 Garden Grove Blvd	Garden Grove	CA	92844	714-530-5773
Panchitos Taqueria (Mexican) 13048 Chapman Ave	Garden Grove	CA	92840	714-748-1590
Perry's (Italian) 6937 Chapman Ave	Garden Grove	CA	92845	714-898-7670
Pinnacle Peak Steak House (Steak) 9100 Trask Ave	Garden Grove	CA	92844	714-892-7311
Red Sea Cafe (Middle Eastern) 12444 Brookhurst St	Garden Grove	CA	92840	714-537-5336
Royal Seafood Restaurant (Chinese/Thai)				
12342 Brookhurst St	Garden Grove	CA	92840	714-636-5028
Spring Garden (Korean) 10022 Garden Grove Blvd	Garden Grove	CA	92844	714-534-1222
Thao Restaurant (Vietnamese) 10082 Chapman Ave	Garden Grove	CA	92840	714-636-1652
Uhsim Japanese Restaurant (Japanese)				
10051 Garden Grove Blvd	Garden Grove	CA	92844	714-638-8820
Venezia Italian Restaurant (Italian)				
12549 Harbor Blvd	Garden Grove	CA	92840	714-537-1710
Waterfront Cafe (American) 12902 Brookhurst St	Garden Grove	CA	92840	714-636-8152

— Goods and Services —

SHOPPING

				Phone	Fax
Brea Mall 1065 Brea Mall	Brea	CA	92821	714-990-2732	990-5048
Buena Park Mall 8308 On The Mall	Buena Park	CA	90620	714-828-7722	761-0748
Garden Grove Shopping Center					
Garden Grove & Harbor Blvds	Garden Grove	CA	92840	949-650-9737	
Garden Promenade					
Chapman Ave & Brookhurst St	Garden Grove	CA	92845		
Harbor Town & Country Center					
12913 Harbor Blvd	Garden Grove	CA	92840	949-650-9737	
Historic Main Street					
Main St & Garden Grove Blvd	Garden Grove	CA	92840		
MainPlace Santa Ana 2800 N Main St	Santa Ana	CA	92705	714-547-7000	547-2643
Mall of Orange 2298 N Orange Mall	Orange	CA	92865	714-998-0440	998-6378
Westminster Mall					
1025 Westminster Mall	Westminster	CA	92683	714-898-2558	892-8824

BANKS

				Phone	Fax
Bank of America 9591 Chapman Ave	Garden Grove	CA	92840	714-778-7425	539-9134
California Center Bank					
8132 Garden Grove Blvd	Garden Grove	CA	92844	714-891-2222	891-7172
California Korea Bank					
9122 Garden Grove Blvd	Garden Grove	CA	92844	714-537-4111	537-4891
Farmers & Merchants Bank					
10422 Garden Grove Blvd	Garden Grove	CA	92843	714-590-3880	537-5349
First State Bank of Southern California					
13011 Brookhurst St	Garden Grove	CA	92843	714-534-3900	534-6801
Hanmi Bank 9820 Garden Grove Blvd	Garden Grove	CA	92844	714-537-4040	537-4168*
**Fax:* Cust Svc					
Sanwa Bank 12976 Main St	Garden Grove	CA	92840	714-530-0820	530-2843
Union Bank of California					
11900 Brookhurst St	Garden Grove	CA	92840	714-534-0300	534-2190

BUSINESS SERVICES

	Phone		Phone
Aim Mail Center	714-539-0949	**Manpower Temporary Services**	714-558-0238
Airborne Express	800-247-2676	**Post Office**	800-275-8777
DHL Worldwide Express	800-225-5345	**Thomas Staffing**	714-891-4768
Federal Express	800-238-5355	**UPS**	800-742-5877
KC Printing	714-638-2011		

— Media —

PUBLICATIONS

				Phone	Fax
Garden Grove Journal					
12866 Main St Suite 203	Garden Grove	CA	92840	714-539-6018	892-7052
Web: www.ggjournal.com					
Orange County Business Journal					
4590 MacArthur Blvd Suite 100	Newport Beach	CA	92660	949-833-8373	833-8751
Orange County Register‡ 625 N Grand Ave	Santa Ana	CA	92701	714-835-1234	565-3681
Web: www.ocregister.com					
Orange County Reporter					
600 W Santa Ana Blvd Suite 205	Santa Ana	CA	92701	714-543-2027	542-6841

‡Daily newspapers

TELEVISION

				Phone	Fax
KABC-TV Ch 7 (ABC) 4151 Prospect Ave	Los Angeles	CA	90027	310-557-3200	557-3360
Web: abcnews.go.com/local/kabc ■ *E-mail:* abc7@abc.com					
KCBS-TV Ch 2 (CBS) 6121 Sunset Blvd	Los Angeles	CA	90028	323-460-3000	460-3733
Web: www.kcbs2.com					
KCET-TV Ch 28 (PBS) 4401 Sunset Blvd	Los Angeles	CA	90027	323-666-6500	953-5523
Web: www.keet.org					
KNBC-TV Ch 4 (NBC) 3000 W Alameda Ave	Burbank	CA	91523	818-840-4444	840-3535
Web: www.knbc4la.com					
KTTV-TV Ch 11 (Fox)					
1999 S Bundy Dr	West Los Angeles	CA	90025	310-584-2000	584-2023
Web: www.fox11la.com ■ *E-mail:* talkback@fox11la.com					

RADIO

				Phone	Fax
KABC-AM 790 kHz (N/T)					
3321 S La Cienega Blvd	Los Angeles	CA	90016	310-840-4900	838-5222
Web: www.kabc.com					
KBIG-FM 104.3 MHz (AC)					
330 N Brand Blvd Suite 800	Glendale	CA	91203	818-546-1043	637-2267*
**Fax:* Sales ■ *Web:* www.kbig104.com					
KCBS-FM 93.1 MHz (CR)					
6121 Sunset Blvd	Los Angeles	CA	90028	323-460-3000	460-3733
Web: www.arrowfm.com					
KFWB-AM 980 kHz (N/T) 6230 Yucca St	Hollywood	CA	90028	323-462-5392	871-4670
Web: www.kfwb.com ■ *E-mail:* quake@kfwb.groupw.wec.com					
KHWY-FM 98.9 MHz (AC) 1611 E Main St	Barstow	CA	92311	760-256-0326	256-9507
KIIS-FM 102.7 MHz (CHR)					
3400 Riverside Dr Suite 800	Burbank	CA	91505	818-845-1027	295-6466
Web: www.kiisfm.com					
KLAX-FM 97.9 MHz (Span)					
10281 W Pico Blvd	Los Angeles	CA	90064	310-203-0900	203-8989*
**Fax:* Sales					
KLOS-FM 95.5 MHz (Rock)					
3321 S La Cienega Blvd	Los Angeles	CA	90016	310-840-4900	558-7685
Web: www.955klos.com					
KNX-AM 1070 kHz (N/T)					
6121 Sunset Blvd	Los Angeles	CA	90028	323-460-3000	460-3275
Web: www.knx1070.com					
KOST-FM 103.5 MHz (AC)					
610 S Ardmore Ave	Los Angeles	CA	90005	213-427-1035	385-0281
TF: 800-929-5678					

Garden Grove — Radio (Cont'd)

				Phone	Fax
KRTH-FM 101.1 MHz (Oldies) 5901 Venice Blvd	Los Angeles	CA	90034	323-937-5230	936-3427
KYSR-FM 98.7 MHz (AC) 3500 W Olive Ave Suite 250 *Web:* www.star987.com	Burbank	CA	91505	818-955-7000	955-6436

— Colleges/Universities —

				Phone	Fax
Azusa Pacific University 1915 W Orangewood Ave	Orange	CA	92868	714-935-9697	935-0356
California State University Fullerton 800 N State College Blvd *Web:* www.fullerton.edu	Fullerton	CA	92831	714-278-2011	278-3990
Chapman University 333 N Glassell St *TF:* 800-282-7759 ■ *Web:* www.chapman.edu ■ *E-mail:* low@chapman.edu	Orange	CA	92866	714-997-6815	997-6713
Santa Ana College Garden Grove Center 11277 Garden Grove Blvd	Garden Grove	CA	92843	714-564-5500	
West Orange College 12865 Main St Suite 105	Garden Grove	CA	92840	714-530-5000	530-5003

— Hospitals —

				Phone	Fax
Anaheim Memorial Hospital 1111 W La Palma Ave	Anaheim	CA	92801	714-774-1450	999-6122
Fountain Valley Regional Hospital & Medical Center 17100 Euclid St	Fountain Valley	CA	92708	714-966-7200	966-8039
Garden Grove Hospital & Medical Center 12601 Garden Grove Blvd *Web:* www.tenethealth.com/GardenGrove	Garden Grove	CA	92843	714-537-5160	741-3322
Vencor Hospital 200 Hospital Cir *Web:* www.vencor.com	Westminster	CA	92683	714-893-4541	894-3407
West Anaheim Medical Center 3033 W Orange Ave	Anaheim	CA	92804	714-827-3000	229-6813

— Attractions —

				Phone	Fax
Atlantis Play Center 9301 Westminster Ave	Garden Grove	CA	92844	714-892-6015	
Buena Park Civic Theater 8150 Knott Ave	Buena Park	CA	90620	714-562-3888	827-9782
Crystal Cathedral 12141 Lewis St *Web:* www.crystalcathedral.org	Garden Grove	CA	92840	714-971-4013	971-2910
Disneyland PO Box 3232 *Web:* disney.go.com/Disneyland	Anaheim	CA	92803	714-781-4565	
Garden Grove Playhouse 12001 Saint Mark St	Garden Grove	CA	92845	714-897-5122	
Grove Theater Center 12852 Main St *Web:* www.gtc.org ■ *E-mail:* gtc@gtc.org	Garden Grove	CA	92840	714-741-9554	741-9560
Historic Main Street Main St & Garden Grove Blvd	Garden Grove	CA	92840		
Knott's Berry Farm 8039 Beach Blvd *Web:* www.knotts.com	Buena Park	CA	90620	714-827-1776	220-5200
Ripley's Believe It or Not! Museum 7850 Beach Blvd *Web:* www.movielandwaxmuseum.com/rip.html	Buena Park	CA	90620	714-522-1152	739-9668
Stanley Ranch Museum 12174 Euclid St PO Box 4297	Garden Grove	CA	92842	714-530-8871	
Westminster Museum 8612 Westminster Blvd	Westminster	CA	92683	714-891-2597	
Yorba Regional Park 7600 E La Palma	Anaheim	CA	92807	714-970-1460	

SPORTS TEAMS & FACILITIES

				Phone	Fax
Los Alamitos Race Course 4961 Katella Ave *Web:* www.webworldinc.com/larace/laqhr	Los Alamitos	CA	90720	714-236-4400	
Orange County Zodiac (soccer) 602 N Flower St Eddie West Field *Web:* www.oczodiac.com ■ *E-mail:* comments@oczodiac.com	Santa Ana	CA	92701	949-348-4880	348-4601

— Events —

	Phone
Crystal Cathedral Glory of Christmas (late November-December)	714-544-5679
Crystal Cathedral Glory of Easter (late March-April)	714-544-5679
Fantasy in the Sky (June-September)	714-781-4560
Garden Grove Strawberry Festival (late May)	714-638-0981
Gogh Van Orange Art & Music Festival (early May)	714-538-3581
Halloween Carnival (late October)	714-741-5200
Korean Festival (early-October)	714-741-3310
Orange County Fair (mid-July)	714-708-3247
Orange County Wine Festival (early October)	714-530-0430
Songs of Christmas (early December)	714-741-5200
Tet Festival (early February)	714-775-6820

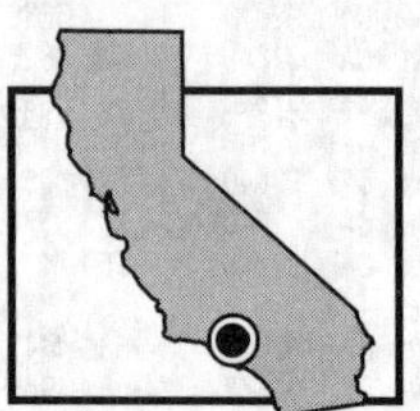

Glendale

Located northeast of Los Angeles in the foothills of the San Gabriel Mountains, Glendale is estimated to be the third largest financial center in the state of California. The city's economic base revolves primarily around retail and service industries, and the Glendale Galleria is Southern California's largest and highest sales tax-generating mall. Glendale has received Certified Local Government Status for its historical preservation efforts; historical sites in Glendale include the Casa Adobe, Verdugo Adobe, Tea House, and Doctor's House.

Population	185,086	**Longitude**	118-15-11 W
Area (Land)	30.6 sq mi	**County**	Los Angeles
Area (Water)	0.0 sq mi	**Time Zone**	PST
Elevation	571 ft	**Area Code/s**	818
Latitude	34-10-36 N		

— Average Temperatures and Precipitation —

TEMPERATURES

	Jan	Feb	Mar	Apr	May	Jun	Jul	Aug	Sep	Oct	Nov	Dec
High	68	70	71	75	78	83	90	90	88	82	73	68
Low	41	44	45	48	53	57	61	62	59	54	46	41

PRECIPITATION

	Jan	Feb	Mar	Apr	May	Jun	Jul	Aug	Sep	Oct	Nov	Dec
Inches	3.0	3.3	3.0	1.2	0.2	0.1	0.0	0.2	0.4	0.5	2.1	2.1

— Important Phone Numbers —

	Phone		Phone
AAA	818-240-2200	**Poison Control Center**	800-876-4766
American Express Travel	818-246-1661	**Time**	310-853-1212
Emergency	911	**Weather**	213-554-1212
Medical Referral	818-502-2378		

— Information Sources —

				Phone	Fax
Better Business Bureau Serving Encino 17609 Ventura Blvd Suite LL03 *Web:* www.la.bbb.org	Encino	CA	91316	818-386-5510	386-5513
Glendale Chamber of Commerce 200 S Louise St *Web:* www.glendalechamber.com ■ *E-mail:* info@glendalechamber.com	Glendale	CA	91205	818-240-7870	240-2872

Glendale — Information Sources (Cont'd)

				Phone	Fax
Glendale City Hall 613 E Broadway *Web:* www.ci.glendale.ca.us	Glendale	CA	91206	818-548-2090	241-5386
Glendale Civic Auditorium 1401 N Verdugo Rd *Web:* www.ci.glendale.ca.us/civicaud/index.html	Glendale	CA	91208	818-548-2147	543-0793
Glendale Community Development & Housing Dept 141 N Glendale Ave Rm 202 *Web:* www.ci.glendale.ca.us/nhood-services/commdev.html ■ *E-mail:* business@glendaleca.com	Glendale	CA	91206	818-548-2060	548-3724
Glendale Mayor 613 E Broadway Suite 200	Glendale	CA	91206	818-548-4844	547-6740
Glendale Public Library 222 E Harvard St *Web:* library.ci.glendale.ca.us	Glendale	CA	91205	818-548-2021	548-7225
Los Angeles County 500 W Temple St. *Web:* www.co.la.ca.us	Los Angeles	CA	90012	213-974-1311	

On-Line Resources

Anthill City Guide Glendale	www.anthill.com/city.asp?city=glendale
City Knowledge Glendale	www.cityknowledge.com/ca_glendale.htm
Glendale City Net	www.excite.com/travel/countries/united_states/california/glendale
Glendale Community Wire	www.cwire.com/glendale/
Glendale On-line	glendale-online.com/
Glendale Theatre District	theatre.glendale.ca.us
GlendaleAccess.com	www.glendaleaccess.com

— Transportation Services —

AIRPORTS

■ Burbank-Glendale-Pasadena Airport (BUR)

	Phone
7 miles W of downtown Glendale (approx 25 minutes) Web: www.bur.com	818-840-8840

Airport Transportation

	Phone
Prime Time Shuttle $19 fare to downtown Glendale	800-733-8267
SuperShuttle $13-15 fare to downtown Glendale	818-556-6600
Taxi $18 fare to downtown Glendale	818-843-8500

Commercial Airlines

	Phone		Phone
America West	800-235-9292	**SkyWest**	800-453-9417
American	800-433-7300	**Southwest**	800-435-9792
American Eagle	800-433-7300	**United**	800-241-6522
Continental	800-525-0280	**United Express**	800-241-6522
Delta	213-386-5510		

Charter Airlines

	Phone
Signature Flight Support	949-263-5800

■ Los Angeles International Airport (LAX)

	Phone
21 miles SW of downtown Glendale (approx 60 minutes) Web: www.lax2015.org	310-646-5252

Airport Transportation

	Phone
California Dream Shuttle $17 fare to downtown Glendale	800-503-7326
Prime Time Shuttle $30-32 fare to downtown Glendale	800-733-8267
SuperShuttle $27 fare to downtown Glendale	818-556-6600
Taxi $50 fare to downtown Glendale	818-242-3131

Commercial Airlines

	Phone		Phone
AccessAir	877-462-2237	**Korean Air**	800-438-5000
Aerolineas Argentinas	800-333-0276	**LACSA**	213-385-9424
Air Canada	800-776-3000	**Lufthansa**	800-645-3880
Air Jamaica	800-523-5585	**Malaysia Airlines**	800-552-9264
Air New Zealand	310-615-1111	**Mexicana**	800-531-7923
Alitalia	800-223-5730	**Midwest Express**	800-452-2022
All Nippon Airways	310-782-3000	**National**	888-757-5387
America West	800-235-9292	**Northwest**	800-225-2525
American	800-433-7300	**Pan Am**	800-359-7262
American Eagle	800-433-7300	**Philippine**	800-435-9725
Avianca	800-284-2622	**Qantas**	800-227-4500
British Airways	800-247-9297	**Scandinavian**	800-221-2350
China Airlines	310-641-8888	**Shuttle by United**	800-748-8853
China Eastern	626-583-1500	**SkyWest**	800-453-9417
Continental	800-525-0280	**Southwest**	800-435-9792
Delta	213-386-5510	**TACA International**	800-535-8780
El Al	800-223-6700	**TWA**	800-221-2000
Hawaiian	310-215-1866	**United**	800-241-6522
Iberia	800-772-4642	**United Express**	800-241-6522
Island Express	562-436-2012	**US Airways**	800-428-4322
Japan	800-525-3663	**Varig Brazilian**	310-646-2190
KLM	800-374-7747	**Virgin Atlantic**	800-862-8621

Charter Airlines

	Phone		Phone
Universal Jet	310-399-7371	**West Coast Charter**	949-852-8340

CAR RENTALS

	Phone		Phone
Alamo	818-840-8045	**Enterprise**	310-649-5400
Avis	818-566-3001	**Hertz**	818-569-3574
Budget	818-841-3922	**National**	800-227-7368
Dollar	310-645-9333	**Thrifty**	310-645-1880

LIMO/TAXI

	Phone		Phone
Alfa Limousine & Shuttle	818-549-1427	**Glendale Taxi**	818-956-5959
Checker Cab	818-843-8500	**Yellow Cab**	818-242-3131
Glendale Limousine Co	818-242-1000		

MASS TRANSIT

	Phone
BeeLine Downtown Shuttle Bus $.25 Base fare	818-548-3960
MetroLink $3.75 Base fare	818-808-5465
MTA $1.35 Base fare	213-626-4455

RAIL/BUS

				Phone
Amtrak Station 400 W Cerritos Ave	Glendale	CA	91204	800-872-7245
Greyhound Bus Station 400 W Cerritos Ave. *TF:* 800-231-2222	Glendale	CA	91204	818-244-7295

— Accommodations —

HOTELS, MOTELS, RESORTS

				Phone	Fax
American Motel 1541 E Colorado St	Glendale	CA	91205	818-242-5572	
Astro Glendale Motel 326 E Colorado St	Glendale	CA	91205	818-246-7401	
Bell Motor Hotel 1130 E Colorado St	Glendale	CA	91205	818-956-7179	
Best Western Golden Key Motor Hotel 123 W Colorado St *TF:* 800-528-1234	Glendale	CA	91204	818-247-0111	545-9393
Chariot Inn Motel 1118 E Colorado St	Glendale	CA	91205	818-507-9600	507-9774
Days Inn 600 N Pacific Ave *TF:* 800-325-2525	Glendale	CA	91203	818-956-0202	502-0843
Doubletree Hotel 100 W Glenoaks Blvd *TF:* 800-222-8733	Glendale	CA	91202	818-956-5466	956-5490
Econo Lodge 1437 E Colorado St	Glendale	CA	91205	818-246-8367	246-8374
El Rio Motel 1515 E Colorado St	Glendale	CA	91205	818-243-3157	
Glen Capri Motel 6700 San Fernando Rd.	Glendale	CA	91201	818-244-8434	240-6911
Glendale Motel 1523 E Colorado St	Glendale	CA	91205	818-243-7126	
Hilton Pasadena 150 S Los Robles Ave. *TF:* 800-445-8667 ■ *Web:* www.hilton.com/hotels/PASPHHH	Pasadena	CA	91101	626-577-1000	584-3148
Manhattan Motel 1523 E Colorado St	Glendale	CA	91205	818-244-8195	
Maryland Hotel 202 E Wilson Ave.	Glendale	CA	91206	818-241-3121	
McKenzie Hotel 339 1/2 N Brand Blvd.	Glendale	CA	91203	818-244-3820	

Glendale — Hotels, Motels, Resorts (Cont'd)

				Phone	Fax
Regalodge Motel 200 W Colorado St	Glendale	CA	91204	818-246-7331	
Ritz-Carlton Huntington Hotel & Spa 1401 S Oak Knoll Ave	Pasadena	CA	91106	626-568-3900	568-3700
TF: 800-241-3333 ■ *Web:* www.ritzcarlton.com/location/NorthAmerica/HuntingtonHotel/main.htm					
Savoy Motel 306 Lafayette St	Glendale	CA	91205	818-956-6170	
Vagabond Inn 120 W Colorado St	Glendale	CA	91204	818-240-1700	548-8428

— Restaurants —

				Phone
100 West American Grill (New American) 100 W Glenoaks Blvd	Glendale	CA	91202	818-956-5466
Acapulco Mexican Restaurant (Mexican) 722 N Pacific Ave	Glendale	CA	91203	818-246-8175
Aoba Japanese Restaurant (Japanese) 239 N Brand Blvd	Glendale	CA	91203	818-247-9789
Barmaky Restaurant (Lebanese) 233 1/2 N Brand Blvd	Glendale	CA	91203	818-240-6133
Black Cow Cafe (American) 2219 Honolulu Ave	Glendale	CA	91214	818-957-5282
Cafe Seoul Restaurant (Korean) 312 1/2 N Brand Blvd.	Glendale	CA	91203	818-247-6955
Casa De Ramos (Mexican) 827 W Glenoaks Blvd	Glendale	CA	91202	818-240-3129
China Garden (Chinese) 217 S Brand Blvd	Glendale	CA	91204	818-240-0119
China Kitchen (Chinese) 1229 E Colorado St.	Glendale	CA	91205	818-507-1185
Cinnabar (California/Asian) 933 S Brand Blvd	Glendale	CA	91204	818-551-1155
Clancy's Crab Broiler (Seafood) 219 N Central Ave	Glendale	CA	91203	818-242-2722
Cuba Cali Restaurant (Cuban) 6604 San Fernando Rd	Glendale	CA	91201	818-247-7703
Elena (Greek/Armenian) 1000 S Glendale Blvd	Glendale	CA	91207	818-241-5730
Far Niente Ristorante (Italian) 204 1/2 N Brand Blvd.	Glendale	CA	91203	818-242-3835
Fortune Inn (Chinese) 117 E Broadway	Glendale	CA	91205	818-547-2833
Fresco Ristorante (Italian) 514 S Brand Blvd	Glendale	CA	91204	818-247-5541
Gennaro's Ristorante (Italian) 1109 N Brand Blvd	Glendale	CA	91202	818-243-6231
Hawaiian BBQ Express (Barbecue) 1135 Glendale Galleria	Glendale	CA	91210	818-242-7768
Hibiscus Cafe (Mediterranean) 3459 N Verdugo Rd.	Glendale	CA	91208	818-541-9918
Il Gazebo Ristorante (Italian) 304 N Brand Blvd	Glendale	CA	91202	818-246-7775
Karuon Restaurant (Persian) 1240 S Glendale Ave.	Glendale	CA	91205	818-500-0008
La Cubana Restaurant (Cuban) 720 E Colorado St.	Glendale	CA	91205	818-243-4398
La Fontana (Italian) 933 N Brand Blvd	Glendale	CA	91202	818-247-6256
Mori Teppan Grill (Japanese) 120 W Stocker St	Glendale	CA	91202	818-548-4227
New Delhi Palace Cuisine (Indian) 119 S Brand Blvd	Glendale	CA	91204	818-265-0666
Orchid Restaurant (Persian) 510 E Broadway	Glendale	CA	91205	818-550-9998
Pacific Seafood Grill (Seafood) 1142 Glendale Galleria	Glendale	CA	91210	818-244-0016
Rusty Pelican (Seafood) 300 Harvey Dr	Glendale	CA	91206	818-242-9191
Shamshiri Restaurant (Persian) 122 W Stocker St.	Glendale	CA	91202	818-246-9541
Sushi on Brand (Japanese) 308 N Brand Blvd.	Glendale	CA	91203	818-241-0133
Tep Thai (Thai) 207 W Wilson Ave.	Glendale	CA	91203	818-956-8626
Varouj's Kabobs (Middle Eastern) 1110 S Glendale Ave	Glendale	CA	91205	818-243-9870
Wazwan Cuisine of India (Indian) 1140 Glendale Galleria	Glendale	CA	91210	818-549-1110
Windsor Club Cafe (Thai) 123 W Windsor Rd	Glendale	CA	91204	818-242-2789
Zono Sushi (Japanese) 139 N Maryland Ave	Glendale	CA	91206	818-507-4819

— Goods and Services —

SHOPPING

				Phone	Fax
Glendale Galleria 2148 Glendale Galleria	Glendale	CA	91210	818-240-9481	547-9398
Web: www.glendalegalleria.com ■ *E-mail:* mallinfo@glendalegalleria.com					
JC Penney 333 W Colorado St	Glendale	CA	91210	818-240-8700	
Media City Center 201 E Magnolia Blvd.	Burbank	CA	91501	818-566-8556	566-7936
Montebello Town Center 2134 Montebello Town Ctr	Montebello	CA	90640	323-722-1776	722-1268
Nordstrom 200 W Broadway	Glendale	CA	91210	818-502-9922	502-0109
Santa Anita Fashion Park 400 S Baldwin Ave	Arcadia	CA	91007	626-445-3116	446-9320
Sears Roebuck & Co 236 N Central Ave	Glendale	CA	91203	818-507-7200	

BANKS

				Phone	Fax
American International Bank 520 N Central Ave.	Glendale	CA	91203	818-545-8800	548-3583
Bank of America 3812 San Fernando Rd	Glendale	CA	91204	818-507-2393	507-0707
California Federal Bank 401 N Brand Blvd.	Glendale	CA	91203	800-843-2265	500-2491*
**Fax Area Code:* 818					
Fidelity Federal Bank 4565 Colorado Blvd.	Los Angeles	CA	90039	818-241-6215	241-2688
TF: 800-434-3354					
Imperial Thrift & Loan Assn 700 N Central Ave.	Glendale	CA	91203	818-551-0600	637-6600

BUSINESS SERVICES

	Phone		Phone
Adecco Employment Personnel Services	818-241-9909	**Mail Boxes Etc**	818-242-4270
DHL Worldwide Express	800-225-5345	**Manpower Temporary Services**	818-242-2185
Federal Express	800-238-5355	**Post Office**	800-275-8777
Kinko's	818-500-1811	**UPS**	800-742-5877

— Media —

PUBLICATIONS

				Phone	Fax
Foothill Leader 3527-A N Verdugo Rd.	Glendale	CA	91208	818-249-8090	249-6563*
**Fax:* News Rm					

TELEVISION

				Phone	Fax
KABC-TV Ch 7 (ABC) 4151 Prospect Ave	Los Angeles	CA	90027	310-557-3200	557-3360
Web: abcnews.go.com/local/kabc ■ *E-mail:* abc7@abc.com					
KCBS-TV Ch 2 (CBS) 6121 Sunset Blvd	Los Angeles	CA	90028	323-460-3000	460-3733
Web: www.kcbs2.com					
KCET-TV Ch 28 (PBS) 4401 Sunset Blvd	Los Angeles	CA	90027	323-666-6500	953-5523
Web: www.keet.org					
KNBC-TV Ch 4 (NBC) 3000 W Alameda Ave	Burbank	CA	91523	818-840-4444	840-3535
Web: www.knbc4la.com					
KTTV-TV Ch 11 (Fox) 1999 S Bundy Dr	West Los Angeles	CA	90025	310-584-2000	584-2023
Web: www.fox11la.com ■ *E-mail:* talkback@fox11la.com					

RADIO

				Phone	Fax
KIEV-AM 870 kHz (N/T) 701 N Brand Blvd Suite 550	Glendale	CA	91203	818-244-8483	551-1110*
**Fax Area Code:* 323					
KKLA-FM 99.5 MHz (N/T/Rel) 701 N Brand Blvd Suite 550	Glendale	CA	91203	818-956-5552	551-1110
Web: www.kkla.com ■ *E-mail:* info@kkla.com					
KLAC-AM 570 kHz (Nost) 330 N Brand Blvd Suite 800	Glendale	CA	91203	818-546-1043	637-2267
KPCC-FM 89.3 MHz (NPR) 1570 E Colorado Blvd	Pasadena	CA	91106	626-585-7000	585-7916
Web: www.kpcc.org					
KSCA-FM 101.9 MHz (Span) 1645 N Vine St.	Hollywood	CA	90028	323-465-3171	461-9973
KZLA-FM 93.9 MHz (Ctry) 7755 Sunset Blvd	Los Angeles	CA	90046	323-882-8000	874-9494
TF: 800-977-1939 ■ *Web:* www.kzla.net ■ *E-mail:* kzla@kzla.net					

— Colleges/Universities —

				Phone	Fax
Azusa Pacific University 901 E Alosta Ave.	Azusa	CA	91702	626-969-3434	969-7180
Web: www.apu.edu					
Glendale Community College 1500 N Verdugo Rd	Glendale	CA	91208	818-240-1000	551-5255
Web: www.glendale.cc.ca.us ■ *E-mail:* gparker@glendale.cc.ca.us					

— Hospitals —

				Phone	Fax
Glendale Adventist Medical Center 1509 Wilson Terr	Glendale	CA	91206	818-409-8000	546-5650*
**Fax:* PR					
Glendale Memorial Hospital & Health Center 1420 S Central Ave.	Glendale	CA	91201	818-502-1900	246-4104
Verdugo Hills Hospital 1812 Verdugo Blvd	Glendale	CA	91208	818-790-7100	952-4616

Glendale (Cont'd)

— Attractions —

				Phone	Fax
Alex Theatre 216 N Brand Blvd	Glendale	CA	91203	818-243-2809	243-3622
Web: theatre.glendale.ca.us/alex/					
Brand Library & Art Center 1601 W Mountain St	Glendale	CA	91201	818-548-2051	
Web: library.ci.glendale.ca.us/brand					
Brand Park 1601 W Mountain St	Glendale	CA	91201	818-548-2147	
Casa Adobe De San Rafael 1330 Dorothy Dr	Glendale	CA	91202	818-548-2147	543-0793
Descanso Gardens 1418 Descanso Dr	La Canada	CA	91011	818-952-4401	790-3291
Web: www.descanso.com/					
Forest Lawn Museum 1712 S Glendale Ave	Glendale	CA	91205	323-254-3131	551-5329
TF: 800-204-3131					
Gene Autry Western Heritage Museum 4700 Western Heritage Way	Los Angeles	CA	90027	323-667-2000	660-5721
E-mail: autry@autry-museum.org					
Glendale Centre Theater 324 N Orange St	Glendale	CA	91203	818-244-8481	244-5042
Glendale Symphony Orchestra 401 N Brand Blvd Suite 520	Glendale	CA	91203	818-500-8720	500-8014
Web: glendale-online.com/entertainment/gso/					
Griffith Observatory 2800 E Observatory Rd Griffith Pk	Los Angeles	CA	90027	323-664-1181	663-4323
Web: www.griffithobs.org					
Kidspace A Participatory Museum 390 S El Molino Ave	Pasadena	CA	91101	626-449-9144	449-9985
Los Angeles Zoo 5333 Zoo Dr	Los Angeles	CA	90027	323-666-4650	662-9786
Web: www.lazoo.org ■ *E-mail:* lazooed@ix.netcom.com					
NBC Studios 3000 W Alameda Ave	Burbank	CA	91523	818-840-3537	
Southwest Museum 234 Museum Dr	Los Angeles	CA	90065	323-221-2164	224-8223
Web: www.southwestmuseum.org ■ *E-mail:* swmuseum@annex.com					

SPORTS TEAMS & FACILITIES

				Phone	Fax
San Fernando Valley Heroes (soccer) 7955 San Fernando Rd	Sun Valley	CA	91352	818-768-0965	768-5213
San Gabriel Valley Highlanders (soccer) 536 N Glen Oaks Blvd	Burbank	CA	91501	818-242-9110	556-6427

— Events —

	Phone
Days of Verdugo Festival (mid-October)	818-240-2464
Tournament of Roses Parade (January 1)	626-795-9311
Valley Fair (mid-June)	818-557-1600

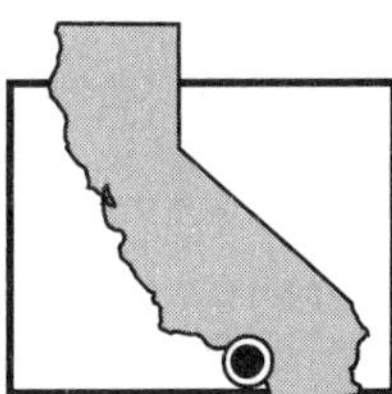

Huntington Beach

Popularly known as "Surf City USA," Huntington Beach is a surfer's paradise, with over eight miles of beaches that provide excellent conditions for surfing and other water sports. The city hosts more than a dozen surfing contests each year, including the world-famous Budweiser Tour and the U.S. Open of Surfing, and it is also home to the International Surfing Museum. Bird watching is also a popular activity in the Huntington Beach area. Prime bird watching spots include the Bolsa Chica Ecological Reserve, and a "Return of the Terns Festival" is held in the city each April. Called "One of America's Safest Cities," Huntington Beach was also named by California Business Magazine in 1993 as the "Best Big City To Do Business In" in the state.

Population	195,316	**Longitude**	118-00-29 W
Area (Land)	26.4 sq mi	**County**	Orange
Area (Water)	5.2 sq mi	**Time Zone**	PST
Elevation	28 ft	**Area Code/s**	714
Latitude	33-41-30 N		

— Average Temperatures and Precipitation —

TEMPERATURES

	Jan	Feb	Mar	Apr	May	Jun	Jul	Aug	Sep	Oct	Nov	Dec
High	67	68	68	72	73	77	83	84	82	78	72	67
Low	45	47	49	52	56	60	63	65	63	58	50	45

PRECIPITATION

	Jan	Feb	Mar	Apr	May	Jun	Jul	Aug	Sep	Oct	Nov	Dec
Inches	2.5	2.5	2.0	0.7	0.2	0.0	0.0	0.1	0.3	0.3	1.7	1.7

— Important Phone Numbers —

	Phone		Phone
AAA	714-848-2227	**Medical Referral**	949-760-2244
American Express Travel	714-540-3611	**Poison Control Center**	800-876-4766
Dental Referral	714-634-8992	**Time**	949-853-1212
Emergency	911	**Weather**	714-550-4636

— Information Sources —

				Phone	Fax
Better Business Bureau Serving Placentia 550 W Orangethorpe Ave	Placentia	CA	92870	714-985-8900	985-8920
Web: www.la.bbb.org					
Huntington Beach Chamber of Commerce 2100 Main St Suite 200	Huntington Beach	CA	92648	714-536-8888	960-7654
Web: www.hbchamber.org					
Huntington Beach City Hall 2000 Main St	Huntington Beach	CA	92648	714-536-5511	374-1557
Web: www.scag.org/homepages/huntington_beach/govt.htm					
Huntington Beach Conference & Visitors Bureau 101 Main St Suite 2A	Huntington Beach	CA	92648	714-969-3492	969-5592
Web: www.hbvisit.com/ ■ *E-mail:* hbvisit@ix.netcom.com					
Huntington Beach Economic Development Dept PO Box 190	Huntington Beach	CA	92648	714-536-5582	375-5087
Web: www.hbbiz.com/home/home.htm ■ *E-mail:* email@hbbiz.com					
Huntington Beach Library 7111 Talbert Ave	Huntington Beach	CA	92648	714-842-4481	375-5180
Huntington Beach Mayor 2000 Main St	Huntington Beach	CA	92648	714-536-5553	536-5233
Orange County 12 Civic Center Plaza	Santa Ana	CA	92701	714-834-2500	834-2675
Web: www.oc.ca.gov					

On-Line Resources

Annual Guide for the Arts	www.guide4arts.com/oc/
City Knowledge Huntington Beach	www.cityknowledge.com/ca_huntington_beach.htm
Excite.com Huntington Beach City Guide	www.excite.com/travel/countries/united_states/california/huntington_beach
Huntington Beach News	hb.quik.com/jperson/
Huntington Beach Online	www.hbonline.com/
Surf & Sun Beach Vacation Guide to Huntington Beach	www.surf-sun.com/ca-huntington-main.htm
Surf City	surfcity.huntington-beach.ca.us/
Surf City Web	www.surfcityweb.com
SurfCity.HuntingtonBeach-Ca.Us	surfcity.huntington-beach.ca.us

— Transportation Services —

AIRPORTS

	Phone
■ **John Wayne Airport/Orange County (SNA)**	
10 miles E of downtown Huntington Beach (approx 10 minutes)	949-252-5200

Airport Transportation

	Phone
Express Shuttle $20 fare to downtown Huntington Beach	800-606-7433
LAXpress Airport Shuttle $20 fare to downtown Huntington Beach	800-427-7483
SuperShuttle $19 fare to downtown Huntington Beach	714-517-6600
Taxi $25 fare to downtown Huntington Beach	714-220-0000

Huntington Beach (Cont'd)

Commercial Airlines

	Phone		Phone
Alaska	800-426-0333	Northwest	800-225-2525
America West	800-235-9292	Southwest	800-435-9792
American	800-433-7300	TWA	800-221-2000
American Eagle	800-433-7300	United	800-241-6522
Continental	800-525-0280	United Express	800-241-6522
Delta	800-221-1212	US Airways	800-428-4322
Delta Connection	800-221-1212	US Airways Express	800-428-4322

Charter Airlines

	Phone		Phone
Alliance Executive Charter Services	800-232-5387	Lenair Aviation Inc	949-756-8546
Ari Worldwide Aircraft Charters	800-426-9110	Regency Air LLC	714-541-3932
Avjet Corp.	800-342-8538	Schubach Aviation	800-214-8215
Clay Lacy Aviation Inc	800-423-2904	Signature Flight Support	949-263-5800
Combs Executive Charter	800-627-8465	Sunbird Aviation LLC	800-434-5150
Corporate America Aviation Inc	800-521-8585	TWC Aviation	888-892-0035
Helistream	714-662-3163	West Coast Charters Inc.	800-352-6153

	Phone
■ **Los Angeles International Airport (LAX)** 24 miles NW of downtown Huntington Beach (approx 60 minutes)	310-646-5252

Web: www.lax2015.org

Airport Transportation

	Phone
Express Shuttle $36 fare to downtown Huntington Beach	800-606-7433
LAXpress Airport Shuttle $34 fare to downtown Huntington Beach	800-427-7483
SuperShuttle $37 fare to downtown Huntington Beach	714-517-6600
Taxi $65 fare to downtown Huntington Beach	323-221-1234

Commercial Airlines

	Phone		Phone
AccessAir	877-462-2237	LACSA	213-385-9424
Aerolineas Argentinas	800-333-0276	LTU International	800-888-0200
Air Canada	800-776-3000	Lufthansa	800-645-3880
Air Jamaica	800-523-5585	Malaysia Airlines	800-552-9264
Air New Zealand	310-615-1111	Mexicana	800-531-7923
Alitalia	800-223-5730	Midwest Express	800-452-2022
All Nippon Airways	310-782-3000	National	888-757-5387
America West	800-235-9292	Northwest	800-225-2525
American	800-433-7300	Pan Am	800-359-7262
American Eagle	800-433-7300	Philippine	800-435-9725
Avianca	800-284-2622	Qantas	800-227-4500
British Airways	800-247-9297	Scandinavian	800-221-2350
China Airlines	310-641-8888	Shuttle by United	800-748-8853
China Eastern	626-583-1500	SkyWest	800-453-9417
Continental	800-525-0280	Southwest	800-435-9792
Delta	213-386-5510	TACA International	800-535-8780
El Al	800-223-6700	TWA	800-221-2000
Hawaiian	310-215-1866	United	800-241-6522
Iberia	800-772-4642	United Express	800-241-6522
Island Express	562-436-2012	US Airways	800-428-4322
Japan	800-525-3663	Varig Brazilian	310-646-2190
KLM	800-374-7747	Virgin Atlantic	800-862-8621
Korean Air	800-438-5000		

Charter Airlines

	Phone		Phone
Universal Jet	310-399-7371	West Coast Charter	949-852-8340

CAR RENTALS

	Phone		Phone
Alamo	949-851-2550	Enterprise	714-841-5011
Budget	714-848-2212	Hertz	310-568-3400
CarTemps USA	714-848-5544	National	310-338-8200
Dollar	949-756-6100	Thrifty	714-841-4887

LIMO/TAXI

	Phone		Phone
American Aristocrat Limousine	714-841-5776	Shooting Star Limousine	714-841-7115
Best Limousine Service	714-375-9128	Sunset Beach Limousines	562-592-3233
California Limousine	714-893-1703	Yellow Cab	714-220-0000

MASS TRANSIT

	Phone
OCTA Bus $1 Base fare	714-636-7433

RAIL/BUS

				Phone
Amtrak Station 1000 E Santa Ana Blvd *TF:* 800-872-7245	Santa Ana	CA	92701	714-547-8389

— Accommodations —

HOTELS, MOTELS, RESORTS

				Phone	Fax
777 Motor Inn 16240 Pacific Coast Hwy **Fax Area Code: 562*	Huntington Beach	CA	92649	714-846-5561	592-9418*
Beach Inn 18112 Beach Blvd	Huntington Beach	CA	92648	714-841-6606	848-9288
Best Western Regency Inn 19360 Beach Blvd *TF:* 800-528-1234	Huntington Beach	CA	92648	714-962-4244	963-4724
Capistrano Surfside Inn 34680 Pacific Coast Hwy	Capistrano Beach	CA	92624	949-240-7681	493-5793
Casa Laguna Inn 2510 S Pacific Coast Hwy *TF:* 800-233-0449	Laguna Beach	CA	92651	949-494-2996	494-5009
Comfort Suites 16301 Beach Blvd *TF:* 800-228-5150	Huntington Beach	CA	92647	714-841-1812	841-0124
Four Seasons Hotel 690 Newport Ctr Dr. *TF:* 800-332-3442 ■ *Web:* www.fourseasons.com/locations/NewportBeach	Newport Beach	CA	92660	949-759-0808	759-0568
Hilton Waterfront Beach Resort 21100 Pacific Coast Hwy *TF:* 800-822-7873 ■ *Web:* www.hilton.com/hotels/HUBWHHF	Huntington Beach	CA	92648	714-960-7873	960-3791
Hotel Huntington Beach 7667 Center Ave	Huntington Beach	CA	92647	714-891-0123	895-4591
Huntington Shores Motel 21002 Pacific Coast Hwy *TF:* 800-554-6799	Huntington Beach	CA	92648	714-536-8861	536-0060
Huntington Suites 727 Yorktown Ave.	Huntington Beach	CA	92648	714-969-0450	960-0280
Hyatt Newporter 1107 Jamboree Rd *TF:* 800-233-1234 ■ *Web:* www.hyatt.com/usa/newport/hotels/hotel_newpo.html	Newport Beach	CA	92660	949-729-1234	644-1552
Newport Beach Marriott Hotel & Tennis Club 900 Newport Center Dr *TF:* 800-228-9290	Newport Beach	CA	92660	949-640-4000	640-5055
Newport Classic Inn 2300 W Coast Hwy *TF:* 800-633-3199	Newport Beach	CA	92663	949-722-2999	631-5659
Quality Inn 800 Pacific Coast Hwy *TF:* 800-228-5151	Huntington Beach	CA	92648	714-536-7500	536-6846
Ritz-Carlton Laguna Niguel 1 Ritz Carlton Dr. *TF:* 800-241-3333 ■ *Web:* www.ritzcarlton.com/location/NorthAmerica/LagunaNiguel/main.htm	Dana Point	CA	92629	949-240-2000	240-0829
Ritz Inn 17251 S Beach Blvd	Huntington Beach	CA	92647	714-375-0250	375-0251
Sheraton Newport Beach Hotel 4545 MacArthur Blvd. *TF:* 800-325-3535	Newport Beach	CA	92660	949-833-0570	833-3927
Sun N' Sands Motel 1102 Pacific Coast Hwy	Huntington Beach	CA	92648	714-536-2543	960-5779
Vacation Village 647 S Coast Hwy *TF:* 800-843-6895	Laguna Beach	CA	92651	949-494-8566	494-1386

— Restaurants —

				Phone
Baci (Italian) 18748 Beach Blvd	Huntington Beach	CA	92648	714-965-1194
Bukhara Cuisine Of India (Indian) 7594 Edinger Ave	Huntington Beach	CA	92647	714-842-3171
El Pollo Loco (Mexican) 19320 Beach Blvd	Huntington Beach	CA	92648	714-962-2097
Fiesta Grill (Mexican) 418 17th St.	Huntington Beach	CA	92648	714-969-7689
Giovanni's (Italian) 16041 Bolsa Chica St	Huntington Beach	CA	92649	714-846-8188
Hijame (Japanese) 15892 Springdale St	Huntington Beach	CA	92647	714-891-4848
Hurricanes Bar & Grill (American) 200 Main St Suite 201	Huntington Beach	CA	92648	714-374-0500
Kikuya Restaurant (Japanese) 8052 Adams Ave	Huntington Beach	CA	92646	714-536-6665
La Capilla (Mexican) 807 E Adams Ave	Huntington Beach	CA	92648	714-374-0342
Longboard Restaurant & Pub (American) 217 Main St.	Huntington Beach	CA	92648	714-960-1896

Huntington Beach — Restaurants (Cont'd)

Name / Address	City	State	Zip	Phone
Louise's Trattoria (Italian) 300 Pacific Coast Hwy	Huntington Beach	CA	92648	714-960-0996
Mario's Restaurant (Mexican) 18603 Main St	Huntington Beach	CA	92648	714-842-5811
Market Broiler (Steak/Seafood) 20111 Brookhurst Street	Huntington Beach	CA	92648	714-963-7796
Matsu Restaurant (Japanese) 18035 Beach Blvd	Huntington Beach	CA	92648	714-848-4404
Old World German Restaurant (German) 7561 Center Ave	Huntington Beach	CA	92647	714-895-8020
Palm Court (Continental) 21100 Pacific Coast Hwy	Huntington Beach	CA	92648	714-960-7873
Randazzo (Italian) 21148 Beach Blvd	Huntington Beach	CA	92648	714-536-2448
Ruby Palace (Chinese) 18330 Beach Blvd	Huntington Beach	CA	92648	714-848-6088
Sea Siam Restaurant (Thai) 16103 Bolsa Chica St	Huntington Beach	CA	92649	714-846-8986
Shorehouse Cafe (Italian) 520 Main St	Huntington Beach	CA	92648	714-960-8091
Silk Thai Cuisine (Thai) 19690 Beach Blvd	Huntington Beach	CA	92648	714-964-1151
Stefano (Italian) 7561 Center Ave	Huntington Beach	CA	92647	714-373-5399
Studio Cafe (California) 300 Pacific Coast Hwy Suite 201	Huntington Beach	CA	92648	714-536-8775
Tosh's (Mediterranean) 16871 Beach Blvd	Huntington Beach	CA	92647	714-842-3315
Trattoria Macaroni (Italian) 18344 Beach Blvd	Huntington Beach	CA	92648	714-841-0059
Vittorio's (Italian) 5921 Warner Ave	Huntington Beach	CA	92649	714-846-9606
Wahoo's Fish Taco (Seafood) 120 Main St	Huntington Beach	CA	92648	714-536-2050

— Goods and Services —

SHOPPING

Name / Address	City	State	Zip	Phone	Fax
Fashion Island Shopping Center 401 Newport Center Dr	Newport Beach	CA	92660	949-721-2000	720-3350
Golden West Swap Meet 15744 Golden West St	Huntington Beach	CA	92647	714-898-7927	895-8944
Huntington Beach Mall 7777 Edinger Ave	Huntington Beach	CA	92647	714-897-2533	894-7686
Huntington Harbour Mall Warner Ave & Algonquin St	Huntington Beach	CA	92649		
Loehmann's Five Points Plaza 18593 Main St	Huntington Beach	CA	92648	714-841-0036	843-5776
Main Street Shopping Pacific Coast Hwy & Main St	Huntington Beach	CA	92648	714-969-3492	
Old World Village 7561 Center Ave	Huntington Beach	CA	92647	714-898-3033	
Peters Landing 16400 Pacific Coast Hwy	Huntington Beach	CA	92649	562-592-2126	592-5382

BANKS

Name / Address	City	State	Zip	Phone	Fax
Bank of America 18691 Main St	Huntington Beach	CA	92648	714-973-8495	
Bank of Yorba Linda 16900 Goldenwest St	Huntington Beach	CA	92647	714-842-9228	842-7164
California Bank & Trust 16041 Goldenwest St	Huntington Beach	CA	92647	714-848-1234	847-3147
California Federal Bank 7222 Edinger Ave **Fax Area Code:* 714	Huntington Beach	CA	92647	800-843-2265	843-0100*
Citibank 7552 Edinger Ave	Huntington Beach	CA	92646	714-848-1131	841-4094
Eldorado Bank 7777 Center Ave *TF:* 800-229-8529	Huntington Beach	CA	92647	714-895-2929	898-4156
Fidelity Federal Bank 19900 Beach Blvd **Fax Area Code:* 714	Huntington Beach	CA	92648	800-434-3354	964-4971*
First Bank & Trust 501 Main St	Huntington Beach	CA	92648	714-536-0096	536-1556
Sanwa Bank 6881 Warner Ave	Huntington Beach	CA	92647	714-842-7741	842-6047
Southern California Bank 9042 Garfield Ave	Huntington Beach	CA	92646	714-963-9802	965-1039
Union Bank 17122 Beach Blvd	Huntington Beach	CA	92647	714-847-9681	842-3073
Washington Mutual Bank 7830 Edinger Ave	Huntington Beach	CA	92647	800-492-2132	
Wells Fargo Bank 7902 Edinger Ave **Fax Area Code:* 714	Huntington Beach	CA	92647	800-869-3557	843-4204*

BUSINESS SERVICES

Name	Phone	Name	Phone
DHL Worldwide Express	800-225-5345	**Mail Boxes Etc**	714-848-8118
Federal Express	800-238-5355	**Manpower Temporary Services**	714-895-8009
Focus on Careers Inc	714-848-1952	**Post Office**	800-275-8777
Kinko's	714-892-1452	**UPS**	800-742-5877

— Media —

PUBLICATIONS

Name / Address	City	State	Zip	Phone	Fax
Huntington Beach Independent 18682 Beach Blvd Suite 160 **Fax:* News Rm ■ *Web:* www.latimes.com/tcn/indynews	Huntington Beach	CA	92648	714-965-3030	965-7174*
Independent The 18682 Beach Blvd Suite 160	Huntington Beach	CA	92648	714-965-3030	965-7174
Orange County Register‡ 625 N Grand Ave *Web:* www.ocregister.com	Santa Ana	CA	92701	714-835-1234	565-3681

‡Daily newspapers

TELEVISION

Name / Address	City	State	Zip	Phone	Fax
KABC-TV Ch 7 (ABC) 4151 Prospect Ave *Web:* abcnews.go.com/local/kabc ■ *E-mail:* abc7@abc.com	Los Angeles	CA	90027	310-557-3200	557-3360
KCBS-TV Ch 2 (CBS) 6121 Sunset Blvd *Web:* www.kcbs2.com	Los Angeles	CA	90028	323-460-3000	460-3733
KCET-TV Ch 28 (PBS) 4401 Sunset Blvd *Web:* www.kcet.org	Los Angeles	CA	90027	323-666-6500	953-5523
KNBC-TV Ch 4 (NBC) 3000 W Alameda Ave *Web:* www.knbc4la.com	Burbank	CA	91523	818-840-4444	840-3535
KTTV-TV Ch 11 (Fox) 1999 S Bundy Dr *Web:* www.fox11la.com ■ *E-mail:* talkback@fox11la.com	West Los Angeles	CA	90025	310-584-2000	584-2023

RADIO

Name / Address	City	State	Zip	Phone	Fax
KABC-AM 790 kHz (N/T) 3321 S La Cienega Blvd *Web:* www.kabc.com	Los Angeles	CA	90016	310-840-4900	838-5222
KBIG-FM 104.3 MHz (AC) 330 N Brand Blvd Suite 800 **Fax:* Sales ■ *Web:* www.kbig104.com	Glendale	CA	91203	818-546-1043	637-2267*
KCBS-FM 93.1 MHz (CR) 6121 Sunset Blvd *Web:* www.arrowfm.com	Los Angeles	CA	90028	323-460-3000	460-3733
KFSG-FM 96.3 MHz (Rel) 1910 W Sunset Blvd Suite 480 *E-mail:* planetrock@rock411.com	Los Angeles	CA	90026	213-483-5374	484-8304
KFWB-AM 980 kHz (N/T) 6230 Yucca St *Web:* www.kfwb.com ■ *E-mail:* quake@kfwb.groupw.wec.com	Hollywood	CA	90028	323-462-5392	871-4670
KIIS-FM 102.7 MHz (CHR) 3400 Riverside Dr Suite 800 *Web:* www.kiisfm.com	Burbank	CA	91505	818-845-1027	295-6466
KLAC-AM 570 kHz (Nost) 330 N Brand Blvd Suite 800	Glendale	CA	91203	818-546-1043	637-2267
KLAX-FM 97.9 MHz (Span) 10281 W Pico Blvd **Fax:* Sales	Los Angeles	CA	90064	310-203-0900	203-8989*
KLOS-FM 95.5 MHz (Rock) 3321 S La Cienega Blvd *Web:* www.955klos.com	Los Angeles	CA	90016	310-840-4900	558-7685
KNX-AM 1070 kHz (N/T) 6121 Sunset Blvd *Web:* www.knx1070.com	Los Angeles	CA	90028	323-460-3000	460-3275
KOST-FM 103.5 MHz (AC) 610 S Ardmore Ave *TF:* 800-929-5678	Los Angeles	CA	90005	213-427-1035	385-0281
KPWR-FM 105.9 MHz (CHR) 2600 W Olive Ave Suite 850	Burbank	CA	91505	818-953-4200	848-0961
KRTH-FM 101.1 MHz (Oldies) 5901 Venice Blvd	Los Angeles	CA	90034	323-937-5230	936-3427
KYSR-FM 98.7 MHz (AC) 3500 W Olive Ave Suite 250 *Web:* www.star987.com	Burbank	CA	91505	818-955-7000	955-6436

— Colleges/Universities —

Name / Address	City	State	Zip	Phone	Fax
Coastline Community College 11460 Warner Ave	Fountain Valley	CA	92708	714-546-7600	241-6288
Golden West College 15744 Golden West St *Web:* www.gwc.cccd.edu ■ *E-mail:* mposner@mail.gwc.cccd.edu	Huntington Beach	CA	92647	714-892-7711	895-8960

Huntington Beach (Cont'd)

— Hospitals —

				Phone	Fax
Huntington Beach Hospital 17772 Beach Blvd	Huntington Beach	CA	92647	714-842-1473	843-5038

— Attractions —

				Phone	Fax
Bolsa Chica Ecological Reserve 3842 Warner Ave	Huntington Beach	CA	92649	714-846-1114	
Gibbs Norma Brandel Park Graham Pl-betw Warner & Heil Sts	Huntington Beach	CA	92649	714-536-5486	
Huntington Beach Arts Center 538 Main St	Huntington Beach	CA	92648	714-374-1650	374-1654
Huntington Beach Central Park Golden West St	Huntington Beach	CA	92648	714-536-5486	
Huntington Beach Pier Pacific Coast Hwy & Main St	Huntington Beach	CA	92648	714-536-5281	
Huntington Beach Playhouse 7111 Talbert Ave. *Web:* www.user-friendly.com/playhouse/hb.html	Huntington Beach	CA	92648	714-375-0696	
International Surfing Museum 411 Olive Ave *Web:* www.surfingmuseum.org	Huntington Beach	CA	92648	714-960-3483	960-1434
Newland House Museum 19820 Beach Blvd	Huntington Beach	CA	92648	714-962-5777	

SPORTS TEAMS & FACILITIES

				Phone	Fax
Orange County Zodiac (soccer) 602 N Flower St Eddie West Field *Web:* www.oczodiac.com ■ *E-mail:* comments@oczodiac.com	Santa Ana	CA	92701	949-348-4880	348-4601
Playa Grande Polo Club 18381 Goldenwest St	Huntington Beach	CA	92648	714-842-7656	

— Events —

	Phone
Civil War Reenactment (Labor Day weekend)	714-962-5777
Concours d'Elegance (early June)	714-842-4481
Cruise of Lights (mid-late December)	714-840-7542
Distance Derby (mid-August)	714-536-5486
Duck-A-Thon (mid-May)	714-374-1951
G-Shock US Open of Surfing (late July)	949-366-4584
Huntington Beach Summer Surf Contest (early September)	714-536-5486
Huntington Harbour Cruise of Lights (mid-December)	714-840-7542
Independence Day Parade (July 4)	714-536-5486
Old World Village Oktoberfest (late September-late October)	714-895-8020
Orange County Fair (mid-July)	714-708-3247
Pacific Shoreline Marathon (late January)	949-661-6062
Rose Show & Sale (late October)	714-897-2533
Summer Horse Classic (early August)	714-536-5258
Surf City Festival (late July)	714-536-8888
Taste of Huntington Beach (early February)	714-842-4481
Tern Island Clean-Up (late March)	714-840-1575

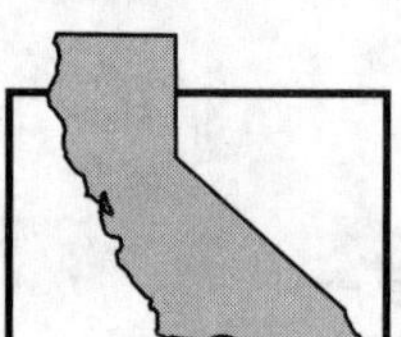

Long Beach

Long Beach takes its name from its five-and-a-half-mile-long stretch of beach. A popular seaside resort in the early 1900s, the city is now reclaiming its former status as the result of an extensive redevelopment program. A star attraction in Long Beach is the Queen Mary, the famous oceanliner that is now a hotel and tourist site. The shops and restaurants of Shoreline Village recapture the charm of a bygone era; and Catalina Island, 26 miles offshore, has been a popular weekend destination since the 1920s.

Population	430,905	**Longitude**	118-26-72 W
Area (Land)	50.0 sq mi	**County**	Los Angeles
Area (Water)	15.4 sq mi	**Time Zone**	PST
Elevation	29 ft	**Area Code/s**	562
Latitude	33-82-31 N		

— Average Temperatures and Precipitation —

TEMPERATURES

	Jan	Feb	Mar	Apr	May	Jun	Jul	Aug	Sep	Oct	Nov	Dec
High	67	68	68	72	73	77	83	84	82	78	72	67
Low	45	47	49	52	56	60	63	65	63	58	50	45

PRECIPITATION

	Jan	Feb	Mar	Apr	May	Jun	Jul	Aug	Sep	Oct	Nov	Dec
Inches	2.5	2.5	2.0	0.7	0.2	0.0	0.0	0.1	0.3	0.3	1.7	1.7

— Important Phone Numbers —

	Phone		Phone
AAA	800-222-4357	**Poison Control Center**	800-876-4766
American Express Travel	310-542-8631	**Time**	323-853-1212
Emergency	911	**Travelers Aid**	562-599-4546
HotelDocs	800-468-3537	**Weather**	213-554-1212

— Information Sources —

				Phone	Fax
Better Business Bureau Serving Los Angeles 3727 W 6th St Suite 607 *Web:* www.la.bbb.org	Los Angeles	CA	90020	213-251-9984	251-9986
Catalina Island Information PO Box 217 *Web:* www.catalina.com ■ *E-mail:* info@catalina.com	Avalon	CA	90704	310-510-1520	510-7606
Downtown Long Beach Associates 1 World Trade Ctr Suite 300	Long Beach	CA	90831	562-436-4259	435-5653
Long Beach Area Chamber of Commerce 1 World Trade Ctr Suite 206 *Web:* www.lbchamber.com	Long Beach	CA	90831	562-436-1251	436-7099
Long Beach City Hall 333 W Ocean Blvd *Web:* www.ci.long-beach.ca.us	Long Beach	CA	90802	562-570-6555	
Long Beach Convention & Entertainment Center 300 E Ocean Blvd *Web:* www.longbeachcc.com	Long Beach	CA	90802	562-436-3636	436-9491
Long Beach Convention & Visitors Bureau 1 World Trade Ctr Suite 300 *TF:* 800-452-7829 ■ *Web:* www.golongbeach.org	Long Beach	CA	90831	562-436-3645	435-5653
Long Beach Economic Development Bureau 200 Pine Ave 4th Fl. *Web:* www.ci.long-beach.ca.us/business	Long Beach	CA	90802	562-570-3800	570-3897
Long Beach Mayor 333 W Ocean Blvd. *Web:* www.ci.long-beach.ca.us/mayor-council/mayor.htm ■ *E-mail:* mayor@ci.long-beach.ca.us	Long Beach	CA	90802	562-570-6309	570-6538
Long Beach Public Library & Information Center 101 Pacific Ave *Web:* www.lbpl.org	Long Beach	CA	90822	562-570-7500	570-7408
Los Angeles County 500 W Temple St. *Web:* www.co.la.ca.us	Los Angeles	CA	90012	213-974-1311	

On-Line Resources

4LongBeach.com	www.4longbeach.com
Anthill City Guide Long Beach	www.anthill.com/city.asp?city=longbeach
Area Guide Long Beach	longbeach.areaguides.net
City Knowledge Long Beach	www.cityknowledge.com/ca_longbeach.htm
Excite.com Long Beach City Guide	www.excite.com/travel/countries/united_states/california/long_beach
Long Beach Jewish Community Web Site	jcclb.org
Long Beach Virtual Village	www.lngbch.com
Surf & Sun Beach Vacation Guide to Long Beach	www.surf-sun.com/ca-long-beach-main.htm

Long Beach (Cont'd)

— Transportation Services —

AIRPORTS

■ **Long Beach Municipal Airport (LGB)**

	Phone
10 miles NE of downtown (approx 20 minutes)	562-570-2600

Airport Transportation

	Phone
Express Shuttle $21 fare to downtown	310-783-4500
SuperShuttle $14 fare to downtown	310-782-6600
Taxi $19 fare to downtown	562-435-6111

Commercial Airlines

	Phone		Phone
American	800-433-7300	**TWA**	800-221-2000
American Eagle	800-433-7300	**United**	800-241-6522
Island Express	562-436-2012	**United Express**	800-241-6522
Pan Am	800-359-7262	**US Airways**	800-428-4322
Spirit	800-772-7117		

Charter Airlines

	Phone		Phone
Aeroplex Aviation	562-426-5500	**Long Beach Air Charter**	562-425-3774
Air Palm Springs	760-322-1104	**Rainbow Air**	562-424-0119
Ari Worldwide Aircraft Charters	800-426-9110	**US Helicopters**	562-497-0390
Island Express Helicopter Service	310-510-2525	**Valley Executive Charter**	562-989-4321
Jet Connection	310-378-1411	**West Coast Charters Inc**	800-352-6153

■ **John Wayne Airport/Orange County (SNA)**

	Phone
15 miles SE of downtown Long Beach (approx 40 minutes)	949-252-5200

Airport Transportation

	Phone
Prime Time $26 fare to downtown Long Beach	800-262-7433
Prime Time Shuttle $34-40 fare to downtown Long Beach	800-733-8267

Commercial Airlines

	Phone		Phone
America West	800-235-9292	**SkyWest**	800-453-9417
American	800-433-7300	**Southwest**	800-435-9792
Continental	714-751-0250	**United**	800-241-6522
Delta	714-534-8468	**United Express**	800-241-6522

Charter Airlines

	Phone		Phone
Alliance Executive Charter Services	800-232-5387	**Lenair Aviation Inc**	949-756-8546
Ari Worldwide Aircraft Charters	800-426-9110	**Regency Air LLC**	714-541-3932
Avjet Corp	800-342-8538	**Schubach Aviation**	800-214-8215
Clay Lacy Aviation Inc	800-423-2904	**Signature Flight Support**	949-263-5800
Combs Executive Charter	800-627-8465	**Sunbird Aviation LLC**	800-434-5150
Corporate America Aviation Inc	800-521-8585	**TWC Aviation**	888-892-0035
Helistream	714-662-3163	**West Coast Charters Inc**	800-352-6153

CAR RENTALS

	Phone		Phone
Avis	562-988-3255	**Enterprise**	562-494-3532
Budget	562-421-7172	**Hertz**	562-420-2322
CarTemps USA	562-426-4064	**National**	562-421-8877

LIMO/TAXI

	Phone		Phone
Integrated Transportation	310-553-6060	**Versaille Limo**	562-498-0844
Tri Star Limousine	800-999-2630	**Yellow Cab**	562-435-6111
United Checker Cab	562-421-7180		

MASS TRANSIT

	Phone
Long Beach Transit $.90 Base fare	562-591-2301
Long Beach Transit Runabout free downtown shuttle	562-591-2301

RAIL/BUS

				Phone
Greyhound Bus Station 464 W 3rd St *TF:* 800-231-2222	Long Beach	CA	90802	562-432-1842

— Accommodations —

HOTELS, MOTELS, RESORTS

				Phone	Fax
Bellamar Corporate Housing 225 W 3rd St	Long Beach	CA	90802	562-437-8889	437-7343
Belmont Shore Inn 3946 E Ocean Blvd	Long Beach	CA	90803	562-434-6236	
Best Western Golden Sails Hotel 6285 E Pacific Coast Hwy *TF:* 800-762-5333	Long Beach	CA	90803	562-596-1631	594-0623
Best Western Long Beach 1725 Long Beach Blvd *TF:* 800-528-1234	Long Beach	CA	90813	562-599-5555	599-1212
Best Western Sunrise Ports O' Call 525 S Harbor Blvd *TF:* 800-356-9609	San Pedro	CA	90731	310-548-1080	519-0380
Comfort Inn 3201 E Pacific Coast Hwy *TF:* 800-228-5150	Long Beach	CA	90804	562-597-3374	985-3142
Comfort Inn 1133 Atlantic Ave *TF:* 800-442-1688	Long Beach	CA	90813	562-590-8858	983-1607
Days Inn City Center 1500 E Pacific Coast Hwy *TF:* 800-329-7466	Long Beach	CA	90806	562-591-0088	591-6390
Days Inn Long Beach 5950 Long Beach Blvd *TF:* 800-882-8883	Long Beach	CA	90805	562-423-9898	423-9898
Extended StayAmerica 4105 E Willow St *TF:* 800-398-7829	Long Beach	CA	90815	562-989-4601	989-4501
GuestHouse Hotel 5325 E Pacific Coast Hwy *TF:* 800-990-9991 ■ *Web:* www.guesthouse.net/lbeach.html	Long Beach	CA	90804	562-597-1341	597-1664
Holiday Inn Long Beach Airport 2640 N Lakewood Blvd *TF:* 800-465-4329	Long Beach	CA	90815	562-597-4401	597-0601
Holiday Inn San Pedro 111 S Gaffey St *TF:* 800-248-3188 ■ *Web:* www.basshotels.com/holiday-inn/?_franchisee=LAXSP	San Pedro	CA	90731	310-514-1414	831-8262
Hotel Queen Mary 1126 Queens Hwy *TF:* 800-437-2934 ■ *Web:* www.queenmary.com/qmweb/html/hotel_c.html ■ *E-mail:* queenmry@gte.net	Long Beach	CA	90802	562-432-6964	437-4531
Hyatt Regency Long Beach 200 S Pine Ave *TF:* 800-233-1234 ■ *Web:* www.hyatt.com/usa/long_beach/hotels/hotel_lgbrl.html	Long Beach	CA	90802	562-491-1234	432-1972
Inn of Long Beach 185 Atlantic Ave *TF:* 800-230-7500	Long Beach	CA	90802	562-435-3791	436-7510
Long Beach Court Yard Marriott 500 E 1st St *TF:* 800-321-2211	Long Beach	CA	90802	562-435-8511	901-0296
Long Beach Hilton 2 World Trade Center	Long Beach	CA	90831	562-983-3400	983-1200
Long Beach Inn 2900 E Pacific Coast Hwy	Long Beach	CA	90804	562-494-4393	
Marriott Hotel 4700 Airport Plaza Dr *TF:* 800-228-9290 ■ *Web:* marriotthotels.com/LGBLB	Long Beach	CA	90815	562-425-5210	425-2744
Renaissance Hotel 111 E Ocean Blvd *TF:* 800-228-9898	Long Beach	CA	90802	562-437-5900	499-2509
Residence Inn by Marriott 4111 E Willow St *TF:* 800-331-3131 ■ *Web:* www.residenceinn.com/LAXBH	Long Beach	CA	90815	562-595-0909	988-0587
Rodeway Inn 50 Atlantic Ave *TF:* 800-228-2000	Long Beach	CA	90802	562-435-8369	432-3799
San Pedro Hilton 2800 Via Cabrillo Marina *TF:* 800-445-8667	San Pedro	CA	90731	310-514-3344	514-8945
Seaport Marina Hotel 6400 E Pacific Coast Hwy *TF:* 800-434-8451 ■ *Web:* www.seaportmarinahotel.com	Long Beach	CA	90803	562-434-8451	598-6028
Sheraton Los Angeles Harbor Hotel 601 S Palos Verdes St *TF:* 800-325-3535	San Pedro	CA	90731	310-519-8200	519-8421
Super 8 Motel 4201 E Pacific Coast Hwy *TF:* 800-800-8000	Long Beach	CA	90804	562-597-7701	494-7373
Travelodge Convention Center 80 Atlantic Ave *TF:* 800-578-7878	Long Beach	CA	90802	562-435-2471	437-1995
WestCoast Long Beach Hotel 700 Queensway Dr *TF:* 800-426-0670	Long Beach	CA	90802	562-435-7676	437-0866

Long Beach — Hotels, Motels, Resorts (Cont'd)

				Phone	Fax
Westin Hotel 333 E Ocean Blvd *TF:* 800-937-8461	Long Beach	CA	90802	562-436-3000	436-9176

— Restaurants —

				Phone
Acapulco Restaurant (Mexican) 6270 E Pacific Coast Hwy	Long Beach	CA	90803	562-596-3371
Aldo & Nikki's Ristorante (Italian) 4007 E Ocean Blvd	Long Beach	CA	90803	562-438-9950
Alegria Cafe & Tapas Bar (Latin American) 115 Pine Ave	Long Beach	CA	90802	562-436-3388
August Moon (Chinese) 6417 E Pacific Coast Hwy	Long Beach	CA	90803	562-596-8882
Babouch Moroccan Restaurant (Moroccan) 810 S Gaffey St	San Pedro	CA	90731	310-831-0246
Belmont Brewing Co (American) 25 39th Pl	Long Beach	CA	90803	562-433-3891
Biba Restaurant (Latin American) 644 Alamitos Ave	Long Beach	CA	90802	562-435-4048
Cafe Terrace (California) 4700 Airport Plaza Dr	Long Beach	CA	90815	562-425-5210
Cha Cha Cha (Caribbean) 762 Pacific Ave	Long Beach	CA	90813	562-436-3900
Clearman's Northwoods Inn (Steak/Seafood) 4911 E 2nd St	Long Beach	CA	90803	562-433-4932
Delius (Continental) 3550 Long Beach Blvd	Long Beach	CA	90807	562-426-0694
Five Five Five East (Steak) 555 E Ocean Blvd	Long Beach	CA	90802	562-437-0626
Frenchy's Bistro (French) 4137 E Anaheim St	Long Beach	CA	90804	562-494-8787
Gazzella (Italian) 525 E Broadway	Long Beach	CA	90802	562-495-7252
Grill Restaurant (Continental) 333 E Ocean Blvd	Long Beach	CA	90802	562-436-3000
Kelly's (American) 5716 E 2nd St	Long Beach	CA	90803	562-433-4983
King's Fish House (Seafood) 100 W Broadway	Long Beach	CA	90802	562-432-7463
L'Opera (Italian) 101 Pine Ave	Long Beach	CA	90802	562-491-0066
La Salsa (Mexican) 245 Pine Ave	Long Beach	CA	90802	562-491-1104
La Trattoria (California) 111 E Ocean Blvd	Long Beach	CA	90802	562-437-5900
Las Brisas (Mexican) 361 Cliff Dr	Laguna Beach	CA	92652	949-497-5434
Legends (American) 5236 E 2nd St	Long Beach	CA	90803	562-433-5743
Long Beach Cafe (American) 615 E Ocean Blvd	Long Beach	CA	90802	562-436-6037
Mama Tina's Cucina (Italian) 329 Pacific Ave	Long Beach	CA	90802	562-432-9718
Mandarin Palace (Chinese) 4074 Hardwick St	Lakewood	CA	90712	562-531-1412
Mum's Restaurant (California) 144 Pine Ave	Long Beach	CA	90802	562-437-7700
Mykonos (Greek) 5374 E 2nd St	Long Beach	CA	90803	562-434-1856
Nino's (Italian) 3853 Atlantic Ave	Long Beach	CA	90807	562-427-1003
Oceana Restaurant (American) 700 Queensway Dr	Long Beach	CA	90802	562-435-7676
Papadakis Taverna (Greek) 301 W 6th St	San Pedro	CA	90731	310-548-1186
Parker's Lighthouse (Seafood) 435 Shoreline Village Dr	Long Beach	CA	90802	562-432-6500
Pasta Presto (Italian) 200 N Pine Ave	Long Beach	CA	90802	562-436-7200
Phil's Angus Grille (Steak/Seafood) 4700 Airport Plaza Dr	Long Beach	CA	90815	562-425-5210
Reef Restaurant (Continental) 880 Harbor Scenic Dr	Long Beach	CA	90802	562-435-0488
Ritz The (Continental) 880 Newport Center Dr	Newport Beach	CA	92660	949-720-1800
Rusty Pelican (Seafood) 6550 Marina Dr	Long Beach	CA	90803	562-594-6551
Sails Restaurant (American) 6285 E Pacific Coast Hwy	Long Beach	CA	90803	562-430-0585
Sarafina (Italian) 135 Pine Ave	Long Beach	CA	90802	562-437-2119
Shenandoah Cafe (American) 4722 E 2nd St	Long Beach	CA	90803	562-434-3469
Sir Winston's (French) 1126 Queens Hwy	Long Beach	CA	90802	562-435-3511
Tequila Jacks (Mexican) 407 Shoreline Village Dr	Long Beach	CA	90802	562-628-0454
Tides (American) 200 S Pine Ave	Long Beach	CA	90802	562-491-1234
Tower Restaurant (American) 2640 Lakewood Blvd	Long Beach	CA	90815	562-597-4401
Yard House (American) 401 Shoreline Village Dr	Long Beach	CA	90802	562-628-0455

— Goods and Services —

SHOPPING

				Phone	Fax
Belmont Shore 2nd St-betw Livingston & Bayshore Drs	Long Beach	CA	90803	562-436-3645	
Del Amo Fashion Center 3525 Carson St *Web:* torranceweb.com/dafc	Torrance	CA	90503	310-542-8525	793-9235
Long Beach Plaza 451 Long Beach Blvd	Long Beach	CA	90802	562-435-8686	
Los Cerritos Center 239 Los Cerritos Ctr	Cerritos	CA	90703	562-860-0341	860-5289
Marina Pacifica 6272 E Pacific Coast Hwy Suite D	Long Beach	CA	90803	562-598-2728	431-8413
Marketplace The 6400 Pacific Coast Hwy	Long Beach	CA	90803	562-431-6282	
Picadilly Circus 1126 Queens Hwy	Long Beach	CA	90802	562-435-3511	
Ports O'Call Village Berth 77 P7A	San Pedro	CA	90731	310-831-0287	831-3686
Queen Mary Seaport 1126 Queens Hwy *TF:* 800-437-2934 ■ *Web:* www.queenmary.com/ ■ *E-mail:* queenmary@qte.net	Long Beach	CA	90802	562-435-3511	437-4531
Shoreline Village 419-R Shoreline Village Dr *Web:* www.shorelinevillage.com ■ *E-mail:* management@shorelinevillage.com	Long Beach	CA	90802	562-435-2668	435-6445

BANKS

				Phone	Fax
Bank of America 150 N Long Beach Blvd	Long Beach	CA	90802	562-868-1448	
City National Bank 11 Golden Shore St	Long Beach	CA	90802	562-624-8600	624-8603
Comerica Bank 301 E Ocean Blvd Suite 1800 *TF Cust Svc:* 800-522-2265*	Long Beach	CA	90802	562-590-2500	595-0901
Farmers & Merchants Bank of Long Beach 302 Pine Ave	Long Beach	CA	90802	562-437-0011	437-8672

BUSINESS SERVICES

	Phone		Phone
Air & Surface Systems	714-832-1212	**Magic Messenger**	562-436-2494
Federal Express	800-463-3339	**Manpower Temporary Services**	562-432-8582
Kelly Services	562-595-6782	**Modern Messengers**	626-575-8500
Kinko's	562-498-1379	**Post Office**	800-275-8777
Labor Ready	562-432-3521	**UPS**	800-742-5877

— Media —

PUBLICATIONS

				Phone	Fax
Orange County Business Journal 4590 MacArthur Blvd Suite 100	Newport Beach	CA	92660	949-833-8373	833-8751
Press-Telegram‡ 604 Pine Ave *Web:* www.ptconnect.com	Long Beach	CA	90844	562-435-1161	437-7892

‡*Daily newspapers*

TELEVISION

				Phone	Fax
KABC-TV Ch 7 (ABC) 4151 Prospect Ave *Web:* abcnews.go.com/local/kabc ■ *E-mail:* abc7@abc.com	Los Angeles	CA	90027	310-557-3200	557-3360
KCBS-TV Ch 2 (CBS) 6121 Sunset Blvd *Web:* www.kcbs2.com	Los Angeles	CA	90028	323-460-3000	460-3733
KCET-TV Ch 28 (PBS) 4401 Sunset Blvd *Web:* www.kcet.org	Los Angeles	CA	90027	323-666-6500	953-5523
KNBC-TV Ch 4 (NBC) 3000 W Alameda Ave *Web:* www.knbc4la.com	Burbank	CA	91523	818-840-4444	840-3535
KTTV-TV Ch 11 (Fox) 1999 S Bundy Dr *Web:* www.fox11la.com ■ *E-mail:* talkback@fox11la.com	West Los Angeles	CA	90025	310-584-2000	584-2023

RADIO

				Phone	Fax
KABC-AM 790 kHz (N/T) 3321 S La Cienega Blvd *Web:* www.kabc.com	Los Angeles	CA	90016	310-840-4900	838-5222
KFI-AM 640 kHz (N/T) 610 S Ardmore Ave **Fax:* News Rm ■ *Web:* www.kfi640.com	Los Angeles	CA	90005	213-385-0101	389-7640*
KIIS-FM 102.7 MHz (CHR) 3400 Riverside Dr Suite 800 *Web:* www.kiisfm.com	Burbank	CA	91505	818-845-1027	295-6466
KLON-FM 88.1 MHz (NPR) 1288 N Bellflower Blvd *Web:* klon.org ■ *E-mail:* jazzave@klon.org	Long Beach	CA	90815	562-985-5566	597-8453
KPWR-FM 105.9 MHz (CHR) 2600 W Olive Ave Suite 850	Burbank	CA	91505	818-953-4200	848-0961

— Colleges/Universities —

				Phone	Fax
Brooks College 4825 E Pacific Coast Hwy *TF:* 800-421-3775 ■ *Web:* www.brookscollege.edu ■ *E-mail:* admin@brookscollege.edu	Long Beach	CA	90804	562-498-2441	597-7412
California State University Long Beach 1250 Bellflower Blvd *Web:* www.csulb.edu	Long Beach	CA	90840	562-985-4111	985-4973
DeVRY Institute of Technology 3880 Kilroy Airport Way *TF:* 800-597-1333 ■ *Web:* www.lb.devry.edu	Long Beach	CA	90806	562-427-4162	427-3512
Long Beach City College 4901 E Carson St *Web:* www.lbcc.cc.ca.us ■ *E-mail:* rschultz@lbcc.cc.ca.us	Long Beach	CA	90808	562-938-4111	420-4118

Long Beach (Cont'd)

— Hospitals —

Name / Address	City	State	ZIP	Phone	Fax
Long Beach Community Medical Center 1720 Termino Ave. *Web:* www.lbcommunity.com	Long Beach	CA	90804	562-498-1000	498-4434
Long Beach Memorial Medical Center 2801 Atlantic Ave	Long Beach	CA	90801	562-933-2000	933-1107
Pacific Hospital of Long Beach 2776 Pacific Ave.	Long Beach	CA	90806	562-595-1911	427-8072
Saint Mary Medical Center 1050 Linden Ave.	Long Beach	CA	90813	562-491-9000	436-6378
Veterans Affairs Medical Center 5901 E 7th St.	Long Beach	CA	90822	562-494-2611	494-5972

— Attractions —

Name / Address	City	State	ZIP	Phone	Fax
Aquarium of the Pacific 100 Aquarium Way *Web:* www.aquariumofpacific.org/	Long Beach	CA	90802	562-590-3100	951-1669
El Dorado East Regional Park & Nature Center 7550 E Spring St	Long Beach	CA	90815	562-570-1745	
El Dorado Park West 2800 Studebaker Rd	Long Beach	CA	90815	562-570-1765	
Found Theatre 251 E 7th St.	Long Beach	CA	90813	562-433-3363	433-3363
General Phineas Banning Residence Museum 401 E M St.	Wilmington	CA	90744	310-548-7777	
International City Theatre 1 World Trade Ctr PO Box 32069 **Fax Area Code: 714*	Long Beach	CA	90832	562-495-4595	960-0639*
Long Beach Arts 447 Long Beach Blvd	Long Beach	CA	90802	562-435-5995	
Long Beach Museum of Art 2300 E Ocean Blvd *Web:* www.lbma.org	Long Beach	CA	90803	562-439-2119	439-3587
Long Beach Opera PO Box 14895	Long Beach	CA	90853	562-439-2580	
Long Beach Playhouse 5021 E Anaheim St. *Web:* www.longbeachplayhouse.com	Long Beach	CA	90804	562-494-1616	494-1014
Long Beach Symphony Orchestra 555 E Ocean Blvd Suite 106 *Web:* www.lbso.org ■ *E-mail:* lbso@lbso.org	Long Beach	CA	90802	562-436-3203	491-3599
Miller Earl Burns Japanese Garden 1250 Bellflower Blvd	Long Beach	CA	90840	562-985-8885	985-8884
Museum of Latin American Art 628 Alamitos Ave *Web:* www.molaa.com	Long Beach	CA	90802	562-437-1689	437-7043
Ports O'Call Village Berth 77 P7A	San Pedro	CA	90731	310-831-0287	831-3686
Queen Mary Seaport 1126 Queens Hwy *TF:* 800-437-2934 ■ *Web:* www.queenmary.com/ ■ *E-mail:* queenmary@qte.net	Long Beach	CA	90802	562-435-3511	437-4531
Rancho Los Alamitos 6400 E Bixby Hill Rd *Web:* www.ci.long-beach.ca.us/park/rancho.htm	Long Beach	CA	90815	562-431-3541	430-9694
Rancho Los Cerritos 4600 Virginia Rd. *Web:* www.ci.long-beach.ca.us/park/ranchlc.htm	Long Beach	CA	90807	562-570-1755	570-1893
Recreation Park 4900 E 7th St.	Long Beach	CA	90804	562-570-3100	
Saint Luke's Episcopal Church Atlantic Ave & 7th St.	Long Beach	CA	90813	562-436-4047	
Shoreline Village 419-R Shoreline Village Dr *Web:* www.shorelinevillage.com ■ *E-mail:* management@shorelinevillage.com	Long Beach	CA	90802	562-435-2668	435-6445
South Coast Botanic Garden 26300 Crenshaw Blvd	Palos Verdes	CA	90274	310-544-6815	544-6820
South Coast Chorale PO Box 92524	Long Beach	CA	90809	562-439-6919	
University Art Museum 1250 Bellflower Blvd CSULB	Long Beach	CA	90840	562-985-5761	985-7602

SPORTS TEAMS & FACILITIES

Name / Address	City	State	ZIP	Phone	Fax
Long Beach Arena 300 E Ocean Blvd	Long Beach	CA	90802	562-436-3636	436-9491
Long Beach Ice Dogs (hockey) 300 E Ocean Blvd Long Beach Arena *Web:* www.icedogshockey.com	Long Beach	CA	90802	562-423-3647	437-5116
Los Alamitos Race Course 4961 Katella Ave. *Web:* www.webworldinc.com/larace/laqhr	Los Alamitos	CA	90720	714-236-4400	

— Events —

	Phone
Aloha Concert Jam (late June)	562-436-3645
Anaheim Street International Festival (early October)	562-436-3645
Beach Charities BeachFest (early May)	949-376-6942
Belmont Shore Car Show (mid-September)	562-434-3066
Belmont Shore Christmas Parade (early December)	562-434-3066
Bob Marley Reggae Festival (mid-February)	562-436-3661
Cajun & Zydeco Festival (late July)	562-427-3713
Grand Prix of Long Beach (early April)	562-436-9953
Grecian Festival (early September)	562-494-8929
Harvest Festival (early September)	562-436-3661
International Sea Festival (August)	562-570-3100
Kaleidoscope Festival (late April)	562-985-2288
KLON Blues Festival (Labor Day weekend)	562-985-1686
Long Beach Blues Festival (early September)	562-985-5566
Long Beach Jazz Festival (early August)	562-436-7794
Long Beach Lesbian & Gay Pride Festival (mid-May)	800-354-7743
Long Beach Renaissance Arts Festival (late August)	562-570-5333
Long Beach Sea Festival (August)	562-570-3100
Martin Luther King Celebration & Parade (mid-January)	562-570-6816
New Year's Eve Blues & Reggae Cruise & Fireworks (December 31)	562-799-7000
New Year's Eve Gala on Queen Mary (December 31)	562-435-3511
New Year's Eve on Pine Square (December 31)	562-436-4259
Orange County Fair (mid-July)	714-708-3247
Parade of a Thousand Lights (late December)	562-435-4093
Queen Mary Scottish Festival (mid-February)	562-435-3511
Whale Watching (January-March)	562-436-3645

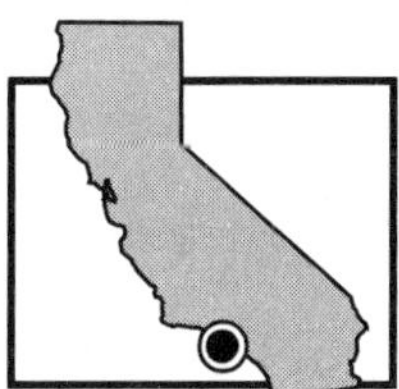

Los Angeles

Originally established as a small Spanish pueblo, the "city of Angels" is now home to more than three million people. El Pueblo de Los Angeles Historic Park, the site of the original pueblo, is located in the downtown area of Los Angeles and contains the restored plaza, the original church from which the city takes its name and which is still in use today, and Olvera Street, an authentic Mexican marketplace. Los Angeles is perhaps best known as the movie and television capital of the world. Visitors can tour both movie and TV studios or take a stroll down the Walk of Fame on Hollywood Boulevard, where the hand- and footprints of famous stars are impressed in the sidewalk outside Mann's Chinese Theatre. Other popular area attractions include the miles of beaches; the Santa Monica Pier, with its vintage 1910 carousel; Chinatown; the Rancho La Brea Tar Pits; and Rodeo Drive in Beverly Hills, known for its exclusive shops and boutiques.

Population	3,597,556	**Longitude**	118-24-28 W
Area (Land)	469.3 sq mi	**County**	Los Angeles
Area (Water)	29.1 sq mi	**Time Zone**	PST
Elevation	330 ft	**Area Code/s**	213, 310, 818, 323
Latitude	34-05-22 N		

— Average Temperatures and Precipitation —

TEMPERATURES

	Jan	Feb	Mar	Apr	May	Jun	Jul	Aug	Sep	Oct	Nov	Dec
High	66	66	66	67	69	72	75	77	77	74	70	66
Low	48	49	51	53	56	60	63	64	63	59	53	48

PRECIPITATION

	Jan	Feb	Mar	Apr	May	Jun	Jul	Aug	Sep	Oct	Nov	Dec
Inches	2.4	2.5	2.0	0.7	0.1	0.0	0.0	0.2	0.3	0.3	1.8	1.7

Los Angeles (Cont'd)

— Important Phone Numbers —

	Phone		Phone
AAA	213-741-3686	**Info Line**	323-686-0950
American Express Travel	310-542-8631	**Poison Control Center**	800-876-4766
Dental Referral	213-380-7669	**Time**	323-853-1212
Emergency	911	**Travelers Aid**	310-646-2270
HotelDocs	800-468-3537	**Weather**	213-554-1212

— Information Sources —

				Phone	Fax
Better Business Bureau Serving Los Angeles 3727 W 6th St Suite 607	Los Angeles	CA	90020	213-251-9984	251-9986
Web: www.la.bbb.org					
Los Angeles Area Chamber of Commerce 350 S Bixel St	Los Angeles	CA	90017	213-580-7500	580-7511
Web: www.lachamber.org					
Los Angeles City Hall 200 N Main St	Los Angeles	CA	90012	213-485-2121	
Web: www.ci.la.ca.us					
Los Angeles Convention & Exhibition Center 1201 S Figueroa St.	Los Angeles	CA	90015	213-741-1151	765-4266
TF: 800-448-7775 ■ *Web:* www.lacclink.com					
Los Angeles Convention & Visitors Bureau 633 W 5th St Suite 6000	Los Angeles	CA	90071	213-624-7300	624-9746
TF: 800-228-2452 ■ *Web:* www.lacvb.com					
Los Angeles County 500 W Temple St.	Los Angeles	CA	90012	213-974-1311	
Web: www.co.la.ca.us					
Los Angeles Mayor 200 N Main St Rm 800	Los Angeles	CA	90012	213-847-2489	485-1286
Web: www.cityofla.org/MAYOR ■ *E-mail:* rriordan@mayor.ci.la.ca.us					
Los Angeles Planning Dept 221 N Figueroa St Rm 1600	Los Angeles	CA	90012	213-580-1168	580-1176
Web: www.cityofla.org/PLN					
Los Angeles Public Library 630 W 5th St	Los Angeles	CA	90071	213-228-7000	228-7429
Web: www.lapl.org					

On-Line Resources

4LA.com	www.4la.com
@LA	www.at-la.com
About Los Angeles	www.thewebstation.com/OgardTravel/losangeles/
Annual Guide for the Arts	www.guide4arts.com/la/
Anthill City Guide Los Angeles	www.anthill.com/city.asp?city=losangeles
Area Guide Los Angeles	losangeles.areaguides.net
ArtScene	artscenecal.com/index.html
Boulevards Los Angeles	www.losangeles.com
Bradmans.com Los Angeles	www.bradmans.com/scripts/display_city.cgi?city=237
Calendar Live	calendarlive.com
City Knowledge Los Angeles	www.cityknowledge.com/ca_losangeles.htm
CityTravelGuide.com Los Angeles	www.citytravelguide.com/los-angeles.htm
CuisineNet Los Angeles	www.cuisinenet.com/restaurant/los_angeles/index.shtml
DigitalCity Los Angeles	home.digitalcity.com/losangeles
Excite.com Los Angeles City Guide	www.excite.com/travel/countries/united_states/california/los_angeles
Gayot's Guide Restaurant Search Los Angeles	www.perrier.com/restaurants/gayot.asp?area=LSA
HotelGuide Los Angeles	losangeles.hotelguide.net
LA2nite.com	www.la2nite.com
LA Dining	ladining.com/
LA Directory	www.ladir.com/
LA Loop	www.smart1.net/laloop/
LA Weekly	www.laweekly.com
La.com	www.la.com
LAHarbor.com	laharbor.com/
Los Angeles California	www.los-angeles-california.com
Los Angeles CityWomen	www.citywomen.com/lawomen.htm
Los Angeles Culture Net	home.lacn.org/LACN/
Los Angeles Downtown News	losangelesdowntown.com/
Los Angeles Graphic City Guide	www.futurecast.com/gcg/la.htm
LosAngeles.TheLinks.com	losangeles.thelinks.com/
NITC Travelbase City Guide Los Angeles	www.travelbase.com/auto/guides/los_angeles-area-ca.html
Open World City Guides Los Angeles	www.worldexecutive.com/cityguides/los_angeles/
Rough Guide Travel Los Angeles	travel.roughguides.com/content/1300/
Savvy Diner Guide to Los Angeles Restaurants	www.savvydiner.com/losangeles/
Search Los Angeles	www.searchla.com
Surf & Sun Beach Vacation Guide to Los Angeles	www.surf-sun.com/ca-los-angeles-main.htm
Time Out Los Angeles	www.timeout.com/losangeles/
Virtual Voyages Los Angeles	www.virtualvoyages.com/usa/ca/l_a/l_a.sht
WeekendEvents.com Los Angeles	www.weekendevents.com/LOSANGEL/la.html
Yahoo! Los Angeles	www.la.yahoo.com

— Transportation Services —

AIRPORTS

■ **Los Angeles International Airport (LAX)** — Phone

17 miles SW of downtown (approx 45 minutes) 310-646-5252
Web: www.lax2015.org ■ *E-mail:* tellus@lax2015.org

Airport Transportation

	Phone
LAXpress Airport Shuttle $12 fare to downtown	800-427-7483
MTA Bus $1.35-$3.35 fare to downtown	213-626-4455
Prime Time Shuttle $13 fare to downtown Los Angeles	800-733-8267
Santa Monica City Bus $1.25 fare to downtown	310-451-5445
Taxi $24 fare to downtown	213-627-7000

Commercial Airlines

	Phone		Phone
AccessAir	877-462-2237	**Korean Air**	800-438-5000
Aerolineas Argentinas	800-333-0276	**LACSA**	213-385-9424
AeroMexico	310-646-0316	**LTU International**	800-888-0200
Air Canada	800-776-3000	**Lufthansa**	800-645-3880
Air Jamaica	800-523-5585	**Malaysia Airlines**	800-552-9264
Air New Zealand	310-615-1111	**Mexicana**	800-531-7923
Alitalia	800-223-5730	**Midwest Express**	800-452-2022
All Nippon Airways	310-782-3000	**National**	888-757-5387
America West	800-235-9292	**Northwest**	800-225-2525
American	800-433-7300	**Pan Am**	800-359-7262
American Eagle	800-433-7300	**Philippine**	800-435-9725
Avianca	800-284-2622	**Qantas**	800-227-4500
British Airways	800-247-9297	**Scandinavian**	800-221-2350
China Airlines	310-641-8888	**Shuttle by United**	800-748-8853
China Eastern	626-583-1500	**SkyWest**	800-453-9417
Continental	800-525-0280	**Southwest**	800-435-9792
Corsair	800-677-0720	**TACA International**	800-535-8780
Delta	213-386-5510	**TWA**	800-221-2000
El Al	800-223-6700	**United**	800-241-6522
Hawaiian	310-215-1866	**United Express**	800-241-6522
Iberia	800-772-4642	**US Airways**	800-428-4322
Island Express	562-436-2012	**Varig Brazilian**	310-646-2190
Japan	800-525-3663	**Virgin Atlantic**	800-862-8621
KLM	800-374-7747		

Charter Airlines

	Phone		Phone
Air Royale International Inc	310-289-9800	**Universal Jet**	310-399-7371
Custom Air Transport Services	310-675-2287	**West Coast Charter**	949-852-8340

■ **Burbank-Glendale-Pasadena Airport (BUR)** — Phone

15 miles NW of downtown Los Angeles (approx 45 minutes) 818-840-8840
Web: www.bur.com

Airport Transportation

	Phone
Prime Time Shuttle $13 fare to downtown Los Angeles	800-733-8267
SuperShuttle $12 fare to downtown Los Angeles	310-782-6600

Commercial Airlines

	Phone		Phone
America West	800-235-9292	**SkyWest**	800-453-9417
American	800-433-7300	**Southwest**	800-435-9792
American Eagle	800-433-7300	**United**	800-241-6522
Continental	800-525-0280	**United Express**	800-241-6522
Delta	213-386-5510		

Charter Airlines

	Phone
Signature Flight Support	949-263-5800

Los Angeles (Cont'd)

CAR RENTALS

	Phone		Phone
Alamo	310-649-2242	**Enterprise**	310-649-5400
Avis	310-646-5600	**Hertz**	310-568-3400
Budget	310-645-4500	**National**	310-338-8200
Dollar	310-645-9333	**Thrifty**	310-645-1880

LIMO/TAXI

	Phone		Phone
Carey Limousine	310-275-4153	**LA Checker Cab**	310-330-3720
Dav El Limousines	800-328-3526	**LA Taxi**	213-627-7000
Diva Limousine	310-278-3482	**Shalimar Limousines**	310-216-9333
ExecuCar	310-410-4020	**Star's Limo**	562-869-6969
Fox Limousine	310-641-9626	**United-Independent Taxi**	323-653-5050
Independent Cabs	213-385-8294	**Yellow Cab**	323-221-1234

MASS TRANSIT

	Phone
MTA Bus $1.35 Base fare	213-626-4455

RAIL/BUS

				Phone
Amtrak Station 800 N Alameda St *TF:* 800-872-7245	Los Angeles	CA	90012	213-683-6729
Greyhound/Trailways Bus Station 1716 E 7th St *TF:* 800-231-2222	Los Angeles	CA	90021	213-629-8401

— Accommodations —

HOTEL RESERVATION SERVICES

	Phone	Fax
Accommodations Express *TF:* 800-444-7666 ■ *Web:* www.accommodationsxpress.com ■ *E-mail:* accomexp@acy.digex.net	609-391-2100	525-0111
California Reservations *TF:* 800-576-0003 ■ *Web:* www.cal-res.com	415-252-1107	252-1483
Central Reservation Service *TF:* 800-548-3311 ■ *Web:* www.reservation-services.com ■ *E-mail:* cenresbos@aol.com	407-740-6442	740-8222
Express Hotel Reservations *TF:* 800-356-1123 ■ *Web:* www.express-res.com ■ *E-mail:* info@express-res.com	303-440-8481	440-0166
Hotel Reservations Network Inc *TF Sales:* 800-964-6835 ■ *Web:* www.hoteldiscount.com	214-361-7311	361-7299
New Otani North America Reservation Center *TF:* 800-421-8795	213-629-1114	620-9808
Oakwood Corporate Housing *TF:* 800-888-0808 ■ *Web:* www.oakwood.com ■ *E-mail:* oakwood@sprynet.com	310-478-1021	444-2210
Quikbook *TF:* 800-789-9887 ■ *Web:* www.quikbook.com	212-532-1660	532-1556
RMC Travel Centre *TF:* 800-782-2674	212-754-6560	754-6571

HOTELS, MOTELS, RESORTS

				Phone	Fax
Best Western 1850 S Pacific Coast Hwy *TF:* 800-528-1234	Redondo Beach	CA	90277	310-540-3700	540-3675
Best Western Dragon Gate Inn 818 N Hill St *TF:* 800-282-9999	Los Angeles	CA	90012	213-617-3077	680-3753
Best Western Mid-Wilshire Plaza Hotel 603 S New Hampshire Ave. *TF:* 800-528-1234	Los Angeles	CA	90005	213-385-4444	380-5413
Best Western Sunset Plaza Hotel 8400 Sunset Blvd *TF:* 800-421-3652	West Hollywood	CA	90069	323-654-0750	650-6146
Beverly Hills Hotel 9641 Sunset Blvd *TF:* 800-283-8885 ■ *Web:* www.thebeverlyhillshotel.com ■ *E-mail:* sales@thebeverlyhillshotel.com	Beverly Hills	CA	90210	310-276-2251	887-2887
Beverly Hills Nikko 465 S La Cienega Blvd *TF:* 800-645-5624	Los Angeles	CA	90048	310-247-0400	247-0315
Beverly Plaza Hotel 8384 W 3rd St *TF:* 800-624-6835 ■ *Web:* www.beverlyplazahotel.com	Los Angeles	CA	90048	323-658-6600	653-3464
Century Plaza Hotel & Tower 2025 Ave of the Stars *TF:* 800-228-3000 ■ *Web:* www.centuryplazala.com ■ *E-mail:* comments@centuryplazala.com	Los Angeles	CA	90067	310-277-2000	551-3355
Century Wilshire Hotel 10776 Wilshire Blvd *TF:* 800-421-7223	Los Angeles	CA	90024	310-474-4506	474-2535
Clarion Hollywood Roosevelt Hotel 7000 Hollywood Blvd. *TF:* 800-252-7466	Hollywood	CA	90028	323-466-7000	462-8056
Continental Plaza Los Angeles Airport 9750 Airport Blvd *TF:* 800-529-4685	Los Angeles	CA	90045	310-645-4600	216-7029
Courtyard by Marriott 6161 W Century Blvd *TF:* 800-529-6161	Los Angeles	CA	90045	310-649-1400	649-0964
Crowne Plaza Los Angeles 5985 W Century Blvd *TF:* 888-315-3700	Los Angeles	CA	90045	310-642-7500	417-3608
Doubletree Hotel 10740 Wilshire Blvd *TF:* 800-472-8556 ■ *Web:* www.doubletreehotels.com/DoubleT/Hotel100/116/116Main.htm	West Los Angeles	CA	90024	310-475-8711	475-5220
Embassy Suites 9801 Airport Blvd *TF:* 800-362-2779	Los Angeles	CA	90045	310-215-1000	215-1952
Embassy Suites Buena Park 7762 Beach Blvd. *TF:* 800-362-2779	Buena Park	CA	90620	714-739-5600	521-9650
Figueroa Hotel 939 S Figueroa St. *TF:* 800-421-9092	Los Angeles	CA	90015	213-627-8971	689-0305
Four Points by Sheraton 530 W Pico Blvd. *TF:* 800-465-4329	Santa Monica	CA	90405	310-399-9344	399-2504
Four Seasons Hotel Beverly Hills 300 S Doheny Dr *TF:* 800-332-3442 ■ *Web:* www.fourseasons.com/locations/LosAngeles	Los Angeles	CA	90048	310-273-2222	859-3824
Furama Hotel 8601 Lincoln Blvd. *TF:* 800-225-8126 ■ *Web:* www.furama-hotels.com/lahome.htm	Los Angeles	CA	90045	310-670-8111	337-1883
Hacienda Hotel 525 N Sepulveda Blvd. *TF:* 800-421-5900 ■ *Web:* www.haciendahotel.com ■ *E-mail:* hacienda4res@earthlink.net	El Segundo	CA	90245	310-615-0015	615-0217
Hilgard House Hotel 927 Hilgard Ave *TF:* 800-826-3934	Los Angeles	CA	90024	310-208-3945	208-1972
Hilton Beverly Hills 9876 Wilshire Blvd. *TF:* 800-445-8667 ■ *Web:* www.hilton.com/hotels/LAXBHHH	Beverly Hills	CA	90210	310-274-7777	285-1313
Hilton Los Angeles Airport 5711 W Century Blvd *TF:* 800-445-8667 ■ *Web:* www.hilton.com/hotels/LAXAHHH	Los Angeles	CA	90045	310-410-4000	410-6250
Hilton Universal City & Towers 555 Universal Terrace Pkwy *TF:* 800-445-8667 ■ *Web:* www.hilton.com/hotels/BURUCHF	Universal City	CA	91608	818-506-2500	509-2058
Holiday Inn 120 Colorado Blvd *TF:* 800-947-9175	Santa Monica	CA	90401	310-451-0676	393-7145
Holiday Inn Convention Center 1020 S Figueroa St *TF:* 800-465-4329	Los Angeles	CA	90015	213-748-1291	748-6028
Holiday Inn Los Angeles Downtown 750 S Garland Ave *TF:* 800-628-5240 ■ *Web:* www.basshotels.com/holiday-inn/?_franchisee=LAXDT	Los Angeles	CA	90017	213-628-5242	628-1201
Hotel Bel-Air 701 Stone Canyon Rd *TF:* 800-648-4097 ■ *Web:* www.bel-air.com ■ *E-mail:* info@hotelbelair.com	Los Angeles	CA	90077	310-472-1211	476-5890
Hotel Inter-Continental 251 S Olive St. *TF:* 800-327-0200	Los Angeles	CA	90012	213-617-3300	617-3399
Hotel Sofitel Los Angeles 8555 Beverly Blvd. *TF:* 800-521-7772	Los Angeles	CA	90048	310-278-5444	657-2816
Hyatt Regency 711 S Hope St *TF:* 800-233-1234 ■ *Web:* www.hyatt.com/usa/los_angeles/hotels/hotel_laxrl.html	Los Angeles	CA	90017	213-683-1234	629-3230
InnTown Hotel Los Angeles 913 S Figueroa St. *TF:* 800-457-8520	Los Angeles	CA	90015	213-628-2222	687-0566
Kawada Hotel 200 S Hill St *TF:* 800-752-9232	Los Angeles	CA	90012	213-621-4455	687-4455
L'Ermitage Hotel 9291 Burton Way. *TF:* 800-800-2113	Beverly Hills	CA	90210	310-278-3344	278-8247
Los Angeles Athletic Club 431 W 7th St *TF:* 800-421-8777 ■ *Web:* www.laac.com	Los Angeles	CA	90014	213-625-2211	689-1194
Los Angeles Marriott Downtown 333 S Figueroa St. *TF:* 800-228-9290	Los Angeles	CA	90071	213-617-1133	613-0291
Malibu Beach Inn 22878 Pacific Coast Hwy *TF:* 800-462-5428	Malibu	CA	90265	310-456-6444	456-1499

Los Angeles — Hotels, Motels, Resorts (Cont'd)

	City	State	ZIP	Phone	Fax
Marriott Hotel Airport 5855 W Century Blvd	Los Angeles	CA	90045	310-641-5700	337-5358
TF: 800-228-9290 ■ *Web:* marriotthotels.com/LAXAP					
Mayfair Hotel 1256 W 7th St	Los Angeles	CA	90017	213-484-9789	484-2769
TF: 800-821-8682					
Metro Plaza Hotel 711 N Main St	Los Angeles	CA	90012	213-680-0200	620-0200
TF: 800-223-2223					
Milner Hotel 813 S Flower St	Los Angeles	CA	90017	213-627-6981	623-9751
TF: 800-827-0411					
Miyako Inn & Spa 328 E 1st St	Los Angeles	CA	90012	213-617-2000	617-2700
TF: 800-228-6596					
Mondrian Hotel 8440 Sunset Blvd	West Hollywood	CA	90069	323-650-8999	650-5215
TF: 800-525-8029 ■ *Web:* www.mondrianhotel.com ■ *E-mail:* mondrian@travelbase.com					
New Otani Hotel & Garden 120 S Los Angeles St	Los Angeles	CA	90012	213-629-1200	622-0980*
**Fax:* Resv ■ *TF:* 800-421-8795					
Oxford Palace 745 S Oxford Ave	Los Angeles	CA	90005	213-389-8000	389-8500
TF: 800-532-7887					
Palos Verdes Inn 1700 S Pacific Coast Hwy	Redondo Beach	CA	90277	310-316-4211	316-4863
TF: 800-421-9241					
Park Hyatt Los Angeles 2151 Ave of the Stars	Los Angeles	CA	90067	310-277-2777	785-9240
TF: 800-233-1234					
Peninsula The Beverly Hills Hotel 9882 S Santa Monica Blvd	Beverly Hills	CA	90212	310-551-2888	788-2304
TF: 800-462-7899 ■ *Web:* www.peninsula.com					
Portofino Hotel & Yacht Club 260 Portofino Way	Redondo Beach	CA	90277	310-379-8481	372-7329
TF: 800-468-4292					
Quality Hotel LAX 5249 W Century Blvd	Los Angeles	CA	90045	310-645-2200	641-8214
TF: 800-266-2200					
Radisson Hotel 3540 S Figueroa St	Los Angeles	CA	90007	213-748-4141	748-0043
TF: 800-333-3333					
Radisson Wilshire Plaza Hotel 3515 Wilshire Blvd	Los Angeles	CA	90010	213-381-7411	386-7379
TF: 800-333-3333					
Ramada Inn Commerce 7272 E Gage Ave	Commerce	CA	90040	562-806-4777	928-2907
TF: 800-547-4777					
Regal Biltmore Hotel 506 S Grand Ave	Los Angeles	CA	90071	213-624-1011	612-1628
TF: 800-222-8888 ■ *Web:* www.thebiltmore.com					
Regent Beverly Wilshire Hotel 9500 Wilshire Blvd	Beverly Hills	CA	90212	310-275-5200	274-2851
TF: 800-545-4000 ■ *Web:* www.fourseasons.com/locations/LosAngelesWilshire					
Renaissance Hotel Los Angeles 9620 Airport Blvd	Los Angeles	CA	90045	310-337-2800	216-6681
TF: 888-293-0523					
Santa Monica Pico Travelodge 3102 Pico Blvd	Santa Monica	CA	90405	310-450-5766	450-8843
TF: 800-231-7679					
Seoul Palace Hotel 620 S Harvard	Los Angeles	CA	90005	213-383-3000	381-0001
TF: 800-974-6600					
Sheraton Gateway 6101 W Century Blvd	Los Angeles	CA	90045	310-642-1111	410-1267
TF: 800-325-3535					
Sheraton Miramar Hotel 101 Wilshire Blvd	Santa Monica	CA	90401	310-576-7777	458-7912
TF: 800-325-3535 ■ *Web:* www.sheraton.com/miramar					
Shutters on the Beach 1 Pico Blvd	Santa Monica	CA	90405	310-458-0030	458-4589
TF: 800-334-9000 ■ *Web:* www.shuttersonthebeach.com					
Stillwell Hotel 838 S Grand Ave	Los Angeles	CA	90017	213-627-1151	622-8940
TF: 800-553-4774					
Summit Hotel Bel-Air 11461 W Sunset Blvd	Los Angeles	CA	90049	310-476-6571	471-6310
TF: 800-468-3541 ■ *Web:* home.earthlink.net/~sumhotel/					
Sunset Marquis Hotel & Villas 1200 N Alta Loma Rd	West Hollywood	CA	90069	310-657-1333	652-5300
TF: 800-858-9758					
Thousand Oaks Inn 75 W Thousand Oaks Blvd	Thousand Oaks	CA	91360	805-497-3701	497-1875
TF: 800-600-6878					
Travelodge LAX Hotel 1804 E Sycamore Ave	El Segundo	CA	90245	310-615-1073	322-4475
TF: 800-421-5781					
Westin Bonaventure Hotel 404 S Figueroa St	Los Angeles	CA	90071	213-624-1000	612-4800
TF: 800-228-3000					
Westin Hotel Airport 5400 W Century Blvd	Los Angeles	CA	90045	310-216-5858	417-4545
TF: 800-937-8461					
Westwood Marquis Hotel & Gardens 930 Hilgard Ave	Los Angeles	CA	90024	310-208-8765	824-0355
TF: 800-421-2317					
Wilshire Grand Hotel & Center 930 Wilshire Blvd	Los Angeles	CA	90017	213-688-7777	612-3989
TF: 888-773-2888 ■ *Web:* www.thewilshiregrand.com ■ *E-mail:* concierge@thewilshiregrand.com					
Wilshire Royale Hotel 2619 Wilshire Blvd	Los Angeles	CA	90057	213-387-5311	380-8174
TF: 800-421-8072 ■ *Web:* www.hotelroyale.com					
Wyndham Bel Age Hotel 1020 N San Vicente Blvd	West Hollywood	CA	90069	310-854-1111	854-0926
TF: 800-996-3426					
Wyndham Checkers Hotel 535 S Grand Ave	Los Angeles	CA	90071	213-624-0000	626-9906
TF: 800-996-3426					
Wyndham Los Angeles Airport 6225 W Century Blvd	Los Angeles	CA	90045	310-670-9000	670-8110
TF: 800-996-3426					

— Restaurants —

	City	State	ZIP	Phone
Barney Greengrass (Jewish) 9570 Wilshire Blvd 5th Fl	Los Angeles	CA	90212	310-777-5877
Beau Rivage (Mediterranean) 26025 Pacific Coast Hwy	Malibu	CA	90265	310-456-5733
Web: www.calendarlive.com/E/V/LAXCA/0001/37/73				
Bel-Air Dining Room (California/French) 701 Stone Canyon Rd	Bel Air	CA	90077	310-472-1211
Belvedere The (California) 9882 Little Santa Monica Blvd	Beverly Hills	CA	90212	310-788-2306
Bernard's (French) 506 S Grand Ave	Los Angeles	CA	90071	213-612-1580
Bistro Garden (Continental) 12950 Ventura Blvd	Studio City	CA	91604	818-501-0202
Ca'Brea (Italian) 346 S La Brea Ave	Los Angeles	CA	90036	323-938-2863
Ca'del Sole (Italian) 4100 Cahuenga Blvd	North Hollywood	CA	91602	818-985-4669
Cafe Bizou (California/French) 14016 Ventura Blvd	Sherman Oaks	CA	91423	818-788-3536
Cafe Del Rey (California) 4451 Admiral T Way	Marina del Rey	CA	90292	310-823-6395
Web: calcafe.com/marinadelrey/				
Cafe Pinot (French/California) 700 W 5th St	Los Angeles	CA	90071	213-239-6500
Web: www.patina-pinot.com				
Campanile (California/Mediterranean) 624 S La Brea Ave	Los Angeles	CA	90036	323-938-1447
Cardini (Italian) 930 Wilshire Blvd	Los Angeles	CA	90017	323-227-3464
Cha Cha Cha (Caribbean) 656 N Virgil Ave	Los Angeles	CA	90004	323-664-7723
Chasen's (Continental) 246 N Canon Dr	Beverly Hills	CA	90210	310-858-1200
Checkers (Continental) 535 S Grand Ave	Los Angeles	CA	90071	213-624-0000
Cheesecake Factory (American) 4142 Via Marina	Marina del Rey	CA	90292	310-306-3344
Chinois on Main (French/Chinese) 2709 Main St	Santa Monica	CA	90405	310-392-9025
Citrus (French) 6703 Melrose Ave	Los Angeles	CA	90038	323-857-0034
Crab Cooker (Seafood) 2200 Newport Blvd	Newport Beach	CA	92663	949-673-0100
Dining Room The (Continental) 9500 Wilshire Blvd Regent Beverly Wilshire	Beverly Hills	CA	90212	310-274-8179
El Cholo (Mexican) 1121 S Western Ave	Los Angeles	CA	90006	323-734-2773
Farm The (American) 439 N Beverly Dr	Los Angeles	CA	90210	310-273-5578
Fenix at the Argyle (French) 8358 Sunset Blvd	West Hollywood	CA	90069	323-848-6677
Four Oaks (French/California) 2181 N Beverly Glen Blvd	Los Angeles	CA	90077	310-470-2265
Garden Terrace (Continental) 930 Hilgard Ave	Los Angeles	CA	90024	310-208-8765
Gardens (Mediterranean) 300 S Doheny Dr	Los Angeles	CA	90048	310-273-2222
Geoffrey's (California) 27400 Pacific Coast Hwy	Malibu	CA	90265	310-457-1519
GiGi Brasserie (French) 8555 Beverly Blvd	Los Angeles	CA	90048	310-278-5444
Harry's Bar & American Grill (Italian) 2020 Ave of the Stars	Los Angeles	CA	90067	310-277-2333
Impresario (California) 135 N Grand Ave Dorothy Chandler Pavilion 5th Fl	Los Angeles	CA	90012	213-972-7333
Ivy The (American) 113 N Robertson Blvd	Los Angeles	CA	90048	310-274-8303
Katsu (Japanese) 1972 N Hillhurst Ave	Los Angeles	CA	90027	323-664-1891
L'Orangerie (French) 903 N La Cienega Blvd	Los Angeles	CA	90069	310-652-9770
Web: www.orangerie.com				
La Cachette (French) 10506 Little Santa Monica Blvd	Los Angeles	CA	90025	310-470-4992
La Scala (Italian) 410 N Canon Dr	Beverly Hills	CA	90210	310-275-0579
Lawry's Prime Rib (Steak) 100 N La Cienega Blvd	Beverly Hills	CA	90211	310-652-2827
Le Chardonnay (French) 8284 Melrose Ave	Los Angeles	CA	90069	323-655-8880
Le Dome (French) 8720 Sunset Blvd	Los Angeles	CA	90069	310-659-6919
Locanda Veneta (Italian) 8638 W 3rd St	Los Angeles	CA	90048	310-274-1893
Mandarin The (Chinese) 430 N Camden Dr	Los Angeles	CA	90210	310-859-0926
Matsuhisa (Asian) 129 N La Cienega Blvd	Beverly Hills	CA	90211	310-659-9639
Michael's (California) 1147 3rd St	Santa Monica	CA	90403	310-451-0843
Muse (California) 7360 Beverly Blvd	Los Angeles	CA	90036	323-934-4400
Nouveau Cafe Blanc (French/Japanese) 9777 Little Santa Monica Blvd	Beverly Hills	CA	90210	310-888-0108
Pacific Dining Car (Steak/Seafood) 1310 W 6th St	Los Angeles	CA	90017	213-483-6000
Pacific Grill (Steak/Seafood) 601 S Figueroa St	Los Angeles	CA	90017	213-485-0927
Palm The (Steak/Seafood) 9001 Santa Monica Blvd	Los Angeles	CA	90069	310-550-8811
Parkway Grill (California) 510 S Arroyo Pkwy	Pasadena	CA	91105	626-795-1001
Patina (French/California) 5955 Melrose Ave	Los Angeles	CA	90038	323-467-1108

Los Angeles — Restaurants (Cont'd)

				Phone
Philippe The Original (American) 1001 N Alameda St *Web:* www.philippes.com	Los Angeles	CA	90012	213-628-3781
Pinot Bistro (French/California) 12969 Ventura Blvd	Studio City	CA	91604	818-990-0500
Spago (New American) 1114 Horn Ave.	West Hollywood	CA	90069	310-652-4025
Swingers (American) 8020 Beverly Blvd	Los Angeles	CA	90048	323-653-5858
Tam O'Shanter Inn (American) 2980 Los Feliz Blvd	Los Angeles	CA	90039	323-664-0228
Three Thirty Three (Continental) 333 S Figueroa St	Los Angeles	CA	90071	213-617-1133
Tower The (Continental) 1150 S Olive St	Los Angeles	CA	90015	213-746-1554
Valentino (Italian) 3115 Pico Blvd	Santa Monica	CA	90405	310-829-4313

— Goods and Services —

SHOPPING

				Phone	Fax
Arco Plaza 505 S Flower St	Los Angeles	CA	90071	213-485-9595	622-5059
Beverly Center 8500 Beverly Blvd	West Hollywood	CA	90048	310-854-0070	
Broadway Plaza 7th & Flower Sts	Los Angeles	CA	90017	213-624-2891	688-0176
Century City Shopping Center & Marketplace 10250 Santa Monica Blvd	West Los Angeles	CA	90067	310-553-5300	553-3812
Citadel Outlet Collection 5675 E Telegraph Rd *Web:* www.citadelfactorystores.com	City of Commerce	CA	90040	323-888-1220	888-0311
Cooper Building 860 S Los Angeles St	Los Angeles	CA	90014	213-622-1139	629-5484
Fox Hills Mall 6000 Sepulveda Blvd	Culver City	CA	90230	310-390-7833	391-9576
Galleria at South Bay 1815 Hawthorne Blvd Suite 201 *Web:* www.sobaygalleria.com	Redondo Beach	CA	90278	310-371-7546	371-0103
Giorgio Beverly Hills 327 N Rodeo Dr. **Fax:* Hum Res	Beverly Hills	CA	90210	310-274-0200	315-3182*
Harris & Frank Inc 17629 Ventura Blvd	Encino	CA	91316	818-783-3125	783-2693
Japanese Village Plaza 335 E 2nd St Suite 220	Los Angeles	CA	90012	213-622-2033	627-9095
Los Angeles City Mall 201 N Los Angeles St	Los Angeles	CA	90012	213-847-5927	847-5891
Oaks The 222 W Hillcrest Dr	Thousand Oaks	CA	91360	805-495-4628	495-9656
Ports O'Call Village Berth 77 P7A	San Pedro	CA	90731	310-831-0287	831-3686
Robinsons-May 920 W 7th St	Los Angeles	CA	90017	213-683-1144	683-2764
Seventh Marketplace 735 S Figueroa St Citicorp Plaza	Los Angeles	CA	90017	213-955-7150	
Talbot's 848 W 7th St	Los Angeles	CA	90017	213-624-2377	

BANKS

				Phone	Fax
Bank of America 555 S Flower St	Los Angeles	CA	90071	213-228-2805	
City National Bank 2029 Century Pk E B-Level *TF:* 800-773-7100	Los Angeles	CA	90067	310-282-7820	282-7815
Mercantile National Bank 1840 Century Pk E	Los Angeles	CA	90067	310-277-2265	201-0862
Union Bank 445 S Figueroa St	Los Angeles	CA	90071	213-236-5000	
Washington Mutual Bank 660 S Figueroa St	Los Angeles	CA	90017	323-965-0400	
Wells Fargo Bank 707 Wilshire Blvd *TF:* 800-869-3557	Los Angeles	CA	90017	213-614-2707	614-2718

BUSINESS SERVICES

	Phone
Century City Messenger Service	310-556-9791
Corporate Express Delivery Systems	323-838-4770
Federal Express	800-463-3339
Kelly Services	323-965-2950
Kinko's	213-747-8341
Messenger Express	310-390-9475
Olsten Staffing Services	310-209-0663
Pacific Express	213-628-3904
Post Office	800-275-8777
UPS	800-742-5877

— Media —

PUBLICATIONS

				Phone	Fax
Beverly Hills 213 9777 Wilshire Blvd Suite 707	Beverly Hills	CA	90212	310-275-8850	275-1341
East Los Angeles/Brooklyn Belvedere Comet 2500 S Atlantic Blvd Bldg A **Fax:* News Rm	Los Angeles	CA	90040	323-263-5743	263-9169*
Hollywood Independent 4201 Wilshire Blvd Suite 600 **Fax:* News Rm	Los Angeles	CA	90010	323-932-6397	932-8285*
La Opinion‡ PO Box 15268 *Web:* www.laopinion.com	Los Angeles	CA	90015	213-622-8332	896-2171
Los Angeles Business Journal 5700 Wilshire Blvd Suite 170 *Web:* www.labiz.com ■ *E-mail:* mtoledo@LAbiz.com	Los Angeles	CA	90036	323-549-5225	549-5255
Los Angeles Downtown News 1264 W 1st St **Fax:* News Rm ■ *Web:* www.ladowntownnews.com ■ *E-mail:* realpeople@downtownnews.com	Los Angeles	CA	90026	213-481-1448	250-4617*
Los Angeles Magazine 11100 Santa Monica Blvd 7th Fl **Fax:* Edit ■ *Web:* www.lamag.com	Los Angeles	CA	90025	310-312-2270	312-2233*
Los Angeles Times‡ Times Mirror Sq *TF:* 800-528-4637 ■ *Web:* www.latimes.com	Los Angeles	CA	90053	213-237-5000	237-4712
Where Los Angeles Magazine 3679 Motor Ave Suite 300 *Web:* www.wherela.com ■ *E-mail:* wherela@aol.com	Los Angeles	CA	90034	310-280-2880	280-2890

‡Daily newspapers

TELEVISION

				Phone	Fax
KABC-TV Ch 7 (ABC) 4151 Prospect Ave *Web:* abcnews.go.com/local/kabc ■ *E-mail:* abc7@abc.com	Los Angeles	CA	90027	310-557-3200	557-3360
KADY-TV Ch 63 (UPN) 950 Flynn Rd	Camarillo	CA	93012	805-388-0081	388-9693
KCAL-TV Ch 9 (Ind) 5515 Melrose Ave *Web:* www.kcal.com ■ *E-mail:* news@kcal.com	Hollywood	CA	90038	323-467-5459	464-2526
KCBS-TV Ch 2 (CBS) 6121 Sunset Blvd *Web:* www.kcbs2.com	Los Angeles	CA	90028	323-460-3000	460-3733
KCET-TV Ch 28 (PBS) 4401 Sunset Blvd *Web:* www.keet.org	Los Angeles	CA	90027	323-666-6500	953-5523
KCOP-TV Ch 13 (UPN) 915 N La Brea Ave *Web:* www.upn13.com	Los Angeles	CA	90038	323-851-1000	850-1265
KDOC-TV Ch 56 (Ind) 18021 Cowan	Irvine	CA	92614	949-442-9800	261-5956
KHIZ-TV Ch 64 (Ind) 15605 Village Dr	Victorville	CA	92394	760-241-5888	241-0056
KJLA-TV Ch 57 (Ind) 18344 Oxnard St Suite 210	Tarzana	CA	91356	818-757-7583	757-7533
KLCS-TV Ch 58 (Ind) 1061 W Temple St *Web:* www.klcs.org ■ *E-mail:* info@klcs.org	Los Angeles	CA	90012	213-625-6958	481-1019
KMEX-TV Ch 34 (Uni) 6701 Center Dr W 15th Fl *Web:* www.kmex.com	Los Angeles	CA	90045	310-216-3434	348-3493
KNBC-TV Ch 4 (NBC) 3000 W Alameda Ave *Web:* www.knbc4la.com	Burbank	CA	91523	818-840-4444	840-3535
KPXN-TV Ch 30 (PAX) 10880 Wilshire Blvd Suite 1200	Los Angeles	CA	90024	310-234-2230	234-4035
KRCA-TV Ch 62 (Ind) 1813 Victory Pl	Burbank	CA	91504	818-563-5722	972-2694
KSCI-TV Ch 18 (Ind) 1990 S Bundy Dr Suite 850 *TF:* 800-841-1818	Los Angeles	CA	90025	310-478-1818	207-1508
KTLA-TV Ch 5 (WB) 5800 W Sunset Blvd *Web:* www.ktla.com	Los Angeles	CA	90028	323-460-5500	460-5333
KTTV-TV Ch 11 (Fox) 1999 S Bundy Dr *Web:* www.fox11la.com ■ *E-mail:* talkback@fox11la.com	West Los Angeles	CA	90025	310-584-2000	584-2023
KVEA-TV Ch 52 (Tele) 1139 Grand Central Ave *Web:* www.kvea.com ■ *E-mail:* airway@kvea.com	Glendale	CA	91201	818-502-5700	247-2561
KWHY-TV Ch 22 (Ind) 5545 Sunset Blvd **Fax:* News Rm	Los Angeles	CA	90028	323-466-5441	466-6418*

RADIO

				Phone	Fax
KABC-AM 790 kHz (N/T) 3321 S La Cienega Blvd *Web:* www.kabc.com	Los Angeles	CA	90016	310-840-4900	838-5222
KACE-FM 103.9 MHz (Oldies) 610 S Ardmore Ave	Los Angeles	CA	90005	213-427-1039	380-4214
KBIG-FM 104.3 MHz (AC) 330 N Brand Blvd Suite 800 **Fax:* Sales ■ *Web:* www.kbig104.com	Glendale	CA	91203	818-546-1043	637-2267*
KBUA-FM 94.3 MHz (Span) 5724 Hollywood Blvd	Hollywood	CA	90028	323-461-9300	461-9946
KBUE-FM 105.5 MHz (Span) 5724 Hollywood Blvd	Hollywood	CA	90028	323-461-9300	461-9946
KCBS-FM 93.1 MHz (CR) 6121 Sunset Blvd *Web:* www.arrowfm.com	Los Angeles	CA	90028	323-460-3000	460-3733
KCLU-FM 88.3 MHz (NPR) 60 W Olsen Rd	Thousand Oaks	CA	91360	805-493-3900	493-3982

Los Angeles — Radio (Cont'd)

				Phone	Fax
KCMG-FM 100.3 MHz (Oldies)					
6500 Wilshire Blvd Suite 650	Los Angeles	CA	90048	323-852-1003	866-1260
Web: www.mega100fm.com					
KCRW-FM 89.9 MHz (NPR)					
1900 Pico Blvd	Santa Monica	CA	90405	310-450-5183	450-7172
Web: kcrw.org ■ *E-mail:* info@kcrw.org					
KFI-AM 640 kHz (N/T)					
610 S Ardmore Ave	Los Angeles	CA	90005	213-385-0101	389-7640*
**Fax:* News Rm ■ *Web:* www.kfi640.com					
KFSG-FM 96.3 MHz (Rel)					
1910 W Sunset Blvd Suite 480	Los Angeles	CA	90026	213-483-5374	484-8304
E-mail: planetrock@rock411.com					
KFWB-AM 980 kHz (N/T) 6230 Yucca St	Hollywood	CA	90028	323-462-5392	871-4670
Web: www.kfwb.com ■ *E-mail:* quake@kfwb.groupw.wec.com					
KHWY-FM 98.9 MHz (AC) 1611 E Main St	Barstow	CA	92311	760-256-0326	256-9507
KIIS-FM 102.7 MHz (CHR)					
3400 Riverside Dr Suite 800	Burbank	CA	91505	818-845-1027	295-6466
Web: www.kiisfm.com					
KJLH-FM 102.3 MHz (Urban)					
161 N La Brea Ave	Inglewood	CA	90301	310-330-5550	330-5555
E-mail: 1023kjlh@earthlink.net					
KKBT-FM 92.3 MHz (Urban)					
5900 Wilshire Blvd Suite 1900	Los Angeles	CA	90036	323-634-1800	634-1888
TF: 888-520-9292 ■ *Web:* www.thebeatla.com					
KKGO-FM 105.1 MHz (Clas)					
1500 Cotner Ave	Los Angeles	CA	90025	310-478-5540	478-4189
KLAC-AM 570 kHz (Nost)					
330 N Brand Blvd Suite 800	Glendale	CA	91203	818-546-1043	637-2267
KLAX-FM 97.9 MHz (Span)					
10281 W Pico Blvd	Los Angeles	CA	90064	310-203-0900	203-8989*
**Fax:* Sales					
KLOS-FM 95.5 MHz (Rock)					
3321 S La Cienega Blvd	Los Angeles	CA	90016	310-840-4900	558-7685
Web: www.955klos.com					
KLSX-FM 97.1 MHz (N/T)					
3580 Wilshire Blvd	Los Angeles	CA	90010	213-383-4222	386-3649
Web: www.realradio.com					
KLVE-FM 107.5 MHz (Span)					
1645 N Vine St Suite 200	Hollywood	CA	90028	323-465-3171	461-9973
KLYY-FM 107.1 MHz (Alt)					
3350 Electronic Dr	Pasadena	CA	91107	626-351-9107	351-6218
KNX-AM 1070 kHz (N/T)					
6121 Sunset Blvd	Los Angeles	CA	90028	323-460-3000	460-3275
Web: www.knx1070.com					
KOST-FM 103.5 MHz (AC)					
610 S Ardmore Ave	Los Angeles	CA	90005	213-427-1035	385-0281
TF: 800-929-5678					
KPWR-FM 105.9 MHz (CHR)					
2600 W Olive Ave Suite 850	Burbank	CA	91505	818-953-4200	848-0961
KROQ-FM 106.7 MHz (Alt) 3500 W Olive Ave	Burbank	CA	91505	818-567-1067	841-5903
KRTH-FM 101.1 MHz (Oldies)					
5901 Venice Blvd	Los Angeles	CA	90034	323-937-5230	936-3427
KSSE-FM 97.5 MHz (Span)					
3450 Wilshire Blvd Suite 820	Los Angeles	CA	90010	213-251-1011	251-1033
KTNQ-AM 1020 kHz (Span)					
1645 N Vine St Suite 200	Hollywood	CA	90028	323-465-3171	461-9973
KTWV-FM 94.7 MHz (NAC)					
8944 Lindblade St	Culver City	CA	90232	310-840-7100	815-1129
KUSC-FM 91.5 MHz (NPR)					
3716 S Hope St	Los Angeles	CA	90007	213-514-1400	747-9400
Web: www.kusc.org ■ *E-mail:* kusc@kusc.org					
KYSR-FM 98.7 MHz (AC)					
3500 W Olive Ave Suite 250	Burbank	CA	91505	818-955-7000	955-6436
Web: www.star987.com					
XTRA-AM 1150 kHz					
3400 Riverside Dr Suite 800	Burbank	CA	91505	818-845-1027	295-6466
Web: www.xtrasports1150.com					

— Colleges/Universities —

				Phone	Fax
American Academy of Dramatic Arts					
600 Playhouse Alley	Pasadena	CA	91101	626-229-9777	229-9977
TF: 800-222-2867 ■ *Web:* www.aada.org					
American Film Institute					
2021 N Western Ave	Los Angeles	CA	90027	323-856-7600	467-4578
TF: 800-999-4234 ■ *Web:* www.afionline.org					
American InterContinental University Los Angeles 12655 W Jefferson Blvd	Los Angeles	CA	90066	310-302-2000	302-2002
TF: 800-333-2652 ■ *Web:* www.aiuniv.edu ■ *E-mail:* info@aiuniv.edu					
Art Center College of Design 1700 Lida St	Pasadena	CA	91103	626-396-2200	405-9104
Web: www.artcenter.edu					
Brooks College 4825 E Pacific Coast Hwy	Long Beach	CA	90804	562-498-2441	597-7412
TF: 800-421-3775 ■ *Web:* www.brookscollege.edu ■ *E-mail:* admin@brookscollege.edu					
California Institute of Technology					
1200 E California Blvd	Pasadena	CA	91125	626-395-6811	683-3026
TF Admissions: 800-568-8324 ■ *Web:* www.caltech.edu ■ *E-mail:* ugadmissions@caltech.edu					
California Institute of the Arts					
24700 McBean Pkwy	Valencia	CA	91355	661-255-1050	254-8352
TF Admissions: 800-545-2787 ■ *Web:* www.calarts.edu					
California International University					
3130 Wilshire Blvd	Los Angeles	CA	90010	213-381-3719	381-6990
Web: www.ciula.edu ■ *E-mail:* dean@ciula.edu					
California State University Los Angeles					
5151 State University Dr	Los Angeles	CA	90032	323-343-3000	343-3888
Web: www.calstatela.edu					
Cerritos College 11110 Alondra Blvd	Norwalk	CA	90650	562-860-2451	467-5068
Web: www.cerritos.edu ■ *E-mail:* info@cerritos.edu					
Chaffey College 5885 Haven Ave	Rancho Cucamonga	CA	91737	909-987-1737	941-2783
Web: www.chaffey.cc.ca.us					
Citrus College 1000 W Foothill Blvd	Glendora	CA	91741	626-963-0323	914-8618
Web: www.citrus.cc.ca.us					
City University of Los Angeles					
PO Box 4277	Inglewood	CA	90309	310-671-0783	671-0572
TF Admissions: 800-262-8388 ■ *Web:* www.cula.edu ■ *E-mail:* info@cula.com					
College of Oceaneering 272 S Fries Ave	Wilmington	CA	90744	310-834-2501	834-7132
TF: 800-432-3483 ■ *Web:* diveco.com ■ *E-mail:* admissions@diveco.com					
College of the Canyons					
26455 N Rockwell Canyon Rd	Santa Clarita	CA	91355	661-259-7800	254-7996
Web: www.coc.cc.ca.us ■ *E-mail:* pio660@coc.cc.ca.us					
Columbia College Hollywood					
18618 Oxnard St	Tarzana	CA	91356	818-345-8414	345-9053
Web: www.columbiacollege.edu					
Compton Community College					
1111 E Artesia Blvd	Compton	CA	90221	310-637-2660	900-1695
Web: www.compton.cc.ca.us					
Cypress College 9200 Valley View St	Cypress	CA	90630	714-484-7000	484-7446
Web: www.cypress.cc.ca.us					
Don Bosco Technical Institute					
1151 San Gabriel Blvd	Rosemead	CA	91770	626-307-6500	940-2000
East Los Angeles College					
1301 Cesar Chavez Ave	Monterey Park	CA	91754	323-265-8650	265-8688
Web: www.laccd.edu/college.htm#EAST ■ *E-mail:* east@laccd.cc.ca.us					
El Camino College 16007 Crenshaw Blvd	Torrance	CA	90506	310-532-3670	660-3818
Web: www.elcamino.cc.ca.us					
Eubanks Conservatory of Music & Arts					
4928 S Crenshaw Blvd	Los Angeles	CA	90043	323-291-7821	
Fashion Institute of Design & Merchandising 919 S Grand Ave	Los Angeles	CA	90015	213-624-1200	624-4777
TF Admissions: 800-421-0127 ■ *Web:* www.fidm.com ■ *E-mail:* fidm@fidm.com					
Glendale Community College					
1500 N Verdugo Rd	Glendale	CA	91208	818-240-1000	551-5255
Web: www.glendale.cc.ca.us ■ *E-mail:* gparker@glendale.cc.ca.us					
Hebrew Union College Los Angeles					
3077 University Ave	Los Angeles	CA	90007	213-749-3424	747-6128
Web: cwis.usc.edu/dept/huc-la/					
International Christian University & Seminary 2853 W 7th St	Los Angeles	CA	90005	213-381-0081	381-0010
ITT Technical Institute					
20050 S Vermont Ave	Torrance	CA	90502	310-380-1555	380-1557
TF: 800-388-3368 ■ *Web:* www.itt-tech.edu					
ITT Technical Institute 12669 Encinitas Ave	Sylmar	CA	91342	818-364-5151	364-5150
TF: 800-363-2086 ■ *Web:* www.itt-tech.edu					
Long Beach City College					
4901 E Carson St	Long Beach	CA	90808	562-938-4111	420-4118
Web: www.lbcc.cc.ca.us ■ *E-mail:* rschultz@lbcc.cc.ca.us					
Los Angeles City College					
855 N Vermont Ave	Los Angeles	CA	90029	323-953-4000	953-4294
Web: citywww.lacc.cc.ca.us					
Los Angeles Community College District					
770 Wilshire Blvd	Los Angeles	CA	90017	213-891-2000	891-2035
Web: www.laccd.edu					
Los Angeles Harbor College					
1111 Figueroa Pl	Wilmington	CA	90744	310-522-8200	834-1882
Web: www.lahc.cc.ca.us ■ *E-mail:* woodg@laccd.cc.ca.us					
Los Angeles Mission College					
13356 Eldridge Ave	Sylmar	CA	91342	818-364-7600	364-7755
Web: www.lamission.cc.ca.us					
Los Angeles Pierce College					
6201 Winnetka Ave	Woodland Hills	CA	91371	818-347-0551	710-9844
Web: www.piercecollege.com					

Los Angeles — Colleges/Universities (Cont'd)

Name / Address	City	State	ZIP	Phone	Fax
Los Angeles Trade-Technical College 400 W Washington Blvd	Los Angeles	CA	90015	213-744-9500	748-7334
Web: www.lattc.cc.ca.us ■ *E-mail:* tradetech@laccd.cc.ca.us					
Los Angeles Valley College 5800 Fulton Ave	Valley Glen	CA	91401	818-947-2600	947-2610
Web: www.lavc.cc.ca.us ■ *E-mail:* jakme@bigfoot.com					
Loyola Marymount University 7900 Loyola Blvd	Los Angeles	CA	90045	310-338-2700	338-2797
Web: www.lmu.edu ■ *E-mail:* bweinste@lmumail.lmu.edu					
Marymount College Palos Verdes 30800 Palos Verdes Dr E	Rancho Palos Verdes	CA	90275	310-377-5501	377-6223
Web: www.marymountpv.edu ■ *E-mail:* admissions@marymountpv.edu					
Mount Saint Mary's College 12001 Chalon Rd	Los Angeles	CA	90049	310-476-2237	954-4259
TF Admissions: 800-999-9893*					
Mount Saint Mary's College Doheny Campus 10 Chester Pl	Los Angeles	CA	90007	213-746-0450	477-2569
Web: www.msmc.la.edu					
Mount San Antonio College 1100 N Grand Ave	Walnut	CA	91789	909-594-5611	468-4068
Web: www.mtsac.edu					
Occidental College 1600 Campus Rd	Los Angeles	CA	90041	323-259-2500	259-2958
TF Admissions: 800-825-5262 ■ *Web:* www.oxy.edu					
Otis College of Art & Design 9045 Lincoln Blvd	Los Angeles	CA	90045	310-665-6820	665-6821
TF: 800-527-6847 ■ *Web:* www.otisart.edu					
Pacific Southern University 9581 W Pico Blvd	Los Angeles	CA	90035	310-551-0304	277-5280
TF: 888-477-8872					
Pacific Western University 600 N Sepulveda Blvd	Los Angeles	CA	90049	310-471-0306	471-6456
TF: 800-423-3244 ■ *Web:* www.pwu.com					
Pasadena City College 1570 E Colorado Blvd	Pasadena	CA	91106	626-585-7123	585-7915
Web: www.paccd.cc.ca.us					
Pepperdine University 24255 Pacific Coast Hwy	Malibu	CA	90263	310-456-4000	456-4758
Web: www.pepperdine.edu					
Rio Hondo College 3600 Workman Mill Rd	Whittier	CA	90601	562-692-0921	692-8318
Web: www.rh.cc.ca.us/					
Ryokan College 11965 Venice Blvd Suite 304	Los Angeles	CA	90066	310-390-7560	391-9756
Web: www.ryokan.edu					
Santa Monica College 1900 Pico Blvd.	Santa Monica	CA	90405	310-450-5150	434-3645
Web: www.smc.edu					
Southern California Institute of Architecture 5454 Beethoven St	Los Angeles	CA	90066	310-574-1123	574-3801
University of California Los Angeles 405 Hilgard Ave	Los Angeles	CA	90095	310-825-4321	206-1206
Web: www.ucla.edu					
University of Judaism 15600 Mulholland Dr.	Los Angeles	CA	90077	310-476-9777	471-3657
TF Admissions: 888-853-6763 ■ *Web:* www.uj.edu ■ *E-mail:* admissions@uj.edu					
University of Southern California University Pk	Los Angeles	CA	90089	213-740-2311	740-6364
Web: www.usc.edu					
University of West Los Angeles 1155 W Arbor Vitae St	Inglewood	CA	90301	310-215-3339	342-5296
West Los Angeles College 4800 Freshman Dr	Culver City	CA	90230	310-287-4200	841-0396
Web: www.wlac.cc.ca.us					
Whittier College 13406 E Philadelphia St.	Whittier	CA	90601	562-907-4200	907-4870
Web: www.whittier.edu					
William Carey International University 1539 E Howard St.	Pasadena	CA	91104	626-797-1200	398-2111
Web: www.wciu.edu ■ *E-mail:* admissions@wciu.edu					
Woodbury University 7500 Glenoaks Blvd	Burbank	CA	91510	818-767-0888	767-7520*
**Fax:* Admissions ■ *TF Admissions:* 800-784-9663 ■ *Web:* www.woodburyu.edu ■ *E-mail:* admissions@vaxb.woodbury.edu					
Yeshiva University of Los Angeles 9760 W Pico Blvd	Los Angeles	CA	90035	310-772-2480	772-7656

— Hospitals —

Name / Address	City	State	ZIP	Phone	Fax
Alhambra Hospital 100 S Raymond Ave	Alhambra	CA	91801	626-570-1606	570-8825
Anaheim Memorial Hospital 1111 W La Palma Ave	Anaheim	CA	92801	714-774-1450	999-6122
Antelope Valley Hospital Medical Center 1600 W Ave J	Lancaster	CA	93534	661-949-5000	949-5510
Arrowhead Regional Medical Center 400 N Pepper Ave	Colton	CA	92324	909-580-1000	580-6196
Bay Harbor Hospital 1437 W Lomita Blvd	Harbor City	CA	90710	310-325-1221	534-3286
Bellflower Doctors Medical Center 9542 E Artesia Blvd	Bellflower	CA	90706	562-925-8355	925-4413
Beverly Hospital 309 W Beverly Blvd	Montebello	CA	90640	323-726-1222	725-4353
Web: www.beverly.org					
Brotman Medical Center 3828 Delmas Terr	Culver City	CA	90231	310-836-7000	202-4141
California Hospital Medical Center 1401 S Grand Ave	Los Angeles	CA	90015	213-748-2411	742-5725
Web: www.chmcla.com					
Cedars-Sinai Medical Center 8700 Beverly Blvd	Los Angeles	CA	90048	310-855-5000	967-0105*
**Fax:* Admitting ■ *TF:* 800-233-2771 ■ *Web:* www.csmc.edu					
Centinela Hospital Medical Center 555 E Hardy St	Inglewood	CA	90301	310-673-4660	673-0400
Century City Hospital 2070 Century Park E	Los Angeles	CA	90067	310-553-6211	201-6723
Web: www.tenethealth.com/CenturyCity					
Chapman Medical Center 2601 E Chapman Ave	Orange	CA	92869	714-633-0011	633-1014*
**Fax:* Admitting					
Children's Hospital of Los Angeles PO Box 54700	Los Angeles	CA	90027	323-660-2450	666-3809
TF Admitting: 800-877-2452 ■ *Web:* www.childrenshospitalla.org					
Children's Hospital of Orange County 455 S Main St	Orange	CA	92868	714-997-3000	289-4559
Web: www.choc.com					
Chino Valley Medical Center 5451 Walnut Ave	Chino	CA	91710	909-464-8600	464-8882
Coastal Communities Hospital 2701 S Bristol St	Santa Ana	CA	92704	714-754-5454	754-5556
Columbia West Hills Medical Center 7300 Medical Center Dr	West Hills	CA	91307	818-712-4100	712-4173
Community Hospital of San Bernardino 1805 Medical Center Dr	San Bernardino	CA	92411	909-887-6333	887-6468
Community Memorial Hospital 147 N Brent St	Ventura	CA	93003	805-652-5011	652-5031
Web: www.cmhhospital.com					
Daniel Freeman Marina Hospital 4650 Lincoln Blvd	Marina del Rey	CA	90292	310-823-8911	574-7854
Daniel Freeman Memorial Hospital 333 N Prairie Ave	Inglewood	CA	90301	310-674-7050	419-8273
Desert Hospital 1150 N Indian Canyon Dr	Palm Springs	CA	92262	760-323-6511	323-6859
Downey Regional Medical Center 11500 Brookshire Ave	Downey	CA	90241	562-904-5000	904-5309
East Los Angeles Doctors Hospital 4060 Whittier Blvd	Los Angeles	CA	90023	323-268-5514	266-1256
Eisenhower Medical Center 39000 Bob Hope Dr	Rancho Mirage	CA	92270	760-340-3911	773-1425*
**Fax:* Mail Rm					
Encino Tarzana Regional Medical Center Encino Campus 16237 Ventura Blvd	Encino	CA	91436	818-995-5000	907-8630
Encino Tarzana Regional Medical Center Tarzana Campus 18321 Clark St	Tarzana	CA	91356	818-881-0800	708-5382
Foothill Presbyterian Hospital Morris L Johnston Memorial 250 S Grand Ave	Glendora	CA	91741	626-963-8411	857-3274
Fountain Valley Regional Hospital & Medical Center 17100 Euclid St	Fountain Valley	CA	92708	714-966-7200	966-8039
Garden Grove Hospital & Medical Center 12601 Garden Grove Blvd	Garden Grove	CA	92843	714-537-5160	741-3322
Web: www.tenethealth.com/GardenGrove					
Garfield Medical Center 525 N Garfield Ave	Monterey Park	CA	91754	626-573-2222	571-8972
Web: www.tenethealth.com/Garfield					
Glendale Adventist Medical Center 1509 Wilson Terr	Glendale	CA	91206	818-409-8000	546-5650*
**Fax:* PR					
Glendale Memorial Hospital & Health Center 1420 S Central Ave	Glendale	CA	91201	818-502-1900	246-4104
Good Samaritan Hospital 1225 Wilshire Blvd	Los Angeles	CA	90017	213-977-2121	482-2770
Web: www.goodsam.org					
Granada Hills Community Hospital 10445 Balboa Blvd	Granada Hills	CA	91344	818-360-1021	360-6451
Greater El Monte Community Hospital 1701 Santa Anita Ave	South El Monte	CA	91733	626-579-7777	350-0368
Hemet Valley Medical Center 1117 E Devonshire Ave	Hemet	CA	92543	909-652-2811	765-4707
Web: www.valleyhealthsystem.com/hemmain.htm					
Henry Mayo Newhall Memorial Hospital 23845 W McBean Pkwy	Valencia	CA	91351	661-253-8000	253-8897

Los Angeles — Hospitals (Cont'd)

Phone *Fax*

Hoag Memorial Hospital Presbyterian
1 Hoag Dr ... Newport Beach CA 92663 949-645-8600 760-5593
Web: www.hoag.org

Huntington East Valley Hospital
150 W Alosta Ave ... Glendora CA 91740 626-335-0231 335-5082

Huntington Memorial Hospital
100 W California Blvd ... Pasadena CA 91109 626-397-5000 397-2980
Web: www.huntingtonhospital.com

Inland Valley Regional Medical Center
36485 Inland Valley Dr ... Wildomar CA 92595 909-677-1111 677-9754
Web: www.ivrmc.com

Irvine Medical Center 16200 Sand Canyon Ave ... Irvine CA 92618 949-753-2000 753-2131
Web: www.tenethealth.com/Irvine

Jerry L Pettis Memorial Veterans Affairs Medical Center 11201 Benton St ... Loma Linda CA 92357 909-825-7084 422-3106

John F Kennedy Memorial Hospital
47-111 Monroe St. ... Indio CA 92201 760-347-6191 775-8014
Web: www.tenethealth.com/JFKMemorial

Kaiser Foundation Hospital
5601 De Soto Ave. ... Woodland Hills CA 91365 818-719-2000 719-2363

Kaiser Permanente Hospital
441 N Lakeview Ave ... Anaheim CA 92807 714-279-4000 279-5590
TF: 800-464-4000

Kaiser Permanente Medical Center
25825 S Vermont Ave ... Harbor City CA 90710 310-325-5111 517-2234
TF: 800-464-4000

Kaiser Permanente Medical Center
9400 E Rosecrans Ave. ... Bellflower CA 90706 562-461-3000 461-5726*
**Fax:* Hum Res

Kaiser Permanente Medical Center
9961 Sierra Ave ... Fontana CA 92335 909-427-5000 427-7359

Kaiser Permanente Medical Center
4867 Sunset Blvd ... Los Angeles CA 90027 323-783-4011 783-5048*
**Fax:* Mail Rm ■ *TF:* 800-954-8000

Kaiser Permanente Medical Center
13652 Cantara St ... Panorama City CA 91402 818-375-2000 375-3480
TF: 800-272-3500

Kaiser Permanente Medical Center-West Los Angeles 6041 Cadillac Ave. ... Los Angeles CA 90034 323-857-2000 857-4501

Kaiser Permanente Riverside Medical Center
10800 Magnolia Ave ... Riverside CA 92505 909-353-2000 353-4611
TF Cust Svc: 800-464-4000*

La Palma Intercommunity Hospital
7901 Walker St. ... La Palma CA 90623 714-670-7400 670-6287

LAC-Harbor-UCLA Medical Center
1000 W Carson St ... Torrance CA 90509 310-222-2345 328-9624*
**Fax:* PR

LAC-King-Drew Medical Center
12021 S Wilmington Ave ... Los Angeles CA 90059 310-668-5011 638-3602

LAC-University of Southern California Medical Center 1200 N State St. ... Los Angeles CA 90033 323-226-2622 226-6518

Lakewood Regional Medical Center
PO Box 6070 ... Lakewood CA 90714 562-531-2550 602-0083
Web: www.tenethealth.com/Lakewood

Lancaster Community Hospital
43830 N 10th St West. ... Lancaster CA 93534 661-948-4781 949-9783

Little Company of Mary Hospital
4101 Torrance Blvd. ... Torrance CA 90503 310-540-7676 540-8408

Loma Linda University Community Medical Center 25333 Barton Rd ... Loma Linda CA 92354 909-796-0167 796-6628*
**Fax:* Admitting

Loma Linda University Medical Center
11234 Anderson St ... Loma Linda CA 92354 909-824-4302 824-4086
Web: www.llu.edu

Long Beach Community Medical Center
1720 Termino Ave. ... Long Beach CA 90804 562-498-1000 498-4434
Web: www.lbcommunity.com

Long Beach Memorial Medical Center
2801 Atlantic Ave ... Long Beach CA 90801 562-933-2000 933-1107

Los Alamitos Medical Center
3751 Katella Ave. ... Los Alamitos CA 90720 562-598-1311 493-2812*
**Fax Area Code:* 310 ■ *Web:* www.tenethealth.com/LosAlamitos

Los Angeles Community Hospital
4081 E Olympic Blvd. ... Los Angeles CA 90023 323-267-0477 261-0809

Los Angeles Metropolitan Medical Center
2231 S Western Ave ... Los Angeles CA 90018 323-737-7372 734-0963

Los Robles Regional Medical Center
215 W Janss Rd. ... Thousand Oaks CA 91360 805-497-2727 370-4666

Memorial Hospital of Gardena
1145 W Redondo Beach Blvd. ... Gardena CA 90247 310-532-4200 538-6680

Methodist Hospital of Southern California
300 W Huntington Dr ... Arcadia CA 91007 626-445-4441 821-6968*
**Fax:* Admitting

Phone *Fax*

Midway Hospital Medical Center
5925 San Vincente Blvd. ... Los Angeles CA 90019 323-938-3161 932-5061*
**Fax:* Admitting ■ *TF:* 800-827-8599

Northridge Hospital Medical Center-Roscoe Blvd Campus 18300 Roscoe Blvd. ... Northridge CA 91328 818-885-8500 885-5365

Northridge Hospital Medical Center-Sherman Way Campus 14500 Sherman Circle ... Van Nuys CA 91405 818-997-0101 908-8607

Olive View Medical Center
14445 Olive View Dr ... Sylmar CA 91342 818-364-1555 364-4206

Orange Coast Memorial Medical Center
9920 Talbert Ave. ... Fountain Valley CA 92708 714-962-4677 378-7079

Orange County Community Hospital of Buena Park 6850 Lincoln Ave ... Buena Park CA 90620 714-827-1161 826-5158*
**Fax:* Admitting

Pacific Hospital of Long Beach
2776 Pacific Ave. ... Long Beach CA 90806 562-595-1911 427-8072

Parkview Community Hospital Medical Center
3865 Jackson St. ... Riverside CA 92503 909-688-2211 352-5471

Placentia-Linda Community Hospital
1301 Rose Dr. ... Placentia CA 92670 714-993-2000 961-8427

Pomona Valley Hospital Medical Center
1798 N Garey Ave. ... Pomona CA 91767 909-865-9500 865-9796

Presbyterian Intercommunity Hospital
12401 E Washington Blvd ... Whittier CA 90602 562-698-0811 698-1728

Providence Holy Cross Medical Center
15031 Rinaldi St. ... Mission Hills CA 91345 818-365-8051 898-4569

Providence Saint Joseph Medical Center
501 S Buena Vista St ... Burbank CA 91505 818-843-5111 843-0641

Queen of Angels Hollywood Presbyterian Medical Center 1300 N Vermont Ave ... Los Angeles CA 90027 323-913-4800 644-4411

Queen of the Valley Hospital
1115 S Sunset Ave ... West Covina CA 91790 626-962-4011 814-2524

Riverside Community Hospital
4445 Magnolia Ave ... Riverside CA 92501 909-788-3000 788-3174

Riverside County Regional Medical Center 26520 Texas Ave ... Moreno Valley CA 92555 909-486-4000 486-4475
TF: 800-900-0888

Robert F Kennedy Medical Center
4500 W 116th St ... Hawthorne CA 90250 310-973-1711 219-3715

Saddleback Memorial Medical Center
24451 Health Center Dr. ... Laguna Hills CA 92653 949-837-4500 452-3467*
**Fax:* Admitting

Saint Bernardine Medical Center
2101 N Waterman Ave. ... San Bernardino CA 92404 909-883-8711 881-4546

Saint Francis Medical Center
3630 E Imperial Hwy. ... Lynwood CA 90262 310-603-6000 604-0864

Saint John's Hospital & Health Center
1328 22nd St. ... Santa Monica CA 90404 310-829-5511 315-6134

Saint John's Regional Medical Center
1600 N Rose Ave ... Oxnard CA 93030 805-988-2500 981-4440

Saint Joseph Hospital 1100 W Stewart Dr. ... Orange CA 92868 714-633-9111 744-8668*
**Fax:* Hum Res

Saint Jude Medical Center
101 E Valencia Mesa Dr. ... Fullerton CA 92835 714-992-3000 992-3029

Saint Luke Medical Center
2632 E Washington Blvd ... Pasadena CA 91107 626-797-1141 797-0948

Saint Mary Medical Center
1050 Linden Ave. ... Long Beach CA 90813 562-491-9000 436-6378

Saint Vincent Medical Center
2131 W 3rd St ... Los Angeles CA 90057 213-484-7111 484-9304
Web: www.stvincentmedicalcenter.com

San Antonio Community Hospital
999 San Bernardino Rd ... Upland CA 91786 909-985-2811 985-7659
Web: www.sach.org

San Dimas Community Hospital
1350 West Covina Blvd ... San Dimas CA 91773 909-599-6811 599-8518

San Gabriel Valley Medical Center
438 W Las Tunas Dr. ... San Gabriel CA 91776 626-289-5454 570-6555

San Pedro Peninsula Hospital
1300 W 7th St ... San Pedro CA 90732 310-832-3311 514-5314

Santa Martha Hospital
319 N Humphreys Ave. ... Los Angeles CA 90022 323-266-6500 260-8641

Santa Monica UCLA Medical Center
1250 16th St ... Santa Monica CA 90404 310-319-4000 319-4534

Santa Teresita Hospital 819 Buena Vista St. ... Duarte CA 91010 626-359-3243 357-7166

Sepulveda Veterans Medical Center
16111 Plummer St ... North Hills CA 91343 818-891-7711 895-9598*
**Fax:* Hum Res

Sherman Oaks Hospital & Health Center
4929 Van Nuys Blvd ... Sherman Oaks CA 91403 818-981-7111 907-4557

Shriners Hospitals for Children Los Angeles Unit 3160 Geneva St. ... Los Angeles CA 90020 213-388-3151 387-7528
Web: www.shrinershq.org/Hospitals/Directry/losangeles.html

Simi Valley Hospital & Health Care Services
2975 N Sycamore Dr. ... Simi Valley CA 93065 805-527-2462 526-9655

South Coast Medical Center
31872 Coast Hwy ... South Laguna CA 92651 949-499-1311 499-7529

Los Angeles — Hospitals (Cont'd)

Name / Address	City	State	ZIP	Phone	Fax
Suburban Medical Center 16453 S Colorado Ave	Paramount	CA	90723	562-531-3110	531-4671
Temple Community Hospital 235 N Hoover St	Los Angeles	CA	90004	213-382-7252	389-4559
Torrance Memorial Medical Center 3330 Lomita Blvd *Web:* torrancememorial.org	Torrance	CA	90505	310-325-9110	784-4801
UCLA Medical Center 10833 Le Conte Ave *Web:* www.medctr.ucla.edu	Los Angeles	CA	90095	310-825-9111	825-9179
University of California Irvine Medical Center 101 City Dr S **Fax:* Library	Orange	CA	92868	714-456-6011	456-7927*
Valley Presbyterian Hospital 15107 Vanowen St	Van Nuys	CA	91405	818-782-6600	902-3974
Ventura County Medical Center 3291 Loma Vista Rd	Ventura	CA	93003	805-652-6058	652-6188
Verdugo Hills Hospital 1812 Verdugo Blvd	Glendale	CA	91208	818-790-7100	952-4616
Veterans Affairs Medical Center 5901 E 7th St	Long Beach	CA	90822	562-494-2611	494-5972
Veterans Affairs Medical Center 110301 Wilshire Blvd	Los Angeles	CA	90073	310-478-3711	268-3494
Victor Valley Hospital 15248 11th St	Victorville	CA	92392	760-245-8691	245-8824
West Anaheim Medical Center 3033 W Orange Ave	Anaheim	CA	92804	714-827-3000	229-6813
Western Medical Center 1001 N Tustin Ave	Santa Ana	CA	92705	714-835-3555	953-3613
White Memorial Medical Center 1720 Cesar E Chavez Ave **Fax:* Admitting ■ *Web:* www.adventisthealthsocal.com/AHSC/hospitals/1WWMC.html	Los Angeles	CA	90033	323-268-5000	265-5065*
Whittier Hospital Medical Center 9080 Colima Rd **Fax:* Admitting	Whittier	CA	90605	562-945-3561	464-2930*

— Attractions —

Name / Address	City	State	ZIP	Phone	Fax
ABC Inc 2040 Ave of the Stars	Century City	CA	90067	310-557-7777	
American Jazz Philharmonic PO Box 34575 *Web:* www.amjazzphil.org	Los Angeles	CA	90034	310-845-1900	845-1909
Angeles National Forest 701 N Santa Anita Ave	Arcadia	CA	91006	626-574-1613	574-5233
Armand Hammer Museum of Art & Cultural Center 10899 Wilshire Blvd *Web:* artscenecal.com/UCLAHammerMsm.html	Los Angeles	CA	90024	310-443-7000	443-7099
Ballet Folklorico de Mexico 10801 National Blvd Suite 220 *Web:* www.balletfolkloricotours.com	Los Angeles	CA	90064	310-474-4443	446-9531
California Plaza 350 S Grand Ave Suite A4 *Web:* www.grandperformances.org ■ *E-mail:* events@grandperformances.org	Los Angeles	CA	90071	213-687-2190	687-2191
California Science Center 700 State Dr *Web:* www.casciencectr.org	Los Angeles	CA	90037	213-744-7400	744-2650
CBS Studio 7800 Beverly Blvd *Web:* www.cbs.com	Los Angeles	CA	90036	323-575-2345	651-5900
Disneyland PO Box 3232 *Web:* disney.go.com/Disneyland	Anaheim	CA	92803	714-781-4565	
Elysian Park 929 Academy Rd	Los Angeles	CA	90012	323-226-1402	
Gene Autry Western Heritage Museum 4700 Western Heritage Way *E-mail:* autry@autry-museum.org	Los Angeles	CA	90027	323-667-2000	660-5721
Getty J Paul Museum 1200 Getty Center Dr *Web:* www.getty.edu	Los Angeles	CA	90049	310-440-7300	440-6949
Grier-Musser Museum 403 S Bonnie Brae St *Web:* www.isi.edu/sims/sheila/gm.html	Los Angeles	CA	90057	213-413-1814	
Griffith Observatory 2800 E Observatory Rd Griffith Pk *Web:* www.griffithobs.org	Los Angeles	CA	90027	323-664-1181	663-4323
Griffith Park Los Feliz Blvd & Riverside Dr	Los Angeles	CA	90027	213-485-8775	485-8775
Heritage Square Museum 3800 Homer St	Los Angeles	CA	90031	626-449-0193	304-9652
Hollywood Bowl 2301 N Highland Ave *Web:* www.hollywoodbowl.org/	Los Angeles	CA	90078	323-850-2000	850-2155
IMAX Theater 700 State Dr Exposition Pk	Los Angeles	CA	90037	213-744-2014	
Japanese American National Museum 369 E 1st St *TF:* 800-461-5266 ■ *Web:* www.lausd.k12.ca.us/janm/	Los Angeles	CA	90012	213-625-0414	625-1770
Kaye Museum of Miniatures 5900 Wilshire Blvd East Wing *Web:* www.museumofminiatures.com	Los Angeles	CA	90036	323-937-6464	937-2126
Knott's Berry Farm 8039 Beach Blvd *Web:* www.knotts.com	Buena Park	CA	90620	714-827-1776	220-5200
Los Angeles Ballet PO Box 712462 **Fax Area Code:* 714	Los Angeles	CA	90071	213-833-3610	991-8050*
Los Angeles Chamber Orchestra 611 W 6th St Suite 2710 *Web:* www.laco.org ■ *E-mail:* lachamber@aol.com	Los Angeles	CA	90017	213-622-7001	955-2071
Los Angeles Children's Museum 310 N Main St	Los Angeles	CA	90012	213-687-8801	687-0319
Los Angeles County Museum of Art 5905 Wilshire Blvd **Fax:* Mktg ■ *Web:* www.lacma.org	Los Angeles	CA	90036	323-857-6111	857-4702*
Los Angeles Farmers Market 6333 W 3rd St *Web:* www.farmersmarketla.com/ ■ *E-mail:* info@farmersmarketla.com	Los Angeles	CA	90036	323-933-9211	
Los Angeles Opera 135 N Grand Ave *Web:* www.laopera.org ■ *E-mail:* contact@laopera.org	Los Angeles	CA	90012	213-972-7219	687-3490
Los Angeles Philharmonic Assn 135 N Grand Ave *Web:* www.laphil.org	Los Angeles	CA	90012	213-972-7300	617-3065
Los Angeles Zoo 5333 Zoo Dr *Web:* www.lazoo.org ■ *E-mail:* lazooed@ix.netcom.com	Los Angeles	CA	90027	323-666-4650	662-9786
Mann's Chinese Theatre 6925 Hollywood Blvd	Hollywood	CA	90028	323-464-8186	
Museum of Contemporary Art 250 S Grand Ave California Plaza *Web:* www.moca.org	Los Angeles	CA	90012	213-621-2766	620-8674
Museum of Neon Art 501 W Olympic Blvd	Los Angeles	CA	90015	213-489-9918	489-9932
Museum of Tolerance 9760 W Pico Blvd Wiesenthal Ctr *Web:* www.wiesenthal.com	Los Angeles	CA	90035	310-553-8403	772-7655
Music Center of Los Angeles 135 N Grand Ave	Los Angeles	CA	90012	213-972-7200	972-7474
My Jewish Discovery Place Children's Museum of JCCA 5870 W Olympic Blvd	Los Angeles	CA	90036	323-857-0072	965-1758
Natural History Museum of Los Angeles County 900 Exposition Blvd *Web:* www.nhm.org ■ *E-mail:* info@nhm.org	Los Angeles	CA	90007	213-763-3466	746-2999
NBC Studio 3000 W Alameda Ave	Burbank	CA	91523	818-840-4444	840-3535
Page George C Museum at La Brea Tar Pits 5801 Wilshire Blvd *Web:* www.tarpits.org	Los Angeles	CA	90036	323-857-6311	933-3974
Paramount Film & TV Studios 5555 Melrose Ave *Web:* www.paramount.com	Los Angeles	CA	90038	323-956-1777	862-8534
Pasadena Center 300 E Green St *Web:* www.pasadenacenter.org	Pasadena	CA	91101	626-793-2122	793-8014
Pasadena Symphony 2500 E Colorado Blvd Suite 260 *Web:* www.pasadenasymphony.org	Pasadena	CA	91107	626-793-7172	793-7180
Petersen Automotive Museum 6060 Wilshire Blvd *Web:* www.petersen.org	Los Angeles	CA	90036	323-930-2277	
Ports O'Call Village Berth 77 P7A	San Pedro	CA	90731	310-831-0287	831-3686
Santa Monica Mountains National Recreation Area 401 W Hillcrest Dr *Web:* www.nps.gov/samo/	Thousand Oaks	CA	91360	805-370-2301	370-1850
Six Flags Hurricane Harbor 26101 Magic Mountain Pkwy	Valencia	CA	91355	661-255-4100	
Six Flags Magic Mountain 26101 Magic Mountain Pkwy	Valencia	CA	91355	661-255-4100	255-4815
Southwest Museum 234 Museum Dr *Web:* www.southwestmuseum.org ■ *E-mail:* swmuseum@annex.com	Los Angeles	CA	90065	323-221-2164	224-8223
Universal Studios Hollywood 100 Universal City Plaza **Fax:* Hum Res ■ *Web:* www.universalstudios.com/unicity/thehill.html ■ *E-mail:* execdesk@mca.com	Universal City	CA	91608	818-622-3801	866-1516*
Warner Bros Studios 4000 Warner Blvd	Burbank	CA	91522	818-954-1744	954-2089
Watts Towers 1727 E 107th St **Fax Area Code:* 323	Los Angeles	CA	90002	213-847-4646	564-7030*
Wells Fargo History Museum 333 S Grand Ave *Web:* www.wellsfargohistory.com	Los Angeles	CA	90071	213-253-7166	680-2269
Wiltern Theatre 3790 Wilshire Blvd	Los Angeles	CA	90010	213-388-1400	388-0242
World Trade Center 350 S Figueroa St Suite 233	Los Angeles	CA	90071	213-489-3337	626-5765

Los Angeles (Cont'd)

SPORTS TEAMS & FACILITIES

				Phone	Fax
Anaheim Angels 2000 Gene Autry Way Edison International Field *Web:* www.angelsbaseball.com	Anaheim	CA	92806	714-940-2000	940-2001
Dodger Stadium 1000 Elysian Park Ave	Los Angeles	CA	90012	323-224-1351	224-1399
Los Angeles Clippers 1111 S Figueroa St Staples Ctr *Web:* www.nba.com/clippers	Los Angeles	CA	90015	213-748-8000	745-0494
Los Angeles Dodgers 1000 Elysian Park Ave Dodger Stadium *Web:* www.dodgers.com	Los Angeles	CA	90012	323-224-1400	224-1269
Los Angeles Galaxy (soccer) 1640 S Sepulveda Blvd Suite 114 *E-mail:* falozano@aol.com	Los Angeles	CA	90025	310-445-1260	445-1270
Los Angeles Kings 865 S Figueroa St Staples Ctr *Web:* www.lakings.com ■ *E-mail:* tickets@lakings.com	Los Angeles	CA	90017	310-419-3160	673-8927
Los Angeles Lakers 865 S Figueroa St Staples Ctr *Web:* www.nba.com/lakers	Los Angeles	CA	90017	213-624-3100	742-7282
Los Angeles Memorial Coliseum & Sports Arena 3939 S Figueroa St	Los Angeles	CA	90037	213-748-6136	746-9346
Los Angeles Sparks (basketball) 3900 W Manchester Blvd Great Western Forum *Web:* www.wnba.com/sparks	Inglewood	CA	90306	310-330-2434	
Mighty Ducks of Anaheim 2695 E Katella Ave Arrowhead Pond of Anaheim *Web:* www.mightyducks.com	Anaheim	CA	92806	714-704-2700	704-2753
San Fernando Valley Heroes (soccer) 7955 San Fernando Rd	Sun Valley	CA	91352	818-768-0965	768-5213
San Gabriel Valley Highlanders (soccer) 536 N Glen Oaks Blvd	Burbank	CA	91501	818-242-9110	556-6427
Santa Anita Park 285 W Huntington Dr *Web:* www.santaanita.com ■ *E-mail:* sainfo@santaanita.com	Arcadia	CA	91007	626-574-7223	446-9565
Staples Center 865 S Figueroa St *Fax: PR ■ *Web:* www.staplescenterla.com	Los Angeles	CA	90017	213-624-3100	742-7282*

— Events —

	Phone
Academy Awards (late March)	310-247-3000
African Marketplace & Cultural Faire (late August-early September)	323-734-1164
Alpine Village Oktoberfest (early September-October)	310-327-4384
California Plaza's Moonlight Concerts (June-October)	213-687-2159
Chinese New Year's Parade in Chinatown (February)	213-617-0396
Christmas Boat Parade (mid-December)	800-831-7678
Cinco de Mayo Celebrations (early May)	213-628-1274
City of Los Angeles Marathon (early March)	310-444-5544
Concours on Rodeo (late June)	310-858-6100
Crystal Cathedral Glory of Easter (late March-April)	714-544-5679
Earth Day Heal the Bay (mid-April)	310-581-4188
Festival of Philippine Arts & Culture (mid-September)	213-389-3050
Fiesta Broadway Cinco de Mayo Celebration (late April)	310-914-0015
Fiesta de las Artes (late May)	310-376-0951
Golden Dragon Parade (mid-February)	213-617-0396
Grammy Awards (February-March)	310-392-3777
Great American Irish Fair & Music Festival (mid-June)	818-503-2511
Griffith Park Light Festival (December)	323-913-4688
Hollywood Christmas Parade (late November)	323-469-8311
Intertribal Marketplace (early November)	323-221-2164
Israeli Festival (late April-early May)	818-757-0123
LA Fiesta Broadway (late April)	310-914-8308
Las Posadas Candlelight Procession (mid-December)	213-628-1274
Los Angeles Bach Festival (mid-March)	213-385-1345
Los Angeles City's Birthday Celebration (early September)	213-680-2821
Los Angeles County Fair (early September-early October)	909-623-3111
Los Angeles Gay & Lesbian Pride Celebration (late June)	323-686-0950
Los Angeles International Film Festival (late October)	323-856-7707
Los Angeles Music Week (early December)	310-670-6898
Lotus Festival (early July)	213-624-7300
Malibu Art Festival (late July)	310-456-9025
Mariachi USA Festival (late June)	323-848-7717
Martin Luther King Celebration & Parade (mid-January)	562-570-6816
Nisei Week Japanese Festival (mid-August)	213-687-7193
Old Pasadena Jazz Fest (early July)	213-624-7300
Old Pasadena Summer Fest (late May)	626-797-6803
Outfest-Los Angeles Gay & Lesbian Film Festival (mid-July)	323-960-9200
Page Museum's Fossil Excavation at La Brea Tar Pits (mid-July-mid-September)	323-934-7243
Pageant of the Masters/Festival of the Arts (early July-late August)	949-494-1145
Playboy Jazz Festival (mid-June)	310-449-4070
Renaissance Pleasure Faire (April-June)	800-523-2473
Rose Bowl Game (early January)	626-449-4100
Sawdust Festival (late June-late August)	949-494-3030
Scandinavian Festival (early October)	323-661-4273
South Bay Greek Festival (early October)	310-540-2434
Spring Fest (mid-May)	626-282-5767
Spring Festival of Flowers (late March-mid-April)	818-952-4400
Summer Nights at the Ford (mid-June-early September)	213-974-1396
Thai Cultural Day (mid-late September)	310-827-2910
Thai New Year Festival (mid-April)	213-624-7300
Tournament of Roses Parade & Rose Bowl (January 1)	626-449-4100
UCLA Jazz & Reggae Festival (late May)	310-825-9912
UCLA Pow Wow (early May)	310-206-7513
Venice Art Walk (mid-May)	310-392-9255

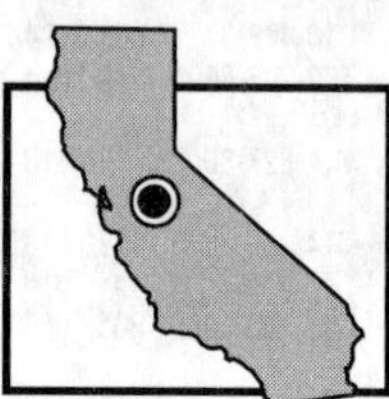

Modesto

Located in the fertile San Joaquin Valley, Modesto is best known as an agricultural center. Visitors to the city can take advantage of a number of "Taste ⁄n Sample" tours offered by local agricultural producers, including Blue Diamond Growers, Hillman Cheese Company, and Hershey's. Historical attractions in Modesto include Miller's California Ranch, which has rare farm equipment and vehicles dating back to the 1880s, as well as an old-fashioned general store. Modesto was founded in 1870, and its settlers intended to name the city "Ralston" after a San Francisco banker who had a major role in its development. When Mr. Ralston declined the honor, the name "Modesto" was chosen instead"Modesto is the Spanish word for "modesty."

Population	182,016	**Longitude**	120-59-38 W
Area (Land)	30.2 sq mi	**County**	Stanislaus
Area (Water)	0.2 sq mi	**Time Zone**	PST
Elevation	87 ft	**Area Code/s**	209
Latitude	37-39-35 N		

— Average Temperatures and Precipitation —

TEMPERATURES

	Jan	Feb	Mar	Apr	May	Jun	Jul	Aug	Sep	Oct	Nov	Dec
High	54	62	67	74	82	89	94	92	88	78	64	53
Low	37	41	43	47	51	57	60	59	56	50	43	37

PRECIPITATION

	Jan	Feb	Mar	Apr	May	Jun	Jul	Aug	Sep	Oct	Nov	Dec
Inches	2.2	1.8	2.1	1.0	0.2	0.1	0.1	0.1	0.3	0.7	1.9	1.7

— Important Phone Numbers —

	Phone		Phone
AAA	209-523-9171	**Medical Referral**	209-523-9151
American Express Travel	209-571-5606	**Poison Control Center**	800-876-4766
Dental Referral	209-522-1530	**Weather**	209-982-1793
Emergency	911		

Modesto (Cont'd)

— Information Sources —

				Phone	Fax
Better Business Bureau Serving the Mid Counties 11 S San Joaquin St Suite 803	Stockton	CA	95202	209-948-4880	465-6302
Web: www.stockton.bbb.org					
Modesto Business Development Office PO Box 642	Modesto	CA	95353	209-571-5566	491-5798
Modesto Centre Plaza 10th & K St	Modesto	CA	95354	209-577-6444	544-6729
Web: www.centreplaza.com					
Modesto Chamber of Commerce PO Box 844	Modesto	CA	95353	209-577-5757	577-2673
Web: www.modchamber.org					
Modesto City Hall 801 11th St	Modesto	CA	95354	209-577-5200	571-5152
Web: www.ci.modesto.ca.us					
Modesto Convention & Visitors Bureau 1114 J St	Modesto	CA	95353	209-571-6480	571-6486
TF: 800-266-4282 ■ *Web:* www.modestocvb.org/ ■ *E-mail:* mcvb@modestocvb.org					
Modesto Mayor 801 11th St	Modesto	CA	95354	209-577-5230	571-5152
Stanislaus County PO Box 1670	Modesto	CA	95353	209-525-5250	525-5210
Web: www.co.stanislaus.ca.us					
Stanislaus County Library 1500 'I' St	Modesto	CA	95354	209-558-7800	529-4779
Web: www.ainet.com/scfl/scfl.htm ■ *E-mail:* library@ainet.com					

On-Line Resources

Anthill City Guide Modesto	www.anthill.com/city.asp?city=modesto
Excite.com Modesto City Guide	www.excite.com/travel/countries/united_states/california/modesto
Modesto	www.cityofmodesto.com

— Transportation Services —

AIRPORTS

■ **Modesto City Airport (MOD)**

	Phone
3 miles E of downtown (approx 10 minutes)	209-577-5318

Airport Transportation

	Phone
BayPorter Express fare varies with destination	415-467-1800
Modesto Cab Co $10 fare to downtown	209-521-7320

Commercial Airlines

	Phone
United Express	800-241-6522

Charter Airlines

	Phone
Modesto Flight Center	209-578-3513
Sky Trek Aviation	209-577-4654

CAR RENTALS

	Phone
Enterprise	209-577-4700
Hertz	209-522-3236
National	209-526-4488

LIMO/TAXI

	Phone
A Touch of Class Limousine	209-527-0328
Modesto Cab Co	209-521-7320
Red Top Taxi	209-524-4741
Stretch Limousine	209-599-6040

MASS TRANSIT

	Phone
MAX Bus $.80 Base fare	209-521-1274

RAIL/BUS

				Phone
Amtrak Station 3243 Talbot Ave	Riverbank	CA	95367	800-872-7245
Greyhound Bus Station 1001 9th St	Modesto	CA	95354	209-526-4314
TF: 800-231-2222				

— Accommodations —

HOTELS, MOTELS, RESORTS

				Phone	Fax
Apex Inn 2225 Yosemite Blvd	Modesto	CA	95354	209-529-4750	577-8146
Best Western Mallard's Inn 1720 Sisk Rd	Modesto	CA	95350	209-577-3825	577-1717
TF: 800-294-4040					
Best Western Townhouse Lodge 909 16th St	Modesto	CA	95354	209-524-7261	579-9546
TF: 800-772-7261					
Budget Inn 581 S 9th St	Modesto	CA	95351	209-522-5151	
Chalet Motel 115 Downey Ave	Modesto	CA	95354	209-529-4370	579-9545
Days Inn 1312 McHenry Ave	Modesto	CA	95350	209-527-1010	527-2033
TF: 800-843-6633					
Doubletree Hotel 1150 9th St	Modesto	CA	95354	209-526-6000	526-6096
TF: 800-222-8733 ■ *Web:* www.doubletreehotels.com/DoubleT/Hotel141/148/148Main.htm					
Econo Lodge 500 Kansas Ave	Modesto	CA	95351	209-578-5400	578-5415
TF: 800-553-2666					
Holiday Inn Express 4100 Salida Blvd	Modesto	CA	95358	209-543-9000	543-9500
TF: 800-768-3500 ■ *Web:* www.hiemodesto.com/					
Holiday Inn/Holidome 1612 Sisk Rd	Modesto	CA	95350	209-521-1612	527-5074
TF: 800-465-4329					
Modesto Inn 807 Needham St	Modesto	CA	95354	209-524-9641	
Motel 6 1920 W Orangeburg Ave	Modesto	CA	95350	209-522-7271	578-0188
TF: 800-466-8356					
Plaza Motel 1522 9th St	Modesto	CA	95354	209-524-2613	
Ramada Inn 2001 W Orangeburg Ave	Modesto	CA	95350	209-521-9000	521-6034
TF: 800-228-2828					
Sundial Lodge 808 McHenry Ave	Modesto	CA	95350	209-523-5642	521-2692
Super 8 Lodge 2025 W Orangeburg Ave	Modesto	CA	95350	209-577-8008	575-4118
TF: 800-800-8000					
Tropics Motor Hotel 936 McHenry Ave	Modesto	CA	95350	209-523-7701	579-9504
Vagabond Inn 1525 McHenry Ave	Modesto	CA	95350	209-521-6340	575-2015

— Restaurants —

				Phone
Acapulco Mexican Restaurant y Cantina (Mexican) 1312 McHenry Ave	Modesto	CA	95350	209-527-1350
Alfonso's El Castillo (Mexican) 1539 Yosemite Ave	Modesto	CA	95354	209-529-3755
Andiamos Bistro (Mediterranean) 5007 McHenry Ave	Modesto	CA	95356	209-571-8600
Beijing Restaurant (Chinese) 3848 McHenry Ave Suite 205	Modesto	CA	95356	209-575-3528
Chevy's Mexican Restaurant (Mexican) 1700 Standiford Ave	Modesto	CA	95350	209-544-2144
Dave Wong's China Express (Chinese) 2240 McHenry Ave	Modesto	CA	95350	209-527-2140
Deva (American) 1202 J St	Modesto	CA	95354	209-572-3382
Dewz (California) 1101 'I' St	Modesto	CA	95354	209-549-1101
Early Dawn Cattle Enterprises (American) 1000 Kansas Ave	Modesto	CA	95351	209-577-5833
Fregoso's El Faro Restaurant (Mexican) 1345 McHenry Ave	Modesto	CA	95350	209-524-2754
Fruit Yard (American) 7948 Yosemite Blvd	Modesto	CA	95351	209-577-3093
Garden Terrace Cafe (American) 1150 9th St	Modesto	CA	95350	209-526-6000
Gervasoni's Restaurant (Italian) 712 9th St	Modesto	CA	95354	209-523-1961
Harvest Moon (American) 1213 'I' St	Modesto	CA	95354	209-523-9723
Hazel's (Continental) 431 12th St	Modesto	CA	95354	209-578-3463
India Oven Restaurant (Indian) 1022 11th St	Modesto	CA	95354	209-572-1805
J Street Cafe (American) 1030 J St	Modesto	CA	95354	209-577-8007
Le's Dynasty (Chinese) 2100 Standiford Ave Suite E-12	Modesto	CA	95350	209-527-1798
Lyon's Restaurant (American) 1445 McHenry Ave	Modesto	CA	95350	209-521-6390
Mallard's Grill (American) 1720 Sisk Rd	Modesto	CA	95350	209-577-3825
Marcella Restaurant (Mexican) 3507 Tully Rd	Modesto	CA	95350	209-577-3777
Maxi's (American) 1150 9th St	Modesto	CA	95354	209-526-6000
Monaco's (Italian) 950 Oakdale Rd	Modesto	CA	95355	209-524-3996
New Hong Kong Restaurant (Chinese) 3430 Tully Rd	Modesto	CA	95350	209-523-6230
Noah's Hof Brau (American) 1311 J St	Modesto	CA	95354	209-527-1090
Old Mill Cafe (Homestyle) 1602 9th St	Modesto	CA	95354	209-577-9858
Pacifica Grill (Mexican) 1700 McHenry Ave	Modesto	CA	95350	209-526-9999
Web: www.expedition.net/pacifica/				
Papachino's (Steak/Seafood) 217 S Golden State Blvd	Modesto	CA	95380	209-668-8095
Pho Viet Restaurant (Vietnamese) 900 Kansas Ave	Modesto	CA	95351	209-524-3032
Portofino Caffe (Italian) 521 McHenry Ave	Modesto	CA	95354	209-549-7761
Rosita's Restaurant (Mexican) 1809 McHenry Ave	Modesto	CA	95350	209-577-6032
Saint Stan's Brewery Pub & Restaurant (German) 821 L St	Modesto	CA	95354	209-524-2337
Web: www.st-stans.com				
Sidelines Pub & Grill (American) 2801 McHenry Ave	Modesto	CA	95350	209-527-4231
Strings Italian Cafe (Italian) 2601 Oakdale Rd	Modesto	CA	95355	209-578-9777
Thailand Restaurant (Thai) 950 10th St	Modesto	CA	95354	209-544-0505
Torii Japanese Restaurant (Japanese) 2401 Orangeburg Ave Suite 590	Modesto	CA	95355	209-529-9881
Tresetti's World Cafe (Continental) 927 11th St	Modesto	CA	95354	209-572-2990

Modesto — Restaurants (Cont'd)

	City	State	ZIP	Phone
Velvet Grill & Creamery (American) 2204 McHenry Ave.	Modesto	CA	95350	209-544-9029
Vineyard Patio Cafe (Continental) 1612 Sisk Rd	Modesto	CA	95350	209-521-1612

— Goods and Services —

SHOPPING

	City	State	ZIP	Phone	Fax
Downtown Improvement District PO Box 1428	Modesto	CA	95353	209-529-9303	529-2143
McHenry Village 1700 McHenry Ave Suite 25	Modesto	CA	95350	209-523-6473	523-1282
Vintage Faire Mall 3401 Dale Rd	Modesto	CA	95356	209-527-3401	525-8827

BANKS

	City	State	ZIP	Phone	Fax
Bank of America 1601 'I' St	Modesto	CA	95354	209-578-6016	578-6060
Bank of the West 1335 Yosemite Blvd.	Modesto	CA	95354	209-529-4355	529-4023
California Federal Bank 2929 McHenry Ave.	Modesto	CA	95354	209-526-9911	522-8858
Delta National Bank 1901 McHenry Ave	Modesto	CA	95350	209-527-3700	527-0820
Farmers & Merchants Bank of California 3001 McHenry Ave	Modesto	CA	95350	209-577-8311	524-3935
Guaranty Federal Bank 1101 J St.	Modesto	CA	95358	209-526-1811	526-8433
Pacific State Bank 2020 Standiford Ave Suite H	Modesto	CA	95350	209-577-2265	571-6095
Sanwa Bank California 3600 McHenry Ave	Modesto	CA	95356	209-521-8060	521-7458
Union Bank of California NA 1124 J St.	Modesto	CA	95354	209-576-2000	576-2025
Union Safe Deposit Bank 901 H St.	Modesto	CA	95354	209-529-9300	521-7761
US Bank 2008 McHenry Ave.	Modesto	CA	95350	209-524-5454	526-0262
Wells Fargo Bank 1120 K St	Modesto	CA	95354	209-578-6805	526-8163
Westamerica Bank 1524 McHenry Ave	Modesto	CA	95350	209-572-8580	572-8593

BUSINESS SERVICES

	Phone		Phone
ABS Presort Inc.	209-523-1606	**Kinko's**	209-577-2679
Adecco Employment Personnel Services	209-521-9233	**Mail Boxes Etc**	209-578-0500
Clark Karen Mailing Service	209-524-0121	**Manpower Temporary Services**	209-529-4821
DHL Worldwide Express	800-225-5345	**Olsten Staffing Services**	209-577-1820
Federal Express	800-238-5355	**Post Office**	800-275-8777
Kelly Services	209-577-4777	**Unishippers Assn**	209-578-0440
		UPS	800-742-5877

— Media —

PUBLICATIONS

	City	State	ZIP	Phone	Fax
Modesto Bee‡ PO Box 5156. *TF:* 800-776-4233 ■ *Web:* www.modbee.com	Modesto	CA	95352	209-578-2000	578-2207

‡Daily newspapers

TELEVISION

	City	State	ZIP	Phone	Fax
KCRA-TV Ch 3 (NBC) 3 Television Cir *Web:* www.kcra.com	Sacramento	CA	95814	916-446-3333	441-4050
KMAX-TV Ch 31 (UPN) 500 Media Pl *Web:* www.paramountstations.com/KMAX	Sacramento	CA	95815	916-925-3100	921-3050
KNSO-TV Ch 51 (WB) 142 N 9th St Suite 8	Modesto	CA	95350	209-529-5100	575-4547
KOVR-TV Ch 13 (CBS) 2713 KOVR Dr *Web:* www.kovr.com	West Sacramento	CA	95605	916-374-1313	374-1304
KTXL-TV Ch 40 (Fox) 4655 Fruitridge Rd.	Sacramento	CA	95820	916-454-4422	739-0559
KVIE-TV Ch 6 (PBS) 2595 Capitol Oaks Dr. *Web:* www.kvie.org ■ *E-mail:* member@kvie.org	Sacramento	CA	95833	916-929-5843	929-7367
KXTV-TV Ch 10 (ABC) 400 Broadway. *Web:* www.kxtv10.com ■ *E-mail:* kxtv10@kxtv10.com	Sacramento	CA	95818	916-441-2345	447-6107

RADIO

	City	State	ZIP	Phone	Fax
KANM-AM 970 kHz (Sports) 1581 Cummins Dr Suite 135	Modesto	CA	95358	209-523-7756	522-2061
KATM-FM 103.3 MHz (Ctry) 1581 Cummins Dr Suite 135 *Web:* www.katm.com	Modesto	CA	95358	209-523-7756	522-2061
KCIV-FM 99.9 MHz (Rel) 1031 15th St Suite 1	Modesto	CA	95354	209-524-8999	524-9088
KFIV-AM 1360 kHz (N/T) 3600 Sisk Rd Suite 2B	Modesto	CA	95356	209-545-5585	545-5588
KHOP-FM 95.1 MHz (Rock) 1581 Cummins Dr Suite 135 *Web:* www.khop.com ■ *E-mail:* feedback@khop.com	Modesto	CA	95358	209-523-7756	522-2061
KJSN-FM 102.3 MHz (AC) 3600 Sisk Rd Suite 2B	Modesto	CA	95356	209-545-5585	545-5588
KLOC-AM 920 kHz (Span) 1620 N Carpenter Rd Suite 341	Modesto	CA	95351	209-521-5562	521-4131
KVFX-FM 96.7 MHz (Rock) 3600 Sisk Rd Suite 2B	Modesto	CA	95356	209-521-9797	521-9844

— Colleges/Universities —

	City	State	ZIP	Phone	Fax
Chapman University 3600 Sisk Rd Suite 5A.	Modesto	CA	95356	209-545-1234	545-0596
Modesto Junior College 435 College Ave.	Modesto	CA	95350	209-575-6498	575-6666
Yosemite Community College District 435 College Ave *Web:* www.yosemite.cc.ca.us	Modesto	CA	95350	209-575-6498	575-6516

— Hospitals —

	City	State	ZIP	Phone	Fax
Doctors Medical Center PO Box 4138 **Fax:* Admitting	Modesto	CA	95352	209-578-1211	576-3896*
Memorial Hospitals Assn 1700 Coffee Rd	Modesto	CA	95355	209-526-4500	569-7417
Stanislaus Medical Center 830 Scenic Dr	Modesto	CA	95350	209-558-7000	558-8320

— Attractions —

	City	State	ZIP	Phone	Fax
Big Bear Park 13400 Yosemite Blvd	Waterford	CA	95386	209-874-1984	874-4544
Blue Diamond Growers Store 4800 Sisk Rd.	Salida	CA	95356	209-545-3222	545-6215
Castle Air Museum 5050 Santa Fe Dr *Web:* www.elite.net/castle-air ■ *E-mail:* cam@elite.net	Atwater	CA	95301	209-723-2178	723-0323
Central California Art League Art Center 1402 'I' St *Web:* www.ainet.com/ccal/	Modesto	CA	95354	209-529-3369	
Central West Ballet Co 3125 McHenry Ave Suite D	Modesto	CA	95350	209-576-8957	576-1308
Delicato Vineyards 12001 S Hwy 99 *Web:* www.delicato.com ■ *E-mail:* wine@delicato.com	Manteca	CA	95336	209-824-3600	824-3400
Great Valley Museum of Natural History 1100 Stoddard Ave	Modesto	CA	95350	209-575-6196	575-6410
Hershey's Visitors Center 120 S Sierra Ave	Oakdale	CA	95361	209-848-8126	847-2622
McHenry Mansion 15th & 'I' Sts.	Modesto	CA	95353	209-577-5344	579-5077
McHenry Museum 1402 'I' St. *Web:* www.invsn.com/mchenry/museum/introduction.html	Modesto	CA	95354	209-577-5366	579-5077
Miller's California Ranch 9425 Yosemite Blvd & Hwy 132	Modesto	CA	95357	209-522-1781	
Modesto Arch 9th & 'I' Sts.	Modesto	CA	95353	209-577-5757	
Modesto Civic Theatre 1307 J St State Theatre	Modesto	CA	95353	209-526-5505	
Modesto Performing Arts 2633 El Greco Dr.	Modesto	CA	95354	209-524-9777	524-5654
Modesto Symphony Orchestra 3509 Coffee Rd Suite D-1 *Web:* www.modestosymphony.org	Modesto	CA	95355	209-523-4156	523-0201
Pure Joy at the Bloomingcamp Ranch 10528 Hwy 120	Oakdale	CA	95361	209-847-1412	845-8519
Saint Stan's Brewery 821 L St	Modesto	CA	95354	209-524-2337	524-4827
State Theatre 1307 J St. *Web:* www.thestate.ainet.com	Modesto	CA	95354	209-527-4697	
Townsend Opera Players 605 H St *Web:* www.townsendoperaplayers.com ■ *E-mail:* top@ainet.com	Modesto	CA	95354	209-572-2867	579-0532
Yosemite National Park PO Box 577 *Web:* www.yosemitepark.com	Yosemite National Park	CA	95389	209-372-0200	

Modesto (Cont'd)

SPORTS TEAMS & FACILITIES

				Phone	Fax
Modesto A's (baseball) 601 Neece Dr John Thurman Field	Modesto	CA	95351	209-572-4487	572-4490
Web: www.minorleaguebaseball.com/teams/cal-mod.php3					
Stanislaus County Cruisers (soccer) 1511 Crows Landing Rd	Modesto	CA	95351	209-531-1403	531-2358
Web: www.wac.com/~modcruz ■ *E-mail:* modcruz@wac.com					

— Events —

	Phone
1st Annual American Graffiti Car Show (mid-June)	888-746-9763
Antiques & Collectibles Show & Sale (mid-February & late November)	209-571-6480
Central Valley Renaissance Festival (mid-May)	209-571-6480
Cinco de Mayo Celebration (early May)	209-571-6480
Delicato Vineyards Grape Stomp (late August)	209-239-1215
Greek Food Festival (mid-September)	209-522-7694
International Festival (late September-early October)	209-521-3852
July 4th Parade & Festival (July 4)	209-571-6480
Knight's Ferry Peddler's Fair (mid April-mid May)	209-881-3217
Manteca Pumpkin Festival (early October)	209-823-6121
Modesto A's Swap Meet (late January)	209-874-5414
Modesto Christmas Parade (early December)	209-571-6480
Modesto Farmers Market (late May-late November)	209-632-9322
Modesto Home Show (mid-September)	209-571-2755
Oakdale Chocolate Festival (mid-May)	209-847-2244
Oktoberfest (late September)	209-577-5757
Ripon Almond Blossom Festival (late February)	209-571-6480
Riverbank Cheese & Wine Exposition (mid-October)	209-869-4541
Saint Patrick's Jazz Bash (mid-March)	209-869-3280
Scandi Fest (late September)	209-667-1452
Scottish Games & Gathering of the Clans (early June)	209-538-0821
Spring Art Show (mid-May)	209-529-3369
Tracy Dry Bean Festival (early August)	209-835-2131
Turlock Poultry & Dairy Festival (mid-September)	209-571-6480

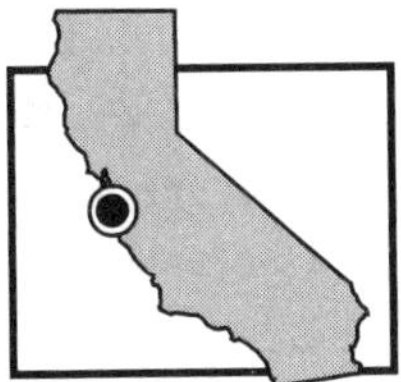

Monterey

Monterey was the capitol of the Spanish territory of Alta California during much of the time between 1775 and 1846. The U.S. Navy took the city in 1846, and California's constitution was written there in 1849. Located on Monterey Bay in the heart of historic Monterey is Cannery Row, which was immortalized by John Steinbeck's novel of the same name. In the 1940s Cannery Row was considered the sardine capital of the world; prior to that it had been the home of Portuguese whalers, and before that it was a Chinese village. Presently, the Row hosts a collection of more than 200 specialty shops, galleries, restaurants, and hotels. Other Monterey attractions include Fisherman's Wharf, once the base of Monterey's active whaling industry and now home to shops, galleries, and seafood restaurants; the Monterey Bay Aquarium, which contains more than 6,500 live creatures, a three-story kelp forest, and a sea otter exhibit; and the Monterey Bay National Marine Sanctuary, the nation's largest marine sanctuary. Monterey County is one of the largest fine wine regions in the U.S., with more than 21 different wine grape varietals on more than 40,000 planted acres. Visitors can sample the various wines at more than 15 different winetasting rooms and vineyards throughout the county. The city of Monterey is also noted for the Monterey Jazz Festival, which it hosts each year in September. The Monterey event is the oldest jazz festival in the world. Located five miles south of Monterey is Carmel-by-the-Sea, a European village overlooking the white sand of Carmel Beach. Visitors to Carmel-by-the Sea can tour the Carmel Mission Basilica and Museum, the second of California's historic missions, built in 1771; and can enjoy more than 90 art galleries and hundreds of unique store fronts along the city's tree-lined streets.

Population	31,106	**Longitude**	121-52-54 W
Area (Land)	8.4 sq mi	**County**	Monterey
Area (Water)	3.3 sq mi	**Time Zone**	PST
Elevation	385 ft	**Area Code/s**	831
Latitude	36-36-04 N		

— Average Temperatures and Precipitation —

TEMPERATURES

	Jan	Feb	Mar	Apr	May	Jun	Jul	Aug	Sep	Oct	Nov	Dec
High	60	62	62	63	64	67	68	69	72	70	65	60
Low	43	45	45	46	48	50	52	53	53	51	47	44

PRECIPITATION

	Jan	Feb	Mar	Apr	May	Jun	Jul	Aug	Sep	Oct	Nov	Dec
Inches	3.5	2.7	3.2	1.7	0.4	0.2	0.1	0.1	0.3	0.9	2.8	2.8

— Important Phone Numbers —

	Phone		Phone
AAA	831-373-3021	**Poison Control Center**	800-876-4766
Dental Referral	831-658-0168	**Time**	831-767-2676
Emergency	911	**Weather**	831-656-1725
Medical Referral	831-455-1008		

— Information Sources —

				Phone	Fax
City of Monterey City Hall Pacific & Madison Sts	Monterey	CA	93940	831-646-3935	646-3702
Web: www.monterey.org					
City of Monterey Mayor Pacific & Madison Sts City Hall	Monterey	CA	93940	831-646-3760	646-3793
Monterey Conference Center 1 Portola Plaza	Monterey	CA	93940	831-646-3770	646-3777
TF: 800-742-8091 ■ *Web:* www.monterey.org/mcc/index.html					
Monterey County PO Box 180	Salinas	CA	93902	831-755-5115	757-5792
Web: www.co.monterey.ca.us					
Monterey County Travel & Tourism Alliance 137 Crossroads Blvd	Carmel	CA	93923	831-626-1424	626-1426
TF: 800-555-6290 ■ *Web:* www.gomonterey.org ■ *E-mail:* mctta@monterey-travel.org					
Monterey Peninsula Chamber of Commerce 380 Alvarado St	Monterey	CA	93940	831-648-5360	649-3502
Web: www.mpcc.com					
Monterey Peninsula Visitors & Convention Bureau PO Box 1770	Monterey	CA	93942	831-649-1770	648-5373
Web: www.monterey.com ■ *E-mail:* info@monterey.com					
Monterey Public Library 625 Pacific St	Monterey	CA	93940	831-646-3932	646-5618
Web: www.monterey.org/lib/lib.html					

On-Line Resources

Access Monterey Peninsula Online	www.mty.com
Area Guide Monterey	monterey.areaguides.net
Cannery Row On-Line Guide	www.cannery-row.com
Coast Weekly	www.coastweekly.com
Excite.com Monterey City Guide	www.excite.com/travel/countries/united_states/california/monterey
Great Places Monterey	monterey.infohut.com
GuestLife Monterey Bay	www.guestlife.com/monterey/
Insiders' Guide to the Monterey Peninsula	www.insiders.com/monterey/
MontereyNet	www.montereynet.com

Monterey (Cont'd)

— Transportation Services —

AIRPORTS

■ **Monterey Peninsula Airport (MRY)**

	Phone
3 miles SE of downtown (approx 10 minutes)	831-648-7000

Web: www.montereyairport.com

Airport Transportation

	Phone
Chartered Limousine Service $45 fare to downtown	831-899-2707
Joe's Taxi $13 fare to downtown	831-624-3885
Yellow Cab $13 fare to downtown	831-646-1234
Your Maitre d' Limousines $85 fare to downtown	831-624-1717

Commercial Airlines

	Phone		Phone
Alaska	800-426-0333	**SkyWest**	800-453-9417
America West	800-235-9292	**United**	800-241-6522
American	800-433-7300	**United Express**	800-241-6522
American Eagle	800-433-7300	**US Airways**	800-428-4322
British Airways	800-247-9297	**US Airways Express**	800-428-4322
Northwest	800-225-2525		

Charter Airlines

	Phone		Phone
Jet Charter International	800-655-5387	**Monterey Airplane Co**	831-375-7518
Million Air Monterey	800-965-8881		

CAR RENTALS

	Phone		Phone
Avis	831-647-7140	**Hertz**	831-373-3318
Budget	831-373-1899	**National**	831-373-4181
Enterprise	831-649-6300		

LIMO/TAXI

	Phone		Phone
Chartered Limousine Service	831-899-2707	**Yellow Cab**	831-646-1234
Joe's Taxi	831-624-3885	**Your Maitre d' Limousines**	831-624-1717

MASS TRANSIT

	Phone
Monterey Salinas Transit $1.50 Base fare	831-899-2555
Waterfront Area Visitors' Express (WAVE) $1 Base fare	831-899-2555

RAIL/BUS

				Phone
Amtrak Station 11 Station Pl *TF:* 800-872-7245	Salinas	CA	93901	831-422-7458
Greyhound Bus Station 1042 Del Monte Ave *TF:* 800-231-2222	Monterey	CA	93940	831-373-4735

— Accommodations —

HOTEL RESERVATION SERVICES

	Phone	Fax
Best Western Monarch Resort *TF:* 800-528-1234	831-646-8885	646-5976
Monterey Peninsula Reservations **Fax Area Code:* 831 ■ *Web:* www.monterey-reservations.com	888-655-3424	655-3488*
Resort Detectives *TF:* 800-566-7188 ■ *Web:* www.resortdetectives.com	831-657-0438	657-9870
Resort II Me *TF:* 800-757-5646 ■ *Web:* www.resort2me.com	831-642-6622	642-6641
Scenic Bay Destinations **Fax Area Code:* 831	888-880-7666	633-6408*
Time to Coast Reservations **Fax Area Code:* 925	800-555-9283	671-4044*
Vacation Center *TF:* 800-466-6283	831-375-2217	375-2210

HOTELS, MOTELS, RESORTS

				Phone	Fax
Bay Park Hotel 1425 Munras Ave *TF:* 800-338-3564 ■ *Web:* www.bayparkhotel.com ■ *E-mail:* info@bayparkhotel.com	Monterey	CA	93940	831-649-1020	373-4258
Best Western Monterey Inn 825 Abrego St *TF:* 800-528-1234	Monterey	CA	93940	831-373-5345	373-3246
Best Western Victorian Inn 487 Foam St *TF:* 800-232-4141 ■ *Web:* www.coastalhotel.com/california/monterey/victorian.html ■ *E-mail:* reservations@innsofmonterey.com	Monterey	CA	93940	831-373-8000	373-4815
Carmel Valley Ranch Resort 1 Old Ranch Rd *TF:* 800-422-7635 ■ *Web:* www.grandbay.com/properties/carmel/default.html	Carmel	CA	93923	831-625-9500	624-2858
Casa Munras Hotel 700 Munras Ave *TF:* 800-222-2558 ■ *Web:* www.casamunras-hotel.com ■ *E-mail:* info@casamunras-hotel.com	Monterey	CA	93940	831-375-2411	375-1365
Comfort Inn 1262 Munras Ave *Web:* www.c8inns.com	Monterey	CA	93940	831-372-8088	373-5829
Cypress Gardens Inn 1150 Munras Ave *TF:* 800-433-4732 ■ *Web:* www.innsbythesea.com	Monterey	CA	93940	831-373-2761	649-1329
Cypress Tree Inn 2227 N Fremont St *TF:* 800-446-8303 ■ *Web:* www.cypresstreeinn.com	Monterey	CA	93940	831-372-7586	372-2940
Deerhaven Inn & Suites 740 Crocker Ave *TF:* 800-525-3373 ■ *Web:* www.montereyinns.com/deerhaven/index.html ■ *E-mail:* deerhaven@montereyinns.com	Pacific Grove	CA	93950	831-373-1114	655-5048
Doubletree Hotel Monterey 2 Portola Plaza *TF:* 800-222-8733 ■ *Web:* www.doubletreemonterey.com	Monterey	CA	93940	831-649-4511	372-0620
Econo Lodge 2042 N Fremont St *TF:* 800-553-2666	Monterey	CA	93940	831-372-5851	372-4228
El Castell Motel 2102 N Fremont St *TF:* 800-628-1094	Monterey	CA	93940	831-372-8176	649-6187
Embassy Suites Monterey Bay-Seaside 1441 Canyon Del Rey *TF:* 800-362-2779	Seaside	CA	93955	831-393-1115	393-1113
Holiday Inn Express Cannery Row 443 Wave St *TF:* 800-248-8442 ■ *Web:* www.basshotels.com/hiexpress/?_franchisee=MRYEX	Monterey	CA	93940	831-372-1800	372-1969
Hotel Pacific 300 Pacific St *TF:* 800-554-5542 ■ *Web:* coastalhotel.com/ourhotels/states/california/pacific/	Monterey	CA	93940	831-373-5700	373-6921
Hyatt Regency Resort & Conference Center 1 Old Golf Course Rd *TF:* 800-233-1234 ■ *Web:* www.montereyhyatt.com ■ *E-mail:* info@montereyhyatt.com	Monterey	CA	93940	831-372-1234	375-3960
Inn at Spanish Bay 2700 17-Mile Dr *TF:* 800-654-9300	Pebble Beach	CA	93953	831-647-7500	644-7955
Lighthouse Lodge & Suites 1150 Lighthouse Ave *TF:* 800-858-1249 ■ *Web:* www.lhls.com	Pacific Grove	CA	93950	831-655-2111	655-4922
Lodge at Pebble Beach 17-Mile Dr *TF:* 800-654-9300	Pebble Beach	CA	93953	831-624-3811	625-8598
Lone Oak Motel 2221 N Fremont St *TF:* 800-283-5663 ■ *Web:* www.loneoakmotel.com	Monterey	CA	93940	831-372-4924	372-4985
Monterey Bay Inn 242 Cannery Row *TF:* 800-424-6242 ■ *Web:* coastalhotel.com/ourhotels/states/california/montereybay/	Monterey	CA	93940	831-373-6242	373-7603
Monterey Downtown Travelodge 675 Munras Ave	Monterey	CA	93940	831-373-1876	373-8693
Monterey Hilton 1000 Aguajito Rd *TF:* 800-445-8667	Monterey	CA	93940	831-373-6141	655-8608
Monterey Hotel 406 Alvarado St *TF:* 800-727-0960 ■ *Web:* www.montereyhotel.com	Monterey	CA	93940	831-375-3184	373-2899
Monterey Marriott Hotel 350 Calle Principal *TF:* 800-228-9290 ■ *Web:* www.marriott.com/marriott/mryca/	Monterey	CA	93940	831-649-4234	372-2968
Monterey Plaza Hotel & Spa 400 Cannery Row *TF:* 800-334-3999 ■ *Web:* www.woodsidehotels.com/monterey/	Monterey	CA	93940	831-646-1700	646-5937
Quality Inn Monterey 1058 Munras Ave *TF:* 800-361-3835 ■ *Web:* www.montereyqualityinn.com ■ *E-mail:* info@montereyqualityinn.com	Monterey	CA	93940	831-372-3381	372-4687
Ramada Limited 2058 N Fremont St *TF:* 800-672-6232 ■ *Web:* www.devi-inc.com/ramada ■ *E-mail:* ramada@devi-inc.com	Monterey	CA	93940	831-375-9511	375-9701
Sand Dollar Inn 755 Abrego St *TF:* 800-982-1986 ■ *Web:* www.sanddollarinn.com	Monterey	CA	93940	831-372-7551	372-0916
Spindrift Inn 652 Cannery Row *TF:* 800-841-1879 ■ *Web:* coastalhotel.com/ourhotels/states/california/spindrift/	Monterey	CA	93940	831-646-8900	373-4815
Super 8 Motel North Fremont 2050 N Fremont St *Web:* www.c8inns.com//super8free/ ■ *E-mail:* super8@c8inns.com	Monterey	CA	93940	831-373-3081	372-6730
Travelodge Monterey/Carmel 2030 N Fremont St	Monterey	CA	93940	831-373-3381	649-8741

Monterey — Hotels, Motels, Resorts (Cont'd)

				Phone	Fax
West Wind Lodge 1046 Munras Ave	Monterey	CA	93940	831-373-1337	372-2451

TF: 800-821-0805 ■ *Web:* www.westwindlodge.com ■ *E-mail:* info@westwindlodge.com

— Restaurants —

				Phone
Abalonetti Seafood Trattoria (Seafood) 57 Fisherman's Wharf Suite 1 .... *Web:* www.restauranteur.com/abalonetti/ ■ *E-mail:* jpisto@redshift.com	Monterey	CA	93940	831-373-1851
Bubba Gump Shrimp Co (Seafood) 720 Cannery Row ..... *Web:* www.bubbagump.com	Monterey	CA	93940	831-373-1884
Cafe Fina (Seafood) 47 Fisherman's Wharf .... *Web:* www.cafefina.com ■ *E-mail:* cafefina@mbayweb.com	Monterey	CA	93940	831-372-5200
California Grill (California) 2 Portola Plaza	Monterey	CA	93940	831-649-4511
Captain's Gig Restaurant (Seafood) 6 Fisherman's Wharf... *E-mail:* larsonsjl@aol.com	Monterey	CA	93940	831-373-5559
Chart House (Steak) 444 Cannery Row................	Monterey	CA	93940	831-372-3362
Cibo Ristorante Italiano (Italian) 301 Alvarado St .... *Web:* www.cibo.com	Monterey	CA	93940	831-649-8151
Crazy Horse Restaurant (American) 1425 Munras Ave	Monterey	CA	93940	831-649-1020
Crocodile Grill (California) 701 Lighthouse Ave.......	Pacific Grove	CA	93950	831-655-3311
Crown & Anchor (English) 150 W Franklin St	Monterey	CA	93940	831-649-6496
Domenico's on the Wharf (Steak/Seafood) 50 Fisherman's Wharf # 1....................... *Web:* www.restauranteur.com/domenicos/ ■ *E mail:* jpisto@redshift.com	Monterey	CA	93940	831-372-3655
El Torito Restaurant (Mexican) 600 Cannery Row .... *Web:* www.eltorito.com	Monterey	CA	93940	831-373-0611
Epsilon Greek Restaurant (Greek) 422 Tyler St	Monterey	CA	93940	831-655-8108
Fandango (Seafood) 223 17th St................. *Web:* www.fandango.com	Pacific Grove	CA	93950	831-372-3456
Fish Hopper (Steak/Seafood) 700 Cannery Row.......... *Web:* www.fishhopper.com	Monterey	CA	93940	831-372-8543
French Cream Restaurant (French) Pacific & Scott Sts Heritage Harbor Bldg 100C	Monterey	CA	93940	831-375-9798
India's Clay Oven (Indian) 150 Del Monte Ave 2nd Fl	Monterey	CA	93940	831-373-2529
Jugem Japanese Restaurant (Japanese) 409 Alvarado St...	Monterey	CA	93940	831-373-6463
Korean Ga San Restaurant (Korean) 2006 Sunset Rd ..	Pacific Grove	CA	93950	831-372-2526
Lugano Swiss Bistro (Swiss) 3670 The Barnyard........... *Web:* www.swissbistro.com	Carmel	CA	93923	831-626-3779
Mighty Duck British Pub (English) 479 Alvarado St	Monterey	CA	93940	831-655-3031
Monterey Jack's Fish House & Sports Bar (American) 711 Cannery Row............................	Monterey	CA	93940	831-655-4947
Monterey Joe's (Italian) 2149 N Fremont St............ *Web:* www.montereyjoes.com	Monterey	CA	93940	831-655-3355
Monterey's Fish House (Seafood) 2114 Del Monte Ave	Monterey	CA	93940	831-373-4647
Montrio (Continental) 414 Calle Principal .... *Web:* www.montrio.com	Monterey	CA	93940	831-648-8880
Old Bath House Restaurant (Continental) 620 Ocean View Blvd	Pacific Grove	CA	93950	831-375-5195
Pacific Grille (California) 1000 Aguajito Rd	Monterey	CA	93940	831-373-6141
Paradiso Trattoria (Mediterranean) 654 Cannery Row	Monterey	CA	93940	831-375-4155
Peninsula Restaurant (California) 1 Old Golf Course Rd....	Monterey	CA	93940	831-372-1234
Peppers MexiCali Cafe (Mexican) 170 Forest Ave	Pacific Grove	CA	93950	831-373-6892
Rappa's Seafood Restaurant (Seafood) 101 Fisherman's Wharf # 1...................... *E-mail:* ton@redshift.com	Monterey	CA	93940	831-372-7562
Rosine's Restaurant (American) 434 Alvarado St.........	Monterey	CA	93940	831-375-1400
Sardine Factory (Seafood) 701 Wave St............... *Web:* www.sardinefactory.com	Monterey	CA	93940	831-373-3775
Schooners Bistro on the Bay (California) 400 Cannery Row..............................	Monterey	CA	93940	831-646-1700
Siamese Bay Thai Restaurant (Thai) 131 Webster St......	Monterey	CA	93940	831-373-1550
Stokes Adobe Restaurant (Mediterranean) 500 Hartnell St..............................	Monterey	CA	93940	831-373-1110
Tarpy's Roadhouse (American) 2999 Monterey-Salinas Hwy...................... *Web:* www.tarpys.com	Monterey	CA	93940	831-647-1444
Tsing Tao China Restaurant (Chinese) 429 Alvarado St	Monterey	CA	93940	831-375-3000
Turtle Bay Taqueria (Seafood) 431 Tyler St	Monterey	CA	93940	831-333-1500
Tutto Buono (Italian) 469 Alvarado St.................	Monterey	CA	93940	831-372-1880
Ventana Vineyards 2999 Monterey-Salinas Hwy..........	Monterey	CA	93940	831-372-7415
Whaling Station Prime Steaks & Seafood (Steak/Seafood) 763 Wave St	Monterey	CA	93940	831-373-3778
Wharfside Restaurant (Seafood) 60 Fisherman's Wharf # 1....................... *Web:* www.wharfside.com ■ *E-mail:* wharfside@montereybay.com	Monterey	CA	93940	831-375-3956

— Goods and Services —

SHOPPING

				Phone	Fax
American Tin Cannery Premium Outlets 125 Ocean View Blvd...............	Pacific Grove	CA	93950	831-372-1442	372-5707
Cannery Row Antique Mall 471 Wave St......	Monterey	CA	93940	831-655-0264	655-0265
Crossroads Shopping Center Hwy 1 & Rio Rd.... *Web:* www.carmelcrossroads.com	Carmel	CA	93923	831-625-4106	
Del Monte Center 1410 Del Monte Ctr........ *Web:* www.delmontecenter.com ■ *E-mail:* info@delmontecenter.com	Monterey	CA	93940	831-373-2705	373-8675
The Barnyard Shopping Village 26400 Carmel Rancho Ln................. *Web:* www.thebarnyard.com ■ *E-mail:* info@thebarnyard.com	Carmel	CA	93923	831-624-8886	624-0549

BANKS

				Phone	Fax
Bank of America 200 E Franklin St..........	Monterey	CA	93940	831-646-5739	646-5880
California Bank & Trust 439 Alvarado St......	Monterey	CA	93940	831-373-4971	372-5299
Comerica Bank California 35 Bonifacio Plaza....................	Monterey	CA	93940	831-655-1779	372-6617
Community Bank 484 Lighthouse Ave Suite 101	Monterey	CA	93940	831-649-5010	649-5018
First National Bank of Central California 495 Washington St...................	Monterey	CA	93942	831-373-4900	646-9748
Monterey Bay Bank 1400 Munras Ave........ *Web:* montereybaybank.com	Monterey	CA	93940	831-373-3755	373-4099
Monterey County Bank 601 Munras Ave	Monterey	CA	93942	831-649-4600	624-6074
World Savings Bank FSB 1100 Del Monte Ctr...................	Monterey	CA	93940	831-373-3215	372-7409

BUSINESS SERVICES

	Phone		Phone
Airborne Express.............	800-247-2676	**Mail Boxes Etc**..............	831-655-0266
Central Coast Press...........	831-372-2123	**Manpower Temporary Services**...	831-646-1200
Copy King..................	831-373-1251	**Nelson Staffing Solutions**.......	831-375-4473
DHL Worldwide Express........	800-225-5345	**Norrell Staffing Services**.......	831-655-0164
Federal Express.............	800-463-3339	**Peninsula Messenger Service**....	831-649-0439
Kelly Services...............	831-372-8188	**Post Office**.................	831-375-8545
Kinko's....................	831-373-2298	**UPS**......................	800-742-5877

— Media —

PUBLICATIONS

				Phone	Fax
Monterey County Herald‡ PO Box 271 .... *Web:* www.montereyherald.com ■ *E-mail:* mheditor@montereyherald.com	Monterey	CA	93942	831-372-3311	372-8401
Monterey County Post 225 Crossroads Blvd Suite 408.............	Carmel	CA	93923	831-624-2222	625-5718

‡Daily newspapers

TELEVISION

				Phone	Fax
KCBA-TV Ch 35 (FOX) 1550 Moffet St.......... *Web:* www.kcba.com	Salinas	CA	93905	831-422-3500	754-1120
KION-TV Ch 46 (CBS) 1550 Moffett St.......... *Web:* www.kiontv.com	Salinas	CA	93905	831-784-1702	646-1973
KNTV-TV Ch 11 (ABC) 645 Park Ave .... *Web:* www.kntv.com	San Jose	CA	95110	408-286-1111	286-1530
KSBW-TV Ch 8 (NBC) 238 John St .... *Web:* www.ksbw.com ■ *E-mail:* info@ksbw.com	Salinas	CA	93901	831-758-8888	424-3750
KSMS-TV Ch 67 (Uni) 67 Garden Ct	Monterey	CA	93940	831-373-6767	373-6700
KTEH-TV Ch 54 (PBS) 1585 Schallenberger Rd................ *Web:* www.kteh.org/	San Jose	CA	95130	408-795-5400	995-5446

RADIO

				Phone	Fax
KBOQ-FM 95.5 MHz (Clas) 2511 Garden Rd Suite C-150 .... *Web:* www.kbach.com ■ *E-mail:* info@kbach.com	Monterey	CA	93940	831-656-9550	656-9551
KBTU-FM 101.7 MHz (CHR) 2511 Garden Rd Suite C-160	Monterey	CA	93940	831-643-1017	657-1349
KCDU-FM 93.5 MHz (AC) 2511 Garden Rd Suite C-160 .... *Web:* www.cd93.com ■ *E-mail:* comments@cd93.com	Monterey	CA	93940	831-643-1017	657-1349

Monterey — Radio (Cont'd)

				Phone	Fax
KCSL-FM 93.9 MHz (Span) 517 S Main St Suite 201	Salinas	CA	93901	831-757-5911	757-9764
KCTY-AM 980 kHz (Span) 517 S Main St Suite 201	Salinas	CA	93901	831-757-5911	757-9764
KDON-AM 1460 kHz (CHR) 903 N Main	Salinas	CA	93906	831-755-8181	755-8193
KDON-FM 102.5 MHz (CHR) 903 N Main *Web:* www.kdon.com	Salinas	CA	93906	831-755-8181	755-8193
KIDD-AM 630 kHz (Nost) 5 Harris Ct Bldg C	Monterey	CA	93940	831-649-0969	649-3335
KLXM-FM 97.9 MHz (Span) 517 S Main St Suite 201	Salinas	CA	93901	831-757-5911	757-9764
KMBY-FM 104.3 MHz (Rock) 2511 Garden Rd Suite C-160 *Web:* www.kmby.com ■ *E-mail:* kmby1043@redshift.com	Monterey	CA	93940	831-643-1017	657-1349
KOCN-FM 105.1 MHz (Oldies) 903 N Main	Salinas	CA	93906	831-755-8181	755-8193
KPTE-AM 1070 kHz (Span) 517 S Main St Suite 201	Salinas	CA	93901	831-757-5911	757-9764
KRAY-FM 103.5 MHz (Span) 517 S Main St Suite 201	Salinas	CA	93901	831-757-5911	757-9764
KRQC-FM 92.7 MHz (Rock) 903 N Main St	Salinas	CA	93906	831-755-8181	755-8193
KTOM-AM 1380 kHz (Sports) 903 N Main St	Salinas	CA	93906	831-755-8181	755-8193
KTOM-AM 1380 kHz (Sports) 903 N Main St *Web:* www.ktom.com ■ *E-mail:* ktom@ktom.com	Salinas	CA	93906	831-755-8181	755-8193
KTOM-FM 100.7 MHz (Ctry) 903 N Main St	Salinas	CA	93906	831-755-8181	757-8193
KWAV-FM 96.9 kHz (AC) 5 Harris Ct Bldg C *Web:* www.kwav.com ■ *E-mail:* kwav97fm@aol.com	Monterey	CA	93940	831-649-0969	649-3335

— Colleges/Universities —

				Phone	Fax
California State University Monterey Bay 100 Campus Ctr *Web:* www.monterey.edu	Seaside	CA	93955	831-582-3518	582-3783
Central Coast College 480 S Main St	Salinas	CA	93901	831-424-6767	753-6485
Chapman University 99 Pacific St Suite 375 Heritage Harbor	Monterey	CA	93940	831-373-0945	648-1326
Golden Gate University 550 Camino El Estero *Web:* www.ggu.edu	Monterey	CA	93940	831-373-4176	655-5750
Monterey Institute of International Studies 425 Van Buren St *Web:* www.miis.edu	Monterey	CA	93940	831-647-4123	647-6400
Monterey Peninsula College 980 Fremont St. *Web:* www.mpc.edu	Monterey	CA	93940	831-646-4000	646-4015

— Hospitals —

				Phone	Fax
Community Hospital of the Monterey Peninsula PO Box HH *Web:* www.chomp.org	Monterey	CA	93942	831-624-5311	625-4948
Monterey Bay Urgent Care Medical Center 245 Washington St	Monterey	CA	93940	831-372-2273	
Natividad Medical Center PO Box 81611 *Web:* www.natividad.com	Salinas	CA	93912	831-755-4111	755-6254
Salinas Valley Memorial Hospital 450 E Romie Ln *Web:* www.svmh.com	Salinas	CA	93901	831-757-4333	754-2638

— Attractions —

				Phone	Fax
A Taste of Monterey 700 Cannery Row Suite KK *TF:* 888-646-5446 ■ *Web:* www.tastemonterey.com ■ *E-mail:* ataste@mbay.net	Monterey	CA	93940	831-646-5446	375-0835
Bargetto Winery Tasting Room 700 L Cannery Row	Monterey	CA	93940	831-373-4053	475-2558
California's First Theatre Pacific Ave & Scott St	Monterey	CA	93940	831-375-4916	
Cannery Row Historic District 640 Wave St.	Monterey	CA	93940	831-373-1902	656-0967
Chateau Julien Wine Estate 8940 Carmel Valley Rd *Web:* www.chateaujulien.com ■ *E-mail:* info@chateaujulien.com	Carmel	CA	93923	831-624-2600	624-6138
Cherry Carl Center for the Arts Guadalupe St & 4th Ave	Carmel	CA	93921	831-624-7491	624-5035
City of Monterey Sports Center 301 E Franklin St	Monterey	CA	93940	831-646-3700	
Cloninger Cellars 1645 River Rd *E-mail:* cloninger@usawines.com	Salinas	CA	93902	831-675-9463	675-1922
Colton Hall Museum 351 Pacific St.	Monterey	CA	93940	831-646-5640	646-3917
El Estero Park Camino El Estero & Fremont St	Monterey	CA	93940	831-646-3860	
Fishermans Wharf 140 W Franklin St *Web:* www.montereywharf.com ■ *E-mail:* info@montereywharf.com	Monterey	CA	93940	831-649-6544	649-4124
Galante Vineyards & Rose Gardens 18181 Cachagua Rd **Fax Area Code:* 415 ■ *Web:* www.galante-vineyards.com ■ *E-mail:* web@galantevineyards.com	Carmel Valley	CA	93924	800-425-2683	331-2039*
Jack's Peak Regional Park Jack's Peak Dr	Monterey	CA	93940	831-647-7799	
Laguna Seca Recreational Area 1021 Hwy 68 N	Monterey	CA	93940	831-647-7795	
Maritime Museum of Monterey 5 Custom House Plaza Stanton Ctr *Web:* www.mhaamm.org ■ *E-mail:* mhaamm@mbay.net	Monterey	CA	93940	831-373-2469	
Monterey Bay Aquarium 886 Cannery Row *Web:* www.mbayaq.org	Monterey	CA	93940	831-648-4800	648-4810
Monterey Bay National Marine Sanctuary 299 Foam St *Web:* bonita.mbnms.nos.noaa.gov/	Monterey	CA	93940	831-647-4201	647-4250
Monterey Bay Sports Museum 883 Lighthouse Ave.	Monterey	CA	93940	831-655-2363	
Monterey County Fairgrounds 2004 Fairgrounds Rd.	Monterey	CA	93940	831-372-5863	
Monterey County Symphony Assn Inc PO Box 3965 *Web:* www.montereysymphony.org ■ *E-mail:* symphony@redshift.com	Carmel	CA	93921	831-624-8511	624-3837
Monterey Museum of Art 559 Pacific St *Web:* www.montereyart.org ■ *E-mail:* mtry_art@mbay.net	Monterey	CA	93940	831-372-5477	372-5680
Monterey Peninsula College Theatre 980 Fremont St.	Monterey	CA	93940	831-646-4213	
Monterey Sport Fishing & Whale Watching 96 Fisherman's Wharf *TF:* 800-200-2203 ■ *Web:* www.montereybaywhalecruise.com ■ *E-mail:* benji@montereybaywhalecruise.com	Monterey	CA	93940	831-372-2203	372-3708
Monterey State Historic Park 20 Custom House Plaza *Web:* www.mbay.net/~mshp/	Monterey	CA	93940	831-649-7118	647-6236
Monterey State Historic Park (Path of History Walking Tours) 20 Custom Plaza *Web:* www.mbay.net/~mshp/	Monterey	CA	93940	831-649-7118	647-6236
My Museum 601 Wave St *Web:* www.mymuseum.org ■ *E-mail:* mymuseum@mbay.net	Monterey	CA	93940	831-649-6444	649-1304
National Steinbeck Center 1 Main St *Web:* www.steinbeck.org	Salinas	CA	93901	831-775-4725	
New Wharf Theatre Fisherman's Wharf Wharf 1	Monterey	CA	93940	831-649-2332	
Old Monterey Market Place Alvarado St	Monterey	CA	93940	831-655-2607	
Pacific Grove Museum of Natural History 165 Forest Ave	Pacific Grove	CA	93950	831-648-3116	372-3256
Pacific Repertory Theater Monte Verde & 8th St *Web:* www.pacrep.org	Carmel	CA	93921	831-622-0100	622-0703
Point Lobos State Reserve Hwy 1 *Web:* pt-lobos.parks.state.ca.us ■ *E-mail:* ptlobos@mbay.net	Carmel	CA	93923	831-624-4909	624-9265
Point Pinos Lighthouse Lighthouse Ave & Asilomer Dr *Web:* www.lhls.com/point.html	Pacific Grove	CA	93950	831-648-3116	372-3256
San Carlos Cathedral 500 Church St.	Monterey	CA	93940	831-373-2628	
Staff Players Repertory Co Mountain View Ave & Santa Rita	Carmel	CA	93921	831-624-1531	
Steinbeck Spirit of Monterey Wax Museum 700 Cannery Row *Web:* www.steinbeckwaxmuseum.com ■ *E-mail:* wmusuem@mbay.net	Monterey	CA	93940	831-375-3770	646-5309
Stowitts Museum & Library 591 Lighthouse Ave. *Web:* www.stowitts.org ■ *E-mail:* stowitts@mbay.net	Pacific Grove	CA	93950	831-655-4488	649-5396
Tor House & Hawk Tower 26304 Ocean View Ave *Web:* www.torhouse.org ■ *E-mail:* thf@torhouse.org	Carmel	CA	93923	831-624-1813	624-3696
Unicorn Theater 320 Hoffman Ave	Monterey	CA	93940	831-649-0259	
Veteran's Memorial Park Skyline Dr & Jefferson St.	Monterey	CA	93940	831-646-3865	
Western Stage Theatre 156 Homestead Ave *Web:* www.westernstage.org ■ *E-mail:* general@westernstage.org	Salinas	CA	93901	831-755-6816	770-6105

SPORTS TEAMS & FACILITIES

				Phone	Fax
Laguna Seca Raceway PO Box 2078 *Web:* www.laguna-seca.com	Monterey	CA	93942	831-648-5111	373-0533

Monterey (Cont'd)

— Events —

	Phone
AT&T Pebble Beach National Pro-Am (late January-early February)	831-649-1533
Best Western Monterey Beach Hotel 2600 Sand Dunes Dr	800-242-8627
Big Sur International Marathon (late April)	831-625-6226
Brewmasters Classic (early July)	831-375-7275
California Chocolate Abalone Dive (June)	831-375-1933
California International Airshow (early October)	888-845-7469
Cannery Row Christmas Tree Lighting (November 25)	831-372-2259
Carmel Beach Bach Festival (mid-July-early August)	831-624-2046
Carmel Performing Arts Festival (early-mid-October)	831-644-8383
Carmel Shakespeare Festival (late July-mid-October)	831-622-0100
Cherry's Jubilee (late September)	831-759-1836
Christmas in the Adobes (mid-December)	831-647-6226
Dixieland Monterey (early March)	888-349-6879
Downtown Celebration (late June)	831-655-8070
Downtown Celebration Sidewalk Sale (early December)	831-655-2607
Festa Italia (mid-September)	831-649-6544
First Night Monterey (December 31)	831-373-4778
First Night Monterey (December31)	831-655-2607
Great Cannery Row Sardine Festival (mid-June)	831-372-2259
Great Monterey Squid Festival (late May)	831-372-2259
Great Wine Escape Weekend (mid-November)	831-375-9400
Greek Festival (early September)	831-424-4434
Honda Grand Prix of Monterey (mid-September)	800-327-7322
Monterey Antique & Collectibles Show (early October)	831-655-0264
Monterey Bay Arts & Crafts Fair (late April)	831-622-0700
Monterey Bay Bird Festival (early October)	831-728-3890
Monterey County Fair (mid-August)	831-372-5863
Monterey Historic Automobile Races (late August)	800-327-7322
Monterey Jazz Festival (mid-September)	800-309-3378
Monterey Wine Festival (early April)	800-656-4282
Northern California Golf Assn Amateur Championship (late August)	831-625-4653
Old Monterey Historic Faire & Festival (early October)	831-655-2607
Old Monterey Market Place (year-round)	831-655-2607
Old Monterey Seafood & Music Festival (mid-April)	831-655-2607
Old Monterey Sidewalk Fine Arts Festival (mid-June)	831-655-2607
Pacific Grove Feast of Lanterns (late July)	831-372-7625
Pebble Beach Concours d'Elegance (late August)	831-659-0663
Pebble Beach Equestrian Classics (late July-early August)	831-624-2756
Pebble Beach Spring Horse Show (late March-early April)	831-624-2756
SRAM Sea Otter Classic (mid-March)	650-306-1414
Steinbeck Festival (early August)	831-796-3833
Stillwell's Snow in the Park (mid-December)	831-373-3304
TheatreFest (early July & early November)	831-622-0700
TomatoFest (September)	831-624-1581
Twelve Days of Christmas (late November-late December)	831-624-1581
Whalefest (mid-late January)	831-644-7588
Wildflower Show (mid-April)	831-648-3116

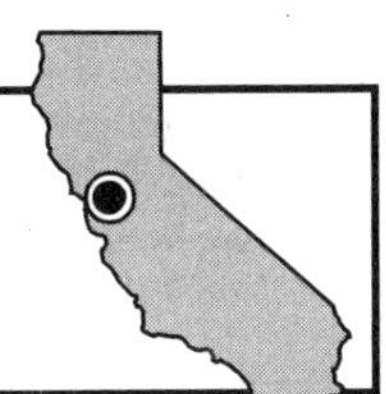

Oakland

Located just across the bay from San Francisco, Oakland has the fourth busiest port in the U.S. Directly on the waterfront are the shops and restaurants of historic Jack London Square; and next to the convention center are the 16 Victorian homes of Preservation Park. Lake Merritt is the site of the annual Festival at the Lake and also the restored Camron-Stanford House, the last remaining Victorian home at the lake. Other local attractions include Chinatown, the Ebony Museum, and the Chabot Obervatory and Science Center.

Population	365,874	**Longitude**	122-21-63 W
Area (Land)	56.1 sq mi	**County**	Alameda
Area (Water)	22.1 sq mi	**Time Zone**	PST
Elevation	42 ft	**Area Code/s**	510
Latitude	37-77-93 N		

— Average Temperatures and Precipitation —

TEMPERATURES

	Jan	Feb	Mar	Apr	May	Jun	Jul	Aug	Sep	Oct	Nov	Dec
High	56	60	61	64	66	69	70	70	72	70	63	57
Low	43	46	47	48	51	53	54	55	56	53	49	44

PRECIPITATION

	Jan	Feb	Mar	Apr	May	Jun	Jul	Aug	Sep	Oct	Nov	Dec
Inches	5.0	3.8	3.7	1.8	0.3	0.2	0.1	0.1	0.4	1.5	3.7	3.8

— Important Phone Numbers —

	Phone		Phone
AAA	510-652-1812	**Time**	925-767-8900
Dental Referral	415-421-1435	**Travelers Aid of Alameda County**	510-444-6834
Emergency	911	**Weather**	510-562-8573
Poison Control Center	800-876-4766		

— Information Sources —

				Phone	Fax
Alameda County 1221 Oak St. *Web:* www.co.alameda.ca.us ■ *E-mail:* dpd@co.alameda.ca.us	Oakland	CA	94612	510-272-6984	272-3784
Better Business Bureau Serving Oakland/San Francisco Area & Northwest Coastal California 510 16th St Suite 550 *Web:* www.oakland.bbb.org	Oakland	CA	94612	510-238-1000	238-1018
Oakland City Hall 1 Frank H Ogawa Plaza 3rd Fl.	Oakland	CA	94612	510-238-3301	238-2223
Oakland Community & Economic Development Agency 250 Frank H Ogawa Plaza 9th Fl *Web:* oaklandnet.com/government/ceda/ceda.html	Oakland	CA	94612	510-238-3015	238-3691
Oakland Convention Center 550 10th St *TF:* 800-262-5526	Oakland	CA	94607	510-451-4000	
Oakland Mayor 1 Frank H Ogawa Plaza 3rd Fl *Web:* oaklandnet.com/government/government41.html ■ *E-mail:* mayor@oaklandnet.com	Oakland	CA	94612	510-238-3141	238-4731
Oakland Metropolitan Chamber of Commerce 475 14th St *Web:* www.oaklandchamber.com	Oakland	CA	94612	510-874-4800	839-8817
Oakland Public Library 125 14th St *Web:* www.ci.oakland.ca.us	Oakland	CA	94612	510-238-3134	238-2232
Visitor Marketing City of Oakland 250 Frank Ogawa Plaza Suite 3330 *Web:* www.ocva.com	Oakland	CA	94612	510-238-2935	839-5924

On-Line Resources

4Oakland.com	www.4oakland.com
Anthill City Guide Oakland	www.anthill.com/city.asp?city=oakland
Area Guide Oakland	oakland.areaguides.net
BayArea.com	www.bayarea.com
Boulevards Oakland	www.oakland.com
City Knowledge Oakland	www.cityknowledge.com/ca_oakland.htm
East Bay Online	www.sftoday.com/eastbay.htm
Excite.com Oakland City Guide	www.excite.com/travel/countries/united_states/california/oakland
Fabulous Oakland	www.sirius.com/~asta/oakland.html
OaklandCA.com	www.oaklandca.com

— Transportation Services —

AIRPORTS

■ **Oakland International Airport (OAK)**

	Phone
10 miles SE of downtown (approx 20 minutes)	510-577-4000

Web: www.flyoakland.com

Airport Transportation

	Phone
AC Transit $1.35 fare to downtown	510-839-2882
Bay Area Rapid Transit (BART) fare varies with destination	510-465-2278
BayPorter Express fare varies with destination	415-467-1800
Taxi $22-25 fare to downtown	510-444-4499

Oakland (Cont'd)

Commercial Airlines

	Phone		Phone
America West	800-235-9292	**Shuttle by United**	800-748-8853
American	800-433-7300	**Southwest**	800-435-9792
Corsair	800-677-0720	**United**	800-241-6522
Delta	800-221-1212	**United Express**	800-241-6522
Martinair Holland	800-627-8462	**US Airways**	800-428-4322
Northwest	800-225-2525		

Charter Airlines

	Phone		Phone
Centurion Flight Services	650-494-7812	**KaiserAir**	510-569-9622
Helinet Aviation Services	800-221-8389	**Kappa Air**	415-388-5559
Jet Aviation Business Jets Inc	818-843-8400	**Professional Pilot Assoc**	925-284-3347

CAR RENTALS

	Phone		Phone
Alamo	800-462-5266	**Dollar**	510-577-4915
Avis	510-577-6360	**Hertz**	510-639-0200
Budget	650-875-6850	**National**	510-632-2225

LIMO/TAXI

	Phone		Phone
Friendly Cab	510-536-3000	**Metro Yellow Cab**	510-444-4499
Metro Taxi	510-532-3000	**Paramount Limousine**	510-569-5466

MASS TRANSIT

	Phone
AC Transit $1.25 Base fare	510-839-2882
Bay Area Rapid Transit (BART) $1.10 Base fare	510-465-2278

RAIL/BUS

Phone

Amtrak Station 245 2nd St Jack London Sq . . . . . Oakland CA 94607 510-238-4320
TF: 800-872-7245

Greyhound/Trailways Bus Station 2103 San Pablo Ave . . . . . Oakland CA 94612 510-834-3213
TF: 800-231-2222

— Accommodations —

HOTELS, MOTELS, RESORTS

Phone Fax

Berkeley Marina Radisson Hotel
200 Marina Blvd . . . . . Berkeley CA 94710 510-548-7920 665-7104
TF: 800-243-0625

Best Western Inn the Square 233 Broadway . . . . Oakland CA 94607 510-452-4565 452-4634

Best Western Sonoma Valley Inn
550 2nd St W . . . . . Sonoma CA 95476 707-938-9200 938-0935
TF: 800-334-5784

Claremont Resort & Spa
Ashby & Domingo Aves . . . . . Oakland CA 94623 510-843-3000 848-6208
TF: 800-551-7266 ■ *Web:* www.claremontresort.com
■ *E-mail:* reservations@clrmntresort.com

Clarion Suites Lake Merritt Hotel
1800 Madison St . . . . . Oakland CA 94612 510-832-2300 832-7150
TF: 800-933-4683

Days Inn Oakland Airport 8350 Edes Ave . . . . . Oakland CA 94621 510-568-1880 569-4652
TF: 800-325-2525

Executive Inn 1755 Embarcadero Dr . . . . . Oakland CA 94606 510-536-6633 536-6006
TF: 800-346-6331

Four Points by Sheraton
5115 Hopyard Rd . . . . . Pleasanton CA 94588 925-460-8800 847-9455
TF: 800-325-3535

Hampton Inn Oakland Airport
8465 Enterprise Way . . . . . Oakland CA 94621 510-632-8900 632-4713
TF: 800-426-7866

Holiday Inn 720 Las Flores Rd . . . . . Livermore CA 94550 925-443-4950 449-9059
TF: 800-465-4329

Holiday Inn Bay Bridge 1800 Powell St . . . . . Emeryville CA 94608 510-658-9300 547-8166
TF: 800-465-4329

Holiday Inn Oakland Airport
500 Hegenberger Rd . . . . . Oakland CA 94621 510-562-5311 636-1539
TF: 800-465-4329

Howard Johnson Chinatown 423 7th St . . . . . Oakland CA 94607 510-451-6316 451-5326
TF: 800-446-4656

Hyatt Rickeys 4219 El Camino Real . . . . . Palo Alto CA 94306 650-493-8000 424-0836
TF: 800-233-1234
■ *Web:* www.hyatt.com/usa/palo_alto/hotels/hotel_sjcri.html

Jack London Inn 444 Embarcadero W . . . . . Oakland CA 94607 510-444-2032 834-3074
TF: 800-549-8780

Marina Village Inn 1151 Pacific Marina . . . . . Alameda CA 94501 510-523-9450 523-6315
TF: 800-345-0304

Marriott Hotel 2355 N Main St . . . . . Walnut Creek CA 94596 925-934-2000 934-6374
TF: 800-228-9290 ■ *Web:* marriotthotels.com/OAKWC

Motel 6 1801 Embarcadero St . . . . . Oakland CA 94606 510-436-0103 436-7428
TF: 800-466-8356

Oakland Airport Hilton 1 Hegenberger Rd . . . . . Oakland CA 94621 510-635-5000 729-0491
TF: 800-445-8667

Oakland Marriott 1001 Broadway . . . . . Oakland CA 94607 510-451-4000 835-3466
TF: 800-228-9290

Park Plaza Hotel 150 Hegenberger Rd . . . . . Oakland CA 94621 510-635-5300 635-9661
TF: 800-635-5301

Washington Inn 495 10th St . . . . . Oakland CA 94607 510-452-1776 452-4436
E-mail: washington@worldnet.att.net

Waterfront Plaza Hotel 10 Washington St . . . . . Oakland CA 94607 510-836-3800 832-5695
TF: 800-729-3638 ■ *Web:* www.waterfrontplaza.com
■ *E-mail:* wfph@ix.netcom.com

Wyndham Hotel 5990 Stoneridge Mall Rd . . . . Pleasanton CA 94588 925-463-3330 463-3315
TF: 800-996-3426

— Restaurants —

Phone

Alameda Tied House Cafe & Brewery (American)
1051 Pacific Marina . . . . . Alameda CA 94501 510-521-4321

Barclay's Restaurant & Pub (English) 5940 College Ave . . . . . Oakland CA 94618 510-654-1650
Web: www.atanda.com/Barclays/ ■ *E-mail:* barclays@atanda.com

Bay Wolf Restaurant (Mediterranean) 3853 Piedmont Ave . . . Oakland CA 94611 510-655-6004

Cafe 817 (Italian) 817 Washington St . . . . . Oakland CA 94607 510-271-7965

Chez Panisse (French/Italian) 1517 Shattuck Ave . . . . . Berkeley CA 94709 510-548-5525
Web: www.chezpanisse.com

Citron (French) 5484 College Ave . . . . . Oakland CA 94618 510-653-5484

City Center Grill (American) 1001 Broadway . . . . . Oakland CA 94607 510-451-4000

Dai Ten Japanese Restaurant (Japanese) 1830 Webster St . . Oakland CA 94612 510-836-3021

El Torito (Mexican) 67 Jack London Sq . . . . . Oakland CA 94607 510-835-9260

Fat Lady (American) 201 Washington St . . . . . Oakland CA 94607 510-465-4996

Ginger Island (California/Asian) 1820 4th St . . . . . Berkeley CA 94710 510-849-0526

Hearts of Palm (Vietnamese) 1000 Broadway Suite A160 . . . . Oakland CA 94607 510-835-4235

Il Pescatore (Italian) 57 Jack London Sq . . . . . Oakland CA 94607 510-465-2188

Jack's Bistro (American) 1 Broadway . . . . . Oakland CA 94607 510-444-7171

Kincaid's Bay House (Seafood) 1 Franklin St . . . . . Oakland CA 94607 510-835-8600
Web: www.kincaids.com/

Le Cheval Restaurant (Vietnamese) 1007 Clay St . . . . . Oakland CA 94607 510-763-8495

Nan Yang Rockridge Restaurant (Burmese)
6048 College Ave . . . . . Oakland CA 94618 510-655-3298

Oakland Grill (Steak/Seafood) 301 Franklin St . . . . . Oakland CA 94607 510-835-1176

Oliveto Cafe & Restaurant (Italian) 5655 College Ave . . . . . Oakland CA 94618 510-547-4381

Oyster Reef (Thai) 1000 Embarcadero . . . . . Oakland CA 94606 510-836-2519

Pacific Coast Brewing Co (American) 906 Washington St . . . . Oakland CA 94607 510-836-2739

Portofino (Chinese) 1422 Broadway . . . . . Oakland CA 94607 510-444-6660

Quinn's Lighthouse (American) 51 Embarcadero Cove . . . . . Oakland CA 94606 510-536-2050

Ratto's Restaurant (Italian) 827 Washington St . . . . . Oakland CA 94607 510-832-6503

Red Sea Restaurant (African) 5200 Claremont Ave . . . . . Oakland CA 94618 510-655-3757

Restaurant Peony (Chinese) 388 9th St Suite 288 . . . . . Oakland CA 94607 510-286-8866

Rosalie's Taste of New Orleans (Cajun/Creole)
1448A High St . . . . . Oakland CA 94607 510-532-8955

Sabina Indian Cuisine (Indian) 1628 Webster St . . . . . Oakland CA 94612 510-268-0170
Web: www.best.com/~bdb/sabina/intro.htm

Sam's Hofbrau (German) 595 Hegenberger Rd . . . . . Oakland CA 94621 510-635-8244

Santa Fe Bar & Grill (California) 1310 University Ave . . . . . Berkeley CA 94702 510-841-4740

Scott's Seafood Restaurant (Seafood)
2 Broadway Jack London Sq . . . . . Oakland CA 94607 510-444-3456

Silver Dragon Restaurant (Chinese) 835 Webster St . . . . . Oakland CA 94607 510-893-3748

Talk of the Town Taqueria Morelia (Mexican)
4493 E 14th St . . . . . Oakland CA 94601 510-535-6034

TJ's Gingerbread House (Cajun) 741 5th St . . . . . Oakland CA 94607 510-444-7373

Trader Vic's (Asian) 9 Anchor Dr . . . . . Emeryville CA 94608 510-653-3400

Yoshi's Japanese Restaurant (Japanese) 510 Embarcadero . . Oakland CA 94618 510-238-9200

Zazoo's (American) 30 Jack London Sq Suite 101 . . . . . Oakland CA 94607 510-893-7440

— Goods and Services —

SHOPPING

Phone Fax

Bayfair Mall 248 Bay Fair Mall . . . . . San Leandro CA 94578 510-357-6000 276-5928

Eastmont Mall 7200 Bancroft Ave . . . . . Oakland CA 94605 510-632-1131 382-0555

Oakland — Shopping (Cont'd)

				Phone	Fax
Jack London Village 30 Jack London Sq	Oakland	CA	94607	510-893-7956	893-0319
Southland Mall 1 Southland Mall	Hayward	CA	94545	510-782-5050	887-9619
Stoneridge Mall 1 Stoneridge Mall	Pleasanton	CA	94588	925-463-2778	463-1467
Sunvalley Mall 1 Sunvalley Mall	Concord	CA	94520	925-825-0400	825-1392
Trans Pacific Centre 1000 Broadway	Oakland	CA	94607	510-839-7651	

BANKS

				Phone	Fax
Bank of Oakland 360 14th St	Oakland	CA	94612	510-763-8486	763-4719
CivicBank of Commerce 2101 Webster St 14th Fl	Oakland	CA	94612	510-836-6500	836-1521
Metropolitan Bank 416 8th St	Oakland	CA	94607	510-834-7534	834-7539
Summit Bank 2969 Broadway	Oakland	CA	94611	510-839-8800	839-8853
Washington Mutual Bank 3310 E 14th St	Oakland	CA	94601	510-535-6585	
World Savings Bank FSB 1970 Broadway	Oakland	CA	94612	510-446-3313	763-5237

BUSINESS SERVICES

	Phone		Phone
ASAP	510-839-4225	**Mail Boxes Etc**	510-835-1209
Capitol Courier Services	510-839-9255	**Manpower Temporary Services**	510-639-0314
Federal Express	510-639-3700	**Olsten Staffing Services**	510-429-8995
Kelly Services	510-444-7804	**Post Office**	800-275-8777
Kinko's	510-465-5209	**UPS**	800-742-5877

— Media —

PUBLICATIONS

				Phone	Fax
Bay Area Press PO Box 10151	Oakland	CA	94610	510-428-2000	
Montclarion The 5707 Redwood Rd Suite 10	Oakland	CA	94619	510-339-8777	339-4066*
**Fax:* News Rm					
Oakland Tribune‡ PO Box 28884	Oakland	CA	94604	510-208-6300	208-6477
Web: www.newschoice.com/newspapers/alameda/tribune					

‡Daily newspapers

TELEVISION

				Phone	Fax
KGO-TV Ch 7 (ABC) 900 Front St	San Francisco	CA	94111	415-954-7777	956-6402
KPIX-TV Ch 5 (CBS) 855 Battery St	San Francisco	CA	94111	415-362-5550	765-8916
Web: www.kpix.com ■ *E-mail:* tvprog@kpix.com					
KQED-TV Ch 9 (PBS) 2601 Mariposa St	San Francisco	CA	94110	415-864-2000	553-2118
Web: www.kqed.org/tv ■ *E-mail:* tv@kqed.org					
KRON-TV Ch 4 (NBC) 1001 Van Ness Ave	San Francisco	CA	94109	415-441-4444	561-8136
Web: www.kron.com					
KTVU-TV Ch 2 (Fox) 2 Jack London Sq	Oakland	CA	94607	510-834-1212	272-9957
Web: www.bayinsider.com/partners/ktvu/index.html ■ *E-mail:* ktvu@team.insider.com					

RADIO

				Phone	Fax
KABL-AM 960 kHz (Nost) 340 Townsend St Suite 5101	San Francisco	CA	94107	415-977-0960	278-0960
KALW-FM 91.7 MHz (NPR) 500 Mansell St	San Francisco	CA	94134	415-841-4121	
Web: www.sfusd.k12.ca.us/programs/kalw/kalw.htm ■ *E-mail:* kalwradio@aol.com					
KBLX-FM 102.9 MHz (NAC) 55 Hawthorne St Suite 900	San Francisco	CA	94105	415-284-1029	764-4959
Web: www.kblxfm.com ■ *E-mail:* info@kblxfm.com					
KCBS-AM 740 kHz (N/T) 1 Embarcadero Ctr 32nd Fl	San Francisco	CA	94111	415-765-4000	765-4080
Web: www.kcbs.com ■ *E-mail:* kcbs@kpix.com					
KGO-AM 810 kHz (N/T) 900 Front St	San Francisco	CA	94111	415-954-8100	362-5827
Web: www.kgoam810.com					
KISQ-FM 98.1 MHz (AC) 750 Battery St Suite 200	San Francisco	CA	94111	415-788-5225	981-2930
Web: www.981kissfm.com ■ *E-mail:* kiss981@aol.com					
KLLC-FM 97.3 MHz (AC) 1 Embarcadero Ctr Suite 3200	San Francisco	CA	94111	415-765-4000	765-4084
Web: www.radioalice.com					
KMEL-FM 106.1 MHz (Urban) 340 Townsend St	San Francisco	CA	94107	415-538-1061	538-1060
Web: www.106kmel.com					
KMKY-AM 1310 kHz (Misc) 384 Embarcadero W 3rd Fl	Oakland	CA	94607	510-251-1400	251-2110

— Colleges/Universities —

				Phone	Fax
Armstrong University 1608 Webster St	Oakland	CA	94612	510-835-7900	835-8935
Web: www.armstrong-u.edu					
California College of Arts & Crafts 5212 Broadway	Oakland	CA	94618	510-653-8118	594-3601
TF Admissions: 800-447-1278 ■ *Web:* www.ccacsf.edu					
California Maritime Academy 200 Maritime Academy Dr	Vallejo	CA	94590	707-654-1000	654-1336
TF Admissions: 800-561-1945 ■ *Web:* www.csum.edu ■ *E-mail:* info@prop.csum.edu					
California State University Hayward 25800 Carlos Bee Blvd	Hayward	CA	94542	510-885-3000	885-3816
Web: www.csuhayward.edu					
Holy Names College 3500 Mountain Blvd	Oakland	CA	94619	510-436-1000	436-1199
Web: www.hnc.edu					
Laney College 900 Fallon St.	Oakland	CA	94607	510-834-5740	466-7394
Web: laney.peralta.cc.ca.us					
Merritt College 12500 Campus Dr	Oakland	CA	94619	510-531-4911	436-2405
Web: www.merritt.edu					
Mills College 5000 MacArthur Blvd.	Oakland	CA	94613	510-430-2255	430-3298
TF Admissions: 800-876-4557 ■ *Web:* www.mills.edu ■ *E-mail:* admission@mills.edu					
Patten College 2433 Coolidge Ave	Oakland	CA	94601	510-533-8300	534-4344
Web: www.patten.edu					
Peralta Community College District (System) 333 E 8th St.	Oakland	CA	94606	510-466-7200	466-7394
Web: www.peralta.cc.ca.us					
Samuel Merritt College 370 Hawthorne Ave	Oakland	CA	94609	510-869-6511	869-6525
TF Admissions: 800-607-6377 ■ *Web:* www.samuelmerritt.edu ■ *E-mail:* information@samuelmerritt.edu					
Shiloh Bible College 3295 School St	Oakland	CA	94602	510-261-1907	261-2002
University of California Berkeley	Berkeley	CA	94720	510-642-6000	643-5499
Web: www.berkeley.edu					

— Hospitals —

				Phone	Fax
Alameda County Medical Center-Highland Campus 1411 E 31st St.	Oakland	CA	94602	510-437-4800	437-5005
Children's Hospital-Oakland 747 52nd St	Oakland	CA	94609	510-428-3000	654-8474
TF: 800-400-7337 ■ *Web:* www.kron.com/kidsfirst					
Summit Medical Center 350 Hawthorne Ave	Oakland	CA	94609	510-655-4000	869-6760
Web: www.summitmed.com ■ *E-mail:* info@summitmed.com					

— Attractions —

				Phone	Fax
Alice Art Center 1428 Alice St	Oakland	CA	94612	510-238-7221	238-7225
Camron-Stanford House 1418 Lakeside Dr.	Oakland	CA	94612	510-444-1876	874-7803
Chabot Observatory & Science Center 4917 Mountain Blvd	Oakland	CA	94619	510-530-3480	879-2194
Web: www.cosc.org					
Children's Fairyland Theme Park 699 Bellevue Ave	Oakland	CA	94610	510-452-2259	
Chinatown Broadway & Alice Sts & 7th to 13th Sts	Oakland	CA	94607	510-893-8979	
Dunsmuir House & Gardens 2960 Peralta Oaks Ct.	Oakland	CA	94605	510-562-0328	562-8294
Ebony Museum 30 Jack London Sq Suite 208	Oakland	CA	94607	510-763-0745	
Eugene O'Neill National Historic Site PO Box 280	Danville	CA	94526	925-838-0249	838-9471
Web: www.nps.gov/euon/					
Jack London Square Broadway & Embarcadero	Oakland	CA	94607	510-814-6000	208-5569
Web: www.jacklondonsquare.com					
Joaquin Miller Park 3590 Sanborn Dr.	Oakland	CA	94602	510-238-6888	
Lake Merritt Boating Center 568 Bellevue Ave	Oakland	CA	94610	510-444-3807	238-7199
Lakeside Park 1520 Lakeside Dr.	Oakland	CA	94610	510-238-3208	
Merritt Museum of Anthropology 12500 Campus Dr.	Oakland	CA	94619	510-531-4911	436-2405
Morcom Amphitheatre of Roses 700 Jean St.	Oakland	CA	94610	510-597-5039	

Oakland — Attractions (Cont'd)

				Phone	Fax
Museum of Children's Art 560 2nd St	Oakland	CA	94607	510-465-8770	465-0772
Web: www.mocha.org					
Napa Valley Wine Train 1275 McKinstry St	Napa	CA	94559	707-253-2111	253-9264
TF: 800-427-4124 ■ *Web:* www.winetrain.com					
New Marine World Theme Park 2001 Marine World Pkwy	Vallejo	CA	94589	707-644-4000	644-0241
Web: www.freerun.com/napavalley/outdoor/marinewo/marinewo.html					
Oakland Asian Cultural Center 388 9th St Suite 290	Oakland	CA	94607	510-208-6080	208-6084
Oakland Ballet 1428 Alice St	Oakland	CA	94612	510-452-9288	452-9557
Web: www.oaklandballet.org/ ■ *E-mail:* oakballet@aol.com					
Oakland Chamber Orchestra 100 Redwood Rd	Oakland	CA	94619	510-533-6145	533-7670
Oakland East Bay Symphony 2025 Broadway Oakland Paramount Theater	Oakland	CA	94612	510-444-0801	444-0863
Web: www.oebs.org ■ *E-mail:* admin@oebs.org					
Oakland Lyric Opera PO Box 20709	Oakland	CA	94612	510-531-4231	531-4989
Oakland Museum of California 1000 Oak St	Oakland	CA	94607	510-238-3401	238-2258
Web: www.museumca.org					
Oakland Museum Sculpture Court 1111 Broadway City Center	Oakland	CA	94607	510-238-3401	238-2258
Oakland Youth Orchestra 1428 Alice St Suite 202A	Oakland	CA	94612	510-832-7710	
Web: www.best.com/~coles/oyo/oyo.shtml					
Oakland Zoo 9777 Golf Links Rd	Oakland	CA	94605	510-632-9525	635-5719
Web: www.oaklandzoo.org					
Paramount Theatre 2025 Broadway	Oakland	CA	94612	510-465-6400	893-5098
Pardee Home Museum 672 11th St	Oakland	CA	94607	510-444-2187	444-7120
Web: www.pardeehome.org					
Port of Oakland Oakland Board of Port Commissioners 530 Water St	Oakland	CA	94607	510-272-1100	839-5104
Web: www.portofoakland.com					
Preservation Park 13th St & ML King Jr Way	Oakland	CA	94607	510-874-7580	
Rotary Nature Center 552 Bellevue Ave	Oakland	CA	94610	510-238-3739	
Savage Jazz Dance Co 530 E 8th St Suite 202	Oakland	CA	94606	510-465-0561	
Web: members.xoom.com/savagejazz					
Sunday Music in the Courtyard 30 Jack London Sq	Oakland	CA	94607	510-893-7956	
USS Potomac Clay St Jack London Sq	Oakland	CA	94604	510-271-8093	839-4729
Web: www.usspotomac.com/ ■ *E-mail:* usspotomac@aol.com					
Western Aerospace Museum Oakland International Airport North Field 8260 Boeing St Bldg 621	Oakland	CA	94614	510-638-7100	638-6530
Web: www.crl.com/~michaelp/wam.html					

SPORTS TEAMS & FACILITIES

				Phone	Fax
Golden State Warriors 66th Ave & Hegenberger Rd Oakland Coliseum Arena	Oakland	CA	94621	510-762-2277	
Web: www.nba.com/warriors					
Network Assoc Coliseum 7000 Coliseum Way	Oakland	CA	94621	510-569-2121	569-4246
E-mail: skoss@netcom.com					
Oakland Athletics 7000 Coliseum Way Network Assoc Coliseum	Oakland	CA	94621	510-638-0500	
Web: www.oaklandathletics.com ■ *E-mail:* info@oaklandathletics.com					
Oakland Raiders 7000 Coliseum Way Network Assoc Coliseum	Oakland	CA	94621	510-569-2121	
Web: www.raiders.com					

— Events —

	Phone
Black Cowboys Parade & Heritage Festival (early October)	510-238-7275
Carijama Oakland Carnival (late May)	510-535-2450
Chinatown StreetFest (late August)	510-893-8979
Christmas at Dunsmuir (December)	510-615-5555
Cinco de Mayo (early May)	510-536-4477
Festival of Greece (mid-May)	510-531-3400
Grand National Roadster Show (mid-January)	415-490-5800
Halloween on the Square (late October)	510-814-6000
Home & Garden Show (early May)	800-222-9351
Italian Fiesta (mid-September)	510-814-6000
Juneteenth Celebration (mid-June)	510-632-9525
Lighted Yacht Parade & Santa Parade (early December)	510-208-4646
Oakland Fourth of July Celebration (July 4)	510-814-6000
Oakland Tree Lighting Ceremony (late November)	510-814-6000
Pacific Power Expo (mid-April)	510-452-6262
Pacific Sail Expo (late April)	800-817-7245
Potomac Public Cruise (mid-March-mid-November)	510-839-7533
Scottish Highland Games (early July)	510-615-5555
Silver Star Pow Wow & Indian Market (mid-June)	415-554-0525
Spring Boat Show (mid-April)	510-452-6262
Stitches Fair & Market (late March)	800-237-7099

Oxnard

Oxnard was named after the Oxnard brothers, founders of the American Beet Sugar Company, which contributed significantly to the development of the city. Today, Oxnard's economy is still based partially on agriculture, but commercial development and tourism are also important to its economy. Heritage Square in Oxnard features renovated turn-of-the-century homes and historic structures, as well as musical performances and cultural programs. The city's museums include the Carnegie Art Museum, Port Hueneme Museum, Seabee Museum, and the Ventura County Maritime Museum. Oxnard's Channel Islands Harbor is a popular site for visitors, with museums, restaurants, and special events. Boat charters also are available there.

Population	154,622	**Longitude**	119-12-49 W
Area (Land)	24.4 sq mi	**County**	Ventura
Area (Water)	11.1 sq mi	**Time Zone**	PST
Elevation	52 ft	**Area Code/s**	805
Latitude	34-11-50 N		

— Average Temperatures and Precipitation —

TEMPERATURES

	Jan	Feb	Mar	Apr	May	Jun	Jul	Aug	Sep	Oct	Nov	Dec
High	66	67	66	68	69	72	74	76	76	75	70	66
Low	44	45	46	48	52	55	58	59	58	54	48	44

PRECIPITATION

	Jan	Feb	Mar	Apr	May	Jun	Jul	Aug	Sep	Oct	Nov	Dec
Inches	3.0	3.1	2.4	0.9	0.1	0.0	0.0	0.1	0.4	0.3	2.0	2.0

— Important Phone Numbers —

	Phone		Phone
AAA	805-644-7171	**Medical Referral**	805-641-1650
American Express Travel	800-221-7282	**Poison Control Center**	800-876-4766
Dental Referral	800-422-8338	**Weather**	805-988-6610
Emergency	911		

— Information Sources —

				Phone	Fax
Better Business Bureau Serving Tri Counties - San Luis Obispo Santa Barbara & Ventura Counties PO Box 129	Santa Barbara	CA	93102	805-963-8657	962-8557
Web: www.santabarbara.bbb.org ■ *E-mail:* info@santabarbara.bbb.org					

Oxnard — Information Sources (Cont'd)

	City	State	Zip	Phone	Fax
Greater Oxnard & Harbors Tourism Bureau 200 W 7th St *TF:* 800-269-6273 ■ *Web:* www.oxnardtourism.com ■ *E-mail:* oxtour@oxnardtourism.com	Oxnard	CA	93030	805-385-7545	385-7571
Oxnard 721 S 'A' St. *TF:* 800-422-6332 ■ *Web:* www.oxnardedc.com	Oxnard	CA	93030	805-385-7444	385-7452
Oxnard Chamber of Commerce 400 S 'A' St *Web:* www.oxnardchamber.org ■ *E-mail:* info@oxnardchamber.org	Oxnard	CA	93030	805-385-8860	487-1763
Oxnard City Hall 305 W 3rd St. *Web:* www.ci.oxnard.ca.us/cityhall.html ■ *E-mail:* oxnardcty@ci.oxnard.ca.us	Oxnard	CA	93030	805-385-7803	385-7806
Oxnard Community Development Dept 305 W 3rd St. *Web:* www.ci.oxnard.ca.us/econdev.html	Oxnard	CA	93030	805-385-7857	385-7408
Oxnard Mayor 300 W 3rd St	Oxnard	CA	93030	805-385-7430	385-7595
Oxnard Public Library 251 S 'A' St *Web:* www.oxnard.org	Oxnard	CA	93030	805-385-7500	385-7526
Ventura County 800 S Victoria Ave *Web:* www.ventura.org/vencnty.htm	Ventura	CA	93009	805-654-2267	662-6343

On-Line Resources

Anthill City Guide Oxnard	www.anthill.com/city.asp?city=oxnard
City Knowledge Oxnard	www.cityknowledge.com/ca_oxnard.htm
Excite.com Oxnard City Guide	www.excite.com/travel/countries/united_states/california/oxnard

— Transportation Services —

AIRPORTS

■ Ventura County Airport (OXR)

	Phone
1 mile W of downtown (approx 5 minutes)	805-388-4274

Airport Transportation

	Phone
Yellow Cab $4-5 fare to downtown	805-483-2444

Commercial Airlines

	Phone
United Express	800-241-6522

Charter Airlines

	Phone		Phone
Aspen Helicopters	805-985-5416	**Sam's Air Service**	805-984-4121
Renown Aviation Inc	805-937-8484		

CAR RENTALS

	Phone		Phone
Avis	805-487-9429	**Enterprise**	805-382-9955
Budget	805-382-8350	**Hertz**	805-985-0911

LIMO/TAXI

	Phone		Phone
Esquire Limousine	805-483-5555	**Yellow Cab**	805-483-2444

MASS TRANSIT

	Phone
Harbor Hopper Water Taxi fare varies with destination	805-985-4677
SCAT Bus $1 Base fare	805-487-4222

RAIL/BUS

	City	State	Zip	Phone
Amtrak Station 201 E 4th St *TF:* 800-872-7245	Oxnard	CA	93030	805-487-8377
Greyhound Bus Station 201 E 4th St Suite 1 *TF:* 800-231-2222	Oxnard	CA	93030	805-487-2706

— Accommodations —

HOTEL RESERVATION SERVICES

	Phone	Fax
Central Reservation Service *TF:* 800-548-3311 ■ *Web:* www.reservation-services.com ■ *E-mail:* cenresbos@aol.com	407-740-6442	740-8222

HOTELS, MOTELS, RESORTS

	City	State	Zip	Phone	Fax
Alisal Guest Ranch 1054 Alisal Rd *TF:* 800-425-4725 ■ *Web:* www.alisal.com ■ *E-mail:* info@alisal.com	Solvang	CA	93463	805-688-6411	688-2510
Ambassador Motel 1631 S Oxnard Blvd	Oxnard	CA	93030	805-486-8404	
Best Western Encina Lodge & Suites 2220 Bath St *TF:* 800-526-2282	Santa Barbara	CA	93105	805-682-7277	563-9319
Best Western Inn 708 E Thompson Blvd *TF:* 800-528-1234	Ventura	CA	93001	805-648-3101	648-4019
Best Western Inn 295 Daily Dr *TF:* 800-528-1234	Camarillo	CA	93010	805-987-4991	388-3679
Best Western Oxnard Inn 1156 S Oxnard Blvd *TF:* 800-469-6273	Oxnard	CA	93030	805-483-9581	483-4072
Best Western Pepper Tree Inn 3850 State St *TF:* 800-338-0030	Santa Barbara	CA	93105	805-687-5511	682-2410
Casa Sirena Marina Resort 3605 Peninsula Rd *TF:* 800-447-3529	Oxnard	CA	93035	805-985-6311	985-4329
Casa Via Mar & Tennis Club 377 W Channel Islands Blvd. *TF:* 800-992-5522	Port Hueneme	CA	93041	805-984-6222	984-9490
Channel Island Shores 1311 Mandalay Beach Rd.	Oxnard	CA	93035	805-985-0621	985-0591
Channel Islands Inn & Suites 1001 E Channel Islands Blvd *TF:* 800-344-5998	Oxnard	CA	93033	805-487-7755	486-1374
Country Inn at Port Hueneme 350 E Hueneme Rd *TF:* 800-447-3529	Port Hueneme	CA	93041	805-986-5363	986-4399
Days Inn 165 Daily Dr *TF:* 800-329-7466	Camarillo	CA	93010	805-482-0761	388-3679
Doubletree Hotels 2055 Harbor Blvd. *TF:* 800-222-8733	Ventura	CA	93001	805-643-6000	643-7137
El Encanto Hotel & Garden Villas 1900 Lasuen Rd *TF:* 800-346-7039	Santa Barbara	CA	93103	805-687-5000	687-3903
Embassy Suites/Mandalay Beach Resort 2101 Mandalay Beach Rd. *TF:* 800-362-2779	Oxnard	CA	93035	805-984-2500	984-8339
Four Points by Sheraton 1050 Schooner Dr.	Ventura	CA	93001	805-658-1212	658-1309
Four Seasons Biltmore Resort 1260 Channel Dr. *TF:* 800-332-3442 ■ *Web:* www.fourseasons.com/locations/SantaBarbara	Santa Barbara	CA	93108	805-969-2261	565-8329
Holiday Inn 450 Harbor Blvd *TF:* 800-465-4329	Ventura	CA	93001	805-648-7731	653-6202
La Quinta Inn 5818 Valentine Rd *TF:* 800-531-5900	Ventura	CA	93003	805-658-6200	642-2840
Miramar Hotel & Resort 1555 S Jameson Ln *TF:* 800-322-6983	Montecito	CA	93108	805-969-2203	969-3163
Oaks at Ojai 122 E Ojai Ave *TF:* 800-753-6257 ■ *Web:* www.keho.com/oaks	Ojai	CA	93023	805-646-5573	640-1504
Ojai Valley Inn & Spa 905 Country Club Rd *TF:* 800-422-6524 ■ *Web:* www.ojairesort.com ■ *E-mail:* info@ojairesort.com	Ojai	CA	93023	805-646-5511	646-7969
Pierpont Inn 550 Sanjon Rd *TF:* 800-285-4667	Ventura	CA	93001	805-643-6144	641-1501
Radisson Hotel 600 Esplanade Dr *TF:* 800-333-3333	Oxnard	CA	93030	805-485-9666	485-2061
Radisson Hotel 1111 E Cabrillo Blvd *TF:* 800-643-1994	Santa Barbara	CA	93103	805-963-0744	962-0985
Ramada Inn 181 E Santa Clara St *TF:* 800-727-1027	Ventura	CA	93001	805-652-0141	643-1432
Regal Lodge 1012 S Oxnard Blvd	Oxnard	CA	93030	805-486-8385	486-1395
Residence Inn by Marriott 2101 W Vineyard Ave **Fax Area Code:* 661 ■ *TF:* 800-331-3131 ■ *Web:* www.residenceinn.com/OXRRI	Oxnard	CA	93030	805-278-2200	983-4470*
Santa Barbara Inn 901 E Cabrillo Blvd. *TF:* 800-231-0431 ■ *Web:* www.santabarbarainn.com	Santa Barbara	CA	93103	805-966-2285	966-6584
Surfside Motel 615 E Hueneme Rd	Port Hueneme	CA	93041	805-488-3686	
Vagabond Inn 1245 N Oxnard Blvd *TF:* 800-522-1555	Oxnard	CA	93030	805-983-0251	988-9638
Wagon Wheel Motel 2751 Wagon Wheel Rd	Oxnard	CA	93030	805-485-3131	981-9937

Oxnard (Cont'd)

— Restaurants —

				Phone
Armando's (Italian) 641 S Ventura Rd	Oxnard	CA	93030	805-984-4500
Bahia Restaurant (Mexican) 349 S Oxnard Blvd	Oxnard	CA	93030	805-487-5166
Buon Appetito Restaurant (Italian) 2721 S Victoria Ave	Oxnard	CA	93035	805-984-8437
Cabo Seafood Grill & Cantina (Seafood) 1041 S Oxnard Blvd	Oxnard	CA	93030	805-487-6933
Capistrano's (California) 2101 Mandalay Beach Rd	Oxnard	CA	93035	805-984-2500
Carrows (American) 1601 N Oxnard Blvd	Oxnard	CA	93030	805-983-0655
China Square Restaurant (Chinese) 141 W Gonzales Rd	Oxnard	CA	93030	805-988-1922
Dominick's (Italian) 477 N Oxnard Blvd	Oxnard	CA	93030	805-483-7933
El Ranchero (Mexican) 131 W 2nd St	Oxnard	CA	93030	805-486-5665
Fisherman's Wharf Seafood (Seafood) 3920 W Channel Islands Blvd	Oxnard	CA	93035	805-382-8171
Green Burrito (Mexican) 1801 E Ventura Blvd	Oxnard	CA	93030	805-983-7117
Hiro-sushi (Japanese) 804 Wagon Wheel Rd	Oxnard	CA	93030	805-485-9898
Hudson's Grill (American) 2091 N Oxnard Blvd	Oxnard	CA	93030	805-485-8607
It's Greek to Me (Greek) 2661 Saviers Rd	Oxnard	CA	93033	805-487-4242
Kampai Japanese Restaurant (Japanese) 2367 N Oxnard Blvd	Oxnard	CA	93030	805-988-0252
Korean Barbeque Swan (Korean) 2061 N Oxnard Blvd	Oxnard	CA	93030	805-278-9611
Lobster Trap Restaurant (Seafood) 3605 Peninsula Rd	Oxnard	CA	93035	805-985-6361
Pilar's Cafe (Mexican) 746 S 'A' St	Oxnard	CA	93030	805-487-1444
Plaza Grill (American) 600 Esplanade Dr	Oxnard	CA	93030	805-485-9666
Quincy Street Ltd (Barbecue) 2405 Roosevelt Blvd	Oxnard	CA	93035	805-984-6262
Sal's Mexican Inn (Mexican) 1450 S Oxnard Blvd	Oxnard	CA	93030	805-483-9015
Sandy's Steak & Seafood (Steak/Seafood) 4238 S Saviers Rd	Oxnard	CA	93033	805-488-1419
Tokyo Sukiyaki (Japanese) 1333 W Gonzales Rd	Oxnard	CA	93030	805-485-7337
Whale's Tail (Seafood) 3950 Bluefin Cir	Oxnard	CA	93035	805-985-2511
Yasubay's (Japanese) 1219 Saviers Rd Suite A	Oxnard	CA	93033	805-483-9611
Yolanda's (Mexican) 2801 Saviers Rd	Oxnard	CA	93033	805-487-3895
Yolie's Mexican Cafe (Mexican) 159 Esplanade Dr	Oxnard	CA	93030	805-983-6100

— Goods and Services —

SHOPPING

Name	City	State	Zip	Phone	Fax
Buenaventura Mall 363 S Mills Rd	Ventura	CA	93003	805-642-5530	654-1521
Centerpoint Mall 2655 Saviers Rd	Oxnard	CA	93033	805-487-1142	
Esplanade Mall 195 W Esplanade Dr	Oxnard	CA	93030	805-485-1146	485-3031
Oxnard Factory Outlet 2000 Outlet Center Dr Suite 222	Oxnard	CA	93030	805-485-2244	485-3303
Ventura Harbor Village 1583 Spinnaker Dr Suite 215	Ventura	CA	93001	805-644-0169	644-1684

BANKS

Name	City	State	Zip	Phone	Fax
American Commercial Bank 155 S 'A' St	Oxnard	CA	93030	805-487-6581	483-6189
Bank of America 2475 Saviers Rd	Oxnard	CA	93033	805-483-4174	
California Federal Bank 2900 Saviers Rd **Fax Area Code: 805*	Oxnard	CA	93033	800-843-2265	483-4882*
Santa Barbara Bank & Trust 2385 N Oxnard Blvd	Oxnard	CA	93030	805-278-1473	278-1479
Washington Mutual Bank 143 W 5th St	Oxnard	CA	93030	805-240-1545	240-1558

BUSINESS SERVICES

	Phone		Phone
DHL Worldwide Express	800-225-5345	**Mail Boxes Etc**	805-983-6034
Federal Express	800-238-5355	**Manpower Temporary Services**	805-445-9663
Interim Personnel Services	805-983-2000	**Post Office**	800-275-8777
Kelly Services	805-485-9779	**UPS**	800-742-5877
Kinko's	805-988-1134		

— Media —

PUBLICATIONS

Name	City	State	Zip	Phone	Fax
Connecticut Post‡ 410 State St *TF Edit:* 800-542-5620 ■ *Web:* www.connpost.com	Bridgeport	CT	06604	203-333-0161	367-8158
Los Angeles Times‡ Times Mirror Sq *TF:* 800-528-4637 ■ *Web:* www.latimes.com	Los Angeles	CA	90053	213-237-5000	237-4712
Ventura County Star‡ 5250 Ralston St *Web:* www.staronline.com	Ventura	CA	93003	805-650-2900	650-2950

‡Daily newspapers

TELEVISION

Name	City	State	Zip	Phone	Fax
KABC-TV Ch 7 (ABC) 4151 Prospect Ave *Web:* abcnews.go.com/local/kabc ■ *E-mail:* abc7@abc.com	Los Angeles	CA	90027	310-557-3200	557-3360
KCBS-TV Ch 2 (CBS) 6121 Sunset Blvd *Web:* www.kcbs2.com	Los Angeles	CA	90028	323-460-3000	460-3733
KCET-TV Ch 28 (PBS) 4401 Sunset Blvd *Web:* www.kcet.org	Los Angeles	CA	90027	323-666-6500	953-5523
KNBC-TV Ch 4 (NBC) 3000 W Alameda Ave *Web:* www.knbc4la.com	Burbank	CA	91523	818-840-4444	840-3535
KTTV-TV Ch 11 (Fox) 1999 S Bundy Dr *Web:* www.fox11la.com ■ *E-mail:* talkback@fox11la.com	West Los Angeles	CA	90025	310-584-2000	584-2023

RADIO

Name	City	State	Zip	Phone	Fax
KCAQ-FM 104.7 MHz (CHR) 2284 S Victoria Ave Suite 2M	Oxnard	CA	93003	805-289-1400	644-4257
KDAR-FM 98.3 MHz (N/T) 500 Esplanade Dr Suite 1500 *Web:* www.kdar.com ■ *E-mail:* info@kdar.com	Oxnard	CA	93030	805-485-8881	656-5330
KDB-FM 93.7 MHz (Clas) 23 W Micheltorena St *Web:* www.kdb.com ■ *E-mail:* info@kdb.com	Santa Barbara	CA	93101	805-966-4131	966-4788
KHAY-FM 100.7 (Ctry) 1376 Walter St	Ventura	CA	93003	805-642-8595	656-5838
KMLT-FM 92.7 MHz (AC) 99 Long Ct Suite 200 *Web:* www.lite92.7fm.com ■ *E-mail:* info@92.7fm.com	Thousand Oaks	CA	91360	805-497-8511	497-8514
KOXR-AM 910 kHz (Span) 418 W 3rd St	Oxnard	CA	93030	805-487-0444	487-2117
KVEN-AM 1450 kHz (N/T) PO Box 699	Ventura	CA	93002	805-642-8595	656-5838
KVTA-AM 1520 kHz (N/T) 2284 S Victoria Ave Suite 2-G	Oxnard	CA	93003	805-289-1400	644-7906

— Colleges/Universities —

Name	City	State	Zip	Phone	Fax
Oxnard College 4000 S Rose Ave *Web:* www.oxnard.cc.ca.us	Oxnard	CA	93033	805-488-0911	986-5806

— Hospitals —

Name	City	State	Zip	Phone	Fax
Saint John's Regional Medical Center 1600 N Rose Ave	Oxnard	CA	93030	805-988-2500	981-4440

— Attractions —

Name	City	State	Zip	Phone	Fax
Albinger Archaeological Museum 113 E Main St	Ventura	CA	93001	805-648-5823	
Art Association Gallery 700 E Santa Clara St	Ventura	CA	93001	805-648-1235	
Carnegie Art Museum 424 S C St *Web:* www.vcnet.com/carnart	Oxnard	CA	93030	805-385-8157	483-3654
Channel Islands Ballet 800 Hobson Way	Oxnard	CA	93030	805-486-2424	648-2827
Channel Islands Harbor 2731 S Victoria Ave Visitor Information *TF:* 800-994-4852	Oxnard	CA	93035	805-985-4852	985-7952
Channel Islands National Park 1901 Spinnaker Dr *Web:* www.nps.gov/chis/ ■ *E-mail:* chis_interpretation@nps.gov	Ventura	CA	93001	805-658-5700	658-5799
Gull Wings Children's Museum 418 W 4th St	Oxnard	CA	93030	805-483-3005	
Heritage Square 715 S 'A' St	Oxnard	CA	93030	805-483-7960	486-2499
New West Symphony 800 Hobson Way	Oxnard	CA	93030	805-486-2424	483-7303
Olivas Adobe Historical Park 4200 Olivas Park Dr	Ventura	CA	93001	805-644-4346	
Oxnard Performing Arts Center 800 Hobson Way	Oxnard	CA	93030	805-486-2424	483-7303
Port Hueneme Museum 220 N Market St	Port Hueneme	CA	93041	805-488-2023	488-6993
Santa Barbara Museum of Art 1130 State St *Web:* www.sbmuseart.org	Santa Barbara	CA	93101	805-963-4364	966-6840

Oxnard — Attractions (Cont'd)

				Phone	Fax
Santa Barbara Museum of Natural History 2559 Puesta Del Sol Rd. *Web:* www.sbnature.org	Santa Barbara	CA	93105	805-682-4711	569-3170
Seabee Museum 1000 23rd Ave Bldg 99	Port Hueneme	CA	93043	805-982-5163	982-5595
Theatre-by-the-Sea 3890 Channel Islands Blvd	Oxnard	CA	93035	805-985-4852	
Ventura County Maritime Museum 2731 S Victoria Ave.	Oxnard	CA	93035	805-984-6260	984-5970
Ventura County Museum of History & Art 100 E Main St	Ventura	CA	93001	805-653-0323	653-5267

— Events —

	Phone
California Strawberry Festival (mid-May)	805-385-7545
Celebration of the Whales (mid-February-mid-March)	805-985-4852
Celtic Lands Faire (early October)	805-486-2424
Channel Islands Harbor Boat Show (late July-early August)	805-985-4852
Cinco de Mayo (early May)	805-486-0266
Fiestas Patrias (mid-September)	805-486-0266
Galaxy of Gems Show (late November)	805-525-5415
Grey Whale Migration (September-December)	805-985-4852
Heritage Square Summer Concert Series (late June-late August)	805-483-7960
Mariachi Festival (early May)	800-269-6273
Multi-Cultural Festival (late October)	805-385-7434
Oasis del Espiritu Santo Convention (late February-early March)	805-486-2424
Obon Festival (mid-July)	805-483-5948
Oxnard's HomeTown Christmas Parade (early December)	805-385-7545
Parade of Lights (early December)	800-269-6273
Point Mugu Air Show (late April)	805-989-8548
Port Hueneme Harbor Days (early October)	800-269-6273
Seabee Days Celebration (late June)	805-982-4493
Ship Model Expo & Sale (December)	805-984-6260
Strawberry Classic Golf Tournament (late April)	805-983-4653
Taste of Ventura County Food & Wine Festival (October)	805-985-4852
Ventura County Boat Show (late July)	805-985-4852
Ventura County Fair (early-mid-August)	805-648-3376

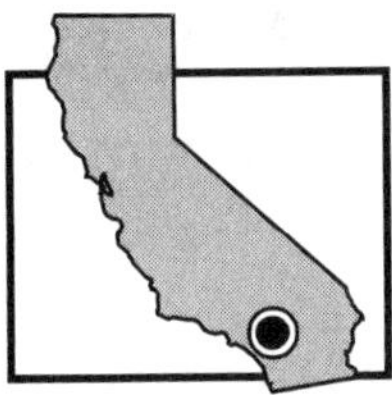

Palm Springs

The city of Palm Springs was made a part of movie history as the setting for Frank Capra's classic 1935 film, Lost Horizon, and may be best known as a playground for the Hollywood rich and famous. However, long before the glitz and glamour of Hollywood arrived, the area was home to the Agua Caliente band of Cahuilla Indians, who knew the canyons and mountains of Palm Springs as la palma de las mano de Dios, the palm of God's hand. Today, visitors to the Agua Caliente Cultural Museum can explore their way of life through exhibits, Indian artifacts, and a full-size kish dwelling. Palm Springs is also home to the Palm Springs Aerial Tramway, the largest vertical cable rise in the United States and the second largest in the world. The 8,516 foot tramway ascent to the top of Mount San Jacinto is two and one-half miles traveled in less than 15 minutes. Once at the mountain station, visitors can enjoy hiking and wilderness trails, picnic areas, and the Alpine Restaurant. Other Palm Springs attractions include the Living Desert, a 1,200-acre wildlife and botanical park featuring rare and endangered desert animals; the Village Green Heritage Center; a group of museums and historical buildings located in the heart of downtown; and the historic Plaza Theater, which was the location of a number of Jack Benny radio broadcasts during the 1940s and is now home to annually sold-out performances of the Fabulous Palm Springs Follies.

Population	43,942	**Longitude**	116-31-43 W
Area (Land)	76.5 sq mi	**County**	Riverside
Area (Water)	0.7 sq mi	**Time Zone**	PST
Elevation	466 ft	**Area Code/s**	760
Latitude	33-46-32 N		

— Average Temperatures and Precipitation —

TEMPERATURES

	Jan	Feb	Mar	Apr	May	Jun	Jul	Aug	Sep	Oct	Nov	Dec
High	70	76	80	87	95	104	109	107	101	92	79	70
Low	43	46	49	54	61	68	75	75	69	60	49	42

PRECIPITATION

	Jan	Feb	Mar	Apr	May	Jun	Jul	Aug	Sep	Oct	Nov	Dec
Inches	1.0	0.8	0.5	0.1	0.1	0.1	0.2	0.4	0.4	0.2	0.7	0.8

— Important Phone Numbers —

	Phone		Phone
AAA	760-320-1121	**Weather**	760-345-3711
Emergency	911		

— Information Sources —

				Phone	Fax
City of Palm Springs City Hall 3200 E Tahquitz Canyon Way *Web:* www.ci.palm-springs.ca.us	Palm Springs	CA	92262	760-323-8299	322-8320
City of Palm Springs Economic Development Dept 3200 E Tahquitz Canyon Way City Hall	Palm Springs	CA	92262	760-323-8259	322-8325
City of Palm Springs Mayor 3200 E Tahquitz Canyon Way City Hall	Palm Springs	CA	92262	760-323-8200	323-8207
Palm Springs Chamber of Commerce 190 W Amado Rd *Web:* www.pschamber.org ■ *E-mail:* pschamber@worldnet.att.net	Palm Springs	CA	92262	760-325-1577	325-8549
Palm Springs Convention Center 277 N Avenida Caballeros **Fax:* Sales ■ *TF:* 800-333-7535 ■ *Web:* www.palmspringscc.com ■ *E-mail:* email@palmspringscc.com	Palm Springs	CA	92262	760-325-6611	322-6921*
Palm Springs Desert Resorts Convention & Visitors Bureau 69-930 Hwy 111 Atrium Design Ctr Suite 201 *TF:* 800-417-3529 ■ *Web:* www.desert-resorts.com/cvb/ ■ *E-mail:* psdrcvb@earthlink.net	Rancho Mirage	CA	92270	760-770-9000	770-9001
Palm Springs Public Library 300 S Sunrise Way *Web:* www.ci.palm-springs.ca.us/library.html	Palm Springs	CA	92262	760-322-7323	320-9834
Riverside County 4080 Lemon St 12th Fl. *Web:* www.co.riverside.ca.us	Riverside	CA	92501	909-955-1100	955-1105

On-Line Resources

4PalmSprings.com	www.4palmsprings.com
About.com Guide to Palm Springs	palmsprings.about.com/local/caus/palmsprings
All Palm Springs.com	www.allpalmsprings.com
Anthill City Guide Palm Springs	www.anthill.com/city.asp?city=palmsprings
Area Guide Palm Springs	palmsprings.areaguides.net
Best Read Guide Palm Springs	www.bestreadguide.com/palmsprings
City Knowledge Palm Springs	www.cityknowledge.com/ca_palmsprings.htm
Desert Concierge	www.desertconcierge.com
Desert Golf & Tennis Guide	www.desertgolfguide.com
Excite.com Palm Springs City Guide	www.excite.com/travel/countries/united_states/california/palm_springs
GuestLife Palm Springs	www.desert-resorts.com
In Palm Springs	www.inpalmsprings.com
NITC Travelbase City Guide Palm Springs	www.travelbase.com/auto/features/palm_springs-area-ca.html
Online City Guide to Palm Springs	www.olcg.com/ca/palmsprings/main.html
Palm Springs CityLink	www.usacitylink.com/citylink/ca/palm-springs
Palm Springs Desert Resorts & Reservations	www.desertresorts.com
Palm Springs Golf	palm-springs-golf.com
Palm Springs.com	palmsprings.com
PalmSpringsGay.com	palmspringsgay.com
Savvy Diner Guide to Palm Springs Restaurants	www.savvydiner.com/palmsprings/

Palm Springs (Cont'd)

— Transportation Services —

AIRPORTS

■ Palm Springs Municipal Airport (PSP)

Phone

2 mi E of downtown (approx 5 minutes) 760-323-8161
Web: www.ci.palm-springs.ca.us/Airport/airport.html

Airport Transportation

	Phone
A Cactus Cab & Shuttle Service $8 fare to downtown	760-324-2158
Airport Taxi $8-15 fare to downtown	760-321-4470
Palm Springs Taxi $10 fare to downtown	760-323-5100

Commercial Airlines

	Phone		Phone
Alaska	800-426-0333	**Northwest**	800-225-2525
America West	800-235-9292	**SkyWest**	800-453-9417
American	800-433-7300	**TWA**	800-221-2000
Canada 3000	877-359-2263	**United**	800-241-6522
Canadian Air	800-426-7000	**US Airways**	800-428-4322
Delta	800-221-1212		

Charter Airlines

	Phone		Phone
Air Palm Springs	760-322-1104	**Corporate America Aviation Inc**	800-521-8585

CAR RENTALS

	Phone		Phone
Alamo	760-778-6271	**Enterprise**	760-327-2699
Avis	760-778-6300	**National**	760-327-1438
Aztec	760-341-1995	**Sears**	760-327-1404
Budget	760-327-1404		

LIMO/TAXI

	Phone		Phone
A Cactus Cab & Shuttle Service	760-324-2158	**Mirage Taxi**	760-322-2008
Country Club Taxi	760-774-9820	**Palm Springs Taxi**	760-323-5100
Desert Resort Transportation	760-836-9223	**Royal Limousine**	760-346-7333
Lone Star Limousine	760-836-0071	**Yellow Cab of the Desert**	760-345-8398

MASS TRANSIT

	Phone
Sun Bus $.75 Base fare	760-343-3451

RAIL/BUS

Phone

Amtrak Station 300 Indian Canyon Dr. . . . . . Palm Springs CA 92263 800-872-7245
Greyhound Bus Station 311 N Indian Canyon Dr . . . . . . Palm Springs CA 92262 760-325-2053
TF: 800-231-2222

— Accommodations —

HOTEL RESERVATION SERVICES

Phone *Fax*

Palm Springs Hotel Reservations 760-778-8418 325-4335
TF: 800-347-7746
Palm Springs Reservations 760-346-8800 341-0707
TF: 800-323-4786

HOTELS, MOTELS, RESORTS

Phone *Fax*

Best Western Las Brisas Hotel
222 S Indian Canyon Dr . . . . . . Palm Springs CA 92262 760-325-4372 320-1371
TF: 800-346-5714 ■ *Web:* www.lasbrisashotel.com
Elizabeth Court Hotel & Spa
288 E Camino Monte Vista. . . . . . Palm Springs CA 92262 760-320-1928 320-0599
TF: 877-324-6835
Estrella Inn & Villas 415 S Belardo Rd . . . . Palm Springs CA 92262 760-320-4117 323-3303
TF: 800-237-3687 ■ *Web:* www.estrella.com
■ *E-mail:* info@estrella.com

Hampton Inn 2000 N Palm Canyon Dr. . . . . Palm Springs CA 92262 760-320-0555 320-2261
TF: 800-732-7755
Hilton Palm Springs Resort
400 E Tahquitz Canyon Way. . . . . . Palm Springs CA 92262 760-320-6868 320-2126
TF: 800-445-8667 ■ *Web:* www.hilton.com/hotels/PSPPSHF
■ *E-mail:* pshilton@aol.com
Historic Oasis Hotel
177 W Tahquitz Canyon Way . . . . . . Palm Springs CA 92262 760-320-7205 320-0985
Holiday Inn Palm Mountain Resort
155 S Belardo Rd . . . . . . Palm Springs CA 92262 760-325-1301 323-8937
TF: 800-622-9451 ■ *Web:* www.palmmountainresort.com
Howard Johnson Resort
701 E Palm Canyon Dr . . . . . . Palm Springs CA 92264 760-320-2700 320-1591
TF: 800-854-4345
Hyatt Regency Suites Palm Springs
285 N Palm Canyon Dr . . . . . . Palm Springs CA 92262 760-322-9000 322-6009
TF: 800-233-1234
Ingleside Inn 200 W Ramon Rd . . . . . . Palm Springs CA 92264 760-325-0046 325-0710
TF: 800-772-6655 ■ *Web:* www.inglesideinn.com
■ *E-mail:* ingleside@earthlink.net
La Mancha Resort Village
444 Avenida Caballeros . . . . . . Palm Springs CA 92262 760-323-1773 323-5928
TF: 800-255-1773 ■ *Web:* www.palmsprings.com/hotels/lamancha/
■ *E-mail:* reservations@la-mancha.com
Le Palmier Inn 200 W Arenas Rd. . . . . . Palm Springs CA 92262 760-320-8866 323-1501
TF: 888-286-8866 ■ *E-mail:* palmierinn@aol.com
Merv Griffin's Resort Hotel & Givenchy Spa 4200 E Palm Canyon Dr . . . . . . Palm Springs CA 92264 760-770-5000 324-6104
TF: 800-276-5000 ■ *Web:* www.palmsprings.com/merv/
Monte Vista Hotel & Spa
414 N Palm Canyon Dr . . . . . . Palm Springs CA 92262 760-325-5641 325-0571
TF: 800-789-3188 ■ *Web:* www.palmsprings.com/hotels/montevista/
Motel 6 Palm Springs Downtown
660 S Palm Canyon Dr . . . . . . Palm Springs CA 92264 760-327-4200 320-9827
TF: 800-466-8356
Musicland Hotel
1342 S Palm Canyon Dr . . . . . . Palm Springs CA 92264 760-325-1326 322-5759
TF: 800-428-3939
Oasis Villa Resort Hotel
4190 E Palm Canyon Dr . . . . . . Palm Springs CA 92264 760-328-1499 328-3359
TF: 800-247-4664 ■ *Web:* www.oasiswaterresort.com
Ocotillo Lodge 1111 E Palm Canyon Dr. . . . Palm Springs CA 92264 760-416-0678 416-0599
Palm Court Inn
1983 N Palm Canyon Dr . . . . . . Palm Springs CA 92262 760-416-2333 416-5425
TF: 800-667-7918
Palm Garden Resort
950 N Indian Canyon Dr . . . . . . Palm Springs CA 92262 760-323-1328 323-2971
Web: www.palmgardenresort.com/palmgarden/palmgarden.html
Palm Springs Marquis Resort
150 S Indian Canyon Dr . . . . . . Palm Springs CA 92262 760-322-2121 778-1263
TF: 800-262-0123 ■ *Web:* www.palmspringsresort.com
Palm Springs Riviera Resort & Racket Club 1600 N Indian Canyon Dr. . . . . . Palm Springs CA 92262 760-327-8311 327-4323
TF: 800-444-8311 ■ *Web:* www.desert-resorts.com/fg/riviera.html
■ *E-mail:* riviera@thegrid.net
Racquet Club of Palm Springs
2743 N Indian Canyon Dr. . . . . . Palm Springs CA 92262 760-325-1281 325-3429
TF: 800-367-0946
■ *Web:* www.palmsprings.com/hotels/racquetclub/index.html
■ *E-mail:* racquetclubps@yahoo.com
Ramada Resort Inn & Conference Center
1800 E Palm Canyon Dr . . . . . . Palm Springs CA 92264 760-323-1711 327-6941
TF: 800-272-6232 ■ *Web:* www.psramada.com
■ *E-mail:* info@psramada.com
Rodeway Inn Tropics
411 E Palm Canyon Dr . . . . . . Palm Springs CA 92264 760-327-1391 323-3493
Royal Sun Inn 1700 S Palm Canyon Dr. . . . Palm Springs CA 92264 760-327-1564 323-9092
TF: 800-619-4786 ■ *Web:* www.royalsuninn.com
■ *E-mail:* royalsun@gte.net
Shilo Inn 1875 N Palm Canyon Dr . . . . . . Palm Springs CA 92262 760-320-7676 320-9543
TF: 800-222-2244
Spa Hotel & Mineral Springs
100 N Indian Canyon Dr . . . . . . Palm Springs CA 92262 760-325-1461 325-3344
TF: 800-854-1279 ■ *Web:* www.spa-hotel.com
■ *E-mail:* spahotel@aol.com
Super 8 Lodge 1900 N Palm Canyon Dr . . . Palm Springs CA 92262 760-322-3757 323-5290
TF: 800-800-8000
Travelodge Palm Springs
333 E Palm Canyon Dr . . . . . . Palm Springs CA 92264 760-327-1211 320-4672
TF: 800-578-7878 ■ *Web:* www.ids2.com/motels/palmspringstl/
■ *E-mail:* pstlps@aol.com
Vagabond Inn Palm Springs
1699 S Palm Canyon Dr . . . . . . Palm Springs CA 92264 760-325-7211 322-9269
TF: 800-522-1555
■ *Web:* vagabondinns.worldres.com/gen_prop.asp?hotel_id=10524
Vista Mirage 400 S Hermosa Dr. . . . . . Palm Springs CA 92262 760-320-5518 320-7679
TF: 800-438-6493

Palm Springs — Hotels, Motels, Resorts (Cont'd)

				Phone	Fax
Wyndham Palm Springs 888 Tahquitz Canyon Way	Palm Springs	CA	92262	760-322-6000	322-5351
TF: 800-996-3426					

— Restaurants —

				Phone
Al Dente Pasta (Italian) 491 N Palm Canyon Dr	Palm Springs	CA	92262	760-325-1160
Appley's (California) 888 Tahquitz Canyon Way	Palm Springs	CA	92262	760-322-6000
Bamboo Lounge (Continental) 2743 N Indian Canyon Dr	Palm Springs	CA	92262	760-325-1281
Blue Angel Bar & Grille (American) 777 E Tahquitz Canyon Way	Palm Springs	CA	92262	760-778-4343
Chen Ling Garden (Chinese) 787 N Palm Canyon Dr	Palm Springs	CA	92262	760-322-0039
Delhi Palace Cuisine of India (Indian) 1422 N Palm Canyon Dr	Palm Springs	CA	92262	760-325-3411
Don Quixote Dining Room & Terrace (Mexican) 444 N Avenida Caballeros	Palm Springs	CA	92263	760-323-1773
Web: www.palmsprings.com/dine/lamancha/ ■ *E-mail:* LaManchaOne@la-mancha.com				
El Mirasol Regional Cuisines of Mexico (Mexican) 140 E Palm Canyon Dr	Palm Springs	CA	92264	760-323-0721
Europa Restaurant (European) 1620 Indian Trail	Palm Springs	CA	92262	760-327-2314
Web: www.palmsprings.com/dine/europa/				
Gigi's (California) 4200 E Palm Canyon Dr	Palm Springs	CA	92264	760-770-5000
Grill The (Southwest) 1600 N Palm Canyon Dr	Palm Springs	CA	92262	760-327-8311
Guacamole's (Mexican) 555 S Sunrise Way	Palm Springs	CA	92264	760-325-9766
Johnny Costa's Ristorante (Italian) 440 S Palm Canyon Dr	Palm Springs	CA	92262	760-325-4556
La Provence (French) 254 N Palm Canyon Dr	Palm Springs	CA	92262	760-416-4418
Le Vallauris (French) 385 W Tahquitz Canyon Way	Palm Springs	CA	92262	760-325-5059
Web: www.palmsprings.com/dine/levallauris/ ■ *E-mail:* vallauris@aol.com				
Left Bank (French) 150 E Vista Chino	Palm Springs	CA	92262	760-320-6116
Leon's Bar & Grill (American) 1800 E Palm Canyon Dr	Palm Springs	CA	92264	760-416-4421
LG's Prime Steakhouse (Steak) 255 S Palm Canyon Dr	Palm Springs	CA	92262	760-416-1779
Livreri's Italian Restaurant (Italian) 350 S Indian Canyon Dr	Palm Springs	CA	92262	760-327-1419
Web: www.palmsprings.com/dine/livreris/ ■ *E-mail:* dago4444@aol.com				
Lobster Co (Seafood) 369 N Palm Canyon Dr	Palm Springs	CA	92262	760-864-1515
Lyons English Grill (European) 233 E Palm Canyon Dr	Palm Springs	CA	92264	760-327-1551
Native Foods (Vegetarian) 1775 E Palm Canyon Dr	Palm Springs	CA	92262	760-416-0070
Palm Springs Cedar Creek Inn (Continental) 1555 S Palm Canyon Dr	Palm Springs	CA	92264	760-325-7300
Web: www.palmsprings.com/dine/cedarcreekinn/ ■ *E-mail:* cedarcreekin@earthlink.net				
Palmie (French) 276 N Palm Canyon Dr	Palm Springs	CA	92262	760-320-3375
Peeraya Thai Restaurant (Thai) 2249 N Palm Canyon Dr	Palm Springs	CA	92262	760-320-8385
Purple Sage (International) 150 S Indian Canyon Dr	Palm Springs	CA	92262	760-322-2121
Saint James at the Vineyard (International) 265 S Palm Canyon Dr	Palm Springs	CA	92262	760-320-8041
Web: www.palmsprings.com/dine/stjames/				
Sorrentino's Seafood House (Steak/Seafood) 1032 N Palm Canyon Dr	Palm Springs	CA	92262	760-325-2944
Web: www.palmsprings.com/dine/sorrentinos/				
Teriyaki Yogi (Japanese) 555 S Palm Canyon Dr	Palm Springs	CA	92264	760-323-1162
Tony's Pasta Mia (Italian) 360 N Palm Canyon Dr	Palm Springs	CA	92262	760-327-1773
Village Pub (International) 266 S Palm Canyon Dr	Palm Springs	CA	92262	760-323-3265
Web: www.palmsprings.com/nightlife/villagepub/				

— Goods and Services —

SHOPPING

				Phone	Fax
Desert Fashion Plaza 123 N Palm Canyon Dr	Palm Springs	CA	92262	760-320-8282	
Desert Hill Premium Outlets 48400 & 48650 Seminole Dr	Cabazon	CA	92230	909-849-6641	
El Paseo Shopping District 73405 El Paseo	Palm Desert	CA	92260	760-568-4500	
Web: www.palmsprings.com/elpaseo/					
La Plaza Palm Canyon & Arenas Drs	Palm Springs	CA	92262	760-325-1347	320-0880
Web: www.laplazaps.com					
Palm Springs Mall 2365 E Tahquitz Canyon Way	Palm Springs	CA	92262	760-327-1319	
Westfield Shoppingtown 72840 US Hwy 111	Palm Desert	CA	92260	760-346-2121	341-7979

BANKS

				Phone	Fax
Bank of America 588 S Palm Canyon Dr	Palm Springs	CA	92262	760-864-8611	864-8618
Canyon National Bank 1711 E Palm Canyon Dr	Palm Springs	CA	92264	760-325-4442	325-1138
Guaranty Bank 420 S Palm Canyon Dr	Palm Springs	CA	92262	760-325-2021	325-3643
Union Bank 500 S Indian Canyon Dr	Palm Springs	CA	92264	760-323-4241	323-5565
Valley Independent Bank 901 E Tahquitz Canyon Way	Palm Springs	CA	92262	760-320-5110	323-2297
Washington Mutual Bank 399 S Palm Canyon Dr	Palm Springs	CA	92262	760-325-1242	325-0341

BUSINESS SERVICES

	Phone		Phone
Airborne Express	800-247-2676	**Post Office**	760-327-1527
C & C Delivery Systems	760-328-1800	**Post Office**	800-275-8777
Desert Delivery	760-340-6233	**Postal Connection**	760-328-9416
DHL Worldwide Express	800-225-5345	**Sun Secretarial Service**	760-325-1259
Federal Express	800-463-3339	**UPS**	800-742-5877
Mail Boxes Etc	760-340-0311		

— Media —

PUBLICATIONS

				Phone	Fax
Desert Sun‡ PO Box 2734	Palm Springs	CA	92263	760-322-8889	778-4654
TF: 800-233-3741 ■ *Web:* www.desertsunonline.com ■ *E-mail:* desunonline@earthlink.net					
Palm Springs Life Magazine 303 N Indian Canyon	Palm Springs	CA	92262	760-325-2333	325-7008
Web: www.desert-resorts.com/indexps.html ■ *E-mail:* admin@desert-resorts.com					

‡*Daily newspapers*

TELEVISION

				Phone	Fax
KCBS-TV Ch 2 (CBS) 6121 Sunset Blvd	Los Angeles	CA	90028	323-460-3000	460-3733
Web: www.kcbs2.com					
KCET-TV Ch 28 (PBS) 4401 Sunset Blvd	Los Angeles	CA	90027	323-666-6500	953-5523
Web: www.keet.org					
KESQ-TV Ch 3 (ABC) 42650 Melanie Pl	Palm Desert	CA	92211	760-568-6830	568-3984
E-mail: kesqtv3@aol.com					
KMIR-TV Ch 6 (NBC) 72920 Parkview Dr	Palm Desert	CA	92260	760-568-3636	568-1176
Web: www.kmir-tv6.com ■ *E-mail:* news@kmir-tv6.com					
KTTV-TV Ch 11 (Fox) 1999 S Bundy Dr	West Los Angeles	CA	90025	310-584-2000	584-2023
Web: www.fox11la.com ■ *E-mail:* talkback@fox11la.com					

RADIO

				Phone	Fax
KCLB-AM 970 kHz (Span) 490 S Farrell Dr Suite C-210	Palm Springs	CA	92262	760-320-6818	320-1493
KCLB-FM 93.7 MHz (Rock) 490 S Farrell Dr Suite C-210	Palm Springs	CA	92262	760-320-6818	320-1493
KCMJ-AM 1140 kHz (AC) 490 S Farrell Dr Suite C-210	Palm Springs	CA	92262	760-320-6818	320-1493
KDES-FM 104.7 MHz (Oldies) 2100 Tahquitz Canyon Way	Palm Springs	CA	92262	760-325-2582	322-3562
KESQ-AM 1400 kHz (N/T) 42-650 Melanie Pl.	Palm Desert	CA	92211	760-568-6830	568-3984
KEZN-FM 103.1 MHz (AC) 72-915 Parkview Dr.	Palm Desert	CA	92260	760-340-9383	340-5756
KJJZ-FM 102.3 MHz (Nost) 441 S Calle Encilia Suite 8	Palm Springs	CA	92262	760-320-4550	320-3037
KKUU-FM 92.7 MHz (CHR) 490 S Farrell Dr Suite C-210	Palm Springs	CA	92262	760-320-6818	320-1493
KLOB-FM 94.7 MHz (Span) 41601 Corporate Way	Palm Desert	CA	92260	760-341-5837	341-0951
KMRJ-FM 99.5 MHz (Alt) 1061 S Palm Canyon Dr	Palm Springs	CA	92264	760-778-6995	778-1249
KNWZ-AM 1010 kHz (N/T) 490 S Farrell Dr Suite C-210	Palm Springs	CA	92262	760-320-6818	320-1493

Palm Springs — Radio (Cont'd)

Name / Address	City	State	ZIP	Phone	Fax
KPLM-FM 106.1 MHz (Ctry) 441 S Calle Encilia Suite 8	Palm Springs	CA	92262	760-320-4550	320-3037
KPSI-AM 920 kHz (N/T) 2100 Tahquitz Canyon Way	Palm Springs	CA	92262	760-325-2582	322-3562
KPSI-FM 100.5 MHz (CHR) 2100 Tahquitz Canyon Way *Web:* www.powerradio.com ■ *E-mail:* kpsi@aol.com	Palm Springs	CA	92262	760-325-2582	322-3562
KYOR-FM 106.9 MHz (AC) 490 S Farrell Dr Suite C-210	Palm Springs	CA	92262	760-320-6818	320-1493

— Colleges/Universities —

Name / Address	City	State	ZIP	Phone	Fax
Chapman University 42600 Cook St	Palm Desert	CA	92211	760-341-8051	346-4628
College of the Desert 43-500 Monterey Ave *Web:* desert.cc.ca.us	Palm Desert	CA	92260	760-346-8041	776-0136

— Hospitals —

Name / Address	City	State	ZIP	Phone	Fax
Desert Hospital 1150 N Indian Canyon Dr.	Palm Springs	CA	92262	760-323-6511	323-6859
John F Kennedy Memorial Hospital 47-111 Monroe St. *Web:* www.tenethealth.com/JFKMemorial	Indio	CA	92201	760-347-6191	775-8014

— Attractions —

Name / Address	City	State	ZIP	Phone	Fax
Adagio Galleries 193 S Palm Canyon Dr *TF:* 800-288-2230 ■ *Web:* www.palmsprings.com/art/adagio/ ■ *E-mail:* adagio1@earthlink.net	Palm Springs	CA	92262	760-320-2230	320-8169
Aerie Art Garden 71-255 Aerie Dr.	Palm Desert	CA	92260	760-568-6366	568-1972
Agua Caliente Cultural Museum 219 S Palm Canyon Dr *Web:* prinet.com/accmuseum/	Palm Springs	CA	92262	760-323-0151	320-0350
Annenberg Theater 100 Museum Dr Palm Springs Desert Museum *Web:* www.palmsprings.com/annenberg/ ■ *E-mail:* info@psmuseum.org	Palm Springs	CA	92262	760-325-4490	322-3246
Big League Dreams Sports Park 33-700 Date Palm Dr. *Web:* www.bigleaguedreams.com	Cathedral City	CA	92234	760-324-5600	770-6541
Cabot's Old Indian Pueblo Museum 67-616 E Desert View Ave	Desert Hot Springs	CA	92240	760-329-7610	
Camelot Park Family Entertainment Center 67-700 E Palm Canyon Dr.	Cathedral City	CA	92234	760-321-9893	
Coachella Valley Museum 82-616 Miles Ave	Indio	CA	92201	760-342-6651	
Desert Holocaust Memorial Fred Waring & San Pablo Sts Palm Desert Civic Ctr. *Web:* www.palmsprings.com/points/holocaust/	Palm Springs	CA	92262	760-325-7281	
Fabulous Palm Springs Follies 128 S Palm Canyon Dr *Web:* www.palmspringsfollies.com	Palm Springs	CA	92262	760-327-0225	
Fantasy Springs Casino 84-245 Indio Springs Dr *TF:* 800-827-2946 ■ *Web:* www.cabazonindians.com/fantasysprings.html ■ *E-mail:* cabpio@gte.net	Indio	CA	92203	760-342-5000	347-7880
Historic Palm Canyon Drive Palm Canyon Dr *Web:* www.palmsprings.com/palmcyn.html	Palm Springs	CA	92262	760-323-8272	
Indian Canyons S Palm Canyon Dr	Palm Springs	CA	92262	760-325-5673	325-0593
Indian Wells Date Gardens Ave 78 & Hwy 86	Oasis	CA	92274	760-346-2914	
J Behman Gallery & Desert Fine Arts Academy 1103 N Palm Canyon Dr *Web:* www.palmsprings.com/art/jbehman/	Palm Springs	CA	92262	760-320-6806	
Joshua Tree National Park 74485 National Park Dr *Web:* www.nps.gov/jotr/	Twentynine Palms	CA	92277	760-367-5500	367-6392
Living Desert 47900 Portola Ave. *Web:* www.livingdesert.org	Palm Desert	CA	92260	760-346-5694	568-9685
McCallum Adobe 221 S Palm Canyon Dr Village Green Heritage Center *Web:* www.palmsprings.com/history ■ *E-mail:* feedback@palmsprings.com	Palm Springs	CA	92262	760-323-8297	320-2561
McCallum Theatre for the Performing Arts 73-000 Fred Waring Dr *Web:* www.mccallum-theatre.org	Palm Desert	CA	92260	760-340-2787	341-9508
Miss Cornelia White's House 221 S Palm Canyon Dr Village Green Heritage Center	Palm Springs	CA	92262	760-323-8297	320-2561
Moorten Botanical Garden 1701 S Palm Canyon Dr	Palm Springs	CA	92264	760-327-6555	
Mountain San Jacinto State Park 1 Tramway Rd	Palm Springs	CA	92262	760-323-3107	
Oasis Waterpark 1500 Gene Autry Trail *TF:* 800-247-4664 ■ *Web:* www.palmsprings.com/hotels/oasis/waterpark.html	Palm Springs	CA	92262	760-327-0499	328-3359
Palm Canyon Theatre 538 N Palm Canyon Dr *Web:* www.palmsprings.com/points/palmcanyontheatre/	Palm Springs	CA	92262	760-323-5123	323-7365
Palm Springs Aerial Tramway 1 Tramway Rd Valley Stn. *TF:* 888-515-8726 ■ *Web:* www.pstramway.com ■ *E-mail:* pstramway@pstramway.com	Palm Springs	CA	92262	760-325-1449	325-6682
Palm Springs Air Museum 745 N Gene Autry Trail *Web:* www.air-museum.org ■ *E-mail:* sales@air-museum.org	Palm Springs	CA	92262	760-778-6262	
Palm Springs Desert Museum 101 Museum Dr *Web:* www.psmuseum.org ■ *E-mail:* info@psmuseum.org	Palm Springs	CA	92262	760-325-7186	327-5069
Palm Springs Walk of Stars Palm Canyon Dr *Web:* www.palmsprings.com/stars/	Palm Springs	CA	92262	760-322-1563	322-0684
Plaza Theater 128 S Palm Canyon Dr	Palm Springs	CA	92262	760-327-0225	
Ruddy's General Store Museum 221 S Palm Canyon Dr Village Green Heritage Center *Web:* www.palmsprings.com/points/heritage/ruddy.html	Palm Springs	CA	92262	760-327-2156	
San Bernardino National Forest 1824 S Commercenter Cir	San Bernardino	CA	92408	909-383-5588	383-5770
Shields Date Gardens 80-255 Hwy 111 *Web:* www.shieldsdates.com ■ *E-mail:* shieldates@aol.com	Indio	CA	92201	760-347-0996	342-3288
Spa Casino 100 N Indian Canyon Dr *TF:* 800-258-2946 ■ *Web:* www.aguacaliente.org/casino/index.html ■ *E-mail:* casino@aguacaliente.org	Palm Springs	CA	92262	760-325-1461	325-3344
Top Hat Playhouse 210 E Arenas Rd.	Palm Springs	CA	92262	760-416-4339	
Village Center for the Arts 538 N Palm Canyon Dr	Palm Springs	CA	92262	760-325-9116	
Village Green Heritage Center 221-223 S Palm Canyon Dr	Palm Springs	CA	92262	760-323-8297	320-2561
Windmill Tours 62-950 20th Ave *TF:* 800-449-9463 ■ *Web:* www.windmilltours.com	North Palm Springs	CA	92258	760-251-1997	323-0688

— Events —

Event	Phone
Black History Festival & Parade (late February)	760-416-5715
Cabazon Band of Mission Indians Anual Pow Wow (March)	800-827-2946
Christmas Craft Show (early December)	760-323-8272
City of Palm Springs Clogging Festival (late April)	760-323-8272
Crossroads Renaissance Festival (late March)	800-320-4736
Desert AIDS Walk (mid-February)	760-323-2118
Desert Arts Festival (late January & late November)	760-323-7973
Festival of Lights Parade (early December)	760-325-5749
Frank Sinatra Celebrity Invitational (mid-February)	760-202-4422
Gay Pride Celebration (early November)	760-416-8711
Halloween Carnival (late October)	760-416-5715
Indio Desert Circuit Horse Shows (late January-mid-March)	760-775-7731
Indio Pow Wow Spring Celebration Festival (late March)	760-342-2593
Indio Pow Wow Thanksgiving Celebration (late November)	760-342-2593
Italian Festival (early February)	760-329-4879
La Quinta Arts Festival (mid-March)	760-564-1244
Nabisco Dinah Shore Golf Tournament (late March)	760-324-4546
Nabisco Mission Hills Desert Junior Golf Tournament (late June)	760-324-4546
NORTEL Palm Springs International Film Festival (mid-late January)	760-778-8979
Palm Desert Golf Cart Parade (early November)	760-346-0611
Palm Springs Bike Weekend (mid-October)	760-323-4141
Palm Springs Car Classic (early April)	760-323-1057
Palm Springs Exotic Car Show & Auction (late October)	760-320-3290
Palm Springs Gay & Lesbian Film Festival (early December)	760-770-2042
Palm Springs International Short Film Festival (early August)	760-778-8979
Palm Springs VillageFest (year-round)	760-320-3781

Palm Springs — Events (Cont'd)

	Phone
Skins Game (late November)	760-776-6688
Tour de Palm Springs (early February)	760-770-4626
Village Arts Festival (early March)	760-325-9116
Wildlights at the Living Desert (late November-early January)	760-346-5694

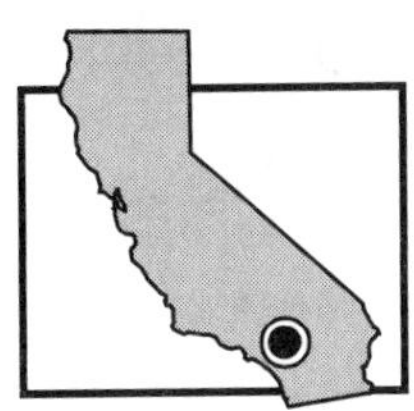

Riverside

Founded in 1870 as a colony dedicated to education and culture, Riverside is home to four major universities, including the University of California at Riverside, and boasts 20 National Register Sites, two National Landmarks, and more than 100 city landmarks. The city's most famous attraction is Mission Inn Museum, a historic hotel that has been frequented throughout the years by presidents, royalty, and movie stars. Riverside has been a top orange producer since the late 1800s, and the California Citrus State Historic Park is a tribute to its prosperous citrus industry. The city also hosts the annual Orange Blossom Festival each year in April.

Population	262,140	**Longitude**	117-23-50 W
Area (Land)	77.7 sq mi	**County**	Riverside
Area (Water)	0.3 sq mi	**Time Zone**	PST
Elevation	858 ft	**Area Code/s**	909
Latitude	33-56-25 N		

— Average Temperatures and Precipitation —

TEMPERATURES

	Jan	Feb	Mar	Apr	May	Jun	Jul	Aug	Sep	Oct	Nov	Dec
High	67	70	71	76	81	88	94	94	90	83	73	67
Low	41	42	44	47	52	57	61	62	59	52	45	40

PRECIPITATION

	Jan	Feb	Mar	Apr	May	Jun	Jul	Aug	Sep	Oct	Nov	Dec
Inches	1.8	1.8	1.8	0.7	0.2	0.0	0.0	0.2	0.4	0.3	1.2	1.2

— Important Phone Numbers —

	Phone		Phone
AAA	909-684-4250	**Time**	909-853-1212
Dental Referral	800-336-8478	**Travelers Aid**	909-986-4988
Emergency	911	**Weather**	213-554-1212
Poison Control Center	800-876-4766		

— Information Sources —

				Phone	Fax
Better Business Bureau Serving Los Angeles Orange Riverside & San Bernardino Counties PO Box 970 *Web:* www.la.bbb.org	Colton	CA	92324	909-825-7280	825-6246
Greater Riverside Chamber of Commerce 3685 Main St Suite 350 *Web:* www.riverside-chamber.com	Riverside	CA	92501	909-683-7100	683-2670
Riverside City & County Public Library 3581 Mission Inn Ave *Web:* www.ci.riverside.ca.us/library/	Riverside	CA	92501	909-782-5213	782-5407
Riverside City Hall 3900 Main St *Web:* www.ci.riverside.ca.us	Riverside	CA	92522	909-782-5312	782-5470
Riverside Convention & Visitors Bureau 3737 6th St *Web:* www.riversidecb.com	Riverside	CA	92501	909-222-4700	222-4712
Riverside Convention Center 3443 Orange St	Riverside	CA	92501	909-787-7950	222-4706
Riverside County 4080 Lemon St 12th Fl. *Web:* www.co.riverside.ca.us	Riverside	CA	92501	909-955-1100	955-1105
Riverside Development Dept 3900 Main St 5th Fl *Web:* www.ci.riverside.ca.us/devdept	Riverside	CA	92522	909-782-5649	782-5744
Riverside Mayor 3900 Main St. *Web:* www.ci.riverside.ca.us/mayor/Default.htm	Riverside	CA	92522	909-782-5551	782-2543

On-Line Resources

4Riverside.com	www.4riverside.com
Anthill City Guide Riverside	www.anthill.com/city.asp?city=riverside
Area Guide Riverside	riverside.areaguides.net
Excite.com Riverside City Guide	www.excite.com/travel/countries/united_states/california/riverside

— Transportation Services —

AIRPORTS

■ **Ontario International Airport (ONT)**

	Phone
18 miles NW of downtown Riverside (approx 30 minutes)	909-937-2700

Airport Transportation

	Phone
Riverside Taxicab Co $34 fare to downtown Riverside	909-684-1234
SuperShuttle $25 fare to downtown Riverside	909-467-9600

Commercial Airlines

	Phone		Phone
America West	800-235-9292	**Southwest**	800-435-9792
American	800-433-7300	**TWA**	800-221-2000
Continental	800-525-0280	**United**	800-241-6522
Delta	800-221-1212	**United Express**	800-241-6522
Northwest	800-225-2525	**US Airways Express**	800-428-4322
Pan Am	800-359-7262		

Charter Airlines

	Phone
KMR Aviation	888-605-6366

CAR RENTALS

	Phone		Phone
Avis	909-689-3114	**Hertz**	909-686-0345
Budget	909-682-2610	**Thrifty**	909-688-7000
Enterprise	909-352-9477		

LIMO/TAXI

	Phone		Phone
A Showcase Limousine Service	909-683-0811	**Riverside Taxicab Co**	909-684-1234
Assured Limousine Service	909-682-5466	**Ultimate Limousine**	909-687-1498
Cloud Nine Limousine	909-699-9151	**Yellow Cab**	909-622-1313

MASS TRANSIT

	Phone
Orange Blossom Express Trolley free	909-682-1234
RTA Bus $.75 Base fare	909-682-1234

RAIL/BUS

				Phone
Greyhound Bus Station 3911 University Ave *TF:* 800-231-2222	Riverside	CA	92501	909-686-2345

— Accommodations —

HOTELS, MOTELS, RESORTS

				Phone
Airport Inn 6759 Arlington Ave	Riverside	CA	92504	909-689-3391
American Inn 11057 Magnolia Ave	Riverside	CA	92505	909-351-0355
Arlington Motor Inn 6843 Arlington Ave.	Riverside	CA	92504	909-351-9990

Riverside — Hotels, Motels, Resorts (Cont'd)

				Phone	Fax
Best Western Motel 10518 Magnolia Ave.	Riverside	CA	92505	909-359-0770	359-6749
TF: 800-528-1234					
Budget Inn of Riverside 1911 University Ave	Riverside	CA	92507	909-686-8888	
Circle Inn Motel 9220 Granite Hill Dr	Riverside	CA	92509	909-360-1132	
Civic Center Motel 3225 Main St	Riverside	CA	92501	909-686-8043	
Courtyard by Marriott 1510 University Ave.	Riverside	CA	92507	909-276-1200	787-6783
TF: 800-321-2200 ■ *Web:* courtyard.com/RALCY					
Days Inn 10545 Magnolia Ave	Riverside	CA	92505	909-358-2808	358-0670
TF: 800-329-7466					
Doral Palm Springs Resort 67967 Vista Chino	Cathedral City	CA	92234	760-322-7000	322-6853
TF: 888-386-4677					
Dynasty Suites 3735 Iowa Ave	Riverside	CA	92507	909-369-8200	341-6486
TF: 800-842-7899					
Econo Lodge 10705 Magnolia Ave.	Riverside	CA	92505	909-351-2424	687-5070
Economy Inn 9878 Magnolia Ave	Riverside	CA	92503	909-687-3090	688-6606
Economy Inn Motel 1971 University Ave	Riverside	CA	92507	909-684-6363	788-8775
Hampton Inn 1590 University Ave.	Riverside	CA	92507	909-683-6000	782-8052
TF: 800-426-7866					
Hampton Inn 2000 N Palm Canyon Dr.	Palm Springs	CA	92262	760-320-0555	320-2261
TF: 800-732-7755					
Hilton Palm Springs Resort 400 E Tahquitz Canyon Way	Palm Springs	CA	92262	760-320-6868	320-2126
TF: 800-445-8667 ■ *Web:* www.hilton.com/hotels/PSPPSHF ■ *E-mail:* pshilton@aol.com					
Holiday Inn Express 11043 Magnolia Ave	Riverside	CA	92505	909-688-5000	785-5655
Holiday Inn Palm Mountain Resort 155 S Belardo Rd	Palm Springs	CA	92262	760-325-1301	323-8937
TF: 800-622-9451 ■ *Web:* www.palmmountainresort.com					
Holiday Inn Riverside 3400 Market St.	Riverside	CA	92501	909-784-8000	369-7127
TF: 800-465-4329					
Hyatt Grand Champions Resort 44-600 Indian Wells Ln	Indian Wells	CA	92210	760-341-1000	568-2236
TF: 800-233-1234 ■ *Web:* www.hyatt.com/usa/indian_wells/hotels/hotel_champ.html					
Indian Wells Resort Hotel 76-661 Hwy 111	Indian Wells	CA	92210	760-345-6466	772-5083
TF: 800-248-3220					
Marriott's Desert Springs Resort & Spa 74855 Country Club Dr	Palm Desert	CA	92260	760-341-2211	341-1872
TF: 800-331-3112 ■ *Web:* marriotthotels.com/CTDCA					
Marriott's Rancho Las Palmas Resort & Conference Center 41000 Bob Hope Dr.	Rancho Mirage	CA	92270	760-568-2727	568-5845
TF: 800-458-8786 ■ *Web:* www.marriott.com/marriott/pspca/default.asp					
Miramonte Resort 76477 Hwy 111	Indian Wells	CA	92210	760-341-2200	568-0541
TF: 800-237-2926 ■ *Web:* www.miramonteresort.com ■ *E-mail:* info@miramonteresort.com					
Mission Inn 3649 Mission Inn Ave	Riverside	CA	92501	909-784-0300	683-1342
TF: 800-843-7755 ■ *Web:* www.missioninn.com ■ *E-mail:* sales@missioninn.com					
Morningside Inn 888 N Indian Canyon Dr	Palm Springs	CA	92262	760-325-2668	322-1532
TF: 800-916-2668 ■ *Web:* www.morningsideinn.com					
Motel 6 3663 La Sierra Ave	Riverside	CA	92505	909-351-0764	687-1430
TF: 800-466-8356					
Motel 6 1260 University Ave.	Riverside	CA	92507	909-784-2131	784-1801
TF: 800-466-8356					
Palm Springs Marquis Resort 150 S Indian Canyon Dr	Palm Springs	CA	92262	760-322-2121	778-1263
TF: 800-262-0123 ■ *Web:* www.palmspringsresort.com					
Palm Springs Riviera Resort & Racket Club 1600 N Indian Canyon Dr.	Palm Springs	CA	92262	760-327-8311	327-4323
TF: 800-444-8311 ■ *Web:* www.desert-resorts.com/fg/riviera.html ■ *E-mail:* riviera@thegrid.net					
Palms at Palm Springs 572 N Indian Canyon Dr	Palm Springs	CA	92262	760-325-1111	327-0867
TF: 800-753-7256 ■ *Web:* www.palmsspa.com					
Ramada Resort Inn & Conference Center 1800 E Palm Canyon Dr	Palm Springs	CA	92264	760-323-1711	327-6941
TF: 800-272-6232 ■ *Web:* www.psramada.com ■ *E-mail:* info@psramada.com					
Rancho Valencia Resort 5921 Valencia Cir	Rancho Santa Fe	CA	92067	858-756-1123	756-0165
TF: 800-548-3664 ■ *Web:* www.ranchovalencia.com					
Renaissance Esmeralda Resort 44-400 Indian Wells Ln	Indian Wells	CA	92210	760-773-4444	346-9308
TF: 800-552-4386					
Ritz-Carlton Resort 68-900 Frank Sinatra Dr.	Rancho Mirage	CA	92270	760-321-8282	321-6928
TF: 800-241-3333 ■ *Web:* www.ritzcarlton.com/location/NorthAmerica/RanchoMirage/main.htm					
Riverside Inn 4045 University Ave	Riverside	CA	92501	909-686-6666	686-6666
Santa Cruz Inn 3425 Market St.	Riverside	CA	92501	909-369-0238	
Shadow Mountain Resort & Racquet Club 45750 San Luis Rey Ave	Palm Desert	CA	92260	760-346-6123	346-6518
TF: 800-472-3713 ■ *Web:* www.shadow-mountain.com					
Sierra Six Motel 10920 Magnolia Ave	Riverside	CA	92505	909-689-0933	
Spa Hotel & Mineral Springs 100 N Indian Canyon Dr	Palm Springs	CA	92262	760-325-1461	325-3344
TF: 800-854-1279 ■ *Web:* www.spa-hotel.com ■ *E-mail:* spahotel@aol.com					
Super 8 Motel 1350 University Ave.	Riverside	CA	92507	909-682-1144	369-6645
TF: 800-800-8000					
Temecula Creek Inn 44501 Rainbow Canyon Rd	Temecula	CA	92592	909-694-1000	676-3422
TF: 800-962-7335 ■ *Web:* www.jcresorts.com/temecula-creek/temecula_creek_inn.html					
University Lodge 1860 University Ave.	Riverside	CA	92507	909-686-8262	788-6262
Welcome Inn of America 1910 University Ave	Riverside	CA	92507	909-684-2400	
Westin Mission Hills Resort 71333 Dinah Shore Dr.	Rancho Mirage	CA	92270	760-328-5955	770-2199
TF: 800-937-8461					

— Restaurants —

				Phone
Anchos Southwest Grill & Bar (Southwest) 10773 Hole Ave	Riverside	CA	92505	909-352-0240
Arts Bar & Grill (American) 3357 University Ave	Riverside	CA	92501	909-683-9520
Bombay Restaurant (Indian) 1725 University Ave.	Riverside	CA	92507	909-788-4994
Cafe Chicago (American) 1960 Chicago Ave	Riverside	CA	92507	909-684-6861
Chan's (Chinese) 1445 University Ave	Riverside	CA	92507	909-788-6360
City Cuisine (American) 3425 Mission Inn Ave	Riverside	CA	92501	909-682-9566
Dragon House (Chinese) 10466 Magnolia Ave	Riverside	CA	92505	909-354-2080
Duane's (American) 3649 Mission Inn Ave	Riverside	CA	92501	909-341-6767
El Trigo (Mexican) 9696 Magnolia Ave	Riverside	CA	92503	909-687-8865
Flo's Farmhouse Cafe (Homestyle) 5620 Van Buren Blvd	Riverside	CA	92503	909-352-2690
Frank's (American) 3221 Iowa Ave.	Riverside	CA	92507	909-788-7630
Gerard's (French) 9814 Magnolia Ave.	Riverside	CA	92503	909-687-4882
Gram's Mission BBQ Palace (Barbecue) 3646 Mission Inn Ave.	Riverside	CA	92501	909-782-8219
Grape Leaves (Mediterranean) 4085 Vine St.	Riverside	CA	92501	909-784-3033
Jose's Mexican Food (Mexican) 3765 La Sierra Ave	Riverside	CA	92505	909-359-8000
Korean Bbq House (Korean) 9844 Magnolia Ave	Riverside	CA	92503	909-359-1019
La Cascada (Mexican) 6154 Magnolia Ave	Riverside	CA	92506	909-684-8614
Mario's Place (Italian) 1725 Spruce St.	Riverside	CA	92507	909-684-7755
Market Broiler (Seafood) 3525 Merrill St	Riverside	CA	92506	909-276-9007
Mex Sea Co (Seafood) 4773 Tyler St	Riverside	CA	92503	909-352-7633
New Tokyo (Japanese) 5180 Arlington Ave	Riverside	CA	92504	909-689-8054
Pho Que Huong (Vietnamese) 10051 Magnolia Ave	Riverside	CA	92503	909-352-9548
Riverside Brewing Co (American) 3397 Mission Inn Ave	Riverside	CA	92501	909-784-2739
Tamale Factory (Mexican) 3850 Main St	Riverside	CA	92501	909-342-3023
Thai Ice Tea Restaurant (Thai) 7207 Arlington Ave	Riverside	CA	92503	909-687-2270
Upper Crust (American) 3573 Main St	Riverside	CA	92501	909-684-1437
Wong's Chinese Restaurant (Chinese) 5537 Van Buren Blvd	Riverside	CA	92503	909-688-8053
Zacatecas Cafe (Mexican) 2472 University Ave	Riverside	CA	92507	909-683-3939

— Goods and Services —

SHOPPING

				Phone	Fax
Canyon Crest Towne Centre 5225 Canyon Crest Dr	Riverside	CA	92507	909-686-8000	
Galleria at Tyler 1299 Galleria at Tyler St	Riverside	CA	92503	909-351-3112	351-3139
Main Street Mall 5th St & University Ave	Riverside	CA	92501	909-781-7335	
Riverside Marketplace Main St.	Riverside	CA	92501	909-715-3400	715-3404
Riverside Plaza 3690 Central Ave	Riverside	CA	92506	909-683-1030	

BANKS

				Phone	Fax
Bank of America 3650 14th St	Riverside	CA	92501	909-686-2590	
TF: 800-441-6437					
California Federal Bank 1651 University Ave	Riverside	CA	92507	800-843-2265	787-8214*
**Fax Area Code:* 909					

Riverside — Banks (Cont'd)

	City	State	Zip	Phone	Fax
City National Bank 3484 Central Ave	Riverside	CA	92506	909-276-8800	276-8816
De Anza National Bank 7710 Limonite Ave	Riverside	CA	92509	909-687-2265	681-1095
Hemet Federal Savings & Loan 3600 Tyler St	Riverside	CA	92503	909-687-0121	687-5546
Inland Empire National Bank 3727 Arlington Ave Suite 202-A	Riverside	CA	92506	909-788-2265	787-0916
Mission Savings Bank 4860 La Sierra Ave	Riverside	CA	92505	909-359-4700	359-3029
Union Bank of California 9380 Magnolia Ave *TF:* 800-796-5656	Riverside	CA	92503	909-352-5560	352-5565
Washington Mutual Bank 3590 Central Ave *TF:* 800-788-7000	Riverside	CA	92506	909-788-1313	276-3284

BUSINESS SERVICES

	Phone		Phone
Airborne Express	800-247-2676	**Kinko's**	909-682-4200
DHL Worldwide Express	800-225-5345	**Manpower Temporary Services**	909-688-5460
Federal Express	800-238-5355	**Post Office**	800-222-1811
Interim Personnel Services	909-787-0771	**UPS**	800-742-5877

— Media —

PUBLICATIONS

	City	State	Zip	Phone	Fax
Inland Empire Magazine 3769 Tibbetts St Suite A	Riverside	CA	92506	909-682-3026	682-0246
Press-Enterprise‡ PO Box 792 *Web:* www.pe.net ■ *E-mail:* comments@pe.net	Riverside	CA	92502	909-684-1200	782-7572
Riverside County Record PO Box 3187 **Fax:* News Rm	Riverside	CA	92519	909-685-6191	685-2961*
Southern California 3769 Tibbetts Ave Suite A	Riverside	CA	92506	909-682-3026	682-0246

‡Daily newspapers

TELEVISION

	City	State	Zip	Phone	Fax
KABC-TV Ch 7 (ABC) 4151 Prospect Ave *Web:* abcnews.go.com/local/kabc ■ *E-mail:* abc7@abc.com	Los Angeles	CA	90027	310-557-3200	557-3360
KCBS-TV Ch 2 (CBS) 6121 Sunset Blvd *Web:* www.kcbs2.com	Los Angeles	CA	90028	323-460-3000	460-3733
KCET-TV Ch 28 (PBS) 4401 Sunset Blvd *Web:* www.keet.org	Los Angeles	CA	90027	323-666-6500	953-5523
KNBC-TV Ch 4 (NBC) 3000 W Alameda Ave *Web:* www.knbc4la.com	Burbank	CA	91523	818-840-4444	840-3535
KTTV-TV Ch 11 (Fox) 1999 S Bundy Dr *Web:* www.fox11la.com ■ *E-mail:* talkback@fox11la.com	West Los Angeles	CA	90025	310-584-2000	584-2023

RADIO

	City	State	Zip	Phone	Fax
KCAL-AM 1410 kHz (Span) 1950 S Sunwest Ln Suite 302	San Bernardino	CA	92408	909-825-5020	884-5844
KCAL-FM 96.7 MHz (Rock) 1940 Orange Tree Ln Suite 200 *Web:* www.kcalfm.com	Redlands	CA	92374	909-793-3554	793-3094
KDIF-AM 1440 kHz (Span) 1465 Spruce St Suite A	Riverside	CA	92507	909-784-4210	784-4213
KFRG-FM 95.1 MHz (Ctry) 900 E Washington St Suite 315 *TF:* 888-560-3764 ■ *Web:* www.kfrog.com ■ *E-mail:* thefrog@kfrog.com	Colton	CA	92324	909-825-9525	825-0441
KGGI-FM 99.1 MHz (CHR) 2001 Iowa Ave Suite 200	Riverside	CA	92507	909-684-1991	274-4949
KMRZ-AM 1290 kHz (Oldies) 2001 Iowa Ave Suite 200	Riverside	CA	92507	909-684-1991	274-4949
KOLA-FM 99.9 MHz (Oldies) 1940 Orange Tree Ln Suite 200 **Fax:* Mktg ■ *Web:* www.kola-fm.com	Redlands	CA	92374	909-793-3554	798-6627*
KPRO-AM 1570 kHz (Rel) 7351 Lincoln Ave	Riverside	CA	92504	909-688-1570	688-7009
KSGN-FM 89.7 MHz (Rel) 11498 Pierce St	Riverside	CA	92505	909-687-5746	785-2288
KSSE-FM 97.5 MHz (Span) 3450 Wilshire Blvd Suite 820	Los Angeles	CA	90010	213-251-1011	251-1033
KSZZ-AM 590 kHz (Span) 1950 S Sunwest Ln Suite 302	San Bernardino	CA	92408	909-825-5020	884-5844
KUCR-FM 88.3 MHz (Misc) University of California	Riverside	CA	92521	909-787-3737	787-3240
KWRP-FM 96.1 MHz (Nost) 475 W Stetson Ave Suite U	Hemet	CA	92543	909-929-5088	658-8822
KXRS-FM 105.7 MHz (Span) 2615 W Devonshire Ave	Hemet	CA	92545	909-925-9000	658-4843
KXSB-FM 101.7 MHz (Span) 2615 W Devonshire Ave	Hemet	CA	92545	909-925-9000	658-4843

— Colleges/Universities —

	City	State	Zip	Phone	Fax
California Baptist College 8432 Magnolia Ave *TF Admissions:* 877-228-8866 ■ *Web:* www.calbaptist.edu	Riverside	CA	92504	909-689-5771	343-4525
La Sierra University 4700 Pierce St *Web:* www.lasierra.edu ■ *E-mail:* dulerodr@lasierra.edu	Riverside	CA	92515	909-785-2000	785-2447
Riverside Community College Riverside City Campus 4800 Magnolia Ave *Web:* www.rccd.cc.ca.us ■ *E-mail:* webmstr@rccd.cc.ca.us	Riverside	CA	92506	909-222-8000	222-8036
University of California Riverside 900 University Ave *Web:* www.ucr.edu	Riverside	CA	92521	909-787-1012	787-5836

— Hospitals —

	City	State	Zip	Phone	Fax
Kaiser Permanente Riverside Medical Center 10800 Magnolia Ave *TF Cust Svc:* 800-464-4000*	Riverside	CA	92505	909-353-2000	353-4611
Parkview Community Hospital Medical Center 3865 Jackson St	Riverside	CA	92503	909-688-2211	352-5471
Riverside Community Hospital 4445 Magnolia Ave	Riverside	CA	92501	909-788-3000	788-3174
Riverside County Regional Medical Center 26520 Texas Ave *TF:* 800-900-0888	Moreno Valley	CA	92555	909-486-4000	486-4475

— Attractions —

	City	State	Zip	Phone	Fax
Ballet Folklorico de Riverside 8859 Philbin Ave	Riverside	CA	92503	909-354-8872	
Benedict Castle 5445 Chicago Ave	Riverside	CA	92507	909-683-4241	682-3754
Box Springs Mountain Park 9699 Box Springs Mountain Rd	Moreno Valley	CA	92557	909-955-4310	
California Botanic Gardens University of California Riverside	Riverside	CA	92521	909-787-4650	787-4437
California Citrus State Historic Park 9400 Dufferin Ave	Riverside	CA	92503	909-780-6222	780-6073
California Museum of Photography 3824 Main St *Web:* www.cmp.ucr.edu	Riverside	CA	92501	909-784-3686	
Castle Amusement Park 3500 Polk St *Web:* www.castlepark.com ■ *E-mail:* info@castlepark.com	Riverside	CA	92505	909-785-4141	785-4177
Fairmount Park 2601 Fairmount Blvd	Riverside	CA	92501	909-715-3440	
First Congregational Church 3504 Mission Inn Ave	Riverside	CA	92501	909-684-2494	778-0309
Heritage House 8193 Magnolia Ave	Riverside	CA	92504	909-689-1333	
Jensen-Alvarado Historic Ranch & Museum 4307 Briggs St	Riverside	CA	92509	909-369-6055	
Joshua Tree National Park 74485 National Park Dr *Web:* www.nps.gov/jotr/	Twentynine Palms	CA	92277	760-367-5500	367-6392
Jurupa Mountains Cultural Center 7621 Granite Hill Dr *E-mail:* jmcc2@dreamsoft.com	Riverside	CA	92509	909-685-5818	685-1240
Just Plain Dancin' & Co 6515 Clay	Riverside	CA	92509	909-681-6930	
Life Arts Center 3485 University Ave	Riverside	CA	92501	909-784-5849	
Main Street Mall 5th St & University Ave	Riverside	CA	92501	909-781-7335	
March Field Air Museum 22550 Van Buren Blvd March Air Force Base *Web:* www.marchfield.org ■ *E-mail:* info@marchfield.org	Riverside	CA	92518	909-697-6600	697-6605
Mission Inn Museum 3649 Mission Inn Ave	Riverside	CA	92501	909-788-9556	
Rancho Jurupa Regional Park 4800 Crestmore Rd	Riverside	CA	92519	909-684-7032	
Riverside Art Museum 3425 Mission Inn Ave	Riverside	CA	92501	909-684-7111	684-7332

Riverside — Attractions (Cont'd)

				Phone	Fax
Riverside Arts Foundation 3485 Mission Inn Ave Municipal Auditorium	Riverside	CA	92501	909-680-1345	680-1348
Web: www.ci.riverside.ca.us/arts_foundation/					
Riverside Ballet Theater 3840 Lemon St Aurea Vista Hotel	Riverside	CA	92501	909-787-7850	686-1240
Riverside Community Players 4026 14th St.	Riverside	CA	92501	909-369-1200	369-1261
Riverside County Philharmonic 3485 Mission Inn Ave Municipal Auditorium	Riverside	CA	92501	909-787-0251	787-8933
Riverside Marketplace Main St.	Riverside	CA	92501	909-715-3400	715-3404
Riverside Municipal Museum 3580 Mission Inn Ave	Riverside	CA	92501	909-782-5273	369-4970
Web: www.ci.riverside.ca.us/museum					
Sherman Indian High School Indian Museum 9010 Magnolia Ave	Riverside	CA	92503	909-276-6719	276-6336
Web: www.sihs.bia.edu/museum.html					
World Museum of Natural History 4700 Pierce St La Sierra University	Riverside	CA	92515	909-785-2209	

SPORTS TEAMS & FACILITIES

				Phone	Fax
California Speedway 9300 Cherry Ave.	Fontana	CA	91719	909-429-5000	429-5500
TF: 800-944-7223					

— Events —

	Phone
Apple Blossom Festival Weekend (April)	909-797-6833
Cherry Valley Cherry Festival (early June)	909-845-8466
Christmas on Main Street (mid-November)	909-781-7335
Cinco de Mayo (early May)	909-340-5906
Concerts in the Park (July-August)	909-780-6222
Family Village Festival (late October)	909-782-5273
Festival of Lights (November)	909-781-7335
Festival of Trees (late November)	909-875-8756
Harvest Festival (mid-September)	707-778-6300
Independence Day Celebration (July 4)	909-683-7100
Mission Inn 5K/10K Run (mid-November)	909-781-8241
Riverside County Fair & National Date Festival (mid-late February)	760-863-8247
Riverside Dickens Festival (early February)	909-781-3168
Riverside Orange Blossom Festival (late April)	909-715-3400

Sacramento

The city of Sacramento began when Captain John Sutter founded the colony of New Helvetia in 1839. After the Gold Rush drove Sutter's workers from the area, his son used a land inheritance to establish the town of Sacramento City. The city's location at the gateway to Gold Rush country helped it to grow and prosper. This history is displayed at the Old Sacramento Historic District, located on the banks of the Sacramento River. The district's shops and restaurants have been restored to their 1800s appearance, and old-time paddlewheelers grace the waterfront. Nearby Sutter's Fort State Historic Park honors the city's original founder.

Population	404,168	**Longitude**	121-49-33 W
Area (Land)	96.3 sq mi	**County**	Sacramento
Area (Water)	2.2 sq mi	**Time Zone**	PST
Elevation	25 ft	**Area Code/s**	916
Latitude	38-58-17 N		

— Average Temperatures and Precipitation —

TEMPERATURES

	Jan	Feb	Mar	Apr	May	Jun	Jul	Aug	Sep	Oct	Nov	Dec
High	53	60	64	71	80	88	93	92	87	78	63	53
Low	38	41	43	46	50	55	58	58	56	50	43	38

PRECIPITATION

	Jan	Feb	Mar	Apr	May	Jun	Jul	Aug	Sep	Oct	Nov	Dec
Inches	3.7	2.9	2.6	1.2	0.3	0.1	0.1	0.1	0.4	1.1	2.7	2.5

— Important Phone Numbers —

	Phone		Phone
AAA	916-331-7610	**Poison Control Center**	800-876-4766
American Express Travel	916-441-1526	**Road Conditions**	800-427-7623
Emergency	911	**Time**	530-767-2676
HotelDocs	800-468-3537	**Weather**	916-646-2000

— Information Sources —

				Phone	Fax
Better Business Bureau Serving North Central California 400 'S' St	Sacramento	CA	95814	916-443-6843	443-0376
Web: www.sacramento.bbb.org					
Downtown Sacramento Partnership Inc 900 J St 2nd Fl.	Sacramento	CA	95814	916-442-8575	442-2053
Sacramento City Hall 915 'I' St Rm 304	Sacramento	CA	95814	916-264-5427	264-7672
Web: www.sacto.org ■ *E-mail:* city@sacto.org					
Sacramento Convention & Visitors Bureau 1303 J St Suite 600	Sacramento	CA	95814	916-264-7777	264-7788
TF: 800-272-2334 ■ *Web:* www.sacramentocvb.org					
Sacramento Convention Center 1400 J St.	Sacramento	CA	95814	916-264-5291	264-7687
Web: www.sacto.org/cvsd/convctr/ ■ *E-mail:* lsu@sacto.org					
Sacramento County 700 H St Rm 7650	Sacramento	CA	95814	916-874-5833	874-5885
Web: www.co.sacramento.ca.us					
Sacramento Mayor 915 'I' St Rm 205	Sacramento	CA	95814	916-264-5300	264-7680
Web: www.ci.sacramento.ca.us/mayor.html					
Sacramento Metro Chamber of Commerce 917 7th St	Sacramento	CA	95814	916-552-6800	443-2672
Web: www.metrochamber.org ■ *E-mail:* chamber@metrochamber.org					
Sacramento Neighborhoods Planning & Development Services Dept 1231 'I' St Suite 300	Sacramento	CA	95814	916-264-5571	264-5328
Web: www.sacto.org/npdsd/about.htm					
Sacramento Public Library 828 'I' St	Sacramento	CA	95814	916-264-2770	264-2755
Web: www.sna.com/saclib					
Visitor Information Center 1303 J St Suite 600	Sacramento	CA	95814	916-264-7777	264-7788
Web: www.sacto.org/cvb/ ■ *E-mail:* cvb@sacto.org					

On-Line Resources

4Sacramento.com	www.4sacramento.com
About.com Guide to Sacramento	sacramento.about.com/local/caus/sacramento
Access Sacramento	www.sacramento.org
Anthill City Guide Sacramento	www.anthill.com/city.asp?city=sacramento
Area Guide Sacramento	sacramento.areaguides.net
City Knowledge Sacramento	www.cityknowledge.com/ca_sacramento.htm
CitySearch Sacramento	sacramento.citysearch.com
DigitalCity Sacramento	home.digitalcity.com/sacramento
Excite.com Sacramento City Guide	www.excite.com/travel/countries/united_states/california/sacramento
InSacramento.com	www.insacramento.com
NITC Travelbase City Guide Sacramento	www.travelbase.com/auto/guides/sacramento-area-ca.html
Sacramento Art Scene Online	sacarts.com/
Sacramento City Information	www.pageweavers.com/sacvisitors.html
Sacramento Fun	www.sactofun.com/
Sacramento Sites	www.worldofweb.com/sacsite.html
Sacramento Valley Online	www.tourvision.com/
Sacramento Web World	www.sacweb.com/sac_world/
Sacramento's InfoVillage	infovillage.com/
Sacramento.TheLinks.com	sacramento.thelinks.com/
SactoFUN.com	www.sactofun.com
SacTown	www.sactown.com

Sacramento (Cont'd)

— Transportation Services —

AIRPORTS

	Phone
■ **Sacramento Metropolitan Airport (SMF)**	
12 miles NW of downtown (approx 20 minutes)	916-929-5411

Web: www.quickaid.com/airports/smf

Airport Transportation

	Phone
Yellow Cab $26 fare to downtown	916-444-2222

Commercial Airlines

	Phone		Phone
America West	800-235-9292	**Shuttle by United**	800-748-8853
American	800-433-7300	**Southwest**	800-435-9792
American Eagle	800-433-7300	**TWA**	800-221-2000
Continental	916-369-2700	**United**	800-241-6522
Delta	800-221-1212	**United Express**	800-241-6522
Delta Connection	800-221-1212	**US Airways**	800-428-4322
Northwest	800-225-2525	**US Airways Express**	800-428-4322

Charter Airlines

	Phone
Horizon Helicopters	916-966-8181

CAR RENTALS

	Phone		Phone
Avis	916-922-5601	**Hertz**	916-927-3882
Budget	916-922-7316	**National**	916-568-2415
Dollar	916-447-4455	**Senator**	916-392-4225
Enterprise	916-349-8000	**Thrifty**	916-447-2847

LIMO/TAXI

	Phone		Phone
California Limousine	916-944-3600	**Shamrock AeroLimo & Taxi**	916-456-2222
Carey Limousine	916-485-7268	**Universal Limousine**	916-920-1123
Sacramento Independent Taxi	916-457-4862	**Yellow Cab**	916-444-2222

MASS TRANSIT

	Phone
Regional Transit $1.25 Base fare	916-321-2877
River Otter Taxi Co $5 Base fare	916-448-4333
Sacramento Hotel Shuttle Free	916-321-2877

RAIL/BUS

				Phone
Amtrak Station 401 'I' St. *TF:* 800-872-7245	Sacramento	CA	95814	916-444-7094
Greyhound Bus Station 715 L St *TF:* 800-231-2222	Sacramento	CA	95814	916-444-7270

— Accommodations —

HOTEL RESERVATION SERVICES

	Phone	Fax
California Reservations *TF:* 800-576-0003 ■ *Web:* www.cal-res.com	415-252-1107	252-1483
California Suites Reservations *TF:* 800-363-9779 ■ *Web:* www.calsuites.com	916-363-9700	363-9465
Oakwood Corporate Housing *TF:* 800-483-1335	916-631-3777	631-3773

HOTELS, MOTELS, RESORTS

				Phone	Fax
Amber House Bed & Breakfast Inn 1315 22nd St *TF:* 800-755-6526	Sacramento	CA	95816	916-444-8085	552-6529
Auberge du Soleil 180 Rutherford Hill Rd *TF:* 800-348-5406 ■ *Web:* www.aubergedusoleil.com ■ *E-mail:* info@aubergedusoleil.com	Rutherford	CA	94573	707-963-1211	963-8764
Best Western Expo Inn 1413 Howe Ave *TF:* 800-528-1234	Sacramento	CA	95825	916-922-9833	922-3384
Best Western John Jay Inn 15 Massie Ct *TF:* 800-528-1234	Sacramento	CA	95823	916-689-4425	689-8045
Best Western Sandman 236 Jibboom St *TF:* 800-528-1234	Sacramento	CA	95814	916-443-6515	443-8346
Best Western Sutter House 1100 H St *TF:* 800-830-1314	Sacramento	CA	95814	916-441-1314	441-5961
Canterbury Inn 1900 Canterbury Rd *TF:* 800-932-3492	Sacramento	CA	95815	916-927-3492	641-8594
Capitol Inn 228 Jibboom St	Sacramento	CA	95814	916-443-4811	443-4907
Capitol Plaza Holiday Inn 300 J St *TF:* 800-465-4329	Sacramento	CA	95814	916-446-0100	446-0117
Clarion Hotel 700 16th St *TF:* 800-443-0880	Sacramento	CA	95814	916-444-8000	442-8129
Days Inn North Highlands 3425 Orange Grove Ave *TF:* 800-329-7466	Sacramento	CA	95660	916-488-4100	489-0286
Delta King Riverboat Hotel 1000 Front St *TF:* 800-825-5464 ■ *Web:* www.deltaking.com/ ■ *E-mail:* dking@deltaking.com	Sacramento	CA	95814	916-444-5464	447-5959
Desert Sand Inn 623 16th St	Sacramento	CA	95814	916-444-7530	444-0640
Doubletree Hotel 2001 Point West Way *TF:* 800-222-8733 ■ *Web:* www.doubletreehotels.com/DoubleT/Hotel121/140/140Main.htm	Sacramento	CA	95815	916-929-8855	564-7706
Econo Lodge 711 16th St. *TF:* 800-553-2666	Sacramento	CA	95814	916-443-6631	442-7251
Executive Inn 2030 Arden Way *TF:* 800-793-2030 ■ *Web:* www.executiveinn.com ■ *E-mail:* executiveinn@worldnet.att.net	Sacramento	CA	95825	916-929-5600	929-2419
Governor's Inn 210 Richards Blvd *TF:* 800-999-6689 ■ *Web:* www.governorsinn.com	Sacramento	CA	95814	916-448-7224	448-7382
Hawthorn Hotel 321 Bercut Dr *TF:* 800-767-1777	Sacramento	CA	95814	916-441-1444	441-6530
Heritage Hotel 1780 Tribute Rd *TF:* 800-972-3976	Sacramento	CA	95815	916-929-7900	921-1326
Hilton Inn Sacramento 2200 Harvard St *TF:* 800-344-4321 ■ *Web:* www.hilton.com/hotels/SMFHIHF/index.html	Sacramento	CA	95815	916-922-4700	922-8418
Holiday Inn Rancho Cordova 11131 Folsom Blvd *TF:* 800-465-4329	Rancho Cordova	CA	95670	916-635-0666	635-3297
Holiday Inn Sacramento Northeast 5321 Date Ave *TF:* 800-388-9284	Sacramento	CA	95841	916-338-5800	334-2868
Host Airport Hotel 6945 Airport Blvd *TF:* 800-903-4678 ■ *Web:* www.hostairporthotel.com ■ *E-mail:* info@hostairporthotel.com	Sacramento	CA	95837	916-922-8071	929-8636
Howard Johnson Hotel & Conference Center 3343 Bradshaw Rd *TF:* 800-446-4656	Sacramento	CA	95827	916-366-1266	366-1266
Hyatt Regency Sacramento 1209 L St. *TF:* 800-233-1234 ■ *Web:* www.hyatt.com/usa/sacramento/hotels/hotel_sacra.html	Sacramento	CA	95814	916-443-1234	321-6699
La Quinta Inn 200 Jibboom St *TF:* 800-531-5900	Sacramento	CA	95814	916-448-8100	447-3621
Madrona Manor 1001 Westside Rd *TF:* 800-258-4003	Healdsburg	CA	95448	707-433-4231	433-0703
Meadowood Resort 900 Meadowood Ln *TF:* 800-458-8080 ■ *Web:* www.relaischateaux.fr/meadowood ■ *E-mail:* meadowood@relaischateaux.fr	Saint Helena	CA	94574	707-963-3646	963-3532
Quality Inn 818 15th St *TF:* 800-228-5151	Sacramento	CA	95814	916-444-3980	444-2991
Radisson Hotel Sacramento 500 Leisure Ln *TF:* 800-333-3333	Sacramento	CA	95815	916-922-2020	922-0391
Ramada Inn Sacramento 2600 Auburn Blvd *TF:* 800-272-6232	Sacramento	CA	95821	916-487-7600	481-7112
Red Lion Hotel 1401 Arden Way *TF:* 800-733-5466	Sacramento	CA	95815	916-922-8041	922-0386
Red Roof Inn 3796 Northgate Blvd *TF:* 800-843-9999	Sacramento	CA	95834	916-927-7117	646-1433
Residence Inn by Marriott 1530 Howe Ave *TF:* 800-331-3131 ■ *Web:* www.residenceinn.com/SACEX	Sacramento	CA	95825	916-920-9111	921-5664
Sheraton Sacremento Rancho Cordova Hotel 11211 Point East Dr *TF:* 800-851-2400	Rancho Cordova	CA	95742	916-638-1100	638-5803
Silverado Country Club & Resort 1600 Atlas Peak Rd *TF:* 800-532-0500 ■ *Web:* www.silveradoresort.com ■ *E-mail:* info@silveradoresort.com	Napa	CA	94558	707-257-5460	257-5425
Sterling Hotel 1300 H St *TF:* 800-365-7660	Sacramento	CA	95818	916-448-1300	448-8066
Travelodge Capitol Center 1111 H St *TF:* 800-578-7878	Sacramento	CA	95814	916-444-8880	447-7540

Sacramento — Hotels, Motels, Resorts (Cont'd)

				Phone	Fax
Vagabond Inn 909 3rd St.	Sacramento	CA	95814	916-446-1481	448-0364
TF: 800-522-1555					
Vizcaya 2019 21st St.	Sacramento	CA	95818	916-455-5243	455-6102
TF: 800-456-2019 ■ *Web:* www.sleepingsacramento.com					

— Restaurants —

				Phone
Aioli Bodega Espanola (Spanish) 1800 L St	Sacramento	CA	95814	916-447-9440
Alamar Restaurant (American) 5999 Garden Hwy	Sacramento	CA	95837	916-922-0200
Amarin Thai Cuisine (Thai) 900 12th St.	Sacramento	CA	95814	916-447-9063
Biba (Italian) 2801 Capitol Ave	Sacramento	CA	95816	916-455-2422
Web: biba-restaurant.com/				
Bonnlair (European) 3651 J St.	Sacramento	CA	95816	916-455-7155
Cafe Vinoteca (Italian) 3535 Fair Oaks Blvd	Sacramento	CA	95864	916-487-1331
California Fats (California) 1015 Front St.	Sacramento	CA	95814	916-441-7966
Chanterelle (Continental) 1300 H St.	Sacramento	CA	95814	916-442-0451
Christophe's (French) 2304 E Bidwell St.	Folsom	CA	95630	916-983-4883
Web: www.christophes.com				
Ciao-Yama Restaurant (Italian/Japanese) 1209 L St	Sacramento	CA	95814	916-443-1234
City Treasure (California) 1730 L St.	Sacramento	CA	95814	916-447-7380
Dawson's (Steak/Seafood) 1209 L St	Sacramento	CA	95814	916-443-1234
Fat City Bar & Cafe (American) 1001 Front St.	Sacramento	CA	95814	916-446-6768
Web: www.pageweavers.com/fatcity/				
Firehouse The (American) 1112 2nd St	Sacramento	CA	95814	916-442-4772
Web: www.firehouseoldsac.com/ ■ *E-mail:* fireno3@aol.com				
Fox & Goose Public House (English) 1001 R St	Sacramento	CA	95814	916-443-8825
Web: foxandgoose.com/				
Frank Fat's (Chinese) 806 L St	Sacramento	CA	95814	916-442-7092
Frasinetti's Winery & Restaurant (Italian) 7395 Frasinetti Rd	Sacramento	CA	95828	916-383-2444
Fuji Sukiyaki (Japanese) 2422 13th St.	Sacramento	CA	95818	916-446-4135
Habanero Cava Latina (Cuban) 2115 J St Suite 101	Sacramento	CA	95816	916-492-0333
Hard Rock Cafe (American) 545 Downtown Plaza Suite C-103.	Sacramento	CA	95814	916-441-5591
Harlow's (Italian) 2708 J St	Sacramento	CA	95816	916-441-4693
Web: www.harlows.com/				
Harvard Street Bar & Grill (California) 2200 Harvard St.	Sacramento	CA	95815	916-922-4700
Hogshead Brew Pub (American) 114 J St.	Sacramento	CA	95814	916-443-2739
Hot & Spicy (Cajun) 1023-A Front St	Sacramento	CA	95814	916-443-5051
Jammin' Salmon Restaurant (Seafood) 1801 Garden Hwy.	Sacramento	CA	95833	916-929-6232
Kip's Kabob (Australian) 1000 'I' St.	Sacramento	CA	95814	916-498-9171
Mace's (American) 501 Pavilion Ln	Sacramento	CA	95825	916-922-0222
Max's Opera Cafe (American) 1735 Arden Way.	Sacramento	CA	95815	916-927-6297
O'Mally's Irish Pub & Restaurant (Irish) 1109 2nd St	Sacramento	CA	95814	916-492-1230
Paragary's Bar & Oven (Italian) 1401 28th St.	Sacramento	CA	95816	916-457-5737
Pilothouse Restaurant (Continental) 1000 Front St	Sacramento	CA	95814	916-441-4440
Rio City Cafe (American) 1110 Front St	Sacramento	CA	95814	916-442-8226
River City Brewing Co (California) 545 Downtown Plaza	Sacramento	CA	95814	916-447-2739
Web: www.rivercitybrewing.com				
Royal Hong King Lum (Chinese) 419 J St.	Sacramento	CA	95814	916-443-1584
Rusty Duck (American) 500 Bercut Dr	Sacramento	CA	95814	916-441-1191
Scott's Seafood Grill & Bar (Seafood) 545 Munroe St	Sacramento	CA	95825	916-489-1822
Slocum House (Continental) 7992 California Ave	Fair Oaks	CA	95628	916-961-7211
Tapa the World (Spanish) 2115 J St	Sacramento	CA	95816	916-442-4353
Texas Bar-B-Que (Barbecue) 180 Otto Cir.	Sacramento	CA	95822	916-424-3520
Tokio Restaurant (Japanese) 428 J St	Sacramento	CA	95814	916-447-7788
Tower Cafe (International) 1518 Broadway	Sacramento	CA	95818	916-441-0222
Twenty-Eight (California) 28th & N Sts.	Sacramento	CA	95816	916-456-2800
Virga's (Italian) 1501 14th St	Sacramento	CA	95814	916-442-8516

— Goods and Services —

SHOPPING

				Phone	Fax
Antique Plaza 11395 Folsom Blvd.	Rancho Cordova	CA	95742	916-852-8517	852-8746
Web: www.antiqueplazaonline.com					
Arden Fair Mall 1689 Arden Way	Sacramento	CA	95815	916-920-1167	920-8652
Web: www.ardenfair.com/ ■ *E-mail:* ardenfair@hotmail.com					
Country Club Plaza 2401 Butano Dr	Sacramento	CA	95825	916-481-6716	481-5350
Downtown Plaza 547 L St	Sacramento	CA	95814	916-442-4000	
Florin Mall 6117 Florin Rd.	Sacramento	CA	95823	916-421-0881	422-1534
Web: www.florinmall.com ■ *E-mail:* info@florinmall.com					
Folsom Premium Outlets 13000 Folsom Blvd.	Folsom	CA	95630	916-985-0313	985-0830
Macy's 414 K St Downtown Plaza Mall	Sacramento	CA	95814	916-444-3333	
Old Sacramento Public Market 1101 2nd St.	Sacramento	CA	95814	916-442-7644	264-8465
Web: www.oldsacramento.com/public_market.htmlx					
■ *E-mail:* oldsac@sacto.org					
Pavilions 563 Pavilions Ln.	Sacramento	CA	95825	916-925-4463	
Sacramento's Antique Row 57th St-betw H & J Sts	Sacramento	CA	95819	916-739-1757	
Sunrise Mall 6041 Sunrise Mall	Citrus Heights	CA	95610	916-961-7150	961-7326
Web: www.sunrise-mall.com					
Town & Country Village 7750 College Town Dr Suite 350	Sacramento	CA	95826	916-383-3333	383-3974

BANKS

				Phone	Fax
Bank of America National Trust & Savings Assn 555 Capitol Mall	Sacramento	CA	95814	916-373-6920	
River City Bank 2485 Natomas Park Dr.	Sacramento	CA	95833	916-920-2265	567-2784
Sacramento Commercial Bank 525 J St	Sacramento	CA	95814	916-443-4700	443-8076
Union Bank 700 L St.	Sacramento	CA	95814	916-321-3164	442-2176*
**Fax:* Cust Svc					
Washington Mutual Bank 930 K St.	Sacramento	CA	95814	916-326-4500	326-4563
TF: 800-788-7000					
Wells Fargo Bank 400 Capitol Mall.	Sacramento	CA	95814	916-440-4342	492-9055*
**Fax:* Cust Svc					

BUSINESS SERVICES

	Phone		Phone
Courier Express	916-922-5820	**Kinko's**	916-731-4012
Express Personnel Services	916-484-0944	**Manpower Temporary Services**	916-569-2710
Federal Express	800-463-3339	**Olsten Staffing Services**	916-924-3161
Interim Industrial Staffing	916-927-7789	**Post Office**	800-275-8777
Kelly Services	916-441-2440	**UPS**	800-742-5877

— Media —

PUBLICATIONS

				Phone	Fax
Sacramento Bee‡ PO Box 15779	Sacramento	CA	95852	916-321-1000	321-1109
TF Circ: 800-876-8700 ■ *Web:* www.sacbee.com					
Sacramento Business Journal 1401 21st St Suite 200	Sacramento	CA	95814	916-447-7661	444-7779
Web: www.amcity.com/sacramento/					
Sacramento Magazine 4471 D St.	Sacramento	CA	95819	916-452-6200	452-6061
Web: www.sacmag.com					

‡Daily newspapers

TELEVISION

				Phone	Fax
KCRA-TV Ch 3 (NBC) 3 Television Cir	Sacramento	CA	95814	916-446-3333	441-4050
Web: www.kcra.com					
KMAX-TV Ch 31 (UPN) 500 Media Pl	Sacramento	CA	95815	916-925-3100	921-3050
Web: www.paramountstations.com/KMAX					
KNSO-TV Ch 51 (WB) 142 N 9th St Suite 8	Modesto	CA	95350	209-529-5100	575-4547
KOVR-TV Ch 13 (CBS) 2713 KOVR Dr	West Sacramento	CA	95605	916-374-1313	374-1304
Web: www.kovr.com					
KQCA-TV Ch 58 (WB) 58 Television Cir	Sacramento	CA	95814	916-447-5858	441-4050
KTXL-TV Ch 40 (Fox) 4655 Fruitridge Rd.	Sacramento	CA	95820	916-454-4422	739-0559
KUVS-TV Ch 19 (Uni) 1710 Arden Way	Sacramento	CA	95815	916-927-1900	614-1906
KVIE-TV Ch 6 (PBS) 2595 Capitol Oaks Dr.	Sacramento	CA	95833	916-929-5843	929-7367
Web: www.kvie.org ■ *E-mail:* member@kvie.org					
KXTV-TV Ch 10 (ABC) 400 Broadway.	Sacramento	CA	95818	916-441-2345	447-6107
Web: www.kxtv10.com ■ *E-mail:* kxtv10@kxtv10.com					

RADIO

				Phone	Fax
KCTC-AM 1320 kHz (Nost) 5345 Madison Ave	Sacramento	CA	95841	916-334-7777	334-1092
KDND-FM 107.9 MHz (CHR) 5345 Madison Ave	Sacramento	CA	95841	916-334-7777	334-1092
KFBK-AM 1530 kHz (N/T) 1440 Ethan Way Suite 200.	Sacramento	CA	95825	916-929-5325	921-5555
Web: www.kfbk.com					
KFIA-AM 710 kHz (Rel) 1425 River Park Dr Suite 520.	Sacramento	CA	95815	916-924-0710	924-1587
KGBY-FM 92.5 MHz (AC) 1440 Ethan Way Suite 200.	Sacramento	CA	95825	916-929-5325	646-6864
Web: www.y92.com ■ *E-mail:* webpage@y92.com					

Sacramento — Radio (Cont'd)

Name / Address	City	State	ZIP	Phone	Fax
KHTK-AM 1140 kHz (Sports)					
5244 Madison Ave	Sacramento	CA	95841	916-338-9200	338-9159
Web: www.khtk.com					
KHYL-FM 101.1 MHz (Oldies)					
1440 Ethan Way Suite 200	Sacramento	CA	95825	916-929-5325	925-0128
KHZZ-FM 104.3 MHz (Oldies)					
298 Commerce Cir	Sacramento	CA	95815	916-641-1043	641-1078
KNCI-FM 105.1 MHz (Ctry)					
5244 Madison Ave	Sacramento	CA	95841	916-338-9200	338-9208*
**Fax:* Sales					
KQPT-FM 100.5 MHz (Oldies)					
280 Commerce Cir	Sacramento	CA	95815	916-635-1005	923-6825
Web: www.radiozone.com					
KRAK-AM 1470 kHz (Ctry)					
5244 Madison Ave	Sacramento	CA	95841	916-338-9200	338-9202
KRXQ-FM 98.5 MHz (Rock)					
5345 Madison Ave	Sacramento	CA	95841	916-334-7777	339-4223
Web: www.krxq98rock.com					
KSEG-FM 96.9 MHz (CR)					
5345 Madison Ave	Sacramento	CA	95841	916-334-9690	339-4280
Web: www.eagle969.com					
KSFM-FM 102.5 MHz (CHR)					
1750 Howe Ave Suite 500	Sacramento	CA	95825	916-920-1025	929-5341
Web: www.ksfm.com					
KSSJ-FM 94.7 MHz (CR)					
5345 Madison Ave	Sacramento	CA	95841	916-334-7777	339-4290
Web: www.kssj.com ■ *E-mail:* comments@kssj.com					
KSTE-AM 650 kHz (N/T)					
1440 Ethan Way Suite 200	Sacramento	CA	95825	916-929-5325	921-5555*
**Fax:* News Rm					
KWOD-FM 106.5 MHz (Alt)					
801 K St 27th Fl	Sacramento	CA	95814	916-448-5000	448-1655
Web: www.kwod.com					
KXJZ-FM 88.9 MHz (NPR)					
3416 American River Dr Suite B	Sacramento	CA	95864	916-480-5900	487-3348
Web: www.csus.edu/npr ■ *E-mail:* npr@csus.edu					
KXPR-FM 90.9 MHz (NPR)					
3416 American River Dr Suite B	Sacramento	CA	95864	916-480-5900	487-3348
TF: 877-480-5900 ■ *Web:* www.csus.edu/npr ■ *E-mail:* npr@csus.edu					
KYMX-FM 96.1 MHz (AC)					
280 Commerce Cir	Sacramento	CA	95815	916-923-6800	923-9696
Web: www.kymx.com					
KZSA-FM 92.1 MHz (Span)					
1436 Auburn Blvd	Sacramento	CA	95815	916-646-4000	646-1688
KZZO-FM 100.5 MHz (AAA)					
280 Commerce Cir	Sacramento	CA	95815	916-923-6800	923-9696
Web: www.thezone.com					

— Colleges/Universities —

Name / Address	City	State	ZIP	Phone	Fax
American River College					
4700 College Oak Dr	Sacramento	CA	95841	916-484-8011	484-8674
Web: www.arc.losrios.cc.ca.us/					
California State University Sacramento					
6000 J St	Sacramento	CA	95819	916-278-6011	278-5603
Web: www.csus.edu					
Cosumnes River College					
8401 Center Parkway	Sacramento	CA	95823	916-688-7410	688-7467
Web: wserver.crc.losrios.cc.ca.us					
D-Q University PO Box 409	Davis	CA	95617	530-758-0470	758-4891
Heald Business College Rancho Cordova 2910 Prospect Park Dr	Rancho Cordova	CA	95670	916-638-1616	853-8282
TF: 800-499-4333					
ITT Technical Institute					
10863 Gold Ctr Dr	Rancho Cordova	CA	95670	916-851-3900	851-9225
TF: 800-488-8466 ■ *Web:* www.itt-tech.edu					
National Center of Continuing Education					
114 N Sunrise Ave Suite 5B	Roseville	CA	95661	916-786-4626	786-4603
TF: 800-824-1254 ■ *Web:* www.nursece.com ■ *E-mail:* ncce@worldnet.att.net					
Sacramento City College					
3835 Freeport Blvd	Sacramento	CA	95822	916-558-2111	558-2190
Web: www.scc.losrios.cc.ca.us/					
Sierra Community College 5000 Rocklin Rd	Rocklin	CA	95677	916-624-3333	781-0455
Web: www.sierra.cc.ca.us					
Trinity Life Bible College					
5225 Hillsdale Blvd	Sacramento	CA	95842	916-348-4689	334-2315

— Hospitals —

Name / Address	City	State	ZIP	Phone	Fax
Kaiser Permanente Medical Center					
2025 Morse Ave	Sacramento	CA	95825	916-973-5000	973-7437*
**Fax:* Admitting					
Kaiser Permanente Medical Center					
6600 Bruceville Rd	Sacramento	CA	95823	916-688-2000	688-2978
TF: 800-464-4000					
Mercy General Hospital 4001 J St	Sacramento	CA	95819	916-453-4545	453-4295*
**Fax:* Admitting					
Mercy San Juan Hospital 6501 Coyle Ave	Carmichael	CA	95608	916-537-5000	537-5427
Methodist Hospital 7500 Hospital Dr.	Sacramento	CA	95823	916-423-3000	423-5954*
**Fax:* Admitting					
Roseville Medical Center 1 Medical Plaza	Roseville	CA	95661	916-781-1000	781-1624*
**Fax:* Admitting					
Sutter General Hospital 2801 L St	Sacramento	CA	95816	916-454-2222	733-8894
Sutter Memorial Hospital 5151 F St	Sacramento	CA	95819	916-454-3333	733-8135*
**Fax:* Admitting					
University of California Davis Medical Center 2315 Stockton Blvd	Sacramento	CA	95817	916-734-3096	734-8080
Web: www.ucdmc.ucdavis.edu					
Woodland Memorial Hospital					
1325 Cottonwood St	Woodland	CA	95695	530-662-3961	666-4363*
**Fax:* Admitting					

— Attractions —

Name / Address	City	State	ZIP	Phone	Fax
Artists' Collaborative Gallery					
1007 2nd St	Sacramento	CA	95814	916-444-3764	
Web: www.gogh.com/acg					
Best of Broadway					
4010 El Camino Ave Hiriam Johnson High School	Sacramento	CA	95821	916-974-6280	974-6281
Big Four Building 111 'I' St	Sacramento	CA	95814	916-445-6645	
California Exposition & State Fair					
1600 Exposition Blvd.	Sacramento	CA	95815	916-263-3247	263-3304
Web: www.calexpo.org					
California Military Museum 1119 2nd St.	Sacramento	CA	95814	916-442-2883	442-7532
California Peace Officers Memorial					
10th St & Capitol Mall	Sacramento	CA	95814	530-676-3315	
California State Archives 1020 'O' St	Sacramento	CA	95814	916-653-7715	653-7134
Web: www.ss.ca.gov/archives/archives.htm					
California State Capitol 10th & L Sts	Sacramento	CA	95814	916-324-0333	445-3628
California State Indian Musuem					
2618 K St	Sacramento	CA	95816	916-324-7405	322-5231
California State Railroad Museum					
111 'I' St	Sacramento	CA	95814	916-445-6645	327-5655
Web: www.csrmf.org ■ *E-mail:* csrmf@csrmf.org					
Camellia Symphony Orchestra					
PO Box 19786	Sacramento	CA	95819	916-929-6655	929-4292
Cathedral of the Blessed Sacrament					
1017 11th St	Sacramento	CA	95814	916-444-3070	
Crest Theatre 1013 K St	Sacramento	CA	95814	916-442-7378	442-5939
Web: www.thecrest.com ■ *E-mail:* info@thecrest.com					
Crocker Art Museum 216 'O' St	Sacramento	CA	95814	916-264-5423	264-7372
Web: capital.sacto.org/crocker ■ *E-mail:* crocker@sacto.org					
Del Paso Park I-80 Old Roseville Rd	Sacramento	CA	95814	916-264-5200	
Del Paso Regional Park					
I-80 & Auburn St	Sacramento	CA	95820	916-566-6581	
di Rosa Preserve 5200 Carneros Hwy	Napa	CA	94559	707-226-5991	255-8934
Discover California Wine Tasting Room					
129 J St	Sacramento	CA	95814	916-443-8275	443-8285
Discovery Museum 101 'I' St	Sacramento	CA	95814	916-264-7057	264-5100
Discovery Museum Learning Center					
3615 Auburn Blvd	Sacramento	CA	95821	916-575-3941	575-3925
Web: www.thediscovery.org					
Fairytale Town 3901 Land Park Dr	Sacramento	CA	95822	916-264-5233	
Governor's Mansion 1520 H St.	Sacramento	CA	95814	916-324-0539	
Governor's Mansion State Historic Park					
1526 H St	Sacramento	CA	95814	916-324-7405	
Historic City Cemetery 1000 Broadway	Sacramento	CA	95818	916-264-5621	
Lassen Volcanic National Park PO Box 100	Mineral	CA	96063	530-595-4444	595-3262
Web: www.nps.gov/lavo/					
McClellan Aviation Museum					
3204 Palm Ave	Sacramento	CA	95652	916-643-3192	643-0389
Napa Valley Wine Train 1275 McKinstry St.	Napa	CA	94559	707-253-2111	253-9264
TF: 800-427-4124 ■ *Web:* www.winetrain.com					
New Marine World Theme Park					
2001 Marine World Pkwy	Vallejo	CA	94589	707-644-4000	644-0241
Web: www.freerun.com/napavalley/outdoor/marinewo/marinewo.html					
Nimbus Fish Hatcheries					
2001 Nimbus Rd.	Rancho Cordova	CA	95670	916-358-2820	

Sacramento — Attractions (Cont'd)

				Phone	Fax
Old Chinatown-Sacramento 'Yee Fow' Chinatown Mall-betw 3rd & 5th Sts.	Sacramento	CA	95814	916-448-6465	448-8969
Old Eagle Theatre 925 Front St	Sacramento	CA	95814	916-323-6343	327-0953
Old Sacramento Historic District 1111 2nd St Suite 300	Sacramento	CA	95814	916-264-7031	264-7286
Web: www.oldsacramento.com ■ *E-mail:* oldsac@sacto.org					
Old Sacramento Public Market 1101 2nd St.	Sacramento	CA	95814	916-442-7644	264-8465
Web: www.oldsacramento.com/public_market.htmlx ■ *E-mail:* oldsac@sacto.org					
Old Sacramento Schoolhouse Front & L Sts	Sacramento	CA	95814	916-483-8818	
Port of Sacramento 3251 Beacon Blvd	West Sacramento	CA	95691	916-371-8000	372-4802
Web: www.portofsacramento.com					
Roseville Telephone Museum 106 Vernon St	Roseville	CA	95678	916-786-1621	786-7170
Sacramento Ballet 1631 K St.	Sacramento	CA	95814	916-552-5800	552-5815
Web: www.sacballet.org					
Sacramento Community Center Theater 13th & L Sts	Sacramento	CA	95814	916-264-5181	264-7317
Sacramento Opera Assn 3811 J St.	Sacramento	CA	95816	916-737-1000	737-1032
Sacramento Philharmonic Orchestra 900 Howe Ave	Sacramento	CA	95825	916-922-9200	
Sacramento Theatre Co 1419 H St.	Sacramento	CA	95814	916-443-6722	446-4066
Web: www.sactheatre.org					
Sacramento Traditional Jazz Society 2787 Del Monte St	West Sacramento	CA	95691	916-372-5277	372-3479
Web: www.sacjazz.com ■ *E-mail:* stjs@earthlink.net					
Sacramento Zoo 3930 W Land Park Dr	Sacramento	CA	95822	916-264-5166	264-5887
Web: www.saczoo.com					
Stanford Leland Mansion 800 N St.	Sacramento	CA	95814	916-324-0575	
Sutter's Fort State Historic Park 2701 L St	Sacramento	CA	95816	916-324-0539	
Web: cal-parks.ca.gov/DISTRICTS/goldrush/sfshp.htm					
Towe Ford Museum of Automotive History 2200 Front St.	Sacramento	CA	95818	916-442-6802	442-2646
Web: www.classicar.com/museums/toweford/toweford.htm					
Waterworld USA 1600 Exposition Blvd	Sacramento	CA	95815	916-924-3747	924-1314
Web: www.waterpark.com					
Wells Fargo History Museum 400 Capitol Mall Wells Fargo Ctr.	Sacramento	CA	95814	916-440-4161	498-0302
William Land Park 11th Ave & Land Park Dr.	Sacramento	CA	95814	916-264-5200	
Yeaw Effie Nature Center Ansel Hoffman Park 6700 Tarshes Dr	Carmichael	CA	95609	916-489-4918	489-4983

SPORTS TEAMS & FACILITIES

				Phone	Fax
Arco Arena 1 Sports Pkwy	Sacramento	CA	95834	916-928-0000	928-0727
Web: www.arcoarena.com					
California Exposition & State Fair 1600 Exposition Blvd.	Sacramento	CA	95815	916-263-3279	263-3198
Web: www.racingfairs.org/lr-calex.html					
Sacramento Geckos (soccer) 3301 Rosin Blvd Natomas High School Stadium	Sacramento	CA	95814	916-448-5425	448-4625
Sacramento Kings 1 Sports Pkwy Arco Arena	Sacramento	CA	95834	916-928-6900	928-0727
Web: www.nba.com/kings					
Sacramento Knights (soccer) 1 Sports Pkwy Arco Arena	Sacramento	CA	95834	916-928-3650	928-6919
Web: www.sacknights.com/					
Sacramento Monarchs (basketball) 1 Sports Pkwy Arco Arena	Sacramento	CA	95834	916-928-3641	
Web: www.wnba.com/monarchs					
Sacramento River Rats (hockey) 1600 Exposition Blvd CalExpo	Sacramento	CA	95852	916-263-3049	

— Events —

	Phone
Autorama (early February)	503-236-0632
Bockbierfest (early April)	916-442-7360
California International Marathon (early December)	916-983-4622
California State Fair (mid-August-early September)	916-263-3093
Chalk it Up to Sacramento! (late April)	916-484-5710
Chinese New Year Celebration (late February)	916-777-5880
Christmas Craft Faire (early December)	916-985-7452
Christmas Memories Celebration (December)	916-323-3047
Cinco de Mayo Celebrations (early May)	916-263-3021
Crawdad Festival (mid-June)	916-777-5880
Downtown Concert Series (early May-late August)	916-442-8575
Elk Grove Western Festival (early May)	916-685-3911
Fair Oaks Fiesta (early May)	916-967-2903
Fair Oaks Renaissance Tudor Fayre (late June)	916-966-1036
Fall Collectors' Faire (mid-September)	916-558-3912
Festa Italiana (mid-August)	916-482-5900
Festival of Cinema (mid-late September)	916-442-5189
Festival of the Arts (mid-April)	916-278-6156
Folsom Championship Rodeo (early July)	916-985-2698
Friday Night Concerts (early May-mid-July)	916-442-8575
Gift & Gourmet Show (mid-November)	916-483-9173
Greek Food Festival (early September)	916-443-2033
Highland Scottish Games (late April)	916-557-0764
International Railfair (early-mid-November)	916-991-4343
Japanese Cultural Bazaar (early August)	916-446-0121
LPGA Longs Drugs Challenge (late March-early April)	916-434-2224
Mardi Gras Parade (early February)	916-443-6223
Martin Luther King Community Celebration (mid-January)	916-395-1895
Native American Arts & Crafts Show (late November)	916-324-0971
Oktoberfest (early October)	916-442-7360
Old Sacramento Oktoberfest (mid-September)	916-558-3912
Pacific Coast Rowing Championship (mid-May)	916-985-7239
Pacific Rim Street Fest (mid-May)	916-264-7031
Pioneer Traders' & Crafts Faire (late April)	916-445-4422
Pony Express Reride (mid-June)	916-264-7031
Renaissance Faire & Tournament (mid-October)	916-355-7285
Sacramento Boat Show (mid-March)	916-263-3218
Sacramento Camellia Show (early March)	916-264-5181
Sacramento County Fair (early May)	916-263-2975
Sacramento Heritage Festival (early June)	916-481-2583
Sacramento Home & Garden Show (late February)	916-924-9934
Sacramento International Festival of Cinema (mid-late September)	916-442-7378
Sacramento Jazz Jubilee (late May)	916-372-5277
Sacramento Shakespeare Festival (July)	916-558-2228
Sacramento Sports Boat & RV Show (mid-February)	916-452-6403
Saint Patrick's Day Parade (mid-March)	916-264-7031
Shakespeare Lite (mid-June-mid-July)	916-442-8575
Spring Collectors' Fair (mid-April)	916-264-7031
Starlight Movie Series (June-August)	916-264-7031
Strauss Festival (late July)	916-685-3911
Sutter Street Antique Market (mid-April & mid-September)	916-985-7452
Sutter Street Arts & Crafts Fair (early May)	916-985-2698
Thursday Night Market (May-September)	916-442-8575
US National Handcar Races (mid-September)	916-445-1018
US Pro Water Ski & Pro Wake Board Tournament (late June)	800-334-6541
Water Festival (early June)	916-985-2698
Waterfront Art Fest (early May)	916-442-7644
Wednesday Farmers' Market (May-November)	916-442-8575

San Bernardino

The seat of the largest county in the contiguous United States, San Bernardino is known as the "Heart of the Inland Empire." The city is surrounded by the San Bernardino National Forest, which offers hiking, horseback riding, and mountain biking opportunities. San Bernardino is also located in close proximity to the San Bernardino Mountains and the San Gabriel Mountains, where visitors can take advantage of a number of ski areas. Each May, the city of San Bernardino hosts the National Orange Show, a two-week-long event featuring exhibits, rides, games, contests, animals, and live entertainment.

Population	186,402	**Longitude**	117-17-32 W
Area (Land)	55.1 sq mi	**County**	San Bernardino
Area (Water)	0.4 sq mi	**Time Zone**	PST
Elevation	1,049 ft	**Area Code/s**	909
Latitude	34-08-23 N		

— Average Temperatures and Precipitation —

TEMPERATURES

	Jan	Feb	Mar	Apr	May	Jun	Jul	Aug	Sep	Oct	Nov	Dec
High	67	69	70	76	81	89	97	96	91	83	73	67
Low	40	43	44	48	52	57	62	63	59	53	45	40

PRECIPITATION

	Jan	Feb	Mar	Apr	May	Jun	Jul	Aug	Sep	Oct	Nov	Dec
Inches	2.9	2.8	2.7	1.2	0.4	0.1	0.0	0.3	0.5	0.6	1.8	2.2

— Important Phone Numbers —

	Phone
AAA	909-381-2211
American Express Travel	909-793-7551
Dental Referral	909-370-2112
Emergency	911
Poison Control Center	800-777-6476
Time	909-853-1212
Travelers Aid	909-986-4988

— Information Sources —

				Phone	Fax
Better Business Bureau Serving Los Angeles Orange Riverside & San Bernardino Counties PO Box 970 *Web:* www.la.bbb.org	Colton	CA	92324	909-825-7280	825-6246
San Bernardino Area Chamber of Commerce PO Box 658	San Bernardino	CA	92402	909-885-7515	384-9979
San Bernardino City Hall 300 N 'D' St *Web:* www.ci.san-bernardino.ca.us	San Bernardino	CA	92418	909-384-5133	384-5067
San Bernardino Convention & Visitors Bureau 201 N 'E' St Suite 103 *TF:* 800-867-8366 ■ *Web:* san-bernardino.org ■ *E-mail:* cvb@san-bernardino.org	San Bernardino	CA	92401	909-889-3980	888-5998
San Bernardino County 351 N Arrowhead Ave 1st Fl *Web:* www.co.san-bernardino.ca.us	San Bernardino	CA	92415	909-387-3922	387-4428
San Bernardino Economic Development Agency 201 N 'E' St Suite 301 *Web:* www.sanbernardino-eda.org	San Bernardino	CA	92401	909-384-5081	888-9413
San Bernardino Mayor 300 N 'D' St	San Bernardino	CA	92418	909-384-5051	384-5067
San Bernardino Public Library 555 W 6th St *Web:* e2.empirenet.com/~sbpl	San Bernardino	CA	92410	909-381-8201	381-8229

On-Line Resources

Anthill City Guide San Bernardino	www.anthill.com/city.asp?city=sanbernardino
Excite.com San Bernardino City Guide	www.excite.com/travel/countries/united_states/california/san_bernardino
San Bernardino.com	www.sanbernardino.com
West Side Story Newspaper	www.westsidestory.com

— Transportation Services —

AIRPORTS

	Phone
■ **Ontario International Airport (ONT)** 20 miles SW of downtown San Bernardino (approx 20 minutes)	909-937-2700

Airport Transportation

	Phone
A-1 Ontario Express $31 fare to downtown	909-484-5757
SuperShuttle $28 fare to downtown San Bernardino	909-467-9600

Commercial Airlines

	Phone
Alaska	800-426-0333
America West	800-235-9292
American	800-433-7300
Continental	800-525-0280
Delta	800-221-1212
Northwest	800-225-2525
Pan Am	800-359-7262
SkyWest	800-453-9417
Southwest	800-435-9792
TWA	800-221-2000
United	800-241-6522
United Express	800-241-6522
US Airways Express	800-428-4322

Charter Airlines

	Phone
KMR Aviation	888-605-6366

CAR RENTALS

	Phone
Budget	909-889-0076
Enterprise	909-482-4800
Hertz	909-884-1808
Thrifty	909-988-8581

LIMO/TAXI

	Phone
Audrie's Tours & Limo	909-792-9229
Jaguar Limousines	909-864-2216
Secure Limousine	909-478-3380
Yellow Cab	909-884-1111

MASS TRANSIT

	Phone
Omnitrans Bus $.85 Base fare	909-889-0811

RAIL/BUS

				Phone
Amtrak Station 1170 W 3rd St *TF:* 800-872-7245	San Bernardino	CA	92410	909-884-1307
Greyhound Bus Station 596 N 'G' St *TF:* 800-231-2222	San Bernardino	CA	92410	909-884-4796

— Accommodations —

HOTELS, MOTELS, RESORTS

				Phone	Fax
Astro Motel 111 S 'E' St	San Bernardino	CA	92401	909-889-0417	888-3067
Claremont Inn 555 W Foothill Blvd *TF:* 800-854-5733	Claremont	CA	91711	909-626-2411	624-0756
Comfort Inn 1909 S Business Center Dr *TF:* 800-228-5150	San Bernardino	CA	92408	909-889-0090	889-9894
Continental 9 Motel 1150 'E' St *TF:* 800-843-5644	San Bernardino	CA	92408	909-885-9941	885-2377
E-Z 8 Motel 1750 S Waterman Ave	San Bernardino	CA	92408	909-888-4827	888-4827
Economy Inn 685 W 6th St	San Bernardino	CA	92410	909-888-5775	
El Patio Hotel 472 N Mt Vernon Ave	San Bernardino	CA	92411	909-885-5562	
La Quinta Inn 205 E Hospitality Ln *TF:* 800-531-5900	San Bernardino	CA	92408	909-888-7571	884-3864
Leisure Inn 777 W 6th St	San Bernardino	CA	92410	909-889-3561	884-7127
Motel 6 111 W Redlands Blvd *TF:* 800-466-8356	San Bernardino	CA	92408	909-825-6666	872-1104
Motel 6 1960 Ostrems Way *TF:* 800-466-8356	San Bernardino	CA	92407	909-887-8191	880-9231
Motel 7 1363 N 'E' St	San Bernardino	CA	92405	909-885-3444	885-0464
Radisson Hotel & Convention Center 295 N 'E' St	San Bernardino	CA	92401	909-381-6181	381-5288
San Bernardino Hilton Hotel 285 E Hospitality Ln *TF:* 800-445-8667	San Bernardino	CA	92408	909-889-0133	381-4299
Shilo Inn Hilltop Suites Hotel 3101 Temple Ave *TF:* 800-222-2244	Pomona	CA	91768	909-598-7666	598-5654
Super 8 Lodge 294 E Hospitality Ln *TF:* 800-800-8000	San Bernardino	CA	92408	909-381-1681	888-5120
Travelodge 225 E Hospitality Ln	San Bernardino	CA	92408	909-888-6777	885-6925
University Inn Motel 1914 S Tippecanoe Ave	San Bernardino	CA	92408	909-796-0254	

— Restaurants —

				Phone
Alfredo's Pizza & Pasta (Italian) 251 W Baseline St	San Bernardino	CA	92410	909-885-0218
Bamboo Garden (Chinese) 228 W Hospitality Ln	San Bernardino	CA	92408	909-890-0077
Bobby McGee's (American) 1905 S Commercenter Dr	San Bernardino	CA	92408	909-884-7233
Bon Appetito (Italian) 246 E Base Line St	San Bernardino	CA	92407	909-884-5054
Castaway The (American) 670 Kendall Dr	San Bernardino	CA	92407	909-881-1502
Chela's Restaurant (Salvadorian) 507 S Mt Vernon Ave	San Bernardino	CA	92410	909-381-3777
Court Street Bar & Grill (American) 440 W Court St	San Bernardino	CA	92401	909-888-3737
Delhi Palace (Indian) 2001 Diners Ct	San Bernardino	CA	92408	909-884-9966
El Paso Restaurant (Mexican) 900 N Mt Vernon Ave	San Bernardino	CA	92411	909-884-4112

San Bernardino — Restaurants (Cont'd)

				Phone
Gazzolo's (German) 132 E Highland Ave	San Bernardino	CA	92404	909-886-3213
Guadalaharry's (Mexican) 280 E Hospitality Ln	San Bernardino	CA	92408	909-889-8555
Hannah's Restaurant (American) 1355 E Highland Ave	San Bernardino	CA	92404	909-883-2242
Isabella's Ristorante Italiano (Italian) 201 N 'E' St	San Bernardino	CA	92401	909-884-2534
Korean Bar-b-que Restaurant (Korean) 127 E Highland Ave	San Bernardino	CA	92404	909-886-7506
Le Rendez Vous (French) 4775 N Sierra Way	San Bernardino	CA	92407	909-883-1231
Lotus Garden (Chinese) 111 E Hospitality Ln.	San Bernardino	CA	92408	909-381-6171
Love's Great Rib Restaurant (Barbecue) 808 W 3rd St.	San Bernardino	CA	92410	909-884-1161
Mazato of Japan (Japanese) 289 E Hospitality Ln	San Bernardino	CA	92408	909-888-3103
Molly's Cafe (American) 350 N 'D' St.	San Bernardino	CA	92401	909-888-1778
Napoli Itailian Restaurant (Italian) 24960 Redlands Blvd	San Bernardino	CA	92408	909-796-3770
Pig's Ear Pub (English) 987 S Diners Ct	San Bernardino	CA	92408	909-889-1442
Potiniere The (American) 285 E Hospitality Ln	San Bernardino	CA	92408	909-889-0133
Ramberto's (Mexican) 1705 S Tippecanoe Ave	San Bernardino	CA	92408	909-799-5451
South Sea Restaurant (Chinese) 204 E Hospitality Ln	San Bernardino	CA	92408	909-885-2338
Spencer's (American) 295 N 'E' St.	San Bernardino	CA	92401	909-381-6181
Spoons California Grill (American) 239 E Hospitality Ln	San Bernardino	CA	92408	909-381-3518
Thai Place (Thai) 1689 Kendall Dr Suite K1	San Bernardino	CA	92407	909-887-7644
Uptowner (Continental) 155 W Highland Ave	San Bernardino	CA	92405	909-882-1189
Vicky's Restaurant (American) 502 S Waterman Ave	San Bernardino	CA	92408	909-888-1171
Wong's Kitchen (Chinese) 2150 N 'E' St.	San Bernardino	CA	92405	909-883-5414

— Goods and Services —

SHOPPING

				Phone	Fax
Carousel Mall 295 Carousel Mall	San Bernardino	CA	92401	909-884-0106	885-6893
Inland Center Mall 500 Inland Center Dr.	San Bernardino	CA	92407	909-884-7268	381-5380
Main Street Downtown 201 N 'E' St	San Bernardino	CA	92401	909-381-5037	888-2576
Ontario Mills 1 Mills Cir. *Web:* ontariomills.com	Ontario	CA	91764	909-484-8300	484-8306
Plaza at West Covina 112 Plaza Dr. *Web:* www.westcovina.shoppingtown.com	West Covina	CA	91790	626-960-1881	337-3337

BANKS

				Phone	Fax
Bank of America 303 N 'D' St	San Bernardino	CA	92401	909-381-2494	
Business Bank of California 505 W 2nd St.	San Bernardino	CA	92401	909-885-0036	381-3975
Community Bank 1175 E Highland Ave.	San Bernardino	CA	92404	909-881-2323	881-3725
Washington Mutual Bank 2020 E Highland Ave.	San Bernardino	CA	92404	909-425-8300	425-8306
Wells Fargo Bank 334 W 3rd St. *TF:* 800-869-3557	San Bernardino	CA	92401	909-384-4805	381-6066

BUSINESS SERVICES

	Phone
DHL Worldwide Express	800-225-5345
Federal Express	800-238-5355
Kelly Services	909-381-4581
Kinko's	909-381-6282
Manpower Temporary Services	909-885-3461
Olsten Staffing Services	909-381-2251
Post Office	800-275-8777
UPS	800-742-5877

— Media —

PUBLICATIONS

				Phone	Fax
Rialto Record PO Box 6247 **Fax:* News Rm	San Bernardino	CA	92412	909-381-9898	384-0406*
Sun The‡ 399 N 'D' St. **Fax:* Edit ■ *Web:* www.sbcsun.com ■ *E-mail:* mail@sbcsun.com	San Bernardino	CA	92401	909-889-9666	885-8741*

‡Daily newspapers

TELEVISION

				Phone	Fax
KABC-TV Ch 7 (ABC) 4151 Prospect Ave *Web:* abcnews.go.com/local/kabc ■ *E-mail:* abc7@abc.com	Los Angeles	CA	90027	310-557-3200	557-3360
KCBS-TV Ch 2 (CBS) 6121 Sunset Blvd *Web:* www.kcbs2.com	Los Angeles	CA	90028	323-460-3000	460-3733
KCET-TV Ch 28 (PBS) 4401 Sunset Blvd *Web:* www.keet.org	Los Angeles	CA	90027	323-666-6500	953-5523
KNBC-TV Ch 4 (NBC) 3000 W Alameda Ave *Web:* www.knbc4la.com	Burbank	CA	91523	818-840-4444	840-3535
KTTV-TV Ch 11 (Fox) 1999 S Bundy Dr *Web:* www.fox11la.com ■ *E-mail:* talkback@fox11la.com	West Los Angeles	CA	90025	310-584-2000	584-2023

RADIO

				Phone	Fax
KABC-AM 790 kHz (N/T) 3321 S La Cienega Blvd. *Web:* www.kabc.com	Los Angeles	CA	90016	310-840-4900	838-5222
KBIG-FM 104.3 MHz (AC) 330 N Brand Blvd Suite 800 **Fax:* Sales ■ *Web:* www.kbig104.com	Glendale	CA	91203	818-546-1043	637-2267*
KCAL-AM 1410 kHz (Span) 1950 S Sunwest Ln Suite 302	San Bernardino	CA	92408	909-825-5020	884-5844
KCBS-FM 93.1 MHz (CR) 6121 Sunset Blvd *Web:* www.arrowfm.com	Los Angeles	CA	90028	323-460-3000	460-3733
KCXX-FM 103.9 MHz (Alt) 740 W 4th St *Web:* www.x1039.com/	San Bernardino	CA	92410	909-384-1039	888-7302
KFSG-FM 96.3 MHz (Rel) 1910 W Sunset Blvd Suite 480 *E-mail:* planetrock@rock411.com	Los Angeles	CA	90026	213-483-5374	484-8304
KFWB-AM 980 kHz (N/T) 6230 Yucca St *Web:* www.kfwb.com ■ *E-mail:* quake@kfwb.groupw.wec.com	Hollywood	CA	90028	323-462-5392	871-4670
KKLA-AM 1240 kHz (N/T) 992 Inland Center Dr.	San Bernardino	CA	92408	909-885-6555	381-9563
KLAX-FM 97.9 MHz (Span) 10281 W Pico Blvd **Fax:* Sales	Los Angeles	CA	90064	310-203-0900	203-8989*
KLOS-FM 95.5 MHz (Rock) 3321 S La Cienega Blvd. *Web:* www.955klos.com	Los Angeles	CA	90016	310-840-4900	558-7685
KNX-AM 1070 kHz (N/T) 6121 Sunset Blvd *Web:* www.knx1070.com	Los Angeles	CA	90028	323-460-3000	460-3275
KOST-FM 103.5 MHz (AC) 610 S Ardmore Ave. *TF:* 800-929-5678	Los Angeles	CA	90005	213-427-1035	385-0281
KPCC-FM 89.3 MHz (NPR) 1570 E Colorado Blvd *Web:* www.kpcc.org	Pasadena	CA	91106	626-585-7000	585-7916
KRTH-FM 101.1 MHz (Oldies) 5901 Venice Blvd	Los Angeles	CA	90034	323-937-5230	936-3427
KSZZ-AM 590 kHz (Span) 1950 S Sunwest Ln Suite 302	San Bernardino	CA	92408	909-825-5020	884-5844
KVCR-FM 91.9 MHz (NPR) 701 Mt Vernon Ave *E-mail:* hometeam@kvcr.pbs.org	San Bernardino	CA	92410	909-888-6511	885-2116

— Colleges/Universities —

				Phone	Fax
California State University San Bernardino 5500 University Pkwy *Web:* www.csusb.edu	San Bernardino	CA	92407	909-880-5000	880-7021
ITT Technical Institute 630 E Brier Dr Suite 150 *TF:* 800-888-3801 ■ *Web:* www.itt-tech.edu	San Bernardino	CA	92408	909-889-3800	888-6970
Loma Linda University 11234 Anderson St *Web:* www.llu.edu	Loma Linda	CA	92354	909-824-4300	824-4577
San Bernardino Valley College 701 S Mt Vernon Ave *Web:* www.sbccd.cc.ca.us/sbvc.htm ■ *E-mail:* pbrubal@sbccd.cc.ca.us	San Bernardino	CA	92410	909-888-6511	889-4988

— Hospitals —

				Phone	Fax
Arrowhead Regional Medical Center 400 N Pepper Ave	Colton	CA	92324	909-580-1000	580-6196

San Bernardino — Hospitals (Cont'd)

				Phone	Fax
Community Hospital of San Bernardino 1805 Medical Center Dr	San Bernardino	CA	92411	909-887-6333	887-6468
Loma Linda University Medical Center 11234 Anderson St	Loma Linda	CA	92354	909-824-4302	824-4086
Web: www.llu.edu					
Saint Bernardine Medical Center 2101 N Waterman Ave	San Bernardino	CA	92404	909-883-8711	881-4546

— Attractions —

				Phone	Fax
Agua Mansa Cemetery Museum 2001 Agua Mansa Rd W	Colton	CA	92324	909-370-2091	
American Wilderness Zoo & Aquarium 4557 Mills Cir	Ontario	CA	91764	909-481-6604	987-9584
Web: www.wildernesszoo.com					
Asistencia Mission 26930 Barton Rd	Redlands	CA	92373	909-793-5402	798-8585
Bear Mountain Ski & Golf Resort 43101 Gold Mine Dr	Big Bear Lake	CA	92315	909-585-2519	585-6805
Web: www.bearmtn.com					
Beattie George F Planetarium 701 S Mt Vernon Ave	San Bernardino	CA	92410	909-888-6511	889-4988
California Theatre of Performing Arts 562 W 4th St	San Bernardino	CA	92401	909-386-7361	885-8672
Web: www.theatricalarts.com					
Crest Kimberly House & Gardens 1325 Prospect Dr	Redlands	CA	92373	909-792-2111	
Fiesta Village 1405 E Washington Rd	Colton	CA	92324	909-824-1111	423-0192
Glen Helen Regional Park 2555 Glen Helen Pkwy	San Bernardino	CA	92407	909-880-2522	880-2659
Heritage House 796 'D' St	San Bernardino	CA	92401	909-883-0750	
Historical Glass Museum 1157 N Orange St	Redlands	CA	92373	909-798-0868	
Inland Empire Symphony Assn 362 W Court St	San Bernardino	CA	92401	909-381-5388	381-5380
Lincoln Memorial Shrine 125 W Vine St	Redlands	CA	92373	909-798-7636	798-7566
Main Street Downtown 201 N 'E' St	San Bernardino	CA	92401	909-381-5037	888-2576
Manzanar National Historic Site PO Box 579	Death Valley	CA	92328	760-786-2331	786-3283
Web: www.nps.gov/manz					
Mojave National Preserve 222 E Main St Suite 202	Barstow	CA	92311	760-255-8800	255-8809
Web: www.nps.gov/moja/					
Pharaoh's Lost Kingdom Theme Park 1101 N California St	Redlands	CA	92374	909-335-7275	307-2622
Web: www.pharaohslostkingdom.com ■ *E-mail:* pharaoh@pharaohslostkingdom.com					
Redlands Bowl PO Box 466	Redlands	CA	92373	909-793-7316	793-5086
San Bernardino County Museum 2024 Orange Tree Ln	Redlands	CA	92374	909-307-2669	307-0539
TF: 888-247-3344 ■ *Web:* www.co.san-bernardino.ca.us/museum					
San Bernardino National Forest 1824 S Commercenter Cir	San Bernardino	CA	92408	909-383-5588	383-5770
San Bernardino Symphony 562 W 4th St California Theatre	San Bernardino	CA	92401	909-381-5388	381-5380
San Manuel Indian Bingo & Casino 5797 N Victoria Ave	Highland	CA	92346	909-864-5050	862-0682*
**Fax:* Hum Res ■ *TF:* 800-359-2464 ■ *Web:* www.sanmanuel.com ■ *E-mail:* slengel@sanmanuel.com					
Special Place A 1003 E Highland Ave	San Bernardino	CA	92404	909-881-1201	
Sturges Center for the Fine Arts 780 N 'E' St	San Bernardino	CA	92410	909-384-5415	384-5449

SPORTS TEAMS & FACILITIES

				Phone	Fax
California Speedway 9300 Cherry Ave	Fontana	CA	91719	909-429-5000	429-5500
TF: 800-944-7223					
San Bernardino Stampede (baseball) 280 'E' St	San Bernardino	CA	92401	909-888-9922	888-5251
Web: www.stampedebaseball.com/ ■ *E-mail:* lerxst@stampedebaseball.com					

— Events —

	Phone
California 500 (early May)	909-429-5000
Cherry Festival (early June)	909-845-9541
Christmas Parade (early December)	909-885-3268
Christmas Tree Lighting & Holiday Kick-off (early December)	909-381-5037
Four Moons Pow Wow (early June)	909-823-6150
Fourth of July Celebration (July 4)	909-384-5031
Grapes & Gourmet Wine & Food Festival (early July)	909-384-5426
Harvest Fair (early-mid-November)	909-384-5426
Miss San Bernardino Pageant (mid-March)	909-889-3980
National Orange Show (late May)	909-888-6788
Parks & Recreation Holiday Craft Fair (early December)	909-381-5037
Red Ribbon Week & Downtown Parade (late October)	909-885-0509
Renaissance Pleasure Faire (April-June)	800-523-2473
Route 66 Rendezvous (mid-September)	909-889-3980
San Bernardino County Fair (mid-May)	760-951-2200
Shakespeare on the Square (August)	909-381-5037
Soap Box Derby (mid-May)	909-888-6788
Village Classic & Vintage Car Show (late May)	909-337-2533
Western Art Show & Sale (late March)	909-270-5632
Western Little League Tournament (mid-August)	909-887-6444

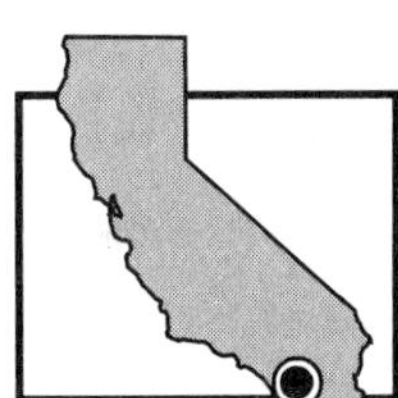

San Diego

The world-famous San Diego Zoo, a 100-acre tropical garden with 3,900 animal inhabitants, is located in Balboa Park, which is also home to a number of museums and the California Tower. The Tower is a prime example of the park's Spanish-Moorish architecture. Sea World is located at another prominent San Diego park, Mission Bay, which has 27 miles of beaches and facilities for boating, fishing, skiing, swimming, and public recreation. Between the winter months of December and February, the gray whales migrate south along the San Diego Coast on their way to Baja, and the Cabrillo National Monument observatory on the tip of Point Loma is an excellent vantage point from which to view them.

Population	1,220,666	**Longitude**	117-16-21 W
Area (Land)	324.0 sq mi	**County**	San Diego
Area (Water)	47.9 sq mi	**Time Zone**	PST
Elevation	42 ft	**Area Code/s**	619
Latitude	32-71-92 N		

— Average Temperatures and Precipitation —

TEMPERATURES

	Jan	Feb	Mar	Apr	May	Jun	Jul	Aug	Sep	Oct	Nov	Dec
High	66	67	66	68	69	72	76	78	77	75	70	66
Low	49	51	53	56	60	62	66	67	66	61	54	49

PRECIPITATION

	Jan	Feb	Mar	Apr	May	Jun	Jul	Aug	Sep	Oct	Nov	Dec
Inches	1.8	1.5	1.8	0.8	0.2	0.1	0.0	0.1	0.2	0.4	1.5	1.6

— Important Phone Numbers —

	Phone		Phone
AAA	619-233-1000	**Poison Control Center**	800-876-4766
American Express Travel	619-297-8101	**Time**	760-853-1212
Dental Referral	619-283-5644	**Travelers Aid**	619-231-7361
Emergency	911	**TravelMed**	800-878-3627
HotelDocs	800-468-3537	**Weather**	858-289-1212
Medical Referral	800-827-4277		

San Diego (Cont'd)

— Information Sources —

Name / Address	City	State	ZIP	Phone	Fax
Better Business Bureau Serving San Diego & Imperial Counties 5050 Murphy Canyon Rd Suite 110 *Web:* www.sandiego.bbb.org	San Diego	CA	92123	858-496-2131	496-2141
Greater San Diego Chamber of Commerce 402 W Broadway Suite 1000 *Web:* www.sddt.com/~chamberofcommerce	San Diego	CA	92101	619-232-0124	234-0571
San Diego City Hall 202 'C' St *Web:* www.sannet.gov	San Diego	CA	92101	619-236-5555	
San Diego Convention & Visitors Bureau 401 'B' St Suite 1400 *Web:* www.sandiego.org	San Diego	CA	92101	619-232-3101	696-9371
San Diego Convention Center 111 W Harbor Dr *Web:* www.sandiegocc.org	San Diego	CA	92101	619-525-5000	525-5005
San Diego County 1600 Pacific Hwy *Web:* www.co.san-diego.ca.us	San Diego	CA	92101	619-531-5507	557-4056
San Diego Development Services 1222 1st Ave *Web:* www.sannet.gov/development-services	San Diego	CA	92101	619-236-6250	236-7092
San Diego Mayor 202 C St 11th Fl *Web:* www.sannet.gov/mayor ■ *E-mail:* mayor@sdmayor.sannet.gov	San Diego	CA	92101	619-236-6330	236-7228
San Diego Public Library 820 'E' St *Web:* www.sannet.gov/public-library ■ *E-mail:* comments@library.sannet.gov	San Diego	CA	92101	619-236-5800	236-5878

On-Line Resources

4SanDiego.com	www.4sandiego.com
About San Diego	www.thewebstation.com/OgardTravel/SanDiego/
About.com Guide to San Diego	sandiego.about.com/local/caus/sandiego/
Accessible San Diego	www.accessandiego.com
All San Diego Travel Guide	www.sandiego.cc/sandiego/
Anthill City Guide San Diego	www.anthill.com/city.asp?city=sandiego
Area Guide San Diego	sandiego.areaguides.net
Boulevards San Diego	www.boulevards.com/cities/sandiego.html
City Knowledge San Diego	www.cityknowledge.com/ca_sandiego.htm
CitySearch San Diego	sandiego.citysearch.com
CuisineNet San Diego	www.menusonline.com/cities/san_diego/locmain.shtml
DigitalCity San Diego	home.digitalcity.com/sandiego
Discovering San Diego	www.discoversd.com/
Excite.com San Diego City Guide	www.excite.com/travel/countries/united_states/california/san_diego
Gaslamp411.com	www.gaslamp411.com
Go San Diego	www.gosandiego.com
Go There San Diego	www.gothere.com
HomePort San Diego	www.homeport-sd.com/
Hometown Free-Press San Diego	emporium.turnpike.net/~walk/hometown/sandiego.htm
HotelGuide San Diego	hotelguide.net/san_diego/
Insiders' Guide to San Diego	www.insiders.com/sandiego/
NITC Travelbase City Guide San Diego	www.travelbase.com/auto/guides/san_diego-area-ca.html
Niteoutsandiego.com	www.niteoutsandiego.com
Rough Guide Travel San Diego	travel.roughguides.com/content/1290/
San Diego 411	www.sandiego411.com
San Diego Black Pages	www.webcom.com/cjcook/SDBP/
San Diego California	san-diego-california.com
San Diego Golf Guide	san-diego-golf.com
San Diego Guide	www.sandiegan.com/
San Diego Historic Tours of America	www.historictours.com/sandiego/index.htm
San Diego Insider.com	www.sandiegoinsider.com
San Diego Online	www.sandiego-online.com/
San Diego Source	www.sddt.com/
San Diego Waterfront	www.sdwaterfront.com/
Sandiego.com	www.sandiego.com/
SanDiego.TheLinks.com	sandiego.thelinks.com/
Search San Diego	searchsd.com/index.html
ShowMEsandiego.com	www.showmesandiego.com/showmesd/index.shtml
Sights of San Diego	www.sightsofsandiego.com
Surf & Sun Beach Vacation Guide to San Diego	www.surf-sun.com/ca-san-diego-main.htm
Tour San Diego	www.toursandiego.com
Virtual Voyages San Diego	www.virtualvoyages.com/usa/ca/s_d/sd.sht
Web San Diego	www.websandiego.com/
Zoom-San Diego Arts & Entertainment	w3.thegroup.net/~zoom/

— Transportation Services —

AIRPORTS

	Phone
■ **San Diego International Airport - Lindbergh Field (SAN)** 3 miles NW of downtown (approx 10 minutes)	619-231-2100

Airport Transportation

	Phone
Cloud Nine Shuttle $5-7 fare to downtown	858-278-8877
Express Shuttle $5 fare to downtown	800-900-7433
San Diego Transit $2 fare to downtown	619-233-3004

Commercial Airlines

	Phone		Phone
AeroMexico	619-238-2090	**Northwest**	800-225-2525
America West	800-235-9292	**Shuttle by United**	800-748-8853
American	800-433-7300	**SkyWest**	800-453-9417
American Eagle	800-433-7300	**Southwest**	800-435-9792
British Airways	800-247-9297	**TWA**	800-221-2000
Continental	800-525-0280	**United**	800-241-6522
Delta	800-221-1212	**US Airways**	800-428-4322

Charter Airlines

	Phone		Phone
Corporate Helicopters of San Diego	619-291-4356	**Lundy Air Charter**	858-505-5660
Jimsair Aviation Services	619-298-7704	**Renown Aviation Inc**	805-937-8484
		Tag Aviation	800-252-6972

CAR RENTALS

	Phone		Phone
Alamo	619-297-0312	**Hertz**	619-220-5222
Avis	619-231-7171	**National**	619-231-7100
Budget	619-542-8686	**Payless**	619-297-7071
Dollar	619-234-3388	**Thrifty**	619-429-5000
Enterprise	619-225-8881		

LIMO/TAXI

	Phone		Phone
Ambassador Limousines	858-457-3333	**Orange Cab**	619-291-3333
American Cab	858-292-1111	**San Diego Cab**	619-226-8294
Old English Livery Service	619-232-6533	**Silver Cab**	619-280-5555

MASS TRANSIT

	Phone
San Diego-Coronado Ferry $2 Base fare	619-234-4111
San Diego Transit $1.75 Base fare	619-233-3004
San Diego Trolley $.75 Base fare	619-595-4949

RAIL/BUS

Name / Address	City	State	ZIP	Phone
Greyhound/Trailways Bus Station 120 W Broadway *TF:* 800-231-2222	San Diego	CA	92101	619-239-8082
San Diego Amtrak Station 1050 Kettner Blvd.	San Diego	CA	92101	619-239-9021

— Accommodations —

HOTEL RESERVATION SERVICES

	Phone	Fax
Accommodations Express *TF:* 800-444-7666 ■ *Web:* www.accommodationsxpress.com ■ *E-mail:* accomexp@acy.digex.net	609-391-2100	525-0111
Advance Reservations Inn Arizona *TF:* 800-456-0682 ■ *Web:* tucson.com/inn ■ *E-mail:* micasa@primenet.com	480-990-0682	990-3390
Bed & Breakfast Directory for San Diego *TF:* 800-619-7666 ■ *Web:* www.sandiegobandb.com	619-297-3130	
California Reservations *TF:* 800-576-0003 ■ *Web:* www.cal-res.com	415-252-1107	252-1483
Hotel Reservations Network Inc *TF Sales:* 800-964-6835 ■ *Web:* www.hoteldiscount.com	214-361-7311	361-7299
Quikbook *TF:* 800-789-9887 ■ *Web:* www.quikbook.com	212-532-1660	532-1556
Reservations Center *TF:* 800-255-6451 ■ *Web:* www.rescenter.com ■ *E-mail:* resnet@rescenter.com	435-649-1592	649-1593
RMC Travel Centre *TF:* 800-782-2674	212-754-6560	754-6571
San Diego Hotel Reservations *TF:* 800-728-3227	858-627-9300	627-9405

San Diego (Cont'd)

HOTELS, MOTELS, RESORTS

Phone *Fax*

Bahia Hotel 998 W Mission Bay Dr. . . . . San Diego CA 92109 858-488-0551 488-7055
TF: 800-288-0770

Balboa Park Inn 3402 Park Blvd . . . . San Diego CA 92103 619-298-0823 294-8070
TF: 800-938-8181 ■ *Web:* www.balboaparkinn.com
■ *E-mail:* info@balboaparkinn.com

Bay Club Hotel & Marina
2131 Shelter Island Dr. . . . . San Diego CA 92106 619-224-8888 225-1604
TF: 800-672-0800 ■ *Web:* www.bayclubhotel.com

Beach Haven Inn 4740 Mission Blvd . . . . San Diego CA 92109 858-272-3812 272-3532
TF: 800-831-6323

Best Western Bayside Inn 555 W Ash St. . . . . San Diego CA 92101 619-233-7500 239-8060
TF: 800-341-1818

Best Western Blue Sea Lodge
707 Pacific Beach Dr. . . . . San Diego CA 92109 858-488-4700 488-7276
TF: 800-258-3732

Best Western Island Palms
2051 Shelter Island Dr. . . . . San Diego CA 92106 619-222-0561 222-9760
TF: 800-528-1234

Bristol Court Hotel 1055 1st Ave . . . . San Diego CA 92101 619-232-6141 232-0118
TF: 800-662-4477

Clarion Hotel Bay View 660 'K' St . . . . San Diego CA 92101 619-696-0234 231-8199
TF: 800-766-0234

Comfort Inn Downtown 719 Ash St. . . . . San Diego CA 92101 619-232-2525 687-3024
TF: 800-221-2222

Comfort Suites Mission Valley
631 Camino del Rio S . . . . San Diego CA 92108 619-294-3444 260-0746
TF: 800-944-5685

Corinthian Suites 1840 4th Ave . . . . San Diego CA 92101 619-236-1600 231-4734

Coronado Island Marriott Resort
2000 2nd St. . . . . .Coronado CA 92118 619-435-3000 435-3032
TF: 800-228-9290

Crown Point View Suite-Hotel
4088 Crown Pt Dr. . . . . San Diego CA 92109 858-272-0676 272-0760
TF: 800-338-3331 ■ *Web:* www.crownpoint-view.com
■ *E-mail:* info@crownpoint-view.com

Days Inn Downtown 1449 9th Ave . . . . San Diego CA 92101 619-239-9113 232-9019
TF: 800-329-7466

Days Inn Harborview 1919 Pacific Hwy . . . . . . San Diego CA 92101 619-232-1077 233-6977
TF: 800-329-7466

Days Inn Oceanside 3170 Vista Way. . . . . Oceanside CA 92056 760-757-2200 757-2389
TF: 800-458-6064

Doubletree Carmel Highland Golf & Tennis Resort 14455 Penasquitos Dr. . . . . San Diego CA 92129 858-672-9100 672-9187
TF: 800-222-8733 ■ *Web:* www.highland.doubletreehotels.com
■ *E-mail:* carmel@highland.doubletreehotels.com

Doubletree Hotel 7450 Hazard Ctr Dr . . . . San Diego CA 92108 619-297-5466 297-5499
TF: 800-222-8733
■ *Web:* www.doubletreehotels.com/DoubleT/Hotel121/122/122Main.htm

Embassy Suites Hotel San Diego Bay
601 Pacific Hwy . . . . San Diego CA 92101 619-239-2400 239-1520
TF: 800-362-2779

Empress Hotel 7766 Fay Ave . . . . La Jolla CA 92037 858-454-3001 454-6387
TF: 888-369-9900 ■ *Web:* www.empress-hotel.com
■ *E-mail:* info@empress-hotel.com

Gaslamp Plaza Suites 520 'E' St . . . . San Diego CA 92101 619-232-9500 238-9945
TF: 800-874-8770

Glorietta Bay Inn 1630 Glorietta Blvd . . . . .Coronado CA 92118 619-435-3101 435-6182
TF: 800-283-9383 ■ *Web:* www.gloriettabayinn.com
■ *E-mail:* info@gloriettabayinn.com

Golden West Hotel 720 4th Ave . . . . San Diego CA 92101 619-233-7596 233-4009

Hanalei Hotel 2270 Hotel Cir N . . . . San Diego CA 92108 619-297-1101 297-6049
TF: 800-882-0858 ■ *Web:* www.hanaleihotel.com
■ *E-mail:* sales@hanaleihotel.com

Handlery Hotel & Resort 950 Hotel Cir N . . . . San Diego CA 92108 619-298-0511 298-9793
TF: 800-676-6567
■ *Web:*www.handlery.com/ONE_SD/ONE_HTML_SD/ONE_main_SD.html

Heritage Park Inn 2470 Heritage Park Row . . . San Diego CA 92110 619-299-6832 299-9465
TF: 800-995-2470

Hilton San Diego Mission Valley
901 Camino del Rio S . . . . San Diego CA 92108 619-543-9000 543-9358
TF: 800-733-2332 ■ *Web:* www.hilton.com/hotels/SANHIHH

Holiday Inn Harbor View 1617 1st Ave . . . . . . San Diego CA 92101 619-239-6171 233-6228
TF: 800-366-3164 ■ *Web:* www.basshotels.com/holiday-inn/?_franchisee=SANHV
■ *E-mail:* holidayinnharborview@sunstonehotels.com

Holiday Inn Mission Bay
3737 Sports Arena Blvd. . . . . San Diego CA 92110 619-226-3711 224-9248
TF: 800-511-1921 ■ *Web:* www.basshotels.com/holiday-inn/?_franchisee=SANSA ■ *E-mail:* dennisb@tarsadia.com

Holiday Inn on the Bay 1355 N Harbor Dr. . . . San Diego CA 92101 619-232-3861 232-4924
TF: 800-877-8920 ■ *Web:* www.basshotels.com/holiday-inn/?_franchisee=SANEM ■ *E-mail:* hi-sandiego@bristolhotels.com

Phone *Fax*

Holiday Inn Rancho Bernardo
17065 W Bernardo Dr . . . . San Diego CA 92127 858-485-6530 485-7819
TF: 800-777-0020

Holiday Inn San Diego Bayside
4875 N Harbor Dr. . . . . San Diego CA 92106 619-224-3621 224-3629
TF: 800-465-4329 ■ *Web:* www.basshotels.com/holiday-inn/?_franchisee=SANBY ■ *E-mail:* reshbs@holinnbayside.com

Horton Grand Hotel 311 Island Ave. . . . . San Diego CA 92101 619-544-1886 544-0058
TF: 800-542-1886 ■ *Web:* www.hortongrand.com

Hotel Del Coronado 1500 Orange Ave . . . . .Coronado CA 92118 619-522-8000 522-8238
TF: 800-468-3533 ■ *Web:* www.hoteldel.com
■ *E-mail:* info@hoteldel.com

Humphrey's Half Moon Inn
2303 Shelter Island Dr. . . . . San Diego CA 92106 619-224-3411 224-3478
TF: 800-542-7400 ■ *Web:* www.halfmooninn.com
■ *E-mail:* res@halfmooninn.com

Hyatt Islandia 1441 Quivira Rd. . . . . San Diego CA 92109 619-224-1234 224-0348
TF: 800-233-1234
■ *Web:* www.hyatt.com/usa/san_diego/hotels/hotel_sanis.html

Hyatt Regency San Diego 1 Market Pl. . . . . . . San Diego CA 92101 619-232-1234 233-6464
TF: 800-233-1234
■ *Web:* www.hyatt.com/usa/san_diego/hotels/hotel_sanrs.html

J Street Inn 222 'J' St. . . . . San Diego CA 92101 619-696-6922 696-1295

La Casa Del Zorro
3845 Yaqui Pass Rd . . . . Borrego Springs CA 92004 760-767-5323 767-5963
TF: 800-824-1884

La Costa Resort & Spa
2100 Costa del Mar Rd . . . . Carlsbad CA 92009 760-438-9111 931-7585
TF: 800-854-5000 ■ *Web:* www.lacosta.com
■ *E-mail:* info@lacosta.com

La Pensione Little Italy 606 W Date St. . . . . . San Diego CA 92101 619-236-8000 236-8088
TF: 800-232-4683

Loews Coronado Bay Resort
4000 Coronado Bay Rd . . . . .Coronado CA 92118 619-424-4000 424-4400
TF: 800-815-6397 ■ *Web:* www.loewshotels.com/coronadohome.html
■ *E-mail:* loewscoronadobay@loewshotels.com

Marriott Mission Valley
8757 Rio San Diego Dr . . . . San Diego CA 92108 619-692-3000 692-0769
TF: 800-228-9290 ■ *Web:* marriotthotels.com/SANMV

Maryland Hotel 630 'F' St . . . . San Diego CA 92101 619-239-9243 235-8968

Motel 6 1546 2nd Ave. . . . . San Diego CA 92101 619-236-9292 236-9988
TF: 800-466-8356

North Miramar Holiday Inn Select
9335 Kearny Mesa Rd . . . . San Diego CA 92126 858-695-2300 578-7925
TF: 800-262-2301

Pala Mesa Resort 2001 Old Hwy 395 . . . . Fallbrook CA 92028 760-728-5881 723-8292
TF: 800-722-4700 ■ *Web:* www.palamesa.com
■ *E-mail:* teeup@palamesa.com

Pickwich Hotel on Broadway
132 W Broadway . . . . San Diego CA 92101 619-234-9200 544-9879
TF: 800-826-0009

Quality Inn & Suites 1430 7th Ave . . . . San Diego CA 92101 619-696-0911 234-9416
TF: 800-404-6835

Radisson Hotel Harbor View 1646 Front St . . . San Diego CA 92101 619-239-6800 238-9461
TF: 800-333-3333

Radisson Hotel San Diego
1433 Camino del Rio S . . . . San Diego CA 92108 619-260-0111 497-0813
TF: 800-333-3333

Radisson Suite Hotel
11520 W Bernardo Ct . . . . San Diego CA 92127 858-451-6600 592-0253
TF: 800-333-3333

Ramada Inn & Suites Downtown
830 6th Ave . . . . San Diego CA 92101 619-531-8877 231-8307
TF: 800-664-4400

Ramada Inn Old Town 3900 Old Town Ave . . . San Diego CA 92110 619-299-7400 299-1619
TF: 800-272-6232

Ramada Plaza 2151 S Hotel Cir . . . . San Diego CA 92108 619-291-6500 294-7531
TF: 800-272-6232

Rancho Bernardo Inn
17550 Bernardo Oaks Dr . . . . San Diego CA 92128 858-675-8500 675-8501
TF: 800-542-6096 ■ *Web:* www.jcresorts.com/rbi/rbi.html

Regency Plaza Hotel 1515 Hotel Cir S . . . . . . San Diego CA 92108 619-291-8790 260-0147
TF: 800-228-8048

San Diego Hilton Beach & Tennis Resort
1775 E Mission Bay Dr . . . . San Diego CA 92109 619-276-4010 275-7991
TF: 800-345-6565

San Diego Marriott Hotel & Marina
333 W Harbor Dr . . . . San Diego CA 92101 619-234-1500 234-8678
TF: 800-228-9290 ■ *Web:* sdmarriott.com/

San Diego Marriott Suites Downtown
701 'A' St . . . . San Diego CA 92101 619-696-9800 696-1555
TF: 800-228-9290

San Diego Princess Resort
1404 W Vacation Rd . . . . San Diego CA 92109 858-274-4630 581-5929
TF: 800-344-2626 ■ *Web:* www.paradisepoint.com

San Diego (Cont'd)

Name / Address	City	State	ZIP	Phone	Fax
San Vicente Inn & Golf Club 24157 San Vicente Rd *TF:* 800-776-1289	Ramona	CA	92065	760-789-8290	788-6115
Sheraton San Diego Hotel & Marina 1380 Harbor Island Dr *TF:* 800-325-3535	San Diego	CA	92101	619-291-2900	692-2337
Singing Hills Resort 3007 Dehesa Rd *TF:* 800-457-5568 ■ *Web:* www.singinghills.com ■ *E-mail:* lodge@singinghills.com	El Cajon	CA	92019	619-442-3425	442-9574
Town & Country Hotel 500 Hotel Cir N *TF:* 800-854-2608 ■ *Web:* www.towncountry.com ■ *E-mail:* atlasres@primenet.com	San Diego	CA	92108	619-291-7131	291-3584
Travelodge Airport 2353 Pacific Hwy *TF:* 800-578-7878	San Diego	CA	92101	619-232-8931	237-0776
Travelodge Hotel Harbor Island 1960 Harbor Island Dr *TF:* 800-578-7878	San Diego	CA	92101	619-291-6700	293-0694
US Grant Hotel A Wyndham Grand Heritage Hotel 326 Broadway *TF:* 800-237-5029 ■ *Web:* www.grandheritage.com/Hotels/Namerican/Usgrant/usgrantindex.html	San Diego	CA	92101	619-232-3121	232-3626
Welk Resort Center 8860 Lawrence Welk Dr *TF:* 800-932-9355 ■ *Web:* www.welkresort.com/	Escondido	CA	92026	760-749-3000	749-9537
Westgate Hotel 1055 2nd Ave *TF:* 800-221-3802	San Diego	CA	92101	619-238-1818	557-3737
Westin Hotel 910 Broadway Cir *TF:* 800-228-3000	San Diego	CA	92101	619-239-2200	239-0509
Wyndham Hotel 400 W Broadway *TF:* 800-889-8846	San Diego	CA	92101	619-239-4500	239-3274

— Restaurants —

Name / Address	City	State	ZIP	Phone
Anthony's Fish Grotto (Seafood) 1360 Harbor Dr	San Diego	CA	92101	619-232-5104
Asti Ristorante (Italian) 728 5th Ave	San Diego	CA	92101	619-232-8844
Athens Market Taverna (Greek) 109 W 'F' St	San Diego	CA	92101	619-234-1955
Baci Ristorante (Italian) 1955 W Morena Blvd	San Diego	CA	92110	619-275-2094
Baja Brewing Co (Mexican) 203 5th Ave	San Diego	CA	92101	619-231-9279
Belgian Lion (French/Belgian) 2265 Bacon St	San Diego	CA	92107	619-223-2700
Bella Luna (Italian) 748 5th Ave	San Diego	CA	92101	619-239-3222
Blue Point Coastal Cuisine (Seafood) 565 5th Ave	San Diego	CA	92101	619-233-6623
Bungalow The (French) 4996 W Point Loma Blvd	San Diego	CA	92107	619-224-2884
Busalacchi's (Italian) 3683 5th Ave N	San Diego	CA	92103	619-298-0119
Cafe Coyote (Mexican) 2461 San Diego Ave	San Diego	CA	92110	619-291-4695
Cafe Japengo (Pan-Asian) 8960 University Center Ln	San Diego	CA	92122	858-450-3355
Cafe Pacifica (Seafood) 2414 San Diego Ave	San Diego	CA	92110	619-291-6666
Cafe Sevilla (Spanish) 555 4th Ave	San Diego	CA	92101	619-233-5979
California Cuisine (California) 1027 University Ave	San Diego	CA	92103	619-543-0790
Casa de Bandini (Mexican) 2754 Calhoun St	San Diego	CA	92110	619-297-8211
Casa de Pico (Mexican) 2754 Calhoun St	San Diego	CA	92110	619-296-3267
Chart House The (Steak/Seafood) 525 E Harbor Dr	San Diego	CA	92101	619-233-7391
China Camp (Chinese) 2137 Pacific Hwy	San Diego	CA	92101	619-232-0686
Cilantros (Southwest) 3702 Via de la Valle	Del Mar	CA	92014	858-259-8777
Croce's (New American) 802 5th Ave *Web:* www.croces.com/	San Diego	CA	92101	619-233-4355
Dakota Grill & Spirits (American) 901 5th Ave	San Diego	CA	92101	619-234-5554
De Medici (Italian) 815 5th Ave	San Diego	CA	92101	619-702-7228
Delicias (California) 6106 Paseo Delicias	Rancho Santa Fe	CA	92067	858-756-8000
Dobson's (French) 956 Broadway Cir	San Diego	CA	92101	619-231-6771
Edgewater Grill (Steak/Seafood) 861 W Harbor Dr	San Diego	CA	92101	619-232-7581
El Bizcocho (French) 17550 Bernardo Oaks Dr	San Diego	CA	92128	858-487-1611
El Tecolote (Mexican) 6110 Friars Rd	San Diego	CA	92108	619-295-2087
Epazote's (Southwest) 1555 Camino del Mar	Del Mar	CA	92014	858-259-9966
Fio's Cucina (Italian) 801 5th Ave *Web:* www.fioscucina.com/	San Diego	CA	92101	619-234-3467
First Avenue Bar & Grill (American) 1055 1st Ave	San Diego	CA	92101	619-232-6141
Fish Market (Seafood) 750 N Harbor Dr	San Diego	CA	92101	619-232-3474
George's at the Cove (California) 1250 Prospect St *Web:* www.georgesatthecove.com/	La Jolla	CA	92037	858-454-4244
Grant Grill (American) 326 Broadway	San Diego	CA	92101	619-239-6806
Harbor House (Steak/Seafood) 831 W Harbor Dr	San Diego	CA	92101	619-232-1141
Hob-Nob Hill (American) 2271 1st Ave	San Diego	CA	92101	619-239-8176
Kelly's (American) 500 Hotel Cir N	San Diego	CA	92108	619-291-7131
L'Escale (American) 2000 2nd St	Coronado	CA	92118	619-435-3000
La Tavola (Mediterranean) 515 5th Ave	San Diego	CA	92101	619-232-3352
Laurel (Mediterranean) 505 Laurel St	San Diego	CA	92101	619-239-2222
Le Fontainbleau (French) 1055 2nd Ave	San Diego	CA	92101	619-238-1818
Mille Fleurs (French) 6009 Paseo Delicias *Web:* www.millefleurs.com/	Rancho Santa Fe	CA	92067	858-756-3085
Mister A's Restaurant (Continental) 2550 5th Ave 12th Fl	San Diego	CA	92103	619-239-1377
Molly's (Steak) 333 W Harbor Dr	San Diego	CA	92101	619-234-1500
Old Town Mexican Cafe (Mexican) 2489 San Diego Ave	San Diego	CA	92110	619-297-4330
Palenque (Mexican) 1653 Garnet Ave	San Diego	CA	92109	858-272-7816
Panda Inn (Chinese) 506 Horton Plaza	San Diego	CA	92101	619-233-7800
Pier Cafe (Seafood) 885 W Harbor Dr	San Diego	CA	92101	619-239-3968
Point Loma Seafoods (Seafood) 2805 Emerson St	San Diego	CA	92106	619-223-1109
Prince of Wales Grill (New American) 1500 Orange Ave	San Diego	CA	92118	619-522-8496
Rainwater's (Steak/Seafood) 1202 Kettner Blvd *Web:* www.rainwaters.com/	San Diego	CA	92101	619-233-5757
Reuben's on Harbor Island (Steak/Seafood) 880 E Harbor Island Dr	San Diego	CA	92101	619-291-5030
Royal Thai Cuisine (Thai) 467 5th Ave	San Diego	CA	92101	619-230-8424
Sally's (Mediterranean) 1 Market Pl	San Diego	CA	92101	619-687-6080
Salvatore's (Italian) 750 Front St	San Diego	CA	92101	619-544-1865
Sushi Bar Nippon (Japanese) 532 4th Ave	San Diego	CA	92101	619-544-9779
Sushi Ota (Japanese) 4529 Mission Bay Dr	San Diego	CA	92109	858-270-5670
Top of the Market (Seafood) 750 N Harbor Dr	San Diego	CA	92101	619-234-4867
Trattoria La Strada (Italian) 702 5th Ave	San Diego	CA	92101	619-239-3400
Trattoria Mamma Anna (Italian) 644 5th Ave	San Diego	CA	92101	619-235-8144
When in Rome (Italian) 1108 1st St	Encinitas	CA	92024	760-944-1771
Winesellar & Brasserie (French) 9550 Waples St Suite 115	San Diego	CA	92121	858-450-9557

— Goods and Services —

SHOPPING

Name / Address	City	State	ZIP	Phone	Fax
Adams Avenue Adams Ave-betw Kensington & Normal Heights *Web:* www.gothere.com/AdamsAve/	San Diego	CA	92116	619-282-7329	
Bazaar del Mundo Inc 2754 Calhoun St *Web:* www.bazaardelmundo.com ■ *E-mail:* customerservice@bazaardelmundo.com	San Diego	CA	92110	619-296-3161	296-3113
Farmers Bazaar 245 7th Ave	San Diego	CA	92101	619-233-0281	235-9702
Fashion Valley Mall 7007 Friars Rd	San Diego	CA	92108	619-688-9113	
Grossmont Center 5500 Grossmont Center Dr	La Mesa	CA	91942	619-465-2900	
Horton Plaza 324 Horton Plaza *Web:* www.hortonplaza.com/ ■ *E-mail:* mstephens@westfieldamerica.com	San Diego	CA	92101	619-238-1596	239-4021
Macy's 275 Fashion Valley Rd	San Diego	CA	92108	619-299-9811	
Marketplace at the Grove Hwy 94 & College Ave	San Diego	CA	92115	619-660-1000	660-0706
Mission Valley Center 1640 Camino del Rio N Suite 1290	San Diego	CA	92108	619-296-6375	692-0555
Neiman Marcus 7027 Friars Rd *Web:* www.neimanmarcus.com	San Diego	CA	92108	619-692-9100	298-8457
Robinsons-May 1702 Camino del Rio N	San Diego	CA	92108	619-297-2511	
San Diego/North County Factory Outlet Center 1050 Los Vallecitos Blvd	San Marcos	CA	92069	760-471-1591	
Seaport Village 849 W Harbor Dr *Web:* www.spvillage.com	San Diego	CA	92101	619-235-4014	696-0025
University Towne Centre 4545 La Jolla Village Dr *Web:* www.shoputc.com	San Diego	CA	92122	858-546-8858	552-9065

BANKS

Name / Address	City	State	ZIP	Phone	Fax
Bank of America 8949 Clairemont Mesa Blvd	San Diego	CA	92123	858-452-8400	
First National Bank 401 W 'A' St	San Diego	CA	92101	619-233-5588	235-1268
General Bank 4688 Convoy St	San Diego	CA	92111	858-277-2030	277-3339
North County Bank 8085 Clairemont Mesa Blvd	San Diego	CA	92111	858-278-3445	278-3069
San Diego National Bank 1420 Kettner Blvd *TF:* 888-724-7362 ■ *Web:* www.sdnb.com ■ *E-mail:* kgregg@sdnb.com	San Diego	CA	92101	619-231-4989	233-7017
Wells Fargo Bank NA 401 'B' St *TF:* 800-869-3557	San Diego	CA	92101	619-702-6949	699-3182

BUSINESS SERVICES

	Phone
Corporate Express Delivery Systems	858-715-1000
Eastridge Temporary Services	619-260-2100
Federal Express	800-463-3339
Hesco Courier	858-571-7395
Kelly Services	619-298-6600
Kinko's	619-287-6188
Mail Dispatch	858-268-9700
Manpower Temporary Services	619-234-6433
Olsten Staffing Services	619-688-0500
Pacific Messengers Service	619-232-3141
Post Office	800-275-8777
UPS	800-742-5877

San Diego (Cont'd)

— Media —

PUBLICATIONS

	City	State	ZIP	Phone	Fax
San Diego Business Journal 4909 Murphy Canyon Rd Suite 200	San Diego	CA	92123	858-277-6359	277-2149
Web: www.sdbj.com ■ *E-mail:* sdbj@sdbj.com					
San Diego Daily Transcript‡ PO Box 85469	San Diego	CA	92816	619-232-4381	236-8126*
**Fax:* Edit ■ *TF:* 800-697-6397 ■ *Web:* www.sddt.com ■ *E-mail:* editor@sddt.com					
San Diego Magazine PO Box 85409	San Diego	CA	92186	619-230-9292	230-9220
Web: www.sandiego-online.com					
San Diego Union-Tribune‡ PO Box 120191	San Diego	CA	92112	619-299-3131	293-1896
TF: 800-244-6397 ■ *Web:* www.uniontrib.com ■ *E-mail:* letters@uniontrib.com					
San Diego Weekly News 7670 Opportunity Rd Suite 100	San Diego	CA	92111	858-565-9135	565-4182*
**Fax:* News Rm					

‡Daily newspapers

TELEVISION

	City	State	ZIP	Phone	Fax
KFMB-TV Ch 8 (CBS) 7677 Engineer Rd	San Diego	CA	92111	858-571-8888	560-0627
Web: www.kfmb.com ■ *E-mail:* news8@kfmb.com					
KGTV-TV Ch 10 (ABC) PO Box 85347	San Diego	CA	92186	619-237-1010	527-0369
Web: www.sandiegoinsider.com/partners/kgtv					
KNSD-TV Ch 7/39 (NBC) 8330 Engineer Rd	San Diego	CA	92171	858-279-3939	279-1076
Web: www.knsd.com ■ *E-mail:* hinczsd@tvsknsd.nbc.com					
KPBS-TV Ch 15 (PBS) 5200 Campanile Dr	San Diego	CA	92182	619-594-1515	265-6417
Web: www.kpbs.org ■ *E-mail:* letters@kpbs.org					
KSWB-TV Ch 69 (WB) 7191 Engineer Rd	San Diego	CA	92111	858-492-9269	268-0401
KUSI-TV Ch 51 (Ind) PO Box 719051	San Diego	CA	92171	858-571-5151	571-4852
XETV-TV Ch 6 (Fox) 8253 Ronson Rd	San Diego	CA	92111	858-279-6666	268-9388
Web: www.fox6.com					
XHAS-TV Ch 33 (Tele) 6048 Cornerstone Ct W Suite A	San Diego	CA	92121	858-558-4646	558-0846

RADIO

	City	State	ZIP	Phone	Fax
KBZT-FM 94.9 MHz (Oldies) 1615 Murray Canyon Rd Suite 710	San Diego	CA	92108	858-452-9595	543-1353*
**Fax Area Code:* 619					
KFMB-AM 760 kHz (N/T) 7677 Engineer Rd	San Diego	CA	92111	858-292-7600	279-7676
KFMB-FM 100.7 MHz (AC) 7677 Engineer Rd	San Diego	CA	92111	858-292-7600	279-3380
Web: www.histar.com					
KFSD-FM 92.1 MHz (Clas) 550 Laguna Dr	Carlsbad	CA	92008	760-729-5946	434-2367
KGB-FM 101.5 MHz (CR) 5745 Kearny Villa Rd Suite M	San Diego	CA	92123	858-565-6006	277-1015
Web: www.101kgb.com					
KHTS-FM 93.3 MHz (CHR) 4891 Pacific Hwy	San Diego	CA	92110	619-291-9191	291-3299
KIFM-FM 98.1 MHz (NAC) 1615 Murray Canyon Rd Suite 710	San Diego	CA	92108	619-297-3698	587-4628*
**Fax Area Code:* 858 ■ *Web:* www.kifm.com ■ *E-mail:* connect@kifm.com					
KIOZ-FM 105.3 MHz (Rock) 5745 Kearny Villa Rd Suite M	San Diego	CA	92123	858-565-6006	560-0742
Web: www.kioz.com					
KJQY-FM 94.1 MHz (AC) 5745 Kearny Villa Rd Suite M	San Diego	CA	92123	858-565-6006	279-9553
KMSX-FM 95.7 MHz (AC) 5745 Kearny Villa Rd Suite M	San Diego	CA	92101	858-565-6006	279-9553
KOGO-AM 600 kHz (N/T) 5050 Murphy Canyon Rd	San Diego	CA	92123	858-278-1130	285-4364*
**Fax Area Code:* 619					
KPBS-FM 89.5 MHz (NPR) 5200 Campanile Dr San Diego State University	San Diego	CA	92182	619-594-8100	265-6478
Web: www.kpbs.org ■ *E-mail:* letters@kpbs.org					
KPLN-FM 103.7 MHz (CR) 8033 Linda Vista Rd	San Diego	CA	92111	858-560-1037	571-0326
Web: www.planetfm.com					
KPOP-AM 1360 kHz (Nost) 5050 Murphy Canyon Rd	San Diego	CA	92123	858-278-1130	285-4372*
**Fax Area Code:* 619					
KSDO-AM 1130 kHz (N/T) 5050 Murphy Canyon Rd	San Diego	CA	92123	858-278-1130	285-4303*
**Fax Area Code:* 619 ■ *Web:* www.ksdoradio.com					
KSON-AM 1240 kHz (Misc) 1615 Murray Canyon Rd Suite 710	San Diego	CA	92108	619-291-9797	543-1353
KSON-FM 97.3 MHz (Ctry) 1615 Murray Canyon Rd Suite 710	San Diego	CA	92108	619-291-9797	543-1353
Web: www.kson.com					
KSPA-AM 1450 kHz (Nost) 550 Laguna Dr	Carlsbad	CA	92008	760-729-5946	434-2367
KXST-FM 102.1 MHz (AAA) PO Box 1021	San Diego	CA	92112	619-286-1170	449-8548
Web: www.sets102.com					
KYXY-FM 96.5 MHz (AC) 8033 Linda Vista Rd	San Diego	CA	92111	858-571-7600	571-0326
Web: www.kyxy.com					
XEMO-AM 860 kHz (Span) 5030 Camino de la Siesta Suite 103	San Diego	CA	92108	619-497-0600	497-1019
XHRM-FM 92.5 MHz (Oldies) 2434 Southport Way Suite A	National City	CA	91950	619-336-4900	336-4925
Web: www.magic92five.com					
XTRA-AM 690 kHz (Sports) 4891 Pacific Hwy	San Diego	CA	92110	619-291-9191	291-5622
Web: www.xtrasports690.com					
XTRA-FM 91.1 MHz (Rock) 4891 Pacific Hwy	San Diego	CA	92110	619-291-9191	291-3299

— Colleges/Universities —

	City	State	ZIP	Phone	Fax
California Pacific University 9683 Tierra Grande St Rm 100	San Diego	CA	92126	858-695-3292	
TF: 800-458-9667 ■ *Web:* www.cpu.edu/					
Cuyamaca College 900 Rancho San Diego Pkwy	El Cajon	CA	92019	619-670-1980	660-4399
Web: michele.gcccd.cc.ca.us/cuyamaca/					
Design Institute of San Diego 8555 Commerce Ave	San Diego	CA	92121	858-566-1200	566-2711
Web: www.disd.edu ■ *E-mail:* disdadm@msn.com					
Grossmont-Cuyamaca Community College District 8800 Grossmont College Dr	El Cajon	CA	92020	619-644-7690	644-7933
Web: www.gcccd.cc.ca.us/					
ITT Technical Institute 9680 Granite Ridge Dr	San Diego	CA	92123	858-571-8500	571-1277
Web: www.itt-tech.edu					
Kelsey-Jenney College 201 'A' St	San Diego	CA	92101	619-233-7418	615-1664
Web: www.kelsey-jenney.com ■ *E-mail:* info@kelsey-jenney.com					
MiraCosta College 1 Barnard Dr	Oceanside	CA	92056	760-757-2121	795-6626
TF: 888-201-8480 ■ *Web:* www.miracosta.cc.ca.us ■ *E-mail:* bhall@mcc.miracosta.cc.ca.us					
National University 11255 N Torrey Pines Rd	La Jolla	CA	92037	858-642-8000	642-8709
TF: 800-628-8648 ■ *Web:* www.nu.edu ■ *E-mail:* mss@nunic.nu.edu					
Palomar College 1140 W Mission Rd	San Marcos	CA	92069	760-744-1150	744-2932
Web: www.palomar.edu					
Point Loma Nazarene University 3900 Lomaland Dr	San Diego	CA	92106	619-849-2200	849-2601
Web: www.ptloma.edu					
San Diego City College 1313 12th Ave	San Diego	CA	92101	619-230-2400	230-2135
Web: www.city.sdccd.cc.ca.us/					
San Diego Mesa College 7250 Mesa College Dr	San Diego	CA	92111	858-627-2600	627-2960
Web: intergate.sdmesa.sdccd.cc.ca.us					
San Diego Miramar College 10440 Black Mountain Rd	San Diego	CA	92126	858-536-7844	693-1899
Web: intergate.miramar.sdccd.cc.ca.us					
San Diego State University 5500 Campanile Dr	San Diego	CA	92182	619-594-5000	594-4902
Web: www.sdsu.edu					
Southern California Bible College 2075 E Madison Ave	El Cajon	CA	92019	619-442-9841	442-4510
TF: 800-554-7222					
Southwestern College 900 Otay Lakes Rd	Chula Vista	CA	91910	619-421-6700	482-6489
Web: swc.cc.ca.us					
United States International University 10455 Pomerado Rd	San Diego	CA	92131	858-271-4300	635-4739
Web: www.usiu.edu					
University of California San Diego 9500 Gilman Dr	La Jolla	CA	92093	858-534-2230	534-5723
Web: www.ucsd.edu ■ *E-mail:* admissionsinfo@ucsd.edu					
University of San Diego 5998 Alcala Pk	San Diego	CA	92110	619-260-4600	260-6836
Web: www.acusd.edu					

— Hospitals —

	City	State	ZIP	Phone	Fax
Alvarado Hospital Medical Center 6655 Alvarado Rd	San Diego	CA	92120	619-287-3270	229-7020
Web: www.tenethealth.com/Alvarado					

San Diego — Hospitals (Cont'd)

Phone Fax

Children's Hospital & Health Center
3020 Children's Way . . . . San Diego CA 92123 858-576-1700 495-4934*
*Fax: Library ■ Web: www.chsd.org

Green Hospital of Scripps Clinic
10666 N Torrey Pines Rd. . . . . La Jolla CA 92037 858-455-9100 554-6869
Web: www.scrippshealth.org/hospitals/green.html

Grossmont Hospital PO Box 158. . . . . .La Mesa CA 91944 619-465-0711 461-7191

Kaiser Permanente Medical Center
4647 Zion Ave . . . . San Diego CA 92120 619-528-5000 528-5317

Mission Bay Memorial Hospital
3030 Bunker Hill St. . . . . San Diego CA 92109 858-274-7721 483-0655*
*Fax: Admitting ■ Web: www.columbia.net/faciliti/ca/mission.html
■ E-mail: mbmh@cts.com

Naval Medical Center
34800 Bob Wilson Dr . . . . San Diego CA 92134 619-532-6400 532-7755
Web: 159.71.170.20/index.html

Palomar Medical Center
555 E Valley Pkwy . . . . Escondido CA 92025 760-739-3000 739-3772*
*Fax: Admitting ■ Web: www.pphs.org/Palomar.htm

Paradise Valley Hospital 2400 E 4th St . . . .National City CA 91950 619-470-4321 470-4209
Web: www.paradisevalleyhospital.org

Pomerado Hospital 15615 Pomerado Rd. . . . . Poway CA 92064 858-485-6511 613-5678*
*Fax: Admitting

Scripps Memorial Hospital-Chula Vista
435 'H' St . . . . .Chula Vista CA 91910 619-691-7000 691-7523*
*Fax: Mail Rm ■ Web: www.scrippshealth.org/hospitals/chula.html

Scripps Memorial Hospital East County
1688 E Main St. . . . . El Cajon CA 92021 619-440-1122 444-5012
Web: www.scrippshealth.org/hospitals/east.html

Scripps Memorial Hospital-Encinitas
PO Box 230817 . . . . Encinitas CA 92023 760-753-6501 633-7356
Web: www.scrippshealth.org/hospitals/encinitas.html

Scripps Memorial Hospital-La Jolla
9888 Genesee Ave . . . . La Jolla CA 92038 858-457-4123 626-6122
Web: www.scrippshealth.org/hospitals/lajolla.html

Scripps Mercy Hospital 4077 5th Ave . . . . San Diego CA 92103 619-294-8111 260-7307
Web: www.scrippshealth.org/hospitals/mercy.html

Sharp Cabrillo Hospital 3475 Kenyon St . . . . . San Diego CA 92110 619-221-3400 221-3704

Sharp Chula Vista Medical Center
751 Medical Center Ct. . . . . .Chula Vista CA 91911 619-482-5800 482-3604*
*Fax: Admitting

Sharp Coronado Hospital & HealthCare Center
250 Prospect Pl . . . . .Coronado CA 92118 619-435-6251 522-3782

Sharp Memorial Hospital 7901 Frost St . . . . . San Diego CA 92123 858-541-3400 541-3714*
*Fax: Admitting

Tri-City Medical Center 4002 Vista Way . . . . . Oceanside CA 92056 760-724-8411 724-1010

University of California San Diego Medical Center 200 W Arbor Dr. . . . . San Diego CA 92103 619-543-6222 543-7277*
*Fax: Admitting ■ Web: health.ucsd.edu
■ E-mail: healthcare@ucsd.edu

Veterans Affairs Medical Center
3350 La Jolla Village Dr. . . . . San Diego CA 92161 858-552-8585 552-7509

— Attractions —

Phone Fax

Anza-Borrego Desert State Park
200 Palm Canyon Dr. . . . . Borrego Springs CA 92004 760-767-5311 767-3427
TF: 800-444-7275 ■ Web: www.anzaborrego.statepark.org
■ E-mail: feedback@desertusa.com

ARCO Olympic Training Center
1750 Wueste Rd. . . . . .Chula Vista CA 91915 619-656-1500 482-6200

Balboa Park 1549 El Prado . . . . San Diego CA 92101 619-239-0512

Barona Casino 1000 Wildcat Canyon Rd . . . . . . Lakeside CA 92040 619-443-2300 443-2856*
*Fax: Mktg ■ Web: www.barona.com

Bazaar del Mundo Inc 2754 Calhoun St. . . . . . San Diego CA 92110 619-296-3161 296-3113
Web: www.bazaardelmundo.com
■ E-mail: customerservice@bazaardelmundo.com

Belmont Park 3146 Mission Blvd . . . . San Diego CA 92109 619-491-2988 488-6658*
*Fax Area Code: 858

Bernardo Winery
13330 Paseo del Verano Norte . . . . San Diego CA 92128 858-487-1866 673-5376

Birch Aquarium at Scripps
2300 Expedition Way. . . . . La Jolla CA 92037 858-534-3474 534-6692
Web: aquarium.ucsd.edu

Cabrillo National Monument
1800 Cabrillo Memorial Dr. . . . . San Diego CA 92106 619-557-5450 557-5469
Web: www.nps.gov/cabr/

California Ballet Co 8276 Ronson Rd . . . . San Diego CA 92111 858-560-5676 560-0072
Web: www.californiaballet.org

Phone Fax

California Center for the Arts
340 N Escondido Blvd. . . . . Escondido CA 92025 760-839-4138 739-0205
TF: 800-988-4253 ■ Web: www.artcenter.org

Children's Museum of San Diego
200 W Island Ave . . . . San Diego CA 92101 619-233-8792 233-8796

Cuyamaca Rancho State Park
12551 Hwy 79 . . . . .Descanso CA 91916 760-765-0755 765-3021

Fern Street Circus
2323 Broadway Suite 108 . . . . San Diego CA 92102 619-235-9756 231-7910

Firehouse Museum 1572 Columbia St. . . . . . . San Diego CA 92101 619-232-3473
Web: www.globalinfo.com/noncomm/firehouse/Firehouse.HTML

Fleet Reuben H Science Center
1875 El Prado . . . . San Diego CA 92101 619-238-1233 685-5771
Web: www.rhfleet.org/

Flower Fields at Carlsbad Ranch
5600 Avenida Encinas . . . . Carlsbad CA 92008 760-930-9123 431-9020
Web: www.theflowerfields.com ■ E-mail: info@theflowerfields.com

Gaslamp Quarter 614 5th Ave Suite E. . . . . . . San Diego CA 92101 619-233-5227 233-4693
Web: www.gaslamp.com/

Junipero Serra Museum 2727 Presidio Dr. . . . San Diego CA 92103 619-297-3258 297-3281

La Jolla Playhouse 2910 La Jolla Village Dr . . . . La Jolla CA 92037 858-550-1010 550-1075
Web: www.lajollaplayhouse.com ■ E-mail: ljplayhouse@ucsd.edu

Los Penasquitos Canyon Preserve
Mercy Rd-W Black Mountain Rd. . . . . San Diego CA 92105 858-538-8122

Mingei International Museum of Folk Art
1439 El Prado . . . . Balboa Park CA 92101 619-239-0003 239-0605
Web: www.mingei.org ■ E-mail: mingei@mingei.org

Mission Bay Park
8 West to W Mission Bay Dr . . . . San Diego CA 92109 619-221-8901

Mission San Diego de Alcala
10818 San Diego Mission Rd. . . . . San Diego CA 92108 619-283-7319 283-7762

Mission Trails Regional Park
1 Father Junipero Serra Trail . . . . San Diego CA 92119 619-685-1350

Museum of Contemporary Art
1001 Kettner Blvd. . . . . San Diego CA 92101 619-234-1001 234-1070
Web: www.mcasandiego.org

Museum of Photographic Arts
1649 El Prado . . . . San Diego CA 92101 619-238-7559 238-8777
Web: www.mopa.org/ ■ E-mail: info@mopa.org

Museum of San Diego History
1649 El Prado Balboa Pk. . . . . San Diego CA 92101 619-232-6203 232-6297
Web: edweb.sdsu.edu/sdhs

Old Globe Theatre/Simon Edison Centre for the Performing Arts Balboa Pk. . . . . San Diego CA 92112 619-239-2255 231-1037
Web: oldglobe.org/

Old Town State Historic Park
4002 Wallace St . . . . San Diego CA 92110 619-220-5422 220-5421

Old Town Trolley Tours 2115 Kurtz St. . . . . . . San Diego CA 92110 619-298-8687
Web: www.historictours.com/sandiego/trolley.htm
■ E-mail: scampbell@historictours.com

Orfila Vineyards & Winery
13455 San Pasqual Rd . . . . Escondido CA 92025 760-738-6500 745-3773
Web: www.orfila.com

San Diego Aerospace Museum
2001 Pan American Plaza Balboa Pk . . . . . . San Diego CA 92101 619-234-8291 233-4526
Web: www.aerospacemuseum.org

San Diego Automotive Museum
2080 Pan American Plaza Balboa Pk . . . . . . San Diego CA 92101 619-231-2886 231-9869
Web: www.sdautomuseum.org

San Diego Civic Light Opera
2005 Pan American Plaza Starlight Bowl . . . San Diego CA 92101 619-544-7800 544-0496

San Diego Hall of Champions Sports Museum
2131 Pan American Plaza Balboa Pk . . . . . . San Diego CA 92101 619-234-2544 234-4543

San Diego Maritime Museum
1306 N Harbor Dr. . . . . San Diego CA 92101 619-234-9153 234-8345
Web: www.sdmaritime.com ■ E-mail: info@sdmaritime.com

San Diego Model Railroad Museum
1649 El Prado Balboa Pk. . . . . San Diego CA 92101 619-696-0199 696-0239
Web: www.sdmodelrailroadm.com/

San Diego Museum of Art
1450 El Prado Balboa Pk. . . . . San Diego CA 92101 619-232-7931 232-9367
Web: www.sdmart.com/

San Diego Museum of Man
1350 El Prado Balboa Pk. . . . . San Diego CA 92101 619-239-2001 239-2749
Web: www.museumofman.org ■ E-mail: contact@museumofman.org

San Diego Natural History Museum
1788 El Prado . . . . San Diego CA 92101 619-232-3821 232-0248
Web: www.sdnhm.org

San Diego Opera Assn
1200 3rd Ave 18th Fl. . . . . San Diego CA 92101 619-232-7636 231-6915
Web: www.sdopera.com ■ E-mail: facts@sdopera.com

San Diego Railroad Museum
1050 Kettner Blvd . . . . San Diego CA 92101 619-595-3030 595-3034
TF: 888-228-9246 ■ Web: www.sdrm.org/
■ E-mail: wolfgang@train.sdrm.org

San Diego Repertory Theatre
79 Horton Plaza . . . . San Diego CA 92101 619-231-3586 235-0939

San Diego — Attractions (Cont'd)

				Phone	Fax
San Diego Wild Animal Park 15500 San Pasqual Valley Rd. *Web:* www.sandiegozoo.org/wap	Escondido	CA	92027	760-747-8702	746-7081
San Diego Zoo 2920 Zoo Dr. *Web:* www.sandiegozoo.org	San Diego	CA	92103	619-231-1515	557-3970
San Luis Rey Mission 4050 Mission Ave. *Web:* sanluisrey.org ■ *E-mail:* mission@slctnet.com	Oceanside	CA	92057	760-757-3651	757-4613
Sea World of California 500 Sea World Dr *Web:* www.seaworld.com/seaworld/sw_california/swcframe.html	San Diego	CA	92109	619-226-3901	226-3996
Seaport Village 849 W Harbor Dr *Web:* www.spvillage.com	San Diego	CA	92101	619-235-4014	696-0025
Spreckels Theatre 121 Broadway	San Diego	CA	92101	619-235-9500	234-8397
Theatre in Old Town 4040 Twiggs St *Web:* www.theatreinoldtown.com ■ *E-mail:* admin@theatreinoldtown.com	San Diego	CA	92110	619-688-2494	688-0960
Timken Museum of Art 1500 El Prado Balboa Pk *Web:* gort.ucsd.edu/sj/timken	San Diego	CA	92101	619-239-5548	233-6629
Torrey Pines State Reserve N Torrey Pines Rd	San Diego	CA	92037	858-755-2063	
Villa Montezuma Museum & Jesse Shepard House 1925 'K' St.	San Diego	CA	92102	619-239-2211	
Wells Fargo History Museum 2733 San Diego Ave *Web:* wellsfargo.com/about/museum/info/	San Diego	CA	92110	619-238-3929	298-8209
Whale Watching 2803 Emerson St H & M Landing *Web:* www.hmlanding.com/nature.htm ■ *E-mail:* hmmail@hmlanding.com	San Diego	CA	92106	619-222-1144	222-0784
Whaley House Museum 2482 San Diego Ave	San Diego	CA	92110	619-298-2482	
White George & Anna Gunn Marston House 3525 7th Ave	San Diego	CA	92103	619-298-3142	232-6297

SPORTS TEAMS & FACILITIES

				Phone	Fax
Del Mar Thoroughbred Club PO Box 700 *Web:* www.dmtc.com	Del Mar	CA	92014	858-755-1141	792-1477
Qualcomm Stadium 9449 Friars Rd *Web:* www.qualcomm.com/stadium	San Diego	CA	92108	619-641-3100	283-0460
San Diego Chargers 9449 Friars Rd Qualcomm Stadium *Web:* www.chargers.com	San Diego	CA	92108	619-280-2121	280-5107
San Diego Flash (soccer) 7250 Mesa College Dr Douglas Stadium *Web:* www.sdflash.com ■ *E-mail:* sdflash@aol.com	San Diego	CA	92111	619-581-2120	581-9419
San Diego Gulls (hockey) 3500 Sports Arena Blvd San Diego Sports Arena *Web:* www.sandiegoarena.com/gulls/gulls.htm	San Diego	CA	92110	619-224-4625	224-3010
San Diego Padres 9449 Friars Rd Qualcomm Stadium *Web:* www.padres.com/ ■ *E-mail:* comments@padres.com	San Diego	CA	92108	619-881-6500	497-5339
San Diego Sports Arena 3500 Sports Arena Blvd *Web:* www.sandiegoarena.com	San Diego	CA	92110	619-225-9813	224-3010
San Jose Municipal Stadium 588 E Alma Ave *Web:* www.sjgiants.com/stadium_info.html	San Jose	CA	95112	408-297-1435	297-1453

— Events —

	Phone
Adams Avenue Street Fair (late September)	619-282-7329
Art Alive (late April)	619-232-7931
Borrego Springs Desert Festival (late October)	760-767-5555
Cabrillo Festival (late September)	619-557-5450
California American Indian Days Celebration (late September)	619-281-5964
Christmas on the Prado (early December)	619-239-0512
Coronado Independence Day Celebration (July 4)	619-437-8788
Culligan Holiday Bowl (late December)	619-236-1212
Del Mar Fair (mid-June-early July)	858-755-1161
Del Mar National Horse Show (late April-early May)	858-792-4288
Fall Village Faire (early November)	760-434-8887
Fiesta Cinco de Mayo (early May)	619-236-1212
First Night San Diego (December 31)	619-280-5838
Harvest Festival (late September)	619-615-4100
Holiday Bowl (late December)	619-283-5808
Hot Air Balloon Classic (July 4)	858-481-6800
La Jolla Festival of the Arts & Food Faire (mid-June)	619-236-1212
Lakeside Western Days & Rodeo (mid-April)	619-236-1212
Mainly Mozart Festival (late May-early June)	619-239-0100
MCAS Miramar Air Show (late July-early August)	619-236-1212
Nations of San Diego International Dance Festival (mid-January)	619-239-9255
Ocean Beach Kite Festival (early March)	619-236-1212
Oceanside Harbor Days (late September)	760-722-1534
Poinsettia Festival (early December)	760-943-1950
Port of San Diego International Triathlon (late June)	619-236-1212
Poway Street Fair (November)	858-748-0022
Ramona Rodeo (mid-May)	619-236-1212
Rancho Bernardo Fall Art & Wine Festival (mid-October)	858-487-1767
Rosarito-Ensenada 50 Mile Fun Bicycle Ride (late September & mid-April)	619-583-3001
San Diego American Indian Cultural Days (mid-May)	619-281-5964
San Diego Boat Show (early January)	858-274-9924
San Diego Crew Classic (late March)	619-236-1212
San Diego Dixieland Jazz Festival (late November)	619-297-5277
San Diego Film Festival (February-May)	858-534-0497
San Diego Harbor Parade of Lights (mid-late December)	619-232-3101
San Diego Marathon (mid-January)	858-792-2900
San Diego New Year Celebration (February)	619-234-4447
San Diego Polo Matches (June-October)	858-481-9217
San Diego Street Scene (mid-September)	619-557-8490
Score Baja 1000 Race (early November)	619-236-1212
Summer Organ Festival (June-August)	619-226-0819
US Open Sandcastle Competition (mid-July)	619-424-6663
Vista Holiday Parade (early December)	760-726-1122
World Body Surfing Championships (mid-August)	760-966-4535
World Championship Over-the-Line Tournament (mid-July)	619-236-1212
World Series of Powerboats Racing (mid-September)	619-236-1212

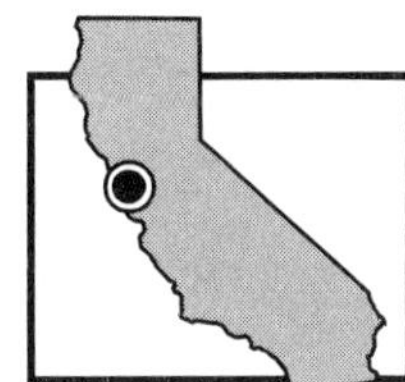

San Francisco

The "City by the Bay" is well-known for its cable cars and the Golden Gate Bridge, plus Lombard Street, which is called the "crookedest street in the world." The area known as The Embarcadero is home to other familiar names like Fisherman's Wharf, The Cannery, and Ghirardelli Square, all known for their shopping and dining venues. The Embarcadero's waterfront promenade extends to the San Francisco-Oakland Bay Bridge, which offers one of the finest views in the city. San Francisco's neighborhoods include Chinatown, the site of the huge Chinese New Year parade; Haight-Ashbury, a quaint Victorian sector and former mecca of 60s counterculture; and Nob Hill, which is home to some of the city's finest hotels and provides the best view of the San Francisco Bay. On the Bay is one of San Francisco's most popular attractions, the infamous Alcatraz, which draws more than 1.1 million visitors annually.

Population	745,774	**Longitude**	122-41-83 W
Area (Land)	46.7 sq mi	**County**	San Francisco
Area (Water)	185.2 sq mi	**Time Zone**	PST
Elevation	63 ft	**Area Code/s**	415
Latitude	37-77-50 N		

— Average Temperatures and Precipitation —

TEMPERATURES

	Jan	Feb	Mar	Apr	May	Jun	Jul	Aug	Sep	Oct	Nov	Dec
High	56	59	61	64	67	70	72	72	74	70	62	56
Low	42	45	46	47	50	53	54	55	55	52	47	43

PRECIPITATION

	Jan	Feb	Mar	Apr	May	Jun	Jul	Aug	Sep	Oct	Nov	Dec
Inches	4.4	3.2	3.1	1.4	0.2	0.1	0.0	0.1	0.2	1.2	2.9	3.1

San Francisco (Cont'd)

— Important Phone Numbers —

	Phone		Phone
AAA	415-565-2012	**Medical Referral**	415-561-0850
American Express Travel	415-908-3500	**Poison Control Center**	800-876-4766
Emergency	911	**Time**	415-767-8900
Events Line	415-391-2001	**Weather**	650-364-7974
HotelDocs	800-468-3537		

— Information Sources —

				Phone	Fax
Better Business Bureau Serving Oakland/San Francisco Area & Northwest Coastal California 510 16th St Suite 550	Oakland	CA	94612	510-238-1000	238-1018
Web: www.oakland.bbb.org					
Moscone Center 747 Howard St	San Francisco	CA	94103	415-974-4000	974-4073
San Francisco Chamber of Commerce 465 California St Suite 900	San Francisco	CA	94104	415-392-4520	392-0485
Web: www.sfchamber.com					
San Francisco City Hall 401 Van Ness Ave.	San Francisco	CA	94102	415-554-4000	554-6160
Web: www.ci.sf.ca.us					
San Francisco Civic Auditorium 99 Grove St	San Francisco	CA	94102	415-974-4000	974-4084
San Francisco Convention & Visitors Bureau 201 3rd St Suite 900	San Francisco	CA	94103	415-974-6900	227-2602
Web: www.sfvisitor.org					
San Francisco County 1 Dr Carleton B Goodlett Pl	San Francisco	CA	94102	415-252-3282	
San Francisco Mayor 1 Dr Carleton B Goodlett Pl Rm 200	San Francisco	CA	94102	415-554-6141	554-6160
Web: www.ci.sf.ca.us/mayor ■ *E-mail:* damayor@ci.sf.ca.us					
San Francisco Planning Commission 1660 Mission St 5th Fl	San Francisco	CA	94103	415-558-6414	558-6409
Web: www.ci.sf.ca.us/planning/index.htm					
San Francisco Public Library 100 Larkin St	San Francisco	CA	94102	415-557-4400	557-4239
Web: sfpl.lib.ca.us					

On-Line Resources

4SanFrancisco.com	www.4sanfrancisco.com
ABAG Online	www.abag.ca.gov
Access America San Francisco	www.accessamer.com/sanfrancisco/
Annual Guide for the Arts	www.guide4arts.com/sf/
Anthill City Guide San Francisco	www.anthill.com/city.asp?city=sanfrancisco
Area Guide San Francisco	sanfrancisco.areaguides.net
Back in San Francisco	www.backinsf.com/
Bay Area Art Source	www.foggy.com/indexf.html
Bay Area eGuide	www.sfgate.com/eguide/
Bay Area Restaurant Guide	dine.com/barg
BayArea.com	www.bayarea.com
BayInsider.com	www.bayinsider.com/
Boulevards San Francisco	www.sanfrancisco.com
Bradmans.com San Francisco	www.bradmans.com/scripts/display_city.cgi?city=242
City Insights San Francisco	cityinsights.com/sanfran.htm
City Knowledge San Francisco	www.cityknowledge.com/ca_sanfrancisco.htm
Cityguide Online	www.ctguide.com/
CitySearch San Francisco	bayarea.citysearch.com
CityTravelGuide.com San Francisco	www.citytravelguide.com/san-francisco.htm
CuisineNet San Francisco	www.cuisinenet.com/restaurant/san_francisco/index.shtml
DigitalCity San Francisco	home.digitalcity.com/sanfrancisco
Essential Guide to San Francisco	www.ego.net/us/ca/sf/index.htm
Excite.com San Francisco City Guide	www.excite.com/travel/countries/united_states/california/san_francisco
Fine Art Museums of San Francisco	www.famsf.org/
Fog City Online	userwww.sfsu.edu/~ped/fogcity.htm
Gayot's Guide Restaurant Search San Francisco	www.perrier.com/restaurants/gayot.asp?area=SFC
HotelGuide San Francisco	sanfrancisco.hotelguide.net
NITC Travelbase City Guide San Francisco	www.travelbase.com/auto/guides/san_francisco-area-ca.html
Open World City Guides San Francisco	www.worldexecutive.com/cityguides/san_francisco/
Q San Francisco Guide	www.qsanfrancisco.com/qsf/guide/
Rough Guide Travel San Francisco	travel.roughguides.com/content/3697/
San Francisco Bay Area CityWomen	www.citywomen.com/sfwomen.htm
San Francisco Bay Area Index	www.sfbayarea.com/index/
San Francisco Bay Guardian	www.sfbayguardian.com
San Francisco Bay Resource Home Page	www.sftoday.com/sfbay.htm
San Francisco California	san-francisco-california.com
San Francisco Graphic City Guide	www.futurecast.com/gcg/sanfran.htm
San Francisco Guide	www.sfguide.com/
San Francisco Home Page	www.wco.com/~chldress/sfhome/
San Francisco Insider	www.theinsider.com/sf
San Francisco Online	www.sfousa.com/
San Francisco Station	www.sfstation.com/
San Francisco.com	sanfrancisco.com
San FranZiskGo	www.transaction.net/sanfran/events/
SanFrancisco.TheLinks.com	sanfrancisco.thelinks.com/
Savvy Diner Guide to San Francisco Restaurants	www.savvydiner.com/sanfrancisco/
SFMission.com	www.sfmission.com
Surf & Sun Beach Vacation Guide to San Francisco	www.surf-sun.com/ca-san-francisco-main.htm
Time Out San Francisco	www.timeout.com/sanfrancisco/
Tourists Guide to San Francisco	www.hooked.net/users/manx/
Ultimate Resource for San Francisco	www.transaction.net/sanfran/ult/index.html
Union Street in San Francisco	www.unionstreet.com
Virtual Voyages San Francisco	www.virtualvoyages.com/usa/ca/s_f/sf.sht
Web Castro	www.webcastro.com/
WeekendEvents.com San Francisco	www.weekendevents.com/sanfrancisco/sanfran.html
World's Online Guide to Castro Street San Francisco	www.castroonline.com
Yahoo! San Francisco	sfbay.yahoo.com
Z San Francisco	www.zpub.com/sf/

— Transportation Services —

AIRPORTS

■ San Francisco International Airport (SFO)

	Phone
14 miles S of downtown (approx 25 minutes)	650-761-0800

Web: www.sfoairport.com

Airport Transportation

	Phone
American Airporter Shuttle $11 fare to downtown	415-546-6689
BayPorter Express fare varies with destination	415-467-1800
Quake City Airport Shuttle $10 fare to downtown	415-255-4899
SAMTRANS $3 fare to downtown	650-508-6200
SFO Airporter $10 fare to downtown	415-495-8404
SuperShuttle $12 fare to downtown.	800-258-3826
Taxi $30 fare to downtown	415-626-2345

Commercial Airlines

	Phone		Phone
Aeroflot	888-686-4949	**Northwest**	800-225-2525
Air Canada	800-776-3000	**Philippine**	800-435-9725
Air China	415-392-2156	**Shuttle by United**	800-748-8853
American	800-433-7300	**Singapore**	800-742-3333
British Airways	800-247-9297	**Southwest**	800-435-9792
China Airlines	415-391-3950	**TACA International**	800-535-8780
Continental	415-397-8818	**TWA**	800-221-2000
Delta	800-221-1212	**United**	800-241-6522
Japan	800-525-3663	**United Express**	800-241-6522
Lufthansa	800-645-3880	**US Airways**	800-428-4322
Mexicana	800-531-7923	**Varig Brazilian**	800-468-2744
National	888-757-5387	**VASP Brazilian Airlines**	800-732-8277

Charter Airlines

	Phone		Phone
Air Share	650-856-3858	**Lasco International Network**	415-668-3770
Clay Lacy Aviation Inc	800-423-2904	**San Francisco Sea Plane Tours**	415-332-4843
KaiserAir	510-569-9622	**Tag Aviation**	800-252-6972

CAR RENTALS

	Phone		Phone
Alamo	650-347-9914	**Hertz**	650-624-6600
Avis	650-877-6780	**National**	650-877-4745
Budget	650-875-6850	**Payless**	650-737-6134
Dollar	650-244-4130	**Thrifty**	415-788-8111
Enterprise	650-697-9200		

San Francisco (Cont'd)

LIMO/TAXI

	Phone		Phone
A-1 Limousine	650-872-8531	**Luxor Cab**	415-282-4141
Associated Limousines	415-563-1000	**Regency Limousine**	415-922-0123
Carey Squire Limousine	650-761-3000	**Uptown Limousine**	650-589-7373
City Wide Cab	415-920-0700	**Veterans Taxicab**	415-552-1300
Ishi Limousine	650-794-1333	**Yellow Cab**	415-626-2345

MASS TRANSIT

	Phone
Bay Area Rapid Transit (BART) $1.10 Base fare	650-992-2278
Municipal Railway (MUNI Bus/Streetcar) $1 Base fare	415-673-6864

RAIL/BUS

				Phone
Amtrak Station 31 Embarcadero & Market	San Francisco	CA	94111	800-872-7245
Greyhound Bus Station 425 Mission St Transbay Stn	San Francisco	CA	94105	800-231-2222

— Accommodations —

HOTEL RESERVATION SERVICES

	Phone	Fax
Accommodations Express	609-391-2100	525-0111

TF: 800-444-7666 ■ *Web:* www.accommodationsxpress.com ■ *E-mail:* accomexp@acy.digex.net

	Phone	Fax
Bed & Breakfast San Francisco	415-899-0060	899-9923

TF: 800-452-8249 ■ *Web:* www.bbsf.com ■ *E-mail:* bbsf@linex.com

	Phone	Fax
California Reservations	415-252-1107	252-1483

TF: 800-576-0003 ■ *Web:* www.cal-res.com

	Phone	Fax
California Suites Reservations	916-363-9700	363-9465

TF: 800-363-9779 ■ *Web:* www.calsuites.com

	Phone	Fax
Central Reservation Service	407-740-6442	740-8222

TF: 800-548-3311 ■ *Web:* www.reservation-services.com ■ *E-mail:* cenresbos@aol.com

	Phone	Fax
Hotel Reservations Network Inc	214-361-7311	361-7299

TF Sales: 800-964-6835 ■ *Web:* www.hoteldiscount.com

	Phone	Fax
Quikbook	212-532-1660	532-1556

TF: 800-789-9887 ■ *Web:* www.quikbook.com

	Phone	Fax
RMC Travel Centre	212-754-6560	754-6571

TF: 800-782-2674

	Phone	Fax
San Francisco Reservations	415-227-1500	227-1520

TF: 800-677-1550 ■ *Web:* www.hotelres.com ■ *E-mail:* sfr@hotelres.com

HOTELS, MOTELS, RESORTS

				Phone	Fax
Andrews Hotel 624 Post St	San Francisco	CA	94109	415-563-6877	928-6919

TF: 800-926-3739

				Phone	Fax
Archbishop's Mansion Inn 1000 Fulton St	San Francisco	CA	94117	415-563-7872	885-3193

TF: 800-543-5820

				Phone	Fax
Argent Hotel 50 3rd St	San Francisco	CA	94103	415-974-6400	543-8268

TF: 877-222-6699 ■ *Web:* www.argenthotel.com ■ *E-mail:* argenthotel@destinationtravel.com

				Phone	Fax
Atherton Hotel 685 Ellis St	San Francisco	CA	94109	415-474-5720	474-8256

TF: 800-474-5720

				Phone	Fax
Best Western Americania 121 7th St	San Francisco	CA	94103	415-626-0200	863-2529

TF: 800-528-1234

				Phone	Fax
Best Western Grosvenor Hotel 380 S Airport Blvd	South San Francisco	CA	94080	650-873-3200	589-3495

TF: 800-722-7141

				Phone	Fax
Britton Hotel 112 7th St	San Francisco	CA	94103	415-621-7001	621-4069

TF: 800-444-5818

				Phone	Fax
Campton Place Hotel 340 Stockton St	San Francisco	CA	94108	415-781-5555	955-5536

TF: 800-235-4300 ■ *Web:* www.camptonplace.com ■ *E-mail:* reserve@campton.com

				Phone	Fax
Canterbury Hotel 750 Sutter St	San Francisco	CA	94109	415-474-6464	474-5856

TF: 800-227-4788

				Phone	Fax
Cathedral Hill Hotel 1101 Van Ness Ave	San Francisco	CA	94109	415-776-8200	441-2841

TF: 800-622-0855 ■ *Web:* www.westcoasthotels.com/cathedralhill

				Phone	Fax
Clarion Hotel Airport 401 E Millbrae Ave	Millbrae	CA	94030	650-692-6363	697-8735

TF: 800-223-7111

				Phone	Fax
Clift Hotel 495 Geary St	San Francisco	CA	94102	415-775-4700	441-4621

TF: 800-652-5438 ■ *Web:* www.travelbase.com/destinations/san-francisco/clift

				Phone	Fax
Crowne Plaza Union Square 480 Sutter St	San Francisco	CA	94108	415-398-8900	989-8823

TF: 800-243-1135

				Phone	Fax
Donatello The 501 Post St	San Francisco	CA	94102	415-441-7100	885-8842

TF: 800-227-3184

				Phone	Fax
Doubletree Hotel San Francisco Airport 835 Airport Blvd	Burlingame	CA	94010	650-344-5500	340-8851

TF: 800-222-8733 ■ *Web:* www.doubletreehotels.com/DoubleT/Hotel/17/17Main.htm

				Phone	Fax
Embassy Suites 150 Anza Blvd	Burlingame	CA	94010	650-342-4600	343-8137

TF: 800-362-2779

				Phone	Fax
Fairmont Hotel 950 Mason St	San Francisco	CA	94108	415-772-5000	837-0587

TF: 800-344-3550 ■ *Web:* www.fairmont.com/sanfrancisco.html ■ *E-mail:* sanfrancisco@fairmont.com

				Phone	Fax
Galleria Park Hotel 191 Sutter St	San Francisco	CA	94104	415-781-3060	433-4409

TF: 800-792-9639 ■ *Web:* 135.145.16.183/galleriapark.com

				Phone	Fax
Grand Hyatt San Francisco 345 Stockton St	San Francisco	CA	94108	415-398-1234	391-1780

TF: 800-233-1234 ■ *Web:* www.hyatt.com/usa/san_francisco/hotels/hotel_sfous.html

				Phone	Fax
Grant Plaza Hotel 465 Grant Ave	San Francisco	CA	94108	415-434-3883	434-3886

TF: 800-472-6899 ■ *Web:* www.grantplaza.com ■ *E-mail:* grantplaza@worldnet.att.net

				Phone	Fax
Half Moon Bay Lodge & Conference Center 2400 S Cabrillo Hwy	Half Moon Bay	CA	94019	650-726-9000	726-7951

TF: 800-368-2468 ■ *Web:* woodsidehotels.com/wlodging/hmbl.html

				Phone	Fax
Handlery Union Square Hotel 351 Geary St	San Francisco	CA	94102	415-781-7800	781-0216

TF: 800-843-4343 ■ *Web:* www.handlery.com/ONE_SF/ONE_HTML_SF/ONE_FRAME_SF.html

				Phone	Fax
Harbor Court 165 Steuart St	San Francisco	CA	94105	415-882-1300	882-1313

TF: 800-346-0555 ■ *Web:* 135.145.16.183/harborcourthotel.com ■ *E-mail:* harborsf@slip.net

				Phone	Fax
Holiday Inn Fisherman's Wharf 1300 Columbus Ave	San Francisco	CA	94133	415-771-9000	771-7006

TF: 800-942-7348 ■ *Web:* www.basshotels.com/holiday-inn/?_franchisee=SFOFW

				Phone	Fax
Hotel Del Sol 3100 Webster St	San Francisco	CA	94123	415-921-5520	931-4137

TF: 877-433-5765 ■ *Web:* www.sftrips.com

				Phone	Fax
Hotel Monaco 501 Geary St	San Francisco	CA	94102	415-292-0100	292-0111

TF: 800-214-4220

				Phone	Fax
Hotel Nikko San Francisco 222 Mason St	San Francisco	CA	94102	415-394-1111	394-1106

TF: 800-645-5687 ■ *Web:* bayarea.citysearch.com/E/V/SFOCA/0001/21/05/

				Phone	Fax
Hotel Rex 562 Sutter St	San Francisco	CA	94102	415-433-4434	433-3695

TF: 800-433-4434

				Phone	Fax
Hotel Triton 342 Grant Ave	San Francisco	CA	94108	415-394-0500	394-0555

TF: 800-433-6611 ■ *Web:* 135.145.16.183/hotel-tritonsf.com

				Phone	Fax
Huntington Hotel Nob Hill 1075 California St	San Francisco	CA	94108	415-474-5400	474-6227

TF: 800-227-4683

				Phone	Fax
Hyatt Fisherman's Wharf 555 N Point St	San Francisco	CA	94133	415-563-1234	749-6122

TF: 800-233-1234 ■ *Web:* www.hyatt.com/usa/san_francisco/hotels/hotel_sfofw.html

				Phone	Fax
Hyatt Regency Airport 1333 Old Bayshore Hwy	Burlingame	CA	94010	650-347-1234	696-2669

TF: 800-233-1234 ■ *Web:* www.hyatt.com/usa/san_francisco/hotels/hotel_sfobu.html

				Phone	Fax
Hyatt Regency San Francisco 5 Embarcadero Ctr	San Francisco	CA	94111	415-788-1234	398-2567

TF: 800-233-1234 ■ *Web:* www.hyatt.com/usa/san_francisco/hotels/hotel_sfors.html

				Phone	Fax
Inn at the Opera 333 Fulton St	San Francisco	CA	94102	415-863-8400	861-0821

TF: 800-325-2708

				Phone	Fax
Inn at Union Square 440 Post St	San Francisco	CA	94102	415-397-3510	989-0529

TF: 800-288-4346 ■ *Web:* www.unionsquare.com/ ■ *E-mail:* inn@unionsquare.com

				Phone	Fax
Kensington Park Hotel 450 Post St	San Francisco	CA	94102	415-788-6400	399-9484

TF: 800-553-1900

				Phone	Fax
Majestic The 1500 Sutter St	San Francisco	CA	94109	415-441-1100	673-7331

TF: 800-869-8966

				Phone	Fax
Mandarin Oriental 222 Sansome St	San Francisco	CA	94104	415-885-0999	433-0289

TF: 800-622-0404

				Phone	Fax
Mark Hopkins Inter-Continental 1 Nob Hill	San Francisco	CA	94108	415-392-3434	421-3302

TF: 800-327-0200

				Phone	Fax
Marriott Fisherman's Wharf 120 Columbus Ave	San Francisco	CA	94133	415-775-7555	474-2099

TF: 800-525-0956 ■ *Web:* marriotthotels.com/SFOFW/

				Phone	Fax
Marriott Hotel San Francisco Airport 1800 Old Bayshore Hwy	Burlingame	CA	94010	650-692-9100	692-8016

TF: 800-228-9290 ■ *Web:* marriotthotels.com/SFOBG

				Phone	Fax
Maxwell Hotel 386 Geary St	San Francisco	CA	94102	415-986-2000	397-2447

TF: 800-738-7477

San Francisco — Hotels, Motels, Resorts (Cont'd)

				Phone	Fax
Miyako Hotel 1625 Post St	San Francisco	CA	94115	415-922-3200	921-0417
TF: 800-333-3333					
Mosser Victorian Hotel 54 4th St	San Francisco	CA	94103	415-986-4400	495-7653
TF: 800-227-3804					
Palace Hotel 2 New Montgomery St	San Francisco	CA	94105	415-512-1111	543-0671
TF: 800-325-3535					
■ *Web:* www.luxurycollection.com/cgi/t3.cgi/property.taf?prop=373					
Pan Pacific Hotel 500 Post St	San Francisco	CA	94102	415-771-8600	398-0267
TF: 800-533-6465					
■ *Web:* www.panpac.com/usa/san_francisco/hotels/hotel.html					
■ *E-mail:* guest@sfo.pan-pacific.com					
Park Plaza Hotel 1177 Airport Blvd	Burlingame	CA	94010	650-342-9200	342-1655
TF: 800-411-7275					
Petite Auberge 863 Bush St	San Francisco	CA	94108	415-928-6000	673-7214
TF: 800-365-3004 ■ *Web:* www.foursisters.com/petite.html					
Phoenix Hotel 601 Eddy St	San Francisco	CA	94109	415-776-1380	885-3109
TF: 800-248-9466					
Pickwick Hotel 85 5th St	San Francisco	CA	94103	415-421-7500	243-8066
TF: 800-227-3282					
Prescott Hotel 545 Post St	San Francisco	CA	94102	415-563-0303	563-6831
TF: 800-283-7322 ■ *Web:* 135.145.16.183/prescotthotel.com					
Queen Anne Hotel 1590 Sutter St	San Francisco	CA	94109	415-441-2828	775-5212
TF: 800-227-3970 ■ *Web:* www.queenanne.com					
■ *E-mail:* stay@queenanne.com					
Ramada Inn 345 Taylor St	San Francisco	CA	94102	415-673-2332	398-0733
Ramada Plaza Hotel Fisherman's Wharf					
590 Bay St	San Francisco	CA	94133	415-885-4700	771-8945
TF: 800-228-8408					
Ramada Plaza Hotel San Francisco					
1231 Market St	San Francisco	CA	94103	415-626-8000	861-1460
TF: 800-227-4747					
Renaissance Parc Fifty Five					
55 Cyril Magnin St	San Francisco	CA	94102	415-392-8000	403-6602
TF: 800-650-7272					
Renaissance Stanford Court Hotel					
905 California St	San Francisco	CA	94108	415-989-3500	391-0513
TF: 800-468-3571					
Residence Inn by Marriott					
2000 Winward Way	San Mateo	CA	94404	650-574-4700	572-9084
TF: 800-331-3131 ■ *Web:* www.residenceinn.com/SFOMV					
Ritz-Carlton San Francisco					
600 Stockton St	San Francisco	CA	94108	415-296-7465	291-0288
TF: 800-241-3333					
■ *Web:* www.ritzcarlton.com/location/NorthAmerica/SanFrancisco/main.htm					
San Francisco Hilton Hotel					
333 O'Farrell St	San Francisco	CA	94102	415-771-1400	771-6807
TF: 800-445-8667					
San Francisco Marriott Hotel					
55 4th St	San Francisco	CA	94103	415-896-1600	777-2799
TF: 800-228-9290 ■ *Web:* www.sfmarriott.com					
■ *E-mail:* info@sfmarriott.com					
Savoy Hotel 580 Geary St	San Francisco	CA	94102	415-441-2700	441-0124
TF: 800-227-4223 ■ *Web:* www.sftrips.com					
Serrano Hotel 405 Taylor St	San Francisco	CA	94102	415-885-2500	474-4879
TF: 877-294-9709 ■ *Web:* 135.145.16.183/serranohotel.com					
Sheraton at Fisherman's Wharf					
2500 Mason St	San Francisco	CA	94133	415-362-5500	956-5275
TF: 800-325-3535					
Sheraton Gateway Hotel 600 Airport Blvd	Burlingame	CA	94010	650-340-8500	343-1546
TF: 800-325-3535					
Sherman House 2160 Green St	San Francisco	CA	94123	415-563-3600	563-1882
TF: 800-424-5777					
Sir Francis Drake Hotel 450 Powell St	San Francisco	CA	94102	415-392-7755	391-8719
TF: 800-227-5480 ■ *Web:* 135.145.16.183/sirfrancisdrake.com					
Suites at Fisherman's Wharf					
2655 Hyde St	San Francisco	CA	94109	415-771-0200	346-8058
TF: 800-227-3608					
Travelodge Fisherman's Wharf					
250 Beach St	San Francisco	CA	94133	415-392-6700	986-7853
TF: 800-578-7878					
Tuscan Inn Best Western					
425 N Point St	San Francisco	CA	94133	415-561-1100	561-1199
TF: 800-648-4626					
Villa Florence Hotel 225 Powell St	San Francisco	CA	94102	415-397-7700	397-1006
TF: 800-553-4411 ■ *Web:* 135.145.16.183/villaflorence.com					
Warwick-Regis Hotel 490 Geary St	San Francisco	CA	94102	415-928-7900	441-8788
TF: 800-827-3447					
Westin Saint Francis Hotel					
335 Powell St	San Francisco	CA	94102	415-397-7000	774-0124
TF: 800-228-3000					
York Hotel 940 Sutter St	San Francisco	CA	94109	415-885-6800	885-2115
TF: 800-808-9675					

— Restaurants —

				Phone
A Sabella's (Seafood) 2766 Taylor St	San Francisco	CA	94133	415-771-6775
Web: www.asabella.com/				
Acquerello (Italian) 1722 Sacramento St	San Francisco	CA	94109	415-567-5432
Aqua (Seafood) 252 California St	San Francisco	CA	94111	415-956-9662
Barcelona (Spanish) 7 Spring St	San Francisco	CA	94104	415-989-1976
Betelnut (Asian) 2030 Union St	San Francisco	CA	94123	415-929-8855
Big Four Restaurant (Continental) 1075 California St	San Francisco	CA	94108	415-771-1140
Black Cat (International) 501 Broadway	San Francisco	CA	94133	415-981-2233
Boulevard (New American) 1 Mission St	San Francisco	CA	94105	415-543-6084
Bruno's (Mediterranean) 2389 Mission St	San Francisco	CA	94110	415-550-7455
Bubba Gump Shrimp Co (Seafood)				
Pier 39 Fisherman's Wharf	San Francisco	CA	94133	415-781-4867
Cafe Adriano (Italian) 3347 Fillmore St	San Francisco	CA	94123	415-474-4180
Cafe Mozart (French) 708 Bush St	San Francisco	CA	94108	415-391-8480
Caffe Sport (Seafood) 574 Green St	San Francisco	CA	94133	415-981-1251
Campton Place Restaurant (New American)				
340 Stockton St	San Francisco	CA	94108	415-781-5555
Capp's Corner (Italian) 1600 Powell St	San Francisco	CA	94133	415-989-2589
Carnelian Room (American) 555 California St	San Francisco	CA	94104	415-433-7500
Charles Nob Hill (French) 1250 Jones St	San Francisco	CA	94109	415-771-5400
Chow (Italian) 215 Church St	San Francisco	CA	94114	415-552-2469
Cityscape (California) 333 O'Farrell St 1 Hilton Sq	San Francisco	CA	94102	415-923-5002
Clementine (French) 126 Clement St	San Francisco	CA	94118	415-387-0408
Cliff House (American) 1090 Point Lobos Ave	San Francisco	CA	94121	415-386-3330
Web: www.cliffhouse.com/				
Cypress Club (California) 500 Jackson St	San Francisco	CA	94133	415-296-8555
Della Torre (Italian) 1349 Montgomery St	San Francisco	CA	94133	415-296-1111
Dining Room The (California/French)				
600 Stockton St	San Francisco	CA	94108	415-296-7465
Empress of China (Chinese) 838 Grant Ave	San Francisco	CA	94108	415-434-1345
Eos (Asian) 901 Cole St	San Francisco	CA	94117	415-566-3063
Web: www.eossf.com/				
Farallon (Seafood) 450 Post St	San Francisco	CA	94102	415-956-6969
Fleur de Lys (French) 777 Sutter St	San Francisco	CA	94109	415-673-7779
Fournou's Ovens (New American) 905 California St	San Francisco	CA	94108	415-989-1910
Fringale (French) 570 4th St	San Francisco	CA	94107	415-543-0573
Gaylord India Restaurant (Indian) 900 N Point St	San Francisco	CA	94109	415-771-8822
Web: www.gaylords.com/				
German Cook Restaurant (German) 612 O'Farrell St	San Francisco	CA	94102	415-776-9022
Globe (Mediterranean) 290 Pacific Ave	San Francisco	CA	94111	415-391-4132
Greens (Vegetarian) Fort Mason Ctr Bldg A	San Francisco	CA	94123	415-771-6222
Harbor Village (Chinese) 4 Embarcadero Ctr	San Francisco	CA	94111	415-781-8833
Hard Rock Cafe (American) 1699 Van Ness Ave	San Francisco	CA	94109	415-885-1699
Harris' Restaurant (Steak) 2100 Van Ness Ave	San Francisco	CA	94109	415-673-1888
Hawthorne Lane (California) 22 Hawthorne St	San Francisco	CA	94105	415-777-9779
Web: www.hawthornelane.com				
Helmand (Afghan) 430 Broadway	San Francisco	CA	94133	415-362-0641
Hong Kong Flower Lounge (Cantonese)				
5322 Geary Blvd	San Francisco	CA	94118	415-668-8998
House of Prime Rib (Steak) 1906 Van Ness Ave	San Francisco	CA	94109	415-885-4605
Hyde Street Seafood House (Seafood) 1509 Hyde St	San Francisco	CA	94109	415-931-3474
Jardiniere (California/French) 300 Grove St	San Francisco	CA	94102	415-861-5555
Julius' Castle (Continental) 1541 Montgomery St	San Francisco	CA	94133	415-362-3042
Kabuto Sushi (Japanese) 5116 Geary Blvd	San Francisco	CA	94118	415-752-5652
Khan Toke Thai House (Thai) 5937 Geary Blvd	San Francisco	CA	94121	415-668-6654
Kuleto's (Italian) 221 Powell St	San Francisco	CA	94102	415-397-7720
Kyo-ya (Japanese) 2 New Montgomery St	San Francisco	CA	94105	415-546-5090
L'Olivier (French) 465 Davis Ct	San Francisco	CA	94111	415-981-7824
L'Osteria del Forno (Italian) 519 Columbus Ave	San Francisco	CA	94133	415-982-1124
La Folie (French) 2316 Polk St	San Francisco	CA	94109	415-776-5577
Le Central (French) 453 Bush St	San Francisco	CA	94108	415-391-2233
Little Joe's (Italian) 523 Broadway St	San Francisco	CA	94133	415-433-4343
LuLu (French) 816 Folsom St	San Francisco	CA	94107	415-495-5775
Mandarin The (Chinese) 900 N Point St	San Francisco	CA	94109	415-673-8812
Web: www.themandarin.com/				
Masa's Restaurant (French) 648 Bush St	San Francisco	CA	94108	415-989-7154
Masons (California) 950 Mason St	San Francisco	CA	94108	415-772-5233
Massawa (African) 1538 Haight St	San Francisco	CA	94117	415-621-4129
Moose's (Mediterranean) 1652 Stockton St	San Francisco	CA	94133	415-989-7800
North Beach Restaurant (Italian) 1512 Stockton St	San Francisco	CA	94133	415-392-1587
One Market (American) 1 Market St	San Francisco	CA	94105	415-777-5577
Pacific Grill (California) 500 Post St	San Francisco	CA	94102	415-771-8600
Palio D'Asti (Italian) 640 Sacramento St	San Francisco	CA	94111	415-395-9800
Pasta Pomodoro (Italian) 2027 Chestnut St	San Francisco	CA	94123	415-474-3400
Pastis (French) 1015 Battery St	San Francisco	CA	94111	415-391-2555
Planet Hollywood (American) 2 Stockton St	San Francisco	CA	94108	415-421-7827
PlumpJack Cafe (French/Mediterranean)				
3127 Fillmore St	San Francisco	CA	94123	415-563-4755
Pompei's Grotto (Seafood) 340 Jefferson St	San Francisco	CA	94133	415-776-9265
PosTrio (Asian/California) 545 Post St	San Francisco	CA	94102	415-776-7825
Web: www.postrio.com ■ *E-mail:* mail@postrio.com				
Rose Pistola (Italian) 532 Columbus Ave	San Francisco	CA	94133	415-399-0499
Rubicon (California) 558 Sacramento St	San Francisco	CA	94111	415-434-4100
Sam's Grill & Seafood Restaurant (Seafood)				
374 Bush St	San Francisco	CA	94104	415-421-0594

San Francisco — Restaurants (Cont'd)

				Phone
Scoma's (Seafood) Fisherman's Wharf Pier 47	San Francisco	CA	94133	415-771-4383
Showley's at Miramonte (California) 1327 Railroad Ave	Saint Helena	CA	94574	707-963-3970
Slanted Door (Vietnamese) 584 Valencia St	San Francisco	CA	94110	415-861-8032
Socca (Continental) 5800 Geary Blvd	San Francisco	CA	94121	415-379-6720
Som Tum (Thai) 1865 Lombard St	San Francisco	CA	94123	415-922-2829
Splendido (Italian) 4 Embarcadero Ctr	San Francisco	CA	94111	415-986-3222
Stars (New American) 555 Golden Gate Ave	San Francisco	CA	94102	415-861-7827
Ti Couz (French) 3108 16th St	San Francisco	CA	94103	415-252-7373
Tommy Toy's Cuisine Chinoise (Chinese) 655 Montgomery St *Web:* www.tommytoys.com/	San Francisco	CA	94111	415-397-4888
Vivande Ristorante (Italian) 670 Golden Gate Ave	San Francisco	CA	94102	415-673-9245
Washington Square Bar & Grill (American) 1707 Powell St	San Francisco	CA	94133	415-982-8123
Yoyo Tsumami Bistro (French/Japanese) 1611 Post St	San Francisco	CA	94115	415-922-7788
Yuet Lee Restaurant (Chinese) 1300 Stockton St	San Francisco	CA	94133	415-982-6020
Zuni Cafe & Grill (Mediterranean) 1658 Market St	San Francisco	CA	94102	415-552-2522

— Goods and Services —

SHOPPING

				Phone	Fax
Anchorage Shopping Center 2800 Leavenworth St	San Francisco	CA	94133	415-775-6000	441-4209
Cannery The 2801 Leavenworth St *Web:* www.thecannery.com	San Francisco	CA	94133	415-771-3112	771-2424
Crocker Galleria 50 Post St	San Francisco	CA	94104	415-393-1505	392-5429
Embarcardero Center 4 Embarcardero Ctr Suite 2600	San Francisco	CA	94111	415-772-0500	982-1780
Ghirardelli Square 900 N Point St *Web:* www.ghirardellisq.com ■ *E-mail:* ghsqmail@aol.com	San Francisco	CA	94109	415-775-5500	775-0912
Hillsdale Shopping Center 60 Hillsdale Mall	San Mateo	CA	94403	650-345-8222	573-5457
Hilltop Mall 2200 Hilltop Mall Rd	Richmond	CA	94806	510-223-6900	223-1453
Neiman Marcus 150 Stockton St *Web:* www.neimanmarcus.com	San Francisco	CA	94108	415-362-3900	291-9616
Nordstrom 865 Market St	San Francisco	CA	94103	415-243-8500	977-5089
Saks Fifth Avenue 384 Post St	San Francisco	CA	94108	415-986-4300	
San Francisco Shopping Center 865 Market St Box A *Web:* www.sanfranciscoshopping.com	San Francisco	CA	94103	415-512-6776	512-6770
Tanforan Park Shopping Center 301 Tanforan Pk	San Bruno	CA	94066	650-873-2000	873-4210

BANKS

				Phone	Fax
Bank of America NT & SA 555 California St **Fax:* Hum Res ■ *TF Cust Svc:* 800-346-7693*	San Francisco	CA	94104	415-622-3456	241-5080*
Bank of the West 295 Bush St *TF:* 800-488-2265	San Francisco	CA	94104	415-765-4886	781-3217
Sanwa Bank California 444 Market St *Web:* www.sanwa-bank-ca.com	San Francisco	CA	94111	415-597-5200	597-5494
Union Bank of California NA 400 California St 1st Fl **Fax:* Hum Res	San Francisco	CA	94104	415-765-3434	705-7088*
Wells Fargo Bank NA 420 Montgomery St *Web:* wellsfargo.com	San Francisco	CA	94163	800-411-4932	

BUSINESS SERVICES

	Phone
Accountemps	415-434-1900
Aero Special Delivery Service Inc.	415-495-8333
Corporate Express Delivery Systems	415-904-4550
Federal Express	800-463-3339
Kelly Services	415-982-2200
Kinko's	415-750-1193
Manpower Temporary Services	415-781-7171
Olsten Staffing Services	415-433-1110
Post Office	800-275-8777
Special-T-Delivery Msgr Svc	415-522-5959
Ultraex	415-243-8600
UPS	800-742-5877
Western Messenger Service	415-864-4100

— Media —

PUBLICATIONS

				Phone	Fax
Nob Hill Gazette 5 3rd St Hearst Bldg Suite 222 *Web:* www.nobhillgazette.com ■ *E-mail:* nobhillnews@nobhillgazette.com	San Francisco	CA	94103	415-227-0190	974-5103
San Francisco 243 Vallejo St *Web:* www.sanfran.com ■ *E-mail:* letters@sanfran.com	San Francisco	CA	94111	415-398-2800	398-6777
San Francisco Business Times Magazine 275 Battery St Suite 940 *Web:* www.amcity.com/sanfrancisco	San Francisco	CA	94111	415-989-2522	398-2494
San Francisco Chronicle‡ 901 Mission St *Web:* www.sfgate.com/chronicle ■ *E-mail:* chronletters@sfgate.com	San Francisco	CA	94103	415-777-7100	896-1107
San Francisco Examiner‡ 110 5th St *Web:* www.examiner.com ■ *E-mail:* letters@examiner.com	San Francisco	CA	94103	415-777-2424	777-2525
San Francisco Independent 1201 Evans Ave **Fax:* News Rm	San Francisco	CA	94124	415-826-1100	826-5371*
Where San Francisco Magazine 74 New Montgomery St Suite 320 *Web:* www.wheremags.com/SanFrancisco.html ■ *E-mail:* wherenews@aol.com	San Francisco	CA	94105	415-546-6101	546-6108

‡Daily newspapers

TELEVISION

				Phone	Fax
KBHK-TV Ch 44 (UPN) 650 California St 7th Fl **Fax:* PR ■ *Web:* www.upn44.com ■ *E-mail:* list@upn44.com	San Francisco	CA	94108	415-249-4444	397-2841*
KBWB-TV Ch 20 (WB) 2500 Marin St *Web:* www.wb20.com	San Francisco	CA	94124	415-821-2020	641-1163
KCNS-TV Ch 38 (Ind) 1550 Bryant St Suite 748	San Francisco	CA	94103	415-863-3800	863-3998
KDTV-TV Ch 14 (Uni) 50 Freemont St 41st Fl	San Francisco	CA	94105	415-641-1400	538-8053
KFTY-TV Ch 50 (Ind) 533 Mendocino Ave	Santa Rosa	CA	95401	707-526-5050	526-7429
KFWU-TV Ch 8 (Ind) 303-B N Main St	Fort Bragg	CA	95437	707-964-8888	964-8150
KGO-TV Ch 7 (ABC) 900 Front St	San Francisco	CA	94111	415-954-7777	956-6402
KICU-TV Ch 36 (Ind) 2102 Commerce Dr *Web:* www.kicu.com	San Jose	CA	95131	408-953-3636	953-3630
KKPX-TV Ch 65 (Ind) 660 Price Ave Suite B	Redwood City	CA	94063	650-369-6565	369-4969
KPIX-TV Ch 5 (CBS) 855 Battery St *Web:* www.kpix.com ■ *E-mail:* tvprog@kpix.com	San Francisco	CA	94111	415-362-5550	765-8916
KQED-TV Ch 9 (PBS) 2601 Mariposa St *Web:* www.kqed.org/tv ■ *E-mail:* tv@kqed.org	San Francisco	CA	94110	415-864-2000	553-2118
KRON-TV Ch 4 (NBC) 1001 Van Ness Ave *Web:* www.kron.com	San Francisco	CA	94109	415-441-4444	561-8136
KSTS-TV Ch 48 (Tele) 2349 Bering Dr	San Jose	CA	95131	408-435-8848	433-5921
KTNC-TV Ch 42 (Ind) 5101 Port Chicago Hwy	Concord	CA	94520	925-686-4242	825-4242
KTSF-TV Ch 26 (Ind) 100 Valley Dr *Web:* www.ktsf.com ■ *E-mail:* ktsf26@ktsf.com	Brisbane	CA	94005	415-468-2626	467-7559
KTVU-TV Ch 2 (Fox) 2 Jack London Sq *Web:* www.bayinsider.com/partners/ktvu/index.html ■ *E-mail:* ktvu@team.insider.com	Oakland	CA	94607	510-834-1212	272-9957

RADIO

				Phone	Fax
KABL-AM 960 kHz (Nost) 340 Townsend St Suite 5101	San Francisco	CA	94107	415-977-0960	278-0960
KALW-FM 91.7 MHz (NPR) 500 Mansell St *Web:* www.sfusd.k12.ca.us/programs/kalw/kalw.htm ■ *E-mail:* kalwradio@aol.com	San Francisco	CA	94134	415-841-4121	
KBLX-FM 102.9 MHz (NAC) 55 Hawthorne St Suite 900 *Web:* www.kblxfm.com ■ *E-mail:* info@kblxfm.com	San Francisco	CA	94105	415-284-1029	764-4959
KCBS-AM 740 kHz (N/T) 1 Embarcadero Ctr 32nd Fl *Web:* www.kcbs.com ■ *E-mail:* kcbs@kpix.com	San Francisco	CA	94111	415-765-4000	765-4080
KCSM-FM 91.1 MHz (NPR) 1700 Hillsdale Blvd *Web:* www.kcsm.org	San Mateo	CA	94402	650-574-6427	574-6675
KDFC-FM 102.1 MHz (Clas) 455 Market St Suite 2300 **Fax Area Code:* 650 ■ *Web:* www.kdfc.com	San Francisco	CA	94105	415-764-1021	777-2291*
KFOG-FM 104.5 MHz (AAA) 55 Hawthorne St Suite 1100 *Web:* www.kfog.com ■ *E-mail:* tweak@a.crl.com	San Francisco	CA	94105	415-543-1045	995-6867

San Francisco — Radio (Cont'd)

	City	State	Zip	Phone	Fax
KFRC-AM 610 kHz (Oldies)					
500 Washington St 2nd Fl	San Francisco	CA	94111	415-391-9970	951-2329
Web: www.kfrc.com					
KFRC-FM 99.7 MHz (Oldies)					
500 Washington St 2nd Fl	San Francisco	CA	94111	415-391-9970	951-2329
Web: www.kfrc.com					
KGO-AM 810 kHz (N/T) 900 Front St	San Francisco	CA	94111	415-954-8100	362-5827
Web: www.kgoam810.com					
KIOI-AM 910 kHz (AC)					
340 Townsend St Suite 5101	San Francisco	CA	94107	415-977-0960	278-0960
KIOI-FM 101.3 MHz (AC)					
340 Townsend St Suite 5101	San Francisco	CA	94107	415-977-0960	278-0960
Web: www.k101radio.com					
KISQ-FM 98.1 MHz (AC)					
750 Battery St Suite 200	San Francisco	CA	94111	415-788-5225	981-2930
Web: www.981kissfm.com ■ *E-mail:* kiss981@aol.com					
KITS-FM 105.3 MHz (Alt)					
730 Harrison St Suite 300	San Francisco	CA	94107	415-512-1053	777-0608
Web: www.live105.com ■ *E-mail:* live105@live105.com					
KKSF-FM 103.7 MHz (NAC)					
340 Townsend St	San Francisco	CA	94107	415-975-5555	975-5573
Web: www.kksf.com ■ *E-mail:* comments@kksf.com					
KLLC-FM 97.3 MHz (AC)					
1 Embarcadero Ctr 32nd Fl	San Francisco	CA	94111	415-765-4000	765-4084
Web: www.radioalice.com					
KMEL-FM 106.1 MHz (Urban)					
340 Townsend St	San Francisco	CA	94107	415-538-1061	538-1060
Web: www.106kmel.com					
KNBR-AM 680 kHz (Sports)					
55 Hawthorne St Suite 1100	San Francisco	CA	94105	415-995-6800	995-6867
Web: www.knbr.com					
KOIT-AM 1260 kHz (AC)					
455 Market St Suite 2300	San Francisco	CA	94105	415-777-0965	896-0965
KOIT-FM 96.5 MHz (AC)					
455 Market St Suite 230	San Francisco	CA	94105	415-777-0965	896-0965
Web: www.koit.com					
KQED-FM 88.5 MHz (NPR)					
2601 Mariposa St	San Francisco	CA	94110	415-553-2129	553-2118
Web: www.kqed.org ■ *E-mail:* sponsor@kqed.org					
KSAN-FM 107.7 MHz (CR)					
55 Hawthorne St	San Francisco	CA	94105	415-995-6904	995-6867
Web: www.ksan.com ■ *E-mail:* ksanradio@aol.com					
KSFO-AM 560 kHz (N/T) 900 Front St	San Francisco	CA	94111	415-954-8100	658-5401
Web: www.ksfo560.com					
KSOL-FM 98.9 MHz (Span)					
55 Green St Suite 200	San Francisco	CA	94111	415-733-5765	733-5766
Web: www.ksol.com					
KUFX-FM 98.5 MHz (CR)					
1420 Koll Cir Suite A	San Jose	CA	95112	408-452-7900	452-8030
KYCY-FM 93.3 MHz (Ctry)					
500 Washington St Suite 450	San Francisco	CA	94111	415-391-9330	951-2325
KYLD-FM 94.9 MHz (CHR)					
340 Townsend Suite 4949	San Francisco	CA	94107	415-356-0949	267-0949
Web: www.wild949.com					
KZOL-FM 99.1 MHz (Span)					
55 Green St Suite 200	San Francisco	CA	94111	415-989-5765	733-5766
Web: www.ksol.com					
KZQZ-FM 95.7 MHz (CHR)					
400 2nd St 3rd Fl	San Francisco	CA	94107	415-957-0957	356-8394

— Colleges/Universities —

	City	State	Zip	Phone	Fax
Academy of Art College					
79 New Montgomery St	San Francisco	CA	94105	415-274-2200	263-4130
TF Admissions: 800-544-2787 ■ *Web:* www.academyart.edu					
Art Institutes International San Francisco					
1170 Market St	San Francisco	CA	94102	888-493-3261	863-6344*
**Fax Area Code:* 415 ■ *TF:* 888-493-3261 ■ *Web:* www.aii.edu					
California Culinary Academy Inc					
625 Polk St	San Francisco	CA	94102	415-771-3536	771-2194
TF: 800-229-2433 ■ *Web:* www.baychef.com					
Canada College 4200 Farm Hill Blvd	Redwood City	CA	94061	650-364-1212	306-3133
Web: www.smcccd.cc.ca.us/smcccd/canada/canada.html					
Chabot College 25555 Hesperian Blvd	Hayward	CA	94545	510-786-6600	723-7510
Web: www.clpccd.cc.ca.us/cc/					
City College of San Francisco					
50 Phelan Ave	San Francisco	CA	94112	415-239-3000	239-3936
Web: www.ccsf.cc.ca.us					
College of Alameda 555 Atlantic Ave	Alameda	CA	94501	510-522-7221	769-6019
Web: www.peralta.cc.ca.us/coa/coa.htm ■ *E-mail:* pio341@peralta.cc.ca.us					
College of Marin 835 College Ave	Kentfield	CA	94904	415-457-8811	460-0773
Web: www.marin.cc.ca.us ■ *E-mail:* pio330@ccc-infonet.edu					
College of Marin Indian Valley Campus					
1800 Ignacio Blvd	Novato	CA	94949	415-883-2211	485-0135
College of San Mateo					
1700 W Hillsdale Blvd	San Mateo	CA	94402	650-574-6161	574-6506
Web: www.smcccd.cc.ca.us/smcccd/csm/					
Contra Costa College 2600 Mission Bell Dr	San Pablo	CA	94806	510-235-7800	236-6768
Contra Costa Community College District					
500 Court St	Martinez	CA	94553	925-229-1000	370-6517
Web: www.collegesofcc.cc.ca.us					
Diablo Valley College 321 Golf Club Rd	Pleasant Hill	CA	94523	925-685-1230	609-8085
Web: www.dvc.edu					
Fashion Institute of Design & Merchandising San Francisco					
55 Stockton St	San Francisco	CA	94108	415-433-6691	296-7299
TF: 800-422-3436 ■ *Web:* www.fidm.com					
Golden Gate University 536 Mission St	San Francisco	CA	94105	415-442-7000	442-7807
TF: 800-448-4968 ■ *Web:* www.ggu.edu					
Heald Business College Concord					
2150 John Glenn Dr Suite 100	Concord	CA	94520	925-827-1300	827-1486
TF: 800-274-7704 ■ *Web:* www.heald.edu/CampusInfo/CampusInfo.asp?campus=ccb					
Heald Business College Hayward					
24301 Southland Dr Suite 500	Hayward	CA	94545	510-784-7000	783-3287
TF: 800-666-9609					
Heald Business College San Francisco					
350 Mission St	San Francisco	CA	94105	415-808-3000	808-3005
TF: 800-999-5455 ■ *Web:* www.heald.edu					
Heald Institute of Technology					
2860 Howe Rd	Martinez	CA	94553	925-228-9000	229-3792
TF: 800-937-7723					
Heald Institute of Technology					
350 Mission St	San Francisco	CA	94105	415-441-5555	808-3005
TF: 800-727-5445 ■ *Web:* www.heald.edu					
Laney College 900 Fallon St	Oakland	CA	94607	510-834-5740	466-7394
Web: laney.peralta.cc.ca.us					
Lincoln University 281 Masonic Ave	San Francisco	CA	94118	415-221-1212	387-9730
Web: www.lincolnuca.edu					
Los Medanos College 2700 E Leland Rd	Pittsburg	CA	94565	925-439-2181	427-1599
Web: www.losmedanos.net					
Merritt College 12500 Campus Dr	Oakland	CA	94619	510-531-4911	436-2405
Web: www.merritt.edu					
Napa Valley College 2277 Napa-Vallejo Hwy	Napa	CA	94558	707-253-3000	253-3064
TF: 800-826-1077 ■ *Web:* nvc.cc.ca.us/nvc/					
New College of California 50 Fell St	San Francisco	CA	94102	415-626-1694	241-9525
TF: 800-335-6262 ■ *Web:* www.newcollege.edu/					
Ohlone College 43600 Mission Blvd	Fremont	CA	94539	510-659-6000	659-5003
Web: www.ohlone.cc.ca.us					
Peralta Community College District (System)					
333 E 8th St	Oakland	CA	94606	510-466-7200	466-7394
Web: www.peralta.cc.ca.us					
Queen of the Holy Rosary College					
43326 Mission Blvd	Fremont	CA	94539	510-657-2468	657-1734
San Francisco Art Institute					
800 Chestnut St	San Francisco	CA	94133	415-771-7020	749-4592
TF: 800-345-7324 ■ *Web:* www.sfai.edu ■ *E-mail:* sfainfo@cdmweb.sfai.edu					
San Francisco College of Mortuary Science 1598 Dolores St	San Francisco	CA	94110	415-567-0674	824-1390
Web: www.sfcms.org					
San Francisco Conservatory of Music					
1201 Ortega St	San Francisco	CA	94122	415-564-8086	759-3499
Web: www.sfcm.edu ■ *E-mail:* cin@sfcm.edu					
San Francisco State University					
1600 Holloway Ave	San Francisco	CA	94132	415-338-1111	338-3880*
**Fax:* Admissions ■ *Web:* www.sfsu.edu ■ *E-mail:* ugadmit@sfsu.edu					
Sequoia Electronics Academy					
1201 Brewster Ave	Redwood City	CA	94062	650-365-6367	367-7593
Web: www.seqacademy.com					
Skyline College 3300 College Dr	San Bruno	CA	94066	650-355-7000	738-4338
Web: www.smcccd.cc.ca.us/smcccd/skyline/skyline.html					
Solano Community College					
4000 Suisun Valley Rd	Suisun City	CA	94585	707-864-7000	864-7175
Web: www.solano.cc.ca.us					
Stanford University	Stanford	CA	94305	650-723-2300	723-6050
Web: www.stanford.edu					
University of California Berkeley	Berkeley	CA	94720	510-642-6000	643-5499
Web: www.berkeley.edu					
University of California San Francisco					
500 Parnassus Ave	San Francisco	CA	94143	415-476-9000	476-9690
Web: www.ucsf.edu					

San Francisco — Colleges/Universities (Cont'd)

				Phone	Fax
University of San Francisco 2130 Fulton St	San Francisco	CA	94117	415-422-6886	422-2217
TF: 800-225-5873 ■ *Web:* www.usfca.edu					
Vista Community College 2020 Milvia St 3rd Fl	Berkeley	CA	94704	510-841-8431	841-7333
Web: www.peralta.cc.ca.us/vista/vista.htm ■ *E-mail:* scoopfoggy@aol.com					

— Hospitals —

				Phone	Fax
Alameda County Medical Center-Highland Campus 1411 E 31st St	Oakland	CA	94602	510-437-4800	437-5005
Alta Bates Medical Center 2450 Ashby Ave	Berkeley	CA	94705	510-540-4444	548-4972
Web: www.altabates.com					
California Pacific Medical Center Davies Campus Castro & Duboce Sts	San Francisco	CA	94114	415-565-6000	565-6523
Web: www.cpmc.org ■ *E-mail:* cpmcadmin@sutterhealth.org					
California Pacific Medical Center Pacific Campus 2333 Buchanan St	San Francisco	CA	94115	415-563-4321	885-8633*
**Fax:* Hum Res ■ *Web:* www.cpmc.org					
Contra Costa Medical Center 2500 Alhambra Ave	Martinez	CA	94553	925-370-5000	370-5138*
**Fax:* Admitting					
John Muir Medical Center 1601 Ygnacio Valley Rd	Walnut Creek	CA	94598	925-939-3000	947-5372*
**Fax:* Admitting					
Kaiser Permanente Hospital 99 Montecillo Rd	San Rafael	CA	94903	415-444-2000	444-2492
TF: 800-464-4000					
Kaiser Permanente Medical Center 1150 Veterans Blvd	Redwood City	CA	94063	650-299-2000	299-2421
TF: 800-464-4000					
Kaiser Permanente Medical Center 1425 S Main St	Walnut Creek	CA	94596	925-295-4000	295-4689
TF: 800-464-4000					
Kaiser Permanente Medical Center 27400 Hesperian Blvd	Hayward	CA	94545	510-784-4000	784-4228*
**Fax:* PR					
Kaiser Permanente Medical Center 2425 Geary Blvd	San Francisco	CA	94115	415-202-2000	202-4567
Kaiser Permanente Medical Center 280 W MacArthur Blvd	Oakland	CA	94611	510-596-1000	596-1554*
**Fax:* Admitting					
Marin General Hospital PO Box 8010	San Rafael	CA	94912	415-925-7000	925-7933
Queen of the Valley Hospital 1000 Trancas St	Napa	CA	94558	707-252-4411	257-4032
Saint Francis Memorial Hospital 900 Hyde St	San Francisco	CA	94109	415-353-6000	353-6203*
**Fax:* Admitting					
Saint Luke's Hospital 3555 Cesar Chavez St	San Francisco	CA	94110	415-647-8600	583-6314
Saint Mary's Medical Center 450 Stanyan St	San Francisco	CA	94117	415-668-1000	668-4531
Web: www.chwbay.org/stmarys					
San Francisco General Hospital Medical Center 1001 Potrero Ave	San Francisco	CA	94110	415-206-8000	206-8535
San Mateo County General Hospital 222 W 39th Ave	San Mateo	CA	94403	650-573-2222	573-2950
Santa Rosa Memorial Hospital PO Box 522	Santa Rosa	CA	95402	707-546-3210	525-5250
Sequoia Hospital 170 Alameda Ave	Redwood City	CA	94062	650-369-5811	780-0532*
**Fax:* Admitting					
Seton Medical Center 1900 Sullivan Ave	Daly City	CA	94015	650-992-4000	991-6817*
**Fax:* Admitting					
Sutter Medical Center of Santa Rosa 3325 Chanate Rd	Santa Rosa	CA	95404	707-576-4000	576-4318
Sutter Solano Medical Center 300 Hospital Dr	Vallejo	CA	94589	707-554-4444	648-3227
UCSF Medical Center 505 Parnassus Ave	San Francisco	CA	94143	415-476-1000	476-2317
Veterans Affairs Medical Center 4150 Clement St	San Francisco	CA	94121	415-221-4810	750-2270
Web: www.va.ucsf.edu					

— Attractions —

				Phone	Fax
Acres of Orchids 914 S Claremont St	San Mateo	CA	94402	650-373-3900	373-3913
Alcatraz Island Pier 41	San Francisco	CA	94133	415-705-5555	433-5402
Web: www.pier39.com					
American Conservatory Theater 30 Grant Ave 6th Fl	San Francisco	CA	94108	415-834-3200	834-3360
Web: www.act-sfbay.org					
Anchor Brewing Co 1705 Mariposa St	San Francisco	CA	94107	415-863-8350	552-7094
Ansel Adams Center for Photography 250 4th St	San Francisco	CA	94103	415-495-7000	495-8517
Web: www.friendsofphotography.org ■ *E-mail:* click@photoarts.com					
Asian Art Museum of San Francisco Golden Gate Pk	San Francisco	CA	94118	415-379-8800	668-8928
Web: www.asianart.org ■ *E-mail:* info@asianart.org					
Bay Area Discovery Museum-Fort Baker 557 McReynolds Rd	Sausalito	CA	94965	415-487-4398	332-9671
Web: www.badm.org ■ *E-mail:* info@badm.org					
Berkeley Art Museum & Pacific Film Archive 2625 Durant Ave	Berkeley	CA	94720	510-642-0808	642-4889
Web: www.uampfa.berkeley.edu					
Best of Broadway 1182 Market St Suite 320	San Francisco	CA	94102	415-551-2050	551-2045
Web: www.bestofbroadway-sf.com					
Cable Car Barn & Museum 1201 Mason St	San Francisco	CA	94108	415-474-1887	929-7546
California Academy of Sciences Golden Gate Pk	San Francisco	CA	94118	415-750-7145	750-7346
Web: www.calacademy.org/					
California Palace of the Legion of Honor Museum 34th Ave & Clement St	San Francisco	CA	94121	415-750-3600	
Web: www.thinker.org/legion					
Cannery The 2801 Leavenworth St	San Francisco	CA	94133	415-771-3112	771-2424
Web: www.thecannery.com					
Cartoon Art Museum 814 Mission St	San Francisco	CA	94103	415-227-8666	243-8666
Web: www.cartoonart.org ■ *E-mail:* toonart@wenet.net					
Center for African & African-American Art & Culture 762 Fulton St	San Francisco	CA	94102	415-928-8546	928-8549
Web: www.caaac.org/2.0/					
Center for the Arts at Yerba Buena Gardens 701 Mission St	San Francisco	CA	94103	415-978-2700	978-9635
Web: www.yerbabuenaarts.org ■ *E-mail:* yerbabuena@aol.com					
Chinatown 832 Grant Ave	San Francisco	CA	94108	415-982-6306	982-6306
Web: www.sfchinatown.com					
Chinese Historical Society of America 644 Broadway St	San Francisco	CA	94133	415-391-1188	391-1150
Web: www.chsa.org/					
Cliff House/Ocean Beach 1090 Point Lobos Ave	San Francisco	CA	94121	415-386-1170	
Coit Tower 1 Telegraph Hill Blvd	San Francisco	CA	94133	415-362-0808	434-1234
Crown Point Press 20 Hawthorne St	San Francisco	CA	94105	415-974-6273	495-4220
Web: www.crownpoint.com ■ *E-mail:* gallery@crownpoint.com					
Exploratorium 3601 Lyon St	San Francisco	CA	94123	415-563-7337	561-0307
Web: www.exploratorium.edu					
Fisherman's Wharf 1873 Market St	San Francisco	CA	94103	415-626-7070	626-4651
Fort Mason Center Buchanan St & Marina Blvd	San Francisco	CA	94123	415-979-3010	441-3405
Fort Point National Historic Site PO Box 29333	Presidio of San Francisco	CA	94129	415-556-1693	556-8474
Web: www.nps.gov/fopo/					
Ghirardelli Square 900 N Point St	San Francisco	CA	94109	415-775-5500	775-0912
Web: www.ghirardellisq.com ■ *E-mail:* ghsqmail@aol.com					
Golden Gate Bridge Presidio Stn	San Francisco	CA	94129	415-257-4563	
Web: www.goldengate.org					
Golden Gate National Recreation Area Fort Mason Bldg 201	San Francisco	CA	94123	415-556-0560	561-4234*
**Fax:* Hum Res ■ *Web:* www.nps.gov/goga/					
Golden Gate Park 501 Stanyan St	San Francisco	CA	94117	415-831-2700	668-3330
Web: www.ci.sf.ca.us/recpark/					
Goode Joe Performance Group 3221 22nd St	San Francisco	CA	94110	415-648-4848	648-5401
E-mail: joegoode@CRL.COM					
Japanese Tea Garden Golden Gate Pk	San Francisco	CA	94117	415-831-2700	668-3330
Japantown	San Francisco	CA		415-395-9353	
Jenkins Margaret Dance Co 3973-A 25th St	San Francisco	CA	94114	415-826-8399	826-8392
E-mail: mjdcinc@aol.com					
Judah L Magnes Museum 2911 Russell St	Berkeley	CA	94705	510-849-2710	849-3673
Web: www.jfed.org/magnes/magnes.htm					
Lake Merced Harding Rd & Skyline Dr	San Francisco	CA	94132	415-753-1101	
Lincoln Park 34th Ave & Clement St	San Francisco	CA	94121	415-831-2700	
LINES Contemporary Ballet 50 Oak St 4th Fl	San Francisco	CA	94102	415-863-3040	863-1180
McLaren John Park University & Woolsey Drs	San Francisco	CA	94117	415-831-2700	
Metreon 101 4th St	San Francisco	CA	94103	415-369-6000	537-3455*
**Fax:* Hum Res ■ *TF Cust Svc:* 888-846-8813 ■ *Web:* www.metreon.com ■ *E-mail:* communityrelations@metreon.com					

San Francisco — Attractions (Cont'd)

				Phone	Fax
Mexican Museum Fort Mason Ctr Bldg D	San Francisco	CA	94123	415-202-9700	441-7683
Web: www.folkart.com/~latitude/museums/m_mexsf.htm					
MH de Young Memorial Museum 75 Tea Garden Dr Golden Gate Pk	San Francisco	CA	94118	415-750-3600	750-7692
Web: www.thinker.org/deyoung					
Mission Dolores 3321 16th St	San Francisco	CA	94114	415-621-8204	621-2294
Morrison Alexander F Planetarium California Academy of Sciences-Golden Gate Pk	San Francisco	CA	94118	415-221-5100	750-7346
Web: www.calacademy.org/planetarium/ ■ *E-mail:* planetarium@calacademy.org					
Muir Woods National Monument	Mill Valley	CA	94941	415-388-2596	389-6957
Web: www.nps.gov/muwo/					
Museo Italo-Americano Fort Mason Ctr Bldg C	San Francisco	CA	94123	415-673-2200	673-2292
Museum of the City of San Francisco 2801 Leavenworth St The Cannery 3rd Fl	San Francisco	CA	94133	415-928-0289	928-6243
Web: www.sfmuseum.org					
Palace of Fine Arts Bay & Lyon Sts	San Francisco	CA	94123	415-567-6642	
Paramount's Great America PO Box 1776	Santa Clara	CA	95052	408-988-1776	986-5855*
**Fax:* Sales ■ *Web:* www.pgathrills.com					
Philharmonia Baroque Orchestra 333 Market St Plaza Suite	San Francisco	CA	94105	415-495-7445	495-7473
Web: www.philharmonia.org ■ *E-mail:* info@philharmonia.org					
Pier 39 Beach & Embarcadero Sts	San Francisco	CA	94119	415-981-7437	981-8808
Web: www.pier39.com/ ■ *E-mail:* info@pier39.com					
Point Reyes National Seashore	Point Reyes	CA	94956	415-663-8522	
Web: www.nps.gov/pore/					
Presidio Museum Presidio Bldg 2	San Francisco	CA	94129	415-561-4331	561-5725
Randall Museum 199 Museum Way	San Francisco	CA	94114	415-554-9604	554-9609
Web: www.wco.com/~dale/randall.html					
Safari West 3115 Porter Creek Rd	Santa Rosa	CA	95404	707-579-2551	579-8777
Web: www.wco.com/~langcos ■ *E-mail:* langcos@wco.com					
San Francisco Ballet 455 Franklin St	San Francisco	CA	94102	415-861-5600	861-2684
Web: www.sfballet.org/ ■ *E-mail:* sfbmktg@sfballet.org					
San Francisco Craft & Folk Art Museum Fort Mason Ctr Bldg A	San Francisco	CA	94123	415-775-0990	775-1861
San Francisco Fire Department Museum 655 Presidio Ave	San Francisco	CA	94115	415-558-3546	
San Francisco Maritime National Historical Park Fort Mason Bldg E Rm 265	San Francisco	CA	94123	415-556-1659	556-1624
Web: www.nps.gov/safr/					
San Francisco Museum of Modern Art 151 3rd St	San Francisco	CA	94103	415-357-4000	357-4037
Web: www.sfmoma.org/					
San Francisco Opera Assn 301 Van Ness Ave	San Francisco	CA	94102	415-861-4008	621-7508
Web: www.sfopera.com ■ *E-mail:* editor@www.sfopera.com					
San Francisco Symphony Van Ness Ave & Grove St Davies Symphony Hall	San Francisco	CA	94102	415-864-6000	
Web: www.sfsymphony.org ■ *E-mail:* messages@sfsymphony.org					
San Francisco War Memorial & Performing Arts Center 401 Van Ness Ave Suite 110	San Francisco	CA	94102	415-621-6600	621-5091
San Francisco Zoological Gardens 1 Zoo Rd	San Francisco	CA	94132	415-753-7080	681-2039
Web: www.sfzoo.com					
Sausalito Information 777 Bridgeway	Sausalito	CA	94965	415-332-0505	
SkyDeck 1 Embarcadero Ctr	San Francisco	CA	94111	888-737-5933	
Web: www.sfskydeck.com					
SS Jeremiah O'Brien Fort Mason Ctr Bldg A	San Francisco	CA	94123	415-441-3101	441-3712
Web: www.crl.com/~wefald/obrien.html					
Steinhart Aquarium California Academy of Sciences Golden Gate Pk	San Francisco	CA	94118	415-750-7247	750-7269
Web: www.calacademy.org/aquarium/					
Strybing Arboretum & Botanical Gardens 9th Ave & Lincoln Way	San Francisco	CA	94122	415-753-7089	661-7427
Web: www.strybing.org					
Underwater World Aquarium Pier 39	San Francisco	CA	94133	415-623-5300	623-5324
TF: 800-623-5300 ■ *Web:* www.underwaterworld.com/					
USS Pampanito Pier 45	San Francisco	CA	94133	415-775-1943	441-0365
Web: www.maritime.org/pamphome.shtml ■ *E-mail:* info@maritime.org					
Wax Museum at Fisherman's Wharf 145 Jefferson St	San Francisco	CA	94133	415-885-4834	771-9248
Web: www.waxmuseum.com ■ *E-mail:* sales@waxmuseum.com					
Wells Fargo History Museum 420 Montgomery St	San Francisco	CA	94163	415-396-2619	391-8644

SPORTS TEAMS & FACILITIES

				Phone	Fax
3Com Park at Candlestick Point Jamestown & Harney	San Francisco	CA	94124	415-467-1994	467-3049
Web: www.3com.com/3compark					
Golden State Warriors 66th Ave & Hegenberger Rd Oakland Coliseum Arena	Oakland	CA	94621	510-762-2277	
Web: www.nba.com/warriors					
San Francisco 49ers 3Com Pk Candlestick Pt	San Francisco	CA	94124	415-468-2249	467-9259
Web: www.sf49ers.com/					
San Francisco Bay Seals (soccer) Stanyon & Frederick Sts Kezar Stadium	San Francisco	CA	94116	415-676-3910	676-3919
Web: www.sfbayseals.com ■ *E-mail:* seals@sfbayseals.com					
San Francisco Giants 3Com Park Candlestick Pt	San Francisco	CA	94124	415-468-3700	467-2143
TF Tickets: 800-734-4268 ■ *Web:* www.sfgiants.com					

— Events —

	Phone
A la Carte A la Park (late August-early September)	415-383-9378
Arts of the Pacific Asian Show (mid-February)	310-455-2886
Bouquets to Art (mid-late March)	415-750-3504
Carnaval (late May)	415-826-1401
Cherry Blossom Festival (mid-April)	415-974-6900
Chinese New Year Celebration (late January)	650-484-1200
Cinco de Mayo Celebrations (early May)	415-826-1401
Contemporary Crafts Market (mid-March & early November)	415-995-4925
Ethnic Dance Festival (mid-late June)	415-392-4400
Festival of the Culinary Arts (mid-September)	800-229-2433
Fillmore Street Festival (early July)	415-249-4625
Fleet Week (mid-October)	415-705-5500
Fourth of July Waterfront Festival (July 4)	415-777-7120
Ghirardelli Square Chocolate Festival (early-mid-September)	415-775-5500
Great Halloween & Pumpkin Festival (mid-October)	415-249-4625
International Asian Film Festival (early-mid-March)	415-863-0814
Jazz & Wine Festival at Embarcadero Center (late July)	800-733-6318
Jazz and All That Art (early July)	415-249-4625
Las Americas (mid-September)	415-705-5500
Macy's Flower Show (late March-early April)	415-393-3724
Nihonmachi Street Fair (early August)	415-771-9861
North Beach Festival (mid-June)	415-989-6426
Norway Day Festival (early May)	925-676-4708
Pacific Orchid Exposition (late February)	415-546-9608
Saint Patrick's Day Parade (mid-March)	415-661-2700
San Francisco Blues Festival (mid-September)	415-979-5588
San Francisco Examiner Bay to Breakers (mid-May)	415-777-7770
San Francisco Fringe Theater Festival (mid-September)	415-673-3847
San Francisco Garden Show (mid-March)	800-829-9751
San Francisco International Film Festival (late April-early May)	415-931-3456
San Francisco International Lesbian & Gay Film Festival (mid-late June)	415-703-8663
San Francisco Jazz Festival (late October-early November)	800-627-5277
San Francisco Shakespeare Festival (July-early October)	415-422-2222
Sports & Boat Show (mid-January)	415-469-6065
Stern Grove Midsummer Music Festival (mid-June-mid-August)	415-252-6252
Street Performers Festival (early June)	415-705-5500
Traditional Music & Dance Festival (mid-May)	415-771-3112

San Jose

The Plaza de Cesar Chavez, with its tree-lined walkways, is the centerpiece of downtown San Jose, the "Capital of Silicon Valley." In the plaza area one can visit the Children's Discovery Museum or the Tech Museum of Innovation, which showcases Silicon Valley technology. Just 30 minutes from San Jose is Santa Cruz, home of the Santa Cruz Beach Boardwalk, California's only remaining seaside amusement park. The city of Monterey, site of the Cannery Row area immortalized by John Steinbeck, is just 70 minutes from San Jose. On the Row is Monterey Bay Aquarium, considered one of the finest aquariums in the nation.

San Jose (Cont'd)

Population	861,284	**Longitude**	121-89-39 W
Area (Land)	171.3 sq mi	**County**	Santa Clara
Area (Water)	3.3 sq mi	**Time Zone**	PST
Elevation	87 ft	**Area Code/s**	408
Latitude	37-33-53 N		

— Average Temperatures and Precipitation —

TEMPERATURES

	Jan	Feb	Mar	Apr	May	Jun	Jul	Aug	Sep	Oct	Nov	Dec
High	58	63	65	70	75	80	82	82	81	75	64	58
Low	41	44	45	47	51	55	57	57	56	52	46	41

PRECIPITATION

	Jan	Feb	Mar	Apr	May	Jun	Jul	Aug	Sep	Oct	Nov	Dec
Inches	2.8	2.2	2.6	1.2	0.3	0.1	0.1	0.1	0.2	0.9	2.1	2.0

— Important Phone Numbers —

	Phone		Phone
AAA	408-985-9300	**HotelDocs**	800-468-3537
American Express Travel	408-244-1015	**Medical Referral**	408-866-4098
Dental Referral	800-917-6453	**Road Conditions**	800-427-7623
Emergency	911	**Time**	831-767-8900
FYI Events Line	408-295-2265	**Weather**	650-364-7974

— Information Sources —

				Phone	Fax
Better Business Bureau Serving the Santa Clara Valley 2100 Forest Ave Suite 110 *Web:* www.sanjose.bbb.org	San Jose	CA	95128	408-278-7400	278-7444
San Jose City Hall 801 N 1st St *Web:* www.ci.san-jose.ca.us	San Jose	CA	95110	408-277-5722	277-3131
San Jose Convention & Visitors Bureau 333 W San Carlos St Suite 1000 *TF:* 800-726-5673	San Jose	CA	95110	408-295-9600	295-3937
San Jose Economic Development Office 50 W San Fernando Suite 900 *Web:* www.ci.san-jose.ca.us/oed/bus_inc_index.html	San Jose	CA	95113	408-277-5880	277-3615
San Jose Mayor 801 N 1st St Rm 600 *Web:* www.sjmayor.org ■ *E-mail:* mayoremail@ci.sj.ca.us	San Jose	CA	95110	408-277-4237	277-3868
San Jose McEnery Convention Center 150 W San Carlos St **Fax:* Mktg ■ *TF:* 800-533-2345 ■ *Web:* www.sjcc.com/sjmcc	San Jose	CA	95113	408-277-3900	277-3535*
San Jose Public Library 180 W San Carlos St *Web:* www.sjpl.lib.ca.us	San Jose	CA	95113	408-277-4822	277-3187
San Jose Silicon Valley Chamber of Commerce 310 S 1st St *Web:* www.sjchamber.com ■ *E-mail:* info@sjchamber.com	San Jose	CA	95113	408-291-5250	286-5019
Santa Clara County 70 W Hedding St *Web:* claraweb.co.santa-clara.ca.us	San Jose	CA	95110	408-299-2424	293-5649
Visitor Information Center 150 W San Carlos McEnery Convention Ctr *TF:* 888-726-5673 ■ *Web:* www.sanjose.org/general_info/html/visitor_info.html ■ *E-mail:* webmaster@sanjose.org	San Jose	CA	95110	408-977-0900	977-0901

On-Line Resources

4SanJose.com	www.4sanjose.com
Anthill City Guide San Jose	www.anthill.com/city.asp?city=sanjose
Area Guide San Jose	sanjose.areaguides.net
BayArea.com	www.bayarea.com
Boulevards San Jose	www.sanjose.com
City Knowledge San Jose	www.cityknowledge.com/ca_sanjose.htm
CitySearch San Jose	sanjose.citysearch.com
Excite.com San Jose City Guide	www.excite.com/travel/countries/united_states/california/san_jose
MetroActive Publishing Inc	www.metroactive.com
San Jose California	san-jose-california.com
San Jose Living	www.sjliving.com/
Savvy Diner Guide to San Jose Restaurants	www.savvydiner.com/sanjose/

— Transportation Services —

AIRPORTS

	Phone
■ **San Jose International Airport (SJC)** 3 miles NW of downtown (approx 15 minutes) Web: www.sjc.org	408-501-7600

Airport Transportation

	Phone
Airport Connection $47 fare to downtown	888-990-5466
Santa Clara Airporter $17 fare to downtown	415-771-7710
South Bay Airport Shuttle $12 fare to downtown	408-559-9477
Taxi $10 fare to downtown	408-293-1234
VIP Airport Shuttle $15 fare to downtown	408-885-1800
VTA $1.10 fare to downtown	408-321-2300

Commercial Airlines

	Phone		Phone
America West	800-235-9292	**SkyWest**	800-453-9417
Continental	800-525-0280	**Southwest**	800-435-9792
Delta	800-221-1212	**TWA**	800-221-2000
Mexicana	800-531-7923	**United**	800-241-6522
Northwest	800-225-2525		

Charter Airlines

	Phone		Phone
ACM Aviation Inc	408-286-3832	**Jet Aviation Business Jets Inc**	818-843-8400
Aris Helicopters LTD	408-998-3266	**Jet Center**	408-297-7552
Centurion Flight Services	650-494-7812	**Silicon Valley Express**	408-292-0677
Executive Jet Management	877-356-5387	**Tag Aviation**	800-252-6972

CAR RENTALS

	Phone		Phone
Able	408-436-6400	**Dollar**	408-808-3655
Alamo	408-288-4662	**Hertz**	408-437-5700
Avis	408-993-2224	**National**	800-227-7368
Budget	408-286-7850	**Thrifty**	408-727-4567

LIMO/TAXI

	Phone		Phone
Alpha Cab	408-295-9500	**Model Limousines**	800-652-3233
Black Tie Transportation	800-445-0444	**Reynolds Carriage Service**	408-988-0445
Champagne Limousine	408-866-1700	**United Cab**	408-971-1111
Cloud 9 Limousines	408-999-0999	**Yellow Cab**	408-293-1234
Espresso Limousine Service	408-395-5466		

MASS TRANSIT

	Phone
VTA $1.10 Base fare	408-321-2300

RAIL/BUS

				Phone
Greyhound/Trailways Bus Station 70 S Almaden Ave *TF:* 800-231-2222	San Jose	CA	95113	408-295-4151
San Jose Amtrak Station 65 Cahill St	San Jose	CA	95110	800-872-7245

— Accommodations —

HOTEL RESERVATION SERVICES

	Phone	Fax
California Reservations *TF:* 800-576-0003 ■ *Web:* www.cal-res.com	415-252-1107	252-1483

HOTELS, MOTELS, RESORTS

				Phone	Fax
Airport Inn International 1355 N 4th St *TF:* 800-453-5340	San Jose	CA	95112	408-453-5340	453-5208
Ambassador Business Inn 910 E Fremont Ave *TF:* 800-538-1600 ■ *Web:* www.abihotels.com	Sunnyvale	CA	94087	408-738-0500	245-4167
Arena Hotel 817 The Alameda *TF:* 800-954-6835 ■ *Web:* www.pacifichotels.com/arena/index.html	San Jose	CA	95126	408-294-6500	294-6585

San Jose — Hotels, Motels, Resorts (Cont'd)

				Phone	Fax
Best Western Gateway Inn 2585 Seaboard Ave *TF:* 800-437-8855	San Jose	CA	95131	408-435-8800	435-8879
Beverly Heritage Hotel 1820 Barber Ln *TF:* 800-443-4455	Milpitas	CA	95035	408-943-9080	432-8617
Biltmore Hotel & Suites 2151 Laurelwood Rd *TF:* 800-255-9925	Santa Clara	CA	95054	408-988-8411	988-0225
Casa Munras Hotel 700 Munras Ave *TF:* 800-222-2558 ■ *Web:* www.casamunras-hotel.com ■ *E-mail:* info@casamunras-hotel.com	Monterey	CA	93940	831-375-2411	375-1365
Chaminade Executive Conference Center 1 Chaminade Ln *TF:* 800-283-6569 ■ *Web:* www.chaminade.com	Santa Cruz	CA	95065	831-475-5600	476-4942
Clarion Inn 3200 Monterey Rd *TF:* 800-252-7466	San Jose	CA	95111	408-972-2200	972-2632
Comfort Inn Airport South 2118 The Alameda	San Jose	CA	95126	408-243-2400	243-5478
Courtyard by Marriott San Jose Airport 1727 Technology Dr *TF:* 800-638-8108 ■ *Web:* courtyard.com/SJCCA	San Jose	CA	95110	408-441-6111	441-8039
Crowne Plaza 777 Bellew Dr *TF:* 800-465-4329	Milpitas	CA	95035	408-321-9500	321-9599
Crowne Plaza San Jose 282 Almaden Blvd *TF:* 800-465-4329	San Jose	CA	95113	408-998-0400	289-9081
Days Inn 2460 Fontaine Rd	San Jose	CA	95121	408-270-7666	270-0714
Dinah's Garden Hotel 4261 El Camino Real *TF:* 800-227-8220 ■ *Web:* www.dinahshotel.com	Palo Alto	CA	94306	650-493-2844	856-4713
Doubletree Hotel 2050 Gateway Pl *TF:* 800-222-8733 ■ *Web:* www.doubletreehotels.com/DoubleT/Hotel141/149/149Main.htm	San Jose	CA	95110	408-453-4000	437-2898
Doubletree Hotel Monterey 2 Portola Plaza *TF:* 800-222-8733 ■ *Web:* www.doubletreemonterey.com	Monterey	CA	93940	831-649-4511	372-0620
Embassy Suites 901 E Calaveras Blvd *TF:* 800-362-2779	Milpitas	CA	95035	408-942-0400	262-8604
Embassy Suites Hotel 2885 Lakeside Dr *TF:* 800-362-2779	Santa Clara	CA	95054	408-496-6400	988-7529
Executive Inn Downtown 1215 S 1st St *TF:* 800-509-7666	San Jose	CA	95110	408-280-5300	280-0569
Executive Inn Suites 3930 Monterey Rd *TF:* 800-453-7755	San Jose	CA	95111	408-281-8700	578-6799
Fairmont Hotel 170 S Market St *TF:* 800-527-4727 ■ *Web:* www.fairmont.com/sanjose.html ■ *E-mail:* sanjose@fairmont.com	San Jose	CA	95113	408-998-1900	287-1648
Hanford Hotel 1755 N 1st St *TF:* 800-793-9121	San Jose	CA	95112	408-453-3133	452-1849
Hayes Renaissance Conference Center 200 Edenvale Ave *TF:* 800-420-3200 ■ *Web:* hayesconferencecenter.com/	San Jose	CA	95136	408-226-3200	362-2377
Hilton & Towers 300 Almaden Blvd *TF:* 800-445-8667 ■ *Web:* www.sjhilton.com ■ *E-mail:* info@sjhilton.com	San Jose	CA	95110	408-287-2100	947-4489
Holiday Inn Express Center City 2660 Monterey Rd *TF:* 800-465-4329	San Jose	CA	95111	408-279-6600	279-1064
Holiday Inn Express San Jose Airport 1350 N 4th St *TF:* 800-465-4329	San Jose	CA	95112	408-467-1789	467-1788
Holiday Inn Silicon Valley 399 Silicon Valley Blvd *TF:* 800-465-4329	San Jose	CA	95138	408-972-7800	972-0157
Homewood Suites Hotel 10 W Trimble Rd *TF:* 800-225-5466	San Jose	CA	95131	408-428-9900	428-0222
Hotel de Anza 233 W Santa Clara St *TF:* 800-843-3700 ■ *Web:* www.hoteldeanza.com ■ *E-mail:* getinfo@hoteldeanza.com	San Jose	CA	95113	408-286-1000	286-0500
Hyatt Hotel 1740 N 1st St *TF:* 800-975-1234 ■ *Web:* www.hyatt.com/usa/san_jose/hotels/hotel_sjcsj.html	San Jose	CA	95112	408-993-1234	453-0259
Hyatt Regency Resort & Conference Center 1 Old Golf Course Rd *TF:* 800-233-1234 ■ *Web:* www.montereyhyatt.com ■ *E-mail:* info@montereyhyatt.com	Monterey	CA	93940	831-372-1234	375-3960
Hyatt Sainte Claire 302 S Market St *TF:* 800-223-1234 ■ *Web:* www.hyatt.com/usa/san_jose/hotels/hotel_clair.html	San Jose	CA	95113	408-295-2000	977-0403
La Playa Hotel & Cottages By The Sea PO Box 900 *TF:* 800-582-8900	Carmel	CA	93921	831-624-6476	624-7966
Marriott Hotel 2700 Mission College Blvd *TF:* 800-228-9290 ■ *Web:* marriotthotels.com/SJCGA	Santa Clara	CA	95054	408-988-1500	727-4353
Monterey Hilton 1000 Aguajito Rd *TF:* 800-445-8667	Monterey	CA	93940	831-373-6141	655-8608
Post Ranch Inn Hwy 1 *TF:* 800-527-2200 ■ *Web:* www.postranchinn.com	Big Sur	CA	93920	831-667-2200	667-2824
Quality Suites Silicon Valley 3100 Lakeside Dr *TF:* 800-345-1554	Santa Clara	CA	95054	408-748-9800	748-1476
Radisson Plaza Hotel San Jose Airport 1471 N 4th St *TF:* 800-333-3333	San Jose	CA	95112	408-452-0200	437-8819
Residence Inn by Marriott 1854 El Camino Real W *TF:* 800-331-3131 ■ *Web:* www.residenceinn.com/residenceinn/SFOMV	Mountain View	CA	94040	650-940-1300	969-4997
Residence Inn by Marriott San Jose 2761 S Bascom Ave *TF:* 800-331-3131 ■ *Web:* www.residenceinn.com/SJCBA	Campbell	CA	95008	408-559-1551	371-9808
San Jose Convention Inn 455 S 2nd St	San Jose	CA	95113	408-298-3500	298-2477
Santa Maria Inn 801 S Broadway *TF:* 800-462-4276 ■ *Web:* www.santamariainn.com ■ *E-mail:* innkeeper@santamariainn.com	Santa Maria	CA	93454	805-928-7777	928-5690
Sheraton Inn Sunnyvale 1100 N Mathilda Ave *TF:* 800-325-3535	Sunnyvale	CA	94089	408-745-6000	734-8276
Sheraton San Jose Hotel 1801 Barber Ln	Milpitas	CA	95035	408-943-0600	943-0484
Summerfield Suites Hotel 1602 Crane Ct *TF:* 800-833-4353	San Jose	CA	95112	408-436-1600	436-1075
Sunnyvale Hilton Hotel 1250 Lakeside Dr *TF:* 800-445-8667	Sunnyvale	CA	94086	408-738-4888	737-7147
Tickle Pink Inn at Carmel Highlands 155 Highlands Dr *TF:* 800-635-4774	Carmel	CA	93923	831-624-1244	626-9516
Travelodge San Jose Arena 1041 The Alameda *TF:* 800-578-7878	San Jose	CA	95126	408-295-0159	998-5509
Vagabond Inn 1488 N 1st St *TF:* 800-522-1555	San Jose	CA	95112	408-453-8822	453-0559
Valley Park Hotel 2404 Stevens Creek *TF:* 800-882-1984	San Jose	CA	95128	408-293-5000	293-5287
Ventana Inn Coast Hwy 1 *TF:* 800-628-6500 ■ *Web:* www.ventanainn.com ■ *E-mail:* reservation@ventanainn.com	Big Sur	CA	93920	831-667-2331	667-2287
Westin Hotel 5101 Great America Pkwy *TF:* 800-937-8461	Santa Clara	CA	95054	408-986-0700	980-3990
Wyndham Hotel 1350 N 1st St *TF:* 800-996-3426	San Jose	CA	95112	408-453-6200	437-9693

— Restaurants —

				Phone
71 Sainte Peter (Mediterranean) 71 N San Pedro St	San Jose	CA	95110	408-971-8523
94th Aero Squadron (Continental) 1160 Coleman Ave	San Jose	CA	95110	408-287-6150
840 North First (American) 840 N 1st St	San Jose	CA	95112	408-282-0840
Agenda Restaurant (New American) 399 S 1st St *Web:* www.agendalounge.com	San Jose	CA	95112	408-287-3991
Amalfi's (Italian) 1740 N 1st St	San Jose	CA	95112	408-993-1234
Bella Mia (Italian) 58 S 1st St *Web:* www.bellamia.com	San Jose	CA	95113	408-280-1993
California Sushi & Grill (Japanese) 1 E San Fernando St	San Jose	CA	95113	408-297-1847
Camau (Vietnamese) 17 S 4th St	San Jose	CA	95112	408-971-2224
Casa Castillo (Mexican) 200 S 1st St	San Jose	CA	95113	408-971-8130
Chevy's (Mexican) 550 S Winchester Blvd	San Jose	CA	95128	408-241-0158
China Chen (Chinese) 400 S 3rd St	San Jose	CA	95112	408-294-2525
City Bar & Grill (American) 300 S Almaden Blvd	San Jose	CA	95110	408-287-2100
Coleman Still The (American) 1240 Coleman Ave	Santa Clara	CA	95050	408-727-4670
Emile's (French) 545 S 2nd St *Web:* www.emiles.com	San Jose	CA	95112	408-289-1960
Eulipia Restaurant (New American) 374 S 1st St *Web:* www.eulipia.com	San Jose	CA	95113	408-280-6161
Fountain The (American) 170 S Market St	San Jose	CA	95113	408-998-1900
Fuji Sushi (Japanese) 56 W Santa Clara St	San Jose	CA	95113	408-298-3854
Garden City (American) 360 S Saratoga Ave	San Jose	CA	95129	408-244-3333
Germania (German) 261 N 2nd St	San Jose	CA	95112	408-295-4484
Gervais Restaurant (French) 1798 Park Ave *Web:* www.eatout.com/	San Jose	CA	95126	408-275-8631
Gordon Biersch Brewery Restaurant (American) 33 E San Fernando St	San Jose	CA	95113	408-294-6785
Grill The (California) 170 S Market St	San Jose	CA	95113	408-294-2244
Henry's Hi-life (Barbecue) 301 W Saint John St	San Jose	CA	95110	408-295-5414
House of Cathay (Chinese) 1339 N 1st St	San Jose	CA	95112	408-453-8148
House of Genji (Japanese) 1335 N 1st St	San Jose	CA	95112	408-453-8120
Inca Gardens (Peruvian) 87 E San Fernando St	San Jose	CA	95113	408-977-0816
Komatsu (Japanese) 300 Orchard City Dr	Campbell	CA	95008	408-379-3000
La Foret (French) 21747 Bertram Rd	San Jose	CA	95120	408-997-3458
La Mere Michelle (Continental) 14467 Big Basin Way	Saratoga	CA	95070	408-867-5272
La Pastaia (Italian) 233 W Santa Clara St	San Jose	CA	95113	408-286-8686
La Penita (Mexican) 601 S 1st St	San Jose	CA	95113	408-295-0434
Le Mouton Noir (French) 14560 Big Basin Way	Saratoga	CA	95070	408-867-7017

San Jose — Restaurants (Cont'd)

				Phone
Le Papillon (French) 410 Saratoga Ave	San Jose	CA	95119	408-296-3730
Lou's Village (Seafood) 1465 W San Carlos St	San Jose	CA	95126	408-293-4570
Web: www.lousvillage.com				
Mariani's Inn (Italian) 2500 El Camino Real	Santa Clara	CA	95051	408-243-1431
Marina Seafood Grotto (Seafood) 995 Elizabeth St	Alviso	CA	95002	408-262-2563
Menara (Moroccan) 41 E Gish Rd	San Jose	CA	95112	408-453-1983
Pagoda The (Chinese) 170 S Market St	San Jose	CA	95113	408-998-3937
Palermo Ristorante Italiano (Italian) 394 S 2nd St	San Jose	CA	95113	408-297-0607
Paolo's (Italian) 333 W San Carlos St Suite 150	San Jose	CA	95110	408-294-2558
Rue de Paris (French) 19 N Market St	San Jose	CA	95113	408-298-0704
Web: www.frenchfood.com				
Scott's Seafood Grill & Bar (Steak/Seafood) 185 Park Ave	San Jose	CA	95113	408-971-1700
Sent Sovi (French) 14583 Big Basin Way	Saratoga	CA	95070	408-867-3110
Sharks Cafe (American) 55 S Market St	San Jose	CA	95113	408-292-7900
Spiedo (Italian) 151 W Santa Clara St	San Jose	CA	95113	408-971-6096
Stratta Grill Cafe (Continental) 71 E San Fernando St	San Jose	CA	95113	408-293-1121
Teske's Germania (German) 255 N 1st St	San Jose	CA	95131	408-292-0291
Thepthai (Thai) 23 N Market St	San Jose	CA	95113	408-292-7515
Tied House Cafe & Brewery (American) 65 N San Pedro St	San Jose	CA	95110	408-295-2739
Web: www.tiedhouse.com/				
Trieu Chau (Vietnamese) 325 S 1st St	San Jose	CA	95113	408-998-3306
West Smokehouse & Saloon (Barbecue) 65 Post St	San Jose	CA	95113	408-885-9283
White Lotus (Vegetarian) 80 N Market St	San Jose	CA	95113	408-977-0540

— Goods and Services —

SHOPPING

				Phone	Fax
Antique Row W San Carlos St	San Jose	CA	95126	408-947-8711	
Eastridge Mall Capitol Expy & Tully Rd	San Jose	CA	95122	408-238-3600	274-9684
Great Mall of the Bay Area 447 Great Mall Dr	Milpitas	CA	95035	408-956-2033	945-4027
TF: 800-625-5229 ■ *Web:* www.greatmallbayarea.com					
Macy's 2801 Stevens Creek Blvd	Santa Clara	CA	95050	408-248-3333	
Oakridge Mall 925-A Blossom Hill Rd	San Jose	CA	95123	408-578-2910	578-1148
Pavilion The 150 S 1st St	San Jose	CA	95113	408-286-2076	286-6899
San Jose Flea Market 1590 Berryessa Rd	San Jose	CA	95133	408-453-1110	437-9011
Web: www.sjfm.com					
Stanford Shopping Center 180 El Camino Real	Palo Alto	CA	94304	650-617-8585	617-8227
TF: 800-772-9332 ■ *Web:* www.stanfordshop.com					
Vallco Fashion Park 10123 N Wolfe Rd	Cupertino	CA	95014	408-255-5660	725-0370
Valley Fair Shopping Center 2855 Stevens Creek Blvd Suite 2178	Santa Clara	CA	95050	408-248-4451	248-8614
Westgate Mall 1600 Saratoga Ave	San Jose	CA	95129	408-379-9350	379-4890
Willow Glen-Lincoln Avenue Shopping District 1275 Lincoln Ave Suite 3A	San Jose	CA	95125	408-298-2100	280-1104

BANKS

				Phone	Fax
Bank of America 32 S 3rd St	San Jose	CA	95113	408-277-7208	277-7905
Bank of the West 50 W San Fernando St	San Jose	CA	95113	408-947-5005	295-0494
TF Cust Svc: 800-488-2265*					
Comerica Bank-California 55 Almaden Blvd	San Jose	CA	95113	408-556-5000	271-4074*
**Fax:* PR					
Heritage Bank of Commerce 150 Almaden Blvd	San Jose	CA	95113	408-947-6900	
San Jose National Bank 1 N Market St	San Jose	CA	95113	408-947-7562	947-7049
Web: www.sjnb.com ■ *E-mail:* the.bank@sjnb.com					
Sanwa Bank of California 220 Almaden Blvd	San Jose	CA	95113	408-998-0800	971-1290
Union Bank 99 Almaden Blvd	San Jose	CA	95113	408-279-7700	292-3981

BUSINESS SERVICES

	Phone
Accountemps	408-293-9040
Adecco Employment Personnel Services	408-296-8414
Blue Ribbon Express	408-945-0312
Federal Express	800-463-3339
Kelly Services	408-261-7000
Kinko's	408-295-4336
Manpower Temporary Services	408-264-5200
Post Office	800-275-8777
Specialized Messenger Services	800-576-1444
UPS	800-742-5877

— Media —

PUBLICATIONS

				Phone	Fax
Business Journal 96 N 3rd St Suite 100	San Jose	CA	95112	408-295-3800	295-5028
Web: www.amcity.com/sanjose					
San Jose City Times 550 S 1st St	San Jose	CA	95113	408-298-8000	298-0602*
**Fax:* News Rm ■ *Web:* metroactive.com/metro ■ *E-mail:* metro@sjmetro.com					
San Jose Mercury News‡ 750 Ridder Park Dr	San Jose	CA	95190	408-920-5000	288-8060
TF Sales: 800-818-6397 ■ *Web:* www.mercurycenter.com ■ *E-mail:* websales@sjmercury.com					

‡Daily newspapers

TELEVISION

				Phone	Fax
KNTV-TV Ch 11 (ABC) 645 Park Ave	San Jose	CA	95110	408-286-1111	286-1530
Web: www.kntv.com					
KPIX-TV Ch 5 (CBS) 855 Battery St	San Francisco	CA	94111	415-362-5550	765-8916
Web: www.kpix.com ■ *E-mail:* tvprog@kpix.com					
KRON-TV Ch 4 (NBC) 1001 Van Ness Ave	San Francisco	CA	94109	415-441-4444	561-8136
Web: www.kron.com					
KTEH-TV Ch 54 (PBS) 1585 Schallenberger Rd	San Jose	CA	95130	408-795-5400	995-5446
Web: www.kteh.org/					
KTVU-TV Ch 2 (Fox) 2 Jack London Sq	Oakland	CA	94607	510-834-1212	272-9957
Web: www.bayinsider.com/partners/ktvu/index.html ■ *E-mail:* ktvu@team.insider.com					

RADIO

				Phone	Fax
KARA-FM 105.7 MHz (AC) 750 Story Rd	San Jose	CA	95122	408-293-8030	995-0823
KBAY-FM 94.5 MHz (AC) 190 Park Center Plaza Suite 200	San Jose	CA	95113	408-287-5775	293-3341
Web: www.kbay.com					
KEZR-FM 106.5 MHz (AC) 190 Park Center Plaza Suite 200	San Jose	CA	95113	408-287-5775	293-3341
KFFG-FM 97.7 MHz (AAA) 55 Hawthorne St Suite 1100	San Francisco	CA	94105	415-543-1045	995-6867
KGO-AM 810 kHz (N/T) 900 Front St	San Francisco	CA	94111	415-954-8100	362-5827
Web: www.kgoam810.com					
KLOK-AM 1170 kHz (Span) 2905 S King Rd	San Jose	CA	95122	408-274-1170	274-1818
KRTY-FM 95.3 MHz (Ctry) 750 Story Rd	San Jose	CA	95122	408-293-8030	995-0823
Web: www.krty.com					
KSJO-FM 92.3 MHz (Rock) 1420 Koll Cir Suite A	San Jose	CA	95112	408-453-5400	452-1330
Web: www.ksjo.com					
KUSP-FM 88.9 MHz (NPR) 203 8th Ave	Santa Cruz	CA	95062	831-476-2800	476-2802
Web: www4.cruzio.com/cruzio/404.html ■ *E-mail:* kusp@cruzio.com					

— Colleges/Universities —

				Phone	Fax
Cogswell Polytechnical College 1175 Bordeaux Dr	Sunnyvale	CA	94089	408-541-0100	747-0764
TF: 800-264-7955 ■ *Web:* www.cogswell.edu ■ *E-mail:* info@gateway.cogswell.edu					
DeAnza College 21250 Stevens Creek Blvd	Cupertino	CA	95014	408-864-8419	864-8329
Web: www.deanza.fhda.edu ■ *E-mail:* deanzainfo@fhda.edu					
Evergreen Valley College 3095 Yerba Buena Rd	San Jose	CA	95135	408-274-7900	223-9351
Web: www.evc.edu ■ *E-mail:* evcinfo@unix.sjeccd.cc.ca.us					
Foothill College 12345 El Monte Rd	Los Altos Hills	CA	94022	650-949-7777	949-7048
Web: www.foothill.fhda.edu					
Heald Institute of Technology 341-A Great Mall Pkwy	Milpitas	CA	95035	408-934-4900	934-7777
TF: 800-967-7576 ■ *Web:* www.heald.edu					
Mission College 3000 Mission College Blvd	Santa Clara	CA	95054	408-988-2200	980-8980
Web: www.wvmccd.cc.ca.us/mc/					
National Hispanic University 14271 Story Rd	San Jose	CA	95127	408-254-6900	254-1369
Web: www.nhu.edu ■ *E-mail:* info@nhu.edu					
San Jose Christian College 790 S 12th St	San Jose	CA	95112	408-293-9058	293-7352
TF: 800-355-7522 ■ *Web:* www.sjchristiancol.edu ■ *E-mail:* sjcc1939@aol.com					
San Jose City College 2100 Moorpark Ave	San Jose	CA	95128	408-298-2181	298-1935
Web: www.sjcc.cc.ca.us					

San Jose — Colleges/Universities (Cont'd)

	City	State	Zip	Phone	Fax
San Jose State University 1 Washington Sq *Web:* www.sjsu.edu	San Jose	CA	95199	408-924-1000	924-2050
Santa Clara University 500 El Camino Real *Web:* www.scu.edu ■ *E-mail:* ugadmissions@scu.edu	Santa Clara	CA	95053	408-554-4764	554-5255

— Hospitals —

	City	State	Zip	Phone	Fax
Community Hospital of Los Gatos 815 Pollard Rd *Web:* www.tenethealth.com/LosGatos	Los Gatos	CA	95032	408-378-6131	866-4003
Good Samaritan Hospital 2425 Samaritan Dr **Fax:* Admitting	San Jose	CA	95124	408-559-2011	559-2661*
O'Connor Hospital 2105 Forest Ave.	San Jose	CA	95128	408-947-2500	947-2710
Regional Medical Center of San Jose 225 N Jackson Ave	San Jose	CA	95116	408-259-5000	729-2884
Santa Clara Valley Medical Center 751 S Bascom Ave **Fax:* Admitting	San Jose	CA	95128	408-885-5000	885-6610*
Santa Teresa Community Hospital 250 Hospital Pkwy **Fax:* Admitting	San Jose	CA	95119	408-972-7000	972-6445*
Stanford University Hospital 300 Pasteur Dr **Fax:* Hum Res ■ *Web:* www-med.stanford.edu/shs	Stanford	CA	94305	650-723-2300	723-8163*

— Attractions —

	City	State	Zip	Phone	Fax
Ainsley House/Campbell Historical Museum 300 Grant St	Campbell	CA	95008	408-866-2119	379-6349
Almaden Lake Park Almaden Expy & Coleman Ave	San Jose	CA	95120	408-277-5130	997-2035
Alum Rock Park 16240 Alum Rock Ave	San Jose	CA	95127	408-259-5477	
American Museum of Quilts & Textiles 110 Paseo de San Antonio *Web:* www.sjquiltmuseum.org/	San Jose	CA	95112	408-971-0323	971-7226
American Musical Theatre of San Jose 1717 Technology Dr *Web:* www.amtsj.org ■ *E-mail:* info@amtsj.org	San Jose	CA	95110	408-453-7108	453-7123
Cannery Row 765 Wave St.	Monterey	CA	93940	831-649-6695	373-4812
Cathedral Basilica of Saint Joseph 80 S Market St *Web:* www.stjosephcathedral.org	San Jose	CA	95113	408-283-8100	283-8110
Center for Beethoven Studies & Museum San Jose State University Library Rm 318	San Jose	CA	95192	408-924-4590	924-4715
Center for the Performing Arts 255 Almaden Blvd	San Jose	CA	95110	408-277-3900	277-3535
Children's Discovery Museum 180 Woz Way *Web:* www.cdm.org ■ *E-mail:* will@cdm.org	San Jose	CA	95110	408-298-5437	298-6826
Chinese Cultural Garden 2145 McKee Rd	San Jose	CA	95116	408-251-3323	251-2865
City Lights Theatre Co 529 S 2nd St. *Web:* www.cltc.org ■ *E-mail:* citylights@cltc.org	San Jose	CA	95112	408-295-4200	295-8318
Fallon House 175 W Saint John St	San Jose	CA	95110	408-993-8182	
Happy Hollow Park & Zoo 1300 Senter Rd Kelley Pk *Web:* www.acoates.com/happyhollow/happyhollow.html ■ *E-mail:* zoovet@netgate.net	San Jose	CA	95112	408-295-8383	277-4470
Intel Museum 2200 Mission College Blvd. *Web:* www.intel.com/intel/intelis/museum/	Santa Clara	CA	95052	408-765-0503	765-1217
J Lohr Winery 1000 Lenzen Ave	San Jose	CA	95126	408-288-5057	993-2276
Japanese-American Museum 535 N 5th St *Web:* www.jarc-m.org	San Jose	CA	95112	408-294-3138	294-1657
Japanese Friendship Garden 1300 Senter Rd	San Jose	CA	95112	408-295-8383	277-4470
Kelley Park 1300 Senter Rd	San Jose	CA	95112	408-277-4191	277-3270
Lake Cunningham Regional Park 2305 S White Rd	San Jose	CA	95148	408-277-4319	
Lick Observatory Mt Hamilton Rd *Web:* www.ucolick.org	San Jose	CA	95140	408-274-5061	
Mirassou Vineyards 3000 Aborn Rd *TF:* 888-647-2776 ■ *Web:* www.mirassou.com ■ *E-mail:* sales@mirassou.com	San Jose	CA	95135	408-274-4000	270-5881
Monterey Bay Aquarium 886 Cannery Row *Web:* www.mbayaq.org	Monterey	CA	93940	831-648-4800	648-4810
Monterey Museum of Art 559 Pacific St *Web:* www.montereyart.org ■ *E-mail:* mtry_art@mbay.net	Monterey	CA	93940	831-372-5477	372-5680
Montgomery Theater San Carlos & Market Sts	San Jose	CA	95110	408-277-3900	
Municipal Rose Garden Naglee & Dana Aves	San Jose	CA	95126	408-277-4191	277-5422
New Marine World Theme Park 2001 Marine World Pkwy. *Web:* www.freerun.com/napavalley/outdoor/marinewo/marinewo.html	Vallejo	CA	94589	707-644-4000	644-0241
Opera San Jose 2149 Paragon Dr. *Web:* operasj.org	San Jose	CA	95131	408-437-4450	437-4455
Overfelt Gardens 2145 McKee Rd	San Jose	CA	95116	408-251-3323	251-2865
Paramount's Great America PO Box 1776 **Fax:* Sales ■ *Web:* www.pgathrills.com	Santa Clara	CA	95052	408-988-1776	986-5855*
Peralta Adobe 175 W Saint John St	San Jose	CA	95110	408-993-8182	
Pinnacles National Monument 5000 Hwy 146 *Web:* www.nps.gov/pinn/	Paicines	CA	95043	831-389-4485	389-4489
Prusch Farm Park 647 S King Rd	San Jose	CA	95116	408-277-4567	277-3820
Raging Waters Aquatic Theme Park 2333 S White Rd *Web:* www.rwsplash.com	San Jose	CA	95148	408-270-8000	270-2022
Rosicrucian Egyptian Museum & Art Gallery 1342 Naglee Ave Rosicrucian Pk. *Web:* www.rcegyptmus.org	San Jose	CA	95191	408-947-3636	947-3638
San Jose Center for the Performing Arts 255 Almaden Ave *TF:* 800-533-2345 ■ *Web:* www.sjcc.com/cftpa/index.html	San Jose	CA	95110	408-277-5277	277-3535
San Jose Children's Musical Theatre 1401 N Parkmoor Ave *Web:* www.sjcmt.com ■ *E-mail:* sjcmt@sjcmt.com	San Jose	CA	95126	408-288-5437	288-6241
San Jose Cleveland Ballet 40 N 1st St 2nd Fl	San Jose	CA	95113	408-288-2820	993-9570
San Jose Flea Market 1590 Berryessa Rd *Web:* www.sjfm.com	San Jose	CA	95133	408-453-1110	437-9011
San Jose Historical Museum 1650 Senter Rd *Web:* www.serve.com/sjhistory/ ■ *E-mail:* sjhistory@mail.serve.com	San Jose	CA	95112	408-287-2290	287-2291
San Jose Museum of Art 110 S Market St. *Web:* www.sjmusart.org ■ *E-mail:* info@sjmusart.org	San Jose	CA	95113	408-271-6840	294-2977
San Jose Repertory Theatre 101 Paseo de San Antonio *E-mail:* The_Rep@Vval.com	San Jose	CA	95113	408-291-2266	367-7237
San Jose Stage Co 490 S 1st St *Web:* www.sanjose-stage.com ■ *E-mail:* rfirst@garlic.com	San Jose	CA	95113	408-283-7142	283-7146
San Jose Symphony Orchestra 495 Almaden Blvd *Web:* www.sanjosesymphony.org	San Jose	CA	95110	408-287-7383	286-6391
Santa Cruz Beach Boardwalk 400 Beach St *Web:* www.beachboardwalk.com	Santa Cruz	CA	95060	831-423-5590	460-3335
Tech Museum of Innovation 201 S Market St *Web:* www.thetech.org	San Jose	CA	95113	408-294-8324	279-7167
Winchester Mystery House 525 S Winchester Blvd *Web:* www.siliconvalley-usa.com/tourist/winchest	San Jose	CA	95128	408-247-2000	
Youth Science Institute 296 Garden Hill Dr *Web:* www.ysi-ca.org ■ *E-mail:* info@ysi-org	Los Gatos	CA	95030	408-356-4945	358-3683

SPORTS TEAMS & FACILITIES

	City	State	Zip	Phone	Fax
Bay Meadows Race Course 2600 S Delaware St. **Fax:* Hum Res ■ *Web:* www.baymeadows.com	San Mateo	CA	94402	650-574-7223	573-4677*
San Jose Arena 525 W Santa Clara St. *TF:* 800-366-4423 ■ *Web:* www.sj-arena.com	San Jose	CA	95113	408-287-7070	999-5797
San Jose Clash (soccer) 3550 Stevens Creek Suite 200 *Web:* www.clash.com ■ *E-mail:* info@clash.com	San Jose	CA	95117	408-241-9922	554-8886
San Jose Giants (baseball) 588 E Alma St Municipal Stadium *Web:* www.sjgiants.com ■ *E-mail:* giantssj@aol.com	San Jose	CA	95112	408-297-1435	297-1453
San Jose Rhinos (roller hockey) 525 W Santa Clara St San Jose Arena *TF:* 800-207-4466 ■ *Web:* www.rhinos.com ■ *E-mail:* alytle.rhinos@sjsharks.com	San Jose	CA	95113	408-287-4442	287-3653
San Jose SaberCats (football) 600 E Brokaw Rd	San Jose	CA	95112	408-573-5577	573-5588
San Jose Sharks 525 W Santa Clara St San Jose Arena *Web:* www.sj-sharks.com	San Jose	CA	95113	408-287-9200	999-5707

San Jose — Sports Teams & Facilities (Cont'd)

				Phone	Fax
Silicon Valley Ambassadors (soccer) 236 Stanford Shopping Ctr Suite 302 *Web:* www.goambassadors.com ■ *E-mail:* soccer@goambassadors.com	Palo Alto	CA	94304	650-618-1523	618-1523
Spartan Stadium 1257 S 10th St	San Jose	CA	95112	408-924-1850	924-1911

— Events —

	Phone
Almaden Art & Wine Festival (late September)	408-268-1133
Arts & Crafts & Music Festival (late March & mid-May)	408-842-9316
Chinese Summer Festival (mid-July)	408-287-2290
Cinco de Mayo Festival (early May)	408-258-0663
CineQuest-San Jose Film Festival (late February-early March)	408-995-5033
Clam Chowder Cook-Off (early February)	831-423-5590
Fiestas Patrias (early May)	408-258-0663
Gay Pride Parade & Festival (mid-June)	408-278-5563
Harvest Festival (late August-December)	800-321-1213
Hoi Tet Festival (mid-February)	408-295-9210
Irish Week Celebration (mid-March)	408-279-6002
Italian American Cultural Festival (early October)	408-293-7122
Juneteenth Festival (mid-June)	408-292-3157
Los Posadas (mid-December)	408-467-9890
Mariachi Conference & Festival (mid-July)	408-292-5197
Metro Fountain Blues Festival (early May)	408-924-6262
Mountain Winery Summer Series (June-September)	408-741-0763
Obon Festival (mid-July)	408-293-9292
Oktoberfest (mid-October)	408-453-1110
San Jose America Festival (early July)	408-298-6861
San Jose Historical Museum Walking Tours (May-October)	408-287-2290
San Jose Holiday Parade (December)	408-995-6635
San Jose International Auto Show (January)	408-277-3900
San Jose Jazz Festival (mid-August)	408-288-7557
San Pedro Square Brew Ha Ha (early October)	408-279-1775
Santa Clara County Fair (late July-early August)	408-494-3247
Santa Cruz Christmas Craft & Gift Festival (late November)	831-423-5590
SoFa Street Fair (mid-September)	408-295-2265
Strawberry Festival (early June)	408-379-3790
Wine & Arts Prune Festival (late May)	408-378-6252

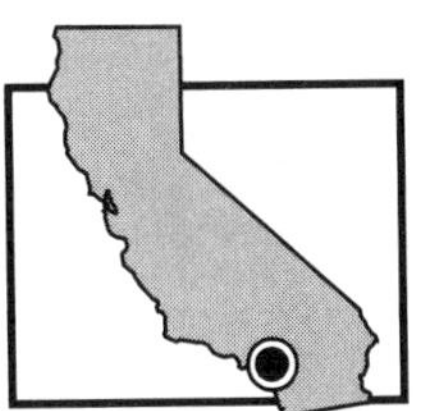

Santa Ana

Located 30 miles southeast of Los Angeles, Santa Ana is the governmental center of Orange County. It was founded in the late 1700s by Spaniards, and the city's Hispanic heritage is evident in its multicultural community and in the architecture of its buildings. Historic Downtown Santa Ana, which is listed in the National Register of Historic Places, features nearly 20 historic buildings, including Santa Ana City Hall, Orange County Courthouse, and Walkers Orange County Theater. The Orange County Center for Contemporary Art is also located in Santa Ana.

Population	305,955	**Longitude**	117-52-55 W
Area (Land)	27.1 sq mi	**County**	Orange
Area (Water)	0.3 sq mi	**Time Zone**	PST
Elevation	110 ft	**Area Code/s**	714
Latitude	33-44-11 N		

— Average Temperatures and Precipitation —

TEMPERATURES

	Jan	Feb	Mar	Apr	May	Jun	Jul	Aug	Sep	Oct	Nov	Dec
High	69	70	70	73	74	78	83	84	83	80	74	69
Low	46	47	49	51	56	59	63	64	62	58	50	45

PRECIPITATION

	Jan	Feb	Mar	Apr	May	Jun	Jul	Aug	Sep	Oct	Nov	Dec
Inches	2.5	2.3	2.2	0.8	0.2	0.1	0.0	0.1	0.4	0.3	1.7	1.8

— Important Phone Numbers —

	Phone		Phone
AAA	714-973-1211	**Medical Referral**	/14-978-1770
American Express Travel	714-541-3318	**Poison Control Center**	800-777-6476
Dental Referral	714-634-8944	**Weather**	858-675-8706
Emergency	911		

— Information Sources —

				Phone	Fax
Better Business Bureau Serving Placentia 550 W Orangethorpe Ave *Web:* www.la.bbb.org	Placentia	CA	92870	714-985-8900	985-8920
Orange County 12 Civic Center Plaza *Web:* www.oc.ca.gov	Santa Ana	CA	92701	714-834-2500	834-2675
Santa Ana Chamber of Commerce 1055 N Main St Suite 904 *Web:* www.santaanacc.com ■ *E-mail:* saccinfo@santaanacc.com	Santa Ana	CA	92701	714-541-5353	541-2238
Santa Ana City Hall 20 Civic Center Plaza *Web:* www.ci.santa-ana.ca.us	Santa Ana	CA	92701	714-647-6900	649-6954
Santa Ana Community Development Agency PO Box 1988	Santa Ana	CA	92702	714-647-5360	647-6549
Santa Ana Mayor 20 Civic Center Plaza *Web:* www.ci.santa-ana.ca.us/mayor/mayor.html	Santa Ana	CA	92701	714-647-6900	647-6954
Santa Ana Public Library 26 Civic Center Plaza *Web:* www.ci.santa-ana.ca.us/library	Santa Ana	CA	92701	714-647-5250	647-5356

On-Line Resources

4SantaAna.com	www.4santaana.com
Annual Guide for the Arts	www.guide4arts.com/oc/
Excite.com Santa Ana City Guide	www.excite.com/travel/countries/united_states/california/santa_ana
InOrangeCounty.com	www.inorangecounty.com

— Transportation Services —

AIRPORTS

■ **John Wayne Airport/Orange County (SNA)**

	Phone
5 miles S of downtown (approx 10 minutes) Web: www.ocair.com	949-252-5200

Airport Transportation

	Phone
Express Shuttle $13 fare to downtown	800-606-7433
LAXpress Airport Shuttle $13 fare to downtown	800-427-7483
Prime Time Shuttle $15 fare to downtown	800-262-7433

Commercial Airlines

	Phone		Phone
America West	800-235-9292	**Malaysia Airlines**	800-552-9264
American	800-433-7300	**SkyWest**	800-453-9417
Continental	800-525-0280	**United**	800-241-6522
Delta	714-534-8468	**United Express**	800-241-6522

Charter Airlines

	Phone		Phone
Alliance Executive Charter Services	800-232-5387	**Lenair Aviation Inc**	949-756-8546
Ari Worldwide Aircraft Charters	800-426-9110	**Regency Air LLC**	714-541-3932
Avjet Corp.	800-342-8538	**Schubach Aviation**	800-214-8215
Clay Lacy Aviation Inc	800-423-2904	**Signature Flight Support**	949-263-5800
Combs Executive Charter	800-627-8465	**Sunbird Aviation LLC**	800-434-5150
Corporate America Aviation Inc	800-521-8585	**TWC Aviation**	888-892-0035
Helistream	714-662-3163	**West Coast Charter**	949-852-8340

■ **Los Angeles International Airport (LAX)**

	Phone
34 miles NW of downtown Santa Ana (approx 75 minutes) Web: www.lax2015.org	310-646-5252

Santa Ana (Cont'd)

Airport Transportation

	Phone
Express Shuttle $38 fare to downtown Santa Ana	800-606-7433
LAXpress Airport Shuttle $33 fare to downtown Santa Ana	800-427-7483
Prime Time $40 fare to downtown Santa Ana	800-262-7433
Yellow Cab $75 fare to downtown Santa Ana	323-221-1234

Commercial Airlines

	Phone		Phone
AccessAir	877-462-2237	**Korean Air**	800-438-5000
Aerolineas Argentinas	800-333-0276	**LACSA**	213-385-9424
Air Canada	800-776-3000	**LTU International**	800-888-0200
Air Jamaica	800-523-5585	**Lufthansa**	800-645-3880
Air New Zealand	310-615-1111	**Mexicana**	800-531-7923
Alitalia	800-223-5730	**Midwest Express**	800-452-2022
All Nippon Airways	310-782-3000	**National**	888-757-5387
America West	800-235-9292	**Northwest**	800-225-2525
American	800-433-7300	**Pan Am**	800-359-7262
American Eagle	800-433-7300	**Philippine**	800-435-9725
Avianca	800-284-2622	**Qantas**	800-227-4500
British Airways	800-247-9297	**Scandinavian**	800-221-2350
China Airlines	310-641-8888	**Shuttle by United**	800-748-8853
China Eastern	626-583-1500	**SkyWest**	800-453-9417
Continental	800-525-0280	**Southwest**	800-435-9792
Delta	213-386-5510	**TACA International**	800-535-8780
El Al	800-223-6700	**TWA**	800-221-2000
Hawaiian	310-215-1866	**United**	800-241-6522
Iberia	800-772-4642	**United Express**	800-241-6522
Island Express	562-436-2012	**US Airways**	800-428-4322
Japan	800-525-3663	**Varig Brazilian**	310-646-2190
KLM	800-374-7747	**Virgin Atlantic**	800-862-8621

Charter Airlines

	Phone		Phone
Helistream	714-662-3163	**West Coast Charter**	949-852-8340
Universal Jet	310-399-7371		

CAR RENTALS

	Phone		Phone
Alamo	949-851-2550	**Dollar**	949-756-6100
Avis	949-852-8608	**Enterprise**	800-325-8007
Budget	714-871-1620	**Hertz**	949-756-8161

LIMO/TAXI

	Phone		Phone
A Taxi	714-547-8000	**Strictly Limousine**	714-543-2861
Ace Limousine	714-957-8023	**Yellow Cab**	714-535-2211
Legacy Limousine Service	714-970-7333		

MASS TRANSIT

	Phone
OCTA Bus $1 Base fare	714-636-7433

RAIL/BUS

				Phone
Amtrak Station 1000 E Santa Ana Blvd *TF:* 800-872-7245	Santa Ana	CA	92701	714-547-8389
Greyhound Bus Station 1000 E Santa Ana Blvd *TF:* 800-231-2222	Santa Ana	CA	92701	714-542-2215

— Accommodations —

HOTELS, MOTELS, RESORTS

				Phone	Fax
Best Inn Motel 609 N Harbor Blvd	Santa Ana	CA	92703	714-554-4040	554-0960
Best Western Inn 2700 Hotel Terrace Dr *TF:* 800-432-0053	Santa Ana	CA	92705	714-432-8888	434-6228
California Lodge Suites 2909 S Bristol St	Santa Ana	CA	92704	714-540-2300	668-0718
California Palms Suites 901 S Harbor Blvd *TF:* 800-660-6761	Santa Ana	CA	92704	714-775-6768	839-6258
Comfort Suites 2620 Hotel Terrace Dr	Santa Ana	CA	92705	714-966-5200	979-9650
Courtyard by Marriott 3002 S Harbor Blvd *Web:* courtyard.com/SNASA	Santa Ana	CA	92704	714-545-1001	545-8439
Days Inn 1104 N Harbor Blvd	Santa Ana	CA	92703	714-554-3268	554-7538
Days Inn 279 S Main St *TF:* 800-329-7466	Orange	CA	92868	714-771-6704	771-5522
Doubletree Club Hotel 7 Hutton Centre Dr *TF:* 800-222-8733 ■ *Web:* www.doubletreehotels.com/DoubleT/Hotel/19/19Main.htm	Santa Ana	CA	92707	714-751-2400	662-7935
Doubletree Hotel Orange County 100 The City Dr *TF:* 800-222-8733 ■ *Web:* www.doubletreehotels.com/DoubleT/Hotel/05/05Main.htm ■ *E-mail:* anaheimdtree@earthlink.net	Orange	CA	92868	714-634-4500	978-3839
El Cortez Lodge 1503 E 1st St	Santa Ana	CA	92701	714-835-2585	
Embassy Suites 1325 E Dyer Rd *TF:* 800-821-0900	Santa Ana	CA	92705	714-241-3800	662-1651
Hilton Suites 400 N State College Blvd *TF:* 800-445-8667 ■ *Web:* www.hilton.com/hotels/SNAORHS	Orange	CA	92868	714-938-1111	938-0930
Holiday Inn 2726 S Grand Ave	Santa Ana	CA	92705	714-966-1955	966-1889
Howard Johnson Lodge 939 E 17th St *TF:* 800-654-8778	Santa Ana	CA	92701	714-558-3700	568-1641
Motel 6 1623 E 1st St *TF:* 800-466-8356	Santa Ana	CA	92701	714-558-0500	558-1574
Quality Suites 2701 Hotel Terrace Dr *TF:* 800-221-2222	Santa Ana	CA	92705	714-957-9200	641-8936
Radisson Suites 2720 Hotel Terrace Dr *TF:* 800-333-3333	Santa Ana	CA	92705	714-556-3838	241-1008
Ramada Inn 1600 E 1st St *TF:* 800-959-4654	Santa Ana	CA	92701	714-835-3051	543-0856
Red Roof Inn 2600 N Main St *TF:* 800-843-7663	Santa Ana	CA	92705	714-542-0311	542-0321
Residence Inn 3101 W Chapman Ave *TF:* 800-331-3131 ■ *Web:* www.residenceinn.com/residenceinn/SNAOR	Orange	CA	92868	714-978-7700	978-6257
Royal Roman Motel 1504 E 1st St	Santa Ana	CA	92701	714-547-8411	547-5647
Saddleback Inn 1660 E 1st St	Santa Ana	CA	92701	714-835-3311	973-1466
Travelodge 1400 SE Bristol St *TF:* 800-578-7878	Santa Ana	CA	92707	714-557-8700	557-9164
Tustin Suites 2151 E 1st St *TF:* 800-558-2772	Santa Ana	CA	92705	714-558-2772	558-7007
Westin South Coast Plaza Hotel 686 Anton Blvd *TF:* 800-228-3000	Costa Mesa	CA	92626	714-540-2500	662-6695
Wooley's Petite Suites 2721 Hotel Terrace Dr *TF:* 800-762-2597	Santa Ana	CA	92705	714-540-1111	662-1643

— Restaurants —

				Phone
Acapulco (Mexican) 1262 SE Bristol St	Santa Ana	CA	92707	714-754-6528
Antonello Ristorante (Italian) 1611 W Sunflower Ave	Santa Ana	CA	92704	714-751-7153
Avila's El Ranchito (Mexican) 2201 E 1st St	Santa Ana	CA	92701	714-547-9129
Bina Ristorante (Italian) 1730 E 17th St	Santa Ana	CA	92701	714-972-3101
Burrell's BBQ (Barbecue) 305 N Hesperian St	Santa Ana	CA	92703	714-547-7441
Carrano's Pasta California (Italian) 1640 E Edinger Ave	Santa Ana	CA	92705	714-835-9678
Carrows (American) 3355 S Bristol St	Santa Ana	CA	92704	714-557-6733
China West (Chinese) 2502 S Bristol St	Santa Ana	CA	92704	714-549-9541
Da Vinci Ristorante (Italian) 2222 E 1st St	Santa Ana	CA	92705	714-285-1130
Dayra Restaurant (Persian) 1611 W Sunflower Ave	Santa Ana	CA	92704	714-557-6600
El Pupusodromo (Salvadorian) 819 S Main St	Santa Ana	CA	92701	714-542-3001
El Siete Mares (Mexican) 1106 S Bristol St	Santa Ana	CA	92704	714-557-4574
Emerald Bay Restaurant (Chinese) 5015 W Edinger Ave	Santa Ana	CA	92704	714-775-5161
Fresca's Mexican Grill (Mexican) 20060 Santa Ana Ave	Santa Ana	CA	92707	714-557-6822
Gustaf Anders (Scandinavian) 1651 Sunflower Ave	Santa Ana	CA	92704	714-668-1737
Hacienda The (Spanish) 1725 College Ave	Santa Ana	CA	92706	714-558-1304
Hankey's Restaurant & Bar (American) 1120 W 17th St	Santa Ana	CA	92706	714-542-9996
Jade Palace (Chinese) 3305 S Bristol St	Santa Ana	CA	92704	714-434-2854
La Perlita (Mexican) 1307 S Main St	Santa Ana	CA	92707	714-543-9033
Mariscos Mi Costa (Mexican) 930 S Main St	Santa Ana	CA	92701	714-542-9463
National Sports Grill (American) 101 Sandpointe Ave	Santa Ana	CA	92707	714-979-0900
Newport Seafood Restaurant (Seafood) 4411 W 1st St	Santa Ana	CA	92703	714-531-5146
Ostioneria Clemente (Mexican) 1473 S Main St	Santa Ana	CA	92707	714-647-9407
Palm Tree Inn (Chinese) 855 S Bristol St	Santa Ana	CA	92704	714-979-3427
Pho Cali (Vietnamese) 120 S Harbor Blvd	Santa Ana	CA	92704	714-531-4556
Rainforest Cafe (American) 3333 Bristol St Suite 1073 *Web:* www.rainforestcafe.com	Costa Mesa	CA	92626	714-424-9200
Rancho De Mendoza (Mexican) 104 E 4th St	Santa Ana	CA	92701	714-547-0345
Restaurant Sui (Japanese) 20070 Santa Ana Ave	Santa Ana	CA	92707	714-429-0141
San Kai (Japanese) 3940 S Bristol St	Santa Ana	CA	92704	714-241-7115
Seoul House (Korean) 1200 W Warner Ave	Santa Ana	CA	92707	714-540-8482
Shelly's Courthouse Bistro (Continental) 400 W 4th St	Santa Ana	CA	92701	714-543-9821
Tacolandia Restaurant (Mexican) 2343 W 1st St	Santa Ana	CA	92703	714-541-4160
Topaz Cafe (American) 2002 N Main St	Santa Ana	CA	92706	714-835-2002
Village Farmer Restaurant (Vegetarian) 1651 W Sunflower Ave	Santa Ana	CA	92704	714-557-8433
Wildflower Cafe (American) 2525 N Grand Ave	Santa Ana	CA	92701	714-532-2750
Yellow Basket Restaurant (American) 2860 S Main St	Santa Ana	CA	92707	714-545-8219

Santa Ana (Cont'd)

— Goods and Services —

SHOPPING

				Phone	Fax
Block at Orange 20 City Blvd W *Web:* www.theblockatorange.com	Orange	CA	92868	714-769-4000	769-4011
MainPlace Santa Ana 2800 N Main St	Santa Ana	CA	92705	714-547-7000	547-2643
South Coast Plaza 3333 Bristol St *Web:* www.southcoastplaza.com ■ *E-mail:* info@southcoastplaza.com	Costa Mesa	CA	92626	714-435-2000	540-7334

BANKS

				Phone	Fax
Bank of America 2800 N Main St	Santa Ana	CA	92701	714-973-8495	
California Federal Bank 518 N Broadway **Fax Area Code:* 714	Santa Ana	CA	92701	800-843-2265	285-2339*
California United Bank 2740 N Grand Ave	Santa Ana	CA	92705	714-771-5050	771-0890
Grand National Bank 1138 S Garfield Ave	Alhambra	CA	91801	626-300-8888	284-8697
Sanwa Bank of California 3931 S Bristol St	Santa Ana	CA	92704	714-540-4660	751-9504
Wells Fargo Bank 2130 E 17th St	Santa Ana	CA	92701	800-869-3557	

BUSINESS SERVICES

	Phone		Phone
Airborne Express	800-247-2676	**Labor Connection**	714-835-8367
DHL Worldwide Express	800-225-5345	**Post Office**	714-662-6200
Federal Express	800-238-5355	**Signature Secretarial Services**	714-543-2723
Kinko's	714-953-2127	**UPS**	800-742-5877

— Media —

PUBLICATIONS

				Phone	Fax
Los Angeles Times Orange County‡ 1375 Sunflower Ave	Costa Mesa	CA	92826	714-966-5600	966-5600
Orange County Business Journal 4590 MacArthur Blvd Suite 100	Newport Beach	CA	92660	949-833-8373	833-8751
Orange County Register‡ 625 N Grand Ave *Web:* www.ocregister.com	Santa Ana	CA	92701	714-835-1234	565-3681
Tustin News PO Box 11626	Santa Ana	CA	92711	714-564-7072	565-6098

‡Daily newspapers

TELEVISION

				Phone	Fax
KABC-TV Ch 7 (ABC) 4151 Prospect Ave *Web:* abcnews.go.com/local/kabc ■ *E-mail:* abc7@abc.com	Los Angeles	CA	90027	310-557-3200	557-3360
KCBS-TV Ch 2 (CBS) 6121 Sunset Blvd *Web:* www.kcbs2.com	Los Angeles	CA	90028	323-460-3000	460-3733
KCET-TV Ch 28 (PBS) 4401 Sunset Blvd *Web:* www.keet.org	Los Angeles	CA	90027	323-666-6500	953-5523
KNBC-TV Ch 4 (NBC) 3000 W Alameda Ave *Web:* www.knbc4la.com	Burbank	CA	91523	818-840-4444	840-3535
KTTV-TV Ch 11 (Fox) 1999 S Bundy Dr *Web:* www.fox11la.com ■ *E-mail:* talkback@fox11la.com	West Los Angeles	CA	90025	310-584-2000	584-2023

RADIO

				Phone	Fax
KABC-AM 790 kHz (N/T) 3321 S La Cienega Blvd *Web:* www.kabc.com	Los Angeles	CA	90016	310-840-4900	838-5222
KBIG-FM 104.3 MHz (AC) 330 N Brand Blvd Suite 800 **Fax:* Sales ■ *Web:* www.kbig104.com	Glendale	CA	91203	818-546-1043	637-2267*
KCBS-FM 93.1 MHz (CR) 6121 Sunset Blvd *Web:* www.arrowfm.com	Los Angeles	CA	90028	323-460-3000	460-3733
KFWB-AM 980 kHz (N/T) 6230 Yucca St *Web:* www.kfwb.com ■ *E-mail:* quake@kfwb.groupw.wec.com	Hollywood	CA	90028	323-462-5392	871-4670
KHWY-FM 98.9 MHz (AC) 1611 E Main St	Barstow	CA	92311	760-256-0326	256-9507
KIIS-FM 102.7 MHz (CHR) 3400 Riverside Dr Suite 800 *Web:* www.kiisfm.com	Burbank	CA	91505	818-845-1027	295-6466
KLAX-FM 97.9 MHz (Span) 10281 W Pico Blvd **Fax:* Sales	Los Angeles	CA	90064	310-203-0900	203-8989*
KNX-AM 1070 kHz (N/T) 6121 Sunset Blvd *Web:* www.knx1070.com	Los Angeles	CA	90028	323-460-3000	460-3275
KOST-FM 103.5 MHz (AC) 610 S Ardmore Ave *TF:* 800-929-5678	Los Angeles	CA	90005	213-427-1035	385-0281
KRTH-FM 101.1 MHz (Oldies) 5901 Venice Blvd	Los Angeles	CA	90034	323-937-5230	936-3427
KWIZ-FM 96.7 MHz (Span) 3101 W 5th St	Santa Ana	CA	92703	714-554-5000	554-9362
KYSR-FM 98.7 MHz (AC) 3500 W Olive Ave Suite 250 *Web:* www.star987.com	Burbank	CA	91505	818-955-7000	955-6436

— Colleges/Universities —

				Phone	Fax
Chapman University 333 N Glassell St *TF:* 800-282-7759 ■ *Web:* www.chapman.edu ■ *E-mail:* low@chapman.edu	Orange	CA	92866	714-997-6815	997-6713
Rancho Santiago Community College District Office 2323 N Broadway *Web:* www.rancho.cc.ca.us	Santa Ana	CA	92706	714-480-7484	796-3939
William Howard Taft University 201 E Sandpointe Ave *TF:* 800-882-4555 ■ *Web:* www.taftu.edu ■ *E-mail:* admissions@taftu.edu	Santa Ana	CA	92707	714-850-4800	708-2082

— Hospitals —

				Phone	Fax
Coastal Communities Hospital 2701 S Bristol St	Santa Ana	CA	92704	714-754-5454	754-5556
Santa Ana Hospital Medical Center 1901 N Fairview St	Santa Ana	CA	92706	714-554-1653	265-3450
Western Medical Center 1001 N Tustin Ave	Santa Ana	CA	92705	714-835-3555	953-3613

— Attractions —

				Phone	Fax
Alternative Repertory Theatre 125 N Broadway Suite B *Web:* www.concentric.net/~glcplt/ ■ *E-mail:* glcplt@concentric.net	Santa Ana	CA	92701	714-836-7929	
Block at Orange 20 City Blvd W *Web:* www.theblockatorange.com	Orange	CA	92868	714-769-4000	769-4011
Bowers Kidseum 1802 N Main St *Web:* www.nativecreative.com/kidseum/	Santa Ana	CA	92706	714-480-1520	480-0053
Bowers Museum of Cultural Art 2002 N Main St *Web:* www.bowers.org/	Santa Ana	CA	92706	714-567-3600	567-3603
Discovery Museum 3101 W Harvard St	Santa Ana	CA	92704	714-540-0404	540-1932
Discovery Science Center 2500 N Main St *Web:* www.go2dsc.org	Santa Ana	CA	92705	714-542-2823	542-2828
Disneyland PO Box 3232 *Web:* disney.go.com/Disneyland	Anaheim	CA	92803	714-781-4565	
Galaxy Concert Theatre 3503 Harbor Blvd *Web:* www.galaxytheatre.com/	Santa Ana	CA	92704	714-957-0600	957-6605
Historic Downtown Santa Ana downtown	Santa Ana	CA	92701	714-558-2791	
Historic French Park 901 N French St	Santa Ana	CA	92702	714-571-4200	
Knott's Berry Farm 8039 Beach Blvd *Web:* www.knotts.com	Buena Park	CA	90620	714-827-1776	220-5200
Old Courthouse Museum 211 W Santa Ana Blvd	Santa Ana	CA	92701	714-834-3703	834-2280
Opera Pacific 18025 Sky Pk E Suite H	Irvine	CA	92614	949-474-4488	474-4442
Orange County Crazies Santa Ana Blvd & Bush St	Santa Ana	CA	92701	714-550-9890	550-0825
Orange County Museum of Art 3333 Bristol St South Coast Plaza	Costa Mesa	CA	92626	714-662-3366	662-3818
Orange County Museum of Art 850 San Clemente Dr *Web:* ocartsnet.org/ocma	Newport Beach	CA	92660	949-759-1122	759-5623
Pacific Chorale 1221 E Dyer Rd Suite 230 *Web:* www.pacific-chorale.org ■ *E-mail:* sing@pacific-chorale.org	Santa Ana	CA	92705	714-662-2345	662-2395

Santa Ana — Attractions (Cont'd)

				Phone	Fax
Pacific Symphony Orchestra 1231 E Dyer Rd Suite 200 *Web:* www.pso.org ■ *E-mail:* pso@pso.org	Santa Ana	CA	92705	714-755-5788	755-5789
Saint Joseph Ballet 220 E 4th St Suite 207	Santa Ana	CA	92701	714-541-8314	541-2150
Santa Ana Historic Preservation Society 500 N Sycamore St	Santa Ana	CA	92706	714-547-9645	
Santa Ana Zoo 1801 E Chestnut Ave *Web:* santaanazoo.org	Santa Ana	CA	92701	714-835-7484	
Tustin Area Historical Society Museum 395 El Camino Real	Tustin	CA	92780	714-731-5701	

SPORTS TEAMS & FACILITIES

				Phone	Fax
Orange County Zodiac (soccer) 602 N Flower St Eddie West Field *Web:* www.oczodiac.com ■ *E-mail:* comments@oczodiac.com	Santa Ana	CA	92701	949-348-4880	348-4601

— Events —

	Phone
Antique Car Parade (August)	714-571-4200
Cinco de Mayo Celebration (early May)	714-571-4200
Fantasy in the Sky (June-September)	714-781-4560
Floral Park Home & Garden Tour (late April)	714-543-3218
Mexican Independence Festival (mid-September)	714-571-4200
Orange County Fair (mid-July)	714-708-3247
Star of Bethlehem (December)	714-547-7000

Stockton

Located in the fertile San Joaquin Valley, Stockton has been a major agricultural center since the 1870s. Stockton's waterways and access to major highways have helped to make the city one of California's fastest developing warehousing and distribution centers as well. A strong environmental consciousness and concern for its urban forest have helped Stockton earn the "Tree City USA" designation by the National Arbor Day Foundation 15 years in a row. Stockton is also home to several institutions of higher education, including University of the Pacific.

Population	240,143	**Longitude**	121-18-24 W
Area (Land)	52.6 sq mi	**County**	San Joaquin
Area (Water)	0.9 sq mi	**Time Zone**	PST
Elevation	13 ft	**Area Code/s**	209
Latitude	37-58-11 N		

— Average Temperatures and Precipitation —

TEMPERATURES

	Jan	Feb	Mar	Apr	May	Jun	Jul	Aug	Sep	Oct	Nov	Dec
High	54	61	66	73	81	87	92	91	87	78	64	54
Low	36	39	42	45	49	54	56	56	53	47	41	36

PRECIPITATION

	Jan	Feb	Mar	Apr	May	Jun	Jul	Aug	Sep	Oct	Nov	Dec
Inches	2.9	2.4	2.4	1.2	0.3	0.1	0.1	0.1	0.4	0.9	2.3	2.4

— Important Phone Numbers —

	Phone		Phone
AAA	209-952-4110	**Medical Referral**	209-952-5299
American Express Travel	209-952-6606	**Poison Control Center**	800-876-4766
Dental Referral	800-422-8338	**Weather**	209-982-1793
Emergency	911		

— Information Sources —

				Phone	Fax
Better Business Bureau Serving the Mid Counties 11 S San Joaquin St Suite 803 *Web:* www.stockton.bbb.org	Stockton	CA	95202	209-948-4880	465-6302
Greater Stockton Chamber of Commerce 445 W Weber Ave Suite 220 *Web:* www.stocktonchamber.org	Stockton	CA	95203	209-547-2770	466-5271
San Joaquin County 24 S Hunter St Rm 304	Stockton	CA	95202	209-468-2362	
Stockton City Hall 425 N El Dorado St *Web:* www.ci.stockton.ca.us	Stockton	CA	95202	209-937-8057	937-8447
Stockton Community Development Dept 425 N El Dorado St *Web:* www.ci.stockton.ca.us/cd	Stockton	CA	95202	209-937-8444	937-8893
Stockton Mayor 425 N El Dorado St *Web:* www.ci.stockton.ca.us/clerk/rstrcncl.htm ■ *E-mail:* mayor@ci.stockton.ca.us	Stockton	CA	95202	209-937-8244	937-8568
Stockton Memorial Civic Auditorium 525 N Center St	Stockton	CA	95202	209-941-8223	941-8262
Stockton-San Joaquin County Public Library 605 N El Dorado St *Web:* www.stockton.lib.ca.us	Stockton	CA	95202	209-937-8415	
Stockton/San Joaquin Convention & Visitors Bureau 46 W Fremont St *TF:* 800-350-1987 ■ *Web:* www.ssjcvb.org	Stockton	CA	95202	209-943-1987	943-6235

On-Line Resources

4Stockton.com	www.4stockton.com
Anthill City Guide Stockton	www.anthill.com/city.asp?city=stockton
Excite.com Stockton City Guide	www.excite.com/travel/countries/united_states/california/stockton
StocktoNet	www.stocktonet.com/
Virtual Stockton.com	www.virtualstockton.com/

— Transportation Services —

AIRPORTS

	Phone
■ **Sacramento Metropolitan Airport (SMF)** 62 miles N of downtown Stockton (approx 75 minutes) Web: www.quickaid.com/airports/smf	916-929-5411

Airport Transportation

	Phone
Sacramento Airport Shuttle $55 fare to downtown Stockton	916-923-3999

Commercial Airlines

	Phone		Phone
America West	800-235-9292	**Shuttle by United**	800-748-8853
American	800-433-7300	**Southwest**	800-435-9792
American Eagle	800-433-7300	**TWA**	800-221-2000
Continental	916-369-2700	**United**	800-241-6522
Delta	800-221-1212	**United Express**	800-241-6522
Delta Connection	800-221-1212	**US Airways**	800-428-4322
Northwest	800-225-2525	**US Airways Express**	800-428-4322

Charter Airlines

	Phone
Horizon Helicopters	916-966-8181

CAR RENTALS

	Phone		Phone
Avis	800-331-1212	**Enterprise**	209-473-7744
Budget	916-922-7317	**Hertz**	209-460-0180
Dollar	916-447-4455		

Stockton (Cont'd)

LIMO/TAXI

	Phone		Phone
Executive Limousine	209-983-0144	**Yellow Cab**	209-465-5721
Gemini Limousine Specialties	209-464-5466	**Yellow Cab**	209-466-7045
Regency Limousine	209-463-6900		

MASS TRANSIT

	Phone
SMART Bus $1.15 Base fare	209-943-1111

RAIL/BUS

				Phone
Amtrak Station 735 S San Joaquin St	Stockton	CA	95203	800-872-7245
Greyhound Bus Station 121 S Center St	Stockton	CA	95202	209-466-1521
TF: 800-231-2222				

— Accommodations —

HOTELS, MOTELS, RESORTS

				Phone	Fax
Alhambra Motel 1565 S El Dorado St	Stockton	CA	95206	209-466-5481	
Arbor Motel 5864 N Hwy 99	Stockton	CA	95212	209-931-2326	
Best Western Inn 550 W Charter Way	Stockton	CA	95206	209-948-0321	436-1638*
**Fax Area Code:* 559 ■ *TF:* 800-545-8388					
Budget Inn 1075 N Wilson Way	Stockton	CA	95205	209-466-6856	
Comfort Inn 3951 Budweiser Ct	Stockton	CA	95215	209-931-9341	931-6243
TF: 800-228-5150					
Concord Hilton Hotel 1970 Diamond Blvd	Concord	CA	94520	925-827-2000	671-0984
TF: 800-826-2644					
Courtyard by Marriott 3252 W March Ln	Stockton	CA	95219	209-472-9700	472-9722
TF: 888-472-9700 ■ *Web:* courtyard.com/SCKST					
Days Inn 33 N Center St	Stockton	CA	95202	209-948-6151	948-1220
TF: 800-325-2525					
Days Inn Lathrop 14750 S Harland Rd	Lathrop	CA	95330	209-982-1959	982-4978
TF: 800-329-7466					
Delta Hotel 241 N San Joaquin St	Stockton	CA	95202	209-465-3732	
Econo Lodge 2210 Manthey Rd	Stockton	CA	95206	209-466-5741	463-1255
TF: 800-553-2666					
Economy Inn 339 S Wilson Way	Stockton	CA	95205	209-466-2951	939-1880
Guest Inn 2533 N Piccoli Rd	Stockton	CA	95215	209-931-6675	931-8351
TF: 800-804-8378					
Holiday Inn Express 16855 Old Harlan Rd	Lathrop	CA	95330	209-858-1234	858-1800
TF: 800-465-4329					
Inn Cal 3473 W Hammer Ln	Stockton	CA	95209	209-473-2000	478-0876
TF: 800-550-0055					
Lafayette Park Hotel 3287 Mt Diablo Blvd	Lafayette	CA	94549	925-283-3700	284-1621
TF: 800-368-2468 ■ *Web:* www.woodsidehotels.com ■ *E-mail:* lph@woodsidehotels.com					
Land Hotel 30 N California St	Stockton	CA	95202	209-464-6313	
LaQuinta Inn 2710 W March Ln	Stockton	CA	95219	209-952-7800	472-0732
TF: 800-531-5900					
Motel 6 6717 Plymouth Rd	Stockton	CA	95207	209-951-8120	474-3829
TF: 800-466-8356					
Radisson Hotel Stockton 2323 Grand Canal Blvd	Stockton	CA	95207	209-957-9090	473-0739
Ramada Inn 111 E March Ln	Stockton	CA	95207	209-474-3301	474-7612
TF: 800-272-6232					
Red Roof Inn 2654 W March Ln	Stockton	CA	95207	209-478-4300	478-1872
TF: 800-843-7663					
Residence Inn by Marriott 3240 W March Ln	Stockton	CA	95219	209-472-9800	472-9888
TF: 800-331-3131 ■ *Web:* www.residenceinn.com/residenceinn/SCKRI					
Sierra Motel 3416 Farmington Rd	Stockton	CA	95205	209-941-9000	
Stockton Inn 4219 E Waterloo Rd	Stockton	CA	95215	209-931-3131	931-0423
TF: 800-528-1234					
Super 8 Motel 2717 W March Ln	Stockton	CA	95219	209-477-5576	477-5968
Town House Motel 1604 N Wilson Way	Stockton	CA	95205	209-466-9667	

— Restaurants —

				Phone
Acapulco Gardens (Mexican) 317 E Charter Way	Stockton	CA	95206	209-464-0233
Angelina's (Italian) 1563 E Fremont St	Stockton	CA	95205	209-948-6609
Arroyo's Cafe (Mexican) 2381 W March Ln	Stockton	CA	85207	209-472-1661
Basil's (American) 2324 Grand Canal Blvd	Stockton	CA	95207	209-478-6290
Best Lumpia Restaurant (Filipino) 9305 Thornton Rd	Stockton	CA	95209	209-952-8300
Bottley's Bar-B-Q & Soul Food (Barbecue) 843 W Fremont St	Stockton	CA	95202	209-944-9514
Bud's Seafood Grill (Steak/Seafood) 314 Lincoln Ctr	Stockton	CA	95207	209-956-0270
Cafe 329 (California) 329 Lincoln Ctr	Stockton	CA	95207	209-474-1804
Casa Flores (Mexican) 201 E Weber Ave	Stockton	CA	95202	209-462-2272
Dave Wong's (Chinese) 5620 N Pershing Ave	Stockton	CA	95207	209-951-4152
De Parsia's Restaurant (Italian) 3404 Delaware Ave	Stockton	CA	95204	209-944-9196
El Tenampa (Mexican) 901 W Church St	Stockton	CA	95203	209-462-9621
Ernie's on the Brick Walk (California) 296 Lincoln Ctr	Stockton	CA	95212	209-951-3311
Far East Restaurant (Chinese) 2211 N Wilson Way	Stockton	CA	95205	209-463-4478
Garlic Brothers (American) 6629 Embarcadero Dr	Stockton	CA	95219	209-474-6585
Jade Palace (Chinese) 1139 E March Ln	Stockton	CA	95210	209-473-8183
Jaws Cafe on the Water (American) 15135 W Eight-Mile Rd	Stockton	CA	95219	209-951-4691
Kazan Japanese Restaurant (Japanese) 7610 Pacific Ave	Stockton	CA	95207	209-957-4202
Kikusui Japanese Restaurant (Japanese) 4555 N Pershing Ave	Stockton	CA	95207	209-952-0164
La Boulangerie (French) 4950 Pacific Ave	Stockton	CA	95207	209-951-0664
Le Bistro (Continental) 3121 W Benjamin Holt Dr	Stockton	CA	95219	209-951-0885
Mallard's Restaurant (American) 3409 Brookside Rd	Stockton	CA	95219	209-952-3825
Matsu (Japanese) 357 E Market St	Stockton	CA	95202	209-946-9018
Mi Ranchito Cafe (Mexican) 425 S Center St	Stockton	CA	95203	209-946-9257
New Kim Tar (Chinese/Thai) 1425 W March Ln	Stockton	CA	95207	209-473-3240
On Lock Sam (Chinese) 333 S Sutter St	Stockton	CA	95203	209-466-4561
Papavo's Greek Cafe (Greek) 7555 Pacific Ave	Stockton	CA	95207	209-477-6855
Peta's Gasthaus (German) 445 W Weber Ave	Stockton	CA	95203	209-941-8605
Pho Bac Hoa Viet Restaurant (Vietnamese) 7945 West Ln	Stockton	CA	95210	209-473-8704
Rozeny's Lumpia (Filipino) 2233 Grand Canal Blvd	Stockton	CA	95207	209-477-2377
Shadows The (Continental) 7555 Pacific Ave	Stockton	CA	95207	209-477-5547
Stockton Joe's (Continental) 1503 St Mark's Plaza	Stockton	CA	95207	209-951-2980
Stuart Anderson's Black Angus Restaurant (Steak) 2605 W March Ln	Stockton	CA	95207	209-951-8900
Summit Steak House (Steak) 111 E March Ln	Stockton	CA	95207	209-474-3301
Sutter Street Bar & Grill (American) 4219 Waterloo Rd	Stockton	CA	95215	209-931-3131
Terminus Tavern (California) 14900 W Hwy 12	Lodi	CA	95242	209-464-0790
Torino's (Italian) 222 N Sutter St	Stockton	CA	95202	209-462-2531
Valley Brewing Co (American) 157 W Adams St	Stockton	CA	95204	209-464-2739
Vincenzo Deli & Restaurant (Italian) 7610 Pacific Ave	Stockton	CA	95207	209-957-4995
Yasso Yani Restaurant (Greek) 326 E Main St	Stockton	CA	95202	209-464-3108
Ye Olde Hoosier Inn (American) 1537 N Wilson Way	Stockton	CA	95205	209-463-0271
Yoneda Japanese Restaurant (Japanese) 1101 E March Ln	Stockton	CA	95210	209-477-1667

— Goods and Services —

SHOPPING

				Phone	Fax
Lincoln Center Pacific Ave & Benjamin Holt St	Stockton	CA	95207	209-477-4868	
Marketplace The 306 E Main St	Stockton	CA	95202	209-943-5222	943-0240
Sherwood Mall 5308 Pacific Ave	Stockton	CA	95207	209-952-6277	952-6282
Tracy Outlet Center 1005 E Pescadero Ave	Tracy	CA	95376	209-833-1895	833-1894
Weberstown Mall 4950 Pacific Ave	Stockton	CA	95207	209-477-0245	952-4671

BANKS

				Phone	Fax
Bank of Agriculture & Commerce 2021 W March Ln	Stockton	CA	95207	209-473-6800	472-1619
Bank of America 503 W Benjamin Holt Dr	Stockton	CA	95207	209-546-0230	944-5007
Bank of Stockton PO Box 1110	Stockton	CA	95201	209-464-8781	465-5483
TF Cust Svc: 800-399-2265*					
Bank of the West 4932 Pacific Ave	Stockton	CA	95204	209-957-2301	957-2434
Pacific State Bank 1889 W March Ln	Stockton	CA	95207	209-943-7400	
Sanwa Bank California 4733-C Quail Lakes Dr	Stockton	CA	95207	209-956-8960	956-9077
Stockton Savings Bank 501 W Weber Ave	Stockton	CA	95203	209-948-1675	547-7773
Union Safe Deposit Bank 317 E Main St	Stockton	CA	95202	209-946-5011	

BUSINESS SERVICES

	Phone		Phone
Adecco Employment Personnel Services	209-957-7167	**Norrell Temporary Services**	209-476-1665
DHL Worldwide Express	800-225-5345	**Pak Mail Centers of America**	209-478-9827
Federal Express	800-238-5355	**Post Office**	800-275-8777
Kelly Services	209-333-1444	**Postal Center**	209-474-6245
Kinko's	209-957-1204	**UPS**	800-742-5877
Mail Boxes Etc	209-474-1731	**Valley Temp & Personnel Services**	209-473-7601
Manpower Temporary Services	209-952-0276		

Stockton (Cont'd)

TELEVISION

				Phone	Fax
KCRA-TV Ch 3 (NBC) 3 Television Cir	Sacramento	CA	95814	916-446-3333	441-4050
Web: www.kcra.com					
KMAX-TV Ch 31 (UPN) 500 Media Pl	Sacramento	CA	95815	916-925-3100	921-3050
Web: www.paramountstations.com/KMAX					
KOVR-TV Ch 13 (CBS) 2713 KOVR Dr	West Sacramento	CA	95605	916-374-1313	374-1304
Web: www.kovr.com					
KTXL-TV Ch 40 (Fox) 4655 Fruitridge Rd	Sacramento	CA	95820	916-454-4422	739-0559
KVIE-TV Ch 6 (PBS) 2595 Capitol Oaks Dr	Sacramento	CA	95833	916-929-5843	929-7367
Web: www.kvie.org ■ *E-mail:* member@kvie.org					
KXTV-TV Ch 10 (ABC) 400 Broadway	Sacramento	CA	95818	916-441-2345	447-6107
Web: www.kxtv10.com ■ *E-mail:* kxtv10@kxtv10.com					

RADIO

				Phone	Fax
KCJH-FM 90.1 MHz (Rel) 9019 West Ln	Stockton	CA	95210	209-477-3690	
KCVR-AM 1570 kHz (Span) 6820 Pacific Ave Suite 3A	Stockton	CA	95207	209-474-0154	474-0316
KJAX-AM 1280 kHz (N/T) 3600 Sisk Rd Suite 2B	Modesto	CA	95356	209-545-5585	545-5587
KJOY-FM 99.3 MHz (AC) 6820 Pacific Ave Suite 2	Stockton	CA	95207	209-478-4993	957-1833
KQOD-FM 100.1 MHz (Oldies) 1120 N San Joaquin St	Stockton	CA	95202	209-462-5367	462-7959
KSTN-AM 1420 kHz (Rel) 2171 Ralph Ave	Stockton	CA	95206	209-948-5786	
KSTN-FM 107.3 MHz (Span) 2171 Ralph Ave	Stockton	CA	95206	209-948-5786	
KUOP-FM 91.3 MHz (NPR) 3601 Pacific Ave	Stockton	CA	95211	209-946-2582	946-2494
TF: 800-800-5867					
KWIN-FM 97.7 MHz (Rel) 6820 Pacific Ave Suite 2	Stockton	CA	95207	209-476-1230	957-1833

— Colleges/Universities —

				Phone	Fax
California State University Stanislaus Stockton Center 612 E Magnolia St	Stockton	CA	95202	209-467-5300	467-5333
Web: www.csustan.edu					
San Joaquin Delta College 5151 Pacific Ave	Stockton	CA	95207	209-954-5151	954-5600
Web: www.sjdccd.cc.ca.us ■ *E-mail:* questions@sjfcc.cc.ca.us					
University of the Pacific 3601 Pacific Ave	Stockton	CA	95211	209-946-2011	946-2413
TF Admissions: 800-959-2867 ■ *Web:* www.uop.edu					

— Hospitals —

				Phone	Fax
Dameron Hospital 525 W Acacia St	Stockton	CA	95203	209-944-5550	461-3108
Saint Joseph's Medical Center 1800 N California St	Stockton	CA	95204	209-943-2000	461-3300*
**Fax:* Admitting ■ *Web:* www.sjrhs.org					
San Joaquin General Hospital PO Box 1020	Stockton	CA	95201	209-468-6000	468-6136

— Attractions —

				Phone	Fax
Asian American Repertory Theatre 3252 Michigan Ave	Stockton	CA	95204	209-464-0347	
Ballet San Joaquin PO Box 70151	Stockton	CA	95267	209-477-4141	
Web: www.stocktonet.com/community/arts/balletsj/					
Children's Museum of Stockton 402 W Weber Ave	Stockton	CA	95203	209-465-4386	465-4394
Clever Planetarium at Delta College 5151 Pacific Ave	Stockton	CA	95207	209-954-5051	
Web: www.sjdccd.cc.ca.us/Planetarium/index.html					
Delicato Vineyards 12001 S Hwy 99	Manteca	CA	95336	209-824-3600	824-3400
Web: www.delicato.com ■ *E-mail:* wine@delicato.com					
Delta Drama Music Dance & the Arts 5151 Pacific Ave	Stockton	CA	95207	209-954-5110	954-5600
Haggin Museum 1201 N Pershing Ave	Stockton	CA	95203	209-462-4116	
John Muir National Historic Site 4202 Alhambra Ave	Martinez	CA	94553	925-228-8860	228-8192
Web: www.nps.gov/jomu/					
Micke Grove Zoo 11793 N Micke Grove Rd	Lodi	CA	95240	209-953-8840	331-7271
Web: www.mgzoo.com					
Oak Ridge Vineyards 6100 E Hwy 12	Lodi	CA	95240	209-369-4758	369-0202
Oakwood Lake Resort 874 E Woodard Ave	Manteca	CA	95337	209-239-2500	239-2060
TF: 800-626-5253					
Phillips Farms 4580 W Hwy 12	Lodi	CA	95242	209-368-7384	368-5801
Pixie Woods Children's Fairyland Monte Diablo & Lewis Park Ave	Stockton	CA	95203	209-937-8220	
San Joaquin County Historical Society & Museum 11793 N Micke Grove Rd	Lodi	CA	95240	209-331-2055	331-2057
Web: www.sanjoaquinhistory.org					
Stockton Chorale PO Box 7711	Stockton	CA	95267	209-466-0540	
Web: www.stocktonet.com/groups/chorale/index.html					
Stockton Civic Theatre 2312 Rose Marie Ln	Stockton	CA	95207	209-473-2400	473-1502
Web: www.californiamall.com/sct					
Stockton Opera 3601 Pacific Ave	Stockton	CA	95211	209-946-2474	946-2800
Stockton Symphony 5151 Pacific Ave Delta College Atherton Auditorium	Stockton	CA	95207	209-951-0196	951-1050
Web: www.stocktonsymphony.org ■ *E-mail:* a-music@inreach.com					
University of the Pacific Drama & Dance 3601 Pacific Ave	Stockton	CA	95211	209-946-2116	
UOP Conservatory of Music 3601 Pacific Ave	Stockton	CA	95211	209-946-2415	946-2770
World Wildlife Museum 1245 W Weber Ave	Stockton	CA	95203	209-465-2834	941-4430
Web: www.worldwildlifemuseum.org ■ *E-mail:* info@worldwildlifemuseum.org					

SPORTS TEAMS & FACILITIES

				Phone	Fax
Mudville Nine (baseball) Alpine & Sutter Sts Billy Hebert Field	Stockton	CA	95204	209-644-1900	644-1922
Winners Gaming & Sports Emporium 1658 S Airport Way	Stockton	CA	95206	209-466-3589	466-5141

— Events —

	Phone
All-American WaterFest (July 4)	209-943-1987
Big Dog Poker Run (early September)	209-369-1041
California Dry Bean Festival (early August)	209-835-2131
Cherry Blossom Festival (mid-April)	209-953-8800
Countywide Art Tour (mid-October)	209-465-6092
Delicata Grape Stomp (late August)	209-239-1215
Dixieland Jazz Festival (early March)	888-474-7407
Eberhardt Bob Memorial Pro-Am Heart Invitational (late July)	209-477-2683
Festa Italiana (early June)	209-368-3077
Lockeford Street Fairs (April)	209-727-3142
Lodi Grape Festival & National Wine Show (mid-September)	209-369-2771
Lodi Spring Wine Show (late March)	209-369-2771
Lodi Street Faires (early May & early October)	209-367-7840
Oktoberfest (mid-October)	209-369-2771
San Joaquin County Fair (mid-late June)	209-466-5041
Stockton Ag Expo (late January)	209-547-2960
Stockton Asparagus Festival (late April)	209-943-1987
Stockton Obon Festival (late July)	209-466-6701
Tower Park Poker Run (late June)	209-369-1041
Wine on the Waterfront (early September)	209-464-7644
Wine Stroll (early October)	209-831-4170
Wine Tasting Event (May)	209-466-0331

Colorado

Population (1999): 4,056,133 **Area (sq mi): 104,100**

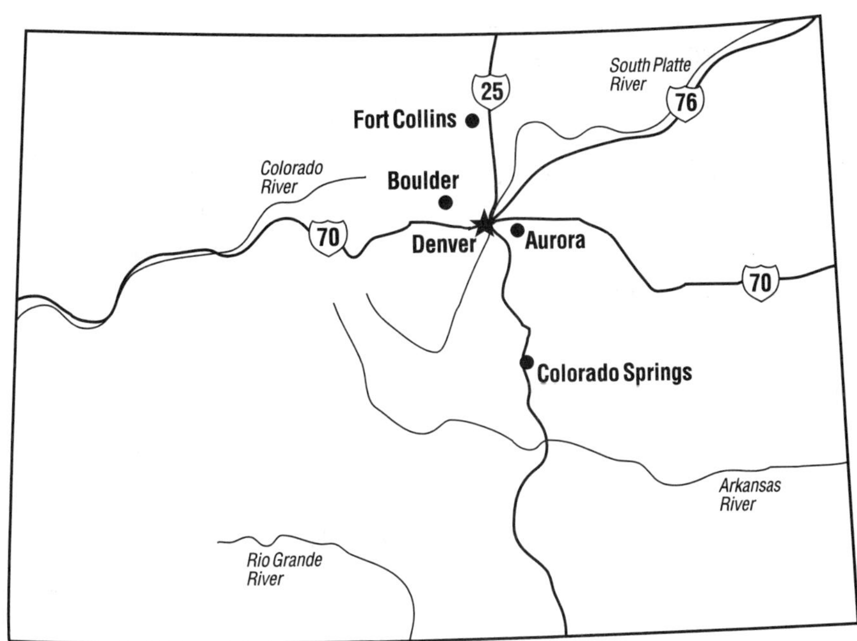

— State Information Sources —

		Phone	Fax
Colorado Assn of Commerce & Industry			
1776 Lincoln St Suite 1200	Denver CO 80203	303-831-7411	860-1439
Web: www.businesscolorado.com ■ *E-mail:* caci@capcon.com			
Colorado Economic Development Commission			
1625 Broadway Suite 1700	Denver CO 80202	303-892-3840	892-3725
Web: www.cde.state.co.us			
Colorado Parks & Outdoor Recreation Div			
1313 Sherman St Rm 618	Denver CO 80203	303-866-3437	866-3206
Web: www.dnr.state.co.us/parks			
Colorado State Government Information		303-866-5000	
Web: www.state.co.us ■ *E-mail:* comments@www.state.co.us			
Colorado State Library			
201 E Colfax Ave Rm 309	Denver CO 80203	303-866-6900	866-6940
Web: www.cde.state.co.us/slindex.htm ■ *E-mail:* parent_k@cde.state.co.us			
Colorado Travel & Tourism Authority			
PO Box 3524	Englewood CO 80155	303-832-6171	296-2015
TF: 800-265-6723 ■ *Web:* www.colorado.com			

ON-LINE RESOURCES

Arts to Zoo Colorado . . . . . www.artstozoo.org
Aspen Snowmass . . . . . aspen.com
Best Read Guide Aspen . . . . . bestreadguide.com/aspen
Colorado Adventure Guide . . . . . www.entertain.com/wedgwood/cag.html
Colorado Cities . . . . . dir.yahoo.com/Regional/U_S__States/Colorado/Cities
Colorado Counties & Regions . . . . . dir.yahoo.com/Regional/U_S__States/Colorado/Counties_and_Regions
Colorado Directory . . . . . www.coloradodirectory.com
Colorado Guide . . . . . www.coloradoguide.com
Colorado Lodging Travel & Recreation . . . . . www.toski.com
Colorado Scenario . . . . . scenariousa.dstylus.com/co/indexf.htm
Colorado Travel & Tourism Guide . . . . . www.travel-library.com/north_america/usa/colorado/
Colorado Vacation Guide . . . . . www.coloradoadventure.net
ColoradoNet . . . . . www.colorado.net
Cybertourist Colorado . . . . . www.cybertourist.com/colorado.shtml
Rough Guide Travel Colorado travel.roughguides.com/content/1045/index.htm
Travel.org-Colorado . . . . . travel.org/colorado.html
What's Up Colorado! . . . . . www.whatsupcolorado.com
Yahoo! Get Local Colorado . . . . . dir.yahoo.com/Regional/U_S__States/Colorado

— Cities Profiled —

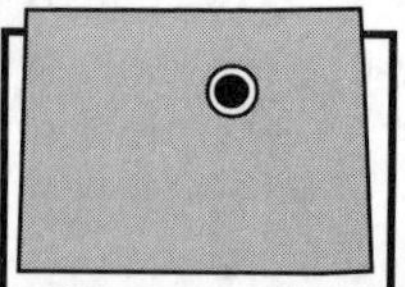

Aurora

Known as the "Gateway to the Rockies," the city of Aurora is located adjacent to Denver, near the new Denver International Airport. The military has had a significant influence on the growth and development of Aurora as a city. During World War I, it was chosen as a site for an Army Recuperation Camp that later became Fitzsimons Army Hospital. Lowry Field, an Army Air Corps training school, was established in Aurora during World War II; and Buckley Airfield and the Rocky Mountain Arsenal in neighboring areas have drawn many residents to Aurora. In recent years, Aurora has been named by Fortune magazine as one of the 10 best metropolitan areas for business. Recreational opportunities in Aurora include fishing, sailing, boating, and hiking at the Aurora Reservoir and Cherry Creek State Park.

Population	250,604	**Longitude**	104-45-43 W
Area (Land)	132.6 sq mi	**County**	Adams, Arapahoe, Douglas
Area (Water)	0.2 sq mi	**Time Zone**	MST
Elevation	5,680 ft	**Area Code/s**	303
Latitude	39-40-29 N		

— Average Temperatures and Precipitation —

TEMPERATURES

	Jan	Feb	Mar	Apr	May	Jun	Jul	Aug	Sep	Oct	Nov	Dec
High	43	47	52	62	71	81	88	86	77	66	53	45
Low	16	20	26	35	44	52	59	57	48	36	25	17

PRECIPITATION

	Jan	Feb	Mar	Apr	May	Jun	Jul	Aug	Sep	Oct	Nov	Dec
Inches	0.5	0.6	1.3	1.7	2.4	1.8	1.9	1.5	1.2	1.0	0.9	0.6

— Important Phone Numbers —

	Phone		Phone
AAA	303-753-8800	**Poison Control Center**	303-739-1123
American Express Travel	303-344-0894	**Road Conditions**	303-639-1234
Dental Referral	303-740-6900	**Time/Temp**	303-443-1910
Emergency	911	**Weather**	303-337-2500
Medical Referral	303-788-6000		

— Information Sources —

				Phone	Fax
Arapahoe County 5334 S Prince St	Littleton	CO	80166	303-795-4200	794-4625
Web: www.co.arapahoe.co.us					
Aurora Chamber of Commerce 562 Sable Blvd Suite 200	Aurora	CO	80011	303-344-1500	344-1564
Web: www.aurorachamber.org ■ *E-mail:* auroracham@aol.com					
Aurora City Hall 1470 S Havana St	Aurora	CO	80012	303-739-7000	739-7520
Web: www.ci.aurora.co.us					
Aurora Economic Development 562 Sable Blvd Suite 240	Aurora	CO	80011	303-340-2101	340-2111
Aurora Mayor 1470 S Havana St 8th Fl	Aurora	CO	80012	303-739-7015	739-7594
Aurora Public Library 14949 E Alameda Dr	Aurora	CO	80012	303-739-6600	340-2237
Web: www.ci.aurora.co.us/library/library.htm					
Better Business Bureau Serving the Denver-Boulder Metro Area 1780 S Bellaire St Suite 700	Denver	CO	80222	303-758-2100	758-8321
Web: www.denver.bbb.org ■ *E-mail:* info@denver.bbb.org					

On-Line Resources

City Knowledge Aurora .... www.cityknowledge.com/co_aurora.htm
Excite.com Aurora City Guide .... www.excite.com/travel/countries/united_states/colorado/aurora
NITC Travelbase City Guide Aurora .... www.travelbase.com/auto/features/aurora-co.html

— Transportation Services —

AIRPORTS

■ **Denver International Airport (DEN)** — *Phone*

15 miles NE of downtown Aurora (approx 30 minutes) 303-342-2000
Web: infodenver.denver.co.us/~aviation/ ■ *E-mail:* aviation@infodenver.denver.co.us

Airport Transportation

	Phone
Dash Shuttle $25 fare to downtown Aurora	800-525-3177
RTD Bus $6 fare to downtown Aurora	303-299-6000
Super Shuttle $25 fare to downtown Aurora	303-342-0295
Taxi $35 fare to downtown Aurora	303-777-7777

Commercial Airlines

	Phone		Phone
America West	800-235-9292	**Midwest Express**	800-452-2022
American	800-433-7300	**Northwest**	800-225-2525
Continental	800-525-0280	**Sun Country**	800-359-5786
Delta	800-221-1212	**TWA**	800-221-2000
Frontier	800-432-1359	**United**	800-241-6522
Martinair Holland	800-366-4655	**United Express**	800-241-6522
Mesa	800-637-2247	**US Airways**	800-428-4322
Mexicana	800-531-7923		

Charter Airlines

	Phone		Phone
Corporate Air Charter	406-248-1541	**Superior Aviation**	800-882-7751
Mayo Aviation Inc	303-790-9777		

CAR RENTALS

	Phone		Phone
Advantage	303-261-8585	**Hertz**	303-342-3800
Alamo	800-327-9633	**National**	303-342-0717
Budget	303-342-9001	**Payless**	303-342-9444
Dollar	303-342-9099	**Thrifty**	303-342-9086
Enterprise	303-342-7350		

LIMO/TAXI

	Phone		Phone
Carey Limousine	303-693-0732	**Yellow Cab**	303-777-7777
Metro Taxi	303-333-3333	**Zone Cab**	303-444-8888
Presidential Limousine	303-286-1114		

MASS TRANSIT

	Phone
RTD Bus $1.25 Base fare	303-299-9000

RAIL/BUS

				Phone
Amtrak Station 1701 Wynkoop St	Denver	CO	80202	800-872-7245
Greyhound Bus Station 9365 Montview Blvd	Aurora	CO	80011	303-340-0501
TF: 800-231-2222				

— Accommodations —

HOTEL RESERVATION SERVICES

	Phone	Fax
All-Colorado Accommodations	877-365-6926	522-0894*

**Fax Area Code:* 719 ■ *Web:* www.rockad.com/aca/ ■ *E-mail:* mountain@frii.com

HOTELS, MOTELS, RESORTS

				Phone	Fax
AmeriSuites 16250 E 40th Ave	Aurora	CO	80011	303-371-0700	371-2223
TF: 800-833-1516					
Aurora Motel & Apartments 11712 E Colfax Ave	Aurora	CO	80010	303-366-7352	
Biltmore Motel 8900 E Colfax Ave	Aurora	CO	80010	303-364-9286	
Comfort Inn 16921 E 32nd Ave	Aurora	CO	80011	303-367-5000	367-5300
TF: 800-228-5150					
Comfort Inn SE 14071 E Iliff Ave	Aurora	CO	80014	303-755-8000	755-4041
TF: 800-228-5150					
Days Inn 5150 S Quebec St	Greenwood Village	CO	80111	303-721-1144	721-1245
TF: 800-329-7466					

Aurora — Hotels, Motels, Resorts (Cont'd)

				Phone	Fax
Doubletree 13696 E Iliff Ave & I-225	Aurora	CO	80014	303-337-2800	752-0296
TF: 800-222-8733 ■ *Web:* www.doubletreehotels.com/DoubleT/Hotel21/25/25Main.htm					
Fairfield Inn Airport 6851 Tower Rd	Denver	CO	80249	303-576-9640	574-9638
TF: 800-228-2800 ■ *Web:* fairfieldinn.com/DENFA					
Family Motel 13280 E Colfax Ave	Aurora	CO	80011	303-344-9150	
Hampton Inn 1500 S Abilene St	Aurora	CO	80012	303-369-8400	369-0324
Holiday Inn Denver Southeast 3200 S Parker Rd	Aurora	CO	80014	303-695-1700	745-6958
TF: 800-465-4329 ■ *Web:* www.basshotels.com/holiday-inn/?_franchisee=DENPK ■ *E-mail:* holidayinnse@denpk.com					
Holtze Executive Village 15196 E Louisiana Dr	Aurora	CO	80012	303-743-5100	743-5119
TF: 888-446-5893 ■ *Web:* www.hotelguide.net/denver/data/h100004.htm					
Homestead Village 13941 E Harvard Ave	Aurora	CO	80014	303-750-9116	750-5013
Web: denver.digitalcity.com/homestead/aurora.htm ■ *E-mail:* Homeaur@aol.com					
La Quinta Inn 1011 S Abilene St	Aurora	CO	80012	303-337-0206	750-9738
TF: 800-687-6667					
Lost Valley Ranch 29555 Goose Creek Rd	Sedalia	CO	80135	303-647-2311	647-2315
Web: www.ranchweb.com/lost ■ *E-mail:* lostranch@aol.com					
Manor House Motel 12700 E Colfax Ave	Aurora	CO	80011	303-364-7651	360-8556
Riveria Motel 9100 E Colfax Ave	Aurora	CO	80010	303-340-1919	367-9559
Sands Motel 13388 E Colfax Ave	Aurora	CO	80011	303-366-3581	360-7476
Super 8 Motel 14200 E 6th Ave	Aurora	CO	80011	303-366-7333	344-1536
TF: 800-800-8000					
Super 8 Motel 5150 S Quebec St	Greenwood Village	CO	80111	303-771-8000	771-0058
TF: 800-800-8000					
Timberline Motel 11818 E Colfax Ave	Aurora	CO	80010	303-344-3000	
Wolf's Motor Inn 15691 E Colfax Ave	Aurora	CO	80011	303-364-7481	344-2265

— Restaurants —

				Phone
America's Bar & Grill (American) 2340 S Chambers Rd	Aurora	CO	80014	303-337-3721
Armadillo The (Mexican) 15001 E Mississippi Ave	Aurora	CO	80012	303-337-2761
Benvenuto's Italian Grill (Italian) 4243 S Buckley Rd	Aurora	CO	80013	303-690-5220
Cafe San Marcos (Mexican) 9935 E Colfax Ave	Aurora	CO	80010	303-341-2939
Chilitos (Mexican) 3133 Peoria St	Aurora	CO	80010	303-366-5144
China Cafe (Chinese) 16950 E Iliff Ave	Aurora	CO	80013	303-369-0330
Dickey's Barbecue Pit (Barbecue) 14050 E Evans Ave	Aurora	CO	80014	303-337-3447
East Cafe (Chinese) 15140 E Mississippi Ave	Aurora	CO	80012	303-369-6103
Empress Of China Restaurant (Chinese) 1535 S Havana St	Aurora	CO	80012	303-337-0514
Fazoli's (Italian) 1012 S Abilene St	Aurora	CO	80012	303-745-6336
Fitzgerald's (American) 13696 E Iliff Ave	Aurora	CO	80014	303-337-2800
TF: 800-243-3112				
Flower Drum (Chinese) 2353 S Havana St	Aurora	CO	80014	303-755-9096
Gazebo Ristorante & Casa Pasta (Italian) 14569 E Alameda Ave	Aurora	CO	80012	303-344-2525
Golden Phoenix Restaurant (Chinese) 15181 E Hampden Ave	Aurora	CO	80014	303-693-2506
Happy Teriyaki (Japanese) 2495 S Havana St	Aurora	CO	80014	303-750-7085
Havana Diner (International) 1050 S Havana St	Aurora	CO	80012	303-341-5594
Helga's German Restaurant (German) 728 Peoria St	Aurora	CO	80011	303-344-5488
Ikaros Restaurant & Lounge (Greek) 1930 S Havana St	Aurora	CO	80014	303-755-2211
Italian Fisherman (Italian) 13250 E Mississippi Ave	Aurora	CO	80012	303-752-2502
Joe's Crab Shack (Seafood) 14025 E Evans Ave	Aurora	CO	80014	303-306-7070
Kangchon Korean Restaurant (Korean) 9915 E Colfax Ave	Aurora	CO	80010	303-367-8816
La Cueva (Mexican) 9742 E Colfax Ave	Aurora	CO	80010	303-367-1422
Las Hadas Mexican Restaurant (Mexican) 15264 E Hampden Ave	Aurora	CO	80014	303-693-9519
Lone Star Steakhouse & Saloon (Steak) 3055 S Parker Rd	Aurora	CO	80014	303-337-7827
Luther's Bar-B-Que (Barbecue) 1595 S Havana St	Aurora	CO	80012	303-750-7200
Oasis Grill (American) 15064 E Mississippi Ave	Aurora	CO	80012	303-696-8000
Paprika Cafe (Mediterranean) 13152 E Mississippi Ave	Aurora	CO	80012	303-755-4150
Restaurant Silla (Barbecue) 3005 S Peoria St	Aurora	CO	80014	303-338-5070
Seoul Korean Barbecue (Barbecue) 12091 E Iliff Ave	Aurora	CO	80014	303-671-0003
Sonoda's (Japanese) 3108 S Parker Rd	Aurora	CO	80014	303-337-3800
Thai Landing Restaurant (Thai) 11101 E Colfax Ave	Aurora	CO	80010	303-367-1504
Tokyoya Bowl N Bowl Restaurant (Japanese) 2210 S Chambers Rd	Aurora	CO	80014	303-368-1668
Village Inn (American) 921 S Havana St	Aurora	CO	80012	303-341-0921

— Goods and Services —

SHOPPING

				Phone	Fax
Aurora Mall 14200 E Alameda Ave	Aurora	CO	80012	303-344-4120	364-0308
Buckingham Square Shopping Center 1306 S Havana St	Aurora	CO	80012	303-755-3232	755-3234

BANKS

				Phone	Fax
City Wide Bank 10660 E Colfax Ave	Aurora	CO	80010	303-365-3600	365-3601
Colorado National Bank 14111 E Alameda Ave	Aurora	CO	80012	303-344-1330	340-1346
Commerce Bank of Aurora 15305 E Colfax Ave	Aurora	CO	80011	303-344-5202	364-7636
Commercial Federal Bank 700 S Abilene St	Aurora	CO	80012	303-337-5311	331-3616
First United Bank 14501 E Alameda Ave	Aurora	CO	80012	303-360-5555	360-6744
Firstbank 2300 S Havana St	Aurora	CO	80014	303-337-2000	337-0586
KeyBank NA 3000 S Peoria Ave	Aurora	CO	80014	303-752-1122	752-1058
Norwest Bank Central 9000 E Colfax Ave	Aurora	CO	80010	303-341-4600	360-4877

BUSINESS SERVICES

	Phone		Phone
Airborne Express	800-247-2676	**Mail Boxes Etc**	303-690-2424
DHL Worldwide Express	800-225-5345	**Olsten Staffing Services**	303-752-9622
Federal Express	800-238-5355	**Pak Mail Centers of America**	303-750-0880
Kelly Services	303-695-9292	**Post Office**	800-275-8777
Kinko's	303-745-2679	**UPS**	800-742-5877

— Media —

PUBLICATIONS

				Phone	Fax
Aurora Sentinel 10730 E Bethany Dr Suite 304	Aurora	CO	80014	303-750-7555	750-7699
Web: www.aurorasentinel.com ■ *E-mail:* editor@aurorasentinel.com					
Denver Business Journal 1700 Broadway Suite 515	Denver	CO	80290	303-837-3500	837-3535
Web: www.amcity.com/denver ■ *E-mail:* denver@amcity.com					
Denver Post‡ 1560 Broadway	Denver	CO	80202	303-820-1010	820-1369
TF: 800-336-7678 ■ *Web:* www.denverpost.com ■ *E-mail:* letters@denverpost.com					
Rocky Mountain News‡ 400 W Colfax Ave	Denver	CO	80204	303-892-5000	892-2568
Web: www.insidedenver.com ■ *E-mail:* letters@denver-rmn.com					

‡Daily newspapers

TELEVISION

				Phone	Fax
KCEC-TV Ch 50 (Uni) 777 Grant St Suite 110	Denver	CO	80203	303-832-0050	832-3410
E-mail: kcecnews@aol.com					
KCNC-TV Ch 4 (CBS) 1044 Lincoln St	Denver	CO	80203	303-861-4444	830-6380
Web: www.kcncnews4.com ■ *E-mail:* mailroom@kcncnews4.com					
KDVR-TV Ch 31 (Fox) 501 Wazee St	Denver	CO	80204	303-595-3131	595-8312
Web: www.fox31.com ■ *E-mail:* feedback@fox31.com					
KMGH-TV Ch 7 (ABC) 123 Speer Blvd	Denver	CO	80203	303-832-7777	832-0119
Web: www.kmgh.com ■ *E-mail:* kmgh7@csn.net					
KPXC-TV Ch 59 (PAX) 3001 S Jamaica Ct	Aurora	CO	80014	303-751-5959	751-5993
Web: www.pax.net/kpxc					
KRMA-TV Ch 6 (PBS) 1089 Bannock St	Denver	CO	80204	303-892-6666	620-5600
Web: www.krma.org ■ *E-mail:* info@krma.org					
KTVD-TV Ch 20 (UPN) 11203 E Peakview Ave	Englewood	CO	80111	303-792-2020	790-4633
KUSA-TV Ch 9 (NBC) 500 Speer Blvd	Denver	CO	80203	303-871-9999	698-4700
Web: www.9news.com ■ *E-mail:* kusa@9news.com					
KWGN-TV Ch 2 (WB) 6160 S Wabash Way	Englewood	CO	80111	303-740-2222	740-2847
Web: www.wb2.com					

RADIO

				Phone	Fax
KCKK-FM 104.3 MHz (Ctry) 1095 S Monaco Pkwy	Denver	CO	80224	303-321-0950	320-0708
KEZW-AM 1430 kHz (Nost) 10200 E Girard Ave Suite B130	Denver	CO	80231	303-696-1714	696-0522
KHOW-AM 630 kHz (N/T) 1380 Lawrence St Suite 1300	Denver	CO	80204	303-893-8500	892-4700
KOA-AM 850 kHz (N/T) 1380 Lawrence St Suite 1300	Denver	CO	80204	303-893-8500	892-4700
KXKL-AM 1280 kHz (Oldies) 1560 Broadway Suite 1100	Denver	CO	80202	303-832-5665	832-7000
KXKL-FM 105.1 MHz (Oldies) 1560 Broadway Suite 1100	Denver	CO	80202	303-832-5665	832-7000

Aurora (Cont'd)

— Colleges/Universities —

				Phone	Fax
Community College of Aurora 16000 E Centretech Pkwy *Web:* www.ccac.edu	Aurora	CO	80011	303-360-4700	360-4761

— Hospitals —

				Phone	Fax
Children's Hospital 14406 E Evans Ave Suite 100	Aurora	CO	80014	303-861-3916	751-3195
Columbia Medical Center of Aurora North Campus 700 Potomac St. **Fax:* Admitting	Aurora	CO	80011	303-363-7200	360-3751*
Medical Center of Aurora South Campus 1501 S Potomac St.	Aurora	CO	80012	303-695-2600	337-9773

— Attractions —

				Phone	Fax
Aurora Fox Arts Center 9900 E Colfax Ave.	Aurora	CO	80010	303-361-2910	361-2909
Aurora History Museum 15001 E Alameda Dr	Aurora	CO	80012	303-739-6660	739-6657
Aurora Reservoir 5800 S Powhaton Rd	Aurora	CO	80016	303-690-1286	690-1654
Belleview Children's Farm 5001 S Inca Ave	Englewood	CO	80110	303-798-6927	
Centennial House 1671 Galena St.	Aurora	CO	80010	303-739-6600	
Cherry Creek State Park 4201 S Parker Rd	Aurora	CO	80014	303-690-1166	699-3864
Colorado State Capitol 200 E Colfax Ave.	Denver	CO	80203	303-866-2604	866-2167
Plains Conservation Center 21901 E Hampden Ave	Aurora	CO	80013	303-693-3621	
Rocky Mountain Arsenal National Wildlife Refuge 72nd & Quebec Sts.	Commerce City	CO	80022	303-289-0232	289-0579

SPORTS TEAMS & FACILITIES

				Phone	Fax
Arapahoe Park Race Track 26000 E Quincy Ave *Web:* www.wembleyusa.com/arapahoe ■ *E-mail:* arapahoe@wembleyusa.com	Aurora	CO	80046	303-690-2400	690-6730
Colorado Comets (soccer) 6200 Dahlia St Wembley Pk Stadium *Web:* www.intermark.com/comets	Commerce City	CO	80022	303-288-1591	289-1640
Colorado Rockies 2001 Blake St Coors Field *TF Sales:* 800-388-7625 ■ *Web:* www.coloradorockies.com	Denver	CO	80205	303-762-5437	312-2219
Denver Broncos 1900 Elliot St Mile High Stadium *Web:* www.denverbroncos.com	Denver	CO	80204	303-433-7466	433-3414
Denver Diamonds (soccer) 7112 W Jefferson Ave Suite 100	Lakewood	CO	80232	303-986-5200	986-5222
Denver Nuggets 1000 Chopper Cir Pepsi Ctr *Web:* www.nba.com/nuggets	Denver	CO	80204	303-893-3865	405-1315

— Events —

	Phone
Gateway to the Rockies Festival (mid-September)	303-361-6169
Kids Spree (late July)	303-739-7546
Men's Masters Slow Pitch-ASA National Championship Tournament (late August)	303-695-7201
Pumpkin Fest (late October)	303-361-2936

Boulder

Boulder is located within an hour's drive of both the Denver International Airport and Rocky Mountain National Park. Several ski areas are close by as well, and limited stakes gaming is available in the towns of Central City and Blackhawk. At the heart of Boulder is Pearl Street Mall, the downtown historic preservation district that serves as the city's center, with restaurants, shops, park areas, and a range of activities and entertainments for both adults and children. Popular annual events include the Colorado Music Festival, Boulder Fall Festival, and the Colorado Shakespeare Festival, a seven-week summer event visited by more than 55,000 people each year.

Population	90,543	**Longitude**	105-20-68 W
Area (Land)	22.6 sq mi	**County**	Boulder
Area (Water)	1.0 sq mi	**Time Zone**	MST
Elevation	5344 ft	**Area Code/s**	303
Latitude	40-04-99 N		

— Average Temperatures and Precipitation —

TEMPERATURES

	Jan	Feb	Mar	Apr	May	Jun	Jul	Aug	Sep	Oct	Nov	Dec
High	45	48	54	63	72	82	88	85	77	67	53	46
Low	20	23	28	36	44	53	59	57	48	39	29	22

PRECIPITATION

	Jan	Feb	Mar	Apr	May	Jun	Jul	Aug	Sep	Oct	Nov	Dec
Inches	0.6	0.7	1.6	2.1	3.0	2.2	2.0	1.3	1.9	1.3	1.1	0.8

— Important Phone Numbers —

	Phone		Phone
AAA	303-442-0383	**Time/Temp**	303-443-1910
Emergency	911	**Weather**	303-337-2500
Poison Control Center	303-739-1123		

— Information Sources —

				Phone	Fax
Better Business Bureau Serving the Denver-Boulder Metro Area 1780 S Bellaire St Suite 700 *Web:* www.denver.bbb.org ■ *E-mail:* info@denver.bbb.org	Denver	CO	80222	303-758-2100	758-8321
Boulder Chamber of Commerce 2440 Pearl St. *Web:* chamber.boulder.net	Boulder	CO	80302	303-442-1044	938-8837
Boulder City Hall 1777 Broadway *Web:* www.ci.boulder.co.us	Boulder	CO	80302	303-441-3388	441-4381
Boulder Convention & Visitors Bureau 2440 Pearl St. *TF:* 800-444-0447 ■ *Web:* visitor.boulder.net/ ■ *E-mail:* visitorsbureau@chamber.boulder.co.us	Boulder	CO	80302	303-442-2911	938-8837
Boulder County PO Box 8020 *Web:* www.boco.co.gov	Boulder	CO	80306	303-441-3515	441-4863
Boulder Mayor PO Box 791 *Web:* www.ci.boulder.co.us/council.html	Boulder	CO	80306	303-441-3002	441-4478
Boulder Planning Dept PO Box 791 *Web:* www.ci.boulder.co.us/planning	Boulder	CO	80306	303-441-3270	441-3241
Boulder Public Library PO Drawer H *Web:* bcn.boulder.co.us/library/bpl/home.html ■ *E-mail:* feedback@boulder.lib.co.us	Boulder	CO	80306	303-441-3100	442-1808

On-Line Resources

About.com Guide to Boulder .... boulder.about.com

Boulder — On-Line Resources (Cont'd)

All of Boulder	www.allofboulder.com
Anthill City Guide Boulder	www.anthill.com/city.asp?city=boulder
Boulder Community Network	bcn.boulder.co.us
Boulder County Guide	www.boulderguide.com/
Boulder Info	www.boulderinfo.com/beta.html
Boulder Weekly	www.boulderweekly.com
City Knowledge Boulder	www.cityknowledge.com/co_boulder.htm
Excite.com Boulder City Guide	www.excite.com/travel/countries/united_states/colorado/boulder
Insiders' Guide to Boulder	www.insiders.com/boulder/index.htm
NITC Travelbase City Guide Boulder	www.travelbase.com/auto/guides/boulder-co.html

— Transportation Services —

AIRPORTS

■ Denver International Airport (DEN)

	Phone
60 miles SE of downtown Boulder (approx 70 minutes)	303-342-2000

Web: infodenver.denver.co.us/~aviation/ ■ *E-mail:* aviation@infodenver.denver.co.us

Airport Transportation

	Phone
Boulder Airporter $18 fare to downtown Boulder	303-444-0808
Skyride $6 fare to downtown Boulder	303-299-6000

Web: www.rtd-denver.com/skyRide

Commercial Airlines

	Phone		Phone
America West	800-235-9292	**Mexicana**	800-531-7923
American	800-433-7300	**Midwest Express**	800-452-2022
Continental	800-525-0280	**Northwest**	800-225-2525
Continental Express	800-525-0280	**Sun Country**	800-359-5786
Delta	800-221-1212	**TWA**	800-221-2000
Frontier	800-432-1359	**United**	800-241-6522
Martinair Holland	800-366-4655	**United Express**	800-241-6522
Mesa	800-637-2247	**US Airways**	800-428-4322

Charter Airlines

	Phone		Phone
Corporate Air Charter	406-248-1541	**Superior Aviation**	800-882-7751
Mayo Aviation Inc	303-790-9777		

CAR RENTALS

	Phone		Phone
Advantage	303-261-8585	**Enterprise**	303-342-7350
Alamo	800-327-9633	**Hertz**	800-654-3131
Avis	303-342-5500	**National**	303-342-0717
Avis-Boulder	303-499-1136	**Payless**	303-342-9444
Budget	303-342-9001	**Thrifty**	303-342-9086
Dollar	303-342-9099		

LIMO/TAXI

	Phone		Phone
Airport Luxury Express	303-938-1234	**Broomfield Taxi**	303-457-9000
Boulder Limousine	303-449-5466	**Prestige Transportation**	303-678-8471
Boulder Yellow Cab	303-442-2277		

MASS TRANSIT

	Phone
RTD Bus $1.25 Base fare	303-299-6000

RAIL/BUS

				Phone
Amtrak Station 1701 Wynkoop St.	Denver	CO	80202	800-872-7245
Greyhound/Trailways Bus Station 1055 19th St.	Denver	CO	80202	800-231-2222

— Accommodations —

HOTEL RESERVATION SERVICES

	Phone	Fax
All-Colorado Accommodations	877-365-6926	522-0894*

**Fax Area Code:* 719 ■ *Web:* www.rockad.com/aca/ ■ *E-mail:* mountain@frii.com

HOTELS, MOTELS, RESORTS

				Phone	Fax
Alps Boulder Canyon Inn 38619 Boulder Canyon Dr *TF:* 800-414-2577	Boulder	CO	80303	303-444-5445	444-5522
Best Western Boulder Inn 770 28th St *TF:* 800-233-8469	Boulder	CO	80303	303-449-3800	402-9118
Best Western Golden Buff Lodge 1725 28th St *TF:* 800-999-2833	Boulder	CO	80301	303-442-7450	442-8788
Best Western Lake Estes Resort 1650 Big Thompson Ave *TF:* 800-292-8439 ■ *Web:* www.lakeestes.com ■ *E-mail:* info@lakeestes.com	Estes Park	CO	80517	970-586-3386	586-9000
Boulder Mountain Lodge 91 Four-Mile Canyon Dr. *TF:* 800-458-0882 ■ *Web:* www.boulderguide.com/Lodge ■ *E-mail:* bldmtnldge@aol.com	Boulder	CO	80302	303-444-0882	541-0665
Boulder Victoria Bed & Breakfast 1305 Pine St *Web:* www.bouldervictoria.com/victoria.html	Boulder	CO	80302	303-938-1300	938-1435
Briar Rose Bed & Breakfast 2151 Arapahoe Ave *Web:* www.globalmall.com/brose ■ *E-mail:* brbbx@aol.com	Boulder	CO	80302	303-442-3007	786-8440
Broker Inn 555 30th St *TF:* 800-338-5407	Boulder	CO	80303	303-444-3330	444-6444
C Lazy U Ranch 3640 Colorado Hwy 125 *Web:* www.clazyu.com ■ *E-mail:* ranch@clazyu.com	Granby	CO	80446	970-887-3344	887-3917
Coburn House 2040 16th St *TF:* 800-858-5811 ■ *Web:* ra.nilenet.com/~coburn	Boulder	CO	80302	303-545-5200	440-6740
Comfort Inn 1450 Big Thompson Ave *TF:* 800-228-5150	Estes Park	CO	80517	970-586-2358	
Courtyard by Marriott 4710 Pearl East Cir *TF:* 800-321-2211 ■ *Web:* courtyard.com/DENBD	Boulder	CO	80301	303-440-4700	440-8975
Days Inn 5397 S Boulder Rd *TF:* 800-329-7466	Boulder	CO	80303	303-499-4422	494-0269
Econo Lodge 2020 Arapahoe Ave *TF:* 888-449-7550	Boulder	CO	80302	303-449-7550	449-1082
Foot of the Mountain Motel 200 Arapahoe Ave	Boulder	CO	80302	303-442-5688	
Gunbarrel Guest House 6901 Lookout Rd *TF:* 800-530-1513 ■ *Web:* www.guest-house.com ■ *E-mail:* ldyhawk@earthlink.net	Boulder	CO	80301	303-530-1513	530-4573
Holiday Inn of Estes Park 101 S St Vrain Hwy *TF:* 800-803-7837 ■ *Web:* www.basshotels.com/holiday-inn/?_franchisee=ESECO ■ *E-mail:* estespk@webaccess.net	Estes Park	CO	80517	970-586-2332	586-2038
Homewood Suites 4950 Baseline Rd *TF:* 800-225-5466	Boulder	CO	80303	303-499-9922	499-6706
Hotel Boulderado 2115 13th St *TF:* 800-433-4344 ■ *Web:* www.boulderado.com ■ *E-mail:* info@boulderado.com	Boulder	CO	80302	303-442-4344	442-4378
Inn on Mapleton Hill 1001 Spruce St *Web:* www.innonmapletonhill.com ■ *E-mail:* maphillinn@aol.com	Boulder	CO	80302	303-449-6528	415-0470
Iron Horse Resort Retreat 257 Winter Park Dr *TF:* 800-621-8190 ■ *Web:* www.ironhorse-resort.com	Winter Park	CO	80482	970-726-8851	726-2321
Lazy-L-Motel 1000 28th St. *TF:* 800-525-1444	Boulder	CO	80303	303-442-7525	
Pearl Street Inn 1820 Pearl St *TF:* 888-810-1302 ■ *Web:* www.pearlstreetinn.com	Boulder	CO	80302	303-444-5584	444-6494
Regal Harvest House Hotel 1345 28th St *TF:* 800-545-6285	Boulder	CO	80302	303-443-3850	443-1480
Residence Inn by Marriott 3030 Center Green Dr *TF:* 800-331-3131 ■ *Web:* www.residenceinn.com/residenceinn/VBOCG	Boulder	CO	80301	303-449-5545	449-2452
Sandy Pointe Inn 6485 Twin Lakes Rd *TF:* 800-322-2939	Boulder	CO	80301	303-530-2939	530-9101
Silver Saddle Motel 90 W Arapahoe Ave *TF:* 800-525-9509	Boulder	CO	80302	303-442-8022	
Silver Saddle Motor Lodge PO Box 1747	Estes Park	CO	80517	970-586-4476	586-4476
Super 8 Motel 970 28th St *TF:* 800-525-2149	Boulder	CO	80303	303-443-7800	
University Inn 1632 Broadway *TF:* 800-258-7917	Boulder	CO	80302	303-442-3830	442-1205

Boulder (Cont'd)

— Restaurants —

				Phone
14th St Bar & Grill (American) 1400 Pearl St	Boulder	CO	80302	303-444-5854
Alexander's (Mexican) 1650 Broadway	Boulder	CO	80302	303-444-6699
Boulder Broker Inn (Steak/Seafood) 555 30th St	Boulder	CO	80303	303-449-1752
Boulder Cafe (American) 1247 Pearl St	Boulder	CO	80302	303-444-4884
Bullfrogs Pub & Grill (English) 1709 Pearl St	Boulder	CO	80302	303-442-2542
Cafe Gondolier (Italian) 2845 28th St	Boulder	CO	80301	303-443-5015
Caffe Antica Roma (Italian) 1308 Pearl St	Boulder	CO	80302	303-442-0378
Casa Alvarez (Mexican) 3161 Walnut St	Boulder	CO	80301	303-546-0630
D'Napoli (Italian) 835 Walnut St	Boulder	CO	80302	303-444-8434
Daddy Bruce's (Barbecue) 2000 Arapahoe Ave	Boulder	CO	80302	303-449-8890
Dagabi (Italian) 3970 N Broadway St	Boulder	CO	80304	303-786-9004
European Cafe (European) 2460 Arapahoe Ave	Boulder	CO	80302	303-938-8250
Fancy Moose (American) 1345 28th St	Boulder	CO	80302	303-443-3850
Flagstaff House (American) 1138 Flagstaff Rd	Boulder	CO	80302	303-442-4640
Web: www.flagstaffhouse.com ■ *E-mail:* flagsta1@ix.netcom.com				
Full Moon Grill & Pasta (European) 2525 Arapahoe Ave	Boulder	CO	80302	303-938-8800
Greenbriar (American) 8735 N Foothills Hwy	Boulder	CO	80302	303-440-7979
Himalayas Restaurant (Indian) 2010 14th St	Boulder	CO	80302	303-442-3230
Jax Fishhouse (Seafood) 928 Pearl St	Boulder	CO	80302	303-444-1811
Korea House (Korean) 2750 Glenwood Dr	Boulder	CO	80304	303-449-1657
Laudisio (Italian) 2785 Iris Ave	Boulder	CO	80304	303-442-1300
Web: www.cuisine.net/Laudisio/				
Little Russian Cafe (Russian) 1430 Pearl St	Boulder	CO	80302	303-449-7696
Mataan Fez (Moroccan) 2226 Pearl St	Boulder	CO	80302	303-440-4167
Mediterranean Inc (Mediterranean) 1002 Walnut St Suite 101B	Boulder	CO	80302	303-444-5335
Nancy's (American) 825 Walnut St	Boulder	CO	80302	303-449-8402
Nepal Restaurant (Tibetan) 1124 Pearl St	Boulder	CO	80302	303-447-2816
Oasis Brewery & Restaurant (American) 1095 Canyon Blvd	Boulder	CO	80302	303-449-0363
Q's Restaurant (Continental) 2115 13th St	Boulder	CO	80302	303-442-4880
Rio Grande Restaurant (Mexican) 1101 Walnut St	Boulder	CO	80302	303-444-3690
Royal Peacock (Indian) 5290 Arapahoe Ave	Boulder	CO	80303	303-447-1409
Siamese Plate (Thai) 1575 Folsom Ave	Boulder	CO	80302	303-447-9718
Sink The (American) 1165 13th St	Boulder	CO	80302	303-444-7465
Sushi Zanmai (Japanese) 1221 Spruce St	Boulder	CO	80302	303-440-0733
Taj Restaurant (Indian) 2630 Baseline Rd	Boulder	CO	80303	303-494-5216
Trios (American) 1155 Canyon Blvd	Boulder	CO	80302	303-442-8400
Web: www.triosgrille.com				
Walnut Brewery (American) 1123 Walnut St	Boulder	CO	80302	303-447-1345
Zolo Grill (Southwest) 2525 Arapahoe Ave	Boulder	CO	80304	303-449-0444

— Goods and Services —

SHOPPING

				Phone	Fax
Boulder Arts & Crafts Cooperative 1421 Pearl St	Boulder	CO	80302	303-443-3683	443-7998
Crossroads Mall 1600 28th St	Boulder	CO	80301	303-444-0265	449-5079
Downtown Boulder Mall Pearl St between 11th & 15th Sts	Boulder	CO	80302	303-449-3774	441-4130

BANKS

				Phone	Fax
Bank One Boulder NA 800 Broadway	Boulder	CO	80302	303-245-6660	245-6692
Community First National Bank 3800 Arapahoe Ave	Boulder	CO	80303	303-444-7771	444-0377
FirstBank of South Boulder 4770 Baseline Rd Suite 100	Boulder	CO	80303	303-499-2200	543-3610
Norwest Bank Colorado NA 1242 Pearl St	Boulder	CO	80306	303-442-0351	440-0285
Vectra Bank of Boulder 1375 Walnut St	Boulder	CO	80302	303-447-5960	449-0119

BUSINESS SERVICES

	Phone
Adecco Employment Personnel Services	303-442-2420
Airborne Express	800-247-2676
BAX Global	800-225-5229
Boulder Executive Services	303-444-3320
DHL Worldwide Express	800-225-5345
Federal Express	800-238-5355
Kinko's	303-494-2622
Mail Boxes Etc	800-789-4623
Post Office	800-275-8777
UPS	800-742-5877

— Media —

PUBLICATIONS

				Phone	Fax
Boulder County Business Report 3180 Sterling Cir Suite 201	Boulder	CO	80301	303-440-4950	440-8954
Web: www.bcbr.com/					
Boulder Daily Camera‡ PO Box 591	Boulder	CO	80306	303-442-1202	449-9358*
**Fax:* Edit ■ *TF:* 800-783-1202 ■ *Web:* www.bouldernews.com/					
Colorado Daily‡ 5505 Central Ave	Boulder	CO	80301	303-443-6272	443-9357*
**Fax:* Fax ■ *Web:* www.codaily.com					

‡*Daily newspapers*

TELEVISION

				Phone	Fax
KBDI-TV Ch 12 (PBS) 2900 Welton St 1st Fl	Denver	CO	80205	303-296-1212	296-6650
Web: www.kbdi.org					
KCEC-TV Ch 50 (Uni) 777 Grant St Suite 110	Denver	CO	80203	303-832-0050	832-3410
E-mail: kcecnews@aol.com					
KCNC-TV Ch 4 (CBS) 1044 Lincoln St	Denver	CO	80203	303-861-4444	830-6380
Web: www.kcncnews4.com ■ *E-mail:* mailroom@kcncnews4.com					
KDVR-TV Ch 31 (Fox) 501 Wazee St	Denver	CO	80204	303-595-3131	595-8312
Web: www.fox31.com ■ *E-mail:* feedback@fox31.com					
KMGH-TV Ch 7 (ABC) 123 Speer Blvd	Denver	CO	80203	303-832-7777	832-0119
Web: www.kmgh.com ■ *E-mail:* kmgh7@csn.net					
KPXC-TV Ch 59 (PAX) 3001 S Jamaica Ct	Aurora	CO	80014	303-751-5959	751-5993
Web: www.pax.net/kpxc					
KRMA-TV Ch 6 (PBS) 1089 Bannock St	Denver	CO	80204	303-892-6666	620-5600
Web: www.krma.org ■ *E-mail:* info@krma.org					
KTVD-TV Ch 20 (UPN) 11203 E Peakview Ave	Englewood	CO	80111	303-792-2020	790-4633
KUSA-TV Ch 9 (NBC) 500 Speer Blvd	Denver	CO	80203	303-871-9999	698-4700
Web: www.9news.com ■ *E-mail:* kusa@9news.com					
KWGN-TV Ch 2 (WB) 6160 S Wabash Way	Englewood	CO	80111	303-740-2222	740-2847
Web: www.wb2.com					

RADIO

				Phone	Fax
KBCO-FM 97.3 MHz (AAA) 2500 Pearl St Suite 315	Boulder	CO	80302	303-444-5600	449-3057
Web: www.kbco.com					
KBPI-FM 106.7 MHz (Rock) 1380 Lawrence St Suite 1300	Denver	CO	80204	303-893-3699	534-7625
Web: www.kbpi.com					
KCKK-FM 104.3 MHz (Ctry) 1095 S Monaco Pkwy	Denver	CO	80224	303-321-0950	320-0708
KEZW-AM 1430 kHz (Nost) 10200 E Girard Ave Suite B130	Denver	CO	80231	303-696-1714	696-0522
KGNU-FM 88.5 MHz (NPR) PO Box 885	Boulder	CO	80306	303-449-4885	
Web: www.kgnu.org					
KHOW-AM 630 kHz (N/T) 1380 Lawrence St Suite 1300	Denver	CO	80204	303-893-8500	892-4700
KWAB-AM 1490 kHz (AAA) 3085 Bluff St	Boulder	CO	80301	303-444-1490	442-6544
KXKL-AM 1280 kHz (Oldies) 1560 Broadway Suite 1100	Denver	CO	80202	303-832-5665	832-7000

— Colleges/Universities —

				Phone	Fax
Naropa University 2130 Arapahoe Ave	Boulder	CO	80302	303-444-0202	444-0410
Web: www.naropa.edu ■ *E-mail:* info@naropa.edu					
University of Colorado Boulder Campus Box 30	Boulder	CO	80309	303-492-1411	492-7115
Web: www.colorado.edu ■ *E-mail:* homepage@colorado.edu					

— Hospitals —

				Phone	Fax
Boulder Community Hospital 1100 Balsam Ave	Boulder	CO	80301	303-440-2273	440-2278*
**Fax:* Admitting ■ *Web:* www.bch.org					

Boulder (Cont'd)

— Attractions —

				Phone	Fax
Arapaho National Forest 2995 Baseline Rd	Boulder	CO	80303	303-444-6600	
Boulder Ballet 2590 W Walnut St	Boulder	CO	80302	303-442-6944	
Web: www.artstozoo.org/bb/					
Boulder Dance Alliance 1600 28th St Crossroads Mall	Boulder	CO	80302	303-444-1357	
Web: www.techmission.com/bda/ ■ *E-mail:* blrdance@dimensional.com					
Boulder Museum of Contemporary Art 1750 13th St	Boulder	CO	80302	303-443-2122	447-1633
Web: www.bmoca.org					
Boulder Museum of History 1206 Euclid Ave	Boulder	CO	80302	303-449-3464	938-8322
Web: bcn.boulder.co.us/arts/bmh/					
Boulder Philharmonic Orchestra 17th St & University Ave Macky Auditorium	Boulder	CO	80309	303-449-1343	443-9203
Web: www.boulderphil.com ■ *E-mail:* bpo@boulderphil.com					
Boulder Reservoir 5100 N 51st St	Boulder	CO	80301	303-441-3461	441-1807
Boulder's Dinner Theater 5501 Arapahoe Ave	Boulder	CO	80303	303-449-6000	442-5671
Celestial Seasonings Tea 4600 Sleepytime Dr.	Boulder	CO	80301	303-581-1202	581-1332*
**Fax:* Hum Res ■ *Web:* www.celestialseasonings.com/whoweare/tourinfo/					
Chautauqua Park 900 Baseline Rd	Boulder	CO	80302	303-442-3282	449-0790
Collage Children's Museum 2065 30th St.	Boulder	CO	80302	303-440-9894	443-8040
Web: bcn.boulder.co.us/arts/collage/					
Colorado Music Festival Orchestra 1525 Spruce St Suite 101	Boulder	CO	80302	303-449-1397	449-0071
Web: www.coloradomusicfest.com					
Dairy Center for the Arts 2590 Walnut St	Boulder	CO	80302	303-449-1343	
Web: www.thedairy.com/nav.htm					
Eldorado Canyon State Park PO Box B.	Eldorado Springs	CO	80025	303-494-3943	499-2729
Web: www.dnr.state.co.us/parks/eldorado					
Fiske Planetarium & Science Center Regent Dr University of Colorado Campus	Boulder	CO	80309	303-492-5001	
Gateway Park Fun Center 4800 N 28th St.	Boulder	CO	80301	303-442-4386	448-0051
Web: www.gatewayfunpark.com ■ *E-mail:* info@gatewayfunpark.com					
Golden Gate Canyon State Park 3873 Hwy 46	Golden	CO	80403	303-582-3707	
Web: www.dnr.state.co.us/parks/golden_gate					
Historic Boulder 646 Pearl St.	Boulder	CO	80302	303-444-5391	444-5309
Historic Boulder Walking Tours 1206 Euclid Ave	Boulder	CO	80302	303-449-3464	
Interweave Dance Theatre Broadway & University Blvd Charlotte York Irey Studio Theatre	Boulder	CO	80309	303-449-0399	
Web: bcn.boulder.co.us/arts/idt/idt.html ■ *E-mail:* montage@juno.com					
Leanin' Tree Museum of Western Art 6055 Longbow Dr.	Boulder	CO	80301	303-530-1442	530-7283
Web: www.leanintree.com ■ *E-mail:* jobs@leanintree.com					
Macky Auditorium 17th St & University Ave.	Boulder	CO	80309	303-492-8423	
National Center for Atmospheric Research PO Box 3000	Boulder	CO	80307	303-497-1000	497-8610*
**Fax:* PR ■ *Web:* www.ncar.ucar.edu					
Rockies Brewing Co 2880 Wilderness Pl	Boulder	CO	80301	303-444-8448	444-4796
Rocky Mountain National Park	Estes Park	CO	80517	970-586-1206	586-1310
Web: www.nps.gov/romo/					
University of Colorado Art Galleries University of Colorado Campus	Boulder	CO	80309	303-492-8300	492-4886
Web: stripe.colorado.edu/~gallery/					
University of Colorado Heritage Center Old Main 3rd Fl.	Boulder	CO	80309	303-492-6329	492-6799
University of Colorado Museum Campus Box 218	Boulder	CO	80309	303-492-6892	492-4195
Web: www.colorado.edu/CUMUSEUM/					
Upstart Crow Theatre Co 2131 Arapahoe Ave.	Boulder	CO	80302	303-442-1415	938-0376
Web: www.serve.com/upstart/					
Youth Ballet Colorado 555 Burbank St Suite J	Broomfield	CO	80020	303-466-5685	
Web: www.artstozoo.org/ybc ■ *E-mail:* ybc@ibm.net					

SPORTS TEAMS & FACILITIES

				Phone	Fax
Colorado Rockies 2001 Blake St Coors Field	Denver	CO	80205	303-762-5437	312-2219
TF Sales: 800-388-7625 ■ *Web:* www.coloradorockies.com					
Denver Broncos 1900 Elliot St Mile High Stadium	Denver	CO	80204	303-433-7466	433-3414
Web: www.denverbroncos.com					
Denver Nuggets 1000 Chopper Cir Pepsi Ctr	Denver	CO	80204	303-893-3865	405-1315
Web: www.nba.com/nuggets					

— Events —

	Phone
Bolder Boulder 10K (late May)	303-444-7223
Boulder Art Fair (mid-July)	303-449-3774
Boulder Artwalk (early December)	303-444-9106
Boulder Bach Festival (late January)	303-494-3159
Boulder Creek Festival (late May)	303-449-3825
Boulder Fall Festival (late September)	303-449-3774
Christmas in July (mid-July)	303-770-0057
Colorado Dance Festival (early July-early August)	303-442-7666
Colorado Mahler Festival (mid-January)	303-447-0513
Colorado Music Festival (late June-early August)	303-449-1397
Colorado Shakespeare Festival (late June-early August)	303-492-0554
Kinetic Conveyance Sculpture Challenge (early May)	303-444-5600
Lights of December Parade (early December)	303-449-3774
Lyric Theatre Festival (July)	303-492-8008

Colorado Springs

In 1893, a trip to the summit of Pikes Peak inspired Katharine Lee Bates to write the words to "America the Beautiful." The 14,110-foot peak, located just outside Colorado Springs, is accessible today by car, cog railway, or hiking path. The region's natural beauty is evident also in the Cave of the Winds, the Garden of the Gods, and the Royal Gorge Bridge area. Buckskin Joe Park, an Old West theme park, has often been used as a movie set, and the Pro Rodeo Hall of Fame chronicles the history of America's original sport. Other attractions in the area include the Cheyenne Mountain Zoological Park, the 46-room Miramont Castle, and the Manitou Cliff Dwellers Museum, a prehistoric Indian preserve located in Manitou Springs.

Population	344,987	**Longitude**	104-82-08 W
Area (Land)	183.2 sq mi	**County**	El Paso
Area (Water)	0.4 sq mi	**Time Zone**	MST
Elevation	6008 ft	**Area Code/s**	719
Latitude	38-83-39 N		

— Average Temperatures and Precipitation —

TEMPERATURES

	Jan	Feb	Mar	Apr	May	Jun	Jul	Aug	Sep	Oct	Nov	Dec
High	41	45	50	60	69	79	84	81	74	64	51	42
Low	16	19	25	33	42	51	57	55	47	36	25	17

PRECIPITATION

	Jan	Feb	Mar	Apr	May	Jun	Jul	Aug	Sep	Oct	Nov	Dec
Inches	0.3	0.4	0.9	1.2	2.2	2.3	2.9	3.0	1.3	0.8	0.5	0.5

— Important Phone Numbers —

	Phone		Phone
AAA	719-591-2222	**Non-emergency Police**	719-444-7000
Emergency	911	**Poison Control Center**	719-776-5333
Events Line	719-635-1723	**Time/Temp**	719-630-1111
Medical Referral	719-444-2273	**Weather**	719-573-6846

Colorado Springs (Cont'd)

— Information Sources —

				Phone	Fax
Better Business Bureau Serving the Pike's Peak Region 25 N Wahsatch Ave. *Web:* www.coloradosprings.bbb.org	Colorado Springs	CO	80903	719-636-1155	636-5078
Colorado Springs Chamber of Commerce PO Box B *Web:* www.cscc.org	Colorado Springs	CO	80901	719-635-1551	635-1571
Colorado Springs City Auditorium 221 E Kiowa St.	Colorado Springs	CO	80903	719-578-6652	635-7806
Colorado Springs City Hall PO Box 1575 *Web:* www.colorado-springs.com ■ *E-mail:* credlightning@ci.colospgs.co.us	Colorado Springs	CO	80901	719-385-5900	578-6601
Colorado Springs Convention & Visitors Bureau 104 S Cascade Ave Suite 104 *TF:* 800-368-4748 ■ *Web:* www.coloradosprings-travel.com ■ *E-mail:* sindt@usa.net	Colorado Springs	CO	80903	719-635-7506	635-4968
Colorado Springs Finance Dept PO Box 1575	Colorado Springs	CO	80901	719-385-5900	578-6601
Colorado Springs Mayor PO Box 1575 *Web:* www.colorado-springs.com/govinfo/reps2.htm	Colorado Springs	CO	80901	719-385-5900	578-6601
El Paso County 200 S Cascade Ave. *Web:* www.co.el-paso.co.us	Colorado Springs	CO	80903	719-520-6200	520-6230
Pikes Peak Library District 5550 N Union Blvd	Colorado Springs	CO	80918	719-531-6333	528-2810

On-Line Resources

4ColoradoSprings.com	www.4coloradosprings.com
About.com Guide to Colorado Springs/Pueblo	coloradospring.about.com/local/mountainus/coloradosprings
Anthill City Guide Colorado Springs	www.anthill.com/city.asp?city=coloradosprings
Area Guide Colorado Springs	coloradosprings.areaguides.net
City Knowledge Colorado Springs	www.cityknowledge.com/co_colorado_springs.htm
Colorado Springs Page	www.cospgs.com/
Excite.com Colorado Springs City Guide	www.excite.com/travel/countries/united_states/colorado/colorado_springs
NITC Travelbase City Guide Colorado Springs	www.travelbase.com/auto/guides/colorado_springs-co.html
Pikes Peak Country Attractions	www.pikes-peak.com/
Surf the Springs	www.csurf.com/
Virtual Voyages Colorado Springs	www.virtualvoyages.com/usa/co/co_spgs/co_spgs.sht
Welcome to Colorado Springs	www.coloradosprings.com/

— Transportation Services —

AIRPORTS

■ Colorado Springs Municipal Airport (COS)

	Phone
14 miles E of downtown (approx 20 minutes)	719-550-1900

Airport Transportation

	Phone
Cloud Nine Limousine $60 fare to downtown	719-599-9199
Colorado Springs Airport Transportation $25 fare to downtown	719-597-4682
My Chauffeur Limousines $85 fare to downtown	719-597-4822
Yellow Cab $22 fare to downtown	719-634-5000

Commercial Airlines

	Phone		Phone
America West	800-235-9292	**Mesa**	800-637-2247
American	800-433-7300	**Northwest**	800-225-2525
Continental	800-525-0280	**TWA**	800-221-2000
Delta	800-221-1212	**United**	800-241-6522

Charter Airlines

	Phone		Phone
Aero Aviation	719-570-9173	**Travelaire Service**	719-948-3316

CAR RENTALS

	Phone		Phone
Alamo	719-574-8579	**Hertz**	719-596-1863
Avis	719-596-2751	**National**	719-596-1519
Budget	719-574-7400	**Xpress**	719-634-1914
Enterprise	719-636-3900		

LIMO/TAXI

	Phone		Phone
American Cab	719-637-1111	**My Chauffeur Limousines**	719-597-4822
Cloud Nine Limousine	719-599-9199	**Yellow Cab**	719-634-5000

MASS TRANSIT

	Phone
Colorado Springs Transit $1 Base fare	719-385-7433

RAIL/BUS

				Phone
TNM & O/Greyhound Bus Station 120 S Weber St *TF:* 800-231-2222	Colorado Springs	CO	80903	719-635-1505

— Accommodations —

HOTEL RESERVATION SERVICES

	Phone	Fax
All-Colorado Accommodations **Fax Area Code:* 719 ■ *Web:* www.rockad.com/aca/ ■ *E-mail:* mountain@frii.com	877-365-6926	522-0894*

HOTELS, MOTELS, RESORTS

				Phone	Fax
Alikar Gardens Resort 1123 Verde Dr *TF:* 800-456-1123	Colorado Springs	CO	80910	719-475-2564	471-5835
Antlers Adam's Mark Hotel 4 S Cascade Ave. *TF:* 800-444-2326	Colorado Springs	CO	80903	719-473-5600	389-0259
Apollo Park Executive Suites 805 S Circle Dr Suite 2B *TF:* 800-279-3620	Colorado Springs	CO	80910	719-634-0286	635-1539
Best Western Le Baron Hotel 314 W Bijou St. *TF:* 800-477-8610	Colorado Springs	CO	80905	719-471-8680	471-0894
Best Western Palmer House 3010 N Chestnut St. *TF:* 800-223-9127	Colorado Springs	CO	80907	719-636-5201	636-3108
Broadmoor The Resort & Country Club 1 Lake Ave. *TF:* 800-634-7711 ■ *Web:* www.broadmoor.com ■ *E-mail:* info@broadmoor.com	Colorado Springs	CO	80906	719-634-7711	577-5700
Cheyenne Mountain Conference Resort 3225 Broadmoor Valley Rd *TF:* 800-428-8886 ■ *Web:* 206.214.55.137	Colorado Springs	CO	80906	719-538-4000	576-4711
Cliff House @ Pikes Peak 306 Canon Ave *TF:* 888-212-7000 ■ *Web:* www.thecliffhouse.com ■ *E-mail:* info@thecliffhouse.com	Manitou Springs	CO	80829	719-685-3000	685-3913
Comfort Inn 2115 Aerotech Dr *TF:* 800-228-5150	Colorado Springs	CO	80916	719-380-9000	596-4738
Comfort Suites Colorado Springs 1055 Kelly Johnson Blvd *TF:* 800-228-5150	Colorado Springs	CO	80920	719-536-0731	536-0152
Days Inn North 4610 Rusina Rd *TF:* 800-329-7466	Colorado Springs	CO	80907	719-598-1700	592-9029
Doubletree Colorado Springs World Arena 1775 E Cheyenne Mountain Blvd *TF:* 800-222-8733 ■ *Web:* www.doubletreehotels.com/DoubleT/Hotel161/166/166Main.htm	Colorado Springs	CO	80906	719-576-8900	576-4450
Drury Inn Pikes Peak 8155 N Academy Blvd *TF:* 800-378-7946	Colorado Springs	CO	80920	719-598-2500	598-2500
Econo Lodge Downtown 714 N Nevada Ave *TF:* 800-553-2666	Colorado Springs	CO	80903	719-636-3385	447-1378
Embassy Suites 7290 Commerce Center Dr. *TF:* 800-362-2779	Colorado Springs	CO	80919	719-599-9100	599-4644

Colorado Springs — Hotels, Motels, Resorts (Cont'd)

Name / Address	City	State	ZIP	Phone	Fax
Express Inn 725 W Cimarron St	Colorado Springs	CO	80905	719-473-5530	473-8763
Fairfield Inn North 7085 Commerce Center Dr.	Colorado Springs	CO	80919	719-533-1903	533-1903
TF: 800-228-2800 ■ *Web:* fairfieldinn.com/COSFI					
Fairfield Inn South 2725 Geyser Dr.	Colorado Springs	CO	80906	719-576-1717	576-4747
TF: 800-228-2800 ■ *Web:* fairfieldinn.com/COSFS					
Garden of the Gods Motel 2922 W Colorado Ave	Colorado Springs	CO	80904	719-636-5271	477-1422
TF: 800-637-0703 ■ *Web:* www.pikes-peak.com/NEWHOME/accomodations/gogmotel/gardenofgodsmotel.htm					
Hampton Inn North 7245 Commerce Center Dr.	Colorado Springs	CO	80919	719-593-9700	598-0563
TF: 800-426-7866					
Holden House 1902 Bed & Breakfast Inn 1102 W Pikes Peak Ave	Colorado Springs	CO	80904	719-471-3980	
Holiday Inn Express 1815 Aeroplaza Dr	Colorado Springs	CO	80916	719-591-6000	591-6100
TF: 800-465-4329					
Holiday Inn Garden of the Gods 505 Popes Bluff Trail	Colorado Springs	CO	80907	719-598-7656	590-9623
TF: 800-465-4329					
Howard Johnson Inn 5056 N Nevada Ave	Colorado Springs	CO	80918	719-598-7793	531-6831
TF: 800-654-2000					
La Quinta Motor Inn 4385 Sinton Rd	Colorado Springs	CO	80907	719-528-5060	598-0360
TF: 800-531-5900					
Marriott Hotel 5580 Tech Center Dr	Colorado Springs	CO	80919	719-260-1800	260-1492
TF: 800-962-6982					
Microtel Inn & Suites 7265 Commerce Center Dr.	Colorado Springs	CO	80919	719-598-7500	598-4975
TF: 888-771-7171					
Monarch Ski Resort 1 Powder Pl	Monarch	CO	81227	719-539-2581	539-3909
TF: 800-332-3668 ■ *Web:* www.skimonarch.com					
Peak View Inn 4950 N Nevada Ave	Colorado Springs	CO	80918	719-598-1545	598-1434
TF: 800-551-2267					
Quality Inn Garden of the Gods 555 W Garden of the Gods Rd	Colorado Springs	CO	80907	719-593-9119	260-0381
TF: 800-228-5151 ■ *Web:* www.qinn.com/					
Radisson Inn Colorado Springs Airport 1645 N Newport Rd	Colorado Springs	CO	80916	719-597-7000	597-4308
TF: 800-333-3333					
Radisson Inn North 8110 N Academy Blvd	Colorado Springs	CO	80920	719-598-5770	598-3434
TF: 800-333-3333					
Ramada Inn North 3125 Sinton Rd	Colorado Springs	CO	80907	719-633-5541	633-3870
TF: 800-272-6232					
Red Roof Inn 8280 Hwy 83	Colorado Springs	CO	80920	719-598-6700	598-3443
TF: 800-843-7663					
Residence Inn by Marriott 3880 N Academy Blvd	Colorado Springs	CO	80917	719-574-0370	574-7821
TF: 800-331-3131 ■ *Web:* www.residenceinn.com/COSSP					
Rodeway Inn S Cheyenne Rd	Colorado Springs	CO	80909	719-471-0990	633-3343
TF: 800-424-4777					
Sheraton Hotel 2886 S Circle Dr.	Colorado Springs	CO	80906	719-576-5900	576-7695
TF: 800-325-3535 ■ *Web:* www.asgusa.com/scsh/					
Sleep Inn 1075 Kelly Johnson Blvd	Colorado Springs	CO	80920	719-260-6969	260-6926
TF: 888-875-3374					
Super 8 Motel 605 Peterson Rd	Colorado Springs	CO	80915	719-597-4100	597-6885
TF: 800-800-8000					
Travelers Uptown Motel 220 E Cimarron St	Colorado Springs	CO	80903	719-473-2774	
Travelodge Inn 2625 Oremill Dr	Colorado Springs	CO	80904	719-632-4600	632-9309
TF: 800-929-5478					
Value Inn 6875 Space Village Ave	Colorado Springs	CO	80915	719-596-5588	596-5588
TF: 800-596-5588					

— Restaurants —

Name / Address	City	State	ZIP	Phone
Alpine Chalet (German) 4608 Rusina Rd	Colorado Springs	CO	80907	719-598-2625
Antonio's Italiano Ristorante (Italian) 4475 Northpark Dr	Colorado Springs	CO	80907	719-531-7177
Briarhurst Manor (Continental) 404 Manitou Ave	Manitou Springs	CO	80829	719-685-1864
Carrabba's Italian Grill (Italian) 2815 Geyser Dr	Colorado Springs	CO	80906	719-527-1126
Castaways The (Steak/Seafood) 107 Manitou Ave	Manitou Springs	CO	80829	719-685-5626
Colorado Springs Fish Market Restaurant (Seafood) 775 W Bijou St	Colorado Springs	CO	80905	719-520-3474
Corbett's (Continental) 817 W Colorado Ave	Colorado Springs	CO	80905	719-471-0004
County Line Steakhouse & Grill (Barbecue) 3350 N Chestnut St	Colorado Springs	CO	80907	719-578-1940
Craftwood Inn (Steak/Seafood) 404 El Paso Blvd	Colorado Springs	CO	80829	719-685-9000
Edelweiss (German) 34 E Ramona Ave	Colorado Springs	CO	80906	719-633-2220
El Tesoro Restaurant (Southwest) 10 N Sierra Madre St	Colorado Springs	CO	80903	719-471-0106
Fargo's Pizza Co (Italian) 2910 E Platte Ave	Colorado Springs	CO	80909	719-473-5540
Flying W Ranch (American) 3330 Chuckwagon Rd	Colorado Springs	CO	80919	719-634-5311
Giuseppe's Old Depot Restaurant (Italian) 10 S Sierra Madre St	Colorado Springs	CO	80903	719-635-3111
Web: www.giuseppes-depot.com/				
Hatch Cover (Steak/Seafood) 252 E Cheyenne Mountain Blvd	Colorado Springs	CO	80906	719-576-5223
Henri's Mexican Food (Mexican) 2427 W Colorado Ave	Colorado Springs	CO	80904	719-634-9031
Howard's Pit BBQ (Barbecue) 114 S Sierra Madre St	Colorado Springs	CO	80903	719-473-7427
Hungry Farmer Restaurant (Homestyle) 575 Garden of the Gods Rd	Colorado Springs	CO	80907	719-598-7622
India Garden Restaurant (Indian) 5644 N Academy Blvd	Colorado Springs	CO	80918	719-535-9196
Jose Muldoons (Mexican) 222 N Tejon St	Colorado Springs	CO	80903	719-636-2311
Judge Baldwin's Brewing Co (American) 4 S Cascade Ave	Colorado Springs	CO	80903	719-473-5600
La Petite Maison (French) 1015 W Colorado Ave	Colorado Springs	CO	80904	719-632-4887
Luigi's (Italian) 947 S Tejon St	Colorado Springs	CO	80903	719-632-0700
Mason Jar (American) 2925 W Colorado Ave	Colorado Springs	CO	80904	719-632-4820
McKenzie's Chop House (American) 128 S Tejon St	Colorado Springs	CO	80903	719-633-3230
Meadow Muffins (American) 2432 W Colorado Ave	Colorado Springs	CO	80904	719-633-0583
Mission Bell Inn (Mexican) 178 Crystal Park Rd	Manitou Springs	CO	80829	719-685-9983
Nemeth's El Tejon (Mexican) 1005 S Tejon St	Colorado Springs	CO	80903	719-471-0240
Old Chicago (Italian) 118 N Tejon St	Colorado Springs	CO	80903	719-634-8812
Olive Branch (Natural/Health) 23 S Tejon St	Colorado Springs	CO	80903	719-475-1199
Penrose Room (Continental) 1 Lake Ave	Colorado Springs	CO	80906	719-634-7711
Phantom Canyon Brewing Co (American) 2 E Pikes Peak Ave	Colorado Springs	CO	80904	719-635-2800
Ritz Grill (Continental) 15 S Tejon St	Colorado Springs	CO	80903	719-635-8484
Steaksmith Restaurant (Steak/Seafood) 3802 Maizeland Rd	Colorado Springs	CO	80909	719-596-9300
Stuart Anderson's Black Angus Restaurant (American) 3330 N Academy Blvd	Colorado Springs	CO	80917	719-574-7500
Uwes (German) 31 N Iowa Ave	Colorado Springs	CO	80909	719-475-1611
Winery Restaurant at Pikes Peak Vineyards (Steak/Seafood) 3901 Janitell Rd	Colorado Springs	CO	80906	719-538-8848

— Goods and Services —

SHOPPING

Name / Address	City	State	ZIP	Phone	Fax
Castle Rock Factory Shops 5050 Factory Shop Blvd.	Castle Rock	CO	80104	303-688-4494	688-2344
Chapel Hills Mall 1710 Briargate Blvd.	Colorado Springs	CO	80920	719-594-0111	594-6439
Citadel Mall 750 Citadel Dr E.	Colorado Springs	CO	80909	719-591-2900	597-4839
Downtown Colorado Springs Shops	Colorado Springs	CO	80901	719-632-0553	
Historical Old Colorado City W Colorado Ave betw 24th & 28th Sts.	Colorado Springs	CO	80934	719-577-4112	
Nevada Avenue Antiques 405 S Nevada Ave.	Colorado Springs	CO	80903	719-473-3351	

BANKS

Name / Address	City	State	ZIP	Phone	Fax
Bank of the Rockies NA 4328 Edison Ave.	Colorado Springs	CO	80915	719-574-8060	574-8075
Bank One Colorado Springs NA 30 E Pikes Peak Ave	Colorado Springs	CO	80903	719-227-6405	227-6420
Cheyenne Mountain Bank 1580 E Cheyenne Mountain Blvd.	Colorado Springs	CO	80906	719-579-9150	576-4534
Colorado Springs National Bank 3100 N Nevada Ave.	Colorado Springs	CO	80907	719-473-2000	473-2025
Norwest Bank Colorado NA PO Box 400	Colorado Springs	CO	80901	719-590-7740	577-5376

Colorado Springs (Cont'd)

BUSINESS SERVICES

	Phone
1 800 Courier	719-594-0043
Add Staff Inc	719-528-8888
Adecco Employment Personnel Services	719-532-9000
Airborne Express	800-247-2676
BAX Global	800-225-5229
DHL Worldwide Express	719-630-7722
Federal Express	800-238-5355
Interim Personnel Services	719-636-1606
Kelly Services	719-528-5811
Kinko's	719-633-6683
Mail Boxes Etc	800-789-4623
Manpower Temporary Services	719-633-7300
Olsten Staffing Services	719-528-5353
Post Office	800-275-8777
UPS	800-742-5877

— Media —

PUBLICATIONS

				Phone	Fax
Gazette The‡ PO Box 1779	Colorado Springs	CO	80901	719-632-5511	636-0202
Web: www.gazette.com ■ *E-mail:* gtnews@usa.net					

‡*Daily newspapers*

TELEVISION

				Phone	Fax
KKTV-TV Ch 11 (CBS) 3100 N Nevada Ave.	Colorado Springs	CO	80907	719-634-2844	634-3741
Web: kktv.cbsnow.com					
KOAA-TV Ch 5 & 30 (NBC) 2200 7th Ave.	Pueblo	CO	81003	719-544-5781	543-5052
Web: www.koaa.com ■ *E-mail:* news@koaa.com					
KRDO-TV Ch 13 (ABC) 399 S 8th St	Colorado Springs	CO	80905	719-632-1515	475-0815
KTSC-TV Ch 8 (PBS) 2200 Bonforte Blvd	Pueblo	CO	81001	719-543-8800	549-2208
KXRM-TV Ch 21 (Fox) 560 Wooten Rd	Colorado Springs	CO	80915	719-596-2100	591-4180
Web: www.kxrm.com					

RADIO

				Phone	Fax
KCMN-AM 1530 kHz (Nost) 5050 Edison Ave Suite 218	Colorado Springs	CO	80915	719-570-1530	570-1007
KEPC-FM 89.7 MHz (AAA) 5675 S Academy Blvd	Colorado Springs	CO	80906	719-540-7490	540-7487
KILO-FM 94.3 MHz (Rock) 1805 E Cheyenne Rd	Colorado Springs	CO	80906	719-634-4896	634-5837
Web: www.kilo943.com					
KKCS-AM 1460 kHz (N/T) 5145 Centennial Blvd Suite 200	Colorado Springs	CO	80919	719-594-9000	594-9006
KKLI-FM 106.3 MHz (AC) 6805 Corporate Dr Suite 130	Colorado Springs	CO	80919	719-593-2700	593-2727
Web: kkli.com ■ *E-mail:* comments@kkli.com					
KRCC-FM 91.5 MHz (NPR) 912 N Weber St	Colorado Springs	CO	80903	719-473-4801	473-7863
Web: www.krcc.org ■ *E-mail:* krcc@cc.colorado.edu					
KRDO-AM 1240 kHz (Sports) 3 S 7th St	Colorado Springs	CO	80905	719-632-1515	635-8455
KRDO-FM 95.1 MHz (AC) 3 S 7th St	Colorado Springs	CO	80905	719-632-1515	635-8455
KSKX-FM 105.5 MHz (NAC) 3 S 7th St	Colorado Springs	CO	80905	719-632-1515	635-8455
KTLF-FM 90.5 MHz (Rel) 1665 Briargate Blvd Suite 100	Colorado Springs	CO	80920	719-593-0600	593-2399
KTWK-AM 740 kHz (Nost) 2864 S Circle Dr Suite 150	Colorado Springs	CO	80906	719-540-9200	527-9253
KVOR-AM 1300 kHz (N/T) 2864 S Circle Dr Suite 150	Colorado Springs	CO	80906	719-540-9200	527-9253

— Colleges/Universities —

				Phone	Fax
Beth-El College of Nursing 1420 Austin Bluffs Pkwy	Colorado Springs	CO	80933	719-262-4422	262-4416
Web: www.uccs.edu/~bethel ■ *E-mail:* admrec@mail.uccs.edu					
Blair College 828 Wooten Rd.	Colorado Springs	CO	80915	719-574-1082	574-4493
Web: www.cci.edu/rci/520ColoradoSprings/f-520.htm					
Colorado Baptist College 3615 Vickers Dr	Colorado Springs	CO	80918	719-593-7887	593-1798
Colorado College 14 E Cache La Poudre St.	Colorado Springs	CO	80903	719-389-6000	389-6816
TF Admissions: 800-542-7214 ■ *Web:* www.cc.colorado.edu/External.asp					
Colorado Technical College 4435 N Chestnut St.	Colorado Springs	CO	80907	719-598-0200	598-3740
Web: www.colotechu.edu ■ *E-mail:* admissions@cos.colotechu.edu					
National American University Colorado Springs Campus 2577 N Chelton Rd.	Colorado Springs	CO	80909	719-471-4205	471-4751
TF: 888-471-4781 ■ *Web:* www.nationalcollege.edu/campussprings.html					
Pikes Peak Community College 5675 S Academy Blvd	Colorado Springs	CO	80906	719-576-7711	540-7092
TF: 800-456-6847 ■ *Web:* www.ppcc.cccoes.edu ■ *E-mail:* cover@ppcc.colorado.edu					
University of Colorado Colorado Springs PO Box 7150	Colorado Springs	CO	80933	719-262-3000	262-3116
TF: 800-990-8227 ■ *Web:* www.uccs.edu ■ *E-mail:* goldmine@uccs.edu					
US Air Force Academy 2304 Cadet Dr Suite 200	USAF Academy	CO	80840	719-333-1110	333-3012
TF Admissions: 800-443-9266 ■ *Web:* www.usafa.af.mil					

— Hospitals —

				Phone	Fax
Memorial Hospital 1400 E Boulder St.	Colorado Springs	CO	80909	719-365-5000	365-6884
Penrose-Saint Francis Healthcare 2215 N Cascade Ave	Colorado Springs	CO	80907	719-776-5000	776-2770

— Attractions —

				Phone	Fax
American Numismatic Assn Money Museum 818 N Cascade Ave	Colorado Springs	CO	80903	719-632-2646	634-4085
TF: 800-367-9723 ■ *Web:* www.money.org/moneymus.html ■ *E-mail:* anamus@money.org					
Bear Creek Nature Center 245 Bear Creek Rd	Colorado Springs	CO	80906	719-520-6387	520-6388
Bent's Old Fort National Historic Site 35110 Hwy 194 E	La Junta	CO	81050	719-383-5010	383-5031
Web: www.nps.gov/beol/					
Black Forest Observatory 12815 Porcupine Ln	Colorado Springs	CO	80908	719-495-3828	
Buckskin Joe Park & Railway 1193 County Rd 3A	Canon City	CO	81212	719-275-5485	275-6270
Carriage House Museum 16 Lake Cir	Colorado Springs	CO	80906	719-634-7711	
Cave of the Winds Hwy 24 W	Manitou Springs	CO	80829	719-685-5444	685-1712
Cheyenne Mountain Zoological Park 4250 Cheyenne Mountain Zoo Rd	Colorado Springs	CO	80906	719-633-9925	633-2254
Web: www.cmzoo.org					
Children's Museum of Colorado Springs 750 Citadel Dr E	Colorado Springs	CO	80909	719-574-0077	574-0077
Web: www.iex.net/cm ■ *E-mail:* museum@usa.net					
Colorado Music Hall 2475 E Pikes Peak Ave	Colorado Springs	CO	80909	719-447-9797	447-1893
Colorado Springs Choral Society PO Box 2304	Colorado Springs	CO	80901	719-634-3737	473-0077
Web: www.cschorale.org					
Colorado Springs Dance Theatre 7 E Bijou St Suite 209	Colorado Springs	CO	80903	719-630-7434	442-2095
Web: www.csdance.org					
Colorado Springs Fine Arts Center 30 W Dale St	Colorado Springs	CO	80903	719-634-5581	634-0570
Web: www.rmi.net/home/tour/colorado/cities/cosprgs/csfac.shtml					
Colorado Springs Pioneers Museum 215 S Tejon St	Colorado Springs	CO	80903	719-578-6650	578-6718
Colorado Springs Symphony Orchestra 619 N Cascade Ave.	Colorado Springs	CO	80903	719-633-4611	633-6699
Web: www.cssymphony.org ■ *E-mail:* csso@access.usa.net					
Curecanti National Recreation Area 102 Elk Creek	Gunnison	CO	81230	970-641-2337	641-3127
Web: www.nps.gov/cure/					
Florissant Fossil Beds National Monument PO Box 185	Florissant	CO	80816	719-748-3253	748-3164
Web: www.nps.gov/flfo/					
Garden of the Gods Park 3190 N 30th St.	Colorado Springs	CO	80904	719-385-5940	578-6934
Web: www.pikes-peak.com/Garden/					
Ghost Town Museum 400 S 21st St	Colorado Springs	CO	80904	719-634-0696	634-2435
Historical Old Colorado City W Colorado Ave betw 24th & 28th Sts.	Colorado Springs	CO	80934	719-577-4112	

Colorado Springs — Attractions (Cont'd)

				Phone	Fax
Magic Town 2418 W Colorado Ave	Colorado Springs	CO	80904	719-471-9391	
Manitou Cliff Dwellings Museum Hwy 24 W *Web:* www.cliffdwellingsmuseum.com ■ *E-mail:* cd@manitousprings.zzn.com	Manitou Springs	CO	80829	719-685-5242	685-1562
May Natural History Museum & Museum of Space Exploration 710 Rock Creek Canyon Rd *TF:* 800-666-3841 ■ *Web:* www.maymuseum-camp-rvpark.com ■ *E-mail:* maymuseum@yahoo.com	Colorado Springs	CO	80926	719-576-0450	576-3644
McAllister House Museum 423 N Cascade Ave	Colorado Springs	CO	80903	719-635-7925	
Miramont Castle Museum 9 Capitol Hill Ave	Manitou Springs	CO	80829	719-685-1011	685-1985
Pike National Forest 601 S Weber St	Colorado Springs	CO	80903	719-636-1602	477-4233
Pikes Peak Auto Hill Climb Museum 135 Manitou Ave *Web:* www.ppihc.com	Manitou Springs	CO	80829	719-685-4400	685-5885
Pikes Peak Cog Railway 515 Ruxton Ave *Web:* www.cograilway.com/ ■ *E-mail:* cogtrain@mail.usa.net	Manitou Springs	CO	80829	719-685-5401	685-9033
Pikes Peak Highway	Cascade	CO	80809	719-684-9383	
Pro Rodeo Hall of Fame & Museum of the American Cowboy 101 Pro Rodeo Dr *Web:* electricstores.com/Rodeo/	Colorado Springs	CO	80919	719-528-4764	548-4876
Rock Ledge Ranch N 30th St & Gateway Rd	Colorado Springs	CO	80904	719-578-6777	
Rocky Mountain Motorcycle Museum & Hall of Fame 302 E Arvada St	Colorado Springs	CO	80906	719-633-6329	633-6329
Seven Falls PO Box 118	Colorado Springs	CO	80901	719-632-0741	632-0781
Smokebrush Center for Arts & Theater 235 S Nevada Ave *Web:* www.smokebrush.org ■ *E-mail:* info@smokebrush.org	Colorado Springs	CO	80903	719-444-0884	471-7351
Starsmore Discovery Center 2120 S Cheyenne Canyon Rd	Colorado Springs	CO	80906	719-578-6147	578-6149
University of Colorado Gallery of Contemporary Art 1420 Austin Bluffs Pkwy	Colorado Springs	CO	80918	719-262-3567	262-3183
US Olympic Center Complex 1 Olympic Plaza	Colorado Springs	CO	80909	719-578-4500	578-4677
US Olympic Hall of Fame 1750 E Boulder St *Web:* www.usoc.org	Colorado Springs	CO	80909	719-578-4618	578-4728
Western Museum of Mining & Industry 1025 N Gate Rd	Colorado Springs	CO	80921	719-488-0880	488-9261
World Figure Skating Museum & Hall of Fame 20 1st St *Web:* www.usfsa.org	Colorado Springs	CO	80906	719-635-5200	635-9548

SPORTS TEAMS & FACILITIES

				Phone	Fax
Colorado Gold Kings (hockey) 3185 Venetucci Blvd *Web:* www.coloradogoldkings.com	Colorado Springs	CO	80906	719-579-9000	579-7609
Colorado Springs Sky Sox (baseball) 4385 Tutt Blvd Sky Sox Stadium *Web:* www.skysox.com/	Colorado Springs	CO	80922	719-597-3000	597-2491
Colorado Springs Stampede (soccer) 31 E Platte Ave Suite 206 *E-mail:* stampedecs@aol.com	Colorado Springs	CO	80903	719-444-8464	633-2722
Pikes Peak International Raceway 16650 Midway Ranch *TF:* 888-306-7223 ■ *Web:* www.ppir.com/	Fountain	CO	80817	719-382-7223	382-9180
Rocky Mountain Greyhound Park 3701 N Nevada Ave *Web:* www.rmgp.com	Colorado Springs	CO	80907	719-632-1391	632-1792
Sky Sox Stadium 4385 Tutt Blvd *Web:* www.skysox.com/boxoffice/index.shtml	Colorado Springs	CO	80922	719-597-3000	597-2491

— Events —

	Phone
Balloon Classic (early September)	719-471-4833
Carnivale & Gumbo Cook-off (early February)	719-685-5089
Cavalcade of Music (early May)	719-520-7469
Cinco de Mayo Celebration (early May)	719-578-6120
Clayfest & Mud Ball (mid-June)	719-685-5795
Colorado Championship Chili Cook-off (mid-July)	719-593-2700
Colorado Springs Opera Festival (late July-early August)	719-520-7469
Donkey Derby Days (late June)	719-689-3315
El Paso County Fair (late July)	719-575-8690
Fabulous Fourth (July 4)	719-633-4611
Family Day & Antique Car Show (late September)	719-488-0880
Farmers' Market (July-September)	719-598-4215
First Night Pikes Peak (December 31)	719-471-9790
Food-A-Rama (early February)	719-576-4228
Gallery of Trees & Lights (December)	719-635-7506
Great Fruitcake Toss (early January)	719-685-5089
Great Pikes Peak Cowboy Poetry Gathering (early October)	719-531-6333
In Their Honor Parade & Air Show (early November)	719-635-8803
Kwanzaa Cultural Celebration (late December-early January)	719-473-6566
Labor Day Arts & Crafts Festival (late August-early September)	719-685-1008
Lone Feather Indian Council Pow Wow (mid-July)	719-495-0798
Madrigal Christmas Celebration (late November-mid-December)	719-594-2237
Mountain Arts Festival (early August)	719-687-7956
National Little Britches Finals Rodeo (late July)	719-520-6711
Oktoberfest (early October)	719-635-7506
Pikes Peak Auto Hill Climb (early July)	719-685-4400
Pikes Peak Bluegrass Festival (mid-October)	719-447-9797
Pikes Peak Highland Games & Celtic Festival (mid-July)	719-481-4597
Pikes Peak Invitational Soccer Tournament (late June-early July)	719-590-9977
Pikes Peak or Bust Rodeo (early August)	719-635-3548
Race to the Clouds (July 4)	719-685-4400
Saint Patrick's Day Parade (mid-March)	719-635-8803
Territory Days (late May)	719-475-0955
Ute Pass Stampede (mid-July)	719-687-6606
Zebulon! A Festival of Arts (mid-June-mid-July)	719-475-2465

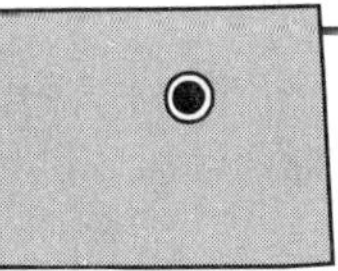

Denver

Denver, the Mile High City, is located 340 miles from the exact center of the continental United States. At the heart of the city is the 16th Street Mall, a tree-lined pedestrian promenade that runs through the center of downtown Denver. The Lower Downtown District (LoDo) features turn-of-the-century streetscaping, with art galleries, antique shops, unique restaurants, and jazz and dance clubs. Denver's City Park is home to the Denver Zoo, which has thousands of exotic animals in a natural setting, and the Denver Museum of Natural History. The Denver Art Museum covers seven floors and has some 40,000 works, including an extensive American Indian collection. Free tours are available of the U.S. Mint in Denver and of the Colorado State Capitol Building, which is modeled after the United States Capitol in Washington, DC, and features a panoramic view of the Rocky Mountains. (The Rockies are located just 12 miles west of the city.) Two other area attractions that feature spectacular views are Buffalo Bill's Grave at the top of Lookout Mountain and Red Rocks Amphitheatre, which is flanked by rugged sandstone rock formations that provide excellent acoustics.

Population	499,055	**Longitude**	104-83-54 W
Area (Land)	153.3 sq mi	**County**	Denver
Area (Water)	1.6 sq mi	**Time Zone**	MST
Elevation	5280 ft	**Area Code/s**	303, 720
Latitude	39-66-77 N		

— Average Temperatures and Precipitation —

TEMPERATURES

	Jan	Feb	Mar	Apr	May	Jun	Jul	Aug	Sep	Oct	Nov	Dec
High	43	47	52	62	71	81	88	86	77	66	53	45
Low	16	20	26	35	44	52	59	57	48	36	25	17

Denver (Cont'd)

PRECIPITATION

	Jan	Feb	Mar	Apr	May	Jun	Jul	Aug	Sep	Oct	Nov	Dec
Inches	0.5	0.6	1.3	1.7	2.4	1.8	1.9	1.5	1.2	1.0	0.9	0.6

— Important Phone Numbers —

	Phone		Phone
AAA	303-753-8800	**Poison Control Center**	303-739-1123
American Express Travel	303-383-5050	**Road Conditions**	303-639-1234
Dental Referral	800-917-6453	**Time/Temp**	303-443-1910
Emergency	911	**Travelers Aid**	303-342-0400
HotelDocs	800-468-3537	**Weather**	303-871-1492
Medical Referral	303-866-8000		

— Information Sources —

Phone *Fax*

Better Business Bureau Serving the Denver-Boulder Metro Area 1780 S Bellaire St Suite 700 ... Denver CO 80222 303-758-2100 758-8321
Web: www.denver.bbb.org ■ *E-mail:* info@denver.bbb.org

Colorado Convention Center 700 14th St. ... Denver CO 80202 303-228-8000 228-8104
Web: denverconvention.com ■ *E-mail:* Info@DenverConvention.com

Denver City Hall 1437 Bannock St ... Denver CO 80202 303-640-5555
Web: www.denvergov.org

Denver County 1437 Bannock St. ... Denver CO 80202 303-640-2628 640-3628

Denver Economic Development & International Trade Office 216 16th St Suite 1000 ... Denver CO 80202 303-640-7100 640-7059
Web: www.denvergov.org/dephome.asp?depid=24
■ *E-mail:* moedit@csi.com

Denver Mayor 1437 Bannock St Rm 350 ... Denver CO 80202 303-640-2721 640-2329
Web: www.denvergov.org/mayor ■ *E-mail:* mayorden@ci.denver.co.us

Denver Metro Convention & Visitors Bureau 1555 California St Suite 300 ... Denver CO 80202 303-892-1112 892-1636
TF: 800-645-3446 ■ *Web:* www.denver.org

Denver Public Library 10 W 14th Ave Pkwy ... Denver CO 80204 303-640-6200 640-6143
Web: www.denver.lib.co.us

Greater Denver Chamber of Commerce 1445 Market St. ... Denver CO 80202 303-534-8500 534-3200
Web: www.den-chamber.org

On-Line Resources

4Denver.com	www.4denver.com
About.com Guide to Denver	denver.about.com/local/mountainus/denver
Anthill City Guide Denver	www.anthill.com/city.asp?city=denver
Area Guide Denver	denver.areaguides.net
Boulevards Denver	www.denver.com
Bradmans.com Denver	www.bradmans.com/scripts/display_city.cgi?city=235
City Knowledge Denver	www.cityknowledge.com/co_denver.htm
CitySearch Denver	denver.citysearch.com
Denver City Pages	denver.thelinks.com/
Denver CityLink	www.usacitylink.com/citylink/denver
Denver Graphic City Guide	www.futurecast.com/gcg/denver.htm
Denver Online	www.denveronline.com/
Denver.sidewalk	denver.sidewalk.citysearch.com
DigitalCity Denver	home.digitalcity.com/denver
Do Denver	www.dodenver.com
Downtown Denver Guide	www.downtown-denver.com/
E.Central Big City Small Planet Denver Guide	www.ecentral.com/
Excite.com Denver City Guide	www.excite.com/travel/countries/united_states/colorado/denver
HotelGuide Denver	hotelguide.net/denver/
Info Denver	infodenver.denver.co.us/
Insiders' Guide to Greater Denver	www.insiders.com/denver/
MetroVille Denver	denver.metroville.com
Mile High City	milehighcity.com/
NITC Travelbase City Guide Denver	www.travelbase.com/auto/guides/denver-area-co.html
Open World City Guides Denver	www.worldexecutive.com/cityguides/denver/
Rough Guide Travel Denver	travel.roughguides.com/content/1046/
Virtual Voyages Denver	www.virtualvoyages.com/usa/co/denver/denver.sht
Westword	www.westword.com

— Transportation Services —

AIRPORTS

Phone

■ **Denver International Airport (DEN)**
25 miles NE of downtown (approx 45 minutes) ... 303-342-2000
Web: infodenver.denver.co.us/~aviation/ ■ *E-mail:* aviation@infodenver.denver.co.us

Airport Transportation

	Phone
Dashabout Roadrunner $10 fare to downtown	800-720-3274
Denver Express Shuttle $15 fare to downtown	303-342-3424
North Denver Airport Shuttle $15 fare to downtown	303-399-3737
RTD Airport Motorcoach $6 fare to downtown	303-299-6000
RTD Bus $8 fare to downtown	303-299-6000
SuperShuttle $17 fare to downtown	303-370-1300

Commercial Airlines

	Phone		Phone
America West	800-235-9292	**Midwest Express**	800-452-2022
American	800-433-7300	**Northwest**	800-225-2525
Continental	800-525-0280	**Sun Country**	800-359-5786
Continental Express	800-525-0280	**TWA**	800-221-2000
Delta	800-221-1212	**United**	800-241-6522
Frontier	800-432-1359	**United Express**	800-241-6522
Martinair Holland	800-366-4655	**US Airways**	800-428-4322
Mesa	800-637-2247	**Vanguard**	800-826-4827
Mexicana	800-531-7923		

Charter Airlines

	Phone		Phone
Corporate Air Charter	406-248-1541	**Superior Aviation**	800-882-7751
Mayo Aviation Inc	303-790-9777		

CAR RENTALS

	Phone		Phone
Advantage	303-261-8585	**Enterprise**	303-342-7350
Alamo	303-342-7373	**Hertz**	800-654-3131
Avis	303-342-5500	**National**	303-342-0717
Budget	303-342-9001	**Payless**	303-342-9444
Dollar	303-342-9099	**Thrifty**	303-342-9086

LIMO/TAXI

	Phone		Phone
Admiral Limousines	303-296-2003	**Limousine Express**	303-299-9099
American Cab	303-321-5555	**Metro Taxi**	303-333-3333
Carey Limousine	303-693-0732	**Presidential Limousine**	303-286-1114
Colorado Limousine	303-832-7155	**Yellow Cab**	303-777-7777
Denver King Limousine Services	303-766-0400	**Zone Cab**	303-444-8888

MASS TRANSIT

	Phone
RTD Bus $1.25 Base fare	303-299-9000

RAIL/BUS

				Phone
Amtrak Station 1701 Wynkoop St.	Denver	CO	80202	800-872-7245
Greyhound/Trailways Bus Station 1055 19th St.	Denver	CO	80202	800-231-2222

— Accommodations —

HOTEL RESERVATION SERVICES

Phone *Fax*

All-Colorado Accommodations ... 877-365-6926 522-0894*
**Fax Area Code:* 719 ■ *Web:* www.rockad.com/aca/
■ *E-mail:* mountain@frii.com

Colorado Reservations ... 800-777-6880

Hotel Reservations Network Inc ... 214-361-7311 361-7299
TF Sales: 800-964-6835 ■ *Web:* www.hoteldiscount.com

Quikbook ... 212-532-1660 532-1556
TF: 800-789-9887 ■ *Web:* www.quikbook.com

Denver (Cont'd)

HOTELS, MOTELS, RESORTS

Phone Fax

Adam's Mark Hotel 1550 Court Pl . . . . .Denver CO 80202 303-893-3333 626-2542
TF: 800-444-2326 ■ *Web:* www.adamsmark.com/denvr.htm
Best Western Central Hotel 200 W 48th Ave . . . . .Denver CO 80216 303-296-4000 296-4000
TF: 800-528-1234
Best Western Executive Hotel 4411 Peoria St . . . .Denver CO 80239 303-373-5730 375-1157
TF: 800-848-4060
Best Western Landmark Inn
455 S Colorado Blvd .Denver CO 80246 303-388-5561 388-0059
TF: 800-528-1234
Brooks Tower 1020 15th St . . . . .Denver CO 80202 303-629-7200 825-6941
Brown Palace Hotel 321 17th St. . . . . .Denver CO 80202 303-297-3111 312-5900
TF: 800-321-2599 ■ *Web:* www.brownpalace.com
■ *E-mail:* marketing@brownpalace.com
Burnsley Hotel 1000 Grant St. . . . . .Denver CO 80203 303-830-1000 830-7676
TF: 800-231-3915
Cambridge Hotel 1560 Sherman St. . . . . .Denver CO 80203 303-831-1252 831-4724
TF: 800-877-1252
Castle Marne 1572 Race St . . . . .Denver CO 80206 303-331-0621 331-0623
Web: www.castlemarne.com ■ *E-mail:* themarne@ix.netcom.com
Comfort Inn Downtown 401 17th St . . . . .Denver CO 80202 303-296-0400 297-0774
TF: 800-221-2222
Courtyard by Marriott Airport 6901 Tower Rd . . . .Denver CO 80249 303-371-0300 371-2480
TF: 800-321-2211 ■ *Web:* courtyard.com/DENCA
Denver Hilton South
7801 E Orchard Rd. . . . . Greenwood Village CO 80111 303-779-6161 689-7080
TF: 800-327-2242
Denver Inn 4765 Federal Blvd. . . . . .Denver CO 80211 303-433-8441 458-0863
Denver Marriott City Center
1701 California St . . . . .Denver CO 80202 303-297-1300 298-7474
TF: 800-228-9290 ■ *Web:* marriotthotels.com/DENDT/
Denver Marriott Southeast
6363 E Hampden Ave . . . . .Denver CO 80222 303-758-7000 691-3418
TF: 800-228-9290
Denver West Marriott Hotel
1717 Denver West Blvd . . . . .Golden CO 80401 303-279-9100 271-0205
TF: 800-228-9290
Doubletree Hotel 3203 Quebec St. . . . . .Denver CO 80207 303-321-3333 329-5233
TF: 800-222-8733
■ *Web:* www.doubletreehotels.com/DoubleT/Hotel161/164/164Main.htm
Drury Inn Airport 4400 Peoria St. . . . . .Denver CO 80239 303-373-1983 373-1983
TF: 800-325-8300
■ *Web:* www.druryinns.com/room/reservation/denver1.htm
Embassy Suites Denver Airport
4444 N Havana St. . . . . .Denver CO 80239 303-375-0400 371-4634
TF: 800-345-0087 ■ *Web:* www.embassysuitesdia.com/
Embassy Suites Downtown 1881 Curtis St. . . . . . .Denver CO 80202 303-297-8888 298-1103
TF: 800-733-3366 ■ *Web:* www.esdendt.com/index.html
Embassy Suites Southeast
7525 E Hampden Ave . . . . .Denver CO 80231 303-696-6644 337-6202
TF: 800-362-2779
Executive Tower Inn 1405 Curtis St . . . . .Denver CO 80202 303-571-0300 825-4301
TF: 800-525-6651
Fairfield Inn Airport 6851 Tower Rd . . . . .Denver CO 80249 303-576-9640 574-9638
TF: 800-228-2800 ■ *Web:* fairfieldinn.com/DENFA
Four Points Hotel by Sheraton
137 Union Blvd. . . . . .Lakewood CO 80228 303-969-9900 989-9847
TF: 800-325-3535
Four Points Hotel Sheridan 3535 Quebec St . . . . .Denver CO 80207 303-333-7711 322-2262
TF: 800-325-3535
Hampton Inn North East 4685 Quebec St. . . . . . . .Denver CO 80216 303-388-8100 333-7710
TF: 800-426-7866
Holiday Chalet 1820 E Colfax Ave. . . . . .Denver CO 80218 303-321-9975 377-6556
TF: 800-626-4497
Holiday Inn Denver Downtown
1450 Glenarm Pl. . . . . .Denver CO 80202 303-573-1450 572-1113
TF: 800-423-5128
Holiday Inn Denver International Airport
15500 E 40th Ave . . . . .Denver CO 80239 303-371-9494 371-9528
TF: 800-465-4329
Holiday Inn North 4849 Bannock St . . . . .Denver CO 80216 303-292-9500 295-3521
TF: 800-638-8941 ■ *Web:* www.holidayinndenver.com
■ *E-mail:* holiday-north@travelbase.com
Holtze Executive Place 818 17th St . . . . .Denver CO 80202 303-607-9000 607-0101
TF: 888-446-5893 ■ *Web:* www.holtze.com
Hyatt Regency 1750 Welton St. . . . . .Denver CO 80202 303-295-1234 292-2472
TF: 800-233-1234
■ *Web:* www.hyatt.com/usa/denver/hotels/hotel_denrd.html
Hyatt Regency Tech Center 7800 E Tufts Ave . . . .Denver CO 80237 303-779-1234 850-7164
TF: 800-233-1234
■ *Web:* www.hyatt.com/usa/denver/hotels/hotel_denve.html

Phone Fax

Inverness Hotel & Golf Club
200 Inverness Dr W . . . . .Englewood CO 80112 303-799-5800 799-5874
TF: 800-346-4891 ■ *Web:* www.invernesshotel.com
■ *E-mail:* staff@invernesshotel.com
La Quinta Inn Airport 3975 Peoria Way. . . . . .Denver CO 80239 303-371-5640 371-7015
TF: 800-531-5900
La Quinta Inn South 1975 S Colorado Blvd . . . . . .Denver CO 80222 303-758-8886 756-2711
TF: 800-687-6667
Loews Giorgio Hotel 4150 E Mississippi Ave . . . . .Denver CO 80246 303-782-9300 758-6542
TF: 800-235-9172 ■ *Web:* www.loewshotels.com/giorgiohome.html
■ *E-mail:* loewsgiorgio@loewshotels.com
Marriott Denver Tech Center
4900 S Syracuse St. .Denver CO 80237 303-779-1100 740-2523
TF: 800-228-9290 ■ *Web:* marriotthotels.com/DENTC
Omni Interlocken Resort
500 Interlocken Blvd . . . . .Broomfield CO 80021 303-438-6600 464-3236
TF: 800-843-6664
Oxford Hotel 1600 17th St. . . . . .Denver CO 80202 303-628-5400 628-5413
TF: 800-228-5838 ■ *Web:* www.theoxfordhotel.com
Quality Inn 6300 Hampden Ave. . . . . .Denver CO 80222 303-758-2211 753-0156
TF: 800-647-1986
Quality Inn Suites 4590 Quebec St . . . . .Denver CO 80216 303-320-0260 320-7595
TF: 800-228-5151
Ramada Inn Denver Airport 3737 Quebec St . . . . .Denver CO 80207 303-388-6161 388-0426
TF: 800-999-8338
Ramada Inn Downtown 1150 E Colfax Ave. . . . . . .Denver CO 80218 303-831-7700 894-9193
TF: 800-524-8603
Ramada Inn Mile High Stadium
1975 Bryant St. . . . . .Denver CO 80204 303-433-8331 455-7061
TF: 800-272-6232
Ramada Limited Denver North
110 W 104th Ave . . . . .Northglenn CO 80234 303-451-1234 451-5189
TF: 800-272-6232
Regency Hotel 3900 Elati St. . . . . .Denver CO 80216 303-458-0808 477-4255
Renaissance Denver Hotel 3801 Quebec St. . . . . .Denver CO 80207 303-399-7500 321-1966
TF: 800-468-3571
Residence Inn by Marriott Denver Downtown
2777 Zuni St . . . . .Denver CO 80211 303-458-5318 458-5318
TF: 800-331-3131 ■ *Web:* residenceinn.com/DENTW
Stapleton Plaza Hotel 3333 Quebec St . . . . .Denver CO 80207 303-321-3500 322-7343
TF: 800-950-6070 ■ *Web:* www.stapletonplaza.com/
Travelodge 6090 Smith Rd. . . . . .Denver CO 80216 303-388-4051 388-8088
TF: 877-336-8372
Warwick Hotel 1776 Grant St. . . . . .Denver CO 80203 303-861-2000 839-8504
TF: 800-525-2888 ■ *Web:* www.warwickhotel.com
Westin Hotel Tabor Center 1672 Lawrence St . . . .Denver CO 80202 303-572-9100 572-7288
TF: 800-228-3000
Wyndham Garden Hotel 1475 S Colorado Blvd. . . .Denver CO 80222 303-757-8797 758-0704
TF: 800-996-3426

— Restaurants —

Phone

Aubergine Cafe (French) 225 E 7th Ave . . . . .Denver CO 80203 303-832-4778
Axum (Ethiopian) 5501 E Colfax Ave. . . . . .Denver CO 80220 303-329-6139
Baby Doe's Matchless Mine (Steak/Seafood)
2520 W 23rd Ave. . . . . .Denver CO 80211 303-433-3386
Barolo Grill (Italian) 3030 E 6th Ave . . . . .Denver CO 80206 303-393-1040
Beacon Grill (Continental) 303 16th St. . . . . .Denver CO 80202 303-592-4745
Breckenridge Brewery (American) 2220 Blake St. . . . . .Denver CO 80205 303-297-3644
Brittany Hill (French) 9350 Grant St. . . . . .Denver CO 80229 303-451-5151
Broker Restaurant (American) 821 17th St . . . . .Denver CO 80202 303-292-5065
Buckhorn Exchange (Steak) 1000 Osage St. . . . . .Denver CO 80204 303-534-9505
Web: www.buckhorn.com/
Cadillac Ranch (American) 1400 Larimer Sq. . . . . .Denver CO 80202 303-820-2288
Casa Bonita (Mexican) 6715 W Colfax Ave . . . . .Denver CO 80214 303-232-5115
Champion Brewing Co (American) 1444 Larimer Sq . . . . .Denver CO 80202 303-534-5444
China Jade (Chinese) 375 S Federal Blvd . . . . .Denver CO 80219 303-935-0033
Cliff Young's (Continental) 700 E 17th Ave. . . . . .Denver CO 80203 303-831-8900
Croc's Cafe (Mexican) 1630 Market St . . . . .Denver CO 80202 303-436-1144
Denver Buffalo Co (American) 1109 Lincoln St . . . . .Denver CO 80203 303-832-0880
El Taco de Mexico (Mexican) 714 Santa Fe Dr . . . . .Denver CO 80204 303-623-3926
European Cafe (Continental) 1060 15th St . . . . .Denver CO 80202 303-825-6555
Fort The (Steak) 19192 Hwy 8. . . . . .Morrison CO 80465 303-697-4771
Web: www.thefort.com/
Gabriel's Restaurant (Italian) 5450 W Hwy 67 . . . . .Denver CO 80135 303-688-2323
Josephina's (Italian) 1433 Larimer Sq . . . . .Denver CO 80202 303-623-0166
La Loma (Mexican) 2527 W 26th Ave . . . . .Denver CO 80211 303-433-8300
Le Central (French) 112 E 8th Ave. . . . . .Denver CO 80203 303-863-8094
McCormick's Fish House & Bar (Seafood) 1659 Wazee St . . . .Denver CO 80202 303-825-1107
Mori Sushi Bar & Tokyo Cuisine (Japanese)
2019 Market St . . . . .Denver CO 80205 303-298-1864
Morton's of Chicago (Steak/Seafood) 1710 Wynkoop St. . . . . .Denver CO 80202 303-825-3353
My Brother's Bar (American) 2376 15th St. . . . . .Denver CO 80202 303-455-9991
New Saigon (Vietnamese) 630 S Federal Blvd. . . . . .Denver CO 80219 303-936-4954

Denver — Restaurants (Cont'd)

	City	State	Zip	Phone
Normandy The (French) 1515 Madison St	Denver	CO	80206	303-321-3311
Palace Arms (American) 321 17th St Brown Palace Hotel	Denver	CO	80202	303-297-3111
Papillon Cafe (French) 250 Josephine St	Denver	CO	80206	303-333-7166
Playa Azul (Mexican) 1500 Curtis St	Denver	CO	80202	303-825-4020
Sfuzzi (Italian) 3000 E 1st Ave	Denver	CO	80206	303-321-4700
Ship Tavern (Steak/Seafood) 321 17th St	Denver	CO	80202	303-297-3111
Sonoda's Sushi (Japanese) 1620 Market St	Denver	CO	80202	303-595-9500
Strings (New American) 1700 Humboldt St	Denver	CO	80281	303-831-7310
Sushi Den (Japanese) 1487 S Pearl St	Denver	CO	80210	303-777-0826
Tante Louise (French) 4900 E Colfax Ave	Denver	CO	80220	303-355-4488
Tommy Tsunami's Pacific Diner (Asian) 1432 Market St	Denver	CO	80202	303-534-5050
Tuscany (Italian) 4150 E Mississippi Ave	Denver	CO	80246	303-782-9300
Wellshire Inn (American) 3333 S Colorado Blvd	Denver	CO	80222	303-759-3333
Wolfe's Barbeque (Barbecue) 333 E Colfax Ave	Denver	CO	80203	303-831-1500
Wynkoop Brewing Co (American) 1634 18th St	Denver	CO	80202	303-297-2700

— Goods and Services —

SHOPPING

	City	State	Zip	Phone	Fax
16th Street Mall 16th St betw Broadway & Market St	Denver	CO	80202	303-534-6161	
Aurora Mall 14200 E Alameda Ave	Aurora	CO	80012	303-344-4120	364-0308
Cherry Creek Shopping Center 3000 E 1st Ave	Denver	CO	80206	303-388-3900	388-8203
Colfax on the Hill District Colfax Ave	Denver	CO	80218	303-832-2086	832-6761
Joslin's 7200 W Almeda Ave	Lakewood	CO	80226	303-922-7575	
Larimer Square 1400 Larimer Sq	Denver	CO	80202	303-534-2367	623-1041
LoDo District Lower Downtown	Denver	CO	80206	303-295-1195	
Shops at Tabor Center 1201 16th St Suite 120	Denver	CO	80202	303-572-6868	
Westminster Mall 5433 W 88th Ave	Westminster	CO	80030	303-428-5634	
Writer Square 1512 Larimer St. *Web:* www.writer-square.com ■ *E-mail:* info@writer-square.com	Denver	CO	80202	303-628-9056	534-4559

BANKS

	City	State	Zip	Phone	Fax
Bank of Denver 1534 California St	Denver	CO	80202	303-572-3600	623-0624
Bank One Colorado NA 1125 17th St **Fax:* Mktg ■ *TF:* 800-372-2651	Denver	CO	80202	303-244-3283	244-5901*
Citywide Bank of Denver 12075 E 45th Ave	Denver	CO	80239	303-365-8000	365-8001
Mountain States Bank 1635 E Colfax Ave	Denver	CO	80218	303-388-3641	329-9415
Norwest Bank Colorado NA 1740 Broadway	Denver	CO	80274	303-861-8811	863-4605
US Bank PO Box 5168 **Fax:* Hum Res ■ *TF Cust Svc:* 800-872-2657*	Denver	CO	80217	303-585-5000	585-4721*

BUSINESS SERVICES

	Phone
Concorde Express Messenger Service	303-771-7288
Corporate Express Delivery Systems	303-371-7100
DHL Worldwide Express	800-225-5345
Express Messenger Systems	303-936-0200
Federal Express	800-238-5355
Kelly Services	303-623-6262
Manpower Temporary Services	303-297-9802
Olsten Staffing Services	303-534-4357
Post Office	800-275-8777
Speedy Messenger Service	303-292-6000
UPS	800-742-5877

— Media —

PUBLICATIONS

	City	State	Zip	Phone	Fax
Denver Business Journal 1700 Broadway Suite 515 *Web:* www.amcity.com/denver ■ *E-mail:* denver@amcity.com	Denver	CO	80290	303-837-3500	837-3535
Denver Post‡ 1560 Broadway *TF:* 800-336-7678 ■ *Web:* www.denverpost.com ■ *E-mail:* letters@denverpost.com	Denver	CO	80202	303-820-1010	820-1369
Rocky Mountain News‡ 400 W Colfax Ave *Web:* www.insidedenver.com ■ *E-mail:* letters@denver-rmn.com	Denver	CO	80204	303-892-5000	892-2568

‡Daily newspapers

TELEVISION

	City	State	Zip	Phone	Fax
KBDI-TV Ch 12 (PBS) 2900 Welton St 1st Fl *Web:* www.kbdi.org	Denver	CO	80205	303-296-1212	296-6650
KCEC-TV Ch 50 (Uni) 777 Grant St Suite 110 *E-mail:* kcecnews@aol.com	Denver	CO	80203	303-832-0050	832-3410
KCNC-TV Ch 4 (CBS) 1044 Lincoln St *Web:* www.kcncnews4.com ■ *E-mail:* mailroom@kcncnews4.com	Denver	CO	80203	303-861-4444	830-6380
KDVR-TV Ch 31 (Fox) 501 Wazee St *Web:* www.fox31.com ■ *E-mail:* feedback@fox31.com	Denver	CO	80204	303-595-3131	595-8312
KMGH-TV Ch 7 (ABC) 123 Speer Blvd *Web:* www.kmgh.com ■ *E-mail:* kmgh7@csn.net	Denver	CO	80203	303-832-7777	832-0119
KPXC-TV Ch 59 (PAX) 3001 S Jamaica Ct *Web:* www.pax.net/kpxc	Aurora	CO	80014	303-751-5959	751-5993
KRMA-TV Ch 6 (PBS) 1089 Bannock St *Web:* www.krma.org ■ *E-mail:* info@krma.org	Denver	CO	80204	303-892-6666	620-5600
KSBS-TV Ch 18 (Ind) 2727 Bryant St Suite 430	Denver	CO	80211	303-477-3031	477-8287
KTVD-TV Ch 20 (UPN) 11203 E Peakview Ave	Englewood	CO	80111	303-792-2020	790-4633
KUSA-TV Ch 9 (NBC) 500 Speer Blvd *Web:* www.9news.com ■ *E-mail:* kusa@9news.com	Denver	CO	80203	303-871-9999	698-4700
KWGN-TV Ch 2 (WB) 6160 S Wabash Way *Web:* www.wb2.com	Englewood	CO	80111	303-740-2222	740-2847
KWHD-TV Ch 53 (Ind) 12999 E Jamison Cir *Web:* www.kwhd.com	Englewood	CO	80112	303-799-8853	792-5303

RADIO

	City	State	Zip	Phone	Fax
KALC-FM 105.9 MHz (AC) 1200 17th St Suite 2300 *Web:* alice106.com	Denver	CO	80202	303-572-7000	615-5393
KBPI-FM 106.7 MHz (Rock) 1380 Lawrence St Suite 1300 *Web:* www.kbpi.com	Denver	CO	80204	303-893-3699	534-7625
KCFR-FM 90.1 MHz (NPR) 2249 S Josephine St	Denver	CO	80210	303-871-9191	733-3319
KCKK-FM 104.3 MHz (Ctry) 1095 S Monaco Pkwy	Denver	CO	80224	303-321-0950	320-0708
KEZW-AM 1430 kHz (Nost) 10200 E Girard Ave Suite B130	Denver	CO	80231	303-696-1714	696-0522
KHIH-FM 95.7 MHz (NAC) 8975 E Kenyon Ave *Web:* www.khih.com	Denver	CO	80237	303-694-6300	694-3498
KHOW-AM 630 kHz (N/T) 1380 Lawrence St Suite 1300	Denver	CO	80204	303-893-8500	892-4700
KIMN-FM 100.3 MHz (AC) 1560 Broadway Suite 11 *Web:* kimn100.com	Denver	CO	80202	303-832-5665	832-7000
KJMN-FM 92.1 MHz (Span) 5660 Greenwood Plaza Blvd Suite 400	Englewood	CO	80111	303-721-9210	721-1435
KKFN-AM 950 kHz (Sports) 1095 S Monaco Pkwy **Fax:* Sales	Denver	CO	80224	303-321-0950	321-3383*
KKHK-FM 99.5 MHz (CR) 10200 E Girard Ave	Denver	CO	80231	303-696-1714	696-0522
KMXA-AM 1090 kHz (Span) 5660 Greenwood Plaza Blvd Suite 400	Englewood	CO	80111	303-721-9210	721-1435
KOA-AM 850 kHz (N/T) 1380 Lawrence St Suite 1300	Denver	CO	80204	303-893-8500	892-4700
KOSI-FM 101.1 MHz (AC) 10200 E Girard Ave Suite B131	Denver	CO	80231	303-696-1714	696-0522
KQKS-FM 107.5 MHz (Urban) 1095 S Monaco Pkwy	Denver	CO	80224	303-321-0950	989-9081
KRFX-FM 103.5 MHz (CR) 1380 Lawrence St Suite 1300 *Web:* www.thefox.com ■ *E-mail:* feedback@thefox.com	Denver	CO	80204	303-893-3699	534-7625
KTCL-FM 93.3 MHz (Alt) 1380 Lawrence St Suite 1300	Denver	CO	80204	303-623-9330	534-7625
KTLK-AM 760 kHz (N/T) 1380 Lawrence St Suite 1300	Denver	CO	80204	303-893-8500	892-4700
KUVO-FM 89.3 MHz (NPR) 2900 Welton St Suite 200 *Web:* www.kuvo.org ■ *E-mail:* info@kuvo.org	Denver	CO	80211	303-480-9272	291-0757
KVOD-FM 92.5 MHz (Clas) 1560 Broadway Suite 1100	Denver	CO	80202	303-832-5665	832-7000
KXKL-AM 1280 kHz (Oldies) 1560 Broadway Suite 1100	Denver	CO	80202	303-832-5665	832-7000
KXKL-FM 105.1 MHz (Oldies) 1560 Broadway Suite 1100	Denver	CO	80202	303-832-5665	832-7000
KXPK-FM 96.5 MHz (Alt) 1560 Broadway Suite 1100 *Web:* www.thepeak.com ■ *E-mail:* radio@thepeak.com	Denver	CO	80202	303-832-5665	832-7000
KYGO-FM 98.5 MHz (Ctry) 1095 S Monaco Pkwy	Denver	CO	80224	303-321-0950	320-0708

Denver (Cont'd)

— Colleges/Universities —

Name / Address	City	State	ZIP	Phone	Fax
Arapahoe Community College 5900 S Santa Fe Dr	Littleton	CO	80160	303-794-1550	797-5935
Bel-Rea Institute of Animal Technology 1681 S Dayton St	Denver	CO	80231	303-751-8700	751-9969
TF: 800-950-8001 ■ *Web:* www.bel-rea.com ■ *E-mail:* admissions@bel-rea.com					
Colorado Christian University 180 S Garrison St	Lakewood	CO	80226	303-963-3103	963-3201
TF: 800-443-2484 ■ *Web:* www.ccu.edu					
Colorado Institute of Art 200 E 9th Ave	Denver	CO	80203	303-837-0825	860-8520
TF: 800-275-2420					
Colorado School of Mines 1500 Illinois St	Golden	CO	80401	303-273-3000	273-3278
TF: 800-446-9488 ■ *Web:* www.mines.colorado.edu					
Community College of Denver PO Box 173363	Denver	CO	80217	303-556-2600	556-2431
Web: www.ccd.cccoes.edu					
Denver Automotive & Diesel College 460 S Lipan St	Denver	CO	80223	303-722-5724	778-8264
TF: 800-347-3232 ■ *Web:* www.denverautodiesel.com					
Denver Technical College 925 S Niagara St	Denver	CO	80224	303-329-3000	329-0955
Web: www.dtc.edu					
Front Range Community College 3645 W 112th Ave	Westminster	CO	80030	303-466-8811	466-1623
Web: frcc.cc.co.us					
Metropolitan State College of Denver 1006 11th St	Denver	CO	80204	303-556-3058	556-6345
Web: www.mscd.edu					
National American University Denver Campus 1325 S Colorado Blvd Suite 100	Denver	CO	80222	303-758-6700	758-6810
Web: www.nationalcollege.edu/campusdenver.html					
Parks Junior College 9065 Grant St	Denver	CO	80229	303-457-2757	457-4030
Red Rocks Community College 13300 W 6th Ave	Lakewood	CO	80228	303-988-6160	914-6666
Web: www.rrcc.cccoes.edu					
Regis University 3333 Regis Blvd	Denver	CO	80221	303-458-4100	964-5534
TF: 800-388-2366 ■ *Web:* www.regis.edu					
University of Colorado Denver PO Box 173364	Denver	CO	80217	303-556-3287	556-4838
Web: www.cudenver.edu					
University of Denver 2199 S University Blvd	Denver	CO	80208	303-871-2000	871-3301
TF Admissions: 800-525-9495 ■ *Web:* www.du.edu					
Westwood College of Technology 7350 N Broadway	Denver	CO	80221	303-650-5050	426-4647
TF: 800-875-6050 ■ *Web:* www.westwood.edu					
Yeshiva Toras Chaim Talmudical Seminary 1555 Stuart St	Denver	CO	80204	303-629-8200	623-5949

— Hospitals —

Name / Address	City	State	ZIP	Phone	Fax
Centura Saint Anthony Hospital Central 4231 W 16th Ave	Denver	CO	80204	303-629-3511	629-2189
Web: www.centura.org/facilities/denver_facilities/st_a_central/st_anth_hosp.html					
Children's Hospital 1056 E 19th Ave	Denver	CO	80218	303-861-8888	861-3992
TF: 800-624-6553 ■ *Web:* www.tchden.org					
Columbia Medical Center of Aurora North Campus 700 Potomac St	Aurora	CO	80011	303-363-7200	360-3751*
**Fax:* Admitting					
Columbia Rose Medical Center 4567 E 9th Ave	Denver	CO	80220	303-320-2121	320-2200
Denver Health Medical Center 777 Bannock St	Denver	CO	80204	303-436-6000	436-5131
Exempla Healthcare/Lutheran Medical Center 8300 W 38th Ave	Wheat Ridge	CO	80033	303-425-4500	425-8198
Healthone Presbyterian-Saint Luke's Medical Center 1719 E 19th Ave	Denver	CO	80218	303-839-6000	839-7779
Medical Center of Aurora South Campus 1501 S Potomac St	Aurora	CO	80012	303-695-2600	337-9773
North Suburban Medical Center 9191 Grant St	Thornton	CO	80229	303-451-7800	457-6701
Porter Memorial Hospital 2525 S Downing St	Denver	CO	80210	303-778-1955	778-5252
Portercare Hospital Littleton 7700 S Broadway	Littleton	CO	80122	303-730-8900	730-5858
Provenant Saint Anthony Hospital North 2551 W 84th Ave	Westminster	CO	80030	303-426-2151	426-2155
Saint Joseph Hospital 1835 Franklin St	Denver	CO	80218	303-837-7111	837-7017
Swedish Medical Center 501 E Hampden Ave	Englewood	CO	80110	303-788-5000	788-6313
University Hospital 4200 E 9th Ave	Denver	CO	80262	303-399-1211	372-9246
Web: www.uchsc.edu/uh					
Veterans Affairs Medical Center 1055 Clermont St	Denver	CO	80220	303-399-8020	393-4656*
**Fax:* Mail Rm					

— Attractions —

Name / Address	City	State	ZIP	Phone	Fax
Arabian Horse Trust Museum 12000 Zuni St	Westminster	CO	80234	303-450-4710	450-4707
Web: www.arabianhorsetrust.com ■ *E-mail:* information@arabianhorsetrust.com					
Arvada Center for the Arts & Humanities 6901 Wadsworth Blvd	Arvada	CO	80003	303-431-3939	431-3083
Web: www.arvadacenter.org					
Ballet Denver 3955 Tennyson St	Denver	CO	80212	303-455-4974	
Black American West Museum & Heritage Center 3091 California St	Denver	CO	80205	303-292-2566	382-1981
Web: www.coax.net/people/lwf/bawcal.htm ■ *E-mail:* bawmhc@aol.com					
Breckinridge Brewery Denver 2220 Blake St	Denver	CO	80205	303-297-3644	297-2341
TF: 800-910-2739					
Broadway Brewing LLC 2441 Broadway	Denver	CO	80205	303-292-5027	296-0164
Buffalo Bill Memorial Museum 987 1/2 Lookout Mountain Rd	Golden	CO	80401	303-526-0744	526-0197
Web: www.buffalobill.org					
Butterfly Pavilion & Insect Center 6252 W 104th Ave	Westminster	CO	80020	303-469-5441	469-5442
Web: www.butterflies.org					
Byers-Evans House & Denver History Museum 1310 Bannock St	Denver	CO	80204	303-620-4933	
Central City Opera House Assn 621 17th St Suite 1601	Denver	CO	80293	303-292-6500	292-4958
TF. 800-851-8175					
Children's Museum of Denver 2121 Children's Museum Dr	Denver	CO	80211	303-433-7444	433-0077
Web: www.artstozoo.org/cmd/					
Colorado Ballet 1278 Lincoln St	Denver	CO	80203	303-837-8888	861-7174
Colorado Governor's Mansion 400 E 8th Ave	Denver	CO	80203	303-866-3682	866-5739
Colorado History Museum 1300 Broadway	Denver	CO	80203	303-866-3682	866-5739
E-mail: chssysop@usa.net					
Colorado Railroad Museum 17155 W 44th Ave	Golden	CO	80402	303-279-4591	279-4229
TF: 800-365-6263					
Colorado Sports Hall of Fame 1445 Market St	Denver	CO	80202	303-620-8083	
Colorado State Capitol 200 E Colfax Ave	Denver	CO	80203	303-866-2604	866-2167
Colorado Symphony Orchestra 821 17th St Suite 700	Denver	CO	80202	303-292-5566	293-2649
Web: www.indra.com/cso ■ *E-mail:* info@coloradosymphony.com					
Comanche Crossing Museum 56060E Colfax Ave	Strasburg	CO	80136	303-622-4690	
Coors Brewery 12th & Ford Sts	Golden	CO	80401	303-279-6565	277-5723*
**Fax:* PR ■ *TF:* 800-642-6116					
Denver Art Museum 100 W 14th Avenue Pkwy	Denver	CO	80204	303-640-2295	640-5627
Web: www.denverartmuseum.org					
Denver Botanic Gardens 1005 York St	Denver	CO	80206	303-331-4000	331-4013
Denver Center Theatre Co 14th & Curtis Sts	Denver	CO	80204	303-893-4100	595-9634
Denver Firefighters Museum 1326 Tremont Pl	Denver	CO	80204	303-892-1436	892-1436
Web: www.colorado2.com/museum					
Denver Museum of Miniatures Dolls & Toys 1880 Gaylord St	Denver	CO	80206	303-322-1053	322-3704
Denver Museum of Natural History 2001 Colorado Blvd	Denver	CO	80205	303-370-6357	331-6492
TF: 800-925-2250 ■ *Web:* www.dmnh.org					
Denver Performing Arts Complex 950 13th St	Denver	CO	80204	303-640-2637	572-4792
Denver Zoological Gardens 2300 Steele St	Denver	CO	80205	303-376-4800	376-4801
Web: www.denverzoo.org					
Elitch Gardens 299 Walnut St	Denver	CO	80204	303-595-4386	534-2221
Web: www.elitchgardens.com					
Four Mile Historic Park 715 S Forest St	Denver	CO	80246	303-399-1859	393-0788
Gates Charles C Planetarium 2001 Colorado Blvd	Denver	CO	80205	303-370-6351	
Golden Pioneer Museum 923 10th St	Golden	CO	80401	303-278-7151	278-2755
Heritage Square Music Hall 18301 W Colfax Ave Bldg D103	Golden	CO	80401	303-279-7800	
Historic Paramount Theatre 1631 Glenarm St	Denver	CO	80202	303-825-4904	741-1831
IMAX Theater 2001 Colorado Blvd Denver Museum of Natural History	Denver	CO	80205	303-370-6322	331-6492
Web: www.dmnh.org/imax.htm					
Lakeside Amusement Park 4601 Sheridan Blvd	Denver	CO	80212	303-477-1621	455-1934
Larimer Square 1400 Larimer Sq	Denver	CO	80202	303-534-2367	623-1041
LoDo District Lower Downtown	Denver	CO	80206	303-295-1195	

Denver — Attractions (Cont'd)

				Phone	Fax
Mizel Museum of Judaica 560 S Monaco Pkwy *Web:* www.mizelmuseum.org ■ *E-mail:* museum@mizelmuseum.org	Denver	CO	80224	303-333-4156	331-8477
Molly Brown House 1340 Pennsylvania St *Web:* www.mollybrown.org/	Denver	CO	80203	303-832-4092	832-2340
Museo de las Americas 861 Santa Fe Dr. *Web:* www.museo.org	Denver	CO	80204	303-571-4401	607-9761
Museum of Outdoor Arts 7600 E Orchard Rd Suite 160	Englewood	CO	80111	303-741-3609	741-1029
Ocean Journey Aquarium 700 Water St US West Pk *Web:* www.oceanjourney.org	Denver	CO	80211	303-561-4450	561-4650
Opera Colorado 695 S Colorado Blvd Suite 20 *Web:* www.operacolo.org ■ *E-mail:* opera@ossinc.net	Denver	CO	80246	303-778-1500	778-6533
Pearce-McAllister Cottage 1880 Gaylord St	Denver	CO	80201	303-322-1053	
Red Rocks Amphitheater 12700 W Alameda Pkwy	Morrison	CO	80465	303-640-2637	640-7330
Robinson Parker Cleo Dance Theater 119 Park Ave W *E-mail:* cleodance@aol.com	Denver	CO	80205	303-295-1759	295-1328
Rocky Mountain Arsenal National Wildlife Refuge 72nd & Quebec Sts.	Commerce City	CO	80022	303-289-0232	289-0579
Rocky Mountain National Park *Web:* www.nps.gov/romo/	Estes Park	CO	80517	970-586-1206	586-1310
Rocky Mountain Quilt Museum 1111 Washington Ave	Golden	CO	80401	303-277-0377	215-1636
Sakura Square 1255 19th St	Denver	CO	80202	303-295-0305	295-0304
Swallow Hill Music Assn 71 E Yale Ave	Denver	CO	80210	303-777-1003	871-0527
Theatre on Broadway 13 S Broadway	Denver	CO	80209	303-777-3292	860-9360
Trianon Museum & Art Gallery 335 14th St.	Denver	CO	80202	303-623-0739	
US Mint 320 W Colfax Ave.	Denver	CO	80204	303-405-4761	405-4604
Wings Over the Rockies Air & Space Museum 7711 E Academy Blvd *Web:* www.dimensional.com/~worm/ ■ *E-mail:* worm@dimensional.com	Denver	CO	80224	303-360-5360	360-5328
Writer Square 1512 Larimer St. *Web:* www.writer-square.com ■ *E-mail:* info@writer-square.com	Denver	CO	80202	303-628-9056	534-4559

SPORTS TEAMS & FACILITIES

				Phone	Fax
Arapahoe Park Race Track 26000 E Quincy Ave *Web:* www.wembleyusa.com/arapahoe ■ *E-mail:* arapahoe@wembleyusa.com	Aurora	CO	80046	303-690-2400	690-6730
Colorado Avalanche 1000 Chopper Cir Pepsi Ctr *Web:* www.coloradoavalanche.com	Denver	CO	80204	303-893-3865	405-1315
Colorado Comets (soccer) 6200 Dahlia St Wembley Pk Stadium *Web:* www.intermark.com/comets	Commerce City	CO	80022	303-288-1591	289-1640
Colorado National Speedway 4281 Weld County Rd 10 *Web:* www.coloradospeedway.com ■ *E-mail:* cns98@earthlink.net	Erie	CO	80516	303-665-4173	291-1901
Colorado Rapids (soccer) 555 17th St Suite 3350 *TF:* 800-844-7777 ■ *Web:* www.intermark.com/Rapids ■ *E-mail:* 103506.1147@compuserve.com	Denver	CO	80202	303-299-1570	299-1580
Colorado Rockies 2001 Blake St Coors Field *TF Sales:* 800-388-7625 ■ *Web:* www.coloradorockies.com	Denver	CO	80205	303-762-5437	312-2219
Coors Field 2001 Blake St *Web:* www.coloradorockies.com/coorsfield/index.html	Denver	CO	80205	303-312-2100	312-2219
Denver Broncos 1900 Eliot St Mile High Stadium *Web:* www.denverbroncos.com	Denver	CO	80204	303-433-7466	433-3414
Denver Coliseum 4600 Humboldt St	Denver	CO	80216	303-295-4444	295-4467
Denver Diamonds (soccer) 7112 W Jefferson Ave Suite 100	Lakewood	CO	80232	303-986-5200	986-5222
Denver Nuggets 1000 Chopper Cir Pepsi Ctr *Web:* www.nba.com/nuggets	Denver	CO	80204	303-893-3865	405-1315
Mile High Greyhound Park 6200 Dahlia St *Web:* www.wembleyusa.com/milehigh ■ *E-mail:* milehigh@wembleyusa.com	Commerce City	CO	80022	303-288-1591	289-1640
Mile High Stadium 1900 Eliot St *Web:* www.denverbroncos.com/offthefield/stadium/milehigh/index.html	Denver	CO	80204	303-458-4850	458-4861
Pepsi Center 1000 Chopper Cir *Web:* www.pepsicenter.com	Denver	CO	80204	303-893-3865	405-1315

— Events —

	Phone
Blossoms of Lights (early December-early January)	303-331-4000
Boo at the Zoo (late October)	303-376-4846
Buffalo Bill's Birthday Celebration (late February)	303-526-0744
Capitol Hill People's Fair (early June)	303-830-1651
Cherry Blossom Festival (mid-July)	303-295-1844
Cherry Creek Arts Festival (July 4)	303-355-2787
Colorado Indian Market & Western Art Roundup (early January & mid-July)	806-355-1610
Colorado Performing Arts Festival (early October)	720-913-8206
Colorado State Fair (late August-early September)	800-876-4567
Denver Auto Show (early February)	303-831-1691
Denver Boat Show (early January)	303-228-8000
Denver International Film Festival (mid-October)	303-321-3456
Denver March Pow Wow (mid-late March)	303-295-4444
Festival of Mountain & Plain: A Taste of Colorado (early September)	303-534-6161
First Night Colorado (December 31)	303-399-9005
Great American Beer Festival (early October)	303-447-0816
Greek Festival (late June)	303-388-9314
Greek Marketplace (mid-June)	303-388-9314
Independence Day Celebration (July 4)	303-399-1859
International Buskerfest (late June)	303-534-6161
Juneteenth Festival (mid-June)	303-399-7138
Lodo Beer Wine & Food Festival (mid-June)	303-458-6685
National Western Stock Show & Rodeo (early-mid-January)	303-297-1166
Oktoberfest (mid-September)	303-534-2367
Parade of Lights (early December)	303-534-6161
Renaissance Festival (early June-early August)	303-688-6010
Rocky Mountain Book Festival (early November)	303-839-8320
Rocky Mountain Children's Book Festival (mid-November)	303-839-8320
Saint Patrick's Day Parade (mid-March)	303-399-9226
Spirits of the Past (late October)	303-399-1859
Summer Nights (late June-late August)	303-534-2367
Theater in the Park (late July-early August)	303-770-2106
Wild Lights (December)	303-331-4110
Winter Park Jazz Festival (mid-July)	970-726-4118
Winterfest Weekends (late November-early January)	303-534-2367
World's Largest Christmas Lighting Display (late November-December)	303-892-1112

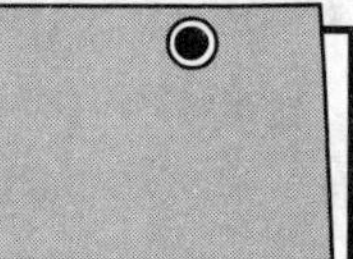

Fort Collins

The area surrounding Fort Collins was first discovered in the early 1800s by French fur trappers. Legend has it that a group of trappers were caught in a snow storm and, to lighten their load, they buried large amounts of gunpowder (poudre) in a hiding place (cache) along the banks of a river, giving it the name Cache La Poudre River. Although Fort Collins had been built in 1862 to provide protection for settlers, its proximity to the Cache La Poudre River, along with the arrival of the Colorado Central Railroad in 1877, contributed to the town's development as the center of a prosperous agricultural region. Today, the 70-mile-long Cache La Poudre is Colorado's only nationally designated "wild and scenic" river on which adventurers can enjoy rafting, fishing, and kayaking. Other natural attractions in the Fort Collins area include Horsetooth Mountain Park, a popular spot for outdoor activities that features more than 50 miles of trails. Rocky Mountain National Park, with 266,906 acres of trails and mountain peaks, is just 35 miles from Fort Collins. For those who prefer indoor activities, the Anheuser-Busch Tour Center offers complimentary brewery tours highlighting the brewing process as well as the chance to see the world-famous Budweiser Clydesdales. Other activities available in Fort Collins include theatrical performances at the Bas Bleu Theatre Company, dance performances by the Canyon Concert Ballet, and classical music productions by the Fort Collins Symphony.

Population	108,905	**Longitude**	105-04-06 W
Area (Land)	41.2 sq mi	**County**	Larimer
Area (Water)	0.5 sq mi	**Time Zone**	MST
Elevation	5003 ft	**Area Code/s**	970
Latitude	40-33-19 N		

Fort Collins (Cont'd)

— Average Temperatures and Precipitation —

TEMPERATURES

	Jan	Feb	Mar	Apr	May	Jun	Jul	Aug	Sep	Oct	Nov	Dec
High	41	46	52	61	70	80	86	83	75	64	51	42
Low	14	19	25	34	43	52	57	55	46	35	24	16

PRECIPITATION

	Jan	Feb	Mar	Apr	May	Jun	Jul	Aug	Sep	Oct	Nov	Dec
Inches	0.4	0.4	1.4	1.8	2.7	1.9	1.8	1.3	1.3	1.0	0.7	0.5

— Important Phone Numbers —

	Phone
AAA	970-223-1111
American Express Travel	970-484-5566
Dental Referral	800-577-7317
Emergency	911
Medical Referral	970-669-4640
Time/Temp	970-226-6060
Weather	970-484-8920

— Information Sources —

				Phone	Fax
Better Business Bureau Serving the Mountain States 1730 S College Ave Suite 303	Fort Collins	CO	80525	970-404-1348	221-1239
Web: www.rockymtn.bbb.org ■ *E-mail:* info@rockymtn.bbb.org					
City of Fort Collins City Hall 300 LaPorte Ave	Fort Collins	CO	80521	970-221-6500	221-6329
Web: www.ci.fort-collins.co.us					
City of Fort Collins City Manager 300 LaPorte Ave	Fort Collins	CO	80521	970-221-6505	224-6107
Web: www.ci.fort-collins.co.us/CITY_HALL/CITY_MANAGER/					
Downtown Business Assn 19 Old Town Sq Suite 230	Fort Collins	CO	80524	970-484-6500	484-2069
Web: www.downtownfortcollins.com					
Fort Collins Area Chamber of Commerce 225 S Meldrum St	Fort Collins	CO	80521	970-482-3746	482-3774
Web: www.fcchamber.org					
Fort Collins Convention & Visitors Bureau 429 S Howes St Suite 101	Fort Collins	CO	80521	970-482-5821	493-8061
TF: 800-274-3678 ■ *Web:* www.ftcollins.com					
Fort Collins Economic Developmment Corp PO Box 1849	Fort Collins	CO	80522	970-221-0861	221-5219
Web: www.fcedc.org ■ *E-mail:* askus@fcedc.org					
Fort Collins Public Library 201 Peterson St	Fort Collins	CO	80524	970-221-6742	221-6398
Web: www.ci.fort-collins.co.us/C_LIBRARY/					
Larimer County PO Box 1280	Fort Collins	CO	80522	970-498-7000	498-7830
Web: www.co.larimer.co.us					

On-Line Resources

Anthill City Guide Fort Collins	www.anthill.com/city.asp?city=fortcollins
Area Guide Fort Collins	fortcollins.areaguides.net
City Knowledge Fort Collins	www.cityknowledge.com/co_fort_collins.htm
Fort Collins Community Online	www.fortcollins.com
FortNet	www.fortnet.org

— Transportation Services —

AIRPORTS

■ Fort Collins/Loveland Municipal Airport (FNL)

	Phone
9 miles SE of downtown (approx 15 minutes)	970-962-2850

Airport Transportation

	Phone
Black Pearl Limousine $30 fare to downtown	970-686-5306
First Class Limousine Service $50 fare to downtown	970-225-0909
Shamrock Yellow Cab $30 fare to downtown	970-686-5555

Commercial Airlines

	Phone
America West	800-235-9292

■ Denver International Airport (DEN)

	Phone
65 miles SE of downtown Fort Collins (approximately 75 minutes)	303-342-2000
Web: infodenver.denver.co.us/~aviation/ ■ *E-mail:* aviation@infodenver.denver.co.us	

Airport Transportation

	Phone
Airport Express $16 fare to downtown Fort Collins	970-482-0505
Shamrock Shuttle $21 fare to downtown Fort Collins	970-686-5555

Commercial Airlines

	Phone
America West	800-235-9292
American	800-433-7300
Continental	800-525-0280
Continental Express	800-525-0280
Delta	800-221-1212
Frontier	800-432-1359
Martinair Holland	800-366-4655
Mesa	800-637-2247
Mexicana	800-531-7923
Midwest Express	800-452-2022
Northwest	800-225-2525
Sun Country	800-359-5786
TWA	800-221-2000
United	800-241-6522
United Express	800-241-6522
US Airways	800-428-4322
Vanguard	800-826-4827

Charter Airlines

	Phone
Corporate Air Charter	406-248-1541
Mayo Aviation Inc	303-790-9777
Superior Aviation	800-882-7751

CAR RENTALS

	Phone
Advantage	970-224-2211
Alamo	303-342-7373
Avis	970-229-9115
Budget	303-342-9001
Dollar	970-203-1809
Econo-Rate	970-221-2722
Enterprise	970-224-2592
National	303-342-0717
Payless	303-342-9444
Thrifty	303-342-9086

LIMO/TAXI

	Phone
Black Pearl Limousine	970-686-5306
Continental Limousine	970-206-9657
Royalty Limousine	970-493-7778
Shamrock Yellow Cab	970-686-5555

MASS TRANSIT

	Phone
Transfort $.90 Base fare	970-221-6620

RAIL/BUS

				Phone
Greyhound Bus Station 501 Riverside Ave	Fort Collins	CO	80524	970-221-1327
TF: 800-231-2222				

— Accommodations —

HOTEL RESERVATION SERVICES

	Phone	Fax
All-Colorado Accommodations	877-365-6926	522-0894*
**Fax Area Code:* 719 ■ *Web:* www.rockad.com/aca/ ■ *E-mail:* mountain@frii.com		

HOTELS, MOTELS, RESORTS

				Phone	Fax
Best Western Kiva Inn 1638 E Mulberry St.	Fort Collins	CO	80524	970-484-2444	221-0967
TF: 888-299-5482					
Best Western University Inn 914 S College Ave.	Fort Collins	CO	80524	970-484-1984	484-1987
TF: 800-528-1234					
Budget Host Inn 1513 N College Ave.	Fort Collins	CO	80524	970-484-0870	224-2998
TF: 800-825-4678 ■ *Web:* www.webaccess.net/~budget					
Cherokee Park Ranch 436 Cherokee Hills Rd.	Livermore	CO	80536	970-493-6522	493-5802
TF: 800-628-0949 ■ *Web:* www.ranchweb.com/cherokeepark ■ *E-mail:* cpranch@gateway.net					

Fort Collins — Hotels, Motels, Resorts (Cont'd)

Name / Address	City	State	Zip	Phone	Fax
Comfort Suites 1415 Oakridge Dr	Fort Collins	CO	80525	970-206-4597	206-4597
TF: 800-228-5150					
Days Inn 3625 E Mulberry St	Fort Collins	CO	80524	970-221-5490	482-4826
TF: 800-325-2525					
El Palomino Motel 1220 N College Ave	Fort Collins	CO	80524	970-482-4555	482-1101
Fort Collins Courtyard by Marriott 1200 Oakridge Dr	Fort Collins	CO	80525	970-282-1700	282-1777
TF: 800-321-2211					
Fort Collins Marriott 350 E Horsetooth Rd	Fort Collins	CO	80525	970-226-5200	226-9708
TF: 800-548-2635					
Fort Collins Plaza Inn 3709 E Mulberry St	Fort Collins	CO	80524	970-493-7800	493-1826
TF: 800-434-5548 ■ *Web:* www.plaza-inn.com					
Fort Collins Ramada 4001 S Mason St	Fort Collins	CO	80525	970-282-9047	282-9047
TF: 800-272-6232					
Hampton Inn 1620 Oakridge Dr	Fort Collins	CO	80525	970-229-5927	229-0854
TF: 800-426-7866					
Helmshire Inn 1204 S College Ave	Fort Collins	CO	80524	970-493-4683	495-0794
Holiday Inn 3836 E Mulberry St	Fort Collins	CO	80524	970-484-4660	484-2326
TF: 800-465-4329					
Home State Bank 303 E Mountain Ave	Fort Collins	CO	80524	970-622-7188	224-4180
Web: www.homestatebank.com ■ *E-mail:* bank@homestatebank.com					
Inn at Fort Collins 2612 S College Ave	Fort Collins	CO	80525	970-226-2600	226-2610
Lamplighter Motel 1809 N College Ave	Fort Collins	CO	80524	970-484-2764	
Montclair Motel 1405 N College Ave	Fort Collins	CO	80524	970-482-5452	221-4328
Mountain Empire Hotel 259 S College Ave	Fort Collins	CO	80524	970-482-5536	
Mulberry Inn 4333 E Mulberry St	Fort Collins	CO	80524	970-493-9000	224-9636
TF: 800-234-5548 ■ *Web:* www.mulberry-inn.com					
Prospect Plaza Motel 304 W Prospect Rd	Fort Collins	CO	80526	970-482-9513	498-8286
Residence Inn by Marriott 1127 Oakridge Dr	Fort Collins	CO	80525	970-223-5700	266-9280
TF: 800-548-2635					
Sky Corral Guest Ranch 8233 Old Flowers Rd	Bellvue	CO	80512	970-484-1362	
TF: 888-323-2531 ■ *Web:* www.skycorral.com ■ *E-mail:* jocon72553@aol.com					
Super 8 Motel 409 Centro Way	Fort Collins	CO	80524	970-493-7701	493-7701
TF: 800-800-8000					
Sylvan Dale Guest Ranch 2939 N County Rd 31	Loveland	CO	80538	970-667-3915	635-9336
TF: 877-667-3999 ■ *Web:* www.sylvandale.com ■ *E-mail:* ranch@sylvandale.com					
University Park Holiday Inn 425 W Prospect Rd	Fort Collins	CO	80526	970-482-2626	493-6265
TF: 800-465-4329					

— Restaurants —

Name / Address	City	State	Zip	Phone
Austin's American Grill (American) 100 W Mountain Ave	Fort Collins	CO	80524	970-224-9691
Bisetti's Italian Restaurant (Italian) 120 S College Ave	Fort Collins	CO	80524	970-493-0086
Cafe Bluebird (International) 524 W Laurel St	Fort Collins	CO	80521	970-484-7755
Canino's Italian Restaurant (Italian) 613 S College Ave	Fort Collins	CO	80524	970-493-7205
CB Potts Restaurant (American) 1415 W Elizabeth St	Fort Collins	CO	80521	970-221-1139
Charco Broiler (Steak) 1716 E Mulberry Ave	Fort Collins	CO	80524	970-482-1472
China Dragon Restaurant (Chinese) 1401 W Elizabeth St	Fort Collins	CO	80521	970-482-1242
CooperSmith's Pub & Brewing (American) 5 Old Town Sq	Fort Collins	CO	80524	970-498-0483
Web: www.coopersmithspub.com ■ *E-mail:* coopland@coopersmithspub.com				
Jay's Bistro (American) 115 S College Ave	Fort Collins	CO	80524	970-482-1876
Johnny Carino's Country Italian Kitchen (Italian) 4235 S College Ave	Fort Collins	CO	80525	970-223-9455
La Luz Mexican Grill (Mexican) 200-B Walnut St	Fort Collins	CO	80524	970-493-1129
Linden's Brewing Co (Cajun) 214 Linden St	Fort Collins	CO	80524	970-482-9291
Web: www.lindensbrewing.com				
Lucky Joe's Sidewalk Saloon (Irish) 25 Old Town Sq	Fort Collins	CO	80524	970-493-2213
Moot House (English) 2626 S College Ave	Fort Collins	CO	80525	970-226-2121
Nate's Steak & Seafood Place (Steak/Seafood) 3620 S Mason St	Fort Collins	CO	80525	970-223-9200
Positano's Pizzeria (Italian) 3645 S College Ave	Fort Collins	CO	80525	970-207-9935
Rainbow Restaurant (Vegetarian) 212 W Laurel St	Fort Collins	CO	80524	970-221-2664
Sports Station (American) 200 Jefferson St	Fort Collins	CO	80524	970-493-4348
SportsCaster Bar & Grill (American) 165 E Boardwalk Dr	Fort Collins	CO	80525	970-223-3553
Sri Thai (Thai) 950 S Taft Hill Rd	Fort Collins	CO	80521	970-482-5115
Sundance Steakhouse (Steak) 2716 E Mulberry Ave	Fort Collins	CO	80524	970-484-1600
Table 65 (New American) 1027 W Horsetooth Rd Suite 111	Fort Collins	CO	80526	970-225-6564
E-mail: table65@aol.com				
Taj Mahal (Indian) 148 W Oak St	Fort Collins	CO	80524	970-493-1105
Thai Pepper (Thai) 109 E Laurel St	Fort Collins	CO	80524	970-221-3260
Tortilla Marissa (Mexican) 2635 S College Ave	Fort Collins	CO	80525	970-225-9222

— Goods and Services —

SHOPPING

Name / Address	City	State	Zip	Phone	Fax
Foothills Fashion Mall 215 E Foothills Pkwy	Fort Collins	CO	80525	970-226-5555	226-5558
Web: www.foothillsfashionmall.com					
The Garment District 633 S College Ave	Fort Collins	CO	80524	970-484-9212	
Town Square Shopping Center 1228 W Elizabeth St	Fort Collins	CO	80521	970-221-1805	

BANKS

Name / Address	City	State	Zip	Phone	Fax
Bank One Colorado NA 2000 S College Ave	Fort Collins	CO	80525	970-662-7603	484-7063
First Community Industrial Bank 2721 S College Ave	Fort Collins	CO	80525	970-226-1080	226-1096
First National Bank 205 W Oak St	Fort Collins	CO	80521	970-482-4861	495-9531
Web: www.1stnationalbank.com					
First State Bank of Fort Collins 2900 S College Ave	Fort Collins	CO	80525	970-223-3535	223-1557
Web: www.firststatebankftc.com ■ *E-mail:* talkback@firststatebankftc.com					
Firstate Bank of Colorado 3131 S College Ave	Fort Collins	CO	80525	970-266-9090	266-1022
FirstBank of Northern Colorado 1013 E Harmony Rd	Fort Collins	CO	80525	970-223-4000	282-3925
KeyBank NA 300 W Oak St	Fort Collins	CO	80521	970-482-3216	495-3310
Norwest Bank Fort Collins 401 S College Ave	Fort Collins	CO	80524	970-482-1100	482-1523

BUSINESS SERVICES

	Phone		Phone
Adecco Employment Services	970-204-4801	**Kelly Services**	970-223-3955
Airborne Express	800-247-2676	**Kinko's**	970-221-2679
Business Express	970-484-9495	**Mail Boxes Etc**	970-221-2133
DHL Worldwide Express	800-225-5345	**Sir Speedy Printing**	970-223-1448
Express Personnel Services	970-226-4300	**Sos Staffing Services**	970-282-4401
Federal Express	800-463-3339	**UPS**	800-742-5877

— Media —

PUBLICATIONS

Name / Address	City	State	Zip	Phone	Fax
Coloradoan The‡ 1212 Riverside Ave	Fort Collins	CO	80524	970-493-6397	224-7899
Web: www.coloradoan.com ■ *E-mail:* news@coloradoan.com					
Loveland Daily Reporter-Herald‡ PO Box 59	Loveland	CO	80539	970-669-5050	667-1111
Web: www.lovelandfyi.com					
Northern Colorado Business Report 201 S College Ave	Fort Collins	CO	80524	970-221-5400	221-5432
Web: www.ncbr.com ■ *E-mail:* ncbr@aol.com					

‡Daily newspapers

TELEVISION

Name / Address	City	State	Zip	Phone	Fax
KBDI-TV Ch 12 (PBS) 2900 Welton St 1st Fl	Denver	CO	80205	303-296-1212	296-6650
Web: www.kbdi.org					
KCEC-TV Ch 50 (Uni) 777 Grant St Suite 110	Denver	CO	80203	303-832-0050	832-3410
E-mail: kcecnews@aol.com					
KCNC-TV Ch 4 (CBS) 1044 Lincoln St	Denver	CO	80203	303-861-4444	830-6380
Web: www.kcncnews4.com ■ *E-mail:* mailroom@kcncnews4.com					
KDVR-TV Ch 31 (Fox) 501 Wazee St	Denver	CO	80204	303-595-3131	595-8312
Web: www.fox31.com ■ *E-mail:* feedback@fox31.com					
KMGH-TV Ch 7 (ABC) 123 Speer Blvd	Denver	CO	80203	303-832-7777	832-0119
Web: www.kmgh.com ■ *E-mail:* kmgh7@csn.net					
KRMA-TV Ch 6 (PBS) 1089 Bannock St	Denver	CO	80204	303-892-6666	620-5600
Web: www.krma.org ■ *E-mail:* info@krma.org					

Fort Collins — Television (Cont'd)

				Phone	Fax
KUSA-TV Ch 9 (NBC) 500 Speer Blvd	Denver	CO	80203	303-871-9999	698-4700
Web: www.9news.com ■ *E-mail:* kusa@9news.com					

RADIO

				Phone	Fax
KCOL-AM 600 kHz (N/T) 1612 La Porte Ave	Fort Collins	CO	80521	970-482-5991	482-5994
Web: www.kcol.com ■ *E-mail:* info@kcol.com					
KGLL-FM 96.1 MHz (Ctry) 1612 La Porte Ave	Fort Collins	CO	80521	970-482-5991	482-5994
Web: www.kgll.com ■ *E-mail:* info@kgll.com					
KIIX-AM 1410 kHz (Sports) 1612 La Porte Ave	Fort Collins	CO	80521	970-482-5991	482-5994
KPAW-FM 107.9 MHz (AC) 1612 La Porte Ave	Fort Collins	CO	80521	970-482-5991	482-5994
Web: www.kpaw.com ■ *E-mail:* info@kpaw.com					

— Colleges/Universities —

				Phone	Fax
Colorado Christian University 3800 Automation Way	Fort Collins	CO	80525	970-223-8505	223-8964
TF: 800-443-2484 ■ *Web:* www.ccu.edu					
Colorado State University	Fort Collins	CO	80523	970-491-1101	491-7799
Web: www.colostate.edu					
Front Range Community College Larimer Campus 4616 S Shields St	Fort Collins	CO	80526	970-226-2500	204-8365*
**Fax Area Code:* 303 ■ *Web:* frcc.cc.co.us/la/index.html					
National Technological University 700 Centre Ave	Fort Collins	CO	80526	970-495-6400	498-0601
TF: 800-582-9976 ■ *Web:* www.ntu.edu					
Regis University 1501 Academy Ct	Fort Collins	CO	80524	970-472-2200	472-2201
TF: 800-390-0891 ■ *Web:* www.regis.edu					

— Hospitals —

				Phone	Fax
McKee Medical Center PO Box 830	Loveland	CO	80539	970-669-4640	635-4066
Poudre Valley Hospital 1024 S Lemay Ave	Fort Collins	CO	80524	970-495-7000	495-7603*
**Fax:* Admitting ■ *TF:* 800-252-5784 ■ *Web:* www.pvhs.org					

— Attractions —

				Phone	Fax
Alpine Family Fun Club 7824 S College Ave	Fort Collins	CO	80525	970-669-4100	
Anheuser-Busch Tour Center 2351 Busch Dr	Fort Collins	CO	80524	970-490-4691	
Web: www.budweisertours.com					
Arapaho & Roosevelt National Forests Visitor Center 1311 S College Ave	Fort Collins	CO	80524	970-498-2770	
Web: www.fs.fed.us//arnf/					
Avery House 328 W Mountain Ave	Fort Collins	CO	80521	970-221-0533	
Web: www.fortnet.org/plf/					
Bas Bleu Theatre Co 216 Pine St	Fort Collins	CO	80524	970-498-8949	
E-mail: basbleu@csn.net					
Big Horn Brewery 1427 W Elizabeth St	Fort Collins	CO	80521	970-221-5954	
Buckhorn Llama Co 7220 N County Rd 27	Loveland	CO	80538	970-667-7411	
Web: www.llamapack.com ■ *E-mail:* buckhorn@llamapack.com					
Canyon Concert Ballet 3720-A S College Ave	Fort Collins	CO	80525	970-229-9191	204-4609
Web: www.ccballet.org ■ *E-mail:* info@ccballet.org					
Carousel Dinner Theatre 3509 S Mason St	Fort Collins	CO	80525	970-225-2555	225-2389
TF: 877-700-2555 ■ *Web:* www.carouseltheatre.com ■ *E-mail:* carousel@carouseltheatre.com					
City Park 1500 W Mulberry St	Fort Collins	CO	80521	970-221-6660	221-6849
Colorado State University Environmental Learning Center 2400 County Rd 9	Fort Collins	CO	80524	970-491-1661	
Colorado State University Hatton Gallery Colorado State University Visual Arts Bldg	Fort Collins	CO	80523	970-491-7634	
Discovery Center Science Museum 703 E Prospect Rd	Fort Collins	CO	80525	970-472-3990	472-3997
Web: www.dcsm.org					
Edora Park 1420 E Stuart St	Fort Collins	CO	80525	970-221-6660	221-6849
Fort Collins Municipal Railway PO Box 635	Fort Collins	CO	80522	970-482-8246	
Fort Collins Museum 200 Matthews St	Fort Collins	CO	80524	970-221-6738	416-2236
Web: www.ci.fort-collins.co.us/arts_culture/museum					
Fort Collins Museum of Contemporary Art 201 S College Ave	Fort Collins	CO	80524	970-482-2787	482-0804
Web: www.fcmoca.org ■ *E-mail:* fcmoca@frii.com					
Fort Collins Symphony 417 W Magnolia Lincoln Ctr	Fort Collins	CO	80521	970-482-4823	482-4858
Web: www.fcsymphony.org					
Front Range Chamber Players 417 W Magnolia St Lincoln Ctr	Fort Collins	CO	80521	970-221-6730	484-0424
Grandview Cemetery 1900 W Mountain Ave	Fort Collins	CO	80524	970-221-6810	
HC Berger Brewing Co 1900 E Lincoln Ave	Fort Collins	CO	80524	970-493-9044	493-4508
Web: www.hcberger.com ■ *E-mail:* info@hcberger.com					
Lincoln Center 417 W Magnolia St	Fort Collins	CO	80521	970-221-6730	484-0424
New Belgium Brewing Co 500 Linden St	Fort Collins	CO	80524	970-221-0524	221-0535
Web: www.newbelgium.com ■ *E-mail:* nbb@newbelgium.com					
Odell Brewing Co 800 E Lincoln Ave	Fort Collins	CO	80524	970-498-9070	498-0706
Web: www.odells.com ■ *E-mail:* odells@odells.com					
Open Stage Theatre & Co 417 W Magnolia St	Fort Collins	CO	80521	970-484-5237	484-0424
Strauss Cabin Horsetooth Rd & Country Rd 7	Fort Collins	CO	80524	970-679-4570	
The Farm at Lee Martinez Park 600 S Sherwood St	Fort Collins	CO	80521	970-221-6665	
Walnut Street Gallery 217 Linden St	Fort Collins	CO	80524	970-221-2383	
TF: 800-562-3387 ■ *Web:* www.walnutst.com ■ *E-mail:* rockout@walnutst.com					
Windswept Farm 5537 N Country Rd 9	Fort Collins	CO	80524	970-484-1124	

— Events —

	Phone
1882 Fort Collins Waterworks Open House (mid-June)	970-221-0533
Anheuser-Busch Pumpkin Carving Contest (late October)	970-490-4691
Annual Garden Tour (late June)	970-224-0430
Boat Show (mid-March)	970-407-1866
Cinco de Mayo Celebration (early May)	970-484-6500
Colorado Brewers' Festival (late June)	970-484-6500
Colorado International Invitational Poster Exhibition (mid-September-late October)	970-491-7634
Concert Under the Stars (June-August)	970-484-6500
First Night Fort Collins (December 31)	970-484-6500
Fourth of July Celebration (July 4)	970-221-6790
Gem & Mineral Show (late March)	970-484-6752
Grateful Disc Spring Frisbee Festival (late April)	970-484-6932
Great Christmas Hall Artisans Fair (mid-November)	970-221-6735
Great Christmas Hall of Trees (mid-November)	970-221-6735
Historic Homes Tour (mid-September)	970-221-0533
Home & Garden Show (early March)	970-407-1866
Magic in the Rockies International Magic Show (early September)	970-484-7014
NewWestFest (late August)	970-484-6500
Northern Colorado Artists Association Annual Juried Art Show (mid-April-late May)	970-223-6450
Rendezvous & Skookum Day (mid-July)	970-221-6738
Saint Patrick's Day Parade (mid-March)	970-484-6500
Taste of Fort Collins (mid-June)	303-777-6887
Thanksgiving Day Run (late November)	970-224-2582
Victorian Christmas Open House (early December)	970-221-0533
WineFest (late May)	970-482-2700

Connecticut

Population (1999): 3,282,031 **Area (sq mi): 5,544**

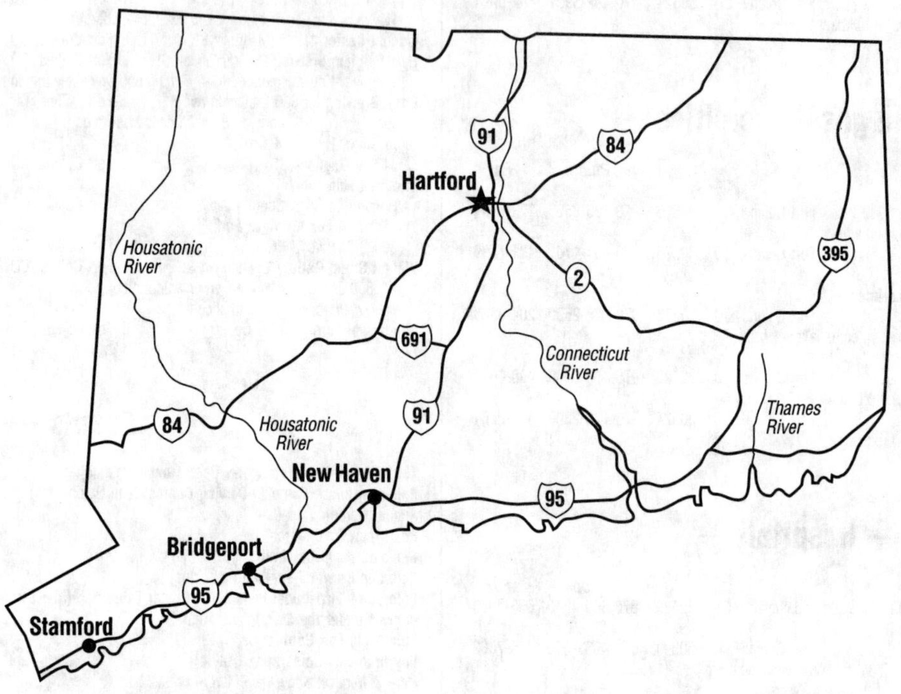

— State Information Sources —

				Phone	Fax
Connecticut Business & Industry Assn 350 Church St	Hartford	CT	06103	860-244-1900	278-8562
Web: www.cbia.com					
Connecticut Economic & Community Development Dept 505 Hudson St	Hartford	CT	06106	860-270-8182	270-8188
Web: www.state.ct.us/ecd ■ *E-mail:* decd@po.state.ct.us					
Connecticut State Government Information				860-566-2211	
Web: www.state.ct.us					
Connecticut State Library 231 Capitol Ave	Hartford	CT	06106	860-566-4301	566-8940
Web: www.cslnet.ctstateu.edu					
Connecticut State Parks Div 79 Elm St	Hartford	CT	06106	860-424-3200	424-4070
Web: dep.state.ct.us/Outdorec/parks.htm					
Connecticut Tourism Div 505 Hudson St	Hartford	CT	06106	860-270-8080	270-8077
TF: 800-282-6863 ■ *Web:* www.ctbound.org					

ON-LINE RESOURCES

Connecticut Cities .... dir.yahoo.com/Regional/U_S__States/Connecticut/Cities
Connecticut Counties & Regions .... dir.yahoo.com/Regional/U_S__States/Connecticut/Counties_and_Regions
Connecticut Passport .... www.ctpassport.com
Connecticut Scenario .... scenariousa.dstylus.com/ct/indexf.htm
Connecticut Travel & Tourism Guide .... www.travel-library.com/north_america/usa/connecticut/index.html
Connecticut.com .... www.connecticut.com
Imbored Connecticut .... www.imbored.com/new/regionct.htm
InConnecticut.com .... www.inconnecticut.com
Net Travel Connecticut .... www.nettx.com/states/ct.htm
PeekABoo Connecticut .... www.peekaboo.net/ct
Rough Guide Travel Connecticut travel.roughguides.com/content/396/index.htm
Search Connecticut .... www.newengland.com/ctmap.html
Town-line State of Connecticut Information .... www.townline.com/common/stateinf.htm
Travel.org-Connecticut .... travel.org/conn.html
Yahoo! Get Local Connecticut .... dir.yahoo.com/Regional/U_S__States/Connecticut

— Cities Profiled —

Bridgeport

Connecticut's largest city, Bridgeport is home to the Barnum Museum and the annual Barnum Festival. It also has Connecticut's only accredited zoo, the Beardsley Zoological Garden. The HMS Rose, a fully-rigged, 24-gun British frigate, is on display at Captain's Cove Seaport, which is located on historic Black Rock Harbor. The Cove also has a full-service marina with charter vessels available for cruises, bareboat charter, diving, or fishing; a fish market; shops along the boardwalk; and a 400-seat restaurant.

Population	137,425	**Longitude**	73-20-53 W
Area (Land)	16.0 sq mi	**County**	Fairfield
Area (Water)	3.4 sq mi	**Time Zone**	EST
Elevation	20 ft	**Area Code/s**	203
Latitude	41-16-69 N		

— Average Temperatures and Precipitation —

TEMPERATURES

	Jan	Feb	Mar	Apr	May	Jun	Jul	Aug	Sep	Oct	Nov	Dec
High	36	38	46	57	67	76	82	81	74	64	53	41
Low	22	23	31	40	50	59	66	65	58	47	38	28

PRECIPITATION

	Jan	Feb	Mar	Apr	May	Jun	Jul	Aug	Sep	Oct	Nov	Dec
Inches	3.2	3.0	3.8	3.8	3.9	3.5	3.8	3.3	3.1	3.1	3.8	3.5

— Important Phone Numbers —

	Phone		*Phone*
AAA	203-765-4222	**Time/Temp**	203-366-4242
Emergency	911	**Weather**	203-366-4242
Poison Control Center	203-576-5178		

— Information Sources —

				Phone	*Fax*
Better Business Bureau Serving Connecticut 821 N Main St Ext Parkside Bldg *Web:* www.connecticut.bbb.org	Wallingford	CT	06492	203-269-2700	269-3124
Bridgeport City Hall 45 Lyon Terr. *Web:* ci.bridgeport.ct.us	Bridgeport	CT	06604	203-576-7081	332-5608
Bridgeport Mayor 45 Lyon Terr. *Web:* ci.bridgeport.ct.us/MAYOROF.HTM	Bridgeport	CT	06604	203-576-7201	576-8383
Bridgeport Planning Dept 45 Lyon Terr	Bridgeport	CT	06604	203-576-7191	332-5568
Bridgeport Public Library 925 Broad St. *Web:* www.futuris.net/bpl	Bridgeport	CT	06604	203-576-7777	576-8255
Bridgeport Regional Business Council 10 Middle St 14th Fl	Bridgeport	CT	04601	203-335-3800	366-0105
Coastal Fairfield County Convention & Visitors Bureau 383 Main Ave Merrittview Bldg 7th Fl. *TF:* 800-473-4868 ■ *Web:* www.visitfairfieldco.org	Norwalk	CT	06851	203-840-0770	840-0771
Coastal Fairfield County Tourism 297 West Ave. *Web:* www.visitconnecticut.com/fairfiel/	Norwalk	CT	06850	203-899-2799	853-7524
Fairfield County 1061 Main St *Web:* ffcol.com	Bridgeport	CT	06604	203-579-6527	382-8406

On-Line Resources

Area Guide Bridgeport	bridgeport.areaguides.net
BridgeNet	access.bridgenet.org
Excite.com Bridgeport City Guide	www.excite.com/travel/countries/united_states/connecticut/bridgeport
I-95 Exit Information Guide Bridgeport	www.usastar.com/i95/cityguide/bridgeport.htm

— Transportation Services —

AIRPORTS

■ **Sikorsky Memorial Airport (BDR)**

	Phone
4 miles NE of downtown (approx 10 minutes)	203-576-8162

Airport Transportation

	Phone
Yellow Cab $8 fare to downtown	203-334-2121

Commercial Airlines

	Phone		*Phone*
Delta Connection	800-221-1212	**US Airways Express**	800-428-4322

Charter Airlines

	Phone		*Phone*
Flight Services Group Inc	800-380-4009	**Three Wing Aviation**	203-375-5795
Panorama Flight Service	914-328-9800	**Wayfarer Aviation**	914-949-3661
Shoreline Aviation Inc	203-468-8639		

■ **LaGuardia Airport (LGA)**

	Phone
66 miles SW of downtown Bridgeport (approx 105 minutes)	718-476-5000

Airport Transportation

	Phone
Connecticut Limousine $36 fare to downtown Bridgeport	203-878-2222

Commercial Airlines

	Phone		*Phone*
AccessAir	877-462-2237	**Midwest Express**	800-452-2022
Air Canada	800-776-3000	**Northwest**	800-225-2525
American	800-433-7300	**TWA**	800-221-2000
American Eagle	800-433-7300	**United**	800-241-6522
Atlantic Coast Airlines	800-241-6522	**US Airways**	800-428-4322
Continental	718-565-1100	**US Airways Express**	800-428-4322
Delta	800-221-1212		

Charter Airlines

	Phone		*Phone*
Atlantic Aviation Charter	201-288-7660	**Northeast Airway**	973-267-2450
Jet Aviation Business Jets Inc	800-736-8538		

CAR RENTALS

	Phone		*Phone*
Avis-Bridgeport	203-377-7390	**Hertz-Bridgeport**	203-378-0513
Avis-La Guardia	718-507-3600	**Hertz-La Guardia**	718-478-5300
Budget-La Guardia	718-639-6400	**Thrifty-Bridgeport**	203-333-2947
Dollar-LaGuardia	718-779-5600		

LIMO/TAXI

	Phone		*Phone*
Ace Cab	203-368-0529	**Nelson Limousine Service**	203-333-9433
Action Cab	203-579-4444	**Quickie Cab**	203-366-4343
Connecticut Limo	203-878-2222	**Reliable Taxi**	203-334-6161
Leisure Limousine	203-371-5466	**Yellow Cab**	203-334-2121

MASS TRANSIT

	Phone
Greater Bridgeport Transit District $1.10 Base fare	203-333-3031

RAIL/BUS

				Phone
Amtrak Station 525 Water St *TF:* 800-872-7245	Bridgeport	CT	06604	203-782-8922
Greyhound/Peter Pan/Arrow Line Bus Terminal 35 John St	Bridgeport	CT	06604	203-335-1123

— Accommodations —

HOTELS, MOTELS, RESORTS

				Phone
Arcade Hotel 1001 Main St	Bridgeport	CT	06604	203-333-9376

Bridgeport — Hotels, Motels, Resorts (Cont'd)

Name / Address	City	State	Zip	Phone	Fax
Bridgeport Holiday Inn 1070 Main St	Bridgeport	CT	06604	203-334-1234	367-1985
Web: www.basshotels.com/holiday-inn/?_franchisee=BGDCT ■ *E-mail:* bgdct@aol.com					
Bridgeport Motor Inn 100 Kings Hwy Cutoff	Fairfield	CT	06430	203-367-4404	
Comfort Inn 278 Old Gate Ln	Milford	CT	06460	203-877-9411	
Ethan Allen Inn 21 Lake Ave Ext	Danbury	CT	06811	203-744-1776	791-9673
TF: 800-742-1776 ■ *Web:* www.ethanalleninn.com					
Fairfield Inn 417 Post Rd	Fairfield	CT	06430	203-255-0491	255-2073
TF: 800-347-0414					
Hampton Inn 129 Plains Rd	Milford	CT	06460	203-874-4400	874-5348
TF: 800-426-7866					
Hilton & Towers Danbury 18 Old Ridgebury Rd	Danbury	CT	06810	203-794-0600	798-2709
TF: 800-327-6646 ■ *Web:* www.hilton.com/hotels/DNBHIHF					
Honeyspot Motor Lodge 360 Honeyspot Rd	Stratford	CT	06497	203-375-5666	378-1509
Howard Johnson Hotel 1052 Boston Post Rd	Milford	CT	06460	203-878-4611	877-6224
TF: 800-654-2000					
Inn at Longshore 260 S Compo Rd	Westport	CT	06880	203-226-3316	226-5723
Inn at National Hall 2 Post Rd W	Westport	CT	06880	203-221-1351	221-0276
TF: 800-628-4255					
Lamp Light Hotel 86 Pequonnock St	Bridgeport	CT	06604	203-576-9667	
Marnick's 10 Washington Pkwy	Stratford	CT	06497	203-377-6288	378-3612
Marriott Hotel Trumbull 180 Hawley Ln	Trumbull	CT	06611	203-378-1400	378-4958
TF: 800-221-9855 ■ *Web:* marriotthotels.com/BDRCT					
Merritt Parkway Motor Inn 4180 Black Rock Tpke	Fairfield	CT	06430	203-259-5264	366-7082
Ramada Inn 780 Bridgeport Ave	Shelton	CT	06484	203-929-1500	929-6711
Ramada Inn Stratford 225 Lordship Blvd	Stratford	CT	06615	203-375-8866	375-2482
TF: 800-272-6232					
Red Roof Inn 10 Rowe Ave	Milford	CT	06460	203-877-6060	374-3287
Residence Inn 1001 Bridgeport Ave	Shelton	CT	06484	203-926-9000	926-9000
Web: www.residenceinn.com/residenceinn/HVNSH					
Susse Chalet 111 Schoolhouse Rd	Milford	CT	06460	203-877-8588	874-3121
Web: www.sussechalet.com/milford.html					
Westport Inn 1595 Post Rd	Westport	CT	06880	203-259-5236	254-8439
TF: 800-446-8997					

— Restaurants —

Name / Address	City	State	Zip	Phone
American Steak House (Steak) 210 Boston Ave	Bridgeport	CT	06610	203-576-9989
Arizona Flats (Southwest) 3001 Fairfield Ave	Bridgeport	CT	06605	203-334-8300
Athena Diner (Greek) 3350 Post Rd	Southport	CT	06490	203-259-0603
Bayamon Barbecue (Barbecue) 537 E Main St	Bridgeport	CT	06608	203-335-6087
Black Rock Castle (Irish) 2895 Fairfield Ave	Bridgeport	CT	06605	203-336-3990
Bloodroot Restaurant (Vegetarian) 85 Ferris St	Bridgeport	CT	06605	203-576-9168
Web: www.bloodroot.com ■ *E-mail:* TheCook@Bloodroot				
Captain's Cove (Seafood) 1 Bostwick Ave	Bridgeport	CT	06605	203-335-7104
Caribbean Kitchen (Caribbean) 375 Pequonnock St	Bridgeport	CT	06604	203-334-3155
Dolphin's Cove Restaurant (Portuguese) 421 Seaview Ave	Bridgeport	CT	06607	203-335-3301
El Cochinito (Spanish) 883 E Main St	Bridgeport	CT	06605	203-334-9496
Fu Wai Kitchen (Chinese) 1199 Stratford Ave	Bridgeport	CT	06607	203-366-8647
Garebaldi Restaurant (Mexican) 1705 Park Ave	Bridgeport	CT	06604	203-368-3434
Kossuth Club (Hungarian) 2931 Fairfield Ave	Bridgeport	CT	06605	203-335-7877
La Caguena Lechonera (Spanish) 2697 Main St	Bridgeport	CT	06606	203-384-2619
La Scogliera Restaurant (Italian) 697 Madison Ave	Bridgeport	CT	06606	203-333-0673
Latino Restaurant (Spanish) 553 Park Ave	Bridgeport	CT	06604	203-366-8221
Little Brazil (Brazilian) 1024 Madison Ave	Bridgeport	CT	06606	203-367-1345
Mako of Japan (Japanese) 941 Black Rock Tpke	Fairfield	CT	06430	203-367-5319
Marisa's Ristorante (Italian) 6540 Main St	Trumbull	CT	06611	203-459-4225
Minabela Restaurant (Seafood) 1282 North Ave	Bridgeport	CT	06604	203-384-1159
Omanel Restaurant (Portuguese) 1909 Main St	Bridgeport	CT	06604	203-335-1676
Ralph 'N Rich's (Italian) 121 Wall St	Bridgeport	CT	06604	203-366-3597
San Jiang (Chinese) 1031 Madison Ave	Bridgeport	CT	06606	203-336-5500
Seven Stars (Chinese) 4175 Main St	Bridgeport	CT	06606	203-371-5656
Sfizio Ristorante (Italian) 746 Madison Ave	Bridgeport	CT	06606	203-367-4640
Solmar (Portuguese) 290 George St	Bridgeport	CT	06604	203-333-2435
Tartaglia's (Italian) 1439 Madison Ave	Bridgeport	CT	06606	203-576-1281
Three Door Restaurant (American) 1775 Madison Ave	Bridgeport	CT	06606	203-374-9438
Vazzy's Brick Oven Restaurant (Italian) 513 Broadbridge Rd	Bridgeport	CT	06610	203-371-8046
Yoshida Japanese Restaurant (Japanese) 439 Boston Post Rd	Milford	CT	06460	203-874-0475

— Goods and Services —

SHOPPING

Name / Address	City	State	Zip	Phone	Fax
Dock Shopping Center 955 Ferry Blvd	Stratford	CT	06614	203-377-2353	
Hawley Lane Mall 100 Hawley Lane	Bridgeport	CT	06611	203-375-9298	
Stratford Antiques Center 400 Honeyspot Rd	Stratford	CT	06497	203-378-7754	
Trumbull Shopping Park 5065 Main St	Trumbull	CT	06611	203-372-4500	372-0197

BANKS

Name / Address	City	State	Zip	Phone	Fax
Chase Manhattan Bank of Connecticut NA 2093 Main St	Bridgeport	CT	06604	203-332-1177	332-0639
TF: 800-242-7333					
Fleet Bank 2091 Boston Ave	Bridgeport	CT	06610	800-579-3211	579-3455*
**Fax Area Code:* 203 ■ **Fax:* Cust Svc ■ *TF:* 800-833-6623					
Lafayette American Bank 1000 Lafayette Blvd	Bridgeport	CT	06604	203-337-4300	337-4309
People's Bank 850 Main St Bridgeport Ctr	Bridgeport	CT	06604	203-338-7171	338-4216*
**Fax:* Cust Svc ■ *Web:* www.peoples.com ■ *E-mail:* custserv@peoples.com					

BUSINESS SERVICES

	Phone		Phone
Airborne Express	800-247-2676	**Mail Boxes Etc**	800-789-4623
BAX Global	800-225-5229	**Olsten Staffing Services**	203-268-9300
DHL Worldwide Express	800-225-5345	**Post Office**	203-332-5338
Express Mail	203-332-5340	**Staff Builders**	203-374-0332
Federal Express	800-238-5355	**Task Force**	203-384-2221
Kelly Services	203-261-4750	**UPS**	800-742-5877

— Media —

PUBLICATIONS

Name / Address	City	State	Zip	Phone	Fax
Bridgeport News PO Box 332	Monroe	CT	06468	203-926-2080	926-2091
Fairfield County Business Journal 3 Gannett Dr	White Plains	NY	10604	914-694-3600	694-3680
TF: 800-784-4564 ■ *Web:* www.businessjrnls.com					

TELEVISION

Name / Address	City	State	Zip	Phone	Fax
WABC-TV Ch 7 (ABC) 7 Lincoln Sq	New York	NY	10023	212-456-7777	456-2381
Web: abcnews.go.com/local/wabc					
WCBS-TV Ch 2 (CBS) 524 W 57th St	New York	NY	10019	212-975-4321	975-9387
Web: www.cbs2ny.com					
WNBC-TV Ch 4 (NBC) 30 Rockefeller Plaza	New York	NY	10112	212-664-4444	664-2994
Web: www.newschannel4.com ■ *E-mail:* nbc4ny@nbc.com					
WNET-TV Ch 13 (PBS) 450 W 33rd St	New York	NY	10001	212-560-1313	582-3297
Web: www.wnet.org ■ *E-mail:* webinfo@www.wnet.org					
WNYW-TV Ch 5 (Fox) 205 E 67th St	New York	NY	10021	212-452-5555	249-1182
WTNH-TV Ch 8 (ABC) 8 Elm St	New Haven	CT	06510	203-784-8888	787-9698
Web: www.wtnh.com ■ *E-mail:* wtnh@aol.com					

RADIO

Name / Address	City	State	Zip	Phone	Fax
WCUM-AM 1450 kHz (Span) 1862 State St	Bridgeport	CT	06605	203-335-1450	331-9378
WDJZ-AM 1530 kHz (Span) 175 Church St	Naugatuck	CT	06770	203-576-6518	723-7565
WEBE-FM 107.9 MHz (AC) 2 Lafayette Sq	Bridgeport	CT	06604	203-366-6000	339-4001
WEZN-FM 99.9 MHz (AC) 10 Middle St Park City Plaza	Bridgeport	CT	06604	203-366-9321	336-9988
Web: www.star999.com					
WICC-AM 600 kHz (AC) 2 Lafayette Sq	Bridgeport	CT	06604	203-366-6000	339-4001
WPKN-FM 89.5 MHz (Misc) 244 University Ave	Bridgeport	CT	06604	203-331-9756	
Web: www.wpkn.org ■ *E-mail:* wpkn@wpkn.org					
WSHU-FM 91.1 MHz (NPR) 5151 Park Ave	Fairfield	CT	06432	203-371-7989	371-7991
Web: www.wshu.org/ ■ *E-mail:* feedback@wshu.org					

— Colleges/Universities —

Name / Address	City	State	Zip	Phone	Fax
Fairfield University 1073 N Benson Rd	Fairfield	CT	06430	203-254-4000	254-4199
Web: www.fairfield.edu					
Fairfield University School of Engineering N Benson Rd	Fairfield	CT	06430	203-254-4147	254-4013
Housatonic Community-Technical College 900 Lafayette Blvd	Bridgeport	CT	06604	203-332-5000	332-5123
Web: www.hctc.commnet.edu					

Bridgeport — Colleges/Universities (Cont'd)

				Phone	Fax
Sacred Heart University 5151 Park Ave. *Web:* www.sacredheart.edu	Fairfield	CT	06432	203-371-7999	365-7609
University of Bridgeport 126 Park Ave. *Web:* www.bridgeport.edu	Bridgeport	CT	06601	203-576-4000	576-4941

— Hospitals —

				Phone	Fax
Bridgeport Hospital 267 Grant St	Bridgeport	CT	06610	203-384-3000	384-3751
Saint Vincent's Medical Center 2800 Main St **Fax:* Admitting ■ *Web:* www.stvincents.org	Bridgeport	CT	06606	203-576-6000	576-5738*

— Attractions —

				Phone	Fax
Barnum Museum 820 Main St *Web:* www.barnum-museum.org	Bridgeport	CT	06604	203-331-1104	339-4341
Beardsley Zoological Gardens 1875 Noble Ave	Bridgeport	CT	06610	203-394-6565	394-6566
Boothe Memorial Park & Museum Main St	Stratford	CT	06497	203-381-2068	
Captain David Judson House 967 Academy Hill	Stratford	CT	06497	203-378-0630	
Connecticut Audubon Society Birdcraft Museum & Sanctuary 314 Unquowa Rd	Fairfield	CT	06430	203-259-0416	259-1344
Connecticut Audubon Society Nature Center 2325 Burr St	Fairfield	CT	06430	203-259-6305	254-7673
Devil's Den Preserve 33 Pent Rd	Weston	CT	06883	203-226-4991	226-4807
Discovery Museum Inc 4450 Park Ave *Web:* www.discoverymuseum.org	Bridgeport	CT	06604	203-372-3521	374-1929
Downtown Cabaret Theatre 263 Golden Hill St.	Bridgeport	CT	06604	203-576-1636	576-1444
Fairfield County Chorale PO Box 124	Green Farms	CT	06436	203-254-1333	319-8273
Fairfield Historical Society Museum 636 Old Post Rd	Fairfield	CT	06430	203-259-1598	255-2716
Fairfield University Quick Center for the Arts N Benson Rd	Fairfield	CT	06430	203-254-4010	254-4113
Greater Bridgeport Symphony 446 University Ave	Bridgeport	CT	06604	203-576-0263	367-0064
HMS Rose & Captain's Cove Seaport 1 Bostwick Ave.	Bridgeport	CT	06605	203-335-1433	
Housatonic Museum of Art Housatonic Community College 900 Lafayette Blvd.	Bridgeport	CT	06604	203-332-5000	
Klein Memorial Auditorium 910 Fairfield Ave.	Bridgeport	CT	06605	203-576-8115	
Levitt Pavilion 110 Myrtle Ave	Westport	CT	06880	203-226-7600	226-2330
Mitchell Catherine Museum 967 Academy Hill	Stratford	CT	06075	203-378-0630	
National Theatre of the Arts 1175 Post Rd E	Westport	CT	06680	203-227-7454	227-5859
Nature Center for Environmental Activities 10 Woodside Ln.	Westport	CT	06880	203-227-7253	227-8909
Ogden House & Gardens 1520 Bronson Rd	Fairfield	CT	06430	203-259-1598	
Ordway Preserve 165 Goodhill Rd	Weston	CT	06883	203-226-4991	226-4807
Polka Dot Playhouse 177 State St	Bridgeport	CT	06604	203-333-3666	
Quick Center for the Arts Fairfield University N Benson Rd.	Fairfield	CT	06430	203-254-4242	254-4113
Rolnick Observatory 182 Bayberry Ln	Westport	CT	06880	203-227-0925	
Sacred Heart University Center for Performing Arts 5151 Park Ave.	Fairfield	CT	06432	203-374-2777	365-7508
Seaside Park Beach Barnum Dyke	Bridgeport	CT	06604	203-576-7233	
Shakespeare Theater State Park 1850 Elm St.	Stratford	CT	06497	203-381-9518	
Sherwood Island State Park 2 miles S of Westport	Greens Farms	CT	06346	203-226-6983	
Westport Arts Center 431 Post Rd E Suite 8.	Westport	CT	06880	203-226-1806	222-7999
Westport Community Theatre 110 Myrtle Ave.	Westport	CT	06880	203-226-1983	
Westport Country Playhouse 25 Powers Ct	Westport	CT	06880	203-227-4177	221-7482
Wheeler House 25 Avery Pl	Westport	CT	06880	203-222-1424	221-0981
Woodcock Nature Center 56 Deer Run Rd	Wilton	CT	06897	203-762-7280	834-0062

SPORTS TEAMS & FACILITIES

				Phone	Fax
Bridgeport Bluefish (baseball) 500 Main St. *Web:* www.bridgeportbluefish.com	Bridgeport	CT	06604	203-345-4800	345-4830
Milford Jai-Alai 311 Old Gate Ln *TF:* 800-243-9660 ■ *Web:* www.jaialai.com	Milford	CT	06460	203-877-4211	878-2317
Shoreline Star Greyhound Park 255 Kossuth St.	Bridgeport	CT	06608	203-576-1976	696-3836

— Events —

	Phone
Barnum Festival (June-early July)	203-367-8495
Fairfield Dogwood Festival (early-May)	203-259-5596
Festival Italiano (early July)	203-227-6279
Fourth of July Celebration & Fireworks (July 4)	203-367-8495
Greatest Bluefish Tournament on Earth (late August)	203-366-2583
Model Railroad Show (late March)	203-259-9592
SoundFest (early September)	203-335-1433
Stratford Day (mid-June)	203-377-0771
Westport Creative Arts Festival (early November)	203-222-1388
Westport Handcrafts Show (late May)	203-227-7844
WICC Greatest Bluefish Tournament on Earth (August)	203-366-6000

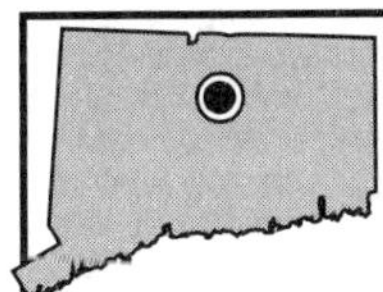

Hartford

From the founding of the Hartford Fire Insurance Company in 1810, Hartford has become known as the insurance capital of the U.S. (Hartford's insurance industry began as a response to the needs of the many factories in the area.) A self-guided walking tour of Hartford includes the Travelers Companies Tower, which offers a clear view of the surrounding area; the Wadsworth Atheneum, the first public art museum in the country; and the 1914 hand-carved Bushnell Park Carousel. Professionally trained Hartford Guides are on duty downtown to assist visitors who lose their way. Among Hartford's famous one-time residents are Samuel Colt, the gun manufacturer, and authors Mark Twain, Harriet Beecher Stowe, and Noah Webster.

Population	131,523	**Longitude**	72-68-56 W
Area (Land)	17.3 sq mi	**County**	Hartford
Area (Water)	0.7 sq mi	**Time Zone**	EST
Elevation	50 ft	**Area Code/s**	860
Latitude	41-76-36 N		

— Average Temperatures and Precipitation —

TEMPERATURES

	Jan	Feb	Mar	Apr	May	Jun	Jul	Aug	Sep	Oct	Nov	Dec
High	33	36	47	60	72	80	85	83	75	64	51	38
Low	16	19	28	38	48	57	62	60	52	41	33	21

PRECIPITATION

	Jan	Feb	Mar	Apr	May	Jun	Jul	Aug	Sep	Oct	Nov	Dec
Inches	3.4	3.2	3.6	3.9	4.1	3.8	3.2	3.7	3.8	3.6	4.0	3.9

— Important Phone Numbers —

	Phone		Phone
AAA	860-236-5864	**HotelDocs**	800-468-3537
Dental Referral	860-523-8657	**Poison Control Center**	800-343-2722
Emergency	911	**Time/Temp**	203-366-4242
Events Line	860-522-6400	**Weather**	203-366-4242

Hartford (Cont'd)

— Information Sources —

Name / Address	City	State	ZIP	Phone	Fax
Better Business Bureau Serving Connecticut 821 N Main St Ext Parkside Bldg *Web:* www.connecticut.bbb.org	Wallingford	CT	06492	203-269-2700	269-3124
Greater Hartford Convention & Visitors Bureau 1 Civic Center Plaza *TF:* 800-446-7811 ■ *Web:* www.grhartfordcvb.com ■ *E-mail:* ghcvb@connix.com	Hartford	CT	06103	860-728-6789	293-2365
Hartford City Hall 550 Main St *Web:* ci.hartford.ct.us	Hartford	CT	06103	860-522-4888	
Hartford Civic Center 1 Civic Center Plaza *Web:* www.hartfordciviccenter.com	Hartford	CT	06103	860-249-6333	241-4226
Hartford Mayor 550 Main St 2nd Fl *Web:* ci.hartford.ct.us/government/mayor/mayormike.htm	Hartford	CT	06103	860-543-8500	722-6606
Hartford Planning Dept 10 Prospect St 4th Fl	Hartford	CT	06103	860-543-8675	722-6402
Hartford Public Library 500 Main St *Web:* www.hartfordpl.lib.ct.us	Hartford	CT	06103	860-543-8628	722-6900
Metro Hartford Chamber of Commerce 250 Constitution Plaza *Web:* www.metrohartford.com ■ *E-mail:* info@metrohartford.com	Hartford	CT	06103	860-525-4451	293-2592

On-Line Resources

4Hartford.com	www.4hartford.com
About.com Guide to Hartford	hartford.about.com/local/newenglandus/hartford
Area Guide Hartford	hartford.areaguides.net
City Knowledge Hartford	www.cityknowledge.com/ct_hartford.htm
DigitalCity Hartford	home.digitalcity.com/hartford
Downtown Hartford Page	hartforddowntown.com/
Excite.com Hartford City Guide	www.excite.com/travel/countries/united_states/connecticut/hartford
Hartford Events Calendar	www.eventscalendar.com
Hartford Home Page	www.state.ct.us/MUNIC/HARTFORD/hartford.htm
XenonArts	www.xenonarts.com/

— Transportation Services —

AIRPORTS

■ Bradley International Airport (BDL)

	Phone
12 miles N of downtown Hartford (approx 15 minutes) Web: www.bradleyairport.com ■ *E-mail:* office@bradleyairport.com	860-292-2000

Airport Transportation

	Phone
Airport Connection $11 fare to downtown Hartford	860-627-3400
Greater Hartford Cab $28 fare to downtown Hartford	860-666-6666

Commercial Airlines

	Phone		Phone
Air Canada	800-776-3000	**MetroJet**	888-638-7653
AirTran	800-247-8726	**Midway**	800-446-4392
American	800-433-7300	**Northwest**	800-225-2525
Continental	800-525-0280	**Southwest**	800-435-9792
Delta	800-221-1212	**TWA**	800-221-2000
Delta Business Express	800-345-3400	**United**	800-241-6522
Delta Connection	800-221-1212	**US Airways**	800-428-4322

Charter Airlines

	Phone		Phone
24th Century Air	800-622-9740	**Million Air**	860-548-9334
Jet Aviation Business Jets Inc	800-736-8538		

CAR RENTALS

	Phone		Phone
Avis	860-627-3500	**Hertz**	860-627-3850
Budget	860-627-3660	**Thrifty**	860-623-8214
Dollar	860-627-9048		

LIMO/TAXI

	Phone		Phone
Carey/Elite Limousines	860-666-9051	**Greater Hartford Cab**	860-666-6666
Essex Limousine	860-767-2152	**Yellow Cab**	860-666-6666
Executive Cab	860-627-5843		

MASS TRANSIT

	Phone
CT Transit $1 Base fare	860-525-9181

RAIL/BUS

Name / Address	City	State	ZIP	Phone
Amtrak Station 1 Union Pl Union Stn *TF:* 800-872-7245	Hartford	CT	06103	860-727-1776
Greyhound Bus Station 1 Union Pl Union Stn *TF:* 800-231-2222	Hartford	CT	06103	860-522-9267

— Accommodations —

HOTELS, MOTELS, RESORTS

Name / Address	City	State	ZIP	Phone	Fax
Baymont Inns & Suites 64 Ella Grasso Tpke *TF:* 800-301-0200	Windsor Locks	CT	06096	860-623-3336	627-6641
Crowne Plaza Hartford 50 Morgan St *TF:* 800-227-6963	Hartford	CT	06120	860-549-2400	527-2746
Days Inn 207 Brainard Rd *TF:* 800-325-2525	Hartford	CT	06114	860-247-3297	249-3297
Days Inn Airport 185 Turnpike Rd *TF:* 800-329-7466	Windsor Locks	CT	06096	860-623-9417	623-5268
Doubletree Hotel 16 Ella Grasso Tpke *TF:* 800-222-8733 ■ *Web:* www.doubletreehotels.com/DoubleT/Hotel200/214/214Main.htm	Windsor Locks	CT	06096	860-627-5171	627-7029
Fairfield Inn 2 Loten Dr *TF:* 800-228-2800 ■ *Web:* fairfieldinn.com/BDLFI	Windsor Locks	CT	06096	860-627-9333	627-9333
Goodwin Hotel 1 Haynes St *TF:* 800-922-5006	Hartford	CT	06103	860-246-7500	247-4576
Great Meadow Inn 1499 Silas Deane Hwy	Rocky Hill	CT	06067	860-257-3140	257-3181
Hastings Hotel & Conference Center 85 Sigourney St	Hartford	CT	06105	860-727-4200	727-4215
Hilton Hartford Hotel 315 Trumbull St. *TF:* 800-445-8667	Hartford	CT	06103	860-728-5151	240-7247
Holiday Inn 363 Roberts St *TF:* 800-465-4329	East Hartford	CT	06108	860-528-9611	289-0270
Homewood Suites 65 Ella Grasso Tpke *TF:* 800-225-5466	Windsor Locks	CT	06096	860-627-8463	627-9313
Imperial Motel 927 Main St.	East Hartford	CT	06108	860-289-7781	291-8992
Manchester Village Inn 100 E Center St *TF:* 800-487-6499	Manchester	CT	06040	860-646-2300	649-6499
Marriott Hotel Farmington 15 Farm Springs Rd *TF:* 800-228-9290 ■ *Web:* marriotthotels.com/BDLCT	Farmington	CT	06032	860-678-1000	677-8849
Marriott Rocky Hill 100 Capital Blvd *TF:* 800-228-9290 ■ *Web:* marriotthotels.com/BDLRH	Rocky Hill	CT	06067	860-257-6000	257-6060
Quality Inn & Conference Center 51 Hartford Tpke. *TF:* 800-228-5151	Vernon	CT	06066	860-646-5700	646-0202
Radisson Hotel & Conference Center 100 Berlin Rd *TF:* 800-333-3333	Cromwell	CT	06416	860-635-2000	635-6970
Ramada Hotel 100 E River Dr *TF:* 800-272-6232	East Hartford	CT	06108	860-528-9703	289-4728
Ramada Inn Airport 5 Ella Grasso Tpke *TF:* 800-272-6232	Windsor Locks	CT	06096	860-623-9494	627-7462
Ramada Inn Capital Hill 440 Asylum St *TF:* 800-272-6232	Hartford	CT	06103	860-246-6591	728-1382
Rsdisson Springfield-Enfield 1 Bright Meadow Blvd *TF:* 800-333-3333	Enfield	CT	06082	860-741-2211	741-6917
Sheraton Hotel Bradley International Airport 1 Bradley International Airport Rd *TF:* 800-325-3535	Windsor Locks	CT	06096	860-627-5311	627-9348
Super 8 Motel 57 W Service Rd *TF:* 800-800-8000	Hartford	CT	06120	860-246-8888	246-8887
Susse Chalet 20 Waterchase Dr *TF:* 800-524-2538 ■ *Web:* www.sussechalet.com/rockyhill.html	Rocky Hill	CT	06067	860-563-7877	257-7417
Wellesley Inn 333 Roberts St. *TF:* 800-444-8888	East Hartford	CT	06108	860-289-4950	289-9258
West Hartford Inn 900 Farmington Ave	West Hartford	CT	06119	860-236-3221	236-3445

Hartford (Cont'd)

— Restaurants —

				Phone
Allegro Cafe (Italian) 347 Franklin Ave	Hartford	CT	06114	860-296-8139
Aqui Me Quedo (Puerto Rican) 622 Park St	Hartford	CT	06106	860-522-1717
Arch Street Tavern (American) 85 Arch St	Hartford	CT	06103	860-246-7610
Black-Eyed Sally's BBQ & Blues (Barbecue) 350 Asylum St	Hartford	CT	06103	860-278-7427
Bombay's Authentic Indian Cuisine (Indian) 89A Arch St	Hartford	CT	06103	860-724-4282
Bourbon Street North (American) 70 Union Pl	Hartford	CT	06103	860-525-1014
Carbone's Ristorante (Italian) 588 Franklin Ave	Hartford	CT	06114	860-296-9646
Casa Lisboa (Portuguese) 1911 Park St	Hartford	CT	06106	860-233-3184
Casa Mia Ristorante (Italian) 381 Franklin Ave	Hartford	CT	06114	860-296-3441
Chale Ipanema (Brazilian) 342 Franklin Ave	Hartford	CT	06114	860-296-2120
Chef Paolino (Italian) 30 State House Sq	Hartford	CT	06103	860-560-1959
Chuck's Steak House (Steak/Seafood) 1 Civic Center Plaza Hartford Civic Ctr	Hartford	CT	06103	860-241-9100
City Fare (American) 86 Franklin Ave	Hartford	CT	06114	860-293-2353
City Steam (American) 942 Main St	Hartford	CT	06103	860-525-1600
Civic Cafe on Trumball (International) 150 Trumball St	Hartford	CT	06103	860-493-7412
Coaches Sports Bar & Grille (American) 187 Allyn St	Hartford	CT	06103	860-522-6224
Corvo (Italian) 494 Franklin Ave	Hartford	CT	06114	860-296-5800
Costa del Sol (Spanish) 901 Wethersfield Ave	Hartford	CT	06114	860-296-1714
Fox & Hound (American) 539 Broad St	Hartford	CT	06106	860-278-7070
Gaetanos (Italian) 1 Civic Center Plaza	Hartford	CT	06103	860-249-1629
Hartford Brewery Ltd (American) 35 Pearl St	Hartford	CT	06103	860-246-2337
Hartford Club (Continental) 46 Prospect St	Hartford	CT	06103	860-522-1271
Hot Tomato's (Italian) 1 Union Station	Hartford	CT	06103	860-249-5100
Ichiban Japanese Steak House (Japanese) 1 Gold St	Hartford	CT	06103	860-560-1414
Kashmir Restaurant (Indian) 481 Wethersfield Ave	Hartford	CT	06114	860-296-9685
Max Downtown (New American) 185 Asylum St	Hartford	CT	06103	860-522-2530
McGregor's Jamaican Cuisine (Jamaican) 1137 Albany Ave	Hartford	CT	06112	860-728-3479
No Fish Today Inc (Seafood) 80 Pratt St	Hartford	CT	06105	860-244-2100
Peking Garden (Chinese) 244 Farmington Ave	Hartford	CT	06105	860-724-3579
Peppercorn's Grill (Italian) 357 Main St	Hartford	CT	06106	860-547-1714
Pierpont's Restaurant (American) 1 Haynes St	Hartford	CT	06103	860-522-4935
Shish Kebab House of Afghanistan (Afghan) 360 Franklin Ave	Hartford	CT	06114	860-296-0301
Skybox Sports Bar & Grill (American) 440 Asylum St	Hartford	CT	06103	860-724-1600
Skywalk Restaurant (American) 242 Trumbull St	Hartford	CT	06103	860-522-7623
Song Hays (Chinese) 93 Asylum St	Hartford	CT	06103	860-525-6388
USS Chowder Pot IV (Seafood) 165 Brainard Rd	Hartford	CT	06114	860-244-3311

— Goods and Services —

SHOPPING

Name	City	State	ZIP	Phone	Fax
Civic Center Mall & Pratt Street Shops 1 Civic Center Plaza	Hartford	CT	06103	860-275-6100	275-6110
Enfield Square Mall 90 Elm St	Enfield	CT	06082	860-745-7000	745-3007
Web: www.enfieldsquaremall.com/ ■ *E-mail:* Email:info@enfieldsquaremall.com					
Pavilion at State House Square 10 State House Sq	Hartford	CT	06103	860-241-0100	549-5301
Richardson Building 942 Main St	Hartford	CT	06103	860-525-9711	
Westfarms Mall 500 Westfarms Mall	Farmington	CT	06032	860-561-3420	521-8682

BANKS

Name	City	State	ZIP	Phone	Fax
Advest Bank & Trust 90 State House Sq	Hartford	CT	06103	860-509-3000	509-3571
TF: 800-541-3566 ■ *Web:* www.advest.com/bank/index.htm					
Bank of Boston Connecticut 100 Pearl St	Hartford	CT	06103	860-727-5000	727-6514
First International Bank 280 Trumbull St	Hartford	CT	06103	860-727-0700	525-2083
Fleet Bank 777 Main St	Hartford	CT	06115	860-986-2000	986-4350
TF Cust Svc: 800-833-6623*					
Mechanics Savings Bank 100 Pearl St	Hartford	CT	06103	860-293-4000	293-4033

BUSINESS SERVICES

	Phone
Accountemps	860-278-7170
Adecco Employment Personnel Services	860-513-5600
Corporate Express Delivery Systems	860-953-1422
Federal Express	800-238-5355
Kinko's	860-233-8245
Manpower Temporary Services	860-676-1320
Post Office	860-524-6001
UPS	800-742-5877

— Media —

PUBLICATIONS

Name	City	State	ZIP	Phone	Fax
East Hartford Gazette 1171 Main St	East Hartford	CT	06108	860-289-6468	289-6469*
**Fax:* News Rm					
Hartford Courant‡ 285 Broad St	Hartford	CT	06115	860-241-6200	241-3865*
**Fax:* News Rm ■ *TF:* 800-472-7377 ■ *Web:* www.courant.com ■ *E-mail:* readerep@courant.com					
Hartford News 191 Franklin Ave	Hartford	CT	06114	860-296-6128	296-8769*
**Fax:* News Rm ■ *Web:* www.hartfordnews.com ■ *E-mail:* ssmedia@townusa.com					

‡Daily newspapers

TELEVISION

Name	City	State	ZIP	Phone	Fax
WBNE-TV Ch 59 (WB) 8 Elm St	New Haven	CT	06510	203-782-5900	782-5995
Web: www.wb59.com ■ *E-mail:* feedback@wb59.com					
WEDH-TV Ch 24 (PBS) 240 New Britain Ave	Hartford	CT	06106	860-278-5310	278-2157
WFSB-TV Ch 3 (CBS) 3 Constitution Plaza	Hartford	CT	06103	860-728-3333	728-0263
Web: www.wfsb.com					
WHPX-TV Ch 26 (PAX) Shaws Cove 3 Suite 226	New London	CT	06320	860-444-2626	440-2601
Web: www.pax.net/whpx					
WTIC-TV Ch 61 (Fox) 1 Corporate Ctr	Hartford	CT	06103	860-527-6161	293-1571
Web: www.fox61.com					
WTNH-TV Ch 8 (ABC) 8 Elm St	New Haven	CT	06510	203-784-8888	787-9698
Web: www.wtnh.com ■ *E-mail:* wtnh@aol.com					
WTXX-TV Ch 20 (UPN) 1 Corporate Ctr	Hartford	CT	06103	860-520-6573	520-6578
WVIT-TV Ch 30 (NBC) 1422 New Britain Ave	West Hartford	CT	06110	860-521-3030	521-4860
Web: www.wvit.com					

RADIO

Name	City	State	ZIP	Phone	Fax
WCCC-AM 1290 kHz (Rock) 1039 Asylum Ave	Hartford	CT	06105	860-525-1069	246-9084
WCCC-FM 106.9 MHz (Rock) 1039 Asylum Ave	Hartford	CT	06105	860-525-1069	246-9084
WDRC-AM 1360 kHz (Nost) 869 BlueHills Ave	Bloomfield	CT	06002	860-243-1115	286-8257
Web: www.wdrc.com					
WDRC-FM 102.9 MHz (Oldies) 869 BlueHills Ave	Bloomfield	CT	06002	860-243-1115	286-8257
Web: www.wdrc.com					
WFAN-AM 660 kHz (Sports) 34-12 36th St	Astoria	NY	11106	718-706-7690	706-6481
WHCN-FM 105.9 MHz (CR) 10 Columbus Blvd	Hartford	CT	06106	860-723-6080	723-6106
WKSS-FM 95.7 MHz (CHR) 10 Columbus Blvd	Hartford	CT	06106	860-723-6160	723-6198
Web: www.kiss957.com					
WLAT-AM 1230 kHz (Span) 86 Cedar St	Hartford	CT	06106	860-524-0001	548-1922
WMRQ-FM 104.1 MHz (Alt) 10 Columbus Blvd	Hartford	CT	06106	860-723-6040	723-6078
Web: www.radio104.com ■ *E-mail:* feedback@radio104.com					
WNEZ-AM 910 kHz (Urban) 86 Cedar St	Hartford	CT	06106	860-524-0001	548-1922
WPKT-FM 90.5 MHz (NPR) 240 New Britain Ave	Hartford	CT	06106	860-278-5310	278-2157
WPOP-AM 1410 kHz (Sports) 10 Columbus Blvd	Hartford	CT	06106	860-723-6160	723-6195
WRCH-FM 100.5 MHz (AC) 10 Executive Dr	Farmington	CT	06032	860-677-6700	678-7053
WTIC-AM 1080 kHz (N/T) 1 Financial Plaza	Hartford	CT	06103	860-522-1080	549-3431
Web: www.wtic.com					
WTIC-FM 96.5 MHz (AC) 1 Financial Plaza	Hartford	CT	06103	860-522-1080	549-3431
Web: www.ticfm.com/ ■ *E-mail:* wticamfm@tiac.net					
WWYZ-FM 92.5 MHz (Ctry) 10 Columbus Blvd	Hartford	CT	06106	860-723-6120	723-6159
Web: www.wwyz.com					
WZMX-FM 93.7 MHz (CR) 10 Executive Dr	Farmington	CT	06032	860-677-6700	677-6799

— Colleges/Universities —

Name	City	State	ZIP	Phone	Fax
Asnuntuck Community-Technical College 170 Elm St	Enfield	CT	06082	860-253-3000	253-3016
Web: www.asctc.commnet.edu					
Capital Community-Technical College 61 Woodland St	Hartford	CT	06105	860-520-7800	520-7906
Web: webster.commnet.edu					

Hartford — Colleges/Universities (Cont'd)

	City	State	Zip	Phone	Fax
Central Connecticut State University 1615 Stanley St; *Web:* www.ccsu.ctstateu.edu	New Britain	CT	06050	860-832-3200	832-2295
Hartford College for Women 1265 Asylum Ave; *Web:* www.hartford.edu/uofh/hcw_s.html	Hartford	CT	06105	860-236-1215	768-5693
Hartford Seminary 77 Sherman St; *Web:* www.hartsem.edu ■ *E-mail:* drollins@ursa.hartnet.org	Hartford	CT	06105	860-509-9500	509-9509
Manchester Community-Technical College PO Box 1046	Manchester	CT	06045	860-646-4900	647-6328
Saint Joseph College 1678 Asylum Ave; *Web:* www.sjc.edu	West Hartford	CT	06117	860-232-4571	233-5695
Trinity College 300 Summit St; *Web:* www.trincoll.edu ■ *E-mail:* publicrelations@trincoll.edu	Hartford	CT	06106	860-297-2000	297-2275
Tunxis Community Technical College 271 Scott Swamp Rd	Farmington	CT	06032	860-677-7701	676-8906
University of Hartford 200 Bloomfield Ave; *Web:* www.hartford.edu	West Hartford	CT	06117	860-768-4100	768-4961

— Hospitals —

	City	State	Zip	Phone	Fax
Bristol Hospital PO Box 977; *Web:* www.bristolhospital.org	Bristol	CT	06011	860-585-3000	585-3058
Connecticut Children's Medical Center 282 Washington St; *Web:* www.ccmckids.org	Hartford	CT	06106	860-545-9000	545-8560
Hartford Hospital 80 Seymour St; *Web:* www.harthosp.org	Hartford	CT	06102	860-545-5000	545-4335
Manchester Memorial Hospital 71 Haynes St	Manchester	CT	06040	860-646-1222	647-4797
Mount Sinai Campus 500 Blue Hills Ave	Hartford	CT	06112	860-714-2611	714-2890
New Britain General Hospital 100 Grand St; *Web:* www.nbgh.org	New Britain	CT	06050	860-224-5011	224-5740
Rockville General Hospital 31 Union St	Vernon	CT	06066	860-872-0501	872-6056
Saint Francis Hospital & Medical Center 114 Woodland St; *Fax: Admitting ■ *TF:* 800-993-4312 ■ *Web:* www.stfranciscare.org/index.htm	Hartford	CT	06105	860-714-4000	714-8026*
University of Connecticut Health Center John Dempsey Hospital 263 Farmington Ave; *Web:* www.uchc.edu	Farmington	CT	06030	860-679-2000	679-4515
Veterans Administration Medical Center 555 Willard Ave	Newington	CT	06111	860-666-6951	667-6764

— Attractions —

	City	State	Zip	Phone	Fax
Artists Collective 1200 Albany Ave	Hartford	CT	06112	860-527-3205	527-2979
Austin Arts Center 300 Summit St; *Web:* www.trincoll.edu/~aac	Hartford	CT	06106	860-297-2199	297-5380
Bushnell Park Carousel Elm & Jewell Sts Bushnell Pk	Hartford	CT	06106	860-246-7739	
Bushnell Performing Arts Center 166 Capitol Ave; *TF:* 888-824-2874 ■ *Web:* www.bushnell.org ■ *E-mail:* info@bushnell.org	Hartford	CT	06106	860-987-5900	987-6080
Center Church & Ancient Burying Ground 60 Gold St	Hartford	CT	06103	860-249-5631	246-3915
Charter Oak Landing Cruises Charter Oak Landing; *Web:* www.deeprivernavigation.com	Hartford	CT		860-526-4954	526-2322
Christ Church Cathedral 45 Church St; *Web:* www.cccathedral.org ■ *E-mail:* ccc@tiac.net	Hartford	CT	06103	860-527-7231	527-5313
Connecticut Historical Society 1 Elizabeth St; *Web:* www.hartnet.org/~chs/ ■ *E-mail:* cthist@ix.netcom.com	Hartford	CT	06105	860-236-5621	236-2664
Connecticut Opera 226 Farmington Ave	Hartford	CT	06105	860-527-0713	293-1715
Connecticut State Capitol 210 Capitol Ave	Hartford	CT	06106	860-240-0222	
Constitution Plaza State & Market Sts	Hartford	CT	06103	860-527-7011	527-6577
Dance Connecticut 224 Farmington Ave	Hartford	CT	06105	860-525-9396	249-8116
Elizabeth Park Rose Gardens Prospect & Asylum Aves	Hartford	CT	06102	860-242-0017	242-0017
Goodwin Park Maple Ave & South St	Hartford	CT	06106	860-547-1426	722-6497
Governor's Residence 990 Prospect Ave	Hartford	CT	06105	860-566-4840	
Harriett Beecher Stowe House 77 Forest St	Hartford	CT	06105	860-525-9317	522-9259
Hartford Children's Theater PO Box 2547	Hartford	CT	06146	860-249-7970	548-0783
Hartford Chorale 200 Bloomfield Ave Hartt School; *Web:* www.hartfordchorale.org ■ *E-mail:* nhinchee@hickoryhill.com	West Hartford	CT	06117	860-547-1982	
Hartford Police Museum 101 Pearl St	Hartford	CT	06103	860-722-6152	
Hartford Stage Co 50 Church St	Hartford	CT	06103	860-527-5151	247-8243
Hartford Symphony Orchestra 166 Capitol Ave Bushnell Memorial Hall	Hartford	CT	06106	860-244-2999	
Isham-Terry House 211 High St	Hartford	CT	06112	860-247-8996	249-4907
King Edward E Museum 840 Main St	East Hartford	CT	06108	860-289-6429	291-9166
Lincoln Theater 200 Bloomfield Ave; *TF:* 800-274-8587	West Hartford	CT	06117	860-768-4228	768-4229
Mark Twain House & Memorial 351 Farmington Ave; *Web:* www.hartnet.org/~twain	Hartford	CT	06105	860-247-0998	
Meadows Music Theatre 61 Savitt Way; *Web:* www.meadowsmusic.com ■ *E-mail:* info@meadowsmusic.com	Hartford	CT	06120	860-548-7370	548-7386
Menczer Museum of Medicine & Dentistry 230 Scarborough St	Hartford	CT	06105	860-236-5613	236-8401
Museum of American Political Life 200 Bloomfield Ave University of Hartford; *Web:* www.hartford.edu/polmus/polmus1.html	West Hartford	CT	06117	860-768-4090	768-5159
New Britain Museum of American Art 56 Lexington St; *Web:* www.nbmaa.org	New Britain	CT	06052	860-229-0257	229-3445
Old State House 800 Main St	Hartford	CT	06103	860-522-6766	522-2812
Pump House Gallery Bushnell Pk	Hartford	CT	06106	860-722-6536	
Raymond E Baldwin Museum of Connecticut History 231 Capitol Ave	Hartford	CT	06106	860-566-3056	566-2133
Soldiers & Sailors Memorial Arch Trinity St Bushnell Pk; *Web:* www.bushnellpark.org/poi/smarch.html	Hartford	CT	06106	860-728-6789	722-6514
TheaterWorks 233 Pearl St	Hartford	CT	06103	860-527-7838	525-0758
Wadsworth Atheneum 600 Main St; *Web:* www.hartnet.org/~wadsworth/	Hartford	CT	06103	860-278-2670	527-0803

SPORTS TEAMS & FACILITIES

	City	State	Zip	Phone	Fax
Connecticut Pride (basketball) 21 Waterville Rd; *TF:* 888-887-7433 ■ *Web:* www.ctpride.com/ ■ *E-mail:* ctpride@ctpride.com	Avon	CT	06001	860-678-8156	674-2639
Connecticut Wolves (soccer) 635 S Main St Veterans Memorial Stadium; *Web:* www.ct-wolves.com ■ *E-mail:* connecticutwolves@yahoo.com	New Britain	CT	06050	860-223-0710	223-2759
Hartford Coliseum 1 Civic Center Plaza Hartford Civic Ctr	Hartford	CT	06103	860-249-6333	241-4226
New Britain Rock Cats (baseball) S Main St New Britain Stadium; *Web:* www.minorleaguebaseball.com/teams/east-nbr.php3	New Britain	CT	06051	860-224-8383	225-6267
Norwich Navigators (baseball) 14 Stott Ave Dodd Stadium; *TF:* 800-644-2867 ■ *Web:* www.gators.com	Yantic	CT	06360	860-887-7962	886-5996

— Events —

	Phone
Annual Daffodil Festival (late March)	860-236-5621
Big Bass Tournaments (late May-early September)	860-713-3131
Connecticut Family Folk Festival (early August)	860-632-7547
Family Day Festival (late August)	860-722-6567
Farmington Antique Weekend (early September)	800-793-4480
Festival of Jazz (early-mid-July)	800-332-7829
Festival of Light (late November-early January)	860-728-6789
First Night (December 31)	860-728-3089
Greater Hartford Marathon (early October)	860-525-3435
Greater Hartford Open (late June-early July)	860-246-4446
Hartford Flower Show (mid-February)	860-529-2123
Hebron Maple Festival (mid-March)	860-244-8181
Music Under the Stars Concert Series (early June-late September)	860-713-3131
Nutmeg State Games (mid-July)	860-528-4588
Podunk Blue Grass Music Festival (mid-August)	860-742-2430
Riverfest (early July)	860-293-0131
Riverfront Recapture Rowing Regatta (late September)	860-713-3131
Taste of Hartford (mid-June)	860-728-3089

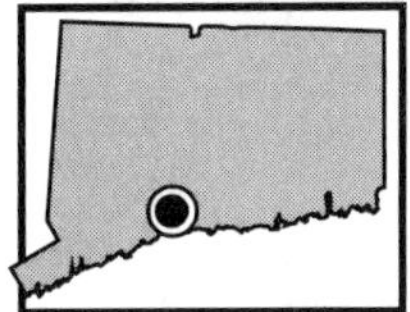

New Haven

The Yale University Art Gallery in New Haven is the nation's oldest college art museum, with 75,000 pieces from ancient Egypt to present day. Yale's Beinecke Rare Book and Manuscript Library features the Gutenberg Bible, a sunken sculpture garden, and translucent marble "windows." Out-of-the-ordinary books, as well as old maps (more than 20,000), prints, and curiosities can be found at the Whitlock Farm Book Barn near New Haven, in Bethany; and visitors can watch the maple syruping process on weekends in February and March at Wayne's Sugarhouse in North Branford.

Population 123,189
Area (Land) .... 18.9 sq mi
Area (Water) .... 1.4 sq mi
Elevation .... 25 ft
Latitude .... 41-30-81 N
Longitude .... 72-92-86 W
County .... New Haven
Time Zone .... EST
Area Code/s 203

— Average Temperatures and Precipitation —

TEMPERATURES

	Jan	Feb	Mar	Apr	May	Jun	Jul	Aug	Sep	Oct	Nov	Dec
High	36	38	46	57	67	76	82	81	74	64	53	41
Low	22	23	31	40	50	59	66	65	58	47	38	28

PRECIPITATION

	Jan	Feb	Mar	Apr	May	Jun	Jul	Aug	Sep	Oct	Nov	Dec
Inches	3.2	3.0	3.8	3.8	3.9	3.5	3.8	3.3	3.1	3.1	3.8	3.5

— Important Phone Numbers —

	Phone
AAA	203-281-1133
American Express Travel	203-772-0060
Emergency	911
HotelDocs	800-468-3537
Poison Control Center	800-343-2722
Time	203-777-4647
Travelers Aid	203-495-7437

— Information Sources —

				Phone	Fax
Better Business Bureau Serving Connecticut 821 N Main St Ext Parkside Bldg *Web:* www.connecticut.bbb.org	Wallingford	CT	06492	203-269-2700	269-3124
Greater New Haven Chamber of Commerce 900 Chapel St 10th Fl *Web:* www.newhavenchamber.com	New Haven	CT	06510	203-787-6735	782-4329
Greater New Haven Convention & Visitors Bureau 59 Elm St *TF:* 800-332-7829 ■ *Web:* www.newhavencvb.org/ ■ *E-mail:* mail@newhavencvb.org	New Haven	CT	06510	203-777-8550	782-7755
New Haven City Hall 165 Church St *Web:* cityofnewhaven.com/	New Haven	CT	06510	203-946-8339	946-6974
New Haven Free Public Library 133 Elm St *Web:* www.nhfpl.lib.ct.us/	New Haven	CT	06511	203-946-8130	946-8699
New Haven Mayor 165 Church St *Web:* cityofnewhaven.com/mayor/index.html	New Haven	CT	06510	203-946-8200	946-7683
New Haven Planning Dept 165 Church St	New Haven	CT	06510	203-946-6353	946-7815

On-Line Resources

Area Guide New Haven .... newhaven.areaguides.net
DigitalCity Hartford .... home.digitalcity.com/hartford
Excite.com New Haven City Guide .... www.excite.com/travel/countries/united_states/connecticut/new_haven
New Haven Web .... www.newhavenweb.com

— Transportation Services —

AIRPORTS

	Phone
■ **Tweed-New Haven Regional Airport (HVN)** 3 1/2 miles SE of downtown (approx 10 minutes)	203-466-8833

Airport Transportation

	Phone
Metro Taxi $10 fare to downtown	203-777-7777
New Haven Taxi $10 fare to downtown	203-877-0000

Commercial Airlines

	Phone
United	800-241-6522
United Express	800-241-6522
US Airways	800-428-4322

Charter Airlines

	Phone
Atlantic Aviation Charter	800-252-5387
Robinson Aviation	203-467-9555
Shoreline Aviation Inc	203-468-8639

CAR RENTALS

	Phone
Avis	203-466-2847
Budget	203-469-1943
Hertz	203-469-8826
Thrifty	203-562-3191

LIMO/TAXI

	Phone
Classic Limousine	203-466-3914
Connecticut Limousine	800-472-5466
Metro Taxi	203-777-7777
New Haven Taxi	203-877-0000
Yellow Cab	203-777-5555

MASS TRANSIT

	Phone
CT Transit $1 Base fare	203-624-0151

RAIL/BUS

				Phone
Greyhound Bus Station 50 Union Ave *TF:* 800-231-2222	New Haven	CT	06519	203-772-2470
Metro-North/Amtrak/Shore Line Railroad 50 Union Ave New Haven Union Stn	New Haven	CT	06519	203-773-6176

— Accommodations —

HOTELS, MOTELS, RESORTS

				Phone	Fax
Best Western Executive Hotel 490 Saw Mill Rd	West Haven	CT	06516	203-933-0344	937-1678
Colony The 1157 Chapel St *TF:* 800-458-8810	New Haven	CT	06511	203-776-1234	772-3929
Duncan Hotel 1151 Chapel St	New Haven	CT	06511	203-787-1273	787-0160
Grand Chalet Long Wharf 400 Sargent Dr *TF:* 800-524-2538	New Haven	CT	06511	203-562-1111	865-7440
Holiday Inn Downtown 30 Whalley Ave *TF:* 800-465-4329	New Haven	CT	06511	203-777-6221	772-1089
Holiday Inn Express 30 Frontage Rd *TF:* 800-465-4329	East Haven	CT	06512	203-469-5321	469-2544
Holiday Inn North Haven 201 Washington Ave *TF:* 800-465-4329	North Haven	CT	06473	203-239-4225	234-1247
Marriott Hotel Trumbull 180 Hawley Ln *TF:* 800-221-9855 ■ *Web:* marriotthotels.com/BDRCT	Trumbull	CT	06611	203-378-1400	378-4958
Motel 6 270 Foxon Blvd *TF:* 800-466-8356	New Haven	CT	06513	203-469-0343	468-0787
New Haven Hotel 229 George St *TF:* 800-644-6835 ■ *Web:* www.nhhotel.com ■ *E-mail:* nhhotel@snet.net	New Haven	CT	06510	203-498-3100	498-0911
Omni New Haven Hotel 155 Temple St *TF:* 800-843-6664	New Haven	CT	06510	203-772-6664	974-6777
Quality Inn 100 Pond Lily Ave *TF:* 800-228-5151	New Haven	CT	06525	203-387-6651	
Regal Inn 1605 Whalley Avenue	New Haven	CT	06515	203-389-9504	387-7099

New Haven — Hotels, Motels, Resorts (Cont'd)

	City	State	Zip	Phone	Fax
Residence Inn by Marriott 3 Long Wharf Dr. *TF:* 800-331-3131 ■ *Web:* www.residenceinn.com/HVNLW	New Haven	CT	06511	203-777-5337	
Three Chimneys Inn 1201 Chapel St *TF:* 800-443-1554	New Haven	CT	06511	203-789-1201	776-7363
Three Judges Motor Lodge 1560 Whalley Ave	New Haven	CT	06515	203-389-2161	397-5177
West Haven Hotel 7 Kimberly Ave	West Haven	CT	06516	203-932-8338	937-8984

— Restaurants —

	City	State	Zip	Phone
500 Blake St (Italian) 500 Blake St	New Haven	CT	06515	203-387-0500
Adriana's (Italian) 771 Grand Ave	New Haven	CT	06511	203-865-6474
Akasaka (Japanese) 1450 Whalley Ave	New Haven	CT	06515	203-387-4898
Bangkok Garden (Thai) 172 York St	New Haven	CT	06511	203-789-8684
Caffe Adulis (Ethiopian) 228 College St	New Haven	CT	06511	203-777-5081
Cape Codder (Seafood) 882 Whalley Ave	New Haven	CT	06515	203-389-8576
Chart House (Seafood) 100 S Water St	New Haven	CT	06519	203-787-3466
El Amigo Felix (Mexican) 8 Whalley Ave	New Haven	CT	06511	203-785-8200
Fireside Restaurant (American) 810 Woodward Ave	New Haven	CT	06512	203-466-1919
Frank Pepe's (Italian) 157 Wooster St	New Haven	CT	06519	203-865-5762
India Palace (Indian) 65 Howe St	New Haven	CT	06511	203-776-9010
Leon's (Italian) 1640 Whitney Ave	New Haven	CT	06517	203-281-5366
Mamoun's Falafel Restaurant (Middle Eastern) 85 Howe St	New Haven	CT	06511	203-562-8444
New West Cafe (American) 879 Whalley Ave	New Haven	CT	06515	203-387-5939
Pad Thai Restaurant (Thai) 1170 Chapel St	New Haven	CT	06511	203-562-0322
Sally's Pizza (Italian) 237 Wooster St	New Haven	CT	06511	203-624-5271
Scoozzi Trattoria (Italian) 1104 Chapel St	New Haven	CT	06510	203-776-8268
Seoul Restaurant (Korean) 341 Crown St	New Haven	CT	06511	203-497-9634
Thai Taste (Thai) 1151 Chapel St	New Haven	CT	06511	203-776-9802
Union League Cafe (French) 1032 Chapel St	New Haven	CT	06510	203-562-4299
York Street Cafe (American) 168 York St	New Haven	CT	06511	203-789-1915

— Goods and Services —

SHOPPING

	City	State	Zip	Phone	Fax
Boulevard Flea Market 520 Ella T Grasso Blvd	New Haven	CT	06519	203-772-1447	
Chapel Square Mall 900 Chapel St	New Haven	CT	06510	203-777-6661	674-2976
Connecticut Post Mall 1201 Boston Post Rd *Web:* connecticutpost.shoppingtown.com	Milford	CT	06460	203-878-6837	874-5812

BANKS

	City	State	Zip	Phone	Fax
Bank of Boston NA 123 Church St **Fax Area Code:* 401 ■ **Fax:* Cust Svc	New Haven	CT	06510	800-788-5000	276-1443*
Citizens Bank 209 Church St	New Haven	CT	06510	203-498-3600	624-0288
First Fidelity Bank 205 Church St	New Haven	CT	06510	203-773-0500	787-1501
Lafayette American Bank 2 Whitney Ave	New Haven	CT	06510	203-776-6033	782-3603
New Haven Savings Bank 195 Church St *Web:* www.nhsb.com	New Haven	CT	06510	203-787-1111	789-2650
Webster Bank 80 Elm St *TF:* 800-325-2424	New Haven	CT	06510	203-782-4588	782-4536

BUSINESS SERVICES

	Phone		Phone
Airborne Express	800-247-2676	**Kinko's**	203-799-2679
BAX Global	800-225-5229	**Mail Boxes Etc**	800-789-4623
DHL Worldwide Express	800-225-5345	**Post Office**	203-782-7000
Federal Express	800-238-5355	**Temporary Labor**	203-865-1151
Interim Personnel	203-624-2255	**UPS**	800-742-5877

— Media —

PUBLICATIONS

	City	State	Zip	Phone	Fax
New Haven Register‡ 40 Sargent Dr. *Web:* www.ctcentral.com	New Haven	CT	06511	203-789-5200	865-7894

‡*Daily newspapers*

TELEVISION

	City	State	Zip	Phone	Fax
WEDH-TV Ch 24 (PBS) 240 New Britain Ave	Hartford	CT	06106	860-278-5310	278-2157
WFSB-TV Ch 3 (CBS) 3 Constitution Plaza *Web:* www.wfsb.com	Hartford	CT	06103	860-728-3333	728-0263
WTIC-TV Ch 61 (Fox) 1 Corporate Ctr *Web:* www.fox61.com	Hartford	CT	06103	860-527-6161	293-1571
WTNH-TV Ch 8 (ABC) 8 Elm St *Web:* www.wtnh.com ■ *E-mail:* wtnh@aol.com	New Haven	CT	06510	203-784-8888	787-9698
WVIT-TV Ch 30 (NBC) 1422 New Britain Ave *Web:* www.wvit.com	West Hartford	CT	06110	860-521-3030	521-4860

RADIO

	City	State	Zip	Phone	Fax
WAVZ-AM 1300 kHz (Nost) 495 Benham St *Web:* www.wavz.com	Hamden	CT	06514	203-248-8814	281-2795
WELI-AM 960 kHz (N/T) 495 Benham St *Web:* www.weli.com	Hamden	CT	06514	203-281-9600	407-4652
WKCI-FM 101.3 MHz (CHR) 495 Benham St *Web:* www.kc101.com ■ *E-mail:* comments@kc101.com	Hamden	CT	06514	203-248-8814	281-2795
WPLR-FM 99.1 MHz (Rock) 1191 Dixwell Ave *Web:* www.wplr.com	Hamden	CT	06514	203-287-9070	287-8997
WYBC-FM 94.3 MHz (Urban) 165 Elm St *Web:* www.wybc.com/fm/index.html	New Haven	CT	06520	203-432-4118	432-4117

— Colleges/Universities —

	City	State	Zip	Phone	Fax
Albertus Magnus College 700 Prospect St *Web:* www.albertus.edu ■ *E-mail:* admissions@albertus.edu	New Haven	CT	06511	203-773-8550	773-3117
Gateway Community-Technical College 60 Sargent Dr. *Web:* www.commnet.edu/gwctc	New Haven	CT	06511	203-789-7071	867-6057
Naugatuck Valley Community-Technical College 750 Chase Pkwy *Web:* www.nvctc.commnet.edu	Waterbury	CT	06708	203-575-8040	575-8096
Paier College of Art Inc 20 Gorham Ave *Web:* www.paierart.com ■ *E-mail:* info@paierart.com	Hamden	CT	06514	203-287-3031	287-3021
Quinnipiac College 275 Mt Carmel Ave *TF:* 800-462-1944 ■ *Web:* www.quinnipiac.edu	Hamden	CT	06518	203-288-5251	281-8906
Southern Connecticut State University 501 Crescent St *Web:* www.scsu.ctstateu.edu	New Haven	CT	06515	203-392-5200	392-5727
University of New Haven 300 Orange Ave *TF:* 800-342-5864 ■ *Web:* www.newhaven.edu	West Haven	CT	06516	203-932-7000	931-6093
Yale University PO Box 208234 Yale Stn. *Web:* www.yale.edu	New Haven	CT	06520	203-432-4771	432-7329

— Hospitals —

	City	State	Zip	Phone	Fax
Hospital of Saint Raphael 1450 Chapel St **Fax:* Hum Res ■ *TF:* 800-662-2366 ■ *Web:* www.srhs.org	New Haven	CT	06511	203-789-3000	789-3359*
Milford Hospital 300 Seaside Ave	Milford	CT	06460	203-876-4000	876-4198
Veterans Affairs Health Care 950 Campbell Ave	West Haven	CT	06516	203-932-5711	937-3868
Yale-New Haven Hospital 20 York St *Web:* info.med.yale.edu/ynhh	New Haven	CT	06504	203-688-4242	688-4319

— Attractions —

	City	State	Zip	Phone	Fax
Alliance Theatre at University of New Haven 300 Orange Ave Dodds Hall	West Haven	CT	06516	203-932-7085	
Ansonia Nature & Recreation Center 10 Deerfield Rd.	Ansonia	CT	06401	203-736-9360	734-1672
Beinecke Rare Book & Manuscript Library at Yale 121 Wall St Yale University	New Haven	CT	06511	203-432-2977	432-4047
Boulevard Flea Market 520 Ella T Grasso Blvd	New Haven	CT	06519	203-772-1447	
Chamber Music Society at Yale 435 College St School of Music	New Haven	CT	06520	203-432-4158	
Connecticut Children's Museum 22 Wall St	New Haven	CT	06511	203-562-5437	
Edgerton Park-Greenbrier Greenhouse & Crosby Conservatory 75 Cliff St	New Haven	CT	06511	203-777-1886	787-7804

New Haven — Attractions (Cont'd)

				Phone	Fax
Eli Whitney Museum 915 Whitney Ave *Web:* www.eliwhitney.org/	Hamden	CT	06517	203-777-1833	777-1229
Ethnic Historical Archives Center 501 Crescent St	New Haven	CT	06515	203-392-6126	
Fairmount Theatre 33 Main St	New Haven	CT	06512	203-467-3832	467-3832
Fort Nathan Hale & Black Rock Fort 36 Woodward Ave	New Haven	CT	06512	203-946-8790	
Knights of Columbus Museum 1 Columbus Plaza	New Haven	CT	06510	203-772-2130	
Lighthouse Point Park 2 Lighthouse Rd	New Haven	CT	06512	203-946-8005	
Long Wharf Theatre 222 Sargent Dr *Web:* www.longwharf.org/	New Haven	CT	06511	203-787-4282	776-2287
Lyman John Performing Arts Center 501 Crescent St	New Haven	CT	06515	203-392-6154	392-6158
Milford's Wharf Lane Complex 34 High St	Milford	CT	06460	203-874-2664	
New England Actors' Theatre 160 Little Meadow Rd	Guilford	CT	06437	203-458-7671	
New Haven Colony Historical Society 114 Whitney Ave	New Haven	CT	06510	203-562-4183	562-2002
New Haven Crypt 250 Temple St	New Haven	CT	06511	203-787-0121	787-2187
New Haven Symphony Orchestra Yale University Woolsey Hall	New Haven	CT	06510	203-776-1444	789-8907
Orchestra New England College & Elm Sts Battell Chapel Yale University	New Haven	CT	06510	203-932-7180	934-8379
Palace Theatre 246 College St	New Haven	CT	06510	203-789-2120	789-0347
Pardee-Morris House 325 Lighthouse Rd	New Haven	CT	06512	203-562-4183	562-2002
Peabody Museum of Natural History 170 Whitney Ave Yale University *Web:* www.peabody.yale.edu/	New Haven	CT	06520	203-432-3750	432-9816
Shore Line Trolley Museum 17 River St *Web:* www.bera.org ■ *E-mail:* berasltm@aol.com	East Haven	CT	06512	203-467-6927	467-7635
Shubert Performing Arts Center 247 College St *Web:* www.shubert.com ■ *E-mail:* shubert@shubert.com	New Haven	CT	06510	203-624-1825	789-2286
West Rock Ridge State Park Wintergreen Ave	New Haven	CT	06515	203-789-7498	789-7498
Yale Center for British Art 1080 Chapel St *Web:* www.yale.edu/ycba	New Haven	CT	06520	203-432-2800	432-9695
Yale University Art Gallery 1111 Chapel St *Web:* www.yale.edu/artgallery	New Haven	CT	06520	203-432-0600	432-7159
Yale University Collection of Musical Instruments 15 Hillhouse Ave	New Haven	CT	06520	203-432-0822	432-8342
Yale University Theatre 222 York St	New Haven	CT	06510	203-432-1234	432-8337

SPORTS TEAMS & FACILITIES

				Phone	Fax
Milford Jai-Alai 311 Old Gate Ln *TF:* 800-243-9660 ■ *Web:* www.jaialai.com	Milford	CT	06460	203-877-4211	878-2317
New Haven Coliseum 275 S Orange St	New Haven	CT	06510	203-772-4200	495-7745
New Haven Ravens (baseball) 252 Derby Ave Yale Field *Web:* www.ravens.com	West Haven	CT	06510	203-782-1666	782-3150

— Events —

	Phone
Blessing of the Fleet (early June)	203-777-8550
Celebrate New Haven Fourth (early July)	203-946-7821
Celebration of American Crafts (early November-late December)	203-562-4927
Cider and Donuts Festival (mid-September)	203-777-8550
Fair on the Green (early June)	203-874-1982
Fall Festival & Chili Cookoff (mid-September)	203-387-7700
Film Fest New Haven (early April)	203-481-6789
Freddie Fixer Parade & Festival (early-mid-May)	203-389-1119
Gem & Mineral Show (mid-June)	203-929-3404
Goldenbells Festival (mid-late April)	203-281-4768
International Festival of Arts & Ideas (mid-June-early July)	203-498-1212
Kite Fly & Spring Festival (early May)	203-230-5226
Meet the Artists & Artisans (mid-May & early October)	203-874-5672
New England Arts and Crafts Festival (mid-July)	203-878-6647
North Haven Agricultural Fair (early-mid-September)	203-239-3700
Pilot Pen International Tennis Tournament (late August)	203-776-7331
Rolling Thunder Monster Truck Tour (early January)	203-772-4200
Saint Andrew's Italian Festival (late June)	203-865-9846
Saint Anthony's Feast (mid-June)	203-624-1418
Saint Barbara Greek Festival (early September)	203-795-1347
Saint Francis Strawberry Festival (mid-June)	203-294-1112
Savin Rock Festival (late July)	203-937-3511
SNET Jazz Festival (August)	203-946-7821
UI Fantasy of Lights (mid-November-early January)	203-777-2000
Winterfest (early February)	203-378-2700
Wooster Square Cherry Blossom Festival (mid-April)	203-865-5842

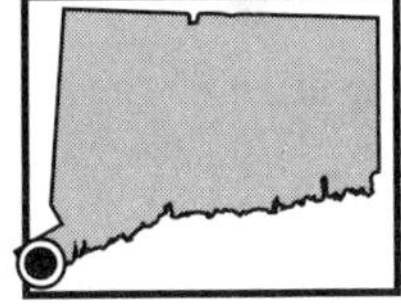

Stamford

Included among the many neighboring communities of coastal Connecticut is the industrial hub city of Stamford. Stamford serves as headquarters for a number of Fortune 500 companies, including GTE, Xerox, Pitney Bowes, and Champion International. The Champion headquarters building also houses the Whitney Museum of Art and its collection of 20th century American paintings and photography, as well as the top-floor Champion Greenhouse. Stamford has many marinas off Long Island Sound, and schooners depart from Stamford Harbor for sunset cruises.

Population	110,689	**Longitude**	73-53-92 W
Area (Land)	37.7 sq mi	**County**	Fairfield
Area (Water)	5.0 sq mi	**Time Zone**	EST
Elevation	10 ft	**Area Code/s**	203
Latitude	41-05-33 N		

— Average Temperatures and Precipitation —

TEMPERATURES

	Jan	Feb	Mar	Apr	May	Jun	Jul	Aug	Sep	Oct	Nov	Dec
High	37	40	50	61	72	80	84	83	76	65	54	41
Low	18	20	28	37	46	55	61	60	52	41	33	24

PRECIPITATION

	Jan	Feb	Mar	Apr	May	Jun	Jul	Aug	Sep	Oct	Nov	Dec
Inches	3.8	3.4	4.2	4.4	4.8	4.0	4.0	4.0	4.1	4.1	4.6	4.2

— Important Phone Numbers —

	Phone		Phone
AAA	203-765-4222	**Emergency**	911
American Express Travel	203-325-9070	**Poison Control Center**	800-343-2722
Dental Referral	203-322-5397	**Weather**	203-366-4242

— Information Sources —

				Phone	Fax
Better Business Bureau Serving Connecticut 821 N Main St Ext Parkside Bldg *Web:* www.connecticut.bbb.org	Wallingford	CT	06492	203-269-2700	269-3124
Coastal Fairfield County Convention & Visitors Bureau 383 Main Ave Merrittview Bldg 7th Fl. *TF:* 800-473-4868 ■ *Web:* www.visitfairfieldco.org	Norwalk	CT	06851	203-840-0770	840-0771
Fairfield County 1061 Main St *Web:* ffcol.com	Bridgeport	CT	06604	203-579-6527	382-8406
Ferguson Library 1 Public Library Plaza *Web:* www.futuris.net/ferg	Stamford	CT	06904	203-964-1000	357-9098
Stamford Chamber of Commerce 733 Summer St Suite 104 *Web:* www.stamfordchamber.com	Stamford	CT	06901	203-359-4761	363-5069
Stamford City Hall 888 Washington Blvd *Web:* www.ci.stamford.ct.us	Stamford	CT	06901	203-977-4056	
Stamford Mayor 888 Washington Blvd.	Stamford	CT	06901	203-977-4150	977-5845
Stamford Planning Board PO Box 10152	Stamford	CT	06904	203-977-4711	977-4100

Stamford (Cont'd)

On-Line Resources

Area Guide Stamford	stamford.areaguides.net
City Knowledge Stamford	www.cityknowledge.com/ct_stamford.htm
Excite.com Stamford City Guide	www.excite.com/travel/countries/united_states/connecticut/stamford
Stamford Home Page	www.gostamford.com
Surf & Sun Beach Vacation Guide to Stamford	www.surf-sun.com/ct-stamford-main.htm

— Transportation Services —

AIRPORTS

■ Westchester County Airport (HPN)

	Phone
13 miles W of downtown Stamford (approx 30 minutes)	914-285-4860

Web: www.co.westchester.ny.us/airport

Airport Transportation

	Phone
DLC Car Service $30 fare to downtown Stamford	914-592-8534

Commercial Airlines

	Phone		Phone
American	800-433-7300	**Pan Am**	800-359-7262
Business Express	603-740-3000	**US Airways**	800-428-4322
Northwest	800-225-2525	**Virgin Atlantic**	800-862-8621

Charter Airlines

	Phone		Phone
Atlantic Aviation Charter	800-252-5387	**Panorama Flight Service**	914-328-9800
Condor Express Corp	203-730-8436	**Pro Jet Charter**	800-422-2233
Diamond Air Charter Inc	800-946-4775	**Summit Aviation**	800-255-4625
Executive Fliteways	800-533-3363	**Tag Aviation**	800-235-9724
Executive Jet Management	877-356-5387	**Wayfarer Aviation**	914-949-3661
Flight Services Group Inc	800-380-4009	**Westchester Air Inc**	914-761-3000
Levetz Group	800-520-6854	**White Cloud Charter**	888-761-4011

■ LaGuardia Airport (LGA)

	Phone
30 miles SW of downtown Stamford (approx 50 minutes)	718-476-5000

Airport Transportation

	Phone
Connecticut Limousine $34 fare to downtown Stamford	800-472-5466

Commercial Airlines

	Phone		Phone
AccessAir	877-462-2237	**Delta**	800-221-1212
Air Canada	800-776-3000	**Midwest Express**	800-452-2022
American Eagle	800-433-7300	**TWA**	800-221-2000
Atlantic Coast Airlines	800-241-6522	**US Airways**	800-428-4322
Continental	718-565-1100	**US Airways Express**	800-428-4322

Charter Airlines

	Phone		Phone
Atlantic Aviation Charter	201-288-7660	**Northeast Airway**	973-267-2450
Jet Aviation Business Jets Inc	800-736-8538		

CAR RENTALS

	Phone		Phone
Avis	914-997-2300	**Budget-White Plains**	914-681-0663
Avis-La Guardia	718-507-3600	**Hertz-Stamford**	203-324-3131
Avis-Stamford	203-964-3200	**Hertz-White Plains**	203-324-3131
Budget-La Guardia	718-639-6400	**National-White Plains**	914-946-9080
Budget-Stamford	203-325-1535	**Sears-Stamford**	203-325-3435

LIMO/TAXI

	Phone		Phone
American Limousine	203-531-0700	**Lincoln Limousine**	203-964-9928
Canaan Parrish Taxi	203-966-6866	**Metropolitan Limousine**	203-323-6008
Connecticut Limo	203-878-2222	**Regency Limousine**	203-357-9717
Darien Yellow Cab	203-655-8779	**Stamford Taxi**	203-325-2611
Greenwich Taxi	203-869-6000	**Yellow Cab**	203-967-3633

MASS TRANSIT

	Phone
Connecticut Transit $1 Base fare	203-327-7433

RAIL/BUS

				Phone
Amtrak Station Washington Blvd & E State St Metro North Stn	Stamford	CT	06902	800-872-7245
Greyhound Bus Station 30 Station Pl *TF:* 800-231-2222	Stamford	CT	06904	203-348-6200

— Accommodations —

HOTELS, MOTELS, RESORTS

				Phone	Fax
Budget Host Hospitality Inn 19 Clarks Hill Ave *TF:* 800-362-7666 ■ *E-mail:* mail@budgethost.com	Stamford	CT	06902	203-327-4300	975-0328
Courtyard by Marriott 474 Main Ave *TF:* 800-321-2211 ■ *Web:* courtyard.com/HPNNW	Norwalk	CT	06851	203-849-9111	849-8144
Doubletree Club Hotel 789 Connecticut Ave *TF:* 888-444-2582	Norwalk	CT	06854	203-853-3477	855-9404
Four Points Hotel 426 Main Ave *TF:* 888-806-4786	Norwalk	CT	06851	203-849-9828	846-6925
Grand Chalet Inn & Suites 135 Harvard Ave *TF:* 800-524-2538	Stamford	CT	06902	203-357-7100	358-9332
Greenwich Harbor Inn 500 Steamboat Rd *TF:* 800-243-8511	Greenwich	CT	06830	203-661-9800	629-4431
Holiday Inn Stamford Downtown 700 Main St *TF:* 800-465-4329 ■ *Web:* www.basshotels.com/holiday-inn/?_franchisee=STMDT ■ *E-mail:* his-stamford@bristolhotels.com	Stamford	CT	06901	203-358-8400	358-8872
Homestead Inn 420 Field Point Rd	Greenwich	CT	06830	203-869-7500	869-7502
Howard Johnson Lodge 150 Ledge Rd *TF:* 800-446-4656	Darien	CT	06820	203-655-3933	655-3084
Howard Johnson Lodge Greenwich 1114 Boston Post Rd *TF:* 800-446-4656	Riverside	CT	06878	203-637-3691	637-0661
Hyatt Regency 1800 E Putnam Ave *TF:* 800-233-1234 ■ *Web:* www.hyatt.com/usa/old_greenwich/hotels/hotel_gwich.html	Old Greenwich	CT	06870	203-637-1234	637-2940
Sheraton Stamford Hotel 2701 Summer St	Stamford	CT	06905	203-359-1300	348-7937
Stamford Marriott 2 Stamford Forum *TF:* 800-228-9290	Stamford	CT	06901	203-357-9555	324-6897
Stamford Motor Inn 1209 E Main St	Stamford	CT	06902	203-325-2655	327-2897
Stamford Suites 720 Bedford St	Stamford	CT	06901	203-359-7300	359-7304
Stanton House Inn 76 Maple Ave	Greenwich	CT	06830	203-869-2110	629-2116
Super 8 Motel 32 Grenhart Rd *TF:* 800-800-8000	Stamford	CT	06902	203-324-8887	964-8465
West Lane Inn 22 West Ln.	Ridgefield	CT	06877	203-438-7323	438-7325
Westin Hotel 1 First Stamford Pl *TF:* 800-937-8461	Stamford	CT	06902	203-967-2222	967-3475

— Restaurants —

				Phone
Abis (Japanese) 381 Greenwich Ave	Greenwich	CT	06830	203-862-9100
Amadeus (International) 201 Summer St	Stamford	CT	06901	203-348-7775
Applausi (Italian) 199 Sound Beach Ave	Old Greenwich	CT	06870	203-637-4447
Bank Street Brewing Co (American) 65 Bank St *Web:* www.bankstreetbrewing.com	Stamford	CT	06901	203-325-2739
Bella Luna Restaurant (Italian) 934 Hope St	Stamford	CT	06907	203-969-1958
Bennett's Steak & Fish House (Steak/Seafood) 24 Spring St	Stamford	CT	06901	203-978-7995
Bonani Indian Cuisine (Indian) 490 Summer St	Stamford	CT	06901	203-348-8138
Cafe Morelli (Italian) 269 Bedford St	Stamford	CT	06901	203-353-3300
Columbus Park Trattoria (Italian) 205 Main St	Stamford	CT	06901	203-967-9191
Crab Shell (Seafood) 46 Southfield Ave	Stamford	CT	06902	203-967-7229
Eclisse Restaurant (Italian) 700 Canal St	Stamford	CT	06902	203-325-3773
Epicure Restaurant (International) 251 Summer St	Stamford	CT	06901	203-323-6229
Fiddler's Green (Irish) 280 Shippan Ave	Stamford	CT	06902	203-356-0906
Fireside Restaurant (International) 847 Hope St	Stamford	CT	06907	203-977-8332
Fjord Fisheries (Seafood) 49 Brown House Rd	Stamford	CT	06902	203-325-0255
Fuji (Chinese) 111 Old Kings Hwy N	Darien	CT	06820	203-655-4995
Great Wall (Chinese) 219 Atlantic St	Stamford	CT	06901	203-327-7188
Hacienda Don Emilio (Mexican) 222 Summer St	Stamford	CT	06901	203-324-0577
Il Mulino Ristorante (Italian) 1078 Hope St	Stamford	CT	06907	203-322-3300
Kujaku (Japanese) 84 W Park Pl	Stamford	CT	06901	203-357-0281
La Bretagne (French) 2010 W Main St	Stamford	CT	06902	203-324-9539
La Maison Indochine (Vietnamese) 107 Greenwich Ave	Greenwich	CT	06830	203-869-2689

Stamford — Restaurants (Cont'd)

				Phone
Mai Thai (Thai) 280 Railroad Ave.	Greenwich	CT	06830	203-625-2602
Mandarin Gourmet (Chinese) 587 Elm St	Stamford	CT	06902	203-975-9788
Meera Cuisine of India (Indian) 227 Summer St	Stamford	CT	06901	203-975-0479
Ole Mole (Mexican) 1030 High Ridge Rd	Stamford	CT	06905	203-461-9962
Paradise Bar and Grille Restaurant (American) 5 Stamford Landing	Stamford	CT	06902	203-323-1116
Pellicci's Restaurant (Italian) 98 Stillwater Ave.	Stamford	CT	06902	203-323-2542
Playwright (Irish) 488 Summer St	Stamford	CT	06901	203-353-1120
Rusty Scupper (California) 183 Harbor Dr.	Stamford	CT	06902	203-964-1235
SoNo Seaport (Seafood) 100 Water St	South Norwalk	CT	06854	203-854-9483
Summer Street Lobster House (Seafood) 222 Summer St *Web:* www.amerimall.com/summerstreet/	Stamford	CT	06901	203-353-9555
Taranto's Restaurant (Italian) 489 Glenbrook Rd.	Stamford	CT	06906	203-324-4735
Uncle Dai's Chinese Restaurant (Chinese) 109 Atlantic St	Stamford	CT	06901	203-327-5757

— Goods and Services —

SHOPPING

				Phone	Fax
Cannondale Village Danbury Rd.	Wilton	CT	06897		
Factory Outlets at Norwalk 230 East Ave.	Norwalk	CT	06855	203-838-1349	
Stamford Town Center 100 Grey Rock Pl.	Stamford	CT	06901	203-324-0935	359-9942
Stratford Antiques Center 400 Honeyspot Rd	Stratford	CT	06497	203-378-7754	

BANKS

				Phone	Fax
Chase Manhattan Bank of Connecticut 274 Hope St.	Stamford	CT	06906	800-242-7324	
Cornerstone Bancorp Inc 550 Summer St *Web:* www.cornerstonebank.com	Stamford	CT	06901	203-356-0111	316-5564
First County Bank 117 Prospect St **Fax:* Mktg	Stamford	CT	06901	203-323-3165	462-4442*
First Union National Bank 300 Main St.	Stamford	CT	06904	203-348-6211	323-4232
People's Bank 350 Bedford St	Stamford	CT	06901	203-359-6009	359-6008

BUSINESS SERVICES

	Phone
Airborne Express	800-247-2676
BAX Global	800-225-5229
DHL Worldwide Express	800-225-5345
Federal Express	800-238-5355
Interim Personnel	203-325-4151
Kinko's	203-968-8100
Mail Boxes Etc	800-789-4623
Manpower Temporary Services	203-348-9241
Olsten Staffing Services	203-327-1550
Post Office	203-323-2092
UPS	800-742-5877

— Media —

PUBLICATIONS

				Phone	Fax
Connecticut Magazine 35 Nutmeg Dr *Web:* www.connecticutmag.com	Trumbull	CT	06611	203-380-6600	380-6610
Stamford Advocate The‡ 75 Tresser Blvd **Fax:* Edit	Stamford	CT	06901	203-964-2200	964-2345*

‡Daily newspapers

TELEVISION

				Phone	Fax
WABC-TV Ch 7 (ABC) 7 Lincoln Sq *Web:* abcnews.go.com/local/wabc	New York	NY	10023	212-456-7777	456-2381
WCBS-TV Ch 2 (CBS) 524 W 57th St *Web:* www.cbs2ny.com	New York	NY	10019	212-975-4321	975-9387
WFSB-TV Ch 3 (CBS) 3 Constitution Plaza *Web:* www.wfsb.com	Hartford	CT	06103	860-728-3333	728-0263
WNBC-TV Ch 4 (NBC) 30 Rockefeller Plaza *Web:* www.newschannel4.com ■ *E-mail:* nbc4ny@nbc.com	New York	NY	10112	212-664-4444	664-2994
WNET-TV Ch 13 (PBS) 450 W 33rd St. *Web:* www.wnet.org ■ *E-mail:* webinfo@www.wnet.org	New York	NY	10001	212-560-1313	582-3297
WNYW-TV Ch 5 (Fox) 205 E 67th St.	New York	NY	10021	212-452-5555	249-1182
WTNH-TV Ch 8 (ABC) 8 Elm St. *Web:* www.wtnh.com ■ *E-mail:* wtnh@aol.com	New Haven	CT	06510	203-784-8888	787-9698
WVIT-TV Ch 30 (NBC) 1422 New Britain Ave *Web:* www.wvit.com	West Hartford	CT	06110	860-521-3030	521-4860

RADIO

Name	City	State	ZIP	Phone	Fax
WEBE-FM 107.9 MHz (AC) 2 Lafayette Sq	Bridgeport	CT	06604	203-366-6000	339-4001
WEDW-FM 88.5 MHz (Clas) 307 Atlantic St.	Stamford	CT	06901	203-965-0440	965-0447
WICC-AM 600 kHz (AC) 2 Lafayette Sq	Bridgeport	CT	06604	203-366-6000	339-4001
WKHL-FM 96.7 MHz (Oldies) 444 Westport Ave. *Web:* www.wkhl.com	Norwalk	CT	06851	203-845-3030	845-3097
WSTC-AM 1400 kHz (N/T) 444 Westport Ave	Norwalk	CT	06851	203-845-3030	845-3097

— Colleges/Universities —

Name	City	State	ZIP	Phone	Fax
Saint Basil's College 195 Glenbrook Rd	Stamford	CT	06902	203-324-4578	967-9948

— Hospitals —

Name	City	State	ZIP	Phone	Fax
Saint Joseph Medical Center 128 Strawberry Hill Ave. **Fax:* Mail Rm	Stamford	CT	06904	203-353-2000	353-2307*
Stamford Hospital Shelburne Rd.	Stamford	CT	06904	203-325-7000	325-7699

— Attractions —

Name	City	State	ZIP	Phone	Fax
Bartlett Arboretum 151 Brookdale Rd University of Connecticut	Stamford	CT	06903	203-322-6971	595-9168
Bates-Scofield Homestead 45 Old King's Hwy N.	Darien	CT	06820	203-655-9233	
Bowman Observatory 1 Museum Dr	Greenwich	CT	06830	203-869-0376	869-0963
Bruce Museum 1 Museum Dr. *Web:* www.brucemuseum.org/	Greenwich	CT	06830	203-869-0376	869-0963
Bush-Holley House 39 Strickland Rd.	Cos Cob	CT	06807	203-869-6899	
Champion Greenhouse Atlantic St & Tresser Blvd 1 Champion Plaza	Stamford	CT	06921	203-358-6533	358-7606
Connecticut Ballet 20 Acosta St	Stamford	CT	06902	203-964-1211	961-1928
Connecticut Grand Opera 4 Landmark Sq	Stamford	CT	06901	203-359-0009	327-1417
Curtain Call 1349 Newfield Ave Sterling Farms Theater Complex.	Stamford	CT	06905	203-329-8207	322-3656
Darien Nature Center 120 Brookside Rd	Darien	CT	06820	203-655-7459	655-3185
Fairfield Orchestra 50 Washington St 10th Fl.	Norwalk	CT	06854	203-838-6995	838-6998
First Presbyterian Church 1101 Bedford St	Stamford	CT	06905	203-324-9522	348-5229
Greenwich Arts Center 299 Greenwich Ave	Greenwich	CT	06830	203-622-3998	622-3980
Greenwich Symphony Orchestra 10 Hillside Rd.	Greenwich	CT	06830	203-869-2664	
Hoyt-Barnum House 713 Bedford St	Stamford	CT	06905	203-329-1183	
IMAX Cinema 10 N Water St	South Norwalk	CT	06854	203-852-0700	838-5416
Lockwood-Mathews Mansion Museum 295 West Ave. *Web:* www.norwalk.com/mansion	Norwalk	CT	06850	203-838-9799	838-1434
Maritime Aquarium at Norwalk 10 N Water St *Web:* www.maritimeaquarium.org/	Norwalk	CT	06854	203-852-0700	838-5416
Mianus River Preserve Westover Rd.	Stamford	CT	06902	203-977-4692	
Mill Hill Historic Park Wall St & East Ave	Norwalk	CT	06851	203-846-0525	
National Audubon Society 613 Riversville Rd.	Greenwich	CT	06831	203-869-5272	869-4437
New Canaan Historical Society Museum 13 Oenoke Ridge	New Canaan	CT	06840	203-966-1776	972-5917
New Canaan Nature Center 144 Oenoke Ridge.	New Canaan	CT	06840	203-966-9577	966-6536
New England Brewing Co 13 Marshall St.	Norwalk	CT	06854	203-866-1339	838-7168
Norwalk Community-Technical College Performing Arts Center 188 Richards Ave	Norwalk	CT	06854	203-857-7271	857-3335
Norwalk Concert Hall 125 East Ave.	Norwalk	CT	06856	203-854-7704	
Norwalk Symphony Orchestra 125 East Ave. *Web:* www.norwalk.com/nso	Norwalk	CT	06856	203-866-2455	866-2290
Palace Theater of the Arts 307 Atlantic St.	Stamford	CT	06901	203-325-4466	358-2313

Stamford — Attractions (Cont'd)

				Phone	Fax
Powerhouse Performing Arts Center 679 South Ave	New Canaan	CT	06840	203-966-7371	
Putnam Cottage 243 E Putname Ave	Greenwich	CT	06830	203-869-9697	
Rainbow Theatre 51 Caprice Dr	Stamford	CT	06902	203-921-1112	
Rowayton Arts Center 145 Rowayton Ave	Rowayton	CT	06853	203-866-2744	866-1123
Sheffield Island Lighthouse 132 Water St *TF:* 888-701-7785 ■ *Web:* www.seaport.org	South Norwalk	CT	06854	203-838-9444	855-1017
Silvermine Guild Arts Center 1037 Silvermine Rd *Web:* www.silvermineart.org	New Canaan	CT	06840	203-966-5617	966-2763
Square One Theatre Co 2422 Main St.	Stramford	CT	06497	203-375-8778	
Stamford Center for the Arts 307 Atlantic St *Web:* www.onlyatsca.com	Stamford	CT	06901	203-358-2305	358-2313
Stamford Historical Society Museum 1508 High Ridge Rd *Web:* www.cslnet.ctstateu.edu/stamford	Stamford	CT	06903	203-329-1183	322-1607
Stamford Museum & Nature Center 39 Scofieldtown Rd *Web:* www.stamfordmuseum.org	Stamford	CT	06903	203-322-1646	322-0408
Stamford Symphony Orchestra 61 Atlantic St Palace Theatre	Stamford	CT	06901	203-325-1407	325-8762
Stamford Theater Works 200 Strawberry Hill Ave	Stamford	CT	06902	203-359-4414	356-1846
Sterling Farms Theatre Complex 1349 Newfield Ave	Stamford	CT	06905	203-329-8207	
Town Players of New Canaan 679 South Ave *Web:* www.tpnc.org ■ *E-mail:* info@tpnc.org	New Canaan	CT	06840	203-966-7084	
Weir Farms National Historic Site 735 Nod Hill Rd *Web:* www.nps.gov/wefa/	Wilton	CT	06897	203-834-1896	834-2421
White Barn Theatre 452 Newtown Ave	Norwalk	CT	06851	203-227-3768	845-8781
Whitney Museum of American Art Atlantic St & Tresser Blvd *Web:* www.echonyc.com/~whitney	Stamford	CT	06921	203-358-7652	358-2975
Wilton Playshop 15 Lovers Ln	Wilton	CT	06897	203-762-7629	
Woodcock Nature Center 56 Deer Run Rd	Wilton	CT	06897	203-762-7280	834-0062
WPA Murals Collection at Norwalk City Hall 125 East Ave	Norwalk	CT	06851	203-854-7900	

— Events —

	Phone
Afternoon of Jazz Festival (late June)	212-290-8600
American Craftsmanship Show (mid-November)	203-762-7257
Antiquarius Christmas Antiques Show (mid-December)	203-869-6899
Antiques Alfresco (mid-September)	203-655-9233
Bruce Museum Outdoor Art Festival (mid-October & late May)	203-869-0376
Cannon Grange Fair (late August)	203-972-0207
Fourth of July Celebration & Fireworks (July 4)	203-977-4150
Gem & Mineral Show (early November)	203-322-4670
Harvest Fair (mid-September)	203-322-1646
Holiday Parade (late November)	203-348-5285
Norwalk Aquarium Society Show (early October)	203-227-7253
Norwalk International In-Water Boat Show (late September)	212-922-1212
Norwalk Oyster Festival (early September)	203-838-9444
Norwalk Seaport's Festival of Crafts (mid-March)	203-838-9444
Outdoor Antiques Fair (May)	203-838-2115
Ox Ridge Summershow (mid-June)	203-655-2559
Round Hill Highland Scottish Games (early July)	203-854-7806
SoNo Arts Celebration Weekend (early August)	203-855-8823
Spring Challenge Rowing Regatta (April)	203-840-0770
Spring on the Farm (late May)	203-322-1646
Stamford Historical Society Quilt Show (late September)	203-329-1183
Victorian Christmas Celebration (mid-December)	203-838-9799
Victorian Ice Cream Social (mid-July)	203-838-9799
Winterbloom (late February)	203-322-6971
Winterfest (late January)	203-322-1646

Delaware

Population (1999): 753,538 **Area (sq mi): 2,489**

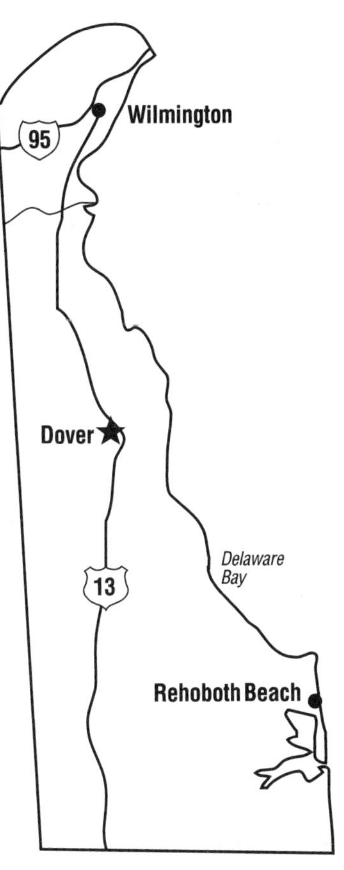

— State Information Sources —

				Phone	Fax
Delaware Div of Libraries 43 S DuPont Hwy..... Web: www.lib.de.us	Dover	DE	19901	302-739-4748	739-6787
Delaware Economic Development Authority 99 Kings Hwy......................... Web: www.state.de.us/dedo	Dover	DE	19903	302-739-4271	739-5749
Delaware Parks & Recreation Div 89 Kings Hwy.. TF: 800-474-4357 ■ Web: www.dnrec.state.de.us/parks/dsp1st.htm ■ E-mail: parkinfo@dnrec.state.de.us	Dover	DE	19901	302-739-4702	739-3817
Delaware State Chamber of Commerce PO Box 671...................... Web: www.inet.net/dscc ■ E-mail: dscc@inet.net	Wilmington	DE	19899	302-655-7221	654-0691
Delaware State Government Information....................... Web: www.state.de.us				302-739-4000	
Delaware Tourism Office 99 Kings Hwy........ TF: 800-441-8846 ■ Web: www.state.de.us/tourism/intro.htm	Dover	DE	19901	302-739-4271	739-5749

ON-LINE RESOURCES

Daily Orbit Delaware.................................... www.dailyorbit.com/delaware
Delaware Beach-Net.. www.beach-net.com
Delaware Cities........................dir.yahoo.com/Regional/U_S__States/Delaware/Cities
Delaware Counties & Regions...............dir.yahoo.com/Regional/U_S__States/Delaware/Counties_and_Regions
Delaware Info Net.................................... www.delmarweb.com/delaware
Delaware Scenario.............................. scenariousa.dstylus.com/de/indexf.htm
Delaware Travel & Tourism Guide...www.travel-library.com/north_america/usa/delaware/index.html
Front Door to Delaware...................................... www.dtcc.edu/delaware
Rough Guide Travel Delaware................. travel.roughguides.com/content/650/index.htm
Southern Delaware Tourism.................................. www.visitdelaware.com
Travel.org-Delaware..travel.org/delaware.html
Yahoo! Get Local Delaware...................dir.yahoo.com/Regional/U_S__States/Delaware

— Cities Profiled —

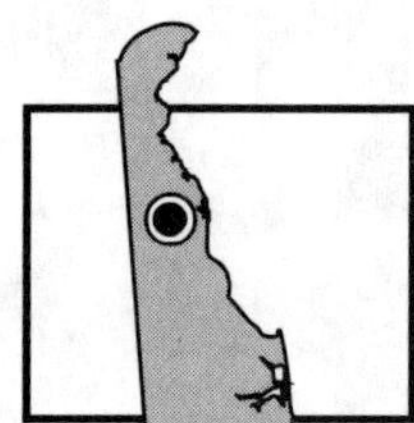

Dover

Delaware's capital is located in Kent County, in the central part of the state, in an area of grand Georgian and Victorian homes. Horse-drawn buggies from nearby Amish communities are a common sight in Dover, but the city is also home to Dover Downs, which hosts both NASCAR and harness racing events. Among the many sites in historic downtown Dover are the Golden Fleece Tavern Site where Delaware became the first state to ratify the United States Constitution in 1787; and the Victrola Museum, a tribute to inventor Eldridge Johnson, founder of the Victor Talking Machine Company (later RCA), which featured the trademark dog "Nipper" listening to "His Master's Voice.'

Population ... 30,369
Area (Land) ... 21.3 sq mi
Area (Water) ... 0.3 sq mi
Elevation ... 36 ft
Latitude ... 39-15-08 N
Longitude ... 75-53-27 W
County ... Kent
Time Zone ... EST
Area Code/s ... 302

— Average Temperatures and Precipitation —

TEMPERATURES

	Jan	Feb	Mar	Apr	May	Jun	Jul	Aug	Sep	Oct	Nov	Dec
High	43	46	56	65	75	84	88	86	80	70	59	48
Low	25	27	35	43	53	62	67	66	59	48	39	30

PRECIPITATION

	Jan	Feb	Mar	Apr	May	Jun	Jul	Aug	Sep	Oct	Nov	Dec
Inches	3.4	2.9	3.8	3.5	4.0	3.9	4.2	4.3	4.3	3.3	3.2	3.5

— Important Phone Numbers —

	Phone
AAA	302-674-8020
American Express Travel	302-678-3747
Dental Referral	302-655-1228
Emergency	911
Medical Referral	302-674-7042
Poison Control Center	800-722-7112
Weather	302-674-9262

— Information Sources —

				Phone	Fax
Better Business Bureau Serving Delaware 1010 Concord Ave Suite 101 *Web:* www.wilmington.bbb.org	Wilmington	DE	19802	302-594-9200	594-1052
Central Delaware Economic Development Council Treadway Towers Suite 2-B *TF:* 800-624-2522 ■ *Web:* www.conway.com/de/cdedc.htm	Dover	DE	19903	302-678-3028	678-0189
Dover City Hall PO Box 475 *Web:* www.cityofdover.com	Dover	DE	19903	302-736-7008	736-7177
Dover Mayor PO Box 475 *Web:* www.cityofdover.com/maycoun.html	Dover	DE	19903	302-736-7004	736-7002
Dover Public Library 45 S State St *Web:* www.cityofdover.com/library.html	Dover	DE	19901	302-736-7030	736-5087
Kent County 414 Federal St	Dover	DE	19901	302-736-2040	736-2279
Kent County/Dover Convention & Visitors Bureau 9 E Loockerman St Suite 203 *TF:* 800-233-5368 ■ *Web:* www.visitdover.com ■ *E-mail:* kctc@visitdover.com	Dover	DE	19901	302-734-1736	734-0167

On-Line Resources

Area Guide Dover ... dover.areaguides.net
Dover ... www.dmv.com/btob/dover/
Excite.com Dover City Guide ... www.excite.com/travel/countries/united_states/delaware/dover

— Transportation Services —

AIRPORTS

	Phone
■ **Philadelphia International Airport (PHL)** 75 miles N of downtown Dover (approx 90 minutes)	215-937-6937

Airport Transportation

	Phone
City Cab $95 fare to downtown Dover	302-734-5968
Galaxy Express Shuttle $55 fare to downtown Dover	302-678-3808

Commercial Airlines

	Phone
Air Jamaica	800-523-5585
American	800-433-7300
American Eagle	800-433-7300
British Airways	800-247-9297
Continental	800-525-0280
Continental Express	800-525-0280
Delta	800-221-1212
Midway	800-446-4392
Northwest	800-225-2525
United	800-241-6522
US Airways	800-428-4322
US Airways Express	800-428-4322

Charter Airlines

	Phone
Northeast Aviation Charter Inc	215-677-5592
Philadelphia Jet Service	800-468-1490
Sterling Helicopters	215-271-2510
Wings Charter	215-646-1800

CAR RENTALS

	Phone
Alamo-Philadelphia	215-492-3960
Avis	302-734-5550
Avis-Philadelphia	215-492-0900
Budget-Philadelphia	215-492-9400
Dollar-Philadelphia	215-365-2700
Enterprise	610-521-3700
Hertz-Philadelphia	215-492-7200
Hertz	302-678-0700
National-Philadelphia	215-492-2750

LIMO/TAXI

	Phone
Adam's Limousine	302-734-8540
Camelot Luxury Limousines	302-736-6510
City Cab	302-734-5968
Galaxy Express Shuttle	302-678-3808

MASS TRANSIT

	Phone
Central Delaware Transit $1.15 Base fare	302-739-3278

RAIL/BUS

				Phone
Trailways Bus Station 650 Bay Court Plaza	Dover	DE	19901	302-734-1417

— Accommodations —

HOTELS, MOTELS, RESORTS

				Phone	Fax
Best Western Galaxy Inn 1700 E Lebanon Rd *TF:* 800-528-1234	Dover	DE	19901	302-735-4700	735-1604
Comfort Inn South 222 S DuPont Hwy *TF:* 800-228-5150	Dover	DE	19901	302-674-3300	674-3300
Comfort Suites 1654 N Dupont Hwy *TF:* 800-228-5150	Dover	DE	19901	302-736-1204	736-1274
Days Inn 272 N DuPont Hwy *TF:* 800-329-7466	Dover	DE	19901	302-674-8002	674-2195
Dover Budget Inn 1426 N DuPont Hwy	Dover	DE	19901	302-734-4433	734-4433
Dover Inn 428 N DuPont Hwy	Dover	DE	19901	302-674-4011	674-5316
Gray's Motel 6232 N Dupont Hwy	Dover	DE	19901	302-734-2857	734-2857
Hampton Inn 1568 N Dupont Hwy *TF:* 800-426-7866	Dover	DE	19901	302-736-3500	736-6402
Howard Johnson Dover 561 N DuPont Hwy *TF:* 800-446-4656	Dover	DE	19901	302-678-8900	678-2245
Kent Budget Motel 383 N Dupont Hwy	Dover	DE	19901	302-674-2211	678-1029
Ramada Inn 348 N DuPont Hwy *TF:* 800-272-6232	Dover	DE	19901	302-734-5701	674-4788
Relax Inn 640 S Dupont Hwy	Dover	DE	19901	302-734-8120	734-3720
Sheraton Inn & Conference Center 1570 N DuPont Hwy *TF:* 800-325-3535	Dover	DE	19901	302-678-8500	678-9073
Super Lodge 246 N DuPont Hwy	Dover	DE	19901	302-678-0160	674-4734

Dover (Cont'd)

— Restaurants —

				Phone
Blue Coat Inn (Seafood) 800 N State St	Dover	DE	19901	302-674-1776
Dolphin Seafood (Seafood) 1417 New Burton Rd	Dover	DE	19901	302-674-3872
El Sombrero (Mexican/Indian) 655 N DuPont Hwy	Dover	DE	19901	302-678-9445
Froggy's Bar & Grille (American) 1036 Lafferty Ln	Dover	DE	19901	302-678-1117
Hibachi Japanese Steak House (Japanese) 691 N DuPont Hwy	Dover	DE	19901	302-734-5900
La Tolteca (Mexican) 245 S DuPont Hwy	Dover	DE	19901	302-734-3444
Orient Express (Chinese) 530 S Bay Rd	Dover	DE	19901	302-674-8410
Roma Italian Restaurant (Italian) 3 President Dr	Dover	DE	19901	302-678-1041
Sambo's Tavern (Seafood) 283 Front St	Dover	DE	19901	302-674-9724
Schucker's Pier 13 Restaurant (Seafood) 889 N DuPont Hwy	Dover	DE	19901	302-674-1190
Shanghai Gardens (Chinese) 561-B N DuPont Hwy	Dover	DE	19901	302-678-0981
Steaming Bean Cafe (American) 25 W Loockerman St	Dover	DE	19904	302-734-2526
Thomas England House (Steak/Seafood) Rt 13	Smyrna	DE	19977	302-653-1420
Three Kings Restaurant (Homestyle) 1171 S Bay Rd	Dover	DE	19901	302-672-6450
Where Pigs Fly (Barbecue) 617 E Loockerman St	Dover	DE	19901	302-678-0586
Win Hing (Chinese) 1618 S Governors Ave	Dover	DE	19901	302-734-8825

— Goods and Services —

SHOPPING

				Phone	Fax
Blue Hen Mall 655 S Bay Rd	Dover	DE	19901	302-678-2209	678-3510
Dover Mall 13 N DuPont Hwy	Dover	DE	19901	302-734-0414	734-9474
Web: www.dovermall.com					
Spence's Bazaar South & New Sts	Dover	DE	19901	302-734-3441	

BANKS

				Phone	Fax
Artisan's Savings Bank 1555 S Governors Ave	Dover	DE	19904	302-674-3214	674-0860
TF: 800-282-8255					
First Union Bank 101 W Loockerman St	Dover	DE	19904	302-736-2910	734-9245
TF: 800-275-3862					
Mellon Bank 8 W Loockerman St	Dover	DE	19901	302-734-0206	734-0204*
**Fax:* Cust Svc ■ *TF:* 800-323-7105					
PNC Bank 3 The Plaza	Dover	DE	19904	302-735-3117	674-3082
TF: 800-926-2265					

BUSINESS SERVICES

	Phone
Airborne Express	800-247-2676
BAX Global	800-225-5229
DHL Worldwide Express	800-225-5345
Federal Express	800-238-5355
Interim Personnel Services	302-452-5600
Kelly Services	302-674-8087
Kinko's	302-678-4850
Mail Boxes Etc	800-789-4623
Manpower Temporary Services	302-674-8600
Olsten Staffing Services	302-734-5379
Post Office	302-734-5821
UPS	800-742-5877

— Media —

PUBLICATIONS

				Phone	Fax
Delaware State News‡ PO Box 737	Dover	DE	19903	302-674-3600	741-8252
Web: www.newszap.com					
Dover Post PO Box 664	Dover	DE	19903	302-678-3616	678-8291*
**Fax:* News Rm ■ *Web:* www.doverpost.com					

‡*Daily newspapers*

TELEVISION

				Phone	Fax
KYW-TV Ch 3 (CBS) 101 S Independence Mall E	Philadelphia	PA	19106	215-238-4700	238-4783
Web: www.kyw.com					
WBOC-TV Ch 16 (CBS) 1729 N Salisbury Blvd	Salisbury	MD	21801	410-749-1111	742-5190
Web: www.wboc.com ■ *E-mail:* wboc@wboc.com					
WCAU-TV Ch 10 (NBC) 10 Monument Rd	Bala Cynwyd	PA	19004	610-668-5510	668-3700
Web: www.nbc10.com					
WHYY-TV Ch 12 (PBS) 150 N 6th St	Philadelphia	PA	19106	215-351-1200	351-0398
Web: whyy.org ■ *E-mail:* talkback@whyy.org					
WMDT-TV Ch 47 (ABC) 202 Downtown Plaza	Salisbury	MD	21801	410-742-4747	742-5767
Web: www.wmdt.com ■ *E-mail:* letters@wmdt.com					
WTXF-TV Ch 29 (Fox) 330 Market St	Philadelphia	PA	19106	215-925-2929	925-2420
Web: www.foxphiladelphia.com					

RADIO

				Phone	Fax
WAFL-FM 97.7 MHz (AC) PO Box 808	Milford	DE	19963	302-422-7575	422-3069
Web: www.eagle977.com					
WDOV-AM 1410 kHz (N/T) 5595 W Denney's Rd	Dover	DE	19904	302-674-1410	674-8621
Web: www.wdov.com					
WDSD-FM 92.9 MHz (Ctry) 5595 W Denney's Rd	Dover	DE	19904	302-674-1410	674-2049
Web: www.wdsd.com					
WXPZ-FM 101.3 MHz (Rel) PO Box K	Milford	DE	19963	302-424-1013	424-2358
Web: www.wxpz.com ■ *E-mail:* lightfm@wxpz.com					
WYUS-AM 930 kHz (Span) PO Box 808	Milford	DE	19963	302-422-7575	422-3069

— Colleges/Universities —

Name	City	State	Zip	Phone	Fax
Delaware State University 1200 N DuPont Hwy	Dover	DE	19901	302-857-6060	857-6352
Web: www.dsc.edu					
Delaware Technical & Community College Terry Campus 1832 N DuPont Pkwy	Dover	DE	19901	302-741-2700	741-2778
Web: www.dtcc.edu					
Wesley College 120 N State St	Dover	DE	19901	302-736-2300	736-2301
TF: 800-937-5398 ■ *Web:* www.wesley.edu					

— Hospitals —

Name	City	State	Zip	Phone	Fax
Kent General Hospital 640 S State St	Dover	DE	19901	302-674-4700	674-7181

— Attractions —

Name	City	State	Zip	Phone	Fax
Allee House 1576 Hay Point Landing Rd	Smyrna	DE	19977	302-653-9345	
Barratt's Chapel Museum 6362 Bay Rd	Frederica	DE	19946	302-335-5544	
Web: hometown.aol.com/barratts/home.html ■ *E-mail:* barratts@aol.com					
Bombay Hook National Wildlife Refuge 2591 Whitehall Neck Rd	Smyrna	DE	19977	302-653-6872	653-0684
E-mail: r5rw_bhnwr@mail.fws.gov					
Christ Episcopal Church S State & Water Sts	Dover	DE	19901	302-734-5731	
Delaware Agricultural Museum & Village 866 N DuPont Hwy	Dover	DE	19901	302-734-1618	734-0457
Web: www.agriculturalmuseum.org					
Delaware State Museum 316 S Governors Ave	Dover	DE	19901	302-739-4266	739-3943
Delaware State Visitors Center 406 Federal St	Dover	DE	19901	302-739-4266	739-3943
Delaware Symphony Orchestra 1200 N DuPont Hwy Delaware State University	Dover	DE	19901	302-652-5577	657-5692
Web: www.desymphony.org ■ *E-mail:* info@desymphony.org					
Dickinson John Plantation 340 Kitts Hummock Rd	Dover	DE	19901	302-739-3277	739-3173
Dover Air Force Base Air Mobility Command Museum 1301 Heritage Rd	Dover AFB	DE	19902	302-677-5938	677-5940
Web: www.amcmuseum.org ■ *E-mail:* museum@dover.af.mil					
Golden Fleece Tavern Site State St & The Green	Dover	DE	19901		
Green The State St & Bank Ln	Dover	DE	19901	302-739-4266	
Harrington Museum 108-110 Fleming St	Harrington	DE	19952	302-398-3698	
Johnson Victrola Museum Bank Ln	Dover	DE	19901	302-739-4266	
Kent County Courthouse 38 The Green	Dover	DE	19901	302-739-4266	
Killens Pond State Park 5025 Killens Pond Rd	Felton	DE	19943	302-284-4526	284-0430
Legislative Hall Legislative Ave	Dover	DE	19901	302-739-5807	739-3815
Meeting House Galleries I & II 316 S Governor's Ave	Dover	DE	19901	302-739-4266	
Messick Agricultural Museum 317 Walt Messick Rd	Harrington	DE	19952	302-398-3729	398-4732
Old State House 406 Federal St The Green	Dover	DE	19901	302-739-4266	
Sewell C Biggs Museum of American Art PO Box 711	Dover	DE	19903	302-674-2111	674-5133
Web: www.biggsmuseum.org					
Silver Lake Park Washington St	Dover	DE	19901	302-736-7050	
Spence's Bazaar South & New Sts	Dover	DE	19901	302-734-3441	
Woodburn-Governor's House 151 Kings Hwy	Dover	DE	19901	302-739-5656	739-6113

Dover (Cont'd)

SPORTS TEAMS & FACILITIES

				Phone	Fax
Dover Downs International Speedway 1131 N DuPont Hwy *Web:* www.doverdowns.com/speedway	Dover	DE	19901	302-674-4600	734-3124
Harrington Raceway US 13 *Web:* www.harringtonraceway.com	Harrington	DE	19952	302-398-7223	398-3056

— Events —

	Phone
African American Festival (late June)	302-736-0101
Delaware State Fair (mid-late July)	302-398-3269
Dover Music Festival (late June)	302-736-7050
Easter Egg Hunt (late March)	302-739-5656
First Night Dover (December 31)	302-674-8581
Governor's Christmas Open House (mid-December)	302-739-5656
Governor's Fall Festival (early October)	302-739-5656
Governor's Haunted House (October 31)	302-739-5656
July 4th Celebration (July 4)	302-734-7513
Old Dover Days (early May)	302-734-1736
SplitFire Spark Plug 200 & 500 (September)	302-734-7223
Summer Performing Arts Series (May-September)	302-736-7050

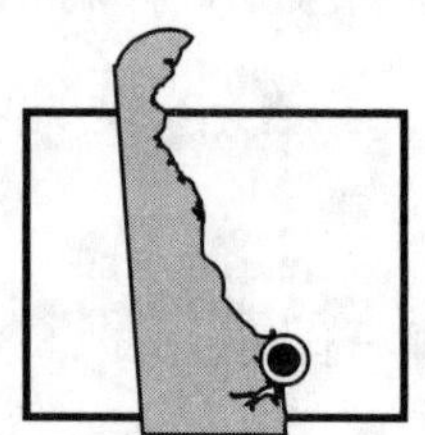

Rehoboth Beach

Rehoboth Beach, located on the shore of southeastern Delaware, is the largest of Delaware's Atlantic resorts. It was originally founded (1873) as a "Christian sea-side resort," but as the railroad was extended to Rehoboth Beach, it brought more and more visitors to the city. Slowly, the city's religious orientation began to disappear, and Rehoboth Beach emerged as a popular vacation destination. The Anna Hazzard Museum is reminiscent of the city's religious history, featuring artifacts and memorabilia housed in a camp meeting-era structure. Attractions in nearby Lewes and Dewey Beach include the Cape Henlopen State Park, a 3,000-acre park with "walking" sand dunes (sand dunes that are constantly moved and reshaped from the wind) and nature trails; and the Lewes Historical Society Complex, which encompasses an area of restored buildings, a country store, and the Maritime Museum. The Cape May-Lewes Ferry offers a three hour scenic tour of the Delaware Bay, as well as ferry trips between Delaware and New Jersey. Rehoboth Beach is also noted for the Rehoboth Outlets, one of the nation's largest outlet centers, and all purchases in the entire state of Delaware are tax-free. Each October, two major events take place in Rehoboth Beach: the Autumn Jazz Fest, with three days of Jazz concerts; and the Sea Witch Halloween and Fiddler's Festival, a local tradition since 1989 that features a parade, a pet costume contest, spook shows, and a number of other events.

Population	1,340	**Longitude**	75-04-51 W
Area (Land)	1.2 sq mi	**County**	Sussex
Area (Water)	0.5 sq mi	**Time Zone**	EST
Elevation	16 ft	**Area Code/s**	302
Latitude	38-43-02 N		

— Average Temperatures and Precipitation —

TEMPERATURES

	Jan	Feb	Mar	Apr	May	Jun	Jul	Aug	Sep	Oct	Nov	Dec
High	43	45	54	64	73	81	85	84	78	68	59	48
Low	26	28	35	43	53	62	67	66	60	49	40	31

PRECIPITATION

	Jan	Feb	Mar	Apr	May	Jun	Jul	Aug	Sep	Oct	Nov	Dec
Inches	3.8	3.3	4.1	3.6	3.8	3.4	4.0	5.2	3.1	3.2	3.3	3.7

— Important Phone Numbers —

	Phone		Phone
AAA	302-674-8020	**Poison Control Center**	800-722-7112
Emergency	911	**Weather**	302-855-9262
Medical Referral	302-645-3332		

— Information Sources —

				Phone	Fax
Better Business Bureau Serving Delaware 1010 Concord Ave Suite 101 *Web:* www.wilmington.bbb.org	Wilmington	DE	19802	302-594-9200	594-1052
Rehoboth Beach City Hall 229 Rehoboth Ave	Rehoboth Beach	DE	19971	302-227-6181	227-4643
Rehoboth Beach Convention Center 229 Rehoboth Ave	Rehoboth Beach	DE	19971	302-227-4641	227-4643
Rehoboth Beach-Dewey Beach Chamber of Commerce PO Box 216 *TF:* 800-441-1329 ■ *Web:* www.beach-fun.com ■ *E-mail:* rehoboth@beach-fun.com	Rehoboth Beach	DE	19971	302-227-2233	227-8351
Rehoboth Beach Main Street Inc PO Box 50 *Web:* www.rehomain.com ■ *E-mail:* rehomain@dol.net	Rehoboth Beach	DE	19971	302-227-2772	227-0149
Rehoboth Beach Mayor 229 Rehoboth Ave	Rehoboth Beach	DE	19971	302-227-4641	
Rehoboth Beach Public Library 226 Rehoboth Ave	Rehoboth Beach	DE	19971	302-227-8044	227-0597
Sussex County PO Box 589	Georgetown	DE	19947	302-855-7743	855-7749

On-Line Resources

At the Beach	www.atbeach.com
Excite.com Rehoboth Beach City Guide	www.excite.com/travel/countries/united_states/delaware/rehoboth_beach
Gay Rehoboth Beach	www.gayrehoboth.com
NITC Travelbase City Guide Rehoboth Beach	www.travelbase.com/auto/features/rehoboth_beach-de.html
Online City Guide to Rehoboth Beach	www.olcg.com/de/rehobothbeach/main.html
Rehoboth Beach	www.rehobothbeachde.com
Rehoboth Beach Delaware	www.badjoad.com/rehoboth.html
Rehoboth Beach-Net	www.beach-net.com/TownsRB.html
Rehoboth Beach Ocean Cam	www.rehobothcam.com
Rehoboth Today	www.rehobothtoday.com
Sunny Day Guide to Rehoboth Beach	www.sunnydayguides.com/rh/default.htm
Surf & Sun Beach Vacation Guide to Rehoboth Beach	www.surf-sun.com/de-rehoboth-main.htm
Welcome to Rehoboth Beach	www.rehoboth.com

— Transportation Services —

AIRPORTS

	Phone
■ **Salisbury-Wicomico County Regional Airport (SBY)** 42 miles SW of downtown Rehoboth Beach (approx 60 minutes)	410-548-4827

Airport Transportation

	Phone
Airport Chauffeur $60 fare to downtown Rehoboth Beach	410-548-0975
Island Shuttle $45-50 fare to downtown Rehoboth Beach	888-524-3401

Rehoboth Beach (Cont'd)

Commercial Airlines

	Phone
US Airways	800-428-4322

Charter Airlines

	Phone		Phone
American Aerospace	302-856-3214	**Bay Land Aviation Inc**	410-749-0323

CAR RENTALS

	Phone		Phone
Avis	410-742-8566	**Hertz**	410-749-2235
CarTemps USA	410-742-4700	**National**	410-749-2450

LIMO/TAXI

	Phone		Phone
Ralph's Taxi Service	302-227-5584	**Surfside Limousine Services**	302-945-7175

MASS TRANSIT

	Phone
Cape May-Lewes Ferry Trolley $3 Base fare	302-644-6030
Jolly Trolley of Rehoboth $1.50 Base fare	302-227-1197

— Accommodations —

HOTELS, MOTELS, RESORTS

Phone Fax

Adams Oceanfront Resort 4 Read St. . . . . . Dewey Beach DE 19971 302-227-3030
TF: 800-448-8080 ■ *Web:* www.adamsoceanfront.com
■ *E-mail:* adamsof@shore.intercom.net

Admiral The 2 Baltimore Ave . . . . Rehoboth Beach DE 19971 302-227-2103 227-3620
TF: 888-882-4188 ■ *Web:* admiralrehoboth.com
■ *E-mail:* admiral@atbeach.net

AmericInn Motel 329-Z Airport Rd . . . . . Rehoboth Beach DE 19971 302-226-0700 226-1037
TF: 800-634-3444 ■ *Web:* beach-net.com/americinn

Atlantic Budget Inn Downtown
154 Rehoboth Ave . . . . Rehoboth Beach DE 19971 302-227-9446 227-9446
TF: 800-245-2112 ■ *Web:* www.rehoboth.com/atlanticbudgetinn

Atlantic Oceanside Motel & Suites
1700 Hwy 1 . . . . Dewey Beach DE 19971 302-227-8811
TF: 800-422-0481 ■ *Web:* www.atlanticoceanside.com
■ *E-mail:* aos@dmv.com

Atlantic Sands Hotel
101 N Boardwalk . . . . Rehoboth Beach DE 19971 302-227-2511 227-9476
TF: 800-422-0600 ■ *Web:* www.atlanticsandshotel.com

Atlantic View Motel 2 Clayton St . . . . Dewey Beach DE 19971 302-227-3878 226-2640
TF: 800-777-4162 ■ *Web:* www.rehobothtoday.com/atlanticview
■ *E-mail:* atlantic@dmv.com

Bay Resort Bellevue St. . . . . Dewey Beach DE 19971 302-227-6400 227-5800
TF: 800-922-9240 ■ *Web:* www.bayresort.com

Beach View Motel 6 Wilmington Ave. . . . Rehoboth Beach DE 19971 302-227-2999 226-2640
TF: 800-288-5962

Beacon Motel 514 E Savannah Rd . . . . Lewes DE 19958 302-645-4888
TF: 800-735-4888 ■ *Web:* www.lewestoday.com/beacon
■ *E-mail:* bconmotel@dmv.com

Bellbuoy Inn 21 Van Dyke St . . . . Dewey Beach DE 19971 302-227-6000

Best Western Gold Leaf 1400 Hwy 1 . . . . . Dewey Beach DE 19971 302-226-1100 226-9785
TF: 800-422-8566 ■ *Web:* www.dmv.com/business/goldleaf
■ *E-mail:* goldleaf@dmv.com

Boardwalk Plaza Hotel 2 Olive Ave . . . . . Rehoboth Beach DE 19971 302-227-7169 227-0561
TF: 800-332-3224 ■ *Web:* www.boardwalkplaza.com
■ *E-mail:* bph@boardwalkplaza.com

Breakers Hotel & Suites 105 2nd St. . . . Rehoboth Beach DE 19971 302-227-6688 227-2013
TF: 800-441-8009 ■ *Web:* www.dmv.com/business/breakers
■ *E-mail:* breakers@dmv.com

Brighton Suites Hotel
34 Wilmington Ave . . . . Rehoboth Beach DE 19971 302-227-5780 227-6815
TF: 800-227-5788 ■ *Web:* www.brightonsuites.com
■ *E-mail:* brighton@brightonsuites.com

Cape Henlopen Motel Savannah Rd . . . . Lewes DE 19958 302-645-2828
TF: 800-447-3158

Comfort Inn Hotel 4439 Hwy 1. . . . . Rehoboth Beach DE 19971 302-226-1515

Crosswinds Motel 312 Rehoboth Ave . . . Rehoboth Beach DE 19971 302-227-7997
TF: 888-581-9463
■ *Web:* www.beach-net.com/crosswindsmotel/index.html
■ *E-mail:* crosswnd@bellatlantic.net

Phone Fax

Dinner Bell Inn 2 Christian St. . . . . Rehoboth Beach DE 19971 302-227-2561
TF: 800-425-2355 ■ *Web:* www.beach-net.com/dinnerbell
■ *E-mail:* bell@ce.net

Econo Lodge 4361 Rt 1 . . . . Rehoboth Beach DE 19971 302-227-0500 227-2170
TF: 800-645-5690 ■ *Web:* www.econolodgerehoboth.com
■ *E-mail:* econolodgede013@worldnet.att.net

Henlopen Hotel 511 N Boardwalk . . . . . . Rehoboth Beach DE 19971 302-227-2551 227-8147
TF: 800-441-8450 ■ *Web:* www.henlopenhotel.com

Holiday Inn Express 4289 Hwy 1 . . . . . . Rehoboth Beach DE 19971 302-227-4030
TF: 800-465-4329 ■ *Web:* www.holiday-rehoboth.com
■ *E-mail:* info@holiday-rehoboth.com

Lord & Hamilton Inn
20 Brooklyn Ave . . . . Rehoboth Beach DE 19971 302-227-6960
TF: 877-227-6960 ■ *Web:* lordhamilton.com
■ *E-mail:* innkeeper@lordhamilton.com

Pirate's Cove Motel
625 Rehoboth Ave . . . . Rehoboth Beach DE 19971 302-227-2844

Rehoboth Inn 3815 Hwy 1 . . . . Rehoboth Beach DE 19971 302-226-2410
TF: 888-666-2609

Royal Rose Inn 41 Baltimore Ave . . . . . . Rehoboth Beach DE 19971 302-226-2535
Web: royalroseinn.com ■ *E-mail:* innkeeper@royalroseinn.com

Sand Palace Motel
Dagsworthy St & Rt 1 . . . . Dewey Beach DE 19971 302-227-4000
TF: 800-775-7263

Sandcastle Motel 123 2nd St. . . . . Rehoboth Beach DE 19971 302-227-0400
TF: 800-372-2112 ■ *Web:* www.thesandcastlemotel.com
■ *E-mail:* sandcastle@dmv.com

Sea-Esta Motel PO Box 394. . . . . Rehoboth Beach DE 19971 302-227-1223
TF: 800-436-6591 ■ *Web:* www.seaesta.com

Sea Ranch Motel 2909 Hwy 1 . . . . Rehoboth Beach DE 19971 302-227-8609 227-0568
TF: 800-639-4430 ■ *Web:* www.delmarweb.com/SeaRanch
■ *E-mail:* searanchmotel@prodigy.net

Sea Voice Inn 14 Delaware Ave . . . . Rehoboth Beach DE 19971 302-226-9435
TF: 800-637-2832 ■ *Web:* www.seavoice.com
■ *E-mail:* innkeeper@seavoice.com

Sea Witch Manor 71 Lake Ave . . . . Rehoboth Beach DE 19971 302-226-9482
Web: www.atbeach.com/lodging/de/bnb/seawitch
■ *E-mail:* seawitch@atbeach.net

Shore Inn 703 Rehoboth Ave . . . . Rehoboth Beach DE 19971 302-227-8487
TF: 800-597-8899 ■ *Web:* www.beach-net.com/shoreinn.html
■ *E-mail:* shoreinn@ce.net

Southwinds Motel 1609 Hwy 1. . . . . Dewey Beach DE 19971 302-227-7800 227-5246
TF: 800-392-8507

Summer Place Hotel 30 Olive Ave . . . . . Rehoboth Beach DE 19971 302-226-0766 226-3350
TF: 800-815-3925
■ *Web:* www.atbeach.com/lodging/de/hotel/summerplace
■ *E-mail:* millerd@dmv.com

Super 8 Motel 4353 Hwy 1 . . . . Rehoboth Beach DE 19971 302-227-0401 227-0401
TF: 800-800-8000 ■ *Web:* www.rehoboth.com/super8

— Restaurants —

Phone

1776 Colonial Club Restaurant & Steakhouse
(Steak/Seafood) 6 Midway Shopping Ctr. . . . . Rehoboth Beach DE 19971 302-645-9355
Web: www.1776ofrehoboth.com

Adriatico Italian Restaurant (Italian)
30 Baltimore Ave . . . . Rehoboth Beach DE 19971 302-227-9255

Ann Marie's Italian & Seafood (Italian)
208 2nd St . . . . Rehoboth Beach DE 19971 302-227-9902
Web: www.beach-net.com/cafe/annmaries/index.html
■ *E-mail:* cafe@beach-net.com

Big Fish Grill (Seafood) 4117 Hwy 1 . . . . Rehoboth Beach DE 19971 302-227-9007

Blue Moon Restaurant (Continental)
35 Baltimore Ave . . . . Rehoboth Beach DE 19971 302-227-6515

Café Italiano (Italian) 4537 Hwy 1. . . . . Rehoboth Beach DE 19971 302-645-6262
Web: www.beach-net.com/cafe/index.html
■ *E-mail:* cafe@beach-net.com

Captain's Table Restaurant (Seafood) 3206 Hwy 1 . . Rehoboth Beach DE 19971 302-227-6203

Catcher's Restaurant & Raw Bar (Seafood)
249 Rehoboth Ave . . . . Rehoboth Beach DE 19971 302-227-1808

Celsius Restaurant (French) 50 Wilmington Ave . . . . Rehoboth Beach DE 19971 302-227-5767

Chez La Mer (Seafood) 210 2nd St . . . . Rehoboth Beach DE 19971 302-227-6494

Crab Barn Restaurant (Steak/Seafood)
4345 Hwy 1. . . . . Rehoboth Beach DE 19971 302-227-6700
Web: www.rehobothtoday.com/CrabBarn

Dos Locos (Mexican) 42 1/2 Baltimore Ave. . . . . Rehoboth Beach DE 19971 302-227-6870

Fusion (American) 50 Wilmington Ave . . . . Rehoboth Beach DE 19971 302-226-1940
Web: www.beach-net.com/fusion/index.html

Iguana Grill (American) 52 Baltimore Ave. . . . . Rehoboth Beach DE 19971 302-227-0948

Jake's Seafood House Restaurant (Seafood)
29 Baltimore Ave . . . . Rehoboth Beach DE 19971 302-227-6237
Web: www.jakesseafood.com ■ *E-mail:* jakes@jakesseafood.com

Lamp Post Seafood Restaurant (Seafood)
4534 Hwy 1. . . . . Rehoboth Beach DE 19971 302-645-9132

Rehoboth Beach — Restaurants (Cont'd)

Name / Address	City	State	ZIP	Phone
Little Greek Boys Restaurant (Greek) 17 Market Place Mall	Rehoboth Beach	DE	19971	302-227-1127
Mama Maria's Italian Restaurant (Italian) PO Box 137	Dewey Beach	DE	19971	302-227-3242
Mulligan's Sports Pub & Restaurant (American) 4443 Hwy 1	Rehoboth Beach	DE	19971	302-644-9288
Ristorante Zebra (Italian) 32 Lake Ave	Rehoboth Beach	DE	19971	302-226-1160
Roadhouse Steak Joint (Steak) 4572 Hwy 1	Rehoboth Beach	DE	19971	302-645-8273
Rusty Rudder Restaurant (Seafood) 113 Dickinson St	Dewey Beach	DE	19971	302-227-3888
Sea Wood Restaurant (American) 32 Rehoboth Ave	Rehoboth Beach	DE	19971	302-227-0700
Summerhouse Restaurant (American) 228 Rehoboth Ave	Rehoboth Beach	DE	19971	302-227-3895
Theo's Family Restaurant (Italian) 2100 Hwy 1	Dewey Beach	DE	19971	302-227-1866
Two Seas Restaurant (Seafood) Van Dyke Ave	Dewey Beach	DE	19971	302-227-2610
Victoria's Restaurant (Continental) 2 Olive Ave Boardwalk Plaza Hotel *Web:* www.boardwalkplaza.com/inside.html ■ *E-mail:* bph@boardwalkplaza.com	Rehoboth Beach	DE	19971	302-227-0615
Yong Hua Chinese Restaurant (Chinese) Hwy 1	Rehoboth Beach	DE	19971	302-227-1549

— Goods and Services —

SHOPPING

Name / Address	City	State	ZIP	Phone	Fax
First Street Station 1st St & Rehoboth Ave	Rehoboth Beach	DE	19971	302-226-1170	
LL Bean Factory Stores 4565 Hwy 1 Suite 208	Rehoboth Beach	DE	19971	302-644-2560	
Rehoboth Mall 4493 Hwy 1	Rehoboth Beach	DE	19971	302-645-6655	
Rehoboth Outlets 1600 Ocean Outlets *TF:* 888-746-7333 ■ *Web:* www.shoprehoboth.com ■ *E-mail:* info@shoprehoboth.com	Rehoboth Beach	DE	19971	302-226-9223	226-9243

BANKS

Name / Address	City	State	ZIP	Phone	Fax
Baltimore Trust Co 4161 Hwy 1 *TF:* 800-522-1199	Rehoboth Beach	DE	19971	302-226-2600	226-2603
County Bank 4299 Hwy 1 Suite A-1	Rehoboth Beach	DE	19971	302-226-9800	226-2265
Delaware National Bank Hwy 1 & Church St	Rehoboth Beach	DE	19971	302-227-0333	227-7972
Mellon Bank NA 8 Rehoboth Beach Plaza *TF:* 800-842-5922	Rehoboth Beach	DE	19971	302-226-1004	226-1006
PNC Bank 4317 Hwy 1	Rehoboth Beach	DE	19971	302-227-5010	227-2469
Wilmington Trust Co 4369 Hwy 1	Rehoboth Beach	DE	19971	302-856-4490	

BUSINESS SERVICES

	Phone
Delmarva Personnel	302-227-1410
Federal Express	800-238-5355
Mr Copy	302-227-4666
Post Office	302-227-8406
Postnet Postal & Business Service	302-644-9034
UPS	800-742-5877

— Media —

PUBLICATIONS

Name / Address	City	State	ZIP	Phone	Fax
Cape Gazette PO Box 213	Lewes	DE	19958	302-645-7700	645-1664
Delaware Beachcomber PO Box 309 *Web:* www.shore-source.com/dbc ■ *E-mail:* dbc@shore-source.com	Rehoboth Beach	DE	19971	302-227-9466	227-9469
Delaware Coast Press PO Box 309	Rehoboth Beach	DE	19971	302-227-9466	
Sussex Post PO Box 37 **Fax:* News Rm	Lewes	DE	19958	302-934-9261	645-2267*

TELEVISION

Name / Address	City	State	ZIP	Phone	Fax
KYW-TV Ch 3 (CBS) 101 S Independence Mall E *Web:* www.kyw.com	Philadelphia	PA	19106	215-238-4700	238-4783
WCAU-TV Ch 10 (NBC) 10 Monument Rd *Web:* www.nbc10.com	Bala Cynwyd	PA	19004	610-668-5510	668-3700
WHYY-TV Ch 12 (PBS) 150 N 6th St *Web:* whyy.org ■ *E-mail:* talkback@whyy.org	Philadelphia	PA	19106	215-351-1200	351-0398
WMDT-TV Ch 47 (ABC) 202 Downtown Plaza *Web:* www.wmdt.com ■ *E-mail:* letters@wmdt.com	Salisbury	MD	21801	410-742-4747	742-5767
WTXF-TV Ch 29 (Fox) 330 Market St *Web:* www.foxphiladelphia.com	Philadelphia	PA	19106	215-925-2929	925-2420

RADIO

Name / Address	City	State	ZIP	Phone	Fax
WAFL-FM 97.7 MHz (AC) PO Box 808 *Web:* www.eagle977.com	Milford	DE	19963	302-422-7575	422-3069
WETT-AM 1590 kHz (N/T) 11500 Coastal Hwy Suite 1	Ocean City	MD	21842	410-723-0900	723-1100
WGBG-FM 98.5 MHz (CR) 701 N Dupont Hwy	Georgetown	DE	19947	302-856-2567	856-6839
WGMD-FM 92.7 MHz (N/T) PO Box 530 *Web:* www.wgmd.com ■ *E-mail:* listen@wgmd.com	Rehoboth Beach	DE	19971	302-945-2050	945-3781
WJWK-AM 1280 kHz (Nost) 701 N Dupont Hwy	Georgetown	DE	19947	302-856-2567	856-6839
WJWL-AM 900 kHz (Nost) 701 N Dupont Hwy	Georgetown	DE	19947	302-856-2567	856-6839
WJYN-FM 103.5 (AC) 701 N Dupont Hwy	Georgetown	DE	19947	302-856-2567	856-6839
WLBW-FM 92.1 MHz (Oldies) 31455 Winterplace Pkwy *Web:* www.delmarvaradio.com/wave.html	Salisbury	MD	21804	410-742-1923	742-2329
WQHQ-FM 104.7 MHz (AC) 31455 Winterplace Pkwy *Web:* www.delmarvaradio.com/q105fm.html	Salisbury	MD	21804	410-742-1923	742-2329
WQJZ-FM 97.1 MHz (NAC) PO Box 909 *Web:* www.wqjz.com	Salisbury	MD	21803	410-219-3500	548-1543
WSBL-FM 97.9 MHz (Ctry) 55 W Church St	Selbyville	DE	19975	302-436-9725	436-9726
WSDL-FM 90.7 MHz (NPR) PO Box 2596	Salisbury	MD	21802	410-543-6895	548-3000
WTGM-AM 960 kHz (Sports) 31455 Winterplace Pkwy *Web:* www.delmarvaradio.com/am960.html	Salisbury	MD	21804	410-742-1923	742-2329
WYUS-AM 930 kHz (Span) PO Box 808	Milford	DE	19963	302-422-7575	422-3069
WZBH-FM 93.5 MHz (Rock) 701 N Dupont Hwy	Georgetown	DE	19947	302-856-2567	856-6839

— Colleges/Universities —

Name / Address	City	State	ZIP	Phone	Fax
Delaware Technical & Community College Southern Campus PO Box 610 *Web:* www.dtcc.edu/southern ■ *E-mail:* info@dtcc.edu	Georgetown	DE	19947	302-856-5400	856-5428
Wilmington College 320 N DuPont Hwy *TF:* 877-967-5464 ■ *Web:* www.wilmcoll.edu	New Castle	DE	19720	302-328-9401	328-5902

— Hospitals —

Name / Address	City	State	ZIP	Phone	Fax
Beebe Medical Center 424 Savannah Rd	Lewes	DE	19958	302-645-3300	645-3405
Rehoboth Health Center 3809 Hwy 1	Rehoboth Beach	DE	19971	302-227-8115	227-2750

— Attractions —

Name / Address	City	State	ZIP	Phone	Fax
Anna Hazzard Museum 17 Christian St	Rehoboth Beach	DE	19971	302-226-1119	
Cape Henlopen State Park 4200 Henlopen Dr *Web:* www.destateparks.com/chsp.htm	Lewes	DE	19958	302-645-8983	645-0588
Cape May-Lewes Ferry PO Box 517 *TF:* 800-643-3779 ■ *Web:* www.capemay-lewesferry.com	Lewes	DE	19958	302-426-1155	
Delaware Seashore State Park Inlet 850 *Web:* www.atbeach.com/destpark/seashorf.html	Rehoboth Beach	DE	19971	302-227-2800	
Funland Delaware Ave & Boardwalk	Rehoboth Beach	DE	19971	302-227-1921	
Henlopen Theater Kings Hwy Little Theatre	Lewes	DE	19958	302-226-4103	226-4104
Indian River Lifesaving Museum Hwy 1 Indian River Inlet	Rehoboth Beach	DE	19971	302-227-0478	227-6438
Midway Speedway Go-Karts Rt 1 Midway Shopping Ctr *Web:* www.rehobothtoday.com/midway ■ *E-mail:* midway@rehobothtoday.com	Rehoboth Beach	DE	19971	302-644-2042	

Rehoboth Beach — Attractions (Cont'd)

	City	State	Zip	Phone	Fax
Nassau Valley Vineyards 36 Nassau Commons	Lewes	DE	19958	302-645-9463	645-6666
Queen Anne's Railroad 730 Kings Hwy	Lewes	DE	19958	302-644-1720	644-9212
TF: 888-456-8668 ■ *Web:* www.ridetherails.com ■ *E-mail:* queenannes@dol.net					
Rehoboth Art League 12 Dodds Ln	Rehoboth Beach	DE	19971	302-227-8408	
Rehoboth Summer Children's Theatre 20 Baltimore Ave United Methodist Church	Rehoboth Beach	DE	19971	302-227-6766	
Web: www.ce.net/rsct ■ *E-mail:* duetpros@aol.com					

— Events —

	Phone
Annual Christmas Shop (early October)	302-227-7202
Annual Sidewalk Sales (mid-May & early October)	302-227-2233
Autumn Faire (mid-November)	302-945-3627
Autumn Jazz Festival (mid-late October)	302-226-2166
Avenue of Lights (late November-early January)	302-227-2233
Best of the Beach Art Auction (mid-June)	302-644-2900
Chocolate Festival (mid-March)	302-227-8259
Christmas Tree Lighting (late November)	302-227-2233
Coast Day (early October)	302-831-8083
Dewey Beach Sprint Triathalon (late September)	302-226-0510
Easter Promenade (late April)	302-227-2233
Fun Fly (early April)	302-227-6996
Greater Delaware Kite Festival (early April)	302-227-6996
Hometown Christmas Parade (mid-December)	302-227-8950
July 4th Fireworks (July 4)	302-227-2772
Make-A-Wish Two Million Dollar Golf Tournament (mid-September)	302-658-9474
Milford Sun Fun Fest (early July)	302-422-3344
Rehoboth Beach Independent Film Festival (mid-November)	302-645-9095
Sea Witch Halloween & Fiddler's Festival (late October)	302-227-2233
Thanksgiving Ball (mid-November)	302-644-2900

Wilmington

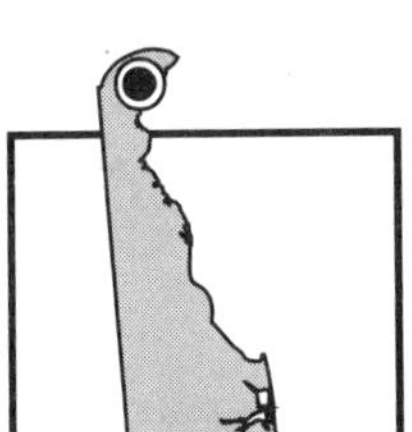

Wilmington and the area known as Greater Wilmington are located in the hills of the Brandywine Valley. The attractions of both are closely linked to the generations of du Pont families that have lived there. Wilmington's Winterthur Museum and Garden is the legacy of Henry Francis du Pont. The Museum contains a premier collection of American decorative arts, including Paul Revere's silver tankards. The Hagley Museum, along the Brandywine River, is made up of the original du Pont mills, gardens, and Eluthierian Mills (the first du Pont family home). North of Wilmington is Nemours, the former estate of Alfred I. du Pont. The estate has 102 rooms, French-style gardens, and a hospital, the Alfred I. du Pont Institute. Just across the Pennsylvania state line is the famous Longwood Garden with more than 11,000 types of plants in both outdoor gardens and indoor conservatories. The Brandywine River Museum in nearby Chadds Ford, Pennsylvania exhibits a sizable collection of Andrew Wyeth paintings.

Population	68,062	**Longitude**	75-54-69 W
Area (Land)	10.8 sq mi	**County**	New Castle
Area (Water)	6.2 sq mi	**Time Zone**	EST
Elevation	100 ft	**Area Code/s**	302
Latitude	39-74-58 N		

— Average Temperatures and Precipitation —

TEMPERATURES

	Jan	Feb	Mar	Apr	May	Jun	Jul	Aug	Sep	Oct	Nov	Dec
High	39	42	52	63	73	81	86	84	78	67	56	44
Low	22	25	33	42	52	62	67	66	58	46	37	28

PRECIPITATION

	Jan	Feb	Mar	Apr	May	Jun	Jul	Aug	Sep	Oct	Nov	Dec
Inches	3.0	2.9	3.4	3.4	3.8	3.6	4.2	3.4	3.4	2.9	3.3	3.5

— Important Phone Numbers —

	Phone		Phone
AAA	302-368-7700	**Time/Temp**	302-475-8463
Emergency	911	**Travelers Aid**	302-656-1696
Medical Referral	302-428-4100	**Weather**	302-429-9000
Poison Control Center	800-722-7112		

— Information Sources —

	City	State	Zip	Phone	Fax
Better Business Bureau Serving Delaware 1010 Concord Ave Suite 101	Wilmington	DE	19802	302-594-9200	594-1052
Web: www.wilmington.bbb.org					
Delaware State Chamber of Commerce PO Box 671	Wilmington	DE	19899	302-655-7221	654-0691
Web: www.inet.net/dscc ■ *E-mail:* dscc@inet.net					
Greater Wilmington Convention & Visitors Bureau 100 W 10th St Suite 20	Wilmington	DE	19801	302-652-4088	652-4726
Web: www.wilmcvb.org/					
New Castle County 800 N French St	Wilmington	DE	19801	302-571-7500	571-7857
Web: www.newcastlecounty.com					
Wilmington City Hall 800 N French St.	Wilmington	DE	19801	302-571-4180	571-4071
Web: www.ci.wilmington.de.us					
Wilmington Library 10th & Market Sts	Wilmington	DE	19801	302-571-7400	654-9132
Wilmington Mayor 800 N French St	Wilmington	DE	19801	302-571-4100	571-4102
Web: www.ci.wilmington.de.us/message.htm					
Wilmington Planning Dept 800 N French St 7th Fl	Wilmington	DE	19801	302-571-4130	571-4119
Web: www.ci.wilmington.de.us/planning.htm					

On-Line Resources

Area Guide Wilmington	wilmingtonde.areaguides.net
I-95 Exit Information Guide Wilmington	www.usastar.com/i95/cityguide/wilmingtondelaware.htm
Wilmington.com	www.wilmington.com

— Transportation Services —

AIRPORTS

■ **Philadelphia International Airport (PHL)**

	Phone
20 miles NE of downtown Wilmington (approx 45 minutes)	215-937-6937

Airport Transportation

	Phone
Airport Shuttle Service $21 fare to downtown Wilmington	302-655-8878
Delaware Express Shuttle $25 fare to downtown Wilmington	302-454-8141

Commercial Airlines

	Phone		Phone
Air Jamaica	800-523-5585	**Mexicana**	800-531-7923
American	800-433-7300	**Midway**	800-446-4392
American Eagle	800-433-7300	**Northwest**	800-225-2525
British Airways	800-247-9297	**United**	800-241-6522
Continental	800-525-0280	**US Airways**	800-428-4322
Continental Express	800-525-0280	**US Airways Express**	800-428-4322
Delta	800-221-1212		

Charter Airlines

	Phone		Phone
Northeast Aviation Charter Inc	215-677-5592	**Sterling Helicopters**	215-271-2510
Philadelphia Jet Service	800-468-1490	**Wings Charter**	215-646-1800

Wilmington (Cont'd)

CAR RENTALS

	Phone		Phone
Alamo	215-492-3960	Dollar	215-365-2700
Avis-Philadelphia	215-492-0900	Enterprise	610-521-3700
Budget	215-492-9400	Hertz	215-492-7200
CarTemps USA	215-334-8800	National	215-492-2750

LIMO/TAXI

	Phone		Phone
Carey Limousine	215-492-8402	King Limousine	302-652-5466
Eagle Limousine	302-325-4200	Yellow Cab	302-656-8151

MASS TRANSIT

	Phone
Dart $1.15 Base fare	302-658-8960

RAIL/BUS

				Phone
Greyhound Bus Station 101 N French St *TF:* 800-231-2222	Wilmington	DE	19801	302-655-6111
Wilmington Amtrak Station ML King Jr Blvd & French St	Wilmington	DE	19801	302-429-6523

— Accommodations —

HOTELS, MOTELS, RESORTS

				Phone	Fax
Best Western Brandywine Valley Inn 1807 Concord Pike *TF:* 800-537-7772 ■ *Web:* www.brandywineinn.com/	Wilmington	DE	19803	302-656-9436	656-8564
Best Western Delaware Inn 260 Chapman Rd *TF:* 800-633-3203	Newark	DE	19702	302-738-3400	738-3414
Brandywine Suites 707 N King St *TF:* 800-756-0070	Wilmington	DE	19801	302-656-9300	656-2459
Christiana Hilton Inn 100 Continental Dr *TF:* 800-348-3133	Newark	DE	19713	302-454-1500	454-0233
Comfort Inn Newark 1120 S College Ave *TF:* 800-441-7564	Newark	DE	19713	302-368-8715	368-6454
Courtyard by Marriott-Christiana 48 Geoffrey Dr *TF:* 800-321-2211 ■ *Web:* courtyard.com/ILGWC	Newark	DE	19713	302-456-3800	456-3824
Doubletree Hotel 4727 Concord Pike *TF:* 800-222-8733	Wilmington	DE	19803	302-478-6000	477-1492
Econo Lodge 232 S Dupont Hwy *TF:* 800-553-2666	New Castle	DE	19720	302-322-4500	322-9612
Hampton Inn-Wilmington/Newark 3 Concord Ln *TF:* 800-426-7866	Newark	DE	19713	302-737-3900	737-2630
Hilton Wilmington 630 Naamans Rd *TF:* 800-445-8667 ■ *Web:* www.hilton.com/hotels/ILGDEHF	Claymont	DE	19703	302-792-2700	798-6182
Holiday Inn Newark 1203 Christiana Rd *TF:* 800-465-4329	Newark	DE	19713	302-737-2700	737-3214
Holiday Inn North 4000 Concord Pike *TF:* 800-465-4329	Wilmington	DE	19803	302-478-2222	479-0850
Homewood Suites Hotel 350 Rocky Run Pkwy *TF:* 800-225-4663	Wilmington	DE	19803	302-479-2000	479-0770
Hotel du Pont 11th & Market Sts *TF:* 800-441-9019	Wilmington	DE	19801	302-594-3100	594-3108
Howard Johnson Lodge & Suites 1119 S College Ave *TF:* 800-446-4656	Newark	DE	19713	302-368-8521	368-9868
McIntosh Inn Newark 100 McIntosh Plaza *TF:* 800-444-2775	Newark	DE	19713	302-453-9100	453-9114
Quality Inn Skyways 147 N DuPont Hwy *TF:* 800-228-5151	New Castle	DE	19720	302-328-6666	322-3791
Ramada Inn Chadd's Ford 1110 Baltimore Pike *TF:* 800-272-6232	Glen Mills	PA	19342	610-358-1700	558-0842
Ramada Inn New Castle I-295 & Rt 13 *TF:* 800-272-6232	New Castle	DE	19720	302-658-8511	658-3071
Red Roof Inn 415 Stanton-Christiana Rd *TF:* 800-843-7663	Newark	DE	19713	302-292-2870	292-2879
Sheraton Suites 422 Delaware Ave *TF:* 800-325-3535	Wilmington	DE	19801	302-654-8300	654-6036
Super 8 Motel 215 S Dupont Hwy *TF:* 800-800-8000	New Castle	DE	19720	302-322-9480	
Tally-Ho Motor Lodge 5209 Concord Pke *TF:* 800-445-0852	Wilmington	DE	19803	302-478-0300	478-2401
Travelodge New Castle 1213 West Ave *TF:* 800-578-7878	New Castle	DE	19720	302-654-5544	652-0146
Wyndham Garden Hotel 700 N King St *TF:* 800-996-3426	Wilmington	DE	19801	302-655-0400	655-0430

— Restaurants —

				Phone
814 Club Restaurant (American) 814 Shipley St	Wilmington	DE	19803	302-657-5730
Air Transport Command (American) 143 N Dupont Hwy	New Castle	DE	19720	302-328-3527
Brandywine Brewing Co (American) 3801 Kennett Pike	Wilmington	DE	19807	302-655-8000
Brandywine Room (American) 11th & Market Sts	Wilmington	DE	19801	302-594-3156
Caffe Bellissimo (Italian) 3421 Kirkwood Hwy	Wilmington	DE	19808	302-994-9200
Casablanca (Middle Eastern) 4010 N DuPont Hwy	New Castle	DE	19720	302-652-5344
Cavanaugh's (American) 703 Market St Mall	Wilmington	DE	19801	302-656-4067
China Palace Restaurant (Chinese) 837 N Market St	Wilmington	DE	19801	302-654-0200
Christina River Club (Continental) 201 A St	Wilmington	DE	19805	302-652-4787
Columbus Inn (American) 2216 Pennsylvania Ave	Wilmington	DE	19806	302-571-1492
Essex Restaurant (American) 219 W 8th St	Wilmington	DE	19801	302-658-8258
Front Door Cafe (American) 1232 N King St	Wilmington	DE	19801	302-654-9977
Genelle's Restaurant (Caribbean) 730 N Market St	Wilmington	DE	19801	302-654-5322
Green Room at the Hotel duPont (French) 11th & Market Sts	Wilmington	DE	19801	302-594-3154
Harry's Savoy Grill (American) 2020 Naamans Rd *Web:* www.harrys-savoy.com/	Wilmington	DE	19801	302-475-3000
Kid Shelleen's (American) 14th & Scott Sts	Wilmington	DE	19801	302-658-4600
Klondike Kate's (American) 158 E Main St	Newark	DE	19711	302-737-6100
Le Chameleon (Continental) 100 Continental Dr	Newark	DE	19713	302-454-1500
Lynnhaven Inn (Steak/Seafood) 154 N Du Pont Hwy	New Castle	DE	19720	302-328-2041
Mediterranean Grill (American) 707 N King St	Wilmington	DE	19801	302-656-9300
Minato Japanese Restaurant (Japanese) 101 W 8th St	Wilmington	DE	19801	302-655-4342
Palett's (American) 4727 Concord Pike	Wilmington	DE	19803	302-478-6000
Pieces Island Cuisine (Jamaican) 1030 S Market St	Wilmington	DE	19801	302-421-9882
Porky's Restaurant (American) 105 Kirkwood Sq	Wilmington	DE	19808	302-633-1944
Ristorante Trevi (Italian) 3100 Naamans Rd	Wilmington	DE	19810	302-478-7434
Sal's Place (French) 603 N Lincoln St	Wilmington	DE	19805	302-652-1200
Shipley Grill Restaurant (American) 913 Shipley St	Wilmington	DE	19801	302-652-7797
Sienna (Continental) 1616 Delaware Ave	Wilmington	DE	19801	302-652-0653
Tavola Toscana (Italian) 1412 N DuPont St	Wilmington	DE	19806	302-654-8001
Walter's Steak House & Saloon (American) 802 N Union St	Wilmington	DE	19801	302-652-6780
Wing Wah (Chinese) 3901-03 Concord Pike	Wilmington	DE	19803	302-478-9500

— Goods and Services —

SHOPPING

				Phone	Fax
Christiana Mall 715 Christiana Mall **Fax Area Code:* 215	Newark	DE	19702	302-731-9815	893-0891*
Concord Mall 4737 Concord Pike	Wilmington	DE	19803	302-478-9271	479-8313
Olde Ridge Village Shoppes Ridge Rd & US Rt 202	Chadds Ford	PA	19317	610-558-0466	
Perryville Outlet Center 68 Heather Ln Suite 46	Perryville	MD	21903	410-378-9399	378-3298
Prices Corner Shopping Center 3202 Kirkwood Hwy	Wilmington	DE	19808	302-999-9758	

BANKS

				Phone	Fax
FCC National Bank 300 N King St *TF Cust Svc:* 800-756-5800*	Wilmington	DE	19801	302-594-8600	594-8625
First Union National Bank 920 N King St Rodney Sq	Wilmington	DE	19801	302-888-7500	888-7513
Mellon Bank Delaware NA 10th & Market Sts **Fax:* Hum Res ■ *TF:* 800-323-7105	Wilmington	DE	19801	302-421-2228	992-7705*
PNC Bank 222 Delaware Ave	Wilmington	DE	19801	302-429-7130	429-2818
Wilmington Trust Co 1100 N Market St **Fax:* Hum Res ■ *TF:* 800-441-7120 ■ *Web:* www.wilmingtontrust.com ■ *E-mail:* info@wilmingtontrust.com	Wilmington	DE	19890	302-651-1000	651-8937*

Wilmington (Cont'd)

BUSINESS SERVICES

	Phone
Airborne Express	800-247-2676
BAX Global	800-225-5229
DHL Worldwide Express	800-225-5345
Federal Express	800-238-5355
Interim Personnel	302-452-5600
Kinko's	302-652-2151
Mail Boxes Etc	800-789-4623
Manpower Temporary Services	302-479-7500
Network Personnel	302-656-5555
Post Office	302-656-0196
UPS	800-742-5877

— Media —

PUBLICATIONS

				Phone	Fax
Dialog The PO Box 2208	Wilmington	DE	19899	302-573-3109	573-2397*
*Fax: News Rm ■ E-mail: thedialog@aol.com					
New Castle Business Ledger 153 E Chestnut Hill Rd Suite 104	Newark	DE	19713	302-737-0923	737-9019
Web: www.ncbl.com/ ■ E-mail: ledger@dca.net					
News Journal‡ 950 W Basin Rd	New Castle	DE	19720	302-324-2617	324-5518
Web: www.delawareonline.com					

‡*Daily newspapers*

TELEVISION

				Phone	Fax
KYW-TV Ch 3 (CBS) 101 S Independence Mall E	Philadelphia	PA	19106	215-238-4700	238-4783
Web: www.kyw.com					
WCAU-TV Ch 10 (NBC) 10 Monument Rd	Bala Cynwyd	PA	19004	610-668-5510	668-3700
Web: www.nbc10.com					
WPVI-TV Ch 6 (ABC) 4100 City Line Ave	Philadelphia	PA	19131	215-878-9700	581-4530
Web: abcnews.go.com/local/wpvi					
WTXF-TV Ch 29 (Fox) 330 Market St	Philadelphia	PA	19106	215-925-2929	925-2420
Web: www.foxphiladelphia.com					

RADIO

				Phone	Fax
WDEL-AM 1150 kHz (N/T) PO Box 7492	Wilmington	DE	19803	302-478-2700	478-0100
Web: www.wdel.com ■ E-mail: wdel@dpnet.net					
WILM-AM 1450 kHz (N/T) 1215 French St	Wilmington	DE	19801	302-656-9800	655-1450
WJBR-FM 99.5 MHz (A/C) 3001 Philadelphia Pike	Claymont	DE	19703	302-791-4110	791-9669
Web: www.wjbr.com					
WMPH-FM 91.7 MHz (Misc) 5201 Washington St Ext	Wilmington	DE	19809	302-762-7199	762-7042
Web: www.wmph.org ■ E-mail: radio@wmph.org					
WSTW-FM 93.7 MHz (CHR) PO Box 7492	Wilmington	DE	19803	302-478-2700	478-0100
Web: www.wstw.com ■ E-mail: wstw@delaware.com					

— Colleges/Universities —

				Phone	Fax
Delaware Technical & Community College **Stanton Campus** 400 Stanton-Christiana Rd	Newark	DE	19713	302-454-3900	368-6620
Web: www.dtcc.edu/stanton-wilmington ■ E-mail: info@dtcc.edu					
Goldey Beacom College 4701 Limestone Rd	Wilmington	DE	19808	302-998-8814	996-5408
TF: 800-833-4877 ■ Web: goldey.gbc.edu ■ E-mail: gbc@goldey.gbc.edu					
University of Delaware Hullihen Hall	Newark	DE	19716	302-831-2000	831-6905
Web: www.udel.edu					
Wilmington College 320 N DuPont Hwy	New Castle	DE	19720	302-328-9401	328-5902
TF: 877-967-5464 ■ Web: www.wilmcoll.edu					

— Hospitals —

				Phone	Fax
DuPont Hospital for Children 1600 Rockland Rd	Wilmington	DE	19803	302-651-4000	651-4055
Web: www.kidshealth.org/ai					
Saint Francis Hospital PO Box 2500	Wilmington	DE	19805	302-421-4800	421-4167*
*Fax: Admitting					
Veterans Affairs Medical Center 1601 Kirkwood Hwy	Wilmington	DE	19805	302-994-2511	633-5415
TF: 800-450-8262					

— Attractions —

				Phone	Fax
Brandywine River Museum Rt 1 & Rt 100	Chadds Ford	PA	19317	610-388-2700	
Web: www.brandywinemuseum.org ■ E-mail: bmuse1@aol.com					
Brandywine Zoo 1001 North Park Dr	Wilmington	DE	19801	302-571-7747	
Chadds John House RR 100	Chadds Ford	PA	19317	610-388-7376	388-7480
Chaddsford Winery 632 Baltimore Pike	Chadds Ford	PA	19317	610-388-6221	388-0360
Web: www.chaddsford.com ■ E-mail: cfwine@chaddsford.com					
Christina Cultural Arts Center 705 Market St	Wilmington	DE	19801	302-652-0101	652-7480
Delaware Art Museum 2301 Kentmere Pkwy	Wilmington	DE	19806	302-571-9590	571-0220
Web: www.delart.mus.de.us ■ E-mail: orangfan@aol.com					
Delaware Center for the Contemporary Arts 103 E 16th St	Wilmington	DE	19801	302-656-6466	656-6944
Delaware Grand Exhibition Hall 800 S Madison St	Wilmington	DE	19801	302-777-1600	655-7844
TF: 888-395-0005					
Delaware History Museum 504 Market St	Wilmington	DE	19801	302-656-0637	655-7844
Web: www.hsd.org/dhm.htm					
Delaware Museum of Natural History 4840 Kenneth Pike	Wilmington	DE	19807	302-658-9111	658-2610
Web: www.delmnh.org					
Delaware Symphony Orchestra 1200 N DuPont Hwy Delaware State University	Dover	DE	19901	302-652-5577	657-5692
Web: www.desymphony.org ■ E-mail: info@desymphony.org					
Delaware Theatre Co 200 Water St	Wilmington	DE	19801	302-594-1100	594-1107
Delaware Toy & Miniature Museum Rt 141	Wilmington	DE	19807	302-427-8697	427-8654
Web: www.thomes.net/toys ■ E-mail: toys@thomes.net					
Fort Delaware State Park 45 Clinton St	Delaware City	DE	19706	302-834-7941	
Grand Opera House 818 N Market St	Wilmington	DE	19801	302-658-7897	652-5346
TF: 800-374-7263 ■ Web: grandoperahouse.org ■ E-mail: grandinfo@grandoperahouse.org					
Hagley Museum & Library 298 Buck Rd	Wilmington	DE	19807	302-658-2400	658-0568
Web: www.hagley.lib.de.us					
Heart Education Center 1096 Old Churchmans Rd	Newark	DE	19713	302-633-0200	633-3964
Henry Francis Winterthur DuPont Museum Rt 52	Winterthur	DE	19735	302-888-4600	888-4880
TF: 800-448-3883 ■ Web: www.winterthur.org ■ E-mail: llock@udel.edu					
Historic Houses of Odessa 2 Main St	Odessa	DE	19730	302-378-4069	
Historical Society of Delaware 505 Market St	Wilmington	DE	19801	302-655-7161	655-7844
Web: www.hsd.org/ ■ E-mail: hsd@dca.net					
Immanuel Episcopal Church 2nd & Harmony Sts On the Green	New Castle	DE	19720	302-328-2413	328-6636
Kalmar Nyckel Shipyard & Museum 1124 E 7th St	Wilmington	DE	19801	302-429-7447	429-0350
Web: www.kalnyc.org					
Lincoln Room of the University of Delaware 2600 Pennsylvania Ave	Wilmington	DE	19806	302-573-4468	
Longwood Gardens 1001 Longwood Rd	Kennett Square	PA	19348	610-388-1000	388-2183
TF: 800-737-5500 ■ Web: www.longwoodgardens.com/					
Nemours Mansion & Gardens PO Box 109	Wilmington	DE	19899	302-651-6912	
Web: www.nemours.org/nf/mansion/index.html					
New Castle Presbyterian Church 25 E 2nd St	New Castle	DE	19720	302-328-3279	328-5670
Old Court House 211 Delaware St	New Castle	DE	19720	302-323-4453	323-5319
Old Swedes Church & Hendrickson House Museum 606 Church St	Wilmington	DE	19801	302-652-5629	652-8615
Web: www.oldswedes.org					
Old Town Hall 512 Market St Mall	Wilmington	DE	19801	302-655-7161	655-7844
Web: www.hsd.org/oth.htm					
OperaDelaware 824 N Market St Suite 200	Wilmington	DE	19801	302-658-8063	658-4991
Web: www.operadel.org ■ E-mail: opinfo@operadel.org					
Phillips Mushroom Place Museum 909 E Baltimore Pike	Kennett Square	PA	19348	610-388-6082	388-3985
Playhouse Theatre 10th & Market Sts DuPont Bldg	Wilmington	DE	19801	302-656-4401	594-1437
TF: 800-338-0881 ■ Web: www.playhousetheatre.com ■ E-mail: tickets.playhouse@usa.dupont.com					

Wilmington — Attractions (Cont'd)

Name / Address	City	State	Zip	Phone	Fax
Quaker Hill Historic Preservation Foundation 521 West St	Wilmington	DE	19801	302-658-4200	658-9075
Read George II House & Garden 42 The Strand	New Castle	DE	19720	302-322-8411	
Web: www.hsd.org/read.htm					
Robinson House Naamans Rd & Philadelphia Pike	Claymont	DE	19703	302-792-0285	
Rockwood Museum 610 Shipley Rd	Wilmington	DE	19809	302-761-4340	764-4570
Web: www.rockwood.org/ ■ *E-mail:* info@rockwood.org					
Russian Ballet Theater of Delaware 728 Philadelphia Pike	Wilmington	DE	19809	302-764-2115	
Sewell C Biggs Museum of American Art PO Box 711	Dover	DE	19903	302-674-2111	674-5133
Web: www.biggsmuseum.org					
University of Delaware Center for Black Culture 192 S College Ave.	Newark	DE	19716	302-831-2991	831-4097
Wilmington & Western Railroad PO Box 5787	Wilmington	DE	19808	302-998-1930	998-7408
Web: www.wwrr.com ■ *E-mail:* schedule@wwrr.com					
Wilmington Drama League Community Theatre 10 W Lea Blvd	Wilmington	DE	19802	302-764-1172	764-7904

SPORTS TEAMS & FACILITIES

Name / Address	City	State	Zip	Phone	Fax
Delaware Genies (soccer) 301 McKennan's Church Rd Randy White Alumni Stadium	New Castle	DE	19808	302-326-1930	326-1932
Delaware Park 777 Delaware Pk Blvd	Wilmington	DE	19804	302-994-2521	993-2355*
**Fax:* Hum Res ■ *Web:* www.delpark.com					
Delaware Wizards (soccer) 301 McKennan's Church Rd Randy White Alumni Stadium	Wilmington	DE	19808	302-326-1930	326-1932
Wilmington Blue Rocks (baseball) 801 S Madison St	Wilmington	DE	19801	302-888-2015	888-2032
Web: www.bluerocks.com ■ *E-mail:* info@bluerocks.com					

— Events —

	Phone
A Christmas Display (mid-November-early January)	610-388-6741
A Day in Old New Castle (mid-late May)	302-322-8411
African Festival (early-mid-July)	302-657-2108
Chrysanthemum Festival (early-late November)	610-388-1000
Civil War Reenactment (late May)	305-655-5704
Clifford Brown Jazz Festival (early June)	302-571-4205
Cool Blues & Micro Brew (early-mid-August)	302-571-4100
DuPont Riverfest (late September)	302-658-1870
Festival of Fountains (May)	610-388-1000
First Night Wilmington (December 31)	302-658-9327
Garrison Days (mid-August)	302-834-7941
Greek Festival (early June)	302-654-4447
Hagley's Craft Fair (mid-October)	302-658-2400
Hagley's Storybook Garden Party (late April)	302-658-2400
Ice Cream Festival (mid-July)	302-761-4340
Jazz Fest (early September)	610-388-6221
Rehoboth Jazz Festival (mid-October)	800-296-8742
Saint Anthony's Italian Festival (mid-June)	302-421-3790
Saint Patrick's Day Parade (March)	302-652-2970
Saint Patrick's Day Tea (mid-March)	302-761-4340
Taste of Wilmington Festival (late September)	302-888-2929
Wilmington Flower Market (early May)	302-995-5699
Wilmington Garden Day (early May)	302-428-6172
Yuletide at Winterthur (mid-November-early January)	800-448-3883

District of Columbia

Population (1999): 519,000 **Area (sq mi): 68**

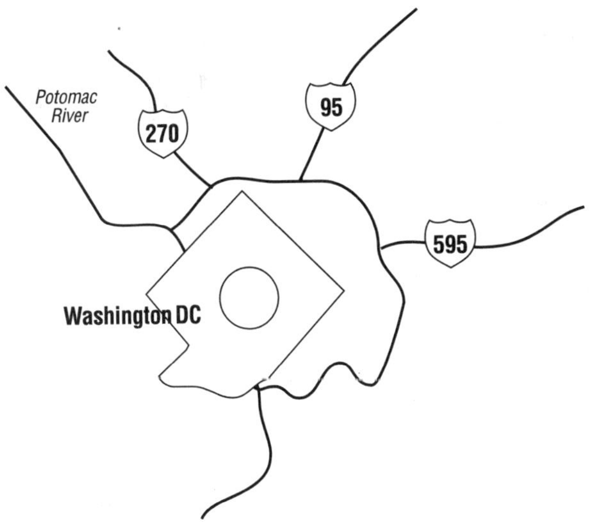

— State Information Sources —

				Phone	Fax
District of Columbia Chamber of Commerce 1301 Pennsylvania Ave NW Suite 309	Washington	DC	20004	202-347-7201	638-6764
Web: www.dcchamber.org					
District of Columbia Committee to Promote Washington 1212 New York Ave Suite 200	Washington	DC	20005	202-724-5644	724-2445
TF: 800-422-8644 ■ *Web:* www.washington.org					
District of Columbia Economic Development 441 4th St NW Suite 1140.	Washington	DC	20001	202-727-6365	727-6703
District of Columbia Government Information				202-727-1000	
Web: www.ci.washington.dc.us					
District of Columbia Recreation & Parks Dept 3149 16th St NW	Washington	DC	20010	202-673-7665	673-2087
US Chamber of Commerce 1615 H St NW. . .	Washington	DC	20062	202-659-6000	887-3437
TF: 800-638-6582 ■ *Web:* www.uschamber.org					

ON-LINE RESOURCES

Destination DC www.washingtonpost.com/wp-srv/local/longterm/tours/guide2.htm
District of Columbia Travel & Tourism Guide. . . . . www.travel-library.com/north_america/usa/dc/index.html
Travel.org-District of Columbia . . . . travel.org/dc.html

Washington

Washington, DC is the nation's capital and seat of government. Visitors to the U.S. Capitol Building, which has been the seat of Congress for almost 200 years, can observe the U.S. government at work. On Capitol Hill also are the Library of Congress and the U.S. Supreme Court, both of which are open to the public. Beginning at the Capitol and continuing on to the Potomac River is a grassy area called The Mall. Located here are museums and art galleries of the Smithsonian Institution, as well as the Washington Monument. The White House, which offers free tours daily, is just north of the Washington Monument, and to the south, on the Tidal Basin, is the Jefferson Memorial. The Lincoln Memorial sits at the west end of The Mall, and close by this area is the Vietnam Veterans Memorial ('The Wall'). Arlington National Cemetery, site of the Tomb of the Unknowns and John F. Kennedy's final resting place, is located on the other side of the Potomac River. Other sights in the Capitol area include the National Archives; the Bureau of Engraving and Printing, where new money is printed and old money is destroyed; the U.S. Holocaust Memorial Museum; Ford's Theatre, where President Lincoln was assassinated; and the National Cathedral. Mount Vernon, the home of George Washington, is in nearby Alexandria, Virginia.

Population 523,124
Area (Land) . . . . . 61.0 sq mi
Area (Water) . . . . . 7.0 sq mi
Elevation . . . . . 420 ft
Latitude . . . . . 38-89-29 N
Longitude . . . . . 77-03-65 W
County . . . . . Independent City
Time Zone . . . . . EST
Area Code/s 202

— Average Temperatures and Precipitation —

TEMPERATURES

	Jan	Feb	Mar	Apr	May	Jun	Jul	Aug	Sep	Oct	Nov	Dec
High	40	44	55	65	74	83	87	86	79	68	57	45
Low	21	23	32	40	50	59	64	63	55	42	34	26

PRECIPITATION

	Jan	Feb	Mar	Apr	May	Jun	Jul	Aug	Sep	Oct	Nov	Dec
Inches	2.7	2.8	3.2	3.1	4.0	3.9	3.5	3.9	3.4	3.2	3.3	3.2

— Important Phone Numbers —

	Phone
AAA	202-331-3000
American Express Travel	202-457-1300
Dental Referral	202-547-7613
Dial-a-Museum	202-357-2020
Emergency	911
Medical Referral	202-877-3627
Poison Control Center	202-625-3333
Time	202-844-1111
Travelers Aid	202-546-3120
Weather	202-936-1212

— Information Sources —

				Phone	*Fax*
Better Business Bureau Serving Metropolitan Washington 1411 K St NW 10th Fl.	Washington	DC	20005	202-393-8000	393-1198
Web: www.dc.bbb.org ■ *E-mail:* sales@dc.bbb.org					
DC Committee to Promote Washington 1212 New York Ave NW Suite 200	Washington	DC	20005	202-724-5644	724-2445
District of Columbia Chamber of Commerce 1301 Pennsylvania Ave NW Suite 309	Washington	DC	20004	202-347-7201	638-6764
Web: www.dcchamber.org					
Martin Luther King Jr Memorial Library 901 G St NW	Washington	DC	20001	202-727-1111	727-1129
Washington City Council 441 4th St NW 7th Fl	Washington	DC	20001	202-724-8000	
Washington Convention Center 900 9th St NW	Washington	DC	20001	202-789-1600	789-8365*
**Fax:* Mktg ■ *TF:* 800-368-9000 ■ *Web:* www.dcconvention.com					
Washington DC Convention & Visitors Assn 1212 New York Ave NW Suite 600	Washington	DC	20005	202-789-7000	789-7037
Web: www.washington.org					
Washington Economic Development Dept 441 4th St NW Rm 1140 N	Washington	DC	20001	202-727-6365	727-6703
Washington Mayor 441 4th St NW	Washington	DC	20001	202-727-2980	727-6526
Web: 208.240.92.159/mayor_williams.html ■ *E-mail:* mayor@dcgov.org					
WETA/CapAccess 2775 S Quincy St	Arlington	VA	22206	703-998-2430	824-7350
Web: www.capaccess.org ■ *E-mail:* info@capaccess.org					

On-Line Resources

4WashingtonDC.com www.4washingtondc.com
About.com Guide to Washington DC . . . . . dc.about.com/local/midlanticus/dc
Annual Guide for the Arts www.guide4arts.com/dc/
Anthill City Guide Washington DC . . . . . www.anthill.com/city.asp?city=washingtondc
Area Guide Washington DC . . . . . washington.areaguides.net
ArtWOW . . . . . www.cais.com/koan/artwow.html
Bradmans.com Washington DC . . . . . www.bradmans.com/scripts/display_city.cgi?city=244
City Knowledge Washington DC . . . . . www.cityknowledge.com/dc.htm
CityTravelGuide.com Washington DC . . . . . www.citytravelguide.com/washington-dc.htm
Columbia Heights . . . . . innercity.org/columbiaheights/
CuisineNet Washington DC . . . . . www.cuisinenet.com/restaurant/washington/index.shtml
DC.TheLinks.com . . . . . dc.thelinks.com/
DigitalCity Washington . . . . . home.digitalcity.com/washington
District The . . . . . www.thedistrict.com
Excite.com Washington DC City Guide . . . . . www.excite.com/travel/countries/united_states/district_of_columbia/washington/
Fiesta Page . . . . . www.fiesta.com
Gayot's Guide Restaurant Search Washington DC . . . . . www.perrier.com/restaurants/gayot.asp?area=WDC
Guide to Washington DC . . . . . www.physics.georgetown.edu/Wash.html
I-95 Exit Information Guide Washington DC www.usastar.com/i95/cityguide/washdc.htm
Insiders' Guide to Washington DC . . . . . www.insiders.com/washington-dc/
Open World City Guides Washington DC . . . . . www.worldexecutive.com/cityguides/washington/
Rough Guide Travel Washington DC travel.roughguides.com/content/552/
Time Out Washington DC . . . . . www.timeout.com/washingtondc/
Washington City Paper . . . . . www.washingtoncitypaper.com
Washington DC City Pages . . . . . www.dcpages.com/
Washington DC CityWomen . . . . . www.citywomen.com/dcwomen.htm
Washington DC Historic Tours of America . . . . . www.historictours.com/washington/index.htm
Washington DC Home Page . . . . . www.ci.washington.dc.us
Washington Web . . . . . www.washweb.net
Yahoo! DC . . . . . dc.yahoo.com

— Transportation Services —

AIRPORTS

■ Washington Dulles International Airport (IAD) — *Phone*

31 miles W of downtown (approx 35 minutes) 703-572-2730
Web: www.mwaa.com/Dulles/index.html

Airport Transportation

	Phone
Taxi $40 fare to downtown	703-534-1111

Commercial Airlines

	Phone
Aeroflot	888-686-4949
AirTran	800-247-8726
All Nippon Airways	800-235-9262
America West	800-235-9292
American	800-433-7300
Atlantic Coast Airlines	800-241-6522
British Airways	800-247-9297
Delta	800-221-1212
Eastwind	888-327-8946
Lufthansa	800-645-3880
MetroJet	888-638-7653
Northwest	800-225-2525
Saudi Arabian	800-472-8342
TWA	800-221-2000
United	800-241-6522
US Airways	800-428-4322

Charter Airlines

	Phone
Extraordinair	800-787-0767
International Jet Management LLC	800-996-0600

■ Washington National Airport (DCA) — *Phone*

4 miles S of downtown (approx 20 minutes) 703-417-8000
Web: www.mwaa.com/National/index.html

Washington (Cont'd)

Airport Transportation

	Phone
Metrorail $1.10 fare to downtown	202-637-7000
Taxi $12-16 fare to downtown	202-544-1212

Commercial Airlines

	Phone		Phone
AccessAir	877-462-2237	**Midway**	800-446-4392
America West	800-235-9292	**Midwest Express**	800-452-2022
American	800-433-7300	**Northwest**	800-225-2525
Continental Express	800-525-0280	**TWA**	800-221-2000
Delta	800-221-1212	**United**	800-241-6522
Delta Business Express	800-345-3400	**US Airways**	800-428-4322

Charter Airlines

	Phone		Phone
Capital Helicopters	703-417-2150	**Martinair Inc**	877-419-5400

CAR RENTALS

	Phone		Phone
Alamo-Dulles	703-260-0182	**Dollar-Dulles**	703-661-6630
Alamo-National	703-684-0086	**Dollar-National**	703-519-8700
Avis	800-331-1212	**Hertz-Dulles**	703-471-6020
Budget-Dulles	703-920-6660	**National**	800-227-7368
Budget-National	703-920-3360	**Thrifty**	703-658-2200

LIMO/TAXI

	Phone		Phone
American Eagle Limousine	703-922-6666	**Manhattan/DC Executive Trans**	202-775-1888
Capital City Limo	202-387-6217	**Red Top Cab**	703-522-3333
DC Express Cab	202-526-5656	**Red Top Executive Sedan Co**	703-525-0900
District Cab	202-636-1600	**Yellow Cab**	202-544-1212
International Limousine Service Inc	202-388-6800		

MASS TRANSIT

	Phone
Metrorail/Metrobus $1.10 Base fare	202-637-7000

RAIL/BUS

				Phone
Amtrak Auto Train 8006 Lorton Rd *TF:* 800-872-7245	Lorton	VA	22079	703-690-3615
Amtrak Station 50 Massachusetts Ave NE Union Station *TF:* 800-872-7245	Washington	DC	20002	202-906-3193
Greyhound Bus Station 1005 NE 1st St *TF:* 800-231-2222	Washington	DC	20002	202-289-5154

— Accommodations —

HOTEL RESERVATION SERVICES

	Phone	Fax
Accommodations Express *TF:* 800-444-7666 ■ *Web:* www.accommodationsxpress.com ■ *E-mail:* accomexp@acy.digex.net	609-391-2100	525-0111
Bed & Breakfast Accommodations *Web:* www.bnbaccom.com ■ *E-mail:* reservations@bnbaccom.com	202-328-3510	332-3885
Capitol Reservations *TF:* 800-847-4832 ■ *Web:* www.visitdc.com ■ *E-mail:* capres@aol.com	202-452-1270	452-0537
Central Reservation Service *TF:* 800-548-3311 ■ *Web:* www.reservation-services.com ■ *E-mail:* cenresbos@aol.com	407-740-6442	740-8222
Hotel Reservations Network Inc *TF Sales:* 800-964-6835 ■ *Web:* www.hoteldiscount.com	214-361-7311	361-7299
Quikbook *TF:* 800-789-9887 ■ *Web:* www.quikbook.com	212-532-1660	532-1556
RMC Travel Centre *TF:* 800-782-2674	212-754-6560	754-6571
Washington DC Accommodations *TF:* 800-554-2220 ■ *Web:* www.dcaccommodations.com	202-289-2220	338-4517

HOTELS, MOTELS, RESORTS

				Phone	Fax
Best Western Capitol Skyline Hotel 10 'I' St SW *TF:* 800-458-7500	Washington	DC	20001	202-488-7500	488-0790
Best Western Downtown Capitol Hill 724 3rd St NW *TF:* 800-242-4831	Washington	DC	20001	202-842-4466	842-4831
Capital Hilton Hotel 16th & K St NW *TF:* 800-445-8667	Washington	DC	20036	202-393-1000	639-5784
Capitol Hill Suites 200 C St SE *TF:* 800-424-9165	Washington	DC	20003	202-543-6000	547-2608
Carlyle Suites Hotel 1731 New Hampshire Ave NW *TF:* 800-964-5377	Washington	DC	20009	202-234-3200	387-0085
Channel Inn Hotel 650 Water St SW *TF:* 800-368-5668 ■ *Web:* www.channelinn.com	Washington	DC	20024	202-554-2400	863-1164
Courtyard by Marriott 1900 Connecticut Ave NW *TF:* 800-842-4211 ■ *Web:* courtyard.com/WASNW	Washington	DC	20009	202-332-9300	328-7039
Courtyard by Marriott Crystal City 2899 Jefferson Davis Hwy *TF:* 800-321-2211 ■ *Web:* courtyard.com/WASCT	Arlington	VA	22202	703-549-3434	549-7440
Crowne Plaza Washington DC 14th & K Sts NW *TF:* 800-637-3788 ■ *E-mail:* crowneplazawashington@meristar.com	Washington	DC	20005	202-682-0111	682-9525
Days Inn Premier Convention Center 1201 K St NW *TF:* 800-325-2525	Washington	DC	20005	202-842-1020	289-0336
Doubletree Hotel Park Terrace 1515 Rhode Island Ave NW *TF:* 800-222-8733 ■ *Web:* www.doubletreehotels.com/DoubleT/Hotel21/29/29Main.htm	Washington	DC	20005	202-232-7000	332-8436
Embassy Row Hilton 2015 Massachusetts Ave NW *TF:* 800-424-2400	Washington	DC	20036	202-265-1600	328-7526
Embassy Square Suites 2000 'N' St NW *TF:* 800-833-4353 ■ *Web:* www.staydc.com/	Washington	DC	20036	202-659-9000	429-9546
Embassy Suites Downtown 1250 22nd St NW *TF:* 800-362-2779	Washington	DC	20037	202-857-3388	293-3173
Four Seasons Hotel 2800 Pennsylvania Ave NW *TF:* 800-332-3442 ■ *Web:* www.fourseasons.com/locations/WashingtonDC	Washington	DC	20007	202-342-0444	944-2076
Georgetown Inn 1310 Wisconsin Ave NW *TF:* 800-424-2979	Washington	DC	20007	202-333-8900	625-1744
Grand Hyatt Washington 1000 H St NW *TF:* 800-233-1234	Washington	DC	20001	202-582-1234	637-4781
Hampshire Hotel 1310 New Hampshire Ave NW *TF:* 800-368-5691	Washington	DC	20036	202-296-7600	293-2476
Hay-Adams Hotel 800 16th St NW *TF:* 800-424-5054	Washington	DC	20006	202-638-6600	638-2716
Henley Park Hotel 926 Massachusetts Ave NW *TF:* 800-222-8474	Washington	DC	20001	202-638-5200	638-6740
Holiday Inn 8120 Wisconsin Ave *TF:* 800-465-4329	Bethesda	MD	20814	301-652-2000	652-4525
Holiday Inn Capitol Smithsonian 550 C St SW *TF:* 800-465-4329 ■ *Web:* www.basshotels.com/holiday-inn/?_franchisee=WASSM ■ *E-mail:* hicapitol@aol.com	Washington	DC	20024	202-479-4000	488-4627
Holiday Inn Georgetown 2101 Wisconsin Ave NW *TF:* 800-465-4329 ■ *Web:* www.basshotels.com/holiday-inn/?_franchisee=WASGT ■ *E-mail:* jorina@ix.netcom.com	Washington	DC	20007	202-338-4600	333-6113
Holiday Inn on the Hill 415 New Jersey Ave NW *TF:* 800-638-1116 ■ *Web:* www.basshotels.com/holiday-inn/?_franchisee=WASCH ■ *E-mail:* mleach@holinnhill.com	Washington	DC	20001	202-638-1616	638-0707
Holiday Inn Washington National Airport 1489 Jefferson Davis Hwy *TF:* 800-465-4329 ■ *Web:* www.basshotels.com/holiday-inn/?_franchisee=WASNA ■ *E-mail:* weadbrock@bfsaulco.com	Arlington	VA	22202	703-416-1600	416-1615
Holidome Conference Center 5400 Holiday Dr *TF:* 800-465-4329	Frederick	MD	21703	301-694-7500	694-0589
Hotel Harrington 11th & 'E' Sts NW *TF:* 800-424-8532 ■ *Web:* www.hotel-harrington.com ■ *E-mail:* reservations@hotel-harrington.com	Washington	DC	20004	202-628-8140	347-3924

Washington — Hotels, Motels, Resorts (Cont'd)

	City	State	Zip	Phone	Fax
Hotel Lombardy 2019 Pennsylvania Ave NW	Washington	DC	20006	202-828-2600	872-0503
TF: 800-424-5486					
Hotel Sofitel 1914 Connecticut Ave NW	Washington	DC	20009	202-797-2000	462-0944
TF: 800-424-2464					
Hotel Washington 515 15th St NW	Washington	DC	20004	202-638-5900	638-4275
TF: 800-424-9540 ■ *Web:* www.hotelwashington.com ■ *E-mail:* reservations@hotelwashington.com					
Howard Johnson Hotel 2650 Jefferson Davis Hwy	Arlington	VA	22202	703-684-7200	684-3217
TF: 800-446-4656					
Hyatt Regency 400 New Jersey Ave NW	Washington	DC	20001	202-737-1234	737-5773
TF: 800-233-1234 ■ *Web:* www.hyatt.com/usa/washington/hotels/hotel_wasrw.html ■ *E-mail:* pr@hyattdc.com					
Jefferson Hotel 1200 16th St NW	Washington	DC	20036	202-347-2200	331-7982
TF: 800-355-8000					
JW Marriott Hotel 1331 Pennsylvania Ave NW	Washington	DC	20004	202-393-2000	626-6991
TF: 800-228-9290					
Latham Hotel 3000 M St NW	Washington	DC	20007	202-726-5000	337-4250
TF: 800-368-5922					
Loews L'Enfant Plaza Hotel 480 L'Enfant Plaza SW	Washington	DC	20024	202-484-1000	646-4456
TF: 800-635-5065 ■ *Web:* www.loewshotels.com/lenfanthome.html					
Madison Hotel 1177 15th St NW	Washington	DC	20005	202-862-1600	785-1255
TF: 800-424-8577					
Marriott Hotel Dulles Airport 45020 Aviation Dr	Dulles	VA	20166	703-471-9500	661-8714
TF: 800-228-9290 ■ *Web:* marriotthotels.com/IADAP					
Marriott Metro Center 775 12th St NW	Washington	DC	20005	202-737-2200	347-5886
TF: 800-228-9290 ■ *Web:* marriotthotels.com/WASMC					
Marriott Suites Dulles International Airport 13101 Worldgate Dr	Herndon	VA	20170	703-709-0400	709-0426
TF: 800-228-9290 ■ *Web:* marriotthotels.com/IADDS					
Marriott Wardman Park 2660 Woodley Rd NW	Washington	DC	20008	202-328-2000	234-0015
TF: 800-228-9290					
Mayflower Renaissance 1127 Connecticut Ave NW	Washington	DC	20036	202-347-3000	776-9182
TF: 800-468-3571					
Omni Shoreham Hotel 2500 Calvert St NW	Washington	DC	20008	202-234-0700	756-5145
TF: 800-843-6664					
One Washington Circle Hotel 1 Washington Cir NW	Washington	DC	20037	202-872-1680	887-4989
TF: 800-424-9671 ■ *Web:* www.onewashcirclehotel.com/					
Park Hyatt Washington 1201 24th St NW	Washington	DC	20037	202-789-1234	457-8823
TF: 800-233-1234					
Phoenix Park Hotel 520 N Capitol St NW	Washington	DC	20001	202-638-6900	393-3236
TF: 800-824-5419					
Radisson Barcelo Hotel 2121 P St NW	Washington	DC	20037	202-293-3100	857-0134
TF: 800-333-3333					
Red Roof Inn Downtown DC 500 H St NW	Washington	DC	20001	202-289-5959	682-9152
TF: 800-843-7663					
Renaissance Hotel 999 9th St NW	Washington	DC	20001	202-898-9000	289-0947
TF: 800-228-9290					
Ritz-Carlton Pentagon City 1250 S Hayes St.	Arlington	VA	22202	703-415-5000	415-5061
TF: 800-241-3333 ■ *Web:* www.ritzcarlton.com/location/NorthAmerica/PentagonCity/main.htm					
River Inn 924 25th St NW	Washington	DC	20037	202-337-7600	337-6520
TF: 800-424-2741 ■ *Web:* www.theriverinn.com/					
Saint Regis Hotel 923 16th St NW	Washington	DC	20006	202-638-2626	638-4231
TF: 800-325-3535					
State Plaza Hotel 2117 'E' St NW	Washington	DC	20037	202-861-8200	659-8601
TF: 800-424-2859					
Washington Court Hotel 525 New Jersey Ave NW	Washington	DC	20001	202-628-2100	879-7918
TF: 800-321-3010					
Washington Hilton & Towers 1919 Connecticut Ave NW	Washington	DC	20009	202-483-3000	232-0438
TF: 800-445-8667					
Washington Monarch The 2401 M St NW	Washington	DC	20037	202-429-2400	457-5010
TF: 877-222-2266 ■ *Web:* www.washingtonmonarch.com ■ *E-mail:* info@destinationtravel.com					
Washington National Airport Hilton 2399 Jefferson Davis Hwy	Arlington	VA	22202	703-418-6800	418-3763
TF: 800-445-8667					
Watergate Hotel 2650 Virginia Ave NW	Washington	DC	20037	202-965-2300	337-7915
TF: 800-424-2736 ■ *Web:* www.thewashingtoninn.com					
Westfields Marriott Center 14750 Conference Center Dr	Chantilly	VA	20151	703-818-0300	818-3655
TF: 800-635-5666					
Westin Fairfax Hotel 2100 Massachusetts Ave NW	Washington	DC	20008	202-293-2100	293-0641
TF: 800-937-8461					
Westin Hotel 2350 M St NW	Washington	DC	20037	202-429-0100	429-9759
TF: 800-228-3000					
Willard Inter-Continental Hotel 1401 Pennsylvania Ave NW	Washington	DC	20004	202-628-9100	637-7326
TF: 800-327-0200 ■ *Web:* www.interconti.com/usa/washington/hotel_waswil.html					
Wyndham Bristol Hotel 2430 Pennsylvania Ave NW	Washington	DC	20037	202-955-6400	955-5765
TF: 800-996-3426					
Wyndham City Centre Hotel 1143 New Hampshire Ave NW	Washington	DC	20037	202-775-0800	331-9491
TF: 800-822-4200					

— Restaurants —

	City	State	Zip	Phone
701 (Continental) 701 Pennsylvania Ave NW	Washington	DC	20004	202-393-0701
America Restaurant (American) 50 Massachusetts Ave NE	Washington	DC	20002	202-682-9555
Aquarelle (French) 2650 Virginia Ave NW Watergate Hotel	Washington	DC	20037	202-298-4455
Asia Nora (New American) 2213 M St NW	Washington	DC	20037	202-797-4860
Austin Grill (Tex Mex) 2404 Wisconsin Ave NW	Washington	DC	20007	202-337-8080
Avenue Cafe & Lounge (American) 1501 Rhode Island Ave NW	Washington	DC	20005	202-483-2000
E-mail: holiday@inn-dc.com				
Bacchus (Lebanese) 1827 Jefferson Pl NW	Washington	DC	20036	202-785-0734
Bertolini's Authentic Trattoria (Italian) 801 Pennsylvania Ave NW	Washington	DC	20004	202-638-2140
Bistro Français (French) 3128 M St NW	Washington	DC	20007	202-338-3830
Bombay Club (Indian) 815 Connecticut Ave NW	Washington	DC	20006	202-659-3727
Bombay Palace (Indian) 2020 K St NW	Washington	DC	20006	202-331-4200
Brickskellar (American) 1523 22nd St NW	Washington	DC	20037	202-293-1885
Brighton on N (Continental) 1733 'N' St NW	Washington	DC	20036	202-393-3000
Busara (Thai) 2340 Wisconsin Ave NW	Washington	DC	20007	202-337-2340
Cafe Mozart (German) 1331 H St NW	Washington	DC	20005	202-347-5732
Cafe on M (European) 2350 M St NW	Washington	DC	20037	202-429-0100
Capital Grille (American) 601 Pennsylvania Ave NW	Washington	DC	20004	202-737-6200
Capitol City Brewing Co (American) 1100 New York Ave NW	Washington	DC	20005	202-628-2222
Web: www.capcitybrew.com/				
Caracalla (Italian) 901 9th St NW	Washington	DC	20001	202-371-0681
Cashion's Eat Place (American) 1819 Columbia Rd NW	Washington	DC	20009	202-797-1819
Childe Harold (American) 1610 20th St NW	Washington	DC	20009	202-483-6700
Citronelle (French) 3000 M St NW	Washington	DC	20007	202-625-2150
Clyde's of Georgetown (American) 3236 M St NW	Washington	DC	20007	202-333-9180
Coco Loco (Mexican) 810 7th St NW	Washington	DC	20001	202-289-2626
Dancing Crab (Seafood) 4611 Wisconsin Ave NW	Washington	DC	20016	202-244-1882
Dubliner Pub (Irish) 520 N Capitol St NW	Washington	DC	20001	202-737-3773
El Caribe (Latin American) 3288 M St NW	Washington	DC	20007	202-338-3121
Enriqueta's (Mexican) 2811 M St NW	Washington	DC	20007	202-338-7772
Filomena Ristorante (Italian) 1063 Wisconsin Ave NW	Washington	DC	20007	202-338-8800
Florentine (Mediterranean) 999 9th St NW	Washington	DC	20001	202-898-9000
Galileo (Italian) 1110 21st St NW	Washington	DC	20036	202-293-7191
Gerard's Place (French) 915 15th St NW	Washington	DC	20005	202-737-4445
Goldoni (Italian) 1120 20th St NW	Washington	DC	20036	202-293-1511
Grill The (Continental) 1250 S Hayes St	Arlington	VA	22202	703-415-5000
Ha' Penny Lion (American) 1101 17th St NW	Washington	DC	20036	202-296-8075
Haad Thai Restaurant (Thai) 1100 New York Ave NW	Washington	DC	20005	202-682-1111
Hard Rock Cafe (American) 999 'E' St NW	Washington	DC	20004	202-737-7625
Hogate's (Seafood) 800 Water St SW	Washington	DC	20024	202-484-6300
i Ricchi (Italian) 1220 19th St NW	Washington	DC	20036	202-835-0459
Inn at Little Washington (French) Middle & Main Sts.	Washington	VA	22747	540-675-3800
Jaleo (Spanish) 480 7th St NW	Washington	DC	20004	202-628-7949
Jandara (Thai) 2606 Connecticut Ave NW	Washington	DC	20008	202-387-8876
Japan Inn (Japanese) 1715 Wisconsin Ave NW	Washington	DC	20007	202-337-3400
Jockey Club (French) 2100 Massachusetts Ave NW	Washington	DC	20008	202-835-2100
Kinkead's (International) 2000 Pennsylvania Ave NW	Washington	DC	20006	202-296-7700
L'Auberge Chez Francois (French) 332 Springvale Rd	Great Falls	VA	22066	703-759-3800
La Bergerie (French) 218 N Lee St.	Alexandria	VA	22314	703-683-1007
La Brasserie (French) 239 Massachusetts Ave NE	Washington	DC	20002	202-546-6066
La Chaumiere (French) 2813 M St NW	Washington	DC	20007	202-338-1784
La Colline (French) 400 N Capitol St NW	Washington	DC	20001	202-737-0400
Le Rivage (French) 1000 Water St SW	Washington	DC	20024	202-488-8111
Lebanese Taverna (Middle Eastern) 2641 Connecticut Ave NW	Washington	DC	20008	202-265-8681
Web: www.lebanese-taverna.com/				
Legal Sea Foods (Seafood) 2020 K St NW	Washington	DC	20006	202-496-1111

Washington — Restaurants (Cont'd)

Name / Address	City	State	ZIP	Phone
Les Halles Restaurant (French) 1201 Pennsylvania Ave NW	Washington	DC	20004	202-347-6848
Maison Blanche (French) 1725 F St NW	Washington	DC	20006	202-842-0070
Marrakesh (Moroccan) 617 New York Ave NW	Washington	DC	20001	202-393-9393
Melrose (Continental) 1201 24th St NW	Washington	DC	20037	202-955-3899
Meskerem (Ethiopian) 2434 18th St NW	Washington	DC	20009	202-462-4100
Metro Center Grille (American) 775 12th St NW	Washington	DC	20005	202-824-6122
Morrison Clark Inn (Southern) 11th St & Massachusetts Ave NW	Washington	DC	20001	202-898-1200
Mr K's (Chinese) 2121 K St NW	Washington	DC	20037	202-331-8868
Murphy's (Irish) 2609 24th St NW	Washington	DC	20008	202-462-7171
Music City Roadhouse (Southern) 1050 30th St NW	Washington	DC	20007	202-337-4444
Mykonos (Greek) 1835 K St NW	Washington	DC	20006	202-331-0370
New Heights (New American) 2317 Calvert St NW	Washington	DC	20008	202-234-4110
Nora (New American) 2132 Florida Ave NW	Washington	DC	20008	202-462-5143
Occidental Grill (American) 1475 Pennsylvania Ave NW	Washington	DC	20004	202-783-1475
Old Ebbitt Grill (American) 675 15th St NW	Washington	DC	20005	202-347-4800
Old Europe Restaurant & Rathskeller (German) 2434 Wisconsin Ave NW	Washington	DC	20007	202-333-7600
Palm The (Steak/Seafood) 1225 19th St NW	Washington	DC	20036	202-293-9091
Petittos (Italian) 2653 Connecticut Ave NW	Washington	DC	20008	202-667-5350
Pier 7 (Seafood) 650 Water St SW	Washington	DC	20024	202-554-2500
Planet Hollywood (American) 1101 Pennsylvania Ave NW	Washington	DC	20004	202-783-7827
Prime Rib The (Steak/Seafood) 2020 K St NW	Washington	DC	20006	202-466-8811
Provence (French) 2401 Pennsylvania Ave NW	Washington	DC	20037	202-296-1166
Raku (Asian) 1900 Q St NW	Washington	DC	20009	202-265-7258
Red River Grill (Mexican) 201 Massachussetts Ave NE	Washington	DC	20002	202-546-7200
Red Sage (Southwest) 605 14th St NW *Web:* town.hall.org/food/sage.html	Washington	DC	20005	202-638-4444
Rocklands Barbecue & Grilling Co (Barbecue) 2418 Wisconsin Ave NW	Washington	DC	20007	202-333-2558
Roxanne & Peyote Cafe (Southwest) 2319 18th St NW	Washington	DC	20009	202-462-8330
Solo Thai (Thai) 2016 P St NW	Washington	DC	20036	202-872-1144
Sam & Harry's (Steak/Seafood) 1200 19th St NW	Washington	DC	20036	202-296-4333
Sea Catch (Seafood) 1054 31st St NW	Washington	DC	20007	202-337-8855
Seasons (Continental) 2800 Pennsylvania Ave NW	Washington	DC	20007	202-342-0810
Sesto Senso (Italian) 1214 18th St NW	Washington	DC	20036	202-785-9525
Sushi-Ko (Japanese) 2309 Wisconsin Ave NW	Washington	DC	20007	202-333-4187
Taberna Del Alabardero (Spanish) 1776 'I' St NW	Washington	DC	20006	202-429-2200
Tahoga (American) 2815 M St NW	Washington	DC	20007	202-338-5380
Thai Town (Thai) 2655 Connecticut Ave NW	Washington	DC	20008	202-667-5115
Tunnicliff's Tavern (American/Cajun) 222 7th St SE	Washington	DC	20003	202-546-3663
Veneziano (Italian) 2305 18th St NW	Washington	DC	20009	202-483-9300
Via Pacifica (Asian/Italian) 1000 H St	Washington	DC	20001	202-582-1234
Vidalia (American) 1990 M St NW	Washington	DC	20036	202-659-1990
Vivaldi's (Italian) 5507 Connecticut Ave NW	Washington	DC	20015	202-244-7774
West End Cafe (American) 1 Washington Cir NW	Washington	DC	20037	202-293-5390
Willard Room (American) 1401 Pennsylvania Ave NW	Washington	DC	20004	202-637-7440
Zed's Ethiopian Cuisine (Ethiopian) 3318 M St NW	Washington	DC	20007	202-333-4710

— Goods and Services —

SHOPPING

Name / Address	City	State	ZIP	Phone	Fax
Chevy Chase Pavilion 5335 Wisconsin Ave NW	Washington	DC	20015	202-686-5335	686-5334
City Place Mall 8661 Colesville Rd	Silver Spring	MD	20910	301-589-1091	589-0581
Fashion Centre at Pentagon City 1100 S Hayes St	Arlington	VA	22202	703-415-2400	415-2175
Georgetown Park 3222 M St NW Suite 140	Washington	DC	20007	202-342-8190	342-1458
Hecht's 1201 G St NW	Washington	DC	20005	202-628-6661	628-0783
Mazza Gallerie 5300 Wisconsin Ave NW	Washington	DC	20015	202-966-6114	362-0471
Montgomery Mall 7101 Democracy Blvd	Bethesda	MD	20817	301-469-6000	469-7612
Pavilion at the Old Post Office 1100 Pennsylvania Ave NW	Washington	DC	20004	202-289-4224	
Potomac Mills 2700 Potomac Mills Cir Suite 307	Prince William	VA	22192	703-643-1855	643-1054
Shops at National Place 1331 Pennsylvania Ave NW Suite 1331	Washington	DC	20004	202-662-1204	662-1212
Tysons Galleria 2001 International Dr	McLean	VA	22102	703-827-7700	827-0976
Union Station 50 Massachusetts Ave NE	Washington	DC	20002	202-371-9441	
White Flint Mall 11301 Rockville Pike	North Bethesda	MD	20895	301-468-5777	816-9231

BANKS

Name / Address	City	State	ZIP	Phone	Fax
Citibank FSB 1775 Pennsylvania Ave NW *Fax Area Code: 202	Washington	DC	20006	800-926-1067	828-5913*
Crestar Bank 11th & G Sts NW *TF:* 800-273-7827	Washington	DC	20005	202-879-6290	879-6316
Crestar Bank NA 1445 New York Ave NW	Washington	DC	20005	202-879-6000	
First Union National Bank 740 15th St NW	Washington	DC	20005	202-637-7652	637-7689
NationsBank 888 17th St NW	Washington	DC	20006	202-624-4400	624-5678
Riggs Bank NA 800 17th St NW *TF:* 800-368-5800	Washington	DC	20006	202-835-4321	835-6734

BUSINESS SERVICES

	Phone		Phone
Choice Courier	301-731-9550	**Manpower Temporary Services**	202-331-8300
Congressional Record Delivery	202-667-5100	**Metropolitan Delivery Inc**	202-387-8200
Dependable Courier Service	202-638-0114	**Olsten Staffing Services**	202-296-5066
Federal Express	800-463-3339	**Post Office**	202-268-2000
Interim Financial Solutions	202-463-4500	**Quick Messenger Service**	202-783-3600
Kelly Services	202-331-8383	**UPS**	800-742-5877
Kinko's	202-686-3331		

— Media —

PUBLICATIONS

Name / Address	City	State	ZIP	Phone	Fax
Washington Business Journal 1555 Wilson Blvd Suite 400 *Web:* www.amcity.com/washington	Arlington	VA	22209	703-875-2200	875-2231
Washington Post‡ 1150 15th St NW *Web:* www.washingtonpost.com	Washington	DC	20071	202-334-6000	334-7502
Washington Times‡ 3600 New York Ave NE *Fax: Edit ■ *Web:* www.americasnewspaper.com	Washington	DC	20002	202-636-3000	269-3419*
Washingtonian 1828 'L' St NW Suite 200 *Web:* www.washingtonian.com	Washington	DC	20036	202-296-3600	

‡Daily newspapers

TELEVISION

Name / Address	City	State	ZIP	Phone	Fax
WBDC-TV Ch 50 (WB) 2121 Wisconsin Ave NW Suite 350	Washington	DC	20007	202-965-5050	965-0050
WDCA-TV Ch 20 (UPN) 5202 River Rd *Web:* www.paramountstations.com/WDCA ■ *E-mail:* programming@upn20email.com	Bethesda	MD	20816	301-986-9322	654-3517
WETA-TV Ch 26 (PBS) 3620 S 27th St *Web:* www.weta.org ■ *E-mail:* info@weta.com	Arlington	VA	22206	703-998-2600	998-3401
WHUT-TV Ch 32 (PBS) 2222 4th St NW	Washington	DC	20059	202-806-3200	806-3300
WJLA-TV Ch 7 (ABC) 3007 Tilden St NW *Web:* www.abc7dc.com	Washington	DC	20008	202-364-7777	364-7734
WPXW-TV Ch 66 (PAX) 6199 Old Arrington Ln	Fairfax Station	VA	22039	703-503-7966	503-1225
WRC-TV Ch 4 (NBC) 4001 Nebraska Ave NW *Web:* www.nbc4dc.com	Washington	DC	20016	202-885-4000	885-4104
WTMW-TV Ch 14 (Ind) 3565 Lee Hwy	Arlington	VA	22207	703-528-0051	528-2956
WTTG-TV Ch 5 (Fox) 5151 Wisconsin Ave NW	Washington	DC	20016	202-244-5151	244-1745
WUSA-TV Ch 9 (CBS) 4100 Wisconsin Ave NW *Web:* www.wusatv9.com ■ *E-mail:* 9news@wusatv.com	Washington	DC	20016	202-895-5999	966-7948

RADIO

Name / Address	City	State	ZIP	Phone	Fax
WAMU-FM 88.5 MHz (NPR) American University *Fax: News Rm ■ *Web:* www.wamu.org ■ *E-mail:* feedback@wamu.org	Washington	DC	20016	202-885-1200	885-1269*
WARW-FM 94.7 MHz (CR) 5912 Hubbard Dr *Web:* www.classicrock947.com	Rockville	MD	20852	301-984-6000	468-2490
WASH-FM 97.1 MHz (AC) 1801 Rockville Pike *Web:* www.washfm.com	Rockville	MD	20852	301-984-9710	255-4344
WBIG-FM 100.3 MHz (Oldies) 1801 Rockville Pike 6th Fl	Rockville	MD	20852	301-468-1800	770-0236
WGAY-FM 99.5 MHz (AC) 1801 Rockville Pike 6th Fl *E-mail:* wgay995@aol.com	Rockville	MD	20852	301-468-9429	770-3541
WGMS-FM 103.5 MHz (Clas) 3400 Idaho Ave NW	Washington	DC	20016	202-895-5000	895-4168
WHFS-FM 99.1 MHz (Alt) 8201 Corporate Dr Suite 550 *Web:* www.whfs.com	Landover	MD	20785	301-306-0991	731-0431

Washington — Radio (Cont'd)

Phone *Fax*

WHUR-FM 96.3 MHz (Urban)
529 Bryant St NW. . . . . Washington DC 20059 202-806-3500 806-3522
WJFK-AM 1300 kHz (N/T)
1 W Pennsylvania Ave Suite 850. . . . . Baltimore MD 21204 410-823-1570 821-5482
WJFK-FM 106.7 MHz (N/T) 10800 Main St . . . . . . Fairfax VA 22030 703-691-1900 352-0111
WJZW-FM 105.9 MHz (NAC)
4400 Jenifer St NW. . . . . Washington DC 20015 202-895-2300 686-3064
WKYS-FM 93.9 MHz (Urban)
5900 Princess Garden Pkwy Suite 800 . . . . . . Lanham MD 20706 301-306-1111 306-9609
WMAL-AM 630 kHz (N/T)
4400 Jenifer St NW. . . . . Washington DC 20015 202-686-3100 686-3061
WMMJ-FM 102.3 MHz (Urban)
5900 Princess Garden Pkwy Suite 800 . . . . . . Lanham MD 20706 301-306-1111 306-9609
WMZQ-FM 98.7 MHz (Ctry)
1801 Rockville Pike 6th Fl . . . . Rockville MD 20852 301-231-8231 984-4895
WOL-AM 1450 kHz (N/T)
5900 Princess Garden Pkwy. . . . . Lanham MD 20706 301-306-1111 306-9609
WPGC-AM 1580 kHz (Rel)
6301 Ivy Ln Suite 800. . . . . Greenbelt MD 20770 301-441-3500 345-9505
WPGC-FM 95.5 MHz (CHR)
6301 Ivy Ln Suite 800. . . . . Greenbelt MD 20770 301-441-3500 345-9505
WRQX-FM 107.3 MHz (AC)
4400 Jenifer St NW. . . . . Washington DC 20015 202-686-3100 686-3091*
**Fax:* New Rm
WTEM-AM 980 kHz (Sports)
11300 Rockville Pike Suite 707. . . . . Rockville MD 20852 301-231-7798 881-8030
Web: www.wtem.com ■ *E-mail:* tcastle@erols.com
WTOP-AM 1500 kHz (N/T)
3400 Idaho Ave NW . . . . Washington DC 20016 202-895-5000 895-5140
WTOP-FM 107.7 MHz (N/T)
3400 Idaho Ave NW . . . . Washington DC 20016 202-895-5000 895-5140
WWVZ-FM 103.9 MHz (CHR)
6633 Mt Philip Rd. Frederick MD 21703 301-662-2148 663-0636
WWZZ-FM 104.1 MHz (CHR)
2000 15th St N Suite 200 . . . . Arlington VA 22201 703-522-1041 526-0250
Web: www.thez.com
WYCB-AM 1340 kHz (Rel)
5900 Princess Garden Pkwy Suite 800 . . . . . . Lanham MD 20706 301-306-1111 306-9609

— Colleges/Universities —

Phone *Fax*

American University
4400 Massachusetts Ave NW. . . . . Washington DC 20016 202-885-1000 885-6014
Web: www.american.edu
Capitol College 11301 Springfield Rd . . . . Laurel MD 20708 301-369-2800 953-3876
TF Admissions: 800-950-1992 ■ *Web:* www.capitol-college.edu
■ *E-mail:* ccinfo@capitol-college.edu
Catholic University of America
620 Michigan Ave NE . . . . Washington DC 20064 202-319-5000 319-6533
TF Admissions: 800-673-2772 ■ *Web:* www.cua.edu
Columbia Union College
7600 Flower Ave. . . . . Takoma Park MD 20912 301-891-4000 891-4167
TF: 800-835-4212 ■ *Web:* www.cuc.edu
Corcoran School of Art 500 17th St NW . . . . Washington DC 20006 202-639-1800 639-1802
Web: www.corcoran.edu/csa
Gallaudet University 800 Florida Ave NE . . . . Washington DC 20002 202-651-5000 651-6107
Web: www.gallaudet.edu
George Mason University
4400 University Dr MSN 3A4 . . . . Fairfax VA 22030 703-993-1000 993-2392
Web: www.gmu.edu ■ *E-mail:* admissions@admissions.gmu.edu
George Washington University
2121 'I' St NW. . . . . Washington DC 20052 202-994-1000 994-0325
TF Admissions: 800-447-3765 ■ *Web:* gwis.circ.gwu.edu
Georgetown University
37th & 'O' Sts NW . . . . Washington DC 20057 202-687-3600 687-5084
Web: www.georgetown.edu
Howard University 2400 6th St NW . . . . Washington DC 20059 202-806-6100 806-4466
Web: www.howard.edu
Maryland College of Art & Design
10500 Georgia Ave . . . . Silver Spring MD 20902 301-649-4454 649-2940
Web: www.mcadmd.org
Marymount University 2807 N Glebe Rd . . . . . . Arlington VA 22207 703-522-5600 522-0349
TF Admissions: 800-548-7638 ■ *Web:* www.marymount.edu
■ *E-mail:* admissions@marymount.edu
Montgomery College Rockville Campus
51 Mannakee St . . . . Rockville MD 20850 301-279-5000 279-5037
Web: www.montgomerycollege.com ■ *E-mail:* arrweb@mc.cc.md.us
Montgomery College Takoma Park Campus
7600 Takoma Ave. . . . . Takoma Park MD 20912 301-650-1501 650-1497

Phone *Fax*

Mount Vernon College
2100 Foxhall Rd NW . . . . Washington DC 20007 202-625-0400 625-4688
TF Admissions: 800-682-4636 ■ *Web:* www.gwu.edu
■ *E-mail:* gwadm@www.gwu.edu
Oblate College 391 Michigan Ave NE . . . . . . Washington DC 20017 202-529-5244 636-9444
Southeastern University 501 'I' St SW . . . . . Washington DC 20024 202-488-8162 488-8093
Web: www.seu.edu ■ *E-mail:* compctr@admin.seu.edu
Strayer University 1025 15th St NW. . . . . . . Washington DC 20005 202-408-2400 289-1831
TF: 888-478-7293 ■ *Web:* www.strayer.edu
Strayer University Arlington Campus
3045 Columbia Pike . . . . Arlington VA 22204 703-892-5100 769-2677
TF: 888-478-7293
Trinity College 125 Michigan Ave NE . . . . . . Washington DC 20017 202-884-9000 884-9229
TF Admissions: 800-492-6882 ■ *Web:* www.trinitydc.edu
University of Maryland College Park . . . . . . College Park MD 20742 301-405-1000 314-9693
TF Admissions: 800-422-5867 ■ *Web:* inform.umd.edu
■ *E-mail:* inform-editor@umail.umd.edu
University of the District of Columbia
4200 Connecticut Ave NW . . . . Washington DC 20008 202-274-5000 274-6073
Web: www.udc.edu
Washington Bible College/Capital Bible
Seminary 6511 Princess Garden Pkwy . . . . . . Lanham MD 20706 301-552-1400 552-2775
TF: 800-787-0256 ■ *Web:* www.bible.edu ■ *E-mail:* info@bible.edu

— Hospitals —

Phone *Fax*

Children's National Medical Center
111 Michigan Ave NW. . . . . Washington DC 20010 202-884-5000 884-5561
TF Billing: 800-787-0080 ■ *Web:* www.cnmc.org
District of Columbia General Hospital
19th St & Massachusetts Ave SE . . . . Washington DC 20003 202-675-5000 675-5650
George Washington University Hospital
901 23rd St NW . . . . Washington DC 20037 202-715-4000 994-0993*
**Fax:* Hum Res
Georgetown University Medical Center
3800 Reservoir Rd NW . . . . Washington DC 20007 202-687-5055 784-2875*
**Fax:* Hum Res ■ *Web:* www.dml.georgetown.edu/gumc.html
Greater Southeast Community Hospital
1310 Southern Ave SE. . . . . Washington DC 20032 202-574-6000 574-7188
Howard University Hospital
2041 Georgia Ave NW. . . . . Washington DC 20060 202-865-6100 865-1360
Web: www.huhosp.org
Providence Hospital 1150 Varnum St NE. . . . Washington DC 20017 202-269-7000 269-7160
Sibley Memorial Hospital
5255 Loughboro Rd NW . . . . Washington DC 20016 202-537-4000 243-2246*
**Fax:* Admissions ■ *Web:* www.sibley.org
Veterans Affairs Medical Center
50 Irving St NW . . . . Washington DC 20422 202-745-8000 745-8530
Washington Hospital Center
110 Irving St NW . . . . Washington DC 20010 202-877-7000 877-7826
E-mail: info@mhg.edu

— Attractions —

Phone *Fax*

African-American Civil War Memorial
10th & U Sts NW . . . . Washington DC 20009 202-667-2667 667-6771
American Sportscasters Assn Hall of Fame
& Museum 601 F St NW. . . . . Washington DC 20004 202-628-3200 661-5172
Anacostia Museum (Smithsonian Institution)
1901 Fort Place SE . . . . Washington DC 20560 202-357-1300 287-3183
Archives of American Art
901 D St SW Suite 704. . . . . Washington DC 20560 202-314-3900 314-3987
Web: www.si.edu/artarchives
Arena Stage 1101 6th St . . . . Washington DC 20024 202-488-3300
Arlington National Cemetery
Arlington Cemetery . . . . Arlington VA 22211 703-697-2131 697-4967
Web: www.mdw.army.mil/cemetery.htm
Arts & Industries Building
900 Jefferson Dr SW. . . . . Washington DC 20560 202-357-2700
B'nai B'rith Klutznick National Jewish
Museum 1640 Rhode Island Ave NW . . . . Washington DC 20036 202-857-6583 857-1099
Bureau of Engraving & Printing
14th & C Sts SW . . . . Washington DC 20228 202-874-2485 874-3177
Capital Children's Museum
800 3rd St NE . . . . Washington DC 20002 202-675-4120 675-4140
Web: www.ccm.org/
Carver George Washington Nature Trail
1901 Fort Place SE Anacostia Museum . . . Washington DC 20020 202-287-3369 287-3183

Washington — Attractions (Cont'd)

Name / Address	City	State	ZIP	Phone	Fax
Chesapeake & Ohio Canal National Historical Park PO Box 4	Sharpsburg	MD	21782	301-739-4200	739-5275
Web: www.nps.gov/choh/ ■ *E-mail:* choh_chief_ranger@nps.gov					
Chevy Chase Pavilion 5335 Wisconsin Ave NW	Washington	DC	20015	202-686-5335	686-5334
Congressional Cemetery 1801 E St SE	Washington	DC	20003	202-543-0539	
Constitution Gardens 900 Ohio Dr SW Survey Lodge	Washington	DC	20242	202-426-6841	426-1844
Web: www.nps.gov/coga/					
Corcoran Gallery of Art 500 17th St NW	Washington	DC	20006	202-639-1700	639-1768
Web: www.corcoran.org/cga ■ *E-mail:* rothschd@access.digex.net					
DAR Museum 1776 D St NW	Washington	DC	20006	202-879-3241	628-0820
Web: www.dar.org/museum/index.html					
Decatur House Museum 748 Jackson Pl NW	Washington	DC	20006	202-842-0920	842-0030
E-mail: decatur-house@nthp.org					
Discovery Creek Children's Museum of Washington DC 5125 MacArthur Blvd NW Suite 10	Washington	DC	20016	202-364-3111	364-3114
Web: www.discoverycreek.org ■ *E-mail:* discovery_creek@capaccess.org					
Discovery Theater 900 Jefferson Dr SW	Washington	DC	20560	202-357-1500	357-2588
Dumbarton House 2715 Q St NW	Washington	DC	20007	202-337-2288	337-0348
Dumbarton Oaks 1703 32nd St NW	Washington	DC	20007	202-339-6401	339-6419
Dumbarton Oaks Research Library & Collection 1703 32nd St NW	Washington	DC	20007	202-339-6400	339-6419
Web: www.doaks.org					
Evans-Tibbs Collection 1910 Vermont Ave NW	Washington	DC	20001	202-234-8164	
Folger Shakespeare Library 201 E Capitol St South East	Washington	DC	20003	202-544-4600	544-4623
Ford's Theatre National Historic Site 511 10th St NW	Washington	DC	20004	202-426-6924	426-1845
Web: www.nps.gov/foth/ ■ *E-mail:* ford's_theatre@nps.gov					
Fort Washington Park 13551 Fort Washington Rd	Fort Washington	MD	20744	301-763-4600	763-1389
Web: www.nps.gov/fowa/					
Franciscan Monastery 1400 Quincy St NE	Washington	DC	20017	202-526-6800	529-9889
Franklin Delano Roosevelt Memorial West Basin Dr SW	Washington	DC	20024	202-619-7222	
Frederick Douglass National Historic Site 1411 'W' St SE	Washington	DC	20020	202-426-5960	426-0880
Web: www.nps.gov/frdo/					
Freer Gallery of Art (Smithsonian Institution) 12th St SW & Jefferson Dr	Washington	DC	20560	202-357-4880	633-9105
Web: www.si.edu/asia/					
Geographica 17th & M Sts NW	Washington	DC	20036	202-857-7588	
Georgetown Historic District Wisconsin Ave betw 29th & 37th Sts	Washington	DC	20007	202-789-7000	
Hillwood Museum & Gardens 4155 Linnean Ave NW	Washington	DC	20008	202-686-8500	966-7846
Hirshhorn Museum & Sculpture Garden (Smithsonian Institution) Independence Ave & 7th St SW	Washington	DC	20560	202-357-3091	786-2682
Web: www.si.edu/hirshhorn/					
Jefferson Memorial 900 Ohio Dr SW National Capital Region	Washington	DC	20242	202-426-6841	426-1844
Web: www.nps.gov/thje/					
Jewish Historical Society of Greater Washington 701 3rd St NW	Washington	DC	20001	202-789-0900	789-0485
John F Kennedy Center for the Performing Arts New Hampshire Ave & F St NW	Washington	DC	20566	202-416-8000	416-8205
Web: kennedy-center.org ■ *E-mail:* comments@kennedy-center.org					
Kenilworth Aquatic Gardens Anacostia Ave & Douglas St NE	Washington	DC	20019	202-426-6905	426-5991
Kennedy Center Opera House Orchestra John F Kennedy Center for the Performing Arts	Washington	DC	20566	202-416-8215	416-8216
Korean War Veterans Memorial 23rd & Independence Ave	Washington	DC	20024	202-619-7222	
Kreeger Museum 2401 Foxhall Rd NW	Washington	DC	20007	202-338-3552	337-3051
Web: www.kreegermuseum.com					
Langley IMAX Theater 6th St & Independence Ave SW	Washington	DC	20560	202-357-1675	
Web: www.nasm.edu/nasm/IMAX/langley.html					
Library of Congress 101 Independence Ave SE	Washington	DC	20540	202-707-5000	707-5844
Web: www.loc.gov					
Lillian & Albert Small Jewish Museum 701 3rd St NW	Washington	DC	20001	202-789-0900	789-0485
Web: www.jewishculture.org/jewishmuseums/small.htm					
Lincoln Memorial 900 Ohio Dr SW National Capitol Park Central	Washington	DC	20024	202-426-6841	426-1844
Web: www.nps.gov/linc/					
Lincoln Theatre 1215 U St NW	Washington	DC	20009	202-328-9177	328-9245
Manassas National Battlefield Park 6511 Sudley Rd	Manassas	VA	20109	703-361-1339	
Web: www.nps.gov/mana/					
Mary McLeod Bethune Council House National Historic Site 1318 Vermont Ave NW	Washington	DC	20005	202-673-2402	673-2414
Web: www.nps.gov/mamc/					
MCI Center 601 'F' St NW	Washington	DC	20001	202-628-3200	661-5083
TF: 800-551-7328 ■ *Web:* www.mcicenter.com					
Mount Vernon Ladies' Assn of the Union PO Box 110	Mount Vernon	VA	22121	703-780-2000	799-8698*
**Fax:* Library ■ *Web:* www.mountvernon.org					
National Air & Space Museum Smithsonian Institution Independence Ave & 6th St SW	Washington	DC	20560	202-357-2700	357-2426
Web: www.nasm.edu ■ *E-mail:* vportway@www.nasm.edu					
National Aquarium 14th & Constitution Ave NW	Washington	DC	20230	202-482-2826	482-4946
E-mail: aqua@doc.gov					
National Archives & Records Administration 8606 Adelphi Rd	College Park	MD	20740	301-713-7360	713-6905
Web: www.nara.gov ■ *E-mail:* inquire@nara.gov					
National Building Museum 401 F St NW	Washington	DC	20001	202-272-2448	272-2564
Web: www.nbm.org					
National Capital Region (NCR) 1100 Ohio Dr SW	Washington	DC	20242	202-619-7222	619-7302
National Cathedral Massachusetts & Wisconsin Aves NW	Washington	DC	20016	202-537-6200	
National Gallery of Art 6th St & Constitution Ave NW	Washington	DC	20565	202-737-4215	842-2356
Web: www.nga.gov					
National Garden to Commemorate Congress's Bicentennial 245 1st St SW	Washington	DC	20024	202-226-4083	225-7910
Web: www.nationalgarden.org					
National Geographic Society 1145 17th St NW	Washington	DC	20036	202-857-7000	775-6141
TF Orders: 800-647-5463 ■ *Web:* www.nationalgeographic.com ■ *E-mail:* askngs@nationalgeographic.com					
National Geographic Society Explorer's Hall 1147 17th St NW	Washington	DC	20036	202-857-7589	
National Law Enforcement Officers Memorial 605 'E' St NW	Washington	DC	20004	202-737-3400	737-3405
National Mall 900 Ohio Dr SW National Capital Region National Park Service	Washington	DC	20024	202-426-6841	426-1844
Web: www.nps.gov/nama/					
National Museum of African Art (Smithsonian Institution) 950 Independence Ave SW	Washington	DC	20560	202-357-4600	357-4879
Web: www.si.edu/organiza/museums/africart/start.htm					
National Museum of American Art (Smithsonian Institution) 8th & G Sts NW	Washington	DC	20560	202-357-2700	357-2528*
**Fax:* PR ■ *Web:* www.nmaa.si.edu					
National Museum of American History (Smithsonian Institution) 14th St & Constitution Ave NW	Washington	DC	20560	202-357-2700	633-8053*
**Fax:* PR ■ *Web:* www.si.edu/organiza/museums/nmah/nmah.htm					
National Museum of Health & Medicine 6825 16th St NW	Washington	DC	20306	202-782-2200	782-3573
Web: natmedmuse.afip.org					
National Museum of Natural History (Smithsonian Institution) 10th St & Constitution Ave NW	Washington	DC	20560	202-357-2664	357-4779
Web: www.mnh.si.edu/nmnhweb.html					
National Museum of Women in the Arts 1250 New York Ave NW	Washington	DC	20005	202-783-5000	393-3245
TF: 800-222-7270 ■ *Web:* www.nmwa.org					
National Portrait Gallery (Smithsonian Institution) F St & 8th NW	Washington	DC	20560	202-357-1915	633-9188*
**Fax:* PR ■ *Web:* www.npg.si.edu					
National Postal Museum (Smithsonian Institution) 2 Massachusetts Ave NE	Washington	DC	20560	202-633-9360	633-9393
Web: www.si.edu/organiza/museums/postal/start.htm					
National Shrine of Immaculate Conception 4th St & Michigan Ave NE	Washington	DC	20017	202-526-8300	526-8313

Washington — Attractions (Cont'd)

Phone | Fax

National Symphony Orchestra
JFK Ctr for the Performing Arts New Hampshire Ave & F St NW | Washington DC | 20566 | 202-416-8100 | 416-8105
TF: 800-444-1324 ■ *Web:* kennedy-center.org/stage/nso/

National Theatre 1321 'E' St NW | Washington DC | 20004 | 202-628-6161 | 638-4830
TF: 800-447-7400 ■ *Web:* www.nationaltheatre.org

National Zoological Park
3001 Connecticut Ave NW | Washington DC | 20008 | 202-673-4717 | 673-4900
Web: www.si.edu/natzoo

Navy Historical Center
901 'M' St SE Washington Navy Yard | Washington DC | 20003 | 202-433-4882 | 433-8200
Web: www.history.navy.mil

Navy Museum
901 'M' St SE Washington Navy Yard | Washington DC | 20003 | 202-433-4882 | 433-8200
Web: www.history.navy.mil

Octagon The Museum
1799 New York Ave NW | Washington DC | 20006 | 202-638-3221 | 879-7764
Web: www.aafpages.org/octabout.htm

Old Stone House 3051 M St NW | Washington DC | 20007 | 202-426-6851 | 426-0215

Old Town Trolley Tours
50 Massachussetts Ave NE Union Stn | Washington DC | 20002 | 202-832-9800 | 832-9040
Web: www.historictours.com/washington/trolley.htm
■ *E-mail:* wdcott@historictours.com

Pavilion at the Old Post Office
1100 Pennsylvania Ave NW | Washington DC | 20004 | 202-289-4224

Pennsylvania Avenue National Historic Site
900 Ohio Dr SW National Capital Park | Washington DC | 20024 | 202-426-6841 | 426-1835
Web: www.nps.gov/paav/

Pentagon The | Arlington VA | 20301 | 703-695-1776
Web: www.defenselink.mil/pubs/pentagon

Phillips Collection 1600 21st St NW | Washington DC | 20009 | 202-387-2151 | 387-2436
Web: www.phillipscollection.org

Piscataway Park
13551 Fort Washington Rd | Fort Washington MD | 20744 | 301-763-4600 | 763-1389
Web: www.nps.gov/pisc/

Potomac Heritage National Scenic Trail
1100 Ohio Dr SW National Capital Region National Park Service | Washington DC | 20242 | 202-619-7025 | 401-0017
Web: www.nps.gov/pohe/

Renwick Gallery of the National Museum of American Art (Smithsonian Institution) Pennsylvania Ave & 17th St NW | Washington DC | 20006 | 202-357-2531 | 786-2810
Web: nmaa-ryder.si.edu/collections/renwick/main.html

Rock Creek Park
3545 Williamsburg Ln NW | Washington DC | 20008 | 202-282-1063 | 282-7612
Web: www.nps.gov/rocr

Sackler Arthur M Gallery (Smithsonian Institution) 1050 Independence Ave SW | Washington DC | 20560 | 202-357-4880 | 357-4911
Web: www.si.edu/asia

Saint Matthew's Cathedral
1725 Rhode Island Ave NW | Washington DC | 20036 | 202-347-3215 | 347-7184

Shakespeare Theatre 450 7th St NW | Washington DC | 20004 | 202-547-1122 | 638-3869
Web: www.shakespearedc.org

Textile Museum 2320 'S' St NW | Washington DC | 20008 | 202-667-0441 | 483-0994
Web: www.textilemuseum.org

Theodore Roosevelt Island
George Washington Pkwy Turkey Run Park | McLean VA | 22101 | 703-289-2530 | 289-2598
Web: www.nps.gov/this/

Thomas Jefferson Memorial & Tidal Basin
900 Ohio Dr SW National Capital Region Mall Operations | Washington DC | 20024 | 202-426-6841 | 426-1844
Web: www.nps.gov/thje/ ■ *E-mail:* national_mall@nps.gov

Tudor Place 1644 31st St NW | Washington DC | 20007 | 202-965-0400 | 965-0164
Web: www.tudorplace.org ■ *E-mail:* ctuggle@tudorplace.org

US Air Force Band Strolling Strings
201 McChord St Bolling Air Force Base | Washington DC | 20332 | 202-767-4224 | 767-0686

US Air Force Concert Band
201 McChord St Bolling Air Force Base | Washington DC | 20332 | 202-767-4224 | 767-0686

US Botanic Garden 245 1st St SW | Washington DC | 20024 | 202-225-8333 | 225-1561

US Capitol 1st St & Independence Ave | Washington DC | 20510 | 202-225-6827
Web: www.aoc.gov ■ *E-mail:* feedback@aoc.gov

US Holocaust Memorial Museum
100 Raoul Wallenburg Pl SW | Washington DC | 20024 | 202-488-0400 | 488-2690
Web: www.ushmm.org ■ *E-mail:* membership@ushmm.org

US National Arboretum
3501 New York Ave NE | Washington DC | 20002 | 202-245-2726 | 245-4575
Web: www.ars-grin.gov/na

US Navy Memorial & Naval Heritage Center
701 Pennsylvania Ave NW | Washington DC | 20004 | 202-737-2300 | 737-2308
TF: 800-723-3557 ■ *Web:* www.history.navy.mil

US Supreme Court
1st St & Maryland Ave NE | Washington DC | 20543 | 202-479-3030
Web: supct.law.cornell.edu/supct

Vietnam Veterans Memorial
Corner Constitution Ave NW & Henry Bacon Dr National Capitol Park Central | Washington DC | 20020 | 202-634-1568
Web: thewall-usa.com

Vietnam Women's Memorial
21st & Constitution Ave NW | Washington DC | 20024 | 202-426-6841

Warner Theatre
1299 Pennsylvania Ave NW | Washington DC | 20004 | 202-783-4000 | 783-0204
Web: www.warnertheatre.com

Washington Ballet
3515 Wisconsin Ave NW | Washington DC | 20016 | 202-362-3606 | 362-1311
Web: www.washingtonballet.org

Washington Design Center
300 D St SW Suite 630 | Washington DC | 20024 | 202-554-5053 | 488-3711

Washington Dolls' House & Toy Museum
5236 44th St NW | Washington DC | 20015 | 202-244-0024 | 237-1659

Washington Monument
15th & Independence Ave NW | Washington DC | 20024 | 202-426-6841 | 426-1844
Web: www.nps.gov/wamo/ ■ *E-mail:* national_mall@nps.gov

Washington National Cathedral
Wisconsin & Massachusetts Aves NW | Washington DC | 20016 | 202-537-6200 | 364-6600
Web: www.cathedral.org/cathedral/

Washington Opera
2600 Virginia Ave NW Suite 104 | Washington DC | 20037 | 202-295-2420 | 295-2479
TF: 800-876-7372 ■ *Web:* www.dc-opera.org
■ *E-mail:* mail@dc-opera.org

White House 1600 Pennsylvania Ave NW | Washington DC | 20500 | 202-208-1631 | 208-1643
Web: www.nps.gov/whho

White House Visitors Center
Pennsylvania Ave | Washington DC | 20500 | 202-456-7041
Web: www.whitehouse.gov/WH/Tours/visitors_center.html

Women in Military Service for America Memorial Arlington National Cemetery | Arlington VA | 22211 | 800-472-5883 | 931-4208*
**Fax Area Code: 703*

Woodrow Wilson House Museum
2340 'S' St NW | Washington DC | 20008 | 202-387-4062 | 483-1466
Web: www.nthp.org/main/sites/wilsonhouse.htm

Woolly Mammoth Theatre Co
1401 Church St NW | Washington DC | 20005 | 202-393-3939 | 667-0904

SPORTS TEAMS & FACILITIES

Phone | Fax

MCI Center 601 'F' St NW | Washington DC | 20001 | 202-628-3200 | 661-5083
TF: 800-551-7328 ■ *Web:* www.mcicenter.com

Robert F Kennedy Memorial Stadium
2400 E Capitol St | Washington DC | 20003 | 202-547-9077 | 547-7460
Web: www.dcsec.dcgov.org

Rosecroft Raceway
6336 Rosecroft Dr | Fort Washington MD | 20744 | 301-567-4000 | 567-9267
Web: www.rosecroft.com

Washington Capitals
601 F St NW MCI Ctr | Washington DC | 20004 | 202-628-3200 | 661-5000

Washington DC United (soccer)
13832 Redskin Dr | Herndon VA | 20171 | 703-478-6600 | 736-9451
Web: www.dcunited.com/ ■ *E-mail:* info@dcunited.com

Washington Mystics (basketball)
601 F St NW MCI Ctr | Washington DC | 20004 | 202-628-3200 | 661-5122
Web: www.wnba.com/mystics/index.html

Washington Redskins
Raljon Rd Redskins Stadium | Raljon MD | 20785 | 301-276-6050 | 276-6001
Web: www.redskins.com

Washington Wizards
601 F St NW MCI Ctr | Washington DC | 20004 | 202-628-3200
TF: 800-551-7328 ■ *Web:* www.nba.com/wizards

— Events —

	Phone
Candlelight Vigil (mid-May)	202-737-3400
Capital Area Auto Show (late December)	202-789-1600
Chinese New Year Parade (mid-February)	202-357-2700
Christmas on 'S' Street (December-early January)	202-387-4062
DC Spring Antiques Fair (early March)	301-924-5002
DC Winter Antiques Fair (early December)	301-924-5002
Dulles International Antiques Show & Sale (mid-April)	703-802-0066
Festival of American Folklife (late June-early July)	202-357-2700
Founder's Day Water Lily Festival (late July)	202-426-6905
Garden Fair & Plant Sale (mid-April)	202-544-8733

Washington — Events (Cont'd)

	Phone
Goodwill Embassy Tour (early May)	202-636-4225
Harambee Carnival (early March)	301-530-3697
Holiday Concert: Bethesdoy Chamber Singers (early December)	202-785-2040
Independence Day Parade (July 4)	202-619-7222
Jazz Art Festival (late June-early August)	202-723-7500
Marine Corps Marathon (late October)	202-789-7000
Martin Luther King Jr Birthday Observance (mid-January)	202-619-7222
Memorial Day Ceremonies at Arlington National Cemetery (late May)	202-685-2892
National Cherry Blossom Festival (late March-early April)	202-728-1137
National Cherry Blossom Parade (early April)	202-728-1137
National Christmas Tree Lighting/Pageant of Peace (December)	202-619-7222
Patuxent Wildlife Art Show & Sale (late March)	301-292-8331
Saint Patrick's Day Parade (mid-March)	301-879-1717
Smithsonian Kite Festival (late March)	202-357-3030
Smithsonian's Craft Show (mid-April)	202-357-2700
Taste of DC (early October)	202-724-4093
Washington Boat Show (mid-February)	202-789-1600
Washington Craft Show (mid-November)	203-254-0486
Washington Flower & Garden Show (early March)	202-789-1600
Washington International Filmfest (late April-early May)	202-724-5613
Washington International Flower & Garden Show (early March)	703-823-7960
Washington National Cathedral Flower Mart (early May)	202-537-6200
Washington Theatre Festival (early July-early August)	202-628-6161
White House Christmas Tours (late December)	202-456-7041
White House Easter Egg Roll (mid-April)	202-456-2200
White House Spring Garden Tours (mid-April)	202-456-2200

Florida

Population (1999): 15,111,244 **Area (sq mi): 65,756**

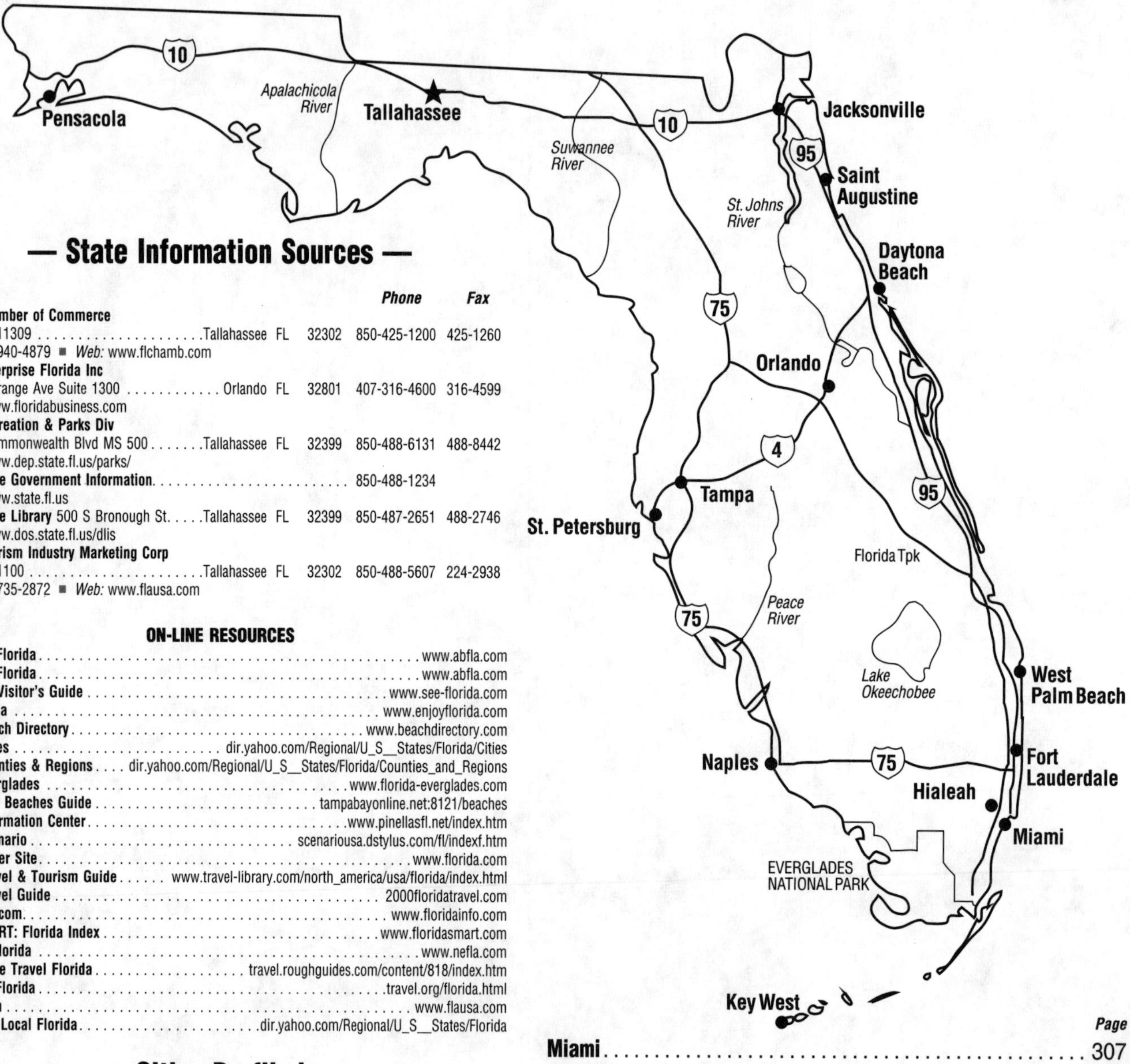

Pensacola
Tallahassee
Apalachicola River
Suwannee River
St. Johns River
Jacksonville
Saint Augustine
Daytona Beach
Orlando
Tampa
St. Petersburg
Florida Tpk
Peace River
Lake Okeechobee
West Palm Beach
Naples
Fort Lauderdale
Hialeah
Miami
EVERGLADES NATIONAL PARK
Key West
10
95
75
4

— State Information Sources —

				Phone	Fax
Florida Chamber of Commerce					
PO Box 11309	Tallahassee	FL	32302	850-425-1200	425-1260
TF: 800-940-4879 ■ *Web:* www.flchamb.com					
Florida Enterprise Florida Inc					
390 N Orange Ave Suite 1300	Orlando	FL	32801	407-316-4600	316-4599
Web: www.floridabusiness.com					
Florida Recreation & Parks Div					
3900 Commonwealth Blvd MS 500	Tallahassee	FL	32399	850-488-6131	488-8442
Web: www.dep.state.fl.us/parks/					
Florida State Government Information				850-488-1234	
Web: www.state.fl.us					
Florida State Library 500 S Bronough St.	Tallahassee	FL	32399	850-487-2651	488-2746
Web: www.dos.state.fl.us/dlis					
Florida Tourism Industry Marketing Corp					
PO Box 1100	Tallahassee	FL	32302	850-488-5607	224-2938
TF: 888-735-2872 ■ *Web:* www.flausa.com					

ON-LINE RESOURCES

Absolutely Florida . . . . . www.abfla.com
Absolutely Florida . . . . . www.abfla.com
All-Florida Visitor's Guide . . . . . www.see-florida.com
Enjoy Florida . . . . . www.enjoyflorida.com
Florida Beach Directory . . . . . www.beachdirectory.com
Florida Cities . . . . . dir.yahoo.com/Regional/U_S__States/Florida/Cities
Florida Counties & Regions . . . . dir.yahoo.com/Regional/U_S__States/Florida/Counties_and_Regions
Florida Everglades . . . . . www.florida-everglades.com
Florida Gulf Beaches Guide tampabayonline.net:8121/beaches
Florida Information Center . . . . . www.pinellasfl.net/index.htm
Florida Scenario . . . . . scenariousa.dstylus.com/fl/indexf.htm
Florida Super Site . . . . . www.florida.com
Florida Travel & Tourism Guide . . . . . www.travel-library.com/north_america/usa/florida/index.html
Florida Travel Guide 2000floridatravel.com
FloridaInfo.com . . . . . www.floridainfo.com
FloridaSMART: Florida Index . . . . . www.floridasmart.com
Northeast Florida . . . . . www.nefla.com
Rough Guide Travel Florida travel.roughguides.com/content/818/index.htm
Travel.org-Florida . . . . . travel.org/florida.html
Visit Florida . . . . . www.flausa.com
Yahoo! Get Local Florida . . . . . dir.yahoo.com/Regional/U_S__States/Florida

— Cities Profiled —

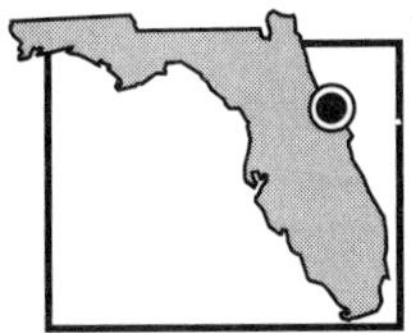

Daytona Beach

As the largest city in Volusia County, Daytona Beach is known internationally as a world center of racing. In early February each year Daytona International Speedway hosts the Rolex 24 Hours at Daytona, the only round-the-clock endurance of its kind held in North America, followed by events that lead up to the world-famous Daytona 500. Race enthusiasts can also visit the newly opened Daytona USA Racing Museum. Located at Daytona International Speedway, Daytona USA is a state-of-the-art interactive motorsports attraction designed to offer a hands-on experience of racing and its history in the Daytona Beach area. Daytona USA allows its visitors to participate in a number of interactive activities, including a NASCAR Winston Cup pit stop, and a 70mm movie depicting race day at the Daytona 500. Other Daytona Beach attractions include the Ponce DeLeon Inlet Lighthouse, which was constructed over 100 years ago and, at 175 feet, is the second tallest lighthouse in the United States; the "world's most famous beach," a specially designated 18-mile stretch of hard-packed sand that visitors can drive on during daylight hours; and the Mary McLeod Bethune Foundation, home of Dr. Mary McLeod Bethune, the noted civil rights leader and educator who founded Bethune-Cookman College.

Population 65,136
Area (Land) . . . . . 32.2 sq mi
Area (Water) . . . . . 4.0 sq mi
Elevation . . . . . 29 ft
Latitude . . . . . 29-10-38 N
Longitude . . . . . 81-03-36 W
County . . . . . Volusia
Time Zone . . . . . EST
Area Code/s 904

— Average Temperatures and Precipitation —

TEMPERATURES

	Jan	Feb	Mar	Apr	May	Jun	Jul	Aug	Sep	Oct	Nov	Dec
High	68	70	75	80	85	88	90	90	87	82	76	70
Low	47	48	54	59	65	71	73	73	72	65	56	50

PRECIPITATION

	Jan	Feb	Mar	Apr	May	Jun	Jul	Aug	Sep	Oct	Nov	Dec
Inches	2.8	3.1	3.0	2.2	3.5	6.0	5.4	6.2	6.3	4.1	2.8	2.6

— Important Phone Numbers —

	Phone
AAA	904-252-0531
American Express Travel	904-672-8113
Emergency	911
HotelDocs	800-468-3537
Medical Referral	904-255-3321
Poison Control Center	800-282-3171
Travelers Aid	904-252-4752
Weather	904-252-8000

— Information Sources —

				Phone	Fax
Better Business Bureau Serving Central Florida 151 Wymore Rd Suite 100 *Web:* www.orlando.bbb.org	Altamonte Springs	FL	32714	407-621-3300	786-2625
Daytona Beach Area Convention & Visitors Bureau 126 E Orange Ave *TF:* 800-544-0415 ■ *Web:* www.daytonabeach.com ■ *E-mail:* info@daytonabeach.com	Daytona Beach	FL	32114	904-255-0415	255-5478
Daytona Beach City Hall 301 S Ridgewood Ave *Web:* www.ci.daytona-beach.fl.us	Daytona Beach	FL	32114	904-258-3168	947-3008
Daytona Beach Economic Development Div 301 S Ridgewood Ave *Web:* www.ci.daytona-beach.fl.us/ecodev	Daytona Beach	FL	32114	904-258-3117	947-3020
Daytona Beach-Halifax Area Chamber of Commerce 126 E Orange Ave. *Web:* www.daytonachamber.com ■ *E-mail:* info@daytonachamber.com	Daytona Beach	FL	32114	904-255-0981	258-5104
Daytona Beach Mayor 301 S Ridgewood Ave *Web:* www.ci.daytona-beach.fl.us	Daytona Beach	FL	32114	904-258-3155	947-3008
Ocean Center Daytona Beach 101 N Atlantic Ave *TF:* 800-858-6444 ■ *Web:* www.oceancenter.com	Daytona Beach	FL	32118	904-254-4500	254-4512
Volusia County 123 W Indiana Ave *Web:* volusia.org	DeLand	FL	32720	904-736-5920	822-5707
Volusia County Business Development Corp 1901 Mason Ave Suite 107 *TF:* 800-554-3801 ■ *Web:* www.floridabusiness.org ■ *E-mail:* info@floridabusiness.org	Daytona Beach	FL	32117	904-274-3800	274-3804
Volusia County Public Library 105 E Magnolia Ave *Web:* merlin.vcpl.lib.fl.us ■ *E-mail:* vcplweb@hotmail.com	Daytona Beach	FL	32114	904-257-6036	257-6026

On-Line Resources

4DaytonaBeach.com www.4daytonabeach.com
Access America Daytona Beach . . . . . www.accessamer.com/daytonabeach/
Area Guide Daytona Beach . . . . . daytonabeach.areaguides.net
Best of Daytona Beach . . . . . www.bestof.net/daytonabeach/
Best Read Guide Daytona Beach . . . . . bestreadguide.com/daytonabeach/
City Knowledge Daytona Beach . . . . . www.cityknowledge.com/fl_daytona_beach.htm
Daytona Beach Area . . . . . www.florida.com/daytona/daytona.htm
Daytona Beach Florida . . . . . www.daytonavisit.com
Daytona Commerce . . . . . www.daytonacommerce.com
Daytona Destinations . . . . . www.daytonadestinations.com
Daytona Internet Pages . . . . . www.daytonainternetpages.com
Daytona.com . . . . . www.daytona.com
Golf Daytona Beach . . . . . www.golf-daytona.com
HotelGuide Daytona Beach . . . . . hotelguide.net/daytona_beach/
Index 411 Daytona Beach www.index411.com/daytona/01002a.htm
Surf & Sun Beach Vacation Guide to Daytona Beach . . . . . www.surf-sun.com/fl-daytona-main.htm
Visit Daytona . . . . . visitdaytona.com

— Transportation Services —

AIRPORTS

■ **Daytona Beach International Airport (DAB)** — Phone

3 Miles SW of downtown (approx 10 minutes) 904-248-8069
Web: www.flydaytonafirst.com

Airport Transportation

	Phone
Daytona Shuttle $7 fare to downtown	904-255-2294
VOTRAN Bus $1 fare to downtown	904-761-7700
Yellow Cab $10 fare to downtown	904-255-5555

Commercial Airlines

	Phone
Casino Airlink	888-464-5465
Continental	800-525-0280
Delta	800-221-1212

Charter Airlines

	Phone
Regional Air Charters Inc	904-248-2485

CAR RENTALS

	Phone
Advantage	904-788-4655
Affordable	904-255-5520
Alamo	904-255-1511
Avis	904-253-8183
Budget	904-252-8594
Enterprise	904-252-1224
Hertz	904-255-3681

LIMO/TAXI

	Phone
All Florida Cab	904-254-3400
Aristocrat Limousine Service	904-253-1959
Southern Comfort Taxi	904-253-9292
Sunshine Cab	904-255-8294
Yellow Cab	904-255-5555

Daytona Beach (Cont'd)

MASS TRANSIT

Phone

VOTRAN Bus $1 Base fare ... 904-761-7700

RAIL/BUS

Phone

Amtrak Station Old New York Ave ... DeLand FL 32720 904-734-2322

Greyhound Bus Station 138 S Ridgewood Ave ... Daytona Beach FL 32114 904-255-3636
TF: 800-231-2222

— Accommodations —

HOTEL RESERVATION SERVICES

Phone *Fax*

Daytona Welcome Center Reservations ... 904-677-3308 677-2542
TF: 800-881-9173 ■ *Web:* www.daytonawelcomecenter.com
■ *E-mail:* info@daytonawelcomecenter.com

HOTELS, MOTELS, RESORTS

Phone *Fax*

Acapulco Inn
2505 S Atlantic Ave ... Daytona Beach Shores FL 32118 904-761-2210 761-2216
TF: 800-245-3580

Adam's Mark Daytona Beach Resort
100 N Atlantic Ave ... Daytona Beach FL 32118 904-254-8200 253-8841
TF: 800-444-2275 ■ *Web:* www.adamsmark.com/dayton.htm

Americano Beach Resort
1260 N Atlantic Ave ... Daytona Beach FL 32118 904-255-7431 253-9513
TF: 800-874-1824

Aqua Terrace Motel
599 S Atlantic Ave ... Ormond Beach FL 32176 904-677-2517 673-1705
TF: 800-726-0678

Bahama House
2001 S Atlantic Ave ... Daytona Beach Shores FL 32118 904-248-2001 248-0991
TF: 800-571-2001

Barefoot Beach Inn
357 S Atlantic Ave ... Daytona Beach FL 32118 904-253-0571
TF: 800-432-7990

Bay View Hotel 124 Orange Ave ... Daytona Beach FL 32114 904-253-6844

Beachcomer Oceanfront Inn
2000 N Atlantic Ave ... Daytona Beach FL 32118 904-252-8513 252-7400
TF: 800-245-3575

Best Western Aku Tiki Inn
2225 S Atlantic Ave ... Daytona Beach Shores FL 32118 904-252-9631 252-1198
TF: 800-258-8454

Best Western LaPlaya
2500 N Atlantic Ave ... Daytona Beach FL 32118 904-672-0990 677-0982
TF: 800-926-5897

Best Western Mayan Inn
103 S Ocean Ave ... Daytona Beach FL 32118 904-252-2378 252-8670
TF: 800-443-5323

Carol Inn 1903 S Atlantic Ave ... Daytona Beach Shores FL 32118 904-253-4556 253-4556
TF: 800-881-8085

Casa Del Mar Beach Resort
621 S Atlantic Ave ... Ormond Beach FL 32176 904-672-4550 253-9935
TF: 800-245-1590

Castaways Beach Resort
2043 S Atlantic Ave ... Daytona Beach Shores FL 32118 904-254-8480 253-6554
TF: 800-407-0342

Comfort Inn Beachside
507 S Atlantic Ave ... Ormond Beach FL 32176 904-677-8550 676-0323
TF: 800-456-8550

Copacabana Motel
1201 S Atlantic Ave ... Daytona Beach FL 32118 904-252-1452 238-6963
TF: 800-839-3061

Coral Beach Motel 711 S Atlantic Ave ... Ormond Beach FL 32176 904-677-4712 677-4712
TF: 800-553-4712 ■ *Web:* coralbeachmotel.com
■ *E-mail:* coralbeachmotel@att.net

Days Inn Oceanfront Central
1909 S Atlantic Ave ... Daytona Beach FL 32118 904-255-4492 238-0632
TF: 800-224-5056

Days Inn Speedway
2900 International Speedway Blvd ... Daytona Beach FL 32124 904-255-0541 253-1468
TF: 800-329-7466

Days Inn Tropical Seas
3357 S Atlantic Ave ... Daytona Beach Shores FL 32118 904-767-8737 756-9612
TF: 800-338-4343

Phone *Fax*

Daytona Beach Resort and Conference Center 2700 N Atlantic Ave ... Daytona Beach FL 32118 904-672-3770 673-7262
TF: 800-654-6216

Daytona Inn Beach Resort
219 S Atlantic Ave ... Daytona Beach FL 32118 904-252-3626 255-3680
TF: 800-874-1822

Desert Inn Resort Motel
900 N Atlantic Ave ... Daytona Beach FL 32118 904-258-6555 238-1635
TF: 800-826-1711 ■ *Web:* desertinnresort.com
■ *E-mail:* di900@desertinnresort.com

Double Stay Inn Oceanfront
905 S Atlantic Ave ... Daytona Beach FL 32118 904-255-5432 254-0885
TF: 888-558-5577

Econo Lodge on the Beach
295 S Atlantic Ave ... Ormond Beach FL 32176 904-672-2651
TF: 800-847-8811

El Caribe Resort & Conference Center 2125 S Atlantic Ave ... Daytona Beach Shores FL 32118 904-252-1558 254-1940
TF: 800-445-9889 ■ *Web:* www.elcaribe.com
■ *E-mail:* elcaribe@elcaribe.com

Esquire Beach Motel
422 N Atlantic Ave ... Daytona Beach FL 32118 904-255-3601 255-2166
TF: 800-535-3601

Grande Resort 1299 S Atlantic Ave ... Daytona Beach FL 32118 904-255-4545 248-0443

Hampton Inn 155 Interchange Blvd ... Ormond Beach FL 32174 904-677-9999 677-0663
TF: 800-426-7866

Hampton Inn Daytona Beach Airport
1715 International Speedway Blvd ... Daytona Beach FL 32114 904-257-4030 257-5721
TF: 800-426-7866

Hawaiian Inn
2301 S Atlantic Ave ... Daytona Beach Shores FL 32118 904-255-5411 253-1209
TF: 800-922-3023

Hilton Daytona Beach Resort
2637 S Atlantic Ave ... Daytona Beach Shores FL 32118 904-767-7350 760-3651
TF: 800-525-7350 ■ *Web:* www.hilton.com/hotels/DABHIHF

Holiday Inn Daytona Beach Shores 3209 S Atlantic Ave ... Daytona Beach Shores FL 32118 904-761-2050 761-3922
TF: 800-722-3297

Howard Johnson Oceanfront
2560 N Atlantic Ave ... Daytona Beach FL 32118 904-672-1440 677-8811
TF: 800-792-7309

Howard Johnson Pirates Cove
3501 S Atlantic Ave ... Daytona Beach Shores FL 32118 904-767-8740 788-8609
TF: 800-272-2683

Howard Johnson Plaza Hotel
701 S Atlantic Ave ... Daytona Beach FL 32118 904-258-8522 257-9122
TF: 800-633-7010 ■ *Web:* www.daytonahojo.com

Indigo Lakes Holiday Inn
2620 W International
Speedway Blvd ... Daytona Beach FL 32114 904-258-6333 254-3698
TF: 800-465-4329

Inn on the Beach 1615 S Atlantic Ave ... Daytona Beach FL 32118 904-255-0921 255-3849
TF: 800-874-0975 ■ *Web:* www.innonthebeach.com
■ *E-mail:* res@innonthbeach.com

La Quinta Inn
2725 International Speedway Blvd ... Daytona Beach FL 32114 904-255-7412 255-5350
TF: 800-639-7666

Landmark Hotel
3135 S Atlantic Ave ... Daytona Beach Shores FL 32118 904-767-8533 788-1609
TF: 800-822-7707

Oceanside Hotel 800 N Atlantic Ave ... Daytona Beach FL 32118 904-252-6491 258-1458
TF: 800-633-7010

Palm Plaza Oceanfront Resort
3301 S Atlantic Ave ... Daytona Beach Shores FL 32118 904-767-1711 756-8394
TF: 800-329-8662 ■ *Web:* www.palmplaza.com
■ *E-mail:* palmplaza@webadept.com

Perry's Ocean Edge Motel
2209 S Atlantic Ave ... Daytona Beach Shores FL 32118 904-255-0581 258-7315
TF: 800-447-0002 ■ *Web:* www.perrysoceanedge.com
■ *E-mail:* relax@perrysoceanedge.com

Plaza Resort and Spa
600 N Atlantic Ave ... Daytona Beach FL 32118 904-255-4471 253-7543
TF: 800-767-4471

Quality Inn and Suites Oceanside
251 S Atlantic Ave ... Ormond Beach FL 32176 904-672-8510 672-7221
TF: 800-227-7220 ■ *Web:* www.qualityinndaytona.com
■ *E-mail:* quality@n-jcenter.com

Radisson Resort Daytona Beach
640 N Atlantic Ave ... Daytona Beach FL 32118 904-239-9800 253-0735
TF: 800-333-3333

Ramada Inn Speedway
1798 W International Speedway ... Daytona Beach FL 32114 904-255-2422 253-1749
TF: 800-352-2722 ■ *Web:* www.ramadaspeedway.com
■ *E-mail:* ramada-speedway@juno.com

Ramada Inn Surfside
3125 S Atlantic Ave ... Daytona Beach Shores FL 32118 904-788-1000 756-9906
TF: 800-255-3838

Daytona Beach — Hotels, Motels, Resorts (Cont'd)

				Phone	Fax
Ramada Limited 1000 N Atlantic Ave *TF:* 800-545-9795	Daytona Beach	FL	32118	904-239-9795	238-7900
Seagarden Inn 3161 S Atlantic Ave. *TF:* 800-245-0575	Daytona Beach Shores	FL	32118	904-761-2335	756-6676
Showboat Inn Oceanfront 1220 N Atlantic Ave. *TF:* 800-452-0932	Daytona Beach	FL	32118	904-255-2745	238-1646
Silver Beach Club 1025 S Atlantic Ave	Daytona Beach	FL	32118	904-252-9681	252-2668
Sleep Inn 170 Williamson Blvd *TF:* 888-280-6030	Ormond Beach	FL	32174	904-673-6030	673-7017
StudioPLUS 255 Bill France Blvd. *TF:* 800-646-8000	Daytona Beach	FL	32114	904-257-4311	257-5034
Sun Viking Lodge 2411 S Atlantic Ave. *TF:* 800-874-4469 ■ *Web:* www.sunviking.com ■ *E-mail:* svl@n-jcenter.com	Daytona Beach Shores	FL	32118	904-252-6252	252-5463
Thunderbird Beach Motel 500 N Atlantic Ave *TF:* 800-234-6543	Daytona Beach	FL	32118	904-253-2562	238-3676
Treasure Island Inn 2025 S Atlantic Ave. *TF:* 800-543-5070	Daytona Beach Shores	FL	32118	904-255-8371	253-4984
Tropical Winds Oceanfront Hotel 1398 N Atlantic Ave. *TF:* 800-245-6099	Daytona Beach	FL	32118	904-258-1016	255-6462

— Restaurants —

				Phone
Adam's Mark Restaurant (Seafood) 100 N Atlantic Ave	Daytona Beach	FL	32118	904-947-8020
Alberto's Restaurant (Italian) 1945 S Ridgewood Ave	Daytona Beach	FL	32119	904-767-1400
Bernkastel Festhaus (German) 100 N Atlantic Ave	Daytona Beach	FL	32118	904-255-8300
Blue Water Grille (American) 2637 S Atlantic Ave	Daytona Beach	FL	32118	904-767-7356
Boondocks Restaurant (American) 3948 S Peninsula Dr	Daytona Beach	FL	32127	904-760-9001
Chart House (Steak/Seafood) 1100 Marina Point Dr	Daytona Beach	FL	32114	904-255-9022
China Dragon Restaurant (Chinese) 145 N Ridgewood Ave	Daytona Beach	FL	32114	904-252-3839
Crabby Joe's Deck & Grill (Seafood) 3701 S Atlantic Ave	Daytona Beach	FL	32118	904-788-3364
Dancing Avocado Kitchen (Vegetarian) 110 S Beach St	Daytona Beach	FL	32114	904-947-2022
Fiesta House Hungarian Village Restaurant (Hungarian) 424 S Ridgewood Ave	Daytona Beach	FL	32114	904-226-0115
Green Turtle Restaurant & Lounge (Steak/Seafood) 2301 S Atlantic Ave	Daytona Beach	FL	32118	904-255-5411
Hog Heaven Bar-B-Q (Barbecue) 37 N Atlantic Ave	Daytona Beach	FL	32118	904-257-1212
Il Bacio (Italian) 631 N Grandview Ave	Daytona Beach	FL	32118	904-255-9822
Lighthouse Landing (American) 4940 S Peninsula Dr	Daytona Beach	FL	32127	904-761-9271
Maria Bonita Authentic Mexican (Mexican) 1435 S Ridgewood Ave	Daytona Beach	FL	32117	904-255-3465
Milano Of Daytona Beach (Italian) 3100 S Atlantic Ave	Daytona Beach	FL	32118	904-767-7273
Neptune's Harvest Seafood (Steak/Seafood) 1130 S Ridgewood Ave	Daytona Beach	FL	32114	904-253-6369
Orient Palace Chinese Restaurant (Chinese) 2116 S Atlantic Ave	Daytona Beach	FL	32118	904-255-4183
Park's Seafood Restaurant (Seafood) 951 N Beach St	Daytona Beach	FL	32117	904-258-7272
Porto-Fino Restaurant (Italian) 3124 S Atlantic Ave	Daytona Beach	FL	32118	904-767-9484
Saint Regis Restaurant (American) 509 Seabreeze Blvd	Daytona Beach	FL	32118	904-252-8743
Sapporo Japanese Steak House (Japanese) 3340 S Atlantic Ave	Daytona Beach	FL	32118	904-756-0480
Seabreeze Cafe (Seafood) 322 Seabreeze Blvd	Daytona Beach	FL	32118	904-258-0510
Songkran Thai Restaurant (Thai) 2309 S Ridgewood Ave	Daytona Beach	FL	32119	904-760-0300
Sophie Kays Waterfall Restaurant (Continental) 3516 S Atlantic Ave	Daytona Beach	FL	32118	904-756-4444
Teauila's Hawaiian Dinner Show (Hawaiian) 2700 N Atlantic Ave	Daytona Beach	FL	32176	904-672-3770
Top Of Daytona Restaurant (French) 2625 S Atlantic Ave	Daytona Beach	FL	32118	904-767-5791
Tydir's Cafe & Snitsel House (Czechoslovakian) 738 Mason Ave	Daytona Beach	FL	32117	904-252-6581
Wild Olive Restaurant (American) 615 Main St	Daytona Beach	FL	32118	904-252-3776

— Goods and Services —

SHOPPING

				Phone	Fax
Bellair Plaza Shopping Center 2411 N Atlantic Ave.	Daytona Beach	FL	32118	904-677-8722	
Daytona Mall 108 N Nova Rd	Daytona Beach	FL	32114	904-252-8652	
Volusia Mall 1700 W International Speedway Blvd	Daytona Beach	FL	32114	904-253-6783	254-8256

BANKS

				Phone	Fax
Bank at Ormond-by-the-Sea 100 Corsair Dr	Daytona Beach	FL	32114	904-257-1791	252-2705
Colonial Bank 1899 S Clyde Morris Blvd	Daytona Beach	FL	32119	904-761-5111	761-8178
First Union National Bank 1300 Beville Rd *TF:* 800-275-3862	Daytona Beach	FL	32114	904-254-7232	254-7246
NationsBank NA 1415 S Nova Rd	Daytona Beach	FL	32114	904-257-1723	
SouthTrust Bank NA 1060 W International Speedway Blvd	Daytona Beach	FL	32114	904-756-6090	756-6091
SunTrust Bank 120 S Ridgewood Ave *TF:* 800-786-8787	Daytona Beach	FL	32114	904-258-2306	258-2650
Surety Bank 1011 Mason Ave	Daytona Beach	FL	32117	904-248-3139	248-2266

BUSINESS SERVICES

	Phone		Phone
Airborne Express	800-247-2676	**Kwik Kopy Printing**	904-756-2201
Daytona Courier Services	904-255-6525	**Mail Boxes Etc**	904-257-9985
Daytona Employment Agency	904-253-3333	**Manpower Temporary Services**	904-760-5100
Daytona Quick Print	904-257-4620	**Post Office**	904-274-3500
DHL Worldwide Express	800-225-5345	**Roltime Courier Services**	904-258-0635
Federal Express	800-463-3339	**Shipping Depot**	904-767-0042
Federal Express	800-238-5355	**UPS**	800-742-5877
Kelly Services	904-255-1661		

— Media —

PUBLICATIONS

				Phone	Fax
Daytona Beach News-Journal‡ PO Box 2831 *Web:* www.n-jcenter.com	Daytona Beach	FL	32120	904-252-1511	258-8465
News-Journal Corp 901 6th St *Web:* www.n-jcenter.com	Daytona Beach	FL	32117	904-252-1511	258-8465

‡Daily newspapers

TELEVISION

				Phone	Fax
WCEU-TV Ch 15 (PBS) 1200 W International Speedway Blvd *Web:* www.wceu.org	Daytona Beach	FL	32114	904-254-4415	254-4427
WESH-TV Ch 2 (NBC) 1021 N Wymore Rd *Web:* www.wesh.com ■ *E-mail:* wesh@intersrv.com	Winter Park	FL	32789	407-645-2222	539-7948
WFTV-TV Ch 9 (ABC) 490 E South St *Web:* www.insidecentralflorida.com/partners/wftv ■ *E-mail:* news@wftv.com	Orlando	FL	32801	407-841-9000	481-2891
WKCF-TV Ch 18 (WB) 31 Skyline Dr *Web:* www.wb18.com ■ *E-mail:* wb18wkcf@wb18.com	Lake Mary	FL	32746	407-670-3018	647-4163
WKMG-TV Ch 6 (CBS) 4466 N John Young Pkwy *Web:* www.wkmg.com	Orlando	FL	32804	407-291-6000	298-2122
WOFL-TV Ch 35 (Fox) 35 Skyline Dr *Web:* www.wofl.com ■ *E-mail:* wofl@wofl.com	Lake Mary	FL	32746	407-644-3535	333-0234
WRBW-TV Ch 65 (UPN) 2000 Universal Studios Plaza Suite 200 *Web:* www.wrbw.com ■ *E-mail:* wrbw@wrbw.com	Orlando	FL	32819	407-248-6500	248-6520

RADIO

				Phone	Fax
WAPN-FM 91.5 MHz (Rel) 1508 State Ave.	Holly Hill	FL	32117	904-677-4272	673-3715
WELE-AM 1380 kHz (N/T) 432 S Nova Rd *Web:* www.wele.com	Ormond Beach	FL	32174	904-677-4122	677-4123

Daytona Beach — Radio (Cont'd)

	City	State	Zip	Phone	Fax
WFKS-FM 99.9 MHz (AC) 801 W Granada Blvd Suite 201 *Web:* www.radiokiss.com	Ormond Beach	FL	32174	904-672-9210	677-2252
WGNE-FM 98.1 MHz (Ctry) 340 S Beach St. *Web:* www.98frog.com	Daytona Beach	FL	32114	904-239-9836	239-0128
WHOG-FM 95.7 MHz (CR) 126 W International Speedway Blvd *Web:* www.whog.com	Daytona Beach	FL	32114	904-257-1150	239-0966
WKRO-FM 93.1 MHz (Rock) 126 W International Speedway Blvd *Web:* www.wkro.com	Daytona Beach	FL	32114	904-255-9300	238-6488
WKTO-FM 88.7 MHz (AC) 1015 10th St	New Smyrna Beach	FL	32168	904-427-1095	427-8970
WNDB-AM 1150 kHz (N/T) 126 W International Speedway Blvd *Web:* www.wndb.com	Daytona Beach	FL	32114	904-257-1150	239-0966
WPUL-AM 1590 kHz (Urban) 2598 S Nova Rd	South Daytona Beach	FL	32119	904-767-1131	254-7510
WROD-AM 1340 kHz (AC) 103 Wilder Blvd	Daytona Beach	FL	32114	904-253-0000	255-3178
WSBB-AM 1230 kHz (Misc) 175 N Causeway *Web:* www.wsbb.com	New Smyrna Beach	FL	32169	904-428-9091	428-7835
WVYB-FM 103.3 MHz (CHR) 126 W International Speedway Blvd	Daytona Beach	FL	32114	904-274-1033	238-6488
WXVQ-AM 1490 kHz (N/T) 220 E Hubbard Ave.	DeLand	FL	32724	904-734-9386	734-9361
WYND-AM 1310 kHz (Rel) 316 E Taylor Rd	DeLand	FL	32724	904-734-1310	734-1315

— Colleges/Universities —

	City	State	Zip	Phone	Fax
Bethune-Cookman College 640 Mary McLeod Bethune Blvd *Web:* www.bethune.cookman.edu ■ *E-mail:* admissions@cookman.edu	Daytona Beach	FL	32114	904-255-1401	257-5338
Daytona Beach Community College 1200 International Speedway Blvd. *Web:* www.dbcc.cc.fl.us	Daytona Beach	FL	32114	904-255-8131	254-4489
Embry-Riddle Aeronautical University Daytona Beach Campus 600 S Clyde Morris Blvd *TF Admissions:* 800-862-2416 ■ *Web:* www.db.erau.edu ■ *E-mail:* admit@db.erau.edu	Daytona Beach	FL	32114	904-226-6000	226-7070
Stetson University 421 N Woodland Blvd. *Web:* www.stetson.edu	DeLand	FL	32720	904-822-7000	822-7112
University of Central Florida Daytona Beach Campus 1200 W International Speedway Blvd	Daytona Beach	FL	32114	904-254-4460	254-3010

— Hospitals —

	City	State	Zip	Phone	Fax
Atlantic Medical Center of Daytona 400 N Clyde Morris Blvd	Daytona Beach	FL	32114	904-239-5000	947-4506
Halifax Medical Center 303 N Clyde Morris Blvd	Daytona Beach	FL	32115	904-254-4000	254-4375
Memorial Hospital Ormond Beach 875 Sterthaus Ave.	Ormond Beach	FL	32174	904-676-6000	673-3462

— Attractions —

	City	State	Zip	Phone	Fax
Adventure Landing 601 Earl St *Web:* www.adventurelanding.com	Daytona Beach	FL	32118	904-258-0071	
African American Museum of the Arts 325 S Clara Ave *E-mail:* aama325idj@aol.com	DeLand	FL	32720	904-736-4004	736-4088
Angell & Phelps Chocolate Factory 154 S Beach St.	Daytona Beach	FL	32114	904-252-6531	
Art League Of Daytona Beach 433 S Palmetto Ave.	Daytona Beach	FL	32114	904-258-3856	
Ashby Acres Wildlife Park 1250 S SR 415	New Smyrna Beach	FL	32168	904-428-1083	
Blue Spring State Park 2001 W French Ave.	Orange City	FL	32736	904-775-3663	775-7794
Boardwalk Amusement Area Boardwalk betw Main & Bandshell	Daytona Beach	FL	32118	904-258-6992	
Bulow Creek State Park Beach St N of Hwy 40	Ormond Beach	FL	32174	904-676-4050	
Bulow Plantation Ruins State Historic Site Old Kings Rd	Flagler Beach	FL	32110	904-517-2084	
Casements The Cultural Center & Museum 25 Riverside Dr	Ormond Beach	FL	32176	904-676-3216	676-3363
Civic Ballet of Volusia County 600 Auditorium Blvd Peabody Auditorium	Daytona Beach	FL	32118	904-677-0375	
Concert Showcase Broadway Productions 600 Auditorium Blvd Peabody Auditorium	Daytona Beach	FL	32118	904-254-4545	
Connor Library Museum 201 Sams Ave	New Smyrna Beach	FL	32170	904-424-2196	
Daytona Beach Kennel Club 2101 International Speedway Blvd.	Daytona Beach	FL	32114	904-252-6484	
Daytona Beach Playhouse 100 Jessamine Blvd	Daytona Beach	FL	32118	904-255-2431	255-2432
Daytona Beach River Cruise 351 Basin St Halifax Harbor Marina	Daytona Beach	FL	32114	904-248-1441	
Daytona Beach Symphony PO Box 2	Daytona Beach	FL	32115	904-253-2901	253-5774
Daytona Flea & Farmer's Market 1425 Tomoka Farms Rd. *Web:* www.volusia.com/daytonafleamarket/	Daytona Beach	FL	32124	904-252-1999	
Daytona IcePlex 2400 S Ridgewood Ave	South Daytona Beach	FL	32119	904-304-8400	760-5537
Daytona USA 1801 W International Speedway Blvd *Web:* www.daytonausa.com	Daytona Beach	FL	32114	904-947-6800	947-6802
DeLeon Springs State Recreation Area 601 Ponce de Leon Blvd	DeLeon Springs	FL	32130	904-985-4212	985-2014
Fred Dana Marsh Museum 2099 N Beach St Tomoka State Pk	Ormond Beach	FL	32174	904-676-4050	
Gamble Rogers Memorial State Recreation Area 3100 S A1A Flagler Beach	Flagler Beach	FL	32136	904-517-2086	
Gillespie Museum Of Minerals 234 E Michigan Ave	DeLand	FL	32724	904-822-7330	
Halifax Historical Museum 252 S Beach St. *Web:* www.halifaxhistorical.org	Daytona Beach	FL	32127	904-255-6976	
Klassix Auto Museum 2909 W International Speedway Blvd *Web:* www.klassixauto.com ■ *E-mail:* www@webadept.com	Daytona Beach	FL	32124	904-252-3800	252-3802
Lake Woodruff National Wildlife Refuge PO Box 488	DeLeon Springs	FL	32130	904-985-4673	985-0926
Lighthouse Point Park and Recreation Area 5000 S Atlantic Ave.	Ponce Inlet	FL	32127	904-756-7488	
Mary McLeod Bethune Foundation 640 Dr Mary McLeod Bethune Blvd.	Daytona Beach	FL	32114	904-255-1401	257-7027
Midway Fun Fair 24 N Ocean Ave.	Daytona Beach	FL	32118	904-253-5007	
Museum of Arts & Sciences 1040 Museum Blvd. *Web:* www.moas.org	Daytona Beach	FL	32114	904-255-0285	255-5040
Oceanfront Bandshell & Park 70 Boardwalk	Daytona Beach	FL	32118	904-258-3169	
Ormond Memorial Art Museum & Gardens 78 E Granada Blvd	Ormond Beach	FL	32176	904-676-3347	676-3244
Palms Gallery 128 S Beach St	Daytona Beach	FL	32114	904-322-7988	
Peabody Auditorium 600 Auditorium Blvd	Daytona Beach	FL	32118	904-258-3169	947-3062
Ponce de Leon Inlet Lighthouse 4931 S Peninsula Dr *Web:* www.ponceinlet.org	Ponce Inlet	FL	32127	904-761-1821	
Seaside Music Theater 454 S Young St *Web:* www.n-jcenter.com/smt/	Ormond Beach	FL	32174	904-252-6200	252-1149
Southeast Museum of Photography 1200 W International Speedway Blvd Daytona Beach Community College Bldg 37	Daytona Beach	FL	32114	904-254-4475	254-4487
Speed Park Motorsports Thrill Park 201 Fentress Blvd *Web:* www.volusiaweb.com/speedpark/	Daytona Beach	FL	32114	904-253-3278	253-3278
Sugar Mill Botanical Gardens 950 Old Sugar Mill Rd.	Port Orange	FL	32129	904-767-1735	
Sugar Mill Ruins 600 Mission Rd.	New Smyrna Beach	FL	32168	904-736-5953	
Swisher Carl S Library 'New Deal' Permanent Exhibit 640 Dr Mary McLeod Bethune Blvd Bethune-Cookman College	Daytona Beach	FL	32114	904-255-1401	

Daytona Beach — Attractions (Cont'd)

Name / Address	City	State	Zip	Phone	Fax
Tomoka State Geological Park 2099 North Beach St.	Ormond Beach	FL	32174	904-676-4050	676-4060
Wright Brothers Flyer 600 S Clyde Morris Blvd Embry-Riddle Aeronautical University	Daytona Beach	FL	32114	904-226-6175	226-6158

SPORTS TEAMS & FACILITIES

Name / Address	City	State	Zip	Phone	Fax
Daytona Cubs (baseball) 105 E Orange Ave. *Web:* www.minorleaguebaseball.com/teams/fsl-day.php3	Daytona Beach	FL	32114	904-257-3172	257-3382
Daytona International Speedway 1801 W International Speedway Blvd *Web:* www.daytonausa.com/dis/index.shtml	Daytona Beach	FL	32114	904-254-2700	257-0281
Volusia Speedway Park 1500 E Hwy 40	DeLeon Springs	FL	32130	904-985-4402	985-6258

— Events —

	Phone
Antique Show & Sale (mid-January)	904-255-0285
Art Fiesta (late February)	904-424-2175
Art in the Park (early May)	904-676-3257
Black Heritage Festival (early February)	904-428-6225
Boardwalk Pier Fireworks (July 4)	904-255-0415
Central Florida Balloon Rally (late March)	904-736-1010
Daytona 500 NASCAR Winston Cup Series Race (mid-February)	904-253-7223
Daytona Beach Biketoberfest (late October)	800-854-1234
Daytona Beach Doll Show (mid-January)	904-672-2341
Daytona Beach Garden Show (mid-March)	904-252-1511
Daytona Bike Week (late February-early March)	904-252-2453
Daytona Turkey Run Car Show & Swap Meet (late November)	904-255-7355
Gatorade 125-Mile Qualifying Races for the Daytona 500 (mid-February)	904-253-7223
Gem & Mineral Show & Sale (mid-January)	904-255-9478
Greater Daytona Beach Striking Fish Tournament (late May)	904-756-7058
Home for the Holidays Parade (mid-December)	904-676-3257
IMAGES-A Festival of the Arts (mid-March)	904-423-4733
Miss Daytona Beach & Miss Volusia County Pageant (mid-January)	904-677-4589
Motorcycle Swap Meet (early March)	904-257-2269
NAPA Auto Parts 300 NASCAR Busch Series Race (mid-February)	904-253-7223
Native American Festival (mid-April)	904-676-3216
Oktoberfest (mid-September)	904-677-0676
Orange City/Blue Spring Manatee Festival (late January)	904-775-9224
Rolex 24 hours of Daytona Race (late January)	904-253-7223
Speedway Spectacular Car Show & Swap Meet (late March)	904-255-7355
Speedweeks (late January-mid-February)	904-253-7223
Very Special Arts Festival (late April)	904-255-6475
World Karting Association Racing (late December)	904-253-7223
World Series of Asphalt Stock Car Racing (early-mid-February)	904-427-4129

Fort Lauderdale

Located on the southeast coast of Florida, the city of Fort Lauderdale, with more than 300 miles of navigable waterways, rivers, and inlets in the area, has become known as the "Venice of America." Fort Lauderdale's Port Everglades is the world's second largest passenger cruise port, and the city's beaches are world famous. The beach area has recently been revitalized with a new boardwalk and a host of new cafes and restaurants. Not far from the beach are the International Swimming Hall of Fame, Fort Lauderdale Museum of Art, and the upscale shops of Las Olas Boulevard. The world's largest outlet mall, Sawgrass Mills, is located in the suburb of Sunrise.

Population	153,728	**Longitude**	80-14-36 W
Area (Land)	31.4 sq mi	**County**	Broward
Area (Water)	4.3 sq mi	**Time Zone**	EST
Elevation	8 ft	**Area Code/s**	954
Latitude	26-12-19 N		

— Average Temperatures and Precipitation —

TEMPERATURES

	Jan	Feb	Mar	Apr	May	Jun	Jul	Aug	Sep	Oct	Nov	Dec
High	77	78	80	83	86	88	90	90	89	86	81	78
Low	58	59	63	66	70	74	75	75	75	71	65	60

PRECIPITATION

	Jan	Feb	Mar	Apr	May	Jun	Jul	Aug	Sep	Oct	Nov	Dec
Inches	2.2	2.8	2.7	3.3	6.6	9.6	6.6	6.8	7.6	6.3	3.9	2.1

— Important Phone Numbers —

	Phone		Phone
AAA	954-748-2700	**Medical Referral**	954-472-8879
Activity Line	954-527-5600	**Poison Control Center**	800-282-3171
Broward Arts Line	954-357-5700	**Time/Temp**	954-748-4444
Emergency	911	**Weather**	954-748-4444
HotelDocs	800-468-3537		

— Information Sources —

Name / Address	City	State	Zip	Phone	Fax
Broward County 115 S Andrews Ave Rm 421 *Web:* www.co.broward.fl.us	Fort Lauderdale	FL	33301	954-357-7000	357-7295
Broward County Convention Center 1950 Eisenhower Blvd *Web:* www.co.broward.fl.us/convention-center.htm	Fort Lauderdale	FL	33316	954-765-5900	763-9551
Broward County Library 100 S Andrews Ave. *Web:* www.co.broward.fl.us/library	Fort Lauderdale	FL	33301	954-357-7444	357-7399
Fort Lauderdale City Hall 100 N Andrews Ave. *Web:* info.ci.ftlaud.fl.us/index.htm	Fort Lauderdale	FL	33301	954-761-5000	761-5122
Fort Lauderdale Mayor 100 N Andrews Ave 8th Fl *Web:* info.ci.ftlaud.fl.us/citygov/Mayorlet.htm	Fort Lauderdale	FL	33301	954-761-5003	761-5667
Fort Lauderdale Planning & Economic Development Dept 101 NE 3rd Ave 3rd Fl *Web:* info.ci.ftlaud.fl.us/citygov/ped/ped.htm	Fort Lauderdale	FL	33301	954-468-1515	468-1500
Greater Fort Lauderdale Chamber of Commerce 512 NE 3rd Ave *Web:* www.ftlchamber.com	Fort Lauderdale	FL	33301	954-462-6000	527-8766
Greater Fort Lauderdale Convention & Visitors Bureau 1850 Eller Dr Suite 303 *TF:* 800-356-1662 ■ *Web:* www.co.broward.fl.us/sunny.htm ■ *E-mail:* gflcvb@co.broward.fl.us	Fort Lauderdale	FL	33316	954-765-4466	765-4467
Seflin Free-Net 100 S Andrews Ave *Web:* www.seflin.org ■ *E-mail:* infodesk@bc.seflin.org	Fort Lauderdale	FL	33301	954-357-7318	357-6998

On-Line Resources

About.com Guide to Fort Lauderdale	fortlauderdale.about.com/local/southeastus/fortlauderdale
Anthill City Guide Fort Lauderdale	www.anthill.com/city.asp?city=ftlauderdale
Area Guide Fort Lauderdale	ftlauderdale.areaguides.net
Broward.com	www.broward.com
City Knowledge Fort Lauderdale	www.cityknowledge.com/fl_fortlauderdale.htm
City Link	www.clinkonline.com
CitySearch Miami/Fort Lauderdale	miami.citysearch.com
Come to the Sun Guide to South Florida	www.cometothesun.com
DigitalCity Fort Lauderdale	home.digitalcity.com/southflorida
DigitalCity South Florida	home.digitalcity.com/southflorida
Essential Guide to Fort Lauderdale	www.ego.net/us/fl/fll/
Excite.com Fort Lauderdale City Guide	www.excite.com/travel/countries/united_states/florida/fort_lauderdale
Fort Lauderdale Connections	www.aesir.com/FtLauderdale/
Fort Lauderdale Florida	fortlauderdale-florida.com
Fort Lauderdale Gay & Lesbian Guide	www.southfloridafun.com/fortlauderdale/index.shtml
Fort Lauderdale Home Page	info.ci.ftlaud.fl.us
Fort Lauderdale Hotels & Discount Guide	www.flhotels.com/ftlauderdale/index.html
Fort Lauderdale Information Access	ft-lauderdale.info-access.com
Fort Lauderdale Information Network	www.gfl.com
Fort Lauderdale Night Guide	ft.lauderdale.nightguide.com/
Fort Lauderdale Restaurant Guide	ft.lauderdale.diningguide.net/
Fort Lauderdale Visitors Guide	www.introweb.com/fortlauderdale/mainmenu.htm

Fort Lauderdale — On-Line Resources (Cont'd)

HotelGuide Fort Lauderdale .... fort.lauderdale.hotelguide.net
InSouthFlorida.com .... www.insouthflorida.com
MetroGuide Fort Lauderdale .... metroguide.net/fll/
NITC Travelbase City Guide Fort Lauderdale .... www.travelbase.com/auto/guides/ft_lauderdale-area-fl.html
SoFla.com .... www.sofla.com
Surf & Sun Beach Vacation Guide to Fort Lauderdale .... www.surf-sun.com/fl-ft-lauderdale-main.htm
Welcome to South Florida .... beachbucks.com/ftl/

— Transportation Services —

AIRPORTS

■ Fort Lauderdale/Hollywood International Airport (FLL)

	Phone
5 miles S of downtown (approx 15 minutes) Web: www.co.broward.fl.us/fll.htm	954-359-6100

Airport Transportation

	Phone
Airport Express $6 fare to downtown	954-561-8888
Tri County Transportation Service $24 fare to downtown	954-561-8886
Yellow Cab $7-9 fare to downtown	954-565-5400

Commercial Airlines

	Phone		Phone
Air Canada	800-776-3000	**Gulfstream International Airlines**	800-525-0280
Air Jamaica	800-523-5585	**Icelandair**	800-223-5500
AirTran	800-247-8726	**MetroJet**	888-638-7653
American	800-433-7300	**Midway**	800-446-4392
American Trans Air	800-225-2995	**Northwest**	800-225-2525
Comair	954-763-2211	**Southwest**	800-435-9792
Continental	800-525-0280	**Spirit**	800-772-7117
Continental Express	800-525-0280	**TWA**	800-221-2000
Delta	800-221-1212	**United**	800-241-6522
Eastwind	888-327-8946	**US Airways**	800-428-4322
Finnair	800-950-5000		

Charter Airlines

	Phone		Phone
Aerojet	954-772-5070	**Heliflight**	954-771-6969
Aircraft Charter Solutions Inc	888-417-1271	**Personal Jet Charter Service**	954-776-4515
Aviator Services Inc	305-893-5874	**United West Airlines Inc**	954-438-9077
Gold Aviation Services Inc	954-359-9919		

■ Palm Beach International Airport (PBI)

	Phone
43 miles N of downtown Fort Lauderdale (approx 60 minutes) Web: www.pbia.org	561-471-7412

Airport Transportation

	Phone
Palm Beach Transportation Taxi $75 fare to downtown Fort Lauderdale	561-684-9900

Commercial Airlines

	Phone		Phone
Air Canada	800-776-3000	**Midway**	800-446-4392
AirTran	800-247-8726	**Northwest**	800-225-2525
American	800-433-7300	**TWA**	800-221-2000
American Eagle	800-433-7300	**United**	800-241-6522
Continental	561-832-5200	**US Airways**	800-428-4322
Delta	561-655-5300	**US Airways Express**	800-428-4322
Gulfstream International Airlines	800-525-0280		

Charter Airlines

	Phone		Phone
Advanced Airways	800-634-2114	**Flight Services Group Inc**	800-380-4009
Aero Taxi	800-362-4401	**Hutt Aviation Inc**	800-488-8247
Alliance Executive Charter Services	800-232-5387	**Jet Aviation Business Jets Inc**	800-736-8538
Atlantic Aviation Charter	800-252-5387	**Jet Aviation Travel Services**	800-422-7242
Chandelle Aviation Corp Ltd	561-683-0830	**RoyalAir Inc**	800-944-3030
Concierge Air Inc	561-616-0809	**Sapphire Aviation Inc**	561-687-7967
Executive Airlink	800-373-0763	**Summit Aviation**	561-683-7334
Executive Jet Management	877-356-5387	**Telford Aviation Inc**	800-639-4809

CAR RENTALS

	Phone		Phone
Alamo	954-525-4713	**Dollar-West Palm Beach**	561-686-3300
Alamo-West Palm Beach	561-684-3840	**Gold Coast**	954-522-0665
Avis	954-359-3250	**Hertz**	954-764-1199
Avis-West Palm Beach	561-233-6400	**Hertz-West Palm Beach**	561-686-4300
Budget	954-359-4747	**National**	954-359-8301
Budget-West Palm Beach	561-683-2400	**National-West Palm Beach**	561-233-7368
Dollar	954-359-7800	**Payless**	954-524-9129

LIMO/TAXI

	Phone		Phone
Absolute Limousine	954-565-2644	**Dolphin Limousine**	954-989-5466
Airport Express	954-565-8900	**Elite Limousine**	954-426-5090
Carey Limousines	954-764-0615	**Jewel Limousines**	954-423-3000
Club Limousine	954-522-0277	**Water Taxi**	954-467-6677
Coastal Limousines	954-749-7433	**Yellow Cab**	954-565-5400

MASS TRANSIT

	Phone
Broward County Transportation Authority $1 Base fare	954-357-8400
Tri-Rail fare varies with destination	800-874-7245
WaterBus $1.75 Base fare	954-522-9333

RAIL/BUS

				Phone
Amtrak Station 200 SW 21st Terr.	Fort Lauderdale	FL	33312	954-587-6692
Greyhound Bus Station 515 NE 3rd St *TF:* 800-231-2222	Fort Lauderdale	FL	33301	954-764-6551

— Accommodations —

HOTEL RESERVATION SERVICES

	Phone	Fax
Accommodations Express *TF:* 800-444-7666 ■ *Web:* www.accommodationsxpress.com ■ *E-mail:* accomexp@acy.digex.net	609-391-2100	525-0111
Accommodations USA	407-931-0003	931-1003
Florida Hotel Network *TF:* 800-538-3616	305-538-3616	538-5858
Florida SunBreak *TF:* 800-786-2732 ■ *Web:* www.lvacation.com/p6802.htm	305-532-1516	532-0564
Hotel Reservations Network Inc *TF Sales:* 800-964-6835 ■ *Web:* www.hoteldiscount.com	214-361-7311	361-7299
IDP Reservations *TF:* 800-436-8611 ■ *Web:* www.idpreservations.com ■ *E-mail:* idpresv@aol.com	305-538-2151	538-1701
Quikbook *TF:* 800-789-9887 ■ *Web:* www.quikbook.com	212-532-1660	532-1556

HOTELS, MOTELS, RESORTS

				Phone	Fax
Airport Inn 2440 SR-84 *TF:* 800-251-1962	Fort Lauderdale	FL	33312	954-792-8181	792-4202
Bahama Hotel 401 N Fort Lauderdale Beach Blvd *TF:* 800-622-9995	Fort Lauderdale	FL	33304	954-467-7315	467-7319
Bahia Cabana Beach Resort 3001 Harbor Dr *TF:* 800-323-2244	Fort Lauderdale	FL	33316	954-524-1555	764-5951
Baymont Inns & Suites 3800 W Commercial Blvd. *TF:* 800-301-0200	Tamarac	FL	33308	954-485-7900	733-5469
Beach Plaza Hotel 625 N Fort Lauderdale Beach Blvd *TF:* 800-451-4711	Fort Lauderdale	FL	33304	954-566-7631	537-9358
Best Inn 2711 N Ocean Blvd. *Web:* www.polymarquis.com ■ *E-mail:* polynesian@travelbase.com	Fort Lauderdale	FL	33308	954-566-3394	
Best Western Beachcomber Hotel & Villas 1200 S Ocean Blvd *TF:* 800-231-2423 ■ *Web:* www.beachcomber-ftlaud.com/	Pompano Beach	FL	33062	954-941-7830	942-7680
Best Western Marina Inn & Yacht Harbor 2150 SE 17th St *TF:* 800-327-1390	Fort Lauderdale	FL	33316	954-525-3484	764-2915
Best Western Oceanside Inn 1180 Seabreeze Blvd *TF:* 800-367-1007	Fort Lauderdale	FL	33316	954-525-8115	527-0957

Fort Lauderdale — Hotels, Motels, Resorts (Cont'd)

Phone *Fax*

Boca Raton Resort & Club
501 E Camino Real . . . . Boca Raton FL 33431 561-447-3000 447-3183
TF: 800-327-0101 ■ *Web:* www.bocaresort.com
■ *E-mail:* reservations@bocaresort.com

Carriage House Resort Motel
250 S Ocean Blvd . . . . Deerfield Beach FL 33441 954-427-7670 428-4790
TF: 800-303-6009 ■ *Web:* www.bocaraton.com/carriagehouse/
■ *E-mail:* carriagehouseresort@worldnet.att.net

Clarion Beach Resort
4660 N Ocean Dr . . . . Lauderdale By The Sea FL 33308 954-776-5660 776-4689
TF: 800-327-5919

Clarion Hotel 4000 S Ocean Dr . . . . Hollywood FL 33019 954-458-1900 458-7222
TF: 800-327-5919

Comfort Inn Airport 2520 Stirling Rd. . . . . Hollywood FL 33020 954-922-1600 923-5363
TF: 800-333-1492

Comfort Suites
1040 E Newport Center Dr . . . . Deerfield Beach FL 33442 954-570-8887 428-7638
TF: 800-538-2777

Comfort Suites & Convention Center
1800 S Federal Hwy . . . . Fort Lauderdale FL 33316 954-767-8700 767-8629
TF: 800-228-5150

Courtyard By Marriott
2440 W Cypress Creek Rd . . . . Fort Lauderdale FL 33309 954-772-7770 772-4780
TF: 800-321-2211

Courtyard by Marriott 7780 SW 16th St . . . . . . Plantation FL 33324 954-475-1100 424-8402
TF: 800-321-2211 ■ *Web:* courtyard.com/FLLPL

Crossroads Motor Lodge 2460 SR-84 . . . . Fort Lauderdale FL 33312 954-792-4700 792-4744

Days Inn 1595 W Oakland Park Blvd . . . . . Fort Lauderdale FL 33311 954-484-9290 485-9025
TF: 800-329-7466

Days Inn 2601 N 29th Ave . . . . Hollywood FL 33020 954-923-7300 921-6706
TF: 800-329-7466

Days Inn Broward Blvd
1700 W Broward Blvd . . . . Fort Lauderdale FL 33312 954-463-2500 763-6404
TF: 800-329-7466

Doubletree Guest Suites
2670 E Sunrise Blvd . . . . Fort Lauderdale FL 33304 954-565-3800 561-0387
TF: 800-222-8733 ■ *Web:* www.galleria.doubletreehotels.com

Doubletree Oceanfront Resort
440 Seabreeze Blvd. . . . . Fort Lauderdale FL 33316 954-524-8733 467-7489
TF: 800-222-8733
■ *Web:* www.doubletreehotels.com/DoubleT/Hotel21/34/34Main.htm

Embassy Suites 1100 SE 17th St . . . . Fort Lauderdale FL 33316 954-527-2700 760-7202
TF: 800-362-2779

Embassy Suites Deerfield Beach Resort
950 SE 20th Ave. . . . . Deerfield Beach FL 33441 954-426-0478 360-0539
TF: 800-362-2779 ■ *Web:* www.embassyflorida.com
■ *E-mail:* suites@embassyflorida.com

Extended StayAmerica
5851 N Andrews Ave Ext . . . . Fort Lauderdale FL 33309 954-776-9447 776-7359
TF: 800-398-7829

Extended StayAmerica
1200 SW 11th Way . . . . Deerfield Beach FL 33441 954-428-5997 428-4934
TF: 800-398-7829

Fairfield Inn by Marriott
5727 N Federal Hwy . . . . Fort Lauderdale FL 33308 954-491-2500 491-7945
TF: 800-228-2800

Fort Lauderdale Airport Hilton
1870 Griffin Rd. . . . . Dania Beach FL 33004 954-920-3300 920-3348
TF: 800-445-8667 ■ *Web:* www.hilton.com/hotels/FLLAHHF

Fort Lauderdale Beach Resort
909 Breakers Ave . . . . Fort Lauderdale FL 33304 954-566-8800 566-8802
TF: 800-424-1943

Four Points Hotel by Sheraton
1208 N Ocean Blvd . . . . Pompano Beach FL 33062 954-782-5300 946-1853

Grand Palms Golf & Country Club
110 Grand Palms Dr . . . . Pembroke Pines FL 33027 954-431-8800 435-5988
TF: 800-327-9246

Hampton Inn & Suites 2500 Stirling Rd. . . . . . Hollywood FL 33020 954-922-0011 929-7118
TF: 800-333-1492

Hampton Inn Cypress Creek
720 E Cypress Creek Rd . . . . Fort Lauderdale FL 33334 954-776-7677 776-0805
TF: 800-426-7866

Hilton Deerfield Beach/Boca Raton
100 Fairway Dr. . . . . Deerfield Beach FL 33441 954-427-7700 427-2308
TF: 800-345-6565 ■ *Web:* www.hilton.com/hotels/DERHIHF

Holiday Inn Airport South
2905 Sheridan St . . . . Hollywood FL 33023 954-925-9100 925-5512
TF: 800-480-7623

Holiday Inn Beach Galleria
999 N Fort Lauderdale Beach Blvd . . . . Fort Lauderdale FL 33304 954-563-5961 564-5261
TF: 800-465-4329

Phone *Fax*

Holiday Inn Express
3355 N Federal Hwy . . . . Fort Lauderdale FL 33306 954-566-4301 565-1472
TF: 800-465-4329

Holiday Inn Lauderdale-By-the Sea 4116 N Ocean Dr . . . . Lauderdale By The Sea FL 33308 954-776-1212 776-1212
TF: 800-465-4329

Holiday Inn Plantation
1711 N University Dr. . . . . Plantation FL 33322 954-472-5600 370-3201
TF: 800-465-4329

Holiday Inn Pompano Beach
1350 S Ocean Blvd . . . . Pompano Beach FL 33062 954-941-7300 941-7300
TF: 800-332-2735

Holiday Inn Sunspree Resort
2711 S Ocean Dr . . . . Hollywood FL 33019 954-923-8700 922-3665
TF: 800-237-4667

Hollywood Beach Resort Hotel
101 N Ocean Dr . . . . Hollywood FL 33019 954-921-0990 920-9480
TF: 800-331-6103 ■ *Web:* florida.com/hollywoodbeach

Howard Johnson Hotel
700 N Fort Lauderdale Beach Blvd . . . . Fort Lauderdale FL 33304 954-563-2451 564-8153
TF: 800-327-8578

Howard Johnson Ocean Resort & Conference Hotel 2096 NE 2nd St . . . . Deerfield Beach FL 33441 954-428-2850 480-9639
TF: 800-426-0084

Howard Johnson Plaza Resort
2501 N Ocean Dr . . . . Hollywood FL 33019 954-925-1411 921-5565
TF: 800-423-9867

Howard Johnson Pompano Beach Plaza Resort 9 N Pompano Beach Blvd . . . . Pompano Beach FL 33062 954-781-1300 782-5585
TF: 800-654-2000

Hyatt Pier 66 Resort & Marina
2301 SE 17th St Cswy Pier 66 . . . . Fort Lauderdale FL 33316 954-525-6666 728-3541
TF: 800-233-1234
■ *Web:* www.hyatt.com/usa/fort_lauderdale/hotels/hotel_ftlhp.html

Inverrary Plaza Resort
3501 Inverrary Blvd. . . . . Fort Lauderdale FL 33319 954-485-0500 733-0236
TF: 800-241-0363

Ireland's Inn Resort Hotel
2220 N Atlantic Blvd . . . . Fort Lauderdale FL 33305 954-565-6661 565-8893
TF: 800-347-7776

La Quinta Hotel 3701 N University Dr . . . . . Coral Springs FL 33065 954-753-9000 755-4012
TF: 800-531-5900

La Quinta Inn
999 W Cypress Creek Rd. . . . . Fort Lauderdale FL 33309 954-491-7666 491-7669
TF: 800-531-5900

La Quinta Inn 351 W Hillsboro Blvd . . . . . Deerfield Beach FL 33441 954-421-1004 427-8069
TF: 800-687-6667

Lago Mar Resort & Yachting Center
1700 S Ocean Ln . . . . Fort Lauderdale FL 33316 954-523-6511 524-6627
TF: 800-255-5246

Lauderdale Beach Hotel
101 S Fort Lauderdale Beach Blvd. . . . . Fort Lauderdale FL 33316 954-764-0088 463-9154
TF: 800-327-7600 ■ *Web:* www.theperfectlocation.com/

Little Inn by the Sea
4546 El Mar Dr. . . . . Lauderdale By The Sea FL 33308 954-772-2450 938-9354
TF: 800-492-0311 ■ *Web:* www.alittleinn.com
■ *E-mail:* alinn@icanect.net

Marina Marriott 1881 SE 17th St . . . . Fort Lauderdale FL 33316 954-463-4000 527-6705
TF: 800-228-9290

Marriott North 6650 N Andrews Ave . . . . . Fort Lauderdale FL 33309 954-771-0440 772-9834
TF: 800-228-9290 ■ *Web:* marriotthotels.com/FLLCC

Marriott's Harbor Beach Resort
3030 Holiday Dr . . . . Fort Lauderdale FL 33316 954-525-4000 766-6152
TF: 800-228-9290 ■ *Web:* marriotthotels.com/FLLSB

Oakland East Motor Lodge
3001 N Federal Hwy . . . . Fort Lauderdale FL 33306 954-565-4601 565-0384
TF: 800-633-6279

Ocean Hacienda Inn
1924 N Fort Lauderdale Beach Blvd. . . . . Fort Lauderdale FL 33305 954-564-7800 396-9971
TF: 800-562-8467 ■ *Web:* www.introweb.com/hacienda
■ *E-mail:* hacienda@gate.net

Ocean Manor Resort
4040 Galt Ocean Dr. . . . . Fort Lauderdale FL 33308 954-566-7500 564-3075
TF: 800-955-0444

Palm Aire Spa Resort
2601 Palm Aire Dr N. . . . . Pompano Beach FL 33069 954-972-3300 968-2711
TF: 888-266-3287

Pelican Beach Resort
2000 N Fort Lauderdale Beach Blvd. . . . . Fort Lauderdale FL 33305 954-568-9431 565-2622
TF: 800-525-6232 ■ *Web:* www.pelicanbeach.com
■ *E-mail:* pelican@aksi.net

Pier Pointe Ocean Resort
4320 El Mar Dr. . . . . Lauderdale By The Sea FL 33308 954-776-5121 491-9084
TF: 800-331-6384

Fort Lauderdale — Hotels, Motels, Resorts (Cont'd)

				Phone	Fax
Pillars Waterfront Inn 111 N Birch Rd. *TF:* 800-800-7666	Fort Lauderdale	FL	33304	954-467-9639	763-2845
Quality Suites 1050 E Newport Center Dr *TF:* 800-538-2777	Deerfield Beach	FL	33442	954-570-8888	570-5346
Radisson Bahia Mar Beach Resort 801 Seabreeze Blvd *TF:* 800-327-8154	Fort Lauderdale	FL	33316	954-764-2233	523-5424
Ramada Inn 2275 SR-84 *TF:* 800-272-6232	Fort Lauderdale	FL	33312	954-584-4000	791-7680
Ramada Inn 1250 W Hillsboro Blvd *TF:* 800-272-6232	Deerfield Beach	FL	33442	954-427-2200	481-2094
Ramada Inn 1401 S Federal Hwy *TF:* 800-283-9946	Deerfield Beach	FL	33441	954-421-5000	426-2811
Ramada Plaza Beach Resort 4060 Galt Ocean Dr. *TF:* 800-678-9022	Fort Lauderdale	FL	33308	954-565-6611	564-7730
Ramada Plaza Resort 5100 N SR-7	Fort Lauderdale	FL	33319	954-739-4000	733-5037
Ramada Sea Club Resort 619 N Fort Lauderdale Beach Blvd *TF:* 800-327-9478	Fort Lauderdale	FL	33304	954-564-3211	568-1825
River Inn 1180 N Federal Hwy *TF:* 800-748-3716	Fort Lauderdale	FL	33304	954-564-6411	566-6477
Riverside Hotel 620 E Las Olas Blvd. *TF:* 800-325-3280 ■ *E-mail:* RiversideHotel@worldnet.att.net	Fort Lauderdale	FL	33301	954-467-0671	462-2148
Riviera Ocean Resort 505 N Fort Lauderdale Beach Blvd *TF:* 800-457-7770	Fort Lauderdale	FL	33304	954-565-4433	568-9118
Rolling Hills Hotel & Golf Resort 3501 W Rolling Hills Cir *TF:* 800-327-7735 ■ *Web:* www.rollinghillsresort.com ■ *E-mail:* sales@rollinghillsresort.com	Fort Lauderdale	FL	33328	954-475-0400	474-9967
Sea Garden Beach & Tennis Resort 615 N Ocean Blvd.	Pompano Beach	FL	33062	954-943-6200	783-0047
Seabonay Beach Resort 1159 Hillsboro Mile *TF:* 800-777-1961	Hillsboro Beach	FL	33062	954-427-2525	427-3228
Sheraton Fort Lauderdale Airport Hotel 1825 Griffin Rd. *TF:* 800-325-3535	Dania Beach	FL	33004	954-920-3500	920-3571
Sheraton Suites 555 NW 62nd St *TF:* 800-325-3535	Fort Lauderdale	FL	33309	954-772-5400	772-5490
Sheraton Suites Plantation 311 N University Dr. *TF:* 888-627-7075	Plantation	FL	33324	954-424-3300	452-8887
Sheraton Yankee Clipper Beach Hotel 1140 Seabreeze Blvd *TF:* 800-958-5551	Fort Lauderdale	FL	33316	954-524-5551	524-0777
Sheraton Yankee Trader Beach Resort 321 N Fort Lauderdale Beach Blvd *TF:* 800-325-3535	Fort Lauderdale	FL	33304	954-467-1111	462-2342
Shore Haven Resort Inn 4433 Ocean Dr *TF:* 800-552-1959	Lauderdale By The Sea	FL	33308	954-776-5555	776-0828
Sunrise Hilton Inn 3003 N University Dr *TF:* 800-445-8667 ■ *Web:* www.hilton.com/hotels/FLLHSHF	Sunrise	FL	33322	954-748-7000	572-0799
Traders Ocean Resort 1600 S Ocean Blvd *TF:* 800-325-5220	Pompano Beach	FL	33062	954-941-8400	941-1024
Travelodge Executive Airport 1500 W Commercial Blvd. *TF:* 800-578-7878	Fort Lauderdale	FL	33309	954-776-4222	771-5026
Villa Caprice Ocean Resort Motel 4110 El Mar Dr *TF:* 800-628-1177 ■ *Web:* www.villacaprice.com ■ *E-mail:* oceanprk@villacaprice.com	Lauderdale By The Sea	FL	33308	954-776-4123	776-2026
Villas By the Sea Resort & Beach Club 4456 El Mar Dr *TF:* 800-247-8963	Lauderdale By The Sea	FL	33308	954-772-3550	772-3835
Wellesley Inn 3100 N University Dr *TF:* 800-444-8888	Coral Springs	FL	33065	954-344-2200	344-7885
Wellesley Inn 7901 SW 6th St *TF:* 800-444-8888	Plantation	FL	33324	954-473-8257	473-9804
Wellesley Inn Fort Lauderdale West 5070 N SR-7 *TF:* 800-444-8888	Fort Lauderdale	FL	33319	954-484-6909	731-2374
Wellesley Inn Sunrise 13600 NW 2nd St *TF:* 800-444-8888	Sunrise	FL	33325	954-845-9929	845-9996
Westin Hotel Cypress Creek 400 Corporate Dr *TF:* 800-228-3000	Fort Lauderdale	FL	33334	954-772-1331	491-9087
Wyndham Resort & Spa 250 Racquet Club Rd *TF:* 800-996-3426 ■ *Web:* www.registryhotels.com ■ *E-mail:* weListen@registryhotels.com	Fort Lauderdale	FL	33326	954-389-3300	384-1416

— Restaurants —

				Phone
15th Street Fisheries (Seafood) 1900 SE 15th St	Fort Lauderdale	FL	33316	954-763-2777
Adobe Gila's (Mexican) 17 S Fort Lauderdale Beach Blvd Suite 214	Fort Lauderdale	FL	33316	954-467-3377
Alfiere Restaurant (Mediterranean) 400 Corporate Dr	Fort Lauderdale	FL	33334	954-772-1331
Armadillo Cafe (Southwest) 4630 SW 64th Ave	Davie	FL	33314	954-791-4866
Aruba Beach Cafe (American) 1 E Commerical Blvd	Lauderdale By The Sea	FL	33308	954-776-0001
Bahia Cabana (Steak/Seafood) 3001 Harbor Dr	Fort Lauderdale	FL	33316	954-524-1555
Bahia Mar Bar & Grill (American) 801 Seabreeze Blvd	Fort Lauderdale	FL	33316	954-764-2233
Bavarian Village (German) 1401 N Federal Hwy	Hollywood	FL	33020	954-922-7321
Betty's Restaurant & Bar-B-Que (Soul) 601 NW 22nd Rd	Fort Lauderdale	FL	33311	954-583-9133
Bimini Boatyard Bar & Grill (American) 1555 SE 17th St.	Fort Lauderdale	FL	33316	954-525-7400
Blue Moon Fish Co (Seafood) 4405 W Tradewinds Ave	Lauderdale By The Sea	FL	33308	954-267-9888
Brasserie La Ferme (French) 1601 E Sunrise Blvd.	Fort Lauderdale	FL	33304	954-764-0987
Brasserie Max (American) 321 N University Dr	Plantation	FL	33324	954-424-8000
Bread of Life (Natural/Health) 2388 N Federal Hwy *E-mail:* breadoflife@cousinrichie.com	Fort Lauderdale	FL	33305	954-565-7423
Brooks (Continental) 500 S Federal Hwy	Deerfield Beach	FL	33441	954-427-9302
Burt & Jacks (American) Port Everglades Berth 23	Fort Lauderdale	FL	33316	954-522-2878
By Word of Mouth (Continental) 3200 NE 12th Ave	Oakland Park	FL	33334	954-564-3663
Cafe Arugula (American) 3110 N Federal Hwy	Lighthouse Point	FL	33064	954-785-7732
Cafe Blue Fish (Seafood) 3134 NE 9th St	Fort Lauderdale	FL	33304	954-563-3474
Cafe Europa (Italian) 726 E Las Olas Blvd.	Fort Lauderdale	FL	33301	954-763-6600
Cafe Iguana (American) 17 S Fort Lauderdale Beach Blvd	Fort Lauderdale	FL	33316	954-763-7222
Cafe La Bonne Crepe (French) 815 E Las Olas Blvd.	Fort Lauderdale	FL	33301	954-761-1515
Cafe Max (Continental) 2601 E Atlantic Blvd	Pompano Beach	FL	33062	954-782-0606
Café Seville (Spanish) 2768 E Oakland Park Blvd	Fort Lauderdale	FL	33306	954-565-1148
California Cafe Bar & Grill (California) 17th St Cswy & Pier 66 *Web:* www.calcafe.com/lauderdale/index.html	Fort Lauderdale	FL	33316	954-728-3500
Cap's Place Island Restaurant (Steak/Seafood) 2765 NE 28th Ct	Lighthouse Point	FL	33064	954-941-0418
Capriccio (Italian) 2424 N University Dr	Pembroke Pines	FL	33024	954-432-7001
Carlos & Pepe's (Mexican) 1302 SE 17th St Cswy	Fort Lauderdale	FL	33316	954-467-7192
Casa D'Angelo (Italian) 1201 N Federal Hwy	Fort Lauderdale	FL	33304	954-564-1234
Casablanca Cafe (Moroccan) Alhambra & A1A	Fort Lauderdale	FL	33304	954-764-3500
Coconuts Restaurant (American) 429 Seabreeze Blvd	Fort Lauderdale	FL	33316	954-467-6788
Cuban Cafe The (Cuban) 3350 NW Boca Raton Blvd	Boca Raton	FL	33431	561-750-8860
Dave & Buster's (American) Oakwood Plaza 3000 Oakwood Blvd	Hollywood	FL	33020	954-923-5505
East City Grille (New American) 505 N Fort Lauderdale Beach Blvd	Fort Lauderdale	FL	33304	954-565-5569
Eduardo de San Angel (Mexican) 2822 E Commercial Blvd	Fort Lauderdale	FL	33308	954-772-4731
Evangeline (Cajun) 211 S Fort Lauderdale Beach Blvd *Web:* www.sofla.com/partners/justsurfit/shooters	Fort Lauderdale	FL	33316	954-522-7001
French Quarter (French) 215 SE 8th Ave.	Fort Lauderdale	FL	33301	954-463-8000
Gibby's Steaks & Seafood (Steak/Seafood) 2900 NE 12th Terr	Fort Lauderdale	FL	33334	954-565-2929
H2O (Italian) 101 S Fort Lauderdale Beach Blvd.	Fort Lauderdale	FL	33316	954-760-7500
Il Tartuffo (Italian) 2400 E Las Olas Blvd	Fort Lauderdale	FL	33301	954-767-9190
Jackson's Steakhouse (American) 450 E Las Olas Blvd	Fort Lauderdale	FL	33301	954-522-4450
Japanese Village (Japanese) 716 E Las Olas Blvd.	Fort Lauderdale	FL	33301	954-763-8163
Jasmine (Chinese) 7860 Glades Rd	Boca Raton	FL	33434	561-483-8888
La Marina (Continental) 1881 SE 17th St	Fort Lauderdale	FL	33316	954-527-6756
La Vieille Maison (French) 770 E Palmetto Park Rd	Boca Raton	FL	33432	561-391-6701
Left Bank The (French) 214 SE 6th Ave	Fort Lauderdale	FL	33301	954-462-5376
Maguires Hill 16 (Irish) 535 N Andrews Ave	Fort Lauderdale	FL	33301	954-764-4453
Mai Kai (Polynesian) 3599 N Federal Hwy	Fort Lauderdale	FL	33308	954-563-3272
Mango's (American) 904 E Las Olas Blvd	Fort Lauderdale	FL	33301	954-523-5001
Mark's on Las Olas (International) 1032 E Las Olas Blvd	Fort Lauderdale	FL	33301	954-463-1000
Martha's Tropical Grill (Caribbean) 6024 N Ocean Dr	Hollywood	FL	33019	954-923-5444
Max's Beach Place (American) 17 S Fort Lauderdale Beach Blvd	Fort Lauderdale	FL	33316	954-525-5022
Max's Grille (Continental) 404 Plaza Real	Boca Raton	FL	33432	561-368-0080
Maxwell's Chophouse (Steak) 501 E Palmetto Park Rd	Boca Raton	FL	33432	561-347-7077

Fort Lauderdale — Restaurants (Cont'd)

Name / Address	City	State	ZIP	Phone
Mistral (Mediterranean) 201 S Fort Lauderdale Beach Blvd	Fort Lauderdale	FL	33316	954-463-4900
Moondance (American) 1825 Griffin Rd	Dania Beach	FL	33004	954-920-3500
Nick & Max (American) 505 Town Center Cir	Boca Raton	FL	33486	561-391-7177
Nick's Italian Fishery (Seafood) 2255 Glades Rd	Boca Raton	FL	33431	561-994-2201
Original Rustic Inn (Seafood) 4331 Anglers Ave	Fort Lauderdale	FL	33312	954-584-1637
Pete's (Steak/Seafood) 7940 Glades Rd	Boca Raton	FL	33434	561-487-1600
Pussar's Landing (Seafood) 3000 E Oakland Park Blvd	Fort Lauderdale	FL	33306	954-563-4123
Rainbow Palace (Chinese) 2787 E Oakland Park Blvd	Fort Lauderdale	FL	33306	954-565-5652
Raindancer (Steak/Seafood) 3031 E Commercial Blvd	Fort Lauderdale	FL	33308	954-772-0337
Rainforest Cafe (American) 12801 W Sunrise Blvd *Web:* www.rainforestcafe.com	Sunrise	FL	33322	954-851-1015
Revolution 2029 (New American) 2029 Harrison St	Hollywood	FL	33020	954-920-4748
River House (Continental) 301 SW 3rd Ave	Fort Lauderdale	FL	33312	954-525-7661
Royal India (Indian) 3801 Griffin Rd	Fort Lauderdale	FL	33312	954-964-0071
Ruth's Chris Steak House (Steak) 2525 N Federal Hwy	Fort Lauderdale	FL	33305	954-565-2338
Sangria (Spanish) 609 E Las Olas Blvd	Fort Lauderdale	FL	33301	954-728-9282
Sea Watch Restaurant (Seafood) 6002 N Ocean Blvd	Fort Lauderdale	FL	33308	954-781-2200
Sheffield's (American) 3030 Holiday Dr	Fort Lauderdale	FL	33316	954-525-4000
Shirttail Charlie's (American) 400 SW 3rd Ave	Fort Lauderdale	FL	33315	954-463-3474
Shooters Waterfront Cafe USA (American) 3033 NE 32nd Ave *Web:* www.justsurfit.com/shooters/	Fort Lauderdale	FL	33308	954-566-2855
Shula's On the Beach (Steak/Seafood) 321 N Fort Lauderdale Beach Blvd	Fort Lauderdale	FL	33304	954-355-4000
Sloppy Joe's (American) 17 S Fort Lauderdale Beach Blvd Beach Pl	Fort Lauderdale	FL	33316	954-522-7553
Southport Raw Bar (Seafood) 1536 Cordova Rd	Fort Lauderdale	FL	33316	954-525-2526
Sushi Blues Cafe (Japanese) 1836 S Young Cir	Hollywood	FL	33020	954-929-9560
Sushi Ray (Japanese) 5250 Town Center Cir Suite 111	Boca Raton	FL	33486	561-394-9506
Thai Spice (Thai) 1514 E Commercial Blvd	Fort Lauderdale	FL	33334	954-771-4535
Tropical Acres (Gourmet) 2500 Griffin Rd	Fort Lauderdale	FL	33312	954-989-2500
Try My Thai (Thai) 2003 Harrison St	Hollywood	FL	33020	954-926-5585
Waxy O'Connor's (Irish) 1095 SE 17th St Cswy	Fort Lauderdale	FL	33316	954-525-9299
Wilt Chamberlain's (American) 8903 Glades Rd Somerset Shoppes	Boca Raton	FL	33434	561-488-8881
Yesterday's (American) 3001 E Oakland Park Blvd	Fort Lauderdale	FL	33306	954-561-4400
Zan Z Bar (South African) 602 E Las Olas Blvd	Fort Lauderdale	FL	33301	954-767-3377

— Goods and Services —

SHOPPING

Name / Address	City	State	ZIP	Phone	Fax
Beach Place Mall 17 S Fort Lauderdale Beach Blvd	Fort Lauderdale	FL	33316	954-764-3460	763-2527
Broward Mall 8000 W Broward Blvd	Plantation	FL	33388	954-473-8100	472-1389
Coral Square Mall 9469 W Atlantic Blvd	Coral Springs	FL	33071	954-755-5550	
Dania Beach Historic Antique Shopping District Federal Hwy	Dania Beach	FL	33004	954-927-1040	
Fashion Mall 321 N University Dr	Plantation	FL	33324	954-370-1884	
Festival Flea Market 2900 W Sample Rd	Pompano Beach	FL	33073	954-979-4555	968-3980
Galleria at Fort Lauderdale 2414 E Sunrise Blvd	Fort Lauderdale	FL	33304	954-564-1015	
Pembroke Lakes Mall 11401 Pines Blvd Suite 546	Pembroke Pines	FL	33026	954-436-3520	436-7992
Pompano Square Mall 1 Pompano Sq	Pompano Beach	FL	33062	954-943-4683	943-5469
Sawgrass Mills 12801 W Sunrise Blvd *TF:* 800-356-4557 ■ *Web:* www.sawgrassmillsmall.com	Sunrise	FL	33323	954-846-2300	846-2312
Town Center at Boca Raton 6000 Glades Rd	Boca Raton	FL	33431	561-368-6000	338-0891

BANKS

Name / Address	City	State	ZIP	Phone	Fax
American National Bank 4301 N Federal Hwy	Oakland Park	FL	33308	954-491-7788	491-2833
BankAtlantic 1750 E Sunrise Blvd *Web:* www.bankatlantic.com ■ *E-mail:* relocat@icanect.net	Fort Lauderdale	FL	33304	954-760-5000	760-5595
Citibank 500 E Broward Blvd	Fort Lauderdale	FL	33394	800-374-9800	
City National Bank of Florida 450 E Las Olas Blvd	Fort Lauderdale	FL	33301	954-467-6667	524-8247
Colonial Bank 600 S Andrews Ave	Fort Lauderdale	FL	33301	954-462-6093	764-6782
Comerica Bank 100 NE 3rd Ave Suite 100 *TF:* 800-225-6077	Fort Lauderdale	FL	33301	954-468-0600	468-0615
First Union National Bank 200 E Broward Blvd *TF:* 800-275-3862	Fort Lauderdale	FL	33301	954-467-5111	467-5240
Gateway American Bank of Florida 1451 NW 62nd St Suite 212	Fort Lauderdale	FL	33309	954-772-0005	772-0254
NationsBank of Florida NA 100 SE 3rd Ave *TF Cust Svc:* 800-299-2265*	Fort Lauderdale	FL	33394	954-765-2000	765-2820
Northern Trust Bank of Florida NA 1100 E Las Olas Blvd	Fort Lauderdale	FL	33301	954-527-0200	
Regent Bank 1100 SE 3rd Ave	Fort Lauderdale	FL	33316	954-474-5000	765-5560
Republic Security Bank 1401 E Broward Blvd.	Fort Lauderdale	FL	33301	954-522-1610	763-1422
Southtrust Bank 225 N Federal Hwy	Pompano Beach	FL	33062	954-786-9400	782-9285
Sunniland Bank 424 W Sunrise Blvd	Fort Lauderdale	FL	33311	954-764-8300	462-7168
SunTrust Bank South Florida NA 501 E Las Olas Blvd **Fax:* Hum Res ■ *TF:* 800-786-2265	Fort Lauderdale	FL	33301	954-467-5000	765-7601*
Washington Mutual Bank 200 S Pine Island Rd **Fax Area Code:* 954	Plantation	FL	33324	800-782-8875	473-0266*

BUSINESS SERVICES

	Phone
Airborne Express	800-247-2676
ASAP Courier	954-527-4444
Certified Courier	954-771-3811
DHL Worldwide Express	800-225-5345
Federal Express	800-238-5355
Girl Friday	954-735-5392
Kelly Services	954-714-3031
Kinko's	954-467-1007
Lincoln Messenger & Courier	954-561-8244
Personnel One	954-563-8000
Post Office	954-527-2077
Sunshine State Messenger	954-975-8100
UPS	800-742-5877

— Media —

PUBLICATIONS

Name / Address	City	State	ZIP	Phone	Fax
Gold Coast 800 E Broward Blvd Cumberland Bldg Suite 506	Fort Lauderdale	FL	33301	954-462-4488	462-5588
Miami Herald Broward Edition‡ 1520 E Sunrise Blvd	Fort Lauderdale	FL	33304	954-527-8940	527-8955
Miami Metro Magazine 1550 Biscayne Blvd Suite 300 *TF:* 800-288-8388 ■ *Web:* miamimetro.com ■ *E-mail:* miametro@bellsouth.net	Miami	FL	33132	305-755-9920	755-9921
South Florida Business Journal 4000 Hollywood Blvd Suite 695 South *Web:* www.amcity.com/southflorida	Hollywood	FL	33021	954-359-2100	359-2135
Sun-Sentinel‡ 200 E Las Olas Blvd *TF Cust Svc:* 800-548-6397 ■ *Web:* www.sun-sentinel.com	Fort Lauderdale	FL	33301	954-356-4000	356-4559

‡Daily newspapers

TELEVISION

Name / Address	City	State	ZIP	Phone	Fax
WBZL-TV Ch 39 (WB) 2055 Lee St *Web:* www.wb39.com ■ *E-mail:* wb39@expressweb.com	Hollywood	FL	33020	954-925-3939	922-3965
WFOR-TV Ch 4 (CBS) 8900 NW 18th Terr *Web:* www.wfor.com ■ *E-mail:* news4@wfor.groupw.wec.com	Miami	FL	33172	305-591-4444	477-3040
WPBF-TV Ch 25 (ABC) 3970 RCA Blvd Suite 7007	Palm Beach Gardens	FL	33410	561-694-2525	624-1089
WPBT-TV Ch 2 (PBS) 14901 NE 20th Ave *Web:* www.channel2.org	Miami	FL	33181	305-949-8321	949-9772
WPEC-TV Ch 12 (CBS) 1100 Fairfield Dr *Web:* www.gopbi.com/partners/news12	West Palm Beach	FL	33407	561-844-1212	881-0731
WPLG-TV Ch 10 (ABC) 3900 Biscayne Blvd *Web:* www.wplg.com/	Miami	FL	33137	305-576-1010	325-2480
WPTV-TV Ch 5 (NBC) 622 N Flagler Dr *Web:* www.wptv.com ■ *E-mail:* wptv@magg.net	West Palm Beach	FL	33401	561-655-5455	653-5719
WSVN-TV Ch 7 (Fox) 1401 79th St Cswy *Web:* www.wsvn.com ■ *E-mail:* 7news@wsvn.com	Miami	FL	33141	305-751-6692	757-2266
WTVJ-TV Ch 6 (NBC) 316 N Miami Ave *Web:* www.nbc6.nbc.com	Miami	FL	33128	305-379-4444	789-4202

Fort Lauderdale (Cont'd)

RADIO

Phone Fax

WAMR-FM 107.5 MHz (Span)
2828 Coral Way Suite 102 .... Miami FL 33145 305-447-1140 643-1075
Web: www.wamr.com ■ *E-mail:* comentarios@wamr.com
WAVS-AM 1170 kHz (Span) 6360 SW 41st Pl .....Davie FL 33314 954-584-1170
WBGG-FM 105.9 MHz (CR) 194 NW 187th St .... Miami FL 33169 305-654-9494 654-9090
Web: www.big106fm.com ■ *E-mail:* big106@big106fm.com
WFLC-FM 97.3 MHz (AC) 2741 N 29th Ave ... Hollywood FL 33020 954-584-7117 847-3223
WFTL-AM 1400 kHz (N/T)
1000 Corporate Dr Suite 330 ....Fort Lauderdale FL 33334 954-776-5300 771-8176
WHQT-FM 105.1 MHz (Urban)
2741 N 29th Ave. .... Hollywood FL 33020 954-584-7117 847-3223
Web: www.hot105fm.com
WHYI-FM 100.7 MHz (CHR)
1975 E Sunrise Blvd Suite 400 ....Fort Lauderdale FL 33304 954-463-9299 522-7002
Web: www.whyi.com
WKIS-FM 99.9 MHz (Ctry)
9881 Sheridan St .... Hollywood FL 33024 954-431-6200 437-2466
Web: www.wkis.com ■ *E-mail:* wkis@sefl.satelnet.org
WKPX-FM 88.5 MHz (Alt) 8000 NW 44th St .... Sunrise FL 33351 954-572-1321 572-1344
WLRN-FM 91.3 MHz (NPR) 172 NE 15th St. ..... Miami FL 33132 305-995-1717 995-2299
Web: www.wlrn.org/radio-fm ■ *E-mail:* radio@wlrn.org
WLVE-FM 93.9 MHz (NAC) 194 NW 187th St. .... Miami FL 33169 305-654-9494 654-9090
Web: www.love94.com
WMGE-FM 103.5 MHz (AC)
1975 E Sunrise Blvd Suite 400 ....Fort Lauderdale FL 33304 954-463-9299 462-5839
WPOW-FM 96.5 MHz (CHR) 20295 NW 2nd Ave .. Miami FL 33169 305-653-6796 770-1456
Web: www.power96.com
WQAM-AM 560 kHz (Sports)
20295 NW 2nd Ave. .... Miami FL 33169 305-653-6796 770-1456
Web: wqam.com
WRMF-FM 97.9 MHz (AC)
2406 S Congress Ave .... West Palm Beach FL 33406 561-432-5100 432-5111
Web: www.gopbi.com/partners/wrmf
WRTO-FM 98.3 MHz (Span)
2828 Coral Way Suite 102 .... Miami FL 33145 305-447-1140 643-1075
Web: www.wrto.com ■ *E-mail:* info@wrto.com
WSUA-AM 1260 kHz (Span) 2100 Coral Way ..... Miami FL 33145 305-285-1260 858-5907
WTMI-FM 93.1 MHz (Clas) 3225 Aviation Ave .... Miami FL 33133 305-856-9393 854-0783
Web: www.wtmi.com ■ *E-mail:* wtmi@safari.net
WXDJ-FM 95.7 MHz (Span)
1001 Ponce de Leon Blvd ....Coral Gables FL 33134 305-447-9595 461-4951
WZTA-FM 94.9 MHz (Rock) 194 NW 187th St .... Miami FL 33169 305-654-9494 654-9090
Web: www.949zeta.com

— Colleges/Universities —

Phone Fax

Art Institute of Fort Lauderdale
1799 SE 17th St. ....Fort Lauderdale FL 33316 954-463-3000 523-7676
TF: 800-275-7603 ■ *Web:* www.aifl.edu
Broward Community College Downtown Center 225 E Las Olas Blvd ....Fort Lauderdale FL 33301 954-475-6500 761-7466
Web: www.broward.cc.fl.us
Broward Community College North Campus 1000 Coconut Creek Pkwy. ... Coconut Creek FL 33066 954-973-2240 973-2247
Web: www.broward.cc.fl.us
Florida Atlantic University
777 Glades Rd .... Boca Raton FL 33431 561-297-3000 297-2758
TF Admissions: 800-299-4328 ■ *Web:* www.fau.edu
■ *E-mail:* barton@fau.edu
Fort Lauderdale College
1040 Bayview Dr. ....Fort Lauderdale FL 33304 954-568-1600 568-2008
TF: 800-468-0168
■ *Web:* 135.145.62.96/fmu/784ftlauderdale/ftlauderdalehome.htm
ITT Technical Institute
3401 S University Dr. ....Fort Lauderdale FL 33328 954-476-9300 476-6889
TF: 800-488-7797 ■ *Web:* www.itt-tech.edu
Lynn University 3601 N Military Trail. ...... Boca Raton FL 33431 561-994-0770 241-3552
TF: 800-544-8035 ■ *Web:* www.lynn.edu
■ *E-mail:* admission@lynn.edu
Nova Southeastern University
3301 College Ave ....Fort Lauderdale FL 33314 954-262-7300 262-3811
TF: 800-541-6682 ■ *Web:* www.nova.edu
■ *E-mail:* benny@nsu.acast.nova.edu
Prospect Hall School of Business
2620 Hollywood Blvd. .... Hollywood FL 33020 954-923-8100 923-4297
Web: www.prospect.edu ■ *E-mail:* prospect@shadow.net

— Hospitals —

Phone Fax

Broward General Medical Center
1600 S Andrews Ave. ....Fort Lauderdale FL 33316 954-355-4400 355-4410
Web: www.nbhd.org/facility/bgmc.htm
Cleveland Clinic Hospital
2835 N Ocean Blvd ....Fort Lauderdale FL 33308 954-568-1000 561-5183
Web: www4.clevelandclinic.org/tour/florida/florida.htm
Columbia Northwest Medical Center
2801 N SR 7 .... Margate FL 33063 954-978-4008 978-4183
Columbia Westside Regional Medical Center
8201 W Broward Blvd ....Plantation FL 33324 954-473-6600 452-2133
Web: www.columbia.net/faciliti/fl/sflorida/west.html
Coral Springs Medical Center
3000 Coral Hills Dr .... Coral Springs FL 33065 954-344-3000 344-3121
Web: www.nbhd.org/facility/csmc.htm
Florida Medical Center Hospital
5000 W Oakland Park Blvd. ....Fort Lauderdale FL 33313 954-735-6000 735-0532
TF Billing: 800-222-9355*
Hollywood Medical Center
3600 Washington St .... Hollywood FL 33021 954-966-4500 985-6322
Web: www.tenethealth.com/Hollywood
Holy Cross Hospital
4725 N Federal Hwy ....Fort Lauderdale FL 33308 954-771-8000 492-5777
Web: www.holy-cross.com
Imperial Point Medical Center
6401 N Federal Hwy ....Fort Lauderdale FL 33308 954-776-8500 776-8609
Memorial Hospital Pembroke
2301 University Dr .... Pembroke Pines FL 33024 954-962-9650 963-8471
Web: www.mhs.net/mhsfpembroke.htm
Memorial Hospital West
703 N Flamingo Rd .... Pembroke Pines FL 33028 954-436-5000 433-7155
Web: www.mhs.net/mhsfwest.htm
Memorial Regional Hospital
3501 Johnson St .... Hollywood FL 33021 954-987-2000 985-3412
Web: www.mhs.net/mhsfregional.htm
North Ridge Medical Center
5757 N Dixie Hwy. ....Fort Lauderdale FL 33334 954-776-6000 938-3230
Plantation General Hospital
401 NW 42nd Ave. ....Plantation FL 33317 954-587-5010 587-3220
University Hospital 7201 N University Dr. ......Tamarac FL 33321 954-721-2200 724-6567

— Attractions —

Phone Fax

Anne Kolb Nature Center 751 Sheridan St.... Hollywood FL 33019 954-926-2410 926-2491
Art & Culture Center of Hollywood
1650 Harrison St .... Hollywood FL 33020 954-921-3275 921-3273
Bailey Hall 3501 SW Davie Rd. ....Fort Lauderdale FL 33314 954-475-6884
Beach Place Mall
17 S Fort Lauderdale Beach Blvd .....Fort Lauderdale FL 33316 954-764-3460 763-2527
Birch Hugh Taylor State Park
3109 E Sunrise Blvd ....Fort Lauderdale FL 33304 954-564-4521 762-3737
Blockbuster 3D IMAX Theater
401 SW 2nd St. ....Fort Lauderdale FL 33312 954-463-4629 467-0046
Web: www.mods.org/imaxpage1.htm
Blockbuster Golf & Games
151 NW 136th Ave .... Sunrise FL 33325 954-846-7650 846-9201
Bonnet House 900 N Birch Rd ....Fort Lauderdale FL 33304 954-563-5393 561-4174
Web: www.bonnethouse.com
Broward Center for the Performing Arts
201 SW 5th Ave. ....Fort Lauderdale FL 33312 954-522-5334 462-3541
TF: 800-564-9539 ■ *Web:* www.curtainup.org
Broward County Historical Commission
151 SW 2nd St. ....Fort Lauderdale FL 33301 954-765-4670 765-4437
Buehler Planetarium 3501 SW Davie Rd ....Davie FL 33314 954-475-6681 475-2858
Web: terra.broward.cc.fl.us/central/buehler
Butterfly World
3600 W Sample Rd Tradewinds Pk S .... Coconut Creek FL 33073 954-977-4400 977-4501
Web: www.butterflyworld.com ■ *E-mail:* gardens@butterflyworld.com
Coral Ridge Concert Series
5555 N Federal Hwy ....Fort Lauderdale FL 33308 954-491-1103 491-7374
Coral Springs City Centre
2855 Coral Springs Dr. .... Coral Springs FL 33065 954-344-5990 344-5980
Everglades Holiday Park
2194 Griffin Rd. ....Fort Lauderdale FL 33332 954-434-8111
Web: www.introweb.com/everglades
Fern Forest Nature Center
201 Lyons Rd S .... Coconut Creek FL 33063 954-970-0150
Flamingo Gardens 3750 Flamingo Rd ....Davie FL 33330 954-473-2955 473-1738
Web: www.flamingogardens.org
Florida Grand Opera 221 SW 3rd Ave....Fort Lauderdale FL 33312 954-728-9700 728-9702

Fort Lauderdale — Attractions (Cont'd)

	City	State	ZIP	Phone	Fax
Florida Philharmonic					
3401 NW 9th Ave	Fort Lauderdale	FL	33309	954-561-2997	561-1390
TF: 800-226-1812 ■ *Web:* www.flaphil.com ■ *E-mail:* admin@flaphil.com					
Fort Lauderdale Beach					
A1A betw 17th St & Sunrise Blvd	Fort Lauderdale	FL	33316	954-468-1595	
Web: www.fortlauderdalebeach.com					
Fort Lauderdale Children's Theater					
640 N Andrews Ave	Fort Lauderdale	FL	33311	954-763-6901	523-0507
Web: www.flct.org ■ *E-mail:* flct@shadow.net					
Fort Lauderdale Historical Museum					
219 SW 2nd Ave	Fort Lauderdale	FL	33301	954-463-4433	463-4434
Fort Lauderdale Historical Society					
219 SW 2nd Ave	Fort Lauderdale	FL	33301	954-463-4431	463-4434
Fort Lauderdale Museum of Art					
1 E Las Olas Blvd	Fort Lauderdale	FL	33301	954-525-5500	524-6011
Fort Lauderdale Players					
617 NE 8th St	Fort Lauderdale	FL	33304	954-761-5374	761-5376
E-mail: flplayers@aol.com					
Fort Lauderdale Swap Shop					
3291 W Sunrise Blvd	Fort Lauderdale	FL	33311	954-791-7927	583-8920
Web: www.floridaswapshop.com					
Fox Observatory					
16001 W SR 84 Markham Pk	Sunrise	FL	33326	954-384-0442	389-2019
Gold Coast Jazz Society					
901 E Las Olas Blvd Suite 201	Fort Lauderdale	FL	33301	954-524-0805	524-7041
Web: www.goldcoastjazz.org ■ *E-mail:* jmackle@omnigraphics.com					
Gold Coast Opera					
2855 Coral Springs Dr	Coral Springs	FL	33065	954-344-5990	344-5980
Grand Prix Race-O-Rama					
1801 NW 1st St	Dania Beach	FL	33004	954-921-1411	923-2604
Web: www.grandprixflorida.com ■ *E-mail:* sales@grandprixflorida.com					
Graves Museum of Archaeology & Natural History 481 S Federal Hwy	Dania Beach	FL	33044	954-925-7770	925-7064
Holiday Park E Sunrise Blvd & US 1	Fort Lauderdale	FL	33304	954-761-5385	
IGFA Fishing Hall of Fame & Museum					
300 Gulf Stream Way	Dania Beach	FL	33004	954-927-2628	924-4299
Web: www.igfa.org/igfahofm					
International Swimming Hall of Fame					
1 Hall of Fame Dr	Fort Lauderdale	FL	33316	954-462-6536	522-4521
Web: www.ishof.org ■ *E-mail:* museum@ishof.org					
John U Lloyd Beach State Recreation Area					
6503 N Ocean Dr	Dania Beach	FL	33004	954-967-1297	923-2904
Jungle Queen					
801 Seabreeze Blvd Bahia Mar Yacht Basin	Fort Lauderdale	FL	33316	954-462-5596	832-9923
Web: www.junglequeen.com					
King-Cromartie House					
229 SW 2nd Ave	Fort Lauderdale	FL	33301	954-463-4431	
Las Olas Boulevard					
downtown Fort Lauderdale	Fort Lauderdale	FL	33301		
Web: www.lasolasonline.com ■ *E-mail:* lasolas@lasolasonline.com					
Lumonics Light/Sound Theater					
3017 NW 60th St	Fort Lauderdale	FL	33309	954-979-3161	972-5802
Web: www.lumonicslightandsound.com					
Markham Park & Range 16001 W SR 84	Sunrise	FL	33326	954-389-2000	389-2019
Morikami Museum & Japanese Gardens					
4000 Morikami Pk Rd	Delray Beach	FL	33446	561-495-0233	499-2557
Web: www.morikami.org ■ *E-mail:* morikami@co.palm-beach.fl.us					
Museum of Discovery & Science					
401 SW 2nd St	Fort Lauderdale	FL	33312	954-467-6637	467-0046
Web: www.mods.org					
Native Indian Village 3551 N SR 7	Hollywood	FL	33021	954-961-4519	
Okalee Museum 5845 S SR-7	Fort Lauderdale	FL	33314	954-792-0745	
Web: www.seminoletribe.com/museum ■ *E-mail:* museum@semtribe.com					
Old Dillard Museum 1009 NW 4th St	Fort Lauderdale	FL	33311	954-765-6952	765-8899
Old Fort Lauderdale Museum of History					
231 SW 2nd Ave	Fort Lauderdale	FL	33301	954-463-4431	463-4434
Parker Playhouse 707 NE 8th St	Fort Lauderdale	FL	33304	954-763-2444	461-3180
Web: www.broadwayseries.com					
Pompano Beach Amphitheater					
NE 6th St & 18th Ave	Pompano Beach	FL	33060	954-946-2402	
Port Everglades 1850 Eller Dr	Fort Lauderdale	FL	33316	954-523-3404	525-1910
Web: www.co.broward.fl.us/port.htm					
Quiet Waters Park					
401 S Powerline Rd	Deerfield Beach	FL	33442	954-360-1315	360-1349
Riverwalk	Fort Lauderdale	FL	33301	954-765-4466	
Sawgrass Park					
US 27 2 miles N of I-75	Fort Lauderdale	FL	33329	954-389-0202	
Sea Screamer Boat Rides					
125 N Riverside Dr Sands Harbor Hotel	Pompano Beach	FL	33062	954-566-9697	
Secret Woods Nature Center					
2701 W SR-84	Fort Lauderdale	FL	33312	954-791-1030	791-1092
Seminole Indian Bingo & Poker Casino					
4150 N SR 7	Hollywood	FL	33021	954-961-3220	961-8958
Stranahan House 335 SE 6th Ave	Fort Lauderdale	FL	33301	954-524-4736	525-2838
Sunrise Musical Theater					
Nob Hill Rd & Commercial Blvd	Sunrise	FL	33351	954-741-8600	749-4032
Topeekeegnee Yugnee Park					
3300 N Park Rd	Hollywood	FL	33021	954-985-1980	961-5950
Tradewinds Park 3600 W Sample Rd	Coconut Creek	FL	33073	954-968-3880	968-3896
Tree Tops Park 3900 SW 100th Ave	Davie	FL	33328	954-370-3750	370-3770
War Memorial Auditorium					
800 NE 8th St	Fort Lauderdale	FL	33304	954-761-5381	761-5361
Young at Art Children's Museum 11584 SR-84	Davie	FL	33325	954-424-0085	370-5057

SPORTS TEAMS & FACILITIES

	City	State	ZIP	Phone	Fax
Baltimore Orioles Spring Training (baseball) 5301 NW 12th Ave	Fort Lauderdale	FL	33309	954-776-1921	776-9116
Dania Jai-Alai 301 E Dania Beach Blvd	Dania Beach	FL	33004	954-927-2841	920-9095
Web: www.dania-jai-alai.com					
Florida Bobcats (football)					
1 Panther Pkwy National Car Rental Ctr	Sunrise	FL	33323	954-577-9009	577-9008
Web: www.floridabobcats.com					
Florida Marlins					
2267 NW 199th St Pro Player Stadium	Miami	FL	33056	305-626-7400	626-7428
Web: www.flamarlins.com					
Florida Panthers					
2555 Panther Pkwy National Car Rental Center	Sunrise	FL	33323	954-835-7000	835-8012
Web: www.flpanthers.com ■ *E-mail:* flpanthers@flpanthers.com					
Gulfstream Park 901 S Federal Hwy	Hallandale	FL	33009	954-454-7000	454-7827
Web: www.gulfstreampark.com					
Hollywood Greyhound Track					
831 N Federal Hwy	Hallandale	FL	33009	954-454-9400	
Miami Dolphins					
2269 NW 199th St Pro Player Stadium	Miami	FL	33056	305-620-2578	
Web: dolphinsendzone.com					
Miami Heat					
1 SE 3rd Ave American Airlines Arena Suite 2300	Miami	FL	33131	305-577-4328	789-5933*
**Fax:* Hum Res ■ *Web:* www.nba.com/heat					
National Car Rental Center					
2555 Panther Pkwy	Sunrise	FL	33323	954-835-8000	835-8012
Web: www.national-ctr.com					
Pompano Park Racing					
1800 SW 3rd St	Pompano Beach	FL	33069	954-972-2000	970-3098
Web: www.pompanopark.com					
Pro Player Stadium 2269 NW 199th St	Miami	FL	33056	305-623-6100	624-6403
Web: www.proplayer.com					

— Events —

	Phone
Air & Sea Show (early May)	954-765-4466
Art a la Carte (October)	954-525-5500
Beethoven by the Beach (early July)	800-226-1812
Broward County Fair (late November)	954-963-3247
Cajun Zydeco Crawfish Festival (early May)	954-489-3255
Canadafest (early February)	954-921-3404
Chris Evert Pro-Celebrity Tennis Classic (early December)	561-394-2400
Christmas on Las Olas (early December)	954-765-4466
Fiesta Tropical Mardi Gras Carnival (late February)	954-922-9959
Florida Renaissance Festival (late January-early March)	954-776-1642
Fort Lauderdale Billfish Tournament (late April)	954-563-0385
Fort Lauderdale International Auto Show (March)	954-765-5933
Fort Lauderdale International Boat Show (late October-early November)	954-764-7642
Fort Lauderdale International Film Festival (late October-mid-November)	954-760-9898
Fort Lauderdale Seafood Festival (early April)	954-463-4431
Fort Lauderdale Spring Boat Show (mid-late April)	954-764-7642
Greek Festival (February)	954-467-1515
Hollywood Beach Latinfest (mid-August)	954-921-3460
Hollywood Jazz Festival (mid-March)	954-921-3404
Irish Fest (mid-March)	954-946-1093
Las Olas Art Fair (early September)	954-472-3755
Las Olas Art Festival (early March)	954-525-5500
Light Up Fort Lauderdale (December 31)	954-765-4466
Micron PC Bowl (early January)	954-564-5000
NationsBank Starlight Musicals (mid-June-late August)	954-627-6500
New River Boat Parade (mid-late December)	954-791-0202
New Riverfest (April)	954-765-4466
Pompano Beach Rainbow Festival (late July)	954-786-4111
Pompano Beach Seafood Festival (late April)	954-941-2940
Promenade in the Park (October)	954-525-5500

Fort Lauderdale — Events (Cont'd)

	Phone
Riverwalk Blues Festival (early November)	954-761-5934
Riverwalk Winter Arts & Crafts Show (mid-January)	954-761-5363
Saint Patrick's Day Parade & Festival (mid-March)	954-921-3404
Seminole Tribal Festival (mid-February)	954-967-3706
Sistrunk Historical Festival (early February)	954-357-7514
Taste of Fort Lauderdale (late February)	954-485-3481
Viva Broward (early October)	954-527-0627
Winterfest Boat Parade (mid-December)	954-767-0686

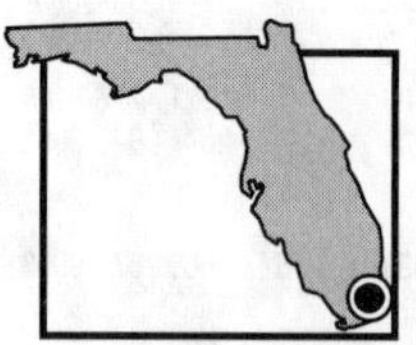

Hialeah

A suburb located northwest of Miami, Hialeah is the fifth largest city in the state of Florida. Primarily an industrial city, Hialeah is home to many manufacturers and distribution centers for large retail companies. Hialeah Park Race Course is known as "one of the world's most beautiful race tracks" and is listed on the National Register of Historic Places. The racetrack has won a number of awards for its architecture, historical significance, and aesthetic appeal.

Population	211,392	**Longitude**	80-17-48 W
Area (Land)	19.2 sq mi	**County**	Dade
Area (Water)	0.5 sq mi	**Time Zone**	EST
Elevation	7 ft	**Area Code/s**	305
Latitude	25-51-42 N		

— Average Temperatures and Precipitation —

TEMPERATURES

	Jan	Feb	Mar	Apr	May	Jun	Jul	Aug	Sep	Oct	Nov	Dec
High	76	77	80	83	86	88	90	90	89	85	81	77
Low	57	58	63	66	70	73	75	75	74	70	65	59

PRECIPITATION

	Jan	Feb	Mar	Apr	May	Jun	Jul	Aug	Sep	Oct	Nov	Dec
Inches	2.4	2.2	2.6	3.4	6.7	10.5	7.1	8.5	8.3	6.3	2.8	2.2

— Important Phone Numbers —

	Phone		Phone
American Express Travel	305-888-1601	**Time/Temp**	305-324-8811
Emergency	911	**Weather**	305-229-4522
Poison Control Center	800-282-3171		

— Information Sources —

				Phone	Fax
Greater Miami Convention & Visitors Bureau 701 Brickell Ave Suite 2700 *TF:* 800-933-8448 ■ *Web:* www.miamiandbeaches.com ■ *E-mail:* gmcvb@miamiandbeaches.com	Miami	FL	33131	305-539-3000	539-3113
Hialeah Chamber of Commerce & Industries 1840 W 49th St Suite 410 *Web:* www.hialeahchamber.com	Hialeah	FL	33012	305-828-9898	828-9777
Hialeah City Council 501 Palm Ave 3rd Fl *Web:* www.ci.hialeah.fl.us/council	Hialeah	FL	33010	305-883-5805	883-5814
Hialeah City Hall 501 Palm Ave *Web:* www.ci.hialeah.fl.us	Hialeah	FL	33010	305-883-5820	883-5814
Hialeah Economic Development Office 501 Palm Ave	Hialeah	FL	33010	305-884-1219	884-1740
Hialeah Mayor 501 Palm Ave *Web:* www.ci.hialeah.fl.us/mayor	Hialeah	FL	33010	305-883-5800	883-5992
Hialeah-Miami Springs-Northwest Dade Area Chamber of Commerce 59 W 5th St *Web:* www.hialeahnwdade.com ■ *E-mail:* hiamscc@bellsouth.net	Hialeah	FL	33010	305-887-1515	887-2453
Kennedy John F Library 190 W 49th St *Web:* www.ci.hialeah.fl.us/library/about/	Hialeah	FL	33012	305-821-2700	818-9144
Miami-Dade County 111 NW 1st St Suite 220 *Web:* www.co.miami-dade.fl.us	Miami	FL	33128	305-375-5124	375-5569

On-Line Resources

NITC Travelbase City Guide Hialeah .... www.travelbase.com/auto/features/hialeah-fl.html

— Transportation Services —

AIRPORTS

■ **Miami International Airport (MIA)**

	Phone
4 miles S of downtown Hialeah (approx 10 minutes)	305-876-7000

Airport Transportation

	Phone
Metrobus $1.25 fare to downtown Hialeah	305-770-3131
SuperShuttle $14 fare to downtown Hialeah	305-871-2000
Yellow Cab $10 fare to downtown Hialeah	305-444-7777

Commercial Airlines

	Phone		Phone
Aerolineas Argentinas	800-333-0276	**LanChile**	305-871-2044
Air Canada	800-776-3000	**Lufthansa**	800-645-3880
Air France	800-321-4538	**MetroJet**	888-638-7653
Air Jamaica	800-523-5585	**Mexicana**	800-531-7923
ALM-Antillean	800-327-7230	**National**	888-757-5387
American	800-433-7300	**Northwest**	800-225-2525
Avianca	305-883-5151	**Pan Am**	800-359-7262
Aviateca	800-327-9832	**Saeta**	800-827-2382
Bahamasair	305-593-1910	**Servivensa**	800-428-3672
Cayman Airways	800-422-9626	**TACA International**	305-223-0312
Continental	305-871-1400	**TransBrasil**	800-872-3153
Delta	305-448-7000	**Turkish Airlines**	800-874-8875
Ecuatoriana	305-476-7837	**TWA**	800-221-2000
El Al	800-223-6700	**United**	800-241-6522
Haiti Air	305-871-5814	**Varig Brazilian**	800-468-2744
Kiwi	800-538-5494	**VASP Brazilian Airlines**	800-732-8277
LAB Airlines	800-327-7407	**Virgin Atlantic**	305-594-0949

Charter Airlines

	Phone		Phone
Action Helicopter	305-358-4723	**Corporate Air Charter Inc**	305-248-0098
Adtech Aircraft Charters	800-511-4016	**Falcon Air Express**	305-592-5672
Air Florida	800-373-9593	**Fox Air International**	800-231-0044
Atlantic Flight Group	305-871-1111	**Miami Air International**	305-871-3300
Biscayne Helicopters	305-252-3883		

CAR RENTALS

	Phone		Phone
Alamo	305-633-6076	**Dollar**	305-887-6000
Avis	305-637-4900	**Hertz**	305-871-0300
Budget	305-871-2722	**National**	305-638-1026

LIMO/TAXI

	Phone		Phone
Central Cab	305-532-5555	**Limousines of South Florida**	305-940-5252
Club Limousine	305-893-9850	**Metro Taxi**	305-888-8888
Corporate Transportation	305-931-3111	**Yellow Cab**	305-444-4444
Diamond Cab	305-545-7575		

MASS TRANSIT

	Phone
Metrobus $1.25 Base fare	305-770-3131
Metromover $.25 Base fare	305-770-3131
Tri-Rail fare varies with destination	800-874-7245

Hialeah (Cont'd)

RAIL/BUS

				Phone
Greyhound Bus Station 5388 W 16th Ave *TF:* 800-231-2222	Hialeah	FL	33012	305-821-6423

— Accommodations —

HOTELS, MOTELS, RESORTS

				Phone	Fax
Cabana Hotel 508 W 1st Ave	Hialeah	FL	33010	305-882-0580	
Chesapeake Hotel 935 W Okeechobee Rd	Hialeah	FL	33010	305-887-7457	
Courtyard by Marriott 15700 NW 77th Ct *TF:* 800-321-2211 ■ *Web:* courtyard.com/MIAML	Hialeah	FL	33016	305-556-6665	556-0282
Don Shula's Hotel & Golf Club 6842 Main St **Fax:* Sales ■ *TF:* 800-247-4852	Miami Lakes	FL	33014	305-821-1150	820-8067*
Hialeah Executive Motel 131 W Okeechobee Rd	Hialeah	FL	33010	305-887-2718	884-1060
Holiday Inn Hialeah/Miami Lakes 6650 W 20th Ave *TF:* 800-465-4329	Hialeah	FL	33016	305-362-7777	826-8107
Okeechobee Inn Motel 699 E Okeechobee Rd	Hialeah	FL	33010	305-885-2999	
Park Plaza 7707 NW 103rd St *TF:* 800-860-3966	Hialeah	FL	33016	305-825-1000	556-6785
Ramada Inn Airport North 1950 W 49th St *TF:* 800-272-6232	Hialeah	FL	33012	305-823-2000	362-4562
Wellesley Inn 7925 NW 154th St *TF:* 800-444-8888	Hialeah	FL	33016	305-821-8274	828-2257

— Restaurants —

				Phone
Alessi Cafe (Cuban) 158 Hialeah Dr	Hialeah	FL	33010	305-887-2281
Alibaba Place (Greek) 1159 W 68th St	Hialeah	FL	33014	305-819-4747
Badias Restaurant (Cuban) 1700 E 4th Ave	Hialeah	FL	33010	305-888-0437
Bak Hee Chinese Restaurant (Chinese) 6500 W 4th Ave	Hialeah	FL	33012	305-823-0280
Beverly Hills Cafe (American) 7321 Miami Lakes Dr	Hialeah	FL	33014	305-558-8201
Cantinas Leidas (Mexican) 468 E 25th St	Hialeah	FL	33013	305-696-0662
Casa Romeu (Cuban) 18620 NW 67th Ave	Miami	FL	33016	305-624-9843
Chicos (Cuban) 4070 W 12th Ave	Hialeah	FL	33012	305-556-8907
Coco Palms (Caribbean) 7707 NW 103rd St	Hialeah	FL	33016	305-825-1000
Di Piazza Italian Restaurant (Italian) 1412 W 49th St	Hialeah	FL	33012	305-558-8412
El Sugundo Viajante (Cuban) 2846 Palm Ave	Hialeah	FL	33010	305-888-5465
Hitching Post Barbecue Ranch (Barbecue) 445 E Okeechobee Rd	Hialeah	FL	33010	305-887-6012
Italian Terrace Restaurant (Italian) 6747 Main St	Miami Lakes	FL	33014	305-556-7800
Kam Kee (Chinese) 3640 Palm Ave	Hialeah	FL	33012	305-825-1300
King & I (Thai/Japanese) 15508 NW 77th	Hialeah	FL	33015	305-823-1095
Koky's Bar-B-Q Ranch (Barbecue) 5350 W 16th Ave	Hialeah	FL	33012	305-823-5200
La Carreta Restaurant (Cuban) 5350 W 16th Ave	Hialeah	FL	33012	305-823-5200
Latin American Cafeteria (Cuban) 1750 W 68th St	Hialeah	FL	33014	305-556-0641
Mar Del Sur (Seafood) 1366 E 4th Ave	Hialeah	FL	33010	305-885-1906
Michael's (Thai) 16927 NW 67th Ave	Miami Lakes	FL	33015	305-556-8094
Nine Dragons (Chinese) 930 E 9th St	Hialeah	FL	33010	305-885-6376
Parrilla Argentina (Argentinean) 5999 W 16th Ave	Hialeah	FL	33012	305-819-7461
Penthouse Cafe (Continental) 2100 W 76th St	Hialeah	FL	33014	305-362-2100
Shima (Japanese) 16873 NW 67th Ave	Miami Lakes	FL	33015	305-821-2310
Stephens Restaurant (Jewish) 1000 E 16th St	Hialeah	FL	33010	305-887-8863
Thai Cafe (Thai) 6845 Main St	Hialeah	FL	33014	305-825-7752
Tiburon (Seafood) 3970 W 16th Ave	Hialeah	FL	33012	305-821-6100
Trattoria Pampered Chef (Italian) 7347 Miami Lakes Dr	Hialeah	FL	33014	305-825-8919
Vichy Cafe & Restaurant (Cuban) 16504 NW 49th Ave	Hialeah	FL	33014	305-621-7117

— Goods and Services —

SHOPPING

				Phone	Fax
Opa Locka Hialeah Flea Market 12705 NW 42nd Ave	Opa Locka	FL	33054	305-688-0500	687-8312
Palm Springs Mile 555 Palm Springs Mile	Hialeah	FL	33012	305-821-7111	
Westland Mall 1675 W 49th St	Hialeah	FL	33012	305-823-9310	

BANKS

				Phone	Fax
Commercebank NA 1601 E 4th Ave	Hialeah	FL	33010	305-885-9302	887-5131
NationsBank 1 E 49th St *TF:* 800-299-2265	Hialeah	FL	33013	305-825-5900	825-6953
Ocean Bank 1801 W 4th Ave	Hialeah	FL	33010	305-884-7400	884-6267
SunTrust Bank 1740 W 49th St	Hialeah	FL	33012	305-591-6711	557-9231
Union Planters Bank of Florida 1975 W 76th St	Hialeah	FL	33012	305-556-5444	827-5157

BUSINESS SERVICES

	Phone		Phone
Accountemps	305-447-1757	**Mail Boxes Etc**	305-821-8898
DHL Worldwide Express	800-225-5345	**Manpower Temporary Services**	305-592-4846
Federal Express	800-238-5355	**Post Office**	305-821-2068
Kelly Services	305-822-8210	**UPS**	800-742-5877

— Media —

PUBLICATIONS

				Phone	Fax
El Sol de Hialeah 436 Palm Ave	Hialeah	FL	33010	305-885-5111	887-8324
La Voz de La Calle 4696 E 10th Ct	Hialeah	FL	33013	305-687-5555	681-0500

TELEVISION

				Phone	Fax
WBFS-TV Ch 33 (UPN) 16550 NW 52nd Ave *Web:* www.paramountstations.com/WBFS	Miami	FL	33014	305-621-3333	628-3448
WFOR-TV Ch 4 (CBS) 8900 NW 18th Terr *Web:* www.wfor.com ■ *E-mail:* news4@wfor.groupw.wec.com	Miami	FL	33172	305-591-4444	477-3040
WPBT-TV Ch 2 (PBS) 14901 NE 20th Ave *Web:* www.channel2.org	Miami	FL	33181	305-949-8321	949-9772
WPLG-TV Ch 10 (ABC) 3900 Biscayne Blvd *Web:* www.wplg.com/	Miami	FL	33137	305-576-1010	325-2480
WSVN-TV Ch 7 (Fox) 1401 79th St Cswy *Web:* www.wsvn.com ■ *E-mail:* 7news@wsvn.com	Miami	FL	33141	305-751-6692	757-2266
WTVJ-TV Ch 6 (NBC) 316 N Miami Ave *Web:* www.nbc6.nbc.com	Miami	FL	33128	305-379-4444	789-4202

RADIO

				Phone	Fax
WAVS-AM 1170 kHz (Span) 6360 SW 41st Pl	Davie	FL	33314	954-584-1170	
WSUA-AM 1260 kHz (Span) 2100 Coral Way	Miami	FL	33145	305-285-1260	858-5907

— Colleges/Universities —

				Phone	Fax
Florida National College 4206 W 12th Ave *Web:* www.florida-national.edu	Hialeah	FL	33012	305-821-3333	362-0595
Miami-Dade Community College North Campus-Hialeah Branch 1775 W 49th St	Hialeah	FL	33012	305-237-1800	237-1812

— Hospitals —

				Phone	Fax
Hialeah Hospital 651 E 25th St	Hialeah	FL	33013	305-693-6100	835-4252
Palm Springs General Hospital 1475 W 49th St	Hialeah	FL	33012	305-558-2500	558-8679
Palmetto General Hospital 2001 W 68th St *Web:* www.tenethealth.com/Palmetto	Hialeah	FL	33016	305-823-5000	364-2173

— Attractions —

SPORTS TEAMS & FACILITIES

				Phone	Fax
Calder Race Course Inc 21001 NW 27th Ave *TF:* 800-333-3227 ■ *Web:* www.calderracecourse.com ■ *E-mail:* marketing@calderracecourse.com	Miami	FL	33056	305-625-1311	620-2569
Flagler Greyhound Track 401 NW 38th Ct	Miami	FL	33126	305-649-3000	631-4525

Hialeah — Sports Teams & Facilities (Cont'd)

	City	State	Zip	Phone	Fax
Florida Panthers 2555 Panther Pkwy National Car Rental Center	Sunrise	FL	33323	954-835-7000	835-8012
Web: www.flpanthers.com ■ *E-mail:* flpanthers@flpanthers.com					
Gulfstream Park 901 S Federal Hwy	Hallandale	FL	33009	954-454-7000	454-7827
Web: www.gulfstreampark.com					
Hialeah Park Race Course 2200 E 4th Ave	Hialeah	FL	33011	305-885-8000	887-8006
Web: www.hialeahpark.com					
Hialeah Speedway 3300 W Okeechobee Rd	Hialeah	FL	33012	305-821-6644	556-9858
Miami Breakers (soccer) Alton Rd & 12th Ave Flamingo Pk.	Miami Beach	FL	33138	305-532-5080	532-0508
Miami Dolphins 2269 NW 199th St Pro Player Stadium	Miami	FL	33056	305-620-2578	
Web: dolphinsendzone.com					
Miami Heat 1 SE 3rd Ave American Airlines Arena Suite 2300	Miami	FL	33131	305-577-4328	789-5933*
**Fax:* Hum Res ■ *Web:* www.nba.com/heat					
Miami Jai-Alai 3500 NW 37th Ave	Miami	FL	33142	305-633-6400	633-4386
Web: www.fla-gaming.com/miami ■ *E-mail:* miajaili@netrunner.net					
Miami Tango (soccer) 10651 NW 19th St	Miami	FL	33172	305-593-6033	594-3973

— Events —

	Phone
Flamingo Stakes (early April)	305-885-8000
Hialeah Spring Festival (late January-mid-February)	305-828-9898
Hispanic Heritage Month (October)	305-687-2671
Holiday Country Craft Show (late-November)	305-821-1130
Widener Handicap (late March)	305-885-8000

Jacksonville

Situated 12 miles inland on a bend in the Saint John's River, the port city of Jacksonville berths vessels ranging from ocean liners to small shrimp boats. Towering skyscrapers give evidence of the city's status as a modern business center, while the many hotels and restaurants along Jacksonville Beach highlight its tourist industry. Jacksonville Landing and the Riverwalk near the Saint John's River are popular sites for festivals and cultural events. North of the city is historic Fernandina Beach with its 19th century mansions; and on Fort George Island, Kingsley Plantation provides a glimpse of life on a 19th century sea island cotton plantation.

Population	693,630	**Longitude**	81-65-62 W
Area (Land)	773.8 sq mi	**County**	Duval
Area (Water)	144.4 sq mi	**Time Zone**	EST
Elevation	19 ft	**Area Code/s**	904
Latitude	30-33-09 N		

— Average Temperatures and Precipitation —

TEMPERATURES

	Jan	Feb	Mar	Apr	May	Jun	Jul	Aug	Sep	Oct	Nov	Dec
High	64	67	73	79	85	89	91	91	87	80	74	67
Low	41	43	49	55	62	69	72	72	69	59	50	43

PRECIPITATION

	Jan	Feb	Mar	Apr	May	Jun	Jul	Aug	Sep	Oct	Nov	Dec
Inches	3.3	3.9	3.7	2.8	3.6	5.7	5.6	7.9	7.1	2.9	2.2	2.7

— Important Phone Numbers —

	Phone		Phone
AAA	904-398-0564	**Poison Control Center**	800-282-3171
American Express Travel	904-642-1701	**Time/Temp**	904-387-4545
Emergency	911	**Weather**	904-741-4311
HotelDocs	800-468-3537		

— Information Sources —

	City	State	Zip	Phone	Fax
Better Business Bureau Serving Northeast Florida 7820 Arlington Expy Suite 147	Jacksonville	FL	32211	904-721-2288	721-7373
Web: www.jacksonville.bbb.org					
Duval County 117 W Duval St	Jacksonville	FL	32202	904-630-1178	
Jacksonville Chamber of Commerce 3 Independent Dr	Jacksonville	FL	32202	904-366-6600	632-0617
Web: www.jacksonvillechamber.org ■ *E-mail:* memberservices@jacksonvillechamber.org					
Jacksonville City Hall 117 W Duval St	Jacksonville	FL	32202	904-630-1178	
Web: www.itd.ci.jax.fl.us/					
Jacksonville Convention & Visitors Bureau 201 E Adams St	Jacksonville	FL	32202	904-798-9111	798-9103
TF: 800-733-2668 ■ *Web:* www.jaxcvb.com ■ *E-mail:* jaxflcvb@jax-inter.net					
Jacksonville Economic Development Div 220 E Bay St 14th Fl	Jacksonville	FL	32202	904-630-1858	630-2919
Web: www.itd.ci.jax.fl.us/pub/jaxbiz.htm					
Jacksonville Mayor 117 W Duval St	Jacksonville	FL	32202	904-630-1776	630-2391
Web: www.itd.ci.jax.fl.us/pub/citygov/mayor.html					
Jacksonville Public Library 122 N Ocean St	Jacksonville	FL	32202	904-630-1994	630-2431
Web: jpl.itd.ci.jax.fl.us/					
Osborn Prime F Convention Center 1000 Water St	Jacksonville	FL	32204	904-630-4000	630-4029
Web: www.jaxevents.com/osborn.html					

On-Line Resources

About.com Guide to Jacksonville	jacksonville.about.com/local/southeastus/jacksonville
Anthill City Guide Jacksonville	www.anthill.com/city.asp?city=jacksonvillefl
Area Guide Jacksonville	jacksonville.areaguides.net
Best Read Guide Jacksonville	bestreadguide.com/jacksonville/
City Knowledge Jacksonville	www.cityknowledge.com/fl_jacksonville.htm
DigitalCity Jacksonville	home.digitalcity.com/jacksonville
Excite.com Jacksonville City Guide	www.excite.com/travel/countries/united_states/florida/jacksonville
HotelGuide Jacksonville	hotelguide.net/jacksonville/
Jacksonville City Info	www.scalise.com/jax/cityinfo.htm
Jacksonville CityLink	www.usacitylink.com/citylink/jackvill
Jacksonville.TheLinks.com	jacksonville.thelinks.com/
NITC Travelbase City Guide Jacksonville	www.travelbase.com/auto/guides/jacksonville-area-fl.html
Planet Jax	www.planetjax.com/
Surf & Sun Beach Vacation Guide to Jacksonville	www.surf-sun.com/fl-jacksonville-main.htm
Welcome to the First Coast	www.welcometo.com

— Transportation Services —

AIRPORTS

■ **Jacksonville International Airport (JAX)**

	Phone
20 miles N of downtown (approx 20 minutes)	904-741-4902

Web: www.jaxport.com/jia.cfm ■ *E-mail:* info@jaxport.com

Airport Transportation

	Phone
Checker Cab $25-30 fare to downtown	904-764-2472
Gator City Shuttle $22 fare to downtown	904-353-8880

Commercial Airlines

	Phone		Phone
American	800-433-7300	**MetroJet**	888-638-7653
Continental	800-525-0280	**TWA**	800-221-2000
Continental Express	800-525-0280	**United**	800-241-6522
Delta	800-221-1212	**US Airways**	800-428-4322

Jacksonville (Cont'd)

Charter Airlines

	Phone		Phone
Alliance Executive Charter Services	800-232-5387	**Corporate Airways**	904-641-0001
		Craig Air Center	904-641-0300

CAR RENTALS

	Phone		Phone
Alamo	904-741-4414	**Dollar**	904-741-4614
Avis	904-741-2327	**Enterprise**	904-388-3553
Budget	904-720-0000	**Hertz**	904-741-2151
CarTemps USA	904-724-8808	**National**	904-641-2445

LIMO/TAXI

	Phone		Phone
Bob's Limo	904-241-1013	**Gator City Taxi**	904-355-8294
Checker Cab	904-764-2472	**Greater Jacksonville Trans.**	904-630-3100
Dana's Limousine Service	904-744-3333	**Yellow Cab**	904-260-1111

MASS TRANSIT

	Phone
Jacksonville Transit Authority Bus $.75 Base fare	904-630-3100

RAIL/BUS

	City	State	Zip	Phone
Amtrak Station 3570 Clifford Ln *TF:* 800-872-7245	Jacksonville	FL	32209	904-766-5110
Greyhound/Trailways Bus Station 10 N Pearl St *TF:* 800-231-2222	Jacksonville	FL	32202	904-356-9976

— Accommodations —

HOTELS, MOTELS, RESORTS

	City	State	Zip	Phone	Fax
Amelia Island Plantation PO Box 3000 *TF:* 800-874-6878 ■ *Web:* aipfl.com ■ *E-mail:* sales@aipfl.com	Fernandina Beach	FL	32035	904-261-6161	277-5159
AmeriSuites 8277 Western Way Cir *TF:* 800-833-1516	Jacksonville	FL	32256	904-737-4477	739-1649
Atlantis The 731 N 1st St	Jacksonville Beach	FL	32250	904-249-5006	
Best Value Inn 1057 Broward Rd	Jacksonville	FL	32218	904-757-0990	757-0990
Candlewood Suites 4990 Belfort Rd *TF:* 800-946-6200	Jacksonville	FL	32256	904-296-7785	296-9281
Clarion Hotel Airport Conference Center 2101 Dixie Clipper Rd *TF:* 800-234-2398	Jacksonville	FL	32218	904-741-1997	741-5520
Comfort Inn Mayport 2401 Mayport Rd *TF:* 800-968-5513	Atlantic Beach	FL	32233	904-249-0313	241-2155
Comfort Inn Oceanfront 1515 N 1st St *TF:* 800-654-8776	Jacksonville Beach	FL	32250	904-241-2311	249-3830
Conch House Marina Resort 57 Comares Ave *TF:* 800-940-6256 ■ *Web:* www.conch-house.com/ ■ *E-mail:* conchhouse@staug.com	Saint Augustine	FL	32084	904-829-8646	829-5414
Courtyard by Marriott 4600 San Pablo Rd *TF:* 800-321-2211 ■ *Web:* courtyard.com/JAXMC	Jacksonville	FL	32224	904-223-1700	223-1026
Courtyard by Marriott 14668 Duval Rd *TF:* 800-321-2211 ■ *Web:* courtyard.com/JAXCA	Jacksonville	FL	32218	904-741-1122	741-0929
Courtyard by Marriott 4670 Lenoir Ave S *TF:* 800-321-2211 ■ *Web:* courtyard.com/JAXCH	Jacksonville	FL	32216	904-296-2828	296-9508
Days Inn Oceanfront Beach Hotel 1031 S 1st St *TF:* 800-321-2037	Jacksonville Beach	FL	32250	904-249-7231	249-7924
Days Inn South 5649 Cagle Rd *TF:* 800-329-7466	Jacksonville	FL	32216	904-733-3890	636-9841
Doubletree Club Hotel 4700 Salisbury Rd *TF:* 800-222-8733	Jacksonville	FL	32256	904-281-9700	281-1957
Econo Lodge 5221 University Blvd W *TF:* 800-553-2666	Jacksonville	FL	32216	904-737-1690	448-5638
Embassy Suites 9300 Baymeadows Rd *TF:* 800-362-2779	Jacksonville	FL	32256	904-731-3555	731-4972
Extended StayAmerica 6961 Lenoir Ave *TF:* 800-398-7829	Jacksonville	FL	32216	904-296-0181	296-0374
Fairfield Inn by Marriott 8050 Baymeadows Cir W *TF:* 800-228-2800 ■ *Web:* fairfieldinn.com/JAXFI	Jacksonville	FL	32256	904-739-0739	739-3080
Hampton Inn Airport 1170 Airport Entrance Rd *TF:* 800-426-7866	Jacksonville	FL	32218	904-741-4980	741-4186
Hampton Inn Central 1331 Prudential Dr *TF:* 800-426-7866	Jacksonville	FL	32207	904-396-7770	396-8044
Hampton Inn Orange Park 6135 Youngerman Cir *TF:* 800-426-7866	Jacksonville	FL	32244	904-777-5313	778-1545
Hampton Inn South 4690 Salisbury Rd *TF:* 800-426-7866	Jacksonville	FL	32256	904-281-0443	281-0144
Holiday Inn 860 A1A Beach Blvd. *TF:* 800-626-7263	Saint Augustine	FL	32084	904-471-2555	461-8450
Holiday Inn 150 Park Ave *TF:* 800-465-4329	Orange Park	FL	32073	904-264-9513	278-1575
Holiday Inn Airport I-95 & Airport Rd *TF:* 800-465-4329	Jacksonville	FL	32229	904-741-4404	741-4907
Holiday Inn Baymeadows 9150 Baymeadows Rd *TF:* 800-465-4329	Jacksonville	FL	32256	904-737-1700	737-0207
Holiday Inn Commonwealth 6802 Commonwealth Ave. *TF:* 800-465-4329	Jacksonville	FL	32205	904-781-6000	781-2784
Holiday Inn Express 4675 Salisbury Rd *TF:* 800-465-4329	Jacksonville	FL	32256	904-332-9500	332-9222
Holiday Inn SunSpree 1617 N 1st St. *TF:* 800-465-4329	Jacksonville Beach	FL	32250	904-249-9071	241-4321
Homestead Village 10020 Skinner Lake Dr	Jacksonville	FL	32246	904-642-9911	642-5673
House on Cherry St 1844 Cherry St	Jacksonville	FL	32205	904-384-1999	
Inns of America 4300 Salisbury Rd. *TF:* 800-826-0778 ■ *Web:* innsofamerica.com/jackson.htm	Jacksonville	FL	32216	904-281-0198	296-3580
Jacksonville Hilton 1201 Riverplace Blvd. *TF:* 800-445-8667	Jacksonville	FL	32207	904-398-8800	398-9170
Jacksonville Marriott 4670 Salisbury Rd *TF:* 800-228-9290	Jacksonville	FL	32256	904-296-2222	296-7561
La Quinta Inn & Suites 4686 Lenoir Ave *TF:* 800-531-5900	Jacksonville	FL	32216	904-296-0703	296-0709
La Quinta Jacksonville North 812 Dunn Ave *TF:* 800-687-6667	Jacksonville	FL	32218	904-751-6960	751-9769
Marriott Sawgrass Resort 1000 PGA Tour Blvd *TF:* 800-457-4653 ■ *Web:* marriotthotels.com/JAXSW	Ponte Vedra Beach	FL	32082	904-285-7777	285-0906
Omni Jacksonville Hotel 245 Water St *TF:* 800-843-6664	Jacksonville	FL	32202	904-355-6664	791-4812
Parkview Inn 901 N Main St.	Jacksonville	FL	32202	904-355-3744	353-3043
Radisson Ponce de Leon Golf & Conference Resort 4000 US 1 N *TF:* 800-333-3333	Saint Augustine	FL	32095	904-824-2821	824-8254
Radisson Riverwalk Hotel 1515 Prudential Dr *TF:* 800-333-3333	Jacksonville	FL	32207	904-396-5100	396-7154
Ramada Conference Center 5865 Arlington Expy *TF:* 800-874-3000	Jacksonville	FL	32211	904-724-3410	727-7606
Ramada Inn & Suites 510 Lane Ave S *TF:* 800-272-6232	Jacksonville	FL	32205	904-786-0500	786-0924
Ramada Inn Mandarin Conference Center 3130 Hartley Rd *TF:* 800-272-6232	Jacksonville	FL	32257	904-268-8080	262-8718
Ramada Resort 1201 N 1st St *TF:* 800-272-6232	Jacksonville Beach	FL	32250	904-241-5333	241-1862
Regency Inn 6237 Arlington Expy	Jacksonville	FL	32211	904-725-5093	720-0378
Residence Inn by Marriott 8365 Dix Ellis Trail *TF:* 800-331-3131 ■ *Web:* www.residenceinn.com/JAXBM	Jacksonville	FL	32256	904-733-8088	731-8354
Sea Turtle Inn 1 Ocean Blvd. *TF:* 800-874-6000	Atlantic Beach	FL	32233	904-249-7402	247-1517
Studio 6 8765 Baymeadows Rd *TF:* 800-466-8356	Jacksonville	FL	32256	904-731-7317	737-8836
Suburban Lodge 8285 Phillips Hwy *TF:* 800-951-7829	Jacksonville	FL	32256	904-448-0021	448-0032

— Restaurants —

	City	State	Zip	Phone
24 Miramar (International) 4446 Hendricks Ave	Jacksonville	FL	32207	904-448-2424
Alhambra Dinner Theatre (American) 12000 Beach Blvd.	Jacksonville	FL	32246	904-641-1212
Amore Cafe (Italian) 1406 Beach Blvd	Jacksonville	FL	32250	904-246-5373
Aqua Grill (Steak/Seafood) 950 Sawgrass Village Dr	Ponte Vedra Beach	FL	32082	904-285-3017

Jacksonville — Restaurants (Cont'd)

Name	Address	City	State	ZIP	Phone
Cafe Carmon (New American)	1986 San Marco Blvd	Jacksonville	FL	32207	904-399-4488
Chart House (Steak/Seafood)	1501 Riverplace Blvd	Jacksonville	FL	32207	904-398-3353
Crawdaddy's (Cajun)	1643 Prudential Dr.	Jacksonville	FL	32207	904-396-3546
De Real Ting Cafe (Jamaican)	45 W Monroe St	Jacksonville	FL	32212	904-633-9738
First Street Grille (Steak/Seafood)	807 N 1st St	Jacksonville Beach	FL	32256	904-246-6555
Island Grille (Seafood)	981 1st St	Jacksonville Beach	FL	32266	904-241-1881
Juliette's (American)	245 W Water St	Jacksonville	FL	32202	904-355-7118
La Cena Ristorante (Italian)	6271-7 St Augustine Rd	Jacksonville	FL	32217	904-737-5350
Longhorn Steaks (Steak)	6015 Argyle Forest Blvd	Jacksonville	FL	32244	904-777-4377
Manatee Ray's (Seafood)	314 1st St N	Jacksonville Beach	FL	32250	904-241-3138
Marker 32 (New American)	14549 Beach Blvd.	Jacksonville Beach	FL	32250	904-223-1534
Max's Place (Mediterranean)	401 Atlantic Blvd	Atlantic Beach	FL	32233	904-247-4422
Mill Brewery (American)	2 Independent Dr Jacksonville Landing	Jacksonville	FL	32202	904-353-3538
Pagoda (Chinese)	8617 Baymeadows Rd	Jacksonville	FL	32256	904-731-0880
Partners (American)	3585 St Johns Ave	Jacksonville	FL	32205	904-387-3585
Ragtime Tavern Seafood & Grill (Seafood)	207 Fort Lauderdale Beach Blvd	Atlantic Beach	FL	32233	904-241-7877
River City Brewing Co (Steak/Seafood)	835 Museum Cir	Jacksonville	FL	32207	904-398-2299
Sebastians (Italian)	10601 San Jose Blvd	Jacksonville	FL	32257	904-268-4458
Sterling Cafe (Continental)	3551 St Johns Ave	Jacksonville	FL	32205	904-387-0700
Wine Cellar (Continental)	1314 Prudential Dr	Jacksonville	FL	32207	904-398-8989

— Goods and Services —

SHOPPING

Name	Address	City	State	ZIP	Phone	Fax
Avenues The	10300 Southside Blvd	Jacksonville	FL	32256	904-363-3054	363-3058
Jacksonville Landing	2 Independent Dr	Jacksonville	FL	32202	904-353-1188	353-1558
Jacobson's	9911 Old Baymeadows Rd.	Jacksonville	FL	32256	904-642-5000	642-7640
Orange Park Mall	1910 Wells Rd	Orange Park	FL	32073	904-269-2422	269-9440
Regency Square Mall	9501 Arlington Expy Suite 100	Jacksonville	FL	32225	904-725-1220	724-7109
Saint Augustine Outlet Center	2700 SR 16	Saint Augustine	FL	32092	904-825-1555	825-0474
Worth Antiques Gallery	1316 Beach Blvd.	Jacksonville	FL	32250	904-249-6000	241-3547

BANKS

Name	Address	City	State	ZIP	Phone	Fax
AmSouth Bank	51 W Bay St.	Jacksonville	FL	32202	904-281-2640	281-2649
Compass Bank	3740 Beach Blvd. **Fax:* Cust Svc	Jacksonville	FL	32207	904-564-8000	564-8050*
First Union-Florida	225 Water St **Fax:* Hum Res	Jacksonville	FL	32202	904-361-3020	361-5888*
NationsBank	50 N Laura St *TF:* 800-299-2265	Jacksonville	FL	32202	904-791-5808	791-7433
SouthTrust Bank of Northeast Florida NA	1301 Riverplace Blvd. **Fax:* Cust Svc	Jacksonville	FL	32207	904-798-6300	798-6858*

BUSINESS SERVICES

	Phone		Phone
Federal Express	800-238-5355	**Modis Professional Services Inc.**	904-360-2000
GDS Worldwide	904-448-1993	**Olsten Staffing Services**	904-737-2400
Kelly Services	904-399-0883	**Post Office**	904-359-2711
Kinko's	904-642-3085	**Reliable Express Service**	904-396-5588
Metro Parcel	904-924-0123	**UPS**	800-742-5877

— Media —

PUBLICATIONS

Name	Address	City	State	ZIP	Phone	Fax
Florida Times-Union‡	PO Box 1949 *TF:* 800-472-6397 ■ *Web:* www.times-union.com	Jacksonville	FL	32231	904-359-4111	359-4478
Jacksonville Business Journal	1200 River Pl Blvd Suite 201 *Web:* www.amcity.com/jacksonville ■ *E-mail:* jacksonville@amcity.com	Jacksonville	FL	32207	904-396-3502	396-5706
Jacksonville Magazine	1032 Hendricks Ave *TF Circ:* 800-962-0214*	Jacksonville	FL	32207	904-396-8666	396-0926

‡*Daily newspapers*

TELEVISION

Name	Address	City	State	ZIP	Phone	Fax
WAWS-TV Ch 30 (Fox)	11700 Central Pkwy	Jacksonville	FL	32224	904-642-3030	646-0115
WJCT-TV Ch 7 (PBS)	100 Festival Park Ave	Jacksonville	FL	32202	904-353-7770	354-6846
WJWB-TV Ch 17 (WB)	9117 Hogan Rd	Jacksonville	FL	32216	904-641-1700	641-0306
WJXT-TV Ch 4 (CBS)	4 Broadcast Pl *Web:* www.wjxt.com ■ *E-mail:* news@wjxt.com	Jacksonville	FL	32247	904-399-4000	393-9822
WJXX-TV Ch 25 (ABC)	PO Box 551000 **Fax:* News Rm ■ *Web:* www.wjxx.com/new ■ *E-mail:* info@wjxx.com	Jacksonville	FL	32255	904-332-2525	332-2418*
WTEV-TV Ch 47 (UPN)	11700 Central Pkwy	Jacksonville	FL	32224	904-646-4747	646-0115
WTLV-TV Ch 12 (NBC)	1070 E Adams St.	Jacksonville	FL	32202	904-354-1212	633-8899

RADIO

Name	Address	City	State	ZIP	Phone	Fax
WAPE-FM 95.1 MHz (CHR)	9090 Hogan Rd *Web:* www.wape951.com ■ *E-mail:* thebigape@wape951.com	Jacksonville	FL	32216	904-725-9273	641-3297
WBWL-AM 600 kHz (Sports)	6869 Lenox Ave *Web:* www.wbwl.com	Jacksonville	FL	32205	904-783-3711	786-1529
WCGL-AM 1360 kHz (Rel)	6050-6 Moncries Rd	Jacksonville	FL	32209	904-766-9955	765-9214
WEJZ-FM 96.1 MHz (AC)	1896 Corporate Square Blvd.	Jacksonville	FL	32216	904-727-9696	721-9322
WFYV-FM 104.5 MHz (Rock)	9090 Hogan Rd *Web:* www.wfyv105.com/ ■ *E-mail:* wfyv105@cybermax.net	Jacksonville	FL	32216	904-642-1055	641-3297
WJAX-AM 1220 kHz (Nost)	5353 Arlington Expy	Jacksonville	FL	32211	904-743-2400	
WJBT-FM 92.7 MHz (Urban)	10592 E Balmoral Cir Suite 1	Jacksonville	FL	32218	904-696-1015	714-4487
WJCT-FM 89.9 MHz (NPR)	100 Festival Pk Ave. *Web:* www.wjct.org/Stereo90 ■ *E-mail:* wjct@wjct.org	Jacksonville	FL	32202	904-353-7770	358-6352
WJGR-AM 1320 kHz (N/T)	5555 Radio Ln	Jacksonville	FL	32205	904-388-7711	384-0859
WKQL-FM 96.9 MHz (Oldies)	6869 Lenox Ave *Web:* www.wkql969.com ■ *E-mail:* coolfm@wkql969.com	Jacksonville	FL	32205	904-783-3711	786-1529
WKTZ-FM 90.9 MHz (B/EZ)	5353 Arlington Expy	Jacksonville	FL	32211	904-743-2400	
WMXQ-FM 103 MHz (AC)	6869 Lenox Ave	Jacksonville	FL	32205	904-783-3711	786-1529
WNZS-AM 930 kHz (Sports)	8386 Baymeadows Rd Suite 107	Jacksonville	FL	32256	904-636-0507	636-7971
WOKV-AM 690 kHz (N/T)	6869 Lenox Ave *Web:* www.wokv.com	Jacksonville	FL	32205	904-783-3711	786-1529
WPLA-FM 93.3 MHz (Alt)	8386 Baymeadows Rd Suite 107 *Web:* www.planet93.com ■ *E-mail:* planet@planet93.com	Jacksonville	FL	32256	904-636-0507	730-5040
WQIK-FM 99.1 MHz (Ctry)	5555 Radio Ln *Web:* www.wqik.com	Jacksonville	FL	32205	904-388-7711	384-0859
WROO-FM 107.3 MHz (Ctry)	8386 Baymeadows Rd Suite 107	Jacksonville	FL	32256	904-636-0507	636-0522
WSOL-FM 101.5 MHz (AC)	10592 Balmoral Cir E Suite 1	Jacksonville	FL	32218	904-696-1015	696-1011
WSVE-AM 1280 kHz (Rel)	4343 Spring Grove	Jacksonville	FL	32209	904-768-1211	768-5115
WVOJ-AM 970 kHz (N/T)	2427 University Blvd N	Jacksonville	FL	32211	904-743-6970	745-0331
WZAZ-AM 1400 kHz (Rel)	10592 Balmoral Cir E Suite 1	Jacksonville	FL	32218	904-696-1015	696-1011

— Colleges/Universities —

Name	Address	City	State	ZIP	Phone	Fax
Edward Waters College	1658 Kings Rd. *Web:* www.ewc.edu	Jacksonville	FL	32209	904-366-6576	366-2760
Florida Community College at Jacksonville Downtown Campus	101 W State St *Web:* www.fccj.cc.fl.us	Jacksonville	FL	32202	904-633-8100	633-8105
ITT Technical Institute	6600 Youngerman Cir Suite 10. *TF:* 800-318-1264 ■ *Web:* www.itt-tech.edu	Jacksonville	FL	32244	904-573-9100	573-0512
Jacksonville University	2800 University Blvd N *TF Admissions:* 800-225-2027 ■ *Web:* junix.ju.edu ■ *E-mail:* admissions@junix.ju.edu	Jacksonville	FL	32211	904-744-3950	745-7012
Jones College	5353 Arlington Expy. *TF:* 800-331-0176 ■ *Web:* www.jones.edu	Jacksonville	FL	32211	904-743-1122	743-4446

Jacksonville — Colleges/Universities (Cont'd)

Name / Address	City	State	Zip	Phone	Fax
University of North Florida 4567 St Johns Bluff Rd S *Web:* www.unf.edu ■ *E-mail:* osprey@unf.edu	Jacksonville	FL	32224	904-620-1000	620-2414

— Hospitals —

Name / Address	City	State	Zip	Phone	Fax
Baptist Medical Center 800 Prudential Dr *Web:* www.baptist-stvincents.com/Hospitals/bmc.htm	Jacksonville	FL	32207	904-393-2000	202-1528
Columbia Memorial Hospital Jacksonville 3625 University Blvd S	Jacksonville	FL	32216	904-399-6111	399-6849
Columbia Orange Park Medical Center 2001 Kingsley Ave	Orange Park	FL	32073	904-276-8500	276-8610
Flagler Hospital 400 Health Park Blvd	Saint Augustine	FL	32086	904-829-5155	825-4472
Saint Luke's Hospital 4201 Belfort Rd.	Jacksonville	FL	32216	904-296-3700	296-4698
Saint Vincent's Medical Center 1800 Barrs St. *Web:* www.baptist-stvincents.com/Hospitals/stvin.htm	Jacksonville	FL	32204	904-308-7300	308-7326
Shands Jacksonville 580 W 8th St.	Jacksonville	FL	32209	904-798-8000	366-7044
University Medical Center 655 W 8th St.	Jacksonville	FL	32209	904-549-5000	549-4027

— Attractions —

Name / Address	City	State	Zip	Phone	Fax
Adventure Landing 1944 Beach Blvd *Web:* www.adventurelanding.com	Jacksonville	FL	32250	904-246-4386	249-1018
Alexander Brest Museum 2800 University Blvd N Jacksonville University	Jacksonville	FL	32211	904-744-3950	
Amelia Island Museum of History 233 S 3rd St *E-mail:* aimh@net-magic.net	Fernandina Beach	FL	32034	904-261-7378	261-9701
Anheuser-Busch Brewery 111 Busch Dr	Jacksonville	FL	32218	904-751-8118	751-8095
Castillo De San Marcos National Monument 1 S Castillo Dr *Web:* www.nps.gov/casa	Saint Augustine	FL	32084	904-829-6506	823-9388
Cumberland Island National Seashore PO Box 806 *Web:* www.nps.gov/cuis/	Saint Marys	GA	31558	912-882-4336	882-6284
Cummer Museum of Art & Gardens 829 Riverside Ave *Web:* www.cummer.org	Jacksonville	FL	32204	904-356-6857	353-4101
Florida Ballet 128 E Forsyth St Florida Theatre of Performing Arts	Jacksonville	FL	32202	904-353-7518	
Florida National Pavilion & Metropolitan Park 1410 Gator Bowl Blvd	Jacksonville	FL	32202	904-630-0837	630-0538
Florida Theatre of Performing Arts 128 E Forsyth St Suite 300 *E-mail:* StillCool@70.fl-theatre-jax.com	Jacksonville	FL	32202	904-355-5661	358-1874
Fort Caroline National Memorial 12713 Fort Caroline Rd *Web:* www.nps.gov/foca/	Jacksonville	FL	32225	904-641-7155	641-3798
Fort Clinch State Park 2601 Atlantic Ave	Fernandina Beach	FL	32034	904-277-7274	277-7225
Fort Matanzas National Monument 8635 A1A S *Web:* www.nps.gov/foma	Saint Augustine	FL	32086	904-471-0116	471-7605
Hanna Kathryn Abbey Park 500 Wonderwood Dr	Jacksonville	FL	32233	904-249-4700	247-8688
Huguenot Memorial Park 10980 Heckscher Dr	Jacksonville	FL	32226	904-251-3335	251-3019
Jacksonville Beach Fishing Pier 3 6th Ave S	Jacksonville Beach	FL	32250	904-246-6001	
Jacksonville Landing 2 Independent Dr	Jacksonville	FL	32202	904-353-1188	353-1558
Jacksonville Maritime Museum 1015 Museum Cir Unit 2 *Web:* www.jaxmarmus.com	Jacksonville	FL	32207	904-398-9011	398-7248
Jacksonville Symphony Orchestra 300 W Water St Suite 200 *Web:* www.jaxsymphony.org	Jacksonville	FL	32202	904-354-5479	354-9238
Jacksonville Zoo 8605 Zoo Pkwy *Web:* www.jaxzoo.org	Jacksonville	FL	32218	904-757-4463	757-4315
Karpeles Manuscript Library Museum 101 W 1st St *Web:* www.rain.org/~karpeles/jax.html	Jacksonville	FL	32206	904-356-2992	356-4338
Kingsley Plantation 11676 Palmetto Ave *Web:* www.cr.nps.gov/nr/21.htm	Jacksonville	FL	32226	904-251-3537	251-3577
Little Talbot Island State Park 12157 Heckscher Dr	Fort George	FL	32226	904-251-2320	
Museum of Science & History of Jacksonville 1025 Museum Cir	Jacksonville	FL	32207	904-396-7062	396-5799
Museum of Southern History 4304 Herschel St	Jacksonville	FL	32210	904-388-3574	
Okefenokee National Wildlife Refuge Rt 2 Box 3330	Folkston	GA	31537	912-496-7836	496-3332
Olustee Battlefield State Historic Site Hwy 90	Olustee	FL	32072	904-397-4331	
Pablo Historical Park 425 Beach Blvd.	Jacksonville Beach	FL	32250	904-246-0093	246-8641
Pope Duval Park 13500 W Beaver St	Jacksonville	FL	32209	904-630-3500	
Riverwalk 1000 Art Museum Dr	Jacksonville	FL	32202	904-632-5578	630-0538
Roosevelt Theodore Area 13165 Mount Pleasant Rd	Jacksonville	FL	32225	904-641-7155	221-5248
Talbot Islands Geopark 12157 Heckscher Dr	Jacksonville	FL	32226	904-251-2320	251-2325
Timucuan Ecological & Historic Preserve 12713 Fort Caroline Rd Fort Caroline National Memorial *Web:* www.nps.gov/timu/	Jacksonville	FL	32225	904-641-7155	641-3798
Tree Hill-Jacksonville's Nature Center 7152 Lone Star Rd	Jacksonville	FL	32211	904-724-4646	724-9132
World Golf Hall of Fame 21 World Golf Pl. *TF:* 800-948-4746 ■ *Web:* www.wgv.com	Saint Augustine	FL	32092	904-940-4000	940-4393

SPORTS TEAMS & FACILITIES

Name / Address	City	State	Zip	Phone	Fax
Alltel Stadium 1 Alltel Stadium Pl *TF:* 800-618-8005 ■ *Web:* www.jaxevents.com/alltel.html ■ *E-mail:* tcharde@ccse.net	Jacksonville	FL	32202	904-633-6000	633-6050
Greyhound Racing 1440 N McDuff Ave *Web:* www.jaxkennel.com/	Jacksonville	FL	32205	904-646-0001	646-0420
Jacksonville Cyclones (soccer) 1201 E Duval St Samuel Wolfson Pk. *Web:* www.cyclonesoccer.com ■ *E-mail:* cyclones@cyclonesoccer.com	Jacksonville	FL	32202	904-278-9232	278-9556
Jacksonville Jade (soccer) 14286-19 Beach Blvd Suite 368 *E-mail:* jacksonvillejade@socceramerica.net	Jacksonville	FL	32250	904-221-6119	221-4674
Jacksonville Jaguars 1 Alltel Stadium Pl Alltel Stadium *Web:* www.jaguarsnfl.com	Jacksonville	FL	32202	904-633-2000	633-6338
Jacksonville Lizard Kings (hockey) 1145 E Adams St Veterans Memorial Coliseum *Web:* www.lizardkings.com/ ■ *E-mail:* lizard@lizardkings.com	Jacksonville	FL	32201	904-358-7825	358-9999
Jacksonville Veterans Memorial Coliseum 1145 E Adams St	Jacksonville	FL	32202	904-630-3905	630-3913

— Events —

	Phone
American Music Festival (late May)	904-354-5479
Caribbean Carnival (early November)	904-798-9111
Gate River Run (early March)	904-739-1917
Gator Bowl (early January)	904-798-9111
Greater Jacksonville Agricultural Fair (mid-late October)	904-353-0535
Greater Jacksonville Kingfish Tournament (mid-July)	904-798-9111
Historic Homes & Gardens Tour (late April)	904-389-2449
Jacksonville Boat-A-Rama (early February)	904-724-3003
Jacksonville Downtown Countdown (December 31)	904-630-3520
Jacksonville Jazz Festival (mid-November)	904-353-7770
Jacksonville Light Parade (late November)	904-798-9111
Jacksonville Pro Rodeo (July)	904-630-3900
Jacksonville Scottish Highland Games (late February)	904-641-1119
Jacksonville Spring Fair (late March-early April)	904-358-6336
Jacksonville Wine Experience (mid-February)	904-358-6336
July Fourth Celebration (July 4)	904-630-3520
King Neptune Seafood Festival (mid-April)	904-249-3972
Kuumba Festival (late May)	904-353-2270
Mayport/Fort George Seafood Festival (mid-March)	904-249-9336
Mug Race (early May)	904-264-4094
Riverside Arts & Music Festival (early September)	904-389-2449
Springing the Blues Festival (early April)	904-249-3972
Tournament Player's Championship (late March)	904-285-7888
World of Nations (early May)	904-630-0837

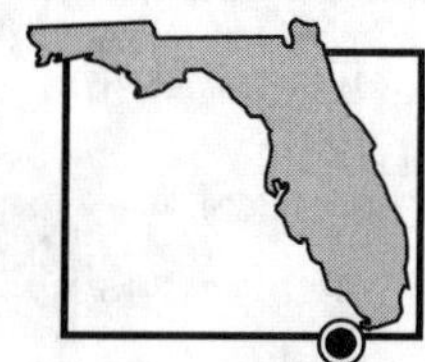

Key West

The southernmost city in the United States, Key West is only four miles long and two miles wide, with the Atlantic Ocean on one side and the Gulf of Mexico on the other. The island is composed mostly of coral rock and, at its southernmost point, is just 90 miles from Cuba ' in fact, it's actually closer to Havana than it is to Miami. America's only living coral reef is located off the shore of Key West, and diving and snorkeling trips on the reef are available. The heart of the city is Old Town, an area of restaurants, shops, art galleries, and historic homes and museums, including the Little White House Museum, which was President Harry Truman's tropical hideaway; the Key West Shipwreck Museum; the Key West Lighthouse Museum; and the Ernest Hemingway Home & Museum. Hemingway lived in Key West from 1931-1940 and produced some of his most famous works there, including A Farewell to Arms and For Whom the Bell Tolls. (Tennessee Williams, Truman Capote, and other famous authors also had homes in Key West, and today the city claims to have more active writers, artists, musicians, artisans per square mile than any other city in the world.) Each evening a crowd gathers at Mallory Square in Old Town to watch the street performers and the famous Key West sunset. Among the special events held in Key West each year is Fantasy Fest, billed as the state's biggest Halloween party.

Population 25,701
Area (Land) . . . . 5.5 sq mi
Area (Water) . . . . 1.4 sq mi
Elevation . . . . 8 ft
Latitude . . . . 24-33-22 N
Longitude . . . . 81-45-34 W
County . . . . Monroe
Time Zone . . . . EST
Area Code/s 305

— Average Temperatures and Precipitation —

TEMPERATURES

	Jan	Feb	Mar	Apr	May	Jun	Jul	Aug	Sep	Oct	Nov	Dec
High	75	75	79	82	85	88	89	89	88	84	80	76
Low	65	66	69	72	76	79	80	79	79	76	71	67

PRECIPITATION

	Jan	Feb	Mar	Apr	May	Jun	Jul	Aug	Sep	Oct	Nov	Dec
Inches	2.0	1.8	1.7	1.8	3.5	5.1	3.6	5.0	5.9	4.4	2.9	2.0

— Important Phone Numbers —

	Phone
Emergency	911
Medical Referral	305-292-3627
Poison Control Center	800-282-3171
Time/Temp	305-292-5000
Weather	305-292-5000

— Information Sources —

				Phone	*Fax*
Consumer Protection Agency 407 S Calhoun St 2nd Fl Mayo Bldg	Tallahassee	FL	32399	850-488-2221	487-4177
Key West Chamber of Commerce 402 Wall St *Web:* www.fla-keys.com/keywest/chambers/kwchamb.htm	Key West	FL	33040	305-294-2587	294-7806
Key West City Hall 525 Angela St. *Web:* www.keywestcity.com ■ *E-mail:* kwcmismgr@aol.com	Key West	FL	33040	305-292-8200	292-8133
Key West Information Center 1601 N Roosevelt Blvd *TF:* 888-222-5090 ■ *Web:* www.keywestinfo.com ■ *E-mail:* reservations@keywestinfo.com	Key West	FL	33040	305-292-5000	295-0900
Key West Mayor PO Box 1409 *E-mail:* kwccomm@aol.com	Key West	FL	33041	305-292-8102	293-6425
Key West Welcome Center 3840 N Roosevelt Blvd *TF:* 800-284-4482 ■ *Web:* www.keywestwelcomecenter.com	Key West	FL	33040	305-296-4444	292-8981
Monroe County PO Box 1980 *Web:* www.state.fl.us/monroe	Key West	FL	33041	305-294-4641	295-3660
Monroe County Public Library System 700 Fleming St	Key West	FL	33040	305-292-3595	295-3626
Monroe County Tourist Development Council 1201 White St Suite 102 *TF:* 800-352-5397 ■ *Web:* www.fla-keys.com	Key West	FL	33040	305-296-1552	296-0788

On-Line Resources

4KeyWest.com www.4keywest.com/
Best of the Florida Keys . . . . www.thefloridakeys.com
Best of the Islands Guide . . . . www.key-west-florida.com
City Knowledge Key West . . . . www.cityknowledge.com/fl_keywest.htm
Come to the Sun Guide to South Florida . . . . www.cometothesun.com
DiningGuide Florida Keys . . . . diningguide.net/eyw/
Discover Key West . . . . key-west.com/
Excite.com Key West City Guide . . . . www.excite.com/travel/countries/united_states/florida/key_west/
Florida Keys On-line . . . . www.flakeysol.com
Florida Keys Travel Guide . . . . fla-keys.com
HotelGuide Florida Keys . . . . hotelguide.net/eyw/
Insiders' Guide to the Florida Keys & Key West . . . . insiders.com/florida-keys/index.htm
Key West Gay & Lesbian Guide . . . . www.southfloridafun.com/keywest/index.shtml
Key West Information Center . . . . www.keywestinfo.com
Key West Paradise . . . . www.keywestparadise.com
NITC Travelbase City Guide Key West . . . . www.travelbase.com/features/key_west-fl.html
Online City Guide to Key West . . . . www.olcg.com/fl/keywest/index.html
Surf & Sun Beach Vacation Guide to Key West . . . . www.surf-sun.com/fl-key-west-main.htm

— Transportation Services —

AIRPORTS

■ **Key West International Airport (EYW)** *Phone*

2 miles E of downtown (approx 8 minutes) 305-296-5439

Airport Transportation

	Phone
Florida Keys Taxi Dispatch $10-11 fare to downtown	305-296-6666
Friendly Cab Co $11-12 fare to downtown	305-292-0000
Maxi Taxi/Yellow Cab $9 fare to downtown	305-296-1800

Commercial Airlines

	Phone
American	800-433-7300
Cape Air	800-352-0714
Comair	800-354-9822
Continental	800-992-8532
US Airways	800-428-4322

CAR RENTALS

	Phone
Alamo	305-294-6675
Avis	305-296-8744
Budget	305-294-8868
Dollar	305-296-9921
Enterprise	305-292-0220
Hertz	305-294-1039
Tropical	305-294-8136

LIMO/TAXI

	Phone
Florida Keys Taxi Dispatch	305-296-6666
Friendly Cab Co	305-292-0000
Maxi Taxi/Yellow Cab	305-296-1800

MASS TRANSIT

	Phone
Key West Dept of Transportation $.75 Base fare	305-292-8160

RAIL/BUS

				Phone
Greyhound Bus Station 3535 S Roosevelt Blvd Key West International Airport *TF:* 800-231-2222	Key West	FL	33040	305-296-9072

Key West (Cont'd)

— Accommodations —

HOTEL RESERVATION SERVICES

	Phone	Fax
AA Accomodation Center Inc	800-732-2006	
Accommodation Finder	305-292-2688	292-8586
TF: 888-453-9937 ■ *Web:* www.keystravel.com		
Accommodations USA	407-931-0003	931-1003
All Keys Reservation Service	305-296-0048	296-7951
TF: 800-255-5397		
Hotel Reservations Network Inc	214-361-7311	361-7299
TF Sales: 800-964-6835 ■ *Web:* www.hoteldiscount.com		
Key West Key	305-294-4357	294-2974
TF: 800-881-7321 ■ *Web:* www.keywestkey.com		
Mystery Isle Reservations	800-985-9916	295-9871*
**Fax Area Code:* 305		
Room Finders USA	504-522-9373	529-1948
TF: 800-473-7829 ■ *Web:* www.roomsusa.com ■ *E-mail:* welcome@roomsusa.com		
USA Hotels	252-331-1555	331-2021
TF: 800-872-4683 ■ *Web:* www.1800usahotels.com ■ *E-mail:* info@1800usahotels.com		

HOTELS, MOTELS, RESORTS

				Phone	Fax
Alexander Palms Court 715 South St	Key West	FL	33040	305-296-6413	292-3975
TF: 800-858-1943 ■ *Web:* www.alexanderpalms.com					
Alexander's Guesthouse 1118 Fleming St	Key West	FL	33040	305-294-9919	295-0357
TF: 800-654-9919 ■ *Web:* www.alexghouse.com/					
Ambrosia House Tropical Lodging 615 Fleming St	Key West	FL	33040	305-296-9838	294-2463
TF: 800-535-9838 ■ *Web:* www.keywest.com/ambrosia.html ■ *E-mail:* ambrosia@bellsouth.net					
Angelina Guest House 302 Angela St	Key West	FL	33040	305-294-4480	294-0621
Artist House 534 Eaton St	Key West	FL	33040	305-296-3977	296-3210
TF: 800-582-7882 ■ *Web:* www.artisthousekeywest.com ■ *E-mail:* artisthse@aol.com					
Atlantic Shores Resort 510 South St	Key West	FL	33040	305-296-2491	294-2753
TF: 800-526-3559 ■ *Web:* www.atlanticshoresresort.com ■ *E-mail:* info@atlanticshoresresort.com					
Authors of Key West 725 White St	Key West	FL	33040	305-294-7381	294-0920
TF: 800-898-6909 ■ *Web:* authors-keywest.com ■ *E-mail:* authorskw@aol.com					
Banana Bay Resort 2319 N Roosevelt Blvd	Key West	FL	33040	305-296-6925	296-2004
TF: 800-226-2621 ■ *Web:* www.bananabay.com ■ *E-mail:* info@bananabay.com					
Banyan Resort 323 Whitehead St	Key West	FL	33040	305-296-7786	294-1107
TF: 800-853-9937 ■ *Web:* www.banyanresort.com					
Best Western Hibiscus Motel 1313 Simonton St	Key West	FL	33040	305-294-3763	293-9243
TF: 800-972-5100					
Best Western Key Ambassador Resort Inn 3755 S Roosevelt Blvd	Key West	FL	33040	305-296-3500	296-9961
TF: 800-432-4315					
Big Ruby's Guesthouse 409 Applerouth Ln	Key West	FL	33040	305-296-2323	296-0281
TF: 800-477-7829 ■ *Web:* www.bigrubys.com/guesthouseinfo.htm ■ *E-mail:* keywest@bigrubys.com					
Blue Marlin Motel 1320 Simonton St	Key West	FL	33040	305-294-2585	296-1209
TF: 800-523-1698					
Blue Parrot Inn 916 Elizabeth St	Key West	FL	33040	305-296-0033	296-5697
Web: www.blueparrotinn.com					
Brass Key Guesthouse 412 Frances St	Key West	FL	33040	305-296-4719	296-1994
TF: 800-932-9119 ■ *Web:* www.brasskey.com/ ■ *E-mail:* keywest@brasskey.com					
Casa Key West Motel 811 Washington St	Key West	FL	33040	305-296-1141	293-0667
TF: 800-248-3033 ■ *Web:* www.casakeywest.com ■ *E-mail:* casakey@aol.com					
Center Court Historic Inn 916 Center St	Key West	FL	33040	305-296-9292	294-4104
TF: 800-797-8787 ■ *Web:* www.centercourtkw.com ■ *E-mail:* kwinn@conch.net					
Cheeca Lodge PO Box 527	Islamorada	FL	33036	305-664-4651	664-5427
TF: 800-327-2893 ■ *Web:* www.cheeca.com ■ *E-mail:* info@cheeca.com					
Chelsea House 707 Truman Ave	Key West	FL	33040	305-296-2211	296-4822
TF: 800-845-8859 ■ *Web:* www.chelseahousekw.com					
Conch House Heritage Inn 625 Truman Ave	Key West	FL	33040	305-293-0020	293-8447
TF: 800-207-5806 ■ *Web:* www.conchhouse.com					
Curry Mansion 511 Caroline St	Key West	FL	33040	305-294-5349	294-4093
TF: 800-253-3466 ■ *Web:* www.currymansion.com					
Cypress House Historic Inn 601 Caroline St	Key West	FL	33040	305-294-6969	296-1174
TF: 800-525-2488 ■ *Web:* www.cypresshousekw.com ■ *E-mail:* cypresskw@aol.com					
Days Inn Key West 3852 N Roosevelt Blvd	Key West	FL	33040	305-294-3742	296-7260
TF: 800-224-5051					
Dewey House 504 South St	Key West	FL	33040	305-296-5611	296-5611
TF: 800-354-4455 ■ *Web:* www.oldtownresorts.com/lamerdewey.htm					
Disney's Yacht & Beach Club 1700 Epcot Resort Blvd	Lake Buena Vista	FL	32830	407-828-3074	934-3450
Web: disney.go.com/DisneyWorld/Resorts/Res611.html					
Douglas House 419 Amelia St	Key West	FL	33040	305-294-5269	292-7665
TF: 800-833-0372 ■ *Web:* www.douglashouse.com ■ *E-mail:* info@douglashouse.com					
Eaton Lodge 511 Eaton St	Key West	FL	33040	305-292-2170	292-4018
TF: 800-294-2170 ■ *Web:* www.eatonlodge.com					
Econo Lodge Key West 3820 N Roosevelt Blvd	Key West	FL	33040	305-294-5511	296-1939
TF: 800-766-7584 ■ *Web:* www.thefloridakeys.com/econolodge					
Eden House 1015 Fleming St	Key West	FL	33040	305-296-6868	294-1221
TF: 800-533-5397 ■ *Web:* www.edenhouse.com					
Fairfield Inn by Marriott 2400 N Roosevelt Blvd	Key West	FL	33040	305-296-5700	292-9840
TF: 800-228-2800					
Galleon Resort & Marina 617 Front St	Key West	FL	33040	305-296-7711	296-0821
TF: 800-544-3030 ■ *Web:* www.galleonresort.com ■ *E-mail:* galleon.res@aol.com					
Gardens Hotel 526 Angela St	Key West	FL	33040	305-294-2661	292-1007
TF: 800-526-2664 ■ *Web:* www.gardenshotel.com ■ *E-mail:* kwgard@travelbase.com					
Halfred Motel 512 Truman Ave	Key West	FL	33040	305-296-5415	
Hampton Inn 2801 N Roosevelt Blvd	Key West	FL	33040	305-294-2917	296-0221
TF: 800-426-7866					
Heron House 512 Simonton St Old Town	Key West	FL	33040	305-294-9227	294-5692
TF: 800-294-1644 ■ *Web:* www.heronhouse.com ■ *E-mail:* heronkw@aol.com					
Hilton Resort & Marina 245 Front St	Key West	FL	33040	305-294-4000	294-4086
TF: 800-621-2193 ■ *Web:* www.hilton.com/hotels/EYWKWHF					
Holiday Inn Beachside 3841 N Roosevelt Blvd	Key West	FL	33040	305-294-2571	296-5659
TF: 800-292-7706 ■ *Web:* www.basshotels.com/holiday-inn/?_franchisee=EYWFL ■ *E-mail:* db_wright@msn.com					
Holiday Inn La Concha Resort Hotel 430 Duval St	Key West	FL	33040	305-296-2991	294-3283
TF: 800-745-2191					
Holiday Isle Beach Resort & Marina 84001 Overseas Hwy	Islamorada	FL	33036	305-664-2321	664-2703
TF: 800-327-7070 ■ *Web:* www.theisle.com					
Hyatt Key West 601 Front St	Key West	FL	33040	305-296-9900	292-1038
TF: 800-554-9288					
Key Lime Inn 725 Truman Ave	Key West	FL	33040	305-294-5229	
TF: 800-594-4430 ■ *Web:* www.keylimeinn.com					
La Mer Hotel 506 South St	Key West	FL	33040	305-296-5611	294-2108
TF: 800-354-4455 ■ *Web:* www.oldtownresorts.com/lamerdewey.htm					
La Pensione Inn 809 Truman Ave	Key West	FL	33040	305-292-9923	296-6509
TF: 800-893-1193 ■ *Web:* www.lapensione.com ■ *E-mail:* info@lapensione.com					
Lightbourn Inn 907 Truman Ave	Key West	FL	33040	305-296-5152	294-9490
TF: 800-352-6011					
Marquesa Hotel 600 Fleming St	Key West	FL	33040	305-292-1919	294-2121
TF: 800-869-4631 ■ *Web:* www.marquesa.com					
Marriott Casa Marina Resort 1500 Reynolds St	Key West	FL	33040	305-296-3535	296-4633
TF: 800-228-9290					
Marriott's Reach Resort 1435 Simonton St	Key West	FL	33040	305-296-5000	296-2830
TF: 800-874-4118					
Mermaid & The Alligator 729 Truman Ave	Key West	FL	33040	305-294-1894	295-9925
TF: 800-773-1894 ■ *Web:* www.kwmermaid.com					
Ocean Key A Noble House Resort Zero Duval St	Key West	FL	33040	305-296-7701	292-7685
TF: 800-328-9815 ■ *Web:* www.oceankeyhouse.com ■ *E-mail:* info@oceankeyhouse.com					
Paradise Inn 819 Simonton St	Key West	FL	33040	305-293-8007	293-0807
TF: 800-888-9648 ■ *Web:* www.theparadiseinn.com					
Pegasus International Hotel 501 Southard St	Key West	FL	33040	305-294-9323	294-4741
TF: 800-397-8148					
Pelican Landing Condominum Resort & Marina 915 Eisenhower Dr	Key West	FL	33040	305-293-9730	292-2997
Pier House Resort 1 Duval St	Key West	FL	33040	305-296-4600	296-7568
TF: 800-327-8340 ■ *Web:* www.pierhouse.com ■ *E-mail:* info@pierhouse.com					
Plantation Yacht Harbor Resort 87000 Overseas Hwy	Islamorada	FL	33036	305-852-2381	853-5357
TF: 800-356-3215 ■ *Web:* www.pyh.com ■ *E-mail:* fun@pyh.com					
Quality Inn Resort 3850 N Roosevelt Blvd	Key West	FL	33040	305-294-6681	294-5618
TF: 800-533-5024					
Ramada Inn Key West 3420 N Roosevelt Blvd	Key West	FL	33040	305-294-5541	294-7932
TF: 800-330-5541					

Key West — Hotels, Motels, Resorts (Cont'd)

Name / Address	City	State	ZIP	Phone	Fax
Santa Maria Motel 1401 Simonton St	Key West	FL	33040	305-296-5678	294-0010
TF: 800-821-5397					
Sheraton Key West 2001 S Roosevelt Blvd	Key West	FL	33040	305-292-9800	294-6009
TF: 800-452-3224 ■ *Web:* www.sheraton.com/cgi/t3.cgi/property.taf?prop=760					
Simonton Court Historic Inn & Cottages 320 Simonton St.	Key West	FL	33040	305-294-6386	293-8446
TF: 800-944-2687 ■ *Web:* www.simontoncourt.com					
South Beach Motel 508 South St	Key West	FL	33040	305-296-5611	294-2108
TF: 800-354-4455					
Southernmost Motel 1319 Duval St.	Key West	FL	33040	305-296-6577	294-8272
TF: 800-354-4455					
Southernmost Point Guest House 1327 Duval St	Key West	FL	33040	305-294-0715	296-0641
Web: www.southernmostpoint.com ■ *E-mail:* info@southernmostpoint.com					
Tamarind Motel 625 South St	Key West	FL	33040	305-296-2829	292-3664
Travelers Palm 815 Catherine St	Key West	FL	33040	305-294-9560	293-9130
TF: 800-294-9560 ■ *Web:* www.travelerspalm.com					
Watson House 525 Simonton St	Key West	FL	33040	305-294-6712	294-7501
TF: 800-621-9405					
William Anthony House 613 Caroline St	Key West	FL	33040	305-294-2887	294-9209
TF: 800-613-2276 ■ *Web:* www.wmanthonyhse.com					

— Restaurants —

Name / Address	City	State	ZIP	Phone
Alexander's Cafe (Italian) 509 Southard St	Key West	FL	33040	305-294-5777
Antonia's (Italian) 615 Duval St	Key West	FL	33040	305-294-6565
Web: www.antoniaskeywest.com ■ *E-mail:* enquire@antoniaskeywest.com				
B's Restaurant (Cuban) 1500 Bertha St	Key West	FL	33040	305-296-3140
Bagatelle (Caribbean) 115 Duval St	Key West	FL	33040	305-296-6609
Banana Cafe (French) 1211 Duval St	Key West	FL	33040	305-294-7227
Web: www.islandtaste.com/french/banana-cafe/bananacafe-index.htm				
Blue Heaven (Caribbean) 729 Thomas St	Key West	FL	33040	305-296-8666
Cafe Bianco (Italian) 917 Duval St	Key West	FL	33040	305-296-7837
Cafe des Artistes (French) 1007 Simonton St	Key West	FL	33040	305-294-7100
Cafe Karumba (Caribbean) 1215 Duval St	Key West	FL	33040	305-296-2644
Cafe Sole (French) 1029 Southard St	Key West	FL	33040	305-294-0230
Camille's (Continental) 703 1/2 Duval St	Key West	FL	33040	305-296-4811
Dim Sum (Pan-Asian) 613 Duval St	Key West	FL	33040	305-294-6230
Web: www.dimsum-fareast.com ■ *E-mail:* dimsum@islandtaste.com				
Duffy's Steak & Lobster House (Steak/Seafood) 1007 Simonton St	Key West	FL	33040	305-296-4900
Dynasty Chinese Restaurant (Chinese) 918 Duval St	Key West	FL	33040	305-294-2943
El Siboney (Cuban) 900 Catherine St	Key West	FL	33040	305-296-4184
Finnegan's Wake (Irish) 320 Grinnell St	Key West	FL	33040	305-293-0222
Flagler's Steakhouse & Lounge (Steak) 1500 Reynolds St Casa Maria Resort	Key West	FL	33040	305-296-3535
Gato Gordo Cafe (Tex Mex) 404 Southard St	Key West	FL	33040	305-294-0888
Harbor Lights Seafood & Raw Bar (Seafood) 711 Eisenhower Dr	Key West	FL	33040	305-294-2727
Hard Rock Cafe (American) 313 Duval St	Key West	FL	33040	305-293-0230
Harpoon Harry's (Homestyle) 832 Caroline St	Key West	FL	33040	305-294-8744
Hog's Breath Saloon (American) 400 Front St Suite C	Key West	FL	33040	305-296-4222
Web: hogsbreath.com				
Kelly's Caribbean Bar Grill & Brewery (Caribbean) 301 Whitehead St	Key West	FL	33040	305-293-8484
Web: www.kellyskeywest.com ■ *E-mail:* kellykeyw@aol.com				
Kyushu Japanese Restaurant (Japanese) 921 Truman Ave	Key West	FL	33040	305-294-2995
La Te Da Restaurant (Continental) 1125 Duval St	Key West	FL	33040	305-296-6706
La Trattoria (Italian) 524 Duval St	Key West	FL	33040	305-296-1075
Louie's Backyard (American) 700 Waddell Ave	Key West	FL	33040	305-294-1061
Web: members.aol.com/lbackyard				
Mangia Mangia (Italian) 900 Southard St	Key West	FL	33040	305-294-2469
Web: www.mangia-mangia.com				
Mangoes (American) 700 Duval St	Key West	FL	33040	305-292-4606
E-mail: mangoeskeywest@aol.com				
Margaritaville (American) 500 Duval St	Key West	FL	33040	305-292-1435
Web: margaritaville.com/				
Marquesa Cafe (New American) 600 Fleming St	Key West	FL	33040	305-292-1244
Web: www.marquesa.com/marquesa/cafe.html				
Martha's Steaks & Seafood (Steak/Seafood) 3591 S Roosevelt Blvd	Key West	FL	33040	305-294-3466
Martin's Cafe Restaurant (German/Irish) 416 Applerouth Ln	Key West	FL	33040	305-296-1183
Ocean Club (Seafood) 1435 Simonton St	Key West	FL	33040	305-296-5000
Pepe's Cafe (American) 806 Caroline St	Key West	FL	33040	305-294-7192
PT's Late Night Bar & Grill (American) 920 Caroline St	Key West	FL	33040	305-296-4245
Quay Restaurant & Lounge (Steak/Seafood) 12 Duval St	Key West	FL	33040	305-294-4446
Rooftop Cafe (American) 310 Front St	Key West	FL	33040	305-294-2042
Siam House (Thai) 829 Simonton St	Key West	FL	33040	305-292-0302
Sloppy Joe's (American) 201 Duval St	Key West	FL	33040	305-294-8585
Web: www.sloppyjoes.com				
Square One (American) 1075 Duval St Duval Square	Key West	FL	33040	305-296-4300
Thai Cuisine (Thai) 513 Greene St	Key West	FL	33040	305-294-9424
Yo Saké (Japanese) 722 Duval St	Key West	FL	33040	305-294-2288

— Goods and Services —

BANKS

Name / Address	City	State	ZIP	Phone	Fax
First National Bank of the Florida Keys 1075 Duval St Suites 7 & 8	Key West	FL	33040	305-294-4817	294-5644
First State Bank of the Florida Keys 1201 Simonton St.	Key West	FL	33040	305-296-8535	294-9203*
**Fax:* Acctg ■ *TF:* 800-451-6556					
First Union 422 Front St	Key West	FL	33040	305-292-6610	292-6628
NationsBank NA 3200 Flagler Ave	Key West	FL	33040	305-294-9593	296-5240
TIB Bank of the Keys 330 Whitehead St	Key West	FL	33040	305-294-6330	294-5982
TF: 800-451-0211					

BUSINESS SERVICES

Name	Phone	Name	Phone
Copy Spot	305-296-5521	**Mail Boxes Etc**	305-292-4177
Creative Services	305-292-0390	**Post Office**	305-294-2557
Federal Express	800-238-5355	**UPS**	800-742-5877
Girl Friday Temporary Services	305-296-9878		

— Media —

PUBLICATIONS

Name / Address	City	State	ZIP	Phone	Fax
Florida Keys Keynoter PO Box 500158	Marathon	FL	33050	305-743-5551	743-9586
Web: www.keynoter.com					
Key West Citizen‡ PO Box 1800	Key West	FL	33041	305-294-6641	294-0768
Web: keysnews.com					

‡Daily newspapers

TELEVISION

Name / Address	City	State	ZIP	Phone	Fax
WEYS-TV Ch 22 (CBS) 527 Southard St	Key West	FL	33040	305-296-4969	296-1669
WPBT-TV Ch 2 (PBS) 14901 NE 20th Ave	Miami	FL	33181	305-949-8321	949-9772
Web: www.channel2.org					
WPLG-TV Ch 10 (ABC) 3900 Biscayne Blvd	Miami	FL	33137	305-576-1010	325-2480
Web: www.wplg.com/					
WSVN-TV Ch 7 (Fox) 1401 79th St Cswy.	Miami	FL	33141	305-751-6692	757-2266
Web: www.wsvn.com ■ *E-mail:* 7news@wsvn.com					
WTVJ-TV Ch 6 (NBC) 316 N Miami Ave	Miami	FL	33128	305-379-4444	789-4202
Web: www.nbc6.nbc.com					
WWFD-TV Ch 8 (Ind) 16502 NW 52nd Ave	Miami	FL	33014	305-621-3688	621-5181

RADIO

Name / Address	City	State	ZIP	Phone	Fax
WAIL-FM 99.5 MHz (Rock) 5016 5th Ave	Key West	FL	33040	305-296-7511	296-0358
Web: www.keysradio.com/wail/wail.html ■ *E-mail:* info@keysradio.com					
WCNK-FM 98.7 MHz (NAC) 30336 Overseas Hwy	Big Pine Key	FL	33043	305-872-0474	872-8930
WEOW-FM 92.5 MHz (CHR) 5016 5th Ave.	Key West	FL	33040	305-294-2523	296-0358
WIIS-FM 107.1 MHz (AAA) 1075 Duval St Suite C17	Key West	FL	33040	305-292-1133	292-6936
WJIR-FM 90.9 MHz (Rel) 1209 United St	Key West	FL	33040	305-296-5773	294-9547
WKRY-FM 93.5 MHz (AC) 3820 N Roosevelt Blvd	Key West	FL	33040	305-296-2435	296-1155
Web: www.keysradio.com/wkry/wkry.html ■ *E-mail:* info@keysradio.com					
WKWF-AM 1600 kHz (Sports) 5016 5th Ave.	Key West	FL	33040	305-296-7511	296-0358
Web: www.keysradio.com/wkwf/wkwf.html ■ *E-mail:* info@keysradio.com					
WWUS-FM 104.7 MHz (CR) 30336 Overseas Hwy	Big Pine Key	FL	33043	305-872-9100	872-8930

Key West (Cont'd)

— Colleges/Universities —

				Phone	Fax
Florida Keys Community College 5901 W Junior College Rd	Key West	FL	33040	305-296-9081	292-5155
Web: www.firn.edu/webfiles/cc/fkcc/ ■ *E-mail:* alo_h@popmail.firn.edu					
Saint Leo College 718 Hornet St Bldg A	Key West	FL	33040	305-293-2847	296-7296

— Hospitals —

				Phone	Fax
Lower Florida Keys Health System 5900 College Rd	Key West	FL	33040	305-294-5531	294-8065

— Attractions —

				Phone	Fax
Audubon House & Tropical Garden 205 Whitehead St	Key West	FL	33040	305-294-2116	294-4513
Web: www.audubonhouse.com ■ *E-mail:* audubon@flakeysol.com					
Bahia Honda State Park 36850 Overseas Hwy	Big Pine Key	FL	33043	305-872-2353	
Web: www.dep.state.fl.us/parks/BahiaHonda/index.html					
Conch Tour Train 1805 Staples Ave Suite 101	Key West	FL	33040	305-294-5161	292-8993
TF: 800-868-7482 ■ *Web:* www.historictours.com/keywest/conchtrain.htm ■ *E-mail:* keyctt@historictours.com					
Curry Mansion 511 Caroline St	Key West	FL	33040	305-294-5349	294-4093
TF: 800-253-3466 ■ *Web:* www.currymansion.com					
Discovery Underseas Tours 251 Margaret St	Key West	FL	33040	305-293-0099	293-0199
TF: 800-262-0099 ■ *Web:* www.key-west.com/tours/discov.htm					
Dry Tortugas National Park Day Trip end of Elizabeth & Greene Sts	Key West	FL	33040	305-296-5556	292-2253
Web: www.sunnydayskeywest.com					
East Martello Museum & Gallery 3501 S Roosevelt Blvd	Key West	FL	33040	305-296-3913	296-6206
Ernest Hemingway Home & Museum 907 Whitehead St	Key West	FL	33040	305-294-1575	294-2755
Web: www.hemingwayhome.com ■ *E-mail:* info@hemingwayhome.com					
Fort Zachary Taylor State Historic Site PO Box 6560	Key West	FL	33041	305-292-6713	
Gallery on Greene 606 Greene St	Key West	FL	33040	305-294-1669	294-7747
Gingerbread Square Gallery 1207 Duval St	Key West	FL	33040	305-296-8900	293-0746
Harry Truman's Little White House Museum 111 Front St Truman Annex	Key West	FL	33040	305-294-9911	294-9988
Heritage House Museum & Robert Frost Cottage 410 Caroline St	Key West	FL	33040	305-296-3573	292-5723
Historic Hauntings Seance Theatre 429 Caroline St Historic Porter Mansion	Key West	FL	33040	305-292-2040	292-2050
Island Arts 1128 Duval St	Key West	FL	33040	305-292-9909	
Kennedy Gallery 1130 Duval St	Key West	FL	33040	305-294-5997	
Key West Aquarium 1 Whitehead St Mallory Square	Key West	FL	33040	305-296-2051	293-7094
TF: 800-868-7482					
Key West Art Center 301 Front St	Key West	FL	33040	305-294-1241	
Key West Cemetery 701 Passover Ln	Key West	FL	33040	305-292-8177	
Key West Ghost Tours 430 Duval St Holiday Inn La Concha	Key West	FL	33040	305-294-9255	
Key West Sunset Celebration Mallory Square End of Duval St	Key West	FL	33040	305-292-5000	
Key West's Shipwreck Historeum 1 Whitehead St	Key West	FL	33040	305-292-8990	293-7898
Web: www.historictours.com/keywest/shipwreck.htm					
Lighthouse Museum 938 Whitehead St	Key West	FL	33040	305-294-0012	294-0012
E-mail: kwahs@aol.com					
Mallory Square Duval St	Key West	FL	33040	305-292-5000	
Mel Fisher Maritime Museum 200 Greene St	Key West	FL	33040	305-294-2633	294-5671
Web: www.melfisher.org					
Nancy Forrester's Secret Garden 1 Free-School Ln	Key West	FL	33040	305-294-0015	
Web: www.hurricanecenter.com/SecretGarden					
Old Town Trolley Tours 6631 Maloney Ave	Key West	FL	33040	305-296-6688	292-8939
TF: 800-868-7482 ■ *Web:* www.historictours.com/keywest/trolley.htm					
Red Barn Theatre 319 Duval St	Key West	FL	33040	305-296-9911	293-3035
Ripley's Believe It or Not! Museum 527 Duval St	Key West	FL	33040	305-293-9686	293-9709
TF: 800-998-4418 ■ *Web:* www.entcon.com/ripleys/rkwhome.htm ■ *E-mail:* ripleyskeywest@entcon.com					
Southernmost Point of the USA Whitehead & South Sts	Key West	FL	33040	305-292-5000	
Tennessee Williams Fine Arts Center 5901 College Rd	Key West	FL	33040	305-296-1520	292-5155
Waterfront Playhouse Mallory Sq	Key West	FL	33040	305-294-5015	296-0174
Wild Side Gallery 291 Front St Suite 9	Key West	FL	33040	305-296-7800	
Wrecker's Museum 322 Duval St	Key West	FL	33040	305-294-9502	
Wyland Galleries 102 Duval St.	Key West	FL	33040	305-294-5240	294-5250
TF: 888-294-5240 ■ *Web:* www.wyland.com ■ *E-mail:* customerservice@wyland.com					

— Events —

	Phone
Big Pine & Lower Keys Dolphin Tournament (mid-June)	305-872-2411
City Christmas Parade (mid-December)	305-292-8100
Civil War Days (early March)	305-292-6713
Conch Republic Independence Celebration (mid-late April)	305-296-0213
Conch Shell Blowing Contest (mid-late March)	305-294-9501
Corvettes in Paradise Show (early November)	305-872-9641
Cuban American Heritage Festival (early November)	305-294-7618
Fantasy Fest (late October)	305-296-1817
Goombay (mid-late October)	305-293-8898
Hemingway Days Festival (mid-late July)	305-294-4440
Historic Seaport Music Festival (late November)	305-296-7182
Hog's Breath 5K Run (late November)	305-296-7182
Hog's Breath Ska King Mackerel Tournament (late January-early February)	305-296-0364
Island Art Fair (mid-late December)	305-872-2411
Key West & Lower Keys Fishing Tournament (mid-late April)	305-745-3332
Key West Crafts Show (late January)	305-294-2587
Key West Garden Club Flower Show (early April)	305-294-3210
Key West Gator Club Dolphin Tournament (mid-late June)	305-296-7511
Key West Literary Seminar (mid-January)	888-293-9291
Key West Songwriters Festival (early-mid-May)	305-294-5015
Key West Theatre Festival (early-mid-October)	305-292-3725
Key West World Championship Race (early-mid-November)	305-296-6166
Lower Keys Golf Tournament (mid-late November)	305-872-2411
Mercury Outboards' SLAM Tournament (mid-September)	305-664-2002
Monroe County Festival of the Seas (early February)	305-296-2454
Oktoberfest (early October)	305-872-2411
Old Island Days Art Festival (mid-late February)	305-294-1241
Pirates in Paradise Festival (late November)	305-743-4386
Red Ribbon Bed Race (late April)	305-296-7511
Reef Relief's Cayo Carnival (mid-November)	305-294-3100
Seven Mile Bridge Run (mid-April)	305-743-8513
Sport Divers Mini Lobster Season (late July)	305-289-2320
Super Boat Races (late May)	305-296-8963
Taste of Key West (mid-April)	305-296-6196
Turtle Kraals 5K Trot (early April)	305-296-7182
Underwater Music Festival (early-mid-July)	305-872-2411
Womenfest Key West (mid-September)	305-296-4238

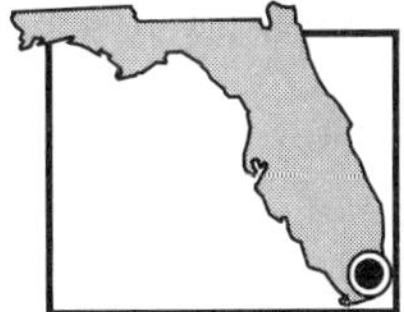

Miami

One of the unique city neighborhoods that make up Miami is Little Havana, with Cuban cuisine and coffees and Calle Ocho, one of the largest Hispanic festivals in the nation. The city's Little Haiti area offers authentic Creole food and a Caribbean Marketplace, while Coconut Grove is home to CocoWalk, a stretch of open air stores, cafes, and bars, and the Coconut Grove Arts Festival, one of the country's largest outdoor art shows. Across Biscayne Bay is Miami's sister city, Miami Beach. This resort area is recognized for its Art Deco District. Designated as a National Historic District, the old art deco buildings here have been restored to their neon and pastel colors. Overlooking the bay is Miami Beach's Bayside, a 16-acre complex with shops, entertainment, and restaurants.

Miami (Cont'd)

Population	368,624	**Longitude**	80-27-80 W
Area (Land)	35.6 sq mi	**County**	Dade
Area (Water)	19.4 sq mi	**Time Zone**	EST
Elevation	11 ft	**Area Code/s**	305, 786
Latitude	25-83-11 N		

— Average Temperatures and Precipitation —

TEMPERATURES

	Jan	Feb	Mar	Apr	May	Jun	Jul	Aug	Sep	Oct	Nov	Dec
High	75	77	79	82	85	88	89	89	88	85	80	77
Low	59	60	64	68	72	75	76	76	76	72	67	62

PRECIPITATION

	Jan	Feb	Mar	Apr	May	Jun	Jul	Aug	Sep	Oct	Nov	Dec
Inches	2.0	2.1	2.4	2.9	6.2	9.3	5.7	7.6	7.6	5.6	2.7	1.8

— Important Phone Numbers —

	Phone		*Phone*
American Express Travel	305-865-5959	**Poison Control Center**	800-282-3171
Emergency	911	**Time/Temp**	305-324-8811
HotelDocs	800-468-3537	**Weather**	305-229-4522
Miami-Dade Consumer Services	305-375-4222		

— Information Sources —

				Phone	*Fax*
Beacon Council 80 SW 8th St Suite 2400	Miami	FL	33130	305-579-1300	375-0271
Greater Miami Chamber of Commerce 1601 Biscayne Blvd *TF:* 888-660-5955 ■ *Web:* www.greatermiami.com	Miami	FL	33132	305-350-7700	374-6902
Greater Miami Convention & Visitors Bureau 701 Brickell Ave Suite 2700 *TF:* 800-933-8448 ■ *Web:* www.miamiandbeaches.com ■ *E-mail:* gmcvb@miamiandbeaches.com	Miami	FL	33131	305-539-3000	539-3113
Miami Beach Chamber of Commerce 1920 Meridian Ave *Web:* www.sobe.com/miamibeachchamber	Miami Beach	FL	33139	305-672-1270	538-4336
Miami Beach Convention Center 1901 Convention Center Dr *Web:* ci.miami-beach.fl.us	Miami Beach	FL	33139	305-673-7311	673-7435
Miami City Hall 3500 Pan American Dr *Web:* ci.miami.fl.us	Miami	FL	33133	305-250-5400	250-5441
Miami Convention Center 400 SE 2nd Ave	Miami	FL	33131	305-579-6341	372-2919
Miami-Dade County 111 NW 1st St Suite 220 *Web:* www.co.miami-dade.fl.us	Miami	FL	33128	305-375-5124	375-5569
Miami-Dade Public Library 101 W Flagler St *Web:* www.mdpls.org	Miami	FL	33130	305-375-2665	375-5232
Miami Mayor 3500 Pan American Dr *Web:* ci.miami.fl.us/co.html	Miami	FL	33133	305-250-5300	854-4001
Miami Planning & Development Dept 444 SW 2nd Ave	Miami	FL	33130	305-416-1400	416-2156

On-Line Resources

4Miami.com	www.4miami.com
Anthill City Guide Miami	www.anthill.com/city.asp?city=miami
Area Guide Miami	miami.areaguides.net
Bradmans.com Miami	www.bradmans.com/scripts/display_city.cgi?city=238
City Knowledge Miami	www.cityknowledge.com/fl_miami.htm
CitySearch Miami/Fort Lauderdale	miami.citysearch.com
CityTravelGuide.com Miami	www.citytravelguide.com/miami.htm
Come to the Sun Guide to South Florida	www.cometothesun.com
CuisineNet Miami	www.cuisinenet.com/restaurant/miami/index.shtml
DigitalCity Miami	home.digitalcity.com/southflorida
DigitalCity South Florida	home.digitalcity.com/southflorida
Dining Guide Miami	miami.diningguide.net/
DiningGuide Miami	miami.diningguide.net
EventGuide Miami	miami.eventguide.com/
Excite.com Miami City Guide	www.excite.com/travel/countries/united_states/florida/miami
Gayot's Guide Restaurant Search Miami	www.perrier.com/restaurants/gayot.asp?area=MIA
Go Miami	www.cnet1.com/gomiami/
Goodnight Miami	www.goodnight.net
Hotel Guide Miami	hotelguide.net/mia/
HotelGuide Miami	miami.hotelguide.net
I-95 Exit Information Guide Miami	www.usastar.com/i95/cityguide/touristguide.htm
InSouthFlorida.com	www.insouthflorida.com
MetroGuide Miami	miami.metroguide.net
Miami Beach Florida	miami-beach-florida.com
Miami City Web Online	www.miamicity.com
Miami CityWomen	www.citywomen.com/miamwomen.htm
Miami Event Guide	eventguide.com/mia/
Miami Gay & Lesbian Guide	www.southfloridafun.com/miami/index.shtml
Miami Information Access	miami.info-access.com/
Miami Metroparks	www.metro-dade.com/parks/
Miami Regional Guide	www.buybeach.com/access/miami.htm
Miami VR	www.miamivr.com/
Miami.com	www.miami.com
Miami.TheLinks.com	miami.thelinks.com/
NITC Travelbase City Guide Miami	www.travelbase.com/auto/guides/miami-area-fl.html
Open World City Guides Miami	www.worldexecutive.com/cityguides/miami/
Rough Guide Travel Miami	travel.roughguides.com/content/819/
SoFla.com	www.sofla.com
Southbeach	southbeach.org/
Southbeach.com	www.southbeach.com/
Surf & Sun Beach Vacation Guide to Miami Beach	www.surf-sun.com/fl-miami-main.htm
Time Out Miami	www.timeout.com/miami/
Virtual Voyages Miami	www.virtualvoyages.com/usa/fl/miami/miami.sht
WeekendEvents.com Miami	www.weekendevents.com/misccity/miami/miami.html
Yahoo! Miami	miami.yahoo.com

— Transportation Services —

AIRPORTS

■ **Miami International Airport (MIA)**

	Phone
7 miles NW of downtown (approx 20 minutes)	305-876-7515

Web: www.miami-airport.com

Airport Transportation

	Phone
Metrobus $1.25 fare to downtown	305-770-3131
SuperShuttle $10 fare to downtown	305-871-2000
Yellow Cab $15 fare to downtown	305-444-4444

Commercial Airlines

	Phone		*Phone*
Aces	800-846-2237	**Haiti Air**	305-871-5814
Aeroflot	888-686-4949	**Iberia**	800-772-4642
Aerolineas Argentinas	800-333-0276	**Kiwi**	800-538-5494
AeroMexico	305-441-0090	**KLM**	800-374-7747
Air Aruba	305-551-1100	**LAB Airlines**	800-327-7407
Air Canada	800-776-3000	**LACSA**	800-225-2272
Air France	800-321-4538	**LanChile**	305-871-2044
Air Jamaica	800-523-5585	**Lauda Air**	800-588-8399
AirTran	800-247-8726	**LTU International**	800-888-0200
Alitalia	800-223-5730	**Lufthansa**	800-645-3880
ALM-Antillean	800-327-7230	**Martinair Holland**	800-627-8462
American	800-433-7300	**MetroJet**	888-638-7653
American Trans Air	800-225-2995	**Mexicana**	800-531-7923
Avianca	305-883-5151	**National**	888-757-5387
Aviateca	800-327-9832	**Northwest**	800-225-2525
Bahamasair	305-593-1910	**Pan Am**	800-359-7262
British Airways	800-247-9297	**Saeta**	800-827-2382
BWIA International	800-538-2942	**Servivensa**	800-428-3672
Cayman Airways	800-422-9626	**TACA International**	305-223-0312
Commonwealth Express	800-995-5555	**Tower Air**	800-348-6937
Continental	305-871-1400	**TransBrasil**	800-872-3153
Continental Express	800-525-0280	**Turkish Airlines**	800-874-8875
Copa	305-871-6331	**TWA**	800-221-2000
Delta	305-448-7000	**United**	800-241-6522
Ecuatoriana	305-476-7837	**US Airways**	800-428-4322
El Al	800-223-6700	**Varig Brazilian**	800-468-2744
Finnair	800-950-5000	**VASP Brazilian Airlines**	800-732-8277
Gulfstream International Airlines	800-525-0280	**Virgin Atlantic**	305-594-0949

Charter Airlines

	Phone		*Phone*
Action Helicopter	305-358-4723	**Corporate Air Charter Inc**	305-248-0098
Adtech Aircraft Charters	800-511-4016	**Falcon Air Express**	305-592-5672
Air Florida	800-373-9593	**Fox Air International**	800-231-0044
Atlantic Flight Group	305-871-1111	**Miami Air International**	305-871-3300
Biscayne Helicopters	305-252-3883		

Miami (Cont'd)

CAR RENTALS

	Phone		Phone
Alamo	305-633-6076	**Hertz**	305-871-0300
Avis	305-637-4900	**Nation's**	305-871-0060
Budget	305-871-2722	**National**	305-638-1026
Dollar	305-887-6000	**Quality**	305-871-7576
Enterprise	305-633-0377	**Specialty**	305-871-2770
Exotic	305-876-9311		

LIMO/TAXI

	Phone		Phone
7 Star Limousines	305-238-2400	**Diamond Cab**	305-545-7575
Carey Limousine	305-666-5466	**Flamingo Taxi**	305-885-7000
Central Cab	305-532-5555	**Limousines of South Florida**	305-940-5252
Club Limousine	305-893-9850	**Metro Taxi**	305-888-8888
Corporate Transportation	305-931-3111	**Yellow Cab**	305-444-4444

MASS TRANSIT

	Phone
Electric Wave Shuttle free	305-535-9160
Metrobus $1.25 Base fare	305-770-3131
Metromover $.25 Base fare	305-770-3131
Tri-Rail fare varies with destination	800-874-7245

RAIL/BUS

Phone

Amtrak Station 8303 NW 37th Ave Miami Station .... Miami FL 33147 305-835-1222
TF: 800-872-7245

Greyhound Bus Station 700 Biscayne Blvd .... Miami FL 33132 305-379-7403
TF: 800-231-2222

— Accommodations —

HOTEL RESERVATION SERVICES

Phone *Fax*

Accommodations Express 609-391-2100 525-0111
TF: 800-444-7666 ■ *Web:* www.accommodationsxpress.com
■ *E-mail:* accomexp@acy.digex.net

Accommodations USA 407-931-0003 931-1003

Central Reservation Service 407-740-6442 740-8222
TF: 800-548-3311 ■ *Web:* www.reservation-services.com
■ *E-mail:* cenresbos@aol.com

Colours Destinations 305-532-9341 534-0362
TF: 800-277-4825 ■ *Web:* www.colours.net
■ *E-mail:* info@colours.net

Florida Hotel Network 305-538-3616 538-5858
TF: 800-538-3616

Florida SunBreak 305-532-1516 532-0564
TF: 800-786-2732 ■ *Web:* www.lvacation.com/p6802.htm

Greater Miami & the Beaches Hotel Assn 305-531-3553 531-8954
TF: 800-531-3553 ■ *Web:* www.gmbha.org ■ *E-mail:* info@gmbha.org

Hotel Reservations Network Inc 214-361-7311 361-7299
TF Sales: 800-964-6835 ■ *Web:* www.hoteldiscount.com

IDP Reservations 305-538-2151 538-1701
TF: 800-436-8611 ■ *Web:* www.idpreservations.com
■ *E-mail:* idpresv@aol.com

Quikbook 212-532-1660 532-1556
TF: 800-789-9887 ■ *Web:* www.quikbook.com

Travel Now 305-532-7273 532-7638
TF: 800-681-1993 ■ *Web:* www.travel-now.com

HOTELS, MOTELS, RESORTS

Phone *Fax*

Abbey Hotel 300 21st St .... Miami Beach FL 33139 305-531-0031 672-1663
TF: 888-612-2239 ■ *Web:* www.abbeyhotel.com

Airport Regency Hotel 1000 NW 42nd Ave ...... Miami FL 33126 305-441-1600 443-0766
TF: 800-367-1039

Albion Hotel 1650 James Ave.......... Miami Beach FL 33139 305-913-1000 674-0507
TF: 888-665-0008

Alexander AllSuite Luxury Hotel
5225 Collins Ave.......... Miami Beach FL 33140 305-865-6500 341-6553
TF: 800-327-6121 ■ *Web:* www.alexanderhotel.com
■ *E-mail:* reservations@alexanderhotel.com

AmeriSuites Miami Airport 3655 NW 82nd Ave ... Miami FL 33166 305-718-8292 718-8295
TF: 800-833-1516

Beachcomber Hotel 1340 Collins Ave ..... Miami Beach FL 33139 305-531-3755 673-8609
TF: 888-305-4683

Beacon Hotel 720 Ocean Dr.......... Miami Beach FL 33139 305-674-8200 674-8976
TF: 800-649-7075

Best Western Airport Inn
1550 NW Le Jeune Rd .... Miami FL 33126 305-871-2345 871-2811
TF: 800-528-1234

Best Western Marina Park Hotel
340 Biscayne Blvd.......... Miami FL 33132 305-371-4400 372-2862
TF: 800-528-1234

Biltmore Hotel 1200 Anastasia Ave........Coral Gables FL 33134 305-445-1926 913-3159
TF: 800-727-1926 ■ *Web:* www.biltmorehotel.com

Breakwater Hotel 940 Ocean Dr......... Miami Beach FL 33139 305-532-1220 532-4451
TF: 800-454-1220 ■ *Web:* www.breakwater-hotel.com

Cavalier Hotel 1320 Ocean Dr .... Miami Beach FL 33139 305-604-5000 531-5543
TF: 800-688-7678 ■ *Web:* www.islandoutpost.com/Cavalier

Clarion Suites Crystal Beach & Health Club 6985 Collins Ave.......... Miami Beach FL 33141 305-865-9555 866-3514
TF: 800-252-7466 ■ *Web:* www.clarionmiamibeach.com
■ *E-mail:* info@clarionmiamibeach.com

Club Hotel & Suites by Doubletree
100 SE 4th St.......... Miami FL 33131 305-374-5100 374-3818
TF: 800-222-8733

Club Hotel by Doubletree 1101 NW 57th Ave .... Miami FL 33126 305-266-0000 266-9179
TF: 888-444-2582

Comfort Inn & Suites Miami Airport
5301 NW 36th St.......... Miami FL 33166 305-871-6000 871-4971
TF: 800-228-5150 ■ *Web:* www.clarcom.com

Crowne Plaza Miami International Airport
950 NW LeJeune Rd.......... Miami FL 33126 305-446-9000 441-0725
TF: 800-465-4329

David William Hotel 700 Biltmore Way.....Coral Gables FL 33134 305-445-7821 913-1933
TF: 800-537-8483

Days Inn Oceanside 4299 Collins Ave..... Miami Beach FL 33140 305-673-1513 538-0727
TF: 800-356-3017

Delano The 1685 Collins Ave.......... Miami Beach FL 33139 305-538-7881 532-0099
TF: 800-555-5001

Dezerland Surfside Beach Hotel
8701 Collins Ave.......... Miami Beach FL 33154 305-865-6661 866-2630
TF: 800-331-9346

Don Shula's Hotel & Golf Club
6842 Main St..........Miami Lakes FL 33014 305-821-1150 820-8067*
**Fax:* Sales ■ *TF:* 800-247-4852

Doral Golf Resort & Spa 4400 NW 87th Ave..... Miami FL 33178 305-592-2000 594-4682
TF: 800-713-6725 ■ *Web:* www.doralgolf.com

Doubletree Grand Hotel Biscayne Bay
1717 N Bayshore Dr.......... Miami FL 33132 305-372-0313 372-9455
TF: 800-222-8733
■ *Web:* www.doubletreehotels.com/DoubleT/Hotel21/36/36Main.htm

Doubletree Hotel Coconut Grove
2649 S Bayshore Dr.......... Miami FL 33133 305-858-2500 858-5776
TF: 800-222-8733
■ *Web:* www.doubletreehotels.com/DoubleT/Hotel21/37/37Main.htm

DuPont Plaza Hotel
300 Biscayne Boulevard Way.......... Miami FL 33131 305-358-2541 377-4049
TF: 800-327-3480

Eden Roc Resort & Spa
4525 Collins Ave.......... Miami Beach FL 33140 305-531-0000 674-5555
TF: 800-327-8337 ■ *Web:* www.edenrocresort.com
■ *E-mail:* sales@ivmonline.com

Embassy Suites 3974 NW South River Dr....... Miami FL 33142 305-634-5000 635-9499
TF: 800-362-2779

Everglades Hotel 244 Biscayne Blvd.......... Miami FL 33132 305-379-5461 577-8390
TF: 800-327-5700 ■ *Web:* www.miamigate.com/everglades
■ *E-mail:* evergladeshotel@worldnet.att.net

Fisher Island Club 1 Fisher Island Dr......Fisher Island FL 33109 305-535-6020 535-6003
TF: 800-537-3708 ■ *Web:* www.fisherisland-florida.com

Fontainebleau Hilton Resort & Towers
4441 Collins Ave.......... Miami Beach FL 33140 305-538-2000 674-4608
TF: 800-548-8886 ■ *Web:* www.hilton.com/hotels/MIAFHHH

Golden Nugget Hotel
18555 Collins Ave..........North Miami Beach FL 33160 305-932-1445 692-8603

Grand Bay Hotel 2669 S Bayshore Dr.......... Miami FL 33133 305-858-9600 859-2026
TF: 888-472-6229
■ *Web:* www.grandbay.com/properties/coconut/default.html
■ *E-mail:* sales@grandbay.com

Grove Isle Club & Resort 4 Grove Isle ... Coconut Grove FL 33133 305-858-8300 858-5908
TF: 800-884-7683

Hilton & Towers Miami Airport
5101 Blue Lagoon Dr.......... Miami FL 33125 305-262-1000 267-0038
TF: 800-445-8667 ■ *Web:* www.hilton.com/hotels/MIAAHHH/index.html

Holiday Inn 21485 NW 27th Ave.......... Miami FL 33056 305-621-5801 624-8202
TF: 800-465-4329

Homestead Village 8720 NW 33rd St.......... Miami FL 33172 305-436-1811 436-1864
TF: 888-782-9473

Miami — Hotels, Motels, Resorts (Cont'd)

Phone / Fax

Hotel Astor 956 Washington Ave. . . . . Miami Beach FL 33139 305-531-8081 531-3193
TF: 800-270-4981 ■ *Web:* www.hotelastor.com
■ *E-mail:* astor@icanect.net

Hotel Sofitel 5800 Blue Lagoon Dr . . . . Miami FL 33126 305-264-4888 262-9049
TF: 800-258-4888

Hotel The 801 Collins Ave . . . . .South Beach FL 33139 305-531-2222 531-3222
TF: 877-843-4683 ■ *Web:* www.thehotelofsouthbeach.com
■ *E-mail:* info@thehotelofsouthbeach.com

Howard Johnson Port of Miami
1100 Biscayne Blvd. Miami FL 33132 305-358-3080 358-8631
TF: 800-654-2000

Hyatt Regency Miami 400 SE 2nd Ave . . . . Miami FL 33131 305-358-1234 358-0529
TF: 800-233-1234
■ *Web:* www.hyatt.com/usa/miami/hotels/hotel_miarm.html

Indian Creek Hotel
2727 Indian Creek Dr . . . . Miami Beach FL 33140 305-531-2727 531-5651

Inter-Continental Hotel Miami
100 Chopin Plaza . . . . Miami FL 33131 305-577-1000 577-0384
TF: 800-327-3005

Key Colony for Guests
240 Crandon Blvd. . . . . Key Biscayne FL 33149 305-361-2170 361-7420

Lido Spa Hotel 40 Island Ave. . . . . Miami Beach FL 33139 305-538-4621 534-3680
TF: 800-327-8363 ■ *Web:* www.lidospa.com
■ *E-mail:* info@lidospa.com

Loews Miami Beach Hotel
1601 Collins Ave. . . . . Miami Beach FL 33139 305-604-1601 531-8677
TF: 800-235-6397 ■ *Web:* www.loewshotels.com

Marina Del Mar Resort & Marina
527 Caribbean Dr . . . . Key Largo FL 33037 305-451-4107 451-1891
TF: 800-451-3483

Marriott Dadeland Miami
9090 S Dadeland Blvd . . . . Kendall FL 33156 305-670-1035 670-7540
TF: 800-228-9290 ■ *Web:* marriotthotels.com/MIADD

Marriott Hotel & Marina Biscayne Bay
1633 N Bayshore Dr . . . . Miami FL 33132 305-374-3900 375-0597
TF: 800-228-9290 ■ *Web:* marriotthotels.com/MIABB

Marseilles Hotel 1741 Collins Ave . . . . Miami Beach FL 33139 305-538-5711 673-1006
TF: 800-327-4739

Mayfair House 3000 Florida Ave. . . . . Coconut Grove FL 33133 305-441-0000 447-9173
TF: 800-341-0809 ■ *Web:* www.mayfairhousehotel.com
■ *E-mail:* mail@mayfairhousehotel.com

Miami Airport Marriott 1201 NW Lejeune Rd . . . . . Miami FL 33126 305-649-5000 642-3369
TF: 800-228-9290 ■ *Web:* marriotthotels.com/MIAAP

Miami Beach Ocean Resort
3025 Collins Ave. . . . . Miami Beach FL 33140 305-534-0505 534-0515
TF: 800-550-0505 ■ *Web:* www.mbor.com
■ *E-mail:* sales@mbor.com

Miami International Airport Hotel
NW 20th St & Le Jeune Rd . . . . Miami FL 33122 305-871-4100 871-0800
TF: 800-327-1276

Newport Beachside Crowne Plaza
16701 Collins Ave. . . . . Miami Beach FL 33160 305-949-1300 956-2733
TF: 800-327-5476 ■ *Web:* www.newportbeachsideresort.com

Quality Inn & Suites Airport
2373 NW LeJeune Rd . . . . Miami FL 33142 305-871-3230 871-1006
TF: 800-228-5151

Radisson Deauville Hotel & Tennis Club
6701 Collins Ave. . . . . Miami Beach FL 33141 305-865-8511 865-8154
TF: 800-327-6656

Radisson Mart Plaza Hotel 711 NW 72nd Ave . . . . Miami FL 33126 305-261-3800 261-7665
TF: 800-333-3333

Ramada Limited 7600 N Kendall Dr . . . . Miami FL 33156 305-595-6000 279-6988
TF: 800-272-6232

Residence Inn by Marriott Miami International Airport 1212 NW 82nd Ave . . . . Miami FL 33126 305-591-2211 591-0902
TF: 800-331-3131 ■ *Web:* www.residenceinn.com/MIACC

Riande Continental Miami Bayside Hotel
146 Biscayne Blvd. . . . . Miami FL 33132 305-358-4555 371-5253

Ritz Plaza Hotel 1701 Collins Ave. . . . . Miami Beach FL 33139 305-534-3500 531-6928
TF: 800-522-6400 ■ *Web:* www.ritzplaza.com
■ *E-mail:* info@ritzplaza.com

Royalton Hotel 131 SE 1st St. . . . . Miami FL 33131 305-374-7451 358-5842

Savoy The 455 Ocean Dr . . . . Miami Beach FL 33139 305-532-0200 534-7436
TF: 800-237-2869 ■ *Web:* www.sunterra.com/resorts/ssb/index.html

Seacoast Suites Hotel 5101 Collins Ave . . . Miami Beach FL 33140 305-865-5152 868-4090
TF: 800-523-3671

Seville Beach Hotel 2901 Collins Ave . . . . . Miami Beach FL 33140 305-532-2511 531-6461
TF: 800-327-1641

Sheraton Bal Harbour Resort
9701 Collins Ave. . . . . Bal Harbour FL 33154 305-865-7511 864-2601
TF: 800-999-9898
■ *Web:* www.sheraton.com/cgi/t3.cgi/property.taf?prop=352

Phone / Fax

Sheraton Biscayne Bay Hotel 495 Brickell Ave . . . . Miami FL 33131 305-373-6000 374-2279
TF: 800-325-3535

Sonesta Beach Resort 350 Ocean Dr. . . . . . Key Biscayne FL 33149 305-361-2021 361-3096
TF: 800-766-3782 ■ *Web:* www.sonesta.com/

South Beach Hotel 2201 Collins Ave . . . . . . Miami Beach FL 33139 305-534-1511 532-1403
TF: 800-356-6902

Suez Resort 18215 Collins Ave. . . . . Miami Beach FL 33160 305-932-0661 937-0058
TF: 800-432-3661 ■ *Web:* www.suezresort.com
■ *E-mail:* ocean@suezresort.com

Traymore Hotel 2445 Collins Ave . . . . Miami Beach FL 33140 305-534-7111 538-2632
TF: 800-445-1512

Turnberry Isle Resort & Club
19999 W Country Club Dr . . . . Aventura FL 33180 305-932-6200 933-6554
TF: 800-327-7028 ■ *Web:* www.turnberryisle.com
■ *E-mail:* reservations@turnberryisle.com

Waldorf Towers Hotel 860 Ocean Dr. . . . . . Miami Beach FL 33139 305-531-7684 672-6836
TF: 800-933-2322

Wellesley Inn Miami Airport 8436 NW 36th St . . . Miami FL 33166 305-592-4799 471-8461
TF: 800-444-8888

Wyndham Hotel 1601 Biscayne Blvd . . . . Miami FL 33132 305-374-0000 374-0020
TF: 800-996-3426

Wyndham Miami Airport 3900 NW 21st St . . . . . . Miami FL 33142 305-871-3800 871-0447
TF: 800-996-3426

Wyndham Resort Miami Beach
4833 Collins Ave. . . . . Miami Beach FL 33140 305-532-3600 534-7409
TF: 800-996-3426

— Restaurants —

Phone

94th Aero Squadron (American) 1395 NW 57th Ave. . . . . Miami FL 33126 305-261-4220

1920 Restaurant (American) 146 Biscayne Blvd. . . . . Miami FL 33132 305-358-4555

Allegro's Restaurant (Continental) 200 SE 2nd Ave . . . . Miami FL 33131 305-374-3000

Astor Place Bar & Grill (American)
956 Washington Ave. . . . . Miami Beach FL 33139 305-672-7217

Bayview Dining Room (American) 300 Biscayne Blvd Way . . . . Miami FL 33131 305-358-2541

Bice (Italian) 2669 S Bayshore Dr . . . . Miami FL 33133 305-858-9600

Big Pink (American) 157 Collins Ave . . . . Miami Beach FL 33139 305-532-4700

Bijan's on the River (Seafood) 64 SE 4th St. . . . . Miami FL 33131 305-381-7778

Brasserie Brickell Key Restaurant (Italian)
601 Brickell Key Dr. . . . . Miami FL 33131 305-577-0907

Cafe Barcelona (French) 3974 NW South River Dr. . . . . Miami FL 33142 305-634-5000

Cafe Brasserie (International) 2649 S Bayshore Dr . . . Coconut Grove FL 33133 305-858-2500

Cafe Tu Tu Tango (International)
3015 Grand Ave Suite 250. . . . . Coconut Grove FL 33133 305-529-2222

Caffe Abbracci (Italian) 318 Aragon Ave . . . . .Coral Gables FL 33134 305-441-0700

Caffe Milano (Italian) 850 Ocean Dr. . . . . Miami Beach FL 33139 305-532-0707

Capital Grille (Steak/Seafood) 444 Brickell Ave . . . . Miami FL 33131 305-374-4500

Caroline's (French) 214 Espanola Way . . . . Miami Beach FL 33139 305-604-0008

Casa Juancho (Spanish) 2436 SW 8th St . . . . Miami FL 33135 305-642-2452
Web: www.casajuancho.com/

Charade Restaurant (Continental) 1850 NW LeJuene Rd . . . . . Miami FL 33126 305-871-4350

Chef Allen's (New American)
19088 NE 29th Ave. . . . . North Miami Beach FL 33180 305-935-2900

China Grill (International) 404 Washington Ave. . . . . . . Miami Beach FL 33139 305-534-2211

Chiyo (Japanese) 3399 Virginia St . . . . Coconut Grove FL 33133 305-445-0865

Christy's (Steak) 3101 Ponce de Leon Blvd. . . . . .Coral Gables FL 33134 305-446-1400

Club Tropigala (Continental) 4441 Collins Ave. . . . . Miami Beach FL 33140 305-672-7469

Cove The (Steak/Seafood) 5101 Blue Lagoon Dr . . . . Miami FL 33126 305-265-3845

Crystal Cafe (Continental) 726 Arthur Godfrey Rd . . . . . Miami Beach FL 33140 305-673-8266

Fishbone Grill (Seafood) 650 S Miami Ave . . . . Miami FL 33136 305-530-1915

Florencia (International) 100 SE 4th St . . . . Miami FL 33131 305-374-5100

Forge The (Continental) 432 Arthur Godfrey Rd. . . . . . . Miami Beach FL 33140 305-538-8533

Hampton Cafe (Italian) 938 Lincoln Rd. . . . . Miami Beach FL 33139 305-531-6542

Hard Rock Cafe (American) 401 Biscayne Blvd . . . . Miami FL 33132 305-377-3110

Il Tulipano (Italian) 11052 Biscayne Blvd . . . . .North Miami FL 33161 305-893-4811

Jeffrey's (American) 1629 Michigan Ave. . . . . Miami Beach FL 33139 305-673-0690

Joe's Stone Crab (Seafood) 227 Biscayne St. . . . . Miami Beach FL 33139 305-673-0365
Web: www.joesstonecrab.com ■ *E-mail:* faq@joesstonecrab.com

La Carreta (Cuban) 3632 SW 8th St. Miami FL 33135 305-444-7501

Le Cafe at Bayside (French) 401 Biscayne Blvd. . . . . Miami FL 33132 305-373-1730

Le Cafe Royal (French) 5800 Blue Lagoon Dr . . . . Miami FL 33126 305-264-4888

Le Festival (French) 2120 Salzedo St. . . . . .Coral Gables FL 33134 305-442-8545

Le Pavillon (International) 100 Chopin Plaza. . . . . Miami FL 33131 305-372-4494

Les Deux Fontaines (French) 1230 Ocean Dr . . . . Miami Beach FL 33139 305-672-7878

Mama Vieja Restaurant (Colombian) 235 23rd St. . . . . Miami Beach FL 33139 305-538-2400

Mango's Tropical Cafe (Latin American)
900 Ocean Dr. . . . . Miami Beach FL 33139 305-673-4422

Mezzaluna (Italian) 834 Ocean Dr . . . . Miami Beach FL 33139 305-674-1330

Mezzanotte (Italian) 1200 Washington Ave . . . . Miami Beach FL 33139 305-673-4343

Mike Gordon's (Seafood) 1201 NE 79th St . . . . Miami FL 33138 305-751-4429

Monty's Stone Crab (Seafood) 2550 S Bayshore Dr . . . Coconut Grove FL 33133 305-858-1431

Naked Earth (Vegetarian) 901 Pennsylvania Ave . . . . . . Miami Beach FL 33139 305-531-2171

Nemo (New American) 100 Collins Ave. . . . . Miami Beach FL 33139 305-532-4550

News Cafe (International) 800 Ocean Dr. . . . . Miami Beach FL 33139 305-538-6397

Norma's on the Beach (Caribbean) 646 Lincoln Rd . . . . Miami Beach FL 33139 305-532-2809

Miami — Restaurants (Cont'd)

	City	State	Zip	Phone
Norman's (International) 21 Almeria Ave	Coral Gables	FL	33134	305-446-6767
Osteria Del Teatro (Italian) 1443 Washington Ave	Miami Beach	FL	33139	305-538-7850
Pacific Time (Asian) 915 Lincoln Rd	Miami	FL	33139	305-534-5979
Palm Restaurant (Steak/Seafood) 9650 E Bay Harbor Dr	Bay Harbor Islands	FL	33154	305-868-7256
Porcao Churrascaria (Brazilian) 801 S Bayshore Dr	Miami	FL	33131	305-373-2777
Rainforest Cafe (American) 19501 Biscayne Blvd	Aventura	FL	33180	305-792-8001
Web: www.rainforestcafe.com				
Red Square (Russian) 411 Washington Ave	Miami Beach	FL	33139	305-672-0200
Regatta Bar & Grill (Continental) 495 Brickell Ave	Miami	FL	33131	305-373-6000
Rib Room (Steak/Seafood) 4833 Collins Ave	Miami Beach	FL	33140	305-532-3600
Riverwalk Cafe (American) 400 SE 2nd Ave	Miami	FL	33132	305-358-1234
Rusty Pelican (Steak/Seafood) 3201 Rickenbacker Cswy	Key Biscayne	FL	33149	305-361-3818
Shula's Steak House (Steak) 5225 Collins Ave	Miami Beach	FL	33140	305-865-6500
Shula's Steak House (Steak/Seafood) 7601 Miami Lakes Dr	Miami Lakes	FL	33014	305-820-8102
Smith & Wollensky (Steak) 1 Washington Ave	Miami Beach	FL	33139	305-673-1708
Soyka (American) 5556 NE 4th Ct	Miami	FL	33137	305-759-3117
Spirit The (American) 7250 NW 11th St	Miami	FL	33126	305-262-9500
Sushi Siam (Thai) 801 Brickell Bay Dr	Miami	FL	33131	305-579-9944
Taisho (Japanese) 2522 Ponce De Leon Blvd	Coral Gables	FL	33134	305-442-0600
Tantra (International) 1445 Pennsylvania Ave	Miami Beach	FL	33139	305-672-4765
Tap Tap (Haitian) 819 5th St	Miami Beach	FL	33139	305-672-2898
Web: www.tap-tap.com ■ *E-mail:* info@tap-tap.com				
Thai House South Beach (Thai) 1137 Washington Ave	Miami Beach	FL	33139	305-531-4841
Tony Chan's Water Club (Chinese) 1717 N Bayshore Dr	Miami	FL	33132	305-374-8888
VanDyke Café (American) 834 Lincoln Rd	Miami Beach	FL	33139	305-534-3600
Versailles (Cuban) 3555 SW 8th St	Miami	FL	33135	305-444-0240
Victor's Cafe (Cuban) 2340 SW 32nd Ave	Miami	FL	33145	305-445-1313
Windows (International) 4400 NW 87th Ave	Miami	FL	33178	305-592-2000
Wish (Vegetarian) 801 Collins Ave	Miami Beach	FL	33139	305-674-9474
Yuca (Cuban) 501 Lincoln Rd	Miami Beach	FL	33139	305-532-9822

— Goods and Services —

SHOPPING

	City	State	Zip	Phone	Fax
Aventura Mall 19501 Biscayne Blvd	Aventura	FL	33180	305-935-1110	935-9360
Web: www.shopaventuramall.com					
Bal Harbour Shops 9700 Collins Ave	Bal Harbour	FL	33154	305-866-0311	866-5235*
**Fax:* Mktg ■ *Web:* www.balharbourshops.com					
Bayside Marketplace 401 Biscayne Blvd	Miami	FL	33132	305-577-3344	577-0306
CocoWalk 3015 Grand Ave Suite 118	Coconut Grove	FL	33133	305-444-0777	441-8936
Web: www.cocowalk.com ■ *E-mail:* comments@cocowalk.com					
Cutler Ridge Mall 20505 S Dixie Hwy	Miami	FL	33189	305-235-8562	235-7956
Dadeland Mall 7535 N Kendall Dr	Miami	FL	33156	305-665-6226	665-5012
Downtown Miami Shopping District Biscayne Blvd to 3rd Ave & SE 1st to NE 3rd Sts	Miami	FL	33131	305-379-7070	379-7222
Falls The Shopping Center US Hwy 1 & 136th St	Miami	FL	33176	305-255-4570	
Web: www.thefallsshoppingcenter.com					
Mall at 163rd Street 1421 NE 163rd St	Miami	FL	33162	305-944-7132	947-1429
Mall of the Americas 7827-B W Flagler St	Miami	FL	33144	305-261-8772	262-4060
Miami International Mall 1455 NW 107th Ave	Miami	FL	33172	305-593-1775	591-4210
Omni International Mall 1601 Biscayne Blvd	Miami	FL	33132	305-374-6664	374-6118
Streets of Mayfair 2911 Grand Ave Suite 2A	Coconut Grove	FL	33133	305-448-1700	448-1641
Web: www.streetsofmayfair.com					

BANKS

	City	State	Zip	Phone	Fax
Citibank 201 S Biscayne Blvd	Miami	FL	33131	800-374-9800	347-1630*
**Fax Area Code:* 305					
First Union National Bank 200 S Biscayne Blvd	Miami	FL	33131	305-789-4710	789-4731
TF Cust Svc: 800-275-3862*					
Hamilton Bank 3750 NW 87th Ave	Miami	FL	33178	305-717-5500	717-5560*
**Fax:* Hum Res					
Mellon United National Bank 1399 SW 1st Ave	Miami	FL	33130	305-358-4334	381-6320
NationsBank 1 SE 3rd Ave	Miami	FL	33131	305-350-6350	
TF: 800-299-2265					
Ocean Bank 780 NW 42nd Ave	Miami	FL	33126	305-442-2660	444-8153
Peoples National Bank of Commerce 3275 NW 79th St	Miami	FL	33147	305-696-0700	835-7345
SunTrust Bank Miami NA 777 Brickell Ave	Miami	FL	33131	305-592-0800	577-5028

BUSINESS SERVICES

	Phone		Phone
Accountemps	305-447-1757	**Kinko's**	305-220-8172
Choice Courier System	305-949-0909	**Manpower Temporary Services**	305-374-3892
Courier Dispatch Group	305-592-0474	**Miami Messenger Service**	305-821-6000
Courthouse Express	305-379-0011	**Post Office**	305-470-0465
Executive Express Couriers	305-854-0565	**Sunshine State Messenger**	954-975-8100
Federal Express	800-238-5355	**UPS**	800-742-5877
Kelly Services	305-822-8210	**Zoom International Couriers**	305-592-3972

— Media —

PUBLICATIONS

	City	State	Zip	Phone	Fax
Daily Business Review 1 SE 3rd Ave Suite 900	Miami	FL	33131	305-347-6672	347-6678
TF: 800-777-7300					
Diario Las Americas‡ 2900 NW 39th St	Miami	FL	33142	305-633-3341	635-7668
TF: 800-327-4210 ■ *Web:* www.diariolasamericas.com					
El Nuevo Herald‡ 1 Herald Plaza	Miami	FL	33132	305-376-3535	376-2378
Web: www.elherald.com ■ *E-mail:* digit@elherald.com					
Kendall News Gazette 6796 SW 62nd Ave	South Miami	FL	33143	305-669-7355	661-0954*
**Fax:* News Rm					
Miami Herald‡ 1 Herald Plaza	Miami	FL	33132	305-350-2111	376-8943
Web: www.herald.com					
Miami Metro Magazine 1550 Biscayne Blvd Suite 300	Miami	FL	33132	305-755-9920	755-9921
TF: 800-288-8388 ■ *Web:* miamimetro.com ■ *E-mail:* miametro@bellsouth.net					
Miami Today PO Box 1368	Miami	FL	33101	305-358-2663	358-4811
Ocean Drive Magazine 404 Washington Ave Suite 650	Miami Beach	FL	33139	305-532-2544	532-4366
Web: www.oceandrive.com					
South Florida Business Journal 4000 Hollywood Blvd Suite 695 South	Hollywood	FL	33021	954-359-2100	359-2135
Web: www.amcity.com/southflorida					

‡*Daily newspapers*

TELEVISION

	City	State	Zip	Phone	Fax
WAMI-TV Ch 69 (USA) 605 Lincoln Rd 2nd Fl	Miami Beach	FL	33139	305-373-6900	604-0406
E-mail: wami@miamiusa.com					
WBFS-TV Ch 33 (UPN) 16550 NW 52nd Ave	Miami	FL	33014	305-621-3333	628-3448
Web: www.paramountstations.com/WBFS					
WBZL-TV Ch 39 (WB) 2055 Lee St	Hollywood	FL	33020	954-925-3939	922-3965
Web: www.wb39.com ■ *E-mail:* wb39@expressweb.com					
WFOR-TV Ch 4 (CBS) 8900 NW 18th Terr	Miami	FL	33172	305-591-4444	477-3040
Web: www.wfor.com ■ *E-mail:* news4@wfor.groupw.wec.com					
WLRN-TV Ch 17 (PBS) 172 NE 15th St	Miami	FL	33132	305-995-1717	995-2299
Web: wlrn.org/wlrn-17/ ■ *E-mail:* info@wlrn.org					
WLTV-TV Ch 23 (Uni) 9405 NW 41st St	Miami	FL	33178	305-470-2323	471-4236
WPBT-TV Ch 2 (PBS) 14901 NE 20th Ave	Miami	FL	33181	305-949-8321	949-9772
Web: www.channel2.org					
WPLG-TV Ch 10 (ABC) 3900 Biscayne Blvd	Miami	FL	33137	305-576-1010	325-2480
Web: www.wplg.com/					
WPXM-TV Ch 35 (PAX) 11900 Biscayne Blvd Suite 760	Miami	FL	33181	305-895-1835	895-7935
Web: www.pax.net/wpxm					
WSCV-TV Ch 51 (Tele) 2340 W 8th Ave	Hialeah	FL	33010	305-888-5151	889-7651
TF: 800-688-8851 ■ *Web:* www.wscv.com ■ *E-mail:* info@wscv.com					
WSVN-TV Ch 7 (Fox) 1401 79th St Cswy	Miami	FL	33141	305-751-6692	757-2266
Web: www.wsvn.com ■ *E-mail:* 7news@wsvn.com					
WTVJ-TV Ch 6 (NBC) 316 N Miami Ave	Miami	FL	33128	305-379-4444	789-4202
Web: www.nbc6.nbc.com					
WWFD-TV Ch 8 (Ind) 16502 NW 52nd Ave	Miami	FL	33014	305-621-3688	621-5181

RADIO

	City	State	Zip	Phone	Fax
WAMR-FM 107.5 MHz (Span) 2828 Coral Way Suite 102	Miami	FL	33145	305-447-1140	643-1075
Web: www.wamr.com ■ *E-mail:* comentarios@wamr.com					
WAQI-AM 710 kHz (N/T) 2828 Coral Way	Miami	FL	33145	305-445-4020	443-3601
Web: www.waqi.com/ ■ *E-mail:* info@waqi.com					
WAVS-AM 1170 kHz (Span) 6360 SW 41st Pl	Davie	FL	33314	954-584-1170	
WCMQ-FM 92.3 MHz (Span) 1001 Ponce de Leon Blvd	Coral Gables	FL	33134	305-444-9292	461-4951
WEDR-FM 99.1 MHz (Urban) PO Box 551748	Miami	FL	33055	305-623-7711	624-2736
Web: www.wedrfm.com					
WFLC-FM 97.3 MHz (AC) 2741 N 29th Ave	Hollywood	FL	33020	954-584-7117	847-3223

Miami — Radio (Cont'd)

Phone | Fax

WHQT-FM 105.1 MHz (Urban)
2741 N 29th Ave. Hollywood FL 33020 954-584-7117 847-3223
Web: www.hot105fm.com

WHYI-FM 100.7 MHz (CHR)
1975 E Sunrise Blvd Suite 400. . . . . . .Fort Lauderdale FL 33304 954-463-9299 522-7002
Web: www.whyi.com

WINZ-AM 940 kHz (N/T) 194 NW 187th St. . . . . . Miami FL 33169 305-654-9494 654-9090

WIOD-AM 610 kHz (N/T) 194 NW 187th St . . . . . . Miami FL 33169 305-654-9494 690-6484
Web: www.wiod.com ■ *E-mail:* wiod610@ix.netcom.com

WKIS-FM 99.9 MHz (Ctry)
9881 Sheridan St . . . . Hollywood FL 33024 954-431-6200 437-2466
Web: www.wkis.com ■ *E-mail:* wkis@sefl.satelnet.org

WLRN-FM 91.3 MHz (NPR) 172 NE 15th St. . . . . . Miami FL 33132 305-995-1717 995-2299
Web: www.wlrn.org/radio-fm ■ *E-mail:* radio@wlrn.org

WLVE-FM 93.9 MHz (NAC) 194 NW 187th St. . . . . Miami FL 33169 305-654-9494 654-9090
Web: www.love94.com

WLYF-FM 101.5 MHz (AC) 20450 NW 2nd Ave . . . Miami FL 33169 305-653-8811 652-5385
Web: www.wlyf.com

WMXJ-FM 102.7 MHz (Oldies)
20450 NW 2nd Ave. Miami FL 33169 305-651-1027 652-1888
Web: www.wmxj.com ■ *E-mail:* majic@gate.net

WPOW-FM 96.5 MHz (CHR) 20295 NW 2nd Ave . . Miami FL 33169 305-653-6796 770-1456
Web: www.power96.com

WQAM-AM 560 kHz (Sports)
20295 NW 2nd Ave. Miami FL 33169 305-653-6796 770-1456
Web: wqam.com

WQBA-AM 1140 kHz (N/T)
2828 Coral Way Suite 102 . . . . Miami FL 33145 305-447-1140 441-2454
Web: www.wqba.com ■ *E-mail:* info@wqba.com

WRMA-FM 106.7 MHz (Span)
1001 Ponce de Leon Blvd . . . . .Coral Gables FL 33134 305-444-9292 461-0987

WRTO-FM 98.3 MHz (Span)
2828 Coral Way Suite 102 . . . . Miami FL 33145 305-447-1140 643-1075
Web: www.wrto.com ■ *E-mail:* info@wrto.com

WSUA-AM 1260 kHz (Span) 2100 Coral Way . . . . . Miami FL 33145 305-285-1260 858-5907

WTMI-FM 93.1 MHz (Clas) 3225 Aviation Ave . . . . Miami FL 33133 305-856-9393 854-0783
Web: www.wtmi.com ■ *E-mail:* wtmi@safari.net

WXDJ-FM 95.7 MHz (Span)
1001 Ponce de Leon Blvd . . . . .Coral Gables FL 33134 305-447-9595 461-4951

WZTA-FM 94.9 MHz (Rock) 194 NW 187th St . . . . Miami FL 33169 305-654-9494 654-9090
Web: www.949zeta.com

— Colleges/Universities —

Phone | Fax

ATI Health Education Center
1395 NW 167 St Suite 200 . . . . Miami FL 33169 305-628-1000 628-1461
TF: 800-275-2725 ■ *Web:* www.aticareertraining.com
■ *E-mail:* ati1@aticareertraining.com

Barry University 11300 NE 2nd Ave . . . . . . Miami Shores FL 33161 305-899-3000 899-2971
TF: 800-756-6000 ■ *Web:* www.barry.edu

Florida International University
11200 SW 8th St . . . . Miami FL 33199 305-348-2000 348-3648
Web: www.fiu.edu

Florida Memorial College 15800 NW 42nd Ave . . . Miami FL 33054 305-626-3600 623-1462
TF: 800-822-1362 ■ *Web:* www.fmc.edu

International Fine Arts College
1737 N Bayshore Dr . . . . Miami FL 33132 305-373-4684 374-7946
TF: 800-225-9023 ■ *Web:* www.ifac.edu

Miami-Dade Community College Kendall Campus
11011 SW 104th St . . . . Miami FL 33176 305-237-2000 237-2964
Web: www.kendall.mdcc.edu

Miami-Dade Community College North Campus
11380 NW 27th Ave . . . . Miami FL 33167 305-237-1000 237-8070
Web: www.mdcc.edu ■ *E-mail:* info@mail.north.mdcc.edu

Miami-Dade Community College North Campus-Hialeah Branch 1775 W 49th St . . . . Hialeah FL 33012 305-237-1800 237-1812

National School of Technology Inc
12000 Biscayne Blvd Suite302 . . . . .North Miami FL 33181 305-893-0005 893-9913
Web: www.national-school-tech.edu

Saint Thomas University 16400 NW 32nd Ave. . . . Miami FL 33054 305-625-6000 628-6591
TF: 800-367-9010 ■ *Web:* www.stu.edu

Trinity International University South Florida Campus 500 NE 1st Ave . . . . Miami FL 33132 305-577-4600 577-4612
Web: www.trin.edu/miami/index.html ■ *E-mail:* tcmadm@tiu.edu

University of Miami 1252 Memorial Dr . . . . .Coral Gables FL 33146 305-284-4323 284-2507
Web: www.miami.edu

Whitman Education Group Inc
4400 Biscayne Blvd. Miami FL 33137 305-575-6514 575-6535
TF: 800-445-6108

— Hospitals —

Phone | Fax

Baptist Hospital of Miami 8900 N Kendall Dr. . . . . Miami FL 33176 305-596-6503 598-5960
Web: www.baptisthealth.net/Hospitals/HomePage/0,1024,1,00.html

Cedars Medical Center 1400 NW 12th Ave . . . . . . Miami FL 33136 305-325-5511 325-5100
Web: www.cedarsmed.com ■ *E-mail:* cedars@hutton.net

Coral Gables Hospital 3100 Douglas Rd . . . .Coral Gables FL 33134 305-445-8461 441-6879

HealthSouth Doctors' Hospital
5000 University Dr . . . . .Coral Gables FL 33146 305-666-2111 669-2289*
**Fax:* Admitting

Jackson Memorial Hospital
1611 NW 12th Ave . . . . Miami FL 33136 305-585-1111 326-1974*
**Fax:* Admitting ■ *Web:* www.um-jmh.org

Kendall Medical Center 11750 Bird Rd. . . . . Miami FL 33175 305-223-3000 229-2444

Mercy Hospital 3663 S Miami Ave . . . . Miami FL 33133 305-854-4400 285-2967*
**Fax:* Admitting ■ *Web:* www.mercymiami.com

Miami Children's Hospital 3100 SW 62nd Ave. . . . Miami FL 33155 305-666-6511 665-1576
Web: www.mch.com ■ *E-mail:* info@mch.com

Mount Sinai Medical Center
4300 Alton Rd . . . . Miami Beach FL 33140 305-674-2121 674-2007
Web: www.mountsinaimiami.org

North Shore Medical Center 1100 NW 95th St. . . . Miami FL 33150 305-835-6000 694-3693

Palm Springs General Hospital
1475 W 49th St . . . . Hialeah FL 33012 305-558-2500 558-8679

Palmetto General Hospital 2001 W 68th St. . . . . Hialeah FL 33016 305-823-5000 364-2173
Web: www.tenethealth.com/Palmetto

Pan American Hospital 5959 NW 7th St . . . . Miami FL 33126 305-264-1000 265-6536
Web: www.pahnet.org/hospital.html

Parkway Regional Medical Center
160 NW 170th St . . . . North Miami Beach FL 33169 305-654-5050 654-5083

South Miami Hospital 6200 SW 73rd St . . . . Miami FL 33143 305-661-4611 663-5025*
**Fax:* Admitting
■ *Web:* www.baptisthealth.net/Hospitals/HomePage/0,1024,2,00.html
■ *E-mail:* corporatepr@baptisthealth.net

South Shore Hospital & Medical Center
630 Alton Rd . . . . Miami Beach FL 33139 305-672-2100 673-1617

Veterans Affairs Medical Center
1201 NW 16th St . . . . Miami FL 33125 305-324-4455 324-3232

— Attractions —

Phone | Fax

American Police Hall of Fame & Museum
3801 Biscayne Blvd. . . . . Miami FL 33137 305-573-0070 573-9819
Web: www.aphf.org ■ *E-mail:* policeinfo@aphf.org

Ancient Spanish Monastery
16711 W Dixie Hwy. . . . . North Miami Beach FL 33160 305-945-1462

Art Deco District & Welcome Center
1001 Ocean Dr. Miami Beach FL 33139 305-672-2014

Art Museum at Florida International University
SW 8th St & 107th Ave University Pk PC110. . . . . Miami FL 33199 305-348-2890 348-2762
Web: www.fiu.edu/museum.html

Atrium Gallery
16400 NW 32nd Ave Saint Thomas University. . . . . Miami FL 33054 305-628-6660 628-6703

Barnacle State Historic Site
3485 Main Hwy . . . . Coconut Grove FL 33133 305-448-9445 448-7484

Bass Museum of Art 2121 Park Ave . . . . . . Miami Beach FL 33139 305-673-7530 673-7062
Web: ci.miami-beach.fl.us/newcity/culture/bass.html

Bayside Marketplace 401 Biscayne Blvd . . . . Miami FL 33132 305-577-3344 577-0306

Biscayne National Park
9700 SW 328th St . . . . .Homestead FL 33033 305-230-1144 230-1190
Web: www.nps.gov/bisc/

Biscayne Nature Center
4000 Crandon Blvd . . . . Key Biscayne FL 33149 305-642-9600

Cape Florida State Recreation Area
1200 S Crandon Blvd . . . . Key Biscayne FL 33149 305-361-5811 365-0003

Coconut Grove Playhouse
3500 Main Hwy . . . . Coconut Grove FL 33133 305-442-4000 443-6369
Web: www.cgplayhouse.com/

CocoWalk 3015 Grand Ave Suite 118 . . . . Coconut Grove FL 33133 305-444-0777 441-8936
Web: www.cocowalk.com ■ *E-mail:* comments@cocowalk.com

Coral Castle 28655 S Dixie Hwy. . . . . .Homestead FL 33030 305-248-6344 248-6344

Crandon Park 4000 Crandon Blvd . . . . Key Biscayne FL 33149 305-361-5421

Dry Tortugas National Park
40001 SR 9336 Everglades National Park . . . . .Homestead FL 33034 305-242-7700 242-7728
Web: www.nps.gov/drto/

Eden of the Everglades
903 Dupont Rd. . . . . .Everglades City FL 34139 941-695-2800 695-4506
TF: 800-543-3367

Miami — Attractions (Cont'd)

Name / Address	City	State	Zip	Phone	Fax
Everglades Alligator Farm 40351 SW 192nd Ave	Homestead	FL	33090	305-247-2628	248-9711
Everglades National Park 40001 SR 9336	Homestead	FL	33034	305-242-7700	242-7711
Web: www.nps.gov/ever/home.htm					
Everglades Safari Park 26700 Tamiami Trail	Miami	FL	33194	305-226-6923	554-5666
Fairchild Tropical Garden 10901 Old Cutler Rd	Miami	FL	33156	305-667-1651	661-8953
Web: www.ftg.org					
Florida Grand Opera 1200 Coral Way	Miami	FL	33145	305-854-1643	856-1042
TF: 800-741-1010 ■ *Web:* www.fgo.org					
Florida Museum of Hispanic & Latin American Art 4006 Aurora St	Coral Gables	FL	33146	305-444-7060	261-6996
Web: www.latinoweb.com/museo/ ■ *E-mail:* hispmuseum@aol.com					
Fruit & Spice Park 24801 SW 187th Ave	Homestead	FL	33031	305-247-5727	245-3369
GableStage 1200 Anastasia Ave Biltmore Hotel	Coral Gables	FL	33134	305-445-1119	445-8645
Gator Park 24050 SW 8th St	Miami	FL	33184	305-559-2255	
TF: 800-559-2205 ■ *Web:* www.gatorpark.com					
Gleason Jackie Theater of the Performing Arts 1700 Washington Ave	Miami Beach	FL	33139	305-673-7300	538-6810
Gold Coast Railroad Museum 12450 SW 152nd St	Miami	FL	33177	305-253-0063	233-4641
Web: www.goldcoast-railroad.org					
Greynolds Park 17530 W Dixie Hwy	North Miami Beach	FL	33160	305-945-3425	
Gusman Center for the Performing Arts 174 E Flagler St	Miami	FL	33131	305-374-2444	374-0303
Historical Museum of Southern Florida 101 W Flagler St	Miami	FL	33130	305-375-1492	375-1609
Web: www.historical-museum.org/ ■ *E-mail:* hasf@ix.netcom.com					
Holocaust Memorial 1933-1945 Meridian Ave	Miami Beach	FL	33139	305-538-1663	538-2423
Ichimura Miami Japan Garden Watson Island & Macarthur Cswy	Miami Beach	FL	33139	305-858-5016	860-3922
IGFA Fishing Hall of Fame & Museum 300 Gulf Stream Way	Dania Beach	FL	33004	954-927-2628	924-4299
Web: www.igfa.org/igfahofm					
Lowe Art Museum University of Miami 1301 Stanford Dr	Coral Gables	FL	33124	305-284-3535	284-2024
Web: www.lowemuseum.org					
Malibu Grand Prix 7775 NW 8th St	Miami	FL	33126	305-266-2100	262-2251
Merrick House 907 Coral Way	Coral Gables	FL	33134	305-460-5361	
Miami Art Museum 101 W Flagler St	Miami	FL	33130	305-375-3000	375-1725
Miami Brewing CMiami Brewing Co 9292 NW 101st St	Miami	FL	33178	305-888-6505	888-8868
E-mail: reef@shadow.net					
Miami Chamber Symphony 1314 Miller Dr Gusman Concert Hall	Coral Gables	FL	33146	305-858-3500	857-5001
Miami Children's Museum 8603 S Dixie Hwy	Miami	FL	33143	305-663-8800	663-8878
Web: www.mcmuseum.org					
Miami City Ballet 905 Lincoln Rd	Miami Beach	FL	33139	305-532-4880	532-2726
Web: www.miamicityballet.org					
Miami Metrozoo 12400 SW 152nd St	Miami	FL	33177	305-251-0401	378-6381
Web: www.metro-dade.com/parks/metrozoo.htm					
Miami Seaquarium 4400 Rickenbacker Cswy	Miami	FL	33149	305-361-5705	361-6077
Web: www.miamiseaquarium.com					
Miccosukee Indian Village & Airboat Tours PO Box 440021	Miami	FL	33144	305-223-8380	223-1011
Monkey Jungle 14805 SW 216th St	Miami	FL	33170	305-235-1611	
Museum of Contemporary Art 770 NE 125th St	North Miami	FL	33161	305-893-6211	891-1472
Museum of Science 3280 S Miami Ave	Miami	FL	33129	305-854-4247	285-5801
Web: www.miamisci.org					
New World Symphony 541 Lincoln Rd	Miami Beach	FL	33139	305-673-3330	673-6749
Oleta River State Recreation Area 3400 NE 163rd St	North Miami Beach	FL	33160	305-919-1846	
Parrot Jungle & Gardens 11000 SW 57th Ave	Miami	FL	33156	305-666-7834	661-2230
Web: parrotjungle.com/ ■ *E-mail:* parrots@parrotjungle.com					
Pennekamp John Coral Reef State Park Mile Marker 102.5	Key Largo	FL	33037	305-451-1202	
South Florida Art Center 924 Lincoln Rd Suite 205	Miami Beach	FL	33139	305-674-8278	
Space Transit Planetarium 3280 S Miami Ave	Miami	FL	33129	305-854-4242	854-2239
Web: www.miamisci.org ■ *E-mail:* bdishong@miamisci.org					
Stardancer Casino Pier B Miami Beach Marina	Miami Beach	FL	33139	305-538-8300	538-2909
Venetian Pool 2701 DeSoto Blvd	Coral Gables	FL	33134	305-460-5356	460-5357
Vizcaya Museum & Gardens 3251 S Miami Ave	Miami	FL	33129	305-250-9133	285-2004
Weeks Air Museum 14710 SW 128th St Tamiami Airport	Miami	FL	33196	305-233-5197	232-4134
Web: www.weeksairmuseum.com					
Wolfsonian Museum 1001 Washington Ave	Miami Beach	FL	33139	305-531-1001	531-2133
Ziff Jewish Museum of Florida 301 Washington Ave	Miami Beach	FL	33139	305-672-5044	672-5933

SPORTS TEAMS & FACILITIES

Name / Address	City	State	Zip	Phone	Fax
American Airlines Arena 1 SE 3rd Ave Suite 2300	Miami	FL	33131	305-577-4328	372-0802*
**Fax:* Acctg ■ *Web:* www.aaarena.com					
Calder Race Course Inc 21001 NW 27th Ave	Miami	FL	33056	305-625-1311	620-2569
TF: 800-333-3227 ■ *Web:* www.calderracecourse.com ■ *E-mail:* marketing@calderracecourse.com					
Flagler Greyhound Track 401 NW 38th Ct	Miami	FL	33126	305-649-3000	631-4525
Florida Panthers 2555 Panther Pkwy National Car Rental Center	Sunrise	FL	33323	954-835-7000	835-8012
Web: www.flpanthers.com ■ *E-mail:* flpanthers@flpanthers.com					
Gulfstream Park 901 S Federal Hwy	Hallandale	FL	33009	954-454-7000	454-7827
Web: www.gulfstreampark.com					
Hialeah Park Race Course 2200 E 4th Ave	Hialeah	FL	33011	305-885-8000	887-8006
Web: www.hialeahpark.com					
Miami Arena 721 NW 1st Ave	Miami	FL	33136	305-530-4400	530-4429
Web: www.miamiarena.com					
Miami Breakers (soccer) Alton Rd & 12th Ave Flamingo Pk	Miami Beach	FL	33138	305-532-5080	532-0508
Miami Dolphins 2269 NW 199th St Pro Player Stadium	Miami	FL	33056	305-620-2578	
Web: dolphinsendzone.com					
Miami Fusion (soccer) 2200 Commercial Blvd Suite 104	Fort Lauderdale	FL	33309	954-739-2501	733-6105
Web: www.miamifusion.com					
Miami Heat 1 SE 3rd Ave American Airlines Arena Suite 2300	Miami	FL	33131	305-577-4328	789-5933*
**Fax:* Hum Res ■ *Web:* www.nba.com/heat					
Miami Jai-Alai 3500 NW 37th Ave	Miami	FL	33142	305-633-6400	633-4386
Web: www.fla-gaming.com/miami ■ *E-mail:* miajaili@netrunner.net					
Miami Tango (soccer) 10651 NW 19th St	Miami	FL	33172	305-593-6033	594-3973
Orange Bowl Stadium 1501 NW 3rd St	Miami	FL	33125	305-643-7100	643-7115
Pro Player Stadium 2269 NW 199th St	Miami	FL	33056	305-623-6100	624-6403
Web: www.proplayer.com					

— Events —

	Phone
4th of July at Bayfront Park (July 4)	305-358-7550
Arabian Nights Festival (early May)	305-688-4611
Art Deco Weekend Festival (mid-January)	305-672-2014
Art Expo (early January)	305-558-1758
Banyan Arts & Crafts Festival (mid-November)	305-444-7270
Beaux Arts Festival of the Arts (mid-January)	305-284-3535
Big Orange New Year's Eve Celebration (December 31)	305-358-7550
Bob Marley Festival (mid-February)	305-358-7550
Calle Ocho Festival (early March)	305-644-8888
Caribbean Festival (mid-October)	305-653-1877
Carnaval Miami (early March)	305-644-8888
Coconut Grove Arts Festival (mid-February)	305-447-0401
Coconut Grove Bed Race (mid-May)	305-444-7270
Colombian Festival (mid-July)	305-448-5558
Columbus Day Regatta (mid-October)	305-539-3000
Dade County Fair & Exposition (mid-March-early April)	305-223-7060
Dade Heritage Days (early April-mid-May)	305-358-9572
Dade Radio Tropical Hamboree Show (early February)	305-223-7060
Doral-Ryder Open (late February-early March)	305-477-4653
Ericsson Open (late March-early April)	305-442-3367
Fairchild Tropical Garden Caribbean Festival (late April)	305-667-1651
February Home Show (early February)	305-666-5944
Festival Miami (mid-September-mid-October)	305-284-4940
Florida Dance Festival (mid-late June)	800-252-0808
Florida Derby (mid-March)	305-931-7223
Freddick Bratcher Florida Dance Festival (late January)	305-448-2021
Grand Prix of Miami (mid-March)	305-539-3000
Great Sunrise Balloon Race & Festival (late May)	305-596-9040
Greater Miami Race for the Cure (mid-October)	305-666-7223
Hispanic Heritage Festival (October)	305-541-5023
Homestead Championship Rodeo (early February)	305-247-3515
International Mango Festival (mid-July)	305-667-1651
Italian Renaissance Festival (mid-March)	305-250-9133
Key Biscayne 4th of July Parade & Fireworks (July 4)	305-365-8901
Key Biscayne Art Festival (late January)	305-361-0049
King Mango Strut (late December)	305-444-7270
King Orange Jamboree Parade (late December)	305-371-4600
Kwanzaa Celebration (late December-early January)	305-936-5805
La Settimana del Cinema Italiano (mid-January)	305-861-2000
Metropolitan South Florida Fishing Tournament (December-mid-May)	305-569-0066

Miami — Events (Cont'd)

	Phone
Miami Beach Festival of the Arts (early February)	305-672-1272
Miami Billfish Tournament (early April)	305-598-2525
Miami Book Fair International (mid-November)	305-237-3258
Miami Film Festival (early February)	305-377-3456
Miami International Boat Show (mid-February)	305-531-8410
Miami International Map Fair (early February)	305-375-1492
Miami International Orchid Show (early March)	305-444-8484
Miami Reggae Festival (early August)	305-891-2944
Miami/Bahamas Goombay Festival (early June)	305-372-9966
Miccosukee Tribe's Indian Arts Festival (early January)	305-223-8380
National Children's Theatre Festival (mid-January)	305-444-9293
Ocean Drive Street Festival (mid-January)	305-672-2014
Orange Bowl (early January)	305-643-7100
Original Miami Beach Antique Show (late January-early February)	305-754-4931
Outdoor Festival of the Arts (early February)	305-673-7730
Puerto Rican Festival (late November)	305-448-5145
Redlands Natural Arts Festival (mid-January)	305-247-5727
Roots & Culture Festival (mid-May)	305-751-4222
Saint Stephen's Arts & Crafts Show (mid-February)	305-558-1758
Santa's Enchanted Forest (late November-early January)	305-893-0090
South Beach Film Festival (mid-late April)	305-532-1233
South Florida International Auto Show (early-mid-November)	305-947-5950
South Miami Art Festival (early November)	305-661-1621
Springtime Harvest Festival (early May)	954-987-4275
Subtropics Music Festival (mid-March-mid-May)	305-758-6676
Taste of the Beach (mid-April)	305-672-1270
Taste of the Grove (late January)	305-444-7270
Tropical Agricultural Fiesta (mid-July)	305-248-3311
West Indian Carnival Extravaganza (mid-October)	305-435-4845

Naples

Located on the west coast of Florida, on the shores of the Gulf of Mexico, Naples is also near the Florida Everglades, which is home to such species of wildlife as manatees, pelicans, Florida panthers, alligators, and sea turtles. These and other animals and birds can be viewed at a number of area attractions, including Big Cypress National Preserve, Corkscrew Swamp Sanctuary, and, of course, Everglades National Park. Airboat or swamp buggy rides offer visitors the opportunity for a close-up look at alligators and shore birds. The area around the Everglades is also home to members of the Seminole tribe, who gather in Naples each year at the first full moon in June for a four-day event, celebrating the Sacred Green Corn Ceremony.Naples is renowned for its pristine beaches along the Gulf, as well as its lakes, rivers, and bays, so it's not surprising that fishing is a popular sport there. Shelling is also a popular local activity, especially in the nearby resort areas of Sanibel and Marco Islands, which are noted for their white sand beaches and abundance of sea shells. Though rare in the rest of the world, left-handed shells (snail shells with openings on the left) are common along beaches in the Naples area. In addition to its many outdoor attractions, Naples features award-winning restaurants and a variety of shopping experiences, from quaint boutiques to upscale shops, as well as an array of downtown houses and buildings in Naples' noted style of architecture. Local resorts, hotels, and clubs offer live music nightly, with jazz as the music of choice.

Population	19,404	**Longitude**	81-47-41 W
Area (Land)	13.5 sq mi	**County**	Collier
Area (Water)	2.4 sq mi	**Time Zone**	EST
Elevation	9 ft	**Area Code/s**	941
Latitude	26-08-41 N		

— Average Temperatures and Precipitation —

TEMPERATURES

	Jan	Feb	Mar	Apr	May	Jun	Jul	Aug	Sep	Oct	Nov	Dec
High	76	77	81	85	88	90	91	92	91	87	82	78
Low	53	54	58	61	66	71	72	73	72	67	61	55

PRECIPITATION

	Jan	Feb	Mar	Apr	May	Jun	Jul	Aug	Sep	Oct	Nov	Dec
Inches	1.7	2.2	2.3	1.5	4.1	8.6	7.8	8.2	8.4	3.1	1.8	1.4

— Important Phone Numbers —

	Phone		Phone
AAA	941-594-5006	**Medical Referral**	941-436-5430
American Express Travel	941-262-3350	**Poison Control Center**	800-282-3171
Dental Referral	813-931-3018	**Time/Temp**	941-594-1234
Emergency	911	**Weather**	941-594-1234

— Information Sources —

				Phone	Fax
Collier County 3301 E Tamiami Trail	Naples	FL	34112	941-774-8383	774-4010
Web: www.naples.net/govern/zgovern.htm					
Collier County Public Library 650 Central Ave	Naples	FL	34102	941-262-4130	649-1293
Web: www.collier-lib.org					
Consumer Protection Agency 407 S Calhoun St 2nd Fl Mayo Bldg	Tallahassee	FL	32399	850-488-2221	487-4177
Economic Development Council 3050 N Horseshoe Dr Suite 120	Naples	FL	34104	941-263-8989	263-6021
Web: www.swfloridabusiness.com					
Naples Area Chamber of Commerce 895 5th Ave S	Naples	FL	34102	941-263-1858	435-9910
Web: www.naples-online.com ■ *E-mail:* chamber@naples-online.com					
Naples City Hall 735 8th St S	Naples	FL	34102	941-434-4717	434-4659
Web: gator.naples.net/govern/city					
Naples Mayor 735 8th St S	Naples	FL	34102	941-434-4601	434-4855
Web: www.naples.net/govern/city/index.htm ■ *E-mail:* naplesmayor&council@gulfcoast.net					

On-Line Resources

Absolute Guide to Naples Florida	www.bestof.net/naples/
Area Guide Naples	naples.areaguides.net
City Knowledge Naples	www.cityknowledge.com/fl_naples.htm
DiningGuide Naples	diningguide.net/apf/
DiningGuide Naples	diningguide.net/apf
Excite.com Naples City Guide	www.excite.com/travel/countries/united_states/florida/naples
HotelGuide Naples	hotelguide.net/naples/
MetroGuide Naples	metroguide.net/naples/
Naples & Southwest Florida Guide	www.naplesnet.com/naples2/index.html
Naples CityLink	usacitylink.com/citylink/fl/naples/default.html
Naples Florida	www.naples-florida.com
Naples Florida Visitor Information	www.azinet.com/Naples
Naples.com	www.naples.com
NITC Travelbase City Guide Naples	www.travelbase.com/auto/guides/naples-area-fl.html
Online City Guide to Naples	www.olcg.com/fl/naples/index.html
Surf & Sun Beach Vacation Guide to Naples	www.surf-sun.com/fl-naples-main.htm
Welcome to Naples Florida	www.naplesnet.com/naples/naples.htm

— Transportation Services —

AIRPORTS

■ **Naples Municipal Airport (APF)**

	Phone
5 miles SE of downtown (approx 15 minutes)	941-643-1415

Web: gator.naples.net/presents/airport

Airport Transportation

	Phone
Airport Connection Inc $5-8 fare to downtown	941-566-1700
Checker Cab $9 fare to downtown	941-455-5555

Naples (Cont'd)

Commercial Airlines

	Phone		Phone
American Eagle	800-433-7300	US Airways Express	800-428-4322
Cape Air	800-352-0714		

Charter Airlines

	Phone		Phone
Ambassador Airways	941-263-4200	Hutt Aviation Inc	800-488-8247
Continental Aviation Services Inc	800-962-0676	Jet 1 Charter	941-643-9700
Corporate America Aviation Inc	800-521-8585	Naples Air Service	800-997-8448
Executive Jet Management	877-356-5387	Regal Aviation	877-359-6520

■ **Southwest Florida International Airport (RSW)** — Phone
35 miles N of downtown Naples (approx 40 minutes) . . . 941-768-4321
Web: www.swfia.com ■ *E-mail:* swfia@swfia.com

Airport Transportation

	Phone
Admiralty Transportation Inc $56 fare to downtown Naples	941-275-7700
Airport Cab $56 fare to downtown Naples	941-489-4990
Airport Express Transportation $48 fare to downtown Naples	941-625-7606
Checker Cab $45 fare to downtown Naples	941-332-1511
Cordially Yours Airport Transportation $44 fare to downtown Naples	941-573-9700
Lou's Airport Transportation $46 fare to downtown Naples	941-549-5272

Commercial Airlines

	Phone		Phone
Air Canada	800-776-3000	LTU International	800-888-0200
AirTran	800-247-8726	Northwest	800-225-2525
American	800-433-7300	Spirit	800-772-7117
American Trans Air	800-225-2995	TWA	800-221-2000
Cape Air	800-352-0714	United	800-241-6522
Continental	800-525-0280	US Airways	800-428-4322
Delta	800-221-1212		

Charter Airlines

	Phone		Phone
Alliance Executive Charter Services	800-232-5387	Corporate America Aviation Inc	800-521-8585

CAR RENTALS

	Phone		Phone
Alamo-Fort Myers	941-768-2424	Hertz	941-643-0265
Avis	941-643-0900	Hertz-Fort Myers	941-768-3100
Avis-Fort Myers	941-768-2121	National	941-643-0200
Budget	941-643-2212	National-Fort Myers	941-768-2100
Budget-Fort Myers	941-768-1500	Sears	941-643-3066
Dollar	941-793-2226	Sears-Fort Myers	941-768-2500
Dollar-Fort Myers	941-768-2223	Thrifty	941-643-4550
Enterprise	941-643-3332	Thrifty-Fort Myers	941-489-3383
Enterprise-Fort Myers	941-332-4558		

LIMO/TAXI

	Phone		Phone
Ace Airport Transportation	941-352-4336	Local Motion Taxi	941-463-4111
Admiralty Transportation Inc	941-275-7700	Maxi Taxi	941-598-2600
Affordable Limousine	941-455-6007	Naples Taxi	941-643-2148
Airline Taxi & Limo	941-643-5757	Platinum Limousine	941-947-2077
Airport Cab	941-489-4990	USA Taxi	941-732-8294
Airport Connection Inc	941-566-1700	Yellow Cab	941-332-1055
Checker Cab	941-455-5555		

RAIL/BUS

				Phone
Greyhound Bus Station 2669 Davis Blvd *TF:* 800-231-2222	Naples	FL	34104	941-774-5660

— Accommodations —

HOTEL RESERVATION SERVICES

	Phone	Fax
Hotel Reservations Network Inc *TF Sales:* 800-964-6835 ■ *Web:* www.hoteldiscount.com	214-361-7311	361-7299
Southwest Florida Reservations *TF:* 800-733-7935	941-768-3633	768-9792

HOTELS, MOTELS, RESORTS

				Phone	Fax
Best Western 2329 9th St *TF:* 800-243-1148 ■ *Web:* www.bestwesternnaples.com/	Naples	FL	34103	941-261-1148	262-4684
Charter Club Resort 1000 10th Ave S *TF:* 800-494-5559 ■ *Web:* www.charterclubresort.com/ ■ *E-mail:* charterclub@worldnet.att.net	Naples	FL	34102	941-261-5559	261-6872
Comfort Inn & Suites 3860 Tollgate Blvd *TF:* 800-277-7517	Naples	FL	34114	941-353-9500	353-0035
Comfort Inn Downtown 1221 5th Ave S *TF:* 800-382-7941 ■ *Web:* www.comfortinnnaples.com	Naples	FL	33940	941-649-5800	649-0523
Courtyard by Marriott 3250 Tamiami Trail N	Naples	FL	34103	941-434-8700	434-7787
Cove Inn 900 Broad Ave S *TF:* 800-255-4365 ■ *Web:* www.bestof.net/naples/hotels/coveinn ■ *E-mail:* coveinn@compuserve.com	Naples	FL	34102	941-262-7161	261-6905
Edgewater Beach Hotel 1901 Gulf Shore Blvd N *TF:* 800-821-0196 ■ *Web:* www.edgewaternaples.com	Naples	FL	34102	941-262-6511	403-2100
Fairways Resort 103 Palm River Blvd *TF:* 800-835-1311	Naples	FL	34110	941-597-8181	597-5413
Hampton Inn 3210 Tamiami Trail N *TF:* 800-426-7866	Naples	FL	33940	941-261-8000	261-7802
Holiday Inn Downtown 1100 9th St N	Naples	FL	34102	941-262-7146	261-3809
Inn at Pelican Bay 800 Vanderbilt Beach Rd *TF:* 800-597-8770 ■ *Web:* www.naplesinn.com/pelicanbay/pbhome.htm ■ *E-mail:* pelicanbay@naplesinn.com	Naples	FL	34108	941-597-8777	597-8012
Inn of Naples 4055 Tamiami Trail N *TF:* 800-237-8858 ■ *Web:* www.flhotels.com/naples/innofnaples.html ■ *E-mail:* info@innofnaples.com	Naples	FL	34103	941-649-5500	430-0422
Inn on Fifth 699 5th Ave S *TF:* 888-403-8778 ■ *Web:* www.naplesinn.com/fifth/fhome.htm ■ *E-mail:* fifth@naplesinn.com	Naples	FL	34102	941-403-8777	403-8778
Knights Inn 6600 Dudley Dr *E-mail:* spinnaker@naplesnet.com	Naples	FL	34105	941-434-0444	434-0414
La Playa Beach Resort 9891 Gulf Shore Dr *TF:* 800-237-6883 ■ *Web:* www.noblehousehotels.com/playa/index.html	Naples	FL	34108	941-597-3123	597-6278
Naples Beach Hotel & Golf Club 851 Gulf Shore Dr N *TF:* 800-237-7600 ■ *Web:* www.naplesbeachhotel.com	Naples	FL	34102	941-261-2222	261-7380
Naples Hotel & Suites 221 9th St S	Naples	FL	34102	941-262-6181	262-0318
Old Naples Trianon 955 7th Ave S *TF:* 800-859-3939 ■ *Web:* www.trianon.com	Naples	FL	34102	941-435-9600	261-0025
Olde Naples Inn & Suites 801 3rd St S *TF:* 800-637-6036 ■ *Web:* www.oldenaplesinn.com ■ *E-mail:* reservations@oldenaplesinn.com	Naples	FL	34102	941-262-5194	262-4876
Park Shore Resort 600 Neapolitan Way *TF:* 800-548-2077 ■ *Web:* www.sunstream.com/parkshore/home.htm	Naples	FL	34103	941-263-2222	263-0946
Quality Inn & Suites Golf Resort 4100 Golden Gate Pkwy *TF:* 800-277-0017	Naples	FL	34116	941-455-1010	455-4038
Quality Inn Gulfcoast 2555 Tamiami Trail N	Naples	FL	34103	941-261-6046	261-5742
Red Roof Inn 1925 Davis Blvd *TF:* 800-843-7663	Naples	FL	34104	941-774-3117	775-5333
Registry Resort 475 Seagate Dr *TF:* 800-247-9810	Naples	FL	34103	941-597-3232	597-3147
Ritz-Carlton Naples 280 Vanderbilt Beach Rd *TF:* 800-241-3333 ■ *Web:* www.ritzcarlton.com/location/NorthAmerica/Naples/main.htm	Naples	FL	34108	941-598-3300	598-6690
Vanderbilt Beach Resort 9225 Gulf Shore Dr N *TF:* 800-243-9076 ■ *Web:* www.vanderbiltbeachresort.com ■ *E-mail:* vbresort@naplesnet.com	Naples	FL	34108	941-597-3144	597-2199
Vanderbilt Inn on the Gulf 11000 Gulf Shore Dr N *TF:* 800-643-8654	Naples	FL	34108	941-597-3151	597-3099
Wellesley Inn 1555 5th Ave S *TF:* 800-444-8888	Naples	FL	34102	941-793-4646	793-5248

— Restaurants —

				Phone
Andre's Steak House (Steak) 2800 Tamiami Trail N	Naples	FL	34103	941-263-5851
Bangkok Cuisine (Thai) 572 9th St N	Naples	FL	34102	941-261-5900
Bayside (Seafood) 4270 Gulf Shore Dr N	Naples	FL	34103	941-649-5552

Naples — Restaurants (Cont'd)

				Phone
Bernard's (Continental) 4300 Royal Wood Blvd	Naples	FL	34112	941-775-4451
Blue Heron (Continental) 387 Capri Blvd.	Naples	FL	34113	941-394-6248
Brown Bag (Barbecue) 4748 Golden Gate Pkwy	Naples	FL	34116	941-455-4366
Chardonnay (French) 2331 Tamiami Trail N.	Naples	FL	34103	941-261-1744
Dock at Crayton Cove (Seafood) 801 12th Ave S	Naples	FL	34102	941-263-9940
Empire China (Chinese) 2085 9th St N	Naples	FL	34102	941-649-1885
Erin's Isle (Irish) 7110 Isle of Capri Rd	Naples	FL	34114	941-774-1880
Fantozzi's of Olde Naples (Gourmet) 1148 3rd St S	Naples	FL	34105	941-262-4808
Farino's (Italian) 4000 N Tamiami Trail	Naples	FL	34103	941-262-2883
Frascatti's (Italian) 1258 N Airport Rd	Naples	FL	34104	941-643-5709
Fujiyama Steak House of Japan (Japanese) 2555 Tamiami Trail N	Naples	FL	34103	941-261-4332
Graf Rudi (German) 870 Neopolitan Way	Naples	FL	34103	941-434-6653
Grecian Gardens (Greek) 3148 Tamiami Trail E	Naples	FL	34112	941-774-4472
Landry's (Seafood) 1355 5th Ave S	Naples	FL	34102	941-793-7700
Le Bistro (French) 842 Neopolitan Way	Naples	FL	34102	941-434-7061
Legends Steakhouse (Steak) 8939 Tamiami Trail N	Naples	FL	34108	941-597-0080
Margaux's (French) 3080 Tamiami Trail N.	Naples	FL	34103	941-434-2773
Maxwell's on the Bay (Steak/Seafood) 4300 Gulf Shore Dr N *Web:* www.naples.com/maxwells	Naples	FL	34103	941-263-1662
McCabe's (Irish) 699 5th Ave S *Web:* www.naplesinn.com/fifth/rest.htm	Naples	FL	34102	941-403-7170
Merriman's Wharf (Steak/Seafood) 1200 5th Ave S	Naples	FL	34102	941-261-1811
Michelbob's Championship Ribs (Barbecue) 371 Airport-Pulling Rd N	Naples	FL	34104	941-643-2877
Midori (Japanese) 885 Vanderbilt Beach Rd	Naples	FL	34108	941-596-9112
Pacific 41 (Steak/Seafood) 173 9th St S	Naples	FL	34102	941-649-5858
Panevino Ristorante (Italian) 8853 Tamiami Trail N *E-mail:* panevino@qpg.com	Naples	FL	34108	941-514-8655
Pazzo! (Italian) 853 5th Ave S	Naples	FL	34102	941-434-8494
Pewter Mug (Steak/Seafood) 12300 Tamiami Trail N	Naples	FL	34110	941-597-3017
Rancho Grande (Mexican) 4859 Golden Gate Pkwy	Naples	FL	34116	941-348-8180
Rib City Grill (Barbecue) 9191 Tamiami Trail N	Naples	FL	34108	941-591-3500
Riverwalk Fish & Ale House (Seafood) 500 5th Ave S Tin City	Naples	FL	34102	941-263-2734
Savannah (New American) 5200 Tamiami Trail N *Web:* www.savannahrestaurant.com ■ *E-mail:* alex@awebstation.net	Naples	FL	34103	941-261-2555
Ship The (Steak/Seafood) 24080 Tamiami Trail N	Bonita Springs	FL	34134	941-947-3333
Szchuan Chinese (Chinese) 3300 Tamiami Trail E	Naples	FL	34112	941-732-1441
Trattoria Milano (Italian) 336 9th St N	Naples	FL	34102	941-643-2030
Truffles (Italian) 8920 Tamiami Trail N *E-mail:* cuisine@sprintmail.com	Naples	FL	34108	941-597-8119

— Goods and Services —

SHOPPING

Name	City	State	ZIP	Phone	Fax
5th Avenue South 720 5th Ave S Suite 111 *Web:* www.fifthavenuesouth.com	Naples	FL	34102	941-435-3742	435-0994
Coastland Center Mall 1900 9th St SW	Naples	FL	34102	941-262-2323	262-5125
Grand Central Station 388 Goodlette Rd S	Naples	FL	34102	941-261-1002	
Greentree Center 2346 Immokalee Rd	Naples	FL	34110	941-566-1100	566-1764
Old Naples Seaport 1001 10th Ave S	Naples	FL	34102	941-434-9300	434-6334
Pavilion Shopping Center 823 Vanderbilt Beach Rd	Naples	FL	34108	941-592-7720	592-7822
Prime Outlets at Naples 7222 Isle of Capri Rd Suite 121 *TF:* 888-545-7196 ■ *Web:* www.primeretail.com/naples	Naples	FL	34114	941-775-8083	775-8415
Tin City Waterfront Marketplace 1200 5th Ave S *Web:* www.tin-city.com ■ *E-mail:* info@tin-city.com	Naples	FL	34102	941-262-4200	262-5966
Village on Venetian Bay 4200 Gulf Shore Blvd.	Naples	FL	34103	941-261-6100	262-6315
Village Plaza Shopping Center 2377 Davis Blvd	Naples	FL	34104	941-774-3338	
Waterside Shops at Pelican Bay 5415 N Tamiami Tr Suite 320	Naples	FL	34108	941-598-1605	598-1773

BANKS

Name	City	State	ZIP	Phone	Fax
AmSouth Bank 4851 Tamiami Trail	Naples	FL	34103	941-261-5522	261-2476
Atlantic States Bank 5010 N Airport Pulling Rd	Naples	FL	34105	941-435-1333	435-1277
Citizens Community Bank of Florida 5101 Tamiami Trail E *Web:* www.ccbank.com	Naples	FL	34113	941-775-0074	775-7854
Community Bank of Naples NA 5150 Tamiami Trail N *TF:* 888-649-1500 ■ *Web:* www.communitybankofnaples.com	Naples	FL	34103	941-649-1500	649-1411
Fifth Third Bank of Florida 4099 Tamiami Trail N *TF:* 800-972-3030 ■ *Web:* www.53.com	Naples	FL	34101	941-430-5300	430-5343
First National Bank of Naples 900 Goodlette Rd N *TF:* 800-262-7600	Naples	FL	34101	941-262-7600	262-5294
First Union National Bank 900 5th Ave S *TF:* 800-275-3862	Naples	FL	34102	941-435-3120	435-3127
Gulf Coast National Bank 3838 Tamiami Trail N *TF:* 800-648-4262	Naples	FL	34103	941-261-4262	261-2990
NationsBank 796 5th Ave S	Naples	FL	34102	941-436-1960	643-4213
PNC Bank FSB 3003 Tamiami Trail N Suite 100	Naples	FL	34103	941-643-7960	643-7966
SouthTrust Bank NA 811 Vanderbilt Beach Rd *TF:* 800-239-9987	Naples	FL	34108	941-598-1001	598-3152
World Savings Bank 8877 Tamiami Trail N	Naples	FL	34108	941-514-1766	

BUSINESS SERVICES

Name	Phone	Name	Phone
AAA Employment	941-262-1755	**Mail Boxes Etc**	941-455-6245
Accu-Temps	941-261-5586	**Manpower Temporary Services**	941-434-5226
Golden Gate Courier	941-352-6677	**Post Office**	800-275-8777
Kelly Services	941-434-9030	**UPS**	800-742-5877
Kinko's	941-643-4477	**Western Staff Services**	941-262-8111

— Media —

PUBLICATIONS

Name	City	State	ZIP	Phone	Fax
Naples Daily News‡ 1075 Central Ave. *Web:* www.naplesnews.com ■ *E-mail:* info@naplesnews.com	Naples	FL	34102	941-262-3161	263-4816
Naples Illustrated 1250 Tamiami Trail N Suite 305 *TF Sales:* 800-308-7346*	Naples	FL	34102	941-434-6966	435-0409

‡Daily newspapers

TELEVISION

Name	City	State	ZIP	Phone	Fax
WBBH-TV Ch 20 (NBC) 3719 Central Ave.	Fort Myers	FL	33901	941-939-2020	936-7771
WEVU-TV Ch 7 (UPN) 301 Tower Rd. *Web:* www.wevutv.com	Naples	FL	34113	941-793-9603	793-3957
WFTX-TV Ch 36 (Fox) 621 SW Pine Island Rd	Cape Coral	FL	33991	941-574-3636	574-2025
WGCU-TV Ch 30 (PBS) 10501 FGCU Blvd	Fort Myers	FL	33965	941-590-2300	590-2310
WINK-TV Ch 11 (CBS) 2824 Palm Beach Blvd.	Fort Myers	FL	33916	941-334-1111	334-0744
WTVK-TV Ch 46 (WB) 3451 Bonita Bay Blvd Suite 101	Bonita Springs	FL	34134	941-498-4600	498-0146
WZVN-TV Ch 26 (ABC) 3719 Central Ave	Fort Myers	FL	33901	941-939-2020	936-7771

RADIO

Name	City	State	ZIP	Phone	Fax
WARO-FM 94.5 MHz (CR) 2824 Palm Beach Blvd.	Fort Myers	FL	33916	941-479-5506	332-0767
WAVV-FM 101.1 MHz (B/EZ) 11800 Tamiami Trail E.	Naples	FL	34113	941-775-9288	793-7000
WAYJ-FM 88.7 MHz (Rel) 1860 Boyscout Dr Suite 202 *TF:* 888-936-1929 ■ *Web:* wayfm.com/wayj ■ *E-mail:* wayj@wayfm.com	Fort Myers	FL	33907	941-936-1929	936-5433
WCKT-FM 107.1 MHz (Ctry) 4110 Center Pointe Dr Suite 212 **Fax:* Hum Res ■ *Web:* www.wckt.com	Fort Myers	FL	33916	941-275-5107	275-8684*
WGCU-FM 90.1 MHz (NPR) 10501 FGCU Blvd *Web:* wgcufm.fgcu.edu	Fort Myers	FL	33965	941-590-2500	590-2511
WGUF-FM 98.9 MHz (AC) 2640 Golden Gate Pkwy Suite 316	Naples	FL	34105	941-435-9100	435-9106
WINK-AM 1240 kHz (N/T) 2824 Palm Beach Blvd.	Fort Myers	FL	33916	941-334-1111	332-0767
WJBX-FM 99.3 MHz (Alt) 12995 S Cleveland Ave Suite 258	Fort Myers	FL	33907	941-275-9980	275-5611
WJST-FM 106.3 MHz (Nost) 12995 S Cleveland Ave Suite 258	Fort Myers	FL	33907	941-275-9980	275-5611
WNOG-AM 1270 kHz (N/T) 333 8th St S	Naples	FL	34102	941-263-4600	263-6525
WODX-AM 1480 kHz (B/EZ) 1112 1/2 N Collier Blvd *Web:* www.wodx.com ■ *E-mail:* wodx@wodx.com	Marco Island	FL	34145	941-394-5353	642-6970

Naples — Radio (Cont'd)

				Phone	Fax
WOLZ-FM 95.3 MHz (Oldies) 7290 College Pkwy Suite 200	Fort Myers	FL	33907	941-275-0095	275-3299
WQNU-FM 105.5 MHz (Ctry) 4110 Center Pointe Dr Suite 212	Fort Myers	FL	33916	941-275-5107	275-8684*
*Fax: Hum Res ■ Web: www.wqnu.com ■ E-mail: mts1055@aol.com					
WSGL-FM 103.1 MHz (AC) 2500 Airport Rd S Suite 211	Naples	FL	34101	941-793-1031	793-7329
WSOR-FM 90.9 MHz (Rel) 940 Tarpon St	Fort Myers	FL	33916	941-334-1393	334-0596
WSRX-FM 89.5 MHz (AC) 2132 Shadowlawn Dr	Naples	FL	34112	941-775-8950	774-5889
WWGR-FM 101.9 MHz (Ctry) 4210 Metro Pkwy Suite 210	Fort Myers	FL	33916	941-936-2599	936-0977
Web: www.gatorcountry1019.com					

— Colleges/Universities —

				Phone	Fax
International College 2654 Tamiami Trail E	Naples	FL	34112	941-774-4700	774-4593
TF: 800-466-8017 ■ *Web:* www.internationalcollege.edu					

— Hospitals —

				Phone	Fax
Naples Community Hospital 350 7th St N	Naples	FL	34102	941-436-5000	436-5914
Web: www.nchhcs.org ■ *E-mail:* info@nchhcs.org					
North Collier Hospital 11190 Health Park Blvd	Naples	FL	34110	941-513-7000	513-7779

— Attractions —

				Phone	Fax
Big Cypress Gallery 52388 Tamiami Trail	Ochopee	FL	34141	941-695-2428	695-2670
TF: 888-999-9113 ■ *Web:* www.clydebutcher.com					
Big Cypress National Preserve Hwy 41 Tamiami Tr.	Ochopee	FL	34141	941-695-4111	695-3007
Web: www.nps.gov/bicy/					
Briggs Nature Center 401 Shell Island Rd	Naples	FL	34113	941-775-8569	775-5139
Web: www.conservancy.org					
Cambier Park 755 Ace Ave S	Naples	FL	34102	941-434-4690	434-3049
Caribbean Gardens 1590 Goodlette-Frank Rd	Naples	FL	34102	941-262-5409	262-6866
Web: www.caribbeangardens.com/					
Clam Pass County Park Seagate Dr.	Naples	FL	34103	941-353-0404	353-1002
Collier County Museum 3301 Tamiami Trail E	Naples	FL	34112	941-774-8476	774-8580
Web: www.colliermuseum.com					
Collier Seminole State Park 20200 Tamiami Trail E.	Naples	FL	34114	941-394-3397	394-5113
Conservancy Nature Center 1450 Merrihue Dr	Naples	FL	34102	941-262-0304	262-0672
Web: www.conservancy.org					
Corkscrew Swamp Sanctuary 375 Sanctuary Rd W.	Naples	FL	34120	941-348-9151	348-9155
Web: www.audubon.org/local/sanctuary/corkscrew/index.html					
DeBruyne Fine Art Gallery 390 Broad Ave S	Naples	FL	34102	941-649-5585	649-5871
TF: 800-967-1268					
Delnor-Wiggins Pass State Recreation Area 11100 Gulfshore Dr.	Naples	FL	34108	941-597-6196	591-8223
East Naples Community Park 3500 Thomasson Dr	Naples	FL	34112	941-793-4414	793-7358
Eden of the Everglades 903 Dupont Rd.	Everglades City	FL	34139	941-695-2800	695-4506
TF: 800-543-3367					
Fleischmann Park 1600 Fleischmann Blvd	Naples	FL	34102	941-434-4692	434-3044
Florida Sports Park PO Box 990010	Naples	FL	34116	941-774-2701	774-4118
TF: 800-897-2701 ■ *Web:* www.florida-sports-park.com					
King Richard's Family Fun Park 6780 N Airport-Pulling Rd	Naples	FL	34109	941-598-1666	514-7164
Lowdermilk Park 1301 Gulf Shore Blvd N	Naples	FL	34102	941-434-4698	
Naples Art Association-Von Leibig Art Center 585 Park St	Naples	FL	34102	941-262-6517	262-5404
Naples Depot 1051 5th Ave S	Naples	FL	34102	941-262-1776	262-5119
Naples Horse & Carriage 1450 Whippoorwill Ln	Naples	FL	34105	941-649-1210	649-6434
Naples Philharmonic Center for the Arts 5833 Pelican Bay Blvd	Naples	FL	34108	941-597-1900	597-7856
Web: www.naplesphilcenter.org					
Naples Players 701 5th Ave S Sugden Community Theatre	Naples	FL	34102	941-263-7990	434-7772
Web: gator.naples.net/presents/theatre ■ *E-mail:* theatre@naples.net					
Naples Princess Cruise Line 1001 10th Ave S	Naples	FL	34102	941-649-2275	649-7357
Web: www.naplesprincesscruises.com ■ *E-mail:* naplesprin@aol.com					
Naples Trolley Tours 1010 6th Ave S	Naples	FL	34102	941-262-7300	262-6967
Palm Cottage 137 12th Ave S	Naples	FL	34102	941-261-8164	435-1438
Philharmonic Center for the Arts Galleries 5833 Pelican Bay Blvd	Naples	FL	34108	941-597-1111	597-8163
Web: www.naplesphilcenter.org					
Shaw Gallery of Fine Art 761 Fifth Ave S	Naples	FL	34102	941-261-7828	261-6108
TF: 888-406-1369 ■ *Web:* www.shawgallery.com ■ *E-mail:* info@shawgallery.com					
Sugden Community Theatre 701 5th Ave S	Naples	FL	34102	941-263-7990	434-7772
Web: gator.naples.net/presents/theatre/np_newth.htm ■ *E-mail:* theatre@naples.net					
Teddy Bear Museum 2511 Pine Ridge Rd	Naples	FL	34109	941-598-2711	598-9239
Web: www.teddymuseum.com					
Tin City Waterfront Marketplace 1200 5th Ave S.	Naples	FL	34102	941-262-4200	262-5966
Web: www.tin-city.com ■ *E-mail:* info@tin-city.com					
Veterans Community Park 1900 Immokalee Rd	Naples	FL	34110	941-566-2367	566-8128
Village on Venetian Bay 4200 Gulf Shore Blvd.	Naples	FL	34103	941-261-6100	262-6315

— Events —

	Phone
American Street Craft Show (early September)	941-435-3742
Art Encounter (February)	941-262-6517
Art in the Park (November-May)	941-262-6517
Christmas Walk & Festival of Lights (early December)	941-435-3742
Classic Swamp Buggy Races (early March & mid-late May & late October)	941-774-2701
Fourth of July Festival (July 4)	941-434-4717
Grand Millenium Parade (early December)	941-435-3742
Lunar Festival (mid-April)	941-992-2184
Millenium Lifestyle & Business Expo (early-mid-May)	941-435-3742
Naples Invitational Art Fest (late January)	941-263-1667
Naples National Art Festival (late February)	941-262-6517
Naples Saint Patrick's Day Parade (mid-March)	941-774-6086
Naples/Fort Myers Bluegrass Jam (mid-March)	941-992-2184
National Art Association Founders Exhibit (March)	941-262-6517
Octoberfest & Sidewalk Sale (late October)	941-435-3742
Summerjazz on the Gulf (May-September)	941-261-2222
Swamp Buggy Parade (mid-late October)	941-774-2701
Thanksgiving Weekend Festival (late November)	941-435-3742
World Orchid Symposium (late October)	941-261-2222

Orlando

Since the opening of Walt Disney World in 1971, Orlando has been a top vacation spot for travelers from all over the world. In addition to the Magic Kingdom and EPCOT, the park area also encompasses Disney-MGM Studios, River Country and Disney's Typhoon Lagoon aquatic parks, and Pleasure Island. Also in the surrounding Orlando area are Universal Studios Florida, the largest working film studio outside Hollywood; Sea World; Cypress Gardens; and Splendid China theme park with more than 60 scaled-down models of the greatest landmarks in China. Besides its many theme parks, restaurants, and hotels, Orlando also has several fine museums, more than 100 golf courses, fishing, water skiing, horseback riding, and hot-air ballooning. The Kennedy Space Center is on the Atlantic coast in nearby Cocoa Beach.

Population	181,175	**Longitude**	81-37-94 W
Area (Land)	67.3 sq mi	**County**	Orange
Area (Water)	4.7 sq mi	**Time Zone**	EST
Elevation	106 ft	**Area Code/s**	407, 321
Latitude	28-53-81 N		

Orlando (Cont'd)

— Average Temperatures and Precipitation —

TEMPERATURES

	Jan	Feb	Mar	Apr	May	Jun	Jul	Aug	Sep	Oct	Nov	Dec
High	71	73	78	83	88	91	92	92	90	85	79	73
Low	49	50	55	59	66	72	73	73	72	66	58	51

PRECIPITATION

	Jan	Feb	Mar	Apr	May	Jun	Jul	Aug	Sep	Oct	Nov	Dec
Inches	2.3	3.0	3.2	1.8	3.6	7.3	7.3	6.8	6.0	2.4	2.3	2.2

— Important Phone Numbers —

	Phone		Phone
AAA	407-894-3333	**Medical Referral**	407-897-1700
American Express Travel	407-843-0004	**Poison Control Center**	800-282-3171
Dental Referral	407-894-9798	**Time**	407-646-3131
Emergency	911	**Weather**	321-255-2900
HotelDocs	800-468-3537		

— Information Sources —

				Phone	Fax
Better Business Bureau Serving Central Florida 151 Wymore Rd Suite 100	Altamonte Springs	FL	32714	407-621-3300	786-2625
Web: www.orlando.bbb.org					
Greater Orlando Chamber of Commerce PO Box 1234	Orlando	FL	32802	407-425-1234	839-5020
Web: www.orlando.org					
Official Visitor Center 8723 International Dr.	Orlando	FL	32819	407-363-5871	
Orange County PO Box 1393	Orlando	FL	32802	407-836-7350	836-5879
Web: www.citizens-first.co.orange.fl.us					
Orange County Convention Center 9800 International Dr.	Orlando	FL	32819	407-345-9800	345-9876*
**Fax:* Mktg ■ *Web:* www.orlandoconvention.com					
Orange County Library System 101 E Central Blvd	Orlando	FL	32801	407-425-4694	648-0523
Web: www.ocls.lib.fl.us					
Orlando Centroplex & Expo Center 500 W Livingston St	Orlando	FL	32801	407-849-2000	423-3482
Web: www.orlandocentroplex.com					
Orlando City Hall 400 S Orange Ave	Orlando	FL	32801	407-246-2221	246-2842
Web: www.ci.orlando.fl.us					
Orlando Mayor 400 S Orange Ave	Orlando	FL	32801	407-246-2221	246-2842
Web: www.ci.orlando.fl.us/welcome/index.html					
Orlando Planning & Development Dept 400 S Orange Ave	Orlando	FL	32801	407-246-2269	246-2895
Web: www.ci.orlando.fl.us/departments/planning_and_development/dir.html					
Orlando/Orange County Convention & Visitors Bureau 6700 Forum Dr Suite 100	Orlando	FL	32821	407-363-5871	370-5022
TF: 800-643-9492 ■ *Web:* www.go2orlando.com					

On-Line Resources

4Orlando.com	www.4orlando.com
Access America Orlando	orlando.accessamer.com/
Area Guide Orlando	orlando.areaguides.net
City Knowledge Orlando	www.cityknowledge.com/fl_orlando.htm
CitySearch Orlando	orlando.citysearch.com
CityTravelGuide.com Orlando	www.citytravelguide.com/orlando.htm
DigitalCity Orlando	home.digitalcity.com/orlando
DiningGuide Orlando	orlando.diningguide.net
Downtown Orlando	www.downtownorlando.com/
Essential Guide to Orlando	www.ego.net/us/fl/orlando/
EventGuide Orlando	orlando.eventguide.com/
Events Guide Orlando	eventguide.com/mco/
Excite.com Orlando City Guide	www.excite.com/travel/countries/united_states/florida/orlando
Go2Orlando	www.go2orlando.com
HotelGuide Orlando	orlando.hotelguide.net
I Love Orlando	www.iloveorlando.com
Index 411 Orlando	www.index411.com/orlando/01003a.htm
Inside Central Florida	www.insidecentralflorida.com
MetroGuide Orlando	metroguide.net/orlando/
NITC Travelbase City Guide Orlando	www.travelbase.com/auto/guides/orlando-area-fl.html
Open World City Guides Orlando	www.worldexecutive.com/cityguides/orlando/
Orl.com	www.orl.com/
Orlando	www.iu.net/orlando/
Orlando Connections	www.aesir.com/Orlando/Welcome.html
Orlando Golf Guide	orlando-golf.com
Orlando Graphic City Guide	www.futurecast.com/gcg/orlando.htm
Orlando Holiday Choice	www.holiday-choice.com
Orlando Hotel Source	www.hotelorlando.com
Orlando Online	orlandoonline.com
Orlando Travel	www.orlandotravel.com/
Slant The	www.theslant.com/
Virtual Voyages Orlando	www.virtualvoyages.com/usa/fl/orlando/orlando.sht

— Transportation Services —

AIRPORTS

	Phone
■ **Orlando International Airport (MCO)**	
8 miles SE of downtown (approx 20 minutes)	407-825-2001
Web: fcn.state.fl.us/goaa	

Airport Transportation

	Phone
Lynx Transportation Authority $1 fare to downtown	407-841-8240
Mears Motor Shuttle $12 fare to downtown	407-423-5566

Commercial Airlines

	Phone		Phone
Aerolineas Argentinas	800-333-0276	**Icelandair**	800-223-5500
Air Canada	800-776-3000	**KLM**	800-374-7747
AirTran	800-247-8726	**MetroJet**	888-638-7653
American	800-433-7300	**Midway**	800-446-4392
American Trans Air	800-225-2995	**Midwest Express**	800-452-2022
British Airways	800-247-9297	**Northwest**	800-225-2525
Comair	800-354-9822	**Southwest**	800-435-9792
Continental	800-231-0856	**Spirit**	800-772-7117
Continental Express	800-525-0280	**TransBrasil**	800-872-3153
Delta	407-849-6400	**TWA**	800-221-2000
Delta Express	800-325-5205	**United**	800-241-6522
Eastwind	888-327-8946	**US Airways**	800-428-4322
Gulfstream International Airlines	800-525-0280	**Virgin Atlantic**	800-862-8621

Charter Airlines

	Phone		Phone
Canada 3000	407-825-3000	**Whisper Airlines Inc**	407-324-4110

CAR RENTALS

	Phone		Phone
Alamo	407-857-8200	**Hertz**	407-859-8400
Avis	407-825-3700	**National**	407-855-4170
Budget	407-850-6700	**Thrifty**	407-380-1002
Dollar	407-825-3265		

LIMO/TAXI

	Phone		Phone
Absolute Limousine	407-857-5466	**Murray Hill Transportation**	407-658-2284
Ace Metro Cab	407-855-1111	**Orlando Limousine**	407-788-0355
Carey Limousine	407-876-9148	**Showtime Limousine**	407-699-6060
Mears Transportation	407-422-5466	**Yellow Cab**	407-422-5151

MASS TRANSIT

	Phone
Tri County Transit Authority $1 Base fare	407-841-8240

RAIL/BUS

				Phone
Amtrak Auto Train 600 Persimmon Ave	Sanford	FL	32771	407-330-6066
TF: 800-872-7245				
Amtrak Station 1400 Sligh Blvd	Orlando	FL	32806	407-425-9411
TF: 800-872-7245				
Greyhound Bus Station 555 John Young Pkwy	Orlando	FL	32805	407-292-3407
TF: 800-231-2222				

Orlando (Cont'd)

— Accommodations —

HOTEL RESERVATION SERVICES

	Phone	Fax
Accommodations Express	609-391-2100	525-0111
TF: 800-444-7666 ■ *Web:* www.accommodationsxpress.com ■ *E-mail:* accomexp@acy.digex.net		
Accommodations USA	407-931-0003	931-1003
Central Reservation Service	407-740-6442	740-8222
TF: 800-548-3311 ■ *Web:* www.reservation-services.com ■ *E-mail:* cenresbos@aol.com		
Hotel Reservations Network Inc	214-361-7311	361-7299
TF Sales: 800-964-6835 ■ *Web:* www.hoteldiscount.com		
Know Before You Go Reservations	407-352-9813	352-9814
TF: 800-749-1993 ■ *Web:* www.1travel.com/knowbeforeyougo		
Quikbook	212-532-1660	532-1556
TF: 800-789-9887 ■ *Web:* www.quikbook.com		

HOTELS, MOTELS, RESORTS

				Phone	Fax
Adam's Mark of Orlando 1500 Sand Lake Rd.	Orlando	FL	32809	407-859-1500	855-1585
TF: 800-444-2326 ■ *Web:* www.adamsmark.com/orland.htm					
Bay Hill Golf Club & Lodge 9000 Bay Hill Blvd	Orlando	FL	32819	407-876-2429	876-1035
TF: 888-422-9445 ■ *Web:* www.bayhill.com					
Best Western 8421 S Orange Blossom Trail	Orlando	FL	32809	407-855-6060	855-7150
TF: 800-327-9742					
Best Western Kissimmee 2261 E Irlo Bronson Memorial Hwy.	Kissimmee	FL	34744	407-846-2221	846-1095
TF: 800-944-0062					
Best Western Lake Buena Vista Hotel 2000 Hotel Plaza Blvd	Lake Buena Vista	FL	32830	407-828-2424	827-6390
TF: 800-348-3765					
Best Western Maingate Hotel 8600 W Irlo Bronson Memorial Hwy	Kissimmee	FL	34747	407-396-0100	396-6718
TF: 800-327-9151					
Best Western Orlando West 2014 W Colonial Dr.	Orlando	FL	32804	407-841-8600	843-7080
TF: 800-645-6386					
Best Western Plaza International 8738 International Dr.	Orlando	FL	32819	407-345-8195	345-1417
TF: 800-654-7160					
Buena Vista Suites 14450 International Dr.	Orlando	FL	32821	407-239-8588	239-1401
TF: 800-537-7737					
Caribe Royale Resort Suites 8101 World Center Dr	Orlando	FL	32821	407-238-8000	238-8400
TF: 800-823-8300					
Castle Doubletree Hotel Orlando 8629 International Dr.	Orlando	FL	32819	407-345-1511	248-8181
TF: 800-952-2785					
Clarion Plaza Hotel 9700 International Dr	Orlando	FL	32819	407-996-9700	354-5774
TF: 800-366-9700					
Clarion Suites Resort World 2800 N Poinciana Blvd	Kissimmee	FL	34746	407-997-5000	997-5225
TF: 800-423-8604					
Comfort Inn Maingate 7571 W Irlo Bronson Memorial Hwy	Kissimmee	FL	34747	407-396-7500	396-7497
TF: 800-223-1628					
Comfort Suites Maingate 7888 W Hwy 192	Kissimmee	FL	34747	407-390-9888	390-0981
TF: 888-390-9888					
Comfort Suites Orlando 9350 Turkey Lake Rd	Orlando	FL	32819	407-351-5050	363-7953
TF: 800-221-2222					
Country Hearth Inn 9861 International Dr.	Orlando	FL	32819	407-352-0008	352-5449
TF: 800-447-1890					
Country Inn & Suites 12191 S Apopka-Vineland Rd	Lake Buena Vista	FL	32830	407-239-1115	239-8882
TF: 800-456-4000					
Courtyard by Marriott 7155 N Frontage Rd	Orlando	FL	32812	407-240-7200	240-8962
TF: 800-321-2211 ■ *Web:* courtyard.com/MCOCH					
Courtyard by Marriott International Drive 8600 Austrian Ct.	Orlando	FL	32819	407-351-2244	351-3306
TF: 800-321-2211 ■ *Web:* courtyard.com/MCOOI					
Courtyard by Marriott Maingate 7675 W Irlo Bronson Memorial Hwy	Kissimmee	FL	34747	407-396-4000	396-0714
TF: 800-568-3352 ■ *Web:* courtyard.com/MCOKS					
Courtyard by Marriott Walt Disney World Village 1805 Hotel Plaza Blvd	Lake Buena Vista	FL	32830	407-828-8888	827-4623
TF: 800-223-9930 ■ *Web:* courtyard.com/MCOLB					
Days Inn Convention Center 9990 International Dr.	Orlando	FL	32819	407-352-8700	363-3965
TF: 800-224-5055					
Days Inn East of Universal Studios 5827 Caravan Ct.	Orlando	FL	32819	407-351-3800	363-0907
TF: 800-327-2111					
Days Inn International Drive 7200 International Dr.	Orlando	FL	32819	407-351-1200	363-1182
TF: 800-224-5057					
Days Inn Lake Buena Vista Village 12490 Apopka-Vineland Rd	Orlando	FL	32836	407-239-4646	239-8469
TF: 800-521-3297					
Days Inn Lakeside 7335 Sand Lake Rd	Orlando	FL	32819	407-351-1900	363-1749
TF: 800-777-3297					
Days Suites East Kissimee 5820 W Irlo Bronson Memorial Hwy	Kissimmee	FL	34746	407-396-7900	396-1789
TF: 800-327-9126					
Delta Orlando Resort Main Gate Universal Studios 5715 Major Blvd	Orlando	FL	32819	407-351-3340	345-2872
TF: 800-634-4763					
Disney's All-Star Movies Resort 1901 W Buena Vista Dr	Lake Buena Vista	FL	32830	407-939-7000	939-7111
Web: 208.218.3.141/DisneyWorld/Resorts/AS_Movies.html					
Disney's All-Star Music Resort 1801 W Buena Vista Dr	Lake Buena Vista	FL	32830	407-939-6000	939-7222
Web: 208.218.3.141/DisneyWorld/Resorts/Res62.html					
Disney's All-Star Sports Resort 1701 W Buena Vista Dr	Lake Buena Vista	FL	32830	407-939-5000	939-7333
Web: 208.218.3.141/DisneyWorld/Resorts/Res601.html					
Disney's Boardwalk Inn 2101 Epcot Resort Blvd	Lake Buena Vista	FL	32830	407-939-5100	939-5150
Web: disney.go.com/DisneyWorld/Resorts/Res69.html					
Disney's Boardwalk Villas 2101 N Epcot Resort Blvd	Lake Buena Vista	FL	32830	407-939-5100	939-5150
Web: disney.go.com/DisneyVacationClub/Boardwalk/index.html					
Disney's Caribbean Beach Resort 900 Cayman Way	Lake Buena Vista	FL	32830	407-934-3400	934-3288
Web: disney.go.com/DisneyWorld/Resorts/Res63.html					
Disney's Contemporary Resort 4600 N World Dr	Lake Buena Vista	FL	32830	407-824-1000	824-3539
Web: disney.go.com/DisneyWorld/Resorts/Res67.html					
Disney's Coronado Springs Resort 1000 W Buena Vista Dr	Lake Buena Vista	FL	32830	407-939-1000	939-1001
Web: disney.go.com/DisneyWorld/Resorts/Coronado.html					
Disney's Dixie Landing Resort 1251 Dixie Dr	Lake Buena Vista	FL	32830	407-934-6000	934-5777
Web: disney.go.com/DisneyWorld/Resorts/Res64.html					
Disney's Grand Floridian Resort & Spa 4401 Grand Floridian Way	Lake Buena Vista	FL	32830	407-824-3000	824-3186
Web: disney.go.com/DisneyWorld/Resorts/Res612.html					
Disney's Old Key West Resort 1510 N Cove Rd	Lake Buena Vista	FL	32830	407-827-7700	827-7710
Web: disney.go.com/DisneyVacationClub/OldKeyWest/index.html					
Disney's Polynesian Village Resort 1600 Seven Seas Dr	Lake Buena Vista	FL	32830	407-824-2000	824-3174
Web: disney.go.com/DisneyWorld/Resorts/Res68.html					
Disney's Port Orleans Resort 2201 Orleans Dr	Lake Buena Vista	FL	32830	407-934-5000	934-5024
Web: disney.go.com/DisneyWorld/Resorts/Res65.html					
Disney's Wilderness Lodge 901 Timberline Dr	Lake Buena Vista	FL	32830	407-824-3200	824-3232
Web: disney.go.com/DisneyWorld/Resorts/Res66.html					
Doubletree Guest Suites Orlando Airport 7550 Augusta National Dr	Orlando	FL	32822	407-240-5555	240-1300
TF: 888-675-2477 ■ *Web:* www.doubletreehotels.com/DoubleT/Hotel21/38/38Main.htm					
Doubletree Guest Suites Orlando Maingate 4787 W Irlo Bronson Memorial Hwy	Kissimmee	FL	34746	407-397-0555	397-1968
TF: 800-222-8733 ■ *Web:* www.doubletreehotels.com/DoubleT/Hotel100/111/111Main.htm					
Doubletree Guest Suites Walt Disney World Village 2305 Hotel Plaza Blvd	Lake Buena Vista	FL	32830	407-934-1000	934-1015
TF: 800-222-8733 ■ *Web:* www.doubletreehotels.com/DoubleT/Hotel41/44/44Main.htm ■ *E-mail:* dtorlando@earthlink.net					
Doubletree Resort & Conference Center 3011 Main Gate Ln	Kissimmee	FL	34747	407-396-1400	396-0660
TF: 800-239-6478					
Econo Lodge Maingate East 4311 Hwy 192	Kissimmee	FL	34746	407-396-7100	239-2636
TF: 800-388-7698					
Econo Lodge Maingate Hawaiian Resort 7514 W Irlo Bronson Memorial Hwy	Kissimmee	FL	34747	407-396-2000	396-1295
TF: 800-365-6935					
Embassy Suites 8978 International Dr.	Orlando	FL	32819	407-352-1400	363-1120
TF: 800-433-7275					

Orlando — Hotels, Motels, Resorts (Cont'd)

				Phone	Fax
Embassy Suites Orlando North 225 E Altamonte Dr. *TF:* 800-362-2779	Altamonte Springs	FL	32701	407-834-2400	834-2117
Embassy Suites Resort Lake Buena Vista 8100 Lake Ave *TF:* 800-257-8483	Orlando	FL	32836	407-239-1144	239-1708
Enclave of Orlando 6165 Carrier Dr *TF:* 800-457-0077 ■ *Web:* www.enclavesuites.com	Orlando	FL	32819	407-351-1155	351-2001
Extended StayAmerica 6451 Westwood Blvd *TF:* 800-398-7829	Orlando	FL	32821	407-352-3454	352-1708
Fairfield Inn by Marriott 8342 Jamaican Ct *TF:* 800-398-7829 ■ *Web:* fairfieldinn.com/MCOFI	Orlando	FL	32819	407-363-1944	363-1944
Gateway Inn 7050 S Kirkman Rd *TF:* 800-327-3808	Orlando	FL	32819	407-351-2000	363-1835
Grenelefe Golf & Tennis Resort 3200 SR-546 *TF:* 800-237-9549	Haines City	FL	33844	863-422-7511	421-5000
Grosvenor Resort at Walt Disney World Village 1850 Hotel Plaza Blvd *TF:* 800-624-4109	Lake Buena Vista	FL	32830	407-828-4444	827-8230
Hampton Inn Airport 5767 TG Lee Blvd *TF:* 800-763-1100	Orlando	FL	32822	407-888-2995	888-2418
Hampton Inn International Drive 6101 Sand Lake Rd. *TF:* 800-763-1100	Orlando	FL	32819	407-363-7886	345-0670
Hawthorn Suites Hotel 6435 Westwood Blvd *TF:* 800-527-1133 ■ *Web:* www.hawthorn.com/reservations/locationdetail.asp?state=FL&facid=242&pagecode=hdir ■ *E-mail:* hawthorno@aol.com	Orlando	FL	32821	407-351-6600	351-1977
Hilton at Walt Disney World Village 1751 Hotel Plaza Blvd *TF:* 800-445-8667 ■ *Web:* www.hilton.com/hotels/ORLDWHH	Lake Buena Vista	FL	32830	407-827-4000	827-6369
Holiday Inn Arena 304 W Colonial Dr *TF:* 800-523-3405	Orlando	FL	32801	407-843-8700	996-0103
Holiday Inn Central Park 7900 S Orange Blossom Trail *TF:* 800-465-4329 ■ *Web:* www.basshotels.com/holiday-inn/?_franchisee=MCOCP	Orlando	FL	32809	407-859-7900	859-7442
Holiday Inn Express 6323 International Dr. *TF:* 800-365-6935	Orlando	FL	32819	407-351-4430	345-0742
Holiday Inn Family Suites Resort 18000 International Dr S *TF:* 877-387-5437 ■ *Web:* www.hifamilysuites.com ■ *E-mail:* jj@hifamilysuites.com	Orlando	FL	32821	407-387-5437	387-1490
Holiday Inn Select 5750 TG Lee Blvd *TF:* 800-465-4329	Orlando	FL	32822	407-851-6400	240-3717
Holiday Inn Universal Studios 5905 S Kirkman Rd. *TF:* 800-327-1364 ■ *Web:* www.basshotels.com/holiday-inn/?_franchisee=MCOUS ■ *E-mail:* 74664.2276@compuserve.com	Orlando	FL	32819	407-351-3333	351-3577
Homewood Suites Maingate 3100 Parkway Blvd *TF:* 800-225-5466	Kissimmee	FL	34747	407-396-2229	396-4833
Hotel Royal Plaza PO Box 22203 *TF:* 800-248-7890	Lake Buena Vista	FL	32830	407-828-2828	827-3977
Howard Johnson South 8700 S Orange Blossom Trail *TF:* 800-327-7460	Orlando	FL	32809	407-851-2330	857-6747
Hyatt Orlando 6375 W Irlo Bronson Memorial Hwy *TF:* 800-233-1234 ■ *Web:* www.hyatt.com/usa/kissimmee/hotels/hotel_mcoor.html ■ *E-mail:* hyattorl@aol.com	Kissimmee	FL	34747	407-396-1234	396-5024
Hyatt Regency Grand Cypress Resort 1 Grand Cypress Blvd *TF:* 800-233-1234 ■ *Web:* www.hyatt.com/pages/v/vistaa.html	Orlando	FL	32836	407-239-1234	239-3800
Knights Inn 221 E Colonial Dr. *TF:* 800-843-5644	Orlando	FL	32801	407-425-9065	423-7647
Knights Inn Maingate 7475 W Irlo Bronson Memorial Hwy *TF:* 800-944-0062	Kissimmee	FL	34746	407-396-4200	396-8838
La Quinta International 8300 Jamaican Ct. *TF:* 800-332-1660	Orlando	FL	32819	407-351-1660	351-9264
La Suite Inn & Suites 5858 International Dr. *TF:* 888-527-8483	Orlando	FL	32819	407-351-4410	351-2481
Langford Hotel 300 E New England Ave.	Winter Park	FL	32789	407-644-3400	628-1952
Larson's Lodge Maingate 6075 W Irlo Bronson Memorial Hwy *TF:* 800-327-9074	Kissimmee	FL	34746	407-396-6100	396-6965
Las Palmas Hotel 6233 International Dr *TF:* 800-327-2114	Orlando	FL	32819	407-351-3900	352-5597
Marriott's Orlando World Center 8701 World Center Dr *TF:* 800-621-0638 ■ *Web:* marriotthotels.com/MCOWC	Orlando	FL	32821	407-239-4200	238-8777
Masters Inn 8222 Jamaican Ct *TF:* 800-633-3434	Orlando	FL	32819	407-345-1172	352-2800
Omni Rosen Hotel 9840 International Dr *TF:* 800-204-7234	Orlando	FL	32819	407-996-9840	996-3169
Orlando Airport Marriott 7499 Augusta National Dr *TF:* 800-228-9290	Orlando	FL	32822	407-851-9000	855-4519
Orlando Marriott Downtown 400 W Livingston St *TF:* 800-228-9290 ■ *Web:* www.marriott.com/marriott/mcodt/default.asp	Orlando	FL	32801	407-843-6664	648-5414
Orlando Renaissance Hotel 5445 Forbes Pl. *TF:* 800-228-9290	Orlando	FL	32812	407-240-1000	240-1005
Peabody Orlando 9801 International Dr. *TF:* 800-732-2639 ■ *Web:* www.peabody-orlando.com/	Orlando	FL	32819	407-352-4000	351-9177
Quality Inn Maingate West 7785 W Irlo Bronson Memorial Hwy *TF:* 800-634-5525	Kissimmee	FL	34747	407-396-1828	396-1305
Quality Inn Plaza 9000 International Dr. *TF:* 800-999-8585	Orlando	FL	32819	407-996-8585	996-6849
Radisson Barcelo Inn 8444 International Dr. *TF:* 800-333-3333	Orlando	FL	32819	407-345-0505	352-5894
Radisson Hotel Airport 5555 Hazeltine National Dr. *TF:* 800-333-3333	Orlando	FL	32812	407-856-0100	855-7991
Radisson Plaza Hotel 60 S Ivanhoe Blvd *TF:* 800-333-3333	Orlando	FL	32804	407-425-4455	425-7440
Radisson Resort Parkway 2900 Parkway Blvd *TF:* 800-634-4774	Kissimmee	FL	34747	407-396-7000	396-6792
Radisson Twin Towers Hotel & Convention Center 5780 Major Blvd. *TF:* 800-327-2110	Orlando	FL	32819	407-351-1000	351-0060
Ramada Resort Florida Center 7400 International Dr. *TF:* 800-327-1363	Orlando	FL	32819	407-351-4600	363-0517
Ramada Resort Maingate 2950 Reedy Creek Blvd *TF:* 800-365-6935	Kissimmee	FL	34747	407-396-4466	396-6418
Ranch House Motor Inn Cypress Gardens 1911 Cypress Gardens Blvd **Fax Area Code:* 800	Winter Haven	FL	33884	863-324-5994	366-5996*
Red Roof Inn Maingate 7491 West Irlo Bronson Memorial Hwy *TF:* 800-669-6753	Kissimmee	FL	34747	407-396-6000	396-7393
Renaissance Orlando Resort 6677 Sea Harbor Dr *TF:* 800-327-6677	Orlando	FL	32821	407-351-5555	351-9991
Riande Continental Plaza Hotel 6825 Visitor's Cir *TF:* 800-511-5388	Orlando	FL	32819	407-352-8211	345-0134
RIU Orlando Hotel 8688 Palm Pkwy *TF:* 888-222-9963	Lake Buena Vista	FL	32836	407-239-8500	239-8591
Shades of Green on Walt Disney World Resort 1950 W Magnolia Palm Dr	Lake Buena Vista	FL	32830	407-824-3600	824-3665
Sheraton Four Points Hotel 151 E Washington St. *TF:* 800-325-3535	Orlando	FL	32801	407-841-3220	849-1839
Sheraton Orlando North Hotel 600 N Lake Destiny Dr *TF:* 800-628-6660	Maitland	FL	32751	407-660-9000	660-2563
Sheraton Safari Resort 12205 Apopka-Vineland Rd *TF:* 800-325-3535	Orlando	FL	32836	407-239-0444	239-1778
Sheraton Studio City Hotel 5905 International Dr. *TF:* 800-327-1366	Orlando	FL	32819	407-351-2100	352-2991
Sheraton World Resort 10100 International Dr. *TF:* 800-327-0363	Orlando	FL	32821	407-352-1100	352-3679
Sierra Suites Hotel 8750 Universal Blvd *TF:* 800-474-3772	Orlando	FL	32819	407-903-1500	903-1555
Silverleaf Suites 5630 Monterey Dr *TF:* 800-664-3633 ■ *Web:* www.silver-leaf.com	Orlando	FL	32811	407-295-0883	295-6585
Star Island Resort & Country Club 5000 Avenue of the Stars. *TF:* 800-423-8604	Kissimmee	FL	34746	407-396-8300	396-6403
Summerfield Suites Hotel 8480 International Dr. *TF:* 800-830-4964	Orlando	FL	32819	407-352-2400	352-4631
Sunrise Motel 801 W Vine St.	Kissimmee	FL	34741	407-846-3224	932-4092
Travelodge 201 Simpson Rd *TF:* 800-816-1530	Kissimmee	FL	34744	407-846-1530	846-2162

Orlando — Hotels, Motels, Resorts (Cont'd)

Name / Address	City	State	Zip	Phone	Fax
Villas at the Disney Institute 1901 Buena Vista Dr	Lake Buena Vista	FL	32830	407-827-1100	827-4100
TF: 800-282-9282					
Villas of Grand Cypress 1 N Jacaranda	Orlando	FL	32836	407-239-4700	239-7219
TF: 800-835-7377 ■ *Web:* www.grandcypress.com					
Vistana Resort 8800 Vistana Ctr Dr	Orlando	FL	32821	407-239-3100	239-3111
TF: 800-847-8262 ■ *Web:* vistanainc.com/Resorts/Vistana/default.htm					
Walt Disney World Dolphin 1500 Epcot Resort Blvd	Lake Buena Vista	FL	32830	407-934-4000	934-4884
TF: 800-227-1500 ■ *Web:* www.swandolphin.com					
Walt Disney World Swan 1200 Epcot Resort Blvd	Lake Buena Vista	FL	32830	407-934-3000	934-4499
TF: 800-248-7926 ■ *Web:* www.swandolphin.com					
Wellesley Inn Orlando 5635 Windhover Dr	Orlando	FL	32819	407-345-0026	345-8809
TF: 800-444-8888					
West Side Inn & Suites 3200 W Colonial Dr	Orlando	FL	32808	407-295-5270	291-2092
TF: 800-828-5270					
Westgate Lakes Resort 10000 Turkey Lake Rd	Orlando	FL	32819	407-352-8051	345-5384
Wyndham Orlando Resort 8001 International Dr	Orlando	FL	32819	407-351-2420	345-5611
TF: 800-996-3426					
Wyndham Place 1900 Buena Vista Dr	Lake Buena Vista	FL	32830	407-827-2727	827-6034
TF: 800-327-2906 ■ *Web:* www.bvp-resort.com					
Wynfield Inn Westwood 6263 Westwood Blvd	Orlando	FL	32821	407-345-8000	345-1508
TF: 800-346-1551					

— Restaurants —

Name / Address	City	State	Zip	Phone
Arthur's 27 (International) 1900 Buena Vista Dr	Lake Buena Vista	FL	32830	407-827-3450
Atlantis (Seafood) 6677 Sea Harbor Dr	Orlando	FL	32821	407-351-5555
Bahama Breeze (New American) 8849 International Dr	Orlando	FL	32819	407-248-2499
Bergamo's Italian Restaurant (Italian) 8445 International Dr Suite 126	Orlando	FL	32819	407-352-3805
Bierstube Pub (German) 5445 Forbes Pl	Orlando	FL	32812	407-240-1000
Bill Wong's Restaurant (Chinese) 5668 International Dr	Orlando	FL	32819	407-352-5373
Cafe Gauguin (American) 9840 International Dr	Orlando	FL	32819	407-996-9840
Cafe Tu Tu Tango (International) 8625 International Dr	Orlando	FL	32819	407-248-2222
California Grill (New American) 4600 N World Dr	Lake Buena Vista	FL	32830	407-824-1576
Capriccio (Italian) 9801 International Dr	Orlando	FL	32819	407-352-4000
Cascade (Continental) 1 Grand Cypress Blvd	Orlando	FL	32836	407-239-1234
Charlie's Lobster House (Seafood) 8445 International Dr Suite 122	Orlando	FL	32819	407-352-6929
Chatham's Place (Continental) 7575 Doctor Philips Blvd	Orlando	FL	32819	407-345-2992
Christini's (Italian) 7600 Dr Phillips Blvd	Orlando	FL	32819	407-345-8770
Ciao Italia (Italian) 6149 Westwood Blvd	Orlando	FL	32821	407-354-0770
Del Frisco's Steakhouse (Steak/Seafood) 729 Lee Rd	Orlando	FL	32810	407-645-4443
Dockside Grill (American) 5494 Central Florida Pkwy	Orlando	FL	32821	407-239-8552
Dux (New American) 9801 International Dr	Orlando	FL	32819	407-345-4550
Everglades Restaurant (American) 9840 International Dr	Orlando	FL	32819	407-996-9840
Finn's Grill (Steak/Seafood) 1751 Hotel Plaza Blvd	Lake Buena Vista	FL	32830	407-827-3838
Forbes Place (Mediterranean) 5445 Forbes Pl	Orlando	FL	32812	407-240-1000
Haifeng (Chinese) 6677 Sea Harbor Dr	Orlando	FL	32721	407-351-5555
Hard Rock Cafe (American) 6050 Universal Blvd	Orlando	FL	32819	407-351-7625
Harvey's Bistro (New American) 390 N Orange Ave	Orlando	FL	32801	407-246-6560
Hemingway's (Seafood) 1 Grand Cypress Blvd	Orlando	FL	32836	407-239-1234
House of Blues (Southern) 1490 E Lake Buena Vista Dr	Lake Buena Vista	FL	32830	407-934-2583
Web: www.hob.com				
India Palace Restaurant (Indian) 8530 Palm Pkwy	Orlando	FL	32836	407-238-2322
Johnson's Diner (American) 692 W Robinson St	Orlando	FL	32805	407-841-0717
Jose O'Days (Tex Mex) 8445 International Dr	Orlando	FL	32819	407-363-0613
Kate O'Brien's Irish Pub (Irish) 42 W Central Blvd	Orlando	FL	32801	407-649-7646
La Coquina (French) 1 Grand Cypress Blvd	Orlando	FL	32819	407-239-1234
La Grille (French) 8445 International Dr Suite 142	Orlando	FL	32819	407-345-0883
La Normandie (French) 2021 E Colonial Dr	Orlando	FL	32803	407-896-9976
Lai Lai Japanese Cuisine (Japanese) 7400 Southland Blvd Suite 116	Orlando	FL	32809	407-857-3740
Le Coq au Vin (French) 4800 S Orange Ave	Orlando	FL	32806	407-851-6980
Le Jardin (American) 1500 Sand Lake Rd	Orlando	FL	32809	407-859-1500
Le Provence (French) 50 E Pine St	Orlando	FL	32801	407-843-1320
Lee's Lakeside (Continental) 431 E Central Blvd	Orlando	FL	32801	407-841-1565
Maison et Jardin (Continental) 430 S Wymore Rd	Altamonte Springs	FL	32714	407-862-4410
Manuel's on the 28th (New American) 390 N Orange Ave 28th Fl	Orlando	FL	32801	407-246-6580
Mikado's (Japanese) 8701 World Center Dr	Orlando	FL	32821	407-239-4200
Ming Court (Chinese) 9188 International Dr	Orlando	FL	32819	407-351-9988
New Punjab (Indian) 7451 International Dr	Orlando	FL	32819	407-352-7887
Nicole Saint Pierre (French) 1300 S Orlando Ave	Maitland	FL	32751	407-647-7575
Ocean Grill (Steak/Seafood) 6432 International Dr	Orlando	FL	32819	407-352-9993
Ohana Feast (Polynesian) Seven Seas Dr	Lake Buena Vista	FL	32830	407-824-2000
Old Munich Restaurant (German) 5731 S Orange Blossom Trail	Orlando	FL	32809	407-438-8997
Olympia Restaurant (Greek) 8505 E Colonial Dr	Orlando	FL	32817	407-273-7836
Park Plaza Gardens (Continental) 319 Park Ave S	Winter Park	FL	32789	407-645-2475
Passage to India (Indian) 5532 International Dr	Orlando	FL	32819	407-351-3456
Pebbles Restaurant (American) 12551 SR 535	Lake Buena Vista	FL	32819	407-827-1111
Planet Hollywood (American) 1506 E Buena Vista Dr	Lake Buena Vista	FL	32830	407-827-7827
Portobello Yacht Club (Italian) 1650 Buena Vista Dr	Lake Buena Vista	FL	32830	407-934-8888
Race Rock (American) 8986 International Dr	Orlando	FL	32819	407-248-9876
Web: www.racerock.com				
Rainforest Cafe (American) 1800 E Buena Vista Dr	Lake Buena Vista	FL	32830	407-827-8500
Web: www.rainforestcafe.com				
Sabor Latino Restaurant (Latin) 8445 International Dr Suite 174	Orlando	FL	32819	407-352-7800
Siam Orchid (Thai) 7575 Republic Dr	Orlando	FL	32819	407-351-0821
Trey Yuen Restaurant (Chinese) 6800 Visitors Cir	Orlando	FL	32819	407-352-6822
Tuscany's (Italian) 8701 World Center Dr	Orlando	FL	32821	407-239-4200
Victoria & Albert's (Continental) 40001 Floridian Way	Lake Buena Vista	FL	32830	407-824-2383
Viet Garden (Thai) 1237-1239 E Colonial Dr	Orlando	FL	32803	407-896-4154
White Wolf Cafe (American) 1829 N Orange Ave	Orlando	FL	32804	407-895-9911

— Goods and Services —

SHOPPING

Name / Address	City	State	Zip	Phone	Fax
Altamonte Mall 451 Altamonte Ave	Altamonte Springs	FL	32701	407-830-4422	830-0872
Web: www.altamontemall.com					
Belz Factory Outlet World 5401 W Oakridge Rd	Orlando	FL	32819	407-352-9611	351-3873
Church Street Market 55 W Church St	Orlando	FL	32801	407-872-3500	
Colonial Plaza Mall 2560 E Colonial Dr	Orlando	FL	32803	407-894-3601	
Crossroads of Lake Buena Vista SR 535 & I-4	Lake Buena Vista	FL	32830	407-827-7300	
Downtown Celebration I-4 & US Hwy 192 E	Orlando	FL	32801	407-566-3448	
Florida Mall 8001 S Orange Blossom Trail	Orlando	FL	32809	407-851-6255	
Goodings International Plaza 8255 International Dr	Orlando	FL	32819	407-354-2200	
Lake Buena Vista Factory Stores 15591 S Apopka Vineland Rd	Orlando	FL	32821	407-238-9301	
Mercado The 8445 International Dr	Orlando	FL	32819	407-345-9337	345-1072
Old Town 5770 W Irlo Bronson Memorial Hwy	Kissimmee	FL	34746	407-396-4888	396-0348
TF: 800-843-4202					
Orlando Fashion Square 3201 E Colonial Dr	Orlando	FL	32803	407-896-1131	894-8381
Park Avenue Shopping District 150 N New York Ave	Winter Park	FL	32789	407-644-8281	644-7826
Seminole Towne Center 200 Towne Center Cir	Sanford	FL	32771	407-323-2262	323-2464
West Oaks Mall 9401 W Colonial Dr	Ocoee	FL	34761	407-294-2775	294-0760

BANKS

Name / Address	City	State	Zip	Phone	Fax
AmSouth Bank of Florida 111 N Orange Ave	Orlando	FL	32801	407-246-8900	849-0034
First Union National Bank 20 N Orange Ave	Orlando	FL	32802	407-649-5079	649-5513
NationsBank 390 N Orange Ave	Orlando	FL	32801	407-420-2800	236-5250
Republic Bank 255 S Orange Ave	Orlando	FL	32801	407-841-3333	649-1620
TF: 800-386-5454					
SunTrust Bank Central Florida NA 200 S Orange Ave	Orlando	FL	32801	407-237-4141	237-6910
TF: 800-432-4760					
Washington Mutual Bank 2700 S Orange Ave	Orlando	FL	32806	800-782-8875	352-5934*
**Fax Area Code:* 407					

BUSINESS SERVICES

Name	Phone
AccuStaff Inc.	407-857-3470
Adecco Employment Personnel Services	407-240-3005
ASAP Courier	407-249-2727
Corporate Express Delivery Systems	407-816-0668
Federal Express	800-238-5355
Florida Courier Service	407-298-9772
Kinko's	407-839-5000
Manpower Temporary Services	407-857-6161
Norrell Temporary Services	407-345-8118
Post Office	407-850-6288
UPS	800-742-5877

Orlando (Cont'd)

— Media —

PUBLICATIONS

	City	State	Zip	Phone	Fax
Orlando Business Journal 315 E Robinson St Suite 250 *Web:* www.amcity.com/orlando	Orlando	FL	32801	407-649-8470	649-8469
Orlando Magazine 260 Maitland Ave Suite 2000 *TF:* 800-243-0609 ■ *E-mail:* orlandomag@aol.com	Altamonte Springs	FL	32701	407-767-8338	767-8348
Orlando Sentinel‡ 633 N Orange Ave *TF Adv:* 800-669-5757 ■ *Web:* www.orlandosentinel.com	Orlando	FL	32801	407-420-5000	420-5350
Osceola News-Gazette PO Box 422068 **Fax:* News Rm ■ *Web:* www.oscnewsgazette.com ■ *E-mail:* osceolang@aol.com	Kissimmee	FL	34742	407-846-7600	846-8516*

‡Daily newspapers

TELEVISION

	City	State	Zip	Phone	Fax
WBSF-TV Ch 43 (Ind) 4450-L Enterprise Ct	Melbourne	FL	32934	321-254-4343	242-0863
WESH-TV Ch 2 (NBC) 1021 N Wymore Rd *Web:* www.wesh.com ■ *E-mail:* wesh@intersrv.com	Winter Park	FL	32789	407-645-2222	539-7948
WFTV-TV Ch 9 (ABC) 490 E South St *Web:* www.insidecentralflorida.com/partners/wftv ■ *E-mail:* news@wftv.com	Orlando	FL	32801	407-841-9000	481-2891
WKCF-TV Ch 18 (WB) 31 Skyline Dr *Web:* www.wb18.com ■ *E-mail:* wb18wkcf@wb18.com	Lake Mary	FL	32746	407-670-3018	647-4163
WKMG-TV Ch 6 (CBS) 4466 N John Young Pkwy *Web:* www.wkmg.com	Orlando	FL	32804	407-291-6000	298-2122
WMFE-TV Ch 24 (PBS) 11510 E Colonial Dr *Web:* www.pbs.org/wmfe/	Orlando	FL	32817	407-273-2300	273-3613
WOFL-TV Ch 35 (Fox) 35 Skyline Dr *Web:* www.wofl.com ■ *E-mail:* wofl@wofl.com	Lake Mary	FL	32746	407-644-3535	333-0234
WOPX-TV Ch 56 (PAX) 7091 Grand National Dr Suite 100 *Web:* www.pax.net/WOPX	Orlando	FL	32819	407-370-5600	370-5656
WRBW-TV Ch 65 (UPN) 2000 Universal Studios Plaza Suite 200 *Web:* www.wrbw.com ■ *E-mail:* wrbw@wrbw.com	Orlando	FL	32819	407-248-6500	248-6520
WTGL-TV Ch 52 (Ind) 653 W Michigan St *Web:* tv52.org	Orlando	FL	32805	407-423-5200	422-0120

RADIO

	City	State	Zip	Phone	Fax
WCFB-FM 94.5 MHz (AC) 4192 N John Young Pkwy	Orlando	FL	32804	407-294-2945	297-7595
WDBO-AM 580 kHz (N/T) 4192 N John Young Pkwy *Web:* www.insidecentralflorida.com/partners/580wdbo	Orlando	FL	32804	407-295-5858	291-4879
WHOO-AM 990 kHz (Nost) 200 S Orange Ave Suite 2240	Orlando	FL	32801	407-422-9696	422-0917
WHTQ-FM 96.5 MHz (CR) 200 S Orange Ave Suite 2240 *Web:* www.whtq.com	Orlando	FL	32801	407-422-9890	425-9696
WJHM-FM 101.9 MHz (Urban) 37 Skyline Dr Suite 4200 *E-mail:* fm102jamz@aol.com	Lake Mary	FL	32746	407-333-0072	333-2342
WJRR-FM 101.1 MHz (Rock) 2500 Maitland Ctr Pkwy Suite 401 *Web:* www.wjrr.com	Maitland	FL	32751	407-916-7800	916-7406
WLOQ-FM 103.1 MHz (NAC) 170 W Fairbanks Ave Suite 200 *Web:* www.wloq.com ■ *E-mail:* general@wloq.com	Winter Park	FL	32789	407-647-5557	647-4495
WMFE-FM 90.7 MHz (NPR) 11510 E Colonial Dr *Web:* www.pbs.org/wmfe ■ *E-mail:* wmfe@magicnet.net	Orlando	FL	32817	407-273-2300	273-8462
WMGF-FM 107.7 MHz (AC) PO Box 107	Maitland	FL	32794	407-916-7800	916-7406
WMMO-FM 98.9 MHz (AC) 200 S Orange Ave Suite 2240 *Web:* www.wmmo.com	Orlando	FL	32801	407-422-9890	423-9666
WOCL-FM 105.9 MHz (Oldies) 2101 W SR 434 Suite 305 *Web:* cool1059.com/	Longwood	FL	32779	407-682-2121	862-1059
WOMX-FM 105.1 MHz (AC) 1800 Pembrook Dr Suite 400 *TF:* 800-282-9649	Orlando	FL	32810	407-919-1000	
WPCV-FM 97.5 MHz (Ctry) 404 W Lime St *Web:* www.wpcv.com ■ *E-mail:* wpcv@wpcv.com	Lakeland	FL	33815	863-682-8184	683-2409
WQTM-AM 540 kHz (Sports) 2500 Maitland Ctr Pkwy Suite 401	Maitland	FL	32751	407-916-7800	916-7406
WSHE-FM 100.3 MHz (AC) 2500 Maitland Ctr Pkwy Suite 401	Maitland	FL	32751	407-916-7800	916-7406
WTKS-FM 104.1 MHz (N/T) 2500 Maitland Ctr Pkwy Suite 401 *Web:* www.wtks.com ■ *E-mail:* real104@magicnet.net	Maitland	FL	32751	407-916-7800	916-7511
WTLN-AM 950 kHz (Rel) 400 W Lake Brantley Rd *Web:* www.wtln.com ■ *E-mail:* am950wtln@aol.com	Altamonte Springs	FL	32714	407-682-9494	682-7005
WUCF-FM 89.9 MHz (NPR) 4000 Central Florida Blvd Bldg 75 Rm 130 *Web:* wucf.ucf.edu ■ *E-mail:* wucf@pegasus.cc.ucf.edu	Orlando	FL	32816	407-823-0899	823-6364
WWKA-FM 92.3 MHz (Ctry) 4192 N John Young Pkwy	Orlando	FL	32804	407-298-9292	291-4879
WWNZ-AM 740 kHz (N/T) 2500 Maitland Ctr Pkwy Suite 401	Maitland	FL	32751	407-916-7800	916-7402
WXXL-FM 106.7 MHz (CHR) 337 S Northlake Blvd Suite 1024 *Web:* www.wxxl.com	Altamonte Springs	FL	32701	407-339-1067	332-9613

— Colleges/Universities —

	City	State	Zip	Phone	Fax
Crane Institute of America Inc 1063 Maitland Ctr Commons Suite 100 *TF:* 800-832-2726 ■ *E-mail:* craneinstitute@msn.com	Maitland	FL	32751	407-875-6969	875-1126
Florida Christian College 1011 Bill Beck Blvd *TF Admissions:* 888-468-6322 ■ *Web:* www.fcc.edu	Kissimmee	FL	34744	407-847-8966	847-3925
Florida Metropolitan University Orlando College-North 5421 Diplomat Cir *TF Admissions:* 800-628-5870 ■ *Web:* 135.145.62.96/fmu/767orlandonorth/orlandonorthhome.htm	Orlando	FL	32810	407-628-5870	628-1344
Full Sail Center for the Recording Arts 3300 University Blvd Suite 160 *TF:* 800-226-7625 ■ *Web:* www.fullsail.com ■ *E-mail:* admissions@fullsail.com	Winter Park	FL	32792	407-679-6333	678-0070
Rollins College 1000 Holt Ave *Web:* www.rollins.edu	Winter Park	FL	32789	407-646-2000	646-1502
Seminole Community College 100 Weldon Blvd *Web:* www.seminole.cc.fl.us	Sanford	FL	32773	407-328-4722	328-2395
Southern College 5600 Lake Underhill Rd *Web:* southern.edu ■ *E-mail:* postmaster@southern.edu	Orlando	FL	32807	407-273-1000	273-0492
University of Central Florida 4000 Central Florida Blvd *Web:* www.ucf.edu	Orlando	FL	32816	407-823-2000	823-5652
Valencia Community College PO Box 3028 *Web:* valencia.cc.fl.us/	Orlando	FL	32802	407-299-5000	293-8839

— Hospitals —

	City	State	Zip	Phone	Fax
Central Florida Regional Hospital 1401 W Seminole Blvd	Sanford	FL	32771	407-321-4500	324-4790
Florida Hospital Altamonte 601 E Altamonte Dr	Altamonte Springs	FL	32701	407-830-4321	767-2399
Florida Hospital East Orlando 7727 Lake Underhill Rd	Orlando	FL	32822	407-277-8110	281-8697
Florida Hospital Medical Center 601 E Rollins St *Web:* www.flhosp.org/locations/FHsouth/index.htm	Orlando	FL	32803	407-896-6611	897-1755
Florida Hospital Waterman 201 N Eustis St.	Eustis	FL	32726	352-589-3333	589-3481
Health Central 10000 W Colonial Dr	Ocoee	FL	34761	407-296-1000	521-3406
Leesburg Regional Medical Center 600 E Dixie Ave *TF Physician Referral:* 800-889-3755*	Leesburg	FL	34748	352-365-4545	323-5009
Orlando Regional Lucerne 818 Main Ln	Orlando	FL	32801	407-649-6111	649-6194
Orlando Regional Medical Center 1414 S Kuhl Ave. **Fax:* Admitting	Orlando	FL	32806	407-841-5111	425-5093*
Orlando Regional South Seminole Hospital 555 W State Rd 434	Longwood	FL	32750	407-767-1200	767-5913
Osceola Regional Medical Center 700 W Oak St.	Kissimmee	FL	34741	407-846-2266	518-3684
Sand Lake Hospital 9400 Turkey Lake Rd	Orlando	FL	32819	407-351-8500	351-8569

Orlando (Cont'd)

— Attractions —

Name / Address	City	State	Zip	Phone	Fax
Amazing Animal Adventure 8990 International Dr.	Orlando	FL	32819	407-354-1400	
Bok Tower Gardens 1151 Tower Blvd	Lake Wales	FL	33853	863-676-1408	676-6770
Web: www.boktower.org					
Canaveral National Seashore 308 Julia St.	Titusville	FL	32796	321-267-1110	264-2906
Web: www.nps.gov/cana					
Carr Bob Performing Arts Centre 401 W Livingston St	Orlando	FL	32801	407-849-2000	843-0758
Web: www.orlandocentroplex.com					
Church Street Station 129 W Church St	Orlando	FL	32801	407-422-2434	872-7960
Web: churchstreetstation.com/					
Cirque du Soleil La Nouba PO Box 22157	Lake Buena Vista	FL	32830	407-934-9200	934-9148
Web: www.cirquedusoleil.com/en/piste/lanouba/index.html					
Civic Theatre of Central Florida 1001 E Princeton St	Orlando	FL	32803	407-896-7365	897-3284
Cornell Fine Arts Museum 1000 Holt Ave	Winter Park	FL	32789	407-646-2526	646-2524
Web: www.rollins.edu/cfam					
Cypress Gardens 2641 S Lake Summit Dr	Cypress Gardens	FL	33884	863-324-2111	324-7946*
*Fax: PR ■ *Web:* www.cypressgardens.com/					
Disney Institute 1960 Magnolia Way	Lake Buena Vista	FL	32830	407-827-1100	827-4100
TF: 800-282-9282 ■ *Web:* disney.go.com/DisneyWorld/DisneyInstitute/index.html					
Disney-MGM Studios Theme Park PO Box 10000	Lake Buena Vista	FL	32830	407-824-4321	
Web: disney.go.com/DisneyWorld/ThemeParks/Par43.html					
Disney's Wide World of Sports 700 Victory Way	Kissimmee	FL	34747	407-939-1500	939-2070
Web: disney.go.com/DisneyWorld/Recreation/worldsports_opener.html					
DisneyQuest PO Box 10000	Lake Buena Vista	FL	32830	407-828-4600	
Web: www.disney.go.com/disneyquest/orlando/home.html					
Downtown Celebration I-4 & US Hwy 192 E	Orlando	FL	32801	407-566-3448	
Downtown Disney Hotel Plaza Blvd	Lake Buena Vista	FL	32830	407-939-7727	
Downtown Farmers' Market Church St	Orlando	FL	32801	407-246-2555	
Enzian Theater 1300 S Orlando Ave	Maitland	FL	32751	407-629-1088	629-6870
Web: www.enzian.org					
Florida Symphony Youth Orchestra PO Box 2328	Winter Park	FL	32790	407-999-7800	999-7849
Flying Tigers Warbird Air Museum 231 N Hoagland Blvd.	Kissimmee	FL	34741	407-933-1942	933-7843
Web: www.warbirdmuseum.com ■ *E-mail:* kittyhwk@earthlink.net					
Fun at Flea World 4311 Hwy 17-92	Sanford	FL	32773	407-330-1792	
Gatorland 14501 S Orange Blossom Trail.	Orlando	FL	32837	407-855-5496	240-9389
TF: 800-393-5297 ■ *Web:* www.i3.net/1-800-FL-VILLA/gatorland/					
Green Meadows Petting Farm 1365 S Poinciana Blvd.	Kissimmee	FL	34746	407-846-0770	
IMAX Theater Kennedy Space Center Visitor Ctr	Kennedy Space Center	FL	32899	321-452-2121	
Web: www.kennedyspacecenter.com/html/imax.html					
Islands of Adventure 1000 Universal Studios Plaza	Orlando	FL	32819	407-363-8000	
TF: 888-837-2273 ■ *Web:* www.uescape.com/islands ■ *E-mail:* guestservices@universalflorida.com					
Jungle Adventures 26205 E Hwy 50	Christmas	FL	32709	407-568-1354	568-0038
Jungleland 4580 W US Hwy 192	Kissimmee	FL	34746	407-396-1012	396-1013
Kennedy Space Center Spaceport USA	Kennedy Space Center	FL	32899	321-452-0300	452-3043
King Henry's Feast 8984 International Dr.	Orlando	FL	32819	407-351-5151	
TF: 800-883-8181					
Leu Harry P Botanical Gardens 1920 N Forest Ave	Orlando	FL	32803	407-246-2620	246-2849
Web: www.ci.orlando.fl.us/departments/leu_gardens/					
Loews Universal Cineplex Universal Studios CityWalk 1000 Universal Studios Plaza	Orlando	FL	32819	407-354-5998	
Web: www.uescape.com/citywalk/cineplex/main.html					
Maitland Art Center 231 W Packwood Ave.	Maitland	FL	32751	407-539-2181	539-1198
Malibu Grand Prix Castle 5863 American Way	Orlando	FL	32819	407-351-7093	363-9133
Mark Two Dinner Theater 3376 Edgewater Dr	Orlando	FL	32804	407-843-6275	
TF: 800-726-6275					
Medieval Times Dinner & Tournament 4510 E Hwy 192	Kissimmee	FL	34746	407-396-1518	
Web: www.medievaltimes.com/FL_realm.htm ■ *E-mail:* kissimmee@medievaltimes.com					
Mercado The 8445 International Dr	Orlando	FL	32819	407-345-9337	345-1072
Morse Charles Hosmer Museum of American Art 445 Park Ave N	Winter Park	FL	32789	407-645-5311	647-1284
Movie Rider 8815 International Dr	Orlando	FL	32819	407-352-0050	
TF: 800-998-4418					
Mystery Fun House 5767 Major Blvd.	Orlando	FL	32819	407-351-3359	351-5657
Nickelodeon Studios 3000 Universal Studios Plaza	Orlando	FL	32819	407-363-8500	363-8590
Web: www.uescape.com/studios					
Old Town 5770 W Irlo Bronson Memorial Hwy	Kissimmee	FL	34746	407-396-4888	396-0348
TF: 800-843-4202					
Orange County Historical Museum 812 E Rollins St	Orlando	FL	32803	407-897-6350	897-6409
Orlando Broadway Series 201 S Orange Ave Suite 101	Orlando	FL	32801	407-423-9999	841-4738
TF: 800-950-4647					
Orlando Museum of Art 2416 N Mills Ave	Orlando	FL	32803	407-896-4231	894-4314
Web: www.omart.org					
Orlando Opera Co 1111 N Orange Ave	Orlando	FL	32804	407-426-1717	426-1705
TF: 800-336-7372 ■ *Web:* www.800net.com/opera					
Orlando Philharmonic Orchestra 812 E Rollins St	Orlando	FL	32803	407-896-6700	
Web: www.orlandophil.org					
Orlando Science Center 777 E Princeton St.	Orlando	FL	32803	407-514-2000	514-2277
Web: www.osc.org ■ *E-mail:* cosmicnews@aol.com					
Petty Richard Driving Experience 3450 N World Dr	Lake Buena Vista	FL	32830	407-939-0130	939-0137
TF: 800-237-3889					
Pleasure Island PO Box 10000	Lake Buena Vista	FL	32830	407-934-7781	
Pointe Orlando 9101 International Dr Suite 1040	Orlando	FL	32819	407-248-2838	248-0078
Web: www.pointeorlandofl.com					
Reilly Tom Vintage Aircraft 231 N Hoagland Blvd.	Kissimmee	FL	34741	407-847-7477	933-7843
Web: www.warbirdmuseum.com ■ *E-mail:* warbirds@warbirdmuseum.com					
Ripley's Believe It or Not! Museum 8201 International Dr.	Orlando	FL	32819	407-363-4418	
Sea World of Florida 7007 Sea World Dr	Orlando	FL	32821	407-351-3600	363-2256*
*Fax: Mktg ■ *TF:* 800-327-2424 ■ *Web:* www.seaworld.com/seaworld/sw_florida/swfframe.html ■ *E-mail:* sea.world@bev.net					
Silver Springs PO Box 370	Silver Springs	FL	34489	352-236-2121	236-1732
TF: 800-234-7458 ■ *Web:* www.silversprings.com					
Skull Kingdom 5933 American Way	Orlando	FL	32819	407-354-1564	354-1567
Southern Ballet Theatre 1111 N Orange Ave Suite 4	Orlando	FL	32804	407-426-1733	426-1734
Web: www.southernballet.org					
Splendid China 3000 Splendid China Blvd	Kissimmee	FL	34747	407-396-7111	
TF: 800-244-6226 ■ *Web:* www.floridasplendidchina.com/					
Terror on Church Street 135 S Orange Ave	Orlando	FL	32801	407-649-1912	
Web: members.tripod.com/~tocs/					
Tosohatchee State Reserve 3365 Taylor Creek Rd	Christmas	FL	32708	407-568-5893	
Universal Studios CityWalk 1000 Universal Studios Plaza	Orlando	FL	32819	407-363-8000	
TF: 888-837-2273 ■ *Web:* www.uescape.com/citywalk ■ *E-mail:* guestservices@universalstudios.com					
Universal Studios Florida 1000 Universal Studios Plaza	Orlando	FL	32819	407-363-8000	363-8006*
*Fax: Hum Res ■ *Web:* www.uescape.com/studios/attractions/					
Walt Disney World Animal Kingdom PO Box 10000	Lake Buena Vista	FL	32830	407-824-4321	
Web: disney.go.com/DisneyWorld/ThemeParks/disney_animal_kingdom.html					
Walt Disney World Blizzard Beach 3250 Buena Vista Dr W	Lake Buena Vista	FL	32830	407-824-4321	
Web: disney.go.com/DisneyWorld/Recreation/Rec51.html					
Walt Disney World Boardwalk 2101 Epcot Resorts Blvd PO Box 10000	Lake Buena Vista	FL	32830	407-939-5100	939-5150
Web: disney.go.com/DisneyWorld/Entertainment/Rec510.html					
Walt Disney World Epcot Center PO Box 10000	Lake Buena Vista	FL	32830	407-824-4321	828-5400
Web: disney.go.com/DisneyWorld/ThemeParks/Par42.html					
Walt Disney World Magic Kingdom PO Box 10000	Lake Buena Vista	FL	32830	407-824-4321	
Web: disney.go.com/DisneyWorld/ThemeParks/Par41.html					
Water Mania 6073 W Hwy 192	Kissimmee	FL	34747	407-396-2626	396-8125
TF: 800-527-3092 ■ *Web:* www.watermania-florida.com					
Wekiwa Springs State Park 1800 Wekiwa Cir	Apopka	FL	32712	407-884-2009	884-2014
Wet 'n Wild Inc 6200 International Dr	Orlando	FL	32819	407-351-1800	363-1147
TF: 800-992-9453 ■ *Web:* www.wetnwild.com ■ *E-mail:* GetWet@WetnWild.com					
WonderWorks 9067 International Dr	Orlando	FL	32819	407-351-8800	352-6624
World of Orchids 2501 Old Lake Wilson Rd	Kissimmee	FL	34747	407-396-1887	

Orlando (Cont'd)

SPORTS TEAMS & FACILITIES

				Phone	Fax
Atlanta Braves Spring Training (baseball) 700 S Victory Way	Kissimmee	FL	34747	407-938-3500	
Central Florida Kraze (soccer) PO Box 621566	Oviedo	FL	32762	407-365-2319	366-9026
Web: www.orlandosoccer.org ■ *E-mail:* weeksend@bellsouth.net					
Cleveland Indians Spring Training (baseball) Chain O'Lakes Park	Winter Haven	FL	33880	863-291-5803	299-4491
Cocoa Expos (soccer) 500 Friday Rd Cocoa Expo Sports Ctr	Cocoa	FL	32926	321-639-3976	504-3716
E-mail: xsoccer@palmnet.net					
Houston Astros Spring Training (baseball) 1000 Bill Beck Blvd	Kissimmee	FL	34744	407-933-6500	847-6237
Kissimmee Cobras (baseball) 1000 Bill Beck Blvd	Kissimmee	FL	34744	407-933-5500	847-6237
Orlando Arena 600 W Amelia St	Orlando	FL	32801	407-849-2000	849-2329
Orlando Jackals (hockey) 600 W Amelia St Orlando Arena	Orlando	FL	32801	561-241-9880	
E-mail: pky@jackals.inspace.net					
Orlando Magic 600 W Amelia St Orlando Arena	Orlando	FL	32801	407-896-2442	428-3201
Web: www.nba.com/magic					
Orlando Nighthawks (soccer) 803 Live Oak Dr N	Rockledge	FL	32955	321-631-0691	631-9656
Orlando Predators (football) 400 W Church St	Orlando	FL	32801	407-648-4444	648-8101
Orlando Rays (baseball) 287 S Tampa Ave Tinker Field	Orlando	FL	32805	407-872-7593	
Web: www.insidecentralflorida.com/sports/orlandorays/ ■ *E-mail:* orays@aol.com					
Orlando-Seminole Jai Alai 6405 S Hwy 17-92	Fern Park	FL	32730	407-339-6221	
Web: www.gentech.net/orlando-jailai					
Orlando Solar Bears (hockey) 600 W Amelia St Orlando Arena	Orlando	FL	32801	407-872-7825	
Sanford-Orlando Kennel Club 301 Dog Track Rd.	Longwood	FL	32750	407-831-1600	831-3997
Seminole Greyhound Park 2000 Seminola Blvd	Casselberry	FL	32707	407-699-4510	695-9115

— Events —

	Phone
Bach Music Festival (late February)	407-646-2182
Central Florida Fair (late February-early March)	407-295-3247
Epcot International Flower & Garden Show (mid April-late May)	407-824-4321
Epcot International Food & Wine Festival (late October-late November)	407-824-4321
Festival of the Masters (mid-November)	407-824-4321
Fiesta in the Park (early November)	407-649-3152
Florida Citrus Bowl (January 1)	407-423-2476
Florida Film Festival (mid-late June)	407-629-1088
Halloween Horror Nights (October)	800-447-0675
International Orchid Fair (late October)	407-396-1887
Maitland Arts & Fine Crafts Festival (mid-April)	407-644-0741
Orlando Craft Fair (early October)	407-860-0092
Orlando Scottish Highland Games (mid-January)	407-699-4510
Orlando-UCF Shakespeare Festival (October-May)	407-245-0985
Orlando's Singing Christmas Trees (mid-December)	407-425-2555
Silver Spurs Rodeo (mid-February & early October)	800-847-4052
Summer Festival (mid-July)	407-943-7992
Surf Expo (early January)	407-345-9800
Walt Disney World Fourth of July Celebration (July 4)	407-824-2222
Walt Disney World Marathon (early January)	407-939-7810
Walt Disney World National Car Rental Golf Classic (late October)	407-824-2250
Winter Park Sidewalk Arts Festival (mid-March)	407-644-8281

Pensacola

Located on Pensacola Bay in Florida's panhandle, the city of Pensacola got its name from the now-extinct Panzacola Indians who greeted Spanish Conquistador Don Tristan de Luna when he arrived, along with 1,400 colonists, in what is now Pensacola Beach in 1559. Pensacola was the first European settlement in the U.S., and five different flags have flown over the city since 1559: Spanish, French, British, Confederate, and American. The Fiesta of Five Flags celebration, one of the oldest and largest festivals in the state, is held each year in June to remember the founding of Pensacola. (The festival has been honored as a "Top 20" event by the Southeast Tourism Society.) Visitors to the city can also get a glimpse of Pensacola's rich history in its restored downtown area and in some of its museums. The T.T. Wentworth Jr. Florida State Museum displays artifacts of the Pensacola area; and the National Aviation Museum presents the history of flight and offers aviation films in the adjoining IMAXâ Theatre. Travelers can also cross the three-mile-long Pensacola Bay Bridge to visit Gulf Islands National Seashore, a natural wonder that preserves barrier islands, harbors, and submerged land in their natural environment. Located also within the Seashore's protection is historic Fort Pickens, the 1,400-acre Naval Live Oaks Reservation.

Population	58,193	**Longitude**	87-11-22 W
Area (Land)	22.6 sq mi	**County**	Escambia
Area (Water)	17.0 sq mi	**Time Zone**	CST
Elevation	32 ft	**Area Code/s**	850
Latitude	30-26-41 N		

— Average Temperatures and Precipitation —

TEMPERATURES

	Jan	Feb	Mar	Apr	May	Jun	Jul	Aug	Sep	Oct	Nov	Dec
High	60	63	69	77	83	89	90	89	86	79	70	63
Low	41	44	51	59	66	72	74	74	70	59	51	44

PRECIPITATION

	Jan	Feb	Mar	Apr	May	Jun	Jul	Aug	Sep	Oct	Nov	Dec
Inches	4.7	5.4	5.6	3.8	4.2	6.4	7.4	7.4	5.3	4.2	3.5	4.3

— Important Phone Numbers —

	Phone		Phone
AAA	850-477-6860	**Medical Referral**	850-434-4080
Emerald Arts Hotline	850-314-2787	**Pensacola Beach Events Hotline**	850-932-2259
Emergency	911	**Time/Temp**	850-432-7411

— Information Sources —

				Phone	Fax
Better Business Bureau Serving Northwest Florida PO Box 1511	Pensacola	FL	32597	850-429-0002	429-0006
Web: www.pensacola.bbb.org					
Downtown Improvement Board 16 Palafox Pl Suite 200	Pensacola	FL	32501	850-434-5371	434-7275
Web: www.downtownpensacola.com ■ *E-mail:* dib@networktel.net					
Escambia County PO Box 1591	Pensacola	FL	32597	850-595-4900	595-4908
Web: www.co.escambia.fl.us					
Pensacola Area Chamber of Commerce PO Box 550	Pensacola	FL	32593	850-438-4081	438-6369
Web: www.chamber.pensacola.fl.us					
Pensacola City Hall 180 Governmental Ctr.	Pensacola	FL	32501	850-435-1600	
Web: www.ci.pensacola.fl.us					
Pensacola City Manager 180 Governmental Ctr City Hall 7th Fl	Pensacola	FL	32501	850-435-1603	435-1611
Web: www.ci.pensacola.fl.us/manager.html ■ *E-mail:* tbonfield@ci.pensacola.fl.us					
Pensacola Civic Center 201 E Gregory St	Pensacola	FL	32501	850-432-0800	432-1707
Web: www.pensacolaciviccenter.com					
Pensacola Convention & Visitors Bureau 1401 E Gregory St	Pensacola	FL	32501	850-434-1234	432-8211
TF: 800-874-1234 ■ *Web:* www.visitpensacola.com					
West Florida Regional Library 200 W Gregory St.	Pensacola	FL	32501	850-435-1760	435-1739

On-Line Resources

4Pensacola.com	www.4pensacola.com
Area Guide Pensacola	pensacola.areaguides.net
City Knowledge Pensacola	www.cityknowledge.com/fl_pensacola.htm

Pensacola — On-Line Resources (Cont'd)

Emerald Coast Web Guide . . . www.ecwebguide.com
Excite.com Pensacola City Guide . . . www.excite.com/travel/countries/united_states/florida/pensacola
HotelGuide Pensacola . . . hotelguide.net/pensacola
NITC Travelbase City Guide Pensacola . . . www.travelbase.com/auto/features/pensacola-fl.html
Online City Guide to Pensacola . . . www.olcg.com/fl/pensacola/main.html
Pensacola Area Community Guide . . . www.pcola.com
Pensacola Beach Splash Page . . . www.pensacolabeach.com
Pensacola CityLink . . . usacitylink.com/citylink/fl/pensacola/default.html
Pensacola Gay Guide . . . www.gaypcola.com
Pensacola Local . . . penlocal.com
Pensacola Online . . . www.pensacola.com/main
Surf & Sun Beach Vacation Guide to Pensacola . . . www.surf-sun.com/fl-pensacola-main.htm
Welcome to Pensacola Beach . . . www.visitpensacolabeach.com

— Transportation Services —

AIRPORTS

■ Pensacola Regional Airport (PNS)

	Phone
3 miles NE of downtown (approx 10 minutes)	850-435-1746

Web: www.flypensacola.com

Airport Transportation

	Phone
Airport Express $25 fare to downtown	850-458-5700
Blue & White Taxi Co $8 fare to downtown	850-438-1497
Elite Taxi $12 fare to downtown	850-455-4410

Commercial Airlines

	Phone		Phone
AirTran	800-247-8726	**Delta**	800-221-1212
America West	800-235-9292	**Northwest Airlink**	800-225-2525
American	800-433-7300	**US Airways**	800-428-4322
Continental	800-525-0280	**US Airways Express**	800-428-4322

Charter Airlines

	Phone
Pensacola Aviation Center Inc	850-434-0636

CAR RENTALS

	Phone		Phone
Avis	850-433-5614	**Hertz**	850-432-2345
Budget	850-432-9744	**National**	850-432-8338
Dollar	850-474-9000		

LIMO/TAXI

	Phone		Phone
Blue & White Taxi Co	850-438-1497	**Yellow Cab**	850-433-3333
Elite Taxi	850-455-4410		

MASS TRANSIT

	Phone
ECAT Bus $1 Base fare	850-595-3228
ECAT Trolley $.25 Base fare	850-595-3228

RAIL/BUS

				Phone
Greyhound Bus Station 505 W Burgess Rd *TF:* 800-231-2222	Pensacola	FL	32504	850-476-4800

— Accommodations —

HOTELS, MOTELS, RESORTS

				Phone	Fax
Beachside Resort & Conference Center 14 Via De Luna Dr *TF:* 800-232-2416 ■ *Web:* www.innisfree.com/bsr	Pensacola Beach	FL	32561	850-932-5331	932-3011
Best Western Pensacola Beach 16 Via De Luna Dr *TF:* 800-934-3301	Pensacola Beach	FL	32561	850-934-3300	934-9780
Best Western Village Inn 8240 N Davis Hwy *TF:* 800-528-1234	Pensacola	FL	32514	850-479-1099	479-9320
Clarion Suites Resort & Conference Center 20 Via De Luna Dr *TF:* 800-874-5303	Pensacola Beach	FL	32561	850-932-4300	934-9112
Comfort Inn NAS/Corry 3 New Warrington Rd *TF:* 800-554-3206	Pensacola	FL	32506	850-455-3233	453-3445
Comfort Inn Pensacola Beach 40 Fort Pickens Rd *TF:* 800-934-5470	Pensacola Beach	FL	32561	850-934-5400	932-7210
Courtyard by Marriott 451 Creighton Rd *TF:* 800-321-2211 ■ *Web:* www.lbaproperties.com/courtyard_pensacola/index.htm	Pensacola	FL	32504	850-857-7744	857-0904
Days Inn Downtown Historic District 710 N Palafox St. *TF:* 800-329-7466	Pensacola	FL	32501	850-438-4922	438-7999
Days Inn North 7051 Pensacola Blvd *TF:* 800-325-2525	Pensacola	FL	32505	850-476-9090	476-9090
Dunes The 333 Fort Pickens Rd *TF:* 800-833-8637 ■ *Web:* www.pensacolabeach.com/dunes ■ *E-mail:* thedunes@gulf.net	Pensacola Beach	FL	32561	850-932-3536	932-7088
Econo Lodge Pensacola 7194 Pensacola Blvd *TF:* 800-553-2666	Pensacola	FL	32505	850-479-8600	479-8600
Executive Inn 6954 Pensacola Blvd	Pensacola	FL	32505	850-478-4015	477-8361
Hampton Inn Pensacola Airport 2187 Airport Blvd *TF:* 800-426-7866	Pensacola	FL	32504	850-478-1123	478-8519
Hampton Inn Pensacola Beach 2 Via De Luna Dr *TF:* 800-320-8108 ■ *Web:* www.hamptonbeachresort.com	Pensacola Beach	FL	32561	850-932-6800	932-6800
Hampton Inn University Mall 7330 Plantation Rd *TF:* 800-426-7866	Pensacola	FL	32504	850-477-3333	477-8163
Holiday Inn Express Pensacola 6501 Pensacola Blvd	Pensacola	FL	32505	850-476-7200	476-1277
Holiday Inn Pensacola Beach 165 Fort Pickens Rd *TF:* 800-465-4329 ■ *Web:* www.pensacolabeach.com/holiday/	Pensacola Beach	FL	32561	850-932-5361	932-7121
Holiday Inn University Mall 7200 Plantation Rd *TF:* 800-465-4329	Pensacola	FL	32504	850-474-0100	477-9821
Hospitality Inn 4910 Mobile Hwy *TF:* 800-321-0052	Pensacola	FL	32506	850-453-3333	455-6008
Hospitality Inn North 6900 Pensacola Blvd. *TF:* 800-321-0052	Pensacola	FL	32505	850-477-2333	479-3575
La Quinta Inn 7750 N Davis Hwy *TF:* 800-687-6667	Pensacola	FL	32514	850-474-0411	474-1521
Motel 6 5829 Pensacola Blvd *TF:* 800-466-8356	Pensacola	FL	32505	850-477-7522	476-7126
Motel 6 Pensacola North 7827 N Davis Hwy *TF:* 800-466-8356	Pensacola	FL	32514	850-476-5386	476-7458
Pensacola Grand Hotel 200 E Gregory St *TF:* 800-348-3336 ■ *Web:* www.pensacolagrandhotel.com ■ *E-mail:* grandhotel@pen.net	Pensacola	FL	32501	850-433-3336	432-7572
Ramada Inn Bayview 7601 Scenic Hwy. *TF:* 800-282-1212 ■ *Web:* www.ramadabayview.com	Pensacola	FL	32504	850-477-7155	477-7155
Ramada Inn North 6550 Pensacola Blvd *TF:* 800-838-7642	Pensacola	FL	32505	850-477-0711	479-1977
Ramada Limited 8060 Lavelle Way *TF:* 800-382-6192	Pensacola	FL	32526	850-944-0333	941-1961
Red Roof Inn 6919 Pensacola Blvd *TF:* 800-843-7663	Pensacola	FL	32505	850-478-4499	857-1250
Red Roof Inn University Mall 7340 Plantation Rd *TF:* 800-843-7663	Pensacola	FL	32504	850-476-7960	479-4706
Residence Inn by Marriott Downtown 601 E Chase St. *TF:* 800-331-3131	Pensacola	FL	32501	850-432-0202	438-7965
Residence Inn by Marriott University Mall 7230 Plantation Rd *TF:* 800-331-3131	Pensacola	FL	32504	850-479-1000	477-3399
Seville Inn 223 E Garden St. *TF:* 800-277-7275	Pensacola	FL	32501	850-433-8331	432-6849
Shoney's Inn & Suites Pensacola 8080 N Davis Hwy *TF:* 800-222-2222	Pensacola	FL	32514	850-484-8070	484-3853
Villager Lodge Pensacola 1953 Northcross Ln *TF:* 800-328-7829	Pensacola	FL	32514	850-477-2554	478-3623

Pensacola (Cont'd)

— Restaurants —

Name / Address	City	State	ZIP	Phone
1912 Restaurant (Continental) 200 E Gregory St	Pensacola	FL	32501	850-433-3336
Angus The (Steak/Seafood) 1101 Scenic Hwy	Pensacola	FL	32503	850-432-0539
Barnhill's Buffet (Homestyle) 8102 N Davis Hwy	Pensacola	FL	32514	850-477-5465
Barracks Street Fish House (Seafood) 600 S Barracks St Suite 108	Pensacola	FL	32501	850-470-0003
Bay Breeze Restaurant (American) 7601 Scenic Hwy	Pensacola	FL	32504	850-477-7155
Bayside Grill (Caribbean/Creole) 14 Via De Luna Dr	Pensacola Beach	FL	32561	850-932-9898
Boy on a Dolphin Restaurant & Lounge (Seafood) 400 Pensacola Beach Blvd	Pensacola Beach	FL	32561	850-932-7954
Chan's Gulfside (New American) 2 1/2 Via De Luna Dr	Pensacola Beach	FL	32561	850-932-3525
Flounder's Chowder & Ale House (Steak/Seafood) 800 Quietwater Beach Rd	Pensacola Beach	FL	32561	850-932-2003
Hall's Seafood (Seafood) 920 E Gregory St	Pensacola	FL	32501	850-438-9019
Hopkins Boarding House (Southern) 900 N Spring St	Pensacola	FL	32501	850-438-3979
Hunan Chinese Restaurant (Chinese) 3102 E Cervantes St	Pensacola	FL	32503	850-438-4787
Jamie's French Restaurant (French) 424 E Zarragossa St *Web:* jamies.pensacola.com ■ *E-mail:* jaimes@pensacola.com	Pensacola	FL	32501	850-434-2911
Jerry's Cajun Cafe (Cajun) 6205 N 9th Ave	Pensacola	FL	32504	850-484-6962
Jubilee Restaurant & Oyster Bar (Seafood) 400 Quietwater Beach Rd	Pensacola Beach	FL	32561	850-934-3108
Marina Oyster Barn (Seafood) 505 Bayou Blvd	Pensacola	FL	32503	850-433-0511
McGuire's Irish Pub (Irish) 600 E Gregory St	Pensacola	FL	32501	850-433-6789
Mesquite Charlie's (Barbecue) 5901 N 'W' St	Pensacola	FL	32505	850-434-0498
Monterrey's Mexican Grill (Mexican) 5030 Bayou Blvd	Pensacola	FL	32503	850-479-7351
Oscar's Restaurant (Steak/Seafood) 2805 W Cervantes St	Pensacola	FL	32505	850-432-8388
Peg Leg Pete's (Cajun) 1010 Fort Pickens Rd	Pensacola Beach	FL	32561	850-932-4139
Pensacola Greyhound Track Restaurant (American) 950 Dog Track Rd	Pensacola	FL	32506	850-455-8595
Sabine Steamer (Caribbean) 715 Pensacola Beach Blvd	Pensacola Beach	FL	32561	850-932-7474
Screaming Coyote (Southwest) 196 Palafox St	Pensacola	FL	32501	850-435-9002
Skopelos on the Bay (Steak/Seafood) 670 Scenic Hwy	Pensacola	FL	32503	850-432-6565
Smokey's Real Pit BBQ (Barbecue) 6475 N Pensacola Blvd	Pensacola	FL	32505	850-478-0860
Sun Ray Restaurante & Cantina (Mexican) 400 Quietwater Beach Rd *Web:* sites.gulf.net/sunray	Pensacola Beach	FL	32561	850-932-0118
Tu-Do Vietnamese Restaurant (Vietnamese) 7130 N Davis Hwy	Pensacola	FL	32504	850-473-8877
Yamato Oriental Cuisine (Japanese) 131 New Warrington Rd *Web:* www.yamato.pen.net	Pensacola	FL	32506	850-453-3461

— Goods and Services —

SHOPPING

Name / Address	City	State	ZIP	Phone	Fax
Cordova Mall 5100 N 9th Ave	Pensacola	FL	32504	850-477-5563	478-4723
Flea Market The 5760 Gulf Breeze Pkwy	Gulf Breeze	FL	32561	850-934-1971	934-5507
University Mall 7171 N Davis Hwy	Pensacola	FL	32504	850-478-3600	479-9162

BANKS

Name / Address	City	State	ZIP	Phone	Fax
Amsouth Bank of Florida 70 N Baylen St *TF:* 800-825-0023	Pensacola	FL	32501	850-444-1000	444-1115
Bank of Pensacola 400 W Garden St	Pensacola	FL	32501	850-436-7800	436-7811
Compass Bank 5055 Bayou Blvd	Pensacola	FL	32501	850-857-5000	857-5049
First American Bank of Pensacola NA 33 W Garden St	Pensacola	FL	32501	850-435-9300	435-8731
First Navy Bank 180 Taylor Rd Naval Air Station *Web:* www.firstnavybank.com	Pensacola	FL	32508	850-453-3411	453-2736
First Union National Bank 21 E Garden St *TF:* 800-275-3862	Pensacola	FL	32501	850-469-4230	469-4205
NationsBank 100 W Garden St	Pensacola	FL	32501	850-444-0469	444-0433
SunTrust Bank 220 W Garden St	Pensacola	FL	32501	850-435-1200	435-1270
Warrington Bank 4093 Barrancas Ave *Web:* www.warringtonbank.com	Pensacola	FL	32507	850-455-7351	456-9959

BUSINESS SERVICES

Name	Phone
AAA Employment	850-494-1614
Airborne Express	800-247-2676
Copy Cat Printing	850-438-5566
DHL Worldwide Express	800-225-5345
Express Personnel	850-494-1776
Federal Express	800-463-3339
Landrum Staffing Services	850-476-5100
Post Office	850-434-9127
Southeast Courier	850-932-2677
Staffing Connections	850-435-8383
UPS	800-742-5877
Vowell's Printing	850-438-7831

— Media —

PUBLICATIONS

Name / Address	City	State	ZIP	Phone	Fax
Islander Newspaper PO Box 721	Gulf Breeze	FL	32562	850-934-3417	932-7230
Pensacola News Journal‡ PO Box 12710 *TF:* 800-288-2021 ■ *Web:* www.gulfcoastgateway.com ■ *E-mail:* pns@gulfsurf.infi.net	Pensacola	FL	32574	850-435-8500	435-8633
Travelhost of Pensacola Magazine PO Box 1463	Gulf Breeze	FL	32562	850-934-9466	934-1668

‡*Daily newspapers*

TELEVISION

Name / Address	City	State	ZIP	Phone	Fax
WALA-TV Ch 10 (Fox) 210 Government St	Mobile	AL	36602	334-434-1010	434-1073
WEAR-TV Ch 3 (ABC) 4990 Mobile Hwy *Web:* www.wear.pensacola.com ■ *E-mail:* news@weartv.com	Pensacola	FL	32506	850-456-3333	455-0159
WJTC-TV Ch 44 (UPN) 661 Azalea Rd *Web:* www.wjtc.com	Mobile	AL	36609	334-602-1544	602-1547
WKRG-TV Ch 5 (CBS) 555 Broadcast Dr *TF:* 800-957-4885 ■ *Web:* www.wkrg.com ■ *E-mail:* tv5@wkrg.com	Mobile	AL	36606	334-479-5555	473-8130
WPAN-TV Ch 53 (Ind) 2105 W Gregory St	Pensacola	FL	32501	850-433-1766	433-1641
WPMI-TV Ch 15 (NBC) 661 Azalea Rd *Web:* www.wpmi.com ■ *E-mail:* nbc15@wpmi.com	Mobile	AL	36609	334-602-1500	602-1550

RADIO

Name / Address	City	State	ZIP	Phone	Fax
WBSR-AM 1450 kHz (CHR) 1601 N Pace Blvd *Web:* www.wbsr.com ■ *E-mail:* wbsr@dotstar.net	Pensacola	FL	32505	850-438-4982	433-7932
WCOA-AM 1370 kHz (N/T) 6565 N 'W' St	Pensacola	FL	32505	850-478-6011	478-3971
WGCX-FM 95.7 MHz (Rel) 2070 N Palafox St	Pensacola	FL	32501	850-434-1230	469-9698
WNVY-AM 1090 kHz (Rel) 2070 N Palafox St	Pensacola	FL	32501	850-434-1230	469-9698
WPCS-FM 89.5 MHz (Rel) 250 Brent Ln	Pensacola	FL	32503	850-479-6570	969-1638
WRNE-AM 980 kHz (Urban) 312 E Nine Mile Rd	Pensacola	FL	32514	850-478-6000	484-8080
WSWL-AM 790 kHz (N/T) 3801 N Pace Blvd	Pensacola	FL	32505	850-433-1141	433-1142
WTKX-FM 101.5 MHz (Rock) 6485 Pensacola Blvd	Pensacola	FL	32505	850-473-0400	473-0907
WUWF-FM 88.1 MHz (NPR) University of West Florida 11000 University Pkwy *Web:* www.uwf.edu/~wuwf	Pensacola	FL	32514	850-474-2327	474-3283
WYCL-FM 107.3 MHz (Oldies) 6485 Pensacola Blvd *Web:* www.cool107.com ■ *E-mail:* newrock@onezeroseven.com	Pensacola	FL	32505	850-473-0400	473-0907

— Colleges/Universities —

Name / Address	City	State	ZIP	Phone	Fax
Pensacola Christian College 250 Brent Ln. *Web:* www.pcci.edu	Pensacola	FL	32503	850-478-8496	479-6571
Pensacola Junior College 1000 College Blvd *Web:* www.pjc.cc.fl.us	Pensacola	FL	32504	850-484-1000	484-1829
University of West Florida 11000 University Pkwy *TF Admissions:* 800-263-1074 ■ *Web:* www.uwf.edu ■ *E-mail:* aturner@uwf.cc.uwf.edu	Pensacola	FL	32514	850-474-2000	474-3360

— Hospitals —

Name / Address	City	State	ZIP	Phone	Fax
Baptist Hospital 1000 W Moreno St	Pensacola	FL	32501	850-434-4011	469-2307

Pensacola — Hospitals (Cont'd)

	City	State	Zip	Phone	Fax
Sacred Heart Children's Hospital 5151 N 9th Ave	Pensacola	FL	32504	850-416-4000	416-6775
Sacred Heart Hospital of Pensacola 5151 N 9th Ave **Fax:* Admitting ■ *Web:* www.sacred-heart.org	Pensacola	FL	32504	850-416-7000	416-6775*
West Florida Regional Medical Center 8383 N Davis Hwy *Web:* www.columbia.net/faciliti/fl/wfla.html	Pensacola	FL	32523	850-494-4000	494-4957

— Attractions —

	City	State	Zip	Phone	Fax
Adventures Unlimited Rt 6 *TF:* 800-239-6864 ■ *Web:* www.adventuresunlimited.com ■ *E-mail:* aunlimited@aol.com	Milton	FL	32570	850-623-6197	626-3124
Arts Council of Northwest Florida 226 S Palafox St 2nd Fl	Pensacola	FL	32501	850-432-9906	469-0786
Bayfront Gallery 713 S Palafox St *Web:* www.bayfrontgallery.com	Pensacola	FL	32501	850-438-7556	438-7556
Choral Society of Pensacola 118 S Palafox St Saenger Theatre *Web:* artsnwfl.org/choralsociety	Pensacola	FL	32501	850-444-7699	444-7684
Fast Eddies Fun Center 505 Michigan Ave *Web:* www.fasteddiesfunctr.com ■ *E-mail:* fasteddiesfunctr@worldnet.att.net	Pensacola	FL	32505	850-433-7735	433-7564
Gulf Islands National Seashore (Florida) 1801 Gulf Breeze Pkwy *Web:* www.nps.gov/guis	Gulf Breeze	FL	32561	850-934-2600	932-9654
IMAX Naval Aviation Memorial Theater 1750 Radford Blvd Suite B **Fax Area Code:* 850 ■ *Web:* www.naval-air.org/Foundation/IMAX%20Theater/IMAX_Theater_Frame.htm ■ *E-mail:* namfimax@naval-air.org	Pensacola	FL	32508	888-627-4629	453-2018*
Jazz Society of Pensacola PO Box 18337 *Web:* artsnwfl.org/jazz	Pensacola	FL	32523	850-433-8382	433-1969
National Museum of Naval Aviation 1750 Radford Blvd Suite C *TF:* 800-327-5002 ■ *Web:* www.naval-air.org ■ *E-mail:* Naval.Museum@smtp.cnet.navy.mil	Pensacola	FL	32508	850-452-3604	452-3296
Northwest Florida Ballet 118 S Palafox Pl Saenger Theatre *Web:* www.nwfl.net/nwfb	Pensacola	FL	32501	850-444-7699	444-7684
Pensacola Bay Fishing Bridge 1750 Bayfront Pkwy *Web:* www.fishthebridge.com	Pensacola	FL	32501	850-444-9811	438-2061
Pensacola Cultural Center 400 S Jefferson St	Pensacola	FL	32501	850-434-0257	438-2787
Pensacola Little Theatre 400 S Jefferson St Pensacola Cultural Ctr. *Web:* www.pensacolalittletheatre.com ■ *E-mail:* tmarsh@pensacolalittletheatre.com	Pensacola	FL	32501	850-432-2042	438-2787
Pensacola Museum of Art 407 S Jefferson St *Web:* artsnwfl.org/pma/	Pensacola	FL	32501	850-432-6247	469-1532
Pensacola Opera Co 118 S Palafox Pl Saenger Theatre *Web:* www.pensacolaopera.com ■ *E-mail:* pensacolaopera@worldnet.att.net	Pensacola	FL	32501	850-444-7699	444-7684
Pensacola Symphony Orchestra 118 S Palafox Pl Saenger Theatre *Web:* artsnwfl.org/symphony	Pensacola	FL	32501	850-444-7699	444-7684
Quayside Art Gallery 15-17 Zarragossa St *Web:* www.virtualpcola.com/quayside	Pensacola	FL	32501	850-438-2363	
Quietwater Beach Boardwalk 400 Quietwater Beach Rd *Web:* www.pcola.com/boardwalk/	Pensacola Beach	FL	32561		
Rod & Reel Marina 10045 Sinton Dr *Web:* www.rod-n-reel.com ■ *E-mail:* rodreel11@aol.com	Pensacola	FL	32507	850-492-0100	492-0200
Saenger Theatre 118 S Palafox Pl *Web:* www.pensacolasaenger.com	Pensacola	FL	32501	850-444-7699	444-7684
Seville Dinner Theater 241 E Garden St	Pensacola	FL	32501	850-469-1111	
Seville Quarter 130 E Government St *Web:* www.rosies.com ■ *E-mail:* info@rosies.com	Pensacola	FL	32501	850-434-6211	
Treehouse Theater 400 S Jefferson St	Pensacola	FL	32501	850-434-0257	438-2787
University of West Florida Center for Fine & Performing Arts 11000 University Pkwy *Web:* www.uwf.edu/~theatre	Pensacola	FL	32514	850-474-2405	
Wildlife Sanctuary of Northwest Florida 105 N 'S' St *Web:* www.pcola.com/wildlife/ ■ *E-mail:* ecase@worldnet.att.net	Pensacola	FL	32505	850-433-9453	438-6168

	City	State	Zip	Phone	Fax
Zoo The 5701 Gulf Breeze Pkwy *Web:* www.the-zoo.com ■ *E-mail:* information@the-zoo.com	Gulf Breeze	FL	32561	850-932-2229	932-8575

SPORTS TEAMS & FACILITIES

	City	State	Zip	Phone	Fax
Pensacola Civic Center 201 E Gregory St *Web:* www.pensacolaciviccenter.com	Pensacola	FL	32501	850-432-0800	432-1707
Pensacola Greyhound Track 950 Dog Track Rd. *Web:* www.pensacolagreyhoundpark.com	West Pensacola	FL	32506	850-455-8595	453-8883
Pensacola Ice Pilots (hockey) 201 E Gregory St *Web:* www.icepilots.com	Pensacola	FL	32501	850-432-7825	432-1929

— Events —

	Phone
Fiesta Fall Antique Show (mid-September)	850-433-6512
Fiesta of Five Flags (early-mid-June)	850-433-6512
Fiesta Of Five Flags Golf Tournament (mid-June)	850-433-6512
Fiesta Of Five Flags Regional Pistol Match (early May)	850-433-6512
Fiesta Spring Antique Show (early May)	850-433-6512
First Night Pensacola (December 31)	850-932-0095
Great Gulf Coast Arts Festival (early November)	850-432-9906
Jubilee's Bushwacker & Music Festival (early August)	850-932-1500
Jubilee's Lobster Fest (early September)	850-932-1500
Pensacola Crawfish Creole Fiesta (early May)	850-433-6512
Pensacola Interstate Fair (late October)	850-944-4500
Pensacola JazzFest (mid-April)	850-433-8382
Pensacola Mardi Gras (early January-early March)	850-473-8858
Pensacola Seafood Festival 5k Run/Walk (late September)	850-433-6512
Pensacola Seafood Festival (mid-September)	850-433-6512
Penwheels/Fiesta Fishing Rodeo (early May)	850-433-6512
SpringFest (mid-May)	850-469-1069

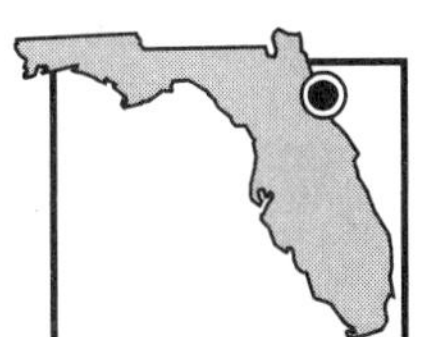

Saint Augustine

Saint Augustine, America's oldest continuously occupied European settlement, is located in northeastern Florida. Founded in 1565, it was under Spanish control until England claimed it as one of the prizes of the French and Indian War. The city has a rich historic heritage that is reflected in its buildings, most of which feature the famous Spanish-style architecture. Other buildings reflect Victorian architecture, but all have a colonial flair. Saint Augustine is home to two defensive forts built by the Spanish: Fort Castillo de San Marcos, which took 23 years to build and is the oldest masonry fort in the continental U.S, and Fort Matanzas, built in the 1740s. Other historic sites include Flagler College, which was formerly the Hotel Ponce de Leon, built by Henry Flagler in 1887, and the Peña-Peck House, which was the original site for the Royal Spanish Treasurer and home of the British Lieutenant Governor of Florida. Two other buildings, the Oldest House Museum and the Oldest Wooden Schoolhouse (in the U.S.), are maintained as living museums. The National Cemetery, used as a burial ground since at least 1763, is Florida's oldest national military cemetery, and the Mission of Nombre de Dios was the site of the first Catholic mass said in what is now the United States. Saint Augustine is also famous for its festivals and reenactments of British and Spanish colonial life. A few of the largest include the Hastings Cabbage and Potato Festival, the EPIC Celebration of Spring, both held in the spring, the Spanish Night Watch in June, and the British Night Watch in December.

Population	12,573	**Longitude**	81-18-39 W
Area (Land)	7.0 sq mi	**County**	Saint John's
Area (Water)	2.1 sq mi	**Time Zone**	EST
Elevation	8 ft	**Area Code/s**	904
Latitude	29-53-31 N		

Saint Augustine (Cont'd)

— Average Temperatures and Precipitation —

TEMPERATURES

	Jan	Feb	Mar	Apr	May	Jun	Jul	Aug	Sep	Oct	Nov	Dec
High	66	68	74	79	84	88	90	89	86	81	74	69
Low	46	47	53	58	64	70	72	72	71	64	55	48

PRECIPITATION

	Jan	Feb	Mar	Apr	May	Jun	Jul	Aug	Sep	Oct	Nov	Dec
Inches	3.1	3.8	3.6	2.4	3.6	5.5	5.5	6.3	6.1	3.7	2.3	3.0

— Important Phone Numbers —

	Phone		Phone
AAA	904-280-8181	**Medical Referral**	904-819-4427
Emergency	911	**Poison Control Center**	800-282-3171

— Information Sources —

				Phone	Fax
Better Business Bureau Serving Northeast Florida 7820 Arlington Expy Suite 147 *Web:* www.jacksonville.bbb.org	Jacksonville	FL	32211	904-721-2288	721-7373
Saint Augustine & Saint Johns County Chamber of Commerce 1 Riberia St *Web:* www.staugustinechamber.com ■ *E-mail:* chamber@aug.com	Saint Augustine	FL	32084	904-829-5681	829-6477
Saint Augustine City Hall 75 King St *Web:* www.ci.st-augustine.fl.us ■ *E-mail:* cosa @aug.com	Saint Augustine	FL	32084	904-825-1010	825-1051
Saint Augustine Mayor 75 King St City Hall *E-mail:* lweeks@aug.com	Saint Augustine	FL	32084	904-824-1626	825-1096
Saint Augustine Visitor Information Center 10 S Castillo Dr	Saint Augustine	FL	32084	904-825-1000	825-1064
Saint Johns County PO Box 300 *Web:* www.co.st-johns.fl.us	Saint Augustine	FL	32085	904-823-2500	823-2294
Saint Johns County Convention & Visitors Bureau 88 Riberia St Suite 400 *TF:* 800-653-2489 ■ *Web:* www.oldcity.com/vcb ■ *E-mail:* inqserv@oldcity.com	Saint Augustine	FL	32084	904-829-1711	829-6149
Saint Johns County Public Library 1960 N Ponce de Leon Blvd	Saint Augustine	FL	32084	904-823-2650	823-2656
Tourist & Development Council 88 Riberia St Suite 400 *TF:* 800-653-2489	Saint Augustine	FL	32084	904-823-2680	829-6149

On-Line Resources

Access America Saint Augustine	www.accessamer.com/staugustine/
All-Florida Visitors Guide to Saint Augustine	www.florida-accommodations.com/StAugustine
Best Read Guide Saint Augustine	www.bestreadguide.com/staugustine
Excite.com Saint Augustine City Guide	www.excite.com/travel/countries/united_states/florida/st_augustine
History of Saint Augustine	macserver.stjohns.k12.fl.us/history/history.html
Info Person Guide to Saint Augustine	www.infoperson.com
NITC Travelbase Guide to Saint Augustine	www.travelbase.com/auto/guides/st_augustine-area-fl.html
Saint Augustine On-Line City Guide	www.onlinecityguide.com/fl/staugustine/
Saint Augustine Travel Guide	www.2000floridatravel.com/staugustine
SaintAugustine.com	www.saintaugustine.com
Surf & Sun Beach Vacation Guide to Saint Augustine	www.surf-sun.com/fl-st-augustine-main.htm
Virtual Saint Augustine	www.aug.com/virtual/virtual.html

— Transportation Services —

AIRPORTS

■ **Jacksonville International Airport (JAX)**

	Phone
48 miles NW of downtown Saint Augustine (approx 60 minutes) Web: www.jaxport.com/jia.cfm ■ *E-mail:* info@jaxport.com	904-741-4902

Airport Transportation

	Phone
Beaches Yellow Cab $70 fare to downtown Saint Augustine	904-246-6667
Gator City Transportation $56-57 fare to downtown Saint Augustine	904-353-8880
Yellow Shuttle $55 fare to downtown Saint Augustine	904-829-2256

Commercial Airlines

	Phone		Phone
American	800-433-7300	**MetroJet**	888-638-7653
Continental	800-525-0280	**TWA**	800-221-2000
Continental Express	800-525-0280	**United**	800-241-6522
Delta	800-221-1212	**US Airways**	800-428-4322

Charter Airlines

	Phone		Phone
Alliance Executive Charter Services	800-232-5387	**Corporate Airways**	904-641-0001
		Craig Air Center	904-641-0300

CAR RENTALS

	Phone		Phone
Alamo-Jacksonville	904-741-4414	**Dollar-Jacksonville**	904-741-4614
Avis	904-829-3700	**Enterprise**	904-829-1662
Avis-Jacksonville	904-741-2327	**Enterprise-Jacksonville**	904-388-3553
Budget	904-794-0708	**Hertz-Jacksonville**	904-741-2151
Budget-Jacksonville	904-720-0000	**National-Jacksonville**	904-641-2445

LIMO/TAXI

	Phone		Phone
Ancient City Cab	904-824-8161	**Yellow Cab**	904-824-6888
Comfort Cab	904-824-8240	**Yellow Shuttle**	904-829-2256

RAIL/BUS

				Phone
Greyhound Bus Station 100 Malaga St *TF:* 800-231-2222	Saint Augustine	FL	32084	904-829-6401

— Accommodations —

HOTELS, MOTELS, RESORTS

				Phone	Fax
Anastasia Inn 218 Anastasia Blvd *Web:* www.anastasiainn.com	Saint Augustine	FL	32084	904-825-2879	825-2724
Bayfront Inn 138 Avenida Menendez *TF:* 800-558-3455 ■ *Web:* www.bayfrontinn.com ■ *E-mail:* info@bayfrontinn.com	Saint Augustine	FL	32084	904-824-1681	829-8721
Beacher's Lodge 6970 US Hwy A1A S *TF:* 800-527-8849 ■ *Web:* yp.bellsouth.com/sites/beacherslodge/	Saint Augustine	FL	32086	904-471-8849	471-3002
Best Western Historical Inn 2010 N Ponce de Leon Blvd *TF:* 800-528-1234	Saint Augustine	FL	32084	904-829-9088	829-6629
Best Western Ocean Inn 3955 US 1 S *TF:* 800-528-1234	Saint Augustine	FL	32084	904-471-8010	460-9124
Casa Monica Hotel 95 Cordova St *TF:* 888-472-6312 ■ *Web:* www.grandthemehotels.com/grandtheme/index-casamonica.htm	Saint Augustine	FL	32084	904-827-1888	827-0426
Clarion Hotel 1300 N Ponce de Leon Blvd	Saint Augustine	FL	32084	904-824-3383	829-0668
Colony Reef Club 4670 A1A S *TF:* 800-624-5965 ■ *Web:* www.travelbase.com/destinations/st-augustine/colony-reef/index.html ■ *E-mail:* colony@aug.com	Saint Augustine	FL	32084	904-471-2233	471-6429
Comfort Inn 901 A1A Beach Blvd	Saint Augustine	FL	32084	904-471-1474	461-9659
Comfort Inn Historic 1111 Ponce de Leon Blvd *TF:* 800-575-5288 ■ *Web:* www.oldcity.com/comfort ■ *E-mail:* windym@aug.com	Saint Augustine	FL	32084	904-824-5554	829-2948
Days Inn 541 A1A Beach Blvd *TF:* 800-329-7466	Saint Augustine	FL	32084	904-461-9990	471-4774
Days Inn Historic 2800 N Ponce de Leon Ave *TF:* 800-331-9995 ■ *Web:* www.oldcity.com/daysinn ■ *E-mail:* daysinn@aug.com	Saint Augustine	FL	32084	904-829-6581	824-0135
Econo Lodge 311 A1A Beach Blvd *TF:* 800-553-2666	Saint Augustine	FL	32084	904-471-2330	471-1018
Edgewater Inn 2 St Augustine Blvd	Saint Augustine	FL	32084	904-825-2697	

Saint Augustine — Hotels, Motels, Resorts (Cont'd)

Name / Address	City	State	ZIP	Phone	Fax
GuestHouse Inn 2365 SR 16 *TF:* 800-214-8378 ■ *Web:* www.guesthouse.net/staug95.html	Saint Augustine	FL	32095	904-824-4306	823-9776
Hampton Inn Historic 2050 N Ponce de Leon Blvd *TF:* 800-426-7866	Saint Augustine	FL	32095	904-829-1996	829-1988
Hampton Inn Oceanfront 430 A1A Beach Blvd *TF:* 800-426-7866 ■ *Web:* www.oldcity.com/hampton	Saint Augustine	FL	32084	904-471-4000	471-4888
Holiday Inn 860 A1A Beach Blvd. *TF:* 800-626-7263	Saint Augustine	FL	32084	904-471-2555	461-8450
Holiday Inn Express 2310 SR 16	Saint Augustine	FL	32095	904-823-8636	823-8728
Holiday Resort Motel 530 A1A Beach Blvd *TF:* 800-249-0282	Saint Augustine	FL	32084	904-471-3505	471-8669
Howard Johnson Express 137 San Marco Ave. *TF:* 800-575-5290 ■ *Web:* www.oldcity.com/hojo	Saint Augustine	FL	32084	904-824-6181	825-2774
Howard Johnson Oceanfront Resort 300 A1A Beach Blvd *TF:* 800-752-4037	Saint Augustine	FL	32084	904-471-2575	471-1247
Inn at Camachee Harbor 201 Yacht Club Dr *TF:* 800-688-5379 ■ *Web:* www.camacheeinn.com ■ *E-mail:* lberg@aug.com	Saint Augustine	FL	32095	904-825-0003	825-0048
La Fiesta Oceanside Inn 810 A1A Beach Blvd *TF:* 800-852-6390	Saint Augustine	FL	32084	904-471-2220	471-0186
Marion Motor Lodge 120 Avenida Menendez *TF:* 800-258-2261	Saint Augustine	FL	32084	904-829-2261	
Merida Motel 2150 N Ponce de Leon Blvd.	Saint Augustine	FL	32084	904-825-2398	824-7822
Monterey Inn 16 Avenida Menendez	Saint Augustine	FL	32084	904-824-4482	829-8854
Ocean Sands Motor Inn 3465 Coastal Hwy *TF:* 800-609-0888 ■ *Web:* www.oceansandsinn.com ■ *E-mail:* osmotorinn@aol.com	Saint Augustine	FL	32095	904-824-1112	824-1112
Old City House Inn 115 Cordova St. *TF:* 800-653-4087 ■ *Web:* www.oldcityhouse.com ■ *E-mail:* jcompton@aug.com	Saint Augustine	FL	32084	904-826-0781	823-8690
Quality Inn 2700 N Ponce de Leon Blvd. *TF:* 800-223-4153	Saint Augustine	FL	32084	904-824-2883	825-0976
Radisson Ponce de Leon Golf & Conference Resort 4000 US 1 N *TF:* 800-333-3333	Saint Augustine	FL	32095	904-824-2821	824-8254
Ramada Inn 116 San Marco Ave. *TF:* 800-575-5289 ■ *Web:* www.oldcity.com/ramada ■ *E-mail:* windym@aug.com	Saint Augustine	FL	32084	904-824-4352	824-2745
Ramada Limited 2535 SR 16. *TF:* 800-272-6232	Saint Augustine	FL	32092	904-829-5643	829-2090
Ramada Limited 894 A1A Beach Blvd.	Saint Augustine	FL	32084	904-471-1440	471-2922
Red Carpet Inn 3101 N Ponce de Leon Blvd.	Saint Augustine	FL	32084	904-829-3461	824-1509
Rodeway Inn 107 Anastasia Blvd *TF:* 800-228-2000	Saint Augustine	FL	32084	904-826-1700	
Saint Augustine Thriftlodge 2500 N Ponce de Leon Blvd.	Saint Augustine	FL	32084	904-824-1341	823-9850
Saint Francis Inn 279 Saint George St *TF:* 800-824-6062 ■ *Web:* www.stfrancisinn.com ■ *E-mail:* innceasd@aug.com	Saint Augustine	FL	32084	904-824-6068	810-5525
San Marco Inn 231 San Marco Ave.	Saint Augustine	FL	32084	904-829-3321	826-0604
Scottish Inn 427 Anastasia Blvd *TF:* 800-251-1962	Saint Augustine	FL	32084	904-824-5055	826-1794
Scottish Inn 110 San Marco Ave. *TF:* 800-251-1962	Saint Augustine	FL	32084	904-824-2871	826-4149
Seabreeze Motel 208 Anastasia Blvd.	Saint Augustine	FL	32084	904-829-8122	
Sunrise Inn 512 Anastasia Blvd.	Saint Augustine	FL	32084	904-829-3888	
Super 8 Motel 3552 N Ponce de Leon Blvd. *TF:* 800-800-8000	Saint Augustine	FL	32084	904-824-6399	823-8687
Travelodge Suites 290 San Marco Ave.	Saint Augustine	FL	32084	904-829-3850	
Vistana Resort 100 Front Nine Dr World Golf Village. *TF:* 800-477-3340 ■ *Web:* www.vistanainc.com/resorts/WGV/	Saint Augustine	FL	32092	904-940-2000	940-2092
Westcott House 146 Avenida Menendez *TF:* 800-513-9814 ■ *Web:* www.westcotthouse.com	Saint Augustine	FL	32084	904-824-4301	824-4301

— Restaurants —

Name / Address	City	State	ZIP	Phone
Acapulco Restaurant (Mexican) 1835 US 1 S Suites 133-135	Saint Augustine	FL	32085	904-826-0191
Alfonso's (Italian) 2443 US 1 S	Saint Augustine	FL	32086	904-797-7597
Alicia's (Italian) 307 Anastasia Blvd	Saint Augustine	FL	32084	904-824-2623
Ann O'Malley's (American) 23 Orange St	Saint Augustine	FL	32084	904-825-4040
Aruanno's (Italian) 105 D St *Web:* www.oldcity.com/aruannos/ ■ *E-mail:* aruannos@aug.com	Saint Augustine	FL	32084	904-471-9373
Athena Restaurant (Greek) 14 Cathedral Pl	Saint Augustine	FL	32084	904-823-9076
Azalea's Cafe (Mediterranean) 4 Aviles St	Saint Augustine	FL	32084	904-824-6465
Barnacle Bill's (Seafood) 14 W Castillo Dr	Saint Augustine	FL	32084	904-824-3663
Barrancotto's Roma Restaurant (Italian) 165 Vilano Rd *Web:* www.oldcity.com/barrancottos	Saint Augustine	FL	32095	904-829-5719
Beach Garden (American) 860 A1A Beach Blvd Holiday Inn	Saint Augustine	FL	32084	904-471-2555
Beachcomber Restaurant (Steak/Seafood) 2 'A' St. *Web:* www.oldcity.com/beachcomber	Saint Augustine	FL	32084	904-471-3744
Black Marlin Grill (Seafood) 1824 A1A S	Saint Augustine	FL	32084	904-471-7976
Bono's (Barbecue) 1001 A1A Beach Blvd	Saint Augustine	FL	32084	904-461-0157
Cafe Alcazar (American) 25 Granada St	Saint Augustine	FL	32084	904-824-7813
Cafe Cortesse (Continental) 172 San Marco Ave	Saint Augustine	FL	32084	904-825-6775
Cafe Latino (Latin American/Caribbean) 900 Anastasia Blvd Suite J	Saint Augustine	FL	32084	904-824-2187
Cap's (Seafood) 4325 Myrtle St.	Saint Augustine	FL	32095	904-824-8794
Captain Jack's (Seafood) 410 Anastasia Blvd	Saint Augustine	FL	32084	904-829-6846
Castanet (Seafood) 2801 Coastal Hwy	Saint Augustine	FL	32095	904-829-3377
Columbia Restaurant (Spanish/Cuban) 98 Saint George St.	Saint Augustine	FL	32084	904-824-3341
Compton's (Seafood) 4100 Coastal Hwy	Saint Augustine	FL	32095	904-824-8051
Conch House Restaurant (Caribbean) 57 Comares Ave Conch House Marina Resort *Web:* www.conch-house.com/restrnt2.htm ■ *E-mail:* conchhouse@staug.com	Saint Augustine	FL	32084	904-829-8646
Dino's (Barbecue) 4508 US 1 N.	Saint Augustine	FL	32095	904-829-2515
Florida Cracker Cafe (American) 81 Saint George St. *Web:* www.oldclty.com/cracker	Saint Augustine	FL	32084	904-829-0397
Fran & Tams (Homestyle) 415 S Ponce de Leon Blvd	Saint Augustine	FL	32084	904-825-2824
Fratelli (Italian) 415 Anastasia Blvd	Saint Augustine	FL	32084	904-826-1601
Fusion Point (New American) 237 San Marco Ave. *Web:* www.fusioncuisine.com	Saint Augustine	FL	32084	904-823-1444
Giggling Gator (American) 121 King St	Saint Augustine	FL	32084	904-824-0444
Good Times Bar & Grill (American) 604 Anastasia Blvd	Saint Augustine	FL	32084	904-829-1005
Gypsy Cab Co (Continental) 828 Anastasia Blvd. *Web:* www.gypsycab.com	Saint Augustine	FL	32084	904-824-8244
Hans Beach House (American) 550 A1A Beach Blvd	Saint Augustine	FL	32084	904-461-8446
Harbor View Cafe (American) 16 Avenida Menendez	Saint Augustine	FL	32084	904-825-0193
Harborside Cafe (Continental) 252 Yacht Club Dr	Saint Augustine	FL	32095	904-826-1667
Harry's Bar & Grill (Cajun) 46 Avenida Menendez *Web:* www.oldcity.com/harrys	Saint Augustine	FL	32084	904-824-7765
JJ's Heritage Cafe (American) 61 Treasury St.	Saint Augustine	FL	32084	904-824-2784
La Parisienne (French) 60 Hypolita St *Web:* www.oldcity.com/parisienne	Saint Augustine	FL	32084	904-829-0055
La Pentola (Continental) 835 S Ponce de Leon Blvd *Web:* www.oldcity.com/lapentola ■ *E-mail:* lilfrog@aug.com	Saint Augustine	FL	32086	904-824-3282
Le Pavillion (Continental) 45 San Marco Ave *Web:* www.lepav.com ■ *E-mail:* lepav@aug.com	Saint Augustine	FL	32084	904-824-6202
Little Harbor Restaurant (Portugese) 1574 US 1 S	Saint Augustine	FL	32086	904-825-0021
Manatee Cafe (Vegetarian) 179-A San Marco Ave *Web:* www.manateecafe.com/ ■ *E-mail:* sthompso@aug.com	Saint Augustine	FL	32084	904-826-0210
Marty's (Steak/Seafood) 2703 N Ponce de Leon Blvd	Saint Augustine	FL	32084	904-829-8679
Matanzas Innlet (Seafood) 8805 A1A S *Web:* www.oldcity.com/innlet ■ *E-mail:* fivej@aug.com	Saint Augustine	FL	32086	904-461-6824
Mikado Steak House (Japanese) 1092 S Ponce de Leon Blvd	Saint Augustine	FL	32086	904-824-7064
O'Steen's (Seafood) 205 Anastasia Blvd	Saint Augustine	FL	32084	904-829-6974
Oasis Deck & Restaurant (American) 4000 A1A S. *Web:* www.jaxadnet.com/oasis	Saint Augustine	FL	32084	904-471-3424
OC White's (Steak/Seafood) 118 Avenida Menendez. *Web:* www.oldcity.com/ocwhite	Saint Augustine	FL	32084	904-824-0808
Oscar's Old Florida Grill (Steak/Seafood) 614 Euclid Ave.	Saint Augustine	FL	32095	904-829-3794
Papagallos (Steak/Seafood) 300 A1A Beach Blvd Howard Johnson Oceanfront Resort.	Saint Augustine	FL	32084	904-471-2575
Raintree (Continental) 102 San Marco Ave	Saint Augustine	FL	32084	904-824-7211
Rendezvous Restaurant (American) 106 Saint George St *Web:* www.oldcity.com/rendezvous ■ *E-mail:* wksmith@aug.com	Saint Augustine	FL	32084	904-824-1090

Saint Augustine — Restaurants (Cont'd)

Name / Address	City	State	ZIP	Phone
Salt Water Cowboy's (Seafood)				
299 Dondanville Rd	Saint Augustine	FL	32084	904-471-2332
Santa Maria Restaurant (Steak/Seafood)				
135 Avenida Menendez	Saint Augustine	FL	32084	904-829-6578
Web: www.oldcity.com/santamaria				
Scarlett O'Hara's (American) 70 Hypolita St	Saint Augustine	FL	32084	904-824-6535
Schooner's (Seafood) 3560 N Ponce de Leon Blvd.	Saint Augustine	FL	32084	904-826-0233
Sea Fair Restaurant (Seafood) 1 Anastasia Blvd	Saint Augustine	FL	32084	904-824-2316
Seaside Shrimp House (Seafood) 5098 A1A S	Saint Augustine	FL	32084	904-471-0550
Sharky's Shrimp Shack (Seafood)				
700 A1A Beach Blvd	Saint Augustine	FL	32084	904-461-9992
South Beach Grill (American) 45 Cubbedge Rd	Saint Augustine	FL	32086	904-471-8700
Web: www.oldcity.com/sbg ■ *E-mail:* sbg@aug.com				
South Seas Restaurant (Seafood)				
841 Anastasia Blvd	Saint Augustine	FL	32084	904-824-9922
Steve's (Italian) 2085 SR 3	Saint Augustine	FL	32084	904-461-7286
Sunset Grill (American) 421 A1A Beach Blvd	Saint Augustine	FL	32084	904-471-5555
Tavern on the Bay (American)				
20 Avenida Menendez	Saint Augustine	FL	32084	904-810-1919
Theo's (Greek) 169 King St	Saint Augustine	FL	32084	904-824-5022
Trader Jack's (Steak/Seafood) 830 Anastasia Blvd	Saint Augustine	FL	32084	904-824-5225
Treasure Ship (Seafood) 7001 A1A S	Saint Augustine	FL	32086	904-471-0889
Two Sisters Cafe (American) 116 San Marco Ave	Saint Augustine	FL	32084	904-810-1961
Verrazano (Italian) 1057 A1A Beach Blvd	Saint Augustine	FL	32084	904-461-9797
Villa Santa Monica Restaurant (Italian)				
120 San Marco Ave	Saint Augustine	FL	32084	904-826-0209
Web: www.cheffranco.com				
Vittoria Trattoria Ristorante (Italian) 4075 A1A S	Saint Augustine	FL	32084	904-471-0081
Waves Cafe (American) 4255 A1A S	Saint Augustine	FL	32084	904-471-7484
White Lion Restaurant (Steak/Seafood) 20 Cuna St.	Saint Augustine	FL	32084	904-829-2388
Web: www.oldcity.com/lion				
Zaharias Restaurant (Steak/Seafood) 3945 A1A S	Saint Augustine	FL	32084	904-471-4799

— Goods and Services —

SHOPPING

Name / Address	City	State	ZIP	Phone	Fax
Lightner Antique Mall 75 King St	Saint Augustine	FL	32085	904-824-2874	824-2712
One King Street 1 King St	Saint Augustine	FL	32084	904-829-6939	
Ponce de Leon Mall					
2121 US Hwy 1 S	Saint Augustine	FL	32086	904-797-5324	797-5324
Saint Augustine Outlet Center					
2700 SR 16	Saint Augustine	FL	32092	904-825-1555	825-0474

BANKS

Name / Address	City	State	ZIP	Phone	Fax
Bank of America 60 Cathedral Pl	Saint Augustine	FL	32084	904-797-1145	819-1304
TF Cust Svc: 800-299-2265*					
Bank of Saint Augustine					
2121 US 1 S	Saint Augustine	FL	32086	904-794-7811	794-7812
BankAtlantic 2355 US 1 S	Saint Augustine	FL	32086	904-794-2550	794-0583
TF: 800-741-1700					
Compass Bank 1695 US 1 S	Saint Augustine	FL	32086	904-824-0101	824-0406
TF: 800-852-6091					
First Federal Savings & Loan					
1578 US 1 S	Saint Augustine	FL	32086	904-808-8572	808-8573
First South Bank 4475 US 1 S	Saint Augustine	FL	32086	904-794-4333	794-4007
TF: 888-950-1888					
First Union National Bank					
24 Cathedral Pl.	Saint Augustine	FL	32084	904-824-7500	824-7527
Prosperity Bank					
790 S Ponce de Leon Blvd.	Saint Augustine	FL	32084	904-824-9111	829-2520
TF: 800-347-9680					
Putnam State Bank					
2300 N Ponce de Leon Blvd.	Saint Augustine	FL	32084	904-825-4555	825-0023
Southtrust Bank 81 King St	Saint Augustine	FL	32084	904-824-0476	824-9229
TF: 800-225-5782					

BUSINESS SERVICES

Name	Phone	Name	Phone
Federal Express	800-238-5355	**Pip Printing**	904-825-2372
Interim Personnel	904-808-1500	**Post Office**	904-829-8716
Mail Boxes Etc	904-824-3444	**UPS**	800-742-5877
Manpower Temporary Services	904-826-3446	**Westaff Inc**	904-824-9221

— Media —

PUBLICATIONS

Name / Address	City	State	ZIP	Phone	Fax
Florida Times-Union‡ PO Box 1949	Jacksonville	FL	32231	904-359-4111	359-4478
TF: 800-472-6397 ■ *Web:* www.times-union.com					
Saint Augustine Record‡					
158 Cordova St.	Saint Augustine	FL	32084	904-824-6105	829-6664
Web: www.staugustine.com					

‡*Daily newspapers*

TELEVISION

Name / Address	City	State	ZIP	Phone	Fax
WAWS-TV Ch 30 (Fox)					
11700 Central Pkwy	Jacksonville	FL	32224	904-642-3030	646-0115
WJWB-TV Ch 17 (WB) 9117 Hogan Rd	Jacksonville	FL	32216	904-641-1700	641-0306
WJXT-TV Ch 4 (CBS) 4 Broadcast Pl.	Jacksonville	FL	32247	904-399-4000	393-9822
Web: www.wjxt.com ■ *E-mail:* news@wjxt.com					
WJXX-TV Ch 25 (ABC) PO Box 551000	Jacksonville	FL	32255	904-332-2525	332-2418*
**Fax:* News Rm ■ *Web:* www.wjxx.com/new ■ *E-mail:* info@wjxx.com					
WTEV-TV Ch 47 (UPN)					
11700 Central Pkwy	Jacksonville	FL	32224	904-646-4747	646-0115
WTLV-TV Ch 12 (NBC) 1070 E Adams St.	Jacksonville	FL	32202	904-354-1212	633-8899

RADIO

Name / Address	City	State	ZIP	Phone	Fax
WAOC-AM 1420 kHz (N/T)					
567 Lewis Point Rd Ext	Saint Augustine	FL	32086	904-797-4444	797-3446
WAYL-FM 91.9 MHz (CHR)					
1485 US 1 S	Saint Augustine	FL	32086	904-829-9200	829-9202
Web: www.wayl.com ■ *E-mail:* waylfm@aug.com					
WFCF-FM 88.5 MHz (Misc)					
PO Box 1027 Flagler College	Saint Augustine	FL	32085	904-829-6481	829-3471
WFKS-FM 99.9 MHz (AC)					
801 W Granada Blvd Suite 201	Ormond Beach	FL	32174	904-672-9210	677-2252
Web: www.radiokiss.com					
WFOY-AM 1240 kHz (N/T)					
PO box 3847	Saint Augustine	FL	32085	904-829-3416	829-8051
Web: www.oldcity.com/wfoy					
WFSJ-FM 97.9 MHz (NAC)					
8386 Baymeadows Rd Suite 107	Jacksonville	FL	32256	904-636-0507	636-0533
Web: www.wfsj.com ■ *E-mail:* sales@wfsj.com					
WIYD-AM 1260 kHz (Ctry) 900 River St.	Palatka	FL	32177	904-325-4556	328-5161
WJQR-FM 105.5 MHz (Ctry)					
567 Lewis Point Rd Ext	Saint Augustine	FL	32086	904-797-4444	797-3446
Web: www.oldcity.com/wjqr ■ *E-mail:* wjqr@aug.com					
WKLN-AM 1170 kHz (N/T)					
2820 Lewis Speedway	Saint Augustine	FL	32095	904-825-0009	825-4371
Web: www.wkln.com ■ *E-mail:* wkln@aug.com					
WPLK-AM 800 kHz (Nost) 1501 Reid St	Palatka	FL	32177	904-325-5800	328-8725
WSOS-FM 94.1 MHz (Nost)					
2715 Stratton Blvd	Saint Augustine	FL	32095	904-824-0833	825-0105

— Colleges/Universities —

Name / Address	City	State	ZIP	Phone	Fax
First Coast Technical Institute					
2980 Collins Ave.	Saint Augustine	FL	32095	904-824-4401	824-6750
Flagler College 74 King St.	Saint Augustine	FL	32084	904-829-6481	826-0094
Web: www.flagler.edu ■ *E-mail:* info@flagler.com					
Saint Johns River Community College					
Saint Augustine Campus					
2990 College Dr	Saint Augustine	FL	32095	904-808-7400	808-7420
Saint Leo College 2990 College Dr	Saint Augustine	FL	32095	904-824-7030	
University of Saint Augustine					
1 University Blvd.	Saint Augustine	FL	32086	904-826-0084	826-0085
TF: 800-241-1027					

— Hospitals —

Name / Address	City	State	ZIP	Phone	Fax
Flagler Hospital 400 Health Park Blvd.	Saint Augustine	FL	32086	904-829-5155	825-4472

— Attractions —

Name / Address	City	State	ZIP	Phone	Fax
3D World 28 San Marco Ave	Saint Augustine	FL	32084	904-824-1220	824-1226

Saint Augustine — Attractions (Cont'd)

			Phone	Fax
Anastasia State Park 1340 A1A S	Saint Augustine FL	32084	904-461-2033	461-2006
Favor-Dykes State Park US 1 S & I-95	Hastings FL		904-794-0997	
Fort Matanzas National Monument 8635 A1A S *Web:* www.nps.gov/foma	Saint Augustine FL	32086	904-471-0116	471-7605
Government House Museum 48 King St	Saint Augustine FL	32084	904-825-5033	825-5096
Guana River State Park 2690 S Ponte Vedra Blvd	Ponte Vedra Beach FL	32082	904-825-5071	825-6829
Historic Villages of St Augustine 254-A San Marco Ave *E-mail:* toursaug@aug.com	Saint Augustine FL	32084	904-824-8874	824-6848
Lightner Museum 75 King St	Saint Augustine FL	32084	904-824-2874	824-2712
Limelight Theatre 1681 US 1 S	Saint Augustine FL	32086	904-825-1164	825-4662
Museum of Weapons & History 81 King St Suite C	Saint Augustine FL	32084	904-829-3727	
Old Jail Museum 167 San Marco Ave *TF:* 800-397-4071	Saint Augustine FL	32084	904-829-3800	829-6678
Oldest House The Gonzales-Alvarez House 14 Saint Francis St *E-mail:* oldhouse@aug.com	Saint Augustine FL	32084	904-824-2872	824-2569
Oldest Wooden School House 14 Saint George St *TF:* 888-653-7245	Saint Augustine FL	32084	904-824-0192	826-1913
Peña-Peck House Museum 143 Saint George St	Saint Augustine FL	32084	904-829-5064	
Ponce de Leon's Fountain of Youth 11 Magnolia Ave *TF:* 800-356-8222	Saint Augustine FL	32084	904-829-3168	826-1913
Potter's Wax Museum 17 King St	Saint Augustine FL	32084	904-829-9056	824-3434
Ripley's Believe It or Not! Museum 19 San Marco Ave	Saint Augustine FL	32084	904-824-1606	829-1790
Saint Augustine Alligator Farm 999 Anastasia Blvd *Web:* www.alligatorfarm.com ■ *E-mail:* alligator@aug.com	Saint Augustine FL	32084	904-824-3337	829-6677
Saint Augustine Ampitheater Hwy A1A S	Saint Augustine FL	32084	904-471-1965	
Saint Augustine Historical Society 271 Charlotte St	Saint Augustine FL	32084	904-824-2872	824-2569
Saint Augustine Historical Trolley Tours 167 San Marco Ave *TF:* 800-397-4071	Saint Augustine FL	32084	904-829-3800	829-6678
Saint Augustine Lighthouse & Museum 81 Lighthouse Ave *Web:* www.stauglight.com/ ■ *E-mail:* stauglh@aug.com	Saint Augustine FL	32084	904-829-0745	829-0745
Saint Augustine National Cemetery 104 Marine St	Saint Augustine FL	32084	352-793-7740	
Saint Augustine Sightseeing Trains 170 San Marco Ave *TF:* 800-226-6545 ■ *Web:* www.redtrains.com/ ■ *E-mail:* trains@aug.com	Saint Augustine FL	32084	904-829-6545	829-6548
Saint Johns Audubon Society PO Box 965	Saint Augustine FL	32094	904-797-5997	
San Sebastian Winery 157 King St *TF:* 888-352-9463	Saint Augustine FL	32084	904-826-1594	826-1595
Spanish Quarter Museum 29 Saint George St	Saint Augustine FL	32084	904-825-6830	825-6874
Washington Oaks State Gardens 6400 N Oceanshore Blvd	Palm Coast FL	32137	904-446-6780	
World Golf Hall of Fame 21 World Golf Pl *TF:* 800-948-4746 ■ *Web:* www.wgv.com	Saint Augustine FL	32092	904-940-4000	940-4393
World Golf Village IMAX Theater 21 World Golf Pl World Golf Village	Saint Augustine FL	32084	904-940-4123	
Zorayda Castle 83 King St	Saint Augustine FL	32084	904-824-3097	

SPORTS TEAMS & FACILITIES

			Phone	Fax
Greyhound Racing 1440 N McDuff Ave *Web:* www.jaxkennel.com/	Jacksonville FL	32205	904-646-0001	646-0420
Saint Augustine Speedway 900 Big Oak Rd *Web:* www.staugustinespeedway.com ■ *E-mail:* info@staugustinespeedway.com	Saint Augustine FL	32095	904-825-2886	824-2889

— Events —

Event	Phone
18th Century Christmas Caroling (mid-December)	904-829-1711
Ancient City King Fish Tournament (early-mid-July)	904-471-2730
Antique Car Show (late May)	904-471-0341
Atlantic Shakespeare Festival (late July-mid-August)	904-471-1965
Beach Bash (early June)	904-461-2000
Blessing of the Fleet (late March)	904-825-1010
Blue Water Tournament (late May)	904-829-5676
British Night Watch (early December)	904-829-1711
Cabbage & Potato Festival (late April)	904-692-1420
Cannon Firing Season (late May-early September)	904-829-6506
Carols by Candlelight (early December)	904-461-2000
Celebrate Ponte Vedra (May)	904-280-0614
Celebration of Centuries (mid-May-mid-June)	800-653-2489
Christmas Tour of Homes (early December)	904-829-1711
Conch House Challenge (late August)	888-463-4742
Confederate Encampment (late January)	904-829-6506
Days In Spain (early September)	904-825-1010
Drake's Raid (early June)	904-829-1711
Earth Day Celebration (late April)	904-808-7009
Easter Parade (early April)	904-829-2992
Easter Sunday Promenade (early April)	904-829-2992
EPIC Celebration of Spring (mid-April)	904-829-3295
Fall Arts & Crafts Festival (late November)	904-829-1711
Fine Art & Jazz Show (early May)	888-352-9463
Flight to Freedom (late February)	904-461-2035
Founder's Day (early September)	904-825-1010
Fourth of July Celebration (July 4)	800-653-2489
Gamble Rogers Folk Festival (late April-early May)	904-794-0222
Grand Illumination (early December)	904-794-7682
Great Chowder Debate (early November)	904-829-8646
Greek Landing Day Festival (late June)	904-829-8205
Halloween Nights (late October)	904-471-9010
Historic Inns & Garden Tour (mid-April)	904-829-3295
Hot Times in the Old Town (early May)	904-829-1711
Kingbuster Fishing Tournament (mid-June)	904-992-9600
La Fiesta de Navidad (mid-December)	904-829-1711
Las Posadas Celebration (mid-December)	904-826-0209
Legends of Golf Tournament (mid-March)	904-940-0321
Lighthouse Festival & 5K Run (mid-March)	904-829-0745
Lincolnville Festival (early November)	904-829-8379
Luminaries in the Plaza (early-mid-December)	904-797-3908
Matanzas 5K & Fun Run (late January)	904-739-1917
Memorial Weekend Cathedral Festival (late May)	904-797-1563
Menendez Day (February 15)	904-825-1010
Menendez Festival (mid-late February)	904-825-5088
Mother's Day Arts & Crafts Show (early May)	904-471-7731
Native American Pow Wow (late February)	904-829-2201
Nature Photo Contest (early May-mid-July)	904-824-3337
Nights of Lights Festival (late November-late January)	904-829-5681
Passion Play (mid-late March-early April)	904-797-5675
Regatta of Lights (mid-December)	800-653-2489
Saint Augustine Beach Run (mid-April)	904-471-4816
Saint Augustine Christmas Parade (early December)	904-829-5681
Saint Augustine Flower, Garden & Art Show (mid-April)	904-829-3295
Saint Johns County Fair (mid-March)	904-829-5681
Seafood Festival (early April)	904-824-1978
Serales' Raid (mid-late March)	904-824-9823
Spanish Night Watch (mid-June)	904-797-7217
Spring Arts & Crafts Festival (late March)	904-829-1711
Taste of Saint Augustine (mid-April)	904-829-3295
Torch Light Tour (early Feb-early April)	904-829-6506
Union Encampment (mid-March)	904-829-6506
Victorian Spring (late April)	904-825-5033
Vilano Bridge Run (early May)	904-824-1761
Voices of the Past (mid-June)	904-824-2056
Winter Dance Festival (mid-January)	904-829-1617

Saint Petersburg

Located just south of Tampa, the city of Saint Petersburg is a collection of beaches, parks, and yacht basins bordered on three sides by bays and the Gulf of Mexico. Saint Petersburg's resort-occupied islands on the Gulf of Mexico form the Saint Pete Beach area. One of the city's best known resorts is the Don CeSar, which was the vacation spot for F. Scott Fitzgerald in the 1920s and '30s. The Salvador Dali Museum in Saint Petersburg houses the largest and most comprehensive collection of the artist's works. The city's ThunderDome is home to the National Hockey League's Tampa Bay Lightning.

Population	236,029	**Longitude**	82-67-94 W
Area (Land)	59.2 sq mi	**County**	Pinellas
Area (Water)	73.5 sq mi	**Time Zone**	EST
Elevation	44 ft	**Area Code/s**	727
Latitude	27-77-06 N		

Saint Petersburg (Cont'd)

— Average Temperatures and Precipitation —

TEMPERATURES

	Jan	Feb	Mar	Apr	May	Jun	Jul	Aug	Sep	Oct	Nov	Dec
High	68	70	75	80	86	89	90	90	88	83	76	71
Low	53	54	60	65	70	75	76	76	75	69	62	55

PRECIPITATION

	Jan	Feb	Mar	Apr	May	Jun	Jul	Aug	Sep	Oct	Nov	Dec
Inches	2.2	3.1	3.6	1.3	3.1	6.2	6.8	8.6	7.1	2.3	2.1	2.4

— Important Phone Numbers —

	Phone		Phone
AAA	727-826-3600	**Medical Referral**	727-341-7555
American Express Travel	727-442-2131	**Poison Control Center**	813-253-4444
Emergency	911	**Travelers Aid**	727-823-4891
HotelDocs	800-468-3537	**Weather**	813-645-2506

— Information Sources —

				Phone	Fax
Better Business Bureau Serving West Florida PO Box 7950	Clearwater	FL	33758	727-535-5522	539-6301
Web: www.clearwater.bbb.org					
Pinellas County 315 Court St	Clearwater	FL	34616	727-464-3000	464-4070
Web: www.co.pinellas.fl.us					
Saint Petersburg Area Chamber of Commerce PO Box 1371	Saint Petersburg	FL	33731	727-821-4069	895-6326
Web: www.stpete.com					
Saint Petersburg City Hall 175 5th St N	Saint Petersburg	FL	33701	727-893-7111	892-5365
Web: www.stpete.org/cityhall.htm					
Saint Petersburg Economic Development Dept PO Box 2842	Saint Petersburg	FL	33731	727-893-7100	892-5465
Web: www.stpete.org/business.htm					
Saint Petersburg Mayor PO Box 2842	Saint Petersburg	FL	33731	727-893-7201	892-5365
Web: www.stpete.org/mayor.htm					
Saint Petersburg Public Library 3745 9th Ave N	Saint Petersburg	FL	33713	727-893-7724	892-5432
Web: www.stpete.org/library.htm					
Saint Petersburg/Clearwater Area Convention & Visitors Bureau 14450 46th St N Suite 108	Clearwater	FL	33762	727-464-7200	464-7222
TF: 800-345-6710 ■ *Web:* www.stpete-clearwater.com ■ *E-mail:* spclwcvb@co.pinellas.fl.us					

On-Line Resources

- **Area Guide Saint Petersburg** ... saintpetersburg.areaguides.net
- **City Knowledge Saint Petersburg** ... www.cityknowledge.com/fl_stpetersburg.htm
- **CitySearch Tampa/Saint Petersburg** ... tampabay.citysearch.com
- **Excite.com Saint Petersburg City Guide** ... www.excite.com/travel/countries/united_states/florida/st_petersburg
- **Hotel Guide Tampa/Saint Petersburg** ... hotelguide.net/tampa/
- **NITC Travelbase City Guide Saint Petersburg** ... www.travelbase.com/auto/guides/st_petersburg-area-fl.html
- **Saint Petersburg Home Page** ... www.stpete.org
- **Surf & Sun Beach Vacation Guide to Saint Petersburg** ... www.surf-sun.com/fl-st-petersburg-main.htm

— Transportation Services —

AIRPORTS

■ **Tampa International Airport (TPA)**

	Phone
5 miles NE of downtown Saint Petersburg (approx 15 minutes)	813-870-8700

Web: www.tampaairport.com/

Airport Transportation

	Phone
Airport Connection $13 fare to downtown Saint Petersburg	727-572-1111
Yellow Cab $30-35 fare to downtown Saint Petersburg	813-253-0121

Commercial Airlines

	Phone		Phone
Air Canada	800-776-3000	**Martinair Holland**	800-627-8462
AirTran	800-247-8726	**MetroJet**	888-638-7653
America West	800-235-9292	**Midway**	800-446-4392
American	800-433-7300	**Midwest Express**	800-452-2022
British Airways	800-247-9297	**Northwest**	800-225-2525
Cayman Airways	800-422-9626	**Southwest**	800-435-9792
Comair	800-354-9822	**Spirit**	800-772-7117
Continental	813-874-7151	**TWA**	800-221-2000
Continental Express	800-525-0280	**United**	800-241-6522
Delta	813-286-1800	**US Airways**	800-428-4322
Eastwind	888-327-8946	**Virgin Atlantic**	800-862-8621
Kiwi	800-538-5494		

Charter Airlines

	Phone		Phone
Biscayne Helicopters	305-252-3883	**Raytheon Aircraft Charter**	800-519-6283
Commander Airways Inc	813-879-9757	**Sovereign Air**	800-473-8008
Corporate Jets Inc	412-466-2500	**Sun Country**	800-733-2692
Gulf Coast Aircraft Charter	813-220-4556	**Tag Aviation**	800-235-9724
Pompano Helicopters Inc	800-957-4374	**Walkabout Air Inc**	813-877-9387

■ **Saint Petersburg-Clearwater International Airport (PIE)**

	Phone
9 miles N of downtown (approx 15 minutes)	727-531-1451

Airport Transportation

	Phone
Yellow Cab $15 fare to downtown	727-821-7777
Yellow Cab $20 fare to downtown	727-573-1111

Commercial Airlines

	Phone		Phone
Air Sunshine	800-435-8900	**Canada 3000**	877-359-2263
American Trans Air	800-225-2995	**World of Vacations**	800-661-8881

Charter Airlines

	Phone		Phone
Execujet Charter Service Inc	888-635-9538	**Global Executive Charter Inc**	800-538-9389
Executive Charters Inc	727-894-2277	**US Aviation**	888-359-8787

CAR RENTALS

	Phone		Phone
Alamo	727-530-5494	**Enterprise**	813-282-1680
Avis	727-530-1406	**Hertz**	727-531-3774
Budget	727-845-1544	**National**	727-530-5491
Dollar	813-396-3640		

LIMO/TAXI

	Phone		Phone
Bay Cab	727-327-8294	**Red Line Limo-Saint Petersburg**	727-535-3391
Blue Star Cab	727-327-4104	**Yellow Cab**	727-821-7777
Rainbow Taxi	727-392-8630		

MASS TRANSIT

	Phone
Pinellas Suncoast Transit Authority $1 Base fare	727-530-9911

RAIL/BUS

				Phone
Greyhound Bus Station 180 9th St N	Saint Petersburg	FL	33705	727-898-1496

TF: 800-231-2222

— Accommodations —

HOTELS, MOTELS, RESORTS

				Phone	Fax
Alden Beach Resort 5900 Gulf Blvd	Saint Pete Beach	FL	33706	727-360-7081	360-5957

TF: 800-237-2530

Saint Petersburg — Hotels, Motels, Resorts (Cont'd)

				Phone	Fax
Bahia Beach Resort 611 Destiny Dr	Ruskin	FL	33570	813-645-3291	641-1589
TF: 800-327-2773					
Bay Plaza Hotel 419 3rd Ave N	Saint Petersburg	FL	33701	727-894-3208	
Best Western Mirage 5005 34th St N	Saint Petersburg	FL	33714	727-525-1181	919-5948
Best Western Sirata Beach Resort 5300 Gulf Blvd	Saint Pete Beach	FL	33706	727-367-2771	360-6799
TF: 800-344-5999					
Broadway Inn 401 44th St N	Saint Petersburg	FL	33713	727-327-5647	327-5647
Colony Beach & Tennis Resort 1620 Gulf of Mexico Dr	Longboat Key	FL	34228	941-383-6464	383-7549
TF: 800-426-5669 ■ *Web:* www.colonybeachresort.com					
Comfort Inn 1400 34th St N	Saint Petersburg	FL	33713	727-323-3100	327-5792
TF: 800-221-2222					
Coral Reef Beach Resort 5800 Gulf Blvd	Saint Pete Beach	FL	33706	727-360-0821	367-3718
TF: 800-352-4874					
Crystal Bay Hotel 7401 Central Ave.	Saint Petersburg	FL	33710	727-384-0220	384-0408
TF: 800-223-8123					
Days Inn Island Beach Resort 6200 Gulf Blvd	Saint Pete Beach	FL	33706	727-367-1902	367-4422
TF: 800-544-4222					
Dolphin Beach Resort 4900 Gulf Blvd	Saint Pete Beach	FL	33706	727-360-7011	367-5909
TF: 800-237-8916 ■ *Web:* www.dolphinbeach.com					
Don CeSar Beach Resort & Spa 3400 Gulf Blvd	Saint Pete Beach	FL	33706	727-360-1881	367-3609*
**Fax:* Sales ■ *TF:* 800-282-1116 ■ *Web:* www.doncesar.com ■ *E-mail:* hotels@silverw.com					
Heritage Holiday Inn 234 3rd Ave N	Saint Petersburg	FL	33701	727-822-4814	823-1644
Hilton Hotel 333 1st St S	Saint Petersburg	FL	33701	727-894-5000	894-7655
TF: 800-944-5500 ■ *Web:* www.hilton.com/hotels/SPTSHHF					
Hilton Longboat Key Beach Resort 4711 Gulf of Mexico Dr	Longboat Key	FL	34228	941-383-2451	383-7979
TF: 800-282-3046 ■ *Web:* www.hilton.com/hotels/SRQHIHF					
Holiday Inn Hotel & Suites 5250 Gulf Blvd	Saint Pete Beach	FL	33706	727-360-1811	360-6919
TF: 800-448-0901					
Holiday Inn SunSpree Resort Marina Cove 6800 Sunshine Skyway Ln	Saint Petersburg	FL	33711	727-867-1151	864-4494
TF: 800-227-8045					
Hosanna Hotel 3000 34th St S	Saint Petersburg	FL	33711	727-867-1111	867-7068
Howard Johnson Lodge 6100 Gulf Blvd	Saint Pete Beach	FL	33706	727-360-7041	360-8941
TF: 800-231-1419					
La Quinta Inn 4999 34th St N	Saint Petersburg	FL	33714	727-527-8421	527-8851
Longboat Key Club 301 Gulf of Mexico Dr	Longboat Key	FL	34228	941-383-8821	383-5396
TF: 800-237-8821 ■ *Web:* www.longboatkeyclub.com ■ *E-mail:* lkres@longboatkeyclub.com					
McCarthy Hotel 326 1st Ave N	Saint Petersburg	FL	33701	727-822-4141	821-0122
Pennsylvania Hotel 300 4th St N	Saint Petersburg	FL	33701	727-822-4045	822-3626
Quality Inn Beach Resort 655 S Gulfview Blvd	Clearwater	FL	33767	727-442-7171	446-7177
TF: 800-228-5151					
Ramada Limited 3601 34th St S	Saint Petersburg	FL	33711	727-867-1377	864-2546
TF: 800-272-6232					
Renaissance Vinoy Resort 501 5th Ave NE	Saint Petersburg	FL	33701	727-894-1000	894-2270
TF: 800-468-3571					
Ritz Club The 711 3rd Ave S	Saint Petersburg	FL	33701	727-893-4663	894-4663
Safety Harbor Spa & Resort 105 N Bayshore Dr	Safety Harbor	FL	34695	727-726-1161	726-4268
TF: 888-237-8772 ■ *Web:* www.safetyharborspa.com					
Sandpiper Beach Resort 6000 Gulf Blvd	Saint Petersburg	FL	33706	727-360-5551	562-1282
TF: 800-237-0707					
TradeWinds Resort on Saint Pete Beach 5500 Gulf Blvd	Saint Pete Beach	FL	33706	727-367-6461	562-1215
TF: 800-237-0707 ■ *Web:* www.tradewindsresort.com					
Travelodge Gateway Inn 6300 Gulf Blvd	Saint Pete Beach	FL	33706	727-367-2711	367-7068
TF: 800-237-8918					

— Restaurants —

				Phone
9 Bangkok Restaurant (Thai) 571 Central Ave	Saint Petersburg	FL	33701	727-894-5990
Adriano's (Italian) 3405 34th St N	Saint Petersburg	FL	33713	727-528-4428
Alfredino's on the Beach (Italian) 7141 Gulf Blvd	Saint Pete Beach	FL	33706	727-367-9999
Apropos (Continental) 300 2nd Ave NE	Saint Petersburg	FL	33701	727-823-8934
Arigato Japanese Steak House (Japanese) 3600 66th St N	Saint Petersburg	FL	33710	727-343-5200
Athenian Garden of Saint Petersburg (Greek) 6940 22nd Ave N	Saint Petersburg	FL	33710	727-345-7040
Babalu (Indian) 9246 4th St N	Saint Petersburg	FL	33702	727-576-7414
Basta's Fine Italian Cuisine (Italian) 1625 4th St S	Saint Petersburg	FL	33701	727-894-7880
Beijing Garden Restaurant & Lounge (Chinese) 8901 4th St N	Saint Petersburg	FL	33701	727-578-0972
Cafe Lido (American) 800 2nd Ave NE	Saint Petersburg	FL	33701	727-898-5800
Carino's Italian Cafe (Italian) 9524 Blind Pass Rd	Saint Pete Beach	FL	33706	727-360-8502
Cockney Rebel Pub (English) 1492 4th St N	Saint Petersburg	FL	33704	727-895-2049
Cody's Original Roadhouse (Steak) 7022 22nd Ave N	Saint Petersburg	FL	33710	727-345-1022
Dogwater Cafe (American) 8300 Bay Pines Blvd	Saint Petersburg	FL	33709	727-347-6190
Durango Steakhouse (Southwest) 5300 Gulf Blvd	Saint Pete Beach	FL	33706	727-367-0706
Four Coins (American) 2700 34th St N	Saint Petersburg	FL	33713	727-526-3150
Fourth Street Shrimp Store (Seafood) 1006 4th St N	Saint Petersburg	FL	33701	727-822-0325
Gigi's Italian Restaurant (Italian) 6852 Gulfport Blvd	Saint Petersburg	FL	33707	727-345-0191
Harvey's 4th Street Grill (American) 3121 4th St N	Saint Petersburg	FL	33704	727-821-6516
Hurricane Seafood Restaurant (Seafood) 807 Gulf Way	Saint Pete Beach	FL	33706	727-360-9558
Johnny Leverock's (Seafood) 10 Corey Ave	Saint Pete Beach	FL	33706	727-367-4588
Julian at the Heritage (Steak/Seafood) 256 2nd St N	Saint Petersburg	FL	33701	727-823-6382
Leverock's Seafood House (Seafood) 54 Corey Ave	Saint Pete Beach	FL	33706	727-367-5671
Maritana Grille (American) 3400 Gulf Blvd	Saint Pete Beach	FL	33706	727-360-1881
Melting Pot Restaurant (American) 2221 4th St N	Saint Petersburg	FL	33704	727-895-6358
Pep's Sea Grill (Seafood) 7610 N 4th St	Saint Petersburg	FL	33702	727-521-1655
Pepin (Spanish) 4125 4th St N	Saint Petersburg	FL	33703	727-821-3773
PJ's Seafood Restaurant (Seafood) 7500 Gulf Blvd	Saint Pete Beach	FL	33706	727-367-3309
Red Mesa Restaurant (Southwest) 4912 4th St N	Saint Petersburg	FL	33703	727-527-8728
Saffron's Restaurant & Catering (Caribbean) 1700 Park St N	Saint Petersburg	FL	33710	727-345-6400
Sea Critters Cafe (Seafood) 2007 Pass-a-Grille Way	Saint Pete Beach	FL	33706	727-360-3706
Sloppy Pelican Saloon (American) 677 75th Ave.	Saint Pete Beach	FL	33706	727-367-5556
Suki's (Chinese) 2901 66th St N	Saint Petersburg	FL	33710	727-345-0559
Tangelo's Grille (Cuban) 226 1st Ave N	Saint Petersburg	FL	33701	727-894-1695
Texas Cattle Co (Steak) 2600 34th St N	Saint Petersburg	FL	33713	727-527-3335
Thai Am Restaurant (Thai) 6040 4th St N	Saint Petersburg	FL	33703	727-522-7813
Three Lions British Pub (English) 4755 Gulf Blvd	Saint Pete Beach	FL	33706	727-367-2748
Wan See Chinese Restaurant (Chinese) 1077 62nd Ave S	Saint Petersburg	FL	33705	727-867-9574

— Goods and Services —

SHOPPING

				Phone	Fax
Bayside Market 5501 Gulf Blvd.	Saint Pete Beach	FL	33706		
Dillard's 6901 22nd Ave N	Saint Petersburg	FL	33710	727-344-4611	
John's Pass Village & Boardwalk 501 150th Ave	Madeira Beach	FL	33708	727-397-1571	391-4259
ParkSide Mall 7200 US 19 N	Pinellas Park	FL	33781	727-527-7241	527-8340
Pier The 800 2nd Ave NE	Saint Petersburg	FL	33701	727-821-6164	
Web: www.stpete-pier.com					
Seminole Mall Seminole & Park Blvds	Seminole	FL	33772	727-392-8174	392-3205
Tyrone Square 6901 22nd Ave N	Saint Petersburg	FL	33710	727-345-0126	345-5699

BANKS

				Phone	Fax
AmSouth Bank 3505 4th St N	Saint Petersburg	FL	33704	727-822-6454	822-6639
TF Cust Svc: 800-267-6844*					
Bank of Saint Petersburg 777 Pasadena Ave S	Saint Petersburg	FL	33707	727-347-3132	381-1692
Colonial Bank 5858 Central Ave	Saint Petersburg	FL	33707	727-347-0197	347-4744
TF Cust Svc: 800-533-8583*					
First State Bank of Pinellas 2832 4th St N	Saint Petersburg	FL	33704	727-898-1000	896-2005
First Union National Bank 410 Central Ave	Saint Petersburg	FL	33701	727-892-7101	892-7199
TF Cust Svc: 800-275-3862*					
Intervest Bank 6750 Gulfport Blvd S	Saint Pasadena	FL	33707	727-344-2265	
Mercantile Bank 425 22nd Ave N	Saint Petersburg	FL	33704	727-822-9444	823-7675
NationsBank 850 Central Ave	Saint Petersburg	FL	33701	727-892-6252	823-0872
TF: 800-299-2265					

Saint Petersburg — Banks (Cont'd)

				Phone	Fax
Premier Community Bank 6850 Central Ave	Saint Petersburg	FL	33707	727-347-7283	381-8135
Republic Bank 111 2nd Ave NE	Saint Petersburg	FL	33701	727-823-7300	896-2444*
*Fax: Hum Res					
Southern Exchange Bank 4105 Gulf Blvd	Saint Petersburg	FL	33706	727-367-4800	363-3305
SouthTrust Bank NA 150 2nd Ave N	Saint Petersburg	FL	33701	727-894-1035	822-2961
TF Cust Svc: 800-225-5782*					
SunTrust Bank 300 1st Ave S	Saint Petersburg	FL	33701	727-823-4181	892-4610
TF Cust Svc: 800-432-4932*					
United Bank & Trust Co 5801 49th St N	Saint Petersburg	FL	33709	727-522-9434	521-2233

BUSINESS SERVICES

	Phone		Phone
Airborne Express	800-247-2676	**Kinko's**	727-381-3118
BAX Global	800-225-5229	**Olsten Staffing Services**	727-573-0003
DHL Worldwide Express	800-225-5345	**Post Office**	727-323-6570
Federal Express	800-238-5355	**UPS**	800-742-5877

— Media —

PUBLICATIONS

				Phone	Fax
Saint Petersburg Times‡ PO Box 1121	Saint Petersburg	FL	33731	727-893-8111	893-8675
TF: 800-333-7505 ■ *Web:* www.sptimes.com ■ *E-mail:* letters@sptimes.com					
Tampa Tribune‡ 202 S Parker St	Tampa	FL	33606	813-259-7711	259-7676
TF: 800-282-5588 ■ *Web:* www.tampatrib.com ■ *E-mail:* tribletters@tampatrib.com					

‡Daily newspapers

TELEVISION

				Phone	Fax
WBHS-TV Ch 50 (Ind) 12425 28th St N Suite 301	Saint Petersburg	FL	33716	727-573-5550	571-1931
WCLF-TV Ch 22 (Ind) 1922 142nd Ave N	Largo	FL	33771	727-535-5622	
WEDU-TV Ch 3 (PBS) 1300 N Blvd	Tampa	FL	33607	813-254-9338	253-0826
Web: www.wedu.org ■ *E-mail:* outreach@wedu.pbs.org					
WFLA-TV Ch 8 (NBC) 905 E Jackson St	Tampa	FL	33602	813-228-8888	225-2770
Web: www.wfla.com					
WFTS-TV Ch 28 (ABC) 4045 N Himes Ave	Tampa	FL	33607	813-354-2800	870-2828
Web: www.wfts.com ■ *E-mail:* 28feedback@wfts.com					
WTOG-TV Ch 44 (UPN) 365 105th Terr NE	Saint Petersburg	FL	33716	727-576-4444	577-1806
WTSP-TV Ch 10 (CBS) 11450 Gandy Blvd N	Saint Petersburg	FL	33702	727-577-1010	576-6924
Web: www.wtsp.com ■ *E-mail:* news@channel10.com					
WTTA-TV Ch 38 (Ind) 5510 W Gray St Suite 38	Tampa	FL	33609	813-289-3838	289-0000
WTVT-TV Ch 13 (Fox) 3213 W Kennedy Blvd	Tampa	FL	33609	813-876-1313	871-3135
Web: www.wtvt.com ■ *E-mail:* 13@wtvt.com					
WUSF-TV Ch 16 (PBS) 4202 Fowler Ave	Tampa	FL	33620	813-974-4000	974-4806
TF: 800-654-3703 ■ *Web:* www.wusftv.usf.edu					
WWWB-TV Ch 32 (WB) 7201 E Hillsborough Ave	Tampa	FL	33610	813-626-3232	622-9032*
*Fax: Sales ■ *Web:* www.wb32.com ■ *E-mail:* mail@wb32.com					
WXPX-TV Ch 66 (PAX) 11300 4th St N Suite 180	Saint Petersburg	FL	33716	727-578-0066	570-8206
Web: www.pax.net/WXPX					

RADIO

				Phone	Fax
WCOF-FM 107.3 MHz (AC) 877 Executive Ctr Dr W Suite 300	Saint Petersburg	FL	33706	813-229-8650	576-8098*
*Fax Area Code: 727 ■ *Web:* www.coast1073.com					
WFJO-FM 101.5 MHz (Oldies) 11300 4th St N Suite 318	Saint Petersburg	FL	33716	727-577-7131	578-2477
WGUL-AM 860 kHz (Nost) 35048 US Hwy 19 The Fountains	Palm Harbor	FL	34684	727-849-2285	781-4375
WGUL-FM 96.1 MHz (Nost) 35048 US Hwy 19 The Fountains	Palm Harbor	FL	34684	727-849-2285	781-4375
WHPT-FM 102.5 MHz (AAA) 11300 4th St N Suite 318	Saint Petersburg	FL	33716	727-577-7131	578-2477
WMNF-FM 88.5 MHz (NPR) 1210 E ML King Blvd	Tampa	FL	33603	813-238-8001	238-1802
Web: www.wmnf.org ■ *E-mail:* wmnf@wmnf.org					
WQYK-AM 1010 kHz (N/T) 9450 Koger Blvd Suite 103	Saint Petersburg	FL	33702	727-576-6055	577-1324
WQYK-FM 99.5 MHz (Ctry) 9450 Koger Blvd Suite 103	Saint Petersburg	FL	33702	727-576-6055	577-1324
WSJT-FM 94.1 MHz (NAC) 11300 4th St N Suite 318	Saint Petersburg	FL	33716	727-577-7131	578-2477
TF: 800-771-7131 ■ *Web:* www.wsjt.com					
WSSR-FM 95.7 MHz (AC) 5510 Gray St Suite 130	Tampa	FL	33609	813-961-9600	261-5957
WSUN-AM 620 kHz (N/T) 877 Executive Center Dr W Suite 300	Saint Petersburg	FL	33702	727-576-1073	576-8098
WSUN-FM 97.1 MHz (Oldies) 877 Executive Ctr Dr W Suite 300	Saint Petersburg	FL	33702	727-841-9797	576-8098
WTBT-FM 105.5 MHz (CR) 13577 Feather Sound Dr Suite 550	Clearwater	FL	34622	727-572-9808	572-0935
Web: thunder1055.com ■ *E-mail:* thunder@1055.com					
WWRM-FM 94.9 MHz (AC) 877 Executive Center Dr W Suite 300	Saint Petersburg	FL	33702	727-576-1073	576-8098
Web: www.warm949.com					
WXTB-FM 97.9 MHz (Rock) 13577 Feather Sound Dr Suite 550	Clearwater	FL	34622	727-572-9808	572-0935
WYUU-FM 92.5 MHz (Oldies) PO Box 42925	Saint Petersburg	FL	33702	813-221-2925	579-9111*
*Fax Area Code: 727					
WZTM-AM 820 kHz (Sports) 11300 4th St N Suite 318	Saint Petersburg	FL	33716	727-577-7131	578-2477

— Colleges/Universities —

				Phone	Fax
Eckerd College 4200 54th Ave S	Saint Petersburg	FL	33711	727-864-8334	866-2304
TF: 800-456-9009 ■ *Web:* www.eckerd.edu ■ *E-mail:* admissions@eckerd.edu					

— Hospitals —

				Phone	Fax
All Children's Hospital 801 6th St S	Saint Petersburg	FL	33701	727-898-7451	892-8500
TF: 800-456-4543 ■ *Web:* www.allkids.org					
Bayfront Medical Center 701 6th St S	Saint Petersburg	FL	33701	727-823-1234	893-6930
Web: www.bayfront.org					
Columbia Northside Medical Center 6000 49th St N	Saint Petersburg	FL	33709	727-521-4411	521-5007
Edward White Hospital 2323 9th Ave N	Saint Petersburg	FL	33713	727-323-1111	328-6135
Palms of Pasadena Hospital 1501 Pasadena Ave S	Saint Petersburg	FL	33707	727-381-1000	341-7690
Web: www.tenethealth.com/PalmsPasadena					
Saint Anthony's Hospital 1200 7th Ave N	Saint Petersburg	FL	33705	727-825-1100	825-1327*
*Fax: Admitting					
Saint Petersburg General Hospital 6500 38th Ave N	Saint Petersburg	FL	33710	727-384-1414	341-4889

— Attractions —

				Phone	Fax
American Stage 211 3rd St S	Saint Petersburg	FL	33701	727-822-8814	823-7529
Bayfront Center/Mahaffey Theater 400 1st St S	Saint Petersburg	FL	33701	727-892-5798	892-5858
TF: 800-874-9015					
Bayside Market 5501 Gulf Blvd	Saint Pete Beach	FL	33706		
Boyd Hill Nature Park 1101 Country Club Way S	Saint Petersburg	FL	33705	727-893-7326	893-7720
Caladesi Island State Park 3 Causeway Blvd	Dunedin	FL	34698	727-469-5918	
De Soto National Memorial PO Box 15390	Bradenton	FL	34280	941-792-0458	792-5094
Web: www.nps.gov/deso/					
Europa SeaKruz 150 B Johns Pass Boardwalk	Madeira Beach	FL	33708	727-393-5110	392-5715
TF: 800-688-7529					

Saint Petersburg — Attractions (Cont'd)

				Phone	Fax
Florida International Museum 100 2nd St N. TF: 800-777-9882 ■ Web: www.floridamuseum.org/	Saint Petersburg	FL	33701	727-821-1448	898-0248
Fort DeSoto Park 3500 Pinellas Bayway S.	Tierra Verde	FL	33715	727-866-2484	866-2485
Great Explorations-The Hands on Museum 1120 4th St S.	Saint Petersburg	FL	33701	727-821-8885	823-7287
Gulf Beaches Historical Museum 115 10th Ave	Saint Pete Beach	FL	33706	727-360-2491	363-6704
John's Pass Village & Boardwalk 501 150th Ave	Madeira Beach	FL	33708	727-397-1571	391-4259
Lyric Opera Assn 1183 85 Terr N	Saint Petersburg	FL	33702	727-578-1657	
Museum of Fine Arts 255 Beach Dr NE Web: www.fine-arts.org	Saint Petersburg	FL	33701	727-896-2667	894-4638
Pier Aquarium 800 2nd Ave NE	Saint Petersburg	FL	33701	727-895-7437	821-6451
Pier The 800 2nd Ave NE. Web: www.stpete-pier.com	Saint Petersburg	FL	33701	727-821-6164	
Ringling John & Mable Museum of Art 5401 Bay Shore Rd. Web: www.ringling.org ■ E-mail: ringling@concentric.net	Sarasota	FL	34243	941-355-5101	359-5745
Saint Petersburg Museum of History 335 2nd Ave NE. Web: www.ij.net/spmh ■ E-mail: spmh@ij.net	Saint Petersburg	FL	33701	727-894-1052	823-7276
Salvador Dali Museum 1000 3rd St S TF: 800-442-3254 ■ Web: www.daliweb.com ■ E-mail: qvbg71a@prodigy.com	Saint Petersburg	FL	33701	727-823-3767	894-6068
Sawgrass Lake Park 7400 25th St N.	Saint Petersburg	FL	33702	727-527-3814	527-3814
Shuffleboard Hall of Fame 559 Mirror Lake Dr N	Saint Petersburg	FL	33701	727-822-2083	
Suncoast Seabird Sanctuary 18328 Gulf Blvd	Indian Shores	FL	33785	727-391-6211	399-2923
Sunken Gardens 1825 4th St N	Saint Petersburg	FL	33701	727 551-3100	
Tampa Bay Holocaust Memorial Museum & Educational Center 55 5th St S Web: www.tampabayholocaust.org ■ E-mail: TampaBayHolo@aol.com	Saint Petersburg	FL	33701	727-820-0100	821-8435
War Veterans' Memorial Park 9600 Bay Pines Blvd	Saint Petersburg	FL	33708	727-392-9575	

SPORTS TEAMS & FACILITIES

				Phone	Fax
Bayfront Center Arena 400 1st St S TF: 800-874-9015 ■ Web: www.stpete.org/bayarena.htm	Saint Petersburg	FL	33701	727-892-5798	892-5858
Clearwater Phillies (baseball) 800 Phillies Dr Web: www.clearwaterphillies.com	Clearwater	FL	33755	727-441-8638	447-3924
Derby Lane Greyhound Racing 10490 Gandy Blvd N Web: www.derbylane.com	Saint Petersburg	FL	33702	727-576-1361	579-4362
Saint Petersburg Devil Rays (baseball) 180 2nd Ave SE Al Lang Stadium Web: www.stpetedevilrays.com	Saint Petersburg	FL	33701	727-822-3384	895-1556
Tropicana Field 1 Tropicana Dr *Fax: Hum Res ■ TF: 800-522-2801 ■ Web: www.devilray.com/home.html	Saint Petersburg	FL	33705	727-825-3120	825-3245*

— Events —

	Phone
4th of July Celebration (July 4)	727-821-6164
American Stage in the Park (mid-April-mid-May)	727-822-8814
Festival of States (late March-early April)	727-898-3654
First Night Saint Petersburg (December 31)	727-823-8906
Holiday Lighted Boat Parade (early December)	727-893-7329
Holiday Show of Fine Arts & Crafts (November)	727-822-7872
International Folk Fair (mid-March)	727-551-3365
July 4th Celebration (July 4)	727-893-7494
Largo Folk Festival (late January)	727-582-2123
Mainsail Arts Festival (mid-April)	727-892-5885
Mid-Winter Regatta (late February)	727-822-3873
Pinellas County Fair (late March)	727-541-6941
Renaissance Festival (early March-mid-April)	727-586-5423
Ribfest (mid-November)	727-896-2727
Sail Expo Saint Petersburg (early November)	727-464-7200
Saint Petersburg Fall Boat Show (November)	727-892-5767
Saint Petersburg-Isla Mujeras Regatta (late April)	727-822-3873
Santa Parade (early December)	727-893-8581
Snowfest (early December)	727-898-3654
Spring Boat Show (March)	727-892-5767
Taste of Pinellas (late May-early June)	727-893-7734
Thistle Mid-Winter Sailboat Races (early March)	727-822-3873

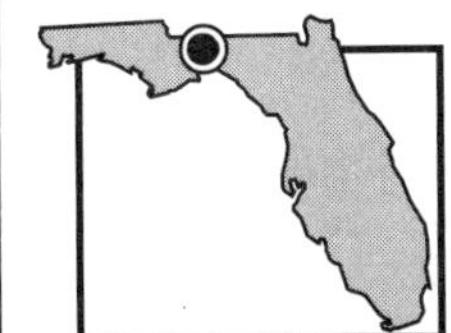

Tallahassee

Tallahassee is located in Florida's "panhandle," in the northern portion of the state. The State Capitol Building in Tallahassee houses an art gallery, and its observation deck provides a panoramic view of the city. The adjacent Historic Old Capitol has been restored to its 1902 appearance, with red-striped awnings and a stained-glass dome. The two major educational institutions in Tallahassee are Florida State University, home of "Seminole" athletics, and Florida A&M University. The Black Archive Research Center and Museum at Florida A&M has an extensive collection of African-American artifacts. Fifteen miles south of Tallahassee, Wakulla Springs State Park's glass-bottom boat and riverboat cruises provide visitors with the opportunity to see alligators, exotic birds, turtles, and various other native animals.

Population	136,628	**Longitude**	84-26-33 W
Area (Land)	63.3 sq mi	**County**	Leon
Area (Water)	1.1 sq mi	**Time Zone**	EST
Elevation	188 ft	**Area Code/s**	850
Latitude	30-42-90 N		

— Average Temperatures and Precipitation —

TEMPERATURES

	Jan	Feb	Mar	Apr	May	Jun	Jul	Aug	Sep	Oct	Nov	Dec
High	63	66	74	80	86	91	91	91	89	82	73	66
Low	38	40	47	52	61	69	71	71	68	56	46	40

PRECIPITATION

	Jan	Feb	Mar	Apr	May	Jun	Jul	Aug	Sep	Oct	Nov	Dec
Inches	4.8	5.6	6.2	3.7	4.8	6.9	8.8	7.5	5.6	2.9	3.9	5.0

— Important Phone Numbers —

	Phone		Phone
AAA	850-878-6000	**Poison Control Center**	800-282-3171
American Express Travel	850-224-6464	**Time/Temp**	850-584-3333
Emergency	911	**Weather**	850-422-1212
HotelDocs	800-468-3537		

— Information Sources —

				Phone	Fax
Leon County 301 S Monroe St Web: www.co.leon.fl.us	Tallahassee	FL	32301	850-488-4710	414-5700
Leon County Public Library System 200 W Park Ave Web: www.co.leon.fl.us/library/index.htm	Tallahassee	FL	32301	850-487-2665	487-1793
Tallahassee Area Convention & Visitors Bureau 106 E Jefferson St. TF: 800-628-2866 ■ Web: www.co.leon.fl.us/visitors/index.htm	Tallahassee	FL	32301	850-413-9200	487-4621
Tallahassee Area Visitor Information Center 401 S Monroe St New Capitol Bldg. TF: 800-628-2866	Tallahassee	FL	32301	850-413-9200	487-4621
Tallahassee Chamber of Commerce 100 N Duval St. Web: www.talchamber.com/	Tallahassee	FL	32301	850-224-8116	561-3860

Tallahassee — Information Sources (Cont'd)

				Phone	Fax
Tallahassee City Hall 300 S Adams St	Tallahassee	FL	32301	850-891-0010	891-8540*
**Fax:* Cust Svc ■ *Web:* www.state.fl.us/citytlh					
Tallahassee-Leon County Civic Center 505 W Pensacola St	Tallahassee	FL	32301	850-487-1691	222-6947
TF: 800-322-3602 ■ *Web:* www.tlccc.org					
Tallahassee Mayor 300 S Adams St	Tallahassee	FL	32301	850-891-8181	891-8542
Web: www.state.fl.us/citytlh/city_commission/maddox.html					
Tallahassee Planning Dept 300 S Adams St	Tallahassee	FL	32301	850-891-8600	891-8734
Web: www.ci.tallahassee.fl.us:/citytlh/planning/tlcpdhp.html					

On-Line Resources

4Tallahassee.com . . . www.4tallahassee.com
About.com Guide to Tallahassee . . . tallahassee.about.com
Anthill City Guide Tallahassee . . . www.anthill.com/city.asp?city=tallahassee
Area Guide Tallahassee . . . tallahassee.areaguides.net
City Knowledge Tallahassee . . . www.cityknowledge.com/fl_tallahassee.htm
Excite.com Tallahassee City Guide . . . www.excite.com/travel/countries/united_states/florida/tallahassee
InTallahassee.com . . . www.intallahassee.com
Tallahassee Freenet . . . www.freenet.scri.fsu.edu/
Tallahassee Online . . . www.tallahasseeonline.com/tlh/index.html
Tastebuds! Internet Guide to Food & Drink . . . www.tastebuds.com

— Transportation Services —

AIRPORTS

■ **Tallahassee Regional Airport (TLH)**

	Phone
8 miles SW of downtown (approx 15 minutes)	850-891-7800

Web: fcn.state.fl.us/citytlh/aviation/aviation.html ■ *E-mail:* boltonb@mn.ci.tlh.fl.us

Airport Transportation

	Phone
Yellow Cab $12-14 fare to downtown	850-222-3070

Commercial Airlines

	Phone		Phone
American Eagle	800-433-7300	**Delta**	800-221-1212
Atlantic Southeast	800-282-3424	**US Airways**	850-574-7141
Continental	800-525-0280		

Charter Airlines

	Phone
Flightline Group Inc	850-574-4444

CAR RENTALS

	Phone		Phone
Alamo	850-576-0211	**Dollar**	850-575-4255
Avis	850-576-4133	**Hertz**	850-576-1154
Budget	850-575-9191	**National**	850-576-4107

LIMO/TAXI

	Phone		Phone
Capital Limousine	850-574-4350	**Premier Transit**	850-574-4350
City Taxi	850-562-4222	**Yellow Cab**	850-222-3070
Classic Limo	850-421-1933		

MASS TRANSIT

	Phone
Old Town Trolley free	850-413-9200
Taltran $.75 Base fare	850-891-5200

RAIL/BUS

				Phone
Amtrak Station 918 1/2 Railroad Ave	Tallahassee	FL	32310	850-224-2779
Greyhound/Trailways Bus Station 112 W Tennessee St	Tallahassee	FL	32301	850-222-4240

— Accommodations —

HOTELS, MOTELS, RESORTS

				Phone	Fax
Best Inns of America 2738 Graves Rd	Tallahassee	FL	32303	850-562-2378	
TF: 800-237-8466					
Best Western Inn 6737 Mahan Dr	Tallahassee	FL	32308	850-656-2938	656-6380
TF: 800-996-6537					
Best Western Pride Inn 2016 Apalachee Pkwy	Tallahassee	FL	32301	850-656-6312	942-4312
TF: 800-827-7390					
Budget Inn 1402 W Tennessee St	Tallahassee	FL	32304	850-224-4174	222-7828
Cabot Lodge 1653 Raymond Diehl Rd	Tallahassee	FL	32308	850-386-7500	386-1136
TF: 800-255-6343					
Cabot Lodge North 2735 N Monroe St	Tallahassee	FL	32303	850-386-8880	386-4254
TF: 800-223-1964					
Collegiate Village Inn 2121 W Tennessee St	Tallahassee	FL	32304	850-576-6121	576-3508
Comfort Inn 2727 Graves Rd	Tallahassee	FL	32303	850-562-7200	562-6335
TF: 800-228-5150					
Courtyard by Marriott 1018 Apalachee Pkwy	Tallahassee	FL	32301	850-222-8822	561-0351
TF: 800-321-2211 ■ *Web:* courtyard.com/TLHCH					
Days Inn 1350 W Tennessee St	Tallahassee	FL	32304	850-222-3219	222-6645
TF: 800-329-7466					
Doubletree Hotel 101 S Adams St	Tallahassee	FL	32301	850-224-5000	513-9516
TF: 800-222-8733 ■ *Web:* www.doubletreehotels.com/DoubleT/Hotel121/131/131Main.htm					
Econo Lodge 2681 N Monroe St	Tallahassee	FL	32303	850-385-6155	385-6155
TF: 800-553-2666					
Executive Suite Motor Inn 522 Scotty's Ln	Tallahassee	FL	32303	850-386-2121	386-3632
TF: 800-324-0090					
Governors Inn 209 S Adams St	Tallahassee	FL	32301	850-681-6855	222-3105
Hampton Inn 3210 N Monroe St	Tallahassee	FL	32303	850-562-4300	562-6735
TF: 800-426-7866					
Heritage Inn Downtown 722 Apalachee Pkwy	Tallahassee	FL	32301	850-224-2181	224-2181
Holiday Inn Northwest 2714 Graves Rd	Tallahassee	FL	32303	850-562-2000	562-8519
TF: 800-465-4329					
Howard Johnson 2726 N Monroe St	Tallahassee	FL	32303	850-386-5000	386-5000
TF: 800-446-4656					
Killearn Country Club & Inn 100 Tyron Cir	Tallahassee	FL	32308	850-893-2186	893-8267
TF: 800-476-4101 ■ *Web:* www.killearncc.com					
La Quinta Inn 2850 Apalachee Pkwy	Tallahassee	FL	32301	850-878-5099	878-6665
TF: 800-531-5900					
La Quinta Inn North 2905 N Monroe St	Tallahassee	FL	32303	850-385-7172	422-2463
TF: 800-687-6667					
Motel 6 1027 Apalachee Pkwy	Tallahassee	FL	32301	850-877-6171	656-6120
TF: 800-466-8356					
Quality Inn & Suites 2020 Apalachee Pkwy	Tallahassee	FL	32301	850-877-4437	878-9964
TF: 800-228-5151					
Radisson Hotel 415 N Monroe St	Tallahassee	FL	32301	850-224-6000	222-0335
TF: 800-333-3333					
Ramada Inn 2900 N Monroe St	Tallahassee	FL	32303	850-386-1027	422-1025
TF: 800-272-6232					
Red Roof Inn 2930 Hospitality St	Tallahassee	FL	32303	850-385-7884	386-8896
TF: 800-843-7663					
Shoney's Inn 2801 N Monroe St	Tallahassee	FL	32303	850-386-8286	
TF: 800-222-2222 ■ *Web:* www.shoneysinn.com/fl3.htm					
Sleep Inn 1695 Capitol Cir NW	Tallahassee	FL	32303	850-575-5885	576-5788
TF: 800-753-3746					
StudioPLUS 1950 Raymond Diehl Rd	Tallahassee	FL	32308	850-383-1700	383-1701
TF: 800-646-8000					
Travelodge 691 W Tennessee St	Tallahassee	FL	32304	850-224-8161	222-5688
TF: 800-578-7878					

— Restaurants —

				Phone
Andrew's Second Act (International) 228 S Adams St	Tallahassee	FL	32308	850-222-3444
Anthony's (Italian) 1950 Thomasville Rd	Tallahassee	FL	32308	850-224-1447
Atlantis (Greek) 220 S Monroe St	Tallahassee	FL	32301	850-224-9711
Bahn Thai Restaurant (Thai) 1319 S Monroe St	Tallahassee	FL	32301	850-224-4765
Bamboo House (Chinese) 112 E 6th Ave	Tallahassee	FL	32303	850-224-9099
Banjo's Bar-B-Q (Barbecue) 2335 Apalachee Pkwy	Tallahassee	FL	32310	850-877-8111
Barnacle Bill's (Seafood) 1830 N Monroe St	Tallahassee	FL	32303	850-385-8734
Bean & Leaf Railroad Cafe (American) 602 Industrial Dr	Tallahassee	FL	32310	850-599-0177
Buckhead Brewery (American) 1900 Capital Cir NE	Tallahassee	FL	32308	850-942-4947
Cafe di Lorenzo (Italian) 1002 N Monroe St	Tallahassee	FL	32303	850-681-3622
Cajun Cafe & Grill (Cajun) 1500 Apalachee Pkwy	Tallahassee	FL	32301	850-877-2131

Tallahassee — Restaurants (Cont'd)

				Phone
Chez Pierre (French) 1215 Thomasville Rd	Tallahassee	FL	32303	850-222-0936
Web: webvista.com/tlh/dine/chezp/				
Crystal River Seafood (Seafood) 1968 W Tennessee St	Tallahassee	FL	32304	850-575-4418
Dragon Room (Chinese) 401 E Tennessee St	Tallahassee	FL	32301	850-224-9686
Driftwood Restaurant (Steak) 2714 Graves Rd	Tallahassee	FL	32303	850-562-2525
El Chico Restaurant (Tex Mex) 2225 N Monroe St	Tallahassee	FL	32301	850-386-1133
Florida Grill & Bar (American) 2840 Apalachee Pkwy	Tallahassee	FL	32301	850-878-6647
Web: www.tastebuds.com/flagrimn.html				
Food Glorious Food (Natural/Health)				
1950 Thomasville Rd Betton Pl	Tallahassee	FL	32303	850-224-9974
Georgio's (Italian) 3425 Thomasville Rd	Tallahassee	FL	33204	850-893-4161
Jacque's Cafe (American) 315 S Calhoun St	Tallahassee	FL	32301	850-224-4164
Julie's Place (Steak) 2901 N Monroe St	Tallahassee	FL	32303	850-386-7181
Kitcho (Japanese) 1415 Timberlane Rd	Tallahassee	FL	32312	850-893-7686
Kool Beanz Cafe (International) 921 Thomasville Rd	Tallahassee	FL	32303	850-224-2466
Longhorn Steaks (Steak/Seafood) 2400 N Monroe St	Tallahassee	FL	32304	850-385-4028
Lucy Ho's (Japanese) 2814 Apalachee Pkwy	Tallahassee	FL	32301	850-878-3365
Lucy Ho's (Chinese/Japanese) 2814 Apalachee Pkwy	Tallahassee	FL	32301	850-878-3366
Melting Pot Restaurant (American) 1832 N Monroe St	Tallahassee	FL	32303	850-386-7440
Mill The (Steak/Seafood) 2329 Apalachee Pkwy	Tallahassee	FL	32301	850-656-2867
Ming Tree Restaurant (Chinese) 1435 E Lafayette St	Tallahassee	FL	32301	850-878-1779
Nino (Italian/German) 6497 Apalachee Pkwy	Tallahassee	FL	32311	850-878-8141
Paradise Grill (Seafood) 1406 N Meridian Rd	Tallahassee	FL	32303	850-224-2742
Plantation Dining Room (Continental)				
415 N Monroe St	Tallahassee	FL	32301	850-224-6000
Po'Boys Creole Cafe (Cajun) 224 E College Ave	Tallahassee	FL	32301	850-224-5400
Samrat Indian Restaurant (Indian)				
2529 Apalachee Pkwy	Tallahassee	FL	32301	850-942-1993
San Miguel (Mexican) 200 W Tharpe St	Tallahassee	FL	32303	850-385-3346
Web: www.tastebuds.com/sanmigmn.html				
Silver Slipper (Steak/Seafood) 531 Scotty's Ln	Tallahassee	FL	32303	850-386-9366
Wakulla Springs Restaurant (Southern)				
550 Wakulla Park Dr	Tallahassee	FL	32305	850-224-5950
Wharf Seafood Restaurant (Seafood)				
1480 Timberlane Rd	Tallahassee	FL	32312	850-894-4443

— Goods and Services —

SHOPPING

				Phone	Fax
Downtown Tallahassee					
Monroe St-betw Park Ave & Jefferson St	Tallahassee	FL	32301	850-413-9200	561-8727
Governor's Square 1500 Apalachee Pkwy	Tallahassee	FL	32301	850-671-4636	942-0136
Parkway Center					
Apalachee Pkwy & Magnolia Dr	Tallahassee	FL	32301		
Pedler's Furniture Hospital					
1114 Carriage Rd	Tallahassee	FL	32312	850-580-2552	
Tallahassee Mall 2415 N Monroe St	Tallahassee	FL	32303	850-385-7145	385-6203
Village Commons					
1400 Village Square Blvd	Tallahassee	FL	32312		

BANKS

				Phone	Fax
Amsouth Bank 201 S Monroe St	Tallahassee	FL	32301	850-222-3727	222-5545
Capital City Bank 2111 N Monroe St	Tallahassee	FL	32303	850-671-0300	878-9135
First Bank of Tallahassee					
1997 Capital Cir NE	Tallahassee	FL	32308	850-668-4034	385-7427
NationsBank 315 S Calhoun St	Tallahassee	FL	32301	850-561-1876	561-1740
TF: 800-299-2265					
SunTrust Bank 3522 Thomasville Rd	Tallahassee	FL	32308	850-298-5111	298-5094*
**Fax:* Cust Svc					
Wakulla Bank 2101 Capital Cir NE	Tallahassee	FL	32308	850-386-2222	385-8231

BUSINESS SERVICES

	Phone
Adecco Employment Personnel Services	850-561-8715
BAX Global	800-225-5229
DHL Worldwide Express	800-225-5345
Federal Express	800-238-5355
Interim Personnel Services	850-671-2345
Kinko's	850-681-6221
Mail Boxes Etc	800-789-4623
Mail Master of Tallahassee	850-224-6245
Post Office	850-222-2862
UPS	800-742-5877

— Media —

PUBLICATIONS

				Phone	Fax
Tallahassee Democrat‡					
277 N Magnolia Dr	Tallahassee	FL	32301	850-599-2100	599-2295
TF: 800-777-2154 ■ *Web:* www.tdo.com					
■ *E-mail:* letters@freenet.fsu.edu					
Tallahassee Magazine					
1932 Miccosukee Rd	Tallahassee	FL	32308	850-878-0554	656-1871

‡Daily newspapers

TELEVISION

				Phone	Fax
WCTV-TV Ch 6 (CBS) County Rd 12	Tallahassee	FL	32312	850-893-6666	668-3851
Web: www.wctv6.com					
WFSU-TV Ch 11 (PBS)					
1600 Red Barber Plaza	Tallahassee	FL	32310	850-487-3170	487-3093
Web: www.fsu.edu/~wfsu_tv/ ■ *E-mail:* wfsu-tv@mailer.fsu.edu					
WTLH-TV Ch 49 (Fox) 950 Commerce Blvd	Midway	FL	32343	850-576-4990	576-0200
Web: www.fox49.com ■ *E-mail:* fox49@fox49.com					
WTWC-TV Ch 40 (NBC) 8440 Deerlake Rd	Tallahassee	FL	32312	850-893-4140	893-6974
WTXL-TV Ch 27 (ABC)					
7927 Thomasville Rd	Tallahassee	FL	32312	850-893-3127	668-1460
Web: www.wtxl.com					

RADIO

				Phone	Fax
WAIB-FM 103.1 MHz (Ctry)					
PO Box 13909	Tallahassee	FL	32317	850-386-5141	422-1897
Web: www.waib103.com					
WBZE-FM 98.9 MHz (AC)					
109B Ridgeland Rd	Tallahassee	FL	32312	850-385-1156	224-8329
Web: www.989breeze.com					
WCVC-AM 1330 kHz (Rel)					
117 1/2 Henderson Rd	Tallahassee	FL	32312	850-386-7133	386-2138
Web: www.mercies.com/wcvc ■ *E-mail:* wcvc@webtv.net					
WFSQ-FM 91.5 MHz (Clas)					
1600 Red Barber Plaza	Tallahassee	FL	32310	850-487-3086	487-3293
Web: www.fsu.edu/~wfsu_fm/915.html					
■ *E-mail:* wfsqfm@freenet.tlh.fl.us					
WFSU-FM 88.9 MHz (NPR)					
1600 Red Barber Plaza	Tallahassee	FL	32310	850-487-3086	487-3293
Web: www.fsu.edu/~wfsu_fm/ ■ *E-mail:* wfsufm@freenet.tlh.fl.us					
WGLF-FM 104.1 MHz (Rock)					
1310 Paul Russell Rd	Tallahassee	FL	32301	850-878-1104	877-1040
Web: www.gulf104.com ■ *E-mail:* jocks@gulf104.com					
WHBX-FM 96.1 MHz (Urban)					
109 B Ridgeland Rd	Tallahassee	FL	32312	850-385-1156	224-8329
WKOL-FM 107.1 MHz (Oldies)					
325 John Knox Rd Suite G	Tallahassee	FL	32303	850-422-3107	383-0748
Web: www.kool1071.com					
WNLS-AM 1270 kHz (N/T)					
325 John Knox Rd Bldg G-200	Tallahassee	FL	32303	850-386-6143	383-0748
WTNT-FM 94.9 MHz (Ctry)					
325 John Knox Rd Bldg E-200	Tallahassee	FL	32303	850-386-6143	385-8789

— Colleges/Universities —

				Phone	Fax
Florida A & M University	Tallahassee	FL	32307	850-599-3000	599-3069
Web: www.famu.edu					
Florida State University					
600 W College Ave	Tallahassee	FL	32306	850-644-2525	644-0170
Web: www.fsu.edu ■ *E-mail:* admissions@mailer.fsu.edu					
Tallahassee Community College					
444 Appleyard Dr	Tallahassee	FL	32304	850-488-9200	922-8205*
**Fax:* Hum Res ■ *Web:* www.tallahassee.cc.fl.us					
■ *E-mail:* enroll@mail.tallahassee.cc.fl.us					

— Hospitals —

				Phone	Fax
Columbia Tallahassee Community Hospital					
2626 Capital Medical Blvd	Tallahassee	FL	32308	850-656-5000	656-5198
TF: 800-882-4556 ■ *Web:* www.ctch.com					

Tallahassee — Hospitals (Cont'd)

				Phone	Fax
Tallahassee Memorial Hospital 1300 Miccosukee Rd *Fax: Admitting ■ Web: www.tmh.org	Tallahassee	FL	32308	850-681-1155	841-6000*

— Attractions —

				Phone	Fax
Apalachicola National Forest 1773 Crawfordville Hwy	Crawfordville	FL	32327	850-926-3561	926-1904
Birdsong Nature Center 2106 Meridian Rd	Thomasville	GA	31792	912-377-4408	377-4408
Black Archives Research Center & Museum Florida A & M University 103 Howard Hall	Tallahassee	FL	32307	850-599-3020	561-2604
Brokaw-McDougall House 329 N Meridian St	Tallahassee	FL	32301	850-891-3900	891-3902
Columns The 100 N Duval St	Tallahassee	FL	32301	850-224-8116	
Downtown Tallahassee Monroe St-betw Park Ave & Jefferson St	Tallahassee	FL	32301	850-413-9200	561-8727
First Presbyterian Church 110 N Adams St	Tallahassee	FL	32301	850-222-4504	222-2215
Florida Agricultural Museum 1850 Princess Pl Rd *Web:* www.flamuseums.org/fam/flamuseums/pages/204.htm	Palm Coast	FL	32137	904-446-7630	446-7631
Florida State University Museum of Fine Arts W Tennessee & Copeland Sts	Tallahassee	FL	32306	850-644-6836	644-8977
Florida State University School of Theatre Copeland & Call Sts	Tallahassee	FL	32306	850-644-6500	644-7420
Forest Capital State Museum 204 Forest Park Dr	Perry	FL	32347	850-584-3227	584-3488
Goodwood Plantation 1600 Miccosukee Rd	Tallahassee	FL	32308	850-877-4202	877-3090
Governor's Mansion 700 N Adams St	Tallahassee	FL	32303	850-488-4661	922-6110
Knott House Museum 301 E Park Ave *Web:* www.freenet.tlh.fl.us/Historic_Preservation/knott.html	Tallahassee	FL	32301	850-922-2459	413-7261
Lake Jackson Mounds State Archaeological Site 3600 Indian Mounds Rd	Tallahassee	FL	32303	850-562-0042	
Lake Talquin State Recreation Area 1022 Desoto Park Dr	Tallahassee	FL	32301	850-922-6007	
LeMoyne Art Foundation 125 N Gadsden St *Web:* www.webvista.com/lemoyne/	Tallahassee	FL	32301	850-222-8800	224-2714
Maclay State Gardens 3540 Thomasville Rd	Tallahassee	FL	32308	850-487-4556	487-8808
Museum of Art Tallahassee 350 S Duval St	Tallahassee	FL	32301	850-513-0700	513-0143
Museum of Florida History 500 S Bronough St RA Gray Bldg *Web:* www.dos.state.fl.us/dhr/museum	Tallahassee	FL	32399	850-488-1484	921-2503
Natural Bridge Battlefield State Historic Site 1022 Desoto Park Dr	Tallahassee	FL	32301	850-922-6007	
Odyssey Science Center 350 S Duval St *Web:* odysseysciencecenter.org ■ *E-mail:* edennis@odysseysciencecenter.org	Tallahassee	FL	32301	850-513-0700	513-0143
Old Capitol 400 S Monroe St	Tallahassee	FL	32399	850-487-1902	921-2540
Pebble Hill Plantation Hwy 319	Thomasville	GA	31792	912-226-2344	226-0780
Saint Marks Historic Railroad State Trail 1022 Desoto Pk Dr	Tallahassee	FL	32301	850-922-6007	488-0366
San Luis Archaeological & Historic Site 2020 W Mission Rd	Tallahassee	FL	32304	850-487-3711	
Tallahassee Antique Car Museum 3550 Mahan Dr	Tallahassee	FL	32308	850-942-0137	942-5134
Tallahassee Ballet Co PO Box 772	Tallahassee	FL	32302	850-222-1287	
Tallahassee Little Theatre 1861 Thomasville Rd *Web:* www.freenet.tlh.fl.us/TLT/	Tallahassee	FL	32304	850-224-4597	
Tallahassee Museum of History & Natural Science 3945 Museum Dr *Web:* www.tallahasseemuseum.org ■ *E-mail:* kcarr@freenet.tlh.fl.us	Tallahassee	FL	32310	850-576-1636	574-8243
Tallahassee Symphony Ruby Diamond Auditorium Florida State University Campus *Web:* www.tsolive.org	Tallahassee	FL	32301	850-224-0461	222-9092
Wakulla Springs State Park 550 Wakulla Springs Park Dr	Wakulla Springs	FL	32305	850-922-3633	222-0451
Young Actors Theatre 609 Glenview Dr	Tallahassee	FL	32303	850-386-6602	422-2084

SPORTS TEAMS & FACILITIES

				Phone	Fax
Tallahassee Scorpions (soccer) 133 N Monroe St	Tallahassee	FL	32301	850-224-7700	224-6300
Tallahassee Tiger Sharks (hockey) 505 W Pensacola St Civic Ctr *Web:* www.tigersharkshockey.com	Tallahassee	FL	32301	850-224-7700	

— Events —

	Phone
Caribbean Carnival (late August)	850-878-2198
Celebrate America (July 4)	850-891-3866
December on the Farm (early November)	850-576-1636
Halloween Howl (late October)	850-575-8684
Havana Music Fest (early March)	850-539-8114
Hernando Desoto Winter Encampment (early January)	850-922-6007
Humanatee Festival (mid-May)	850-922-6007
Jazz & Blues Festival (mid-March)	850-576-1636
Knott House Candlelight Tour (early December)	850-922-2459
Market Days (early December)	850-575-8684
Native American Heritage Festival (September)	850-576-8684
Natural Bridge Battle Reenactment (March)	850-925-6216
North Florida Fair (early November)	850-878-3247
Rose Festival (late April)	800-704-2350
Southern Shakespeare Festival (early May)	850-513-3087
Spring Farm Days (April)	850-575-8684
Springtime Tallahassee (late March-early April)	850-224-5012
Summer Swamp Stomp (mid-July)	850-575-8684
Tallahassee Marathon (mid-January)	850-893-9739
Watermelon Festival (late June)	850-997-5552
Winter Festival (mid-late December)	850-413-9200
Zoobilee (early October)	850-575-8684

Tampa

One hundred and ten blocks of historic buildings make up Tampa's Ybor City, once the "cigar capital of the world." Old cigar factories have now been restored, and the influence of Ybor's Spanish, Cuban, Italian, and German immigrants can be seen in its shops, restaurants, and festivals. On Tampa's waterfront is the new $84 million Florida Aquarium, a glass-domed structure with 4,350 specimens of fish, marine animals, and plants. The African-themed entertainment park, Busch Gardens, is also located in Tampa. Each February, the city hosts its own version of Mardi Gras, the annual Gasparilla Pirate Fest. Tampa extends its pirate theme to sports, as the home of the National Football League's Tampa Bay Buccaneers.

Population	289,156	**Longitude**	82-45-86 W
Area (Land)	108.7 sq mi	**County**	Hillsborough
Area (Water)	58.6 sq mi	**Time Zone**	EST
Elevation	48 ft	**Area Code/s**	813
Latitude	27-94-72 N		

— Average Temperatures and Precipitation —

TEMPERATURES

	Jan	Feb	Mar	Apr	May	Jun	Jul	Aug	Sep	Oct	Nov	Dec
High	70	71	77	82	87	90	90	90	89	84	78	72
Low	50	52	57	61	68	73	75	75	73	65	57	52

PRECIPITATION

	Jan	Feb	Mar	Apr	May	Jun	Jul	Aug	Sep	Oct	Nov	Dec
Inches	2.0	3.1	3.0	1.2	3.1	5.5	6.6	7.6	6.0	2.0	1.8	2.2

Tampa (Cont'd)

— Important Phone Numbers —

	Phone		Phone
AAA	813-289-5000	Medical Referral	813-254-3484
American Express Travel	813-273-0310	Poison Control Center	813-253-4444
Dental Referral	800-511-8663	Travelers Aid	813-273-5936
Emergency	911	Weather	813-645-2506
HotelDocs	800-468-3537		

— Information Sources —

				Phone	Fax
Better Business Bureau Serving West Florida PO Box 7950 *Web:* www.clearwater.bbb.org	Clearwater	FL	33758	727-535-5522	539-6301
Greater Tampa Chamber of Commerce 401 E Jackson St Suite 2100 *TF:* 800-298-2672 ■ *Web:* www.tampachamber.com	Tampa	FL	33602	813-228-7777	223-7899
Hillsborough County 601 E Kennedy Blvd 13th Fl *Web:* www.hillsboroughcounty.org	Tampa	FL	33602	813-272-5900	
Suncoast Free-Net 900 N Ashley Dr Tampa-Hillborough County Public Library *Web:* scfn.thpl.lib.fl.us ■ *E-mail:* infodesk@scfn.thpl.lib.fl.us	Tampa	FL	33602	813-273-3711	
Tampa Business & Community Services Dept 306 E Jackson St	Tampa	FL	33602	813-274-8091	274-7410
Tampa City Hall 306 E Jackson St *Web:* www.ci.tampa.fl.us	Tampa	FL	33602	813-223-8211	
Tampa Convention Center 333 S Franklin St *TF:* 800-426-5630	Tampa	FL	33602	813-274-8511	274-7430
Tampa-Hillsborough County Public Library 900 N Ashley Dr *Web:* scfn.thpl.lib.fl.us/thpl/thpl.htm	Tampa	FL	33602	813-273-3652	273-3707
Tampa Mayor 306 E Jackson St *Web:* www.ci.tampa.fl.us/dept_Mayor	Tampa	FL	33602	813-274-8251	247-7050
Tampa/Hillsborough Convention & Visitors Assn 400 N Tampa St Suite 1010 *TF:* 800-826-8358 ■ *Web:* www.thcva.com	Tampa	FL	33602	813-223-1111	229-6616

On-Line Resources

4Tampa.com	www.4tampa.com
About.com Guide to Tampa Bay	tampa.about.com/local/southeastus/tampa
Access America Tampa	www.accessamer.com/tampa/
Area Guide Tampa	tampa.areaguides.net
City Knowledge Tampa	www.cityknowledge.com/fl_tampa.htm
Cityhits Tampa	www.cityhits.com/tampa/
CitySearch Tampa/Saint Petersburg	tampabay.citysearch.com
DigitalCity Tampa Bay	home.digitalcity.com/tampabay
Essential Guide to Tampa Bay	www.ego.net/us/fl/tampa
Excite.com Tampa City Guide	www.excite.com/travel/countries/united_states/florida/tampa
Go Tampa Bay	www.gotampabay.com
Hotel Guide Tampa/Saint Petersburg	hotelguide.net/tampa/
Insiders' Guide to Tampa Bay	www.insiders.com/tampa/
NITC Travelbase City Guide Tampa	www.travelbase.com/auto/guides/tampa-area-fl.html
Surf & Sun Beach Vacation Guide to Tampa Bay	www.surf-sun.com/fl-tampa-bay-main.htm
Tampa Bay Online	www.tampabayonline.net/home.htm
Tampa CityLink	www.usacitylink.com/citylink/tampa
Tampa Guide	www.tampaguide.com/
Tampa.TheLinks.com	tampa.thelinks.com/
WebCoast-Tampa Bay's Online Information Magazine	webcoast.tampa.fl.us/

— Transportation Services —

AIRPORTS

■ **Tampa International Airport (TPA)**

	Phone
4 miles W of downtown (approx 10 minutes) Web: www.tampaairport.com/	813-870-8700

Airport Transportation

	Phone
HARTline $1.15 fare to downtown	813-254-4278
Limo The $13 fare to downtown	727-572-1111
Taxi $15 fare to downtown	813-253-0121

Commercial Airlines

	Phone		Phone
Air Canada	800-776-3000	Kiwi	800-538-5494
AirTran	800-247-8726	Martinair Holland	800-627-8462
America West	800-235-9292	MetroJet	888-638-7653
American	800-433-7300	Midway	800-446-4392
British Airways	800-247-9297	Midwest Express	800-452-2022
Cayman Airways	800-422-9626	Northwest	800-225-2525
Comair	800-354-9822	Southwest	800-435-9792
Continental	813-874-7151	Spirit	800-772-7117
Continental Express	800-525-0280	TWA	800-221-2000
Delta	813-286-1800	United	800-241-6522
Delta Express	800-325-5205	US Airways	800-428-4322
Eastwind	888-327-8946	Virgin Atlantic	800-862-8621

Charter Airlines

	Phone		Phone
Biscayne Helicopters	305-252-3883	Raytheon Aircraft Charter	800-519-6283
Commander Airways Inc	813-879-9757	Sovereign Air	800-473-8008
Corporate Jets Inc	412-466-2500	Sun Country	800-733-2692
Gulf Coast Aircraft Charter	813-220-4556	Tag Aviation	800-235-9724
Pompano Helicopters Inc	800-957-4374	Walkabout Air Inc	813-877-9387

CAR RENTALS

	Phone		Phone
Alamo	813-289-4323	Hertz	813-874-3232
Avis	813-396-3500	National	800-227-7368
Budget	813-877-6051	Payless	813-289-6554
Dollar	813-396-3640	Thrifty	813-289-4006
Enterprise	813-282-1680		

LIMO/TAXI

	Phone		Phone
Allstar Limousine/Luxury Transportation	727-345-6614	Embassy Limousine Service	727-447-4656
Alpha Limousine	813-247-6190	Royal Limousine	813-288-9116
Carey Limousine	813-228-7927	TaxiPlus	813-228-7587
Central Florida Limousines	813-396-3730	United Cab	813-253-2424
		Yellow Cab	813-253-8871

MASS TRANSIT

	Phone
HARTline $1.15 Base fare	813-254-4278

RAIL/BUS

				Phone
Amtrak Station 601 Nebraska Ave *TF:* 800-872-7245	Tampa	FL	33602	813-221-7602
Greyhound Bus Station 610 E Polk St *TF:* 800-231-2222	Tampa	FL	33602	813-229-2174

— Accommodations —

HOTEL RESERVATION SERVICES

	Phone	Fax
Hotel Reservations Network Inc *TF Sales:* 800-964-6835 ■ *Web:* www.hoteldiscount.com	214-361-7311	361-7299

HOTELS, MOTELS, RESORTS

				Phone	Fax
Adam's Mark Caribbean Gulf Resort 430 S Gulfview Blvd *TF:* 800-444-2326 ■ *Web:* www.adamsmark.com/clear.htm	Clearwater Beach	FL	33767	727-443-5714	298-5008
AmeriSuites Tampa/Busch Gardens 11408 N 30th St *TF:* 800-833-1516	Tampa	FL	33612	813-979-1922	979-1926
AmeriSuites Westshore 4811 W Main St *TF:* 800-833-1516	Tampa	FL	33607	813-282-1037	282-1148
Bahia Beach Resort 611 Destiny Dr *TF:* 800-327-2773	Ruskin	FL	33570	813-645-3291	641-1589
Baymont Inns 4811 Hwy 301 N *TF:* 800-301-0200	Tampa	FL	33610	813-626-0885	623-3321
Biltmore Resort & Spa 25 Belleview Blvd *TF:* 800-237-8947	Clearwater	FL	33756	727-442-6171	441-4173
Courtyard by Marriott 3805 W Cypress St *TF:* 800-321-2211 ■ *Web:* courtyard.com/TPAWT	Tampa	FL	33607	813-874-0555	870-0685
Crowne Plaza Hotel 700 N Westshore Blvd *TF:* 800-227-6963	Tampa	FL	33609	813-289-8200	289-9166

Tampa — Hotels, Motels, Resorts (Cont'd)

	City	State	ZIP	Phone	Fax
Days Inn 2522 N Dale Mabry Hwy *TF:* 800-448-4373	Tampa	FL	33607	813-877-6181	875-6171
Days Inn Busch Gardens East 2520 N 50th St *TF:* 800-523-7513	Tampa	FL	33619	813-247-3300	247-3893
Days Inn Busch Gardens Maingate 2901 E Busch Blvd *TF:* 800-329-7466	Tampa	FL	33612	813-933-6471	931-0261
Days Inn Busch Gardens North 701 E Fletcher Ave *TF:* 800-329-7466	Tampa	FL	33612	813-977-1550	977-6556
Days Inn Rocky Point Island 7627 Courtney Campbell Cswy *TF:* 800-237-2555	Tampa	FL	33607	813-281-0000	281-1067
Doubletree Guest Suites 11310 N 30th St *TF:* 800-222-8733 ■ *Web:* www.doubletreehotels.com/DoubleT/Hotel21/40/40Main.htm	Tampa	FL	33612	813-971-7690	972-5525
Doubletree Guest Suites Tampa Bay 3050 North Rocky Point Dr W *TF:* 800-222-8733 ■ *Web:* www.doubletreehotels.com/DoubleT/Hotel21/39/39Main.htm	Tampa	FL	33607	813-888-8800	888-8743
Doubletree Hotel 4500 W Cypress St *TF:* 800-222-8733	Tampa	FL	33607	813-879-4800	873-1832
Econo Lodge Busch Gardens 1701 E Busch Blvd *TF:* 800-783-7681	Tampa	FL	33612	813-933-7681	935-3301
Embassy Suites Tampa Airport 555 N Westshore Blvd *TF:* 800-362-2779	Tampa	FL	33609	813-875-1555	287-3664
Fairfield Inn by Marriott 10150 Palm River Rd *TF:* 800-228-2800 ■ *Web:* fairfieldinn.com/TPAFI	Tampa	FL	33619	813-661-9719	661-0416
Hampton Inn 4817 W Laurel St *TF:* 800-426-7866	Tampa	FL	33607	813-287-0778	282-0882
Holiday Inn 400 E Bearss Ave *TF:* 800-537-1591	Tampa	FL	33613	813-961-1000	961-5704
Holiday Inn Ashley Plaza Convention Center 111 W Fortune St *TF:* 800-465-4329	Tampa	FL	33602	813-223-1351	221-2000
Holiday Inn Busch Gardens 2701 E Fowler Ave *TF:* 800-465-4329	Tampa	FL	33612	813-971-4710	977-0155
Holiday Inn Express Tampa Stadium/Airport 4732 N Dale Mabry Hwy *TF:* 800-465-4329	Tampa	FL	33614	813-877-6061	876-1531
Holiday Inn State Fair 2708 N 50th St *TF:* 800-237-1510	Tampa	FL	33619	813-621-2081	626-4387
Howard Johnson Main Gate 4139 E Busch Blvd *TF:* 800-446-4656	Tampa	FL	33617	813-988-9191	989-3544
Howard Johnson's Airport/Stadium 2055 N Dale Mabry Hwy *TF:* 800-874-8819	Tampa	FL	33607	813-875-8818	876-4964
Hyatt Regency Tampa 211 N Tampa St *TF:* 800-233-1234 ■ *Web:* www.hyatt.com/usa/tampa/hotels/hotel_tpart.html	Tampa	FL	33602	813-225-1234	224-0148
Hyatt Regency Westshore 6200 Courtney Campbell Cswy *TF:* 800-233-1234 ■ *Web:* www.hyatt.com/usa/tampa/hotels/hotel_tparw.html	Tampa	FL	33607	813-874-1234	281-9168
La Quinta Inn & Suites 3701 E Fowler Ave *TF:* 800-687-6667	Tampa	FL	33612	813-910-7500	910-7600
La Quinta Inn Busch Gardens 2904 Melbourne Blvd *TF:* 800-687-6667	Tampa	FL	33605	813-623-3591	620-1375
La Quinta Inn Tampa Airport 4730 Spruce St *TF:* 800-531-5900	Tampa	FL	33607	813-287-0440	286-7399
Marriott Hotel Airport Tampa International Airport *TF:* 800-228-9290 ■ *Web:* marriotthotels.com/TPAAP	Tampa	FL	33607	813-879-5151	873-0945
Masters Inn 6606 E ML King Blvd *TF:* 800-826-0778	Tampa	FL	33619	813-623-6667	623-1495
Plantation Inn & Golf Resort 9301 W Fort Island Trail *TF:* 800-632-6262 ■ *Web:* www.plantationinn.com	Crystal River	FL	34429	352-795-4211	795-1368
Quality Hotel Airport Plaza 1200 N Westshore Blvd *TF:* 800-449-4343	Tampa	FL	33607	813-282-3636	282-0055
Quality Suites Hotel USF 3001 University Center Dr *TF:* 800-786-7446	Tampa	FL	33612	813-971-8930	971-8935
Radisson Bay Harbor Inn 7700 W Courtney Campbell Cswy *TF:* 800-333-3333	Tampa	FL	33607	813-281-8900	281-0189
Radisson Hotel Tampa 10221 Princess Palm Ave *TF:* 800-333-3333	Tampa	FL	33610	813-623-6363	621-7224
Radisson Riverwalk Hotel 200 N Ashley Dr *TF:* 800-333-3333	Tampa	FL	33602	813-223-2222	273-0839
Ramada Airport Hotel & Conference Center 5303 W Kennedy Blvd *TF:* 800-272-6232	Tampa	FL	33609	813-289-1950	286-2563
Ramada Bayside Inn 6414 Surfside Blvd *TF:* 800-627-2322	Apollo Beach	FL	33572	813-641-2700	645-9294
Ramada Inn Plant City 2011 N Wheeler St *TF:* 800-772-6232	Plant City	FL	33565	813-752-3141	754-5657
Residence Inn by Marriott Airport 3075 North Rocky Pt Dr *TF:* 800-331-3131 ■ *Web:* www.residenceinn.com/TPAFL	Tampa	FL	33607	813-281-5677	289-0266
Residence Inn Tampa North 13420 N Telecom Pkwy *TF:* 800-331-3131 ■ *Web:* residenceinn.com/TPARI	Tampa	FL	33637	813-972-4400	972-3376
Saddlebrook Resort 5700 Saddlebrook Way *TF:* 800-729-8383 ■ *Web:* www.saddlebrookresort.com ■ *E-mail:* info@saddlebrookresort.com	Wesley Chapel	FL	33543	813-973-1111	973-4504
Safety Harbor Spa & Resort 105 N Bayshore Dr *TF:* 888-237-8772 ■ *Web:* www.safetyharborspa.com	Safety Harbor	FL	34695	727-726-1161	726-4268
Sailport Resort 2506 Rocky Point Dr. *TF:* 800-255-9599	Tampa	FL	33607	813-281-9599	281-9510
Sheraton Four Points Hotel 7401 E Hillsborough Ave *TF:* 800-325-3535	Tampa	FL	33610	813-626-0999	622-7893
Sheraton Suites 4400 W Cypress St *TF:* 800-325-3535	Tampa	FL	33607	813-873-8675	879-7196
Shoney's Inn 8602 Morris Bridge Rd *TF:* 800-222-2222 ■ *Web:* www.shoneysinn.com/fl3.htm	Tampa	FL	33617	813-985-8525	988-3552
Sumner Suites 10007 Princess Palm Ave. *TF:* 800-747-8483	Tampa	FL	33619	813-622-8557	620-4866
Sun City Center Inn 1335 Rickenbacker Dr *TF:* 800-237-8200	Sun City Center	FL	33573	813-634-3331	634-2053
Tampa Airport Hilton at Metrocenter 2225 N Lois Ave *TF:* 800-345-6565	Tampa	FL	33607	813-877-6688	879-3264
Tampa Marriott 1001 N Westshore Blvd *TF:* 800-228-9290	Tampa	FL	33607	813-287-2555	289-5464
Travelodge 820 E Busch Blvd. *TF:* 800-578-7878	Tampa	FL	33612	813-933-4011	915-0816
Wyndham Harbour Island Hotel 725 S Harbour Island Blvd *TF:* 800-996-3426	Tampa	FL	33602	813-229-5000	229-5322
Wyndham West Shore 4860 W Kennedy Blvd *TF:* 800-966-3426	Tampa	FL	33609	813-286-4400	286-4053

— Restaurants —

	City	State	ZIP	Phone
Armani's (Italian) 6200 Courtney Campbell Cswy	Tampa	FL	33607	813-281-9165
Backstage Restaurant (Steak/Seafood) 111 W Fortune St.	Tampa	FL	33602	813-223-1351
Bay Cafe (Continental) 555 N Westshore Blvd	Tampa	FL	33609	813-875-1555
Bella's Italian Cafe (Italian) 1413 S Howard Ave	Tampa	FL	33603	813-254-3355
Bern's Steak House (Steak) 1208 S Howard Ave	Tampa	FL	33606	813-251-2421
Cactus Club (Southwest) 1601 Snow Ave	Tampa	FL	33606	813-251-4089
Cafe Creole (Cajun/Creole) 1330 E 9th Ave.	Tampa	FL	33605	813-247-6283
Cafe de Siam (Thai) 11242 W Hillsborough Ave	Tampa	FL	33635	813-855-1108
Caffe Firenze (Italian) 719 N Franklin St.	Tampa	FL	33602	813-282-9200
Camberley's Restaurant (American) 10221 Princess Palm Ave	Tampa	FL	33610	813-623-6363
Carmine's Restaurant (Spanish/Italian) 1802 7th Ave	Tampa	FL	33602	813-248-3834
Castaways The (Steak/Seafood) 7720 Courtney Campbell Cswy	Tampa	FL	33607	813-281-0770
City Center Cafe (Continental) 211 N Tampa St.	Tampa	FL	33602	813-225-1234
CK's Revolving Restaurant (Continental) Tampa International Airport	Tampa	FL	33607	813-879-5151
Colonnade Restaurant The (Steak/Seafood) 3401 Bayshore Blvd	Tampa	FL	33629	813-839-7558
Columbia Restaurant (Spanish) 2117 E 7th Ave	Ybor City	FL	33605	813-248-4961
Courtyard Cafe (Italian) 4860 W Kennedy Blvd	Tampa	FL	33609	813-286-4400
Crawdaddy's (Steak/Seafood) 2500 Rocky Point Dr	Tampa	FL	33607	813-281-0407
Creviche (Spanish) 2109 Bayshore Blvd	Tampa	FL	33629	813-250-0203
Cypress Landing (Steak/Seafood) 7401 E Hillsborough Ave	Tampa	FL	33610	813-626-0999
Cypress Room (Continental) 5700 Saddlebrook Way	Wesley Chapel	FL	33543	813-973-1111
Donatello (Italian) 232 N Dale Mabry Hwy	Tampa	FL	33609	813-875-6660
Four Green Fields (Irish) 205 W Platt St.	Tampa	FL	33602	813-254-4444
Galerie Restaurant (Continental) 3050 N Rocky Point Dr	Tampa	FL	33607	813-888-8800
Green Iguana Bar & Grill (American) 1708 E 7th Ave	Tampa	FL	33605	813-248-9555
Harbour View (American) 725 S Harbour Island Blvd	Tampa	FL	33602	813-229-5000

Tampa — Restaurants (Cont'd)

				Phone
Hemingway's (Continental) 2225 N Lois Ave	Tampa	FL	33607	813-877-6688
Ho Ho Chinois Restaurant (Chinese) 720 S Howard Ave	Tampa	FL	33606	813-254-9557
Latams at the Centro (Mediterranean) 1913 Nebraska Ave	Tampa	FL	33602	813-223-7338
Lauro Ristorante Italiano (Italian) 3915 Henderson Blvd	Tampa	FL	33629	813-281-2100
Le Bordeaux (French) 1502 S Howard Ave	Tampa	FL	33606	813-254-4387
Lobster Pot (Seafood) 17814 Gulf Blvd	Redington Shores	FL	33708	727-391-8592
Michael's On East (Continental) 1212 East Ave S	Sarasota	FL	34239	941-366-0007
Miguel's Mexican Cafe (Mexican) 3035 W Kennedy Blvd	Tampa	FL	33609	813-876-2587
Mise-En-Place (New American) 442 W Kennedy Blvd	Tampa	FL	33606	813-254-5373
Oystercatchers (Seafood) 6200 W Courtney Campbell Cswy	Tampa	FL	33607	813-281-9116
Petey Brown's Restaurant (Continental) 6200 W Courtney Campbell Cswy	Tampa	FL	33607	813-874-1234
Rio Bravo Cantina (Mexican) 1102 N Dale Mabry Hwy	Tampa	FL	33607	813-877-4211
Rumpelmayer's (German) 4812 E Busch Blvd	Tampa	FL	33617	813-989-9563
Seafood Shack Restaurant (Steak/Seafood) 4110 127th St W	Cortez	FL	34215	941-794-1235
Shula's Steak House (Steak/Seafood) 4860 W Kennedy Blvd	Tampa	FL	33609	813-286-4366
Tampa Bay Brewing Co (American) 1812 N 15th St	Tampa	FL	33605	813-247-1422
Tropics Steak & Seafood (Steak/Seafood) 611 Destiny Dr	Ruskin	FL	33570	813-645-8119
Tuscan Oven (Italian) 808 S Howard Ave	Tampa	FL	33606	813-251-0619
Valencia Gardens (Spanish) 811 W Kennedy Blvd	Tampa	FL	33606	813-253-3773
Wine Cellar Restaurant (Continental) 17307 Gulf Blvd *Web:* www.thewinecellar.com	Redington Beach	FL	33708	727-393-3491

— Goods and Services —

SHOPPING

				Phone	Fax
Brandon Town Center 459 Brandon Town Center	Brandon	FL	33511	813-661-6255	
Countryside Mall 27001 US 19 N	Clearwater	FL	33761	727-796-1079	791-8470
Old Hyde Park Village 1507 W Swann Ave	Tampa	FL	33606	813-251-3500	251-4158
Tampa Bay Center 3302 W Dr ML King Blvd	Tampa	FL	33607	813-879-6070	871-5146
University Mall 2200 E Fowler Ave	Tampa	FL	33612	813-971-3465	971-0923
West Shore Plaza 250 West Shore Plaza *Web:* www.westshoreplaza.com	Tampa	FL	33609	813-286-0790	289-1250
Ybor Square 1901 N 13th St	Tampa	FL	33605	813-247-4497	248-8938

BANKS

				Phone	Fax
AmSouth Bank 100 N Tampa St *TF Cust Svc:* 800-267-6884*	Tampa	FL	33602	813-226-1100	226-1101
Bank of Tampa 4400 N Armenia Ave	Tampa	FL	33603	813-872-1200	875-5092
Central Bank of Tampa 2307 W Kennedy Blvd	Tampa	FL	33609	813-253-3302	253-8826
Colonial Bank 400 N Tampa St Suite 130	Tampa	FL	33602	813-223-2832	229-3074
First Union National Bank 100 S Ashley St	Tampa	FL	33602	813-276-6000	276-6515
NationsBank 101 E Kennedy Blvd **Fax Area Code:* 813	Tampa	FL	33602	800-299-2265	225-8528*
SunTrust Bank of Tampa Bay 401 E Jackson St	Tampa	FL	33602	813-224-2121	224-2541

BUSINESS SERVICES

	Phone		Phone
Corporate Courier	813-837-9198	**Kelly Services**	813-289-9452
Corporate Express Delivery Systems	813-243-1200	**Kinko's**	813-988-3950
Crosstown Couriers	813-286-3085	**Manpower Temporary Services**	727-541-5581
Express-It Messenger Service	813-968-5757	**Office Specialist**	813-875-1050
Federal Express	800-238-5355	**Post Office**	800-275-8777
		UPS	800-742-5877

— Media —

PUBLICATIONS

				Phone	Fax
Business Journal The 4350 W Cypress St Suite 400 *Web:* www.amcity.com/tampabay	Tampa	FL	33607	813-873-8225	876-1827
Carrollwood News 5501 W Waters Ave Suite 404 **Fax:* News Rm	Tampa	FL	33634	813-249-5603	249-5316*
Community Connections 3210 E 7th Ave **Fax:* News Rm	Tampa	FL	33605	813-248-3921	247-5357*
Tampa Tribune‡ 202 S Parker St *TF:* 800-282-5588 ■ *Web:* www.tampatrib.com ■ *E-mail:* tribletters@tampatrib.com	Tampa	FL	33606	813-259-7711	259-7676
Town 'n Country News 5501 W Waters Ave Suite 404 **Fax:* News Rm	Tampa	FL	33634	813-249-5603	249-5316*

‡*Daily newspapers*

TELEVISION

				Phone	Fax
WBHS-TV Ch 50 (Ind) 12425 28th St N Suite 301	Saint Petersburg	FL	33716	727-573-5550	571-1931
WCLF-TV Ch 22 (Ind) 1922 142nd Ave N	Largo	FL	33771	727-535-5622	
WEDU-TV Ch 3 (PBS) 1300 N Blvd *Web:* www.wedu.org ■ *E-mail:* outreach@wedu.pbs.org	Tampa	FL	33607	813-254-9338	253-0826
WFLA-TV Ch 8 (NBC) 905 E Jackson St *Web:* www.wfla.com	Tampa	FL	33602	813-228-8888	225-2770
WFTS-TV Ch 28 (ABC) 4045 N Himes Ave *Web:* www.wfts.com ■ *E-mail:* 28feedback@wfts.com	Tampa	FL	33607	813-354-2800	870-2828
WTOG-TV Ch 44 (UPN) 365 105th Terr NE	Saint Petersburg	FL	33716	727-576-4444	577-1806
WTSP-TV Ch 10 (CBS) 11450 Gandy Blvd N *Web:* www.wtsp.com ■ *E-mail:* news@channel10.com	Saint Petersburg	FL	33702	727-577-1010	576-6924
WTTA-TV Ch 38 (Ind) 5510 W Gray St Suite 38	Tampa	FL	33609	813-289-3838	289-0000
WTVT-TV Ch 13 (Fox) 3213 W Kennedy Blvd *Web:* www.wtvt.com ■ *E-mail:* 13@wtvt.com	Tampa	FL	33609	813-876-1313	871-3135
WUSF-TV Ch 16 (PBS) 4202 Fowler Ave *TF:* 800-654-3703 ■ *Web:* www.wusftv.usf.edu	Tampa	FL	33620	813-974-4000	974-4806
WWWB-TV Ch 32 (WB) 7201 E Hillsborough Ave **Fax:* Sales ■ *Web:* www.wb32.com ■ *E-mail:* mail@wb32.com	Tampa	FL	33610	813-626-3232	622-9032*
WXPX-TV Ch 66 (PAX) 11300 4th St N Suite 180 *Web:* www.pax.net/WXPX	Saint Petersburg	FL	33716	727-578-0066	570-8206

RADIO

				Phone	Fax
KISS-FM 100.7 MHz (AC) 4002-A Gandy Blvd **Fax Area Code:* 813	Tampa	FL	33611	727-446-9352	832-6235*
WDAE-AM 1250 kHz (Sports) 4002 Gandy Blvd	Tampa	FL	33611	813-839-9393	831-6397
WDUV-FM 103.5 MHz (B/EZ) 4002-A Gandy Blvd *TF:* 800-932-6100	Tampa	FL	33611	813-839-9393	837-0300
WFJO-FM 101.5 MHz (Oldies) 11300 4th St N Suite 318	Saint Petersburg	FL	33716	727-577-7131	578-2477
WFLA-AM 970 kHz (N/T) 4002-A Gandy Blvd *Web:* www.970wfla.com ■ *E-mail:* wfla97b@prodigy.com	Tampa	FL	33611	813-839-9393	831-3299
WFLZ-FM 93.3 MHz (CHR) 4002-A Gandy Blvd *Web:* www.933flz.com ■ *E-mail:* bj933flz@aol.com	Tampa	FL	33611	813-839-9393	831-3299
WGUL-AM 860 kHz (Nost) 35048 US Hwy 19 The Fountains	Palm Harbor	FL	34684	727-849-2285	781-4375
WGUL-FM 96.1 MHz (Nost) 35048 US Hwy 19 The Fountains	Palm Harbor	FL	34684	727-849-2285	781-4375
WMNF-FM 88.5 MHz (NPR) 1210 E ML King Blvd *Web:* www.wmnf.org ■ *E-mail:* wmnf@wmnf.org	Tampa	FL	33603	813-238-8001	238-1802
WRBQ-AM 1380 kHz (Urban) 5510 W Gray St Suite 130	Tampa	FL	33609	813-287-1047	289-2851
WRBQ-FM 104.7 MHz (Ctry) 5510 W Gray St Suite 130 *Web:* www.wrbq.com ■ *E-mail:* qalm19b@prodigy.com	Tampa	FL	33609	813-287-1047	289-2851
WSSR-FM 95.7 MHz (AC) 5510 Gray St Suite 130	Tampa	FL	33609	813-961-9600	261-5957
WSUN-FM 97.1 MHz (Oldies) 877 Executive Ctr Dr W Suite 300	Saint Petersburg	FL	33702	727-841-9797	576-8098
WTBT-FM 105.5 MHz (CR) 13577 Feather Sound Dr Suite 550 *Web:* thunder1055.com ■ *E-mail:* thunder@1055.com	Clearwater	FL	34622	727-572-9808	572-0935
WTMP-AM 1150 kHz (Urban) 5207 Washington Blvd *Web:* www.wtmp-am1150.com ■ *E-mail:* wtmpjams@gte.net	Tampa	FL	33619	813-620-1300	628-0713
WUSF-FM 89.7 MHz (NPR) 4202 E Fowler Ave University of South Florida	Tampa	FL	33620	813-974-4890	974-5016
WXTB-FM 97.9 MHz (Rock) 13577 Feather Sound Dr Suite 550	Clearwater	FL	34622	727-572-9808	572-0935
WZTM-AM 820 kHz (Sports) 11300 4th St N Suite 318	Saint Petersburg	FL	33716	727-577-7131	578-2477

Tampa (Cont'd)

— Colleges/Universities —

				Phone	Fax
Florida College 119 N Glen Arven Ave	Temple Terrace	FL	33617	813-988-5131	899-6772
TF: 800-326-7655 ■ *Web:* www.flcoll.edu					
Hillsborough Community College Dale Mabry Campus PO Box 30030	Tampa	FL	33630	813-253-7000	253-7400
Web: www.hcc.cc.fl.us					
International Academy of Design 5225 Memorial Hwy	Tampa	FL	33634	813-881-0007	881-0008
TF: 800-222-3369 ■ *Web:* www.academy.edu					
ITT Technical Institute 4809 Memorial Hwy	Tampa	FL	33634	813-885-2244	888-6078
TF: 800-825-2831 ■ *Web:* www.itt-tech.edu					
Saint Petersburg Junior College 6605 5th Ave N	Saint Petersburg	FL	33710	727-341-3239	341-4792
Web: www.spjc.cc.fl.us					
Tampa Technical Institute 2410 E Bush Blvd	Tampa	FL	33612	813-935-5700	935-7415
TF: 800-992-4850					
University of South Florida Tampa Campus 4202 E Fowler Ave	Tampa	FL	33620	813-974-2011	974-9689
Web: www.usf.edu ■ *E-mail:* www@usf.edu					
University of Tampa 401 W Kennedy Blvd	Tampa	FL	33606	813-253-3333	258-7398
TF: 800-733-4773 ■ *Web:* www.utampa.edu					

— Hospitals —

				Phone	Fax
All Children's Hospital 801 6th St S	Saint Petersburg	FL	33701	727-898-7451	892-8500
TF: 800-456-4543 ■ *Web:* www.allkids.org					
Bayfront Medical Center 701 6th St S	Saint Petersburg	FL	33701	727-823-1234	893-6930
Web: www.bayfront.org					
Columbia Clearwater Community Hospital 1521 E Druid Rd	Clearwater	FL	33756	727-447-4571	444-4914
Edward White Hospital 2323 9th Ave N	Saint Petersburg	FL	33713	727-323-1111	328-6135
James A Haley Veterans Hospital 13000 Bruce B Downs Blvd	Tampa	FL	33612	813-972-2000	972-7680
Mease Hospital Dunedin 601 Main St	Dunedin	FL	34698	727-733-1111	734-6977
Web: www.mpmhealth.com/abou2.B.stm					
Memorial Hospital of Tampa 2901 Swann Ave	Tampa	FL	33609	813-873-6400	874-8685
Morton Plant Hospital 323 Jeffords St	Clearwater	FL	33756	727-462-7000	461-8860*
**Fax:* Admitting ■ *Web:* www.mpmhealth.com					
Palms of Pasadena Hospital 1501 Pasadena Ave S	Saint Petersburg	FL	33707	727-381-1000	341-7690
Web: www.tenethealth.com/PalmsPasadena					
Saint Anthony's Hospital 1200 7th Ave N	Saint Petersburg	FL	33705	727-825-1100	825-1327*
**Fax:* Admitting					
Saint Joseph's Hospital 3001 W Dr ML King Blvd	Tampa	FL	33607	813-870-4000	870-4946*
**Fax:* Admitting					
Shriners Hospitals for Children Tampa Unit 12502 N Pine Dr	Tampa	FL	33612	813-972-2250	978-9442
TF: 888-665-5437 ■ *Web:* www.shrinershq.org/Hospitals/Directry/tampa.html					
South Florida Baptist Hospital 301 N Alexander St	Plant City	FL	33566	813-757-1200	757-8301
Sun Coast Hospital 2025 Indian Rocks Rd	Largo	FL	33774	727-581-9474	587-7604*
**Fax:* Admitting					
Tampa General Hospital Davis Islands	Tampa	FL	33606	813-251-7551	251-7008*
**Fax:* Admitting					
Town & Country Hospital 6001 Webb Rd	Tampa	FL	33615	813-885-6666	887-5112
University Community Hospital 3100 E Fletcher Ave	Tampa	FL	33613	813-971-6000	979-7313
University Community Hospital Carrollwood 7171 N Dale Mabry Hwy	Tampa	FL	33614	813-932-2222	558-8049*
**Fax:* Admitting					

— Attractions —

				Phone	Fax
Adventure Island 4500 Bougainvillea Ave	Tampa	FL	33617	813-987-5600	987-5654
Big Top Flea Market 9250 E Fowler Ave	Thonotosassa	FL	33592	813-986-4004	986-6296
Bobby's Indian Village 5221 N Orient Rd	Tampa	FL	33610	813-620-3077	620-1767
Busch Gardens 3605 Bougainvillea Ave	Tampa	FL	33674	813-987-5082	987-5374*
**Fax:* Hum Res ■ *Web:* www.buschgardens.com/buschgardens/bg_tampa/frame.html					
Caladesi Island State Park 3 Causeway Blvd	Dunedin	FL	34698	727-469-5918	
Celebration Station Entertainment Complex 10230 Palm River Rd	Tampa	FL	33619	813-661-4557	661-2023
Children's Museum of Tampa 7550 North Blvd	Tampa	FL	33604	813-935-8441	915-0063
Falk Theatre 428 W Kennedy Blvd	Tampa	FL	33606	813-253-6238	258-7211
Florida Aquarium 701 Channelside Dr	Tampa	FL	33602	813-273-4000	224-9583
TF: 800-353-4741 ■ *Web:* www2.sptimes.com/Aquarium/Default.html					
Florida Orchestra PO Box 23647	Tampa	FL	33623	813-286-1170	286-2316
TF: 800-662-7286 ■ *Web:* www.fl-orchestra.org ■ *E-mail:* florida_orchestra@juno.com					
Lettuce Lake Park 6920 E Fletcher Ave	Tampa	FL	33637	813-987-6204	
Lowry Park Zoo 7530 North Blvd	Tampa	FL	33604	813-935-8552	935-9486
Web: www.the-solution.com/zoo					
MOSIMAX-IMAX Dome Theater 4801 E Fowler Ave	Tampa	FL	33617	813-987-6300	987-6310
Web: www.mosi.org/mosimax.htm ■ *E-mail:* tjcouch@mosi.org					
Museum of Science & Industry 4801 E Fowler Ave	Tampa	FL	33617	813-987-6300	987-6310
TF: 800-995-6674 ■ *Web:* www.mosi.org					
Old Hyde Park Village 1507 W Swann Ave	Tampa	FL	33606	813-251-3500	251-4158
Plant Henry B Museum 401 W Kennedy Blvd	Tampa	FL	33606	813-254-1891	258-7272
Web: www.plantmuseum.com					
Seminole Indian Casino 5223 N Orient Rd	Tampa	FL	33610	813-621-1302	623-6862
TF: 800-282-7016					
Suncoast Seabird Sanctuary 18328 Gulf Blvd	Indian Shores	FL	33785	727-391-6211	399-2923
Tampa Bay History Center 225 S Franklin St	Tampa	FL	33602	813-228-0097	223-7021
Web: www2.sptimes.com/Holocaust_museum/default.html					
Tampa Bay Performing Arts Center 1010 N WC MacInnes Pl	Tampa	FL	33602	813-222-1000	222-1057
TF: 800-955-1045 ■ *Web:* www.tampacenter.com ■ *E-mail:* thecenter@tampacenter.com					
Tampa Museum of Art 600 N Ashley Dr	Tampa	FL	33602	813-274-8130	274-8732
Web: www.ci.tampa.fl.us/museum ■ *E-mail:* museum@ci.tampa.fl.us					
Tampa Rico Cigar Co 1901 N 13th St	Tampa	FL	33605	813-247-6738	247-2422
Tampa Theater 711 N Franklin St	Tampa	FL	33602	813-274-8286	274-8978
Web: www.tampabayonline.com/tour/tpatheat.htm					
USF Contemporary Art Museum 4202 E Fowler Ave Bldg CAM101	Tampa	FL	33620	813-974-2849	974-5130
Web: www.arts.usf.edu/museum/					
Wild Life on Easy Street 12802 Easy St	Tampa	FL	33625	813-920-4130	920-5924
Ybor City 2 miles E of downtown	Tampa	FL	33605		
Ybor City State Museum 1818 9th Ave	Tampa	FL	33605	813-247-6323	
Ybor Market 1632 E 7th Ave	Tampa	FL	33605	813-231-2720	237-6874

SPORTS TEAMS & FACILITIES

				Phone	Fax
Expo Hall 4800 US Hwy 301 N	Tampa	FL	33610	813-621-7821	740-3505
Ice Palace 401 Channelside Dr	Tampa	FL	33602	813-223-6100	223-0095
Web: www.tampabaylightning.com/guide.html					
New York Yankees Spring Training (baseball) 1 Steinbrenner Dr Legends Field	Tampa	FL	33614	813-875-7753	673-3199
Web: www.yankees.com ■ *E-mail:* yankees@yankees.com					
Raymond James Stadium 4201 N Dale Mabry Hwy	Tampa	FL	33607	813-350-6500	673-4312
Web: www.raymondjames.com/stadium					
Tampa Bay Buccaneers 4201 N Dale Mabry Hwy Raymond James Stadium	Tampa	FL	33607	813-673-4300	
Tampa Bay Devil Rays 1 Tropicana Dr	Saint Petersburg	FL	33705	727-825-3137	825-3111
Web: www.devilray.com/					
Tampa Bay Downs Inc PO Box 2007	Oldsmar	FL	34677	813-855-4401	854-3539
TF: 800-200-4434					
Tampa Bay Lightning 401 Channelside Dr Ice Palace	Tampa	FL	33602	813-229-8800	229-3350
Tampa Bay Mutiny (soccer) 4042 N Himes Ave	Tampa	FL	33607	813-288-0096	353-3837
Web: www.tampabaymutiny.com ■ *E-mail:* mlsmutiny@aol.com					
Tampa Bay Storm (football) 401 Channelside Dr Ice Palace	Tampa	FL	33602	813-276-7300	276-7301
Web: tampastorm.com					
Tampa Greyhound Track 8300 N Nebraska Ave	Tampa	FL	33604	813-932-4313	932-5048
Tampa Yankees (baseball) 1 Steinbrenner Dr Legends Field	Tampa	FL	33614	813-879-2244	673-3199
Web: www.yankees.com					

— Events —

	Phone
All Makes Auto Swap Meet (early April)	419-478-5292

Tampa — Events (Cont'd)

	Phone
Brandon Balloon Classic (late April)	813-689-1221
Celebrate America (early July)	727-562-4800
Country Folk Art Show (early January & mid-October)	800-345-3247
Fiesta Day (mid-February)	813-248-3712
First Night Tampa (late December)	813-223-1111
Florida State Fair (February)	813-621-7821
Florida Strawberry Festival (mid-March)	813-752-9194
Freedom Fest (early July)	813-223-1111
Gasparilla Distance Classic (mid-February)	813-229-7866
Gasparilla Festival of the Arts (early March)	813-876-1747
Gasparilla Pirate Fest (early February)	813-223-1111
Greek Festival (mid-September)	419-243-9189
GTE Classic (mid-February)	813-948-4653
Guavaweeen (late October)	813-248-3712
Hillsborough County Fair (late October-early November)	813-223-1111
Illuminated Night Parade (mid-February)	813-248-3712
Krewe of the Knights of Sant' Yago Illuminated Night Parade (mid-February)	813-248-3712
Old Hyde Park Village Art Festival (early October & late February)	813-251-3500
Old Hyde Park Village Live Music Series (May-October)	813-251-3500
Outback Bowl (January 1)	813-874-2695
President's Cup Regatta (early March)	813-253-6241
Ruskin Seafood & Arts Festival (early November)	813-645-3808
Sun 'n Fun EAA Fly-In (mid-April)	863-644-2431
Tampa Recreation's International Festival (mid-November)	813-931-2106
Taste of Florida (early October)	813-259-7376
Winter Equestrian Festival (late January-early April)	813-623-5801

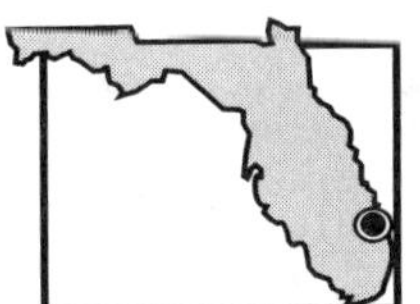

West Palm Beach

Henry Flagler arrived in South Florida in 1893 intent on making Palm Beach the most "highfalutin" resort in the world. Inspired by Flagler's dream, the City of West Palm Beach was incorporated in 1894. A developing tourist industry and rapid economic expansion led West Palm Beach to become the largest city in Palm Beach County, and the city is now home to the county government, international airport, and a thriving business district. Located in the heart of downtown West Palm Beach and marking the entrance to the city is the newly constructed Raymond F. Kravis Center for the Performing Arts, which offers both concerts and Broadway productions. A number of regional performing groups, including the Palm Beach Opera, Palm Beach Pops, and the Florida Philharmonic Orchestra, make their home at the Kravis Center. West Palm Beach is also home to the Norton Gallery of Art; Dreher Park Zoo, a 22-acre tropical zoological garden with 128 species and more than 500 animals; Palm Beach Kennel Club, a greyhound track established in 1932; and South Florida Science Museum.

Population	76,308	**Longitude**	80-07-34 W
Area (Land)	49.3 sq mi	**County**	Palm Beach
Area (Water)	3.0 sq mi	**Time Zone**	EST
Elevation	21 ft	**Area Code/s**	561
Latitude	26-44-51 N		

— Average Temperatures and Precipitation —

TEMPERATURES

	Jan	Feb	Mar	Apr	May	Jun	Jul	Aug	Sep	Oct	Nov	Dec
High	75	76	79	82	86	88	90	90	89	85	80	76
Low	56	57	61	65	70	73	75	75	75	71	65	59

PRECIPITATION

	Jan	Feb	Mar	Apr	May	Jun	Jul	Aug	Sep	Oct	Nov	Dec
Inches	2.8	2.7	3.7	2.9	6.1	8.1	6.1	6.0	8.5	6.6	4.7	2.5

— Important Phone Numbers —

	Phone		Phone
AAA	800-926-4222	**Medical Referral**	800-466-3726
Artsline	800-882-2787	**Poison Control Center**	800-282-3171
Emergency	911	**Time/Temp**	561-832-3801
HotelDocs	800-468-3537		

— Information Sources —

				Phone	Fax
Better Business Bureau Serving the Palm Beach Area 580 Village Blvd Suite 340	West Palm Beach	FL	33409	561-686-2200	686-2775
Web: www.westpalm.bbb.org					
Chamber of Commerce of the Palm Beaches 401 N Flagler Dr	West Palm Beach	FL	33401	561-833-3711	833-5582
Web: palmbeaches.com/					
Palm Beach County PO Box 1989	West Palm Beach	FL	33401	561-355-2030	355-3990
Web: www.co.palm-beach.fl.us					
Palm Beach County Convention & Visitors Bureau 1555 Palm Beach Lakes Blvd Suite 204	West Palm Beach	FL	33401	561-471-3995	471-3990
Web: www.palmbeachfl.com					
Palm Beach County Public Library System 3650 Summit Blvd	West Palm Beach	FL	33406	561-233-2600	233-2622
Web: www.seflin.org/pbcls/ ■ *E-mail:* pbcls@pb.seflin.org					
West Palm Beach City Hall 200 2nd St	West Palm Beach	FL	33401	561-659-8000	659-8039
West Palm Beach Housing & Community Development Dept PO Box 3366	West Palm Beach	FL	33402	561-835-7060	835-7012
West Palm Beach Mayor PO Box 3366	West Palm Beach	FL	33402	561-659-8025	659-8066

On-Line Resources

About.com Guide to West Palm Beach	westpalmbeach.about.com/local/southeastus/westpalmbeach
Anthill City Guide West Palm Beach	www.anthill.com/city.asp?city=westpalmbeach
Area Guide West Palm Beach	westpalmbeach.areaguides.net
Boca Raton	bocaraton.com/
City Knowledge West Palm Beach	www.cityknowledge.com/fl_west_palm_beach.htm
Come to the Sun Guide to South Florida	www.cometothesun.com
DigitalCity South Florida	home.digitalcity.com/southflorida
DiningGuide Palm Beaches	diningguide.net/pbi/
HotelGuide Palm Beaches	hotelguide.net/pbi/
Insiders' Guide to Boca Raton & the Palm Beaches	www.insiders.com/boca
InSouthFlorida.com	www.insouthflorida.com
LDS iAmerica Boca Raton	boca-raton.iamerica.net
MetroGuide Palm Beaches	metroguide.net/palm_beaches/
NITC Travelbase City Guide Palm Beaches	www.travelbase.com/auto/guides/palm_beaches-area-fl.html
Palm Beach Interactive	www.gopbi.com
West Palm Beach Florida	westpalmbeach.com
West Palm Beach Gay & Lesbian Guide	www.southfloridafun.com/westpalmbeach/index.shtml

— Transportation Services —

AIRPORTS

	Phone
■ **Palm Beach International Airport (PBI)**	
3 miles W of downtown (approx 10 minutes)	561-471-7412

Airport Transportation

	Phone
Airport Service $10 fare to downtown	561-684-9900
Carey Limousine $50-53 fare to downtown	561-471-5466
Palm Beach Transportation Taxi $10 fare to downtown	561-684-9900
Yellow Cab $4-6 fare to downtown	561-689-2222

West Palm Beach (Cont'd)

Commercial Airlines

	Phone		Phone
Air Canada	800-776-3000	**Delta Express**	800-325-5205
AirTran	800-247-8726	**Finnair**	800-950-5000
America West	800-235-9292	**Gulfstream International Airlines**	800-525-0280
American	800-433-7300	**Kiwi**	800-538-5494
American Eagle	800-433-7300	**Lufthansa**	800-645-3880
American Trans Air	800-225-2995	**Midway**	800-446-4392
Bahamasair	800-222-4262	**Northwest**	800-225-2525
British Airways	800-247-9297	**Spirit**	800-772-7117
Canadian Air	800-426-7000	**SwissAir**	800-221-4750
Comair	800-354-9822	**TWA**	800-221-2000
Continental	800-525-0280	**United**	800-241-6522
Delta	800-221-1212	**US Airways**	800-428-4322

Charter Airlines

	Phone		Phone
Advanced Airways	800-634-2114	**Flight Services Group Inc**	800-380-4009
Aero Taxi	800-362-4401	**Hutt Aviation Inc**	800-488-8247
Alliance Executive Charter Services	800-232-5387	**Jet Aviation Business Jets Inc**	800-736-8538
Atlantic Aviation Charter	800-252-5387	**Jet Aviation Travel Services**	800-422-7242
Chandelle Aviation Corp Ltd	561-683-0830	**RoyalAir Inc**	800-944-3030
Concierge Air Inc	561-616-0809	**Sapphire Aviation Inc**	561-687-7967
Executive Airlink	800-373-0763	**Summit Aviation**	561-683-7334
Executive Jet Management	877-356-5387	**Telford Aviation Inc**	800-639-4809

CAR RENTALS

	Phone		Phone
Admiral	561-586-2277	**Dollar**	561-686-3300
Alamo	561-684-6806	**Enterprise**	561-689-8585
Ambassador	561-533-5005	**Hertz**	561-686-4300
Avis	561-233-6400	**National**	561-233-7368
Budget	561-683-2400	**Thrifty**	561-686-7900
CarTemps USA	561-471-9444		

LIMO/TAXI

	Phone		Phone
Americoach Limousine	561-744-9984	**Limo Limo**	561-687-5466
Black Tie Limo	561-793-2877	**Palm Beach Transportation**	561-689-4222
Carey Limousine	561-471-5466	**Park Limousine**	561-832-2222
Classy Coach Limousine	561-688-1111	**Yellow Cab**	561-689-2222
Everglades Taxi & Limo	561-655-6551		

MASS TRANSIT

	Phone
Palm Tran Bus Service $1 Base fare	561-233-4287
Tri-Rail fare varies with destination	800-874-7245

RAIL/BUS

				Phone
Amtrak 201 S Tamarind Ave *TF:* 800-872-7245	West Palm Beach	FL	33401	561-832-6169
Greyhound Bus Station 205 S Tamarind Ave *TF:* 800-231-2222	West Palm Beach	FL	33401	561-833-8534

— Accommodations —

HOTEL RESERVATION SERVICES

	Phone	Fax
Accommodations USA	407-931-0003	931-1003
Hotel Reservations Network Inc *TF Sales:* 800-964-6835 ■ *Web:* www.hoteldiscount.com	214-361-7311	361-7299

HOTELS, MOTELS, RESORTS

				Phone	Fax
Best Western Palm Beach Lakes 1800 Palm Beach Lakes Blvd *TF:* 800-331-9569	West Palm Beach	FL	33401	561-683-8810	478-2580
Boca Raton Marriott 5150 Town Center Cir	Boca Raton	FL	33486	561-392-4600	395-8258
Boca Raton Resort & Club 501 E Camino Real *TF:* 800-327-0101 ■ *Web:* www.bocaresort.com ■ *E-mail:* reservations@bocaresort.com	Boca Raton	FL	33431	561-447-3000	447-3183
Breakers The 1 S County Rd *TF:* 800-833-3141 ■ *Web:* www.thebreakers.com	Palm Beach	FL	33480	561-659-8404	659-8403
Club Med Sandpiper 3500 Morningside Blvd SE *TF:* 800-258-2633 ■ *Web:* www.clubmed.com/ID-NrCtpdFDAckAAECiA58/Villages/	Port Saint Lucie	FL	34952	561-335-4400	398-5101
Colony Hotel 155 Hammon Ave *TF:* 800-521-5525	Palm Beach	FL	33480	561-655-5430	832-7318
Colony Hotel 525 E Atlantic Ave *TF:* 800-552-2363	Delray Beach	FL	33483	561-276-4123	276-0123
Comfort Inn Palm Beach Lakes 1901 Palm Beach Lakes Blvd *TF:* 800-228-5150	West Palm Beach	FL	33409	561-689-6100	686-6177
Courtyard by Marriott 600 Northpoint Pkwy *Web:* courtyard.com/PBICH	West Palm Beach	FL	33407	561-640-9000	471-0122
Courtyard by Marriott 2000 NW Executive Ctr *TF:* 800-321-2211 ■ *Web:* courtyard.com/PBIBC	Boca Raton	FL	33431	561-241-7070	241-7080
Crowne Plaza Hotel 1601 Belvedere Rd *TF:* 800-227-6963	West Palm Beach	FL	33406	561-689-6400	683-7150
Days Inn 6255 Okeechobee Blvd *TF:* 800-286-5801	West Palm Beach	FL	33417	561-686-6000	687-0415
Days Inn 2300 W 45th St *TF:* 800-329-7466	West Palm Beach	FL	33407	561-689-0450	686-7439
Days Inn 6651 Darter Ct *TF:* 800-329-7466	Fort Pierce	FL	34945	561-466-4066	468-3260
Delray Beach Marriott 10 N Ocean Ave *TF:* 800-228-9290	Delray Beach	FL	33483	561-274-3200	274-3202
Doubletree Guest Suites Boca Raton 701 NW 53rd St *TF:* 800-222-8733 ■ *Web:* www.doubletreehotels.com/DoubleT/Hotel21/30/30Main.htm	Boca Raton	FL	33487	561-997-9500	994-3565
Doubletree in the Gardens 4431 PGA Blvd *TF:* 800-222-8733 ■ *Web:* www.doubletreehotels.com/DoubleT/Hotel200/203/203Main.htm	Palm Beach	FL	33410	561-622-2260	624-1043
Embassy Suites Boca Raton 661 NW 53rd St *TF:* 800-362-2779	Boca Raton	FL	33487	561-994-8200	994-9518
Fairfield Inn 5981 Okeechobee Blvd *TF:* 800-228-2800 ■ *Web:* fairfieldinn.com/PBIFI	West Palm Beach	FL	33417	561-697-3388	697-2834
Four Seasons Resort Palm Beach 2800 S Ocean Blvd *TF:* 800-432-2335 ■ *Web:* www.fourseasons.com/locations/PalmBeach	Palm Beach	FL	33480	561-582-2800	547-1374
Hampton Inn 1505 Belvedere Rd *TF:* 800-426-7866	West Palm Beach	FL	33406	561-471-8700	689-7385
Harbor House 124 Marine Way	Delray Beach	FL	33483	561-276-4221	276-4122
Helen Wilkes Hotel 201 N Flagler Dr	West Palm Beach	FL	33401	561-655-8520	655-8520
Hilton Oceanfront Resort 2842 S Ocean Blvd *TF:* 800-433-1718 ■ *Web:* www.hilton.com/hotels/PBIPHHF	Palm Beach	FL	33480	561-586-6542	585-0188
Holiday Inn Airport 1301 Belvedere Rd *TF:* 800-465-4329	West Palm Beach	FL	33405	561-659-3880	655-8886
Holiday Inn Catalina Center 1601 N Congress Ave *TF:* 800-465-4329	Boynton Beach	FL	33426	561-737-4600	734-6523
Holiday Inn Express 480 W Boynton Beach Blvd	Boynton Beach	FL	33435	561-734-9100	738-7193
Indian River Plantation Beach Resort 555 NE Ocean Blvd *TF:* 800-775-5936	Stuart	FL	34996	561-225-3700	225-0003
Jupiter Beach Resort 5 N Hwy A1A *TF:* 800-228-8810	Jupiter	FL	33477	561-746-2511	744-1741
Knights Inn 2200 45th St *TF:* 800-843-5644	West Palm Beach	FL	33407	561-478-1554	478-7813
Palm Beach Gardens Marriott 4000 RCA Blvd *TF:* 800-228-9290	Palm Beach Gardens	FL	33410	561-622-8888	622-0052
Palm Beach Resort & Club 3031 S Ocean Blvd *TF:* 800-215-7256	Palm Beach	FL	33480	561-586-8898	533-6664
PGA National Resort & Spa 400 Ave of Champions *TF:* 800-633-9150 ■ *Web:* www.pga-resorts.com	Palm Beach Gardens	FL	33418	561-627-2000	622-0261
Radisson Bridge Hotel 999 E Camino Real *TF:* 800-333-3333	Boca Raton	FL	33432	561-368-9500	362-0492

West Palm Beach — Hotels, Motels, Resorts (Cont'd)

				Phone	Fax
Radisson Suite Inn 1808 Australian Ave S TF: 800-333-3333	West Palm Beach	FL	33409	561-689-6888	683-5783
Red Carpet Inn 8605 SE Federal Hwy TF: 800-251-1962	Hobe Sound	FL	33455	561-546-3600	546-3610
Residence Inn Boca Raton 525 NW 77th St Web: www.residenceinn.com/residenceinn/PBIBO	Boca Raton	FL	33487	561-994-3222	994-3339
Ritz-Carlton Palm Beach 100 S Ocean Blvd *Fax: PR ■ TF: 800-241-3333 ■ Web:www.ritzcarlton.com/location/NorthAmerica/PalmBeach/main.htm	Manalapan	FL	33462	561-533-6000	588-4020*
Sheraton Boca Raton 2000 NW 19th St. TF: 800-394-7829	Boca Raton	FL	33431	561-368-5252	750-5437
Sheraton West Palm Beach Hotel 630 Clearwater Pk Rd TF: 800-833-3775 ■ Web: www.pb-sheraton.com ■ E-mail: salesoffice@pb-sheraton.com	West Palm Beach	FL	33401	561-833-1234	833-4689
Spanish River Resort 1111 E Atlantic Ave. TF: 800-543-7946	Delray Beach	FL	33483	561-243-7946	276-9634
Wellesley Inn & Suites 1910 Palm Beach Lakes Blvd TF: 800-444-8888	West Palm Beach	FL	33409	561-689-8540	687-8090

— Restaurants —

				Phone
4 Brothers Uptown Cafe (Italian) 221 Datura Ave	West Palm Beach	FL	33401	561-655-5044
Arezzo (Italian) 400 Avenue of the Champions	Palm Beach Gardens	FL	33418	561-627-2000
Bice (Italian) 313 1/2 Worth Ave	Palm Beach	FL	33480	561-835-1600
Boston's on the Beach (American) 40 S Ocean Blvd	Delray Beach	FL	33483	561-278-3364
Bull English Pub (English) 801 Village Blvd.	West Palm Beach	FL	33409	561-697-2855
Cafe Chardonnay (American) 4533 PGA Blvd	Palm Beach Gardens	FL	33418	561-627-2662
Cafe L'Europe (French) 331 S Country Rd	Palm Beach	FL	33480	561-655-4020
Cafe Protege (New American) 2400 Metrocentre Blvd	West Palm Beach	FL	33407	561-687-2433
Carrabba's Italian Grill (Italian) 2224 Palm Beach Lakes Blvd.	West Palm Beach	FL	33409	561-615-8900
Casablanca Cafe Americain (Continental) 101 N County Rd	Palm Beach	FL	33480	561-655-1115
Chef Reto's Restaurant (International) 41 E Palmetto Park Rd	Boca Raton	FL	33432	561-395-0633
Chez Moustache (French) 1659 Forum Pl	West Palm Beach	FL	33401	561-689-4110
Contented Sole (Seafood) 3815 S Dixie Hwy	West Palm Beach	FL	33405	561-835-0300
Cucina del Arte (Italian) 257 Royal Poinciana Way	Palm Beach	FL	33480	561-655-0770
Galaxy Grille (Mediterranean) 350 S Country Rd.	Palm Beach	FL	33480	561-833-9909
Gatsby's (International) 5970 SW 18th St.	Boca Raton	FL	33433	561-393-3900
Hong Kong Cafe (Chinese) 2100 45th St.	West Palm Beach	FL	33407	561-845-6698
Hong Kong Express (Chinese) 330 Clematis St	West Palm Beach	FL	33401	561-832-2388
Indian Garden Restaurant (Indian) 7504 S Dixie Hwy.	West Palm Beach	FL	33405	561-586-9579
Jerk Island Jamaican Restaurant (Jamaican) 1739 45th St	West Palm Beach	FL	33407	561-881-4444
La Finestra (Italian) 171 E Palmetto Park Rd	Boca Raton	FL	33432	561-392-1838
La Sirena (Italian) 6316 S Dixie Hwy	West Palm Beach	FL	33405	561-585-3128
La Taqueria (Mexican) 419 Clematis St	West Palm Beach	FL	33401	561-655-5450
Maya Azteca (Mexican) 1771 S Congress Ave.	West Palm Beach	FL	33406	561-964-8894
My Martini (Steak) 225 Claremont St	West Palm Beach	FL	33401	561-832-8333
No Anchovies (Italian) 1901 Palm Beach Lakes Blvd	West Palm Beach	FL	33409	561-684-0040
O'Shea's Pub (Irish) 531 Clematis St	West Palm Beach	FL	33401	561-833-3865
Orchids of Siam (Thai) 3027 A-1 Forest Hill Blvd.	West Palm Beach	FL	33406	561-969-2444
Pescatore (Italian) 200 Clematis	West Palm Beach	FL	33401	561-837-6633
Raindancer Steak House (Steak/Seafood) 2300 Palm Beach Lakes Blvd	West Palm Beach	FL	33409	561-684-2810
Rockwell's Restaurant (Continental) 515 N Flagler Dr.	West Palm Beach	FL	33401	561-835-8061
Rosie's Key West Grill (American) 4068 Forest Hill Blvd	West Palm Beach	FL	33406	561-966-0815
Saigon Tokyo (Japanese) 2902 Jog Rd.	West Palm Beach	FL	33467	561-966-2802
Sforza (Italian) 223 Clematis St	West Palm Beach	FL	33401	561-832-8819
Shula's Steak House (Steak) 400 Avenue of the Champions	Palm Beach Gardens	FL	33418	561-627-2000
Singing Bamboo (Chinese) 2845 N Military Trail	West Palm Beach	FL	33409	561-686-9100
Snappers (Seafood) 398 N Congress Ave	Boynton Beach	FL	33435	561-375-8600
Spangles Restaurant (American) 1808 Australian Ave S.	West Palm Beach	FL	33709	561-689-6888
Splendid Blendeds Cafe (International) 432 E Atlantic Ave	Delray Beach	FL	33483	561-265-1035
Taboo (American) 221 Worth Ave	Palm Beach	FL	33480	561-835-3500
Tavern in the Greenery (American) 301 Yamato Rd.	Boca Raton	FL	33441	561-241-9214
Thirty Two East (New American) 32 E Atlantic Ave	Delray Beach	FL	33444	561-276-7868
This Is It Pub (European) 424 24th St	West Palm Beach	FL	33407	561-833-4997

— Goods and Services —

SHOPPING

				Phone	Fax
Atlantic Avenue downtown-betw Swinton Ave & A1A	Delray Beach	FL	33483	561-278-0424	278-0555
Boynton Beach Mall 801 N Congress Ave	Boynton Beach	FL	33426	561-736-7900	736-7907
Farmers Market Mall 1200 S Congress Ave	West Palm Beach	FL	33406	561-965-1500	965-0433
Gardens of the Palm Beaches 3101 PGA Blvd.	Palm Beach Gardens	FL	33410	561-622-2115	694-9380
Mizner Park 407 Plaza Real	Boca Raton	FL	33432	561-362-0606	750-8825
Palm Beach Mall 1801 Palm Beach Lakes Blvd	West Palm Beach	FL	33401	561-683-9186	683-9266
Town Center at Boca Raton 6000 Glades Rd	Boca Raton	FL	33431	561-368-6000	338-0891
Uptown Downtown Flea Market & Outlet Mall 5700 Okeechobee Blvd	West Palm Beach	FL	33417	561-684-5700	697-3734

BANKS

				Phone	Fax
Colonial Bank 2000 Palm Beach Lakes Blvd	West Palm Beach	FL	33409	561-683-1600	683-4532
Community Savings FA 971 Village Blvd	West Palm Beach	FL	33409	561-478-9100	478-9488
Fidelity Federal Savings Bank of Florida 218 Datura St *Fax: Mktg ■ Web: www.fidfed.com	West Palm Beach	FL	33401	561-659-9900	659-9968*
First Union National Bank 303 Banyan Blvd. *Fax: Hum Res	West Palm Beach	FL	33401	561-838-5364	838-4918*
Mackinac Savings Bank FSB 2901-A N Military Trail *Fax: Lendings	West Palm Beach	FL	33409	561-686-2352	686-2768*
NationsBank NA 2881 N Military Trail	West Palm Beach	FL	33409	561-683-6000	683-8225
Republic Security Bank 4400 Congress Ave	West Palm Beach	FL	33407	561-840-1200	881-9225
Republic Security Bank 450 S Australian Ave. *Fax: Hum Res	West Palm Beach	FL	33401	561-840-8726	650-2431*
Sterling Bank FSB 1661 Congress Ave	West Palm Beach	FL	33406	561-968-1000	968-1220
SunTrust Bank South Florida NA 422 Belvedere Rd	West Palm Beach	FL	33405	561-655-4481	832-3359
Union Planters Bank 6080 Okeechobee Blvd *Fax Area Code: 561	West Palm Beach	FL	33417	877-848-2265	478-4590*
Washington Mutual Bank 2959 N Military Trail Crosstown Plaza TF: 800-782-8875	West Palm Beach	FL	33409	561-478-9101	478-4162

BUSINESS SERVICES

	Phone		Phone
Airborne Express	800-247-2676	**Mail Boxes Etc**	561-835-9791
BAX Global	800-225-5229	**Manpower Temporary Services**	561-659-0991
DHL Worldwide Express	800-225-5345	**Office Specialists**	561-697-2510
Federal Express	800-238-5355	**Post Office**	800-275-8777
IKON Office Solutions	561-655-5590	**Sir Speedy Printing**	561-833-9661
Kelly Services	561-694-0116	**Snelling Personnel Services**	561-689-5400
Kinko's	561-478-0600	**UPS**	800-742-5877

— Media —

PUBLICATIONS

				Phone	Fax
Miami Metro Magazine 1550 Biscayne Blvd Suite 300 TF: 800-288-8388 ■ Web: miamimetro.com ■ E-mail: miametro@bellsouth.net	Miami	FL	33132	305-755-9920	755-9921

West Palm Beach — Publications (Cont'd)

Name / Address	City	State	Zip	Phone	Fax
Palm Beach Daily Business Review 330 Clematis St Suite 114	West Palm Beach	FL	33401	561-820-2060	820-2077
Palm Beach Illustrated 1000 N Dixie Hwy Suite C	West Palm Beach	FL	33401	561-659-0210	659-1736
Palm Beach Post‡ PO Box 24700 — *Web:* www.pbpost.com ■ *E-mail:* letters@pbpost.com	West Palm Beach	FL	33416	561-820-4100	820-4407
South Florida Business Journal 4000 Hollywood Blvd Suite 695 South — *Web:* www.amcity.com/southflorida	Hollywood	FL	33021	954-359-2100	359-2135

‡Daily newspapers

TELEVISION

Name / Address	City	State	Zip	Phone	Fax
WFGC-TV Ch 61 (Ind) 2406 S Congress Ave Suite 2	West Palm Beach	FL	33406	561-642-3361	967-5961
WFLX-TV Ch 29 (Fox) 4119 W Blue Heron Blvd	West Palm Beach	FL	33404	561-845-2929	863-1238
WPEC-TV Ch 12 (CBS) 1100 Fairfield Dr — *Web:* www.gopbi.com/partners/news12	West Palm Beach	FL	33407	561-844-1212	881-0731
WPTV-TV Ch 5 (NBC) 622 N Flagler Dr — *Web:* www.wptv.com ■ *E-mail:* wptv@magg.net	West Palm Beach	FL	33401	561-655-5455	653-5719
WPXP-TV Ch 67 (PAX) 500 Australian Ave S Suite 510 — *Web:* www.pax.net/WPXP	West Palm Beach	FL	33401	561-686-6767	682-3475
WTVX-TV Ch 34 (UPN) 4411 Beacon Cir Majestic Plaza Suite 5	West Palm Beach	FL	33407	561-841-3434	848-9150

RADIO

Name / Address	City	State	Zip	Phone	Fax
WAYF-FM 88.1 MHz (AC) 800 Northpointe Pkwy Suite 881 — *Web:* www.wayfm.com	West Palm Beach	FL	33407	561-881-1929	840-1929
WBZT-AM 1290 kHz (N/T) 3071 Continental Dr	West Palm Beach	FL	33407	561-439-1111	881-8880
WDBF-AM 1420 kHz (Nost) 2710 W Atlantic Ave	Delray Beach	FL	33445	561-278-1420	278-1898
WEAT-FM 104.3 MHz (AC) 701 Northpoint Pkwy Suite 500 — *Web:* www.sunny1043.com ■ *E-mail:* veras@veras.com	West Palm Beach	FL	33407	561-686-9505	689-4043
WIRK-FM 107.9 MHz (Ctry) 701 Northpoint Pkwy Suite 500 — *Web:* www.wirk.com ■ *E-mail:* wirk@quinncom.net	West Palm Beach	FL	33407	561-686-9505	686-0157
WJBW-FM 99.5 MHz (Nost) 6699 N Federal Hwy Suite 200	Boca Raton	FL	33487	561-997-0074	997-0476
WJNA-AM 1230 kHz (Nost) 2406 S Congress Ave	West Palm Beach	FL	33409	561-432-5100	432-5111
WKGR-FM 98.7 MHz (CR) 3071 Continental Dr — *Web:* www.gater.com	West Palm Beach	FL	33407	561-439-1111	881-8880
WLDI-FM 95.5 MHz (CHR) 3071 Continental Dr — *Web:* www.wild955.com ■ *E-mail:* wild955@aol.com	West Palm Beach	FL	33407	561-616-6600	616-6677
WLVJ-AM 640 kHz (Rel) 1601 Belvedere Rd Suite 204E	West Palm Beach	FL	33406	561-688-9585	688-9601
WMBX-FM 102.3 MHz (AC) 701 Northpoint Pkwy Suite 501 — *Web:* www.mix1023.com	West Palm Beach	FL	33407	561-616-4600	684-6311
WPBZ-FM 103.1 MHz (Alt) 701 Northpoint Pkwy Suite 501 — *Web:* www.buzz103.com ■ *E-mail:* buzz103@quinncom.net	West Palm Beach	FL	33407	561-616-4600	688-0209
WPOM-AM 1600 kHz (Urban) 5033 Okeechobee Blvd	West Palm Beach	FL	33417	561-687-1960	687-4221
WRLX-FM 92.1 MHz (AC) 2406 S Congress Ave	West Palm Beach	FL	33406	561-432-5100	432-5111
WRMF-FM 97.9 MHz (AC) 2406 S Congress Ave — *Web:* www.gopbi.com/partners/wrmf	West Palm Beach	FL	33406	561-432-5100	432-5111
WWLV-FM 94.3 MHz (Nost) 3071 Continental Dr — *Web:* www.943beach.com ■ *E-mail:* radio1@radio-1.com	West Palm Beach	FL	33407	561-439-1111	881-8880
WXEL-TV Ch 42 (PBS) PO Box 6607 — *Web:* www.wxel.org ■ *E-mail:* comments@wxel.org	West Palm Beach	FL	33405	561-737-8000	369-3067
WZZR-FM 92.7 MHz (Rock) PO Box 0093 — *Web:* www.wzzr.com ■ *E-mail:* lovedocs@wzzr.com	Port Saint Lucie	FL	34985	561-335-9300	335-3291

— Colleges/Universities —

Name / Address	City	State	Zip	Phone	Fax
Barry University 701 N Congress Ave	Boynton Beach	FL	33426	561-364-8220	364-8113
Florida Atlantic University 777 Glades Rd — *TF Admissions:* 800-299-4328 ■ *Web:* www.fau.edu ■ *E-mail:* barton@fau.edu	Boca Raton	FL	33431	561-297-3000	297-2758
Institute of Career Education 1750 45th St — *Web:* www.vocedu.com	West Palm Beach	FL	33407	561-881-0220	881-3831
Lynn University 3601 N Military Trail — *TF:* 800-544-8035 ■ *Web:* www.lynn.edu ■ *E-mail:* admission@lynn.edu	Boca Raton	FL	33431	561-994-0770	241-3552
New England Institute of Technology 1126 53rd Ct — *TF:* 800-826-9986	West Palm Beach	FL	33407	561-842-8324	842-9503
Northwood University Florida Campus 2600 N Military Trail — *TF:* 800-458-8325 ■ *Web:* www.northwood.edu ■ *E-mail:* info@northwood.edu	West Palm Beach	FL	33409	561-478-5510	640-3328
Palm Beach Atlantic College PO Box 24708 — *TF:* 888-468-6722 ■ *Web:* www.pbac.edu ■ *E-mail:* admit@pbac.edu	West Palm Beach	FL	33416	561-803-2000	803-2155
Palm Beach Community College Central Campus 4200 Congress Ave — *Web:* www.pbcc.cc.fl.us ■ *E-mail:* dill s@popmail.firn.edu	Lake Worth	FL	33461	561-439-8000	439-8255
South College 1760 N Congress Ave	West Palm Beach	FL	33409	561-697-9200	697-9944

— Hospitals —

Name / Address	City	State	Zip	Phone	Fax
Bethesda Memorial Hospital 2815 S Seacrest Blvd — *Web:* www.bethesdaweb.com	Boynton Beach	FL	33435	561-737-7733	735-7057
Boca Raton Community Hospital 800 Meadows Rd — *Web:* www.brch.com	Boca Raton	FL	33486	561-395-7100	750-4715
Delray Medical Center 5352 Linton Blvd — *Web:* www.tenethealth.com/Delray	Delray Beach	FL	33484	561-498-4440	495-3103
Good Samaritan Medical Center 1309 N Flagler Dr	West Palm Beach	FL	33401	561-655-5511	650-6127
JFK Medical Center 5301 Congress Ave	Atlantis	FL	33462	561-965-7300	642-3623
Jupiter Medical Center 1210 S Old Dixie Hwy — *Web:* www.jupitermed.com ■ *E-mail:* jupitermed@aol.com	Jupiter	FL	33458	561-747-2234	744-4493
Palm Beach Gardens Medical Center 3360 Burns Rd — *Web:* www.tenethealth.com/PalmBeachGardens	Palm Beach Gardens	FL	33410	561-622-1411	694-7160
Saint Mary's Medical Center 901 45th St — **Fax:* Admitting	West Palm Beach	FL	33407	561-844-6300	881-0903*
Veterans Affairs Medical Center 7305 N Military Trail	West Palm Beach	FL	33410	561-882-8262	882-7353
West Boca Medical Center 21644 State Rd 7 — **Fax:* Admitting ■ *Web:* www.tenethealth.com/WestBoca	Boca Raton	FL	33428	561-488-8000	883-7020*

— Attractions —

Name / Address	City	State	Zip	Phone	Fax
Armory Art Center 1703 S Lake Ave	West Palm Beach	FL	33401	561-832-1776	832-0191
Atlantic Avenue downtown-betw Swinton Ave & A1A	Delray Beach	FL	33483	561-278-0424	278-0555
Ballet Florida 500 Fern St — *TF:* 800-540-0172 ■ *Web:* www.balletflorida.com ■ *E-mail:* georgepb@ix.netcom.com	West Palm Beach	FL	33401	561-659-1212	659-2222
Boca Pops 100 NE 1st Ave — *TF:* 888-876-7677 ■ *Web:* www.bocapops.org	Boca Raton	FL	33432	561-393-7677	393-7364
Boca Raton Museum of Art 801 W Palmetto Park Rd — *Web:* www.bocamuseum.org ■ *E-mail:* bocart@gate.net	Boca Raton	FL	33486	561-392-2500	391-6410
Caldwell Theatre Co 7873 N Federal Hwy — *Web:* www.caldwelltheatre.com	Boca Raton	FL	33487	561-241-7380	997-6917
Callery-Judge Grove 4001 Seminole-Pratt Whitney Rd — *TF Cust Svc:* 800-967-2643*	Loxahatchee	FL	33470	561-793-1676	790-5466
Cason Cottage Museum 5 NE 1st St	Delray Beach	FL	33444	561-243-0223	
Children's Museum 498 Crawford Blvd	Boca Raton	FL	33432	561-368-6875	395-7764
Dickinson Jonathan State Park 16450 SE Federal Hwy	Hobe Sound	FL	33455	561-546-2771	744-7604

West Palm Beach — Attractions (Cont'd)

	City	State	ZIP	Phone	Fax
Flagler Henry M Museum 1 Whitehall Way *Web:* www.flagler.org ■ *E-mail:* flagler@flagler.org	Palm Beach	FL	33480	561-655-2833	655-2826
Florida History Center & Museum 805 N US 1 Burt Reynolds Park	Jupiter	FL	33477	561-747-6639	575-3292
Florida Philharmonic Orchestra 701 Okeechobee Blvd Raymond Kravis Center for the Performing Arts *TF:* 800-226-1812	West Palm Beach	FL	33401	561-655-7228	655-7287
Gaines Park 1501 N Australian Ave	West Palm Beach	FL	33401	561-835-7090	
Gumbo Limbo Nature Center 1801 N Ocean Blvd	Boca Raton	FL	33432	561-338-1473	338-1483
Hibel Museum of Art 150 Royal Poinciana Plaza	Palm Beach	FL	33480	561-833-6870	
International Museum of Cartoon Art 201 Plaza Real Mizner Pk *Web:* www.cartoon.org ■ *E-mail:* correspondence@cartoon.org	Boca Raton	FL	33432	561-391-2200	391-2721
Knollwood Groves & Hallapatee Indian Village 8053 Lawrence Rd *TF:* 800-222-9696 ■ *Web:* www.knollwoodgroves.com	Boynton Beach	FL	33436	561-734-4800	737-6700
Lion Country Safari 2003 Lion Country Safari Rd *Web:* www.lioncountrysafari.com	Loxahatchee	FL	33470	561-793-1084	793-9603
Loxahatchee National Wildlife Refuge 10216 Lee Rd	Boynton Beach	FL	33437	561-734-8303	
Marine Life Center 14200 US Hwy 1 Loggerhead Pk *Web:* www.marinelife.org	Juno Beach	FL	33408	561-627-8280	627-8305
Morikami Museum & Japanese Gardens 4000 Morikami Pk Rd *Web:* www.morikami.org ■ *E-mail:* morikami@co.palm-beach.fl.us	Delray Beach	FL	33446	561-495-0233	499-2557
Mounts Botanical Gardens 531 N Military Trail *Web:* www.mounts.org ■ *E-mail:* jeterjm@gate.net	West Palm Beach	FL	33415	561-233-1700	233-1782
Northwood University Art Gallery 2600 N Military Trail	West Palm Beach	FL	33409	561-478-5555	640-3328
Norton Ann Sculpture Gardens 253 Barcelona Rd	West Palm Beach	FL	33401	561-832-5328	835-9305
Norton Museum of Art 1451 S Olive Ave *Web:* www.norton.org/ ■ *E-mail:* museum@norton.org	West Palm Beach	FL	33401	561-832-5194	659-4689
Okeeheelee Park 7715 Forest Hill Blvd	West Palm Beach	FL	33413	561-964-4420	233-1406
Old School Square Cultural Arts Center 51 N Swinton Ave *Web:* www.oldschool.org	Delray Beach	FL	33444	561-243-7922	243-7018
Palm Beach Opera 415 S Olive Ave	West Palm Beach	FL	33401	561-833-7888	833-8294
Palm Beach Photographic Centre 55 NE 2nd Ave *Web:* www.workshop.org ■ *E-mail:* pbphoto@workshop.org	Delray Beach	FL	33444	561-276-9797	276-1932
Palm Beach Pops 701 Okeechobee Blvd Raymond Kravis Center for the Performing Arts *TF:* 800-448-2472	West Palm Beach	FL	33401	561-832-7469	832-9686
Palm Beach Zoo at Dreher Park 1301 Summit Blvd *Web:* www.palmbeachzoo.org ■ *E-mail:* pbzoo@palmbeachzoo.org	West Palm Beach	FL	33405	561-533-0887	585-6085
Pine Jog Environmental Education Center 6301 Summit Blvd *E-mail:* pinejog@aol.com	West Palm Beach	FL	33415	561-686-6600	687-4968
Rapids Water Park 6566 N Military Trail *Web:* www.rapidswaterpark.com	West Palm Beach	FL	33407	561-848-6272	848-2822
Raymond F Kravis Center for the Performing Arts 701 Okeechobee Blvd **Fax:* Mktg ■ *TF:* 800-572-8471 ■ *Web:* www.kravis.org ■ *E-mail:* kravis@kravis.org	West Palm Beach	FL	33401	561-832-7469	835-0738*
Royal Poinciana Playhouse 70 Royal Poinciana Plaza	Palm Beach	FL	33480	561-659-3310	659-7141
Society of the Four Arts 2 Four Arts Plaza	Palm Beach	FL	33480	561-655-7226	655-7233
South Florida Science Museum 4801 Dreher Trail N *Web:* www.sfsm.org	West Palm Beach	FL	33405	561-832-1988	833-0551
Spanish River Park 3001 N Ocean Blvd	Boca Raton	FL	33431	561-393-7815	
Sports Immortals Museum 6830 N Federal Hwy *Web:* www.sportsimmortals.com	Boca Raton	FL	33487	561-997-2575	997-6949
Will Lawrence E Museum 530 S Main St	Belle Glade	FL	33430	561-996-3453	996-2304

SPORTS TEAMS & FACILITIES

	City	State	ZIP	Phone	Fax
Florida Bobcats (football) 1 Panther Pkwy National Car Rental Ctr *Web:* www.floridabobcats.com	Sunrise	FL	33323	954-577-9009	577-9008
Jupiter Hammerheads (baseball) Roger Dean Stadium 4751 Main St	Jupiter	FL	33458	561-775-1818	
Moroso Motor Sports Park 17047 Beeline Hwy	Palm Beach Gardens	FL	33410	561-622-1400	626-2053
Palm Beach Kennel Club 1111 N Congress Ave *Web:* www.pbkennelclub.com	West Palm Beach	FL	33409	561-683-2222	683-4361
Palm Beach Polo 11199 Polo Club Rd	West Palm Beach	FL	33414	561-793-1113	798-7345
Palm Beach Polo & Country Club 11199 Polo Club Rd *Web:* www.pbpolo.com ■ *E-mail:* info@pbpolo.com	Wellington	FL	33414	561-798-7000	798-7330
Royal Palm Polo Sports Club 18000 Jog Rd	Boca Raton	FL	33496	561-734-7656	994-2553

— Events —

	Phone
$25,000 Arthur J Rooney Sr-St Patrick's Invitational (mid-March)	561-683-2222
$25,000 Bob Balfe/Molyneux Cup Puppy Stakes (late April)	561-683-2222
$25,000 Fall Futurity (late October)	561-683-2222
$25,000 He's My Man Royal Palm Classic (late January)	561-683-2222
$25,000 James W Paul 3/8th Mile Derby (late February)	561-683-2222
$25,000 Palm Beach Invitational (late March)	561-683-2222
All Florida Exhibit (late May-mid-July)	561-392-2500
All Ford Show (early October)	561-622-1400
Antiques Show & Sale (mid-February)	561-243-0223
Artigras (mid-February)	561-694-2300
Boca Festival Days (August)	561 395-4433
Boca Raton Outdoor Art Festival (late February)	561-392-2500
Bon Festival (August)	561-495-0233
Boynton Beach's GALA (late March)	561-375-6236
Challenge Cup Polo Tournament (early-mid-January)	561-793-1440
Chris Evert Pro-Celebrity Tennis Classic (early December)	561-394-2400
Delray Affair (early April)	561-278-0424
Downtown Delray Craft Festival (late February-early March)	954-472-3755
Festival of Trees (December)	561-243-7356
Fiesta of Arts (early February)	561-393-7806
Fine Arts Festival (late November)	561-746-3101
Florida Winter Equestrian Festival (January-March)	561-793-5867
FOTOFusion (late January)	561-276-9797
Fourth on Flagler (July 4)	561-659-8004
Gold Cup of the Americas (early-mid-March)	561-793-1440
Harvest Fest (mid-November)	561-278-0424
Hatsume Fair (late February)	561-495-0233
Holiday Street Parade (early December)	561-393-7806
Indian River Native American Festival (late February)	561-978-4500
Jet Car Nationals (mid-May)	561-622-1400
Moroso Chrysler Classic Show (mid-September)	561-622-1400
Oktoberfest (mid-late October)	561-967-6464
Old-time Street Celebration (early February)	561-393-7806
Oshogatsu Japanese New Year Celebration (early January)	561-495-0233
Palm Beach Boat Show (late March)	800-940-7642
Palm Beach International Art & Antiques Fair (late January-early February)	561-659-8007
Palm Beach International Food & Wine Festival (late February-early March)	561-220-2690
Palm Beach Renaissance Festival (early-mid-February)	800-676-7333
Palm Beach Seafood Festival (early February)	561-832-6397
Palm Beach Tropical Flower Show (late February)	561-655-5522
PGA Seniors' Championship (mid-April)	561-627-1800
Pioneer Days Festival (late May)	561-793-0333
Seafare (October)	561-747-6639
South Florida Fair (mid-January-early February)	561-793-0333
Spring Fling (late March)	561-393-7806
Sterling Cup Polo Tournament (late January-mid-February)	561-793-1440
SunFest of Palm Beach County (late April-early May)	561-659-5980
Tropical Fruit Festival (late June)	561-233-1759
US Croquet National Championship (late September & early October)	561-753-9141
US Open Polo Championship (mid-March-early April)	561-793-1440
West Palm Beach Italian Festival (early April)	561-832-6397
Wine & All That Jazz (late July)	561-395-4433
Winter Fantasy on the Waterway (mid-December)	561-395-4433
Winter Festival (late February)	561-451-4485

Georgia

Population (1999): 7,788,240 **Area (sq mi): 59,441**

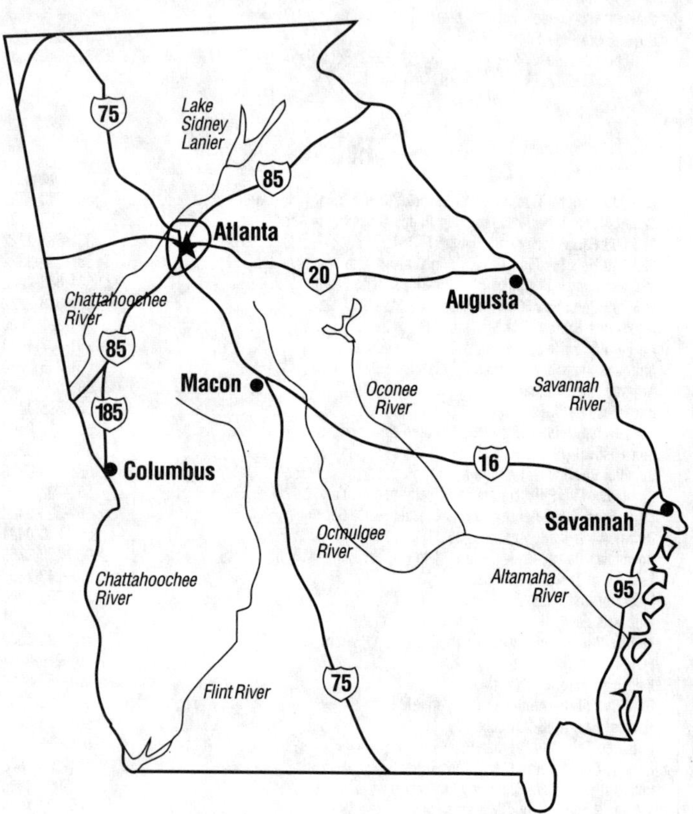

— State Information Sources —

				Phone	Fax
Georgia Chamber of Commerce					
233 Peachtree St NE Suite 200	Atlanta	GA	30303	404-223-2264	223-2290
Web: www.gachamber.org ■ *E-mail:* staff@gachamber.org					
Georgia Industry Trade & Tourism Dept					
285 Peachtree Ctr Ave NE Suite 1000	Atlanta	GA	30303	404-656-3545	656-3567
TF: 800-847-4842 ■ *Web:* www.georgia.org					
Georgia Parks Recreation & Historic Sites Div					
205 Butler St SE Floyd Tower East Suite 1352	Atlanta	GA	30334	404-656-3530	651-5871
TF: 800-869-8420 ■ *Web:* www.georgianet.org/dnr/parks					
Georgia Public Library Services					
1800 Century Pl Suite 150	Atlanta	GA	30345	404-982-3560	982-3563
Web: www.gpls.public.lib.ga.us					
Georgia State Government Information				404-656-2000	
Web: www.state.ga.us					
Georgia Tourism Div					
285 Peachtree Center Ave Suite 100	Atlanta	GA	30303	404-656-3589	651-9063
TF: 800-847-4842 ■ *Web:* www.georgia.org/itt/tourism					

ON-LINE RESOURCES

Coastal Georgia Destinations . . . . www.gacoast.com/navigator/destinations.html
Georgia Cities . . . . dir.yahoo.com/Regional/U_S__States/Georgia/Cities
Georgia Counties & Regions . . dir.yahoo.com/Regional/U_S__States/Georgia/Counties_and_Regions
Georgia Information . . . . valuecom.com/georgia/info.htm
Georgia on My Mind . . . . www.gomm.com
Georgia Scenario . . . . scenariousa.dstylus.com/ga/indexf.htm
Georgia Travel & Tourism Guide . . . . www.travel-library.com/north_america/usa/georgia/index.html
Georgia's Best Online . . . . www.georgiasbest.com
InGeorgia.com . . . . www.ingeorgia.com
Rough Guide Travel Georgia travel.roughguides.com/content/702/index.htm
Travel.org-Georgia . . . . travel.org/georgia.html
Welcome to North Georgia . . . . www.ngeorgia.com
Wiregrass Trail . . . . www.wiregrasstrail.com
Yahoo! Get Local Georgia . . . . dir.yahoo.com/Regional/U_S__States/Georgia

— Cities Profiled —

Atlanta

The metropolitan area of Atlanta encompasses five distinct counties - Clayton, Cobb, DeKalb, Fulton, and Gwinnett - each with its own unique activities and attractions.Primarily located in Fulton County, the City of Atlanta is home to the trendy neighborhood of Buckhead; CNN Center, which is also the world headquarters for Turner Broadcasting System; Underground Atlanta, a restored below-street-level marketplace, and the adjacent World of Coca-Cola; the shops and galleries of Antebellum Roswell; and Zoo Atlanta. Atlanta's Martin Luther King, Jr. Center for Nonviolent Social Change includes the Center itself, the home where Dr. King was born, his grave site, and the Ebenezer Baptist Church where he preached. The area south of downtown Atlanta, in Clayton County, was the setting for the novel "Gone With the Wind." Other notable attractions in Atlanta's metro area include Kennesaw Mountain National Battlefield Park and the Confederate Cemetery; and the 3,200-acre Stone Mountain Park, featuring the world's largest bas relief sculpture. In 1996, Atlanta hosted the Summer Olympic Games.

Population 403,819
Area (Land) . . . . 124.9 sq mi
Area (Water) . . . . 0.7 sq mi
Elevation . . . . 1050 ft
Latitude . . . . 33-74-89 N
Longitude . . . . 84-38-81 W
County . . . . Fulton
Time Zone . . . . EST
Area Code/s 404, 678, 770

— Average Temperatures and Precipitation —

TEMPERATURES

	Jan	Feb	Mar	Apr	May	Jun	Jul	Aug	Sep	Oct	Nov	Dec
High	50	55	64	73	80	86	89	87	82	73	64	54
Low	32	35	43	50	59	66	70	69	64	52	43	35

PRECIPITATION

	Jan	Feb	Mar	Apr	May	Jun	Jul	Aug	Sep	Oct	Nov	Dec
Inches	4.8	4.8	5.8	4.3	4.3	3.6	5.0	3.7	3.4	3.1	3.9	4.3

— Important Phone Numbers —

	Phone
AAA	404-843-4500
American Express Travel	404-262-7561
Dental Referral	404-636-7553
Emergency	911
HotelDocs	800-468-3537
Medical Referral	404-881-1714
Poison Control Center	404-616-9000
Time	770-455-7141
Travelers Aid	404-817-7070
Weather	770-603-3333

— Information Sources —

	City	State	ZIP	Phone	Fax
Atlanta Chamber of Commerce PO Box 1740 *Web:* www.forward-atlanta.com	Atlanta	GA	30301	404-880-9000	586-8464
Atlanta City Hall 55 Trinity Ave SW *Web:* www.ci.atlanta.ga.us	Atlanta	GA	30335	404-330-6000	658-6454
Atlanta Convention & Visitors Bureau 233 Peachtree St NE Suite 100 **Fax:* Sales ■ *TF:* 800-285-2682 ■ *Web:* www.acvb.com/ ■ *E-mail:* acvb@atlanta.com	Atlanta	GA	30303	404-521-6600	577-3293*
Atlanta-Fulton Public Library 1 Margaret Mitchell Sq NW *Web:* www.af.public.lib.ga.us	Atlanta	GA	30303	404-730-1700	730-1990
Atlanta Mayor 55 Trinity Ave SW Suite 2400 *Web:* www.ci.atlanta.ga.us/MAYOR/Mayor.htm	Atlanta	GA	30335	404-330-6100	658-7361
Atlanta Planning Development & Neighborhood Conservation Dept 55 Trinity Ave SW Suite 1450 *Web:* www.ci.atlanta.ga.us/dept/pdnc/pdnc.htm	Atlanta	GA	30335	404-330-6070	658-7638
Better Business Bureau Serving Metropolitan Atlanta PO Box 2707 *Web:* www.atlanta.bbb.org	Atlanta	GA	30301	404-688-4910	688-8901
Fulton County 141 Pryor St SW *Web:* www.co.fulton.ga.us ■ *E-mail:* feedback@co.fulton.ga.us	Atlanta	GA	30303	404-730-4000	730-4237
Georgia International Convention Center 1902 Sullivan Rd	College Park	GA	30337	770-997-3566	994-8559

On-Line Resources

4Atlanta.com www.4atlanta.com
About.com Guide to Atlanta . . . . atlanta.about.com/local/southeastus/atlanta
Access Atlanta . . . . www.accessatlanta.com
ACME Atlanta . . . . www.acme-atlanta.com
Area Guide Atlanta . . . . atlanta.areaguides.net
Atlanta by Moonlight . . . . www.suspensionofdisbelief.com/atlanta/
Atlanta CityLink . . . . www.usacitylink.com/citylink/atlanta/
Atlanta CityWomen . . . . www.citywomen.com/atlwomen.htm
Atlanta Graphic City Guide . . . . www.futurecast.com/gcg/atlanta.htm
Atlanta Guidebook . . . . clever.net/qms/atl-page.htm
Atlanta Information Systems . . . . www.atlnta.com/
Atlanta Web Guide . . . . www.webguide.com
Atlanta.TheLinks.com . . . . atlanta.thelinks.com/
AtlantaEntertainment.com . . . . www.atlantaentertainment.com/ATLANTA/index.htm
BestAtlanta.com . . . . www.bestatlanta.com
Boulevards Atlanta . . . . www.boulevards.com/cities/atlanta.html
Bradmans.com Atlanta . . . . www.bradmans.com/scripts/display_city.cgi?city=231
Buckhead . . . . www.buckhead.org/
City Knowledge Atlanta . . . . www.cityknowledge.com/ga_atlanta.htm
CitySearch Atlanta . . . . atlanta.citysearch.com
CityTravelGuide.com Atlanta . . . . www.citytravelguide.com/atlanta.htm
Creative Loafing Atlanta . . . . web.cln.com
CuisineNet Atlanta . . . . www.cuisinenet.com/restaurant/atlanta/
DigitalCity Atlanta . . . . home.digitalcity.com/atlanta
E2Atlanta www.e2atlanta.com/
Excite.com Atlanta City Guide . . . . www.excite.com/travel/countries/united_states/georgia/atlanta
Gay Atlanta . . . . www.gayatlanta.org/
Golf Atlanta . . . . www.golfatlanta.com
Hot Atlanta . . . . zaphod.cc.ttu.ee/vrainn/Atlanta/ahome.html
HotelGuide Atlanta . . . . atlanta.hotelguide.net
Info Atlanta . . . . travel.to/atlanta
Insiders' Guide to Atlanta . . . . www.insiders.com/atlanta/
Metroscope Atlanta . . . . metroscope.com/atlanta.html
Net Atlanta . . . . www.netatlanta.com
NITC Travelbase City Guide Atlanta . . . . www.travelbase.com/auto/guides/atlanta-area-ga.html
On-line Menus Atlanta . . . . menus.atlanta.com
Open World City Guides Atlanta . . . . www.worldexecutive.com/cityguides/atlanta/
Restaurant Row Atlanta . . . . www.restaurantrow.com/atlanta.htm
Rough Guide Travel Atlanta travel.roughguides.com/content/703/
Savvy Diner Guide to Atlanta Restaurants . . . . www.savvydiner.com/atlanta/
Surf Atlanta . . . . surfatlanta.com
Traveler Information Showcase . . . . www.atlanta-traveler.com/
Virtual Voyages Atlanta . . . . www.virtualvoyages.com/usa/ga/atlanta/atlanta.sht
WeekendEvents.com Atlanta . . . . www.weekendevents.com/Atlanta/atlanta.html
Yahoo! Atlanta . . . . atlanta.yahoo.com

— Transportation Services —

AIRPORTS

■ Hartsfield Atlanta International Airport (ATL)

10 miles S of downtown (approx 20 minutes) . . . . Phone: 404-530-6600
Web: www.atlanta-airport.com

Airport Transportation

	Phone
Airport Shuttle $10 fare to downtown	404-524-3400
Atlanta Airport Northside Shuttle $10 fare to downtown	404-768-7600
Taxi $18 fare to downtown	404-521-0200

Commercial Airlines

	Phone
AeroMexico	404-767-4822
Air Jamaica	800-523-5585
AirTran	800-247-8726
America West	800-235-9292
American	800-433-7300
British Airways	800-247-9297
Cayman Airways	800-422-9626
Continental	800-525-0280
Continental Express	800-525-0280
Delta	404-765-5000
Iberia	800-772-4642
Japan	800-525-3663
Kiwi	800-538-5494
KLM	800-374-7747
Lufthansa	800-645-3880
Midwest Express	800-452-2022
Northwest	800-225-2525
Sabena	800-955-2000
Singapore	800-742-3333
SwissAir	404-814-6300
TWA	800-221-2000
United	800-241-6522
US Airways	800-428-4322

Atlanta (Cont'd)

Charter Airlines

	Phone		Phone
Air Group Inc	800-233-8890	**Piedmont Aviation Services Inc**	800-548-1978
Corpjet Inc	800-267-7538	**Smithair Inc**	800-899-2538
Epps Aviation	770-458-9851	**Universal Air Service**	770-454-8900

CAR RENTALS

	Phone		Phone
Alamo	404-768-4161	**Enterprise**	404-261-7337
Avis	404-530-2700	**Hertz**	404-530-2925
Budget	404-530-3000	**National**	404-530-2800
Dollar	404-766-0244	**Thrifty**	770-996-2350

LIMO/TAXI

	Phone		Phone
Atlanta Limousine	404-351-5466	**Greene Classic Limousines**	404-875-3866
Avanti Limousine	404-233-6100	**Safeway Cab Co**	770-457-4023
Carey Limousine	404-681-3366	**Style Taxi**	404-522-8294
Checker Cab	404-351-1111	**Yellow Cab**	404-521-0200
Cosmopolitan Limousine	404-696-9800		

MASS TRANSIT

	Phone
MARTA $1.50 Base fare	404-848-4711

RAIL/BUS

Phone

Amtrak Station 1688 Peachtree St NW . . . . . . Atlanta GA 30309 800-872-7245
TF: 800-872-7245

Greyhound/Trailways Bus Station 232 Forsyth St. . . . . . Atlanta GA 30303 800-231-2222

— Accommodations —

HOTEL RESERVATION SERVICES

Phone Fax

Accommodations Express 609-391-2100 525-0111
TF: 800-444-7666 ■ *Web:* www.accommodationsxpress.com
■ *E-mail:* accomexp@acy.digex.net

Bed & Breakfast Atlanta Reservation Services 404-875-0525 875-8198
TF: 800-967-3224

Central Reservation Service 407-740-6442 740-8222
TF: 800-548-3311 ■ *Web:* www.reservation-services.com
■ *E-mail:* cenresbos@aol.com

Hotel Reservations Network Inc 214-361-7311 361-7299
TF Sales: 800-964-6835 ■ *Web:* www.hoteldiscount.com

Quikbook 212-532-1660 532-1556
TF: 800-789-9887 ■ *Web:* www.quikbook.com

HOTELS, MOTELS, RESORTS

Phone Fax

AmeriSuites Atlanta 3242 Peachtree Rd NE . . . . . . Atlanta GA 30305 404-869-6161 869-6093
TF: 800-833-1516

Ansley Inn 253 15th St NE . . . . . . Atlanta GA 30309 404-872-9000 892-2318
TF: 800-446-5416 ■ *Web:* www.ansleyinn.com
■ *E-mail:* reservations@ansleyinn.com

Atlanta Airport Hilton & Towers
1031 Virginia Ave . . . . . . Atlanta GA 30354 404-767-9000 768-0185
TF: 800-445-8667 ■ *Web:* www.hilton.com/hotels/ATLAAHH

Best Western Airport East 301 N Central Ave. . . . . . Atlanta GA 30354 404-763-8777 761-1171
TF: 800-733-0298

Best Western Inn at the Peachtrees
330 W Peachtree St NW . . . . . . Atlanta GA 30308 404-577-6970 659-3244
TF: 800-242-4642

Castlegate Hotel & Conference Center
1750 Commerce Dr NW. . . . . . Atlanta GA 30318 404-351-6100 351-9954

Clarion Hotel 3601 N Desert Dr . . . . . . Atlanta GA 30344 404-762-5141 761-9121
TF: 800-252-7466

ClubHouse Inn & Suites
5945 Oakbrook Pkwy. . . . . . Norcross GA 30093 770-368-9400 416-7370
TF: 800-258-2466 ■ *E-mail:* info@clubhouseinn.com

Phone Fax

Comfort Inn Downtown
101 International Blvd NW . . . . . . Atlanta GA 30303 404-524-5555 524-0218
TF: 800-535-0707

Courtyard by Marriott Atlanta Airport South 2050 Sullivan Rd. . . . . . College Park GA 30337 770-997-2220 994-9743
TF: 800-321-2211 ■ *Web:* courtyard.com/ATLCA

Courtyard by Marriott Downtown
175 Piedmont Ave. . . . . . Atlanta GA 30303 404-659-2727 688-6332
TF: 800-321-2211 ■ *Web:* courtyard.com/ATLCD

Courtyard by Marriott Windy Hill
2045 S Park Pl NW. . . . . . Atlanta GA 30339 770-955-3838 933-0394
TF: 800-321-2211 ■ *Web:* courtyard.com/ATLWH

Crowne Plaza 1325 Virginia Ave . . . . . . Atlanta GA 30344 404-768-6660 766-6121
TF: 800-227-6963

Crowne Plaza Ravinia
4355 Ashford-Dunwoody Rd . . . . . . Atlanta GA 30346 770-395-7700 392-9503
TF: 800-554-0055

Days Inn 4300 Snapfinger Woods Dr. . . . . . Decatur GA 30035 770-981-5670 322-9854
TF: 800-329-7466

Days Inn Atlanta Airport 4601 Best Rd . . . . . . Atlanta GA 30337 404-761-6500 763-3267

Days Inn Downtown 300 Spring St . . . . . . Atlanta GA 30308 404-523-1144 577-8495
TF: 800-329-7466

Doubletree Guest Suites
2780 Windy Ridge Pkwy . . . . . . Atlanta GA 30339 770-980-1900 980-1528
TF: 800-843-5858
■ *Web:* www.doubletreehotels.com/DoubleT/Hotel121/138/138Main.htm

Doubletree Guest Suites Perimeter
6120 Peachtree Dunwoody Rd . . . . . . Atlanta GA 30328 770-668-0808 668-0008
TF: 800-222-8733
■ *Web:* www.doubletreehotels.com/DoubleT/Hotel41/45/45Main.htm

Drury Inn & Suites Atlanta Airport
1270 Virginia Ave . . . . . . Atlanta GA 30344 404-761-4900 761-4900
TF: 800-378-7946

Embassy Suites at Centennial Olympic Park
267 Marietta St. . . . . . Atlanta GA 30313 404-223-2300 223-0925
TF: 800-362-2779

Embassy Suites Atlanta Airport
4700 Southport Rd . . . . . . Atlanta GA 30337 404-767-1988 768-2080
TF: 800-362-2779

Embassy Suites Hotel Buckhead
3285 Peachtree Rd NE. . . . . . Atlanta GA 30305 404-261-7733 261-6857
TF: 800-362-2779

Evergreen Conference Center & Resort
1 Lakeview Dr . . . . . . Stone Mountain GA 30083 770-879-9900 465-3258*
**Fax:* Cust Svc ■ *Web:* www.evergreen.org
■ *E-mail:* evergreen@evergreen.org

Extended StayAmerica 3115 Clairmont Rd. . . . . . Atlanta GA 30329 404-679-4333 679-0777
TF: 800-398-7829

Fairfield Inn 175 Piedmont Ave NE. . . . . . Atlanta GA 30303 404-659-7777 688-6518
TF: 800-228-2800 ■ *Web:* fairfieldinn.com/ATLFD

Forrest Hills Mountain Hideaway
135 Forrest Hills Rd . . . . . . Dahlonega GA 30533 706-864-6456 864-0757
TF: 800-654-6313 ■ *Web:* www.foresths.com

Four Points Hotel 3387 Lenox Rd NE . . . . . . Atlanta GA 30326 404-261-5500 261-6140
TF: 800-241-0200

Four Seasons Hotel Atlanta 75 14th St. . . . . . Atlanta GA 30309 404-881-9898 873-4692

Georgian Terrace 659 Peachtree St. . . . . . Atlanta GA 30308 404-897-1991 724-9116
TF: 800-651-2316

Grand Hyatt Atlanta 3300 Peachtree Rd. . . . . . Atlanta GA 30305 404-365-8100 233-5686
TF: 800-233-1234

Hampton Inn & Suites Downtown
161 Spring St. . . . . . Atlanta GA 30303 404-589-1111 589-8999
TF: 800-426-7866

Hampton Inn Downtown Stadium
759 Pollard St SW . . . . . . Atlanta GA 30315 404-658-1961 223-3521
TF: 800-426-7866

Hilton & Towers 255 Courtland St NE . . . . . . Atlanta GA 30309 404-659-2000 221-6368
TF: 800-445-8667 ■ *Web:* www.hilton.com/hotels/ATLAHHH

Holiday Inn Airport North 1380 Virginia Ave. . . . . . Atlanta GA 30344 404-762-8411 767-4963
TF: 800-465-4329
■ *Web:* www.basshotels.com/holiday-inn/?_franchisee=ATLAP
■ *E-mail:* lspinaci@bristolhotels.com

Howard Johnson 330 Peachtree St NE. . . . . . Atlanta GA 30308 404-577-1980 688-3706
TF: 800-446-4656

Hyatt Regency 265 Peachtree St NE . . . . . . Atlanta GA 30303 404-577-1234 588-4137
TF: 800-233-1234
■ *Web:* www.hyatt.com/usa/atlanta/hotels/hotel_atlra.html

JW Marriott Hotel at Lenox
3300 Lenox Rd NE . . . . . . Atlanta GA 30326 404-262-3344 262-8689
TF: 800-228-9290

Marque of Atlanta 111 Perimeter Ctr W. . . . . . Atlanta GA 30346 770-396-6800 399-5514
TF: 800-683-6100

Marriott Hotel Atlanta Airport
4711 Best Rd. . . . . . College Park GA 30337 404-766-7900 209-6808
TF: 800-228-9290 ■ *Web:* marriotthotels.com/ATLAP

Atlanta — Hotels, Motels, Resorts (Cont'd)

	City	State	Zip	Phone	Fax
Marriott Marquis Hotel Atlanta 265 Peachtree Center Ave	Atlanta	GA	30303	404-521-0000	586-6299
TF: 800-228-9290 ■ *Web:* marriotthotels.com/ATLMQ					
Marriott Perimeter Center 246 Perimeter Center Pkwy NE	Atlanta	GA	30346	770-394-6500	394-4338
TF: 800-228-9290 ■ *Web:* marriotthotels.com/ATLPC					
Masters Economy Inn 4120 Fulton Industrial Blvd	Atlanta	GA	30336	404-696-4690	696-8432
TF: 800-633-3434					
Omni Hotel at CNN Center 100 CNN Ctr	Atlanta	GA	30335	404-659-0000	525-5050
TF: 800-843-6664					
Quality Inn Hotel 89 Luckie St	Atlanta	GA	30303	404-524-7991	524-0672
TF: 800-228-5151					
Radisson Hotel 5010 Old National Hwy	Atlanta	GA	30349	404-761-4000	763-0181
TF: 800-333-3333					
Ramada Inn 70 John Wesley Dobbs Ave	Atlanta	GA	30303	404-659-2660	524-5390
TF: 800-272-6232					
Regency Suites Hotel 975 W Peachtree St.	Atlanta	GA	30309	404-876-5003	817-7511
TF: 800-642-3629					
Renaissance Atlanta Hotel 590 W Peachtree St NW	Atlanta	GA	30308	404-881-6000	815-5010
TF: 800-228-9898					
Renaissance Atlanta Hotel Concourse 1 Hartsfield Centre Pkwy	Atlanta	GA	30354	404-209-9999	209-7031
TF: 800-228-9290					
Renaissance Waverly Hotel 2450 Galleria Pkwy NW	Atlanta	GA	30339	770-953-4500	953-0740
TF: 800-468-3571					
Residence Inn by Marriott Downtown 134 Peachtree St	Atlanta	GA	30303	404-522-0950	577-3235
TF: 800-331-3131 ■ *Web:* www.residenceinn.com/ATLDT					
Ritz-Carlton Atlanta 181 Peachtree St NE	Atlanta	GA	30303	404-659-0400	688-0400
TF: 800-241-3333 ■ *Web:* www.ritzcarlton.com/location/NorthAmerica/Atlanta/main.htm					
Ritz-Carlton Buckhead 3434 Peachtree Rd NE	Atlanta	GA	30326	404-237-2700	239-0078
TF: 800-241-3333 ■ *Web:* www.ritzcarlton.com/location/NorthAmerica/Buckhead/main.htm					
Sheraton Colony Square Hotel 188 14th St NE	Atlanta	GA	30361	404-892-6000	872-9192
TF: 800-325-3535					
Sheraton Gateway Hotel 1900 Sullivan Rd	College Park	GA	30337	770-997-1100	991-5906
TF: 800-325-3535					
Spirit of Atlanta Hotel 165 Courtland St NE	Atlanta	GA	30303	404-659-6500	524-1259
TF: 800-833-8624					
StudioPLUS 2474 Cumberland Pkwy SE	Atlanta	GA	30339	770-436-1511	436-1512
TF: 800-646-8000					
Sugar Magnolia 804 Edgewood Ave NE	Atlanta	GA	30307	404-222-0226	681-1067
Suite Hotel Underground Atlanta 54 Peachtree St	Atlanta	GA	30303	404-223-5555	223-0467
TF: 800-304-0828					
Sumner Suites Atlanta Airport 1899 Sullivan Rd	College Park	GA	30337	770-994-2997	994-8626
TF: 800-747-8483					
Super 8 Hotel Downtown 111 Cone St	Atlanta	GA	30303	404-524-7000	659-7521
TF: 800-800-8000					
Swissotel 3391 Peachtree Rd NE	Atlanta	GA	30326	404-365-0065	365-8787
TF: 800-637-9477					
Terrace Garden Inn Buckhead 3405 Lenox Rd NE	Atlanta	GA	30326	404-261-9250	848-7391
TF: 800-241-8260					
Travelodge Downtown 311 Courtland St NE	Atlanta	GA	30303	404-659-4545	659-5934
TF: 800-578-7878					
Westin Atlanta Airport 4736 Best Rd.	College Park	GA	30337	404-762-7676	763-4199
TF: 800-228-3000					
Westin Hotel North 7 Concourse Pkwy	Atlanta	GA	30328	770-395-3900	395-3918*
**Fax:* Sales ■ *TF:* 800-937-8461					
Westin Peachtree Plaza Hotel 210 Peachtree St NW	Atlanta	GA	30303	404-659-1400	589-7424
TF: 800-228-3000					
Wyndham Garden Hotel 1775 Parkway Pl NW	Marietta	GA	30067	770-428-4400	424-5756
TF: 800-996-3426					
Wyndham Hotel Atlanta 160 Spring St NW	Atlanta	GA	30303	404-688-8600	686-3327*
**Fax Area Code:* 678 ■ *TF:* 800-996-3426					
Wyndham Hotel Buckhead 3340 Peachtree Rd NE	Atlanta	GA	30326	404-231-1234	231-5236
TF: 800-996-3426					
Wyndham Midtown Hotel 125 10th St NE	Atlanta	GA	30309	404-873-4800	870-1530
TF: 800-996-3426					
Wyndham Peachtree Conference Center 2443 Hwy 54 W	Peachtree City	GA	30269	770-487-2000	487-8599
TF: 800-996-3426					
Wynfield Inn Atlanta Airport 1808 Phoenix Blvd	Atlanta	GA	30349	770-991-1099	991-1076
TF: 800-669-8888					

— Restaurants —

	City	State	Zip	Phone
103 West Restaurant (Continental) 103 West Paces Ferry Rd NW	Atlanta	GA	30305	404-233-5993
Abbey Restaurant The (Continental) 163 Ponce De Leon Ave	Atlanta	GA	30308	404-876-8532
Web: www.theabbeyrestaurant.com				
Abruzzi (Italian) 2355 Peachtree Rd NE	Atlanta	GA	30305	404-261-8186
Annie's Thai Castle (Thai) 3195 Roswell Rd	Atlanta	GA	30305	404-264-9546
Anthony's Plantation Restaurant (American) 3109 Piedmont Rd NE	Atlanta	GA	30305	404-262-7379
Atlanta Fish Market (Seafood) 265 Pharr Rd	Atlanta	GA	30305	404-262-3165
Bacchanalia (New American) 3125 Piedmont Rd NE	Atlanta	GA	30305	404-365-0410
Bai Tong (Thai) 2329 Cheshire Bridge Rd	Atlanta	GA	30324	404-728-9040
Blue Ridge Grill (American) 1261 W Paces Ferry Rd	Atlanta	GA	30327	404-233-5030
Bone's Restaurant (American) 3130 Piedmont Rd NE	Atlanta	GA	30305	404-237-2663
Brasserie Le Coze (French) 3393 Peachtree Rd	Atlanta	GA	30326	404-266-1440
Buckhead Diner (American) 3073 Piedmont Rd NE	Atlanta	GA	30305	404-262-3336
Cafe The (Continental) Ritz-Carlton Buckhead 3434 Peachtree Rd NE	Atlanta	GA	30326	404-237-2700
Cafe The (Continental) Ritz-Carlton Atlanta 181 Peachtree St NE	Atlanta	GA	30303	404-659-0400
Canoe (American) 4199 Paces Ferry Rd NW	Atlanta	GA	30339	770-432-2808
Cassis (Mediterranean) 3300 Peachtree Rd	Atlanta	GA	30305	404-365-8100
Chops (Steak/Seafood) 70 West Paces Ferry Rd NW	Atlanta	GA	30305	404-262-2675
Ciboulette (French) 1529 Piedmont Ave	Atlanta	GA	30324	404-874-7600
City Grill (American) 50 Hurt Plaza Suite 200	Atlanta	GA	30303	404-524-2489
Coco Loco (Caribbean) 2625 Piedmont Rd Suite G40	Atlanta	GA	30324	404-364-0212
Coohill's Steakhouse (Steak) 1100 Peachtree St	Atlanta	GA	30309	404-724-0901
Dailey's Restaurant & Bar (American) 17 International Blvd	Atlanta	GA	30303	404-681-3303
Dusty's (Barbecue) 1815 Briarcliff Rd	Atlanta	GA	30329	404-320-6264
Eclipse di Luna (Spanish) 764 Miami Cir	Atlanta	GA	30324	404-846-0449
Fado's Irish Pub (Irish) 3035 Peachtree Rd	Atlanta	GA	30305	404-841-0066
Fairlie Poplar Cafe & Grill (Mediterranean) 85 Poplar St.	Atlanta	GA	30305	404-827-0040
Fat Matt's Rib Shack (Barbecue) 1811 Piedmont Ave	Atlanta	GA	30324	404-607-1622
First China (Chinese) 5295 Buford Hwy NE	Doraville	GA	30340	770-457-6788
Flying Biscuit Cafe (American) 1655 McLendon Ave	Atlanta	GA	30307	404-687-8888
Web: www.flyingbiscuit.com				
Food Studio (New American) 887 W Marietta St NW	Atlanta	GA	30318	404-815-6677
Georgia Grille (American) 2290 Peachtree Rd	Atlanta	GA	30309	404-352-3517
Hedgerose Heights Inn (American) 490 E Paces Ferry Rd NE	Atlanta	GA	30305	404-233-7673
Horseradish Grill (Southern) 4320 Powers Ferry Rd	Atlanta	GA	30342	404-255-7277
Hsu's Gourmet Chinese Restaurant (Chinese) 192 Peachtree Center Ave	Atlanta	GA	30303	404-659-2788
Imperial Fez (Moroccan) 2285 Peachtree Rd	Atlanta	GA	30309	404-351-0870
Kamogawa (Japanese) 3300 Peachtree Rd	Atlanta	GA	30305	404-841-0314
La Grotta (Italian) 2637 Peachtree Rd	Atlanta	GA	30305	404-231-1368
Luna Si (New American) 1931 Peachtree Rd	Atlanta	GA	30309	404-355-5993
Mama Ninfa's (Mexican) 231 Peachtree St NE	Atlanta	GA	30303	404-521-3500
Max Lager's American Grill & Brewery (American) 320 Peachtree St	Atlanta	GA	30308	404-525-4400
Mumbo Jumbo Bar & Grill (New American) 89 Park Pl	Atlanta	GA	30303	404-523-0330
Nava (Southwest) 3060 Peachtree Rd	Atlanta	GA	30305	404-240-1984
Nikolai's Roof (Continental) 255 Courtland St	Atlanta	GA	30303	404-221-6362
E-mail: nikolaislouis@msn.com				
Nuevo Laredo (Mexican) 1495 Chattahoochee Ave	Atlanta	GA	30318	404-352-9009
Old South Barbecue (American) 601 Burbank Cir	Smyrna	GA	30080	770-435-4215
Pano's & Paul's (Continental) 1232 W Paces Ferry Rd NW	Atlanta	GA	30327	404-261-3662
Pasta da Pulcinella (Italian) 1027 Peachtree St.	Atlanta	GA	30309	404-892-6195
Pittypat's Porch (Southern) 25 International Blvd	Atlanta	GA	30303	404-525-8228
Pleasant Peasant (Continental) 555 Peachtree St NE	Atlanta	GA	30308	404-874-3223
Polaris (Continental) 265 Peachtree St NE	Atlanta	GA	30303	404-577-1234
Pricci (Italian) 500 Pharr Rd	Atlanta	GA	30305	404-237-2941
Righteous Room (American) 1051 Ponce de Leon Ave	Atlanta	GA	30307	404-874-0939
Ritz-Carlton Dining Room (Continental) 3434 Peachtree Rd NE	Atlanta	GA	30326	404-237-2700
Rose & Crown (English) 288 E Paces Ferry Rd	Atlanta	GA	30305	404-233-8168
Savannah Fish Co (Seafood) 210 Peachtree St NW	Atlanta	GA	30303	404-589-7456
Seeger's (Continental) 111 W Paces Ferry Rd	Atlanta	GA	30305	404-846-9779
Soto Japanese Restaurant (Japanese) 3330 Piedmont Rd	Atlanta	GA	30305	404-233-2005
South City Kitchen (Southern) 1144 Crescent Ave	Atlanta	GA	30309	404-873-7358
Sundown Cafe (Southwest) 2165 Cheshire Bridge Rd	Atlanta	GA	30324	404-321-1118
Sylvia's of Atlanta (Southern) 241 Central Ave	Atlanta	GA	30305	404-529-9692
Tap Room (Italian) 231 Peachtree St Suite A5	Atlanta	GA	30303	404-577-7860
Thai Chili (Thai) 2169 Briarcliff Rd NE	Atlanta	GA	30329	404-315-6750
Tom Tom (New American) 3393 Peachtree Rd	Atlanta	GA	30329	404-264-1163
Van Gogh's (American) 70 W Crossville Rd	Roswell	GA	30075	770-993-1156
Veni-Vidi-Vici (Italian) 41 14th St	Atlanta	GA	30309	404-875-8424

Atlanta (Cont'd)

— Goods and Services —

SHOPPING

				Phone	Fax
Atlanta State Farmers' Market 16 Forest Pkwy	Forest Park	GA	30297	404-366-6910	362-4564
Buckhead Village Peachtree & E Paces Ferry Rds	Atlanta	GA	30305	404-233-2228	812-8222
Cumberland Mall 1000 Cumberland Mall	Atlanta	GA	30339	770-435-2206	438-0432
Galleria Specialty Mall 1 Galleria Pkwy	Atlanta	GA	30339	770-955-9100	955-0792
Greenbriar Mall 2841 Greenbriar Pkwy SW	Atlanta	GA	30331	404-344-6611	344-6631
Gwinnett Place Mall 2100 Pleasant Hill Rd	Duluth	GA	30109	770-476-5160	476-9355
Lenox Square Mall 3393 Peachtree Rd NE	Atlanta	GA	30326	404-233-6767	233-7868
North DeKalb Mall 2050 Lawrenceville Hwy	Decatur	GA	30033	404-320-7960	728-1942
Northlake Mall 1000 Northlake Mall	Atlanta	GA	30345	770-938-3564	938-5850
Northpoint Mall 1000 Northpoint Cir	Alpharetta	GA	30022	770-740-9273	442-8295
Peachtree Center 225 Peachtree St	Atlanta	GA	30303	404-524-3787	654-1200
Perimeter Mall 4400 Ashford-Dunwoody Rd	Atlanta	GA	30346	770-394-4270	396-4732
Web: www.perimetermall.com ■ *E-mail:* management@perimetermall.com					
Phipps Plaza 3500 Peachtree Rd NE	Atlanta	GA	30326	404-261-7910	
Web: www.phippsplaza.com					
Rich's/Goldsmith's/Lazarus Co 223 Perimeter Ctr Pkwy	Atlanta	GA	30346	770-396-2611	913-5114*
**Fax:* Hum Res					
Shannon Southpark Mall 1000 Shannon Southpark	Union City	GA	30291	770-964-2200	969-1273
South DeKalb Mall 2801 Candler Rd	Atlanta	GA	30034	404-241-2431	241-1831
Southlake Mall 1000 Southlake Mall	Morrow	GA	30260	770-961-1050	961-1113
Stone Mountain Village 891 Main St	Stone Mountain	GA	30083	770-879-4971	879-4972
Town Center at Cobb 400 Ernest Barrett Pkwy NW	Kennesaw	GA	30144	770-424-0915	424-7917
Underground Atlanta 50 Upper Alabama St	Atlanta	GA	30303	404-523-2311	523-0507
Web: www.underatl.com/					
Vinings Jubilee 4300 Paces Ferry Rd NW Suite 500	Atlanta	GA	30339	770-438-8080	438-8181

BANKS

				Phone	Fax
Amtrade International Bank of Georgia 1360 Peachtree St NE Suite 1105	Atlanta	GA	30309	404-898-1100	898-1110
Citizens Trust Bank 75 Piedmont Ave NE	Atlanta	GA	30303	404-659-5959	653-2877
Fidelity National Bank 3490 Piedmont Rd NE	Atlanta	GA	30305	404-639-6530	639-6534
Web: www.fidelitynational.com					
First Union National Bank 999 Peachtree St Suite 100	Atlanta	GA	30309	404-865-3010	865-3012
Mutual Federal Savings Bank 205 Auburn Ave NE	Atlanta	GA	30305	404-659-0701	659-3916
NationsBank 1800 Peachtree St NW	Atlanta	GA	30305	404-870-3040	870-3041
Web: www.nationsbank.com					
SouthTrust Bank of Georgia NA 2000 Riveredge Pkwy NW	Atlanta	GA	30328	770-951-4000	951-4496
TF: 800-606-0634					
SunTrust Bank 25 Park Pl NE	Atlanta	GA	30303	404-588-7711	827-6001*
**Fax:* Mktg					
Wachovia Bank NA 191 Peachtree St NE	Atlanta	GA	30303	404-332-4116	332-4139

BUSINESS SERVICES

	Phone
Any Time Service	404-763-0142
Central Delivery Service	404-209-5300
Corporate Express Delivery Systems	404-767-7930
Executive Courier	404-249-9000
Federal Express	800-463-3339
Georgia Messenger Service	404-681-3278
Kelly Services	404-607-7575
Kinko's	404-876-4752
Manpower Temporary Services	404-724-0780
MLQ Express	770-984-7000
Olsten Staffing Services	770-650-8101
Post Office	800-275-8777
UPS	800-742-5877

— Media —

PUBLICATIONS

				Phone	Fax
Atlanta Business Chronicle 1801 Peachtree St NE Suite 150	Atlanta	GA	30309	404-249-1000	249-1048
Web: www.amcity.com/atlanta					
Atlanta Constitution‡ PO Box 4689	Atlanta	GA	30302	404-526-5151	526-5746
Web: www.accessatlanta.com/ajc/ ■ *E-mail:* constitution@ajc.com					
Atlanta Journal‡ PO Box 4689	Atlanta	GA	30302	404-526-5151	526-5746
Web: www.accessatlanta.com/ajc ■ *E-mail:* info@cim.accessatlanta.com					
Atlanta Magazine 1330 W Peachtree St NE Suite 450	Atlanta	GA	30309	404-872-3100	870-6230
Web: atlantamagazine.com ■ *E-mail:* atlmag@atlanta.com					
Decatur/Tucker/Stone Mountain-DeKalb Neighbor 3060 Mercer University Dr Suite 210	Atlanta	GA	30341	770-454-9388	454-9131*
**Fax:* News Rm					

‡Daily newspapers

TELEVISION

				Phone	Fax
WAGA-TV Ch 5 (Fox) 1551 Briarcliff Rd NE	Atlanta	GA	30306	404-875-5555	898-0169
Web: wagatv.com ■ *E-mail:* feedback@wagatv.com					
WATL-TV Ch 36 (WB) 1 Monroe Pl	Atlanta	GA	30324	404-881-3600	881-3635
Web: www.wb36.com					
WGNX-TV Ch 46 (CBS) 1810 Briarcliff Rd NE	Atlanta	GA	30329	404-325-4646	327-3003
Web: www.wgnx.com					
WGTV-TV Ch 8 (PBS) 260 14th St NW	Atlanta	GA	30318	404-685-2400	685-2417
Web: www.gpb.org/gptv/gptv.htm ■ *E-mail:* viewerservices@gpb.org					
WPBA-TV Ch 30 (PBS) 740 Bismark Rd NE	Atlanta	GA	30324	404-827-8900	827-8956
Web: www.wpba.org					
WPXA-TV Ch 14 (PAX) 200 N Cobb Pkwy Suite 114	Marietta	GA	30062	770-528-1400	528-1403
Web: www.pax.net/WPXA					
WSB-TV Ch 2 (ABC) 1601 W Peachtree St NE	Atlanta	GA	30309	404-897-7000	897-7370
Web: www.wsbtv.com					
WTBS-TV Ch 17 (Ind) 1050 Techwood Dr NW	Atlanta	GA	30348	404-827-1717	827-1947
Web: tbssuperstation.com ■ *E-mail:* tbssuperstation@turner.com					
WUPA-TV Ch 69 (UPN) 2700 Northeast Expy Bldg A	Atlanta	GA	30345	404-325-6929	633-4567
Web: www.paramountstations.com/WUPA ■ *E-mail:* upn69@paramount.com					
WXIA-TV Ch 11 (NBC) 1611 W Peachtree St NE	Atlanta	GA	30309	404-892-1611	881-0182
Web: www.11alive.com					

RADIO

				Phone	Fax
WABE-FM 90.1 MHz (NPR) 740 Bismark Rd NE	Atlanta	GA	30324	404-827-8900	827-8956
Web: www.wabe.org/wabe.html					
WALR-AM 1340 kHz (Urban) 2970 Peachtree Rd Suite 700	Atlanta	GA	30305	404-688-0068	688-4262
WALR-FM 104.7 MHz (Urban) 2970 Peachtree Rd Suite 700	Atlanta	GA	30305	404-688-0068	688-4262
Web: www.kiss1047.com					
WAOK-AM 1380 kHz (Rel) 1201 Peachtree St NE Suite 800	Atlanta	GA	30361	404-898-8900	898-8916
WCLK-FM 91.9 MHz (NPR) 111 James P Brawley Dr SW	Atlanta	GA	30314	404-880-8273	880-8869
Web: www.cau-wclk.com ■ *E-mail:* gnsales@globolnet.com					
WCNN-AM 680 kHz (N/T) 1601 W Peachtree St	Atlanta	GA	30309	404-897-7500	897-7363
WFOX-FM 97.1 MHz (Oldies) 2000 Riveredge Pkwy Suite 797	Atlanta	GA	30328	770-953-9369	955-5483
Web: www.fox97.com					
WGST-AM 640 kHz (N/T) 1819 Peachtree St Suite 700	Atlanta	GA	30309	404-367-0640	367-1057
TF: 800-776-4638 ■ *Web:* www.wgst.com					
WGST-FM 105.7 MHz (N/T) 1819 Peachtree St Suite 700	Atlanta	GA	30309	404-367-0640	367-1057
TF: 800-776-4638 ■ *Web:* www.wgst.com ■ *E-mail:* wgst.feedback@sid.net					
WHTA-FM 97.5 MHz (Urban) 5526 Old National Hwy Bldg B-C	College Park	GA	30349	404-765-9750	765-0071
WJSP-FM 88.1 MHz (NPR) 260 14th St NW	Atlanta	GA	30318	404-685-2400	685-2684
Web: www.gpb.org/pspr					
WJZF-FM 104.1 MHz (NAC) 5520 Old National Hwy Suite B	College Park	GA	30349	404-761-2823	761-2839
WKHX-AM 590 kHz (Ctry) 210 I-North Pkwy 6th Fl	Atlanta	GA	30339	770-955-0101	953-4612
Web: www.wkhx.com					
WKHX-FM 101.5 MHz (Ctry) 210 I-North Pkwy 6th Fl	Atlanta	GA	30339	770-955-0101	953-4612
Web: www.wkhx.com					
WKLS-FM 96.1 MHz (Rock) 1800 Century Blvd Suite 1200	Atlanta	GA	30345	404-325-0960	325-8715
WNNX-FM 99.7 MHz (Alt) 3405 Piedmont Rd Suite 500	Atlanta	GA	30305	404-266-0997	364-5855
Web: www.99x.com					
WPCH-FM 94.9 MHz (AC) 1819 Peachtree Rd NE Suite 700	Atlanta	GA	30309	404-367-0949	367-9490
Web: www.peach949.com/					

Atlanta — Radio (Cont'd)

				Phone	Fax
WSB-AM 750 kHz (N/T) 1601 W Peachtree St NE	Atlanta	GA	30309	404-897-7500	897-7363
WSB-FM 98.5 MHz (AC) 1601 W Peachtree St NE	Atlanta	GA	30309	404-897-7500	897-7363
WSTR-FM 94.1 MHz (CHR) 3350 Peachtree Rd NE Suite 1800 *Web:* www.star94.com	Atlanta	GA	30326	404-261-2970	365-9026
WVEE-FM 103.3 MHz (Urban) 1201 Peachtree St NE Suite 800 *Web:* www.v-103.com	Atlanta	GA	30361	404-898-8900	898-8916
WYAY-FM 106.7 MHz (Ctry) 210 I-N Pkwy 6th Fl	Atlanta	GA	30339	770-955-0106	953-4612
WZGC-FM 92.9 MHz (CR) 1100 Johnson Ferry Rd Suite 593 *Web:* www.z93.com ■ *E-mail:* feedback@z93.com	Atlanta	GA	30342	404-851-9393	843-3541

— Colleges/Universities —

				Phone	Fax
Agnes Scott College 141 E College Ave *TF Admissions:* 800-868-8602 ■ *Web:* www.agnesscott.edu ■ *E-mail:* admission@agnesscott.edu	Decatur	GA	30030	404-471-6000	471-6414
American InterContinental University Atlanta 3330 Peachtree Rd NE *TF:* 800-255-6839 ■ *Web:* www.aiuniv.edu	Atlanta	GA	30326	404-965-5700	965-5701
Art Institute of Atlanta 6600 Peachtree Dunwoody Rd 100 Embassy Row *TF:* 800-275-4242 ■ *Web:* www.aii.edu	Atlanta	GA	30328	770-394-8300	394-0008
Atlanta Christian College 2605 Ben Hill Rd *Web:* www.acc.edu ■ *E-mail:* chargers777@juno.com	East Point	GA	30344	404-761-8861	669-2024
Atlanta College of Art 1280 Peachtree St NE *TF:* 800-832-2104 ■ *E-mail:* acainfo@woodruff-arts.org	Atlanta	GA	30309	404-733-5001	733-5107
Atlanta Metropolitan College 1630 Metropolitan Pkwy SW *Web:* www.atlm.peachnet.edu/	Atlanta	GA	30310	404-756-4004	756-4407
Bauder College 3500 Peachtree Rd NE *TF:* 800-241-3797 ■ *Web:* www.bauder.edu	Atlanta	GA	30326	404-237-7573	237-1642
Carver Bible Institute & College 437 Nelson St SW	Atlanta	GA	30313	404-527-4520	527-4526
Clark Atlanta University 223 James P Brawley Dr SW *TF Admissions:* 800-688-3228 ■ *Web:* www.cau.edu	Atlanta	GA	30314	404-880-8000	880-6174
DeVRY Institute of Technology 250 N Arcadia Ave *TF:* 800-221-4771	Decatur	GA	30030	404-292-7900	292-7011
Emory University 200 Jones Ctr *TF Admissions:* 800-727-6036 ■ *Web:* www.emory.edu	Atlanta	GA	30322	404-727-6036	727-4303
Georgia Baptist Bible College PO Box 429	Senoia	GA	30276	770-252-4004	
Georgia Institute of Technology 225 North Ave NW *Web:* www.gatech.edu ■ *E-mail:* admissions@success.gatech.edu	Atlanta	GA	30332	404-894-2000	894-9511
Georgia State University University Plaza *Web:* www.gsu.edu ■ *E-mail:* Admissions@GSU.edu	Atlanta	GA	30303	404-651-2000	651-4811
Gupton-Jones College of Funeral Service 5141 Snapfinger Woods Dr *TF:* 800-848-5352 ■ *Web:* www.gupton-jones.edu	Decatur	GA	30035	770-593-2257	593-1891
Herzing College 3355 Lenox Rd Suite 100 *TF:* 800-573-4533	Atlanta	GA	30326	404-816-4533	816-5576
Kennesaw State University 1000 Chastain Rd *Web:* www.kennesaw.edu	Kennesaw	GA	30144	770-423-6000	423-6541
Mercer University Cecil B Day Campus 3001 Mercer University Dr *Web:* www.mercer.edu/cbd ■ *E-mail:* postmaster@mercer.edu	Atlanta	GA	30341	770-986-3000	986-3135
Morehouse College 830 Westview Dr SW *TF Admissions:* 800-851-1254 ■ *Web:* www.morehouse.edu	Atlanta	GA	30314	404-681-2800	659-6536
Morris Brown College 643 ML King Jr Dr NW	Atlanta	GA	30314	404-220-0270	220-0371
Oglethorpe University 4484 Peachtree Rd NE *TF Admissions:* 800-428-4484 ■ *Web:* www.oglethorpe.edu	Atlanta	GA	30319	404-261-1441	364-8491
Southern Polytechnic State University 1100 S Marietta Pkwy *TF Admissions:* 800-635-3204 ■ *Web:* www.sct.edu	Marietta	GA	30060	770-528-7281	528-7292
Spelman College 350 Spelman Ln SW *TF Admissions:* 800-982-2411 ■ *Web:* www.spelman.edu ■ *E-mail:* admiss@spelman.edu	Atlanta	GA	30314	404-681-3643	215-7788
State University of West Georgia 1600 Maple St **Fax:* Hum Res ■ *Web:* www.westga.edu	Carrollton	GA	30118	770-836-6500	836-4637*

— Hospitals —

				Phone	Fax
Atlanta Medical Center 303 Parkway Dr NE **Fax:* Admitting	Atlanta	GA	30312	404-265-4000	265-4595*
Baptist Medical Center 1200 Medical Center Dr	Cumming	GA	30041	770-887-2355	844-4327
Crawford Long Hospital of Emory University 550 Peachtree St NE *Web:* www.ect.enron.com/products/assets/louisiana.fset.html	Atlanta	GA	30365	404-686-4411	686-2848
DeKalb Medical Center 2701 N Decatur Rd *Web:* www.drhs.org	Decatur	GA	30033	404-501-1000	501-5147
Dunwoody Medical Center 4575 N Shallowford Rd	Atlanta	GA	30338	770-454-2000	454-4279
Eastside Medical Center 1700 Medical Way	Snellville	GA	30078	770-979-0200	736-2395
Egleston Children's Hospital at Emory University 1405 Clifton Rd NE	Atlanta	GA	30322	404-325-6000	315-2347
Emory Northlake Regional Medical Center 1455 Montreal Rd	Tucker	GA	30084	770-270-3000	270-3446
Emory University Hospital 1364 Clifton Rd NE	Atlanta	GA	30322	404-712-7021	712-7801
Grady Memorial Hospital 80 Butler St **Fax:* Admitting	Atlanta	GA	30335	404-616-4307	616-9208*
Henry Medical Center 1133 Eagle's Landing Pkwy	Stockbridge	GA	30281	770-389-2200	389-2083
Hughes Spalding Children's Hospital 35 Butler St	Atlanta	GA	30335	404-616-6600	616-5006
Mountainside Medical Center 1266 E Church St	Jasper	GA	30143	706-692-2441	692-6754
Newnan Hospital 80 Jackson St *Web:* www.newnanhospital.com	Newnan	GA	30263	770-253-2330	254-0566
Newton General Hospital 5126 Hospital Dr NE	Covington	GA	30014	770-786-7053	787-9059
North Fulton Regional Hospital 3000 Hospital Blvd **Fax:* Cust Svc ■ *Web:* www.tenethealth.com/NorthFulton	Roswell	GA	30076	770-751-2545	751-2767*
Northside Hospital 1000 Johnson Ferry Rd NE *Web:* www.northside.com	Atlanta	GA	30342	404-851-8000	303-3333
Parkway Medical Center 1000 Thornton Rd	Lithia Springs	GA	30122	770-732-7777	732-7896
Peachtree Regional Hospital 60 Hospital Rd	Newnan	GA	30263	770-253-1912	304-4244
Piedmont Hospital 1968 Peachtree Rd NW	Atlanta	GA	30309	404-605-5000	609-6832
Promina Gwinnett Medical Center 1000 Medical Center Blvd *Web:* www.gwinnetthealth.org	Lawrenceville	GA	30045	770-995-4321	682-2257
Rockdale Hospital 1412 Milstead Ave NE	Conyers	GA	30012	770-918-3000	918-3104
Saint Joseph's Hospital of Atlanta 5665 Peachtree Dunwoody Rd NE *TF:* 800-678-5637	Atlanta	GA	30342	404-851-7001	851-7339
Scottish Rite Children's Medical Center 1001 Johnson Ferry Rd NE **Fax:* Admitting ■ *Web:* www.scottishritechildrens.org	Atlanta	GA	30342	404-256-5252	250-2799*
South Fulton Medical Center 1170 Cleveland Ave	East Point	GA	30344	404-305-3500	305-4418
Southern Regional Medical Center 11 Upper Riverdale Rd SW **Fax:* Acctg	Riverdale	GA	30274	770-991-8000	991-8644*
Southwest Hospital & Medical Center 501 Fairburn Rd SW **Fax:* Hum Res	Atlanta	GA	30331	404-699-1111	505-5379*
Spalding Regional Hospital 601 S 8th St	Griffin	GA	30224	770-228-2721	229-6489
Tanner Medical Center 705 Dixie St	Carrollton	GA	30117	770-836-9666	836-9897
Veterans Affairs Medical Center 1670 Clairmont Rd	Decatur	GA	30033	404-321-6111	728-5000
Walton Medical Center 330 Alcovy St	Monroe	GA	30655	770-267-8461	267-1888
Wellstar Cobb Hospital 3950 Austell Rd **Fax:* Admitting	Austell	GA	30106	770-732-4000	732-3703*
Wellstar Douglas Hospital 8954 Hospital Dr	Douglasville	GA	30134	770-949-1500	920-6413
Wellstar Kennestone Hospital 677 Church St	Marietta	GA	30060	770-793-5000	793-7966
WellStar Paulding Hospital 600 W Memorial Dr	Dallas	GA	30132	770-445-4411	443-7049
West Paces Medical Center 3200 Howell Mill Rd NW **Fax:* Admitting	Atlanta	GA	30327	404-351-0351	350-4417*

— Attractions —

				Phone	Fax
14th Street Playhouse 173 14th St	Atlanta	GA	30309	404-733-4750	733-4756
Academy Theatre 501 Means St	Atlanta	GA	30318	404-525-4111	525-5659
African-American Panoramic Experience 135 Auburn Ave NE	Atlanta	GA	30303	404-521-2739	523-3248
Alliance Theatre Co 1280 Peachtree St NE Woodruff Arts Ctr *Web:* www.alliancetheatre.org	Atlanta	GA	30309	404-733-5000	733-4625

Atlanta — Attractions (Cont'd)

Name / Address	City	State	ZIP	Phone	Fax
American Adventures White Water Park					
250 N Cobb Pkwy	Marietta	GA	30062	770-424-9283	424-7565
Web: www.whitewaterpark.com					
■ *E-mail:* whitewaterpark@mindspring.com					
Antebellum Roswell Historic District					
Canton St & Town Sq	Roswell	GA	30075	770-640-3253	640-3252
Artist's Colony Main St	Buford	GA	30518	770-945-9718	
Asian Square 5150 Buford Hwy NE	Doraville	GA	30340	770-458-8899	
Atlanta Ballet 1400 W Peachtree St NW	Atlanta	GA	30309	404-873-5811	874-7905
Web: www.atlantaballet.com/					
Atlanta Botanical Garden 1345 Piedmont Ave	Atlanta	GA	30309	404-876-5859	876-7472
Web: www.atlgarden.com					
Atlanta China Town					
5379 New Peachtree Rd	Chamblee	GA	30341	770-458-4624	451-4462
Atlanta Cyclorama 800-C Cherokee Ave SE	Atlanta	GA	30315	404-658-7625	658-7045
Atlanta History Center 130 W Paces Ferry Rd	Atlanta	GA	30305	404-814-4000	814-4186
Web: www.atlhist.org					
Atlanta International Museum of Art & Design					
285 Peachtree Center Ave	Atlanta	GA	30303	404-688-2467	521-9311
Web: www.atlinternationalmuseum.org					
Atlanta Opera					
728 West Peachtree St NW Suite 620	Atlanta	GA	30308	404-881-8801	881-1711
TF: 800-356-7372 ■ *Web:* www.atlantaopera.org					
Atlanta Preservation Center 537 Peachtree St	Atlanta	GA	30308	404-876-2040	876-2618
Atlanta Symphony Orchestra					
1293 Peachtree St NE Suite 300	Atlanta	GA	30309	404-733-4900	733-4901
Web: www.atlantasymphony.org					
Buckhead Village					
Peachtree & E Paces Ferry Rds	Atlanta	GA	30305	404-233-2228	812-8222
Callanwolde Fine Arts Center					
980 Briarcliff Rd NE	Atlanta	GA	30306	404-872-5338	872-5175
Web: www.mindspring.com/~callanwolde/					
■ *E-mail:* callanwolde@mindspring.com					
Carlos Michael C Museum					
571 S Kilgo St Carlos Hall	Atlanta	GA	30322	404-727-4282	727-4292
Web: www.cc.emory.edu/CARLOS					
Centennial Olympic Park					
International Blvd & Techwood Dr	Atlanta	GA	30313	404-222-7275	223-4499
Web: www.gwcc.com					
Center for Puppetry Arts 1404 Spring St NW	Atlanta	GA	30309	404-873-3089	873-9907
Web: www.puppet.org/ ■ *E-mail:* puppet@mindspring.com					
Chastain Memorial Park 135 W Wieuca Rd	Atlanta	GA	30342	404-817-6788	
Chateau Elan Winery 100 Tour de France	Braselton	GA	30517	770-932-0900	271-6005
TF: 800-233-9463 ■ *Web:* www.chateauelan.com					
■ *E-mail:* chateau@chateaelan.com					
Chattahoochee Nature Center					
9135 Willeo Rd	Roswell	GA	30075	770-992-2055	552-0926
Chattahoochee River National Recreation Area					
1978 Island Ford Pkwy	Atlanta	GA	30350	770-399-8070	392-7045
Web: www.nps.gov/chat/					
Children's Museum of Atlanta					
1 Park Tower Suite 2055	Atlanta	GA	30303	404-659-5437	223-3675
Clayton County International Park					
2300 Hwy 138 SE	Jonesboro	GA	30236	770-478-1932	477-1696
CNN Center/CNN Studio Tours					
1 CNN Ctr Box 105366	Atlanta	GA	30348	404-827-2400	
Web: www.cnn.com/StudioTour/ ■ *E-mail:* cnn.studio.tour@cnn.com					
Concord Covered Bridge & Historic District					
Concord Rd	Smyrna	GA	30080	404-656-3590	
Dad's Garage Theatre Co 280 Elizabeth St	Atlanta	GA	30307	404-523-3141	688-6644
Web: www.dadsgarage.com ■ *E-mail:* info@dadsgarage.com					
Ebenezer Baptist Church 407 Auburn Ave NE	Atlanta	GA	30312	404-688-7263	521-1129
Web: www.ebenezer.org					
Federal Reserve Bank Monetary Museum					
104 Marietta St NW	Atlanta	GA	30303	404-521-8784	521-8050
Fernbank Museum of Natural History					
767 Clifton Rd NE	Atlanta	GA	30307	404-378-0127	370-8087
Web: www.fernbank.edu/museum/index.html					
Fernbank Science Center					
156 Heaton Park Dr NE	Atlanta	GA	30307	404-378-4311	370-1336
Web: www.fernbank.edu/fsc/fsc.html					
Fox Theatre 660 Peachtree St NE	Atlanta	GA	30365	404-881-2100	872-2972
Web: www.thefoxtheater.com					
■ *E-mail:* foxmanagement@mindspring.com					
Frabel Studio & Galleries 695 Antone St NW	Atlanta	GA	30318	404-351-9794	351-1491
Georgia State Capitol	Atlanta	GA	30334	404-656-2844	
Goethe Institut Atlanta/German Cultural Center					
1197 Peachtree St NE	Atlanta	GA	30361	404-892-2388	892-3832
Web: www.goethe.de/uk/atl/ ■ *E-mail:* goetheatlanta@mindspring.com					
Governor's Mansion 391 W Paces Ferry Rd	Atlanta	GA	30305	404-261-1776	231-8621
Grant Park 537 Park Ave SE	Atlanta	GA	30312	404-624-0697	
Hammonds House 503 Peeples St SW	Atlanta	GA	30310	404-752-8730	752-8733
Herndon House 587 University Pl NW	Atlanta	GA	30314	404-581-9813	
High Museum of Art 1280 Peachtree St NE	Atlanta	GA	30309	404-733-4200	733-4502
Web: www.high.org					
High Museum of Art Folk Art & Photography					
Galleries 30 John Wesley Dobbs Ave NE	Atlanta	GA	30303	404-577-6940	653-0916
Web: www.high.org					
Historic Marietta Square 4 Depot St	Marietta	GA	30060	770-429-1115	428-3443
Historic Oakland Cemetery					
248 Oakland Ave SE	Atlanta	GA	30312	404-688-2107	658-6092
IMAX Theater					
767 Clifton Rd NE Fernbank Museum of					
Natural History	Atlanta	GA	30307	404-378-0127	378-8140
Jimmy Carter Library & Museum					
441 Freedom Pkwy	Atlanta	GA	30307	404-331-3942	730-2215
Web: carterlibrary.galileo.peachnet.edu					
Kennesaw Mountain National Battlefield Park					
900 Kennesaw Mountain Dr	Kennesaw	GA	30152	770-427-4686	528-8399
Web: www.nps.gov/kemo/					
Lillie Glassblowers 3431 Lake Dr SE	Smyrna	GA	30082	770-436-8959	435-0695
Martin Luther King Jr Center for Nonviolent					
Social Change Inc 449 Auburn Ave NE	Atlanta	GA	30312	404-524-1956	526-8901
Martin Luther King Jr National Historic Site					
450 Auburn Ave NE	Atlanta	GA	30312	404-331-3920	331-7620
Web: www.nps.gov/malu/					
Mitchell Margaret House					
999 Peachtree St Suite 775	Atlanta	GA	30309	404-249-7012	249-9388
Web: www.gwtw.org					
Nexus Contemporary Art Center 535 Means St	Atlanta	GA	30318	404-688-2500	577-5856
Web: www.nexusart.org					
Oglethorpe University Museum					
4484 Peachtree Rd NE	Atlanta	GA	30319	404-364-8555	364-8556
Web: museum.oglethorpe.edu					
Omenala-Griot Afrocentric Teaching Museum					
337 Dargan Pl SW	Atlanta	GA	30310	404-755-8403	
Piedmont Park 400 Park Dr	Atlanta	GA	30306	404-817-6788	
Rhodes Hall 1516 Peachtree St NW	Atlanta	GA	30309	404-881-9980	875-2205
Rialto Center for the Performing Arts					
80 Forsyth St	Atlanta	GA	30303	404-651-1234	651-1332
Web: www.rialtocenter.org					
SciTrek Science & Technology Museum					
395 Piedmont Ave NE	Atlanta	GA	30308	404-522-5500	659-1861
Web: scitrek.org					
Shakespeare Tavern 499 Peachtree Street NE	Atlanta	GA	30308	404-874-5299	
Sibley's Christine Urban Nirvana					
15 Waddell St NE	Atlanta	GA	30307	404-688-3329	688-0665
Six Flags Over Georgia 7561 Six Flags Pkwy	Austell	GA	30168	770-948-9290	948-4378
Web: www.sixflags.com/georgia					
Smith Plantation Home 935 Alpharetta St	Roswell	GA	30075	770-641-3978	641-3974
Southface Energy & Environmental Resource					
Center 241 Pine St	Atlanta	GA	30308	404-872-3549	872-5009
Web: www.southface.org					
Stately Oaks Plantation PO Box 922	Jonesboro	GA	30237	770-473-0197	473-9855
Stone Mountain Park					
6867 Memorial Dr	Stone Mountain	GA	30087	770-498-5690	498-5607
Web: www.stonemountainpark.org					
■ *E-mail:* mail@stonemountainpark.org					
Stone Mountain Village 891 Main St	Stone Mountain	GA	30083	770-879-4971	879-4972
Swan House & Tullie Smith Farm					
130 W Paces Ferry Rd	Atlanta	GA	30305	404-814-4000	
Telephone Museum					
675 W Peachtree St NE Southern Bell Ctr	Atlanta	GA	30375	404-223-3661	
Theater of the Stars 4469 Stella Dr	Atlanta	GA	30327	404-252-8960	252-1460
Underground Atlanta 50 Upper Alabama St	Atlanta	GA	30303	404-523-2311	523-0507
Web: www.underatl.com/					
Vines Botanical Gardens					
3500 Oak Grove Rd	Loganville	GA	30052	770-466-7532	466-7854
William Breman Jewish Heritage Museum					
1440 Spring St NW	Atlanta	GA	30309	404-873-1661	881-4009
Williams Robert C American Museum of					
Papermaking 500 10th St NW	Atlanta	GA	30318	404-894-7840	894-4778
Web: www.ipst.edu/amp/					
Woodruff Robert W Arts Center					
1280 Peachtree St NE	Atlanta	GA	30309	404-733-4200	733-4281
Web: www.woodruff-arts.org					
World of Coca-Cola Pavilion					
55 ML King Jr Dr	Atlanta	GA	30303	404-676-5151	676-5432
Web: www.cocacola.com/museum/					
Yellow River Game Ranch 4525 Hwy 78	Lilburn	GA	30247	770-972-6643	985-0150
Zoo Atlanta 800 Cherokee Ave	Atlanta	GA	30315	404-624-5600	627-7514
Web: www.zooatlanta.org					

SPORTS TEAMS & FACILITIES

Name / Address	City	State	ZIP	Phone
Alexander Memorial Coliseum 965 Fowler St	Atlanta	GA	30332	404-894-2000

Atlanta — Sports Teams & Facilities (Cont'd)

				Phone	Fax
Atlanta Braves 755 Hank Aaron Dr Turner Field	Atlanta	GA	30315	404-522-7630	614-1329*
**Fax:* Mktg ■ *Web:* www.atlantabraves.com/ ■ *E-mail:* braves@atlantabraves.com					
Atlanta Classics N Druid Hills Rd Adams Stadium	Atlanta	GA	30319	770-879-3668	879-7110
Web: www.atlantaclassics.com ■ *E-mail:* news@atlantaclassics.com					
Atlanta Falcons 1 Falcon Pl	Suwanee	GA	30024	770-945-1111	271-1221
TF: 800-241-3489 ■ *Web:* www.atlantafalcons.com					
Atlanta Hawks 1 CNN Ctr	Atlanta	GA	30303	404-827-3865	827-3806*
**Fax:* Sales ■ *Web:* www.nba.com/hawks					
Atlanta Motor Speedway 1500 Hwys 19 & 41 S	Hampton	GA	30228	770-946-3920	946-3928
Web: www.atlantamotorspeedway.com					
Atlanta Silverbacks (soccer) 116 E Howard Ave	Decatur	GA	30030	404-377-5575	377-5558
Web: www.atlantasilverbacks.com/home.html ■ *E-mail:* tickets@atlantasilverbacks.com					
Atlanta Trojans (basketball) 3640 Burnette Rd	Suwanee	GA	30024	770-614-6686	614-6993
Web: www.usbl.com/atlanta.html					
Colorado Silver Bullets (baseball) 1575 Sheridan Rd NE Suite 200	Atlanta	GA	30324	404-636-8200	636-0530
TF: 800-278-2772 ■ *E-mail:* sbulletsi@aol.com					
Georgia Dome 1 Georgia Dome Dr NW	Atlanta	GA	30313	404-223-9200	223-8011
Web: www.gwcc.com/domeinfo.htm					
Road Atlanta Raceway 5300 Winder Hwy	Braselton	GA	30517	770-967-6143	967-2668
Web: www.roadatlanta.com					
Turner Field 755 Hank Aaron Dr	Atlanta	GA	30315	404-522-7630	614-1329
Web: www.atlantabraves.com/turnerfield					

— Events —

	Phone
Art of the Season (late November-early December)	404-220-2659
Atlanta Boat Show (early January)	770-951-2500
Atlanta Caribbean Folk Festival (late May)	404-753-3497
Atlanta Dogwood Festival (early April)	404-329-0501
Atlanta Film & Video Festival (mid-May)	404-352-4254
Atlanta Garden & Patio Show (late January)	770-998-9800
Atlanta Greek Festival (late September)	404-633-5870
Atlanta Home Show (late March)	770-998-9800
Atlanta Jazz Festival (late May)	404-817-6851
Atlanta Marathon (late November)	404-231-9064
Atlanta Renaissance Festival (late April-early June)	770-964-8575
Atlanta Steeplechase (early April)	404-222-6688
CNN Center Tuba Christmas (mid-December)	770-887-5856
Down to Earth Day Celebration (April 22)	404-873-3173
Festival of Trees (early December)	404-325-6635
First Night Atlanta (December 31)	404-881-0400
Fright Fest (October)	770-948-9290
Georgia Renaissance Festival (late April-early June)	770-964-8575
Georgia Shakespeare Festival (early June-late December)	404-264-0020
Holiday Celebration (late November-late December)	770-498-5600
Inman Park Spring Festival & Tour of Homes (late April)	770-242-4895
Labor Day Weekend Festival (early September)	404-523-2311
Montreaux Atlanta International Jazz Festival (early September)	404-521-6600
National Black Arts Festival (late July-early August)	404-730-7315
National King Week (January)	404-524-1956
New Year's Eve Peach Drop (December 31)	404-523-2311
Peach Bowl (December 31)	404-586-8500
Peachtree International Film Festival (early-mid-November)	770-729-8487
PGA BellSouth Classic (late March-early April)	770-951-8777
Rose Show & Sale (early May)	404-876-5859
Roswell Arts Festival (late September)	770-640-3253
Saint Patrick's Day Celebration (mid-March)	404-523-2311
Salute 2 America Parade (July 4)	404-521-6600
Scottish Festival & Highland Games (mid-October)	770-498-5702
Southeastern Flower Show (mid-February)	404-888-5638
Springfest Festival (early May)	770-498-5702
Stone Mountain Village Arts & Crafts Festival (mid-June)	770-498-2097
Super Bowl XXXIV (late January)	404-223-9200
Thunder over Atlanta Fireworks (July 4)	404-523-2311
Tour of Southern Ghosts (mid-late October)	770-469-1105
Vinings Fall Festival (early October)	770-438-8080
Yellow Daisy Festival (early September)	770-498-5702

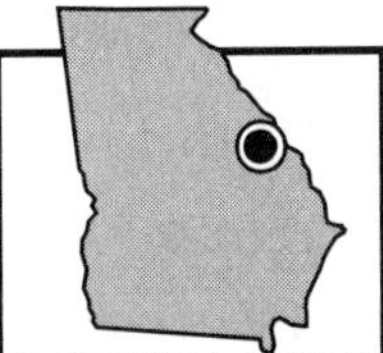

Augusta

The second oldest city in Georgia, Augusta is part of the state's Classic South travel region. Visitors to its historic districts can tour antebellum plantations, the Cotton Exchange that was built in 1886 as headquarters for Augusta's cotton industry, and other historic sites dating from colonial times to the present. In downtown Augusta, on the banks of the Savannah River, is Augusta Riverwalk, which has fairs, festivals, shopping, nightlife, museums, and restaurants. The river is also the city's main attraction for boating events. The prestigious Masters Golf Tournament is held annually in April at the Augusta National Golf Club.

Population	187,689	**Longitude**	82-01-67 W
Area (Land)	19.7 sq mi	**County**	Richmond
Area (Water)	1.3 sq mi	**Time Zone**	EST
Elevation	414 ft	**Area Code/s**	706
Latitude	33-46-67 N		

— Average Temperatures and Precipitation —

TEMPERATURES

	Jan	Feb	Mar	Apr	May	Jun	Jul	Aug	Sep	Oct	Nov	Dec
High	56	61	69	77	84	89	92	90	86	77	68	60
Low	32	35	42	49	58	66	70	70	63	50	42	35

PRECIPITATION

	Jan	Feb	Mar	Apr	May	Jun	Jul	Aug	Sep	Oct	Nov	Dec
Inches	4.1	4.3	4.7	3.3	3.8	4.1	4.2	4.5	3.0	2.8	2.5	3.4

— Important Phone Numbers —

	Phone		Phone
AAA	706-738-6611	**Riverwalk Special Events**	706-821-1754
Emergency	911	**Weather**	706-724-0056
Poison Control Center	800-282-5846		

— Information Sources —

				Phone	Fax
Augusta City Hall 530 Greene St.	Augusta	GA	30911	706-821-2300	821-2819
Web: augusta.co.richmond.ga.us ■ *E-mail:* lb6764@supct.co.richmond.ga.us					
Augusta Mayor 530 Greene St Rm 801	Augusta	GA	30911	706-821-1831	821-1838
Web: augusta.co.richmond.ga.us/mayor/default.htm ■ *E-mail:* mayoryoung@co.richmond.ga.us					
Augusta Metropolitan Convention & Visitors Bureau 1450 Greene St Suite 110	Augusta	GA	30901	706-823-6600	823-6609
TF: 800-726-0243 ■ *Web:* www.augustaga.org ■ *E-mail:* august-cvb@groupz.net					
Augusta-Richmond County 530 Greene St	Augusta	GA	30911	706-821-2300	821-2520
Augusta-Richmond County Civic Center 601 7th St	Augusta	GA	30901	706-722-3521	724-7545
Web: www.augustaciviccenter.com ■ *E-mail:* info@arccc.com					
Augusta-Richmond County Library 902 Greene St	Augusta	GA	30901	706-821-2600	724-6762
Web: ecgrl.home.duesouth.net					
Better Business Bureau Serving Northeast Georgia & Southwest South Carolina PO Box 2085	Augusta	GA	30903	706-722-1574	724-0969
Web: www.augusta-ga.bbb.org					
Historic Augusta Inc 111 10th St	Augusta	GA	30903	706-724-0436	724-3083
Metro Augusta Chamber of Commerce 600 Broad Street Plaza	Augusta	GA	30903	706-821-1300	821-1330
Web: www.metroaugusta.com ■ *E-mail:* augustausa@aol.com					

Augusta (Cont'd)

On-Line Resources

4Augusta.com www.4augusta.com
About.com Guide to Augusta . . . . augustaga.about.com
Anthill City Guide Augusta . . . . www.anthill.com/city.asp?city=augusta
Area Guide Augusta . . . . augustaga.areaguides.net
Augusta Georgia . . . . augusta-georgia.com
Best Read Guide Augusta . . . . bestreadguide.com/augusta
City Knowledge Augusta . . . . www.cityknowledge.com/ga_augusta.htm
Excite.com Augusta City Guide . . . . www.excite.com/travel/countries/united_states/georgia/augusta/

— Transportation Services —

AIRPORTS

■ **Bush Field (AGS)** — *Phone*
8 miles S of downtown (approx 20 minutes) 706-798-2656

Airport Transportation

	Phone
Radio Cab $18 fare to downtown	706-722-3501
Yellow Cab $25 fare to downtown	706-722-7711

Commercial Airlines

	Phone		*Phone*
Delta	800-221-1212	**US Airways**	800-428-4322
Delta Connection	800-221-1212	**US Airways Express**	800-428-4322

Charter Airlines

	Phone
Augusta Aviation	706-733-8970

CAR RENTALS

	Phone		*Phone*
Avis	706-798-1383	**Hertz**	706-798-3970
Budget	706-790-6901	**National**	706-798-5835
Economy	706-863-8101		

LIMO/TAXI

	Phone		*Phone*
A Touch of Class Limousine	706-869-1120	**Queens Limousine**	706-793-4715
Augusta Limousine	706-724-3543	**Radio Cab**	706-722-3501
Bentley Production	706-793-8880	**Simons Limousine**	706-793-4896
Curtis Cab	706-722-9925	**Yellow Cab**	706-722-7711

MASS TRANSIT

	Phone
Augusta Public Transit $.75 Base fare	706-821-1719

RAIL/BUS

				Phone
Greyhound Bus Station 1128 Greene St *TF:* 800-231-2222	Augusta	GA	30901	706-722-6411

— Accommodations —

HOTEL RESERVATION SERVICES

	Phone
Georgia Room Reservations	800-554-2778

HOTELS, MOTELS, RESORTS

				Phone	*Fax*
AmeriSuites 1062 Claussen Rd. *TF:* 800-833-1516	Augusta	GA	30907	706-733-4656	736-1133
Augusta Airport Inn 1520 Aviation Way	Augusta	GA	30906	706-798-5501	792-0200
Augusta Lodge 1520 Gordon Hwy.	Augusta	GA	30906	706-798-2230	796-3823
Azalea Inn 316 Greene St *Web:* www.azaleainn.com	Augusta	GA	30901	706-724-3454	
Best Western 452 Park West Dr *TF:* 800-528-1234	Grovetown	GA	30813	706-651-9100	651-0514
Budget Inn Augusta 441 Broad St.	Augusta	GA	30901	706-722-0212	722-8706
Comfort Inn 629 Frontage Rd NW *TF:* 800-228-5150	Augusta	GA	30907	706-855-6060	855-8008
Courtyard by Marriott 1045 Stevens Creek Rd *TF:* 800-321-2211 ■ *Web:* courtyard.com/AGSCH	Augusta	GA	30907	706-737-3737	738-7851
Days Inn 3026 Washington Rd *TF:* 800-328-6466	Augusta	GA	30907	706-738-0131	738-0131
Days Inn Wheeler Rd 3654 Wheeler Rd *TF:* 800-329-7466	Augusta	GA	30909	706-868-8610	868-8610
Econo Lodge 444 Broad St. *TF:* 877-326-6634	Augusta	GA	30901	706-724-8100	
Econo Lodge 4090 Belair Rd *TF:* 800-424-4777	Augusta	GA	30909	706-863-0777	863-0777
Econo Lodge 2852 Washington Rd *TF:* 800-446-6900	Augusta	GA	30909	706-736-0707	736-0707
Fairfield Inn Augusta 201 Boy Scout Rd *TF:* 800-228-2800 ■ *Web:* fairfieldinn.com/AGSFI	Augusta	GA	30909	706-733-8200	733-8200
Gateway Inn 3061 Deans Bridge Rd	Augusta	GA	30906	706-798-8480	560-2903
Hampton Inn 3030 Washington Rd *TF:* 800-426-7866	Augusta	GA	30907	706-737-1122	738-9988
Holiday Inn Express 1103 15th St. *TF:* 800-465-4329	Augusta	GA	30901	706-724-5560	774-6821
Holiday Inn West 1075 Stevens Creek Rd *TF:* 800-465-4329	Augusta	GA	30907	706-738-8811	737-3600
Homewood Suites 1049 Stevens Creek Rd. *TF:* 800-225-5466	Augusta	GA	30907	706-650-5858	736-6562
Howard Johnson Inn 1238 Gordon Hwy.	Augusta	GA	30901	706-724-9613	724-9613
Knights Inn 210 Boy Scout Rd *TF:* 800-843-5644	Augusta	GA	30909	706-737-3166	731-9204
La Quinta Motor Inn 3020 Washington Rd. *TF:* 800-687-6667	Augusta	GA	30907	706-733-2660	738-3637
Masters Economy Inn 3027 Washington Rd. *TF:* 800-633-3434	Augusta	GA	30907	706-863-5566	863-5566
Partridge Inn 2110 Walton Way *TF:* 800-476-6888	Augusta	GA	30904	706-737-8888	731-0826
Perrin Guest House Inn 208 LaFayette Dr	Augusta	GA	30909	706-731-0920	731-9009
Radisson Riverfront Hotel Augusta 2 10th St. *TF:* 800-333-3333	Augusta	GA	30901	706-722-8900	823-6513
Radisson Suites 3038 Washington Rd. *TF:* 800-333-3333	Augusta	GA	30907	706-868-1800	868-9300
Ramada Limited 2154 Gordon Hwy *TF:* 800-272-6232	Augusta	GA	30909	706-733-8115	733-8115
Ramada Limited 4324 Frontage Rd. *TF:* 800-272-6232	Augusta	GA	30909	706-860-8840	860-8840
Ramada Plaza 640 Broad St *TF:* 800-257-5060	Augusta	GA	30901	706-722-5541	724-0053
Red Carpet Inn 1455 Walton Way *TF:* 800-228-5160	Augusta	GA	30901	706-722-2224	722-4212
Sheraton Hotel Augusta 2651 Perimeter Pkwy *TF:* 800-325-3535	Augusta	GA	30909	706-855-8100	860-1720
Shoney's Inn Augusta 3023 Washington Rd. *TF:* 800-222-2222 ■ *Web:* www.shoneysinn.com/ga1.htm	Augusta	GA	30907	706-736-2595	733-1524
Sunset Inn 3034 Washington Rd.	Augusta	GA	30907	706-860-8485	860-3567
Super 8 Motel 2137 Gordon Hwy *TF:* 800-800-8000	Augusta	GA	30909	706-738-5018	738-5018
Valu Lodge 1365 Gordon Hwy *TF:* 800-580-8258	Augusta	GA	30901	706-722-4344	724-4437
Wingate Inn 4087 Belair Rd *TF:* 800-228-1000	Augusta	GA	30909	706-860-8223	860-5520

— Restaurants —

				Phone
Andrew's Sea Grille (Seafood) 2651 Perimeter Pkwy	Augusta	GA	30909	706-855-8100
Augustino's (Italian) 2 10th St.	Augusta	GA	30901	706-823-6521
Beamie's (Seafood) 9th & Reynolds Sts	Augusta	GA	30901	706-724-6593
Cadwalladers Cafe (Continental) 106-A Davis Rd	Augusta	GA	30907	706-860-7444
California Dreaming (American) 3241 Washington Rd	Augusta	GA	30907	706-860-6206
Calvert's (Continental) 475 Highland Ave	Augusta	GA	30909	706-738-4514
Cotton Patch (American) 816 Cotton Ln	Augusta	GA	30901	706-724-4511
Cotton Row Cafe (American) 2 8th St.	Augusta	GA	30901	706-828-2100
Formosa's (Chinese) 3830 Washington Rd	Augusta	GA	30907	706-855-8998
French Market Grille (Cajun) 425 Highland Ave.	Augusta	GA	30909	706-737-4865
King George Restaurant & Riverwalk Brewery (English) 2 8th St	Augusta	GA	30901	706-724-4755
Le Cafe du Teau (Continental) 1855 Central Ave	Augusta	GA	30904	706-733-3505
Le Maison (International) 404 Telfair St	Augusta	GA	30901	706-722-4805
Michael's Fine Food & Entertainment (American) 2860 Washington Rd	Augusta	GA	30909	706-733-2860
Mikoto Japanese Restaurant (Japanese) 3102 Washington Rd	Augusta	GA	30907	706-855-0009
Ming Wah (Chinese) 920 Baker Ave	Augusta	GA	30904	706-733-0740
Partridge Inn Dining Room (New American) 2110 Walton Way	Augusta	GA	30904	706-737-8888
S & S Cafeteria (American) 1616 Walton Way	Augusta	GA	30904	706-736-2972

Augusta — Restaurants (Cont'd)

				Phone
Silla Cafe (Japanese) 855 Broad St	Augusta	GA	30901	706-722-1800
Williams Seafood of Augusta (Seafood) 3160 Wrightsboro Rd	Augusta	GA	30909	706-737-9415

— Goods and Services —

SHOPPING

				Phone	Fax
Augusta Mall 3450 Wrightsboro Rd	Augusta	GA	30909	706-733-1001	733-7980
Downtown Antique Mall 1243 Broad St	Augusta	GA	30901	706-722-3571	
Downtown Augusta Broad St	Augusta	GA	30901	706-724-0436	
Fairway Square Shopping Center 2825 Washington Rd	Augusta	GA	30909	706-737-3381	
Regency Mall 1700 Gordon Hwy	Augusta	GA	30904	706-790-6535	790-0437
Southgate Plaza Shopping Center 1631 Gordon Hwy	Augusta	GA	30906	706-793-2094	
Westtown Market 3830 Washington Rd	Martinez	GA	30907	706-860-3966	855-5359

BANKS

				Phone	Fax
First Union Direct Bank NA 699 Broad St *TF Cust Svc:* 800-413-7898*	Augusta	GA	30901	706-823-2500	823-2505
Georgia Bank & Trust Co of Augusta 3530 Wheeler Rd	Augusta	GA	30909	706-738-6990	737-3106
NationsBank of Georgia NA 1450 Walton Way *TF:* 800-299-2265	Augusta	GA	30901	706-849-0660	
Regions Bank 700 Broad St	Augusta	GA	30901	706-821-3905	821-3906
Southtrust Bank of Georgia 1 10th St	Augusta	GA	30901	706-849-3200	821-8816
SunTrust Bank of Augusta 801 Broad St *TF:* 800-688-7878	Augusta	GA	30901	706-821-2000	821-2071
Wachovia Bank NA 1268 Broad St	Augusta	GA	30901	706-821-6710	821-6696

BUSINESS SERVICES

	Phone		Phone
Airborne Express	800-247-2676	**Kinko's**	706-733-1002
BAX Global	800-225-5229	**Mail Boxes Etc**	800-789-4623
DHL Worldwide Express	800-225-5345	**Post Office**	706-823-3100
Federal Express	800-238-5355	**UPS**	800-742-5877

— Media —

PUBLICATIONS

				Phone	Fax
Augusta Chronicle‡ PO Box 1928 *Web:* www.augustachronicle.com	Augusta	GA	30903	706-724-0851	722-7403
Augusta Focus 1143 Laney Walker Blvd	Augusta	GA	30901	706-722-4222	724-6969
Metropolitan Spirit PO Box 3809 **Fax:* News Rm ■ *Web:* www.metspirit.com	Augusta	GA	30914	706-738-1142	733-6663*

‡Daily newspapers

TELEVISION

				Phone	Fax
WAGT-TV Ch 26 (NBC) PO Box 1526 *Web:* www.wagt.com	Augusta	GA	30903	706-826-0026	724-4028
WCES-TV Ch 20 (PBS) 2316 Miller Place Rd	Wrens	GA	30833	706-547-2107	
WFXG-TV Ch 54 (Fox) 3933 Washington Rd *Web:* www.wfxg.com	Augusta	GA	30907	706-650-5400	650-8411
WJBF-TV Ch 6 (ABC) PO Box 1404 *Web:* www.wjbf.com	Augusta	GA	30903	706-722-6664	722-0022
WRDW-TV Ch 12 (CBS) PO Box 1212 *Web:* www.wrdw.com	Augusta	GA	30903	803-278-1212	279-8316

RADIO

				Phone	Fax
WAKB-FM 96.9 MHz (Urban) 104 Bennett Ln	North Augusta	GA	30901	803-279-2330	819-3781
WBBQ-FM 104.3 MHz (AC) 500 Carolina Springs Rd *Web:* www.wbbq.com ■ *E-mail:* wbbq@csra.net	North Augusta	SC	29841	803-279-6610	279-1175
WFAM-AM 1050 kHz (Rel) 552 Laney Walker Blvd	Augusta	GA	30901	706-722-6077	722-7066
WGOR-FM 93.9 MHz (AC) PO Box 211045 *Web:* www.gabn.net/coolfm/ ■ *E-mail:* coolfm@gabn.net	Augusta	GA	30917	706-855-9494	860-9343
WRXR-FM 96.3 MHz (Urban) 500 Carolina Springs Rd	North Augusta	SC	29841	803-279-1977	279-1175
WZNY-FM 105.7 MHz (CHR) 500 Carolina Springs Rd *Web:* www.y105augusta.com	North Augusta	SC	29841	803-279-6610	279-1175

— Colleges/Universities —

				Phone	Fax
Augusta State University 2500 Walton Way *TF:* 800-341-4373 ■ *Web:* www.aug.edu	Augusta	GA	30904	706-737-1400	667-4355
Medical College of Georgia 1120 15th St *Web:* www.mcg.edu ■ *E-mail:* hbuchana@mail.mcg.edu	Augusta	GA	30912	706-721-0211	721-7028
Paine College 1235 15th St *Web:* www.paine.edu	Augusta	GA	30901	706-821-8200	821-8293

— Hospitals —

				Phone	Fax
Dwight David Eisenhower Army Medical Center Hospital Rd Bldg 300	Fort Gordon	GA	30905	706-787-5811	787-7211
Medical College of Georgia Hospital & Clinics 1120 15th St	Augusta	GA	30912	706-721-0211	721-6126
Saint Joseph Hospital 2260 Wrightsboro Rd	Augusta	GA	30904	706-481-7000	481-7599
University Hospital 1350 Walton Way	Augusta	GA	30901	706-722-9011	774-8699
Veterans Affairs Medical Center 1 Freedom Way	Augusta	GA	30904	706-733-0188	481-6726

— Attractions —

				Phone	Fax
Augusta Ballet 1301 Greene St	Augusta	GA	30901	706-826-4721	826-4716
Augusta Choral Society 1301 Greene St	Augusta	GA	30901	706-826-4713	
Augusta Opera 1301 Greene St Suite 100	Augusta	GA	30901	706-826-4710	826-4732
Augusta Players 1301 Greene St Suite 304 *Web:* www.sdirect.com/theatre/ ■ *E-mail:* players@sdirect.com	Augusta	GA	30901	706-826-4707	826-4708
Augusta Richmond County Museum 560 Reynolds St	Augusta	GA	30901	706-722-8454	724-5192
Augusta Symphony Orchestra 1301 Greene St Suite 200	Augusta	GA	30903	706-826-4705	826-4735
Confederate Powerworks Downtown on Goodrich St	Augusta	GA	30904	706-724-0436	
Cotton Exchange Museum 32 8th St *TF:* 800-726-0243 ■ *Web:* www.augustaga.org/frames-tour.htm ■ *E-mail:* amcvb@augustaga.org	Augusta	GA	30901	706-724-4067	262-0287
Enterprise Mill 1450 Greene St Suite 170 *Web:* www.enterprisemill.com	Augusta	GA	30901	706-774-6424	774-6426
Fort Discovery National Science Center Riverwalk & 7th St *TF:* 800-325-5445 ■ *Web:* www.nscdiscovery.org/	Augusta	GA	30901	706-821-0200	821-0269
Georgia Golf Hall of Fame 1 10th St Suite 745 *Web:* www.gghf.org/	Augusta	GA	30901	706-724-4443	724-4428
Gertrude Herbert Institute of Art 506 Telfair St	Augusta	GA	30901	706-722-5495	722-3670
Greater Augusta Arts Council PO Box 1776	Augusta	GA	30903	706-826-4702	826-4723
Harris Ezekiel House 1822 Broad St	Augusta	GA	30904	706-724-0436	724-3083
Imperial Theatre 745 Broad St	Augusta	GA	30901	706-722-8293	
Krystal River Water Park 799 Industrial Park Dr	Evans	GA	30809	706-855-0061	855-0667
Lucy Craft Laney Museum 116 Phillips St	Augusta	GA	30901	706-724-3576	724-3576
Meadow Garden 1320 Independence Dr	Augusta	GA	30901	706-724-4174	
Morris Museum of Art 1 10th St *Web:* www.themorris.org ■ *E-mail:* mormuse@themorris.org	Augusta	GA	30901	706-724-7501	724-7612
Old Government House 432 Telfair St	Augusta	GA	30901	706-821-1812	
Riverwalk 15 8th St	Augusta	GA	30901	706-821-1754	821-1756
Riverwalk Marina 1 5th St	Augusta	GA	30901	706-722-1388	724-4787
Sacred Heart Cultural Center 1301 Greene St	Augusta	GA	30901	706-826-4700	722-2222
Saint Paul's Episcopal Church 605 Reynolds St	Augusta	GA	30901	706-724-2485	
Savannah Rapids Park 3300 Evans-to-Locks Rd	Martinez	GA	30907	706-868-3349	
Springfield Baptist Church 114 12th St	Augusta	GA	30901	706-724-1056	
Wilson Woodrow Boyhood Home 419 7th St	Augusta	GA	30901	706-724-0436	

Augusta (Cont'd)

SPORTS TEAMS & FACILITIES

				Phone	Fax
Augusta Greenjackets (baseball) 78 Milledge Rd	Augusta	GA	30904	706-736-7889	736-1122
Augusta Motor Speedway 3157 Gordon Hwy	Augusta	GA	30909	706-868-1060	863-1882

— Events —

	Phone
Arts in the Heart of Augusta (mid-September)	706-826-4702
Augusta Cutting Horse Futurity & Festival (late January)	706-724-4067
Augusta Southern National Drag Boat Races (mid-July)	706-724-2452
Boshears' Memorial Fly In (late September)	706-733-1647
Christmas Made in The South (mid-November)	706-722-3521
Craft Festival (mid-April)	706-541-0321
Fall Fest (early October)	803-278-5404
Festival of Lights (late November)	706-821-1754
Garden City Folk Festival (early May)	706-826-4702
Gem & Mineral Show (mid-March)	706-796-5025
Grecian Festival (early October)	706-821-1755
Hispanic Festival (mid-October)	706-821-1754
Historic Augusta Antique Show & Sale (mid-September)	706-724-0436
June Jazz Candlelight Concert Series (May)	706-821-1754
Masters Tournament (April)	706-667-6000
Oktoberfest (early October)	706-860-0935
Regatta Fest (late March)	706-724-4439
River Race Augusta (mid-August)	706-724-4148
Riverwalk Bluegrass Festival (late May)	706-821-1754
Riverwalk Fourth Celebration (July 4)	706-821-1754
Sacred Heart Garden & Flower Show (late March)	706-826-4700
Saint Patrick's Day Celebration (mid-March)	706-821-1754
Springtime Made in The South (early March)	706-722-3521
Taste of Augusta (late September)	706-868-7683
West Paint Party (early June & mid-October)	706-826-4702

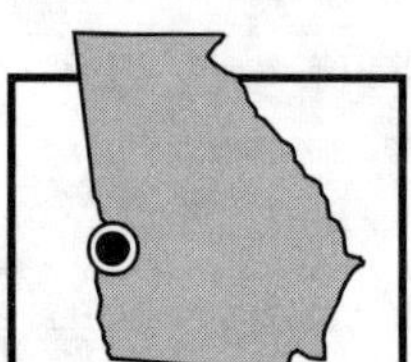

Columbus

Columbus is located along the banks of the Chattahoochee River on the Georgia/Alabama border, adjacent to Fort Benning, "the Best Army Base in the World." The city's military history dates back to the Civil War, when the city was a major center for medical care as well as a manufacturer of many items"from weapons to uniforms"for the Confederacy. The influence of the military on the city's history can also be seen at the National Infantry Museum, the Confederate Naval Museum, and the unique Columbus Iron Works Convention and Trade Center, a Confederate cannon manufacturing facility which has been transformed into a convention center. Many of Columbus' attractions, including the Columbus Iron Works and Coca-Cola Space Science Center, are located along the city's Riverwalk. The Riverwalk is also the site of Riverfest, held each year during the last weekend in April, which features arts and crafts, live music and entertainment, a children's carnival, a barbecue cook-off, and other activities.

Population	182,219	**Longitude**	84-52-29 W
Area (Land)	216.1 sq mi	**County**	Muscogee
Area (Water)	4.7 sq mi	**Time Zone**	EST
Elevation	250 ft	**Area Code/s**	706
Latitude	32-30-38 N		

— Average Temperatures and Precipitation —

TEMPERATURES

	Jan	Feb	Mar	Apr	May	Jun	Jul	Aug	Sep	Oct	Nov	Dec
High	34	38	51	62	73	80	84	82	76	65	51	39
Low	19	21	31	40	50	58	63	61	55	43	34	25

PRECIPITATION

	Jan	Feb	Mar	Apr	May	Jun	Jul	Aug	Sep	Oct	Nov	Dec
Inches	2.2	2.2	3.3	3.2	3.9	4.0	4.3	3.7	3.0	2.2	3.2	2.9

— Important Phone Numbers —

	Phone		Phone
AAA	706-324-7121	**HotelDocs**	800-468-3537
American Express Travel	800-528-4800	**Medical Referral**	706-596-4170
Contact 24-Hour Help Line	706-327-3999	**Poison Control Center**	800-282-5846
Emergency	911	**Visitor Information Hotline**	706-322-3181

— Information Sources —

				Phone	Fax
Better Business Bureau Serving West Georgia & East Alabama PO Box 2587	Columbus	GA	31902	706-324-0712	324-2181
Web: www.columbus-ga.bbb.org ■ *E-mail:* info@columbus-ga.bbb.org					
Columbus Chamber of Commerce 901 Front Ave.	Columbus	GA	31901	706-327-1566	327-7512
Web: www.columbusga.com/chamber					
Columbus City Hall 100 10th St	Columbus	GA	31901	706-653-4000	
Web: www.columbusga.com					
Columbus Civic Center 400 4th St	Columbus	GA	31901	706-653-4472	653-4481
TF: 800-711-3986 ■ *Web:* www.columbusga.com/civiccenter ■ *E-mail:* info@columbusga.com					
Columbus Community & Economic Development Dept PO Box 1340	Columbus	GA	31902	706-653-4116	653-4120
Columbus Convention & Visitors Bureau 1000 Bay Ave	Columbus	GA	31901	706-322-1613	322-0701
TF: 800-999-1613					
Columbus Ironworks Convention & Trade Center 801 Front Ave	Columbus	GA	31901	706-327-4522	327-0162
Columbus Mayor 100 10th St Government Ctr Tower	Columbus	GA	31902	706-653-4712	653-4970
WC Bradley Memorial Library 1120 Bradley Dr	Columbus	GA	31906	706-649-0780	649-1914

On-Line Resources

Area Guide Columbus	columbusga.areaguides.net
City Knowledge Columbus	www.cityknowledge.com/ga_columbus.htm
Columbus City Net	www.excite.com/travel/countries/united_states/georgia/columbus
MetroVille Columbus	columbus.metroville.com

— Transportation Services —

AIRPORTS

■ **Columbus Metropolitan Airport (CSG)**	Phone
4 miles NE of downtown (approx 10 minutes)	706-324-2449

Airport Transportation

	Phone
Columbus Shuttle $15 fare to downtown	706-322-9036
Taxi $10 fare to downtown	706-322-1616

Commercial Airlines

	Phone		Phone
American	800-433-7300	**Northwest**	800-225-2525
Atlantic Southeast	800-282-3424	**Northwest Airlink**	706-323-0790
Continental	800-525-0280	**US Airways Express**	800-428-4322

Columbus (Cont'd)

Charter Airlines

	Phone
Total Flight Inc	706-660-0251

CAR RENTALS

	Phone		Phone
Avis	706-322-2539	**Enterprise**	706-568-3400
Budget	706-327-5501	**Hertz**	706-324-2725
Economy	706-568-0808	**National**	706-322-4586

LIMO/TAXI

	Phone		Phone
Ambiance Limousine	706-571-9888	**Co-op Taxi**	706-323-5575
American Cab	706-689-6367	**Independent Taxi Cab Co**	706-689-1234
Benning Taxi Co	706-322-5411	**Radio Cab**	706-322-5411
Beverly Hills Limousine	706-321-9884	**Yellow Cab**	706-322-1616

MASS TRANSIT

	Phone
METRA Bus $1 Base fare	706-653-4413

RAIL/BUS

				Phone
Greyhound Bus Station 818 Veterans Pkwy	Columbus	GA	31901	706-322-7391
TF: 800-231-2222				

— Accommodations —

HOTELS, MOTELS, RESORTS

				Phone	Fax
Baymont Inns & Suites 2919 Warm Springs Rd	Columbus	GA	31909	706-323-4344	596-9622
TF: 800-301-0200					
Candlelight Motel 3456 Victory Dr	Columbus	GA	31903	706-689-2750	
Colony Inn 4300 Victory Dr	Columbus	GA	31903	706-689-1590	687-0203
Columbus Hilton Hotel 800 Front Ave	Columbus	GA	31901	706-324-1800	327-8042
TF: 800-524-4020					
Comfort Inn 3443-B Macon Rd	Columbus	GA	31907	706-568-3300	563-2388
TF: 800-228-5150					
Comfort Suites 5236 Armour Rd	Columbus	GA	31904	706-322-6666	322-2553
TF: 800-228-5160					
Courtyard by Marriott 3501 Courtyard Way	Columbus	GA	31909	706-323-2323	327-6030
TF: 800-321-2211 ■ *Web:* courtyard.com/CSGCH					
Days Inn 3452 Macon Rd	Columbus	GA	31907	706-561-4400	568-3075
TF: 800-325-2525					
Econo Lodge 4483 Victory Dr	Columbus	GA	31903	706-682-3803	687-9128
TF: 800-446-6900					
Edgewood Motel 4265 Macon Rd	Columbus	GA	31907	706-561-2170	
Extended StayAmerica 5020 Armour Rd	Columbus	GA	31904	706-653-0131	653-0133
TF: 800-398-7829					
Georgian Motel 3461 Victory Dr	Columbus	GA	31903	706-689-5712	
Hampton Inn 5585 Whitesville Rd	Columbus	GA	31904	706-576-5303	596-8076
TF: 800-426-7866					
Holiday Inn 1325 Veterans Pkwy	Columbus	GA	31901	706-322-2522	322-9059
TF: 800-465-4329					
Holiday Inn North 2800 Manchester Expy	Columbus	GA	31904	706-324-0231	596-0248
TF: 800-465-4329					
Howard Johnson Express Inn 1011 Veterans Pkwy	Columbus	GA	31901	706-322-6641	322-1999
TF: 800-697-7293					
LaQuinta Motor Inn 3201 Macon Rd	Columbus	GA	31906	706-568-1740	569-7434
TF: 800-531-5900					
Motel 6 3050 Victory Dr	Columbus	GA	31903	706-687-7214	682-2362
TF: 800-466-8356					
Plaza Motel 3540 Victory Dr	Columbus	GA	31903	706-689-0599	
Sheraton Airport 5351 Sidney Simons Blvd	Columbus	GA	31904	706-327-6868	327-0041
TF: 800-325-3535					
Southgate Suites 2339 Ft Benning Rd	Columbus	GA	31903	706-221-2330	685-8071
Sunset Motel 3464 Victory Dr	Columbus	GA	31903	706-689-0240	
Super 8 Motel 2935 Warm Springs Rd	Columbus	GA	31907	706-322-6580	322-6580
TF: 800-800-8000					
Villager Lodge 1024 Veterans Pkwy	Columbus	GA	31901	706-324-3694	322-5785

— Restaurants —

				Phone
Atrium Restaurant (American) 5351 Simons Blvd	Columbus	GA	31904	706-327-6868
Brittania Pub & Restaurant (English) 3709 Gentian Blvd	Columbus	GA	31907	706-563-6266
Buckhead Grill (American) 5010 Armour Rd	Columbus	GA	31904	706-571-9995
Butler's Pantry (American) 2533 Auburn Ave	Columbus	GA	31906	706-561-1733
Coach's Corner (American) 3709 Gentian Blvd Suite 12	Columbus	GA	31907	706-568-7228
Country's Barbecue (Barbecue) 3137 Mercury Dr	Columbus	GA	31906	706-563-7604
Crystal River Seafood (Seafood) 2606 Manchester Expy	Columbus	GA	31904	706-324-0055
Deorio's (Italian) 3201 Macon Rd	Columbus	GA	31907	706-563-5887
El Vaquero Restaurant (Mexican) 3135 Cross Country Plaza	Columbus	GA	31906	706-569-1420
Goetchius House (Continental) 405 Broadway	Columbus	GA	31901	706-324-4863
Hunan Chinese Restaurant (Chinese) 4553 Woodruff Rd	Columbus	GA	31904	706-327-2248
Los Amigos (Mexican) 5592 Whitesville Rd	Columbus	GA	31904	706-322-1993
Louie Louie's (American) 6298 Veteran's Pkwy	Columbus	GA	31909	706-660-9900
Macon Road Barbecue (Barbecue) 2703 Avalon Rd	Columbus	GA	31907	706-563-0542
Mikata Japanese Steakhouse (Japanese) 5300 Sidney Simons Blvd	Columbus	GA	31904	706-327-5100
Minnie's (Southern) 104 8th St	Columbus	GA	31901	706-322-2766
Pemberton's (American) 800 Front Ave	Columbus	GA	31901	706-324-1800
Rose Hill Seafood Restaurant (Seafood) 2621 Hamilton Rd	Columbus	GA	31904	706-322-4410
Tavern On The Square (American) 14 11th St	Columbus	GA	31901	706-324-2238
Terrace Cafe Restaurant (American) 2800 Manchester Expy	Columbus	GA	31904	706-324-0231

— Goods and Services —

SHOPPING

				Phone	Fax
Columbus Square Mall 3050 Macon Rd	Columbus	GA	31906	706-561-6305	561-8068
Cross Country Plaza 2010 Auburn Ave	Columbus	GA	31906	706-563-2223	563-2227
Main Street Village 6298 Veterans Pkwy	Columbus	GA	31909	706-322-1100	
Peachtree Mall 3131 Manchester Expy	Columbus	GA	31909	706-327-1578	327-8715
Warm Springs Village GA 85 & US 27	Warm Springs	GA	31830	706-655-9093	
TF: 800-337-1927					

BANKS

				Phone	Fax
Columbus Bank & Trust Co 1148 Broadway	Columbus	GA	31902	706-649-2311	649-2481*
**Fax:* Cust Svc ■ *TF:* 800-282-1205					
First Union National Bank 101 13th St	Columbus	GA	31901	706-571-6500	571-6579
Regions Bank of Georgia 201 13th St	Columbus	GA	31901	706-324-3421	660-3791
South Trust Bank 1237 1st Ave	Columbus	GA	31908	706-571-7300	571-7230
SunTrust Bank-West Georgia NA 1246 1st Ave	Columbus	GA	31902	706-649-3600	649-3759

BUSINESS SERVICES

	Phone		Phone
Columbus Air Freight	706-563-9496	**Manpower Temporary Services**	706-596-1512
DHL Worldwide Express	800-225-5345	**Post Office**	706-562-1760
Federal Express	800-238-5355	**Randstad Staffing Services**	706-596-8344
Interim Personnel Services	706-571-2400	**Staffing Solutions**	706-327-7877
Kelly Services	706-321-0444	**UPS**	800-742-5877
Mail Boxes Etc	706-568-1600		

— Media —

PUBLICATIONS

				Phone	Fax
Columbus Ledger-Enquirer‡ PO Box 711	Columbus	GA	31902	706-324-5526	576-6290
TF: 800-282-7859 ■ *Web:* www.l-e-o.com ■ *E-mail:* leonline@leo.infi.net					

‡Daily newspapers

TELEVISION

				Phone	Fax
WLTZ-TV Ch 38 (NBC) 6140 Buena Vista Rd	Columbus	GA	31907	706-561-3838	563-8467
WRBL-TV Ch 3 (CBS) 1350 13th Ave	Columbus	GA	31901	706-323-3333	323-0841
WTVM-TV Ch 9 (ABC) 1909 Wynnton Rd	Columbus	GA	31906	706-324-6471	322-7527
Web: www.wtvm.com ■ *E-mail:* newsleader@wtvm.com					
WXTX-TV Ch 54 (Fox) 6524 Buena Vista Rd	Columbus	GA	31907	706-561-5400	561-6505

RADIO

				Phone	Fax
WAGH-FM 98.3 MHz (Urban) PO Box 687	Columbus	GA	31902	706-576-3000	576-3010
WCGQ-FM 107.3 MHz (AC) 1353 13th Ave	Columbus	GA	31901	706-327-1217	596-4600
WDAK-AM 540 MHz (N/T) PO Box 687	Columbus	GA	31902	706-576-3000	576-3010

Columbus — Radio (Cont'd)

				Phone	Fax
WFXE-FM 104.9 MHz (Urban) 1115 14th St.	Columbus	GA	31902	706-576-3565	576-3683
WGSY-FM 100.1 MHz (A/C) 1826 Wynnton Rd.	Columbus	GA	31906	706-576-3000	576-3005*
**Fax:* Sales					
WKCN-FM 99.3 MHz (Ctry) 1353 13th Ave.	Columbus	GA	31901	706-596-9000	660-4634
WOKS-AM 1340 kHz (Urban) 1115 14th St	Columbus	GA	31902	706-576-3565	576-3683
WPNX-AM 1460 kHz (Rel) 1826 Wynnton Rd.	Columbus	GA	31906	706-576-3000	576-3005*
**Fax:* Sales					
WRCG-AM 1420 kHz (N/T) 1353 13th Ave	Columbus	GA	31901	706-324-0338	596-4600
WSTH-FM 106 MHz (Ctry) PO Box 687	Columbus	GA	31902	706-576-3000	576-3010
WVRK-FM 102.9 MHz (Rock) 1826 Wynnton Rd.	Columbus	GA	31906	706-576-3000	576-3005*
**Fax:* Sales ■ *Web:* www.rock103online.com ■ *E-mail:* rock103@mindspring.com					

— Colleges/Universities —

				Phone	Fax
Columbus State University 4225 University Ave	Columbus	GA	31907	706-568-2001	568-2462
Web: www.colstate.edu					

— Hospitals —

				Phone	Fax
Columbia Doctors Hospital PO Box 2188.	Columbus	GA	31901	706-571-4262	571-4156
Columbus Regional Hospital 707 Center St.	Columbus	GA	31901	706-660-6100	571-1216
Medical Center The 710 Center St	Columbus	GA	31902	706-571-1000	571-1216
Saint Francis Hospital 2122 Manchester Expy	Columbus	GA	31904	706-596-4000	596-4481
West Central Georgia Hospital 3000 Schatulga Rd	Columbus	GA	31901	706-568-5000	568-5339

— Attractions —

				Phone	Fax
Andersonville National Historic Site Rt 1 Box 800	Andersonville	GA	31711	912-924-0343	928-9640
Web: www.nps.gov/ande/					
Bradley Theater 1241 Broadway	Columbus	GA	31901	706-321-9098	321-8425
Callaway Gardens Resort US Hwy 27	Pine Mountain	GA	31822	706-663-2281	663-5080
TF: 800-225-5292 ■ *Web:* www.callawaygardens.com					
Challenger Learning Center 701 Front Ave Coca-Cola Space Science Ctr.	Columbus	GA	31901	706-649-1470	649-1478
Web: www.ccssc.org					
Chattahoochee Princess Riverboat 1 Bay Ave	Columbus	GA	31901	706-324-4499	
Coca-Cola Space Science Center 701 Front Ave.	Columbus	GA	31901	706-649-1470	649-1478
Web: www.ccssc.org ■ *E-mail:* info@ccssc.org					
Columbus Black Heritage Tour Uptown Area	Columbus	GA		706-322-1613	
Columbus Museum 1251 Wynnton Rd.	Columbus	GA	31906	706-649-0713	649-1070
Web: www.columbusmuseum.com ■ *E-mail:* colmuse@leo.infi.net					
Columbus Symphony Orchestra 1029 Talbotton Rd Three Arts Theatre	Columbus	GA	31904	706-323-5059	323-7051
Web: www.csoga.org ■ *E-mail:* columbussymphony@mindspring.com					
Heritage Corner Tour Historic District	Columbus	GA		706-322-0756	
Human Experience Theatre 1037 Broadway	Columbus	GA	31901	706-323-3689	
Jimmy Carter National Historic Site 300 N Bond St	Plains	GA	31780	912-824-3413	824-3441
Web: www.nps.gov/jica/					
Liberty Theater 823 8th Ave.	Columbus	GA	31901	706-653-7566	
E-mail: libtheater@aol.com					
Little White House GA 85 W	Warm Springs	GA	31830	706-655-5870	655-5872
Ma Rainey House 805 5th Ave.	Columbus	GA	31901	706-322-1613	
National Infantry Museum Baltzell Ave Bldg 396.	Fort Benning	GA	31905	706-545-2958	545-5158
Web: www.benningmwr.com/museum.htm					
Ocmulgee National Monument 1207 Emery Hwy	Macon	GA	31217	912-752-8257	752-8259
Web: www.nps.gov/ocmu/					
Oxbow Meadows Environmental Park 3491 S Lumpkin Rd	Columbus	GA	31907	706-687-4090	
Pine Mountain Wild Animal Park 1300 Oak Grove Rd.	Pine Mountain	GA	31822	706-663-8744	663-8880
TF: 800-367-2751 ■ *Web:* www.animalsafari.com ■ *E-mail:* info@animalsafari.com					
Providence Canyon State Park Hwy 39C	Lumpkin	GA	31815	912-838-6202	
Rankin House 1440 2nd Ave	Columbus	GA	31901	706-327-3588	
Riverwalk 12th St to S Commons	Columbus	GA	31901	706-322-1613	
TF: 800-999-1613					
Roosevelt State Park GA 190	Pine Mountain	GA	31822	706-663-4858	
Spencer House 4th Ave & 8th St	Columbus	GA	31901	706-322-1613	
Springer Opera House 103 10th St.	Columbus	GA	31902	706-327-3688	324-4681
Three Arts Theater 1029 Talbotton Rd.	Columbus	GA	31904	706-653-4183	
Warm Springs Village GA 85 & US 27	Warm Springs	GA	31830	706-655-9093	
TF: 800-337-1927					
Westville 1850's Village ML King Dr	Lumpkin	GA	31815	912-838-6310	838-4000
Web: www.westville.org					
Woodruff Museum of Civil War Naval History PO Box 1022	Columbus	GA	31902	706-327-9798	

SPORTS TEAMS & FACILITIES

				Phone	Fax
Columbus Cottonmouths (hockey) 400 4th St Columbus Civic Ctr	Columbus	GA	31901	706-571-0086	571-0080
Web: www.cottonmouths.com/					
Columbus RedStixx (baseball) 100 4th St Golden Pk	Columbus	GA	31901	706-571-8866	571-9107
Web: www.redstixx.com ■ *E-mail:* info@redstixx.com					
Memorial Stadium 400 4th St	Columbus	GA	31901	706-653-4482	653-4481
TF: 800-711-3986					
New South Commons Complex 400 4th St PO Box 1340	Columbus	GA	31901	706-653-4482	653-4481
TF: 800-711-3986					

— Events —

	Phone
Autumn Adventure (October)	706-663-2281
Bi-City Christmas Parade (mid-December)	334-291-4719
Buick Challenge PGA Golf Tournament (early October)	706-663-2281
Chill Out Columbus Style Jazz Festival (early May)	706-323-3687
Christmas Parade (early December)	706-322-1613
Columbus Day Uptown Jam (early October)	706-596-0111
Columbus-Fort Benning Shrine Circus (September)	706-561-5448
Fantasy in Lights (late November-late December)	706-663-2281
Miss Georgia Pageant (late June)	706-322-2315
Riverfest Weekend (late April)	706-322-0756
Spring Celebration (late March-mid-April)	706-663-2281
Steeplechase at Callaway Gardens (early November)	706-324-6252

Macon

Located in central Georgia, Macon has a rich architectural and archaeological history and has more acreage listed on the National Register of Historic Places than any other city in Georgia. The Downtown Historic District alone includes over 48 buildings cited for architectural excellence and listed on the National Register. Other historic sites in Macon include the Rose Hill Cemetery, established in 1839, which is one of the oldest surviving public cemetery parks in the U.S; and the Sidney Lanier Cottage, once home to poet Sidney Clopton Lanier, author of "The Marshes of Glynn" and "Song of the Chatahoochee." The beautiful Hay House, a magnificent Italian Renaissance Revival mansion, is a National Landmark. Woodruff House served as Union General Wilson's residence in 1865 and hosted

Macon (Cont'd)

Confederate President Jefferson Davis in 1887. Relics of Macon and the Confederacy can be found at the Cannonball House and Confederate Museum, which was named after it was struck by a cannonball during the Civil War. The Tubman African American Museum is Georgia's largest museum dedicated to preserving African-American history. Macon is also home to Wesleyan College, which was founded in 1836 and was the first college in the world chartered to grant degrees to women. Native American Indian heritage is studied at the Ocmulgee National Monument, the largest archaeological development east of the Mississippi. Otis Redding, Cab Calloway, and Little Richard were discovered at the Douglass Theatre, which was recently restored and reopened. The Georgia Music Hall of Fame, as well as the Georgia Sports Hall of Fame, can also be found in Macon.

Population	114,336	**Longitude**	83-38-57 W
Area (Land)	47.9 sq mi	**County**	Bibb
Area (Water)	0.3 sq mi	**Time Zone**	EST
Elevation	354 ft	**Area Code/s**	912
Latitude	32-41-34 N		

— Average Temperatures and Precipitation —

TEMPERATURES

	Jan	Feb	Mar	Apr	May	Jun	Jul	Aug	Sep	Oct	Nov	Dec
High	57	61	70	78	85	90	92	91	86	78	69	60
Low	34	37	44	51	59	67	71	70	64	52	43	37

PRECIPITATION

	Jan	Feb	Mar	Apr	May	Jun	Jul	Aug	Sep	Oct	Nov	Dec
Inches	4.6	4.7	4.8	3.5	3.6	3.6	4.3	3.6	2.8	2.2	2.7	4.3

— Important Phone Numbers —

	Phone		Phone
AAA	912-471-0800	**Medical Referral**	912-757-8200
Emergency	911	**Poison Control Center**	800-282-5846

— Information Sources —

				Phone	Fax
Better Business Bureau Serving Central Georgia 277 ML King Jr Blvd Suite 102 *Web:* www.macon.bbb.org	Macon	GA	31201	912-742-7999	742-8191
Bibb County PO Box 4708	Macon	GA	31208	912-749-6400	749-6329
Edgar H Wilson Convention Centre 200 Coliseum Dr. *Web:* www.maconcentreplex.com	Macon	GA	31217	912-751-9152	751-9154
Greater Macon Chamber of Commerce 305 Coliseum Dr. *Web:* www.maconchamber.org ■ *E-mail:* macon@mto.infi.net	Macon	GA	31217	912-741-8000	741-8021
Macon-Bibb County Convention/Visitors Bureau PO Box 6354 *TF:* 800-768-3401 ■ *Web:* www.maconga.org ■ *E-mail:* maconcvb@macon.com	Macon	GA	31208	912-743-3401	745-2022
Macon City Auditorium 200 Coliseum Dr.	Macon	GA	31217	912-751-9152	751-9154
Macon City Hall 700 Poplar St. *Web:* www.macon.ga.us	Macon	GA	31298	912-751-7170	751-7931
Macon Economic & Community Development Dept 439 Cotton Ave.	Macon	GA	31201	912-751-7190	751-7390
Macon Mayor 700 Poplar St.	Macon	GA	31298	912-751-7170	751-7931
Middle Georgia Regional Library System 1180 Washington Ave	Macon	GA	31201	912-744-0800	744-0840

On-Line Resources

4Macon.com	www.4macon.com
Anthill City Guide Macon	www.anthill.com/city.asp?city=macon
Area Guide Macon	macon.areaguides.net
City Knowledge Macon	www.cityknowledge.com/ga_macon.htm
Excite.com Macon City Guide	www.excite.com/travel/countries/united_states/georgia/macon
Macon.com	www.macon.com
Meetmacon.com	www.meetmacon.com
NITC Travelbase City Guide Macon	www.travelbase.com/auto/features/macon-ga.html
Online City Guide to Macon	www.olcg.com/ga/macon/index.html
Virtual Macon	www.maconga.com/

— Transportation Services —

AIRPORTS

■ **Middle Georgia Regional Airport (MCN)**	Phone
9 miles S of downtown (approx 13 minutes)	912-788-3760

Airport Transportation

	Phone
A All Star Limousine Service $50 fare to downtown	912-757-0267
Yellow Cab $12-15 fare to downtown	912-742-6464

Commercial Airlines

	Phone
Atlantic Southeast	800-282-3424

Charter Airlines

	Phone		Phone
Aviance International Inc	800-228-9388	**Lowe Aviation Co**	912-788-3491

CAR RENTALS

	Phone		Phone
Avis	912-788-3840	**Enterprise**	912-784-8633
Budget	912-784-7130	**Hertz**	912-788-3600
Economy	912-742-4316	**National**	912-788-5385

LIMO/TAXI

	Phone		Phone
A All Star Limousine Service	912-757-0267	**Royal Limousine**	912-755-9838
Radio Cab	912-781-0076	**Yellow Cab**	912-742-6464

MASS TRANSIT

	Phone
Macon-Bibb County Transit Authority $.75 Base fare	912-746-1318

RAIL/BUS

				Phone
Greyhound Bus Station 65 Spring St *TF:* 800-231-2222	Macon	GA	31201	912-746-5046

— Accommodations —

HOTEL RESERVATION SERVICES

	Phone	Fax
Reservations USA *TF:* 800-251-4444 ■ *Web:* www.reservationsusa.com ■ *E-mail:* reserve@lodging4u.com	865-453-1000	453-7484
USA Hotels *TF:* 800-872-4683 ■ *Web:* www.1800usahotels.com ■ *E-mail:* info@1800usahotels.com	252-331-1555	331-2021

HOTELS, MOTELS, RESORTS

				Phone	Fax
1842 Inn 353 College St. *TF:* 800-336-1842	Macon	GA	31201	912-741-1842	741-1842
Ambassador Inn Riverside 2772 Riverside Dr	Macon	GA	31204	912-742-3687	750-9913
Ambassador Inn South 4546 Harley Bridge Rd.	Macon	GA	31206	912-788-7500	788-7512
Best Western Inn 4681 Chambers Rd	Macon	GA	31206	912-781-5300	784-8111
Best Western Riverside Inn 2400 Riverside Dr. *TF:* 888-454-4565	Macon	GA	31204	912-743-6311	743-9420
Budget Inn Suites 2737 Sheraton Dr.	Macon	GA	31204	912-745-8521	743-4917
Comfort Inn 2690 Riverside Dr *TF:* 800-847-6453	Macon	GA	31204	912-746-8855	746-8881

Macon — Hotels, Motels, Resorts (Cont'd)

				Phone	Fax
Comfort Inn West 4951 Eisenhower Pkwy	Macon	GA	31206	912-788-5500	785-9237
TF: 800-228-5150					
Courtyard by Marriott 3990 Sheraton Dr	Macon	GA	31210	912-477-8899	477-4684
TF: 800-321-2211					
Crowne Plaza Macon 108 1st St.	Macon	GA	31201	912-746-1461	738-2460
TF: 800-465-4329					
Days Inn West 6000 Harrison Rd	Macon	GA	31206	912-784-1000	784-1000
TF: 800-329-7468					
Discovery Inn 4604 Chambers Rd	Macon	GA	31206	912-781-2810	781-4782
TF: 800-251-1962					
Econo Lodge 1990 Riverside Dr	Macon	GA	31201	912-746-6221	745-0548
Econo Lodge 4951 Romeiser Dr	Macon	GA	31206	912-474-1661	474-4340
TF: 800-553-2666					
Economy Inn 4717 Chambers Rd	Macon	GA	31206	912-781-0088	
Fairfield Inn 110 Plantation Inn Dr	Macon	GA	31210	912-474-9922	476-8353
TF: 800-228-2800					
Family Inns of America 4173 Interstate Pkwy	Macon	GA	31220	912-474-8800	474-8338
TF: 800-251-9752					
Hampton Inn 3680 Riverside Dr	Macon	GA	31210	912-471-0660	471-2528
TF: 800-426-7866					
Holiday Inn 4755 Chambers Rd	Macon	GA	31206	912-788-0120	788-0122
TF: 800-465-4329					
Holiday Inn 3590 Riverside Dr	Macon	GA	31210	912-474-2610	471-0712
TF: 888-781-7666					
Holiday Inn Express 2720 Riverside Dr	Macon	GA	31204	912-743-1482	745-3967
Howard Johnson 2566 Riverside Dr.	Macon	GA	31204	912-746-7671	746-7671
TF: 800-446-4656					
Jameson Inns 150 Plantation Inn Dr	Macon	GA	31210	912-474-8004	475-9005
TF: 800-526-3766					
Knights Inn 4952 Romeiser Rd	Macon	GA	31206	912-471-1230	477-5125
La Quinta Inn 3944 River Place Dr	Macon	GA	31210	912-475-0206	475-8577
Macon Inn 1044 Riverside Dr	Macon	GA	31201	912-746-3561	746-3561
TF: 800-342-1933					
Magnolia Court Motel 4727 Houston Rd	Macon	GA	31216	912-784-0428	
Masters Economy Inn 4295 Pio Nono Ave	Macon	GA	31206	912-788-8910	781-9550
TF: 800-633-3434					
Motel 6 4991 Harrison Rd	Macon	GA	31206	912-474-2870	477-4889
TF: 800-466-8356					
Quality Inn 4630 Chambers Rd	Macon	GA	31206	912-781-7000	781-7000
TF: 800-228-5158					
Quality Inn & Suites 115 Riverside Pkwy	Macon	GA	31210	912-474-4000	474-1220
TF: 800-228-5151					
Ramada Inn 5009 Harrison Rd	Macon	GA	31206	912-474-0871	474-5763
Red Roof Inn 3950 River Place Dr	Macon	GA	31210	912-477-7477	477-3278
TF: 800-843-7667					
Residence Inn 3900 Sheraton Dr	Macon	GA	31210	912-475-4280	475-4290
TF: 800-331-3131					
Rodeway Inn 4999 Eisenhower Pkwy.	Macon	GA	31206	912-781-4343	784-8140
TF: 800-228-2000					
Royal Inn 4709 Chambers Rd.	Macon	GA	31206	912-781-6680	788-2912
Scottish Inn 5022 Romeiser Dr.	Macon	GA	31206	912-474-2665	474-2402
TF: 800-251-1962					
Sleep Inn 3928 River Place Dr	Macon	GA	31210	912-757-8300	757-0991
TF: 800-221-2222					
Southwind Motel 3010 Riggins Mill Rd	Macon	GA	31217	912-742-4208	
Super 8 Motel 6007 Harrison Rd	Macon	GA	31206	912-788-8800	788-2327
TF: 800-800-8000					
Super 8 Motel North 3935 Arkwright Rd	Macon	GA	31210	912-757-8688	471-8526
TF: 800-800-8000					
Travelodge 5000 Harrison Rd.	Macon	GA	31206	912-471-6116	474-5506
TF: 800-578-7878					

— Restaurants —

				Phone
Bourbon Street Grill (American) 3661 Eisenhower Pkwy.	Macon	GA	31206	912-474-0109
Buffalo's Cafe (American) 5990 Zebulon Rd	Macon	GA	31210	912-471-0200
Carrabba's Grill (Italian) 3913 River Place Dr	Macon	GA	31210	912-474-5115
Casa Maria (Mexican) 4357 Forsyth Rd	Macon	GA	31210	912-471-0111
Downtown Grill (American) 562 Mulberry Street Ln	Macon	GA	31201	912-742-5999
El Sombrero (Mexican) 4646 Forsyth Rd	Macon	GA	31210	912-471-6535
El Zarape (Mexican) 5022 Romeiser Dr	Macon	GA	31206	912-474-6244
Finches Restaurant (Barbecue) 5631 Houston Rd	Macon	GA	31216	912-781-6998
H&H Restaurant (Soul) 807 Forsyth St	Macon	GA	31201	912-742-9810
Harbour Pointe Restaurant (Seafood) 6420 Moseley Dixon Rd	Macon	GA	31220	912-471-0393
Inn Cahoots Steakhouse (Steak/Seafood) 7275 Hawkinsville Rd	Macon	GA	31216	912-781-7700
Jeneane's Cafe (Southern) 524 Mulberry St	Macon	GA	31201	912-743-5267
Johnny V's Restaurant (Homestyle) 4326 Mercer University Dr.	Macon	GA	31206	912-474-0488
Julia's Kitchen (Homestyle) 3254 Jeffersonville Rd	Macon	GA	31217	912-741-1700
Laney's (Soul) 2863 Napier Ave	Macon	GA	31204	912-746-0350
Midtown Grill (American) 3065 Vineville Ave.	Macon	GA	31204	912-745-8595
Natalia's (Italian) 2720 Riverside Plaza	Macon	GA	31204	912-741-1380
Papouli's (Greek/Mediterranean) 121 Tom Hill Sr Blvd	Macon	GA	31210	912-474-0204
Rookery (American) 543 Cherry St.	Macon	GA	31201	912-746-8658
Sakkio Japan (Japanese) 3661 Eisenhower Pkwy	Macon	GA	31206	912-477-1100
Satterfield's (Barbecue) 120 New St	Macon	GA	31201	912-742-0352
Shamrock (Irish) 881 Wimbish Rd	Macon	GA	31210	912-475-0077
T's International (International) 717 Riverside Dr	Macon	GA	31201	912-746-8360
Traditions (Continental) 3590 Riverside Dr Holiday Inn	Macon	GA	31210	912-474-2610
Voncell's (Soul) 504 2nd St	Macon	GA	31201	912-743-3655

— Goods and Services —

SHOPPING

				Phone	Fax
Macon Mall 3661 Eisenhower Pkwy	Macon	GA	31206	912-477-8840	474-5238
Westgate Center 2525 Pio Nono Ave.	Macon	GA	31206	912-781-2000	784-7110

BANKS

				Phone	Fax
Colonial Bank 501 Walnut St	Macon	GA	31201	912-746-7000	743-5241
Colony Bank 3080 Riverside Dr.	Macon	GA	31210	912-722-9500	722-9506
First Colony Bank 159 Tom Hill Sr Blvd.	Macon	GA	31210	912-476-9911	476-9922
First Liberty Bank 1302 Gray Hwy	Macon	GA	31211	912-743-9212	743-9125
TF Cust Svc: 888-454-2243*					
First South Bank 502 Mulberry St.	Macon	GA	31201	912-744-2400	750-7979
First Union 3710 Northside Dr	Macon	GA	31210	912-749-8070	749-8074
TF Cust Svc: 800-275-3862*					
NationsBank 1250 Gray Hwy	Macon	GA	31211	912-746-0681	745-6826
Rivoli Bank & Trust 515 Mulberry St.	Macon	GA	31201	912-475-5200	750-7790
TF: 800-745-5203					
Security National Bank 4100 Riverside Dr Suite 100	Macon	GA	31210	912-722-6300	722-6338
SunTrust Bank 1104 Gray Hwy	Macon	GA	31211	912-741-2265	751-5819
Wachovia Bank 484 Mulberry St.	Macon	GA	31201	912-750-2021	742-5110

BUSINESS SERVICES

	Phone
Interim Personnel	912-405-0000
Kelly Services	912-745-8663
Mail Boxes Etc	912-471-9006
Manpower Temporary Services	912-471-9182
Pip Printing	912-742-0077
Post Office	912-752-8400
UPS	800-742-5877

— Media —

PUBLICATIONS

				Phone	Fax
Macon Magazine 227 Orange St.	Macon	GA	31201	912-746-7779	743-4608
Web: www.maconmagazine.com ■ *E-mail:* jwoolf@maconmagazine.com					
Macon Telegraph‡ PO Box 4167	Macon	GA	31208	912-744-4200	744-4385
TF: 800-677-4110 ■ *Web:* www.macontelegraph.com					

‡Daily newspapers

TELEVISION

				Phone	Fax
WGNM-TV Ch 64 (UPN) 2525 Beech Ave.	Macon	GA	31204	912-746-6464	745-2367
WGXA-TV Ch 24 (Fox) 599 MLK Jr Blvd	Macon	GA	31201	912-745-2424	745-4347
Web: www.fox24.com					
WMAZ-TV Ch 13 (CBS) 1314 Gray Hwy.	Macon	GA	31211	912-752-1313	752-1331
Web: www.13wmaz.com ■ *E-mail:* suggestions@13wmaz.com					
WMGT-TV Ch 41 (NBC) 6525 Ocmulgee E Blvd	Macon	GA	31217	912-745-4141	742-2626
Web: www.wmgt.com					
WPGA-TV Ch 58 (ABC) 1691 Forsyth St.	Macon	GA	31201	912-745-5858	745-5800
Web: www.58abc.com					

RADIO

				Phone	Fax
WALJ-FM 107.1 MHz (Urban) Rt 6 Box 735	Macon	GA	31217	912-745-3301	742-2293
Web: www.j107.com ■ *E-mail:* j107@j107.com					
WAYS-FM 99.1 MHz (Oldies) 544 Mulberry St Suite 700	Macon	GA	31201	912-746-6286	742-8061
WBAF-AM 1090 kHz (Rel) 645 Forsyth St	Barnesville	GA	30204	770-358-1090	

Macon — Radio (Cont'd)

				Phone	Fax
WBML-AM 900 kHz (Rel) 735 Reese St.	Macon	GA	31217	912-743-5453	743-9265
WBNM-AM 1120 kHz (Rel) Rt 6 Box 735.	Macon	GA	31217	912-745-3301	742-2293
WCOP-AM 1350 kHz (Rel) 1350 Radio Loop Rd	Warner Robins	GA	31088	912-923-3416	
E-mail: wcop@cyberhighway.net					
WDDO-AM 1240 kHz (Rel) 544 Mulberry St Suite 700	Macon	GA	31201	912-745-3375	742-8061
WDEN-AM 1500 kHz (Ctry) 544 Mulberry St Suite 700	Macon	GA	31201	912-745-3383	741-8811
WDEN-FM 105.3 MHz (Ctry) 544 Mulberry St Suite 700	Macon	GA	31201	912-745-3383	741-8811
WIBB-FM 97.9 MHz (Urban) 7080 Industrial Hwy	Macon	GA	31216	912-781-1063	781-6711
WJTG-FM 91.3 MHz (Rel) 3214 Richardson Mill Rd	Fort Valley	GA	31030	912-825-0085	825-9911
E-mail: wjtg@accucomm.net					
WKGQ-AM 1060 kHz (AC) 156 Lake Laurel Rd NE	Milledgeville	GA	31061	912-453-9406	453-3298
Web: accucomm.net/~z97 ■ *E-mail:* z97@accucomm.net					
WLCG-AM 1280 kHz (Rel) 7080 Industrial Hwy	Macon	GA	31216	912-781-1063	781-6711
WLCG-FM 102.5 MHz (Rel) 7080 Industrial Hwy	Macon	GA	31216	912-781-1063	781-6711
WMAC-AM 940 kHz (N/T) 544 Mulberry St Suite 700	Macon	GA	31201	912-746-6286	742-8061
WMGB-FM 93.7 MHz (CHR) 544 Mulberry St Suite 700	Macon	GA	31201	912-746-6286	742-8061
WMKS-FM 92.3 MHz (CR) 544 Mulberry St Suite 700	Macon	GA	31201	912-746-6286	742-8061
WMVG-AM 1450 kHz (Rel) 1250 W Charlton St.	Milledgeville	GA	31061	912-452-0586	452-5886
Web: www.accucomm.net/~wmvgwkzr/am1450.htm ■ *E-mail:* wmvgwkzr@accucomm.net					
WPEZ-FM 107.9 MHz (AC) 544 Mulberry St Suite 700	Macon	GA	31201	912-745-3375	742-8061
Web. www.z108.com					
WPGA-AM 980 kHz (Misc) 1691 Forsyth St	Macon	GA	31201	912-745-5858	745-5800
WPGA-FM 100.9 MHz (AC) 1691 Forsyth St.	Macon	GA	31201	912-745-5858	745-5800
WQBZ-FM 106.3 MHz (Rock) 7080 Industrial Pkwy	Macon	GA	31216	912-781-1063	781-6711
Web: www.q106online.com					
WRBV-FM 101.7 MHz (Urban) 7080 Industrial Hwy	Macon	GA	31216	912-781-1063	781-6711
WRNC-AM 1670 kHz (Ctry) 7080 Industrial Hwy	Macon	GA	31216	912-781-1063	781-6711
WRNC-FM 96.5 MHz (Ctry) 7080 Industrial Hwy	Macon	GA	31216	912-781-1063	781-6711
WXKO-AM 1150 kHz (Rel) 1675 Hwy 341 N.	Fort Valley	GA	31030	912-825-5547	827-1273

— Colleges/Universities —

				Phone	Fax
Georgia College & State University Macon Campus 100 College Dr Bldg E.	Macon	GA	31206	912-471-2898	471-2985
Web: www.gcsu.edu					
Macon State College 100 College Station Dr	Macon	GA	31206	912-471-2700	471-2846
TF: 800-272-7619 ■ *Web:* www.mc.peachnet.edu ■ *E-mail:* mcinfo@cennet.mc.peachnet.edu					
Macon Technical Institute 3300 Macon Tech Dr.	Macon	GA	31206	912-757-3400	757-3454
Web: www.macontech.org ■ *E-mail:* info@macon.tec.ga.us					
Mercer University 1400 Coleman Ave	Macon	GA	31207	912-301-2700	752-2828
TF: 800-637-2378 ■ *Web:* www.mercer.edu ■ *E-mail:* info@mercer.edu					
Wesleyan College 4760 Forsyth Rd	Macon	GA	31210	912-477-1110	757-4030
TF Admissions: 800-447-6610 ■ *Web:* www.wesleyan-college.edu					

— Hospitals —

				Phone	Fax
Columbia Coliseum Medical Center 350 Hospital Dr	Macon	GA	31217	912-765-7000	742-1247
TF: 800-277-4221					
Macon Northside Hospital 400 Charter Blvd.	Macon	GA	31210	912-757-8200	757-5995
Medical Center of Central Georgia 777 Hemlock St	Macon	GA	31201	912-633-1000	633-1702
Web: www.mccg.org					
Middle Georgia Hospital 888 Pine St	Macon	GA	31201	912-751-1111	751-0412

— Attractions —

				Phone	Fax
Cannonball House & Confederate Museum 856 Mulberry St	Macon	GA	31201	912-745-5982	745-5944
Douglass Theatre 355 ML King Jr Blvd	Macon	GA	31201	912-742-2000	742-0270
Georgia Music Hall of Fame 200 ML King Jr Blvd	Macon	GA	31202	912-750-8555	750-0350
TF: 888-427-6257 ■ *Web:* www.gamusichall.com					
Georgia Sports Hall of Fame 301 Cherry St.	Macon	GA	31201	912-752-1585	752-1587
Web: www.gshf.org					
Grand Opera House 651 Mulberry St.	Macon	GA	31201	912-301-5460	301-5469
Web: www.mercer.edu/thegrand					
Hay House 934 Georgia Ave.	Macon	GA	31201	912-742-8155	745-4277
Lake Tobesofkee Recreation Area 6600 Moseley Dixon Rd.	Macon	GA	31220	912-474-8770	474-8996
Lanier Sidney Cottage 935 High St.	Macon	GA	31201	912-743-3851	745-3132
Macon Little Theater 4220 Forsyth Rd	Macon	GA	31210	912-477-3342	471-8711
Museum of Arts & Sciences 4182 Forsyth Rd	Macon	GA	31210	912-477-3232	477-3251
Web: www.masmacon.com ■ *E-mail:* masmacon@mindspring.com					
Ocmulgee National Monument 1207 Emery Hwy	Macon	GA	31217	912-752-8257	752-8259
Web: www.nps.gov/ocmu/					
Reid Neel Garden Center 730 College St.	Macon	GA	31201	912-742-0921	
Rose Hill Cemetery 1071 Riverside Dr	Macon	GA	31201	912-751-9119	
Tubman African American Museum 340 Walnut St	Macon	GA	31201	912-743-8544	743-9063
Web: www.tubmanmuseum.com ■ *E-mail:* tubman@mindspring.com					
Woodruff House 988 Bond St.	Macon	GA	31201	912-752-2715	752-4124
TF: 800-837-2911					

SPORTS TEAMS & FACILITIES

				Phone	Fax
Macon Braves (baseball) 7th St Central City Pk	Macon	GA	31201	912-745-8943	743-5559
Web: www.macontelegraph.com/braves/index.htm					
Macon Centreplex Coliseum 200 Coliseum Dr	Macon	GA	31217	912-751-9152	751-9154
Web: www.maconcentreplex.com/coliseum/index.html					
Macon Whoopee (hockey) 200 Coliseum Dr Macon Centreplex Coliseum	Macon	GA	31217	912-741-1000	464-0655
Web: www.maconwhoopee.com ■ *E-mail:* hockey@maconwhoopee.com					

— Events —

	Phone
Arrowhead Arts & Crafts Festival (late October)	912-474-8770
Cherry Blossom Festival (mid-March)	912-751-7429
Christmas in Macon (late Novemer-late December)	912-743-3401
First Night Macon (late December)	912-741-8000
Georgia Music Festival (mid-September)	912-743-3401
Georgia State Fair (late October)	912-746-7184
Midsummer Macon (early-late July)	912-477-1110
Ocmulgee Indian Celebration (mid-September)	912-743-3401
Tubman Museum Pan African Festival (early May)	912-743-8544

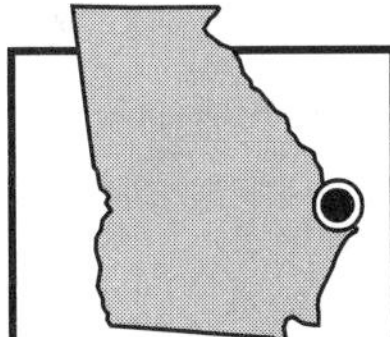

Savannah

Situated at the confluence of the Savannah River and the Atlantic Ocean, Savannah is considered by many to be one of the most beautiful cities in the U.S. Its Historic District is the country's largest historic urban landmark, with more than two thousand architecturally and historically significant buildings and 24 public squares featuring azaleas, camellias, fountains, and monuments. Many of the historic homes in this area are private residences, but others are occupied by businesses, shops, or restaurants. Some of the houses now serve as museums, including the home that

Savannah (Cont'd)

was the birthplace of Girl Scouts founder Juliette Gordon Low. Each March the city hosts a four-day event that includes a walking tour of private residences, churches, museums, and gardens in the Historic District. Thirty minutes from Savannah is Tybee Island, with white sand beaches and resort facilities that draw visitors for day trips as well as vacations. Georgia's oldest (1736) and tallest (154 ft.) lighthouse is located on the island. Fort Pulaski National Monument, which commemorates the site of an 1862 Civil War battle, is also located in the area. During the summer of 1996 Savannah hosted Olympic yachting and beach volleyball events.

Population 131,674
Area (Land) .... 62.6 sq mi
Area (Water) .... 3.3 sq mi
Elevation .... 42 ft
Latitude .... 32-08-33 N
Longitude .... 81-10-00 W
County .... Chatham
Time Zone .... EST
Area Code/s 912

— Average Temperatures and Precipitation —

TEMPERATURES

	Jan	Feb	Mar	Apr	May	Jun	Jul	Aug	Sep	Oct	Nov	Dec
High	60	62	70	78	84	89	91	90	85	78	70	62
Low	38	41	48	55	63	69	72	72	68	57	48	41

PRECIPITATION

	Jan	Feb	Mar	Apr	May	Jun	Jul	Aug	Sep	Oct	Nov	Dec
Inches	3.6	3.2	3.8	3.0	4.1	5.7	6.4	7.5	4.5	2.4	2.2	3.0

— Important Phone Numbers —

	Phone
Artsline	912-236-7284
Emergency	911
Medical Referral	912-350-9355
Poison Control Center	800-282-5846
Time/Temp	912-369-1234
Travelers Aid	912-651-5310
Weather	912-964-1700

— Information Sources —

				Phone	Fax
Better Business Bureau Serving Southeast Georgia & Southeast South Carolina 6606 Abercorn St Suite 108C	Savannah	GA	31405	912-354-7521	354-5068
Web: www.savannah.bbb.org					
Chatham County PO Box 8161	Savannah	GA	31412	912-652-7175	652-7874
Web: www.co.chatham.ga.us/chatham/chatham.htm					
Chatham-Effingham-Liberty Regional Library 2002 Bull St	Savannah	GA	31401	912-652-3600	652-3638
Web: www.co.chatham.ga.us					
Savannah Area Chamber of Commerce 101 E Bay St	Savannah	GA	31401	912-644-6400	944-0468
TF: 800-444-2427 ■ *E-mail:* cvb@smvga.com					
Savannah Area Convention & Visitors Bureau PO Box 1628	Savannah	GA	31402	912-644-6401	944-0468
TF: 800-444-2427 ■ *Web:* www.savcvb.com					
Savannah City Hall PO Box 1027	Savannah	GA	31402	912-651-6790	651-6408*
**Fax:* PR ■ *Web:* www.ci.savannah.ga.us					
Savannah Civic Center Liberty & Montgomery Sts	Savannah	GA	31401	912-651-6550	651-6552
Savannah Mayor PO Box 1027	Savannah	GA	31402	912-651-6444	651-6805

On-Line Resources

Anthill City Guide Savannah .... www.anthill.com/city.asp?city=savannah
Area Guide Savannah .... savannah.areaguides.net
Best Read Guide Savannah .... bestreadguide.com/savannah
City Knowledge Savannah .... www.cityknowledge.com/ga_savannah.htm
Creative Loafing Online Savannah .... www.cln.com/savannah/newsstand/current/
Excite.com Savannah City Guide .... www.excite.com/travel/countries/united_states/georgia/savannah/
Insiders' Guide to Savannah .... www.insiders.com/savannah/
Insiders' Guide to Savannah .... www.insiders.com/savannah/index.htm
NITC Travelbase City Guide Savannah .... www.travelbase.com/auto/guides/savannah-area-ga.html
Savannah Online .... savannah-online.com
Savannah.com .... www.savannahgeorgia.com

— Transportation Services —

AIRPORTS

■ **Savannah International Airport (SAV)** — Phone
8 miles NW of downtown (approx 20 minutes) 912-964-0514
Web: www.savapt.com ■ *E-mail:* info@savapt.com

Airport Transportation

	Phone
McCall's Airport Shuttle $16 fare to downtown	912-966-5364
Taxi $18 fare to downtown	912-269-5586

Commercial Airlines

	Phone
AirTran	800-247-8726
American Eagle	800-433-7300
Delta	800-221-1212
Midway	800-446-4392
US Airways	800-428-4322
US Airways Express	800-428-4322

Charter Airlines

	Phone
Air Savannah	912-964-5655
Savannah Aviation	912-964-1022
Signature Flight Support	912-964-1557

CAR RENTALS

	Phone
Alamo	912-964-7364
Budget	912-964-9186
Enterprise	912-966-1177
Federal	912-234-5307
Hertz	912-964-9595
Joe Thompson Auto Rental	912-925-6444
Thrifty	912-966-2277

LIMO/TAXI

	Phone
AAA Adam Cab	912-927-7466
Downtown Taxi	912-965-0213
Luxury Limousine	912-354-2982
Pooler Courier Service Inc	912-748-5685
Savannah Cab	912-236-2424
Yellow Cab	912-236-1133

MASS TRANSIT

	Phone
Chatham Area Transit Authority $.75 Base fare	912-236-2111

RAIL/BUS

				Phone
Amtrak Station 2611 Seaboard Coastline Dr	Savannah	GA	31401	800-872-7245
Greyhound Bus Station 610 W Oglethorpe Ave	Savannah	GA	31401	800-231-2222

— Accommodations —

HOTELS, MOTELS, RESORTS

				Phone	Fax
Ballastone Inn & Townhouse 14 E Oglethorpe Ave	Savannah	GA	31401	912-236-1484	236-4626
TF: 800-822-4553					
Baymont Inns & Suites 8484 Abercorn St	Savannah	GA	31406	912-927-7660	927-6392
TF: 800-301-0200					
Best Western Motel Central 45 Eisenhower Dr	Savannah	GA	31406	912-355-1000	352-1671
Best Western Savannah Historic District 412 W Bay St	Savannah	GA	31401	912-233-1011	234-3963
TF: 800-528-1234					
Budget Inn Savannah 3702 Ogeechee Rd.	Savannah	GA	31405	912-233-3633	238-1488
TF: 800-949-7666					
ClubHouse Inn 6800 Abercorn St	Savannah	GA	31405	912-356-1234	352-2828
TF: 800-258-2466 ■ *Web:* www.clubhouseinn.com/3.SAV.shtml ■ *E-mail:* info@clubhouseinn.com					
Courtyard by Marriott 6703 Abercorn St	Savannah	GA	31405	912-354-7878	354-1432
TF: 800-321-2211 ■ *Web:* courtyard.com/SAVCH					
Days Inn 114 Mall Blvd	Savannah	GA	31406	912-352-4455	352-0395
TF: 800-329-7466					

Savannah — Hotels, Motels, Resorts (Cont'd)

				Phone	Fax
Days Inn I-95 & Hwy 204	Savannah	GA	31419	912-925-3680	925-3680
TF: 800-329-7466					
Days Inn Airport 2500 Dean Forest Rd	Savannah	GA	31408	912-966-5000	966-5842
TF: 800-329-7466					
Days Inn Richmond Hill 3926 Hwy 17	Richmond Hill	GA	31324	912-756-3371	756-4157
TF: 800-329-7466					
Days Inn Riverfront 201 W Bay St	Savannah	GA	31401	912-236-4440	232-2725
TF: 800-329-7466 ■ *Web:* www.aladv.com/disv/ ■ *E-mail:* savbay@aol.com					
East Bay Inn 225 E Bay St	Savannah	GA	31401	912-238-1225	232-2709
TF: 800-500-1225					
Econo Lodge 7500 Abercorn St	Savannah	GA	31406	912-352-1657	352-1657
TF: 800-553-2666					
Econo Lodge Gateway 7 Gateway Blvd W	Savannah	GA	31419	912-925-2280	925-1075
TF: 800-673-7301					
Fairfield Inn by Marriott 2 Lee Blvd	Savannah	GA	31405	912-353-7100	353-7100
TF: 800-228-2800 ■ *Web:* fairfieldinn.com/SAVFI					
Foley House Inn 14 W Hull St	Savannah	GA	31401	912-232-6622	231-1218
TF: 800-647-3708 ■ *Web:* www.foleyinn.com ■ *E-mail:* foleyinn@aol.com					
Forsyth Park Inn 102 W Hall St	Savannah	GA	31401	912-233-6800	
Gastonian Inn 220 E Gaston St	Savannah	GA	31401	912-232-2869	232-0710
TF: 800-322-6603 ■ *Web:* www.gastonian.com					
Guesthouse Inn 390 Canebreak Rd	Savannah	GA	31419	912-927-2999	927-9830
TF: 800-214-8378 ■ *E-mail:* Travel@sysconn.com					
Hampton Inn 201 Stevenson Ave	Savannah	GA	31405	912-355-4100	356-5385
TF: 800-426-7866					
Hampton Inn 17007 Abercorn St	Savannah	GA	31419	912-925-1212	925-1227
TF: 800-426-7866					
Hampton Inn Historic District 201 E Bay St	Savannah	GA	31401	912-231-9700	231-0440
TF: 800-426-7866					
Hilton Savannah Desoto 15 E Liberty St	Savannah	GA	31401	912-232-9000	232-6018
TF: 800-445-8667 ■ *Web:* www.savannah-online.com/hilton/					
Holiday Inn Midtown 7100 Abercorn St	Savannah	GA	31406	912-352-7100	355-6408
TF: 800-255-8268					
Holiday Inn Mulberry 601 E Bay St	Savannah	GA	31401	912-238-1200	236-2184
TF: 800-465-4329 ■ *Web:* www.savannahhotel.com					
Homewood Suites Hotel 5820 White Bluff Rd	Savannah	GA	31405	912-353-8500	354-3821
TF: 800-225-5466					
Howard Johnson 224 W Boundary St	Savannah	GA	31401	912-232-4371	232-4371
TF: 800-446-4656					
Hyatt Regency 2 W Bay St	Savannah	GA	31401	912-238-1234	944-3678
TF: 800-233-1234 ■ *Web:* www.savannah-online.com/hyatt/					
Kehoe House 123 Habersham St	Savannah	GA	31401	912-232-1020	231-0208
TF: 800-820-1020					
King & Prince Beach Hotel & Villas 201 Arnold Rd	Saint Simons Island	GA	31522	912-638-3631	634-1720
TF: 800-342-0212					
La Quinta Motor Inn 6 Gateway Blvd	Savannah	GA	31419	912-925-9505	925-3495
TF: 800-687-6667					
La Quinta Motor Inn 6805 Abercorn St	Savannah	GA	31405	912-355-3004	355-0143
TF: 800-687-6667					
Liberty Inn 4005 Ogeechee Rd	Savannah	GA	31405	912-236-8236	234-6733
Magnolia Place Inn 503 Whitaker St	Savannah	GA	31401	912-236-7674	236-1145
TF: 800-238-7674 ■ *Web:* www.magnoliaplaceinn.com ■ *E-mail:* info@magnoliaplaceinn.com					
Masters Inn Suites 7110 Hodgson Memorial Dr	Savannah	GA	31406	912-354-8560	356-1438
TF: 800-344-4378					
Olde Harbour Inn 508 E Factors Walk	Savannah	GA	31401	912-234-4100	233-5979
TF: 800-553-6533 ■ *Web:* www.oldeharbourinn.com					
Planters Inn 29 Abercorn St	Savannah	GA	31401	912-232-5678	232-8893
TF: 800-554-1187 ■ *Web:* www.plantersinnsavannah.com					
Presidents' Quarters 225 E Presidents St	Savannah	GA	31401	912-233-1600	238-0849
TF: 800-233-1776 ■ *Web:* www.presidentsquarters.com ■ *E-mail:* info@presidentsquarters.com					
Quail Run Lodge 1130 Bob Harman Rd	Savannah	GA	31408	912-964-1421	966-5646
TF: 800-627-7035					
Quality Inn 300 W Bay St	Savannah	GA	31401	912-236-6321	234-5317
TF: 800-228-5151					
Quality Inn & Suites 6 Gateway Blvd E	Savannah	GA	31419	912-925-6666	927-3110
TF: 800-228-5151					
River Street Inn 115 E River St	Savannah	GA	31401	912-234-6400	234-1478
TF: 800-253-4229					
Savannah Marriott Riverfront 100 General McIntosh Blvd	Savannah	GA	31401	912-233-7722	233-3765
TF: 800-228-9290 ■ *Web:* www.marriott.com/marriott/savrf ■ *E-mail:* customerservice@marriott.com					
Sea Palms Golf & Tennis Resort 5445 Frederica Rd	Saint Simons Island	GA	31522	912-638-3351	634-8029
TF: 800-841-6268 ■ *Web:* www.seapalms.com					
Suburban Lodge of Savannah 10614 Abercorn St	Savannah	GA	31419	912-920-7700	920-9599
TF: 800-951-7829					
Westin Savannah Harbor Resort 410 E Bay St	Savannah	GA	31401	912-239-9999	238-0607
TF: 800-228-3000					

— Restaurants —

				Phone
17 Hundred 90 Restaurant (Continental) 307 E President St	Savannah	GA	31401	912-236-7122
45 South (Continental) 20 E Broad St	Savannah	GA	31401	912-233-1881
Bistro Savannah (Southern) 309 W Congress St	Savannah	GA	31401	912-233-6266
Chart House (Steak/Seafood) 202 W Bay St	Savannah	GA	31401	912-234-6686
Chiang Mai Orchids Thai Cafe (Thai) 215 W Broughton St	Savannah	GA	31401	912-231-0789
Churchill's Pub (English) 9 Drayton St	Savannah	GA	31401	912-232-8501
City Market Cafe (International) 224 W Saint Julian St	Savannah	GA	31401	912-236-7133
Clary's Cafe (American) 404 Abercorn St	Savannah	GA	31401	912-233-0402
Debi's Restaurant (Homestyle) 10 W State St	Savannah	GA	31401	912-236-3322
Dockside Seafood Restaurant (Seafood) 201 W River St	Savannah	GA	31401	912-236-9253
Elizabeth on 37th (Southern) 105 E 37th St	Savannah	GA	31401	912-236-5547
Exchange Tavern & Restaurant (American) 201 E River St	Savannah	GA	31401	912-232-7088
Garibaldi Cafe (Italian) 315 W Congress St	Savannah	GA	31401	912-232-7118
Huey's (Cajun) 115 E River St	Savannah	GA	31401	912-234-7385
Il Pasticcio (Italian) 2 E Broughton St	Savannah	GA	31401	912-231-8888
Johnny Harris (Southern) 1651 E Victory Dr	Savannah	GA	31404	912-354-7810
Kevin Barry's (Irish) 117 W River St	Savannah	GA	31401	912-233-9626
Kyoto Japanese Steak & Seafood House (Japanese) 7805 Abercorn Ext	Savannah	GA	31406	912-355-9800
Mrs Wilkes Dining Room (Homestyle) 107 W Jones St	Savannah	GA	31401	912-232-5997
Musashi Japanese Steak House (Japanese) 7312 Hodgson Memorial Dr	Savannah	GA	31406	912-352-2128
Nita's Place (Homestyle) 140 Abercorn St	Savannah	GA	31401	912-238-8233
Olde Pink House (Continental) 23 Abercorn St	Savannah	GA	31401	912-232-4286
Olympia Cafe (Greek) 5 E River St	Savannah	GA	31401	912-233-3131
Pearl's Elegant Pelican (Steak/Seafood) 7000 LaRoche Ave	Savannah	GA	31406	912-352-8221
Pirates' House (Seafood) 20 E Broad St	Savannah	GA	31401	912-233-5757
River House (Steak/Seafood) 125 W River St	Savannah	GA	31401	912-234-1900
Web: www.riverhouseseafood.com/river.htm				
Seasons (Steak/Seafood) 315 W Saint Julian St	Savannah	GA	31401	912-233-2626
Shrimp Factory (Seafood) 313 E River St	Savannah	GA	31401	912-236-4229
Six Pence Pub (English) 245 Bull St	Savannah	GA	31404	912-233-3156

— Goods and Services —

SHOPPING

				Phone	Fax
City Market 204 West Saint Julian St	Savannah	GA	31401	912-232-4903	232-2142
Historic Railroad Shops 601 W Harris St	Savannah	GA	31401	912-651-6823	651-3691
E-mail: hrs@gnet.net					
Oglethorpe Mall 7804 Abercorn St	Savannah	GA	31406	912-354-7038	352-3365
Web: www.omall.com					
River Street Historic District River St-betw ML King Blvd & President St	Savannah	GA	31401	912-234-0295	234-4904
Savannah Festival Factory Stores 11 Gateway Blvd S	Savannah	GA	31419	912-925-3089	925-3163
Savannah Mall 14045 Abercorn St	Savannah	GA	31419	912-927-7467	927-0018
Twelve Oaks Shopping Center 5500 Abercorn St	Savannah	GA	31405	912-355-1311	355-1168

BANKS

				Phone	Fax
AmeriBank NA 7393 Hodgson Memorial Dr	Savannah	GA	31406	912-921-7100	921-1661
Web: www.ameribank.net					
Carver State Bank 701 ML King Blvd	Savannah	GA	31401	912-233-9971	232-8666
Coastal Bank 27 Bull St	Savannah	GA	31401	912-235-4400	233-2433
First Liberty Bank 18 W Bryan St	Savannah	GA	31401	912-351-2201	351-2270
TF Cust Svc: 888-454-2243*					
First Union National Bank 20 Bank St	Savannah	GA	31404	912-651-5916	651-5983
TF Cust Svc: 800-733-4008*					
Savannah Bank NA 25 Bull St	Savannah	GA	31401	912-651-8200	232-3733
SunTrust Bank 33 Bull St	Savannah	GA	31401	912-944-1000	944-1168*
**Fax:* Hum Res ■ *TF:* 800-688-7878					

Savannah — Banks (Cont'd)

				Phone	Fax
Wachovia Bank NA 5354 Reynolds St	Savannah	GA	31405	912-353-1010	353-1016

TF Cust Svc: 800-922-4684*

BUSINESS SERVICES

	Phone		Phone
Airborne Express	800-247-2676	**Kelly Services**	912-354-3050
BAX Global	800-225-5229	**Kinko's**	912-927-8119
DHL Worldwide Express	800-225-5345	**Mail Boxes Etc**	800-789-4623
Federal Express	800-238-5355	**Post Office**	912-235-4653
Interim Personnel	912-353-7966	**UPS**	800-742-5877

— Media —

PUBLICATIONS

				Phone	Fax
Savannah Morning News‡ 111 W Bay St	Savannah	GA	31401	912-236-9511	234-6522

Web: www.savanews.com

‡Daily newspapers

TELEVISION

				Phone	Fax
WJCL-TV Ch 22 (ABC) 10001 Abercorn Ext	Savannah	GA	31406	912-925-0022	921-2235
WSAV-TV Ch 3 (NBC) 1430 E Victory Dr	Savannah	GA	31404	912-651-0300	651-0304
Web: www.wsav.com ■ *E-mail:* wsav@ix.netcom.com					
WTGS-TV Ch 28 (Fox) 10001 Abercorn St	Savannah	GA	31420	912-925-2287	921-2235
WTOC-TV Ch 11 (CBS) PO Box 8086	Savannah	GA	31412	912-234-1111	232-4945
Web: www.wtoctv.com ■ *E-mail:* wtoctv@sava.gulfnet.com					
WVAN-TV Ch 9 (PBS) 86 Vandiver St	Pembroke	GA	31321	912-653-4996	

RADIO

				Phone	Fax
WAEV-FM 97.3 MHz (AC) 24 W Henry St	Savannah	GA	31401	912-232-0097	232-6144
E-mail: mix97@wce.com					
WCHY-FM 94.1 MHz (Ctry) 245 Alfred St	Savannah	GA	31408	912-964-7794	964-9414
WEAS-AM 900 kHz (Rel) PO Box 60789	Savannah	GA	31420	912-234-7264	233-7247
WEAS-FM 93.1 MHz (Urban) 214 Television Cir	Savannah	GA	31401	912-961-9000	231-1722
WGCO-FM 98.3 & 103.1 MHz (Oldies) 401 Mall Blvd Suite 201F	Savannah	GA	31406	912-351-9830	352-4821
WIXV-FM 95.5 MHz (Rock) 1 Riverview Rd	Savannah	GA	31410	912-897-1529	897-4047
Web: www.rockofsavannah.com					
WJCL-FM 96.5 MHz (Ctry) PO Box 60789	Savannah	GA	31420	912-921-0965	921-2218
WMCD-FM 100.1 MHz (AC) PO Box 958	Statesboro	GA	30459	912-764-5446	764-8827
WRHQ-FM 105.3 MHz (Rock) 1102 E 52nd St	Savannah	GA	31404	912-234-1053	354-6600
Web: www.wrhq.com ■ *E-mail:* wrhq1053@aol.com					
WSVH-FM 91.1 MHz (NPR) 12 Ocean Science Cir	Savannah	GA	31411	912-598-3300	598-3306
TF: 800-673-7332 ■ *Web:* www.wsvh.org					
WWNS-AM 1240 kHz (N/T) PO Box 958	Statesboro	GA	30459	912-764-5446	764-8827

— Colleges/Universities —

				Phone	Fax
Armstrong Atlantic State University 11935 Abercorn St	Savannah	GA	31419	912-927-5275	921-5462
TF Admissions: 800-633-2349 ■ *Web:* www.armstrong.edu					
Savannah College of Art & Design 342 Bull St	Savannah	GA	31401	912-238-2483	525-5983
Web: www.scad.edu ■ *E-mail:* admin@scad.edu					
Savannah State University 3219 College St	Savannah	GA	31404	912-356-2186	356-2253
South College 709 Mall Blvd	Savannah	GA	31406	912-691-6000	691-6070
Web: www.southcollege.edu					

— Hospitals —

				Phone	Fax
Candler Hospital 5353 Reynolds St	Savannah	GA	31405	912-354-9211	692-6350
Memorial Medical Center 4700 Waters Ave	Savannah	GA	31404	912-350-8000	350-7073
Web: www.memorialcares.com					
Saint Joseph's Hospital 11705 Mercy Blvd	Savannah	GA	31419	912-925-4100	927-5188

— Attractions —

				Phone	Fax
Atlantic Star Casino Cruise 1 Old Hwy 80 Lazaretto Creek Marina	Savannah	GA	31328	912-786-7827	786-7828
Beach Institute African American Cultural Center 502 E Harris St	Savannah	GA	31401	912-234-8000	234-8001
Chatham County Garden Center & Botanical Gardens 1388 Eisenhower Dr	Savannah	GA	31405	912-355-3883	
City Lights Theatre Co 125 E Broughton St	Savannah	GA	31401	912-234-9860	
City Market 204 West Saint Julian St	Savannah	GA	31401	912-232-4903	232-2142
City Market Art Center 219 W Bryan St Suite 202	Savannah	GA	31401	912-234-2327	232-2142
Davenport House Museum 324 E State St	Savannah	GA	31401	912-236-8097	
First African Baptist Church 23 Montgomery St Franklin Sq	Savannah	GA	31401	912-233-6597	234-7950
Fort Frederica National Monument Rt 9 Box 286-C	Saint Simons Island	GA	31522	912-638-3639	638-3639
Web: www.nps.gov/fofr/ ■ *E-mail:* fofr_superintendent@nps.gov					
Fort Pulaski National Monument US Hwy 80 E	Savannah	GA	31410	912-786-5787	786-6023
Web: www.nps.gov/fopu/					
Gilbert Ralph Mark Civil Rights Museum 460 ML King Jr Blvd	Savannah	GA	31401	912-231-8900	234-2577
Hamilton-Turner House & Museum 330 Abercorn St	Savannah	GA	31401	912-233-4800	233-9800
Historic Railroad Shops 601 W Harris St	Savannah	GA	31401	912-651-6823	651-3691
E-mail: hrs@gnet.net					
King-Tisdale Cottage Black History Museum 502 E Harris St	Savannah	GA	31401	912-234-8000	234-8001
Low Andrew House 329 Abercorn St	Savannah	GA	31401	912-233-6854	
Lowe Juliette Gordon Birthplace 142 Bull St	Savannah	GA	31401	912-233-4501	233-4659
Mighty Eighth Airforce Heritage Museum 175 Bourne Ave	Pooler	GA	31322	912-748-8888	748-0209
TF: 800-421-9428 ■ *Web:* www.mighty8thmuseum.com ■ *E-mail:* mighty8cur@aol.com					
Oatland Island Education Center 711 Sandtown Rd	Savannah	GA	31410	912-897-3773	898-7402
Old Fort Jackson 1 Old Fort Jackson Rd	Savannah	GA	31404	912-232-3945	236-5126
Web: www.chsgeorgia.org/site/ftjack/right.htm ■ *E-mail:* ofs@g-net.net					
Old Town Trolley Tours 341 ML King Blvd	Savannah	GA	31401	912-233-0083	
Web: www.historictours.com/savannah/trolley.htm ■ *E-mail:* savott@historictours.com					
Owens-Thomas House 124 Abercorn St	Savannah	GA	31401	912-233-9743	233-0102
E-mail: olivia alison@worldnet.att.net					
River Street Historic District River St-betw ML King Blvd & President St	Savannah	GA	31401	912-234-0295	234-4904
Savannah History Museum 303 ML King Jr Blvd	Savannah	GA	31401	912-238-1779	651-6827
Web: www.chsgeorgia.org					
Savannah National Wildlife Refuge 1000 Business Center Dr Suite 10	Savannah	GA	31405	912-652-4415	652-4385
E-mail: r4rw_ga.scr@fws.gov					
Savannah River Queen & Georgia Queen Riverboats 9 E River St	Savannah	GA	31412	912-232-6404	234-7881
TF: 800-786-6404 ■ *Web:* www.savannah-riverboat.com ■ *E-mail:* sales@savannah-riverboat.com					
Savannah Symphony Orchestra 225 Abercorn St	Savannah	GA	31401	912-236-9536	234-1450
Web: www.savannahsymphony.org ■ *E-mail:* feedback@savannahsymphony.org					
Savannah Theatre Co 222 Bull St	Savannah	GA	31401	912-233-7764	
Web: www.savtheatre.org ■ *E-mail:* stc@savtheatre.org					
Ships of the Sea Maritime Museum 41 ML King Blvd	Savannah	GA	31401	912-232-1511	234-7363
Web: www.shipsofthesea.org ■ *E-mail:* info@shipsofthesea.org					
Telfair Museum of Art 121 Barnard St	Savannah	GA	31401	912-232-1177	232-6954
Web: www.telfair.org					
Tybee Island	Tybee Island	GA	31328	912-786-5444	
Web: www.tybeeisland.com					
Tybee Island Lighthouse & Museum 30 Meddin Dr	Tybee Island	GA	31328	912-786-5801	786-6538
Web: www.tybeeisland.com/tourinfo/museum/timuseum.htm					
Tybee Marine Science Foundation 1510 Strand 14th St Parking Lot 10	Tybee Island	GA	31328	912-786-5917	786-5917
Web: www.tybeeisland.com/tourinfo/tybeemsc/tybeemsc.htm					
University of Georgia Aquarium 30 Ocean Science Cir	Savannah	GA	31411	912-598-2496	598-2302

Savannah — Attractions (Cont'd)

				Phone	Fax
Wormsloe Historic Site 7601 Skidaway Rd *Web:* www.gastateparks.org	Savannah	GA	31406	912-353-3023	353-3023

SPORTS TEAMS & FACILITIES

				Phone	Fax
Grayson Stadium 1401 E Victory Dr	Savannah	GA	31414	912-351-9150	352-9722
Martin Luther King Jr Arena Liberty at Montgomery St	Savannah	GA	31401	912-651-6550	651-6552
Oglethorpe Speedway 267 Raymond Rd	Pooler	GA	31322	912-964-8200	964-9501
Savannah Sand Gnats (baseball) 1401 E Victory Dr Grayson Stadium	Savannah	GA	31414	912-351-9150	352-9722

— Events —

	Phone
4th of July Celebration (July 4)	912-234-0295
Arts-on-the-River Weekend (mid-May)	912-651-6417
Christmas on the River (early December)	912-234-0295
Christmas Tour of Homes (mid-December)	800-627-5030
City Market Blues Festival (early June)	912-232-4903
Georgia Heritage Celebration (early February)	912-651-2128
Hidden Gardens (mid-late April)	912-238-0248
Jazz Festival (late September)	912-232-2222
New Years Eve at City Market (December 31)	912-232-4903
Nogs Tour of Hidden Gardens (mid-April)	912-644-6401
Oktoberfest on the River (early October)	912-234-0295
Saint Patrick's Day Celebration on the River (mid-March)	912-234-0295
Savannah Greek Festival (mid-October)	912-236-8256
Savannah Irish Festival (mid-February)	912-927-0331
Savannah Jazz Festival (late September)	912-232-2222
Savannah Maritime Festival (late August)	912-238-4434
Savannah Onstage International Arts Festival (early March)	912-236-5745
Savannah Tour of Homes & Gardens (late March)	912-234-8054
Scottish Games & Highland Gathering (mid-May)	912-644-6401
Seafood Festival (early May)	912-234-0295
Siege & Reduction Weekend (mid-April)	912-786-5787
Southern Home Show (early March)	912-354-6193
Spring Fling (mid-April)	912-232-4903
Telfair Art Fair (early-mid-October)	912-232-1177

Hawaii

Population (1999): 1,185,497 **Area (sq mi): 10,932**

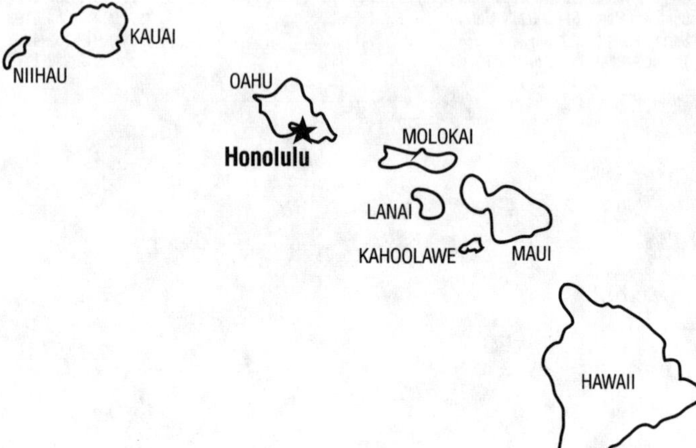

— State Information Sources —

				Phone	Fax
Hawaii Business Economic Development & Tourism Dept PO Box 2359	Honolulu	HI	96804	808-586-2355	586-2377
Web: www.hawaii.gov/dbedt ■ *E-mail:* library@pixi.com					
Hawaii Chamber of Commerce 1132 Bishop St Suite 402	Honolulu	HI	96813	808-545-4300	545-4369
Web: www.cochawaii.com ■ *E-mail:* info@cochawaii.org					
Hawaii State Government Information				808-586-2211	
Web: www.hawaii.gov					
Hawaii State Parks Div PO Box 621	Honolulu	HI	96809	808-587-0300	587-0311
Web: www.hawaii.gov/dlnr/dsp/dsp.html ■ *E-mail:* dlnr@pixi.com					
Hawaii State Public Library 478 S King St	Honolulu	HI	96813	808-586-3505	
Web: www.hcc.hawaii.edu/hspls					
Hawaii Tourism Office 250S Hotel St Rm 435	Honolulu	HI	96813	808-586-2550	586-2549
Web: www.gohawaii.com					

ON-LINE RESOURCES

4Hawaii.com 4hawaii.com
Access America Hawaii . . . . . . www.accessamer.com/hawaii
Aloha from Hawaii . . . . . . www.aloha-hawaii.com/home.shtml
Alternative Hawaii . . . . . . www.alternative-hawaii.com
AreaTravel.net Hawaii . . . . . . www.hawaii.areatravel.net/hawaii/
Best of Hawaii . . . . . . www.bestofhawaii.com
Discover Hawaii . . . . . . discoverhawaii.com/index.html
Extreme Hawaii Fun . . . . . . www.extreme-hawaii.com
Hawaii Cities . . . . . . dir.yahoo.com/Regional/U_S__States/Hawaii/Cities
Hawaii Guide . . . . . . www.hawaiiguide.com
Hawaii Home Page . . . . . . www.hawaii.net
Hawaii Islands & Regions . . . . . . dir.yahoo.com/Regional/U_S__States/Hawaii/Islands_and_Regions
Hawaii Online Highways . . . . . . www.hiohwy.com
Hawaii Scenario . . . . . . scenariousa.dstylus.com/hi/indexf.htm
Hawaii State Vacation Planner . . . . . . www.hshawaii.com
Hawaii Travel & Tourism Guide . . . . . . www.travel-library.com/pacific/hawaii/index.html
Hawaii Visitor Guide . . . . . . www.visit-hawaii.com
Planet Hawaii . . . . . . planet-hawaii.com
Rough Guide Travel Hawaii travel.roughguides.com/content/1621/index.htm
Travel.org-Hawaii . . . . . . travel.org/hawaii.html
Ultimate Hawaii . . . . . . www.ultimatehawaii.com
Virtually Hawaii . . . . . . hawaii.ivv.nasa.gov/space/hawaii/index.html
Yahoo! Get Local Hawaii . . . . . . dir.yahoo.com/Regional/U_S__States/Hawaii

— Cities Profiled —

Honolulu

Located on the island of Oahu, Honolulu attracts close to five million visitors a year. The city and surrounding areas offer a variety of attractions, including world-famous Waikiki Beach, Diamond Head State Park, and Waimea Falls Park, with archaeological sites and several varieties of exotic tropical flora. Outdoor recreational activities such as rainforest hikes, outrigger canoe rides, and volcano climbs are all available within an hour from Honolulu. At Pearl Harbor, one can see the USS Arizona Memorial and USS Bowfin, an actual WWII submarine. The National Memorial of the Pacific, the resting place for more than 25,000 servicemen and women, provides a panoramic view of the Harbor, Waikiki, and Honolulu.

Population	395,789	**Longitude**	156-44-75 W
Area (Land)	82.8 sq mi	**County**	Honolulu
Area (Water)	19.4 sq mi	**Time Zone**	Hawaii
Elevation	18 ft	**Area Code/s**	808
Latitude	20-73-46 N		

— Average Temperatures and Precipitation —

TEMPERATURES

	Jan	Feb	Mar	Apr	May	Jun	Jul	Aug	Sep	Oct	Nov	Dec
High	80	81	82	83	85	87	88	89	89	87	84	81
Low	66	65	67	69	70	72	74	74	74	72	70	67

PRECIPITATION

	Jan	Feb	Mar	Apr	May	Jun	Jul	Aug	Sep	Oct	Nov	Dec
Inches	3.6	2.2	2.2	1.5	1.1	0.5	0.6	0.4	0.8	2.3	3.0	3.8

— Important Phone Numbers —

	Phone		Phone
AAA	808-593-2221	**Medical Referral**	808-536-7702
American Express Travel	808-946-7741	**Poison Control Center**	808-941-4411
Dental Referral	808-593-7956	**Travelers Aid**	808-926-8274
Emergency	911	**Weather**	808-973-5286
HotelDocs	800-468-3537		

— Information Sources —

				Phone	Fax
Better Business Bureau Serving Hawaii 1132 Bishop St Suite 1507 *Web:* www.hawaii.bbb.org	Honolulu	HI	96813	808-536-6956	523-2335
Hawaii Chamber of Commerce 1132 Bishop St Suite 402 *Web:* www.cochawaii.com ■ *E-mail:* info@cochawaii.org	Honolulu	HI	96813	808-545-4300	545-4369
Hawaii Visitors & Convention Bureau 2270 Kalakaua Ave Suite 801 *TF:* 800-464-2924 ■ *Web:* www.visit.hawaii.org	Honolulu	HI	96815	808-923-1811	924-0290
Honolulu City Hall 530 S King St *Web:* www.co.honolulu.hi.us	Honolulu	HI	96813	808-523-4385	
Honolulu County 530 S King St	Honolulu	HI	96813	808-523-4352	527-6888
Honolulu Mayor 530 S King St *Web:* www.co.honolulu.hi.us/Mayor ■ *E-mail:* mayor@co.honolulu.hi.us	Honolulu	HI	96813	808-523-4141	527-5552
Honolulu Planning & Permitting Dept 650 S King St 8th Fl *Web:* www.co.honolulu.hi.us/planning ■ *E-mail:* dpp@co.honolulu.hi.us	Honolulu	HI	96813	808-523-4713	523-4950

On-Line Resources

4Honolulu.com	www.4honolulu.com
About.com Guide to Honolulu/Oahu	honolulu.about.com/local/alaskahawaii/honolulu
Access America Honolulu	www.accessamer.com/honolulu_oahu/
Area Guide Honolulu	honolulu.areaguides.net
Boulevards Honolulu	www.honolulu.com
City Knowledge Honolulu	www.cityknowledge.com/hi_honolulu.htm
Excite.com Honolulu City Guide	www.excite.com/travel/countries/united_states/hawaii/honolulu
Gayot's Guide Restaurant Search Hawaii	www.perrier.com/restaurants/gayot.asp?area=HAW
HotelGuide Honolulu	hotelguide.net/honolulu/
Rough Guide Travel Honolulu	travel.roughguides.com/content/1623/

— Transportation Services —

AIRPORTS

	Phone
■ **Honolulu International Airport (HNL)**	
5 miles NW of downtown (approx 15 minutes) Web: kumu.icsd.hawaii.gov/dot/hono.htm	808-836-6413

Airport Transportation

	Phone
Bus The $1 fare to downtown	808-848-4500
Taxi $15-20 fare to downtown	808-591-8830

Commercial Airlines

	Phone		Phone
Air New Zealand	800-262-1234	**Islandair**	808-484-2222
Aloha	808-484-1111	**Japan**	808-521-1441
American	800-433-7300	**Korean Air**	800-438-5000
China Airlines	808-955-0088	**Northwest**	808-955-2255
Continental	808-523-0000	**Philippine**	800-435-9725
Delta	800-221-1212	**TWA**	800-221-2000
Hawaiian	808-838-1555	**United**	800-241-6522

Charter Airlines

	Phone		Phone
Air Group Inc	800-233-8890	**Makani Kai Helicopters**	808-834-5813
Call Air	808-839-1499		

CAR RENTALS

	Phone		Phone
Alamo	808-833-4585	**Hertz**	808-831-3500
Avis	808-834-5536	**National**	808-831-3800
Budget	808-537-3600	**VIP**	808-922-4605
Dollar	808-944-1544		

LIMO/TAXI

	Phone		Phone
Aloha State Cab	808-847-3566	**Diamond Taxi**	808-926-4466
Americabs	808-973-2950	**Elite Limousine**	808-735-2431
Cab The	808-422-2222	**Exclusive Limousines**	808-591-1975
Carey Limousine	808-735-2431	**North Shore Limousines**	808-293-1447
City Taxi	808-524-2121	**Pacific Viking Limousine**	808-946-5525

MASS TRANSIT

	Phone
Bus The $1 Base fare	808-848-4500

— Accommodations —

HOTEL RESERVATION SERVICES

	Phone	Fax
All Islands Bed & Breakfast *TF:* 800-542-0344 ■ *Web:* home.hawaii.rr.com/allislands ■ *E-mail:* cac@hawaii.rr.com	808-263-2342	263-0308
Bed & Breakfast Honolulu *TF:* 800-288-4666 ■ *Web:* www.hawaiibnb.com ■ *E-mail:* rainbow@hawaiibnb.com	808-595-7533	595-2030
Bed & Breakfast of Hawaii *TF:* 800-733-1632 ■ *Web:* www.bandb-hawaii.com/ ■ *E-mail:* reservations@bandb-hawaii.com	808-822-7771	822-2723
Hawaii's Best Bed & Breakfasts *TF:* 800-262-9912 ■ *Web:* www.bestbnb.com/	808-885-4550	885-0559
Hotel Reservations Network Inc *TF Sales:* 800-964-6835 ■ *Web:* www.hoteldiscount.com	214-361-7311	361-7299

HOTELS, MOTELS, RESORTS

				Phone	Fax
Ala Moana Hotel 410 Atkinson Dr. *TF:* 800-367-6025 ■ *Web:* www.alamoanahotel.com/	Honolulu	HI	96814	808-955-4811	944-2974
Aspen Pacific Monarch 2427 Kuhio Ave *TF:* 800-922-7866	Honolulu	HI	96815	808-923-9805	924-3220

Honolulu — Hotels, Motels, Resorts (Cont'd)

	City	State	ZIP	Phone	Fax
Aston Island Colony Hotel 445 Seaside Ave. *TF:* 800-922-7866	Honolulu	HI	96815	808-923-2345	921-7105
Aston Waikiki Beach Tower 2470 Kalakaua Ave *TF:* 800-922-7866 ■ *Web:* www.aston-hotels.com	Honolulu	HI	96815	808-926-6400	926-7380
Aston Waikiki Circle Hotel 2464 Kalakaua Ave *TF:* 800-922-7866	Honolulu	HI	96815	808-923-1571	926-8024
Aston Waikiki Terrace Hotel 2045 Kalakaua Ave *TF:* 800-922-7866	Honolulu	HI	96815	808-955-6000	943-8555
Best Western Outrigger Waikiki Tower 200 Lewers St *TF:* 800-462-6262 ■ *Web:* www.outrigger.com	Honolulu	HI	96815	808-922-6424	923-7437
Best Western Plaza Hotel 3253 N Nimitz Hwy *TF:* 800-800-4683	Honolulu	HI	96819	808-836-3636	834-7406
Breakers The 250 Beach Walk *TF:* 800-426-0494 ■ *Web:* www.breakers-hawaii.com	Honolulu	HI	96815	808-923-8894	923-7174
Doubletree Alana Waikiki Hotel 1956 Ala Moana Blvd *TF:* 800-367-6070 ■ *Web:* www.doubletreehotels.com/DoubleT/Hotel121/123/123Main.htm	Honolulu	HI	96815	808-941-7275	949-0996
Executive Centre Hotel 1088 Bishop St *TF:* 800-949-3932	Honolulu	HI	96813	808-539-3000	523-1088
Halekulani Hotel 2199 Kalia Rd *TF:* 800-367-2343 ■ *Web:* www.halekulani.com	Honolulu	HI	96815	808-923-2311	926-8004
Hawaii Prince Hotel 100 Holomoana St. *TF:* 800-321-6248	Honolulu	HI	96815	808-956-1111	946-0811
Hawaiian Inn Waikiki Beach 2570 Kalakaua Ave *TF:* 800-877-7666	Honolulu	HI	96815	808-922-2511	923-3656
Hawaiian Regent 2552 Kalakaua Ave. *TF:* 800-367-5370 ■ *Web:* www.hawaiianregent.com ■ *E-mail:* info@hawaiianregent.com	Honolulu	HI	96815	808-922-6611	921-5255
Hilton Hawaiian Village 2005 Kalia Rd *TF:* 800-445-8667 ■ *Web:* www.hilton.com/hotels/HNLHVHH	Honolulu	HI	96815	808-949-4321	951-5458
Hilton Waikoloa Village 425 Waikoloa Beach Dr *TF:* 800-445-8667 ■ *Web:* www.hilton.com/hotels/KOAHWHH	Waikoloa	HI	96738	808-885-1234	886-2900
Honolulu Airport Hotel 3401 N Nimitz Hwy *TF:* 800-800-4377	Honolulu	HI	96819	808-836-0661	833-1738
Honolulu Prince 415 Nahua St *TF:* 800-922-7866	Honolulu	HI	96815	808-922-1616	922-6223
Hotel Southern Cross 444 Kanekapolei St *TF:* 800-423-4514	Honolulu	HI	96815	808-923-5532	924-7160
Hyatt Regency Waikiki Resort 2424 Kalakaua Ave *TF:* 800-233-1234 ■ *Web:* www.hyattwaikiki.com ■ *E-mail:* info@hyattwaikiki.com	Honolulu	HI	96815	808-923-1234	924-3356
Ilikai Hotel Nikko Waikiki 1777 Ala Moana Blvd *TF:* 800-245-4524 ■ *Web:* www.nikkohotels.com/americas/ilikai.html	Honolulu	HI	96815	808-949-3811	947-4523
Imperial Waikiki Resort 205 Lewers St. *TF:* 800-347-2582 ■ *Web:* www.imperialofwaikiki.com	Honolulu	HI	96815	808-923-1827	921-7586
Inn on the Park 1920 Ala Moana Blvd *TF:* 800-367-5004	Honolulu	HI	96815	808-946-8355	946-4839
Kahala Mandarin Oriental Hotel 5000 Kahala Ave. *TF:* 800-367-2525 ■ *Web:* www.mohnl.com	Honolulu	HI	96816	808-734-2211	739-8800
Marine Surf Waikiki Hotel 364 Seaside Ave. *TF:* 888-456-7873	Honolulu	HI	96815	808-923-0277	926-5915
Miramar Hotel At Waikiki 2345 Kuhio Ave. *TF:* 800-367-2303	Honolulu	HI	96815	808-922-2077	922-4601
New Otani Kaimana Beach Hotel 2863 Kalakaua Ave *TF:* 800-356-8264 ■ *Web:* www.kaimana.com	Honolulu	HI	96815	808-923-1555	922-9404
Ocean Resort Hotel Waikiki 175 Paoakalani Ave *TF:* 800-367-2317	Honolulu	HI	96815	808-922-3861	924-1982
Ohana Hotel of Hawaii 225 Saratoga Rd *TF:* 800-462-6262 ■ *Web:* www.outrigger.com	Honolulu	HI	96815	808-923-3881	923-3823
Outrigger Ala Wai Tower 1700 Ala Moana Blvd *TF:* 800-688-7444 ■ *Web:* www.outrigger.com/details/property.asp?code=phx	Honolulu	HI	96815	808-942-7722	943-7272
Outrigger Coral Seas 250 Lewers St. *TF:* 800-462-6262 ■ *Web:* www.outrigger.com/details/property.asp?code=ocs	Honolulu	HI	96815	808-923-3881	924-6361
Outrigger East Hotel 150 Kaiulani Ave. *TF:* 800-688-7444	Honolulu	HI	96815	808-922-5353	926-4334
Outrigger Edgewater Hotel 2168 Kalia Rd *TF:* 800-688-7444	Honolulu	HI	96815	808-922-6424	924-6354
Outrigger Hobron Hotel 343 Hobron Ln. *TF:* 800-688-7444	Honolulu	HI	96815	808-942-7777	943-7373
Outrigger Maile Sky Court 2058 Kuhio Ave *TF:* 800-688-7444	Honolulu	HI	96815	808-947-2828	943-0504
Outrigger Malia Hotel 2211 Kuhio Ave *TF:* 800-688-7444	Honolulu	HI	96815	808-923-7621	921-4804
Outrigger Prince Kuhio Hotel 2500 Kuhio Ave *TF:* 800-688-7474 ■ *Web:* www.outrigger.com	Honolulu	HI	96815	808-922-0811	923-0330
Outrigger Reef Hotel 2169 Kalia Rd *TF:* 800-462-6262 ■ *Web:* www.outrigger.com	Honolulu	HI	96815	808-923-3111	924-4957
Outrigger Reef Towers 227 Lewers St. *TF:* 800-688-7444	Honolulu	HI	96815	808-924-8844	924-6042
Outrigger Royal Islander Hotel 2164 Kalia Rd. *TF:* 800-688-7444 ■ *Web:* www.outrigger.com	Honolulu	HI	96815	808-922-1961	923-4632
Outrigger Surf 2280 Kuhio Ave. *TF:* 800-688-7444	Honolulu	HI	96815	808-922-5777	921-3677
Outrigger Village Hotel 240 Lewers St *TF:* 800-462-6262 ■ *Web:* www.outrigger.com	Honolulu	HI	96815	808-923-3881	922-2330
Outrigger Waikiki Hotel 2335 Kalakaua Ave. *TF:* 800-688-7444	Honolulu	HI	96815	808-923-0711	921-9749
Outrigger Waikiki Surf 2200 Kuhio Ave. *TF:* 800-688-7444	Honolulu	HI	96815	808-923-7671	921-4959
Outrigger Waikiki Surf East Hotel 422 Royal Hawaiian Ave. *TF:* 800-688-7444 ■ *Web:* www.outrigger.com	Honolulu	HI	96815	808-923-7671	921-4141
Outrigger Waikoloan Beach Resort 69-275 Waikoloan Beach Dr. *TF:* 800-922-5533 ■ *Web:* www.outrigger.com	Waikoloa	HI	96738	808-886-6789	886-7852
Outrigger West Hotel 2330 Kuhio Ave. *TF:* 800-688-7444	Honolulu	HI	96815	808-922-5022	924-6414
Pacific Beach Hotel 2490 Kalakaua Ave. *TF:* 800-367-6060 ■ *Web:* www.pacificbeachhotel.com	Honolulu	HI	96815	808-922-1233	922-0129
Park Shore Hotel 2586 Kalakaua Ave. *TF:* 800-367-2377 ■ *Web:* www.westcoasthotels.com/parkshore/	Honolulu	HI	96815	808-923-0411	923-0311
Princeville Hotel 5520 Kahaku Rd *TF:* 800-325-3589 ■ *Web:* www.princeville.com	Princeville	HI	96722	808-826-9644	826-1166
Queen Kapiolani Hotel 150 Kapahulu Ave *TF:* 800-367-5004	Honolulu	HI	96815	808-922-1941	922-2694
Royal Garden Hotel 440 Olohana St *TF:* 800-367-5666 ■ *Web:* www.royalgardens.com ■ *E-mail:* hotel-info@royalgardens.com	Honolulu	HI	96815	808-943-0202	946-8777
Royal Grove Hotel 151 Uluniu Ave *Web:* www.royalgrovehotel.com	Honolulu	HI	96815	808-923-7691	922-7508
Royal Hawaiian Hotel 2259 Kalakaua Ave *Web:* www.royal-hawaiian.com/	Honolulu	HI	96815	808-923-7311	924-7098
Sheraton Moana Surfrider 2365 Kalakaua Ave *TF:* 800-325-3535 ■ *Web:* www.moana-surfrider.com/	Honolulu	HI	96815	808-922-3111	923-0308
Sheraton Princess Kaiulani 120 Kaiulani Ave. *TF:* 800-325-3535 ■ *Web:* www.princess-kaiulani.com	Honolulu	HI	96815	808-922-5811	931-4577
Sheraton Waikiki Hotel 2255 Kalakaua Ave *TF:* 800-325-3535 ■ *Web:* www.sheraton-waikiki.com/	Honolulu	HI	96815	808-922-4422	923-8785
Turtle Bay Hilton Golf & Tennis Resort 57-091 Kamehameha Hwy *TF:* 800-445-8667 ■ *Web:* www.hilton.com/hotels/KHKTBHH	Kahuku	HI	96731	808-293-8811	293-9147
Waikiki Beachcomber Hotel 2300 Kalakaua Ave *TF:* 800-622-4646 ■ *Web:* dps.net/~beachcomber/	Honolulu	HI	96815	808-922-4646	923-4889
Waikiki Gateway Hotel 2070 Kalakaua Ave *TF:* 800-247-1903	Honolulu	HI	96815	808-955-3741	955-1313
Waikiki Parc Hotel 2233 Helumoa Rd *TF:* 800-422-0450 ■ *Web:* www.waikikiparchotel.com/	Honolulu	HI	96815	808-921-7272	923-1336
Waikiki Parkside Hotel 1850 Ala Moana Blvd *TF:* 800-237-9666	Honolulu	HI	96815	808-955-1567	955-6010
Waikiki Resort Hotel 2460 Koa Ave *TF:* 800-367-5116	Honolulu	HI	96815	808-922-4911	922-9468

— Restaurants —

	City	State	ZIP	Phone
3660 on the Rise (Pan-Asian) 3660 Waialae Ave	Honolulu	HI	96816	808-737-1177
Alan Wong's Restaurant (Continental) 1857 S King St.	Honolulu	HI	96826	808-949-2526
Alfred's (French) 1750 Kalakaua Ave *Web:* www.lava.net/alfreds/	Honolulu	HI	96826	808-955-5353
All Star Cafe (American) 2080 Kalakaua Ave.	Honolulu	HI	96815	808-955-8326
Bali By-the-Sea (Continental) 2005 Kalia Rd.	Honolulu	HI	96815	808-949-4321
Beachcomber Restaurant (American) 2300 Kalakaua Ave	Honolulu	HI	96815	808-922-4646
Bird of Paradise (American) 91-1200 Fort Weaver Rd	Honolulu	HI	96706	808-689-2230
Cascada Restaurant (European) 440 Olohana St	Honolulu	HI	96815	808-945-0270
Chez Michel (French/California) 444 Hobron Ln Eaton Sq	Honolulu	HI	96815	808-955-7866
Ciao Mein (Chinese/Italian) 2424 Kalakaua Ave.	Honolulu	HI	96815	808-923-2426
Ciao! (Italian) 2255 Kalakaua Ave	Honolulu	HI	96815	808-922-4422

Honolulu — Restaurants (Cont'd)

Name	City	State	ZIP	Phone
Duc's Bistro (Vietnamese) 1188 Maunakea St	Honolulu	HI	96817	808-531-6325
Golden Dragon (Chinese) 2005 Kalia Rd	Honolulu	HI	96815	808-946-5336
Gordon Biersch Brewery Restaurant (American) 101 Ala Moana Blvd	Honolulu	HI	96813	808-599-4877
Hard Rock Cafe (American) 1837 Kapiolani Blvd	Honolulu	HI	96826	808-955-7383
Hawaii Seafood Paradise (Seafood) 1830 Ala Moana Blvd	Honolulu	HI	96815	808-946-4514
Hee Hing (Chinese) 449 Kapahulu Ave	Honolulu	HI	96815	808-735-5544
Hoku's (Continental) 5000 Kahala Ave	Honolulu	HI	96816	808-739-8780
House of Hong (Chinese) 260-A Lewers St	Honolulu	HI	96815	808-923-0202
Hy's Steak House (Continental) 2440 Kuhio Ave	Honolulu	HI	96815	808-922-5555
Indigo (International) 1121 Nuuanu Ave *Web:* places.com/indigo/	Honolulu	HI	96817	808-521-2900
John Dominis (Continental) 43 Ahui St	Honolulu	HI	96813	808-523-0955
Kacho (Japanese) 2233 Helumoa Rd	Honolulu	HI	96815	808-921-7272
Kahala Moon (Pan-Asian) 4614 Kilauea Ave	Honolulu	HI	96816	808-732-7777
Kaka'ako Kitchen (Gourmet) 1216 Waimanu St	Honolulu	HI	96814	808-596-7488
Kim Chee II (Korean) 3569 Waialae Ave	Honolulu	HI	96816	808-737-7733
La Mer (French) 2199 Kalia Rd Halekulani Hotel	Honolulu	HI	96815	808-923-2311
Legend Seafood Restaurant (Cantonese) 100 N Beretania St Suite108	Honolulu	HI	96817	808-532-1868
Mariposa (International) 1450 Ala Moana Blvd	Honolulu	HI	96814	808-951-3420
Mekong Thai (Thai) 1295 S Beretania St	Honolulu	HI	96814	808-591-8841
Michel's (French) 2895 Kalakaua Ave Colony Surf Hotel	Honolulu	HI	96815	808-923-6553
Nicholas Nickolas (Steak/Seafood) 410 Atkinson Dr	Honolulu	HI	96814	808-955-4466
Nick's Fishmarket (Seafood) 2070 Kalakaua Ave	Honolulu	HI	96815	808-955-6333
Orchids (Pan-Asian) 2199 Kalia Rd Halekulani Hotel	Honolulu	HI	96815	808-923-2311
Pacific Cafe (Pan-Asian) 1200 Ala Moana Blvd Ward Ctr	Honolulu	HI	96814	808-593-0035
Peacock Pavilion Restaurant (Polynesian) 59-864 Kamehameha Hwy Waimea Valley	Haleiwa	HI	96712	808-638-8531
Prince Court Restaurant (Hawaiian) 100 Holomoana St	Honolulu	HI	96815	808-956-1111
Roy's Restaurant (Pan-Asian) 6600 Kalanianaole Hwy	Honolulu	HI	96825	808-396-7697
Ruth's Chris Steak House (Steak) 500 Ala Moana Blvd.	Honolulu	HI	96813	808-599-3860
Sam Choy's Diamond Head (Hawaiian) 449 Kapahulu Ave Suite 201	Honolulu	HI	96815	808-732-8645
Shorebird Beach Broiler (Seafood) 2169 Kalia Rd Outrigger Reef Hotel	Honolulu	HI	96815	808-922-2887
Swiss Inn (Continental) 5730 Kalanianaole Hwy	Honolulu	HI	96821	808-377-5447

— Goods and Services —

SHOPPING

Name	City	State	ZIP	Phone	Fax
Ala Moana Shopping Center 1450 Ala Moana Blvd *Web:* www.alamoana.com	Honolulu	HI	96814	808-955-9517	946-2216
Aloha Tower Marketplace 1 Aloha Tower Dr *Web:* www.alohatower.com/ ■ *E-mail:* olc@olaha.net	Honolulu	HI	96813	808-528-5700	524-8334
Hilo Hattie Store of Hawaii 700 N Nimitz Hwy	Honolulu	HI	96817	808-537-2926	
International Marketplace 2330 Kalakaua Ave Suite 200	Honolulu	HI	96815	808-923-9871	924-3670
Koko Marina Shopping Center 7192 Kalanianaole Hwy Suite G205	Honolulu	HI	96825	808-395-4737	396-8656
Liberty House of Hawaii 1450 Ala Moana Blvd *TF:* 800-654-9970 ■ *Web:* www.libertyhouse.com ■ *E-mail:* customer.service@libertyhouse.com	Honolulu	HI	96814	808-941-2345	945-8700
Pearlridge Center 231 Pearlridge Ctr.	Aiea	HI	96701	808-488-0981	488-9456
Royal Hawaiian Heritage Jewelry 1525 Kalakaua Ave *Web:* www.rhhj.com	Honolulu	HI	96826	808-942-7474	942-5454
Royal Hawaiian Shopping Center 2201 Kalakaua Ave	Honolulu	HI	96815	808-922-0588	922-0961
Waikele Premium Outlet 94790 Lumiana St	Waipahu	HI	96797	808-676-5656	676-9700
Waikiki Town Center 2301 Kuhio Ave Suite 304	Honolulu	HI	96815	808-922-2724	924-7168
Ward Centre 1200 Ala Moana Blvd *Web:* www.victoriaward.com	Honolulu	HI	96814	808-591-8411	596-4919

BANKS

Name	City	State	ZIP	Phone	Fax
Bank of Hawaii 111 S King St *Web:* www.boh.com	Honolulu	HI	96813	808-538-4171	538-4145
Bank of Honolulu 841 Bishop St.	Honolulu	HI	96813	808-543-3700	543-3747
Central Pacific Bank 220 S King St. *Web:* www.cpbi.com	Honolulu	HI	96813	808-544-0500	531-2982
City Bank 201 Merchant St.	Honolulu	HI	96813	808-535-2500	546-2435
First Hawaiian Bank 999 Bishop St. **Fax:* Mktg ■ *TF:* 800-843-8411 ■ *Web:* www.fhb.com	Honolulu	HI	96813	808-525-7153	525-8708*
Hawaii National Bank 45 N King St	Honolulu	HI	96817	808-528-7711	528-7773

BUSINESS SERVICES

Name	Phone	Name	Phone
Kelly Services	808-536-9343	**Post Office**	800-275-8777
Kinko's	808-943-0005	**Rabbit Transit**	808-524-4273
Manpower Temporary Services	808-524-3630	**UPS**	800-742-5877

— Media —

PUBLICATIONS

Name	City	State	ZIP	Phone	Fax
Honolulu Advertiser‡ PO Box 3110 *Web:* www.thehonoluluadvertiser.com	Honolulu	HI	96802	808-525-8000	525-8037
Honolulu Magazine 36 Merchant St *TF:* 800-272-5245 ■ *Web:* honpub.com/hnl/hnlintro.htm ■ *E-mail:* honmag@pixi.com	Honolulu	HI	96813	808-524-7400	531-2306
Honolulu Star-Bulletin‡ PO Box 3080 *Web:* www.starbulletin.com ■ *E-mail:* editor@starbulletin.com	Honolulu	HI	96802	808-525-8000	523-8509
Island Business 36 Merchant St *TF:* 800-788-4230 ■ *Web:* www.honpub.com	Honolulu	HI	96813	808-524-7400	531-2306

‡Daily newspapers

TELEVISION

Name	City	State	ZIP	Phone	Fax
KBFD-TV Ch 32 (Ind) 1188 Bishop St PH 1 *Web:* www.kbfd.com	Honolulu	HI	96813	808-521-8066	521-5233
KGMB-TV Ch 9 (CBS) 1534 Kapiolani Blvd *Web:* www.kgmb.com	Honolulu	HI	96814	808-973-5462	941-8153
KHET-TV Ch 11 (PBS) 2350 Dole St *Web:* www.khet.org ■ *E-mail:* e_mail@khet.pbs.org	Honolulu	HI	96822	808-973-1000	973-1090
KHNL-TV Ch 13 (NBC) 150-B Puuhale Rd *Web:* www.khnl.com	Honolulu	HI	96819	808-847-3246	845-3616
KHON-TV Ch 2 (Fox) 1170 Auahi St *Web:* www.khon.com ■ *E-mail:* khon@pixi.com	Honolulu	HI	96814	808-591-4278	593-2418
KIKU-TV Ch 20 (Ind) 197 Sand Island Access Rd Suite 2021 *Web:* www.kikutv.com ■ *E-mail:* kikutv@lava.net	Honolulu	HI	96819	808-847-2021	841-3326
KITV-TV Ch 4 (ABC) 1290 Ala Moana Blvd. *Web:* www.kitv.com ■ *E-mail:* news4@kitv.com	Honolulu	HI	96814	808-593-4444	593-9446
KPXO-TV Ch 66 (PAX) 875 Waimanu St Suite 601 *Web:* www.pax.net/KPXO	Honolulu	HI	96813	808-591-1275	591-1409

RADIO

Name	City	State	ZIP	Phone	Fax
KCCN-AM 1420 kHz (Misc) 900 Fort St Mall Suite 400	Honolulu	HI	96813	808-536-2728	536-2528
KHNR-AM 650 kHz (NPR) 560 N Nimitz Hwy Suite 114-B	Honolulu	HI	96817	808-533-0065	528-5467
KHPR-FM 88.1 MHz (NPR) 738 Kaheka St. *Web:* www.hawaiipublicradio.org ■ *E-mail:* hpr@lava.net	Honolulu	HI	96814	808-955-8821	942-5477
KHVH-AM 830 kHz (N/T) 345 Queen St Suite 601	Honolulu	HI	96813	808-521-8383	531-0083
KIKI-FM 93.9 MHz (CHR) 345 Queen St Suite 601	Honolulu	HI	96813	808-531-4602	531-4606
KLHT-AM 1040 kHz (Rel) 1190 Nuuanu Ave.	Honolulu	HI	96817	808-524-1040	524-0998
KPOI-FM 97.5 MHz (Alt) 711 Kapiolani Blvd Suite 1193	Honolulu	HI	96813	808-591-9369	591-9349
KQMQ-AM 690 kHz (CHR) 711 Kapiolani Blvd Suite 1100 *Web:* www.hawaiiradio.com	Honolulu	HI	96813	808-591-9369	591-9349
KQMQ-FM 93.1 MHz (CHR) 711 Kapiolani Blvd Suite 1100 *Web:* www.hawaiiradio.com	Honolulu	HI	96813	808-591-9369	591-9349
KSSK-AM 590 kHz (AC) 1505 Dillingham Blvd Suite 208 *Web:* www.ksskradio.com ■ *E-mail:* kssk@pixi.com	Honolulu	HI	96817	808-841-8300	841-9259
KSSK-FM 92.3 MHz (AC) 1505 Dillingham Blvd Suite 208 *Web:* www.ksskradio.com	Honolulu	HI	96817	808-841-8300	841-9259
KUCD-FM 101.9 MHz (Jazz) 1505 Dillingham Blvd Suite 208	Honolulu	HI	96817	808-841-8300	842-1019
KUMU-FM 94.7 MHz (B/EZ) 765 Amana St Suite 206 *Web:* www.kumu.com	Honolulu	HI	96814	808-947-1500	947-1506

Honolulu (Cont'd)

— Colleges/Universities —

				Phone	Fax
Chaminade University 3140 Waialae Ave *TF:* 800-735-3733 ■ *Web:* www.chaminade.edu ■ *E-mail:* cuhadm@lava.net	Honolulu	HI	96816	808-735-4711	739-4647
Hawaii Pacific University 1164 Bishop St Suite 200 *TF Admissions:* 800-669-4724 ■ *Web:* www.hpu.edu ■ *E-mail:* admissions@hpu.edu	Honolulu	HI	96813	808-544-0237	544-1136
Heald Business College Honolulu 1500 Kapiolani Blvd.	Honolulu	HI	96814	808-955-1500	955-6964
Kapiolani Community College 4303 Diamond Head Rd. *Web:* www.kcc.hawaii.edu	Honolulu	HI	96816	808-734-9559	734-9545
University of Hawaii Honolulu Community College 874 Dillingham Blvd *Web:* www.hcc.hawaii.edu	Honolulu	HI	96817	808-845-9129	845-9173
University of Hawaii Manoa 2444 Dole St. **Fax:* Admissions ■ *TF:* 800-823-9771 ■ *Web:* www.uhm.hawaii.edu	Honolulu	HI	96822	808-956-8111	956-4148*

— Hospitals —

				Phone	Fax
Kaiser Permanente Medical Center 3288 Moanalua Rd	Honolulu	HI	96819	808-834-5333	834-3990
Kuakini Medical Center 347 N Kuakini St	Honolulu	HI	96817	808-536-2236	547-9547
Queen's Medical Center 1301 Punchbowl St *Web:* www.queens.org	Honolulu	HI	96813	808-538-9011	537-7851
Saint Francis Medical Center 2230 Liliha St *Web:* www.sfhs-hi.org	Honolulu	HI	96817	808-547-6011	547-6616
Straub Clinic & Hospital 888 S King St. *Web:* www.straubhealth.com	Honolulu	HI	96813	808-522-4000	522-4111

— Attractions —

				Phone	Fax
Ala Moana Regional Park 1201 Ala Moana Blvd	Honolulu	HI	96814	808-523-4182	
Aloha Tower Marketplace 1 Aloha Tower Dr *Web:* www.alohatower.com/ ■ *E-mail:* olc@olaha.net	Honolulu	HI	96813	808-528-5700	524-8334
Bishop Museum 1525 Bernice St *Web:* www.bishop.hawaii.org	Honolulu	HI	96817	808-847-3511	841-8968
Children's Discovery Center 111 Ohe St	Honolulu	HI	96813	808-592-5437	592-5433
Diamond Head State Park Diamond Head Rd & 18th Ave	Honolulu	HI	96809	808-587-0300	587-0311
Dole Cannery Square 650 Iwilei Rd	Honolulu	HI	96817	808-528-2236	531-3159
Dole Plantation 64-1550 Kamehameha Hwy.	Wahiawa	HI	96786	808-621-8408	621-1926
Foster Botanical Garden 50 N Vineyard Blvd	Honolulu	HI	96817	808-522-7066	522-7050
Hawaii Army Museum Society Fort Derussy *Web:* www.aloha-lestweforget.com	Honolulu	HI	96815	808-955-9552	941-3617
Hawaii Contemporary Museum 2411 Makiki Heights Dr	Honolulu	HI	96822	808-526-0232	536-5973
Hawaii IMAX Theatre 325 Seaside Ave	Honolulu	HI	96815	808-923-4629	923-2707
Hawaii Okinawa Center 94-587 Ukee St	Waipahu	HI	96797	808-676-5400	
Hawaii Opera Theatre 987 Waimanu St.	Honolulu	HI	96814	808-596-7372	596-0379
Hawaii State Ballet 1418 Kaplolani Blvd	Honolulu	HI	96814	808-947-2755	
Hawaii's Plantation Village 94-695 Waipahu St	Waipahu	HI	96797	808-677-0110	676-6727
Honolulu Academy of Arts 900 S Beretania St *Web:* www.honoluluacademy.org/	Honolulu	HI	96814	808-532-8700	532-8787
Honolulu Botanical Gardens 50 N Vineyard Blvd	Honolulu	HI	96817	808-522-7060	522-7050
Honolulu Dance Theatre 3041 Manoa Rd *Web:* www.pixi.com/~hdt ■ *E-mail:* htd@pixi.com	Honolulu	HI	96822	808-988-3202	988-5199
Honolulu Symphony Orchestra 650 Iwilei Rd Suite 202	Honolulu	HI	96817	808-524-0815	524-1507
Honolulu Zoo 151 Kapahulu Ave *Web:* www.hawaii.rr.com/zoo/	Honolulu	HI	96815	808-971-7175	971-7173
Iolani Palace PO Box 2259 *Web:* alaike.lcc.hawaii.edu/openstudio/iolani	Honolulu	HI	96804	808-538-1471	532-1051
Japanese Cultural Center of Hawaii 2454 S Beretania St *Web:* www.jcch.com	Honolulu	HI	96826	808-945-7633	944-1123
Judiciary History Center 417 S King St. *Web:* www.jhchawaii.org	Honolulu	HI	96813	808-539-4999	539-4996
Kapiolani Regional Park 2805 Monsarrat Ave	Honolulu	HI	96815	808-523-4182	
Mission Houses Museum 553 S King St *Web:* www.lava.net/~mhm/main.htm ■ *E-mail:* mlm@lava.net	Honolulu	HI	96813	808-531-0481	545-2280
Neal S Blaisdell Center Concert Hall 777 Ward Ave *Web:* www.co.honolulu.hi.us/Depts/aud/blaisd/concert	Honolulu	HI	96814	808-527-5400	527-5499
Pacific Aerospace Museum Honolulu International Airport	Honolulu	HI	96819	808-839-0777	836-3267
Paradise Cove Luau 92-1089 Aliinui Dr. *TF:* 800-775-2683 ■ *Web:* www.paradisecovehawaii.com	Kapolei	HI	96707	808-973-5828	679-0007
Polynesian Cultural Center 55-370 Kamehameha Hwy *Web:* www.polynesia.com	Laie	HI	96762	808-293-3000	293-3027
Pu'uhonua O Honaunau National Historical Park PO Box 129 *Web:* www.nps.gov/puho/	Honaunau	HI	96726	808-328-2326	328-9485
Queen Emma Summer Palace 2913 Pali Hwy	Honolulu	HI	96817	808-595-3167	595-4395
Royal Hawaiian Hotel Luau 2259 Kalakaua Ave *TF:* 800-325-3535	Honolulu	HI	96815	808-931-7194	931-7188
Sea Life Park 41-202 Kalanianaole Hwy.	Waimanalo	HI	96795	808-259-7933	259-7373
Sheraton's Spectacular Polynesian Revue 120 Kaiulani Ave 2nd Fl	Honolulu	HI	96815	808-931-4660	931-4653
Tropic Lightning Museum Schofield Barracks Carter Hall Waianae Ave.	Honolulu	HI	96857	808-655-0438	655-8301
US Army Museum of Hawaii Fort DeRussy	Waikiki	HI	96815	808-438-2821	438-2819
USS Arizona Memorial (Pearl Harbor) 1 Arizona Memorial Pl *Web:* www.nps.gov/usar/	Honolulu	HI	96818	808-422-2772	541-3168
USS Bowfin Submarine Museum & Park 11 Arizona Memorial Dr. *Web:* www.aloha.net/~bowfin/ ■ *E-mail:* bowfin@aloha.net	Honolulu	HI	96818	808-423-1341	422-5201
Waikiki Aquarium 2777 Kalakaua Ave *Web:* waquarium.mic.hawaii.edu	Honolulu	HI	96815	808-923-9741	923-1771
Waikiki Beach	Honolulu	HI	96815	808-923-1811	924-2120
Waimea Valley Park 59-864 Kamehameha Hwy	Haleiwa	HI	96712	808-638-8511	638-7900
Wyland Galleries Hawaii 66-150 Kamehameha Hwy	Haleiwa	HI	96712	808-637-7498	637-3700

SPORTS TEAMS & FACILITIES

				Phone	Fax
Blaisdell Center Arena 777 Ward Ave *Web:* www.co.honolulu.hi.us/Depts/aud/blaisd/arena/index.htm	Honolulu	HI	96814	808-527-5400	527-5499
Hawaii Island Movers (baseball) Rainbow Stadium University of Hawaii	Honolulu	HI	96817	808-832-4805	841-2321

— Events —

	Phone
Aloha Bowl (December 25)	808-947-4141
Aloha Festivals (September-late October)	808-589-1771
Bank of Hawaii Ki Ho Alu Festival (mid-August)	808-537-8615
Bankoh Nawahineokekai Championship Long Distance Canoe Races (September-October)	808-537-8658
Bud Light Tin Man Triathalon (mid-July)	808-923-1811
Cherry Blossom Festival Culture & Craft Fair (early March)	808-949-2255
Downtown Faire (early May)	808-521-8941
Fancy Fair (mid-June)	808-531-0481
Hawaii International Film Festival (November)	808-528-3456
Hawaii International Jazz Festival (mid-July)	808-941-9974
Hawaii Mardi Gras Celebration (late February)	808-923-1811
Honolulu Festival (mid-March)	808-922-0254
Honolulu International Bed Race (late April)	808-923-1811
Honolulu Marathon (mid-December)	808-734-7200
Hula Bowl (late January)	808-947-4141
Ironman Triathlon (October)	808-329-0063
King Kamehameha Celebration Floral Parade (mid-June)	808-586-0333
King Kamehameha Day Celebration (mid-June)	808-935-9338
Lei Day Celebration (early May)	808-266-7654
Matsuri in Hawaii Festival (mid-June)	808-926-0647
Merrie Monarch Festival (early April)	808-935-9168
Narcissus Festival (January-February)	808-923-1811
Narcissus Festival/Night in Chinatown (late January)	808-533-3181
NFL Pro Bowl (early February)	808-486-9500
Outrigger Hotels Hawaiian Oceanfest (late May-early June)	808-521-4322
Rainbow Classic (late December)	808-956-6501
Royal Hawaiian Rowing Challenge (late December-early January)	604-272-1060
Saint Patrick's Day Parade (March 17)	808-923-1811
Triple Crown of Surfing (mid-November-mid-December)	808-637-4558
Warrior Society Pow Wow (early May)	808-947-3206
World Invitational Hula Festival (early November)	808-486-3185

Idaho

Population (1999): 1,251,700 **Area (sq mi): 83,574**

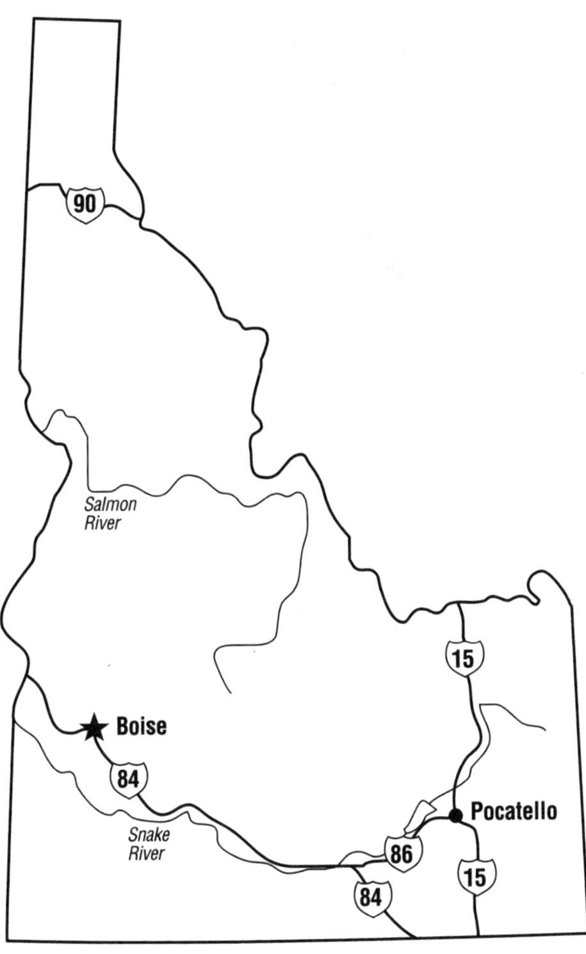

— State Information Sources —

				Phone	Fax
Idaho Assn of Commerce & Industry PO Box 389 . . Boise *Web:* www.iaci.org ■ *E-mail:* iaci@iaci.org	ID	83701		208-343-1849	338-5623
Idaho Economic Development Div PO Box 83720. . . Boise *Web:* www.idoc.state.id.us	ID	83720		208-334-2470	334-2631
Idaho Parks & Recreation Dept 5657 Warm Springs Ave . . . . Boise *Web:* www.idoc.state.id.us/irti/StateParks/spdir.html	ID	83712		208-334-4199	334-3741
Idaho State Government Information. . . . . *Web:* www2.state.id.us ■ *E-mail:* www@adm.state.id.us				208-334-2411	
Idaho State Library 325 W State St . . . . Boise *Web:* www.state.id.us/isl/hp.htm	ID	83702		208-334-2150	334-4016
Idaho Tourism Div PO Box 83720. . . . . Boise *TF:* 800-635-7820 ■ *Web:* www.visitid.org	ID	83720		208-334-2470	334-2631

ON-LINE RESOURCES

Cybertourist Idaho . . . . www.cybertourist.com/idaho.shtml
Destination Northwest: Idaho . . . . www.destinationnw.com/idaho
East Idaho Online Guide . . . . .www.eastidaho.com
Idaho @ Travel Notes . . . . www.travelnotes.org/NorthAmerica/idaho.htm
Idaho Cities . . . . dir.yahoo.com/Regional/U_S__States/Idaho/Cities
Idaho Counties & Regions . . . . . . dir.yahoo.com/Regional/U_S__States/Idaho/Counties_and_Regions
Idaho Scenario . . . . scenariousa.dstylus.com/id/indexf.htm
Idaho Travel & Tourism Guide . . . . www.travel-library.com/north_america/usa/idaho/index.html
Online Highways Travel Guide to Idaho . . . . www.ohwy.com/id/homepage.htm
Rough Guide Travel Idaho travel.roughguides.com/content/1124/index.htm
Surf Idaho . . . . .www.surfidaho.com
Travel.org-Idaho . . . . travel.org/idaho.html
Unofficial Idaho . . . . www.cs.uidaho.edu/~beers/Idaho
What's Up Idaho! . . . . .www.whatsupidaho.com
Yahoo! Get Local Idaho . . . . dir.yahoo.com/Regional/U_S__States/Idaho

— Cities Profiled —

Page

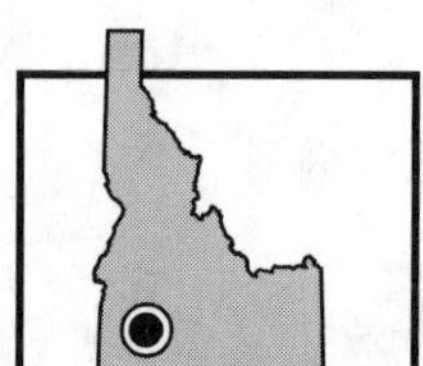

Boise

Known as the "City of Trees," Boise is not only the capital of Idaho but also the largest metropolitan area in the state. The Boise River flows through the heart of the city, and 14 miles of riverside have been developed into a Greenbelt with a network of parks and outdoor recreational areas. Less than an hour's drive from the city is Bogus Basin Ski Area, with both alpine and cross-country skiing, as well as night-lighted runs. Near Boise also is the Snake River Birds of Prey Area, which has an especially large concentration of eagles, falcons, hawks, and owls.

Population	157,452	**Longitude**	116-20-25 W
Area (Land)	46.1 sq mi	**County**	Ada
Area (Water)	0.2 sq mi	**Time Zone**	MST
Elevation	2726 ft	**Area Code/s**	208
Latitude	43-61-36 N		

— Average Temperatures and Precipitation —

TEMPERATURES

	Jan	Feb	Mar	Apr	May	Jun	Jul	Aug	Sep	Oct	Nov	Dec
High	36	44	53	61	71	81	90	88	77	65	49	38
Low	22	28	32	37	44	52	58	57	48	39	31	23

PRECIPITATION

	Jan	Feb	Mar	Apr	May	Jun	Jul	Aug	Sep	Oct	Nov	Dec
Inches	1.5	1.1	1.3	1.2	1.1	0.8	0.4	0.4	0.8	0.8	1.5	1.4

— Important Phone Numbers —

	Phone		Phone
AAA	208-342-9391	**Poison Control Center**	800-860-0620
American Express Travel	208-343-7915	**Weather**	208-342-8303
Emergency	911		

— Information Sources —

				Phone	Fax
Ada County 650 Main St	Boise	ID	83702	208-364-2333	364-2331
Web: adaweb.co.ada.id.us					
Better Business Bureau Serving Southwest Idaho & Eastern Oregon 4619 Emerald St Suite A2	Boise	ID	83706	208-342-4649	342-5116
Web: www.boise.bbb.org ■ *E-mail:* info@boise.bbb.org					
Boise Centre on the Grove 850 W Front St	Boise	ID	83702	208-336-8900	336-8803
Web: www.boise.org/tour/bcg.html					
Boise City Hall PO Box 500	Boise	ID	83701	208-384-3700	384-3750
Web: www.ci.boise.id.us/city_of_boise					
Boise Convention & Visitors Bureau 168 N 9th St Suite 200	Boise	ID	83702	208-344-7777	344-6236
TF: 800-635-5240 ■ *Web:* www.boise.org/bcvb/index.html					
Boise Mayor PO Box 500	Boise	ID	83701	208-384-4422	384-4420
Web: www.ci.boise.id.us/city_of_boise/mayor					
Boise Metro Chamber of Commerce PO Box 2368	Boise	ID	83701	208-472-5205	472-5201
Web: www.boise.org					
Boise Planning & Development Services Dept PO Box 500	Boise	ID	83701	208-384-3830	384-3753
Web: www.ci.boise.id.us/city_of_boise/planning_and_development					
Boise Public Library 715 S Capitol Blvd	Boise	ID	83702	208-384-4238	384-4025
Web: www.ci.boise.id.us/library					

On-Line Resources

4Boise.com	www.4boise.com
Anthill City Guide Boise	www.anthill.com/city.asp?city=boise
Area Guide Boise	boise.areaguides.net
Boise CityLink	www.usacitylink.com/citylink/boise
Boise Online	www.boiseonline.com
City Knowledge Boise	www.cityknowledge.com/id_boise.htm
Destination Northwest-Boise	www.destinationnw.com/idaho/boise.htm
Excite.com Boise City Guide	www.excite.com/travel/countries/united_states/idaho/boise
Insiders' Guide to Boise	www.insiders.com/boise/
NITC Travelbase City Guide Boise	www.travelbase.com/auto/guides/boise-id.html
Onroute Destinations-Boise	www.onroute.com/destinations/idaho/boise.html

— Transportation Services —

AIRPORTS

	Phone
■ **Boise Air Terminal (BOI)**	
4 miles SW of downtown (approx 15 minutes)	208-383-3110
Web: www.boise-airport.com	

Airport Transportation

	Phone
ABC Taxi $10-12 fare to downtown	208-344-4444
Boise Urban Stages $.75 fare to downtown	208-336-1010
Web: www.tellmewye.com/alttrans/thebus	
Yellow Cab $10 fare to downtown	208-345-5555

Commercial Airlines

	Phone		Phone
Delta	800-221-1212	**SkyWest**	800-453-9417
Delta Connection	800-221-1212	**Southwest**	800-435-9792
Horizon	800-547-9308	**United**	800-241-6522
Northwest	800-225-2525		

Charter Airlines

	Phone		Phone
Boise Cascade Aviation	208-384-7580	**Sawtooth Flying Service**	208-342-7888
Conyan Aviation	208-342-1042	**SP Aircraft**	208-383-3323
Crew Concepts Inc	208-344-4691	**Turbo Air**	208-343-3300
Idaho Helicopters Inc	208-344-4361		

CAR RENTALS

	Phone		Phone
Alamo	800-327-9633	**Enterprise**	208-336-8777
Budget	208-383-3090	**Hertz**	208-383-3100
Dollar	208-345-9727		

LIMO/TAXI

	Phone		Phone
ABC Taxi	208-344-4444	**Boise City Taxi**	208-377-3333
Airway Taxi	208-866-3767	**Koala Cab**	208-385-7600
Beautiful Adventure Limousine	208-939-8927	**Yellow Cab**	208-345-5555

MASS TRANSIT

	Phone
The BUS $.75 Base fare	208-336-1010

RAIL/BUS

				Phone
Greyhound/Trailways Bus Station 1212 W Bannock St	Boise	ID	83702	208-343-3681

— Accommodations —

HOTELS, MOTELS, RESORTS

				Phone	Fax
Ameritel Inn 7965 W Emerald St	Boise	ID	83704	208-378-7000	378-7040
TF: 800-600-6001					
Best Rest Inn 8002 Overland Rd	Boise	ID	83709	208-322-4404	322-7487
TF: 800-733-1418					
Best Western Airport Motor Inn 2660 Airport Way	Boise	ID	83705	208-384-5000	388-5566
TF: 800-727-5004					
Best Western Safari Inn 1070 Grove	Boise	ID	83702	208-344-6556	344-7240
TF: 800-541-6556					
Best Western Vista Inn 2645 Airport Way	Boise	ID	83705	208-336-8100	342-3060
TF: 800-727-5006					

Boise — Hotels, Motels, Resorts (Cont'd)

				Phone	Fax
Budget Inn 2600 Fairview Ave.	Boise	ID	83702	208-344-8617	331-3330
Cavanaugh's Park Center Suites 424 E Park Center Blvd	Boise	ID	83706	208-342-1044	342-2763
TF: 800-342-1044					
Comfort Inn Airport 2526 Airport Way	Boise	ID	83705	208-336-0077	342-6592
TF: 800-228-5150					
Courtyard by Marriott 222 Broadway Ave.	Boise	ID	83702	208-331-2700	331-3296
TF: 800-321-2211 ■ *Web:* courtyard.com/BOICY					
Doubletree Boise Downtown 1800 Fairview Ave	Boise	ID	83702	208-344-7691	336-3652
TF: 800-222-8733 ■ *Web:* www.doubletreehotels.com/DoubleT/Hotel141/142/142Main.htm					
Doubletree Club Hotel 475 W Park Ctr Blvd.	Boise	ID	83706	208-345-2002	345-8354
TF: 800-222-8733 ■ *Web:* www.doubletreehotels.com/ClubHtls/properties/229/229_default.html					
Doubletree Hotel 2900 Chinden Blvd.	Boise	ID	83714	208-343-1871	344-1079
TF: 800-222-8733 ■ *Web:* www.doubletreehotels.com/DoubleT/Hotel141/141/141Main.htm					
Econo Lodge 4060 Fairview Ave	Boise	ID	83706	208-344-4030	342-1635
TF: 800-553-2666					
Extended StayAmerica 2500 S Vista Ave	Boise	ID	83705	208-363-9040	363-9039
TF: 800-398-7829					
Fairfield Inn 3300 S Shoshone St.	Boise	ID	83705	208-331-5656	424-3169
TF: 800-228-2800 ■ *Web:* fairfieldinn.com/BOIFI					
Grandview Motel 1315 Federal Way	Boise	ID	83705	208-342-8676	
Grove Hotel 245 S Capitol Blvd	Boise	ID	83702	208-333-8000	333-8800
TF: 800-426-0670 ■ *Web:* www.westcoasthotels.com/grove ■ *E-mail:* fourdiamond@msn.com					
Hampton Inn 3270 S Shoshone St	Boise	ID	83705	208-331-5600	389-1220
TF: 800-426-7866					
Holiday Inn Airport 3300 Vista Ave	Boise	ID	83705	208-344-8365	343-9635
TF: 800-465-4329					
Holiday Inn Express 2613 Vista Ave	Boise	ID	83705	208-388-0800	388-0846
TF: 800-465-4329					
Inn America 2275 Airport Way	Boise	ID	83705	208-389-9800	338-1303
TF: 800-469-4667					
Motel 6 2323 Airport Way	Boise	ID	83705	208-344-3506	344-6264
TF: 800-466-8356					
Owyhee Plaza Hotel 1109 Main St	Boise	ID	83702	208-343-4611	336-3860
TF: 800-233-4611					
Plaza Suite Hotel 409 S Cole Rd	Boise	ID	83709	208-375-7666	376-3608
TF: 800-376-3608					
Quality Inn 2717 Vista Ave.	Boise	ID	83705	208-343-7505	342-4319
TF: 800-221-2222					
Residence Inn by Marriott 1401 Lusk Pl	Boise	ID	83706	208-344-1200	384-5354
TF: 800-331-3131 ■ *Web:* www.residenceinn.com/BOIID					
River Inn 1140 Colorado Ave	Boise	ID	83706	208-344-9988	336-9471
Rodeway Inn 1115 N Curtis Rd	Boise	ID	83706	208-376-2700	377-0324
TF: 800-228-2000					
Shilo Inn Airport 4111 Broadway Ave	Boise	ID	83705	208-343-7662	344-0318
TF: 800-222-2244					
Shilo Inn Riverside 3031 Main St.	Boise	ID	83702	208-344-3521	384-1217
TF: 800-222-2244					
Shore Lodge 501 W Lake St.	McCall	ID	83638	208-634-2244	634-7504
TF: 800-657-6464					
Sleep Inn 2799 Airport Way	Boise	ID	83705	208-336-7377	336-2035
TF: 800-753-3746					
Statehouse Inn 981 Grove St	Boise	ID	83702	208-342-4622	344-5751
TF: 800-243-4622					
Super 8 Lodge 2773 Elder St	Boise	ID	83705	208-344-8871	344-8871
TF: 800-800-8000					
Travelodge Boise Center 1314 Grove St	Boise	ID	83702	208-342-9351	336-5828
TF: 800-578-7878					
University Inn 2360 University Dr	Boise	ID	83706	208-345-7170	345-5118
TF: 800-345-7170					

— Restaurants —

				Phone
Angell's Bar & Grill (Steak/Seafood) 999 Main St One Capital Ctr	Boise	ID	83702	208-342-4900
Blue Coyote Cafe (Southwest) 650 E Boise Ave.	Boise	ID	83706	208-345-3381
Cazba (Mediterranean) 211 N 8th St	Boise	ID	83702	208-381-0222
Chapala IV (Mexican) 105 S 6th St	Boise	ID	83702	208-331-7866
Chart House (Steak/Seafood) 2288 N Garden St	Boise	ID	83706	208-336-9370
Desert Sage (New American) 750 W Idaho St.	Boise	ID	83702	208-333-8400
Web: www.idahodesertsage.com				
El Cazador (Mexican) 5900 Fairview Ave.	Boise	ID	83704	208-323-1801
Fletchers (American) 160 N 8th St.	Boise	ID	83702	208-345-6262
Gamekeeper Restaurant (Steak/Seafood) 1109 Main St	Boise	ID	83702	208-343-4611
Golden Star Restaurant (Chinese) 1142 N Orchard St	Boise	ID	83706	208-336-0191
Joe's All American Bar & Grill (American) 100 S 6th St	Boise	ID	83702	208-344-4146
Lock Stock & Barrel (Steak/Seafood) 4705 Emerald St.	Boise	ID	83706	208-336-4266
Milford's (Seafood) 405 S 8th St	Boise	ID	83702	208-342-8382
Onati (French/Spanish) 3544 Chinden Blvd	Garden City	ID	83714	208-343-6464
Peter Schott's (New American) 928 Main St	Boise	ID	83702	208-336-9100
Radio Room Club & Grill (Steak/Seafood) 802 W Bannock St	Boise	ID	83702	208-345-1551
Renaissance (Italian) 110 5th St	Boise	ID	83702	208-344-6776
Sandpiper (Steak) 1100 W Jefferson St	Boise	ID	83702	208-344-8911
Shige Japanese Cuisine (Japanese) 215 N 8th St.	Boise	ID	83702	208-338-8423
Tepanyaki Japanese Steak House (Japanese) 2197 N Garden St	Boise	ID	83706	208-343-3515

— Goods and Services —

SHOPPING

				Phone	Fax
Boise Factory Outlets 6852 S Eisenman Rd	Boise	ID	83716	208-331-5000	331-5002
Boise Towne Square Mall 350 N Milwaukee St	West Boise	ID	83788	208-378-4400	378-4933

BANKS

				Phone	Fax
Bank of America 421 N Cole Rd	Boise	ID	83704	208-323-8700	323-8757
TF: 800-442-5002					
Farmers & Merchants State Bank 209 N 12th St	Boise	ID	83702	208-343-7848	343-7979
First Security Bank of Idaho NA 119 N 9th St	Boise	ID	83702	208-393-4000	393-4708*
**Fax:* Hum Res ■ *TF:* 800-574-4200					
KeyBank NA Boise District 702 W Idaho St	Boise	ID	83702	208-334-7000	364-8540
TF: 800-777-5391					
Washington Federal Savings & Loan Assn PO Box 1460	Boise	ID	83701	208-343-1833	338-7374
Wells Fargo Bank 877 W Main St.	Boise	ID	83702	800-869-3557	389-4016*
**Fax Area Code:* 208					

BUSINESS SERVICES

	Phone		Phone
Airborne Express	800-247-2676	**Kinko's**	208-331-5100
BAX Global	800-225-5229	**Mail Boxes Etc**	800-789-4623
Copytime	208-377-3350	**Parcel & Post**	208-342-7678
DHL Worldwide Express	800-225-5345	**Post Office**	800-275-8777
Federal Express	800-238-5355	**UPS**	800-742-5877

— Media —

PUBLICATIONS

				Phone	Fax
Idaho Statesman‡ PO Box 40	Boise	ID	83707	208-377-6200	377-6449
TF: 800-635-8934 ■ *Web:* www.idahostatesman.com					

‡Daily newspapers

TELEVISION

				Phone	Fax
KAID-TV Ch 4 (PBS) 1455 N Orchard St	Boise	ID	83706	208-373-7220	373-7245
TF: 800-543-6868 ■ *Web:* idptv.state.id.us ■ *E-mail:* iptv@idptv.idbsu.edu					
KBCI-TV Ch 2 (CBS) 140 N 16th St.	Boise	ID	83702	208-336-5222	472-2212
Web: www.2online.com					
KIVI-TV Ch 6 (ABC) 1866 E Chisholm Dr	Nampa	ID	83687	208-336-0500	381-6682
KNIN-TV Ch 9 (UPN) 816 W Bannock St Suite 402	Boise	ID	83702	208-331-0909	344-0119
KTRV-TV Ch 12 (Fox) 679 6th St N Ext	Nampa	ID	83687	208-466-1200	467-6958
Web: ktrv.com					
KTVB-TV Ch 7 (NBC) 5407 Fairview Ave	Boise	ID	83707	208-375-7277	378-1762
TF: 800-559-7277 ■ *Web:* www.ktvb.com					

RADIO

				Phone	Fax
KBSU-FM 90.3 MHz (NPR) 1910 University Dr BSU	Boise	ID	83725	208-385-3663	344-6631
TF: 888-859-5278 ■ *Web:* www.idbsu.edu/bsuradio/ ■ *E-mail:* akbradio@idbsu.idbsu.edu					
KBSW-FM 91.7 MHz (NPR) 1910 University Dr	Boise	ID	83725	208-385-3663	344-6631
TF: 888-859-5278 ■ *Web:* www.idbsu.edu/bsuradio/ ■ *E-mail:* akbradio@idbsu.idbsu.edu					

Boise — Radio (Cont'd)

				Phone	Fax
KBSX-FM 91.5 MHz (NPR) 1910 University Dr *TF:* 888-859-5278 ■ *Web:* www.idbsu.edu/bsuradio/ ■ *E-mail:* akbradio@idbsu.idbsu.edu	Boise	ID	83725	208-385-3663	344-6631
KBXL-FM 94.1 MHz (Rel) 1477 S Five-Mile Rd	Boise	ID	83709	208-377-3790	377-3792
KCIX-FM 105.9 MHz (AC) 5257 Fairview Ave Suite 250	Boise	ID	83706	208-376-6666	323-7918
KGEM-AM 1140 kHz (Nost) 5601 Cassia St	Boise	ID	83705	208-344-3511	336-3264
KIZN-FM 92.3 MHz (Ctry) 1419 W Bannock St *Web:* www.kizn.com	Boise	ID	83702	208-336-3670	336-3734
KJHY-FM 101.9 MHz (Span) PO Box 1600	Nampa	ID	83653	208-322-3437	322-3438
KJOT-FM 105.1 MHz (CR) 5601 Cassia St	Boise	ID	83705	208-344-3511	336-3264
KKGL-FM 96.9 MHz (Rock) 1419 W Bannock St	Boise	ID	83702	208-336-3670	336-3734
KLTB-FM 104.3 MHz (Oldies) PO Box 63 *Web:* www.oldies1043.com	Boise	ID	83707	208-384-5483	385-9064
KTIK-AM 1340 kHz (N/T) 5257 Fairview Ave Suite 250 *Web:* ktik.com/	Boise	ID	83706	208-377-5845	375-9248
KXLT-FM 107.9 MHz (AC) 5257 Fairview Ave Suite 250	Boise	ID	83706	208-376-6666	323-7918

— Colleges/Universities —

Name / Address	City	State	Zip	Phone	Fax
Albertson College of Idaho 2112 Cleveland Blvd *TF Admissions:* 800-224-3246 ■ *Web:* www.acofi.edu	Caldwell	ID	83605	208-459-5011	459-5757
Boise Bible College 8695 Marigold St *TF Admissions:* 800-893-7755 ■ *Web:* netnow.micron.net/~boibible ■ *E-mail:* biobible@micron.net	Boise	ID	83714	208-376-7731	376-7743
Boise State University 1910 University Dr *TF Admissions:* 800-824-7017 ■ *Web:* www.idbsu.edu	Boise	ID	83725	208-426-1156	426-3765
ITT Technical Institute 12302 W Explorer Dr *TF:* 800-666-4888 ■ *Web:* www.itt-tech.edu	Boise	ID	83713	208-322-8844	322-0173
Northwest Nazarene College 623 Holly St *TF:* 800-584-9812 ■ *Web:* www.nnc.edu	Nampa	ID	83686	208-467-8011	467-8645

— Hospitals —

Name / Address	City	State	Zip	Phone	Fax
Saint Alphonsus Regional Medical Center 1055 N Curtis Rd **Fax:* Admitting ■ *Web:* www.sarmc.org	Boise	ID	83706	208-367-2121	367-3971*
Saint Luke's Regional Medical Center 190 E Bannock St **Fax:* Admitting ■ *Web:* www.slrmc.org	Boise	ID	83712	208-381-2222	381-3060*
Veterans Affairs Medical Center 500 W Fort St **Fax:* Admitting	Boise	ID	83702	208-422-1000	422-1148*

— Attractions —

Name / Address	City	State	Zip	Phone	Fax
Ballet Idaho 501 S 8th St Esther Simplot Annex Suite A *Web:* www.balletidaho.org	Boise	ID	83702	208-343-0556	424-3129
Basque Museum & Cultural Center 611 Grove St *E-mail:* basqmusm@micron.net	Boise	ID	83702	208-343-2671	336-4801
Bishop's House 2420 Old Penitentiary Rd	Boise	ID	83712	208-342-3279	
Bogus Basin Ski Area 2405 Bogus Basin Rd *TF:* 800-367-4397 ■ *Web:* www.bogusbasin.com ■ *E-mail:* info@bogusbasin.com	Boise	ID	83702	208-332-5100	332-5102
Boise Art Museum 670 Julia Davis Dr *Web:* www.boiseartmuseum.org ■ *E-mail:* boiseart@micron.net	Boise	ID	83702	208-345-8330	345-2247
Boise Philharmonic 516 S 9th St Suite C *Web:* www.philharmonic.boise.id.us	Boise	ID	83702	208-344-7849	336-9078
BSU Pavilion 1910 University Dr *Web:* www.bsupavilion.com	Boise	ID	83725	208-426-1900	426-1998
Discovery Center of Idaho 131 E Myrtle St	Boise	ID	83702	208-343-9895	343-0105
Hagerman Fossil Beds National Monument 221 N State St *Web:* www.nps.gov/hafo/	Hagerman	ID	83332	208-837-4793	837-4857
Idaho Botanical Garden 2355 N Penitentiary Rd *Web:* www.avocet.net/ibg	Boise	ID	83712	208-343-8649	343-3601
Idaho Dance Theatre 1700 University Dr Boise State University Special Events Ctr *Web:* theatre.boisestate.edu/idahodance ■ *E-mail:* idt@micron.net	Boise	ID	83725	208-331-9592	331-8205
Idaho State Capitol 700 W Jefferson St	Boise	ID	83720	208-334-3468	
Idaho State Historical Museum 610 Julia Davis Dr	Boise	ID	83702	208-334-2120	334-4059
Idaho Theatre for Youth 404 S 8th St Suite 232	Boise	ID	83702	208-345-0060	345-6433
Morrison Center for the Performing Arts 2201 Campus Ln Boise State University *Web:* mc.idbsu.edu	Boise	ID	83725	208-426-1609	426-3021
Morrison-Knudsen Nature Center 600 S Walnut St *Web:* www.state.id.us/fishgame/mknc.htm	Boise	ID	83706	208-334-2225	334-2148
Mountain Home Air Force Base 366 Gunfighter Ave Suite 152 *Web:* www.mountainhome.af.mil ■ *E-mail:* bleleoj@cs366.mountainhome.af.mil	Mountain Home AFB	ID	83648	208-828-2111	828-6387
National Interagency Fire Center 3833 S Development Ave *Web:* www.nifc.gov	Boise	ID	83705	208-387-5512	387-5730
Old Idaho Territorial Penitentiary 2445 Old Penitentiary Rd *E-mail:* oldpen@rmci.net	Boise	ID	83712	208-334-2844	334-3225
Opera Idaho 501 S 8th St Suite B Morrison Centre	Boise	ID	83702	208-345-3531	342-7566
Snake River Birds of Prey Area Swan Falls Rd	Kuna	ID	83634	208-384-3300	
Stage Coach Theatre Orchard St & Overland Rd *Web:* nssnet.com/stagecoach/	Boise	ID	83705	208-342-2000	
Warhawk Air Museum 4917 Aviation Way	Caldwell	ID	83605	208-454-2854	
Western Idaho Fairgrounds 5610 Glenwood	Boise	ID	83714	208-376-3247	375-9972
World Center for Birds of Prey 5666 W Flying Hawk Ln *Web:* www.peregrinefund.org	Boise	ID	83709	208-362-8687	362-2376
Zoo Boise 355 N Julia Davis Dr *Web:* www.sunvalleyski.com/zooboise/	Boise	ID	83702	208-384-4260	384-4194

SPORTS TEAMS & FACILITIES

Name / Address	City	State	Zip	Phone	Fax
Boise Hawks (baseball) 5600 Glenwood St Memorial Stadium *Web:* www.diamondsportsworld.com/hawks	Boise	ID	83714	208-322-5000	322-7432
Les Bois Horse Racing Park 5610 Glenwood Rd *TF:* 800-376-3991 ■ *Web:* www.lesboisracing.com	Boise	ID	83714	208-376-7223	376-7227

— Events —

	Phone
Art in the Park (early September)	208-345-8330
Boise River Festival (late June)	208-338-8887
Boise Tour Train & Trolley (June-October)	208-342-4796
Festival of Trees (late November-early December)	208-367-2797
Hewlett-Packard LaserJet Women's Challenge (early June)	208-345-7223
Idaho Business Expo (late January)	208-323-4464
Idaho City Arts & Crafts Festival (early June)	208-392-4553
Idaho Great Potato Marathon (early May)	208-344-5501
Idaho Shakespeare Festival (mid-June-September)	208-323-9700
National Oldtime Fiddlers' Contest (mid-June)	208-549-0452
Nike Open Golf Tournament (mid-September)	208-939-6028
Race to Robie Creek (mid-April)	208-368-9990
Snake River Stampede (mid-July)	208-466-8497
Western Idaho Fair (mid-August)	208-376-3247
Womens Fitness Celebration (late September)	208-331-2221

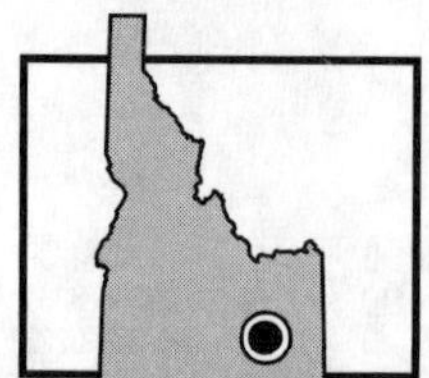

Pocatello

Idaho State University in Pocatello has two of the city's major cultural attractions, Theatre ISU and the Idaho State Civic Symphony, both of which perform on the University's campus. Between Pocatello and Blackfoot is Fort Hall Indian Reservation, which is home to the Shoshone and Bannock tribes who have lived in the area for hundreds of years. (The Shoshone chief who granted the railroad the right-of-way through Fort Hall also gave the city of Pocatello its name.) Mt. Bonneville and Pebble Creek Ski Area is just

Pocatello (Cont'd)

15 miles southeast of Pocatello, and the American Falls Reservoir, one of Idaho's top boating and fishing areas, is less than 30 miles west of the city. Caribou National Forest is near Pocatello as well.

Population	53,074	**Longitude**	112-43-79 W
Area (Land)	22.4 sq mi	**County**	Bannock
Area (Water)	0 sq mi	**Time Zone**	MST
Elevation	4464 ft	**Area Code/s**	208
Latitude	43-03-50 N		

— Average Temperatures and Precipitation —

TEMPERATURES

	Jan	Feb	Mar	Apr	May	Jun	Jul	Aug	Sep	Oct	Nov	Dec
High	32	38	47	58	68	78	88	86	75	63	45	34
Low	14	20	26	32	40	47	53	51	43	34	26	16

PRECIPITATION

	Jan	Feb	Mar	Apr	May	Jun	Jul	Aug	Sep	Oct	Nov	Dec
Inches	1.0	0.9	1.3	1.2	1.4	1.0	0.7	0.7	0.9	0.9	1.2	1.1

— Important Phone Numbers —

	Phone		Phone
AAA	208-522-8495	**Poison Control Center**	800-860-0620
Emergency	911	**Road Conditions**	208-336-6600
Medical Referral	208-239-2057	**Time/Temp**	208-234-4000

— Information Sources —

				Phone	Fax
Bannock County PO Box 4016 *Web:* www.co.bannock.id.us	Pocatello	ID	83205	208-236-7210	236-7363
Better Business Bureau Serving Eastern Idaho & Western Wyoming 1575 South Blvd *Web:* www.idahofalls.bbb.org	Idaho Falls	ID	83404	208-523-9754	524-6190
Greater Pocatello Chamber of Commerce PO Box 626 *Web:* www.pocatelloidaho.com ■ *E-mail:* pocchamber@ida.net	Pocatello	ID	83204	208-233-1525	233-1527
Pocatello City Hall PO Box 4169 *Web:* www.ci.pocatello.id.us	Pocatello	ID	83205	208-234-6163	234-6297
Pocatello Mayor PO Box 4169 *Web:* www.ci.pocatello.id.us/mayorltr.html ■ *E-mail:* andegreg@ci.pocatello.id.us	Pocatello	ID	83205	208-234-6163	234-6297
Pocatello Public Library 113 S Garfield St. *Web:* www.lili.org/marshall/	Pocatello	ID	83204	208-232-1263	232-9266

On-Line Resources

Anthill City Guide Pocatello	www.anthill.com/city.asp?city=pocatello
Area Guide Pocatello	pocatello.areaguides.net
Excite.com Pocatello City Guide	www.excite.com/travel/countries/united_states/idaho/pocatello

— Transportation Services —

AIRPORTS

■ **Pocatello Regional Airport (PIH)**

	Phone
8 miles NW of downtown (approx 15 minutes) E-mail: airport@ci.pocatello.id.us	208-234-6154

Airport Transportation

	Phone
Taxi Service $15 fare to downtown	208-232-1115

Commercial Airlines

	Phone		Phone
Horizon	208-233-1731	**SkyWest**	800-453-9417

Charter Airlines

	Phone		Phone
D & D Aviation	800-532-0991	**Pocatello AvCenter**	208-234-2141

CAR RENTALS

	Phone		Phone
Avis	208-232-3244	**Hertz**	208-233-2970
Budget	208-233-0600	**U-Save Auto**	208-237-9010
Enterprise	208-232-1444		

LIMO/TAXI

	Phone
Taxi Dispatch	208-232-1115

MASS TRANSIT

	Phone
Pocatello Regional Transit $.60 Base fare	208-234-2287

RAIL/BUS

				Phone
Amtrak Station 215 W Bonneville St	Pocatello	ID	83204	800-872-7245
Greyhound Bus Station 215 W Bonneville St *TF:* 800-231-2222	Pocatello	ID	83204	208-232-5365

— Accommodations —

HOTELS, MOTELS, RESORTS

				Phone	Fax
Ameritel Inn 1440 Bench Rd *TF:* 800-600-6001	Pocatello	ID	83201	208-234-7500	234-0000
Best Western Cotton Tree Inn 1415 Bench Rd. *TF:* 800-662-6886	Pocatello	ID	83201	208-237-7650	238-1355
Black Swan Inn 746 E Center St *Web:* www.blackswaninn.com	Pocatello	ID	83201	208-233-3051	232-9046
Cavanaugh's Pocatello Hotel 1555 Pocatello Creek Rd *TF:* 800-325-4000	Pocatello	ID	83201	208-233-2200	234-4524
Comfort Inn 1333 Bench Rd *TF:* 800-228-5150	Pocatello	ID	83201	208-237-8155	237-5695
Days Inn 133 W Burnside Ave	Pocatello	ID	83202	208-237-0020	237-3216
Econo Lodge 835 S 5th Ave *TF:* 800-377-0451	Pocatello	ID	83201	208-233-0451	233-5548
Holiday Inn 1399 Bench Rd *TF:* 800-200-8944	Pocatello	ID	83201	208-237-1400	238-0225
Motel 6 291 W Burnside Ave *TF:* 800-466-8356	Chubbuck	ID	83202	208-237-7880	237-3115
Pine Ridge Inn 4333 Yellowstone Ave	Pocatello	ID	83202	208-237-3100	238-0038
Super 8 Motel 1330 Bench Rd *TF:* 800-800-8000	Pocatello	ID	83201	208-234-0888	232-0347
Thunderbird Motel 1415 S 5th Ave *TF:* 888-978-2473	Pocatello	ID	83201	208-232-6330	232-6330

— Restaurants —

				Phone
Arctic Circle (American) 198 Yellowstone Ave	Pocatello	ID	83201	208-232-0523
Bamboo Garden (Chinese) 1200 Yellowstone Ave	Pocatello	ID	83201	208-238-2331
Brass Rail (American) 1399 Bench Rd	Pocatello	ID	83201	208-237-1400
Butterburrs (American) 917 Yellowstone Ave	Pocatello	ID	83201	208-232-3296
Center Street Clubhouse (American) 542 E Center St	Pocatello	ID	83201	208-232-9654
Continental Bistro (Continental) 140 S Main St	Pocatello	ID	83204	208-233-4433
Eduardo's Mexican Restaurant (Mexican) 612 Yellowstone Ave	Pocatello	ID	83201	208-233-9440
Food for Thought (American) 504 E Center St	Pocatello	ID	83201	208-233-7267
JJ North's (American) 850 W Quinn Rd	Pocatello	ID	83202	208-237-6235
Jumbo's Cafe (Homestyle) 3122 Poleline Rd	Pocatello	ID	83201	208-237-2158
La Paloma (Mexican) 323 N Main St	Pocatello	ID	83204	208-232-7712
Mama Inez (Mexican) 390 Yellowstone Ave	Pocatello	ID	83201	208-234-7674
Mandarin House (Chinese) 990 Yellowstone Ave	Pocatello	ID	83201	208-233-6088
Melina's (Mexican) 714 N 5th Ave	Pocatello	ID	83201	208-232-0014
Oliver's (American) 130 S 5th Ave	Pocatello	ID	83201	208-234-0672

Pocatello — Restaurants (Cont'd)

	City	State	Zip	Phone
Pilot House (American) 1625 N Arthur Ave	Pocatello	ID	83204	208-233-2332
Remo's Steak Seafood & Pasta (Continental) 160 W Cedar St	Pocatello	ID	83201	208-233-1710
Sandpiper (American) 1400 Bench Rd	Pocatello	ID	83201	208-233-1000
Shanghai Cafe (Chinese) 247 E Center St	Pocatello	ID	83201	208-233-2036
Skipper's Seafood 'N Chowder House (Seafood) 303 E Alameda Rd	Pocatello	ID	89201	208-233-7751
Whistle Stop (American) 200 S Main St	Pocatello	ID	83201	208-233-1037

— Goods and Services —

SHOPPING

	City	State	Zip	Phone	Fax
Pine Ridge Mall 4155 Yellowstone Hwy	Chubbock	ID	83202	208-237-7160	237-0591
Pocatello Mall 800 Yellowstone Ave	Pocatello	ID	83201	208-232-7061	
Westwood Mall 1800 Garrett Way	Pocatello	ID	83201	208-234-0022	234-1483

BANKS

	City	State	Zip	Phone	Fax
Bank of America 860 Yellowstone Ave.	Pocatello	ID	83201	208-232-1564	232-0301
Bank of Idaho 333 Yellowstone Ave	Pocatello	ID	83201	208-232-1700	235-3796
First Security Bank of Idaho 333 S Main St. **Fax Area Code:* 208	Pocatello	ID	83204	800-574-4200	235-3358*
Ireland Bank 2715 Poleline Rd	Pocatello	ID	83201	208-233-1816	233-1840
US Bank 120 N Arthur St. *TF:* 800-872-2657	Pocatello	ID	83204	208-234-5500	234-5549
Wells Fargo Bank 950 Yellowstone Ave. *TF:* 800-869-3557 ■ *Web:* www.wellsfargo.com	Pocatello	ID	83201	208-233-8180	233-8188

BUSINESS SERVICES

	Phone
Airborne Express	800-247-2676
BAX Global	800-225-5229
DHL Worldwide Express	800-225-5345
Federal Express	800-238-5355
Kinko's	208-232-6646
Mail Boxes Etc	800-789-4623
Post Office	800-275-8777
SOS Staffing Service	208-234-7221
Sunshine Secretarial Service	208-233-4815
UPS	800-742-5877

— Media —

PUBLICATIONS

	City	State	Zip	Phone	Fax
Idaho State Journal‡ PO Box 431 *Web:* www.journalnet.com	Pocatello	ID	83204	208-232-4161	233-8007

‡Daily newspapers

TELEVISION

	City	State	Zip	Phone	Fax
KIDK-TV Ch 3 (CBS) PO Box 33 *Web:* www.kidk.com	Pocatello	ID	83204	208-233-3333	233-3337
KIFI-TV Ch 8 (ABC) 150 S Main St Suite C *Web:* www.idaho8.com ■ *E-mail:* idaho8@aol.com	Pocatello	ID	83204	208-233-8888	233-8932
KISU-TV Ch 10 (PBS) PO Box 8111 *Web:* www.idahoptv.org/about/stations/kisu.html	Pocatello	ID	83209	208-236-2857	236-2848
KPVI-TV Ch 6 (NBC) 902 E Sherman St. *E-mail:* news6@kpvi.com	Pocatello	ID	83201	208-232-6666	233-6678

RADIO

	City	State	Zip	Phone	Fax
KMGI-FM 102.5 MHz (CR) 544 N Arthur Ave	Pocatello	ID	83204	208-233-2121	234-7682
KOUU-AM 1290 kHz (Ctry) 436 N Main St	Pocatello	ID	83204	208-234-1290	234-9451
KPKY-FM 94.9 MHz (Oldies) PO Box 998	Pocatello	ID	83204	208-233-1133	232-1240
KWIK-AM 1240 kHz (N/T) PO Box 998. *E-mail:* kwik@gemstate.net	Pocatello	ID	83204	208-233-1133	232-1240
KZBQ-FM 93.7 MHz (Ctry) 436 N Main St	Pocatello	ID	83204	208-234-1290	234-9451

— Colleges/Universities —

	City	State	Zip	Phone	Fax
Idaho State University 741 S 7th Ave *Web:* www.isu.edu	Pocatello	ID	83209	208-236-0211	236-4231

— Hospitals —

	City	State	Zip	Phone	Fax
Bannock Regional Medical Center 651 Memorial Dr. *Web:* www.brmc.org	Pocatello	ID	83201	208-239-1000	239-1938
Pocatello Regional Medical Center 777 Hospital Way	Pocatello	ID	83201	208-234-0777	239-3708
Portneuf Valley Hospital 2200 E Terry St *TF:* 800-471-2570	Pocatello	ID	83201	208-232-2570	233-6769

— Attractions —

	City	State	Zip	Phone	Fax
American Falls Reservoir 1035 N Lincoln Ave	Jerome	ID	83338	208-324-8835	
Bannock County Historical Museum Ross Pk Upper Level	Pocatello	ID	83204	208-233-0434	
Caribou National Forest	Pocatello	ID	83201	208-236-7500	236-7503
Cherry Springs Nature Area Caribou National Forest	Pocatello	ID	83201	208-236-7500	236-7503
City of Rocks National Reserve PO Box 169 *Web:* www.nps.gov/ciro/	Almo	ID	83312	208-824-5519	824-5563
Craters of the Moon National Monument US 20-26 18 Miles SW *Web:* www.nps.gov/crmo/	Arco	ID	83213	208-527-3257	527-3073
Fort Hall Indian Reservation	Fort Hall	ID	83203	208-238-3700	237-0797
Idaho Museum of Natural History Idaho State University	Pocatello	ID	83209	208-236-3317	236-4600
Idaho State Civic Symphony 1010 S 5th Fine Arts Bldg 11	Pocatello	ID	83209	208-236-3479	236-4529
Lava Hot Springs 430 E Main St. *TF:* 800-423-8597	Lava Hot Springs	ID	83246	208-776-5221	776-5273
Massacre Rocks State Park 3592 N Park Ln	American Falls	ID	83211	208-548-2672	
Pebble Creek Ski Area at Mount Bonneville 3340 E Green Canyon Rd.	Inkom	ID	83245	208-775-4452	
Pocatello Art Center 401 1/2 N Main St	Pocatello	ID	83204	208-232-0970	
Pocatello Zoo 2900 S 2nd Ave	Pocatello	ID	83205	208-234-6264	
Theater ISU Idaho State University Frazier Auditorium	Pocatello	ID	83209	208-236-3695	236-4598
Willow Bay Recreational Area American Falls Reservoir	American Falls	ID	83211	208-226-2688	

SPORTS TEAMS & FACILITIES

	City	State	Zip	Phone	Fax
Drag City Raceway 1249 E County Rd.	Pocatello	ID	83201	208-766-2711	766-2711
Pocatello Super Speedway 1421 Municipal Airport	Pocatello	ID	83204	208-232-5615	232-5615

— Events —

	Phone
Bannock County Fair & Rodeo (August)	208-237-1340
Black Powder Shoot & Trapper Rendezvous (mid-June)	208-233-1525
Christmas in Nightime Skies (late November)	208-233-1525
Dodge National Circuit Finals Rodeo (mid-March)	208-233-1525
Duck Race & Riverfest (mid-June)	208-233-1525
Eastern Idaho Agriculture Show (mid-January)	208-233-1525
Eastern Idaho State Fair (early September)	208-785-0510
Festival of Trees (late November)	208-233-1525
Greek Festival (mid-August)	208-232-5519
Health Line Classic (early August)	208-239-1818
Idaho State High School Rodeo (mid-June)	208-233-1525
Iris Festival (late May-early June)	208-233-1525
Night Lights of Christmas Parade (late November)	208-232-7545
Pocatello Stock Car Racing (late May-early September)	208-233-1525
Shoshone-Bannock Indian Festival (August)	208-238-3700
Spring Fair (March)	208-233-1525
Wild West Nationals Moto Cross (mid-July)	208-237-1340

Illinois

Population (1999): 12,128,370 **Area (sq mi): 57,918**

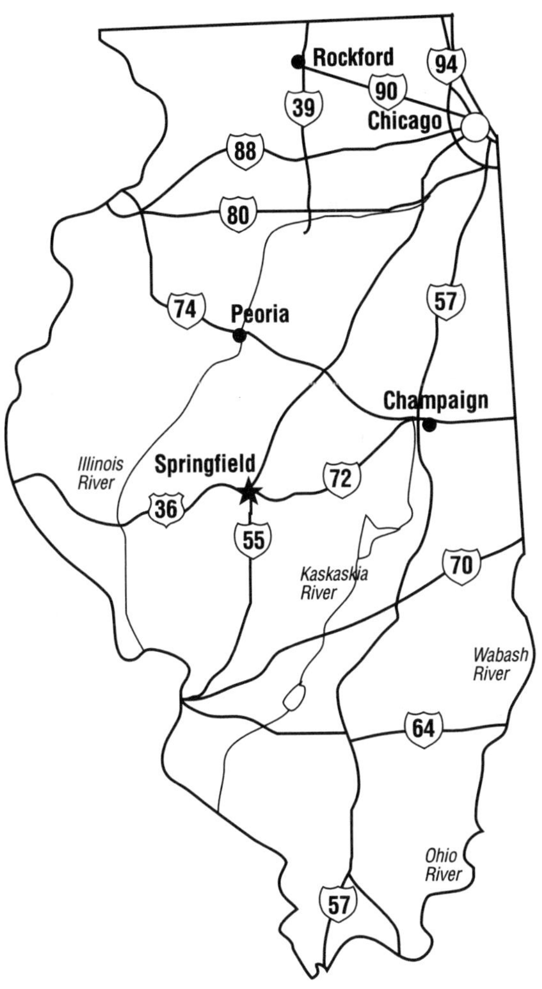

— State Information Sources —

				Phone	Fax
Illinois Business Development Bureau 100 W Randolf St Suite 3-400	Chicago	IL	60601	312-814-2811	814-6732
Illinois Natural Resources Dept 524 S 2nd St Lincoln Tower Plaza *Web:* dnr.state.il.us	Springfield	IL	62701	217-782-6302	782-0179
Illinois State Chamber of Commerce 311 S Wacker Dr Suite 1500 *Web:* www.ilchamber.org	Chicago	IL	60606	312-983-7100	983-7101
Illinois State Government Information *Web:* www.state.il.us				217-782-2000	
Illinois State Library 300 S 2nd St *Web:* www.sos.state.il.us/depts/library/isl_home.html	Springfield	IL	62701	217-782-2994	785-4326
Illinois Tourism Bureau 100 W Randolph St Suite 3-400 *TF.* 800-226-6632 ■ *Web:* www.enjoyillinois.com	Chicago	IL	60601	312-814-4732	814-6175

ON-LINE RESOURCES

Illinois Cities .... dir.yahoo.com/Regional/U_S__States/Illinois/Cities
Illinois Community Information .... www.outfitters.com/illinois
Illinois Counties & Regions .... dir.yahoo.com/Regional/U_S__States/Illinois/Counties_and_Regions
Illinois Online Highways .... www.ilohwy.com
Illinois Scenario .... scenariousa.dstylus.com/il/indexf.htm
Illinois Travel & Tourism Guide ...... www.travel-library.com/north_america/usa/illinois/index.html
Rough Guide Travel Illinois travel.roughguides.com/content/510/index.htm
Southern Illinois Tourist Council .... www.sitc.org
ThisIsFun.com Southern Illinois .... www.thisisfun.com
Travel.org-Illinois .... travel.org/illinois.html
Yahoo! Get Local Illinois .... dir.yahoo.com/Regional/U_S__States/Illinois

— Cities Profiled —

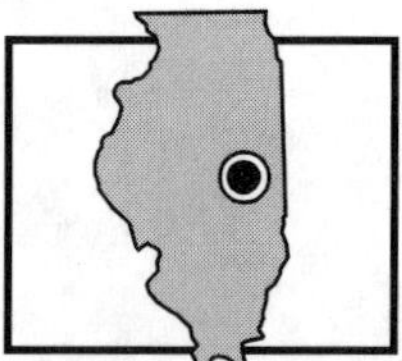

Champaign

Champaign is home to the University of Illinois, which was chartered in 1867 as a state-supported land grant institution. Originally called Illinois Industrial University, UI today is one of the nation's leading universities. Visitors to Champaign have access to many campus sites, including the University of Illinois Library, which is the sixth largest library, and the third largest academic library, in the U.S.; Assembly Hall, a venue for sporting events, conferences, and trade shows; and Memorial Stadium, which was constructed in 1923 to house the "Fighting Illini" football team. The newly constructed University Arboretum offers tours of its gardens, collections, and habitats, all of which are located on 160 acres of the campus grounds. Visitors to this midwestern university town can also enjoy a production of the Champaign-Urbana symphony at the Krannert Center for the Performing Arts, or enjoy an evening of star gazing at the William M. Staerkel Planetarium.

Population 64,280
Area (Land) . . . . 13.0 sq mi
Area (Water) . . . . 0.0 sq mi
Elevation . . . . 754 ft
Latitude . . . . 40-02-21 N
Longitude . . . . 88-16-41 W
County . . . . Champaign
Time Zone . . . . CST
Area Code/s 217

— Average Temperatures and Precipitation —

TEMPERATURES

	Jan	Feb	Mar	Apr	May	Jun	Jul	Aug	Sep	Oct	Nov	Dec
High	32	36	49	62	74	83	85	83	78	65	50	37
Low	16	20	31	41	52	61	65	62	55	44	34	22

PRECIPITATION

	Jan	Feb	Mar	Apr	May	Jun	Jul	Aug	Sep	Oct	Nov	Dec
Inches	1.8	2.0	3.3	3.9	4.0	4.0	4.5	4.0	3.4	2.7	3.1	3.0

— Important Phone Numbers —

	Phone
American Express Travel	217-359-2525
Emergency	911
Poison Control Center	800-942-5969
Weather	217-351-2900
What's Happening Hotline	217-351-1772

— Information Sources —

				Phone	Fax
Assembly Hall 1800 S 1st St *Web:* www.assembly.uiuc.edu ■ *E-mail:* webcom@ahmail.assembly.uiuc.edu	Champaign	IL	61824	217-333-5000	
Better Business Bureau Serving Central Illinois 3024 W Lake Ave Suite 200 *TF:* 800-500-3780 ■ *Web:* www.peoria.bbb.org ■ *E-mail:* bbb@heart.net	Peoria	IL	61615	309-688-3741	681-7290
Champaign City Hall 102 N Neil St Champaign City Bldg *Web:* www.city.champaign.il.us	Champaign	IL	61820	217-351-4400	351-6910
Champaign County 1776 E Washington St *Web:* www.prairienet.org/champco ■ *E-mail:* cconline@prairienet.org	Urbana	IL	61802	217-384-3720	384-1241
Champaign County Chamber of Commerce 1817 S Neil St Suite 201 *Web:* www.ccchamber.org ■ *E-mail:* chamberinfo@ccchamber.org	Champaign	IL	61820	217-359-1791	359-1809
Champaign Mayor 102 N Neil St Champaign City Bldg 2nd Fl *Web:* www.city.champaign.il.us/government/mayor.html	Champaign	IL	61820	217-351-4417	351-6910
Champaign Public Library 505 S Randolph St *Web:* www.champaign.org	Champaign	IL	61820	217-356-7243	356-1131
Champaign-Urbana Convention & Visitors Bureau 1817 S Neil St Suite 201 *TF:* 800-369-6151 ■ *Web:* www.cupartnership.org/cvb	Champaign	IL	61820	217-351-4133	351-0906
Greater Champaign-Urbana Economic Partnership 1817 S Neil St Suite 201 *TF:* 800-369-6151 ■ *Web:* www.cupartnership.org	Champaign	IL	61820	217-351-4133	351-0906
Urbana Civic Center 108 E Water St	Urbana	IL	61801	217-384-2375	384-2313

On-Line Resources

Anthill City Guide Champaign . . . . www.anthill.com/city.asp?city=champaign
Chambana Web Pages . . . . www.chambana.com
Champaign Urbana Dining World . . . . www.diningworld.com
Champaign Urbana Home Page . . . . www.champaign.com
E-Magazine: Champaign-Urbana's Free Community Guide . . . . www.e-magazine.com
University of Illinois Visitors Guide www.uiuc.edu/admin2/vguide.html

— Transportation Services —

AIRPORTS

■ **University of Illinois Willard Airport (CMI)**

	Phone
6 miles SW of downtown (approx 15 minutes)	217-244-8600

Airport Transportation

	Phone
Corky's Cab $9 fare to downtown	217-352-3121
D&D Cab $11 fare to downtown	217-377-0621

Commercial Airlines

	Phone
American Eagle	800-433-7300
Northwest Airlink	800-225-2525
TWA Express	800-221-2000
US Airways Express	800-428-4322

Charter Airlines

	Phone
Flightstar Corp	217-351-7700

CAR RENTALS

	Phone
Avis	217-359-5441
Enterprise	217-351-1400
Ford	217-356-8366
Hertz	217-359-5413
National	217-352-2775

LIMO/TAXI

	Phone
Corky's Cab	217-352-3121
D&D Cab	217-377-0621
Yellow Cab	217-355-3553

MASS TRANSIT

	Phone
MTD Bus $.75 Base fare	217-384-8188

RAIL/BUS

				Phone
Amtrak Station 45 E University Ave Illinois Terminal Bldg *TF:* 800-872-7245	Champaign	IL	61820	217-352-5905
Greyhound Bus Station 45 E University Ave *TF:* 800-231-2222	Champaign	IL	61820	217-352-4150

— Accommodations —

HOTELS, MOTELS, RESORTS

				Phone	Fax
Baymont Inn & Suites 302 W Anthony Dr *TF:* 800-301-0200	Champaign	IL	61822	217-356-8900	356-9253
Best Western Inn Cunningham Place 1907 N Cunningham Ave *TF:* 800-253-8331	Urbana	IL	61802	217-367-8331	384-3370
Best Western Lincoln Lodge 403 W University Ave *TF:* 800-528-1234	Urbana	IL	61801	217-367-1111	367-8233

Champaign — Hotels, Motels, Resorts (Cont'd)

				Phone	Fax
Clarion Hotel & Convention Center 1501 S Neil St	Champaign	IL	61820	217-352-7891	352-8108
TF: 800-257-6667 ■ *Web:* www.stadiumview.com					
Comfort Inn 305 W Marketview Dr	Champaign	IL	61821	217-352-4055	352-4055
TF: 800-228-5150					
Courtyard by Marriott 1811 Moreland Blvd	Champaign	IL	61820	217-355-0411	355-0411
TF: 800-321-2211					
Days Inn 1019 W Bloomington Rd	Champaign	IL	61821	217-356-6873	356-6950
TF: 800-325-2525					
Drury Inn 905 W Anthony Dr	Champaign	IL	61821	217-398-0030	398-0030
TF: 800-378-7946					
Extended StayAmerica 610 W Marketview Dr	Champaign	IL	61820	217-351-8899	351-8811
TF: 800-398-7829					
Fairfield Inn by Marriott 1807 Moreland Blvd	Champaign	IL	61820	217-355-0604	355-0604
TF: 800-228-2800					
Hampton Inn 1200 W University Ave	Urbana	IL	61801	217-337-1100	337-1143
TF: 800-426-7866					
Holiday Inn 1001 W Killarney St	Urbana	IL	61801	217-328-7900	328-7941
TF: 800-465-4329					
Howard Johnson 1505 N Neil St	Champaign	IL	61820	217-359-1601	359-2062
TF: 800-599-7622					
Jumer's Castle Lodge 209 S Broadway Ave	Urbana	IL	61801	217-384-8800	384-9001
TF: 800-285-8637 ■ *Web:* www.jumers.com/documents/urbindex.htm					
La Quinta Motor Inn 1900 Center Dr	Champaign	IL	61820	217-356-4000	352-7783
TF: 800-687-6667					
Motel 6 1906 N Cunningham Ave	Urbana	IL	61802	217-344-1082	328-4108
TF: 800-466-8356					
Park Inn & Illini Conference Center 2408 N Cunningham Ave	Urbana	IL	61802	217-344-8000	344-0013
TF: 800-437-7275					
Quality Hotel University Center 302 E John St	Champaign	IL	61820	217-384-2100	384-2298
TF: 800-322-8282 ■ *Web:* www.stadiumview.com					
Radisson Suite Hotel 101 Trade Centre Dr	Champaign	IL	61820	217-398-3400	398-6147
TF: 800-333-3333					
Ramada Limited 902 W Killarney St	Urbana	IL	61801	217-328-4400	328-6623
TF: 800-272-6232					
Red Roof Inn 212 W Anthony Dr	Champaign	IL	61820	217-352-0101	352-1891
TF: 800-843-7663					
Sleep Inn Champaign-Urbana 1908 N Lincoln Ave	Urbana	IL	61801	217-367-6000	367-6000
TF: 800-753-3746					
Super 8 Motel 202 W Marketview Dr	Champaign	IL	61820	217-359-2388	359-2388
TF: 800-800-8000					
TraveLodge 409 W University Ave	Urbana	IL	68201	217-328-3521	328-0802
TF: 800-578-7878					

— Restaurants —

				Phone
A-Ri-Rang (Korean) 607 S Wright St	Champaign	IL	61820	217-355-5569
Alexander's Steak House (Steak/Seafood) 202 W Anthony Dr	Champaign	IL	61821	217-359-1789
Asiana (Japanese) 408 E Green St	Champaign	IL	61820	217-398-3344
Basmati Restaurant (Indian) 302 S 1st St	Champaign	IL	61820	217-351-8877
Bread Co (American) 706 Goodwin Ave	Urbana	IL	61801	217-383-1007
Cancun Mexican Restaurant (Mexican) 1717 Philo Rd	Urbana	IL	61802	217-337-6919
Chef Jean-Louis (French) 115 W Main St	Urbana	IL	61801	217-328-2433
Fiesta Cafe (Mexican) 216 1st St	Champaign	IL	61820	217-352-5902
Galileo's (Steak/Seafood) 302 E John St	Champaign	IL	61820	217-384-7171
Great American Seafood Co (Seafood) 1711 W Kirby Ave	Champaign	IL	61821	217-352-0986
Hong Kong Restaurant (Chinese) 1410 N Prospect Ave	Champaign	IL	61820	217-352-1422
Kennedy's (Continental) 1717 Philo Rd	Urbana	IL	61801	217-384-8111
Longhorn Smokehouse (Steak) 1104 N Cunningham Ave	Urbana	IL	61802	217-337-1656
Main Addition (American) 119 W Main St	Urbana	IL	61801	217-367-0096
Manzella's Italian Patio (Italian) 115 S 1st St	Champaign	IL	61820	217-352-7624
Milo's Restaurant (Continental) 156-D Lincoln Square Mall	Urbana	IL	61801	217-344-8946
Ned Kelley's Steakhouse (Steak) 1601 N Cunningham Ave	Urbana	IL	61802	217-344-8201
Prime Room (Steak/Seafood) 1501 S Neil St	Champaign	IL	61820	217-352-8178
Radio Maria (Middle Eastern) 119 N Walnut St	Champaign	IL	61820	217-398-7729
Sea Boat Restaurant (Seafood) 1114 N Market St	Champaign	IL	61820	217-351-6209
Texas Roadhouse (Steak) 204 N Country Fair Dr	Champaign	IL	61821	217-355-9901
Timpone's (Italian) 710 S Goodwin Ave	Urbana	IL	61801	217-344-7619
Yen Ching (Chinese) 510 N Cunningham Ave	Urbana	IL	61802	217-384-0799
Zorba's Greek Restaurant (Greek) 627 E Green St	Champaign	IL	61820	217-344-0710

— Goods and Services —

SHOPPING

				Phone	Fax
Lincoln Square Mall 1 Lincoln Sq	Urbana	IL	61801	217-367-4092	367-0557
Market Place Mall 2000 N Neil St	Champaign	IL	61820	217-356-2700	359-3385

BANKS

				Phone	Fax
Bank Champaign NA 2101 S Neil St	Champaign	IL	61820	217-351-2870	351-2879
Bank One Illinois NA 306 S Mattis Ave	Champaign	IL	61821	217-351-1601	351-7993
BankIllinois 100 W University Ave	Champaign	IL	61820	217-351-6500	351-2810
Busey Bank 201 W Main	Urbana	IL	61801	217-384-4500	
Central Ilinois Bank 1514 N Cunningham Ave	Urbana	IL	61801	217-366-7000	328-7940
First Federal Savings Bank of Champaign-Urbana 1311 S Neil St	Champaign	IL	61820	217-356-2265	356-2502
First Mid-Illinois Bank & Trust NA 601 S Vine St	Urbana	IL	61801	217-367-8451	367-7717
National City 30 Main St	Champaign	IL	61820	217-351-0500	363-4108

BUSINESS SERVICES

	Phone
Adecco Employment Service	217-355-2342
Airborne Express	800-247-2676
DHL Worldwide Express	800-225-5345
Federal Express	800-238-5355
Federal Express	800-463-3339
Kelly Services	217-351-0937
Kinko's	217-398-0003
Kinko's	217-355-3400
Kwik Kopy Printing	217-359-1191
Mail Boxes Etc	217-359-6233
Norrell Services	217-359-4488
Post Office	217-373-6078
UPS	800-742-5877
Westaff	217-351-6372

— Media —

PUBLICATIONS

				Phone	Fax
News Gazette‡ PO Box 677	Champaign	IL	61824	217-351-5252	351-5374
Web: www.news-gazette.com					
Octopus The PO Box 344	Champaign	IL	61824	217-398-3049	
Web: www.cuoctopus.com ■ *E-mail:* octopus@cuoctopus.com					

‡Daily newspapers

TELEVISION

				Phone	Fax
WAND-TV Ch 17 (ABC) 904 South Side Dr	Decatur	IL	62521	217-424-2500	424-2583
Web: www.wandtv.com ■ *E-mail:* wandtv@aol.com					
WCIA-TV Ch 3 (CBS) 509 S Neil St	Champaign	IL	61824	217-356-8333	373-3663
Web: www.wcia.com					
WICS-TV Ch 20 (NBC) 2680 E Cook St	Springfield	IL	62703	217-753-5620	753-5681
Web: www.fgi.net/news20/ ■ *E-mail:* news20@fgi.net					
WILL-TV Ch 12 (PBS) 300 N Goodwin Ave	Urbana	IL	61801	217-333-1070	244-6386
Web: www.will.uiuc.edu/WILL/tvc12.html					
WRSP-TV Ch 55 (Fox) 3003 Old Rochester Rd	Springfield	IL	62703	217-523-8855	523-4410
Web: www.wrsptv.com					

RADIO

				Phone	Fax
WBCP-AM 1580 kHz (Urban) 904 N 4th St Suite D	Champaign	IL	61820	217-359-1580	359-1583
WBGL-FM 91.7 MHz (Rel) 2108 W Springfield Rd	Champaign	IL	61821	217-359-8232	359-7374
Web: www.wbgl.org ■ *E-mail:* wbgl@wbgl.org					
WCRT-FM 88.5 MHz (Rel) 2108 W Springfield Rd	Champaign	IL	61821	217-359-8232	359-7374
WDWS-AM 1400 kHz (N/T) 2301 S Neil St	Champaign	IL	61820	217-351-5300	351-5385
Web: www.wdws.com ■ *E-mail:* 1400@wdws.com					
WEFT-FM 90.1 MHz (NPR) 113 N Market St	Champaign	IL	61820	217-359-9338	
WHMS-FM 97.5 MHz (AC) 2301 S Neil St	Champaign	IL	61820	217-351-5300	351-5385
Web: www.whms.com ■ *E-mail:* 975@whms.com					
WIXY-FM 100.3 MHz (Ctry) 2603 W Bradley Ave	Champaign	IL	61821	217-355-2222	352-1256
Web: www.wixy.com ■ *E-mail:* rw@wixy.com					
WKIO-FM 92.5 MHz (Oldies) 504 S Neil St	Champaign	IL	61820	217-352-1040	356-3330
Web: www.wkio.com ■ *E-mail:* feedback@wkio.com					
WLRW-FM 94.5 MHz (AC) 2603 W Bradley Ave	Champaign	IL	61821	217-352-4141	352-1256
Web: www.mix945.com					

Champaign — Radio (Cont'd)

	City	State	Zip	Phone	Fax
WNLD-FM 88.1 MHz (Rel) 2108 W Springfield Rd	Champaign	IL	61821	217-359-8232	359-7374
WPCD-FM 88.7 MHz (CR) 2400 W Bradley Ave	Champaign	IL	61821	217-351-2450	351-2450
Web: www.parkland.cc.il.us/wpcd ■ *E-mail:* wpcd@eudoramail.com					
WPGU-FM 107.1 MHz (Alt) 24 E Green St Suite 107	Champaign	IL	61820	217-244-3000	244-3001
Web: www.wpgu.com ■ *E-mail:* wpgu@wpgu.com					

— Colleges/Universities —

	City	State	Zip	Phone	Fax
Parkland College 2400 W Bradley Ave	Champaign	IL	61821	217-351-2200	351-2581
TF Admissions: 800-346-8089 ■ *Web:* www.parkland.cc.il.us					
University of Illinois Urbana-Champaign 901 W Illinois St.	Urbana	IL	61801	217-333-1000	244-4614
Web: www.uiuc.edu					

— Hospitals —

	City	State	Zip	Phone	Fax
Carle Foundation Hospital 611 W Park St	Urbana	IL	61801	217-383-3311	383-3018
Web: www.carle.com					
Covenant Medical Center 1400 W Park St.	Urbana	IL	61801	217-337-2000	337-4541
Pavilion Hospital 809 W Church St.	Champaign	IL	61820	217-373-1700	373-1737
TF: 800-373-1700					

— Attractions —

	City	State	Zip	Phone	Fax
Arboretum The S Lincoln Ave University of Illinois at Urbana-Champaign	Urbana	IL	61801	217-333-2126	244-3469
Web: w3.aces.uiuc.edu/advancement/GivingOps/Arboretum.html					
Chanute Octave Aerospace Museum 1011 Pacesetter Dr	Rantoul	IL	61866	217-893-1613	892-5774
Web: www.cu-online.com/~leonhard/chanute/					
Curtis Orchard 3902 S Duncan Rd	Champaign	IL	61822	217-359-5565	
Early American Museum 600 N Lombard St Route 47 Museum Annex	Mahomet	IL	61853	217-586-2612	586-3491
Web: www.advancenet.net/~early/					
Krannert Art Museum 500 E Peabody Dr University of Illinois	Champaign	IL	61820	217-333-1860	333-0883
Web: www.art.uiuc.edu/kam					
Krannert Center for the Performing Arts 500 S Goodwin Ave.	Urbana	IL	61801	217-333-6280	244-7469
TF: 800-527-2849 ■ *Web:* www.kcpa.uiuc.edu/kcpa					
Mabery Gelvin Botanical Gardens N Rt 47	Mahomet	IL	68153	217-586-4630	
Olympic Tribute N Mattis Ave Dodds Pk	Champaign	IL	61821	217-398-2550	
Orpheum Children's Science Museum 354 N Neil St	Champaign	IL	61820	217-352-5895	352-5895
Web: www.m-crossroads.org//orpheum/ ■ *E-mail:* orpheum@c-u.net					
Parkland College Art Gallery 2400 W Bradley Ave	Champaign	IL	61821	217-351-2485	373-3899
Parkland College Theatre 2400 W Bradley Ave	Champaign	IL	61821	217-351-2528	
Web: www.parkland.cc.il.us/theatre/ ■ *E-mail:* theatre@parkland.cc.il.us					
Prairie Farm W Kirby Ave Centennial Pk	Champaign	IL	61820	217-398-2550	
Purves Anita Nature Center 1505 N Broadway	Urbana	IL	61801	217-384-4062	384-1052
Web: www.prairienet.org/rec/park/urbana/apnc.htm					
Sousa John Philip Library & Museum 1103 S 6th St Harding Band Bldg 2nd Fl	Champaign	IL	61820	217-244-9309	333-2868
Web: www.library.uiuc.edu/sousa/					
Staerkel William M Planetarium 2400 W Bradley Ave Parkland College	Champaign	IL	61821	217-351-2446	
Web: www.parkland.cc.il.us/coned/pla/staerkel.html					
Station Theatre 223 N Broadway Ave	Urbana	IL	61801	217-384-4000	
Web: www.8am.com/station/index.html ■ *E-mail:* custationtheatre@listbot.com					
Sunshine Dinner Playhouse 1501 S Neil St	Champaign	IL	61820	217-359-4503	
Virginia Theatre 203 W Park St	Champaign	IL	61820	217-356-9053	356-5729
Web: www.thevirginia.org ■ *E-mail:* events@thevirginia.org					
White Street Arts Center 304 1/2 E White St	Champaign	IL	61820	217-359-1862	
Web: www.prairienet.org/white-street/ ■ *E-mail:* white-street@prairienet.org					

— Events —

	Phone
Annual Duck Race (early May)	217-352-4229
British Car Festival (late May)	217-367-4092
Candles over the Prairie Grove (December)	217-367-1536
Carol Concerts (December)	217-333-6280
Champaign County Fair (July)	217-351-4133
Champaign County Town & Country Amateur Art Show (mid-late May)	217-398-2376
Champaign-Urbana Home Show (March)	217-333-5000
Chris Cringle Craft Show & Sale (November)	217-333-5000
Christmas Past (November)	217-586-2612
Dinosaur Day (early May)	217-384-4062
Drum Corps International (July)	217-351-4133
Fall Arts & Crafts Bazaar (October)	217-351-4133
Fourth of July Celebrations (July 4)	217-351-4133
Halloween Fun Fest (late October)	217-356-2700
Hit the Streets Festival (early May)	217-351-4070
Land of Lincoln Hunting & Fishing Show (January)	217-893-1613
Market at the Square (late May-October)	217-367-4092
Mayor's Race Duathlon (September)	217-351-4133
Midwest Regional Firefighters Combat Challenge (June)	217-351-4133
Model Railroad Show & Swap Session (late March)	217-367-4092
Sounds of Summer Concerts (July)	217-367-1536
Strawberry Moon Shine Social (June)	217-384-4062
Sweetcorn Festival (August)	217-351-4133
Taste of Champaign-Urbana (June)	217-351-4133
Turkey Trot (late November)	217-367-1536
US National Hot Air Balloon Championships (August)	217-351-4133

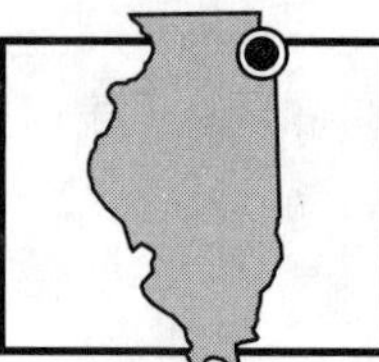

Chicago

The cold winds off Lake Michigan have earned Chicago its famous nickname as "The Windy City." The city is composed of many diverse neighborhoods, each offering different types of attractions. Its excellence in the arts is reflected in The Loop/Downtown area, which is home to the Chicago Architectural Foundation, Art Institute, Chicago Symphony, and many theaters. Along Lake Shore Drive one can visit the Museum of Science and Industry's thousands of exhibits demonstrating scientific principles and technical advances. The Chicago Cubs' Wrigley Field and the Lincoln Park Zoo are located in the Lincoln Park area. With its many department stores, North Michigan Avenue is known as "The Magnificent Mile" of shopping. The Second City comedy group is located in the Old Town area, and one of the oldest art fairs in America is held here each summer. The world's largest marketplace, the Chicago Mercantile Exchange, and the world's largest oceanarium/aquarium, the Shedd Aquarium, and Navy Pier are also popular sites to visit. Just twenty minutes from Chicago is the Village of Oak Brook, which features the renowned architectural style of Frank Lloyd Wright.

Population	2,802,079	**Longitude**	87-65-00 W
Area (Land)	224.9 sq mi	**County**	Cook
Area (Water)	6.8 sq mi	**Time Zone**	CST
Elevation	596 ft	**Area Code/s**	312, 630, 708, 773, 847
Latitude	41-88-50 N		

Chicago (Cont'd)

— Average Temperatures and Precipitation —

TEMPERATURES

	Jan	Feb	Mar	Apr	May	Jun	Jul	Aug	Sep	Oct	Nov	Dec
High	29	34	46	59	70	80	84	82	75	63	48	34
Low	13	17	29	39	48	58	63	62	54	42	32	19

PRECIPITATION

	Jan	Feb	Mar	Apr	May	Jun	Jul	Aug	Sep	Oct	Nov	Dec
Inches	1.5	1.4	2.7	3.6	3.3	3.8	3.7	4.2	3.8	2.4	2.9	2.5

— Important Phone Numbers —

	Phone
AAA	312-372-1818
American Express Travel	312-435-2595
Chicago Dance Coalition Hotline	312-419-8383
Chicago Fine Arts Hotline	312-346-3278
Chicago Music Alliance Hotline	312-987-1123
Chicago Sun-Times Infoline	630-231-4600
Dental Referral	312-836-7300
Emergency	911
HotelDocs	800-468-3537
Jazz Hotline	312-427-3300
Medical Referral	312-670-2550
Poison Control Center	800-942-5969
Special Events Hotline	312-744-3370
Travelers Aid	773-626-9076
Weather	815-834-0675

— Information Sources —

				Phone	Fax
Accenting Chicago Events & Tours Inc 111 E Wacker Dr 1 Illinois Ctr Suite 1400	Chicago	IL	60601	312-616-8811	616-8813
Better Business Bureau Serving Chicago & Northern Illinois 330 N Wabash Ave Suite 2006 *Web:* www.chicago.bbb.org	Chicago	IL	60611	312-832-0500	832-9985
Chicago City Hall 121 N La Salle St *Web:* www.cityofchicago.org	Chicago	IL	60602	312-744-4000	744-4149
Chicago Convention & Tourism Bureau 2301 S Lake Shore Dr *Web:* www.chicago.il.org	Chicago	IL	60616	312-567-8500	567-8533
Chicago Department of Tourism 78 E Washington Cultural Ctr	Chicago	IL	60602	312-744-2400	744-2359
Chicago International Visitors Center 820 N Michigan Ave Suite 515 *E-mail:* info@ivcc.org	Chicago	IL	60611	312-915-6380	915-6381
Chicago Mayor 121 N La Salle St Rm 507 *Web:* www.cityofchicago.org/Mayor ■ *E-mail:* mayordaley@cityofchicago.org	Chicago	IL	60602	312-744-3300	744-2324
Chicago Office of Tourism 78 E Washington St *Web:* www.ci.chi.il.us/Tourism ■ *E-mail:* feedback@ci.chi.il.us	Chicago	IL	60602	312-744-2400	744-2359
Chicago Planning & Development Dept 121 N La Salle St Rm 1000 *Web:* www.cityofchicago.org/PlanAndDevelop ■ *E-mail:* planning@ci.chi.il.us	Chicago	IL	60602	312-744-4471	744-2271
Chicago Public Library 400 S State St *Web:* www.chipublib.org ■ *E-mail:* comments@chipublib.org	Chicago	IL	60605	312-747-4999	747-4962
Chicagoland Chamber of Commerce 330 N Wabash Ave 1 IBM Plaza Suite 2800 *Web:* www.chicagolandchamber.org	Chicago	IL	60611	312-494-6700	494-0196
Cook County 118 N Clark St Rm 537 *Web:* www.co.cook.il.us	Chicago	IL	60602	312-443-6400	443-4397
McCormick Place 2301 S Lake Shore Dr **Fax:* Mktg ■ *Web:* www.mccormickplace.com	Chicago	IL	60616	312-791-7000	791-6227*

On-Line Resources

4Chicago.com	www.4chicago.com
About.com Guide to Chicago North & Suburbs	chicagonorth.about.com/local/midwestus/chicagonorth
About.com Guide to Chicago West & Suburbs	chicagowest.about.com/local/midwestus/chicagowest
Anthill City Guide Chicago	www.anthill.com/city.asp?city=chicago
Area Guide Chicago	chicago.areaguides.net
Boulevards Chicago	www.boulevards.com/chicago/
Bradmans.com Chicago	www.bradmans.com/scripts/display_city.cgi?city=233
Chicago City Page	chicago.thelinks.com/
Chicago CityLink	www.usacitylink.com/citylink/chicago
Chicago CityWomen	www.citywomen.com/chiwomen.htm
Chicago Footlights Performing Arts Guide	www.footlights.com
Chicago Graphic City Guide	www.futurecast.com/gcg/chicago.htm
Chicago Guide	www.chicago-guide.com/
Chicago Home Page	www.city-life.com/chicago
Chicago Metromix Arts & Entertainment Guide	www.metromix.com
Chicago NewCityNet	www.newcitynet.com
Chicago Reader	www.chireader.com
Chicago Web	www.chiweb.com/
City Insights Chicago	www.cityinsights.com/chicago.htm
City Knowledge Chicago	www.cityknowledge.com/il_chicago.htm
Cityhits Chicago	www.cityhits.com/chicago/
CitySearch Chicago	chicago.citysearch.com
CityTravelGuide.com Chicago	www.citytravelguide.com/chicago.htm
CuisineNet Chicago	www.cuisinenet.com/restaurant/chicago/index.shtml
DigitalCity Chicago	home.digitalcity.com/chicago
Excite.com Chicago City Guide	www.excite.com/travel/countries/united_states/illinois/chicago
Gayot's Guide Restaurant Search Chicago	www.perrier.com/restaurants/gayot.asp?area=CHI
HotelGuide Chicago	chicago.hotelguide.net
NITC Travelbase City Guide Chicago	www.travelbase.com/auto/guides/chicago-area-il.html
Open World City Guides Chicago	www.worldexecutive.com/cityguides/chicago/
OutChicago Resource Guide	www.outchicago.org
Rough Guide Travel Chicago	travel.roughguides.com/content/511/
Savvy Diner Guide to Chicago Restaurants	www.savvydiner.com/chicago/
Time Out Chicago	www.timeout.com/chicago/
Virtual Voyages Chicago	www.virtualvoyages.com/usa/il/chicago/chicago.sht
WeekendEvents.com Chicago	www.weekendevents.com/CHICAGO/CHICAGO.HTM
Windy City Electronic Village	www.thewindycity.com/
Windy-City.com	www.windy-city.com/
Yahoo! Chicago	chi.yahoo.com

— Transportation Services —

AIRPORTS

■ Chicago O'Hare International Airport (ORD)

	Phone
25 miles NW of downtown (approx 30-45 minutes)	773-686-2200

Web: www.cityofchicago.org/Aviation/OHare

Airport Transportation

	Phone
Continental Airport Express $16 fare to downtown	312-454-7800
CTA Train $1.50 fare to downtown	312-836-7000
Smart Cars $36 fare to downtown	312-433-7627
Taxi $26-30 fare to downtown	312-829-4222

Commercial Airlines

	Phone
Aer Lingus	800-223-6537
Aeroflot	888-686-4949
Air Canada	800-776-3000
Air Jamaica	800-523-5585
Alitalia	800-223-5730
America West	800-235-9292
American	800-433-7300
American Eagle	800-433-7300
British Airways	800-247-9297
Cayman Airways	800-422-9626
Continental	800-525-0280
Continental Express	800-525-0280
Delta	800-221-1212
El Al	800-223-6700
Great Lakes	800-554-5111
Japan	773-686-4584
KLM	800-374-7747
Lufthansa	800-645-3880
Mexicana	800-531-7923
Northwest	800-225-2525
Philippine	800-435-9725
Qantas	800-227-4500
Royal Jordanian	800-223-0470
Sabena	800-955-2000
Scandinavian	800-221-2350
Southwest	800-435-9792
SwissAir	800-221-4750
TWA	800-221-2000
United	800-241-6522
United Express	800-241-6522
US Airways	800-428-4322

Charter Airlines

	Phone
Midwest Helicopter Airways Inc	630-325-7860

■ Midway Airport (MDW)

	Phone
8 miles SW of downtown (approx 30 minutes)	773-838-0600

Web: www.cityofchicago.org/Aviation/Midway

Airport Transportation

	Phone
CTA Train $1.50 fare to downtown	312-836-7000
Smart Cars $36 fare to downtown	312-433-7627
Taxi $22-25 fare to downtown	312-829-4222

Chicago (Cont'd)

Commercial Airlines

	Phone		Phone
AirTran	800-247-8726	**Delta**	800-221-1212
America West	800-235-9292	**National**	888-757-5387
American Trans Air	800-225-2995	**Northwest**	800-225-2525
Cayman Airways	800-422-9626	**Southwest**	800-435-9792
Continental	773-686-6500	**United**	800-241-6522
Continental Express	800-525-0280	**US Airways**	800-428-4322

Charter Airlines

	Phone		Phone
Aero Services	773-582-5720	**Jet Aviation Business Jets Inc**	800-736-8538
Corporate Aviation Services Inc	918-834-8348	**Jet Charter International**	800-655-5387
Executive Flight Management	773-735-6906	**Planemasters Ltd**	630-513-2100
Executive Jet Management	877-356-5387	**Scott Aviation**	630-513-2222
Helicopter Transport Services Inc	773-585-9800	**Sunbird Air Services**	937-322-2711
Helicopters Inc	800-466-2903	**WSG Executive Air Service**	888-974-3932

CAR RENTALS

Company	Phone	Company	Phone
Alamo	847-671-7662	**Enterprise**	847-298-3600
Avis-O'Hare	773-825-4600	**Enterprise-Midway**	773-581-2200
Budget	773-686-4951	**Hertz-O'Hare**	773-686-7272
Budget-O'Hare	773-686-6800	**National-O'Hare**	773-694-4640
Dollar-Midway	773-735-7200	**Thrifty-O'Hare**	847-928-2000

LIMO/TAXI

Company	Phone	Company	Phone
American Limousine	630-920-8888	**Delaware Limousines**	312-337-2800
Blue Ribbon Taxi	773-878-5400	**Flash Cab**	773-561-1444
Carey Limousine	312-663-1220	**O'Hare Midway Limousine Service**	312-558-1111
Checker Taxi	312-243-2537	**Yellow Cab**	312-829-4222
Chicago Limousine	312-726-1035		

MASS TRANSIT

	Phone
Chicago Transit Authority $1.50 Base fare	312-836-7000
L-Train $1.50 Base fare	312-836-7000

RAIL/BUS

	City	State	Zip	Phone
Amtrak Station 225 S Canal St Union Stn *TF:* 800-872-7245	Chicago	IL	60606	800-872-7245
Greyhound Bus Station 630 W Harrison St *TF:* 800-231-2222	Chicago	IL	60607	312-408-5971

— Accommodations —

HOTEL RESERVATION SERVICES

	Phone	Fax
Accommodations Express *TF:* 800-444-7666 ■ *Web:* www.accommodationsxpress.com ■ *E-mail:* accomexp@acy.digex.net	609-391-2100	525-0111
Central Reservation Service *TF:* 800-548-3311 ■ *Web:* www.reservation-services.com ■ *E-mail:* cenresbos@aol.com	407-740-6442	740-8222
Chicago Bed & Breakfast Reservations *TF:* 800-375-7084	773-248-0005	248-7090
Hot Rooms **Fax Area Code:* 312 ■ *TF:* 800-468-3500 ■ *Web:* www.hotrooms.com ■ *E-mail:* hotrooms@wwa.com	773-468-7666	649-0559*
Hotel Reservations Network Inc *TF Sales:* 800-964-6835 ■ *Web:* www.hoteldiscount.com	214-361-7311	361-7299
Quikbook *TF:* 800-789-9887 ■ *Web:* www.quikbook.com	212-532-1660	532-1556
RMC Travel Centre *TF:* 800-782-2674	212-754-6560	754-6571
Room Finders USA *TF:* 800-473-7829 ■ *Web:* www.roomsusa.com ■ *E-mail:* welcome@roomsusa.com	504-522-9373	529-1948

HOTELS, MOTELS, RESORTS

	City	State	Zip	Phone	Fax
Allerton Crowne Plaza 701 N Michigan Ave *TF:* 800-227-6963	Chicago	IL	60611	312-440-1500	440-1819
Ambassador West 1300 N State Pkwy *TF:* 800-300-9378	Chicago	IL	60610	312-787-3700	640-2967
Arlington Park Hilton 3400 W Euclid Ave *TF:* 800-344-3434	Arlington Heights	IL	60005	847-394-2000	394-2095
Best Western Grant Park Hotel 1100 S Michigan Ave *TF:* 800-528-1234	Chicago	IL	60605	312-922-2900	922-8812
Best Western Inn of Chicago 162 E Ohio St. *TF:* 800-557-2378	Chicago	IL	60611	312-787-3100	573-3136
Blackstone Hotel 636 S Michigan Ave *TF:* 800-622-6330	Chicago	IL	60605	312-427-4300	427-4300
Chicago Downtown Marriott Hotel 540 N Michigan Ave *TF:* 800-228-0265	Chicago	IL	60611	312-836-0100	836-6139
Chicago Hilton & Towers 720 S Michigan Ave *TF:* 800-445-8667	Chicago	IL	60605	312-922-4400	922-5240
Chicago Marriott O'Hare 8535 W Higgins Rd. *TF:* 800-228-9290	Chicago	IL	60631	773-693-4444	693-3164
Comfort Inn O'Hare 2175 E Touhy Ave *TF:* 800-222-7666	Des Plaines	IL	60018	847-635-1300	635-7572
Congress Plaza Hotel and Convention Center 520 S Michigan Ave *TF:* 800-635-1666	Chicago	IL	60605	312-427-3800	427-3972
Days Inn Lake Shore Drive 644 N Lake Shore Dr. *TF:* 800-325-2525	Chicago	IL	60611	312-943-9200	255-4411
Doubletree Guest Suites 198 E Delaware Pl. *TF:* 800-222-8733 ■ *Web:* www.doubletreehotels.com/DoubleT/Hotel41/48/48Main.htm	Chicago	IL	60611	312-664-1100	664-9881
Doubletree North Shore 9599 Skokie Blvd *TF:* 800-222-8733 ■ *Web:* www.doubletreehotels.com/DoubleT/Hotel121/133/133Main.htm	Skokie	IL	60077	847-679-7000	679-9841
Drake Hotel 140 E Walton Pl *TF:* 800-553-7253	Chicago	IL	60611	312-787-2200	787-1431
Drake Oak Brook Hotel 2301 York Rd *TF:* 800-555-8000	Oak Brook	IL	60523	630-574-5700	574-0830
Embassy Suites 600 N State St *TF:* 800-362-2779	Chicago	IL	60610	312-943-3800	943-7629
Essex Inn 800 S Michigan Ave *TF:* 800-621-6909	Chicago	IL	60605	312-939-2800	922-6153
Executive Plaza Hotel 71 E Wacker Dr *TF:* 800-621-4005	Chicago	IL	60601	312-346-7100	346-1721
Fairmont Hotel 200 N Columbus Dr *TF:* 800-526-2008 ■ *Web:* www.fairmont.com/chicago.html ■ *E-mail:* chicago@fairmont.com	Chicago	IL	60601	312-565-8000	856-1032
Four Points Hotel by Sheraton 10249 W Irving Park Rd *TF:* 800-323-1239	Schiller Park	IL	60176	847-671-6000	671-0371
Four Seasons Hotel 120 E Delaware Pl *TF:* 800-332-3442 ■ *Web:* www.fourseasons.com/locations/Chicago	Chicago	IL	60611	312-280-8800	280-1748
Harrison Conference Center 136 Greenbay Rd	Lake Bluff	IL	60044	847-295-1100	295-9307
Hickory Ridge Conference Center 1195 Summerhill Dr *TF:* 800-225-4722	Lisle	IL	60532	630-971-5000	971-6956
Hilton Hotel & Conference Centre 9333 S Cicero Ave *TF:* 800-445-9333 ■ *Web:* www.hilton.com/hotels/OALHIHF	Oak Lawn	IL	60453	708-425-7800	425-8111
Hilton Northbrook 2855 N Milwaukee Ave *Web:* www.hilton.com/hotels/CHINBHF	Northbrook	IL	60062	847-480-7500	480-0827
Holiday Inn 1801 N Naper Blvd *TF:* 800-465-4329	Naperville	IL	60563	630-505-4900	505-8239
Holiday Inn & Conference Center Evanston 1501 Sherman Ave *TF:* 800-465-4329 ■ *Web:* www.basshotels.com/holiday-inn/?_franchisee=CHIES ■ *E-mail:* chies@worldnet.att.net	Evanston	IL	60201	847-491-6400	328-3090
Holiday Inn Mart Plaza 350 N Orleans St *TF:* 800-465-4329 ■ *Web:* www.basshotels.com/holiday-inn/?_franchisee=CHIPL	Chicago	IL	60654	312-836-5000	222-9508
Holiday Inn O'Hare International Airport 5440 N River Rd. *TF:* 800-465-4329 ■ *Web:* www.basshotels.com/holiday-inn/?_franchisee=CHIOK ■ *E-mail:* hiohare@enteract.com	Rosemont	IL	60018	847-671-6350	671-5406
Holiday Inn Oak Lawn 4140 W 95th St. *TF:* 800-362-5529 ■ *Web:* www.basshotels.com/holiday-inn/?_franchisee=CHISW ■ *E-mail:* chisw@ameritech.net	Oak Lawn	IL	60453	708-425-7900	425-7918
Hotel Allegro 171 W Randolph St. *TF:* 800-643-1500	Chicago	IL	60601	312-236-0123	236-0917
Hotel Inter-Continental Chicago 505 N Michigan Ave *TF:* 800-628-2112	Chicago	IL	60611	312-944-4100	944-3050

Chicago — Hotels, Motels, Resorts (Cont'd)

Name / Address	City	State	Zip	Phone	Fax
Hotel Sofitel Chicago 5550 N River Rd *TF:* 800-763-4835	Rosemont	IL	60018	847-678-4488	678-4244
House of Blues 330 N State St	Chicago	IL	60610	312-923-2000	527-3072
Howard Johnson Hotel 306 S Lincolnway St *TF:* 800-446-4656	North Aurora	IL	60542	630-892-6481	892-1630
Hyatt on Printers Row 500 S Dearborn St *TF:* 800-233-1234 ■ *Web:* www.hyatt.com/usa/chicago/hotels/hotel_chipr.html	Chicago	IL	60605	312-986-1234	939-2468
Hyatt Regency Chicago 151 E Wacker Dr *TF:* 800-233-1234 ■ *Web:* www.hyatt.com/usa/chicago/hotels/hotel_chirc.html	Chicago	IL	60601	312-565-1234	565-2966
Hyatt Regency O'Hare 9300 Bryn Mawr Ave *TF:* 800-233-1234 ■ *Web:* www.hyatt.com/usa/rosemont/hotels/hotel_chiro.html	Rosemont	IL	60018	847-696-1234	698-0139
Hyatt Regency Oak Brook 1909 Spring Rd *TF:* 800-233-1234 ■ *Web:* www.hyatt.com/usa/chicago/hotels/hotel_chiob.html	Oak Brook	IL	60523	630-573-1234	573-1133
Hyatt University Village 625 S Ashland Ave *TF:* 800-233-1234 ■ *Web:* www.hyatt.com/usa/chicago/hotels/hotel_chiuv.html	Chicago	IL	60607	312-491-1234	529-6095
Lenox Suites 616 N Rush St *TF:* 800-445-3669	Chicago	IL	60611	312-337-1000	337-7217
Midland Hotel 172 W Adams St *TF:* 800-621-2360	Chicago	IL	60603	312-332-1200	917-5771
Motel 6 162 E Ontario St *TF:* 800-466-8356	Chicago	IL	60611	312-787-3580	787-1299
Oak Brook Hills Resort& Conference Center 3500 Midwest Rd *TF:* 800-445-3315	Oak Brook	IL	60523	630-850-5555	850-5569
Oak Brook Marriott Hotel 1401 W 22nd St *TF:* 800-228-9290	Oak Brook	IL	60523	630-573-8555	573-1026
Omni Ambassador East 1301 N State Pkwy *TF:* 800-843-6664	Chicago	IL	60610	312-787-7200	707-4760
Omni Chicago Hotel 676 N Michigan Ave *TF:* 800-843-6664	Chicago	IL	60611	312-944-6664	266-3015
Palmer House Hilton Hotel 17 E Monroe St *TF:* 800-445-8667	Chicago	IL	60603	312-726-7500	917-1707
Pheasant Run Resort 4051 E Main St *TF:* 800-999-3319 ■ *Web:* www.pheasantrun.com ■ *E-mail:* reservations@pheasantrun.com	Saint Charles	IL	60174	630-584-6300	584-4693
Quality Inn Chicago Downtown 1 S Halsted St	Chicago	IL	60661	312-829-5000	829-8151
Radisson Hotel 160 E Huron St *TF:* 800-333-3333	Chicago	IL	60611	312-787-2900	787-6093
Ramada Hotel O'Hare Airport 6600 N Mannheim Rd *TF:* 800-272-6232	Rosemont	IL	60018	847-827-5131	827-5659
Ramada Inn & Conference Center 200 N Green Bay Rd *TF:* 800-272-6232	Waukegan	IL	60085	847-244-2400	249-9716
Ramada Inn Lake Shore Hotel & Conference Center 4900 S Lake Shore Dr	Chicago	IL	60615	773-288-5800	288-5745
Raphael Hotel 201 E Delaware Pl *TF:* 800-821-5343	Chicago	IL	60611	312-943-5000	943-9483
Regal Knickerbocker Hotel 163 E Walton Pl *TF:* 800-621-8140	Chicago	IL	60611	312-867-7500	751-9205
Renaissance Chicago Hotel 1 W Wacker Dr *TF:* 800-228-9290	Chicago	IL	60601	312-372-7200	372-0093
Renaissance Oak Brook Hotel 2100 Spring Rd *TF:* 800-468-3571	Oak Brook	IL	60523	630-573-2800	573-7134
Ritz-Carlton Chicago 160 E Pearson St *TF:* 800-621-6906 ■ *Web:* www.fourseasons.com/locations/ChicagoRitzCarlton	Chicago	IL	60611	312-266-1000	266-1194
Seneca Hotel 200 E Chestnut St *TF:* 800-800-6261	Chicago	IL	60611	312-787-8900	988-4438
Sheraton Chicago Hotel & Towers 301 E North Water St *TF:* 800-325-3535	Chicago	IL	60611	312-464-1000	464-9140
Sheraton Gateway Suites 6501 N Mannheim Rd *TF:* 800-325-3535	Rosemont	IL	60018	847-699-6300	699-0391
Summerfield Suites 166 E Superior St *TF:* 800-833-4353	Chicago	IL	60611	312-787-6000	787-4331
Sutton Place Hotel 21 E Bellevue Pl *TF:* 800-810-6888 ■ *Web:* www.travelweb.com/TravelWeb/000063/common/sutton.html ■ *E-mail:* info@chi.suttonplace.com	Chicago	IL	60611	312-266-2100	266-2103
Swissotel Chicago 323 E Wacker Dr *TF:* 800-654-7263	Chicago	IL	60601	312-565-0565	565-0540
Talbott Hotel 20 E Delaware Pl *TF:* 800-825-2688	Chicago	IL	60611	312-944-4970	944-7241
Tremont Hotel 100 E Chestnut St *TF:* 800-621-8133	Chicago	IL	60611	312-751-1900	751-8691
Union League Club 65 W Jackson Blvd *TF:* 800-443-0578	Chicago	IL	60604	312-427-7800	427-8117
Westin Hotel Chicago 909 N Michigan Ave *TF:* 800-228-3000	Chicago	IL	60611	312-943-7200	397-5580
Westin Hotel O'Hare 6100 N River Rd *TF:* 800-228-3000	Rosemont	IL	60018	847-698-6000	698-3522
Westin River North 320 N Dearborn St *TF:* 800-937-8461	Chicago	IL	60610	312-744-1900	527-2650
Whitehall Hotel 105 E Delaware Pl *TF:* 800-323-7500 ■ *Web:* www.whitehall-chicago.com	Chicago	IL	60611	312-944-6300	944-8552

— Restaurants —

Name / Address	City	State	Zip	Phone
65 Restaurant (Chinese) 2414 S Wentworth Ave	Chicago	IL	60616	312-225-7060
302 West (American) 302 W State St	Geneva	IL	60134	630-232-9302
Ambria (French) 2300 N Lincoln Park West	Chicago	IL	60614	773-472-5959
Arun's (Thai) 4156 N Kedzie Ave	Chicago	IL	60618	773-539-1909
Bando Restaurant (Korean) 2200 W Lawrence Ave	Chicago	IL	60625	773-728-7400
Berghoff (German) 17 W Adams St	Chicago	IL	60603	312-427-3170
Biggs (Continental) 1150 N Dearborn Pkwy	Chicago	IL	60610	312-787-0900
Bistro 110 (French) 110 E Pearson St	Chicago	IL	60611	312-266-3110
Blackhawk Lodge (American) 41 E Superior St	Chicago	IL	60611	312-280-4080
Bob Chinn's Crab House (Steak/Seafood) 393 S Milwaukee Ave	Wheeling	IL	60090	847-520-3633
Brasserie Jo (French) 59 W Hubbard St	Chicago	IL	60610	312-595-0800
Buckingham's (Steak/Seafood) 720 S Michigan Ave	Chicago	IL	60605	312-922-4400
Cafe Ba-Ba Reeba (Spanish) 2024 N Halsted St	Chicago	IL	60614	773-935-5000
Cafe Bernard (French) 2100 N Halsted St	Chicago	IL	60614	773-871-2100
Cafe La Cave (French) 2777 Mannheim Rd	Des Plaines	IL	60018	847-827-7818
Cape Cod Room (Seafood) 140 E Walton St	Chicago	IL	60611	312-787-2200
Carlos' (French) 429 Temple Ave	Highland Park	IL	60035	847-432-0770
Carlucci (Italian) 2901 N Sheffield St	Chicago	IL	60657	773-281-1220
Carson's The Place for Ribs (Barbecue) 612 N Wells St *Web:* www.ribs.com/	Chicago	IL	60610	312-280-9200
Celebrity Cafe (American) 320 N Dearborn St	Chicago	IL	60610	312-836-5499
Charlie Trotter's (American) 816 W Armitage Ave *Web:* www.charlietrotters.com/	Chicago	IL	60614	773-248-6228
Chicago Brauhaus (German) 4732-34 N Lincoln Ave	Chicago	IL	60625	773-784-4444
Chicago Chop House (Steak) 60 W Ontario	Chicago	IL	60610	312-787-7100
Coco Pazzo (Italian) 300 W Hubbard St	Chicago	IL	60610	312-836-0900
Como Inn (Italian) 546 N Milwaukee Ave	Chicago	IL	60622	312-421-5222
Cuisine's (Mediterranean/Italian) 1 W Wacker Dr	Chicago	IL	60601	312-372-7200
Earth (American) 738 N Wells St	Chicago	IL	60610	312-335-5475
Eli's The Place for Steak (Steak) 215 E Chicago Ave	Chicago	IL	60611	312-642-1393
Emilio's Tapas (Spanish) 444 W Fullerton Pkwy	Chicago	IL	60603	773-327-5100
Entre Nous (French) 200 N Columbus Dr	Chicago	IL	60601	312-565-8000
Erwin (New American) 2925 N Halsted St	Chicago	IL	60657	773-528-7200
Everest (French) 440 S La Salle St 40th Fl	Chicago	IL	60605	312-663-8920
Fado's Irish Pub (Irish) 100 W Grand Ave	Chicago	IL	60610	312-836-0066
Frontera Grill (Mexican) 445 N Clark St	Chicago	IL	60610	312-661-1434
Gabriel's (Italian/French) 310 Green Bay Rd	Chicago	IL	60040	847-433-0031
Gene & Georgetti (Steak) 500 N Franklin St	Chicago	IL	60610	312-527-3718
Giordanos (Italian) 730 N Rush St	Chicago	IL	60611	312-951-0747
Goose Island Brewing Co (American) 1800 N Clybourn Ave	Chicago	IL	60614	312-915-0071
Gordon (New American) 500 N Clark St	Chicago	IL	60610	312-467-9780
Grazie (Italian) 1050 E Oakton St	Des Plaines	IL	60018	847-299-0011
Green Dolphin Street (New American) 2200 N Ashland Ave	Chicago	IL	60614	773-395-0066
Hard Rock Cafe (American) 63 W Ontario St	Chicago	IL	60610	312-943-2252
Harry Caray's (Italian) 33 W Kinzie *Web:* www.harrycarays.com/	Chicago	IL	60610	773-465-9269
Hatsuhana (Japanese) 160 E Ontario St	Chicago	IL	60611	312-280-8808
Hickory Pit (Barbecue) 2801 Halsted St	Chicago	IL	60608	312-842-7600
Jaipur Palace (Indian) 22 E Hubbard St	Chicago	IL	60611	312-595-0911
Klay Oven (Indian) 414 N Orleans St	Chicago	IL	60610	312-527-3999
La Luce (Italian) 1393 W Lake St	Chicago	IL	60606	312-850-1900
La Strada (Italian) 155 N Michigan Ave *Web:* members.aol.com/lastrada/home	Chicago	IL	60601	312-565-2200
Lawry's Prime Rib (American) 100 E Ontario St	Chicago	IL	60611	312-787-5000
Le Colonial (French/Vietnamese) 937 N Rush St	Chicago	IL	60611	312-255-0088
Le Francais (French) 269 S Milwaukee Ave	Wheeling	IL	60090	847-541-7470
Le Titi de Paris (French) 1015 W Dundee Rd	Arlington Heights	IL	60004	847-506-0222
Leona's (Italian) 3215 N Sheffield Ave	Chicago	IL	60657	773-327-8861
Les Nomades (French) 222 E Ontario St	Chicago	IL	60611	312-649-9010
Maggiano's Little Italy (Italian) 516 N Clark St	Chicago	IL	60610	312-644-7700
Mandar-Inn (Chinese) 2249 S Wentworth Ave	Chicago	IL	60616	312-842-4014
Mango (American) 712 N Clark St	Chicago	IL	60610	312-337-5440
Mia Francesca (Italian) 3311 N Clark St	Chicago	IL	60657	773-281-3310
Mon Ami Gabi (French) 2300 N Lincoln Park West	Chicago	IL	60614	773-348-8886
Morton's of Chicago (Steak) 1050 N State St	Chicago	IL	60610	312-266-4820

Chicago — Restaurants (Cont'd)

Name	City	State	ZIP	Phone
Nick's Fishmarket (Seafood) 1 First National Plaza	Chicago	IL	60603	312-621-0200
North Pond Cafe (American) Lincoln Park	Chicago	IL	60657	773-477-5845
Omega Pancake House (Greek) 9100 Golf Rd	Niles	IL	60714	847-296-7777
Papagus Greek Taverna (Greek) 620 N State St	Chicago	IL	60610	312-642-8450
Parthenon (Greek) 314 S Halsted St	Chicago	IL	60661	312-726-2407
Pattaya (Thai) 114 W Chicago Ave	Chicago	IL	60610	312-944-3753
Philander's (Seafood) 1120 Pleasant St	Oak Park	IL	60302	708-848-4250
Prairie (American) 500 S Dearborn St	Chicago	IL	60605	312-663-1143
Printer's Row (American) 550 S Dearborn St	Chicago	IL	60605	312-461-0780
Pump Room (American) 1301 N State Pkwy	Chicago	IL	60610	312-266-0360
Rainforest Cafe (American) 605 N Clark St	Chicago	IL	60610	312-787-1501
Web: www.rainforestcafe.com				
Restaurant Suntory (Japanese) 13 E Huron St	Chicago	IL	60611	312-664-3344
Rhumba Brazilian Eatery (Brazilian) 3631 N Halsted St	Chicago	IL	60613	773-975-2345
Ritz-Carlton Dining Room (French) 160 E Pearson St	Chicago	IL	60611	773-227-5866
Riva (Steak/Seafood) 700 E Grand Ave	Chicago	IL	60611	312-644-7482
Rivers (American) 30 S Wacker Dr	Chicago	IL	60606	312-559-1515
Rosebud Cafe (Italian) 1500 W Taylor St	Chicago	IL	60607	312-942-1117
Scoozi (Italian) 410 W Huron St	Chicago	IL	60610	312-943-5900
Seasons (American) 120 E Delaware Pl 7th Fl	Chicago	IL	60611	312-649-2349
Shaw's Crab House (Seafood) 21 E Hubbard St	Chicago	IL	60611	312-527-2722
Signature Room 95th Floor (American) 875 N Michigan Ave	Chicago	IL	60611	312-787-9596
Soul Kitchen (Continental) 1576 N Milwaukee Ave	Chicago	IL	60622	773-342-9742
Spiaggia (Italian) 980 N Michigan Ave	Chicago	IL	60611	312-280-2750
Spruce (New American) 238 E Ontario St	Chicago	IL	60611	312-642-3757
Su Casa (Mexican) 49 E Ontario St	Chicago	IL	60611	312-943-4041
Topolobampo (Mexican) 445 N Clark St	Chicago	IL	60610	312-661-1434
Trader Vic's (Polynesian) 17 E Monroe St	Chicago	IL	60603	312-917-7317
Trattoria No 10 (Italian) 10 N Dearborn	Chicago	IL	60602	312-984-1718
Vivere (Italian) 71 W Monroe St	Chicago	IL	60603	312-332-4040
Voila (French) 33 W Monroe St	Chicago	IL	60603	312-580-9500
Wildfire (American) 159 W Erie St	Chicago	IL	60610	312-787-9000
Yoshi's Cafe (French/Oriental) 3257 N Halsted St	Chicago	IL	60657	773-248-6160
Zinfandel (American) 59 W Grand Ave	Chicago	IL	60610	312-527-1818

— Goods and Services —

SHOPPING

Name	City	State	ZIP	Phone	Fax
900 North Michigan Shops 900 N Michigan Ave	Chicago	IL	60611	312-915-3916	
Atrium Mall 100 W Randolph St	Chicago	IL	60601	312-346-0777	
Bloomingdale's 900 N Michigan Ave	Chicago	IL	60611	312-440-4460	440-4394
Carson Pirie Scott 1 S State St	Chicago	IL	60603	312-641-8000	
Century Shopping Centre 2828 N Clark St	Chicago	IL	60657	773-929-8100	
Charlestowne Mall 3800 E Main St	Saint Charles	IL	60174	630-513-1120	513-1459
Chicago Place 700 N Michigan Ave	Chicago	IL	60611	312-266-7710	
Chicago Ridge Mall 444 Chicago Ridge Mall Dr	Chicago Ridge	IL	60415	708-422-0897	499-0840
Evergreen Plaza 9730 S Western Ave	Evergreen Park	IL	60805	708-422-5454	422-9780
Fox Valley Center 195 Fox Valley Ctr	Aurora	IL	60504	630-851-3000	851-3683
Golf Mill Center 239 Golf Mill Ctr	Niles	IL	60714	847-699-1070	699-1593
Gurnee Mills 6170 W Grand Ave	Gurnee	IL	60031	847-263-7500	263-2423
TF: 800-937-7467 ■ *Web:* www.gurneemillsmall.com					
Hawthorn Center 122 Hawthorn Ctr	Vernon Hills	IL	60061	847-362-2600	362-2689
Lakehurst Mall 199 Lakehurst Rd	Waukegan	IL	60085	847-473-0234	
Lincoln Mall 208 Lincoln Mall Dr	Matteson	IL	60443	708-747-5600	747-5629
Lord & Taylor 835 N Michigan Ave	Chicago	IL	60611	312-787-7400	
Marshall Field & Co 111 N State St	Chicago	IL	60602	312-781-1000	781-4594*
**Fax:* PR					
Navy Pier 600 E Grand Ave	Chicago	IL	60611	312-595-7437	
Web: www.navypier.com ■ *E-mail:* npgeninfo@mpea.com					
Neiman Marcus 737 N Michigan Ave	Chicago	IL	60611	312-642-5900	642-9622
Web: www.neimanmarcus.com					
Northbrook Court 2171 Northbrook Cr	Northbrook	IL	60062	847-498-1770	498-5194
Oakbrook Shopping Center 100 Oakbrook Ctr	Oak Brook	IL	60523	630-573-0250	573-0710
Web: www.oldorachard.com ■ *E-mail:* info@oldorchard.com					
Old Orchard Center 34 Old Orchard Ctr	Skokie	IL	60077	847-674-7070	674-7083
Orland Square 288 Orland Sq	Orland Park	IL	60462	708-349-6936	349-8419
Randhurst Shopping Center 999 N Elmhurst Rd	Mount Prospect	IL	60056	847-259-0500	259-0228
Web: www.randhurstmall.com					
River Oaks Center 96 River Oaks Dr	Calumet City	IL	60409	708-868-0600	868-1402
Saks Fifth Avenue 700 N Michigan Ave	Chicago	IL	60611	312-944-6500	944-3138
Shops at the Mart 222 Merchandise Mart Plaza	Chicago	IL	60654	312-527-7990	527-7058
Spring Hill Mall 1072 Spring Hill Mall	West Dundee	IL	60118	847-428-2200	428-2219
Stratford Square Mall 152 Stratford Sq	Bloomingdale	IL	60108	630-351-9400	
Water Tower Place 835-845 N Michigan Ave	Chicago	IL	60611	312-440-3165	
Woodfield Mall 5 Woodfield Mall	Schaumburg	IL	60173	847-330-1537	330-0251
Yorktown Shopping Center 203 Yorktown	Lombard	IL	60148	630-629-7330	629-7334
Web: www.yorktowncenter.com					

BANKS

Name	City	State	ZIP	Phone	Fax
Amalgamated Bank of Chicago 1 W Monroe St	Chicago	IL	60603	312-822-3000	822-3258
TF: 800-991-4254					
American National Bank & Trust Co of Chicago 120 S La Salle St	Chicago	IL	60603	312-661-5000	661-6417
Banco Popular 4000 W North Ave	Chicago	IL	60639	773-772-8665	292-4609
Bank of America NT & SA 231 S La Salle St	Chicago	IL	60697	312-828-2345	828-1974
Bank of Tokyo-Mitsubishi Ltd 227 W Monroe St Suite 2300	Chicago	IL	60606	312-696-4500	696-4530
Cole Taylor Bank 1965 N Milwaukee Ave	Chicago	IL	60647	773-278-6800	278-2183
Web: www.ctbnk.com ■ *E-mail:* ctbnk@coletaylor.com					
Corus Bank 4800 N Western Ave	Chicago	IL	60625	773-388-5100	388-5158
Firstar Bank Illinois 30 N Michigan Ave	Chicago	IL	60602	312-641-1000	641-2103
Harris Trust & Savings Bank 111 W Monroe St	Chicago	IL	60603	312-461-2121	461-6640
Web: www.harrisbank.com ■ *E-mail:* newaccounts@harrisbank.com					
La Salle Bank NA 5250 N Harlem Ave	Chicago	IL	60656	773-775-6800	594-3027
LaSalle National Bank 135 S LaSalle St	Chicago	IL	60603	312-443-2000	904-6521*
**Fax:* Mktg ■ *Web:* www.lsnb.com ■ *E-mail:* lsnb@ivi.net					
Manufacturers Bank 1200 N Ashland Ave	Chicago	IL	60622	773-278-4040	278-4066
Web: www.manbk.com					
Mid-City National Bank of Chicago 801 W Madison St	Chicago	IL	60607	312-421-7600	421-7612
Northern Trust Bank O'Hare NA 8501 W Higgins Rd	Chicago	IL	60631	773-693-5555	714-6209
Old Kent Bank Chicago 233 S Wacker Dr	Chicago	IL	60606	312-876-4200	876-4184*
**Fax:* PR					
Pullman Bank & Trust Co 1000 E 111th St	Chicago	IL	60628	773-602-8200	785-9755
Saint Paul Federal Bank for Savings 6700 W North Ave	Chicago	IL	60707	773-622-5000	804-2110
Web: www.stpaulbank.com					
TCF National Bank 4192 S Archer Ave	Chicago	IL	60632	773-847-1140	847-7791

BUSINESS SERVICES

Name	Phone
Accountemps	312-616-8367
Adecco Employment Personnel Services	312-372-6783
Arrow Messenger Service	773-489-6688
Cannonball Messenger Service	312-829-1234
Chicago Messenger Service	312-666-6800
Comet Messenger Service	312-786-2288
Dynamex	312-527-0100
Federal Express	800-463-3339
Interim Office Professionals	312-781-7220
Kelly Services	312-853-3434
Kinko's	773-528-0500
Manpower Temporary Services	312-263-5144
Olsten Staffing Services	312-782-1014
Post Office	312-654-3788
Quicksilver Messenger Service	312-726-3736
UPS	800-742-5877

— Media —

PUBLICATIONS

Name	City	State	ZIP	Phone	Fax
Bridgeport News 3252 S Halstead St	Chicago	IL	60608	312-842-5883	842-5097*
**Fax:* News Rm					
Chicago Life Magazine PO Box 11311	Chicago	IL	60611	773-528-2737	
E-mail: chgolife@mcs.com					
Chicago Magazine 500 N Dearborn Ave Suite 1200	Chicago	IL	60610	312-222-8999	222-0699
Web: www.chicagomag.com					
Chicago Sun-Times‡ 401 N Wabash Ave	Chicago	IL	60611	312-321-3000	321-3084
Web: www.suntimes.com ■ *E-mail:* letters@suntimes.com					
Chicago Tribune‡ 435 N Michigan Ave	Chicago	IL	60611	312-222-3232	
Web: www.chicago.tribune.com					
Chicago's Northwest Side Press 4937 N Milwaukee Ave	Chicago	IL	60630	773-286-6100	286-8151
Crain's Chicago Business 740 N Rush St	Chicago	IL	60611	312-649-5200	649-5415
TF: 800-678-2724 ■ *Web:* www.crainschicagobusiness.com					
Inside Lake View 4710 N Lincoln Ave	Chicago	IL	60625	773-878-7333	878-0959*
**Fax:* News Rm					
Key: This Week in Chicago 226 E Ontario Suite 300	Chicago	IL	60611	312-943-0838	664-6113
Web: www.keymag.com					
Morningstar Inc 225 W Wacker Dr	Chicago	IL	60606	312-696-6000	696-6001
TF Orders: 800-735-0700 ■ *Web:* www.morningstar.net ■ *E-mail:* joe@morningstar.net					

Chicago — Publications (Cont'd)

				Phone	Fax
North Loop News 6008 W Belmont Ave *Fax: News Rm	Chicago	IL	60634	773-283-7900	283-7761*
Where Chicago 1165 N Clark St Suite 302 *Web:* www.wheremags.com/chicago.html ■ *E-mail:* wherechicago@insnet.com	Chicago	IL	60610	312-642-1896	642-5467

‡*Daily newspapers*

TELEVISION

				Phone	Fax
WBBM-TV Ch 2 (CBS) 630 N McClurg Ct *E-mail:* wbbmch2@aol.com	Chicago	IL	60611	312-944-6000	951-3878
WCIU-TV Ch 26 (Ind) 26 N Halsted St	Chicago	IL	60661	312-705-2600	705-2656
WCPX-TV Ch 38 (PAX) 541 N Fairbanks Ct Suite 800 *Web:* www.pax.net/WCPX	Chicago	IL	60611	312-410-9038	467-9318
WFLD-TV Ch 32 (Fox) 205 N Michigan Ave *Web:* www.foxchicago.com	Chicago	IL	60601	312-565-5532	819-1332
WGBO-TV Ch 66 (Uni) 541 N Fairbanks Ct 11th Fl	Chicago	IL	60611	312-670-1000	494-6492
WGN-TV Ch 9 (WB) 2501 W Bradley Pl *Fax: News Rm ■ *Web:* www.wgntv.com ■ *E-mail:* wgn-tv@tribune.com	Chicago	IL	60618	773-528-2311	528-6050*
WJYS-TV Ch 62 (Ind) 18600 S Oak Park Ave	Tinley Park	IL	60477	708-633-0001	633-0040
WLS-TV Ch 7 (ABC) 190 N State St	Chicago	IL	60601	312-750-7777	899-8019
WMAQ-TV Ch 5 (NBC) 454 N Columbus Dr NBC Tower *Web:* www.nbc5.com	Chicago	IL	60611	312-836-5555	527-5925
WPWR-TV Ch 50 (UPN) 2151 N Elston Ave	Chicago	IL	60614	773-276-5050	276-6477
WSNS-TV Ch 44 (Tele) 430 W Grant Pl	Chicago	IL	60614	773-929-1200	929-8153
WTTW-TV Ch 11 (PBS) 5400 N St Louis Ave *Web:* www.wttw.com ■ *E-mail:* viewermail@wttw.com	Chicago	IL	60625	773-583-5000	583-3046
WYCC-TV Ch 20 (Ind) 7500 S Pulaski Rd	Chicago	IL	60652	773-838-7878	581-2071

RADIO

				Phone	Fax
WAIT-AM 850 kHz (Nost) 8800 Rt 14 *Fax Area Code: 312	Crystal Lake	IL	60012	815-459-7000	755-1059*
WBBM-AM 780 kHz (N/T) 630 N McClurg Ct	Chicago	IL	60611	312-944-6000	951-3674
WBBM-FM 96.3 MHz (CHR) 630 N McClurg Ct	Chicago	IL	60611	312-944-6000	951-1773
WBEZ-FM 91.5 MHz (NPR) 848 E Grand Ave *Web:* www.a2z.com/wbez	Chicago	IL	60611	312-832-9150	832-3100
WCKG-FM 105.9 MHz (N/T) 2 Prudential Plaza Suite 1059	Chicago	IL	60601	312-240-7900	565-3181
WFMT-FM 98.7 MHz (Clas) 5400 N St Louis Ave *Web:* www.wfmt.com ■ *E-mail:* fine.arts@wfmt.com	Chicago	IL	60625	773-279-2000	279-2199
WGCI-AM 1390 kHz (Urban) 332 S Michigan Ave Suite 600	Chicago	IL	60604	312-427-4800	427-7410
WGCI-FM 107.5 MHz (Urban) 332 S Michigan Ave Suite 600	Chicago	IL	60604	312-427-4800	427-7410
WGN-AM 720 kHz (N/T) 435 N Michigan Ave *Web:* www.wgnradio.com ■ *E-mail:* WGNfanAMU@aol.com	Chicago	IL	60611	312-222-4700	222-5165
WIND-AM 560 kHz (Span) 625 N Michigan Ave Suite 300	Chicago	IL	60611	312-751-5560	654-0092
WJMK-FM 104.3 MHz (Oldies) 180 N Michigan Ave Suite 1200 *Web:* www.wjmk.com ■ *E-mail:* wjmk@aol.com	Chicago	IL	60601	312-977-1800	977-1859
WKQX-FM 101.1 MHz (Alt) Merchandise Mart Suite 1700	Chicago	IL	60654	312-527-8348	245-0073
WLEY-FM 107.9 MHz (Span) 150 N Michigan Ave Suite 1040	Chicago	IL	60601	312-920-9500	920-9515
WLIT-FM 93.9 MHz (AC) 150 N Michigan Ave Suite 1135	Chicago	IL	60601	312-329-9002	346-2649
WLS-AM 890 kHz (N/T) 190 N State St *Web:* www.wlsam.com ■ *E-mail:* wlslam@wlsam.com	Chicago	IL	60601	312-984-0890	984-5305
WLUP-FM 97.9 MHz (Rock) 875 N Michigan Ave Suite 3750 *Web:* www.979theloop.com ■ *E-mail:* wlup@aol.com	Chicago	IL	60611	312-440-5270	440-9377
WMAQ-AM 670 kHz (Sports) 455 N Cityfront Plaza NBC Tower 6th Fl	Chicago	IL	60611	312-670-6767	245-6098
WMVP-AM 1000 kHz (Sports) 875 N Michigan Ave Suite 1510	Chicago	IL	60611	312-980-1000	440-1993
WNIB-FM 97.1 MHz (Clas) 1140 W Erie St	Chicago	IL	60622	312-633-9700	633-9710
WNND-FM 100.3 MHz (AC) 1 Prudential Plaza Suite 2780	Chicago	IL	60601	312-297-5100	297-5155
WNUA-FM 95.5 MHz (NAC) 444 N Michigan Ave Suite 300	Chicago	IL	60611	312-645-9550	645-9645
WOJO-FM 105.1 MHz (Span) 625 N Michigan Ave Suite 300	Chicago	IL	60611	312-751-5560	664-2472
WSCR-AM 1160 kHz (Sports) 4949 W Belmont Ave	Chicago	IL	60641	773-777-1700	777-5031
WTMX-FM 101.9 MHz (AC) 1 Prudential Plaza Suite 2700 *Web:* www.wtmx.com	Chicago	IL	60601	312-946-1019	946-4747
WUBT-FM 103.5 MHz (Oldies) 875 N Michigan Ave Suite 4000	Chicago	IL	60611	312-861-8100	440-9143
WUSN-FM 99.5 MHz (Ctry) 875 N Michigan Ave Suite 1310	Chicago	IL	60611	312-649-0099	664-3999
WVAZ-FM 102.7 MHz (Urban) 800 S Wells St Suite 250	Chicago	IL	60607	312-360-9000	360-9070
WXCD-FM 94.7 MHz (CR) 190 N State St 8th Fl	Chicago	IL	60601	312-984-0890	984-5357
WXRT-FM 93.1 MHz (Alt) 4949 W Belmont Ave *Web:* www.wxrt.com ■ *E-mail:* comments@wxrt.com	Chicago	IL	60641	773-777-1700	777-5031

— Colleges/Universities —

				Phone	Fax
American Academy of Art 332 S Michigan Ave Suite 300	Chicago	IL	60604	312-461-0600	294-9570
American Conservatory of Music 36 S Wabash Ave Suite 800 *E-mail:* otto@shell.portal.com	Chicago	IL	60603	312-263-4161	263-5832
American Islamic College 640 W Irving Park Rd	Chicago	IL	60613	773-281-4700	281-8552
Career Colleges of Chicago 11 E Adams St	Chicago	IL	60603	312-895-6300	895-6301
Chicago State University 9501 S King Dr *Web:* www.csu.edu	Chicago	IL	60628	773-995-2000	995-3820
College of DuPage 425 22nd St *Web:* www.cod.edu	Glen Ellyn	IL	60137	630-858-2800	790-2686
College of Lake County 19351 W Washington St *Web:* www.clc.cc.il.us	Grayslake	IL	60030	847-223-6601	543-3061
Columbia College 600 S Michigan Ave *Web:* www.colum.edu	Chicago	IL	60605	312-663-1600	344-8024
Concordia University 7400 Augusta St *Web:* www.curf.edu ■ *E-mail:* crfadmis@crf.cuis.edu	River Forest	IL	60305	708-771-8300	209-3176
DePaul University 1 E Jackson Blvd 9th Fl *TF:* 800-433-7285 ■ *Web:* www.depaul.edu	Chicago	IL	60604	312-362-8000	362-5749
DeVRY Institute of Technology 3300 N Campbell Ave *TF:* 800-659-4588 ■ *Web:* www.chi.devry.edu	Chicago	IL	60618	773-929-8500	348-1780
Dominican University 7900 W Division St *Web:* www.dom.edu	River Forest	IL	60305	708-366-2490	524-5990
East-West University 816 S Michigan Ave *Web:* www.eastwest.edu ■ *E-mail:* seeyou@eastwest.edu	Chicago	IL	60605	312-939-0111	939-0083
Elgin Community College 1700 Spartan Dr *Web:* www.elgin.cc.il.us	Elgin	IL	60123	847-697-1000	608-5458
Elmhurst College 190 S Prospect Ave *TF Admissions:* 800-697-1871 ■ *Web:* www.elmhurst.edu ■ *E-mail:* info@elmhurst.edu	Elmhurst	IL	60126	630-617-3500	617-5501
Harold Washington College 30 E Lake St *Web:* cccweb.ccc.edu/hwashington	Chicago	IL	60601	312-553-6000	553-6084
Harrington Institute of Interior Design 410 S Michigan Ave *TF Admissions:* 877-939-4975 ■ *Web:* www.interiordesign.edu	Chicago	IL	60605	312-939-4975	939-8005
Harry S Truman College 1145 W Wilson Ave *Web:* www.ccc.edu/truman/home.htm	Chicago	IL	60640	773-878-1700	907-4464
Illinois Institute of Art 350 N Orleans St Suite 136-L *Web:* www.ilia.aii.edu	Chicago	IL	60654	312-280-3500	280-3528
Illinois Institute of Technology 3300 S Federal St *TF Admissions:* 800-448-2329 ■ *Web:* www.iit.edu	Chicago	IL	60616	312-567-3000	567-6939
Industrial Engineering College 18 S Michigan Ave Suite 1006	Chicago	IL	60603	312-372-1360	236-2221
International Academy of Merchandising & Design 1 N State St *TF:* 800-222-3369 ■ *Web:* www.iamd.edu	Chicago	IL	60602	312-980-9200	541-3929
ITT Technical Institute 375 W Higgins Rd *Web:* www.itt-tech.edu	Hoffman Estates	IL	60195	847-519-9300	519-0153
Joliet Junior College 1215 Houbolt Rd *Web:* www.jjc.cc.il.us	Joliet	IL	60431	815-729-9020	280-6740
Kendall College 2408 Orrington Ave *Web:* www.kendall.edu	Evanston	IL	60201	847-866-1300	733-7450
Kennedy-King College 6800 S Wentworth Ave *Web:* www.ccc.edu/kennedyking/	Chicago	IL	60621	773-602-5000	602-5247
Lewis University Rt 53 *Fax: Library ■ *TF Admissions:* 800-897-9000 ■ *Web:* www.lewisu.edu	Romeoville	IL	60446	815-838-0500	838-9456*

Chicago — Colleges/Universities (Cont'd)

				Phone	Fax
Lexington College 10840 S Western Ave	Chicago	IL	60643	773-779-3800	779-7450
E-mail: lexcollege@ameritech.net					
Loyola University Chicago 820 N Michigan Ave	Chicago	IL	60611	312-915-6000	915-6449
TF Admissions: 800-262-2373 ■ *Web:* www.luc.edu/ ■ *E-mail:* admissions@luc.edu					
Loyola University Chicago Mallinckrodt Campus 1041 Ridge Rd.	Wilmette	IL	60091	847-853-3000	853-3375
MacCormac College 506 S Wabash Ave	Chicago	IL	60605	312-922-1884	922-3196
Malcolm X College 1900 W Van Buren St	Chicago	IL	60612	312-942-3000	850-7092
Web: cccweb.ccc.edu/malcolmx					
Moody Bible Institute 820 N La Salle St	Chicago	IL	60610	312-329-4000	329-2099*
**Fax:* PR ■ *TF:* 800-356-6639 ■ *Web:* www.moody.edu					
Moraine Valley Community College 10900 S 88th Ave	Palos Hills	IL	60465	708-974-4300	974-0974
Web: www.moraine.cc.il.us					
Morton College 3801 S Central Ave	Cicero	IL	60804	708-656-8000	656-9592
Web: www.morton.cc.il.us					
Mundelein College 6525 N Sheridan Rd	Chicago	IL	60626	773-262-8100	508-8008
TF: 800-756-9652 ■ *Web:* www.luc.edu/schools/mundelein					
NAES College 2838 W Peterson Ave	Chicago	IL	60659	773-761-5000	761-3808
Web: naes.indian.com					
National College of Chiropractic 200 E Roosevelt Rd.	Lombard	IL	60148	630-629-2000	889-6554
TF Admissions: 800-826-6285 ■ *Web:* www.national.chiropractic.edu ■ *E-mail:* HomePage@national.chiropractic.edu					
National-Louis University 2840 Sheridan Rd	Evanston	IL	60201	847-475-1100	256-1057
TF: 800-443-5522 ■ *Web:* www.nl.edu					
National-Louis University Chicago Campus 122 S Michigan Ave	Chicago	IL	60603	312-621-9650	621-1205
TF: 800-443-5522					
North Central College 30 N Brainard St.	Naperville	IL	60566	630-637-5100	637-5819
TF: 800-411-1861 ■ *Web:* www.noctrl.edu ■ *E-mail:* ncadm@noctrl.edu					
North Park University 3225 W Foster Ave	Chicago	IL	60625	773-244-6200	244-4953
TF Admissions: 800-888-6728 ■ *Web:* www.npcts.edu					
Northeastern Illinois University 5500 N St Louis Ave	Chicago	IL	60625	773-583-4050	794-6243
Web: www.neiu.edu					
Northwestern Business College 4829 N Lipps Ave	Chicago	IL	60630	773-777-4220	777-2861
TF: 800-396-5613					
Northwestern University 1801 Hinman Ave	Evanston	IL	60208	847-491-3741	491-5136*
**Fax:* Hum Res ■ *Web:* www.nwu.edu ■ *E-mail:* nuinfo@nwu.edu					
Oakton Community College 1600 E Golf Rd.	Des Plaines	IL	60016	847-635-1600	635-1706
Web: www.oakton.edu					
Olive-Harvey College 10001 S Woodlawn Ave	Chicago	IL	60628	773-568-3700	291-6185
Web: cccweb.ccc.edu/oliveharvey					
Prairie State College 202 S Halsted St.	Chicago Heights	IL	60411	708-709-3500	709-3951
Web: www.prairie.cc.il.us					
Richard J Daley College 7500 S Pulaski Rd	Chicago	IL	60652	773-838-7500	838-7605
Web: www.ccc.edu/daley/					
Robert Morris College Chicago Campus 401 S State St	Chicago	IL	60605	312-935-6800	935-4440
TF: 800-225-1520 ■ *Web:* www.rmcil.edu ■ *E-mail:* enroll@rmcil.edu					
Roosevelt University 430 S Michigan Ave	Chicago	IL	60605	312-341-3500	341-3523
Web: www.roosevelt.edu					
Rush University 600 S Paulina St Rm 440	Chicago	IL	60612	312-942-7100	942-2219
Web: www.rushu.rush.edu ■ *E-mail:* rushu@rush.edu					
Saint Augustine College 1333-1345 W Argyle	Chicago	IL	60640	773-878-8756	878-0932
Web: www.staugustinecollege.edu ■ *E-mail:* info@staugustinecollege.edu					
Saint Xavier University 3700 W 103rd St	Chicago	IL	60655	773-298-3000	779-9061
Web: www.sxu.edu					
School of the Art Institute of Chicago 37 S Wabash Ave	Chicago	IL	60603	312-899-5100	899-1840
TF Admissions: 800-232-7242*					
South Suburban College 15800 State St	South Holland	IL	60473	708-596-2000	210-5758
TF Admissions: 800-248-4772 ■ *Web:* www.ssc.cc.il.us/					
Triton College 2000 N 5th Ave	River Grove	IL	60171	708-456-0300	583-3108
Web: www.triton.cc.il.us ■ *E-mail:* triton@triton.cc.il.us					
University of Chicago 5801 S Ellis Ave	Chicago	IL	60637	773-702-1234	702-4199
Web: www.uchicago.edu					
University of Illinois Chicago 1200 W Harrison St	Chicago	IL	60607	312-996-3000	413-7628
Web: www.uic.edu					
VanderCook College of Music 3140 S Federal St	Chicago	IL	60616	312-225-6288	225-5211
TF: 800-448-2655 ■ *Web:* www.mcs.net/~vcmusic/ ■ *E-mail:* ami@mcs.com					
West Suburban College of Nursing Erie St & Austin Blvd.	Oak Park	IL	60302	708-763-6530	763-1531
Web: www.curf.edu/~wscasseyp/wscn.htm ■ *E-mail:* wsadmis@crf.cuis.edu					
Wilbur Wright College 4300 N Narragansett Ave	Chicago	IL	60634	773-777-7900	481-8185
Web: www.ccc.edu/wright/					
William Rainey Harper College 1200 W Algonquin Rd	Palatine	IL	60067	847-925-6000	925-6044*
**Fax:* Admissions ■ *Web:* www.harper.cc.il.us					

— Hospitals —

				Phone	Fax
Bethany Hospital 3435 W Van Buren St	Chicago	IL	60624	773-265-7700	265-3558
Web: www.advocatehealth.com/sites/hospitals/beth/index.html					
Children's Memorial Hospital 2300 Children's Plaza	Chicago	IL	60614	773-880-4000	880-6954
Web: www.childmmc.edu					
Christ Hospital & Medical Center 4440 W 95th St	Oak Lawn	IL	60453	708-425-8000	346-5012
Web: www.advocatehealth.com/sites/hospitals/chmc/index.html					
Columbia Grant Hospital of Chicago 550 W Webster Ave	Chicago	IL	60614	773-883-3800	883-5168
Columbia Michael Reese Hospital & Medical Center 2929 S Ellis Ave.	Chicago	IL	60616	312-791-2000	791-2299
Columbus Hospital 2520 N Lakeview Ave	Chicago	IL	60614	773-883-7300	665-3861
Web: www.cath-health.org/columbushospita3618.cfm					
Cook County Hospital 1835 W Harrison St.	Chicago	IL	60612	312-633-6000	633-3068*
**Fax:* Hum Res					
Doctors Hospital of Hyde Park 5800 S Stony Island Ave	Chicago	IL	60637	773-643-9200	643-7461
Edgewater Medical Center 5700 N Ashland Ave	Chicago	IL	60660	773-878-6000	878-4431
Holy Cross Hospital 2701 W 68th St.	Chicago	IL	60629	773-471-8000	471-7460
Illinois Masonic Medical Center 836 W Wellington Ave.	Chicago	IL	60657	773-975-1600	296-5101
Web: www.immc.org					
Loretto Hospital 645 S Central Ave.	Chicago	IL	60644	773-626-4300	626-2613
Louis A Weiss Memorial Hospital 4646 N Marine Dr.	Chicago	IL	60640	773-878-8700	878-7146
Loyola University Chicago Medical Center 2160 S 1st Ave.	Maywood	IL	60153	708-216-9000	216-4918*
**Fax:* Hum Res ■ *Web:* www.lumc.edu					
Lutheran General Hospital 1775 W Dempster St.	Park Ridge	IL	60068	847-696-2210	723-2285
Web: www.advocatehealth.com/sites/hospitals/luth/index.html					
Mercy Hospital & Medical Center 2525 S Michigan Ave	Chicago	IL	60616	312-567-2000	328-7745*
**Fax:* Admitting ■ *Web:* www.mercy-chicago.org					
Methodist Hospital of Chicago 5025 N Paulina St.	Chicago	IL	60640	773-271-9040	989-1537
Mount Sinai Hospital Medical Center of Chicago California Ave & 15th St	Chicago	IL	60608	773-542-2000	257-6208*
**Fax:* PR ■ *Web:* www.sinai.org ■ *E-mail:* shs@sinai.org					
Naval Hospital 3001-A 6th St.	Great Lakes	IL	60088	847-688-4560	688-2856
Northwestern Memorial Hospital 251 E Huron St.	Chicago	IL	60611	312-908-2000	926-6199
Web: www.nmh.org					
Our Lady of Resurrection Medical Center 5645 W Addison St.	Chicago	IL	60634	773-282-7000	794-7651
Ravenswood Hospital Medical Center 4550 N Winchester Ave	Chicago	IL	60640	773-878-4300	279-3133
Web: www.advocatehealth.com/sites/hospitals/ravn/index.html					
Resurrection Medical Center 7435 W Talcott Ave.	Chicago	IL	60631	773-774-8000	594-7987
Roseland Community Hospital 45 W 111th St	Chicago	IL	60628	773-995-3000	995-3100
Rush-Presbyterian-Saint Luke's Medical Center 1653 W Congress Pkwy.	Chicago	IL	60612	312-942-5000	942-3212*
**Fax:* Hum Res ■ *Web:* www.rpslmc.edu					
Saint Bernard Hospital & Health Care Center 326 W 64th St	Chicago	IL	60621	773-962-3900	602-3849
Saint Elizabeth's Hospital 1431 N Claremont Ave.	Chicago	IL	60622	773-278-2000	850-5970*
**Fax Area Code:* 312					
Saint Joseph Hospital & Health Care Center 2900 N Lake Shore Dr.	Chicago	IL	60657	773-665-3000	665-3255*
**Fax:* Admitting ■ *Web:* www.cath-health.org/saintjosephhosp3617.cfm					

Chicago — Hospitals (Cont'd)

Phone *Fax*

Saint Mary of Nazareth Hospital Center
2233 W Division St. . . . . Chicago IL 60622 312-770-2000 770-3389

Shriners Hospitals for Children Chicago Unit
2211 N Oak Pk Ave. . . . . Chicago IL 60707 773-622-5400 385-5453
TF: 800-237-5055
■ *Web:* www.shrinershq.org/Hospitals/Directory/chicago.html

South Shore Hospital 8012 S Crandon Ave . . . . . Chicago IL 60617 773-768-0810 768-0332

Trinity Hospital 2320 E 93rd St . . . . . Chicago IL 60617 773-978-2000 933-6435
Web: www.advocatehealth.com/sites/hospitals/trin/index.html

University of Chicago Hospitals
5841 S Maryland Ave . . . . . Chicago IL 60637 773-702-1000 702-9005
Web: www.uchospitals.edu

University of Illinois Hospital & Clinics
1740 W Taylor St Suite 1400. . . . . Chicago IL 60612 312-996-7000 996-7049
Web: www.uic.edu/hsc ■ *E-mail:* comments@cerulean.bvis.uic.edu

Veterans Affairs Edward Hines Jr Hospital
PO Box 5000 . . . . . Hines IL 60141 708-202-8387 202-7998

Veterans Affairs Westside Medical Center
PO Box 8195 . . . . . Chicago IL 60680 312-666-6500 633-2195

— Attractions —

Phone *Fax*

ABA Museum of Law 750 N Lake Shore Dr . . . . . Chicago IL 60611 312-988-6222

Adler Planetarium 1300 S Lake Shore Dr . . . . . Chicago IL 60605 312-922-7827 322-2257
Web: www.adlerplanetarium.org ■ *E-mail:* pr@adlernet.org

American Police Center & Museum
1717 S State St . . . . . Chicago IL 60616 312-431-0005 939-1122

Art Institute of Chicago Museum
111 S Michigan Ave . . . . . Chicago IL 60603 312-443-3600 443-0849
Web: www.artic.edu/aic/

Auditorium Theatre 50 E Congress Pkwy. . . . . Chicago IL 60605 312-922-4046

Ballet Chicago
185 N Wabash Ave Suite 2300. . . . . Chicago IL 60601 312-251-8838 251-8840

Balzekas Museum of Lithuanian Culture
6500 S Pulaski Rd . . . . . Chicago IL 60629 773-582-6500 582-5133

Brookfield Zoo 1st Ave & 31st St. . . . . Brookfield IL 60513 708-485-2200 485-3532
Web: hereandnow.nwu.edu/ev-chi/parks/brookfield

Buckingham Fountain
Columbus Dr & Congress Pkwy . . . . . Chicago IL 60605 312-747-2200

Burnham Park 1559 S Lake Shore Dr . . . . . Chicago IL 60605 312-747-7009

Chicago Academy of Sciences Nature Museum
2430 Cannon Dr . . . . . Chicago IL 60614 773-549-0606 755-5199
Web: www.chias.org/ ■ *E-mail:* cas@chias.org

Chicago Athenaeum Museum of Architecture & Design 6 N Michigan Ave . . . . . Chicago IL 60602 312-251-0175 251-0176
Web: www.chi-athenaeum.org

Chicago Board of Trade 141 W Jackson Blvd. . . . . Chicago IL 60604 312-435-3500 341-3392
TF: 800-572-3276 ■ *Web:* www.cbot.com

Chicago Botanic Garden 1000 Lake Cook Rd . . . . Glencoe IL 60022 847-835-5440 835-4484
Web: www.chicago-botanic.org ■ *E-mail:* cbglib@nslsilus.org

Chicago Chamber Orchestra
78 E Washington St Chicago Cultural Ctr. . . . . Chicago IL 60602 312-922-5570 922-9290

Chicago Children's Museum
700 E Grand Ave Suite 127 . . . . . Chicago IL 60611 312-527-1000 527-9082
Web: www.chichildrensmuseum.org

Chicago Cultural Center 78 E Washington St. . . . Chicago IL 60602 312-346-3278
Web: www.ci.chi.il.us/Tourism/CultureCenterTour/

Chicago Historical Society 1601 N Clark St. . . . . Chicago IL 60614 312-642-4600 266-2077
Web: www.chicagohs.org

Chicago Mercantile Exchange
30 S Wacker Dr . . . . . Chicago IL 60606 312-930-1000 930-3016
Web: www.cme.com ■ *E-mail:* info@cme.com

Chicago Music Mart
333 S State St DePaul Ctr . . . . . Chicago IL 60604 312-362-6700 362-5838

Chicago Opera Theater 70 E Lake St. . . . . Chicago IL 60601 312-704-8420 704-8421

Chicago Sinfonietta
105 W Adams St Suite 3330 . . . . . Chicago IL 60603 312-857-1062 857-1007

Chicago Sports Hall of Fame
1150 N River Rd. . . . . Des Plaines IL 60016 847-294-1700 635-1571

Chicago Stock Exchange 440 S LaSalle St. . . . . Chicago IL 60605 312-663-2222 663-2232
Web: www.chicagostockex.com

Chicago Symphony Orchestra
220 S Michigan Ave . . . . . Chicago IL 60604 312-294-3000 294-3035
Web: www.chicagosymphony.org ■ *E-mail:* info@chicagosymphony.org

Chicago Zoological Park 3300 S Golf Rd. . . . . Brookfield IL 60513 708-485-0263 485-3532
Web: www.brookfield-zoo.mus.il.us

Chinatown
2169B S China Pl Chinatown Square. . . . . Chicago IL 60616 312-326-5320 326-5668

Civic Opera House 20 N Wacker Dr . . . . . Chicago IL 60606 312-332-2244 332-8120

Phone *Fax*

Clarke House Museum
18th St & S Indiana Ave . . . . . Chicago IL 60616 312-745-0040 745-0077

Crown Henry Space Center OMNIMAX Theater
57th St & Lake Shore Dr. . . . . Chicago IL 60637 773-684-1414
Web: www.msichicago.org ■ *E-mail:* omnimax@msichicago.org

DisneyQuest 10 W Ohio. . . . . Chicago IL 60610 312-222-1300

Dusable Museum of African American History
740 E 56th Pl. . . . . Chicago IL 60637 773-947-0600 947-0677
Web: www.dusablemuseum.org

Field Museum of Natural History
Roosevelt Rd & Lake Shore Dr. . . . . Chicago IL 60605 312-922-9410 427-7269
Web: www.fmnh.org

Frank Lloyd Wright Home & Studio
931 Chicago Ave. . . . . Oak Park IL 60302 708-848-1976 848-1248
Web: www.wrightplus.org

Garfield Park Conservatory
300 N Central Park Blvd . . . . . Chicago IL 60624 312-746-5100

Glessner House Museum 1800 S Prairie Ave. . . . Chicago IL 60616 312-326-1480 326-1397

Goodman Theatre 200 S Columbus Dr . . . . . Chicago IL 60603 312-443-3800 443-9201

Grant Park Symphony Orchestra
425 E McFetridge Dr. . . . . Chicago IL 60605 312-742-7638 742-7662

Hancock John Center 875 N Michigan Ave. . . . . Chicago IL 60611 312-751-3681
Web: www.hancock-observatory.com

Hancock Observatory 875 N Michigan Ave. . . . . Chicago IL 60611 888-875-8439

Hellenic Museum & Cultural Center
168 N Michigan Ave 4th Fl. . . . . Chicago IL 60601 312-726-1234 726-8539

Hemingway Ernest Museum
200 N Oak Park Ave . . . . . Oak Park IL 60303 708-848-2222

Historic Pullman District
11111 S Forrestville Ave . . . . . Chicago IL 60628 773-785-8181 785-8182

House of Blues 330 N State St. . . . . Chicago IL 60610 312-923-2000 527-3072

Hubbard Street Dance Co
1147 W Jackson Blvd . . . . . Chicago IL 60607 312-850-9744 455-8240

Hull Jane Adams House 800 S Halsted St. . . . . Chicago IL 60607 312-413-5353 413-2092

Irish American Heritage Center
4626 N Knox Ave . . . . . Chicago IL 60630 773-282-7035 282-0380

Jackson Park 6401 S Stony Island Ave . . . . . Chicago IL 60637 312-747-6187

Joffrey Ballet of Chicago
70 E Lake St Suite 1300 . . . . . Chicago IL 60601 312-739-0120 739-0119
Web: www.joffrey.com ■ *E-mail:* information@joffrey.com

John G Shedd Aquarium
1200 S Lake Shore Dr. . . . . Chicago IL 60605 312-939-2426 939-8069
Web: www.sheddnet.org

Lifeline Theatre 6912 N Glenwood Ave . . . . . Chicago IL 60626 773-761-1772 761-4582
Web: www.theatrechicago.com/lifeline

Lincoln Park Conservatory
2400 N Stockton Dr . . . . . Chicago IL 60614 312-742-7736 742-5619

Lincoln Park Zoo 2001 N Clark St. . . . . Chicago IL 60614 312-742-2000 742-2137
Web: www.lpzoo.com

Loews Cineplex IMAX Theatre
600 E Grand Ave Navy Pier . . . . . Chicago IL 60611 312-595-0090 595-9212
Web: www.cineplexodeon.com

Loop The Downtown District State St . . . . . Chicago IL 60602

Lyric Opera of Chicago
20 N Wacker Dr Civic Opera House
Suite 860. . . . . Chicago IL 60606 312-332-2244 419-1459

Marriott's Lincolnshire Theatre
10 Marriott Dr . . . . . Lincolnshire IL 60069 847-634-0200 634-7022
Web: marriotthotels.com/CHILN

Mayfair Theatre 636 S Michigan Ave. . . . . Chicago IL 60605 312-786-9120 786-9174

Mexican Fine Arts Center Museum
1852 W 19th St . . . . . Chicago IL 60608 312-738-1503 738-9740
Web: www.mfacmchicago.org ■ *E-mail:* coronel@mfacmchicago.org

Mordine & Co Dance Theatre
4730 N Sheridan Rd . . . . . Chicago IL 60640 773-989-3310 344-8036*
**Fax Area Code:* 312

Morton Arboretum 4100 Illinois Rt 53 . . . . . Lisle IL 60532 630-968-0074 719-2463
Web: www.mortonarb.org ■ *E-mail:* trees@mortonarb.org

Museum of Broadcast Communications
78 E Washington Ave Chicago Cultural Ctr. . . . Chicago IL 60602 312-629-6000 629-6009
Web: www.mbcnet.org

Museum of Contemporary Art
220 E Chicago Ave . . . . . Chicago IL 60611 312-280-2660 397-4095
Web: www.mcachicago.org

Museum of Contemporary Photography
600 S Michigan Ave Columbia College. . . . . Chicago IL 60605 312-663-5554 360-1656

Museum of Holography
1134 W Washington Blvd. . . . . Chicago IL 60607 312-226-1007
Web: www.museumofholography.com ■ *E-mail:* hologram@flash.net

Museum of Science & Industry
5700 S Lake Shore Dr. . . . . Chicago IL 60637 773-684-1414 684-7141
TF: 800-468-6674 ■ *Web:* www.msichicago.org
■ *E-mail:* msi@msichicago.org

Museum of the Chicago Academy of Sciences
2430 N Cannon Dr . . . . . Chicago IL 60614 773-549-0606 755-5199
Web: www.chias.org ■ *E-mail:* cas@chias.org

Chicago — Attractions (Cont'd)

				Phone	Fax
Music of the Baroque Chorus & Orchestra 100 N LaSalle St Suite 1610	Chicago	IL	60602	312-551-1415	551-1444
National Vietnam Veterans Art Museum 1801 S Indiana Ave	Chicago	IL	60616	312-326-0270	
Navy Pier 600 E Grand Ave	Chicago	IL	60611	312-595-7437	
Web: www.navypier.com ■ *E-mail:* npgeninfo@mpea.com					
North Lakeside Cultural Center 6219 N Sheridan Rd	Chicago	IL	60660	773-743-4477	
North Pier 401 E Illinois St	Chicago	IL	60611	312-836-4300	836-4329
Old Saint Patrick's Church 700 W Adams St	Chicago	IL	60661	312-648-1021	648-9025
Old Town Wells St.	Chicago	IL	60614		
Old Town School of Folk Music 4544 N Lincoln Ave.	Chicago	IL	60625	773-728-6000	728-6999
Orchestra Hall 220 S Michigan Ave.	Chicago	IL	60604	312-294-3333	294-3329
TF: 800-223-7114					
Oriental Institute Museum 1155 E 58th St University of Chicago	Chicago	IL	60637	773-702-9521	702-9853
Web: www-oi.uchicago.edu					
Osaka Garden 5900 S Lake Shore Dr	Chicago	IL	60637	312-747-2474	
Paramount Arts Centre 8 E Galena Blvd Suite 230	Aurora	IL	60506	630-896-7676	892-1084
Web: www.paramountarts.com					
Peace Museum 314 W Institute Pl	Chicago	IL	60610	312-440-1860	440-1267
Web: www.peacemuseum.org					
Performing Arts Chicago 410 S Michigan Ave Suite 911	Chicago	IL	60605	312-663-1628	663-1043
Web: www.pachicago.org					
Polish Museum of America 984 N Milwaukee Ave	Chicago	IL	60622	773-384-3352	384-3799
TF: 800-772-8632					
Porter Pullman Museum Gallery 10406 S Maryland Ave	Chicago	IL	60628	773-928-3935	
Pullman Historic District/Hotel Florence Museum 11111 S Forrestville Ave.	Chicago	IL	60628	773-785-8181	785-8182
Web: www.pullmanil.org					
Rosehill Cemetery 5800 N Ravenswood Ave	Chicago	IL	60660	773-561-5940	
Royal George Theatre Center 1641 N Halsted St.	Chicago	IL	60614	312-944-5626	944-5627
Sears Tower 233 S Wacker Dr	Chicago	IL	60684	312-875-9696	
Second City Chicago 1608 N Wells St.	Chicago	IL	60614	312-337-3992	664-9837
Web: www.secondcity.com ■ *E-mail:* bmk1616@aol.com					
Shattered Globe Theatre 2856 N Halsted St.	Chicago	IL	60608	773-404-1237	
Six Flags Great America 542 N Rt 21	Gurnee	IL	60031	847-249-2133	249-2390
South Shore Cultural Center 7059 S Shore Dr.	Chicago	IL	60649	312-747-2536	747-6666
Spertus Museum 618 S Michigan Ave.	Chicago	IL	60605	312-922-9012	922-3934
Web: www.spertus.edu/Museum.html					
Steppenwolf Theatre 1650 N Halsted St	Chicago	IL	60614	312-335-1650	335-0440
Swedish American Museum 5211 N Clark St.	Chicago	IL	60640	773-728-8111	728-8870
Web: www.samac.org					
Terra Museum of American Art 664 N Michigan Ave	Chicago	IL	60611	312-664-3939	664-2052
Ukranian National Museum 721 N Oakley St	Chicago	IL	60612	312-421-8020	
Water Tower Place 835-845 N Michigan Ave	Chicago	IL	60611	312-440-3165	

SPORTS TEAMS & FACILITIES

				Phone	Fax
Arlington International Racecourse Euclid & Wilke Rd.	Arlington Heights	IL	60006	847-255-4300	255-4331
Web: www.arlington-intl.com					
Chicago Bears Soldier Field	Chicago	IL	60616	847-615-2327	
Web: www.nfl.com/bears/					
Chicago Blackhawks 1901 W Madison St United Ctr.	Chicago	IL	60612	312-455-7000	455-7041*
**Fax:* PR ■ *Web:* www.chicagoblackhawks.com					
Chicago Bluesmen (roller hockey) 1996 S Kirk Rd Fox Valley Ice Arena	Geneva	IL	60134	630-262-8881	262-9025
Web: www.chicagobluesmen.com ■ *E-mail:* chicagobluesmen@earthlink.net					
Chicago Bulls 1901 W Madison St United Ctr	Chicago	IL	60612	312-455-4000	455-4198*
**Fax:* PR ■ *Web:* www.nba.com/bulls					
Chicago Cubs 1060 W Addison St Wrigley Field	Chicago	IL	60613	773-404-2827	
Web: www.cubs.com ■ *E-mail:* comments@mail.cubs.com					
Chicago Fire (soccer) 311 W Superior St Suite 444	Chicago	IL	60610	312-705-7200	705-7393
TF: 888-657-3473 ■ *Web:* www.chicago-fire.com					
Chicago Freeze (hockey) PO Box 1000	Batavia	IL	60510	630-262-0010	262-9025
Web: www.chicagofreeze.com ■ *E-mail:* chgofreeze@aol.com					
Chicago Sockers (soccer) 2121 S Goebbert Chicago Stingers Stadium	Arlington Heights	IL	60005	847-670-5425	670-5427
Chicago Stingers (soccer) 545 Consumers Ave	Palatine	IL	60067	847-394-9860	394-9942
Web: www.chicagosoccer.com ■ *E-mail:* stingers@chicagosoccer.com					
Chicago White Sox 333 W 35th St Comiskey Park	Chicago	IL	60616	312-674-1000	674-5140*
**Fax:* Sales ■ *Web:* www.chisox.com					
Chicago Wolves (hockey) 6920 N Manheim Rd Rosemont Horizon	Rosemont	IL	60018	847-390-0404	
Comiskey Park 333 W 35th St	Chicago	IL	60616	312-674-1000	674-5103
Web: www.chisox.com/comiskey/comiskey-main.asp					
Hawthorne Race Course 3501 S Laramie Ave	Cicero	IL	60804	708-780-3700	780-3677
TF: 800-780-0701 ■ *Web:* www.hawthorneracecourse.com					
Soldier Field 425 E McFetridge Dr	Chicago	IL	60605	312-747-1285	747-6694
Sportsman's Park Racetrack 3301 S Laramie Ave	Cicero	IL	60804	773-242-1121	652-0015
United Center 1901 W Madison St	Chicago	IL	60612	312-455-4500	455-4511
Web: www.unitedcenter.com					
Wrigley Field 1060 W Addison St.	Chicago	IL	60613	773-404-2827	404-4129

— Events —

	Phone
Belmont Street Fair (early June)	773-868-3010
Berghoff Oktoberfest (mid-September)	312-427-3170
Celebrate on State Street (mid-June)	312-782-9160
Celtic Fest (mid-September)	312-744-3315
Chicago Air & Water Show (late August)	312-744-3370
Chicago Auto Show (mid-February)	312-744-3315
Chicago Blues Festival (early June)	312-744-3370
Chicago Country Music Festival (late June)	312-744-3315
Chicago Earth Day (April 22)	773-549-0606
Chicago Flower & Garden Show (mid-March)	312-321-0077
Chicago Gospel Festival (mid-June)	312-744-3315
Chicago International Film Festival (mid-October)	312-425-9400
Chicago Jazz Festival (early September)	312-744-3370
Chicago Park District Spring Flower Show (late March-early May)	312-742-7737
Chicago Underground Film Festival (mid-August)	773-327-3456
Chinese New Year Parade (late February)	312-225-0303
Fiesta de Hemingway (mid-July)	708-848-2222
Gold Coast Art Fair (early August)	312-787-2677
Grant Park Music Festival (mid-June-mid-August)	312-742-7638
LaSalle Banks Chicago Marathon (mid-October)	312-243-0003
Latin Music Festival (late August)	312-744-3370
Magnificent Mile Lights Festival (mid-November)	312-642-3570
Maple Syrup Festival (late March)	847-824-8360
Medinah Shrine Circus (late February-mid-March)	312-266-5050
National Sporting Goods Assn World Sports Expo (early-mid-July)	847-439-4000
Old Town Art Fair (mid-June)	312-337-1938
Oz Festival (late July-early August)	312-744-3315
Printers Row Book Fair (early June)	312-987-1980
Saint Patrick's Day Celebration & Fireworks (mid-March)	312-942-9188
SOFA-Sculpture Objects & Fundamental Art (early November)	312-654-0870
South Side Irish Saint Patrick's Day Parade (mid-March)	773-239-7755
Taste of Chicago (late June-early July)	312-744-3370
Taste of Lincoln Avenue (late July)	773-975-1022
Taste of Polonia Festival (early September)	773-777-8898
Venetian Night (late July)	312-744-3315
Wells Street Art Festival (mid-June)	312-951-6106
WinterBreak (February)	312-744-3315

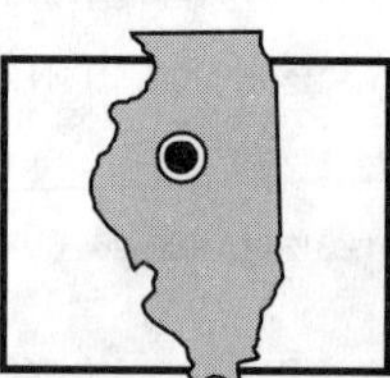

Peoria

Founded in 1819 and incorporated as a city in 1845, Peoria was the first European settlement in Illinois and one of the earliest in middle America. Native Americans called the river valley now known as Peoria Lake "Pimiteoui," which means 'the land of great abundance' or 'fat lake.' A marker commemorating the lake and overlooking the river valley is located on Grandview Drive (which is famous in itself for Teddy Roosevelt's reference to the road as "the world's most beautiful drive'). Visitors to Peoria are invited to attend the annual Return to Pimiteoui Intertribal Pow Wow, which is held each June to celebrate traditional ceremonies, dances, ethnic foods, and crafts. Other area attractions include the John C. Flannagan house, an American Federalist style building built in 1837 that is thought to be the oldest standing home in Peoria; and the Wildlife Prairie Park, a 2,000-acre park home to animals that roamed the prairies before Illinois was settled.

Peoria (Cont'd)

Population	111,148	**Longitude**	89-36-66 W
Area (Land)	40.9 sq mi	**County**	Peoria
Area (Water)	2.2 sq mi	**Time Zone**	CST
Elevation	650 ft	**Area Code/s**	309
Latitude	40-44-41 N		

— Average Temperatures and Precipitation —

TEMPERATURES

	Jan	Feb	Mar	Apr	May	Jun	Jul	Aug	Sep	Oct	Nov	Dec
High	30	35	48	62	73	82	86	83	77	65	50	35
Low	13	18	30	41	51	61	65	63	55	43	33	19

PRECIPITATION

	Jan	Feb	Mar	Apr	May	Jun	Jul	Aug	Sep	Oct	Nov	Dec
Inches	1.5	1.4	2.9	3.8	3.7	4.0	4.2	3.1	3.9	2.7	2.7	2.4

— Important Phone Numbers —

	Phone		Phone
AAA	309-693-1066	**Poison Control Center**	800-942-5969
Dental Referral	309-685-5339	**Road Conditions**	800-452-4368
Emergency	911	**Time/Temp**	309-347-6161
Medical Referral	309-691-1050	**Weather**	309-697-8620
Peoria Area Community Events	309-681-0696		

— Information Sources —

				Phone	Fax
Better Business Bureau Serving Central Illinois 3024 W Lake Ave Suite 200 *TF:* 800-500-3780 ■ *Web:* www.peoria.bbb.org ■ *E-mail:* bbb@heart.net	Peoria	IL	61615	309-688-3741	681-7290
Economic Development Council for the Peoria Area Inc 124 SW Adams St Suite 300 *Web:* edc.peoria.il.us ■ *E-mail:* info@edc.peoria.il.us	Peoria	IL	61602	309-676-7500	676-7534
Peoria Area Chamber of Commerce 124 SW Adams St Suite 300 *TF:* 800-676-7500 ■ *Web:* www.peoriachamber.org ■ *E-mail:* chamber@chamber.h-p.org	Peoria	IL	61602	309-676-0755	676-7534
Peoria Area Convention & Visitors Bureau 403 NE Jefferson St *TF:* 800-747-0302 ■ *Web:* www.peoria.org ■ *E-mail:* info@peoria.org	Peoria	IL	61603	309-676-0303	676-8470
Peoria City Hall 419 Fulton St *Web:* www.ci.peoria.il.us	Peoria	IL	61602	309-494-8565	494-8574
Peoria Civic Center 201 SW Jefferson St *Web:* www.peoriaciviccenter.com	Peoria	IL	61602	309-673-8900	673-9223
Peoria County 324 Main St	Peoria	IL	61602	309-672-6059	672-6063
Peoria Economic Development Office 419 Fulton St City Hall Suite 303 *E-mail:* econdev@ci.peoria.il.us	Peoria	IL	61602	309-494-8640	494-8658
Peoria Mayor 419 Fulton St City Hall Rm 207 *E-mail:* mayor@ci.peoria.il.us	Peoria	IL	61602	309-494-8519	494-8559
Peoria Public Library 107 NE Monroe St *Web:* www.peoria.lib.il.us	Peoria	IL	61602	309-672-8835	674-0116

On-Line Resources

Anthill City Guide Peoria	www.anthill.com/city.asp?city=peoria
City Knowledge Peoria	www.cityknowledge.com/il_peoria.htm
Peoria Area Community Events	www.mtco.com/~pace/
Peoria Illinois	www.villageprofile.com/illinois/peoria
Peoria Online	www.peoriaonline.com
Peoria Pages	www.peoriapages.com

— Transportation Services —

AIRPORTS

■ **Greater Peoria Regional Airport (PIA)**

	Phone
5 miles W of downtown (approx 15 minutes) Web: www.flypia.com	309-697-8272

Airport Transportation

	Phone
DeluxeTransportation $12 fare to downtown	309-637-5466
Elite Taxi $9 fare to downtown	309-674-8294
Pearlene Bell Cab $12 fare to downtown	309-674-5956
River City Cab $11 fare to downtown	309-685-2227
Yellow Cab $12 fare to downtown	309-676-0731

Commercial Airlines

	Phone		Phone
AccessAir	877-462-2237	**Northwest Airlink**	800-225-2525
American Eagle	800-433-7300	**TWA**	800-221-2000

Charter Airlines

	Phone
Mt Hawley Air Charter Inc	309-693-1987

CAR RENTALS

	Phone		Phone
Avis	309-673-3081	**Enterprise**	309-673-4100
Budget	309-697-1565	**Hertz**	309-697-0650

LIMO/TAXI

	Phone		Phone
Cassano Limousine Services	309-452-2237	**River City Cab**	309-685-2227
Elite Taxi	309-674-8294	**Yellow Cab**	309-676-0731
Pearlene Bell Cab	309-674-5956	**Yellow-Checker Cab**	309-676-2075
Peoria Cab	309-673-9101		

MASS TRANSIT

	Phone
Greater Peoria Mass Transit District $.75 Base fare	309-676-4040
Greater Peoria Mass Transit Trolley $.50 Base fare	309-676-4040

— Accommodations —

HOTELS, MOTELS, RESORTS

				Phone	Fax
Baymont Inns & Suites 300 E Light Ct *TF:* 800-301-0200	East Peoria	IL	61611	309-694-4959	694-4727
Comfort Suites of Peoria 4021 War Memorial Dr *TF:* 800-228-5150	Peoria	IL	61614	309-688-3800	688-3800
Courtyard by Marriott 4125 N War Memorial Dr *TF:* 800-321-2211	Peoria	IL	61614	309-686-1900	686-1900
Days Inn Peoria 2726 W Lake Ave *TF:* 800-325-2525	Peoria	IL	61615	309-688-7000	688-7049
Fairfield Inn by Marriott 4203 N War Memorial Dr *TF:* 800-228-2800	Peoria	IL	61614	309-686-7600	686-0686
Grandview Hotel 5901 N Prospect Ave	Peoria	IL	61614	309-691-6800	691-6891
Hampton Inn of East Peoria 11 Winners Way *TF:* 800-426-7866	East Peoria	IL	61611	309-694-0711	694-0407
Holiday Inn Brandywine 4400 N Brandywine Dr *TF:* 800-465-4329	Peoria	IL	61614	309-686-8000	682-8237
Holiday Inn City Centre 500 Hamilton Blvd *TF:* 800-474-2501 ■ *Web:* www.holidayinnpeoria.com	Peoria	IL	61602	309-674-2500	674-1205
Hotel Pere Marquette 501 Main St *TF:* 800-447-1676 ■ *Web:* www.hotelperemarquette.com	Peoria	IL	61602	309-637-6500	671-9445
Jumer's Castle Lodge 117 N Western Ave *TF:* 800-285-8637 ■ *Web:* www.jumers.com	Peoria	IL	61604	309-673-8040	673-9782
Mark Twain Hotel Downtown Peoria 225 NE Adams St *TF:* 800-325-6351	Peoria	IL	61602	309-676-3600	636-6259

Peoria — Hotels, Motels, Resorts (Cont'd)

				Phone	Fax
Par-A-Dice Hotel 7 Blackjack Blvd.	East Peoria	IL	61611	309-699-7711	699-9317
TF: 800-727-2342 ■ *Web:* www.par-a-dice.com					
Peoria/Washington Super 8 1884 Washington Rd.	Washington	IL	61571	309-444-8881	444-8881
Red Roof Inn 4031 N War Memorial Dr.	Peoria	IL	61614	309-685-3911	685-3941
TF: 800-843-7663					
Residence Inn By Marriott 4201 N War Memorial Dr.	Peoria	IL	61614	309-681-9000	681-9000
TF: 800-331-3131					
Signature Inn Brandywine 4112 N Brandywine Dr	Peoria	IL	61614	309-685-2556	685-2556
TF: 800-822-5252					
Sleep Inn 4244 Brandywine Dr.	Peoria	IL	61614	309-682-3322	682-3031
Stoney Creek Inn & Conference Center 101 Mariner's Way	East Peoria	IL	61611	309-694-1300	
Super 8 Motel 4025 W War Memorial Dr.	Peoria	IL	61614	309-688-8074	688-8284
TF: 800-800-8000					
Super 8 Motel East Peoria 725 Taylor St	East Peoria	IL	61611	309-698-8889	698-8885
Towne House Motel 1519 N Knoxville Ave.	Peoria	IL	61603	309-688-8646	688-8666
TF: 800-747-5337					

— Restaurants —

				Phone
American Cafe (American) 501 Main St	Peoria	IL	61602	309-637-6500
Avanti's Italian Ristorante (Italian) 1301 W Main St	Peoria	IL	61606	309-674-4923
Carnegie's (Continental) 501 Main St.	Peoria	IL	61602	309-637-6500
Cheddar's Casual Cafe (American) 4027 N War Memorial Dr	Peoria	IL	61614	309-685-7832
Crooked Waters Brewery & Pub (American) 330 SW Water St.	Peoria	IL	61602	309-673-2739
Web: www.crookedwaters.com				
El Ranchera (Mexican) 1615 N Knoxville Ave	Peoria	IL	61603	309-681-1833
Fitzpatrick's North Beach (American) 2229 Poplar Ln	Peoria Heights	IL	61614	309-685-1808
Grill on Fulton (Continental) 456 Fulton St.	Peoria	IL	61602	309-674-6870
Jim's Downtown Steakhouse (Steak/Seafood) 110 SW Jefferson St.	Peoria	IL	61602	309-673-5300
Jonah's Seafood House (Seafood) 2601 N Main St	East Peoria	IL	61611	309-694-0946
Jumer's Restaurant (Continental) 117 N Western Ave	Peoria	IL	61604	309-673-8040
Lindsey's on Liberty (Continental) 330 Liberty St	Peoria	IL	61602	309-497-3300
Martini's Angus Barn (Steak) 3300 Willow Knolls Rd.	Peoria	IL	61614	309-692-9030
Peking Restaurant (Chinese) 430 W Main St.	Peoria	IL	61606	309-676-0282
Peppertree Restaurant (American) 4400 N Brandywine Dr	Peoria	IL	61614	309-686-8000
River Station (Steak/Seafood) 212 Water St	Peoria	IL	61602	309-676-7100
Senor Serrano's Mexican Bar & Grill (Mexican) 100 NE Water St	Peoria	IL	61602	309-673-7737
Sky Harbor Steakhouse (Steak) 1321 N Park Rd.	Peoria	IL	61604	309-674-5532
Steamers New Orleans Grille (Cajun/Creole) 225 NE Adams St.	Peoria	IL	61602	309-676-4100
Sully's Irish Pub (Irish) 121 SW Adams St.	Peoria	IL	61602	309-674-0238
Vonachen's Old Place (American) 5934 N Knoxville Ave	Peoria	IL	61614	309-692-7033

— Goods and Services —

SHOPPING

				Phone	Fax
Crafter's Marketplace 4125 N Sheridan Rd	Peoria	IL	61614	309-688-1144	688-7388
Duryea Center 4623 N University St	Peoria	IL	61614	309-676-7600	676-8119
Metro Center 4700 N University Ave	Peoria	IL	61614	309-692-6690	692-6692
Web: www.shopmetrocentre.com					
Northwoods Mall 4501 War Memorial Dr.	Peoria	IL	61613	309-688-0443	688-9726
Washington Specialty Shops 123 Washington Sq.	Washington	IL	61571	309-444-7355	444-2146

BANKS

				Phone	Fax
Associated Bank 125 NE Jefferson St	Peoria	IL	61602	309-671-1700	671-1787
Bank One 124 SW Adams St	Peoria	IL	61602	309-672-6123	672-7786
Commerce Bank 416 Main St.	Peoria	IL	61602	309-676-1311	999-3416
National City Bank 301 SW Adams St.	Peoria	IL	61652	309-655-5000	655-5844
South Side Trust & Savings Bank 2119 SW Adams.	Peoria	IL	61602	309-676-0521	
Union Planters Bank 107 SW Jefferson	Peoria	IL	61602	309-655-7500	

BUSINESS SERVICES

	Phone
Adecco Employment Services	309-692-4300
Airborne Express	800-247-2676
Alphagraphics	309-689-1874
Central Illinois Courier	309-697-5152
DHL Worldwide Express	800-225-5345
Express Personnel Services	309-682-2888
Federal Express	800-463-3339
Horizon Printing Co	309-699-4287
Kelly Services	309-692-7562
Kinko's	309-637-6140
Kwik Copy Printing	309-688-2155
Manpower Temporary Services	309-674-4163
Pip Mail Services	309-689-6856
Post Office	309-671-8800
Tandem Staffing	309-637-8130
UPS	800-742-5877

— Media —

PUBLICATIONS

				Phone	Fax
Observer The‡ 1616 W Pioneer Pkwy	Peoria	IL	60615	309-692-4910	692-6447
Peoria Journal Star‡ 1 News Plaza	Peoria	IL	61643	309-686-3000	686-3296
TF: 800-225-5757 ■ *Web:* pjstar.com					

‡Daily newspapers

TELEVISION

				Phone	Fax
WEEK-TV Ch 25 (NBC) 2907 Springfield Rd	East Peoria	IL	61611	309-698-2525	698-9335
Web: www.week.com ■ *E-mail:* xxweek@heartland.bradley.edu					
WHOI-TV Ch 19 (ABC) 500 N Stewart St	Creve Coeur	IL	61611	309-698-1919	698-0008
Web: www.hoinews.com ■ *E-mail:* whoitv@aol.com					
WMBD-TV Ch 31 (CBS) 3131 N University St.	Peoria	IL	61604	309-688-3131	686-8650
Web: www.wmbd.com ■ *E-mail:* wmbdtv@wmbd.com					
WTVP-TV Ch 47 (PBS) 1501 W Bradley Ave.	Peoria	IL	61625	309-677-4747	677-3518
Web: www.wtvp.com					
WYZZ-TV Ch 43 (FOX) 2714 E Lincoln St	Bloomington	IL	61704	309-662-4373	663-6943

RADIO

				Phone	Fax
WBGE-FM 92.3 MHz (Urban) 4234 N Brandywine Dr Suite D.	Peoria	IL	61614	309-686-0101	686-0111
Web: www.b92.com					
WBNQ-FM 101.5 MHz (CHR) 236 Greenwood Ave	Bloomington	IL	61704	309-829-1221	827-8071
Web: www.wbnq.com					
WBWN-FM 104.1 MHz (Ctry) 236 Greenwood Ave	Bloomington	IL	61704	309-829-1221	827-8071
WFXF-FM 94.3 MHz (AC) 3641 Meadowbrook Rd	Peoria	IL	61604	309-685-1111	685-1049
WJBC-AM 1230 kHz (N/T) 236 Greenwood Ave	Bloomington	IL	61704	309-829-1221	827-8071
Web: www.wjbc.com ■ *E-mail:* wjbc@wjbc.com					
WJPL-FM 96.5 MHz (NAC) 4234 N Brandywine Dr Suite D.	Peoria	IL	61614	309-686-0101	686-0111
Web: www.smoothjazz965.com ■ *E-mail:* studio@smoothjazz965.com					
WKSO-FM 94.3 MHz (AC) 3641 Meadowbrook Rd	Peoria	IL	61604	309-685-1111	685-7150
Web: www.kiss94.com					
WMBD-AM 1470 kHz (N/T) 3131 N University St.	Peopria	IL	61604	309-688-3131	686-8655
Web: www.wmbdradio.com					
WPBG-FM 93.3 MHz (Oldies) 3131 N University St.	Peoria	IL	61604	309-688-3131	686-8655
WTAZ-FM 102.3 MHz (N/T) 3641 Meadowbrook Rd	Peoria	IL	61604	309-685-1111	685-7150
WXCL-FM 104.9 MHz (Ctry) 3641 Meadowbrook Rd	Peoria	IL	61604	309-685-1111	685-7150
Web: www.wxcl.com					

— Colleges/Universities —

				Phone	Fax
Bradley University 1501 W Bradley Ave.	Peoria	IL	61625	309-676-7611	677-2797
TF: 800-677-3501 ■ *Web:* www.bradley.edu					
Illinois Central College 1 College Dr.	East Peoria	IL	61635	309-694-5011	694-8461
Web: www.icc.cc.il.us					
Midstate College 411 W Northmoor Rd.	Peoria	IL	61614	309-692-4092	692-3893
TF: 800-251-4299 ■ *Web:* www.midstate.edu					

Peoria (Cont'd)

— Hospitals —

				Phone	Fax
Children's Hospital of Illinois 530 NE Glen Oak Ave OSF Saint Francis Medical Ctr. *Web:* www.osfsaintfrancis.org/child.htm	Peoria	IL	61637	309-655-2000	
Methodist Medical Center of Illinois 221 NE Glen Oak Ave **Fax:* Admitting ■ *Web:* www.mmci.org ■ *E-mail:* marketing@mmci.org	Peoria	IL	61636	309-672-5522	672-4228*
OSF Saint Francis Medical Center 530 NE Glen Oak Ave **Fax:* Admitting ■ *TF:* 888-627-5673 ■ *Web:* www.osfsaintfrancis.org	Peoria	IL	61637	309-655-2000	655-2950*

— Attractions —

				Phone	Fax
African American Museum Hall Of Fame 309 Du Sable St	Peoria	IL	61605	309-673-2206	
Apollo Fine Arts & Entertainment Centre 311 Main St	Peoria	IL	61602	309-673-4343	673-2387
Artistic Community Theatre 3500 Court St	Pekin	IL	61554	309-346-9203	
Ballance-Herschel House 256 NE Randolph Ave	Peoria	IL	61606	309-685-9312	685-4857
Corn Stock Theatre 1700 Park Rd *Web:* www.cornstocktheatre.com ■ *E-mail:* cst@ocs.link.com	Peoria	IL	61604	309-676-2196	676-9036
Dickson Mounds State Museum 10956 N Dickson Mounds Rd *Web:* www.museum.state.il.us/ismsites/dickson/	Lewistown	IL	61542	309-547-3721	547-3189
Dragonland Water Park Mineral Springs Pk	Pekin	IL	61554	309-347-4000	
Eastlight Theatre 1401 E Washington	East Peoria	IL	61611	309-699-7469	
Flanagan John C House 942 NE Glen Oak Ave	Peoria	IL	61603	309-674-1921	
Forest Park Nature Center 5809 Forest Park Dr	Peoria Heights	IL	61614	309-686-3360	686-8820
Glen Oak Zoo 2218 N Prospect Rd *Web:* hometown.aol.com/gozookeep/	Peoria	IL	61603	309-686-3365	685-6240
Haberdasher's Dinner Playhouse 619-B SW Water St	Peoria	IL	61602	309-676-9552	676-9545
Illinois American Historical Water Museum 100 Lorentz St	Peoria	IL	61614	309-671-3701	671-3701
Jubilee College State Historic Site 11817 Jubilee College Rd	Brimfield	IL	61517	309-243-9489	
Lakeview Museum of Arts & Sciences 1125 W Lake Ave *Web:* www.cyberdesic.com/lakeview	Peoria	IL	61614	309-686-7000	686-0280
Luthy George L Memorial Botanical Gardens 2218 N Prospect Rd	Peoria	IL	61603	309-686-3362	685-6240
McGlothlin Farm Park Museum & Petting Zoo 305 Neuman Dr	East Peoria	IL	61611	309-699-3923	699-3419
Opera Illinois 331 Fulton St Suite 309	Peoria	IL	61602	309-673-7253	673-7211
Owens Recreation Center 1019 W Lake St	Peoria	IL	61614	309-686-3369	681-0610
Par-A-Dice Riverboat Casino 21 Blackjack Blvd *Web:* www.par-a-dice.com	East Peoria	IL	61611	309-698-7711	698-7705
Peoria Area Civic Chorale 6720 N Upper Skyline Dr *Web:* www.peoriacivicchorale.org	Peoria	IL	61614	309-693-6725	693-6725
Peoria Art Guild 203 Harrison St	Peoria	IL	61602	309-637-2787	637-7334
Peoria Ballet 416 Hamilton Blvd *Web:* www.peoriaballet.com ■ *E-mail:* peoriaballet@juno.com	Peoria	IL	61602	309-673-3680	672-2031
Peoria Players Theatre 4300 N University Dr	Peoria	IL	61614	309-688-4473	688-4483
Peoria Symphony Orchestra 203 Harrison St *Web:* www.peoriasymphony.org	Peoria	IL	61602	309-637-2787	637-7388
Pettengill Morron House 1212 W Moss Ave	Peoria	IL	61606	309-674-4745	
River Trail of Illinois 201 Veterans Dr	East Peoria	IL	61611	309-699-3923	
Riverfront The 200 NE Water St	Peoria	IL	61602	309-689-3019	
Ronald Reagan Museum 300 E College Ave	Eureka	IL	61530	309-467-6407	467-6437
Saint Martin de Porres Historic Landmark 103 S Sheridan Rd	Peoria	IL	61605	309-676-0726	676-4090
Saint Mary's Cathedral 607 NE Madison	Peoria	IL	61603	309-671-1568	671-5079
Spirit of Peoria Sternwheeler 100 NE Water St	Peoria	IL	61602	309-699-7232	676-3667
Splashdown at Eastside 1 Eastside Dr	East Peoria	IL	61611	309-694-1867	694-1973
Tanners Orchard 740 SR 40	Speer	IL	61479	309-493-5442	
Wheels O'Time Museum 11923 N Knoxville Ave	Peoria	IL	61612	309-243-9020	
Wildlife Prairie Park 3826 N Taylor Rd *Web:* www.wildlifepark.org	Peoria	IL	61615	309-676-0998	676-7783

SPORTS TEAMS & FACILITIES

				Phone	Fax
Peoria Chiefs (baseball) 1524 W Nebraska Ave Pete Vonachen Stadium *Web:* www.chiefsnet.com	Peoria	IL	61604	309-688-1622	686-4516
Peoria Civic Center Arena 201 SW Jefferson St *Web:* www.peoriaciviccenter.com	Peoria	IL	61602	309-673-8900	673-9223
Peoria Pirates (football) 331 Fulton St Suite 405	Peoria	IL	61602	309-637-7777	637-7778
Peoria Rivermen (hockey) 201 SW Jefferson St Peoria Civic Center Arena *Web:* www.rivermen.net	Peoria	IL	61602	309-676-1040	676-2488
Peoria Speedway 3520 W Farmington Rd	Peoria	IL	61604	309-673-3342	673-3332

— Events —

	Phone
Antique Car Show (late July)	309-927-3345
Central Illinois Black Expo (mid-September)	309-673-8900
Chillifest & Corn Boil (early August)	309-274-4556
East Peoria Festival Of Lights (late November-late December)	800-365-3743
Fall Family Riverfest (late October)	309-685-9312
Gospel Jubilee (late October)	309-681-0696
Greater Peoria Farm Show (late November-early December)	309-673-8900
Greater Peoria Open (late September)	309-673-7161
Hall-zoo-een (late October)	309-681-0696
Home Living Show (late September)	309-673-8900
Italian American Summer Fiesta (mid-August)	309-681-8665
Julep's Closet (early November)	309-685-9312
Metro Centre Fine Arts Fair (mid-June)	309-692-6690
Mid-America Waterfowl Expo (early October)	309-673-8900
Pekin Marigold Festival (early September)	309-346-2106
Peoria Jaycees Annual Haunted House (mid-late October)	309-676-5292
Rib Fest (mid-July)	309-681-0696
Santa Parade (late November)	309-681-0696
Steamboat Festival (mid-June)	309-681-0696
Taste of Peoria (mid-August)	309-681-0696
Tremont Turkey Festival (mid-June)	309-925-4331
Yule Like Peoria (late November)	309-681-0696

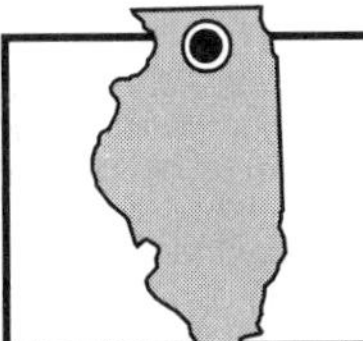

Rockford

Rockford is home to three attractions listed on the National Register of Historic Places: the Graham Ginestra House, built in 1957, which showcases restored murals and a six-foot stained glass window; the Stephen Mack Home and Whitman Trading Post, home of the first settler in Winnebago County; and, set on a limestone bluff overlooking Kent Creek, the Tinker Swiss Cottage Museum, which was home to Robert H. Tinker, Rockford industrialist and co-creator of the city's park system. Rockford also has shopping in a historical setting at Victorian Village, an area of homes and businesses restored and developed by private citizens. In addition, Rockford's East State Street Antique Malls are the largest antiques malls in the Midwest.

Population	143,656	**Longitude**	89-09-39 W
Area (Land)	45.0 sq mi	**County**	Winnebago
Area (Water)	0.6 sq mi	**Time Zone**	CST
Elevation	721 ft	**Area Code/s**	815
Latitude	42-27-11 N		

Rockford (Cont'd)

— Average Temperatures and Precipitation —

TEMPERATURES

	Jan	Feb	Mar	Apr	May	Jun	Jul	Aug	Sep	Oct	Nov	Dec
High	27	32	44	58	71	80	84	81	74	62	46	32
Low	10	14	26	37	47	57	63	60	52	41	30	16

PRECIPITATION

	Jan	Feb	Mar	Apr	May	Jun	Jul	Aug	Sep	Oct	Nov	Dec
Inches	1.3	1.1	2.5	3.7	3.7	4.5	4.1	4.2	3.8	2.9	2.6	2.1

— Important Phone Numbers —

	Phone
AAA	815-229-5363
Dental Referral	815-399-1797
Emergency	911
Medical Referral	815-971-3737
Poison Control Center	800-942-5969
Time/Temp	815-968-2311
Weather	815-963-5913

— Information Sources —

				Phone	Fax
Rockford Area Chamber of Commerce 515 N Court St. Web: www.rockfordchamber.com ■ E-mail: cservice@rockfordchamber.com	Rockford	IL	61103	815-987-8100	987-8122
Rockford Area Convention & Visitors Bureau 211 N Main St. TF: 800-521-0849 ■ Web: www.gorockford.com ■ E-mail: rcfdcvb@wwa.com	Rockford	IL	61101	815-963-8111	963-4298
Rockford City Hall 425 E State St. Web: www.ci.rockford.il.us/	Rockford	IL	61104	815-987-5500	967-6952
Rockford Community Development Dept 425 E State St Web: www.ci.rockford.il.us/CD/CD.htm	Rockford	IL	61104	815-987-5600	967-6933
Rockford Mayor 425 E State St. Web: www.ci.rockford.il.us/Mayor/Mayor.htm	Rockford	IL	61104	815-987-5590	967-6952
Rockford Public Library 215 N Wyman St	Rockford	IL	61101	815-965-6731	965-6739
Winnebago County 404 Elm St.	Rockford	IL	61101	815-987-3050	969-0259

On-Line Resources

Anthill City Guide Rockford	www.anthill.com/city.asp?city=rockford
Area Guide Rockford	rockford.areaguides.net
ComPortOne of Rockford	www.comportone.com
Excite.com Rockford City Guide	www.excite.com/travel/countries/united_states/illinois/rockford
Rockford Area Launch Pad	www.rockford.il.us/LaunchPad/
Sinnissippi Valley Information Network	sinnfree.org

— Transportation Services —

AIRPORTS

■ **Greater Rockford Airport (RFD)**

	Phone
5 miles S of downtown (approx 15 minutes)	815-965-8639

Web: www.rockfordairport.com ■ *E-mail:* rfd@rockfordairport.com

Airport Transportation

	Phone
On Time Taxi $7-9 fare to downtown	815-962-5511

Commercial Airlines

	Phone
American Eagle	800-433-7300
Midwest Express	800-452-2022
Northwest	800-225-2525

Charter Airlines

	Phone
Alpine Aviation	815-962-8504

CAR RENTALS

	Phone
Avis	815-962-8447
Budget	815-963-0441
Hertz	815-963-5318
National	815-965-4466

LIMO/TAXI

	Phone
Black Cadillac	815-547-4328
D & E Limousine	815-946-3933
Easy Rider Limousine	815-968-5995
On Time Taxi	815-962-5511
Park Avenue Limousine	815-229-5466
Spee-Dee Taxi	815-963-3322

MASS TRANSIT

	Phone
Rockford Mass Transit $1 Base fare	815-961-9000

RAIL/BUS

				Phone
Greyhound/Trailways Bus Station 542 N Lyford Rd	Rockford	IL	61107	815-964-8671

— Accommodations —

HOTELS, MOTELS, RESORTS

				Phone	Fax
Airport Inn 4419 S 11th St.	Rockford	IL	61109	815-397-4000	397-4821
Baymont Inns & Suites 662 N Lyford Rd. TF: 800-301-0200	Rockford	IL	61107	815-229-8200	229-8220
Best Western Clock Tower Resort & Conference Center 7801 E State St. TF: 800-358-7666	Rockford	IL	61108	815-398-6000	398-0443
Best Western Colonial Inn 4850 E State St TF: 800-528-1234	Rockford	IL	61108	815-398-5050	
Candlewood Hotel 7555 Walton St TF: 888-226-3539	Rockford	IL	61108	815-229-9300	229-9323
Comfort Inn 7392 Argus Dr TF: 800-228-5150	Rockford	IL	61107	815-398-7061	398-7061
Courtyard by Marriott 7676 E State St. TF: 800-321-2211 ■ Web: courtyard.com/RFDCH	Rockford	IL	61108	815-397-6222	397-6254
Eagle Ridge Inn & Resort 444 Eagle Ridge Dr. TF: 800-892-2269 ■ Web: www.eagleridge.com	Galena	IL	61036	815-777-2444	777-4502
Edgewater Resort 10 E Riverside Blvd.	Loves Park	IL	61111	815-877-1122	633-7983
Exel Inn 220 S Lyford Rd. TF: 800-367-3935	Rockford	IL	61108	815-332-4915	332-4843
Fairfield Inn by Marriott 7712 Potawatomi Trail TF: 800-228-2800 ■ Web: fairfieldinn.com/RFDFI	Rockford	IL	61107	815-397-8000	397-8183
Gold Star Motel 7885 W State St	Rockford	IL	61102	815-968-0631	968-0631
Hampton Inn 615 Clark Dr TF: 800-426-7866	Rockford	IL	61107	815-229-0404	229-0175
Holiday Inn Rockford 7550 E State St TF: 800-383-7829 ■ Web: www.basshotels.com/holiday-inn/?_franchisee=RFDIL	Rockford	IL	61108	815-398-2200	229-3122
Howard Johnson 3909 11th St TF: 800-446-4656	Rockford	IL	61109	815-397-9000	397-4669
Lafayette Hotel 411 Mulberry St.	Rockford	IL	61101	815-964-5651	
Paramount Motel 733 E State St.	Rockford	IL	61104	815-961-9345	961-9300
Ramada Suites 200 S Bell School Rd TF: 800-272-6232	Rockford	IL	61108	815-226-2100	229-3070
Red Roof Inn 7434 E State St. TF: 800-843-7663	Rockford	IL	61108	815-398-9750	398-9761
Residence Inn by Marriott 7542 Colosseum Dr. TF: 800-331-3131 ■ Web: www.residenceinn.com/RFDIL	Rockford	IL	61107	815-227-0013	
Six Penny Inn 4205 11th St	Rockford	IL	61109	815-398-0066	
StudioPLUS 747 N Bell School Rd TF: 888-788-3467	Rockford	IL	61107	815-397-8316	397-8373
Super 8 Motel 7646 Colosseum Dr TF: 800-800-8000	Rockford	IL	61107	815-229-5522	229-5547
Sweden House 4605 E State St TF: 800-886-4138	Rockford	IL	61108	815-398-4130	398-9203
Villager Lodge 4404 E State St TF: 800-399-3580	Rockford	IL	61108	815-399-1890	399-1898

— Restaurants —

				Phone
Bellamy's (Continental) 7801 E State St.	Rockford	IL	61108	815-398-6000

Rockford — Restaurants (Cont'd)

	City	State	ZIP	Phone
Box's Bar-B-Q (Barbecue) 815 Marchesano Dr	Rockford	IL	61102	815-962-9629
Cafe Patou (French) 3929 Broadway	Rockford	IL	61108	815-227-4100
Cliffbreakers River Restaurant (American) 700 W Riverside Blvd	Rockford	IL	61103	815-282-3033
El Reboso (Mexican) 2648 11th St	Rockford	IL	61109	815-227-4262
Giordanos (Italian) 333 Executive Pkwy	Rockford	IL	61107	815-398-5700
Giovanni's (American) 610 N Bell School Rd	Rockford	IL	61107	815-398-6411
Great Wall Restaurant (Chinese) 4228 E State St	Rockford	IL	61108	815-226-0982
Hoffman House (Continental) 7550 E State St	Rockford	IL	61108	815-397-5800
Imperial Palace (Chinese) 3415 E State St	Rockford	IL	61108	815-227-1442
J & J Fish (Seafood) 217 7th St	Rockford	IL	61104	815-969-9575
JMK Nippon (Japanese) 2615 N Mulford Rd	Rockford	IL	61114	815-877-0505
Lucerne's Fondue & Spirits (American) 845 N Church St	Rockford	IL	61103	815-968-2665
Mary's Market Bistro (Homestyle) 4431 E State St	Rockford	IL	61108	815-397-6461
Mayflower (Continental) 5040 N 2nd St	Loves Park	IL	61111	815-877-5701
New Mill Restaurant (American) 6030 11th St	Rockford	IL	61109	815-874-5356
Oakview Restaurant (American) 7470 Harrison Ave	Rockford	IL	61112	815-332-4390
Paesano's Italian Restaurant (Italian) 1401 N Main St	Rockford	IL	61103	815-965-5111
Rathskeller The (German) 1132 Auburn St	Rockford	IL	61103	815-963-2922
Riverboat Restaurant (American) 4414 Charles St	Rockford	IL	61108	815-395-0977
Sammy's Restaurant (American) 307 S Main St	Rockford	IL	61101	815-968-2218
Stockholm Inn (Scandinavian) 2420 Charles St	Rockford	IL	61108	815-397-3534
Trattoria Fantini (Italian) 1313 Auburn St	Rockford	IL	61103	815-961-3674
Tumbleweed Mexican Food (Mexican) 5494 E State St	Rockford	IL	61108	815-227-0192
Yen Ching (Chinese) 5555 E State St	Rockford	IL	61108	815-397-5555
Ziltzie's Restaurant (American) 3600 N Main St	Rockford	IL	61103	815-282-0800

— Goods and Services —

SHOPPING

	City	State	ZIP	Phone	Fax
Brynwood Square 2601 N Mulford Rd	Rockford	IL	61104		
CherryVale Mall 7200 Harrison Ave	Rockford	IL	61112	815-332-2451	
Colonial Village Shopping Mall 1100 S Alpine Rd	Rockford	IL	61108	815-398-3350	398-8980
East State Street Antique Malls 5301 & 5411 E State St	Rockford	IL	61108	815-229-4004	
Machesney Park Mall 8750 N 2nd St	Rockford	IL	61115	815-654-9880	965-9564

BANKS

	City	State	ZIP	Phone	Fax
AMCORE Bank NA Rockford 501 7th St	Rockford	IL	61110	815-968-1259	961-7748*
**Fax:* Mktg					
Associated Bank 612 N Main St	Rockford	IL	61103	815-987-3500	987-3536
Bank One Rockford NA 6000 E State St	Rockford	IL	61108	815-962-3771	962-0946
Mercantile Bank 1107 E State St	Rockford	IL	61104	815-987-2200	987-2227
National City Bank 120 W State St	Rockford	IL	61101	815-987-2000	987-2005

BUSINESS SERVICES

	Phone
Airborne Express	800-247-2676
BAX Global	800-225-5229
DHL Worldwide Express	800-225-5345
Federal Express	800-238-5355
Gaffney Services	815-962-4880
Kinko's	815-229-0033
Mail Boxes Etc	800-789-4623
Norrell Temporary Services	815-397-5075
Post Office	815-229-4811
Staff Management Inc	815-282-3900
UPS	800-742-5877

— Media —

PUBLICATIONS

	City	State	ZIP	Phone	Fax
Rockford Register Star‡ 99 E State St	Rockford	IL	61104	815-987-1200	987-1365
TF: 800-383-7827 ■ *Web:* www.rrstar.com ■ *E-mail:* advertising@www.rrstar.com					

‡*Daily newspapers*

TELEVISION

	City	State	ZIP	Phone	Fax
WIFR-TV Ch 23 (CBS) 2523 N Meridian Rd	Rockford	IL	61101	815-987-5300	965-0981
Web: www.wifr.com					
WQRF-TV Ch 39 (Fox) 401 S Main St	Rockford	IL	61101	815-987-3950	964-9974
Web: www.fox39.com					
WREX-TV Ch 13 (NBC) 10322 Auburn Rd	Rockford	IL	61103	815-335-2213	335-2297*
**Fax:* News Rm ■ *Web:* www.wrex.com					
WTTW-TV Ch 11 (PBS) 5400 N St Louis Ave	Chicago	IL	60625	773-583-5000	583-3046
Web: www.wttw.com ■ *E-mail:* viewermail@wttw.com					
WTVO-TV Ch 17 (ABC) 1917 N Meridian Rd	Rockford	IL	61101	815-963-5413	963-6113

RADIO

	City	State	ZIP	Phone	Fax
WGSL-FM 91.1 MHz (Rel) PO Box 2730	Rockford	IL	61132	815-654-1200	282-7779
Web: www.radio91.com ■ *E-mail:* home@radio91.com					
WKMQ-FM 95.3 MHz (Oldies) 2830 Sandy Hollow Rd	Rockford	IL	61109	815-874-7861	874-2202
WLUV-FM 96.7 MHz (Ctry) 2272 Elmwood Rd	Rockford	IL	61103	815-877-9588	877-9649
WNIJ-FM 90.5 MHz (NPR) 801 N 1st St	De Kalb	IL	60115	815-753-9000	753-9938
WNTA-AM 1330 kHz (N/T) 2830 Sandy Hollow Rd	Rockford	IL	61109	815-874-7861	874-2202
E-mail: wnta@aol.com					
WQFL-FM 100.9 MHz (Rel) PO Box 2730	Rockford	IL	61132	815-654-1200	282-7779
Web: www.101qfl.com ■ *E-mail:* positive@101qfl.com					
WROK-AM 1440 kHz (N/T) 3901 Brendenwood Rd	Rockford	IL	61107	815-399-2233	399-8148
Web: www.wrok.com					
WXRX-FM 104.9 MHz (CR) 2830 Sandy Hollow Rd	Rockford	IL	61109	815-874-7861	874-2202
Web: www.wxrx.com					
WXXQ-FM 98.5 MHz (Ctry) 3901 Brendenwood Rd	Rockford	IL	61107	815-399-2233	399-8148
WZOK-FM 97.5 MHz (CHR) 3901 Brendenwood Rd	Rockford	IL	61107	815-399-2233	399-8148

— Colleges/Universities —

	City	State	ZIP	Phone	Fax
Rock Valley College 3301 N Mulford Rd	Rockford	IL	61114	815-654-4250	654-5568
Web: www.rvc.cc.il.us					
Rockford College 5050 E State St	Rockford	IL	61108	815-226-4000	226-4119
TF Admissions: 800-892-2984 ■ *Web:* www.rockford.edu					

— Hospitals —

	City	State	ZIP	Phone	Fax
Rockford Memorial Hospital 2400 N Rockton Ave	Rockford	IL	61103	815-971-5000	968-3812*
**Fax:* Admitting ■ *Web:* www.rhsnet.org					
Saint Anthony Medical Center 5666 E State St	Rockford	IL	61108	815-226-2000	395-5449
TF: 800-343-3185					
SwedishAmerican Hospital 1400 Charles St	Rockford	IL	61104	815-968-4400	966-3981*
**Fax:* Admitting					

— Attractions —

	City	State	ZIP	Phone	Fax
Burpee Museum of Natural History 813 N Main St	Rockford	IL	61103	815-965-3433	965-2703
Discovery Center Museum 711 N Main St	Rockford	IL	61103	815-963-6769	968-0164
Web: www.discoverycentermuseum.org/					
Erlander Home Museum 404 S 3rd St	Rockford	IL	61104	815-963-5559	
Ethnic Heritage Museum 1129 S Main St	Rockford	IL	61101	815-962-7402	962-7402
Forest City Queen 324 N Madison St	Rockford	IL	61107	815-987-8894	
Graham Ginestra House 1115 S Main St	Rockford	IL	61101	815-964-8333	
Harlem Hills Nature Preserve Nimtz Rd & Flora Dr	Loves Park	IL	61111	815-964-6666	
Klehm Arboretum & Botanical Garden 2701 Clifton Ave	Rockford	IL	61102	815-965-8146	965-5914
E-mail: botanical@aol.com					
Mack Stephen Home & Whitman Trading Post 2221 Freeport Rd	Rockton	IL	61072	815-877-6100	
Mendelssohn Club 415 N Church St	Rockford	IL	61103	815-964-9713	964-9929
Midway Village & Museum Center 6799 Guilford Rd	Rockford	IL	61107	815-397-9112	397-9156
New American Theater 118 N Main St	Rockford	IL	61101	815-964-8023	963-7215
Rockford Art Museum 711 N Main St	Rockford	IL	61103	815-968-2787	968-0164
Web: ram-artmuseum.rockford.org					
Rockford College Art Gallery 5050 E State St	Rockford	IL	61108	815-226-4034	

Rockford — Attractions (Cont'd)

				Phone	Fax
Rockford Symphony Orchestra 711 N Main St Riverfront Museum Pk 2nd Fl	Rockford	IL	61103	815-965-0049	
Severson Dells Environmental Education Center 8786 Montague Rd	Rockford	IL	61102	815-335-2915	335-2471
Web: www.seversondells.org ■ *E-mail:* sevdells01@sprynet.com					
Sinnissippi Gardens Greenhouse & Lagoon 1300 N 2nd St	Rockford	IL	61107	815-987-8858	
Tinker Swiss Cottage Museum 411 Kent St	Rockford	IL	61102	815-964-2424	964-2466
Web: www.tinkercottage.com					

SPORTS TEAMS & FACILITIES

				Phone	Fax
Arlington in Rockford 5011 E State St	Rockford	IL	61108	815-398-2300	226-0762
Blackhawk Farms Raceway 15538 Prairie Rd	South Beloit	IL	61080	815-389-3323	
MetroCentre Arena 300 Elm St	Rockford	IL	61105	815-968-5600	968-5451
Web: www.metrocentre.com					
Rockford Dactyls (soccer) 8800 E Riverside Blvd Russell E Wedgbury Soccer Complex	Loves Park	IL	61011	815-885-1135	885-3302
Rockford Lightning (basketball) 300 Elm St MetroCentre	Rockford	IL	61101	815-968-5222	
Rockford Raptors (soccer) 8800 E Riverside Blvd Russell E Wedgbury Soccer Complex	Loves Park	IL	61011	815-885-1135	885-3302
Rockford Speedway 9500 Forest Hills Rd	Rockford	IL	61111	815-633-1500	633-7093
Web: www.rockfordspeedway.com ■ *E-mail:* rkfdspdwy@aol.com					

— Events —

	Phone
Boat Vacation & Fishing Show (late February)	815-877-8043
Civil War Days (late June)	815-397-9112
First Night Rockford (December 31)	815-963-6765
Northern Illinois Farm Show (early January)	815-968-5600
On the Waterfront Festival (early September)	815-963-8111
Rockford Home Show (late February-early March)	815-877-8043
Saint Patrick's Day Celebration (mid-March)	815-624-6694
Splendor & Majesty Christmas Musical (early December)	815-963-8111
Spring Folk Craft & Art Expo (mid-March)	815-968-5600
Winnebago County Fair (mid-August)	815-239-1641
Young at Heart Festival (late May)	815-633-3999

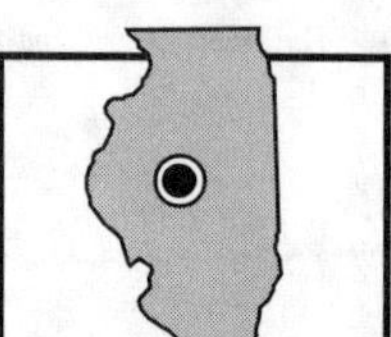

Springfield

With what may be the highest concentration of sites in America devoted to Abraham Lincoln, Springfield, Illinois provides a complete look at the life of the nation's 16th president. The home of the Lincoln family and the Lincoln-Herndon Law Offices are both located in the city. In addition, one can see the Lincoln Tomb and the Lincoln Depot, which even includes his ledger. At the five miles of wooded trails known as Lincoln Memorial Gardens, Maple Syrup Time is a featured event. Twenty miles northwest of Springfield is the reconstructed historic village of New Salem where Lincoln spent six years studying law and working various jobs. The Great American People Show, a group created to "pursue a passion for Lincoln," performs at New Salem, focusing both on Lincoln's life as well as other historical subjects.

Population	117,098	**Longitude**	89-64-36 W
Area (Land)	42.5 sq mi	**County**	Sangamon
Area (Water)	6.3 sq mi	**Time Zone**	CST
Elevation	600 ft	**Area Code/s**	217
Latitude	39-80-17 N		

— Average Temperatures and Precipitation —

TEMPERATURES

	Jan	Feb	Mar	Apr	May	Jun	Jul	Aug	Sep	Oct	Nov	Dec
High	33	37	50	64	75	84	87	84	79	67	52	37
Low	16	20	32	43	52	62	66	63	56	44	34	22

PRECIPITATION

	Jan	Feb	Mar	Apr	May	Jun	Jul	Aug	Sep	Oct	Nov	Dec
Inches	1.5	1.8	3.2	3.7	3.6	3.4	3.5	3.3	3.3	2.6	2.5	2.7

— Important Phone Numbers —

	Phone		Phone
AAA	217-787-0741	**HotelDocs**	800-468-3537
American Express Travel	217-523-2525	**Time/Temp**	217-747-1212
Emergency	911	**Weather**	217-753-3000

— Information Sources —

				Phone	Fax
Better Business Bureau Serving Central Illinois 3024 W Lake Ave Suite 200	Peoria	IL	61615	309-688-3741	681-7290
TF: 800-500-3780 ■ *Web:* www.peoria.bbb.org ■ *E-mail:* bbb@heart.net					
Central Illinois Tourism Development Office 700 E Adams St	Springfield	IL	62701	217-525-7980	525-8004
Lincoln Library 326 S 7th St	Springfield	IL	62701	217-753-4900	753-5329
Web: www.springfield.il.us/city_gov/library/library.htm					
Prairie Capital Convention Center 1 Convention Ctr Plaza	Springfield	IL	62701	217-788-8800	788-0811
Web: www.springfield-pccc.com					
Sangamon County 200 S 9th St	Springfield	IL	62701	217-753-6706	753-6672
Springfield Chamber of Commerce 3 S Old State Capitol Plaza	Springfield	IL	62701	217-525-1173	525-8768
Web: www.gscc.org					
Springfield City Hall 300 S 7th St	Springfield	IL	62701	217-789-2000	
Web: www.springfield.il.us					
Springfield Convention & Visitors Bureau 109 N 7th St	Springfield	IL	62701	217-789-2360	544-8711
TF: 800-545-7300 ■ *Web:* www.springfield.il.us/visit/ ■ *E-mail:* mailbox@springfield.il.us					
Springfield Mayor 800 E Monroe St Suite 300 Municipal Ctr E	Springfield	IL	62701	217-789-2200	789-2109
Web: www.springfield.il.us/mayor/mayor.htm					

On-Line Resources

About.com Guide to Springfield	springfieldil.about.com
Anthill City Guide Springfield	www.anthill.com/city.asp?city=springfield
Area Guide Springfield	springfieldil.areaguides.net
City Knowledge Springfield	www.cityknowledge.com/il_springfield.htm
Online Springfield	www.online-springfield.com
Springfield City Net	www.excite.com/travel/countries/united_states/illinois/springfield
Springfield Concert & Entertainment Web	www.springfieldmusic.com
Springfield-Illinois.com	www.springfield-illinois.com

— Transportation Services —

AIRPORTS

■ **Capital Airport (SPI)**

	Phone
3 miles NW of downtown (approx 10 minutes)	217-788-1063

Airport Transportation

	Phone
A-Diamond Cab $8 fare to downtown	217-788-5828
Airport Cab $7.50 fare to downtown	217-741-3029

Commercial Airlines

	Phone		Phone
American Eagle	800-433-7300	**TWA Express**	800-221-2000
Midway	800-446-4392	**United Express**	800-241-6522

Springfield (Cont'd)

Charter Airlines

Name	Phone	Name	Phone
Capital Aircraft	217-525-6988	**McClelland Aviation**	217-544-9027
Lobo Air Service	217-525-0097		

CAR RENTALS

Name	Phone	Name	Phone
Avis	217-522-7728	**Hertz**	217-525-8820
Budget	217-523-7000		

LIMO/TAXI

Name	Phone	Name	Phone
A-Diamond Cab	217-788-5828	**Mid-State Cab**	217-522-9039
Dan's Cab	217-525-8370	**Yellow Cab**	217-523-4545
Liberty Cab	217-525-1982		

MASS TRANSIT

Name	Phone
Springfield Mass Transit $.75 Base fare	217-522-5531

RAIL/BUS

				Phone
Amtrak Station 3rd & Washington Sts *TF:* 800-872-7245	Springfield	IL	62701	217-753-2013
Greyhound Bus Station 2351 S Dirksen Pkwy *TF:* 800-231-2222	Springfield	IL	62704	217-544-8466

— Accommodations —

HOTELS, MOTELS, RESORTS

Name	City	State	Zip	Phone	Fax
Baymont Inns & Suites 5871 S 6th St. *TF:* 800-301-0200	Springfield	IL	62707	217-529-6655	529-6510
Best Inns of America 500 N 1st St *TF:* 800-237-8466	Springfield	IL	62702	217-522-1100	753-8589
Best Western Lincoln Plaza Hotel 101 E Adams St *TF:* 800-528-1234	Springfield	IL	62701	217-523-5661	523-5675
Budget Inn 3125 Wide Track Dr	Springfield	IL	62703	217-789-9471	789-9010
Capitol Plaza Hotel 5th & Jefferson Sts	Springfield	IL	62701	217-525-1700	525-9037
Comfort Inn 3442 Freedom Dr *TF:* 800-228-5150	Springfield	IL	62704	217-787-2250	
Comfort Suites 2620 Dirksen Pkwy *TF:* 800-228-5150	Springfield	IL	62703	217-753-4000	753-4166
Courtyard by Marriott Springfield 3462 Freedom Dr *TF:* 800-321-2211 ■ *Web:* courtyard.com/SPICY	Springfield	IL	62704	217-793-5300	793-5300
Crowne Plaza Hotel 3000 S Dirksen Pkwy *TF:* 800-589-2769	Springfield	IL	62703	217-529-7777	529-6666
Days Inn 3000 Stevenson Dr *TF:* 800-329-7466	Springfield	IL	62703	217-529-0171	529-9431
Drury Inn 3180 Dirksen Pkwy *TF:* 800-378-7946	Springfield	IL	62703	217-529-3900	529-3900
Fairfield Inn 3446 Freedom Dr *TF:* 800-228-2800 ■ *Web:* fairfieldinn.com/SPIFI	Springfield	IL	62704	217-793-9277	793-9277
Hampton Inn 3185 S Dirksen Pkwy *TF:* 800-426-7866	Springfield	IL	62703	217-529-1100	529-1105
Holiday Inn East 3100 S Dirksen Pkwy *TF:* 800-465-4329	Springfield	IL	62703	217-529-7171	529-5063
Holiday Inn Select Decatur Conference Center 4191 US Rt 36 W *TF:* 800-465-4329 ■ *Web:* www.basshotels.com/holiday-inn/?_franchisee=DECIL ■ *E-mail:* decil@aol.com	Decatur	IL	62522	217-422-8800	422-9155
Mansion View Inn & Suites 529 S 4th St *TF:* 800-252-1083 ■ *Web:* www.mansionview.com ■ *E-mail:* Mansionview@cnsnet.net	Springfield	IL	62701	217-544-7411	544-6211
Motel 6 6010 S 6th Street Rd. *TF:* 800-466-8356	Springfield	IL	62707	217-529-1633	585-1271
Parkview Motel 3121 Clear Lake Ave.	Springfield	IL	62702	217-789-1682	523-3479
Pear Tree Inn 3190 Dirksen Pkwy. *TF:* 800-282-8733	Springfield	IL	62703	217-529-9100	529-9100
Ramada Limited 3281 Northfield Dr *TF:* 800-272-6232	Springfield	IL	62702	217-523-4000	523-4080
Ramada South Plaza 625 E Saint Joseph St *TF:* 800-272-6232	Springfield	IL	62703	217-529-7131	529-7160
Red Roof Inn 3200 Singer Ave *TF:* 800-843-7663	Springfield	IL	62703	217-753-4302	753-4391
Renaissance Hotel 701 E Adams St *TF:* 800-468-3571	Springfield	IL	62701	217-544-8800	544-8079
Signature Inn Springfield 3090 Adlai Stevenson Dr *TF:* 800-822-5252 ■ *Web:* www.signature-inns.com/locations/springfield	Springfield	IL	62703	217-529-6611	529-6611
Sky Harbor Inn 1701 J David Jones Pkwy *TF:* 800-349-4081	Springfield	IL	62702	217-541-8762	541-8774
Sleep Inn 3470 Freedom Dr *TF:* 800-753-3746	Springfield	IL	62704	217-787-6200	787-6200
Springfield Hilton Hotel 700 E Adams St. *TF:* 800-445-8667	Springfield	IL	62701	217-789-1530	789-0709
Super 8 Lodge East 1330 S Dirksen Pkwy *TF:* 800-800-8000	Springfield	IL	62703	217-528-8889	529-4354
Super 8 Lodge South 3675 S 6th St *TF:* 800-800-8000	Springfield	IL	62703	217-529-8898	
Travelodge 3751 S 6th St	Springfield	IL	62703	217-529-5511	529-1541

— Restaurants —

				Phone
20's Hideout Steakhouse (Steak) 2660 S Dirksen Pkwy	Springfield	IL	62703	217-753-0200
Alexander's (Steak) 620 Bruns Ln	Springfield	IL	62702	217-793-0440
Arturo's (Continental) 517 S 4th St *Web:* www.arturosdining.com	Springfield	IL	62701	217-522-5359
Augie's Front Burner (New American) 2 W Old State Capitol Plaza	Springfield	IL	62701	217-544-6979
Black Angus (Steak) 1645 Wabash	Springfield	IL	62704	217-793-9995
Bombay Bicycle Club (American) 2690 S Dirksen Pkwy	Springfield	IL	62703	217-529-8250
Bourbon Street Rhythm & Ribs (Barbecue) 1031 S Grand Ave East	Springfield	Il	62703	217-788-5808
Cafe Brio (International) 524 E Monroe St	Springfield	IL	62701	217-544-0574
Chesapeake Seafood House (Seafood) 3045 Clear Lake Ave	Springfield	IL	62702	217-522-5220
China Gate II (Chinese) 2001 W Washington St	Springfield	IL	62702	217-793-9680
Den Chili Parlor (Mexican) 3419 Freedom Dr	Springfield	IL	62704	217-698-4477
El Rancherito (Mexican) 1825 W Jefferson St	Springfield	IL	62702	217-787-3162
Filia's (Greek) 2501 Wabash Ave	Springfield	IL	62704	217-787-9197
Floreale (American) 701 E Adams St	Springfield	IL	62701	217-544-8800
Gabatoni's Restaurant (Italian) 300 E Laurel St	Springfield	IL	62703	217-528-9629
La Sorella (Italian) 3325 Robbins Rd	Springfield	IL	62704	217-546-1680
Lime Street Cafe (American) 951 S Durkin Dr	Springfield	IL	62704	217-793-1905
Magic Kitchen (Thai) 4112 Peoria Rd	Springfield	IL	62702	217-525-2230
Maldaner's (American) 222 S 6th St	Springfield	IL	62701	217-522-4313
New England Lobster House (Seafood) 1710 S MacArthur Blvd	Springfield	IL	62704	217-544-7171
Old Luxemburg Inn (Steak/Seafood) 1900 S 15th St	Springfield	IL	62703	217-528-0503
Romanesque (Italian) 115 N Lewis St	Springfield	IL	62702	217-789-4241
Sebastian's Hide-Out (New American) 221 S 5th St	Springfield	IL	62701	217-789-8988
Sunrise Cafe (American) 1201 S 2nd St	Springfield	IL	62704	217-753-1311
Taste Of Thai Restaurant (Thai) 3053 S Dirksen Pkwy	Springfield	IL	62703	217-529-8393
Tokyo of Japan (Japanese) 2225 Stevenson Dr	Springfield	IL	62703	217-585-0088

— Goods and Services —

SHOPPING

Name	City	State	Zip	Phone	Fax
Capital City Shopping Center 3095 S Dirksen Pkwy	Springfield	IL	62703	217-529-3581	529-3594
Fairhills Mall 1911 W Monroe St *Fax Area Code: 314 ■ *TF:* 888-790-4177	Springfield	IL	62704	217-787-9636	972-0006*
Town & Country Shopping Center 2403 S MacArthur Blvd	Springfield	IL	62704	217-698-7511	698-7540
White Oaks Mall 2501 W Wabash Ave	Springfield	IL	62704	217-787-8560	787-8579

BANKS

Name	City	State	Zip	Phone	Fax
Bank One Illinois NA E Old State Capitol Plaza *TF Cust Svc:* 800-528-2870*	Springfield	IL	62701	217-525-9600	525-2756
Illini Bank 120 S Chatham Rd	Springfield	IL	62704	217-787-1651	787-9718
Mercantile Bank 205 S 5th St *Fax: Cust Svc	Springfield	IL	62701	217-753-7530	753-7432*

Springfield (Cont'd)

BUSINESS SERVICES

	Phone		Phone
Airborne Express	800-247-2676	**Kinko's**	217-793-6888
BAX Global	800-225-5229	**Mail Boxes Etc**	800-789-4623
DHL Worldwide Express	800-225-5345	**Post Office**	217-788-7200
Federal Express	800-238-5355	**UPS**	800-742-5877
Kelly Services	217-793-1226	**Westaff**	217-698-8396

— Media —

PUBLICATIONS

				Phone	Fax
State Journal-Register‡ PO Box 219	Springfield	IL	62705	217-788-1300	788-1551

TF: 800-397-6397 ■ *Web:* www.sj-r.com ■ *E-mail:* sjr@sj-r.com

‡*Daily newspapers*

TELEVISION

				Phone	Fax
WAND-TV Ch 17 (ABC) 904 South Side Dr	Decatur	IL	62521	217-424-2500	424-2583
Web: www.wandtv.com ■ *E-mail:* wandtv@aol.com					
WCIA-TV Ch 3 (CBS) 509 S Neil St	Champaign	IL	61824	217-356-8333	373-3663
Web: www.wcia.com					
WICS-TV Ch 20 (NBC) 2680 E Cook St	Springfield	IL	62703	217-753-5620	753-5681
Web: www.fgi.net/news20/ ■ *E-mail:* news20@fgi.net					
WRSP-TV Ch 55 (Fox) 3003 Old Rochester Rd	Springfield	IL	62703	217-523-8855	523-4410
Web: www.wrsptv.com					
WSEC-TV Ch 14 (PBS) PO Box 6248	Springfield	IL	62708	217-206-6647	206-7267
Web: www.convocom.org ■ *E-mail:* viewer@wmec.pbs.org					

RADIO

				Phone	Fax
WCVS-FM 96.7 MHz (CR) 3055 S 4th St	Springfield	IL	62703	217-544-9855	528-5348
Web: www.fgi.net/wcvs ■ *E-mail:* wcvs@fgi.net					
WDBR-FM 103.7 MHz (CHR) 3501 E Sangamon Ave	Springfield	IL	62707	217-753-5400	753-7902
WFMB-AM 1450 kHz (Sports) 3055 S 4th St	Springfield	IL	62703	217-544-9855	528-5348
Web: www.fgi.net/wfmbam ■ *E-mail:* wfmbam@fgi.net					
WFMB-FM 104.5 MHz (Ctry) 3055 S 4th St	Springfield	IL	62703	217-544-9855	528-5348
Web: www.fgi.net/wfmbfm					
WNNS-FM 98.7 MHz (AC) PO Box 460	Springfield	IL	62705	217-629-7077	629-7952
WQLZ-FM 92.7 MHz (Rock) PO Box 460	Springfield	IL	62705	217-629-7077	629-7952
WQQL-FM 101.9 MHz (Oldies) 1030 Durkin Dr	Springfield	IL	62704	217-546-9000	546-4388
WTAX-AM 1240 kHz (N/T) 3501 E Sangamon Ave	Springfield	IL	62707	217-753-5400	753-7902
WUIS-FM 91.9 MHz (NPR) University of Illinois Bldg 130 PO Box 19243	Springfield	IL	62794	217-206-6516	206-6527
Web: www.uis.edu/~wuis/wuis2.htm ■ *E-mail:* wuis@uis.edu					
WYMG-FM 100.5 MHz (Rock) 1030 Durkin Dr	Springfield	IL	62704	217-546-9000	546-4388
WYXY-FM 93.9 MHz (Ctry) 3501 E Sangamon Ave	Springfield	IL	62707	217-753-5400	753-7902

— Colleges/Universities —

				Phone	Fax
Lincoln Land Community College 5250 Shepherd Rd	Springfield	IL	62794	217-786-2200	786-2492
Web: www.llcc.cc.il.us					
Robert Morris College Springfield Campus 3101 Montvale Dr	Springfield	IL	62704	217-793-2500	793-4210
Web: www.rmcil.edu					
Springfield College Illinois 1500 N 5th St	Springfield	IL	62702	217-525-1420	789-1698
TF Admissions: 800-635-7289 ■ *Web:* www.sci.edu					
University of Illinois Springfield	Springfield	IL	62794	217-206-6174	786-7280
TF: 800-252-8533 ■ *Web:* www.uis.edu					

— Hospitals —

				Phone	Fax
Doctors Hospital 5230 S 6th St	Springfield	IL	60794	217-529-7151	529-9472
Memorial Medical Center 701 N 1st St	Springfield	IL	62781	217-788-3000	788-5591
Saint John's Hospital 800 E Carpenter St	Springfield	IL	62769	217-544-6464	525-5659*
**Fax:* Admitting ■ *Web:* www.st-johns.org					

— Attractions —

				Phone	Fax
Adams Wildlife Sanctuary 2315 E Clear Lake Ave	Springfield	IL	62703	217-544-5781	
Camp Butler National Cemetery 5063 Camp Butler Rd	Springfield	IL	62707	217-492-4070	492-4072
Dana-Thomas House 301 E Lawrence Ave	Springfield	IL	62703	217-782-6776	788-9450
Web: www.online-springfield.com/sites/dth.html					
Daughters of the Union Veterans of the Civil War Museum 503 S Walnut St	Springfield	IL	62704	217-544-0616	
Edward's Place 700 N 4th St	Springfield	IL	62702	217-523-2631	523-3866
Executive Mansion 410 E Jackson St	Springfield	IL	62701	217-782-6450	782-2771
Grand Army of the Republic Memorial Museum 629 S 7th St	Springfield	IL	62703	217-522-4373	
Illinois State Capitol 2nd St & E Capitol Ave	Springfield	IL	62701	217-782-2099	
Illinois State Military Museum 1301 N MacArthur Camp Lincoln Bldg 41	Springfield	IL	62702	217-761-3910	761-3709
Illinois State Museum Spring & Edwards Sts	Springfield	IL	62706	217-782-7386	782-1254
Web: www.museum.state.il.us					
Illinois Vietnam Veterans Memorial Oak Ridge Cemetery	Springfield	IL	62702	217-782-2717	
Knight's Action Park 1700 Recreation Dr	Springfield	IL	62707	217-546-8881	546-8995
TF: 800-421-4386 ■ *Web:* www.knightsactionpark.com					
Lawrence Memorial Library 101 E Laurel St	Springfield	IL	62704	217-525-3144	525-3090
Lincoln Depot 10th & Monroe Sts	Springfield	IL	62703	217-544-8695	
Lincoln Home National Historic Site 413 S 8th St	Springfield	IL	62701	217-492-4241	492-4673
Web: www.nps.gov/liho/					
Lincoln Memorial Garden 2301 E Lake Shore Dr	Springfield	IL	62707	217-529-1111	529-0134
Lincoln Tomb Oak Ridge Cemetery	Springfield	IL	62702	217-782-2717	
Lincoln's New Salem 20 miles NW on Rt 97	Petersburg	IL	62675	217-632-4000	
Old State Capitol Old State Capitol Mall	Springfield	IL	62701	217-785-7961	
Parks Telephone Museum 529 S 7th St	Springfield	IL	62721	217-789-5303	
Rees Thomas Memorial Carillon Washington Pk	Springfield	IL	62704	217-544-1751	
Robinson Henson Zoo 1100 E Lake Dr	Springfield	IL	62707	217-753-6217	529-8748
Web: www.hensonrobinsonzoo.org					
Springfield Ballet Co 2820 S MacArthur Blvd	Springfield	IL	62704	217-544-1967	544-1968
Springfield Children's Museum 619 E Washington St	Springfield	IL	62701	217-789-0679	789-0682
Springfield Muni Opera 815 E Lake Dr	Springfield	IL	62705	217-793-6864	
Web: www.themuni.org ■ *E-mail:* TheMuni@TheMuni.org					
Springfield Theatre Centre 101 E Lawrence	Springfield	IL	62704	217-523-0878	
State Fairgrounds Amusement Park Sangamon Ave & Peoria Rd	Springfield	IL	62702	217-528-9207	
Washington Park Botanical Gardens Fayette & Chatham Rds	Springfield	IL	62704	217-753-6228	546-0257

SPORTS TEAMS & FACILITIES

				Phone	Fax
Springfield Capitals (baseball) 1351 North Grant Ave E Lanphier Stadium	Springfield	IL	62702	217-525-5500	525-5508
Web: www.springfieldcapitals.com					

— Events —

	Phone
Bluegrass Festival (early September)	217-632-4000
Brinkerhoff Fall Fair (early September)	217-789-2360
Capital City Farm Show (mid-January)	217-498-9404
Central Illinois Blues Fest (early September)	217-546-8881
Central Illinois Polka Festival (late October)	800-545-7300
Christmas Parade (early December)	217-528-8669

Springfield — Events (Cont'd)

	Phone
Christmas Walk (early December)	217-544-1723
Chrysanthemum Festival (mid-late November)	217-753-6228
Dana-Thomas House Christmas (mid-late December)	217-782-6776
Edwards Place Fine Crafts Fair (late September)	217-523-2631
Ethnic Festival (early September)	217-529-8189
Festival of Trees (late November)	217-788-3293
First Night Springfield (December 31)	800-545-7300
Harvest Feast at New Salem (early November)	217-632-4000
Holiday Lights at the Zoo (mid-late December)	217-753-6217
Holiday Market (mid-late November)	217-529-1111
Illinois State Fair (mid-August)	800-545-7300
Indian Summer Festival (mid-October)	217-529-1111
International Carillon Festival (early June)	217-753-6219
International Ethnic Festival (early September)	217-529-8189
Keepsake Country Craft Show (late January & mid-July)	217-787-8560
Maple Syrup Time (late February)	217-529-1111
Motorcycle Show & Swap Meet (late February)	217-788-8800
Old Capitol Art Fair (late May)	800-545-7300
Springfield Air Rendezvous (mid-August)	800-545-7300
Springfield All Sports Show (late February-early March)	217-629-7077
Springfield Scottish Highland Games & Celtic Festival (mid-May)	217-546-5802
Summer Festival (mid-July)	217-632-4000
Theatre in the Park (June)	217-632-4000
Traditional Music Festival (early September)	217-632-4000

Indiana

Population (1999): 5,942,901 **Area (sq mi): 36,420**

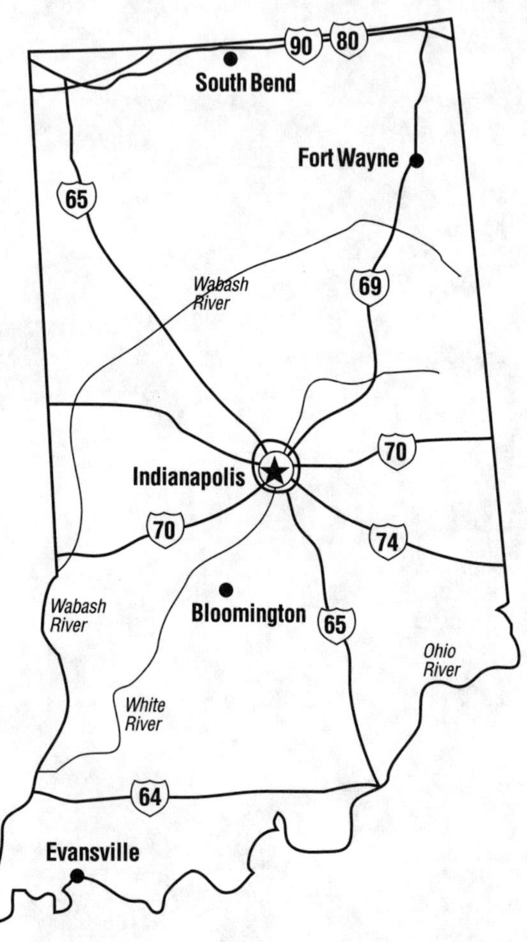

— State Information Sources —

				Phone	Fax
Indiana Business Development Div					
1 N Capitol Ave Suite 700	Indianapolis	IN	46204	317-232-8888	232-4146
Web: www.ai.org/bdev					
Indiana State Chamber of Commerce					
115 W Washington St Suite 850 S	Indianapolis	IN	46204	317-264-3110	264-6855
Web: www.indianachamber.com/					
Indiana State Government Information				317-232-1000	
Web: www.state.in.us					
Indiana State Library 140 N Senate Ave	Indianapolis	IN	46204	317-232-3675	232-3728
Web: www.statelib.lib.in.us ■ *E-mail:* john@statelib.lib.in.us					
Indiana State Parks Div					
402 W Washington Rm W-298.	Indianapolis	IN	46204	317-232-4124	232-4132
TF: 800-622-4931 ■ *Web:* www.dnr.state.in.us/statepar/other/index.htm					
Indiana Tourism Div					
1 N Capitol Ave Suite 700	Indianapolis	IN	46204	317-232-8860	233-6887
TF: 800-289-6646 ■ *Web:* www.indianatourism.com					

ON-LINE RESOURCES

Access Indiana Information Network . . . . www.ai.org
Area Links for Central Northwest Indiana . . . . www.arealinks.net
Enjoy Indiana . . . . www.enjoyindiana.com
Indiana Cities . . . . dir.yahoo.com/Regional/U_S__States/Indiana/Cities
Indiana Counties & Regions . . . . dir.yahoo.com/Regional/U_S__States/Indiana/Counties_and_Regions
Indiana Scenario . . . . scenariousa.dstylus.com/in/indexf.htm
Indiana Travel & Tourism Guide . . . . . . www.travel-library.com/north_america/usa/indiana/index.html
Indiana Virtual Tourist . . . . www.cica.indiana.edu/news/servers/tourist/index.html
Indiana.com . . . . www.indiana.com
Rough Guide Travel Indiana travel.roughguides.com/content/504/index.htm
Travel.org-Indiana . . . . travel.org/indiana.html
VisitIndiana.net . . . . www.visitindiana.net
Yahoo! Get Local Indiana . . . . dir.yahoo.com/Regional/U_S__States/Indiana

— Cities Profiled —

Page

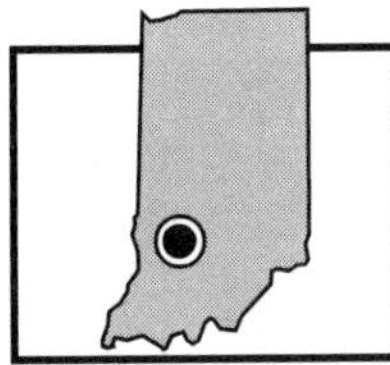

Bloomington

Bloomington is the home of Indiana University, which is the oldest state university west of the Alleghenies (it was founded in 1820) and has been rated as one of the five most beautiful campuses in the United States. The University's Musical Arts Center has the longest continuously running opera program in the Western Hemisphere, and the newly-renovated Indiana University Auditorium offers Broadway plays and other performances throughout the year. In addition to its Fine Arts Museum, the University is home to the Hoagy Carmichael Room, which contains such memorabilia as the songwriter's piano and records. The city's Downtown Square offers 11 blocks of specialty shops, restaurants, and music clubs and includes a three-story antique mall with over 100 dealers. About 15 miles southeast of Bloomington is the Hoosier National Forest, which surrounds Lake Monroe, the state's largest inland lake. A firetower in the park may be climbed for a spectacular view of the area and lake.

Population 65,065
Area (Land) . . . . . . 15.1 sq mi
Area (Water) . . . . . . 1.9 sq mi
Elevation . . . . . . 846 ft
Latitude . . . . . . 39-10-00 N
Longitude . . . . . . 86-31-17 W
County . . . . . . Monroe
Time Zone . . . . . . EST
Area Code/s 812

— Average Temperatures and Precipitation —

TEMPERATURES

	Jan	Feb	Mar	Apr	May	Jun	Jul	Aug	Sep	Oct	Nov	Dec
High	37	41	52	64	74	82	86	84	78	67	54	41
Low	18	21	32	43	52	62	66	63	56	45	35	24

PRECIPITATION

	Jan	Feb	Mar	Apr	May	Jun	Jul	Aug	Sep	Oct	Nov	Dec
Inches	2.4	2.6	4.1	3.9	4.8	3.6	4.8	3.9	3.3	2.8	3.5	3.6

— Important Phone Numbers —

	Phone
AAA	812-336-1700
American Express Travel	812-333-3360
Emergency	911
Medical Referral	812-332-4033
Poison Control Center	800-382-9097

— Information Sources —

				Phone	*Fax*
Better Business Bureau Serving Central Indiana 22 E Washington St Suite 200	Indianapolis	IN	46204	317-488-2222	488-2224

Web: www.indianapolis.bbb.org

Bloomington City Hall 401 N Morton St	Bloomington	IN	47404	812-339-2261	349-3455

Web: www.city.bloomington.in.us

Bloomington Convention Center 302 S College Ave	Bloomington	IN	47403	812-336-3681	349-2981

Web: www.kiva.net/~downtown ■ *E-mail:* downtown@kiva.net

Bloomington Economic Development Corp 400 W 7th St Suite 101	Bloomington	IN	47404	812-335-7346	335-7348

TF: 800-319-2983 ■ *Web:* www.bedc.bloomington.in.us ■ *E-mail:* lwilliam@bedc.bloomington.in.us

Bloomington Mayor 401 N Morton St	Bloomington	IN	47404	812-349-3406	349-3455

Web: www.city.bloomington.in.us/mayor ■ *E-mail:* mayor@city.bloomington.in.us

Bloomington/Monroe County Convention & Visitors Bureau 2855 N Walnut St	Bloomington	IN	47404	812-334-8900	334-2344

TF: 800-800-0037 ■ *Web:* www.visitbloomington.com

Greater Bloomington Chamber of Commerce 400 W 7th St Suite 102	Bloomington	IN	47404	812-336-6381	336-0651

Web: www.chamber.bloomington.in.us

				Phone	*Fax*
Monroe County PO Box 547	Bloomington	IN	47402	812-349-2612	349-2610
Monroe County Public Library 303 E Kirkwood Ave	Bloomington	IN	47408	812-349-3050	349-3051

Web: www.monroe.lib.in.us

On-Line Resources

4Bloomington.com	www.4bloomington.com
Anthill City Guide Bloomington	www.anthill.com/city.asp?city=bloomingtonin
Area Guide Bloomington	bloomington.areaguides.net
BloomingtonGuide	www.geocities.com/~bloomingguide
Excite.com Bloomington City Guide	www.excite.com/travel/countries/united_states/indiana/bloomington
HoosierNet	www.bloomington.in.us
NITC Travelbase City Guide Bloomington	www.travelbase.com/auto/guides/bloomington-in.html
Online City Guide to Bloomington	www.olcg.com/in/bloomington/index.html

— Transportation Services —

AIRPORTS

■ **Indianapolis International Airport (IND)**

	Phone
47 miles NE of downtown Bloomington (approx 60 minutes)	317-487-9594

Web: indianapolisairport.com

Airport Transportation

	Phone
A1 Taxi $90 fare to downtown Bloomington	317-856-8666
A American Cab $70-80 fare to downtown Bloomington	317-821-8000
Bloomington Shuttle Service $18 fare to downtown Bloomington	800-589-6004
Lildouth's Cab $75 fare to downtown Bloomington	317-243-8800
Yellow Cab $104 fare to downtown Bloomington	317-487-7777

Commercial Airlines

	Phone		*Phone*
America West	800-235-9292	**Northwest**	800-225-2525
American	800-433-7300	**Southwest**	800-435-9792
American Trans Air	800-225-2995	**TWA**	800-221-2000
Continental	800-525-0280	**United**	800-241-6522
Delta	800-221-1212	**US Airways**	800-428-4322
Midway	800-446-4392		

Charter Airlines

	Phone		*Phone*
Alliance Executive Charter Services	800-232-5387	**Direct Airway**	800-257-9424
Aviation Charter Services	317-244-7200	**IndianAero Inc**	317-487-5936
Corporate Aviation Services Inc	918-834-8348	**Indianapolis Aviation**	317-849-0840
		Raytheon Aircraft Charter	800-519-6283

CAR RENTALS

	Phone		*Phone*
Ace	317-243-6336	**Enterprise**	317-243-8988
Alamo	317-856-5572	**Hertz**	317-243-9321
Avis	317-244-3307	**National**	317-243-1159
Budget	317-248-1100	**Thrifty**	317-243-2282

LIMO/TAXI

	Phone		*Phone*
Classic Touch Limousine	812-339-7269	**Yellow Cab**	812-339-9744
Signature Limousine	812-332-6045		

MASS TRANSIT

	Phone
Bloomington Transit $.75 Base fare	812-336-7433

RAIL/BUS

				Phone
Greyhound Bus Station 219 W 6th St	Bloomington	IN	47401	812-332-1522

TF: 800-231-2222

Bloomington (Cont'd)

— Accommodations —

HOTEL RESERVATION SERVICES

	Phone	Fax
USA Hotels	252-331-1555	331-2021

TF: 800-872-4683 ■ *Web:* www.1800usahotels.com
■ *E-mail:* info@1800usahotels.com

HOTELS, MOTELS, RESORTS

	City	State	Zip	Phone	Fax
Century Suites Hotel 300 S SR-446	Bloomington	IN	47401	812-336-7777	336-0436
TF: 800-766-5446					
College Motor Inn 509 N College Ave	Bloomington	IN	47404	812-336-6881	
Comfort Inn 1722 N Walnut St	Bloomington	IN	47401	812-339-1919	339-2052
TF: 800-221-2222 ■ *Web:* home.bluemarble.net/~comfort/comfort.htm ■ *E-mail:* comfort@bluemarble.net					
Courtyard by Marriott 310 S College Ave	Bloomington	IN	47403	812-335-8000	336-9997
TF: 800-321-2211					
Days Inn 200 E Matlock Rd	Bloomington	IN	47402	812-336-0905	336-0905
TF: 800-329-7466					
Eagle Pointe Golf Resort 2250 E Pointe Rd	Bloomington	IN	47401	812-824-4040	824-6666
Web: www.eaglepointe.com ■ *E-mail:* info@eaglepointe.com					
Economy Inn 4805 Old Hwy 37 S	Bloomington	IN	47401	812-824-8311	824-1041
Fairfield Inn by Marriott 120 Fairfield Dr	Bloomington	IN	47404	812-331-1122	323-1133
TF: 800-228-2800					
Hampton Inn 2100 N Walnut St	Bloomington	IN	47404	812-334-2100	334-8433
TF: 800-426-7866					
Holiday Inn 1710 N Kinser Pike	Bloomington	IN	47404	812-334-3252	333-1702
TF: 800-465-4329					
Indiana Memorial Union 900 E 7th St	Bloomington	IN	47405	812-856-6381	855-3426
TF: 800-209-8145					
Motel 6 University 1800 N Walnut St	Bloomington	IN	47404	812-332-0820	337-1526
TF: 800-466-8356					
Motel 6 West 126 Franklin Rd	Bloomington	IN	47404	812-332-0337	332-1967
TF: 800-466-8356					
Ramada Inn 2601 N Walnut St	Bloomington	IN	47402	812-332-9453	333-1303
TF: 800-272-6232					
Super 8 Motel 1000 W SR 46	Bloomington	IN	47404	812-323-8000	323-8000
TF: 800-800-8000					
Travelodge 2615 E 3rd St	Bloomington	IN	47401	812-339-6191	332-8556
TF: 800-578-7878					

— Restaurants —

	City	State	Zip	Phone
A&W Family Restaurant (American) 2816 E 3rd St	Bloomington	IN	47408	812-339-3134
Bear's Place (American) 1316 E 3rd St	Bloomington	IN	47401	812-339-3460
Beijing Chinese Restaurant (Chinese) 220 Williamsburg Dr Suite 1	Bloomington	IN	47408	812-332-5867
Carmella's (Italian) 1600 N Walnut St	Bloomington	IN	47404	812-339-2962
Chapman's Restaurant (American) 300 SR 446	Bloomington	IN	47401	812-337-9999
China Star Restaurant (Chinese) 4641 W Richland Plaza	Bloomington	IN	47404	812-876-5778
Cloverleaf Family Restaurant (Homestyle) 2500 W 3rd St	Bloomington	IN	47404	812-334-1077
Colorado Steakhouse (Steak/Seafood) 1800 N College Ave	Bloomington	IN	47404	812-339-9979
Crazy Horse (American) 214 W Kirkwood Ave	Bloomington	IN	47404	812-336-8877
Dragon Restaurant (Chinese) 3261 W 3rd St	Bloomington	IN	47404	812-332-6610
Ekimae Restaurant (Japanese) 825 N Walnut St	Bloomington	IN	47404	812-334-1661
Encore Cafe (American) 316 W 6th St	Bloomington	IN	47404	812-333-7312
Gable's Restaurant (American) 114 S Indiana Ave	Bloomington	IN	47408	812-323-1950
Gib & Denzil's Restaurant (Homestyle) 2130 S Walnut St	Bloomington	IN	47401	812-332-7810
Grisanti's Restaurant (Italian) 850 Auto Mall Rd	Bloomington	IN	47401	812-339-9391
Hong Kong Restaurant (Chinese) 430 E Kirkwood Ave 2nd Fl	Bloomington	IN	47408	812-339-4296
Irish Lion (Irish) 212 W Kirkwood Ave	Bloomington	IN	47404	812-336-9076
Web: www.kiva.net/~irishl ■ *E-mail:* irishl@kiva.net				
Johnny Angel's (American) 830 W 17th St	Bloomington	IN	47404	812-332-4646
Kaya Restaurant (Japanese) 1500 E 3rd St	Bloomington	IN	47401	812-339-7868
Kilroy's (American) 502 E Kirkwood Ave	Bloomington	IN	47408	812-339-3006
Web: www.kiva.net/~kilroys/				
King Gyros Restaurant (Greek) 2000 S Walnut St	Bloomington	IN	47401	812-334-4144
La Bamba Restaurant (Mexican) 520 E Kirkwood Ave	Bloomington	IN	47408	812-332-5970
La Charreada (Mexican) 1720 N Walnut St	Bloomington	IN	47404	812-332-2343
La Rosa (Mexican) 416 E 4th St	Bloomington	IN	47408	812-323-8962
Le Petit Cafe (French) 308 W 6th St	Bloomington	IN	47404	812-334-9747
Lennie's Restaurant (Italian) 1795 E 10th St	Bloomington	IN	47404	812-323-2112
Little Zagreb (Steak/Seafood) 223 W 6th St	Bloomington	IN	47404	812-332-0694
Malibu Grill (California) 106 N Walnut St	Bloomington	IN	47402	812-332-4334
Mikado (Japanese) 895 S College Mall Rd	Bloomington	IN	47401	812-333-1950
Mustard's (American) 300 S College Mall Rd	Bloomington	IN	47401	812-334-3344
Peterson's (American) 1811 E 10th St	Bloomington	IN	47408	812-336-5450
Princess Restaurant (Moroccan/Mediterranean) 206 N Walnut St	Bloomington	IN	47404	812-336-8821
Puccini's Ristorante (Italian) 420 E 4th St	Bloomington	IN	47408	812-333-5522
Red Sea (Ethiopian) 404 E 4th St	Bloomington	IN	47408	812-331-8366
Rib Cage (Barbecue) 813 N Walnut St	Bloomington	IN	47404	812-332-0136
Shanti (Indian) 221 E Kirkwood Ave Suite G	Bloomington	IN	47408	812-333-0303
Siam House (Thai) 430 E 4th St	Bloomington	IN	47401	812-331-1233
Snow Lion (Tibetan/Asian) 113 S Grant St	Bloomington	IN	47408	812-336-0835
Tortilla Flat (Mexican) 501 N Walnut St	Bloomington	IN	47404	812-330-1212
Trojan Horse (Greek) 100 E Kirkwood Ave	Bloomington	IN	47408	812-332-1101
Yen Ching Restaurant (Chinese) 1143 S College Mall Rd	Bloomington	IN	47401	812-334-1334
Yogi's Grill & Bar (American) 519 E 10th St	Bloomington	IN	47408	812-323-9644
Web: www.yogis.com ■ *E-mail:* yogi@yogis.com				

— Goods and Services —

SHOPPING

	City	State	Zip	Phone	Fax
Antique Mall 311 W 7th St	Bloomington	IN	47401	812-332-2290	
College Mall 2896 E 3rd St	Bloomington	IN	47401	812-339-3054	339-3374
Ellettsville Antique Mall 1416 SR 46	Ellettsville	IN	47429	812-876-4527	
Fountain Square Mall 100 Fountain Square	Bloomington	IN	47404	812-336-7100	
Shoppes on College Mall Road 8600 College Mall Rd	Bloomington	IN	47401	812-332-9575	332-0261
Walnut Park Shopping Center 2400 South Walnut St	Bloomington	IN	47401	812-332-9575	332-0162

BANKS

	City	State	Zip	Phone	Fax
Bank One 100 S College Ave	Bloomington	IN	47404	812-323-3859	331-6387
TF: 800-349-6317					
Bloomfield State Bank 2111 Liberty Dr	Bloomington	IN	47403	812-334-1980	323-1931
TF: 800-319-6110					
Citizens Bank 200 S Washington St	Bloomington	IN	47408	812-339-1131	323-3624
Civitas Bank 3200 E 3rd St	Bloomington	IN	47401	812-332-2293	323-3618
TF Cust Svc: 800-449-8362*					
Key Bank 418 S College Mall Rd	Bloomington	IN	47401	812-331-0600	331-0379
TF: 800-762-4389					
Monroe County Bank 306 E Kirkwood Ave	Bloomington	IN	47408	812-331-3510	331-3469
NBD Bank 2421 S Walnut St	Bloomington	IN	47401	812-334-2147	334-2170
TF: 800-433-8248					
ONB Bank Bloomington 2718 E 3rd St	Bloomington	IN	47401	812-332-2158	331-4022
Peoples State Bank 202 W 17th St	Bloomington	IN	47404	812-332-9228	323-3207
TF: 800-800-5861					

BUSINESS SERVICES

	Phone		Phone
Airborne Express	800-247-2676	**Kelly Services**	812-332-1003
Collegiate Copies	812-339-3769	**Mail Boxes Etc**	812-331-9990
DHL Worldwide Express	800-225-5345	**Post Office**	812-334-4030
Federal Express	800-238-5355	**UPS**	800-742-5877
Interim Personnel	812-330-1525		

— Media —

PUBLICATIONS

	City	State	Zip	Phone	Fax
Bloomington Independent 217 S Dunn St	Bloomington	IN	47408	812-331-0963	337-3314*
**Fax:* Edit ■ *Web:* www.indepen.com ■ *E-mail:* lsorg@indepen.com					
Herald-Times‡ 1900 S Walnut St	Bloomington	IN	47401	812-332-4401	331-4383
TF: 800-422-0670 ■ *Web:* www.hoosiertimes.com ■ *E-mail:* circulation@heraldt.com					
Inside Indiana 4615 E Morningside Dr	Bloomington	IN	47408	812-334-9722	334-9756
TF: 800-282-4648 ■ *Web:* indiana.rivals.com					

‡*Daily newspapers*

TELEVISION

	City	State	Zip	Phone	Fax
WISH-TV Ch 8 (CBS) 1950 N Meridian St	Indianapolis	IN	46202	317-923-8888	931-2242
Web: www.wish-tv.com ■ *E-mail:* wishmail@wish-tv.com					

Bloomington — Television (Cont'd)

				Phone	Fax
WNDY-TV Ch 23 (UPN) 451 W 16th St *Web:* www.paramountstations.com/WNDY	Indianapolis	IN	46222	317-241-2388	381-6975
WRTV-TV Ch 6 (ABC) 1330 N Meridian St *Web:* www.6news.com	Indianapolis	IN	46202	317-635-9788	269-1445
WTHR-TV Ch 13 (NBC) 1000 N Meridian St *Web:* www.wthr.com ■ *E-mail:* 13news@wthr.com	Indianapolis	IN	46204	317-636-1313	636-3717
WTIU-TV Ch 30 (PBS) 1229 E 7th St *Web:* www.wtiu.indiana.edu ■ *E-mail:* wtiu@indiana.edu	Bloomington	IN	47405	812-855-5900	855-0729
WTTV-TV Ch 4 (WB) 3490 Bluff Rd *Web:* www.ttv.com ■ *E-mail:* wb4@wb4.com	Indianapolis	IN	46217	317-782-4444	780-5464
WXIN-TV Ch 59 (Fox) 1440 N Meridian St *Web:* www.wxin.com	Indianapolis	IN	46202	317-632-5900	687-6534

RADIO

				Phone	Fax
WBIW-AM 1340 kHz (CR) 424 Heltonville Rd	Bedford	IN	47421	812-275-7555	279-8046
WBWB-FM 96.7 MHz (AC) 304 SR-446 *Web:* www.wbwb.com ■ *E-mail:* wbwb@wbwb.com	Bloomington	IN	47401	812-336-8000	336-7000
WCBK-FM 102.3 MHz (Ctry) 1639 Burton Ln	Martinsville	IN	46151	765-342-3394	342-5020
WFHB-FM 91.3 MHz (Misc) 108 W 4th St *Web:* www.wfhb.com	Bloomington	IN	47404	812-323-1200	323-0320
WFIU-FM 103.7 MHz (NPR) Indiana University *Web:* www.wfiu.indiana.edu ■ *E-mail:* wfiu@indiana.edu	Bloomington	IN	47405	812-855-1357	855-0729
WGCL-AM 1370 kHz (N/T) 400 One City Ctr	Bloomington	IN	47404	812-332-3366	331-4570
WGCT-FM 105.1 MHz (Ctry) 304 SR-446	Bloomington	IN	47401	812-336-8000	336-7000
WMCB-AM 1540 kHz (Ctry) 1639 Burton Ln	Martinsville	IN	46151	765-342-3394	342-5020
WQKC-FM 93.7 MHz (Ctry) 1534 Ewing St	Seymour	IN	47274	812-522-1390	522-9541
WTTS-FM 92.3 MHz (AAA) 400 One City Centre	Bloomington	IN	47404	812-332-3366	331-4570
WVNI-FM 95.1 MHz (Rel) 2620 N Walnut St	Bloomington	IN	47404	812-335-9500	335-8880

— Colleges/Universities —

				Phone	Fax
Indiana University 601 E Kirkwood Ave *Web:* www.indiana.edu/campus/iu-bloomington.html	Bloomington	IN	47405	812-855-4848	855-5102
Ivy Tech State College Bloomington 3116 Canterbury Ct *Web:* 168.91.42.5/ivytech	Bloomington	IN	47404	812-332-1559	332-8147

— Hospitals —

				Phone	Fax
Bloomington Hospital PO Box 1149	Bloomington	IN	47402	812-336-6821	336-9339

— Attractions —

				Phone	Fax
Butler Winery 15th St & College Ave	Bloomington	IN	47404	812-339-7233	
Dagom Gaden Tensung Ling Monastery 102 Clubhouse Dr Cascades Pk	Bloomington	IN	47408	812-339-0857	
Griffy Lake Park 3500 N Hinkle Rd	Bloomington	IN	47408	812-349-3732	
Hilltop Garden & Nature Center 2301 E 10th St Indiana University Campus	Bloomington	IN	47405	812-855-5715	855-3998
Hoosier National Forest 811 Constitution Ave	Bedford	IN	47421	812-275-5987	279-3423
Indiana University Auditorium 1211 E 7th St *Web:* iuauditorium.indiana.edu	Bloomington	IN	47405	812-855-1103	855-4244
Indiana University Fine Arts Gallery 7th St Indiana University Campus Fine Arts Bldg	Bloomington	IN	47405	812-855-8490	
John Waldron Arts Center 122 S Walnut St *Web:* www.artlives.org ■ *E-mail:* jwaldron@bluemarble.net	Bloomington	IN	47404	812-334-3100	323-2787
Lilly Library 1200 E 7th St Fine Arts Plaza *Web:* www.indiana.edu/~liblilly ■ *E-mail:* liblilly@indiana.edu	Bloomington	IN	47405	812-855-2452	855-3143
Mathers William Hammond Museum 601 E 8th St *Web:* www.indiana.edu/~mathers	Bloomington	IN	47405	812-855-6873	855-0205
Monroe County Historical Museum 202 E 6th St *Web:* www.kiva.net/~mchm/museum.htm	Bloomington	IN	47408	812-332-2517	355-5593
Musical Arts Center Jordan Ave	Bloomington	IN	47405	812-855-7433	855-2753
Oliver Winery 8024 N SR-37 *TF:* 800-258-2783	Bloomington	IN	47404	812-876-5800	876-9309
Tibetan Cultural Center 3655 Snoddy Rd	Bloomington	IN	47401	812-334-7046	335-9054
Wapehani Mountain Bike Park Weimer Rd betw Bloomfield & Tapp Rds *Web:* www.bloomington.in.us/~bicycle/wapehani/wapehani.html	Bloomington	IN	47403	812-349-3736	349-3705
Wylie House Museum 317 E 2nd St	Bloomington	IN	47401	812-855-6224	

SPORTS TEAMS & FACILITIES

				Phone	Fax
Bloomington Speedway 5185 S Fairfax Rd *Web:* www.bloomingtonspeedway.com	Bloomington	IN	47401	812-825-9614	824-7400

— Events —

	Phone
Antique Show (late March)	812-332-5233
Art Fair on the Square (mid-late June)	812-334-8900
Bloomington Early Music Festival (late May)	812-334-8900
Chocolate Fest (early February)	812-334-8900
Coin Show (early-mid-March)	812-332-3432
Easter Egg Hunt (early April)	812-336-3681
Fair for the Arts (June-August)	812-349-3737
Gold Wing Road Riders Convention (late May)	812-334-8900
Hometown Cinema Film Festival (early-mid-April)	812-337-1091
Indiana Heritage Quilt Show (early March)	812-334-8900
Mini-Play Festival (early March)	812-332-4401
SummerFest (mid-June)	812-349-2800
Taste of Bloomington (mid-late June)	812-334-8900

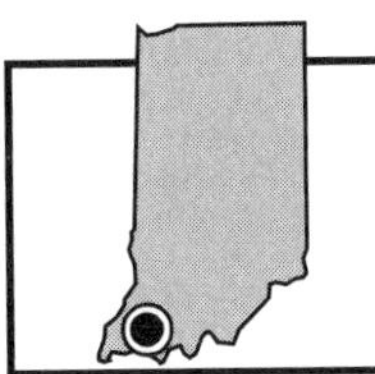

Evansville

Located on a horseshoe bend along the Ohio River, Evansville is home to the annual Thunder on the Ohio Boat Races, one of the many events that make up the city's annual Freedom Festival. Located also on the banks of the Ohio River is the Angel Mounds Historic Site, which was occupied by a large tribe of Middle Mississippian Indians from about 1250-1450 AD. Another popular attraction in the Evansville area is historic New Harmony. Originally founded in 1814 by the Harmony Society, a utopian religious community, New Harmony was sold to Robert Owen in 1824. He attracted scholars, scientists, and educators to his commune, and together they had a profound impact on American science, literature, and art. Historic sites located in the city of Evansville itself include the Old Courthouse Center built in 1891. The building is an example of Beaux-Arts architecture, and its ornate interior now houses shops, galleries, restored meeting rooms, and offices. Evansville's Willard Library, which opened in 1885, is the oldest public library building in Indiana.

Population	122,779	**Longitude**	87-55-58 W
Area (Land)	40.7 sq mi	**County**	Vanderburgh
Area (Water)	0.1 sq mi	**Time Zone**	CST
Elevation	388 ft	**Area Code/s**	812
Latitude	37-97-47 N		

Evansville (Cont'd)

— Average Temperatures and Precipitation —

TEMPERATURES

	Jan	Feb	Mar	Apr	May	Jun	Jul	Aug	Sep	Oct	Nov	Dec
High	39	44	56	67	77	86	89	87	81	70	56	44
Low	21	25	36	45	54	63	68	65	58	45	37	27

PRECIPITATION

	Jan	Feb	Mar	Apr	May	Jun	Jul	Aug	Sep	Oct	Nov	Dec
Inches	2.7	3.1	4.7	4.0	4.8	3.5	4.0	3.1	3.0	2.9	3.7	3.7

— Important Phone Numbers —

	Phone		*Phone*
AAA	812-477-9966	**Poison Control Center**	800-382-9097
Emergency	911	**Time/Temp**	812-464-9211
Entertainment Hotline	812-422-2600	**Weather**	812-425-5549

— Information Sources —

				Phone	*Fax*
Better Business Bureau Serving Tri-State - Southwest Indiana 1139 Washington Sq Mall *Web:* www.evansville.bbb.org	Evansville	IN	47715	812-473-0202	473-3080
Civic Center Complex 1 NW ML King Blvd. **Fax:* Hum Res	Evansville	IN	47708	812-435-5000	425-1105*
Evansville Area Plan Commission 1 NW ML King Jr Blvd 312 Admin Bldg *Web:* www.evansville.net/mayor/joint.htm#apc	Evansville	IN	47708	812-435-5226	435-5237
Evansville City Hall 1 NW ML King Jr Blvd *Web:* www.evansville.net/eville ■ *E-mail:* citygov@evansville.net	Evansville	IN	47708	812-436-4962	436-4999
Evansville Convention & Visitors Bureau 401 SE Riverside Dr *TF:* 800-433-3025 ■ *Web:* www.evansvillecvb.org/ ■ *E-mail:* tourism@evansvillecvb.org	Evansville	IN	47713	812-425-5402	421-2207
Evansville Mayor 1 NW ML King Jr Blvd Rm 302 *Web:* www.evansville.net/mayor	Evansville	IN	47708	812-426-5581	436-4926
Evansville-Vanderburgh County Public Library 22 SE 5th St *Web:* www.evcpl.lib.in.us ■ *E-mail:* comments@evans.evcpl.lib.in.us	Evansville	IN	47708	812-428-8218	422-4718
Metropolitan Evansville Chamber of Commerce 100 NW 2nd St Suite 100 *Web:* www.mevcc.org	Evansville	IN	47708	812-425-8147	421-5883
Vanderburgh County PO Box 3356	Evansville	IN	47732	812-435-5000	435-5849

On-Line Resources

Anthill City Guide Evansville .... www.anthill.com/city.asp?city=evansville
Area Guide Evansville .... evansville.areaguides.net
Evansville Online .... www.evansville.net/
Excite.com Evansville City Guide ... www.excite.com/travel/countries/united_states/indiana/evansville
News4U Magazine www.news-4u.com/

— Transportation Services —

AIRPORTS

■ **Evansville Regional Airport (EVV)** — *Phone*

6 miles NE of downtown (approx 20 minutes) 812-421-4401
Web: www.evvairport.com ■ *E-mail:* evvndb@evansville.net

Airport Transportation

	Phone
River City-Yellow Cab $13 fare to downtown	812-429-0000
Sunset Limousine Service $45 fare to downtown	812-424-9297

Commercial Airlines

	Phone		*Phone*
American Eagle	800-433-7300	**Northwest**	800-225-2525
Atlantic Southeast	800-282-3424	**TWA Express**	800-221-2000
Chicago Express	800-435-9282	**US Airways**	800-428-4322
Comair	800-354-9822	**US Airways Express**	800-428-4322
Delta Connection	800-221-1212		

Charter Airlines

	Phone		*Phone*
Executive Jet Management	877-356-5387	**Tri-State Aero**	812-426-1221
Million Air	812-425-4700		

CAR RENTALS

	Phone		*Phone*
Avis	812-423-5645	**National**	812-425-2426
Budget	812-428-7880	**Premiere**	812-479-0232
Hertz	812-425-7141		

LIMO/TAXI

	Phone		*Phone*
ASAP Limo	812-423-3200	**River City-Yellow Cab**	812-429-0000
Auto Haus Limousine Service	812-476-5700	**Sunset Limousine Service**	812-424-9297
Comaier Limousine Service	812-422-8515	**Yellow Cab**	812-425-9091
Limousine Co	812-425-5700		

MASS TRANSIT

	Phone
Metro Evansville Transit $.75 Base fare	812-423-4856

RAIL/BUS

				Phone
Greyhound Bus Station 100 NW 3rd St *TF:* 800-231-2222	Evansville	IN	47708	812-425-8274

— Accommodations —

HOTELS, MOTELS, RESORTS

				Phone	*Fax*
Arrowhead Lodge 2021 Business Hwy 41 N.	Evansville	IN	47711	812-425-1531	
Best Western Expressway Inn 8015 Division St *TF:* 800-528-1234	Evansville	IN	47715	812-471-3414	471-3414
Casino Aztar Hotel 421 NW Riverside Dr *TF:* 800-544-0120	Evansville	IN	47708	812-433-4444	433-4384
Comfort Inn 5006 E Morgan Ave *TF:* 800-228-5150	Evansville	IN	47715	812-477-2211	477-2211
Days Inn Airport 5701 Hwy 41 N *TF:* 800-329-7466	Evansville	IN	47711	812-464-1010	464-2742
Days Inn East 4819 Tecumseh Ln *TF:* 800-325-2525	Evansville	IN	47715	812-473-7944	473-0099
Drury Inn 3901 Hwy 41 N *TF:* 800-378-7946	Evansville	IN	47711	812-423-5818	423-5818
Esquire Inn 1817 Business Hwy 41 N	Evansville	IN	47711	812-422-6000	
Fairfield Inn East 7879 Eagle Crest Blvd *TF:* 800-228-2800 ■ *Web:* fairfieldinn.com/EVVIN	Evansville	IN	47715	812-471-7000	471-7000
Fairfield Inn West 5400 Weston Rd *TF:* 800-228-2800 ■ *Web:* fairfieldinn.com/EVVFW	Evansville	IN	47712	812-429-0900	429-0900
Hampton Inn 8000 Eagle Crest Blvd *TF:* 800-426-7866	Evansville	IN	47715	812-473-5000	479-1664
Holiday Inn Airport 4101 Hwy 41 N *TF:* 800-465-4329	Evansville	IN	47711	812-424-6400	424-6409
Holiday Inn East 100 S Green River Rd *TF:* 800-465-4329	Evansville	IN	47715	812-473-0171	473-5021
Holiday Inn Express 19600 Elpers Rd *TF:* 800-465-4329	Evansville	IN	47711	812-867-1100	867-2170
Lees Inn 5538 E Indiana St *TF:* 800-733-5337	Evansville	IN	47715	812-477-6663	477-1471
Marriott Evansville Airport 7101 Hwy 41 N *TF:* 800-228-9290 ■ *Web:* marriotthotels.com/EVVAP	Evansville	IN	47711	812-867-7999	867-0241
Motel 6 4321 Hwy 41 N *TF:* 800-466-8356	Evansville	IN	47711	812-424-6431	424-7803
Oak Meadow Lodge 11503 Browning Rd *TF:* 800-933-1920	Evansville	IN	47711	812-867-6431	867-6400
Quality Hotel & Suites 20 Walnut St *TF:* 800-824-6710 ■ *Web:* www.theriverhouse.com	Evansville	IN	47708	812-425-3176	423-7216
Radisson Hotel 600 Walnut St *TF:* 800-333-3333	Evansville	IN	47708	812-424-8000	426-2320
Ramada Limited 2508 Hwy 41 N	Evansville	IN	47711	812-425-1092	426-1462

Evansville — Hotels, Motels, Resorts (Cont'd)

				Phone	Fax
Signature Inn Evansville 1101 N Green River Rd. TF: 800-822-5252 ■ Web: www.signature-inns.com/locations/evansville ■ E-mail: feedback@signature-inns.com	Evansville	IN	47715	812-476-9626	
StudioPLUS 301 Eagle Crest Dr. TF: 800-646-8000	Evansville	IN	47715	812-479-0103	469-7172
Super 8 Motel 4600 E Morgan Ave. TF: 800-800-8000	Evansville	IN	47715	812-476-4008	476-4008
Travelodge 701 1st Ave. TF: 800-578-7878	Evansville	IN	47710	812-424-3886	424-0256

— Restaurants —

				Phone
Canton Inn (Chinese) 915 N Park Dr	Evansville	IN	47710	812-428-6611
Chili Peppers (Mexican) 600 Walnut St	Evansville	IN	47708	812-424-8000
Clouds Restaurant (American) 7101 Hwy 41 N	Evansville	IN	47711	812-867-7999
Como (Lebanese/Italian) 2700 S Kentucky Ave	Evansville	IN	47714	812-422-0572
Cork'N Cleaver (Steak/Seafood) 650 S Hebron Ave	Evansville	IN	47714	812-479-6974
DiLegge's Restaurant (Italian) 607 N Main St	Evansville	IN	47711	812-428-3004
Elliott's (Steak/Seafood) 4701 E Powell Ave	Evansville	IN	47714	812-473-3378
Hacienda (Mexican) 711 1st Ave	Evansville	IN	47710	812-423-6355
Hilltop Inn (American) 1100 Harmony Way	Evansville	IN	47720	812-422-1757
Jaya's Authentic Foods (Korean) 119 SE 4th St	Evansville	IN	47708	812-422-6667
Landmark The (Middle Eastern) 216 E Riverside Dr	Evansville	IN	47713	812-422-7701
Lone Star Steak House & Saloon (Steak) 943 N Green River Rd	Evansville	IN	47715	812-473-5468
Merry-Go-Round Restaurant (American) 2101 Hwy 41 N	Evansville	IN	47711	812-423-6388
Old Mill (Steak/Seafood) 5031 New Harmony Rd	Evansville	IN	47720	812-963-6000
Passaggio Italian Gardens (Italian) 423 NW Riverside Dr	Evansville	IN	47708	812-433-4230
Raffi's (Italian) 4025 E Morgan Ave	Evansville	IN	47715	812-479-9166
Red Geranium (American) 504 North St	New Harmony	IN	47631	812-425-1314
Shing Lee (Chinese) 215 Main St	Evansville	IN	47708	812-464-2769
Steeple Chase Cafe (Steak) 4101 Hwy 41 N	Evansville	IN	47711	812-424-6400
Sunset Restaurant (American) 20 Walnut St	Evansville	IN	47708	812-425-6500
Wolf's Bar-B-Q Restaurant (Barbecue) 6600 1st Ave	Evansville	IN	47710	812-424-8891
Yen Ching (Chinese) 406 S Green River Rd	Evansville	IN	47715	812-474-0181

— Goods and Services —

SHOPPING

				Phone	Fax
Downtown Walkway Main St	Evansville	IN	47708		
Eastland Mall 800 N Green River Rd	Evansville	IN	47715	812-477-4848	474-1691
Fairlawn Shopping Center S Weinbach & Pollack	Evansville	IN	47714	812-424-4851	424-9242
North Park Shopping Center 4492 1st Ave	Evansville	IN	47710	812-428-0005	421-8145
Village Commons 5300 E Indiana	Evansville	IN	47715	812-424-4851	424-9242
Washington Square Mall 1138 Washington Sq	Evansville	IN	47715	812-477-5041	473-5130
Westgate Shopping Center S Barker Ave	Evansville	IN	47712	812-424-4851	

BANKS

				Phone	Fax
National City Bank of Evansville PO Box 868	Evansville	IN	47705	812-464-9800	464-9825
Old National Bank Evansville 420 Main St. *Fax: Cust Svc ■ TF: 800-731-2265	Evansville	IN	47708	812-464-1200	464-1551*
Peoples Bank 132 S 3rd St	Boonville	IN	47601	812-897-0230	897-6227
Permanent FSB 101 SE 3rd St. *Fax: Hum Res	Evansville	IN	47708	812-428-6800	421-2604*

BUSINESS SERVICES

	Phone
Airborne Express	800-247-2676
BAX Global	800-225-5229
DHL Worldwide Express	800-225-5345
Federal Express	800-238-5355
Kelly Services	812-423-8080
Mail Boxes Etc	800-789-4623
Norrell Temporary Services	812-473-3838
Post Office	812-429-3400
UPS	800-742-5877
Workload Temporary Services	812-422-8367

— Media —

PUBLICATIONS

				Phone	Fax
Evansville Courier‡ PO Box 268. TF: 800-288-3200 ■ Web: courier.evansville.net/	Evansville	IN	47702	812-424-7711	422-8196

‡*Daily newspapers*

TELEVISION

				Phone	Fax
WEHT-TV Ch 25 (ABC) 800 Marywood Dr. TF: 800-879-8549 ■ Web: www.abc25.com	Henderson	KY	42420	270-826-9566	827-0561
WEVV-TV Ch 44 (CBS) 44 Main St. Web: www.wevv.com ■ E-mail: info@wevv.com	Evansville	IN	47708	812-464-4444	465-4559
WFIE-TV Ch 14 (NBC) 1115 Mt Auburn Rd. TF: 800-832-0014 ■ Web: www.nbc14.com/ ■ E-mail: wfie@nbc14.com	Evansville	IN	47720	812-426-1414	426-1945
WNIN-TV Ch 9 (PBS) 405 Carpenter St. Web: www.wnin.org	Evansville	IN	47708	812-423-2973	428-7548
WTSN-TV Ch 63 (Ind) 44 Main St	Evansville	IN	47708	812-464-4463	465-4559
WTVW-TV Ch 7 (Fox) 477 Carpenter St. TF: 800-511-6009 ■ Web: www.wtvw.com	Evansville	IN	47708	812-424-7777	421-4040
WWAZ-TV Ch 19 (WB) 1277 N St Joseph Ave	Evansville	IN	47720	812-425-1900	423-3405

RADIO

				Phone	Fax
WIKY-FM 104.1 MHz (AC) PO Box 3848. Web: www.wiky.com	Evansville	IN	47736	812-424-8284	426-7928
WJPS-FM 93.5 MHz (Oldies) PO Box 3848. Web: www.wjps.com	Evansville	IN	47736	812-424-8284	426-7928
WNIN-FM 88.3 MHz (NPR) 405 Carpenter St. Web: www.wnin.org/	Evansville	IN	47708	812-423-2973	428-7548
WSTO-FM 96.1 MHz (CHR) PO Box 1390. Web: www.wsto.com	Owensboro	KY	42302	270-686-0096	685-7098
WTRI-FM 94.9 MHz (CR) PO Box 78	Evansville	IN	47701	812-425-4226	428-5895
WYNG-FM 105.3 MHz (Ctry) PO Box 78. Web: www.wyng.com	Evansville	IN	47728	812-425-4226	421-0005

— Colleges/Universities —

				Phone	Fax
Ivy Tech State College Southwest 3501 N 1st Ave. Web: www.ivytech12.cc.in.us	Evansville	IN	47710	812-426-2865	429-1483
University of Evansville 1800 Lincoln Ave. *Fax: Admissions ■ TF: 800-423-8633 ■ Web: www.evansville.edu ■ E-mail: admisweb@evansville.edu	Evansville	IN	47722	812-479-2000	474-4076*
University of Southern Indiana 8600 University Blvd. TF Admin: 800-467-1965 ■ Web: www.usi.edu	Evansville	IN	47712	812-464-8600	465-7154

— Hospitals —

				Phone	Fax
Deaconess Hospital 600 Mary St. *Fax: Admissions	Evansville	IN	47747	812-450-5000	450-2155*
Saint Mary's Medical Center of Evansville 3700 Washington Ave. *Fax: Admitting	Evansville	IN	47750	812-485-4000	485-4094*
Welborn Baptist Hospital 401 SE 6th St. Web: www.welborn.com	Evansville	IN	47713	812-426-8000	426-8757

— Attractions —

				Phone	Fax
Angel Mounds State Historic Site 8215 Pollack Ave. Web: www.angelmounds.org ■ E-mail: curator@angelmounds.org	Evansville	IN	47715	812-853-3956	853-6271
Burdette Park 5301 Nurrenbern Rd	Evansville	IN	47712	812-435-5602	435-5949
Casino Aztar 421 NW Riverside Dr. TF: 800-342-5386 ■ Web: www.casinoaztar.com/	Evansville	IN	47708	812-433-4000	433-4384
Engelbrecht Orchards 600 Christ Rd	Evansville	IN	47711	812-423-1079	
Evansville Civic Theatre 717 N Fulton Ave	Evansville	IN	47710	812-423-2616	423-2616

Evansville — Attractions (Cont'd)

	City	State	Zip	Phone	Fax
Evansville Dance Theatre 333 N Plaza East Blvd Suite E *Web:* www.evansville.net/~nagivon/	Evansville	IN	47715	812-473-8937	473-8937
Evansville Museum of Arts & Science 411 SE Riverside Dr *Web:* www.emuseum.org	Evansville	IN	47713	812-425-2406	421-7509
Evansville Philharmonic Orchestra 530 Main St *Web:* philharmonic.evansville.net/ ■ *E-mail:* evphil@evansville.net	Evansville	IN	47708	812-425-5050	426-7008
George Rogers Clark National Historical Park 401 S 2nd St *Web:* www.nps.gov/gero/	Vincennes	IN	47591	812-882-1776	882-7270
Historic New Harmony 506 1/2 Main St	New Harmony	IN	47631	812-682-4474	682-4313
Historic Newburgh 9 W Jennings St *TF:* 800-636-9489	Newburgh	IN	47630	812-853-2815	853-2815
Holiday World Theme Park & Splashin' Safari Hwys 162 & 245 **Fax Area Code:* 812 ■ *TF:* 800-467-2682 ■ *Web:* www.holidayworld.com ■ *E-mail:* hwadmin@holidayworld.com	Santa Claus	IN	47579	800-467-2682	937-4405*
John James Audubon Museum 3100 US Hwy 41 N	Henderson	KY	42419	270-826-2247	826-2286
Lincoln Boyhood National Memorial Hwy 162 *Web:* www.nps.gov/libo/	Lincoln City	IN	47552	812-937-4541	937-9929
Mesker Park Zoo 2421 Bement Ave *Web:* www.meskerparkzoo.org ■ *E-mail:* mpzoo@evansville.net	Evansville	IN	47720	812-428-0715	422-9673
Old Courthouse Preservation Society 201 NW 4th St Suite 101	Evansville	IN	47708	812-423-3361	423-5260
Reitz Home Museum 224 SE 1st St *Web:* reitzhome.evansville.net/	Evansville	IN	47713	812-426-1871	426-2179
Wesselman Woods Nature Preserve 551 N Boeke Rd	Evansville	IN	47711	812-479-0771	479-7573
Willard Library of Evansville 21 1st Ave *Web:* www.evansville.net/eville/education/willard.html	Evansville	IN	47710	812-425-4309	421-9742

SPORTS TEAMS & FACILITIES

	City	State	Zip	Phone	Fax
Ellis Park Race Course 3300 Hwy 41 N *TF:* 800-333-8110	Henderson	KY	42420	812-425-1456	425-3725
Evansville Otters (baseball) 1701 N Main St Bosse Field *TF:* 800-435-8681 ■ *Web:* www.otters.evansville.net ■ *E-mail:* ottersbb@evansville.net	Evansville	IN	47711	812-435-8686	435-8688

— Events —

	Phone
Arts & Crafts Show (late September)	812-867-4935
Big Rivers Arts & Crafts Festival (early October)	270-926-4433
Boo at the Zoo (mid-October)	812-428-0715
Christmas Main Street Parade (mid-November)	812-424-2986
Collector's Carnival (late January & late April & late October)	812-471-9419
Fantasy of Lights (late November-late December)	812-474-2348
First Night Evansville (December 31)	812-422-2111
Germania Mannerchor Volksfest (early August)	812-422-1915
Golden Harvest Arts & Crafts Show (early October)	812-422-5600
Haunted Hay Rides (late October)	812-479-0771
Heritage Week (late April)	812-682-4488
Kite Day (late April)	812-853-3956
Mid-States Arts Exhibition (early December-late January)	812-425-2406
Native American Days (late September)	812-853-3956
Pioneer Days Festival (early May)	812-479-0771
Sugarbush Festival (early March)	812-479-0771
Thunder Festival (mid-June-early July)	812-464-9576
Victorian Christmas (November-December)	812-426-1871
West Side Nut Club Fall Festival (early October)	812-464-5993
Winter Carnival (late November)	812-867-6217

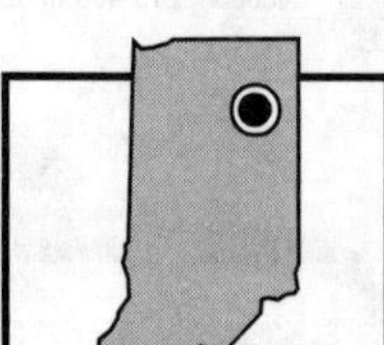

Fort Wayne

Named for the fort built by General "Mad" Anthony Wayne at the confluence of the Maumee, Saint Joseph, and Saint Marys rivers, Fort Wayne is the second largest city in Indiana. In recent years the city has received an "All American City" award and has been designated as one of America's most livable cities. It has also been called the "City of Restaurants" for its more than 400 eating establishments, ranging from fast food to four-star dining. One of the many shopping areas in Fort Wayne is Glenbrook Square, Indiana's largest indoor mall. The Allen County Public Library in Fort Wayne has the second-largest genealogy department in the U.S. Indiana's largest employer, Lincoln National Corporation, which is home of the world's largest private collection of President Lincoln memorabilia, has its headquarters in Fort Wayne.

Population	185,716	**Longitude**	85-12-89 W
Area (Land)	62.7 sq mi	**County**	Allen
Area (Water)	0.2 sq mi	**Time Zone**	EST
Elevation	781 ft	**Area Code/s**	219
Latitude	41-13-06 N		

— Average Temperatures and Precipitation —

TEMPERATURES

	Jan	Feb	Mar	Apr	May	Jun	Jul	Aug	Sep	Oct	Nov	Dec
High	30	34	46	60	71	81	85	82	76	63	49	36
Low	15	18	29	39	49	59	63	61	54	43	34	22

PRECIPITATION

	Jan	Feb	Mar	Apr	May	Jun	Jul	Aug	Sep	Oct	Nov	Dec
Inches	1.9	1.9	2.9	3.4	3.4	3.6	3.5	3.4	2.7	2.5	2.8	2.9

— Important Phone Numbers —

	Phone		Phone
AAA	219-484-1541	**Poison Control Center**	800-382-9097
Dental Referral	219-483-4684	**Time/Temp**	219-422-0123
Emergency	911	**Weather**	219-424-5050

— Information Sources —

	City	State	Zip	Phone	Fax
Allen County 715 S Calhoun St County Courthouse Rm 201	Fort Wayne	IN	46802	219-449-7245	449-7929
Allen County Public Library 900 Webster St. *Web:* www.acpl.lib.in.us	Fort Wayne	IN	46801	219-421-1200	422-9688
Allen County War Memorial Coliseum 4000 Parnell Ave. *Web:* www.memorialcoliseum.com ■ *E-mail:* info@memorialcoliseum.com	Fort Wayne	IN	46805	219-482-9502	484-1637
Better Business Bureau Serving Northeastern Indiana 1203 Webster St *Web:* www.fortwayne.bbb.org	Fort Wayne	IN	46802	219-423-4433	423-3301
Fort Wayne City Hall 1 Main St *Web:* www.ci.ft-wayne.in.us	Fort Wayne	IN	46802	219-427-1111	427-1115
Fort Wayne Community & Economic Development Div 1 Main St Rm 910 *Web:* www.ci.ft-wayne.in.us/ced	Fort Wayne	IN	46802	219-427-1131	427-1115
Fort Wayne Mayor 1 Main St *Web:* www.ci.ft-wayne.in.us/mayors_office/index.htm ■ *E-mail:* mayor@ci.ft-wayne.in.us	Fort Wayne	IN	46802	219-427-1111	427-1115
Fort Wayne/Allen County Convention & Visitors Bureau 1021 S Calhoun St. *TF:* 800-767-7752 ■ *Web:* www.fwcvb.org ■ *E-mail:* fwcvb@fwai.org	Fort Wayne	IN	46802	219-424-3700	424-3914
Grand Wayne Center 120 W Jefferson Blvd	Fort Wayne	IN	46802	219-426-4100	420-9080
Greater Fort Wayne Chamber of Commerce 826 Ewing St *Web:* www.fwchamber.org	Fort Wayne	IN	46802	219-424-1435	426-7232

On-Line Resources

4FortWayne.com	www.4fortwayne.com
Anthill City Guide Fort Wayne	www.anthill.com/city.asp?city=fortwayne
Area Guide Fort Wayne	fortwayne.areaguides.net
City Knowledge Fort Wayne	www.cityknowledge.com/in_fortwayne.htm

Fort Wayne — On-Line Resources (Cont'd)

Excite.com Fort Wayne City Guide .... www.excite.com/travel/countries/united_states/indiana/fort_wayne
Fort Wayne Area InfoNet .... www.ft-wayne.com
Fort Wayne Guide .... www.srspub.com
InFortWayne.com .... www.inftwayne.com/

— Transportation Services —

AIRPORTS

■ Fort Wayne International Airport (FWA)

	Phone
7 miles SW of downtown (approx 15 minutes)	219-747-4146

Web: www.ftwayneintlairport.com ■ *E-mail:* info@ftwayneintlairport.com

Airport Transportation

	Phone
Deluxe Cab $22 fare to downtown	219-482-3634

Commercial Airlines

	Phone		Phone
American Eagle	800-433-7300	**TWA Express**	800-221-2000
Comair	800-354-9822	**United Express**	800-241-6522
Delta	800-221-1212	**US Airways**	800-428-4322
Northwest	800-225-2525		

Charter Airlines

	Phone		Phone
Bowman Aviation Inc	219-927-4040	**Fort Wayne Air Service Inc**	219-747-1565
Consolidated Charter Service	219-747-1626		

CAR RENTALS

	Phone		Phone
Ace	219-482-8546	**CarTemps USA**	219-482-7777
Avis	219-747-7438	**Enterprise**	219-482-2662
Budget	219-478-2507	**Hertz**	219-747-6108

LIMO/TAXI

	Phone		Phone
AAA Fort Wayne Connection	219-436-5466	**Fort Wayne Limo**	219-436-5466
Checker Cab	219-426-8555	**JJR Corp**	219-423-2486
Deluxe Cab	219-482-3634		

MASS TRANSIT

	Phone
PTC Bus $1 Base fare	219-432-4546

RAIL/BUS

				Phone
Greyhound/Trailways Bus Station 929 Lafayette St.	Fort Wayne	IN	46802	219-423-9525

— Accommodations —

HOTELS, MOTELS, RESORTS

				Phone	Fax
Baymont Inns & Suites 1005 W Washington Center Rd.	Fort Wayne	IN	46825	219-489-2220	489-4579
TF: 800-301-0200					
Best Western Airport Plaza 3939 Ferguson Rd	Fort Wayne	IN	46809	219-747-9171	747-1848
TF: 800-528-1234					
Best Western Luxbury Inn 5501 Coventry Ln	Fort Wayne	IN	46804	219-436-0242	436-2256
Canterbury Green Executive Suites 2613 Abbey Dr	Fort Wayne	IN	46835	219-485-9619	485-7699
Coliseum Inn 1020 N Coliseum Blvd	Fort Wayne	IN	46805	219-424-0975	424-0975
Comfort Suites 5575 Coventry Ln	Fort Wayne	IN	46804	219-436-4300	436-2030
TF: 800-228-5150					
Corporate Housing Systems 6517 Constitution Dr	Fort Wayne	IN	46804	219-436-7171	436-8281
TF: 800-430-7171					
Courtyard by Marriott Hotel 1619 W Washington Ctr Rd	Fort Wayne	IN	46818	219-489-1500	489-3273
TF: 800-321-2211 ■ *Web:* courtyard.com/FWACY					
Days Inn 3730 E Washington Blvd	Fort Wayne	IN	46803	219-424-1980	422-6525
TF: 800-329-7466					
Days Inn North 5250 Distribution Dr	Fort Wayne	IN	46825	219-484-9681	483-2217
TF: 800-829-7466					
Don Hall's Guesthouse 1313 W Washington Center Rd.	Fort Wayne	IN	46825	219-489-2524	489-7067
TF: 800-348-1999 ■ *Web:* www.donhalls.com					
Economy Inn 1401 W Washington Center Rd.	Fort Wayne	IN	46825	219-489-3588	489-3588
Extended StayAmerica 8309 W Jefferson Blvd	Fort Wayne	IN	46804	219-432-1916	432-0757
TF: 800-398-7829					
Fairfield Inn 5710 Challenger Pkwy	Fort Wayne	IN	46818	219-489-0050	489-0050
TF: 800-228-2800 ■ *Web:* fairfieldinn.com/FWAFI					
Hampton Inn 8219 W Jefferson Blvd	Fort Wayne	IN	46804	219-459-1999	432-4087
TF: 800-426-7866					
Hampton Inn & Suites 5702 Challenger Pkwy	Fort Wayne	IN	46818	219-489-0908	489-9295
TF: 800-426-7866					
Hilton Hotel 1020 S Calhoun St	Fort Wayne	IN	46802	219-420-1100	424-7775
TF: 800-448-8667 ■ *Web:* www.hilton.com/hotels/FWAFHHF					
Holiday Inn Downtown 300 E Washington Blvd	Fort Wayne	IN	46802	219-422-5511	424-1511
TF: 800-465-4329					
Holiday Inn Northwest 3330 W Coliseum Blvd	Fort Wayne	IN	46808	219-484-7711	482-7429
TF: 800-465-4329 ■ *Web:* www.basshotels.com/holiday-inn/?_franchisee=FWANW ■ *E-mail:* hifwa@aol.com					
Hometown Inn 6910 Hwy 930 E	Fort Wayne	IN	46803	219-749-5058	493-2283
Knights Inn North 2901 Goshen Rd	Fort Wayne	IN	46808	219-484-2669	484-1209
TF: 800-843-5644					
Lees Inn 5707 Challenger Pkwy	Fort Wayne	IN	46818	219-489-8888	489-4354
TF: 800-733-5337					
Marriott Hotel Fort Wayne 305 E Washington Ctr Rd	Fort Wayne	IN	46825	219-484-0411	483-2892
TF: 800-228-9290 ■ *Web:* marriotthotels.com/FWAIN					
Potawatomi Inn 6 Lane 100A Lake James	Angola	IN	46703	219-833-1077	833-4087
TF: 877-768-2928					
Red Carpet Inn 1212 Magnavox Way	Fort Wayne	IN	46804	219-436-8600	432-9764
TF: 800-251-1962					
Red Roof Inn 2920 Goshen Rd	Fort Wayne	IN	46808	219-484-8641	484-3441
TF: 800-843-7663					
Residence Inn by Marriott 4919 Lima Rd	Fort Wayne	IN	46808	219-484-4700	484-9772
TF: 800-331-3131 ■ *Web:* www.residenceinn.com/FWALM					
Signature Inn Fort Wayne 1734 Washington Ctr Rd	Fort Wayne	IN	46818	219-489-5554	489-5554
TF: 800-822-5252 ■ *Web:* www.signature-inns.com/locations/ft_wayne ■ *E-mail:* feedback@signature-inns.com					
StudioPLUS 5810 Challenger Pkwy	Fort Wayne	IN	46818	219-490-0500	497-6472
TF: 800-646-8000					
Sumner Suites 111 W Washington Center Rd	Fort Wayne	IN	46825	219-471-8522	471-9223
TF: 800-747-8483					
Traveler's Inn 4606 Lincoln Hwy	Fort Wayne	IN	46803	219-422-9511	422-9511
Willows of Coventry Corporate Lodging 4499 Coventry Pkwy	Fort Wayne	IN	46804	219-432-9566	436-5591

— Restaurants —

				Phone
Acme Bar (American) 1105 E State Blvd	Fort Wayne	IN	46805	219-484-5098
Bagatelle Bistro & Bar (Steak/Seafood) 6421 W Jefferson Blvd	Fort Wayne	IN	46804	219-436-9115
Bandido's (Mexican) 6536 E State Blvd	Fort Wayne	IN	46815	219-749-0485
Bill's Bistro (Steak/Seafood) 1802 Spy Run	Fort Wayne	IN	46805	219-422-7012
Cafe Johnell (French) 2529 S Calhoun St	Fort Wayne	IN	46807	219-456-1939
Casa D'Angelo (Italian) 4111 Parnell Ave	Fort Wayne	IN	46805	219-483-0202
Chappell's Coral Grill & Seafood Market (Seafood) 2723 Broadway	Fort Wayne	IN	46807	219-456-9652
Cindy's Diner (American) 830 S Harrison St	Fort Wayne	IN	46802	219-422-1957
Columbia Street West (American) 135 W Columbia St	Fort Wayne	IN	46802	219-422-5055
Cork'N Cleaver (Steak/Seafood) 211 E Washington Center Rd	Fort Wayne	IN	46825	219-484-7772
D & G's Just Ribs (Barbecue) 2115 S Lafayette St	Fort Wayne	IN	46803	219-456-3232
Don Hall's Factory (American) 5811 Coldwater Rd	Fort Wayne	IN	46825	219-484-8693
Don Hall's Old Gas House (American) 305 E Superior St	Fort Wayne	IN	46802	219-426-3411
El Azteca (Mexican) 535 E State St	Fort Wayne	IN	46805	219-482-2172
El Charro (Mexican) 2419 W Jefferson Blvd	Fort Wayne	IN	46804	219-432-6038
Elegant Farmer (Steak) 1820 Coliseum Blvd N	Fort Wayne	IN	46805	219-482-1976
Firehouse Cafe (American) 226 W Washington Blvd	Fort Wayne	IN	46806	219-426-0051

Fort Wayne — Restaurants (Cont'd)

				Phone
Hilgers Farm Restaurant (Homestyle) 13210 US Hwy 30 W	Fort Wayne	IN	46818	219-625-4181
La Hacienda (Mexican) 3938 W Jefferson Blvd	Fort Wayne	IN	46804	219-432-9721
Lombard's (Italian) 1020 S Calhoun St	Fort Wayne	IN	46802	219-420-1100
Mandarian (Chinese) 5978 Stellhorn Plaza	Fort Wayne	IN	46815	219-485-9175
Oyster Bar (Seafood) 1830 S Calhoun St	Fort Wayne	IN	46802	219-744-9490
Park Place Grill (American) 200 E Main St Suite 120	Fort Wayne	IN	46802	219-420-7275
Sidewalk Cafe (American) 300 E Washington Blvd	Fort Wayne	IN	46802	219-422-5511
Takaoka of Japan (Japanese) 305 E Superior St	Fort Wayne	IN	46802	219-424-3183
Taste of India (Indian) 4614 Coldwater Rd	Fort Wayne	IN	46825	219-482-1612
Triangle Park Bar & Grille (Steak/Seafood) 3010 Trier Rd	Fort Wayne	IN	46815	219-482-4342

— Goods and Services —

SHOPPING

				Phone
Georgetown Mall 6426 Georgetown Ln	Fort Wayne	IN	46815	219-749-0461
Glenbrook Square 4201 Coldwater Rd	Fort Wayne	IN	46805	219-483-2119
Southtown Mall 7800 S Anthony Blvd	Fort Wayne	IN	46816	219-447-4594

BANKS

				Phone	Fax
Bank One PO Box 2345	Fort Wayne	IN	46801	219-427-8333	427-8189
Home Loan Bank SB PO Box 989	Fort Wayne	IN	46801	219-422-3502	426-7027
National City Bank PO Box 110 **Fax:* Cust Svc	Fort Wayne	IN	46802	219-426-0555	461-6209*
Norwest Bank Indiana NA PO Box 960	Fort Wayne	IN	46801	219-461-6000	461-6392
Star Financial Bank 5854 N Clinton St	Fort Wayne	IN	46825	219-431-5534	431-5537

BUSINESS SERVICES

	Phone
Airborne Express	800-247-2676
An Office Alternative	219-482-4032
BAX Global	800-225-5229
DHL Worldwide Express	800-225-5345
Federal Express	800-238-5355
Interim Personnel Services	219-483-9590
Mail Boxes Etc	800-789-4623
Post Office	219-427-7310
UPS	800-742-5877

— Media —

PUBLICATIONS

				Phone	Fax
Journal Gazette‡ 600 W Main St — *TF:* 800-444-3303 ■ *Web:* www.jg.net/jg/	Fort Wayne	IN	46802	219-461-8222	461-8648
News-Sentinel‡ 600 W Main St — *Web:* www.news-sentinel.com/ns	Fort Wayne	IN	46802	219-461-8222	461-8817

‡Daily newspapers

TELEVISION

				Phone	Fax
WANE-TV Ch 15 (CBS) 2915 W State Blvd — *Web:* www.wane.com ■ *E-mail:* wane-tv@cris.com	Fort Wayne	IN	46808	219-424-1515	424-6054
WFFT-TV Ch 55 (Fox) 3707 Hillegas Rd — *Web:* www.wfft.com ■ *E-mail:* wfft@mail.fwi.com	Fort Wayne	IN	46808	219-471-5555	484-4331
WFWA-TV Ch 39 (PBS) 3632 Butler Rd — *E-mail:* tv39@wfwa.pbs.org	Fort Wayne	IN	46808	219-484-8839	482-3632
WKJG-TV Ch 33 (NBC) 2633 W State Blvd — *Web:* www.nbc33.com	Fort Wayne	IN	46808	219-422-7474	422-7702
WPTA-TV Ch 21 (ABC) 3401 Butler Rd — *Web:* www.wpta.com ■ *E-mail:* wpta@wpta.com	Fort Wayne	IN	46808	219-483-0584	484-8240

RADIO

				Phone	Fax
WAJI-FM 95.1 MHz (AC) 347 W Berry St Suite 600 — *Web:* www.waji.com	Fort Wayne	IN	46802	219-423-3676	422-5266
WBCL-FM 90.3 MHz (Rel) 1025 W Rudisill Blvd — *Web:* www.wbcl.org ■ *E-mail:* mail@wbcl.org	Fort Wayne	IN	46807	219-745-0576	745-2001
WBNI-FM 89.1 MHz (NPR) 3204 Clairmont Ct — *Web:* www.wbni.org	Fort Wayne	IN	46808	219-452-1189	452-1188
WBTU-FM 93.3 MHz (Ctry) 2100 Goshen Rd Suite 232 — *Web:* www.wbtu.com ■ *E-mail:* wbtu@wbtu.com	Fort Wayne	IN	46808	219-482-9288	482-8655
WBYR-FM 98.9 MHz (Rock) 1005 Production Rd — *Web:* www.wbyr.com	Fort Wayne	IN	46808	219-471-5100	471-5224
WMEE-FM 97.3 MHz (AC) 2915 Maples Rd — *Web:* www.wmee.com	Fort Wayne	IN	46816	219-447-5511	447-7546
WXKE-FM 103.9 MHz (Rock) 2541 Goshen Rd	Fort Wayne	IN	46808	219-484-0580	482-5151

— Colleges/Universities —

				Phone	Fax
Indiana Institute of Technology 1600 E Washington Blvd — *Web:* www.indtech.edu	Fort Wayne	IN	46803	219-422-5561	422-7696
Indiana University-Purdue University Fort Wayne 2101 E Coliseum Blvd — *Web:* www.ipfw.indiana.edu ■ *E-mail:* violette@ipfw.indiana.edu	Fort Wayne	IN	46805	219-481-6100	481-6880
International Business College 3811 Illinois Rd	Fort Wayne	IN	46804	219-432-8702	436-1896
ITT Technical Institute 4919 Coldwater Rd — *TF:* 800-866-4488 ■ *Web:* www.itt-tech.edu	Fort Wayne	IN	46825	219-484-4107	484-0860
Ivy Tech State College Fort Wayne 3800 N Anthony Blvd — *Web:* www.ivy.tec.in.us/FortWayne	Fort Wayne	IN	46805	219-482-9171	480-4177
Taylor University Fort Wayne Campus 1025 W Rudisill Blvd — *TF:* 800-233-3922 ■ *Web:* www.tayloru.edu/fw/	Fort Wayne	IN	46807	219-456-2111	456-2119
University of Saint Francis 2701 Spring St — *TF Admissions:* 800-729-4732 ■ *Web:* www.sfc.edu ■ *E-mail:* admiss@sf.edu	Fort Wayne	IN	46808	219-434-3100	434-3183

— Hospitals —

				Phone	Fax
Lutheran Hospital of Indiana 7950 W Jefferson Blvd — *Web:* www.lutheran-hosp.com	Fort Wayne	IN	46804	219-435-7001	435-7632
Parkview Hospital 2200 Randallia Dr — **Fax:* Admitting ■ *TF:* 888-856-2522 ■ *Web:* www.parkview.com	Fort Wayne	IN	46805	219-484-6636	480-5965*
Saint Joseph Medical Center 700 Broadway	Fort Wayne	IN	46802	219-425-3000	425-3222
Veterans Affairs Medical Center 2121 Lake Ave	Fort Wayne	IN	46805	219-426-5431	460-1410

— Attractions —

				Phone	Fax
Allen County Courthouse 715 S Calhoun St — **Fax:* County Clerk	Fort Wayne	IN	46802	219-449-7211	449-7929*
Arena Dinner Theater 719 Rockhill St	Fort Wayne	IN	46802	219-493-1384	
Artlink Visual Arts Gallery 437 E Berry St	Fort Wayne	IN	46802	219-424-7195	
Arts United of Greater Fort Wayne 114 E Superior St	Fort Wayne	IN	46802	219-424-0646	424-2783
Auburn Cord-Duesenberg Museum 1600 S Wayne St — *Web:* www.clearlake.com/auburn/	Auburn	IN	46706	219-925-1444	925-6266
Cathedral of the Immaculate Conception & Museum 1122 S Clinton St	Fort Wayne	IN	46802	219-424-1485	
Concordia Theological Seminary 6600 N Clinton St — *Web:* www.ctsfw.edu	Fort Wayne	IN	46825	219-452-2100	452-2121
Embassy Theatre 125 W Jefferson Blvd	Fort Wayne	IN	46802	219-424-6287	424-4806
Firefighters' Museum 226 W Washington Blvd — *Web:* www.fwcvb.org/fire.html	Fort Wayne	IN	46802	219-426-0051	
First Presbyterian Theater 300 W Wayne St	Fort Wayne	IN	46802	219-426-7421	422-6329

Fort Wayne — Attractions (Cont'd)

				Phone	Fax
Foellinger-Freimann Botanical Conservatory 1100 S Calhoun St	Fort Wayne	IN	46802	219-427-6440	427-6450
Fort Wayne Ballet 303 E Main St Performing Arts Center	Fort Wayne	IN	46802	219-484-9646	484-9647
Fort Wayne Children's Zoo 3411 Sherman Blvd **Fax:* Mail Rm ■ *Web:* www.kidszoo.com	Fort Wayne	IN	46808	219-427-6800	427-6820*
Fort Wayne Civic Theater 303 E Main St Performing Arts Ctr *Web:* www.fwcivic.org ■ *E-mail:* civic@fwa.cioe.com	Fort Wayne	IN	46802	219-422-8641	422-6699
Fort Wayne Dance Collective 437 E Berry St	Fort Wayne	IN	46802	219-424-6574	422-8712
Fort Wayne Historical Museum 302 E Berry St *Web:* www.fwcvb.org/history.html ■ *E-mail:* fwcvb@fwcvb.org	Fort Wayne	IN	46802	219-426-2882	424-4419
Fort Wayne Museum of Art 311 E Main St *Web:* www.art-museum-ftwayne.org	Fort Wayne	IN	46802	219-422-6467	422-1374
Fort Wayne Philharmonic Orchestra 303 E Main St Performing Arts Ctr	Fort Wayne	IN	46802	219-744-1700	456-8555
Fort Wayne Youtheatre 303 E Main St	Fort Wayne	IN	46802	219-422-6900	422-6900
Fox Island 7324 Yohne Rd	Fort Wayne	IN	46809	219-449-3180	449-3181
Headwaters Park Superior & Clinton Sts	Fort Wayne	IN	46802	219-425-5745	425-5158
Heritage Trail Walking Tour Downtown Ft Wayne	Fort Wayne	IN	46802	219-426-5117	422-8712
Jack D Diehm Museum of Natural History 600 Franke Park Dr	Fort Wayne	IN	46808	219-427-6708	
Lakeside Rose Garden 1400 Lake Ave	Fort Wayne	IN	46805	219-427-6000	427-6020
Lincoln Museum 200 E Berry St *Web:* www.thelincolnmuseum.org	Fort Wayne	IN	46802	219-455-3864	455-6922
Macedonian Tribune Museum 124 W Wayne St Suite 204 *Web:* www.macedonian.org ■ *E-mail:* mtfw@macedonian.org	Fort Wayne	IN	46802	219-422-5900	422-1348
Science Central 1950 N Clinton St *TF:* 800-442-6376	Fort Wayne	IN	46805	219-424-2413	422-2899
Swinney Homestead 1424 W Jefferson Blvd	Fort Wayne	IN	46802	219-424-7212	

SPORTS TEAMS & FACILITIES

				Phone	Fax
Fort Wayne Fury (basketball) 4000 Parnell Ave Allen County War Memorial Coliseum *Web:* www.furyhoops.com	Fort Wayne	IN	46805	219-471-3879	471-9716
Fort Wayne Komets (hockey) 4000 Parnell Ave Allen County War Memorial Coliseum *Web:* www.komets.com/	Fort Wayne	IN	46805	219-483-0011	483-3899
Fort Wayne Wizards (baseball) 4000 Parnell Ave Memorial Stadium *Web:* www.fwi.com/wizards/ ■ *E-mail:* info@wizzardsbaseball.com	Fort Wayne	IN	46805	219-482-6400	

— Events —

	Phone
Allen County Fair (late July)	219-637-5818
Auburn Cord-Duesenberg Festival (early September)	219-925-1444
Berne Swiss Days (late July)	219-589-3632
Festival of Gingerbread (late November-mid-December)	219-426-2882
Festival of Trees (late November-early December)	219-424-6287
Fort Wayne Hoosier Marathon (early-June)	219-749-7288
Gathering of the People (late July)	219-244-7702
Germanfest (mid-June)	219-436-4064
Greek Fest (late June)	219-426-9706
Hispanic American Festival (early-mid-September)	219-744-5129
Indiana Black Expo (early June)	219-422-6486
Indiana Highland Games (late July)	219-486-9543
Irish Fest (mid-August)	219-423-3343
Johnny Appleseed Festival (mid-September)	219-424-3700
National Print Exhibition (late May-early July)	219-424-7195
New Haven Canal Days (early June)	219-749-2972
Three Rivers Festival (mid-July)	219-745-5556

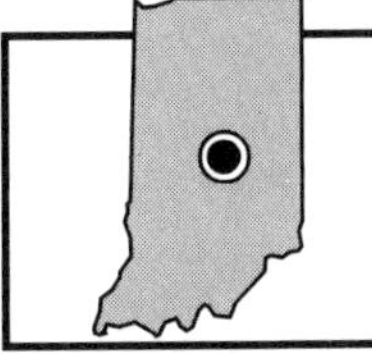

Indianapolis

The world-renowned Indy 500 automobile race attracts more than 350,000 spectators to Indianapolis every May, and the Brickyard 400 is held there each August. Indianapolis is also home to the world's largest Children's Museum; and the Eiteljorg Museum of American Indians and Western Art, the President Benjamin Harrison Memorial Home, Murat Temple, and Connor Prairie Pioneer Settlement (a living history museum set in a restored 1836 village) are also a part of the Indianapolis cultural scene. Eli Lilly and Co., a leading pharmaceutical manufacturer, is headquartered in the city as well. The 60,500 seat RCA Dome (formerly called the Hoosier Dome) is home to the Indianapolis Colts football team and the National Track and Field Hall of Fame, and the new Indiana Basketball Hall of Fame is just 48 miles from Indianapolis, in the city of New Castle.

Population	741,304	**Longitude**	86-09-35 W
Area (Land)	361.7 sq mi	**County**	Marion
Area (Water)	6.6 sq mi	**Time Zone**	EST
Elevation	717 ft	**Area Code/s**	317
Latitude	39-71-43 N		

— Average Temperatures and Precipitation —

TEMPERATURES

	Jan	Feb	Mar	Apr	May	Jun	Jul	Aug	Sep	Oct	Nov	Dec
High	34	38	51	63	74	83	86	84	78	66	52	39
Low	17	21	32	42	52	61	65	63	56	44	34	23

PRECIPITATION

	Jan	Feb	Mar	Apr	May	Jun	Jul	Aug	Sep	Oct	Nov	Dec
Inches	2.3	2.5	3.8	3.7	4.0	3.5	4.5	3.6	2.9	2.6	3.2	3.3

— Important Phone Numbers —

	Phone		Phone
AAA	317-923-1500	**HotelDocs**	800-468-3537
American Express Travel	317-237-2230	**Poison Control Center**	317-929-2323
Dental Referral	317-923-8421	**Time/Temp**	317-635-5959
Emergency	911	**Weather**	317-635-5959

— Information Sources —

				Phone	Fax
Better Business Bureau Serving Central Indiana 22 E Washington St Suite 200 *Web:* www.indianapolis.bbb.org	Indianapolis	IN	46204	317-488-2222	488-2224
Indiana Convention Center & RCA Dome 100 S Capitol Ave *Web:* www.iccrd.com	Indianapolis	IN	46225	317-262-3410	262-3685
Indianapolis Chamber of Commerce 320 N Meridian St Suite 200 *Web:* www.indychamber.com ■ *E-mail:* chamber@indylink.com	Indianapolis	IN	46204	317-464-2200	464-2217
Indianapolis City Center 201 S Capitol Ave Pan Am Plaza Suite 200 *TF:* 800-323-4639 ■ *Web:* www.indy.org ■ *E-mail:* icva@indianapolis.org	Indianapolis	IN	46225	317-237-5200	237-5211
Indianapolis City Hall 200 E Washington St. *Web:* www.ci.indianapolis.in.us	Indianapolis	IN	46204	317-327-4348	
Indianapolis Convention & Visitors Assn 200 S Capitol Ave 1 RCA Dome Suite 100 *TF:* 800-323-4639 ■ *Web:* www.indy.org ■ *E-mail:* icva@indianapolis.org	Indianapolis	IN	46225	317-639-4282	639-5273

Indianapolis — Information Sources (Cont'd)

				Phone	Fax
Indianapolis-Marion County Public Library 40 E Saint Clair St *Web:* www.imcpl.lib.in.us	Indianapolis	IN	46206	317-269-1700	269-1768
Indianapolis Mayor 200 E Washington St Suite 2501 *Web:* www.ci.indianapolis.in.us/mayor	Indianapolis	IN	46204	317-327-3601	327-5424
Indianapolis Planning Div 200 E Washington St Suite 2041	Indianapolis	IN	46204	317-327-5151	327-7883
Marion County 200 E Washington St W-122 City County Bldg *Web:* www.ci.indianapolis.in.us/county	Indianapolis	IN	46204	317-327-3200	327-3893

On-Line Resources

4Indianapolis.com . . . www.4indianapolis.com
About.com Guide to Indianapolis . . . indianapolis.about.com/local/midwestus/indianapolis
Anthill City Guide Indianapolis . . . www.anthill.com/city.asp?city=indianapolis
Area Guide Indianapolis . . . indianapolis.areaguides.net
Boulevards Indianapolis . . . www.indianapolis.com
City Knowledge Indianapolis . . . www.cityknowledge.com/in_indianapolis.htm
DigitalCity Indianapolis . . . home.digitalcity.com/indianapolis
Excite.com Indianapolis City Guide . . . www.excite.com/travel/countries/united_states/indiana/indianapolis
Front Page . . . www.indianapolis.org/menu1.htm
Gateway to Greater Indianapolis . . . www.bit-wise.com/magic
Gay & Lesbian Indianapolis . . . www.gayindy.org/
Go Indy . . . www.goindy.com/
Indianapolis Connect . . . www.indplsconnect.com/
Indianapolis Home Page . . . www.indygov.org
Indianapolis Online . . . www.indianapolis.in.us/
Indy Links . . . www.indylinks.com
Indy.com . . . www.indy.com
IndyMall . . . www.indymall.com/
IndySearch . . . www.indysearch.com/
InIndianapolis.com . . . www.inindy.com/
NITC Travelbase City Guide Indianapolis . . . www.travelbase.com/auto/guides/indianapolis-area-in.html

— Transportation Services —

AIRPORTS

■ Indianapolis International Airport (IND)

	Phone
7 miles SW of downtown (approx 12 minutes)	317-487-9594

Web: indianapolisairport.com

Airport Transportation

	Phone
Metro Bus $1 fare to downtown	317-635-3344
Taxi $17 fare to downtown	317-487-7777

Commercial Airlines

	Phone		Phone
Air Canada	800-776-3000	**Continental Express**	800-525-0280
America West	800-235-9292	**Delta**	800-221-1212
American	800-433-7300	**Northwest**	800-225-2525
American Eagle	800-433-7300	**Southwest**	800-435-9792
American Trans Air	317-248-8308	**TWA**	800-221-2000
Comair	800-354-9822	**United**	800-241-6522
Continental	800-525-0280	**US Airways**	800-428-4322

Charter Airlines

	Phone		Phone
Alliance Executive Charter Services	800-232-5387	**IndianAero Inc**	317-487-5936
Aviation Charter Services	317-244-7200	**Indianapolis Aviation**	317-849-0840
Direct Airway	800-257-9424	**Raytheon Aircraft Charter**	800-519-6283

CAR RENTALS

	Phone		Phone
Ace	317-243-6336	**Enterprise**	317-243-8988
Alamo	317-856-5572	**Hertz**	317-243-9321
Avis	317-244-3307	**National**	317-243-1159
Budget	317-248-1100	**Thrifty**	317-243-2282

LIMO/TAXI

	Phone		Phone
Indy Connection Limousine	317-241-6700	**Yellow Cab**	317-487-7777
VIP Limousine	317-686-4626		

MASS TRANSIT

	Phone
Metro $1 Base fare	317-632-1900

RAIL/BUS

				Phone
Greyhound/Trailways Bus Station 350 S Illinois St. *TF:* 800-231-2222	Indianapolis	IN	46204	317-267-3076
Indianapolis Amtrak Station 350 S Illinois St	Indianapolis	IN	46225	317-263-0550

— Accommodations —

HOTELS, MOTELS, RESORTS

				Phone	Fax
Adam's Mark Hotel 2544 Executive Dr *TF:* 800-444-2326 ■ *Web:* www.adamsmark.com/indin.htm	Indianapolis	IN	46241	317-248-2481	381-6159
American Inn North 7202 E 82nd St	Indianapolis	IN	46256	317-849-6910	849-6783
AmeriSuites 9104 Keystone Crossing *TF:* 800-833-1516	Indianapolis	IN	46240	317-843-0064	843-1851
Baymont Inns & Suites 2349 N Post Dr *TF:* 800-301-0200	Indianapolis	IN	46219	317-897-2300	897-2266
Best Western Fireside Inn 4501 E 3rd St. *TF:* 800-528-1234	Bloomington	IN	47401	812-332-2141	332-8441
Best Western Waterfront Plaza 2930 Waterfront Pkwy W Dr *TF:* 800-528-1234	Indianapolis	IN	46214	317-299-8400	299-9257
Brickyard Crossing Golf Resort & Inn 4400 W 16th St	Indianapolis	IN	46222	317-241-2500	227-2715
Budget Inn of America 6850 E 21st St *TF:* 800-863-2838	Indianapolis	IN	46219	317-353-9781	353-8688
Canterbury Hotel 123 S Illinois St. *TF:* 800-538-8186	Indianapolis	IN	46225	317-634-3000	685-2519
Clarion Fourwinds Resort 9301 Fairfax Rd *TF:* 800-538-1187	Bloomington	IN	47401	812-824-9904	824-9816
Comfort Inn Indianapolis Downtown 530 S Capitol Ave *TF:* 800-228-5150	Indianapolis	IN	46225	317-631-9000	631-9999
Courtyard by Marriott 320 N Senate Ave *TF:* 800-321-2211 ■ *Web:* courtyard.com/INDCD	Indianapolis	IN	46204	317-684-7733	684-7734
Courtyard by Marriott 8670 Allisonville Rd. *TF:* 800-321-2211 ■ *Web:* courtyard.com/INDCS	Indianapolis	IN	46250	317-576-9559	576-0695
Courtyard by Marriott Downtown 501 W Washington St *TF:* 800-321-2211 ■ *Web:* courtyard.com/INDDC	Indianapolis	IN	46204	317-635-4443	687-0029
Crowne Plaza Union Station 123 W Louisiana St. *TF:* 800-227-6963	Indianapolis	IN	46225	317-631-2221	236-7474
Days Inn Airport 5860 Fortune Cir W. *TF:* 800-329-7466	Indianapolis	IN	46241	317-248-0621	247-7637
Days Inn Downtown 401 E Washington St. *TF:* 800-329-7466	Indianapolis	IN	46204	317-637-6464	637-0242
Days Inn Suites 8275 Craig St *TF:* 800-329-7466	Indianapolis	IN	46250	317-841-9700	576-0795
Doubletree Guest Suites 11355 N Meridian St *TF:* 800-222-8733	Carmel	IN	46032	317-844-7994	844-2118
Econo Lodge 4505 S Harding St *TF:* 800-424-4777	Indianapolis	IN	46217	317-788-9361	788-9361
Embassy Suites Downtown 110 W Washington St *TF:* 800-362-2779	Indianapolis	IN	46204	317-236-1800	236-1816
Embassy Suites Hotel North 3912 W Vincennes Rd *TF:* 800-362-2779	Indianapolis	IN	46268	317-872-7700	872-2974
Fairfield Inn Airport 5220 W Southern Ave *TF:* 800-228-2800 ■ *Web:* fairfieldinn.com/INDFA	Indianapolis	IN	46241	317-244-1600	244-1600
Fairfield Inn by Marriott 8325 Bash Rd *TF:* 800-228-2800 ■ *Web:* fairfieldinn.com/INDFC	Indianapolis	IN	46250	317-577-0455	577-0455
Four Points by Sheraton 7701 E 42nd St. *TF:* 800-325-3535	Indianapolis	IN	46226	317-897-4000	897-8100
Hampton Inn Airport 5601 Fortune Circle W. *TF:* 800-426-7866	Indianapolis	IN	46241	317-244-1221	247-4573

Indianapolis — Hotels, Motels, Resorts (Cont'd)

				Phone	Fax
Hampton Inn Downtown 105 S Meridian St.	Indianapolis	IN	46225	317-261-1200	261-1030
TF: 800-426-7866					
Holiday Inn 2500 N Lafayette Rd	Crawfordsville	IN	47933	765-362-8700	
TF: 800-465-4329					
Holiday Inn Conference Center 2480 W Jonathan Moore Pike-Rd 46	Columbus	IN	47201	812-372-1541	378-9049
Web: www.basshotels.com/holiday-inn/?_franchisee=CLUIN ■ E-mail: hisales1@hsonline.net					
Holiday Inn East 6990 E 21st St.	Indianapolis	IN	46219	317-359-5341	351-1666
TF: 800-465-4329					
Holiday Inn Select Airport 2501 S High School Rd.	Indianapolis	IN	46241	317-244-6861	243-1059
TF: 800-465-4329					
Holiday Inn Select North 3850 DePauw Blvd	Indianapolis	IN	46268	317-872-9790	871-5608
TF: 800-465-4329					
Homewood Suites at the Crossing 2501 E 86th St.	Indianapolis	IN	46240	317-253-1919	255-8223
TF: 800-225-5466					
Howard Johnson East 7050 E 21st St	Indianapolis	IN	46219	317-352-0481	353-0194
TF: 800-446-4656					
Hyatt Regency Indianapolis 1 S Capitol Ave.	Indianapolis	IN	46204	317-632-1234	231-7569
TF: 800-233-1234 ■ Web: www.hyatt.com/pages/i/indria.html					
Indianapolis Marriott 7202 E 21st St	Indianapolis	IN	46219	317-352-1231	352-1231
TF: 800-228-9290					
Motel 6 6330 Debonair Ln	Speedway	IN	46224	317-293-3220	329-7644
TF: 800-466-8356					
Omni North 8181 N Shadeland Ave	Indianapolis	IN	46250	317-849-6668	849-4936
TF: 800-843-6664					
Omni Severin Hotel 40 W Jackson Pl	Indianapolis	IN	46225	317-634-6664	687-3612
TF: 800-843-6664					
Pickwick Farms Airport 25 Beachway Dr Suite A-3	Indianapolis	IN	46224	317-240-3567	240-3568
TF: 800-736-8390					
Pickwick Farms North 9300 N Ditch Rd.	Indianapolis	IN	46260	317-872-6506	879-7380
TF: 800-869-7368					
Quality Inn Suites Pyramids 9090 Wesleyan Rd	Indianapolis	IN	46268	317-875-7676	875-9051
TF: 800-228-5151					
Radisson Plaza Hotel 31 W Ohio St	Indianapolis	IN	46204	317-635-2000	638-0782
TF: 800-333-3333					
Ramada Hotel Airport 2500 S High School Rd.	Indianapolis	IN	46251	317-244-3361	241-9202
TF: 800-272-6232					
Ramada Inn 3400 S Madison St.	Muncie	IN	47302	765-288-1911	282-9458
TF: 800-465-4329					
Ramada Inn South 4514 S Emerson Ave	Indianapolis	IN	46203	317-787-3344	788-8616
TF: 800-272-6232					
Renaissance Tower Historic Inn 230 E 9th St.	Indianapolis	IN	46204	317-261-1652	262-8648
TF: 800-676-7786					
Residence Inn by Marriott North 3553 Founders Rd	Indianapolis	IN	46268	317-872-0462	876-8829
TF: 800-331-3131 ■ Web: www.residenceinn.com/INDAP					
Saint Vincent Marten House 1801 W 86th St	Indianapolis	IN	46260	317-872-4111	415-5245
TF: 800-736-5634					
Signature Inn Northwest 3910 Payne Branch Rd	Indianapolis	IN	46268	317-875-5656	875-5656
TF: 800-822-5252 ■ Web: www.signature-inns.com/locations/indy_nw ■ E-mail: feedback@signature-inns.com					
Signature Inn West 3850 Eagle View Dr	Indianapolis	IN	46254	317-299-6165	299-6165
TF: 800-822-5252 ■ Web: www.signature-inns.com/locations/indy_w ■ E-mail: feedback@signature-inns.com					
StudioPLUS 9750 Lakeshore Dr	Indianapolis	IN	46280	317-843-1181	575-4463
TF: 800-646-8000					
StudioPLUS 9030 Wesleyan Rd.	Indianapolis	IN	46268	317-872-3090	471-6262
TF: 800-646-8000					
StudioPLUS 4715 N Main St.	Mishawaka	IN	46545	219-255-8031	255-8041
TF: 800-646-8000					
University Place Conference Center & Hotel 850 W Michigan St.	Indianapolis	IN	46206	317-269-9000	231-5168
TF: 800-627-2700 ■ Web: www.iupui.edu/it/univplac/uplace.html					
Westin Hotel 50 S Capitol Ave	Indianapolis	IN	46204	317-262-8100	231-3928
TF: 800-228-3000					
Westin Suites 8787 Keystone Crossing	Indianapolis	IN	46240	317-574-6770	574-6775
TF: 800-937-8461					
Wyndham Garden Hotel 251 E Pennsylvania Pkwy.	Indianapolis	IN	46280	317-574-4600	574-4633
TF: 800-996-3426					

— Restaurants —

				Phone
Acapulco Joe's (Mexican) 365 N Illinois St.	Indianapolis	IN	46201	317-637-5160
Alcatraz Brewing Co (Continental) 49 W Maryland St Circle Ctr	Indianapolis	IN	46204	317-488-1230
Web: calcafe.com/alcatraz/				
Amici's (Italian) 601 E New York St.	Indianapolis	IN	46204	317-634-0440
Bazbeaux (Italian) 334 Massachusetts Ave	Indianapolis	IN	46204	317-636-7662
Brother Juniper's Restaurant (American) 339 Massachusetts Ave.	Indianapolis	IN	46204	317-636-3115
California Cafe Bar & Grill (California) 49 W Maryland St	Indianapolis	IN	46204	317-488-8686
Web: www.calcafe.com/indy/index.html				
Canterbury Restaurant (Continental) 123 S Illinois St	Indianapolis	IN	46225	317-634-3000
Chanteclair (French) 2501 S High School Rd	Indianapolis	IN	46241	317-243-1040
Chez Jean Restaurant Francais (French) 8821 SR-67	Camby	IN	46113	317-831-0870
Dodd's Town House (Steak/Seafood) 5694 N Meridian St	Indianapolis	IN	46208	317-257-1872
Eagle's Nest Restaurant (American) 1 S Capitol Ave	Indianapolis	IN	46204	317-632-1234
Elbow Room (American) 605 N Pennsylvania St	Indianapolis	IN	46204	317-635-3354
English's Cafe (American) 31 W Ohio St	Indianapolis	IN	46205	317-635-2000
Gibson's American Grill (American) 49 W Maryland St 4th Fl	Indianapolis	IN	46204	317-951-1621
Glass Chimney (French) 12901 N Old Meridian St	Carmel	IN	46032	317-844-0921
Greek Islands Restaurant (Greek) 906 S Meridian St	Indianapolis	IN	46225	317-636-0700
Hollyhock Hill (American) 8110 N College Ave	Indianapolis	IN	46240	317-251-2294
Hot Tuna (Seafood) 10 W Jackson Pl	Indianapolis	IN	46225	317-634-6664
Iaria's Italian Restaurant (Italian) 317 S College Ave.	Indianapolis	IN	46202	317-638-7706
Iron Skillet (American) 2489 W 30th St	Indianapolis	IN	46222	317-923-6353
Keystone Grill (Seafood) 8650 Keystone Crossing	Indianapolis	IN	46240	317-848-5202
Web: www.keystonegrill.com				
Loughmiller's Pub & Eatery (American) 301 W Washington St.	Indianapolis	IN	46204	317-638-7380
Majestic Restaurant (Seafood) 47 S Pennsylvania St	Indianapolis	IN	46204	317-636-5418
Milano Inn (Italian) 231 S College Ave	Indianapolis	IN	46202	317-264-3585
New Orleans House (Seafood) 8845 Township Line Rd	Indianapolis	IN	46260	317-872-9670
Palomino Euro Bistro (Mediterranean) 49 W Maryland St Suite 189	Indianapolis	IN	46204	317-974-0400
Peppy Grill (American) 1004 Virginia Ave	Indianapolis	IN	46203	317-637-1158
Peter's Restaurant & Bar (American) 8505 Keystone Crossing	Indianapolis	IN	46240	317-465-1155
Web: www.peters-restaurant.com				
Plump's Last Shot (American) 6416 Cornell Ave	Indianapolis	IN	46220	317-257-5867
Porch (Continental) 1 S Capitol Ave	Indianapolis	IN	46204	317-632-1234
Rathskeller Restaurant (German) 401 E Michigan St	Indianapolis	IN	46204	317-636-0396
Web: www.rathskeller.com				
Rick's Cafe Boatyard (Continental) 4050 Dandy Trail	Indianapolis	IN	46254	317-290-9300
Ruth's Chris Steak House (Steak) 96 N Keystone Ave	Indianapolis	IN	46240	317-844-1155
Saint Elmo Steak House (Steak) 127 S Illinois St	Indianapolis	IN	46225	317-637-1811
Shapiro's (Jewish) 808 S Meridian St.	Indianapolis	IN	46225	317-631-4041
Shula's Steak House (Steak) 50 S Capitol Ave	Indianapolis	IN	46224	317-262-8100
Slippery Noodle Inn (American) 372 S Meridian St	Indianapolis	IN	46225	317-631-6974

— Goods and Services —

SHOPPING

				Phone	Fax
Ayres LS & Co 6020 E 82nd St	Indianapolis	IN	46250	317-579-2900	
Castleton Square Mall 6020 E 82nd St	Indianapolis	IN	46250	317-849-9993	849-4689
Circle Centre Mall 49 W Maryland St	Indianapolis	IN	46204	317-681-8000	681-5697
Glendale Center 6101 N Keystone Ave	Indianapolis	IN	46220	317-251-9281	255-5107
Greenwood Park Mall 1251 US Hwy 31	Greenwood	IN	46142	317-881-6758	887-8606
Indianapolis City Market 222 E Market St	Indianapolis	IN	46204	317-634-9266	637-6814
Indianapolis Downtown Antique Mall 1044 Virginia Ave	Indianapolis	IN	46203	317-635-5336	635-5336
Keystone at the Crossing 8701 Keystone Crossing Blvd	Indianapolis	IN	46240	317-574-4000	
Lafayette Square Mall 3919 Lafayette Rd	Indianapolis	IN	46254	317-291-6390	
Shops at 52nd Street 652 E 52nd St.	Indianapolis	IN	46205	317-283-3753	283-0053
Southport Antique Mall 2028 E Southport Rd.	Indianapolis	IN	46227	317-786-8246	786-9926
Washington Square Mall 10202 E Washington St.	Indianapolis	IN	46229	317-899-4567	897-9428

BANKS

				Phone	Fax
Bank One Indianapolis NA 111 Monument Cir	Indianapolis	IN	46277	317-321-3000	321-8200
First Chicago NBD Bank 1 Indiana Sq	Indianapolis	IN	46266	317-266-6000	266-5626*
*Fax: Hum Res ■ TF: 800-548-3600					

Indianapolis — Banks (Cont'd)

				Phone	Fax
First Indiana Bank 135 N Penn St First Indiana Plaza *TF:* 800-888-8586	Indianapolis	IN	46204	317-269-1200	269-1341
National City Bank Indiana 101 W Washington St **Fax:* Hum Res	Indianapolis	IN	46255	317-267-7000	267-6156*
Peoples Bank & Trust Co 130 E Market St	Indianapolis	IN	46204	317-237-8000	237-8150
Union Federal Savings Bank of Indianapolis 45 N Pennsylvania St *TF:* 800-284-2104 ■ *Web:* www.unionfedbank.com	Indianapolis	IN	46204	317-269-4700	269-4857

BUSINESS SERVICES

	Phone		Phone
Dunhill Staffing Systems	317-247-1775	**Now Courier Messenger Service**	317-638-7071
Federal Express	800-238-5355	**Olsten Staffing Services**	317-237-7991
Kelly Services	317-634-3600	**Post Office**	317-464-6000
Kinko's	317-849-9683	**UPS**	800-742-5877
Manpower Temporary Services	317-262-1122		

— Media —

PUBLICATIONS

				Phone	Fax
Indiana Business Magazine 1000 Waterway Blvd *Web:* www.indianabusiness.com ■ *E-mail:* info@indianabusiness.com	Indianapolis	IN	46202	317-692-1200	692-4250
Indianapolis Business Journal 41 E Washington St Suite 200 *Web:* www.ibj.com	Indianapolis	IN	46204	317-634-6200	263-5406
Indianapolis Monthly 40 Monument Cir Suite 100 *TF Circ:* 888-403-9005*	Indianapolis	IN	46204	317-237-9288	684-2080
Indianapolis News‡ 307 N Pennsylvania St *TF:* 800-669-7827 ■ *Web:* www.starnews.com ■ *E-mail:* NewsEditor@starnews.com	Indianapolis	IN	46204	317-633-1240	633-1038
Indianapolis Star‡ 307 N Pennsylvania St *TF:* 800-669-7827 ■ *Web:* www.starnews.com ■ *E-mail:* StarEditor@starnews.com	Indianapolis	IN	46204	317-633-1240	633-1038

‡Daily newspapers

TELEVISION

				Phone	Fax
WAV-TV Ch 53 (Ind) 6264 Lapas Tr	Indianapolis	IN	46268	317-293-9600	328-3870
WFYI-TV Ch 20 (PBS) 1401 N Meridian St *Web:* www.wfyi.org	Indianapolis	IN	46202	317-636-2020	633-7418
WHMB-TV Ch 40 (Ind) 10511 Greenfield Ave *Web:* www.lesea.com/whmb.htm	Noblesville	IN	46060	317-773-5050	776-4051
WISH-TV Ch 8 (CBS) 1950 N Meridian St *Web:* www.wish-tv.com ■ *E-mail:* wishmail@wish-tv.com	Indianapolis	IN	46202	317-923-8888	931-2242
WNDY-TV Ch 23 (UPN) 451 W 16th St *Web:* www.paramountstations.com/WNDY	Indianapolis	IN	46222	317-241-2388	381-6975
WRTV-TV Ch 6 (ABC) 1330 N Meridian St *Web:* www.6news.com	Indianapolis	IN	46202	317-635-9788	269-1445
WTBU-TV Ch 69 (Ind) 2835 N Illinois St	Indianapolis	IN	46208	317-940-9828	940-5971
WTHR-TV Ch 13 (NBC) 1000 N Meridian St *Web:* www.wthr.com ■ *E-mail:* 13news@wthr.com	Indianapolis	IN	46204	317-636-1313	636-3717
WTTV-TV Ch 4 (WB) 3490 Bluff Rd *Web:* www.ttv.com ■ *E-mail:* wb4@wb4.com	Indianapolis	IN	46217	317-782-4444	780-5464
WXIN-TV Ch 59 (Fox) 1440 N Meridian St *Web:* www.wxin.com	Indianapolis	IN	46202	317-632-5900	687-6534

RADIO

				Phone	Fax
WBKS-FM 106.7 MHz (Urban) 6264 LaPas Trail	Indianapolis	IN	46268	317-293-9600	328-3870
WENS-FM 97.1 MHz (AC) 40 Monument Cir Suite 600 *Web:* www.wens.com	Indianapolis	IN	46204	317-266-9700	684-2021
WFBQ-FM 94.7 MHz (CR) 6161 Fall Creek Rd *TF:* 888-262-8661 ■ *Web:* www.wfbq.com	Indianapolis	IN	46220	317-257-7565	253-6501
WFMS-FM 95.5 MHz (Ctry) 6810 N Shadeland Ave *Web:* www.wfms.com ■ *E-mail:* info@wfms.com	Indianapolis	IN	46220	317-842-9550	577-3361
WFYI-FM 90.1 MHz (NPR) 1401 N Meridian St *Web:* www.wfyi.org	Indianapolis	IN	46202	317-636-2020	633-7433
WGLD-FM 104.5 MHz (Oldies) 6810 N Shadeland Ave	Indianapolis	IN	46220	317-842-9550	921-1996
WGRL-FM 93.9 MHz (Ctry) 6810 N Shadeland Ave *Web:* www.939thebear.com	Indianapolis	IN	46220	317-842-9550	577-3361
WHHH-FM 96.3 MHz (CHR) 6264 La Pas Trail	Indianapolis	IN	46268	317-293-9600	328-3870
WIBC-AM 1070 kHz (N/T) 40 Monument Cir Suite 400 *Web:* www.wibc.com	Indianapolis	IN	46204	317-266-9422	684-2022
WKKG-FM 101.5 MHz (Ctry) 3212 Washington St *Web:* www.wkkg.com	Columbus	IN	47203	812-372-4448	372-1061
WMYS-AM 1430 kHz (Nost) 9245 N Meridian St 3rd Fl *Web:* www.wmys.com	Indianapolis	IN	46260	317-816-4000	816-4030
WNAP-FM 93.1 MHz (CR) 950 N Meridian St Suite 1293	Indianapolis	IN	46204	317-236-9300	684-2024
WNDE-AM 1260 kHz (Sports) 6161 Fall Creek Rd *Web:* www.wnde.com	Indianapolis	IN	46220	317-257-7565	253-6501
WRZX-FM 103.3 MHz (Alt) 6161 Fall Creek Rd *Web:* www.wrzx.com	Indianapolis	IN	46220	317-257-7565	253-6501
WSYW-FM 107.1 MHz (NAC) 8203 Indy Ct	Indianapolis	IN	46214	317-271-9799	273-1507
WTLC-AM 1310 kHz (Urban) 40 Monument Cir 1 Emmis Plaza Suite 500 *Web:* www.wtlc.com	Indianapolis	IN	46204	317-955-9852	684-2010
WTLC-FM 105.7 MHz (Urban) 40 Monument Cir 1 Emmis Plaza Suite 500 *Web:* www.wtlc.com	Indianapolis	IN	46204	317-955-9852	684-2010
WTPI-FM 107.9 MHz (AC) 9245 N Meridian St Suite 300 *Web:* www.wtpi.com	Indianapolis	IN	46260	317-816-4000	816-4060
WTTS-FM 92.3 MHz (AAA) 400 One City Centre	Bloomington	IN	47404	812-332-3366	331-4570
WXIR-FM 98.3 MHz (Rel) 4802 E 62nd St	Indianapolis	IN	46220	317-255-5484	255-4452
WZPL-FM 99.5 MHz (CHR) 9245 N Meridian St Suite 300 *Web:* www.wzpl.com	Indianapolis	IN	46260	317-816-4000	816-4060

— Colleges/Universities —

				Phone	Fax
Butler University 4600 Sunset Ave *TF:* 800-368-6852 ■ *Web:* www.butler.edu ■ *E-mail:* Admission@Butler.edu	Indianapolis	IN	46208	317-940-8000	940-8150
Franklin College 501 E Monroe St *TF:* 800-852-0232 ■ *Web:* www.franklincoll.edu ■ *E-mail:* broshears@delta.franklincoll.edu	Franklin	IN	46131	317-738-8000	736-6030
Indiana Business College 802 N Meridian St *TF:* 800-999-9229	Indianapolis	IN	46204	317-264-5656	634-0471
Indiana University-Purdue University Indianapolis 425 University Blvd *Web:* www.iupui.edu	Indianapolis	IN	46202	317-274-5555	278-1862
ITT Technical Institute 9511 Angola Ct *TF:* 800-937-4488	Indianapolis	IN	46268	317-875-8640	875-8641
Ivy Tech State College Central Indiana 1 W 26th St *Web:* www.ivy.tec.in.us/Indianapolis	Indianapolis	IN	46208	317-921-4882	921-4753
Lincoln Technical Institute 1201 Stadium Dr *TF:* 800-554-4465 ■ *Web:* www.lincolntech.com	Indianapolis	IN	46202	317-632-5553	687-0475
Marian College 3200 Cold Spring Rd *Web:* www.marian.edu	Indianapolis	IN	46222	317-955-6000	955-6401
Martin University 2171 Avondale Pl *Web:* www.martin.edu	Indianapolis	IN	46218	317-543-3235	543-4790
University of Indianapolis 1400 E Hanna Ave *TF:* 800-232-8634 ■ *Web:* www.uindy.edu	Indianapolis	IN	46227	317-788-3368	788-3300

Indianapolis (Cont'd)

— Hospitals —

				Phone	Fax
Community Hospital South 1402 E County Line Rd S	Indianapolis	IN	46227	317-887-7000	877-7178
Community Hospitals East 1500 N Ritter Ave *Web:* www.commhospindy.org	Indianapolis	IN	46219	317-355-1411	351-7723
Indiana University Medical Center 550 N University Blvd *Web:* www.iupui.edu/home/medcentr.html ■ *E-mail:* cio@iupui.edu	Indianapolis	IN	46202	317-274-5000	274-6777
Methodist Hospital of Indiana 1701 N Senate Blvd. *TF:* 800-248-1199	Indianapolis	IN	46202	317-929-2000	929-6188
Richard L Roudebush Veterans Affairs Medical Center 1481 W 10th St.	Indianapolis	IN	46202	317-554-0000	554-0028
Saint Francis Hospital & Health Centers 1600 Albany St. *Web:* www.stfrancis-indy.org	Beech Grove	IN	46107	317-787-3311	782-6731
Saint Vincent Carmel Hospital 13500 N Meridian St.	Carmel	IN	46032	317-573-7000	582-7492
Saint Vincent Hospital & Health Systems 2001 W 86th St *Web:* www.stvincent.org	Indianapolis	IN	46260	317-338-2345	338-7005
Westview Hospital 3630 Guion Rd	Indianapolis	IN	46222	317-924-6661	920-7551
Winona Memorial Hospital 3232 N Meridian St. **Fax:* Admitting	Indianapolis	IN	46208	317-924-3392	927-2875*
Wishard Health Services 1001 W 10th St	Indianapolis	IN	46202	317-639-6671	630-6947
Women's Hospital 8111 Township Line Rd.	Indianapolis	IN	46260	317-875-5994	554-6807

— Attractions —

				Phone	Fax
American Cabaret Theatre 401 E Michigan St *TF:* 800-375-8887 ■ *Web:* www.americancabarettheatre.com	Indianapolis	IN	46204	317-631-0334	686-5443
Anthenaeum The 401 E Michigan St.	Indianapolis	IN	46204	317-630-4569	
Ballet International 502 N Capitol Ave Suite B	Indianapolis	IN	46204	317-637-8979	637-1637
Billie Creek Village & Inn RR 2 Box 27	Rockville	IN	47872	765-569-3430	569-3582
Children's Museum of Indianapolis 3000 N Meridian St. *Web:* www.childrensmuseum.org ■ *E-mail:* tcmi@childrensmuseum.org	Indianapolis	IN	46208	317-924-5431	921-4019
Christ Church Cathedral 125 Monument Cir *Web:* www.christcathedralindy.com	Indianapolis	IN	46204	317-636-4577	635-1040
Clowes Memorial Hall at Butler University 4600 Sunset Ave.	Indianapolis	IN	46208	317-940-6444	940-8456
Conner Prairie Pioneer Settlement 13400 Allisonville Rd. *TF:* 800-966-1836 ■ *Web:* www.connerprairie.org	Fishers	IN	46038	317-776-6000	776-6014
Crispus Attucks Museum 1140 ML King Jr St	Indianapolis	IN	46202	317-226-4611	
Deer Creek Music Center 12880 E 146th St	Noblesville	IN	46060	317-776-3337	773-5996
DeHaan Christel Fine Arts Center 1400 E Hanna Ave University of Indianapolis *TF:* 800-232-8634	Indianapolis	IN	46227	317-788-3211	788-3300
Eagle Creek Park 7840 W 56th St	Indianapolis	IN	46254	317-327-7110	327-7122
Easley Winery 205 N College Ave.	Indianapolis	IN	46202	317-636-4516	
Edyvean Repertory Theatre 1400 E Hanna Ave Ransburg Auditorium. *TF:* 800-807-7732 ■ *Web:* www.edyvean.org ■ *E-mail:* ert@indy.net	Indianapolis	IN	46227	317-788-2072	788-2079
Eiteljorg Museum of American Indian & Western Art 500 W Washington St	Indianapolis	IN	46204	317-636-9378	264-1724
Fountain Square 1105 E Prospect St. *Web:* www.fountainsquareindy.com	Indianapolis	IN	46203	317-686-6010	686-6002
Freetown Village 202 N Alabama St Indianapolis State Museum	Indianapolis	IN	46204	317-631-1870	
Garfield Park 2345 Pagoda Dr	Indianapolis	IN	46203	317-327-7220	
Garfield Park Conservatory & Sunken Gardens 2450 Shelby St	Indianapolis	IN	46203	317-327-7184	327-7268
Hilbert Circle Theatre 45 Monument Cir *TF:* 800-366-8457	Indianapolis	IN	46204	317-262-1110	262-1159
Historic Lockerbie Square College Ave & New York Michigan & East Sts.	Indianapolis	IN	46202	317-638-5264	
Holcomb Jl Observatory & Planetarium 4600 Sunset Ave Butler University	Indianapolis	IN	46208	317-940-9333	940-9951
Hook's Historical Drug Store & Pharmacy Museum 1180 E 38th St Indiana State Fairgrounds	Indianapolis	IN	46205	317-924-1503	
IMAX 3D Theater 650 W Washington St White River State Pk.	Indianapolis	IN	46204	317-233-4629	232-0749
Indiana Basketball Hall of Fame 1 Hall of Fame Ct *Web:* www.hoopshall.com	New Castle	IN	47362	765-529-1891	529-0273
Indiana Historical Society 315 W Ohio St *Web:* www.indianahistory.org	Indianapolis	IN	46202	317-232-1882	233-3109
Indiana Medical History Museum 3045 W Vermont St *Web:* www.imhm.org	Indianapolis	IN	46222	317-635-7329	635-7349
Indiana Repertory Theatre 140 W Washington St *Web:* indianarep.com ■ *E-mail:* indianarep@indianarep.com	Indianapolis	IN	46204	317-635-5277	236-0767
Indiana State Capitol 200 W Washington St	Indianapolis	IN	46204	317-233-5293	
Indiana State House 200 W Washington St Rm 206	Indianapolis	IN	46204	317-232-4567	232-3443
Indiana State Museum 202 N Alabama St *Web:* www.ai.org/ism/	Indianapolis	IN	46204	317-232-1637	232-7090
Indianapolis Art Center 820 E 67th St. *Web:* www.indplsartcenter.org	Indianapolis	IN	46220	317-255-2464	254-0486
Indianapolis Artsgarden 110 W Washington St *Web:* www.indyarts.org	Indianapolis	IN	46204	317-631-3301	624-2559
Indianapolis Civic Theatre 1200 W 38th St *Web:* www.civictheatre.org	Indianapolis	IN	46208	317-923-4597	923-3548
Indianapolis Motor Speedway & Hall of Fame Museum 4790 W 16th St *Web:* www.indyracingleague.com	Indianapolis	IN	46222	317-484-6747	484 6449
Indianapolis Museum of Art 1200 W 38th St *Web:* www.ima-art.org ■ *E-mail:* ima@starnews.com	Indianapolis	IN	46208	317-923-1331	926-8931
Indianapolis Opera 250 E 38 St	Indianapolis	IN	46205	317-283-3531	923-5611
Indianapolis Symphony Orchestra 45 Monument Cir *TF:* 800-366-8457 ■ *Web:* www.indyorch.org ■ *E-mail:* cello@in.net	Indianapolis	IN	46204	317-262-1100	262-1159
Indianapolis Zoo 1200 W Washington St. *Web:* www.indyzoo.com	Indianapolis	IN	46222	317-630-2001	630-5153
Madame Walker Theatre Center 617 Indiana Ave *Web:* www.mmewalkertheatre.org	Indianapolis	IN	46202	317-236-2099	236-2097
Morris Butler House 1204 N Park Ave.	Indianapolis	IN	46202	317-636-5409	636-2630
Murat Temple 510 N New Jersey St	Indianapolis	IN	46204	317-635-2433	686-4199
National Art Museum of Sport 850 W Michigan St University Pl	Indianapolis	IN	46202	317-274-3627	274-3878
NCAA Hall of Champions Visitors Center 1802 Alonzo Watford Sr Dr *TF:* 800-735-6222	Indianapolis	IN	46202	317-917-6222	917-6888
Philharmonic Orchestra of Indianapolis PO Box 503 *Web:* www.iupui.edu/it/dentlib/concerts.html	Indianapolis	IN	46206	317-916-0178	
President Benjamin Harrison Memorial Home 1230 N Delaware St. *Web:* www.surf-ici.com/harrison ■ *E-mail:* harrison@surf-ici.com	Indianapolis	IN	46202	317-631-1898	
Riley James Whitcomb Museum Home 528 Lockerbie St.	Indianapolis	IN	46202	317-631-5885	
Scottish Rite Cathedral 650 N Meridian St. *TF:* 800-489-3579	Indianapolis	IN	46204	317-262-3100	262-3124
USS Indianapolis Memorial Walnut St Footbridge	Indianapolis	IN	46204	317-232-7615	233-4285
War Memorials Plaza 431 N Meridian St.	Indianapolis	IN	46204	317-232-7615	233-4285
Warren Performing Arts Center 9301 E 18th St.	Indianapolis	IN	46229	317-898-9722	532-6440
White River State Park 801 W Washington St *Web:* www.inwhiteriver.com/	Indianapolis	IN	46204	317-634-4567	634-4508

SPORTS TEAMS & FACILITIES

				Phone	Fax
Indiana Blast (soccer) 1502 W 16th St Kuntz Memorial Stadium. *Web:* indianablast.com/blast/ ■ *E-mail:* blastblaze@aol.com	Indianapolis	IN	46250	317-585-9203	585-9205

Indianapolis — Sports Teams & Facilities (Cont'd)

				Phone	Fax
Indiana Blaze 1502 W 16th St Kuntz Memorial Stadium	Indianapolis	IN	46250	317-585-9203	585-9205
Web: www.indianablast.com ■ *E-mail:* blastblaze@aol.com					
Indiana Pacers 300 E Market St Market Square Arena	Indianapolis	IN	46204	317-639-2112	261-6299
Web: www.nba.com/pacers					
Indianapolis Colts 100 S Capitol Ave RCA Dome	Indianapolis	IN	46225	317-297-7000	297-7010
Web: www.colts.com					
Indianapolis Ice (hockey) 300 E Market St Market Square Arena	Indianapolis	IN	46204	317-239-5151	
Web: theihl.com/teams/indianapolis/Indianapolis.htm					
Indianapolis Indians (baseball) 501 W Maryland St	Indianapolis	IN	46225	317-269-3545	269-3541
Web: www.indyindians.com ■ *E-mail:* indians@indyindians.com					
Indianapolis Motor Speedway 4790 W 16th St	Indianapolis	IN	46222	317-484-6747	484-6759
Web: www.indyracingleague.com					
Indianapolis Raceway Park 10267 Hwy 136	Indianapolis	IN	46234	317-293-7223	291-4220
Web: www.goracing.com/indy					
Market Square Arena 300 E Market St	Indianapolis	IN	46204	317-639-6411	261-6299
Web: www.marketsquarearena.com					
Pepsi Coliseum 1202 E 38th St Indiana State Fairgrounds	Indianapolis	IN	46205	317-927-7500	927-7695
RCA Dome 100 S Capitol Ave	Indianapolis	IN	46225	317-262-3410	262-3685
Web: www.iccrd.com					

— Events —

	Phone
4th Fest (July 4)	317-633-6363
500 Festival (May)	800-638-4296
Africafest (mid-August)	317-923-1331
Animals & All that Jazz (August)	317-630-2001
Brickyard 400 (early August)	317-481-8500
Broad Ripple Art Fair (early May)	317-255-2464
Carquest World of Wheels (early February)	317-236-6515
Celebration of Lights (late November)	317-237-2222
Circle City Classic (early October)	317-237-5222
Circle City Grand National Rodeo (early January)	317-639-6411
Circlefest (late July)	317-237-2222
Earth Day Indiana Festival (April 22)	317-767-3672
Fall Home Show (late October)	317-927-7500
Greek Festival (mid-September)	317-283-3816
Halloween ZooBoo (late October)	317-630-2001
Harrison Victorian Christmas (December)	317-631-1898
Heartland Film Festival (late October)	317-464-9405
Hoosier Classic (late December)	317-917-2727
Hoosier Horse Fair & Expo (mid-April)	317-927-7500
Hoosier Storytelling Festival (late September)	317-255-7628
Indian Market (late June)	317-636-9378
Indiana Avenue Jazz Festival (mid-August)	317-236-2099
Indiana Black Expo (mid-July)	317-925-2702
Indiana Flower & Patio Show (mid-March)	317-576-9933
Indiana Motorcycle & Watercraft Expo (late January)	317-546-4344
Indiana State Fair (mid-August)	317-927-7500
Indianapolis 500 (late May)	317-481-8500
Indianapolis Boat Sport & Travel Show (late February)	317-543-4344
Indianapolis Home Show (late January-early February)	317-927-7500
Indy Festival (May)	317-237-3400
Italian Festival (mid-June)	317-636-4478
IU Basketball Classic (early December)	317-262-3410
Maple Fair (late February-early March)	765-569-3430
Merry Prairie Days (December)	317-773-0666
Middle Eastern Festival (mid-June)	317-547-9356
Oktoberfest (early-mid-September)	317-888-6940
Penrod Arts Fair (mid-September)	317-252-9895
RCA Championships (mid-August)	317-632-4100
Saint Patrick's Day Parade (mid-March)	317-236-6515
Strawberry Festival (mid-June)	317-636-4577
Talbott Street Art Fair (mid-June)	800-323-4639
Winterland Holiday Light Display (late November-early January)	765-664-3918

South Bend

The 150-year-old University of Notre Dame in South Bend, known for its "Fighting Irish" football, is also noted for its beautiful "Golden Dome" Administration Building. Other buildings of interest in South Bend include Copshaholm, the former home of industrialist J.D. Oliver and the first home in South Bend to have electricity; the Studebaker National Museum built in 1919; and the 1889 home of Clement Studebaker, which is now Tippecanoe Place Restaurant. East Race Waterway in South Bend, which was once an old race mill that gave power to the city in the mid-1800s, is now one of only six artificial whitewater courses in the world. East Race is located in the city's downtown area, on the east side of the Saint Joseph River at the South Bend Dam, and one can walk along the paved riverbanks. South Bend is also close to attractions of Northern Indiana Amish Country.

Population	99,417	**Longitude**	86-25-00 W
Area (Land)	36.4 sq mi	**County**	Saint Joseph
Area (Water)	0.4 sq mi	**Time Zone**	EST
Elevation	725 ft	**Area Code/s**	219
Latitude	41-68-33 N		

— Average Temperatures and Precipitation —

TEMPERATURES

	Jan	Feb	Mar	Apr	May	Jun	Jul	Aug	Sep	Oct	Nov	Dec
High	30	34	46	59	70	80	83	81	74	62	49	35
Low	16	19	29	39	49	59	63	61	54	43	33	22

PRECIPITATION

	Jan	Feb	Mar	Apr	May	Jun	Jul	Aug	Sep	Oct	Nov	Dec
Inches	2.2	1.9	3.1	3.9	3.2	4.1	3.8	3.7	3.6	3.1	3.3	3.3

— Important Phone Numbers —

	Phone		Phone
AAA	219-277-5790	**Poison Control Center**	800-382-9097
Emergency	911	**Time/Temp**	219-234-7121
Events Line	219-674-0900	**Weather**	219-232-1121
Guest Hotline	219-277-1115		

— Information Sources —

				Phone	Fax
Better Business Bureau Serving Michiana 207 Dixie Way N Suite 130	South Bend	IN	46637	219-277-9121	273-6666*
**Fax:* Acctg ■ *Web:* www.gary.bbb.org					
Century Center 120 S Saint Joseph St	South Bend	IN	46601	219-235-9711	235-9185
Web: centurycenter.org/ ■ *E-mail:* centuryc@pipeline.com					
Chamber of Commerce of Saint Joseph County PO Box 1677	South Bend	IN	46634	219-234-0051	289-0358
Web: www.sjchamber.org ■ *E-mail:* info@sjchamber.org					
Saint Joseph County 101 S Main St	South Bend	IN	46601	219-235-9635	235-9838
Saint Joseph County Public Library 304 S Main St	South Bend	IN	46601	219-282-4630	282-4651
Web: sjcpl.lib.in.us					
South Bend City Hall 1400 County-City Bldg	South Bend	IN	46601	219-235-9261	235-9892
Web: www.ci.south-bend.in.us					
South Bend Community & Economic Development Dept 227 W Jefferson Blvd 1200 County City Bldg	South Bend	IN	46601	219-235-9371	235-9021
South Bend Mayor 1400 County-City Bldg	South Bend	IN	46601	219-235-9261	235-9892
E-mail: sluecke@ci.south-bend.in.us					

South Bend — Information Sources (Cont'd)

				Phone	Fax
South Bend/Mishawaka Convention & Visitors Bureau PO Box 1677 *TF:* 800-828-7881 ■ *Web:* www.cdiguide.com/IN/219/b_com/southben.html ■ *E-mail:* cvbsjco@aol.com	South Bend	IN	46634	219-234-0051	289-0358

On-Line Resources

4SouthBend.com . . . www.4southbend.com
About.com Guide to South Bend . . . southbend.about.co
Anthill City Guide South Bend . . . www.anthill.com/city.asp?city=southbend
Area Guide South Bend . . . southbend.areaguides.net
Excite.com South Bend City Guide . . . www.excite.com/travel/countries/united_states/indiana/south_bend/

— Transportation Services —

AIRPORTS

	Phone
■ **Michiana Regional Airport (SBN)** 4 miles NW of downtown (approx 15 minutes)	219-233-2185

Airport Transportation

	Phone
A-Yellow Cab $8 fare to downtown	219-233-9333
Airport Taxi $8 fare to downtown	219-277-1095

Commercial Airlines

	Phone		Phone
American Eagle	800-433-7300	**TWA**	800-221-2000
Delta	800-221-1212	**United Express**	800-241-6522
Delta Connection	800-221-1212	**US Airways**	800-428-4322
Midwest Express	800-452-2022	**US Airways Express**	800-428-4322
Northwest	800-225-2525		

CAR RENTALS

	Phone		Phone
Avis	219-234-1024	**Hertz**	219-234-3712
Budget	219-282-3708	**National**	219-234-4878

LIMO/TAXI

	Phone		Phone
A-Yellow Cab	219-233-9333	**McGann's Executive Limousine**	219-232-1418

MASS TRANSIT

	Phone
Transpo $.75 Base fare	219-233-2131

RAIL/BUS

				Phone
Amtrak Station 2702 W Washington Ave	South Bend	IN	46628	800-872-7245
Greyhound/Trailways Bus Station 4671 Terminal Dr	South Bend	IN	46628	219-287-6541

— Accommodations —

HOTELS, MOTELS, RESORTS

				Phone	Fax
Best Inn 425 US Hwy 31/33 N *TF:* 800-237-8466	South Bend	IN	46637	219-277-7700	277-7700
Courtyard by Marriott 4825 N Main St *TF:* 800-321-2211 ■ *Web:* courtyard.com/SBNCY	Mishawaka	IN	46545	219-273-9900	272-0143
Fairfield Inn Mishawaka 425 University Dr *TF:* 800-228-2800 ■ *Web:* fairfieldinn.com/SBNFI	Mishawaka	IN	46545	219-273-2202	273-2202
Hampton Inn & Suites 52709 US 31 N *TF:* 800-426-7866	South Bend	IN	46637	219-277-9373	243-0128
Hampton Inn Mishawaka 445 Univeristy Dr *TF:* 800-426-7866	Mishawaka	IN	46545	219-273-2309	273-0258
Holiday Inn 515 Dixie Way N *TF:* 800-465-4329	South Bend	IN	46637	219-272-6600	272-5553
Holiday Inn City Center 213 W Washington St *TF:* 800-465-4329	South Bend	IN	46601	219-232-3941	284-3715
Howard Johnson 130 Dixie Way S *TF:* 800-446-4656	South Bend	IN	46637	219-272-7900	272-7944
Inn at Saint Mary's 53993 US 31-33 N *TF:* 800-947-8627 ■ *Web:* www.lodginghost.com/inn-at-saint-marys/ ■ *E-mail:* iasm@worldnet.att.net	South Bend	IN	46637	219-232-4000	289-0986
Jamison Inn 1404 N Ivy Rd	South Bend	IN	46637	219-277-9682	277-9682
Knights Inn 236 Dixie Hwy *TF:* 800-843-5644	South Bend	IN	46637	219-277-2960	277-0203
Mishawaka Inn 2754 Lincoln Way E	Mishawaka	IN	46544	219-256-2300	255-3519
Morris Inn Notre Dame Ave University of Notre Dame	Notre Dame	IN	46556	219-631-2000	631-2017
Ramada Inn 52890 US Hwy 33 N *TF:* 800-272-6232	South Bend	IN	46637	219-272-5220	272-3956
Residence Inn by Marriott 716 N Niles Ave *TF:* 800-331-3131 ■ *Web:* www.residenceinn.com/SBNRI	South Bend	IN	46617	219-289-5555	288-4531
Signature Inn South Bend 215 Dixie Way S *TF:* 800-822-5252 ■ *Web:* www.signature-inns.com/locations/south_bend ■ *E-mail:* feedback@signature-inns.com	South Bend	IN	46637	219-277-3211	277-3211
South Bend Marriott Hotel 123 N Saint Joseph St *TF:* 800-228-9290	South Bend	IN	46601	219-234-2000	234-0677
Varsity Clubs of America Hotel 3800 N Main St *TF:* 800-946-4822	Mishawaka	IN	46545	219-277-0500	277-9977
Weston Plaza Hotel & Conference Center 2725 Cassopolis St *TF:* 800-521-8400	Elkhart	IN	46514	219-264-7502	264-0042

— Restaurants —

				Phone
1140 Cafe (American) 1140 W Western Ave	South Bend	IN	46601	219-287-5472
Carriage House (Continental) 24460 Adams Rd	South Bend	IN	46628	219-272-9220
Doc Pierce's (Steak/Seafood) 120 N Main St	Mishawaka	IN	46544	219-255-7737
East Bank Emporium Restaurant (American) 121 S Niles Ave	South Bend	IN	46617	219-234-9000
Four Seasons Restaurant (Greek) 22858 US Hwy 20	South Bend	IN	46628	219-237-0691
Frankie's Barbecue (Barbecue) 1621 Circle Ave	South Bend	IN	46628	219-287-8993
Hacienda Mexican Restaurant (Mexican) 1290 Scottsdale Mall Suite 2000 *Web:* www.haciendafiesta.com	South Bend	IN	46614	219-291-2566
Honkers (American) 3939 S Michigan St	South Bend	IN	46614	219-291-2115
LaSalle Grill (Steak/Seafood) 115 W Colfax Ave *Web:* www.lasallegrill.com	South Bend	IN	46601	219-288-1155
Locos (Mexican) 3801 Western Ave	South Bend	IN	46619	219-287-0200
Macadoo's Kitchen (American) 2714 Mishawaka Ave	South Bend	IN	46615	219-289-7374
Malabar Cuisine Of India (Indian) 1640 S Bend Ave	South Bend	IN	46617	219-282-2977
Mishawaka Brewing Co (American) 3703 N Main St	Mishawaka	IN	46545	219-256-9993
Morris Inn (American) Notre Dame Dr University of Notre Dame	South Bend	IN	46556	219-631-2020
Nicola's Restaurant (American) 1705 S Bend Ave	South Bend	IN	46637	219-277-5666
No 1 Chinese Restaurant (Chinese) 301-303 S Michigan St	South Bend	IN	46601	219-234-8888
Parisi's Italian Ristorante (Italian) 1412 S Bend Ave	South Bend	IN	46617	219-232-4244
Rosie's Kazbar (Hungarian) 2644 W Western Ave	South Bend	IN	46619	219-288-3725
Siam Thai Restaurant (Thai) 211 N Main St	South Bend	IN	46601	219-232-4445
Silver Tower Seafood House (Steak/Seafood) 1536 Lincoln Way W	South Bend	IN	46628	219-233-0304
Tippecanoe Place (Steak) 620 W Washington St	South Bend	IN	46601	219-234-9077
Toyo (Japanese) 620 W Edison Rd	Mishawaka	IN	46545	219-254-9120
Volcano Restaurant (Italian) 3700 Lincoln Way W	South Bend	IN	46628	219-287-5775

— Goods and Services —

SHOPPING

				Phone	Fax
North Village Mall US 33 & Darden Rd	South Bend	IN	46637	219-272-8080	272-8080
Scottsdale Mall 1290 Scottsdale Mall Suite 3000	South Bend	IN	46614	219-299-7300	
Unique Antique Mall 50981 US 31 N	South Bend	IN	46637	219-271-1799	
University Park Mall 6501 N Grape Rd	Mishawaka	IN	46545	219-277-2223	272-5924

South Bend (Cont'd)

BANKS

				Phone	Fax
1st Source Bank PO Box 1602 *Fax: Mktg ■ Web: www.1stsource.com	South Bend	IN	46634	219-235-2000	235-2948*
KeyBank NA South Bend District 202 S Michigan St *Fax: Cust Svc ■ TF: 800-348-2243	South Bend	IN	46601	219-237-5200	237-5227*
National City Bank 101 N Main St	South Bend	IN	46601	219-237-4733	237-4711
Norwest Bank 112 W Jefferson Blvd TF: 800-688-8510	South Bend	IN	46601	219-237-3385	237-3370

BUSINESS SERVICES

	Phone		Phone
Airborne Express	800-247-2676	**Kinko's**	219-271-0398
BAX Global	800-225-5229	**Mail Boxes Etc**	800-789-4623
Corporate Staffing Resources	219-234-2224	**Manpower Temporary Services**	219-234-0157
DHL Worldwide Express	800-225-5345	**Norell Staffing Services**	219-282-2761
Federal Express	800-238-5355	**Post Office**	219-282-8400
Interim Personnel	219-234-6700	**UPS**	800-742-5877

— Media —

PUBLICATIONS

				Phone	Fax
South Bend Tribune‡ 225 W Colfax Ave TF: 800-552-2795 ■ Web: www.sbtinfo.com ■ E-mail: mclein@sbt.sbtinfo.com	South Bend	IN	46626	219-235-6161	236-1765

‡Daily newspapers

TELEVISION

				Phone	Fax
WBND-TV Ch 58 (ABC) 431 E Colfax Ave Suite 120	South Bend	IN	46617	219-287-9263	287-5769
WNDU-TV Ch 16 (NBC) 54516 US 31 N. Web: www.wndu.com	South Bend	IN	46637	219-631-1616	631-1639
WNIT-TV Ch 34 (PBS) 2300 Charger Blvd Web: www.wnit.org ■ E-mail: wnit@wnit.org	Elkhart	IN	46514	219-674-5961	262-8497
WSBT-TV Ch 22 (CBS) 300 W Jefferson Blvd TF: 800-872-3141 ■ Web: www.wsbt.com/tvwelcom.htm ■ E-mail: wsbtnews@wsbt.com	South Bend	IN	46601	219-233-3141	288-6630
WSJV-TV Ch 28 (Fox) PO Box 28 Web: www.fox28.com ■ E-mail: fox28@fox28.com	South Bend	IN	46624	219-674-5106	294-1267

RADIO

				Phone	Fax
WBYT-FM 100.7 MHz (Ctry) 237 Edison Rd Suite 200 Web: www.b100.com ■ E-mail: b100@b100.com	Mishawaka	IN	46545	219-258-5483	258-0930
WFRN-AM 1270 kHz (Rel) PO Box 307 TF: 800-522-9376 ■ Web: www.wfrn.com	Elkhart	IN	46515	219-875-5166	875-6662
WGTC-FM 102.3 MHz (Rel) 61300 Ironwood Rd	South Bend	IN	46614	219-291-8200	291-9043
WHME-FM 103.1 MHz (Rel) 61300 Ironwood Rd	South Bend	IN	46614	219-291-8200	291-9043
WNDU-AM 1490 kHz (Oldies) 3371 Cleveland Rd Suite 310	South Bend	IN	46628	219-273-9300	273-9090
WNDU-FM 92.9 MHz (CHR) 3371 Cleveland Rd Suite 310	South Bend	IN	46628	219-273-9300	273-9090
WNSN-FM 101.5 MHz (AC) 202 S Michigan St 7th Fl. Web: www.wsbt.com/fmwelcom.htm	South Bend	IN	46601	219-239-4230	239-4231
WSBT-AM 960 kHz (N/T) 300 W Jefferson Blvd TF: 800-872-3141 ■ Web: www.wsbt.com/amwelcom.htm ■ E-mail: wsbtnews@wsbt.com	South Bend	IN	46601	219-233-3141	289-7382
WTRC-AM 1340 kHz (N/T) 58096 County Rd 7 Web: www.am1340.com	Elkhart	IN	46517	219-293-5611	295-2329
WVPE-FM 88.1 MHz (NPR) 2424 California Rd. TF: 888-399-9873 ■ Web: www.wvpe.org ■ E-mail: wvpe@wvpe.org	Elkhart	IN	46514	219-262-5660	262-5700

— Colleges/Universities —

				Phone	Fax
Bethel College 1001 W McKinley Ave TF Admissions: 800-422-4101 ■ Web: www.bethel-in.edu ■ E-mail: admissions@bethel-in.edu	Mishawaka	IN	46545	219-259-8511	257-3326
Indiana Christian University 530 E Ireland Rd.	South Bend	IN	46614	219-291-3292	299-4248
Indiana University South Bend Campus 1700 Mishawaka Ave Box 7111 Web: www.iusb.edu	South Bend	IN	46634	219-237-4111	237-4834
Ivy Tech State College South Bend 1534 W Sample St TF: 888-489-5463 ■ Web: www.ivy.tec.in.us/SouthBend	South Bend	IN	46619	219-289-7001	236-7165
Michiana College 1030 E Jefferson Blvd TF: 800-743-2447	South Bend	IN	46617	219-237-0774	237-3585
Saint Mary's College Web: www.saintmarys.edu	Notre Dame	IN	46556	219-284-4587	284-4841
University of Notre Dame Web: www.nd.edu	Notre Dame	IN	46556	219-631-5000	631-3180

— Hospitals —

				Phone	Fax
Memorial Hospital of South Bend 615 N Michigan St	South Bend	IN	46601	219-234-9041	284-3670
Saint Joseph's Regional Medical Center 801 E La Salle Ave *Fax: Admitting ■ Web: www.sjmed.com	South Bend	IN	46617	219-237-7111	237-7789*

— Attractions —

				Phone	Fax
Amish Acres 1600 W Market St *Fax Area Code: 219 ■ Web: www.amishacres.com	Nappanee	IN	46550	800-800-4942	773-4180*
Colfax Cultural Center Galleries 914 Lincoln Way W.	South Bend	IN	46616	219-289-1066	289-4550
Copshaholm 808 W Washington St.	South Bend	IN	46601	219-235-9664	
East Race Waterway 126 N Niles Ave	South Bend	IN	46617	219-235-9401	235-9331
Hannah Lindahl Children's Museum 1402 S Main St Web: www.hlcm.org	Mishawaka	IN	46544	219-254-4540	258-3075
Indiana Dunes National Lakeshore 1100 N Mineral Springs Rd Web: www.nps.gov/indu/	Porter	IN	46304	219-926-7561	
Moreau Center for the Arts Hwy 31 N St Mary's College	Notre Dame	IN	46556	219-284-4655	284-4716
Morris-Ellis Conservatory 2105 Michawaka Ave.	South Bend	IN	46615	219-235-9442	
Morris Performing Arts Center Colfax Ave & Michigan St TF: 800-537-6415	South Bend	IN	46601	219-235-9190	235-5945
Northern Indiana Center for History 808 W Washington St.	South Bend	IN	46601	219-235-9664	
Potawatomi Zoo 500 S Greenlawn Ave	South Bend	IN	46615	219-235-9800	235-9080
Snite Museum of Art University of Notre Dame Web: www.nd.edu/~sniteart/	Notre Dame	IN	46556	219-631-5466	631-8501
South Bend Chamber Singers St Mary's College Dept of Music Web: users.michiana.org/sbcs1/	Notre Dame	IN	46556	219-284-4632	
South Bend Civic Theatre 701 Portage Ave The Firehouse Web: members.aol.com/SBCTheatre/sbct.html	South Bend	IN	46634	219-234-1112	
South Bend Regional Museum of Art 120 S Saint Joseph St. Web: mh102.infi.net/~sbrma ■ E-mail: sbrma@sbt.infi.net	South Bend	IN	46601	219-235-9102	235-5782
South Bend Symphony Orchestra 211 N Michigan Morris Civic Auditorium Web: www.sbsymphony.org ■ E-mail: tickets@sbinet.com	South Bend	IN	46601	219-232-6343	232-6627
Studebaker National Museum 525 S Main St Web: www.classicar.com/MUSEUMS/STUDE/STUDE.HTM	South Bend	IN	46601	219-235-9714	235-5522

SPORTS TEAMS & FACILITIES

				Phone	Fax
Indiana Invaders (soccer) 55900 Bittersweet Rd Penn High Stadium E-mail: ininvaders@aol.com	Mishawaka	IN	46545	219-232-2595	232-3285

South Bend — Sports Teams & Facilities (Cont'd)

				Phone	*Fax*
South Bend Silver Hawks (baseball) 501 W South St Coveleski Regional Stadium	South Bend	IN	46601	219-235-9988	235-9950

— Events —

	Phone
Amish Acres Arts & Crafts Festival (mid-August)	800-800-4942
Downtown for the Holidays (early December)	219-235-9951
Ethnic Festival (mid-June)	219-235-9952
Firefly Festival (early August)	219-288-3472
Junior Irish Memorial Day Soccer Tournament (late May)	219-273-1209
Midwest RV Super Show (mid-August)	317-247-6258
Mishawaka Summerfest (late June)	219-258-1664
Saint Joseph County 4-H Fair (early August)	219-291-4870
Saint Patrick's Day Celebration (mid-March)	219-235-9951
Studebaker Swap (early May)	219-287-3381
Swap Meet & Car Show (late May)	219-289-2292
ZooBoo Halloween (late October)	219-288-4639
Zooltide-Light Up a Heart (late November-late December)	219-288-4639

Iowa

Population (1999): 2,869,413 **Area (sq mi): 56,276**

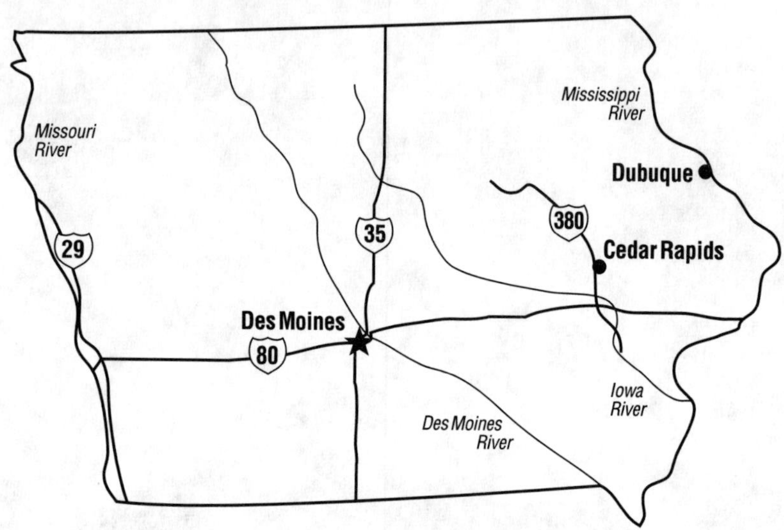

— State Information Sources —

				Phone	Fax
Iowa Assn of Business & Industry 904 Walnut St Suite 100 *TF:* 800-383-4224 ■ *Web:* www.iowaabi.org	Des Moines	IA	50309	515-280-8000	244-8907
Iowa Economic Development Dept 200 E Grand Ave. *Web:* www.state.ia.us/government/ided	Des Moines	IA	50309	515-242-4700	242-4809
Iowa Parks Recreation & Preservation Div Wallace State Office Bldg *Web:* www.state.ia.us/dnr/organiza/ppd/parksdiv.htm	Des Moines	IA	50319	515-281-5145	281-6794
Iowa State Government Information *Web:* www.state.ia.us/				515-281-5011	
Iowa State Library E 12th & Grand Aves *Web:* www.silo.lib.ia.us	Des Moines	IA	50319	515-281-4105	281-6191
Iowa Tourism Div 200 E Grand Ave *TF:* 800-345-4692 ■ *Web:* www.traveliowa.com	Des Moines	IA	50309	515-242-4705	242-4749

ON-LINE RESOURCES

Eastern Iowa Tourism .... www.easterniowatourism.org
Heart of Iowa .... www.heartofiowa.com
Iowa Cities .... dir.yahoo.com/Regional/U_S__States/Iowa/Cities
Iowa Counties & Regions ....dir.yahoo.com/Regional/U_S__States/Iowa/Counties_and_Regions
Iowa Information Network .... www.iowa.net
Iowa Scenario .... scenariousa.dstylus.com/ia/indexf.htm
Iowa Travel & Tourism Guide ....www.travel-library.com/north_america/usa/iowa/index.html
Iowa Virtual Tourist .... www.iowacity.com/tourist
Rough Guide Travel Iowa travel.roughguides.com/content/991/index.htm
Travel.org-Iowa .... travel.org/iowa.html
Visit Iowa .... www.visitiowa.org
Welcome Traveler Iowa .... www.welcometraveler.com
Yahoo! Get Local Iowa .... dir.yahoo.com/Regional/U_S__States/Iowa

— Cities Profiled —

Page

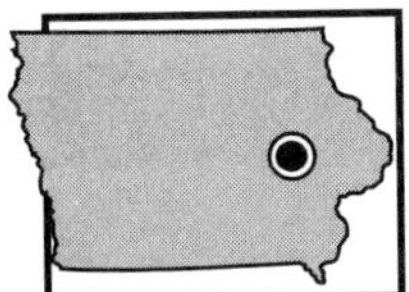

Cedar Rapids

Located in eastern Iowa, in the heart of the Midwest, Cedar Rapids is the second largest city in the state. The center for the city's government is on Mays Island (also known as Municipal Island), a narrow strip of land in the main channel of the Cedar River. Among the major manufacturing industries in Cedar Rapids are the Quaker Oats Company (originally established as the North Star Oatmeal Mill in 1872), General Mills, and Amana Refrigeration. The Amana Colonies are just 19 miles south of Cedar Rapids. Famous for their woolen mills, wineries, bakeries, and hand-made furniture, all seven Amana villages are Registered National Landmarks. Visitors to the villages will find inns and bed and breakfast establishments, shops, restaurants, and craft centers, as well as some 475 historic sites and museums.

Population 114,563
Area (Land) .... 53.5 sq mi
Area (Water) .... 1.2 sq mi
Elevation .... 730 ft
Latitude .... 42-00-83 N
Longitude .... 91-64-39 W
County .... Linn
Time Zone .... CST
Area Code/s 319

— Average Temperatures and Precipitation —

TEMPERATURES

	Jan	Feb	Mar	Apr	May	Jun	Jul	Aug	Sep	Oct	Nov	Dec
High	26	32	44	60	72	81	85	82	74	63	46	31
Low	9	14	27	39	50	60	64	61	52	41	29	15

PRECIPITATION

	Jan	Feb	Mar	Apr	May	Jun	Jul	Aug	Sep	Oct	Nov	Dec
Inches	1.1	1.0	2.3	3.4	4.2	5.1	4.4	4.4	4.2	2.6	2.2	1.6

— Important Phone Numbers —

	Phone
AAA	319-393-0400
Emergency	911
Poison Control Center	800-352-2222
Time/Temp	319-366-7212
Weather	319-393-0500

— Information Sources —

				Phone	Fax
Better Business Bureau Serving Central & Eastern Iowa 505 5th Ave Suite 950	Des Moines	IA	50309	515-243-8137	243-2227
TF: 800-222-1600 ■ *Web:* www.desmoines.bbb.org ■ *E-mail:* info@dm.bbb.org					
Cedar Rapids Area Chamber of Commerce 424 1st Ave NE	Cedar Rapids	IA	52401	319-398-5317	398-5228
Web: www.cedarrapids.org/iowa					
Cedar Rapids Area Convention & Visitors Bureau PO Box 5339	Cedar Rapids	IA	52406	319-398-5009	398-5089
TF: 800-735-5557 ■ *Web:* www.fyiowa.com/iowa/cvb/ ■ *E-mail:* visitors@fyiowa.infi.net					
Cedar Rapids City Hall 50 2nd Avenue Bridge	Cedar Rapids	IA	52401	319-286-5000	286-5144
Web: www.fyiowa.com/iowa/cityofcr					
Cedar Rapids Development Div 50 2nd Ave Bridge 6th Fl	Cedar Rapids	IA	52401	319-286-5041	286-5141
Cedar Rapids Mayor 50 2nd Avenue Bridge City Hall 3rd Fl	Cedar Rapids	IA	52401	319-286-5051	286-5144
Web: www.fyiowa.com/iowa/cityofcr/mayor.htm					
Cedar Rapids Public Library 500 1st St SE	Cedar Rapids	IA	52401	319-398-5123	398-0476
Web: www.cedar-rapids.lib.ia.us/crpl					
Five Seasons Center 370 1st Ave NE	Cedar Rapids	IA	52401	319-398-5211	362-2102
Web: www.5seasons.com					
Linn County 3rd Ave Bridge	Cedar Rapids	IA	52401	319-398-3412	398-4054

On-Line Resources

Anthill City Guide Cedar Rapids .... www.anthill.com/city.asp?city=cedarrapids
Area Guide Cedar Rapids .... cedarrapids.areaguides.net
City Knowledge Cedar Rapids .... www.cityknowledge.com/ia_cedar_rapids.htm
Excite.com Cedar Rapids City Guide .... www.excite.com/travel/countries/united_states/iowa/cedar_rapids

— Transportation Services —

AIRPORTS

■ **Eastern Iowa Airport (CID)**

10 miles SW of downtown (approx 15 minutes) 319-362-3131
Web: www.crairport.org ■ *E-mail:* crairprt@fyiowa.infi.net

Airport Transportation

	Phone
Cedar Rapids Airport Shuttle $10 fare to downtown	319-365-0655
Yellow Cab $15 fare to downtown	319-365-1444

Commercial Airlines

	Phone
American	800-433-7300
American Eagle	800-433-7300
Chicago Express	800-435-9282
Northwest	800-225-2525
TWA	800-221-2000
TWA Express	800-221-2000
United	800-241-6522
United Express	800-241-6522
US Airways Express	800-428-4322

Charter Airlines

	Phone
Cedar Rapids Flying Service	319-365-2000
PS Air	319-846-3600

CAR RENTALS

	Phone
Avis	319-366-6418
Budget	319-363-9595
Dollar	800-800-4000
Hertz	319-365-9408
National	319-363-0249

LIMO/TAXI

	Phone
A Royal Executive Limousine	319-373-2174
Alpha Taxi	319-390-3440
Century Cab	319-365-0505
Harris Limousines	319-396-5981
Limo Service by Crystal Elegance	319-378-1650
Yellow Cab	319-365-1444

MASS TRANSIT

	Phone
Five Seasons Transportation $.50 Base fare	319-286-5573

RAIL/BUS

				Phone
Greyhound/Trailways Bus Station 145 Transit Way SE	Cedar Rapids	IA	52401	319-364-4167

— Accommodations —

HOTELS, MOTELS, RESORTS

				Phone	Fax
Best Western 100 'F' Ave NW	Cedar Rapids	IA	52405	319-366-5323	366-5323
TF: 800-858-5511					
Best Western Canterbury Inn & Suites 704 1st Ave	Coralville	IA	52241	319-351-0400	351-1657
TF: 800-798-0400					
Best Western Longbranch Motor Inn 90 Twixt Town Rd NE	Cedar Rapids	IA	52402	319-377-6386	
TF: 800-528-1234					
Budget Inn 3100 16th Ave SW	Cedar Rapids	IA	52404	319-363-8101	363-8101
Cedar Express Inn 3233 Southridge Dr SW	Cedar Rapids	IA	52404	319-363-9999	363-9050
Cedar Rapids Conference Center 2501 Williams Blvd SW	Cedar Rapids	IA	52404	319-365-9441	365-0255

Cedar Rapids — Hotels, Motels, Resorts (Cont'd)

Name / Address	City	State	ZIP	Phone	Fax
Collins Plaza Hotel 1200 Collins Rd NE *TF:* 800-541-1067	Cedar Rapids	IA	52402	319-393-6600	393-2308
Comfort Inn 390 33rd Ave SW *TF:* 800-228-5150	Cedar Rapids	IA	52404	319-363-7934	363-7934
Comfort Inn North 5055 Rockwell Dr NE *TF:* 800-228-5150	Cedar Rapids	IA	52402	319-393-8247	393-8247
Country Inn 2216 N Dodge St *TF:* 800-456-4000	Iowa City	IA	52240	319-351-1010	351-1802
Country Inn by Carlson 4747 1st Ave SE *TF:* 800-456-4000	Cedar Rapids	IA	52403	319-393-8800	378-3505
Crowne Plaza Hotel 350 1st Ave NE *TF:* 800-227-6963	Cedar Rapids	IA	52401	319-363-8161	363-3804
Days Inn 2214 'U' Ave *TF:* 800-329-7466	Williamsburg	IA	52361	319-668-2097	
Days Inn South 3245 Southgate Pl SW *TF:* 800-329-7466	Cedar Rapids	IA	52404	319-365-4339	365-4339
Econo Lodge 622 33rd Ave SW *TF:* 800-553-2666	Cedar Rapids	IA	52404	319-363-8888	363-7504
Exel Inn 616 33rd Ave SW *TF:* 800-367-3935	Cedar Rapids	IA	52404	319-366-2475	366-5712
Fairfield Inn by Marriott 3243 Southridge Dr SW *TF:* 800-228-2800 ■ *Web:* fairfieldinn.com/CIDFI	Cedar Rapids	IA	52404	319-364-2000	364-2000
Hampton Inn 3265 6th St SW *TF:* 800-426-7866	Cedar Rapids	IA	52404	319-364-8144	399-1877
Heartland Inn 3315 Southgate Ct SW *TF:* 800-334-3277	Cedar Rapids	IA	52404	319-362-9012	362-9694
Holiday Inn Express 1230 Collins Rd NE *TF:* 800-465-4329	Cedar Rapids	IA	52402	319-294-9407	294-8551
Holiday Inn Express Hotel & Suites 3320 Southgate Ct SW *TF:* 800-465-4329	Cedar Rapids	IA	52404	319-399-5025	399-5199
Ramada 4011 16th Ave SW *TF:* 800-272-6232	Cedar Rapids	IA	52404	319-396-5000	396-5000
Ramada Suites 2025 Werner Rd NE *TF:* 800-272-6232	Cedar Rapids	IA	52402	319-378-8888	378-9399
Red Roof Inn 3325 Southgate Ct SW *TF:* 800-843-7663	Cedar Rapids	IA	52404	319-366-7523	366-7639
Residence Inn by Marriott 1900 Dodge Road NE *TF:* 800-331-3131 ■ *Web:* residenceinn.com/CIDRI	Cedar Rapids	IA	52402	319-395-0111	395-0111
Sheraton Hotel Four Points 525 33rd Ave SW *TF:* 800-325-3535 ■ *Web:* members.aol.com/CRsheraton/index.htm	Cedar Rapids	IA	52404	319-366-8671	362-1420
Shoney's Inn & Suites 2215 Blairs Ferry Rd NE *TF:* 800-222-2222 ■ *Web:* www.shoneysinn.com/ia1.htm	Cedar Rapids	IA	52402	319-378-3948	378-4012
Super 8 Motel 400 33rd Ave SW *TF:* 800-800-8000	Cedar Rapids	IA	52404	319-363-1755	363-1755
Super 8 Motel 720 33rd Ave SW *TF:* 800-800-8000	Cedar Rapids	IA	52404	319-362-6002	362-6002

— Restaurants —

Name / Address	City	State	ZIP	Phone
Al & Irene's Barbecue House (Barbecue) 2020 N Towne Ln NE	Cedar Rapids	IA	52402	319-393-6242
Al's Red Frog (American) 88 16th Ave SW	Cedar Rapids	IA	52404	319-369-3940
Amana Barn Restaurant (German) 4709 220th Trail	Amana	IA	52203	319-622-3214
Cafe de Klos (European) 821 3rd Ave SE	Cedar Rapids	IA	52403	319-362-9340
Carlos O'Kelly's (Mexican) 3320 Armar Dr	Marion	IA	52302	319-373-1451
Cedar Brewing Co (American) 500 Blairs Ferry Rd NE *Web:* www.beerstuff.com/cbc/	Cedar Rapids	IA	52402	319-378-9090
Colony Inn (German) 741 47th Ave	Amana	IA	52203	319-622-6270
Dockside (American) 1895 Ellis Blvd NW	Cedar Rapids	IA	52405	319-365-7049
Dos Gringo's (Mexican) 215 1st Ave SE	Cedar Rapids	IA	52401	319-363-8883
Dragon Restaurant (Chinese) 329 2nd Ave SE	Cedar Rapids	IA	52401	319-362-9716
Hacienda Las Glorias (Mexican) 715 1st Ave SW	Cedar Rapids	IA	52405	319-363-7344
Irish Democrat Pub & Grill (Irish) 3207 1st Ave SE	Cedar Rapids	IA	52403	319-364-9896
Park Place (American) 1200 Collins Rd NE	Cedar Rapids	IA	52402	319-393-6600
Pei's Mandarin (Chinese) 5131 Council St NE	Cedar Rapids	IA	52402	319-395-9741
Taj Mahal Cuisine of India (Indian) 5454 Blairs Forest Way NE	Cedar Rapids	IA	52402	319-393-4500
Teddy's Steakhouse (Steak) 200 1st Ave NE	Cedar Rapids	IA	52401	319-364-2333
Tic Toc (American) 600 17th St NE	Cedar Rapids	IA	52402	319-364-9685
Top of the Five (American) 350 1st Ave NE	Cedar Rapids	IA	52401	319-363-8161
Vernon Inn (Greek) 2663 Mount Vernon Rd SE	Cedar Rapids	IA	52403	319-366-7817
Winifred's (Steak/Seafood) 3847 First Ave SE	Cedar Rapids	IA	52402	319-364-6125
Xavier's (American) 1401 1st Ave SE	Cedar Rapids	IA	52406	319-364-9313
Zindrick Czech Restaurant (Czechoslovakian) 86 16th Ave SW	Cedar Rapids	IA	52404	319-369-3940

— Goods and Services —

SHOPPING

Name / Address	City	State	ZIP	Phone	Fax
Czech Village 16th Ave SW	Cedar Rapids	IA	52404	319-866-9801	
Lindale Mall 4444 1st Ave NE	Cedar Rapids	IA	52402	319-393-9393	393-5819
Wellington Square Antique Mall 1200 2nd Ave SE	Cedar Rapids	IA	52403	319-368-6640	
Westdale Mall 2600 Edgewood Rd SW	Cedar Rapids	IA	52404	319-396-0740	

BANKS

Name / Address	City	State	ZIP	Phone	Fax
Brenton Bank & Trust Co 150 1st Ave NE	Cedar Rapids	IA	52407	319-398-3000	365-2736
Commercial Federal Bank 700 1st Ave NE	Cedar Rapids	IA	52407	319-366-1851	369-5653
Firstar Bank Cedar Rapids NA 222 2nd Ave SE *TF:* 800-236-6717	Cedar Rapids	IA	52401	319-368-4444	368-4052
Guaranty Bank & Trust Co 302 3rd Ave SE	Cedar Rapids	IA	52401	319-362-2111	362-7894
Mercantile Bank 1100 Old Marion Rd NE	Cedar Rapids	IA	52406	319-393-9210	393-3536

BUSINESS SERVICES

Name	Phone	Name	Phone
Airborne Express	800-247-2676	**Mail Boxes Etc**	800-789-4623
BAX Global	800-225-5229	**Norrell Temporary Services**	319-395-7548
DHL Worldwide Express	800-225-5345	**Post Office**	319-399-2900
Federal Express	800-238-5355	**UPS**	800-742-5877

— Media —

PUBLICATIONS

Name / Address	City	State	ZIP	Phone	Fax
Gazette‡ 500 3rd Ave SE *TF:* 800-397-8212 ■ *Web:* www.gazetteonline.com ■ *E-mail:* gazette@fyiowa.infi.net	Cedar Rapids	IA	52401	319-398-8313	398-5846

‡*Daily newspapers*

TELEVISION

Name / Address	City	State	ZIP	Phone	Fax
KCRG-TV Ch 9 (ABC) PO Box 816 *Web:* www.kcrg.com ■ *E-mail:* newsroom@kcrg.com	Cedar Rapids	IA	52406	319-398-8422	398-8378
KDIN-TV Ch 11 (PBS) PO Box 6450	Johnston	IA	50131	515-242-3100	242-5830
KFXA-TV Ch 28 (Fox) 605 Boyson Rd NE	Cedar Rapids	IA	52402	319-393-2800	395-7028
KGAN-TV Ch 2 (CBS) 600 Old Marion Rd NE *Web:* www.kgan.com ■ *E-mail:* kgan@kgan.com	Cedar Rapids	IA	52402	319-395-9060	395-0113
KPXR-TV Ch 48 (PAX) 1957 Blairs Ferry Rd NE *Web:* www.pax.net/KPXR	Cedar Rapids	IA	52402	319-366-4848	378-9587
KWWL-TV Ch 7 (NBC) 500 E 4th St **Fax:* News Rm ■ *Web:* www.kwwl.com ■ *E-mail:* comments@kwwl.com	Waterloo	IA	50703	319-291-1200	291-1233*

RADIO

Name / Address	City	State	ZIP	Phone	Fax
KCCK-FM 88.3 MHz (Nost) PO Box 2068	Cedar Rapids	IA	52406	319-398-5446	398-5492
KCRG-AM 1600 kHz (N/T) 2nd Ave & 5th St SE *Web:* www.kcrg.com/1600/k1600.htm ■ *E-mail:* newsroom@kcrg.com	Cedar Rapids	IA	52401	319-398-8422	398-8378
KHAK-FM 98.1 MHz (Ctry) 425 2nd St SE Suite 450 *Web:* www.khak.com ■ *E-mail:* khak@khak.com	Cedar Rapids	IA	52401	319-365-9431	363-8062
KKRQ-FM 100.7 MHz (CR) PO Box 2388	Iowa City	IA	52244	319-354-9500	354-9504
KRNA-FM 94.1 MHz (Rock) 425 2nd St SE 4th Fl *Web:* www.krna.com/	Cedar Rapids	IA	52401	319-365-9431	363-8062
KZIA-FM 102.9 MHz (CHR) 1110 26th Ave SW	Cedar Rapids	IA	52404	319-363-2061	363-2948
WMT-AM 600 kHz (N/T) PO Box 2147	Cedar Rapids	IA	52406	319-395-0530	393-0918
WMT-FM 96.5 MHz (AC) PO Box 2147 *Web:* www.wmtradio.com ■ *E-mail:* wmt@wmtradio.com	Cedar Rapids	IA	52406	319-395-0530	393-0918

Cedar Rapids (Cont'd)

— Colleges/Universities —

				Phone	Fax
Coe College 1220 1st Ave NE	Cedar Rapids	IA	52402	319-399-8000	399-8816*
**Fax:* Admissions ■ *TF:* 800-332-8404 ■ *Web:* www.coe.edu ■ *E-mail:* admission@coe.edu					
Cornell College 600 1st St W	Mount Vernon	IA	52314	319-895-4000	895-4492
TF Admissions: 800-747-1112 ■ *Web:* www.cornell-iowa.edu ■ *E-mail:* postmaster@cornell-iowa.edu					
Kirkwood Community College 6301 Kirkwood Blvd SW	Cedar Rapids	IA	52406	319-398-5411	398-5492
TF: 800-332-2055 ■ *Web:* www.kirkwood.cc.ia.us ■ *E-mail:* info@kirkwood.cc.ia.us					
Mount Mercy College 1330 Elmhurst Dr NE	Cedar Rapids	IA	52402	319-363-8213	363-5270
TF Admissions: 800-248-4504 ■ *Web:* www.mtmercy.edu ■ *E-mail:* admission@mmc.mtmercy.edu					
University of Iowa	Iowa City	IA	52242	319-353-2121	335-1535
Web: www.uiowa.edu					

— Hospitals —

				Phone	Fax
Mercy Medical Center 701 10th St SE	Cedar Rapids	IA	52403	319-398-6011	398-6912
Web: www.mercycare.org					
Saint Luke's Hospital 1026 A Ave NE	Cedar Rapids	IA	52402	319-369-7211	398-5585

— Attractions —

				Phone	Fax
Amana Colonies	Amana	IA	52203	319-622-3828	
Bever Park Zoo 2700 Bever Ave SE	Cedar Rapids	IA	52403	319-286-5080	
Brucemore 2160 Linden Dr SE	Cedar Rapids	IA	52403	319-362-7375	362-9481
Web: www.brucemore.org/					
Cedar Rapids Area Cultural Alliance 427 First St SE	Cedar Rapids	IA	52407	319-366-4739	366-4590
Web: www.crculture.org/ ■ *E-mail:* craca@crculture.org					
Cedar Rapids Museum of Art 410 3rd Ave SE	Cedar Rapids	IA	52401	319-366-7503	366-4111
Web: www.crma.org/					
Cedar Rapids Symphony Orchestra 205 2nd Ave SE	Cedar Rapids	IA	52401	319-366-8203	366-5206
Web: www.crsymphony.org ■ *E-mail:* symphony@crsymphony.org					
Cedar Valley Nature Trail	Hiawatha	IA	52233	319-398-3505	
Coe College Permanent Collection of Art 1220 1st Ave NE	Cedar Rapids	IA	52402	319-399-8585	
Web: www.public.coe.edu/departments/Art/title.html					
Czech Village 16th Avenue SW betw E & C Sts	Cedar Rapids	IA	52405	319-362-2846	
Duffy's Collectible Cars 250 Classic Car Ct SW	Cedar Rapids	IA	52404	319-364-7000	364-4036
Web: www.duffys.com/					
Granger House Museum 970 10th St	Marion	IA	52302	319-377-6672	
Web: members.aol.com/Grangerhou/index.html					
Herbert Hoover National Historic Site PO Box 607	West Branch	IA	52358	319-643-2541	643-5367
Web: www.nps.gov/heho/					
Indian Creek Nature Center 6665 Otis Rd SE	Cedar Rapids	IA	52403	319-362-0664	362-2876
Iowa Masonic Library & Museum 813 1st Ave SE	Cedar Rapids	IA	52402	319-365-1438	365-1439
Legion Arts 1103 Third St SE	Cedar Rapids	IA	52401	319-364-1580	362-9156
Web: www.legionarts.org/ ■ *E-mail:* legion@artswire.org					
Linn County History Center 615 1st Ave SE	Cedar Rapids	IA	52401	319-362-1501	362-6790
National Czech & Slovak Museum & Library 30 16th Ave SW	Cedar Rapids	IA	52404	319-362-8500	363-2209
Web: www.ncsml.org ■ *E-mail:* giftstor@ncsml.org					
Paramount Theatre 123 3rd Ave SE	Cedar Rapids	IA	52401	319-398-5211	
Riverside Roadhouse Farmers Market 1350 'A' St SW	Cedar Rapids	IA	52404	319-286-5731	
Science Station 427 1st St SE	Cedar Rapids	IA	52401	319-366-0968	366-4590
Web: www.netins.net/showcase/scistation/					
Seminole Valley Farm Seminole Valley Pk	Cedar Rapids	IA	52411	319-378-9240	
Theatre Cedar Rapids 102 3rd St SE	Cedar Rapids	IA	52401	319-366-8592	366-8593
University of Iowa Museum of Art 150 N Riverside Dr	Iowa City	IA	52242	319-335-1727	335-3677
Web: www.uiowa.edu/~artmus/					
Ushers Ferry Historic Village 5925 Seminole Valley Trail	Cedar Rapids	IA	52401	319-286-5763	286-5764

SPORTS TEAMS & FACILITIES

				Phone	Fax
Cedar Rapids Kernels (baseball) 950 Rockford Rd SW	Cedar Rapids	IA	52404	319-363-3887	363-5631
Web: www.kernels.com ■ *E-mail:* kernels@ia.net					
Hawkeye Downs 4400 6th St SW	Cedar Rapids	IA	52404	319-365-8656	365-1735

— Events —

	Phone
All Iowa Fair (mid-July)	319-365-8656
Art & Craft Show Weekend (late November)	319-364-1641
Art on the Fence (mid-May)	319-363-4942
Autumnfest Arts & Craft Show (early November)	319-365-8656
Bluegrass Festival-Amana (mid-July)	800-245-5465
Cedar Rapids Antique Show & Collectors Fair (early April & early October)	319-362-1729
Cedar Rapids BBQ Round Up (late June)	319-398-5211
Cedar Rapids Ethnic Fest (late May)	319-362-1302
Cedar Rapids Freedom Festival (late June-early July)	319-398-5009
Celebration of the Arts (late June)	319-398-5322
Christmas on the River Arts & Crafts Sale (late November)	319-362-8070
Fantasy of Lights (late November-early January)	319-398-5009
Festival of Trees (mid-November)	319-369-8733
Firstar Eve (December 31)	319-368-4444
Grant Wood Art Festival (mid-June)	319-462-4267
Greater Iowa Boat & Sports Show (mid-January)	319-377-7660
Heritage Days Celebration (early July)	319-895-8214
Hiawatha Hog Wild Days (mid-June)	319-393-3668
Maple Syrup Festival (early March)	319-362-0664
Marion Arts Festival (mid-May)	319-377-6316
Old Time Country Fair (late August)	319-286-5763
Olde World Faire (early May)	319-895-6862
Saint Patrick's Day Parade (mid-March)	319-390-3501
Springfest Arts & Crafts Sale (late February-early March)	319-377-7660
Swamp Fox Festival Heritage Celebration (early September)	319-377-6316
Tanager Place Hot Air Balloon Festival (early August)	319-365-9164
Taste of Iowa (early September)	319-398-5009
Ushers Ferry Civil War Reenactment (mid-July)	319-286-5763
Wild West Weekend (mid-August)	319-286-5763
Winterfest (early February)	319-398-5009
World's Toughest Rodeo (mid-February)	319-363-1888

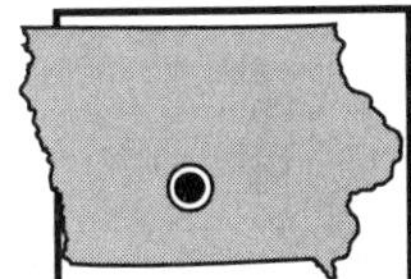

Des Moines

Iowa's capital and largest city is also the birthplace of John Wayne and Mamie Doud Eisenhower. Agriculture has long been the primary industry in Des Moines, but as the headquarters of more than 50 insurance companies, it is also the third largest insurance center in the world. The city's skywalks, three miles of enclosed glass and concrete bridges connected at the second story level, make getting around downtown easy in any kind of weather. The Civic Center is home to the Des Moines Symphony and Ballet Iowa, and the Des Moines Art Center is noted for its collection of 20th century art. Living History Farms in nearby Urbandale recreates Iowa's past in a 600-acre open-air museum. In Pella, the shops, homes, festivals, and events give visitors a taste of life in an Old World Dutch village.

Population	191,293	**Longitude**	93-60-89 W
Area (Land)	75.3 sq mi	**County**	Polk
Area (Water)	1.5 sq mi	**Time Zone**	CST
Elevation	803 ft	**Area Code/s**	515
Latitude	41-60-06 N		

Des Moines (Cont'd)

— Average Temperatures and Precipitation —

TEMPERATURES

	Jan	Feb	Mar	Apr	May	Jun	Jul	Aug	Sep	Oct	Nov	Dec
High	28	34	47	62	73	82	87	84	76	64	48	33
Low	11	16	28	40	52	61	67	64	55	43	30	16

PRECIPITATION

	Jan	Feb	Mar	Apr	May	Jun	Jul	Aug	Sep	Oct	Nov	Dec
Inches	1.0	1.1	2.3	3.4	3.7	4.5	3.8	4.2	3.5	2.6	1.8	1.3

— Important Phone Numbers —

	Phone
AAA	515-223-4104
American Express Travel	515-247-7131
Dental Referral	800-243-4444
Emergency	911
HotelDocs	800-468-3537
Iowa Guest Hotline	515-278-6710
Poison Control Center	712-277-2222
Road Conditions	515-288-1047
Time/Temp	515-244-5611
Travelers Aid	515-286-2088
Weather	515-270-2614

— Information Sources —

				Phone	Fax
Better Business Bureau Serving Central & Eastern Iowa 505 5th Ave Suite 950 *TF:* 800-222-1600 ■ *Web:* www.desmoines.bbb.org ■ *E-mail:* info@dm.bbb.org	Des Moines	IA	50309	515-243-8137	243-2227
Des Moines City Hall 400 E 1st St *Web:* www.ci.des-moines.ia.us	Des Moines	IA	50309	515-283-4500	283-1300
Des Moines Economic Development Office 400 E 1st St. *Web:* www.ci.des-moines.ia.us/economy	Des Moines	IA	50309	515-283-4004	237-1667
Des Moines Mayor 400 E 1st St 2nd Fl. *Web:* www.ci.des-moines.ia.us/mayor	Des Moines	IA	50309	515-283-4944	237-1645
Des Moines Public Library 100 Locust St *Web:* www.pldminfo.org ■ *E-mail:* dsmlib@netins.net	Des Moines	IA	50309	515-283-4152	237-1654
Greater Des Moines Chamber of Commerce Federation 601 Locust St Suite 100 *Web:* www.dmchamber.com	Des Moines	IA	50309	515-286-4950	286-4974
Greater Des Moines Convention & Visitors Bureau 601 Locust St Suite 222 *TF:* 800-451-2625 ■ *Web:* www.desmoinesia.com	Des Moines	IA	50309	515-286-4960	244-9757
Iowa Tourism Div 200 E Grand Ave *TF:* 800-345-4692 ■ *Web:* www.traveliowa.com	Des Moines	IA	50309	515-242-4705	242-4749
Polk County 111 Court Ave.	Des Moines	IA	50309	515-286-3000	286-3082
Polk County Convention Complex 501 Grand Ave	Des Moines	IA	50309	515-242-2500	242-2530

On-Line Resources

4DesMoines.com	www.4desmoines.com
Anthill City Guide Des Moines	www.anthill.com/city.asp?city=desmoines
Area Guide Des Moines	desmoines.areaguides.net
City Knowledge Des Moines	www.cityknowledge.com/ia_desmoines.htm
Excite.com Des Moines City Guide	www.excite.com/travel/countries/united_states/iowa/des_moines
Metro Arts Alliance	www.metroarts.org/

— Transportation Services —

AIRPORTS

■ **Des Moines International Airport (DSM)**

	Phone
5 miles SE of downtown (approx 10-15 minutes) Web: www.dsmairport.com	515-256-5050

Airport Transportation

	Phone
Ruan Cab Co $10 fare to downtown	515-263-0122
Unique Courtesy Service $15 fare to downtown	515-240-4563

Commercial Airlines

	Phone
AccessAir	877-462-2237
American	800-433-7300
Midwest Express	800-452-2022
Northwest	800-225-2525
TWA	800-221-2000
United	800-241-6522
US Airways	800-428-4322
Vanguard	800-826-4827

Charter Airlines

	Phone
Charter Star	515-256-5270
Elliott Aviation Inc	515-285-6551

CAR RENTALS

	Phone
Avis	515-245-2585
Budget	515-287-2612
Dewey Ford	515-282-2828
Hertz	515-285-9650
National	515-256-5353

LIMO/TAXI

	Phone
AJ's Best Stretch Limousine	515-222-1826
Allbee's Old Market Limousine	515-253-9589
Capitol Cab	515-282-8111
Continental Limousine	515-243-5466
Old Market Limousine	515-277-5512
Ruan Cab Co.	515-263-0122
Smithson Limousine	515-285-6346
Yellow Cab	515-243-1111

MASS TRANSIT

	Phone
Des Moines Metropolitan Transit Authority $1 Base fare	515-283-8100

RAIL/BUS

				Phone
Greyhound/Trailways Bus Station 1107 Keosauqua Way	Des Moines	IA	50309	800-231-2222

— Accommodations —

HOTELS, MOTELS, RESORTS

				Phone	Fax
14th Street Inn 4685 NE 14th St.	Des Moines	IA	50313	515-265-5671	262-7469
Adventureland Inn PO Box 3355 *TF:* 800-532-1286	Des Moines	IA	50316	515-265-7321	265-3506
Best Western Airport Inn 1810 Army Post Rd. *TF:* 800-383-6462	Des Moines	IA	50315	515-287-6464	287-5818
Best Western Colonial Inn 5020 NE 14th St. *TF:* 800-528-1234	Des Moines	IA	50313	515-265-7511	265-7511
Best Western Regency Inn 3303 S Center St *TF:* 800-241-2974	Marshalltown	IA	50158	515-752-6321	752-4412
Best Western Starlite Village 929 3rd St *TF:* 800-903-0009	Des Moines	IA	50309	515-282-5251	282-6871
Best Western Walnut Creek Inn 1258 8th St *TF:* 800-792-5688	West Des Moines	IA	50265	515-223-1212	223-1235
Comfort Inn Airport 5231 Fleur Dr. *TF:* 800-228-5150	Des Moines	IA	50321	515-287-3434	287-3434
Comfort Suites Living History Farms 11167 Hickman Rd *TF:* 800-395-7675	Urbandale	IA	50322	515-276-1126	276-8969
Courtyard by Marriott 1520 NW 114th St *TF:* 800-321-2211 ■ *Web:* courtyard.com/DSMCH	Clive	IA	50325	515-225-1222	225-3773
Days Inn 4845 Merle Hay Rd *TF:* 800-329-7466	Des Moines	IA	50322	515-278-5511	278-5511
Des Moines Marriott Hotel 700 Grand Ave *TF:* 800-228-9290	Des Moines	IA	50309	515-245-5500	245-5567
Embassy Suites on the River 101 E Locust St *TF:* 800-362-2779	Des Moines	IA	50309	515-244-1700	244-2537
Executive Inn 3530 Westown Pkwy *TF:* 800-998-9669	West Des Moines	IA	50266	515-225-1144	225-6463
Fairfield Inn by Marriott 1600 NW 114th St. *TF:* 800-228-2800 ■ *Web:* fairfieldinn.com/DSMFI	Clive	IA	50325	515-226-1600	226-1600
Hampton Inn Airport 5001 Fleur Dr *TF:* 800-426-7866	Des Moines	IA	50321	515-287-7300	287-6343
Hampton Inn West Des Moines 7060 Lake Dr *TF:* 800-426-7866	West Des Moines	IA	50266	515-223-4700	221-1010
Holiday Inn 5000 Merle Hay Rd *TF:* 800-465-4329	Des Moines	IA	50322	515-278-0271	276-8172

Des Moines — Hotels, Motels, Resorts (Cont'd)

	City	State	Zip	Phone	Fax
Holiday Inn Airport 6111 Fleur Dr. *TF:* 800-248-4013 ■ *E-mail:* holidayinndsm@mindspring.com	Des Moines	IA	50321	515-287-2400	287-4811
Holiday Inn Downtown 1050 6th Ave. *TF:* 800-465-4329	Des Moines	IA	50314	515-283-0151	283-0151
Holiday Inn Express 1700 W 19th St S *TF:* 888-249-1468	Newton	IA	50208	515-792-7722	792-1787
Holiday Inn Express at Drake 1140 24th St *TF:* 800-252-7838	Des Moines	IA	50311	515-255-4000	255-1192
Holiday Inn University Park 1800 50th St *TF:* 800-465-4329	West Des Moines	IA	50266	515-223-1800	223-0894
Hotel Fort Des Moines 1000 Walnut St *TF:* 800-532-1466 ■ *Web:* www.hotelfortdm.com/ ■ *E-mail:* sales@hotelfortdm.com	Des Moines	IA	50309	515-243-1161	243-4317
Kirkwood Civic Center Hotel 400 Walnut St *TF:* 800-798-9191	Des Moines	IA	50309	515-244-9191	282-7004
Marriott West Des Moines 1250 74th St *TF:* 800-228-9290 ■ *Web:* marriotthotels.com/DSMWD	West Des Moines	IA	50266	515-267-1500	223-1687
Residence Inn by Marriott 11428 Forest Ave *TF:* 800-331-3131 ■ *Web:* www.residenceinn.com/DSMWE	Clive	IA	50325	515-223-7700	223-7222
Savery Hotel & Spa 401 Locust St *TF:* 800-798-2151	Des Moines	IA	50309	515-244-2151	244-1408
Sheraton Four Points Hotel 11040 Hickman Rd *TF:* 800-325-3535	Des Moines	IA	50325	515-278-5575	278-4078
Sheraton Four Points Hotel 4800 Merle Hay Rd *TF:* 800-325-3535	Des Moines	IA	50322	515-278-4755	278-2846
StudioPLUS 2701 Westown Pkwy *TF:* 800-646-8000	West Des Moines	IA	50266	515-327-9100	327-9200
Valley West Inn 3535 Westown Pkwy *TF:* 800-833-6755	West Des Moines	IA	50266	515-225-2524	225-9058

— Restaurants —

	City	State	Zip	Phone
801 Steak & Chop House Ltd (Steak/Seafood) 801 Grand Ave Suite 201	Des Moines	IA	50309	515-288-6000
Anna's Restaurant (American) 401 Locust St	Des Moines	IA	50309	515-244-2151
Bavarian Haus Restaurant (German) 5220 NE 14th St	Des Moines	IA	50313	515-266-1173
Cheddar's Casual Cafe (American) 1301 NW 114th St	Clive	IA	50325	515-222-3129
Christopher's (Italian) 2816 Beaver Ave	Des Moines	IA	50310	515-274-3694
Court Avenue Brewing Co (American) 309 Court Ave	Des Moines	IA	50309	515-282-2739
Crimmins Cattle Co (Steak) 4901 Fleur Dr	Des Moines	IA	50321	515-287-6611
Crystal Tree Restaurant (American) 6111 Fleur Dr	Des Moines	IA	50321	515-287-2032
Doozies (American) 101 E Locust St	Des Moines	IA	50309	515-244-1700
El Patio (Mexican) 611 37th St	Des Moines	IA	50312	515-274-2303
Genevieve's (American) 1050 6th Ave	Des Moines	IA	50314	515-283-0151
Gotham Club (Steak/Seafood) 1000 Walnut St	Des Moines	IA	50309	515-243-1161
Great China Restaurant (Chinese) 8569 Hickman Rd	Des Moines	IA	50325	515-270-1688
Greenbrier Restaurant (Continental) 5810 Merle Hay Rd	Johnston	IA	50131	515-253-0124
Iowa Beef Steakhouse (Steak) 1201 E Euclid Ave	Des Moines	IA	50316	515-262-1138
Iowa Machine Shed Restaurant (American) 11151 Hickman Rd	Urbandale	IA	50312	515-270-6818
Jesse's Embers (Steak/Seafood) 3301 Ingersoll Ave	Des Moines	IA	50312	515-255-6011
Julio's (Tex Mex) 308 Court Ave	Des Moines	IA	50309	515-244-1710
King Ying Low (Chinese) 223 4th St	Des Moines	IA	50309	515-243-7049
Mandarin (Chinese) 3520 Beaver Ave	Des Moines	IA	50310	515-277-6263
Nacho Mammas (Mexican) 216 Court Ave	Des Moines	IA	50309	515-280-6262
Noah's Ark Restaurant (Italian) 2400 Ingersoll Ave	Des Moines	IA	50312	515-288-2246
Ohana Steakhouse (Japanese) 2900 University Ave	Des Moines	IA	50311	515-225-3325
Quenelles (Continental) 700 Grand Ave	Des Moines	IA	50309	515-245-5500
Raccoon River Brewing Co (American) 200 10th St	Des Moines	IA	50309	515-283-1941
Spaghetti Works (Italian) 310 Court Ave	Des Moines	IA	50309	515-243-2195
Taste of Thailand (Thai) 215 E Walnut St	Des Moines	IA	50309	515-243-9521
Trattoria The (Italian) 207 4th St	Des Moines	IA	50312	515-288-6821
Tursi's Latin King (Italian) 2200 Hubbell Ave	Des Moines	IA	50317	515-266-4466
Waterfront Seafood Market (Seafood) 2900 University Ave	West Des Moines	IA	50266	515-223-5106
Winston's Pub & Grille (American) 601 Locust St Suite 200	Des Moines	IA	50309	515-245-5454

— Goods and Services —

SHOPPING

	City	State	Zip	Phone	Fax
Historic Valley Junction 217 5th St	West Des Moines	IA	50265	515-222-3642	222-3644
Kaleidoscope at the Hub 555-655 Walnut St	Des Moines	IA	50309	515-243-3228	
Locust Mall 700 Locust St	Des Moines	IA	50309	515-244-1005	
Merle Hay Mall 3800 Merle Hay Rd	Des Moines	IA	50310	515-276-8551	276-9309
Southridge Mall 1111 E Army Post Rd	Des Moines	IA	50315	515-287-3880	287-0983
Valley West Mall 1551 Valley West Dr	West Des Moines	IA	50266	515-225-3631	224-9935

BANKS

	City	State	Zip	Phone	Fax
Brenton Bank 400 Locust St Suite 200 **Fax Area Code:* 515	Des Moines	IA	50309	800-820-0088	237-5221*
Commercial Federal Bank 801 Grand Suite 300	Des Moines	IA	50309	515-246-0141	246-0280
Firstar Bank Iowa NA PO Box 906 *TF:* 800-236-4462	Des Moines	IA	50304	515-245-6100	245-6351
West Des Moines State Bank 1601 22nd St	West Des Moines	IA	50266	515-222-2300	222-2346

BUSINESS SERVICES

	Phone
A-1 Speed Delivery	515-266-1022
Accountemps	515-282-8367
Advance Delivery	515-288-8220
DHL Worldwide Express	800-225-5345
Express Messenger Systems	800-736-8310
Federal Express	800-238-5355
Kelly Services	515-282-0264
Kinko's	515-282-5955
Manpower Temporary Services	515-288-6745
Olsten Staffing Services	515-223-6440
Post Office	515-283-7505
Priority Express	515-243-3900
UPS	800-742-5877

— Media —

PUBLICATIONS

	City	State	Zip	Phone	Fax
Des Moines Business Record 100 4th St *E-mail:* pbc@mail.commonlink.com	Des Moines	IA	50309	515-288-3336	288-0309
Des Moines Register‡ PO Box 957 *Web:* www.dmregister.com	Des Moines	IA	50304	515-284-8000	286-2504
Midwest Living 1912 Grand Ave *TF:* 800-678-8093	Des Moines	IA	50309	515-284-2662	284-3836

‡Daily newspapers

TELEVISION

	City	State	Zip	Phone	Fax
KCCI-TV Ch 8 (CBS) 888 9th St *Web:* www.kcci.com ■ *E-mail:* kcci@kcci.com	Des Moines	IA	50309	515-247-8888	244-0202
KDIN-TV Ch 11 (PBS) PO Box 6450	Johnston	IA	50131	515-242-3100	242-5830
KDSM-TV Ch 17 (Fox/UPN) 4023 Fleur Dr *Web:* www.kdsmtv.com ■ *E-mail:* kdsm@commonlink.com	Des Moines	IA	50321	515-287-1717	287-0064
WHO-TV Ch 13 (NBC) 1801 Grand Ave *Web:* www.whotv.com ■ *E-mail:* newscenter13@netins.net	Des Moines	IA	50309	515-242-3500	242-3796
WOI-TV Ch 5 (ABC) 3903 Westown Pkwy **Fax:* Sales ■ *Web:* www.woi-tv.com/ ■ *E-mail:* woitv@ecity.net	West Des Moines	IA	50266	515-457-9645	457-1034*

RADIO

	City	State	Zip	Phone	Fax
KBGG-AM 1700 kHz (N/T) 5161 Maple Dr	Des Moines	IA	50317	515-262-9200	261-6192
KDFR-FM 91.3 MHz (Rel) PO Box 57023	Des Moines	IA	50317	515-262-0449	
KGGO-FM 94.9 MHz (CR) 3900 NE Broadway *Web:* www.kggo.com ■ *E-mail:* kggo@kggo.com	Des Moines	IA	50317	515-265-6181	265-9005
KIOA-FM 93.3 MHz (Oldies) 1416 Locust St	Des Moines	IA	50309	515-280-1350	280-3011
KLYF-FM 100.3 MHz (AC) 1801 Grand Ave	Des Moines	IA	50309	515-242-3500	242-3711
KSTZ-FM 102.5 MHz (AC) 1416 Locust St	Des Moines	IA	50309	515-280-1350	280-3011
KWKY-AM 1150 kHz (Rel) PO Box 662	Des Moines	IA	50303	515-981-0981	981-0840

— Colleges/Universities —

	City	State	Zip	Phone	Fax
American Institute of Business 2500 Fleur Dr *TF:* 800-444-1921	Des Moines	IA	50321	515-244-4221	244-6773

Des Moines — Colleges/Universities (Cont'd)

				Phone	Fax
Des Moines Area Community College 2006 S Ankeny Blvd	Ankeny	IA	50021	515-964-6200	965-7054
Web: www.dmacc.cc.ia.us ■ *E-mail:* marketing@dmacc.cc.ia.us					
Drake University 2507 University Ave	Des Moines	IA	50311	515-271-2011	271-2831
TF: 800-443-7253 ■ *Web:* www.drake.edu					
Grand View College 1200 Grandview Ave	Des Moines	IA	50316	515-263-2800	263-2974
TF: 800-444-6083 ■ *Web:* www.gvc.edu					
Simpson College 701 N 'C' St	Indianola	IA	50125	515-961-6251	961-1870
TF Admissions: 800-362-2454 ■ *Web:* www.simpson.edu					

— Hospitals —

				Phone	Fax
Broadlawns Medical Center 1801 Hickman Rd	Des Moines	IA	50314	515-282-2200	282-5785
Web: www.broadlawns.org					
Dallas County Hospital 610 10th St	Perry	IA	50220	515-465-3547	465-2922
Des Moines General Hospital 603 E 12th St	Des Moines	IA	50309	515-263-4200	263-4699
Iowa Lutheran Hospital 700 E University Ave	Des Moines	IA	50316	515-263-5612	263-5295
Iowa Methodist Medical Center 1200 Pleasant St	Des Moines	IA	50309	515-241-6212	241-5994
Madison County Memorial Hospital 300 W Hutchings St	Winterset	IA	50273	515-462-2373	462-5008
Mary Greeley Medical Center 1111 Duff Ave	Ames	IA	50010	515-239-2011	239-2060
Mercy Hospital Medical Center 400 University Ave	Des Moines	IA	50314	515-247-3121	643-8880
TF: 800-637-2993 ■ *Web:* www.mercydesmoines.org					
Veterans Affairs Medical Center 3600 30th St	Des Moines	IA	50310	515-699-5999	699-5869

— Attractions —

				Phone	Fax
Adventure Lands of America Inc 5091 NE 56th St	Altoona	IA	50009	515-266-2121	266-9831
TF: 800-532-1286					
Blank Park Zoo 7401 SW 9th St	Des Moines	IA	50315	515-285-4722	285-1487
Web: www.des-moines.ia.us/zoo					
Boone & Scenic Valley Railroad 225 10th St	Boone	IA	50036	515-432-4249	432-4253
TF: 800-626-0319					
Civic Music Assn 221 Walnut St	Des Moines	IA	50309	515-288-8919	243-1588
Web: www.civicmusic.org					
Court Avenue District 204 4th St	Des Moines	IA	50309	515-243-2195	
Des Moines Art Center 4700 Grand Ave	Des Moines	IA	50312	515-277-4405	271-0357
Web: www.desmoinesartcenter.org					
Des Moines Botanical Center 909 E River Dr	Des Moines	IA	50316	515-242-2934	242-2797
Des Moines Metro Opera 106 W Boston Ave	Indianola	IA	50125	515-961-6221	961-2994
E-mail: dmmopera@aol.com					
Des Moines Symphony 221 Walnut St	Des Moines	IA	50309	515-243-1140	243-1588
Web: www.dmsymphony.org					
Eisenhower Mamie Doud Birthplace 709 Carroll St	Boone	IA	50036	515-432-1896	
Hoyt Sherman Place 1501 Woodland Ave	Des Moines	IA	50309	515-243-0913	237-3582
Iowa Gold Star Museum 7700 NW Beaver Dr Camp Dodge	Johnston	IA	50131	515-252-4531	252-4139
Web: www.guard.state.ia.us/pages/history/museum/iowa_gold_star_museumestablished.html					
Iowa Historical Building 600 E Locust St	Des Moines	IA	50319	515-281-5111	282-0502
Web: www.culturalaffairs.org					
Iowa State Capitol E 9th St & Grand Ave	Des Moines	IA	50319	515-281-5591	
John Wayne Birthplace 216 S 2nd St	Winterset	IA	50273	515-462-1044	
Web: www.johnwaynebirthplace.org					
Jordan House 2001 Fuller Rd	West Des Moines	IA	50265	515-225-1286	
Lake Red Rock 1105 Hwy T-15	Knoxville	IA	50138	515-828-7522	
Living History Farms 2600 NW 111th St	Urbandale	IA	50322	515-278-5286	278-9808
Web: www.ioweb.com/lhf/index.html					
National Balloon Museum 1601 N Jefferson St	Indianola	IA	50125	515-961-3714	
National Sprint Car Hall of Fame & Museum 1 Sprint Capital Pl	Knoxville	IA	50138	515-842-6176	842-6177
Web: www.classicar.com/museums/sprint/sprint.htm					
Pella Historical Village 507 Franklin St	Pella	IA	50219	515-628-4311	628-9192
Web: www.kdsi.net/~pellatt/ ■ *E-mail:* pellatt@kdsi.net					
Polk County Heritage Gallery 111 Court Ave Polk County Office Bldg	Des Moines	IA	50309	515-286-3215	
Salisbury House Foundation 4025 Tonawanda Dr	Des Moines	IA	50312	515-274-1777	274-0184
Web: www.salisburyhouse.org					
Saylorville Lake 5600 NW 78th Ave	Johnston	IA	50131	515-964-0672	
Science Center of Iowa 4500 Grand Ave Greenwood Pk	Des Moines	IA	50312	515-274-6868	274-3404
Web: www.sciowa.org					
Sherman Hill National Historic District 756 16th St	Des Moines	IA	50314	515-284-5717	
Sleepy Hollow Sports Park 4051 Dean Ave	Des Moines	IA	50317	515-262-4100	
Smith Neal National Wildlife Refuge 9981 Pacific St	Prairie City	IA	50228	515-994-3400	994-3459
Terrace Hill-Governor's Mansion 2300 Grand Ave	Des Moines	IA	50312	515-281-3604	
Wallace House Foundation 756 16th St	Des Moines	IA	50314	515-243-7063	243-8927
Women's Army Corps Museum at Fort Des Moines 225 E Army Post Rd	Des Moines	IA	50315	515-284-6005	284-6125

SPORTS TEAMS & FACILITIES

				Phone	Fax
Des Moines Buccaneers (hockey) 7201 Hickman Rd Metro Arena	Urbandale	IA	50322	515-278-9757	278-5401
Web: www.bucshockey.org/					
Des Moines Menace (soccer) 50th St & Aurora Ave Cara McGrane Memorial Stadium	Des Moines	IA	50325	515-226-9890	226-1595
Web: www.dmmenace.com ■ *E-mail:* soccer@dmmenace.com					
Iowa Barnstormers (football) 833 5th Ave Veterans Memorial Auditorium	Des Moines	IA	50309	515-282-3596	282-6449
TF: 888-786-7637 ■ *Web:* www.iowabarnstormers.com/					
Iowa Cubs (baseball) 350 SW 1st St Sec Taylor Stadium	Des Moines	IA	50309	515-243-6111	243-5152
Web: www.iowacubs.com/					
Knoxville Raceway 1000 N Lincoln St	Knoxville	IA	50138	515-842-5431	
Prairie Meadows Racetrack 1 Prairie Meadows Dr	Altoona	IA	50009	515-967-1000	967-1253
TF: 800-325-9015 ■ *Web:* www.prairiemeadows.com					

— Events —

	Phone
Annual Herb Sale (early May)	515-242-2934
Appaloosa Horse Show (mid-September)	515-262-3111
Autumn Festival & Craft Show (late October)	515-323-5444
Bass Masters Fishermen's Swap Meet & Boat Show (late February)	515-262-3111
Block & Bridle Horse Show (late April)	515-262-3111
Christmas Walk (mid-November-late December)	515-628-2409
Covered Bridge Festival (mid-October)	515-462-1185
Craft Festival (late January)	515-276-8551
Des Moines Boat Tackle & Sports Show (mid-January)	515-262-3111
Des Moines Home & Garden Show (late February)	515-323-5444
Drake Relays Week (late April)	515-271-3711
Fall Antique Jamboree (mid-June & mid-August)	515-222-3642
Fall Classic Horse Show (early October)	515-262-3111
Fall Festival (late September)	515-628-2409
Festival of Lanterns (mid-January-early February)	515-242-2934
Festival of Trees & Lights (late November)	515-241-6494
Firstar Eve (December 31)	515-245-6100
Fox Family Fair (early February)	515-323-5444
Governor & First Lady Easter Egg Hunt (late April)	515-281-7205
Happily Haunted Halloween Treasure Trail (mid-late October)	515-242-2934
Holiday Lights & Holiday Wonderland (December)	515-242-2934
Iowa Horse Fair (mid-April)	515-262-3111
Iowa Pork Congress (late January)	515-323-5444
Iowa Renaissance Festival (mid-September)	515-262-3111
Iowa Sports & Vacation Show (early March)	515-323-5444
Iowa State Fair (early-mid-August)	515-262-3111
Iowa Winter Beef Expo (mid-February)	515-262-3111
Kids Fest (mid-March)	515-288-1981
Latinos Unidos Fiesta (mid-September)	515-242-2934
Mayor's Annual Ride for Trails (mid-April)	515-283-4500
Monster Jam (early January)	515-323-5444
National Balloon Classic (early August)	515-961-8415
Potpourri Painters Craft Show (late March)	515-262-3111
Pufferbilly Days (mid-September)	800-266-6312
Skywalk Open Golf Tournament (early February)	515-243-6625
Spring into the Past (late March)	515-281-6412
Two Rivers Art Expo (mid-November)	515-277-1511
Valley Arts Festival (late September)	515-225-6009
Wings Wheels & Water Festival (late September)	515-964-0685

Des Moines — Events (Cont'd)

	Phone
World of Wheels (late January)	515-323-5444
World's Toughest Rodeo (late March)	515-323-5444

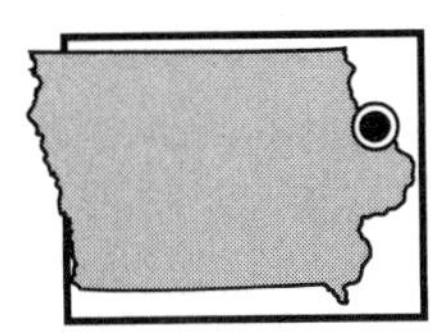

Dubuque

Named for Julien Dubuque, a French Canadian fur trader who settled in the area in the 1780s, the city of Dubuque is located in northeastern Iowa, along the Mississippi River. The river is the site of some of the city's main attractions, including paddleboat rides, sightseeing and dinner cruises, and the Mississippi River Museum. Spectacular views of Iowa, Wisconsin, and Illinois can be seen from Eagle Point Park, a 164-acre park overlooking the Mississippi, and from the Fenelon Place Elevator, the world's shortest, steepest, scenic railway. Another area attraction is Crystal Lake Cave, which is a natural living cave full of intricate, rare formations. The National Farm Toy Museum is also located in Dubuque. The movie site for the Field of Dreams is located in nearby Dyersville and is open daily to the public, and the historic city of Galena, IL is located just 15 miles from Dubuque. Among the sites in Galena is the Ulysses S. Grant Historic Home, which was presented to Grant on his return from the Civil War.

Population	56,467	**Longitude**	90-42-33 W
Area (Land)	23.1 sq mi	**County**	Dubuque
Area (Water)	1.2 sq mi	**Time Zone**	CST
Elevation	675 ft	**Area Code/s**	319
Latitude	42-24-10 N		

— Average Temperatures and Precipitation —

TEMPERATURES

	Jan	Feb	Mar	Apr	May	Jun	Jul	Aug	Sep	Oct	Nov	Dec
High	24	30	43	58	69	78	82	80	72	61	45	29
Low	8	13	25	37	48	57	62	60	51	40	28	14

PRECIPITATION

	Jan	Feb	Mar	Apr	May	Jun	Jul	Aug	Sep	Oct	Nov	Dec
Inches	1.3	1.3	2.9	3.7	4.3	4.1	4.0	4.7	4.7	2.7	2.7	2.0

— Important Phone Numbers —

	Phone		Phone
AAA	319-556-0202	**Poison Control Center**	800-272-6477
Emergency	911	**Time**	319-556-7000
Medical Referral	319-583-7915	**Weather**	319-583-9955

— Information Sources —

				Phone	Fax
Better Business Bureau Serving Central & Eastern Iowa 505 5th Ave Suite 950 *TF:* 800-222-1600 ■ *Web:* www.desmoines.bbb.org ■ *E-mail:* info@dm.bbb.org	Des Moines	IA	50309	515-243-8137	243-2227
Carnegie-Stout Public Library 360 W 11th St *Web:* www.dubuque.lib.ia.us	Dubuque	IA	52001	319-589-4225	589-4306
Dubuque Area Chamber of Commerce PO Box 705 *TF:* 800-798-4748 ■ *Web:* www.dubuque.org	Dubuque	IA	52004	319-557-9200	557-1591
Dubuque City Hall 50 W 13th St.	Dubuque	IA	52001	319-589-4110	589-4149
Dubuque Convention & Visitors Bureau 770 Town Clock Plaza *TF:* 800-798-4748 ■ *Web:* www.dubuque.org	Dubuque	IA	52001	319-557-9200	557-1591
Dubuque County 720 Central Ave	Dubuque	IA	52001	319-589-4418	
Dubuque Five Flags Center 405 Main St	Dubuque	IA	52001	319-589-4254	589-4351
Dubuque Mayor 50 W 13th St City Hall	Dubuque	IA	52001	319-556-2525	556-2347
Greater Dubuque Development 770 Town Clock Plaza *Web:* www.greaterdubuque.org ■ *E-mail:* gddc@mwci.net	Dubuque	IA	52001	319-557-9049	557-1059

On-Line Resources

4Dubuque.com	www.4dubuque.com
Area Guide Dubuque	dubuque.areaguides.net
City Knowledge Dubuque	www.cityknowledge.com/ia_dubuque.htm
Dubuque CityGuide	cityguide.lycos.com/midwest/DubuqueIAa.html
Excite.com Dubuque City Guide	www.excite.com/travel/countries/united_states/iowa/dubuque
NITC Travelbase Guide to Dubuque	www.travelbase.com/auto/guides/dubuque-ia.html
Online City Guide to Dubuque	www.olcg.com/ia/dubuque/
Our Dubuque	www.dubuque-ia.com/

— Transportation Services —

AIRPORTS

	Phone
■ **Dubuque Regional Airport (DBQ)**	
8 miles S of downtown (approx 15 minutes)	319-589-4127

Airport Transportation

	Phone
A-OK Yellow Cab $11 fare to downtown	319-582-1818

Commercial Airlines

	Phone		Phone
American	800-433-7300	**United**	800-241-6522
Northwest	800-225-2525		

Charter Airlines

	Phone
Chartaire Inc	319-557-6087

CAR RENTALS

	Phone		Phone
Avis	319-556-0656	**National**	319-583-6729
Enterprise	319-583-8000		

LIMO/TAXI

	Phone		Phone
A-OK Yellow Cab	319-582-1818	**Starlight Limo & Taxi**	319-552-2028
Nite Star Limousines	319-583-5700		

MASS TRANSIT

	Phone
Dubuque Keyline Transit $1 Base fare	319-589-4196

RAIL/BUS

				Phone
Greyhound Bus Station 200 Main St Suite 1B *TF:* 800-231-2222	Dubuque	IA	52001	319-583-3397

— Accommodations —

HOTELS, MOTELS, RESORTS

				Phone	Fax
Best Western Dubuque Inn 3434 Dodge St *TF:* 800-747-7760	Dubuque	IA	52003	319-556-7760	556-4003
Best Western Midway 3100 Dodge St. *TF:* 800-336-4392	Dubuque	IA	52003	319-557-8000	557-7692
Comfort Inn 4055 McDonald Dr *TF:* 800-228-5150	Dubuque	IA	52003	319-556-3006	556-3006

Dubuque — Hotels, Motels, Resorts (Cont'd)

Name / Address	City	State	Zip	Phone	Fax
Days Inn 1111 Dodge St	Dubuque	IA	52003	319-583-3297	583-5900
TF: 800-772-3297					
Fairfield by Marriott 3400 Dodge St	Dubuque	IA	52003	319-588-2349	588-2349
TF: 800-228-2800					
Glenview Motel 1050 Rockdale Rd	Dubuque	IA	52003	319-556-2661	
Heartland Inn South 2090 Southpark Ct	Dubuque	IA	52003	319-556-6555	556-0542
TF: 800-334-3277					
Heartland Inn West 4025 McDonald Dr	Dubuque	IA	52003	319-582-3752	582-0113
TF: 800-334-3277					
Holiday Inn 450 Main St	Dubuque	IA	52001	319-556-2000	556-2303
TF: 800-421-1213					
Hotel Canfield 36 W 4th St	Dubuque	IA	52001	319-556-4331	556-4331
Julien Inn 200 Main St	Dubuque	IA	52001	319-556-4200	582-5023
TF: 800-798-7098					
Redstone Inn 504 Bluff St	Dubuque	IA	52001	319-582-1894	582-1893
Richards House 1492 Locust St	Dubuque	IA	52001	319-557-1492	
Web: www.the-richards-house.com					
Super 8 Motel 2730 Dodge St	Dubuque	IA	52003	319-582-8898	582-8898
TF: 800-800-8000					

— Restaurants —

Name / Address	City	State	Zip	Phone
Bridge Restaurant (American) 31 Locust St	Dubuque	IA	52001	319-557-7280
Country Kitchen (Homestyle) 3187 University Ave	Dubuque	IA	52001	319-556-8405
Dempsey's (Steak/Seafood) 395 W 9th St	Dubuque	IA	52001	319-582-7057
Dottie's Cafe (American) 504 Central Ave	Dubuque	IA	52001	319-556-9617
Dougherty's (Homestyle) 131 Security Rd Town Clock Plaza	Dubuque	IA	52001	319-556-6840
Dubuque Family Restaurant (Homestyle) 2600 Dodge St	Dubuque	IA	52003	319-557-8800
Eichman's Bar & Grill (American) 11941 Rt 52 N	Sageville	IA	52002	319-552-2494
Europa Haus Restaurant (German) 1301 Rhomberg Ave	Dubuque	IA	52001	319-588-0361
Finney's Bar & Grill (American) 2155 Southpark Ct	Dubuque	IA	52003	319-583-3211
Grandma's Pantry (Homestyle) 2660 Dodge St	Dubuque	IA	52003	319-556-6577
Hoffman House (American) 3100 Dodge St Best Western Midway	Dubuque	IA	52003	319-557-8900
Hooligan's Sports Bar & Grill (American) 2600 Dodge St	Dubuque	IA	52003	319-588-9770
Kalmes Breaktime Bar & Grill (American) 1097 Jackson St	Dubuque	IA	52001	319-582-8566
Ken Fenelon's Finer Foods (Homestyle) 3130 Jackson St	Dubuque	IA	52001	319-582-4252
La Mesa (Mexican) 2700 Dodge St	Dubuque	IA	52003	319-583-8828
Marco's (Italian) 22 Central Ave	Dubuque	IA	52001	319-588-0007
Mario's Restaurant (Italian) 1298 Main St	Dubuque	IA	52001	319-556-9424
Moracco (American) 1413 Rockdale Rd	Dubuque	IA	52001	319-582-2947
Nana's Cafe (Homestyle) 605 Bluff St	Dubuque	IA	52001	319-557-1544
Nicholas Perrot's (American) 3434 Dodge St Best Western Dubuque Inn	Dubuque	IA	52003	319-556-7767
Office Grill (American) 909 Main St Suite 7B	Dubuque	IA	52001	319-588-1620
Papa Sarducci's (Italian) 1895 JFK Rd	Dubuque	IA	52002	319-583-1371
Porter's Steakhouse (Steak) 450 Main St Holiday Inn	Dubuque	IA	52001	319-556-2000
Pusateri's (Italian) 2400 Central Ave	Dubuque	IA	52001	319-583-9104
Ryan House (Continental) 1375 Locust St	Dubuque	IA	52001	319-556-5000
Sfikas Restaurant (Greek) 401 Central Ave	Dubuque	IA	52001	319-582-8140
Spirits Bar & Grill (American) 1111 Dodge St Days Inn	Dubuque	IA	52003	319-583-3297

— Goods and Services —

SHOPPING

Name / Address	City	State	Zip	Phone
Cable Car Square 391 Bluff St	Dubuque	IA	52001	319-583-5000
Ice Harbor Emporium 2600 Dodge St	Dubuque	IA	52003	319-556-8902
Kennedy Mall Shopping Center 555 JFK Rd	Dubuque	IA	52002	319-556-1994

BANKS

Name / Address	City	State	Zip	Phone	Fax
American Trust & Savings Bank 895 Town Clock Plaza	Dubuque	IA	52001	319-582-1841	589-0835*
**Fax:* Cust Svc					
Dubuque Bank & Trust Co 500 N Grandview Ave	Dubuque	IA	52001	319-589-2160	589-2060
First Star Bank 1865 JFK Rd	Dubuque	IA	52002	319-557-3213	583-2799
TF Cust Svc: 800-236-5800*					
General Drivers Credit Union 1828 Central Ave	Dubuque	IA	52001	319-556-2114	556-0990
Mercantile Bank 2201 Jackson St	Dubuque	IA	52001	319-589-2285	589-2206
TF Cust Svc: 800-747-2265*					
Premier Bank 1975 JFK Rd	Dubuque	IA	52002	319-588-1000	588-3352

BUSINESS SERVICES

Name	Phone
Copyworks	319-557-2679
Federal Express	800-238-5355
Kelly Services	319-583-6038
Mail Boxes Etc	319-582-3030
Manpower Temporary Services	319-588-2021
Post Office	319-582-3674
UPS	800-742-5877

— Media —

PUBLICATIONS

Name / Address	City	State	Zip	Phone	Fax
Telegraph Herald‡ 801 Bluff St	Dubuque	IA	52001	319-588-5611	588-5745*
**Fax:* Edit ■ *TF:* 800-553-4801 ■ *Web:* www.thonline.com ■ *E-mail:* thonline@wcinet.com					

‡Daily newspapers

TELEVISION

Name / Address	City	State	Zip	Phone	Fax
KCRG-TV Ch 9 (ABC) PO Box 816	Cedar Rapids	IA	52406	319-398-8422	398-8378
Web: www.kcrg.com ■ *E-mail:* newsroom@kcrg.com					
KFXB-TV Ch 40 (Fox) 744 Main St	Dubuque	IA	52001	319-556-4040	557-3118
KGAN-TV Ch 2 (CBS) 600 Old Marion Rd NE	Cedar Rapids	IA	52402	319-395-9060	395-0113
Web: www.kgan.com ■ *E-mail:* kgan@kgan.com					
KPXR-TV Ch 48 (PAX) 1957 Blairs Ferry Rd NE	Cedar Rapids	IA	52402	319-366-4848	378-9587
Web: www.pax.net/KPXR					
KWWL-TV Ch 7 (NBC) 500 E 4th St	Waterloo	IA	50703	319-291-1200	291-1233*
**Fax:* News Rm ■ *Web:* www.kwwl.com ■ *E-mail:* comments@kwwl.com					

RADIO

Name / Address	City	State	Zip	Phone	Fax
KATF-FM 92.9 MHz (AC) 346 8th St	Dubuque	IA	52001	319-588-5700	588-5688
Web: www.katfm.com ■ *E-mail:* katfm@wcinet.com					
KDTH-AM 1370 kHz (N/T) 346 8th St	Dubuque	IA	52001	319-588-5700	588-5688
Web: www.kdth.com ■ *E-mail:* kdth@wcinet.com					
KGRR-FM 97.3 MHz (CR) 2115 JFK Rd	Dubuque	IA	52002	319-556-7625	556-3994
KLYV-FM 105.3 MHz (CHR) 5490 Saratoga Rd	Dubuque	IA	52002	319-557-1040	583-4535
E-mail: klyv@dubuque.net					
KXGE-FM 102.3 MHz (CR) 5490 Saratoga Rd	Dubuque	IA	52002	319-557-1040	583-4535
WDBQ-AM 1490 kHz (N/T) 5490 Saratoga Rd	Dubuque	IA	52002	319-557-1040	583-4535
WDBQ-FM 107.5 MHz (Oldies) 5490 Saratoga Rd	Dubuque	IA	52002	319-557-1040	583-4535
WJOD-FM 103.3 MHz (Ctry) 5490 Saratoga Rd	Dubuque	IA	52002	319-557-1040	583-4535

— Colleges/Universities —

Name / Address	City	State	Zip	Phone	Fax
Clarke College 1550 Clarke Dr	Dubuque	IA	52001	319-588-6300	588-6789
Web: www.clarke.edu ■ *E-mail:* jolson@keller.clarke.edu					
Emmaus Bible College 2570 Asbury Rd	Dubuque	IA	52001	319-588-8000	588-1216
TF: 800-397-2425 ■ *Web:* www.emmaus.edu					
Loras College 1450 Alta Vista St	Dubuque	IA	52001	319-588-7100	588-7964
TF Admissions: 800-245-6727 ■ *Web:* www.loras.edu					
Northeast Iowa Community College Dubuque Campus 700 Main St Suite 1	Dubuque	IA	52001	319-557-8271	557-8353
TF: 800-728-7367 ■ *Web:* www.nicc.cc.ia.us/					
University of Dubuque 2000 University Ave	Dubuque	IA	52001	319-589-3000	589-3690
TF Admissions: 800-722-5583 ■ *Web:* www.dbq.edu					

— Hospitals —

Name / Address	City	State	Zip	Phone	Fax
Finley Hospital 350 N Grandview Ave	Dubuque	IA	52001	319-582-1881	589-2562
TF: 800-397-2467					
Mercy Medical Center 250 Mercy Dr	Dubuque	IA	52001	319-589-8000	589-9005*
**Fax:* Admitting ■ *Web:* www.mercydubuque.com					

Dubuque (Cont'd)

— Attractions —

				Phone	Fax
Brownstone Gallery 1172 Main St.	Dubuque	IA	52001	319-582-1561	583-2663
Crystal Lake Cave 7699 Crystal Lake Cave Dr.	Dubuque	IA	52003	319-556-6451	
Diamond Jo Casino 400 E 3rd St *TF:* 800-582-5956 ■ *Web:* www.diamondjo.com	Dubuque	IA	52001	319-583-7005	583-7516
Dubuque Arboretum & Botanical Gardens 3800 Arboretum Dr.	Dubuque	IA	52001	319-556-2100	
Dubuque County Historical Society 400 E 3rd St	Dubuque	IA	52001	319-557-9545	583-1241
Dubuque Greyhound Park & Casino 1855 Greyhound Park Rd. *TF:* 800-373-3647	Dubuque	IA	52001	319-582-3647	582-9074
Dubuque Museum of Art 36 E 8th St	Dubuque	IA	52001	319-557-1851	557-7826
Dubuque Symphony Orchestra PO Box 881	Dubuque	IA	52004	319-557-1677	557-9841
Eagle Point Park 2601 Shiras Ave.	Dubuque	IA	52001	319-589-4263	
Fenelon Place Elevator 512 Fenelon Pl	Dubuque	IA	52001	319-582-6496	
Field of Dreams Movie Site 28963 Lansing Rd. *TF:* 888-875-8404 ■ *Web:* www.fieldofdreamsmoviesite.com ■ *E-mail:* shoelessjoe@fieldofdreamsmoviesite.com	Dyersville	IA	52040	319-875-8404	875-7253
Five Flags Theater 405 Main St *TF Sales:* 888-412-9758*	Dubuque	IA	52001	319-589-4254	589-4351
Grand Opera House 135 W 8th St	Dubuque	IA	52001	319-588-1305	588-3497
Julien Dubuque Monument Grandview Ave & Julien Dubuque Dr.	Dubuque	IA	52001	319-556-0620	
Mathias Ham House Historic Site 2241 Lincoln Ave	Dubuque	IA	52001	319-557-9545	
National Farm Toy Museum 1110 16th Ave SE.	Dyersville	IA	52040	319-875-2727	875-8467
National Rivers Hall of Fame & Mississippi River Museum 400 E 3rd St Ice Harbor *TF:* 800-226-3369	Dubuque	IA	52004	319-557-9545	583-1241
Spirit of Dubuque PO Box 1276 *TF:* 800-747-8093 ■ *Web:* www.spiritofdubuque.com ■ *E-mail:* spirit@mwci.net	Dubuque	IA	52004	319-583-8093	583-8093
Trolleys of Dubuque PO Box 1322 *TF:* 800-408-0077	Dubuque	IA	52004	319-552-2896	

SPORTS TEAMS & FACILITIES

				Phone	Fax
Dubuque Fairgrounds Speedway 14583 Old Highway Rd	Dubuque	IA	52002	319-588-1406	588-1162
Dubuque Fighting Saints (hockey) 405 Main St Dubuque Five Flags Ctr *E-mail:* dbgfghtsts@mwci.net	Dubuque	IA	52004	319-556-9199	556-9215
Dubuque Greyhound Park & Casino 1855 Greyhound Park Rd. *TF:* 800-373-3647	Dubuque	IA	52001	319-582-3647	582-9074

— Events —

	Phone
Arbor Day Celebration (late April)	319-556-2100
Arts & Crafts Fair (mid-March)	319-556-1994
Arts & Crafts Festival (early August)	319-582-9269
Arts & Crafts Show (mid-late March)	319-589-4254
BestFest (late March)	319-583-3755
Catfish Festival (late June)	319-583-8535
Christmas Candlewalk (late November)	319-582-3320
City Expo (mid-late April)	319-589-4116
Dragon Boat Festival (mid-September)	319-557-1429
Dubuque County Fair (late July-early August)	319-588-1406
Dubuquefest (mid-May)	319-557-9200
Dubuquefest House Tour (mid-May)	319-557-2556
Dyersville Independence Day Celebration (July 3)	319-875-2311
Farmer's Market (early May-late October)	319-588-4400
Fireworks Spectacular (July 3)	319-588-5700
Four Mounds Blues Fest (early-mid-August)	319-557-7292
Heartland Creative Arts & Crafts Fair (mid-October)	319-556-1994
High School Alumni Basketball Tournament (June)	319-589-4263
Historic Old Main Event (late May)	319-588-4400
Home Show (mid-March)	319-589-4254
Home Show & Arts & Crafts Fair (late September)	319-556-1994
Jazz Fest (mid-June)	319-557-1677
Racing Collectibles Show (early-mid-July)	319-875-2727
Rose Festival (mid-June)	319-556-2100
Saint Patrick's Day Parade & Gaelic Gallop (mid-March)	319-875-2311
Senior Fair (mid-June)	319-556-1994
Summerfest (mid-August)	319-582-8804
Taste of Dubuque: A County Celebration (early August)	800-226-3369

Kansas

Population (1999): 2,654,052 **Area (sq mi): 82,282**

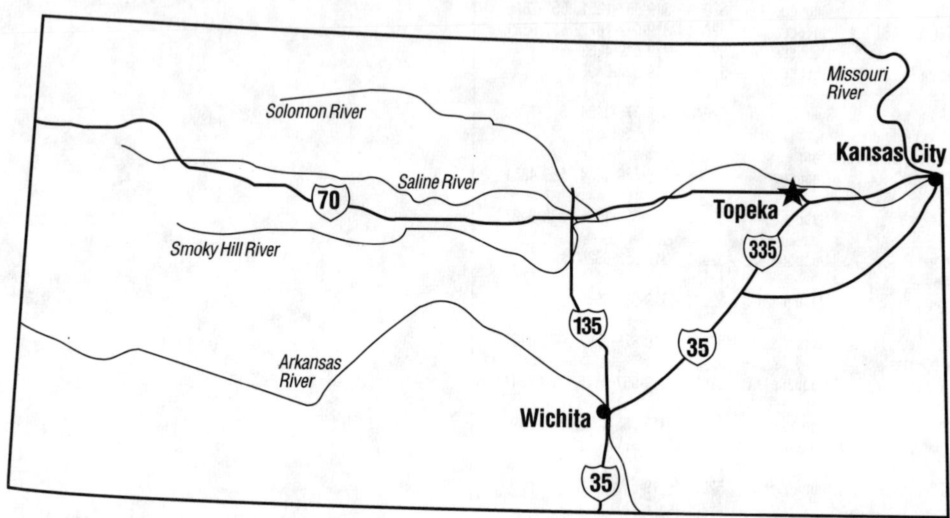

— State Information Sources —

				Phone	Fax
Kansas Chamber of Commerce & Industry					
835 SW Topeka Blvd.	Topeka	KS	66612	785-357-6321	357-4732
Web: www.kansaschamber.org ■ *E-mail:* kcci@kansaschamber.org					
Kansas Kansas Inc					
632 SW Van Buren Suite 100	Topeka	KS	66603	785-296-1460	296-1463
Web: www.state.ks.us/public/ks-inc					
Kansas Parks Div 512 SE 25th Ave.	Pratt	KS	67124	316-672-5911	672-6020
Web: www.kdwp.state.ks.us/parks/parks.html					
Kansas State Government Information				785-296-0111	
Web: www.state.ks.us					
Kansas State Library					
300 SW 10th Ave Capitol Bldg Rm 343 N	Topeka	KS	66612	785-296-3296	296-6650
Web: skyways.lib.ks.us/kansas/library.html					
Kansas Travel & Tourism Development Div					
611 S Kansas Ave Suite 100	Topeka	KS	66603	785-296-7091	296-2422
TF: 800-252-6727					
■ *Web:* www.ink.org/public/kicin/kdoch/html/tour1.html					

ON-LINE RESOURCES

Kansas Cities . . . . dir.yahoo.com/Regional/U_S__States/Kansas/Cities
Kansas Counties & Regions . . . . dir.yahoo.com/Regional/U_S__States/Kansas/Counties_and_Regions
Kansas Scenario . . . . scenariousa.dstylus.com/ks/indexf.htm
Kansas Travel & Tourism Guide . . . . www.travel-library.com/north_america/usa/kansas/index.html
Rough Guide Travel Kansas travel.roughguides.com/content/984/index.htm
Sights of Kansas . . . . surf.to/kansas
Travel.org-Kansas . . . . travel.org/kansas.html
Welcome to the Sights of Kansas . . . . raven.cc.ukans.edu/heritage/kssights
What's Up Kansas! . . . . www.whatsupkansas.com
Yahoo! Get Local Kansas . . . . dir.yahoo.com/Regional/U_S__States/Kansas

— Cities Profiled —

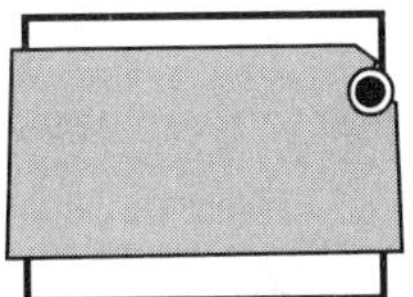

Kansas City

The smaller of the two cities which make up the Greater Kansas City Metropolitan Area, Kansas City, Kansas is the second largest city in the state. Located at the junction of the Kansas and Missouri Rivers, Kansas City has been dubbed an "All-America City," and agriculture (primarily livestock and grain) is an important part of its economy. Visitors can learn about Kansas City's Eastern European heritage at the Strawberry Hill Museum and Cultural Center, and families with children can enjoy hands-on learning at the Children's Museum of Kansas City. The Missouri River Queen at River City USA, a paddle-wheel boat which offers several types of short cruises and sightseeing trips up and down the river, is also based in Kansas City.

Population	141,297	**Longitude**	94-43-37 W
Area (Land)	107.8 sq mi	**County**	Wyandotte
Area (Water)	3.5 sq mi	**Time Zone**	CST
Elevation	740 ft	**Area Code/s**	913
Latitude	39-07-06 N		

— Average Temperatures and Precipitation —

TEMPERATURES

	Jan	Feb	Mar	Apr	May	Jun	Jul	Aug	Sep	Oct	Nov	Dec
High	35	41	53	65	74	83	89	86	78	68	53	39
Low	17	22	33	44	54	63	68	66	57	46	34	22

PRECIPITATION

	Jan	Feb	Mar	Apr	May	Jun	Jul	Aug	Sep	Oct	Nov	Dec
Inches	1.1	1.1	2.5	3.1	5.0	4.7	4.4	4.0	4.9	3.3	1.9	1.6

— Important Phone Numbers —

	Phone		Phone
AAA	816-931-5252	**Medical Referral**	913-588-1227
American Express Travel	816-531-9114	**Poison Control Center**	913-588-6633
Emergency	911	**Weather**	913-384-5555

— Information Sources —

	City	State	Zip	Phone	Fax
Better Business Bureau Serving Greater Kansas City 306 E 12th St Suite 1024 *Web:* www.kansascity.bbb.org	Kansas City	MO	64106	816-421-7800	472-5442
Kansas City City Hall 701 N 7th St Municipal Office Bldg *Web:* www.wycokck.org	Kansas City	KS	66101	913-573-5000	573-5005
Kansas City Economic Development 701 N 7th St Rm 421	Kansas City	KS	66101	913-573-5730	573-5745
Kansas City Kansas Area Chamber of Commerce PO Box 171337 *Web:* www.kckacc.com ■ *E-mail:* kckacc@enterway.net	Kansas City	KS	66117	913-371-3070	371-3732
Kansas City Kansas/Wyandotte County Convention & Visitors Bureau 727 Minnesota Ave *TF:* 800-264-1563	Kansas City	KS	66117	913-321-5800	371-3732
Kansas City Information & Research Dept 701 N 7th St	Kansas City	KS	66101	913-573-5150	573-5160
Kansas City Main Library 625 Minnesota Ave *Web:* www.kckpl.lib.ks.us	Kansas City	KS	66101	913-551-3280	551-3216
Kansas City Mayor 701 N 7th St Municipal Office Bldg Suite 926 *Web:* www.wycokck.org/html/officials.htm	Kansas City	KS	66101	913-573-5010	573-5020
Reardon Civic Center 500 Minnesota Ave	Kansas City	KS	66101	913-371-1610	342-6160
Wyandotte County 710 N 7th St *Web:* www.wyandottecountyks.com	Kansas City	KS	66101	913-573-2800	321-0237

On-Line Resources

Anthill City Guide Kansas City	www.anthill.com/city.asp?city=kansascity
DigitalCity Kansas City	www.digitalcity.com/kansascity
Kansas City Visual Arts Connection	www.kcvac.com

— Transportation Services —

AIRPORTS

■ **Kansas City International Airport (MCI)**

	Phone
18 miles NW of downtown Kansas City KS (approx 30 minutes)	816-243-5237

Airport Transportation

	Phone
La Plant Airport Transportation $25-28 fare to downtown Kansas City KS	816-421-7611
We Serve Cab Co $25 fare to downtown Kansas City KS	913-371-5464

Commercial Airlines

	Phone		Phone
Air Canada	800-776-3000	**Northwest**	800-225-2525
America West	800-235-9292	**Redwing Airways**	660-665-6607
American	800-433-7300	**Southwest**	800-435-9792
Continental	800-525-0280	**TWA**	800-221-2000
Continental Express	800-525-0280	**United**	800-241-6522
Delta	800-221-1212	**US Airways**	800-428-4322
Midwest Express	800-452-2022	**Vanguard**	800-826-4827

Charter Airlines

	Phone		Phone
Executive Beechcraft	816-842-8484	**Spirit Aviation**	816-221-3192

CAR RENTALS

	Phone		Phone
Avis	816-243-5760	**Hertz**	816-243-5765
Budget	816-243-5757	**National**	816-243-5770
Dollar	816-243-5600	**Thrifty**	816-464-5670
Enterprise	913-371-0070		

LIMO/TAXI

	Phone		Phone
Custom Limousine	913-441-2674	**We Serve Cab Co**	913-371-5464
King Transportation	913-299-3849		

MASS TRANSIT

	Phone
Bus The $1 Base fare	913-551-0485
Johnson County Transit Bus $1.25 Base fare	913-541-8450
Metro $.90 Base fare	816-221-0660

RAIL/BUS

	City	State	Zip	Phone
Amtrak Station 2200 Main St *TF:* 800-872-7245	Kansas City	MO	64108	816-421-3622
Greyhound Bus Station 1101 Troost St *TF:* 800-231-2222	Kansas City	MO	64106	816-221-2885

— Accommodations —

HOTELS, MOTELS, RESORTS

	City	State	Zip	Phone	Fax
American Motel 7949 Splitlog St *TF:* 800-905-6343	Kansas City	KS	66112	913-299-2999	299-0308
Best Western Flamingo Motel 4725 State Ave *TF:* 800-528-1234	Kansas City	KS	66102	913-287-5511	287-1021
Best Western Inn & Conference Center 501 Southwest Blvd *TF:* 800-368-1741	Kansas City	KS	66103	913-677-3060	677-7065

Kansas City — Hotels, Motels, Resorts (Cont'd)

Name / Address	City	State	Zip	Phone	Fax
Clark Motel 1807 Merriam Ln.	Kansas City	KS	66106	913-262-9960	
Comfort Inn 78th St & 1-70	Kansas City	KS	66112	913-299-5555	299-5505
TF: 800-228-5150					
Days Inn 3930 Rainbow Blvd	Kansas City	KS	66103	913-236-6880	236-6880
TF: 800-766-6521					
Doubletree Hotel at Corporate Woods					
10100 College Blvd	Overland Park	KS	66210	913-451-6100	451-3873
TF: 800-222-8733					
■ *Web:* www.doubletreehotels.com/DoubleT/Hotel41/51/51Main.htm					
Eagle Inn 199 S 18th St	Kansas City	KS	66102	913-342-8592	342-5332
Gables Motel 6831 State Ave	Kansas City	KS	66102	913-299-8111	
Harvest Moon Hotel 7933 State Ave	Kansas City	KS	66112	913-788-9170	
Holiday Inn Express I-70 & Hwy 7	Bonner Springs	KS	66012	913-721-5300	721-5445
TF: 888-206-2066					
Holiday Inn Overland Park					
7240 Shawnee Mission Pkwy	Overland Park	KS	66202	913-262-3010	262-6180
TF: 800-465-4329					
Marriott Hotel Overland Park					
10800 Metcalf Ave	Overland Park	KS	66210	913-451-8000	451-5914
TF: 800-228-9290 ■ *Web:* marriotthotels.com/MCIOP					
Penrod Motel 224 S 86th St.	Kansas City	KS	66111	913-788-9143	
Radisson Hotel 8787 Reeder Rd	Overland Park	KS	66214	913-888-8440	888-3438
TF: 800-333-3333					
Relax Inn 3228 State Ave.	Kansas City	KS	66102	913-342-3333	
White Haven Motor Lodge					
8039 Metcalf Ave	Overland Park	KS	66204	913-649-8200	649-8200
TF: 800-752-2892					

— Restaurants —

Name / Address	City	State	Zip	Phone
Board Room Bar & Grill (American)				
8123 Parallel Pkwy	Kansas City	KS	66112	913-299-0022
Dagwood's Cafe (Homestyle) 1117 Southwest Blvd	Kansas City	KS	66103	913-677-0747
Evergreen (Chinese) 7648 State Ave.	Kansas City	KS	66112	913-334-7648
Frontier Restaurant (American) 9338 State Ave.	Kansas City	KS	66112	913-788-9159
Greek Kafeneo (Greek) 852 Minnesota Ave	Kansas City	KS	66101	913-321-4120
Italian Delight (Italian) 4601 State Ave.	Kansas City	KS	66102	913-287-4323
King Dragon (Chinese) 4929 State Ave	Kansas City	KS	66102	913-287-0707
La Hacienda Restaurant (Mexican) 320 Kansas Ave	Kansas City	KS	66105	913-371-1324
Los Amigos (Mexican) 2808 State Ave	Kansas City	KS	66102	913-281-4547
Michael Forbes Grill (American) 7539 Wornall Rd	Kansas City	MO	64114	816-444-5445
Mrs Peters Chicken Dinners (Southern) 4960 State Ave	Kansas City	KS	66102	913-287-7711
Rosedale Barbeque (Barbecue) 600 Southwest Blvd	Kansas City	KS	66103	913-262-0343
Seventh Street Cafe (American) 210 S 7th St	Kansas City	KS	66101	913-281-0838
Tao Tao (Chinese) 1300 Minnesota Ave	Kansas City	KS	66102	913-342-1331
Victory Junction Restaurant (American)				
13832 Parallel Ave	Kansas City	KS	66102	913-721-2171

— Goods and Services —

SHOPPING

Name / Address	City	State	Zip	Phone	Fax
Great Mall of the Great Plains					
20700 W 151st St.	Olathe	KS	66061	888-386-6255	
Indian Springs Shopping Center					
4601 State Ave	Kansas City	KS	66102	913-287-9393	287-4367
TF: 800-287-9459					
Metcalf South Shopping Center					
9635 Metcalf Ave	Overland Park	KS	66212	913-649-2277	649-2295
Mission Center Mall					
4801 Johnson Dr	Shawnee Mission	KS	66205	913-262-3000	262-3622
Oak Park Mall 11461 W 95th St.	Overland Park	KS	66214	913-888-4400	888-0843

BANKS

Name / Address	City	State	Zip	Phone	Fax
Bank Midwest NA 444 Minnesota Ave	Kansas City	KS	66101	913-321-3333	321-1194
Brotherhood Bank & Trust Co					
756 Minnesota Ave	Kansas City	KS	66101	913-321-4241	321-1585
Douglass National Bank 1314 N 5th St	Kansas City	KS	66101	913-321-7200	321-7519
First Community Bank 1300 N 78th St	Kansas City	KS	66112	913-299-6200	299-4758
First State Bank 650 Kansas Ave	Kansas City	KS	66105	913-371-1242	371-7516
Guaranty Bank & Trust					
1000 Minnesota Ave	Kansas City	KS	66101	913-371-1200	342-8532
Industrial State Bank					
32nd St & Strong Ave	Kansas City	KS	66106	913-831-2000	831-2013
Mercantile Bank of Kansas					
700 Central Ave	Kansas City	KS	66101	913-279-5223	279-5282
TF Cust Svc: 800-963-6372*					
Security Bank Kansas City					
701 Minnesota Ave	Kansas City	KS	66101	913-281-3165	621-8409*
**Fax:* Mktg ■ *TF:* 800-332-0088					
UMB Bank Kansas PO Box 17-1427	Kansas City	KS	66117	913-371-0035	573-1015
TF: 800-234-8301					

BUSINESS SERVICES

Name	Phone	Name	Phone
DHL Worldwide Express	800-225-5345	**Olsten Staffing Services**	913-596-1442
Federal Express	800-238-5355	**Post Office**	913-621-8216
Kelly Services	913-722-3644	**UPS**	800-742-5877

— Media —

PUBLICATIONS

Name / Address	City	State	Zip	Phone	Fax
Kansas City Business Journal					
1101 Walnut St Suite 800	Kansas City	MO	64106	816-421-5900	472-4010
Web: www.amcity.com/kansascity ■ *E-mail:* kansascity@amcity.com					
Kansas City Star‡ 1729 Grand Blvd	Kansas City	MO	64108	816-234-4141	234-4926
Web: www.kcstar.com ■ *E-mail:* starstaff@kcstar.com					

‡*Daily newspapers*

TELEVISION

Name / Address	City	State	Zip	Phone	Fax
KCPT-TV Ch 19 (PBS) 125 E 31st St.	Kansas City	MO	64108	816-756-3580	931-2500
Web: www.kcpt.org ■ *E-mail:* kcpt@tv19.kcpt.org					
KCTV-TV Ch 5 (CBS) PO Box 5555	Kansas City	MO	64109	913-677-5555	677-7243
Web: www.kctv.com ■ *E-mail:* kctv@kctv.com					
KCWE-TV Ch 29 (UPN) 1049 Central	Kansas City	MO	64105	816-221-2900	760-9149*
**Fax:* Sales					
KMBC-TV Ch 9 (ABC) 1049 Central St	Kansas City	MO	64105	816-221-9999	421-4163
Web: www.kmbc.com					
KMCI-TV Ch 38 (Ind) 2951 Four Wheel Dr	Lawrence	KS	66047	785-749-3388	749-3377
KPXE-TV Ch 50 (PAX)					
3101 Broadway Suite 570	Kansas City	MO	64111	816-924-5050	931-1818
KSHB-TV Ch 41 (NBC) 4720 Oak St	Kansas City	MO	64112	816-753-4141	932-4145
Web: www.kshb.com ■ *E-mail:* news@kshb.com					
KSMO-TV Ch 62 (WB)					
10 E Cambridge Dr Suite 300	Kansas City	KS	66103	913-621-6262	621-4703
WDAF-TV Ch 4 (Fox) 3030 Summit St.	Kansas City	MO	64108	816-753-4567	561-4181
Web: www.wdaftv4.com					

RADIO

Name / Address	City	State	Zip	Phone	Fax
KCFX-FM 101.1 MHz (Rock)					
5800 Foxridge Dr	Mission	KS	66202	913-514-3000	514-3003
KCIY-FM 106.5 MHz (Nost)					
5800 Foxridge Dr Suite 600	Mission	KS	66202	913-514-3000	514-3003
KCMO-AM 710 kHz (N/T) 4935 Belinder Rd	Westwood	KS	66205	913-677-8998	677-8901
KCMO-FM 94.9 MHz (Oldies)					
4935 Belinder Rd	Westwood	KS	66205	913-677-8998	677-8901*
**Fax:* News Rm					
KCUR-FM 89.3 MHz (NPR)					
4825 Troost Ave Suite 202	Kansas City	MO	64110	816-235-1551	235-2864
Web: www.umkc.edu/kcur ■ *E-mail:* kcur@smtpgate.umkc.edu					
KFEZ-AM 1340 kHz (Nost)					
1212 Baltimore St	Kansas City	KS	64105	816-421-1900	471-1320
TF: 800-266-1190 ■ *E-mail:* mail@kphn1190.com					
KFKF-FM 94.1 MHz (Ctry)					
4717 Grand Ave Suite 600	Kansas City	MO	64112	816-753-4000	753-4045
Web: sites.kansascity.com/kfkf ■ *E-mail:* kfkf@kansascity.com					
KMBZ-AM 980 kHz (N/T) 4935 Belinder Rd	Westwood	KS	66205	913-236-9800	677-8901
KPRS-FM 103.3 MHz (Urban)					
11131 Colorado Ave	Kansas City	MO	64137	816-763-2040	966-1055
Web: www.kprs.com ■ *E-mail:* 103@kprs.com					
KQRC-FM 98.9 MHz (Rock)					
4350 Shawnee Mission Pkwy Suite 99	Mission	KS	66202	913-514-3000	384-9911
Web: www.989therock.com					
KYYS-FM 99.7 MHz (Rock)					
4935 Belinder Rd	Westwood	KS	66205	913-677-8998	677-8901
WDAF-AM 610 kHz (Ctry) 4935 Belinder Rd	Westwood	KS	66205	913-677-8998	677-8901

Kansas City (Cont'd)

— Colleges/Universities —

	City	State	Zip	Phone	Fax
Brown Mackie College 100 E Santa Fe St Suite 300	Olathe	KS	66061	913-768-1900	768-0555
TF: 800-635-9101 ■ *Web:* www.bmcaec.com					
Donnelly College 608 N 18th St	Kansas City	KS	66102	913-621-6070	621-0354
Web: www.donnelly.cc.ks.us					
Kansas City Kansas Community College 7250 State Ave	Kansas City	KS	66112	913-334-1100	596-9648
Web: www.kckcc.cc.ks.us					
MidAmerica Nazarene University 2030 E College Way	Olathe	KS	66062	913-782-3750	791-3481
TF Admissions: 800-800-8887 ■ *Web:* www.mnu.edu					

— Hospitals —

	City	State	Zip	Phone	Fax
Providence Medical Center 8929 Parallel Pkwy	Kansas City	KS	66112	913-596-4000	596-4098
University of Kansas Medical Center 3901 Rainbow Blvd	Kansas City	KS	66160	913-588-1270	588-1280
Web: www.kumc.edu/Pulse					

— Attractions —

	City	State	Zip	Phone	Fax
Brown John Statue 27th St & Sewell Ave	Kansas City	KS	66104	913-371-7489	
Children's Museum of Kansas City 4601 State Ave	Kansas City	KS	66102	913-287-8888	287-8888
Web: www.geocities.com/~kidmuzm					
Grinter Place Museum 1420 S 78th St	Kansas City	KS	66111	913-299-0373	
Harry S Truman Presidential Library & Museum 500 W Hwy 24	Independence	MO	64050	816-833-1400	833-4368
Web: www.trumanlibrary.org ■ *E-mail:* library@truman.nara.gov					
Huron Indian Cemetery 7th & Ann Sts	Kansas City	KS	66101	913-321-5800	
Kansas City Symphony 1020 Central St Suite 300	Kansas City	MO	64105	816-471-1100	471-0976
Web: www.kcsymphony.org ■ *E-mail:* symphony-info@kcsymphony.org					
Kansas City Zoological Gardens 6700 Zoo Dr	Kansas City	MO	64132	816-871-5700	822-8903
Web: www.kansascityzoo.org					
Korean-Vietnam War Memorial 91st & Leavenworth Rd	Kansas City	KS	66109	913-299-0550	
Lyric Opera of Kansas City 1029 Central St.	Kansas City	MO	64105	816-471-4933	471-0602
Web: kc-opera.org ■ *E-mail:* mail@kc-opera.org					
Missouri Repertory Theatre 4949 Cherry St	Kansas City	MO	64110	816-235-2700	235-5367
TF: 888-502-2700 ■ *Web:* cctr.umkc.edu/user/gkeathley/missouri.htm					
National Agricultural Center & Hall of Fame 630 Hall of Fame Dr	Bonner Springs	KS	66012	913-721-1075	721-1202
Quindaro Ruins & Underground Railroad 27th St & Sewell Ave	Kansas City	KS	66104	913-342-8683	
Rosedale Memorial Arch 35th St & Booth	Kansas City	KS	66103	913-677-5097	
Soldiers & Sailors Memorial Hall 600 N 7th St	Kansas City	KS	66101	913-371-7555	371-2025
Spencer Museum of Art 1301 Mississippi St University of Kansas	Lawrence	KS	66045	785-864-4710	864-3112
Web: www.ukans.edu/~sma/					
State Ballet of Missouri 1601 Broadway	Kansas City	MO	64108	816-931-2232	931-1172
Web: www.stateballetofmissouri.org					
Strawberry Hill Museum & Cultural Center 720 N 4th St	Kansas City	KS	66101	913-371-3264	
Wyandotte County Historical Society & Museum 631 N 126th St	Bonner Springs	KS	66012	913-721-1078	721-1394
E-mail: wycomus@toto.net					
Wyandotte County Lake & Park 91st & Leavenworth Rd	Kansas City	KS	66109	913-299-0550	299-9051
Wyandotte Players 7250 State Ave	Kansas City	KS	66112	913-596-9690	

SPORTS TEAMS & FACILITIES

	City	State	Zip	Phone	Fax
Kansas City Attack (soccer) 1800 Genessee St Kemper Arena	Kansas City	MO	64102	816-474-2255	474-2255
Web: www.kcattack.com ■ *E-mail:* info@kcattack.com					
Kansas City Blades (hockey) 1800 Genessee St Kemper Arena	Kansas City	MO	64102	816-842-1063	842-5610
Web: www.kcblades.com					
Kansas City Chiefs 1 Arrowhead Dr Arrowhead Stadium	Kansas City	MO	64129	816-920-9300	920-4315
Web: www.kcchiefs.com					
Kansas City Royals 1 Royal Way Kauffman Stadium	Kansas City	MO	64129	816-921-8000	921-5775
Kansas City Wizards (soccer) 706 Broadway St Suite 100	Kansas City	MO	64105	816-472-4625	472-0299
Web: www.kcwizards.com					
Lakeside Speedway 5615 Wolcott Dr	Kansas City	KS	66109	913-299-2040	299-1105
Web: www.lakesidespeedway.com ■ *E-mail:* I70Lake@discoverynet.com					
Woodlands Race Track 9700 Leavenworth Rd	Kansas City	KS	66109	913-299-9797	299-9804

— Events —

	Phone
Avenue Area Christmas Lighting Ceremony (mid-November)	913-371-0065
Blue Devil Barbecue Cookoff (early May)	913-321-5800
Central Avenue Parade (late September)	913-371-4511
Farm Heritage Days (mid-July)	913-721-1075
Grinter Applefest (late September)	913-299-0373
Highland Games & Scottish Festival (early June)	913-432-6823
Kansas Day at the American Royal (early-November)	816-221-9800
National Wildlife Art Show (mid-February)	913-888-6927
Polski Day (early May)	913-321-5800
Renaissance Festival (early September-mid-October)	800-373-0357
Santa's Express (mid-December)	913-721-1075
Silver City Celebration (early October)	913-321-5800
Tiblow Days (late August)	913-321-5800
Turner Days (mid-October)	913-287-7500
Wyandotte County Fair (late July-early August)	913-788-7898
Wyandotte Days (mid-October)	913-321-5800

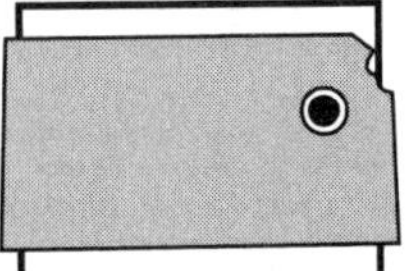

Topeka

Topeka, the capital of Kansas, lies in the fertile Kansas River Valley, where area reservoirs are plentiful. These reservoirs frequently are bordered by state parks; Perry State Park, near Topeka, is an excellent spot for fishing. The Mulvane Art Museum, located at Washburn University in Topeka, features international print and American art, Kansas art, and mountain-plains art. The museum extends onto the campus grounds with sculptures by Mountain-Plains Region artists. Between Topeka and Lawrence is Big Springs, a former rest stop for Oregon Trail emigrants. Visitors to Serenata Farms in Big Springs can participate in different Historic Oregon Trail expeditions.

Population	118,977	**Longitude**	95-67-78 W
Area (Land)	55.2 sq mi	**County**	Shawnee
Area (Water)	1.0 sq mi	**Time Zone**	CST
Elevation	1000 ft	**Area Code/s**	785
Latitude	39-04-83 N		

— Average Temperatures and Precipitation —

TEMPERATURES

	Jan	Feb	Mar	Apr	May	Jun	Jul	Aug	Sep	Oct	Nov	Dec
High	37	43	55	67	76	84	89	88	80	69	54	41
Low	16	22	32	43	53	63	68	65	56	44	32	21

Topeka (Cont'd)

PRECIPITATION

	Jan	Feb	Mar	Apr	May	Jun	Jul	Aug	Sep	Oct	Nov	Dec
Inches	1.0	1.0	2.5	3.1	4.5	5.5	3.6	3.9	3.8	3.1	1.9	1.4

— Important Phone Numbers —

	Phone
AAA	785-233-0222
Ask-A-Nurse	785-295-8333
Emergency	911
HotelDocs	800-468-3537
Poison Control Center	800-332-6633
Time/Temp	785-271-7575
Weather	785-271-7575

— Information Sources —

	City	State	Zip	Phone	Fax
Better Business Bureau Serving Northeast Kansas 501 SE Jefferson St Suite 24 *Web:* www.topeka.bbb.org	Topeka	KS	66607	785-232-0454	232-9677
Greater Topeka Chamber of Commerce 120 SE 6th St Suite 110 *Web:* www.topekachamber.org ■ *E-mail:* topekainfo@topekachamber.org	Topeka	KS	66603	785-234-2644	234-8656
Kansas Expocentre 1 Expocentre Dr	Topeka	KS	66612	785-235-1986	235-2967
Shawnee County 200 SE 7th St	Topeka	KS	66603	785-233-8200	291-4912
Topeka & Shawnee County Public Library 1515 SW 10th Ave *Web:* www.tscpl.org/ ■ *E-mail:* smarchan@tscpl.lib.ks.us	Topeka	KS	66604	785-233-2040	231-0519
Topeka City Hall 215 SE 7th St *Web:* www.topeka.org	Topeka	KS	66603	785-368-3754	368-3940
Topeka Civic Theatre 3028 SW 8th Ave *Web:* www.topekacivictheatre.com	Topeka	KS	66606	785-357-5211	357-0719
Topeka Community & Economic Development Dept 515 S Kansas St Suite 405 *Web:* www.topeka.org/departmt/ecdev.htm	Topeka	KS	66603	785-295-3711	368-2546
Topeka Convention & Visitors Bureau 1275 SW Topeka Blvd *TF:* 800-235-1030 ■ *Web:* www.topekacvb.org/ ■ *E-mail:* tcvb@topekacvb.org	Topeka	KS	66612	785-234-1030	234-8282
Topeka Mayor 215 SE 7th St Rm 352 *Web:* www.topeka.org/departmt/mayor.htm	Topeka	KS	66603	785-368-3895	368-3850

On-Line Resources

Anthill City Guide Topeka .... www.anthill.com/city.asp?city=topeka
Area Guide Topeka .... topeka.areaguides.net
City Knowledge Topeka .... www.cityknowledge.com/ks_topeka.htm
Excite.com Topeka City Guide .... www.excite.com/travel/countries/united_states/kansas/topeka

— Transportation Services —

AIRPORTS

■ Forbes Field (FOE)

	Phone
6 miles S of downtown (approx 15 minutes)	785-862-2362

Airport Transportation

	Phone
Capital City Taxi $13-15 fare to downtown	785-267-3777
Yellow Cab $13 fare to downtown	785-357-4444

Commercial Airlines

	Phone
US Airways Express	800-428-4322

Charter Airlines

	Phone
Godfrey Ken Aviation Inc	785-233-6677
Spicer Aircraft Inc	785-862-4010

■ Kansas City International Airport (MCI)

	Phone
72 miles NE of downtown Topeka (approx 90 minutes)	816-243-5237

Airport Transportation

	Phone
Roadrunner Express $28 fare to downtown Topeka	800-747-2524

Commercial Airlines

	Phone
America West	800-235-9292
American	800-433-7300
Continental	800-525-0280
Continental Express	800-525-0280
Northwest	800-225-2525
Southwest	800-435-9792
TWA	800-221-2000
United	800-241-6522
US Airways	800-428-4322

Charter Airlines

	Phone
Executive Beechcraft	816-842-8484
Spirit Aviation	816-221-3192

CAR RENTALS

	Phone
Alamo	816-464-5151
Avis	816-243-5760
Budget	816-243-5757
Dollar	816-243-5600
Hertz	816-243-5765
National	816-243-5770
Thrifty	816-464-5670

LIMO/TAXI

	Phone
Capital City Taxi	785-267-3777
Crescent Limo	785-232-2236
Yellow Cab	785-357-4444

MASS TRANSIT

	Phone
Topeka Metropolitan Transit Authority $.80 Base fare	785-233-2011

RAIL/BUS

	City	State	Zip	Phone
Amtrak Station SE 5th & Holliday Sts	Topeka	KS	66607	800-872-7245
Greyhound Bus Station 200 SE 3rd St *TF:* 800-231-2222	Topeka	KS	66603	785-233-2301

— Accommodations —

HOTELS, MOTELS, RESORTS

	City	State	Zip	Phone	Fax
AmeriSuites 6021 SW 6th St *TF:* 800-833-1516	Topeka	KS	66615	785-273-0066	273-1423
Best Western Candlelight Inn 2831 SW Fairlawn Rd *TF:* 800-223-8892	Topeka	KS	66614	785-272-9550	272-8242
Best Western Meadow Acres 2950 S Topeka Ave *TF:* 800-432-3949	Topeka	KS	66611	785-267-1681	267-1681
Capitol Plaza Hotel 1717 SW Topeka Blvd *TF:* 800-579-7937	Topeka	KS	66612	785-431-7200	431-7206
ClubHouse Inn 924 SW Henderson Rd *TF:* 800-258-2466 ■ *Web:* www.clubhouseinn.com/3.TOP.shtml ■ *E-mail:* info@clubhouseinn.com	Topeka	KS	66615	785-273-8888	273-5809
Comfort Inn 1518 SW Wanamaker Rd *TF:* 800-228-5150	Topeka	KS	66604	785-273-5365	273-5365
Country Inn 601 NW US Hwy 24	Topeka	KS	66608	785-233-7704	233-1514
Days Inn 1510 SW Wanamaker Rd *TF:* 800-329-7466	Topeka	KS	66604	785-272-8538	272-8538
Days Inn 1024 S Washington St *TF:* 800-329-7466	Junction City	KS	66441	785-762-2727	762-2751
Elderberry Bed & Breakfast 1035 SW Fillmore St	Topeka	KS	66604	785-235-6309	
Fairfield Inn by Marriott 1530 SW Westport Dr *TF:* 800-228-2800 ■ *Web:* fairfieldinn.com/FOETO	Topeka	KS	66604	785-273-6800	273-6800
Hampton Inn 1401 SW Ashworth Pl *TF:* 800-426-7866	Topeka	KS	66604	785-273-0003	273-3030
Heritage House 3535 SW 6th St *TF:* 800-582-1937	Topeka	KS	66606	785-233-3800	233-9793
Holiday Inn 530 Richards Dr *TF:* 800-465-4329	Manhattan	KS	66502	785-539-5311	539-8368
Holiday Inn City Center 914 SE Madison St *TF:* 800-465-4329	Topeka	KS	66607	785-232-7721	232-7721
Holiday Inn West 605 SW Fairlawn Rd *TF:* 800-822-0216	Topeka	KS	66606	785-272-8040	272-8065
Liberty Inn 3839 S Topeka Blvd	Topeka	KS	66609	785-266-4700	

Topeka — Hotels, Motels, Resorts (Cont'd)

				Phone	Fax
Lincoln Inn 904 SW Lincoln St	Topeka	KS	66606	785-233-4200	233-4201
TF: 800-520-8513					
Motel 6 1224 SW Wanamaker Rd	Topeka	KS	66604	785-273-9888	273-0665
TF: 800-466-8356					
Motel 6 709 SW Fairlawn Rd	Topeka	KS	66606	785-272-8283	271-1341
TF: 800-466-8356					
Plaza Inn Topeka 3802 S Topeka Blvd	Topeka	KS	66609	785-266-8880	266-4591
TF: 800-833-8033					
Quality Inn 1240 SW Wanamaker Rd	Topeka	KS	66604	785-273-6969	273-6036
TF: 800-228-5151					
Raceway Inn 6700 S Topeka Blvd	Topeka	KS	66619	785-862-1414	862-0087
TF: 800-657-7215					
Ramada Inn 2222 W 6th St	Lawrence	KS	66049	785-842-7030	842-9668
TF: 800-272-6232					
Ramada Inn 1641 Anderson Ave	Manhattan	KS	66502	785-539-7531	539-3909
TF: 800-962-0014					
Ramada Inn Downtown 420 SE 6th Ave	Topeka	KS	66607	785-234-5400	233-0460
TF: 800-272-6232					
Residence Inn by Marriott 1620 SW Westport Dr	Topeka	KS	66604	785-271-8903	271-8903
TF: 800-331-3131 ■ *Web:* residenceinn.com/FOERI					
Saint Gregory Suites 635 SW Harrison St	Topeka	KS	66603	785-233-8347	354-7564
TF: 800-337-4109					
Senate Luxury Suites 900 SW Tyler St	Topeka	KS	66612	785-233-5050	233-1614
TF: 800-488-3188					
Sunflower Bed & Breakfast 915 SW Munson Ave	Topeka	KS	66604	785-357-7509	
Super 8 Motel 5968 SW 10th St	Topeka	KS	66604	785-273-5100	273-5100
TF: 800-800-8000					
Tabor Arms 700 SW Washburn Ave	Topeka	KS	66606	785-232-3551	
Travelodge 3846 SW Topeka Blvd	Topeka	KS	66609	785-267-1222	267-0418
TF: 800-578-7878					
Travelodge 801 Iowa St	Lawrence	KS	66049	785-842-5100	842-9623
TF: 800-578-7878					
Woodward House 1272 SW Fillmore St	Topeka	KS	66604	785-354-7111	354-4166

— Restaurants —

				Phone
Annie's Place (American) 4014 SW Gage Center Dr	Topeka	KS	66604	785-273-0848
Augustina's (Mexican) 309 S Kansas Ave	Topeka	KS	66601	785-233-4500
Baldwin Bar-B-Que (Barbecue) 5900 SW Topeka Blvd	Topeka	KS	66619	785-862-7427
Blind Tiger Brewery & Restaurant (American) 417 SW 37th St	Topeka	KS	66611	785-267-2739
Web: www.blindtiger.com/				
Carlos O'Kelly's (Mexican) 3425 S Kansas Ave	Topeka	KS	66611	785-266-3457
Casa (Mexican) 3320 S Topeka Blvd	Topeka	KS	66611	785-266-4503
Catch The (Seafood) 1929 S Kansas Ave	Topeka	KS	66612	785-232-6165
Downtowner (American) 119 SE 6th St	Topeka	KS	66603	785-232-5775
Dutch Goose (American) 3203 SW 10th St	Topeka	KS	66604	785-357-8474
El Cazador (Mexican) 1521 SW 21st St	Topeka	KS	66604	785-232-3842
Grand Beijing (Chinese) 115 SE 29th St	Topeka	KS	66605	785-267-9888
Grazie The Italian Bistro (Italian) 435 S Kansas Ave	Topeka	KS	66604	785-357-6545
Heartland Cafe (American) 5701 SW Topeka Blvd	Topeka	KS	66619	785-862-8328
Heidelberger Cafe (German) 1409 NW Topeka Blvd	Topeka	KS	66608	785-233-9065
Heritage House (Seafood) 3535 SW 6th St	Topeka	KS	66606	785-233-3800
Imperial Garden (Chinese) 934 S Kansas Ave	Topeka	KS	66612	785-357-1688
JJ's Bistro (American) 2121 SW Bell Ave	Topeka	KS	66604	785-272-3100
La Siesta (Mexican) 201 NE Woodruff St	Topeka	KS	66616	785-354-1325
Lane's Bar-B-Que (Barbecue) 1306 S Kansas Ave	Topeka	KS	66612	785-232-3610
McFarland's (American) 4133 Gage Center Dr	Topeka	KS	66604	785-272-6909
Paisano's (Italian) 4043 SW 10th St	Topeka	KS	66604	785-273-0100
Pore Richards (American) 705 S Kansas Ave	Topeka	KS	66603	785-233-4276
Topeka Steak House (Steak) 526 Dupont Rd	Topeka	KS	66542	785-379-9994
Vintage The (Steak/Seafood) 1301 SW Gage Blvd	Topeka	KS	66604	785-271-6276
Yesterday's (American) 914 SE Madison	Topeka	KS	66607	785-232-7721

— Goods and Services —

SHOPPING

				Phone	Fax
Topeka Antique Mall 5247 SW 28th Ct	Topeka	KS	66614	785-273-2969	
Wal-Mart Supercenter 1501 SW Wanamaker Rd	Topeka	KS	66604	785-271-6444	
West Ridge Mall 1801 SW Wanamaker Rd	Topeka	KS	66604	785-272-5119	272-1483
White Lakes Mall 3600 S Topeka Blvd	Topeka	KS	66611	785-266-4548	

BANKS

				Phone	Fax
Bank of America 534 S Kansas Ave	Topeka	KS	66603	785-295-3400	295-3426
TF: 800-444-2410					
Capitol City Bank 3710 S Topeka Blvd	Topeka	KS	66609	785-266-4575	266-7680
Central National Bank 800 SE Quincy St	Topeka	KS	66612	785-234-2265	234-9660
Commerce Bank & Trust Co 3035 S Topeka Ave	Topeka	KS	66611	785-267-0123	267-8473
Community National Bank 5431 SW 29th St	Topeka	KS	66614	785-271-6696	271-6623
Fidelity State Bank & Trust Co 600 S Kansas Ave	Topeka	KS	66603	785-233-3465	233-7571
E-mail: fidelity@smartnet.net					
Kaw Valley State Bank & Trust Co 1110 N Kansas Ave	Topeka	KS	66608	785-232-6062	232-6513
Mercantile Bank 800 SW Jackson St	Topeka	KS	66612	785-291-1000	291-1244

BUSINESS SERVICES

	Phone		Phone
Airborne Express	800-247-2676	**Kinko's**	785-232-0023
BAX Global	800-225-5229	**Mail Boxes Etc**	800-789-4623
DHL Worldwide Express	800-225-5345	**Post Office**	800-275-8777
Federal Express	800-238-5355	**UPS**	800-742-5877

— Media —

PUBLICATIONS

				Phone	Fax
Topeka Capitol-Journal‡ 616 SE Jefferson St	Topeka	KS	66607	785-295-1111	295-1230
TF: 800-777-7171 ■ *Web:* www.cjonline.com ■ *E-mail:* letters@cjnetworks.com					

‡Daily newspapers

TELEVISION

				Phone	Fax
KSNT-TV Ch 27 (NBC) 6835 NW Hwy 24	Topeka	KS	66618	785-582-4000	582-5283
Web: www.ksnt.com ■ *E-mail:* 27news@ksnt.com					
KTKA-TV Ch 49 (ABC) PO Box 4949	Topeka	KS	66601	785-273-4949	273-7811
Web: www.newssource49.com ■ *E-mail:* 49email@newssource49.com					
KTWU-TV Ch 11 (PBS) 1700 College Ave	Topeka	KS	66621	785-231-1111	231-1112
Web: ktwu.wuacc.edu					
WIBW-TV Ch 13 (CBS) PO Box 119	Topeka	KS	66601	785-272-3456	272-0117
Web: www.wibw.com ■ *E-mail:* wibwtv@wibw.com					

RADIO

				Phone	Fax
KANU-FM 91.5 MHz (NPR) Broadcasting Hall University of Kansas	Lawrence	KS	66045	785-864-4530	864-5278
Web: www.ukans.edu/~kanu-fm					
KDVV-FM 100.3 MHz (CR) 5315 SW 7th St	Topeka	KS	66606	785-272-2122	272-6219
KJTY-FM 88.1 MHz (Rel) 1005 SW 10th St	Topeka	KS	66604	785-357-8888	357-0100
Web: www.joy88.org ■ *E-mail:* joy88@cjnetworks.com					
KMAJ-AM 1440 kHz (N/T) 5315 SW 7th St	Topeka	KS	66606	785-272-2122	272-6219
Web: www.kmaj.com					
KMAJ-FM 107.7 MHz (AC) 5315 SW 7th St	Topeka	KS	66606	785-272-2122	272-6219
Web: www.kmaj.com					
KTPK-FM 106.9 MHz (Ctry) 2121 SW Chelsea Dr	Topeka	KS	66614	785-273-1069	273-0123
Web: www.twister1069.com					
WIBW-AM 580 kHz (N/T) PO Box 1818	Topeka	KS	66601	785-272-3456	272-3536
WIBW-FM 97.3 MHz (Ctry) PO Box 1818	Topeka	KS	66601	785-272-3456	272-3536
Web: www.97country.com					

— Colleges/Universities —

				Phone	Fax
University of Kansas	Lawrence	KS	66045	785-864-2700	864-5006
TF Admissions: 888-686-7323 ■ *Web:* www.ukans.edu					
Washburn University 1700 SW College Ave	Topeka	KS	66621	785-231-1010	231-1089
TF: 800-332-0291 ■ *Web:* www.washburn.edu ■ *E-mail:* zzdpadm@washburn.edu					

Topeka (Cont'd)

— Hospitals —

				Phone	Fax
Colmery-O'Neil Veterans Affairs Medical Center 2200 SW Gage Blvd	Topeka	KS	66622	785-350-3111	350-4336
Saint Francis Hospital & Medical Center 1700 SW 7th St	Topeka	KS	66606	785-295-8000	295-8199*
**Fax:* Admissions ■ *TF:* 800-444-2954 ■ *Web:* www.stfrancistopeka.org ■ *E-mail:* cr@stfrancistopeka.org					
Stormont-Vail Regional Health Center 1500 SW 10th St	Topeka	KS	66604	785-354-6000	354-6874*
**Fax:* Admitting ■ *TF:* 800-432-2951 ■ *Web:* www.stormontvail.org					

— Attractions —

				Phone	Fax
Brown Versus Board of Education National Historic Site 424 South Kansas Ave Suite 220	Topeka	KS	66603	785-354-4273	354-7213
Web: www.nps.gov/brvb/					
Carousel in the Park Gage Pk	Topeka	KS	66606	785-273-1191	228-6065
Cedar Crest Governor's Mansion 1 SW Cedar Crest Rd	Topeka	KS	66606	785-296-3636	272-9024
Combat Air Museum Hanger 602 Forbes Field	Topeka	KS	66619	785-862-3303	
Web: www.cjnetworks.com/~superbatics/					
Gage Park 635 SW Gage Blvd	Topeka	KS	66606	785-368-3700	
Harrah's Prairie Band Casino & Bingo Hall Hwy 75 & 150th Rd	Mayetta	KS	66509	785-966-7777	966-7640
Hocker Helen Theater 700 SW Zoo Pkwy Gage Pk	Topeka	KS	66606	785-273-1191	228-6065
Kansas Museum of History 6425 SW 6th St	Topeka	KS	66615	785-272-8681	272-8682
Web: www.kshs.org/places/museum.htm					
Kansas National Guard Museum 6700 S Topeka Blvd Forbes Field Bldg 301	Topeka	KS	66619	785-862-1020	862-1066
Kansas State Capitol 10th & Jackson St	Topeka	KS	66612	785-296-3966	
Lake Shawnee 3137 SE 29th St	Topeka	KS	66605	785-267-1156	266-0308
Menninger Museum 5800 SW 6th Ave	Topeka	KS	66606	785-350-5000	273-9150
Mulvane Art Museum 1700 SW College Ave Washburn University	Topeka	KS	66621	785-231-1010	234-2703
Perry State Park 5441 W Lake Rd	Ozawkie	KS	66070	785-246-3449	246-0224
Phoenix Gallery 2900 Oakley Ave Brookwood Shopping Ctr	Topeka	KS	66614	785-272-3999	
Reinisch Rose Garden 6th & Gage Blvd Gage Pk	Topeka	KS	66606	785-272-6150	
Serenata Farms 1895 E 56 Rd Big Springs	Lecompton	KS	66050	785-887-6660	
Topeka Performing Arts Center 214 SE 8th Ave.	Topeka	KS	66603	785-297-9000	234-2307
Web: www.tpactix.org					
Topeka Symphony 727 S Campus Ave.	Topeka	KS	66603	785-232-2032	232-6204
Web: www.topekasymphony.org ■ *E-mail:* tso@topekasymphony.org					
Topeka Zoological Park 635 SW Gage Blvd.	Topeka	KS	66606	785-272-5821	272-2539
Web: www.topeka.org/activity/zoo.htm					
Ward Meade Park 124 N Fillmore St.	Topeka	KS	66606	785-295-3888	
Web: www.topeka.org/activity/wmeade.htm ■ *E-mail:* wardmead@ksnews.com					

SPORTS TEAMS & FACILITIES

				Phone	Fax
Heartland Park Topeka 1805 SW 71st St	Topeka	KS	66619	785-862-4781	862-2016
TF: 800-437-2237					
Landon Arena Kansas Expocentre 1 Expocentre Dr	Topeka	KS	66612	785-235-1986	235-2967

— Events —

	Phone
Apple Festival (early October)	785-295-3888
Cider Days (late September)	785-235-1986
Combat Air Museum & Pancake Feed & Fall Fling (late April)	785-862-3303
Fall Parade of Homes (early-mid-October)	785-273-1260
Festival of Beers (early October)	785-862-3303
Festival of Trees (early December)	785-233-2566
Fiesta Mexicana (mid-July)	785-232-5088
Gem & Mineral Show (mid-October)	785-235-1986
Holiday Happenings (early December)	785-368-3888
Huff N' Puff Balloon Rally (mid-September)	785-234-1030
Kansas River Valley Art Fair (late July)	785-295-3888
KBHA Quarter Horse Show (late July)	785-235-1986
KSHSAA Rodeo (mid-June)	785-235-1986
Miracle on Kansas Avenue Parade (late November)	785-234-9336
Mountain Plains Art Fair (early June)	785-231-1010
NHRA Parts America Nationals (late September-early October)	800-437-2237
Sunflower Music Festival (June)	785-231-1010
Topeka Boat & Outdoor Show (late January)	785-235-1986
Topeka Farm Show (early January)	785-235-1986
Topeka Railroad Days (late August-early September)	785-232-5533

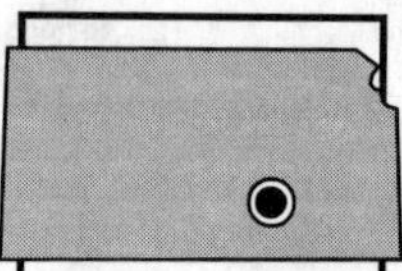

Wichita

In the mid-1800s, James R. Mead established the trading post from which the city of Wichita grew as a cowtown on the Chisholm Trail. A pictorial display of this trail, made famous by Jesse Chisholm (Mead's assistant), is located at the Wichita-Sedgwick County Historical Museum. Life in Wichita between 1865-1880 is illustrated in the open-air exhibit areas of the Old Cowtown Museum, which includes in its complex Wichita's first jail, six historic houses, and a working blacksmith shop. The sculptures of native artist Gina Salerno, created from the trunks of dead and dying trees, can be seen in Wichita's parks and recreation areas; more than 40 of these creations are scattered throughout the city. On the fringe of downtown Wichita is Botanica, the Wichita Gardens. Among its exhibits are a Shakespeare garden, a terrace garden with cascading pools, and formal gardens with native plants. Wichita is called the "air capital of the world" as Beech, Learjet, and Cessna aircraft companies all started here and continue to maintain their headquarters in the city.

Population	329,211	**Longitude**	97-33-72 W
Area (Land)	115.1 sq mi	**County**	Sedgwick
Area (Water)	2.2 sq mi	**Time Zone**	CST
Elevation	1035 ft	**Area Code/s**	316
Latitude	37-69-22 N		

— Average Temperatures and Precipitation —

TEMPERATURES

	Jan	Feb	Mar	Apr	May	Jun	Jul	Aug	Sep	Oct	Nov	Dec
High	40	46	57	68	77	87	93	91	81	71	55	43
Low	19	24	34	45	54	65	70	68	59	47	34	23

PRECIPITATION

	Jan	Feb	Mar	Apr	May	Jun	Jul	Aug	Sep	Oct	Nov	Dec
Inches	0.8	1.0	2.4	2.4	3.8	4.3	3.1	3.0	3.5	2.2	1.6	1.2

— Important Phone Numbers —

	Phone		Phone
AAA	316-685-5241	**HotelDocs**	800-468-3537
American Express Travel	316-686-7375	**Poison Control Center**	316-688-2277
Emergency	911	**Time/Temp**	316-436-1200
Fun Fone Events Recording	316-262-7474	**Weather**	316-681-1371

Wichita (Cont'd)

— Information Sources —

				Phone	Fax
Better Business Bureau Serving Kansas (Except the Northeast) 328 Laura St	Wichita	KS	67211	316-263-3146	263-3063
Web: www.wichita.bbb.org					
Century II Convention & Cultural Center 225 W Douglas Ave.	Wichita	KS	67202	316-264-9121	268-9268
Sedgwick County 525 N Main St Rm 211	Wichita	KS	67203	316-383-7666	383-7961
Web: www.southwind.net/sedgwick/					
Wichita Area Chamber of Commerce 350 W Douglas Ave.	Wichita	KS	67202	316-265-7771	265-7502
Web: www.wacc.org					
Wichita City Hall 455 N Main St.	Wichita	KS	67202	316-268-4531	268-4286*
**Fax:* Hum Res ■ *Web:* www.ci.wichita.ks.us					
Wichita Convention & Visitors Bureau 100 S Main St Suite 100	Wichita	KS	67202	316-265-2800	265-0162
TF: 800-288-9424 ■ *Web:* www.wichita-cvb.org					
Wichita Economic Development Office 455 N Main St 12th Fl.	Wichita	KS	67202	316-268-4502	268-4656
Wichita Mayor 455 N Main St 1st Fl.	Wichita	KS	67202	316-268-4331	268-4333
Wichita Public Library 223 S Main St.	Wichita	KS	67202	316-261-8500	262-4540
Web: www.wichita.lib.ks.us					

On-Line Resources

4Wichita.com	www.4wichita.com
About.com Guide to Wichita	wichita.about.com/local/midwestus/wichita
Anthill City Guide Wichita	www.anthill.com/city.asp?city=wichita
Area Guide Wichita	wichita.areaguides.net
City Knowledge Wichita	www.cityknowledge.com/ks_wichita.htm
Excite.com Wichita City Guide	www.excite.com/travel/countries/united_states/kansas/wichita
Wichita CityLink	www.usacitylink.com/citylink/wichita/
Wichita Kansas Cyberguide	www2.southwind.net/~vic/Wichita/index.html
Wichita.TheLinks.com	wichita.thelinks.com/

— Transportation Services —

AIRPORTS

■ Midcontinent Airport (ICT)

	Phone
6 miles SW of downtown (approx 12 minutes)	316-946-4700

Airport Transportation

	Phone
Taxi $10 fare to downtown	316-262-7511

Commercial Airlines

	Phone		Phone
America West	800-235-9292	**TWA**	800-221-2000
American	800-433-7300	**United**	800-241-6522
Continental	800-525-0280	**US Airways**	800-428-4322
Delta	800-221-1212	**Vanguard**	800-826-4827
Northwest	800-225-2525		

Charter Airlines

	Phone		Phone
Ballard Aviation Inc	316-946-4855	**Oliver Aviation Inc**	316-267-6712
Executive Aircraft Corp	316-946-4990	**Yingling Aircraft Inc**	316-943-3246
Midwest Corp Aviation	316-636-9700		

CAR RENTALS

	Phone		Phone
Avis	316-946-4882	**Hertz**	316-946-4860
Budget	316-946-4444	**National**	316-946-4851
CarTemps USA	316-945-3944	**Thrifty**	316-721-9552
Dollar	316-943-2333		

LIMO/TAXI

	Phone		Phone
American Cab	316-262-7511	**Cheetah Express**	316-734-6862
Best Cabs	316-838-2233	**Executive Limousine**	316-262-5466

MASS TRANSIT

	Phone
Metropolitan Transit Authority Bus $1 Base fare	316-265-7221

RAIL/BUS

				Phone
Greyhound/Trailways Bus Station 312 S Broadway	Wichita	KS	67202	316-265-7711

— Accommodations —

HOTEL RESERVATION SERVICES

	Phone	Fax
Reservations USA	865-453-1000	453-7484
TF: 800-251-4444 ■ *Web:* www.reservationsusa.com ■ *E-mail:* reserve@lodging4u.com		

HOTELS, MOTELS, RESORTS

				Phone	Fax
Best Western Airport Red Coach Inn 6815 W Kellogg St	Wichita	KS	67209	316-942-5600	943-1549
TF: 888-942-5666					
Best Western Red Coach Inn 915 E 53rd St N	Wichita	KS	67219	316-832-9387	832-9443
TF: 800-362-0095					
Cambridge Suites 120 W Orme St	Wichita	KS	67213	316-263-1061	263-3817
TF: 800-946-6200					
Candlewood Suites Northeast 3141 N Webb Rd	Wichita	KS	67226	316-634-6070	634-6575
TF: 888-226-3539					
Castle Inn Riverside 1155 N River Blvd.	Wichita	KS	67203	316-263-9300	
TF: 800-580-1131 ■ *Web:* www.castleinnriverside.com ■ *E-mail:* 1castle@gte.net					
Clarion Hotel Airport 5805 W Kellogg St	Wichita	KS	67209	316-942-7911	942-0854
TF: 800-835-2913					
Comfort Inn 4849 S Laura St	Wichita	KS	67216	316-522-1800	522-5273
TF: 800-228-5160					
Comfort Suites Airport 658 Westdale Dr	Wichita	KS	67209	316-945-2600	945-5033
TF: 800-318-2607					
Days Inn 9100 E Kellogg St	Wichita	KS	67207	316-685-0371	685-4668
TF: 800-329-4766					
Days Inn North 901 E 53rd St North	Wichita	KS	67219	316-832-1131	832-0591
TF: 800-329-7466					
Econo Lodge 6245 W Kellogg St.	Wichita	KS	67209	316-945-5261	945-0077
TF: 800-553-2666					
English Village Motor Inn 6727 E Kellogg Dr.	Wichita	KS	67207	316-683-5613	684-3530
Fairfield Inn by Marriott 333 S Webb Rd	Wichita	KS	67207	316-685-3777	685-3777
TF: 800-228-2800 ■ *Web:* fairfieldinn.com/ICTFI					
Four Points by Sheraton 549 S Rock Rd.	Wichita	KS	67207	316-686-7131	686-0018
TF: 800-325-3535					
Guild Plaza Hotel 125 N Market St	Wichita	KS	67202	316-265-9800	265-9830
Hampton Inn Hotel 3800 W Kellogg St	Wichita	KS	67213	316-945-4100	945-4611
TF: 800-426-7866					
Hilton & Executive Conference Center Wichita Airport 2098 Airport Rd.	Wichita	KS	67209	316-945-5272	945-7620
TF: 800-445-8667 ■ *Web:* www.hilton.com/hotels/ICTAHHF					
Holiday Inn Airport 5500 W Kellogg Dr	Wichita	KS	67209	316-943-2181	943-6587
TF: 800-465-4329					
Holiday Inn Express 4848 S Laura St	Wichita	KS	67216	316-529-4848	529-8585
TF: 800-465-4329					
Hotel at Oldtown 830 E 1st St	Wichita	KS	67202	316-267-4800	267-4840
TF: 888-226-3539 ■ *Web:* www.hotelatoldtown.com					
Hyatt Regency Wichita 400 W Waterman St	Wichita	KS	67202	316-293-1234	293-1200
TF: 800-233-1234 ■ *Web:* www.hyatt.com/usa/wichita/hotels/hotel_wicrw.html					
Inn at Tallgrass 2280 N Tara Cir.	Wichita	KS	67226	316-684-3466	685-3466
Inn at the Park 3751 E Douglas Ave	Wichita	KS	67218	316-652-0500	652-0610
TF: 800-258-1951					
Inn at Willowbend 3939 Comotara St	Wichita	KS	67226	316-636-4032	634-2190
TF: 800-553-5775					
La Quinta Motor Inn 7700 E Kellogg St.	Wichita	KS	67207	316-681-2881	681-0568
TF: 800-687-6667					
Marriott Wichita 9100 Corporate Hills Dr.	Wichita	KS	67207	316-651-0333	651-0990
TF: 800-228-9290 ■ *Web:* marriotthotels.com/ICTWE					
Quality Inn 600 S Holland St	Wichita	KS	67209	316-722-8730	722-8732
TF: 800-926-0721					
Ramada Inn 7335 E Kellogg Dr	Wichita	KS	67207	316-685-1281	685-8621
TF: 800-272-6232					
Ramada Inn 1400 N Lorraine St.	Hutchinson	KS	67501	316-669-9311	669-9830
TF: 800-362-5018					
Red Coach Inn 2111 E Kansas Ave	McPherson	KS	67460	316-241-6960	241-4340
TF: 800-835-0117					
Royal Lodge 320 E Kellogg St	Wichita	KS	67202	316-263-8877	

Wichita — Hotels, Motels, Resorts (Cont'd)

	City	State	Zip	Phone	Fax
Scotsman Inn East 465 S Webb Rd *TF:* 800-477-7268	Wichita	KS	67207	316-684-6363	684-6363
Scotsman Inn West 5922 W Kellogg St *TF:* 800-950-7268	Wichita	KS	67209	316-943-3800	943-3800
The Broadview Grand Heritage Hotel 400 W Douglas St. *TF:* 800-362-2929	Wichita	KS	67202	316-262-5000	262-6175
Wichita Suites Hotel 5211 E Kellogg St. *TF:* 800-243-5953	Wichita	KS	67218	316-685-2233	685-4152
Williamsburg Inn 8300 E Kellog St.	Wichita	KS	67207	316-684-0541	684-4295
Wyndham Garden Hotel 515 S Webb Rd. *TF:* 800-996-3426	Wichita	KS	67207	316-684-1111	684-0538

— Restaurants —

	City	State	Zip	Phone
Abe's Steak House (Steak) 1044 W 29th St North	Wichita	KS	67204	316-838-9933
Albert's Restaurant (Chinese) 6425 E Kellogg St.	Wichita	KS	67207	316-684-1861
Angelo's (Italian) 3105 E Harry St	Wichita	KS	67211	316-682-1473
Azteca Restaurant (Mexican) 605 W 13th St.	Wichita	KS	60623	316-263-1204
Bangkok Thai Restaurant (Thai) 2020 S Rock Rd Suite 50	Wichita	KS	67207	316-685-6333
Champs Bar & Grill (Mexican) 1106 S Seneca	Wichita	KS	67213	316-262-1284
Chelsea's Bar & Grill (American) 2949 N Rock Rd	Wichita	KS	67226	316-636-1100
Chisholm's Bar & Grill (American) 400 W Douglas St	Wichita	KS	67202	316-262-5000
Joe Kelly's Oyster Dock & Restaurant (Steak/Seafood) 7700 E Kellogg St	Wichita	KS	67207	316-682-0443
Kan-Tex Barbeque (Barbecue) 2345 N Broadway St.	Wichita	KS	67219	316-838-1031
La Chinita (Mexican) 1451 N Broadway St	Wichita	KS	67214	316-267-1552
Larkspur Restaurant (California) 904 E Douglas St	Wichita	KS	67202	316-262-5275
Le Parc Restaurant (American) 400 W Douglas St.	Wichita	KS	67202	316-262-5000
Legends (American) 2098 Airport Rd	Wichita	KS	67209	316-945-5272
Old Town Barbecue (Barbecue) 111 N Washington St	Wichita	KS	67202	316-269-4000
Olive Tree (Continental) 2949 N Rock Rd	Wichita	KS	67226	316-636-1100
River City Brewing Co (New American) 150 N Mosley St	Wichita	KS	67202	316-263-2739
Savute's (Italian) 3303 N Broadway	Wichita	KS	67219	316-838-0455
Scotch & Sirloin (Steak/Seafood) 5325 E Kellogg St	Wichita	KS	67218	316-685-8701
Upper Crust The (New American) 7038 E Lincoln St	Wichita	KS	67211	316-683-8088

— Goods and Services —

SHOPPING

	City	State	Zip	Phone	Fax
Clifton Square 3700 E Douglas Ave Suite 12	Wichita	KS	67208	316-686-2177	
Delano Township Square 915 W Douglas Ave	Wichita	KS	67213	316-263-2323	
Eastgate Plaza Shopping Center 8235 E Kellogg St.	Wichita	KS	67207	316-682-6787	
Old Town District Douglas St-betw Washington & 2nd Sts	Wichita	KS	67202	316-265-2800	
Town West Square 4600 W Kellogg St	Wichita	KS	67209	316-945-9374	945-8617
Towne East Square 7700 E Kellogg St.	Wichita	KS	67207	316-686-3341	684-0740
Wichita Mall 4165 E Harry.	Wichita	KS	67218	316-686-9072	

BANKS

	City	State	Zip	Phone	Fax
Bank of America 100 N Broadway St. *TF:* 888-279-3121	Wichita	KS	67202	316-261-4251	261-2241
Commerce Bank 150 N Main St *TF:* 800-866-9095	Wichita	KS	67202	316-261-4700	261-3627
Emprise Bank PO Box 2970 *TF:* 800-201-7118	Wichita	KS	67201	316-383-4400	383-4399
Intrust Bank NA 105 N Main St. **Fax:* Hum Res ■ *Web:* www.intrustbank.com ■ *E-mail:* intrust@intrustbank.com	Wichita	KS	67202	316-383-1111	383-5805*
Southwest National Bank of Wichita 400 E Douglas Ave *TF:* 800-747-5303	Wichita	KS	67202	316-291-5303	291-5274

BUSINESS SERVICES

	Phone		Phone
City Wide Courier Service	316-264-2619	**Metro Courier Service**	316-522-8008
DHL Worldwide Express	800-225-5345	**Norrell Temporary Services**	316-262-1560
Express Mail	316-946-4545	**Olsten Staffing Services**	316-263-9283
Federal Express	800-238-5355	**Pony Express Courier Corp**	316-943-9888
Kelly Services	316-267-2885	**Post Office**	316-262-6245
Kinko's	316-682-1327	**UPS**	800-742-5877

— Media —

PUBLICATIONS

	City	State	Zip	Phone	Fax
Wichita Business Journal 110 S Main St Suite 200 *Web:* www.amcity.com/wichita	Wichita	KS	67202	316-267-6406	267-8570
Wichita Eagle‡ PO Box 820 *Web:* www.wichitaeagle.com/ ■ *E-mail:* eaglenws@aol.com	Wichita	KS	67201	316-268-6000	268-6627

‡Daily newspapers

TELEVISION

	City	State	Zip	Phone	Fax
KAKE-TV Ch 10 (ABC) 1500 N West St *Web:* www.kake.com	Wichita	KS	67203	316-943-4221	943-5374
KPTS-TV Ch 8 (PBS) PO Box 288 *E-mail:* tv8@kpts.org	Wichita	KS	67201	316-838-3090	838-8586
KSAS-TV Ch 24 (Fox) 316 N West St *Web:* www.ksasfox24.com ■ *E-mail:* foxfeedback@foxkansas.com	Wichita	KS	67203	316-942-2424	292-1195
KSNW-TV Ch 3 (NBC) 833 N Main St *Web:* www.ksnw.com ■ *E-mail:* ksnw@aol.com	Wichita	KS	67203	316-265-3333	292-1195
KWCH-TV Ch 12 (CBS) 2815 E 37th North *Web:* www.kwch.com/ ■ *E-mail:* news@kwch.com	Wichita	KS	67219	316-838-1212	831-6193

RADIO

	City	State	Zip	Phone	Fax
KEYN-FM 103.7 MHz (Oldies) 2120 N Woodlawn St Suite 352	Wichita	KS	67208	316-685-2121	685-1287
KFDI-FM 101.3 MHz (Ctry) 4200 N Old Lawrence Rd. *Web:* www.kfdi.com ■ *E-mail:* spike@kfdi.com	Wichita	KS	67219	316-838-9141	838-3607
KHCC-FM 90.1 MHz (NPR) 815 N Walnut St Suite 300 *Web:* www.radioks.org	Hutchinson	KS	67501	316-662-6646	
KICT-FM 95.1 MHz (Rock) 734 N Maize Rd *Web:* www.t95.com ■ *E-mail:* staff@t95.com	Wichita	KS	67212	316-722-5600	722-0722
KKRD-FM 107.3 MHz (CHR) 2402 E 37th St N. *E-mail:* kkrd@southwind.net	Wichita	KS	67219	316-832-9600	832-0112
KMUW-FM 89.1 MHz (NPR) 3317 E 17th St *E-mail:* kmuw@twsu.edu	Wichita	KS	67208	316-978-6789	978-3946
KNSS-AM 1240 kHz (N/T) 2402 E 37th St N. *Web:* www.southwind.net/knss ■ *E-mail:* knss@southwind.net	Wichita	KS	67219	316-832-9600	832-9688
KZSN-FM 102.1 MHz (Ctry) 2120 N Woodlawn Suite 352 *Web:* www.kzsn.com	Wichita	KS	67208	316-685-2121	685-1287

— Colleges/Universities —

	City	State	Zip	Phone	Fax
Friends University 2100 University St *TF:* 800-794-6945 ■ *Web:* www.friends.edu	Wichita	KS	67213	316-295-5000	295-5701
Newman University 3100 McCormick Ave *TF:* 877-639-6268 ■ *Web:* www.newmanu.edu	Wichita	KS	67213	316-942-4291	942-4483
Wichita Area Technical College 301 S Grove St.	Wichita	KS	67211	316-973-8400	973-8489
Wichita State University 1845 N Fairmount St. *TF Admissions:* 800-362-2594 ■ *Web:* www.twsu.edu	Wichita	KS	67260	316-978-3456	978-3174

— Hospitals —

	City	State	Zip	Phone	Fax
Columbia Wesley Medical Center 550 N Hillside Ave	Wichita	KS	67214	316-688-2000	688-7410
Veterans Affairs Medical Center 5500 E Kellogg St.	Wichita	KS	67218	316-685-2221	651-3666
Via Christi Regional Medical Center 929 N Saint Francis St. **Fax:* Admitting ■ *TF:* 800-362-0070	Wichita	KS	67214	316-268-5000	291-7971*

Wichita (Cont'd)

— Attractions —

Name / Address	City	State	Zip	Phone	Fax
Allen-Lambe House Museum & Study Center 255 N Roosevelt St	Wichita	KS	67208	316-687-1027	687-2991
Web: www2.southwind.net/~allenlam/ ■ *E-mail:* allenlam@southwind.net					
Barnacle Bill's Fanta Sea Water Park 3330 N Woodlawn	Wichita	KS	67220	316-682-8656	
Botanica The Wichita Gardens 701 Amidon St	Wichita	KS	67203	316-264-0448	264-0587
Web: www.botanica.org ■ *E-mail:* botanica@southwind.net					
Cheney State Park & Wildlife Area 16000 NE 50th St	Cheney	KS	67025	316-542-3664	
Coleman Factory Outlet Store & Museum 235 N Saint Francis St	Wichita	KS	67202	316-264-0836	264-6526
Crown-Uptown Professional Dinner Theatre 3207 E Douglas St	Wichita	KS	67218	316-681-1566	681-1925
Eberly Farm 13111 W 21st St North	Wichita	KS	67235	316-722-3580	722-3591
Fort Larned National Historic Site Route 3	Larned	KS	67550	316-285-6911	285-3571
Web: www.nps.gov/fols/					
Great Plains Nature Center 6232 East 29th St N	Wichita	KS	67220	316-683-5499	688-9555
Great Plains Transportation Museum 700 E Douglas St	Wichita	KS	67202	316-263-0944	
Indian Center Museum 650 N Seneca St	Wichita	KS	67203	316-262-5221	262-4216
Web: www2.southwind.net/~icm/museum/museum.html ■ *E-mail:* icm@southwind.net					
Joyland Amusement Park 2801 S Hillside St	Wichita	KS	67216	316-684-0179	684-1478
Kansas African American Museum 601 N Water St	Wichita	KS	67203	316-262-7651	
Kansas Aviation Museum 3350 S George Washington Blvd	Wichita	KS	67210	316-683-9242	683-0573
Web: www.saranap.com/kam.html ■ *E-mail:* craner@ccnet.com					
Kansas Wildlife Exhibit Nims & Murdock Sts Central Riverside Pk	Wichita	KS	67202	316-683-5499	688-9555
Keeper of the Plains Statue 650 N Seneca St	Wichita	KS	67203	316-262-5221	262-4216
Lake Afton Public Observatory 24600 West 39th St S	Goddard	KS	67215	316-794-8995	
Web: www.twsu.edu/~obswww/ ■ *E-mail:* Facsme@wsuhub.uc.twsu.edu					
Metropolitan Ballet Century II Concert Hall	Wichita	KS	67202	316-687-5880	
Music Theatre of Wichita 225 W Douglas Century II Concert Hall	Wichita	KS	67202	316-265-3107	265-8708
Old Cowtown Museum 1871 Sim Park Dr	Wichita	KS	67203	316-264-0671	264-2937
Web: www.old-cowtown.org ■ *E-mail:* cowtown@southwind.net					
Old Town District Douglas St-betw Washington & 2nd Sts	Wichita	KS	67202	316-265-2800	
Omnisphere & Science Center 220 S Main St	Wichita	KS	67202	316-337-9178	
Sedgwick County Park 6501 West 21st St N	Wichita	KS	67212	316-943-0192	942-3127
Sedgwick County Zoo 5555 Zoo Blvd	Wichita	KS	67212	316-942-2213	942-3781
Web: www.scz.org ■ *E-mail:* director@scz.org					
Society of Decorative Painters Museum 393 N McLean Blvd	Wichita	KS	67203	316-269-9300	269-9191
Ulrich Edwin A Museum of Art 1845 Fairmount St Wichita State University	Wichita	KS	67208	316-978-3664	978-3898
Web: www.twsu.edu/~ulrich ■ *E-mail:* ulrichma@twsuvm.uc.twsu.edu					
Watson Park 3055 S Lawrence Rd	Wichita	KS	67217	316-529-9940	
Wichita Art Museum 619 Stackman Dr	Wichita	KS	67203	316-268-4921	268-4980
Web: www.feist.com/~wam/ ■ *E-mail:* wam@feist.com					
Wichita Center for the Arts 9112 E Central	Wichita	KS	67206	316-634-2787	634-0593
Wichita-Sedgewick County Historical Museum 204 S Main St	Wichita	KS	67202	316-265-9314	265-9319
Wichita Symphony Orchestra 225 W Douglas Suite 207	Wichita	KS	67202	316-267-7658	267-1937
Web: www.wso.org ■ *E-mail:* symphony@louverture.com					

SPORTS TEAMS & FACILITIES

Name / Address	City	State	Zip	Phone	Fax
Wichita Greyhound Park 1500 East 77th St N	Valley Center	KS	67147	316-755-4000	755-2405
TF: 800-872-2894					
Wichita Thunder (hockey) 1229 East 85th St N Kansas Coliseum	Valley Center	KS	67147	316-264-4625	264-3037
Web: www.wichitathunder.com/					
Wichita Wings (soccer) 1229 East 85th St N Kansas Coliseum	Wichita	KS	67147	316-262-3545	263-8531
Web: www.wichita-wings.com/					
Wichita Wranglers (baseball) 300 S Sycamore St Lawrence-Dumont Stadium	Wichita	KS	67213	316-267-3372	267-3382
Web: www.wichitawranglers.com					

— Events —

	Phone
Asian Festival (late October)	316-689-8729
Celebrate (early July)	316-943-4221
Cinco De Mayo Festival (early May)	800-288-9424
Holiday Wreath Festival (mid-November)	316-264-3386
Kansas Day Celebration (late January)	316-265-3933
Mexican Independence Weekend (mid-September)	316-265-2800
Mid-America All-Indian Center Pow Wow (late July)	316-524-1210
Old Sedgwick County Fair (early October)	316-264-0671
Polkatennial (early May)	316-722-4201
Saint Patrick's Day Parade (mid-March)	316-946-1322
Sand Creek Folklife Festival (late April)	316-283-7925
Tulip Festival (mid-April)	316-264-0448
Wichita Black Arts Festival (early September)	316-691-1499
Wichita Indian Art Market & Exhibition (mid-April)	316-262-5221
Wichita Jazz Festival (late April)	316-684-1100
Wichita River Festival (early-mid-May)	316-267-2817
Wichita Winter Fest (early December)	316-946-1323

Kentucky

Population (1999): 3,960,825 **Area (sq mi): 40,411**

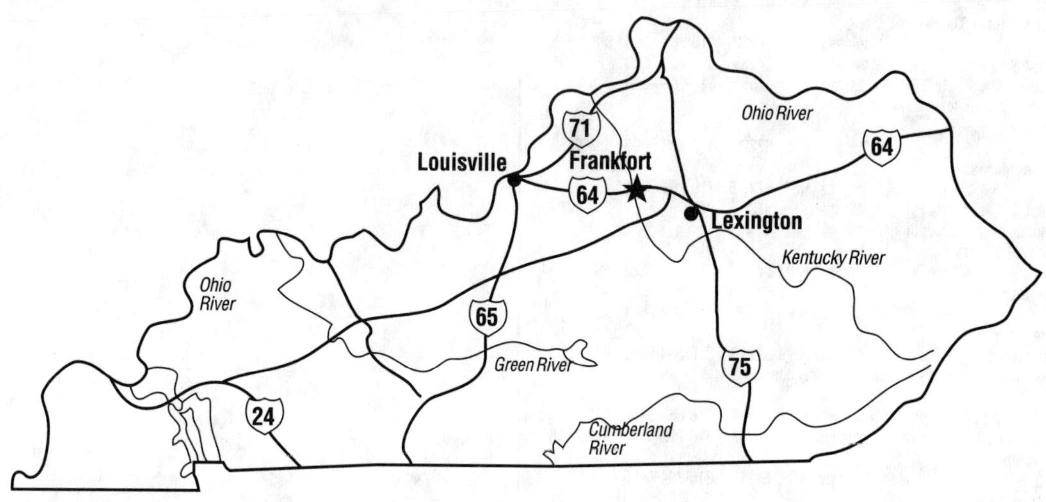

— State Information Sources —

				Phone	Fax
Kentucky Chamber of Commerce					
464 Chenault Rd.	Frankfort	KY	40602	502-695-4700	695-6824
Web: www.kychamber.com					
Kentucky Dept for Libraries & Archives					
300 Coffee Tree Rd	Frankfort	KY	40601	502-564-8300	564-5773
Web: www.kdla.state.ky.us					
Kentucky Economic Development Cabinet					
500 Mero St.	Frankfort	KY	40601	502-564-7670	564-3256
Web: www.state.ky.us/edc/cabmain.htm ■ *E-mail:* econdev@mail.state.ky.us					
Kentucky Parks Dept 500 Mero St 11th Fl	Frankfort	KY	40601	502-564-2172	564-6100
TF: 800-255-7275 ■ *Web:* www.state.ky.us/agencies/parks/parkhome.htm					
Kentucky State Government Information				502-564-2500	
Web: www.state.ky.us					
Kentucky Travel Dept 500 Mero St Suite 2200	Frankfort	KY	40601	502-564-4930	564-5695
TF: 800-225-8747 ■ *Web:* www.kentuckytourism.com ■ *E-mail:* travel@mail.state.ky.us					

ON-LINE RESOURCES

Best Read Guide Kentucky . . . www.bestreadguide.com/kentucky
Kentucky Cities . . . dir.yahoo.com/Regional/U_S__States/Kentucky/Cities
Kentucky Cities By County . . . dir.yahoo.com/Regional/U_S__States/Kentucky/Counties_and_Regions
Kentucky Tourism Council . . . www.tourky.com
Kentucky Travel & Tourism Guide . . . www.travel-library.com/north_america/usa/kentucky/index.html
Kentucky Travel Guide . . . www.kytravel.com
Kentucky's Western Waterland . . . www.tokentucky.com
Rough Guide Travel Kentucky . . . travel.roughguides.com/content/724/index.htm
Travel.org-Kentucky . . . travel.org/kentucky.html
WestKentucky.com Tourism . . . www.westkentucky.com
Yahoo! Get Local Kentucky . . . dir.yahoo.com/Regional/U_S__States/Kentucky

— Cities Profiled —

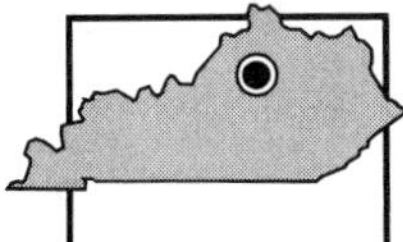

Frankfort

The capital of Kentucky is located in the Bluegrass Region of the state, in the valley of the Kentucky River. Attractions in Frankfort include both the State Capitol Building and the Old State Capitol, a Greek revival structure that features a self-supporting spiral staircase. The Floral Clock on the West Lawn behind the State Capitol is planted with thousands of colorful flowering plants and has a face 34 feet in diameter. Two of the sites featured on the Old Frankfort Walking Tour are shopping areas - the Olde Capitol Shoppes in the downtown area, which feature antiques, books, Kentucky handcrafts, and collectibles; and Saint Clair Mall, located in front of the Old State House, with specialty and antique shops, boutiques, and restaurants. Daniel Boone's gravesite is at the Frankfort Cemetery, overlooking the city.

Population	26,418	**Longitude**	84-86-69 W
Area (Land)	14.6 sq mi	**County**	Franklin
Area (Water)	0.3 sq mi	**Time Zone**	EST
Elevation	510 ft	**Area Code/s**	502
Latitude	38-19-72 N		

— Average Temperatures and Precipitation —

TEMPERATURES

	Jan	Feb	Mar	Apr	May	Jun	Jul	Aug	Sep	Oct	Nov	Dec
High	40	44	56	67	76	83	87	86	80	69	57	45
Low	19	22	31	40	50	59	64	62	55	42	34	25

PRECIPITATION

	Jan	Feb	Mar	Apr	May	Jun	Jul	Aug	Sep	Oct	Nov	Dec
Inches	2.6	3.0	4.3	3.8	4.7	3.6	4.3	3.6	3.4	2.5	3.3	3.5

— Important Phone Numbers —

	Phone		Phone
AAA	502-227-9613	**Poison Control Center**	800-722-5725
Emergency	911	**Time/Temp**	502-227-2588
Medical Referral	502-226-7681		

— Information Sources —

				Phone	Fax
Farnham Dudgeon Civic Center 405 Mero St.	Frankfort	KY	40601	502-564-5335	564-3310
Frankfort Chamber of Commerce 100 Capitol Ave *Web:* www.frankfortky.org ■ *E-mail:* info@frankfortky.org	Frankfort	KY	40601	502-223-8261	223-5942
Frankfort City Hall PO Box 697	Frankfort	KY	40602	502-875-8500	875-8502
Frankfort Mayor PO Box 697	Frankfort	KY	40602	502-875-8500	875-8502
Frankfort Planning Dept PO Box 697.	Frankfort	KY	40602	502-875-8513	875-8502
Frankfort Visitors Center 100 Capitol Ave	Frankfort	KY	40601	502-875-8687	227-2604
Frankfort/Franklin County Tourist & Convention Commission 100 Capital Ave. *TF:* 800-960-7200 ■ *Web:* www.frankfortky.org	Frankfort	KY	40601	502-875-8687	227-2604
Franklin County PO Box 338	Frankfort	KY	40602	502-875-8702	875-8718
Kentucky Consumer Protection Div 1024 Capital Ctr Dr *Web:* www.law.state.ky.us/cp/default.htm	Frankfort	KY	40601	502-696-5389	573-8317
Sawyier Paul Public Library 305 Wapping St	Frankfort	KY	40601	502-223-1658	227-2250

On-Line Resources

Anthill City Guide Frankfort	www.anthill.com/city.asp?city=frankfort
Area Guide Frankfort	frankfort.areaguides.net
Excite.com Frankfort City Guide	www.excite.com/travel/countries/united_states/kentucky/frankfort
Frankfort	www.frankfortky.org

— Transportation Services —

AIRPORTS

	Phone
■ **Blue Grass Airport (LEX)** 25 miles SE of downtown Frankfort (approx 35 minutes)	606-425-3114

Airport Transportation

	Phone
Capital City Cab $40 fare to downtown Frankfort	502-875-5078
United Transportation $40 fare to downtown Frankfort	606-225-2227

Commercial Airlines

	Phone		Phone
Comair	606-231-7571	**TWA Express**	800-221-2000
Northwest	606-277-0245	**United Express**	606-253-3800

Charter Airlines

	Phone		Phone
Blue Grass Charter	606-233-2152	**TAC Air**	606-255-7724
Comair Jet Express	606-767-3500	**United Transportation Co**	606-233-4890
Executive Express Inc	606-225-5449	**Wilkinson Flying Service Inc**	606-293-2999
Richmor Aviation Inc	800-359-2299	**Wombles Charters**	606-887-4611
Sprite Flite Jets	800-354-9232		

CAR RENTALS

	Phone		Phone
Avis	606-252-5581	**Enterprise-Frankfort**	502-695-5542
Avis-Frankfort	502-875-4469	**Hertz**	606-254-3496
Budget	606-254-5400	**Local-Frankfort**	502-875-7413
Budget-Frankfort	502-695-4189	**National**	606-254-8806

LIMO/TAXI

	Phone		Phone
Capital City Cab	502-875-5078	**Taxi Service**	606-231-8294
Gold Shield Transportation	800-205-7330		

MASS TRANSIT

	Phone
Frankfort Transit $.50 Base fare	502-875-8563

RAIL/BUS

				Phone
Greyhound Bus Station 477 New Circle Rd *TF:* 800-231-2222	Lexington	KY	40511	606-299-8804

— Accommodations —

HOTELS, MOTELS, RESORTS

				Phone	Fax
Best Western Parkside Inn 80 Chanult Dr *TF:* 800-528-1234	Frankfort	KY	40601	502-695-6111	695-6111
Bluegrass Inn 635 Versailles Rd *TF:* 800-322-1802	Frankfort	KY	40601	502-695-1800	
Days Inn 1051 US 127 S *TF:* 800-329-7466	Frankfort	KY	40601	502-875-2200	875-3574
Holiday Inn Capital Plaza 405 Wilkinson Blvd *TF:* 800-465-4329	Frankfort	KY	40601	502-227-5100	875-7147
Knights Inn 855 Louisville Rd *TF:* 800-843-5644	Frankfort	KY	40601	502-227-2282	223-5159
Red Carpet Inn 711 E Main St *TF:* 800-251-1962	Frankfort	KY	40601	502-223-2041	223-2043
Super 8 Motel 1225 US 127 S *TF:* 800-800-8000	Frankfort	KY	40601	502-875-3220	875-2342

— Restaurants —

				Phone
Arandas Mexican Restaurant (Mexican) 193 Versailles Rd	Frankfort	KY	40601	502-695-4002
Capital Bar-B-Q (Barbecue) US 127 S Anderson Rd.	Frankfort	KY	40601	502-223-8110
Casa Fiesta (Mexican) 801 Louisville Rd	Frankfort	KY	40601	502-226-5010

Frankfort — Restaurants (Cont'd)

				Phone
China Wok (Chinese) Versailles Rd Eastwood Shopping Ctr	Frankfort	KY	40601	502-695-9388
Cliffside Restaurant (Homestyle) Old Lawrenceburg/420 Rd	Frankfort	KY	40601	502-223-3173
Columbia's Steak House (Steak) 1371 US 127 S	Frankfort	KY	40601	502-227-2380
Jim's Seafood (Seafood) 950 Wilkinson Blvd	Frankfort	KY	40601	502-223-7448
Jubilee Dragon (Chinese) 1232 US 127 S	Frankfort	KY	40601	502-875-5111
Kelley's Garden (American) 334 Saint Clair St	Frankfort	KY	40601	502-227-7287
La Fiesta Grande (Mexican) 314 Versailles Rd	Frankfort	KY	40601	502-695-8378
Market Cafe (American) 1420 Versailles Rd Suite 2	Frankfort	KY	40601	502-695-4871
Marshall's (American) 232 W Main St	Frankfort	KY	40601	502-223-5006
New China (Chinese) 1389 US Hwy 127 S	Frankfort	KY	40601	502-226-3400
Pink Pig Bar-B-Q (Barbecue) 581 E Main St	Frankfort	KY	40601	502-223-7343
Rio's Steak House (Steak) 1100 US 127 S	Frankfort	KY	40601	502-227-1185
Saylor's (Continental) 900 Louisville Rd	Frankfort	KY	40601	502-227-9282
Smile of Siam (Thai) 19 Century Plaza	Frankfort	KY	40601	502-227-9934
Tumbleweed Mexican Food & Mesquite Grill (Mexican) 105 Brighton Pk	Frankfort	KY	40601	502-695-8889

— Goods and Services —

SHOPPING

				Phone
Eastwood Shopping Center Versailles Rd	Frankfort	KY	40601	502-695-9340
Franklin Square Shopping Center US 127 S	Frankfort	KY	40601	
Old Capital Antique Mall 231 W Broadway	Frankfort	KY	40601	502-223-3879
Old Capitol Shop State Capitol Bldg	Frankfort	KY	40601	
Saint Clair Mall Old State Capitol Mall	Frankfort	KY	40601	

BANKS

				Phone	Fax
Bankers Bank of Kentucky 107 Progress Dr	Frankfort	KY	40602	502-695-3000	227-2715
Farmers Bank & Capital Trust Co PO Box 309	Frankfort	KY	40602	502-227-1600	227-1680
Fifth Third Bank of Kentucky 475 Versailles Rd	Frankfort	KY	40601	502-695-4958	695-0624
First Federal Savings Bank of Frankfort 216 W Main St	Frankfort	KY	40601	502-223-1638	223-7136
Republic Bank 100 Hwy 676	Frankfort	KY	40601	502-875-4300	223-8849

BUSINESS SERVICES

	Phone		Phone
Airborne Express	800-247-2676	**Mail Boxes Etc**	800-789-4623
BAX Global	800-225-5229	**Olsten Staffing Services**	502-875-0195
DHL Worldwide Express	800-225-5345	**Post Office**	502-223-3447
Federal Express	800-238-5355	**Precision Staffing**	502-227-7000
Kelly Services	502-227-9502	**UPS**	800-742-5877

— Media —

PUBLICATIONS

				Phone	Fax
State Journal‡ PO Box 368	Frankfort	KY	40602	502-227-4556	227-2831

‡*Daily newspapers*

TELEVISION

				Phone	Fax
WDKY-TV Ch 56 (Fox) 836 Euclid Ave	Lexington	KY	40502	606-269-5656	269-3774
WKLE-TV Ch 46 (PBS) 600 Cooper Dr	Lexington	KY	40502	606-258-7000	258-7399
WKYT-TV Ch 27 (CBS) 2851 Winchester Rd *Web:* www.wkyt.com ■ *E-mail:* fbme52a@prodigy.com	Lexington	KY	40509	606-299-0411	293-1578
WLEX-TV Ch 18 (NBC) 1065 Russell Cave Rd *Web:* www.wlextv.com ■ *E-mail:* wlex@mis.net	Lexington	KY	40505	606-255-4404	255-2418
WTVQ-TV Ch 36 (ABC) 6940 Man O War Blvd *Web:* www.wtvq.com	Lexington	KY	40509	606-233-3600	293-5002

RADIO

				Phone	Fax
WFKY-AM 1490 kHz (Oldies) PO Box 4130	Frankfort	KY	40604	502-223-8281	875-1225
WKED-AM 1130 kHz (Nost) 306 W Main St Suite 509 *E-mail:* wked@kih.net	Frankfort	KY	40601	502-875-1130	875-1225
WKED-FM 103.7 MHz (AC) 306 W Main St Suite 509 *E-mail:* wked@kih.net	Frankfort	KY	40601	502-875-1130	875-1225
WKYL-FM 102.1 MHz (Rel) 88 C Michael Davenport Blvd Suite 2	Frankfort	KY	40601	502-696-9595	227-1021
WKYW-FM 104.9 MHz (CR) PO Box 4130	Frankfort	KY	40604	502-223-8281	875-1225

— Colleges/Universities —

				Phone	Fax
Georgetown College 400 E College St *TF Admissions:* 800-788-9985 ■ *Web:* www.georgetowncollege.edu ■ *E-mail:* admissions@gtc.georgetown.ky.us	Georgetown	KY	40324	502-863-8000	868-8891
Kentucky State University 400 E Main St *Web:* www.kysu.edu	Frankfort	KY	40601	502-227-6000	227-6239
Midway College 512 E Stephens St *TF Admissions:* 800-755-0031 ■ *Web:* www.midway.edu	Midway	KY	40347	606-846-4421	846-5823

— Hospitals —

				Phone	Fax
Frankfort Regional Medical Center 299 King's Daughters Dr **Fax:* Admitting ■ *Web:* www.frankfortregional.com	Frankfort	KY	40601	502-875-5240	226-7966*
Woodford Hospital 360 Amsden Ave	Versailles	KY	40383	606-873-3111	873-1016

— Attractions —

				Phone	Fax
Berry Hill Mansion 700 Louisville Rd *E-mail:* berryhillmusicroom@mail.state.ky.us	Frankfort	KY	40601	502-564-3000	564-6505
Brown Orlando House 202 Wilkinson St	Frankfort	KY	40601	502-227-2560	227-3348
Buckley Clyde E Wildlife Sanctuary 1305 Germany Rd	Frankfort	KY	40601	606-873-5711	873-5711
Buffalo Trace Distillery 1001 Wilkinson Blvd	Frankfort	KY	40601	502-223-7641	
Canoe Kentucky 7323 Peaks Mill Rd *TF:* 800-522-6631 ■ *Web:* www.canoeky.com ■ *E-mail:* canoeky@aol.com	Frankfort	KY	40601	502-227-4492	227-8086
Capital Gallery of Contemporary Art 314 Lewis St	Frankfort	KY	40601	502-223-2649	
Capital View Park Hwy 676	Frankfort	KY	40601	502-695-0865	
Daniel Boone's Grave 215 E Main St	Frankfort	KY	40601	502-227-2403	
East Frankfort Park Myrtle Ave	Frankfort	KY	40601	502-875-8575	875-8577
Executive Mansion Capitol Ave	Frankfort	KY	40601	502-564-2500	
Frank Lloyd Wright Zeigler House 509 Shelby St	Frankfort	KY	40601	502-227-7164	
Juniper Hill Park 800 Louisville Rd	Frankfort	KY	40601	502-875-8575	875-8577
Kentucky Dept of Fish & Wildlife Game Farm 1 Game Farm Rd	Frankfort	KY	40601	502-564-5448	
Kentucky History Museum 100 W Broadway	Frankfort	KY	40601	502-564-3016	564-4701
Kentucky Military History Museum E Main St & Capitol Ave *Web:* www.kyhistory.org	Frankfort	KY	40601	502-564-3265	564-4054
Kentucky State Capitol & Floral Clock Capitol Ave	Frankfort	KY	40601	502-564-3449	
Lakeview Park Georgetown Rd & Steadmantown Ln	Frankfort	KY	40601	502-695-8431	
Liberty Hall 218 Wilkinson St	Frankfort	KY	40601	502-227-2560	227-3348
Lieutenant Governor's Mansion 420 High St	Frankfort	KY	40601	502-564-5500	564-4099
Old State Capitol Museum 300 W Broadway	Frankfort	KY	40601	502-564-3016	564-4701
Rebecca Ruth Candies 112 E 2nd St *TF:* 800-444-3766	Frankfort	KY	40601	502-223-7475	226-3204
South Frankfort Park Murray St	Frankfort	KY	40601	502-875-8575	
Still Waters Marina & Canoe Trails 249 Strohmeier Rd	Frankfort	KY	40601	502-223-8896	
Switzer Covered Bridge Hwy 1262	Switzer	KY			
Vest-Lindsay House 401 Wapping St	Frankfort	KY	40601	502-564-6980	

— Events —

	Phone
Candlelight Tour & Christmas 'Round the Fountain (late November)	502-223-2261

Frankfort — Events (Cont'd)

	Phone
Capital City Bass Classic (late September)	502-223-8261
Capital Expo Festival (early June)	502-875-8687
Christmas Arts & Crafts Expo (early December)	502-695-9179
Deafestival (late May)	800-372-2907
Franklin County Fair & Horse Show (late July)	502-695-9035
Governor's Derby Breakfast (early May)	502-564-2611
Great Pumpkin Festival (mid-October)	502-223-2261
Kentucky Book Fair (late November)	502-227-4556
Kentucky Folklife Festival (mid-September)	502-564-3016
Kentucky Herb Festival (mid-June)	502-695-8431
Kentucky's Capital Christmas (early December)	502-875-8687
Switzer Covered Bridge Day (late September)	502-875-8687

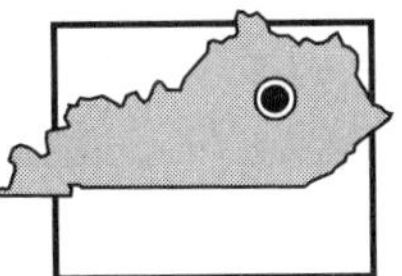

Lexington

Lexington is located about 75 miles from Louisville, in the heart of Kentucky's Bluegrass region. The Kentucky Horse Park at Lexington is a 1,032-acre working farm and park devoted to the horse. Features there include two museums, films, a stable of equine champions, walking and horse-drawn tours, and year-round shows and events. One such event is the Southern Lights Holiday Festival, which begins the day after Thanksgiving and runs through January 1 each year, featuring some 750,000 lights with animated holiday and horse scenes along a two-and-a-half-mile drive. Thoroughbred racing is available at Keeneland Race Course in Lexington, with harness racing at the Red Mile Harness Track. A number of historic sites in Lexington offer guided tours to visitors, including: Ashland, the Henry Clay Estate; Hopemont, the Hunt-Morgan House; the Mary Todd Lincoln house, where President Lincoln's wife spent her girlhood; and Waveland, an antebellum plantation house built in the 1840s. Lexington also has several shopping areas, including Victorian Square in the downtown area and Dudley Square, a restored 1881 school building with shops featuring antiques, prints, quilts, collectibles, and other unique items.

Population	241,749	**Longitude**	84-50-03 W
Area (Land)	284.5 sq mi	**County**	Fayette
Area (Water)	1.0 sq mi	**Time Zone**	EST
Elevation	983 ft	**Area Code/s**	606
Latitude	38-04-92 N		

— Average Temperatures and Precipitation —

TEMPERATURES

	Jan	Feb	Mar	Apr	May	Jun	Jul	Aug	Sep	Oct	Nov	Dec
High	39	44	55	66	74	83	86	85	78	67	55	44
Low	22	25	35	44	54	62	66	64	58	46	37	28

PRECIPITATION

	Jan	Feb	Mar	Apr	May	Jun	Jul	Aug	Sep	Oct	Nov	Dec
Inches	2.9	3.2	4.4	3.9	4.5	3.7	5.0	3.9	3.2	2.6	3.4	4.0

— Important Phone Numbers —

	Phone		Phone
AAA	606-233-1111	**Poison Control Center**	800-722-5725
Emergency	911	**Time/Temp**	606-259-2333
Medical Referral	606-278-3444	**Weather**	606-253-4444

— Information Sources —

				Phone	Fax
Better Business Bureau Serving Central & Eastern Kentucky 410 W Vine St Suite 340 *Web:* www.lexington.bbb.org	Lexington	KY	40507	606-259-1008	259-1639
Fayette County 162 E Main St	Lexington	KY	40507	606-253-3344	231-9619
Lexington Chamber of Commerce 330 E Main St Suite 100 *Web:* www.lexingtonchamber.com ■ *E-mail:* lexchamb@lex.infi.net	Lexington	KY	40507	606-254-4447	233-3304
Lexington City Hall 200 E Main St Fayette Government Ctr *Web:* www.lfucg.com	Lexington	KY	40507	606-258-3000	258-3250
Lexington Convention & Visitors Bureau 301 E Vine St. *TF:* 800-845-3959 ■ *Web:* www.visitlex.com/ ■ *E-mail:* vacation@visitlex.com	Lexington	KY	40507	606-233-7299	254-4555
Lexington Convention Center 430 W Vine St	Lexington	KY	40507	606-233-4567	253-2718
Lexington Mayor 200 E Main St Fayette Government Ctr *Web:* www.lfucg.com/ucg1.htm	Lexington	KY	40507	606-258-3100	258-3194
Lexington Planning Div 200 E Main St Fayette Government Ctr *Web:* www.lfucg.com/adserv.htm#plannin	Lexington	KY	40507	606-258-3160	258-3163
Lexington Public Library 140 E Main St *Web:* www.lexpublib.org	Lexington	KY	40507	606-231-5500	231-5598

On-Line Resources

4Lexington.com	www.4lexington.com
About.com Guide to Lexington	lexington.about.com/local/southeastus/lexington
Anthill City Guide Lexington	www.anthill.com/city.asp?city=lexington
Area Guide Lexington	lexington.areaguides.net
City Knowledge Lexington	www.cityknowledge.com/ky_lexington.htm
DigitalCity Lexington	home.digitalcity.com/lexington
Excite.com Lexington City Guide	www.excite.com/travel/countries/united_states/kentucky/lexington
Insiders' Guide to Greater Lexington	www.insiders.com/lexington-ky
Insiders' Guide to Lexington	www.insiders.com/lexington-ky/
Lex Info	www.lexinfo.com/
Lexington CityLink	www.usacitylink.com/citylink/lexing
Lexington Kentucky	lexington-kentucky.com
Lexington Online	www.lexington-on-line.com/
METROSPIN	www.metrospin.com

— Transportation Services —

AIRPORTS

■ **Blue Grass Airport (LEX)**

	Phone
5 miles W of downtown (approx 15 minutes)	606-425-3114

Airport Transportation

	Phone
Gold Shield Limo $17 fare to downtown	606-255-6388
Taxi Service $12 fare to downtown	606-231-8294

Commercial Airlines

	Phone		Phone
Atlantic Southeast	800-282-3424	**Northwest**	606-277-0245
Comair	606-231-7571	**TWA Express**	800-221-2000
Continental	800-525-0280	**United Express**	606-253-3800
Delta	800-221-1212		

Charter Airlines

	Phone		Phone
Blue Grass Charter	606-233-2152	**TAC Air**	606-255-7724
Comair Jet Express	606-767-3500	**United Transportation Co**	606-233-4890
Executive Express Inc	606-225-5449	**Wilkinson Flying Service Inc**	606-293-2999
Richmor Aviation Inc	800-359-2299	**Wombles Charters**	606-887-4611
Sprite Flite Jets	800-354-9232		

CAR RENTALS

	Phone		Phone
Avis	606-252-5581	**Enterprise**	606-271-9697
Budget	606-254-5400	**Hertz**	606-254-3496
CarTemps USA	606-273-2366	**National**	606-254-8806

Lexington (Cont'd)

LIMO/TAXI

	Phone
Gold Shield Limo	606-255-6388
Happy's Limousine	606-252-1541
Taxi Service	606-231-8294

MASS TRANSIT

	Phone
LexTran $.80 Base fare	606-252-4936

RAIL/BUS

				Phone
Greyhound Bus Station 477 New Circle Rd TF: 800-231-2222	Lexington	KY	40511	606-299-8804

— Accommodations —

HOTELS, MOTELS, RESORTS

				Phone	Fax
American Inn 826 New Circle Rd NE	Lexington	KY	40505	606-231-5890	
Best Western Regency Inn 2241 Elkhorn Rd TF: 800-528-1234	Lexington	KY	40505	606-293-2202	293-1821
Blue Grass Suites 2400 Buena Vista Rd	Lexington	KY	40505	606-293-6113	299-1424
Bryan Station Inn 273 E New Circle Rd	Lexington	KY	40505	606-299-4162	
Campbell House Inn 1375 Harrodsburg Rd TF: 800-354-9235	Lexington	KY	40504	606-255-4281	254-4368
Carter Caves State Resort Park 344 Caveland Dr TF: 800-325-0059	Olive Hill	KY	41164	606-286-4411	286-8165
Comfort Inn 2381 Buena Vista Dr TF: 800-228-5150	Lexington	KY	40505	606-299-0302	299-2306
Comfort Suites 5527 Athens-Boonesboro Rd TF: 800 228-5150	Lexington	KY	40509	606-263-0777	263-0781
Congress Inn 1700 N Broadway	Lexington	KY	40505	606-299-6226	
Continental Inn 801 New Circle Rd TF: 800-432-9388	Lexington	KY	40505	606-299-5281	293-5905
Courtyard by Marriott 775 Newtown Ct TF: 800-321-2582 ■ *Web:* courtyard.com/LEXNO	Lexington	KY	40511	606-253-4646	253-9118
Day's Inn South 5575 Athens-Boonesboro Rd TF: 800-329-7466	Lexington	KY	40509	606-263-3100	263-3120
Days Inn Lexington 1987 N Broadway TF: 800-333-9843	Lexington	KY	40505	606-299-1202	299-5760
Econo Lodge North 925 Newtown Pike TF: 800-394-8402	Lexington	KY	40511	606-231-6300	231-0651
Econo Lodge South 5527 Athens-Boonesboro Rd TF: 800-553-2666	Lexington	KY	40509	606-263-5101	263-5101
Extended StayAmerica 2650 Wilhite Dr TF: 800-398-7829	Lexington	KY	40503	606-278-9600	278-9900
Fairfield Inn by Marriott 3050 Lakecrest Cir TF: 800-228-2800 ■ *Web:* fairfieldinn.com/LEXSW	Lexington	KY	40513	606-224-3338	224-3338
Gratz Park Inn 120 W 2nd St TF: 800-752-4166	Lexington	KY	40507	606-231-1777	233-7593
Greenleaf Inn 2280 Nicholasville Rd TF: 800-354-9096	Lexington	KY	40503	606-277-1191	277-1191
Hampton Inn 2251 Elkhorn Rd TF: 800-426-7866	Lexington	KY	40505	606-299-2613	299-9664
Hampton Inn South 3060 Lakecrest Cir TF: 800-296-0064	Lexington	KY	40513	606-223-0088	223-0088
Hilton Suites of Lexington Green 245 Lexington Green Cir TF: 800-445-8667	Lexington	KY	40503	606-271-4000	273-2975
Holiday Inn Express 2221 Elkhorn Rd TF: 800-465-4329	Lexington	KY	40505	606-293-0047	293-6544
Holiday Inn North 1950 Newtown Pike TF: 800-465-4329	Lexington	KY	40511	606-233-0512	231-9285
Holiday Inn South 5532 Athens-Boonesboro Rd TF: 800-465-4329	Lexington	KY	40509	606-263-5241	263-4333
Hyatt Regency 401 W High St TF: 800-233-1234 ■ *Web:* www.hyatt.com/usa/lexington/hotels/hotel_lexrl.html	Lexington	KY	40507	606-253-1234	233-7974
Kentucky Inn 525 Waller Ave TF: 800-221-6652	Lexington	KY	40504	606-254-1177	252-4913
Knights Inn 1935 Stanton Way TF: 800-843-5644	Lexington	KY	40511	606-231-0232	231-0511
La Quinta Inn 1919 Stanton Way TF: 800-531-5900	Lexington	KY	40511	606-231-7551	281-6002
Marriott's Griffin Gate Resort 1800 Newtown Pike TF: 800-228-9290 ■ *Web:* marriotthotels.com/LEXKY	Lexington	KY	40511	606-231-5100	255-9944
Microtel 2240 Buena Vista Dr TF: 800-844-8608	Lexington	KY	40505	606-299-9600	299-8719
Quality Inn Northwest 1050 Newtown Pike TF: 800-228-5151	Lexington	KY	40511	606-233-0561	231-6125
Radisson Plaza Hotel Lexington 369 W Vine St TF: 800-333-3333	Lexington	KY	40507	606-231-9000	281-3737
Ramada Inn 2143 N Broadway St TF: 800-272-6232	Lexington	KY	40505	606-299-1261	293-0048
Red Roof Inn North 1980 Haggard Ct TF: 800-843-7663	Lexington	KY	40505	606-293-2626	299-8353
Residence Inn by Marriott 1080 Newtown Pike TF: 800-331-3131 ■ *Web:* www.residenceinn.com/LEXNN	Lexington	KY	40511	606-231-6191	231-6191
Sheraton Suites 2601 Richmond Rd TF: 800-325-3535	Lexington	KY	40509	606-268-0060	268-6209
Springs Inn 2020 Harrodsburg Rd TF: 800-354-9503	Lexington	KY	40503	606-277-5751	277-3142
StudioPLUS 3575 Tates Creek Rd TF: 800-646-8000 ■ *Web:* www.studioplus.com	Lexington	KY	40517	606-271-6160	245-8936
StudioPLUS 2750 Gribbin Dr TF: 888-788-3467	Lexington	KY	40517	606-266-4800	268-6565
Travelodge 2250 Elkhorn Rd TF: 800-578-7878	Lexington	KY	40505	606-299-8481	293-2472
Wyndham Garden Hotel 1938 Stanton Way TF: 800-996-3426	Lexington	KY	40511	606-259-1311	233-3658

— Restaurants —

				Phone
A La Lucie (Continental) 159 N Limestone St	Lexington	KY	40507	606-252-5277
Alfalfa (Vegetarian) 557 S Limestone St	Lexington	KY	40508	606-253-0014
AP Suggins Bar & Grill (American) 345 Romany Rd	Lexington	KY	40502	606-268-0709
Atomic Cafe (Caribbean) 265 N Limestone St	Lexington	KY	40503	606-254-1969
Billy's Bar B-Q (Barbecue) 101 Cochran Rd	Lexington	KY	40502	606-269-9593
Cheapside Bar & Grill (Southwest) 131 Cheapside St	Lexington	KY	40507	606-254-0046
Coach House The (Continental) 855 S Broadway	Lexington	KY	40504	606-252-7777
DeSha's (American) 109 N Broadway	Lexington	KY	40507	606-259-3771
Dudley's (Continental) 380 S Mill St	Lexington	KY	40508	606-252-1010
Jalapeno's (Mexican) 285 New Circle Rd NW	Lexington	KY	40505	606-299-8299
Joe Bologna's (Italian) 120 W Maxwell St	Lexington	KY	40508	606-252-4933
Ketch The (Seafood) 2012 Regency Rd	Lexington	KY	40503	606-277-5919
La Petite Rose (French) 121 N Mill St	Lexington	KY	40507	606-254-1907
Lexington City Brewery (American) 1050 S Broadway	Lexington	KY	40502	606-259-2739
Mansion at Griffin Gate (Continental) 1800 Newtown Pike	Lexington	KY	40511	606-288-6142
Marikka's (German) 411 Southland Dr	Lexington	KY	40503	606-275-1925
Mason's (Continental) 438 S Ashland Ave	Lexington	KY	40502	606-266-8382
Merrick Inn (Continental) 3380 Tates Creek Rd	Lexington	KY	40502	606-269-5417
Oasis The (Mediterranean) 868 E High St	Lexington	KY	40508	606-268-0414
Phil Dunn's Cookshop (American) 431 Old Vine St	Lexington	KY	40507	606-231-0099
Rafferty's (American) 2420 Nicholasville Rd	Lexington	KY	40503	606-278-9427
Ramsey's (American) 496 E High St	Lexington	KY	40507	606-259-2708
Siam (Thai) 126 New Circle Rd	Lexington	KY	40505	606-231-7975
Zuni (French) 890 E High St	Lexington	KY	40502	606-266-8357

— Goods and Services —

SHOPPING

				Phone	Fax
Bluegrass Bazaar 246 Walton Ave	Lexington	KY	40502	606-259-0303	
Civic Center Shops 410 West Vine St	Lexington	KY	40507	606-233-4567	
Dudley Square 380 S Mill & Maxwell St	Lexington	KY	40508		
Factory Stores of America 401 Outlet Center Dr *Web:* www.factorystores.com/	Georgetown	KY	40324	502-868-0682	
Fayette Mall 3401 Nicholasville Rd	Lexington	KY	40503	606-272-3493	273-6376
Lexington Mall 2349 Richmond Rd	Lexington	KY	40502	606-269-5393	
Mall at Lexington Green 3199 Nicholasville Rd	Lexington	KY	40503	606-245-1513	
Patchen Village 153-154 Patchen Dr	Lexington	KY	40517	606-266-6664	
Triangle Center 325 W Main St	Lexington	KY	40507	606-231-1085	
Turfland Mall 2033 Turfland Mall	Lexington	KY	40504	606-276-4411	277-2892
Victorian Square 401 W Main St	Lexington	KY	40507	606-252-7575	254-4496

BANKS

				Phone	Fax
Bank One Lexington NA 201 E Main St	Lexington	KY	40507	606-231-2696	231-2175

Lexington — Banks (Cont'd)

	City	State	ZIP	Phone	Fax
Central Bank & Trust Co 300 W Vine St	Lexington	KY	40507	606-253-6222	253-6100
TF: 800-637-6884					
Community Trust Bank 100 E Vine St	Lexington	KY	40507	606-389-5350	233-1320
Firstar Bank 2020 Nicholasville Rd	Lexington	KY	40503	606-232-8199	232-8164
National City Bank Kentucky 301 E Main St	Lexington	KY	40507	606-281-5100	281-5238
PNC Bank 200 W Vine St	Lexington	KY	40507	606-281-0400	281-0459

BUSINESS SERVICES

	Phone
Adecco Employment Personnel Services	606-263-1212
Airborne Express	800-247-2676
BAX Global	800-225-5229
Dacher Express	606-255-3884
DHL Worldwide Express	800-225-5345
Federal Express	800-238-5355
Interim Personnel Services	606-231-0801
Kelly Services	606-223-2416
Kinko's	606-253-1360
Mail Boxes Etc	800-789-4623
Post Office	606-231-6700
Snelling Personnel Services	606-223-1115
UPS	800-742-5877
Zip Express	606-254-0001

— Media —

PUBLICATIONS

	City	State	ZIP	Phone	Fax
Lexington Herald-Leader‡ 100 Midland Ave	Lexington	KY	40508	606-231-3100	254-9738
TF: 800-274-7355 ■ *Web:* www.kentuckyconnect.com/heraldleader ■ *E-mail:* hledit@lex.infi.net					

‡*Daily newspapers*

TELEVISION

	City	State	ZIP	Phone	Fax
WDKY-TV Ch 56 (Fox) 836 Euclid Ave	Lexington	KY	40502	606-269-5656	269-3774
WKLE-TV Ch 46 (PBS) 600 Cooper Dr	Lexington	KY	40502	606-258-7000	258-7399
WKYT-TV Ch 27 (CBS) 2851 Winchester Rd	Lexington	KY	40509	606-299-0411	293-1578
Web: www.wkyt.com ■ *E-mail:* fbme52a@prodigy.com					
WLEX-TV Ch 18 (NBC) 1065 Russell Cave Rd	Lexington	KY	40505	606-255-4404	255-2418
Web: www.wlextv.com ■ *E-mail:* wlex@mis.net					
WTVQ-TV Ch 36 (ABC) 6940 Man O War Blvd	Lexington	KY	40509	606-233-3600	293-5002
Web: www.wtvq.com					

RADIO

	City	State	ZIP	Phone	Fax
WBUL-FM 98.1 MHz (Ctry) 3549 Russell Cave Rd	Lexington	KY	40511	606-293-0563	299-3898
WEKU-FM 88.9 MHz (NPR) 521 Lancaster Ave 102 Perkins Bldg-EKU	Richmond	KY	40475	606-622-1660	622-6276
TF: 800-621-8890 ■ *Web:* www.weku.org ■ *E-mail:* weku@acs.eku.edu					
WGKS-FM 96.9 MHz (AC) PO Box 11788	Lexington	KY	40578	606-233-1515	233-1517
WKQQ-FM 100.1 MHz (CR) 1498 Trade Ctr Dr	Lexington	KY	40505	606-252-6694	252-8505
Web: www.wkqq.com ■ *E-mail:* catduvh@aol.com					
WLAP-AM 630 kHz (N/T) 3549 Russell Cave Rd	Lexington	KY	40511	606-293-0563	299-3898
WLRO-FM 101.5 MHz (Oldies) 300 W Vine St	Lexington	KY	40507	606-253-5900	253-5903
WMXL-FM 94.5 MHz (AC) 3549 Russell Cave Rd	Lexington	KY	40511	606-293-0563	299-3898
WUKY-FM 91.3 MHz (NPR) 340 McVey Hall University of Kentucky	Lexington	KY	40506	606-257-3221	257-6291
Web: wuky.uky.edu ■ *E-mail:* wuky913@ukcc.uky.edu					
WVLK-FM 92.9 MHz (Ctry) 300 W Vine St	Lexington	KY	40507	606-253-5900	253-5903
Web: www.k93.com ■ *E-mail:* k93@mis.net					

— Colleges/Universities —

	City	State	ZIP	Phone	Fax
Asbury College 1 Macklem Dr	Wilmore	KY	40390	606-858-3511	858-3921
TF Admissions: 800-888-1818 ■ *Web:* www.asbury.edu ■ *E-mail:* admissions@asbury.edu					
Berea College 101 Chestnut St	Berea	KY	40403	606-986-9341	986-7476
TF Admissions: 800-326-5948 ■ *Web:* www.berea.edu ■ *E-mail:* Claude_Hammond@berea.edu					
Centre College of Kentucky 600 W Walnut St	Danville	KY	40422	606-238-5200	238-5373
TF Admissions: 800-423-6236 ■ *Web:* www.centre.edu ■ *E-mail:* admission@centre.edu					
Eastern Kentucky University 521 Lancaster Ave	Richmond	KY	40475	606-622-1000	622-1020
TF: 800-465-9191 ■ *Web:* www.eku.edu					
Fugazzi College 407 Marquis Ave	Lexington	KY	40502	606-266-0401	268-2118
Georgetown College 400 E College St	Georgetown	KY	40324	502-863-8000	868-8891
TF Admissions: 800-788-9985 ■ *Web:* www.georgetowncollege.edu ■ *E-mail:* admissions@gtc.georgetown.ky.us					
Kentucky College of Business 628 E Main St	Lexington	KY	40508	606-253-0621	233-3054
Lexington Community College Cooper Dr 203 Oswald Bldg	Lexington	KY	40506	606-257-4872	257-2634
Web: www.uky.edu/LCC ■ *E-mail:* lccweb@pop.uky.edu					
Transylvania University 300 N Broadway	Lexington	KY	40508	606-233-8300	233-8797
TF Admissions: 800-872-6798 ■ *Web:* www.transy.edu ■ *E-mail:* admsapp@music.transy.edu					
University of Kentucky 100 Funkhouser Bldg	Lexington	KY	40506	606-257-9000	257-3823
Web: www.uky.edu ■ *E-mail:* rmills@pop.uky.edu					

— Hospitals —

	City	State	ZIP	Phone	Fax
Central Baptist Hospital 1740 Nicholasville Rd	Lexington	KY	40503	606-275-6100	260-6935*
**Fax:* Admitting					
Chandler Medical Center University of Kentucky	Lexington	KY	40536	606-323-5000	257-2184*
**Fax:* Admitting ■ *Web:* www.mc.uky.edu					
Saint Joseph Hospital 1 St Joseph Dr	Lexington	KY	40504	606-278-3436	260-8000
Saint Joseph Hospital 150 N Eagle Creek Dr	Lexington	KY	40509	606-268-4800	268-3766
Samaritan Hospital 310 S Limestone St	Lexington	KY	40508	606-252-6612	259-1627
Shriners Hospitals for Children Lexington Unit 1900 Richmond Rd	Lexington	KY	40502	606-266-2101	268-5636
TF: 800-668-4634 ■ *Web:* www.shrinershq.org/Hospitals/Directry/lexington.html					
Veterans Affairs Medical Center Lexington 2250 Leestown Rd	Lexington	KY	40511	606-233-4511	281-4970

— Attractions —

	City	State	ZIP	Phone	Fax
American Saddle Horse Museum 4093 Iron Works Pkwy	Lexington	KY	40511	606-259-2746	255-4909
TF: 800-829-4438 ■ *Web:* www.lexinfo.com/museum/saddle.html ■ *E-mail:* asbfan@aol.com					
ArtsPlace 161 N Mill St	Lexington	KY	40507	606-255-2951	255-2787
Ashland-The Henry Clay Estate 120 Sycamore Rd	Lexington	KY	40502	606-266-8581	
Web: www.henryclay.org					
Aviation Museum of Kentucky Hangar Dr Blue Grass Airport	Lexington	KY	40544	606-231-1219	277-7118
Web: www.dynasty.net/users/rawham/kyairmus.htm					
Bluegrass Scenic Railroad & Museum Beasley Rd Woodford County Pk	Versailles	KY	40383	606-873-2476	223-2363
Cathedral of Christ the King 299 Colony Blvd	Lexington	KY	40502	606-268-2861	
Flag Fork Herb Farms 900 N Broadway	Lexington	KY	40505	606-233-7381	
Headley-Whitney Museum 4435 Old Frankfort Pike	Lexington	KY	40510	606-255-6653	255-8375
Web: www.headley-whitney.org					
Hopemont-The Hunt-Morgan House 201 N Mill St	Lexington	KY	40508	606-253-0362	
Hummel Arnim D Planetarium Eastern Kentucky University	Richmond	KY	40475	606-622-1547	622-6205
Jacobson Park Richmond Rd	Lexington	KY	40515	606-288-2900	
Kentucky Horse Center 3380 Paris Pike	Lexington	KY	40511	606-293-1853	299-1284
Kentucky Horse Park 4089 Iron Works Pike	Lexington	KY	40511	606-233-4303	254-0253
Web: www.imh.org/khp/hp1.html					
Kentucky Theater 214 E Main St	Lexington	KY	40507	606-231-6997	231-7924
E-mail: kytheatr@mis.net					
Labrot & Graham Distillery 7855 McCracken Pike	Versailles	KY	40383	606-879-1812	879-1946
TF: 800-542-1812					

Lexington — Attractions (Cont'd)

				Phone	Fax
Lexington Ballet 161 N Mill St	Lexington	KY	40507	606-233-3925	
Lexington Cemetery 833 W Main St	Lexington	KY	40508	606-255-5522	
Lexington Children's Museum 401 W Main St Suite 309	Lexington	KY	40507	606-258-3253	258-3255
Lexington Opera House 401 W Short St *Web:* www.lfucg.com/opera.htm	Lexington	KY	40508	606-233-4567	253-2718
Lexington Philharmonic 161 N Mill St.	Lexington	KY	40507	606-233-4226	233-7896
Loudoun House 209 Castlewood Dr.	Lexington	KY	40505	606-254-7024	254-7214
Mary Todd Lincoln House 578 W Main St	Lexington	KY	40501	606-233-9999	
Masterson Station Park Leestown Rd	Lexington	KY	40511	606-288-2900	
McConnell Springs 416 Quarry Dr	Lexington	KY	40504	606-225-4073	
Raven Run Nature Sanctuary 588 Jacks Creek Pike	Lexington	KY	40515	606-272-6105	
Senator John Pope House 326 Grosvenor Ave	Lexington	KY	40508	606-253-0362	
Shaker Village of Pleasant Hill 3501 Lexington Rd *TF:* 800-734-5611 ■ *Web:* www.shakervillageky.org	Harrodsburg	KY	40330	606-734-5411	
Shillito Park Reynolds Rd	Lexington	KY	40503	606-288-2900	
University of Kentucky Art Museum Rose & Euclid Sts	Lexington	KY	40506	606-257-5716	323-1994
University of Kentucky Museum of Anthropology 211 Lafferty Hall	Lexington	KY	40506	606-257-1944	323-3686
Waveland Historical Site 225 Waveland Museum Ln	Lexington	KY	40514	606-272-3611	245-4269
Woodland Park Woodland Ave	Lexington	KY	40508	606-288-2900	

SPORTS TEAMS & FACILITIES

				Phone	Fax
Keeneland Race Course 4201 Versailles Rd *TF:* 800-456-3412 ■ *Web:* www.keeneland.com ■ *E-mail:* keeneland@keeneland.com	Lexington	KY	40510	606-254-3412	288-4348
Kentucky Thoroughblades (hockey) 430 W Vine St Rupp Arena *TF:* 888-259-1996 ■ *Web:* www.thoroughblades.com/ ■ *E-mail:* hockey@thoroughblades.com	Lexington	KY	40507	606-259-1996	252-3684
Red Mile Harness Track 1200 Red Mile Rd *Web:* www.tattersallsredmile.com	Lexington	KY	40504	606-255-0752	231-0217

— Events —

	Phone
All-Arabian Combined Classic I & II (early September)	606-233-4303
Bluegrass Classic Dog Show (early September)	606-527-3865
Bluegrass Festival Hunter/Jumper Show (mid-late August)	606-266-6937
Bluegrass State Games (mid-January & mid-late July)	606-255-0336
Boy's Sweet Sixteen Tournament (early March)	606-233-3535
Breyerfest (late July)	606-233-4303
Champagne Run Hunter/Jumper Show (late March)	606-263-4638
Festival of the Bluegrass (mid-June)	606-846-4995
Festival of the Horse (mid-September)	502-863-2547
Great American Brass Band Festival (mid-June)	800-755-0076
Harvest Festival (late September)	606-257-3221
High Hope Steeplechase (mid-May)	606-255-5727
July 4th Festival (early July)	606-258-3123
Kentucky Arabian Horse Assn Annual Show (early April)	502-241-5244
Kentucky Guild of Artists & Craftsmen Spring Fair (mid-May & early October)	606-986-3192
Kentucky High School Rodeo Assn Annual Rodeo (late May)	270-395-4889
Kentucky Hunter/Jumper Assn Show (late August)	606-266-6937
Kentucky National Hunter/Jumper Show (late September)	606-233-4303
Lexington Christmas Parade (early December)	606-231-7335
Lexington Egyptian Event (mid-June)	606-231-0771
Lexington Lions Club Bluegrass Fair (early March)	606-233-1465
Lexington Shakespeare Festival (July)	606-266-4423
Mayfest (early May)	606-231-7335
Memorial Stakes Day Chili Cook-off (late May)	606-255-0752
Mid-America Miniature Horse Assn Julep Cup (mid-July)	800-848-1224
Mid-South Regional Pony Club Rally (late June)	502-244-1797
Paso Fino Festival of the Bluegrass (mid-June)	513-724-3220
Polo at the Park (June-September)	606-233-4303
Red Mile Harness Racing Grand Circuit Meet (late September-early October)	606-255-0752
Rolex Kentucky Three Day Event (late April)	606-254-8123
Roots & Heritage Festival (mid-September)	606-231-2611
Saint Patrick's Day Parade (mid-March)	606-278-7349
Sheiks & Shreiks Arabian Fun Show (early November)	606-988-0805
Southern Lights Holiday Festival (mid-November-late December)	606-255-5727
Woodland Art Fair (mid-August)	606-254-7024

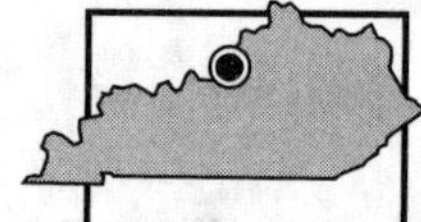

Louisville

Nicknamed the "Run for the Roses" and known as "the greatest two minutes in sports," the Kentucky Derby is held at Louisville's Churchill Downs each year on the first Saturday in May. Long known as the city's main social event, the oldest race in continuous existence in the U.S. is preceded by the two-week-long Kentucky Derby Festival, which includes parades, concerts, sports tournaments, and the Great Steamboat Race. The Kentucky Derby Museum is located next to Churchill Downs and has an outdoor paddock for the thoroughbreds on its grounds. The University of Louisville is home to interesting sites of its own, including the Photo Archives, one of the largest collections of photographs in the country; and the original town charter signed by Thomas Jefferson. Slugger Park, manufacturer of Louisville Slugger baseball bats, and the Belle of Louisville, the oldest Mississippi sternwheeler in the country, are also located in Louisville. Cultural attractions include the Museum of Nebraska History, Lincoln Botanical Garden and Arboretum, and the Great Plains Art Collection.

Population	255,045	**Longitude**	85-75-94 W
Area (Land)	62.1 sq mi	**County**	Jefferson
Area (Water)	4.5 sq mi	**Time Zone**	EST
Elevation	462 ft	**Area Code/s**	502
Latitude	38-25-42 N		

— Average Temperatures and Precipitation —

TEMPERATURES

	Jan	Feb	Mar	Apr	May	Jun	Jul	Aug	Sep	Oct	Nov	Dec
High	40	45	56	67	76	84	87	86	80	69	57	45
Low	23	27	36	45	55	63	67	66	59	46	37	29

PRECIPITATION

	Jan	Feb	Mar	Apr	May	Jun	Jul	Aug	Sep	Oct	Nov	Dec
Inches	2.9	3.3	4.7	4.2	4.6	3.5	4.5	3.5	3.2	2.7	3.7	3.6

— Important Phone Numbers —

	Phone		Phone
AAA	502-582-2222	**Medical Referral**	502-587-4912
American Express Travel	502-585-2368	**Poison Control Center**	502-589-8222
Dental Referral	502-459-7971	**Time/Temp**	502-585-5961
Emergency	911	**Travelers Aid**	502-584-8186
HotelDocs	800-468-3537	**Weather**	502-585-1212

— Information Sources —

				Phone	Fax
Better Business Bureau Serving Louisville Southern Indiana & Western Kentucky 844 S 4th St *Web:* www.ky-in.bbb.org	Louisville	KY	40203	502-583-6546	589-9940
Commonwealth Convention Center 221 4th St *TF:* 800-701-5831	Louisville	KY	40202	502-595-4381	584-9711
Greater Louisville Inc 600 W Main St *Web:* www.lacc.org	Louisville	KY	40202	502-625-0000	625-0010
Jefferson County 527 W Jefferson St *Web:* www.co.jefferson.ky.us	Louisville	KY	40202	502-574-5700	574-5566
Louisville & Jefferson County Convention & Visitors Bureau 400 S 1st St *TF:* 800-792-5595 ■ *Web:* www.louisville-visitors.com	Louisville	KY	40202	502-582-3732	584-6697
Louisville City Hall 601 W Jefferson St	Louisville	KY	40202	502-574-3333	
Louisville Economic Development Dept 600 W Main St	Louisville	KY	40202	502-625-0000	625-0211

Louisville — Information Sources (Cont'd)

				Phone	Fax
Louisville Mayor 601 W Jefferson St 1st Fl	Louisville	KY	40202	502-574-3061	574-4201
Louisville Public Library 301 York St *Web:* lfpl.org	Louisville	KY	40203	502-574-1600	574-1657

On-Line Resources

4Louisville.com	www.2louisville.com
About.com Guide to Louisville	louisville.about.com/local/southeastus/louisville
Anthill City Guide Louisville	www.anthill.com/city.asp?city=louisville
Area Guide Louisville	louisville.areaguides.net
City Knowledge Louisville	www.cityknowledge.com/ky_louisville.htm
Excite.com Louisville City Guide	www.excite.com/travel/countries/united_states/kentucky/louisville
Insiders' Guide to Greater Louisville	www.insiders.com/louisville/index.htm
Links @ Louisville	www.johnpaul.com/links/
Louisville Kentucky	louisville-kentucky.com
Louisville Scene	www.louisvillescene.com/
Louisville.com	www.louisville.com/
Louisville.net	www.louisville.net/
LouisvilleOnLine	www.louonline.com

— Transportation Services —

AIRPORTS

■ Louisville International Airport (SDF)

	Phone
5 miles S of downtown (approx 5 minutes) Web: louintlairport.com ■ *E-mail:* raa@louintlairport.com	502-368-6524

Airport Transportation

	Phone
Louisville Cab $8-12 fare to downtown	502-636-5511
TARC $1 fare to downtown	502-585-1234
Yellow Cab $12-15 fare to downtown	502-636-5511

Commercial Airlines

	Phone		Phone
American	800-433-7300	**Northwest**	800-225-2525
American Eagle	800-433-7300	**Southwest**	800-435-9792
Comair	800-354-9822	**United**	800-241-6522
Delta	502-361-6805	**US Airways**	800-428-4322

Charter Airlines

	Phone		Phone
Alliance Executive Charter Services	800-232-5387	**James Flying Service**	800-556-4221
Grand Aire Express Inc	800-704-7263	**Tag Aviation**	800-235-9724

CAR RENTALS

	Phone		Phone
Avis	502-368-5851	**Hertz**	502-361-0181
Budget	502-363-4300	**National**	502-361-2515
Dollar	502-366-1600	**Thrifty**	502-368-5287
Enterprise	502-458-5522		

LIMO/TAXI

	Phone		Phone
Ambassador Capital Limousine	502-964-7139	**Miller Transportation**	502-368-5644
Cosmopolitan Limousine	502-966-5466	**Supreme Limousine Service**	502-772-0200
Louisville Cab	502-636-5511		

MASS TRANSIT

	Phone
TARC $1 Base fare	502-585-1234

RAIL/BUS

				Phone
Greyhound Bus Station 720 W Muhammad Ali Blvd *TF:* 800-231-2222	Louisville	KY	40203	502-561-2801

— Accommodations —

HOTELS, MOTELS, RESORTS

				Phone	Fax
AmeriSuites 701 S Hurstbourne Pkwy *TF:* 800-833-1516	Louisville	KY	40222	502-426-0119	426-3013
Best Western Ashton Inn Suites 653 Phillips Ln *TF:* 888-527-4866	Louisville	KY	40209	502-375-2233	375-2237
Best Western Brownsboro Inn 4805 Brownsboro Rd *TF:* 800-528-1234	Louisville	KY	40207	502-893-2551	895-2417
Best Western Regency Louisville 1301 Kentucky Mills Dr *TF:* 800-528-1234	Louisville	KY	40299	502-267-8100	267-8100
Breckinridge Inn 2800 Breckinridge Ln	Louisville	KY	40220	502-456-5050	451-1577
Camberley Brown Hotel 335 W Broadway St *TF:* 800-555-8000	Louisville	KY	40202	502-583-1234	587-7006
Club Hotel by Doubletree 101 E Jefferson St *TF:* 888-444-2582	Louisville	KY	40202	502-585-2200	584-5657
Comfort Inn Airport 571 Phillips Ln *TF:* 800-228-5150	Louisville	KY	40209	502-361-5008	361-0037
Comfort Suites 1850 Resource Way *TF:* 800-228-5150	Louisville	KY	40299	502-266-6509	266-9014
Courtyard by Marriott 9608 Blairwood Rd *TF:* 800-321-2211 ■ *Web:* courtyard.com/SDFCH	Louisville	KY	40222	502-429-0006	429-5926
Days Inn Central 1620 Arthur St *TF:* 800-329-7466	Louisville	KY	40217	502-636-3781	634-9544
Doubletree Hotel 9700 Bluegrass Pkwy *TF:* 800-222-8733	Louisville	KY	40299	502-491-4830	499-2893
Executive Inn 978 Phillips Ln *TF:* 800-626-2706 ■ *E-mail:* executiveinn@att.net	Louisville	KY	40209	502-367-6161	363-1880
Executive West Hotel 830 Phillips Ln *TF:* 800-626-2708 ■ *Web:* wl.iglou.com/exwest/	Louisville	KY	40209	502-367-2251	363-2087
Extended StayAmerica 6101 Dutchmans Ln *TF:* 800-398-7029	Louisville	KY	40205	502-895-7707	895-6900
Fairfield Inn Hurstbourne 9400 Blairwood Rd *TF:* 800-228-2800 ■ *Web:* fairfieldinn.com/SDFFI	Louisville	KY	40222	502-339-1900	339-2494
Galt House East 141 N 4th Ave *TF:* 800-626-1814 ■ *Web:* www.galthouse.com ■ *E-mail:* info@galthouse.com	Louisville	KY	40202	502-589-5200	585-4266
Galt House Hotel 140 N 4th Ave *TF:* 800-626-1814 ■ *Web:* www.galthouse.com ■ *E-mail:* info@galthouse.com	Louisville	KY	40202	502-589-5200	585-4266
Hampton Inn 1902 Embassy Square Blvd *TF:* 800-426-7866	Louisville	KY	40299	502-491-2577	491-1325
Holiday Inn Airport East 1465 Gardiner Ln *TF:* 800-465-4329	Louisville	KY	40213	502-452-6361	451-1541
Holiday Inn Airport South 3317 Fern Valley Rd *TF:* 800-465-4329 ■ *Web:* www.basshotels.com/holiday-inn/?_franchisee=SDFSO ■ *E-mail:* dos4hias@aol.com	Louisville	KY	40213	502-964-3311	966-4874
Holiday Inn Downtown 120 W Broadway St *TF:* 800-626-1558	Louisville	KY	40202	502-582-2241	584-8591
Holiday Inn Hurstbourne 1325 Hurstbourne Pkwy *TF:* 800-465-4329 ■ *Web:* www.basshotels.com/holiday-inn/?_franchisee=SDFEA ■ *E-mail:* sdfea@ix.netcom.com	Louisville	KY	40222	502-426-2600	423-1605
Hyatt Regency 320 W Jefferson St *TF:* 800-233-1234 ■ *Web:* www.hyatt.com/usa/louisville/hotels/hotel_sdfrl.html	Louisville	KY	40202	502-587-3434	581-0133
Inn & Suites 3315 Bardstown Rd *TF:* 800-228-5151	Louisville	KY	40218	502-452-1501	452-1501
Inn at Jewish Hospital 100 E Jefferson St	Louisville	KY	40202	502-582-2481	582-3511
Marriott Hotel East 1903 Embassy Square Blvd *TF:* 800-228-9290 ■ *Web:* marriotthotels.com/SDFEA	Louisville	KY	40299	502-499-6220	499-2480
Microtel Inn 1221 Kentucky Mills Dr *TF:* 888-333-8188	Louisville	KY	40299	502-266-6590	266-6467
Park Mammoth Resort I-65 & Hwy 31 W	Park City	KY	42160	270-749-4101	749-2524
Ramada Hotel Airport East 1921 Bishop Ln *TF:* 800-272-6232	Louisville	KY	40218	502-456-4411	456-2592
Red Carpet Inn 1640 S Hurstbourne Pkwy *TF:* 800-251-1962	Louisville	KY	40220	502-491-7320	499-7617
Red Roof Inn 4704 Preston Hwy *TF:* 800-843-7663	Louisville	KY	40213	502-968-0151	968-0194
Residence Inn by Marriott 120 N Hurstbourne Pkwy *TF:* 800-331-3131 ■ *Web:* www.residenceinn.com/SDFHF	Louisville	KY	40222	502-425-1821	425-1672
Royal Inn 4444 Dixie Hwy	Louisville	KY	40216	502-448-9502	
Seelbach Hilton Hotel 500 S 4th St *TF:* 800-333-3399	Louisville	KY	40202	502-585-3200	585-9239

Louisville — Hotels, Motels, Resorts (Cont'd)

				Phone	Fax
Signature Inn South 6515 Signature Dr	Louisville	KY	40213	502-968-4100	968-4100
TF: 800-822-5252 ■ *Web:* www.signature-inns.com/locations/louisville_s ■ *E-mail:* feedback@signature-inns.com					
Sleep Inn 3330 Preston Hwy	Louisville	KY	40213	502-368-9597	375-0698
TF: 800-753-3746					
StudioPLUS 1401 Browns Ln	Louisville	KY	40207	502-897-2559	894-2369
TF: 888-788-3467					
StudioPLUS 9801 Bunsen Pkwy	Louisville	KY	40299	502-499-6215	495-3551
TF: 800-398-7829					
Travelodge 401 S 2nd St	Louisville	KY	40202	502-583-2841	583-2629
TF: 800-578-7878					
Travelodge 9340 Blairwood Rd	Louisville	KY	40222	502-425-8010	425-2689
TF: 800-578-7878					
Wilson Inn Airport 3200 Kemmons Dr	Louisville	KY	40218	502-473-0000	473-0000
TF: 800-945-7667					

— Restaurants —

				Phone
100 East (American) 100 E Jefferson St	Louisville	KY	40208	502-582-2481
211 Clover Lane (International) 211 Clover Ln	Louisville	KY	40207	502-896-9570
610 Magnolia (Continental) 610 Magnolia St	Louisville	KY	40208	502-636-0783
Asiana Restaurant (Korean) 2039 Frankfort Ave	Louisville	KY	40206	502-893-0380
Asiatique (Pan-Asian) 106 Sears Ave	Louisville	KY	40207	502-899-3578
Azalea (New American) 3612 Brownsboro Rd	Louisville	KY	40207	502-895-5493
Bluegrass Brewing Co (American) 3929 Shelbyville Rd	Louisville	KY	40207	502-899-7070
Brasserie Deitrich (International) 2862 Frankfort Ave	Louisville	KY	40206	502-897-6076
Buck's (Continental) 425 W Ormsby Ave	Louisville	KY	40203	502-637-5284
Cafe Kilimanjaro (International) 649 S 4th St	Louisville	KY	40202	502-583-4332
Cafe Metro (Continental) 1700 Bardstown Rd	Louisville	KY	40205	502-458-4830
China Inn (Chinese) 1925 S 4th St	Louisville	KY	40208	502-636-2020
Chung King Palace (Chinese) 110 E Market St	Louisville	KY	40202	502-584-8880
Clark's Bar-B-Que (Barbecue) 6728 Johnsontown Rd	Louisville	KY	40272	502-933-5577
Cottage Inn (American) 570 Eastern Pkwy	Louisville	KY	40217	502-637-4325
Darryl's 1815 Restaurant (American) 3110 Bardstown Rd	Louisville	KY	40205	502-458-1815
De La Torre's (Spanish) 1606 Bardstown Rd	Louisville	KY	40205	502-456-4955
Delta Restaurant (Mexican) 434 W Market St	Louisville	KY	40202	502-584-0860
Dillon's Steakhouse (Steak) 2101 S Hurstbourne Pkwy	Louisville	KY	40220	502-499-7106
Ditto's Food & Drink (American) 1114 Bardstown Rd	Louisville	KY	40204	502-581-9129
El Mundo (Mexican) 2345 Frankfort Ave	Louisville	KY	40206	502-899-9930
English Grill (American) 335 W Broadway St	Louisville	KY	40202	502-583-1234
Equus (American) 122 Sears Ave	Louisville	KY	40207	502-897-9721
Ferd Grisanti's (Italian) 10212 Taylorsville Rd	Louisville	KY	40299	502-267-0050
Fifth Quarter (American) 1241 Durrett Ln	Louisville	KY	40213	502-361-2363
Fishhouse (Seafood) 1310 Winter Ave	Louisville	KY	40204	502-568-2993
Flagship at the Galt House (American) 140 N 4th Ave	Louisville	KY	40202	502-589-5200
Gasthaus (German) 4812 Brownsboro Ctr	Louisville	KY	40207	502-899-7177
Hungry Pelican (Seafood) 400 S 4th St	Louisville	KY	40202	502-581-1481
Irish Rover The (Irish) 2319 Frankfort Ave	Louisville	KY	40206	502-899-3544
Jillian's (American) 630 Barret Ave	Louisville	KY	40204	502-589-2739
Judge Roy Bean's (Southwest) 1801 Bardstown Rd	Louisville	KY	40205	502-451-4982
Kunz's (Continental) 115 S 4th Ave	Louisville	KY	40202	502-585-5555
Le Relais (French) 2817 Taylorsville Rd Bowman Field	Louisville	KY	40205	502-451-9020
Lilly's (Southern) 1147 Bardstown Rd	Louisville	KY	40204	502-451-0447
Lynn's Paradise Cafe (American) 984 Barret Ave	Louisville	KY	40204	502-583-3447
Market Place Grill (American) 301 W Market St	Louisville	KY	40202	502-584-8337
Mayan Gypsy (Mayan) 813 E Market St	Louisville	KY	40206	502-583-3300
Oakroom The (American) 500 4th Ave	Louisville	KY	40202	502-585-3200
Pat's Steak House (Steak) 2437 Brownsboro Rd	Louisville	KY	40206	502-896-9234
Pete's Cajun 99 (Cajun) 1616 Grinstead Dr	Louisville	KY	40204	502-561-9551
Restaurant at Actors Theatre (American) 316 W Main St	Louisville	KY	40202	502-584-1205
Rib Tavern (Barbecue) 4157 Bardstown Rd	Louisville	KY	40218	502-499-1515
Rudyard Kipling (International) 422 W Oak St	Louisville	KY	40203	502-636-1311
Shariat's (Continental) 2901 Brownsboro Rd	Louisville	KY	40206	502-899-7878
Spire Restaurant & Bar (American) 320 W Jefferson St	Louisville	KY	40202	502-587-3434
Szechuan Garden (Chinese/Thai) 9850 Linn Station Rd	Louisville	KY	40223	502-426-6767
Timothy's (Continental) 826 E Broadway	Louisville	KY	40204	502-561-0880
Veranda The (International) 15206 Shelbyville Rd	Louisville	KY	40245	502-253-0580
Vince Staten's Old Time Barbecue (Barbecue) 9291 US 42	Louisville	KY	40059	502-228-7427
Vincenzo's (Continental) 150 S 5th St	Louisville	KY	40202	502-580-1350
Zephyr Cove (New American) 2330 Frankfort Ave	Louisville	KY	40206	502-897-1030

— Goods and Services —

SHOPPING

				Phone	Fax
Bashford Manor Mall 3600 Bardstown Rd & Hikes Ln	Louisville	KY	40218	502-459-9600	
Galleria The 4th Ave & Liberty St	Louisville	KY	40202	502-584-7170	
Jefferson Mall 4801 Outerloop Rd	Louisville	KY	40219	502-968-4101	
Kentucky Art & Craft Gallery 609 W Main St	Louisville	KY	40202	502-589-0102	589-0154
Lazarus 7900 Shelbyville Rd	Louisville	KY	40222	502-423-3212	423-3317
Louisville Antique Mall 900 Goss Ave	Louisville	KY	40217	502-635-2852	
Mall Saint Matthews 5000 Shelbyville Rd	Louisville	KY	40207	502-893-0311	897-5849
Oxmoor Center 7900 Shelbyville Rd	Louisville	KY	40222	502-426-3000	425-3417

BANKS

				Phone	Fax
Bank One Kentucky NA 416 W Jefferson St	Louisville	KY	40202	502-566-2000	566-3614
Firstar Bank 1 Financial Sq	Louisville	KY	40202	502-562-6000	562-6659
Mid-America Bank of Louisville & Trust Co 500 W Broadway St	Louisville	KY	40202	502-589-3351	562-5402
TF: 800-925-0810					
National City Bank PO Box 36000	Louisville	KY	40233	502-581-4200	581-4015*
**Fax:* Cust Svc ■ *TF:* 800-727-8686					
PNC Bank Kentucky 500 W Jefferson St	Louisville	KY	40202	502-581-2100	581-2792
Stock Yards Bank & Trust Co 1040 E Main St	Louisville	KY	40206	502-582-2571	589-2855
TF: 800-625-9066					

BUSINESS SERVICES

	Phone		Phone
Federal Express	800-238-5355	**Olsten Staffing Services**	502-499-2442
Kelly Services	502-585-2171	**Post Office**	502-454-1650
Kinko's	502-429-8421	**UPS**	800-742-5877
Manpower Temporary Services	502-583-1674	**Zip Express Courier Service Inc**	502-587-3487

— Media —

PUBLICATIONS

				Phone	Fax
Business First 501 S 4th St Suite 130	Louisville	KY	40202	502-583-1731	587-1703
Web: www.amcity.com/louisville					
Courier-Journal‡ PO Box 740031	Louisville	KY	40201	502-582-4011	582-4200
TF: 800-765-4011 ■ *Web:* www.courier-journal.com					
Louisville Magazine 137 W Muhammad Ali Blvd Suite 101	Louisville	KY	40202	502-625-0100	625-0109
Web: www.louisville.com/loumag ■ *E-mail:* loumag@louisville.com					

‡Daily newspapers

TELEVISION

				Phone	Fax
WAVE-TV Ch 3 (NBC) 725 S Floyd St	Louisville	KY	40203	502-585-2201	561-4105
Web: www.wave3.com ■ *E-mail:* wave3mail@msn.com					
WBNA-TV Ch 21 (WB) 3701 Fern Valley Rd	Louisville	KY	40219	502-964-2121	966-9692
Web: www.wbna.com ■ *E-mail:* info@wbna.com					
WDRB-TV Ch 41 (Fox) 1 Independence Sq	Louisville	KY	40203	502-584-6441	589-5559
Web: www.fox41.com ■ *E-mail:* administration@fox41.com					
WFTE-TV Ch 58 (UPN) 5257 S Skyline Dr	Floyds Knobs	IN	47119	812-948-5800	949-9365
WHAS-TV Ch 11 (ABC) PO Box 1100	Louisville	KY	40201	502-582-7840	582-7279
Web: www.whas11.com ■ *E-mail:* info@whas11.com					
WKMJ-TV Ch 68 (PBS) 600 Cooper Dr	Lexington	KY	40502	606-258-7000	258-7390
TF: 800-432-0951					
WKPC-TV Ch 15 (PBS) 600 Cooper Dr	Lexington	KY	40502	606-258-7000	258-7390
WLKY-TV Ch 32 (CBS) PO Box 6205	Louisville	KY	40206	502-893-3671	896-0725
Web: www.wlky.com/ ■ *E-mail:* wlky@iglou.com					

RADIO

				Phone	Fax
WAMZ-FM 97.5 MHz (Ctry) 4000 One Radio Rd	Louisville	KY	40218	502-479-2222	479-2227
WAVG-AM 1450 kHz (Ctry) PO Box 726	Jeffersonville	IN	47130	812-285-5055	285-5060
WDJX-FM 99.7 MHz (AC) 612 S 4th Ave Suite 100	Louisville	KY	40202	502-589-4800	587-0212
WFIA-AM 900 kHz (Rel) 612 4th Ave Suite 100	Louisville	KY	40202	502-583-4811	583-4820
WFPK-FM 91.9 MHz (NPR) 301 York St	Louisville	KY	40203	502-574-1640	574-1671
E-mail: wfpk@iglou.com					
WFPL-FM 89.3 MHz (NPR) 301 York St	Louisville	KY	40203	502-574-1640	574-1671
E-mail: wfpl@iglou.com					
WGZB-FM 96.5 MHz (Urban) 1300 S 4th St Suite 200	Louisville	KY	40203	502-636-0600	636-0401
WHAS-AM 840 kHz (N/T) 4000 One Radio Rd	Louisville	KY	40218	502-479-2222	582-7837
Web: www.whas.com ■ *E-mail:* info@whas.com					

Louisville — Radio (Cont'd)

				Phone	Fax
WLLV-AM 1240 kHz (Rel) 2001 W Broadway Suite 13	Louisville	KY	40203	502-776-1240	776-1250
WLOU-AM 1350 kHz (Rel) 2001 W Broadway Dale Plaza	Louisville	KY	40203	502-776-1350	776-1250
WLRS-FM 102.3 MHz (Alt) 612 4th Ave Suite 100	Louisville	KY	40202	502-585-5178	587-0212
WMHX-FM 103.9 (NAC) 612 S 4th Ave Suite 100	Louisville	KY	40202	502-589-4800	587-0212
WMJM-FM 101.3 MHz (AC) 1300 S 4th St Suite 200	Louisville	KY	40203	502-636-0600	636-0401
WQMF-FM 95.7 MHz (CR) 4000 One Radio Rd. *Web:* www.wqmf.com	Louisville	KY	40218	502-479-2222	479-2227
WRKA-FM 103.1 MHz (Oldies) 10001 Linn Stn Rd *Web:* www.wrka.com	Louisville	KY	40223	502-423-9752	423-0231
WRVI-FM 105.9 MHz (AC) 10001 Linn Station Rd.	Louisville	KY	40223	502-423-9752	423-0231
WSFR-FM 107.7 MHz (CR) 612 S 4th Ave Suite 100	Louisville	KY	40202	502-589-4800	587-0212
WTFX-FM 100.5 MHz (Rock) 4000 One Radio Rd.	Louisville	KY	40218	502-479-2222	479-2227
WTMT-AM 620 kHz (Sports) 162 W Broadway	Louisville	KY	40202	502-583-6200	589-2979
WVEZ-FM 106.9 MHz (AC) 612 S 4th Ave Suite 100	Louisville	KY	40202	502-589-4800	587-0212
WWKY-AM 790 kHz (N/T) 4000 One Radio Rd.	Louisville	KY	40218	502-479-2222	479-2227

— Colleges/Universities —

				Phone	Fax
Bellarmine College 2001 Newburg Rd *TF:* 800-274-4723 ■ *Web:* www.bellarmine.edu	Louisville	KY	40205	502-452-8000	452-8002
Indiana University Southeast Campus 4201 Grant Line Rd. *Web:* www.ius.indiana.edu ■ *E-mail:* dcampbel@ius.indiana.edu	New Albany	IN	47150	812-941-2000	941-2595
Jefferson Community College 109 E Broadway *Web:* www.jcc.uky.edu	Louisville	KY	40202	502-584-0181	585-4425
Louisville Bible College PO Box 91046 *E-mail:* loubibcol@juno.com	Louisville	KY	40291	502-231-5221	231-5222
Louisville Technical Institute 3901 Atkinson Square Dr. *TF:* 800-844-6528 ■ *Web:* www.louisvilletech.com	Louisville	KY	40218	502-456-6509	456-2341
RETS Electronic Institute 300 Highrise Dr *TF:* 800-999-7387 ■ *Web:* www.retsaec.com	Louisville	KY	40213	502-968-7191	968-1727
Simmons Bible College 1811 Dumesnil St.	Louisville	KY	40210	502-776-1443	776-2227
Spalding University 851 S 4th St *TF:* 800-896-8941 ■ *Web:* www.spalding.edu	Louisville	KY	40203	502-585-9911	585-7128
Sullivan College 3101 Bardstown Rd *TF:* 800-844-1354	Louisville	KY	40205	502-456-6504	456-0040
University of Louisville 2301 S 3rd St *TF:* 800-334-8635 ■ *Web:* www.louisville.edu ■ *E-mail:* admitme@ulkyvm.louisville.edu	Louisville	KY	40292	502-852-5555	852-6526

— Hospitals —

				Phone	Fax
Baptist Hospital East 4000 Kresge Way	Louisville	KY	40207	502-897-8100	897-8500
Caritas Medical Center 1850 Bluegrass Ave.	Louisville	KY	40215	502-361-6000	361-6799
Columbia Audubon Hospital PO Box 17550	Louisville	KY	40217	502-636-7111	636-7216
Jewish Hospital 217 E Chestnut St *Web:* www.jhhs.org ■ *E-mail:* info@jhhs.org	Louisville	KY	40202	502-587-4011	587-4537
Norton Hospital 200 E Chestnut St	Louisville	KY	40202	502-629-8000	629-7591
Norton Southwest Hospital 9820 3rd Street Rd	Louisville	KY	40272	502-933-8100	933-8278
Norton Suburban Hospital 4001 Dutchmans Ln	Louisville	KY	40207	502-893-1000	893-1289
Tri-County Baptist Hospital 1025 New Moody Ln.	LaGrange	KY	40031	502-222-5388	222-3411
University of Louisville Hospital 545 S Jackson St	Louisville	KY	40202	502-562-3000	562-3831
Vencor Hospital Louisville 1313 St Anthony Pl.	Louisville	KY	40204	502-587-7001	587-0060
Veterans Affairs Medical Center 800 Zorn Ave	Louisville	KY	40206	502-895-3401	894-6155

— Attractions —

				Phone	Fax
Actors Theatre of Louisville 316 W Main St. *Web:* www.actorstheatre.org ■ *E-mail:* actors@aye.net	Louisville	KY	40202	502-584-1265	561-3300
American Printing House for the Blind 1839 Frankfort Ave *TF:* 800-223-1839 ■ *Web:* www.aph.org ■ *E-mail:* info@aph.org	Louisville	KY	40206	502-895-2405	899-2274
Belle of Louisville 401 W River Rd. *Web:* www.co.jefferson.ky.us/AttractionsBelle.html	Louisville	KY	40214	502-574-2355	574-3030
Brennan House Historic Home 631 S 5th St	Louisville	KY	40202	502-540-5145	587-6481
Broadway Series 611 W Main St *Web:* www.broadwayseries.com	Louisville	KY	40202	502-584-7469	584-2703
Brown Theater 315 W Broadway	Louisville	KY	40202	502-562-0188	
Bunbury Theatre 112 S 7th St	Louisville	KY	40202	502-585-5306	
Cathedral Heritage Foundation 429 W Muhammad Ali Blvd Suite 100 *Web:* www.cathedral-heritage.org	Louisville	KY	40202	502-583-3100	583-8524
Cave Hill Cemetery & Arboretum 701 Baxter Ave	Louisville	KY	40204	502-451-5630	451-5655
Cherokee Park Eastern Pkwy & Cherokee Pk	Louisville	KY	40233	502-456-8100	
Colonel Harland Sanders Museum 1441 Gardiner Ln	Louisville	KY	40213	502-874-8353	874-2195
Conrad-Caldwell House 1402 St James Ct.	Louisville	KY	40208	502-636-5023	
Farmington Historic Home 3033 Bardstown Rd.	Louisville	KY	40205	502-452-9920	456-1976
Filson Club Historical Society 1310 S 3rd St *Web:* www.filsonclub.org	Louisville	KY	40208	502-635-5083	635-5086
IMAX Theater 727 W Main St. *Web:* www.lsclouienet.org/imax.htm	Louisville	KY	40202	502-561-6100	561-6145
Iroquois Park Taylor Blvd & South Pkwy	Louisville	KY	40233	502-456-8100	
Kentucky Art & Craft Gallery 609 W Main St.	Louisville	KY	40202	502-589-0102	589-0154
Kentucky Center for the Arts 5 Riverfront Plaza *TF:* 800-775-7777 ■ *Web:* www.kca.org ■ *E-mail:* kca@sitesonthe.net	Louisville	KY	40202	502-562-0100	562-0150
Kentucky Derby Museum 704 Central Ave *TF:* 800-273-3729 ■ *Web:* www.derbymuseum.org ■ *E-mail:* info@derbymuseum.org	Louisville	KY	40208	502-634-0676	636-5855
Kentucky Opera Assn 101 S 8th St.	Louisville	KY	40202	502-584-4500	584-7484
Locust Grove Historic Home 561 Blankenbaker Ln. *Web:* www.locustgrove.org ■ *E-mail:* lghh@locustgrove.org	Louisville	KY	40207	502-897-9845	897-0103
Louisville Ballet 315 E Main St *Web:* www.louisvilleballet.org ■ *E-mail:* louballet1@ka.net	Louisville	KY	40202	502-583-3150	583-0006
Louisville Chorus 6303 Fern Valley Pass	Louisville	KY	40228	502-968-6300	962-1094
Louisville Fire History & Learning Center 3228 River Park Dr	Louisville	KY	40211	502-574-3731	
Louisville Nature Center 3745 Illinois Ave.	Louisville	KY	40213	502-458-1328	458-0232
Louisville Orchestra 300 W Main St Suite 100. *Web:* www.louisvilleorchestra.org	Louisville	KY	40202	502-587-8681	589-7870
Louisville Science Center 727 W Main St *Web:* www.lsclouienet.org/	Louisville	KY	40202	502-561-6100	561-6145
Louisville Slugger Museum 800 W Main St. *Web:* www.slugger.com/museum	Louisville	KY	40202	502-588-7228	585-1179
Louisville Zoological Garden 1100 Trevilian Way *Web:* www.iglou.com/louzoo	Louisville	KY	40213	502-459-2181	459-2196
Music Theatre Louisville 624 W Main St.	Louisville	KY	40202	502-589-4060	589-0741
Old Louisville Historic District 1340 S 4th St.	Louisville	KY	40208	502-635-5244	
Palace Theatre 625 4th Ave. *Web:* www.louisvillepalace.com	Louisville	KY	40202	502-583-4555	583-9955
Riverside Farnsley-Moremen House 7410 Moorman Rd *Web:* www.co.jefferson.ky.us/AttractionsRiverside.html	Louisville	KY	40272	502-935-6809	
Shawnee Park Broadway & SW Pkwy	Louisville	KY	40233	502-456-8100	
Six Flags Kentucky Kingdom 937 Phillips Ln *TF:* 800-727-3267 ■ *Web:* www.sixflags.com/kentuckykingdom	Louisville	KY	40209	502-366-2231	366-8746
Speed JB Art Museum 2035 S 3rd St *Web:* www.speedmuseum.org/	Louisville	KY	40208	502-634-2700	636-2899
Thomas Edison House 729-31 E Washington St	Louisville	KY	40202	502-585-5247	
University of Louisville Photo Archives Ekstrom Library University of Louisville	Louisville	KY	40292	502-852-6752	852-8734
Whitehall 3110 Lexington Rd	Louisville	KY	40206	502-897-2944	

SPORTS TEAMS & FACILITIES

				Phone	Fax
Cardinal Stadium/Freedom Hall 937 Phillips Ln Kentucky Fair & Exposition Ctr.	Louisville	KY	40209	502-367-5000	367-5139

Louisville — Sports Teams & Facilities (Cont'd)

				Phone	Fax
Churchill Downs Inc 700 Central Ave. *Web:* www.churchilldowns.com	Louisville	KY	40208	502-636-4400	636-4430
Kentucky Fair & Expo Center 937 Phillips Ln *Web:* www.kyfairexpo.org	Louisville	KY	40209	502-367-5000	367-5139
Louisville Motor Speedway 1900 Outer Loop *Web:* www.louisvillespeedway.com ■ *E-mail:* info@louisvillespeedway.com	Louisville	KY	40219	502-966-2277	969-8582
Louisville Riverbats (baseball) 937 Phillips Ln Cardinal Stadium	Louisville	KY	40213	502-367-9121	

— Events —

	Phone
Autumn Fest (early October)	502-583-3577
Cherokee Triangle Art Fair (late April)	502-451-3534
Corn Island Storytelling Festival (mid-September)	502-582-3732
Derby City Square Dance Festival (mid-May)	502-367-5000
Derby Festival Great Balloon Glow (late April)	502-584-6383
Derby Festival Great Balloon Race (late April)	502-584-6383
Derby Festival Great Steamboat Race (late April)	502-584-6383
Derby Festival KyDzFest (late April)	502-584-6383
Derby Festival Pegasus Parade (late April)	502-584-6383
Derby Festival Planes of Thunder (mid-April)	502-584-6383
Dickens on Main Street (late November)	502-574-3333
DinnerWorks (mid-January-mid-February)	502-896-2146
Humana Festival of New American Plays (late February-late March)	502-584-1265
Kentucky Derby (early May)	502-582-3732
Kentucky Derby Festival (late March-early May)	800-928-3378
Kentucky Golf Show (mid-January)	502-367-5000
Kentucky Oaks (early May)	502-636-4400
Kentucky Reggae Festival (late May)	502-583-0333
Kentucky Shakespeare Festival (mid-June-mid-July)	502-583-8738
Kentucky State Fair (late August)	502-582-3732
Light Up Louisville International Festival (late November)	502-584-2121
Mid-America Trucking Show (late March)	502-367-5000
National City Music Weekend (late July)	502-348-5237
National Farm Machinery Show & Tractor Pull (mid-February)	502-367-5000
National Gun Days (early February & early June)	502-367-5000
Revolutionary War Encampment (mid-April)	502-896-2433
Saint James Art Fair (early October)	502-635-1842
Sport Boat & Vacation Show (late January-early February)	502-367-5000
Strassenfest (early July)	502-561-3440
Strictly Bluegrass Festival (mid-September)	502-582-3732
Thunder over Louisville (mid-April)	502-584-6383
Waterside Art & Blues Festival (early July)	502-896-2146

Louisiana

Population (1999): 4,372,035 **Area (sq mi): 51,843**

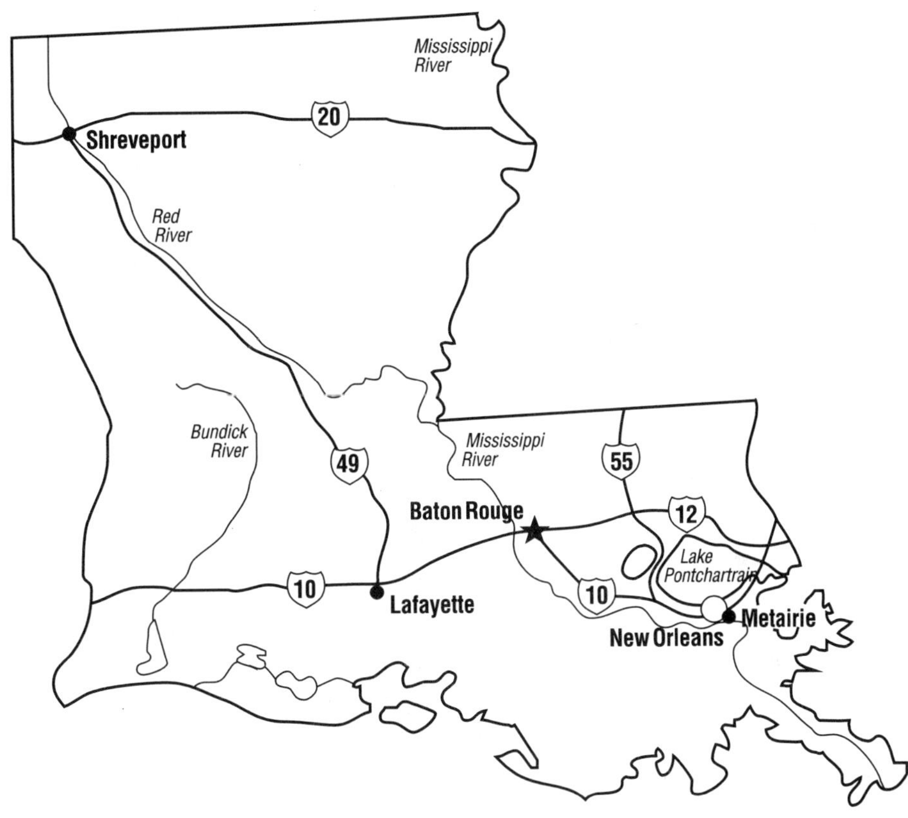

— State Information Sources —

				Phone	Fax
Louisiana Assn of Business & Industry PO Box 80258	Baton Rouge	LA	70898	225-928-5388	929-6054
Louisiana Economic Development Dept PO Box 94185 *Web:* www.lded.state.la.us	Baton Rouge	LA	70804	225-342-3000	342-5389
Louisiana State Government Information *Web:* www.state.la.us				225-342-6600	
Louisiana State Library PO Box 131 *Web:* smt.state.lib.la.us/statelib.htm	Baton Rouge	LA	70821	225-342-4915	342-3547
Louisiana State Parks Office PO Box 44426 *TF:* 888-677-1400 ■ *Web:* crt.state.la.us/crt/spintro.htm	Baton Rouge	LA	70804	225-342-8111	342-8107
Louisiana Tourism Office PO Box 94291 *TF:* 800-334-8626 ■ *Web:* www.louisianatravel.com	Baton Rouge	LA	70804	225-342-8100	342-8390

ON-LINE RESOURCES

4 OK Links . . . www.4oklinks.com
Cajun Concierge . . . www.lacajun.com
Cajun Life . . . www.cajunlife.com
Louisiana Cities . . . dir.yahoo.com/Regional/U_S__States/Louisiana/Cities
Louisiana Home Page . . . www.wisdom.com/la
Louisiana Images . . . laimages.com
Louisiana Page Locale . . . www.lapage.com/page
Louisiana Parishes & Regions . . . dir.yahoo.com/Regional/U_S__States/Louisiana/Parishes_and_Regions
Louisiana Profiles . . . www.state.la.us/state/profiles.htm
Louisiana Scenario . . . scenariousa.dstylus.com/la/indexf.htm
Louisiana Travel & Tourism Guide . . . www.travel-library.com/north_america/usa/louisiana/index.html
Louisiana.com . . . www.louisiana.com
Mobetta in Louisiana . . . www.fortunecity.com/meltingpot/aerodrome/457
Rough Guide Travel Louisiana . . . travel.roughguides.com/content/882/index.htm
Travel.org-Louisiana . . . travel.org/louisian.html
Yahoo! Get Local Louisiana . . . dir.yahoo.com/Regional/U_S__States/Louisiana

— Cities Profiled —

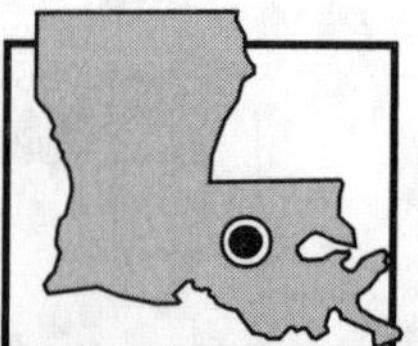

Baton Rouge

The French founders of Baton Rouge, the capital of Louisiana, named the city for a red post that marked the boundary between the lands of two Native American tribes. The 19th century plantations that surround this Mississippi River port city include the Houmas House Plantation and Gardens where the movie "Hush Hush Sweet Charlotte" was filmed. The Southern mansions of nearby Saint Francisville include Oakley Plantation, which was once the home of John James Audubon. It was here that more than 80 birds in his "Birds of America" series were painted. Oakley is also part of the Audubon State Commemorative Area, a 100-acre wildlife sanctuary.

Population	211,551	**Longitude**	91-15-44 W
Area (Land)	73.9 sq mi	**County**	East Baton Rouge
Area (Water)	2.2 sq mi	**Time Zone**	CST
Elevation	58 ft	**Area Code/s**	225
Latitude	30-45-06 N		

— Average Temperatures and Precipitation —

TEMPERATURES

	Jan	Feb	Mar	Apr	May	Jun	Jul	Aug	Sep	Oct	Nov	Dec
High	60	64	72	80	86	91	91	91	87	80	71	63
Low	40	43	50	58	65	70	73	73	69	57	49	43

PRECIPITATION

	Jan	Feb	Mar	Apr	May	Jun	Jul	Aug	Sep	Oct	Nov	Dec
Inches	4.9	5.5	4.8	5.4	4.9	4.5	6.7	6.0	4.9	3.5	4.3	5.5

— Important Phone Numbers —

	Phone		Phone
AAA	225-293-1200	**HotelDocs**	800-468-3537
American Express Travel	225-927-6002	**Poison Control Center**	800-256-9822
Emergency	911	**Time/Temp**	225-387-5411

— Information Sources —

				Phone	Fax
Baton Rouge Area Convention & Visitors Commission 730 North Blvd *TF:* 800-527-6843 ■ *Web:* www.bracvb.com	Baton Rouge	LA	70802	225-383-1825	346-1253
Baton Rouge City Hall PO Box 1471 *Web:* www.ci.baton-rouge.la.us	Baton Rouge	LA	70821	225-389-3100	389-5203
Baton Rouge Community & Economic Development Dept PO Box 1471 *Web:* www.ci.baton-rouge.la.us/dept/ocd ■ *E-mail:* ocd@ci.baton-rouge.la.us	Baton Rouge	LA	70821	225-389-3039	389-3939
Baton Rouge Mayor PO Box 1471 *Web:* www.ci.baton-rouge.la.us/Dept/Mayor	Baton Rouge	LA	70821	225-389-3100	389-5203
Better Business Bureau Serving South Central Louisiana 748 Main St. *Web:* www.batonrouge.bbb.org	Baton Rouge	LA	70802	225-346-5222	346-1029
East Baton Rouge Parish 1755 Florida St. **Fax:* Hum Res	Baton Rouge	LA	70821	225-389-3000	389-4962*
East Baton Rouge Parish Library 7711 Goodwood Blvd	Baton Rouge	LA	70806	225-231-3700	231-3759
Greater Baton Rouge Chamber of Commerce PO Box 3217 *Web:* www.brchamber.org ■ *E-mail:* info@brchamber.org	Baton Rouge	LA	70821	225-381-7125	336-4306
Riverside Centroplex 275 S River Rd	Baton Rouge	LA	70802	225-389-3030	389-4954

On-Line Resources

Area Guide Baton Rouge	batonrouge.areaguides.net
Baton Rouge Net	www.brnet.com
Baton Rouge On-line	www.br-online.com
Baton Rouge Town Planner	www.townplannerbr.com
City Knowledge Baton Rouge	www.cityknowledge.com/la_batonrouge.htm
Excite.com Baton Rouge City Guide	www.excite.com/travel/countries/united_states/louisiana/baton_rouge
Greater Baton Rouge Internet Rest Area	www.baton-rouge.com/BatonRouge
LDS iAmerica Baton Rouge	baton-rouge.iamerica.net
Rhythm City Magazine Online	www.rhythmcitymag.com/

— Transportation Services —

AIRPORTS

	Phone
■ **Baton Rouge Metropolitan Airport (BTR)** 8 miles N of downtown (approx 20 minutes)	225-355-0333

Airport Transportation

	Phone
AAA Taxi Cab $12 fare to downtown	225-357-2521
Taxi $15 fare to downtown	225-926-6400

Commercial Airlines

	Phone		Phone
American	800-433-7300	**Delta**	800-221-1212
Continental	225-387-4911	**Northwest**	800-225-2525

Charter Airlines

	Phone		Phone
Baton Rouge Air Charter	225-358-0055	**Louisiana Aircraft**	225-356-1401
Baton Rouge Helicopters Inc	225-755-6090		

CAR RENTALS

	Phone		Phone
Audubon	225-296-7213	**Hertz**	225-357-5992
Avis	225-355-4702	**Thrifty**	225-356-2576
Budget	225-355-0312		

LIMO/TAXI

	Phone		Phone
AAA Taxi Cab	225-357-2521	**Lunden Limousine Service**	225-275-5466
Baton Rouge Limousine Service	225-927-4908	**Riverside Limousine**	225-928-5466
Blue Streak Cab Co	225-272-9884	**Smitty's Airport Cab**	225-357-2500
Capital City Limousine	225-753-1577	**Yellow Cab**	225-926-6400

MASS TRANSIT

	Phone
Capitol Transportation $1.25 Base fare	225-389-8920

RAIL/BUS

				Phone
Amtrak Station Railroad Ave	Hammond	LA	70401	800-872-7245
Greyhound/Trailways Bus Station 1253 Florida St	Baton Rouge	LA	70802	225-383-3124

— Accommodations —

HOTEL RESERVATION SERVICES

	Phone	Fax
Bed & Breakfast Reservation Service *TF:* 800-926-4320 ■ *Web:* www.bnbtravel.com ■ *E-mail:* bnb@bnbtravel.com	225-923-2337	923-2374

HOTELS, MOTELS, RESORTS

				Phone	Fax
Alamo Plaza Motel 4243 Florida Blvd	Baton Rouge	LA	70806	225-924-7231	
Allround Suites 2045 N 3rd St	Baton Rouge	LA	70802	225-344-6000	387-2878
AmeriSuites 6080 Bluebonnet Blvd *TF:* 800-833-1516	Baton Rouge	LA	70809	225-769-4400	769-7444
Baton Rouge Hilton Hotel 5500 Hilton Ave *TF:* 800-445-8667	Baton Rouge	LA	70808	225-924-5000	926-8152
Baymont Inns 10555 Reiger Rd *TF:* 800-301-0200	Baton Rouge	LA	70808	225-291-6600	926-0474

Baton Rouge — Hotels, Motels, Resorts (Cont'd)

Name / Address	City	State	Zip	Phone	Fax
Bellemont Hotel & Convention Center 7370 Airline Hwy	Baton Rouge	LA	70805	225-357-8612	357-4974
Best Western Chateau Louisianne Suite Hotel 710 N Lobdell Ave	Baton Rouge	LA	70806	225-927-6700	927-6709
TF: 800-528-1234					
Comfort Inn University 2445 S Acadian Thwy	Baton Rouge	LA	70808	225-927-5790	925-0084
TF: 800-228-5150					
Corporate Inn 2365 College Dr	Baton Rouge	LA	70808	225-925-2451	926-8168
TF: 800-695-0077					
Courtyard by Marriott Baton Rouge 2421 S Acadian Thwy	Baton Rouge	LA	70808	225-924-6400	923-3041
TF: 800-321-2211 ■ *Web:* courtyard.com/BTRCH					
Crosslands Economy Studios 11140 Boardwalk Dr	Baton Rouge	LA	70816	225-274-8997	274-9134
TF: 888-802-7677 ■ *Web:* www.extstay.com/loc/la_batonrouge_sherwoodforest_crs.html					
Days Inn 10245 Airline Hwy	Baton Rouge	LA	70816	225-291-8152	292-9566
TF: 800-325-2525					
Embassy Suites 4914 Constitution Ave	Baton Rouge	LA	70808	225-924-6566	923-3712
TF: 800-362-2779					
Hampton Inn 10045 Gwenadele Ave	Baton Rouge	LA	70816	225-924-4433	927-4008
TF: 800-426-7866					
Hampton Inn College Drive 4646 Constitution Ave	Baton Rouge	LA	70808	225-926-9990	923-3007
TF: 800-426-7866					
Holiday Inn East 10455 Reiger Rd	Baton Rouge	LA	70809	225-293-6880	293-6880
TF: 800-465-4329					
Holiday Inn Express College Drive 4924 Constitution Ave	Baton Rouge	LA	70808	225-930-0600	930-0673
TF: 800-465-4329					
Holiday Inn South Holidome 9940 Airline Hwy	Baton Rouge	LA	70816	225-924-7021	924-7021
TF: 800-465-4329					
Homewood Suites 5860 Corporate Blvd	Baton Rouge	LA	70808	225-927-1700	927-1700
TF: 800-225-5466					
La Quinta Motor Inn 2333 S Acadian Thwy	Baton Rouge	LA	70808	225-924-9600	924-2609
TF: 800-531-5900					
Microtel Inn & Suites 10645 Rieger Rd	Baton Rouge	LA	70884	225-291-6200	291-6202
TF: 888-771-7171					
Motel 6 Airline Highway 9901 Gwenadele Ave	Baton Rouge	LA	70816	225-924-2130	929-7150
TF: 800-466-8356					
Plantation Inn 10330 Airline Hwy	Baton Rouge	LA	70816	225-293-4100	295-3733
Prince Murat Inn 1480 Nicholson Dr	Baton Rouge	LA	70802	225-387-1111	343-5323
TF: 800-916-8728					
Quality Inn 10920 Mead Rd	Baton Rouge	LA	70816	225-293-9370	293-8889
TF: 800-228-5151					
Quality Suites Hotel 9138 Bluebonnet Centre Blvd	Baton Rouge	LA	70809	225-293-1199	296-5014
TF: 800-228-5151					
Radisson Baton Rouge Hotel 4728 Constitution Ave	Baton Rouge	LA	70808	225-925-2244	930-0140
TF: 800-333-3333					
Red Roof Inn 11314 Boardwalk Dr	Baton Rouge	LA	70816	225-275-6600	275-6792
TF: 800-843-7663					
Residence Inn by Marriott 5522 Corporate Blvd	Baton Rouge	LA	70808	225-927-5630	926-2317
TF: 800-331-3131 ■ *Web:* www.residenceinn.com/BTRBR					
Shoney's Inn 9919 Gwenadele Ave	Baton Rouge	LA	70816	225-925-8399	927-1731
TF: 800-222-2222					
Sleep Inn Baton Rouge 10332 Plaza Americana Dr	Baton Rouge	LA	70816	225-926-8488	926-7989
TF: 800-753-3746					
Super 8 Suites 11444 Reulet Ave	Baton Rouge	LA	70816	225-275-8878	275-1134
TF: 800-800-8000					
Wilson Inn & Suites 3045 Valley Creek Rd	Baton Rouge	LA	70808	225-923-3377	924-7044
TF: 800-945-7667					

— Restaurants —

Name / Address	City	State	Zip	Phone
Black Forest Restaurant (German) 321 North Blvd.	Baton Rouge	LA	70801	225-334-0059
Bonanno's Seafood Restaurant (Seafood) 10270 Airline Hwy	Baton Rouge	LA	70816	225-293-1150
Branberrys (Continental) 4914 Constitution Ave.	Baton Rouge	LA	70808	225-924-6566
Brunet's Cajun Restaurant (Cajun) 135 S Flannery Rd	Baton Rouge	LA	70815	225-272-6226
Cabin The (Cajun) Hwy 44 & Hwy 22	Burnside	LA	70738	225-473-3007
Cafe Acadian (Cajun) 5500 Hilton Ave	Baton Rouge	LA	70708	225-924-5000
Cafe' Mediterranean (Greek/Lebanese) 151 3rd St	Baton Rouge	LA	70802	225-336-4501
Caila's Fine Cuisine (Continental) 427 Lafayette St	Baton Rouge	LA	70802	225-343-6233
Chalet Brandt (Continental) 7655 Old Hammond Hwy	Baton Rouge	LA	70809	225-927-6040
Chimes Restaurant & Oyster Bar (Seafood) 3357 Highland Rd.	Baton Rouge	LA	70802	225-383-1754
Copelands of New Orleans (Cajun/Creole) 4957 Essen Ln.	Baton Rouge	LA	70809	225-769-1800
Da Jo Nel's (Continental) 7327 Jefferson Hwy	Baton Rouge	LA	70806	225-924-7537
Dino's (Mediterranean) 1803 S Sherwood Forest Blvd	Baton Rouge	LA	70816	225-275-9911
Don's Seafood & Steak House (Cajun) 6823 Airline Hwy	Baton Rouge	LA	70805	225-357-0601
Frank's Restaurant (American) 8353 Airline Hwy.	Baton Rouge	LA	70815	225-926-5977
Giamanco's (Italian) 4624 Government St.	Baton Rouge	LA	70806	225-928-5045
India Cuisine Restaurant (Indian) 5230 Essen Ln	Baton Rouge	LA	70809	225-769-0600
Juban's Restaurant (Creole) 3739 Perkins Rd	Baton Rouge	LA	70808	225-346-8422
Lafitte's Landing (Cajun/Creole) 404 Clairborne Ave Bittersweet Plantation	Donaldson	LA	70346	225-473-1232
LaFonda Restaurant (Mexican) 7838 Airline Hwy.	Baton Rouge	LA	70815	225-927-2535
Magnolia Cafe (Steak/Seafood) 3535 S Sherwood Forest Blvd	Baton Rouge	LA	70816	225-291-2233
Maison Lacour (French) 11025 N Harrell's Ferry Rd.	Baton Rouge	LA	70816	225-275-3755
Mansur's (Cajun/Creole) 3044 College Dr	Baton Rouge	LA	70806	225-923-3366
Web: www.explore-br.com/mansurs/				
Mike Anderson's (Seafood) 1031 W Lee Dr	Baton Rouge	LA	70820	225-766-3728
Mulate's (Cajun) 8322 Bluebonnet Blvd	Baton Rouge	LA	70810	225-767-4794
Ninfa's Restaurant (Mexican) 4738 Constitution Ave	Baton Rouge	LA	70808	225-924-0377
Nottoway Plantation (Cajun) Hwy 1	White Castle	LA	70788	225-545-2992
On Stage Cafe (American) 10920 Mead Rd.	Baton Rouge	LA	70816	225-293-9370
Patio Grill & Bar (American) 4728 Constitution Ave.	Baton Rouge	LA	70808	225-930-0104
Place The (Steak/Seafood) 5255 Florida Blvd	Baton Rouge	LA	70806	225-924-5069
Rafferty's (International) 9940 Airline Hwy	Baton Rouge	LA	70816	225-924-7021
Richoux's (American) 302 3rd St.	Baton Rouge	LA	70801	225-387-0253
Ruth's Chris Steak House (Steak) 4836 Constitution Ave.	Baton Rouge	LA	70808	225-925-0163
Serop's Restaurant (Lebanese) 4065 Government St	Baton Rouge	LA	70806	225-383-3658
Silver Spoon (Caribbean/Latin American) 7731 Jefferson Hwy	Baton Rouge	LA	70809	225-926-1172
Superior Grill (Mexican) 5435 Government St.	Baton Rouge	LA	70806	225-927-2022
Thai Kitchen (Thai) 5958 Florida Blvd.	Baton Rouge	LA	70806	225-923-1230
Zee Zee Gardens (American) 2904 Perkins Rd	Baton Rouge	LA	70808	225-346-1291
Zorba's (Greek) 9990 Perkins Rd	Baton Rouge	LA	70810	225-769-8833

— Goods and Services —

SHOPPING

Name / Address	City	State	Zip	Phone	Fax
Bon Marche Mall 7359 Florida Blvd	Baton Rouge	LA	70806	225-926-4546	926-3457
Cortana Mall 9401 Cortana Pl	Baton Rouge	LA	70815	225-923-1412	928-7920
Web: www.cortanamall.com					
Dillard's 1500 Main St.	Baton Rouge	LA	70802	225-389-7000	382-3129
Landmark Mall 832 St Phillip St.	Baton Rouge	LA	70802	225-383-4867	383-9325
Mall of Louisiana 6401 Bluebonnet Blvd	Baton Rouge	LA	70836	225-761-7228	761-7225
Tanger Factory Outlet Center 2200 Tanger Blvd	Gonzales	LA	70737	225-647-0521	

BANKS

Name / Address	City	State	Zip	Phone	Fax
Bank One Louisiana NA 451 Florida St	Baton Rouge	LA	70821	225-332-7000	332-3336*
**Fax:* Hum Res ■ *TF Cust Svc:* 800-777-0142*					
First National Banker's Bank PO Box 80579	Baton Rouge	LA	70898	225-924-8015	952-0899
Hancock Bank of Louisiana 301 Main St.	Baton Rouge	LA	70801	225-346-6380	346-6326
Hibernia National Bank 440 3rd St.	Baton Rouge	LA	70801	225-381-2201	381-2006
Regions Bank of Louisiana 5353 Essen Ln Suite 500	Baton Rouge	LA	70809	225-767-0000	767-0187
Union Planters Bank of Louisiana 8440 Jefferson Hwy	Baton Rouge	LA	70809	225-924-9400	936-7930*
**Fax:* Mktg					
Whitney National Bank 617 North Blvd	Baton Rouge	LA	70821	800-326-3503	381-0416*
**Fax Area Code:* 225					

BUSINESS SERVICES

Name	Phone	Name	Phone
AAA Temporaries	225-925-9060	**Kinko's**	225-344-7296
American Printing Center	225-925-5000	**Mail Boxes Etc**	225-766-8810
City Courier Service	225-756-8009	**Manpower Temporary Services**	225-924-4281
Express Courier Services	225-924-9990	**Metro Mail Express**	225-926-9999
Federal Express	800-238-5355	**Olsten Staffing Services**	225-924-0200
Interim Personnel	225-925-5686	**Post Office**	225-381-0713
Kelly Services	225-767-6177	**UPS**	800-742-5877

Baton Rouge (Cont'd)

— Media —

PUBLICATIONS

				Phone	Fax
Advocate The‡ PO Box 588	Baton Rouge	LA	70821	225-383-1111	388-0371
Web: www.theadvocate.com ■ *E-mail:* comments@theadvocate.com					
Greater Baton Rouge Business Report 5757 Corporate Blvd Suite 402	Baton Rouge	LA	70808	225-928-1700	926-1329*
**Fax:* Sales ■ *Web:* www.businessreport.com ■ *E-mail:* editors@businessreport.com					

‡*Daily newspapers*

TELEVISION

				Phone	Fax
WAFB-TV Ch 9 (CBS) 844 Government St	Baton Rouge	LA	70802	225-383-9999	379-7880
E-mail: wafb@aol.com					
WBRZ-TV Ch 2 (ABC) PO Box 2906	Baton Rouge	LA	70821	225-387-2222	336-2347
Web: www.wbrz.com ■ *E-mail:* mis@wbrz.com					
WBTR-TV Ch 19 (UPN) 914 N Foster Dr	Baton Rouge	LA	70806	225-928-3146	923-2822*
**Fax:* News Rm					
WGMB-TV Ch 44 (Fox) 5220-B Essen Ln	Baton Rouge	LA	70809	225-769-0044	769-9462
E-mail: feedback@fox44.com					
WLPB-TV Ch 27 (PBS) 7733 Perkins Rd	Baton Rouge	LA	70810	225-767-5660	767-4277
Web: www.lpb.org					
WTNC-TV Ch 21 (Ind) 914 N Foster Dr	Baton Rouge	LA	70806	225-928-2121	928-5097
WVLA-TV Ch 33 (NBC) 5220 Essen Ln	Baton Rouge	LA	70809	225-766-3233	768-9191

RADIO

				Phone	Fax
KQXL-FM 106.5 MHz (Urban) 650 Woodale Blvd	Baton Rouge	LA	70806	225-926-1106	928-1606
KRVE-FM 96.1 MHz (AC) 5555 Hilton Ave Suite 500	Baton Rouge	LA	70808	225-231-1860	231-1873*
**Fax:* News Rm					
WDGL-FM 98.1 MHz (CR) PO Box 2231	Baton Rouge	LA	70821	225-388-9898	499-9800
WIBR-AM 1300 kHz (Sports) 650 Wooddale Blvd	Baton Rouge	LA	70806	225-499-1300	928-1606
Web: www.team1300.com					
WJBO-AM 1150 kHz (N/T) 5555 Hilton Ave Suite 500	Baton Rouge	LA	70808	225-231-1860	231-1873
Web: www.wjbo.com					
WLSS-FM 102.5 MHz (CHR) 5555 Hilton Ave Suite 500	Baton Rouge	LA	70808	225-231-1860	231-1873
TF: 888-235-6673					
WRKF-FM 89.3 MHz (NPR) 3050 Valley Creek Dr	Baton Rouge	LA	70808	225-926-3050	926-3105
Web: www.wrkf.org ■ *E-mail:* wrkf@aol.com					
WTGE-FM 100.7 MHz (Oldies) 929-B Government St	Baton Rouge	LA	70821	225-388-9898	499-9800
WXOK-AM 1460 kHz (Misc) 650 Woodale Blvd	Baton Rouge	LA	70806	225-499-1460	928-1606
WYNK-AM 1380 kHz (Misc) 5555 Hilton Ave Suite 500	Baton Rouge	LA	70808	225-231-1860	231-1873

— Colleges/Universities —

				Phone	Fax
Louisiana State University 3810 W Lake Shore Dr	Baton Rouge	LA	70808	225-388-2111	388-4433
Web: www.lsu.edu					
Louisiana State University A & M College	Baton Rouge	LA	70803	225-388-3202	388-4433
E-mail: help@unix1.sncc.lsu.edu					
Louisiana State University Baton Rouge Campus Tower Dr	Baton Rouge	LA	70803	225-388-3202	388-5991
Web: unix1.sncc.lsu.edu					
Southern University & A & M College Main Branch Post Office	Baton Rouge	LA	70813	225-771-4500	771-2500
TF: 800-256-1531 ■ *Web:* www.subr.edu					

— Hospitals —

				Phone	Fax
Baton Rouge General Medical Center 3600 Florida Blvd	Baton Rouge	LA	70806	225-387-7000	387-7661
Web: www.generalhealth.org/brgmc.html					
Columbia Medical Center 17000 Medical Center Dr	Baton Rouge	LA	70816	225-752-2470	755-4883
Earl K Long Medical Center 5825 Airline Hwy	Baton Rouge	LA	70805	225-358-1000	358-1003
Lane Memorial Hospital 6300 Main St	Zachary	LA	70791	225-658-4000	658-4287
TF: 800-737-5263					
Our Lady of the Lake Regional Medical Center 5000 Hennessy Blvd	Baton Rouge	LA	70808	225-765-6565	765-8759
Web: www.ololrmc.com ■ *E-mail:* mail@ololrmc.com					
Woman's Hospital PO Box 95009	Baton Rouge	LA	70895	225-927-1300	924-8777
Web: www.womans.com ■ *E-mail:* mktphp@womans.com					

— Attractions —

				Phone	Fax
Afton Villa Gardens 9247 Hwy 61	Saint Francisville	LA	70775	225-635-6773	861-7365
Audubon State Commemorative Area & Oakley Plantation Hwy 965	Saint Francisville	LA	70775	225-635-3739	635-3739
Baton Rouge Ballet Theatre 275 S River Rd Centroplex Theatre	Baton Rouge	LA	70884	225-766-8379	766-8230
E-mail: ballet@aol.com					
Baton Rouge Little Theater 7155 Florida Blvd	Baton Rouge	LA	70806	225-924-6496	924-9972
Baton Rouge Symphony Orchestra 275 S River Rd Centroplex Theatre	Baton Rouge	LA	70809	225-927-2776	923-2772
Web: www.brso.org					
Belle of Baton Rouge Casino 103 France St	Baton Rouge	LA	70802	225-378-5825	344-8056
TF: 800-378-5825 ■ *Web:* www.argosycasinos.com					
Blue Bayou Water Park 18142 Perkins Rd	Baton Rouge	LA	70810	225-753-3333	751-4228
Bluebonnet Swamp Nature Center 10503 N Oak Hills Pkwy	Baton Rouge	LA	70810	225-757-8905	757-9390
Blythewood Plantation 400 Daniel St	Amite	LA	70422	504-345-6419	748-6246
Brec's Baton Rouge Zoo PO Box 60	Baker	LA	70704	225-775-3877	775-3931
Casino Rouge 1717 River Rd N	Baton Rouge	LA	70802	225-709-7777	709-7770
TF: 800-447-6843 ■ *Web:* www.casinorouge.com/ ■ *E-mail:* mail@casinorouge.com					
Celebration Station Entertainment Complex 10111 Gwenadele Ave	Baton Rouge	LA	70816	225-924-7888	928-1952
Web: www.celebrationstation.com					
Cohn Laurens Sr Memorial Plant Arboretum 12206 Foster Rd	Baton Rouge	LA	70811	225-775-1006	273-6404
Cottage Plantation 10528 Cottage Ln	Saint Francisville	LA	70775	225-635-3674	
Enchanted Mansion Doll Museum 190 Lee Dr	Baton Rouge	LA	70808	225-769-0005	766-6822
Firefighters Museum 427 Laurel St	Baton Rouge	LA	70801	225-344-8558	344-7777
Fun Fair Park 8475 Florida Blvd	Baton Rouge	LA	70806	225-924-6266	
Global Wildlife Center 26389 Hwy 40	Folsom	LA	70437	504-796-3585	796-9487
Web: www.globalwildlife.com					
Greenwood Plantation 6838 Highland Rd	Saint Francisville	LA	70775	225-655-4475	655-3292
TF: 800-259-4475					
Heritage Museum & Cultural Center 1606 Main St	Baker	LA	70714	225-774-1776	
Hilltop Arboretum Louisiana State University 11855 Highland Rd	Baton Rouge	LA	70810	225-767-6916	768-7710
Houmas House Plantation & Gardens 40136 Hwy 942	Darrow	LA	70725	225-473-7841	474-0480
Independence Park Botanic Garden 7500 Independence Blvd	Baton Rouge	LA	70806	225-928-2270	
Louisiana Arts & Science Center PO Box 3373	Baton Rouge	LA	70821	225-344-5272	344-9477
Louisiana Governor's Mansion 1001 Capitol Access Rd	Baton Rouge	LA	70802	225-342-5855	379-2043
Louisiana Naval War Memorial 305 S River Rd	Baton Rouge	LA	70802	225-342-1942	342-2039
Web: www.premier.net/~uss_kidd/home.html ■ *E-mail:* kidd661@aol.com					
Louisiana State Archives 3851 Essen Ln	Baton Rouge	LA	70809	225-922-1206	922-0433
Web: www.sec.state.la.us/arch-1.htm					
Louisiana State Capitol Building State Capitol Dr	Baton Rouge	LA	70804	225-342-7317	
Louisiana State University Museum of Art Memorial Tower Louisiana State University	Baton Rouge	LA	70803	225-388-4003	334-4016

Baton Rouge — Attractions (Cont'd)

				Phone	Fax
Louisiana State University Rural Life Museum 5640 Essen Ln	Baton Rouge	LA	70808	225-765-2437	765-2639
Web: rurallife.lsu.edu ■ *E-mail:* lhin@unix1.sncc.lsu.edu					
Louisiana State University Theater Dalrymple Dr 217 Music and Dramatic Arts Bldg	Baton Rouge	LA	70803	225-388-4174	388-4135
Magnolia Mound Plantation 2161 Nicholson Dr	Baton Rouge	LA	70802	225-343-4955	343-6739
Nottoway Plantation PO Box 160	White Castle	LA	70788	225-346-8263	545-8632
Old Arsenal Museum PO Box 94125	Baton Rouge	LA	70804	225-342-0401	
Web: www.sec.state.la.us/arsnl-1.htm					
Old Capitol Gallery 303 North Blvd.	Baton Rouge	LA	70801	225-343-7333	343-7334
Old Govenor's Mansion 502 North Blvd.	Baton Rouge	LA	70802	225-387-2464	344-9477
Old State Capitol 100 North Blvd	Baton Rouge	LA	70801	225-342-0500	342-0316
Web: www.sec.state.la.us/osc-1.htm					
Pentagon Barracks 959 3rd St	Baton Rouge	LA	70802	225-342-1866	
Plaquemine Lock Museum 57730 Main St.	Plaquemine	LA	70764	225-687-7158	687-8933
Port Hudson State Commemorative Area 756 W Plains-Port Hudson Rd	Zachary	LA	70791	225-654-3775	654-1048
River Bend Energy Center 5485 US Hwy 61	Saint Francisville	LA	70775	225-635-6094	381-4870
Rosedown Plantation & Historic Gardens 12501 Hwy 10	Saint Francisville	LA	70775	225-635-3332	
Saint James Episcopal Church 208 N 4th St	Baton Rouge	LA	70801	225-387-5141	387-1443
Saint Joseph's Cathedral 412 North St.	Baton Rouge	LA	70802	225-387-5928	387-5929
Tezcuco Plantation 3138 Hwy 44	Burnside	LA	70725	225-562-3929	562-3923
USS Kidd & Nautical Center 305 S River Rd.	Baton Rouge	LA	70802	225-342-1942	342-2039
E-mail: rvnwolf@aol.com					
West Baton Rouge Museum 845 N Jefferson Avo	Port Allen	LA	70767	225-336-2422	336-2448
Web: www.lapage.com/wbrm					
White Oak Plantation 17660 George O'Neal Rd	Baton Rouge	LA	70817	225-751-1882	751-0767

SPORTS TEAMS & FACILITIES

				Phone	Fax
Baton Rouge Kingfish (hockey) 275 S River Rd Riverside Centroplex.	Baton Rouge	LA	70801	225-336-4625	336-4011
Web: www.kingfish-hockey.com ■ *E-mail:* brkingfish@i-55.com					
Baton Rouge Raceway Plank Rd.	Baker	LA	70714	225-275-5040	
Evangeline Downs Race Track 3620 NW Evangeline Thruway	Carencro	LA	70520	337-896-7223	896-5445
Web: www.evangelinedowns.com ■ *E-mail:* info@evangelinedowns.com					
State Capitol Dragway PO Box 159.	Erwinville	LA	70729	225-627-4574	627-4408

— Events —

	Phone
Audubon Pilgrimage (mid-March)	225-383-1825
Baton Rouge BREC Rodeo (mid-February)	225-769-7805
Baton Rouge Earth Day Festival (mid-April)	225-383-1825
Big Easy Charity Horse Show (mid-June)	225-388-2255
Boo at the Zoo (late October)	225-775-3877
Breaux Bridge Crawfish Festival (early May)	225-383-1825
Christmas on the River (December)	225-383-1825
Creole Christmas at Magnolia Mound (mid-December-early January)	225-343-4955
Dixie Jubilee Horse Show (early November)	225-388-2255
FestForAll (early March)	225-383-1825
Greater Baton Rouge State Fair (late October)	225-383-1825
Jackson Assembly Antique Festival (late March)	225-383-1825
July 4th Celebration (July 4)	225-383-1825
June Quarter Horse Show (early June)	225-388-2255
Junior Livestock Show (mid-February)	225-388-2255
Krewe Mystic Mardi Gras Parade (early February)	225-383-1825
Magnolia Mound Market Days Festival (early April)	225-383-1825
PRCA Rodeo (mid-February)	225-388-2255
Spring Junior Livestock Show (mid-February)	225-383-1825
State Horse Show (mid-July)	225-388-2255
Zippity Zoo Day (late March)	225-775-3877

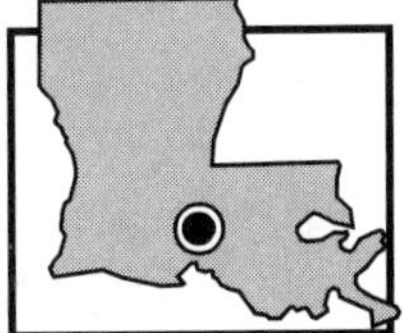

Lafayette

Louisiana is the only state in the U.S. with a dominant French culture, dating back to the 1700s. Acadian immigrants from Canada, now known as Cajuns, and migrants direct from French countries have kept their French heritage alive, preserving their culture in language, music, and food. This heritage is celebrated each April at the Festival International de Louisiane in Lafayette, Louisiana. One of Louisiana's biggest festivals, it features international musicians, artists, storytellers, theater performers, and crafters, each celebrating the French heritage and influence in Louisiana. Lafayette also hosts numerous Mardi Gras festivals in February, and in August of 1999, the Congrès Mondial Acadien, hailed as the largest gathering of the Acadian people since 1755, was held in Lafayette. The Cajun and Creole culture is also showcased at Vermilionville, a 23-acre attraction in Lafayette that features a living history exhibit, Cajun music, a gift shop, and an art gallery.

Population	113,615	**Longitude**	91-59-15 W
Area (Land)	40.9 sq mi	**County**	Lafayette Parish
Area (Water)	0.1 sq mi	**Time Zone**	CST
Elevation	42 ft	**Area Code/s**	337
Latitude	30-12-19 N		

— Average Temperatures and Precipitation —

TEMPERATURES

	Jan	Feb	Mar	Apr	May	Jun	Jul	Aug	Sep	Oct	Nov	Dec
High	60	63	71	79	85	90	91	90	87	80	71	64
Low	41	44	51	59	65	71	74	73	69	58	50	44

PRECIPITATION

	Jan	Feb	Mar	Apr	May	Jun	Jul	Aug	Sep	Oct	Nov	Dec
Inches	5.0	4.3	4.1	4.1	5.2	5.1	7.0	5.4	5.4	3.8	3.8	5.4

— Important Phone Numbers —

	Phone		Phone
AAA	504-838-7500	**Poison Control Center**	504-345-5554
American Express Travel	337-233-6990	**Time/Temp**	337-394-9744
Emergency	911		

— Information Sources —

				Phone	Fax
Better Business Bureau Serving Acadiana 100 Huggins Rd	Lafayette	LA	70506	337-981-3497	981-7559
Web: www.lafayette.bbb.org ■ *E-mail:* lafayecb@gte.net					
Greater Lafayette Chamber of Commerce 804 E St Mary Blvd.	Lafayette	LA	70503	337-233-2705	234-8671
Web: www.lafchamber.org					
Lafayette City Hall 705 W University Ave.	Lafayette	LA	70502	337-291-8200	
Web: www.lafayettegov.org					
Lafayette City-Parish President 705 W University Ave City Hall.	Lafayette	LA	70502	337-291-8300	291-8399
Lafayette Community Development 705 W University Ave 2nd Fl	Lafayette	LA	70506	337-291-8400	291-8415
Lafayette Convention & Visitors Commission PO Box 52066	Lafayette	LA	70505	337-232-3737	232-0161
TF: 800-346-1958 ■ *Web:* www.lafayettetravel.com					
Lafayette Parish PO Box 2009	Lafayette	LA	70502	337-233-0150	269-6392
Lafayette Parish Public Library 301 W Congress St.	Lafayette	LA	70501	337-261-5775	261-5782

Lafayette (Cont'd)

On-Line Resources

4Lafayette.com www.4lafayette.com
Area Guide Lafayette .... lafayettela.areaguides.net
CajunFun.com .... www.cajunfun.com
Excite.com Lafayette City Guide .... www.excite.com/travel/countries/united_states/louisiana/lafayette
Guide to Acadiana .... www.webcom.com/~gumbo/cajun-home.html
NITC Travelbase City Guide Lafayette .... www.travelbase.com/auto/guides/lafayette-la.html
Online City Guide to Lafayette .... www.olcg.com/la/lafayette/index.html
USA Hotel Guide Lafayette .... www.usahotelguide.com/states/louisiana/lafayette

— Transportation Services —

AIRPORTS

■ **Lafayette Regional Airport (LFT)** — Phone
1 mile SE of downtown (approx 5-10 minutes) 337-266-4400

Airport Transportation

	Phone
Acadiana Cab $5 fare to downtown	337-264-9707
City Cab Inc $5 fare to downtown	337-235-7515
Yellow Checker Cab $5 fare to downtown	337-237-5701

Commercial Airlines

	Phone		Phone
American Eagle	800-433-7300	**Continental**	800-525-0280
Atlantic Southeast	800-221-1212	**Northwest Airlink**	800-225-2525

Charter Airlines

	Phone		Phone
Alliance Executive Charter Services	800-232-5387	**American Aviation Charter LLC**	800-449-1677
		Petroleum Helicopters Inc	337-235-2452

CAR RENTALS

	Phone		Phone
Avis	337-234-6944	**Enterprise**	337-993-8444
Budget	337-233-8888	**Hertz**	337-233-7010

LIMO/TAXI

	Phone		Phone
Acadiana Cab	337-264-9707	**City Cab Inc**	337-235-7515
Affordable Cabs of Acadiana	337-234-2111	**Yellow Checker Cab**	337-237-5701

MASS TRANSIT

	Phone
Lafayette Transit System $.45 Base fare	337-291-8570

RAIL/BUS

Greyhound Bus Station 315 Lee Ave. .... Lafayette LA 70501 — Phone 337-233-6750
TF: 800-231-2222

— Accommodations —

HOTEL RESERVATION SERVICES

	Phone	Fax
Hotel Reservations Network Inc	214-361-7311	361-7299
TF Sales: 800-964-6835 ■ *Web:* www.hoteldiscount.com		
USA Hotels	252-331-1555	331-2021
TF: 800-872-4683 ■ *Web:* www.1800usahotels.com ■ *E-mail:* info@1800usahotels.com		

HOTELS, MOTELS, RESORTS

Name / Address	City	State	Zip	Phone	Fax
Acadian Motel 120 N University Ave	Lafayette	LA	70506	337-234-3268	
Bendel Executive Suites 213 Bendel Rd	Lafayette	LA	70503	337-261-0604	233-4296
Best Western Hotel Acadiana 1801 W Pinhook Rd	Lafayette	LA	70508	337-233-8120	234-9667
TF: 800-826-8368					
Comfort Inn 1421 SE Evangeline Thwy.	Lafayette	LA	70501	337-232-9000	233-8629
TF: 800-800-8752 ■ *Web:* www.comfortinnlafayette.com ■ *E-mail:* cbreaux@eatel.net					
Courtyard by Marriott 214 E Kaliste Saloom Rd	Lafayette	LA	70508	337-232-5005	231-0049
TF: 800-321-2211					
Days Inn 1620 N University Ave	Lafayette	LA	70506	337-237-8880	235-1386
TF: 800-329-7466					
Executive House Hotel 115 Sycamore Dr.	Lafayette	LA	70506	337-988-1750	988-1882
Fairfield Inn by Marriott 2225 NW Evangeline Thwy.	Lafayette	LA	70501	337-235-9898	235-9898
TF: 800-228-2800					
Hampton Inn 2144 W Willow St	Scott	LA	70583	337-236-6161	235-8768
TF: 800-426-7886 ■ *E-mail:* kirkcomo@aol.com					
Hilton Lafayette & Towers 1521 W Pinhook Rd	Lafayette	LA	70503	337-235-6111	261-0311
TF: 800-332-2586					
Holiday Inn 2032 NE Evangeline Thwy.	Lafayette	LA	70501	337-233-6815	235-1954
TF: 800-942-4868					
Holiday Inn Express 2503 SE Evangeline Thwy	Lafayette	LA	70508	337-234-2000	234-6373
TF: 888-234-1143					
La Quinta Motor Inn 2100 NE Evangeline Thwy	Lafayette	LA	70501	337-233-5610	235-2104
TF: 800-531-5900					
Lafayette Inn 2615 Cameron St	Lafayette	LA	70506	337-235-9442	235-9442
Lighthouse Inn 2111 NW Evangeline Thwy.	Lafayette	LA	70501	337-235-4591	235-4591
Microtel Inns & Suites 301 Ambassador Caffery Pkwy	Scott	LA	70583	337-235-9010	235-9019
TF: 888-889-7190					
Motel 6 2724 NE Evangeline Thwy	Lafayette	LA	70507	337-233-2055	269-9267
Plantation Motor Inn 2810 NE Evangeline Thwy	Lafayette	LA	70507	337-232-7285	232-7285
TF: 800-723-8228					
Quality Inn 1605 N University Ave.	Lafayette	LA	70506	337-232-6131	232-2682
TF: 800-752-2682					
Ramada Executive Plaza 120 Kaliste Saloom Rd	Lafayette	LA	70508	337-235-0858	235-4586
TF: 800-272-6232					
Ramada Inn 2716 NE Evangeline Thwy	Lafayette	LA	70507	337-233-0003	233-0360
TF: 800-473-0360					
Red Roof Inn 1718 N University Ave	Lafayette	LA	70507	337-233-3339	233-7206
TF: 800-843-7663					
Rodeway Inn 1801 NW Evangeline Thwy	Lafayette	LA	70501	337-233-5500	235-7376
TF: 800-228-2000					
Saint Francis Motel 1604 N University Ave	Lafayette	LA	70501	337-234-1454	
Super 8 Motel 2224 NE Evangeline Thwy.	Lafayette	LA	70501	337-232-8826	232-8826
TF: 800-800-8000					
Travel Host Inn South 1314 NW Evangeline Thwy.	Lafayette	LA	70501	337-233-2090	233-2090
TF: 800-677-1466					
Travelodge 1101 W Pinhook Rd	Lafayette	LA	70503	337-234-7402	234-7404
TF: 800-578-7878					

— Restaurants —

Name / Address	City	State	Zip	Phone
Acadiana's Catfish Shak (Seafood) 5818 Johnston St	Lafayette	LA	70503	337-988-2200
Alesi's Restaurant (Italian) 4110 Johnston St.	Lafayette	LA	70503	337-984-9064
Antoni's Italian Cafe (Italian) 1118 Coolidge Blvd Suite A	Lafayette	LA	70503	337-232-8384
Baracca's Grill (Italian) 3502 Ambassador Caffery Pkwy	Lafayette	LA	70503	337-988-6119
Blair House Restaurant (Cajun) 1316 Surrey St.	Lafayette	LA	70501	337-234-0357
Bubba Moe Betta Barbecue (Barbecue) 1426 N Bertrand Dr	Lafayette	LA	70506	337-269-9717
Cafe Jardin (New American) 1521 W Pinhook Rd Hilton Lafayette	Lafayette	LA	70503	337-235-6111
Cafe Vermilionville (French) 1304 W Pinhook Rd	Lafayette	LA	70503	337-237-0100
Web: www.cafev.com ■ *E-mail:* mikecafe@globalreach.net				
Cajun Pier (Cajun/Creole) 1601 W Pinhook Rd	Lafayette	LA	70508	337-233-8640
Casa Ole (Mexican) 2312 Kaliste Saloom Rd.	Lafayette	LA	70508	337-993-9900
Charley G's Seafood Grill (Seafood) 3809 Ambassador Caffery Pkwy.	Lafayette	LA	70503	337-981-0108
Web: www.charleygs.com ■ *E-mail:* info@charleygs.com				
Chopsticks Chinese Restaurant (Chinese) 1901 NW Evangeline Thwy	Lafayette	LA	70501	337-269-9898
Country Cuisine (Creole) 709 N University Ave	Lafayette	LA	70506	337-269-1653
Don's Seafood & Steakhouse (Steak/Seafood) 301 E Vermilion St	Lafayette	LA	70501	337-235-3551
Edie's Restaurant (Homestyle) 1895 W Pinhook Rd.	Lafayette	LA	70508	337-234-2485
Evangeline Steakhouse (Steak/Seafood) 2633 SE Evangeline Thwy	Lafayette	LA	70508	337-233-2658
Gallagher's Restaurant (Homestyle) 407 Brook Ave.	Lafayette	LA	70506	337-261-0493
Great American Steak & More (Steak) 5725 Johnston St.	Lafayette	LA	70503	337-981-8234
Green Olive Restaurant (Lebanese) 2441 W Congress St.	Lafayette	LA	70506	337-234-0004
Imonelli Italian Restaurant (Italian) 4017 Johnston St.	Lafayette	LA	70503	337-989-9291

Lafayette — Restaurants (Cont'd)

Name	Address	City	State	ZIP	Phone
John's Seafood (Seafood)	4501 Johnston St	Lafayette	LA	70503	337-989-9020
Lagneaux's Restaurant (Seafood)	445 Ridge Rd	Lafayette	LA	70506	337-984-1415
Little China Restaurant (Chinese)	4510 Ambassador Caffery Pkwy Suite G	Lafayette	LA	70508	337-981-9388
Nigril Jamaican Cuisine (Jamaican)	1402 Jefferson St	Lafayette	LA	70501	337-232-9499
Oxford Street Restaurant (Continental)	3561 Ambassador Caffery Pkwy	Lafayette	LA	70503	337-989-8017
Picante Mexican Restaurant (Mexican)	3235 NW Evangeline Thwy	Lafayette	LA	70507	337-896-1200
Pimon Thai (Thai)	3904 Johnston St	Lafayette	LA	70503	337-993-8424
Poseidon's Greek Restaurant (Greek)	103 Kaliste Saloom Rd	Lafayette	LA	70508	337-235-9154
Prejean's Restaurant (Cajun)	3480 I-49 N	Lafayette	LA	70507	337-896-3247
	Web: www.prejeans.com ■ *E-mail:* prejeans@prejeans.com				
Rick's Family Restaurant (Homestyle)	3701 Cameron St	Lafayette	LA	70506	337-232-7462
Ruby's Restaurant (Cajun/Homestyle)	1601 Eraste Landry Rd	Lafayette	LA	70506	337-235-2046
Sahara Restaurant (Mediterranean)	1103 W Pinhook Rd	Lafayette	LA	70503	337-269-1434

— Goods and Services —

SHOPPING

Name	Address	City	State	ZIP	Phone	Fax
Acadiana Mall	5725 Johnston St	Lafayette	LA	70503	337-984-8240	981-4896
Acadiana Market	1693 Creswell Ln	Lafayette	LA	70570	337-942-6111	
Jefferson Street Market	538 Jefferson St.	Lafayette	LA	70501	337-233-2589	237-8882
Lafayette Antique Market	3108 Johnston St	Lafayette	LA	70503	337-981-9884	

BANKS

Name	Address	City	State	ZIP	Phone	Fax
Bank One	800 W Pinhook Rd	Lafayette	LA	70503	337-236-7118	236-7280
	TF Cust Svc: 800-777-8837*					
First Louisiana National Bank	2701 Moss St.	Lafayette	LA	70501	337-268-9600	268-5112
Gulf Coast Bank	4310 Johnston St	Lafayette	LA	70503	337-989-1133	989-2172
	TF: 800-722-5363					
Hibernia National Bank	213 W Vermilion St	Lafayette	LA	70501	337-268-4521	268-4564
	TF: 800-562-9007					
Iberia Bank	2130 W Kaliste Saloom Rd	Lafayette	LA	70508	337-988-4438	981-5987
Mid South National Bank	320 Heymann Blvd	Lafayette	LA	70503	337-237-8343	234-4671
	TF: 800-213-2265					
Regions Bank	5711 S Johnston St	Lafayette	LA	70593	337-988-0703	988-2358
	TF Cust Svc: 800-734-4667*					

BUSINESS SERVICES

Name	Phone	Name	Phone
Corporate Express	337-269-9955	**Mail Boxes Etc**	337-232-2442
Federal Express	800-238-5355	**Manpower Temporary Services**	337-237-6007
Hard Copy Inc	337-235-7503	**Post Office**	337-269-4800
Kelly Services	337-988-2010	**UPS**	800-742-5877
Kwik Kopy Printing	337-261-0139		

— Media —

PUBLICATIONS

Name	Address	City	State	ZIP	Phone	Fax
Lifestyle Lafayette	1720 Kaliste Saloom Rd Suite B-1	Lafayette	LA	70508	337-988-4607	983-0150
	E-mail: lifestyle@1stnet.com					
Times of Arcadia Newspaper	201 Jefferson St	Lafayette	LA	70501	337-237-3560	233-7484

TELEVISION

Name	Address	City	State	ZIP	Phone	Fax
KADN-TV Ch 15 (Fox)	1500 Eraste Landry Rd	Lafayette	LA	70506	337-237-1500	237-2237
	Web: www.kadn.com					
KATC-TV Ch 3 (ABC)	1103 Eraste Landry Rd	Lafayette	LA	70506	337-235-3333	234-3580
	Web: www.katc.com					
KLFY-TV Ch 10 (CBS)	1808 Eraste Landry Rd	Lafayette	LA	70506	337-981-4823	984-8323*
	**Fax:* Sales ■ *Web:* www.klfy.com					
KLPB-TV Ch 24 (PBS)	7733 Parkins Rd	Baton Rouge	LA	70810	225-767-5660	767-4277
	Web: www.lpb.org ■ *E-mail:* comments@lpb.org					
KPLC-TV Ch 7 (NBC)	PO Box 1490	Lake Charles	LA	70602	337-439-9071	437-7600
	E-mail: kplc@aol.com					

RADIO

Name	Address	City	State	ZIP	Phone	Fax
KAJN-FM 102.9 MHz (Rel)	110 W 3rd St	Crowley	LA	70526	337-783-1560	783-1674
KANE-AM 1240 kHz (Oldies)	2316 E Main St.	New Iberia	LA	70560	337-365-3434	367-5385
KEUN-AM 1490 kHz (Ctry)	330 W Laurel Ave	Eunice	LA	70535	337-457-3041	457-3081
KFMV-FM 105.5 MHz (Urban)	413 Jefferson St.	Lafayette	LA	70501	337-233-4262	235-9681
KFRA-AM 1390 kHz (Rel)	413 Jefferson St	Lafyaette	LA	70501	337-233-4262	235-9681
KFTE-FM 96.5 MHz (Rock)	1749 Bertrand Dr	Lafayette	LA	70506	337-232-2242	235-4181
KFXZ-FM 106.3 MHz (Rel)	3225 Ambassador Caffrey Pkwy	Lafayette	LA	70506	337-981-0106	988-0443
KJCB-AM 770 kHz (Urban)	413 Jefferson St.	Lafayette	LA	70501	337-233-4262	235-9681
KMDL-FM 97.3 MHz (Ctry)	1749 Bertrand Dr	Lafayette	LA	70506	337-232-2242	235-4181
KNEK-FM 104.7 MHz (Urban)	3225 Ambassador Caffery Pkwy	Lafayette	LA	70506	337-981-0106	988-0443
KNIR-AM 1360 kHz (Nost)	145 W Main St.	New Iberia	LA	70560	337-365-6651	365-6314
KPEL-AM 1420 kHz (N/T)	1749 Bertrand Dr	Lafayette	LA	70506	337-233-7003	234-7360
KROF-AM 960 kHz (B/EZ)	9525 US Hwy 167	Abbeville	LA	70510	337-893-2531	893-2569
KROF-FM 105.1 MHz (Oldies)	9525 US Hwy 167	Abbeville	LA	70510	337-893-2531	893-2569
KRRQ-FM 95.5 MHz (Urban)	3225 Ambassador Caffrey Pkwy	Lafayette	LA	70506	337-981-0106	988-0443
KRVS-FM 88.7 MHz (NPR)	PO Box 42171	Lafayette	LA	70504	337-482-5668	482-6101
	Web: krvs.usl.edu ■ *E-mail:* krvs@usl.edu					
KRXZ-FM 107.9 MHz (CR)	1749 Bertrand Dr	Lafayette	LA	70506	337-233-7003	234-7360
KSIG-AM 1450 kHz (B/EZ)	320 N Parkerson Ave.	Crowley	LA	70526	337-783-2520	783-5744
KSJY-FM 90.9 MHz (Rel)	614 Acadian Hills Ln	Lafayette	LA	70507	337-572-9909	572-9920
KSLO-AM 1230 kHz (Ctry)	PO Box 1150	Opelousas	LA	70571	337-942-2633	942-2635
KSMB-FM 94.5 MHz (CHR)	202 Galbert Rd	Lafayette	LA	70506	337-232-2632	233-3779
	Web: www.ksmb.com					
KTDY-FM 99.9 MHz (AC)	1749 Bertrand Dr	Lafayette	LA	70506	337-233-6000	234-7360
	E-mail: ktdy@aol.com					
KVOL-AM 1330 kHz (Sports)	202 Galbert Rd	Lafayette	LA	70506	337-233-1330	233-3779
KVOL-FM 105.9 MHz (Sports)	202 Galbert Rd	Lafayette	LA	70506	337-233-1330	233-3779
KXKC-FM 99.1 MHz (Ctry)	145 W Main St.	New Iberia	LA	70560	337-365-6651	365-6314
	Web: www.kxkc.com ■ *E-mail:* kxkc@kxkc.com					

— Colleges/Universities —

Name	Address	City	State	ZIP	Phone	Fax
University of Southwestern Louisiana	104 University Cir	Lafayette	LA	70504	337-482-1000	482-6195
	TF Admissions: 800-752-6553 ■ *Web:* www.usl.edu					

— Hospitals —

Name	Address	City	State	ZIP	Phone	Fax
Lafayette General Medical Center	1214 Coolidge Blvd	Lafayette	LA	70503	337-289-7991	289-7911
Our Lady of Lourdes Regional Medical Center	611 Saint Landry St	Lafayette	LA	70506	337-289-2000	289-2681*
	**Fax:* Admitting ■ *Web:* www.lourdes.net ■ *E-mail:* info@lourdes.net					

— Attractions —

Name	Address	City	State	ZIP	Phone	Fax
Acadian Village	200 Greenleaf St	Lafayette	LA	70506	337-981-2489	988-4554
	TF: 800-962-9133					
Alexandre Mouton House/Lafayette Museum	1122 Lafayette St	Lafayette	LA	70501	337-234-2208	
Artists Alliance Gallery	551 Jefferson St.	Lafayette	LA	70501	337-233-7518	
	Web: www.metacadiana.com/alliance					
Artists of Acadiana Gallery	1600 Surrey St Vermilionville	Lafayette	LA	70508	337-233-4077	

Lafayette — Attractions (Cont'd)

				Phone	Fax
Children's Museum of Acadiana 201 E Congress St	Lafayette	LA	70501	337-232-8500	232-8167
Chretien Point Plantation 665 Chretien Point Rd *TF:* 800-880-7050	Sunset	LA	70584	337-662-5876	662-5876
Girard Park 500 Girard Park Dr.	Lafayette	LA	70503	337-291-8379	291-8389
Heymann Performing Arts Center 1373 S College Rd	Lafayette	LA	70503	337-291-5540	291-5580
Jean Lafitte National Historical Park/Acadian Cultural Center 501 Fisher Rd *Web:* www.nationalparks.org/guide/parks/jean-lafitte-1780.htm	Lafayette	LA	70508	337-232-0789	232-5740
Kart Ranch Family Fun Center 508 Youngsville Hwy 89 *Web:* www.kartranch.com	Lafayette	LA	70592	337-837-5278	837-4078
Lafayette Art Gallery 412 Travis St Acadiana Symphony Cultural Ctr.	Lafayette	LA	70503	337-269-0363	
Lafayette Museum 1122 Lafayette St.	Lafayette	LA	70501	337-234-2208	234-2208
Lafayette Natural History Museum & Planetarium 637 Girard Park Dr. *Web:* www.lnhm.org ■ *E-mail:* magasin@1stnet.com	Lafayette	LA	70503	337-291-5544	291-5464
Rodrigue Gallery 1206 Jefferson St	Lafayette	LA	70501	337-232-6398	
Saint John Cathedral & Museum 914 Saint John St.	Lafayette	LA	70502	337-232-1322	232-1379
University Art Museum E Lewis St USL Campus Fletcher Hall	Lafayette	LA	70504	337-231-5326	482-5907
Vermilionville 1600 Surrey St *TF:* 800-992-2968	Lafayette	LA	70508	337-233-4077	233-1694
Zoo of Arcadiana 116 Lakeview Dr	Broussard	LA	70518	337-837-4325	837-4253

SPORTS TEAMS & FACILITIES

				Phone	Fax
Bayou Bullfrogs (baseball) 201 Reinhardt Dr ML Tigue Moore Field *Web:* www.txproball.com/frogs ■ *E-mail:* frogs@txproball.com	Lafayette	LA	70506	337-233-0998	237-3539
Cajundome 444 Cajundome Blvd.	Lafayette	LA	70506	337-265-2100	265-2311
Louisiana Hockeyplex 3067 NW Evangeline Thwy. *Web:* www.lahockeyplex.com ■ *E-mail:* administrator@lahockeyplex.com	Carencro	LA	70520	337-896-2042	896-2047
Louisiana IceGators (hockey) 444 Cajundome Blvd Cajundome. *Web:* www.icegators.com	Lafayette	LA	70506	337-234-4423	232-1254

— Events —

	Phone
Acadiana Culinary Classic (early November)	337-265-2100
Cajun & Creole Christmas (December)	337-232-3808
Cajun Fun Fest (mid-March)	337-365-1540
Cajun Heatland State Fair (late May-early June)	337-265-2100
Carencro Boudin & Cracklin Festival (mid-late February)	337-896-3378
Children's Carnival (late February)	337-845-4217
Children's Mardi Gras Parade (mid-February)	337-232-3808
Christmas at Vermilionville (December)	337-233-4077
Christmas Renaissance 'Festival of Light' (early December)	337-232-1267
Christmas Under the Lamppost (early December)	337-828-3817
Downtown Alive! (April-June & September-November)	337-291-5566
Festival du Courtableau (mid-late March)	337-826-3627
Festival International de Louisiane (late April)	337-232-8086
Festivals Acadiens (mid-late September)	337-232-3808
Fourth Futurity Festival (early July)	337-896-7223
Herb Fest (mid-April)	337-232-3737
King's Court (mid-February)	337-291-5566
King's Parade (mid-February)	337-232-3808
Kwanzaa Celebration (early January)	337-233-4758
La Fete de Vermilionville (mid-April)	337-233-4077
Lafayette Christmas Parade (early December)	337-232-3808
Le Cajun Music Awards Festival (mid-August)	337-232-3808
Le Festival de Mardi Gras à Lafayette (mid-February)	337-265-3904
Mardi Gras Association Parade (mid-February)	337-232-3808
Saint Ignatius Rainbeau Festival (mid-late March)	337-662-3325
Tour d'Acadiana (mid-April)	337-232-3808
Zydeco Extravaganza (late May)	337-234-9695

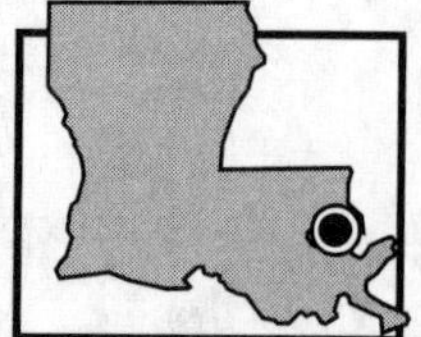

Metairie

Founded in 1825, Metairie has evolved from a residential community into one of the thriving business sectors of the New Orleans subdivision of Jefferson Parish. Located on the east bank of the Mississippi River, Metairie includes many parks, theaters, and shopping areas. It also is home to the longest bridge over water in the world, the Lake Pontchartrain Causeway. Due to its saltwater content, the 610-square-mile Lake Pontchartrain is technically an estuary, the largest in the United States. It features thousands of purple martins, a favorite of birdwatchers, who enjoy the aerial acrobatics as the birds fly in huge formations throughout the summer.

Population	149,428	**Longitude**	90-10-38 W
Area (Land)	23.3 sq mi	**County**	Jefferson Parish
Area (Water)	0.0 sq mi	**Time Zone**	CST
Elevation	5 ft	**Area Code/s**	504
Latitude	29-59-51 N		

— Average Temperatures and Precipitation —

TEMPERATURES

	Jan	Feb	Mar	Apr	May	Jun	Jul	Aug	Sep	Oct	Nov	Dec
High	61	64	72	79	84	89	91	90	87	79	71	64
Low	42	44	52	58	65	71	73	73	70	59	51	45

PRECIPITATION

	Jan	Feb	Mar	Apr	May	Jun	Jul	Aug	Sep	Oct	Nov	Dec
Inches	5.1	6.0	4.9	4.5	4.6	5.8	6.1	6.2	5.5	3.1	4.4	5.8

— Important Phone Numbers —

	Phone		Phone
AAA	504-838-7500	**Medical Referral**	504-456-5000
American Express Travel	504-586-8201	**Poison Control Center**	800-256-9822
Dental Referral	504-834-6449	**Weather**	504-828-4000
Emergency	911		

— Information Sources —

				Phone	Fax
Better Business Bureau Serving Greater New Orleans 1539 Jackson Ave Suite 400 *Web:* www.neworleans.bbb.org	New Orleans	LA	70130	504-581-6222	524-9110
Jefferson Parish PO Box 9 *Web:* www.jeffparish.net	Gretna	LA	70054	504-364-2600	364-2633
Jefferson Parish Library 4747 W Napoleon Ave *Web:* www.jefferson.lib.la.us	Metairie	LA	70001	504-838-1100	838-1117
Jefferson Parish Tourist Information Center 300 Veterans Memorial Blvd.	Kenner	LA	70062	504-468-7527	
Metairie Community Development Dept 1221 Elmwood Pk Blvd Suite 605 *Web:* www.jeffparish.net/departments/d-cdev.html	Jefferson	LA	70123	504-736-6262	736-6425
Metairie Parish President 1221 Elmwood Pk Blvd Suite 1002	Jefferson	LA	70123	504-736-6400	736-6638
New Orleans & River Region Chamber of Commerce 601 Poydras St Suite 1700 *Web:* chamber.gnofn.org ■ *E-mail:* chamber@gnofn.org	New Orleans	LA	70130	504-527-6900	527-6950

On-Line Resources

Metairie.com .... www.metairie.com
NITC Travelbase City Guide Metairie .... www.travelbase.com/auto/features/metairie-la.html

Metairie (Cont'd)

— Transportation Services —

AIRPORTS

■ New Orleans International Airport (MSY)

	Phone
10 miles W of downtown Metairie (approx 20 minutes)	504-464-0831

Airport Transportation

	Phone
Service Cab $18 fare to downtown Metairie	504-834-1400
Taxi $21 fare to downtown Metairie	504-835-2227

Commercial Airlines

	Phone		Phone
American	800-433-7300	**Northwest**	800-225-2525
Aviateca	800-327-9832	**Southwest**	800-435-9792
Continental	504-581-2965	**TACA International**	800-535-8780
Continental Express	800-525-0280	**TWA**	800-221-2000
Delta	800-221-1212	**United**	800-241-6522
LACSA	504-468-3948	**US Airways**	800-428-4322

Charter Airlines

	Phone
Trans-Gulf Seaplane Service Inc.	504-254-0621

CAR RENTALS

	Phone		Phone
Alamo	504-469-0532	**Hertz**	504-400-3695
Avis	504-464-9511	**National**	504-466-4335
Budget	504-467-2277		

LIMO/TAXI

	Phone		Phone
Classic Cab	504-835-2227	**Metry Cab Service**	504-833-1511
King Cab	504-469-5464	**Service Cab**	504-834-1400

MASS TRANSIT

	Phone
Mass Transit RTA $1 Base fare	504-248-3900

RAIL/BUS

	City	State	Zip	Phone
Amtrak Station 1001 Loyola Ave *TF:* 800-872-7245	New Orleans	LA	70113	504-528-1610
Greyhound/Trailways Bus Station 1001 Loyola Ave *TF:* 800-231-2222	New Orleans	LA	70113	504-524-7571

— Accommodations —

HOTELS, MOTELS, RESORTS

	City	State	Zip	Phone	Fax
Best Western Inn 2438 Veterans Memorial Blvd *TF:* 800-528-1234	Kenner	LA	70062	504-469-2800	469-4177
Best Western Landmark Hotel 2601 Severn Ave. *TF:* 800-277-7575	Metairie	LA	70002	504-888-9500	885-8474
Brent House Hotel 1512 Jefferson Hwy *TF:* 800-535-3986	Jefferson	LA	70121	504-835-5411	842-4160
Contempra Inn 2820 Williams Blvd	Kenner	LA	70062	504-468-7700	468-7500
Doubletree Lakeside New Orleans 3838 N Causeway Blvd *TF:* 800-222-8733 ■ *Web:* www.doubletreehotels.com/DoubleT/Hotel41/53/53Main.htm	Metairie	LA	70002	504-836-5253	846-4562
Evergreen Plaza Inn 6590 Veterans Memorial Blvd.	Metairie	LA	70003	504-885-4800	887-6607
Famous Plaza Inn 4801 Airline Hwy	Metairie	LA	70001	504-455-9300	454-6199
Hilton New Orleans Airport 901 Airline Hwy *Web:* www.hilton.com/hotels/MSYAHHH	Kenner	LA	70062	504-469-5000	466-5473
Holiday Inn Metairie 3400 S I-10 Service Rd & Cswy *TF:* 800-747-3279 ■ *Web:* www.basshotels.com/holiday-inn/?_franchisee=MSYFC	Metairie	LA	70001	504-833-8201	838-6829
Holiday Inn New Orleans 6401 Veterans Memorial Blvd *TF:* 800-465-4329 ■ *Web:* www.basshotels.com/holiday-inn/?_franchisee=MSYAT	Metairie	LA	70003	504-885-5700	454-8294
Holiday Inn Select New Orleans Airport 2929 Williams Blvd *TF:* 800-465-4329 ■ *Web:* www.basshotels.com/holiday-inn/?_franchisee=MSYAP ■ *E-mail:* gdc836a@aol.com	Kenner	LA	70062	504-467-5611	469-4915
La Quinta Inn 2610 Williams Blvd *TF:* 800-531-5900	Kenner	LA	70062	504-466-1401	466-0319
La Quinta Inn 3100 I-10 Service Rd *TF:* 800-531-5900	Metairie	LA	70001	504-835-8511	837-3383
La Quinta Inn 5900 Veterans Memorial Blvd. *TF:* 800-531-5900	Metairie	LA	70003	504-456-0003	888-0863
Orleans Courtyard Inn 3800 Hessmer Ave *TF:* 800-258-2514 ■ *Web:* www.neworleans.com/court.html	Metairie	LA	70002	504-455-6110	455-0940
Park Plaza Inn 2125 Veterans Memorial Blvd *TF:* 800-504-7275	Kenner	LA	70062	504-464-6464	464-7532
Quality Hotel 2261 N Causeway Blvd. *TF:* 800-228-5151	Metairie	LA	70001	504-833-8211	833-8213
Quality Inn 100 Westbank Expy *TF:* 800-635-7787	Gretna	LA	70053	504-366-8531	362-9502
Quality Inn Marina 5353 Paris Rd. *TF:* 800-228-5151	Chalmette	LA	70044	504-277-5353	279-6442
Radisson Inn Airport 2150 Veterans Memorial Blvd. *TF:* 800-333-3333	Kenner	LA	70062	504-467-3111	469-4634
Ramada Limited 2713 N Causeway Blvd *TF:* 800-874-1280	Metairie	LA	70002	504-835-4141	833-6942
Shoney's Inn 2421 S Clearview Pkwy *TF:* 800-222-2222 ■ *Web:* www.shoneysinn.com/la1.htm	Metairie	LA	70001	504-456-9081	455-6287
Trade Winds Motel 3616 Airline Dr.	Metairie	LA	70001	504-835-4221	
Travelodge 5733 Airline Dr.	Metairie	LA	70003	504-733-1550	733-1554
Travelodge Airport 2240 Veterans Memorial Blvd. *TF:* 800-578-7878	Kenner	LA	70062	504-469-7341	469-7922

— Restaurants —

	City	State	Zip	Phone
Andrea's (Italian) 3100 19th St	Metairie	LA	70002	504-834-8583
Barreca's Restaurant (Italian) 3100 Metairie Rd	Metairie	LA	70001	504-831-4546
Caffe Fresco (Italian) 2007 Clearview Pkwy.	Metairie	LA	70001	504-887-2010
Carmine's Italian Grill (Italian) 4101 Veterans Blvd.	Metairie	LA	70002	504-455-7904
Churros Cafe (Cuban) 3100 Kingman St	Metairie	LA	70006	504-885-6516
Corky's (Barbecue) 4243 Veterans Memorial Blvd	Metairie	LA	70006	504-887-5000
Crozier's (French) 3216 West Esplanade N	Metairie	LA	70002	504-833-8108
Don's Seafood Hut (Seafood) 4801 Veterans Memorial Blvd	Metairie	LA	70006	504-889-1550
Dragon's Garden (Chinese) 3100 17th St	Metairie	LA	70002	504-834-9065
Eggroll House Restaurant (Chinese) 3507 Veterans Memorial Blvd	Metairie	LA	70002	504-887-9364
Fausto's Kitchen (Italian) 530 Veterans Memorial Blvd.	Metairie	LA	70005	504-833-7121
Galley Seafood Restaurant (Seafood) 2535 Metairie Rd	Metairie	LA	70001	504-832-0955
Hobnobbers Cafe & Grill (American) 4441 W Metairie Ave.	Metairie	LA	70001	504-456-0013
Impastato's (Italian) 3400 16th St	Metairie	LA	70002	504-455-1545
India Palace (Indian) 3322 N Turnball Dr	Metairie	LA	70002	504-889-2436
Jade Moon Chinese Restaurant (Chinese) 4337 Airline Dr	Metairie	LA	70001	504-831-0555
Jalapeno's Mexican Cafe (Mexican) 2320 Veterans Memorial Blvd	Metairie	LA	70002	504-837-6696
Johnny's Po' Boys (American) 4445 Veterans Memorial Blvd	Metairie	LA	70002	504-888-7888
La Riviera (Italian) 4506 Shores Dr	Metairie	LA	70006	504-888-6238
Luther's Bar-B-Q (Barbecue) 2750 Severn Ave	Metairie	LA	70002	504-888-6370
New Orleans Hamburger & Seafood Co (American/Seafood) 817 Veterans Memorial Blvd	Metairie	LA	70005	504-837-8580
O'Henry's Food & Spirits (American) 3020 Severn Ave	Metairie	LA	70002	504-888-9383
Parran's Po Boys (Cajun/Creole) 3939 B Veterans Memorial Blvd	Metairie	LA	70002	504-885-3416
Peppermill Restaurant (Creole/Italian) 3524 Severn Ave	Metairie	LA	70002	504-455-2266
Ralph & Kacoo's Seafood (Cajun) 601 Veterans Memorial Blvd	Metairie	LA	70005	504-831-3177
Saia's Beef Room (Steak) 2645 N Causeway Blvd	Metairie	LA	70002	504-835-8555
Sal & Sam's (Italian) 4300 Veterans Memorial Blvd.	Metairie	LA	70006	504-885-5566
Siamese Restaurant (Thai) 6601 Veterans Memorial Blvd.	Metairie	LA	70003	504-454-8752
Straya California Creole Cafe (California) 4517 Veterans Memorial Blvd *Web:* www.yatcom.com/neworl/dining/straya/	Metairie	LA	70006	504-887-8873
Texas Bar-B-Que (Barbecue) 3320 Houma Blvd.	Metairie	LA	70006	504-456-2832
Vega Tapas Cafe (Spanish) 2051 Metairie Rd	Metairie	LA	70005	504-836-2007
Yoshi's Sushi (Japanese) 3205 Edenborn Ave.	Metairie	LA	70002	504-885-7363

Metairie (Cont'd)

— Goods and Services —

SHOPPING

				Phone	Fax
Clearview Shopping Center 4436 Veterans Memorial Blvd	Metairie	LA	70006	504-885-0202	885-4100
Esplanade The 1401 W Esplanade	Kenner	LA	70065	504-468-6116	466-9502
Lakeside Shopping Center 3301 Veterans Memorial Blvd	Metairie	LA	70002	504-835-8000	831-1170
Rosedale Mall 3780 Veterans Memorial Blvd	Metairie	LA	70002	504-455-3678	455-3373
Westgate Shopping Center 4941 Yale St	Metairie	LA	70006	504-455-1283	

BANKS

				Phone	Fax
Deposit Guaranty National Bank 3525 N Causeway Blvd *Web:* www.dgb.com	Metairie	LA	70002	504-837-3333	838-6609
Greater New Orleans Homestead FSB 1600 Veterans Memorial Blvd	Metairie	LA	70005	504-834-1190	835-2373
Hibernia National Bank 4466 Veterans Memorial Blvd	Metairie	LA	70006	504-533-3787	533-5365
Metairie Bank & Trust Co 3344 Metairie Rd. *Web:* www.metairiebank.com ■ *E-mail:* info@metairiebank.com	Metairie	LA	70001	504-834-6330	835-4385
Omni Bank 2900 Ridgelake Dr *Web:* www.omnibk.com	Metairie	LA	70002	504-833-2900	841-2059
Regions Bank 5055 Veterans Memorial Blvd *TF:* 800-888-9293	Metairie	LA	70006	504-561-7354	455-7082
Whitney National Bank 4845 Veterans Memorial Blvd	Metairie	LA	70006	504-838-6393	838-6351

BUSINESS SERVICES

	Phone		Phone
ATS Personnel Services	504-468-6771	**Mail Boxes Etc**	504-835-0470
DHL Worldwide Express	800-225-5345	**Norrell Staffing**	504-455-6565
Federal Express	800-238-5355	**Post Office**	800-275-8777
Interim Personnel Services	504-831-3552	**Preferred Temporary Services**	504-835-8085
Key Temporary Services	504-889-0722	**UPS**	800-742-5877
Kinko's	504-831-8720		

— Media —

PUBLICATIONS

				Phone	Fax
Louisiana Life 111 Veterans Blvd Suite 1810 *TF:* 800-739-8836 ■ *Web:* www.neworleans.com/lalife/	Metairie	LA	70005	504-834-9698	838-7700
New Orleans City Business 111 Veterans Blvd Suite 1810 *Web:* www.neworleans.com/citybusiness/ ■ *E-mail:* citybiz@nopg.com	Metairie	LA	70005	504-834-9292	832-3550
Times-Picayune‡ 3800 Howard Ave *TF:* 800-925-0000 ■ *Web:* www.nola.com	New Orleans	LA	70140	504-826-3279	826-3007

‡Daily newspapers

TELEVISION

				Phone	Fax
WDSU-TV Ch 6 (NBC) 846 Howard *Web:* www.wdsu.com ■ *E-mail:* wdsu@comm.net	New Orleans	LA	70113	504-679-0600	679-0733
WLAE-TV Ch 32 (PBS) 2929 S Carrollton Ave *Web:* www.pbs.org/wlae/ ■ *E-mail:* info@wlae.pbs.org	New Orleans	LA	70118	504-866-7411	861-5186
WNOL-TV Ch 38 (WB) 1661 Canal St *Web:* www.wnol.com ■ *E-mail:* wnol@comm.net	New Orleans	LA	70112	504-525-3838	569-0908
WUPL-TV Ch 54 (UPN) 3850 N Causeway Blvd Suite 454 *Web:* www.paramountstations.com/WUPL	Metairie	LA	70002	504-828-5454	828-5455
WVUE-TV Ch 8 (Fox) 1025 S Jefferson Davis Pkwy	New Orleans	LA	70125	504-486-6161	483-1212
WWL-TV Ch 4 (CBS) 1024 N Rampart St. *Web:* www.wwltv.com	New Orleans	LA	70116	504-529-4444	529-6472
WYES-TV Ch 12 (PBS) 916 Navarre Ave *Web:* www.pbs.org/wyes/ ■ *E-mail:* assist@wyes.pbs.org	New Orleans	LA	70124	504-486-5511	483-8408

RADIO

				Phone	Fax
KUMX-FM 104.1 MHz (CHR) 929 Howard Ave 2nd Fl *Web:* www.themix1041.com ■ *E-mail:* request@themixmail.com	New Orleans	LA	70113	504-679-7300	679-7358
WCKW-FM 92.3 MHz (Rock) 3501 N Causeway Blvd Suite 700 *Web:* www.wckw.com	Metairie	LA	70002	504-831-8811	831-8885
WGSO-AM 990 kHz (N/T) 111 Veterans Memorial Blvd Suite 1800	Metairie	LA	70005	504-834-9292	838-7700
WLTS-FM 105.3 MHz (AC) 3525 N Causeway Blvd Suite 1053	Metairie	LA	70002	504-834-9587	833-8560
WTIX-FM 94.3 MHz (Oldies) 4539 I-10 Service Rd	Metairie	LA	70006	504-454-9000	454-9506
WTKL-FM 95.7 MHz (Oldies) 1450 Poydras Suite 440	New Orleans	LA	70112	504-593-6376	593-1865
WVOG-AM 600 kHz (Rel) 2730 Loumor Ave.	Metairie	LA	70001	504-831-6941	

— Colleges/Universities —

				Phone	Fax
Concordia University 3229 36th St	Metairie	LA	70001	504-828-3802	828-2008
Southeast College of Technology 321 Veterans Memorial Blvd *Web:* www.sctno.com	Metairie	LA	70005	504-948-7246	831-6803

— Hospitals —

				Phone	Fax
Doctors Hospital of Jefferson 4320 Houma Blvd *Web:* www.tenethealth.com/DoctorsJefferson	Metairie	LA	70006	504-849-4000	846-3010
East Jefferson General Hospital 4200 Houma Blvd *Web:* www.eastjeffhospital.org	Metairie	LA	70006	504-454-4000	456-8151
Lakeside Hospital 4700 I-10 Service Rd	Metairie	LA	70001	504-885-3333	780-4374

— Attractions —

				Phone	Fax
Bayou Segnette State Park 7777 Westbank Expy	Westwego	LA	70094	504-736-7140	436-0695
Cannes Brulee Native American Center 303 Williams Blvd Rivertown *TF:* 800-473-6789	Kenner	LA	70062	504-468-7231	471-2159
Celebration Station Entertainment Complex 5959 Veterans Memorial Blvd	Metairie	LA	70003	504-887-7888	888-8404
Children's Castle 501 Williams Blvd Rivertown *TF:* 800-473-6789	Kenner	LA	70062	504-469-3236	471-2159
Cytec Louisiana Wildlife & Fisheries Museum 303 Williams Blvd Rivertown	Kenner	LA	70062	504-468-7231	471-2159
Daily Living Science Center 409 Williams Blvd	Kenner	LA	70062	504-468-7231	468-7599
Delta Festival Ballet 3850 N Causeway Blvd Suite 119	Metairie	LA	70002	504-836-7166	836-7167
Freeport Memoran Daily Living Science Center 409 Williams Blvd Rivertown *TF:* 800-473-6789	Kenner	LA	70062	504-468-7231	471-2159
Jean Lafitte National Historical Park & Preserve 365 Canal St Suite 2400 *Web:* www.nps.gov/jela/	New Orleans	LA	70130	504-589-3882	589-3851
Lil' Cajun Swamp Tours Hwy 301 *TF:* 800-689-3213	Crown Point	LA	70072	504-689-3213	689-3213
Longue Vue House & Gardens 7 Bamboo Rd *Web:* www.longuevue.com	New Orleans	LA	70124	504-488-5488	486-7015
Louisiana Toy Train Museum 519 Williams Blvd Rivertown	Kenner	LA	70062	504-468-7231	471-2159
Louisiana Wildlife Museum 303 Williams Blvd Rivertown	Kenner	LA	70062	504-468-7231	471-2159
Pontchartrain Astronomy Society Observatory 409 Williams Blvd Rivertown *TF:* 800-473-6789	Kenner	LA	70062	504-468-7229	471-2159
Rivertown USA 405 Williams Blvd. *Web:* www.kenner.la.us	Kenner	LA	70062	504-468-7231	
Saints Hall of Fame Museum 409 Williams Blvd Rivertown *Web:* www.kenner.la.us/saints.html	Kenner	LA	70062	504-468-7231	471-2159

Metairie — Attractions (Cont'd)

				Phone	Fax
Treasure Chest Casino 5050 Williams Blvd	Kenner	LA	70065	504-443-8000	443-8104
TF: 800-298-0711 ■ *Web:* www.treasurechest.com					
Treasure Chest Casino Presents Mardi Gras Museum 421 Williams Blvd Rivertown	Kenner	LA	70062	504-468-7231	471-2159
TF: 800-473-6789					

SPORTS TEAMS & FACILITIES

				Phone	Fax
New Orleans Brass (hockey) 1201 Saint Peter St Municipal Auditorium	New Orleans	LA	70116	504-522-7825	523-7295
New Orleans Storm (soccer) 6000 Airline Dr Zephyr Field	Metairie	LA	70003	504-734-5155	734-5118
New Orleans Zephyrs (baseball) 6000 Airline Dr Zephyr Field	Metairie	LA	70003	504-734-5155	734-5118
Web: www.insideneworleans.com/zephyrs					

— Events —

	Phone
Chinese New Year Festival (late January)	504-482-6682
Christmas in July (late July)	504-465-9985
Christmas Tree Lighting (early December)	504-363-1580
Christmas Village (late November-mid-December)	504-468-7293
Collector's Festival (late September)	504-363-1580
Family Day (early October)	504-468-7293
Gretna Heritage Festival (early October)	504-363-1580
Gumbo Festival (mid-October)	504-436-4712
Holly Jolly Christmas Bonfires (mid-December)	504-468-7293
Jeff Fest (late October)	504-888-2900
Louisiana Railroad Festival (mid-November)	504-363-1580
Mensaje's Spanish Festival (late March-early April)	504-468-7527
Pet Fest (late September)	504-734-7590
Veteran's Day Program (November 11)	504-363-1580
Westwego Festival (mid-September)	504-436-0812

New Orleans

New Orleans is a unique blend of several distinct cultures, and the legacy of its Cajun, Creole, and Santo Domingan heritage is reflected in the city's music, food, architecture, and religion. The 100 square blocks of the Historic French Quarter, with its wrought iron balconies and secluded courtyards, offer exotic Creole cuisine and some of the area's finest jazz, especially along Bourbon Street. The Saint Charles Avenue streetcar travels to the more formal Uptown area, with its Garden District of pre-Civil War homes. Along River Avenue, as well as in outlying areas, are many restored plantations and "Louisiana cottages." Each year people come from all over the country to celebrate Mardi Gras in New Orleans, and the two weeks before Lent are filled with non-stop parties, parades, costume balls, and street festivals. In late April, the city hosts the annual Jazz and Heritage Festival.

Population	465,538	**Longitude**	90-07-50 W
Area (Land)	180.6 sq mi	**County**	Orleans Parish
Area (Water)	169.6 sq mi	**Time Zone**	CST
Elevation	5 ft	**Area Code/s**	504
Latitude	29-95-44 N		

— Average Temperatures and Precipitation —

TEMPERATURES

	Jan	Feb	Mar	Apr	May	Jun	Jul	Aug	Sep	Oct	Nov	Dec
High	61	64	72	79	84	89	91	90	87	79	71	64
Low	42	44	52	58	65	71	73	73	70	59	51	45

PRECIPITATION

	Jan	Feb	Mar	Apr	May	Jun	Jul	Aug	Sep	Oct	Nov	Dec
Inches	5.1	6.0	4.9	4.5	4.6	5.8	6.1	6.2	5.5	3.1	4.4	5.8

— Important Phone Numbers —

	Phone		Phone
AAA	800-926-4222	**Medical Referral**	504-456-5000
American Express Travel	504-586-8201	**Poison Control Center**	800-256-9822
Dental Referral	504-834-6449	**Travelers Aid Society**	504-525-8726
Emergency	911	**Weather**	504-828-4000
HotelDocs	800-468-3537		

— Information Sources —

				Phone	Fax
Better Business Bureau Serving Greater New Orleans 1539 Jackson Ave Suite 400	New Orleans	LA	70130	504-581-6222	524-9110
Web: www.neworleans.bbb.org					
Ernest N Morial Convention Center 900 Convention Center Blvd	New Orleans	LA	70130	504-582-3023	582-3088
New Orleans & River Region Chamber of Commerce 601 Poydras St Suite 1700	New Orleans	LA	70130	504-527-6900	527-6950
Web: chamber.gnofn.org ■ *E-mail:* chamber@gnofn.org					
New Orleans City Hall 1300 Perdido St	New Orleans	LA	70112	504-565-6000	
Web: www.new-orleans.la.us					
New Orleans Economic Development Dept 1515 Poydras St Suite 1200	New Orleans	LA	70112	504-565-8100	565-8108
New Orleans Mayor 1300 Perdido St	New Orleans	LA	70112	504-565-6400	565-8076
Web: www.new-orleans.la.us/cnoweb/mayor/index.html					
New Orleans Metropolitan Convention & Visitors Bureau 1520 Sugar Bowl Dr	New Orleans	LA	70112	504-566-5011	566-5046
TF: 800-672-6124 ■ *Web:* www.neworleanscvb.com					
New Orleans Public Library 219 Loyola Ave	New Orleans	LA	70112	504-596-2550	596-2609
Web: www.gnofn.org/~nopl					
New Orleans Visitor Center 1520 Sugar Bowl Dr	New Orleans	LA	70112	504-566-5011	566-5046
Web: www.neworleanscvb.com					
Orleans Parish 1300 Perdido St Rm 9-E-06	New Orleans	LA	70112	504-565-6570	

On-Line Resources

4NewOrleans.com	www.4neworleans.com
About.com Guide to New Orleans	neworleans.about.com/local/southeastus/neworleans
Area Guide New Orleans	neworleans.areaguides.net
Big Easy New Orleans Guide	www.big-easy.com
City Knowledge New Orleans	www.cityknowledge.com/la_neworleans.htm
CitySearch New Orleans	neworleans.citysearch.com
CityTravelGuide.com New Orleans	www.citytravelguide.com/new-orleans.htm
CrescentCity.com	www.crescentcity.com/
CuisineNet New Orleans	www.menusonline.com/cities/new_orleans/locmain.shtml
DigitalCity New Orleans	home.digitalcity.com/neworleans
Discover New Orleans	www.discoverneworleans.com/
Excite.com New Orleans City Guide	www.excite.com/travel/countries/united_states/louisiana/new_orleans
Experience New Orleans	www.neworleansweb.org/
French Quarter	www.frenchquarter.com/
Gambit Weekly	www.bestofneworleans.com
Gateway New Orleans	www.gatewayno.com/
Gay New Orleans	www.gayneworleans.com/
Gayot's Guide Restaurant Search New Orleans	www.perrier.com/restaurants/gayot.asp?area=NOR
Gumbo Pages	www.gumbopages.com/
HotelGuide New Orleans	new.orleans.hotelguide.net
LDS iAmerica New Orleans	new-orleans.iamerica.net/
New Orleans 2fun.com	www.2fun.com
New Orleans a la Net	www.alanet.com/
New Orleans CityLink	www.usacitylink.com/citylink/new-orleans/
New Orleans Connection	www.neworleansla.com/

New Orleans — On-Line Resources (Cont'd)

New Orleans from A to Z . . . www.neworleansatoz.com/home.htm
New Orleans Guide . . . nola.accesscom.net
New Orleans Home Page . . . www.neworleans.com
New Orleans LA Live . . . www.nolalive.com
New Orleans Online . . . www.neworleansonline.com/
New Orleans Times & Directory . . . www.gna.com/
New Orleans Visitors Guide . . . www.compucast.com/acquaint.html
NITC Travelbase City Guide New Orleans . . . www.travelbase.com/auto/guides/new_orleans-area-la.html
Nitebeat Guide to Nightlife . . . www.nitebeat.com/
OffBeat Magazine . . . www.offbeat.com
Open World City Guides New Orleans . . . www.worldexecutive.com/cityguides/new_orleans/
Rough Guide Travel New Orleans . . . travel.roughguides.com/content/883/
Time Out New Orleans . . . www.timeout.com/neworleans/
Virtual New Orleans . . . www.virtualneworleans.com/
Virtual Voyages New Orleans . . . www.virtualvoyages.com/usa/la/n_o/n_o.sht
WeekendEvents.com New Orleans . . . www.weekendevents.com/neworleans/norleans.html

— Transportation Services —

AIRPORTS

■ New Orleans International Airport (MSY)

	Phone
14 miles NW of downtown New Orleans (approx 20 minutes)	504-464-0831

Web: home.gnofn.org/~airport ■ *E-mail:* airport@chamber.gnofn.org

Airport Transportation

	Phone
Airport Shuttle $10 fare to downtown New Orleans	504-592-0555
Louisiana Transit Co $1.50 fare to downtown New Orleans	504-818-1077
Taxi $21 fare to downtown New Orleans	504-525-3311

Commercial Airlines

	Phone		Phone
AeroMexico	800-237-6639	**MetroJet**	888-638-7653
American	800-433-7300	**Northwest**	800-225-2525
Aviateca	800-327-9832	**Southwest**	800-435-9792
Continental	504-581-2965	**TACA International**	800-535-8780
Continental Express	800-525-0280	**TWA**	800-221-2000
Delta	800-221-1212	**United**	800-241-6522
LACSA	504-468-3948	**US Airways**	800-428-4322

Charter Airlines

	Phone
Trans-Gulf Seaplane Service Inc.	504-254-0621

CAR RENTALS

	Phone		Phone
Alamo	504-469-0532	**Dollar**	504-467-2285
Avis	504-464-9511	**Hertz**	504-468-3695
Budget	504-467-2277	**National**	504-466-4335

LIMO/TAXI

	Phone		Phone
A Touch of Class Limousine	504-522-7565	**New Orleans Limousine**	504-529-5226
Carey Limousine	504-522-0778	**Orleans Limousines**	504-831-7433
Golden Dragon Limousine	800-521-9336	**United Cab**	504-522-9771
Landry's Limousine	504-244-0127	**White Fleet Cabs**	504-948-6605
Lanusse Limousine	504-595-8922	**Yellow Checker Cab**	504-525-3311

MASS TRANSIT

	Phone
Mass Transit RTA $1 Base fare	504-248-3900

RAIL/BUS

				Phone
Amtrak Station 1001 Loyola Ave	New Orleans	LA	70113	504-528-1610
TF: 800-872-7245				
Greyhound/Trailways Bus Station 1001 Loyola Ave	New Orleans	LA	70113	504-524-7571
TF: 800-231-2222				

— Accommodations —

HOTEL RESERVATION SERVICES

	Phone	Fax
AAA Reservation Services *TF:* 888-840-2331	504-522-1785	566-0405
Accommodations Express *TF:* 800-444-7666 ■ *Web:* www.accommodationsxpress.com ■ *E-mail:* accomexp@acy.digex.net	609-391-2100	525-0111
Bed & Breakfast & Beyond Reservation Service *TF:* 800-886-3709 ■ *Web:* www.nolabandb.com	504-896-9977	896-2482
Bed & Breakfast Inc-A Reservation Service *TF:* 800-729-4640	504-488-4640	488-4639
Big Easy/Gulf Coast Reservation Service *TF:* 800-368-4876 ■ *Web:* www.crescentcity.com/fql/ ■ *E-mail:* bigeasy3@bellsouth.net	504-433-2563	391-1903
Central Reservation Service *TF:* 800-548-3311 ■ *Web:* www.reservation-services.com ■ *E-mail:* cenresbos@aol.com	407-740-6442	740-8222
Corporate Lodging Service *TF:* 800-995-0137	504-828-0380	467-3037
Greater New Orleans Hotel-Motel Assn **Fax Area Code:* 504	800-695-2264	525-9327*
Hotel Reservations Network Inc *TF Sales:* 800-964-6835 ■ *Web:* www.hoteldiscount.com	214-361-7311	361-7299
New Orleans Accommodations Bed & Breakfast Service *TF:* 888-340-0070 ■ *Web:* www.neworleansbandb.com/ ■ *E-mail:* info@neworleansbandb.com	504-838-0071	838-0140
Oakwood Corporate Housing *TF:* 800-259-2086 ■ *Web:* www.oakwood.com	504-733-7033	733-8393
Quikbook *TF:* 800-789-9887 ■ *Web:* www.quikbook.com	212-532-1660	532-1556
Reservations USA *TF:* 800-251-4444 ■ *Web:* www.reservationsusa.com ■ *E-mail:* reserve@lodging4u.com	865-453-1000	453-7484
Room Finders USA *TF:* 800-473-7829 ■ *Web:* www.roomsusa.com ■ *E-mail:* welcome@roomsusa.com	504-522-9373	529-1948

HOTELS, MOTELS, RESORTS

				Phone	Fax
Ambassador Hotel 535 Tchoupitoulas St *TF:* 888-527-5271 ■ *Web:* www.neworleans.com/ambassador/	New Orleans	LA	70130	504-527-5271	527-5270
Avenue Plaza Hotel & Spa 2111 St Charles Ave *TF:* 800-535-9575	New Orleans	LA	70130	504-566-1212	525-6899
Bally's Casino Lakeshore Resort 1 Stars & Stripes Blvd **Fax:* Hum Res ■ *TF:* 800-572-2559 ■ *Web:* www.ballysno.com	New Orleans	LA	70126	504-248-3200	248-3283*
Best Western Inn on Bourbon 541 Bourbon St *TF:* 800-535-7891 ■ *Web:* www.innonbourbon.com/	New Orleans	LA	70130	504-524-7611	568-9427
Bienville House Hotel 320 Decatur St *TF:* 800-535-7836 ■ *Web:* www.bienvillehouse.com	New Orleans	LA	70130	504-529-2345	525-6079
Bourbon Orleans Hotel 717 Orleans Ave *TF:* 800-521-5338 ■ *Web:* www.bourbonorleans.com ■ *E-mail:* bourbonorleans@msn.com	New Orleans	LA	70116	504-523-2222	525-8166
Chateau Hotel 1001 Chartres St	New Orleans	LA	70116	504-524-9636	525-2989
Chateau Lemoyne Holiday Inn 301 Rue Dauphine *TF:* 800-747-3279 ■ *Web:* www.basshotels.com/holiday-inn/?_franchisee=MSYCL ■ *E-mail:* hi-neworleans-chateau@bristolhotels.com	New Orleans	LA	70112	504-581-1303	523-5709
Chateau Sonesta Hotel 800 Iberville St *TF:* 800-766-3782 ■ *Web:* www.sonestano.com	New Orleans	LA	70112	504-586-0800	586-1987
Columns Hotel 3811 St Charles Ave *TF:* 800-445-9308	New Orleans	LA	70115	504-899-9308	899-8170
Comfort Inn Downtown Superdome 1315 Gravier St *TF:* 800-535-9141	New Orleans	LA	70112	504-586-0100	527-5663
Comfort Suites 346 Baronne St *TF:* 800-524-1140	New Orleans	LA	70112	504-524-1140	523-4444
Courtyard by Marriott 124 St Charles Ave *TF:* 800-321-2211 ■ *Web:* courtyard.com/MSYCY	New Orleans	LA	70130	504-581-9005	581-6264
Dauphine Orleans Hotel 415 Dauphine St *TF:* 800-521-7111 ■ *Web:* www.dauphineorleans.com/	New Orleans	LA	70112	504-586-1800	586-1409
Days Inn Canal 1630 Canal St *TF:* 800-329-7466	New Orleans	LA	70112	504-586-0110	581-2253
Doubletree Hotel New Orleans 300 Canal St *TF:* 800-222-8733 ■ *Web:* www.doubletreehotels.com/DoubleT/Hotel41/52/52Main.htm	New Orleans	LA	70130	504-581-1300	522-4100

New Orleans — Hotels, Motels, Resorts (Cont'd)

	City	State	ZIP	Phone	Fax
Embassy Suites 315 Julia St	New Orleans	LA	70130	504-525-1993	525-3437
TF: 800-362-2779					
Fairmont Hotel 123 Baronne St	New Orleans	LA	70112	504-529-7111	522-2303
TF: 800-635-4440 ■ *Web:* www.fairmont.com/neworleans.html ■ *E-mail:* neworleans@fairmont.com					
Four Points Sheraton 333 Poydras St	New Orleans	LA	70130	504-525-9444	581-7179
TF: 800-235-3535					
Grand Boutique Hotel 2001 St Charles Ave	New Orleans	LA	70130	504-558-9966	571-6464
TF: 800-976-1755					
Grenoble House 329 Dauphine St	New Orleans	LA	70112	504-522-1331	524-4968
TF: 800-722-1834					
Hampton Inn 226 Carondelet St	New Orleans	LA	70130	504-529-9990	529-9996
TF: 800-292-0653					
Historic French Market Inn 501 Decatur St	New Orleans	LA	70130	504-561-5621	569-0619
TF: 888-211-3447 ■ *Web:* www.neworleanscollection.com/HistoricFrenchMarket.htm					
Holiday Inn Downtown Superdome 330 Loyola Ave	New Orleans	LA	70112	504-581-1600	586-0833
TF: 800-535-7830 ■ *Web:* www.basshotels.com/holiday-inn/?_franchisee=MSYDT ■ *E-mail:* superdom@sprynet.com					
Holiday Inn Select New Orleans Convention Center 881 Convention Ctr Blvd	New Orleans	LA	70130	504-524-1881	528-1005
TF: 888-524-1881 ■ *Web:* www.basshotels.com/holiday-inn/?_franchisee=MSYCT					
Hotel de la Poste 316 Chartres St	New Orleans	LA	70130	504-581-1200	523-2910
TF: 800-448-4927					
Hotel Inter-Continental New Orleans 444 St Charles Ave	New Orleans	LA	70130	504-525-5566	523-7310
TF: 800-445-6563 ■ *Web:* www.interconti.com/usa/new_orleans/hotel_newic.html ■ *E-mail:* neworleans@interconti.com					
Hotel Provincial 1024 Chartres St	New Orleans	LA	70116	504-581-4995	581-1018
TF: 800-535-7922 ■ *Web:* www.hotelprovincial.com					
Hotel Saint Marie 827 Toulouse St	New Orleans	LA	70112	504-561-8951	571-2802
TF: 800-366-2743 ■ *Web:* www.hotelstmarie.com/					
Hotel Saint Pierre 911 Burgundy St	New Orleans	LA	70116	504-524-4401	524-6800
TF: 800-225-4040					
Hyatt Regency New Orleans 500 Poydras Plaza	New Orleans	LA	70113	504-561-1234	587-4141
TF: 800-233-1234 ■ *Web:* www.hyatt.com/usa/new_orleans/hotels/hotel_msyrn.html					
La Salle Hotel 1113 Canal St	New Orleans	LA	70112	504-523-5831	523-2531
TF: 800-521-9450					
Lafayette Hotel 600 St Charles Ave	New Orleans	LA	70130	504-524-4441	523-7327
TF: 888-524-4441 ■ *Web:* www.neworleanscollection.com/LafayetteHotel.htm					
Lamothe House 621 Esplanade Ave	New Orleans	LA	70116	504-947-1161	943-6536
TF: 800-367-5858					
Landmark French Quarter Hotel 920 N Rampart St	New Orleans	LA	70116	504-524-3333	552-8044
TF: 800-535-7862					
Le Meridien New Orleans 614 Canal St	New Orleans	LA	70130	504-525-6500	525-8068
TF: 800-543-4300 ■ *Web:* www.neworleans.com/lemeridien/					
Le Pavillon Hotel 833 Poydras St	New Orleans	LA	70112	504-581-3111	522-5543
TF: 800-535-9095 ■ *Web:* www.lepavillon.com/					
Le Richelieu Hotel 1234 Chartres St	New Orleans	LA	70116	504-529-2492	524-8179
TF: 800-535-9653					
Maison de Ville Hotel 727 Toulouse St	New Orleans	LA	70130	504-561-5858	528-9939
TF: 800-634-1600 ■ *Web:* www.maisondeville.com/					
Maison Dupuy 1001 Toulouse St	New Orleans	LA	70112	504-586-8000	525-5334
TF: 800-535-9177 ■ *Web:* www.maisondupuy.com					
Monteleone Hotel 214 Royal St	New Orleans	LA	70140	504-523-3341	561-5803
TF: 800-535-9595 ■ *Web:* www.hotelmonteleone.com ■ *E-mail:* sales@hotelmonteleone.com					
New Orleans Hilton Riverside 2 Poydras St	New Orleans	LA	70140	504-561-0500	568-1721
TF: 800-445-8667 ■ *Web:* www.hilton.com/hotels/MSYNHHH/					
New Orleans Marriott 555 Canal St	New Orleans	LA	70130	504-581-1000	523-6755
TF: 800-228-9290					
Omni Royal Crescent Hotel 535 Gravier St	New Orleans	LA	70130	504-527-0006	523-0806
TF: 800-843-6664					
Omni Royal Orleans 621 Saint Louis St	New Orleans	LA	70140	504-529-5333	523-5046
TF: 800-843-6664					
Parc Saint Charles 500 St Charles Ave	New Orleans	LA	70130	504-522-9000	522-9060
TF: 800-521-7551 ■ *Web:* www.neworleanscollection.com/ParcStCharles.htm					
Pelham Hotel 444 Common St	New Orleans	LA	70130	504-522-4444	539-9010
TF: 888-211-3447 ■ *Web:* www.neworleanscollection.com/Pelhamhotel.htm					
Place D'Armes Hotel 625 Saint Ann St	New Orleans	LA	70116	504-524-4531	571-2803
TF: 800-366-2743 ■ *Web:* www.placedarmes.com/					
Pontchartrain Hotel 2031 St Charles Ave	New Orleans	LA	70140	504-524-0581	529-1165
TF: 800-777-6193 ■ *Web:* www.grandheritage.com/Hotels/Namerican/Pontch/pontchindex.html					
Prince Conti Hotel 830 Conti St	New Orleans	LA	70112	504-529-4172	581-3802
TF: 800-366-2743 ■ *Web:* www.princeconti.com/					
Queen & Crescent Hotel 344 Camp St	New Orleans	LA	70130	504-587-9700	587-9701
TF: 800-975-6652 ■ *Web:* www.queenandcrescent.com					
Radisson Hotel New Orleans 1500 Canal St	New Orleans	LA	70112	504-522-4500	525-2644
TF: 800-333-3333					
Ramada Inn 6324 Chef Menteur Hwy	New Orleans	LA	70126	504-241-2900	241-5697
TF: 800-228-2828					
Ramada Inn 1732 Canal St	New Orleans	LA	70112	504-412-4000	529-1609
TF: 800-236-6119					
Residence Inn by Marriott 345 St Joseph	New Orleans	LA	70130	504-522-1300	522-6060
TF: 800-331-3131 ■ *Web:* www.residenceinn.com/residenceinn/MSYRI					
Ritz-Carlton New Orleans 921 Canal St	New Orleans	LA	70112	504-524-1331	524-7233
Royal Sonesta Hotel 300 Bourbon St	New Orleans	LA	70140	504-586-0300	586-0335
TF: 800-766-3782 ■ *Web:* www.royalsonestano.com					
Saint Ann Marie Antoinette Hotel 717 Conti St	New Orleans	LA	70130	504-581-1881	544-6180
TF: 800-537-8483 ■ *Web:* www.stannmarieantoinette.com					
Saint Louis The 730 Bienville St	New Orleans	LA	70130	504-581-7300	679-5013
TF: 800-535-9111 ■ *Web:* www.stlouishotel.com/					
Sheraton New Orleans Hotel 500 Canal St	New Orleans	LA	70130	504-525-2500	592-8017
TF: 800-325-3535					
Westin Canal Place 100 Rue Iberville	New Orleans	LA	70130	504-566-7006	553-5120
TF: 800-228-3000					
Windsor Court Hotel 300 Gravier St	New Orleans	LA	70130	504-523-6000	596-4513
TF: 800-262-2662 ■ *Web:* www.windsorcourthotel.com					
Wyndham Riverfront Hotel 701 Convention Center Blvd	New Orleans	LA	70130	504-524-8200	681-1018
TF: 800-996-3426					

— Restaurants —

	City	State	ZIP	Phone
Acme Oyster House (Seafood) 724 Iberville St	New Orleans	LA	70130	504-522-5973
Allegro Bistro (New American) 1100 Poydras St	New Orleans	LA	70163	504-582-2350
Andrea's (Italian) 3100 19th St	Metairie	LA	70002	504-834-8583
Antoine's (French/Creole) 713 Saint Louis St	New Orleans	LA	70130	504-581-4044
Web: www.antoines.com/				
Arnaud's (French/Creole) 813 Bienville St	New Orleans	LA	70112	504-523-5433
Bacco (Italian) 310 Chartres St	New Orleans	LA	70130	504-522-2426
Web: www.bacco.com/				
Bangkok Thai Restaurant (Thai) 513 S Carrollton Ave	New Orleans	LA	70118	504-861-3932
Bayona (French) 430 Dauphine St	New Orleans	LA	70112	504-525-4455
Web: www.bayona.com/				
Bella Luna (Continental) 914 N Peters St	New Orleans	LA	70116	504-529-1583
Bizou (French/Creole) 701 St Charles Ave	New Orleans	LA	70130	504-524-4114
Bon Ton Cafe (Cajun) 401 Magazine St	New Orleans	LA	70130	504-524-3386
Breakwater Bistro (American) 8550 Ponchartrain Blvd	New Orleans	LA	70124	504-283-8301
Brennan's Restaurant (French/Creole) 417 Royal St	New Orleans	LA	70130	504-525-9711
Web: www.brennansneworleans.com/				
Brigsten's (Cajun/Creole) 723 Dante St	New Orleans	LA	70118	504-861-7610
Broussard's Restaurant (French/Creole) 819 Conti St	New Orleans	LA	70112	504-581-3866
Web: www.broussards.com/				
Cafe Degas (French) 3127 Esplanade Ave	New Orleans	LA	70119	504-945-5635
Cafe Rue Bourbon (Cajun/French) 241 Bourbon St	New Orleans	LA	70130	504-524-0114
Web: www.neworleans.com/rue_bourbon/				
Cafe Sbisa (Creole) 1011 Decatur St	New Orleans	LA	70116	504-522-5565
Camellia Grill (American) 626 S Carrollton Ave	New Orleans	LA	70118	504-866-9573
Cannon's Uptown (American) 4141 St Charles Ave	New Orleans	LA	70115	504-891-3200
Christian's (French/Creole) 3835 Iberville St	New Orleans	LA	70119	504-482-4924
Commander's Palace (Creole) 1403 Washington Ave	New Orleans	LA	70130	504-899-8221
Web: www.commanderspalace.com/				
Court of Two Sisters (French/Creole) 613 Royal St	New Orleans	LA	70130	504-522-7273
Web: www.courtoftwosisters.com/				
Crescent City Brewhouse (American) 527 Decatur St	New Orleans	LA	70130	504-522-0571
Crescent City Steak House (Steak) 1001 N Broad St	New Orleans	LA	70119	504-821-3271
Crozier's (French) 3216 West Esplanade N	Metairie	LA	70002	504-833-8108
Delmonico Restaurant (Creole) 1300 St Charles Ave	New Orleans	LA	70130	504-525-4937
Dooky Chase's (Creole) 2301 Orleans Ave	New Orleans	LA	70119	504-821-0600
Emeril's (Creole) 800 Tchoupitoulas St	New Orleans	LA	70130	504-528-9393
Web: www.emerils.com				
Ernst Cafe (American) 600 S Peters St	New Orleans	LA	70130	504-525-8544
Five Happiness Restaurant (Chinese) 3605 S Carrollton Ave	New Orleans	LA	70118	504-482-3935
French Market (Cajun) 1001 Decatur St	New Orleans	LA	70116	504-581-9855
G & E Courtyard Grill (European) 1113 Decatur St	New Orleans	LA	70116	504-528-9376
Gabrielle (Creole) 3201 Esplanade Ave	New Orleans	LA	70119	504-948-6233

New Orleans — Restaurants (Cont'd)

				Phone
Galatoire's (French/Creole) 209 Bourbon St	New Orleans	LA	70130	504-525-2021
Gautreau's (French) 1728 Soniat St	New Orleans	LA	70115	504-899-7397
Grill Room (New American) 300 Gravier St	New Orleans	LA	70130	504-523-6000
Gumbo Shop (Creole) 630 Saint Peter St	New Orleans	LA	70116	504-525-1486
K-Paul's Louisiana Kitchen (Cajun) 416 Chartres St *Web:* www.kpauls.com/	New Orleans	LA	70130	504-524-7394
La Provence (French) 25020 Hwy 190 E *Web:* www.laprovencerestaurant.com	Lacombe	LA	70445	504-626-7662
Liborio's (Cuban) 321 Magazine St	New Orleans	LA	70130	504-581-9680
Liuzza's Restaurant (Homestyle) 3636 Bienville St	New Orleans	LA	70119	504-482-9120
Louis XVI (French) 730 Bienville St	New Orleans	LA	70130	504-581-7000
Maximos Italian Grill (Italian) 1117 Decatur St	New Orleans	LA	70116	504-586-8883
Metro Bistro (French) 200 Magazine St	New Orleans	LA	70130	504-529-1900
Mike Anderson's (Seafood) 215 Bourbon St *Web:* www.mikeandersons.com/	New Orleans	LA	70130	504-524-3884
Mike's On the Avenue (Asian/Southwest) 628 Saint Charles Ave	New Orleans	LA	70130	504-523-1709
Mother's (Homestyle) 401 Poydras St *Web:* www.mothersrestaurant.com/	New Orleans	LA	70130	504-523-9656
Mr B's Bistro (Creole) 201 Royal St *Web:* www.mrbsbistro.com/	New Orleans	LA	70130	504-523-2078
Mulate's (Cajun) 201 Julia St	New Orleans	LA	70130	504-522-1492
Nola (Creole) 534 Saint Louis St	New Orleans	LA	70130	504-522-6652
O'Flaherty's Irish Channel Pub (Irish) 514 Toulouse St	New Orleans	LA	70130	504-529-4570
Pascal's Manale Restaurant (Italian) 1838 Napoleon Ave	New Orleans	LA	70115	504-895-4877
Pelican Club (New American) 312 Exchange Alley	New Orleans	LA	70130	504-523-1504
Peristyle (French) 1041 Dumaine St	New Orleans	LA	70016	504-593-9535
Petunias (Cajun) 817 Saint Louis St	New Orleans	LA	70112	504-522-6440
Planet Hollywood (Cajun/Creole) 620 Decatur St Suite 100	New Orleans	LA	70130	504-522-7826
Praline Connection (Homestyle) 542 Frenchman St	New Orleans	LA	70116	504-943-3934
Red Room (California) 2040 St Charles Ave	New Orleans	LA	70130	504-528-9759
Remoulade (Cajun) 309 Bourbon St	New Orleans	LA	70130	504-523-0377
Rib Room (Continental) 621 Saint Louis St	New Orleans	LA	70140	504-529-7045
Ristorante Carmelo (Italian) 541 Decatur St	New Orleans	LA	70130	504-586-1414
Royal Cafe (Creole) 700 Royal St *Web:* www.royalcafe.com/	New Orleans	LA	70116	504-528-9086
Santa Fe (Southwest) 801 Frenchman St	New Orleans	LA	70116	504-944-6854
Sazerac (Continental) 123 Baronne St	New Orleans	LA	70112	504-529-4733
Seaport Cafe & Bar (Seafood) 424 Bourbon St	New Orleans	LA	70172	504-568-0981
Shalimar (Indian) 535 Wilkinson Row	New Orleans	LA	70130	504-523-0099
Snug Harbor Jazz Bistro (Steak/Seafood) 626 Frenchman St *Web:* www.snugjazz.com	New Orleans	LA	70116	504-949-0696
Straya (Creole) 2001 St Charles Ave	New Orleans	LA	70130	504-593-9955
Tujague's Restaurant (Creole) 823 Decatur St	New Orleans	LA	70116	504-525-8676
Uglesich's (Seafood) 1238 Baronne St	New Orleans	LA	70113	504-523-8571
Upperline (Creole) 1413 Upperline St *Web:* www.upperline.com/	New Orleans	LA	70115	504-891-9822
Veranda Restaurant (Continental) 444 St Charles Ave	New Orleans	LA	70130	504-525-5566

— Goods and Services —

SHOPPING

				Phone	Fax
Canal Place 365 Canal St Suite 2070	New Orleans	LA	70130	504-522-9200	522-0866
Esplanade The 1401 W Esplanade	Kenner	LA	70065	504-468-6116	466-9502
French Market Corp 1008 N Peters St	New Orleans	LA	70116	504-522-2621	596-3419
Jackson Brewery Mall 600 Decatur St	New Orleans	LA	70130	504-566-7245	
Macy's 1400 Poydras St	New Orleans	LA	70112	504-592-5985	
New Orleans Centre 1400 Poydras St	New Orleans	LA	70112	504-568-0000	595-8870
Plaza Shopping Center 5700 Read Blvd	New Orleans	LA	70127	504-246-1500	246-9222
Riverwalk Marketplace 1 Poydras St *Web:* www.riverwalkmarketplace.com	New Orleans	LA	70130	504-522-1555	586-8532
Royal Street District 828 Royal St	New Orleans	LA	70116	504-524-1260	891-1228
Saks Fifth Avenue 301 Canal St	New Orleans	LA	70130	504-524-2200	529-2323
Slidell Factory Stores 1000 Caruso Blvd	Slidell	LA	70461	504-646-0756	
Uptown Square 200 Broadway St	New Orleans	LA	70118	504-866-4513	

BANKS

				Phone	Fax
Bank of Louisiana 300 St Charles Ave	New Orleans	LA	70130	504-592-0600	592-0606
Bank One 201 St Charles Ave *TF:* 800-777-8837	New Orleans	LA	70170	504-558-1164	558-1188
Crescent Bank & Trust 1100 Poydras St Suite 100	New Orleans	LA	70130	504-556-5950	552-4467
Deposit Guaranty National Bank 321 St Charles Ave	New Orleans	LA	70130	504-838-4533	525-4072
Dryades Savings Bank FSB 233 Carondelet St Suite 200	New Orleans	LA	70130	504-581-5891	598-7233
Federal Reserve Bank 525 St Charles Ave **Fax:* Cust Svc ■ *TF:* 800-562-9023	New Orleans	LA	70130	504-593-3200	593-5831*
First Bank & Trust 909 Poydras St	New Orleans	LA	70112	504-584-5900	584-5902
Greater New Orleans Homestead FSB 5435 Magazine St	New Orleans	LA	70115	504-897-9751	
Gulf Coast Bank & Trust 200 St Charles Ave	New Orleans	LA	70130	504-581-4561	581-3583
Hibernia National Bank 313 Carondelet St *TF:* 800-562-9007 ■ *Web:* www.hiberniabank.com ■ *E-mail:* mailus@hiberniabank.com	New Orleans	LA	70130	504-533-3333	533-2367
Iberia Bank 9300 Jefferson Hwy	New Orleans	LA	70123	504-363-7873	363-7973
Liberty Bank & Trust Co 1950 St Bernard Ave	New Orleans	LA	70116	504-941-6471	483-6654
Omni Bank 330 Carondelet St	New Orleans	LA	70130	504-833-2900	841-2183
Regions Bank 301 St Charles Ave *TF Cust Svc:* 800-888-1655*	New Orleans	LA	70130	504-584-1382	565-3109
Schwegmann Bank & Trust Co 6600 Franklin Ave	New Orleans	LA	70122	504-883-5132	883-5135
United Bank & Trust Co 2714 Canal St Suite 100	New Orleans	LA	70119	504-827-0060	827-0059
Whitney National Bank 228 St Charles Ave *TF:* 800-347-7272	New Orleans	LA	70130	504-586-7272	586-7383

BUSINESS SERVICES

	Phone
Choice Courier Systems Inc	504-466-3111
Federal Express	800-238-5355
Kelly Services	504-529-1451
Kenner Courier	504-469-7657
Kinko's	504-861-8016
Manpower Temporary Services	504-523-6381
New Orleans Messenger Service	504-586-0036
Olsten Staffing Services	504-581-1888
Post Office	504-589-1111
UPS	800-742-5877
World Courier	504-586-0036

— Media —

PUBLICATIONS

				Phone	Fax
Louisiana Life 111 Veterans Blvd Suite 1810 *TF:* 800-739-8836 ■ *Web:* www.neworleans.com/lalife/	Metairie	LA	70005	504-834-9698	838-7700
New Orleans City Business 111 Veterans Blvd Suite 1810 *Web:* www.neworleans.com/citybusiness/ ■ *E-mail:* citybiz@nopg.com	Metairie	LA	70005	504-834-9292	832-3550
New Orleans Magazine 111 Veterans Memorial Blvd Suite 1810 *Web:* www.neworleans.com/no_magazine/	Metairie	LA	70005	504-831-3731	832-3550
Times-Picayune‡ 3800 Howard Ave *TF:* 800-925-0000 ■ *Web:* www.nola.com	New Orleans	LA	70140	504-826-3279	826-3007
Where New Orleans Magazine 528 Wilkinson Row *Web:* www.whereneworleans.com ■ *E-mail:* wneworlean@aol.com	New Orleans	LA	70130	504-522-6468	522-0018

‡Daily newspapers

TELEVISION

				Phone	Fax
WDSU-TV Ch 6 (NBC) 846 Howard *Web:* www.wdsu.com ■ *E-mail:* wdsu@comm.net	New Orleans	LA	70113	504-679-0600	679-0733
WGNO-TV Ch 26 (ABC) 2 Canal St World Trade Ctr Suite 2800 *Web:* www.abc26.com ■ *E-mail:* wgno-tv@tribune.com	New Orleans	LA	70130	504-581-2600	619-6332
WHNO-TV Ch 20 (Ind) 1100 S Jefferson Davis Pkwy *Web:* www.whno.com	New Orleans	LA	70125	504-822-1920	822-2060
WLAE-TV Ch 32 (PBS) 2929 S Carrollton Ave *Web:* www.pbs.org/wlae/ ■ *E-mail:* info@wlae.pbs.org	New Orleans	LA	70118	504-866-7411	861-5186
WNOL-TV Ch 38 (WB) 1661 Canal St *Web:* www.wnol.com ■ *E-mail:* wnol@comm.net	New Orleans	LA	70112	504-525-3838	569-0908
WPXL-TV Ch 49 (PAX) 3900 Veterans Blvd Suite 202 *Web:* www.pax.net/WPXL	Metairie	LA	70002	504-887-9795	887-1518
WVUE-TV Ch 8 (Fox) 1025 S Jefferson Davis Pkwy	New Orleans	LA	70125	504-486-6161	483-1212
WWL-TV Ch 4 (CBS) 1024 N Rampart St *Web:* www.wwltv.com	New Orleans	LA	70116	504-529-4444	529-6472
WYES-TV Ch 12 (PBS) 916 Navarre Ave *Web:* www.pbs.org/wyes/ ■ *E-mail:* assist@wyes.pbs.org	New Orleans	LA	70124	504-486-5511	483-8408

New Orleans (Cont'd)

RADIO

Name / Address	City	State	ZIP	Phone	Fax
KKND-FM 106.7 MHz (Alt) 929 Howard Ave 2nd Fl	New Orleans	LA	70113	504-679-7300	679-7345
KMEZ-FM 102.9 MHz (Urban) 201 Saint Charles Suite 201	New Orleans	LA	70170	504-581-7002	566-4857
WBOK-AM 1230 kHz (Rel) 1639 Gentilly Blvd	New Orleans	LA	70119	504-943-4600	944-4662
WBYU-AM 1450 kHz (B/EZ) 201 St Charles Ave	New Orleans	LA	70170	504-581-7002	566-4857
WEZB-FM 97.1 MHz (CHR) 3525 N Causeway Blvd Suite 1053	New Orleans	LA	70002	504-834-9587	566-4857
WLMG-FM 101.9 MHz (AC) 3525 N Causeway Blvd Suite 1053 *Web:* www.magic1019.com ■ *E-mail:* info@magic1019.com	New Orleans	LA	70002	504-834-9587	833-8560
WNOE-FM 101.1 MHz (Ctry) 929 Howard Ave	New Orleans	LA	70113	504-679-7300	679-7345
WODT-AM 1280 kHz (Urban) 2228 Gravier St	New Orleans	LA	70119	504-827-6000	827-6048
WQUE-FM 93.3 MHz (Urban) 2228 Gravier St	New Orleans	LA	70119	504-827-6000	827-6045
WRNO-FM 99.5 MHz (CR) 201 St Charles Ave Suite 201 **Fax:* Sales ■ *Web:* www.wrno.com	New Orleans	LA	70170	504-581-7002	566-4857*
WSMB-AM 1350 kHz (N/T) 1450 Poydras St Suite 440	New Orleans	LA	70112	504-593-2100	593-1850
WWL-AM 870 kHz (N/T) 1450 Poydras St Suite 440 *Web:* www.wwl870am.com	New Orleans	LA	70112	504-593-6376	593-1850
WWNO-FM 89.9 MHz (NPR) University of New Orleans Lake Front Campus *Web:* wwno.uno.edu ■ *E-mail:* wwno@www.uno.edu	New Orleans	LA	70148	504-280-7000	280-6061
WWOZ-FM 90.7 MHz (Urban) 1201 St Philip St *Web:* www.wwoz.org/ ■ *E-mail:* wwoz@gnofn.org	New Orleans	LA	70116	504-568-1239	558-9332
WYLD-AM 940 kHz (Rel) 2228 Gravier St	New Orleans	LA	70119	504-827-6000	827-6045
WYLD-FM 98.5 MHz (Urban) 2228 Gravier St	New Orleans	LA	70119	504-827-6000	827-6045

— Colleges/Universities —

Name / Address	City	State	ZIP	Phone	Fax
Delgado Community College 615 City Park Ave *Web:* www.dcc.edu	New Orleans	LA	70119	504-483-4216	483-4386
Dillard University 2601 Gentilly Blvd *TF:* 877-240-3838 ■ *Web:* www.dillard.edu	New Orleans	LA	70122	504-283-8822	286-4895
Elaine P Nunez Community College 3710 Paris Rd	Chalmette	LA	70043	504-278-7350	278-7353
Loyola University 6363 St Charles Ave *TF:* 800-456-9652 ■ *Web:* www.loyno.edu	New Orleans	LA	70118	504-865-2011	865-3383
Nicholls State University 906 E 1st St *TF:* 877-642-4655 ■ *Web:* www.nich.edu ■ *E-mail:* nichweb@mail.nich.edu	Thibodaux	LA	70301	504-446-8111	448-4929
Our Lady of Holy Cross College 4123 Woodland Dr *TF:* 800-259-7744 ■ *Web:* www.olhcc.edu	New Orleans	LA	70131	504-394-7744	391-2421
Southern University New Orleans 6400 Press Dr *Web:* www.suno.edu	New Orleans	LA	70126	504-286-5000	286-5131
Tulane University 6823 St Charles Ave *Web:* www.tulane.edu ■ *E-mail:* Undergrad.Admission@tulane.edu	New Orleans	LA	70118	504-865-5000	862-8715
University of New Orleans 2000 Lake Front *TF Admissions:* 800-256-5866 ■ *Web:* www.uno.edu ■ *E-mail:* help_desk@uno.edu	New Orleans	LA	70148	504-280-6000	280-5522
Xavier University of Louisiana 7325 Palmetto St **Fax:* Admissions ■ *Web:* www.xula.edu ■ *E-mail:* apply@mail.xula.edu	New Orleans	LA	70125	504-486-7411	482-1508*

— Hospitals —

Name / Address	City	State	ZIP	Phone	Fax
Chalmette Medical Center 9001 Patricia St	Chalmette	LA	70043	504-620-6000	620-6162
Children's Hospital 200 Henry Clay Ave *Web:* www.chnola.org ■ *E-mail:* info@chnola.org	New Orleans	LA	70118	504-899-9511	896-9708
Columbia Lakeland Medical Center 6000 Bullard Ave	New Orleans	LA	70128	504-241-6335	243-3370
Doctors Hospital of Jefferson 4320 Houma Blvd *Web:* www.tenethealth.com/DoctorsJefferson	Metairie	LA	70006	504-849-4000	846-3010
East Jefferson General Hospital 4200 Houma Blvd *Web:* www.eastjeffhospital.org	Metairie	LA	70006	504-454-4000	456-8151
Kenner Regional Medical Center 180 W Esplanade Ave	Kenner	LA	70065	504-468-8600	464-8256
Meadowcrest Hospital 2500 Belle Chasse Hwy *Web:* www.tenethealth.com/Meadowcrest	Gretna	LA	70056	504-392-3131	391-5498
Medical Center 3419 St Claude Ave	New Orleans	LA	70117	504-948-8200	948-8208
Medical Center of Louisiana at New Orleans 1532 Tulane Ave	New Orleans	LA	70112	504-568-2311	568-2028
Memorial Medical Center 2700 Napoleon Ave Baptist Campus **Fax:* Admitting	New Orleans	LA	70115	504-899-9311	897-4418*
Ochsner Foundation Hospital 1516 Jefferson Hwy **Fax:* Admitting ■ *TF:* 800-928-6247 ■ *Web:* www.ochsner.org	New Orleans	LA	70121	504-842-3000	842-3434*
Pendleton Memorial Methodist Hospital 5620 Read Blvd	New Orleans	LA	70127	504-244-5100	244-5841
River Parishes Hospital 500 Rue de Sante	LaPlace	LA	70068	504-652-7000	652-5161
Saint Charles General Hospital 3700 St Charles Ave *Web:* www.tenethealth.com/StCharles	New Orleans	LA	70115	504-899-7441	899-3174
Touro Infirmary 1401 Foucher St **Fax:* Admitting	New Orleans	LA	70115	504-897-7011	897-8446*
Tulane University Medical Center 1415 Tulane Ave *TF:* 800-588-5800 ■ *Web:* www.mcl.tulane.edu	New Orleans	LA	70112	504-588-5263	582-7973
University Hospital of Medical Center of Louisiana 2021 Perdido St	New Orleans	LA	70112	504-588-3000	524-7584
Veterans Affairs Medical Center 1601 Perdido St	New Orleans	LA	70146	504-568-0811	589-5904
West Jefferson Medical Center 1101 Medical Center Blvd **Fax:* Admitting	Marrero	LA	70072	504-347-5511	349-1319*

— Attractions —

Name / Address	City	State	ZIP	Phone	Fax
American Italian Renaissance Foundation Museum 537 S Peters St *Web:* www.airf.com	New Orleans	LA	70130	504-522-7294	522-1657
Aquarium of the Americas 1 Canal St *TF:* 800-774-7394	New Orleans	LA	70130	504-565-3035	565-3010
Audubon Institute PO Box 4327 *Web:* www.auduboninstitute.org	New Orleans	LA	70178	504-861-2537	866-0819
Audubon Park St Charles Ave	New Orleans	LA	70178	504-565-3020	
BAND-Black Arts National Diaspora Inc 1530 N Claiborne Ave	New Orleans	LA	70116	504-949-2263	949-0807
Cajun Queen Riverboat Canal St Wharf *TF:* 800-445-4109	New Orleans	LA	70130	504-529-4567	524-6265
Cane River Creole National Historical Park & Heritage Area PO Box 536 *Web:* www.nps.gov/cari/	Natchitoches	LA	71457	318-352-0383	352-4549
Cannes Brulee Native American Center 303 Williams Blvd Rivertown *TF:* 800-473-6789	Kenner	LA	70062	504-468-7231	471-2159
Carousel Gardens in City Park Dreyfus Ave	New Orleans	LA	70124	504-482-4888	483-9412
Celebration Station Entertainment Complex 5959 Veterans Memorial Blvd	Metairie	LA	70003	504-887-7888	888-8404
Children's Castle 501 Williams Blvd Rivertown *TF:* 800-473-6789	Kenner	LA	70062	504-469-3236	471-2159
City Park 1 Palm Dr	New Orleans	LA	70124	504-482-4888	483-9412
Confederate Museum 929 Camp St *Web:* www.confederatemuseum.com	New Orleans	LA	70130	504-523-4522	
Contemporary Arts Center 900 Camp St *Web:* www.cacno.org	New Orleans	LA	70130	504-523-1216	528-3828
Daily Living Science Center 409 Williams Blvd	Kenner	LA	70062	504-468-7231	468-7599
Delta Queen Steamboat Co 1380 Port of New Orleans Pl Robin Street Wharf *TF:* 800-543-7637 ■ *Web:* www.deltaqueen.com	New Orleans	LA	70130	504-586-0631	585-0630
Destrehan Plantation 13034 River Rd	Destrehan	LA	70047	504-764-9315	725-1929
Entergy IMAX Theater 1 Canal St Aquarium of the Americas *Web:* www.auduboninstitute.org/html/aa_imaxmain.html	New Orleans	LA	70130	504-565-3033	

New Orleans — Attractions (Cont'd)

	City	State	ZIP	Phone	Fax
Fine Arts Gallery of New Orleans 636 Burdette St	New Orleans	LA	70118	504-866-4287	522-0693
Web: www.fineartsgallery.com					
Freeport Memoran Daily Living Science Center 409 Williams Blvd Rivertown	Kenner	LA	70062	504-468-7231	471-2159
TF: 800-473-6789					
Gallery for Fine Photography 322 Royal St	New Orleans	LA	70130	504-568-1313	568-1322
Gallier House Museum 1132 Royal St.	New Orleans	LA	70116	504-525-5661	568-9735
Web: www.gnofn.org/~hggh/ ■ *E-mail:* hggh@gnofn.org					
Harrah's Casino Hotel New Orleans 512 S Peter St	New Orleans	LA	70130	504-533-6000	
TF: 800-427-7247 ■ *Web:* www.harrahsneworleans.com					
Hermann-Grima House 820 Saint Louis St	New Orleans	LA	70112	504-525-5661	568-9735
Historic New Orleans Collection 533 Royal St	New Orleans	LA	70130	504-523-4662	598-7108
Web: www.hnoc.org/ ■ *E-mail:* hnocinfo@hnoc.org					
House of Broel's Historic Mansion & Dollhouse Museum 2220 St Charles Ave	New Orleans	LA	70130	504-525-1000	524-6775
Web: www.houseofbroel.com					
Jackson Barracks Military Museum 6400 St Claude Ave.	New Orleans	LA	70146	504-278-8242	278-8614
Web: www.la.ngb.army.mil/jbmm.htm ■ *E-mail:* jbmuseum@cmq.com					
Jean Lafitte National Historical Park & Preserve 365 Canal St Suite 2400	New Orleans	LA	70130	504-589-3882	589-3851
Web: www.nps.gov/jela/					
Lakeshore Park Lakeshore & Leon C Simon Drs	New Orleans	LA	70126	504-243-4048	
Longue Vue House & Gardens 7 Bamboo Rd	New Orleans	LA	70124	504-488-5488	486-7015
Web: www.longuevue.com					
Louisiana Children's Museum 420 Julia St	New Orleans	LA	70130	504-523-1357	529-3666
Web: www.lcm.org					
Louisiana Nature Center PO Box 870610	New Orleans	LA	70187	504-246-5672	242-1889
Web: www.auduboninstitute.org/html/aa_lancmain.html					
Louisiana Philharmonic Orchestra 305 Baronne St Suite 600	New Orleans	LA	70112	504-523-6530	595-8468
Web: www.gnofn.org/~lpo/index.html ■ *E-mail:* lpo@gnofn.org					
Louisiana State Museum 751 Chartres St	New Orleans	LA	70116	504-568-6968	568-4995
TF: 800-568-6968 ■ *Web:* lsm.crt.state.la.us					
Louisiana Toy Train Museum 519 Williams Blvd Rivertown	Kenner	LA	70062	504-468-7231	471-2159
Louisiana Wildlife Museum 303 Williams Blvd Rivertown	Kenner	LA	70062	504-468-7231	471-2159
Mahalia Jackson Theatre of Performing Arts 801 N Rampart St	New Orleans	LA	70116	504-565-7470	565-7477
Mardi Gras World 233 Newton St Take free ferry from Canal St.	New Orleans	LA	70114	504-361-7821	361-3164
Web: www.mardigrasday.com/world.html					
Mississippi River Cruises Toulouse St Wharf	New Orleans	LA	70130	800-233-2628	
Musee Conti-Wax Museum of Louisiana Legends 917 Conti St French Quarter	New Orleans	LA	70112	504-525-2605	566-7636
Web: www.get-waxed.com ■ *E-mail:* sales@get-waxed.com					
Natchez Steamboat 2 Canal St	New Orleans	LA	70130	504-586-8777	587-0708
TF: 800-233-2628 ■ *Web:* www.nosteamboat.com ■ *E-mail:* natchez@nosteamboat.com					
New Orleans Historic Voodoo Museum 724 Dumaine St	New Orleans	LA	70116	504-522-5223	523-8591
Web: www.voodoomuseum.com/ ■ *E-mail:* voodoo@voodoomuseum.com					
New Orleans Museum of Art 1 Collins Dibol Cir.	New Orleans	LA	70124	504-488-2631	484-6662
Web: www.noma.org					
New Orleans Opera Assn 305 Baronne St Suite 500	New Orleans	LA	70112	504-529-2278	529-7668
Web: www.neworleansopera.org					
New Orleans Pharmacy Museum 514 Chartres St	New Orleans	LA	70130	504-565-8027	565-8028
Web: www.pharmacymuseum.org ■ *E-mail:* info@pharmacymuseum.org					
New Orleans School of Glass Works & Printmaking Studio 727 Magazine St	New Orleans	LA	70130	504-529-7277	539-5417
Old Absinthe House Bar 400 Bourbon St.	New Orleans	LA	70130	504-525-8108	568-1144
Pitot House Museum 1440 Moss St	New Orleans	LA	70119	504-482-0312	482-0312
Web: www.neworleans.com/museum/pitot/					
Pontchartrain Astronomy Society Observatory 409 Williams Blvd Rivertown	Kenner	LA	70062	504-468-7229	471-2159
TF: 800-473-6789					
Preservation Hall 726 Saint Peters St	New Orleans	LA	70116	504-522-2841	558-9192
Web: www.preservationhall.com					
Rivertown USA 405 Williams Blvd.	Kenner	LA	70062	504-468-7231	
Web: www.kenner.la.us					
Riverwalk 2 Canal St Suite 2300 E	New Orleans	LA	70130	504-522-1555	586-8532
Saenger Theatre of the Creative & Performing Arts 143 N Rampart St.	New Orleans	LA	70112	504-525-1052	569-1533
Saint Louis Cathedral 615 Pere Antoine Alley	New Orleans	LA	70116	504-525-9585	525-9583
Saints Hall of Fame Museum 409 Williams Blvd Rivertown	Kenner	LA	70062	504-468-7231	471-2159
Web: www.kenner.la.us/saints.html					
Southern Rep Theatre 333 Canal St	New Orleans	LA	70130	504-861-8163	861-5875
Web: www.southernrep.com					
Treasure Chest Casino Presents Mardi Gras Museum 421 Williams Blvd Rivertown.	Kenner	LA	70062	504-468-7231	471-2159
TF: 800-473-6789					

SPORTS TEAMS & FACILITIES

	City	State	ZIP	Phone	Fax
Fair Grounds Race Course 1751 Gentilly Blvd.	New Orleans	LA	70119	504-944-5515	944-1211
TF: 800-786-0010 ■ *Web:* www.fgno.com					
Kiefer Uno Lakefront Arena 6801 Franklin Ave	New Orleans	LA	70122	504-280-7222	280-7178
New Orleans Brass (hockey) 1201 Saint Peter St Municipal Auditorium.	New Orleans	LA	70116	504-522-7825	523-7295
New Orleans Fair Grounds Horse Racing 1751 Gentilly Blvd.	New Orleans	LA	70119	504-944-5515	944-2511
TF: 800-262-7983					
New Orleans Saints 5800 Airline Hwy	Metairie	LA	70003	504-731-1700	731-1888*
**Fax:* PR ■ *TF:* 800-241-3011 ■ *Web:* www.nfl.com/saints					
New Orleans Storm (soccer) 6000 Airline Dr Zephyr Field	Metairie	LA	70003	504-734-5155	734-5118
New Orleans Zephyrs (baseball) 6000 Airline Dr Zephyr Field	Metairie	LA	70003	504-734-5155	734-5118
Web: www.insideneworleans.com/zephyrs					
Superdome Sugar Bowl Dr.	New Orleans	LA	70112	504-587-3663	587-3848
TF: 800-756-7074 ■ *Web:* www.superdome.com					

— Events —

	Phone
Bayou Classic Football Game (late November)	504-587-3663
Boo at the Zoo (late October)	504-861-2537
Celebration in the Oaks (late November-early January)	504-488-2896
Celtic Nations Heritage Festival of Louisiana (late October)	504-486-1113
Compaq Classic of New Orleans (late March-early April)	504-831-4653
Crescent City Classic (early April)	504-861-8686
Destrehan Plantation Fall Festival (mid-November)	504-764-9315
French Quarter Festival (mid-April)	504-522-5730
Go 4th on the River (July 4)	504-528-9994
Great French Market Tomato Festival (early June)	504-522-2621
Greek Festival (late May)	504-282-0259
Gumbo Festival (mid-October)	504-436-4712
Halloween in New Orleans (late October)	800-672-6124
Jeff Fest (late October)	504-888-2900
Los Islenos Festival (late March)	504-682-2713
Louisiana Black Heritage Festival (mid-March)	504-827-0112
Louisiana Crawfish Festival (early May)	337-332-6655
Lundi Gras (mid-February)	504-566-5005
Mardi Gras (late February)	504-566-5011
New Orleans Boat & Sportsfishing Show (early February)	504-846-4446
New Orleans Christmas (December)	504-522-5730
New Orleans Film & Video Festival (early-mid-October)	504-523-3818
New Orleans Jazz & Heritage Festival (late April-early May)	504-522-4786
New Orleans Wine & Food Experience (mid-July)	504-529-9463
New Years Eve Countdown (December 31)	504-566-5011
Nokia Sugar Bowl Mardi Gras Marathon (early February)	504-525-8573
Oktoberfest (October)	504-566-5011
Reggae Riddums International Arts Festival (mid-June)	504-367-1313
Saint Joseph's Day Festivities (mid-March)	504-522-7294
Saint Patrick's Day Parade (mid-March)	504-525-5169
Spring Fiesta (mid-March)	504-566-5011
Sugar Bowl (January)	504-525-8573
Swamp Festival (early-mid-October)	504-861-2537
Sweet Arts & Beaux Arts Ball (mid-February)	504-528-3805
Tennessee Wiliams/New Orleans Literary Festival (late March)	504-286-6680
Winn-Dixie Showdown (late February)	504-587-3663

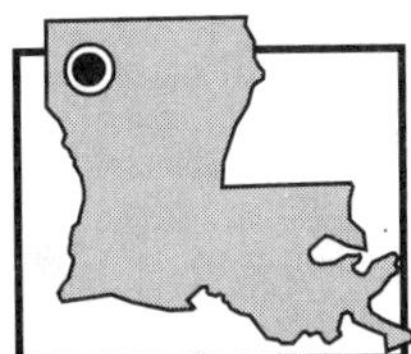

Shreveport

Separated by the Red River, Shreveport and neighboring Bossier City comprise the largest metro area in North Louisiana. The laser and neon-adorned Texas Street Bridge connects the two cities. Shreveport-Bossier is the trade and cultural center of a 200-mile radius extending into Arkansas, Louisiana, and Texas, known as the Ark-La-Tex. Riverboat gambling is popular entertainment in both cities, and new riverboat casinos include Harrah's and the Horseshoe Riverboat. Shreveport's American Rose Center, headquarters of the American Rose Society, has over 20,000 roses in more than 60 individual gardens on display, while Bossier City is home to one of the nation's top thoroughbred racetracks, Louisiana Downs.

Population 188,319
Area (Land) . . . . . 97.1 sq mi
Area (Water) . . . . . 14.5 sq mi
Elevation . . . . . 204 ft
Latitude . . . . . 32-50-52 N
Longitude . . . . . 93-74-85 W
County . . . . . Caddo Parish
Time Zone . . . . . CST
Area Code/s 318

— Average Temperatures and Precipitation —

TEMPERATURES

	Jan	Feb	Mar	Apr	May	Jun	Jul	Aug	Sep	Oct	Nov	Dec
High	55	61	69	77	83	90	93	93	87	79	68	59
Low	35	38	46	54	62	69	72	71	66	54	45	37

PRECIPITATION

	Jan	Feb	Mar	Apr	May	Jun	Jul	Aug	Sep	Oct	Nov	Dec
Inches	3.9	3.9	3.6	3.8	5.1	4.3	3.7	2.4	3.1	3.7	4.5	4.1

— Important Phone Numbers —

	Phone
AAA	800-222-4357
Emergency	911
Events Line	318-226-9227
HotelDocs	800-468-3537
Poison Control Center	800-256-9822
Time/Temp	318-425-0211
Weather	318-635-7575

— Information Sources —

				Phone	Fax
Better Business Bureau Serving Ark-La-Tex 3612 Youree Dr *Web:* www.shreveport.bbb.org	Shreveport	LA	71105	318-868-5146	861-6426
Bossier Chamber of Commerce 710 Benton Rd *Web:* www.bossierchamber.com ■ *E-mail:* bcchamber@aol.com	Bossier City	LA	71111	318-746-0252	746-0357
Bossier Civic Center 620 Benton Rd *TF:* 800-522-4842	Bossier City	LA	71111	318-741-8900	741-8910
Caddo Parish 525 Marshall St Suite 300	Shreveport	LA	71101	318-226-6900	429-7630
Greater Shreveport Chamber of Commerce 400 Edwards St *TF:* 800-448-5432 ■ *Web:* www.shreveportchamber.org	Shreveport	LA	71101	318-677-2500	677-2541
Shreve Memorial Library 424 Texas St	Shreveport	LA	71101	318-226-5897	226-4780
Shreveport-Bossier Convention & Tourist Bureau PO Box 1761 *TF:* 800-551-8682 ■ *Web:* www.shreveport-bossier.org/ ■ *E-mail:* tourism@shreveport.bossier.org	Shreveport	LA	71166	318-222-9391	222-0056
Shreveport-Bossier Visitor Center 100 John Wesley Blvd	Bossier City	LA	71112	318-226-8884	429-0647
Shreveport City Hall 1234 Texas Ave *Web:* www.ci.shreveport.la.us	Shreveport	LA	71101	318-673-2489	673-5055
Shreveport Community Development Dept 1237 Murphy St *Web:* www.ci.shreveport.la.us/dept/cd ■ *E-mail:* community@ci.shreveport.la.us	Shreveport	LA	71101	318-673-7500	673-7512
Shreveport Mayor PO Box 31109 *Web:* www.ci.shreveport.la.us/dept/mayor/index.htm ■ *E-mail:* mayor@ci.shreveport.la.us	Shreveport	LA	71130	318-673-5050	673-5085

On-Line Resources

Area Guide Shreveport . . . . . shreveport.areaguides.net
City Knowledge Shreveport . . . . . www.cityknowledge.com/la_shreveport.htm
Excite.com Shreveport City Guide . . . . . www.excite.com/travel/countries/united_states/louisiana/shreveport
LDS iAmerica Shreveport . . . . . shreveport.iamerica.net
Shreveport-Bossier Online . . . . . www.shreveport.com
Shreveport Home Page . . . . . www.shreveport.net

— Transportation Services —

AIRPORTS

■ **Shreveport Regional Airport (SHV)**

	Phone
5 miles SW of downtown (approx 15 minutes)	318-673-5370

Airport Transportation

	Phone
Casino Cab $12 fare to downtown	318-425-3325
Yellow Checker Cab $12 fare to downtown	318-425-7000

Commercial Airlines

	Phone
American Eagle	800-433-7300
Continental	318-636-1111
Delta	800-221-1212
Northwest	800-225-2525
TWA	800-221-2000
US Airways Express	800-428-4322

Charter Airlines

	Phone
Executive Travel Air	318-424-9191
TAC Air	800-233-5987

CAR RENTALS

	Phone
AIR	318-631-3040
Avis	318-631-1839
Budget	318-636-2846
Enterprise	318-797-9100
Hertz	318-636-1212
National	318-636-2734

LIMO/TAXI

	Phone
A-1 Charter	318-621-0700
Casino Cab	318-425-3325
G & H Limo	318-632-9007
Louisa's Limousine	318-635-8967
Royal Limousine	318-925-1972
Yellow Checker Cab	318-425-7000

MASS TRANSIT

	Phone
Sportran City Transit $.90 Base fare	318-221-7433

RAIL/BUS

				Phone
Greyhound Bus Station 2225 Beckett St *TF:* 800-231-2222	Bossier City	LA	71111	318-746-7511
Greyhound/Trailways Bus Station 408 Fannin St	Shreveport	LA	71101	318-221-4205

— Accommodations —

HOTELS, MOTELS, RESORTS

				Phone	Fax
Best Value Inn & Suites 4915 Monkhouse Dr	Shreveport	LA	71109	318-631-5566	631-5008
Best Western Chateau Suite Hotel 201 Lake St *TF:* 800-845-9334 ■ *Web:* www.bestwestern.com/chateausuitehotelshreveport	Shreveport	LA	71101	318-222-7620	424-2014

Shreveport — Hotels, Motels, Resorts (Cont'd)

Name / Address	City	State	Zip	Phone	Fax
Best Western Richmond Suites Hotel 5101 Monkhouse Dr	Shreveport	LA	71109	318-635-6431	635-6040
TF: 800-447-2582					
Comfort Inn 1100 Delhi St	Bossier City	LA	71111	318-221-2400	221-2909
TF: 800-228-5150					
Country Inn 8489 Greenwood Rd	Shreveport	LA	71033	318-938-7952	938-7958
Crossland Economy Studios 3070 E Texas St	Bossier City	LA	71111	318-747-5800	747-5805
TF: 888-802-7677 ■ *Web:* www.extstay.com/loc/la_shreveport_bossiercity_crs.html					
Days Inn 4935 Monkhouse Dr	Shreveport	LA	71109	318-636-0080	635-4517
TF: 800-329-7466					
Econo Lodge 4911 Monkhouse Dr.	Shreveport	LA	71109	318-636-0771	636-0771
TF: 800-424-4777					
Emerald Hills Resort Hwy 171 S	Florien	LA	71429	318-586-4661	586-4804
TF: 800-533-5031					
Fairfield Inn by Marriott 6245 Westport Ave	Shreveport	LA	71129	318-686-0102	686-8791
TF: 800-228-2800 ■ *Web:* fairfieldinn.com/SHVFI					
Fairfield Place 2221 Fairfield Ave	Shreveport	LA	71104	318-222-0048	226-0631
Hampton Inn 1005 Gould Dr.	Bossier City	LA	71111	318-752-1112	752-1405
TF: 800-426-7866					
Holiday Inn 2015 Old Minden Rd	Bossier City	LA	71111	318-742-9700	747-4651
TF: 800-465-4329					
Holiday Inn Downtown 102 Lake St	Shreveport	LA	71101	318-222-7717	221-5951
TF: 800-465-4329					
Holiday Inn Express Airport 5101 Westwood Park Dr	Shreveport	LA	71109	318-631-2000	631-2800
TF: 800-465-4329					
Holiday Inn Holidome Financial Plaza 5555 Financial Plaza	Shreveport	LA	71129	318-688-3000	687-4462
TF: 800-465-4329					
Howard Johnson 1906 N Market St.	Shreveport	LA	71107	318-424-6621	221-1028
TF: 800-446-4656					
Isle of Capri Hotel 3033 Hilton Dr	Bossier City	LA	71111	318-747-2400	747-6822
TF: 800-221-4095					
La Quinta Inn & Suites 6700 Financial Plaza	Shreveport	LA	71129	318-671-1100	671-1600
TF: 800-531-5900					
LeBossier Hotel 4000 Industrial Dr	Bossier City	LA	71111	318-747-0711	742-3346
TF: 800-789-0711					
Mid-Continent Inn 8580 Greenwood Rd	Shreveport	LA	71033	318-938-5423	938-5426
Pelican Inn 5215 Monkhouse Dr.	Shreveport	LA	71109	318-636-6011	635-7955
TF: 800-430-5275					
Plantation Inn 4901 Greenwood Rd.	Shreveport	LA	71109	318-635-0500	631-1329
TF: 800-356-3410					
Quality Inn 4300 Industrial Dr	Bossier City	LA	71112	318-746-5050	742-6154
TF: 800-228-5151					
Ramada Inn 5116 Monkhouse Dr	Shreveport	LA	71109	318-635-7531	635-1600
TF: 800-228-2828					
Red Roof Inn 7296 Greenwood Rd	Shreveport	LA	71119	318-938-5342	938-5348
TF: 800-843-7663					
Remington Suite Hotel 220 Travis St	Shreveport	LA	71101	318-425-5000	
TF: 800-444-6750					
Residence Inn by Marriott 1001 Gould Dr	Bossier City	LA	71111	318-747-6220	747-3424
TF: 800-331-3131 ■ *Web:* residenceinn.com/SHVBB					
Rodeway Inn 3101 Hilton Dr	Bossier City	LA	71111	318-747-7010	747-6927
TF: 800-228-2000					
Ryder Inn Hwy 1 S Bypass	Natchitoches	LA	71457	318-357-8281	352-9907
TF: 888-252-8281 ■ *E-mail:* ryderinn@worldnetla.net					
Sheraton Hotel 1419 E 70th St.	Shreveport	LA	71105	318-797-9900	798-2923
TF: 800-635-3304					
Shoney's Inn 1836 Old Minden Rd	Bossier City	LA	71111	318-747-7700	742-2779
TF: 800-222-2222 ■ *Web:* www.shoneysinn.com/la1.htm					
Sundowner Inn West 2134 Greenwood Rd	Shreveport	LA	71103	318-425-7467	425-7030
Super 8 Lodge 5204 Monkhouse Dr	Shreveport	LA	71109	318-635-8888	
TF: 800-800-8000					

— Restaurants —

Name / Address	City	State	Zip	Phone
Brocato's (Italian) 189 E Kings Hwy	Shreveport	LA	71104	318-865-2352
Chadwick's Restaurant (Homestyle) 102 Lake St.	Shreveport	LA	71101	318-222-7717
Chianti Restaurant (Italian) 6535 Line Ave	Shreveport	LA	71106	318-868-8866
Country Tavern (Barbecue) 823 Brookhollow Dr	Shreveport	LA	71105	318-797-4477
Crescent Landing Catfish Restaurant (Seafood) 7601 Pines Rd	Shreveport	LA	71129	318-686-4450
Don's Seafood & Steak House (Steak/Seafood) 3100 Highland Ave	Shreveport	LA	71104	318-865-4291
Dudley's on the Lake (Steak/Seafood) 5765 S Lakeshore Dr	Shreveport	LA	71105	318-621-0095
Earthereal Restaurant (Vegetarian) 3309 Line Ave.	Shreveport	LA	71104	318-865-8947
Ernest's Orleans Restaurant (Continental) 1601 Spring St S	Shreveport	LA	71101	318-226-1325
Fertitta's 6301 Restaurant (Steak/Seafood) 6301 Line Ave	Shreveport	LA	71106	318-865-6301
Grandy's (Homestyle) 6811 Pines Rd	Shreveport	LA	71129	318-687-0718
Joe's Bar & Grill (American) 163 E Kings Hwy	Shreveport	LA	71105	318-868-5637
Kon Tiki (Chinese) 5815 Youree Dr	Shreveport	LA	71105	318-869-2316
Monjunis (Italian) 1315 Louisiana Ave	Shreveport	LA	71101	318-227-0847
Monsieur Patou (French) 855 Pierremont Rd Suite 135	Shreveport	LA	71106	318-868-9822
Murrell's (Homestyle) 539 E Kings Hwy	Shreveport	LA	71105	318-868-2620
Noble Savage Tavern (American) 417 Texas St.	Shreveport	LA	71101	318-221-1781
Olive Street Bistro (Mediterranean) 1027 Olive St.	Shreveport	LA	71101	318-221-4517
Oxford Street Restaurant & Pub (American) 8905 Mansfield Rd	Shreveport	LA	71118	318-687-1681
Pete Harris Cafe (Seafood) 1355 Milam St	Shreveport	LA	71101	318-425-4277
Rennick's Restaurant (American) 1419 E 70th St	Shreveport	LA	71105	318-797-9900
Savoie's (Cajun) 2400 E 70th St	Shreveport	LA	71105	318-797-3014
Shogun Steak House (Japanese) 1409 E 70th St.	Shreveport	LA	71129	318-798-1001
Smith's Cross Lake Inn (Steak/Seafood) 5301 S Lakeshore Dr	Shreveport	LA	71105	318-631-0919
Stumpwater Inn (Seafood) 9294 Blanchard Furrh Rd	Shreveport	LA	71107	318-929-3725
Superior Bar & Grill (Mexican) 6123 Line Ave	Shreveport	LA	71106	318-869-3243

— Goods and Services —

SHOPPING

Name / Address	City	State	Zip	Phone	Fax
Libbey Glass Factory Outlet 4302 Jewella Ave	Shreveport	LA	71109	318-621-0265	621-0351
Mall Saint Vincent 1133 St Vincent Ave Suite 200	Shreveport	LA	71104	318-227-9880	424-0454
Pierre Bossier Mall 2950 E Texas St.	Bossier City	LA	71111	318-747-5700	742-4739
Pierremont Mall 4801 Line Ave	Shreveport	LA	71106	318-222-3119	222-0566
South Park Mall 8924 Jewella Ave	Shreveport	LA	71118	318-686-7627	688-5744

BANKS

Name / Address	City	State	Zip	Phone	Fax
Bank One 400 Texas St	Shreveport	LA	71101	318-226-2345	226-2191*
**Fax:* Mktg					
Deposit Guaranty National Bank 333 Texas St	Shreveport	LA	71101	318-429-1000	429-1117*
**Fax:* Mktg ■ *TF Cust Svc:* 800-748-8501 ■ *Web:* www.dgb.com					
Hibernia National Bank 333 Travis St	Shreveport	LA	71101	318-221-5406	675-5109

BUSINESS SERVICES

Name	Phone	Name	Phone
Airborne Express	800-247-2676	**Kinko's**	318-869-2197
BAX Global	800-225-5229	**Mail Boxes Etc**	800-789-4623
Creative Staffing	318-868-2010	**Manpower Temporary Services**	318-631-4242
DHL Worldwide Express	800-225-5345	**Post Office**	800-275-8777
Federal Express	800-238-5355	**Snelling Temporaries**	318-865-2696
Kavanaugh Group	318-424-9754	**UPS**	800-742-5877

— Media —

PUBLICATIONS

Name / Address	City	State	Zip	Phone	Fax
Times‡ PO Box 30222	Shreveport	LA	71130	318-459-3200	459-3301
TF: 800-551-8892 ■ *Web:* www.nwlouisiana.com					

‡Daily newspapers

TELEVISION

Name / Address	City	State	Zip	Phone	Fax
KLTS-TV Ch 24 (PBS) 72733 Perkins Rd	Baton Rouge	LA	70810	225-767-5660	767-4299
KMSS-TV Ch 33 (Fox) 3519 Jewella Ave	Shreveport	LA	71109	318-631-5677	631-4195
Web: www.kmssfox33.com ■ *E-mail:* kmss@kmsstv.com					
KSHV-TV Ch 45 (Ind) 3519 Jewella Ave	Shreveport	LA	71109	318-631-4545	631-4195
KSLA-TV Ch 12 (CBS) 1812 Fairfield Ave	Shreveport	LA	71101	318-222-1212	677-6703
Web: www.ksla.com					
KTAL-TV Ch 6 (NBC) 3150 N Market St	Shreveport	LA	71107	318-425-2422	425-2488
Web: www.ktal.com					
KTBS-TV Ch 3 (ABC) 312 E Kings Hwy	Shreveport	LA	71104	318-861-5800	862-9434
Web: www.ktbs.com ■ *E-mail:* ktbsnews@ktbs.com					

Shreveport (Cont'd)

RADIO

	City	State	ZIP	Phone	Fax
KBCL-AM 1070 kHz (Rel) 316 B Gregg St	Shreveport	LA	71104	318-861-1070	861-1230
KDAQ-FM 89.9 MHz (NPR) 1 University Pl. *Web:* www.npr.org/members/KDAQ ■ *E-mail:* kdaq@aol.com	Shreveport	LA	71115	318-797-5150	797-5153
KEEL-AM 710 kHz (N/T) 6341 Westport Ave	Shreveport	LA	71129	318-688-1130	687-8574
KITT-FM 93.7 MHz (Ctry) 6341 Westport Ave *Web:* www.catcountry937.com	Shreveport	LA	71129	318-688-1130	687-8574
KLKL-FM 92.1 MHz (Oldies) 1300 Grimmett Dr	Shreveport	LA	71107	318-222-3122	459-1493
KRMD-AM 1340 kHz (Sports) 3109 Alexander Ave	Shreveport	LA	71104	318-865-5173	865-3657
KRMD-FM 101.1 MHz (Ctry) 3109 Alexander Ave *Web:* www.krmd.com	Shreveport	LA	71104	318-865-5173	631-4195
KTAL-FM 98.1 MHz (CR) 3150 N Market St	Shreveport	LA	71107	318-425-2422	425-2486
KTUX-FM 98.9 MHz (Rock) 6341 Wesstport Ave *Web:* www.rebelrocker99x.com ■ *E-mail:* ktux@broadcast.com	Shreveport	LA	71129	318-688-1130	687-8574
KWKH-AM 1130 kHz (Ctry) 6341 Westport Ave	Shreveport	LA	71129	318-688-1130	687-8574

— Colleges/Universities —

	City	State	ZIP	Phone	Fax
Bossier Parish Community College 2719 Airline Dr N *Web:* www.bpcc.cc.la.us	Bossier City	LA	71111	318-746-9851	742-8664
Centenary College 2911 Centenary Blvd *TF Admissions:* 800-234-4448 ■ *Web:* alpha.centenary.edu ■ *E-mail:* postmaster@beta.centenary.edu	Shreveport	LA	71104	318-869-5011	869-5026
East Texas Baptist University 1209 N Grove St. *Web:* www.etbu.edu	Marshall	TX	75670	903-935-7963	938-1705
Louisiana State University Shreveport Campus 1 University Pl *Web:* www.lsus.edu	Shreveport	LA	71115	318-797-5000	798-4138
Wiley College 711 Wiley Ave *TF:* 800-658-6889	Marshall	TX	75670	903-927-3300	938-8100

— Hospitals —

	City	State	ZIP	Phone	Fax
Bossier Medical Center 2105 Airline Dr. **Fax:* Admitting ■ *Web:* www.bossiermed.org	Bossier City	LA	71111	318-741-6000	741-6585*
Columbia Highland Hospital 1453 E Bert Kouns Industrial Loop	Shreveport	LA	71105	318-798-4300	798-4375
Louisiana State University Medical Center 1541 Kings Hwy **Fax:* Admitting ■ *Web:* www.lsumc.edu	Shreveport	LA	71130	318-675-5000	675-7065*
Overton Brooks Veterans Affairs Medical Center 510 E Stoner Ave	Shreveport	LA	71101	318-221-8411	424-6156
Schumpert Medical Center 1 St Mary Pl **Fax:* Admitting	Shreveport	LA	71120	318-681-4500	681-4465*
Shriners Hospitals for Children Shreveport Unit 3100 Samford Ave *Web:* www.shrinershq.org/Hospitals/Directry/shreveport.html	Shreveport	LA	71103	318-222-5704	424-7610
Willis Knighton Medical Center 2600 Greenwood Rd **Fax:* Admitting	Shreveport	LA	71103	318-632-4600	632-8630*

— Attractions —

	City	State	ZIP	Phone	Fax
Ark-La-Tex Antique & Classic Vehicle Museum 601 Spring St *Web:* www.softdisk.com/comp/classic/	Shreveport	LA	71101	318-222-0227	222-5042
Barnwell Garden & Art Center 601 Clyde Fant Pkwy	Shreveport	LA	71101	318-673-7703	673-7707
Bickham Dickson Park 2283 E Bert Kouns Loop	Shreveport	LA	71105	318-673-7808	
East Bank Theatre 630 Barksdale Blvd.	Bossier City	LA	71111	318-741-8310	741-8312
Eighth Air Force Museum Barksdale Air Force Base	Bossier City	LA	71110	318-456-3067	456-5558
Gardens of the American Rose Center 8877 Jefferson-Paige Rd	West Shreveport	LA	71119	318-938-5402	
Harrah's Casino Shreveport PO Box 1114 *TF:* 800-427-7247	Shreveport	LA	71163	318-424-7777	424-5650
Horseshoe Riverboat Casino 7111 Horseshoe Blvd **Fax:* Hum Res ■ *TF:* 800-895-0711 ■ *Web:* www.horseshoecasinos.com/	Bossier City	LA	71171	318-742-0711	742-1541*
Isle of Capri Casino 711 Isle of Capri Blvd *TF:* 800-843-4753	Bossier City	LA	71111	318-678-7777	226-1782
Jacobs Walter B Memorial Nature Park 8012 Blanchard-Furrh Rd	Blanchard	LA	71107	318-929-2806	929-3718
Louisiana State Exhibit Museum 3015 Greenwood Rd	Shreveport	LA	71109	318-632-2020	632-2056
Meadows Museum of Art of Centenary College 2911 Centenary Blvd	Shreveport	LA	71104	318-869-5169	869-5730
Norton RW Art Gallery 4747 Creswell Ave *Web:* www.softdisk.com/comp/norton ■ *E-mail:* norton@softdisk.com	Shreveport	LA	71106	318-865-4201	869-0435
Olde Covered Bridge Garden 6905 Greenwood Rd	Shreveport	LA	71119	318-635-6296	635-0020
Pioneer Heritage Center 1 University Pl Louisiana State University	Shreveport	LA	71115	318-797-5332	797-5395
Poverty Point National Monument 6859 Hwy 577 *Web:* www.nps.gov/popo/	Pioneer	LA	71266	318-926-5492	
Sci-Port Discovery Center Lake St & Clyde Fant Pkwy *Web:* www.sciport.org	Shreveport	LA	71101	318-424-3466	
Shreveport Civic Theatre 400 Clyde Fant Pkwy	Shreveport	LA	71101	318-673-5100	673-5105
Shreveport Entertainment District Downtown Shreveport Riverfront	Shreveport	LA	71101	318-222-9391	
Shreveport Little Theatre 812 Maragret Pl.	Shreveport	LA	71101	318-424-4439	424-4440
Shreveport Metropolitan Ballet 600 Clyde Fant Pkwy Civic Theatre	Shreveport	LA	71101	318-865-8242	
Shreveport Opera 600 Clyde Fant Pkwy Civic Theatre	Shreveport	LA	71101	318-227-9503	227-9518
Shreveport Regional Arts Council 800 Snow St	Shreveport	LA	71101	318-673-6500	673-6515
Shreveport Symphony 600 Clyde Fant Pkwy Civic Theatre	Shreveport	LA	71101	318-227-8863	222-7490
SPAR Planetarium 2820 Pershing Blvd	Shreveport	LA	71109	318-673-7827	
Sports Museum of Champions 700 Clyde Fant Pkwy	Shreveport	LA	71101	318-221-0712	221-7366
Spring Street Museum 525 Spring St	Shreveport	LA	71101	318-424-0964	
Strand Theatre 619 Louisiana Ave. *Web:* thestrandtheatre.com	Shreveport	LA	71101	318-226-1481	424-5434
Texas Street Bridge	Shreveport	LA		318-222-9391	
Theatre of Performing Arts 4005 Lakeshore Dr	Shreveport	LA	71109	318-525-0740	525-0720
Touchstone Wildlife & Art Museum 3386 Hwy 80 E.	Haughton	LA	71037	318-949-2323	
Water Town USA 7670 W 70th St.	Shreveport	LA	71129	318-938-5473	938-1183

SPORTS TEAMS & FACILITIES

	City	State	ZIP	Phone	Fax
Boothill Speedway I-20 W to Exit 3	West Shreveport	LA	71102	318-938-5373	
Hirsch Coliseum 3207 Pershing Blvd.	Shreveport	LA	71109	318-635-1361	631-4909
Independence Stadium 3301 Pershing Blvd.	Shreveport	LA	71109	318-673-7758	673-7786
Louisiana Downs 8000 E Texas St *TF:* 800-648-0712 ■ *Web:* www.ladowns.com	Bossier City	LA	71111	318-742-5555	741-2615
Shreveport Captains (baseball) 2901 Pershing Blvd Fairgrounds Field *Web:* www.shreveportcaptains.com ■ *E-mail:* shvcaps@iamerica.net	Shreveport	LA	71109	318-636-5555	636-5555
Shreveport Mudbugs (hockey) 3701 Hudson St 2nd Fl *Web:* www.mudbugshockey.com ■ *E-mail:* info@mudbugshockey.com	Shreveport	LA	71109	318-636-2847	636-2280

— Events —

	Phone
Artbreak (early May)	318-673-6500
Champion Lake Pro Classic (mid-June)	318-222-7442
Christmas in Roseland (late November-early January)	318-938-5402
December on the Red (late November-late December)	318-222-9391
Downtown Neon Saturday Nights (June-September)	318-673-6500
First Bloom Festival (late April)	318-938-5402
Fourth of July Celebration (July 4)	318-459-3515
Holiday in Dixie (early-mid-April)	318-865-5555

Shreveport — Events (Cont'd)

	Phone
Jazz & Gumbo Music Festival (mid-May)	318-226-4552
Let the Good Times Roll Festival (mid-June)	318-222-7403
Louisiana State Fair (late October-early November)	318-635-1361
Mardi Gras in the Ark-La-Tex (late February-early March)	318-746-0252
Mudbug Madness (late May)	318-222-7403
Nike Shreveport Open Golf Tournament (mid-April)	318-798-6463
Pioneer Days (late September)	318-938-7289
Rackets Over the Red (late November-late December)	318-222-7403
Red River Rally (early October)	318-222-9391
Red River Revel (early October)	318-424-4000
Redbud Festival (mid-March)	318-226-8884
Sanford Independence Bowl (late December)	318-221-0712

Maine

Population (1999): 1,253,040 **Area (sq mi): 35,387**

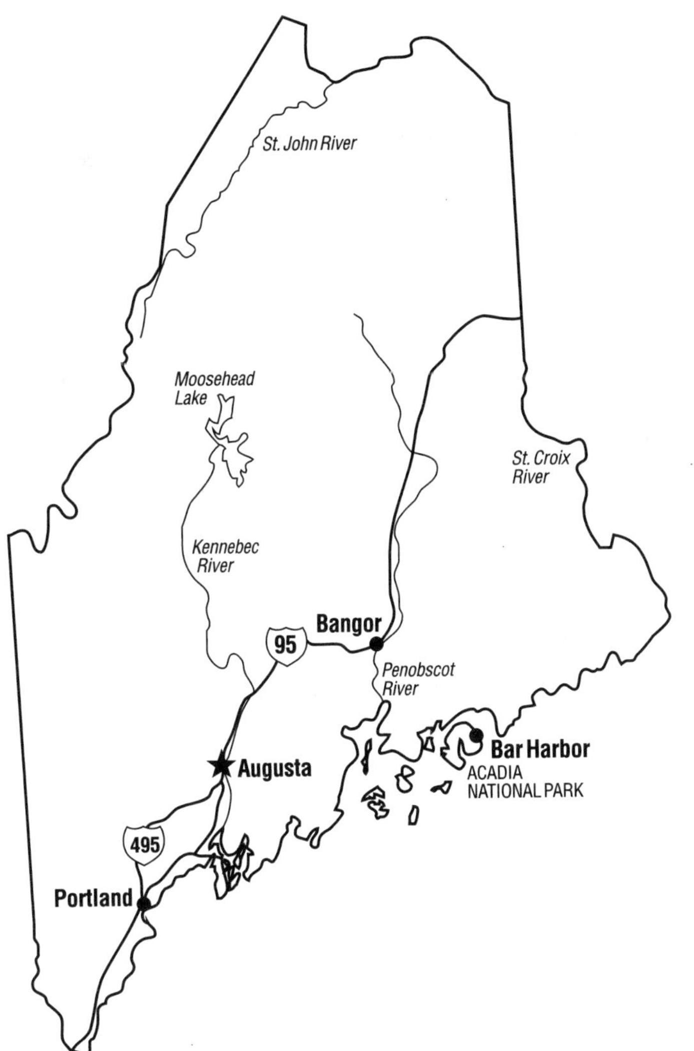

— State Information Sources —

				Phone	Fax
Maine Chamber of Commerce & Business Alliance 7 Community Dr	Augusta	ME	04330	207-623-4568	622-7723
Maine Economic & Community Development Dept 59 State House Stn *Web:* www.econdevmaine.com	Augusta	ME	04333	207-287-2656	287-2861
Maine Parks & Land Bureau 22 State House Stn *Web:* www.state.me.us/doc/prkslnds/prkslnds.htm#parks	Augusta	ME	04333	207-287-3821	287-3823
Maine State Government Information *Web:* www.state.me.us				207-624-9494	
Maine State Library 64 State House Stn *Web:* www.state.me.us/msl ■ *E-mail:* edna.comstock@state.me.us	Augusta	ME	04333	207-287-5600	287-5615
Maine Tourism Office 59 State House Stn *TF:* 888-624-6345 ■ *Web:* www.visitmaine.com	Augusta	ME	04333	207-287-5711	287-8070

ON-LINE RESOURCES

Coastal Maine Vacation Information . . . . www.coastalmaine.net
Destination Maine . . . . www.destinationmaine.com
GORP Maine Travel & Recreation Guide . . . . www.gorp.com/gorp/location/me/me.htm
Imbored Maine www.imbored.com/new/rme01.htm
Maine Accommodations Links . . . . www.nettx.com/states/me.htm
Maine Cities . . . . dir.yahoo.com/Regional/U_S__States/Maine/Cities
Maine Counties & Regions . . . . dir.yahoo.com/Regional/U_S__States/Maine/Counties_and_Regions
Maine Event Scheduler . . . . maineevents.com
Maine Lobster.net . . . . www.chickadee.com/lobster
Maine Outdoors Sporting Guide . . . . maineoutdoors.com
Maine Resource Guide . . . . www.maineguide.com
Maine Scenario . . . . scenariousa.dstylus.com/me/indexf.htm
Maine Sunshine . . . . www.mainesunshine.com
Maine Travel & Tourism Guide . . . . www.travel-library.com/north_america/usa/maine/index.html
PeekABoo Maine . . . . www.peekaboo.net/me
Rough Guide Travel Maine travel.roughguides.com/content/440/index.htm
Search Maine . . . . www.newengland.com/memap.html
Travel.org-Maine . . . . travel.org/maine.html
VisitMaine.com . . . . www.visit-maine.com
VisitMaine.com Unofficial Maine State Directory . . . . www.visitmaine.net
Yahoo! Get Local Maine . . . . dir.yahoo.com/Regional/U_S__States/Maine

— Cities Profiled —

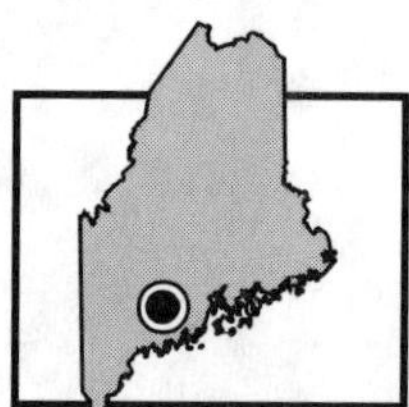

Augusta

Originally settled in 1628 as a trading post on the site of an Indian village, Augusta has been the capital of Maine since 1827. The Maine State House, built in 1829, was designed by Charles Bulfinch. Its dome rises above Capitol Park and the Kennebec River. The city encompasses both sides of the Kennebec River, which is the site of an annual Whatever Week Festival, a 12-day event featuring more than 50 family fun events, a carnival, fireworks, concerts, and a "Wacky River Race."

Population	19,978	**Longitude**	69-77-50 W
Area (Land)	55.4 sq mi	**County**	Kennebec
Area (Water)	2.9 sq mi	**Time Zone**	EST
Elevation	153 ft	**Area Code/s**	207
Latitude	44-31-53 N		

— Average Temperatures and Precipitation —

TEMPERATURES

	Jan	Feb	Mar	Apr	May	Jun	Jul	Aug	Sep	Oct	Nov	Dec
High	28	31	40	52	65	74	79	77	69	58	45	32
Low	10	12	24	34	45	54	60	58	50	40	31	16

PRECIPITATION

	Jan	Feb	Mar	Apr	May	Jun	Jul	Aug	Sep	Oct	Nov	Dec
Inches	2.9	2.8	3.2	3.7	3.8	3.3	3.2	3.3	3.1	3.9	4.5	3.8

— Important Phone Numbers —

	Phone		Phone
AAA	207-622-2221	**Medical Referral**	207-596-8200
Emergency	911	**Poison Control Center**	207-871-4720

— Information Sources —

				Phone	Fax
Augusta City Hall 16 Cony St. *Web:* www.ci.augusta.me.us	Augusta	ME	04330	207-626-2310	626-2304
Augusta Civic Center Community Dr *E-mail:* ACC@biddeford.com	Augusta	ME	04330	207-626-2405	626-5968
Augusta Economic & Community Development Office 16 Cony St	Augusta	ME	04330	207-626-2336	626-2338
Augusta Mayor 16 Cony St.	Augusta	ME	04330	207-626-2300	626-2304
Better Business Bureau Serving Maine 812 Stevens Ave *Web:* www.bosbbb.org	Portland	ME	04103	207-878-2715	797-5818
Kennebec County 125 State St	Augusta	ME	04330	207-622-0971	623-4083
Kennebec Valley Chamber of Commerce PO Box 676 *Web:* www.augustamaine.com ■ *E-mail:* kvcc@mint.net	Augusta	ME	04332	207-623-4559	626-9342
Lithgow Public Library Winthrop St *Web:* www.ci.augusta.me.us/service/community/lithgow/	Augusta	ME	04330	207-626-2415	626-2419

On-Line Resources

Area Guide Augusta .... augustame.areaguides.net
Excite.com Augusta (ME) City Guide .... www.excite.com/travel/countries/united_states/maine/augusta
NITC Travelbase City Guide Augusta .... www.travelbase.com/auto/features/augusta-me.html

— Transportation Services —

AIRPORTS

■ **Augusta State Airport (AUG)**

	Phone
1 mile NW of downtown (approx 5 minutes)	207-626-2306

Airport Transportation

	Phone
Al's Taxi $3-6 fare to downtown	207-622-5846
B Line Taxi $2-3 fare to downtown	207-623-7702
Romeo's Taxi $3 fare to downtown	207-621-0489

Commercial Airlines

	Phone
Colgan Air	207-623-7527

Charter Airlines

	Phone
Maine Beechcraft	207-622-1211

■ **Portland International Jetport (PWM)**

	Phone
75 Miles SW of downtown Augusta (approx 90 minutes)	207-774-7301

Airport Transportation

	Phone
Airport Car Service $75 fare to downtown Augusta	800-362-6795
Medallion Coach $65 fare to downtown Augusta	800-887-4185

Commercial Airlines

	Phone		Phone
Continental	800-525-0280	**United**	800-241-6522
Continental Express	800-525-0280	**United Express**	800-241-6522
Delta	800-221-1212	**US Airways**	800-428-4322
Delta Connection	800-221-1212	**US Airways Express**	800-428-4322
Northwest	800-225-2525		

Charter Airlines

	Phone		Phone
Charter Fleet International	800-355-5387	**Maine Aviation**	207-780-1811
Gray Webster Aviation	207-865-0083	**Telford Aviation Inc**	800-639-4809

CAR RENTALS

	Phone		Phone
Alamo	207-775-0855	**Hertz**	207-774-4544
Budget	207-622-0210	**National**	207-773-0036
Enterprise	207-772-0030		

LIMO/TAXI

	Phone		Phone
Al's Taxi	207-622-5846	**Double R's Taxi**	207-623-3431
B Line Taxi	207-623-7702	**Mid-Coast Limo**	207-236-2424
Classy Taxi & Limousine	800-499-0663	**Romeo's Taxi**	207-621-0489
Custom Coach Limousine	207-797-9100		

MASS TRANSIT

	Phone
Kennebec Valley Transit $.75 Base fare	207-622-4761

RAIL/BUS

				Phone
Greyhound Bus Station 312 Water St *TF:* 800-231-2222	Augusta	ME	04330	207-622-1601

— Accommodations —

HOTELS, MOTELS, RESORTS

				Phone	Fax
Augusta Hotel 390 Western Ave *TF:* 888-636-2463	Augusta	ME	04330	207-622-6371	621-0349
Best Western Senator Inn 284 Western Ave. *TF:* 800-528-1234	Augusta	ME	04330	207-622-5804	622-5804

Augusta — Hotels, Motels, Resorts (Cont'd)

				Phone	Fax
Bethel Inn & Country Club PO Box 49	Bethel	ME	04217	207-824-2175	824-2233
TF: 800-654-0125 ■ *Web:* www.bethelinn.com ■ *E-mail:* info@bethelinn.com					
Comfort Inn 281 Civic Center Dr	Augusta	ME	04330	207-623-1000	623-3505
TF: 800-228-5150					
Fairway Motor Lodge Rt 202	Manchester	ME	04351	207-623-3902	623-3902
Holiday Inn Civic Center 110 Community Dr	Augusta	ME	04330	207-622-4751	622-3108
TF: 800-465-4329 ■ *Web:* www.basshotels.com/holiday-inn/?_franchisee=AUGCC ■ *E-mail:* tmeagher@fine-hotels.com					
Maple Hill Farm Bed & Breakfast Inn Outlet Rd	Hollowell	ME	04330	207-622-2708	622-0655
TF: 800-622-2708 ■ *Web:* www.maplebb.com					
Motel 6 18 Edison Dr	Augusta	ME	04330	207-622-0000	622-1048
TF: 800-466-8356					
Ramada Inn Conference Center 490 Pleasant St	Lewiston	ME	04240	207-784-2331	784-2332
TF: 800-228-2828					
Samoset Resort 220 Warrenton Ave	Rockport	ME	04856	207-594-2511	594-0722
TF: 800-341-1650 ■ *Web:* www.samoset.com ■ *E-mail:* info@samoset.com					
Scandinavian Inn Rt 202	Manchester	ME	04351	207-623-4583	623-4583
Super 8 Motel 395 Western Ave	Augusta	ME	04330	207-626-2888	623-8468
TF: 800-800-8000					
Susse Chalet Motor Lodge Whitten Rd	Augusta	ME	04330	207-622-3776	622-3778
TF: 800-524-2538 ■ *Web:* www.sussechalet.com/augusta.html					

— Restaurants —

				Phone
Canton Express (Chinese) 102 Bangor St	Augusta	ME	04330	207-623-0039
Capital Cafe (Chinese) 208 Western Ave	Augusta	ME	04330	207-623-8878
Captain Cote's Seafood (Seafood) Civic Center Dr	Augusta	ME	04330	207-622-4625
Crossroads Restaurant & Pub (American) 115 Whitten Rd	Augusta	ME	04330	207-621-0132
David's Restaurant (American) 390 Brunswick Ave	Gardiner	ME	04345	207-582-6656
Ground Round (American) 110 Community Dr	Augusta	ME	04330	207-623-0022
Hill Top Family Restaurant (Steak/Seafood) Augusta State Airport	Augusta	ME	04330	207-623-2044
Margaritas (Mexican) 390 Western Ave	Augusta	ME	04330	207-622-7874
Rebecca's Place (American) 434 Eastern Ave	Augusta	ME	04330	207-623-8142
River Cafe (Lebanese) 119 Water St	Augusta	ME	04330	207-622-2190
Roseland Restaurant (American) 780 Riverside Dr	Augusta	ME	04330	207-623-9640
Sally's Steak House (American) 281 Civic Center Dr	Augusta	ME	04330	207-621-0100
Sandollar Restaurant (American) 272 Water St	Hallowell	ME	04347	207-622-9020
Senator Restaurant (American) 284 Outer Western Ave	Augusta	ME	04330	207-622-0320
Tea House (Chinese) 475 Western Ave	Augusta	ME	04330	207-622-7500
Tina's (Italian) Rt 9	Chelsea	ME	04330	207-582-4020
Vickery Cafe (American) 261 Water St	Augusta	ME	04330	207-623-7670
Wicked Good Restaurant (American) Rt 27 Civic Center Dr	Augusta	ME	04330	207-622-2515

— Goods and Services —

SHOPPING

				Phone	Fax
Dealers' Choice Antique Mall 108 Water St	Hallowell	ME	04347	207-622-5527	
Sears 10 Whitten Rd	Augusta	ME	04330	207-621-2000	621-2047*
**Fax:* Hum Res					

BANKS

				Phone	Fax
Augusta Federal Savings Bank 22 Western Ave	Augusta	ME	04332	207-622-5885	622-5941
Fleet Bank 21 Armory St	Augusta	ME	04330	207-621-2283	621-2262
TF: 800-841-4000					
Kennebec Savings Bank 150 State St	Augusta	ME	04330	207-622-5801	626-2858
KeyBank NA 286 Water St	Augusta	ME	04330	207-623-5579	623-5500
TF: 800-539-2968					
Northeast Bank 1 Bangor St	Augusta	ME	04332	207-623-1700	623-8528
TF: 800-284-5989					
Peoples Heritage Bank 101 Western Ave	Augusta	ME	04330	207-622-1790	

BUSINESS SERVICES

	Phone
Airborne Express	800-247-2676
BAX Global	800-225-5229
DHL Worldwide Express	800-225-5345
Federal Express	800-463-3339
Kelly Services	207-623-1118
Manpower Temporary Services	207-622-1535
Olsten Staffing Services	207-622-4662
Post Office	207-622-6114
UPS	800-742-5877

— Media —

PUBLICATIONS

				Phone	Fax
Kennebec Journal‡ 274 Western Ave	Augusta	ME	04332	207-623-3811	623-2220

‡Daily newspapers

TELEVISION

				Phone	Fax
WABI-TV Ch 5 (CBS) 35 Hildreth St	Bangor	ME	04401	207-947-8321	941-9378
Web: www.wabi-tv.com ■ *E-mail:* wabi@wabi-tv.com					
WCSH-TV Ch 6 (NBC) 1 Congress Sq	Portland	ME	04101	207-828-6666	828-6630
TF: 800-464-1213 ■ *Web:* www.wcsh6.com ■ *E-mail:* info@wcsh6.com					
WGME-TV Ch 13 (CBS) 1335 Washington Ave	Portland	ME	04103	207-797-9330	878-3505
Web: www.wgme-tv.com ■ *E-mail:* tvmail@wgme-tv.com					
WMTW-TV Ch 8 (ABC) 99 Danville Corner Rd	Auburn	ME	04210	207-782-1800	783-7371
Web: www.wmtw.com ■ *E-mail:* wmtw@wmtw.com					
WPXT-TV Ch 51 (Fox) 2320 Congress St	Portland	ME	04102	207-774-0051	774-6849
Web: www.wpxt.com					

RADIO

				Phone	Fax
WABK-FM 104.3 MHz (Oldies) PO Box 280	Gardiner	ME	04345	207-582-3303	582-8144
WBCI-FM 105.9 MHz (N/T) 122 Main St	Topsham	ME	04086	207-725-9224	725-2686
Web: www.lifechangingradio.com/wbci.htm					
WEBB-FM 98.5 MHz (Ctry) 52 Western Ave	Augusta	ME	04330	207-623-4735	626-5948
WFAU-AM 1280 kHz (Nost) PO Box 280	Gardiner	ME	04345	207-582-3303	582-8144
WJTO-AM 730 kHz (B/EZ) PO Box 308	Bath	ME	04530	207-443-6673	386-0388
WKCG-FM 101.3 MHz (AC) PO Box 280	Gardiner	ME	04345	207-582-3313	582-8144

— Colleges/Universities —

				Phone	Fax
Colby College 4000 Mayflower Hill Lunder House	Waterville	ME	04901	207-872-3000	872-3555
TF Admissions: 800-723-3032 ■ *Web:* www.colby.edu					
Thomas College 180 W River Rd	Waterville	ME	04901	207-859-1111	859-1114
TF Admissions: 800-339-7001 ■ *Web:* www.thomas.edu ■ *E-mail:* admiss@host2.thomas.edu					
University of Maine Augusta 46 University Dr	Augusta	ME	04330	207-621-3000	621-3116
Web: www.uma.maine.edu ■ *E-mail:* jbolduc@maine.maine.edu					

— Hospitals —

				Phone	Fax
Inland Hospital 200 Kennedy Memorial Dr	Waterville	ME	04901	207-861-3000	861-3039
Maine General Medical Center 6 E Chestnut St	Augusta	ME	04330	207-626-1000	626-1090*
**Fax:* Admitting ■ *Web:* www.mainegeneral.org ■ *E-mail:* public@mainegeneral.org					

— Attractions —

				Phone	Fax
Acadia National Park PO Box 177	Bar Harbor	ME	04609	207-288-9561	288-5507
Web: www.nps.gov/acad					
Blaine House 192 State St	Augusta	ME	04330	207-287-2121	623-7878
Cony Cemetery Hospital St	Augusta	ME	04330		
Maine State Museum 83 State House Stn	Augusta	ME	04333	207-287-2301	287-6633
Old Fort Western 16 Cony St	Augusta	ME	04330	207-626-2385	626-2304
Web: www.oldfortwestern.org ■ *E-mail:* fone@mint.net					
Pine Tree State Arboretum 153 Hospital St	Augusta	ME	04330	207-621-0031	621-8245
State House Museum State & Capitol Sts	Augusta	ME	04333	207-287-2301	287-6633

Augusta (Cont'd)

— Events —

	Phone
Mile of Art (late July)	207-623-4559
Whatever Week Festival (mid-June-early July)	207-623-4559
Windsor Fair (mid-late August)	207-623-4559

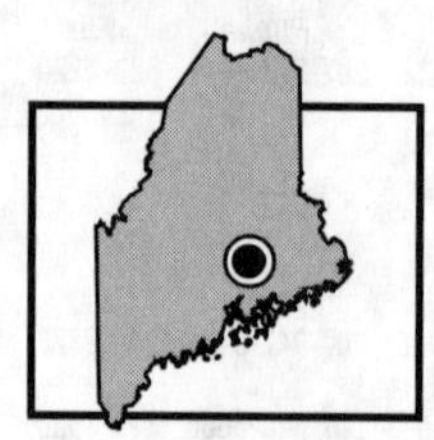

Bangor

During the 19th century Bangor was known as the lumber capital of the world. Today a statue of Bangor's legendary lumberjack, Paul Bunyan, towers over Main Street, and noted author Stephen King lives and writes in Bangor in a former lumber baron's mansion. The city is located in the lower Penobscot Valley, within 50 miles of Bar Harbor and Acadia National Park, which features a spectacular drive on the Park Loop. The Penobscot Indian Reservation is part of Greater Bangor; and Moosehead Lake is within an hour's drive. Nearby also is Orono, home of the University of Maine.

Population	30,508	**Longitude**	68-78-07 W
Area (Land)	34.5 sq mi	**County**	Penobscot
Area (Water)	0.3 sq mi	**Time Zone**	EST
Elevation	158 ft	**Area Code/s**	207
Latitude	44-81-46 N		

— Average Temperatures and Precipitation —

TEMPERATURES

	Jan	Feb	Mar	Apr	May	Jun	Jul	Aug	Sep	Oct	Nov	Dec
High	27	29	39	51	64	73	78	76	68	57	44	31
Low	8	10	22	33	43	53	58	57	48	39	29	15

PRECIPITATION

	Jan	Feb	Mar	Apr	May	Jun	Jul	Aug	Sep	Oct	Nov	Dec
Inches	3.0	2.9	3.1	3.3	3.6	3.3	3.3	3.4	3.4	3.4	4.6	4.0

— Important Phone Numbers —

	Phone		Phone
AAA	207-942-8287	**Poison Control Center**	207-871-4720
Emergency	911	**Time/Temp**	207-942-2026
Medical Referral	207-942-6414	**Weather**	207-942-2026

— Information Sources —

				Phone	Fax
Bangor City Hall 73 Harlow St	Bangor	ME	04401	207-945-4400	945-4449
Bangor Civic Center 100 Dutton St	Bangor	ME	04401	207-942-9000	947-5105
Web: www.maineguide.com/bangor/basspark/ ■ *E-mail:* basstar1@acadia.net					
Bangor Convention & Visitors Bureau 519 Main St	Bangor	ME	04401	207-947-5205	990-1427
TF: 800-916-6673 ■ *Web:* www.bangorcvb.org ■ *E-mail:* info@bangorcvb.org					
Bangor Economic Development Dept 73 Harlow St	Bangor	ME	04401	207-945-4400	945-4449
Bangor Mayor 73 Harlow St	Bangor	ME	04401	207-945-4400	945-4449
Bangor Public Library 145 Harlow St	Bangor	ME	04401	207-947-8336	945-6694
Web: www.bpl.lib.me.us					
Bangor Region Chamber of Commerce PO Box 1443	Bangor	ME	04402	207-947-0307	990-1427
Web: www.bangorregion.com ■ *E-mail:* chamber@bangorregion.com					
Better Business Bureau Serving Maine 812 Stevens Ave	Portland	ME	04103	207-878-2715	797-5818
Web: www.bosbbb.org					
Penobscot County 97 Hammond St	Bangor	ME	04401	207-942-8535	945-6027

On-Line Resources

About.com Guide to Bangor	bangorme.about.com
Area Guide Bangor	bangor.areaguides.net
Bangor Online	www.bangorme.com
Excite.com Bangor City Guide	www.excite.com/travel/countries/united_states/maine/bangor
Greater Bangor Region Resource Guide	www.maineguide.com/bangor/
I-95 Exit Information Guide Bangor	www.usastar.com/i95/cityguide/Bangor.htm

— Transportation Services —

AIRPORTS

■ **Bangor International Airport (BGR)**

	Phone
2 miles NW of downtown (approx 10 minutes)	207-947-0384

Web: www.flybangor.com ■ *E-mail:* admin@flybangor.com

Airport Transportation

	Phone
Bus The $.75 fare to downtown	207-947-0536
Town Taxi $5 fare to downtown	207-945-5671

Commercial Airlines

	Phone		Phone
Business Express	207-947-5757	**Northwest**	800-225-2525
Continental	800-525-0280	**United**	800-241-6522
Continental Express	800-525-0280	**US Airways Express**	800-428-4322
Delta	800-221-1212		

Charter Airlines

	Phone		Phone
KT Aviation	207-945-5087	**Telford Aviation Inc**	800-639-4809
Snug Harbor Airways	207-947-0824		

CAR RENTALS

	Phone		Phone
Avis	207-947-8383	**Hertz**	207-942-5519
Budget	207-945-9429	**National**	207-947-0158
Enterprise	207-990-0745		

LIMO/TAXI

	Phone		Phone
Gosselin Limo	207-942-1111	**Tally-Ho Limo**	207-942-2002
Perfection Limo	207-945-1439	**Town Taxi**	207-945-5671
Royal Coach Limousine	207-942-2002		

MASS TRANSIT

	Phone
The Bus $.75 Base fare	207-947-0536

RAIL/BUS

				Phone
Concord Trailways Bus Station 1039 Union St	Bangor	ME	04401	207-945-4000
Cyr Bus Lines Station 160 Gilman Falls Ave	Old Town	ME	04468	207-827-2335
Greyhound/Trailways Bus Station 158 Main St	Bangor	ME	04401	207-945-3000

— Accommodations —

HOTELS, MOTELS, RESORTS

				Phone	Fax
Bangor Motor Inn 701 Hogan Rd	Bangor	ME	04401	207-947-0355	947-0350
Best Western White House Inn 155 Littlefield Ave	Bangor	ME	04401	207-862-3737	862-6465
TF: 800-528-1234					

Bangor — Hotels, Motels, Resorts (Cont'd)

	City	State	Zip	Phone	Fax
Comfort Inn 750 Hogan Rd. *TF:* 800-228-5150	Bangor	ME	04401	207-942-7899	942-6463
Country Inn at the Mall 936 Stillwater Ave. *TF:* 800-244-3961	Bangor	ME	04401	207-941-0200	942-1167
Days Inn Bangor 250 Odlin Rd *TF:* 800-329-7466	Bangor	ME	04401	207-942-8272	942-1382
Fairfield Inn by Marriott 300 Odlin Rd *TF:* 800-228-2800 ■ *Web:* fairfieldinn.com/BGRFI	Bangor	ME	04401	207-990-0001	990-0917
Hampton Inn 10 Bangor Mall Blvd. *TF:* 800-998-7829 ■ *Web:* www.maineguide.com/bangor/hampton/	Bangor	ME	04401	207-990-4400	990-0577
Holiday Inn 500 Main St *TF:* 800-465-4329	Bangor	ME	04401	207-947-8651	942-2848
Holiday Inn 404 Odlin Rd. *TF:* 800-914-0101	Bangor	ME	04401	207-947-0101	947-7619
Howard Johnson Lodge 336 Odlin Rd *TF:* 800-446-4656	Bangor	ME	04401	207-942-5251	942-4227
Main Street Inn 480 Main St *TF:* 800-928-9877	Bangor	ME	04401	207-942-5281	947-8733
Motel 6 1100 Hammond St *TF:* 800-466-8356	Bangor	ME	04401	207-947-6921	941-8543
Phoenix Inn 20 Broad St	Bangor	ME	04401	207-947-0411	947-0255
Ramada Inn 357 Odlin Rd *TF:* 800-445-7787	Bangor	ME	04401	207-947-6961	945-9428
Riverside Inn 495 State St. *TF:* 800-252-4044	Bangor	ME	04401	207-973-4100	973-4110
Rodeway Inn 482 Odlin Rd. *TF:* 800-214-2152	Bangor	ME	04401	207-942-6301	941-0949
Sheraton Four Points Hotel 308 Godfrey Blvd *TF:* 800-228-4609	Bangor	ME	04401	207-947-6721	941-9761
Super 8 Motel 462 Odlin Rd. *TF:* 800-800-8000	Bangor	ME	04401	207-945-5681	945-5682

— Restaurants —

	City	State	Zip	Phone
Barnaby's (American) 357 Odlin Rd	Bangor	ME	04401	207-947-6961
Captain Nick's (Steak/Seafood) 1165 Union St	Bangor	ME	04401	207-942-6444
Dana's Grill (American) 290 State St *Web:* www.maineguide.com/bangor/danasgrill/	Bangor	ME	04401	207-945-6428
Geaghan's Roundhouse (American) 570 Main St.	Bangor	ME	04401	207-945-3730
Governor's (American) 643 Broadway	Bangor	ME	04401	207-947-3113
Harborside Restaurant (American) 9 S Main St.	Brewer	ME	04412	207-989-2040
Killarney's (Irish) 500 Main St.	Bangor	ME	04401	207-947-8651
Legends Restaurant & Sports Bar (American) 16 Union St.	Bangor	ME	04401	207-941-1181
Lemon Tree (Southwest) 167 Center St *Web:* www.maineguide.com/bangor/food/lemon.html ■ *E-mail:* lemongod@aol.com	Bangor	ME	04401	207-945-3666
Margarita's (Mexican) 15 Mill St.	Orono	ME	04473	207-866-4863
Nicky's Restaurant (Homestyle) 957 Union St. *Web:* www.maineguide.com/bangor/nickys/	Bangor	ME	04401	207-942-3430
Oriental Jade (Chinese) 555 Stillwater Ave *Web:* www.orientaljade.com/	Bangor	ME	04401	207-947-6969
Panda Garden (Chinese) 123 Franklin St.	Bangor	ME	04401	207-942-2704
Paul's Restaurant & Speakeasy (American) 605 Hogan Rd	Bangor	ME	04401	207-942-6726
Pilots Grill Restaurant (American) 1528 Hammond St.	Bangor	ME	04401	207-942-6325
Sea Dog Brewing Co (American) 26 Front St	Bangor	ME	04401	207-947-8004
Siam Garden (Thai) 40 Broadway	Bangor	ME	04401	207-947-7911
Thailand Restaurant (Thai) 28 Mill St.	Orono	ME	04473	207-866-4200
Thistle's (Continental) 175 Exchange St *Web:* www.maineguide.com/bangor/thistles/	Bangor	ME	04401	207-945-5480
West Side Restaurant (Seafood) 1575 Hammond St	Bangor	ME	04401	207-947-0030

— Goods and Services —

SHOPPING

	City	State	Zip	Phone	Fax
Bangor Mall 663 Stillwater Ave.	Bangor	ME	04401	207-947-7333	
Broadway Shopping Center 649 Broadway.	Bangor	ME	04401	207-947-8713	945-3366
Center Mall 39 Center St.	Brewer	ME	04412	207-989-9842	
Historic Downtown Shopping Area Main St	Bangor	ME	04401	207-947-5205	

BANKS

	City	State	Zip	Phone	Fax
Bangor Savings Bank PO Box 930 **Fax:* Cust Svc ■ *TF:* 800-432-1591	Bangor	ME	04402	207-942-5211	942-3682*
Fleet Bank 80 Exchange St.	Bangor	ME	04401	207-941-6000	941-6108
KeyBank NA 23 Water St	Bangor	ME	04401	207-945-0600	945-0717
Merrill Merchants Bank 201 Main St.	Bangor	ME	04401	207-942-4801	942-9255
Peoples Heritage Bank 74 Hammond St	Bangor	ME	04401	207-945-6445	945-6448
United Bank 145 Exchange St.	Bangor	ME	04401	207-942-5263	945-4651

BUSINESS SERVICES

	Phone		Phone
Airborne Express	800-247-2676	**Mail Boxes Etc**	800-789-4623
BAX Global	800-225-5229	**Manpower Temporary Services**	207-942-6178
DHL Worldwide Express	800-225-5345	**Pagemployment**	207-945-3301

— Media —

PUBLICATIONS

	City	State	Zip	Phone	Fax
Bangor Daily News‡ PO Box 1329 **Fax:* Edit ■ *Web:* www.bangornews.com	Bangor	ME	04402	207-990-8000	941-9476*
Weekly The 34 Summer St **Fax:* News Rm	Bangor	ME	04401	207-942-2913	947-7508*

‡Daily newspapers

TELEVISION

	City	State	Zip	Phone	Fax
WABI-TV Ch 5 (CBS) 35 Hildreth St *Web:* www.wabi-tv.com ■ *E-mail:* wabi@wabi-tv.com	Bangor	ME	04401	207-947-8321	941-9378
WLBZ-TV Ch 2 (NBC) PO Box 415 *Web:* www.wlbz.com	Bangor	ME	04402	207-942-4821	942-2109
WMEB-TV Ch 12 (PBS) 65 Texas Ave *Web:* www.mpbc.org	Bangor	ME	04401	207-941-1010	942-2857
WVII-TV Ch 7 (ABC) 371 Target Industrial Cir.	Bangor	ME	04401	207-945-6457	945-6864

RADIO

	City	State	Zip	Phone	Fax
WABI-AM 910 kHz (Oldies) 27 State St.	Bangor	ME	04401	207-947-9100	947-2346
WBFB-FM 104.7 MHz (Ctry) 12 Acme Rd Suite 207	Brewer	ME	04412	207-989-7364	989-8321
WHCF-FM 88.5 MHz (Rel) PO Box 5000 *E-mail:* fm885@midmaine.com	Bangor	ME	04402	207-947-2751	947-0010
WHSN-FM 89.3 MHz (Alt) 1 College Cir. *Web:* www.nescom.org/whsn	Bangor	ME	04401	207-941-7116	947-3987
WKIT-FM 100.3 MHz (Rock) 861 Broadway *Web:* www.zoneradio.com/wkit ■ *E-mail:* wkit@zoneradio.com	Bangor	ME	04401	207-990-2800	990-2444
WKSQ-FM 94.5 MHz (AC) PO Box 9494	Ellsworth	ME	04605	207-667-7573	667-9494
WMEH-FM 90.9 MHz (NPR) 65 Texas Ave.	Bangor	ME	04401	207-941-1010	942-2857
WQCB-FM 106.5 MHz (Ctry) 49 Acme Rd *Web:* www.telplus.net/q1065/ ■ *E-mail:* q1065@telplus.net	Brewer	ME	04412	207-989-5631	989-5685
WWBX-FM 97.1 MHz (AC) 27 State St	Bangor	ME	04401	207-947-9100	947-2346
WZON-AM 620 kHz (Sports) PO Box 1929 *Web:* www.zoneradio.com/wzon ■ *E-mail:* wzon@zoneradio.com	Bangor	ME	04402	207-942-4656	990-2444

— Colleges/Universities —

	City	State	Zip	Phone	Fax
Beal College 629 Main St *TF:* 800-660-7351	Bangor	ME	04401	207-947-4591	947-0208
Eastern Maine Technical College 354 Hogan Rd *Web:* www.mtcs.tec.me.us/emtchome.htm	Bangor	ME	04401	207-941-4600	941-4683
Husson College 1 College Cir. *TF Admissions:* 800-448-7766 ■ *Web:* www.husson.edu ■ *E-mail:* jgoodwin@husson.husson.edu	Bangor	ME	04401	207-941-7000	941-7935
University of Maine System 107 Maine Ave. *Web:* www.maine.edu	Bangor	ME	04401	207-973-3200	947-7556

— Hospitals —

	City	State	Zip	Phone	Fax
Eastern Maine Medical Center 489 State St *Web:* www.emh.org/emmc.html	Bangor	ME	04402	207-945-7000	973-7139
Saint Joseph Hospital 360 Broadway *Web:* www.stjoseph-me.org ■ *E-mail:* comments@stjoseph-me.org	Bangor	ME	04401	207-262-1000	262-1922

Bangor (Cont'd)

— Attractions —

				Phone	Fax
Acadia National Park PO Box 177	Bar Harbor	ME	04609	207-288-9561	288-5507
Web: www.nps.gov/acad					
Bangor Historical Society Museum					
159 Union St	Bangor	ME	04401	207-942-5766	941-0266
Bangor Symphony Orchestra 44 Central St	Bangor	ME	04402	207-942-5555	990-1272
TF: 800-639-3220 ■ *Web:* www.bangorsymphony.com ■ *E-mail:* symphony@bangorsymphony.com					
Blackbeard's USA Family Fun Park					
339 Odlin Rd	Bangor	ME	04401	207-945-0233	
Web: www.blackbeardsusa.com ■ *E-mail:* info@blackbeardsusa.com					
Cole Land Transportation Museum					
405 Perry Rd	Bangor	ME	04401	207-990-3600	990-2653
Web: www.classicar.com/museums/coleland/cole.htm					
Fort Knox Historical Site Rt 174	Prospect	ME	04981	207-469-7719	
Grotto Cascade Park State St	Bangor	ME	04401	207-947-1018	947-1605
Hudson Museum University of Maine MS 5746	Orono	ME	04469	207-581-1901	581-1950
Isaac Farrar Mansion 17 2nd St	Bangor	ME	04401	207-941-2808	
Leonard's Mills Museum Rt 178	Bradley	ME	04411	207-581-2871	
Maine Center for the Arts					
5746 Maine Center for the Arts University of Maine	Orono	ME	04469	207-581-1804	581-1837
TF: 800-622-8499					
Maine Folklife Center University of Maine	Orono	ME	04469	207-581-1891	581-1823
Web: www.ume.maine.edu/~folklife/					
Maynard Jordan F Planetarium & Observatory					
University of Maine 5781 Wingate Hall	Orono	ME	04469	207-581-1341	581-1314
Web: www.ume.maine.edu/~lookup/					
Old Town Museum 138 S Main St	Old Town	ME	04468	207-827-7256	
Ornamental Test Gardens University of Maine	Orono	ME	04469	207-581-2918	581-2999
Paul Bunyan Statue Main St	Bangor	ME	04401	207-947-0307	
Penobscot High Stakes Bingo PO Box 46	Old Town	ME	04468	207-827-7750	827-0237
TF: 800-255-1293					
Penobscot Indian Reservation					
6 River Rd Indian Island	Old Town	ME	04468	207-827-7776	827-6042
Penobscot Marine Museum					
US Rt 1 & Church St	Searsport	ME	04974	207-548-2529	548-2520
Web: www.acadia.net/pmmuseum ■ *E-mail:* pmmuseum@acadia.net					
Penobscot Theatre Co 183 Main St	Bangor	ME	04401	207-942-3333	947-6678
Web: ptc.maineguide.com					
Robinson Ballet Co 107 Union St	Bangor	ME	04401	207-942-1990	
Roger Clapp Greenhouses University of Maine	Orono	ME	04469	207-581-3112	
Saint Croix Island International Historic Site					
PO Box 177	Bar Harbor	ME	04609	207-288-3338	288-5507
Web: www.nps.gov/sacn/					
Saint John's Catholic Church 207 York St	Bangor	ME	04401	207-942-6941	
Sunkhaze Meadows National Wildlife Refuge					
1033 S Main St	Old Town	ME	04468	207-827-6138	827-6099
University of Maine Museum of Art					
Carnegie Hall	Orono	ME	04469	207-581-3255	

SPORTS TEAMS & FACILITIES

				Phone	Fax
Bangor Raceway 100 Dutton St	Bangor	ME	04402	207-947-6744	990-2199

— Events —

	Phone
Bangor Boating and Marine Exposition (late March)	207-947-5555
Bangor Garden Show (early April)	207-947-5555
Bangor Home and Better Living Show (mid-April)	207-947-5555
Bangor State Fair (late July-early August)	207-947-5205
Downtown Christmas Parade (late November)	207-947-5205
Fourth of July Celebration (July 4)	207-947-5205
Kenduskeag Canoe Race (mid-April)	207-947-5205
Living History Days (early October)	207-581-2871
Shakespeare Festival (late July)	207-947-5205
Shrine Circus (early May)	207-947-5555
Sidewalk Art Festival (early August)	207-947-5205
United Maine Craftsman Show (mid-October)	207-942-9000
World's Largest Garage Sale (mid-June)	207-942-9000
YWCA Spring Fair (mid-March)	207-947-5555

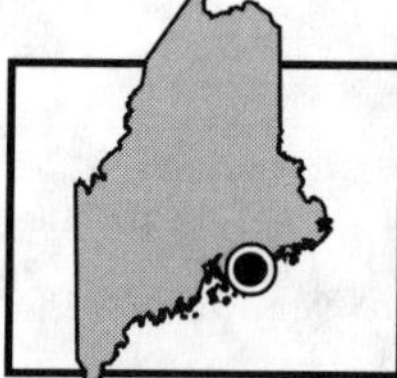

Bar Harbor

Located on the east side of Mount Desert Island, Bar Harbor was ravaged in a month-long fire in 1947 that destroyed most of the island. Today, the town is rebuilt and is surrounded by its biggest attraction, the 41,000-acre Acadia National Park, which draws more visitors per acre than any other national park in the U.S. The carriage roads in the park, a gift of John D. Rockefeller, Jr. and constructed between 1913 and 1940, are the best examples of hand cut stone roads in America today. Wildlife-watching"especially whale-watching"is a popular activity on the island. A number of species of whales can be seen in the area, but the humpback whale is most often sighted. Puffins and peregrine falcons, who were once nearly extinct, are making a comeback due to conservation efforts on the island. The 27-mile Park Loop Scenic Drive includes such sites as Otter Cliffs, Cadillac Mountain, and Thunder Hole, which is one of the most popular stops along the drive. When water surges into the chasm, it compresses the air which cannot escape, creating a resounding boom. Located in Bar Harbor is the Abbe Museum, featuring a collection of Native American artifacts that represent 10,000 years of Maine's ancestry. Located a short distance away from Bar Harbor is Campobello Island, Franklin Roosevelt's summer home, and the Schoodic Peninsula, the mainland part of Acadia National Park.

Population	4,443	**Longitude**	68-15-36 W
Area (Land)	42.2 sq mi	**County**	Hancock
Area (Water)	28.2 sq mi	**Time Zone**	EST
Elevation	20 ft	**Area Code/s**	207
Latitude	44-22-29 N		

— Average Temperatures and Precipitation —

TEMPERATURES

	Jan	Feb	Mar	Apr	May	Jun	Jul	Aug	Sep	Oct	Nov	Dec
High	30	33	41	52	63	73	78	77	69	58	46	34
Low	11	12	23	32	42	51	57	56	48	39	31	17

PRECIPITATION

	Jan	Feb	Mar	Apr	May	Jun	Jul	Aug	Sep	Oct	Nov	Dec
Inches	3.6	3.4	3.7	4.1	3.9	3.2	3.3	3.1	3.7	3.9	5.2	4.7

— Important Phone Numbers —

	Phone		Phone
AAA	207-942-8287	**Medical Referral**	207-667-8095
Emergency	911	**Poison Control Center**	207-871-4720

— Information Sources —

				Phone	Fax
Bar Harbor Chamber of Commerce					
93 Cottage St	Bar Harbor	ME	04609	207-288-5103	288-2565
Web: www.barharborinfo.com ■ *E-mail:* bhcc@acadia.net					
Bar Harbor City Hall 93 Cottage St	Bar Harbor	ME	04609	207-288-4098	288-4461
Bar Harbor Public Library 34 Mt Desert St	Bar Harbor	ME	04609	207-288-4245	288-9067
Bar Harbor Town Manager					
93 Cottage St City Hall	Bar Harbor	ME	04609	207-288-4098	288-4461
Better Business Bureau Serving Eastern Massachusetts Maine & Vermont 20 Park Plaza Suite 820	Boston	MA	02116	617-426-9000	426-7813
Web: www.bosbbb.org ■ *E-mail:* info@bosbbb.org					

Bar Harbor — Information Sources (Cont'd)

				Phone	Fax
Coastal Acadia Development Corp PO Box 554	Ellsworth	ME	04605	207-667-3897	
TF: 800-696-2540 ■ *Web:* www.acadia.net/cadc ■ *E-mail:* cadc@acadia.net					
Hancock County 60 State St	Ellsworth	ME	04605	207-667-9542	667-1412
Hulls Cove Visitor Center Rt 3	Bar Harbor	ME	04609	207-288-5262	
Mount Desert Island Visitor Center Rt 3	Thompson Island	ME	04609	207-288-3411	

On-Line Resources

Acadia Guide . . . www.acadiaguide.com/
Acadia Information Center . . . palermo.org/acadiainfo/acadia.htm
Area Guide Bar Harbor . . . barharbor.areaguides.net
Bar Harbor Maine USA . . . maineusa.com/barharbor
BarHarbor.com . . . www.barharbor.com
Downeast Guide . . . www.downeastguide.com
Excite.com Bar Harbor City Guide . . . www.excite.com/travel/countries/united_states/maine/bar_harbor
NITC Travelbase City Guide Bar Harbor . . . www.travelbase.com/auto/features/bar_harbor-me.html
Online City Guide to Bar Harbor . . . olcg.com/me/barharbor/index.html

— Transportation Services —

AIRPORTS

■ Hancock County Airport (BHB)

	Phone
12 miles NW of downtown (approx 18 minutes)	207-667-7329

Airport Transportation

	Phone
Bar Harbor Cab $20 fare to downtown	207-288-4020

Commercial Airlines

	Phone
Continental Connection	800-523-3273

Charter Airlines

	Phone
Acadia Air	207-667-5534

■ Bangor International Airport (BGR)

	Phone
50 miles NW of downtown Bar Harbor (approx 60 minutes)	207-947-0384

Web: www.flybangor.com ■ *E-mail:* admin@flybangor.com

Airport Transportation

	Phone
Concord Trailways Shuttle $20 fare to downtown Bar Harbor	888-741-8686
Downeast Transportation $9 fare to downtown Bar Harbor	207-667-5796
Town Taxi $60-70 fare to downtown Bar Harbor	207-945-5671

Commercial Airlines

	Phone		Phone
Business Express	207-947-5757	**Northwest**	800-225-2525
Continental	800-525-0280	**Northwest Airlink**	800-225-2525
Continental Express	800-525-0280	**United**	800-241-6522
Delta	800-221-1212	**US Airways Express**	800-428-4322

Charter Airlines

	Phone		Phone
KT Aviation	207-945-5087	**Telford Aviation Inc**	800-639-4809
Snug Harbor Airways	207-947-0824		

CAR RENTALS

	Phone		Phone
Avis-Bangor	207-947-8383	**Enterprise-Bangor**	207-990-0745
Budget	207-667-1200	**Hertz**	207-667-5017
Budget-Bangor	207-945-9429	**Hertz-Bangor**	207-942-5519
Enterprise	207-667-1217	**National-Bangor**	207-947-0158

LIMO/TAXI

	Phone
Bar Harbor Cab	207-288-4020

MASS TRANSIT

	Phone
Island Explorer Free	207-667-5796

— Accommodations —

HOTELS, MOTELS, RESORTS

				Phone	Fax
Acadia Hotel 20 Mt Desert St	Bar Harbor	ME	04609	207-288-5721	288-5789
Web: www.acadiahotel.com ■ *E-mail:* acadiahotel@acadia.net					
Acadia Inn 98 Eden St	Bar Harbor	ME	04609	207-288-3500	288-8424
TF: 800-638-3636 ■ *Web:* www.acadiainn.com ■ *E-mail:* acadiainn@acadia.net					
Anchorage Motel 51 Mt Desert St	Bar Harbor	ME	04609	207-288-3959	288-5588
TF: 800-336-3959					
Asticou Inn Rt 3	Northeast Harbor	ME	04662	207-276-3344	276-3373
TF: 800-258-3373 ■ *Web:* www.asticou.com ■ *E-mail:* asticou@acadia.net					
Atlantic Eyrie Lodge 6 Norman Rd	Bar Harbor	ME	04609	207-288-9786	288-8500
TF: 800-422-2883 ■ *Web:* www.barharbor.com/eyrie ■ *E-mail:* eyrie@barharbor.com					
Atlantic Oakes Motel PO Box 3	Bar Harbor	ME	04609	207-288-5801	288-8402
TF: 800-336-2463 ■ *Web:* www.barharbor.com/mansion.html ■ *E-mail:* oakes@acadia.net					
Aurora Motel 51 Holland Ave	Bar Harbor	ME	04609	207-288-3771	
TF: 800-841-8925 ■ *Web:* www.theaurora.com ■ *E-mail:* rc@theaurora.com					
Balance Rock Inn 21 Albert Meadow	Bar Harbor	ME	04609	207-288-2610	288-5534
TF: 800-753-0494 ■ *Web:* www.barharborvacations.com/welcomebri.htm					
Bar Harbor Hotel-Bluenose Inn 90 Eden St	Bar Harbor	ME	04609	207-288-3348	288-2183
TF: 800-445-4077 ■ *Web:* www.acadia.net/bluenose ■ *E-mail:* reservations@bluenoseinn.com					
Bar Harbor Inn Oceanfront Resort Newport Dr Box 7	Bar Harbor	ME	04609	207-288-3351	288-5296
TF: 800-248-3351 ■ *Web:* www.barharborinn.com ■ *E-mail:* bhinn@acadia.net					
Bar Harbor Motel 100 Eden St	Bar Harbor	ME	04609	207-288-3453	288-3598
TF: 800-388-3453 ■ *Web:* www.barharbormotel.com					
Bayview Hotel 111 Eden St	Bar Harbor	ME	04609	207-288-5861	288-3173
TF: 800-356-3585 ■ *Web:* www.barharbor.com/bayview					
Belle Isle Motel RR 1 Box 1880	Bar Harbor	ME	04609	207-288-5726	288-5726
TF: 877-782-9235					
Best Western Inn RR 2 Box 1127	Bar Harbor	ME	04609	207-288-5823	288-9827
E-mail: bestwestern@acadia.net					
Bradley Inn 3063 Bristol Rd	New Harbor	ME	04554	207-677-2105	677-3367
TF: 800-942-5560 ■ *Web:* www.bradleyinn.com					
Cadillac Motor Inn 336 Main St	Bar Harbor	ME	04609	207-288-3831	288-9370
TF: 888-207-2593 ■ *Web:* www.cadillacmotorinn.com ■ *E-mail:* cadillac@acadia.net					
Castlemaine Inn 39 Holland Ave	Bar Harbor	ME	04609	207-288-4563	288-4525
TF: 800-338-4563 ■ *Web:* www.acadia.net/castle					
Chiltern Inn 3 Cromwell Harbor Rd	Bar Harbor	ME	04609	207-288-0114	288-0124
TF: 800-404-0114 ■ *Web:* www.chilterninn.com ■ *E-mail:* chiltern@acadia.net					
Cleftstone Manor 92 Eden St	Bar Harbor	ME	04609	207-288-4951	288-2089
TF: 888-288-4951 ■ *Web:* www.acadia.net/cleftstone ■ *E-mail:* cleftstone@acadia.net					
Colony The Rt 3	Hulls Cove	ME	04644	207-288-3383	
TF: 800-524-1159 ■ *Web:* www.acadia.net/thecolony ■ *E-mail:* thecolony@acadia.net					
Cromwell Harbor Motel 359 Main St	Bar Harbor	ME	04609	207-288-3201	
TF: 800-544-3201 ■ *Web:* www.acadia.net/cromwellharbormotel ■ *E-mail:* thomi@acadia.net					
Cromwell Harbor Suites 9 Cromwell Harbor Rd	Bar Harbor	ME	04609	207-288-4118	288-0158
Dreamwood Pines Motel Rt 3 Box 1100	Bar Harbor	ME	04609	207-288-9717	288-4194
Web: www.acadia.net/dreamwood					
Edenbrook Motel 96 Eden St	Bar Harbor	ME	04609	207-288-4975	
TF: 800-323-7819 ■ *Web:* www.acadia.net/edenbrook					
Edgewater Motel Old Bar Harbor Rd	Salisbury Cove	ME	04672	207-288-3491	
TF: 888-310-9920 ■ *Web:* www.acadia.net/edgewater					
Fairfield Inn by Marriott 125 Eden St	Bar Harbor	ME	04609	207-288-8983	288-8983
Golden Anchor Inn 55 West St	Bar Harbor	ME	04609	207-288-5033	288-4577
TF: 800-328-5033 ■ *Web:* www.goldenanchorinn.com					
Graycote Inn 40 Holland Avenue	Bar Harbor	ME	04609	207-288-3044	288-2719
Web: www.graycoteinn.com ■ *E-mail:* innkeepers@graycoteinn.com					

Bar Harbor — Hotels, Motels, Resorts (Cont'd)

	City	State	ZIP	Phone	Fax
Hanscom's Motel RR 1 Box 1070 *Web:* hanscomsmotel.com	Bar Harbor	ME	04609	207-288-3744	
Higgins Holiday Motel 43 Holland Ave *TF:* 800-345-0305 ■ *Web:* www.mainetravelguide.com/higginsholidaymotel	Bar Harbor	ME	04609	207-288-3829	
High Seas Motel RR 2 Box 1085 *TF:* 800-959-5836	Bar Harbor	ME	04609	207-288-5836	
Highbrook Motel 94 Eden St *TF:* 800-338-9688 ■ *Web:* www.highbrookmotel.amtg.com	Bar Harbor	ME	04609	207-288-3591	
Holiday Inn SunSpree Resort 123 Eden St. *TF:* 800-465-4329 ■ *Web:* www.barharborholidayinn.com	Bar Harbor	ME	04609	207-288-9723	288-3089
Ledgelawn Inn 66 Mt Desert St *TF:* 800-274-5334 ■ *Web:* www.barharborvacations.com/welcomelli.htm	Bar Harbor	ME	04609	207-288-4596	288-9968
Maine Street Motel 315 Main St. *TF:* 800-333-3188 ■ *Web:* www.acadia.net/mainestreet/ ■ *E-mail:* cwitham@acadia.net	Bar Harbor	ME	04609	207-288-3188	288-2317
Manor House Inn 106 West St *TF:* 800-437-0088 ■ *Web:* www.acadia.net/manorhouse ■ *E-mail:* manor@acadia.net	Bar Harbor	ME	04609	207-288-3759	288-2974
Maples Inn 16 Roberts Ave *Web:* www.acadia.net/maples ■ *E-mail:* maplesinn@acadia.net	Bar Harbor	ME	04609	207-288-3443	288-0356
Mira Monte Inn & Suites 69 Mt Desert St *TF:* 800-553-5109	Bar Harbor	ME	04609	207-288-4263	288-3115
Park Entrance Oceanfront Motel RR1 Box 180 *TF:* 800-288-9703 ■ *Web:* www.acadia.net/parkentrance	Bar Harbor	ME	04609	207-288-9703	288-9703
Primrose Inn 73 Mt Desert St. *TF:* 800-543-7842 ■ *Web:* www.primroseinn.com ■ *E-mail:* primrose@acadia.net	Bar Harbor	ME	04609	207-288-4031	
Quality Inn 40 Kebo St *TF:* 800-282-5403 ■ *Web:* www.acadia.net/quality ■ *E-mail:* quality@acadia.net	Bar Harbor	ME	04609	207-288-5403	288-5473
Quimby House Inn 109 Cottage St *TF:* 800-344-5811 ■ *Web:* www.quimbyhouse.com ■ *E-mail:* quimbyhouse@acadia.net	Bar Harbor	ME	04609	207-288-5811	288-5811
Rockhurst Motel 68 Mt Desert St	Bar Harbor	ME	04609	207-288-3140	
Sea Breeze Motel RR 2 Box 1080 *TF:* 800-441-3123 ■ *Web:* www.acadia.net/sea_breeze ■ *E-mail:* seabreeze@acadia.net	Bar Harbor	ME	04609	207-288-3565	288-9587
Seacroft Inn 18 Albert Meadow *TF:* 800-824-9694 ■ *E-mail:* seacroft@acadia.net	Bar Harbor	ME	04609	207-288-4669	
Snell House 21 Atlantic Ave *Web:* www.snellhouse.com ■ *E-mail:* egg@acadia.net	Bar Harbor	ME	04609	207-288-8004	
Stratford House Inn 45 Mt Desert St *Web:* portland.maine.com/people/stratford ■ *E-mail:* inkeeper@downeast.net	Bar Harbor	ME	04609	207-288-5189	288-5181
Sunnyside Motel & Cottages RR 3 Box 2150	Bar Harbor	ME	04609	207-288-3602	
Town Motel 12 Atlantic Ave *TF:* 800-458-8644 ■ *Web:* www.mainesunshine.com/townmotl	Bar Harbor	ME	04609	207-288-5548	288-9406
Villager Motel 207 Main St *Web:* www.acadia.net/villager ■ *E-mail:* villager@acadia.net	Bar Harbor	ME	04609	207-288-3211	288-2270
Wonder View Inn 50 Eden St *TF:* 888-439-8439 ■ *Web:* www.wonderviewinn.com ■ *E-mail:* wonderview@acadia.net	Bar Harbor	ME	04609	207-288-3358	288-2005
Yankee Lady Inn 18 Roberts Ave *TF:* 800-971-4999 ■ *Web:* www.acadia.net/yankeelady ■ *E-mail:* yankeelady@acadia.net	Bar Harbor	ME	04609	207-288-5176	

— Restaurants —

	City	State	ZIP	Phone
124 Cottage Street (Continental) 124 Cottage St *Web:* www.amtg.com/northeast/maine/ads/124cottagest/index.htm	Bar Harbor	ME	04609	207-288-4383
Anthony's (Italian) 191 Main St	Bar Harbor	ME	04609	207-288-3377
Bar Harbor Lobster Bakes (Seafood) Rt 3	Hulls Cove	ME	04644	207-288-4055
Blackboards Restaurant (American) 101 Cottage St	Bar Harbor	ME	04609	207-288-9098
Bubba's (American) 30 Cottage St	Bar Harbor	ME	04609	207-288-5871
Cafe Blue Fish (Seafood) 122 Cottage St	Bar Harbor	ME	04609	207-288-3696
Cafe This Way (American) 14 1/2 Mt Desert St	Bar Harbor	ME	04609	207-288-4483
Carlo Pizza Ristorante (Italian) 15 Cottage St	Bar Harbor	ME	04609	207-288-4889
Chartroom Restaurant (Steak/Seafood) Rt 3 *Web:* www.thechartroom.com ■ *E-mail:* jeff@thechartroom.com	Hulls Cove	ME	04644	207-288-9740
Duffy's Quarterdeck (American) 1 Main St	Bar Harbor	ME	04609	207-288-5292
Elaine's Cafe (Vegetarian) 78 West St *Web:* www.starlightoasis.com	Bar Harbor	ME	04609	207-288-3287
Fish House Grill (Seafood) 1 West St	Bar Harbor	ME	04609	207-288-3070
Freddies Route 66 (American) 21 Cottage St	Bar Harbor	ME	04609	207-288-3708
Galyn's Galley Restaurant (Seafood) 17 Main St	Bar Harbor	ME	04609	207-288-9706
Geddy's Pub (American) 19 Main St	Bar Harbor	ME	04609	207-288-5077
George's (Mediterranean) 7 Stephens Ln *Web:* www.georgesbarharbor.com ■ *E-mail:* gayann@acadia.net	Bar Harbor	ME	04609	207-288-4505
Island Chowder House (Seafood) 38 Cottage St	Bar Harbor	ME	04609	207-288-4905
Jordan Pond House (American) Park Loop Rd. *Web:* www.jordanpond.com	Seal Harbor	ME	04675	207-276-3316
Jordan's (American) 80 Cottage St	Bar Harbor	ME	04609	207-288-3586
Lompoc Cafe & Brew Pub (American) 36 Rodick St	Bar Harbor	ME	04609	207-288-9392
Maggie's Classic Scales (Steak/Seafood) 6 Summer St	Bar Harbor	ME	04609	207-288-9007
Maine Menu (Steak/Seafood) 58 Cottage St	Bar Harbor	ME	04609	207-288-9938
Maine Street Restaurant (American) 297 Main St	Bar Harbor	ME	04609	207-288-3040
Mama Di Matteo's (Italian) 34 Kennebec St	Bar Harbor	ME	04609	207-288-3666
Miguel's (Mexican) 51 Rodick St	Bar Harbor	ME	04609	207-288-5117
Opera House (Continental) 27 Cottage St	Bar Harbor	ME	04609	207-288-3509
Parkside Restaurant (American) 185 Main St	Bar Harbor	ME	04609	207-288-3700
Pier Restaurant (Seafood) 55 West St Golden Anchor Inn *Web:* www.goldenanchorinn.com/restaurant.html	Bar Harbor	ME	04609	207-288-2110
Porcupine Grill (American) 123 Cottage St	Bar Harbor	ME	04609	207-288-3884
Rosalie's (Italian) 46 Cottage St	Bar Harbor	ME	04609	207-288-5666
Rupununi Bar & Grill (American) 119 Main St *Web:* www.rupununi.com ■ *E-mail:* info@runpnuni.com	Bar Harbor	ME	04609	207-288-2886
Testa's (Italian) 53 Main St	Bar Harbor	ME	04609	207-288-3327
Thirsty Whale (Seafood) 40 Cottage St	Bar Harbor	ME	04609	207-288-9335
West Street Cafe (American) 76 West St *Web:* www.acadia.net/weststreetcafe ■ *E-mail:* weststcafe@aol.com	Bar Harbor	ME	04609	207-288-5242

— Goods and Services —

SHOPPING

	City	State	ZIP	Phone
Maine Coast Mall 225 High St	Ellsworth	ME	04605	207-667-9905

BANKS

	City	State	ZIP	Phone	Fax
Bar Harbor Banking & Trust Co 82 Main St. *TF:* 800-924-7787 ■ *Web:* www.bhbt.com	Bar Harbor	ME	04609	207-288-3314	288-5440
First National Bank of Bar Harbor 102 Main St *TF:* 800-244-3341 ■ *Web:* www.fnbbh.com ■ *E-mail:* teller@fnbbh.com	Bar Harbor	ME	04609	207-288-3341	288-2455
Machias Savings Bank 64 Mt Desert St. *TF:* 800-339-3347	Bar Harbor	ME	04609	207-288-5826	288-3005
Union Trust Co 43 Cottage St	Bar Harbor	ME	04609	207-288-2300	244-8220

BUSINESS SERVICES

	Phone		Phone
DHL Worldwide Express	800-225-5345	**Post Office**	207-288-3122
Downeast Printing	207-667-5582	**UPS**	800-742-5877
Federal Express	800-238-5355	**Worksource**	207-667-1939
Mail Boxes Etc	207-667-7601		

— Media —

PUBLICATIONS

	City	State	ZIP	Phone	Fax
Bar Harbor Times 76 Cottage St. *TF:* 800-499-4401	Bar Harbor	ME	04609	207-288-3311	288-5813

TELEVISION

	City	State	ZIP	Phone	Fax
WABI-TV Ch 5 (CBS) 35 Hildreth St *Web:* www.wabi-tv.com ■ *E-mail:* wabi@wabi-tv.com	Bangor	ME	04401	207-947-8321	941-9378
WLBZ-TV Ch 2 (NBC) PO Box 415 *Web:* www.wlbz.com	Bangor	ME	04402	207-942-4821	942-2109
WMEB-TV Ch 12 (PBS) 65 Texas Ave *Web:* www.mpbc.org	Bangor	ME	04401	207-941-1010	942-2857
WVII-TV Ch 7 (ABC) 371 Target Industrial Cir.	Bangor	ME	04401	207-945-6457	945-6864

RADIO

	City	State	ZIP	Phone	Fax
WABI-AM 910 kHz (Oldies) 27 State St	Bangor	ME	04401	207-947-9100	947-2346
WDEA-AM 1370 kHz (Nost) PO Box 100	Brewer	ME	04412	207-989-5631	667-2436
WERU-FM 89.9 MHz (Misc) PO Box 170 *Web:* www.weru.org	East Orland	ME	04431	207-469-6600	469-8961
WKSQ-FM 94.5 MHz (AC) PO Box 9494	Ellsworth	ME	04605	207-667-7573	667-9494

Bar Harbor — Radio (Cont'd)

				Phone	Fax
WMDI-FM 107.7 MHz (AAA) 53 Main St Suite 202	Bar Harbor	ME	04609	207-288-4166	288-4902
Web: www.1077.com ■ *E-mail:* wmdi@1077.com					
WWMJ-FM 95.7 MHz (Oldies) PO Box 100	Brewer	ME	04412	207-989-5631	667-2436

— Colleges/Universities —

				Phone	Fax
College of the Atlantic 105 Eden St	Bar Harbor	ME	04609	207-288-5015	288-4126
TF Admissions: 800-528-0025 ■ *Web:* www.coa.edu					

— Hospitals —

				Phone	Fax
Mount Desert Island Hospital 10 Wayman Ln	Bar Harbor	ME	04609	207-288-5081	288-5874
Web: www.mdihospital.org ■ *E-mail:* admin@mdihospital.org					

— Attractions —

				Phone	Fax
Abbe Museum 26 Mount Desert St	Bar Harbor	ME	04609	207-288-3519	288-8979
Web: www.abbemuseum.org ■ *E-mail:* abbe@midmaine.com					
Acadia National Park PO Box 177	Bar Harbor	ME	04609	207-288-9561	288-5507
Web: www.nps.gov/acad					
Acadia Zoological Park RD 1 Box 113	Trenton	ME	04605	207-667-3244	
Acadian Whale Watcher Co 52 West St Bar Harbor Whale Museum	Bar Harbor	ME	04609	207-288-9794	288-3738
TF: 800-421-3307					
Arcady Music Society PO Box 780	Bar Harbor	ME	04609	207-288-2141	
Atlantic Brewing Co RR 1 Box 2810 Knox Rd	Bar Harbor	ME	04609	207-288-2337	288-2589
Web: www.atlanticbrewing.com ■ *E-mail:* atlantic@acadia.net					
Atlantis Whale Watch 1 West St	Bar Harbor	ME	04609	207-288-3322	288-5626
TF: 800-508-1499 ■ *Web:* www.atlantiswhale.com					
Bar Harbor Brewing Co RR 2 Box 61	Bar Harbor	ME	04609	207-288-4592	
E-mail: suzi@acadia.net					
Bar Harbor Historical Society 33 Ledgelawn Ave	Bar Harbor	ME	04609	207-288-0000	
Bar Harbor Whale Museum & Gift Shop 52 West St	Bar Harbor	ME	04609	207-288-2025	
Web: www.whalesandpuffins.com/web					
Bar Harbor Whale Watch Co 39 Cottage St	Bar Harbor	ME	04609	207-288-2386	288-4393
TF: 800-942-5374 ■ *Web:* www.whalesrus.com ■ *E-mail:* humpback@acadia.net					
Bass Cottage 14 The Field	Bar Harbor	ME	04609	207-288-3705	
Birdsnest Gallery 12 Mt Desert St	Bar Harbor	ME	04609	207-288-4054	
Echo Lake Rt 102	Bar Harbor	ME	04609	207-288-5262	
Eclipse Gallery 12 Mt Desert St	Bar Harbor	ME	04609	207-288-9048	
Evergreen Pottery Gallery 4 Mt Desert St	Bar Harbor	ME	04609	207-288-3221	
Web: www.evergreenpottery.com ■ *E-mail:* info@evergreenpottery.com					
Island Artisans Art Gallery 99 Main St	Bar Harbor	ME	04609	207-288-4214	
Lady's Slipper Gallery 4 York St	Bar Harbor	ME	04609	207-288-9053	
Web: www.ladyslippergallery.com					
Lone Moose Crafts Gallery 78 West St	Bar Harbor	ME	04609	207-288-4229	
Web: www.finemainecrafts.com ■ *E-mail:* finecrafts@acadia.net					
Nature Center & Wild Gardens of Acadia Park Loop Rd Sieur de Mont Springs	Bar Harbor	ME	04609	207-288-3003	
Oceanarium/Lobster Hatchery Rt 3	Bar Harbor	ME	04609	207-288-5005	
Park Loop Road Scenic Drive Park Loop Rd	Bar Harbor	ME	04609	207-288-5262	
Pirate's Cove Amusement Center RR1 Box 1150	Bar Harbor	ME	04609	207-288-2133	
Web: www.piratescove.net/barharbor.html					
Spruce Grove Gallery 29 Cottage St	Bar Harbor	ME	04609	207-288-2002	288-9410
Thuya Gardens Peabody Dr	Northeast Harbor	ME	04609	207-276-5130	

— Events —

	Phone
Acadia Crossing Cross Country Ski Race (early February)	207-288-3511
Acadia Triathalon (early October)	207-288-3511
Annual Book Fair (late August)	207-288-4245
Arcady Music Festival (mid-July-late August)	207-288-2141
Art & Photography Show (late July)	207-288-5103
Bar Harbor Days & Chowder Cookoff (mid-June)	207-288-5103
Bar Harbor Film Festival (early-mid-September)	207-288-3686
Bar Harbor Half Marathon (October)	207-288-3511
Bar Harbor Music Festival (early July-early August)	212-222-1026
Bar Harbor Village Holidays (December)	207-288-5103
Blessing of the Boats & Seaman's Memorial Day (mid-June)	207-288-5571
Children's Christmas Bazaar (mid-December)	207-288-5008
Christmas Village Holiday B&B & Inn Tour (early-mid-December)	207-288-5103
Downeast Church Fair (mid-July)	207-288-5103
Downeast Dulcimer & Folk Harp Festival (early-mid-July)	207-288-5653
Early Bird Sale (mid-late November)	207-288-5103
Fireworks Over Frenchman Bay (early July)	207-288-5103
Island Arts Association Holiday Fair (early December)	207-288-5008
Island Arts Association Summer Fair in the Park (early August)	207-288-5008
July 4th Festivities Seafood Festival (early July)	207-288-5103
July 4th Independence Day Parade (early July)	207-288-5103
Maine War Canoe & Sea Kayak Championship (early-mid-October)	207-288-3519
Mount Desert Island Tour de Cure (May)	207-623-2232
Native American Festival (mid-July)	207-288-3519
Penobscot Valley Craft Show (late July)	207-794-3543
Spring 5K Race & 1 Mile Fun Run (mid-June)	207-288-3511
Step Back in Time (early July-October)	207-288-9605
Walktoberfest (early October)	207-623-2232

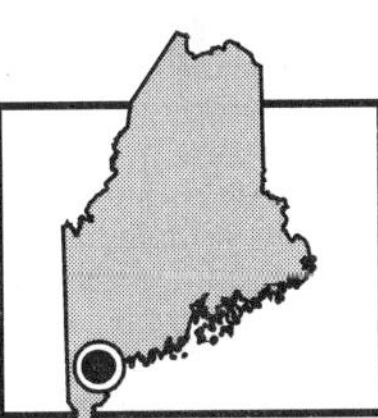

Portland

The city of Portland, Maine is surrounded by water on three sides and extends into Casco Bay. Some of the water-related excursions available include tour boats that cruise the Calendar Islands of Casco Bay, day-long boat tours around the Bay that include a lobsterbake, and whale watching and deep sea fishing expeditions out of Portland Harbor. Four miles from Portland in the Casco Bay region is Cape Elizabeth, home to the most photographed lighthouse in America, Portland Head Light. From the lighthouse one can view the entire Portland skyline. The nearby towns of Freeport and Kittery are well-known for their factory outlets, including L.L. Bean.

Population	62,786	**Longitude**	70-25-58 W
Area (Land)	22.6 sq mi	**County**	Cumberland
Area (Water)	40.5 sq mi	**Time Zone**	EST
Elevation	50 ft	**Area Code/s**	207
Latitude	43-66-14 N		

— Average Temperatures and Precipitation —

TEMPERATURES

	Jan	Feb	Mar	Apr	May	Jun	Jul	Aug	Sep	Oct	Nov	Dec
High	30	33	41	52	63	73	79	77	69	59	47	35
Low	11	14	25	34	43	52	58	57	49	38	30	18

PRECIPITATION

	Jan	Feb	Mar	Apr	May	Jun	Jul	Aug	Sep	Oct	Nov	Dec
Inches	3.5	3.3	3.7	4.1	3.6	3.4	3.1	2.9	3.1	3.9	5.2	4.5

— Important Phone Numbers —

	Phone		Phone
AAA	207-780-6800	**Medical Referral**	207-871-2196
American Express Travel	207-772-8450	**Poison Control Center**	207-871-4720
Emergency	911	**Time/Temp**	207-775-4321
HotelDocs	800-468-3537	**Weather**	207-688-3216

Portland (Cont'd)

— Information Sources —

				Phone	Fax
Better Business Bureau Serving Maine 812 Stevens Ave	Portland	ME	04103	207-878-2715	797-5818
Web: www.bosbbb.org					
Convention & Visitors Bureau of Greater Portland 305 Commercial St	Portland	ME	04101	207-772-5800	874-9043
Web: www.visitportland.com					
Cumberland County 142 Federal St Rm 102	Portland	ME	04101	207-871-8380	871-8292
Cumberland County Civic Center 1 Civic Ctr Sq	Portland	ME	04101	207-775-3481	828-8344
Web: www.theciviccenter.com					
Greater Portland Chambers of Commerce 60 Pearl St	Portland	ME	04101	207-772-2811	772-1179
Web: www.portlandregion.com					
Portland City Hall 389 Congress St	Portland	ME	04101	207-874-8300	874-8669
Web: www.ci.portland.me.us ■ *E-mail:* jar@ci.portland.me.us					
Portland Mayor 389 Congress St	Portland	ME	04101	207-874-8300	874-8669
Web: www.ci.portland.me.us/citycou.htm					
Portland Planning & Urban Development Dept 389 Congress St	Portland	ME	04101	207-874-8719	756-8258
Portland Public Library 5 Monument Sq	Portland	ME	04101	207-871-1700	871-1714
Web: www.portlandlibrary.com					

On-Line Resources

About.com Guide to Portland	portlandme.about.com
Area Guide Portland	portlandme.areaguides.net
Boulevards Portland	www.boulevards.com/cities/portland-me.html
Casco Bay Weekly	www.cascobayweekly.com
City Knowledge Portland	www.cityknowledge.com/me_portland.htm
Discover Portland First	www.portlandmaine.com/
Portland City Net	www.excite.com/travel/countries/united_states/maine/portland
Portland CityLink	www.usacitylink.com/citylink/portland/
Portland Resource & Vacation Guide	www.maineguide.com/portland/
Rough Guide Travel Portland	travel.roughguides.com/content/445/

— Transportation Services —

AIRPORTS

■ **Portland International Jetport (PWM)**

	Phone
2 miles W of downtown (approx 10 minutes)	207-774-7301

Airport Transportation

	Phone
A Airport Limo & Taxi $14 fare to downtown	800-517-9442
Metro Bus Service $1 fare to downtown	207-774-0351
Town Taxi $10 fare to downtown	207-772-0111

Commercial Airlines

	Phone		Phone
Continental	800-525-0280	**United**	800-241-6522
Continental Express	800-525-0280	**United Express**	800-241-6522
Delta	800-221-1212	**US Airways**	800-428-4322
Delta Connection	800-221-1212	**US Airways Express**	800-428-4322
Northwest	800-225-2525		

Charter Airlines

	Phone
Maine Aviation	207-780-1811

CAR RENTALS

	Phone		Phone
Alamo	207-775-0855	**Enterprise**	207-772-0030
Avis	207-874-7500	**Hertz**	207-774-4544
Budget	207-775-6508	**National**	207-773-0036

LIMO/TAXI

	Phone		Phone
A Airport Limo & Taxi	800-517-9442	**Kleen Taxi**	207-773-0055
ABC Taxi	207-772-8685	**Mid-Coast Limo**	207-236-2424
Anthony's Taxi	207-761-7949	**Oldport Taxi**	207-874-7872
Custom Coach Limousine	207-797-9100	**Pine State Taxi**	207-775-4843
Excalibur Limousine & Town Car	503-380-7228	**South Portland Taxi**	207-767-5200
Friendly Taxi	207-879-7238	**Town Taxi**	207-772-0111
Heritage Limousine	503-238-3966		

MASS TRANSIT

	Phone
Metro Bus Service $1 Base fare	207-774-0351

RAIL/BUS

				Phone
Concord Trailways Bus Station 100 Sewall St	Portland	ME	04103	207-828-1151

— Accommodations —

HOTELS, MOTELS, RESORTS

				Phone	Fax
Best Western Merry Manor Inn 700 Main St	South Portland	ME	04106	207-774-6151	871-0537
TF: 800-528-1234					
Brown Brothers Wharf Motel PO Box 460	Boothbay Harbor	ME	04538	207-633-5440	633-5440
TF: 800-334-8110					
Captain Briggs House Inn 8 Maple Ave	Freeport	ME	04032	207-865-1868	
Carleton Inn 46 Carleton St	Portland	ME	04102	207-775-1910	761-0956
TF: 800-639-1779					
Coastline Inn 80 John Roberts Rd	South Portland	ME	04106	207-772-3838	772-4238
TF: 800-470-9404					
Comfort Inn 90 Maine Mall Rd	South Portland	ME	04106	207-775-0409	775-1755
TF: 800-368-6485					
Days Inn 461 Maine Mall Rd	South Portland	ME	04106	207-772-3450	780-9748
TF: 800-329-7466					
Doubletree Hotel 1230 Congress St	Portland	ME	04102	207-774-5611	761-1560
TF: 800-222-8733 ■ *Web:* www.doubletreehotels.com/DoubleT/Hotel181/198/198Main.htm					
Econo Lodge 738 Main St	South Portland	ME	04106	207-774-5891	761-0407
TF: 800-553-2666					
Embassy Suites 1050 Westbrook St	Portland	ME	04102	207-775-2200	775-4052
TF: 800-753-8767 ■ *Web:* www.embassysuitesportland.com ■ *E-mail:* embassy@embassysuitesportland.com					
Fisherman's Wharf Inn & Motel 22 Commercial St	Boothbay Harbor	ME	04538	207-633-5090	633-5092
TF: 800-628-6872 ■ *Web:* www.fishermanswharfinn.com					
Hampton Inn 171 Philbrook Ave	South Portland	ME	04106	207-773-4400	773-6786
TF: 800-426-7866					
Harraseeket Inn 162 Main St	Freeport	ME	04032	207-865-9377	865-1684
TF: 800-342-6423					
Holiday Inn 81 Riverside St	Portland	ME	04103	207-774-5601	774-2103
TF: 800-465-4329					
Holiday Inn By the Bay 88 Spring St	Portland	ME	04101	207-775-2311	761-8224
TF: 800-465-4329 ■ *Web:* www.innbythebay.com ■ *E-mail:* sales@innbythebay.com					
Howard Johnson 675 Main St	South Portland	ME	04106	207-775-5343	772-8789
TF: 800-446-4656					
Howard Johnson Hotel 155 Riverside St	Portland	ME	04103	207-774-5861	774-5861
TF: 800-446-4656					
Inn at Saint John 939 Congress St	Portland	ME	04102	207-773-6481	756-7629
TF: 800-636-9127					
Inn by the Sea 40 Bowery Beach Rd	Cape Elizabeth	ME	04107	207-799-3134	799-4779
TF: 800-888-4287					
Maine Motel 606 Main St	South Portland	ME	04106	207-774-8284	
Marriott at Sable Oaks 200 Sable Oaks Dr	South Portland	ME	04106	207-871-8000	871-7971
TF: 800-228-9290 ■ *Web:* marriotthotels.com/PWMAP					
Motel 6 1 Riverside St	Portland	ME	04103	207-775-0111	775-0449
TF: 800-466-8356					
Oak Leaf Inn 51A Oak St	Portland	ME	04101	207-773-7882	879-0949
Web: www.oakleafinn.com ■ *E-mail:* oakleaf@maine.rr.com					
Portland Regency Hotel 20 Milk St	Portland	ME	04101	207-774-4200	775-2150
TF: 800-727-3436 ■ *Web:* www.theregency.com					
Radisson Eastland Hotel 157 High St	Portland	ME	04101	207-775-5411	775-0148
TF: 800-333-3333					
Sheraton Hotel 363 Maine Mall Rd	South Portland	ME	04106	207-775-6161	775-0196
TF: 800-325-3535					
Spruce Point Inn Resort PO Box 237	Boothbay Harbor	ME	04538	207-633-4152	633-7138
TF: 800-553-0289 ■ *Web:* www.sprucepointinn.com ■ *E-mail:* thepoint@sprucepointinn.com					

Portland — Hotels, Motels, Resorts (Cont'd)

Name / Address	City	State	Zip	Phone	Fax
Susse Chalet 1200 Brighton Ave	Portland	ME	04102	207-774-6101	772-8697
TF: 800-524-2538 ■ *Web:* www.sussechalet.com/portland.html					
Susse Chalet Inn 340 Park Ave	Portland	ME	04102	207-871-0611	871-8243
TF: 800-524-2538 ■ *Web:* www.sussechalet.com/portland2.html					
West End Inn 146 Pine St	Portland	ME	04102	207-772-1377	828-0984
TF: 800-338-1377					

— Restaurants —

Name / Address	City	State	Zip	Phone
Aubergine Bistro & Wine Bar (French) 555 Congress St	Portland	ME	04101	207-874-0680
Audubon Room (New American) 40 Bowery Beach Rd	Cape Elizabeth	ME	04107	207-767-0888
Back Bay Grill (American) 65 Portland St	Portland	ME	04101	207-772-8833
Bellacucina (Italian) 653 Congress St	Portland	ME	04101	207-828-4033
Boone's (Steak/Seafood) 6 Custom House Wharf	Portland	ME	04101	207-774-5725
Clay Oven (Indian) 565 Congress St	Portland	ME	04101	207-773-1444
Cotton Street Cantina (Caribbean/Asian) 10 Cotton St	Portland	ME	04101	207-775-3222
David's Creative Cuisine (Continental) 22 Monument Sq	Portland	ME	04101	207-773-4340
DiMillo's Floating Restaurant (Seafood) 25 Long Wharf	Portland	ME	04101	207-772-2216
Dry Dock Restaurant & Tavern (Seafood) 84 Commercial St	Portland	ME	04101	207-774-3550
Esposito's Restaurant (Italian) 1335 Congress St	Portland	ME	04102	207-774-7923
F Parker Reidy's (Steak/Seafood) 83 Exchange St	Portland	ME	04101	207-773-4731
Federal Spice (International) 225 Federal St	Portland	ME	04101	207-774-6404
Free Street Taverna (Greek) 128 Free St	Portland	ME	04101	207-774-1114
Fresh Market Pasta (Italian) 43 Exchange St	Portland	ME	04101	207-773-7146
G'vanni's (Italian) 37 Wharf St	Portland	ME	04101	207-775-9061
Gilbert's Chowder House (Seafood) 92 Commercial St	Portland	ME	04101	207-871-5636
Good Table (American) Rt 77	Cape Elizabeth	ME	04107	207-799-4663
Great Lost Bear (American) 540 Forest Ave	Portland	ME	04104	207-772-0300
Gritty McDuff's (English) 396 Fore St	Portland	ME	04101	207-772-2739
Web: www.grittys.com				
J's Oyster (Seafood) 5 Portland Pier	Portland	ME	04101	207-772-4828
Jan Mee Restaurant (Chinese) 280 Saint John St	Portland	ME	04102	207-761-4335
Katahdin Restaurant (American) 106 High St	Portland	ME	04101	207-774-1740
Latte Cafe & Bistro (American) 486 Congress St	Portland	ME	04101	207-828-8755
Margarita's Mexican Restaurant & Watering Hole (Mexican) 242 Saint John St Union Station Plaza	Portland	ME	04102	207-874-6444
Norm's Bar-B-Q (Barbecue) 43 Middle St	Portland	ME	04101	207-774-6711
Nu's Restaurant Market (Vietnamese) 44-46 Washington Ave	Portland	ME	04101	207-773-9734
Oriental Table (Chinese) 106 Exchange St	Portland	ME	04101	207-775-3388
Panda Garden (Chinese) 1041 Brighton Ave	Portland	ME	04102	207-874-6935
Perfetto's (Italian) 28 Exchange St	Portland	ME	04101	207-828-0001
Porthole The (American) 20 Custom House Wharf	Portland	ME	04101	207-761-7634
Rachel's Wood Grill (American) 90 Exchange St	Portland	ME	04101	207-774-1192
Raoul's (Southwest) 865 Forest Ave	Portland	ME	04103	207-773-6886
Roma The (Italian) 769 Congress St	Portland	ME	04102	207-773-9873
Sapporo (Japanese) 230 Commercial St	Portland	ME	04112	207-772-1233
Shalimar of India Restaurant (Indian) 675 Congress St	Portland	ME	04101	207-874-6342
Snow Squall Restaurant (Steak/Seafood) 18 Ocean St	South Portland	ME	04106	207-799-2232
Web: www.snowsquall.com				
Stone Coast Brewing Co (American) 14 York St	Portland	ME	04101	207-773-2337
Web: www.stonecoast.com				
Street & Co (Seafood) 33 Wharf St	Portland	ME	04101	207-775-0887
Tortilla Flat (Mexican) 1871 Forest Ave	Portland	ME	04103	207-797-8729
Uncle Billy's Restaurant (Barbecue) 69 Newbury St	Portland	ME	04101	207-871-5631
Valle's Steak House (American) 1140 Brighton Ave	Portland	ME	04102	207-774-4551
Village Cafe (Italian) 112 Newbury St	Portland	ME	04101	207-772-5320
Wharf Street Cafe (Seafood) 38 Wharf St	Portland	ME	04101	207-773-6667

— Goods and Services —

SHOPPING

Name / Address	City	State	Zip	Phone	Fax
LL Bean Inc 15 Casco St	Freeport	ME	04033	207-865-4761	552-2802
TF Cust Svc: 800-341-4341 ■ *Web:* www.llbean.com ■ *E-mail:* llbean@llbean.com					
Maine Mall 364 Maine Mall Rd	South Portland	ME	04106	207-774-0303	
Web: www.mainemall.com					
Old Port 195 Middle St Stein Gallery	Portland	ME	04101	207-772-9072	
Saco Valley Shopping Center Scammon St & Rt 1	Saco	ME	04072	207-283-3222	

BANKS

Name / Address	City	State	Zip	Phone	Fax
Acadia Trust NA 511 Congress St Suite 900	Portland	ME	04101	207-774-3333	775-5174
Bank of Boston 65 Gannett Dr	South Portland	ME	04106	207-842-5000	842-5120
Bath Savings Institution 239 US Rt 1	Falmouth	ME	04105	207-781-7131	781-7410
TF Cust Svc: 800-447-4559*					
Coastal Bank 120 Exchange St	Portland	ME	04101	207-879-4307	761-9692
Fleet Bank of Maine 1 City Ctr	Portland	ME	04104	207-874-5000	874-5569
TF: 800-841-4000					
KeyBank NA Maine District 1 Monument Sq	Portland	ME	04101	207-776-7720	776-7421
Maine Bank & Trust Co 467 Congress St	Portland	ME	04101	207-828-3000	828-3175
Maine Merchant Bank 2 Monument Sq 5th Fl	Portland	ME	04101	207-772-8141	761-4464
Peoples Heritage Bank PO Box 9540	Portland	ME	04112	207-761-8500	761-8536*
**Fax:* Hum Res ■ *TF Cust Svc:* 800-462-3666 ■ *Web:* www.peoplesheritage.com					
State Street Bank 75 Pearl St	Portland	ME	04101	207-772-6241	

BUSINESS SERVICES

Name	Phone	Name	Phone
Airborne Express	800-247-2676	**Mail Boxes Etc**	800-789-4623
BAX Global	800-225-5229	**Manpower Temporary Services**	207-774-8258
DHL Worldwide Express	800-225-5345	**Olsten Staffing Services**	207-772-2882
Federal Express	800-238-5355	**Post Office**	207-871-8449
Initial Staffing Services	207-774-5300	**Springborn Staffing Service**	207-761-8367
Kinko's	207-773-3177	**UPS**	800-742-5877

— Media —

PUBLICATIONS

Name / Address	City	State	Zip	Phone	Fax
Portland Press Herald‡ PO Box 1460	Portland	ME	04104	207-791-6650	791-6920
Web: www.portland.com ■ *E-mail:* letters@portland.com					

‡Daily newspapers

TELEVISION

Name / Address	City	State	Zip	Phone	Fax
WCBB-TV Ch 10 (PBS) 1450 Lisbon St	Lewiston	ME	04240	207-783-9101	783-5193
Web: www.mpbc.org ■ *E-mail:* Comments@mpbc.org					
WCSH-TV Ch 6 (NBC) 1 Congress Sq	Portland	ME	04101	207-828-6666	828-6630
TF: 800-464-1213 ■ *Web:* www.wcsh6.com ■ *E-mail:* info@wcsh6.com					
WGME-TV Ch 13 (CBS) 1335 Washington Ave	Portland	ME	04103	207-797-9330	878-3505
Web: www.wgme-tv.com ■ *E-mail:* tvmail@wgme-tv.com					
WMTW-TV Ch 8 (ABC) 99 Danville Corner Rd	Auburn	ME	04210	207-782-1800	783-7371
Web: www.wmtw.com ■ *E-mail:* wmtw@wmtw.com					
WPXT-TV Ch 51 (Fox) 2320 Congress St	Portland	ME	04102	207-774-0051	774-6849
Web: www.wpxt.com					

RADIO

Name / Address	City	State	Zip	Phone	Fax
WBAE-AM 1490 kHz (B/EZ) 420 Western Ave	South Portland	ME	04106	207-774-4561	774-3788
E-mail: wpor@aol.com					
WBLM-FM 102.9 MHz (Rock) 1 City Ctr	Portland	ME	04101	207-774-6364	774-8707
Web: www.wblm.com					
WCYY-FM 94.3 MHz (Alt) 1 City Ctr	Portland	ME	04101	207-774-6364	774-8707
Web: www.wcyy.com ■ *E-mail:* wcyyfm@aol.com					
WHOM-FM 94.9 MHz (AC) 583 Warren Ave	Portland	ME	04103	207-773-0200	773-5770
WJAB-AM 1440 kHz (Sports) 583 Warren Ave	Portland	ME	04103	207-775-6321	772-8087
E-mail: bigjab@compuserve.com					
WJBQ-FM 97.9 MHz (AC) 583 Warren Ave	Portland	ME	04103	207-775-6321	772-8087
Web: www.wjbq.com					
WLOB-AM 1310 kHz (Rel) 779 Warren Ave	Portland	ME	04103	207-775-1310	
WMEA-FM 90.1 MHz (NPR) 309 Marginal Way	Portland	ME	04101	207-874-6570	761-0318
Web: www.mpbc.org ■ *E-mail:* comments@mpbc.pbs.org					
WPOR-FM 101.9 MHz (Ctry) 420 Western Ave	South Portland	ME	04106	207-774-4561	774-3788
Web: www.wpor.com ■ *E-mail:* wpor@aol.com					
WTHT-FM 107.5 MHz (Ctry) 1335 Washington Ave	Portland	ME	04103	207-797-0780	797-0368

— Colleges/Universities —

Name / Address	City	State	Zip	Phone	Fax
Andover College 901 Washington Ave	Portland	ME	04103	207-774-6126	774-1715
TF: 800-639-3110 ■ *Web:* www.andovercollege.com ■ *E-mail:* enroll@andovercollege.com					

Portland — Colleges/Universities (Cont'd)

				Phone	Fax
Bowdoin College 6000 College Station *Web:* www.bowdoin.edu	Brunswick	ME	04011	207-725-3000	725-3101
Maine College of Art 97 Spring St *Web:* www.meca.edu ■ *E-mail:* admsns@mesa.edu	Portland	ME	04101	207-775-3052	772-5069
New England Baptist Bible College 879 Sawyer St *TF Admissions:* 800-286-1859 ■ *Web:* www.nebc.edu ■ *E-mail:* nebc@main.rr.com	South Portland	ME	04116	207-799-5979	799-6586
Saint Joseph's College 278 Whites Bridge Rd **Fax:* Admissions ■ *TF:* 800-338-7057 ■ *Web:* www.sjcme.edu	Standish	ME	04084	207-892-6766	893-7862*
Southern Maine Technical College 2 Fort Rd *Web:* ctech.smtc.mtcs.tec.me.us ■ *E-mail:* dpratt@ctech.smtc.mtcs.tec.me.us	South Portland	ME	04106	207-767-9500	767-9671
University of New England 11 Hills Beach Rd *Web:* www.une.edu	Biddeford	ME	04005	207-283-0171	286-3678
University of Southern Maine PO Box 9300 *Web:* www.usm.maine.edu	Portland	ME	04104	207-780-4141	780-4933
Westbrook College 716 Stevens Ave	Portland	ME	04103	207-797-7261	797-7225

— Hospitals —

				Phone	Fax
Brighton Medical Center 335 Brighton Ave	Portland	ME	04102	207-879-8000	879-8198
Maine Medical Center 22 Bramhall St. *Web:* www.mmc.org	Portland	ME	04102	207-871-0111	761-4294
Mercy Hospital 144 State St. **Fax:* Admitting	Portland	ME	04101	207-879-3000	879-3343*

— Attractions —

Name/Address	City	State	ZIP	Phone	Fax
Acadia National Park PO Box 177 *Web:* www.nps.gov/acad	Bar Harbor	ME	04609	207-288-9561	288-5507
Bowdoin College Museum of Art Walker Art Bldg 9400 College Stn	Brunswick	ME	04011	207-725-3275	725-3762
Center for Maine History 485 Congress St. *Web:* www.mainehistory.com	Portland	ME	04101	207-774-1822	775-4301
Children's Museum of Maine 142 Free St *Web:* www.childrensmuseumofme.org	Portland	ME	04101	207-828-1234	828-5726
Desert of Maine 95 Desert Rd *Web:* www.desertofmaine.com ■ *E-mail:* info@desertofmaine.com	Freeport	ME	04032	207-865-6962	865-1678
First Parish Church 425 Congress St.	Portland	ME	04101	207-773-5747	
Geary DL Brewing Co Inc 38 Evergreen Dr	Portland	ME	04103	207-878-2337	878-2388
Institute of Contemporary Art 522 Congress St Maine College of Art	Portland	ME	04101	207-879-5742	
Maine Maritime Museum 243 Washington St *Web:* www.bathmaine.com ■ *E-mail:* maritime@bathmaine.com	Bath	ME	04530	207-443-1316	443-1665
Maine Narrow Gauge Railroad Co & Museum 58 Fore St	Portland	ME	04101	207-828-0814	879-6132
Merrill Auditorium 20 Myrtle St	Portland	ME	04101	207-874-8200	842-0810
Museum at Portland Headlight 1000 Shore Rd *Web:* www.portlandheadlight.com	Cape Elizabeth	ME	04107	207-799-2661	767-2616
Neal Dow Memorial 714 Congress St	Portland	ME	04102	207-773-7773	
Portland Fire Museum 157 Spring St	Portland	ME	04101	207-772-2040	
Portland Harbor Museum SMTC-Fort Rd *Web:* www.portlandharbormuseum.org ■ *E-mail:* info@portlandharbormuseum.org	South Portland	ME	04106	207-799-6337	799-6337
Portland Headlight Fort Williams Park	Cape Elizabeth	ME	04107	207-799-2661	
Portland Museum of Art 7 Congress Sq *Web:* www.portlandmuseum.org/	Portland	ME	04101	207-775-6148	773-7324
Portland Stage Co 25A Forest Ave *Web:* www.portlandstage.com ■ *E-mail:* portstage@aol.com	Portland	ME	04101	207-774-1043	774-0576
Portland Symphony Orchestra 20 Myrtle St Merrill Auditorium *Web:* www.portlandsymphony.com ■ *E-mail:* psobox@portlandsymphony.com	Portland	ME	04101	207-842-0800	773-6089
Tate House 1270 Westbrook St	Portland	ME	04102	207-774-9781	
University of Southern Maine Art Gallery 37 College Ave	Gorham	ME	04038	207-780-5008	
US Custom House 312 Fore St	Portland	ME	04101	207-771-3600	771-3627
Victoria Mansion 109 Danforth St. *Web:* www.portlandarts.com/victoriamansion ■ *E-mail:* victoria@maine.rr.com	Portland	ME	04101	207-772-4841	772-6290
Wadsworth-Longfellow House 487 Congress St.	Portland	ME	04101	207-879-0427	

SPORTS TEAMS & FACILITIES

Name/Address	City	State	ZIP	Phone	Fax
George I Lewis Auditorium 1 Civic Center Sq Cumberland County Civic Ctr.	Portland	ME	04101	207-775-3481	828-8344
Portland Pirates (hockey) 1 Civic Center Sq Cumberland County Civic Ctr. *Web:* www.portlandpirates.com ■ *E-mail:* pirates@ime.net	Portland	ME	04101	207-828-4665	773-3278
Portland Sea Dogs (baseball) 271 Park Ave Hadlock Stadium *Web:* www.portlandseadogs.com ■ *E-mail:* seadogs@portlandseadogs.com	Portland	ME	04102	207-874-9300	879-9520

— Events —

	Phone
Art in the Park (mid-August)	207-767-7660
Bluegrass Festival (early September)	207-725-6009
Cumberland Fair (late September)	207-287-3221
Family Fun Day (late July)	207-772-2811
Greek Heritage Festival (late June)	207-774-0281
Italian Street Festival (mid-August)	207-773-0748
Maine Boat Builders Show (mid-March)	207-774-1067
Maine Festival (early August)	207-772-9012
Maine Marathon (early October)	207-741-2084
New Year's Eve Portland (December 31)	207-772-9012
Old Port Festival (early June)	207-772-6828
Portland Chamber Music Festival (late August)	800-320-0257
Sidewalk Art Show (mid-August)	207-828-6666
Yarmouth Clam Festival (mid-July)	207-846-3984

Maryland

Population (1999): 5,171,634 **Area (sq mi): 12,407**

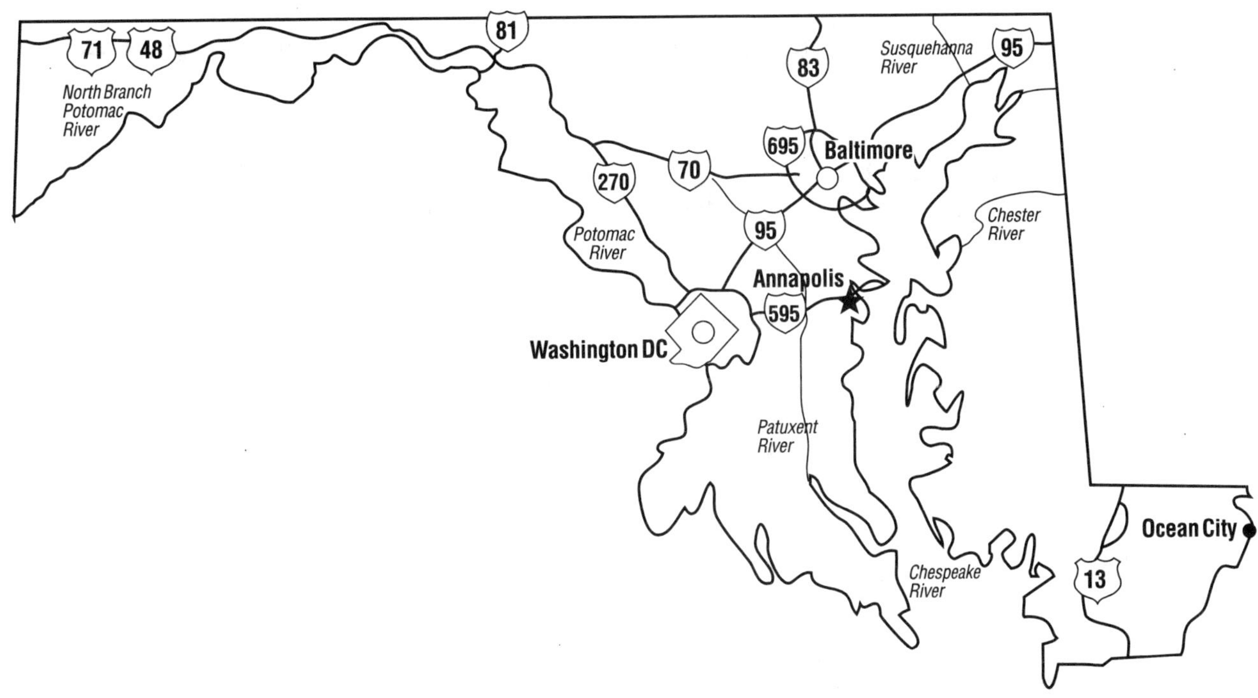

— State Information Sources —

		Phone	Fax
Federal Information Center PO Box 600	Cumberland	800-688-9889	
Web: fic.info.gov			
Federal Information Center TDD/TTY Line PO Box 600	Cumberland	800-326-2996	
Web: www.gsa.gov/et/fic-firs/ttynbrs/ttyhome.htm			
Maryland Business & Economic Development Dept 217 E Redwood St	Baltimore MD 21202	410-767-6300	333-6911
Web: www.dbed.state.md.us/dbed/			
Maryland Chamber of Commerce 60 West St Suite 100	Annapolis MD 21401	410-269-0642	269-5247
Maryland State Forest & Park Service Tawes State Office Bldg 580 Taylor Ave Rm E3	Annapolis MD 21401	410-260-8186	260-8191
TF: 800-830-3974 ■ *Web:* www.dnr.state.md.us/publiclands ■ *E-mail:* dnr@gacc.com			
Maryland Tourism Development Office 217 E Redwood St 9th Fl	Baltimore MD 21202	410-767-3400	333-6643
TF: 800-543-1036 ■ *Web:* www.mdisfun.org/travel/index.htm			

ON-LINE RESOURCES

Daily Orbit Maryland . . . . . www.dailyorbit.com/maryland
DelMarWeb-Maryland's Info Net . . . . . delmarweb.com/maryland
Maryland Cities . . . . . dir.yahoo.com/Regional/U_S__States/Maryland/Cities
Maryland Counties & Regions . . . . . dir.yahoo.com/Regional/U_S__States/Maryland/Counties_and_Regions
Maryland Scenario . . . . . scenariousa.dstylus.com/md/indexf.htm
Maryland Travel & Tourism Guide . . www.travel-library.com/north_america/usa/maryland/index.html
Maryland's Best . . . . . mdbest.com
Maryland's Eastern Shore & Chesapeake Bay Home Page . . . . . www.covesoft.com/Eastern
Rough Guide Travel Maryland travel.roughguides.com/content/626/index.htm
Sailor: Maryland's Online Public Information Network . . . . . www.sailor.lib.md.us
Skipjack.net: Maryland's Lower Eastern Shore . . . . . skipjack.net
Travel.org-Maryland . . . . . travel.org/maryland.html
Yahoo! Get Local Maryland . . . . . dir.yahoo.com/Regional/U_S__States/Maryland

— Cities Profiled —

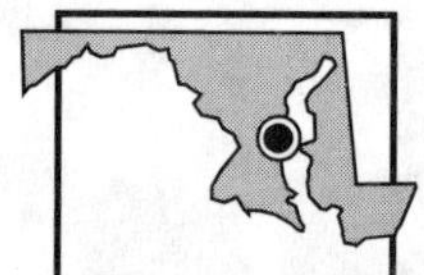

Annapolis

Perhaps best known by many today as the home of the U.S. Naval Academy, Annapolis was originally settled in 1649 and became the state capital in 1694. Early in its history, the city served for about nine months as the capital of the U.S., and it was at Annapolis that George Washington resigned as Commander-in-Chief of the Continental Armies. Today Annapolis serves both as the capital of Maryland and the seat of Anne Arundel County. Its National Historic Landmark District reflects its colonial beginnings, with many of its historic homes and other landmarks now used as shops and stores. The city is situated at the confluence of Chesapeake Bay and the Severn River, and the City Dock, located in downtown Annapolis, is a popular site for visitors. Historic homes and other landmarks, food, and entertainment all are within convenient walking distance.

Population 33,585
Area (Land) . . . . . . 6.3 sq mi
Area (Water) . . . . . . 0.9 sq mi
Elevation . . . . . . 57 ft
Latitude . . . . . . 38-97-83 N
Longitude . . . . . . 76-49-25 W
County . . . . . . Anne Arundel
Time Zone . . . . . . EST
Area Code/s 410, 443

— Average Temperatures and Precipitation —

TEMPERATURES

	Jan	Feb	Mar	Apr	May	Jun	Jul	Aug	Sep	Oct	Nov	Dec
High	42	45	55	66	76	84	88	86	80	69	58	47
Low	25	27	35	44	54	63	68	67	60	48	39	30

PRECIPITATION

	Jan	Feb	Mar	Apr	May	Jun	Jul	Aug	Sep	Oct	Nov	Dec
Inches	3.3	3.2	3.6	3.4	4.1	3.4	3.6	3.9	3.3	3.3	3.5	3.4

— Important Phone Numbers —

	Phone
AAA	410-757-8900
American Express Travel	410-224-4200
Emergency	911
Medical Referral	410-544-0312
Poison Control Center	800-492-2414
Time	410-844-2525
Weather	410-936-1212

— Information Sources —

		Phone	*Fax*
Annapolis & Anne Arundel County Chamber of Commerce 151 West St *Web:* www.annapolischamber.com	Annapolis MD 21401	410-757-6709	974-1536
Annapolis & Anne Arundel County Conference & Visitors Bureau 26 West St *Web:* visit-annapolis.org	Annapolis MD 21401	410-268-8687	263-9591
Annapolis City Hall 160 Duke of Gloucester St *Web:* www.ci.annapolis.md.us	Annapolis MD 21401	410-263-7942	280-1853
Annapolis Economic Development & Public Info 160 Duke of Gloucester St *Web:* www.ci.annapolis.md.us/citizens/depts/econdev.htm ■ *E-mail:* econdev@ci.annapolis.md.us	Annapolis MD 21401	410-263-7940	216-9284
Annapolis Mayor 160 Duke of Gloucester St *Web:* www.ci.annapolis.md.us/citizens/depts/mayoff.htm	Annapolis MD 21401	410-263-7997	216-9284
Anne Arundel County PO Box 71	Annapolis MD 21404	410-222-7000	
Anne Arundel County Public Library 5 Harry S Truman Pkwy *Web:* web.aacpl.lib.md.us	Annapolis MD 21401	410-222-7371	222-7188
Better Business Bureau Serving Greater Maryland 2100 Huntingdon Ave *Web:* www.baltimore.bbb.org	Baltimore MD 21211	410-347-3990	347-3936

On-Line Resources

About.com Guide to Annapolis . . . . . . annapolis.about.com
Annapolis1.com www.annapolis1.com
Annapolis Home Page . . . . . . sl001.infi.net/~city/
Annapolis Maryland Area Information . . . . . . www.azinet.com/annaarea.html
Anthill City Guide Annapolis . . . . . . www.anthill.com/city.asp?city=annapolis
Area Guide Annapolis . . . . . . annapolis.areaguides.net
City Knowledge Annapolis . . . . . . www.cityknowledge.com/md_annapolis.htm
Excite.com Annapolis City Guide . . . . . . www.excite.com/travel/countries/united_states/maryland
Visit Annapolis . . . . . . www.visit-annapolis.org

— Transportation Services —

AIRPORTS

■ **Baltimore-Washington International Airport (BWI)**

	Phone
20 miles NW of downtown Annapolis (approx 45 minutes)	410-859-7111

Airport Transportation

	Phone
Colonial Cab $35 fare to downtown Annapolis	410-263-2555
SuperShuttle $17 fare to downtown Annapolis	410-859-0800

Commercial Airlines

	Phone
Air Canada	800-776-3000
Air Jamaica	800-523-5585
America West	800-235-9292
American	800-433-7300
Continental	800-525-0280
Continental Express	800-525-0280
Delta	800-221-1212
El Al	800-223-6700
Icelandair	800-223-5500
MetroJet	888-638-7653
Northwest	800-225-2525
Southwest	800-435-9792
TWA	800-221-2000
United	800-241-6522
US Airways	800-428-4322

Charter Airlines

	Phone
Liberty Air Management Inc	800-739-4401
Piedmont Aviation Services Inc	800-548-1978

CAR RENTALS

	Phone
Alamo	410-850-5011
Avis	410-859-1680
Budget	410-859-1050
Dollar	410-684-3316
Enterprise	410-268-7751
Hertz	410-850-7400
National	410-859-8860
Thrifty	410-859-4900

LIMO/TAXI

	Phone
Carey Limousine	410-269-5500
Colonial Cab	410-263-2555
Extraordinair Limousine	410-437-8200
Imperial Limousines	410-295-0000
Parran Limousine	410-586-2424
Private Car	410-519-0000
Reliable Cab	410-268-4714
Robin's Limousine	888-242-0432
Yellow Checker Cab	410-268-3737

MASS TRANSIT

	Phone
Annapolis Transit $.75 Base fare	410-263-7964

RAIL/BUS

		Phone
Amtrak Station 1500 N Charles St *TF:* 800-872-7245	Baltimore MD 21240	410-291-4260

Annapolis (Cont'd)

— Accommodations —

HOTEL RESERVATION SERVICES

	Phone	Fax
Annapolis Accommodations *TF:* 800-715-1000	410-280-0900	263-1703

HOTELS, MOTELS, RESORTS

				Phone	Fax
American Heritage Bed & Breakfast 108 Charles St	Annapolis	MD	21401	410-280-1620	280-2540
Coggeshall House 198 King George St	Annapolis	MD	21401	410-263-5068	
College House Suites 1 College Ave *Web:* www.bbonline.com/md/college	Annapolis	MD	21401	410-263-6124	
Comfort Inn 76 Old Mill Bottom Rd N *TF:* 800-228-5150	Annapolis	MD	21401	410-757-8500	757-4409
Comfort Inn Hotel & Conference Center 4500 Crain Hwy *TF:* 800-228-5150	Bowie	MD	20718	301-464-0089	805-5563
Courtyard by Marriott 2559 Riva Rd *TF:* 800-321-2211 ■ *Web:* courtyard.com/BWIAN	Annapolis	MD	21401	410-266-1555	266-6376
Days Inn 1542 Whitehall Rd *TF:* 800-329-7466	Annapolis	MD	21401	410-974-4440	757-6419
Days Inn Historic Annapolis 2520 Riva Rd *TF:* 800-329-7466	Annapolis	MD	21401	410-224-2800	266-5539
Econo Lodge Annapolis 2451 Riva Rd *TF:* 800-424-4777	Annapolis	MD	21401	410-224-4317	224-6010
Governor Calvert House 58 State Cir *TF:* 800-847-8882	Annapolis	MD	21401	410-263-2641	268-3613
Hampton Inn Suites 124 Womack Dr *TF:* 800-426-7866	Annapolis	MD	21401	410-571-0200	571-0333
Harbortown Golf Resort Rt 33 & Martingham Dr *TF:* 800-446-9066	Saint Michaels	MD	21663	410-745-9066	745-9124
Historic Inns of Annapolis 58 State Cir *TF:* 800-847-8882	Annapolis	MD	21401	410-263-2641	
Loews Annapolis Hotel 126 West St *TF:* 800-526-2593 ■ *Web:* www.loewshotels.com/annapolishome.html ■ *E-mail:* loewsannapolis@loewshotels.com	Annapolis	MD	21401	410-263-7777	263-0084
MainStay Suites 10750 Columbia Pike **Fax Area Code:* 301	Silver Spring	MD	20901	800-547-0007	592-6184*
Marriott Waterfront Hotel 80 Compromise St *TF:* 800-336-0072 ■ *Web:* marriotthotels.com/BWIAW	Annapolis	MD	21401	410-268-7555	269-5864
Maryland Inn 16 Church Cir *TF:* 800-847-8882	Annapolis	MD	21401	410-263-2641	268-3813
Radisson Hotel Annapolis 210 Holiday Ct *TF:* 800-465-4329	Annapolis	MD	21401	410-224-3150	224-3413
Residence Inn by Marriott 170 Admiral Cochrane Dr *TF:* 800-331-3131 ■ *Web:* www.residenceinn.com/BWIRA	Annapolis	MD	21401	410-573-0300	573-0316
Saint Michael's Harbour Inn & Marina 101 N Harbor Rd *TF:* 800-955-9001	Saint Michaels	MD	21663	410-745-9001	745-9150
Super 8 Motel 74 Old Mill Bottom Rd *TF:* 800-800-8000	Annapolis	MD	21401	410-757-2222	757-6920
Tidewater Inn & Conference Center 101 E Dover St *TF:* 800-237-8775	Easton	MD	21601	410-822-1300	820-8847
Town Center Hotel 8727 Colesville Rd *TF:* 800-228-5151	Silver Spring	MD	20901	301-589-5200	588-1841
William Page Bed & Breakfast 8 Martin St *TF:* 800-364-4160 ■ *Web:* www.williampageinn.com ■ *E-mail:* wmpageinn@aol.com	Annapolis	MD	21401	410-626-1506	263-4841
Wyndham Garden Hotel 173 Jennifer Rd *TF:* 800-351-9209	Annapolis	MD	21401	410-266-3131	266-6247

— Restaurants —

				Phone
49 West (American) 49 West St	Annapolis	MD	21401	410-626-9796
Acme Bar & Grill (American) 163 Main St	Annapolis	MD	21401	410-280-6486
Armadillo's (Mexican) 132 Dock St	Annapolis	MD	21401	410-268-6680
Buddy's Crabs & Ribs (Steak/Seafood) 100 Main St *Web:* www.sevarez.com/buddys/	Annapolis	MD	21401	410-626-1100
Cafe Normandie (French) 185 Main St	Annapolis	MD	21401	410-263-3382
Carrol's Creek (Seafood) 410 Severn Ave	Eastport	MD	21403	410-263-8102
Chart House (Steak/Seafood) 300 2nd St	Annapolis	MD	21403	410-268-7166
Corinthian Restaurant (Steak/Seafood) 126 West St	Annapolis	MD	21401	410-263-1299
Court of Shanghai (Chinese) 1971 West St	Annapolis	MD	21401	410-266-5990
Davis' Pub (American) 400 Chester Ave	Annapolis	MD	21401	410-268-7432
Fergie's Waterfront Restaurant (American) 2840 Solomons Island Rd	Edgewater	MD	21037	410-573-1371
Griffin's West Street (American) 2049 West St	Annapolis	MD	21401	410-266-7662
Griffin's (American) 22 Market Space *Web:* www.griffins-citydock.com	Annapolis	MD	21401	410-268-2576
Harry Browne's (American) 66 State Cir	Annapolis	MD	21401	410-263-4332
Joss Cafe & Sushi Bar (Japanese) 195 Main St	Annapolis	MD	21401	410-263-4688
Lewnes' Steakhouse (Steak) Severn Ave & 4th St	Annapolis	MD	21403	410-263-1617
Maria's Italian Ristorante (Italian) 12 Market Space	Annapolis	MD	21401	410-268-2112
McGarvey's Saloon and Oyster Bar (American) 8 Market Space *Web:* www.mcgarveyssaloon.com	Annapolis	MD	21401	410-263-5700
Middleton Tavern (Seafood) 2 Market Space & Randall St	Annapolis	MD	21401	410-263-3323
Northwoods (Continental) 609 Melvin Ave	Annapolis	MD	21401	410-268-2609
O'Brien's Oyster Bar & Grill (Seafood) 113 Main St	Annapolis	MD	21401	410-268-6288
Papazee's Authentic Thai Cuisine (Thai) 257 West St	Annapolis	MD	21401	410-263-8424
Rams Head Tavern (International) 33 West St	Annapolis	MD	21401	410-268-4545
Riordan's Saloon and Restaurant (American) 26 Market Space *Web:* www.riordans.com	Annapolis	MD	21401	410-263-5449
Sam's Waterfront Cafe (Seafood) Chesapeake Harbour Marina	Annapolis	MD	21403	410-263-3600
Treaty of Paris (Continental) 16 Church Cir	Annapolis	MD	21401	410-263-2641
Vespucci's Restaurant & Bistro (Italian) City Dock	Annapolis	MD	21401	410-571-0100

— Goods and Services —

SHOPPING

				Phone	Fax
Annapolis Antique Gallery 2009 West St	Annapolis	MD	21401	410-266-0635	
Annapolis Harbour Shopping Center 2512A Solomon's Island Rd **Fax Area Code:* 301	Annapolis	MD	21401	410-266-5857	970-2508*
Harbour Square Mall 110 Dock St	Annapolis	MD	21401	410-268-8687	
Maryland Avenue & State Circle Assn 80 Maryland Ave	Annapolis	MD	21401	410-269-1965	269-1965
Westfield Shopping Town Annapolis 2002 Annapolis Mall	Annapolis	MD	21401	410-266-5432	266-3572

BANKS

				Phone	Fax
Annapolis National Bank 900 Bestgate Rd Suite 100	Annapolis	MD	21401	410-224-4483	224-6737
Bank of Maryland 37 Parole Plaza	Annapolis	MD	21401	410-841-1947	841-1967
Farmers Bank of Maryland 5 Church Cir **Fax:* Mktg	Annapolis	MD	21401	410-263-2603	626-9687*
Sandy Spring National Bank 2024 West St	Annapolis	MD	21401	410-266-3000	266-0664
Severn Savings Bank 1919-A West St	Annapolis	MD	21401	410-268-4554	841-6296

BUSINESS SERVICES

	Phone		Phone
Airborne Express	800-247-2676	**Kinko's**	410-573-5600
BAX Global	800-225-5229	**Mail Boxes Etc**	800-789-4623
Bayside Office Support	410-267-6407	**Post Office**	410-573-1889
DHL Worldwide Express	800-225-5345	**Todays Temporary**	410-266-9191
Federal Express	800-238-5355	**UPS**	800-742-5877

— Media —

PUBLICATIONS

				Phone	Fax
Capital The‡ 2000 Capital Dr *Web:* www.capitalonline.com ■ *E-mail:* capletts@annap.infi.net	Annapolis	MD	21401	410-268-5000	268-4643
Inside Annapolis Magazine 519 Burnside St	Annapolis	MD	21403	410-263-6300	263-8518

‡Daily newspapers

TELEVISION

				Phone	Fax
WBAL-TV Ch 11 (NBC) 3800 Hooper Ave *Web:* wbaltv.com	Baltimore	MD	21211	410-467-3000	338-6460
WJLA-TV Ch 7 (ABC) 3007 Tilden St NW *Web:* www.abc7dc.com	Washington	DC	20008	202-364-7777	364-7734

Annapolis — Television (Cont'd)

Name / Address	City	State	ZIP	Phone	Fax
WJZ-TV Ch 13 (CBS) 3725 Malden Ave TV Hill	Baltimore	MD	21211	410-466-0013	578-7502
Web: www.wjz.com/ ■ *E-mail:* ridalld@wjz.groupw.wec.com					
WMAR-TV Ch 2 (ABC) 6400 York Rd	Baltimore	MD	21212	410-377-2222	377-0493
Web: www.insidebaltimore.com/wmar/ ■ *E-mail:* wmartv2@aol.com					
WMPT-TV Ch 22 (PBS) 11767 Owings Mills Blvd	Owings Mills	MD	21117	410-356-5600	581-4338
Web: www.mpt.org					
WRC-TV Ch 4 (NBC) 4001 Nebraska Ave NW	Washington	DC	20016	202-885-4000	885-4104
Web: www.nbc4dc.com					
WTTG-TV Ch 5 (Fox) 5151 Wisconsin Ave NW	Washington	DC	20016	202-244-5151	244-1745
WUSA-TV Ch 9 (CBS) 4100 Wisconsin Ave NW	Washington	DC	20016	202-895-5999	966-7948
Web: www.wusatv9.com ■ *E-mail:* 9news@wusatv.com					

RADIO

Name / Address	City	State	ZIP	Phone	Fax
WBIS-AM 1190 kHz (N/T) 1081 Bay Ridge Rd	Annapolis	MD	21403	410-269-0700	269-0692
WFSI-FM 107.9 MHz (Rel) 918 Chesapeake Ave	Annapolis	MD	21403	410-268-6200	
Web: www.wfsiradio.com					
WNAV-AM 1430 kHz (AC) PO Box 829	Annapolis	MD	21404	410-263-1430	268-5360
Web: www.wnav.com					
WRNR-FM 103.1 MHz (AAA) 112 Main St 3rd Fl	Annapolis	MD	21401	410-626-0103	267-7634
Web: www.wrnr.com					
WYRE-AM 810 kHz (Oldies) 112 Main St 3rd Fl	Annapolis	MD	21401	410-626-0103	267-7634
Web: www.wyreradio.com					

— Colleges/Universities —

Name / Address	City	State	ZIP	Phone	Fax
Anne Arundel Community College 101 College Pkwy	Arnold	MD	21012	410-647-7100	541-2827
Web: www.aacc.cc.md.us					
Saint John's College PO Box 2800	Annapolis	MD	21404	410-263-2371	263-4828
TF Admissions: 800-727-9238 ■ *Web:* www.sjca.edu					
US Naval Academy 117 Decatur Rd	Annapolis	MD	21402	410-293-1000	293-4348
TF Admissions: 800-638-9156 ■ *Web:* www.usna.edu ■ *E-mail:* pao@nadn.navy.mil					

— Hospitals —

Name / Address	City	State	ZIP	Phone	Fax
Anne Arundel Medical Center 64 Franklin St	Annapolis	MD	21401	410-267-1000	267-1624
Web: www.aa-healthsystem.org					

— Attractions —

Name / Address	City	State	ZIP	Phone	Fax
Annapolis Chamber Orchestra 801 Chase St Maryland Hall for the Creative Arts	Annapolis	MD	21401	410-263-1906	
Annapolis Naval Station 58 Bennion Rd	Annapolis	MD	21402	410-293-2385	293-9021
Annapolis Opera Inc 801 Chase St Maryland Hall for the Creative Arts Suite 304	Annapolis	MD	21401	410-267-8135	
Annapolis Summer Garden Theatre 143 Compromise St	Annapolis	MD	21401	410-268-9212	
Annapolis Symphony Orchestra 801 Chase St Maryland Hall	Annapolis	MD	21401	410-269-1132	263-0616
Ballet Theatre of Annapolis 801 Chase St Maryland Hall	Annapolis	MD	21401	410-263-8289	
Banneker-Douglas Museum 84 Franklin St	Annapolis	MD	21401	410-974-2893	974-2553
Barge House Museum 2nd St & Bay Shore Dr	Eastport	MD	21403	410-268-1802	
Barracks The 43 Pinkney St	Annapolis	MD	21401	410-267-7619	
Brice House 42 East St	Annapolis	MD	21401	202-383-3910	
Charles Carroll House 107 Duke of Gloucester St	Annapolis	MD	21401	410-269-1737	269-1746
Chase-Lloyd House 22 Maryland Ave	Annapolis	MD	21401	410-263-2723	
Chesapeake Music Hall 339 Busch's Frontage Rd	Annapolis	MD	21401	410-626-7515	626-7215
TF: 800-406-0306					
Colonial Players of Annapolis 108 East St	Annapolis	MD	21401	410-268-7373	
Web: www.geocities.com/Broadway/9057/ ■ *E-mail:* cplayers@toad.net					
Governor's Mansion State Cir & School St	Annapolis	MD	21401	410-974-3531	974-5155
Hammond-Harwood House 19 Maryland Ave	Annapolis	MD	21401	410-269-1714	267-6891
Historic Annapolis Foundation Museum Store & Welcome Center 77 Main St	Annapolis	MD	21401	410-268-5576	267-6189
Web: www.annapolis.org					
Main Street Gallery 109 Main St	Annapolis	MD	21401	410-280-2787	
Maryland Hall for the Creative Arts 801 Chase St	Annapolis	MD	21401	410-263-5544	263-5114
Web: www.mdhallarts.org					
Maryland State Archives 350 Rowe Blvd	Annapolis	MD	21401	410-260-6400	974-3895
Web: www.mdarchives.state.md.us ■ *E-mail:* archives@mdarchives.state.md.us					
Maryland State House 91 State Cir	Annapolis	MD	21401	410-974-3400	974-5598
Myers Elizabeth Mitchell Art Gallery 60 College Ave	Annapolis	MD	21404	410-626-2556	
Pennsylvania Dutch Farmers Market 2472 Harbor Ctr	Annapolis	MD	21401	410-573-0770	
Quiet Waters Park Forest & Hillsmere Dr	Annapolis	MD	21403	410-222-1777	222-1545
Saint Anne's Parish Duke of Gloucester St	Annapolis	MD	21401	410-267-9333	280-3181
Saint Mary's Church 109 Duke of Gloucester St	Annapolis	MD	21403	410-263-2396	
Sandy Point State Park 1100 E College Pkwy	Annapolis	MD	21401	410-974-2149	974-2647
Schooner Woodwind PO Box 3254	Annapolis	MD	21403	410-267-6333	
TF: 800-638-5139					
Shiplap House Museum 18 Pinkney St	Annapolis	MD	21401	410-267-7619	267-6189
Web: www.annapolis.org/shiplap.htm					
Tawes Helen Avalynne Garden Taylor Ave & Rowe Blvd	Annapolis	MD	21401	410-260-8189	260-8191
Web: www.dnr.state.md.us/programs/tawesgarden.html					
Three Centuries Tours of Annapolis 48 Maryland Ave	Annapolis	MD	21401	410-263-5401	263-1901
Web: www.annapolis-tours.com					
Tobacco Prise House 4 Pinkney St	Annapolis	MD	21401	410-267-7619	
US Naval Academy Museum 118 Maryland Ave	Annapolis	MD	21402	410-293-2108	293-5220
William Paca House & Garden 186 Prince George St	Annapolis	MD	21401	410-263-5553	
Web: www.annapolis.org/paca.htm					

SPORTS TEAMS & FACILITIES

Name / Address	City	State	ZIP	Phone	Fax
Baltimore Orioles 333 W Camden St	Baltimore	MD	21201	410-685-9800	547-6272
Web: www.theorioles.com					
Maryland Pride (soccer) 303 Najoles Rd Suite 112	Millersville	MD	21108	410-729-1100	729-1604
TF: 888-592-5425 ■ *Web:* mdpride.com ■ *E-mail:* info@mdpride.com					

— Events —

	Phone
Annapolis Heritage Antique Show (late January)	410-222-1919
Annapolis Rotary Crab Feast (early August)	410-841-2841
Annapolis Waterfront Festival (mid-June)	410-268-8828
Anne Arundel County Fair (mid-September)	410-923-3400
Anne Arundel County Fair Rodeo (mid-September)	410-923-3400
Anne Arundel Scottish Highland Games (early October)	410-849-2849
Candlelight Pub Crawl (early-mid-December)	410-263-5401
Christmas in Annapolis (late November-early January)	410-268-8687
Fall Craft Show (early October)	410-255-5632
First Night Annapolis (December 31)	410-268-8553
Fourth of July Celebration (July 4)	410-263-1183
Kunta Kinte Heritage Festival (mid-August)	410-349-0338
Maryland Renaissance Festival (August-October)	410-266-7304
Maryland Seafood Festival (early September)	410-268-7682
Mid-Atlantic Wine Festival (mid-June)	410-280-3306
US Powerboat Show (mid-October)	410-268-8828
US Sailboat Show (early October)	410-268-8828

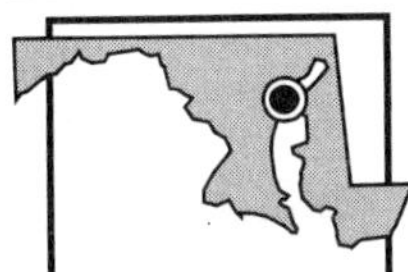

Baltimore

The heart of the seaport city of Baltimore is the Inner Harbor area, which features shops, restaurants, and festivals, as well as cultural attractions such as the Baltimore Maritime Museum, National Aquarium, and the Maryland Science Center. Baltimore also has six public markets, including Lexington Market, the nation's oldest continuously operating market. Baltimore's colleges and universities include Johns Hopkins University, a major center of medical research. Baltimore is also the home of Fort McHenry, where a battle in 1814 inspired Francis Scott Key to compose "The Star-Spangled Banner.'

Population . . . 645,593
Area (Land) . . . 80.8 sq mi
Area (Water) . . . 11.3 sq mi
Elevation . . . 32 ft
Latitude . . . 39-29-51 N
Longitude . . . 76-62-31 W
County . . . Independent City
Time Zone . . . EST
Area Code/s . . . 410, 443

— Average Temperatures and Precipitation —

TEMPERATURES

	Jan	Feb	Mar	Apr	May	Jun	Jul	Aug	Sep	Oct	Nov	Dec
High	40	44	54	64	74	83	87	85	79	67	57	45
Low	23	26	34	43	53	62	67	66	58	46	37	28

PRECIPITATION

	Jan	Feb	Mar	Apr	May	Jun	Jul	Aug	Sep	Oct	Nov	Dec
Inches	3.1	3.1	3.4	3.1	3.7	3.7	3.7	3.9	3.4	3.0	3.3	3.4

— Important Phone Numbers —

	Phone
AAA	410-821-1458
American Express Travel	410-837-3100
Dental Referral	410-964-2880
Emergency	911
HotelDocs	800-468-3537
Medical Referral	410-625-0022
Poison Control Center	410-528-7701
Time	410-844-1212
Weather	410-936-1212

— Information Sources —

				Phone	Fax
Baltimore Area Convention & Visitors Assn 100 Light St 12th Fl	Baltimore	MD	21202	410-659-7300	727-2308

TF: 800-343-3468 ■ *Web:* www.baltconvstr.com

Baltimore City Chamber of Commerce 3 W Baltimore St	Baltimore	MD	21201	410-837-7101	837-7104

Web: www.baltocitychamber.com

Baltimore City Hall 100 N Holliday St	Baltimore	MD	21202	410-396-3100	396-9568

Web: www.ci.baltimore.md.us

Baltimore Convention Center 1 W Pratt St.	Baltimore	MD	21201	410-649-7000	649-7008

TF: 800-207-1175

Baltimore Mayor 100 N Holliday St Rm 250	Baltimore	MD	21202	410-396-4892	576-9425

Web: www.ci.baltimore.md.us/mayor/index.html

Baltimore Planning Dept 417 E Fayette St 8th Fl	Baltimore	MD	21202	410-396-4329	244-7358
Baltimore Visitors Center 301 E Pratt St	Baltimore	MD	21202	410-837-4636	727-6769

TF: 800-282-6632

Better Business Bureau Serving Greater Maryland 2100 Huntingdon Ave	Baltimore	MD	21211	410-347-3990	347-3936

Web: www.baltimore.bbb.org

Enoch Pratt Free Library 400 Cathedral St.	Baltimore	MD	21201	410-396-5430	396-1351

Web: www.pratt.lib.md.us/ ■ *E-mail:* helpdesk@epfl1.epflbalto.org

On-Line Resources

4Baltimore.com . . . www.4baltimore.com
About.com Guide to Baltimore . . . baltimore.about.com/local/midlanticus/baltimore
Anthill City Guide Baltimore . . . www.anthill.com/city.asp?city=baltimore
Area Guide Baltimore . . . baltimore.areaguides.net
Baltimore City Paper . . . www.citypaper.com
Baltimore CityLink . . . www.usacitylink.com/citylink/baltimor/
Baltimore Collegetown Network . . . www.colltown.org
Baltimore Marketplace . . . www.markpoint.com/index.htm
Baltimore on the WWW . . . www.baltimore.com/
Baltimore What2Do Entertainment Guide . . . www.hyperstuff.com/md/balt/
BaltimoreMD.com . . . www.baltimoremd.com
Best of Baltimore.com . . . www.bestofbaltimore.com
Boulevards Baltimore . . . www.boulevards.com/cities/baltimore.html
City Knowledge Baltimore . . . www.cityknowledge.com/md_baltimore.htm
Cityhits Baltimore . . . www.cityhits.com/baltimore/
CityTravelGuide.com Baltimore . . . www.citytravelguide.com/baltimore.htm
DigitalCity Baltimore . . . home.digitalcity.com/baltimore
Encore Baltimore . . . encorebaltimore.org/
Excite.com Baltimore City Guide . . . www.excite.com/travel/countries/united_states/maryland/baltimore
InBaltimore.com . . . www.inbaltimore.com
Insiders' Guide to Baltimore . . . www.insiders.com/baltimore/
My Baltimore.net . . . www.mybaltimore.net
NITC Travelbase City Guide Baltimore . . . www.travelbase.com/auto/guides/baltimore-area-md.html
Rough Guide Travel Baltimore . . . travel.roughguides.com/content/627/
VisitBaltimore.com . . . www.visitbaltimore.com

— Transportation Services —

AIRPORTS

	Phone
■ **Baltimore-Washington International Airport (BWI)** 8 miles SW of downtown (approx 15 minutes)	410-859-7111

Web: baltwashintlairport.com

Airport Transportation

	Phone
Airport Taxi $17 fare to downtown	410-859-1100
Baltimore Airport Shuttle $16 fare to downtown	410-821-5387
SuperShuttle $11 fare to downtown	410-859-0800

Commercial Airlines

	Phone
Air Canada	800-776-3000
Air Jamaica	800-523-5585
America West	800-235-9292
American	800-433-7300
American Trans Air	800-225-2995
Continental	800-525-0280
Continental Express	800-525-0280
Delta	800-221-1212
El Al	800-223-6700
Frontier	800-432-1359
Icelandair	800-223-5500
KLM	800-374-7747
MetroJet	888-638-7653
Northwest	800-225-2525
Southwest	800-435-9792
TWA	800-221-2000
United	800-241-6522
US Airways	800-428-4322

Charter Airlines

	Phone
Liberty Air Management Inc	800-739-4401
Piedmont Aviation Services Inc	800-548-1978

CAR RENTALS

	Phone
Alamo	410-850-5011
Avis	410-859-1680
Budget	410-859-1050
Dollar	410-684-3316
Enterprise	410-268-7751
Hertz	410-850-7400
National	410-859-8860
Thrifty	410-859-4900

LIMO/TAXI

	Phone
Arrow Cab	410-358-9696
Carey Limousine	410-880-0999
Celebrity Limousine	410-496-1303
Diamond Cab	410-947-3333
Harford Limousines	410-426-7780
Presidential Limousine	410-780-8181
Royal Cab	410-327-0330
Sun Cab	410-235-0300
Triple Crown Limousine	410-850-4100
Yellow Cab	410-727-7300

MASS TRANSIT

	Phone
Harbor Shuttle $3 Base fare	410-675-2900
Metrorail $1.35 Base fare	410-539-5000
Water Taxi $3.50 Base fare	410-563-3901

Baltimore (Cont'd)

RAIL/BUS

Phone

Amtrak Station 1500 N Charles St . . . . Baltimore MD 21240 410-291-4260
TF: 800-872-7245

Pennsylvania Station 1500 N Charles St. . . . . Baltimore MD 21201 410-291-4261

— Accommodations —

HOTEL RESERVATION SERVICES

Phone *Fax*

Amanda's Bed & Breakfast Reservation Service. 410-225-0001 728-8957
TF: 800-899-7533 ■ *Web:* www.amandas-bbrs.com

Hotel Reservations Network Inc 214-361-7311 361-7299
TF Sales: 800-964-6835 ■ *Web:* www.hoteldiscount.com

Quikbook. 212-532-1660 532-1556
TF: 800-789-9887 ■ *Web:* www.quikbook.com

Room Finders USA 504-522-9373 529-1948
TF: 800-473-7829 ■ *Web:* www.roomsusa.com
■ *E-mail:* welcome@roomsusa.com

HOTELS, MOTELS, RESORTS

Phone *Fax*

Abbey Schaefer Hotel 723 Saint Paul St . . . . . . Baltimore MD 21202 410-332-0405

Admiral Fell Inn 888 S Broadway. . . . . Baltimore MD 21231 410-522-7377 522-0707
TF: 800-292-4667 ■ *Web:* www.admiralfell.com
■ *E-mail:* Inn@AdmiralFell.com

AmeriSuites Hotel Airport
940 International Dr . . . . .Linthicum MD 21090 410-859-3366 859-3331
TF: 800-833-1516

Baltimore Clarion Hotel 612 Cathedral St . . . . . Baltimore MD 21201 410-727-7101 789-3312
TF: 800-292-5500

Baltimore Hilton & Towers
20 W Baltimore St . . . . Baltimore MD 21201 410-539-8400 625-1060
TF: 800-445-8667

Best Inn & Suites
5701 Baltimore National Pike . . . . Baltimore MD 21228 410-747-8900 747-7375
TF: 800-237-8466

Best Western Inn 5625 Odonnell St . . . . Baltimore MD 21224 410-633-9500 633-4314
TF: 800-528-1234

Best Western Washington Gateway Hotel
1251 W Montgomery Ave . . . . Rockville MD 20850 301-424-4940 424-1047
TF: 800-366-1251

Biltmore Suites 205 W Madison St. . . . . Baltimore MD 21201 410-728-6550 728-5829

Brookshire Inner Harbor Suite Hotel
120 E Lombard St. Baltimore MD 21202 410-625-1300 625-0912
TF: 800-647-0013

Comfort Inn 8 N Howard St . . . . Baltimore MD 21201 410-539-1188 539-6411

Comfort Inn 6700 Security Blvd . . . . Baltimore MD 21207 410-281-1800 281-9148
TF: 800-228-5150

Comfort Inn 6921 Baltimore Annapolis Blvd . . . . Baltimore MD 21225 410-789-9100 355-2854
TF: 800-228-5150

Comfort Suites BWI Airport
815 Elkridge Landing Rd . . . . .Linthicum MD 21090 410-691-1000 691-1275

Days Inn Baltimore East
8801 Loch Raven Blvd. . . . . Towson MD 21286 410-882-0900 882-4176
TF: 800-329-7466

Days Inn Inner Harbor 100 Hopkins Pl . . . . Baltimore MD 21201 410-576-1000 659-0257
TF: 800-329-7466

Doubletree Guest Suites BWI
1300 Concourse Dr. . . . . .Linthicum Heights MD 21090 410-850-0747 859-0816
TF: 800-222-8733
■ *Web:* www.doubletreehotels.com/DoubleT/Hotel41/54/54Main.htm

Doubletree Inn at the Colonnade
4 W University Pkwy. . . . . Baltimore MD 21218 410-235-5400 235-5572
TF: 800-222-8733
■ *Web:* www.doubletreehotels.com/DoubleT/Hotel41/55/55Main.htm

Downtown Hotel 3 W Preston St. . . . . Baltimore MD 21201 410-837-1846

Embassy Suites 213 International Cir . . . . . . .Hunt Valley MD 21030 410-584-1400 584-7306
TF: 800-362-2779

Hampton Inn 8225 Town Center Dr. . . . . Baltimore MD 21236 410-931-2200 931-2215
TF: 800-426-7866

Hampton Inn BWI Airport
829 Elkridge Landing Rd . . . . .Linthicum MD 21090 410-850-0600 691-2119
TF: 800-426-7866

Harbor Court Hotel 550 Light St. . . . . Baltimore MD 21202 410-234-0550 659-5925
TF: 800-824-0076 ■ *Web:* www.harborcourt.com

Harbor Inn Pier 5 Hotel 711 Eastern Ave. . . . . . Baltimore MD 21201 410-539-2000 783-1469
TF: 800-539-2000

Phone *Fax*

Henderson's Wharf Inn 1000 Fell St . . . . Baltimore MD 21231 410-522-7777 522-7087
TF: 800-522-2088 ■ *Web:* www.hendersonswharf.com
■ *E-mail:* info@hendersonswharf.com

Holiday Inn 8120 Wisconsin Ave. . . . . Bethesda MD 20814 301-652-2000 652-4525
TF: 800-465-4329

Holiday Inn 1800 Belmont Ave . . . . Baltimore MD 21244 410-265-1400 281-9569
TF: 800-465-4329

Holiday Inn Airport
890 Elkridge Landing Rd . . . . .Linthicum Heights MD 21090 410-859-8400 684-6778
TF: 800-465-4329

Holiday Inn Cromwell Bridge
1100 Cromwell Bridge Rd . . . . Baltimore MD 21286 410-823-4410 296-6618
TF: 800-465-4329

Holiday Inn Express 1401 Bloomfield Ave . . . . . Baltimore MD 21227 410-646-1700 368-1341
TF: 800-465-4329

Holiday Inn Inner Harbor
301 W Lombard St . . . . Baltimore MD 21201 410-685-3500 727-6169
TF: 800-465-4329

Holiday Inn Select Baltimore North
2004 Greenspring Dr. . . . . .Timonium MD 21093 410-252-7373 561-0182
TF: 800-465-4329
■ *Web:* www.basshotels.com/holiday-inn/?_franchisee=BALLT
■ *E-mail:* sales@hiselectbaltimore.com

Homewood Suites BWI Airport
1181 Winterson Rd. . . . . .Linthicum MD 21090 410-684-6100 684-6810
TF: 800-225-5466

Hyatt Regency Baltimore 300 Light St . . . . Baltimore MD 21202 410-528-1234 685-3362
TF: 800-233-1234
■ *Web:* www.hyatt.com/usa/baltimore/hotels/hotel_bwirb.html

Knights Inn 6422 Baltimore National Pike. . . . . . Baltimore MD 21228 410-788-3900 788-4288
TF: 800-843-5644

Marriott Hotel BWI Airport
1743 W Nursery Rd . . . . Baltimore MD 21240 410-859-8300 691-4555
TF: 800-228-9290 ■ *Web:* marriotthotels.com/BWIAP

Marriott Inner Harbor 110 S Eutaw St. . . . . Baltimore MD 21201 410-962-0202 625-7832
TF: 800-228-9290 ■ *Web:* marriotthotels.com/BWIIH

Mount Vernon Hotel 24 W Franklin St. . . . . Baltimore MD 21201 410-727-2000 576-9300
TF: 800-245-5256

North Avenue Motel 110 W North Ave. . . . . Baltimore MD 21201 410-752-2000 539-7927

Omni Inner Harbor Hotel 101 W Fayette St . . . . Baltimore MD 21201 410-752-1100 625-9646
TF: 800-843-6664

Park Plaza Motel 4810 Ritchie Hwy . . . . Baltimore MD 21225 410-789-0500 636-1516

Pikesville Hilton Inn 1726 Reisterstown Rd. . . . Pikesville MD 21208 410-653-1100 415-6231
TF: 800-445-8667

Quality Inn 1701 Russell St . . . . Baltimore MD 21230 410-727-3400 547-0586
TF: 800-221-2222

Radisson Hotel at Cross Keys
5100 Falls Rd. . . . . Baltimore MD 21210 410-532-6900 532-2403
TF: 800-532-5397 ■ *Web:* www.crosskeysinn.com

Ramada Inn 8712 Loch Raven Blvd . . . . Baltimore MD 21286 410-823-8750 823-8644
TF: 800-272-6232

Red Roof Inn BWI Airport
827 Elkridge Landing Rd . . . . .Linthicum MD 21090 410-850-7600 850-7611
TF: 800-843-7663

Regal Inn 8005 Pulaski Hwy. . . . . Baltimore MD 21237 410-686-0010 686-0010

Sheraton Inner Harbor Hotel
300 S Charles St. Baltimore MD 21201 410-962-8300 962-8211
TF: 800-325-3535

Sheraton International BWI Hotel
7032 Elm Rd . . . . Baltimore MD 21240 410-859-3300 859-0565
TF: 800-638-5858

Stouffer Renaissance Harborplace Hotel
202 E Pratt St . . . . Baltimore MD 21202 410-547-1200 539-5780
TF: 800-468-3571

Susse Chalet 4 Philadelphia Ct . . . . Baltimore MD 21237 410-574-8100 574-8100
TF: 800-524-2538 ■ *Web:* www.sussechalet.com/baltimore.html

Susse Chalet Inn BWI Airport
1734 W Nursery Rd . . . . .Linthicum MD 20708 410-859-2333 859-2357
TF: 800-524-2538 ■ *Web:* www.sussechalet.com/bwiairport.html

Tremont Hotel 8 E Pleasant St . . . . Baltimore MD 21202 410-576-1200 244-1154
TF: 800-873-6668

Tremont Plaza 222 St Paul Pl. . . . . Baltimore MD 21202 410-727-2222 685-4215
TF: 800-873-6668

Turf Valley Hotel & Country Club
2700 Turf Valley Rd . . . . .Ellicott City MD 21042 410-465-1500 465-8280
TF: 800-666-8873

— Restaurants —

Phone

A-1 Crab Haven (Seafood) 1600 Old Eastern Ave. . . . . Baltimore MD 21221 410-687-6000
Web: a1crab.skyline.net

Akbar (Indian) 823 N Charles St. . . . . Baltimore MD 21201 410-539-0944
Web: sbachman.com/akbar/indexs.htm

Al Pacino Cafe (Middle Eastern) 542 E Belvedere Ave . . . . . Baltimore MD 21212 410-323-7060

Baltimore — Restaurants (Cont'd)

				Phone
Amiccis (Italian) 231 S High St	Baltimore	MD	21202	410-528-1096
Angelina's of Baltimore (Seafood) 7135 Hartford Rd	Baltimore	MD	21234	410-444-5545
Web: www.crabcake.com				
Atlantic (Seafood) 2400 Boston St	Baltimore	MD	21224	410-675-4565
Azeb's Ethiopian Restaurant (Ethiopian) 322 N Charles St	Baltimore	MD	21201	410-625-9787
Baltimore Brewing Co (American) 104 Albemarle St	Baltimore	MD	21202	410-837-5000
Web: www.degroens.com				
Ban Thai (Thai) 340 N Charles St	Baltimore	MD	21201	410-727-7971
Banjara (Indian) 1017 S Charles St	Baltimore	MD	21230	410-962-1554
Bertha's Dining Room (Seafood) 734 S Broadway	Baltimore	MD	21231	410-327-5795
Birds of a Feather (New American) 1712 Aliceanna St	Baltimore	MD	21231	410-675-8466
Web: www.abs.net/~scotchjh/				
Black Olive (Mediterranean) 814 S Bond St	Baltimore	MD	21231	410-276-7141
Boomerang Pub & Restaurant (Australian) 1110 S Charles St	Baltimore	MD	21230	410-727-2333
Brass Elephant (Italian) 924 N Charles St	Baltimore	MD	21201	410-547-8480
Burke's Cafe (Steak/Seafood) 36 Light St	Baltimore	MD	21202	410-752-4189
Cafe 100 (International) 100 S Charles St	Baltimore	MD	21201	410-685-7676
Web: members.aol.com/cafe100/				
Cafe Bombay (Indian) 114 E Lombard St	Baltimore	MD	21202	410-539-2233
Cafe Hon (American) 1002 W 36th St	Baltimore	MD	21211	410-243-1230
Capitol City Brewing Co (American) 301 S Light St	Baltimore	MD	21202	410-539-7468
Capriccio (Italian) 846 Fawn St	Baltimore	MD	21202	410-685-2710
Casa Mia (International) 8601 Honeygo Blvd	Baltimore	MD	21236	410-931-0200
Web: www.casamias.com				
Charleston (Southern) 1000 Lancaster St	Baltimore	MD	21202	410-332-7373
Chart House (Steak/Seafood) 601 E Pratt St	Baltimore	MD	21202	410-539-6616
Chiapparelli's Restaurant (Italian) 237 S High St	Baltimore	MD	21202	410-837-0309
City Lights (Seafood) 301 Light St 2nd Fl	Baltimore	MD	21202	410-244-8811
Cork's (American) 1026 S Charles St	Baltimore	MD	21230	410-752-3810
Dalesio's of Little Italy (Italian) 829 Eastern Ave	Baltimore	MD	21202	410-539-1965
Dougherty's Pub (American) 223 W Chase St	Baltimore	MD	21201	410-752-4059
Edo Japan (Japanese) 825 Dulaney Valley Rd	Baltimore	MD	21204	410-823-2653
Eight East Restaurant (American) 8 E Pleasant St	Baltimore	MD	21202	410-576-1200
Faidley's Seafood (Seafood) 400 W Lexington St	Baltimore	MD	21201	410-727-4898
Geckos (Southwest) 2318 Fleet St	Baltimore	MD	21224	410-732-1961
Germano's Trattoria Petrucci (Italian) 300 S High St	Baltimore	MD	21202	410-752-4515
Gunnings Crab House (Seafood) 3901 S Hanover St	Baltimore	MD	21225	410-354-0085
Hamilton's (New American) 888 S Broadway	Baltimore	MD	21231	410-522-2195
Hampton's (Continental) 550 Light St	Baltimore	MD	21202	410-234-0550
Hard Rock Cafe (American) 601 E Pratt St	Baltimore	MD	21202	410-347-7625
Helmand The (Afghan) 806 N Charles St	Baltimore	MD	21201	410-752-0311
Hull Street Blues (American) 1222 Hull St	Baltimore	MD	21230	410-727-7476
Ikaros (Greek) 4805 Eastern Ave	Baltimore	MD	21224	410-633-3750
Indian Pavilion (Indian) 635 W Pratt St	Baltimore	MD	21201	410-752-5700
Jeannier's (French) 105 W 39th St	Baltimore	MD	21210	410-889-3303
Joy America Cafe (New American) 800 Key Hwy	Baltimore	MD	21230	410-244-6500
Kawasaki (Japanese) 413 N Charles St	Baltimore	MD	21201	410-659-7600
La Tavola (Italian) 248 Albemarle St	Baltimore	MD	21202	410-685-1859
Web: www.mbd.com/latavola.html				
Lighthouse Restaurant (Seafood) 10 Park Ave	Baltimore	MD	21201	410-727-3814
Linwood's Cafe-Grille (American) 25 Crossroads Dr	Owings Mills	MD	21117	410-356-3030
Louie's Bookstore Cafe (American) 518 N Charles St	Baltimore	MD	21201	410-962-1224
Maison Marconi (Continental) 106 W Saratoga St	Baltimore	MD	21201	410-727-9522
Mamie's Cafe (American) 911 W 36th St	Baltimore	MD	21211	410-366-2996
Matsuri (Japanese) 1105 S Charles St	Baltimore	MD	21230	410-752-8561
Milton Inn (Continental) 14211 York Rd	Sparks	MD	21152	410-771-4366
Nam Kang (Korean) 2126 Maryland Ave	Baltimore	MD	21218	410-685-6237
Nichiban of Federal Hill (Japanese) 1035-37 S Charles St	Baltimore	MD	21201	410-837-0816
Web: angritt.com/nichiban.html				
Obrycki's Crab House (Seafood) 1727 E Pratt St	Baltimore	MD	21231	410-732-6399
Web: www.obryckis.com/				
One World Cafe (Vegetarian) 904 S Charles St	Baltimore	MD	21230	410-234-0235
Web: www.oneworldcafe.com				
PaperMoon Diner (American) 227 W 29th St	Baltimore	MD	21209	410-889-4444
Web: www.charm.net/~diner/				
Peter's Inn (Steak/Seafood) 504 S Ann St	Baltimore	MD	21231	410-675-7313
Phillips Harborplace (Seafood) 301 Light Street	Baltimore	MD	21202	410-685-6600
Web: www.phillipsfoods.com				
Polo Grill (American) 4 W University Pkwy	Baltimore	MD	21218	410-235-8200
Prime Rib (American) 1101 N Calvert St	Baltimore	MD	21202	410-539-1804
Purple Orchid (French) 419 N Charles St	Baltimore	MD	21201	410-837-0080
Ristorante Pecora (Italian) 1012 Eastern Ave	Baltimore	MD	21202	410-727-3437
Web: www.bemyguest.com/pecora/				
Rusty Scupper (Seafood) 402 Key Hwy	Baltimore	MD	21230	410-727-3678
Silk Road (Afghan) 336 N Charles St	Baltimore	MD	21201	410-385-9013
Sisson's Restaurant & Brewery (Cajun/Creole) 36 E Cross St	Baltimore	MD	21230	410-539-2093
Sotto Sopra (Italian) 405 N Charles St	Baltimore	MD	21201	410-625-0534
Sushi Chalet (Japanese/Korean) 105 N Charles St	Baltimore	MD	21202	410-625-7811
Tapestry (American) 1705 Aliceanna St	Baltimore	MD	21231	410-327-7037
Tersiguel (French) 8293 Main St	Ellicott City	MD	21043	410-465-4004
Tex Mex Grill (Mexican) 201 E Pratt St	Baltimore	MD	21201	410-783-2970
Thai Bangkok Place (Thai) 5230 York Rd	Baltimore	MD	21212	410-433-0040
Tio Pepe (Spanish) 10 E Franklin St	Baltimore	MD	21202	410-539-4675
Tony Cheng's Szechuan (Chinese) 801 N Charles St	Baltimore	MD	21201	410-539-6666
Uncle Lee's Harbor Restaurant (Chinese) 44 South St	Baltimore	MD	21202	410-727-6666
Velleggia's Restaurant (Italian) 829 E Pratt St	Baltimore	MD	21202	410-685-2620
Viccino Bistro (Italian) 1317 N Charles St	Baltimore	MD	21201	410-347-0349
Washington Cafe (American) 24 W Franklin St	Baltimore	MD	21201	410-727-2000
Water Street Exchange (American) 110 Water St	Baltimore	MD	21202	410-332-4060
Wayne's Barbeque (Barbecue) 201 E Pratt St	Baltimore	MD	21202	410-539-3810

— Goods and Services —

SHOPPING

				Phone	Fax
Antique Warehouse @ 1300 1300 Jackson St	Baltimore	MD	21230	410-659-0663	685-7934
Brokerage The 34 Market Pl Suite 329	Baltimore	MD	21202	410-752-0173	685-8204
Golden Ring Mall 6400 Rossville Blvd	Baltimore	MD	21237	410-391-8400	687-2389
Harborplace & The Gallery 200 E Pratt St	Baltimore	MD	21202	410-332-4191	547-7317
Web: www.harborplace.com ■ *E-mail:* comments@harborplace.com					
Hunt Valley Mall 118 Shawan Rd	Cockeysville	MD	21030	410-785-3770	785-0812
Lexington Market 400 W Lexington St	Baltimore	MD	21201	410-685-6169	
Owings Mills Mall 10300 Mill Run Cir	Owings Mills	MD	21117	410-363-7000	363-7999
Security Square Mall 6901 Security Blvd	Baltimore	MD	21244	410-265-6000	281-1473
Towson Marketplace 1238 Putty Hill Ave	Baltimore	MD	21286	410-337-0505	321-7348
Towson Town Center 825 Dulaney Valley Rd	Towson	MD	21204	410-296-6800	296-6803
Village of Cross Keys 5100 Falls Rd The Gatehouse	Baltimore	MD	21210	410-323-1000	377-0876
Westview Mall 5748 Baltimore National Pike Suite 104	Baltimore	MD	21228	410-744-5650	747-1631
White Marsh Mall 8200 Perry Hall Blvd	Baltimore	MD	21236	410-931-7100	931-7120

BANKS

				Phone	Fax
Allfirst Bank PO Box 1596	Baltimore	MD	21203	410-244-4000	347-6989*
**Fax:* Hum Res					
Crestar Bank 1300 N Charles St	Baltimore	MD	21201	410-986-1540	986-1505
First Union Bank 7 Saint Paul St	Baltimore	MD	21201	410-468-1600	752-2769
First Union National Bank 1 E Baltimore St	Baltimore	MD	21202	410-244-3412	752-8961
First United National Bank & Trust Co PO Box 9	Oakland	MD	21550	301-334-9471	334-8351
Harbor Bank of Maryland 25 W Fayette St	Baltimore	MD	21201	410-528-1800	528-1420
TF: 800-423-7503					

BUSINESS SERVICES

	Phone
Able Temporaries	410-685-8189
Acme Delivery & Messenger	410-945-3900
Atlantic Courier Co	410-244-7243
Corporate Express Delivery Systems	410-761-1234
DocuPrint Imaging	410-539-3127
Federal Express	800-463-3339
Global Messenger	410-234-3100
Imtek Office Solutions	410-576-9110
Kinko's	410-625-5862
Magic Messengers	410-625-2600
Mail Boxes Etc	410-659-9360
Manpower Temporary Services	410-685-0697
Maryland Messenger Service	410-837-5550
Olsten Staffing Services	410-685-7955
Post Office	410-347-4425
UPS	800-742-5877

— Media —

PUBLICATIONS

				Phone	Fax
Baltimore Business Journal 111 Market Pl Suite 720	Baltimore	MD	21202	410-576-1161	752-3112
Web: www.amcity.com/baltimore					
Baltimore Magazine 1000 Lancaster St Suite 400	Baltimore	MD	21202	410-752-4200	625-0280
TF Cust Svc: 800-935-0838 ■ *Web:* www.baltimoremag.com/ ■ *E-mail:* bmag@abs.net					
Baltimore Sun‡ 501 N Calvert St	Baltimore	MD	21278	410-332-6000	332-6455
TF: 800-829-8000 ■ *Web:* www.sunspot.net ■ *E-mail:* baltsun@clark.net					
Where Baltimore Magazine 516 N Charles St Suite 300	Baltimore	MD	21201	410-539-4373	539-4381

‡*Daily newspapers*

Baltimore (Cont'd)

TELEVISION

Phone *Fax*

WBAL-TV Ch 11 (NBC) 3800 Hooper Ave...... Baltimore MD 21211 410-467-3000 338-6460
Web: wbaltv.com

WBFF-TV Ch 45 (Fox) 2000 W 41st St....... Baltimore MD 21211 410-467-4545 467-5090
Web: www.wbff45.com/ ■ *E-mail:* wbff45@aol.com

WJZ-TV Ch 13 (CBS)
3725 Malden Ave TV Hill............... Baltimore MD 21211 410-466-0013 578-7502
Web: www.wjz.com/ ■ *E-mail:* ridalld@wjz.groupw.wec.com

WMAR-TV Ch 2 (ABC) 6400 York Rd........ Baltimore MD 21212 410-377-2222 377-0493
Web: www.insidebaltimore.com/wmar/ ■ *E-mail:* wmartv2@aol.com

WMPB-TV Ch 67 (PBS)
11767 Owings Mills Blvd............ Owings Mills MD 21117 410-356-5600 581-4338
TF: 800-223-3678 ■ *Web:* www.mpt.org/mpt/
■ *E-mail:* comments@mpt.org

WNUV-TV Ch 54 (WB)
711 W 40th St Suite 301............... Baltimore MD 21211 410-662-9688 662-0816
Web: www.wnuv54.com

RADIO

Phone *Fax*

WBAL-AM 1090 kHz (N/T) 3800 Hooper Ave ... Baltimore MD 21211 410-889-0098 338-6675
Web: wbal.com

WCAO-AM 600 kHz (Rel)
1829 Reisterstown Rd Suite 420.......... Baltimore MD 21208 410-653-2200 486-8057

WCBM-AM 680 kHz (N/T)
11 Music Fair Rd.................. Owings Mills MD 21117 410-356-3003 581-0150
Web: www.wcbm.com ■ *E-mail:* hottalk@wcbm.com

WERQ-FM 92.3 MHz (CHR)
100 Saint Paul St.................... Baltimore MD 21202 410-332-8200 783-4791

WGRX-FM 100.7 MHz (Ctry)
11350 McCormick Rd Executive Plaza
3 Suite 701........................Hunt Valley MD 21031 410-771-8484 771-1616

WIYY-FM 97.9 MHz (Rock)
3800 Hooper Ave.................... Baltimore MD 21211 410-889-0098 467-3291
Web: 98online.com

WJHU-FM 88.1 MHz (NPR)
2216 N Charles St..................... Baltimore MD 21218 410-516-9548 516-1976
Web: www.wjhu.org/ ■ *E-mail:* mail@wjhu.org

WLIF-FM 101.9 MHz (AC)
1 W Pennsylvania Ave Suite 850.......... Baltimore MD 21204 410-823-1570 821-5482

WOCT-FM 104.3 MHz (Oldies)
1829 Reisterstown Rd Suite 420.......... Baltimore MD 21208 410-825-1043 602-8104
Web: www.thecolt.com

WPOC-FM 93.1 MHz (Ctry) 711 W 40th St.... Baltimore MD 21211 410-366-3693 235-3899
Web: www.wpoc.com ■ *E-mail:* wpoc93fm@prodigy.com

WQSR-FM 105.7 MHz (Oldies)
600 Washington Ave.................. Baltimore MD 21204 410-825-1000 337-2772*
**Fax:* Sales

WRBS-FM 95.1 MHz (Rel)
3600 Georgetown Rd.................. Baltimore MD 21227 410-247-4100 247-4533
TF: 800-899-0951 ■ *Web:* www.wrbs.com ■ *E-mail:* info@wrbs.com

WWDC-FM 101.1 MHz (Rock)
8750 Brookville Rd................ Silver Spring MD 20910 301-587-7100 587-5267
Web: www.dc101.com

WWIN-AM 1400 kHz (Rel) 100 Saint Paul St... Baltimore MD 21202 410-332-8200 539-4550

WWIN-FM 95.9 MHz (Urban)
100 Saint Paul St.................... Baltimore MD 21202 410-332-8200 783-4791

WWLG-AM 1360 kHz (Nost)
1726 Reisterstown Rd Hilton Plaza
Suite 117.......................... Baltimore MD 21208 410-580-6800 580-6810

WWMX-FM 106.5 MHz (AC)
600 Washington Ave Suite 201............ Towson MD 21204 410-825-5400 583-1065
Web: www.wwmxfm.com

WXYV-FM 102.7 MHz (Urban)
600 Washington Ave Suite 201............ Towson MD 21204 410-828-7722 821-8256

— Colleges/Universities —

Phone *Fax*

Baltimore City Community College
2901 Liberty Heights Ave................ Baltimore MD 21215 410-462-8000 462-7677

Baltimore Hebrew University
5800 Park Heights Ave................ Baltimore MD 21215 410-578-6900 578-6940
TF: 888-248-7420 ■ *Web:* www.bhu.edu ■ *E-mail:* bhu@bhu.edu

Baltimore International College
17 Commerce St...................... Baltimore MD 21202 410-752-4710 752-3730
TF: 800-624-9926 ■ *Web:* www.bic.edu
■ *E-mail:* publicaffairs@bic.edu

Phone *Fax*

Capitol College 11301 Springfield Rd.......... Laurel MD 20708 301-369-2800 953-3876
TF Admissions: 800-950-1992 ■ *Web:* www.capitol-college.edu
■ *E-mail:* ccinfo@capitol-college.edu

Catonsville Community College
800 S Rolling Rd................... Catonsville MD 21228 410-455-6050 719-6546
Web: www.cat.cc.md.us

College of Notre Dame of Maryland
4701 N Charles St................... Baltimore MD 21210 410-435-0100 532-6287
TF Admissions: 800-435-0300 ■ *Web:* www.ndm.edu

Coppin State College 2500 W North Ave...... Baltimore MD 21216 410-383-5400 523-7238*
**Fax:* Admissions ■ *TF:* 800-635-3674 ■ *Web:* www.coppin.edu
■ *E-mail:* rkannan@coe.coppin.umd.edu

Dundalk Community College
7200 Sollers Point Rd................. Baltimore MD 21222 410-282-6700 285-9903
Web: www.dundalk.cc.md.us

Essex Community College
7201 Rossville Blvd................... Baltimore MD 21237 410-682-6000 780-6211
Web: www.essex.cc.md.us

Goucher College 1021 Dulaney Valley Rd..... Baltimore MD 21204 410-337-6000 337-6354*
**Fax:* Admissions ■ *TF:* 800-468-2437 ■ *Web:* www.goucher.edu

Howard Community College
10901 Little Patuxent Pkwy............ Columbia MD 21044 410-772-4800 772-4589
Web: www.howardcc.edu

Johns Hopkins University
3400 N Charles St.................... Baltimore MD 21218 410-516-8000 516-6025
Web: www.jhu.edu

Loyola College 4501 N Charles St.......... Baltimore MD 21210 410-617-2000 617-5097
TF: 800-221-9107 ■ *Web:* www.loyola.edu

Maryland Institute College of Art
1300 W Mt Royal Ave................. Baltimore MD 21217 410-669-9200 669-9206
TF Admissions: 800-293-5757 ■ *Web:* www.mica.edu

Morgan State University
1700 E Cold Spring Ln................ Baltimore MD 21251 443-885-3333 885-3000
TF Admissions: 800-332-6674 ■ *Web:* www.morgan.edu

Peabody Conservatory of Music
1 E Mt Vernon Pl..................... Baltimore MD 21202 410-659-8110 659-8102
TF Admissions: 800-368-2521 ■ *Web:* www.peabody.jhu.edu

Sojourner-Douglass College
500 N Caroline St.................... Baltimore MD 21205 410-276-0306 675-1810
TF: 800-732-2630 ■ *Web:* host.sdc.edu

University of Baltimore 1420 N Charles St..... Baltimore MD 21201 410-837-4200 837-4793
TF Admissions: 877-277-5982 ■ *Web:* www.ubalt.edu

University of Maryland Baltimore County
1000 Hilltop Cir..................... Baltimore MD 21250 410-455-2902 455-1094
TF Admissions: 800-862-2482 ■ *Web:* www.umbc.edu

— Hospitals —

Phone *Fax*

Bon Secours Liberty Medical Center
2000 W Baltimore St.................. Baltimore MD 21223 410-362-3000 362-3450

Church Hospital Corp 100 N Broadway....... Baltimore MD 21231 410-522-8000 563-6599
Web: www.helixhealth.com/church/index.htm

Franklin Square Hospital Center
9000 Franklin Sq Dr.................. Baltimore MD 21237 410-682-7000 682-7904
Web: www.helixhealth.com/fsquare/index.htm

Good Samaritan Hospital of Maryland
5601 Loch Raven Blvd................. Baltimore MD 21239 410-532-8000 532-4599
Web: www.helixhealth.com/goodsam/index.htm

Greater Baltimore Medical Center
6701 N Charles St.................... Baltimore MD 21204 410-828-2000 825-1272
Web: www.gbmc.org/

Harbor Hospital Center 3001 S Hanover St.... Baltimore MD 21225 410-350-3200 355-2853
Web: www.helixhealth.com/harbor/index.htm

John Hopkins Bayview Medical Center
4940 Eastern Ave.................... Baltimore MD 21224 410-550-0100 550-2700
Web: www.jhbmc.jhu.edu

Johns Hopkins Hospital 600 N Wolfe St...... Baltimore MD 21287 410-955-5000 955-0890
Web: www.med.jhu.edu ■ *E-mail:* www@www.med.jhu.edu

Kennedy Krieger Institute 707 N Broadway.... Baltimore MD 21205 410-502-9000 550-9524

Maryland General Hospital 827 Linden Ave.... Baltimore MD 21201 410-225-8000 462-5834

Mercy Medical Center 301 St Paul Pl........ Baltimore MD 21202 410-332-9000 962-8392*
**Fax:* Admitting ■ *Web:* www.mercymed.com

Mount Washington Pediatric Hospital
1708 W Rogers Ave................... Baltimore MD 21209 410-578-8600 466-1715
Web: www.mwph.org ■ *E-mail:* MWPH@mwph.org

Sinai Hospital of Baltimore
2401 W Belvedere Ave................. Baltimore MD 21215 410-601-5678 601-8356
TF: 800-444-8233 ■ *Web:* www.sinai-balt.com

Union Memorial Hospital
201 E University Pkwy................. Baltimore MD 21218 410-554-2000 554-2652
TF: 800-647-7864 ■ *Web:* www.helixhealth.com/union/index.htm

Baltimore — Hospitals (Cont'd)

				Phone	Fax
University of Maryland Medical System 22 S Greene St	Baltimore	MD	21201	410-328-8667	328-0117*
*Fax: Hum Res ■ *Web:* www.umm.edu/system/hospital/univ-hosp-1.html					
Veterans Affairs Medical Center 10 N Greene St	Baltimore	MD	21201	410-605-7000	605-7901

— Attractions —

				Phone	Fax
American Visionary Art Museum 800 Key Hwy	Baltimore	MD	21230	410-244-1900	244-5858
Web: www.avam.org					
Antietam National Battlefield 5831 Dunker Church Rd	Sharpsburg	MD	21782	301-432-5124	432-4590
Web: www.nps.gov/anti/					
Antique Row 807 N Howard St	Baltimore	MD	21201	410-383-2881	
B & O Railroad Museum 901 W Pratt St	Baltimore	MD	21223	410-752-2490	752-2499
Web: www.borail.org/ ■ *E-mail:* webinfo@borail.org					
Babe Ruth Birthplace Museum 216 Emory St	Baltimore	MD	21230	410-727-1539	727-1652
Web: www.baberuthmuseum.com/					
Baltimore Center for the Performing Arts 1 N Charles St	Baltimore	MD	21201	410-625-4230	625-4250
Baltimore Civil War Museum & President Street Station 601 President St	Baltimore	MD	21202	410-385-5188	385-5189
Baltimore Harbor Promenade Pier 5 & Pratt St	Baltimore	MD	21230	410-396-3228	396-3393
Baltimore Maritime Museum Pratt St Pier 3	Baltimore	MD	21202	410-396-3453	396-3393
Web: www.livingclassrooms.org					
Baltimore Museum of Art 10 Art Museum Dr	Baltimore	MD	21218	410-396-7100	396-6562
Web: www.artbma.org					
Baltimore Museum of Industry 1415 Key Hwy	Baltimore	MD	21230	410-727-4808	727-4869
Web: www.charm.net/~bmi/ ■ *E-mail:* bmi@mailhost.charm.net					
Baltimore Opera Co 110 W Mt Royal Ave Suite 306	Baltimore	MD	21201	410-625-1600	625-6474
Web: www.baltimoreopera.com					
Baltimore Public Works Museum 751 Eastern Ave	Baltimore	MD	21202	410-396-5565	545-6781
Baltimore Streetcar Museum 1901 Falls Rd	Baltimore	MD	21211	410-547-0264	
Web: www.baltimoremd.com/streetcar					
Baltimore Symphony Orchestra 1212 Cathedral St	Baltimore	MD	21201	410-783-8000	783-8131
Web: www.baltimoresymphony.org					
Baltimore Zoo Druid Hill Pk	Baltimore	MD	21217	410-396-7102	396-6464
Web: www.baltimorezoo.org					
Basilica of the Assumption Cathedral & Mulberry Sts	Baltimore	MD	21201	410-727-3565	539-0407
Catoctin Mountain Park 6602 Foxville Rd	Thurmont	MD	21788	301-663-9343	271-2764
Web: www.nps.gov/cato/					
Center Stage 700 N Calvert St	Baltimore	MD	21202	410-685-3200	539-3912
Web: www.erols.com/cntrstage/index.html					
Chesapeake & Ohio Canal National Historical Park PO Box 4	Sharpsburg	MD	21782	301-739-4200	739-5275
Web: www.nps.gov/choh/ ■ *E-mail:* choh_chief_ranger@nps.gov					
Cole B Olive Pharmacy Museum 650 W Lombard St	Baltimore	MD	21201	410-727-0746	727-2253
Contemporary Museum The 100 W Centre St	Baltimore	MD	21201	410-783-5720	783-5722
Cylburn Arboretum 4915 Greenspring Ave	Baltimore	MD	21209	410-396-0180	367-8039
Druid Hill Park I-83 & Exit 7	Baltimore	MD	21217	410-396-6106	
Edgar Allan Poe House 203 N Amity St	Baltimore	MD	21223	410-396-7932	
Web: www.comnet.ca/~forrest/museum1.html					
Eubie Blake National Museum & Cultural Center 34 Market Pl Suite 323	Baltimore	MD	21202	410-625-3113	385-2916
Web: www.eubieblake.org ■ *E-mail:* eblake847@aol.com					
Evergreen House 4545 N Charles St	Baltimore	MD	21210	410-516-0341	
Web: www.jhu.edu/news_info/to_do/evergreen/					
Fire Museum of Maryland 1301 York Rd	Lutherville	MD	21093	410-321-7500	769-8433
Web: www.firemuseummd.org ■ *E-mail:* info@firemuseummd.org					
Fort McHenry National Monument & Historic Shrine E Fort Ave	Baltimore	MD	21230	410-962-4290	962-2500
Web: www.nps.gov/fomc/					
Gordon Center for Performing Arts 3506 Gwynnbrook Ave	Owings Mills	MD	21117	410-356-5200	581-0561
Web: www.gordoncenter.com/ ■ *E-mail:* gordon-center@kohnet.com					
Great Blacks in Wax Museum 1601-03 E North Ave	Baltimore	MD	21213	410-563-3404	675-5040
Gwynn's Falls/Leakin Park 4921 Windsor Mill Rd	Baltimore	MD	21207	410-396-0010	
Hampton National Historic Site 535 Hampton Ln	Towson	MD	21286	410-823-1309	823-8394
Web: www.nps.gov/hamp/					
Harborplace & The Gallery 200 E Pratt St	Baltimore	MD	21202	410-332-4191	547-7317
Web: www.harborplace.com ■ *E-mail:* comments@harborplace.com					
Homewood House Museum 3400 N Charles St Johns Hopkins University	Baltimore	MD	21218	410-516-5589	516-7859
E-mail: homewood@jhunix.hcf.jhu.edu					
IMAX Theater 601 Light St Maryland Science Ctr	Baltimore	MD	21230	410-685-5225	545-5974
Inner Harbor Ice Rink 200 W Key Hwy	Baltimore	MD	21201	410-385-0673	385-0361
Web: www.bop.org					
James E Lewis Museum of Art 1700 E Coldspring Ln Morgan State University	Baltimore	MD	21251	443-885-3030	319-4024
Web: www.morgan.edu/ACADEMIC/SCHOOLS/FineArts/gallery.htm					
Joseph Meyerhoff Symphony Hall 1212 Cathedral St	Baltimore	MD	21201	410-783-8100	783-8077
TF: 800-442-1198					
Lacrosse Hall of Fame Museum 113 W University Pkwy	Baltimore	MD	21210	410-235-6882	366-6735
Web: lacrosse.org/museum/hall.cfm					
Lloyd Street Synagogue/Jewish Historical Society of Maryland 15 Lloyd St	Baltimore	MD	21202	410-732-6400	732-6451
Long Robert House 812 S Ann St	Baltimore	MD	21231	410-675-6750	675-6769
Lovely Lane United Methodist Church & Museum 2200 Saint Paul St	Baltimore	MD	21218	410-889-1512	889-1501
Lyric Opera House 100 W Mt Royal Ave	Baltimore	MD	21201	410-685-5086	332-8234
Maryland Art Place 218 W Saratoga St	Baltimore	MD	21201	410-962-8565	244-8017
E-mail: map@charm.net					
Maryland Historical Society Museum & Library 201 W Monument St	Baltimore	MD	21201	410-685-3750	385-2105
Web: mdhs.org					
Maryland Science Center 601 Light St	Baltimore	MD	21230	410-685-2370	545-5974
Web: www.mdsci.org/ ■ *E-mail:* info@mdsci.org					
Mechanic Morris A Theatre 25 Hopkins Plaza	Baltimore	MD	21201	410-752-1200	625-4224
Web: www.themechanic.org ■ *E-mail:* subs@themechanic.org					
Monocacy National Battlefield 4801 Urbana Pike	Frederick	MD	21704	301-662-3515	662-3420
Web: www.nps.gov/mono/					
Mother Seton House 600 N Paca St	Baltimore	MD	21201	410-523-3443	
Mount Clare Museum House 1500 Washington Blvd Carroll Pk	Baltimore	MD	21230	410-837-3262	837-0251
Mount Vernon Cultural District 217 N Charles St	Baltimore	MD	21201	410-244-1030	234-2733
National Aquarium 501 E Pratt St Pier 3	Baltimore	MD	21202	410-576-3800	576-8238
Web: www.aqua.org					
National Museum of Dentistry 31 S Greene St	Baltimore	MD	21201	410-706-8314	706-8313
Web: www.dentalmuseum.umaryland.edu					
Oriole Park 333 W Camden St	Baltimore	MD	21201	410-547-6234	547-6279
Web: www.fred.net/fredrick/f-camden.html					
Peabody Conservatory & Library 1 E Mount Vernon Pl	Baltimore	MD	21202	410-659-8179	783-8576*
*Fax: PR ■ *Web:* www.peabody.jhu.edu					
Port Discovery Kid-Powered Museum 35 Market Pl	Baltimore	MD	21202	410-727-8120	727-3042
Potters Guild of Baltimore 3600 Clipper Mill Rd	Baltimore	MD	21211	410-235-4884	
Power Plant Entertainment Complex 601 E Pratt St	Baltimore	MD	21202	410-752-5444	659-9491
Rosenberg Gallery Kraushaar Auditorium & Merrick Hall Goucher College	Baltimore	MD	21204	410-337-6333	
Web: www.goucher.edu/rosenberg/Welcome.htm					
Six Flags America PO Box 4210	Largo	MD	20775	301-249-1500	249-8853
Web: www.adventureworld.com ■ *E-mail:* info@adventure-world.net					
SS John W Brown Clinton St Pier 1	Baltimore	MD	21224	410-558-0646	558-1737
Star-Spangled Banner Flag House & 1812 Museum 844 E Pratt St	Baltimore	MD	21202	410-837-1793	837-1812
Web: www.flaghouse.org ■ *E-mail:* info@flaghouse.org					
Top of the World Observation Level & Museum 401 E Pratt St World Trade Ctr 27th Fl	Baltimore	MD	21202	410-837-8439	837-0845
Web: www.bop.org/totw/index.html					
Walters Art Gallery 600 N Charles St	Baltimore	MD	21201	410-547-9000	783-7969
Web: www.thewalters.org					
War Memorial Building 101 N Gay St	Baltimore	MD	21202	410-752-6474	783-2939
Westminster Hall & Burying Ground Fayette & Green Sts	Baltimore	MD	21201	410-706-2072	706-0596

Baltimore (Cont'd)

SPORTS TEAMS & FACILITIES

				Phone	Fax
Baltimore Arena 201 W Baltimore St.	Baltimore	MD	21201	410-347-2020	347-2042
Baltimore Blast (soccer) 1801 S Clinton St	Baltimore	MD	21224	410-732-5278	732-1737
Web: www.baltimoreblast.com ■ *E-mail:* questions@baltimorespirit.com					
Baltimore Orioles 333 W Camden St.	Baltimore	MD	21201	410-685-9800	547-6272
Web: www.theorioles.com					
Baltimore Ravens 1101 Russell St PSINet Stadium	Baltimore	MD	21230	410-654-6200	654-6212
Web: www.nfl.com/ravens					
Baltimore Thunder (lacrosse) 210 W Pennsylvania Ave Suite 700	Towson	MD	21204	410-321-1908	321-1901
Web: www.baltimorethunder.com					
Maryland Jockey Club of Baltimore City Inc 5201 Park Heights Ave	Baltimore	MD	21215	410-542-9400	466-2521
TF: 800-638-3811 ■ *Web:* www.marylandracing.com ■ *E-mail:* mjc@smart.net					
Maryland Pride (soccer) 303 Najoles Rd Suite 112	Millersville	MD	21108	410-729-1100	729-1604
TF: 888-592-5425 ■ *Web:* mdpride.com ■ *E-mail:* info@mdpride.com					
Oriole Park at Camden Yards 555 Russell St Suite A	Baltimore	MD	21230	410-576-0300	539-7640
Pimlico Race Course 5201 Park Heights Ave	Baltimore	MD	21215	410-542-9400	542-1221

— Events —

	Phone
ACC Craft Fair (late February)	800-836-3470
Artscape (late July)	410-396-4575
Baltimore Holiday Tree Lighting (early December)	410-837-4636
Baltimore on Ice (January-March)	800-282-6632
Baltimore's New Year's Eve Extravaganza (December 31)	410-837-4636
Christmas at Harborplace (December)	410-332-4191
Christmas Music at Lexington Marketplace (December)	410-685-6169
Kennedy Krieger Institute Festival of Trees (late November)	410-502-9460
Lighted Boat Parade (early December)	410-837-4636
Maryland Million Day (mid-October)	410-252-2100
Maryland State Fair (late August-early September)	410-252-0200
Orioles Winter Carnival (mid-January)	410-685-9800
PJI National ArenaCross (late January)	410-347-2010
Portfest (early October)	410-752-8632
Preakness Celebration Week (early May)	410-837-3030
Rhythm Festival (mid-September)	410-664-6322
Zoo Lights (late November-early January)	410-396-7102

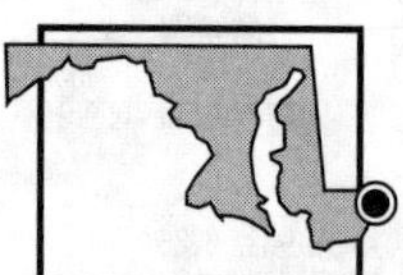

Ocean City

Founded in 1875 as a small fishing village, Ocean City today is considered by many to be the White Marlin Capital of the World. Each year, in August, Ocean City holds its premier fishing tournament, the White Marlin Open, which has long been known as the "World's Largest Billfish Tournament." Although the city is probably best known for its sportfishing opportunities, it is also a prime destination for golf enthusiasts. Ten championship golf courses are located in the Ocean City area, including the city's own course, Eagle's Landing, which has been named one of the top 10 municipal golf courses in the U.S. The three-mile-long Boardwalk in Ocean City is lined with shops, restaurants, entertainment venues, and museums, and draws large crowds daily. Located on the Boardwalk is the Ocean City Life-Saving Museum, a building constructed in 1891 that has since become a museum to preserve the history of the U.S. Life-Saving Service and the town of Ocean City. In addition to the annual billfish tournament, a number of other events attract visitors to Ocean City as well. The Arts Atlantica fine arts show and festival is held on the Boardwalk each June, and in August visitors can attend the Sunfest, an annual celebration of summer's end and fall's beginning. The festival includes musical performances, arts, and crafts, and has been listed as a top 100 event in the U.S.

Population	5,095	**Longitude**	75-02-11 W
Area (Land)	433.2 sq mi	**County**	Worcester
Area (Water)	31.8 sq mi	**Time Zone**	EST
Elevation	8 ft	**Area Code/s**	410
Latitude	38-22-46 N		

— Average Temperatures and Precipitation —

TEMPERATURES

	Jan	Feb	Mar	Apr	May	Jun	Jul	Aug	Sep	Oct	Nov	Dec
High	45	48	57	67	76	83	87	86	80	70	60	50
Low	27	29	36	44	54	62	67	66	59	48	40	31

PRECIPITATION

	Jan	Feb	Mar	Apr	May	Jun	Jul	Aug	Sep	Oct	Nov	Dec
Inches	3.8	3.5	4.2	3.3	3.5	3.7	4.0	5.0	3.6	3.2	3.1	3.5

— Important Phone Numbers —

	Phone		Phone
AAA	410-749-0303	**Poison Control Center**	800-492-2414
Beach Patrol	410-250-0125	**Time**	410-844-1212
Emergency	911	**Weather**	410-742-8400
Medical Referral	410-629-1500		

— Information Sources —

				Phone	Fax
Better Business Bureau Serving Greater Maryland 2100 Huntingdon Ave	Baltimore	MD	21211	410-347-3990	347-3936
Web: www.baltimore.bbb.org					
Ocean City Branch Library 200 14th St.	Ocean City	MD	21842	410-289-7297	289-5577
Ocean City Chamber of Commerce 12320 Ocean Gateway	Ocean City	MD	21842	410-213-0144	213-7521
Web: www.oceancity.org ■ *E-mail:* ocbeach@shore.intercom.net					
Ocean City City Hall 301 N Baltimore Ave	Ocean City	MD	21842	410-289-8221	289-7385
Ocean City Convention & Visitors Bureau 4001 Coastal Hwy	Ocean City	MD	21842	410-289-8181	723-8655
TF: 800-626-2326 ■ *Web:* www.ocean-city.com ■ *E-mail:* ochmra@mail.dmv.com					
Ocean City Convention Center 4001 Coastal Hwy	Ocean City	MD	21842	410-289-8311	289-0058
TF: 800-626-2326 ■ *Web:* www.ocean-city.com/convention/ ■ *E-mail:* mnoah@ococean.com					
Ocean City Downtown Assn 1101-B Philadelphia Ave	Ocean City	MD	21842	410-289-1413	289-4900
Web: www.ocean-city.com/downtown/ ■ *E-mail:* downtown@beachin.net					
Ocean City Mayor 301 N Baltimore Ave	Ocean City	MD	21842	410-289-3300	289-7385
Ocean City Planning & Zoning 301 N Baltimore Ave	Ocean City	MD	21842	410-289-8855	289-7385
Worcester County 1 W Market St County Courthouse Suite 112	Snow Hill	MD	21863	410-632-1194	632-3131

On-Line Resources

At the Beach	www.atbeach.com
City Knowledge Ocean City	www.cityknowledge.com/md_oceancity.htm
Ocean City Maryland Regional Information Page	www.ocmaryland.com/index.html
Oceancity-md.com	www.oceancity-md.com
Sunny Day Guide Ocean City	www.sunnydayguides.com/oc/
Surf & Sun Beach Vacation Guide to Ocean City	www.surf-sun.com/md-ocean-city-main.htm

Ocean City (Cont'd)

— Transportation Services —

AIRPORTS

■ Salisbury-Wicomico County Regional Airport (SBY)

	Phone
27 miles W of downtown Ocean City (approx 30 minutes)	410-548-4827

Airport Transportation

	Phone
Atlantic Taxi $35 fare to downtown Ocean City	410-289-1313
Bayside Taxi $35 fare to downtown Ocean City	410-632-1800
Beach Bound Shuttle $50 fare to downtown Ocean City	410-749-9029

Commercial Airlines

	Phone
US Airways	800-428-4322

Charter Airlines

	Phone
Bay Land Aviation Inc	410-749-0323

CAR RENTALS

	Phone		Phone
Avis-Salisbury	410-742-8566	**Hertz**	410-213-2400
CarTemps USA-Salisbury	410-742-4700	**Hertz-Salisbury**	410-749-2235
Enterprise	410-213-0886	**National-Salisbury**	410-749-2450

LIMO/TAXI

	Phone		Phone
Atlantic Taxi	410-289-1313	**Sunshine Cab Co**	410-208-2828
Bayside Taxi	410-632-1800	**White's Taxi**	410-250-8294
Coast to Coast Limousine	410-723-5466		

MASS TRANSIT

	Phone
Boardwalk Train $2 Base fare	410-289-5311
Ocean City Municipal Bus $1 Base fare	410-723-1607

RAIL/BUS

	Phone
Carolina Trailways Bus Station 2nd St & Philadelphia Ave . Ocean City MD 21842	410-289-9307

— Accommodations —

HOTEL RESERVATION SERVICES

	Phone	Fax
Ocean City Hotel-Motel-Restaurant Assn	410-289-6733	289-5645

TF: 800-626-2326 ■ *Web:* www.ocean-city.com/ochmra.htm

HOTELS, MOTELS, RESORTS

Phone / Fax

Admiral Hotel 813 Baltimore Ave . . . . Ocean City MD 21843 410-289-4805 289-4823
TF: 800-292-6280

Beachmark Motel 7300 Coastal Hwy . . . . Ocean City MD 21842 410-524-7300
TF: 800-638-1600 ■ *Web:* www.ocean-city.com/beachmark.htm

Best Western Hotel Flagship
2600 Baltimore Ave . . . . Ocean City MD 21842 410-289-3384 289-1743
TF: 800-837-3585 ■ *Web:* www.ocmdhotels.com/bestwestern
■ *E-mail:* bwestern@beachin.net

Best Western Sea Bay Inn
6007 Coastal Hwy . . . . Ocean City MD 21842 410-524-6100 524-1619
TF: 800-888-2229 ■ *Web:* www.bestwesternoc.com
■ *E-mail:* cybercom@intercom.net

Breakers Hotel 3rd St & Boardwalk . . . . Ocean City MD 21842 410-289-9165 289-3590
TF: 800-283-9165

Buckingham Hotel 1405 Baltimore Ave . . . . Ocean City MD 21842 410-289-6246 289-8746
TF: 800-787-6246
■ *Web:* www.atbeach.com/lodging/md/buckingham/index.html
■ *E-mail:* buckhotel@aol.com

Candlelight Motor Lodge
8100 Coastal Hwy . . . . Ocean City MD 21842 410-524-1401
TF: 800-553-2013 ■ *Web:* www.ocean-city.com/candlelight.htm

Casa Blanca Motel 2408 Baltimore Ave . . . . Ocean City MD 21842 410-289-8273
TF: 800-770-9773

Castle in the Sand Hotel
37th St & Oceanfront . . . . Ocean City MD 21842 410-289-6846 289-9446
TF: 800-552-7263 ■ *Web:* www.castleinthesand.com
■ *E-mail:* castle@beachin.net

Cayman Suites Hotel 12500 Coastal Hwy . . . . Ocean City MD 21842 410-250-7600 250-7603
TF: 800-546-0042 ■ *Web:* www.caymansuites.com

Coconut Malorie Resort 200 59th St . . . . Ocean City MD 21842 410-723-6100 524-9327
TF: 800-767-6060 ■ *Web:* www.coconutmalorie.com
■ *E-mail:* ocmalori@beachin.net

Comfort Inn Boardwalk
5th St & Boardwalk . . . . Ocean City MD 21843 410-289-5155 289-6547
TF: 800-282-5155 ■ *Web:* www.comfortinnboardwalk.com

Comfort Inn Gold Coast
11201 Coastal Hwy . . . . Ocean City MD 21842 410-524-3000 524-8255
TF: 800-221-2222 ■ *Web:* www.comfortgoldcoast.com
■ *E-mail:* comfort@ezy.net

Commander Hotel 1401 Atlantic Ave . . . . Ocean City MD 21842 410-289-6166 289-3998
TF: 888-289-6166 ■ *Web:* www.commanderhotel.com
■ *E-mail:* cmdrhotel@aol.com

Days Inn Boardwalk 23rd St & Boardwalk . . . . Ocean City MD 21842 410-289-7161 289-6525
TF: 800-926-1122 ■ *Web:* www.daysinnboardwalk.com

Dunes Manor Hotel 2800 Baltimore Ave . . . . Ocean City MD 21842 410-289-1100 289-4905
TF: 800-523-2888 ■ *Web:* www.dunesmanor.com
■ *E-mail:* dunes@dmv.com

Dunes Motel 27th St & Boardwalk . . . . Ocean City MD 21842 410-289-4414 289-0891
Web: www.ocean-city.com/dunes.htm

Econo Lodge Oceanfront
45th St & Boardwalk . . . . Ocean City MD 21842 410-289-6424 289-8729
TF: 800-638-3244
■ *Web:* www.purnellproperties.com/econolodgeoceanfront/

Econo Lodge Oceanside
145th St & Coastal Hwy . . . . Ocean City MD 21843 410-250-1155 250-1155
TF: 800-443-4557
■ *Web:* www.purnellproperties.com/econolodgeoceanblock

Eden Roc Motel 2000 Baltimore Ave . . . . Ocean City MD 21842 410-289-6022
TF: 800-800-4826 ■ *Web:* www.ocean-city.com/edenroc.htm

Executive Motel 30th St & Baltimore Ave . . . . Ocean City MD 21842 410-289-3101
TF: 800-638-1600

Fenwick Inn 13801 Coastal Hwy . . . . Ocean City MD 21842 410-250-1100 250-0087
TF: 800-492-1873 ■ *Web:* www.fenwickinn.com
■ *E-mail:* fenwick@shore.intercom.net

Flamingo Motel 3100 Baltimore Ave . . . . Ocean City MD 21842 410-289-6464 289-4472
TF: 800-394-7465 ■ *Web:* www.flamingo-ocmd.com
■ *E-mail:* flam@intercom.net

Francis Scott Key Motel
12806 Ocean Gateway . . . . West Ocean City MD 21843 410-213-0088 213-2854
TF: 800-213-0088 ■ *Web:* www.fskmotel.com
■ *E-mail:* fskinoc@aol.com

Gateway Resort Hotel 4800 Coastal Hwy . . . . Ocean City MD 21842 410-524-6500 524-5374
TF: 800-382-2582 ■ *Web:* www.gatewayoc.com
■ *E-mail:* frontdesk@gatewayoc.com

Georgia Belle Hotel Suites
12004 Coastal Hwy . . . . Ocean City MD 21842 410-250-4000
TF: 800-542-4444 ■ *Web:* www.ocean-city.com/georgia-belle.htm

Hampton Inn 4201 Coastal Hwy . . . . Ocean City MD 21842 410-289-6488 289-1617
Web: www.ocean-city.com/hampton.htm
■ *E-mail:* hampton@beachin.net

Harrison Hall Hotel 15th St & Boardwalk . . . . Ocean City MD 21843 410-289-6222 289-0467
TF: 800-638-2106 ■ *Web:* www.ocmdhotels.com/harrisonhall.htm
■ *E-mail:* oceanres@beachin.net

Holiday Inn Oceanfront 6600 Coastal Hwy . . . . Ocean City MD 21842 410-524-1600 524-1135
TF: 800-837-3588 ■ *Web:* www.ocmdhotels.com/holiday-inn.htm
■ *E-mail:* hiocean@beachin.net

Howard Johnson Oceanfront Inn
2401 Atlantic Ave . . . . Ocean City MD 21842 410-289-6401 289-2365
TF: 800-926-1122 ■ *Web:* www.hojoexpress.com/
■ *E-mail:* ochotels@aol.com

Howard Johnson Oceanfront Plaza Hotel
1109 Atlantic Ave . . . . Ocean City MD 21842 410-289-7251 289-4901
TF: 800-926-1122 ■ *Web:* www.hjoceanfrontplaza.com
■ *E-mail:* ochotels@aol.com

Islander Motel 20th St & Philadelphia Ave . . . . Ocean City MD 21842 410-289-9179 289-9179

King Charles Hotel 1209 Baltimore Ave . . . . Ocean City MD 21842 410-289-6141 289-6218
TF: 800-498-0356 ■ *E-mail:* kchotel@aol.com

Lighthouse Club Hotel 201 60th St . . . . Ocean City MD 21842 410-524-5400 524-3928
TF: 888-371-5400 ■ *Web:* www.fagers.com/lghtmain.htm
■ *E-mail:* llthouse@dmv.com

Monticello Hotel 216 N Baltimore Ave . . . . Ocean City MD 21842 410-289-7101
Web: www.atbeach.com/lodging/md/monticello/index.html

Nassau Motel 6002 Coastal Hwy . . . . Ocean City MD 21842 410-524-6451
Web: www.ocean-city.com/nassau.htm ■ *E-mail:* nassauocmd@aol.com

Ocean City — Hotels, Motels, Resorts (Cont'd)

Phone Fax

Ocean Voyager Motel 3201 Baltimore Ave.... Ocean City MD 21842 410-289-6414 289-0488
TF: 800-338-6113

Oceanic Motel 106 S 1st St.............. Ocean City MD 21842 410-289-6494 289-2120
TF: 800-638-2106

Paradise Plaza Inn 9th St & Boadwalk ...... Ocean City MD 21842 410-289-6381 289-1303
TF: 888-678-4111 ■ *Web:* www.paradiseplazainn.com
■ *E-mail:* ddouglas@paradiseplazainn.com

Phillips Beach Plaza Hotel
1301 Atlantic Ave .... Ocean City MD 21842 410-289-9121 289-3041
TF: 800-492-5834
■ *Web:* www.ocean-city.com/phillips-beach-plaza.htm

Plim Plaza Hotel
2nd St & Boardwalk PO Box 160 .... Ocean City MD 21842 410-289-6181 289-0714
TF: 800-837-3587 ■ *Web:* www.ocmdhotels.com/plimplaza
■ *E-mail:* oceanres@beachin.net

Princess Bayside Beach Hotel & Golf Center
4801 Coastal Hwy................... Ocean City MD 21842 410-723-2900 723-0207
TF: 888-622-9743 ■ *Web:* www.princessbayside.com
■ *E-mail:* pbayside@dmv.com

Princess Royale Oceanfront Hotel & Conference Center 9100 Coastal Hwy..... Ocean City MD 21842 410-524-7777 524-7787
TF: 800-476-9253 ■ *Web:* www.princessroyale.com
■ *E-mail:* princess@dmv.com

Quality Inn Beachfront
33rd St & Oceanfront .... Ocean City MD 21842 410-289-1234

Quality Inn Boardwalk 1601 Atlantic Ave..... Ocean City MD 21842 410-289-4401 289-8620
TF: 800-837-3584 ■ *Web:* www.ocmdhotels.com/qualityinn.htm
■ *E-mail:* qiboard@beachin.net

Quality Inn Oceanfront 5401 Atlantic Ave..... Ocean City MD 21842 410-524-7200 723-0018
TF: 800-837-3586 ■ *Web:* www.ocmdhotels.com/quality.htm
■ *E-mail:* tropics@beachin.net

Ramada Limited Oceanfront
3200 Baltimore Ave.................. Ocean City MD 21842 410-289-6444 289-0108
TF: 800-837-3589 ■ *Web:* www.ocmdhotels.com/ramada.htm
■ *E-mail:* ramada@beachin.net

Rodeway Inn Oceanfront
2910 Baltimore Ave.................. Ocean City MD 21843 410-289-7291 289-7691
TF: 800-531-9700 ■ *Web:* www.rodewayinnoceanfront.com

Royalton Hotel on the Boardwalk
1101 Atlantic Ave .... Ocean City MD 21842 410-289-7145
Web: www.atbeach.com/lodging/md/royalton/index.html

Sahara Motel 19th St & Boardwalk......... Ocean City MD 21843 410-289-8101 289-2894
TF: 800-638-1600 ■ *Web:* www.saharamotel.com

Santa Maria Motel 1500 Baltimore Ave...... Ocean City MD 21843 410-289-7191 289-8609
TF: 800-237-4566 ■ *Web:* www.santamariahotel.com
■ *E-mail:* santa@shore.intercom.net

Sheraton Fontainebleau Hotel
10100 Coastal Hwy................. Ocean City MD 21842 410-524-3535 524-3834
TF: 800-638-2100 ■ *Web:* www.sheratonoc.com
■ *E-mail:* webconcierge@sheratonoc.com

Spinnaker Motel 18th St & Baltimore Ave .... Ocean City MD 21842 410-289-5444 289-0741
TF: 800-638-3244 ■ *Web:* www.purnellproperties.com/spinnaker
■ *E-mail:* ocmotels@aol.com

Wellington Hotel 900 N Baltimore Ave ...... Ocean City MD 21842 410-289-9189 289-4108
Web: www.ocean-city.com/wellington.htm
■ *E-mail:* hotelwell1@aol.com

— Restaurants —

Phone

48th Street Seafood & Crab House (Seafood)
4801 Coastal Hwy........................... Ocean City MD 21842 410-723-3150

Adolfo's Restaurant (Italian) 806 S Baltimore Ave....... Ocean City MD 21842 410-289-4001

Angelo's Restaurant (Italian) 27th St & Coastal Hwy..... Ocean City MD 21842 410-289-6522

Angler Restaurant (Seafood) 312 Talbot St........... Ocean City MD 21843 410-289-7424

Anna Maria's Italian Ristorante (Italian)
116th St & Oceanfront .... Ocean City MD 21842 410-723-3675

Atrium Cafe & Bar (American)
54th St & Oceanfront Quality Inn .... Ocean City MD 21842 410-723-1646

Bahama Mamas (Steak/Seafood) 221 Wicomico St...... Ocean City MD 21842 410-289-0291
Web: www.bahama-mamas.com/restaurant.htm

Bj's On The Water (American) 75th St & Bay.......... Ocean City MD 21843 410-524-7575
Web: www.ocean-city.com/bjs.htm

Bonfire Restaurant (Seafood) 7009 Coastal Hwy........ Ocean City MD 21842 410-524-7171

Brass Balls Saloon (American)
Boardwalk betw 11th & 12th Sts .... Ocean City MD 21842 410-289-0069

Captain Bob's Steak & Seafood (Steak/Seafood)
105 64th St.................................. Ocean City MD 21842 410-524-7070

Captain's Table Restaurant (Steak/Seafood)
1500 Baltimore Ave Santa Maria Motel .... Ocean City MD 21842 410-289-7191

Charlie Chiang's Restaurant (Chinese)
5401 Coastal Hwy............................ Ocean City MD 21842 410-723-4600

Phone

Christopher's Tutti Gusti (Italian) 3322 Coastal Hwy ..... Ocean City MD 21842 410-289-3318
Web: www.ocean-city.com/tuttigusti.htm

Cottage Café (American) 14505-B Coastal Hwy......... Ocean City MD 21842 410-250-1460
Web: www.cottagecafe.com ■ *E-mail:* cottage@shore.intercom.net

Davinci's Restaurant (Italian) 1401 Atlantic Ave .... Ocean City MD 21842 410-289-2974

Duffy's Love Shack (American) 102 Worcester St .... Ocean City MD 21842 410-289-1400
Web: www.duffysloveshack.com

Embers Restaurant (Continental) 2305 Philadelphia Ave... Ocean City MD 21842 410-289-3322
Web: www.embers.com

English Diner (English) 21st St & Philadelphia Ave ...... Ocean City MD 21843 410-289-7288

Fager's Island Restaurant (Pan-Asian) 201 60th St...... Ocean City MD 21842 410-524-5500
Web: www.fagers.com ■ *E-mail:* island@dmv.com

Greene Turtle (American) 11601 Coastal Hwy.......... Ocean City MD 21842 410-723-2128
Web: www.greeneturtle.com ■ *E-mail:* gturtle@beachinet.com

Hall's Restaurant (Steak/Seafood) 5909 Coastal Hwy..... Ocean City MD 21842 410-524-2305
Web: www.halls-oc.com

Harrison's Harbor Watch Restaurant (American)
Boardwalk S Boardwalk Six Inlet .... Ocean City MD 21842 410-289-5121

La Hacienda Restaurant (Mexican)
80th St & Coastal Hwy .... Ocean City MD 21842 410-524-8080

Marios Restaurant (Italian) 2204 Philadelphia Ave....... Ocean City MD 21842 410-289-9445

Mo's Seafood Factory (Seafood) 8203 Coastal Hwy...... Ocean City MD 21842 410-723-2500
Web: www.ocean-city.com/mos-seafood.htm
■ *E-mail:* tony.assadi@ismart.com

Mulligans Restaurant (American) 12445 Ocean Gateway .. Ocean City MD 21842 410-213-7717
Web: www.funatmulligans.com

Nick's Original House of Ribs (Barbecue)
14410 Coastal Hwy........................... Ocean City MD 21842 410-250-1984
Web: www.nickshouseofribs.com ■ *E-mail:* original@beachinnet.com

Phillips by the Sea Restaurant (Continental)
1301 Atlantic Ave Phillips Beach Plaza Hotel .... Ocean City MD 21842 410-289-9121
Web: www.ocean-city.com/pbpmenu2.htm

Reflections Restaurant & Wine Bar (Continental)
67th St & Boardwalk.......................... Ocean City MD 21842 410-524-5252

Ristorante Antipasti (Italian) 3303 Coastal Hwy.......... Ocean City MD 21842 410-289-4588
Web: www.ocean-city.com/antipasti.htm

Seacrets (Jamaican) 49th St & Bay .... Ocean City MD 21842 410-524-4900
Web: www.seacrets.com

Shenanigan's Irish Pub (Irish) 4th St & Boardwalk ...... Ocean City MD 21842 410-289-7181
Web: www.ocean-city.com/shenanigans.htm

Smoker's Bbq Pit (Barbecue) 611 Stephen Decatur Rd.... Ocean City MD 21842 410-213-0040

Victorian Room Restaurant (Continental)
2800 Baltimore Ave Dunes Manor Hotel .... Ocean City MD 21842 410-289-1100

Waterman's Seafood Co (Seafood)
Rt 50 & Bonita St....................... West Ocean City MD 21842 410-213-1020

Wharf Restaurant (Steak/Seafood) 12801 Coastal Hwy.... Ocean City MD 21842 410-250-1001

— Goods and Services —

SHOPPING

Phone Fax

45th Street Village Shopping
45th St & Coastal Hwy .... Ocean City MD 21842 410-524-1110

Gold Coast Mall 11427-A Coastal Hwy ...... Ocean City MD 21842 410-524-9000 524-5520
Web: www.ocean-city.com/gold-coast-mall.htm

Montego Bay Shopping Center
12829 Coastal Hwy................. Ocean City MD 21842 410-250-8130 250-1146

Ocean City Factory Outlets
Rt 50 & Golf Course Rd .... Ocean City MD 21842 410-213-1538
TF: 800-625-6696 ■ *Web:* www.ocfactoryoutlets.com

Ocean City Square Shopping Center
11805 Coastal Hwy.................. Ocean City MD 21842 410-524-2523
Web: www.ocean-city.com/ocsquare.htm

Ocean Plaza Mall 9701 Coastal Hwy........ Ocean City MD 21842 410-723-0805 723-5064

Shantytown Waterfront Shopping Village
Rt 50 & Shantytown Rd.............. Ocean City MD 21842 410-213-0926
Web: www.shantytownvillage.com

BANKS

Phone Fax

Atlantic Bank 4604 Coastal Hwy........... Ocean City MD 21842 410-524-7333 524-1843

Bank of Ocean City 10005 Golf Course Rd.... Ocean City MD 21842 410-213-0173 213-2422

Crestar Bank 5702 Coastal Hwy .... Ocean City MD 21842 410-524-7272 524-1120

NationsBank NA 4401 Coastal Hwy......... Ocean City MD 21842 410-289-6818 289-0235

Peninsula Bank 3409 Coastal Hwy .... Ocean City MD 21842 410-289-3444 289-2431

Susquehanna Bank 9403 Coastal Hwy....... Ocean City MD 21842 410-524-5757 723-2649

Taylor Calvin B Banking Co
14200 Coastal Hwy.................. Ocean City MD 21842 410-250-1405 250-1379

Wilmington Trust FSB 7900 Coastal Hwy..... Ocean City MD 21842 410-219-3061 219-3090
TF Cust Svc: 800-523-2378*

Ocean City (Cont'd)

BUSINESS SERVICES

	Phone		Phone
Airborne Express	800-247-2676	Kinko's	410-546-1991
Beach Copy	410-250-0255	Mailers Plus	410-213-7420
Coastal Printing	410-289-3329	Post Office	410-289-7819
Federal Express	800-463-3339	UPS	800-742-5877

— Media —

PUBLICATIONS

				Phone	Fax
Maryland Beachcomber PO Box 479	Ocean City	MD	21842	410-289-6834	289-6838*
*Fax: News Rm					
Ocean City Today 5901 Coastal Hwy Suite C	Ocean City	MD	21842	410-723-6397	723-6511
Oceana Magazine 146th St & Jarvis Ave	Ocean City	MD	21842	410-250-5512	539-6815
TF: 888-539-7717 ■ *Web:* www.oceanamagazine.com ■ *E-mail:* oceana@beachin.net					

TELEVISION

				Phone	Fax
WBOC-TV Ch 16 (CBS) 1729 N Salisbury Blvd	Salisbury	MD	21801	410-749-1111	742-5190
Web: www.wboc.com ■ *E-mail:* wboc@wboc.com					
WCPB-TV Ch 9 (PBS) 11767 Owings Mills Blvd	Owings Mills	MD	21117	410-356-5600	581-4338
WJZ-TV Ch 13 (CBS) 3725 Malden Ave TV Hill	Baltimore	MD	21211	410-466-0013	578-7502
Web: www.wjz.com/ ■ *E-mail:* rldalld@wjz.groupw.wec.com					
WMAR-TV Ch 2 (ABC) 6400 York Rd	Baltimore	MD	21212	410-377-2222	377-0493
Web: www.insidebaltimore.com/wmar/ ■ *E-mail:* wmartv2@aol.com					
WMDT-TV Ch 47 (ABC/NBC) 202 Downtown Plaza	Salisbury	MD	21801	410-742-4747	742-5767
Web: www.wmdt.com ■ *E-mail:* letters@wmdt.com					
WTTG-TV Ch 5 (Fox) 5151 Wisconsin Ave NW	Washington	DC	20016	202-244-5151	244-1745

RADIO

				Phone	Fax
WICO-AM 1320 kHz (N/T) 919 Ellegood St	Salisbury	MD	21801	410-742-3212	548-1543
Web: www.radiocenter.com/wico_index.htm ■ *E-mail:* wico@radiocenter.com					
WICO-FM 94.3 MHz (Ctry) 919 Ellegood St	Salisbury	MD	21801	410-742-3212	548-1543
WLBW-FM 92.1 MHz (Oldies) 31455 Winterplace Pkwy	Salisbury	MD	21804	410-742-1923	742-2329
Web: www.delmarvaradio.com/wave.html					
WLVW-FM 105.5 MHz (Oldies) 31455 Winterplace Pkwy	Salisbury	MD	21804	410-742-1923	742-2329
WOSC-FM 95.9 MHz (Rock) 2326 Goddard Pkwy	Salisbury	MD	21801	410-860-2200	860-0599
WQHQ-FM 104.7 MHz (AC) 31455 Winterplace Pkwy	Salisbury	MD	21804	410-742-1923	742-2329
Web: www.delmarvaradio.com/q105fm.html					
WTGM-AM 960 kHz (Sports) 31455 Winterplace Pkwy	Salisbury	MD	21804	410-742-1923	742-2329
Web: www.delmarvaradio.com/am960.html					
WWFG-FM 99.9 MHz (Ctry) 2326 Goddard Pkwy	Salisbury	MD	21801	410-860-2200	860-0599
Web: www.delmarvaradio.com/froggy.html					
WXJN-FM 105.9 MHz (Ctry) 919 Ellegood St	Salisbury	MD	21801	410-742-3212	548-1543
Web: www.radiocenter.com/cat_right.htm ■ *E-mail:* catcountry@radiocenter.com					

— Colleges/Universities —

				Phone	Fax
Salisbury State University 1101 Camden Ave	Salisbury	MD	21801	410-543-6000	543-6068
Web: www.ssu.edu					
Wor-Wic Community College 32000 Campus Dr	Salisbury	MD	21804	410-334-2895	334-2954
Web: www.worwic.cc.md.us					
Wor-Wic Community College Berlin Campus 10452 Old Ocean City Blvd	Berlin	MD	21811	410-641-4134	334-2952

— Hospitals —

				Phone	Fax
Atlantic General Hospital 9733 Healthway Dr	Berlin	MD	21811	410-641-1100	641-9670

— Attractions —

				Phone	Fax
65th Street Slide & Ride Water Park 65th St & Bay	Ocean City	MD	21842	410-524-5270	
Assateague Island National Seashore 7206 National Seashore Ln	Berlin	MD	21811	410-641-1441	
Web: www.nps.gov/asis					
Assateague State Park 7307 Stephen Decatur Hwy	Berlin	MD	21811	410-641-2120	641-3615
Baja Amusements 12639 Ocean Gateway	West Ocean City	MD	21842	410-213-2252	213-1997
Web: www.ocean-city.com/baja.htm					
Calvin B Taylor House Museum 208 N Main St	Berlin	MD	21811	410-641-1019	
Frontier Town Western Theme Park Rt 611	Ocean City	MD	21842	410-289-7877	
Web: www.frontiertown.com					
Furnace Town Old Furnace Rd PO Box 207	Snow Hill	MD	21863	410-632-2032	
Web: www.dol.net/~ebola/Ftown.htm					
Jolly Roger Amusement Park 2901 Coastal Hwy	Ocean City	MD	21842	410-289-4902	289-0450
Web: www.jollyrogerpark.com					
Mid-Atlantic Symphony 12806 Old Bridge Rd	West Ocean City	MD	21842	410-213-2806	213-0282
TF: 888-889-0980					
Ocean City Fishing Center Rt 50 & Shantytown Rd	Ocean City	MD	21842	410-213-1121	
TF: 800-322-3065					
Ocean City Jamboree 12600 Marjan Ln & Rt 611	Ocean City	MD	21842	410-213-7581	
Ocean City Life-Saving Station Museum 813 S Boardwalk	Ocean City	MD	21842	410-289-4991	
Web: www.ocmuseum.org ■ *E-mail:* curator@ocmuseum.org					
Ocean City Pier Rides & Amusements 401 S Boardwalk Boardwalk Pier	Ocean City	MD	21842	410-289-3031	289-0450
Web: www.ocean-city.com/pierrides					
Ocean City Town Skate Park 302 St Louis Ave	Ocean City	MD	21842	410-289-2695	
Ocean Gallery World Center 201 N Boardwalk	Ocean City	MD	21842	410-289-5300	
Web: www.oceangallery.com					
Planet Maze & Laser Storm 3305 Coastal Hwy	Ocean City	MD	21842	410-524-4386	723-3866
Pocomoke River State Park 3461 Worcester Hwy	Snow Hill	MD	21863	410-632-2566	
Q-ZAR Entertainment Center 401 S Boardwalk	Ocean City	MD	21842	410-289-2266	289-7946
Web: www.ocean-city.com/q-zar.htm					
Salisbury Zoological Park PO Box 2979	Salisbury	MD	21802	410-548-3188	860-0919
Trimpers Rides & Amusements S 1st St & Boardwalk	Ocean City	MD	21842	410-289-8617	289-2779
Web: www.beach-net.com/trimpers/index.html ■ *E-mail:* trimpers@ce.net					
Wheels Of Yesterday Antique & Classic Cars Museum 12708 Ocean Gateway	Ocean City	MD	21842	410-213-7329	
Worcester County Arts Council 6 Jefferson St	Berlin	MD	21811	410-641-0809	641-3947

SPORTS TEAMS & FACILITIES

				Phone	Fax
Bally's at Ocean Downs 10218 Racetrack Rd	Berlin	MD	21811	410-641-0600	641-2711
Web: www.oceandowns.com ■ *E-mail:* info@oceandowns.com					
Delmarva Shorebirds (baseball) 6400 Hobbs Rd Arthur W Perdue Stadium	Salisbury	MD	21802	410-219-3112	
Web: www.theshorebirds.com					
Eastern Shore Sharks (soccer) 10311 Old Ocean City Blvd	Berlin	MD	21811	410-334-6991	334-6992

— Events —

	Phone
Antiques by the Sea (mid-August)	410-289-3453
Arts Atlantica (early June)	800-626-2326
Barbershop Singers Annual Jamboree (early October)	800-626-2326
Christmas Craft Expo (late October)	410-524-9177
Cruisin' Ocean City (late May)	410-798-6304

Ocean City — Events (Cont'd)

	Phone
Endless Summer Cruisin' (mid-October)	410-798-6304
Fall Fest of Fine Art (late October)	410-524-9177
Fireworks Jubilee (July 4)	800-626-2326
Holiday Shopper's Fair (late November)	410-289-8311
International Auto Show of the Eastern Shore (mid-March)	800-345-1487
Jamboree in the Park (July 4)	410-250-0125
Jesus at the Beach Music & Ministry Festival (late July)	410-289-1296
Labor Day Weekend Arts & Crafts Festival (early September)	410-352-5851
Maryland International Kite Festival (late April)	410-289-7855
Mid-Atlantic Surf Fishing Tournament (early October)	410-213-2042
Nautical & Wildlife Art Festival (mid-January)	410-524-9177
North American Craft Show (mid-January)	410-524-9177
Ocean City Hot Rod & Custom Car Show (early January)	800-626-2326
Ocean City Tuna Tournament (mid-July)	800-322-3065
Oktoberfest (mid-October)	800-626-2326
Quota Club Antique Show (mid-March)	410-289-8311
Saint Patrick's Day Parade & Festival (mid-March)	410-289-6156
Seaside Boat Show (mid-February)	410-641-6301
Slovenian Festival & Polka Beach Party (late June)	410-524-6440
Spring Amateur Golf Classic (mid-April)	410-798-6304
Springfest (early May)	410-289-2800
Springfest Boat Show (early May)	800-322-3065
Sunfest (late September)	410-289-2800
Sunfest Boat Show (late September)	800-322-3065
Sunfest Kite Festival (late September)	410-289-7855
Victorian Christmas (early-late January)	800-523-2888
Ward World Championship Wildfowl Carving Competition (late April)	410-742-4988
White Marlin Open Fishing Tournament (early August)	410-289-9229
White Marlin Parade (early May)	410-289-1413
Winefest on the Beach (early October)	800-626-2326
Winterfest of Lights (mid-late November-late January)	410-289-2800
World of Wheels (early January)	410-798-6304

Massachusetts

Population (1999): 6,175,169 **Area (sq mi): 10,555**

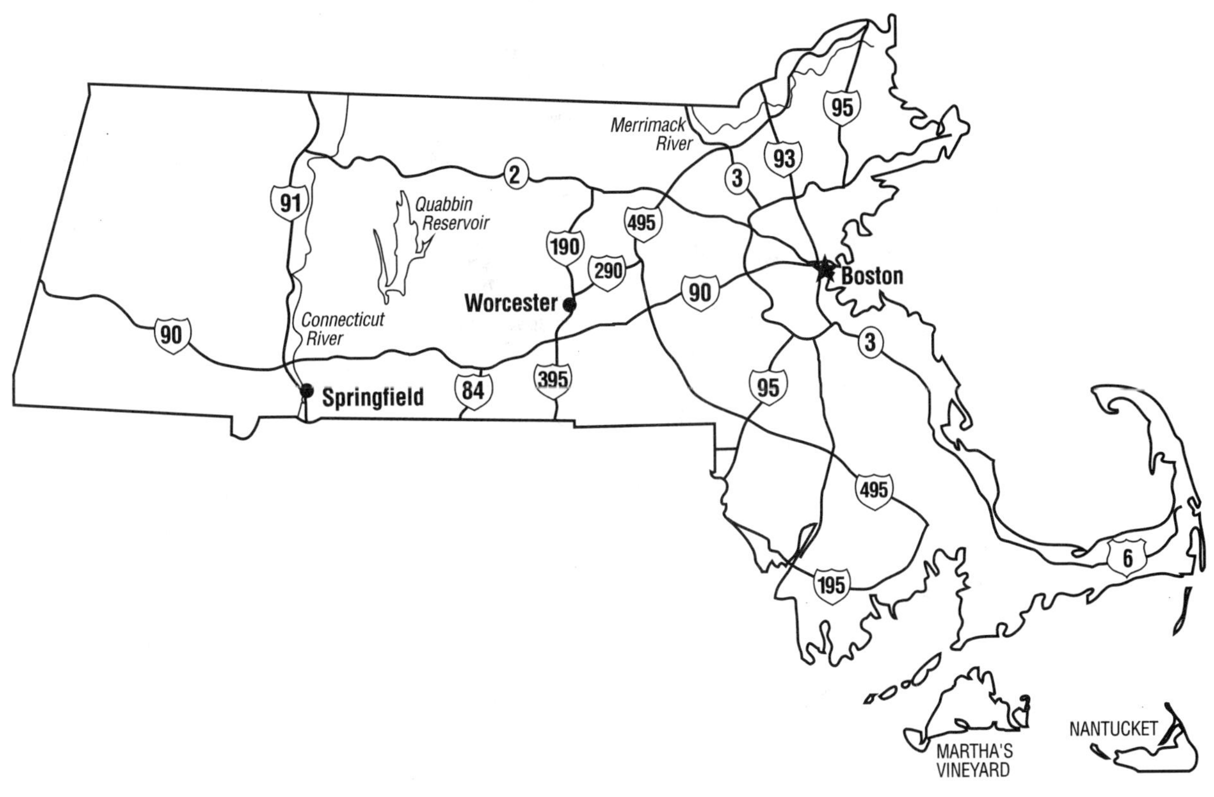

— State Information Sources —

				Phone	Fax
Massachusetts Board of Library Commissioners 648 Beacon St	Boston	MA	02215	617-267-9400	421-9833
Web: www.mlin.lib.ma.us					
Massachusetts Economic Development Dept 1 Ashburton Pl Rm 2101	Boston	MA	02108	617-727-8380	727-4426
Web: www.state.ma.us/econ					
Massachusetts Forests & Parks Div 100 Cambridge St Suite 1905	Boston	MA	02202	617-727-3180	727-9402
Web: www.state.ma.us/dem/forparks.htm					
Massachusetts State Government Information				617-727-2121	
Web: www.state.ma.us					
Massachusetts Travel & Tourism Office 10 Park Plaza State Transportation Bldg Suite 4510	Boston	MA	02116	617-727-3201	973-8525
Web: www.mass-vacation.com ■ *E-mail:* vacationinfo@state.ma.us					
New England Council Inc 250 Boylston St	Boston	MA	02116	617-437-0304	437-6279
E-mail: newenglandcouncil@msn.com					

ON-LINE RESOURCES

FindTheFun.com . . . . . www.findthefun.com
HotList Helper: Eastern Massachusetts Edition . . . . . www.tiac.net/users/dinitto/hlh/maeast
Imbored Massachusetts www.imbored.com/new/rma05.htm
Massachusetts Cities . . . . . dir.yahoo.com/Regional/U_S__States/Massachusetts/Cities
Massachusetts Counties & Regions . . . . . dir.yahoo.com/Regional/U_S__States/Massachusetts/Counties_and_Regions
Massachusetts Scenario . . . . . scenariousa.dstylus.com/ma/indexf.htm
Massachusetts Travel & Tourism Guide . . . . . www.travel-library.com/north_america/usa/massachusetts/index.html
Neighborhoods.net . . . . . www.neighborhoods.net
Net Travel Massachusetts . . . . . www.nettx.com/states/ma.htm
PeekABoo Massachusetts . . . . . www.peekaboo.net/ma
Rough Guide Travel Massachusetts travel.roughguides.com/content/366/index.htm
Search Massachusetts . . . . . www.newengland.com/mamap.html
Travel.org-Massachusetts . . . . . travel.org/massachu.html
Virtual Valley . . . . . virtual-valley.com
Visit Massachusetts . . . . . www.visit-massachusetts.com
Yahoo! Get Local Massachusetts . . . . . dir.yahoo.com/Regional/U_S__States/Massachusetts

— Cities Profiled —

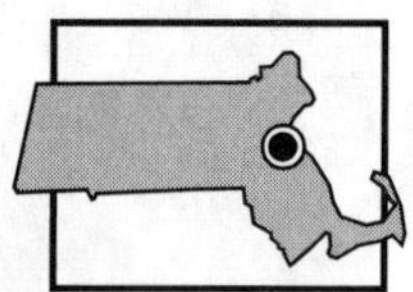

Boston

Boston's Freedom Trail winds throughout the city, beginning at Boston Common and ending in Charlestown at the Bunker Hill Monument. Along the Trail are Paul Revere's home, Old North Church, King's Chapel (the nation's first public school), the USS Constitution ('Old Ironsides'), and the Old South Meeting House, where patriots gathered before launching the Boston Tea Party. Also on the Trail, at the Boston Waterfront, are the Faneuil Hall and Quincy Market areas. Other areas of interest in Boston include Beacon Hill, Copley Square with the John Hancock Observatory, and Harvard University, which is located in the suburb of Cambridge. Boston is also a travel gateway to Nantucket, Martha's Vineyard, and Cape Cod. The Boston Marathon is held in the city each April.

Population	578,364	**Longitude**	71-06-03 W
Area (Land)	48.4 sq mi	**County**	Suffolk
Area (Water)	41.2 sq mi	**Time Zone**	EST
Elevation	20 ft	**Area Code/s**	617, 781
Latitude	42-35-83 N		

— Average Temperatures and Precipitation —

TEMPERATURES

	Jan	Feb	Mar	Apr	May	Jun	Jul	Aug	Sep	Oct	Nov	Dec
High	36	38	46	56	67	76	82	80	73	63	52	40
Low	22	23	31	40	50	59	65	64	57	47	38	27

PRECIPITATION

	Jan	Feb	Mar	Apr	May	Jun	Jul	Aug	Sep	Oct	Nov	Dec
Inches	3.6	3.6	3.7	3.6	3.3	3.1	2.8	3.2	3.1	3.3	4.2	4.0

— Important Phone Numbers —

	Phone		Phone
AAA	781-871-5880	**Medical Referral**	800-488-5959
American Express Travel	617-723-8400	**Poison Control Center**	617-232-2120
Boston By Phone	888-733-2678	**Time/Temp**	617-637-1234
Dental Referral	508-651-7511	**Travelers Aid Society of Boston**	617-542-7286
Emergency	911	**Weather**	617-936-1234
HotelDocs	800-468-3537		

— Information Sources —

Phone *Fax*

Better Business Bureau Serving Eastern Massachusetts Maine & Vermont 20 Park Plaza Suite 820 . . . . . Boston MA 02116 617-426-9000 426-7813
Web: www.bosbbb.org ■ *E-mail:* info@bosbbb.org

Boston City Hall 1 City Hall Plaza . . . . . Boston MA 02201 617-635-4000
Web: www.ci.boston.ma.us

Boston Mayor 1 City Hall Plaza 5th Fl . . . . . Boston MA 02201 617-635-4500 635-4090
Web: www.ci.boston.ma.us/mayor/

Boston Public Library
700 Boylston St Copley Sq. . . . . . Boston MA 02117 617-536-5400 236-4306
Web: www.bpl.org

Boston Redevelopment Authority
1 City Hall Sq. . . . . . Boston MA 02201 617-722-4300 367-5916
Web: www.ci.boston.ma.us/economicdevelopment

Greater Boston Chamber of Commerce
1 Beacon St 4th Fl . . . . . Boston MA 02108 617-227-4500 227-7505
Web: www.gbcc.org ■ *E-mail:* chamber@gbcc.org

Greater Boston Convention & Visitors Bureau
2 Copley Pl Suite 105 . . . . . Boston MA 02116 617-536-4100 424-7664
TF: 888-433-2673 ■ *Web:* www.bostonusa.com

John B Hynes Veterans Memorial Convention Center 900 Boylston St . . . . . Boston MA 02115 617-954-2000 954-2125
TF: 800-845-8800 ■ *Web:* www.mccahome.com

Suffolk County
55 Pemberton Sq Government Ctr. . . . . . Boston MA 02108 617-725-8000 725-8137

On-Line Resources

4Boston.com	www.4boston.com
About.com Guide to Boston: North Suburbs	bostonnorth.about.com
About.com Guide to Boston: South Suburbs	bostonsouth.about.com/local/newenglandus/bostonsouth
Area Guide Boston	boston.areaguides.net
ArtsAround Boston	www.artsaroundboston.com/
Boston Alternative Life	lexicon.psy.tufts.edu/alternative/
Boston Cambridge Best Guide	www.bostonbest.com
Boston City Central	www.enn2.com/ccbos.htm
Boston City Page	boston.thelinks.com/
Boston CityWomen	www.citywomen.com/boswomen.htm
Boston Graphic City Guide	www.futurecast.com/gcg/boston.htm
Boston Historic Tours of America	www.historictours.com/boston/index.htm
Boston Insider	www.theinsider.com/boston
Boston Phoenix	www.bostonphoenix.com
Boston Restaurant Guide	www.bostondine.com
Boston Web	www.bweb.com
Boston.com	www.boston.com
Boulevards Boston	www.boulevards.com/cities/boston.html
Bradmans.com Boston	www.bradmans.com/scripts/display_city.cgi?city=232
City Insights Boston	www.cityinsights.com/boston.htm
City Knowledge Boston	www.cityknowledge.com/ma_boston.htm
CityBuzz Boston	www.citybuzz.com/
CitySearch Boston	boston.citysearch.com
CityTravelGuide.com Boston	www.citytravelguide.com/boston.htm
CuisineNet Boston	www.cuisinenet.com/restaurant/boston/index.shtml
DigitalCity Boston	home.digitalcity.com/boston
Excite.com Boston City Guide	www.excite.com/travel/countries/united_states/massachusetts/boston
HotelGuide Boston	boston.hotelguide.net
Open World City Guides Boston	www.worldexecutive.com/cityguides/boston/
Rough Guide Travel Boston	travel.roughguides.com/content/4603/
Time Out Boston	www.timeout.com/boston/
Tonite in Boston	www.2nite.com
Underground Guide to Boston	www.newbury.com/guide.htm
Virtual Voyages Boston	www.virtualvoyages.com/usa/ma/boston/boston.sht
Virtually Boston	www.vboston.com/
WeekendEvents.com Boston	www.weekendevents.com/BOSTON/boston.html
Yahoo! Boston	boston.yahoo.com

— Transportation Services —

AIRPORTS

■ **Logan International Airport (BOS)**

	Phone
3 miles NE of downtown (approx 10 minutes)	617-561-1818

Web: www.massport.com/logan

Airport Transportation

	Phone
Back Bay Coach $7.50 fare to downtown	617-728-8686
City Transportation $7.50 fare to downtown	617-561-9000
MBTA Train $.85 fare to downtown	617-722-3200
Taxi $12-14 fare to downtown	617-734-5000

Commercial Airlines

	Phone		Phone
Aer Lingus	800-474-7424	**MetroJet**	888-638-7653
Air Canada	800-776-3000	**Midway**	800-446-4392
Alitalia	800-223-5730	**Northwest**	800-225-2525
American	800-433-7300	**Pan Am**	800-359-7262
American Eagle	800-433-7300	**SwissAir**	800-221-4750
British Airways	800-247-9297	**TAP Air Portugal**	800-221-7370
Continental	800-525-0280	**TWA**	800-221-2000
Delta	617-567-4100	**United**	800-241-6522
Eastwind	888-327-8946	**US Airways**	800-428-4322
Lufthansa	800-645-3880		

Charter Airlines

	Phone		Phone
Charter Fleet International	800-355-5387	**Knighthawk Express**	800-544-4295
Jet Aviation	800-736-8538		

Boston (Cont'd)

CAR RENTALS

	Phone		Phone
Alamo	617-561-4100	**Enterprise**	781-289-1683
Avis	617-561-3500	**Hertz**	617-569-7272
Budget	617-497-1800	**National**	617-569-6700
Dollar	617-634-0006	**Thrifty**	617-634-7350

LIMO/TAXI

	Phone		Phone
Boston Beats Limo	617-267-5856	**Coopers Limousine Service**	617-482-1000
Boston Cab	617-536-5010	**Independent Taxi**	617-426-8700
Carey Limousine	617-623-8700	**Luxury Limousine**	617-742-2223
Checker Cab	617-536-7000	**Red Cab**	617-734-5000
City Cat Limousine	617-364-8388	**Town Taxi**	617-536-5000
Commonwealth Limousine	617-787-5575		

MASS TRANSIT

	Phone
MBTA Bus $.60 Base fare	617-722-3200
MBTA Train $.85 Base fare	617-722-3200

RAIL/BUS

				Phone
Amtrak South Station Atlantic Ave & Summer St *TF:* 800-872-7245	Boston	MA	02210	617-345-7591
Greyhound Bus Station 700 Atlantic Ave *TF:* 800-231-2222	Boston	MA	02110	617-526-1808

— Accommodations —

HOTEL RESERVATION SERVICES

	Phone	Fax
ABC: Accommodations of Boston & Cambridge *TF:* 800-253-5542	617-491-0274	547-5478
Accommodations Express *TF:* 800-444-7666 ■ *Web:* www.accommodationsxpress.com ■ *E-mail:* accomexp@acy.digex.net	609-391-2100	525-0111
B & B Agency of Boston *TF:* 800-248-9262 ■ *Web:* www.boston-bnbagency.com	617-720-3540	523-5761
Bed & Breakfast Assoc Bay Colony Ltd **Fax Area Code:* 781 ■ *Web:* www.bnbboston.com/ ■ *E-mail:* info@bnbboston.com	888-486-6018	449-5958*
Bed & Breakfast-Cambridge & Greater Boston *TF:* 800-888-0178 ■ *E-mail:* bandb@gis.net	617-262-1155	227-0021
Bed & Breakfast Reservations *TF:* 800-832-2632 ■ *Web:* www.bbreserve.com/ ■ *E-mail:* bnbinc@ix.netcom.com	617-964-1606	332-8572
Boston & New England Reservation Service *TF:* 800-754-7470	508-393-7470	393-9199
Central Reservation Service *TF:* 800-548-3311 ■ *Web:* www.reservation-services.com ■ *E-mail:* cenresbos@aol.com	407-740-6442	740-8222
Citywide Reservation Services *TF:* 800-468-3593 ■ *Web:* www.cityres.com	617-267-7424	267-9408
Hotel Reservations Network Inc *TF Sales:* 800-964-6835 ■ *Web:* www.hoteldiscount.com	214-361-7311	361-7299
Quikbook *TF:* 800-789-9887 ■ *Web:* www.quikbook.com	212-532-1660	532-1556
RMC Travel Centre *TF:* 800-782-2674	212-754-6560	754-6571
Taylor-Made Reservations *TF:* 800-848-8848 ■ *Web:* www.enjoy-newport.com	401-848-0300	848-0301

HOTELS, MOTELS, RESORTS

				Phone	Fax
Back Bay Hilton Hotel 40 Dalton St *TF:* 800-445-8667	Boston	MA	02115	617-236-1100	867-6104
Battle Green Inn 1720 Massachusetts Ave *TF:* 800-343-0235	Lexington	MA	02420	781-862-6100	861-9485
Best Western Boston-Inn at Children's 342 Longwood Ave *TF:* 800-468-2378	Boston	MA	02115	617-731-4700	731-6273
Best Western Terrace Inn 1650 Commonwealth Ave *TF:* 800-242-8377	Boston	MA	02135	617-566-6260	731-3543
Boston Harbor Hotel 70 Rowes Wharf *TF:* 800-752-7077	Boston	MA	02110	617-439-7000	330-9450
Boston Marriott Copley Place 110 Huntington Ave *TF:* 800-228-9290 ■ *Web:* marriotthotels.com/BOSCO	Boston	MA	02116	617-236-5800	236-5885
Boston Milner Hotel 78 Charles St S *TF:* 800-453-1731	Boston	MA	02116	617-426-6220	350-0360
Boston Park Plaza Hotel & Towers 64 Arlington St *TF:* 800-225-2008	Boston	MA	02116	617-426-2000	426-5545
Buckminster The 645 Beacon St *TF:* 800-727-2825	Boston	MA	02115	617-236-7050	262-0068
Chandler Inn Hotel 26 Chandler St *TF:* 800-842-3450 ■ *Web:* www.chandlerinn.com	Boston	MA	02116	617-482-3450	542-3428
Charles Hotel 1 Bennett St *TF:* 800-882-1818	Cambridge	MA	02138	617-864-1200	864-5715
Colonnade Hotel 120 Huntington Ave *TF:* 800-962-3030	Boston	MA	02116	617-424-7000	424-1717
Copley Square Hotel 47 Huntington Ave *TF:* 800-225-7062	Boston	MA	02116	617-536-9000	267-3547
Days Inn Boston on the Charles 1234 Soldiers Field Rd *TF:* 800-325-2525	Boston	MA	02135	617-254-1234	254-1234
Doubletree Guest Suites 400 Soldiers Field Rd *TF:* 800-222-8733 ■ *Web:* www.doubletreehotels.com/DoubleT/Hotel41/57/57Main.htm	Boston	MA	02134	617-783-0090	783-0897
Eliot Hotel Suites 370 Commonwealth Ave *TF:* 800-443-5468 ■ *Web:* www.eliothotel.com ■ *E-mail:* hoteleliot@aol.com	Boston	MA	02115	617-267-1607	536-9114
Fairmont Copley Plaza Hotel 138 St James Ave *TF:* 800-795-3906 ■ *Web:* www.fairmont.com/boston.html ■ *E-mail:* boston@fairmont.com	Boston	MA	02116	617-267-5300	375-9648
Fifteen Beacon Hotel 15 Beacon St *Web:* www.xvbeacon.com	Boston	MA	02108	617-670-1500	670-2525
Four Seasons Hotel 200 Boylston St *TF:* 800-332-3442 ■ *Web:* www.fourseasons.com/locations/Boston	Boston	MA	02116	617-338-4400	423-0154
Harvard Square Hotel 110 Mt Auburn St *TF:* 800-458-5886	Cambridge	MA	02138	617-864-5200	864-2409
Hawthorne Hotel 18 Washington Sq W *TF:* 800-729-7829	Salem	MA	01970	978-744-4080	745-9842
Hilton Dedham Place 25 Allied Dr *TF:* 800-445-8667 ■ *Web:* www.hilton.com/hotels/DDHDHHF	Dedham	MA	02026	781-329-7900	329-5552
Holiday Inn Boston-Logan Airport 225 McClellan Hwy *TF:* 800-465-4329 ■ *Web:* www.basshotels.com/holiday-inn/?_franchisee=BOSAP ■ *E-mail:* bdama@msn.com	East Boston	MA	02128	617-569-5250	569-5159
Holiday Inn Brookline 1200 Beacon St *TF:* 800-465-4329 ■ *Web:* www.basshotels.com/holiday-inn/?_franchisee=BKLMA ■ *E-mail:* brk_sales@fine-hotels.com	Brookline	MA	02446	617-277-1200	734-6991
Holiday Inn Express 69 Boston St *TF:* 800-465-4329	Boston	MA	02125	617-288-3030	265-6543
Holiday Inn Government Center 5 Blossom St *TF:* 800-465-4329 ■ *Web:* www.basshotels.com/holiday-inn/?_franchisee=BOSGC ■ *E-mail:* his-boston@bristolhotels.com	Boston	MA	02114	617-742-7630	742-4192
Howard Johnson Hotel Kenmore Square 575 Commonwealth Ave *TF:* 800-654-2000	Boston	MA	02215	617-267-3100	424-1045
Howard Johnson Lodge 1271 Boylston St *TF:* 800-654-2000	Boston	MA	02215	617-267-8300	267-2763
Hyatt Harborside 101 Harborside Dr *TF:* 800-233-1234 ■ *Web:* www.hyatt.com/usa/boston/hotels/hotel_bosha.html	Boston	MA	02128	617-568-1234	567-8856
Hyatt Regency Cambridge 575 Memorial Dr *TF:* 800-233-1234 ■ *Web:* www.hyatt.com/usa/cambridge/hotels/hotel_bosrc.html	Cambridge	MA	02139	617-492-1234	491-6906
John Hancock Conference Center 40 Trinity Pl	Boston	MA	02116	617-572-7700	572-7709
Kimball's By the Sea Hotel 124 Elm St *TF:* 800-252-5287 ■ *Web:* www.kimballsbythesea.com	Cohasset	MA	02025	781-383-6650	383-2872
Le Meridien Boston 250 Franklin St *TF:* 800-543-4300	Boston	MA	02110	617-451-1900	423-2844
Lenox Hotel 710 Boylston St *TF:* 800-225-7676 ■ *Web:* www.lenoxhotel.com	Boston	MA	02116	617-536-5300	267-1237
Logan Airport Ramada Hotel 75 Service Rd *TF:* 800-272-6232	East Boston	MA	02128	617-569-9300	569-3981
Marriott Custom House 3 McKinley Sq *TF:* 800-228-9290	Boston	MA	02109	617-310-6300	310-6301
Marriott Hotel Cambridge 2 Cambridge Ctr *TF:* 800-228-9290 ■ *Web:* marriotthotels.com/BOSCB	Cambridge	MA	02142	617-494-6600	494-0036

Boston — Hotels, Motels, Resorts (Cont'd)

Name / Address	City	State	Zip	Phone	Fax
Marriott Hotel Long Wharf 296 State St *TF:* 800-228-9290 ■ *Web:* marriotthotels.com/BOSLW	Boston	MA	02109	617-227-0800	227-2867
Marriott Newton 2345 Commonwealth Ave. *TF:* 800-228-9290 ■ *Web:* marriotthotels.com/BOSNT/	Newton	MA	02466	617-969-1000	527-6914
Midtown Hotel 220 Huntington Ave. *TF:* 800-343-1177	Boston	MA	02115	617-262-1000	262-8739
Newbury Guest House 261 Newbury St. *TF:* 800-437-7668	Boston	MA	02116	617-437-7666	262-4243
Omni Parker House 60 School St *TF:* 800-843-6664	Boston	MA	02108	617-227-8600	742-5729
Quality Inn King's Grant Rt 128 N Trask Ln. *TF:* 800-782-7841	Danvers	MA	01923	978-774-6800	774-6502
Radisson Hotel 200 Stuart St. *TF:* 800-333-3333	Boston	MA	02116	617-482-1800	451-2750
Ramada Hotel 311 Lowell St *TF:* 800-272-6232	Andover	MA	01810	978-475-5400	470-1108
Regal Bostonian Hotel 40 N St Faneuil Hall Marketplace *TF:* 800-222-8888	Boston	MA	02109	617-523-3600	523-2454
Renaissance Bedford Hotel 44 Middlesex Tpke *TF:* 800-468-3571	Bedford	MA	01730	781-275-5500	275-8956
Ritz-Carlton Boston 15 Arlington St. *TF:* 800-241-3333 ■ *Web:* www.ritzcarlton.com/location/NorthAmerica/Boston/main.htm	Boston	MA	02117	617-536-5700	536-1335
Royal Sonesta Hotel Cambridge 5 Cambridge Pkwy *TF:* 800-766-3782 ■ *Web:* www.sonesta.com	Cambridge	MA	02142	617-491-3600	806-4232
Seaport Hotel at World Trade Center 1 Seaport Ln *TF:* 888-982-4683 ■ *Web:* www.seaporthotel.com	Boston	MA	02210	617-385-4000	385-5090
Seaward Inn 44 Marmion Way *TF:* 800-648-7733 ■ *Web:* www.seawardinn.com ■ *E-mail:* info@seawardinn.com	Rockport	MA	01966	978-546-3471	546-7661
Shawmut Inn 280 Friend St *TF:* 800-350-7784	Boston	MA	02114	617-720-5544	723-7784
Sheraton Boston Hotel & Towers 39 Dalton St. *TF:* 800-325-3535	Boston	MA	02199	617-236-2000	236-1702
Sheraton Commander Hotel 16 Garden St. *TF:* 800-325-3535	Cambridge	MA	02138	617-547-4800	868-8322
Sheraton Needham Hotel 100 Cabot St. *TF:* 800-325-3535 ■ *Web:* www.sheraton.com/cgi/t3.cgi/property.taf?prop=015	Needham	MA	02494	781-444-1110	449-3945
Sheraton Newton Hotel 320 Washington St. *TF:* 800-325-3535 ■ *Web:* www.sheratonnyc.com	Newton	MA	02458	617-969-3010	244-5894
Sheraton Tara Inn 727 Marrett Rd *TF:* 800-325-3535	Lexington	MA	02421	781-862-8700	863-0404
Susse Chalet 800-900 Morrissey Blvd *TF:* 800-258-1980 ■ *Web:* www.bostonhotel.com	Boston	MA	02122	617-287-9100	265-9287
Swissotel 1 Avenue de Lafayette *TF:* 800-621-9200 ■ *Web:* www.swissotel.com	Boston	MA	02111	617-451-2600	451-0054
Tremont House Hotel 275 Tremont St. *TF:* 800-331-9998	Boston	MA	02116	617-426-1400	482-6730
Westford Regency Inn & Conference Center 219 Littleton Rd *TF:* 800-543-7801	Westford	MA	01886	978-692-8200	692-7403
Westin Hotel Copley Place 10 Huntington Ave. *TF:* 800-937-8461	Boston	MA	02116	617-262-9600	424-7483

— Restaurants —

Name / Address	City	State	Zip	Phone
Ambrosia on Huntington (French) 116 Huntington Ave.	Boston	MA	02116	617-247-2400
Anthony's Pier 4 (Seafood) 140 Northern Ave Pier 4	Boston	MA	02210	617-482-6262
Atasca (Portuguese) 279-A Broadway	Cambridge	MA	02139	617-354-4355
Aujourd'hui (Continental) 200 Boylston St	Boston	MA	02116	617-451-1392
Bangkok Blue (Thai) 651 Boylston St	Boston	MA	02116	617-266-1010
Bay Tower Room (Continental) 60 State St.	Boston	MA	02109	617-723-1666
Biba (American) 272 Boylston St.	Boston	MA	02116	617-426-7878
Blue Room (American) 1 Kendall Sq	Cambridge	MA	02139	617-494-9034
Boodle's (American) 40 Dalton St	Boston	MA	02115	617-266-3537
Boston Chart House (Steak/Seafood) 60 Long Wharf	Boston	MA	02110	617-227-1576
Brew Moon (American) 115 Stuart St. *Web:* www.brewmoon.com	Boston	MA	02115	617-523-6467
Bristol Lounge (American) 200 Boylston St.	Boston	MA	02116	617-338-4400
Cafe Budapest (Hungarian) 90 Exeter St.	Boston	MA	02116	617-734-3388
Cafe Fleuri (American) 250 Franklin St.	Boston	MA	02110	617-451-1900
Cafe Suisse (American) 1 Lafayette Ave	Boston	MA	02111	617-451-2600
Capital Grille (Steak/Seafood) 359 Newbury St.	Boston	MA	02115	617-262-8900
Centre Street Cafe (International) 669 Centre St	Boston	MA	02130	617-524-9217
Chateau Restaurant (Italian) 195 School St	Waltham	MA	02451	781-894-3339
Cheers Bull & Finch Pub (American) 84 Beacon St	Boston	MA	02108	617-227-9600
China Pearl (Chinese) 9 Tyler St	Boston	MA	02111	617-426-4338
Ciao Bella Cafe & Restaurant (Italian) 242 Newbury St. *Web:* www.concierge.org/ciaobella/	Boston	MA	02116	617-536-2626
Clio (French) 370 A Commonwealth Ave	Boston	MA	02215	617-536-7200
Davio's (Italian) 269 Newbury St.	Boston	MA	02116	617-262-4810
Durgin-Park (American) 340 N Market St *Web:* www.durginpark.com	Boston	MA	02109	617-227-2038
East Coast Grill & Raw Bar (Seafood) 1271 Cambridge St. *Web:* www.eastcoastgrill.com	Cambridge	MA	02114	617-491-6568
Elephant Walk (Cambodian/French) 900 Beacon St	Boston	MA	02215	617-247-1500
Emporio Armani Cafe (Italian) 214 Newbury St.	Boston	MA	02116	617-437-0909
Galeria Italiana (Italian) 177 Tremont St	Boston	MA	02111	617-423-2092
Ginza (Japanese) 16 Hudson St.	Boston	MA	02111	617-338-2261
Green Dragon Tavern (Irish) 11 Marshall St	Boston	MA	02108	617-367-0055
Grill 23 & Bar (Steak/Seafood) 161 Berkeley St.	Boston	MA	02116	617-542-2255
Hamersley's Bistro (French) 553 Tremont St.	Boston	MA	02116	617-423-2700
Hampshire House (American) 84 Beacon St	Boston	MA	02108	617-227-9600
Hilltop Steak House (American) 855 Broadway	Saugus	MA	01906	781-233-7700
Icarus (New American) 3 Appleton St.	Boston	MA	02116	617-426-1790
Il Panino (Italian) 295 Franklin St	Boston	MA	02110	617-338-1000
Jabob Wirth's (German) 31-37 Stuart St.	Boston	MA	02116	617-338-8586
Joe's American Bar & Grill (American) 279 Dartmouth St	Boston	MA	02116	617-536-4200
Julien (French) 250 Franklin St	Boston	MA	02110	617-451-1900
Kowloon (Chinese/Thai) 948 Broadway	Saugus	MA	01906	781-233-0077
L'Espalier (French) 30 Gloucester St	Boston	MA	02115	617-262-3023
Lala Rokh (Persian) 97 Mt Vernon St.	Boston	MA	02108	617-720-5511
Legal Seafoods (Seafood) 35 Columbus Ave.	Boston	MA	02116	617-426-4444
Locke-Ober (Continental) 3 Winter Pl	Boston	MA	02108	617-542-1340
Maison Robert (French) 45 School St.	Boston	MA	02108	617-227-3370
Mamma Maria's (Italian) 3 North Sq	Boston	MA	02113	617-523-0077
Mercury Bar (Mediterranean) 116 Boylston St.	Boston	MA	02166	617-482-7799
Mistral (New American) 223 Columbus Ave	Boston	MA	02116	617-867-9300
Mr Dooley's Boston Tavern (Irish) 77 Broad St	Boston	MA	02109	617-338-5656
New Shanghai (Chinese) 21 Hudson St	Boston	MA	02111	617-338-6688
No Name Restaurant (Seafood) 17 Fish Pier	Boston	MA	02110	617-338-7539
Oak Room (Steak) 138 St James Ave	Boston	MA	02116	617-267-5300
Olives (Mediterranean) 10 City Sq	Boston	MA	02129	617-242-1999
Omonia (Greek) 75 S Charles St	Boston	MA	02116	617-426-4310
Parish Cafe (American) 361 Boylston St.	Boston	MA	02116	617-247-4777
Parker's Restuarant (New American) 60 School St	Boston	MA	02108	617-227-8600
Piccola Venezia (Italian) 263 Hanover St	Boston	MA	02113	617-523-3888
Pignoli (Italian) 79 Park Plaza	Boston	MA	02116	617-338-7500
Red Raven's Love Noodle (International) 75 Congress St	Salem	MA	01970	978-745-8558
Rialto (International) 1 Bennett St	Cambridge	MA	02138	617-661-5050
Ristorante Toscano (Italian) 47 Charles St	Boston	MA	02114	617-723-4090
Ritz-Carlton Dining Room (French) 15 Arlington St	Boston	MA	02116	617-536-5700
Rowes Wharf (Seafood) 70 Rowes Wharf	Boston	MA	02110	617-439-7000
Salamander (Asian) 1 Athenaeum St *Web:* www.salamander-restaurant.com	Boston	MA	02142	617-225-2121
Salts Restaurant (European) 798 Main St.	Cambridge	MA	02139	617-876-8444
Seasons (New American) Faneuil Hall Marketplace	Boston	MA	02109	617-523-3600
Sonsie (Continental) 327 Newbury St.	Boston	MA	02115	617-351-2500
Thai House (Thai) 1033 Commonwealth Ave	Boston	MA	02215	617-787-4242
Upstairs at the Pudding (Continental) 10 Holyoke St	Cambridge	MA	02138	617-864-1933
Wisteria House (Chinese) 264 Newbury St	Boston	MA	02116	617-437-7396
Ye Olde Union Oyster House (Seafood) 41 Union St	Boston	MA	02108	617-227-2750

— Goods and Services —

SHOPPING

Name / Address	City	State	Zip	Phone	Fax
Atrium Mall 300 Boylston St	Chestnut Hill	MA	02167	617-527-1400	969-7438
Bloomingdale's 175 Boylston St. **Fax:* Cust Svc	Chestnut Hill	MA	02167	617-630-6000	630-6028*
CambridgeSide Galleria 1st St.	Cambridge	MA	02149	617-621-8666	621-6078
Charles Street Beacon Hill	Boston	MA	02116		
Copley Place 2 Copley Pl Suite 100	Boston	MA	02116	617-262-6600	369-5002
Dedham Mall 300 Providence Hwy	Dedham	MA	02026	781-329-1210	329-0513
Downtown Crossing 59 Temple Pl.	Boston	MA	02111	617-482-2139	482-1932
Faneuil Hall Marketplace 4 S Market Bldg *Web:* www.faneuilhallmarketplace.com	Boston	MA	02109	617-523-1300	523-1779
Filene's Co 426 Washington St *Web:* www.mayco.com/may/fi_home.html	Boston	MA	02108	617-357-2978	357-2996
Hanover Mall 1775 Washington St *Web:* www.hanovermall.com	Hanover	MA	02339	781-826-4392	826-1575
Harvard Co-op Society 1400 Massachusetts Ave *TF:* 800-242-1882 ■ *Web:* www.thecoop.com	Cambridge	MA	02238	617-499-2000	499-2016
Liberty Tree Mall 100 Independence Way	Danvers	MA	01923	978-777-0794	777-9857
Macy's 450 Washington St.	Boston	MA	02111	617-357-3000	357-3102
Mall at Chestnut Hill 199 Boylston St.	Chestnut Hill	MA	02167	617-965-3037	

Boston — Shopping (Cont'd)

				Phone	Fax
North Shore Mall Rts 128 & 114	Peabody	MA	01960	978-531-3440	532-9115
Prudential Center Shops 800 Boylston St	Boston	MA	02199	800-746-7778	
Web: www.prudentialcenter.com					
Quincy Market betw Chatham & Clinton Sts	Boston	MA	02109	617-338-2323	
South Shore Plaza 250 Granite St	Braintree	MA	02184	781-843-8200	843-4708
Square One Mall 1277 Broadway	Saugus	MA	01906	781-233-8787	231-9787

BANKS

				Phone	Fax
Bank of Boston 460 W Broadway	Boston	MA	02127	617-434-5873	268-0635
TF Cust Svc: 800-788-5000*					
BankBoston NA 100 Federal St	Boston	MA	02110	617-434-2200	434-1632*
**Fax:* Mail Rm					
Boston Safe Deposit & Trust Co 1 Boston Pl	Boston	MA	02108	617-722-7000	248-3132*
**Fax:* Sales					
Citizens Bank of Massachusetts 28 State St	Boston	MA	02109	617-725-5900	734-0722
TF: 800-922-9999					
Eastern Bank 101 Federal St	Boston	MA	02110	617-345-0441	345-0441
Web: www.easternbank.com					
Fleet National Bank 1 Federal St	Boston	MA	02211	800-841-4000	
USTrust Bank 40 Court St	Boston	MA	02108	617-726-7000	723-9414
Web: www.ustrustboston.com					

BUSINESS SERVICES

	Phone		Phone
Accountemps	617-951-4000	**Kinko's**	617-262-6188
Airborne Express	800-247-2676	**Mail Boxes Etc**	617-437-9303
American Personnel Service	617-350-0080	**Manpower Temporary Services**	617-443-4100
Boston Bicycle Couriers	617-426-7575	**Middlesex Courier Service**	781-272-0000
Choice Courier Systems	617-868-1425	**Olsten Staffing Services**	617-523-5030
Corporate Express Delivery Systems	617-770-9800	**Post Office**	617-654-5326
DHL Worldwide Express	800-225-5345	**Sir Speedy Printing**	617-267-9711
Federal Express	800-463-3339	**Skill Bureau**	617-423-2986
Kelly Services	617-482-8833	**UPS**	800-742-5877

— Media —

PUBLICATIONS

				Phone	Fax
Boston Business Journal 200 High St	Boston	MA	02110	617-330-1000	330-1016
Web: www.amcity.com/boston/index.html					
Boston Globe‡ PO Box 2378	Boston	MA	02107	617-929-2000	929-3192
Web: www.globe.com					
Boston Herald‡ PO Box 2096	Boston	MA	02106	617-426-3000	542-1315
Web: www.bostonherald.com ■ *E-mail:* letterstoeditor@bostonherald.com					
Boston Magazine 300 Massachusetts Ave	Boston	MA	02115	617-262-9700	262-4925
Web: www.bostonmagazine.com					

‡Daily newspapers

TELEVISION

				Phone	Fax
WABU-TV Ch 68 (Ind) 1660 Soldiers Field Rd	Boston	MA	02135	617-787-6868	562-4280
Web: www.wabu.com					
WBZ-TV Ch 4 (CBS) 1170 Soldiers Field Rd	Boston	MA	02134	617-787-7000	254-6383
Web: www.wbz.com					
WCVB-TV Ch 5 (ABC) 5 TV Pl	Needham	MA	02492	781-449-0400	449-6681
Web: www.wcvb.com ■ *E-mail:* wcvb@aol.com					
WFXT-TV Ch 25 (Fox) 25 Fox Dr	Dedham	MA	02026	781-326-8825	467-7213
WGBH-TV Ch 2 (PBS) 125 Western Ave	Boston	MA	02134	617-492-2777	787-0714
Web: www.wgbh.org					
WHDH-TV Ch 7 (NBC) 7 Bulfinch Pl	Boston	MA	02114	617-725-0777	723-6117
Web: www.whdh.com ■ *E-mail:* stationmanagement@whdh.com					
WLVI-TV Ch 56 (WB) 75 Morrissey Blvd	Boston	MA	02125	617-265-5656	287-2872
Web: www.wb56.com ■ *E-mail:* wlvitv@tribune.com					
WNDS-TV Ch 50 (Ind) 50 Television Pl	Derry	NH	03038	603-434-8850	434-8627
Web: www.wndsnews.com					
WSBK-TV Ch 38 (UPN) 83 Leo Birmingham Pkwy	Boston	MA	02135	617-783-3838	783-1875
Web: www.paramountstations.com/WSBK ■ *E-mail:* upn38@paramount.com					
WUNI-TV Ch 27 (Uni) 33 4th Ave	Needham	MA	02494	781-433-2727	433-2750

RADIO

				Phone	Fax
WBCN-FM 104.1 MHz (Alt) 1265 Boylston St	Boston	MA	02215	617-266-1111	247-2266
Web: www.wbcn.com					
WBMX-FM 98.5 MHz (AC) 116 Huntington Ave	Boston	MA	02116	617-236-6898	236-6832
WBOS-FM 92.9 MHz (AAA) 55 Morrissey Blvd	Boston	MA	02125	617-822-9600	822-6759
Web: www.wbos.com					
WBUR-FM 90.9 MHz (NPR) 890 Commonwealth Ave	Boston	MA	02215	617-353-2790	353-4747
TF: 800-909-9287 ■ *Web:* www.wbur.org ■ *E-mail:* info@wbur.bu.edu					
WBZ-AM 1030 kHz (N/T) 1170 Soldiers Field Rd	Boston	MA	02134	617-787-7000	787-7060
Web: www.wbz.com					
WCRB-FM 102.5 MHz (Clas) 750 South St	Waltham	MA	02453	781-893-7080	893-0038
Web: www.wcrb.com ■ *E-mail:* wcrb-feedback@utopia.com					
WEEI-AM 850 kHz (Sports) 116 Huntington Ave.	Boston	MA	02116	617-375-8000	375-8905
Web: www.weei.com					
WEGQ-FM 93.7 MHz (CR) 116 Huntington Ave.	Boston	MA	02116	617-375-8900	375-8921
Web: www.eagle937.com					
WFNX-FM 101.7 MHz (Alt) 25 Exchange St	Lynn	MA	01901	781-595-6200	595-3810
Web: fnxradio.com					
WGBH-FM 89.7 MHz (NPR) 125 Western Ave	Boston	MA	02134	617-492-2777	787-0714
Web: www.boston.com/wgbh/radio/ ■ *E-mail:* feedback@wgbh.org					
WILD-AM 1090 kHz (Urban) 90 Warren St	Boston	MA	02119	617-427-2222	427-2677
WJMN-FM 94.5 MHz (CHR) 235 Bear Hill Rd	Waltham	MA	02451	781-290-0009	290-0722
Web: www.jamn.com ■ *E-mail:* jamn@jamn.com					
WKLB-FM 99.5 MHz (Ctry) 55 Morrissey Blvd	Boston	MA	02125	617-822-9600	822-6854
Web: www.wklb.com					
WMJX-FM 106.7 MHz (AC) 55 Morrissey Blvd	Boston	MA	02125	617-822-9600	822-6571
Web: www.magic1067.com					
WODS-FM 103.3 MHz (Oldies) 1170 Soldiers Field Rd	Boston	MA	02134	617-787-7000	787-7524
Web: www.oldies1033.com					
WRKO-AM 680 kHz (N/T) 116 Huntington Ave	Boston	MA	02116	617-236-6800	236-6890
Web: www.wrko.com					
WROR-FM 105.7 MHz (Oldies) 55 Morrissey Blvd.	Boston	MA	02125	617-822-9600	822-6471
Web: www.wror.com					
WSJZ-FM 96.9 MHz (NAC) 55 Morrissey Blvd	Boston	MA	02125	617-822-9600	822-6859
Web: www.smoothjazz969.com ■ *E-mail:* wsjz@aol.com					
WXKS-AM 1430 kHz (Nost) 99 Revere Beach Pkwy	Medford	MA	02155	781-396-1430	391-8345
WXKS-FM 107.9 MHz (CHR) 99 Revere Beach Pkwy	Medford	MA	02155	781-396-1430	391-3064
Web: www.kissfm.com					
WZLX-FM 100.7 MHz (CR) 800 Boylston St Prudential Tower Suite 2450	Boston	MA	02199	617-267-0123	421-9305
Web: www.wzlx.com					

— Colleges/Universities —

				Phone	Fax
Aquinas College at Milton 303 Adams St	Milton	MA	02186	617-696-3100	696-8706
Web: www.aquinas-college.net					
Babson College	Babson Park	MA	02457	781-235-1200	239-4006
Web: www.babson.edu					
Bay State College 122 Commonwealth Ave	Boston	MA	02116	617-236-8000	536-1735
TF: 800-815-3276					
Bentley College 175 Forest St	Waltham	MA	02452	781-891-2000	891-3414
TF Admissions: 800-523-2354 ■ *Web:* www.bentley.edu ■ *E-mail:* moreinfo@bentley.edu					
Berklee College of Music 1140 Boylston St	Boston	MA	02215	617-266-1400	536-2632
TF Admissions: 800-421-0084 ■ *Web:* www.berklee.edu					
Boston Architectural Center 320 Newbury St	Boston	MA	02115	617-536-3170	536-5829
Web: www.the-bac.edu					
Boston College 140 Commonwealth Ave	Chestnut Hill	MA	02467	617-552-8000	552-0798
TF Admissions: 800-860-2522 ■ *Web:* www.bc.edu ■ *E-mail:* admissions@bcvms.bc.edu					
Boston Conservatory of Music Dance & Theater 8 Fenway	Boston	MA	02215	617-536-6340	536-3176
Web: www.bostonconservatory.edu ■ *E-mail:* admissions@bostonconservatory.edu					
Boston University 881 Commonwealth Ave	Boston	MA	02215	617-353-2000	353-9695
Web: web.bu.edu					
Brandeis University PO Box 9110	Waltham	MA	02454	781-736-2000	736-3536
TF Admissions: 800-622-0622 ■ *Web:* www.brandeis.edu ■ *E-mail:* admitme@brandeis.edu					
Bunker Hill Community College 250 New Rutherford Ave	Boston	MA	02129	617-228-2000	228-2082
Web: www.bhcc.state.ma.us					
Curry College 1071 Blue Hill Ave	Milton	MA	02186	617-333-0500	333-2114
TF: 800-669-0686 ■ *Web:* www.curry.edu:8080					

Boston — Colleges/Universities (Cont'd)

				Phone	Fax
Eastern Nazarene College 23 E Elm Ave *TF:* 800-883-6288 ■ *Web:* www.enc.edu	Quincy	MA	02170	617-773-6350	745-3907
Emerson College 100 Beacon St. *Web:* www.emerson.edu ■ *E-mail:* admission@emerson.edu	Boston	MA	02116	617-824-8500	824-8609
Emmanuel College 400 The Fenway *Web:* www.emmanuel.edu	Boston	MA	02215	617-277-9340	735-9801
Endicott College 376 Hale St *TF Admissions:* 800-325-1114 ■ *Web:* www.endicott.edu	Beverly	MA	01915	978-927-0585	927-0084
Fisher College 118 Beacon St *TF:* 800-446-1226 ■ *Web:* www.fisher.edu	Boston	MA	02116	617-236-8800	236-8858
Franklin Institute of Boston 41 Berkeley St *Web:* www.franklin-fib.edu	Boston	MA	02116	617-423-4630	482-3706
Harvard University 1350 Massachusetts Ave Holyoke Ctr *Web:* www.harvard.edu ■ *E-mail:* www-admin@harvard.edu	Cambridge	MA	02138	617-495-1000	495-8821
Hebrew College 43 Hawes St. *Web:* www.hebrewcollege.edu	Brookline	MA	02446	617-232-8710	264-9264
Hellenic College-Holy Cross 50 Goddard Ave	Brookline	MA	02445	617-731-3500	850-1460
Katharine Gibbs School 126 Newbury St. *TF:* 800-675-4557	Boston	MA	02116	617-578-7100	262-2610
Laboure College 2120 Dorchester Ave.	Boston	MA	02124	617-296-8300	296-7947
Lasell College 1844 Commonwealth Ave. *Web:* www.lasell.edu	Newton	MA	02166	617-243-2000	796-4343
Lesley College 29 Everett St *Web:* www.lesley.edu ■ *E-mail:* communic@mail.lesley.edu	Cambridge	MA	02138	617-868-9600	349-8150
Massachusetts Bay Community College 50 Oakland St. *Web:* www.mbcc.mass.edu ■ *E-mail:* mbccinfo@mbcc.mass.edu	Wellesley Hills	MA	02481	781-237-1100	239-1047
Massachusetts College of Art 621 Huntington Ave. *Web:* www.massart.edu ■ *E-mail:* admissions@massart.edu	Boston	MA	02115	617-232-1555	739-9744
Massachusetts College of Pharmacy & Allied Health Sciences 179 Longwood Ave. *TF:* 800-225-5506 ■ *Web:* www.mcp.edu	Boston	MA	02115	617-732-2800	732-2801
Massachusetts Institute of Technology 77 Massachusetts Ave. *Web:* web.mit.edu ■ *E-mail:* admissions@mit.edu	Cambridge	MA	02139	617-253-1000	258-8304
Mount Ida College 777 Dedham St. *TF:* 800-769-7001 ■ *Web:* www.mountida.edu	Newton Center	MA	02459	617-928-4500	928-4760
New England College of Finance 89 South St 1 Lincoln Plaza *TF:* 888-696-6323	Boston	MA	02111	617-951-2350	951-2533
New England Conservatory of Music 290 Huntington Ave. *Web:* www.newenglandconservatory.edu	Boston	MA	02115	617-585-1100	262-0500
Newbury College 129 Fisher Ave *TF Admissions:* 800-639-2879 ■ *Web:* www.newbury.edu ■ *E-mail:* info@newbury.edu	Brookline	MA	02445	617-730-7000	731-9618
Northeastern University 360 Huntington Ave *Web:* www.northeastern.edu	Boston	MA	02115	617-373-2000	373-8780
Pine Manor College 400 Heath St. *TF Admissions:* 800-762-1357 ■ *Web:* www.pmc.edu	Chestnut Hill	MA	02467	617-731-7000	731-7199
Quincy College 34 Coddington St. *Web:* www.quincycollege.com	Quincy	MA	02169	617-984-1600	984-1669
Radcliffe College 10 Garden St *Web:* www.radcliffe.edu	Cambridge	MA	02138	617-495-8601	495-8821
Regis College 235 Wellesley St *TF Admissions:* 800-456-1820 ■ *Web:* www.regiscollege.edu	Weston	MA	02493	781-768-7000	768-7071
Roxbury Community College 1234 Columbus Ave	Roxbury Crossing	MA	02120	617-541-5310	427-5316
Salem State College 352 Lafayette St. *Web:* www.salem-ma.edu	Salem	MA	01970	978-741-6000	542-6893
School of the Museum of Fine Arts 230 Fenway *Web:* www.smfa.edu ■ *E-mail:* smfa_info@flo.org	Boston	MA	02115	617-267-6100	369-3679
Simmons College 300 Fenway *TF:* 800-345-8468 ■ *Web:* www.simmons.edu	Boston	MA	02115	617-521-2000	521-3190
Suffolk University 8 Ashburton Pl *TF:* 800-678-3365 ■ *Web:* www.suffolk.edu ■ *E-mail:* admission@admin.suffolk.edu	Boston	MA	02108	617-573-8000	742-4291
Tufts University *Web:* www.tufts.edu ■ *E-mail:* uadmiss_inquiry@infonet.tufts.edu	Medford	MA	02155	617-628-5000	627-3860
University of Massachusetts Boston 100 Morrissey Blvd Quinn Bldg *Web:* www.umb.edu ■ *E-mail:* adminfo@umbsky.cc.umb.edu	Boston	MA	02125	617-287-5000	287-5999
Wellesley College 106 Central St. *Web:* www.wellesley.edu	Wellesley	MA	02181	781-283-1000	283-3678
Wentworth Institute of Technology 550 Huntington Ave. *TF Admissions:* 800-556-0610 ■ *Web:* www.wit.edu ■ *E-mail:* info@everyware.edu	Boston	MA	02115	617-442-9010	989-4010
Wheelock College 200 The Riverway *TF:* 800-734-5212 ■ *Web:* www.wheelock.edu ■ *E-mail:* undergrad@wheelock.edu	Boston	MA	02215	617-734-5200	566-4453

— Hospitals —

				Phone	Fax
Beth Israel Deaconess Medical Center 330 Brookline Ave. **Fax:* Hum Res ■ *TF:* 800-535-3556 ■ *Web:* www.bih.harvard.edu	Boston	MA	02215	617-667-8000	632-9430*
Beverly Hospital 85 Herrick St	Beverly	MA	01915	978-922-3000	921-7070
Boston Medical Center 1 Boston Medical Ctr Pl. *Web:* www.bmc.org	Boston	MA	02118	617-638-8000	638-6905
Brigham & Women's Hospital 75 Francis St *Web:* www.partners.org/bwh	Boston	MA	02115	617-732-5500	732-7452
Brockton Hospital 680 Centre St. *Web:* www.brocktonhospital.com	Brockton	MA	02302	508-941-7000	941-6100
Carney Hospital 2100 Dorchester Ave	Boston	MA	02124	617-296-4000	296-9513
Children's Hospital 300 Longwood Ave. *Web:* www.childrenshospital.org ■ *E-mail:* famres@a1.tch.harvard.edu	Boston	MA	02115	617-355-6000	355-6434
Franciscan Children's Hospital & Rehabilitation Center 30 Warren St *Web:* www.fch.com ■ *E-mail:* fch@fch.com	Brighton	MA	02135	617-254-3800	254-6842
Good Samaritan Medical Center 235 N Pearl St	Brockton	MA	02301	508-427-3000	427-3010
Lowell General Hospital 295 Varnum Ave *Web:* www.lowellgeneral.org	Lowell	MA	01854	978-937-6000	452-4169
Massachusetts General Hospital 32 Fruit St *Web:* www.mgh.harvard.edu	Boston	MA	02114	617-726-2000	726-2093
MetroWest Medical Center 115 Lincoln St **Fax:* Admitting ■ *Web:* www.mwmc.com ■ *E-mail:* mwmc_mis@mwmc.com	Framingham	MA	01702	508-383-1000	383-1166*
Mount Auburn Hospital 330 Mt Auburn St.	Cambridge	MA	02238	617-492-3500	499-5575
New England Baptist Hospital 125 Parker Hill Ave *TF:* 800-340-6324 ■ *Web:* www.nebh.org	Boston	MA	02120	617-754-5800	754-6397
New England Medical Center 750 Washington St *Web:* www.nemc.org	Boston	MA	02111	617-636-5000	636-5353
Newton-Wellesley Hospital 2014 Washington St *Web:* www.nwh.org	Newton	MA	02462	617-243-6000	243-6630
Saint Elizabeth's Medical Center 736 Cambridge St. *Web:* www.semc.org ■ *E-mail:* shagop@aol.com	Brighton	MA	02135	617-789-3000	789-3154
South Shore Hospital 55 Fogg Rd.	South Weymouth	MA	02190	781-340-8000	331-8947

— Attractions —

				Phone	Fax
Adams National Historical Park 135 Adams St *Web:* www.nps.gov/adam	Quincy	MA	02169	617-773-1177	471-9683
American Jewish Historical Society 2 Thornton Rd *Web:* www.ajhs.org ■ *E-mail:* ajhs@ajhs.org	Waltham	MA	02453	781-891-8110	899-9208
Black Heritage Trail 46 Joy St *Web:* www.nps.gov/boaf/home.htm	Boston	MA	02114	617-742-5415	720-0848
Boston African-American National Historic Site 14 Beacon St Rm 503 *Web:* www.nps.gov/boaf/	Boston	MA	02108	617-742-5415	720-0848
Boston Athenaeum 10 1/2 Beacon St *Web:* www.bostonathenaeum.org	Boston	MA	02108	617-227-0270	227-5266
Boston Ballet 19 Clarendon St *Web:* www.boston.com/bostonballet	Boston	MA	02116	617-695-6950	695-6954
Boston Beer Co 75 Arlington St *TF:* 800-372-1131 ■ *Web:* www.samadams.com ■ *E-mail:* info@samadams.com	Boston	MA	02116	617-368-5000	368-5500
Boston Center for the Arts 539 Tremont St	Boston	MA	02116	617-426-5000	426-5336
Boston Chamber Ensemble 6 Summer St *Web:* www.mit.edu:8001/people/jcb/BCE/	Hyde Park	MA	02136	617-361-5975	364-1944
Boston Conservatory of Music Dance & Theater 8 Fenway *Web:* www.bostonconservatory.edu ■ *E-mail:* admissions@bostonconservatory.edu	Boston	MA	02215	617-536-6340	536-3176
Boston Harbor Cruises 1 Long Wharf	Boston	MA	02110	617-227-4321	723-2011
Boston Harbor Islands National Recreation Area 408 Atlantic Ave Suite 228 *Web:* www.nps.gov/boha/	Boston	MA	02110	617-223-8666	223-8671

Boston — Attractions (Cont'd)

	City	State	Zip	Phone	Fax
Boston Lyric Opera Co 45 Franklin St 4th Fl.	Boston	MA	02110	617-542-4912	542-4913
Web: www.blo.org					
Boston Museum of Fine Arts 465 Huntington Ave.	Boston	MA	02115	617-267-9300	247-6880
Web: www.mfa.org					
Boston National Historical Park Charlestown Navy Yard	Boston	MA	02129	617-242-5601	241-5797
Web: www.nps.gov/bost/					
Boston Pops 301 Massachusetts Ave Symphony Hall	Boston	MA	02115	617-266-1492	638-9367
Web: www.bso.org					
Boston Symphony Hall 301 Massachusetts Ave	Boston	MA	02115	617-266-1492	638-9367
Boston Symphony Orchestra 301 Massachusetts Ave Symphony Hall	Boston	MA	02115	617-266-1200	
Web: www.bso.org					
Boston Tea Party Ship & Museum Congress Street Bridge	Boston	MA	02210	617-338-1773	338-1974
Web: www.historictours.com ■ *E-mail:* bosott@historictours.com					
Bunker Hill Monument Monument Sq	Charlestown	MA	02129	617-242-5641	
Web: www.nps.gov/bost/					
Busch-Reisinger Museum 32 Quincy St Harvard University Art Museums	Cambridge	MA	02138	617-495-9400	496-2359
Web: www.artmuseums.harvard.edu/Busch_Pages/BuschMain.html					
Cape Cod National Seashore 99 Marconi Site Rd.	Wellfleet	MA	02667	508-349-3785	349-9052
Web: www.nps.gov/caco/					
Cheers/Bull & Finch Bar 84 Beacon St	Boston	MA	02108	617-227-9600	723-1898
Web: www.cheersbos.com					
Children's Museum 300 Congress St Museum Wharf	Boston	MA	02210	617-426-6500	426-1944
Web: www.bostonkids.org					
Colonial Theatre 106 Boylston St.	Boston	MA	02116	617-426-9366	482-8899
Web: www.broadwayinboston.com					
Commonwealth Shakespeare Co 17 Harcourt St	Boston	MA	02116	617-624-6780	
Emerson Majestic Theatre 219 Tremont St	Boston	MA	02116	617-824-8000	824-8725
Web: www.maj.org ■ *E-mail:* majestic@emerson.edu					
Faneuil Hall Marketplace 4 S Market Bldg	Boston	MA	02109	617-523-1300	523-1779
Web: www.faneuilhallmarketplace.com					
Fogg Art Museum 32 Quincy St Harvard University	Cambridge	MA	02138	617-495-9400	495-9936
Web: www.artmuseums.harvard.edu/Fogg_Pages/FoggMain.html					
Fort Warren Boston Harbor	Boston	MA	02110	617-727-5290	727-7059
Franklin Park Blue Hill Ave & Columbia Rd	Boston	MA	02118	617-635-4505	
Franklin Park Zoo 1 Franklin Pk Rd.	Boston	MA	02121	617-442-2002	989-2025
Web: www.zoonewengland.com/fpzoo.html					
Frederick Law Olmsted National Historic Site 99 Warren St	Brookline	MA	02245	617-566-1689	232-3964
Web: www.nps.gov/frla/					
Freedom Trail 2 1/2 Miles	Boston	MA	02124	617-536-4100	
Gardner Isabella Stewart Museum 280 The Fenway	Boston	MA	02115	617-566-1401	278-5175
Web: www.boston.com/gardner/					
Gibson House Museum 137 Beacon St	Boston	MA	02116	617-267-6338	
Hancock John Observatory 200 Clarendon St 60th Fl	Boston	MA	02116	617-247-1977	
Handel & Haydn Society 300 Massachusetts Ave Horticultural Hall	Boston	MA	02115	617-262-1815	266-4217
Web: www.handelandhaydn.org ■ *E-mail:* handlhaydn@aol.com					
Harvard University Art Museums 32 Quincy St	Cambridge	MA	02138	617-495-9400	496-2359
Web: www.artmuseums.harvard.edu					
Hayden Charles Planetarium Science Pk	Boston	MA	02114	617-723-2500	589-0362
Web: www.mos.org					
Huntington Theatre Co 264 Huntington Ave Boston University Theatre	Boston	MA	02115	617-266-0800	421-9674
Web: www.bu.edu/huntington/reachus/mail.htm					
John F Kennedy Library & Museum Columbia Point	Boston	MA	02125	617-929-4500	929-4538
Web: www.cs.umb.edu/jfklibrary/index.htm					
John F Kennedy National Historic Site 83 Beals St	Brookline	MA	02146	617-566-7937	730-9884
King's Chapel 64 Beacon St.	Boston	MA	02108	617-227-2155	227-4101
E-mail: kchapel@kings-chapel.org					
Longfellow National Historic Site 105 Brattle St.	Cambridge	MA	02138	617-876-4491	876-6014
Web: www.nps.gov/long/					
Longwood Symphony Orchestra 290 Huntinton Ave Jordan Hall	Boston	MA	02146	617-332-7011	
Web: www.longwoodsymphony.org/					
Lowell National Historical Park 67 Kirk St	Lowell	MA	01852	978-970-5000	275-1762
Web: www.nps.gov/lowe/					
Mass Bay Brewing Co 306 Northern Ave	Boston	MA	02210	617-574-9551	482-9361
Minute Man National Historical Park 174 Liberty St	Concord	MA	01742	978-369-6993	371-2483
Web: www.nps.gov/mima/					
MIT Museum 265 Massachusetts Ave	Cambridge	MA	02139	617-253-4444	253-8994
Web: web.mit.edu/museum					
Mugar OMNI Theater Museum of Science Science Pk	Boston	MA	02114	617-723-2500	
Web: www.mos.org					
Museum of Afro-American Artists 300 Walnut Ave	Boston	MA	02119	617-442-8614	445-5525
Museum of Science Science Pk	Boston	MA	02114	617-589-0100	589-0454
Web: www.mos.org					
New England Aquarium Central Wharf	Boston	MA	02110	617-973-5200	720-5098
Web: www.neaq.org ■ *E-mail:* bwyman@neaq.org					
New England Conservatory of Music 290 Huntington Ave.	Boston	MA	02115	617-585-1100	262-0500
Web: www.newenglandconservatory.edu					
New England Sports Museum 1175 Soldiers Field Rd	Boston	MA	02134	617-787-7678	787-8152
Nichols House Museum 55 Mt Vernon St	Boston	MA	02108	617-227-6993	
Nostalgia Factory 51 N Margin St.	Boston	MA	02113	617-236-8754	720-5587
TF: 800-479-8754 ■ *Web:* www.nostalgia.com					
Old North Church 193 Salem St	Boston	MA	02113	617-523-6676	720-2854
Web: www.oldnorth.com					
Old South Meeting House 310 Washington St	Boston	MA	02108	617-482-6439	
Old Statehouse 206 Washington St.	Boston	MA	02109	617-720-1713	720-3289
Web: www.bostonhistory.org/osh.html					
Old Town Trolley Tours 380 Dorchester Ave	Boston	MA	02127	617-269-7150	
Web: www.historictours.com/boston/bostrolley.htm ■ *E-mail:* bosott@historictours.com					
Paul Revere House 19 North Sq.	Boston	MA	02113	617-523-2338	523-1775
Web: www.paulreverehouse.org					
Peabody Essex Museum E India Sq	Salem	MA	01970	978-745-1876	741-8951
TF: 800-745-4054 ■ *Web:* www.pem.org/ ■ *E-mail:* pem@pem.org					
Peabody Museum of Archaeology & Ethnology 11 Divinity Ave	Cambridge	MA	02138	617-496-1027	495-7535
Web: www.peabody.harvard.edu					
Public Garden Charles, Boylestown, Arlington & Beacon Sts.	Boston	MA	02118	617-635-4505	
Quincy Market betw Chatham & Clinton Sts.	Boston	MA	02109	617-338-2323	
Salem Maritime National Historic Site 193 Derby St	Salem	MA	01970	978-740-1660	740-1685
Web: www.nps.gov/sama/					
Salem Witch Museum 19 1/2 Washington Sq N	Salem	MA	01970	978-744-1692	745-4414
TF: 800-544-1692 ■ *Web:* www.salemwitchmuseum.com					
Samuel Adams Boston Beer Co 30 Germania St.	Boston	MA	02130	617-522-9080	368-5564*
**Fax:* Hum Res ■ *Web:* www.samadams.com					
Saugus Iron Works National Historic Site 244 Central St	Saugus	MA	01906	781-233-0050	231-9012
Web: www.nps.gov/sair/					
Shubert Theatre 265 Tremont St.	Boston	MA	02116	617-482-9393	451-1436
Web: www.boston.com/wangcenter/					
Sports Museum of New England 25 Shattuck St	Lowell	MA	01852	978-452-6775	
Web: www.lowellarea.com/lowellpage/museums.htm#sportsmuseum					
USS Constitution Museum Charlestown Navy Yard Bldg 22	Boston	MA	02129	617-426-1812	242-0496
Web: www.ussconstitutionmuseum.org ■ *E-mail:* info@ussconstitutionmuseum.org					
Wang Center for the Performing Arts 270 Tremont St	Boston	MA	02116	617-482-9393	451-1436
Wilburt Theatre 246 Tremont St.	Boston	MA	02116	617-423-4008	423-3054

SPORTS TEAMS & FACILITIES

	City	State	Zip	Phone	Fax
Boston Bruins 1 Fleet Ctr FleetCenter	Boston	MA	02114	617-624-1900	523-7184
Web: www.bostonbruins.com					
Boston Bulldogs (soccer) 475 Union Ave Bowditch Stadium	Framingham	MA	01702	508-872-8998	872-8822
Web: www.bostonbulldogs.com					
Boston Celtics 1 Fleet Ctr FleetCenter	Boston	MA	02114	617-523-3030	
Web: www.bostonceltics.com					
Boston Red Sox 4 Yawkey Way Fenway Pk	Boston	MA	02215	617-267-9440	236-6797
Web: www.redsox.com					
Boston Renegades (soccer) 175 Union Ave Bowditch Field	Framingham	MA	01702	508-872-8998	870-0884
Brewster Whitecaps (baseball) 1 Boston Pl Suite 3620	Boston	MA	02108	617-720-7870	720-7877

Boston — Sports Teams & Facilities (Cont'd)

				Phone	Fax
Cape Cod Crusaders (soccer) 35 Winter St Suite 101 *Web:* www.capecodcrusaders.com ■ *E-mail:* pgorham@capecodcrusaders.com	Hyannis	MA	02601	508-790-4782	778-8446
Fenway Park 4 Yawkey Way *Web:* www.redsox.com/fenway/index.html	Boston	MA	02215	617-267-9440	236-6797
FleetCenter 1 Fleet Ctr. *Web:* www.fleetcenter.com	Boston	MA	02114	617-624-1050	624-1818
New England Patriots Rt 1 Foxboro Stadium *Web:* www.patriots.com	Foxboro	MA	02035	508-543-1776	
New England Revolution (soccer) 60 Washington St *Web:* www.nerevolution.com	Foxboro	MA	02035	508-543-5001	384-9128
Suffolk Downs 111 Waldemar Ave. *TF:* 800-225-3460 ■ *Web:* www.suffolkdowns.com ■ *E-mail:* sufflkdown@aol.com	East Boston	MA	02128	617-567-3900	567-5140

— Events —

	Phone
Art Festival Newbury Street (early-mid-September)	617-267-2224
Auto Zone World of Wheels (early January)	617-367-3555
Boston Antique & Classic Boat Festival (mid-July)	617-666-8530
Boston Common Tree Lighting (early December)	617-635-4505
Boston Film Festival (mid-September)	781-925-1373
Boston Globe Jazz Festival (mid-June)	617-929-2649
Boston Harborfest (late June-early July)	617-227-1528
Boston International Festival (late October)	781-861-9729
Boston Marathon (mid-April)	617-236-1652
Boston Tea Party Reenactment (mid-December)	617-338-1773
Boston Wine Expo (early February)	617-385-5015
Boston Wine Festival (January-April)	617-330-9355
Cambridge River Festival (early September)	617-349-4380
Caribbean Carnival (mid-late August)	781-380-7559
Celebrate Seaport (early August)	617-385-4200
Central Square World's Fair (early June)	617-876-1655
Christmas Craft Show (late November)	617-367-3555
Christmas Festival (mid-November)	617-742-3973
Concerts on the Hatch Shell (late March-early November)	617-727-9547
Crafts at the Castle (early December)	617-523-6400
First Night Boston (December 31)	617-542-1399
Fourth of July on the Esplanade (July 4)	617-267-2400
Halloween on the Harbor (late October)	617-727-7676
Halloween Prowl (late October)	781-784-5691
Harvard Square Oktoberfest (mid-October)	617-491-3434
Head of the Charles Regatta (mid-October)	617-782-8889
Honey Harvest (mid-October)	617-333-0690
New England Home Show (late February)	617-385-5000
New England International Auto Show (early November)	617-474-6000
New England Spring Flower Show (early March)	617-536-9280
Newburyport Waterfront Festival (early September)	978-462-6680
Regattabar Jazz Festival (late January-late May)	617-536-4100
Saint Patrick's Day Celebration (mid-March)	617-536-4100
Skating on Frog Pond (late February-mid-March)	617-635-4505
Tree Lighting & Carol Festival (early December)	617-236-3744
World of Wheels (mid-January)	617-474-6000

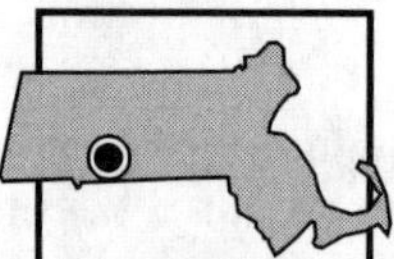

Springfield

Springfield, Massachusetts, the "Crossroads of New England," was the first English settlement in the Pioneer Valley and home to the first federal armory. The Springfield Armory (now a National Historic Site) was founded by George Washington in 1779 and brought many artisans and new types of manufacturing to Springfield. Today the Armory is famous for its extensive weapons collection. Another popular stop for tourists is the Basketball Hall of Fame - 101 years ago Dr. James Naismith invented the game in Springfield. The city's main cultural resources are located in the area known as the Quadrangle. Among these are Springfield's Museum of Fine Arts, Central Library, and Science Museum.

Population	148,144	**Longitude**	72-59-03 W
Area (Land)	32.1 sq mi	**County**	Hampden
Area (Water)	1.1 sq mi	**Time Zone**	EST
Elevation	70 ft	**Area Code/s**	413
Latitude	42-10-14 N		

— Average Temperatures and Precipitation —

TEMPERATURES

	Jan	Feb	Mar	Apr	May	Jun	Jul	Aug	Sep	Oct	Nov	Dec
High	36	39	48	61	72	81	85	84	76	65	53	39
Low	18	20	29	38	48	57	63	61	53	43	35	23

PRECIPITATION

	Jan	Feb	Mar	Apr	May	Jun	Jul	Aug	Sep	Oct	Nov	Dec
Inches	3.2	3.0	3.5	3.9	4.1	4.1	3.6	3.5	3.5	3.6	4.1	3.8

— Important Phone Numbers —

	Phone		Phone
AAA	413-785-1381	**Poison Control Center**	800-682-9211
Emergency	911	**Weather**	413-499-2627
HotelDocs	800-468-3537		

— Information Sources —

				Phone	Fax
Better Business Bureau Serving Western Massachusetts 293 Bridge St Suite 320 *Web:* www.springfield-ma.bbb.org	Springfield	MA	01103	413-734-3114	734-2006
Greater Springfield Chamber of Commerce 1441 Main St *Web:* www.gschamber.org	Springfield	MA	01103	413-787-1555	731-8530
Greater Springfield Convention & Visitors Bureau 1441 Main St *TF:* 800-723-1548 ■ *Web:* www.valleyvisitor.com	Springfield	MA	01103	413-787-1548	781-4607
Hampden County 50 State St	Springfield	MA	01103	413-748-8600	737-1611
Springfield City Hall 36 Court St **Fax:* Hum Res ■ *Web:* www.ci.springfield.ma.us	Springfield	MA	01103	413-787-7500	787-6010*
Springfield City Library 220 State St. *Web:* www.springfieldlibrary.org	Springfield	MA	01103	413-739-3871	263-6825
Springfield Civic Center 1277 Main St *TF:* 800-639-8602 ■ *Web:* www.civic-center.com	Springfield	MA	01103	413-787-6600	787-6645
Springfield Mayor 36 Court St *Web:* www.ci.springfield.ma.us/mayor.htm ■ *E-mail:* mayor@largo.ci.springfield.ma.us	Springfield	MA	01103	413-787-6100	787-6104
Springfield Planning Dept 36 Court St *Web:* www.ci.springfield.ma.us/plan/planning.htm	Springfield	MA	01103	413-787-6020	787-6524

On-Line Resources

4Springfield.com	www.4springfield.com
Area Guide Springfield	springfieldma.areaguides.net
DigitalCity Springfield	www.digitalcity.com/springfield
Mass Live	www.masslive.com/
Springfield Advocate	springfieldadvocate.com
Springfield City Guide	www.ci.springfield.ma.us/visitors.htm
Springfield City Net	www.excite.com/travel/countries/united_states/massachusetts/springfield

— Transportation Services —

AIRPORTS

■ **Bradley International Airport (BDL)**

	Phone
18 miles S of downtown Springfield (approx 40 minutes)	860-292-2000

Web: www.bradleyairport.com ■ *E-mail:* office@bradleyairport.com

Springfield (Cont'd)

Airport Transportation

	Phone
Bradway's Town Car $41 fare to downtown Springfield	413-786-1976
Longmeadow Limousine $39 fare to downtown	413-567-9355
Valley Transporter $24 fare to downtown Springfield	413-253-1350

Commercial Airlines

	Phone		Phone
Air Canada	800-776-3000	**Delta Connection**	800-221-1212
AirTran	800-247-8726	**Northwest**	800-225-2525
American	800-433-7300	**Southwest**	800-435-9792
Continental	800-525-0280	**TWA**	800-221-2000
Delta	800-221-1212	**United**	800-241-6522
Delta Business Express	800-345-3400	**US Airways**	800-428-4322

Charter Airlines

	Phone		Phone
24th Century Air	800-622-9740	**Million Air**	860-548-9334
Jet Aviation Business Jets Inc	800-736-8538		

CAR RENTALS

	Phone		Phone
Avis	860-627-3500	**Hertz**	860-627-3850
Budget	860-627-3660	**Thrifty**	860-623-8214
Dollar	860-627-9048		

LIMO/TAXI

	Phone		Phone
Bradway's Limousine	413-786-1976	**Longmeadow Limousine**	413-567-9355
City Cab	413-734-8294	**Yellow Cab**	413-732-1101
Dial-A-Ride	413-731-8485		

MASS TRANSIT

	Phone
Pioneer Valley Transit Authority $.75 Base fare	413-781-7882

RAIL/BUS

				Phone
Amtrak Station 66 Lyman St Union Station	Springfield	MA	01103	413-785-4230
Peter Pan Bus Station 1776 Main St	Springfield	MA	01102	413-781-2900

— Accommodations —

HOTELS, MOTELS, RESORTS

				Phone	Fax
Bel Air Motel 387 Riverdale St	West Springfield	MA	01089	413-781-7825	746-2937
Best Western Chicopee Motor Lodge 463 Memorial Dr. *TF:* 800-528-1234	Chicopee	MA	01020	413-592-6171	598-8351
Best Western Sovereign Hotel 1080 Riverdale St *TF:* 800-870-0486	West Springfield	MA	01089	413-781-8750	733-8652
Campus Center Hotel Campus Ctr Way University of Massachusetts	Amherst	MA	01003	413-549-6000	545-1210
Comfort Inn Parwick Centre 450 Memorial Dr. *TF:* 800-228-5150	Chicopee	MA	01020	413-739-7311	594-5005
Econo Lodge 1533 Elm St *TF:* 800-553-2666	West Springfield	MA	01089	413-734-8278	736-7690
Hampton Inn 1011 Riverdale St *TF:* 800-426-7866	West Springfield	MA	01089	413-732-1300	732-9883
Holiday Inn 711 Dwight St. *TF:* 800-465-4329	Springfield	MA	01104	413-781-0900	785-1410
Holiday Inn Holidome & Conference Center 245 Whiting Farms Rd. *TF:* 800-465-4329 ■ *Web:* www.basshotels.com/holiday-inn/?_franchisee=HLYMA ■ *E-mail:* hlyma@aol.com	Holyoke	MA	01040	413-534-3311	533-8443
Howard Johnson 1356 Boston Rd *TF:* 800-446-4656	Springfield	MA	01119	413-783-2111	783-7750
Inn at Northampton 1 Atwood Dr *TF:* 800-582-2929	Northampton	MA	01060	413-586-1211	586-0630
Plantation Inn 295 Burnett Rd *TF:* 800-248-8495	Chicopee	MA	01020	413-592-8200	592-9671
Quality Inn 1150 Riverdale St. *TF:* 800-228-5151	West Springfield	MA	01089	413-739-7261	737-8410
Ramada Inn 357 Burnett Rd. *TF:* 800-272-6232	Chicopee	MA	01020	413-592-9101	594-8333
Ramada Limited 21 Baldwin St *TF:* 800-839-6260	West Springfield	MA	01089	413-781-2300	732-1231
Sheraton Springfield Monarch Place 1 Monarch Pl *TF:* 800-426-9004	Springfield	MA	01144	413-781-1010	734-3249
Springfield Marriott Hotel 1500 Main St *TF:* 800-228-9290	Springfield	MA	01115	413-781-7111	731-8932
Super 8 Motel 1500 Riverdale St *TF:* 800-800-8000	West Springfield	MA	01089	413-736-8080	747-9214

— Restaurants —

				Phone
Angelina's Ristorante (Italian) 340 Main St	Springfield	MA	01105	413-734-4662
Aqui-me-quedo Restaurant (Spanish) 13 Locust St	Springfield	MA	01108	413-737-2827
Athens Restaurant (Greek) 1659 Main St	Springfield	MA	01103	413-733-6045
Big Mamou (Cajun) 63 Liberty St.	Springfield	MA	01103	413-732-1011
Cafe Eurasia (Japanese/Chinese) 1373 Main St	Springfield	MA	01103	413-747-8000
Cafe Lebanon (Middle Eastern) 141 State St.	Springfield	MA	01103	413-746-5667
Cafe Manhattan (Continental) 301 Bridge St	Springfield	MA	01103	413-737-7913
Capaccio's (Italian) 135 Cooper St.	Agawam	MA	01001	413-789-1267
Center Court Restaurant (American) 1 Monarch Pl	Springfield	MA	01144	413-781-1010
Debbie Wong (Chinese) 1053 Riverdale St	West Springfield	MA	01089	413-781-1711
Delaney House (American) Rt 5 Smith's Ferry	Holyoke	MA	01040	413-532-1800
Eats West Indian Restaurant (Caribbean) 494 Central St	Springfield	MA	01105	413-736-6365
Grill Room (American) 1500 Main St	Springfield	MA	01115	413-781-7111
House Of Huang (Chinese) 506 Armory St	Springfield	MA	01104	413-788-8967
Hu Ke Lau (Hawaiian) 705 Memorial Dr	Chicopee	MA	01020	413-593-5222
Lido's (Italian) 555 Worthington St	Springfield	MA	01115	413-736-9433
Mulino's (Italian) 280 Bridge St.	Springfield	MA	01103	413-736-8900
Peking Duck House (Chinese) 1535 Main St	Springfield	MA	01103	413-734-5604
Pioneer Valley Brew Pub (American) 57 Taylor St.	Springfield	MA	01103	413-732-2739
Ray's Seafood Market (Seafood) 646 Page Blvd	Springfield	MA	01104	413-739-1219
Sabor Latino (Spanish) 194 Chestnut St	Springfield	MA	01103	413-734-7878
Sitar Restaurant (Indian) 1688 Main St	Springfield	MA	01103	413-732-8011
Spaghetti Freddy's (Italian) 1500 Main St.	Springfield	MA	01115	413-787-2113
Storrowton Tavern & Carriage House (Continental) 1305 Memorial Ave.	West Springfield	MA	01089	413-732-4188
Student Prince & Fort Restaurant (German) 8 Fort St	Springfield	MA	01103	413-734-7475
Tavern Inn (Steak/Seafood) 25 Mill St	Springfield	MA	01105	413-781-2882
Tilly's (American) 1390 Main St	Springfield	MA	01103	413-732-3613
Trumpet (American) 450 Memorial Dr	Chicopee	MA	01020	413-739-7311
Yankee Pedlar (American) 1866 Northampton St.	Holyoke	MA	01040	413-532-9494
Zaffino's Italian Restaurant (Italian) 711 Dwight St.	Springfield	MA	01104	413-781-0900

— Goods and Services —

SHOPPING

				Phone	Fax
Holyoke Mall at Ingleside 50 Holyoke St. *Web:* www.holyokemall.com	Holyoke	MA	01040	413-536-1440	536-5740
Shops at Baystate West 1500 Main St	Springfield	MA	01115	413-733-2171	

BANKS

				Phone	Fax
Bank of Western Massachusetts 29 State St. *TF:* 800-331-5003 ■ *Web:* www.bankwmass.com ■ *E-mail:* info@bankwmass.com	Springfield	MA	01103	413-781-2265	736-8626
Peoples Savings Bank 314 High St.	Holyoke	MA	01040	413-538-9500	536-4072
SIS Bank 1441 Main St **Fax:* Cust Svc ■ *TF:* 800-747-7000	Springfield	MA	01103	413-748-8000	748-8451*
United Co-Operative Bank 95 Elm St. *Web:* www.bankatunited.com	West Springfield	MA	01089	413-787-1700	788-5599

BUSINESS SERVICES

	Phone		Phone
Airborne Express	800-247-2676	**Mail Boxes Etc**	800-789-4623
BAX Global	800-225-5229	**Olsten Staffing Services**	413-781-1555
DHL Worldwide Express	800-225-5345	**Post Office**	413-731-0396
Federal Express	800-238-5355	**United Personnel Services**	413-736-0800
Kelly Services	413-737-1157	**UPS**	800-742-5877

Springfield (Cont'd)

— Media —

PUBLICATIONS

Name / Address	City	State	ZIP	Phone	Fax
Sunday Republican 1860 Main St	Springfield	MA	01101	413-788-1000	788-1301
Union News‡ 1860 Main St	Springfield	MA	01103	413-788-1000	788-1301
Web: www.masslive.com/unionnews/index.html ■ *E-mail:* unews-letters@union-news.com					

‡*Daily newspapers*

TELEVISION

Name / Address	City	State	ZIP	Phone	Fax
WFSB-TV Ch 3 (CBS) 3 Constitution Plaza	Hartford	CT	06103	860-728-3333	728-0263
Web: www.wfsb.com					
WGBY-TV Ch 57 (PBS) 44 Hampden St	Springfield	MA	01103	413-781-2801	731-5093
Web: www.wgby.org/ ■ *E-mail:* wgby_feedback@wgbh.org					
WGGB-TV Ch 40 (ABC) 1300 Liberty St	Springfield	MA	01104	413-733-4040	781-1363
Web: www.wggb.com					
WTIC-TV Ch 61 (Fox) 1 Corporate Ctr	Hartford	CT	06103	860-527-6161	293-1571
Web: www.fox61.com					
WWLP-TV Ch 22 (NBC) PO Box 2210	Springfield	MA	01102	413-786-2200	786-7144
Web: www.wwlp.com ■ *E-mail:* news@wwlp.com					

RADIO

Name / Address	City	State	ZIP	Phone	Fax
WACE-AM 730 kHz (Rel) 326 Chicopee St	Chicopee	MA	01013	413-594-6654	
WACM-AM 1490 kHz (Span) 34 Sylvan St	West Springfield	MA	01089	413-781-5200	734-2240
WAQY-FM 102.1 MHz (CR) 45 Fisher Ave	East Longmeadow	MA	01028	413-525-4141	525-4334
Web: www.rock102.com					
WFCR-FM 88.5 MHz (NPR) PO Box 33630 Hampshire House	Amherst	MA	01003	413-545-0100	545-2546
Web: www.wfcr.org ■ *E-mail:* radio@wfcr.org					
WHMP-FM 99.3 MHz (Rock) 15 Hampton Ave	Northampton	MA	01060	413-586-7400	585-0927
Web: www.993.com					
WMAS-AM 1450 kHz (Nost) 101 West St	Springfield	MA	01104	413-737-1414	737-1488
Web: www.947wmas.com ■ *E-mail:* wmas@947wmas.com					
WMAS-FM 94.7 MHz (AC) 101 West St	Springfield	MA	01104	413-737-1414	737-1488
Web: www.947wmas.com ■ *E-mail:* wmas@947wmas.com					
WNNZ-AM 640 kHz (N/T) PO Box 15640	Springfield	MA	01105	413-736-6400	858-1958
Web: www.wnnz.com ■ *E-mail:* talk@wnnz.com					
WPKX-FM 97.9 MHz (Ctry) 1 Monarch Pl Suite 220	Springfield	MA	01144	413-732-5353	732-7851
TF: 800-345-9759 ■ *Web:* www.kix979.com ■ *E-mail:* kix979@kix979.com					
WSCB-FM 89.9 MHz (Misc) 263 Alden St	Springfield	MA	01109	413-748-3131	748-3712
WTCC-FM 90.7 MHz (Span) 1 Armory Sq	Springfield	MA	01105	413-736-2781	781-3747

— Colleges/Universities —

Name / Address	City	State	ZIP	Phone	Fax
American International College 1000 State St	Springfield	MA	01109	413-737-7000	737-2803
TF Admissions: 800-242-3142 ■ *Web:* www.aic.edu					
Amherst College PO Box 2231	Amherst	MA	02002	413-542-2000	542-2040
Web: www.amherst.edu ■ *E-mail:* admissio@unix.amherst.edu					
Bay Path College 588 Longmeadow St	Longmeadow	MA	01106	413-567-0621	565-1103
TF: 800-782-7284 ■ *Web:* www.baypath.edu					
Elms College 291 Springfield St	Chicopee	MA	01013	413-592-3189	594-2781
TF Admissions: 800-255-3567 ■ *Web:* www.elms.edu					
Holyoke Community College 303 Homestead Ave	Holyoke	MA	01040	413-538-7000	552-2192
Web: www.hcc.mass.edu					
Mount Holyoke College 50 College St	South Hadley	MA	01075	413-538-2000	538-2409
Web: www.mtholyoke.edu ■ *E-mail:* admissions@mtholyoke.edu					
Smith College	Northampton	MA	01063	413-584-2700	585-2527
Web: www.smith.edu					
Springfield College 263 Alden St	Springfield	MA	01109	413-748-3000	748-3694
TF: 800-343-1257 ■ *Web:* www.spfldcol.edu ■ *E-mail:* admissions@spfldcol.edu					
Springfield Technical Community College 1 Armory Sq	Springfield	MA	01101	413-781-7822	746-0344
Web: www.stcc.mass.edu					
University of Massachusetts	Amherst	MA	01003	413-545-0111	545-2114
Web: www.umass.edu ■ *E-mail:* beaubien@admin.umass.edu					
Western New England College 1215 Wilbraham Rd	Springfield	MA	01119	413-782-3111	782-1777
TF: 800-325-1122 ■ *Web:* www.wnec.edu					

— Hospitals —

Name / Address	City	State	ZIP	Phone	Fax
Baystate Medical Center 759 Chestnut St	Springfield	MA	01199	413-784-0000	794-8274*
**Fax:* Hum Res					
Cooley Dickinson Hospital 30 Locust St	Northampton	MA	01060	413-582-2000	586-9333
Franklin Medical Center 164 High St	Greenfield	MA	01301	413-772-0211	773-2100
Holyoke Hospital 575 Beech St	Holyoke	MA	01040	413-534-2500	534-2633
Web: www.holyokehealth.com					
Mercy Hospital 271 Carew St	Springfield	MA	01104	413-748-9000	748-7078*
**Fax:* Admitting					

— Attractions —

Name / Address	City	State	ZIP	Phone	Fax
Bellamy Homestead 91-93 Church St	Chicopee	MA	01020	413-594-6496	
Chicopee Memorial State Park 570 Burnett Rd	Chicopee Falls	MA	01020	413-594-9416	
Children's Museum at Holyoke Inc 444 Dwight St	Holyoke	MA	01040	413-536-7048	533-2999
Connecticut Valley Historical Museum 194 State St	Springfield	MA	01103	413-263-6800	263-6898
Web: www.quadrangle.org/CVHM.htm					
George Walter Vincent Smith Art Museum 220 State St	Springfield	MA	01103	413-263-6800	
Web: www.quadrangle.org/GWVS.htm					
Historic Deerfield Inc PO Box 321	Deerfield	MA	01342	413-774-5581	773-7415
Indian Motocycle Museum & Hall of Fame 33 Hendee St	Springfield	MA	01139	413-737-2624	
Web: www.sidecar.com/indian/					
Lake Lorraine State Park 44 Lake Dr	Springfield	MA	01151	413-543-6628	
Web: www.state.ma.us/dem/parks/llor.htm					
Museum of Fine Arts 49 Chestnut St	Springfield	MA	01103	413-263-6800	263-6889
TF: 800-554-4812 ■ *Web:* www.quadrangle.org/MFA.htm					
Naismith Memorial Basketball Hall of Fame 1150 W Columbus Ave	Springfield	MA	01101	413-781-6500	781-1939
Web: www.hoophall.com ■ *E-mail:* info@hoophall.com					
New England Peace Pagoda 100 Cave Hill Rd	Leverett	MA	01054	413-367-2202	367-9369
Quadrangle The-Springfield Library & Museum Assn 220 State St	Springfield	MA	01103	413-263-6800	263-6807
Web: www.quadrangle.org					
Rand Jasper Art Museum 6 Elm St	Westfield	MA	01085	413-568-7833	
Riverside Park PO Box 307	Agawam	MA	01001	413-786-9300	786-4682*
**Fax:* Mktg ■ *TF:* 800-370-7488 ■ *Web:* www.riversideparkspeedway.com					
Robinson State Park North St	Agawam	MA	01030	413-786-2877	
Web: www.state.ma.us/dem/parks/robn.htm					
Springfield Armory National Historic Site 1 Armory Sq	Springfield	MA	01105	413-734-6477	747-8062
Web: www.nps.gov/spar/ ■ *E-mail:* SPAR_INTERPRETATION@NPS.GOV					
Springfield Library & Museums 220 State St	Springfield	MA	01103	413-263-6800	263-6889
Web: www.spfldlibmus.org					
Springfield Symphony Hall 1277 Main St	Springfield	MA	01103	413-787-6610	787-6645
TF: 800-639-8602 ■ *Web:* www.symphonyhall.com					
Springfield Symphony Orchestra Court St Symphony Hall	Springfield	MA	01103	413-733-2291	
Stagewest 1 Columbus Ctr	Springfield	MA	01103	413-781-2340	
Storrowtown Village Museum 1305 Memorial Ave	West Springfield	MA	01089	413-787-0136	787-0127
Titanic Museum 208 Main St	Indian Orchard	MA	01151	413-543-4770	
Volleyball Hall of Fame Heritage State Pk 444 Dwight St	Holyoke	MA	01040	413-536-0926	539-6673
Web: www.volleyhall.org ■ *E-mail:* info@volleyhall.org					
Westover Air Reserve Base 100 Lloyd St Suite 103	WestoverAir Reserve Base	MA	01022	413-557-1110	
Web: www.afres.af.mil/units/439AW/Default.htm					
Wistariahurst Museum 238 Cabot St	Holyoke	MA	01040	413-534-2216	534-2344
Zoo in Forest Park Rt 83	Springfield	MA	01138	413-733-2251	
Web: www.the-spa.com/zoo/					

Springfield (Cont'd)

SPORTS TEAMS & FACILITIES

				Phone	Fax
Southwick Motorcross 46 Powder Mill Rd	Southwick	MA	01077	413-569-6801	
Springfield Falcons (hockey) 1277 Main St Springfield Civic Ctr	Springfield	MA	01103	413-787-6600	
Springfield Sirens (soccer) Bay St Fred Berte Stadium *Web:* www.springfieldsirens.com ■ *E-mail:* spfldsiren@aol.com	Springfield	MA	01108	413-783-9158	783-9158
Western Massachusetts Pioneers (soccer) Winsor St Lusitano Stadium *E-mail:* wmpioneers@aol.com	Ludlow	MA	01056	413-583-4814	583-8192

— Events —

	Phone
ACC Craft Fair (mid-June)	413-737-2443
Antique-A-Rama (January)	413-737-2443
Bright Nights at Forest Park (November-January)	413-733-3800
Columbus Day Parade (early October)	413-732-7449
Glendi Festival (mid-September)	413-737-1496
Holiday Gala (early December)	413-263-6800
Holyoke Saint Patrick's Parade (mid-March)	413-536-1646
Old Sturbridge Agricultural Fair (late September)	508-347-3362
Parade of the Big Balloons (late November)	413-733-3800
Peachbasket Festival & Hall of Fame Tip-Off Classic (late November)	413-781-6500
Peter Pan Taste of Springfield (mid-June)	413-733-3800
Puerto Rican Cultural Festival (late July)	413-737-7450
Star Spangled Springfield (July 4)	413-733-3800
The Big E-New England Great State Fair (September)	413-737-2443
Westfest (May)	413-568-2904

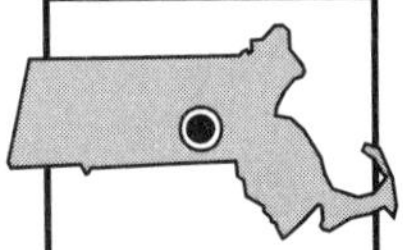

Worcester

The city of Worcester is called the "Heart of New England" because of its proximity to cities in Massachusetts, Vermont, New Hampshire, and Connecticut. Within Worcester is the American Antiquarian Society, a national research library that preserves the largest single collection of printed materials related to the literature, history, and culture of the first 250 years of the United States; and the Higgins Armory Museum, which contains a sizable collection of medieval and Renaissance armor and weaponry in a Gothic castle setting. Worcester also is home to the New England Science Center and the world-class art collection of the Worcester Art Museum. Outdoor attractions in Worcester include the Broad Meadow Brook Wildlife Sanctuary, the largest urban sanctuary in New England; and Row Worcester, a series of collegiate crew events held each May at Lake Quinsigamond.

Population	166,535	**Longitude**	71-79-79 W
Area (Land)	37.6 sq mi	**County**	Worcester
Area (Water)	1.0 sq mi	**Time Zone**	EST
Elevation	480 ft	**Area Code/s**	508
Latitude	42-25-74 N		

— Average Temperatures and Precipitation —

TEMPERATURES

	Jan	Feb	Mar	Apr	May	Jun	Jul	Aug	Sep	Oct	Nov	Dec
High	31	33	42	54	66	75	79	77	70	60	47	35
Low	15	17	25	35	45	54	60	59	51	41	31	20

PRECIPITATION

	Jan	Feb	Mar	Apr	May	Jun	Jul	Aug	Sep	Oct	Nov	Dec
Inches	3.7	3.5	4.0	3.9	4.3	3.9	3.9	3.8	4.0	4.3	4.5	4.1

— Important Phone Numbers —

	Phone		Phone
AAA	508-853-7000	**Medical Referral**	781-893-4610
American Express Travel	508-755-4375	**Poison Control Center**	800-682-9211
Dental Referral	508-753-5276	**Weather**	508-792-9600
Emergency	911		

— Information Sources —

				Phone	Fax
Better Business Bureau Serving Central Massachusetts & Northeast Connecticut PO Box 16555 *Web:* www.worcester.bbb.org	Worcester	MA	01601	508-755-2548	754-4158
Central Massachusetts Regional Library System 8 Flagg Rd *Web:* www.cmrls.org ■ *E-mail:* cmrls@cmrls.org	Worcester	MA	01545	508-757-4110	757-4370
Worcester Area Chamber of Commerce 33 Waldo St *Web:* chamber.worcester.ma.us	Worcester	MA	01608	508-753-2924	754-8560
Worcester City Hall 455 Main St *Web:* www.ci.worcester.ma.us	Worcester	MA	01608	508-799-1000	799-1015
Worcester County 2 Main St County Courthouse	Worcester	MA	01608	508-798-7700	798-7741
Worcester County Convention & Visitors Bureau 33 Waldo St *TF:* 800-231-7557 ■ *Web:* www.worcester.org	Worcester	MA	01608	508-753-2920	754-2703
Worcester Mayor 455 Main St	Worcester	MA	01608	508-799-1153	799-1156
Worcester Planning & Community Development Office 418 Main St *Web:* www.ci.worcester.ma.us/develop ■ *E-mail:* opcd@ci.worcester.ma.us	Worcester	MA	01608	508-799-1400	799-1406
Worcester's Centrum Centre 50 Foster St *Web:* www.centrumcentre.com	Worcester	MA	01608	508-755-6800	929-0111

On-Line Resources

4Worcester.com	www.4worcester.com
About.com Guide to Worcester	worcester.about.com
Area Guide Worcester	worcester.areaguides.net
City Knowledge Worcester	www.cityknowledge.com/ma_worcester.htm
Excite.com Worcester City Guide	www.excite.com/travel/countries/united_states/massachusetts/worcester
Welcome to Worcester	www.worcester.ma.us
Worcester Web	speed.city-net.com/~lmann/ww/

— Transportation Services —

AIRPORTS

	Phone
■ **Worcester Regional Airport (ORH)** 4 miles W of downtown (approx 15 minutes)	508-799-1741

Airport Transportation

	Phone
Knight's Airport Limousine $26 fare to downtown	508-839-6252

Commercial Airlines

	Phone		Phone
Continental	508-757-4478	**US Airways Express**	800-428-4322
US Airways	800-428-4322		

Charter Airlines

	Phone		Phone
Airwest Inc	800-277-9768	**Bullock Charter**	978-464-2706

Worcester (Cont'd)

CAR RENTALS

	Phone		Phone
Avis	508-754-7004	**Enterprise**	508-752-4100
Budget	508-852-0361	**Hertz**	508-753-7203
CarTemps USA	508-756-1740	**National**	508-791-1345

LIMO/TAXI

	Phone		Phone
Flick's Limousine	508-752-3991	**Red & White Cab Co**	508-756-5184
Little Daddy Limousine	508-987-8295	**Red Cab Taxi**	508-792-9999
Professional Limousine	508-754-1205	**Yellow Cab**	508-754-3211

MASS TRANSIT

	Phone
Worcester Regional Transit Authority $1 Base fare	508-791-9782

RAIL/BUS

				Phone
Amtrak Station 45 Shrewsbury St	Worcester	MA	01604	508-755-0356
Greyhound Bus Station 75 Madison St *TF:* 800-231-2222	Worcester	MA	01608	508-754-3247

— Accommodations —

HOTELS, MOTELS, RESORTS

				Phone	Fax
Baymont Inns & Suites 444 Southbridge St *TF:* 800-301-0200	Auburn	MA	01501	508-832-7000	832-5790
Beechwood Inn 363 Plantation St *TF:* 800-344-2589	Worcester	MA	01605	508-754-5789	752-2060
Best Western Royal Plaza Hotel & Trade Center 181 Boston Post Rd W	Marlborough	MA	01752	508-460-0700	480-8218
Comfort Inn Westboro 399 Worcester Turnpike Rd	Westborough	MA	01581	508-366-0202	836-4226
Crowne Plaza 10 Lincoln Sq *TF:* 800-628-4240	Worcester	MA	01608	508-791-1600	791-1796
Days Inn Shrewsbury 889 Boston Tpke *TF:* 800-329-7466	Shrewsbury	MA	01545	508-842-8500	842-3042
Days Lodge of Worcester 50 Oriol Dr *TF:* 800-932-3297	Worcester	MA	01605	508-852-2800	852-4605
Embassy Suites 123 Boston Post Rd	Marlborough	MA	01752	508-485-5900	481-3110
Hampton Inn 110 Summer St *TF:* 800-426-7866	Worcester	MA	01608	508-757-0400	831-9839
Holiday Inn Worcester 500 Lincoln St *TF:* 800-782-7306	Worcester	MA	01605	508-852-4000	852-8521
Marriott Westborough Hotel 5400 Computer Dr *TF:* 800-228-9290	Westborough	MA	01581	508-366-5511	870-5965
Publick House Historic Resort PO Box 187 *TF:* 800-782-5425 ■ *Web:* www.publickhouse.com ■ *E-mail:* info@publickhouse.com	Sturbridge	MA	01566	508-347-3313	347-5073
Ramada Inn 624 Southbridge St *TF:* 800-528-5012	Auburn	MA	01501	508-832-3221	832-8366
Red Roof Inn 367 Turnpike Rd *TF:* 800-843-7663	Southborough	MA	01772	508-481-3904	481-3909
Regency Suites 70 Southbridge St *TF:* 800-221-2220	Worcester	MA	01608	508-753-3512	755-7104
Sheraton Four Points Hotel 99 Erdman Way *TF:* 800-325-3535	Leominster	MA	01453	978-534-9000	534-0891
Sturbridge Host Hotel & Conference Center 366 Main St *TF:* 800-582-3232	Sturbridge	MA	01566	508-347-7393	347-3944
Super 8 Motel 358 Main St	Sturbridge	MA	01566	508-347-9000	347-5658

— Restaurants —

				Phone
99 Restaurant & Pub (American) 900 W Boylston St	Worcester	MA	01606	508-852-2999
Aku-aku Restaurant (Chinese) 11 E Central St	Worcester	MA	01605	508-792-1124
Biagio's (Italian) 257 Park Ave	Worcester	MA	01609	508-756-7995
Cactus Pete's Steak House & Saloon (Steak) 400 Park Ave	Worcester	MA	01610	508-752-3038
Caesar's Bistro (American) 70 S Bridge St	Worcester	MA	01608	508-753-3512
Chestnuts Cafe (American) 10 Chestnut St	Worcester	MA	01608	508-757-7984
Chopsticks (Chinese) 1083 Main St	Worcester	MA	01603	508-755-1075
City Lights Pub & Restaurant (Italian) 395 Grafton St	Worcester	MA	01604	508-752-6660
Coral Seafood Restaurant & Fish Market (Seafood) 112-114 Green St	Worcester	MA	01604	508-755-8331
Dalat Restaurant (Asian) 425 Park Ave	Worcester	MA	01610	508-753-6036
El-basha (Lebanese) 424 Belmont St	Worcester	MA	01604	508-797-0884
El Palazzo (Italian) 100 Wall St	Worcester	MA	01604	508-756-7117
Firehouse Cafe Co (American) 1 Exchange Pl	Worcester	MA	01608	508-753-7899
House of India (Indian) 439 Park Ave	Worcester	MA	01610	508-752-1330
La Scala Restaurant (Italian) 183 Shrewsbury St	Worcester	MA	01604	508-753-9912
Leo's Ristorante (Italian) 11 Bracket Ct	Worcester	MA	01605	508-753-9490
Maxwell-Silverman's Toolhouse (Steak/Seafood) 25 Union St	Worcester	MA	01608	508-755-1200
Millbrook Restaurant (American) 36 Millbrook St	Worcester	MA	01606	508-752-7442
Northworks (American) 106 Grove St	Worcester	MA	01605	508-755-9657
O'Connor's Restaurant & Bar (American) 1160 W Boylston St	Worcester	MA	01606	508-853-0789
Ping's Garden Restaurant (Chinese) 60 Madison St	Worcester	MA	01608	508-791-9577
Porto Bello (Italian) 156 Shrewsbury St	Worcester	MA	01604	508-753-9865
Quan Yin (Asian) 56 Hamilton St	Worcester	MA	01604	508-831-1322
Saigon Restaurant (Chinese/Vietnamese) 976 Main St Suite B	Worcester	MA	01603	508-799-5250
Shorah's Ristorante (Italian) 27 Foster St	Worcester	MA	01607	508-797-0007
Sole Proprietor (Seafood) 118 Highland St	Worcester	MA	01609	508-798-3474
Struck Cafe (Continental) 415 Chandler St	Worcester	MA	01602	508-757-1670
Sweetheart (Indian) 270 Shrewsbury St	Worcester	MA	01604	508-752-3700
Thai Cha-Da (Thai) 266 Park Ave	Worcester	MA	01603	508-752-2211
Thai Orchid (Thai) 271 Worcester Rd	Framingham	MA	01701	508-626-0248
Tiano's (Italian) 108 Grove St	Worcester	MA	01605	508-752-8901
Tortilla Sams (Mexican) 107 Highland St	Worcester	MA	01609	508-791-1746
Toyama (Japanese) 100 Front St	Worcester	MA	01608	508-831-1168
Webster House Restaurant (American) 1 Webster St	Worcester	MA	01603	508-757-7208

— Goods and Services —

SHOPPING

				Phone	Fax
Auburn Mall 385 Southbridge St	Auburn	MA	01501	508-832-3488	832-6250
Greendale Mall 7 Neponset St	Worcester	MA	01606	508-856-9400	852-5294
Olde Shrewsbury Village 1000 Boston Tpke	Shrewsbury	MA	01545	508-842-7467	842-6100
Worcester Common Fashion Outlet 110 Front St	Worcester	MA	01608	508-755-4381	

BANKS

				Phone	Fax
Bank of Boston 100 Front St	Worcester	MA	01608	508-770-7000	770-7784
Bay State Savings Bank 28-32 Franklin St	Worcester	MA	01608	508-791-8161	792-5217
Commerce Bank & Trust Co 386 Main St *TF:* 800-698-2265 ■ *Web:* www.bankatcommerce.com ■ *E-mail:* branchadmin@bankatcommerce.com	Worcester	MA	01608	508-797-6800	797-6834
Family Bank 200 Commercial St	Worcester	MA	01608	508-791-6271	797-5062
First Massachusetts Bank 295 Park Ave *TF Cust Svc:* 800-390-6443 ■ *Web:* firstmass.banknorth.com ■ *E-mail:* firstmass@banknorth.com	Worcester	MA	01609	508-752-2584	751-8090
Flagship Bank & Trust Co 120 Front St	Worcester	MA	01608	508-799-4321	797-4628

BUSINESS SERVICES

	Phone		Phone
Airborne Express	800-247-2676	**Mail Boxes Etc**	800-789-4623
BAX Global	800-225-5229	**Post Office**	508-795-3666
DHL Worldwide Express	800-225-5345	**Talent Tree Staffing Service**	508-831-7604
Federal Express	800-238-5355	**UPS**	800-742-5877
Kelly Services	508-753-2954	**Westaff**	508-756-3409

— Media —

PUBLICATIONS

				Phone	Fax
Telegram & Gazette‡ PO Box 15012 *TF:* 800-678-6680 ■ *Web:* www.telegram.com ■ *E-mail:* info@telegram.com	Worcester	MA	01615	508-793-9100	793-9281

‡Daily newspapers

TELEVISION

				Phone	Fax
WBZ-TV Ch 4 (CBS) 1170 Soldiers Field Rd *Web:* www.wbz.com	Boston	MA	02134	617-787-7000	254-6383
WCVB-TV Ch 5 (ABC) 5 TV Pl *Web:* www.wcvb.com ■ *E-mail:* wcvb@aol.com	Needham	MA	02492	781-449-0400	449-6681

Worcester — Television (Cont'd)

				Phone	Fax
WFXT-TV Ch 25 (Fox) 25 Fox Dr.	Dedham	MA	02026	781-326-8825	467-7213
WGBH-TV Ch 2 (PBS) 125 Western Ave.	Boston	MA	02134	617-492-2777	787-0714
Web: www.wgbh.org					
WHDH-TV Ch 7 (NBC) 7 Bulfinch Pl	Boston	MA	02114	617-725-0777	723-6117
Web: www.whdh.com ■ *E-mail:* stationmanagement@whdh.com					
WJAR-TV Ch 10 (NBC) 23 Kenney Dr	Cranston	RI	02920	401-455-9100	455-9140
Web: www.nbc10wjar.com ■ *E-mail:* mail.box10@nbc.com					
WWLP-TV Ch 22 (NBC) PO Box 2210	Springfield	MA	01102	413-786-2200	786-7144
Web: www.wwlp.com ■ *E-mail:* news@wwlp.com					

RADIO

				Phone	Fax
WAAF-FM 107.3 MHz (Rock)					
200 Friberg Pkwy Suite 4000	Westborough	MA	01581	508-836-9223	366-0745
Web: www.waaf.com					
WCHC-FM 88.1 MHz (Alt)					
1 College St College of the Holy Cross	Worcester	MA	01610	508-793-2474	793-3643
Web: carver.holycross.edu/studentorgs/wchc					
■ *E-mail:* wchcfm_bag@hotmail.com					
WCUW-FM 91.3 MHz (Misc) 910 Main St	Worcester	MA	01610	508-753-1012	
WICN-FM 90.5 MHz (NPR) 6 Chatham St	Worcester	MA	01609	508-752-0700	752-7518
Web: www.wicn.org					
WKOX-AM 1200 kHz (Span)					
100 Mount Wayte Ave	Framingham	MA	01702	508-820-2400	820-2458
WORC-AM 1310 kHz (N/T) 27 Douglas Rd	Webster	MA	01570	508-799-0581	943-0405
Web: www.worcradio.com ■ *E-mail:* worcradio@aol.com					
WSRS-FM 96.1 MHz (Rock) 96 Stereo Ln	Paxton	MA	01612	508-795-0580	757-1779
WTAG-AM 580 kHz (N/T) 96 Stereo Ln	Paxton	MA	01612	508-795-0580	757-1779
Web: www.wtag.com					
WVNE-AM 760 kHz (Rel)					
70 James St Suite 201	Worcester	MA	01603	508-831-9863	831-7964
Web: www.lifechangingradio.com ■ *E-mail:* wvne@aol.com					
WXLO-FM 104.5 MHz (AC)					
250 Commercial St	Worcester	MA	01608	508-752-1045	793-0824
Web: www.wxlo.com ■ *E-mail:* wxlo@wxlo.com					

— Colleges/Universities —

				Phone	Fax
Anna Maria College 50 Sunset Ln	Paxton	MA	01612	508-849-3300	849-3362*
**Fax:* Admissions ■ *TF:* 800-344-4586 ■ *Web:* www.anna-maria.edu					
Assumption College 500 Salisbury St	Worcester	MA	01609	508-767-7000	756-1780
Web: www.assumption.edu ■ *E-mail:* amahoney@eve.assumption.edu					
Becker College 61 Sever St	Worcester	MA	01609	508-791-9241	890-1500
Clark University 950 Main St	Worcester	MA	01610	508-793-7711	793-8821
TF: 800-462-5275 ■ *Web:* www.clarku.edu					
■ *E-mail:* admissions@vax.clarku.edu					
College of the Holy Cross 1 College St	Worcester	MA	01610	508-793-2011	793-3888
TF Admissions: 800-442-2421 ■ *Web:* www.holycross.edu					
■ *E-mail:* admission@holycross.edu					
Quinsigamond Community College					
670 W Boylston St	Worcester	MA	01606	508-853-2300	852-6943
Web: www.qcc.mass.edu					
Worcester Polytechnic Institute					
100 Institute Rd	Worcester	MA	01609	508-831-5000	831-5875
Web: www.wpi.edu					
Worcester State College 486 Chandler St	Worcester	MA	01602	508-793-8000	929-8183
Web: www.worc.mass.edu					

— Hospitals —

				Phone	Fax
Clinton Hospital 201 Highland St	Clinton	MA	01510	978-368-3000	368-1360
Harrington Memorial Hospital					
100 South St	Southbridge	MA	01550	508-765-9771	764-2464
Web: www.harringtonhospital.org					
Health Alliance Leominster Hospital					
60 Hospital Rd	Leominster	MA	01453	978-537-4811	466-4395
Web: www.healthalliance.com/lh_history.htm					
Heywood Hospital 242 Green St	Gardner	MA	01440	978-632-3420	630-6595
Hubbard Regional Hospital					
340 Thompson Rd	Webster	MA	01570	508-943-2600	949-1544
Marlborough Hospital 157 Union St	Marlborough	MA	01752	508-485-1121	485-9123
Memorial Health Care Hahnemann Campus					
119 Belmont St.	Worcester	MA	01605	508-792-8000	793-6006
MetroWest Medical Center					
115 Lincoln St	Framingham	MA	01702	508-383-1000	383-1166*
**Fax:* Admitting ■ *Web:* www.mwmc.com					
■ *E-mail:* mwmc_mis@mwmc.com					
Milford-Whitinsville Regional Hospital					
14 Prospect St	Milford	MA	01757	508-473-1190	473-7460*
**Fax:* Admitting					
Saint Vincent Hospital 25 Winthrop St	Worcester	MA	01604	508-798-1234	798-1119*
**Fax:* Admitting					
UMass Memorial Health Care Memorial Campus 119 Belmont St	Worcester	MA	01605	508-793-6611	334-0333
University of Massachusetts Medical Center					
55 Lake Ave N	Worcester	MA	01655	508-856-0011	856-1825*
**Fax:* Admitting ■ *Web:* www.ummed.edu					
Worcester Memorial Hospital					
119 Belmont St.	Worcester	MA	01605	508-793-6611	334-5049

— Attractions —

				Phone	Fax
American Antiquarian Society					
185 Salisbury St	Worcester	MA	01609	508-755-5221	753-3311
Web: www.americanantiquarian.org ■ *E-mail:* library@mwa.org					
American Textile History Museum					
491 Dutton St.	Lowell	MA	01854	978-441-0400	441-1412
Web: www.athm.org					
ARTworks Gallery 261 Park Ave	Worcester	MA	01609	508-755-7808	756-7684
Broad Meadow Brook Wildlife Sanctuary					
414 Massasoit Rd	Worcester	MA	01604	508-753-6087	755-0148
Cantor Iris & B Gerald Art Gallery					
1 College St	Worcester	MA	01610	508-793-3356	793-3030
Web: www.holycross.edu/departments/cantor/website/					
Capen Hill Nature Sanctuary					
PO Box 218	Charlton City	MA	01508	508-248-5516	248-5516
E-mail: capenhill@gis.net					
Central Massachusetts Symphony Orchestra					
10 Tuckerman St Tuckerman Hall	Worcester	MA	01609	508-754-1234	754-5329
EcoTarium 222 Harrington Way	Worcester	MA	01604	508-929-2700	929-2701
Web: www.ecotarium.org ■ *E-mail:* info@ecotarium.org					
Foothills Theater 100 Front St Suite 137	Worcester	MA	01608	508-754-3314	767-0676
Hebert Candy Mansion 575 Hartford Pike	Shrewsbury	MA	01545	508-845-8051	842-3065
Hellenic Sports Hall of Fame					
180 Bolton St.	Marlborough	MA	01752	508-485-0736	481-7532
Higgins Armory Museum 100 Barber Ave	Worcester	MA	01606	508-853-6015	852-7697
Web: www.higgins.org ■ *E-mail:* higgins@higgins.org					
Mechanics Hall 321 Main St	Worcester	MA	01608	508-752-5608	754-8442
Web: www.mechanicshall.org					
Old Sturbridge Village					
1 Old Sturbridge Village Rd	Sturbridge	MA	01566	508-347-3362	347-0375
Web: www.osv.org					
Olde Shrewsbury Village					
1000 Boston Tpke.	Shrewsbury	MA	01545	508-842-7467	842-6100
Opera Worcester Inc					
486 Chandler St Sullivan Auditorium	Worcester	MA	01602	508-752-8201	752-0766
Quinsigamond State Park 10 N Lake Ave	Worcester	MA	01605	508-755-6880	
Salisbury Lyric Opera					
11 Chamberlain Pkwy	Worcester	MA	01602	508-799-3848	799-3848
Salisbury Mansion 40 Highland St	Worcester	MA	01609	508-753-8278	753-9070
Spooky World 100 River Rd.	Berlin	MA	01503	978-838-0200	
Tower Hill Botanical Gardens PO Box 598	Boylston	MA	01505	508-869-6111	869-0314
Web: www.towerhillbg.org					
Tuckerman Hall 10 Tuckerman St.	Worcester	MA	01609	508-754-1234	754-5329
Willard House & Clock Museum					
11 Willard St	Grafton	MA	01536	508-839-3500	
Web: www.nawcc.org/museum/willard/willard.htm					
Worcester Art Museum 55 Salisbury St.	Worcester	MA	01609	508-799-4406	798-5646
Web: www.worcesterart.org					
Worcester Center for Crafts					
25 Sagamore Rd.	Worcester	MA	01605	508-753-8183	797-5626
Web: www.craftcenter.worcester.org					
Worcester Forum Theatre Ensemble					
6 Chatham St.	Worcester	MA	01609	508-799-9166	799-9558
Worcester Historical Museum 30 Elm St.	Worcester	MA	01609	508-753-8278	
E-mail: theworchistmu@aol.com					

SPORTS TEAMS & FACILITIES

				Phone	Fax
Boston Renegades (soccer)					
175 Union Ave Bowditch Field	Framingham	MA	01702	508-872-8998	870-0884
Worcester IceCats (hockey)					
50 Foster St The Centrum	Worcester	MA	01608	508-798-5400	799-5267
Web: www.worcestericecats.com					

Worcester (Cont'd)

— Events —

	Phone
A Celebration of Craftmanship (mid-August)	508-347-3362
AppleFest (October)	978-464-2300
Beginning of a New England Christmas The (early-mid-December)	508-347-3362
Brimfield Outdoor Antique Shows (early September)	800-628-8379
First Night Worcester (December 31)	508-799-1400
Harvest Festival (September)	978-779-5521
Longsjo Bike Race (early July)	978-464-2300
New England Rowing Championships (early May)	508-753-2920
New England Summer Nationals (early July)	508-987-3375
Spencer Fair (September)	508-753-2920
Taste of Massachusetts (August)	978-779-5521
Worcester Music Festival (October-April)	508-754-3231

Michigan

Population (1999): 9,863,775 **Area (sq mi): 96,705**

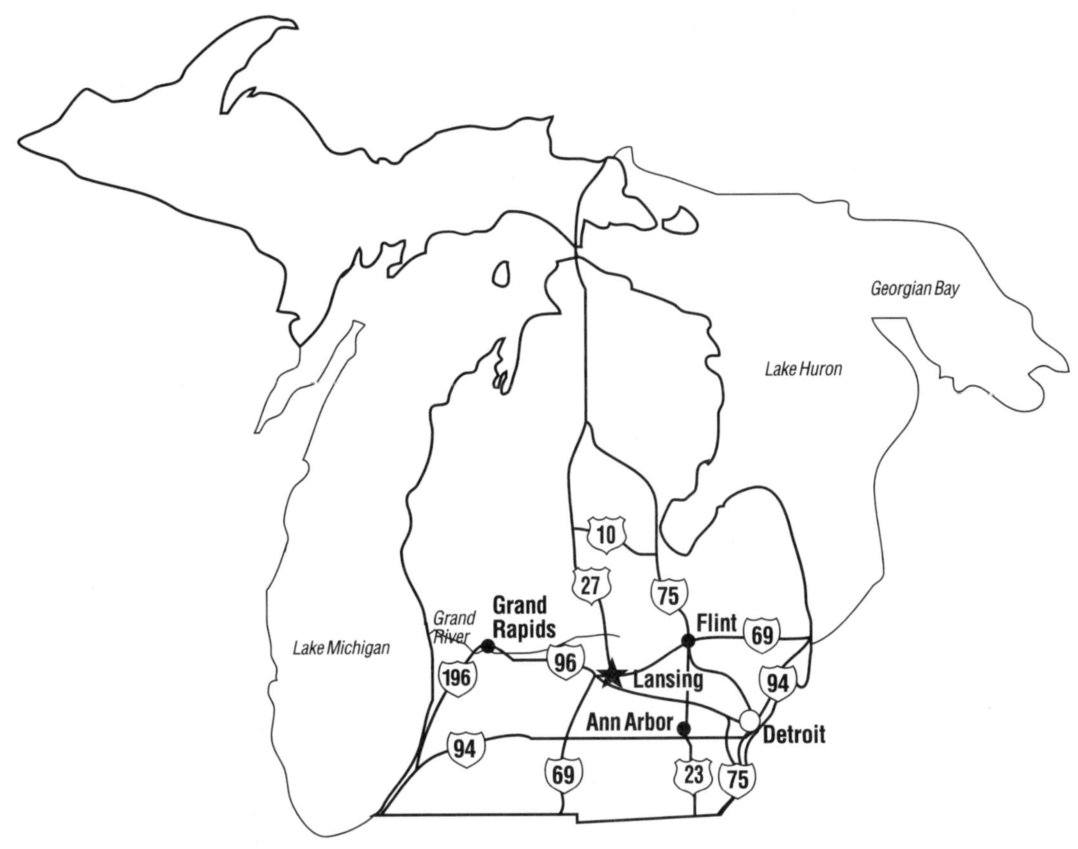

— State Information Sources —

				Phone	Fax
Michigan Chamber of Commerce 600 S Walnut St. *TF:* 800-748-0266 ■ *Web:* www.michamber.com	Lansing	MI	48933	517-371-2100	371-7224
Michigan Jobs Commission 201 N Washington Sq 4th Fl *Web:* www.state.mi.us/mjc/ceo	Lansing	MI	48913	517-373-6508	373-0314
Michigan Library 717 W Allegan St. *Web:* www.libofmich.lib.mi.us ■ *E-mail:* info@libofmich.lib.mi.us	Lansing	MI	48909	517-373-5400	373-5700
Michigan Parks & Recreation Div PO Box 30257 *TF:* 800-447-2757 ■ *Web:* www.dnr.state.mi.us/www/parks/index.htm	Lansing	MI	48909	517-373-9900	373-4625
Michigan State Government Information *Web:* www.migov.state.mi.us ■ *E-mail:* migov@mail.state.mi.us				517-373-1837	
Michigan Travel Michigan PO Box 30226 *TF:* 888-784-7328 ■ *Web:* www.michigan.org	Lansing	MI	48909	517-373-0670	373-0059

ON-LINE RESOURCES

Go! Michigan . . . . . www.gomichigan.com
Guide to Bed & Breakfast Inns in Michigan . . . . . www.michiganweb.com/BedandBreakfast
Michigan Cities . . . . . dir.yahoo.com/Regional/U_S__States/Michigan/Cities
Michigan Counties & Regions . . . . . dir.yahoo.com/Regional/U_S__States/Michigan/Counties_and_Regions
Michigan Live . . . . . state.mlive.com
Michigan Recreation Guide . . . . . www.mirecreationguide.com
Michigan Scenario . . . . . scenariousa.dstylus.com/mi/indexf.htm
Michigan Travel & Tourism Guide . . . www.travel-library.com/north_america/usa/michigan/index.html
Michigan Travel Companion . . . . . www.yesmichigan.com
Northern Michigan Connection . . . . . www.michiweb.com
Ring! OnLine: Michigan's Internet SuperStation . . . . . www.ring.com/minews.htm
Ring!OnLine Michigan . . . . . www.ring.com/michigan.htm
Rough Guide Travel Michigan travel.roughguides.com/content/482/index.htm
Travel.org-Michigan . . . . . travel.org/michigan.html
Virtual Michigan . . . . . www.virtualmichigan.com
Yahoo! Get Local Michigan . . . . . dir.yahoo.com/Regional/U_S__States/Michigan

— Cities Profiled —

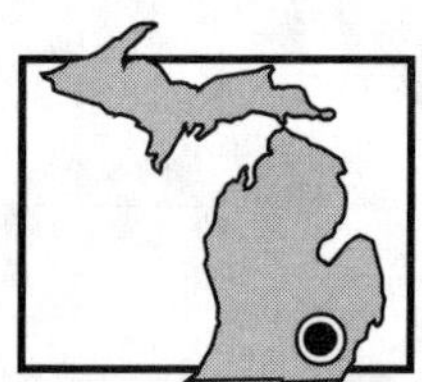

Ann Arbor

Ann Arbor is the home of the University of Michigan, which has the largest college-owned football stadium in the U.S. Bentley Historical Library on the University's North Campus contains the Michigan Historical Collections and the University of Michigan archives. Just a few blocks from the University, visitors will find the Courtyard Shops at North Campus Plaza, an eclectic collection of specialty shops and restaurants in a park-like setting. Additional shopping can be found at the Kerrytown Artisans Market, which features hand-made arts and crafts; and downtown's Main Street Area, the shopping, restaurant, and theater district of Ann Arbor. The nearby city of Ypsilanti, named for the Greek hero Demetrius Ypsilanti, is noted for its Greek Revival-styled architecture. Its historic business district, Depot Town, features antique shops and an antique car dealer.

Population	109,967	**Longitude**	83-78-21 W
Area (Land)	25.9 sq mi	**County**	Washtenaw
Area (Water)	0.7 sq mi	**Time Zone**	EST
Elevation	840 ft	**Area Code/s**	734
Latitude	42-27-90 N		

— Average Temperatures and Precipitation —

TEMPERATURES

	Jan	Feb	Mar	Apr	May	Jun	Jul	Aug	Sep	Oct	Nov	Dec
High	30	34	45	59	71	80	84	81	74	62	48	35
Low	16	18	27	38	49	58	62	61	54	43	33	22

PRECIPITATION

	Jan	Feb	Mar	Apr	May	Jun	Jul	Aug	Sep	Oct	Nov	Dec
Inches	1.7	1.7	2.6	3.2	2.9	3.5	3.0	3.4	3.1	2.2	2.8	2.8

— Important Phone Numbers —

	Phone		*Phone*
AAA	734-662-9350	**Poison Control Center**	313-745-5711
Dental Referral	734-761-2445	**Time**	734-665-1212
Emergency	911	**Washtenaw County Events Hotline**	734-930-6300
Medical Referral	734-668-6241	**Weather**	734-973-2929

— Information Sources —

				Phone	*Fax*
Ann Arbor Area Chamber of Commerce 425 S Main St Suite 103	Ann Arbor	MI	48104	734-665-4433	665-4191
Web: www.annarborchamber.org/ ■ *E-mail:* gen@annarborchamber.org					
Ann Arbor Area Convention & Visitors Bureau 120 W Huron St	Ann Arbor	MI	48104	734-995-7281	995-7283
TF: 800-888-9487 ■ *Web:* www.annarbor.org ■ *E-mail:* a2info@annarbor.org					
Ann Arbor City Hall 100 N 5th Ave	Ann Arbor	MI	48107	734-994-2700	994-8296
Web: www.ci.ann-arbor.mi.us					
Ann Arbor Community Development Dept PO Box 8647	Ann Arbor	MI	48107	734-994-2912	994-2915
Web: www.ci.ann-arbor.mi.us/framed/commdev/Default.htm					
Ann Arbor Mayor PO Box 8647	Ann Arbor	MI	48107	734-994-2766	994-8297
Ann Arbor Public Library 343 S 5th Ave	Ann Arbor	MI	48104	734-994-2333	994-4762
Web: www.annarbor.lib.mi.us					
Better Business Bureau Serving Detroit & Eastern Michigan 30555 Southfield Rd Suite 200	Southfield	MI	48076	248-644-9100	644-5026
Web: www.detroit.bbb.org					
Washtenaw County PO Box 8645	Ann Arbor	MI	48107	734-996-3055	994-2952
Web: www.co.washtenaw.mi.us					

On-Line Resources

4AnnArbor.com	www.4annarbor.com
Ann Arbor Home Page	ann-arbor.com
Anthill City Guide Ann Arbor	www.anthill.com/city.asp?city=annarbor
Arborweb	www.arborweb.com/
Area Guide Ann Arbor	annarbor.areaguides.net
City Knowledge Ann Arbor	www.cityknowledge.com/mi_annarbor.htm
Electric Current Entertainment Magazine	www.ecurrent.com
Excite.com Ann Arbor City Guide	www.excite.com/travel/countries/united_states/michigan/ann_arbor
Living in Ann Arbor	www.liaa.com/liaa.shtml

— Transportation Services —

AIRPORTS

■ **Detroit Metropolitan Airport (DTW)**

	Phone
25 miles E of downtown Ann Arbor (approx 50 minutes)	734-942-3550
Web: www.metroairport.com	

Airport Transportation

	Phone
Commuter Transportation $15 fare to downtown Ann Arbor	800-488-7433
Scheduled Airport/Hotel Shuttle $41 fare to downtown Ann Arbor	734-941-3252

Commercial Airlines

	Phone		*Phone*
American	800-433-7300	**Southwest**	800-435-9792
British Airways	800-247-9297	**Sun Country**	800-359-5786
Continental	800-525-0280	**TWA**	800-221-2000
Continental Express	800-525-0280	**United**	800-241-6522
Delta	800-221-1212	**US Airways**	800-428-4322
Northwest	800-225-2525		

Charter Airlines

	Phone		*Phone*
Aero Charter Inc	800-535-1445	**Corporate Flight Inc**	800-767-2473
Charter Airlines Inc	702-876-1166	**DaimlerChrysler Aviation**	248-666-3630
Corporate America Aviation Inc	800-521-8585	**Direct Airway**	800-257-9424

CAR RENTALS

	Phone		*Phone*
Avis	734-942-3450	**Hertz**	734-941-4747
Avis-Ann Arbor	734-677-2300	**Hertz-Ann Arbor**	734-761-1176
CarTemps USA	734-434-6999	**National**	734-941-7000
Dollar	734-942-4777	**National-Ann Arbor**	734-769-8437
Enterprise-Ann Arbor	734-971-1221	**Thrifty**	734-946-7830

LIMO/TAXI

	Phone		*Phone*
A & J Travel Service	734-665-3878	**C & J Limousine Service**	734-480-2033
Acme Sedan Service	734-665-8283	**Executive Limousine**	734-971-9240
Ann Arbor Taxi	734-741-9000	**Golden Limousine**	734-668-8282
Arbor Limousine	734-663-5959	**Reliable City Cab**	734-481-0141
Black & White Cab	734-722-4114	**Veterans Cab**	734-485-7797
Blue Cab	734-547-2222	**Yellow Cab**	734-663-3355

MASS TRANSIT

	Phone
Ann Arbor Transportation Authority $.75 Base fare	734-996-0400

RAIL/BUS

				Phone
Amtrak Station 325 Depot St	Ann Arbor	MI	48104	734-994-4906
TF: 800-872-7245				
Greyhound/Trailways Bus Station 116 W Huron St	Ann Arbor	MI	48104	734-662-5511

— Accommodations —

HOTELS, MOTELS, RESORTS

				Phone	*Fax*
Ann Arbor Inn 3750 Washtenaw Ave	Ann Arbor	MI	48104	734-971-2000	971-1149

Ann Arbor — Hotels, Motels, Resorts (Cont'd)

	City	State	ZIP	Phone	Fax
Bell Tower Hotel 300 S Thayer St	Ann Arbor	MI	48104	734-769-3010	769-4339
TF: 800-562-3559					
Campus Inn 615 E Huron St	Ann Arbor	MI	48104	734-769-2200	769-6222
TF: 800-666-8693					
Clarion Atrium & Conference Center 2900 Jackson Rd	Ann Arbor	MI	48103	734-665-4444	665-5558
Comfort Inn 2455 Carpenter Rd	Ann Arbor	MI	48105	734-973-6100	973-6142
TF: 800-221-2222					
Courtyard by Marriott 3205 Boardwalk	Ann Arbor	MI	48108	734-995-5900	995-2937
TF: 800-321-2211 ■ *Web:* courtyard.com/ARBCH					
Crowne Plaza Hotel 610 Hilton Blvd	Ann Arbor	MI	48108	734-761-7800	761-1040
TF: 800-465-4329					
Days Inn 2380 Carpenter Rd	Ann Arbor	MI	48108	734-971-0700	971-1492
TF: 800-329-7466					
Doubletree Hotel 31500 Wick Rd	Romulus	MI	48174	734-467-8000	721-8870
TF: 800-669-0221					
Embassy Hotel 200 E Huron St	Ann Arbor	MI	48104	734-662-7100	662-4520
Extended StayAmerica 1501 Briarwood Circle Dr	Ann Arbor	MI	48108	734-332-1980	332-1998
TF: 800-398-7829					
Fairfield Inn by Marriott 3285 Boardwalk	Ann Arbor	MI	48108	734-995-5200	995-5394
TF: 800-228-2800 ■ *Web:* fairfieldinn.com/ARBFI					
Hampton Inn North 2300 Green Rd	Ann Arbor	MI	48105	734-996-4444	996-0196
TF: 800-426-7866					
Hampton Inn South 925 Victors Way	Ann Arbor	MI	48108	734-665-5000	665-8452
Holiday Inn Ann Arbor North Campus 3600 Plymouth Rd	Ann Arbor	MI	48105	734-769-9800	761-1290
TF: 800-800-5560 ■ *Web:* www.basshotels.com/holiday-inn/?_franchisee=ARBNC					
Lamp Post Inn 2424 E Stadium Blvd	Ann Arbor	MI	48104	734-971-8000	971-7483
Motel 6 3764 S State St	Ann Arbor	MI	48108	734-665-9900	665-2202
TF: 800-466-8356					
Red Roof Inn 3505 S State St	Ann Arbor	MI	48108	734-665-3500	665-3517
TF: 800-766-4023					
Red Roof Inn 3621 Plymouth Rd	Ann Arbor	MI	48105	734-996-5800	996-5707
TF: 800-843-7663					
Residence Inn by Marriott 800 Victors Way	Ann Arbor	MI	48108	734-996-5666	996-1919
TF: 800-331-3131 ■ *Web:* www.residenceinn.com/residenceinn/ARRMI					
Sheraton Inn 3200 Boardwalk St	Ann Arbor	MI	48108	734-996-0600	996-8136
TF: 800-848-2770					
StudioPLUS 3265 Boardwalk St	Ann Arbor	MI	48108	734-997-7623	997-7633
TF: 800-646-8000					
Weber's Inn 3050 Jackson Ave	Ann Arbor	MI	48103	734-769-2500	769-4743
TF: 800-443-3050 ■ *Web:* webersinn.com/					
Ypsilanti Marriott 1275 S Huron St	Ypsilanti	MI	48197	734-487-2000	481-0700
TF: 800-228-9290					

— Restaurants —

	City	State	ZIP	Phone
Amadeus (European) 122 E Washington St	Ann Arbor	MI	48104	734-665-8767
Arbor Brewing Co (American) 114 E Washington	Ann Arbor	MI	48104	734-213-1393
Argiero's (Italian) 300 Detroit St	Ann Arbor	MI	48104	734-665-0444
Arriba (Mexican) 314 S 4th Ave	Ann Arbor	MI	48104	734-662-8485
Bella Ciao (Italian) 118 W Liberty St	Ann Arbor	MI	48104	734-995-2107
Blue Nile (Ethiopian) 221 E Washington St	Ann Arbor	MI	48104	734-998-4746
Champion House (Japanese) 120 E Liberty Ave	Ann Arbor	MI	48104	734-741-8100
Earle The (French/Italian) 121 W Washington St	Ann Arbor	MI	48104	734-994-0211
Escoffier (French) 300 S Thayer St	Ann Arbor	MI	48104	734-995-3800
Fuji (Japanese) 327 Braun Ct	Ann Arbor	MI	48104	734-663-3111
Gandy Dancer (Seafood) 401 Depot St	Ann Arbor	MI	48104	734-769-0592
Gratzi (Italian) 326 S Main St	Ann Arbor	MI	48104	734-663-5555
Grizzly Peak Brewing Co (American) 120 W Washington	Ann Arbor	MI	48104	734-741-7325
Heidelberg Restaurant (German) 215 N Main St	Ann Arbor	MI	48104	734-663-7758
Kai Garden (Chinese) 116 S Main St	Ann Arbor	MI	48104	734-995-1786
Kana Korean Restaurant (Korean) 114 W Liberty St	Ann Arbor	MI	48104	734-662-9303
Kerrytown Bistro (French) 415 N 5th Ave	Ann Arbor	MI	48104	734-994-6424
Middle Kingdom (Chinese) 332 S Main St	Ann Arbor	MI	48104	734-668-6638
Miki Japanese Restaurant (Japanese) 106 S 1st St	Ann Arbor	MI	48104	734-665-8226
Movable Feast (French) 326 W Liberty St	Ann Arbor	MI	48103	734-663-3278
Parthenon (Greek) 226 S Main St	Ann Arbor	MI	48104	734-994-1012
Prickly Pear Southwest Cafe (Southwest) 328 S Main St	Ann Arbor	MI	48104	734-930-0047
Raja Rani (Indian) 400 S Division St	Ann Arbor	MI	48104	734-995-1545
Real Seafood Co (Seafood) 341 S Main St	Ann Arbor	MI	48104	734-769-5960
Seva Restaurant (Vegetarian) 314 E Liberty St	Ann Arbor	MI	48104	734-662-1111
Siam Cuisine (Thai) 313 N 4th Ave	Ann Arbor	MI	48104	734-663-4083
Sweet Lorraine's Cafe (American) 303 Detroit St	Ann Arbor	MI	48104	734-665-0700
West End Grill (New American) 120 W Liberty Ave	Ann Arbor	MI	48104	734-747-6260

— Goods and Services —

SHOPPING

	City	State	ZIP	Phone	Fax
Antiques Mall of Ann Arbor 2739 Plymouth Rd	Ann Arbor	MI	48105	734-663-8200	
Briarwood Mall 100 Briarwood Cir	Ann Arbor	MI	48108	734-769-9610	769-2521
Depot Town E Cross & River Sts	Ypsilanti	MI	48198	734-483-4444	
Kerrytown Shops 407 N 5th Ave	Ann Arbor	MI	48104	734-662-5008	
Main Street Area Main St betw William & Huron	Ann Arbor	MI	48104		

BANKS

	City	State	ZIP	Phone	Fax
Ann Arbor Commerce Bank 2950 S State St	Ann Arbor	MI	48104	734-995-3130	995-9717
Bank of Ann Arbor 125 S 5th Ave	Ann Arbor	MI	48103	734-662-1600	662-0934
Great Lakes National Bank 401 E Liberty St	Ann Arbor	MI	48104	734-769-8300	930-6740*
**Fax:* Mktg ■ *TF:* 800-362-5555					
KeyBank NA 100 S Main St	Ann Arbor	MI	48104	734-741-6582	747-7448
Michigan National Bank 201 S Main St	Ann Arbor	MI	48105	734-747-7600	747-7613
TF: 800-225-5662					
National City Bank 101 S Main St	Ann Arbor	MI	48104	734-995-7801	995-5240
TF Cust Svc: 800-832-9184*					
Republic Bank 2100 S Main St Suite E	Ann Arbor	MI	49103	734-665-4080	665-4184
University Bank 959 Maiden Ln	Ann Arbor	MI	48105	734-741-5858	741-5859

BUSINESS SERVICES

	Phone		Phone
Airborne Express	800-247-2676	**Mail Boxes Etc**	734-665-7981
BAX Global	800-225-5229	**Personal Scribe**	734-996-8585
DHL Worldwide Express	800-225-5345	**Post Office**	734-665-1100
Federal Express	800-238-5355	**UPS**	800-742-5877
Kinko's	734-761-4539		

— Media —

PUBLICATIONS

	City	State	ZIP	Phone	Fax
Ann Arbor News‡ PO Box 1147	Ann Arbor	MI	48106	734-994-6989	994-6879
TF: 800-466-6989 ■ *Web:* aa.mlive.com					

‡Daily newspapers

TELEVISION

	City	State	ZIP	Phone	Fax
WDIV-TV Ch 4 (NBC) 550 W Lafayette Blvd	Detroit	MI	48231	313-222-0444	222-0592
Web: www.wdiv.com					
WJBK-TV Ch 2 (Fox) PO Box 2000	Southfield	MI	48037	248-557-2000	552-0280
Web: www.wjbk.com ■ *E-mail:* contact@fox2detroit.com					
WKAR-TV Ch 23 (PBS) MSU 212 Communications Arts Bldg	East Lansing	MI	48824	517-432-9527	353-7124
Web: www.wkar.msu.edu/tv/index.htm ■ *E-mail:* mail@wkar.msu.edu					
WTVS-TV Ch 56 (PBS) 7441 2nd Ave	Detroit	MI	48202	313-873-7200	876-8118
Web: www.wtvs.org ■ *E-mail:* viewer_services@wtvs.pbs.org					
WXYZ-TV Ch 7 (ABC) 20777 W 10-Mile Rd	Southfield	MI	48037	248-827-7777	827-4454
Web: www.detnow.com ■ *E-mail:* talkback@wxyztv.com					

RADIO

	City	State	ZIP	Phone	Fax
WAAM-AM 1600 kHz (N/T) 4230 Packard Rd	Ann Arbor	MI	48108	734-971-1600	973-2916
WCBN-FM 88.3 MHz (Misc) 530 Student Activities Bldg	Ann Arbor	MI	48109	734-763-3500	647-3885
Web: wcbn.org					
WDEO-AM 1290 kHz (Rel) 24 Frank Lloyd Wright Dr	Ann Arbor	MI	48106	734-930-3177	930-3179
WIQB-FM 102.9 MHz (Alt) 24 Frank Lloyd Wright Dr Lobby D	Ann Arbor	MI	48106	734-930-0103	741-1071
Web: www.rock103wiqb.com ■ *E-mail:* rock103wiqb.com					
WQKL-FM 107.1 MHz (AC) 24 Frank Lloyd Wright Dr Lobby D	Ann Arbor	MI	48106	734-930-0107	741-1071
Web: www.kool107.com					
WTKA-AM 1050 kHz (N/T) 24 Frank Lloyd Wright Dr Lobby D	Ann Arbor	MI	48106	734-930-0107	741-1071
Web: www.wtka.com					
WUOM-FM 91.7 MHz (NPR) 5000 LSA Bldg	Ann Arbor	MI	48109	734-764-9210	647-3488
Web: www.umich.edu/~wuom/ ■ *E-mail:* annat@umich.edu					

Ann Arbor (Cont'd)

— Colleges/Universities —

Name / Address	City	State	Zip	Phone	Fax
Cleary College 2170 Washtenaw Ave	Ypsilanti	MI	48197	734-332-4477	483-0090
TF Admissions: 800-589-1979 ■ *Web:* www.cleary.edu					
Concordia College 4090 Geddes Rd	Ann Arbor	MI	48105	734-995-7300	995-4610
TF: 800-253-0680 ■ *Web:* www.ccaa.edu ■ *E-mail:* admissions@ccaa.edu					
Eastern Michigan University	Ypsilanti	MI	48197	734-487-1849	487-1484
Web: www.emich.edu					
University of Michigan 503 Thompson St	Ann Arbor	MI	48109	734-764-1817	936-0740
Web: www.umich.edu					
Washtenaw Community College 4800 E Huron River Dr	Ann Arbor	MI	48106	734-973-3300	677-5414
Web: www.washtenaw.cc.mi.us					

— Hospitals —

Name / Address	City	State	Zip	Phone	Fax
Chelsea Community Hospital 955 W Eisenhower Cir	Ann Arbor	MI	48103	734-665-5070	665-6487
University of Michigan Medical Center 1500 E Medical Center Dr	Ann Arbor	MI	48109	734-936-4000	647-3273
Web: www.med.umich.edu					
Veterans Affairs Medical Center 2215 Fuller Rd	Ann Arbor	MI	48105	734-769-7100	761-7870

— Attractions —

Name / Address	City	State	Zip	Phone	Fax
Alber's Orchard 13011 Bethel Church Rd.	Manchester	MI	48158	734-428-7758	428-8873
Ann Arbor Art Center 117 W Liberty St	Ann Arbor	MI	48104	734-994-8004	994-3610
Ann Arbor Artisans & Farmers' Market Catherine & 4th Ave	Ann Arbor	MI	48104	734-994-3276	
Web: goblin.arborlink.com/artisanmarket					
Ann Arbor Civic Ballet 525 E Liberty St.	Ann Arbor	MI	48104	734-668-8066	668-8066
Ann Arbor Civic Theatre 2275 Platt Rd	Ann Arbor	MI	48104	734-971-2228	971-2769
Web: www.a2ct.org					
Ann Arbor Hands-On Museum 219 E Huron St.	Ann Arbor	MI	48104	734-995-5439	995-1188
Web: www.aahom.org					
Ann Arbor Ice Cube 2121 Oak Valley Dr	Ann Arbor	MI	48103	734-213-1600	213-7614
Web: www.emich.edu/public/hockey/icecube.html					
Ann Arbor Symphony Orchestra 527 E Liberty St Michigan Theater	Ann Arbor	MI	48104	734-994-4801	994-3949
Web: www.wwnet.net/~a2so					
Argus Planetarium 601 W Stadium Blvd	Ann Arbor	MI	48103	734-994-1771	994-2198
ArtVentures Art Center 117 W Liberty	Ann Arbor	MI	48104	734-994-8004	994-3610
Bentley Historical Library 1150 Beal Ave.	Ann Arbor	MI	48109	734-764-3482	936-1333
E-mail: bentley.ref@umich.edu					
Chelsea Milling Co PO Box 460	Chelsea	MI	48118	734-475-1361	475-4630
Web: www.jiffymix.com					
Cobblestone Farm Museum 2781 Packard Rd	Ann Arbor	MI	48108	734-994-2928	971-9415
Comic Opera Guild 227 S Ingalls St University of Michigan Mendelssohn Theatre	Ann Arbor	MI	48109	734-973-3264	973-6281
Domino's Farm Petting Zoo 24 Frank Lloyd Wright Dr.	Ann Arbor	MI	48106	734-930-5032	930-3012
Eddy Geology Center 16345 McClure Rd	Chelsea	MI	48118	734-475-3170	475-1830
Exhibit Museum of Natural History 1109 Geddes Ave University of Michigan	Ann Arbor	MI	48109	734-764-0478	647-2767
Web: www.exhibits.lsa.umich.edu					
Gallup Park 3000 Fuller	Ann Arbor	MI	48104	734-994-2778	
Gerald R Ford Library 1000 Beal Ave	Ann Arbor	MI	48109	734-741-2218	741-2341
Web: www.ford.utexas.edu ■ *E-mail:* library@fordlib.nara.gov					
Herbarium of the University of Michigan North University Bldg Rm 2001	Ann Arbor	MI	48109	734-764-2407	
Historic Hack House Museum 775 County St.	Milan	MI	48160	734-439-7522	439-7522
Kelsey Museum of Archaeology 434 S State St University of Michigan	Ann Arbor	MI	48109	734-763-3559	763-8976
Web: www.umich.edu/~kelseydb					
Kempf House 312 S Division St	Ann Arbor	MI	48104	734-994-4898	
Kerrytown Concert House 415 N 4th Ave.	Ann Arbor	MI	48104	734-769-2999	769-7791
Leslie Science Center 1831 Traver Rd	Ann Arbor	MI	48105	734-662-7802	997-1072
Lillie Park Platt Rd	Ann Arbor	MI	48108	734-996-3056	
Matthaei Botanical Gardens 1800 N Dixboro Rd	Ann Arbor	MI	48105	734-998-7061	998-6205
Web: www.lsa.umich.edu/mbg/index.html					
Michigan Theater 603 E Liberty	Ann Arbor	MI	48104	734-668-8397	668-7136
Web: www.michtheater.com/mt/					
Nichols Aboretum 1827 Geddes Rd University of Michigan	Ann Arbor	MI	48109	734-763-6632	936-2195
Web: www.umich.edu/~snrewww/arb/					
Parker Mill 4650 Geddes Rd	Ann Arbor	MI	48105	734-971-6337	971-6386
Performance Network 408 W Washington	Ann Arbor	MI	48103	734-663-0681	
Web: comnet.org/PNetwork/ ■ *E-mail:* oops@ izzy.net					
Power Center for the Performing Arts Huron & Fletcher	Ann Arbor	MI	48109	734-763-3333	
Riverside Arts Center 76 N Huron St	Ypsilanti	MI	48197	734-480-2787	
Sharon Mills Winery 5701 Sharon Hollow Rd.	Manchester	MI	48158	734-428-9160	
Spring Valley Trout Farm 12190 Island Lake Rd	Dexter	MI	48130	734-426-4772	426-2238
Stearn's Collection of Musical Instruments 1100 Baits Dr University of Michigan School of Music	Ann Arbor	MI	48109	734-763-4389	763-5097
Towsley Margaret Dow Sports Museum 1000 S State St Schembechler Hall	Ann Arbor	MI	48109	734-647-2583	
University of Michigan Museum of Art 525 S State St	Ann Arbor	MI	48109	734-764-0395	764-3731
Web: www.umich.edu/~umma/					
Veterans Memorial Park 2150 Jackson Rd	Ann Arbor	MI	48103	734-761-7240	994-8988
Washtenaw County Park Platt Rd	Ann Arbor	MI	48107	734-971-6337	971-6386
Waterloo Recreation Area 16345 McClure Rd	Chelsea	MI	48118	734-475-8307	475-1830
Wild Swan Theater 416 W Huron St.	Ann Arbor	MI	48103	734-995-0530	668-7292
Web: comnet.org/wildswan ■ *E-mail:* WildSwanTh@aol.com					
Yankee Air Museum Willow Run Airport	Ypsilanti	MI	48197	734-483-4030	
Ypsilanti Automotive Heritage Collection 100-112 E Cross St.	Ypsilanti	MI	48198	734-482-5200	482-5200
Ypsilanti Historical Museum 220 N Huron St	Ypsilanti	MI	48197	734-482-4990	483-7481
Web: www.hvcn.org/info/libyhma.html					

SPORTS TEAMS & FACILITIES

Name / Address	City	State	Zip	Phone	Fax
Detroit Lions 1200 Featherstone Rd Pontiac Silverdome	Pontiac	MI	48342	248-335-4151	322-2283
Web: www.detroitlions.com					
Detroit Pistons 2 Championship Dr Palace of Auburn Hills	Auburn Hills	MI	48326	248-377-0100	377-4262
Web: www.nba.com/pistons					
Detroit Red Wings 600 Civic Ctr Dr Joe Louis Arena	Detroit	MI	48226	313-396-7544	567-0296
Web: www.detroitredwings.com					
Detroit Rockers (soccer) 600 Civic Ctr Dr Joe Louis Arena	Detroit	MI	48226	313-396-7070	396-7944
Web: www.concentric.net/~jibanes/rockers					
Detroit Tigers 2121 Trumbull Ave Tiger Stadium	Detroit	MI	48216	313-962-4000	
TF: 800-221-2324 ■ *Web:* www.detroittigers.com ■ *E-mail:* tigers@detroittigers.com					
Detroit Vipers (hockey) 2 Championship Dr Palace at Auburn Hills	Auburn Hills	MI	48326	248-377-0100	377-2695
Web: www.detroitvipers.com/ ■ *E-mail:* info@detroitvipers.com					
Michigan International Speedway US-12	Brooklyn	MI	49230	517-592-6672	592-3848
TF: 800-354-1010					
Milan International Dragway 10860 Plank Rd	Milan	MI	48160	734-439-7368	
Web: www.milandragway.com					

— Events —

	Phone
Ann Arbor Antiques Market (April-November)	734-995-7281
Ann Arbor Art Fair Extravaganza (mid-late July)	734-995-7281
Ann Arbor Blues & Jazz Festival (early September)	734-747-9955
Ann Arbor Film Festival (early March)	734-668-8397
Ann Arbor Folk Music Festival (late January)	734-763-5750
Ann Arbor Street Art Fair (mid-July)	734-995-7281
Ann Arbor Summer Festival (late June-mid-July)	734-647-2278
Ann Arbor Winter Art Fair (late October)	734-995-7281
Big Ten Run (late September)	734-973-6730
Festival of Lights (December 31)	734-483-4444
Frog Island Festival (late June)	734-761-1800
Heritage Festival (mid-August)	734-327-2051
New Year Jubilee (December 31)	734-483-4444
Pow Wow (early-mid-March)	734-764-9044
Summer Symphony (June-August)	734-677-4831
Winter Carnival (mid-February)	734-994-2780

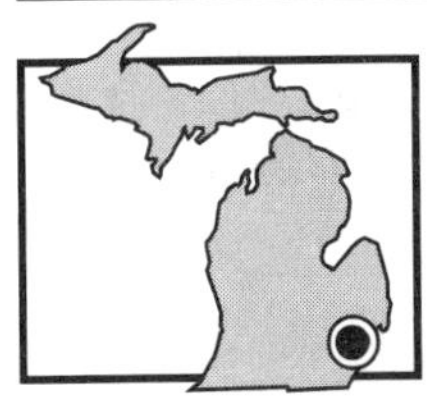

Detroit

The downtown skyline of Detroit is dominated by the Renaissance Center, which has six office towers and the 73-story Westin Hotel, one of the tallest hotels in the world. Located in southeast downtown is Greektown, one of the "Motor City's" most popular entertainment districts. Trappers Alley, at the center of Greektown, was once a leading fur center of the Midwest. Today it is a shopping center made up of five century-old buildings enclosed under one roof. Three miles southeast of the city center is Belle Isle, a 1,000-acre park in the Detroit River. The park has a Zoo, Aquarium, and Whitcomb Conservatory, known for its orchid collections. Near Detroit in the city of Dearborn is the Henry Ford Museum and Greenfield Village. The Village is an indoor-outdoor museum which preserves 80 famous historic structures, among them Thomas Edison's laboratory, the bikeshop where the Wright Brothers' first airplane was built, and the farm where Henry Ford was born.

Population	970,196	**Longitude**	83-04-39 W
Area (Land)	138.7 sq mi	**County**	Wayne
Area (Water)	4.2 sq mi	**Time Zone**	EST
Elevation	600 ft	**Area Code/s**	313
Latitude	42-34-01 N		

— Average Temperatures and Precipitation —

TEMPERATURES

	Jan	Feb	Mar	Apr	May	Jun	Jul	Aug	Sep	Oct	Nov	Dec
High	30	33	44	58	70	79	83	81	74	62	48	35
Low	16	18	27	37	47	56	61	60	53	41	32	21

PRECIPITATION

	Jan	Feb	Mar	Apr	May	Jun	Jul	Aug	Sep	Oct	Nov	Dec
Inches	1.8	1.7	2.6	3.0	2.9	3.6	3.2	3.4	2.9	2.1	2.7	2.8

— Important Phone Numbers —

	Phone		Phone
AAA	313-336-1234	**Medical Referral**	313-567-1640
American Express Travel	248-642-3350	**Poison Control Center**	313-745-5711
Dental Referral	313-871-3500	**Time**	248-472-1212
Emergency	911	**Travelers Aid**	313-962-6740
Greater Detroit Activity Line	248-597-1010	**Visitor Information Line**	800-338-7648
HotelDocs	800-468-3537	**Weather**	313-961-8686

— Information Sources —

				Phone	Fax
Better Business Bureau Serving Detroit & Eastern Michigan 30555 Southfield Rd Suite 200 *Web:* www.detroit.bbb.org	Southfield	MI	48076	248-644-9100	644-5026
Cobo Conference & Exhibition Center 1 Washington Blvd *Web:* www.cobocenter.com	Detroit	MI	48226	313-877-8777	877-8577
Detroit City Hall 2 Woodward Ave *Web:* www.ci.detroit.mi.us	Detroit	MI	48226	313-224-3270	
Detroit Mayor 2 Woodward Ave Suite 1126 *Web:* www.ci.detroit.mi.us/mayor/ ■ *E-mail:* archerd@mayor.ci.detroit.mi.us	Detroit	MI	48226	313-224-3400	224-4433
Detroit Planning & Development Dept 65 Cadillac Tower Suite 2300 *Web:* www.ci.detroit.mi.us/plandevl	Detroit	MI	48226	313-224-2560	224-1629
Detroit Public Library 5201 Woodward Ave *Web:* www.detroit.lib.mi.us	Detroit	MI	48202	313-833-1000	832-0877
Greater Detroit Chamber of Commerce 1 Woodward Ave *Web:* www.detroitchamber.com	Detroit	MI	48226	313-964-4000	964-0531
Metropolitan Detroit Convention & Visitors Bureau 211 W Fort St Suite 1000 *TF:* 800-225-5389 ■ *Web:* www.visitdetroit.com	Detroit	MI	48226	313-202-1800	202-1808
Wayne County 211 City-County Bldg *Web:* www.waynecounty.com	Detroit	MI	48226	313-224-6262	224-5364

On-Line Resources

4Detroit.com	www.4detroit.com
About.com Guide to Detroit	detroit.about.com/local/midwestus/detroit
Anthill City Guide Detroit	www.anthill.com/city.asp?city=detroit
Area Guide Detroit	detroit.areaguides.net
Boulevards Detroit	www.detroit.com
City Knowledge Detroit	www.cityknowledge.com/mi_detroit.htm
CitySearch Detroit	detroit.citysearch.com
Detroit City Pages	detroit.thelinks.com/
Detroit CityLink	www.usacitylink.com/citylink/detroit
Detroit On-line Metro Directory	detroit.net/
Detroit's Internet Metro Guide	www.metroguide.com/
DigitalCity Detroit	home.digitalcity.com/detroit
Excite.com Detroit City Guide	www.excite.com/travel/countries/united_states/michigan/detroit
Fabulous Ruins of Detroit	bhere.com/ruins/home.htm
InDetroit.com	www.indetroit.com
iNetDetroit	www.inetdetroit.com
Metro Detroit Area Guide	www.citysidewalks.com/detroitnew/frames17.htm
Metro On-Line Magazine	www.ddsi.com/metro/
MetroDine Detroit	www.metrodine.com/MetroDetroit/
Rough Guide Travel Detroit	travel.roughguides.com/content/483/

— Transportation Services —

AIRPORTS

■ **Detroit Metropolitan Airport (DTW)**

	Phone
20 miles SW of downtown (approx 30 minutes) Web: www.metroairport.com	734-942-3685

Airport Transportation

	Phone
Commuter Transportation $19 fare to downtown	734-941-3252
Luxury Sedan Transportation Service $35 fare to downtown	313-331-1211
Metropolitan Shuttlebus $22 fare to downtown	734-942-7452
Taxi $25-30 fare to downtown	313-582-6900

Commercial Airlines

	Phone		Phone
American	800-433-7300	**Southwest**	800-435-9792
British Airways	800-247-9297	**Sun Country**	800-359-5786
Continental	800-525-0280	**TWA**	800-221-2000
Continental Express	800-525-0280	**United**	800-241-6522
Delta	800-221-1212	**US Airways**	800-428-4322
Northwest	800-225-2525		

Charter Airlines

	Phone		Phone
Aero Charter Inc	800-535-1445	**Corporate Flight Inc**	800-767-2473
Corporate America Aviation Inc	800-521-8585	**Direct Airway**	800-257-9424

■ **Detroit City Airport (DET)**

	Phone
6 miles E of downtown (approx 20 minutes)	313-852-6400

Airport Transportation

	Phone
Commuter Transportation $15 fare to downtown	734-941-3252
Luxury Sedan Transportation Service $40 fare to downtown	313-331-1211
Taxi $15 fare to downtown	313-582-6900

Commercial Airlines

	Phone
Pro Air	313-245-4706

Charter Airlines

	Phone		Phone
Helicopters Inc	800-466-2903	**Signature Flight Support**	313-527-6620

Detroit (Cont'd)

CAR RENTALS

	Phone		Phone
Alamo	734-941-8420	**Hertz**	734-941-4747
Avis	734-942-3450	**National**	734-941-7000
Dollar	734-942-4777	**Thrifty**	734-946-7830
Enterprise	734-467-8054		

LIMO/TAXI

	Phone		Phone
Checker Cab	313-963-5005	**Michigan Limousine Service**	248-546-6112
Larry's Limousine	313-834-1087	**Southfield Cab**	888-757-1090
Lorraine Cab	313-582-6900	**Taylor Winfield Limousine Service**	313-833-2266
Metro Cars	734-946-5700		

MASS TRANSIT

	Phone
Detroit Department of Transportation Bus $1.25 Base fare	313-933-1300
Detroit Trolley $.50 Base Fare	313-224-6449
People Mover $.50 Base fare	313-962-7245
SMART $1.50 Base fare	313-962-5515

RAIL/BUS

				Phone
Amtrak Station 11 W Baltimore Ave	Detroit	MI	48202	800-872-7245
Greyhound/Trailways Bus Station 1001 Howard St.	Detroit	MI	48226	800-231-2222

— Accommodations —

HOTELS, MOTELS, RESORTS

				Phone	Fax
Atheneum Suite Hotel 1000 Brush Ave *TF:* 800-772-2323	Detroit	MI	48226	313-962-2323	962-2424
Best Western Sterling Inn 34911 Van Dyke Ave *TF:* 800-528-1234	Sterling Heights	MI	48312	810-979-1400	979-0430
Courtyard by Marriott 17200 N Laurel Park Dr. *TF:* 800-321-2211 ■ *Web:* courtyard.com/DETLV	Livonia	MI	48152	734-462-2000	462-5907
Courtyard by Marriott 333 E Jefferson Ave. *TF:* 800-321-2211	Detroit	MI	48226	313-222-7700	222-6509
Courtyard by Marriott Metro Airport 30653 Flynn Dr. *TF:* 800-321-2211 ■ *Web:* courtyard.com/DTWCA	Romulus	MI	48174	734-721-3200	721-1304
Crowne Plaza Detroit 8000 Merriman Rd. *TF:* 800-227-6963	Romulus	MI	48174	734-729-2600	729-9414
Dearborn Inn 20301 Oakwood Blvd *TF:* 800-228-9290	Dearborn	MI	48124	313-271-2700	271-7464
Detroit Airport Marriott Hotel Detroit Metropolitan Airport *TF:* 800-228-9290	Detroit	MI	48242	734-941-9400	941-2522
Detroit Marriott Renaissance Center Jefferson & Brush Sts *TF:* 800-228-9290	Detroit	MI	48243	313-568-8000	568-8666
Doubletree Guest Suites 28100 Franklin Rd. *TF:* 800-222-8733 ■ *Web:* www.doubletreehotels.com/DoubleT/Hotel41/59/59Main.htm	Southfield	MI	48034	248-350-2000	350-1185
Georgian Inn 31327 Gratiot Ave *TF:* 800-477-1466 ■ *Web:* www.thegeorgianinn.com ■ *E-mail:* sales@thegeorgianinn.com	Roseville	MI	48066	810-294-0400	294-1020
Hampton Inn Metro 30847 Flynn Dr *TF:* 800-426-7866	Romulus	MI	48174	734-721-1100	721-9915
Hilton Hotel Northfield 5500 Crooks Rd *TF:* 800-445-8667 ■ *Web:* www.hilton.com/hotels/DETNHHF	Troy	MI	48098	248-879-2100	879-6054
Hilton Suites Metro Airport 8600 Wickham Rd *TF:* 800-445-8667 ■ *Web:* www.hilton.com/hotels/DETHSHF	Romulus	MI	48174	734-728-9200	728-9278
Hotel Pontchartrain 2 Washington Blvd *TF:* 800-537-8483	Detroit	MI	48226	313-965-0200	965-9464
Hotel Saint Regis New Center Area 3071 W Grand Blvd. *TF:* 800-848-4810	Detroit	MI	48202	313-873-3000	873-2574
Hyatt Regency Dearborn Fairlane Town Ctr *TF:* 800-233-1234 ■ *Web:* www.hyatt.com/usa/detroit/hotels/hotel_dttrd.html	Dearborn	MI	48126	313-593-1234	593-3366
Kingsley Hotel & Suites 1475 N Woodward Ave *TF:* 800-544-6835	Bloomfield Hills	MI	48304	248-644-1400	644-5449
Marriott Hotel Romulus 30559 Flynn Dr *TF:* 800-228-9290 ■ *Web:* marriotthotels.com/DTWRM	Romulus	MI	48174	734-729-7555	729-8634
Michigan Inn 16400 JL Hudson Dr *TF:* 800-800-5112	Southfield	MI	48075	248-559-6500	559-3625
Milner Hotel 1538 Centre St. *TF:* 800-521-0592 ■ *Web:* www.milner-hotels.com/milnerdetroit.html ■ *E-mail:* milnerht@ix.netcom.com	Detroit	MI	48226	313-962-5400	962-0847
Novi Hilton Hotel 21111 Haggerty Rd *TF:* 800-445-8667	Novi	MI	48375	248-349-4000	349-4066
Omni Hotel 1000 Stroh River Pl *TF:* 800-843-6664 ■ *Web:* www.grandheritage.com/htmlcode/hus_riverpal.html	Detroit	MI	48207	313-259-9500	567-2439
Ramada Inn Metro Airport 8270 Wickham Rd *TF:* 800-272-6232	Romulus	MI	48174	734-729-6300	729-6491
Ramada International Hotel & Convention Center 17017 W Nine-Mile Rd *TF:* 800-272-6232	Southfield	MI	48075	248-552-7777	552-7778
Residence Inn by Marriott 2600 Livernois Rd *TF:* 800-331-3131 ■ *Web:* www.residenceinn.com/DTTTY	Troy	MI	48083	248-689-6856	689-3788
Residence Inn by Marriott 5777 Southfield Service Dr. *TF:* 800-331-3131	Detroit	MI	48228	313-441-1700	441-4144
Ritz-Carlton Dearborn 300 Town Ctr Dr. *TF:* 800-241-3333 ■ *Web:* www.ritzcarlton.com/location/NorthAmerica/Dearborn/main.htm	Dearborn	MI	48126	313-441-2000	441-2051
Saint Clair Inn 500 N Riverside Ave *TF:* 800-482-8327	Saint Clair	MI	48079	810-329-2222	329-2348
Somerset Inn Hotel 2601 W Big Beaver Rd *TF:* 800-228-8769	Troy	MI	48084	248-643-7800	643-2296
Town Apartments & Suites 1511 1st St. *TF:* 800-385-5333	Detroit	MI	48226	313-962-0674	962-2724
Townsend Hotel 100 Townsend St *TF:* 800-548-4172	Birmingham	MI	48009	248-642-7900	645-9061
Van Dyke Park Hotel & Conference Center 31800 Van Dyke Ave	Warren	MI	48093	810-939-2860	268-4880
Westin Hotel 1500 Town Ctr Dr *TF:* 800-894-8300	Southfield	MI	48075	248-827-4000	827-1364
Wyndham Garden Hotel 8600 Merriman Rd. *TF:* 800-996-3426	Romulus	MI	48174	734-728-7900	728-6518

— Restaurants —

				Phone
Atwater Block Brewery (American) 237 Joseph Campau St.	Detroit	MI	48207	313-393-2337
Blue Nile (Ethiopian) 508 Monroe St	Detroit	MI	48226	313-964-6699
Cadieux Cafe (Belgian) 4300 Cadieux St.	Detroit	MI	48224	313-882-8560
Cafe Bon Homme (European) 844 Penniman	Plymouth	MI	48170	734-453-6260
Carl's Chop House (Steak/Seafood) 3020 Grand River Ave	Detroit	MI	48201	313-833-0700
Caucus Club (Continental) 150 W Congress St	Detroit	MI	48226	313-965-4970
Charley's Crab (Seafood) 5498 Crooks Rd	Troy	MI	48098	248-879-2060
Chung's Restaurant (Chinese) 3177 Cass Ave	Detroit	MI	48201	313-831-1100
Clique The (American) 1326 E Jefferson Ave.	Detroit	MI	48207	313-259-0922
Courthouse Brasserie (American) 1436 E Brush St	Detroit	MI	48226	313-963-8887
Dakota Inn Rathskeller (German) 17324 John R St	Detroit	MI	48203	313-867-9722
Duet at Orchestra Place (American) 3663 Woodward Ave	Detroit	MI	48201	313-831-3838
Dunleavy'z River Place (American) 267 Jos Campau	Detroit	MI	48207	313-259-0909
Fishbone's Rhythm Kitchen Cafe (Cajun) 400 Monroe St	Detroit	MI	48226	313-965-4600
Foran's Irish Pub (Irish) 612 Woodward Ave	Detroit	MI	48226	313-961-3043
Frankenmuth Bavarian Inn (German) 713 S Main St	Frankenmuth	MI	48734	517-652-9941
Franklin Street Brewing Co (American) 1560 Franklin St	Detroit	MI	48207	313-568-0390
Giovanni's Ristorante (Italian) 330 S Oakwood Blvd	Detroit	MI	48217	313-841-0122
Golden Mushroom (Continental) 18100 W 10-Mile Rd	Southfield	MI	48075	248-559-4230
Intermezzo (Italian) 1435 Randolph St	Detroit	MI	48226	313-961-0707
Ja Da (Barbecue) 546 E Larned St	Detroit	MI	48226	313-965-1700
Lark Restaurant (European) 6430 Farmington Rd.	West Bloomfield	MI	48322	248-661-4466
Lelli's Inn (Italian) 7618 Woodward Ave.	Detroit	MI	48202	313-871-1590
MacKinnon's (American) 126 E Main St	Northville	MI	48167	248-348-1991
Majestic Cafe (Mediterranean) 4140 Woodward Ave	Detroit	MI	48201	313-833-0120
New Hellas Cafe (Greek) 583 Monroe St	Detroit	MI	48226	313-961-5544
New Parthenon (Greek) 547 Monroe St	Detroit	MI	48226	313-963-8888
Nippon Kai (Japanese) 511 W 14-Mile Rd	Clawson	MI	48017	248-288-3210
Opus One (American) 565 E Larned St	Detroit	MI	48226	313-961-7766
Pegasus Taverna (Greek) 558 Monroe St	Detroit	MI	48226	313-964-6800
Rattlesnake Club (New American) 300 River Pl.	Detroit	MI	48207	313-567-4400
Risata (Italian) 2301 Woodward Ave	Detroit	MI	48201	313-965-9500
Roma Cafe (Italian) 3401 Riopelle	Detroit	MI	48207	313-831-5940
Rumors on the River (American) 8900 E Jefferson Ave	Detroit	MI	48214	313-824-1000
Summit Restaurant (Continental) Renaissance Ctr	Detroit	MI	48243	313-568-8600
Too Chez (American) 27155 Sheraton Dr	Novi	MI	48377	248-348-5555
Tres Vite (New American) 2203 Woodward Ave	Detroit	MI	48201	313-471-3500
Tribute Restaurant (French/Asian) 31425 W 12 Mile Rd *Web:* www.tribute-restaurant.com ■ *E-mail:* tribute@earthlink.net	Farmington Hills	MI	48334	248-848-9393
Whitney The (Steak/Seafood) 4421 Woodward Ave *Web:* www.thewhitney.com/	Detroit	MI	48201	313-832-5700

Detroit (Cont'd)

— Goods and Services —

SHOPPING

				Phone	Fax
Eastland Center 18000 Vernier Rd	Harper Woods	MI	48225	313-371-1501	371-3511
Fairlane Town Center 18900 Michigan Ave	Dearborn	MI	48126	313-593-3330	593-0572
Lakeside Mall 14000 Lakeside Cir	Sterling Heights	MI	48312	800-334-5573	
Laurel Park Place 37700 6 Mile Rd	Livonia	MI	48152	734-462-1100	462-6210
Macomb Mall 32100 Beaconsfield St.	Roseville	MI	48066	810-294-2816	
New Center Place 3031 W Grand Blvd	Detroit	MI	48202	313-874-4444	
Northland Shopping Center 21500 Northwestern Hwy.	Southfield	MI	48075	248-557-0460	569-0861
Oakland Mall 412 W 14 Mile Rd.	Troy	MI	48083	248-585-6000	585-2440
Renaissance Center 200 Renaissance Ctr Suite 1200	Detroit	MI	48243	313-568-5600	568-5606
Somerset Collection 2800 W Big Beaver Rd	Troy	MI	48084	248-643-6360	643-4633
Summitt Place 315 N Telegraph Rd	Waterford	MI	48328	248-682-0123	682-1188
Tel Twelve Mall 28690 Telegraph Rd	Southfield	MI	48034	248-354-0002	353-1857
Twelve Oaks Mall 27500 Novi Rd.	Novi	MI	48377	248-348-9400	348-9411

BANKS

				Phone	Fax
Comerica Bank 500 Woodward Ave	Detroit	MI	48226	800-643-4418	222-4667*
**Fax Area Code:* 313 ■ *Web:* www.comerica.com					
First State Bank of East Detroit 16100 E Nine-Mile Rd	Eastpointe	MI	48021	810-775-5000	773-7233
Michigan National Bank 25001 Michigan Ave	Dearborn	MI	48124	800-225-5662	274-5460*
**Fax Area Code:* 313					
National City Bank PO Box 2659	Detroit	MI	48231	800-925-9259	596-8239*
**Fax Area Code:* 313					
NBD Bank 611 Woodward Ave	Detroit	MI	48226	313-225-3774	225-3334*
**Fax:* Cust Svc ■ *TF:* 800-225-5623					

BUSINESS SERVICES

	Phone		Phone
Expeditors of Michigan	313-961-3877	**Manpower Temporary Services**	313-871-1010
Federal Express	800-463-3339	**Olsten Staffing Services**	313-875-4300
Kelly Services	313-259-1400	**Post Office**	313-226-8302
Kinko's	313-259-8344	**UPS**	800-742-5877

— Media —

PUBLICATIONS

				Phone	Fax
Connection The 96 Kercheval Ave	Grosse Pointe	MI	48236	313-882-0294	882-1585*
**Fax:* News Rm					
Crain's Detroit Business 1400 Woodbridge St	Detroit	MI	48207	313-446-6000	446-1687
Web: www.crainsdetroit.com					
Detroit Free Press‡ 600 W Fort St	Detroit	MI	48226	313-222-6400	222-5981
TF: 800-678-6400 ■ *Web:* www.freep.com					
Detroit News‡ 615 W Lafayette Blvd	Detroit	MI	48226	313-222-6400	222-2335
TF: 800-678-6400 ■ *Web:* www.detnews.com					
Michigan Living 1 Auto Club Dr	Dearborn	MI	48126	313-336-1506	336-0986
Web: www.leelanau.com/nmj/living ■ *E-mail:* info@aaamich.com					

‡Daily newspapers

TELEVISION

				Phone	Fax
WADL-TV Ch 38 (Fox) 22590 15-Mile Rd.	Clinton Township	MI	48035	810-790-3838	790-3841
WDIV-TV Ch 4 (NBC) 550 W Lafayette Blvd	Detroit	MI	48231	313-222-0444	222-0592
Web: www.wdiv.com					
WDWB-TV Ch 20 (WB) 27777 Franklin Rd Suite 1220	Southfield	MI	48034	248-355-2020	355-0368
Web: www.wb20detroit.com					
WJBK-TV Ch 2 (Fox) PO Box 2000	Southfield	MI	48037	248-557-2000	552-0280
Web: www.wjbk.com ■ *E-mail:* contact@fox2detroit.com					
WKBD-TV Ch 50 (UPN) 26905 W 11-Mile Rd.	Southfield	MI	48034	248-350-5050	358-0977
Web: www.paramountstations.com/WKBD					
WPXD-TV Ch 31 (PAX) 3975 Varsity Dr.	Ann Arbor	MI	48108	734-973-7900	973-7906
Web: www.pax.net/WPXD					
WTVS-TV Ch 56 (PBS) 7441 2nd Ave	Detroit	MI	48202	313-873-7200	876-8118
Web: www.wtvs.org ■ *E-mail:* viewer_services@wtvs.pbs.org					
WWJ-TV Ch 62 (CBS) 300 River Pl Suite 6200	Detroit	MI	48207	313-259-6288	259-4585
WXYZ-TV Ch 7 (ABC) 20777 W 10-Mile Rd	Southfield	MI	48037	248-827-7777	827-4454
Web: www.detnow.com ■ *E-mail:* talkback@wxyztv.com					

RADIO

				Phone	Fax
CIDR-FM 93.9 MHz (AAA) 1640 Ouellette Ave	Windsor	ON	N8X1L1	313-961-9811	961-1603
Web: www.smoothrock939.com ■ *E-mail:* sales@theriver939.com					
CIMX-FM 88.7 MHz (Alt) 1640 Ouellette Ave	Windsor	ON	N8X1L1	313-961-9811	961-1603
CKLW-AM 800 kHz (N/T) 1640 Ouellette Ave	Windsor	ON	N8X1L1	313-961-9811	961-1603
CKWW-AM 580 kHz (Nost) 1640 Ouellette Ave	Windsor	ON	N8X1L1	313-961-9811	961-1603
WCHB-FM 105.9 MHz (Urban) 2994 E Grand Blvd	Detroit	MI	48202	313-871-0590	871-8770
WCSX-FM 94.7 MHz (CR) 28588 Northwestern Hwy Suite 200	Southfield	MI	48034	248-945-9470	355-3485
Web: www.wcsx.com					
WDET-FM 101.9 MHz (NPR) 4600 Cass Ave	Detroit	MI	48201	313-577-4146	577-1300
Web: www.wdetfm.org					
WDFN-AM 1130 kHz (Sports) 2930 E Jefferson Ave	Detroit	MI	48207	313-259-5440	259-0560
Web: www.wdfn.com					
WDRQ-FM 93.1 MHz (AC) 28411 Northwestern Hwy Suite 1000	Southfield	MI	48034	248-354-9300	354-1474
WEMU-FM 89.1 MHz (NPR) PO Box 980350	Ypsilanti	MI	48198	734-487-2229	487-1015
TF: 888-299-8910 ■ *Web:* www.wemu.org					
WGPR-FM 107.5 MHz (Urban) 3146 E Jefferson Ave	Detroit	MI	48207	313-259-8862	259-6662
WJLB-FM 97.9 MHz (Urban) 645 Griswold St Suite 633	Detroit	MI	48226	313-965-2000	965-3965
WJR-AM 760 kHz (N/T) 2100 Fisher Bldg.	Detroit	MI	48202	313-875-4440	875-9022
Web: www.760wjr.com					
WKQI-FM 95.5 MHz (AC) 15401 W 10-Mile Rd	Detroit	MI	48237	248-967-3750	967-0840
Web: www.q955.com					
WKRK-FM 97.1 MHz (Rock) 16550 W Nine-Mile Rd	Southfield	MI	48075	248-423-3300	423-3326
Web: www.wkrk.com ■ *E-mail:* wkrk@wkrk.com					
WMUZ-FM 103.5 MHz (Rel) 12300 Radio Pl	Detroit	MI	48228	313-272-3434	272-5045
WMXD-FM 92.3 MHz (AC) 645 Griswold St Suite 633	Detroit	MI	48226	313-965-2000	965-3965
WNIC-FM 100.3 MHz (AC) 15001 Michigan Ave	Dearborn	MI	48126	313-846-8500	846-1068
Web: www.wnic.com					
WOMC-FM 104.3 MHz (Oldies) 2201 Woodward Heights	Detroit	MI	48220	248-546-9600	546-5446
WPLT-FM 96.3 MHz (Alt) 2100 Fisher Bldg	Detroit	MI	48202	313-871-3030	875-9636
Web: www.planet963.com ■ *E-mail:* theplanet@planet963.com					
WQBH-AM 1400 kHz (Urban) 645 Griswold Ave Suite 2050	Detroit	MI	48226	313-965-4500	965-4608
WRIF-FM 101.1 MHz (Rock) 1 Radio Plaza	Ferndale	MI	48220	248-547-0101	542-8800
Web: www.wrif.com					
WVMV-FM 98.7 MHz (NAC) 31555 W 14-Mile Rd Suite 102	Farmington Hills	MI	48334	248-855-5100	855-1302
WWBR-FM 102.7 MHz (AC) 850 Stephenson Hwy Suite 405	Troy	MI	48083	248-589-7900	589-8295
WWJ-AM 950 kHz (N/T) 16550 W Nine-Mile Rd	Southfield	MI	48075	248-423-3300	423-3326
Web: wwj.com					
WWWW-FM 106.7 MHz (Ctry) 2930 E Jefferson Ave	Detroit	MI	48207	313-259-4323	259-9817
WXDG-FM 105.1 MHz (Alt) 1 Radio Plaza	Detroit	MI	48220	248-414-5600	355-3485
WXYT-AM 1270 kHz (N/T) 15600 W 12-Mile Rd.	Southfield	MI	48076	248-569-8000	569-9866
WYCD-FM 99.5 MHz (Ctry) 26555 Evergreen Suite 675	Southfield	MI	48076	248-799-0600	358-9216
Web: www.wycd.com					

— Colleges/Universities —

				Phone	Fax
Baker College Auburn Hills Campus 1500 University Dr	Auburn Hills	MI	48326	248-340-0600	340-0608
TF: 888-429-0410 ■ *Web:* www.baker.edu/visit/auburn.html ■ *E-mail:* adm-ah@baker.edu					
Center for Creative Studies College of Art & Design 201 E Kirby St.	Detroit	MI	48202	313-872-3118	872-2739
TF Admissions: 800-952-2787 ■ *Web:* www.ccscad.edu					
Detroit College of Business 4801 Oakman Blvd	Dearborn	MI	48126	313-581-4400	581-6822
Web: www.dcb.edu					
Detroit College of Business Warren Campus 27500 Dequindre Rd	Warren	MI	48092	810-558-8700	558-7868

Detroit — Colleges/Universities (Cont'd)

Phone *Fax*

Lawrence Technological University
21000 W 10-Mile Rd Southfield MI 48075 248-204-4000 204-3188
TF: 800-225-5588 ■ *Web:* www.ltu.edu
Lewis College of Business 17370 Meyers Rd Detroit MI 48235 313-862-6300 862-1027
Web: www.lewiscollege.edu/index.html
Macomb Community College South Campus
14500 E 12-Mile Rd Warren MI 48093 810-445-7000 445-7140
Web: www.macomb.cc.mi.us ■ *E-mail:* answer@macomb.cc.mi.us
Madonna University 36600 Schoolcraft Rd Livonia MI 48150 734-432-5300 432-5393
TF: 800-852-4951 ■ *Web:* www.munet.edu
Marygrove College 8425 W McNichols Rd Detroit MI 48221 313-927-1200 927-1345
Web: www.marygrove.edu
Monroe County Community College
1555 S Raisinville Rd Monroe MI 48161 734-242-7300 242-9711
Web: www.monroe.cc.mi.us
Oakland Community College
2480 Opdyke Rd Bloomfield Hills MI 48304 248-540-1500 540-1841
Web: www.occ.cc.mi.us
Oakland Community College Auburn Hills Campus 2900 Featherstone Rd Auburn Hills MI 48326 248-340-6500 340-6507
Web: www.occ.cc.mi.us/occ/ah.htm
Oakland Community College Royal Oak Campus 739 S Washington Ave Royal Oak MI 48067 248-544-4900 544-5517
Web: www.occ.cc.mi.us/occ/ro.htm
Oakland Community College Southfield Campus 22322 Rutland Ave Southfield MI 48075 248-552-2600 552-2661
Web: www.occ.cc.mi.us/occ/sf.htm
Oakland University
Walton Blvd & Squirrel Rd Rochester MI 48309 248-370-2100 370-4462
Web: www.acs.oakland.edu
Rochester College 800 W Avon Rd Rochester Hills MI 48307 248-651-5800 218-2035
TF: 800-521-6010 ■ *Web:* www.rc.edu
Saint Mary's College 3535 Indian Trail Orchard Lake MI 48324 248-682-1885 683-0402
Schoolcraft College 18600 Haggerty Rd Livonia MI 48152 734-462-4400 462-4553
Web: www.schoolcraft.cc.mi.us
University of Detroit Mercy PO Box 19900 Detroit MI 48219 313-993-1000 993-3326
TF Admissions: 800-635-5020 ■ *Web:* www.udmercy.edu
University of Michigan Dearborn
4901 Evergreen Rd Dearborn MI 48128 313-593-5100 436-9167
Web: www.umd.umich.edu
Washtenaw Community College
4800 E Huron River Dr Ann Arbor MI 48106 734-973-3300 677-5414
Web: www.washtenaw.cc.mi.us
Wayne County Community College
801 W Fort St Detroit MI 48226 313-496-2500 961-7842
Web: www.wccc.edu
Wayne State University 6050 Cass Ave Detroit MI 48202 313-577-2424 577-7536
Web: www.wayne.edu ■ *E-mail:* dsynder@cms.cc.wayne.edu
William Tyndale College
35700 W 12-Mile Rd Farmington Hills MI 48331 248-553-7200 553-5963
TF: 800-483-0707

— Hospitals —

Phone *Fax*

Bon Secours Hospital 468 Cadieux Rd Grosse Pointe MI 48230 313-343-1000 343-1297
Children's Hospital of Michigan
3901 Beaubien Blvd Detroit MI 48201 313-745-0073 993-0389
Web: www.dmc.org/chm
Detroit Receiving Hospital & University Health Center 4201 Saint Antoine St Detroit MI 48201 313-745-3100 966-7206
Garden City Osteopathic Hospital
6245 N Inkster Rd Garden City MI 48135 734-421-3300 421-3530
Greater Detroit Hospital 3105 Carpenter Ave Detroit MI 48212 313-369-3000 369-3015
Harper Hospital 3990 John R St Detroit MI 48201 313-745-8040 993-0635
Web: www.harperhospital.org/harper
Henry Ford Hospital 2799 W Grand Blvd Detroit MI 48202 313-876-2600 916-1410
Huron Valley Hospital
1 William Carls Dr Commerce Township MI 48382 248-360-3300 360-5022
Hutzel Hospital 4707 Saint Antoine St Detroit MI 48201 313-745-7552 993-0693
Mercy Hospital 5555 Conner St Detroit MI 48213 313-579-4000 579-4491*
**Fax:* Admitting ■ *Web:* www.mercyhealth.com/detroit
Providence Hospital
16001 W Nine-Mile Rd Southfield MI 48075 248-424-3000 424-3035
Web: www.providence-hospital.org
Saint John Detroit Riverview Hospital
7733 E Jefferson Ave Detroit MI 48214 313-499-3000 499-4908
Saint John Health System Oakland Hospital 27351 Dequindre Madison Heights MI 48071 248-967-7000 967-7619
Saint John Hospital & Medical Center
22101 Moross Rd Detroit MI 48236 313-343-4000 343-7532
Web: stjohn.org/StJohn/stjohnhospitalandmedicalcenter.cfm
Saint John Northeast Community Hospital
4777 E Outer Dr Detroit MI 48234 313-369-9100 369-5650
Saint Joseph Mercy-Oakland
900 Woodward Ave Pontiac MI 48341 248-858-3000 858-3155
Web: www.mercyhealth.com/oakland
Sinai Grace Hospital 6071 W Outer Dr Detroit MI 48235 313-966-3300 966-3351*
**Fax:* Admitting
Sinai Grace Hospital 6071 W Outer Dr Detroit MI 48235 313-493-6800 493-5400*
**Fax:* Admitting
Vencor Hospital 2700 ML King Jr Blvd Detroit MI 48208 313-361-8000 361-8001
William Beaumont Hospital
3601 W 13-Mile Rd Royal Oak MI 48073 248-551-5000 551-8446
Web: www.beaumont.edu

— Attractions —

Phone *Fax*

ACT 35 E Grand River Ave Detroit MI 48226 313-961-4336
Anna Scripps Whitcomb Conservatory
Belle Isle Pk Detroit MI 48207 313-852-4065 852-4074
Automotive Hall of Fame
21400 Oakwood Blvd Dearborn MI 48124 313-240-4000 240-8641
TF: 888-298-4748
Belle Isle Park E Grand Blvd & Jefferson Ave Detroit MI 48207 313-267-7133
Belle Isle Zoo & Aquarium Belle Isle Pk Detroit MI 48204 313-852-4083
Web: www.ring.com/zoo/belle.htm
Bonstelle Theatre 3424 Woodward Ave Detroit MI 48202 313-577-2960
Charles H Wright Museum of African American History 315 E Warren St Detroit MI 48201 313-494-5800 494-5855
Web: www.maah-detroit.org
Chene Park 2600 E Atwater St Detroit MI 48207 313-393-0292
Children's Museum 67 E Kirby St Detroit MI 48202 313-873-8100 873-3384
Cranbrook House & Gardens
380 Lone Pine Rd Bloomfield Hills MI 48303 248-645-3149 645-3085
Web: www.cranbrook.edu/museum/house.html
Cranbrook Institute of Science
1221 N Woodward Ave Bloomfield Hills MI 48303 248-645-3260 645-3050
Detroit Artists Market
300 River Pl Suite 1650 Detroit MI 48207 313-393-1770 393-1772
E-mail: detroitartists@juno.com
Detroit Chamber Winds & Strings
755 W Big Beaver Rd Suite 214 Troy MI 48084 248-362-9329 362-2628
E-mail: chambermusic@juno.com
Detroit Film Theatre
5200 Woodward Ave Detroit Institute of Arts Detroit MI 48202 313-833-2323 833-9169
Web: www.dia.org
Detroit Gallery of Contemporary Crafts
Fisher Bldg Suite 104 Detroit MI 48202 313-873-7888
Detroit Historical Museum
5401 Woodward Ave Detroit MI 48202 313-833-1805 833-5342
Web: www.detroithistorical.org/
Detroit Institute of Arts 5200 Woodward Ave Detroit MI 48202 313-833-7900 833-2357
Web: www.dia.org
Detroit Opera House 1526 Broadway Detroit MI 48226 313-961-3500 237-3412
Detroit Repertory Theatre
13103 Woodrow Wilson St Detroit MI 48238 313-868-1347 868-1705
E-mail: DetRepTh@aol.com
Detroit Science Center 5020 John R St Detroit MI 48202 313-577-8400 832-1623
Web: www.sciencedetroit.org/
Detroit Symphony Orchestra
3711 Woodward Ave Orchestra Hall Detroit MI 48201 313-576-5111 576-5109
Web: www.detnews.com/DSO
Detroit Symphony Orchestra Hall
3711 Woodward Ave Detroit MI 48201 313-576-5100 576-5101
E-mail: info@detroitsymphonyorchestra.com
Detroit Zoo 8450 W Ten-Mile Rd Royal Oak MI 48068 248-398-0903 398-0504
Web: www.detroitzoo.org
Dossin Great Lakes Museum
100 Strand Dr Belle Isle Detroit MI 48207 313-852-4051 822-4610
Web: www.detroithistorical.org/
Eastern Market 2934 Russell St Detroit MI 48207 313-833-1560
Fisher Mansion 383 Lenox Ave Detroit MI 48215 313-331-6740 822-3748
Fisher Theatre 3011 W Grand Blvd Detroit MI 48202 313-872-1000 872-0632
Web: www.fisherdetroit.com/frame1.html
Ford Edsel & Eleanor House
1100 Lake Shore Rd Grosse Pointe Shores MI 48236 313-884-4222 884-5977
Web: bizserve.com/fordhouse/
Ford Henry Estate-University of Michigan
4901 Evergreen Rd Dearborn MI 48128 313-593-5590 593-5243
Web: www.umd.umich.edu/fairlane/

Detroit — Attractions (Cont'd)

				Phone	Fax
Fox Theatre 2211 Woodward Ave	Detroit	MI	48201	313-983-6611	965-3599
Gallerie 454 15105 Kercheval Ave	Grosse Pointe Park	MI	48230	313-822-4454	822-3768
Gem Theater 333 Madison Ave	Detroit	MI	48226	313-963-9800	963-0889
Graystone International Jazz Museum 1249 Washington Blvd Suite 201	Detroit	MI	48226	313-963-3813	
Greektown 400 Monroe St	Detroit	MI	48226	313-963-3357	963-2333
Greenfield Village 20900 Oakwood Blvd	Dearborn	MI	48124	313-271-1620	982-6230*
*Fax: Cust Svc ■ *Web:* www.hfmgv.org					
Heidelberg Project 3680 Heidelberg St	Detroit	MI	48207	313-537-8037	
Web: www.heidelberg.org					
Henry Ford Museum 20900 Oakwood Blvd.	Dearborn	MI	48124	313-271-1620	982-6244
TF: 800-343-1929 ■ *Web:* www.hfmgv.org					
Holocaust Memorial Center 6602 W Maple Rd	West Bloomfield	MI	48322	248-661-0840	661-4204
Web: holocaustcenter.org ■ *E-mail:* info@holocaustcenter.org					
IMAX Dome Theater 5020 John R St	Detroit	MI	48202	313-577-8400	832-1623
Web: www.sciencedetroit.org/imax.html					
Institute of African-American Arts 2641 W Grand Blvd.	Detroit	MI	48208	313-872-0332	872-7855
International Institute of Metropolitan Detroit 111 E Kirby St	Detroit	MI	48202	313-871-8600	871-1651
Isle Royale National Park 800 East Lakeshore Dr	Houghton	MI	49931	906-482-0986	487-7170
Web: www.nps.gov/isro/					
Masonic Temple 500 Temple Ave	Detroit	MI	48201	313-832-7100	832-2922
Masonic Temple Theatre 500 Temple St	Detroit	MI	48201	313-832-5900	832-1047
Web: www.fisherdetroit.com/frame3.html					
Meadow Brook Art Gallery Oakland University Wilson Hall Rm 208	Rochester	MI	48309	248-370-3005	370-3108
Meadow Brook Hall Oakland University	Rochester Hills	MI	48309	248-370-3140	370-4260
Michigan Opera Theatre 1526 Broadway	Detroit	MI	48226	313-961-3500	237-3412
Web: detnews.com/mot					
Michigan Sports Hall of Fame 1 Washington Blvd Cobo Conference Ctr	Detroit	MI	48226	248-848-0252	
Moross House/Detroit Garden Center 1460 E Jefferson Ave	Detroit	MI	48207	313-259-6363	259-0107
Motown Museum 2648 W Grand Blvd	Detroit	MI	48208	313-875-2264	875-2267
E-mail: motownmus@aol.com					
Music Hall Center for the Performing Arts 350 Madison St	Detroit	MI	48226	313-963-7622	963-2462
Old Mariners' Church 170 E Jefferson Ave.	Detroit	MI	48226	313-259-2206	
Palmer Park 900 Merrill Plaisance	Detroit	MI	48203	313-578-7600	
Pewabic Pottery 10125 E Jefferson Ave.	Detroit	MI	48214	313-822-0954	
Web: www.pewabic.com					
Plowshares Theatre Co 315 E Warren St.	Detroit	MI	48201	313-872-0279	
Renaissance Center 200 Renaissance Ctr Suite 1200	Detroit	MI	48243	313-568-5600	568-5606
River Rouge Park 22000 Joy Rd.	Detroit	MI	48239	313-852-4520	
Saint Aubin Park & Marina 1900 E Atwater St	Detroit	MI	48207	313-259-4677	
Second City Detroit 2301 Woodward Ave.	Detroit	MI	48201	313-965-2222	964-5833
Web: www.secondcity.com ■ *E-mail:* SCDet@aol.com					
Summit Observation Deck Renaissance Ctr	Detroit	MI	48243	313-568-8600	
Youtheatre 350 Madison Ave	Detroit	MI	48226	313-963-7663	963-2462

SPORTS TEAMS & FACILITIES

				Phone	Fax
Cobo Arena 300 Civic Center Dr	Detroit	MI	48226	313-983-6616	396-7994
Detroit Compuware Ambassadors (hockey) 14900 Beck Rd Compuware Sports Arena	Plymouth	MI	48170	734-453-6400	453-3427
Web: www.compuwareambassadors.com					
Detroit Lions 1200 Featherstone Rd Pontiac Silverdome	Pontiac	MI	48342	248-335-4151	322-2283
Web: www.detroitlions.com					
Detroit Pistons 2 Championship Dr Palace of Auburn Hills	Auburn Hills	MI	48326	248-377-0100	377-4262
Web: www.nba.com/pistons					
Detroit Red Wings 600 Civic Ctr Dr Joe Louis Arena	Detroit	MI	48226	313-396-7544	567-0296
Web: www.detroitredwings.com					
Detroit Rockers (soccer) 600 Civic Ctr Dr Joe Louis Arena	Detroit	MI	48226	313-396-7070	396-7944
Web: www.concentric.net/~jibanes/rockers					
Detroit Shock (basketball) 2 Championship Dr Palace at Auburn Hills	Auburn Hills	MI	48326	248-377-8696	377-3260
Web: www.wnba.com/shock/index.html					
Detroit Tigers 2121 Trumbull Ave Tiger Stadium	Detroit	MI	48216	313-962-4000	
TF: 800-221-2324 ■ *Web:* www.detroittigers.com ■ *E-mail:* tigers@detroittigers.com					
Detroit Vipers (hockey) 2 Championship Dr Palace at Auburn Hills	Auburn Hills	MI	48326	248-377-0100	377-2695
Web: www.detroitvipers.com/ ■ *E-mail:* info@detroitvipers.com					
Joe Louis Arena 600 Civic Ctr Dr	Detroit	MI	48226	313-396-7444	396-7994
Palace at Auburn Hills 2 Championship Dr	Auburn Hills	MI	48326	248-377-8222	377-3260
Plymouth Whalers (hockey) 14900 Beck Rd Compuware Sports Arena	Plymouth	MI	48170	734-453-8400	453-4201
Web: www.canoe.com/OHLStatsSeason/detroithome.html ■ *E-mail:* hockey@compuworld.com					

— Events —

	Phone
African World Festival (mid-August)	313-494-5800
America's Thanksgiving Day Parade (late November)	313-923-7400
APBA Gold Cup Thunderfest Races (early July)	313-331-7770
Art & Apples Craft Show (mid-September)	248-651-4110
Art on the Pointe (mid-June)	313-884-4222
Builders Home & Detroit Flower Show (mid-March)	248-737-4477
Christmas Flower Show & Open House (December-mid-January)	313-852-4064
Detroit Aglow (mid-November)	313-961-1403
Detroit Autorama (mid-March)	248-650-5560
Detroit Boat Show (late January-early February)	734-261-0123
Detroit Festival of the Arts (mid-September)	313-577-5088
Detroit Riverfront Festivals (May-September)	313-202-1800
Eastern Market Flower Day (mid-May)	313-833-1560
Fall Chrysanthemum Show (mid-October-late November)	313-852-4064
Fall Harvest Days (early-mid-October)	313-271-1620
Festival of Trees (late November-early December)	313-745-0178
Ford Fleet Festival (early December)	313-852-4051
Ford House Holiday Tours (November-December)	313-884-4222
Greektown Art Fair (mid-May)	734-662-3382
International Freedom Festival (late June-early July)	313-923-7400
Meadow Brook Music Festival (June-August)	248-377-0100
Mexicantown Mercado (mid-June-early September)	313-842-0450
Michigan All-Morgan Horse Show (early July)	810-793-4583
Michigan State Fair (late August-early September)	313-369-8250
Michigan Tastefest (early July)	313-872-0188
Montreux Detroit Jazz Festival (early September)	313-963-7622
North American International Auto Show (mid-January)	248-643-0250
Old Car Festival (mid-September)	313-271-1620
Original Old World Market (mid-October)	313-871-8600
Plymouth International Ice Sculpture Spectacular (mid-January)	734-459-6969
Spirit of Detroit Thunderfest (mid-July)	313-331-7770
Tenneco Automotive Grand Prix of Detroit (early June)	313-393-7749
Traditions of the Season (December-early January)	313-271-1620
Zoo Boo-The Nighttime Zoo (late October)	248-541-5835

Flint

The seat of Genesee County, Flint was the original home of several American auto manufacturers, including General Motors. The city is currently home to GM's Buick and Cadillac/Luxury Car divisions. Flint's Crossroads Village features 30 historic structures dating back to the mid-late 1800s where costumed performers demonstrate various facets of life in the 19th century. Visitors can tour the area by steam train or a paddlewheel river boat. Flint's Alfred P. Sloan Museum presents the city's history as an automotive center in a variety of exhibitions and special events, including the annual Summer Antique Auto Fair. Flint is also home to Michigan's largest planetarium, the Longway Planetarium, which features star shows and laser shows for visitors.

Population	131,668	**Longitude**	83-41-34 W
Area (Land)	33.8 sq mi	**County**	Genesee
Area (Water)	0.4 sq mi	**Time Zone**	EST
Elevation	750 ft	**Area Code/s**	810
Latitude	43-01-22 N		

Flint (Cont'd)

— Average Temperatures and Precipitation —

TEMPERATURES

	Jan	Feb	Mar	Apr	May	Jun	Jul	Aug	Sep	Oct	Nov	Dec
High	29	31	42	56	68	77	82	79	72	60	47	34
Low	14	16	26	36	46	55	60	58	51	41	32	21

PRECIPITATION

	Jan	Feb	Mar	Apr	May	Jun	Jul	Aug	Sep	Oct	Nov	Dec
Inches	1.4	1.3	2.2	2.9	2.7	3.2	2.7	3.5	3.6	2.2	2.6	2.1

— Important Phone Numbers —

	Phone
AAA	810-230-8890
American Express Travel	248-642-3350
Dental Referral	810-230-3790
Emergency	911
Entertainment Hot Line	810-232-2211
Medical Referral	810-733-6260
Poison Control Center	313-745-5711
Time/Temp	810-743-4200
Weather	810-232-3333

— Information Sources —

	City	State	Zip	Phone	Fax
Better Business Bureau Serving Detroit & Eastern Michigan 30555 Southfield Rd Suite 200 *Web:* www.detroit.bbb.org	Southfield	MI	48076	248-644-9100	644-5026
Flint Area Chamber of Commerce 519 S Saginaw St Suite 200 *Web:* www.flintchamber.org ■ *E-mail:* flintchamber@flint.org	Flint	MI	48502	810-232-7101	233-7437
Flint Area Convention & Visitors Bureau 519 S Saginaw St *TF Sales:* 800-253-5468 ■ *Web:* flint.org ■ *E-mail:* staff@flint.org	Flint	MI	48502	810-232-8900	232-1515
Flint City Hall 1101 S Saginaw St *Web:* www.ci.flint.mi.us	Flint	MI	48502	810-766-7015	766-7218
Flint Community & Economic Development Dept 1101 S Saginaw St *Web:* www.ci.flint.mi.us/economic/economic.html	Flint	MI	48502	810-766-7436	766-7351
Flint Mayor 1101 S Saginaw St *Web:* www.ci.flint.mi.us/mayor/mayor.html	Flint	MI	48502	810-766-7346	766-7218
Flint Public Library 1026 E Kearsley St *Web:* www.flint.lib.mi.us/fpl.html	Flint	MI	48502	810-232-7111	767-6740
Genesee County 900 S Saginaw St	Flint	MI	48502	810-257-3282	257-3464

On-Line Resources

Anthill City Guide Flint .... www.anthill.com/city.asp?city=flint
Area Guide Flint .... flint.areaguides.net
Excite.com Flint City Guide .... www.excite.com/travel/countries/united_states/michigan/flint

— Transportation Services —

AIRPORTS

■ Bishop International Airport (FNT)

	Phone
5 miles SW of downtown (approx 10 minutes) Web: www.voyager.net/bishopairport	810-235-6560

Airport Transportation

	Phone
CLD Transport Systems $20 fare to downtown	810-659-7436
Taxi $10 fare to downtown	810-238-7450

Commercial Airlines

	Phone
AirTran	800-247-8726
Continental	800-525-0280
Midwest Express	800-452-2022
Northwest	800-225-2525
US Airways Express	800-428-4322

Charter Airlines

	Phone
Flint Air Service	810-235-0681

CAR RENTALS

	Phone
Avis	810-234-7847
Budget	810-238-8300
Celebrity	810-715-5000
Enterprise	810-742-1433
Hertz	810-234-2041
National	810-239-4341
Thrifty	810-234-4616

LIMO/TAXI

	Phone
Dynasty Limousine	810-232-7199
International Cab	810-238-7450
William Allen Co Inc	810-743-4158

MASS TRANSIT

	Phone
Mass Transportation Authority $1 Base fare	810-767-0100

RAIL/BUS

	City	State	Zip	Phone
Amtrak Station 1407 S Dort Hwy *TF:* 800-872-7245	Flint	MI	48503	810-234-2659
Greyhound Bus Station 615 N Harrison St *TF:* 800-231-2222	Flint	MI	48502	810-232-1114

— Accommodations —

HOTELS, MOTELS, RESORTS

	City	State	Zip	Phone	Fax
Amerihost Inn 9040 Holly Rd *TF:* 800-434-5800 ■ *Web:* www.amerihostinn.com/127-main.html ■ *E-mail:* 127@amerihostinn.com	Grand Blanc	MI	48439	810-694-0000	694-0155
Avon House 518 Avon St *TF:* 888-832-0627	Flint	MI	48503	810-232-6861	
Bay Valley Hotel & Resort 2470 Old Bridge Rd *TF:* 800-292-5028	Bay City	MI	48706	517-686-3500	686-6931
Baymont Inns & Suites 4160 Pier North Blvd *TF:* 800-301-0200	Flint	MI	48504	810-732-2300	732-9777
Comfort Inn-Davison 10082 Lapeer Rd *TF:* 800-228-5150	Davison	MI	48423	810-658-2700	658-2640
Comfort Inn-Flint 2361 Austin Pkwy	Flint	MI	48507	810-232-4222	232-9625
Days Inn 2207 W Bristol Rd	Flint	MI	48507	810-239-4681	239-4022
Four Points Hotel by Sheraton 4960 Towne Centre Rd *TF:* 800-325-3535	Saginaw	MI	48604	517-790-5050	790-1466
Holiday Inn Express 1150 Robert T Longway Blvd *TF:* 800-465-4329	Flint	MI	48503	810-238-7744	233-7444
Holiday Inn Gateway Centre 5353 Gateway Centre *TF:* 800-465-4329	Flint	MI	48507	810-232-5300	232-9806
Howard Johnson Lodge G-3277 Miller Rd *TF:* 800-446-4656	Flint	MI	48507	810-733-5910	733-2713
Knights Inn G-4380 W Pierson Rd *TF:* 800-843-5644	Flint	MI	48504	810-733-7570	733-0040
Lowhelen Baha'I Conference Center 3208 S State Rd	Davison	MI	48423	810-653-5033	653-7181
Metro Inn 2435 W Grand Blanc Rd *TF:* 800-578-7878	Grand Blanc	MI	48439	810-655-2300	655-2547
Ramada Inn 4300 W Pierson Rd *TF:* 800-272-6232 ■ *Web:* www.ramadaflint.com	Flint	MI	48504	810-732-0400	732-2811
Ramada Plaza Hotel 1 Riverfront Ctr W *TF:* 800-272-6232	Flint	MI	48502	810-239-1234	239-5843
Red Roof Inn G-3219 Miller Rd *TF:* 800-843-7663	Flint	MI	48507	810-733-1660	733-6310
Super 8 Motel 3033 Claude Ave *TF:* 800-800-8000	Flint	MI	48507	810-230-7888	230-7888
Travelodge 932 S Center Rd *TF:* 800-542-4037	Flint	MI	48503	810-744-0200	744-2954
Walli's W Super 8 4160 W Pierson Rd *TF:* 800-800-8000	Flint	MI	48504	810-789-0400	789-6562

— Restaurants —

	City	State	Zip	Phone
Angelo's Coney Island & Grill (American) 1816 Davison Rd	Flint	MI	48506	810-238-3761

Flint — Restaurants (Cont'd)

	City	State	Zip	Phone
Bavarian Inn (German) 713 S Main St	Flint	MI	48507	800-228-2742
Beech Tree American Grill (American) 1519 W Bristol Rd	Flint	MI	48507	810-232-7811
Bill's Steak House (Steak) 4300 W Pierson Rd	Flint	MI	48504	810-732-0400
Bonaparte's Eatery (American) 4000 S Saginaw St	Flint	MI	48507	810-767-3411
Bubba's Roadside Inn (American) 5311 Corunna Rd	Flint	MI	48532	810-732-4600
Canton Chinese Restaurant (Chinese) 5313 Fenton Rd.	Flint	MI	48507	810-232-8710
Grand Blanc Inn (American) 5313 S Dort Hwy	Flint	MI	48507	810-694-0010
Halo Burger (American) 800 S Saginaw St	Flint	MI	48502	810-238-4607
Hill Street Bar & Grille (American) 5353 Gateway Centre	Flint	MI	48507	810-232-5300
Latina Restaurant & Pizzeria (Italian) 1370 W Bristol Rd.	Flint	MI	48507	810-767-8491
Redwood Lodge (American) 5304 Gateway Ctr	Flint	MI	48507	810-233-8000
Riverfront Café (American) 1 Riverfront Ctr W	Flint	MI	48502	810-767-4321
Roma Pizzeria & Restaurant (Italian) 5227 N Saginaw St	Flint	MI	48505	810-787-1061
Ruggero's Restaurant (Italian) 2055 Linden Rd.	Flint	MI	48532	810-733-7633
Salvatore Scallopini Restaurant (Italian) G-3227 Miller Rd.	Flint	MI	48507	810-732-1070
Shap's Family Restaurant (Barbecue) G-2520 W Hill Rd at Torrey Rd	Flint	MI	48507	810-232-8677
Walli's Supper Club (Seafood) 4160 W Pierson Rd	Flint	MI	48506	810-785-5511
White Horse Tavern (American) 621 W Court St.	Flint	MI	48503	810-234-3811

— Goods and Services —

SHOPPING

	City	State	Zip	Phone	Fax
Courtland Center 4190 E Court St.	Burton	MI	48509	810-744-0742	742-6866
Genesee Valley Center 3341 Linden Rd S	Flint	MI	48507	810-732-4000	732-5437

BANKS

	City	State	Zip	Phone	Fax
Chemical Bank Key State 3501 S Linden Rd	Flint	MI	48507	810-733-6330	733-7254
Citizens Bank 328 S Saginaw St 1 Citizens Banking Ctr. **Fax:* Mktg ■ *TF:* 800-999-6949	Flint	MI	48502	810-766-7500	766-7634*
D & N Bank G-6120 Fenton Rd. *TF Cust Svc:* 800-950-5540*	Flint	MI	48507	810-232-3810	232-2622
Michigan National Bank 503 S Saginaw St **Fax Area Code:* 810	Flint	MI	48502	800-225-5662	762-5543*
NBD Bank 1 E 1st St. **Fax Area Code:* 810	Flint	MI	48502	800-225-5623	760-8082*
Old Kent Bank 3302 Corunna Rd	Flint	MI	48532	810-762-4844	
Republic Bank 3200 Beecher Rd.	Flint	MI	48532	810-732-3300	732-3202
State Bank 1 Fenton Sq	Fenton	MI	48430	800-729-6283	629-9331*

**Fax Area Code:* 810

BUSINESS SERVICES

	Phone
DHL Worldwide Express	800-225-5345
Federal Express	800-463-3339
Interim Personnel Services	810-733-1996
Kelly Services	810-230-1644
Kinko's	810-230-1180
Mail Boxes Etc	810-733-0055
Manpower Temporary Services	810-733-1520
Olsten Staffing Services	810-742-9675
Post Office	810-257-1521
Q-Temps Temporary Services Inc	810-230-6944
UPS	800-742-5877

— Media —

PUBLICATIONS

	City	State	Zip	Phone	Fax
Flint Journal‡ 200 E 1st St **Fax:* Edit ■ *TF Circulation:* 800-875-6300 ■ *Web:* fl.mlive.com ■ *E-mail:* fj@flintj.com	Flint	MI	48502	810-766-6100	767-7518*

‡Daily newspapers

TELEVISION

	City	State	Zip	Phone	Fax
WEYI-TV Ch 25 (NBC) 2225 W Willard Rd *E-mail:* weyi@aol.com	Clio	MI	48420	810-687-1000	687-4925
WFUM-TV Ch 28 (PBS) University of Michigan *Web:* www.flint.umich.edu/wfum/index.htm ■ *E-mail:* wfum@list.flint.umich.edu	Flint	MI	48502	810-762-3028	233-6017
WJRT-TV Ch 12 (ABC) 2302 Lapeer Rd *E-mail:* wjrt@crif.com	Flint	MI	48503	810-233-3130	257-2812
WNEM-TV Ch 5 (CBS) 107 N Franklin *Web:* www.wnem.com ■ *E-mail:* wnem@concentric.net	Saginaw	MI	48607	517-755-8191	758-2110
WSMH-TV Ch 66 (Fox) 3463 W Pierson Rd	Flint	MI	48504	810-785-8866	785-8963

RADIO

	City	State	Zip	Phone	Fax
WCRZ-FM 107.9 MHz (AC) 3338 Bristol Rd *E-mail:* wcrz@aol.com	Burton	MI	48529	810-743-1080	742-5170
WDZZ-FM 92.7 MHz (Urban) 120 E 1st St Suite 1830	Flint	MI	48502	810-238-7300	238-7310
WFDF-AM 910 kHz (N/T) 120 E 1st St Suite 1830	Flint	MI	48502	810-238-7300	238-7310
WFLT-AM 1420 kHz (Rel) 317 S Averill Ave.	Flint	MI	48506	810-239-5733	239-7134
WFNT-AM 1470 kHz (N/T) 3338 Bristol Rd.	Burton	MI	48529	810-743-1080	742-5170
WKCQ-FM 98.1 MHz (Ctry) 2000 Whittier *TF:* 800-262-0098	Saginaw	MI	48601	517-752-8161	752-8102
WWBN-FM 101.7 MHz (Rock) 3338 Bristol Rd.	Burton	MI	48529	810-743-1080	742-5170
WWCK-AM 1570 kHz (CHR) 3217 Lapeer Rd	Flint	MI	48503	810-744-1570	743-2500
WWCK-FM 105.5 MHz (CHR) 3217 Lapeer Rd	Flint	MI	48503	810-744-1570	743-2500

— Colleges/Universities —

	City	State	Zip	Phone	Fax
Baker College Flint Campus 1050 W Bristol Rd *Web:* www.baker.edu/visit/flint.html ■ *E-mail:* adm-fl@baker.edu	Flint	MI	48507	810-767-7600	766-4049
Mott Community College 1401 E Court St. *Web:* www.mcc.edu	Flint	MI	48503	810-762-0200	232-9442
University of Michigan Flint 303 E Kearsley St. *TF:* 800-942-5636 ■ *Web:* www.flint.umich.edu	Flint	MI	48502	810-762-3000	762-3272

— Hospitals —

	City	State	Zip	Phone	Fax
Genesys Regional Medical Center Flint Osteopathic Campus 3921 Beecher Rd	Flint	MI	48532	810-762-4000	606-6605
Genesys Regional Medical Center Saint Joseph Campus 302 Kensington Ave *TF:* 888-606-6556 ■ *Web:* www.genesys.org/homegen.htm	Flint	MI	48503	810-762-8000	762-8094
Hurley Medical Center 1 Hurley Plaza **Fax:* Admitting ■ *Web:* www.hurleymc.com	Flint	MI	48503	810-257-9000	257-9473*
McLaren Regional Medical Center 401 S Ballenger Hwy **Fax:* Admitting ■ *TF:* 800-821-6517	Flint	MI	48532	810-762-2000	342-4912*

— Attractions —

	City	State	Zip	Phone	Fax
Buckham Alley Theater 512 Buckham Alley	Flint	MI	48502	810-239-4477	
Children's Museum 1602 W 3rd Ave.	Flint	MI	48503	810-767-5437	767-4936
Crossroads Village & Huckleberry Railroad 6140 Bray Rd. *TF:* 800-648-7275	Flint	MI	48506	810-736-7100	
Flint City Market 420 East Blvd	Flint	MI	48502	810-766-7449	
Flint Community Players 1220 E Kearsley St Bower Theater	Flint	MI	48503	810-235-6963	
Flint Cultural Center 1241 E Kearsley St Whiting Auditorium *TF:* 888-823-6837	Flint	MI	48503	810-760-1138	760-5016
Flint Institute of Arts 1120 E Kearsley St. *Web:* www.flintarts.org/	Flint	MI	48503	810-234-1695	234-1692
Flint Symphony Orchestra 1241 E Kearsley St Whiting Auditorium *TF:* 800-395-4849	Flint	MI	48503	810-238-1350	238-6385
Flint Youth Theater 1220 E Kearsley St.	Flint	MI	48503	810-760-1018	760-7420
For-Mar Nature Preserve & Arboretum 2142 N Genesee Rd	Burton	MI	48509	810-789-8567	
Genesee Belle 6140 Bray Rd. *TF:* 800-648-7275	Flint	MI	48506	810-736-7100	736-7220
Left Bank Gallery 503 East St	Flint	MI	48503	810-239-2921	
Longway Robert T Planetarium 1310 E Kearsley St *Web:* flint.org/longway/	Flint	MI	48503	810-760-1181	760-6774
Montrose Historical & Telephone Pioneer Museum 144 E Hickory St.	Montrose	MI	48457	810-639-6644	
Museum of Afrikan American History 2712 N Saginaw Suite 13.	Flint	MI	48505	810-233-5606	
Penny Whistle Place 5500 Bray Rd	Flint	MI	48505	810-736-7100	736-7220

Flint — Attractions (Cont'd)

				Phone	Fax
Sloan Alfred P Museum 1221 E Kearsley St. *Web:* www.classicar.com/museums/sloan/sloan.htm	Flint	MI	48503	810-760-1169	760-5339
Stepping Stone Falls 5161 Branch Rd.	Flint	MI	48506	810-736-7100	
University of Michigan-Flint Theater 303 E Kearsley St	Flint	MI	48502	810-762-3230	762-3687
Whaley Historical House 624 E Kearsley St.	Flint	MI	48503	810-235-6841	235-4626

SPORTS TEAMS & FACILITIES

				Phone	Fax
Flint Generals (hockey) 3501 Lapeer Rd IMA Sports Arena *Web:* www.flintgenerals.com	Flint	MI	48503	810-742-9422	742-5892
Mid-Michigan Bucks (soccer) 505 N Center Dr White Pines Stadium *Web:* home.att.net/~mmbucks ■ *E-mail:* mmbucks@worldnet.att.net	Saginaw Township	MI	48706	517-781-6888	
Sports Creek Raceway 4290 Morrish Rd	Swartz Creek	MI	48473	810-635-3333	635-9711

— Events —

	Phone
Antique Machine Show (early August)	800-648-7275
Civil War Weekend (late June)	800-648-7275
Country Music Fest (mid-June)	810-732-2040
Crim Festival of Races (late August)	810-235-3396
Flint Art Fair (early-June)	810-234-1695
Flint Jazz Festival (mid-August)	810-736-7017
Flint's Juneteenth Festival (mid-June)	810-766-7144
Fourth of July Festival (early July)	810-766-7463
Genesee County Fair (mid-late August)	810-687-0953
Honoring the Eagle Pow Wow (mid-July)	810-736-7100
Huckleberry Ghost Train (October)	810-736-7100
Michigan Renaissance Festival (mid-August-late September)	800-601-4848
Mott Community College Student Art Show (May)	810-762-0474
Railfans Weekend (mid-August)	800-648-7275
Saint John Festival of Flags (late June)	810-653-2377
Septemberfest (mid-September)	810-686-9861
Summer Antique Auto Fair (late June)	810-760-1169

Grand Rapids

Named for the rapids in the Grand River, which flows through the heart of the city, Grand Rapids became known as a center for furniture making. Examples of this work can be seen at the Grand Rapids Art Museum and at the Van Andel Museum Center in the city's Public Museum. Among the various exhibits there is a large collection of furniture that includes designs by Frank Lloyd Wright. In addition, a completely restored Wright home can be seen at the Meyer May House in Grand Rapids. Originally built in 1908, this prairie style house has been reproduced in exact detail by its present owner, Steelcase, Inc. The Gerald R. Ford Museum honors the nation's 38th president, who was raised in Grand Rapids.

Population	185,437	**Longitude**	85-68-44 W
Area (Land)	44.3 sq mi	**County**	Kent
Area (Water)	0.7 sq mi	**Time Zone**	EST
Elevation	657 ft	**Area Code/s**	616
Latitude	42-95-80 N		

— Average Temperatures and Precipitation —

TEMPERATURES

	Jan	Feb	Mar	Apr	May	Jun	Jul	Aug	Sep	Oct	Nov	Dec
High	29	32	43	57	69	79	83	81	72	60	46	34
Low	15	16	25	35	46	55	60	58	50	39	30	21

PRECIPITATION

	Jan	Feb	Mar	Apr	May	Jun	Jul	Aug	Sep	Oct	Nov	Dec
Inches	1.8	1.4	2.6	3.4	3.1	3.7	3.2	3.6	4.2	2.8	3.3	2.9

— Important Phone Numbers —

	Phone		Phone
AAA	616-364-6111	**Poison Control Center**	800-764-7661
Emergency	911	**Time**	616-459-1212
Grand Rapids Events Line	616-451-3866	**Weather**	616-776-1234
HotelDocs	800-468-3537		

— Information Sources —

				Phone	Fax
Better Business Bureau Serving Western Michigan 40 Pearl St NW Suite 354 *Web:* www.grandrapids.bbb.org ■ *E-mail:* info@grandrapids.bbb.org	Grand Rapids	MI	49503	616-774-8236	774-2014
Grand Center 245 Monroe Ave NW *Web:* www.grandcenter.com/grand.htm	Grand Rapids	MI	49503	616-742-6600	742-6590
Grand Rapids Area Chamber of Commerce 111 Pearl St NW *TF:* 800-376-6437 ■ *Web:* www.grandrapids.org	Grand Rapids	MI	49503	616-771-0300	771-0318
Grand Rapids City Hall 300 Monroe Ave NW *Web:* www.grand-rapids.mi.us	Grand Rapids	MI	49503	616-456-3000	456-3111
Grand Rapids Mayor 300 Monroe Ave NW *E-mail:* mayor@grand-rapids.mi.us	Grand Rapids	MI	49503	616-456-3168	456-3111
Grand Rapids Planning Dept 300 Monroe Ave NW *Web:* www.grand-rapids.mi.us/planning/plandpt.html	Grand Rapids	MI	49503	616-456-3031	456-4568
Grand Rapids Public Library 60 Library Plaza NE *Web:* www.grapids.lib.mi.us ■ *E-mail:* gr_web@lakeland.lib.mi.us	Grand Rapids	MI	49503	616-456-3600	456-3619
Grand Rapids/Kent County Convention & Visitors Bureau 140 Monroe Ctr Suite 300 *TF:* 800-678-9859 ■ *Web:* www.grcvb.org	Grand Rapids	MI	49503	616-459-8287	459-7291
Kent County 300 Monroe Ave NW *Web:* www.co.kent.mi.us/	Grand Rapids	MI	49503	616-336-3550	

On-Line Resources

4GrandRapids.com	www.4grandrapids.com
Anthill City Guide Grand Rapids	www.anthill.com/city.asp?city=grandrapids
Area Guide Grand Rapids	grandrapids.areaguides.net
City Knowledge Grand Rapids	www.cityknowledge.com/mi_grandrapids.htm
DigitalCity Grand Rapids	www.digitalcity.com/grandrapids
Excite.com Grand Rapids City Guide	www.excite.com/travel/countries/united_states/michigan/grand_rapids
Grand Happenings Community Calendar	www.grand-rapids.mi.us/calendar/

— Transportation Services —

AIRPORTS

■ **Kent County International Airport (GRR)**

	Phone
6 miles SE of downtown (approx 15 minutes) Web: www.grr.org	616-336-4500

Airport Transportation

	Phone
Calder City Cab $25 fare to downtown	616-454-8080
Executive Coach Service $54 fare to downtown	616-393-9595
Port City Cab $22 fare to downtown	616-243-5314

Grand Rapids (Cont'd)

Commercial Airlines

	Phone		Phone
American	800-433-7300	**Midwest Express**	800-452-2022
Chicago Express	800-435-9282	**Northwest**	800-225-2525
Continental Express	616-233-6140	**United**	800-241-6522
Delta	800-221-1212	**US Airways**	800-428-4322

Charter Airlines

	Phone		Phone
Northern Air	616-336-4700	**Rapid Air Service**	616-957-5050
Northern Jet Management	800-462-7709	**Superior Aviation**	800-882-7751

CAR RENTALS

	Phone		Phone
Avis	616-949-1720	**Hertz**	616-233-6351
Budget	616-942-1905	**National**	616-949-3510
Enterprise	616-475-1300	**Thrifty**	616-940-3333

LIMO/TAXI

	Phone		Phone
Calder City Cab	616-454-8080	**Verhey Limo**	616-459-2788
Port City Cab	616-243-5314	**Vets Taxi**	616-459-4646

MASS TRANSIT

	Phone
Grand Rapids Area Transit Authority (GRATA) $1.25 Base fare	616-776-1100

RAIL/BUS

				Phone
Amtrak Station Market & Wealthy Sts	Grand Rapids	MI	49503	800-872-7245
Greyhound Bus Station 190 Wealthy St SW *TF:* 800-231-2222	Grand Rapids	MI	49503	616-456-1709

— Accommodations —

HOTELS, MOTELS, RESORTS

				Phone	Fax
Amerihost Inn Grand Rapids 7625 Caterpillar Ct *TF:* 800-434-5800 ■ *Web:* www.amerihostinn.com/165-main.html ■ *E-mail:* 165@amerihostinn.com	Grand Rapids	MI	49548	616-827-9900	827-9998
Amway Grand Plaza Hotel 187 Monroe Ave NW *TF:* 800-253-3590 ■ *Web:* www.amwaygrand.com ■ *E-mail:* 2090598@mcimail.com	Grand Rapids	MI	49503	616-774-2000	776-6489
Baymont Inns 2873 Kraft Ave SE *TF:* 800-301-0200	Grand Rapids	MI	49512	616-956-3300	956-5561
Best Western Midway Hotel 4101 28th St *TF:* 800-528-1234	Grand Rapids	MI	49512	616-942-2550	942-2446
Clarion Hotel 3600 E Cork St *TF:* 800-252-7466	Kalamazoo	MI	49001	616-385-3922	385-2747
Comfort Inn 4155 28th St SE *TF:* 800-228-5150	Grand Rapids	MI	49512	616-957-2080	957-9712
Country Inn & Suites 5399 28th Street SE *TF:* 800-456-4000	Grand Rapids	MI	49512	616-977-0909	977-0909
Courtyard by Marriott 11 Monroe Ave NW *TF:* 800-321-2211 ■ *Web:* courtyard.com/GRRDT	Grand Rapids	MI	49503	616-242-6000	242-6605
Crowne Plaza Grand Rapids 5700 28th St SE *TF:* 888-957-9575	Grand Rapids	MI	49546	616-957-1770	957-0629
Days Inn Airport 5500 28th St SE *TF:* 800-329-7466	Grand Rapids	MI	49512	616-949-8400	949-8400
Days Inn Downtown 310 Pearl St NW *TF:* 800-329-7466	Grand Rapids	MI	49504	616-235-7611	235-1995
Econo Lodge 5175 28th St SE *TF:* 800-553-2666	Grand Rapids	MI	49512	616-956-6601	940-3589
Exel Inn 4855 28th St SE *TF:* 800-356-8013	Grand Rapids	MI	49512	616-957-3000	957-0194
Fairfield Inn 3930 Stahl Drive SE *TF:* 800-228-2800 ■ *Web:* fairfieldinn.com/GRRPA	Grand Rapids	MI	49546	616-940-2700	940-2700
Hampton Inn 4981 28th St *TF:* 800-426-7266	Grand Rapids	MI	49512	616-956-9304	956-6617
Hawthorn Suites Hotel 2985 Kraft Ave SE *TF:* 800-784-8371	Grand Rapids	MI	49512	616-940-1777	940-9809
Heritage Residential Suites 303 Madison Ave SE	Grand Rapids	MI	49503	616-454-3232	
Hilton Inn Airport 4747 28th St SE *TF:* 800-445-8667 ■ *Web:* www.hilton.com/hotels/GRRHIHF	Grand Rapids	MI	49512	616-957-0100	957-2977
Holiday Inn East 3333 28th St SE *TF:* 800-465-4329 ■ *Web:* www.basshotels.com/holiday-inn/?_franchisee=GRREA ■ *E-mail:* bboll@voyager.net	Grand Rapids	MI	49512	616-949-9222	949-3841
Holiday Inn North 270 Ann St NW *TF:* 800-465-4329 ■ *Web:* www.basshotels.com/holiday-inn/?_franchisee=GRRNO ■ *E-mail:* hinorth@voyager.net	Grand Rapids	MI	49504	616-363-9001	363-0670
Holiday Inn South 255 28th St SW *TF:* 800-465-4329 ■ *Web:* www.basshotels.com/holiday-inn/?_franchisee=GRRSS ■ *E-mail:* higrrso@voyager.net	Grand Rapids	MI	49548	616-241-6444	241-1807
Homewood Suites 3920 Stahl Dr *TF:* 800-225-5466	Grand Rapids	MI	49546	616-285-7100	285-1505
Lexington Hotel Suites 5401 28th Ct SE *TF:* 800-441-9628	Grand Rapids	MI	49546	616-940-8100	940-0914
Motel 6 3524 28th St SE *TF:* 800-466-8356	Grand Rapids	MI	49512	616-957-3511	957-4369
President Inn 3221 Plainfield Ave NE *TF:* 800-445-5004	Grand Rapids	MI	49525	616-363-0800	363-6940
Quality Inn Terrace Club 4495 28th St SE *TF:* 800-228-5151	Grand Rapids	MI	49512	616-956-8080	956-0619
Radisson Plaza Hotel Kalamazoo Center 100 W Michigan Ave *TF:* 800-333-3333	Kalamazoo	MI	49007	616-343-3333	381-1560
Ramada Limited 65 28th St SW *TF:* 800-272-6232	Grand Rapids	MI	49548	616-452-1461	452-5115
Red Roof Inn 5131 28th St SE *TF:* 800-843-7663	Grand Rapids	MI	49512	616-942-0800	942-8341
Residence Inn by Marriott 2701 E Beltline SE *TF:* 800-331-3131 ■ *Web:* www.residenceinn.com/GRRGR	Grand Rapids	MI	49546	616-957-8111	957-3699
Sleep Inn 4284 29th St SE *TF:* 800-627-5337	Grand Rapids	MI	49512	616-975-9000	954-6767
Travelodge 4041 Cascade Rd SE *TF:* 800-578-7878	Grand Rapids	MI	49546	616-949-8800	949-4303

— Restaurants —

				Phone
1913 Room (American) 187 Monroe St NW	Grand Rapids	MI	49503	616-774-2000
Bentham's Riverfront Restaurant (American) 187 Monroe St NW	Grand Rapids	MI	49503	616-774-2000
Bistro Bella Vita (Italian) 44 Grandville Ave	Grand Rapids	MI	49503	616-222-4600
Brann's Steakhouse (Steak) 401 Leonard NW	Grand Rapids	MI	49504	616-454-9368
Charley's Crab Restaurant (Seafood) 63 Market St SW	Grand Rapids	MI	49503	616-459-2500
Cherie Inn (European) 969 Cherry St	Grand Rapids	MI	49506	616-458-0588
Cottage Bar & Restaurant (American) 8 LaGrave Ave SE	Grand Rapids	MI	49503	616-454-9088
Cygnus (Continental) 187 Monroe Ave NW	Grand Rapids	MI	49503	616-776-6425
Duba's (American) 420 East Beltline Ave NE	Grand Rapids	MI	49506	616-949-1011
Flanagan's (Irish) 139 Pearl St NW	Grand Rapids	MI	49503	616-454-7852
Gibson's Restaurant (Continental) 1033 Lake Dr SE	Grand Rapids	MI	49506	616-774-8535
Grand River Saloon (American) 151 Ottawa Ave *Web:* www.foodquest.com/grandriver.html	Grand Rapids	MI	49503	616-458-2229
Hong Kong Inn (Chinese) 121 Monroe Ctr	Grand Rapids	MI	49503	616-451-3835
One Trick Pony (Mediterranean) 136 E Fulton St	Grand Rapids	MI	49503	616-235-7669
Rembrandt's at Bridgewater (American) 333 Bridge St NW Suite 205 *Web:* www.foodquest.com/Rembrandts.html	Grand Rapids	MI	49504	616-459-8900
Rhythm Kitchen Cafe (American) 100 Monroe Ctr *Web:* www.foodquest.com/Rythm_Kitchen.html	Grand Rapids	MI	49503	616-774-4199
San Chez (Spanish) 38 W Fulton St	Grand Rapids	MI	49503	616-774-8272
Sayfee's (Continental) 3555 Lake Eastbrook Blvd SE	Grand Rapids	MI	49506	616-949-5750
Schnitzelbank (German) 342 Jefferson Ave SE *Web:* www.schnitzel.kvi.net/	Grand Rapids	MI	49506	616-459-9527
Taps Sports Bar (American) 8 Ionia Ave SW	Grand Rapids	MI	49503	616-774-3338
Three Crowns Bistro (European) 29 Pearl St NW	Grand Rapids	MI	49503	616-454-4525
Tillman's (Steak) 1245 Monroe Ave NW	Grand Rapids	MI	49505	616-451-9266
Yen Ching (Chinese) 57 Monroe Ctr NW	Grand Rapids	MI	49503	616-235-6969

Grand Rapids (Cont'd)

— Goods and Services —

SHOPPING

				Phone	Fax
Breton Village Shopping Center 1830 Breton Rd SE	Grand Rapids	MI	49506	616-949-4141	949-0414
Gaslight Village Wealthy St-betw Bretton Rd & Lovett Ave	East Grand Rapids	MI	49506	616-459-8287	
Holland Outlet Center 12330 James St	Holland	MI	49424	616-396-1808	396-5993
Monroe Mall Pearl St & Monroe Ave.	Grand Rapids	MI	49503	616-459-8287	
Woodland Shopping Center 3195 28th St SE	Grand Rapids	MI	49512	616-949-0010	949-7348

BANKS

				Phone	Fax
Bank West 2185 Three-Mile Rd NW	Grand Rapids	MI	49544	616-785-3400	785-3590
Comerica Bank 99 Monroe Ave NW Campau Sq **Fax Area Code:* 616	Grand Rapids	MI	49503	800-654-4456	451-9298*
Grand Bank 126 Ottawa Ave NW Suite 100	Grand Rapids	MI	49503	616-235-7000	235-2160
Huntington Bank 173 Ottawa Ave NW *TF:* 800-480-2265	Grand Rapids	MI	49503	616-771-6256	235-5904
National City Corp 171 Monroe Ave NW	Grand Rapids	MI	49503	616-771-8800	771-8790
Old Kent Bank 1 Vandenberg Ctr. *TF:* 800-652-2657	Grand Rapids	MI	49503	616-771-5000	771-4672

BUSINESS SERVICES

	Phone		Phone
Airborne Express	800-247-2676	**Kinko's**	616-957-7888
BAX Global	800-225-5229	**Mail Boxes Etc**	800-789-4623
DHL Worldwide Express	800-225-5345	**Office Staffing Inc**	616-949-2525
Elaine's Secretarial Service	616-361-0916	**Post Office**	616-776-1415
Federal Express	800-238-5355	**UPS**	800-742-5877

— Media —

PUBLICATIONS

				Phone	Fax
Grand Rapids Business Journal 549 Ottawa Ave NW *Web:* www.grbj.com	Grand Rapids	MI	49503	616-459-0555	459-4800
Grand Rapids Press‡ 155 Michigan St NW *Web:* gr.mlive.com	Grand Rapids	MI	49503	616-459-1400	222-5409

‡Daily newspapers

TELEVISION

				Phone	Fax
WGVU-TV Ch 35 (PBS) 301 W Fulton St *Web:* www.wgvu.org/tv.html	Grand Rapids	MI	49504	616-771-6666	771-6625
WLLA-TV Ch 64 (Ind) PO Box 3157	Kalamazoo	MI	49003	616-345-6421	345-5665
WOOD-TV Ch 8 (NBC) PO Box B. *Web:* www.woodtv.com ■ *E-mail:* woodtv8@aol.com	Grand Rapids	MI	49501	616-456-8888	456-5755
WOTV-TV Ch 41 (ABC) 5200 W Dickman Rd *Web:* www.wotv.com ■ *E-mail:* wotv@wotv.com	Battle Creek	MI	49015	616-968-9341	966-6837
WTLJ-TV Ch 54 (Ind) 10290 48th Ave.	Allendale	MI	49401	616-895-4154	892-4401
WWMT-TV Ch 3 (CBS) 590 W Maple St. *Web:* www.wwmt.com	Kalamazoo	MI	49008	616-388-3333	388-8322
WXMI-TV Ch 17 (Fox) 3117 Plaza Dr NE *Web:* www.wxmi.com	Grand Rapids	MI	49505	616-364-8722	364-8506
WZPX-TV Ch 43 (Ind) 2610 Horizon Dr Suite E *Web:* www.wzpxtv.com	Grand Rapids	MI	49546	616-222-4343	493-2677
WZZM-TV Ch 13 (ABC) 645 Three-Mile Rd NW *E-mail:* wzzmtv@aol.com	Grand Rapids	MI	49544	616-785-1313	785-1301

RADIO

				Phone	Fax
WBBL-AM 1340 kHz (Sports) 60 Monroe Ctr 10th Fl. *Web:* www.wbbl.com	Grand Rapids	MI	49503	616-456-5461	451-3299
WBCT-FM 93.7 MHz (Ctry) 77 Monroe Ctr Suite 1000 *Web:* www.b93.com	Grand Rapids	MI	49503	616-459-1919	732-3330
WCSG-FM 91.3 MHz (Rel) 1159 E Beltline Ave NE *TF:* 800-968-4543 ■ *Web:* www.wcsg.org ■ *E-mail:* wcsgfm@aol.com	Grand Rapids	MI	49525	616-942-1500	942-7078
WCUZ-FM 101.3 kHz (Ctry) 77 Monroe Ctr NW Suite 1000 *Web:* www.wcuz.com	Grand Rapids	MI	49503	616-459-1919	242-9373
WGRD-FM 97.9 MHz (Rock) 38 W Fulton St *Web:* www.wgrd.com	Grand Rapids	MI	49503	616-459-4111	454-5530
WGVU-AM 1480 kHz (NPR) Grand Valley State University 301 W Fulton St *TF:* 800-442-2771 ■ *Web:* www.wgvu.org/radio.html ■ *E-mail:* wgvu@gvsu.edu	Grand Rapids	MI	49504	616-771-6666	336-7204
WGVU-FM 88.5 MHz (NPR) 301 W Fulton St *Web:* www.wgvu.org/radio.html ■ *E-mail:* wgvu@gvsu.edu	Grand Rapids	MI	49504	616-771-6666	336-7204
WKLQ-FM 94.5 MHz (Rock) 60 Monroe Ctr *TF:* 800-968-9450 ■ *Web:* www.wklq.com	Grand Rapids	MI	49503	616-774-8461	774-0351
WMFN-AM 640 kHz (Sports) 2422 Burton SE *TF:* 800-380-0064	Grand Rapids	MI	49546	616-949-8585	949-9262
WMJH-AM 810 kHz (Nost) 2422 Burton St. *TF:* 800-380-0064	Grand Rapids	MI	49546	616-949-8585	949-9262
WOOD-FM 105.7 MHz (AC) 77 Monroe Ctr 10th Fl. *Web:* www.woodradio.com	Grand Rapids	MI	49503	616-459-1919	732-3330

— Colleges/Universities —

				Phone	Fax
Aquinas College 1607 Robinson Rd SE *TF:* 800-678-9593 ■ *Web:* www.aquinas.edu	Grand Rapids	MI	49506	616-459-8281	732-4487
Calvin College 3201 Burton St SE *TF Admissions:* 800-688-0122 ■ *Web:* www.calvin.edu ■ *E-mail:* admissions@calvin.edu	Grand Rapids	MI	49546	616-957-6000	957-8551
Cornerstone College 1001 E Beltline Ave NE *TF:* 800-787-9778 ■ *Web:* www.cornerstone.edu	Grand Rapids	MI	49525	616-949-5300	222-1400
Davenport College 415 E Fulton St. **Fax:* Admissions ■ *TF Admissions:* 800-632-9569 ■ *Web:* www.davenport.edu/grandrapids	Grand Rapids	MI	49503	616-451-3511	732-1167*
Grace Bible College PO Box 910 *TF:* 800-968-1887 ■ *Web:* www.gbcol.edu ■ *E-mail:* info@gbcol.edu	Grand Rapids	MI	49509	616-538-2330	538-0599
Grand Rapids Community College 143 Bostwick Ave NE *Web:* www.grcc.cc.mi.us	Grand Rapids	MI	49503	616-234-4000	234-4107
Kendall College of Art & Design 111 Division Ave N *TF:* 800-676-2787	Grand Rapids	MI	49503	616-451-2787	451-9867
Reformed Bible College 3333 East Beltline Ave NE *Web:* www.reformed.edu ■ *E-mail:* admissions@reformed.edu	Grand Rapids	MI	49525	616-222-3000	222-3045

— Hospitals —

				Phone	Fax
Holland Community Hospital 602 Michigan Ave *Web:* www.hoho.org	Holland	MI	49423	616-392-5141	394-3528
Metropolitan Hospital 1919 Boston St SE **Fax:* Admitting	Grand Rapids	MI	49506	616-252-7200	252-7365*
Saint Mary's Health Services 200 Jefferson St SE **Fax:* Admitting ■ *Web:* www.mercyhealth.com/smhs	Grand Rapids	MI	49503	616-752-6090	732-3082*
Spectrum Health DeVos Children's Hospital 100 Michigan St NE **Fax:* Admitting ■ *Web:* www.spectrum-health.org/devos/dvchindex2.htm	Grand Rapids	MI	49503	616-391-1774	391-1720*

Grand Rapids — Hospitals (Cont'd)

				Phone	Fax
Spectrum Health East Campus 1840 Wealthy St SE	Grand Rapids	MI	49506	616-774-7444	774-7894*

*Fax: Admitting ■ Web: www.spectrum-health.org

— Attractions —

				Phone	Fax
Amway Corp Tours 7575 Fulton St E	Ada	MI	49355	616-787-6701	787-7102
Blandford Nature Center 1715 Hillburn Ave NW	Grand Rapids	MI	49504	616-453-6192	559-3130
Web: www.grmuseum.org/blnfrd.htm ■ E-mail: staff@grmuseum.org					
BOB The (Big Old Building) 20 Monroe Ave	Grand Rapids	MI	49503	616-356-2000	493-2011
Web: www.thebob.com/ ■ E-mail: thebob@thebob.com					
Broadway Theatre Guild 50 Monroe Pl Suite 620	Grand Rapids	MI	49503	616-235-6285	235-6282
Web: www.bwaygr.org ■ E-mail: live@iserv.net					
Calvin College Center Art Gallery Calvin College	Grand Rapids	MI	49546	616-957-6271	957-8551
Chaffee Roger B Planetarium 272 Pearl Ave NW	Grand Rapids	MI	49504	616-456-3977	456-3873
Web: www.grmuseum.org/chaffee.htm ■ E-mail: staff@grmuseum.org					
Community Circle Theatre 1300 W Fulton St	Grand Rapids	MI	49504	616-456-5929	456-8540
DeGraaf Nature Center 600 Graafschap Rd	Holland	MI	49423	616-355-1057	
Fish Ladder Sculpture Scribner Ave	Grand Rapids	MI	49503	616-459-8287	
Gaslight Village Wealthy St-betw Bretton Rd & Lovett Ave	East Grand Rapids	MI	49506	616-459-8287	
Gerald R Ford Museum 303 Pearl St NW Suite 126	Grand Rapids	MI	49504	616-451-9263	451-9570
Web: www.ford.utexas.edu ■ E-mail: information.museum@fordmus.nara.gov					
Grand Lady Riverboat Indian Mounds Dr	Grandville	MI	49418	616-457-4837	457-2231
Web: www.river-boat.com					
Grand Rapids Art Museum 155 Division Ave N	Grand Rapids	MI	49503	616-459-4677	459-8491
Web: www.gram.mus.mi.us ■ E-mail: gram@iserv.net					
Grand Rapids Ballet Co 233 E Fulton St Suite 126	Grand Rapids	MI	49503	616-454-4771	454-0672
Web: www.grballet.org ■ E-mail: grballet@grballet.org					
Grand Rapids Children's Museum 22 Sheldon Ave NE	Grand Rapids	MI	49503	616-235-4726	235-4728
Web: www.grcm.org ■ E-mail: grcm@hotmail.com					
Grand Rapids Civic Theatre 30 N Division Ave	Grand Rapids	MI	49503	616-222-6650	222-6660
Web: www.grct.org					
Grand Rapids Symphony Orchestra 169 Louis Campau Promenade Suite 1	Grand Rapids	MI	49503	616-454-9451	454-7477
Web: www.grsymphony.org/					
Heritage Hill Historic District 126 College Ave SE	Grand Rapids	MI	49503	616-459-8950	
Web: www.heritagehill.gen.mi.us/ ■ E-mail: heritage@iserv.net					
John Ball Zoological Garden 1300 W Fulton	Grand Rapids	MI	49504	616-336-4300	336-3907
Web: www.ring.com/zoo/ballzoo5.htm					
LeMontueux Vineyard & Winery 2365 8 Mile Road NW	Grand Rapids	MI	49544	616-784-4554	784-4554
Meijer Frederik Gardens 3411 Bradford St NE	Grand Rapids	MI	49525	616-957-1580	957-5792
Web: www.meijergardens.org/home.html					
Meyer May House 450 Madison Ave SE	Grand Rapids	MI	49503	616-246-4821	
Monroe Mall Pearl St & Monroe Ave	Grand Rapids	MI	49503	616-459-8287	
Opera Grand Rapids 161 Ottawa Ave NW Suite 207	Grand Rapids	MI	49503	616-451-2741	451-4587
Public Museum of Grand Rapids 272 Pearl St NW Van Andel Museum Ctr	Grand Rapids	MI	49504	616-456-3977	456-3873
Web: www.grmuseum.org ■ E-mail: staff@grmuseum.org					
Saugatuck Dune Rides 6495 Washington Rd	Saugutuck	MI	49453	616-857-2253	
Urban Institute for Contemporary Arts 41 Sheldon Blvd SE	Grand Rapids	MI	49503	616-454-7000	454-7013
Web: www.uica.org/					
Voigt House Victorian Museum 115 College Ave SE	Grand Rapids	MI	49503	616-456-4600	456-4603
Web: www.grmuseum.org/voigt.htm ■ E-mail: staff@grmuseum.org					
Windmill Island 7th & Lincoln Aves	Holland	MI	49423	616-355-1030	355-1035

SPORTS TEAMS & FACILITIES

				Phone	Fax
Grand Rapids Griffins (hockey) 130 W Fulton St Van Andel Arena	Grand Rapids	MI	49503	616-774-4585	336-5464
TF: 800-246-2539 ■ Web: www.grgriffins.com/ ■ E-mail: info@grgriffins.com					
Grand Rapids Hoops (basketball) 130 W Fulton St Van Andel Arena	Grand Rapids	MI	49503	616-458-7788	458-2123
Web: www.grhoops.com ■ E-mail: admin@grhoops.com					
Grand Rapids Rampage (soccer) 25 Ionia Ave SW Suite 300	Grand Rapids	MI	49503	616-559-1871	774-2337
Web: www.grrampage.com/					
Grattan Raceway Park 7201 Lessiter	Belding	MI	48809	616-691-7221	691-7449
Van Andel Arena 130 W Fulton St	Grand Rapids	MI	49503	616-742-6600	742-6197
Web: www.vanandelarena.com					
West Michigan Explosion (soccer) 1001 E Beltline SE Cornerstone College Soccer Field	Grand Rapids	MI	49505	616-957-2500	957-0369
West Michigan Whitecaps (baseball) 4500 W River Dr Old Kent Pk	Comstock Park	MI	49321	616-784-4131	784-4911
Web: www.whitecaps-baseball.com/ ■ E-mail: whitecaps@gr.cns.net					

— Events —

	Phone
African American Festival (mid-July)	616-245-5756
Buffalo Days (mid-June)	616-784-4853
Celebration on the Grand (mid-September)	616-456-3696
Christmas Around the World (late November-late December)	616-957-1580
Downtown Discovery Days (mid-October)	616-774-7124
East Rotary Antique Fair & Sale (mid-April)	616-243-5333
Festa Italiana (early August)	616-456-3178
Festival of the Arts (June)	616-459-2787
Foremost Insurance Championship (early September)	616-235-0943
Germanfest (early September)	616-364-0456
Grand Center Boat Show (February)	616-530-1919
Grand Rapids Jazz & Blues Festival (late July)	616-774-7124
Grand Regatta (mid-July)	616-364-5150
Grand Valley Artist Reeds Lake Art Festival (late June)	616-458-0315
Grand Valley Indian Pow Wow (early September)	616-364-4697
Hispanic Festival (mid-September)	616-742-0200
Kent Harvest Trails (late September-mid-October)	616-452-4647
Klein Rodeo (early September)	616-887-9945
Labor Day Parade and Rally (early September)	616-241-6555
Meijer Food Fair (mid-September)	616-791-3257
Parade of Homes (late May-early June)	616-281-2021
Polish Harvest Festival (late July)	616-452-3363
Pulaski Days Celebration (early October)	616-459-8287
Riverside Arts & Craft Fair (mid-August)	616-454-7900
Saint Patrick's Day Parade (mid-March)	616-247-5127
Saladin Shrine Circus (mid-late March)	616-957-4100
Summer in the City (mid-June-late August)	616-774-7124
Three Fires Indian Pow Wow (mid-June)	616-458-8759
Thunder on the Grand Championship Drag Boat Race (late August)	616-795-0065
Tulip Time (early-mid-May)	800-822-2770
Victorian Christmas at Voigt House (mid-November-early January)	616-456-4600
West Michigan Grand Prix (late August)	616-222-4000
West Michigan Home & Garden Show (mid-March)	616-530-1919
Zoo Goes Boo (late October)	616-336-4300

Lansing

One of the top science museums in the United States, Impression 5 Science Museum, is situated along Museum Drive in downtown Lansing. This is also the starting point for Planet Walk, a model of the solar system that stretches across 8,000 feet of the River Trail along the Grand River in Lansing. Other attractions in this area include the Riverwalk Theatre, Michigan Museum of Surveying, and R.E. Olds Transportation Museum. The State Capitol Building, originally designed by architect Elijah E. Meyers, has recently undergone extensive renovation in order to restore its original Victorian design, thereby earning its new designation as a National Historic Landmark. East Lansing is the home of Michigan State University, and the Michigan Festival, one of the region's largest events, is held on the MSU campus.

Lansing (Cont'd)

Population 127,825
Area (Land) ....32.8 sq mi
Area (Water).......0.2 sq mi
Elevation ....860 ft
Latitude ....42-72-43 N
Longitude.......84-56-13 W
County ....Ingham
Time Zone ....EST
Area Code/s 517

— Average Temperatures and Precipitation —

TEMPERATURES

	Jan	Feb	Mar	Apr	May	Jun	Jul	Aug	Sep	Oct	Nov	Dec
High	29	32	43	57	69	78	83	80	72	59	46	34
Low	13	14	25	35	45	55	59	57	50	39	31	19

PRECIPITATION

	Jan	Feb	Mar	Apr	May	Jun	Jul	Aug	Sep	Oct	Nov	Dec
Inches	1.5	1.4	2.3	2.8	2.6	3.7	2.5	3.2	3.6	2.1	2.6	2.3

— Important Phone Numbers —

	Phone
AAA	517-882-5111
American Express Travel	517-787-5200
Artsline	517-372-4636
Emergency	911
Medical Referral	517-334-2145
Poison Control Center	800-764-7661
Time	517-487-1212
Weather	517-321-7576

— Information Sources —

				Phone	Fax
Better Business Bureau Serving Western Michigan 40 Pearl St NW Suite 354	Grand Rapids	MI	49503	616-774-8236	774-2014
Web: www.grandrapids.bbb.org ■ *E-mail:* info@grandrapids.bbb.org					
Greater Lansing Convention & Visitors Bureau 1223 Turner St	Lansing	MI	48906	517-487-6800	487-5151
TF: 800-648-6630 ■ *Web:* www.lansing.org ■ *E-mail:* glcvb-info@lansing.org					
Ingham County PO Box 179	Mason	MI	48854	517-676-7204	676-7254
Lansing Center 333 E Michigan Ave	Lansing	MI	48933	517-483-7400	483-7439
Lansing City Hall 124 W Michigan Ave	Lansing	MI	48933	517-483-4000	
Web: ci.lansing.mi.us					
Lansing Mayor 124 W Michigan Ave 9th Fl	Lansing	MI	48933	517-483-4141	483-6066
Web: ci.lansing.mi.us/depts/mayor/mayor.html ■ *E-mail:* mayor@ci.lansing.mi.us					
Lansing Planning & Neighborhood Development Dept 316 N Capitol Ave Suite D-1	Lansing	MI	48933	517-483-4066	483-6036
Lansing Public Library 401 S Capitol Ave	Lansing	MI	48933	517-325-6400	367-6333
E-mail: morrowl@mlc.lib.mi.us					
Lansing Regional Chamber of Commerce 300 E Michigan Ave Suite 300	Lansing	MI	48933	517-487-6340	484-6910
Web: www.lansingchamber.org/					

On-Line Resources

4Lansing.com www.4lansing.com
Anthill City Guide Lansing ....www.anthill.com/city.asp?city=lansing
Area Guide Lansing.......lansing.areaguides.net
City Knowledge Lansing.......www.cityknowledge.com/mi_lansing.htm
Excite.com Lansing City Guide.......www.excite.com/travel/countries/united_states/michigan/lansing
Lansing.com.......lansing.com/
Lansing.TheLinks.com.......lansing.thelinks.com/

— Transportation Services —

AIRPORTS

■ **Capital City Airport (LAN)** — *Phone*

4 miles NW of downtown (approx 10 minutes) 517-321-6121

Airport Transportation

	Phone
Airport Transportation $10 fare to downtown	517-482-1444
Spartan Cab $8-10 fare to downtown	517-485-4400

Commercial Airlines

	Phone
Continental Express	800-525-0280
Delta Connection	800-221-1212
Northwest	800-225-2525
United	800-241-6522
United Express	800-241-6522
US Airways	800-428-4322
US Airways Express	800-428-4322

Charter Airlines

	Phone
Aerogenesis Aviation Inc	800-669-7305
Superior Aviation	800-882-7751

CAR RENTALS

	Phone
Enterprise	517-374-2880
Hertz	517-321-1445
National	517-321-6777
Thrifty	517-372-8900

LIMO/TAXI

	Phone
Champagne Limousine	517-372-2822
Classic Caddy Limousine	517-372-5466
Grand Limousine	517-371-1940
Lansing Limousine	517-349-4300
Majestic Limousine	517-332-7970
Spartan Cab	517-485-4400
Yellow Cab	517-482-1444

MASS TRANSIT

	Phone
Capital Area Transportation Authority $1 Base fare	517-394-1000

RAIL/BUS

				Phone
Amtrak Station 1240 S Harrison Rd	East Lansing	MI	48823	517-332-5051
TF: 800-872-7245				
Greyhound Bus Station 420 S Grand Ave	Lansing	MI	48933	517-332-2569
TF: 800-231-2222				

— Accommodations —

HOTELS, MOTELS, RESORTS

				Phone	Fax
Apex One Motel 15749 S US Hwy 27	Lansing	MI	48906	517-484-2241	
Battle Creek Inn 5050 Beckley Rd	Battle Creek	MI	49015	616-979-1100	979-1899
TF: 800-232-3405 ■ *Web:* www.battle-creek.com/bcinn/ ■ *E-mail:* bcinn@iserv.net					
Best Western Governor's Inn & Conference Center 6133 S Pennsylvania	Lansing	MI	48911	517-393-5500	393-5500
TF: 800-528-1234					
Best Western Midway Hotel & Conference Center 7711 W Saginaw Hwy	Lansing	MI	48917	517-627-8471	627-8597
TF: 800-528-1234					
ClubHouse Inn 2710 Lake Lansing Rd	Lansing	MI	48912	517-482-0500	482-0557
TF: 800-258-2466 ■ *Web:* www.clubhouseinn.com/3.LAN.shtml ■ *E-mail:* info@clubhouseinn.com					
Comfort Inn & Executive Suites 2209 University Park Dr	Okemos	MI	48864	517-349-8700	349-5638
TF: 800-228-5150					
Days Inn South 6501 S Pennsylvania Ave	Lansing	MI	48911	517-393-1650	393-9633
TF: 800-329-7466					
Econo Lodge 1100 Ramada Dr	Lansing	MI	48911	517-394-7200	394-0826
TF: 800-553-2666					
Fairfield Inn 810 Delta Commerce Dr	Lansing	MI	48917	517-886-1066	886-1066
TF: 800-228-2800 ■ *Web:* fairfieldinn.com/LANFW					
Hampton Inn 525 N Canal Rd	Lansing	MI	48917	517-627-8381	627-5502
TF: 800-426-7866					
Harley Hotel 3600 Dunckel Dr	Lansing	MI	48910	517-351-7600	351-4640
TF: 800-321-2323					
Hawthorn Suites Hotel 901 Delta Commerce Dr	Lansing	MI	48917	517-886-0600	886-0103
TF: 800-456-6431					
Holiday Inn 2590 Capital Ave SW	Battle Creek	MI	49015	616-965-3201	965-0740
TF: 800-465-4329					
Holiday Inn Conference Center 7501 W Saginaw Hwy	Lansing	MI	48917	517-627-3211	627-5240
TF: 800-465-4329					
Holiday Inn Lansing 6820 S Cedar St	Lansing	MI	48911	517-694-8123	699-3753
TF: 800-333-8123					

Lansing — Hotels, Motels, Resorts (Cont'd)

				Phone	Fax
Kellogg Hotel & Conference Center S Harrison Rd Michigan State University Campus	East Lansing	MI	48824	517-432-4000	353-1872
TF: 800-875-5090 ■ *Web:* www.hfs.msu.edu/kellogg					
Marriott University Place 300 MAC Ave	East Lansing	MI	48823	517-337-4440	337-5001
TF: 800-228-9290 ■ *Web:* marriotthotels.com/LANEA					
McCamly Plaza Hotel 50 Capital Ave SW	Battle Creek	MI	49017	616-963-7050	963-4335
TF: 888-622-2659 ■ *Web:* www.mccamlyplazahotel.com					
Motel 6 7326 W Saginaw Hwy	Lansing	MI	48917	517-321-1444	886-2024
TF: 800-466-8356					
Radisson Hotel 111 N Grand Ave	Lansing	MI	48933	517-482-0188	487-6646
TF: 800-333-3333					
Ramada Inn 1100 Trowbridge Rd	East Lansing	MI	48823	517-351-5500	351-5509
TF: 800-272-6232					
Ramada Limited 6741 S Cedar St	Lansing	MI	48911	517-694-0454	694-7087
TF: 800-272-6232					
Red Roof Inn East 3615 Dunckel Rd	Lansing	MI	48910	517-332-2575	332-1459
TF: 800-843-7663					
Red Roof Inn West 7412 W Saginaw Hwy	Lansing	MI	48917	517-321-7246	321-2831
TF: 800-843-7663					
Residence Inn by Marriott 1600 E Grand River	East Lansing	MI	48823	517-332-7711	
TF: 800-331-3131 ■ *Web:* www.residenceinn.com/residenceinn/LANMI					
Sheraton Hotel 925 S Creyts Rd	Lansing	MI	48917	517-323-7100	323-2180
TF: 800-325-3535					
Super 8 Motel 910 American Rd	Lansing	MI	48911	517-393-8008	
TF: 800-800-8000					
Town & Country Motel 16262 S US Hwy 27	Lansing	MI	48906	517-372-2710	372-2710
University Quality Inn 3121 E Grand River Ave	Lansing	MI	48912	517-351-1440	351-6220
TF: 800-228-5151					

— Restaurants —

				Phone
Aldaco Restaurant (Mexican) 902 E Grand River Ave	Lansing	MI	48906	517-372-9758
Austin's Cafe (American) 320 S Walnut St	Lansing	MI	48933	517-372-6263
Bangkok House Restaurant (Thai) 420 E Saginaw Hwy	Lansing	MI	48906	517-487-6900
Beggar's Banquet (Continental) 218 Abbott Rd	East Lansing	MI	48823	517-351-4573
Blue Coyote Brewing Co (Southwest) 113 Pere Marquette	Lansing	MI	48912	517-485-2583
Bonnie's Place (American) 326 N Cedar St	Lansing	MI	48912	517-372-1559
Christies (Continental) 925 S Creyts Rd	Lansing	MI	48917	517-323-4190
Clara's (American) 637 E Michigan Ave	Lansing	MI	48912	517-372-7120
Coscarelli's (Italian) 2400 S Cedar St	Lansing	MI	48910	517-482-4919
Web: www.coscarellis.com				
Downtown Hobie's (American) 115 S Washington Sq	Lansing	MI	48901	517-482-1383
Dusty's Wine Bar (American) 1839 E Grand River Ave	Okemos	MI	48864	517-349-8680
El Azteco (Mexican) 1016 W Saginaw St	Lansing	MI	48915	517-485-4589
Emil's (Italian) 2012 E Michigan Ave	Lansing	MI	48912	517-482-4430
Frank's Press Box (American) 7216 W Saginaw Rd	Lansing	MI	48917	517-886-1330
Golden Harvest Restaurant (Homestyle) 1625 N Turner St	Lansing	MI	48906	517-485-3663
Hershey's (Continental) 2682 E Grand River	East Lansing	MI	48823	517-337-7324
House of Ing (Chinese) 4113 S Cedar St	Lansing	MI	48910	517-393-4848
Irish Pub (American) 1910 W Saginaw St	Lansing	MI	48915	517-482-3916
Kelly's Downtown (American) 203 S Washington Ave	Lansing	MI	48933	517-484-5007
Knight Cap (American) 320 E Michigan Ave	Lansing	MI	48933	517-484-7676
La Senorita (Mexican) 2706 Lake Lansing Rd	Lansing	MI	48912	517-485-0166
Madison Street Bistro (American) 207 W Madison St	Lansing	MI	48910	517-485-7017
Mountain Jack's (Steak) 5800 W Saginaw Hwy	Lansing	MI	48917	517-321-2770
Murasaki Restaurant (Japanese) 116 Bailey St Stonehouse Village	East Lansing	MI	48823	517-332-7766
New China Restaurant (Chinese) 6250 S Cedar St	Lansing	MI	48911	517-882-7755
Nuthouse Sports Grill (American) 420 E Michigan Ave	Lansing	MI	48933	517-484-6887
Olympic Broil Restaurant (American) 1320 N Grand River Ave	Lansing	MI	48906	517-485-8584
Parthenon (Greek) 227 S Washington Sq	Lansing	MI	48933	517-484-0573
Piazzano's (Italian) 1825 N Grand River	Lansing	MI	48906	517-484-0150
Pistachios for Fish (Seafood) 2827 E Grand River Ave	East Lansing	MI	48823	517-351-1551
Regent Cafe (Homestyle) 5600 S Pennsylvania Ave	Lansing	MI	48911	517-887-2466
Rum Runners (American) 601 E Michigan Ave	Lansing	MI	48912	517-482-4949
Seville's (American) 111 N Grand Ave	Lansing	MI	48933	517-482-9427
Signatures American Grill (American) 5900 Park Lake Rd	East Lansing	MI	48823	517-339-0755

— Goods and Services —

SHOPPING

				Phone	Fax
Central Park Place 5100 Marsh Rd	Okemos	MI	48864	517-349-5450	349-7192
Lansing Factory Outlet Stores 1161 E Clark Rd	DeWitt	MI	48820	517-669-2624	
Lansing Mall 5330 W Saginaw Hwy	Lansing	MI	48917	517-321-3534	
Web: www.lansingmall.com					
Meridian Mall 1982 W Grand River Ave	Okemos	MI	48864	517-349-2030	349-7737
Web: www.meridianmall.com					
Washington Square Mall Washington Sq & Michigan Ave	Lansing	MI	48933	517-487-3322	487-5889
Williamston Area Antique District E & W Grand River Ave & N & S Putnam St	Williamston	MI	48895	517-655-2622	

BANKS

				Phone	Fax
Bank One 201 Washington Sq S	Lansing	MI	48933	517-487-1037	487-5472
Capitol National Bank 200 Washington Sq N	Lansing	MI	48933	517-484-5080	374-2559
Citizens Bank 2201 E Grand River	Lansing	MI	48912	517-371-8870	371-8869
Michigan National Bank 124 W Allegan St	Lansing	MI	48933	800-225-5662	377-3037*
**Fax Area Code: 517*					
National City Bank PO Box 30120	Lansing	MI	48909	517-334-1600	334-5370
Old Kent Bank 112 E Allegan St	Lansing	MI	48933	517-371-2911	371-1491
TF: 800-304-0434					
Old Kent Bank 111 S Capitol Ave	Lansing	MI	48933	517-372-7500	372-7616

BUSINESS SERVICES

	Phone
Airborne Express	800-247-2676
BAX Global	800-225-5229
DHL Worldwide Express	800-225-5345
Federal Express	800-238-5355
Kinko's	517-394-1410
Mail Boxes Etc	800-789-4623
Manpower Temporary Services	517-372-0880
Olsten Staffing Services	517-371-5790
Post Office	517-337-8711
Protemps	517-371-3023
UPS	800-742-5877

— Media —

PUBLICATIONS

				Phone	Fax
Greater Lansing Business Monthly 614 Seymour Ave Suite 580	Lansing	MI	48933	517-487-1714	487-9597
Web: www.businessmonthly.com/ ■ *E-mail:* glbm@lansing.net					
Lansing State Journal‡ 120 E Lenawee St	Lansing	MI	48919	517-377-1000	377-1298
TF: 800-433-6946 ■ *Web:* www.lansingstatejournal.com					
Michigan Out-of-Doors PO Box 30235	Lansing	MI	48909	517-371-1041	371-1505
TF: 800-777-6720 ■ *Web:* www.mucc.org/michigan_out_of_doors/mood.html					

‡Daily newspapers

TELEVISION

				Phone	Fax
WILX-TV Ch 10 (NBC) 500 American Rd	Lansing	MI	48911	517-393-0110	393-9180
Web: www.wilxnbc10.com					
WKAR-TV Ch 23 (PBS) MSU 212 Communications Arts Bldg	East Lansing	MI	48824	517-432-9527	353-7124
Web: www.wkar.msu.edu/tv/index.htm ■ *E-mail:* mail@wkar.msu.edu					
WLAJ-TV Ch 53 (ABC) 5815 S Pennsylvania Ave	Lansing	MI	48911	517-394-5300	887-0077
Web: www.wlaj.com/					
WLNS-TV Ch 6 (CBS) 2820 E Saginaw St	Lansing	MI	48912	517-372-8282	374-7610
Web: www.wlns.com					
WSYM-TV Ch 47 (Fox) 600 W Saint Joseph St Suite 47	Lansing	MI	48933	517-484-7747	484-3144
WZPX-TV Ch 43 (Ind) 2610 Horizon Dr Suite E	Grand Rapids	MI	49546	616-222-4343	493-2677
Web: www.wzpxtv.com					

RADIO

				Phone	Fax
WILS-AM 1320 kHz (Nost) PO Box 25008	Lansing	MI	48909	517-393-1320	393-0882
WJIM-AM 1240 kHz (N/T) 3420 Pine Tree Rd	Lansing	MI	48911	517-394-7272	394-3388
TF: 800-286-9546					
WKAR-AM 870 kHz (NPR) Michigan State University 283 Communication Arts Bldg	East Lansing	MI	48824	517-355-6540	353-7124
Web: wkar.msu.edu/					
WKAR-FM 90.5 MHz (NPR) 283 Communications Arts & Sciences Michigan State University	Lansing	MI	48824	517-355-6540	353-7124
Web: wkar.msu.edu/radio/index.htm ■ *E-mail:* mail@wkar.msu.edu					

Lansing — Radio (Cont'd)

	City	State	Zip	Phone	Fax
WMMQ-FM 94.9 MHz (CR) 3200 Pine Tree Rd	Lansing	MI	48911	517-393-1010	393-4041
WVFN-AM 730 kHz (Sports) 3420 Pine Tree Rd	Lansing	MI	48911	517-394-7272	393-9757
WXIK-FM 94.1 MHz (Ctry) 2495 N Cedar St *TF:* 800-786-7106	Holt	MI	48842	517-699-0994	699-1880
WXLA-AM 1180 kHz (AC) 1011 Northcrest Rd Suite 4	Lansing	MI	48906	517-484-9600	484-9699

— Colleges/Universities —

	City	State	Zip	Phone	Fax
Davenport College 220 E Kalamazoo St *TF:* 800-686-1600 ■ *Web:* www.davenport.edu/lansing ■ *E-mail:* laadmissions@davenport.edu	Lansing	MI	48933	517-484-2600	484-9719
Great Lakes Christian College 6211 W Willow Hwy *TF:* 800-937-4522 ■ *Web:* www.glcc.edu ■ *E-mail:* glcc@glcc.edu	Lansing	MI	48917	517-321-0242	321-5902
Lansing Community College 521 N Washington Sq *TF:* 800-644-4522 ■ *Web:* www.lansing.cc.mi.us	Lansing	MI	48901	517-483-1957	483-9668
Michigan State University 250 Administration Bldg. *Web:* wxweb.msu.edu ■ *E-mail:* admis@pilot.msu.edu	East Lansing	MI	48824	517-355-1855	353-1647

— Hospitals —

	City	State	Zip	Phone	Fax
Ingham Regional Medical Center 401 W Greenlawn Ave *Web:* www.irmc.org	Lansing	MI	48910	517-334-2121	334-2230
Ingham Regional Medical Center Pennsylvania Campus 2727 S Pennsylvania	Lansing	MI	48910	517-372-8220	372-5006
Saint Lawrence Hospital & Healthcare Services 1210 W Saginaw St. **Fax:* Admitting ■ *Web:* www.mercyhealth.com/stl	Lansing	MI	48915	517-372-3610	377-0467*
Sparrow Health System 1215 E Michigan Ave **Fax:* Admitting ■ *Web:* www.sparrow.com ■ *E-mail:* sparrow@www.sparrow.com	Lansing	MI	48912	517-483-2700	483-3747*

— Attractions —

	City	State	Zip	Phone	Fax
Abrams Planetarium Shaw Ln & Science Rd Michigan State University *Web:* www.pa.msu.edu/abrams	East Lansing	MI	48824	517-355-4676	432-3838
Adado Louis F Riverfront Park & Trail System 201 E Shiawasee St.	Lansing	MI	48933	517-483-4277	483-6062
Arts Council of Greater Lansing 425 S Grand Ave Center for the Arts *Web:* www.lansing.com/artscouncil ■ *E-mail:* artscouncil@lansing.com	Lansing	MI	48933	517-372-4636	484-2564
BoarsHead Michigan Public Theater 425 S Grand Ave Center for the Arts	Lansing	MI	48933	517-484-7805	484-2564
Burchfield Park 881 Grovenburg Rd	Holt	MI	48842	517-676-2233	694-2958
Cooley Gardens 225 W Main St	Lansing	MI	48933	517-483-4277	
Country Mill 4648 Otto Rd	Charlotte	MI	48813	517-543-1019	
Fenner Carl G Nature Center 2020 E Mt Hope Rd	Lansing	MI	48910	517-483-4224	377-0012
Frances Park 2600 Moores River Dr	Lansing	MI	48911	517-483-4277	483-6062
Greater Lansing Symphony Orchestra 230 N Washington Sq Suite 100	Lansing	MI	48933	517-487-5001	487-0210
Impression 5 Science Center 200 Museum Dr *Web:* www.impression5.org	Lansing	MI	48933	517-485-8116	485-8125
Ingham County Courthouse PO Box 319	Mason	MI	48854	517-676-7213	676-7230
Kresge Art Museum Michigan State University *Web:* www.msu.edu/unit/kamuseum/	East Lansing	MI	48824	517-355-7631	355-6577
Lansing Art Gallery 425 S Grand Ave Center for the Arts	Lansing	MI	48933	517-374-6400	484-2564
Lansing Civic Players 2300 E Michigan Ave.	Lansing	MI	48912	517-484-9115	484-7440
Ledges The 133 Fitzgerald Park Dr	Grand Ledge	MI	48837	517-627-7351	
Malcolm X Homesite ML King Jr Blvd.	Lansing	MI	48911		
Meridian Historical Village 5151 Marsh Rd Meridian Township Central Park	Okemos	MI	48864	517-347-7300	
Michigan Library & Historical Center 717 W Allegan St *Web:* www.sos.state.mi.us/history/history.html	Lansing	MI	48918	517-373-3559	373-0851
Michigan Museum of Surveying 220 S Museum Dr	Lansing	MI	48933	517-484-6605	
Michigan State Capitol Capitol & Michigan Aves	Lansing	MI	48913	517-373-2348	
Michigan State University Greenhouse & Butterfly House East Circle Dr	Lansing	MI	48824	517-355-0348	353-4354
Michigan State University Museum W Circle Dr *Web:* museum.cl.msu.edu	East Lansing	MI	48824	517-355-2370	432-2846
Michigan Women's Historical Center & Hall of Fame 213 W Main St *Web:* scnc.leslie.k12.mi.us/~mwhfame ■ *E-mail:* mwhfame@leslie.k12.mi.us	Lansing	MI	48933	517-484-1880	372-0170
Nokomis Learning Center 5153 Marsh Rd *Web:* www.nokomis.org ■ *E-mail:* cameron@nokomis.org	Okemos	MI	48864	517-349-5777	349-8560
Olds RE Transportation Museum 240 Museum Dr *Web:* www.reolds.com	Lansing	MI	48933	517-372-0422	372-2901
Opera Co of Mid-Michigan 215 S Washington Sq	Lansing	MI	48933	517-482-1431	482-3761
Planet Walk	Lansing	MI	48933	517-487-6800	
Potter Park Zoo 1301 S Pennsylvania Ave *Web:* www.ci.lansing.mi.us/depts/zoo/zoo.html ■ *E-mail:* potterpark@ci.lansing.mi.us	Lansing	MI	48912	517-483-4221	483-6065
Riverwalk Theatre 228 Museum Dr. *Web:* www.comnet.org/riverwalktheatre	Lansing	MI	48933	517-482-5700	482-9812
Snow's Sugar Bush 3188 Plains Rd	Mason	MI	48854	517-676-2442	
Spotlight Theatre Jefferson Hwy Fitzgerald Pk	Grand Ledge	MI	48837	517-627-5444	627-2977
Telephone Pioneer Museum 221 N Washington Sq	Lansing	MI	48933	517-487-6800	
Turner-Dodge House & Park 100 E North St	Lansing	MI	48906	517-483-4220	483-6081
Wharton Center for the Performing Arts Michigan State University *TF:* 800-942-7866 ■ *Web:* web.msu.edu/wharton/ ■ *E-mail:* wharton@pilot.msu.edu	East Lansing	MI	48824	517-432-2000	353-5329
WJ Beal Botanical Garden Michigan State University *Web:* www.cpp.msu.edu/beal	East Lansing	MI	48824	517-355-9582	432-1090
Woldumar Nature Center 5739 Old Lansing Rd. *Web:* www.woldumar.org	Lansing	MI	48917	517-322-0030	322-9394

SPORTS TEAMS & FACILITIES

	City	State	Zip	Phone	Fax
Lansing Lugnuts (baseball) 505 E Michigan Ave Oldsmobile Pk *TF:* 800-945-6887 ■ *Web:* www.lansinglugnuts.com ■ *E-mail:* lugnuts@tcimet.net	Lansing	MI	48912	517-485-4500	485-4518

— Events —

	Phone
Bluegrass Music Festival (late August)	517-589-8097
Car/Capital Celebration (late August)	517-372-0529
Central Michigan Boat Show (late January)	517-485-2309
Festeve (late December)	517-487-3322
Festival of Trees (late November)	517-483-7400
Home & Garden Show (mid-March)	517-686-0660
Ingham County Fair (late July-early August)	517-676-2428
Island Art Fair (early August)	517-627-9843
Lansing Art Festival (late May)	517-337-1731
Lansing Jazzfest (early August)	517-371-4600
LPGA Tournament (late August)	517-372-4653
Mexican Fiesta (Memorial Day Weekend)	517-394-4639
Michigan Parades Into the 21st Century (mid-May)	517-323-2000
National Folk Festival (mid-August)	517-355-2370
Old Town Lansing Art & Octoberfest (mid-October)	517-487-3322
Riverfest (early September)	517-483-4499
Wonderland of Lights (late November-late December)	517-371-3926

Minnesota

Population (1999): 4,775,508 **Area (sq mi): 86,943**

— State Information Sources —

				Phone	Fax
Minnesota Chamber of Commerce					
30 E 7th St Suite 1700	Saint Paul	MN	55101	651-292-4650	292-4656
TF: 800-821-2230 ■ *Web:* www.mnchamber.com					
Minnesota Parks & Recreation Div					
500 Lafayette Rd.	Saint Paul	MN	55155	651-296-9223	297-1157
Web: www.dnr.state.mn.us/parks_and_recreation/index.html					
Minnesota State Government Information				651-296-6013	
Web: www.state.mn.us ■ *E-mail:* info@state.mn.us					
Minnesota State Library Agency					
550 Cedar St Rm 440	Saint Paul	MN	55101	651-296-2821	296-5418
Web: www.state.mn.us/libraries/calco.html ■ *E-mail:* mmatters@library.leg.state.mn.us					
Minnesota Tourism Office					
121 E 7th Pl Suite 500	Saint Paul	MN	55101	651-296-5029	296-2000
TF: 800-657-3700 ■ *Web:* www.exploreminnesota.com					
Minnesota Trade & Economic Development Dept					
121 E 7th Pl Suite 500	Saint Paul	MN	55101	651-297-1291	296-4772
Web: www.dted.state.mn.us ■ *E-mail:* dted@state.mn.us					

ON-LINE RESOURCES

KAZAM Upper Midwest Web Guide .... www.kazam.com
Minnesota Cities .... dir.yahoo.com/Regional/U_S__States/Minnesota/Cities
Minnesota Counties & Regions .... dir.yahoo.com/Regional/U_S__States/Minnesota/Counties_and_Regions
Minnesota Online .... www.mnonline.org
Minnesota Page .... deckernet.com/minn
Minnesota Scenario .... scenariousa.dstylus.com/mn/indexf.htm
Minnesota Travel .... www.minntravel.com
Minnesota Travel & Tourism Guide .... www.travel-library.com/north_america/usa/minnesota/index.html
Minnesota's Great Northwest .... www.mngreatnw.org
Rough Guide Travel Minnesota travel.roughguides.com/content/537/index.htm
Travel.org-Minnesota .... travel.org/minnesot.html
Uffda! Search Minnesota .... www.mnonline.org/uffda
Where 2Havefun in Minnesota www.2havefun.com
Yahoo! Get Local Minnesota .... dir.yahoo.com/Regional/U_S__States/Minnesota

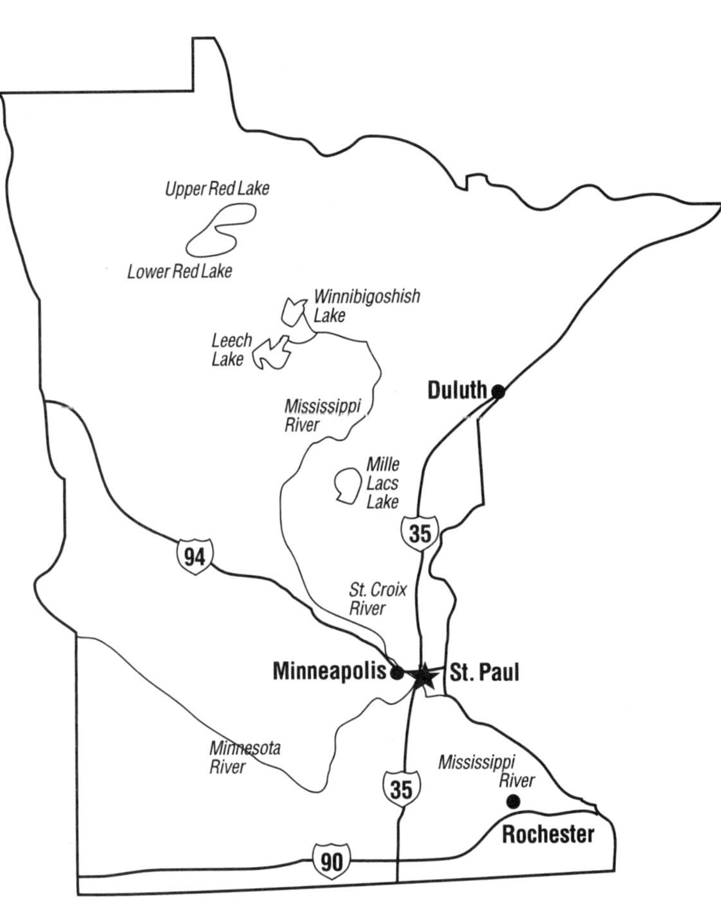

— Cities Profiled —

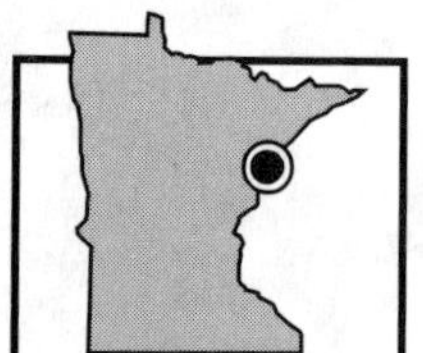

Duluth

Duluth is located just north of the Wisconsin state line on the shores of Lake Superior, and the lake is the focus of many of Duluth's attractions. The North Shore Scenic Drive is a 22-mile stretch that affords a view of lake vistas as well as secluded stops where one can walk down to the water's edge. Superb views of the lake are also found on Skyline Drive, which runs 600 feet above the shoreline for 30 miles. Another waterfront attraction is the SS William A. Irvin, once the flagship of the USS Great Lakes Fleet, which is now a floating museum permanently docked at the Duluth Convention Center. The North Shore Scenic Railroad offers scenic trips through the city, along the shoreline, and deep into the North Woods in a vintage train from the historic Lakefront Line, as well as other types of train rides. One of the area's most visited attractions is The Depot, which is home to five performing arts organizations and four museums. One of the museums there is the Lake Superior Railroad Museum, which contains one of the nation's finest collections of railroad equipment. Duluth is also home to the Karpeles Manuscript Library Museum, one of the world's largest private holdings of original manuscripts, including the U.S. Bill of Rights, the Emancipation Proclamation Amendment, and Handel's Messiah, all of which are on display in their original handwriting.

Population 81,228
Area (Land) . . . . 67.6 sq mi
Area (Water) . . . . 19.4 sq mi
Elevation . . . . 1428 ft
Latitude . . . . 46-46-51 N
Longitude . . . . 92-07-04 W
County . . . . Saint Louis
Time Zone . . . . CST
Area Code/s 218

— Average Temperatures and Precipitation —

TEMPERATURES

	Jan	Feb	Mar	Apr	May	Jun	Jul	Aug	Sep	Oct	Nov	Dec
High	16	22	33	48	62	71	77	74	64	52	35	21
Low	-2	3	16	29	40	49	55	53	45	35	22	5

PRECIPITATION

	Jan	Feb	Mar	Apr	May	Jun	Jul	Aug	Sep	Oct	Nov	Dec
Inches	1.2	0.8	1.9	2.3	3.0	3.8	3.6	4.0	3.8	2.5	1.8	1.2

— Important Phone Numbers —

	Phone
AAA	218-723-8055
Emergency	911
Medical Referral	218-727-3325
Poison Control Center	888-779-7921
Time/Temp	218-727-9000
Weather	218-729-6697

— Information Sources —

	City	State	Zip	Phone	Fax
Better Business Bureau Serving Minnesota & North Dakota 2706 Gannon Rd. *Web:* www.minnesota.bbb.org	Saint Paul	MN	55116	651-699-1111	699-7665
Duluth Area Chamber of Commerce 118 E Superior St.	Duluth	MN	55802	218-722-5501	722-3223
Duluth City Hall 411 W 1st St *Web:* www.ci.duluth.mn.us	Duluth	MN	55802	218-723-3340	723-3336
Duluth Convention & Visitors Bureau 100 Lake Place Dr. *TF:* 800-438-5884 ■ *Web:* www.visitduluth.com ■ *E-mail:* cvb@visit.duluth.mn.us	Duluth	MN	55802	218-722-4011	722-1322
Duluth Economic Development Dept 411 W 1st St Suite 400 *TF:* 800-444-6610 ■ *Web:* www.ci.duluth.mn.us/city/economic/ ■ *E-mail:* tcotruvo@ci.duluth.mn.us	Duluth	MN	55802	218-725-0697	
Duluth Entertainment Convention Center 350 Harbor Dr *TF:* 800-628-8385 ■ *Web:* www.decc.org ■ *E-mail:* decc@decc.org	Duluth	MN	55802	218-722-5573	722-4247
Duluth Mayor 411 W 1st St	Duluth	MN	55802	218-723-3295	723-3540
Duluth Public Library 520 W Superior St. *Web:* www.duluth.lib.mn.us ■ *E-mail:* webmail@duluth.lib.mn.us	Duluth	MN	55802	218-723-3800	723-3815
Saint Louis County 100 North 5th Ave W Rm 214 **Fax:* Acctg	Duluth	MN	55802	218-726-2380	725-5060*
Thompson Hill Information Center 8525 W Skyline Pkwy	Duluth	MN	55810	218-723-4938	

On-Line Resources

4Duluth.com www.4duluth.com
About.com Guide to Duluth . . . . duluth.about.com/local/midwestus/duluth
Area Guide Duluth . . . . duluth.areaguides.net
City Knowledge Duluth . . . . www.cityknowledge.com/mn_duluth.htm
Duluth Links . . . . www.duluthlinks.com
Duluth Search Directory . . . . duluthinfo.com
Duluth.com . . . . www.duluth.com
Excite.com Duluth City Guide . . . . www.excite.com/travel/countries/united_states/minnesota/duluth
NITC Travelbase City Guide Duluth . . . . www.travelbase.com/auto/features/duluth-mn.html
Online City Guide to Duluth . . . . www.olcg.com/mn/duluth/index.html

— Transportation Services —

AIRPORTS

■ **Duluth International Airport (DLH)**

	Phone
7 miles NW of downtown (approx 12 minutes)	218-727-2968

Airport Transportation

	Phone
Ace-Hi Taxi $11 fare to downtown	218-722-2929
Allied Taxicab $11 fare to downtown	218-722-3311
DLM Taxi $10-12 fare to downtown.	218-724-7557
Yellow Cab $10-12 fare to downtown	218-727-1515

Commercial Airlines

	Phone
American Eagle	800-433-7300
Northwest	800-225-2525

Charter Airlines

	Phone
Air DirectCharters	218-751-1880
Executive Aviation	800-486-5387
North Country Aviation	218-727-2911

CAR RENTALS

	Phone
Avis	218-727-7233
Budget	218-727-7685
Enterprise	218-722-5800
Hertz	218-722-7418
National	218-727-7426

LIMO/TAXI

	Phone
Ace-Hi Taxi	218-722-2929
Allied Taxicab	218-722-3311
DLM Taxi	218-724-7557
Fantasy Limousine	218-628-3372
Yellow Cab	218-727-1515

MASS TRANSIT

	Phone
Duluth Transit Authority $1 Base fare	218-722-7283
Port Town Trolley $.50 Base fare	218-722-4426

RAIL/BUS

	City	State	Zip	Phone
Greyhound Bus Station 4426 Grand Ave *TF:* 800-231-2222	Duluth	MN	55807	218-722-5591

Duluth (Cont'd)

— Accommodations —

HOTELS, MOTELS, RESORTS

Phone | Fax

A Charles Weiss Inn 1615 E Superior St. . . . . Duluth MN 55812 218-724-7016
TF: 800-525-5423 ■ *Web:* www.visitduluth.com/acweissinn/
■ *E-mail:* dglee@uslink.net
Airliner Motel 5002 Miller Trunk Hwy . . . . . . Hermantown MN 55811 218-729-6628
TF: 800-777-7478
Allyndale Motel 510 North 66th Ave W. . . . . Duluth MN 55807 218-628-1061
TF: 800-806-1061
AmericInn Lodge & Suites
1088 Hwy 61 N . . . . Two Harbors MN 55616 218-834-3000
TF: 800-634-3444
AmericInn Motel & Suites 185 Hwy 2. . . . . Duluth MN 55810 218-624-1026 624-2818
TF: 800-634-3444 ■ *Web:* www.visitduluth.com/Americinn/
Best Western Downtown Motel 131 W 2nd St . . . . Duluth MN 55802 218-727-6851 727-6779
TF: 800-528-1234
Best Western Edgewater 2400 London Rd. . . . . . . Duluth MN 55812 218-728-3601 728-3727
TF: 800-777-7925
Best Western Edgewater West
2211 London Rd. . . . . Duluth MN 55812 218-728-3601 728-3727
Buena Vista Motel 1144 Mesaba Ave . . . . Duluth MN 55811 218-722-7796 722-7796
TF: 800-569-8124
Canal Park Inn 250 Canal Park Dr. . . . . Duluth MN 55802 218-727-8821 723-7164
TF: 800-777-8560 ■ *E-mail:* canal@computerpro.com
Casa Motel 923 E Central Entrance Dr. . . . . Duluth MN 55805 218-727-9229
Chalet Motel 1801 London Rd . . . . Duluth MN 55812 218-728-4238
TF: 800-235-2957
Cody Inn 6716 Cody St . . . . Duluth MN 55807 218-628-2380
Comfort Inn West 3900 W Superior St . . . . Duluth MN 55807 218-628-1464 624-7263
TF: 800-228-5150
Comfort Suites 408 Canal Park Dr. . . . . Duluth MN 55802 218-727-1378 727-1947
TF: 800-228-5150 ■ *Web:* www.duluth.com/comfortsuites
Country Inn & Suites 9330 W Skyline Pkwy. . . . . . Duluth MN 55810 218-628-0668 628-3095
TF: 800-456-4000
Days Inn 909 Cottonwood Ave . . . . Duluth MN 55811 218-727-3110 727-3110
Duluth Motel 4415 Grand Ave . . . . Duluth MN 55807 218-628-1008
Eagle's Nest Resort 6103 LaVaque Rd . . . . Duluth MN 55803 218-721-4147
TF: 800-348-4575
Econo Lodge Airport 4197 Haines Rd . . . . Duluth MN 55811 218-722-5522 722-8316
TF: 800-922-0569
Edgetown Motel 5150 Miller Trunk Hwy . . . . Hermantown MN 55811 218-729-9806
Ellery House Inn 28 South 21st Ave E. . . . . Duluth MN 55812 218-724-7639
TF: 800-355-3794 ■ *Web:* www.visitduluth.com/elleryhouse/
Fairfield Inn by Marriott 901 Joshua Ave . . . . Duluth MN 55811 218-723-8607 723-8607
TF: 800-228-2800
Fitger's Inn 600 E Superior St . . . . Duluth MN 55802 218-722-8826 722-8826
TF: 800-726-2982 ■ *Web:* www.fitgers.com
■ *E-mail:* fitgers@fitgers.com
Gardenwood Motel 5107 North Shore Dr. . . . . Duluth MN 55804 218-525-1738
TF: 888-950-8036
Grand Motel 4312 Grand Ave. . . . . Duluth MN 55807 218-624-4821
TF: 800-472-0841
Hampton Inn 310 Canal Park Dr . . . . Duluth MN 55802 218-720-3000 722-3969
TF: 800-426-7866
Hawthorn Suites 325 Lake Ave S . . . . Duluth MN 55802 218-727-4663 722-0572
TF: 800-527-1133 ■ *Web:* www.hawthornsuitesduluth.com
■ *E-mail:* hawthorn@hawthornsuitesduluth.com
Heinz Beachway Motel & Cabin
5119 North Shore Dr. Duluth MN 55804 218-525-5191
Web: www.lakesuperiorresorts.com/bm_index.html
Holiday Inn Hotel & Suites 200 W 1st St . . . . Duluth MN 55802 218-722-1202 722-0233
TF: 800-477-7089 ■ *Web:* www.duluth.com/holidayinn/
■ *E-mail:* holiday@duluth.com
Inn on Gitche Gumee 8517 Congdon Blvd . . . . Duluth MN 55804 218-525-4979
TF: 800-317-4979 ■ *Web:* www.visitduluth.com/GitcheGumee/
Inn on Lake Superior 350 Canal Park Dr . . . . Duluth MN 55802 218-726-1111 727-3976
TF: 888-668-4352 ■ *Web:* www.duluth.com/iols
■ *E-mail:* iols@cpinternet.com
Lake Breeze Motel Resort 9000 Congdon Blvd. . . . Duluth MN 55804 218-525-6808
TF: 800-738-5884 ■ *Web:* www.lakebreeze.com/
■ *E-mail:* eklundlake@aol.com
Lakeview Castle Motel 5135 North Shore Dr . . . . . Duluth MN 55804 218-525-1014 525-1121
Motel 6 200 South 27th Ave W . . . . Duluth MN 55806 218-723-1123 720-3084
TF: 800-466-8356
North Shore Motel & Cottages
7717 Congdon Blvd. . . . . Duluth MN 55804 218-525-2812
TF: 800-926-6268 ■ *Web:* www.northshoremotel.com
■ *E-mail:* nsc@gateway.net
Radisson Hotel Duluth-Harborview
505 W Superior St . . . . Duluth MN 55802 218-727-8981 727-0162
TF: 800-333-3333 ■ *Web:* www.duluth.com/Radisson

Phone | Fax

Skyline Court Motel
4880 Miller Trunk Hwy . . . . Hermantown MN 55811 218-727-1563
TF: 800-554-0621
Spirit Mountain Lodge 9315 Westgate Blvd . . . . . . Duluth MN 55810 218-628-3691 628-2076
TF: 800-777-8530 ■ *Web:* www.duluth.com/spiritmtnlodge
Stanford Inn 1415 E Superior St. . . . . Duluth MN 55805 218-724-3044
Web: www.visitduluth.com/stanford
■ *E-mail:* stanford_inn@hotmail.com
Sundown Motel 5310 Thompson Hill Rd . . . . Duluth MN 55810 218-628-3613
Super 8 Motel 4100 W Superior St. . . . . Duluth MN 55807 218-628-2241 628-2570
TF: 800-800-8000 ■ *E-mail:* duluthgrps@aol.com
Voyageur Lakewalk Inn 333 E Superior St. . . . . . . Duluth MN 55802 218-722-3911 722-3124
TF: 800-258-3911 ■ *Web:* www.visitduluth.com/Voyageur/
■ *E-mail:* voyageur@visitduluth.com
Willard Munger Inn 7408 Grand Ave. . . . . Duluth MN 55807 218-624-4814
TF: 800-982-2453 ■ *Web:* www.mungerinn.com
■ *E-mail:* munger@computerpro.com

— Restaurants —

Phone

Beijing Restaurant (Chinese) 1219 E Superior St. . . . . Duluth MN 55802 218-724-2627
Bellisio's (Italian) 405 Lake Ave S. . . . . Duluth MN 55802 218-727-4921
Black Woods Grill & Bar (Steak/Seafood) 2525 London Rd . . . Duluth MN 55812 218-724-1612
Blue Max Restaurant (American) 6139 LaVaque Rd. . . . . Duluth MN 55803 218-721-4235
Bridgeman's Restaurant (American)
2202 Mountain Shadow Dr . . . . Duluth MN 55811 218-727-0196
Buena Vista Restaurant (American) 1144 Mesaba Ave. . . . . . . Duluth MN 55811 218-722-9047
Buffalo House (Barbecue) 2590 Guss Rd . . . . Duluth MN 55810 218-624-9901
Web: www.2havefun.com/BuffaloHouse
Cantonese House (Cantonese) 28 W 1st St. . . . . Duluth MN 55802 218-722-0778
Diane's Family Restaurant (Homestyle)
9058 W Central Entrance Dr . . . . Duluth MN 55811 218-727-4153
Dry Dock Bar & Restaurant (Steak/Seafood)
2820 Midway Rd . . . . Duluth MN 55810 218-624-5512
Duluth Grill (American) 118 South 27th Ave W. . . . . Duluth MN 55806 218-727-1527
Fitger's Brewery Complex (American) 600 E Superior St . . . . . Duluth MN 55802 218-722-8826
Web: www.brewhouse.net ■ *E-mail:* brew@brewhouse.net
Gallagher's Country Café (Homestyle)
5671 Miller Trunk Hwy . . . . Duluth MN 55811 218-729-7100
Gopher Restaurant & Lounge (American) 402 N Central Ave . . Duluth MN 55807 218-624-9793
Grandma's Saloon & Grill (American) 522 Lake Ave S. . . . . . . Duluth MN 55802 218-727-4192
Grizzly's Grill 'n Saloon (American) 1722 Miller Trunk Hwy . . . Duluth MN 55811 218-722-9231
Hacienda del Sol (Mexican) 319 E Superior St . . . . Duluth MN 55802 218-722-7296
Web: www.hacienda-del-sol.com ■ *E-mail:* hacienda@wwcoinc.com
Helen's Place (American) 1314 Commonwealth Ave . . . . Duluth MN 55808 218-626-1824
Island Lake Inn (American) 7153 Rice Lake Rd. . . . . Duluth MN 55803 218-721-4604
Jade Fountain (Chinese) 305 N Central Ave . . . . Duluth MN 55807 218-624-4212
Keglers Bar & Grill (American) 601 W Superior St . . . . Duluth MN 55802 218-722-0671
Ketola's Kafe (American) 3901 Grand Ave . . . . Duluth MN 55807 218-624-2725
Lake Avenue Café (New American) 394 Lake Ave S. . . . . Duluth MN 55802 218-722-2355
Little Angie's Cantina & Grill (Southwest) 11 Buchanan St . . . Duluth MN 55802 218-727-6117
Louis' Café & Restaurant (Greek) 1500 London Rd. . . . . Duluth MN 55812 218-728-4370
Mr D's Bar & Grill (American) 5622 Grand Ave. . . . . Duluth MN 55807 218-628-3793
Mr Nick's Restaurant (American) 220 W Superior St. . . . . Duluth MN 55802 218-722-5373
Northern Lights Restaurant (American) Main St . . . . Beaver Bay MN 55601 218-226-3012
Old Chicago Pizza & Pasta (American) 327 Lake Ave S . . . . . . Duluth MN 55802 218-720-2966
Pickwick (American) 508 E Superior St. . . . . Duluth MN 55802 218-727-8901
Porter's (Continental) 207 W Superior St . . . . Duluth MN 55802 218-727-6746
Saigon Café (Vietnamese)
915 W Central Entrance Dr Suite 2400 . . . . Duluth MN 55802 218-727-3987
Scenic Café (New American) 5461 North Shore Dr . . . . Duluth MN 55804 218-525-6274
Web: www.sceniccafe.com ■ *E-mail:* scenic@cpinternet.com
Sherry's Courtyard Café (American)
100 North 5th Ave W . . . . Duluth MN 55802 218-727-5442
Sir Benedict's Tavern (American) 805 E Superior St . . . . Duluth MN 55802 218-728-1192
Sneakers Sports Bar & Grill (American) 207 W 1st St. . . . . . . Duluth MN 55802 218-727-7494
Sunshine Café (American) 5719 Grand Ave. . . . . Duluth MN 55807 218-624-7013
Taste of Saigon (Vietnamese) 394 Lake Ave S . . . . Duluth MN 55802 218-727-1598
Timberlodge Steakhouse (Steak) 325 Lake Ave S . . . . Duluth MN 55802 218-722-2624
Top of the Harbor (American)
505 W Superior St Radisson Hotel Duluth Harborview . . . . . Duluth MN 55802 218-727-8981
Tradewinds Restaurant (American)
250 Canal Park Dr Canal Park Inn . . . . Duluth MN 55802 218-727-8821
Uncle Louie's Café (American) 520 E 4th St. . . . . Duluth MN 55805 218-727-4518
Z's Restaurant (Greek) 3904 Grand Ave . . . . Duluth MN 55805 218-624-3131

— Goods and Services —

SHOPPING

Phone

Antiques Off Broadway Antique Mall
103 Ave C . . . . Cloquet MN 55720 218-879-5284
Canal Park Antique Mall 310 Lake Ave S . . . . Duluth MN 55802 218-720-3940

Duluth — Shopping (Cont'd)

	City	State	ZIP	Phone
Dewitt-Seitz Marketplace 394 Lake Ave S Canal Pk	Duluth	MN	55802	218-722-0047
Holiday Center 207 W Superior St	Duluth	MN	55802	218-727-7765
Miller Hill Mall 1600 Miller Trunk Hwy	Duluth	MN	55811	218-727-8301

BANKS

	City	State	ZIP	Phone	Fax
North Shore Bank of Commerce 131 W Superior St **Fax:* Hum Res	Duluth	MN	55802	218-722-4784	722-7904*
Norwest Bank Minnesota North NA 230 W Superior St	Duluth	MN	55802	218-723-2600	
Park State Bank 1106 88th Ave W	Duluth	MN	55808	218-626-2755	626-2758
Pioneer National Bank 331 N Central Ave *Web:* www.pioneer-bank.com ■ *E-mail:* money@pioneer-bank.com	Duluth	MN	55807	218-624-3676	624-9066
Republic Bank Inc 306 W Superior St *Web:* www.republic-bank-inc.com ■ *E-mail:* bankers@republic-bank-inc.com	Duluth	MN	55802	218-722-3445	722-6901
TCF National Bank Minnesota 1530 Woodland Ave	Duluth	MN	55803	218-728-9080	728-9081
Western National Bank 5629 Grand Ave	Duluth	MN	55807	218-723-5100	723-5101

BUSINESS SERVICES

	Phone
Federal Express	800-238-5355
Insty-Prints	218-727-1311
Interim Personnel	218-722-8003
Kelly Services	218-727-5663
Mail Boxes Etc	218-727-5550
Manpower Temporary Services	218-727-8891
Olsten Staffing Services	218-720-3265
Post Office	218-723-2590
UPS	800-742-5877

— Media —

PUBLICATIONS

	City	State	ZIP	Phone	Fax
Budgeteer Press 5807 Grand Ave **Fax:* News Rm ■ *Web:* www.duluth.com/placed ■ *E-mail:* budgeteer@mx3.com	Duluth	MN	55807	218-624-3665	624-7927*
Duluth News-Tribune‡ 424 W 1st St *TF Circ:* 800-456-8080 ■ *Web:* www.duluthnews.com ■ *E-mail:* online@duluth.infi.net	Duluth	MN	55802	218-723-5281	720-4120
Duluth Shipping News 525 Lake Ave S *Web:* www.duluthshippingnews.com ■ *E-mail:* knewhams@duluthshippingnews.com	Duluth	MN	55802	218-722-3119	
Lake Superior Magazine 325 Lake Ave S Suite 600 *TF:* 888-244-5253 ■ *Web:* www.lakesuperior.com ■ *E-mail:* reader@lakesuperior.com	Duluth	MN	55802	218-722-5002	722-4096
North Life Magazine 5302 Ramsey St	Duluth	MN	55802	218-624-4949	624-1541
Proctor Journal 215 5th St *Web:* www.computerpro.com/~pjournal ■ *E-mail:* pjournal@computerpro.com	Proctor	MN	55810	218-624-3344	624-7037
Star Tribune Duluth Bureau 500 Medical Arts Bldg *TF:* 800-827-8742 ■ *Web:* www.startribune.com	Duluth	MN	55802	218-727-7344	727-7901
Twin Ports People 2711 W Superior St	Duluth	MN	55806	218-726-1610	

‡Daily newspapers

TELEVISION

	City	State	ZIP	Phone	Fax
KBJR-TV Ch 6 (NBC) 246 S Lake Ave *Web:* www.kbjr.com ■ *E-mail:* comments@kbjr.com	Duluth	MN	55802	218-727-8484	720-9699
KDLH-TV Ch 3 (CBS) 425 W Superior St *Web:* www.kdlh.com ■ *E-mail:* news3@kdlh.com	Duluth	MN	55802	218-733-0303	727-7515
WDIO-TV Ch 10 (ABC) 10 Observation Rd *E-mail:* wdio@aol.com	Duluth	MN	55811	218-727-6864	727-4415
WDSE-TV Ch 8 (PBS) 1202 E University Cir *Web:* www.wdse.org ■ *E-mail:* email@wdse.org	Duluth	MN	55811	218-724-8568	724-4269

RADIO

	City	State	ZIP	Phone	Fax
KDAL-AM 610 kHz (AC) 715 E Central Entrance	Duluth	MN	55811	218-722-4321	722-5423
KDAL-FM 95.7 MHz (AC) 715 E Central Entrance *Web:* www.96litefm.com	Duluth	MN	55811	218-722-4321	722-5423
KDDS-AM 1490 kHz (CR) 2001 London Rd	Duluth	MN	55812	218-728-6421	728-5809
KDNI-FM 90.5 MHz (Rel) 1101 E Central Entrance	Duluth	MN	55811	218-722-6700	722-1092
KDNW-FM 97.3 MHz (Rel) 1101 E Central Entrance *E-mail:* kdnw@juno.com	Duluth	MN	55811	218-722-6700	722-1092
KKCB-FM 105.1 MHz (Ctry) 14 E Central Entrance *Web:* www.kkcb.com ■ *E-mail:* country@kkcb.com	Duluth	MN	55811	218-727-4500	727-9356
KLDJ-FM 101.7 MHz (Oldies) 14 E Central Entrance *Web:* www.kool1017.com ■ *E-mail:* oldies@kool1017.com	Duluth	MN	55811	218-727-4500	727-9356
KQDS-FM 94.9 MHz (CR) 2001 London Rd	Duluth	MN	55812	218-728-6421	728-5809
KRBR-FM 102.5 MHz (Rock) 715 E Central Entrance *Web:* www.krbr.com ■ *E-mail:* thebear@krbr.com	Duluth	MN	55811	218-722-4321	722-5423
KTCO-FM 98.9 MHz (Ctry) 715 E Central Entrance	Duluth	MN	55811	218-722-4321	722-5423
KUMD-FM 103.3 MHz (NPR) 130 Humanities Bldg Suite 130 *Web:* www.d.umn.edu/kumd ■ *E-mail:* kumd@d.umn.edu	Duluth	MN	55812	218-726-7181	726-6571
KUSZ-FM 107.7 MHz (CR) 14 E Central Entrance	Duluth	MN	55811	218-727-4500	727-9356
KUWS-FM 91.3 MHz (NPR) PO Box 2000 *E-mail:* kuws@iname.com	Superior	WI	54880	715-394-8530	394-8404
KZIO-FM 104.3 MHz (Oldies) 501 Lake Ave S Suite 200-A	Duluth	MN	55802	218-723-1043	723-1499
WDSM-AM 710 kHz (Sports) 715 E Central Entrance *Web:* www.allsports710.com ■ *E-mail:* sports@discover-net.net	Duluth	MN	55811	218-722-4321	722-5423
WEBC-AM 560 kHz (N/T) 14 E Central Entrance *Web:* www.56webc.com ■ *E-mail:* talk@56webc.com	Duluth	MN	55811	218-727-4500	727-9356
WIRN-FM 92.5 MHz (NPR) 224 Holiday Ctr	Duluth	MN	55802	218-722-9411	720-4900
WKLK-AM 1230 kHz (Oldies) 1104 Cloquet Ave	Cloquet	MN	55720	218-879-4534	879-1962
WKLK-FM 96.5 MHz (Oldies) 1104 Cloquet Ave	Cloquet	MN	55720	218-879-4534	879-1962
WNCB-FM 89.3 MHz (Rel) 425 W Superior St Suite 300 *Web:* wncb.com ■ *E-mail:* airstaff@wncb.com	Duluth	MN	55802	218-722-3017	722-1650
WSCD-FM 92.9 MHz (NPR) 224 Holiday Ctr	Duluth	MN	55802	218-722-9411	720-4900
WSCN-FM 100.5 MHz (NPR) 224 Holiday Ctr	Duluth	MN	55802	218-722-9411	720-4900
WWAX-FM 92.1 MHz (AC) 501 Lake Ave S Suite 200-A	Duluth	MN	55802	218-723-1043	723-1499
WWJC-AM 850 kHz (Rel) 1120 E McCuen St *Web:* www.wwjc.com ■ *E-mail:* radio@wwjc.com	Duluth	MN	55808	218-626-2738	626-2585

— Colleges/Universities —

	City	State	ZIP	Phone	Fax
College of Saint Scholastica 1200 Kenwood Ave *TF:* 800-447-5444 ■ *Web:* www.css.edu	Duluth	MN	55811	218-723-6000	723-5991
Duluth Business University Inc 412 W Superior St *TF:* 800-777-8406 ■ *Web:* www.dbumn.com	Duluth	MN	55802	218-722-4000	722-8376
Lake Superior College 2101 Trinity Rd *TF:* 800-432-2884 ■ *Web:* www.lsc.cc.mn.us	Duluth	MN	55811	218-733-7600	723-4921
University of Minnesota Duluth 10 University Dr *TF:* 800-232-1339 ■ *Web:* www.d.umn.edu ■ *E-mail:* fsimmons@d.umn.edu	Duluth	MN	55812	218-726-8000	726-6144

— Hospitals —

	City	State	ZIP	Phone	Fax
Miller-Dwan Medical Center 502 E 2nd St *TF:* 800-766-8762 ■ *Web:* www.miller-dwan.com ■ *E-mail:* webrequest@mdmcduluth.com	Duluth	MN	55805	218-727-8762	720-1492
Saint Luke's Hospital & Regional Trauma Center 915 E 1st St *TF:* 800-321-3790	Duluth	MN	55805	218-726-5555	726-5100
Saint Mary's Medical Center 407 E 3rd St **Fax:* Admissions ■ *Web:* www.smdc.org	Duluth	MN	55805	218-726-4000	726-4170*

— Attractions —

	City	State	ZIP	Phone
Bennett's Dinner Theater 600 E Superior St *Web:* www.fitgers.com/dining/bennetts/theater	Duluth	MN	55802	218-722-2829

Duluth — Attractions (Cont'd)

				Phone	Fax
Black Bear Casino 1785 Hwy 210 *TF:* 888-771-0777	Carlton	MN	55718	218-878-2327	878-2414
Depot The Saint Louis County Heritage & Arts Center 506 W Michigan St *TF:* 888-733-5833 ■ *Web:* www.computerpro.com/~depot	Duluth	MN	55802	218-727-8025	733-7585
Duluth Children's Museum 506 W Michigan St	Duluth	MN	55802	218-733-7543	
Duluth Playhouse 506 W Michigan St	Duluth	MN	55802	218-733-7555	733-7554
Duluth-Superior Entertainment League 317 W Superior St *TF:* 800-622-2003	Duluth	MN	55802	218-722-2000	
Duluth-Superior Symphony Orchestra 350 Harbor Dr Duluth Entertainment Convention Ctr *Web:* computerpro.com/~dsso ■ *E-mail:* dsso@computerpro.com	Duluth	MN	55802	218-733-7577	733-7537
Fairlawn Museum 906 E 2nd St	Superior	WI	54880	715-394-5712	
Fitger's Brewery Complex Museum 600 E Superior St *Web:* www.fitgers.com ■ *E-mail:* fitgers@fitgers.com	Duluth	MN	55802	218-722-8826	722-8826
Fond du Luth Casino 129 E Superior St *TF:* 800-873-0280	Duluth	MN	55802	218-722-0280	722-7505
Glensheen Mansion 3300 London Rd *TF:* 888-454-4536 ■ *Web:* www.d.umn.edu/glen ■ *E-mail:* glen@d.umn.edu	Duluth	MN	55804	218-726-8910	726-8911
Grand Slam Family Fun Center 395 Lake Ave S	Duluth	MN	55802	218-722-5667	
Great Lakes Aquarium 6008 London Rd Lake Superior Ctr *Web:* www.glaquarium.org ■ *E-mail:* info@glaquarium.org	Duluth	MN	55804	218-525-2265	525-2827
Ironworld Discovery Center W Hwy 169 *TF:* 800-372-6437 ■ *Web:* www.ironworld.com ■ *E-mail:* janette@ironworld.com	Chisholm	MN	55719	218-254-3321	254-5235
Irvin William A Museum 350 Harbor Dr *Web:* www.decc.org/attractions/Irvin.htm	Duluth	MN	55802	218-722-7876	722-9206
Karpeles Manuscript Library Museum 902 E 1st St *Web:* www.rain.org/~karpeles/dulfrm.html ■ *E-mail:* kmuseumdul@aol.com	Duluth	MN	55805	218-728-0630	
Lake Shore Scenic Railroad 506 W Michigan St *TF:* 800-423-1273 ■ *Web:* www.duluth.com/lsrm ■ *E-mail:* lsrm@cpinternet.com	Duluth	MN	55802	218-722-1273	733-7590
Lake Superior & Mississippi Railroad Grand & 17th Aves	Duluth	MN	55807	218-624-7549	728-6303
Lake Superior Brewing Co 2711 W Superior St	Duluth	MN	55806	218-723-4000	
Lake Superior Maritime Visitors Center 600 Lake Ave S	Duluth	MN	55802	218-727-2497	720-5270
Lake Superior Museum of Transportation 506 W Michigan St *Web:* www.duluth.com/lsrm ■ *E-mail:* lsrm@cpinternet.com	Duluth	MN	55802	218-733-7590	733-7596
Lake Superior Zoological Gardens 7210 Fremont St	Duluth	MN	55807	218-733-3777	723-3750
Mariner Mall 69 N 28th St *Web:* www.marinermall-wi.com	Superior	WI	54880	715-392-7117	
Minnesota Ballet 301 W 1st St Suite 800 *Web:* www.minnesotaballet.org	Duluth	MN	55802	218-529-3742	529-3744
Minnesota Repertory Theatre 10 University Dr Marshall Performing Arts Ctr	Duluth	MN	55812	218-726-8564	
North Shore Scenic Drive Hwy 61 *Web:* www.northshorescenicdrive.com ■ *E-mail:* nssda@yahoo.com	Duluth	MN	55802	218-722-4011	
Omnimax Theatre 301 Harbor Dr	Duluth	MN	55802	218-727-0022	722-9206
Port of Duluth Seaway Port Authority of Duluth 1200 Port Terminal Dr *TF:* 800-232-0703 ■ *Web:* www.duluthport.com ■ *E-mail:* admin@duluthport.com	Duluth	MN	55802	218-727-8525	727-6888
Renegade Comedy Theatre 105 Holiday Ctr *TF:* 888-722-6627 ■ *Web:* www.renegadecomedy.org ■ *E-mail:* rencomedy@aol.com	Duluth	MN	55802	218-722-6775	
Rivers Bend Carriage Service 7864 Arkola Rd *E-mail:* riversbend1@juno.com	Cotton	MN	55724	218-482-5552	
Rose Garden at Leif Erikson Park London Rd betw E 12th & 13th Aves	Duluth	MN	88502	218-723-3337	
Sacred Heart Memorial Center 201 W 4th St	Duluth	MN	55806	218-723-1895	
Saint Louis County Historical Society 506 W Michigan St	Duluth	MN	55802	218-733-7580	
Spirit Mountain Ski Area 9500 Spirit Mountain Pl **Fax:* Mktg ■ *TF:* 800-642-6377 ■ *Web:* www.spiritmt.com ■ *E-mail:* spiritmt@cp.duluth.mn.us	Duluth	MN	55810	218-628-2891	624-0213*
Superior Hiking Trail 731 7th Ave	Two Harbors	MN	55616	218-834-2700	834-4436
Tom's Logging Camp 5797 North Shore Dr *Web:* www.tomsloggingcamp.com ■ *E-mail:* tomscamp@computerpro.com	Duluth	MN	55804	218-525-4120	
Tweed Museum of Art 10 University Dr *Web:* www.d.umn.edu/tma ■ *E-mail:* tma@d.umn.edu	Duluth	MN	55812	218-726-8222	726-8503
Waterfront Sculpture Walk Duluth Waterfront	Duluth	MN	55802	218-722-4011	

SPORTS TEAMS & FACILITIES

				Phone	Fax
Duluth Lumberjacks (football) 350 Harbor Dr Duluth Entertainment Convention Ctr	Duluth	MN	55802	218-722-5573	
Duluth-Superior Dukes (baseball) 207 W Superior St Suite 206 *Web:* www.dsdukes.com ■ *E-mail:* hitnrum@dsdukes.com	Duluth	MN	55802	218-727-4525	727-4533
Proctor Speedway 800 N Boundary Ave	Proctor	MN	55810	218-624-0606	
Superior Speedway 4700 Tower Ave *Web:* www.racewissota.com/superior	Superior	WI	74880	715-394-7848	

— Events —

	Phone
4th of July Pike Lake Boat Parade (July 4)	218-722-4011
Annual Volunteer Get-Together (early-mid-April)	218-723-3724
Bayfront Blues Festival (mid-August)	715-394-6831
Boo at the Zoo (late October)	218-723-3748
Christmas at Glensheen (late November-late December)	218-726-8910
Duluth International Folk Festival (early August)	218-733-7543
Duluth Lions Club Apple Harvest Festival (late September)	218-722-4011
Duluth National Snocross (late November)	218-722-4011
Duluth Winter Festival (early-late January)	218-722-4011
Duluth Yesterdays (late April-early May)	218-722-4011
Easter Egg Hunt (early April)	218-723-3748
Fallfest (mid-late September)	218-724-9832
Father's Day at the Zoo (mid-late June)	218-723-3748
Feast with the Beasts Food Festival (late July)	218-723-3748
Festival of Lights (late November-early January)	218-722-4011
FourthFest (July 4)	218-722-4011
Fun Fair (early March)	218-722-5573
Gingerbread Craft Show (late March)	218-722-5573
Glensheen Festival of Fine Art & Craft (late August)	218-726-8910
Grandma's Marathon (mid-June)	218-727-0947
Grandparent's Day at the Zoo (mid-September)	218-723-3748
Heritage Preservation Fair (mid-May)	218-722-8826
Hermantown Summerfest (mid-July)	218-727-7667
John Beargrease Sled Dog Marathon (early February)	218-722-7631
Lake Superior Paper Industries Tours (early June-early September)	218-628-5100
Martin Luther King Day Gathering (mid-January)	218-722-5573
Mayflower Festival (late May)	218-724-9832
Memorial Day Parade (May 31)	218-624-5518
Memorial Park Winter Carnival (late January)	218-723-3567
Mid-Winter Blues Fest (late January)	218-727-8981
Mother's Day at the Zoo (early May)	218-723-3748
North Saint Louis County Fair (early August)	800-372-6437
Northshore Inline Marathon (mid-September)	218-723-1503
Octoberfest (late September)	218-723-3748
Park Point Art Fair (late June)	715-398-5970
Polar Bear Picnic (late February-early March)	218-723-3748
President's Day Snow Festival (mid-February)	218-724-9832
Ragtime Music Festival (mid-September)	218-724-7696
Red Flannel Days (early-mid-February)	218-722-4651
Scandanavian Festival (early October)	715-392-2773
Semester Day Snow Festival (late January)	218-724-9832
Ship of Ghouls (late October)	218-722-7876
Taste of the Nation (early April)	218-722-8826
Two Harbors Folk Festival (mid-July)	218-834-2600
YWCA Mother's Day Walk/Run (early May)	218-722-7425
Zoo Year's Eve (December 31)	218-723-3748

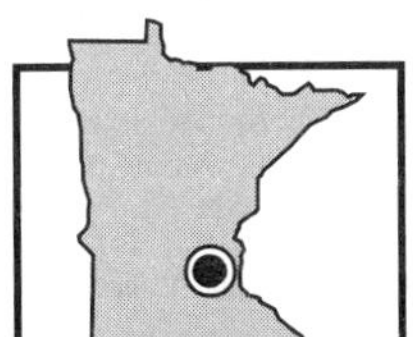

Minneapolis

The Mississippi Mile winds through downtown Minneapolis, with parkways, biking and walking paths, and picnic areas all along the banks of the River. From the James J. Hill Stone Bridge one can view the Mississippi, Saint Anthony Falls, and the surrounding historic district. Fort Snelling State Park, a stone fortress where guides recreate army life of the 1820s, also overlooks the River. In the nearby city of Bloomington is the Mall of America,

Minneapolis (Cont'd)

the largest shopping complex in the U.S. A total of 32 Fortune 500 companies, including Honeywell and General Mills, have their corporate headquarters in Minneapolis and the surrounding Twin Cities area.

Population	351,731	**Longitude**	93-26-36 W
Area (Land)	54.9 sq mi	**County**	Hennepin
Area (Water)	3.5 sq mi	**Time Zone**	CST
Elevation	838 ft	**Area Code/s**	612, 651
Latitude	44-98-00 N		

— Average Temperatures and Precipitation —

TEMPERATURES

	Jan	Feb	Mar	Apr	May	Jun	Jul	Aug	Sep	Oct	Nov	Dec
High	21	27	39	57	69	79	84	81	71	59	41	26
Low	3	9	23	36	48	58	63	60	50	39	25	10

PRECIPITATION

	Jan	Feb	Mar	Apr	May	Jun	Jul	Aug	Sep	Oct	Nov	Dec
Inches	1.0	0.9	1.9	2.4	3.4	4.1	3.5	3.6	2.7	2.2	1.6	1.1

— Important Phone Numbers —

	Phone		*Phone*
AAA	612-927-2727	**Medical Referral**	651-697-3333
American Express Travel	612-343-5500	**Poison Control Center**	612-347-3141
Connection The	612-922-9000	**Road Conditions**	651-405-6030
Dental Referral	612-892-5050	**Time**	612-512-1111
Emergency	911	**Weather**	612-512-1111
HotelDocs	800-468-3537		

— Information Sources —

				Phone	*Fax*
Better Business Bureau Serving Minnesota & North Dakota 2706 Gannon Rd.	Saint Paul	MN	55116	651-699-1111	699-7665
Web: www.minnesota.bbb.org					
Greater Minneapolis Chamber of Commerce 81 S 9th St Suite 200	Minneapolis	MN	55402	612-370-9132	370-9195
Web: www.tc-chamber.org ■ *E-mail:* info@tc-chamber.org					
Greater Minneapolis Convention & Visitors Assn 33 S 6th St Multifoods Tower Suite 4000	Minneapolis	MN	55402	612-661-4700	335-5839
TF: 800-445-7412 ■ *Web:* www.minneapolis.org					
Hennepin County 300 S 6th St.	Minneapolis	MN	55487	612-348-3000	
Web: www.co.hennepin.mn.us					
Minneapolis City Hall 350 S 5th St	Minneapolis	MN	55415	612-673-2215	673-2185
Web: www.ci.mpls.mn.us ■ *E-mail:* opa@ci.minneapolis.mn.us					
Minneapolis Convention Center 1301 2nd Ave S	Minneapolis	MN	55403	612-335-6000	335-6757
Web: www.mplsconvctr.org ■ *E-mail:* mplscc@mplsconvctr.org					
Minneapolis Mayor 350 S 5th St Rm 331	Minneapolis	MN	55415	612-673-2100	673-2305
Web: www.ci.mpls.mn.us/citywork/mayor ■ *E-mail:* mayor@ci.minneapolis.mn.us					
Minneapolis Planning Dept 350 S 5th St Rm 210	Minneapolis	MN	55415	612-673-2597	673-2728
Web: www.ci.mpls.mn.us/citywork/planning ■ *E-mail:* opa@ci.minneapolis.mn.us					
Minneapolis Public Library 300 Nicollet Mall	Minneapolis	MN	55401	612-630-6000	630-6210
Web: www.mpls.lib.mn.us					

On-Line Resources

4Minneapolis.com	www.4minneapolis.com
About.com Guide to Minneapolis/Saint Paul	minneapolis.about.com/local/midwestus/minneapolis
Area Guide Minneapolis	minneapolis.areaguides.net
Boulevards Minneapolis	www.boulevards.com/cities/minneapolis.html
City Knowledge Minneapolis	www.cityknowledge.com/mn_minneapolis.htm
City Wide Guide	www.citywideguide.com/
CitySearch Twin Cities	twincities.citysearch.com
DigitalCity Twin Cities	home.digitalcity.com/twincities
Excite.com Minneapolis City Guide	www.excite.com/travel/countries/united_states/minnesota/minneapolis
Insiders' Guide to the Twin Cities	www.insiders.com/twin-cities/
Minneapolis City Pages	minneapolis.thelinks.com/
Minneapolis FAQ	scc.net/~peter/MPLSFAQ.html
Minneapolis-Saint Paul City Guide	www.tgimaps.com/marketplace/cityguide/
Minneapolis-Saint Paul CityWomen	www.citywomen.com/minnwomen.htm
Mpls.com	www.mpls.com/
NITC Travelbase City Guide Twin Cities	www.travelbase.com/auto/guides/twin_cities-area-mn.html
Rough Guide Travel Minneapolis	travel.roughguides.com/content/538/
Savvy Diner Guide to Minneapolis-Saint Paul Restaurants	www.savvydiner.com/minneapolis/
Twin Cities Global Connection	www.tcglobal.com/
Twin Cities Internet Guide & Directory	www.tcigd.com/
Twin Cities Just Go	www.justgo.com/twincities/
Twin Cities Restaurant Guide	dine.com/twin
TwinCities.com	www.twincities.com
Yahoo! Twin Cities	minn.yahoo.com

— Transportation Services —

AIRPORTS

■ **Minneapolis-Saint Paul International Airport (MSP)** — *Phone*

10 miles SE of downtown Minneapolis (approx 20 minutes) 612-726-5500
Web: www.mspairport.com

Airport Transportation

	Phone
Airport Express $10 fare to downtown Minneapolis	612-827-7777
Boston Coach $47.50 fare to downtown Minneapolis	800-672-7676
Premier Transportation $35 fare to downtown Minneapolis	612-331-7433

Commercial Airlines

	Phone		*Phone*
America West	800-235-9292	**Northwest**	800-225-2525
American	800-433-7300	**Sun Country**	800-359-5786
Continental	800-525-0280	**TWA**	800-221-2000
Delta	800-221-1212	**United**	800-241-6522
KLM	800-374-7747	**US Airways**	800-428-4322
Mesaba Airlines	612-726-5151	**Vanguard**	800-826-4827

Charter Airlines

	Phone		*Phone*
Air Direct Charter	800-332-7133	**Regent Aviation**	651-227-7801
Dwyer Air Charter	612-726-5150	**Superior Aviation**	800-882-7751

CAR RENTALS

	Phone		*Phone*
Alamo	612-726-5323	**CarTemps USA**	612-881-7816
Americar	612-866-4918	**Dollar**	612-854-3003
Avis	612-726-5220	**Hertz**	651-698-9585
Budget	612-727-2000	**National**	612-830-2121

LIMO/TAXI

	Phone		*Phone*
Blue & White Taxi	612-333-3331	**Red & White Taxi**	612-871-1600
Carey Limousine	612-623-0565	**Town Taxi**	612-331-8294
Henderson Limousine	612-871-5466	**Yellow Cab**	612-824-4444

MASS TRANSIT

	Phone
Como-Harriet Streetcar Line $1.25 Base fare	651-228-0263
Metropolitan Transit $1 Base fare	612-373-3333

RAIL/BUS

				Phone
Greyhound Bus Station 1100 Hawthorne Ave.	Minneapolis	MN	55403	612-371-3325
TF: 800-231-2222				

Minneapolis (Cont'd)

— Accommodations —

HOTELS, MOTELS, RESORTS

Name / Address	City	State	Zip	Phone	Fax
Best Western American Inn 3924 Excelsior Blvd.	Minneapolis	MN	55416	612-927-7731	927-7731
Best Western Downtown 405 S 8th St. *TF:* 800-372-3131	Minneapolis	MN	55404	612-370-1400	370-0351
Best Western Kelly Inn 2705 Annapolis Ln N. *TF:* 800-528-1234	Plymouth	MN	55441	612-553-1600	553-9108
Best Western Seville Plaza Hotel 8151 Bridge Rd *TF:* 800-328-7947	Bloomington	MN	55437	612-830-1300	830-1535
Best Western Thunderbird Hotel & Convention Center 2201 E 78th St *TF:* 800-328-1931	Bloomington	MN	55425	612-854-3411	854-1183
Best Western University Inn 2600 University Ave SE	Minneapolis	MN	55414	612-379-2313	378-2382
Comfort Inn Airport 1321 E 78th St. *TF:* 800-228-5150	Bloomington	MN	55425	612-854-3400	854-2234
Crowne Plaza Northstar Hotel 618 2nd Ave S *TF:* 800-227-6963	Minneapolis	MN	55402	612-338-2288	673-1157
Days Inn Airport 1901 Killebrew Dr. *TF:* 800-329-7466	Bloomington	MN	55425	612-854-8400	854-3331
Doubletree Grand Hotel Mall of America 7901 24th Ave S. *TF:* 800-222-8733 ■ *Web:* www.doubletreehotels.com/DoubleT/Hotel61/61/61Main.htm	Bloomington	MN	55425	612-854-2244	854-4421
Doubletree Guest Suites 1101 LaSalle Ave *TF:* 800-222-8733 ■ *Web:* www.doubletreehotels.com/DoubleT/Hotel121/130/130Main.htm	Minneapolis	MN	55403	612-332-6800	332-8246
Doubletree Park Place Hotel 1500 Park Pl Blvd. *TF:* 800-222-8733 ■ *Web:* www.doubletreehotels.com/DoubleT/Hotel121/139/139Main.htm	Minneapolis	MN	55416	612-542-8600	542-8063
Embassy Suites 425 S 7th St. *TF:* 800-362-2779	Minneapolis	MN	55415	612-333-3111	333-7984
Embassy Suites 2800 W 80th St. *TF:* 800-362-2779	Bloomington	MN	55431	612-884-4811	884-8137
Embassy Suites South Airport 7901 34th Ave S. *TF:* 800-362-2779	Bloomington	MN	55425	612-854-1000	854-6557
Hampton Inn Bloomington 4201 W 80th St *TF:* 800-426-7866	Bloomington	MN	55437	612-835-6643	835-7217
Hawthorn Suites Hotel 3400 Edinborough Way *TF:* 800-527-1133 ■ *Web:* www.hawthorn.com/reservations/locationdetail.asp?state=MN&facid=238&pagecode=hdir ■ *E-mail:* hsedina@internetmci.com	Edina	MN	55435	612-893-9300	893-9885
Holiday Inn 1201 W County Rd E *TF:* 800-777-2232	Saint Paul	MN	55112	651-636-4123	636-2526
Holiday Inn Airport I 35W 1201 W 94th St *TF:* 800-465-4329	Bloomington	MN	55431	612-884-8211	881-5574
Holiday Inn Express Airport 814 E 79th St. *TF:* 800-465-4329	Bloomington	MN	55420	612-854-5558	854-4623
Holiday Inn Express Hotel & Suites 225 S 11th St. *TF:* 800-465-4329	Minneapolis	MN	55403	612-341-3300	341-1174
Holiday Inn Metrodome 1500 Washington Ave S *TF:* 800-448-3663 ■ *Web:* www.metrodome.com	Minneapolis	MN	55454	612-333-4646	333-7910
Holiday Inn Minneapolis North 1501 Freeway Blvd *TF:* 800-465-4329	Minneapolis	MN	55430	612-566-4140	561-9614
Holiday Inn Select International Airport 3 Appletree Sq *TF:* 800-465-4329 ■ *Web:* www.basshotels.com/holiday-inn/?_franchisee=MSPIA	Bloomington	MN	55425	612-854-9000	854-9000
Hotel Sofitel 5601 W 78th St. *TF:* 800-876-6303	Bloomington	MN	55439	612-835-1900	835-2696
Hyatt Regency 1300 Nicollet Mall *TF:* 800-233-1234 ■ *Web:* www.hyatt.com/usa/minneapolis/hotels/hotel_msprm.html	Minneapolis	MN	55403	612-370-1234	370-1463
Hyatt Whitney Hotel 150 Portland Ave.	Minneapolis	MN	55401	612-339-9300	339-1333
Izatys Golf & Yacht Club 40005 85th Ave *TF:* 800-533-1728	Onamia	MN	56359	320-532-3101	532-3208
Marquette Hotel 710 Marquette Ave *TF:* 800-328-4782	Minneapolis	MN	55402	612-332-2351	288-2188
Marriott City Center 30 S 7th St. *TF:* 800-228-9290 ■ *Web:* marriotthotels.com/MSPCC	Minneapolis	MN	55402	612-349-4000	332-7165
Marriott Hotel Southwest 5801 Opus Pkwy. *TF:* 800-228-9290 ■ *Web:* marriotthotels.com/MSPWE	Minnetonka	MN	55343	612-935-5500	935-0753
Marriott Minneapolis Airport Hotel 2020 E 79th St. *TF:* 800-228-9290 ■ *Web:* marriotthotels.com/MSPMN	Bloomington	MN	55425	612-854-7441	854-7671
Minneapolis Hilton & Towers 1001 Marquette Ave *TF:* 800-445-8667	Minneapolis	MN	55403	612-376-1000	397-4875
Minneapolis-Saint Paul Airport Hilton 3800 E 80th St *TF:* 800-445-8667	Bloomington	MN	55425	612-854-2100	854-5507
Nicollet Island Inn 95 Merriam St. *TF:* 800-331-6528 ■ *Web:* www.theunionstation.com/nicolletislandinn/	Minneapolis	MN	55401	612-331-3035	331-6528
Park Inn Suites 7770 Johnson Ave	Minneapolis	MN	55435	612-893-9999	893-1316
Quality Inn Suites 41 10th St N	Minneapolis	MN	55403	612-339-9311	339-4765
Radisson Hotel Metrodome 615 Washington Ave SE *TF:* 800-333-3333 ■ *Web:* www.radisson.com/hotels/minneapolismn_metrodome/	Minneapolis	MN	55414	612-379-8888	379-8682
Radisson Hotel South & Plaza Tower 7800 Normandale Blvd *TF:* 800-333-3333 ■ *Web:* www.radisson.com/hotels/minneapolismn_south/	Bloomington	MN	55439	612-835-7800	893-8419
Radisson Plaza Hotel 35 S 7th St. *TF:* 800-333-3333 ■ *Web:* www.radisson.com/hotels/minneapolismn_plaza/	Minneapolis	MN	55402	612-339-4900	337-9766
Ramada Hotel 2540 N Cleveland Ave *TF:* 800-272-6232	Roseville	MN	55113	651-636-4567	636-7110
Regal Minneapolis Hotel 1313 Nicollet Mall. *TF:* 800-522-8856	Minneapolis	MN	55403	612-332-0371	359-2160
Residence Inn by Marriott 7780 Flying Cloud Dr. *TF:* 800-331-3131 ■ *Web:* www.residenceinn.com/residenceinn/MSPEP	Eden Prairie	MN	55344	612-829-0033	829-1935
Sheraton Inn Airport 2500 E 79th St. *TF:* 800-325-3535	Bloomington	MN	55425	612-854-1771	854-5898
Sheraton Metrodome 1330 Industrial Blvd NE. *TF:* 800-777-3277	Minneapolis	MN	55413	612-331-1900	331-6827
Wyndham Garden Hotel 4460 W 78th Cir. *TF:* 800-996-3426	Bloomington	MN	55435	612-831-3131	831-6372

— Restaurants —

Name / Address	City	State	Zip	Phone
8th Street Grill (American) 800 Marquette Ave	Minneapolis	MN	55402	612-349-5717
510 Restaurant (American) 510 Groveland Ave	Minneapolis	MN	55403	612-874-6440
Allie's Grill (American) 30 S 7th St.	Minneapolis	MN	55402	612-349-4000
Anthony's Wharf (Seafood) 201 Main St SE	Minneapolis	MN	55414	612-378-7058
Aquavit (Scandanavian) 75 S 7th St. *Web:* www.aquavit.org	Minneapolis	MN	55402	612-343-3333
Atrium International Cafe (American) 275 Market St	Minneapolis	MN	55405	612-330-9425
Basil's (American) 710 Marquette Ave	Minneapolis	MN	55402	612-376-7404
Black Forest Inn (German) 1 E 26th St.	Minneapolis	MN	55404	612-872-0812
Brit's Pub & Eating Establishment (English) 1110 Nicollet Mall.	Minneapolis	MN	55403	612-332-3908
Buca Di Beppo (Italian) 1204 Harmon Pl	Minneapolis	MN	55403	651-638-2225
Cafe Brenda (Vegetarian) 300 1st Ave N	Minneapolis	MN	55401	612-342-9230
Cafe Havana (Cuban) 119 Washington Ave N	Minneapolis	MN	55401	612-338-8484
Cafe Luxx (Continental) 1101 LaSalle Ave.	Minneapolis	MN	55401	612-332-6800
Cafe Un Deux Trois (French) 114 S 9th St	Minneapolis	MN	55402	612-673-0686
Carver's (American) 1001 Marquette Ave	Minneapolis	MN	55403	612-376-1000
Champs Sports Cafe (American) 790 W 66th St	Richfield	MN	55423	612-861-3333
Christo's (Greek) 2632 Nicollet Ave S.	Minneapolis	MN	55404	612-871-2111
Cornell's (American) 425 S 7th St.	Minneapolis	MN	55415	612-333-3111
D'Amico Cucina (Italian) 100 N 6th St	Minneapolis	MN	55403	612-338-2401
Dan Kelly's (American) 212 S 7th St	Minneapolis	MN	55402	612-333-2644
Festival (Steak/Seafood) 35 S 7th St	Minneapolis	MN	55402	612-337-9760
Figlio (Italian) 3001 Hennepin Ave S	Minneapolis	MN	55408	612-822-1688
Georgio's (Italian) 2451 Hennepin Ave	Minneapolis	MN	55405	612-374-5131
Gluek's Restaurant (American) 16 N 6th St	Minneapolis	MN	55403	612-338-6621
Goodfellow's (American) 40 S 7th St.	Minneapolis	MN	55402	612-332-4800
Gustino's (Italian) 30 S 7th St.	Minneapolis	MN	55402	612-349-4000
Ichiban Japanese Steak House (Japanese) 1333 Nicollet Mall.	Minneapolis	MN	55403	612-339-0540
Jax Cafe (Continental) 1928 University Ave NE	Minneapolis	MN	55418	612-789-7297
JD Hoyt's (Cajun) 301 N Washington Ave	Minneapolis	MN	55401	612-338-1560
Joe's Garage (New American) 1610 Harmon Pl.	Minneapolis	MN	55403	612-904-1163
Kieran's Irish Pub (Irish) 330 S 2nd Ave	Minneapolis	MN	55401	612-339-4499
Kincaid's Steak Chop & Fish House (Steak/Seafood) 8400 Normandale Lake Blvd	Bloomington	MN	55437	612-921-2255

Minneapolis — Restaurants (Cont'd)

Restaurant	City	State	Zip	Phone
King The & I (Thai) 1034 Nicollet Mall	Minneapolis	MN	55403	612-332-6928
La Cucaracha (Mexican) 533 Hennepin Ave.	Minneapolis	MN	55405	612-339-1161
Leeann Chin (Chinese) 9th St & 2nd Ave S	Minneapolis	MN	55402	612-338-8488
Linguini & Bob (Italian) 100 N 6th St.	Minneapolis	MN	55403	612-332-1600
Loon Cafe (American) 504 1st Ave N	Minneapolis	MN	55403	612-332-8342
Lord Fletcher's of the Lake (American) 3746 Sunset Dr	Spring Park	MN	55384	612-471-8513
Lowell Inn (American) 102 N 2nd St	Stillwater	MN	55082	651-439-1100
Lyon's Pub (American) 16 S 6th St	Minneapolis	MN	55402	612-333-6612
Manny's Steak House (Steak) 1300 Nicollet Mall	Minneapolis	MN	55403	612-339-9900
Market Bar-B-Que (Barbecue) 1414 Nicollet Ave S.	Minneapolis	MN	55403	612-872-1111
Meadows (Continental) 615 Washington Ave.	Minneapolis	MN	55414	612-379-8888
Morton's of Chicago (Steak) 555 Nicollet Mall.	Minneapolis	MN	55402	612-673-9700
Mpls Cafe (French) 1110 Hennepin Ave S.	Minneapolis	MN	55403	612-672-9100
Murray's (Steak) 26 S 6th St.	Minneapolis	MN	55402	612-339-0909
New French Cafe (French) 128 N 4th St.	Minneapolis	MN	55401	612-338-3790
Origami (Japanese) 30 N 1st St	Minneapolis	MN	55401	612-333-8430
Palomino Euro Bistro (Mediterranean) 825 Hennepin Ave	Minneapolis	MN	55402	612-339-3800
Pracna on Main (American) 117 Main St	Minneapolis	MN	55414	612-379-3200
Rainforest Cafe (American) 102 South Ave. *Web:* www.rainforestcafe.com	Bloomington	MN	55425	612-854-7500
Rock Bottom Brewery (American) 825 Hennepin Ave	Minneapolis	MN	55402	612-332-2739
Rosewood Room (Continental) 618 2nd Ave S	Minneapolis	MN	55402	612-338-2288
Rudolph's Bar-B-Que (Barbecue) 1933 Lyndale Ave S	Minneapolis	MN	55403	612-871-8969
Singapore Chinese Cuisine (Chinese) 1715-A Beam Ave.	Maplewood	MN	55109	651-777-7999
Table of Contents (New American) 1310 Hennepin Ave	Minneapolis	MN	55403	612-339-1133
Village Wok (Chinese) 610 Washington Ave SE.	Minneapolis	MN	55414	612-331-9041

— Goods and Services —

SHOPPING

Name	City	State	Zip	Phone	Fax
Burnsville Center 1178 Burnsville Ctr *Web:* www.burnsvillecenter.com	Burnsville	MN	55306	612-435-8182	892-5073
Calhoun Square Shopping Center 3001 Hennepin Ave S *Web:* www.calhounsquare.com/	Minneapolis	MN	55408	612-824-1240	824-4930
City Center 33 S 6th St	Minneapolis	MN	55402	612-372-1234	
Dayton's 700 Nicollet Mall **Fax:* Cust Svc	Minneapolis	MN	55402	612-375-2200	375-3878*
Gaviidae Common 651 Nicollet Mall	Minneapolis	MN	55402	612-372-1222	372-1239
Knollwood Mall 8332 Hwy 7	Saint Louis Park	MN	55426	612-933-8041	933-7660
Mall of America 60 E Broadway *Web:* www.mallofamerica.com ■ *E-mail:* info@mallofamerica.com	Bloomington	MN	55425	612-883-8810	
Minneapolis City Center 40 S 7th St.	Minneapolis	MN	55402	612-372-1200	
Ridgedale Center 12401 Wayzata Blvd *Web:* www.ridgedalecenter.com	Minnetonka	MN	55305	612-541-4864	540-0154
Rosedale Center 10 Rosedale Ctr *Web:* www.rosedalecenter.com ■ *E-mail:* shop@rosedalecenter.com	Roseville	MN	55113	651-638-3553	638-3599
Saint Anthony Main Shopping & Entertainment Center 125 SE Main St. **Fax Area Code:* 651	Minneapolis	MN	55414	612-378-1226	646-0230*
Southdale Center 10 Southdale Ctr *Web:* www.southdalecenter.com ■ *E-mail:* shopping@southdalecenter.com	Edina	MN	55435	612-925-7874	925-7856

BANKS

Name	City	State	Zip	Phone	Fax
Franklin National Bank 2100 Blaisdell Ave.	Minneapolis	MN	55404	612-874-6000	874-7978
National City Bank of Minneapolis 651 Nicollet Mall.	Minneapolis	MN	55402	612-904-8000	904-8010
Norwest Bank Minnesota NA 6th St & Marquette Ave. **Fax:* Hum Res	Minneapolis	MN	55479	612-667-1234	667-0288*
Resource Trust Bank 900 2nd Ave S Suite 300.	Minneapolis	MN	55402	612-371-9332	336-1388
Ridgedale State Bank 1200 Nicollet Mall.	Minneapolis	MN	55403	612-332-8890	333-8547
Riverside Bank 1801 Riverside Ave.	Minneapolis	MN	55454	612-341-3505	341-3576
US Bank NA 601 2nd Ave S **Fax:* Mail Rm	Minneapolis	MN	55402	612-973-1111	973-4645*

BUSINESS SERVICES

Name	Phone
Accountemps	612-339-5521
Corporate Express Delivery Systems	612-374-9002
Express Messenger Services	651-628-3200
Federal Express	800-463-3339
Kelly Services	612-339-7154
Kinko's	612-379-2452
Manpower Temporary Services	612-375-9200
Olsten Staffing Services	612-339-7981
Post Office	612-349-4711
Road Runner Parcel Service	651-644-8444
Skywalkers Courier Service	612-371-8778
Street Fleet Express	612-340-0059
UPS	800-742-5877

— Media —

PUBLICATIONS

Name	City	State	Zip	Phone	Fax
Corporate Report Minnesota 527 Marquette Ave S Suite 300	Minneapolis	MN	55402	612-338-4288	573-6300
Finance & Commerce 730 2nd Ave S Peavey Bldg Suite 100. *Web:* www.finance-commerce.com	Minneapolis	MN	55402	612-333-4244	333-3243
Minneapolis-Saint Paul 220 S 6th St Suite 500	Minneapolis	MN	55402	612-339-7571	339-5806
Minneapolis-Saint Paul CityBusiness 527 Marquette Ave Suite 400 *Web:* www.amcity.com/twincities ■ *E-mail:* twincities@amcity.com	Minneapolis	MN	55402	612-288-2141	288-2121
Skyway News 15 S 5th St Suite 800 **Fax:* News Rm	Minneapolis	MN	55402	612-375-9222	375-9208*
Star Tribune‡ 425 Portland Ave S. *TF:* 800-827-8742 ■ *Web:* www.startribune.com ■ *E-mail:* roberts@startribune.com	Minneapolis	MN	55488	612-673-4000	673-4359

‡*Daily newspapers*

TELEVISION

Name	City	State	Zip	Phone	Fax
KARE-TV Ch 11 (NBC) 8811 Olson Memorial Hwy *Web:* www.kare11.com	Minneapolis	MN	55427	612-546-1111	546-8606
KMSP-TV Ch 9 (UPN) 11358 Viking Dr *Web:* www.kmsp.com ■ *E-mail:* upn9@kmsp9.com	Eden Prairie	MN	55344	612-944-9999	942-0286
KMWB-TV Ch 23 (WB) 1640 Como Ave.	Saint Paul	MN	55108	651-646-2300	646-1220
KPXM-TV Ch 41 (PAX) PO Box 407 *Web:* www.pax.net/kpxm	Big Lake	MN	55309	612-263-8666	263-6600
KSTP-TV Ch 5 (ABC) 3415 University Ave SE *Web:* www.kstp.com	Saint Paul	MN	55114	651-646-5555	642-4409
KTCA-TV Ch 2 (PBS) 172 E 4th St *Web:* www.ktca.org	Saint Paul	MN	55101	651-222-1717	229-1282
KTCI-TV Ch 17 (PBS) 172 E 4th St	Saint Paul	MN	55101	651-222-1717	229-1282
WCCO-TV Ch 4 (CBS) 90 S 11th St. *Web:* www.wcco.com/partners/tv/index.html ■ *E-mail:* wccotv@wcco.com	Minneapolis	MN	55403	612-339-4444	330-2767
WFTC-TV Ch 29 (Fox) 1701 Broadway St NE *Web:* www.fox29.com ■ *E-mail:* feedback@fox29.com	Minneapolis	MN	55413	612-379-2929	379-2900

RADIO

Name	City	State	Zip	Phone	Fax
KDWB-FM 101.3 MHz (CHR) 100 N 6th St Suite 306C	Minneapolis	MN	55403	612-340-9000	340-9560
KEEY-FM 102.1 MHz (Ctry) 7900 Xerxes Ave S Suite 102 *Web:* www.k102.com ■ *E-mail:* k102@pclink.com	Minneapolis	MN	55409	612-820-4200	820-4223
KFAN-AM 1130 kHz (Sports) 7900 Xerxes Ave S Suite 102 *Web:* www.kfan.com ■ *E-mail:* kfan@pclink.com	Minneapolis	MN	55431	612-820-4300	820-4256
KQQL-FM 107.9 MHz (Oldies) 60 S 6th St Suite 930 *Web:* www.kool108.com	Minneapolis	MN	55402	612-333-8118	333-1616
KQRS-FM 92.5 MHz (CR) 917 N Lilac Dr. *Web:* www.92kqrs.com ■ *E-mail:* kqcrew@mnvirtmall.com	Golden Valley	MN	55422	612-545-5601	595-4940
KSTP-AM 1500 kHz (N/T) 2792 Maplewood Dr *TF:* 877-615-1500 ■ *Web:* www.am1500.com	Maplewood	MN	55109	651-481-9333	481-9324
KSTP-FM 94.5 MHz (AC) 3415 University Ave	Saint Paul	MN	55114	651-642-4141	642-4148
KTCJ-AM 690 kHz (Ctry) 7900 Xerxes Ave S Suite 102	Minneapolis	MN	55431	612-820-4200	820-4223
KTCZ-FM 97.1 MHz (AAA) 100 N 6th St Suite 306-C *Web:* www.cities97.com	Minneapolis	MN	55403	612-339-0000	333-2997
KXXR-FM 93.7 MHz (Rock) 917 N Lilac Dr *Web:* www.93x.com ■ *E-mail:* 93x@sidewalk.com	Golden Valley	MN	55422	612-545-5601	595-4940

Minneapolis — Radio (Cont'd)

Phone / Fax

WCAL-FM 89.3 MHz (NPR)
1520 St Olaf Ave. . . . . Northfield MN 55057 612-798-9225 798-8614
Web: www.stolaf.edu/wcal/ ■ *E-mail:* wcal@stolaf.edu

WCCO-AM 830 kHz (N/T) 625 2nd Ave S. . . . Minneapolis MN 55402 612-370-0611 370-0410
Web: www.wcco.com ■ *E-mail:* wcco830@ibsys.com

WLTE-FM 102.9 MHz (AC)
625 2nd Ave S Suite 500. . . . . Minneapolis MN 55402 612-339-1029 339-5653
Web: www.wlte.com

WRQC-FM 100.3 MHz (Rock)
60 S 6th St Suite 930 . . . . . Minneapolis MN 55402 612-330-0100 330-0897

WWTC-AM 1280 kHz (N/T)
5501 Excelsior Blvd. . . . . Minneapolis MN 55416 612-926-1280 926-8014

WXPT-FM 104.1 MHz (Alt)
7001 France Ave S Suite 200. . . . . Edina MN 55435 612-836-1041 915-6781

— Colleges/Universities —

Phone / Fax

Anoka-Ramsey Community College
11200 Mississippi Blvd NW . . . . . Coon Rapids MN 55433 612-427-2600 422-3341
Web: www.an.cc.mn.us ■ *E-mail:* trallela@an.cc.mn.us

Art Institute of Minnesota 15 S 9th St. . . . . Minneapolis MN 55402 612-332-3361 332-3934
TF: 800-777-3643 ■ *Web:* www.aii.edu

Augsburg College 2211 Riverside Ave. . . . . Minneapolis MN 55454 612-330-1000 330-1649
TF: 800-788-5678 ■ *Web:* www.augsburg.edu
■ *E-mail:* admissions@augsburg.edu

Brown Institute 1440 Northland Dr . . . . . Mendota Heights MN 55120 651-905-3400 905-3550
TF: 800-627-6966 ■ *Web:* www.brown-institute.com

Century College 3300 Century Ave . . . . . White Bear Lake MN 55110 651-779-3200 773-1796
TF: 800-228-1978 ■ *Web:* www.century.cc.mn.us

College of Saint Catherine Minneapolis
601 25th Ave S. . . . . Minneapolis MN 55454 651-690-7700 690-7849

Inver Hills Community College
2500 80th St E. . . . . Inver Grove Heights MN 55076 651-450-8501 450-8677
Web: www.ih.cc.mn.us

Medical Institute of Minnesota
5503 Green Valley Dr . . . . . Bloomington MN 55437 612-844-0064 844-0472
Web: www.mim.tec.mn.us ■ *E-mail:* info@mim.tec.mn.us

Minneapolis College of Art & Design
2501 Stevens Ave S . . . . . Minneapolis MN 55404 612-874-3760 874-3702
TF: 800-874-6223 ■ *Web:* www.mcad.edu
■ *E-mail:* admissions@mn.mcad.edu

Minneapolis Community College
1501 Hennepin Ave. . . . . Minneapolis MN 55403 612-341-7000 341-7075
Web: www.mctc.tec.mn.us/ ■ *E-mail:* mctcinfo@mi.cc.mn.us

NEI College of Technology
825-41st Ave NE. . . . . Columbia Heights MN 55421 612-781-4881 782-7329
TF: 800-777-7634 ■ *Web:* www.neicoltech.org

Normandale Community College
9700 France Ave S . . . . . Bloomington MN 55431 612-832-6000 832-6571
Web: www.nr.cc.mn.us

North Central University 910 Elliot Ave S . . . Minneapolis MN 55404 612-332-3491 343-4778
TF Admissions: 800-289-6222 ■ *Web:* www.northcentral.edu
■ *E-mail:* postmaster@northcentral.edu

North Hennepin Community College
7411 85th Ave N. . . . . Brooklyn Park MN 55445 612-424-0702 424-0929
Web: www.nh.cc.mn.us

Northwest Technical Institute
11995 Singletree Ln . . . . . Eden Prairie MN 55344 612-944-0080 944-9274
TF: 800-443-4223 ■ *Web:* www.nwtech.org

Saint Paul Technical College
235 Marshall Ave . . . . . Saint Paul MN 55102 651-221-1300 221-1416
TF: 800-227-6029 ■ *Web:* www.sptc.tec.mn.us

University of Minnesota Twin Cities
231 Pillsbury Dr SE. . . . . Minneapolis MN 55455 612-625-5000 625-2008
TF Admissions: 800-752-1000 ■ *Web:* www.umn.edu
■ *E-mail:* admissions@tc.umn.edu

— Hospitals —

Phone / Fax

Abbott-Northwestern Hospital
800 E 28th St. . . . . Minneapolis MN 55407 612-863-4000 863-5667
Web: www.abbottnorthwestern.com ■ *E-mail:* askabby@allina.com

Children's Hospitals & Clinics Minneapolis
2525 Chicago Ave. . . . . Minneapolis MN 55404 612-813-6100 813-6531
Web: www.childrenshc.org ■ *E-mail:* web.comments@childrenshc.org

Children's Hospitals & Clinics Saint Paul
345 N Smith Ave . . . . . Saint Paul MN 55102 651-220-6000 220-7180
Web: www.childrenshc.org ■ *E-mail:* web.comments@childrenshc.org

Fairview Riverside Medical Center
2450 Riverside Ave. . . . . Minneapolis MN 55454 612-672-6000 672-4098

Fairview University Medical Center
420 SE Delaware St. . . . . Minneapolis MN 55455 612-626-3000 626-3028
TF: 800-688-5252

Healtheast Saint John's Hospital
1575 Beam Ave . . . . . Maplewood MN 55109 651-232-7000 232-7697*
**Fax:* Admitting ■ *Web:* www.healtheast.org

Healtheast Saint Joseph's Hospital
69 W Exchange St . . . . . Saint Paul MN 55102 651-232-3000 232-4352
Web: www.healtheast.org

Hennepin County Medical Center
701 Park Ave . . . . . Minneapolis MN 55415 612-347-2121 904-4216
Web: www.co.hennepin.mn.us/wmedctr.html

Methodist Hospital HealthSystem
Minnesota 6500 Excelsior Blvd. . . . . Saint Louis Park MN 55426 612-993-5000 993-5273*
**Fax:* Admitting
■ *Web:* www.healthsystemminnesota.com/methodist-main.htm

North Memorial Health Care
3300 Oakdale Ave N . . . . . Robbinsdale MN 55422 612-520-5200 520-1454*
**Fax:* Admitting ■ *Web:* www.nmmc.com
■ *E-mail:* leo@central.nmmc.com

Regions Hospital 640 Jackson St. . . . . Saint Paul MN 55101 651-221-3456 221-3643*
**Fax:* Admitting ■ *TF:* 800-332-5720

Ridgeview Medical Center 500 S Maple St . . . . . Waconia MN 55387 612-442-2191 442-6543

United Hospital 333 N Smith Ave. . . . . Saint Paul MN 55102 651-220-8000 220-5189
TF: 800-869-1220

Unity Hospital 550 Osborne Rd NE. . . . . Fridley MN 55432 612-421-2222 780-6783

Veterans Affairs Medical Center
1 Veterans Dr. . . . . Minneapolis MN 55417 612-725-2000 725-2049
Web: pet.med.va.gov:8080 ■ *E-mail:* dar@pet.med.va.gov

— Attractions —

Phone / Fax

American Swedish Institute
2600 Park Ave . . . . . Minneapolis MN 55407 612-871-4907 871-8682
TF Sales: 800-579-3336 ■ *Web:* www.americanswedishinst.org/
■ *E-mail:* information@americanswedishinst.org

Bakken Library & Museum
3537 Zenith Ave S . . . . . Minneapolis MN 55416 612-927-6508 927-7265
Web: www.thebakken.org

Baseball Hall of Fame 910 3rd Ave S. . . . . Minneapolis MN 55415 612-375-9707
TF: 888-375-9707

Children's Theatre Co 2400 3rd Ave S . . . . . Minneapolis MN 55404 612-874-0400 874-8119
Web: www.childrenstheatre.org/ ■ *E-mail:* info@childrenstheatre.org

Ethnic Dance Theatre
2337 Central Ave NE. . . . . Minneapolis MN 55418 612-782-3970 782-3970

Fort Snelling State Park Hwys 5 & 55 . . . . . Minneapolis MN 55111 612-725-2413
Web: www.mnhs.org/places/sites/hfs/index.html

Foshay Tower Observation Deck & Museum
821 Marquette Ave . . . . . Minneapolis MN 55402 612-341-2522 359-3034

Godfrey Ard House 28 University Ave SE. . . . Minneapolis MN 55414 612-870-8001

Guthrie Theater 725 Vineland Pl. . . . . Minneapolis MN 55403 612-377-2224 397-8177
TF: 877-447-8243

Hennepin History Museum
2303 3rd Ave S . . . . . Minneapolis MN 55404 612-870-1329 870-1320

Hey City Theater 824 Hennepin Ave . . . . . Minneapolis MN 55403 612-333-9202 333-9195
TF: 800-476-2786 ■ *E-mail:* heycitythr@aol.com

Historic Orpheum Theatre
910 Hennepin Ave. . . . . Minneapolis MN 55403 612-339-0075 339-3909

Historic State Theatre 805 Hennepin Ave. . . . Minneapolis MN 55403 612-339-0075 339-3909

Humphrey Forum 301 19th Ave S. . . . . Minneapolis MN 55455 612-624-5799 625-3513

James Ford Bell Museum of Natural History
10 Church St SE. . . . . Minneapolis MN 55455 612-624-7083 626-7704
Web: www.umn.edu/bellmuse/

Jungle Theater 709 W Lake St. . . . . Minneapolis MN 55408 612-822-7063 822-9408

Knott's Camp Snoopy 5000 Center Ct . . . . . Bloomington MN 55425 612-883-8500 883-8683
Web: www.campsnoopy.com

Lake Calhoun 3000 E Calhoun Pkwy . . . . . Minneapolis MN 55415 612-370-4964

Lake Harriet 4135 W Lake Harriet Pkwy . . . . Minneapolis MN 55415 612-661-4806

Macphail Center for the Arts
1128 LaSalle Ave . . . . . Minneapolis MN 55403 612-321-0100 321-9740

Mall of America 60 E Broadway. . . . . Bloomington MN 55425 612-883-8810
Web: www.mallofamerica.com ■ *E-mail:* info@mallofamerica.com

Minneapolis Grain Exchange
400 S 4th St Rm 130 . . . . . Minneapolis MN 55415 612-338-6212 339-1155
TF: 800-827-4746 ■ *Web:* www.mgex.com
■ *E-mail:* mgex@ix.netcom.com

Minneapolis — Attractions (Cont'd)

				Phone	Fax
Minneapolis Institute of Arts 2400 3rd Ave S *TF:* 888-642-2787 ■ *Web:* www.artsmia.org ■ *E-mail:* miagen@artsMIA.org	Minneapolis	MN	55404	612-870-3000	870-3004
Minneapolis Planetarium 300 Nicollet Mall *Web:* ast1.spa.umn.edu/Outreach/planetarium.html	Minneapolis	MN	55401	612-630-6150	630-6180
Minneapolis Sculpure Garden 726 Vineland Pl	Minneapolis	MN	55403	612-370-3996	370-4882
Minnehaha Falls 4825 Minnehaha Ave S	Minneapolis	MN	55417	612-661-4800	
Minnehaha Princess Depot 4926 Hiawatha Ave Minnehaha Falls	Minneapolis	MN	55417	651-227-5171	227-5171
Minnesota Opera Co 620 N 1st St *Web:* www.bitstream.net/theatre/opera.htm	Minneapolis	MN	55401	612-333-2700	333-0869
Minnesota Orchestra 1111 Nicollet Mall Orchestra Hall *Web:* www.mnorch.org ■ *E-mail:* info@mnorch.org	Minneapolis	MN	55403	612-371-5600	371-0838
Minnesota Sinfonia 1820 Stevens Ave S Suite E	Minneapolis	MN	55403	612-871-1701	871-1701
Minnesota Transportation Museum 1310 Spruce Pl *TF:* 800-711-2591 ■ *Web:* www.mtmuseum.org	Mound	MN	55364	651-228-0263	
Minnesota Valley National Wildlife Refuge 3815 E 80th St *Web:* www.fws.gov/r3pao/mn_vall	Bloomington	MN	55425	612-854-5900	725-3279
Minnesota Zoo 13000 Zoo Blvd *TF:* 800-366-7811 ■ *Web:* www.mnzoo.com	Apple Valley	MN	55124	612-431-9200	431-9300
Mississippi Mile 125 SE Main St	Minneapolis	MN	55414	612-673-5123	
Museum of Questionable Medical Devices 219 SE Main St *Web:* www.mtn.org/~quack ■ *E-mail:* quack@mtn.org	Minneapolis	MN	55414	612-379-4046	540-9999
Music Box Theatre 1407 Nicollet Ave	Minneapolis	MN	55403	612-871-1414	
Mystic Lake Casino 2400 Mystic Lake Blvd *TF:* 800-262-7799 ■ *Web:* www.mysticlake.com	Prior Lake	MN	55372	612-445-9000	496-7280
Our Lady of Lourdes Church 1 Lourdes Pl	Minneapolis	MN	55414	612-379-2259	
Pavek Museum of Broadcasting 3515 Raleigh Ave *Web:* www.pavekmuseum.org	Saint Louis Park	MN	55416	612-926-8198	926-9761
Purcell Cutts House 2328 Lake Pl	Minneapolis	MN	55405	612-870-3131	
Riverplace 1 Main St SE Suite 204	Minneapolis	MN	55414	612-379-2438	379-4120
Saint Anthony Main Shopping & Entertainment Center 125 SE Main St **Fax Area Code:* 651	Minneapolis	MN	55414	612-378-1226	646-0230*
Stevens John H House 4901 Minnehaha Ave	Minneapolis	MN	55417	612-722-2220	
Valleyfair 1 Valleyfair Dr *TF:* 800-386-7433 ■ *Web:* www.valleyfair.com	Shakopee	MN	55379	612-445-7600	445-1539
Walker Art Center 725 Vineland Pl *Web:* www.walkerart.org	Minneapolis	MN	55403	612-375-7600	375-7618
Weisman Art Museum 333 E River Rd *Web:* hudson.acad.umn.edu/	Minneapolis	MN	55455	612-625-9494	625-9630
Westwood Hills Nature Center 8300 Franklin Ave W	Saint Louis Park	MN	55426	612-924-2544	797-9691
Wirth Theodore Park Wirth Pkwy & Plymouth Ave N	Minneapolis	MN	55422	612-661-4806	661-4789
Zenon Dance Co 528 Hennepin Ave Suite 400	Minneapolis	MN	55403	612-338-1101	338-2479

SPORTS TEAMS & FACILITIES

				Phone	Fax
Metrodome 900 S 5th St *E-mail:* 105521.764@compuserve.com	Minneapolis	MN	55415	612-332-0386	332-8334
Minnesota Blue Ox (roller hockey) 5612 Doron Dr *Web:* www.minnblueox.com ■ *E-mail:* index@minnblueox.com	Edina	MN	55439	612-941-7446	996-0884
Minnesota Thunder (soccer) 1700 105th Ave NE National Sports Ctr *Web:* www.mnthunder.com ■ *E-mail:* info@mnthunder.com	Blaine	MN	55126	612-785-3668	785-5999
Minnesota Timberwolves 600 1st Ave N *Web:* www.nba.com/timberwolves	Minneapolis	MN	55403	612-337-3865	673-1699
Minnesota Twins 34 Kirby Puckett Pl *TF:* 800-338-9467 ■ *Web:* www.mntwins.com ■ *E-mail:* twins@mntwins.com	Minneapolis	MN	55415	612-338-9467	375-7473
Minnesota Vikings 500 11th Ave S Hubert H Humphrey Metrodome *Web:* www.nfl.com/vikings	Minneapolis	MN	55415	612-333-8828	333-0458
Raceway Park 1 Checkered Flag Blvd	Shakopee	MN	55379	612-445-2257	445-5500
Target Center 600 1st Ave N *Web:* www.targetcenter.com ■ *E-mail:* mail@targetcenter.com	Minneapolis	MN	55403	612-673-1300	673-1370

— Events —

	Phone
Alive After Five Concerts (June)	612-338-3807
Bloomington Jazz Festival (mid-August)	612-948-8877
Cedarfest (mid-August)	612-673-0401
Civil War Weekend (mid-June)	612-726-1171
Country Folk Art Show (late September)	651-642-2200
Dayton's Bachman's Flower Show (mid-late March)	612-375-3018
Eagle Creek Rendezvous (late May)	612-445-6900
Easter Egg-Stravaganza (mid-April)	612-883-8600
Fall Home & Garden Show (early October)	612-335-6000
Farmers Market on Nicollet Mall (May-October)	612-338-3807
Holidays at the Zoo (December)	612-431-9298
Hollidazzle Parades (late November-December)	612-338-3807
International Film Fest (late April-early May)	202-724-5613
Juneteenth Festival (mid-June)	612-375-7622
Main Street Days (mid-May)	612-931-0132
Mayday Parade & Festival (early May)	612-721-2535
Midsommar Celebration & Scandinavian Art Fair (mid-June)	612-871-4907
Midwest Fall Antique Auto Show (early October)	651-642-2200
Minneapolis Aquatennial (mid-late July)	612-661-4700
Minnesota 4-H Horse Show (mid-September)	651-642-2200
Minnesota Fringe Theater Festival (late July-early August)	612-823-6005
Minnesota Renaissance Festival (mid-August-late September)	612-445-7361
Minnesota State Fair (late August-early September)	651-642-2200
New Year's Eve Fireworks Celebration (December 31)	612-673-5123
Northwest Sports Show (early-mid-March)	612-827-5833
Oyster & Guinness Festival (late August)	612-904-1000
Semstone Truck Rodeo (mid-September)	651-642-2200
Ski Snowmobile & Winter Sports Show (mid-November)	612-335-6000
Sommerfest (early July)	612-661-4700
Spring Festival Arts & Crafts Affair (early April)	612-445-7223
Stone Arch Festival of the Arts (mid-June)	612-378-1226
Summit Avenue Walking Tours (May-September)	651-297-2555
Twin Cities Juneteenth Celebration (mid-June)	612-529-5553
Twin Cities Marathon (early October)	612-673-0778
Twin Cities Ribfest (late July)	612-338-3807
Uptown Art Fair (early August)	612-661-4700
Viennese Sommerfest (July)	612-371-5656
Warehouse District Art Walk (mid-May)	612-344-1700
Western Saddle Club Horse Show (late September)	651-642-2200

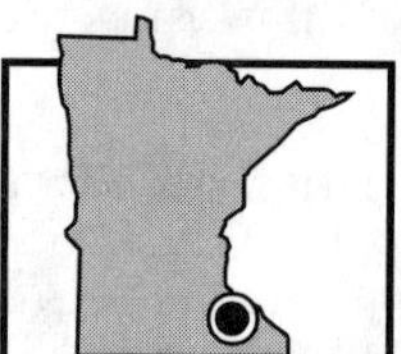

Rochester

Rochester is located in the Zumbro River Valley in southeast Minnesota, about 75 miles from Minneapolis/Saint Paul. Doctor William Worrall Mayo settled there in 1863 and, together with his sons William and Charles, pioneered the group practice of medicine. Today, Rochester's Mayo Clinic is considered one of the top medical facilities in the world. The Clinic facilities include 30 buildings and employ 1,041 doctors. The 19-story Mayo Building stretches for one block and serves as the Clinic's diagnosis and treatment facility. Both the Mayo Clinic and Mayowood, the former home of Mayo's sons, are open for tours. Included in the tour of the Clinic is a "gallery" of original art donated by former patients and benefactors and displayed throughout the facility. The mansion is set on 15 acres and features works of art and French, Spanish, and English period antiques.

Population	78,173	**Longitude**	92-48-39 W
Area (Land)	29.5 sq mi	**County**	Olmsted
Area (Water)	0.1 sq mi	**Time Zone**	CST
Elevation	1297 ft	**Area Code/s**	507
Latitude	44-04-34 N		

— Average Temperatures and Precipitation —

TEMPERATURES

	Jan	Feb	Mar	Apr	May	Jun	Jul	Aug	Sep	Oct	Nov	Dec
High	20	26	38	55	68	78	82	79	70	58	41	25
Low	3	8	21	35	46	55	60	58	49	38	24	9

Rochester (Cont'd)

PRECIPITATION

	Jan	Feb	Mar	Apr	May	Jun	Jul	Aug	Sep	Oct	Nov	Dec
Inches	0.8	0.7	1.8	2.7	3.4	3.7	4.2	3.9	3.5	2.3	1.6	1.0

— Important Phone Numbers —

	Phone
AAA	507-289-1851
American Express Travel	507-281-3652
Emergency	911
Poison Control Center	507-372-3109
Time	507-356-2222
Weather	507-281-8888

— Information Sources —

				Phone	Fax
Better Business Bureau Serving Minnesota & North Dakota 2706 Gannon Rd.	Saint Paul	MN	55116	651-699-1111	699-7665
Web: www.minnesota.bbb.org					
Mayo Civic Center 30 Civic Center Dr SE	Rochester	MN	55904	507-281-6184	281-6277
TF: 800-422-2199 ■ *Web:* www.ci.rochester.mn.us/mcc ■ *E-mail:* mayocivic@ci.rochester.mn.us					
Olmsted County 151 4th St SE	Rochester	MN	55904	507-285-8115	287-2693
Web: www.olmstedcounty.com					
Rochester Chamber of Commerce 220 S Broadway Suite 100	Rochester	MN	55904	507-288-1122	282-8960
Rochester City Hall 201 4th St SE	Rochester	MN	55904	507-285-8082	285-8256
Web: www.ci.rochester.mn.us ■ *E-mail:* cityhall@ci.rochester.mn.us					
Rochester Convention & Visitors Bureau 150 S Broadway Suite A	Rochester	MN	55904	507-288-4331	288-9144
TF: 800-634-8277 ■ *Web:* www.rochestercvb.org ■ *E-mail:* info@rochestercvb.org					
Rochester Economic Development Administration 220 S Broadway Suite 100	Rochester	MN	55904	507-288-0208	282-8960
Rochester Mayor 201 4th St SE	Rochester	MN	55904	507-285-8080	287-7979
Web: www.ci.rochester.mn.us/city/mayor.html ■ *E-mail:* ccanfield@ci.rochester.mn.us					
Rochester Public Library 101 2nd St SE	Rochester	MN	55904	507-285-8000	287-1910
Web: mcls.rochester.lib.ny.us/central ■ *E-mail:* cdoyle@mcls.rochester.lib.ny.us					

On-Line Resources

City Knowledge Rochester	www.cityknowledge.com/mn_rochester.htm
Mayo's Visitor Guide to Rochester	www.mayo.edu/location/rst/rst.html
Rochester Area Visitor	visitor-guide.com/rochester
Rochester City Net	www.excite.com/travel/countries/united_states/minnesota/rochester/
Rochester User's Guide	www.web-site.com/guide/
Rochester, MN HomePage	www.hps.com/Rochester/Welcome.html

— Transportation Services —

AIRPORTS

■ **Rochester Municipal Airport (RST)**

	Phone
10 miles S of downtown (approx 20 minutes)	507-282-2328

Airport Transportation

	Phone
RTS Bus $9 fare to downtown	507-282-2222
Yellow Cab $15 fare to downtown	507-282-2222

Commercial Airlines

	Phone
American	800-433-7300
Northwest	800-225-2525
TWA Express	800-221-2000

Charter Airlines

	Phone
Neuman Aviation	507-288-9594
Rochester Aviation Inc	507-282-1717

CAR RENTALS

	Phone
Affordable	507-280-8660
Avis	507-288-5655
Enterprise	507-282-9190
Hertz	507-288-2244
National	507-288-1155
Sears	507-280-2500

LIMO/TAXI

	Phone
Yellow Cab	507-282-2222

MASS TRANSIT

	Phone
Rochester City Line $1 Base fare	507-288-4353

RAIL/BUS

				Phone
Jefferson Bus Station 405 1st Ave SW	Rochester	MN	55902	507-289-4037

— Accommodations —

HOTELS, MOTELS, RESORTS

				Phone	Fax
Alpine Inn 1231 2nd St SW	Rochester	MN	55902	507-288-2055	
TF: 800-448-7583					
Bell Tower Inn 1235 2nd St SW	Rochester	MN	55902	507-289-2233	
TF: 800-448-7583					
Best Western Apache 1517 16th St SW	Rochester	MN	55902	507-289-8866	292-0000
TF: 800-552-7224					
Best Western Fifth Avenue 20 NW 5th Ave	Rochester	MN	55901	507-289-3987	289-3987
TF: 800-528-1234					
Best Western Soldier's Field Tower & Suites 401 6th St SW	Rochester	MN	55902	507-288-2677	282-2042
TF: 800-366-2067					
Blondell's Crown Square 1406 2nd St SW	Rochester	MN	55902	507-282-9444	282-8683
TF: 800-441-5209					
Brentwood Motor Inn 123 4th Ave NW	Rochester	MN	55901	507-288-8011	288-6163
TF: 800-658-7045 ■ *Web:* www.brentwoodinn.com ■ *E-mail:* info@brentwoodinn.com					
Colonial Inn 114 2nd St SW	Rochester	MN	55902	507-289-3363	289-3363
TF: 800-533-2226					
Comfort Inn 1625 S Broadway	Rochester	MN	55904	507-281-2211	288-8979
TF: 800-305-8470					
Country Inn & Suites 4323 Hwy 52 N	Rochester	MN	55901	507-285-3335	285-3335
TF: 800-456-4000					
Courtesy Inn 510 17th Ave NW	Rochester	MN	55901	507-289-1801	289-1801
TF: 800-658-7046					
Days Inn 111 28th St SE	Rochester	MN	55904	507-286-1001	286-1001
TF: 800-329-7466					
Days Inn Downtown 6 1st Ave NW	Rochester	MN	55901	507-282-3801	282-3801
TF: 800-325-2525					
Econo Lodge 519 3rd Ave SW	Rochester	MN	55902	507-288-1855	288-1855
TF: 800-553-2666					
Economy Inn by Kahler 9 3rd Ave NW	Rochester	MN	55901	507-285-9200	282-4478
TF: 800-533-1655					
Executive Inn 116 5th St SW	Rochester	MN	55902	507-289-1628	289-1628
TF: 888-233-9470					
Fiksdal Motel 1215 2nd St SW	Rochester	MN	55902	507-288-2671	285-9325
TF: 800-366-3451					
Hampton Inn 1755 S Broadway	Rochester	MN	55904	507-287-9050	287-9139
TF: 800-465-4329					
Holiday Inn City Centre Rochester 220 S Broadway	Rochester	MN	55904	507-288-3231	288-6602
TF: 800-241-1597 ■ *Web:* www.basshotels.com/holiday-inn/?_franchisee=RSTDT ■ *E-mail:* rochesterhi@sunstonehotels.com					
Holiday Inn South 1630 S Broadway	Rochester	MN	55904	507-288-1844	288-1844
TF: 800-465-4329					
Howard Johnson Express Inn 111 17th Ave SW	Rochester	MN	55902	507-289-1617	289-8380
TF: 800-322-8388					
Kahler Hotel 20 2nd Ave SW	Rochester	MN	55902	507-282-2581	285-2701
TF: 800-533-1655					
Motel 6 2107 W Frontage Rd	Rochester	MN	55901	507-282-6625	280-7987
TF: 800-466-8356					
Quality Inn & Suites 1620 1st Ave SE	Rochester	MN	55904	507-282-8091	282-8091
TF: 800-544-2717					
Radisson Hotel Centerplace 150 S Broadway	Rochester	MN	55904	507-281-8000	281-4280
TF: 800-333-3333					
Ramada Limited 435 16th Ave NW	Rochester	MN	55901	507-288-9090	292-9442
TF: 800-305-8470					

Rochester — Hotels, Motels, Resorts (Cont'd)

				Phone	Fax
Red Carpet Inn 2214 S Broadway *TF:* 800-658-7048	Rochester	MN	55904	507-282-7448	282-7448
Rochester Inn 1837 S Broadway *TF:* 800-890-3871	Rochester	MN	55904	507-288-2031	288-2031
Rochester Marriott 101 1st Ave SW *TF:* 800-228-9290	Rochester	MN	55902	507-280-6000	280-8531
Super 8 Motel 1850 S Broadway *TF:* 800-800-8000	Rochester	MN	55904	507-282-9905	
Super 8 Motel South 1230 S Broadway *TF:* 800-800-8000	Rochester	MN	55904	507-288-8288	
Super 8 South Broadway 106 21st St SE *TF:* 800-800-8000	Rochester	MN	55904	507-282-1756	282-1756
Travelodge Downtown 426 2nd St SW *TF:* 800-255-3050	Rochester	MN	55901	507-289-4095	289-4095

— Restaurants —

				Phone
Aviary (American) 4320 N US 52	Rochester	MN	55901	507-281-5141
Bilotti's Italian Village (Italian) 304 1st Ave SW	Rochester	MN	55902	507-282-8668
Brass Lantern (American) 1828 14th St NW	Rochester	MN	55901	507-289-9399
Broadstreet Cafe (Continental) 300 1st Ave NW	Rochester	MN	55901	507-281-2451
Brothers Bar & Grill (American) 812 S Broadway	Rochester	MN	55904	507-281-8902
Canadian Honker (American) 1239 2nd St SW	Rochester	MN	55902	507-282-6572
Chardonnay (French) 723 2nd St SW	Rochester	MN	55902	507-252-1310
China Dynasty (Chinese) 701 S Broadway	Rochester	MN	55904	507-289-2333
Daube's German Restaurant (German) 14 SW 3rd St	Rochester	MN	55906	507-280-6446
Fazoli's (Italian) 5550 Hwy 52 E	Rochester	MN	55901	507-286-8763
Great China (Chinese) 4214 N Hwy 52	Rochester	MN	55901	507-280-9092
Henry Wellington (Steak/Seafood) 216 1st Ave SW	Rochester	MN	55902	507-289-1949
Hubbell House (American) Hwy 57 & 5th Ave	Mantorville	MN	55955	507-635-2331
Hunan Garden (Chinese) 1120 NW 7th St	Rochester	MN	55901	507-285-1438
John Barleycorn (Steak) 2804 S Broadway	Rochester	MN	55904	507-285-0178
Mac's Downtown Restaurant (Greek) 20 1st St SW	Rochester	MN	55902	507-289-4219
Michael's (American) 15 S Broadway	Rochester	MN	55904	507-288-2020
Oak Room (Steak) 101 1st Ave SW	Rochester	MN	55902	507-280-6000
Pannekoeken Restaurant (Dutch) 1201 S Broadway	Rochester	MN	55904	507-287-0717
Rainbow Cafe (American) 1217 2nd St SW	Rochester	MN	55902	507-289-9601
Ranch Family Restaurant (American) 1705 S Broadway	Rochester	MN	55902	507-288-6551
Redwood Room (American) 300 1st Ave NW	Rochester	MN	55901	507-281-2978
Sam & Mickey's Embers America (American) 108 SW 17th Ave	Rochester	MN	55902	507-288-8994
Sandy Point (Steak/Seafood) 18 Sandy Point Ct NE	Rochester	MN	55906	507-367-4983
Smiling Moose (American) 1829 Hwy 52 N	Rochester	MN	55901	507-288-1689
Tasos Restaurant (American) 1223 2nd St SW	Rochester	MN	55902	507-289-2690
Valentino's (Italian) 130 Elton Hills Dr NW Suite 200	Rochester	MN	55901	507-281-2100
Wong's Cafe (Chinese) 4 3rd St SW	Rochester	MN	55902	507-282-7545
Zorba's (Greek) 924 7th St NW	Rochester	MN	55901	507-281-1540

— Goods and Services —

SHOPPING

				Phone	Fax
Antique Mall 18 SW 3rd St	Rochester	MN	55902	507-287-0684	
Apache Mall 333 Apache Mall SW	Rochester	MN	55902	507-288-8056	281-2543
Centerplace Galleria Mall 111 S Broadway	Rochester	MN	55904	507-281-4119	
Crossroads Shopping Center 1201 S Broadway	Rochester	MN	55904	507-288-5306	
Miracle Mile 115 NW 16th Ave	Rochester	MN	55901	507-288-2455	288-6164
Northbrook Shopping Center 1593-1655 N Broadway	Rochester	MN	55906	507-280-9885	
Old Rooster Antique Mall 106 N Broadway	Rochester	MN	55906	507-287-6228	

BANKS

				Phone	Fax
Marquette Bank Rochester 206 S Broadway	Rochester	MN	55904	507-285-2600	285-2601
Norwest Bank Minnesota South NA 21 1st St SW **Fax:* Hum Res	Rochester	MN	55902	507-285-2800	285-2974*
Premier Bank 421 1st Ave SW	Rochester	MN	55902	507-285-3700	285-3735
Rochester Bank & Trust 4th St & 16th Ave NW	Rochester	MN	55901	507-288-0224	288-5816

BUSINESS SERVICES

	Phone
Airborne Express	800-247-2676
BAX Global	800-225-5229
DHL Worldwide Express	800-225-5345
Federal Express	800-238-5355
Kelly Services	507-282-1584
Mail Boxes Etc	800-789-4623
Post Office	507-287-1240
Pro Staff Personnel Services	507-288-8878
Quality Temp	507-285-0321
UPS	800-742-5877

— Media —

PUBLICATIONS

				Phone	Fax
Post-Bulletin‡ 18 1st Ave SE *TF:* 800-562-1758 ■ *Web:* www.postbulletin.com/ ■ *E-mail:* feedback@postbulletin.com	Rochester	MN	55904	507-285-7600	285-7772

‡*Daily newspapers*

TELEVISION

				Phone	Fax
KAAL-TV Ch 6 (ABC) 1701 10th Pl NE *TF:* 800-234-0776 ■ *Web:* www.kaaltv.com	Austin	MN	55912	507-437-6666	433-9560
KIMT-TV Ch 3 (CBS) 112 N Pennsylvania Ave. *Web:* www.kimt.com	Mason City	IA	50401	515-423-2540	423-9309
KSMQ-TV Ch 15 (PBS) 2000 8th Ave NW *Web:* www.ksmq.org ■ *E-mail:* ksmq@ksmq.org	Austin	MN	55912	507-433-0678	433-0670
KSTP-TV Ch 5 (ABC) 3415 University Ave SE *Web:* www.kstp.com	Saint Paul	MN	55114	651-646-5555	642-4409
KTCA-TV Ch 2 (PBS) 172 E 4th St *Web:* www.ktca.org	Saint Paul	MN	55101	651-222-1717	229-1282
KTCI-TV Ch 17 (PBS) 172 E 4th St	Saint Paul	MN	55101	651-222-1717	229-1282
KTTC-TV Ch 10 (NBC) 601 1st Ave SW *TF:* 800-288-1656 ■ *Web:* www.kttc.com ■ *E-mail:* kttc@kttc.com	Rochester	MN	55902	507-288-4444	288-6324
KXLT-TV Ch 47 (Fox) 6301 Bandel Rd NW Suite 47	Rochester	MN	55901	507-252-4747	252-5050
WCCO-TV Ch 4 (CBS) 90 S 11th St. *Web:* www.wcco.com/partners/tv/index.html ■ *E-mail:* wccotv@wcco.com	Minneapolis	MN	55403	612-339-4444	330-2767
WFTC-TV Ch 29 (Fox) 1701 Broadway St NE *Web:* www.fox29.com ■ *E-mail:* feedback@fox29.com	Minneapolis	MN	55413	612-379-2929	379-2900

RADIO

				Phone	Fax
KNFX-AM 970 kHz (N/T) 1530 Greenview Dr SW Suite 200	Rochester	MN	55902	507-288-3888	288-7815
KOLM-AM 1520 kHz (Oldies) 1220 4th Ave SW *TF:* 888-599-5965 ■ *Web:* www.ocbradio.com/KOLM/kolmframe.html	Rochester	MN	55902	507-288-1971	288-1520
KRCH-FM 101.7 MHz (CR) 1530 Greenview Dr SW Suite 200	Rochester	MN	55902	507-288-3888	288-7815
KROC-AM 1340 kHz (N/T) 122 SW 4th St *Web:* www.kroc.com/am.html	Rochester	MN	55902	507-286-1010	280-0000
KROC-FM 106.9 MHz (CHR) 122 SW 4th St. *Web:* www.kroc.com/fm.html	Rochester	MN	55902	507-286-1010	280-0000
KWEB-AM 1270 kHz (Sports) 1530 Greenview Dr SW Suite 200 *E-mail:* kweb@radiominnesota.com	Rochester	MN	55902	507-288-3888	288-7815
KWWK-FM 96.5 MHz (Ctry) 1220 4th Ave SW	Rochester	MN	55902	507-288-1971	288-1520

— Colleges/Universities —

				Phone	Fax
Minnesota Bible College 920 Mayowood Rd SW *Web:* www.mnbc.edu ■ *E-mail:* admissions@mnbc.edu	Rochester	MN	55902	507-288-4563	288-9046
Rochester Community & Technical College 851 30th Ave SE. *Web:* www.roch.edu/rctc/	Rochester	MN	55904	507-285-7210	285-7496
University of Minnesota Rochester Center 855 30th Ave SE. *TF:* 800-947-0117	Rochester	MN	55904	507-280-2828	280-2839

Rochester (Cont'd)

— Hospitals —

				Phone	Fax
Rochester Methodist Hospital 201 W Center St *Fax: Admitting	Rochester	MN	55902	507-286-7890	266-7467*
Saint Marys Hospital of Rochester 1216 2nd St SW *Fax: Admissions	Rochester	MN	55902	507-255-5123	255-3125*

— Attractions —

				Phone	Fax
Assisi Heights Convent 1001 14th St NW	Rochester	MN	55901	507-282-7441	282-7762
Forestville/Mystery Cave State Park Hwy 16 E to County Rd 5	Spring Valley	MN	55965	507-937-3251	937-3252
Heritage House 225 1st Ave NW Central Pk.	Rochester	MN	55901	507-289-2104	
Historic Mantorville 501 Clay St.	Mantorville	MN	55955	507-635-3231	
Masque Youth Theatre 14 4th St SW	Rochester	MN	55904	507-287-0704	
Mayo Clinic 200 1st St SW *Web:* www.mayo.edu	Rochester	MN	55905	507-284-2511	284-0161
Mayowood Mansion 3720 Mayowood Rd SW	Rochester	MN	55902	507-282-9447	
Olmstead County History Center & Museum 1195 W Circle Dr SW	Rochester	MN	55902	507-282-9447	289-5481
Oxbow Park & Zollman Zoo 5731 County Rd 105 NW *Web:* www.oxbowpark.com ■ *E-mail:* info@oxbowpark.com	Byron	MN	55920	507-775-2451	
Plummer House 1091 SW Plummer Ln	Rochester	MN	55902	507-281-6160	
Quarry Hill Nature Center 701 NE Silver Creek Rd	Rochester	MN	55906	507-281-6114	287-1345
Rochester Art Center 320 E Center St	Rochester	MN	55904	507-282-8629	282-7737
Rochester Civic Theater 220 E Center St	Rochester	MN	55904	507-282-8481	282-0608
Rochester Community College Theatre 851 30th Ave SE	Rochester	MN	55904	507-285-7200	285-7469
Rochester Orchestra & Chorale PO Box 302 *Web:* www.web-site.com/roc/index.htm ■ *E-mail:* wahzoo@worldnet.att.com	Rochester	MN	55903	507-286-8742	280-4136
Rochester Repertory Theatre 314 1/2 S Broadway	Rochester	MN	55904	507-289-1737	
SEMVA Gallery 16 1st St SW	Rochester	MN	55902	507-281-4920	
Skyline Raceway & Waterslide 2250 40th St SW	Rochester	MN	55902	507-287-6289	
Southeast Minnesota Youth Orchestra 214 1st Ave Wellington Sq. *Web:* www.semyo.org ■ *E-mail:* semyo@rconnect.com	Rochester	MN	55902	507-282-1718	282-1718
Wild Wings Gallery 111 S Broadway	Rochester	MN	55904	507-281-3022	281-1712

SPORTS TEAMS & FACILITIES

				Phone	Fax
Rochester Honkers (baseball) 403 East Center St SE Mayo Field	Rochester	MN	55904	507-289-1170	289-1866
Rochester Mustangs (hockey) 21 Elton Hills Dr Recreation Ctr *E-mail:* rmustangs@aol.com	Rochester	MN	55901	507-282-3301	287-9022

— Events —

	Phone
Berne Swissfest (early August)	507-635-5420
Fall Harvest Festival (mid-September)	507-281-6114
Festival of Trees (late November)	507-287-2222
Gold Rush of Olmsted County (early May-late September)	507-288-0320
Mantorville Melodramas (mid-June-late August)	507-635-5420
Marigold Days (early September)	507-635-5420
Mayowood Holiday Tours (early November)	507-282-9447
Old Tyme Days (late June)	507-635-5420
Polka Party (mid-November)	800-533-1655
Rochesterfest (mid-late June)	507-285-8769
Three Rivers Rendezvous (late September)	507-282-9447
Yule-Fest (early December)	507-285-8076

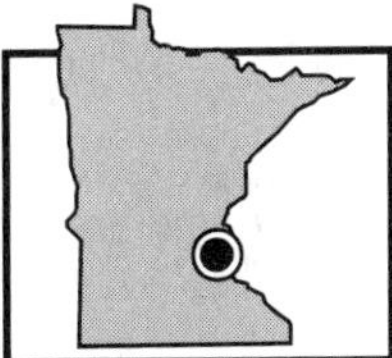

Saint Paul

Saint Paul is the state capital of Minnesota and the "Twin City" of Minneapolis. Originally a French village known as "Pig's Eye Landing," the city was renamed in 1841 at the request of Father Lucien Galtier, who built a chapel in the city dedicated to Saint Paul. The city is known for its magnificent architecture, and the State Capitol building boasts the largest unsupported marble dome in the world. Summit Avenue in Saint Paul is known for its beautiful Victorian mansions, and the architecture of the acclaimed Ordway Music Theatre has been compared to the great concert halls of Europe. Saint Paul is also home to the largest fairgrounds in the United States, the Minnesota State Fairgrounds, where the city hosts the annual Minnesota State Fair each August.

Population	257,284	**Longitude**	93-09-31 W
Area (Land)	52.8 sq mi	**County**	Ramsey
Area (Water)	3.4 sq mi	**Time Zone**	CST
Elevation	874 ft	**Area Code/s**	651
Latitude	44-94-44 N		

— Average Temperatures and Precipitation —

TEMPERATURES

	Jan	Feb	Mar	Apr	May	Jun	Jul	Aug	Sep	Oct	Nov	Dec
High	24	30	42	59	72	80	85	82	73	61	43	28
Low	6	12	24	37	48	58	63	61	52	41	28	12

PRECIPITATION

	Jan	Feb	Mar	Apr	May	Jun	Jul	Aug	Sep	Oct	Nov	Dec
Inches	0.9	0.9	1.9	2.6	3.6	4.7	3.9	3.8	3.2	2.5	1.7	1.1

— Important Phone Numbers —

	Phone		Phone
AAA	651-292-0323	**Poison Control Center**	800-764-7661
Emergency	911	**Road Conditions**	651-405-6030
HotelDocs	800-468-3537	**Time**	612-512-1111
Jazz Line	651-633-0329		

— Information Sources —

				Phone	Fax
Better Business Bureau Serving Minnesota & North Dakota 2706 Gannon Rd. *Web:* www.minnesota.bbb.org	Saint Paul	MN	55116	651-699-1111	699-7665
Ramsey County 15 W Kellogg Blvd Rm 250 *Web:* www.co.ramsey.mn.us	Saint Paul	MN	55102	651-266-8000	266-8039
RiverCentre 175 W Kellogg Blvd. *Web:* www.rivercentre.org	Saint Paul	MN	55102	651-265-4800	265-4899
Saint Paul Area Chamber of Commerce 332 Minnesota St Suite N-205 *Web:* www.saintpaulchamber.com	Saint Paul	MN	55101	651-223-5000	223-5119
Saint Paul City Hall 15 W Kellogg Blvd *Web:* www.stpaul.gov	Saint Paul	MN	55102	651-266-8500	
Saint Paul Convention & Visitors Bureau 175 W Kellogg Blvd RiverCentre Suite 502 *TF:* 800-627-6101 ■ *Web:* www.stpaulcvb.org ■ *E-mail:* spcvb@pioneerplanet.infi.net	Saint Paul	MN	55102	651-265-4900	265-4999
Saint Paul Mayor 15 W Kellogg Blvd Rm 390 *Web:* www.stpaul.gov/mayor ■ *E-mail:* norm.coleman@stpaul.gov	Saint Paul	MN	55102	651-266-8510	266-8513
Saint Paul Planning & Economic Development Dept 25 W 4th St *Web:* www.stpaul.gov/depts/ped	Saint Paul	MN	55102	651-266-6700	228-3261

Saint Paul — Information Sources (Cont'd)

				Phone	Fax
Saint Paul Public Library 90 W 4th St	Saint Paul	MN	55102	651-266-7000	292-6141

Web: www.stpaul.lib.mn.us

On-Line Resources

About.com Guide to Minneapolis/Saint Paul	minneapolis.about.com/local/midwestus/minneapolis
Area Guide Saint Paul	stpaul.areaguides.net
City Knowledge Saint Paul	www.cityknowledge.com/mn_stpaul.htm
City Search Twin Cities	twincities.citysearch.com
City Wide Guide	www.citywideguide.com/
DigitalCity Twin Cities	home.digitalcity.com/twincities
Excite.com Saint Paul City Guide	www.excite.com/travel/countries/united_states/minnesota/saint_paul
Insiders' Guide to the Twin Cities	www.insiders.com/twin-cities/
Minneapolis-Saint Paul CityWomen	www.citywomen.com/minnwomen.htm
NITC Travelbase City Guide Twin Cities	www.travelbase.com/auto/guides/twin_cities-area-mn.html
Rough Guide Travel Saint Paul	travel.roughguides.com/content/11184/
Saint Paul City Guide	www.saint-paul.com
Saint Paul Neighborhood Network	www.spnn.org/
Savvy Diner Guide to Minneapolis-Saint Paul Restaurants	www.savvydiner.com/minneapolis/
Twin Cities Internet Guide & Directory	www.tcigd.com/
Twin Cities Just Go	www.justgo.com/twincities
TwinCities.com	www.twincities.com
Yahoo! Twin Cities	minn.yahoo.com

— Transportation Services —

AIRPORTS

■ **Minneapolis-Saint Paul International Airport (MSP)**

	Phone
9 miles SW of downtown Saint Paul (approx 20 minutes)	612-726-5500

Web: www.mspairport.com/

Airport Transportation

	Phone
Airport Express $8 fare to downtown Saint Paul	612-827-7777
Boston Coach $43 fare to downtown Saint Paul	612-888-6600
Premier Transportation $39 fare to downtown Saint Paul	612-331-7433

Commercial Airlines

	Phone		Phone
America West	800-235-9292	**Northwest**	800-225-2525
American	800-433-7300	**Sun Country**	800-359-5786
Continental	800-525-0280	**TWA**	800-221-2000
Delta	800-221-1212	**United**	800-241-6522
KLM	800-374-7747	**US Airways**	800-428-4322
Mesaba Airlines	612-726-5151	**Vanguard**	800-826-4827

Charter Airlines

	Phone		Phone
Air Direct Charter	800-332-7133	**Regent Aviation**	651-227-7801
Dwyer Air Charter	612-726-5150	**Superior Aviation**	800-882-7751

CAR RENTALS

	Phone		Phone
Alamo	612-726-5323	**Hertz**	651-698-9585
Avis	612-726-5220	**National**	612-726-5600
Budget	612-727-2000	**Thrifty**	651-227-7690
Dollar	612-854-3003		

LIMO/TAXI

	Phone		Phone
Blue & White Taxi	612-333-3331	**Red & White Taxi**	612-871-1600
Carey Limousine	612-623-0565	**Town Taxi**	612-331-8294
Diamond Cab Co	651-642-1188	**Yellow Cab**	612-824-4444
Henderson Limousine	612-871-5466		

MASS TRANSIT

	Phone
Metropolitan Transit $1 Base fare	612-373-3333

RAIL/BUS

				Phone
Amtrak Station 730 Transfer Rd	Saint Paul	MN	55114	651-644-6012
Greyhound/Trailways Bus Station 166 W University Ave (*TF:* 800-231-2222)	Saint Paul	MN	55103	651-222-0507

— Accommodations —

HOTELS, MOTELS, RESORTS

				Phone	Fax
Best Western Drovers Inn 701 Concord St S (*TF:* 800-528-1234)	South Saint Paul	MN	55075	651-455-3600	455-0282
Best Western Kelly Inn 161 St Anthony Blvd (*TF:* 800-528-1234)	Saint Paul	MN	55103	651-227-8711	227-1698
Country Inn by Carlson-Woodbury 6003 Hudson Rd (*TF:* 800-456-4000)	Woodbury	MN	55125	651-739-7300	731-4007
Days Inn at River Center 175 W 7th St (*TF:* 800-329-7466)	Saint Paul	MN	55102	651-292-8929	292-1749
Embassy Suites 175 E 10th St (*TF:* 800-362-2779)	Saint Paul	MN	55101	651-224-5400	224-0957
Exel Inn 1739 Old Hudson Rd (*TF:* 800-356-8013)	Saint Paul	MN	55106	651-771-5566	771-1262
Hampton Inn Woodbury 1450 Weir Dr. (*TF:* 800-426-7866)	Woodbury	MN	55125	651-578-2822	578-8692
Holiday Inn East 2201 Burns Ave (*TF:* 800-465-4329)	Saint Paul	MN	55119	651-731-2220	731-0243
Holiday Inn Express 1010 W Bandana Blvd (*TF:* 800-465-4329)	Saint Paul	MN	55108	651-647-1637	647-0244
Holiday Inn Express & Suites 9840 Norma Ln (*TF:* 877-702-0200)	Woodbury	MN	55125	651-702-0200	702-0066
Lowell Inn 102 N 2nd St (*TF:* 888-569-3554)	Stillwater	MN	55082	651-439-1100	439-4686
Radisson Hotel Saint Paul 11 Kellogg Blvd E (*TF:* 800-333-3333)	Saint Paul	MN	55101	651-292-1900	224-8999
Radisson Inn Saint Paul 411 Minnesota St (*TF:* 800-333-3333)	Saint Paul	MN	55101	651-291-8800	292-8845
Ramada Inn & Conference Center 1870 Old Hudson Rd (*TF:* 800-272-6232)	Saint Paul	MN	55119	651-735-2330	735-1953
Saint James Hotel 406 Main St (*TF:* 800-252-1875 ■ *Web:* www.st-james-hotel.com)	Red Wing	MN	55066	651-388-2846	388-5226
Saint Paul Hotel 350 Market St (*TF:* 800-292-9292 ■ *Web:* www.stpaulhotel.com/ ■ *E-mail:* Concierge@stpaulhotel.com)	Saint Paul	MN	55102	651-292-9292	228-9506
Sheraton Inn Midway 400 N Hamline Ave (*TF:* 800-535-2339)	Saint Paul	MN	55104	651-642-1234	642-1126
Springhill Suites 3635 Crestridge Dr. (*TF:* 888-287-9400)	Eagan	MN	55122	651-686-0600	686-7771

— Restaurants —

				Phone
Boca Chica Restorante (Mexican) 11 Concord St.	Saint Paul	MN	55107	651-222-8499
Buca di Beppo (Italian) 2728 Gannon Rd	Saint Paul	MN	55116	651-772-4388
Cafe da Vinci (Italian) 400 Sibley St	Saint Paul	MN	55101	651-222-4050
Cafe Latte (Continental) 850 Grand Ave	Saint Paul	MN	55105	651-224-5687
Cafe Minnesota (Gourmet) 345 Kellogg Blvd W.	Saint Paul	MN	55102	651-297-4097
Cafe The (American) 350 Market St.	Saint Paul	MN	55102	651-228-3855
Caravan Serai (Afghan) 2175 Ford Pkwy.	Saint Paul	MN	55116	651-690-1935
Carousel (Continental) 11 E Kellogg Blvd	Saint Paul	MN	55101	651-292-0408
Christos (Greek) 214 E 4th St	Saint Paul	MN	55101	651-224-6000
Dakota Bar & Grill (American) 1021 E Bandana Blvd	Saint Paul	MN	55108	651-642-1442
Day by Day Cafe (Homestyle) 477 W 7th St	Saint Paul	MN	55102	651-227-0654
Forepaugh's (French) 276 S Exchange St	Saint Paul	MN	55102	651-224-5606
Gallivan's (Steak/Seafood) 354 N Wabasha St	Saint Paul	MN	55102	651-227-6688
Great Waters Brewing Co (American) 426 St Peter St	Saint Paul	MN	55102	651-224-2739
Hunan Garden (Chinese) 380 Cedar St	Saint Paul	MN	55101	651-224-7588
Jamy's Pioneer Grill (American) 336 N Roberts St	Saint Paul	MN	55101	651-224-6435
La Belle Vie (Mediterranean) 312 S Main St	Stillwater	MN	55082	651-430-3545
Le Carrousel Restaurant (Continental) 11 E Kellogg Blvd	Saint Paul	MN	55101	651-292-1900
Leeann Chin (Chinese) 214 E 4th St	Saint Paul	MN	55101	651-224-8814
Lexington (American) 1096 Grand Ave	Saint Paul	MN	55105	651-222-5878
Mancini's Char House (Steak) 531 W 7th St.	Saint Paul	MN	55102	651-224-7345
Muffuletta Cafe (European) 2260 Como Ave SE.	Saint Paul	MN	55108	651-644-9116
No Wake Cafe (American) Pier 1 Harriet Island Suite B3	Saint Paul	MN	55107	651-292-1411
Patrick McGovern's Pub (American) 225 W 7th St.	Saint Paul	MN	55102	651-224-5821
Rainforest Cafe (American) 102 South Ave. (*Web:* www.rainforestcafe.com)	Bloomington	MN	55425	612-854-7500
Rio Bravo (Tex Mex) 389 Hamline Ave	Saint Paul	MN	55104	651-647-5870
Ruam Mit Thai Cafe (Thai) 475 Saint Peter St.	Saint Paul	MN	55102	651-290-0067
Saint Paul Grill (American) 350 Market St	Saint Paul	MN	55102	651-224-7455

Saint Paul — Restaurants (Cont'd)

Name	City	State	ZIP	Phone
Sakura Japanese Restaurant (Japanese) 34 W 6th St	Saint Paul	MN	55102	651-224-0185
Sawatdee Thai Restaurant (Thai) 289 E 5th St	Saint Paul	MN	55101	651-222-5859
Table of Contents (New American) 1648 Grand Ave.	Saint Paul	MN	55105	651-699-6595
Tavern on Grand (American) 656 Grand Ave	Saint Paul	MN	55105	651-228-9030
Tulips Restaurant (French) 452 Selby Ave	Saint Paul	MN	55102	651-221-1061
Venetian Inn (Italian) 2814 Rice St	Saint Paul	MN	55113	651-484-7215
Wooley's (American) 175 E 10th St	Saint Paul	MN	55101	651-224-5111
Zander Café (American) 525 Selby Ave.	Saint Paul	MN	55102	651-222-5224
Zephyr Cafe (American) 214 E 4th St	Saint Paul	MN	55101	651-222-4053

— Goods and Services —

SHOPPING

Name	City	State	ZIP	Phone	Fax
Burnsville Center 1178 Burnsville Ctr	Burnsville	MN	55306	612-435-8182	892-5073
Web: www.burnsvillecenter.com					
Carriage Hill Plaza 350 Saint Peter St.	Saint Paul	MN	55102	651-848-0533	
Dayton's 411 Cedar St.	Saint Paul	MN	55101	651-292-5222	
Galtier Plaza 175 5th St E Suite 315	Saint Paul	MN	55101	651-297-6734	297-6287
Grand Avenue 1043 Grand Ave Box 315	Saint Paul	MN	55105	651-699-0029	699-7775
Web: www.grandave.com/					
Horizon Outlet Center Hwy I-94 & County Rd 19	Woodbury	MN	55129	651-735-9060	735-9235
Lafayette Square Shopping Center 1990 Christensen Ave	West Saint Paul	MN	55118	651-455-7100	
Mall of America 60 E Broadway	Bloomington	MN	55425	612-883-8810	
Web: www.mallofamerica.com ■ *E-mail:* info@mallofamerica.com					
Mall of Saint Paul 1817 Selby Ave	Saint Paul	MN	55104	651-647-6163	
Maplewood Mall I-694 & White Bear Ave	Saint Paul	MN	55106	651-770-5020	
Norwest Center 55 E 5th St	Saint Paul	MN	55101	651-221-1949	221 0540
Oakdale Mall 7166 10th St N.	Saint Paul	MN	55128	651-739-4893	
Phalen Shopping Center 5101 Vernon Ave S	Edina	MN	55436	651-771-2504	771-1063
Rosedale Center 10 Rosedale Ctr	Roseville	MN	55113	651-638-3553	638-3599
Web: www.rosedalecenter.com ■ *E-mail:* shop@rosedalecenter.com					
Town Square 445 Minnesota St	Saint Paul	MN	55101	651-291-5900	291-5922
World Trade Center 30 E 7th St Suite 2600	Saint Paul	MN	55101	651-291-5900	291-5922

BANKS

Name	City	State	ZIP	Phone	Fax
Bank of Saint Paul 6 W 5th St	Saint Paul	MN	55102	651-222-5551	222-5554
Capital Bank 1020 Rice St	Saint Paul	MN	55117	651-488-2516	488-7212
Cherokee State Bank 607 S Smith Ave	Saint Paul	MN	55107	651-227-7071	290-6968
Eastern Heights Bank 670 McKnight Rd N.	Saint Paul	MN	55119	651-736-9900	737-1553
Firstar Bank 35 W 5th St.	Saint Paul	MN	55102	651-291-6800	291-9524
Firstar Bank of Minnesota NA 101 E 5th St.	Saint Paul	MN	55101	651-298-6000	229-6518
TF: 800-264-2265					
Liberty State Bank 176 Smelling Ave N.	Saint Paul	MN	55104	651-646-8681	646-2951
Midway National Bank of Saint Paul 1578 University Ave W	Saint Paul	MN	55104	651-628-2661	643-8518
Norwest Bank Minnesota 875 E Minnehaha Ave	Saint Paul	MN	55106	651-778-2700	205-8412
US Bank NA 332 Minnesota Ave	Saint Paul	MN	55119	651-973-1111	739-2752
Western State Bank 663 University Ave.	Saint Paul	MN	55104	651-290-8100	290-8118
TF: 800-219-9894					

BUSINESS SERVICES

Name	Phone	Name	Phone
Airborne Express	800-247-2676	**Olsten Staffing Services**	651-631-0092
BAX Global	800-225-5229	**Post Office**	651-293-3099
Federal Express	800-238-5355	**Pro Staff**	651-291-7811
Kelly Services	651-221-0006	**Romac International**	651-225-1000
Kinko's	651-699-9671	**UPS**	800-742-5877

— Media —

PUBLICATIONS

Name	City	State	ZIP	Phone	Fax
Minneapolis-Saint Paul 220 S 6th St Suite 500	Minneapolis	MN	55402	612-339-7571	339-5806
Minneapolis-Saint Paul CityBusiness 527 Marquette Ave Suite 400	Minneapolis	MN	55402	612-288-2141	288-2121
Web: www.amcity.com/twincities ■ *E-mail:* twincities@amcity.com					
Saint Paul Pioneer Press‡ 345 Cedar St.	Saint Paul	MN	55101	651-222-5011	228-5500
Web: www.pioneerplanet.com					
■ *E-mail:* feedback@pioneerplanet.infi.net					

‡Daily newspapers

TELEVISION

Name	City	State	ZIP	Phone	Fax
KARE-TV Ch 11 (NBC) 8811 Olson Memorial Hwy	Minneapolis	MN	55427	612-546-1111	546-8606
Web: www.kare11.com					
KMSP-TV Ch 9 (UPN) 11358 Viking Dr	Eden Prairie	MN	55344	612-944-9999	942-0286
Web: www.kmsp.com ■ *E-mail:* upn9@kmsp9.com					
KMWB-TV Ch 23 (WB) 1640 Como Ave.	Saint Paul	MN	55108	651-646-2300	646-1220
KPXM-TV Ch 41 (PAX) PO Box 407	Big Lake	MN	55309	612-263-8666	263-6600
Web: www.pax.net/kpxm					
KSTP-TV Ch 5 (ABC) 3415 University Ave SE	Saint Paul	MN	55114	651-646-5555	642-4409
Web: www.kstp.com					
KTCA-TV Ch 2 (PBS) 172 E 4th St	Saint Paul	MN	55101	651-222-1717	229-1282
Web: www.ktca.org					
KTCI-TV Ch 17 (PBS) 172 E 4th St	Saint Paul	MN	55101	651-222-1717	229-1282
WCCO-TV Ch 4 (CBS) 90 S 11th St.	Minneapolis	MN	55403	612-339-4444	330-2767
Web: www.wcco.com/partners/tv/index.html					
■ *E-mail:* wccotv@wcco.com					
WFTC-TV Ch 29 (Fox) 1701 Broadway St NE	Minneapolis	MN	55413	612-379-2929	379-2900
Web: www.fox29.com ■ *E-mail:* feedback@fox29.com					

RADIO

Name	City	State	ZIP	Phone	Fax
KDWB-FM 101.3 MHz (CHR) 100 N 6th St Suite 306C	Minneapolis	MN	55403	612-340-9000	340-9560
KEEY-FM 102.1 MHz (Ctry) 7900 Xerxes Ave S Suite 102	Minneapolis	MN	55409	612-820-4200	820-4223
Web: www.k102.com ■ *E-mail:* k102@pclink.com					
KLBB-AM 1400 kHz (Nost) 611 Frontenac Pl.	Saint Paul	MN	55104	651-603-5720	603-5701
KNOW-FM 91.1 MHz (NPR) 45 E 7th St	Saint Paul	MN	55101	651-290-1500	290-1295
KSTP-AM 1500 kHz (N/T) 2792 Maplewood Dr	Maplewood	MN	55109	651-481-9333	481-9324
TF: 877-615-1500 ■ *Web:* www.am1500.com					
KSTP-FM 94.5 MHz (AC) 3415 University Ave	Saint Paul	MN	55114	651-642-4141	642-4148
WCAL-FM 89.3 MHz (NPR) 1520 St Olaf Ave.	Northfield	MN	55057	612-798-9225	798-8614
Web: www.stolaf.edu/wcal/ ■ *E-mail:* wcal@stolaf.edu					
WCCO-AM 830 kHz (N/T) 625 2nd Ave S	Minneapolis	MN	55402	612-370-0611	370-0410
Web: www.wcco.com ■ *E-mail:* wcco830@ibsys.com					
WLOL-AM 1470 kHz (Nost) 611 Frontenac Pl.	Saint Paul	MN	55401	651-603-5720	603-5701
WLTE-FM 102.9 MHz (AC) 625 2nd Ave S Suite 500	Minneapolis	MN	55402	612-339-1029	339-5653
Web: www.wlte.com					
WWTC-AM 1280 kHz (N/T) 5501 Excelsior Blvd.	Minneapolis	MN	55416	612-926-1280	926-8014

— Colleges/Universities —

Name	City	State	ZIP	Phone	Fax
Apostolic Bible Institute Inc 6944 Hudson Blvd N.	Saint Paul	MN	55128	651-739-7686	730-8669
Web: www.apostolic.org ■ *E-mail:* abi@mm.com					
Bethel College & Seminary 3900 Bethel Dr	Saint Paul	MN	55112	651-638-6400	638-6001
TF: 800-255-8706 ■ *Web:* www.bethel.edu					
■ *E-mail:* mrussell@homer.bethel.edu					
College of Saint Catherine 2004 Randolph Ave.	Saint Paul	MN	55105	651-690-6000	690-6024
TF: 800-945-4599 ■ *Web:* www.stkate.edu					
■ *E-mail:* admissions@stkate.edu					
Concordia University 275 Syndicate St N.	Saint Paul	MN	55104	651-641-8278	659-0207
TF Admissions: 800-333-4705 ■ *Web:* www.csp.edu					
Hamline University 1536 Hewitt Ave.	Saint Paul	MN	55104	651-523-2800	523-2458
TF Admissions: 800-753-9753 ■ *Web:* www.hamline.edu					
■ *E-mail:* admis@seq.hamline.edu					
Macalester College 1600 Grand Ave.	Saint Paul	MN	55105	651-696-6000	696-6724
TF Admissions: 800-231-7974 ■ *Web:* www.macalstr.edu					
■ *E-mail:* admissions@macalstr.edu					
Metropolitan State University 700 E 7th St.	Saint Paul	MN	55106	651-772-7777	772-7738
Web: www.metro.msus.edu					

Saint Paul — Colleges/Universities (Cont'd)

Name / Address	City	State	ZIP	Phone	Fax
National American University Saint Paul Campus 1380 Energy Ln Suite 13	Saint Paul	MN	55108	651-644-1265	644-0690
Web: www.nationalcollege.edu/campuspaul.html					
Northwestern College 3003 Snelling Ave N	Saint Paul	MN	55113	651-631-5100	631-5680
TF Admissions: 800-827-6827 ■ *Web:* www.nwc.edu					
Saint Paul Technical College 235 Marshall Ave	Saint Paul	MN	55102	651-221-1300	221-1416
TF: 800-227-6029 ■ *Web:* www.sptc.tec.mn.us					
University of Saint Thomas 2115 Summit Ave	Saint Paul	MN	55105	651-962-5000	962-6160
TF Admissions: 800-328-6819 ■ *Web:* www.stthomas.edu					

— Hospitals —

Name / Address	City	State	ZIP	Phone	Fax
Children's Hospitals & Clinics Saint Paul 345 N Smith Ave	Saint Paul	MN	55102	651-220-6000	220-7180
Web: www.childrenshc.org ■ *E-mail:* web.comments@childrenshc.org					
Healtheast Saint John's Hospital 1575 Beam Ave	Maplewood	MN	55109	651-232-7000	232-7697*
**Fax:* Admitting ■ *Web:* www.healtheast.org					
Healtheast Saint Joseph's Hospital 69 W Exchange St	Saint Paul	MN	55102	651-232-3000	232-4352
Web: www.healtheast.org					
Regions Hospital 640 Jackson St	Saint Paul	MN	55101	651-221-3456	221-3643*
**Fax:* Admitting ■ *TF:* 800-332-5720					
United Hospital 333 N Smith Ave	Saint Paul	MN	55102	651-220-8000	220-5189
TF: 800-869-1220					

— Attractions —

Name / Address	City	State	ZIP	Phone	Fax
Carriage Hill Plaza 350 Saint Peter St.	Saint Paul	MN	55102	651-848-0533	
Como Ordway Memorial Japanese Garden 1325 Aida Pl	Saint Paul	MN	55103	651-487-8240	487-8255
Como Park Lexington Pkwy & Como	Saint Paul	MN	55102	651-266-6400	
Como Park Zoo & Conservatory Midway Pkwy & Kaufman Dr	Saint Paul	MN	55103	651-487-8200	487-8203
Crosby Park Shepard Rd & Gannon	Saint Paul	MN	55104	651-645-5713	645-7822
Dakota County Historical Museum 130 3rd Ave N	South Saint Paul	MN	55075	651-451-6260	552-7265
Dodge Nature Center 365 W Marie Ave	West Saint Paul	MN	55118	651-455-4531	455-2575
Farmers' Market 290 E 5th St	Saint Paul	MN	55101	651-227-8101	
Web: www.stpaulfarmersmarket.com ■ *E-mail:* spmkweb@aol.com					
Fitzgerald Theater 10 E Exchange St.	Saint Paul	MN	55101	651-290-1200	290-1195
Gibbs Farm Museum 2097 W Larpenteur Ave	Saint Paul	MN	55113	651-646-8629	
Governor's Residence 1006 Summit Ave	Saint Paul	MN	55115	651-297-8177	
Great American History Theatre 30 10th St E.	Saint Paul	MN	55101	651-292-4323	292-4322
Web: www.historytheatre.com ■ *E-mail:* info@historytheatre.com					
Harriet Island Lilydale Regional Park Plato Ave & Waubasha St	Saint Paul	MN	55102	651-266-6400	
Hidden Falls Park 2400 Crosby Farm Rd.	Saint Paul	MN	55116	651-488-7291	
Hidden Falls Regional Park Mississippi River Blvd & Magoffin	Saint Paul	MN	55104	651-645-5713	645-7822
Hidden Falls/Crosby Farm Park Magoffin & Mississippi River Blvd.	Saint Paul	MN	55102	651-266-6400	
Hill James J House 240 Summit Ave	Saint Paul	MN	55102	651-297-2555	297-5655
Historic Fort Snelling Hwy 55 E of Airport	Saint Paul	MN	55111	612-726-1171	
Imation IMAX Theatre 12000 Zoo Blvd	Apple Valley	MN	55124	612-431-4629	997-9744
Web: www.imax3d.com					
Indian Mounds Park Mounds Blvd & Earl St	Saint Paul	MN	55106	651-266-6400	292-7405
Landmark Center 75 W 5th St	Saint Paul	MN	55102	651-292-3225	292-3272
Lowertown District Downtown Saint Paul-E of Jackson St	Saint Paul	MN	55101	651-227-9131	
Mall of America 60 E Broadway	Bloomington	MN	55425	612-883-8810	
Web: www.mallofamerica.com ■ *E-mail:* info@mallofamerica.com					
McKnight William L 3M Omnitheater 30 E 10th St.	Saint Paul	MN	55101	651-221-9444	221-9433
Web: www.sci.mus.mn.us/explore_zone/virtual_nm/v_omni.html					
Mears Park 6th St & Sibley	Saint Paul	MN	55101	651-266-6400	
Minnesota Air Guard Museum 670 General Miller Dr Minnesota Air Guard Base	Saint Paul	MN	55111	612-713-2523	713-2525
Web: www.mnangmuseum.org					
Minnesota Brewing Co 882 W 7th St	Saint Paul	MN	55102	651-228-9173	290-8211
Web: www.grainbelt.com ■ *E-mail:* info@grainbelt.com					
Minnesota Children's Museum 10 W 7th St	Saint Paul	MN	55102	651-225-6001	225-6006
Minnesota Historical Society 345 Kellogg Blvd W.	Saint Paul	MN	55102	651-296-6126	296-1004
TF: 800-657-3773 ■ *Web:* www.mnhs.org					
Minnesota Museum of American Art 75 W 5th St Landmark Ctr.	Saint Paul	MN	55102	651-292-4355	292-4340
Web: www.mtn.org/MMAA					
Minnesota Opera 345 Washington St Ordway Music Theatre	Saint Paul	MN	55102	612-333-6669	333-0869
Web: www.mnopera.org ■ *E-mail:* mithu@mnopera.org					
Minnesota State Capitol 75 Constitution Ave	Saint Paul	MN	55155	651-296-2739	297-2739
Minnesota Valley National Wildlife Refuge 3815 E 80th St	Bloomington	MN	55425	612-854-5900	725-3279
Web: www.fws.gov/r3pao/mn_vall					
Minnesota Vietnam Veterans' Memorial State Capitol Grounds	Saint Paul	MN	55082	651-777-0686	
Music in the Park Series 1333 Chelmsford St	Saint Paul	MN	55108	651-644-4234	644-8152
Web: www.sap.org/foodfun/musicinpark.html ■ *E-mail:* jahchamber@aol.com					
Mystic Lake Casino 2400 Mystic Lake Blvd	Prior Lake	MN	55372	612-445-9000	496-7280
TF: 800-262-7799 ■ *Web:* www.mysticlake.com					
North Star Opera 312 N Hamline Ave EM Pearson Theatre	Saint Paul	MN	55104	651-698-5386	
Old Muskego Church 2481 Como Ave	Saint Paul	MN	55108	651-641-3456	
Ordway Music Theatre 345 Washington St	Saint Paul	MN	55102	651-224-4222	224-1051
Web: www.ordway.org/					
Park Square Theatre Co 20 W 7th Pl	Saint Paul	MN	55102	651-291-7005	291-9180
Penumbra Theatre 270 N Kent St.	Saint Paul	MN	55102	651-224-4601	224-7074
Plymouth Music Series of Minnesota 1900 Nicollet Ave	Minneapolis	MN	55403	612-547-1451	547-1484
Ramsey Alexander House 265 S Exchange St	Saint Paul	MN	55102	651-296-0100	296-0100
Web: www.mnhs.org					
Rice Park 5th & Market Sts	Saint Paul	MN	55102	651-266-6400	
Saint Paul Chamber Orchestra 408 Saint Peter St Hamm Bldg Suite 500	Saint Paul	MN	55102	651-292-3248	292-3281
Web: www1.stpaul.gov/spco/					
Saint Paul's Cathedral 239 Selby Ave	Saint Paul	MN	55102	651-228-1766	
Schubert Club Musical Instrument Museum 75 W 5th St	Saint Paul	MN	55102	651-292-3267	292-4317
Web: www.schubert.org/SCmuseum.html					
Science Museum of Minnesota 120 W Kellogg Blvd.	Saint Paul	MN	55102	651-221-9448	
Web: www.sci.mus.mn.us ■ *E-mail:* 2us@sci.mus.mn.us					
Seventh Place Plaza 7th Pl-betw Wabasha & Saint Peter Sts.	Saint Paul	MN	55102	651-225-9002	
Summit Brewing Co 910 Montreal Cir	Saint Paul	MN	55102	651-265-7800	265-7801
Town Square 445 Minnesota	Saint Paul	MN	55101	651-291-5900	291-5922
Town Square Park 7th & Cedar Sts.	Saint Paul	MN	55101	651-227-3307	227-5908
Wabasha Street Caves 215 S Wabasha St.	Saint Paul	MN	55107	651-224-1191	224-0059
World Trade Center 30 E 7th St Suite 2600	Saint Paul	MN	55101	651-291-5900	291-5922

SPORTS TEAMS & FACILITIES

Name / Address	City	State	ZIP	Phone	Fax
Midway Stadium 1771 Energy Park Dr	Saint Paul	MN	55108	651-644-6512	644-1627
Raceway Park 1 Checkered Flag Blvd	Shakopee	MN	55379	612-445-2257	445-5500
Saint Paul Saints (baseball) 1771 Energy Park Dr Midway Stadium	Saint Paul	MN	55108	651-644-6659	
Web: spsaints.com/ ■ *E-mail:* funsgood@spsaints.com					

— Events —

	Phone
American Craft Council Craft Expo (mid-April)	651-224-7361
An Irish Celebration (mid-March)	651-292-3225
Bavarian Sommerfest (late June)	651-439-7128
Capital City Lights (November-February)	651-297-6985
Capital New Year (December 31)	612-920-9054
Cinco de Mayo Mexican Fiesta (early May)	651-222-6347
Classic Cars on Wabasha (June-mid-October)	651-266-8989
Fall Colors Art Festival (early October)	651-439-4001
Festival of Nations (early May)	651-647-0191
Fur Trade Weekend 1827 (late August)	612-725-2413
Gaslight Tours (late January-early February)	651-297-2555
Grand Meander (early December)	651-699-0029

Saint Paul — Events (Cont'd)

	Phone
Hill House Holidays (mid-late December)	651-297-2555
Holiday Bazaar (early December)	651-292-3230
Holidays at the Zoo (December)	612-431-9298
Minnesota State Fair (late August-early September)	651-642-2200
Oktoberfest (mid-late September)	651-439-7128
Rondo Days Festival (mid-July)	651-646-6597
Saint Paul Art Crawl (early October & mid-April)	651-292-4373
Saint Paul Ice Fishing & Winter Sports Show (early December)	651-297-6985
Saint Paul Winter Carnival (late January-early February)	651-223-4710
Scottish Ramble & Highland Dance Competition (mid-February)	651-292-3276
Spring Babies (early-mid-April)	612-431-9213
Taste of Minnesota (early July)	651-772-9980
Thursday Night Live Outdoor Concerts (July)	651-774-5422
Twin Cities Juneteenth Celebration (mid-June)	612-529-5553
Twin Cities Marathon (early October)	612-673-0778
Winter on the Hill (late January-early February)	651-297-2555

Mississippi

Population (1999): 2,768,619 **Area (sq mi): 48,434**

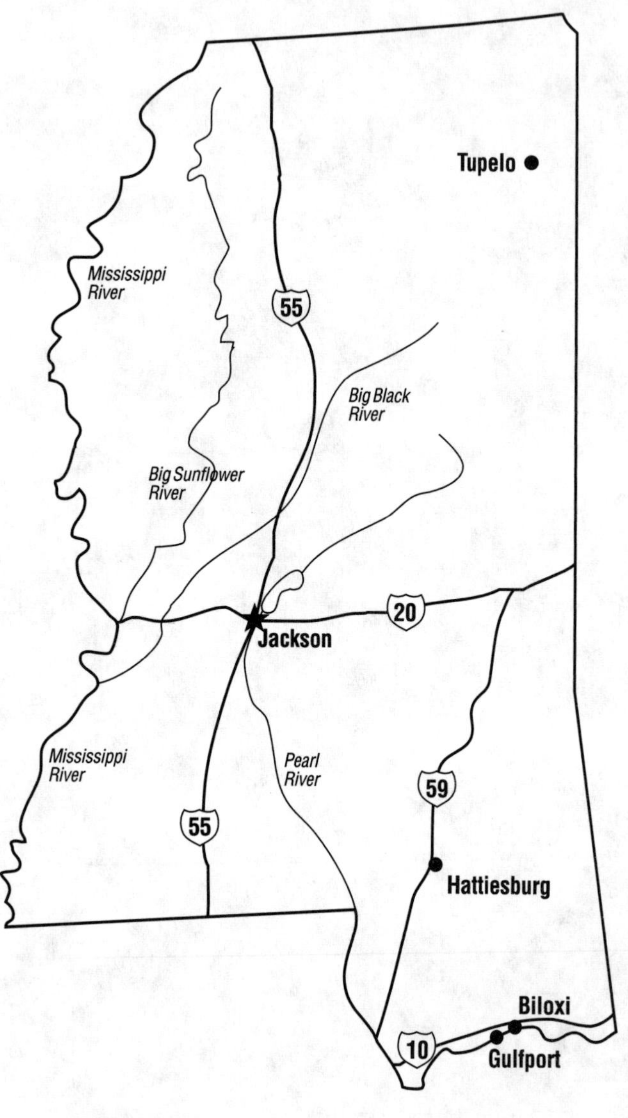

— State Information Sources —

	Phone	Fax
Mississippi Economic & Community Development Dept PO Box 849 . . . . Jackson MS 39205	601-359-3449	359-3613
Web: www.mississippi.org		
Mississippi Economic Council PO Box 23276 . . . Jackson MS 39225	601-969-0022	353-0247
TF: 800-748-7626 ■ *E-mail:* mcouncil@bellsouth.net		
Mississippi Library Commission PO Box 10700 . . . . Jackson MS 39289	601-961-4111	354-4181
TF: 800-647-7542 ■ *Web:* www.mlc.lib.ms.us		
Mississippi Parks & Recreation Div PO Box 451 . . . . Jackson MS 39205	601-364-2163	364-2008
TF: 800-467-2757 ■ *Web:* www.decd.state.ms.us/outdoors/PUBOUT.htm		
Mississippi State Government Information	601-359-1000	
Web: www.state.ms.us		
Mississippi Tourism Development Div PO Box 1705 . . . . Ocean Springs MS 39566	228-214-4493	214-4494
TF: 800-927-6378 ■ *Web:* www.mississippi.org		

ON-LINE RESOURCES

InMississippi.com . . . . www.inmississippi.com
Mississippi Cities . . . . dir.yahoo.com/Regional/U_S__States/Mississippi/Cities
Mississippi Counties & Regions . . . . dir.yahoo.com/Regional/U_S__States/Mississippi/Counties_and_Regions
Mississippi Gulf Coast . . . . www.gulf-coast.com
Mississippi Scenario . . . . scenariousa.dstylus.com/ms/indexf.htm
Mississippi Travel & Tourism Guide . . . . www.travel-library.com/north_america/usa/mississippi/index.html
Mississippi Web Sites by County . . . . www.allrednet.com/mscounty/index.html
Mississippi.com . . . . www.mississippi.com
Rough Guide Travel Mississippi travel.roughguides.com/content/781/index.htm
Travel.org-Mississippi . . . . travel.org/mississi.html
Yahoo! Get Local Mississippi . . . . dir.yahoo.com/Regional/U_S__States/Mississippi

— Cities Profiled —

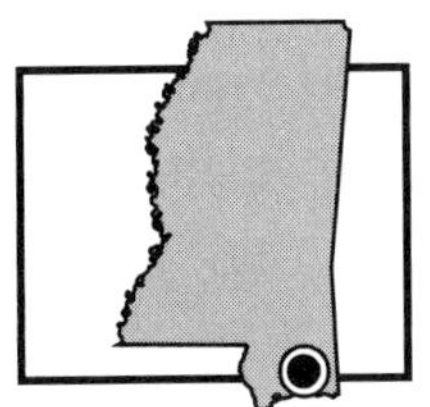

Gulfport/Biloxi

The cities of Gulfport and Biloxi are situated on the Mississippi Gulf Coast, along a 26-mile area of white sand beaches known for its sportfishing as well as its fine shrimp, oysters, and crabs. A French explorer, d'Iberville, first claimed the region in 1699, and during the following decades at least eight other countries laid claim to the area. The influence of these varied cultures can be seen today in Gulfport, Biloxi, and the other Gulf coast communities of Mississippi. This diversity is perhaps most evident in the architecture of the area, which ranges from Victorian and Greek Revival to the influence of Frank Lloyd Wright. Nearly 100 historic homes are included in a driving tour of the area, more than 20 of which can be viewed on a walking tour of Biloxi. The Biloxi homes include the Brielmaier House, which is in a three-room, T-shape design; and the Foretich House, a lateral-wing structure called a 'shotgun' from the saying that a shot fired through the front door would exit the rear door without touching a wall. In Gulfport, the Marine Life Oceanarium features trained dolphins and sea lions and a giant reef tank. Gulfport also has a number of interesting specialty shops where the works of local potters, painters, and crafts of all kinds are available. New in the area are Las Vegas-style gaming casinos which are open all along the Gulf Coast 24 hours a day, seven days a week.

GULFPORT

Population	64,762	**Longitude**	89-09-29 W
Area (Land)	22.6 sq mi	**County**	Harrison
Area (Water)	6.9 sq mi	**Time Zone**	CST
Elevation	25 ft	**Area Code/s**	228
Latitude	30-38-66 N		

— Average Temperatures and Precipitation —

TEMPERATURES

	Jan	Feb	Mar	Apr	May	Jun	Jul	Aug	Sep	Oct	Nov	Dec
High	60	64	70	78	84	90	91	91	87	80	71	63
Low	41	44	51	59	66	71	73	73	69	58	51	44

PRECIPITATION

	Jan	Feb	Mar	Apr	May	Jun	Jul	Aug	Sep	Oct	Nov	Dec
Inches	5.5	6.1	5.4	4.8	4.9	4.8	6.5	6.0	5.8	3.3	4.2	5.5

BILOXI

Population	47,316	**Longitude**	88-89-10 W
Area (Land)	19.6 sq mi	**County**	Harrison
Area (Water)	7.1 sq mi	**Time Zone**	CST
Elevation	25 ft	**Area Code/s**	228
Latitude	30-40-13 N		

— Average Temperatures and Precipitation —

TEMPERATURES

	Jan	Feb	Mar	Apr	May	Jun	Jul	Aug	Sep	Oct	Nov	Dec
High	60	69	69	76	83	88	90	90	87	80	71	63
Low	42	45	52	60	67	73	75	74	71	60	52	46

PRECIPITATION

	Jan	Feb	Mar	Apr	May	Jun	Jul	Aug	Sep	Oct	Nov	Dec
Inches	5.4	5.9	5.3	4.4	4.8	5.0	6.5	6.6	5.3	3.3	4.1	5.4

— Important Phone Numbers —

	Phone		Phone
AAA	800-926-4222	**Poison Control Center**	601-354-7660
Emergency	911	**Time/Temp**	228-868-9600
Medical Referral	228-865-3627	**Weather**	601-693-5311

— Information Sources —

				Phone	Fax
Better Business Bureau Serving Mississippi PO Box 12745	Jackson	MS	39236	601-987-8282	987-8285
Web: www.bbbmississippi.org ■ *E-mail:* info@bbbmississippi.org					
Biloxi Chamber of Commerce 1048 Beach Blvd	Biloxi	MS	39530	228-374-2717	374-2764
Web: www.biloxi.org ■ *E-mail:* exec@biloxi.org					
Biloxi City Hall 140 Lameuse St	Biloxi	MS	39530	228-435-6254	435-6129
Web: www.biloxi.ms.us ■ *E-mail:* biloxi@biloxi.ms.us					
Biloxi Community & Economic Development Dept PO Box 508	Biloxi	MS	39533	228-435-6280	435-6188
Web: www.biloxi.ms.us/economic.html					
Biloxi Mayor PO Box 429	Biloxi	MS	39533	228-435-6254	435-6129
Biloxi Public Library 139 Lameuse St	Biloxi	MS	39530	228-374-0330	374-0375
Web: www.harrison.lib.ms.us:/harrison/public_html/bcmain.htm					
Biloxi Visitors Center 710 Beach Blvd	Biloxi	MS	39530	228-374-3105	435-6248
TF: 800-245-6943 ■ *Web:* www.biloxi.ms.us ■ *E-mail:* biloxi@biloxi.ms.us					
Gulfport City Hall PO Box 1780	Gulfport	MS	39502	228-868-5700	868-5800
Web: www.ci.gulfport.ms.us					
Gulfport Mayor PO Box 1780	Gulfport	MS	39502	228-868-5810	868-5800
Web: www.ci.gulfport.ms.us/mayor.htm					
Gulfport Urban Development Dept PO Box 59	Gulfport	MS	39502	228-868-5736	868-5708
Harrison County PO Drawer CC	Gulfport	MS	39502	228-865-4036	868-1480
Harrison County Library System 1300 21st Ave	Gulfport	MS	39501	228-868-1383	863-7433
Web: www.harrison.lib.ms.us					
Mississippi Coast Coliseum & Convention Center 2350 Beach Blvd	Biloxi	MS	39531	228-594-3700	594-3812
TF: 800-726-2781 ■ *Web:* www.mscoastcoliseum.com ■ *E-mail:* coliseum@mscoastcoliseum.com					
Mississippi Gulf Coast Convention & Visitors Bureau PO Box 6128	Gulfport	MS	39506	228-896-6699	896-6788
TF: 800-237-9493 ■ *Web:* www.gulfcoast.org/					

On-Line Resources

Area Guide Biloxi	biloxi.areaguides.net
Area Guide Gulfport	gulfport.areaguides.net
Biloxi CityLink	www.usacitylink.com/citylink/biloxi
City Knowledge Biloxi	www.cityknowledge.com/ms_biloxi.htm
City Knowledge Gulfport	www.cityknowledge.com/ms_gulfport.htm
Excite.com Biloxi City Guide	www.excite.com/travel/countries/united_states/mississippi/biloxi
Gulf Coast Information Systems	www.gulf-coast.com/
NITC Travelbase City Guide Gulf Coast	www.travelbase.com/auto/guides/gulf_coast-area-ms.html

— Transportation Services —

AIRPORTS

■ **Gulfport/Biloxi Regional Airport (GPT)**

	Phone
4 miles NE of downtown Gulfport (approx 15 minutes)	228-863-5951

Web: www.gulfcoast.org/gpt/ ■ *E-mail:* gpt@gulfcoast.org

Airport Transportation

	Phone
Airport Limousine $7.50 fare to downtown Gulfport/Biloxi	228-432-8000

Commercial Airlines

	Phone		Phone
American Eagle	800-433-7300	**Delta**	800-221-1212
Atlantic Southeast	800-282-3424	**Northwest**	800-225-2525
Continental Express	800-525-0280		

Gulfport/Biloxi (Cont'd)

Charter Airlines

	Phone
US Aviation Corp	228-863-2570

CAR RENTALS

	Phone
Avis-Gulfport	228-864-7182
Budget-Gulfport	228-864-5181
Emerald Coast-Gulfport	228-863-8020
Hertz-Gulfport	228-863-2761
National-Gulfport	228-863-5548

LIMO/TAXI

	Phone
Celebrity Limousine-Biloxi	228-388-1384
Classic Limousine	228-864-0862
Golden Gulf Limousine-Biloxi	228-374-5466
Sunshine Cab-Gulfport	228-863-8002
VIP Limousine-Biloxi	228-392-7715
Yellow Cab	228-436-4655
Yellow Cab-Biloxi	228-436-3788
Yellow Cab-Gulfport	228-863-1511

MASS TRANSIT

	Phone
Coast Area Transit System $1 Base fare	228-896-8080

RAIL/BUS

				Phone
Amtrak Station 860 Esters Blvd	Biloxi	MS	39530	800-872-7245
Amtrak Station 1419 27th Ave	Gulfport	MS	39501	800-872-7245
Greyhound/Trailways Bus Station 2805 13th St. *TF:* 800-231-2222	Gulfport	MS	39501	228-863-1022
Greyhound/Trailways Bus Station 166 Main St	Biloxi	MS	39530	228-436-4335

— Accommodations —

HOTEL RESERVATION SERVICES

	Phone	Fax
Gulf Coast Hotel Reservations *TF:* 888-388-1006 ■ *Web:* www.biloxi-ms.com	228-875-1006	875-7641

HOTELS, MOTELS, RESORTS

				Phone	Fax
Balmoral Inn 120 Balmoral Ave *TF:* 800-393-9131 ■ *Web:* www.gcww.com/balmoralinn	Biloxi	MS	39531	228-388-6776	388-5450
Beach Resort Inn 2736 Beach Blvd *TF:* 800-345-1570	Biloxi	MS	39531	228-388-3310	388-8387
Beau Rivage Resort & Casino 875 Beach Blvd. *TF:* 800-239-2771 ■ *Web:* www.beaurivage.com	Biloxi	MS	39530	228-386-7171	386-7179
Best Western Beach View Inn 2922 W Beach Blvd. *TF:* 800-748-8969	Gulfport	MS	39501	228-864-4650	863-6867
Best Western Oak Manor Inn 886 Beach Blvd *TF:* 800-591-9057	Biloxi	MS	39530	228-435-4331	374-7631
Best Western Seaway Inn 9475 Hwy 49 & I-10 *TF:* 800-822-4141	Gulfport	MS	39503	228-864-0050	864-0739
Best Western Swan Motel 1726 Beach Blvd. *TF:* 800-528-1234	Biloxi	MS	39531	228-432-0487	374-3547
Breakers Inn 2506 Beach Blvd *TF:* 800-624-5031	Biloxi	MS	39531	228-388-6320	388-7185
Broadwater Beach Resort 2110 Beach Blvd *TF:* 800-647-3964 ■ *Web:* www.broadwater.com ■ *E-mail:* broadwater@southwind.com	Biloxi	MS	39531	228-388-2211	385-1801
Chateau de La Mer Resort Inn 1410 Beach Blvd. *TF:* 800-257-5551	Gulfport	MS	39507	228-896-1703	896-6934
Comfort Inn 1648 Beach Blvd *TF:* 800-228-5150	Biloxi	MS	39531	228-432-1993	432-2297
Comfort Inn Gulfport 9343 Hwy 49 *TF:* 800-228-5150	Gulfport	MS	39503	228-863-5500	863-7341
Comfort Suites Biloxi 1634 Beach Blvd *TF:* 800-228-5150	Biloxi	MS	39531	228-435-1995	435-1981
Crowne Plaza Resort 151 Beach Blvd *TF:* 800-843-4753	Biloxi	MS	39530	228-435-5400	436-7834
Crystal Inn 9379 Canal Rd *TF:* 888-822-9600	Gulfport	MS	39503	228-822-9600	822-0666
Days Inn 2046 Beach Blvd *TF:* 800-526-5656	Biloxi	MS	39531	228-385-1155	385-2532
Days Inn Gulfport 15250 Poole St. *TF:* 800-329-7466	Gulfport	MS	39503	228-864-5135	864-7194
Deep South Motel 940 Beach Blvd	Gulfport	MS	39507	228-896-7808	897-2088
Diamond Inn 100 Brady Dr. *TF:* 800-576-5781	Biloxi	MS	39531	228-388-7321	385-9878
Economy Inn in Gulfport 4120 W Beach Blvd	Gulfport	MS	39501	228-863-3700	863-3700
Economy Resort Inn 1716 Beach Blvd *TF:* 888-613-5313	Biloxi	MS	39531	228-374-8888	374-8888
Fairfield Inn Hwy 49 & Airport Blvd *TF:* 800-228-2800 ■ *Web:* fairfieldinn.com/GPTFI	Gulfport	MS	39503	228-822-9000	822-9000
Grand Casino Biloxi Hotel 245 Beach Blvd *TF:* 800-354-2450 ■ *Web:* www.grandcasinos.com/biloxi	Biloxi	MS	39530	228-436-2946	435-8901
Grand Casino Gulfport Hotel 3215 W Beach Blvd. *TF:* 800-354-2450 ■ *Web:* www.grandcasinos.com/gulfport	Gulfport	MS	39501	228-870-7777	867-5610
Gulf Hills Resort 13701 Paso Rd *TF:* 877-875-4211	Ocean Springs	MS	39564	228-875-4211	872-4211
Hampton Inn 9445 Hwy 49. *TF:* 800-984-7489	Gulfport	MS	39503	228-868-3300	864-3347
Holiday Inn Airport 9415 Hwy 49 N *TF:* 800-441-0892	Gulfport	MS	39503	228-868-8200	865-9164
Holiday Inn Beachfront 1600 E Beach Blvd *TF:* 800-441-0887	Gulfport	MS	39501	228-864-4310	865-0525
Holiday Inn Coliseum 2400 Beach Blvd *TF:* 800-441-0882	Biloxi	MS	39531	228-388-3551	385-2032
Holiday Inn Express 2416 Beach Blvd *TF:* 800-468-2102	Biloxi	MS	39531	228-388-1000	388-6048
Howard Johnson Express 1712 Beach Blvd *TF:* 800-446-4656	Biloxi	MS	39531	228-432-2000	435-9975
Imperial Palace Hotel & Casino 850 Bayview Ave. *TF:* 800-436-3000 ■ *Web:* www.ipbiloxi.com	Biloxi	MS	39530	228-436-3000	432-3271
La Font Inn Hwy 90 E *TF:* 800-647-6077	Pascagoula	MS	39567	228-762-7111	934-4324
Motel 6 2476 Beach Blvd *TF:* 800-466-8356	Biloxi	MS	39531	228-388-5130	388-8819
Motel 6 9355 Hwy 49 *TF:* 800-466-8356	Gulfport	MS	39503	228-863-1890	868-2445
Ocean Manor Inn 2484 Beach Blvd	Biloxi	MS	39531	228-388-2579	388-2579
Ocean View Inn 1842 Beach Blvd	Biloxi	MS	39531	228-388-4384	388-4384
Quality Inn Emerald Beach 1865 Beach Blvd *TF:* 800-342-7519	Biloxi	MS	39531	228-388-3212	388-6541
Ramada Limited 960 E Beach Blvd *TF:* 800-900-3139	Gulfport	MS	39507	228-896-5555	896-5852
Ramada Limited Biloxi Beach 1768 Beach Blvd *TF:* 800-272-6232	Biloxi	MS	39531	228-432-1997	435-9934
Red Carpet Inn 2752 Beach Blvd *TF:* 800-251-1962	Biloxi	MS	39531	228-388-2610	388-7782
Royal Holiday Beach Resort 1980 Beach Blvd *TF:* 800-874-0402	Biloxi	MS	39531	228-388-7553	388-8959
Sahara Inn 530 E Beach Blvd	Gulfport	MS	39507	228-896-7211	
Shoney's Inn 9375 Hwy 49 N. *TF:* 800-222-2222 ■ *Web:* www.shoneysinn.com/ms1.htm	Gulfport	MS	39503	228-868-8500	865-0054
Super 8 Motel 1678 Beach Blvd *TF:* 800-800-8000	Biloxi	MS	39531	228-432-1984	435-5971
Travel Inn Biloxi 2030 Beach Blvd *TF:* 800-676-4465	Biloxi	MS	39531	228-388-5531	388-5272
Travelodge Gulf Beach 2428 Beach Blvd *TF:* 800-323-9164	Biloxi	MS	39531	228-385-5555	388-9015
Treasure Bay Resort & Casino 1980 Beach Blvd. *TF:* 800-747-2839 ■ *Web:* treasurebay.com/	Biloxi	MS	39531	228-388-6610	385-6067

— Restaurants —

				Phone
Alberti's (Italian) 2028 Beach Blvd	Biloxi	MS	39531	228-388-9507
Amazing Randolphs (Steak/Seafood) 195 E Beach Blvd	Biloxi	MS	39530	228-386-3045
Annie's (Southern) 120 W Bayview.	Pass Christian	MS	39571	228-452-2062
Bernie's (American) 2800 Hwy 90	Gautier	MS	39581	228-497-5700
Blow Fly Inn (Steak/Seafood) 1201 Washington Ave	Gulfport	MS	39507	228-896-9812
Bombay Bicycle Club (American) 830 Beach Blvd	Biloxi	MS	39530	228-374-4101
Brullo's New Orleans Seafood Co (Seafood) 265 E Beach Blvd	Biloxi	MS	39530	228-436-2946
Cafe Joni (American) 765 16th St	Gulfport	MS	39507	228-897-2003
Cafe New Orleans (Cajun) 1621 30th Ave.	Gulfport	MS	39501	228-863-3402
Captain Al's (Steak/Seafood) 11268 E Dedeaux Ave.	Gulfport	MS	39507	228-831-5751
Chimneys The (Steak/Seafood) 213 E Beach Blvd	Long Beach	MS	39560	228-868-7020
China Palace (Chinese) 4110 W Beach Blvd	Gulfport	MS	39501	228-868-5439
Cuco's Border Cafe (Mexican) 1851 Beach Blvd	Biloxi	MS	39531	228-388-1982
El Mexicano Inn (Mexican) 1215 30th Ave	Gulfport	MS	39501	228-863-3691
Farraday's (International) 151 Beach Blvd.	Biloxi	MS	39530	228-435-5400
Fishermans Harbor (Seafood) 749 Beach Blvd.	Biloxi	MS	39530	228-435-0087
Fountain The (American/French) 111 Rue Magnolia	Biloxi	MS	39530	228-435-1106

Gulfport/Biloxi — Restaurants (Cont'd)

Name / Address	City	State	Zip	Phone
French Connection (French) 1891 Pass Rd	Biloxi	MS	39531	228-388-6367
Hong Kong Palace (Chinese) 523 Broad Ave	Gulfport	MS	39501	228-864-6250
Hook Line & Sinker Restaurant (Seafood) 2010 W Beach Blvd	Biloxi	MS	39531	228-388-3757
Hugo's (Italian) 1067 Division St	Biloxi	MS	39530	228-374-0045
Jappeppis (Italian) 195 Porter Ave	Biloxi	MS	39530	228-374-9660
Keppner's Gasthaus (German) 1789 Beach Blvd	Biloxi	MS	39531	228-436-4878
Web: www.gcww.com/keppners ■ *E-mail:* keppner@earthlink.com				
Landry's Seafood House (Seafood) 2694 Beach Blvd	Biloxi	MS	39531	228-385-2220
Los Tres Amigos (Mexican) 603 E Pass Rd	Gulfport	MS	39507	228-896-6905
Magnolias (American) 3215 W Beach Blvd	Gulfport	MS	39501	228-870-7777
Mary Mahoney's Old French House (Steak/Seafood) 116 Rue Magnolia & Beach Blvd	Biloxi	MS	39530	228-374-0163
McElroy's Harbor House Restaurant (Steak/Seafood) 695 Beach Blvd	Biloxi	MS	39530	228-435-5001
O'Charley's (Steak/Seafood) 2590 Beach Blvd	Biloxi	MS	39531	228-388-7883
Port-O-Call Seafood Restaurant (Seafood) 15200 Lemoyne Blvd	Biloxi	MS	39532	228-392-0335
RC Korean Restaurant (Korean) 1670 E Pass Rd	Biloxi	MS	39531	228-432-7666
Sho-ya Japanese Restaurant (Japanese) 2511 25th Ave	Gulfport	MS	39501	228-868-7333
Vrazel's (Continental) 3206 W Beach Blvd	Gulfport	MS	39501	228-863-2229
White Cap Restaurant (Seafood) 1411 28th Ave	Gulfport	MS	39501	228-863-4652

— Goods and Services —

SHOPPING

Name / Address	City	State	Zip	Phone	Fax
Beauvoir Antique Mall & Flea Market 190 Beauvoir Rd	Biloxi	MS	39531	228-388-5506	
Edgewater Mall 2600 Beach Blvd	Biloxi	MS	39531	228-388-4636	
Edgewater Village Shopping Center 2650 Beach Blvd	Biloxi	MS	39531	228-896-1631	388-5141
Gulfport Factory Shops 10000 Factory Shops Blvd	Gulfport	MS	39503	228-867-6100	864-8130*
**Fax:* Cust Svc ■ *TF:* 888-260-7609 ■ *Web:* www.primeoutlets.com/Gulfport					
Singing River Mall 2800 Hwy 90	Gautier	MS	39553	228-497-6160	

BANKS

Name / Address	City	State	Zip	Phone	Fax
BancorpSouth 524 Courthouse Rd	Gulfport	MS	39507	228-896-6862	897-3388
TF: 888-797-7711					
Hancock Bank PO Box 4019	Gulfport	MS	39502	228-868-4000	868-4675*
**Fax:* Mktg ■ *TF:* 800-522-6542 ■ *E-mail:* employment@hancockbank.com					
Peoples Bank 152 Lameuse St	Biloxi	MS	39530	228-435-5511	435-8417
Southtrust Bank 854 W Howard Ave	Biloxi	MS	39530	228-374-4616	436-8689*
**Fax:* Mktg					
Whitney National Bank of Mississippi 1300 25th Ave	Gulfport	MS	39501	228-864-7332	864-7974

BUSINESS SERVICES

Name	Phone
Airborne Express	800-247-2676
BAX Global	800-225-5229
DHL Worldwide Express	800-225-5345
Federal Express	800-238-5355
Kelly Services	228-896-1980
Mail Boxes Etc	800-789-4623
Post Office-Biloxi	228-432-0312
Post Office-Gulfport	228-863-1633
UPS	800-742-5877

— Media —

PUBLICATIONS

Name / Address	City	State	Zip	Phone	Fax
Sun Herald‡ PO Box 4567	Biloxi	MS	39535	228-896-2100	896-2104
TF: 800-346-5022 ■ *Web:* www.sunherald.com ■ *E-mail:* maildrop@sunherald.infi.net					

‡Daily newspapers

TELEVISION

Name / Address	City	State	Zip	Phone	Fax
WDSU-TV Ch 6 (NBC) 846 Howard	New Orleans	LA	70113	504-679-0600	679-0733
Web: www.wdsu.com ■ *E-mail:* wdsu@comm.net					
WKRG-TV Ch 5 (CBS) 555 Broadcast Dr	Mobile	AL	36606	334-479-5555	473-8130
TF: 800-957-4885 ■ *Web:* www.wkrg.com ■ *E-mail:* tv5@wkrg.com					
WLOX-TV Ch 13 (ABC) 208 Debuys Rd	Biloxi	MS	39531	228-896-1313	896-0749
Web: www.wlox.com ■ *E-mail:* wlox@wlox.com					
WMAH-TV Ch 19 (PBS) 3825 Ridgewood Rd	Jackson	MS	39211	601-982-6565	982-6746
Web: www.etv.state.ms.us					
WWL-TV Ch 4 (CBS) 1024 N Rampart St	New Orleans	LA	70116	504-529-4444	529-6472
Web: www.wwltv.com					
WXXV-TV Ch 25 (Fox) PO Box 2500	Gulfport	MS	39505	228-832-2525	832-4442

RADIO

Name / Address	City	State	Zip	Phone	Fax
WGCM-AM 1240 kHz (Ctry) PO Box 2639	Gulfport	MS	39505	228-832-5111	896-0458
WKNN-FM 99.1 MHz (Ctry) 286 DeBuys Rd	Biloxi	MS	39531	228-762-3113	388-2362
Web: www.k99fm.com ■ *E-mail:* online@k99fm.com					
WLRK-FM 96.7 MHz (Rock) 212 DeBuys Rd	Biloxi	MS	39531	228-388-1490	388-1966
Web: www.wlrk.com					
WMJY-FM 93.7 MHz (AC) 286 DeBuys Rd	Biloxi	MS	39531	228-388-2323	388-2362
Web: www.magic937.com ■ *E-mail:* info@magic937.com					
WVMI-AM 570 kHz (N/T) PO Box 1459	Biloxi	MS	39533	228-374-1570	374-1576
Web: www.wvmi.com ■ *E-mail:* wvmi@wvmi.com					
WXBD-AM 1490 kHz (Nost) 212 DeBuys Rd	Biloxi	MS	39531	228-388-1490	388-1966
WZKX-FM 108 MHz (Ctry) PO Box 2639	Gulfport	MS	39505	228-832-5111	896-0458
Web: www.kicker108.com					

— Colleges/Universities —

Name / Address	City	State	Zip	Phone	Fax
University of Southern Mississippi 2701 Hardy St	Hattiesburg	MS	39406	601-266-7011	266-5816
Web: www.usm.edu					
William Carey College 498 Tuscan Ave	Hattiesburg	MS	39401	601-582-5051	582-6454
TF: 800-962-5991 ■ *Web:* www.wmcarey.edu ■ *E-mail:* admiss@wmcarey.edu					

— Hospitals —

Name / Address	City	State	Zip	Phone	Fax
Gulf Coast Medical Center 180-A Debuys Rd	Biloxi	MS	39531	228-388-6711	388-0358

— Attractions —

Name / Address	City	State	Zip	Phone	Fax
Beauvoir-Jefferson Davis Home 2244 Beach Blvd	Biloxi	MS	39531	228-388-1313	
Web: www.beauvoir.org					
Biloxi Beach Amusement Park 1785 Beach Blvd	Biloxi	MS	39531	228-432-0635	868-7526
Biloxi Lighthouse Porter Ave & Hwy 90	Biloxi	MS	39530	228-435-6293	
Biloxi Little Theatre 220 Lee St	Biloxi	MS	39530	228-432-8543	
Boomtown Casino 676 Bayview Ave	Biloxi	MS	39533	228-435-7000	436-7560
TF: 800-627-0777 ■ *Web:* www.boomtownbiloxi.com ■ *E-mail:* btbxmk@datasync.com					
Brielmaier House 710 Beach Blvd	Biloxi	MS	39530	228-374-3105	
Casino Magic Bay Saint Louis 711 Casino Magic Dr	Bay Saint Louis	MS	39520	228-467-9257	467-3080*
**Fax:* Hum Res ■ *TF:* 800-562-4425 ■ *Web:* www.casinomagic.com/html/bsl.html					
Casino Magic Biloxi 195 E Beach Blvd	Biloxi	MS	39530	228-435-2559	435-1559
TF: 800-562-4425 ■ *Web:* www.casinomagic.com/html/biloxi.html					
Center Stage 240 Eisenhower Dr	Biloxi	MS	39531	228-388-6258	388-6238
Web: www.lillypr.com/centerstage					
Cirque du Soleil Alegría c/o Beau Rivage PO Box 7777	Biloxi	MS	39532	228-386-7790	386-7876
Web: www.cirquedusoleil.com/en/piste/alegria/index.html					
Copa Casino 777 Copa Blvd	Gulfport	MS	39502	228-863-3330	863-3127
TF: 800-946-2672					
Crosby Arboretum 370 Ridge Rd	Picayune	MS	39466	601-799-2311	799-2372
Foretich House & Brielmaier House 710 Beach Blvd	Biloxi	MS	39530	228-374-3105	
Grand Casino Biloxi 265 Beach Blvd	Biloxi	MS	39530	228-436-2946	436-2801
TF: 800-946-2946 ■ *Web:* www.grandcasinos.com/biloxi/index.html					
Grand Casino Gulfport 3215 W Beach Blvd	Gulfport	MS	39501	228-870-7777	867-5601
TF: 800-946-7777 ■ *Web:* www.grandcasinos.com/gulfport/index.html					
Gulf Coast Opera Theatre Inc 170 Reynoir St Saenger Theatre	Biloxi	MS	39533	228-374-4200	374-2005
Gulf Coast Winery 1306 29th Ave	Gulfport	MS	39501	228-863-0790	863-0115

Gulfport/Biloxi — Attractions (Cont'd)

				Phone	Fax
Gulf Islands National Seashore 3500 Park Rd	Ocean Springs	MS	39564	228-875-9057	872-2954
Gulfport Little Theatre 2600 13th Ave	Gulfport	MS	39501	228-864-7983	
Imperial Palace Hotel & Casino 850 Bayview Ave. *TF:* 800-436-3000 ■ *Web:* www.ipbiloxi.com	Biloxi	MS	39530	228-436-3000	432-3271
Isle of Capri Crown Plaza Resort & Casino 151 Beach Blvd. *TF:* 800-843-4753	Biloxi	MS	39530	228-435-5400	436-7834
Mardi Gras Museum 119 Rue Magnolia	Biloxi	MS	39530	228-435-6245	435-6246
Marine Life Oceanarium Joseph T Jones Memorial Pk *Web:* www.dolphinsrus.com	Gulfport	MS	39501	228-864-2511	863-3673
Maritime & Seafood Industry Museum 115 1st St *Web:* www.maritimemuseum.org/	Biloxi	MS	39530	228-435-6320	435-6309
Mississippi Sandhill Crane National Wildlife Refuge Gautier VanCleave Rd *Web:* www.fws.gov/r4mis	Gautier	MS	39553	228-497-6322	497-5407
Ohr George E Arts & Cultural Center 136 George E Ohr St. *Web:* www.georgeohr.org ■ *E-mail:* info@georgeohr.org	Biloxi	MS	39530	228-374-5547	436-3641
Old Biloxi Cemetery 1166 Irish Hill Dr	Biloxi	MS	39530	228-435-6247	
Old Brick House 622 Bayview Ave. *TF:* 800-245-6943	Biloxi	MS	39530	228-435-6308	435-6246
Ole' Biloxi Train Tour Porter Ave Biloxi Lighthouse	Biloxi	MS	39530	228-374-8687	
Palace Casino 182 Howard Ave **Fax:* Mktg ■ *TF:* 800-725-2239	Biloxi	MS	39530	228-432-8888	432-0261*
President Casino at the Broadwater 2110 Beach Blvd. *TF:* 800-624-3000	Biloxi	MS	39531	228-388-2270	385-3637
Saenger Theatre for the Performing Arts 170 Reynoir St. *Web:* www.biloxi.ms.us/saenger	Biloxi	MS	39533	228-435-6291	435-6211
Scott JL Marine Education Center & Aquarium 115 Beach Blvd. *Web:* www.foolscap.com/jlscott/	Biloxi	MS	39530	228-374-5550	374-5559
Tullis-Toledano Manor 360 Beach Blvd	Biloxi	MS	39530	228-435-6293	

SPORTS TEAMS & FACILITIES

				Phone	Fax
Mississippi Sea Wolves (hockey) 2350 Beach Blvd Mississippi Coast Coliseum *Web:* www.msseawolves.com ■ *E-mail:* jady@msseawolves.com	Biloxi	MS	39531	228-388-6151	388-5848

— Events —

	Phone
Biloxi Blessing of the Fleet (early May)	228-435-5578
Biloxi Christmas City USA (mid-November)	228-896-9336
Biloxi Oyster Festival (mid-March)	228-374-2330
Biloxi Seafood Festival (mid-September)	228-374-2717
Biloxi Shrimp Festival (early May)	228-435-5578
Bull Bash (mid-September)	228-832-0080
Christmas on the Water (early December)	228-374-3105
Christmas on the Water Boat Parade (early December)	228-374-3611
Country Cajun Crawfish Festival (mid-April)	228-594-3700
Crab Festival (early July)	228-467-6509
Crusin' the Coast (mid-October)	228-896-6699
Fall Muster (late October)	228-388-1313
George Ohr's Fall Festival of Arts (late October)	228-435-6308
Great Biloxi Schooner Races (early May)	228-435-6320
Gulf Coast Spring Pilgrimage (mid-late March)	228-863-0550
July 4th Celebration (July 4)	228-374-3105
Juneteenth Celebration (mid-June)	228-388-4038
Mardi Gras (February)	800-237-9493
Mississippi Coast Pro Rodeo (mid-August)	228-594-3700
Mississippi Deep Sea Fishing Rodeo (early July)	228-863-2713
Mississippi Gulf Coast Blues Festival (early September)	228-497-5615
Mississippi Gulf Coast Fair & Expo (June)	228-594-3700
Oktoberfest (late September-early October)	228-436-4878
Peter Anderson Art Festival (early November)	228-875-4424
Saint Patrick's Day Parade (mid-March)	228-864-2551
Scottish Games & Celtic Festival (early October)	228-864-8055
Sun Herald Sand Sculpture Contest (mid-September)	228-896-2434
Victorian Christmas (mid-December)	228-388-9074

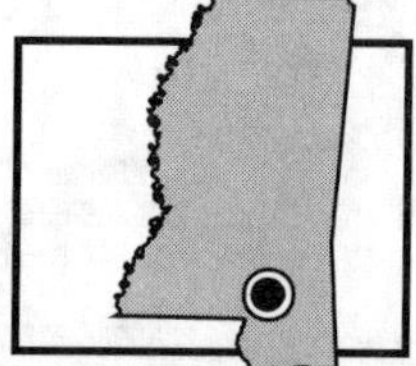

Hattiesburg

Hattiesburg's rich architectural heritage is showcased in four historic districts: the Hattiesburg Historic Neighborhood District, which is one of the largest, most intact historic districts in southeast Mississippi, covering over 115 acres and featuring a variety of styles dated between 1884 to 1930; the North Main District, which features large Victorian, Colonial Revival, and smaller Folk Victorian cottages, with some Prairie-style homes; the Oaks Historic District, which features mainly Bungalow-style homes and is the site of Pinehurst, a Neoclassical-style home built on the site of what had been the city founder's 1895 estate; and the Mobile Street District, which was a major African-American business district from 1895 to 1910. Museums in Hattiesburg include the Armed Forces Museum at Camp Shelby, which houses memorabilia from the Civil War, both world wars, and the Korean, Vietnam, and Persian Gulf wars. The Library of Hattiesburg is home to "The Spirit that Builds" by William Baggett, a circular 167-foot mural of South Mississippi painted on sandblasted steel. The 10,000-square foot Lauren Rogers Museum of Art is noted for its collection of English Georgian silver, an extensive collection of Japanese woodblock prints, and one of the finest collections of Native American baskets in the world. The city is also home to two colleges, the University of Southern Mississippi and William Carey College. The McCain Library & Archives, located on the USM Campus, houses genealogical material that dates back to the beginning of the United States (with more extensive records of the southern states) as well as a collection of Forrest County Cemetery Census books.

Population	48,806	**Longitude**	89-17-25 W
Area (Land)	25.4 sq mi	**County**	Forrest
Area (Water)	0.2 sq mi	**Time Zone**	CST
Elevation	161 ft	**Area Code/s**	601
Latitude	31-19-37 N		

— Average Temperatures and Precipitation —

TEMPERATURES

	Jan	Feb	Mar	Apr	May	Jun	Jul	Aug	Sep	Oct	Nov	Dec
High	58	62	70	78	84	90	92	92	88	79	70	62
Low	34	37	45	54	61	68	71	70	65	52	44	38

PRECIPITATION

	Jan	Feb	Mar	Apr	May	Jun	Jul	Aug	Sep	Oct	Nov	Dec
Inches	5.8	5.7	6.3	4.8	5.2	4.2	5.5	5.2	3.6	3.2	4.8	6.3

— Important Phone Numbers —

	Phone		Phone
AAA	601-957-8484	**Poison Control Center**	601-354-7660
Emergency	911	**Time/Temp**	601-545-2841
Medical Referral	601-261-3463		

— Information Sources —

				Phone	Fax
Area Development Partnership 1 Convention Center Plaza *TF:* 800-238-4288 ■ *Web:* www.hattiesburg-adp.org ■ *E-mail:* adp@hattiesburg-adp.org	Hattiesburg	MS	39401	601-296-7500	296-7505
Better Business Bureau Serving Mississippi PO Box 12745 *Web:* www.bbbmississippi.org ■ *E-mail:* info@bbbmississippi.org	Jackson	MS	39236	601-987-8282	987-8285

Hattiesburg — Information Sources (Cont'd)

Name / Address	City	State	Zip	Phone	Fax
Forrest County 630 N Main St	Hattiesburg	MS	39401	601-582-3213	545-6065
Hattiesburg City Hall 200 Forrest St *Web:* www.hattiesburgms.com	Hattiesburg	MS	39401	601-545-4501	545-4608
Hattiesburg Convention & Visitors Bureau 1 Convention Center Plaza *TF:* 800-638-6877 ■ *Web:* www.hattiesburg.org ■ *E-mail:* kgodwin@hattiesburg.org	Hattiesburg	MS	39401	601-268-3220	268-3249
Hattiesburg Convention Center 1 Convention Center Plaza	Hattiesburg	MS	39401	601-268-3220	
Hattiesburg Mayor 200 Forrest St 3rd Fl *Web:* www.hattiesburgms.com/m.html	Hattiesburg	MS	39401	601-545-4501	545-4608
Library of Hattiesburg Petal & Forrest County 329 Hardy St *Web:* www.hpfc.lib.ms.us	Hattiesburg	MS	39401	601-582-4461	582-5338

On-Line Resources

Area Guide Hattiesburg .... hattiesburg.areaguides.net
City Knowledge Hattiesburg .... www.cityknowledge.com/ms_hattiesburg.htm
Excite.com Hattiesburg City Guide .... www.excite.com/travel/countries/united_states/mississippi/hattiesburg
Hattiesburg Tour .... www.missbiz.com/hattiesburgtour
Hattiesburg.net Information Hub .... www.hattiesburg.net/info.shtml
NITC Travelbase City Guide Hattiesburg .... www.travelbase.com/auto/guides/hattiesburg-ms.html
Online City Guide to Hattiesburg .... www.olcg.com/ms/hattiesburg/index.html

— Transportation Services —

AIRPORTS

■ Hattiesburg-Laurel Regional Airport (PIB)

	Phone
12 miles NE of downtown Hattiesburg (approx 18 minutes) E-mail: hlra@cgate.net	601-649-2444

Airport Transportation

	Phone
AAA Cab Co $13 fare to downtown Hattiesburg	601-582-2301
City Cab Co $13 fare to downtown Hattiesburg	601-584-8411
Yellow Taxicabs Inc $20 fare to downtown Hattiesburg	601-544-5090

Commercial Airlines

	Phone
Northwest Airlink	800-225-2525

CAR RENTALS

	Phone		Phone
Enterprise	601-544-0022	**Hertz**	601-544-4914

LIMO/TAXI

	Phone		Phone
AAA Cab Co	601-582-2301	**Coleman's Limousine Service**	601-649-3623
City Cab Co	601-584-8411	**Yellow Taxicabs Inc**	601-544-5090

MASS TRANSIT

	Phone
Hattiesburg Public Transit $.50 Base fare	601-545-4671

RAIL/BUS

Name / Address	City	State	Zip	Phone
Amtrak 308 Newman St	Hattiesburg	MS	39401	800-872-7245
Greyhound Bus Station 6657 Hwy 49 *TF:* 800-231-2222	Hattiesburg	MS	39401	601-271-6500

— Accommodations —

HOTELS, MOTELS, RESORTS

Name / Address	City	State	Zip	Phone	Fax
Best Western Northgate Inn 6757 Hwy 49	Hattiesburg	MS	39402	601-268-8816	268-8816
Broadway Inn 1818 Broadway Dr	Hattiesburg	MS	39401	601-268-3717	
Budget Inn 6574 Hwy 49	Hattiesburg	MS	39401	601-544-3475	544-3475
Cabot Lodge 6541 Hwy 49 *TF:* 800-225-9429	Hattiesburg	MS	39401	601-264-1881	268-3226
Carriage Inn 914 Broadway Dr	Hattiesburg	MS	39401	601-544-5100	544-5100
Comfort Inn 6595 Hwy 49 N *TF:* 800-228-5150	Hattiesburg	MS	39401	601-268-2170	261-2170
Comfort Suites 122 Plaza Dr *TF:* 800-228-5160	Hattiesburg	MS	39402	601-261-5555	261-5555
Days Inn 6518 Hwy 49 *TF:* 800-329-7466	Hattiesburg	MS	39401	601-544-6300	544-6300
Dru's Inn 558 Southgate Rd	Hattiesburg	MS	39401	601-544-6837	544-9758
Econo Lodge 3501 Hardy St	Hattiesburg	MS	39401	601-264-0010	264-0010
Hampton Inn 4301 Hardy St	Hattiesburg	MS	39402	601-264-8080	268-9916
Holiday Inn 6563 Hwy 49 N	Hattiesburg	MS	39401	601-268-2850	268-2823
Howard Johnson 6553 Hwy 49 N *TF:* 800-332-5565	Hattiesburg	MS	39401	601-268-2251	264-7283
Motel 6 6508 Hwy 49 N *TF:* 800-466-8356	Hattiesburg	MS	39401	601-544-6096	582-7743
Ramada Inn 6528 Hwy 49 N *TF:* 800-272-6232	Hattiesburg	MS	39401	601-544-4530	544-4530
Ramada Inn 900 Broadway Dr *TF:* 800-272-6232	Hattiesburg	MS	39401	601-582-7101	582-7101
Scottish Inn 6560 Hwy 49 *TF:* 800-251-1962	Hattiesburg	MS	39401	601-582-1211	544-5228
Super 8 Motel 6529 Hwy 49	Hattiesburg	MS	39401	601-264-2885	264-2885

— Restaurants —

Name / Address	City	State	Zip	Phone
Bea's Broiler (Seafood) 3616 Hwy 42	Hattiesburg	MS	39402	601-261-0133
Breeze (American) 2663 Oak Grove Rd	Hattiesburg	MS	39402	601-268-3675
Burkett's Restaurant (American) 910 Timothy Ln	Hattiesburg	MS	39401	601-583-0541
Cane Creek Restaurant (Seafood) 3200 Lakeview Rd	Hattiesburg	MS	39401	601-582-7637
Chesterfield's (Continental) 2507 Hardy St	Hattiesburg	MS	39401	601-582-2778
Conestoga Steak House (Steak/Seafood) 6313 Hwy 49	Hattiesburg	MS	39401	601-264-8816
Crescent City Grill (American) 3810 Hardy St	Hattiesburg	MS	39401	601-264-0657
Donanelle's Bar & Grill (Steak/Seafood) 4321 Hwy 49	Hattiesburg	MS	39401	601-545-3860
Down Home Cooking (Homestyle) 522 Eastside Ave	Hattiesburg	MS	39401	601-545-1266
Front Porch (Barbecue) 205 Thornhill Dr	Hattiesburg	MS	39402	601-264-3536
Gus' Cafe (American) 144 E Front St	Hattiesburg	MS	39401	601-544-4939
La Fiesta Brava (Mexican) 4404 Hardy St	Hattiesburg	MS	39401	601-271-6070
Mack's Country Catfish Restaurant (Seafood) 6094 Hwy 98	Hattiesburg	MS	39402	601-268-7036
Mandarin House (Chinese) 4400 Hardy St	Hattiesburg	MS	39402	601-264-5511
Mexican Kitchen (Mexican) 5697 Hwy 49	Hattiesburg	MS	39401	601-544-4811
Nanny's Country Kitchen (Homestyle) 907 Edwards St	Hattiesburg	MS	39401	601-583-1117
O'Charley's (American) 4640 Hardy St	Hattiesburg	MS	39402	601-268-1193
Our Place Bar & Grill (American) 1900 Lincoln Rd	Hattiesburg	MS	39401	601-296-0303
Parker's Kitchen (Soul) 80 J M Tatum Industrial Dr	Hattiesburg	MS	39401	601-582-1204
Peking Garden (Chinese) 4700 Hardy St Suite A	Hattiesburg	MS	39402	601-271-6000
Purple Parrot Cafe (Continental) 3810 Hardy St	Hattiesburg	MS	39401	601-264-0656
Rayner's Seafood House (Seafood) 7343 Hwy 49	Hattiesburg	MS	39402	601-268-2639
Shenanigans (Amercian) 2100 W Pine St	Hattiesburg	MS	39401	601-261-0730
Ward's Restaurant (American) 101 Thornhill Dr	Hattiesburg	MS	39402	601-264-4758

— Goods and Services —

SHOPPING

Name / Address	City	State	Zip	Phone	Fax
Antique Mall 2103 W Pine St	Hattiesburg	MS	39402	601-268-2511	
Calico Antique Mall 309 E Pine St	Hattiesburg	MS	39401	601-582-4351	
Cloverleaf Mall 5912 Hwy 49	Hattiesburg	MS	39401	601-582-5281	544-5852
Riverwalk Marketplace 5619 Hwy 42	Hattiesburg	MS	39401	601-545-7001	545-8417
Sawmill Square Mall 910 Sawmill Rd *Web:* www.sawmillsquare.com	Laurel	MS	39440	601-426-6320	426-2693
Turtle Creek Mall 1000 Turtle Creek Dr *Web:* www.turtlecreekmall.com	Hattiesburg	MS	39402	601-261-3032	261-2526

BANKS

Name / Address	City	State	Zip	Phone	Fax
Bank of Mississippi 713 Broadway Dr	Hattiesburg	MS	39401	601-545-6800	545-6808
Community Bank 3707 Hardy St	Hattiesburg	MS	39402	601-268-0299	268-0289
Deposit Guaranty National Bank 700 Broadway Dr	Hattiesburg	MS	39401	601-261-4290	261-4293
First National Bank 6480 Hwy 98	Hattiesburg	MS	39402	601-268-8998	268-8904
Grand Bank for Savings 14 Plaza Dr *TF:* 800-300-1467	Hattiesburg	MS	39402	601-264-1467	264-5805
Great Southern National Bank 1300 Hardy St	Hattiesburg	MS	39401	601-545-2700	545-5446

Hattiesburg — Banks (Cont'd)

				Phone	Fax
Lamar Bank 1000 Turtle Creek Dr.	Hattiesburg	MS	39402	601-268-7510	268-7631
TF Cust Svc: 800-794-8026*					
Trustmark National Bank 951 Broadway Dr	Hattiesburg	MS	39401	601-583-5204	583-5339
Union Planters Bank 130 W Front St.	Hattiesburg	MS	39401	601-545-4743	545-4897
TF: 800-748-8679					

BUSINESS SERVICES

	Phone		Phone
Federal Express	800-238-5355	**Post Office**	601-544-8711
Kelly Services	601-268-3895	**Snelling Personnel Services**	601-544-0821
Kinko's	601-264-6434	**UPS**	800-742-5877
Mail Boxes Etc	601-261-0068		

— Media —

PUBLICATIONS

				Phone	Fax
Hattiesburg American‡ 825 N Main St	Hattiesburg	MS	39401	601-582-4321	584-3130
TF: 800-844-2637 ■ *E-mail:* HBAmerican@aol.com					
Lamar Times 6504 Hwy 98 W	Hattiesburg	MS	39402	601-268-2331	268-2965
WDAM-TV Ch 7 (NBC) PO Box 16269	Hattiesburg	MS	39404	601-544-4730	584-9302
Web: www.wdam.com ■ *E-mail:* info@wdam.com					

‡Daily newspapers

TELEVISION

				Phone	Fax
WHLT-TV Ch 22 (CBS) 5912 Hwy 49 Cloverleaf Mall Suite A.	Hattiesburg	MS	39401	601-545-2077	545-3589
WLOX-TV Ch 13 (ABC) 208 Debuys Rd	Biloxi	MS	39531	228-896-1313	896-0749
Web: www.wlox.com ■ *E-mail:* wlox@wlox.com					
WXXV-TV Ch 25 (Fox) PO Box 2500	Gulfport	MS	39505	228-832-2525	832-4442

RADIO

				Phone	Fax
WAML-AM 1340 kHz (Rel) 1425 Ellisville Blvd	Laurel	MS	39440	601-425-0011	425-0016
WBBN-FM 95.9 MHz (Ctry) 4580 Hwy 15 N.	Laurel	MS	39440	601-649-0095	649-8199
Web: www.b95country.com					
WBKH-AM 950 kHz (Rel) 63 Braswell Rd.	Hattiesburg	MS	39401	601-582-9595	
WCJU-AM 1450 kHz (N/T) PO Box 452	Columbia	MS	39429	601-736-2616	736-2617
WEEZ-AM 890 kHz (Rel) 51 Victory Rd	Laurel	MS	39443	601-425-1491	426-8255
WFFF-AM 1360 kHz (Ctry) 11 Gardner Shopping Ctr	Columbia	MS	39429	601-736-1360	736-1361
WFOR-AM 1400 kHz (Oldies) 2414 W 7th St	Hattiesburg	MS	39401	601-544-1400	582-5481
WHER-FM 103.7 MHz (Oldies) 2414 W 7th St	Hattiesburg	MS	39401	601-544-1400	582-5481
WJMG-FM 92.1 MHz (Urban) 1204 Graveline St.	Hattiesburg	MS	39401	601-544-1941	544-1947
WKNZ-FM 107.1 MHz (Oldies) 7501 Hwy 49 N	Hattiesburg	MS	39402	601-264-0443	264-5733
Web: www.zoo107.com					
WMFM-FM 106.3 MHz (AC) 2571 Old Richton Rd.	Petal	MS	39465	601-545-1063	
Web: www.access-net.com/lite106 ■ *E-mail:* lite1063@aol.com					
WMXI-FM 98.1 MHz (Rel) 113 Fairfield Dr.	Hattiesburg	MS	39402	601-649-0898	261-3798
WNSL-FM 100.3 MHz (CHR) 51 Victory Rd	Laurel	MS	39443	601-425-1491	426-8255
Web: www.sl100.com					
WORV-AM 1580 kHz (Rel) 1204 Graveline St.	Hattiesburg	MS	39401	601-544-1941	544-1947
WUSM-FM 88.5 MHz (Misc) PO Box 10045	Hattiesburg	MS	39406	601-266-4287	266-4288
WXHB-FM 96.5 MHz (Misc) 7501 Hwy 49 N	Hattiesburg	MS	39403	601-268-6965	264-5733
WXRR-FM 104.5 MHz (Rock) PO Box 16596	Hattiesburg	MS	39404	601-544-0095	545-8199
Web: www.rock104fm.com					

— Colleges/Universities —

				Phone	Fax
University of Southern Mississippi 2701 Hardy St	Hattiesburg	MS	39406	601-266-7011	266-5816
Web: www.usm.edu					
William Carey College 498 Tuscan Ave.	Hattiesburg	MS	39401	601-582-5051	582-6454
TF: 800-962-5991 ■ *Web:* www.wmcarey.edu ■ *E-mail:* admiss@wmcarey.edu					

— Hospitals —

				Phone	Fax
Forrest General Hospital PO Box 16389	Hattiesburg	MS	39404	601-288-7000	288-4441
Wesley Medical Center 5001 Hardy St	Hattiesburg	MS	39402	601-268-8000	268-8406
Web: www.wesley.com					

— Attractions —

				Phone	Fax
All-American Rose Garden University of Southern Mississippi Campus.	Hattiesburg	MS	39406	601-266-4491	
Armed Forces Museum Hwy 49	Camp Shelby	MS	39407	601-558-2757	
Bay Street Presbyterian Church 204 Short Bay St	Hattiesburg	MS	39401	601-582-1584	582-1584
Carey Dinner Theater 498 Tuscan Ave	Hattiesburg	MS	39401	601-582-6221	582-6454
Chain Garden Thomas Hall William Carey College	Hattiesburg	MS	39401	601-582-6192	
Checker Flag Speedway Hwy 49 N.	Hattiesburg	MS	39402	601-261-9029	
Hall George Robert Air Park Academy Dr Municipal Airport	Hattiesburg	MS	39402	601-544-8661	
Hattiesburg Area Historical Society Museum 107 S Park Ave.	Hattiesburg	MS	39401	601-545-4582	
Hattiesburg Zoo 107 S 17th Ave Kamper Park	Hattiesburg	MS	39401	601-545-4576	545-4653
E-mail: hattzoo@aol.com					
International Checker Hall of Fame 220 Lynn Ray Rd	Petal	MS	39465	601-582-7090	583-9761
Isaac Carter Cabin 1701 Old Richton Rd	Petal	MS	39465	800-638-6877	
Johnson Paul B State Park 319 Geiger Lake Rd.	Hattiesburg	MS	39401	601-582-7721	
Kamper Park 107 S 17th Ave	Hattiesburg	MS	39401	601-545-4576	545-4653
Landrum's Homestead & Village 1356 Hwy 15 S.	Laurel	MS	39443	601-649-2546	428-1663
Parker Lucille Art Gallery 498 Tuscan Ave William Carey College	Hattiesburg	MS	39401	601-582-6192	
Pep's Point 382 Pep's Point Rd	Hattiesburg	MS	39401	601-582-8461	
Roberts MM Schoolhouse Owings-McQuagge Hall University of Southern Mississippi	Hattiesburg	MS	39406	601-266-4571	
Rogers Lauren Museum of Art PO Box 1108	Laurel	MS	39441	601-649-6374	649-6379
Web: www.lrma.org					
Ross House 416 Bay St.	Hattiesburg	MS	39401	800-638-6877	
Studio The 117 E Front St	Hattiesburg	MS	39403	601-545-8534	
Turner House 500 Bay St.	Hattiesburg	MS	39401	601-582-4249	
Woods Art Gallery Box 5033 University of Southern Mississippi	Hattiesburg	MS	39406	601-266-5200	266-6379

— Events —

	Phone
A Day in the Park (early May)	601-649-1206
Children's Book Festival (mid-late March)	601-266-4186
Fireworks Spectacular (early July)	601-426-6320
Hattiesburg Historic Downtown Holiday (mid-December)	601-545-4503
Holiday Fantasy (mid-late November)	601-296-7500
Holiday Lights Safari (mid-December)	601-545-4576
Hub City Hustle Triathalon (late May)	601-268-5010
Hub Fest (mid-October)	601-296-7500
Mississippi Pecan Festival (late September)	601-525-3792
Okatoma Festival (early May)	601-765-6012
Old Time Festival (early May)	601-296-7500
Paul B Johnson Fireworks (July 4)	601-582-7721

Hattiesburg — Events (Cont'd)

	Phone
Pinebelt Expo (mid August)	601-296-7500
Taste of the Pinebelt (mid-August)	601-296-7500
Victorian Candelit Christmas (mid-December)	601-583-8723
Zoo Boo (late October)	601-545-4576

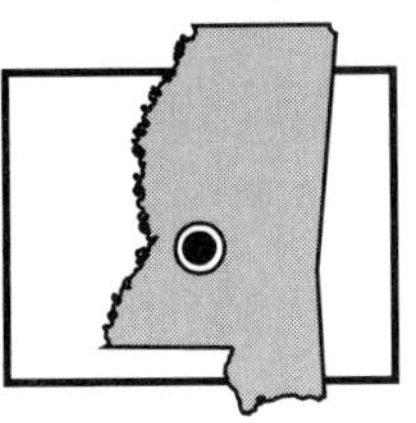

Jackson

Many of Jackson's museums are located in the downtown area of the city, including the Mississippi Museum of Art and Jim Buck Ross Mississippi Agriculture and Forestry Museum. The Ross Museum has ten old Mississippi farm buildings, a working farm, and a 1920s crossroads town on the premises. Jackson is the capital of Mississippi, and the Governor's Mansion, which has served as the official home of the Mississippi first family since its completion in 1841, is also open for public tours. The Natchez Trace Parkway runs through Jackson, and the Ross R. Barnett Reservoir is located on this portion of the 400-mile parkway. The Reservoir offers a wide range of water sports and picnic areas for travelers.

Population	188,419	**Longitude**	90-18-96 W
Area (Land)	100.6 sq mi	**County**	Hinds
Area (Water)	1.9 sq mi	**Time Zone**	CST
Elevation	294 ft	**Area Code/s**	601
Latitude	32-29-32 N		

— Average Temperatures and Precipitation —

TEMPERATURES

	Jan	Feb	Mar	Apr	May	Jun	Jul	Aug	Sep	Oct	Nov	Dec
High	56	60	69	77	84	91	92	92	88	79	69	60
Low	33	36	44	52	60	67	71	70	64	50	42	36

PRECIPITATION

	Jan	Feb	Mar	Apr	May	Jun	Jul	Aug	Sep	Oct	Nov	Dec
Inches	5.2	4.7	5.8	5.6	5.1	3.2	4.5	3.8	3.6	3.3	4.8	5.9

— Important Phone Numbers —

	Phone		Phone
AAA	601-957-8484	**Poison Control Center**	601-354-7660
Emergency	911	**Time/Temp**	601-355-9311
HotelDocs	800-468-3537	**Weather**	601-936-2189

— Information Sources —

				Phone	Fax
Better Business Bureau Serving Mississippi PO Box 12745	Jackson	MS	39236	601-987-8282	987-8285
Web: www.bbbmississippi.org ■ *E-mail:* info@bbbmississippi.org					
Hinds County PO Box 686	Jackson	MS	39205	601-968-6501	968-6794
Jackson City Hall 219 S President St	Jackson	MS	39201	601-960-1084	960-2193
Web: www.city.jackson.ms.us					
Jackson Mayor 219 S President St	Jackson	MS	39201	601-960-1084	960-2193
Web: www.city.jackson.ms.us/Govt/mayor.html					
Jackson Planning & Development Dept 200 S President St 2nd Fl	Jackson	MS	39201	601-960-1993	960-2208
Web: www.city.jackson.ms.us/Govt/planning_dev.html					
Jackson/Hinds Library System 300 N State St	Jackson	MS	39201	601-968-5811	968-5806
Web: www.jhls.lib.ms.us					
Metro Jackson Convention & Visitors Bureau 921 N President St	Jackson	MS	39202	601-960-1891	960-1827
TF: 800-354-7695 ■ *Web:* www.visitjackson.com ■ *E-mail:* info@visitjackson.com					
MetroJackson Chamber of Commerce PO Box 22548	Jackson	MS	39225	601-948-7575	352-5539
Mississippi Trade Mart 1200 E Mississippi St	Jackson	MS	39205	601-354-7051	

On-Line Resources

Area Guide Jackson	jacksonms.areaguides.net
City Knowledge Jackson	www.cityknowledge.com/ms_jackson.htm
Excite.com Jackson City Guide	www.excite.com/travel/countries/united_states/mississippi/jackson

— Transportation Services —

AIRPORTS

	Phone
■ **Jackson International Airport (JAN)**	
10 miles E of downtown (approx 20 minutes)	601-939-5631
Web: www.jmaa.com	

Airport Transportation

	Phone
Deluxe Cab $20 fare to downtown	601-948-4761
United Yellow Taxi $20 fare to downtown	601-922-3782

Commercial Airlines

	Phone		Phone
American Eagle	800-433-7300	**Delta Connection**	800-221-1212
Continental Express	800-525-0280	**Northwest**	800-225-2525
Delta	800-221-1212	**US Airways Express**	800-428-4322

Charter Airlines

	Phone
Jackson Air Center	601-939-9366

CAR RENTALS

	Phone		Phone
Avis	601-939-5853	**Hertz**	601-939-5312
Budget	601-939-0571	**National**	601-939-5713
Enterprise	601-981-4446	**Sears**	601-948-5050

LIMO/TAXI

	Phone		Phone
Act One Limousine	601-952-0000	**LeFleur's Limousine**	601-956-5466
Citi-Cab	601-355-8319	**United Yellow Taxi**	601-922-3782
Deluxe Cab	601-948-4761	**Veterans Cab**	601-977-1000

MASS TRANSIT

	Phone
JATRAN $1 Base fare	601-948-3840

RAIL/BUS

				Phone
Amtrak Station 300 W Capitol St	Jackson	MS	39201	601-355-6350
TF: 800-872-7245				
Greyhound/Trailways Bus Station 201 S Jefferson St	Jackson	MS	39201	601-353-6342

— Accommodations —

HOTELS, MOTELS, RESORTS

				Phone	Fax
Best Suites of America 5411 I-55 N	Jackson	MS	39206	601-899-9000	899-8316
TF: 800-237-8466					
Best Western Metro Inn 1520 Ellis Ave	Jackson	MS	39204	601-355-7483	355-7483
TF: 800-528-1234					

Jackson — Hotels, Motels, Resorts (Cont'd)

Name / Address	City	State	ZIP	Phone	Fax
Comfort Inn 2800 Greenway Dr.	Jackson	MS	39204	601-922-5600	922-0768
TF: 800-756-1362					
Comfort Inn 235 N Pearson Rd.	Jackson	MS	39208	601-932-6009	939-6922
TF: 888-214-7255					
Courtyard by Marriott 6820 Ridgewood Ct.	Jackson	MS	39211	601-956-9991	956-9994
TF: 800-321-2211 ■ *Web:* courtyard.com/JANCY					
Crown Plaza Resort 200 E Amite St	Jackson	MS	39201	601-969-5100	353-4333
Web: www.basshotels.com/crowneplaza/?_franchisee=JANDT ■ *E-mail:* cp-jackson-dwntn@bristolhotels.com					
Days Inn 804 Larson St.	Jackson	MS	39202	601-352-7387	352-7387
TF: 800-329-7466					
Dollar Save Inn 3740 I-55 S	Jackson	MS	39212	601-373-1040	
Econo Lodge 2450 Hwy 80 W	Jackson	MS	39204	601-353-0340	353-0340
TF: 800-553-2666					
Economy Inn 3016 W Northside Dr.	Jackson	MS	39213	601-982-0092	
Edison Walthall Hotel 225 E Capitol St.	Jackson	MS	39201	601-948-6161	948-0088
TF: 800-932-6161					
Extended StayAmerica 5354 N Hwy 55	Jackson	MS	39206	601-956-4312	956-7135
TF: 800-398-7829					
Fairview Inn 734 Fairview St	Jackson	MS	39202	601-948-3429	948-1203
TF: 888-948-1908					
French Quarter Inn 1865 Lakeland Dr	Jackson	MS	39216	601-366-6661	366-2434
TF: 800-931-6661					
Hampton Inn 320 Greymont Ave.	Jackson	MS	39202	601-352-1700	352-9988
TF: 800-426-7866					
Hampton Inn 465 Briarwood Dr	Jackson	MS	39206	601-956-3611	956-4999
TF: 800-426-7866					
Holiday Inn 310 Greymont Ave.	Jackson	MS	39202	601-948-4466	352-9368
TF: 800-465-4329					
Holiday Inn 3330 Clay St.	Vicksburg	MS	39180	601-636-4551	636-4552
TF: 800-465-4329					
Holiday Inn 5075 I-55 N	Jackson	MS	39206	601-366-9411	366-6688
TF: 800-465-4329					
Holiday Inn Southwest 2649 Hwy 80 W	Jackson	MS	39204	601-355-3472	355-3020
TF: 800-465-4329					
Jackson Hilton & Convention Center 1001 E County Line Rd	Jackson	MS	39211	601-957-2800	957-3191
TF: 888-263-0524					
La Quinta Inn 150 Angle St	Jackson	MS	39204	601-373-6110	373-6115
TF: 800-531-5900					
Luxury Inn 5709 Medgar Evers Blvd	Jackson	MS	39213	601-981-0877	
Millsaps-Buie House 628 N State St.	Jackson	MS	39202	601-352-0221	
Motel 6 6145 I-55 N.	Jackson	MS	39213	601-956-8848	956-1378
TF: 800-466-8356					
Parkside Inn 3720 I-55 N.	Jackson	MS	39211	601-982-1122	
Ramada Inn Coliseum 400 Greymont Ave	Jackson	MS	39202	601-969-2141	355-1704
TF: 800-272-6232					
Ramada Inn Southwest Conference Center 1525 Ellis Ave	Jackson	MS	39204	601-944-1150	355-3602
TF: 800-272-6232					
Red Roof Inn 700 Larson St.	Jackson	MS	39202	601-969-5006	969-5159
TF: 800-843-7663					
Relax Inn 2355 Hwy 80 W.	Jackson	MS	39204	601-948-0680	948-0680
Residence Inn by Marriott 881 E River Pl	Jackson	MS	39202	601-355-3599	355-5127
TF: 800-331-3131 ■ *Web:* www.residenceinn.com/residenceinn/JANRP					
Rodeway Inn 3880 I-55 S	Jackson	MS	39212	601-373-1244	373-9349
TF: 800-228-2000					
Scottish Inns 2263 Hwy 80 W	Jackson	MS	39204	601-969-1144	353-6658
TF: 800-251-1962					
Sleep Inn 2620 Hwy 80 W.	Jackson	MS	39204	601-354-3900	354-3900
TF: 800-753-3746					
Super 8 Motel 2655 I-55 S	Jackson	MS	39204	601-372-1006	372-1414
TF: 800-800-8000					
Super 8 North 4641 I-55 N	Jackson	MS	39206	601-982-1044	366-3381
TF: 800-800-8000					
Travelodge 5925 I-55 N.	Jackson	MS	39213	601-957-5500	957-2473
TF: 800-578-7878					
Value Inn & Suites 5035 I-55 N.	Jackson	MS	39206	601-982-1011	982-1011
Vieux Carre Corporate Apartments 3975 I-55 N	Jackson	MS	39216	601-982-3182	982-1082

— Restaurants —

Name / Address	City	State	ZIP	Phone
Barbalina's Barbeque (Barbecue) 975 W Northside Dr.	Jackson	MS	39213	601-982-1707
Big Apple (American) 509 N Farish St	Jackson	MS	39202	601-354-9371
Bonsai Japanese Steak House (Japanese) 1855 Lakeland Dr Bldg E.	Jackson	MS	39216	601-981-0606
Bravo (Italian) 244 Highland Village	Jackson	MS	39211	601-982-8111
Bristol Grill (American) 200 E Amite St	Jackson	MS	39201	601-969-5100
Chimneyville Bbq Smoke House (Barbecue) 970 High St.	Jackson	MS	39202	601-354-4665
Cock of the Walk (Seafood) 141 Madison Landing Cir	Ridgeland	MS	31957	601-856-5500
Dennery's (Steak/Seafood) 330 Greymont St.	Jackson	MS	39202	601-354-2527
El Chico (Tex Mex) 4240 Robinson Rd	Jackson	MS	39209	601-969-5997
Elite Restaurant (Homestyle) 141 E Capitol St.	Jackson	MS	39201	601-352-5606
Fenian's (American) 901 E Fortification St	Jackson	MS	39202	601-948-0055
Field's Cafe (American) 100 W Griffith St.	Jackson	MS	39201	601-353-1400
Fish Hut The (Seafood) 1041 W Woodrow Wilson Ave.	Jackson	MS	39213	601-353-0830
Gallery Grill (American) 105 E Capitol St	Jackson	MS	39201	601-355-8666
India Palace (Indian) 5101 I-55 N	Jackson	MS	39206	601-366-9680
Iron Horse Grill (Southwest) 320 W Pearl St.	Jackson	MS	39203	601-355-8419
Kathryn's (Steak/Seafood) 6800 Old Canton Rd.	Ridgeland	MS	39157	601-956-2803
Keifer's (Greek) 705 Poplar Blvd	Jackson	MS	39202	601-355-6825
Little Toyko (Japanese) 4800 I-55 N LeFleur's Gallery	Jackson	MS	39211	601-982-3035
Mayflower The (Continental) 123 W Capitol St	Jackson	MS	39201	601-355-4122
Museum Cafe (American) 1150 Lakeland Dr	Jackson	MS	39216	601-981-1465
Nick's (American) 1501 Lakeland Dr.	Jackson	MS	39216	601-981-8017
On the Border (Mexican) 6352 Ridgewood Ct	Jackson	MS	39211	601-977-9447
Palette The (Continental) 201 E Pascagoula St	Jackson	MS	39201	601-960-2003
Peaches Cafe (American) 327 N Farish St	Jackson	MS	39201	601-354-9267
Poets (Continental) 1855 Lakeland Dr.	Jackson	MS	39216	601-982-9711
Primos Restaurant at Northgate (Steak/Seafood) 4330 N State St.	Jackson	MS	39206	601-982-2064
Punchy's Live Charcoal (Steak/Seafood) 1102 Raymond Rd	Jackson	MS	39204	601-373-1776
Que Sera Sera (Cajun) 2801 N State St	Jackson	MS	39216	601-981-2520
Remington's (Southern) 2649 Hwy 80 W	Jackson	MS	39204	601-355-3472
Scrooges (Southern) 4450 I-55 N.	Jackson	MS	39211	601-362-2131
Tai Hong Restaurant (Chinese) 1601 Terry Rd	Jackson	MS	39204	601-352-3470
Thai House Restaurant (Thai) 2665 I-55 S	Jackson	MS	39204	601-373-8154
Tico's (Steak/Seafood) 1536 E County Line Rd	Ridgeland	MS	39157	601-956-1030
Two Sisters' Kitchen (Southern) 707 N Congress.	Jackson	MS	39202	601-353-1180
Valley Street Fish House (Seafood) 1234 Valley St	Jackson	MS	39203	601-354-0939

— Goods and Services —

SHOPPING

Name / Address	City	State	ZIP	Phone
Fairground Antique Flea Market 900 High St.	Jackson	MS	39225	601-353-5327
Highland Village Shopping Center 4500 I-55 N	Jackson	MS	39211	601-982-5861
Metrocenter Mall 3645 Hwy 80 W	Jackson	MS	39209	601-969-7633
Northpark Mall 1200 E County Line Rd	Ridgeland	MS	39157	601-957-3744
Westland Plaza Shopping Center Ellis & Robinson Rds	Jackson	MS	39204	601-948-7786

BANKS

Name / Address	City	State	ZIP	Phone	Fax
BancorpSouth Bank 525 E Capitol St.	Jackson	MS	39201	601-354-4500	944-3621
Deposit Guaranty National Bank 210 E Capitol Dr 1 Deposit Guaranty Plaza.	Jackson	MS	39215	601-354-8211	354-8192
Web: www.dgb.com					
First American Bank 200 S Lamar St	Jackson	MS	39201	601-355-4600	355-0600*
**Fax:* Cust Svc					
Trustmark National Bank 248 E Capitol St.	Jackson	MS	39201	601-354-5111	354-5030
TF: 800-844-2000 ■ *Web:* www.trustmark.com					
Union Planters Bank of Central Mississippi 329 E Capital St	Jackson	MS	39201	601-969-6100	969-6173

BUSINESS SERVICES

Name	Phone	Name	Phone
Airborne Express	800-247-2676	**Kinko's**	601-957-3311
BAX Global	800-225-5229	**Mail Boxes Etc**	800-789-4623
DHL Worldwide Express	800-225-5345	**Manpower Temporary Services**	601-981-2000
Federal Express	800-238-5355	**Post Office**	601-968-0520
Kelly Services	601-977-0911	**UPS**	800-742-5877

— Media —

PUBLICATIONS

Name / Address	City	State	ZIP	Phone	Fax
Clarion-Ledger‡ 201 S Congress St	Jackson	MS	39201	601-961-7000	961-7211
TF: 800-367-3384 ■ *Web:* www.clarionledger.com					
Mississippi 5 Lakeland Cir	Jackson	MS	39216	601-982-8418	982-8447
Mississippi Business Journal 5120 Galaxie Dr	Jackson	MS	39206	601-364-1000	364-1007
Web: www.msbusiness.com ■ *E-mail:* mbj@msbusiness.com					

Jackson — Publications (Cont'd)

Name / Address	City	State	ZIP	Phone	Fax
Northside Sun PO Box 16709	Jackson	MS	39236	601-957-1122	957-1533

‡*Daily newspapers*

TELEVISION

Name / Address	City	State	ZIP	Phone	Fax
WAPT-TV Ch 16 (ABC) PO Box 10297	Jackson	MS	39289	601-922-1607	922-1663
Web: www.wapt.com ■ *E-mail:* wapt@misnet.com					
WDBD-TV Ch 40 (Fox) 7440 Channel 16 Way	Jackson	MS	39209	601-922-1234	922-0268
Web: www.fox40wdbd.com					
WJTV-TV Ch 12 (CBS) 1820 TV Rd	Jackson	MS	39204	601-372-6311	373-8401
Web: www.wjtv.com					
WLBT-TV Ch 3 (NBC) 715 S Jefferson St	Jackson	MS	39201	601-948-3333	355-7830
Web: www.wlbt.com ■ *E-mail:* news@wlbt.com					
WMPN-TV Ch 29 (PBS) 3825 Ridgewood Rd	Jackson	MS	39211	601-982-6565	982-6746
Web: www.etv.state.ms.us					

RADIO

Name / Address	City	State	ZIP	Phone	Fax
WIIN-AM 780 kHz (Oldies) 265 High Point Dr	Ridgeland	MS	39157	601-956-0102	978-3980
WJDS-AM 620 kHz (N/T) PO Box 31999	Jackson	MS	39286	601-982-1062	362-1905
WJKK-FM 98.7 MHz (AC) 269 High Point Dr	Ridgeland	MS	39157	601-956-0102	978-3980
WJNT-AM 1180 kHz (N/T) PO Box 1248	Jackson	MS	39215	601-366-1150	366-1627
Web: www.wjnt.com					
WJSU-FM 88.5 MHz (NPR) 1400 Lynch St	Jackson	MS	39217	601-968-2140	968-2878
WJXN-FM 92.9 kHz (Rel) PO Box 24387	Jackson	MS	39205	601-944-1450	944-1450
WMPN-FM 91.3 MHz (NPR) 3825 Ridgewood Rd	Jackson	MS	39211	601-982-6565	982-6746
WMPR-FM 90.1 MHz (Urban) 1018 Pecan Park Cir	Jackson	MS	39209	601-948-5835	948-6162
WMSI-FM 102.9 MHz (Ctry) PO Box 31999	Jackson	MS	39286	601-982-1062	362-1905
WSTZ-FM 106.7 MHz (CR) 1375 Beasley Rd	Jackson	MS	39206	601-982-2106	362-1905
Web: www.z106.com					
WTYX-FM 94.7 MHz (CR) 222 Beasley Rd	Jackson	MS	39206	601-957-3000	956-0370
Web: www.arrow94.com ■ *E-mail:* mail94@arrow94.com					
WYOY-FM 101.7 MHz (CHR) 265 High Point Dr	Ridgeland	MS	39157	601-956-0102	978-3980

— Colleges/Universities —

Name / Address	City	State	ZIP	Phone	Fax
Belhaven College 1500 Peachtree St	Jackson	MS	39202	601-968-5928	968-8946
TF Admissions: 800-960-5940 ■ *Web:* www.belhaven.edu					
Jackson College of Ministries 1555 Beasley Rd	Jackson	MS	39206	601-981-1611	982-5121
Web: www.jcm.edu ■ *E-mail:* jcm@jcm.edu					
Jackson State University 1325 John R Lynch St	Jackson	MS	39217	601-968-2121	264-6234
TF: 800-682-5390 ■ *Web:* ccaix.jsums.edu ■ *E-mail:* gblakley@ccaix.jsums.edu					
Millsaps College 1701 N State St	Jackson	MS	39210	601-974-1000	974-1059
TF: 800-352-1050 ■ *Web:* www.millsaps.edu ■ *E-mail:* hinesfw@okra.millsaps.edu					
Mississippi College 200 College St	Clinton	MS	39058	601-925-3000	925-3950
TF: 800-738-1236 ■ *Web:* www.mc.edu ■ *E-mail:* admissions@mc.edu					
Tougaloo College 500 W County Line Rd	Tougaloo	MS	39174	601-977-7700	977-6185
TF: 888-424-2566 ■ *Web:* www.tougaloo.edu ■ *E-mail:* information@mail.tougaloo.edu					

— Hospitals —

Name / Address	City	State	ZIP	Phone	Fax
Baptist Health Systems Inc 1225 N State St	Jackson	MS	39202	601-968-1000	968-1149*
**Fax:* Admitting ■ *TF:* 800-948-6262 ■ *Web:* www.mbhs.org					
Central Mississippi Medical Center 1850 Chadwick Dr	Jackson	MS	39204	601-376-1000	376-2821*
**Fax:* Admitting ■ *TF:* 800-844-0919 ■ *Web:* www.hma-corp.com/ms7.html					
River Oaks Hospital PO Box 5100	Jackson	MS	39296	601-932-1030	936-2275
Saint Dominic-Jackson Memorial Hospital 969 Lakeland Dr	Jackson	MS	39216	601-982-0121	364-5871
Web: www.health-futures.org/stdom.html					
University of Mississippi Medical Center 2500 N State St	Jackson	MS	39216	601-984-1000	984-4125
Web: umcnews.com					
Veterans Affairs Medical Center 1500 E Woodrow Wilson Dr	Jackson	MS	39216	601-362-4471	364-1286*
**Fax:* Hum Res ■ *Web:* www.health-futures.org/va.html					

— Attractions —

Name / Address	City	State	ZIP	Phone	Fax
Alamo Theater 333 N Farish St	Jackson	MS	39202	601-352-3365	
Armed Forces Museum Hwy 49	Camp Shelby	MS	39407	601-558-2757	
Ballet Magnificat 5406 I-55 N	Jackson	MS	39211	601-977-1001	977-8948
Web: www.balletmagnificat.com ■ *E-mail:* bmag@teclink.net					
Ballet Mississippi PO Box 1787	Jackson	MS	39215	601-960-1560	960-2135
City of Jackson Fire Museum 355 Woodrow Wilson Blvd	Jackson	MS	39213	601-960-2433	960-2432
Web: www.city.jackson.ms.us/Fire/pfsed_museum.html					
Davis Planetarium 201 E Pascagoula St	Jackson	MS	39201	601-960-1550	960-1555
Farish Street Historical District Mill to Lamar Sts	Jackson	MS	39202	601-949-4000	
Governor's Mansion 300 E Capitol St	Jackson	MS	39201	601-359-3175	359-6473
Jackson Municipal Art Gallery 839 N State St	Jackson	MS	39202	601-960-1582	
Jackson Zoological Park 2918 W Capitol St	Jackson	MS	39209	601-352-2580	
Web: www.ayrix.net/jacksonzoo					
LeFleur's Bluff State Park 2140 Riverside Dr	Jackson	MS	39202	601-987-3923	354-6930
Manship House 420 E Fortification St	Jackson	MS	39202	601-961-4724	354-6043
Mara Thalia Hall 255 E Pascagoula St	Jackson	MS	39205	601-960-1537	960-1583
Mississippi Archives & History Library 100 S State St	Jackson	MS	39201	601-359-6876	359-6964
Mississippi Museum of Art 201 E Pascagoula St	Jackson	MS	39201	601-960-1515	960-1505
Web: www.msmuseumart.org					
Mississippi Museum of Natural Science 111 N Jefferson St	Jackson	MS	39202	601-354-7303	354-7227
Web: www.mdwfp.state.ms.us/museum/					
Mississippi Opera 201 E Pascagoula St Thalia Mara Hall	Jackson	MS	39201	601-960-2300	960-1526
Mississippi Petrified Forest US 49 N	Jackson	MS	39209	601-879-8189	
Mississippi Sports Hall of Fame 1152 Lakeland Dr	Jackson	MS	39216	601-982-8264	982-4702
TF: 800-280-3263					
Mississippi State Capitol 400 High St	Jackson	MS	39201	601-359-3114	
Mississippi State Historical Museum 100 S State St	Jackson	MS	39201	601-359-6920	359-6981
Web: www.mdah.state.ms.us/musetxt.html#capitol					
Mississippi Symphony Orchestra PO Box 2052	Jackson	MS	39225	601-960-1565	960-1564
Municipal Art Gallery 839 N State St	Jackson	MS	39202	601-960-1582	
Museum of the Southern Jewish Experience PO Box 16528	Jackson	MS	39236	601-362-6357	366-6293
Web: www.msje.org ■ *E-mail:* information@msje.org					
Mynelle Gardens 4736 Clinton Blvd	Jackson	MS	39209	601-960-1894	922-5759
Web: www.lnstar.com/mynelle/					
New Stage Theatre 1100 Carlisle St	Jackson	MS	39202	601-948-3531	948-3538
Web: www.newstagetheatre.com					
Oaks House Museum 823 N Jefferson St	Jackson	MS	39202	601-353-9339	
Rapids on the Reservoir PO Box 6020	Brandon	MS	39047	601-992-0500	992-0531
Web: www.rapidswaterpark.net					
Ross Jim Buck Mississippi Agriculture & Forestry Museum/National Agricultural Aviation Museum 1150 Lakeland Dr	Jackson	MS	39216	601-354-6113	
Web: www.lnstar.com/agmuseum/					
Smith Robertson Museum & Cultural Center 528 Bloom St	Jackson	MS	39202	601-960-1457	960-2070
Vicksburg National Military Park 3201 Clay St	Vicksburg	MS	39180	601-636-0583	636-9497
Web: www.nps.gov/vick/					
War Memorial Building 100 State St	Jackson	MS	39201	601-354-7207	

SPORTS TEAMS & FACILITIES

Name / Address	City	State	ZIP	Phone	Fax
Coliseum The Mississippi State Fairgrounds 1207 Mississippi St	Jackson	MS	39202	601-961-4000	354-6545
Web: www.mdac.state.ms.us/coliseum.htm					
Jackson Calypso (soccer) 4408 Ridgewood Rd Jackson Academy Stadium	Jackson	MS	39211	601-969-0936	961-9810
Web: www.angelfire.com/ms/JacksonCalypso/ ■ *E-mail:* hrayburn@netdoor.com					

Jackson — Sports Teams & Facilities (Cont'd)

				Phone	Fax
Jackson Chargers (soccer) 2240 E Westbrook Dr Sports Club Stadium	Jackson	MS	39211	601-991-0047	956-7529
Web: members.aol.com/JxnCharger/index.html ■ *E-mail:* ajd-ins@teclink.net					
Jackson Generals (baseball) 1200 Lakeland Dr Smith-Wills Stadium	Jackson	MS	39216	601-981-4664	
Web: www.jacksongenerals.com ■ *E-mail:* generals@jacksongenerals.com					
Veterans Memorial Stadium 2531 N State St.	Jackson	MS	39296	601-354-6021	354-6019
Web: www.ms-veteransstadium.com					

— Events —

	Phone
Capital City Football Classic (mid-November)	601-960-1891
Celtic Fest (early September)	601-960-1891
Chimneyville Crafts Festival (early December)	601-981-0019
Christmas at the New Capitol (December)	601-359-3114
Dixie National Livestock Show & Rodeo (early-mid-February)	601-961-4000
Farish Street Festival (late September)	601-960-2384
Festival of Christmas Trees (December)	601-960-1457
Gem & Mineral Show (late February)	601-961-4000
Harvest Festival (November)	601-354-6113
Hog Wild In June (late June)	601-354-6113
Holiday Jubilee (early December)	601-960-1891
Hot Air Balloon Race (early July)	601-859-1307
International Crawfish Festival (early May)	601-354-6113
Jackson County Fair (early October)	601-948-7575
Jubilee Jam (mid-May)	601-960-2008
Mal's Saint Paddy's Day Parade (March)	601-984-1109
Mississippi Heritage Festival (late May)	601-960-1891
Mississippi State Fair (early October)	601-961-4000
Mistletoe Marketplace (early November)	601-960-1891
Natives & Pioneers Heritage Fair (early October)	601-856-7546
Old Fashion Independence Day (July 4)	601-354-6113
Pioneer & Indian Festival (late October)	601-856-7546
Scottish Highland Games (mid-August)	601-960-1891
Sky Parade (late August-early September)	601-982-8088
Spring Festival at Mynelle Garden (late March)	601-960-1894
WellsFest (late September)	601-353-0658
Zoo Blues (mid-April)	601-960-1891

Tupelo

Tupelo is the headquarters from which the U.S. Department of the Interior manages the Natchez Trace Parkway, considered one of the nation's most unique national parks. The Chickasaw Indians are credited with creating the now-historic Natchez Trace when they established a trade route with the Natchez Indians to the south. (When the Spanish explorer Hernando De Soto passed through the Tupelo area in the 1540s, he found there an established Chickasaw Indian civilization.) Today the historic 400-mile Natchez Trace highway links Natchez, Mississippi with Nashville, Tennessee. Travelers can stop at the Natchez Trace Parkway Visitors Center in Tupelo to view displays and exhibits, and to obtain information about the parkway. Four miles south of the visitors center is a Chickasaw village that is the site of an 18th Century Chickasaw settlement and contains exhibits describing the Indians' daily life and early history. The most significant landmark of Tupelo's modern history is the Elvis Presley Birthplace and Museum. Visitors can view the two-room house where Presley was born on January 8, 1935 and tour the museum, which contains one of the most unique private collections of Elvis memorabilia in the world.

Population	35,589	**Longitude**	88-43-55 W
Area (Land)	51.1 sq mi	**County**	Lee
Area (Water)	0.3 sq mi	**Time Zone**	CST
Elevation	290 ft	**Area Code/s**	601
Latitude	34-15-48 N		

— Average Temperatures and Precipitation —

TEMPERATURES

	Jan	Feb	Mar	Apr	May	Jun	Jul	Aug	Sep	Oct	Nov	Dec
High	49	55	64	74	81	88	91	90	85	75	64	53
Low	31	34	43	51	60	67	71	69	63	50	42	34

PRECIPITATION

	Jan	Feb	Mar	Apr	May	Jun	Jul	Aug	Sep	Oct	Nov	Dec
Inches	4.9	4.7	6.1	5.3	5.7	3.8	4.3	3.1	3.6	3.4	4.9	6.2

— Important Phone Numbers —

	Phone		Phone
Emergency	911	**Time/Temp**	662-842-8422
Medical Referral	800-882-6274	**Tupelo Info Line**	662-842-8422
Poison Control Center	901-528-6048	**Weather**	662-842-8422

— Information Sources —

				Phone	Fax
Better Business Bureau Serving Mississippi PO Box 12745	Jackson	MS	39236	601-987-8282	987-8285
Web: www.bbbmississippi.org ■ *E-mail:* info@bbbmississippi.org					
Community Development Foundation 300 W Main St	Tupelo	MS	38801	662-842-4521	841-0693
Lee County PO Box 7127	Tupelo	MS	38802	662-841-9100	680-6091
Lee County Agri-Center 5395 Hwy 145	Verona	MS	38879	662-566-5600	566-5604
Lee County Library 219 N Madison St.	Tupelo	MS	38801	662-841-9027	740-7615
Tupelo City Hall 117 N Broadway St	Tupelo	MS	38801	662-841-6505	840-2075
Web: www.ci.tupelo.ms.us					
Tupelo Convention & Visitors Bureau 399 E Main St	Tupelo	MS	38801	662-841-6521	841-6558
TF: 800-533-0611 ■ *Web:* tupelo.net ■ *E-mail:* tour20@tsixroads.com					
Tupelo Mayor 117 N Broadway St City Hall	Tupelo	MS	38801	662-841-6513	840-2075

On-Line Resources

Area Guide Tupelo	tupelo.areaguides.net
City Knowledge Tupelo	www.cityknowledge.com/ms_tupelo.htm

— Transportation Services —

AIRPORTS

	Phone
■ **Tupelo Regional Airport (TUP)**	
3 miles W of downtown (approx 10 minutes)	662-841-6570

Airport Transportation

	Phone
Limousine Connection $25 fare to downtown	662-840-9484
Tupelo Cab $10 fare to downtown	662-842-1513

Commercial Airlines

	Phone		Phone
Northwest Airlink	800-225-2525	**US Airways**	800-428-4322

CAR RENTALS

	Phone		Phone
Budget	662-840-3710	**Hertz**	662-842-3174
Enterprise	662-842-2237		

LIMO/TAXI

	Phone		Phone
Limousine Connection	662-840-9484	**Tupelo Cab**	662-842-1513

RAIL/BUS

				Phone
Greyhound Bus Station 201 Commerce St.	Tupelo	MS	38801	662-842-4557
TF: 800-231-2222				

Tupelo (Cont'd)

— Accommodations —

HOTELS, MOTELS, RESORTS

Name / Address	City	State	ZIP	Phone	Fax
All American Coliseum Motel 767 E Main St	Tupelo	MS	38801	662-844-5610	844-8546
Amerihost Inn 625 Spicer Dr	Tupelo	MS	38801	662-844-7660	844-3009
TF: 800-434-5800 ■ *Web:* www.amerihostinn.com/176-fram.html					
Best Western 897 Harmony Ln	Tupelo	MS	38801	662-842-4403	842-5362
TF: 800-528-1234					
Comfort Inn Tupelo 1190 N Gloster St	Tupelo	MS	38801	662-842-5100	844-0554
TF: 800-221-2222					
Courtyard by Marriott 1320 N Gloster St	Tupelo	MS	38801	662-841-9960	841-9907
TF: 800-321-2211					
Days Inn 1015 N Gloster St	Tupelo	MS	38801	662-842-0088	842-3659
TF: 800-329-7466					
Economy Inn 708 N Gloster St	Tupelo	MS	38801	662-842-1213	840-2400
Executive Inn 1011 N Gloster St	Tupelo	MS	38802	662-841-2222	844-7836
TF: 800-533-3220					
Gumtree Inn 101 Thompson St	Tupelo	MS	38801	662-680-8000	842-8195
TF: 800-530-7779					
Hampton Inn 1516 McCullough Blvd	Tupelo	MS	38801	662-840-8300	840-8307
TF: 800-426-7866					
Holiday Inn Express 923 N Gloster St	Tupelo	MS	38802	662-842-8811	844-6884
TF: 800-465-4329					
Microtel Inn & Suites 1532 McCullough Blvd	Tupelo	MS	38801	662-840-2111	840-0077
TF: 888-771-7171					
Ramada Inn & Convention Center 854 N Gloster St	Tupelo	MS	38801	662-844-4111	844-4111
TF: 800-228-2828					
Red Roof Inn Tupelo 1500 McCullough Blvd	Tupelo	MS	38804	662-844-1904	844-0139
TF: 800-843-7663					
Rex Plaza Suites 619 N Gloster St	Tupelo	MS	38804	662-840-8000	840-1116
TF: 800-203-5917					
Scottish Inn 401 N Gloster St	Tupelo	MS	38801	662-842-1961	
TF: 800-251-1962					
Super 8 Motel 3898 McCullough Blvd	Tupelo	MS	38801	662-842-0448	842-0448
Town House Motel 931 S Gloster St	Tupelo	MS	38801	662-842-5411	840-1686
Trace Inn 3400 W Main St	Tupelo	MS	38801	662-842-5555	844-3105
Travelers Motel 915 N Gloster St	Tupelo	MS	38801	662-844-2221	

— Restaurants —

Name / Address	City	State	ZIP	Phone
Back Yard Burgers (American) 405 S Gloster St	Tupelo	MS	38801	662-840-5999
Bar-B-Que by Jim (Barbecue) 203 Commerce St	Tupelo	MS	38801	662-840-8800
Cafe Bravo (American) 854 N Gloster St	Tupelo	MS	38801	662-844-5371
Cancun Mexican Restaurant (Mexican) 201 N Gloster St	Tupelo	MS	38801	662-842-9557
Casa Monterry Grill & Cantina (Mexican) 700 W Main St	Tupelo	MS	38801	662-844-0440
Chadwicks (Steak/Seafood) 1721 N Gloster St	Tupelo	MS	38801	662-840-5106
China Capital (Chinese) 530 N Gloster St	Tupelo	MS	38801	662-841-0484
China House Restaurant (Chinese) 3654 N Gloster St	Tupelo	MS	38801	662-680-5666
Gloster 205 Restaurant (Steak/Seafood) 205 N Gloster St	Tupelo	MS	38801	662-842-7205
Gold Star Chinese Restaurant (Chinese) 1153 S Gloster St	Tupelo	MS	38801	662-840-6849
Hunan Chinese Restaurant (Chinese) 365 S Gloster St	Tupelo	MS	38801	662-842-8888
Jefferson Place (Steak) 823 Jefferson St	Tupelo	MS	38801	662-844-8696
Las Margaritas (Mexican) 123 Industrial Rd	Tupelo	MS	38801	662-844-7399
Legend Steakhouse (Steak) 2901 S Eason Blvd	Tupelo	MS	38801	662-844-1936
Mulberry Alley (American) 102 Cockrell St	Tupelo	MS	38801	662-841-2818
Omar's Ranch House (Steak/Seafood) 712 S Gloster St	Tupelo	MS	38801	662-840-1009
Rib Cage (Barbecue) 206 Troy St	Tupelo	MS	38801	662-840-5400
Russell's Beef House (Steak/Seafood) 3400 W Main St	Tupelo	MS	38801	662-680-8673
Stables Restaurant (Steak/Seafood) 206 N Spring St	Tupelo	MS	38801	662-791-0440
Vanelli's (Greek/Italian) 1302 N Gloster St	Tupelo	MS	38801	662-844-4410
Woody's (Steak/Seafood) 619 N Gloster St	Tupelo	MS	38801	662-840-0460

— Goods and Services —

SHOPPING

Name / Address	City	State	ZIP	Phone	Fax
Black's Department Store 207 W Main St	Tupelo	MS	38801	662-842-5801	842-7930
Gloster Creek Village 499 Gloster Creek Village	Tupelo	MS	38801	662-844-2032	840-4903
Mall at Barnes Crossing 1001 Barnes Crossing Rd	Tupelo	MS	38801	662-844-6255	
Web: www.barnescrossing.com					

BANKS

Name / Address	City	State	ZIP	Phone	Fax
BancorpSouth Bank 1 Mississippi Plaza	Tupelo	MS	38804	662-680-2000	680-2570
Community Federal Savings Bank 333 Court St	Tupelo	MS	38802	662-842-3981	842-3187
Deposit Guaranty National Bank 431 W Main St	Tupelo	MS	38801	662-842-7072	841-5283
Peoples Bank & Trust 209 Troy St	Tupelo	MS	38801	662-680-1001	680-1234
Trustmark National Bank 216 S Broadway St	Tupelo	MS	38801	662-841-2983	841-8727
Union Planter's Bank 331 W Main St	Tupelo	MS	38801	662-842-2666	842-7864

BUSINESS SERVICES

Name	Phone	Name	Phone
AAA Employment	662-844-8448	**Mail Boxes Etc**	662-840-7222
Airborne Express	800-247-2676	**Manpower Temporary Services**	662-680-6100
DHL Worldwide Express	800-225-5345	**Post Office**	662-841-1286
Express Personnel Service	662-842-5500	**Sir Speedy Printing**	662-841-0004
Federal Express	800-463-3339	**Sprint Print of Tupelo**	662-841-9292
Kelly Services	662-842-9602	**UPS**	800-742-5877

— Media —

PUBLICATIONS

Name / Address	City	State	ZIP	Phone	Fax
Northeast Mississippi Daily Journal‡ PO Box 909	Tupelo	MS	38802	662-842-2611	842-2233
TF News Rm: 800-270-2612 ■ *Web:* www.djournal.com					

TELEVISION

Name / Address	City	State	ZIP	Phone	Fax
WBUY-TV Ch 40 (TBN) PO Box 38421	Memphis	TN	38183	901-521-9289	521-9989
WCBI-TV4 (CBS) 201 5th St S	Columbus	MS	39701	662-327-4444	328-5222
Web: wcbi.com					
WHBQ-TV Ch 13 (Fox) 485 S Highland St	Memphis	TN	38111	901-320-1313	320-1366
Web: www.fox13whbq.com ■ *E-mail:* news@fox13whbq.com					
WKNO-TV Ch 10 (PBS) 900 Getwell Rd	Memphis	TN	38111	901-458-2521	325-6505
Web: www.wkno.org ■ *E-mail:* wknopi@wkno.org					
WLMT-TV Ch 30 (UPN) 2701 Union Ave Ext.	Memphis	TN	38112	901-323-2430	452-1820
Web: www.upn30memphis.com					
WLOV-TV Ch 27 (Fox) 1359 Rd 681	Tupelo	MS	38801	662-842-7620	844-7061
WPTY-TV Ch 24 (ABC) 2701 Union Ave	Memphis	TN	38112	901-323-2430	452-1820
Web: www.abc24.com ■ *E-mail:* newsdesk@abc24.com					
WTVA-TV Ch 9 (NBC) 1359 Rd 681	Tupelo	MS	38801	662-842-7620	844-7061
Web: www.wtva.com ■ *E-mail:* wtva@netdoor.com					

RADIO

Name / Address	City	State	ZIP	Phone	Fax
KAVW-FM 90.7 MHz (Rel) 107 Parkgate Dr	Tupelo	MS	38803	601-844-8888	842-6791
WAFR-FM 88.3 MHz (Rel) 107 Parkgate Dr	Tupelo	MS	38803	601-844-8888	842-6791
Web: www.afr.net					
WESE-FM 92.5 MHz (Urban) 5026 Cliff Gookin Blvd	Tupelo	MS	38801	662-842-1067	842-0725
WFTA-FM 101.9 MHz (AC) 1241 Cliff Gookin Blvd	Tupelo	MS	38801	601-862-3191	842-9568
WFTO-AM 1330 kHz (Ctry) 1241 Cliff Gookin Blvd	Tupelo	MS	38801	601-862-3191	842-9568
WNRX-AM 1060 kHz (Rel) 5026 Cliff Gookin Blvd	Tupelo	MS	38801	662-842-1067	842-0725
WRBO-FM 103.5 MHz (Oldies) 3200 W Main	Tupelo	MS	38801	601-844-2134	844-2887
WSEL-FM 96.7 MHz (Rel) PO Box 3788	Tupelo	MS	38803	601-489-0297	488-9735
WSYE-FM 93.3 MHz (AC) 1705 S Gloster Suite H	Tupelo	MS	38802	601-844-9793	844-7400
Web: www.wsyesunny93.com ■ *E-mail:* sunny93@network-one.com					
WTUP-AM 1490 kHz (N/T) 5026 Cliff Gookin Blvd	Tupelo	MS	38801	662-842-1067	842-0725
WWKZ-FM 105.3 MHz (CHR) 3200 W Main	Tupelo	MS	38801	601-844-2134	844-2887
Web: www.kz105.com					
WWZD-FM 106.7 MHz (Ctry) 5026 Cliff Gookin Blvd	Tupelo	MS	38801	662-842-1067	842-0725

— Colleges/Universities —

Name / Address	City	State	ZIP	Phone	Fax
Itawamba Community College Tupelo Campus 2176 S Eason Blvd	Tupelo	MS	38804	662-620-5000	620-5315

Tupelo — Colleges/Universities (Cont'd)

				Phone	Fax
University of Mississippi Tupelo 2170 Eason Blvd.	Tupelo	MS	38804	662-844-5622	844-5625
Web: www.olemiss.edu/tupelo ■ *E-mail:* info@olemiss.edu					

— Hospitals —

				Phone	Fax
Barnes Crossing Medical Clinic 903 Mississippi Dr	Tupelo	MS	38804	662-841-4652	
North Mississippi Medical Center 830 S Gloster St.	Tupelo	MS	38801	662-841-3000	841-3552*
**Fax:* Hum Res					

— Attractions —

				Phone	Fax
Amory Regional Museum 3rd St & 8th Ave S	Tupelo	MS	38821	662-256-2761	
Brices Cross Roads National Battlefield Site 2680 Natchez Trace Pkwy	Tupelo	MS	38804	662-680-4025	680-4033
TF: 800-305-7417 ■ *Web:* www.nps.gov/brcr/					
Dunn Oren Museum of Tupelo 689 Rutherford Rd	Tupelo	MS	38803	662-841-6438	841-6458
Elvis Presley Birthplace & Museum 306 Elvis Presley Dr	Tupelo	MS	38801	662-841-1245	841-1245
Elvis Presley Lake 272 Rd 995	Tupelo	MS	38801	662-841-1304	
Lyric Theatre N Broadway & Court Sts	Tupelo	MS	38801	662-844-1935	
Web: www.ebicom.net/~tct/lyric.htm					
Private John Allen National Fish Hatchery 111 Elizabeth St	Tupelo	MS	38802	662-842-1341	842-1341
Tombigbee State Park 264 Cabin Dr	Tupelo	MS	38804	662-842-7669	840-5597
Tupelo Artist Guild Gallery 211 W Main St	Tupelo	MS	38801	662-844-2787	844-9751
Tupelo Ballet Co 1009 Varsity Dr Tupelo Civic Auditorium	Tupelo	MS	38801	662-844-1928	844-1951
Tupelo Community Theatre 200 N Broadway St Lyric Theatre	Tupelo	MS	38801	662-844-1935	
Web: www.ebicom.net/~tct/					
Tupelo Lee Acres Park 902 Lawndale Dr	Tupelo	MS	38801	662-841-6452	
Tupelo National Battlefield 2680 Natchez Trace Pkwy	Tupelo	MS	38804	662-680-4025	680-4033
TF: 800-305-7417 ■ *Web:* www.nps.gov/tupe/					
Tupelo Symphony Orchestra Assn 1009 Varsity Dr Tupelo Civic Auditorium	Tupelo	MS	38801	662-842-8433	842-9565
Web: www.tupsymp.com ■ *E-mail:* tupsymp@tsixroads.com					

SPORTS TEAMS & FACILITIES

				Phone	Fax
Tupelo Coliseum 375 E Main St	Tupelo	MS	38801	662-841-6573	841-6413
Web: www.tupelocoliseum.com					

— Events —

	Phone
Bodock Festival (late August)	662-489-5042
Calhoun City Arts And Crafts Festival (late May)	662-628-6990
Elvis Presley Festival (early August)	662-841-1245
Gum Tree Arts Festival (early May)	662-841-6521
Hancock Fabric Show (late August-early September)	662-844-1473
Heritage Day Festival (early June)	662-423-9571
North Mississippi Fair (mid-September)	662-566-5600
Oleput Mardi Gras Festival (June)	662-841-6521
Oxford Conference for the Book (early April)	662-232-5993
Tupelo Gigantic Flea Market And Craft Show (year-round)	662-842-4442

Missouri

Population (1999): 5,468,338　　**Area (sq mi): 69,709**

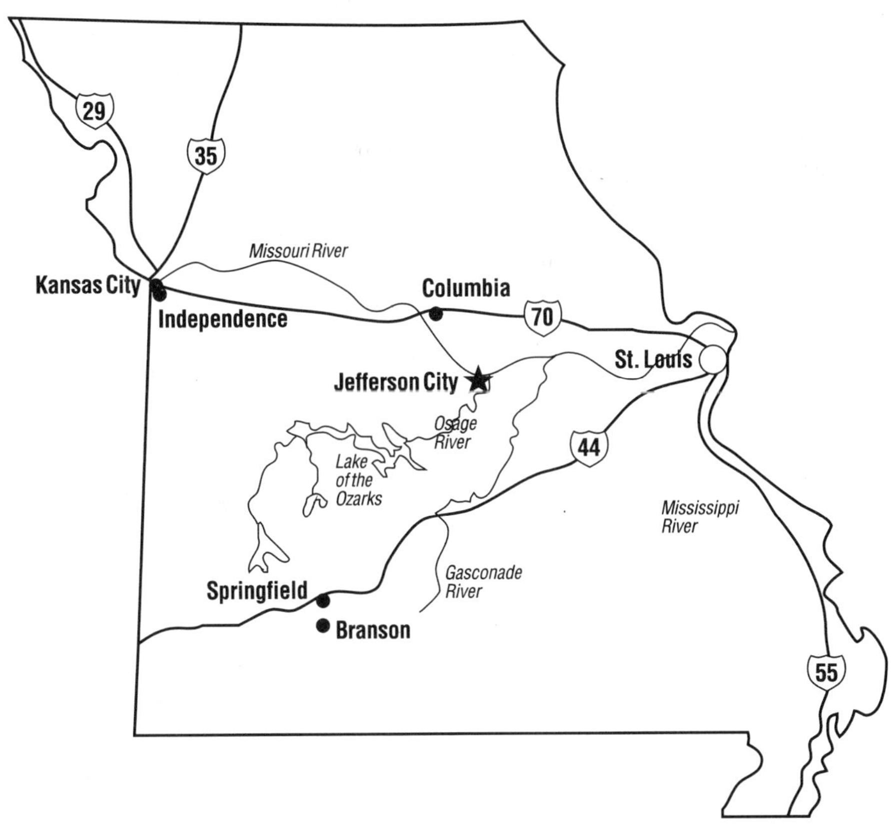

— State Information Sources —

					Phone	Fax
Missouri Chamber of Commerce						
PO Box 149	Jefferson City	MO	65102		573-634-3511	634-8855
Web: www.computerland.net/~mchamber/ ■ *E-mail:* mchamber@computerland.net						
Missouri Economic Development Dept						
PO Box 1157	Jefferson City	MO	65102		573-751-3946	751-7258
TF: 800-523-1435 ■ *Web:* www.ecodev.state.mo.us/ded ■ *E-mail:* ecodev@mail.state.mo.us						
Missouri State Government Information					573-751-2000	
Web: www.state.mo.us/ ■ *E-mail:* stategov@mail.state.mo.us						
Missouri State Library PO Box 387	Jefferson City	MO	65102		573-751-3615	526-1142
Web: mosl.sos.state.mo.us/lib-ser/libser.html						
Missouri State Parks Div PO Box 176	Jefferson City	MO	65102		573-751-2479	751-8656
TF: 800-334-6946 ■ *Web:* www.dnr.state.mo.us/parks.htm						
Missouri Tourism Div PO Box 1055	Jefferson City	MO	65102		573-751-4133	751-5160
TF: 800-877-1234 ■ *Web:* www.missouritourism.org ■ *E-mail:* tourism@mail.state.mo.us						

ON-LINE RESOURCES

Guide2Missouri guide2america.com/missouri
Missouri @ Travel Notes . . . . . www.travelnotes.org/NorthAmerica/missouri.htm
Missouri Cities . . . . . dir.yahoo.com/Regional/U_S__States/Missouri/Cities
Missouri Counties & Regions . . . . . dir.yahoo.com/Regional/U_S__States/Missouri/Counties_and_Regions
Missouri Scenario . . . . . scenariousa.dstylus.com/mo/indexf.htm
Missouri Travel & Tourism Guide . . . . . www.travel-library.com/north_america/usa/missouri/index.html
Missouri USA . . . . . www.missouriusa.com
Photohaven Missouri . . . . . members.aol.com/photohaven/missouri.htm
Rough Guide Travel Missouri travel.roughguides.com/content/968/index.htm
Show Me Missouri . . . . . www.show-me-missouri.com
Travel.org-Missouri . . . . . travel.org/missouri.html
Truman Lake Directory . . . . . www.trumanlake.com
Wine Country of Missouri . . . . . www.wine-mo.com
Yahoo! Get Local Missouri . . . . . dir.yahoo.com/Regional/U_S__States/Missouri

— Cities Profiled —

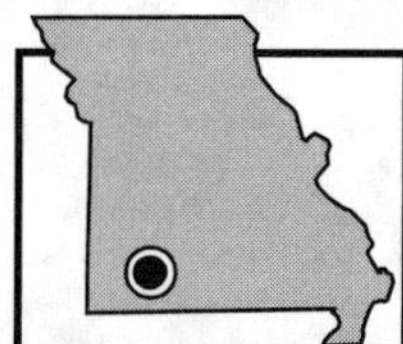

Branson

The Branson/Lakes area is located in the heart of the Ozark Mountains, only 35 minutes from Springfield, Missouri. The city of Branson was founded in 1881, and the downtown area has more than 20 historic sites dating back to the early 1900s. Two such buildings include the old Branson Hotel and the Main Street Railroad Depot. Known for country music, the city has more than three dozen venues for musical performances, comedy acts, and magic shows. The Baldknobbers Jamboree, founded in 1959, is the original Branson music show, and the Presleys' Country Jubilee has been performed there since 1967. The completion of Table Rock Dam in 1958 created Table Rock Lake, which, along with Lake Tanycomo and Bull Shoals Lake, offers the opportunity for boating, year-round fishing, and other water sports. Known as "The Smithsonian of the Ozarks", the Ralph Foster Museum contains more than 750,000 objects celebrating the history of the Ozarks, including weapons, stuffed animals, and the original Beverly Hillbillies' car. Other area attractions include the Shepherd of the Hills Homestead, where native actors perform America's longest running outdoor drama based on Harold Bell Wright's novel "The Shepherd of the Hills," and Silver Dollar City, an 1890s theme park with rides, entertainment, and local artisans & crafters.

Population 4,991
Area (Land) . . . . 10.6 sq mi
Area (Water) . . . . 3.5 sq mi
Elevation . . . . 722 ft
Latitude . . . . 36-38-37 N
Longitude . . . . 93-13-06 W
County . . . . Taney
Time Zone . . . . CST
Area Code/s 417

— Average Temperatures and Precipitation —

TEMPERATURES

	Jan	Feb	Mar	Apr	May	Jun	Jul	Aug	Sep	Oct	Nov	Dec
High	43	48	58	69	77	84	90	88	81	71	58	47
Low	19	23	32	42	52	60	65	63	56	43	33	24

PRECIPITATION

	Jan	Feb	Mar	Apr	May	Jun	Jul	Aug	Sep	Oct	Nov	Dec
Inches	2.3	3.0	4.6	4.4	4.5	4.3	3.1	3.6	3.9	3.2	4.2	4.0

— Important Phone Numbers —

	Phone
AAA	417-334-3222
Dental Referral	417-882-4117
Emergency	911
Medical Referral	417-887-1017
Time/Temperature	417-866-1010
Weather	417-866-1010

— Information Sources —

Phone *Fax*

Better Business Bureau Serving Southwest Missouri 205 Park Central E Suite 509 . . . . Springfield MO 65806 417-862-4222 869-5544
Web: www.springfield-mo.bbb.org
Branson City Hall 110 West Maddux . . . . Branson MO 65616 417-334-3345 335-4354
Web: www.bransoncourier.com/city/ ■ *E-mail:* cityhall@branson.com
Branson Mayor 110 West Maddux . . . . Branson MO 65616 417-334-3345 334-6095
Branson Planning Dept 110 W Maddux St. . . . . Branson MO 65616 417-337-8568 334-2391
Branson Regional Economic Development Assn
PO Box 2282 . . . . Branson MO 65615 417-334-4149 335-3140
Web: www.branson.com/breda ■ *E-mail:* breda@branson.com
Branson/Lakes Area Chamber of Commerce
PO Box 1897 . . . . Branson MO 65615 417-334-4136 334-4139
TF: 800-214-3661 ■ *E-mail:* chamber@branson.com
Branson/Lakes Area Convention & Visitors Bureau PO Box 1897 . . . . Branson MO 65615 417-334-4080 334-4139
TF: 800-214-3661 ■ *Web:* www.bransoncvb.com
■ *E-mail:* answerdesk@branson.com
Downtown Branson Betterment Assn
120 S Veterans Blvd . . . . Branson MO 65616 417-334-1548 335-3643
TF: 800-322-2786 ■ *Web:* www.branson.com/dbba
■ *E-mail:* dbba@branson.com
Taney County PO Box 156 . . . . Forsyth MO 65653 417-546-7201 546-2519
Taneyhills Library 200 S 4th St . . . . Branson MO 65616 417-334-1418 334-1470

On-Line Resources

Access America Branson . . . . branson.accessamer.com
Access Branson . . . . www.travelnow.com/branson/
Anthill City Guide Branson . . . . www.anthill.com/city.asp?city=bransonozarkpkwy
Best Read Guide Branson . . . . bestreadguide.com/branson
Branson . . . . www.bransonmo.com
Branson Connection . . . . www.bransonconnection.com
Branson Courier . . . . www.bransoncourier.com
Branson Information Network . . . . www.bransoninfo.com
Branson Now . . . . www.bransonnow.com
Branson Trip . . . . branson.tripusa.com
Branson-USA Online . . . . www.branson.com
Branson Webzine . . . . www.bransonwebzine.com
BransonLive . . . . www.bransonlive.com
BransonMissouri.com . . . . www.bransonmissouri.com
Excite.com Branson City Guide . . . . www.excite.com/travel/countries/united_states/missouri/branson
Insiders' Guide to Branson . . . . www.insiders.com/branson/
Sunny Day Guide Branson . . . . www.sunnydayguides.com/br/

— Transportation Services —

AIRPORTS

■ **Springfield-Branson Regional Airport (SGF)** *Phone*

40 miles N of downtown Branson (approx 60 minutes) 417-869-0300
E-mail: flysgf@dialnet.net

Airport Transportation

Phone

A-1 Airport Shuttle $50 fare to downtown Branson 417-335-6001
A-Ok Shuttle $48 fare to downtown Branson 417-334-8687

Commercial Airlines

	Phone
American Eagle	800-433-7300
Atlantic Southeast	800-282-3424
Delta	800-221-1212
Northwest	800-225-2525
TWA	800-221-2000
TWA Express	800-221-2000
United	800-241-6522
United Express	800-241-6522
US Airways Express	800-428-4322

Charter Airlines

	Phone
Pro Flight Air	800-743-9698
Springfield Aircraft Charter	800-944-5555

CAR RENTALS

	Phone
Avis	417-865-6226
Budget	417-831-2662
Dollar	417-862-6090
Enterprise	417-338-2280
Hertz	417-865-1681
National	417-865-5311
Thrifty	417-866-8777

LIMO/TAXI

	Phone
Branson City Cab	417-334-5678
Fisk Limousines	417-862-2900
Maxi Taxi	417-336-2996
Noble Limousine Service	417-334-5466
Yellow Cab	417-862-5511

Branson (Cont'd)

— Accommodations —

HOTEL RESERVATION SERVICES

Phone | Fax

Branson Nights Reservations 417-335-6971 335-6025
TF: 800-329-9999 ■ *Web:* www.branson-nights.com

Branson Vacation Reservations 417-335-8747 335-2254
TF: 800-221-5692 ■ *Web:* www.bransonvacation.com
■ *E-mail:* cindibarr@aol.com

Branson's Best Reservations 417-339-2204 339-4051
TF: 800-800-2019 ■ *Web:* www.bransonbest.com
■ *E-mail:* info@bransonbest.com

Branson/Lakes Area Lodging Assn 417-332-1400 239-1400
TF: 888-238-6782

Show Me Hospitality B&B Reservations 417-335-4063 336-6772
TF: 800-348-5210

HOTELS, MOTELS, RESORTS

Phone | Fax

Best Western Branson Inn 448 Hwy 248 Branson MO 65616 417-334-5121 334-6039
TF: 800-334-5121

Best Western Knight's Inn 3215 W Hwy 76 Branson MO 65616 417-334-1894 334-3437
TF: 800-528-1234

Best Western Music Capital Inn
3257 Shepherd of the Hills Expy Branson MO 65616 417-334-8378 334-8855
TF: 800-528-1234

Best Western Rustic Oak Motor Inn
403 W Main St Branson MO 65616 417-334-6464 334-6470
TF: 800-828-0404

Blue Haven Resort 1851 Lake Shore Dr Branson MO 65616 417-334-3917 334-9103

Cascades Inn
3226 Shepherd of the Hills Expy Branson MO 65616 417-335-8424 334-1927
TF: 800-588-8424

Classic Motor Inn
2384 Shepherd of the Hills Expy Branson MO 65616 417-334-6991 336-4468
TF: 800-334-6991

Cobblestone Inn 275 Tanger Blvd Branson MO 65616 417-336-2152 339-3178
TF: 800-641-5660

Comfort Inn 203 S Wildwood Dr Branson MO 65616 417-335-4727 335-4748
TF: 800-228-5150

Country Hearth Inn 1360 W Hwy 76 Branson MO 65616 417-334-0040 336-3618
TF: 800-324-8745

Days Inn 3524 Keeter St Branson MO 65616 417-334-5544 334-2935
TF: 800-325-2525

Dogwood Inn 1420 W Hwy 76 Branson MO 65616 417-334-5101 334-0789
TF: 888-334-3649

Eagles Inn 3221 Shepherd of the Hills Expy Branson MO 65616 417-336-2666 334-7358
TF: 800-728-2664

Econo Lodge 230 S Wildwood Dr Branson MO 65616 417-336-4849 336-4862
TF: 800-553-2666

Fairfield Inn 220 State Hwy 165 Branson MO 65616 417-336-5665 336-5665
TF: 800-228-2800 ■ *Web:* fairfieldinn.com/SGFBN

Family Inn 208 Old County Rd Branson MO 65616 417-334-2113
TF: 800-798-2113

Grand Country Inn 1945 W Hwy 76 Branson MO 65616 417-335-3535 336-6286
TF: 800-828-9068

Grand Oaks Hotel 2315 Green Mountain Dr Branson MO 65616 417-336-6423 334-6264
TF: 800-553-6423

Grand Ramada Branson 245 N Wildwood Dr Branson MO 65616 417-336-6646 337-5535
TF: 800-850-6646

Hampton Inn Central
2350 Green Mountain Dr Branson MO 65616 417-334-6500 334-6506
TF: 800-443-6504

Howard Johnson 3027 W Hwy 76 Branson MO 65616 417-336-5151 337-7007
TF: 800-446-4656

Indian Point Lodge Indian Point Rd Branson MO 65616 417-338-2250 338-3507
Web: www.indianpoint.com

Lilleys' Landing Resort 367 River Ln Branson MO 65616 417-334-6380 334-6311
TF: 888-545-5397

Lodge of the Ozarks 3431 W Hwy 76 Branson MO 65616 417-334-7535 334-6861
TF: 800-213-2584 ■ *Web:* www.bransonlodging.net
■ *E-mail:* lodge@gte.net

Motel 9 210 N Gretna Rd Branson MO 65616 417-334-4836 335-5406
TF: 800-304-4881

Ozark Valley Inn
2693 Shephard of the Hills Expy Branson MO 65616 417-336-4666 336-4750
TF: 800-947-4666

Plantation Inn 3470 Keeter St Branson MO 65616 417-334-3600 334-8166
TF: 800-324-8748

Quality Inn 3269 Shepherd of the Hills Expy Branson MO 65616 417-335-6776 335-6762
TF: 800-245-3308

Quality Inn & Suites 2834 W Hwy 76 Branson MO 65616 417-334-1194 334-6670
TF: 800-826-0368

Ramada Limited
2316 Shepherd of the Hills Expy Branson MO 65616 417-337-5207 335-4258
TF: 800-856-0730

Residence Inn 280 S Wildwood Dr Branson MO 65616 417-336-4077 336-5837
TF: 800-331-3131 ■ *Web:* www.residenceinn.com/residenceinn/SGFBR

Settle Inn Resort & Conference Center
3050 Green Mountain Dr Branson MO 65616 417-335-4700 335-3906
TF: 800-677-6906 ■ *Web:* www.bransonsettleinn.com

Shady Lane Resort 404 N Sycamore St Branson MO 65616 417-334-3823
TF: 800-282-8099 ■ *Web:* www.branson.com/shadylane
■ *E-mail:* shadylane@branson.com

Sunterra Plantation at Fall Creek Resort
1-A Fall Creek Dr Branson MO 65616 417-334-6404 336-1218
TF: 800-562-6636

Super 8 Motel Hwy 76 & Hwy 13 Branson MO 65737 417-272-8195 272-8271
TF: 800-343-2769

Taneycomo Resort 365 Velencia Ave Branson MO 65616 417-334-7375
TF: 800-949-9975

Tara Inn 245 Shepherd of the Hills Expy Branson MO 65616 417-334-8272 335-3029
TF: 800-525-8272

Thousand Hills Golf Resort
245 S Wildwood Dr Branson MO 65616 417-336-5873 337-5740
TF: 800-864-4145 ■ *Web:* www.thousandhills.com

Travelodge 1415 W Hwy 76 Branson MO 65616 417-334-8300 337-5749
TF: 800-732-6664

Welk Resort Center 1984 State Hwy 165 Branson MO 65616 417-336-3575 337-3470
TF: 800-505-9355 ■ *Web:* www.welkresort.com
■ *E-mail:* welkresv@aol.com

Woods Resort 2201 Roark Valley Rd Branson MO 65616 417-334-2324 334-0834
TF: 800-935-2345
■ *Web:* bransonnow.com/lodging/woodsresort/index.html
■ *E-mail:* Woods65616@aol.com

— Restaurants —

Phone

Aunt Mollies Restaurant (Homestyle) 5586 W Hwy 76 Branson MO 65616 417-334-4191

Beijing Chinese Restaurant (Chinese)
118 N Commercial St Branson MO 65616 417-335-8609

Beverly's Steakhouse & Saloon (Steak) 225 Violyn Dr Branson MO 65616 417-334-6508

Branson Cafe (Homestyle) 120 W Main St Branson MO 65616 417-334-3021

Candlestick Inn (Continental) 127 Taney St Branson MO 65616 417-334-3633

Casa Fuentes (Mexican) 1107 W Hwy 76 Branson MO 65616 417-339-3888

China Garden (Chinese) 448 State Hwy 248 Branson MO 65616 417-339-4311

Dimitri's Restaurant (Greek) 500 E Main St Branson MO 65616 417-334-0888

Downtown Restaurant (American) 103 S Commercial St Branson MO 65616 417-334-4444

Farmhouse Restaurant (American) 119 W Main St Branson MO 65616 417-334-9701

Gilley's Texas Cafe (Tex Mex) 3457 W State Hwy 76 Branson MO 65616 417-335-2755

Green Mountain Cafe (American) 3524 Keeter St Branson MO 65616 417-339-2219

Happy Days (American) 20602 W Hwy 76 Branson MO 65616 417-334-6410

Indian Point Floating Cafe (American) Indian Point Rd Indian Point MO 65616 417-338-2101

Lotus Valley (Chinese) 3129 W Hwy 76 Branson MO 65616 417-334-3427

Lowe's Fall Creek Steak House (Steak)
977 State Hwy 165 Branson MO 65616 417-336-5060

Mesquite Charlie's Steaks (Steak) 2849 Gretna Rd Branson MO 65616 417-334-0498

Noodles Pizza & Pub (Italian) 1000 Pat Nash Dr Branson MO 65616 417-335-3040

Pasta Grill (Italian) 2690 Green Mountain Dr Branson MO 65616 417-337-9882

Pepper Bellies (Mexican) 305 E Main St Branson MO 65616 417-339-4096

Planet Branson (American) 440 Hwy 248 Branson MO 65616 417-332-2234

Plantation Restaurant (American) 3460 W State Hwy 76 Branson MO 65616 417-334-7800

Pzazz (American) 158 Pointe Royale Dr Branson MO 65616 417-335-2798

Raftors Restaurant (American) 3431 W State Hwy 76 Branson MO 65616 417-334-7535

Rocky's Italian Restaurant (Italian) 120 N Sycamore St Branson MO 65616 417-335-4765

Sadies Sideboard Restaurant (Southern) 2830 W Hwy 76 Branson MO 65616 417-334-3619

Uncle Joe's Bar-b-q (Barbecue) 2819 W State Hwy 76 Branson MO 65616 417-334-4548

Whipper Snapper's (American)
236 Shepherd of the Hills Expy Branson MO 65616 417-334-3282

— Goods and Services —

SHOPPING

Phone | Fax

76 Mall Shops 1945 W 76 Country Blvd Branson MO 65616 417-335-3535

Branson Mall 2206 W Hwy 76 Branson MO 65616 417-334-5412 337-5489

Carolina Mills Factory Outlet
3615 W Hwy 76 Branson MO 65616 417-334-2291

Factory Merchants Branson
1000 Pat Nash Dr Branson MO 65616 417-335-6686 335-4595

Branson — Shopping (Cont'd)

Name / Address	City	State	Zip	Phone	Fax
Grand Country Square					
1945 W 76 Country Blvd	Branson	MO	65616	417-334-3919	334-1647
Grand Village The					
2800 W 76 Country Music Blvd	Branson	MO	65616	417-336-7280	336-7293
TF: 800-952-6626 ■ *Web:* www.gvshops.com					
Historic Downtown Branson					
120 S Veterans Blvd	Branson	MO	65615	417-334-1548	335-3643
Web: www.branson.com/dbba ■ *E-mail:* dbba@branson.com					
Shoppes of Branson Meadows					
4562 Gretna Rd	Branson	MO	65616	417-339-2580	336-3275
Tanger Factory Outlet Center					
300 Tanger Blvd	Branson	MO	65616	417-337-9328	337-9331
TF: 800-407-2762 ■ *Web:* www.tangeroutlets.com					
Village Shopping Mall					
3044 Shepherd of the Hills Expy	Branson	MO	65616	417-334-6625	334-5866

BANKS

Name / Address	City	State	Zip	Phone	Fax
Commerce Bank NA 2210 W Hwy 76	Branson	MO	65616	417-335-5684	335-5730
TF: 800-746-8704					
First Community Bank of Taney County					
121 S Commercial St	Branson	MO	65616	417-336-6310	336-5637
Great Southern Bank FSB 1729 W Hwy 76	Branson	MO	65616	417-334-6424	334-8094
Mercantile Bank of South Central Missouri					
520 W Main St	Branson	MO	65616	417-335-2122	335-2570
NationsBank 510 N Business Hwy 65	Branson	MO	65616	417-336-6363	336-6368
Ozark Mountain Bank 400 S Commercial St	Branson	MO	65616	417-334-4125	334-5428*
**Fax:* Mktg					
Union Planters Bank NA					
203 N Commercial St	Branson	MO	65616	417-334-2191	334-0356

BUSINESS SERVICES

Name	Phone	Name	Phone
Airborne Express	800-247-2676	**Mail Boxes Etc**	417-336-5776
Copy Run	417-334-6611	**Manpower Temporary Services**	417-334-1727
Creative Printing	417-337-5450	**Ozark Postal Express**	417-335-4306
DHL Worldwide Express	800-225-5345	**Post Office**	417-334-3366
Express Personnel Services	417-339-2464	**Professional Services**	417-334-0094
Express Printing	417-334-1953	**Sir Speedy Printing**	417-339-2397
Federal Express	800-463-3339	**UPS**	800-742-5877

— Media —

PUBLICATIONS

Name / Address	City	State	Zip	Phone	Fax
Branson Tri-Lakes Daily News‡					
PO Box 1900	Branson	MO	65615	417-334-3161	335-3933
Springfield News Leader‡ PO Box 798	Springfield	MO	65801	417-836-1100	837-1381
TF Circ: 800-695-2005 ■ *Web:* www.ozarksgateway.com/nl.htm					

‡Daily newspapers

TELEVISION

Name / Address	City	State	Zip	Phone	Fax
KDEB-TV Ch 27 (Fox) 3000 E Cherry St	Springfield	MO	65802	417-862-2727	831-4209
Web: www.fox27.com					
KOJQ-TV Ch 5 (UPN) 118 State Dr	Hollister	MO	65672	417-336-5545	336-6431
KOLR-TV Ch 10 (CBS) 2650 E Division St	Springfield	MO	65803	417-862-1010	862-6439
Web: www.kolr10.com					
KOZK-TV Ch 21 (PBS) 821 Washington Ave	Springfield	MO	65802	417-865-2100	863-1599
KSPR-TV Ch 33 (ABC) 1359 Saint Louis St	Springfield	MO	65802	417-831-1333	831-4125
Web: www.kspr33.com ■ *E-mail:* admin@kspr33.com					
KYTV-TV Ch 3 (NBC) PO Box 3500	Springfield	MO	65808	417-268-3000	268-3100
Web: www.ky3.com ■ *E-mail:* ky3news@ky3.com					

RADIO

Name / Address	City	State	Zip	Phone	Fax
KBCN-FM 104.3 MHz (Ctry) 100 Fall Creek Dr	Branson	MO	65616	417-335-2261	335-2377
KGBX-FM 105.9 MHz (AC)					
1856 S Glenstone Ave	Springfield	MO	65804	417-890-5555	890-5050
Web: www.kgbx.com					
KHOZ-FM 102.9 MHz (Ctry)					
2527 Hwy 248 Mel Tillis Theater	Branson	MO	65616	417-334-6750	334-6756
TF: 800-553-6103 ■ *Web:* khoz.com					
KLFC-FM 88.1 MHz (Rel) 205 W Atlantic St	Branson	MO	65616	417-334-5532	335-2437
KOMC-AM 1220 kHz (Nost) 202 Courtney St	Branson	MO	65616	417-334-6003	334-7141
KOMC-FM 100.1 MHz (Nost) 202 Courtney St	Branson	MO	65616	417-334-6003	334-7141
KRZK-FM 106.3 MHz (Ctry) 202 Courtney St	Branson	MO	65616	417-334-6003	334-7141
KTXR-FM 101.3 MHz (B/EZ)					
3000 E Chestnut Expy	Springfield	MO	65802	417-862-3751	869-7675
Web: www.ktxrfm.com ■ *E-mail:* ktxrfm@ktxrfm.com					

— Colleges/Universities —

Name / Address	City	State	Zip	Phone	Fax
Branson Performing Arts Academy					
PO Box 1264	Branson	MO	65615	417-336-2223	335-8850
College of the Ozarks	Point Lookout	MO	65726	417-334-6411	335-2618
TF: 800-222-0525 ■ *Web:* www.cofo.edu					

— Hospitals —

Name / Address	City	State	Zip	Phone	Fax
Branson West Medical Care Hwy 13	Branson	MO	65737	417-272-8911	272-3900
Skaggs Community Health Center					
PO Box 650	Branson	MO	65615	417-335-7000	334-1505
Web: www.skaggs.net					

— Attractions —

Name / Address	City	State	Zip	Phone	Fax
76 Music Hall					
1945 W 76 Country Music Blvd	Branson	MO	65616	417-335-2484	334-1647
Baldknobbers Jamboree 2835 W Hwy 76	Branson	MO	65616	417-334-4528	334-4526
Web: www.baldknobbers.com					
Bonniebrook Park 485 Rose O'Neill Dr	Walnut Shade	MO	65771	417-336-3230	561-2220
TF: 800-539-7437 ■ *Web:* www.bonniebrookpark.com					
BoxCar Willie Theatre & Museum					
3454 W Hwy 76	Branson	MO	65616	417-334-8696	337-5539
TF: 800-942-4626					
Branson Mall Music Theatre					
2206 W Hwy 76	Branson	MO	65616	417-335-5300	337-5489
Branson Scenic Railway 206 E Main St.	Branson	MO	65616	417-334-6110	336-3909
TF: 800-287-2462					
Cadwell Classic Car Museum Hwy 248	Branson	MO	65616	417-336-2277	
Champagne Theatre					
1984 Hwy 165 Welk Resort Ctr	Branson	MO	65616	800-505-9355	
Web: branson.welkresort.com/welkshow					
Cool Off Water Chutes 2115 W Hwy 76	Branson	MO	65616	417-334-1919	
Cosmic Cavern 6386 Hwy 21 N	Berryville	AR	72616	870-749-2298	
Country Tonite Theatre 4080 W Hwy 76	Branson	MO	65616	417-334-2422	334-2466
TF: 800-468-6648 ■ *Web:* www.countrytonite.com					
Dixie Stampede Dinner Attraction					
1525 W Hwy 76	Branson	MO	65616	417-336-3000	339-4360
TF: 800-520-5544					
■ *Web:* www.branson.com/branson/dixie/default.html					
Fairchild Barbara Show					
3044 Shepherd of the Hills Exwy	Branson	MO	65616	417-334-6400	335-4053
Web: www.barbarafairchild.com					
Foster Ralph Museum					
College of the Ozarks	Point Lookout	MO	65726	417-334-6411	
Grand Palace The					
2700 W 76 Country Music Blvd	Branson	MO	65616	417-336-1220	337-5170
TF: 800-884-4536					
Historic Downtown Branson					
120 S Veterans Blvd	Branson	MO	65615	417-334-1548	335-3643
Web: www.branson.com/dbba ■ *E-mail:* dbba@branson.com					
Historic Walking Tours					
110 S Commercial St Downtown Branson	Branson	MO	65616	417-334-1548	
Hollywood Wax Museum 3030 W Hwy 76	Branson	MO	65616	417-337-8277	334-8202
TF: 800-720-4110					
Jennifer's Americana Theatre					
2905 W Hwy 76	Branson	MO	65616	417-335-8176	335-8105
Web: www.jennifer.com					
Lane Sammy Pirate Cruise 280 N Lake Dr	Branson	MO	65616	417-334-3015	335-3014
Military Museum of the Ozarks					
2320 W Hwy 76	Branson	MO	65616	417-335-5337	334-5382

Branson — Attractions (Cont'd)

				Phone	Fax
Newton Wayne Theatre 464 State Hwy 248	Branson	MO	65616	417-335-2000	335-2773
Osmond Family Theater 3216 W Hwy 76	Branson	MO	65616	417-336-6100	336-6110
Ozarks Discovery IMAX Theater 3562 Shepherd of the Hills Expy	Branson	MO	65616	417-335-3533	336-5348
TF: 800-419-4832 ■ *Web:* members.aol.com/OzarksIMAX/index1.html					
Polynesian Princess 1358 Long Creek Rd	Branson	MO	65739	417-337-8366	339-2941
TF: 800-653-6288 ■ *Web:* www.branson.com/branson/princess/princess.htm					
Positive Country Theater 3069 Shepherd of the Hills Expy	Branson	MO	65615	417-334-7272	334-1975
TF: 800-811-6555					
Presleys' Country Jubilee 2920 W Hwy 76	Branson	MO	65616	417-334-4874	334-5779
Web: www.presleys.com					
Promise The 755 Gretna Rd	Branson	MO	65616	417-336-4202	335-8317
Web: www.thepromise.com					
Remington Theatre 3701 W Hwy 76	Branson	MO	65616	417-336-6220	336-6226
TF: 888-371-3701 ■ *Web:* www.remingtontheatre.com ■ *E-mail:* cast@remingtontheatre.com					
Ride The Ducks 2320 W Hwy 76	Branson	MO	65616	417-334-3825	334-5382
Ripley's Believe It or Not! Museum 3326 W Hwy 76	Branson	MO	65616	417-337-5300	337-5229
TF: 800-998-4418					
Shepherd of the Hills Fish Hatchery 483 Hatchery Rd	Branson	MO	65616	417-334-4865	334-4996
Shepherd of the Hills Outdoor Theatre 5586 W Hwy 76	Branson	MO	65616	417-334-4191	334-4617
TF: 800-653-6288 ■ *Web:* www.branson.com/branson/shepherd/shepherd.htm					
Showboat Branson Belle 4800 State Hwy 165	Branson	MO	65616	417-336-7171	336-7410
TF: 800-227-8587 ■ *Web:* www.silverdollarcity.com/showboat ■ *E-mail:* tickets@silverdollarcity.com					
Stafford Jim Theatre 3440 Hwy 76	Branson	MO	65616	417-335-8080	335-2482
Web: www.jimstafford.com					
Stone Hill Winery 601 State Hwy 165	Branson	MO	65616	417-334-1897	334-1942
Table Rock State Park 5272 State Hwy 165	Branson	MO	65616	417-334-4704	334-4782
Tillis Mel Theater 2527 Hwy 248	Branson	MO	65616	417-335-6635	335-3735
Web: www.meltillis.com/theater					
White Water 3505 W Hwy 76	Branson	MO	65616	417-334-7488	334-7421
Williams Andy Moon River Theatre 2500 W Hwy 76	Branson	MO	65616	417-334-4500	334-3200
TF: 800-666-6094					

— Events —

	Phone
Adoration Parade & Lighting Ceremony (early December)	417-334-4136
Autumn Daze Craft Festival (mid-September)	417-334-1548
Band Choral & Orchestra Festival (late April-early May)	417-335-3554
Branson Area Festival of Lights (early November-late December)	417-334-4136
Branson Fest (late March)	417-334-4136
Buddy Bass Tournament (mid-February)	417-546-2741
Candlelight Christmas Open House (early December)	417-334-1548
Central Pro-Am Bass Tournament (early November)	417-881-2158
Christian Family Week (mid-June)	417-334-4191
Crusin' Branson Lights Automobile Festival (mid-August)	417-334-4136
Fall Harvest Festival (early September-late October)	417-334-4191
Farm Family Week (August)	417-334-4084
Great American Music Festival (mid-May-early June)	800-952-6626
Harvest Moon Festival (early October)	417-546-2741
Independence Day Celebration & Fireworks Display (July 4)	417-334-3050
Lawrence Welk Polka Fest (early June)	800-505-9355
National Children's Festival (mid-June-late August)	800-952-6626
National Church Choir Festival (late April)	417-335-3554
National Festival of Craftsmen (early September-late October)	800-952-6626
Old Time Country Christmas (early November-late December)	800-952-6626
Old Time Fiddle Contest (mid-August)	417-334-1548
Ozark Mountain Christmas (November-late December)	800-214-3661
Ozark Mountain Country Fall Foliage Drive (late September-early November)	800-519-1600
Plumb Nellie Festival & Craft Show (late May)	417-334-1548
Spirit of '76 Independence Day Celebration (early July)	417-337-8387
State of the Ozarks Fiddlers Convention (mid-September)	417-338-2911
Taney County Fair (mid-late July)	417-546-2741
Veterans Homecoming (early-mid-November)	417-334-4136
White Bass Round Up (mid-March)	417-546-2741
White River Valley Arts & Crafts Fair (early August)	417-546-2741
World-Fest (mid-April-mid-May)	800-952-6626

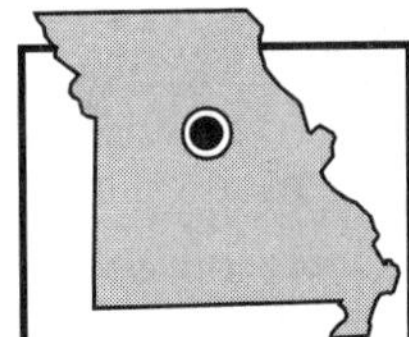

Columbia

Three major colleges are located in Columbia (Stephens College, Columbia College, and the University of Missouri) and the city has been called one of America's great college towns. Stephens College, founded in 1833, is the second oldest women's college in the United States. Columbia College was founded in 1851 as Christian Female and was the first women's college chartered by a state legislature west of the Mississippi River. In 1970 the college changed its name to Columbia College and became a private co-educational institution. The University of Missouri-Columbia, founded in 1839, is the state's flagship university and represents the birth of public higher education west of the Mississippi River. The three college campuses border Downtown Columbia, which has unique restaurants, specialty shops, museums, and galleries. A popular attraction in Columbia is the historic Katy Trail. Originally the Missouri Kansas Texas Railroad, built in the 1890s, it ran between Sedalia and Saint Charles, MO. In 1986, it stopped running and was converted into the Katy Trail State Park, one of the longest rails-to-trails conversions in the U.S.

Population	78,915	**Longitude**	92-13-10 W
Area (Land)	44.3 sq mi	**County**	Boone
Area (Water)	0.2 sq mi	**Time Zone**	CST
Elevation	889 ft	**Area Code/s**	573
Latitude	38-49-05 N		

— Average Temperatures and Precipitation —

TEMPERATURES

	Jan	Feb	Mar	Apr	May	Jun	Jul	Aug	Sep	Oct	Nov	Dec
High	37	41	53	66	74	83	89	87	79	68	54	40
Low	19	23	33	44	53	61	66	64	57	46	35	23

PRECIPITATION

	Jan	Feb	Mar	Apr	May	Jun	Jul	Aug	Sep	Oct	Nov	Dec
Inches	1.5	1.8	3.2	3.8	5.0	4.3	3.7	3.3	3.9	3.2	2.9	2.5

— Important Phone Numbers —

	Phone		Phone
AAA	573-874-1909	**Poison Control Center**	800-366-8888
Columbia Community Line	573-874-7650	**Road Conditions**	573-526-8828
Emergency	911	**Time/Temp**	573-449-0655
Entertainment & Activities Hotline	573-443-2222	**Weather**	573-442-5171
Medical Referral	573-875-9400		

— Information Sources —

				Phone	Fax
Better Business Bureau Serving Eastern Missouri & Southern Illinois 12 Sunnen Dr Suite 121	Saint Louis	MO	63143	314-645-3300	645-2666
Web: www.stlouis.bbb.org					
Boone County 801 E Walnut St	Columbia	MO	65201	573-886-4295	886-4300
Web: boone.county.missouri.org/ ■ *E-mail:* stephdp@ccmail.mo-boone.org					
Columbia Chamber of Commerce PO Box 1016	Columbia	MO	65205	573-874-1132	443-3986
Web: chamber.columbia.mo.us					
Columbia City Hall 701 E Broadway	Columbia	MO	65201	573-874-7111	442-8828
Web: www.ci.columbia.mo.us					
Columbia Convention & Visitors Bureau 300 S Providence Rd	Columbia	MO	65203	573-875-1231	443-3986
Web: www.ammultimedia.com/visitcolumbiamo.com/ ■ *E-mail:* cvb@socket.net					

Columbia — Information Sources (Cont'd)

				Phone	Fax
Columbia Economic Development 300 S Providence Rd.	Columbia	MO	65203	573-442-8303	443-3986
Columbia Expo Center 2200 I-70 Dr SW	Columbia	MO	65203	573-446-3976	446-1159
Columbia Mayor 701 E Broadway City Hall *E-mail:* mayor@ci.columbia.mo.us	Columbia	MO	65201	573-874-7222	874-7359
Daniel Boone Regional Library 100 W Broadway *Web:* www.dbrl.library.missouri.org ■ *E-mail:* dbrlpr@mail.coin.missouri.edu	Columbia	MO	65203	573-443-3161	443-3281
Hearnes Center 600 Stadium Blvd	Columbia	MO	65211	573-882-2056	882-4298

On-Line Resources

Anthill City Guide Columbia . . . www.anthill.com/city.asp?city=columbiamo
Area Guide Columbia . . . columbiamo.areaguides.net
Columbia Community Network . . . www.columbiamo.com
Columbia Online Information Network . . . www.coin.missouri.edu
Digital Missourian . . . digmo.com/community
Excite.com Columbia City Guide . . . www.excite.com/travel/countries/united_states/missouri/columbia
NITC Travelbase City Guide Columbia . . . www.travelbase.com/auto/features/columbia-mo.html
Online Columbia . . . www.onlinecolumbia.com

— Transportation Services —

AIRPORTS

■ Columbia Regional Airport (COU)

	Phone
12 miles S of downtown (approx 15 minutes)	573-442-9770

Airport Transportation

	Phone
Columbia Regional Airport Shuttle $17 fare to downtown	573-874-4048
Smart Taxi $12-15 fare to downtown	573-449-4961

Commercial Airlines

	Phone
TWA	800-221-2000

Charter Airlines

	Phone
Central Missouri Aviation	573-443-1576

CAR RENTALS

	Phone		Phone
Enterprise	573-442-0555	**National**	573-443-4611
Hertz	573-449-0077		

LIMO/TAXI

	Phone		Phone
Smart Taxi	573-449-4961	**White Knight Limousine**	573-875-2936

MASS TRANSIT

	Phone
Columbia Area Transit System $.50 Base fare	573-874-7282

RAIL/BUS

				Phone
Greyhound Bus Station 200 Business Loop 70 W *TF:* 800-231-2222	Columbia	MO	65201	573-449-2416

— Accommodations —

HOTELS, MOTELS, RESORTS

				Phone	Fax
Arrow Head Motel 1411 Business Loop 70 E	Columbia	MO	65201	573-442-1141	256-1901
Best Value 1718 N Providence Rd	Columbia	MO	65202	573-442-9390	875-5477
Best Western Columbia Inn 3100 I-70 Dr SE *TF:* 800-362-3185	Columbia	MO	65203	573-474-6161	474-9323
Campus Inn 1112 E Stadium Blvd	Columbia	MO	65201	573-449-2731	449-6691
Columbia Centre Ramada Inn 1100 Vandiver Dr *TF:* 800-228-2828	Columbia	MO	65202	573-449-0051	874-8963
Comfort Inn 901 Conley Rd *TF:* 800-228-5150	Columbia	MO	65201	573-443-4141	443-4049
Crossroads West Shopping Center 2101 W Broadway *TF:* 800-487-8606	Columbia	MO	65203	573-445-8606	446-2489
Days Inn Conference Center 1900 I-70 Dr SW *TF:* 800-329-7466	Columbia	MO	65203	573-445-8511	445-7991
Deluxe Inn 2112 Business Loop 70 E	Columbia	MO	65201	573-449-3771	449-3771
Drury Inns 1000 Knipp St. *TF:* 800-325-8300	Columbia	MO	65203	573-445-1800	445-1800
Eastwood Motel 2518 Business Loop 70 E. *TF:* 800-274-3278	Columbia	MO	65201	573-443-8793	443-7722
Econo Lodge 900 I-70 Dr SW. *TF:* 800-553-2666	Columbia	MO	65203	573-442-1191	449-2633
Fairfield Inn by Marriott 2904 Clark Ln *TF:* 877-814-2727	Columbia	MO	65202	573-814-2727	814-2828
Holiday Inn East 1612 N Providence Rd	Columbia	MO	65202	573-449-2491	874-6720
Holiday Inn Select Executive Center 2200 I-70 Dr SW *TF:* 800-465-4329	Columbia	MO	65203	573-445-8531	445-7607
Howard Johnson 3402 I-70 Dr SE *TF:* 800-446-4656	Columbia	MO	65201	573-815-0123	815-9772
Ramada Inn 1111 E Broadway *TF:* 800-272-6232	Columbia	MO	65201	573-443-2090	443-2190
Red Roof Inn 201 E Texas Ave *TF:* 800-843-7663	Columbia	MO	65202	573-442-0145	449-9588
Super 8 Motel 3216 Clark Ln *TF:* 800-800-8000	Columbia	MO	65202	573-474-8488	474-4180
Travelodge 900 Vandiver Dr *TF:* 800-456-1065	Columbia	MO	65202	573-449-1065	442-6266

— Restaurants —

				Phone
Alexander's (Steak) 301 N Stadium Blvd	Columbia	MO	65201	573-445-1282
Angelo's (Italian) 4107 S Providence Rd	Columbia	MO	65203	573-443-6100
Atomic Cafe (American) 38 N 8th St	Columbia	MO	65201	573-442-7881
Bangkok Gardens (Thai) 26 N 9th St	Columbia	MO	65201	573-874-3284
Block & Barrell (American) 1612 N Providence Rd Holiday Inn East	Columbia	MO	65202	573-449-2491
Blue Cactus Cafe (Southwest) 3915 S Providence Rd	Columbia	MO	65203	573-443-2583
Boone Tavern & Restaurant (American) 811 E Walnut St	Columbia	MO	65201	573-442-5123
Bren's Place (Homestyle) 300 E Ash St	Columbia	MO	65201	573-442-6685
Bull Pen Cafe (American) 2310 Business Loop 70	Columbia	MO	65201	573-442-8113
Churchill's (Continental) 2200 I-70 Dr SW Holiday Inn Select Executive Ctr	Columbia	MO	65203	573-445-8531
CJ's (American) 704 E Broadway	Columbia	MO	65201	573-442-7777
Country Kitchen (Homestyle) 1712 N Providence Rd	Columbia	MO	65202	573-875-1333
Dino's Steak House (Steak) 1802 Paris Rd	Columbia	MO	65201	573-874-3400
Ernie's Restaurant (Steak) 1005 E Walnut St	Columbia	MO	65201	573-874-7804
Everett's Restaurant & Lounge (Continental) 1601 Rangeline St	Columbia	MO	65201	573-443-6200
Flat Branch Pub & Brewing Co (American) 115 S 5th St *Web:* www.flatbranch.com ■ *E-mail:* tsmith@flatbranch.com	Columbia	MO	65201	573-499-0400
Formosa Restaurant (Chinese) 913 E Broadway Suite A	Columbia	MO	65201	573-449-3339
Forum Smokehouse (American) 1412 Forum Blvd *Web:* www.onlinecolumbia.com/menus/restaurants/smokehouse.html	Columbia	MO	65203	573-446-6424
G&D Steakhouse (Steak) 2001 W Worley St	Columbia	MO	65203	573-445-3504
Garfield's Restaurant & Pub (American) 2300 Bernadette Dr.	Columbia	MO	65203	573-446-5100
George's (Steak) 200 Business Loop 70 E	Columbia	MO	65202	573-449-6006
Glenn's Cafe (American) 29 S 9th St	Columbia	MO	65201	573-443-3094
Harpo's Bar & Grill (American) 29 S 10th St	Columbia	MO	65201	573-443-5418
Heidelberg Restaurant (American) 410 S 9th St	Columbia	MO	65201	573-449-6927
Hong Kong Restaurant (Chinese) 106 Business Loop 70 W	Columbia	MO	65203	573-442-7350
India's Rasoi (Indian) 1101 E Broadway	Columbia	MO	65201	573-817-2009
International Cafe (Greek) 209 Hitt St	Columbia	MO	65201	573-449-4560
Jimmy's Family Steak House (Steak) 3101 S Providence Rd	Columbia	MO	65203	573-443-1796
Le Petit Bouchon (French/Italian) 700 E Broadway	Columbia	MO	65201	573-499-9463
Los Bandidos (Mexican) 220 S 8th St	Columbia	MO	65201	573-443-2419
Osaka (Japanese) 120 E Nifong Blvd Suite A	Columbia	MO	65203	573-875-8588
Ozark Mountain Bar & Grill (American) 2715 Burrwood Dr	Columbia	MO	65203	573-442 0045
T&H Restaurant (American) 609 N Garth Ave	Columbia	MO	65203	573-449-1777
TP's Bar & Grill (American) 119 S 7th St	Columbia	MO	65201	573-449-0132

Columbia — Restaurants (Cont'd)

				Phone
Trattoria Strada Nova (Italian/French) 21 N 9th St	Columbia	MO	65201	573-442-8992
Widman's Bar & Grill (American) 800 E Broadway	Columbia	MO	65201	573-874-1515
Yen Ching (Chinese) 600 Business Loop 70 W	Columbia	MO	65203	573-875-4636

— Goods and Services —

SHOPPING

				Phone	Fax
Columbia Mall 2300 Bernadette	Columbia	MO	65203	573-445-8458	445-0255
Ice Chalet Antique Mall 3411 Old 63 S	Columbia	MO	65202	573-442-6893	449-9434
Itchy's Stop-n-Scratch Flea Market 1907 N Providence Rd	Columbia	MO	65202	573-443-8275	

BANKS

				Phone	Fax
Boone County National Bank 720 E Broadway	Columbia	MO	65201	573-874-8490	874-8432
Commerce Bank NA 3709 Sandman Ln *TF:* 800-292-7977	Columbia	MO	65201	573-886-5250	886-5354
First National Bank & Trust Co 10 N Garth Ave	Columbia	MO	65203	573-499-7365	875-8627
Merchants & Farmers Bank 4000 Rangeline St	Columbia	MO	65202	573-499-0955	499-0647
NationsBank 800 Cherry St	Columbia	MO	65201	573-876-6000	876-6302
Premier Bank 15 S 5th St	Columbia	MO	65201	573-441-1500	
UMB Bank NA 1516 Chapel Hill Rd	Columbia	MO	65203	573-445-4600	
Union Planters Bank 2114 Paris Rd *TF:* 800-761-2265	Columbia	MO	65202	573-446-0662	474-4275

BUSINESS SERVICES

	Phone
Federal Express	800-238-5355
Interim Personnel	573-874-1800
Kelly Services	573-875-0605
Kinko's	573-449-5021
Mail Boxes Etc	573-442-2380
Manpower Temporary Services	573-817-2552
On Time Delivery	573-874-5282
Post Office	573-876-7800
UPS	800-742-5877

— Media —

PUBLICATIONS

				Phone	Fax
Columbia Daily Tribune‡ 101 N 4th St *TF:* 800-333-6799 ■ *Web:* www.trib.net	Columbia	MO	65201	573-449-3811	815-1701
Columbia Missourian‡ 221 S 8th St *Web:* digmo.org ■ *E-mail:* editor@digmo.org	Columbia	MO	65201	573-882-5700	884-5293
Mid-Missouri Business Journal 4250 E Broadway Suite 1043	Columbia	MO	65201	573-443-1311	875-1149

‡*Daily newspapers*

TELEVISION

				Phone	Fax
KMIZ-TV Ch 17 (ABC) 501 Business Loop 70 E *Web:* www.kmiz.com	Columbia	MO	65201	573-449-0917	875-7078
KMOS-TV Ch 6 (PBS) Central Missouri State University *Web:* www.kmos.cmsu.edu/TV	Warrensburg	MO	64093	660-543-4155	543-8863
KNLJ-TV Ch 25 (Ind) 9810 SR-AE	New Bloomfield	MO	65063	573-896-5105	896-4376
KOMU-TV Ch 8 (NBC) 5550 Hwy 63 S *Web:* www.komu.com	Columbia	MO	65201	573-884-6397	884-5353
KRCG-TV Ch 13 (CBS) PO Box 659 *Web:* www.krcg.com ■ *E-mail:* krcg@socketis.net	Jefferson City	MO	65102	573-896-5144	896-5193

RADIO

				Phone	Fax
KBIA-FM 91.3 MHz (NPR) 409 Jesse Hall *Web:* www.kbia.org ■ *E-mail:* kbiaog@showme.missouri.edu	Columbia	MO	65211	573-882-3431	882-2636
KBXR-FM 102.3 MHz (AAA) 503 Old 63 N *Web:* www.bxr.com ■ *E-mail:* bxr@bxr.com	Columbia	MO	65201	573-449-1520	449-7770
KCLR-FM 99.3 MHz (Ctry) 3215 Lemone Industrial Blvd Suite 200	Columbia	MO	65201	573-875-1099	875-2439
KCMQ-FM 96.7 MHz (CR) 3215 Lemone Industrial Blvd Suite 200	Columbia	MO	65201	573-875-1099	875-2439
KFAL-AM 900 kHz (Ctry) 1805 Westminster *TF:* 800-769-5274 ■ *Web:* www.kfal.com ■ *E-mail:* kfal@sockets.net	Fulton	MO	65251	573-642-3341	642-3343
KFMZ-FM 98.3 MHz (Alt) 1101 E Walnut St	Columbia	MO	65201	573-874-3000	443-1460
KFRU-AM 1400 kHz (N/T) 503 Old 63 N *Web:* www.kfru.com ■ *E-mail:* news@kfru.com	Columbia	MO	65201	573-449-4141	449-7770
KLSC-FM 93.9 MHz (AC) 3215 Lemone Industrial Blvd Suite 200	Columbia	MO	65201	573-875-1099	875-2439
KMFC-FM 92.1 MHz (Rel) 1249 E Hwy 22 *Web:* www.kmfc.com ■ *E-mail:* info@kmfc.com	Centralia	MO	65240	573-682-5525	682-2744
KOPN-FM 89.5 MHz (NPR) 915 E Broadway *Web:* www.kopn.org ■ *E-mail:* mail@kopn.org	Columbia	MO	65201	573-874-5676	499-1662
KOQL-FM 106.1 MHz (Oldies) 503 Old 63 N *Web:* www.koql.com ■ *E-mail:* kool@koql.com	Columbia	MO	65201	573-443-1524	449-7770
KPLA-FM 101.5 MHz (AC) 503 Old 63 N *Web:* www.kpla.com ■ *E-mail:* studio@kpla.com	Columbia	MO	65201	573-449-4141	449-7770
KREL-AM 1420 kHz (Ctry) 100 E Buchanan Suite A	California	MO	65018	573-796-3139	796-4131
KTGR-AM 1580 kHz (Sports) 3215 Lemone Industrial Blvd Suite 200	Columbia	MO	65201	573-875-1099	875-2439
KTXY-FM 106.9 MHz (AC) 3215 Lemone Industrial Blvd Suite 200	Columbia	MO	65201	573-875-1099	875-2439
KWOS-AM 1240 kHz (N/T) 3109 S Ten-Mile Dr	Jefferson City	MO	65109	573-893-5100	893-4137
KWRT-AM 1370 kHz (Misc) 1600 Radio Hill Rd	Boonville	MO	65233	660-882-6686	882-6688
KWWC-FM 90.5 MHz (Nost) 1405 E Broadway	Columbia	MO	65201	573-876-7297	876-7248
KWWR-FM 95.7 MHz (Ctry) 1705 E Liberty	Mexico	MO	65265	573-581-5500	581-1801

— Colleges/Universities —

				Phone	Fax
Columbia College 1001 Rogers St *TF:* 800-231-2391 ■ *Web:* www.ccis.edu ■ *E-mail:* admissions@email.ccis.edu	Columbia	MO	65216	573-875-8700	875-7506
Columbia Regional Hospital 404 Keene St *TF Cust Svc:* 800-233-5779*	Columbia	MO	65201	573-875-9200	499-6237
Stephens College 1200 E Broadway **Fax:* Admissions ■ *TF Admissions:* 800-876-7207 ■ *Web:* www.stephens.edu ■ *E-mail:* apply@sc.stephens.edu	Columbia	MO	65215	573-442-2211	876-7237*
University of Missouri 230 Jesse Hall *Web:* www.missouri.edu ■ *E-mail:* mu4u@showme.missouri.edu	Columbia	MO	65211	573-882-2121	882-7887

— Hospitals —

				Phone	Fax
Boone Hospital Center 1600 E Broadway *TF:* 800-872-9008 ■ *Web:* www.boone.org	Columbia	MO	65201	573-815-8000	815-2638
Harry S Truman Memorial Veterans Hospital 800 Hospital Dr	Columbia	MO	65201	573-443-2511	814-6431

— Attractions —

				Phone	Fax
Albert-Oakland Park 1900 Blue Ridge Rd	Columbia	MO	65202	573-874-7460	
Bingham George Caleb Gallery A-126 Fine Arts Bldg University of Missouri-Columbia Campus	Columbia	MO	65211	573-882-3555	
Bluestem Missouri Crafts Gallery 13 S 9th St	Columbia	MO	65201	573-442-0211	
Columbia Art League Gallery 1013 E Walnut St *Web:* midwest-arts.com/cal	Columbia	MO	65201	573-443-8838	
Historical Society of Missouri 1020 Lowry St	Columbia	MO	65201	573-882-7083	884-4950
Maplewood Barn Theater Nifong Blvd Nifong Pk	Columbia	MO	65201	573-449-7517	
Martin Luther King Jr Memorial Garden 800 S Stadium Blvd	Columbia	MO	65203	573-874-7460	
Missouri Art Gallery 9 N 10th St	Columbia	MO	65201	573-443-5010	
Missouri Symphony Society 203 S 9th St	Columbia	MO	65201	573-875-0600	449-4214
Missouri Theatre PO Box 1121	Columbia	MO	65205	573-875-0600	449-4214
Montminy Gallery Boone County Historical Society 3801 Ponderosa Dr	Columbia	MO	65201	573-443-8936	

Columbia — Attractions (Cont'd)

				Phone	Fax
Museum of Anthropology 104 Swallow Hall University of Missouri	Columbia	MO	65211	573-882-3573	884-1435
Museum of Art & Archaeology Pickard Hall University of Missouri *Web:* www.research.missouri.edu/museum/ ■ *E-mail:* muswww@showme.missouri.edu	Columbia	MO	65211	573-882-3591	884-4039
Nifong Park 2900 E Nifong Blvd	Columbia	MO	65201	573-874-7460	
Rhynsburger Theatre 129 Fine Arts Building University of Missouri-Columbia Campus	Columbia	MO	65211	573-882-7529	
Shelter Gardens 1817 W Broadway	Columbia	MO	65218	573-874-4715	446-5720
Stephens College Playhouse 100 Willis St Stephens College Campus	Columbia	MO	65215	573-876-7199	
Twin Lakes Recreation Area 2500 Chapel Hill Rd	Columbia	MO	65203	573-445-8839	
Walters-Boone County Historical Museum 3801 Ponderosa St	Columbia	MO	65201	573-443-8936	875-5268

— Events —

	Phone
Annual Business Expo (late March)	573-874-1132
Art in the Park (early June)	573-443-8838
Boone County Fair (late July)	573-474-9435
Boone County Heritage Festival (mid-September)	573-875-1231
Christmas Candlelight Tour (early December)	573-875-1231
Columbia Festival of the Arts (late September)	573-874-1132
Columbia Values Diversity Celebration (mid-January)	573-874-7488
Downtown Holiday Festival (early December)	573-442-6816
Earth Day (April 22)	573-875-0539
Fall Craft Show (early November)	573-882-2056
Fire in the Sky Fireworks Extravaganza (July 4)	573-449-0917
First Night Columbia (December 31)	573-817-2781
Holiday Parade (late November)	573-442-6816
Home & Garden Show (late February)	573-882-2056
International Buckskin Horse World Championship Show (late July)	573-445-8338
JW Boone Ragtime Festival (early June)	573-875-1231
Lions Antique Show (early September)	573-882-2056
Memorial Day Weekend Celebration (late May)	573-443-2651
Salute to Veterans Airshow (late May)	573-443-2651
Salute to Veterans Parade (late May)	573-443-2651
Show-Me State Games (mid-late July)	573-882-2101
Spring Craft Show (mid-late March)	573-882-2056
Thursdays Downtown Twilight Festivals (June & September)	573-442-6816
US Cellular Balloon Classic (late August)	573-814-4000

Independence

Located just east of Kansas City, Independence is perhaps best known as the hometown of Harry S. Truman. Among the many Truman-related sites in Independence are the Harry S. Truman home; the Truman Depot, where the 1948 Whistlestop tour ended; and the Truman Library and Museum, which is one of only 11 presidential libraries in the U.S. Independence is also a historic frontier town, and the National Frontier Trails Center is the only museum in the country devoted to the three primary frontier trails, the Santa Fe, California, and Oregon Trails. In addition, every year on Labor Day week-end the city celebrates its frontier past with Santa-Cali-Gon, a street festival that features major country music artists in concert as well as one of the nation's largest juried craft shows. The heart of the city is Independence Square, which had become the county seat in 1827 and soon thereafter turned into an outfitting post from which thousands of settlers started their journeys to the West. One of the city's restored homes, the Marshal's home, is located on the Square, at the 1859 jail. Two other restored homes from the 19th Century are the 30-room Vaile Mansion, built in 1881, and the Bingham-Waggoner Estate, built in 1855. The Vaile Mansion is a Second Empire Victorian mansion with hand-painted and stenciled ceilings and elaborate hand graining on woodwork. The Bingham-Waggoner Estate, which was once the home of Missouri artist George Caleb Bingham, was remodeled around 1890 and many of the furnishings and accessories from that era remain intact. Independence is also the home of the world headquarters of the Reorganized Church of Jesus Christ of Latter Day Saints. The RLDS World Headquarters complex includes a domed Auditorium and a Temple that spirals 300 feet above the city's skyline.

Population	116,832	**Longitude**	94-21-02 W
Area (Land)	77.9 sq mi	**County**	Jackson
Area (Water)	0.0 sq mi	**Time Zone**	CST
Elevation	756 ft	**Area Code/s**	816
Latitude	39-05-28 N		

— Average Temperatures and Precipitation —

TEMPERATURES

	Jan	Feb	Mar	Apr	May	Jun	Jul	Aug	Sep	Oct	Nov	Dec
High	35	41	53	65	74	83	89	86	78	68	53	39
Low	17	22	33	44	54	63	68	66	57	46	34	22

PRECIPITATION

	Jan	Feb	Mar	Apr	May	Jun	Jul	Aug	Sep	Oct	Nov	Dec
Inches	1.1	1.1	2.5	3.1	5.0	4.7	4.4	4.0	4.9	3.3	1.9	1.6

— Important Phone Numbers —

	Phone		Phone
AAA	816-373-1717	**Medical Referral**	816-531-8432
Dental Referral	816-737-5353	**Poison Control Center**	816-234-3434
Emergency	911	**Time/Temp**	816-461-4636
HotelDocs	800-468-3537		

— Information Sources —

				Phone	Fax
Better Business Bureau Serving Greater Kansas City 306 E 12th St Suite 1024 *Web:* www.kansascity.bbb.org	Kansas City	MO	64106	816-421-7800	472-5442
Independence Chamber of Commerce PO Box 1077 *Web:* www.independencechamber.com ■ *E-mail:* rchamber@independencechamber.com	Independence	MO	64051	816-252-4745	252-4917
Independence City Hall 111 E Maple Ave. *Web:* www.ci.independence.mo.us	Independence	MO	64050	816-325-7000	
Independence Community Development 111 E Maple Ave City Hall	Independence	MO	64050	816-325-7425	325-7400
Independence Mayor 111 E Maple Ave City Hall	Independence	MO	64050	816-325-7027	325-7012
Jackson County 200 S Main St 2nd Fl	Independence	MO	64050	816-881-1626	881-4473
Mid-Continent Public Library 15616 E 24 Hwy *Web:* www.mcpl.lib.mo.us ■ *E-mail:* info@mcpl.lib.mo.us	Independence	MO	64050	816-836-5200	521-7253
Missouri Assn of Convention & Visitors Bureau 109 S 4th St *TF:* 800-785-0360	Saint Joseph	MO	64501	816-233-6688	233-9120

On-Line Resources

4Independence.com	www.4independence.com
Anthill City Guide Independence	www.anthill.com/city.asp?city=independence
Area Guide Independence	independence.areaguides.net
City Knowledge Independence	www.cityknowledge.com/mo_independence.htm
Excite.com Independence City Guide	www.excite.com/travel/countries/united_states/missouri/independence
Gazette Weekly Newspaper Online	www.gazetteweekly.com
Independence Bed & Breakfast Directory	bbchannel.previewtravel.com/USA/Missouri/Independence.asp
Independence-Missouri.com	www.independence-missouri.com
NITC Travelbase City Guide Independence	www.travelbase.com/auto/guides/independence-mo.html

Independence (Cont'd)

— Transportation Services —

AIRPORTS

■ **Kansas City International Airport (MCI)**

	Phone
25 miles NW of downtown Independence (approx 35 minutes)	816-243-5237

Web: www.kcairports.org

Airport Transportation

	Phone
Yellow Cab $38-46 fare to downtown Independence	816-254-1222

Commercial Airlines

	Phone		Phone
Air Canada	800-776-3000	**Northwest**	800-225-2525
AirTran	800-247-8726	**Redwing Airways**	660-665-6607
America West	800-235-9292	**Southwest**	800-435-9792
American	800-433-7300	**TWA**	800-221-2000
Continental	800-525-0280	**United**	800-241-6522
Continental Express	800-525-0280	**US Airways**	800-428-4322
Delta	800-221-1212	**Vanguard**	800-826-4827
Midwest Express	800-452-2022		

Charter Airlines

	Phone		Phone
Executive Beechcraft	816-842-8484	**Spirit Aviation**	816-221-3192

CAR RENTALS

	Phone		Phone
Alamo	816-464-5151	**Enterprise**	816-836-3200
Avis	816-243-5760	**Hertz**	816-243-5765
Budget	816-243-5757	**National**	816-243-5770
Dollar	816-243-5600	**Thrifty**	816-464-5670

LIMO/TAXI

	Phone		Phone
Checker Cab	816-461-0700	**Yellow Cab**	816-254-1222

MASS TRANSIT

	Phone
Metro $.90 Base fare	816-221-0660

RAIL/BUS

				Phone
Amtrak Station 600 S Grand St	Independence	MO	64050	800-872-7245
Greyhound Bus Station 1101 Troost St *TF:* 800-231-2222	Kansas City	MO	64106	816-221-2885

— Accommodations —

HOTELS, MOTELS, RESORTS

				Phone	Fax
American Inn 4141 S Noland Rd *TF:* 800-905-6343	Independence	MO	64055	816-373-8300	373-8300
Beauty Rest Motel 1631 Salisbury Rd	Independence	MO	64050	816-252-5778	
Blue Bird Motel Hwy 40 E	Independence	MO	64055	816-252-5488	
Budget Inn 9900 Hwy 40 E	Independence	MO	64055	816-737-1922	
Crossland 14800 E 42nd St	Independence	MO	64055	816-350-2151	
Deluxe Inn 10301 Hwy 40 E	Independence	MO	64055	816-313-1200	
Great Western Motel 15912 E 24 Hwy	Independence	MO	64050	816-833-0880	
Howard Johnson Lodge East 4200 S Noland Rd *TF:* 800-338-3752	Independence	MO	64055	816-373-8856	373-3312
Hyline Inn 15008 E 40 Hwy	Independence	MO	64050	816-373-0956	
Queen City Motel 11402 E 24 Hwy	Independence	MO	64054	816-254-1077	
Red Roof Inn 13712 42nd Terr *TF:* 800-843-7663	Independence	MO	64055	816-373-2800	373-0067
Serendipity Bed & Breakfast 116 S Pleasant St *TF:* 800-203-4299	Independence	MO	64050	816-833-4719	833-4719
Shoney's Inn 4048 S Lynn Court Dr *TF:* 800-222-2222	Independence	MO	64055	816-254-0100	254-6796
Sports Stadium Motel 9803 E 40 Hwy	Independence	MO	64055	816-353-0005	
Super 8 Motel 4032 S Lynn Court Dr *TF:* 800-800-8000	Independence	MO	64055	816-833-1888	833-1888
Woodstock Inn 1212 W Lexington St *Web:* www.independence-missouri.com ■ *E-mail:* woodstock@independence-missouri.com	Independence	MO	64050	816-833-2233	

— Restaurants —

				Phone
Backstage Barbecue & Grill (Barbecue) 17005 E 24 Hwy	Independence	MO	64056	816-257-1313
Bamboo Hut (American) 10111 E 40 Hwy	Independence	MO	64055	816-353-9472
Country Kitchen (Homestyle) 4140 S Noland Rd	Independence	MO	64055	816-373-8702
Courthouse Exchange Restaurant & Lounge (American) 113 W Lexington St	Independence	MO	64050	816-252-0344
Dragon House Restaurant (Chinese) 1003 E 23rd St	Independence	MO	64055	816-461-7272
El Maguey (Mexican) 3738 S Noland Rd	Independence	MO	64055	816-252-6868
Englewood Cafe (American) 10904 E Winner Rd	Independence	MO	64050	816-461-9588
Fat Chance Bar & Grill (American) 2560 Hwy 291 S	Independence	MO	64057	816-478-9898
Fazoli's (Italian) 19008 E 39th St	Independence	MO	64057	816-795-0063
Garozzo's Ristorante (Italian) 12801 E 40 Hwy	Independence	MO	64057	816-737-2400
Gates Bar-B-Q (Barbecue) 10440 E 40 Hwy	Independence	MO	64050	816-353-5880
Gold Lion Restaurant (Chinese) 2411 Hwy 291 S	Independence	MO	64057	816-478-8886
Golden Rice Restaurant (Chinese) 1435 S Noland Rd	Independence	MO	64055	816-254-8898
Harry T's Restaurant (American) 408 Hwy 24 W	Independence	MO	64050	816-254-5860
Hickory Smoke Pit Bar-B-Q (Barbecue) 203 W 23rd St	Independence	MO	64055	816-252-3355
Hwang's Restaurant (Chinese) 9401 E 35th St	Independence	MO	64052	816-353-2229
Jerry's Restaurant (American) 10219 E Independence Ave	Independence	MO	64053	816-252-0900
Jim's Family Restaurant (Homestyle) 11220 E 24 Hwy	Sugar Creek	MO	64054	816-461-9390
Kross Lounge & Restaurant (American) 605 N Sterling Ave	Sugar Creek	MO	64054	816-254-9494
Lucia's Taquera (Mexican) 641 Hwy 24 E	Independence	MO	64050	816-252-0762
Miles' Coyote Cantina (Mexican) 4815 Noland Rd	Kansas City	MO	64133	816-350-2000
Old Country Buffet (Homestyle) 13720 E 40 Hwy	Independence	MO	64055	816-478-1012
Old Mexico Restaurant (Mexican) 11600 E 23rd St	Independence	MO	64050	816-461-1848
Pioneer Restaurant (American) 17000 E 24 Hwy	Independence	MO	64056	816-257-4778
Red Mule Restaurant (American) 16506 E 40 Hwy	Independence	MO	64050	816-478-1810
Rheinland Restaurant (German) 208 N Main St	Independence	MO	64050	816-461-5383
Rio Bravo Cantina (Mexican) 4001 Bolger Rd	Independence	MO	64055	816-478-2113
Rosie's Cafe (American) 10690 E 40 Hwy	Independence	MO	64055	816-353-5835
Rustler's Hickory Pit Bar-B-Q (Barbecue) 14220 E 42nd St	Independence	MO	64055	816-373-4226
Shinny's Cave Cafe (American) 3005 W Geospace Dr	Independence	MO	64056	816-257-5655
Stephenson's Apple Farm Restaurant (American) 16401 E 40 Hwy	Kansas City	MO	64136	816-373-5400
Tokyo Steak House (Japanese) 14310 E 42nd St	Independence	MO	64055	816-478-8858
Trolley Inn (Homestyle) 11400 E Truman Rd	Independence	MO	64050	816-461-9857
Waid's Restaurant (American) 600 E 24 Hwy	Independence	MO	64050	816-836-0800
Waldron's Country Inn (Homestyle) 16703 E 23rd St	Independence	MO	64055	816-252-3880
Winstead's (American) 1428 S Noland Rd	Independence	MO	64055	816-252-9363

— Goods and Services —

SHOPPING

				Phone	Fax
Independence Center 2035 Independence Center Dr	Independence	MO	64057	816-795-8600	795-7836
Independence Square Main St betw Walnut St & Truman Rd	Independence	MO	64050		

BANKS

				Phone	Fax
American Sterling Bank 11206 E 24 Hwy	Independence	MO	64054	816-521-2500	252-7988
Bank of Jacomo 10801 E 23rd St	Independence	MO	64052	816-836-0200	521-4518
Bank Ten 220 W White Oak St	Independence	MO	64050	816-252-5000	252-5001
Commerce Bank 300 N Osage St	Independence	MO	64050	816-234-8855	254-0834
First Federal Bank FSB 3500 S Noland Rd	Independence	MO	64055	816-254-2225	254-2227
Hillcrest Bank 201 W Lexington Ave	Independence	MO	64050	816-257-5212	833-3091
Mercantile Bank 110 E 24 Hwy	Independence	MO	64050	816-833-2800	521-3476
Midland Bank 4610 S Noland Rd	Independence	MO	64055	816-373-6500	373-4535
Midwest Heritage Bank 1525 E 23rd St South	Independence	MO	64055	816-254-6500	254-6768

Independence — Banks (Cont'd)

Name	Address	City	State	Zip	Phone	Fax
NationsBank	129 W Lexington Ave	Independence	MO	64050	816-252-4000	
North American Savings Bank	11221 E 23rd St South	Independence	MO	64052	816-254-4000	254-4003
UMB Bank	13813 E 39th St South	Independence	MO	64055	816-836-1200	836-1783

BUSINESS SERVICES

Name	Phone	Name	Phone
CopyMax	816-461-7084	**Mail Boxes Etc**	816-373-1155
Excel Personnel	816-478-6505	**Mail Unlimited**	816-257-5422
Federal Express	800-238-5355	**Post Office**	800-275-8777
Interim Personnel	816-358-3838	**UPS**	800-742-5877
Larmil Business Service	816-252-0728		

— Media —

PUBLICATIONS

Name	Address	City	State	Zip	Phone	Fax
Examiner The‡	410 S Liberty St	Independence	MO	64050	816-254-8600	836-3805
Web: examiner.net						

‡*Daily newspapers*

TELEVISION

Name	Address	City	State	Zip	Phone	Fax
KCPT-TV Ch 19 (PBS)	125 E 31st St	Kansas City	MO	64108	816-756-3580	931-2500
Web: www.kcpt.org ■ *E-mail:* kcpt@tv19.kcpt.org						
KCTV-TV Ch 5 (CBS)	PO Box 5555	Kansas City	MO	64109	913-677-5555	677-7243
Web: www.kctv.com ■ *E-mail:* kctv@kctv.com						
KCWE-TV Ch 29 (UPN)	1049 Central	Kansas City	MO	64105	816-221-2900	760-9149*
**Fax:* Sales						
KMBC-TV Ch 9 (ABC)	1049 Central St	Kansas City	MO	64105	816-221-9999	421-4163
Web: www.kmbc.com						
KSHB-TV Ch 41 (NBC)	4720 Oak St	Kansas City	MO	64112	816-753-4141	932-4145
Web: www.kshb.com ■ *E-mail:* news@kshb.com						
WDAF-TV Ch 4 (Fox)	3030 Summit St	Kansas City	MO	64108	816-753-4567	561-4181
Web: www.wdaftv4.com						

RADIO

Name	Address	City	State	Zip	Phone	Fax
KBEQ-FM 104.3 MHz (Ctry)	4717 Grand Ave Suite 600	Kansas City	MO	64112	816-531-2535	531-7327
Web: www.kbeq.com						
KCCV-AM 760 kHz (Rel)	10550 Barkley St Suite 112	Overland Park	KS	66212	913-642-7600	642-2424
KCFX-FM 101.1 MHz (Rock)	5800 Foxridge Dr	Mission	KS	66202	913-514-3000	514-3003
KCIY-FM 106.5 MHz (Nost)	5800 Foxridge Dr Suite 600	Mission	KS	66202	913-514-3000	514-3003
KCMO-AM 710 kHz (N/T)	4935 Belinder Rd	Westwood	KS	66205	913-677-8998	677-8901
KCMO-FM 94.9 MHz (Oldies)	4935 Belinder Rd	Westwood	KS	66205	913-677-8998	677-8901*
**Fax:* News Rm						
KCTE-AM 1510 kHz (Sports)	10841 E 28th St	Independence	MO	64052	816-836-8326	836-2111
KCUR-FM 89.3 MHz (NPR)	4825 Troost Ave Suite 202	Kansas City	MO	64110	816-235-1551	235-2864
Web: www.umkc.edu/kcur ■ *E-mail:* kcur@smtpgate.umkc.edu						
KCXL-AM 1140 kHz (N/T)	310 S La Frenz Rd	Liberty	MO	64068	816-792-1140	792-8258
Web: www.kcxl.com ■ *E-mail:* kcxl@kcxl.com						
KEXS-AM 1090 kHz (Rel)	201 Industrial Park Rd	Excelsior Springs	MO	64024	816-630-1090	630-6063
KFKF-FM 94.1 MHz (Ctry)	4717 Grand Ave Suite 600	Kansas City	MO	64112	816-753-4000	753-4045
Web: sites.kansascity.com/kfkf ■ *E-mail:* kfkf@kansascity.com						
KGGN-AM 890 kHz (Rel)	1734 E 63rd St Suite 600	Kansas City	MO	64110	816-333-0092	363-8120
KKFI-FM 90.1 MHz (Misc)	900 1/2 Westport Rd 2nd Fl	Kansas City	MO	64111	816-931-3122	931-7078
KKLO-AM 1410 kHz (Rel)	481 Muncie Rd	Leavenworth	KS	66048	913-351-1410	
Web: www.kklo.com ■ *E-mail:* kklo@tfs.net						
KLJC-FM 88.5 MHz (Rel)	15800 Calvary Rd	Kansas City	MO	64147	816-331-8700	303-1553
Web: www.kljc.org ■ *E-mail:* kljc@kljc.org						
KMBZ-AM 980 kHz (N/T)	4935 Belinder Rd	Westwood	KS	66205	913-236-9800	677-8901
KMXV-FM 93.3 MHz (CHR)	508 Westport Rd	Kansas City	MO	64111	816-756-5698	531-2550
Web: www.mix93.com						
KPHN-AM 1190 kHz (N/T)	1212 Baltimore St	Kansas City	KS	64105	816-421-1900	266-1190
Web: www.kphn1190.com ■ *E-mail:* mail@kphn1190.com						
KPRS-FM 103.3 MHz (Urban)	11131 Colorado Ave	Kansas City	MO	64137	816-763-2040	966-1055
Web: www.kprs.com ■ *E-mail:* 103@kprs.com						
KPRT-AM 1590 kHz (Rel)	11131 Colorado Ave	Kansas City	MO	64137	816-763-2040	966-1055
KQRC-FM 98.9 MHz (Rock)	4350 Shawnee Mission Pkwy Suite 99	Mission	KS	66202	913-514-3000	384-9911
Web: www.989therock.com						
KSRC-FM 102.1 MHz (AC)	508 Westport Rd Suite 202	Kansas City	MO	64111	816-561-9102	531-2550
KUDL-FM 98.1 MHz (AC)	4935 Belinder Rd	Westwood	KS	66205	913-236-9800	677-8981
Web: www.kudl.com						
KXTR-FM 96.5 MHz (Clas)	5800 Foxridge Dr	Mission	KS	66202	913-514-3000	514-3003
KYYS-FM 99.7 MHz (Rock)	4935 Belinder Rd	Westwood	KS	66205	913-677-8998	677-8901
WDAF-AM 610 kHz (Ctry)	4935 Belinder Rd	Westwood	KS	66205	913-677-8998	677-8901
WHB-AM 810 kHz (Ctry)	1600 Genesee St Suite 925	Kansas City	MO	64102	816-221-7170	221-7944

— Colleges/Universities —

Name	Address	City	State	Zip	Phone	Fax
Concorde Career Colleges Inc	5800 Foxridge Dr Mission Corporate Ctr Suite 500	Mission	KS	66202	913-831-9977	831-6556
TF: 800-515-1007 ■ *Web:* www.concordecareercolleges.com						
Graceland College	1401 W Truman Rd	Independence	MO	64050	816-833-0524	833-2990
TF: 800-833-0524						
Longview Community College	500 SW Longview Rd	Lees Summit	MO	64081	816-672-2000	672-2040
Web: www.longview.cc.mo.us						
Park College Independence Campus	2200 Hwy 291 S	Independence	MO	64057	816-252-9065	252-4161
Web: www.park.edu						
Vatterott College	210 S Main St	Independence	MO	64050	816-252-3997	252-0645
TF: 800-466-3997 ■ *Web:* www.vatterott-college.com						

— Hospitals —

Name	Address	City	State	Zip	Phone	Fax
Columbia Independence Regional Health Center	1509 W Truman Rd	Independence	MO	64050	816-836-8100	836-6003
Medical Center of Independence	17203 E 23rd St	Independence	MO	64057	816-478-5000	478-5383
Web: www.healthmidwest.org/Hospitals_and_Services/Medical_Center_of_Independence						

— Attractions —

Name	Address	City	State	Zip	Phone	Fax
1827 Log Courthouse	107 W Kansas Ave	Independence	MO	64050	816-325-7111	
1859 Jail Marshal's Home & Museum	217 N Main St	Independence	MO	64050	816-252-1892	461-1510
American Jazz Museum	1616 E 18th St	Kansas City	MO	64108	816-474-8463	474-0074
Web: www.kcjazz.org/jazz.htm ■ *E-mail:* postmaster@kcjazz.org						
American Royal Museum & Visitors Center	1701 American Royal Ct	Kansas City	MO	64102	816-221-9800	221-8189
Web: www.americanroyal.com ■ *E-mail:* mericanroyal@americanroyal.com						
Arabia Steamboat Museum	400 Grand Blvd	Kansas City	MO	64106	816-471-1856	471-1616
TF: 800-471-1856 ■ *Web:* www.1856.com ■ *E-mail:* info@1856.com						
Bingham-Waggoner Estate	313 W Pacific Ave	Independence	MO	64050	816-461-3491	
Bingham-Waggoner Historical Society	313 W Pacific Ave	Independence	MO	64050	816-461-3491	
Black Archives of Mid-America	2033 Vine St	Kansas City	MO	64108	816-483-1300	483-1341
Web: www.blackarchives.org						
Cave Spring Interpretive Center	8701 E Gregory Blvd	Kansas City	MO	64133	816-358-2283	
Cool Crest Family Fun Center	10735 Hwy 40 E	Independence	MO	64050	816-358-0088	358-7980

Independence — Attractions (Cont'd)

Name / Address	City	State	Zip	Phone	Fax
Fleming Park/Lake Jacomo 22807 Woods Chapel Rd Jackson County Parks & Recreation	Blue Springs	MO	64015	816-795-8200	795-1234
Fort Osage National Historic Landmark 105 Osage St	Sibley	MO	64088	816-795-8200	795-7938
Harry S Truman Home 219 N Delaware St	Independence	MO	64050	816-254-9929	
Harry S Truman National Historic Site 223 N Main St *Web:* www.nps.gov/hstr	Independence	MO	64050	816-254-2720	254-4491
Harry S Truman Presidential Library & Museum 500 W Hwy 24 *Web:* www.trumanlibrary.org ■ *E-mail:* library@truman.nara.gov	Independence	MO	64050	816-833-1400	833-4368
Independence Square Main St betw Walnut St & Truman Rd	Independence	MO	64050		
Jackson County Historical Society Archives 112 W Lexington Ave Rm 103 *Web:* www.jchs.org ■ *E-mail:* info@jchs.org	Independence	MO	64050	816-252-7454	
James Country Mercantile 111 N Main St	Liberty	MO	64068	816-781-9473	
Kansas City Museum 3218 Gladstone Blvd *TF:* 800-556-9372 ■ *Web:* www.kcmuseum.com	Kansas City	MO	64123	816-483-8300	483-9912
Kansas City Zoological Gardens 6700 Zoo Dr. *Web:* www.kansascityzoo.org	Kansas City	MO	64132	816-871-5700	822-8903
Leila's Hair Museum 815 W 23rd St.	Independence	MO	64050	816-252-4247	
Longview Lake Park I-470 & 109 S Raytown Rd	Blue Springs	MO	64015	816-795-8200	
Majors Alexander Historic House & Museum 8201 State Line Rd	Kansas City	MO	64114	816-333-5556	
Missouri Town 1855 22807 Woods Chapel Rd Fleming Pk.	Blue Springs	MO	64015	816-795-8200	
Mormon Visitors Center 937 W Walnut St	Independence	MO	64050	816-836-3466	252-6256
National Frontier Trails Center 318 W Pacific Ave. *Web:* www.frontiertrailscenter.com ■ *E-mail:* fdesk@indepmo.org	Independence	MO	64050	816-325-7575	325-7479
Negro Leagues Baseball Museum 1616 E 18th St.	Kansas City	MO	64108	816-221-1920	221-8424
Osage Honey Farms Inc 222 Santa Fe St.	Sibley	MO	64088	816-650-5637	
Owens George Nature Park 1601 S Speck Rd	Independence	MO	64057	816-257-4654	
Pioneer Spring Cabin Truman & Noland Rds.	Independence	MO	64050	816-325-7111	
Powell Gardens Hwy 50 W *Web:* www.powellgardens.org	Kingsville	MO	64061	816-697-3600	697-3576
Save a Connie Museum 480 NW Richards Rd. *TF:* 800-513-9484 ■ *Web:* www.saveaconnie.org	Kansas City	MO	64116	816-421-3401	421-3421
Toy & Minature Museum 5235 Oak St	Kansas City	MO	64112	816-333-2055	333-2055
Vaile Mansion 1500 N Liberty Ave	Independence	MO	64050	816-325-7430	

SPORTS TEAMS & FACILITIES

Name / Address	City	State	Zip	Phone	Fax
Lakeside Speedway 5615 Wolcott Dr *Web:* www.lakesidespeedway.com ■ *E-mail:* I70Lake@discoverynet.com	Kansas City	KS	66109	913-299-2040	299-1105
Woodlands Race Track 9700 Leavenworth Rd	Kansas City	KS	66109	913-299-9797	299-9804

— Events —

	Phone
Best Little Arts & Crafts Show in Independence (mid-late November)	816-325-7370
Bingham-Waggoner Antique & Craft Fair (mid-July)	816-461-3491
Bingham-Waggoner Fashion Show (mid-March)	816-461-3491
Bingham-Waggoner Quilt Show (September)	816-461-3491
Children's Day at Fort Osage National Historic Landmark (early August)	816-795-8200
Children's Day at Missouri Town 1855 (early June)	816-795-8200
Dawg Days Animal Fair Craft Show & Flea Market (early August)	816-252-0608
Enchanted Forest (late October)	816-257-4654
Farm & Flower Festival (late April)	816-252-0608
Farmer's Market Saturdays (early May-late October)	816-252-0608
Flint Knap-In (mid-May & mid-September)	816-795-8200
Fort Osage Militia Muster (mid-October)	816-795-8200
Fort Osage Rendezvous (mid-September)	816-795-8200
Frontier Christmas (early December)	816-795-8200
Frontier Fright Night (late October)	816-795-8200
Harry S Truman Appreciation Ceremony (early August)	816-833-1400
Historic Site Trolley Tours (early May)	816-325-7111
Holiday Open House (early November)	816-252-0608
Independence Day at Fort Osage National Historic Landmark (July 4)	816-795-8200
Independence Day at Missouri Town 1855 (July 4)	816-795-8200
Lighting of Jackson County Courthouse & Queen City Christmas Tree (early November)	816-252-0608
Missouri Town Christmas Celebration (mid-December)	816-795-8200
Missouri Town Fall Festival (early October)	816-795-8200
Presidential Wreath Laying (May 8)	816-833-1400
Santa-Cali-Gon Days Festival (early September)	816-252-4745
Santa-Cali-Gon Quilt Show (early September)	816-325-7370
Spirit of Christmas Past Homes Tour (late November-late December)	816-461-3491
Spirits of the Past (late October)	816-795-8200
Strawberry Festival (early June)	816-252-9098
Trick 'n Treat & Halloween Parade (late October)	816-252-4745
Truman Birthday Celebration (May 8)	816-252-0608
Truman Health Walk (early May)	816-833-2088
Truman Walking Tours (late May-early September)	816-254-7199
Vaile Tea Party (late March)	816-461-5135
Windows on the Past (mid-December)	816-795-8200

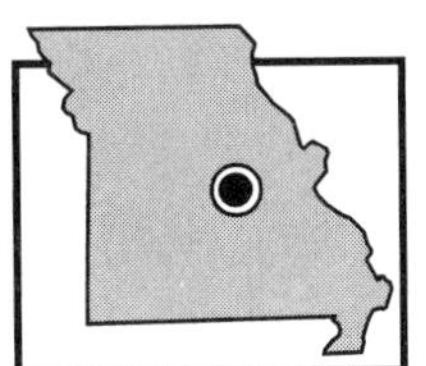

Jefferson City

Jefferson City takes its name from the third President of the United States, Thomas Jefferson. The scenic drive along the 50-mile Jefferson City-to-Franklin section of Katy Trail State Park is bordered by towering limestone and dolomite bluffs and includes wetlands, glades, and bottomland forests. This area is excellent for bird watching, and during the winter American bald eagles can be seen along the Trail. Jefferson City also has an exceptionally large park system which encompasses ten area parks. The Missouri Highway Patrol Safety Education Center in Jefferson City contains exhibits on famous criminals Bonnie and Clyde and Pretty Boy Floyd. The center also displays five patrol cars dating from 1931 to the present, law enforcement antiques, and criminals' weapons.

Population	34,911	**Longitude**	92-16-30 W
Area (Land)	23.1 sq mi	**County**	Cole
Area (Water)	0.6 sq mi	**Time Zone**	CST
Elevation	702 ft	**Area Code/s**	573
Latitude	38-54-76 N		

— Average Temperatures and Precipitation —

TEMPERATURES

	Jan	Feb	Mar	Apr	May	Jun	Jul	Aug	Sep	Oct	Nov	Dec
High	40	44	56	68	76	84	90	88	81	70	56	43
Low	15	19	30	41	51	60	65	62	54	42	31	21

PRECIPITATION

	Jan	Feb	Mar	Apr	May	Jun	Jul	Aug	Sep	Oct	Nov	Dec
Inches	1.4	1.7	3.3	3.6	4.9	4.4	3.0	3.1	4.0	3.5	2.9	2.6

— Important Phone Numbers —

	Phone		Phone
AAA	573-634-3322	**Poison Control Center**	800-366-8888
Emergency	911	**Time/Temp**	573-636-2121
Events Line	573-634-6485	**Weather**	573-442-2222

Jefferson City (Cont'd)

— Information Sources —

				Phone	Fax
Better Business Bureau Serving Eastern Missouri & Southern Illinois 12 Sunnen Dr Suite 121 *Web:* www.stlouis.bbb.org	Saint Louis	MO	63143	314-645-3300	645-2666
Cole County 301 E High St. *Web:* www.primelink.com/cole/	Jefferson City	MO	65101	573-634-9100	634-8031
Jefferson City Area Chamber of Commerce 213 Adams St *TF:* 800-769-4183 ■ *Web:* www.jcchamber.org	Jefferson City	MO	65102	573-634-3616	634-3805
Jefferson City City Hall 320 E McCarty St *Web:* www.jeffcity.com/cityclerk/cityhall.html ■ *E-mail:* clerkofjc@aol.com	Jefferson City	MO	65101	573-634-6303	634-6329
Jefferson City Convention & Visitors Bureau 213 Adams St. *TF:* 800-769-4183 ■ *Web:* www.jcchamber.org/cvb	Jefferson City	MO	65102	573-634-3616	634-3805
Jefferson City Mayor 320 E McCarty St.	Jefferson City	MO	65101	573-634-6303	634-6329
Jefferson City Planning Dept 320 E McCarty St	Jefferson City	MO	65101	573-634-6409	634-6457
Missouri River Regional Library 214 Adams St	Jefferson City	MO	65101	573-634-2464	634-7028

On-Line Resources

Area Guide Jefferson City	jeffersoncity.areaguides.net
City Knowledge Jefferson City	www.cityknowledge.com/mo_jefferson_city.htm
Directory of Jefferson City	www.jeffcity.net/web
Excite.com Jefferson City Guide	www.excite.com/travel/countries/united_states/missouri/jefferson_city

— Transportation Services —

AIRPORTS

■ **Columbia Regional Airport (COU)**

	Phone
14 miles N of downtown Jefferson City (approx 20 minutes)	573-442-9770

Airport Transportation

	Phone
Airport Shuttle $30 fare to downtown Jefferson City	573-874-4048
Yellow Cab $30 fare to downtown Jefferson City	573-636-7101

Commercial Airlines

	Phone
TWA Express	800-221-2000

Charter Airlines

	Phone
Central Missouri Aviation	573-443-1576
Jefferson City Flying Service	573-636-5118

CAR RENTALS

	Phone
Alamo	800-327-9633
Avis	800-831-2847
Enterprise	573-635-9000
Hertz	573-761-3535
Payless	800-729-5377

LIMO/TAXI

	Phone
Chase Limousine	573-635-8966
Mr T's Limousine	800-456-0261
Yellow Cab	573-636-7101

MASS TRANSIT

	Phone
Jefferson City Transit $.50 Base fare	573-634-6477

RAIL/BUS

				Phone
Amtrak Station 101 Jefferson St. *TF:* 800-872-7245	Jefferson City	MO	65101	573-636-8414
Sho-Me Bus Station 620 W McCarty St	Jefferson City	MO	65102	573-635-0183

— Accommodations —

HOTELS, MOTELS, RESORTS

				Phone	Fax
Best Western Inn 1937 Christy Dr. *TF:* 800-528-1234	Jefferson City	MO	65101	573-635-4175	635-6769
Best Western State Fair Motor Inn 3120 S Limit Ave *TF:* 800-528-1234	Sedalia	MO	65301	660-826-6100	827-3850
Capitol Plaza Hotel & Convention Center 415 W McCarty St *TF:* 800-338-8088	Jefferson City	MO	65101	573-635-1234	635-4565
Comfort Inn 1926 Jefferson St *TF:* 800-228-5150	Jefferson City	MO	65109	573-636-2797	636-2797
First Value Inn 808 Stadium Dr	Jefferson City	MO	65109	573-634-2848	635-5329
Holiday Inn Express 1716 Jefferson St *TF:* 800-465-4329	Jefferson City	MO	65109	573-634-4040	634-4200
Hotel DeVille 319 W Miller St *TF:* 800-392-3366	Jefferson City	MO	65101	573-636-5231	636-5260
Howard Johnson Plaza 422 Monroe St *TF:* 800-575-5101	Jefferson City	MO	65101	573-636-5101	636-9664
Lakeside Motel 5629 Highway 50 W	Jefferson City	MO	65109	573-893-2512	
Motel 6 1624 Jefferson St *TF:* 800-466-8356	Jefferson City	MO	65109	573-634-4220	635-5284
Ramada Inn 1510 Jefferson St. *TF:* 800-272-6232	Jefferson City	MO	65110	573-635-7171	635-8006
Super 8 Motel 1710 Jefferson St *TF:* 800-800-8000	Jefferson City	MO	65110	573-636-5456	636-0441
Veit's Village Motel 1309 Jefferson St	Jefferson City	MO	65109	573-636-6167	636-5749

— Restaurants —

				Phone
Alexandro's (Continental) 2125 Missouri Blvd	Jefferson City	MO	65109	573-634-7740
Bingham's (American) 1510 Jefferson St	Jefferson City	MO	65109	573-635-5388
Cajun Catfish House (Cajun) 6819 Hwy 50 W	Jefferson City	MO	65109	573-893-4665
Capital Sports Bar & Grill (American) 1508 E McCarty St	Jefferson City	MO	65101	573-635-0462
China Garden (Chinese) 211 E High St.	Jefferson City	MO	65101	573-634-4715
Domenico's (Italian) 3702 W Truman Blvd	Jefferson City	MO	65109	573-893-5454
Fazoli's (Italian) 2333 Missouri Blvd	Jefferson City	MO	65109	573-635-3744
High Street Pub (American) 209 E High St	Jefferson City	MO	65101	573-634-6033
Hunan Restaurant (Chinese) 1416 Missouri Blvd	Jefferson City	MO	65109	573-634-5253
La Casa Mexican Restaurant (Mexican) 1102 Missouri Blvd.	Jefferson City	MO	65109	573-636-7868
Mo & Waldo's (American) 126 E Dunklin St	Jefferson City	MO	65101	573-634-8887
Mortimer Kegley's (American) 115 E High St	Jefferson City	MO	65101	573-635-7848
Park Place Restaurant (Cajun) 415 W McCarty St.	Jefferson City	MO	65101	573-635-1234
Ryan's Steakhouse (Steak) 730 W Stadium Blvd	Jefferson City	MO	65109	573-636-7926
Santacruz (Mexican) 242 Jaycee Dr	Jefferson City	MO	65109	573-635-6500
Stein House (European) 1436 South Ridge Dr.	Jefferson City	MO	65109	573-634-3869
Veit's Diamond Restaurant (Steak/Seafood) 2001 Missouri Blvd.	Jefferson City	MO	65109	573-635-1213
Yen Ching Restaurant (Chinese) 2208 Missouri Blvd	Jefferson City	MO	65109	573-635-5225

— Goods and Services —

SHOPPING

				Phone
Capital Mall 3600 Country Club Dr	Jefferson City	MO	65109	573-893-5323
Downtown Shopping District High St-betw Broadway & Lafayette St	Jefferson City	MO	65101	573-634-7267

BANKS

				Phone	Fax
Central Trust Bank 238 Madison St.	Jefferson City	MO	65101	573-634-1234	635-1434
Exchange National Bank 132 E High St. **Fax:* Mktg	Jefferson City	MO	65101	573-761-6100	761-6242*
Jefferson Bank of Missouri 700 Southwest Blvd **Fax:* Hum Res ■ *Web:* www.jefferson-bank.com/index.html	Jefferson City	MO	65109	573-634-0800	634-0874*
Midwest Independent Bank 910 Weathered Rock Rd *TF Cust Svc:* 800-347-4642*	Jefferson City	MO	65110	573-636-9555	636-8470

Jefferson City (Cont'd)

BUSINESS SERVICES

	Phone		Phone
Airborne Express	800-247-2676	**Kinko's**	573-635-2202
BAX Global	800-225-5229	**Mail Boxes Etc**	800-789-4623
DHL Worldwide Express	800-225-5345	**Post Office**	573-636-4186
Federal Express	800-238-5355	**UPS**	800-742-5877

— Media —

PUBLICATIONS

				Phone	Fax
Daily Capital News‡ 210 Monroe St	Jefferson City	MO	65101	573-636-3131	761-0235*
**Fax:* News Rm ■ *E-mail:* newstrib@mail.ultraweb.net					
Post-Tribune‡ 210 Monroe St.	Jefferson City	MO	65101	573-636-3131	761-0235

‡Daily newspapers

TELEVISION

				Phone	Fax
KMIZ-TV Ch 17 (ABC) 501 Business Loop 70 E	Columbia	MO	65201	573-449-0917	875-7078
Web: www.kmiz.com					
KMOS-TV Ch 6 (PBS) Central Missouri State University	Warrensburg	MO	64093	660-543-4155	543-8863
Web: www.kmos.cmsu.edu/TV					
KOMU-TV Ch 8 (NBC) 5550 Hwy 63 S.	Columbia	MO	65201	573-884-6397	884-5353
Web: www.komu.com					
KRCG-TV Ch 13 (CBS) PO Box 659	Jefferson City	MO	65102	573-896-5144	896-5193
Web: www.krcg.com ■ *E-mail:* krcg@socketis.net					

RADIO

				Phone	Fax
KBIA-FM 91.3 MHz (NPR) 409 Jesse Hall	Columbia	MO	65211	573-882-3431	882-2636
Web: www.kbia.org ■ *E-mail:* kbiaog@showme.missouri.edu					
KFMZ-FM 98.3 MHz (Alt) 1101 E Walnut St.	Columbia	MO	65201	573-874-3000	443-1460
KJLU-FM 88.9 MHz (Misc) 1004 E Dunklin St.	Jefferson City	MO	65102	573-681-5301	681-5299
Web: www.lincolnu.edu/~kjlu/					
KJMO-FM 100.1 MHz (AC) 3109 S Ten-Mile Dr.	Jefferson City	MO	65109	573-893-5100	893-4137
KLIK-AM 950 kHz (Ctry) 3605 Country Club Dr	Jefferson City	MO	65109	573-893-5696	893-8330
KOPN-FM 89.5 MHz (NPR) 915 E Broadway	Columbia	MO	65201	573-874-5676	499-1662
Web: www.kopn.org ■ *E-mail:* mail@kopn.org					
KPLA-FM 101.5 MHz (AC) 503 Old 63 N	Columbia	MO	65201	573-449-4141	449-7770
Web: www.kpla.com ■ *E-mail:* studio@kpla.com					
KWOS-AM 1240 kHz (N/T) 3109 S Ten-Mile Dr.	Jefferson City	MO	65109	573-893-5100	893-4137

— Colleges/Universities —

				Phone	Fax
Columbia College-Jefferson City 315 Ellis Blvd	Jefferson City	MO	65101	573-634-3250	634-8507
TF: 800-231-2391					
Lincoln University PO Box 29	Jefferson City	MO	65102	573-681-5000	681-5566
TF Admissions: 800-521-5052 ■ *Web:* www.lincolnu.edu/					
Westminster College 501 Westminster Ave	Fulton	MO	65251	573-642-3361	592-5255
TF Admissions: 800-475-3361 ■ *Web:* www.wcmo.edu					
William Woods University 200 W 12th St	Fulton	MO	65251	573-642-2251	592-1146
TF: 800-995-3159 ■ *Web:* www.wmwoods.edu					

— Hospitals —

				Phone	Fax
Capital Region Medical Center Madison PO Box 1125	Jefferson City	MO	65101	573-635-7141	635-5146
Capitol Region Medical Center Southwest 1125 Madison St	Jefferson City	MO	65101	573-632-5000	632-5880
Saint Mary's Health Center 100 St Mary's Medical Plaza	Jefferson City	MO	65101	573-635-7642	636-5733
Web: www.stmarys-jeffcity.com					

— Attractions —

				Phone	Fax
Cole County Historical Museum 109 Madison St	Jefferson City	MO	65101	573-635-1850	
Deutschheim State Historic Site 109 W 2nd St.	Hermann	MO	65041	573-486-2200	
Finger Lakes State Park 1505 E Peabody Rd.	Columbia	MO	65202	573-443-5315	
Governor's Mansion 100 Madison St.	Jefferson City	MO	65101	573-751-7929	751-9219
Graham Cave State Park off I-70 on Hwy TT	Montgomery City	MO	63361	573-564-3476	
TF: 800-334-6946					
Jefferson Landing Historic Site	Jefferson City	MO	65101	573-751-3475	
Jewell Cemetery State Historic Site Hwy 163	Columbia	MO	65203	573-449-7402	
Lohman Building	Jefferson City	MO	65101	573-751-3475	
Missouri State Capitol Main St Capitol Bldg	Jefferson City	MO	65102	573-751-4127	
Missouri State Highway Patrol Safety Education Center 1510 E Elm St	Jefferson City	MO	65101	573-751-3313	
Missouri State Museum Capitol Bldg Room B2	Jefferson City	MO	65101	573-751-2854	526-2927
Missouri Veterans Memorial Capitol Building Complex Box 176	Jefferson City	MO	65102	573-751-3330	
Missouri Veterinary Medical Foundation Museum 2500 Country Club Dr	Jefferson City	MO	65109	573-636-8612	659-7175
Rock Bridge Memorial State Park 5901 S Hwy 163	Columbia	MO	65203	573-449-7402	
Runge Nature Center 2901 W Truman Blvd	Jefferson City	MO	65109	573-526-5544	

— Events —

	Phone
Capital Jazz Fest (early September)	573-681-5000
Christmas Parade (early December)	573-634-3616
Cole County Fair (late July-early August)	573-634-3616
Fall Festival & Crafts Fair (early September)	573-634-2824
Hartsburg Pumpkin Festival (early October)	573-657-4556
Independence Day Celebration (July 4)	573-634-3616
Luck of the Irish 5K Run & Walk (mid-March)	573-761-9000
Missouri Shakespeare Festival (early July)	573-634-6482
Old Car Roundup & Show (late May)	573-636-6666
Old Fashioned Christmas Celebration (early December)	573-634-7267
Show-Me State Games (mid-late July)	573-882-2101
State High School Track Championships (mid-late May)	573-445-4443
Super Cruise Car Show (late May)	573-634-3616
Washington Park Winter Skating Recital (mid-December)	573-634-6482

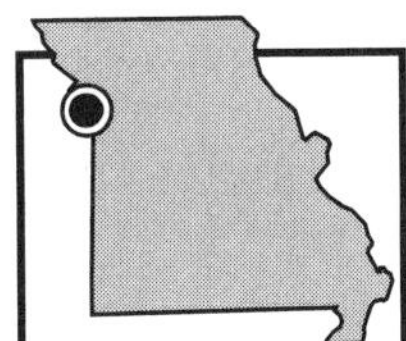

Kansas City

Some of the oldest buildings in Kansas City are located in the unique historic district of Westport. A center for outfitting and Indian trade in the 1850s, Westport is now home to shopping areas built from preserved old building facades. Its Pioneer Park traces the district's role in the founding of Kansas City. In contrast, Kansas City's ultramodern Crown Center complex is a "city within a city," with live theater, 80 shops and restaurants, ice-skating facilities, and the Hallmark Visitors Center. An event which brings thousands of visitors to Kansas City each November is the American Royal Livestock Horse Show and Rodeo, the largest combined show of its kind in the country. The home of President Harry S Truman and his Library and Museum are located in the nearby town of Independence.

Population	441,574	**Longitude**	94-57-00 W
Area (Land)	154.7 sq mi	**County**	Jackson
Area (Water)	2.4 sq mi	**Time Zone**	CST
Elevation	800 ft	**Area Code/s**	816
Latitude	39-09-00 N		

Kansas City (Cont'd)

— Average Temperatures and Precipitation —

TEMPERATURES

	Jan	Feb	Mar	Apr	May	Jun	Jul	Aug	Sep	Oct	Nov	Dec
High	35	41	53	65	74	83	89	86	78	68	53	39
Low	17	22	33	44	54	63	68	66	57	46	34	22

PRECIPITATION

	Jan	Feb	Mar	Apr	May	Jun	Jul	Aug	Sep	Oct	Nov	Dec
Inches	1.1	1.1	2.5	3.1	5.0	4.7	4.4	4.0	4.9	3.3	1.9	1.6

— Important Phone Numbers —

	Phone
AAA	816-931-5252
American Express Travel	816-531-9114
Dental Referral	816-737-5353
Emergency	911
Events Bureau Fun Phone	816-691-3800
HotelDocs	800-468-3537
Jazz Hotline	816-753-5277
Medical Referral	816-531-8432
Poison Control Center	816-234-3434
Time/Temp	816-844-4444
Weather	913-384-5555

— Information Sources —

				Phone	Fax
Better Business Bureau Serving Greater Kansas City 306 E 12th St Suite 1024 *Web:* www.kansascity.bbb.org	Kansas City	MO	64106	816-421-7800	472-5442
Convention & Visitors Bureau of Greater Kansas City 1100 Main St Suite 2550 *TF:* 800-767-7700 ■ *Web:* www.visitkc.com	Kansas City	MO	64105	816-221-5242	691-3805
Greater Kansas City Chamber of Commerce 911 Main St Suite 2600 *Web:* www.kcity.com	Kansas City	MO	64105	816-221-2424	221-7440
Jackson County 415 E 12th St	Kansas City	MO	64106	816-881-3522	
Kansas City City Hall 414 E 12th St *Web:* www.kcmo.org	Kansas City	MO	64106	816-274-2000	
Kansas City Convention Center 301 W 13th St *TF:* 800-821-7060 ■ *Web:* www.kcconvention.com	Kansas City	MO	64105	816-871-3700	871-3710
Kansas City Mayor 414 E 12th St 29th Fl *Web:* www.kcmo.org/mayor/home.htm ■ *E-mail:* mayor@kcmo.org	Kansas City	MO	64106	816-274-2595	274-1991
Kansas City Planning & Development Dept 414 E 12th St 15th Fl *Web:* www.kcmo.org/planning/home.htm	Kansas City	MO	64106	816-274-1841	274-1840
Kansas City Public Library 311 E 12th St *Web:* www.kcpl.lib.mo.us ■ *E-mail:* postmaster@kcpl.lib.mo.us	Kansas City	MO	64106	816-221-2685	842-6839

On-Line Resources

4KansasCity.com	www.4kansascity.com
About.com Guide to Kansas City	kansascity.about.com
Access America Kansas City	www.accessamer.com/kansascity/
Anthill City Guide Kansas City	www.anthill.com/city.asp?city=kansascity
Area Guide Kansas City	kansascity.areaguides.net
City Knowledge Kansas City	www.cityknowledge.com/mo_kansascity.htm
CuisineNet Kansas City	www.menusonline.com/cities/kansas_city/locmain.shtml
Excite.com Kansas City City Guide	www.excite.com/travel/countries/united_states/missouri/kansas_city
Greater Kansas City Civic Center	worldmall.com/wmcc/wmcc.htm
Kansas City Jazz Ambassador Magazine	www.kansascity.com/kcjazz
Kansas City.Com	www.kansascity.com/
KansasCity.TheLinks.com	kansascity.thelinks.com/
Virtual Kansas City	www.virtualkansascity.com/
Webcrafter's KC Metro	webcrafters.com/kcmetro

— Transportation Services —

AIRPORTS

■ **Kansas City International Airport (MCI)**

	Phone
25 miles NW of downtown (approx 30 minutes)	816-243-5237

Web: www.kcairports.org

Airport Transportation

	Phone
KCI Shuttle $11 fare to downtown	816-243-5000
Taxi $26-28 fare to downtown	816-471-5000

Commercial Airlines

	Phone
Air Canada	800-776-3000
AirTran	800-247-8726
America West	800-235-9292
American	800-433-7300
Continental	800-525-0280
Continental Express	800-525-0280
Delta	800-221-1212
Midwest Express	800-452-2022
Northwest	800-225-2525
Redwing Airways	660-665-6607
Southwest	800-435-9792
TWA	800-221-2000
United	800-241-6522
US Airways	800-428-4322
Vanguard	800-826-4827

Charter Airlines

	Phone
Executive Beechcraft	816-842-8484
Spirit Aviation	816-221-3192

CAR RENTALS

	Phone
Alamo	816-464-5151
Avis	816-243-5760
Budget	816-243-5757
Dollar	816-243-5600
Hertz	816-243-5765
National	816-243-5770
Thrifty	816-464-5670

LIMO/TAXI

	Phone
Adrienne Exclusive Limousines	816-822-7919
Armour Limousine	816-942-5959
Corporate Coach	913-432-1700
Metropolitan Transportation	816-471-6050
Overland Limousine	913-381-3504
Superior One Limousine	816-737-1180
Yellow Cab	816-471-5000

MASS TRANSIT

	Phone
Kansas City Trolley $9 Base fare	816-221-3399
Metro $.90 Base fare	816-221-0660

RAIL/BUS

				Phone
Amtrak Station 2200 Main St *TF:* 800-872-7245	Kansas City	MO	64108	816-421-3622
Greyhound Bus Station 1101 Troost St *TF:* 800-231-2222	Kansas City	MO	64106	816-221-2885

— Accommodations —

HOTELS, MOTELS, RESORTS

				Phone	Fax
Adam's Mark Hotel 9103 E 39th St *TF:* 800-444-2326 ■ *Web:* www.adamsmark.com/kcity.htm	Kansas City	MO	64133	816-737-0200	737-4712
Best Western 6101 E 87th St *TF:* 800-532-6338	Kansas City	MO	64138	816-765-4331	765-7395
Best Western Country Inn 7100 NE Parvin Rd	Kansas City	MO	64117	816-453-3355	453-0242
Broadway Plaza Suites 4615 Broadway	Kansas City	MO	64112	816-753-1044	753-3074
Courtyard by Marriott Airport 7901 NW Tiffany Springs Pkwy *TF:* 800-321-2211 ■ *Web:* courtyard.com/MCICA	Kansas City	MO	64153	816-891-7500	891-8855
Crowne Plaza Kansas City 4445 Main St *TF:* 800-465-4329	Kansas City	MO	64111	816-531-3000	531-3007
Embassy Suites 7640 NW Tiffany Springs Pkwy *TF:* 800-362-2779	Kansas City	MO	64153	816-891-7788	891-7513
Embassy Suites Country Club Plaza 220 W 43rd St *TF:* 800-362-2779	Kansas City	MO	64111	816-756-1720	756-3260
Extended StayAmerica 11712 NW Plaza Cir *TF:* 800-398-7829	Kansas City	MO	64153	816-270-7829	270-3872
Extended StayAmerica 550 E 105th St *TF:* 800-398-7829	Kansas City	MO	64131	816-943-1315	943-1322
Hampton Inn 1051 N Cambridge *TF:* 800-426-7866	Kansas City	MO	64120	816-483-7900	483-8887
Hampton Inn Airport 11212 N Newark Cir *TF:* 800-426-7866	Kansas City	MO	64153	816-464-5454	464-5416
Hilton Hotel Airport 8801 NW 112th St *TF:* 800-525-6322 ■ *Web:* www.hilton.com/hotels/MCIAPHF	Kansas City	MO	64153	816-891-8900	891-8030

Kansas City — Hotels, Motels, Resorts (Cont'd)

				Phone	Fax
Historic Suites 612 Central St	Kansas City	MO	64105	816-842-6544	842-0656
TF: 800-733-0612 ■ *Web:* www.historicsuites.com					
Holiday Inn Airport 11832 NW Plaza Cir	Kansas City	MO	64153	816-464-2345	464-2543
TF: 800-465-4329					
Holiday Inn City Centre					
1215 Wyandotte St	Kansas City	MO	64105	816-471-1333	421-4820
TF: 800-465-4329					
■ *Web:* www.basshotels.com/holiday-inn/?_franchisee=MKCCC					
■ *E-mail:* hicc@swbell.net					
Holiday Inn Express Airport					
11130 NW Ambassador Dr	Kansas City	MO	64153	816-891-9111	891-8811
TF: 800-465-4329					
Holiday Inn South 5701 Longview Rd	Kansas City	MO	64137	816-765-4100	765-6399
TF: 800-465-4329					
Holiday Inn Sports Complex					
4011 Blue Ridge Cutoff	Kansas City	MO	64133	816-353-5300	353-1199
TF: 800-465-4329					
Homewood Suites 7312 NW Polo Dr	Kansas City	MO	64153	816-880-9880	880-9461
TF: 800-225-5466					
Hotel Phillips 106 W 12th St	Kansas City	MO	64105	816-221-7000	221-3477
TF: 800-537-8483					
Hotel Savoy 219 W 9th St	Kansas City	MO	64105	816-842-3575	842-3575
TF: 800-728-6922					
Howard Johnson Lodge East					
4200 S Noland Rd	Independence	MO	64055	816-373-8856	373-3312
TF: 800-338-3752					
Hyatt Regency Crown Center					
2345 McGee St	Kansas City	MO	64108	816-421-1234	435-4190
TF: 800-233-1234					
■ *Web:* www.hyatt.com/usa/kansas_city/hotels/hotel_mkcrk.html					
Marriott Hotel Airport 775 Brasilia Ave	Kansas City	MO	64153	816-464-2200	464-5915
TF: 800-228-9290					
Marriott Hotel Downtown 200 W 12th St	Kansas City	MO	64105	816-421-6800	855-4418
TF: 800-228-9290 ■ *Web:* marriotthotels.com/MCIDT					
Park Place Hotel 1601 N Universal Ave	Kansas City	MO	64120	816-483-9900	231-1418
TF: 800-821-8532					
Quarterage Hotel 560 Westport Rd	Kansas City	MO	64111	816-931-0001	931-8891
TF: 800-942-4233 ■ *Web:* www.quarteragehotel.com					
■ *E-mail:* info@quarteragehotel.com					
Ramada Hotel Kansas City Airport					
7301 NW Tiffany Springs Rd	Kansas City	MO	64153	816-741-9500	741-0655
TF: 800-234-9501					
Raphael Hotel 325 Ward Pkwy	Kansas City	MO	64112	816-756-3800	802-2131
TF: 800-821-5343					
Residence Inn by Marriott					
9900 NW Prairie View Rd	Kansas City	MO	64153	816-891-9009	891-8623
TF: 800-331-3131 ■ *Web:* www.residenceinn.com/residenceinn/MKCAA					
Ritz-Carlton Kansas City 401 Ward Pkwy	Kansas City	MO	64112	816-756-1500	756-1635
TF: 800-241-3333					
■ *Web:*www.ritzcarlton.com/location/NorthAmerica/KansasCity/main.htm					
Sheraton Suites Country Club Plaza					
770 W 47th St	Kansas City	MO	64112	816-931-4400	561-7330
TF: 800-325-3535					
Southmoreland on the Plaza					
116 E 46th St	Kansas City	MO	64112	816-531-7979	531-2407
Station Casino Hotel Kansas City					
3200 N Station Dr	Kansas City	MO	64161	816-414-7000	414-7250
TF: 800-499-4961 ■ *Web:* www.kansascitystation.com/rooms.html					
Westin Crown Center Hotel					
1 Pershing Rd	Kansas City	MO	64108	816-474-4400	391-4438
TF: 800-228-3000					
Wyndham Garden Hotel					
11828 NW Plaza Cir	Kansas City	MO	64153	816-464-2423	464-2560
TF: 800-996-3426					
Wyndham Garden Hotel 1 E 45th St	Kansas City	MO	64111	816-753-7400	753-0359
TF: 800-996-3426					

— Restaurants —

				Phone
American Restaurant (American) 2500 Grand Ave	Kansas City	MO	64108	816-426-1133
Arthur Bryant Barbeque (Barbecue) 1727 Brooklyn Ave	Kansas City	MO	64127	816-231-1123
BB's Lawnside Bar-B-Q (Barbecue) 1205 E 85th St	Kansas City	MO	64131	816-822-7427
Bluebird The (Vegetarian) 1700 Summit	Kansas City	MO	64108	816-221-7559
Boulevard Cafe (Mediterranean) 703 Southwest Blvd	Kansas City	MO	64108	816-842-6984
Cafe Allegro (New American) 1815 W 39th St	Kansas City	MO	64111	816-561-3663
Cafe Barcelona (Spanish) 520 Southwest Blvd	Kansas City	MO	64111	816-471-4944
Californos (American) 4124 Pennsylvania Ave	Kansas City	MO	64111	816-531-7878
Classic Cup (Continental) 301 W 47th St	Kansas City	MO	64112	816-753-1840
EBT (American) 1310 Carondelet Dr	Kansas City	MO	64114	816-942-8870
Fedora Cafe & Bar (Continental) 210 W 47th St	Kansas City	MO	64112	816-561-6565
Gates & Sons Bar-B-Q (Barbecue) 3201 Main St	Kansas City	MO	64110	816-753-0828
Genghis Khan (Chinese) 3906 Bell St	Kansas City	MO	64111	816-753-3600
Golden Ox Restaurant & Lounge (Steak)				
1600 Genessee St	Kansas City	MO	64102	816-842-2866
Grand Street Cafe (American) 4740 Grand Ave	Kansas City	MO	64112	816-561-8000
Guacamole Grill (Mexican) 11134 Holmes Rd	Kansas City	MO	64131	816-943-1299
Hannah Bistro Café (American) 3895 Stateline Rd	Kansas City	MO	64111	816-960-1300
Hereford House (Steak) 2 E 20th St	Kansas City	MO	64108	816-842-1080
Web: www.herefordhouse.com ■ *E-mail:* beef@herefordhouse.com				
Houston's (American) 4640 Wornall Rd	Kansas City	MO	64112	816-561-8542
Japengo (Pan-Asian) 600 Ward Pkwy	Kansas City	MO	64112	816-931-6600
Jasper's (Continental) 1201 W 103rd St	Kansas City	MO	64114	816-941-6600
Jazz Restaurant (Cajun/Creole) 1823 W 39th St	Kansas City	MO	64111	816-531-5556
Web: www.jazzkitchen.com				
JJ's (Continental) 910 W 48th St	Kansas City	MO	64112	816-561-7136
Jules' Seafood on the Plaza (Seafood)				
4740 Jefferson St	Kansas City	MO	64112	816-561-4004
Kabuki (Japanese) 2450 Grand Ave Suite 110	Kansas City	MO	64108	816-472-1717
KC Masterpiece Barbecue & Grill (Barbecue)				
4747 Wyandotte St	Kansas City	MO	64112	816-531-3332
La Mediterranee (French) 9058 MetCalf Ave	Kansas City	MO	64112	816-561-2916
Las Chiquitas (Mexican) 1656 Broadway	Kansas City	MO	64108	816-421-9229
LC's BBQ (Barbecue) 5800 Blue Pkwy	Kansas City	MO	64129	816-923-4484
Le Fou Frog (French) 400 E 5th St	Kansas City	MO	64106	816-474-6060
Lidia's Kansas City (Italian) 101 W 22nd St	Kansas City	MO	64108	816-221-3722
Macaluso's (Italian) 1403 W 39th St	Kansas City	MO	64111	816-561-0100
Madry's Dash of Flavor (Soul) 26 E 39th St	Kansas City	MO	64111	816-753-3274
Marco Polo's Italian Market (Italian) 1201 W 103rd St	Kansas City	MO	64114	816-941-6600
Margarita's (Mexican) 2829 Southwest Blvd	Kansas City	MO	64108	816-931-4849
Metropolis American Grill (American)				
303 Westport Rd	Kansas City	MO	64111	816-753-1550
Milano (Italian) 2450 Grand Ave	Kansas City	MO	64108	816-426-1130
Mill Creek Brewery (American) 4050 Pennsylvania Ave	Kansas City	MO	64111	816-931-4499
Papagallo Restaurant (Mediterranean) 3535 Broadway	Kansas City	MO	64111	816-756-3227
Phoenix Piano Bar & Grill (American) 302 W 8th St	Kansas City	MO	64105	816-472-0001
Plaza III Steakhouse (Steak) 4749 Pennsylvania Ave	Kansas City	MO	64112	816-753-0000
Raphael Restaurant (Continental) 325 Ward Pkwy	Kansas City	MO	64112	816-756-3800
Red Dragon House (Chinese) 312 W 8th St	Kansas City	MO	64105	816-221-1388
Rembrandt Restaurant (New American)				
2820 NW Barry Rd	Kansas City	MO	64154	816-436-8700
Web: www.rembrandt-s.com/				
River Market Brewing Co (American) 500 Walnut St	Kansas City	MO	64106	816-471-6300
Savoy Grill (Steak/Seafood) 219 W 9th St	Kansas City	MO	64105	816-842-3890
Skies (American) 2345 McGee St	Kansas City	MO	64108	816-435-4199
Starker's (American) 201 W 47th St	Kansas City	MO	64112	816-753-3565
Stephenson's Apple Farm Restaurant (American)				
16401 E 40 Hwy	Kansas City	MO	64136	816-373-5400
Stolen Grill (American) 904 Westport Rd	Kansas City	MO	64111	816-960-1450
Streetcar Named Desire (American) 2450 Grand Ave	Kansas City	MO	64108	816-472-5959
Walt Bodine's Steakhouse (Steak) 106 W 12th St	Kansas City	MO	64105	816-221-7000
Winslow's City Market Smoke House (Barbecue)				
20 E 5th St	Kansas City	MO	64106	816-471-7427

— Goods and Services —

SHOPPING

				Phone	Fax
39th Street Corridor 39th & Bell Sts	Kansas City	MO	64111	816-561-5411	
Antioch Shopping Center					
5307 Center Mall	Kansas City	MO	64119	816-454-1200	
Bannister Mall 5600 E Bannister Rd	Kansas City	MO	64137	816-763-6900	763-3920
Web: www.augustamall.com					
City Market/River Market					
20 E 5th St Suite 201	Kansas City	MO	64106	816-842-1271	
Country Club Plaza 450 Ward Pkwy	Kansas City	MO	64112	816-753-0100	753-4625
Crown Center 2450 Grand Ave	Kansas City	MO	64108	816-274-8444	545-6595
Web: www.crowncenter.com					
Dillard's 8800 Ward Pkwy	Kansas City	MO	64114	816-363-8800	
Great Mall of the Great Plains					
20700 W 151st St	Olathe	KS	66061	888-386-6255	
Hall's 200 E 25th St	Kansas City	MO	64108	816-274-8111	274-4471
Independence Center					
2035 Independence Center Dr	Independence	MO	64057	816-795-8600	795-7836
Jones Store 9757 Metcalf	Overland Park	KS	66212	913-652-8651	652-7438
TF: 800-821-2146					
Metro North Mall 400 NW Barry Rd	Kansas City	MO	64155	816-436-7800	436-9952
Saks Fifth Avenue 444 Nichols Rd	Kansas City	MO	64112	816-931-6000	753-4564
Town Pavilion 1111 Main St Suite 218	Kansas City	MO	64105	816-472-9600	474-0693
Ward Parkway Shopping Center					
8600 Ward Pkwy	Kansas City	MO	64114	816-363-3545	
Westport Historic District					
Broadway & Westport Rd	Kansas City	MO	64111	816-756-2789	
Westport Square 4123 Mill St	Kansas City	MO	64111	816-756-2789	

Kansas City (Cont'd)

BANKS

Name / Address	City	State	Zip	Phone	Fax
Blue Ridge Bank & Trust Co 4240 Blue Ridge Blvd Suite 100	Kansas City	MO	64133	816-358-5000	356-7530
Commerce Bank NA 1000 Walnut St	Kansas City	MO	64106	816-234-2000	234-2799
TF Cust Svc: 800-453-2265 ■ *Web:* www.commercebank.com ■ *E-mail:* mymoney@commercebank.com					
Mercantile Bank 4901 Main St	Kansas City	MO	64112	816-472-6372	360-6182
Mercantile Bank of Kansas City 1101 Walnut Tower	Kansas City	MO	64106	816-842-2000	871-2326
Web: www.mercantile.com/kansas					
NationsBank 14 W 10th St	Kansas City	MO	64105	816-221-2800	979-7424
TF: 800-366-6364					
UMB Bank NA 1010 Grand Blvd	Kansas City	MO	64106	816-860-7000	421-5411
TF: 800-821-2171 ■ *Web:* www.umb.com					

BUSINESS SERVICES

Name	Phone
AB Express	816-461-4040
Accountemps	816-474-4583
Action Delivery	816-241-3300
Adecco Employment Personnel Services	816-756-0340
Direct Messenger Service	913-631-7515
Federal Express	800-463-3339
Kelly Services	913-661-0402
Kinko's	816-444-0500
Manpower Temporary Services	816-224-5122
Post Office	800-275-8777
Today's Office Staffing	816-471-4972
UPS	800-742-5877

— Media —

PUBLICATIONS

Name / Address	City	State	Zip	Phone	Fax
Kansas City Business Journal 1101 Walnut St Suite 800	Kansas City	MO	64106	816-421-5900	472-4010
Web: www.amcity.com/kansascity ■ *E-mail:* kansascity@amcity.com					
Kansas City Star‡ 1729 Grand Blvd	Kansas City	MO	64108	816-234-4141	234-4926
Web: www.kcstar.com ■ *E-mail:* starstaff@kcstar.com					
Raytown Dispatch-Tribune 7007 NE Parvin Rd	Kansas City	MO	64117	816-454-9660	452-5889*
**Fax:* News Rm					
Wednesday Magazine 20 E Gregory St	Kansas City	MO	64114	816-454-9660	822-1856

‡Daily newspapers

TELEVISION

Name / Address	City	State	Zip	Phone	Fax
KCPT-TV Ch 19 (PBS) 125 E 31st St	Kansas City	MO	64108	816-756-3580	931-2500
Web: www.kcpt.org ■ *E-mail:* kcpt@tv19.kcpt.org					
KCTV-TV Ch 5 (CBS) PO Box 5555	Kansas City	MO	64109	913-677-5555	677-7243
Web: www.kctv.com ■ *E-mail:* kctv@kctv.com					
KCWE-TV Ch 29 (UPN) 1049 Central	Kansas City	MO	64105	816-221-2900	760-9149*
**Fax:* Sales					
KMBC-TV Ch 9 (ABC) 1049 Central St	Kansas City	MO	64105	816-221-9999	421-4163
Web: www.kmbc.com					
KSHB-TV Ch 41 (NBC) 4720 Oak St	Kansas City	MO	64112	816-753-4141	932-4145
Web: www.kshb.com ■ *E-mail:* news@kshb.com					
WDAF-TV Ch 4 (Fox) 3030 Summit St	Kansas City	MO	64108	816-753-4567	561-4181
Web: www.wdaftv4.com					

RADIO

Name / Address	City	State	Zip	Phone	Fax
KBEQ-FM 104.3 MHz (Ctry) 4717 Grand Ave Suite 600	Kansas City	MO	64112	816-531-2535	531-7327
Web: www.kbeq.com					
KCFX-FM 101.1 MHz (Rock) 5800 Foxridge Dr	Mission	KS	66202	913-514-3000	514-3003
KCIY-FM 106.5 MHz (Nost) 5800 Foxridge Dr Suite 600	Mission	KS	66202	913-514-3000	514-3003
KCMO-AM 710 kHz (N/T) 4935 Belinder Rd	Westwood	KS	66205	913-677-8998	677-8901
KCMO-FM 94.9 MHz (Oldies) 4935 Belinder Rd	Westwood	KS	66205	913-677-8998	677-8901*
**Fax:* News Rm					
KCTE-AM 1510 kHz (Sports) 10841 E 28th St	Independence	MO	64052	816-836-8326	836-2111
KCUR-FM 89.3 MHz (NPR) 4825 Troost Ave Suite 202	Kansas City	MO	64110	816-235-1551	235-2864
Web: www.umkc.edu/kcur ■ *E-mail:* kcur@smtpgate.umkc.edu					
KFKF-FM 94.1 MHz (Ctry) 4717 Grand Ave Suite 600	Kansas City	MO	64112	816-753-4000	753-4045
Web: sites.kansascity.com/kfkf ■ *E-mail:* kfkf@kansascity.com					
KGGN-AM 890 kHz (Rel) 1734 E 63rd St Suite 600	Kansas City	MO	64110	816-333-0092	363-8120
KKFI-FM 90.1 MHz (Misc) 900 1/2 Westport Rd 2nd Fl.	Kansas City	MO	64111	816-931-3122	931-7078
KLJC-FM 88.5 MHz (Rel) 15800 Calvary Rd	Kansas City	MO	64147	816-331-8700	303-1553
Web: www.kljc.org ■ *E-mail:* kljc@kljc.org					
KMBZ-AM 980 kHz (N/T) 4935 Belinder Rd	Westwood	KS	66205	913-236-9800	677-8901
KMXV-FM 93.3 MHz (CHR) 508 Westport Rd	Kansas City	MO	64111	816-756-5698	531-2550
Web: www.mix93.com					
KNRX-FM 107.3 MHz (Urban) 4240 Blue Ridge Blvd Suite 820	Kansas City	MO	64133	816-353-7600	353-2300
Web: www.1073thex.com ■ *E-mail:* comments@1073thex.com					
KPHN-AM 1190 kHz (N/T) 1212 Baltimore St	Kansas City	KS	64105	816-421-1900	266-1190
Web: www.kphn1190.com ■ *E-mail:* mail@kphn1190.com					
KPRS-FM 103.3 MHz (Urban) 11131 Colorado Ave	Kansas City	MO	64137	816-763-2040	966-1055
Web: www.kprs.com ■ *E-mail:* 103@kprs.com					
KPRT-AM 1590 kHz (Rel) 11131 Colorado Ave	Kansas City	MO	64137	816-763-2040	966-1055
KQRC-FM 98.9 MHz (Rock) 4350 Shawnee Mission Pkwy Suite 99	Mission	KS	66202	913-514-3000	384-9911
Web: www.989therock.com					
KSRC-FM 102.1 MHz (AC) 508 Westport Rd Suite 202	Kansas City	MO	64111	816-561-9102	531-2550
KUDL-FM 98.1 MHz (AC) 4935 Belinder Rd	Westwood	KS	66205	913-236-9800	677-8981
Web: www.kudl.com					
KXTR-FM 96.5 MHz (Clas) 5800 Foxridge Dr	Mission	KS	66202	913-514-3000	514-3003
KYYS-FM 99.7 MHz (Rock) 4935 Belinder Rd	Westwood	KS	66205	913-677-8998	677-8901
WDAF-AM 610 kHz (Ctry) 4935 Belinder Rd	Westwood	KS	66205	913-677-8998	677-8901
WHB-AM 810 kHz (Ctry) 1600 Genesee St Suite 925	Kansas City	MO	64102	816-221-7170	221-7944

— Colleges/Universities —

Name / Address	City	State	Zip	Phone	Fax
Avila College 11901 Wornall Rd	Kansas City	MO	64145	816-942-8400	942-3362
TF: 800-462-8452 ■ *Web:* www.avila.edu ■ *E-mail:* admissions@mail.avila.edu					
Calvary Bible College & Seminary 15800 Calvary Rd	Kansas City	MO	64147	816-322-0110	331-4474
TF Admissions: 800-326-3960 ■ *Web:* www.calvary.edu					
Concorde Career Colleges Inc 5800 Foxridge Dr Mission Corporate Ctr Suite 500	Mission	KS	66202	913-831-9977	831-6556
TF: 800-515-1007 ■ *Web:* www.concordecareercolleges.com					
DeVRY Institute of Technology 11224 Holmes Rd	Kansas City	MO	64131	816-941-0430	941-0896
TF: 800-821-3766 ■ *Web:* www.kc.devry.edu					
Finlay Engineering College 7 E 79th Terr	Kansas City	MO	64114	816-523-6030	
Graceland College 1401 W Truman Rd	Independence	MO	64050	816-833-0524	833-2990
TF: 800-833-0524					
Kansas City Art Institute 4415 Warwick Blvd	Kansas City	MO	64111	816-472-4852	802-3309
TF Admissions: 800-522-5224*					
Longview Community College 500 SW Longview Rd	Lees Summit	MO	64081	816-672-2000	672-2040
Web: www.longview.cc.mo.us					
Maple Woods Community College 2601 NE Barry Rd	Kansas City	MO	64156	816-437-3000	437-3049
Web: www.kcmetro.cc.mo.us/maplewoods/mwhome.html					
MidAmerica Nazarene University 2030 E College Way	Olathe	KS	66062	913-782-3750	791-3481
TF Admissions: 800-800-8887 ■ *Web:* www.mnu.edu					
National American University Kansas City Campus 4200 Blue Ridge Blvd	Kansas City	MO	64133	816-353-4554	353-1176
Web: www.nationalcollege.edu/campuskansas.html					
Penn Valley Community College 3201 SW Trafficway	Kansas City	MO	64111	816-759-4000	759-4161
Web: www.kcmetro.cc.mo.us/pennvalley					
Rockhurst College 1100 Rockhurst Rd	Kansas City	MO	64110	816-501-4000	501-4588
TF Admissions: 800-842-6776 ■ *Web:* www.rockhurst.edu ■ *E-mail:* wadsworth@vax2.rockhurst.edu					
University of Missouri Kansas City 5100 Rockhill Rd	Kansas City	MO	64110	816-235-1000	235-5544
Web: www.umkc.edu ■ *E-mail:* catalog-admin@smtpgate.umkc.edu					

Kansas City (Cont'd)

— Hospitals —

				Phone	Fax
Baptist Medical Center 6601 Rockhill Rd.	Kansas City	MO	64131	816-276-7000	926-2266
Web: www.healthmidwest.org/Hospitals_and_Services/Baptist_Medical_Center/					
Bethany Medical Center 51 N 12th St.	Kansas City	KS	66102	913-281-8400	281-8494
Children's Mercy Hospital 2401 Gillham Rd.	Kansas City	MO	64108	816-234-3000	842-6107
Web: www.cmh.edu					
Columbia Independence Regional Health Center 1509 W Truman Rd	Independence	MO	64050	816-836-8100	836-6003
Liberty Hospital 2525 Glenn Hendren Dr	Liberty	MO	64069	816-781-7200	792-7117
Medical Center of Independence 17203 E 23rd St.	Independence	MO	64057	816-478-5000	478-5383
Web: www.healthmidwest.org/Hospitals_and_Services/Medical_Center_of_Independence					
Menorah Medical Center 5721 W 119th St	Overland Park	KS	66209	913-498-6000	498-7106
Web: www.healthmidwest.org/Hospitals_and_Services/Menorah_Medical_Center/					
North Kansas City Hospital 2800 Clay Edwards Dr.	North Kansas City	MO	64116	816-691-2000	346-7192*
**Fax:* Library					
Olathe Medical Center 20333 W 151st St	Olathe	KS	66061	913-791-4200	791-4454
Web: www.omci.com					
Overland Park Regional Medical Center 10500 Quivira Rd	Overland Park	KS	66215	913-541-5000	541-5484
Providence Medical Center 8929 Parallel Pkwy	Kansas City	KS	66112	913-596-4000	596-4098
Research Medical Center 2316 E Meyer Blvd	Kansas City	MO	64132	816-276-4000	276-4387
Saint Joseph Health Center 1000 Carondelet Dr.	Kansas City	MO	64114	816-942-4400	943-2840
Saint Luke's Hospital 4401 Wornall Rd.	Kansas City	MO	64111	816-932-2000	932-3884
Web: www.saint-lukes.org/about/stlukes.html					
Saint Mary's Hospital of Blue Springs 201 W RD Mize Rd.	Blue Springs	MO	64014	816-228-5900	655-5408
Shawnee Mission Medical Center 9100 W 74th St	Shawnee Mission	KS	66204	913-676-2000	789-3178
Web: www.saintlukes.org					
Trinity Lutheran Hospital 3030 Baltimore Ave.	Kansas City	MO	64108	816-751-4600	751-4590*
**Fax:* Admitting ■ *Web:* www.healthmidwest.org/Hospitals_and_Services/Trinity_Lutheran_Hospital					
Truman Medical Center East 7900 Lee's Summit Rd	Kansas City	MO	64139	816-373-4415	478-7500
Truman Medical Center West 2301 Holmes St	Kansas City	MO	64108	816-556-3000	556-3882*
**Fax:* Hum Res					
University of Kansas Medical Center 3901 Rainbow Blvd.	Kansas City	KS	66160	913-588-1270	588-1280
Web: www.kumc.edu/Pulse					
Veterans Affairs Medical Center 4801 E Linwood Blvd	Kansas City	MO	64128	816-861-4700	922-3329*
**Fax:* Hum Res					

— Attractions —

				Phone	Fax
39th Street Corridor 39th & Bell Sts	Kansas City	MO	64111	816-561-5411	
American Heartland Theatre 2450 Grand Blvd Suite 314	Kansas City	MO	64108	816-842-0202	842-1881
American Jazz Museum 1616 E 18th St	Kansas City	MO	64108	816-474-8463	474-0074
Web: www.kcjazz.org/jazz.htm ■ *E-mail:* postmaster@kcjazz.org					
American Royal Museum & Visitors Center 1701 American Royal Ct	Kansas City	MO	64102	816-221-9800	221-8189
Web: www.americanroyal.com ■ *E-mail:* mericanroyal@americanroyal.com					
Arabia Steamboat Museum 400 Grand Blvd.	Kansas City	MO	64106	816-471-1856	471-1616
TF: 800-471-1856 ■ *Web:* www.1856.com ■ *E-mail:* info@1856.com					
Benjamin Ranch on the Santa Fe Trail 6401 E 87th St.	Kansas City	MO	64138	816-761-5055	761-7400
TF: 800-437-2624					
Benton Thomas Hart Home & Studio Historic Site 3616 Belleview St	Kansas City	MO	64111	816-931-5722	
Black Archives of Mid-America 2033 Vine St	Kansas City	MO	64108	816-483-1300	483-1341
Web: www.blackarchives.org					
Boulevard Brewing Co 2501 Southwest Blvd.	Kansas City	MO	64108	816-474-7095	474-1722
Cave Spring Interpretive Center 8701 E Gregory Blvd.	Kansas City	MO	64133	816-358-2283	
Coterie Theatre 2450 Grand Blvd	Kansas City	MO	64108	816-474-6552	474-7112
Web: www.crowncenter.com/coterie.html					
Country Club Plaza 450 Ward Pkwy	Kansas City	MO	64112	816-753-0100	753-4625
Crown Center 2450 Grand Ave	Kansas City	MO	64108	816-274-8444	545-6595
Web: www.crowncenter.com					
Excelsior Springs Historical Museum 101 E Broadway	Excelsior Springs	MO	64024	816-630-3712	630-3712
Federal Reserve Bank Visitors Center 925 Grand Ave	Kansas City	MO	64198	816-881-2200	881-2568
Flamingo Hilton Casino 1800 E Front St	Kansas City	MO	64120	816-855-7777	855-4188
TF: 800-946-8711					
Folly Theater 300 W 12th St	Kansas City	MO	64105	816-474-4444	842-8709
Gem Theater Cultural & Performing Arts Center 1615 E 18th St.	Kansas City	MO	64108	816-842-4538	842-8379
Hallmark Visitors Center 2501 McGee.	Kansas City	MO	64108	816-274-3613	274-3148
Harrah's Casino Hotel North Kansas City 1 Riverboat Dr.	North Kansas City	MO	64116	816-472-7777	472-7778
TF: 800-427-7247					
Harris-Kearney House 4000 Baltimore St.	Kansas City	MO	64111	816-561-1821	
Harry S Truman National Historic Site 223 N Main St	Independence	MO	64050	816-254-2720	254-4491
Web: www.nps.gov/hstr					
Harry S Truman Presidential Library & Museum 500 W Hwy 24	Independence	MO	64050	816-833-1400	833-4368
Web: www.trumanlibrary.org ■ *E-mail:* library@truman.nara.gov					
Hodge Park 7000 NE Barry Rd	Kansas City	MO	64156	816-792-2655	
Kaleidoscope PO Box 419580	Kansas City	MO	64141	816-274-8301	274-3148
Kansas City Board of Trade 4800 Main St Suite 303.	Kansas City	MO	64112	816-753-7500	753-3944
TF: 800-821-5228 ■ *Web:* www.kcbt.com ■ *E-mail:* kcbt@kcbt.com					
Kansas City Museum 3218 Gladstone Blvd	Kansas City	MO	64123	816-483-8300	483-9912
TF: 800-556-9372 ■ *Web:* www.kcmuseum.com					
Kansas City Music Hall 301 W 13th St.	Kansas City	MO	64105	816-871-3700	871-3710
TF: 800-821-7060					
Kansas City Symphony 1020 Central St Suite 300	Kansas City	MO	64105	816-471-1100	471-0976
Web: www.kcsymphony.org ■ *E-mail:* symphony-info@kcsymphony.org					
Kansas City Zoological Gardens 6700 Zoo Dr.	Kansas City	MO	64132	816-871-5700	822-8903
Web: www.kansascityzoo.org					
Kemper Museum of Contemporary Art 4420 Warwick Blvd	Kansas City	MO	64111	816-753-5784	753-5806
Web: www.kemperart.org					
Lakeside Nature Center 4701 E Gregory Blvd Swope Park	Kansas City	MO	64132	816-545-5525	545-5533
Liberty Memorial Museum & Archives 100 W 26th St	Kansas City	MO	64108	816-221-1918	221-8981
Lyric Opera of Kansas City 1029 Central St.	Kansas City	MO	64105	816-471-4933	471-0602
Web: kc-opera.org ■ *E-mail:* mail@kc-opera.org					
Majors Alexander Historic House & Museum 8201 State Line Rd	Kansas City	MO	64114	816-333-5556	
Martin City Melodrama 13440 Holmes Rd.	Kansas City	MO	64145	816-942-7576	
Midland Theatre 1228 Main St.	Kansas City	MO	64105	816-471-8600	221-1127
Web: www.amctheatres.com/theatres/kc_midland/index.html					
Missouri Repertory Theatre 4949 Cherry St.	Kansas City	MO	64110	816-235-2700	235-5367
TF: 888-502-2700 ■ *Web:* cctr.umkc.edu/user/gkeathley/missouri.htm					
Museums at 18th & Vine 1616 E 18th St	Kansas City	MO	64108	816-474-8463	474-0074
Web: www.kcmo.org/18&Vine/home.htm ■ *E-mail:* postmaster@kcjazz.org					
Negro Leagues Baseball Museum 1616 E 18th St.	Kansas City	MO	64108	816-221-1920	221-8424
Nelson-Atkins Museum of Art 4525 Oak St.	Kansas City	MO	64111	816-561-4000	561-7154
Web: www.nelson-atkins.org/					
Oceans of Fun 8600 NE Parvin Rd	Kansas City	MO	64161	816-454-4545	
Plaza Riverwalk Boat Cruise Wyandotte St & Ward Pkwy.	Kansas City	MO	64112	816-741-3410	
Powell Gardens Hwy 50 W	Kingsville	MO	64061	816-697-3600	697-3576
Web: www.powellgardens.org					
Quality Hill Playhouse 303 W 10th St.	Kansas City	MO	64141	816-421-1700	221-6556
Web: www.qhpkc.org					
Saint Mary's Episcopal Church 1307 Holmes St	Kansas City	MO	64106	816-842-0975	221-2371
Save a Connie Museum 480 NW Richards Rd.	Kansas City	MO	64116	816-421-3401	421-3421
TF: 800-513-9484 ■ *Web:* www.saveaconnie.org					
Shoal Creek Living History Museum 7000 NE Barry Rd Hodge Pk	Kansas City	MO	64156	816-792-2655	792-3469
Spencer Museum of Art 1301 Mississippi St University of Kansas.	Lawrence	KS	66045	785-864-4710	864-3112
Web: www.ukans.edu/~sma/					

Kansas City — Attractions (Cont'd)

				Phone	Fax
Sprint IMAX Theater 6800 Zoo Dr Deramus Education Pavilion	Kansas City	MO	64132	816-871-5800	871-5850
Starlight Theatre 4600 Starlight Rd Swope Pk	Kansas City	MO	64132	816-363-7827	361-6398
State Ballet of Missouri 1601 Broadway *Web:* www.stateballetofmissouri.org	Kansas City	MO	64108	816-931-2232	931-1172
Station Casino Kansas City 3200 N Station Dr **Fax:* Mktg ■ *TF:* 800-499-4961 ■ *Web:* www.kansascitystation.com	Kansas City	MO	64161	816-414-7000	414-7221*
Swope Park Swope Pkwy & Meyer Blvd	Kansas City	MO	64132	816-221-5242	
Toy & Minature Museum 5235 Oak St	Kansas City	MO	64112	816-333-2055	333-2055
Unicorn Theatre 3828 Main St	Kansas City	MO	64111	816-531-7529	531-0421
University of Missouri-Kansas City Gallery of Art 5100 Rockhill Rd	Kansas City	MO	64110	816-235-1502	
Vietnam Veterans Memorial 43rd St & Broadway	Kansas City	MO	64111	816-561-8387	
Watkins Bruce R Cultural Heritage Center 3700 Blue Pkwy	Kansas City	MO	64130	816-923-6226	921-0538
Westport Historic District Broadway & Westport Rd	Kansas City	MO	64111	816-756-2789	
Westport Square 4123 Mill St	Kansas City	MO	64111	816-756-2789	
Worlds of Fun 4545 Worlds of Fun Ave *Web:* www.worldsoffun.com	Kansas City	MO	64161	816-454-4545	454-4655
Wornall John House Museum 146 W 61st Terr *E-mail:* jwornall@crn.org	Kansas City	MO	64113	816-444-1858	361-8165

SPORTS TEAMS & FACILITIES

				Phone	Fax
Arrowhead Stadium 1 Arrowhead Dr *Web:* www.kcchiefs.com/fanfair/arrowhead.asp	Kansas City	MO	64129	816-920-9300	923-4719
Ewing M Kauffman Stadium 1 Royal Way *Web:* www.kcroyals.com/kauffmanstadium/kauffman_stadium.html	Kansas City	MO	64129	816-921-8000	924-0347
Kansas City Attack (soccer) 1800 Genessee St Kemper Arena *Web:* www.kcattack.com ■ *E-mail:* info@kcattack.com	Kansas City	MO	64102	816-474-2255	474-2255
Kansas City Blades (hockey) 1800 Genessee St Kemper Arena *Web:* www.kcblades.com	Kansas City	MO	64102	816-842-1063	842-5610
Kansas City Chiefs 1 Arrowhead Dr Arrowhead Stadium *Web:* www.kcchiefs.com	Kansas City	MO	64129	816-920-9300	920-4315
Kansas City Explorers (tennis) 1800 Genessee St Hale Arena	Kansas City	MO	64102	913-362-9944	362-9953
Kansas City Royals 1 Royal Way Kauffman Stadium	Kansas City	MO	64129	816-921-8000	921-5775
Kansas City Wizards (soccer) 706 Broadway St Suite 100 *Web:* www.kcwizards.com	Kansas City	MO	64105	816-472-4625	472-0299
Kemper Arena 1800 Genessee St *TF:* 800-634-3942	Kansas City	MO	64102	816-274-6222	472-0306
Lakeside Speedway 5615 Wolcott Dr *Web:* www.lakesidespeedway.com ■ *E-mail:* I70Lake@discoverynet.com	Kansas City	KS	66109	913-299-2040	299-1105
Municipal Auditorium Arena 301 W 13th St Suite 100 *TF:* 800-821-7060	Kansas City	MO	64105	816-871-3700	871-3710
Woodlands Race Track 9700 Leavenworth Rd	Kansas City	KS	66109	913-299-9797	299-9804

— Events —

	Phone
Abdallah Shrine Rodeo (mid-August)	913-362-5300
American Royal Barbecue Contest (early October)	816-221-9800
American Royal Livestock Horse Show & Rodeo (late October-early November)	800-821-5857
Brookside Art Annual (late April-early May)	816-523-0091
Cinco de Mayo Celebration (early May)	816-221-4747
Ethnic Enrichment Festival (late August)	816-842-7530
Excelsior Springs Waterfest (October)	816-792-7691
Fiesta Hispana (late September)	816-765-1992
Greater Kansas City Auto Show (early March)	816-871-3700
Greek Festival (September)	816-942-9100
Heartland of America Shakespeare Festival (late June-mid-July)	816-531-7728
Highland Games & Scottish Festival (early June)	913-432-6823
Juneteenth Celebrations (mid-June)	816-483-1300
Kansas City Blues & Jazz Festival (late July)	800-530-5266
Kansas City Home Show (mid-April-early May)	816-942-8800
Kansas City Jaycees Rodeo (early July)	816-761-5055
Kansas City River Valley Festival (late June)	816-960-0800
Kansas City Saint Patrick's Day Parade (March 17)	816-931-7373
Kiki's Crawfish Fiesta (early June)	816-842-1271
Plaza Fine Arts Fair (late September)	816-753-0100
Plaza Lighting Ceremony (late November)	816-753-0100
Renaissance Festival (early September-mid-October)	800-373-0357
Settlers' Day (early June)	816-792-2655
Shrimp Festival (late April-early May)	904-277-0717
Spirit Festival (Labor Day weekend)	816-221-4444

Saint Louis

The eastern Saint Louis skyline is dominated by the Gateway Arch, designed by Eero Saarinen and opened in 1965 as a symbol of the city's historic role as Gateway to the West. The Arch rises some 630 feet above the Mississippi in the riverfront area of Saint Louis. Along the north edge of the riverfront is Laclede's Landing, a 19th century neighborhood complete with cobblestone streets and cast iron street lamps that now serves as an entertainment district. In downtown Saint Louis is Union Station. Once the busiest passenger rail terminal in the U.S., the train shed is now a festival marketplace with more than 100 shops, as well as a major hotel, restaurants, and clubs. Just south of downtown is the headquarters of Anheuser-Busch, the world's largest brewer. A tour of its facilities includes the stables of the Budweiser Clydesdales. The city's Forest Park, which has been named one of the top ten urban parks in the country, is the site of the Saint Louis Art Museum, History Museum, Science Center, and the Saint Louis Zoo, a world-class facility with more than 6,000 animals. The Missouri Botanical Garden in Saint Louis has the nation's largest authentic Japanese garden, as well as woodland and scented gardens and a Climatron greenhouse that is a geodesic dome. The New Cathedral of Saint Louis is a Romanesque-Byzantine structure containing the world's largest collection of mosaic art.

Population	339,316	**Longitude**	90-19-78 W
Area (Land)	61.9 sq mi	**County**	Independent City
Area (Water)	4.2 sq mi	**Time Zone**	CST
Elevation	470 ft	**Area Code/s**	314
Latitude	38-62-72 N		

— Average Temperatures and Precipitation —

TEMPERATURES

	Jan	Feb	Mar	Apr	May	Jun	Jul	Aug	Sep	Oct	Nov	Dec
High	38	43	55	67	76	85	89	87	80	69	55	42
Low	21	25	36	46	56	66	70	68	61	48	38	26

PRECIPITATION

	Jan	Feb	Mar	Apr	May	Jun	Jul	Aug	Sep	Oct	Nov	Dec
Inches	1.8	2.1	3.6	3.5	4.0	3.7	3.9	2.9	3.1	2.7	3.3	3.0

— Important Phone Numbers —

	Phone		Phone
AAA	314-576-7373	**HotelDocs**	800-468-3537
American Express Travel	314-241-6400	**Poison Control Center**	314-772-5200
Dental Referral	314-965-5960	**Special Events**	314-421-2100
Disabled Accessibility Information	314-622-3686	**Time/Temp**	314-321-2522
Emergency	911	**Travelers Aid Society**	314-241-5820
		Weather	314-321-2222

Saint Louis (Cont'd)

— Information Sources —

				Phone	Fax
Better Business Bureau Serving Eastern Missouri & Southern Illinois 12 Sunnen Dr Suite 121 *Web:* www.stlouis.bbb.org	Saint Louis	MO	63143	314-645-3300	645-2666
Cervantes Convention Center at America's Center 701 Convention Plaza	Saint Louis	MO	63101	314-342-5036	342-5040
Regional Commerce & Growth Assn 1 Metropolitan Sq Suite 1300 *TF:* 800-444-7653 ■ *Web:* www.stlrcga.org ■ *E-mail:* rcginfo@stlrcga.org	Saint Louis	MO	63102	314-231-5555	444-1122
Saint Louis City Hall 1200 Market St *Web:* stlouis.missouri.org	Saint Louis	MO	63103	314-622-4000	
Saint Louis Community Development Agency 1015 Locust St Suite 1200	Saint Louis	MO	63101	314-622-3400	622-3413
Saint Louis Convention & Visitors Commission 1 Metropolitan Sq Suite 1100 *TF:* 800-325-7962 ■ *Web:* www.st-louis-cvc.com	Saint Louis	MO	63102	314-421-1023	421-0039
Saint Louis County 41 S Central Ave *Web:* www.co.st-louis.mo.us	Clayton	MO	63105	314-889-2000	889-2890
Saint Louis Mayor 1200 Market St Rm 200	Saint Louis	MO	63103	314-622-3201	622-4955
Saint Louis Public Library 1301 Olive St *Web:* www.slpl.lib.mo.us	Saint Louis	MO	63103	314-241-2288	241-3840

On-Line Resources

4SaintLouis.com	www.4stlouis.com
About.com Guide to Saint Louis	stlouis.about.com/local/midwestus/stlouis
Access America Saint Louis	www.accessamer.com/stlouis/
Area Guide Saint Louis	stlouis.areaguides.net
Boulevards Saint Louis	www.stlouis.com
City Knowledge Saint Louis	www.cityknowledge.com/mo_stlouis.htm
Cityhits Saint Louis	www.cityhits.com/index.shtml
CitySearch Saint Louis	stlouis.citysearch.com
DigitalCity St Louis	home.digitalcity.com/stlouis
Excite.com Saint Louis City Guide	www.excite.com/travel/countries/united_states/missouri/st_louis
Gay Saint Louis	www.gaystlouis.com/
Hill The	www.thehill-stl.com
MetroVille Saint Louis	stlouis.metroville.com
Riverfront Times	www.rftstl.com
Rough Guide Travel Saint Louis	travel.roughguides.com/content/972/
Saint Louis Community Information Network	stlouis.missouri.org/
Saint Louis Front Page	www.mooredesign.com/
StLouis.TheLinks.com	stlouis.thelinks.com/

— Transportation Services —

AIRPORTS

■ Lambert Saint Louis International Airport (STL)

	Phone
10 miles NW of downtown (approx 20 minutes) Web: www.lambert-stlouis.com	314-426-8000

Airport Transportation

	Phone
Air Flight Cab $25 fare to downtown	636-477-0108
Airport Express $10 fare to downtown	314-429-4950
Bi-State Transit $1.25 fare to downtown	314-231-2345
Taxi $19 fare to downtown	314-361-2345

Commercial Airlines

	Phone		Phone
America West	800-235-9292	**Northwest**	800-225-2525
American	800-433-7300	**Southwest**	800-435-9792
American Trans Air	800-225-2995	**TWA**	800-221-2000
Continental	314-241-7205	**United**	800-241-6522
Continental Express	800-525-0280	**US Airways**	800-428-4322
Delta	800-221-1212		

Charter Airlines

	Phone		Phone
Archway Aviation	314-576-5499	**Saint Louis Helicopter Airways Inc**	636-532-1177

CAR RENTALS

	Phone		Phone
Alamo	314-428-1405	**Hertz**	314-426-7555
Avis	314-426-7766	**National**	314-426-6272
Budget	314-423-3000	**Payless**	314-429-5657
Dollar	314-423-4004	**Thrifty**	314-423-3737
Enterprise	314-427-7757		

LIMO/TAXI

	Phone		Phone
Admiral Limousine Service	314-731-1707	**Harris Taxi**	314-371-7111
Allen Cab	314-241-7722	**Laclede Cab**	314-652-3456
Carey Limousine	636-946-4114	**LeCompte Limousine**	636-537-9996
County Cab	314-991-5300	**Style Limousine**	314-521-6506
Gem Transportation	314-731-1707	**Yellow Cab**	314-361-2345

MASS TRANSIT

	Phone
Bi-State Transit System $1.25 Base fare	314-231-2345
MetroLink $1.25 Base fare	314-231-2345

RAIL/BUS

				Phone
Amtrak Station 550 S 16th St Amtrak Stn	Saint Louis	MO	63103	800-872-7245
Greyhound Bus Station 1450 N 13th St *TF:* 800-231-2222	Saint Louis	MO	63106	314-231-4485

— Accommodations —

HOTELS, MOTELS, RESORTS

				Phone	Fax
Adam's Mark Hotel 4th & Chestnut Sts *TF:* 800-444-2326 ■ *Web:* www.adamsmark.com/stlou.htm	Saint Louis	MO	63102	314-241-7400	241-6618
Baymont Inns & Suites 1425 S 5th St *TF:* 800-301-0200	Saint Charles	MO	63301	636-946-6936	946-9640
Best Western Airport Inn 10232 Natural Bridge Rd *TF:* 800-872-0070	Saint Louis	MO	63134	314-427-5955	427-3079
Cheshire Inn & Lodge 6300 Clayton Rd *TF:* 800-325-7378 ■ *Web:* www.cheshirelodge.com	Saint Louis	MO	63117	314-647-7300	647-0442
Club Hotel by Doubletree 9600 Natural Bridge Rd *TF:* 888-444-2582	Saint Louis	MO	63134	314-427-7600	427-1614
Courtyard by Marriott 2340 Market St *TF:* 800-321-2211	Saint Louis	MO	63103	314-241-9111	241-8113
Daniele Hotel 216 N Meramec Ave *TF:* 800-325-8302	Clayton	MO	63105	314-721-0101	721-0609
Days Inn 333 Washington Ave *TF:* 800-329-7466	Saint Louis	MO	63127	314-821-3000	821-2441
Doubletree Club Hotel Riverport 13735 Riverport Dr *TF:* 800-222-8733 ■ *Web:* www.doubletreehotels.com/DoubleT/Hotel61/63/63Main.htm	Saint Louis	MO	63043	314-298-3400	298-9646
Doubletree Hotel & Conference Center 16625 Swingley Ridge Rd *TF:* 800-222-8733 ■ *Web:* www.doubletreehotels.com/DoubleT/Hotel61/65/65Main.htm	Saint Louis	MO	63017	636-532-5000	532-9984
Drury Inn Convention Center 711 N Broadway *TF:* 800-325-8300	Saint Louis	MO	63102	314-231-8100	621-6568
Drury Inn Union Station 201 S 20th St *TF:* 800-378-7946 ■ *Web:* www.drury-inn.com/room/reservation/st_louis_9.htm ■ *E-mail:* info@drury-inn.com	Saint Louis	MO	63103	314-231-3900	231-3900
Embassy Suites 901 N 1st St *TF:* 800-362-2779	Saint Louis	MO	63102	314-241-4200	241-6513
Hampton Inn Union Station 2211 Market St *TF:* 800-426-7866	Saint Louis	MO	63103	314-241-3200	241-9351
Harrah's Saint Louis Riverport 777 Casino Center Dr *TF:* 800-427-7247 ■ *Web:* www.harrahs.com/tour/tour_stlouis.html	Maryland Heights	MO	63043	314-770-8100	770-8399
Henry VIII Hotel & Conference Center 4690 N Lindbergh Blvd *TF:* 800-325-1588	Saint Louis	MO	63044	314-731-3040	731-4210
Hilton Hotel Frontenac 1335 S Lindbergh Blvd *TF:* 800-445-8667 ■ *Web:* www.hilton.com/hotels/STLFHHF	Saint Louis	MO	63131	314-993-1100	993-8546
Holiday Inn Airport North 4545 N Lindbergh Blvd *TF:* 800-785-6202	Bridgeton	MO	63044	314-731-2100	731-4970

Saint Louis — Hotels, Motels, Resorts (Cont'd)

				Phone	Fax
Holiday Inn Convention Center 811 N 9th St	Saint Louis	MO	63101	314-421-4000	421-5974
TF: 800-289-8338					
Holiday Inn Southwest 10709 Watson Rd	Saint Louis	MO	63127	314-821-6600	821-4673
TF: 800-682-6338					
Holiday Inn Westport 1973 Craigshire Rd	Saint Louis	MO	63146	314-434-0100	434-6619
TF: 800-682-6338 ■ *Web:* www.holidayinn-wp.com					
Hyatt Regency Saint Louis Union Station 1 Saint Louis Union Stn.	Saint Louis	MO	63103	314-231-1234	923-3970
TF: 800-233-1234 ■ *Web:* www.hyattstlouis.com					
Marriott Hotel Airport I-70 at Lambert Airport	Saint Louis	MO	63134	314-423-9700	423-0213
TF: 800-228-9290 ■ *Web:* marriotthotels.com/STLAP					
Marriott Saint Louis West 660 Maryville Ctr Dr	Saint Louis	MO	63141	314-878-2747	878-3005
TF: 800-352-1175 ■ *Web:* marriotthotels.com/STLWE					
Mayfair Grand Heritage 806 Saint Charles St	Saint Louis	MO	63101	314-421-2500	421-0770
Omni Majestic Hotel 1019 Pine St	Saint Louis	MO	63101	314-436-2355	436-0223
TF: 800-843-6664					
Radisson Hotel Saint Louis Airport 11228 Lone Eagle Dr.	Bridgeton	MO	63044	314-291-6700	770-1205
TF: 800-333-3333					
Radisson Suites 200 N 4th St	Saint Louis	MO	63102	314-621-8200	621-8073
TF: 800-925-1395					
Regal Riverfront Hotel 200 S 4th St	Saint Louis	MO	63102	314-241-9500	241-9977
TF: 800-222-8888					
Renaissance Saint Louis Hotel 9801 Natural Bridge Rd	Berkeley	MO	63134	314-429-1100	429-3625
TF: 800-228-9290					
Ritz-Carlton Saint Louis 100 Carondelet Plaza	Saint Louis	MO	63105	314-863-6300	863-3525
TF: 800-241-3333 ■ *Web:* www.ritzcarlton.com/location/NorthAmerica/StLouis/main.htm					
Saint Louis Airport Hilton 10330 Natural Bridge Rd	Saint Louis	MO	63134	314-426-5500	426-3429
TF: 800-345-5500					
Saint Louis Marriott Pavilion Hotel 1 S Broadway	Saint Louis	MO	63102	314-421-1776	331-9029
TF: 800-228-9290					
Seven Gables Inn 26 N Meremac Ave	Saint Louis	MO	63105	314-863-8400	863-8846
TF: 800-433-6590 ■ *Web:* www.sevengablesinn.com					
Sheraton Plaza Hotel 900 Westport Plaza	Saint Louis	MO	63146	314-434-5010	434-0140
TF: 800-822-3535					
Sheraton West Port Inn 191 W Port Plaza Dr	Saint Louis	MO	63146	314-878-1500	878-2837
TF: 800-325-3535					

— Restaurants —

				Phone
Agostino's Colosseum (Italian) 15846 Manchester Rd	Ellisville	MO	63011	636-391-5480
Al's (Italian) 1200 N 1st St	Saint Louis	MO	63102	314-421-6399
Backstage Bistro (American) 3536 Washington Ave	Saint Louis	MO	63103	314-534-3663
Balaban's (American) 405 N Euclid Ave	Saint Louis	MO	63108	314-361-8085
Bar Italia (Italian) 4656 Maryland Ave	Saint Louis	MO	63108	314-361-7010
BB's Jazz, Blues & Soups (Cajun) 700 S Broadway	Saint Louis	MO	63102	314-436-5222
Benedetto's (Italian) 10411 Clayton Rd.	Frontenac	MO	63131	314-432-8585
Blue Owl Restaurant (American) 2nd & Mill Sts	Kimmswick	MO	63053	636-464-3128
Blue Water Grill (Seafood) 343 S Kirkwood Rd	Saint Louis	MO	63122	314-821-5757
Broadway Oyster Bar (Seafood) 736 S Broadway	Saint Louis	MO	63102	314-621-8811
Bruno's Little Italy (Italian) 5901 Southwest Ave	Saint Louis	MO	63139	314-781-5988
Cafe de France (French) 410 Olive St	Saint Louis	MO	63102	314-231-2204
Caleco's Bar & Grill (American) 101 N Broadway	Saint Louis	MO	63102	314-421-0708
Cardwell's (American) 8100 Maryland Ave	Clayton	MO	63105	314-726-5055
Cheshire Inn (Steak/Seafood) 7036 Clayton Rd	Saint Louis	MO	63117	314-647-7300
Dierdorf & Hart's Steak House (Steak) 701 Market St	Saint Louis	MO	63101	314-421-1772
Dominic's (Italian) 5101 Wilson Ave	South Saint Louis	MO	63110	314-771-1632
Faust's (American) 4th & Chestnut Sts	Saint Louis	MO	63102	314-241-7400
Fio's La Fourchette (French) 7515 Forsyth Blvd	Saint Louis	MO	63105	314-863-6866
Flaco's Tacos (Mexican) 6th & Pine Sts	Saint Louis	MO	63101	314-231-8226
Gian Peppe's (Italian) 2126 Marconi Ave	Saint Louis	MO	63110	314-772-3303
Giovanni's (Italian) 5201 Shaw Ave	Saint Louis	MO	63110	314-772-5958
Harvest (American) 1059 S Big Bend Blvd	Saint Louis	MO	63117	314-645-3522
Hot Locust Cantina (Southwest) 2005 Locust St	Saint Louis	MO	63103	314-231-3666
Hunan Manor (Chinese) 606 Pine St	Saint Louis	MO	63101	314-231-2867
Jackie's (Continental) 26 N Meremac Ave	Saint Louis	MO	63105	314-863-8400
Jake's Steaks (Steak) 708 N 2nd St	Saint Louis	MO	63102	314-621-8184
John Mineo's (Italian) 13490 Clayton Rd	Saint Louis	MO	63131	314-434-5244
Kemoll's (Italian) 211 N Broadway	Saint Louis	MO	63102	314-421-0555
Key West Cafe (American) 1820 Market St	Saint Louis	MO	63103	314-241-2566
Kreis' Restaurant (Steak/Seafood) 535 S Lindbergh Blvd	Saint Louis	MO	63131	314-993-0735
La Sala (Mexican) 513 Olive St	Saint Louis	MO	63101	314-231-5620
Lombardo's Trattoria (Italian) 201 S 20th St.	Saint Louis	MO	63103	314-621-0666
Malmaison (French) Saint Albans Rd	Saint Albans	MO	63073	636-458-0131
Mandarin House (Chinese) 9150 Oberland Plaza	Saint Louis	MO	63114	314-427-8070
McMurphy's Grill (American) 614 N 11th St	Saint Louis	MO	63101	314-231-3006
Morgan Street Brewery (American) 721 N 2nd St	Saint Louis	MO	63102	314-231-9970
Norton's Cafe (Cajun/Creole) 808 Geyer St	Saint Louis	MO	63104	314-436-0828
Planet Hollywood (American) 800 N 3rd St	Saint Louis	MO	63102	314-588-1717
Restaurant The (Italian) 100 Carondelet Plaza	Saint Louis	MO	63105	314-863-6300
Robata of Japan (Japanese) 111 W Port Plaza Gold Tower Bldg 12th Fl	Saint Louis	MO	63146	314-434-1007
Safari Cafe (Continental) 201 N 6th St	Saint Louis	MO	63101	314-231-5888
Schneithorst's (German) 1600 S Lindbergh Blvd	Saint Louis	MO	63131	314-993-5600
Web: www.schneithorst.com/				
Seventh Inn (Continental) 100 7th Trail Dr	Ballwin	MO	63011	636-227-6686
Soulard's Restaurant (Continental) 1731 S 7th St	Saint Louis	MO	63104	314-241-7956
Station Grille (American) 1 Union Stn	Saint Louis	MO	63103	314-231-1234
Tony's (Italian) 410 Market St	Saint Louis	MO	63102	314-231-7007
Tornatore's (Italian) 12315 Natural Bridge Rd	Bridgeton	MO	63044	314-739-6644
Verandas (American) 10330 Natural Bridge Rd	Saint Louis	MO	63134	314-426-5500
Westerfield House (American) 8059 Jefferson Rd	Freeburg	IL	62243	618-539-5643
Zinnia (New American) 7491 Big Bend Blvd	Saint Louis	MO	63119	314-962-0572

— Goods and Services —

SHOPPING

				Phone	Fax
Cherokee Street Antique Row 2125 Cherokee St	Saint Louis	MO	63118	314-773-8810	664-8787
Chesterfield Mall 291 Chesterfield Mall	Chesterfield	MO	63017	636-532-0777	532-9728
Crestwood Plaza 164 Crestwood Plaza	Saint Louis	MO	63126	314-962-2395	962-2384
Web: www.crestwood.shoppingtown.com					
Dillard's 601 Washington Ave	Saint Louis	MO	63101	314-231-5080	
Famous-Barr 601 Olive St	Saint Louis	MO	63101	314-444-3111	
TF Orders: 800-528-2345*					
Grand South Grand 311 S Grand Blvd	Saint Louis	MO	63118	314-773-7733	773-1942
Jamestown Mall 175 Jamestown Mall	Florissant	MO	63034	314-355-3500	355-8785
Laclede's Landing 801 N 2nd St	Saint Louis	MO	63102	314-241-5875	241-5862
Northwest Plaza 650 Northwest Plaza	Saint Louis	MO	63074	314-298-0071	298-3481
TF: 800-264-7841					
Plaza Frontenac 1701 S Lindbergh Blvd	Frontenac	MO	63131	314-432-0604	
Saint Louis Centre 515 N 6th St.	Saint Louis	MO	63101	314-231-5522	231-4837
Saint Louis Galleria 1155 St Louis Galleria	Saint Louis	MO	63117	314-863-6633	863-8665
Web: www.saintlouisgalleria.com/ ■ *E-mail:* info@saintlouisgalleria.com					
Saint Louis Union Station 1820 Market St.	Saint Louis	MO	63103	314-421-6655	421-3314
Saks Fifth Avenue 1 Plaza Frontenac	Frontenac	MO	63131	314-567-9200	

BANKS

				Phone	Fax
Commerce Bank NA 8000 Forsyth Blvd	Clayton	MO	63105	314-726-2255	746-8738*
**Fax:* Cust Svc ■ *TF Cust Svc:* 800-746-8704*					
Heartland Savings Bank FSB 312 N 6th St	Saint Louis	MO	63101	314-512-8800	621-4789
TF: 800-557-2781					
Jefferson Bank & Trust Co 2301 Market St.	Saint Louis	MO	63103	314-621-0100	621-1267
TF: 800-737-0018					
Mercantile Bank of Saint Louis NA 721 Locust St.	Saint Louis	MO	63101	314-966-2530	
NationsBank 800 Market St	Saint Louis	MO	63101	314-466-6000	466-5050*
**Fax:* Hum Res ■ *TF Cust Svc:* 800-944-0404*					
South Side National Bank in Saint Louis 3606 Gravois Ave	Saint Louis	MO	63116	314-776-7000	776-2332
Southern Commercial Bank 5515 S Grand Blvd	Saint Louis	MO	63111	314-481-6800	481-0173
Southwest Bank of Saint Louis 2301 S Kingshighway Blvd.	Saint Louis	MO	63110	314-776-5200	776-2146
TF: 888-680-2172					
UMB of Saint Louis NA 2 S Broadway	Saint Louis	MO	63102	314-621-1000	621-8492

BUSINESS SERVICES

	Phone
Accountemps	314-621-8367
Associated Couriers	314-739-0400
Federal Express	800-463-3339
Kelly Services	314-421-4111
Kinko's	314-842-5676
Manpower Temporary Services	314-241-1356
Olsten Staffing Services	314-421-3858
Post Office	800-275-8777
Special Dispatch	314-731-2288
UPS	800-742-5877

Saint Louis (Cont'd)

— Media —

PUBLICATIONS

Name / Address	City	State	ZIP	Phone	Fax
Chesterfield Journal 1714 Deer Tracks Trail	Saint Louis	MO	63131	314-821-2462	821-0843
Citizen Journal 1714 Deer Tracks Trail	Saint Louis	MO	63131	314-821-2462	821-0843
Community News 5748 Helen Ave. **Fax:* News Rm	Saint Louis	MO	63136	314-261-5555	261-2776*
County Star Journal East 7751 N Lindbergh Rd **Fax:* News Rm ■ *Web:* www.yourjournal.com	Hazelwood	MO	63042	314-972-1111	831-7643*
North County East Journal 7751 N Lindbergh Rd **Fax:* News Rm	Hazelwood	MO	63042	314-972-1111	831-7643*
Press Journal 1714 Deer Tracks Trail **Fax:* News Rm ■ *Web:* www.yourjournal.com	Saint Louis	MO	63131	314-821-2462	821-0843*
Saint Louis Business Journal 1 Metropolitan Sq Suite 2170 *Web:* www.amcity.com/stlouis	Saint Louis	MO	63102	314-421-6200	621-5031
Saint Louis Post-Dispatch‡ 900 N Tucker Blvd *TF:* 800-365-0820 ■ *Web:* www.stlnet.com ■ *E-mail:* vtipton@stlnet.com	Saint Louis	MO	63101	314-340-8000	340-3050
South City Journal 4210 Chippewa St **Fax:* News Rm	Saint Louis	MO	63116	314-664-2700	664-8533*
Where Saint Louis 1750 S Brentwood Blvd Suite 511 *E-mail:* info@wheremags.com	Saint Louis	MO	63144	314-968-4940	968-0813

‡Daily newspapers

TELEVISION

Name / Address	City	State	ZIP	Phone	Fax
KDNL-TV Ch 30 (ABC) 1215 Cole St	Saint Louis	MO	63106	314-436-3030	259-5569
KETC-TV Ch 9 (PBS) 3655 Olive St *Web:* www.ketc.org ■ *E-mail:* letters@ketc.pbs.org	Saint Louis	MO	63108	314-725-2460	512-9005
KMOV-TV Ch 4 (CBS) 1 Memorial Dr. *Web:* www.kmov.com	Saint Louis	MO	63102	314-621-4444	621-4775
KNLC-TV Ch 24 (Ind) 1411 Locust St *Web:* www.hereshelpnet.org	Saint Louis	MO	63103	314-436-2424	436-2434
KPLR-TV Ch 11 (WB) 4935 Lindell Blvd. *Web:* www.kplr.com	Saint Louis	MO	63108	314-367-7211	454-6430
KSDK-TV Ch 5 (NBC) 1000 Market St	Saint Louis	MO	63101	314-421-5055	444-5164
KTVI-TV Ch 2 (Fox) 5915 Berthold Ave	Saint Louis	MO	63110	314-647-2222	647-8960

RADIO

Name / Address	City	State	ZIP	Phone	Fax
KATZ-AM 1600 kHz (Rel) 10155 Corporate Square Dr	Saint Louis	MO	63132	314-692-5108	692-5134
KATZ-FM 100.3 MHz (Urban) 10155 Corporate Sq Dr	Saint Louis	MO	63132	314-692-5108	692-5131
KDHX-FM 88.1 MHz (NPR) 3504 Magnolia St *Web:* www.kdhxfm88.org	Saint Louis	MO	63118	314-664-3955	664-1020
KEZK-AM 590 kHz (AC) 3100 Market St.	Saint Louis	MO	63103	314-531-0000	969-7638
KEZK-FM 102.5 MHz (AC) 3100 Market St. *Web:* www.kezk.com	Saint Louis	MO	63103	314-531-0000	969-7638
KFNS-AM 590 kHz (Sports) 8045 Big Bend Blvd. **Fax:* Sales ■ *Web:* www.kfns.com/ ■ *E-mail:* kfns@kfns.com	Saint Louis	MO	63119	314-962-0590	962-7576*
KFUO-FM 99.1 MHz (Clas) 85 Founders Ln *Web:* www.classic99.com	Clayton	MO	63105	314-725-3030	725-3801
KIHT-FM 96.3 MHz (B/EZ) 8081 Manchester Rd *Web:* www.k-hits.com	Saint Louis	MO	63144	314-781-9600	781-3298
KLOU-FM 103.3 MHz (Oldies) 1910 Pine St Suite 225 *Web:* www.klou.com	Saint Louis	MO	63103	314-533-1033	533-2103
KMJM-FM 104.9 MHz (Urban) 10155 Corporate Sq Dr *TF:* 888-426-9105 ■ *Web:* www.majic105fm.com ■ *E-mail:* majic@majic105fm.com	Saint Louis	MO	63132	314-692-5108	692-5127
KMOX-AM 1120 kHz (N/T) 1 Memorial Dr *Web:* www.kmox.com ■ *E-mail:* kmox@kmox.com	Saint Louis	MO	63102	314-621-2345	444-3230
KPNT-FM 105.7 MHz (Alt) 1215 Cole St *Web:* www.kpnt.com ■ *E-mail:* webdude@kpnt.com	Saint Louis	MO	63106	314-231-1057	259-5598
KSD-FM 93.7 MHz (CR) 1910 Pine St *Web:* www.ksd.com ■ *E-mail:* hey937ksd@ksd.com	Saint Louis	MO	63103	314-436-9370	231-7625
KSHE-FM 94.7 MHz (Rock) 700 St Louis Union Stn Annex Suite 101 *Web:* www.kshe95.com	Saint Louis	MO	63103	314-621-0095	621-3428
KSLZ-FM 107.7 MHz (CHR) 10155 Corporate Sq Dr *Web:* www.z1077.com	Saint Louis	MO	63132	314-969-1077	969-3299
KTRS-AM 550 kHz (N/T) 638 W Port Plaza *Web:* www.ktrs.com	Saint Louis	MO	63146	314-453-5500	453-9704
KWMU-FM 90.7 MHz (NPR) 8001 Natural Bridge Rd **Fax:* News Rm ■ *Web:* www.kwmu.org ■ *E-mail:* kwmu@umsl.edu	Saint Louis	MO	63121	314-516-5968	516-6397*
KXOK-FM 97.1 MHz (Rock) 1215 Cole St	Saint Louis	MO	63106	314-231-9710	
KYKY-FM 98.1 MHz (AC) 3100 Market St *Web:* www.y98.com	Saint Louis	MO	63103	314-531-9898	531-9810
WEW-AM 770 kHz (Nost) 2740 Hampton Ave *Web:* www.wewradio.com ■ *E-mail:* wewradio@aol.com	Saint Louis	MO	63139	314-781-9397	781-8545
WIL-FM 92.3 MHz (Ctry) 8081 Manchester Rd *Web:* www.wil92.com	Saint Louis	MO	63144	314-781-9600	781-3298
WKKX-FM 106.5 MHz (Ctry) 800 St Louis Union Station The Power House	Saint Louis	MO	63103	314-621-4106	621-3000
WRTH-AM 1430 kHz (Nost) 8081 Manchester Rd *Web:* www.wrth-am.com	Saint Louis	MO	63144	314-781-9600	781-3298
WVRV-FM 101.1 MHz (AAA) 1215 Cole St.	Saint Louis	MO	63106	314-231-3699	259-5598
WXTM-FM 104.1 MHz (Rock) 800 Union Station *Web:* www.extremeradio1041.com	Saint Louis	MO	63103	314-621-0400	621-3000

— Colleges/Universities —

Name / Address	City	State	ZIP	Phone	Fax
Deaconess College of Nursing 6150 Oakland Ave *Web:* www.tenethealth.com/deaconessnursing ■ *E-mail:* info@tenethealth.com	Saint Louis	MO	63139	314-768-3044	768-5673
Fontbonne College 6800 Wydown Blvd *Web:* www.fontbonne.edu	Saint Louis	MO	63105	314-862-3456	889-1451
Harris-Stowe State College 3026 Laclede Ave *Web:* www.hssc.edu	Saint Louis	MO	63103	314-340-3366	340-3555
Lindenwood University 209 S Kingshighway *Web:* www.lindenwood.edu	Saint Charles	MO	63301	636-949-2000	949-4949
Maryville University of Saint Louis 13550 Conway Rd. *TF Admissions:* 800-627-9855 ■ *Web:* www.maryvillestl.edu ■ *E-mail:* admissions@maryville.edu	Saint Louis	MO	63141	314-529-9300	529-9927
Missouri Baptist College 1 College Pk Dr *TF Admissions:* 888-484-1115 ■ *Web:* www.mobap.edu	Saint Louis	MO	63141	314-434-1115	434-7596
Saint Louis Christian College 1360 Grandview Dr	Florissant	MO	63033	314-837-6777	837-8291
Saint Louis College of Pharmacy 4588 Parkview Pl *Web:* www.stlcop.edu	Saint Louis	MO	63110	314-367-8700	367-2784
Saint Louis Community College 300 S Broadway *Web:* www.stlcc.cc.mo.us ■ *E-mail:* info@ccm.stlcc.cc.mo.us	Saint Louis	MO	63102	314-539-5000	539-5170
Saint Louis Community College Florissant Valley 3400 Pershall Rd *Web:* www.stlcc.cc.mo.us/fv/	Ferguson	MO	63135	314-595-4200	595-2224
Saint Louis Community College Forest Park 5600 Oakland Ave *Web:* www.stlcc.cc.mo.us/fp/	Saint Louis	MO	63110	314-644-9100	644-9752
Saint Louis Community College Meramec 11333 Big Bend Blvd. *Web:* www.stlcc.cc.mo.us/mcdocs/	Kirkwood	MO	63122	314-984-7500	984-7051
Saint Louis Symphony Community Music School 560 Trinity Ave	Saint Louis	MO	63130	314-863-3033	286-4421
Saint Louis University 221 N Grand Blvd. *Web:* www.slu.edu ■ *E-mail:* admitme@sluvca.slu.edu	Saint Louis	MO	63103	314-977-2222	977-7136
University of Missouri Saint Louis 8001 Natural Bridge Rd *Web:* www.umsl.edu	Saint Louis	MO	63121	314-516-5000	516-5310
Washington University 1 Brookings Dr *TF Admissions:* 800-638-0700 ■ *Web:* www.wustl.edu	Saint Louis	MO	63130	314-935-5000	935-4290
Webster University 470 E Lockwood Ave. *Web:* www.webster.edu	Saint Louis	MO	63119	314-968-6900	968-7115

Saint Louis (Cont'd)

— Hospitals —

Name / Address	City	State	ZIP	Phone	Fax
Alexian Brothers Hospital 3933 S Broadway	Saint Louis	MO	63118	314-865-3333	865-7934
Alton Memorial Hospital 1 Memorial Dr	Alton	IL	62002	618-463-7311	463-7850
Barnes-Jewish Hospital 216 S Kings Hwy	Saint Louis	MO	63110	314-362-5000	362-8877
Barnes Saint Peters Hospital 10 Hospital Dr	Saint Peters	MO	63376	636-447-6600	916-9414
Bethesda General Hospital 3655 Vista Ave	Saint Louis	MO	63110	314-772-9200	772-1819
Christian Hospital Northeast 11133 Dunn Rd	Saint Louis	MO	63136	314-355-2300	653-5399
DePaul Health Center 12303 De Paul Dr	Bridgeton	MO	63044	314-344-6000	344-6840
Doctors Hospital Wentzville 500 Medical Dr	Wentzville	MO	63285	636-327-1000	327-5413
Forest Park Hospital 6150 Oakland Ave	Saint Louis	MO	63139	314-768-3000	768-3136
Forest Park Hospital 6150 Oakland Ave	Saint Louis	MO	63139	314-768-3000	768-5663
Jefferson Memorial Hospital PO Box 350	Crystal City	MO	63019	636-933-1000	933-1119
Lafayette Grand Hospital 3545 Lafayette Ave	Saint Louis	MO	63104	314-865-6813	
Memorial Hospital 4500 Memorial Dr	Belleville	IL	62226	618-233-7750	257-5658
Missouri Baptist Medical Center 3015 N Ballas Rd	Saint Louis	MO	63131	314-996-5000	996-5373*
*Fax: Admitting					
Saint Anthony's Health Center PO Box 340	Alton	IL	62002	618-465-2571	465-4569
Saint Anthony's Medical Center 10010 Kennerly Rd	Saint Louis	MO	63128	314-525-1000	525-4065*
*Fax: Admitting					
Saint Elizabeth's Hospital 211 S 3rd St	Belleville	IL	62222	618-234-2120	234-2180
Web: www.apci.net/~ste					
Saint John's Mercy Medical Center 615 S New Ballas Rd	Saint Louis	MO	63141	314-569-6000	569-6135*
*Fax: Admitting ■ *TF:* 800-876-3729					
Saint Joseph Health Center 300 1st Capitol Dr	Saint Charles	MO	63301	636-947-5000	947-5611*
*Fax: Admitting					
Saint Louis Children's Hospital 1 Children's Pl	Saint Louis	MO	63110	314-454-6000	454-2870
Web: www.ihc.com/primary					
Saint Louis ConnectCare 5535 Delmar Blvd	Saint Louis	MO	63112	314-361-2273	879-6488*
*Fax: Admitting					
Saint Louis University Hospital PO Box 15250	Saint Louis	MO	63110	314-577-8000	268-5109*
*Fax: Admitting ■ *TF:* 800-268-5880 ■ *Web:* www.slucare.edu ■ *E-mail:* slucare@slucare1.sluh.edu					
Saint Luke's Hospital 232 S Woods Mill Rd	Chesterfield	MO	63017	314-434-1500	205-6865
Saint Mary's Health Center 6420 Clayton Rd	Richmond Heights	MO	63117	314-768-8000	768-8829*
*Fax: Admitting ■ *TF:* 800-284-2854					
Shriners Hospitals for Children Saint Louis Unit 2001 S Lindbergh Blvd	Saint Louis	MO	63131	314-432-3600	432-2930
Web: www.shrinershq.org/Hospitals/Directry/stlouis.html					
SouthPointe Hospital 2639 Miami St	Saint Louis	MO	63118	314-268-6000	268-6156*
*Fax: Admitting ■ *Web:* www.tenethealth.com/Lutheran ■ *E-mail:* lmc-community.relations@tenethealth.com					
SSM Cardinal Glennon Children's Hospital 1465 S Grand Blvd	Saint Louis	MO	63104	314-577-5600	268-6468
Web: www.cardinalglennon.com					
SSM Saint Joseph Hospital of Kirkwood 525 Couch Ave	Kirkwood	MO	63122	314-966-1500	822-6302*
*Fax: Admitting ■ *Web:* www.stjosephkirkwood.com/internet/home/stjokirk.nsf					
Veterans Affairs Medical Center 915 N Grand Blvd	Saint Louis	MO	63106	314-487-0400	894-6682

— Attractions —

Name / Address	City	State	ZIP	Phone	Fax
American Kennel Club Museum of the Dog 1721 S Mason Rd	Saint Louis	MO	63131	314-821-3647	821-7381
Web: commerce.bizonthe.net/intro.asp?company=amerkennelclubmuseum					
American Theatre 416 N 9th St	Saint Louis	MO	63101	314-962-4000	
Anheuser-Busch Brewery 1 Busch Pl	Saint Louis	MO	63118	314-577-2626	577-7715
Arch Odyssey Theatre 11 N 4th St Underground at Gateway Arch	Saint Louis	MO	63102	314-982-1410	982-1527
Black Madonna Shrine St Joseph's Rd	Eureka	MO	63025	636-938-5361	
Black World History Wax Museum 2505 St Louis Ave	Saint Louis	MO	63106	314-241-7057	241-7058
Campbell House Museum 1508 Locust St	Saint Louis	MO	63103	314-421-0325	421-0113
Carondelet Park Grand & Loughborough	Saint Louis	MO	63110	314-535-0400	
Casino Queen 200 S Front St	East Saint Louis	IL	62201	618-874-5000	874-5008
TF: 800-777-0777 ■ *Web:* www.casinoqueen.com ■ *E-mail:* queen@casinoqueen.com					
Cathedral of Saint Louis (New Cathedral) 4431 Lindell Blvd	Saint Louis	MO	63108	314-533-2824	533-2844
Center of Contemporary Arts 524 Trinity Ave	Saint Louis	MO	63130	314-725-6555	725-6222
Chatillon-DeMenil Mansion 3352 DeMenil Pl	Saint Louis	MO	63118	314-771-5828	
City Museum 701 N 15th St	Saint Louis	MO	63103	314-231-2489	231-1009
Web: www.citymuseum.org					
Concordia Historical Institute 801 DeMun Ave	Saint Louis	MO	63105	314-505-7900	505-7901
Web: chi.lcms.org/					
Craft Alliance Gallery 6640 Delmar Blvd	Saint Louis	MO	63130	314-725-1177	725-2068
Dance Saint Louis 634 N Grand Blvd Suite 1102	Saint Louis	MO	63103	314-534-5000	534-5001
DeMenil Mansion & Museum 3352 DeMenil Pl	Saint Louis	MO	63118	314-771-5828	771-3475
Field Eugene House & Saint Louis Toy Museum 634 S Broadway	Saint Louis	MO	63102	314-421-4689	421-4689
Forest Park 5600 Clayton Ave	Saint Louis	MO	63110	314-535-0100	535-3901
Forum for Contemporary Art 3540 Washington Ave	Saint Louis	MO	63108	314-535-4660	535-1226
Fox Theatre 527 N Grand Blvd	Saint Louis	MO	63103	314-534-1678	534-8702
Web: www.fabulousfox.com/					
General Daniel Bissell House 10225 Bellefontaine Rd	Saint Louis	MO	63137	314-868-0973	868-8435
Golden Eagle River Museum Bee Tree Pk	Saint Louis	MO	63129	314-846-9073	
Grand Center 634 N Grand Ave	Saint Louis	MO	63103	800-572-7776	533-3345*
*Fax Area Code: 314 ■ *TF:* 800-572-7776					
Grand South Grand 311 S Grand Blvd	Saint Louis	MO	63118	314-773-7733	773-1942
Grant's Farm 10501 Gravois Rd	Saint Louis	MO	63123	314-843-1700	525-0822
Web: www.grantsfarm.com					
Hawken House 1155 S Rock Hill Rd	Saint Louis	MO	63119	314-968-1857	
Historic Hanley House 7600 Westmoreland St	Saint Louis	MO	63105	314-746-0426	746-0494
Historic Samuel Cupples House 3673 W Pine Blvd	Saint Louis	MO	63108	314-977-3575	977-3581
Holocaust Museum & Learning Center 12 Millstone Campus Dr	Saint Louis	MO	63146	314-432-0020	432-1277
International Bowling Museum & Hall of Fame 111 Stadium Plaza	Saint Louis	MO	63102	314-231-6340	231-4054
TF: 800-966-2695 ■ *Web:* www.bowlingmuseum.com/					
Jefferson Barracks Historic Park 533 Grant Rd	Saint Louis	MO	63125	314-544-5714	638-5009
Jefferson National Expansion Memorial & Gateway Arch 11 N 4th St	Saint Louis	MO	63102	314-655-1600	655-1641
Web: www.nps.gov/jeff/arch-home/					
Jewel Box Forest Pk	Saint Louis	MO	63110	314-531-0080	
Joplin Scott House 2658 Delmar St	Saint Louis	MO	63103	314-340-5790	340-5793
Laclede's Landing 801 N 2nd St	Saint Louis	MO	63102	314-241-5875	241-5862
Laumeier Sculpture Park & Museum 12580 Rott Rd	Saint Louis	MO	63127	314-821-1209	821-1248
Web: www.laumeier.com/					
Magic House/Saint Louis Children's Museum 516 S Kirkwood Rd	Saint Louis	MO	63122	314-822-8900	822-8930
Web: www.magichouse.com					
Maryland Heights Family Aquatic Center 2344 McKelvey Rd	Saint Louis	MO	63043	314-291-6550	434-6365
Meyers John B House 180 Dunn Rd	Saint Louis	MO	63031	314-837-7661	
Mid-America Aquacenter 416 Hanley Industrial Ct	Brentwood	MO	63144	314-647-9594	647-7874
Web: hometown.aol.com/lsaquaman/myhomepage/index.html					
Missouri Botanical Garden PO Box 299	Saint Louis	MO	63166	314-577-5100	577-9597*
*Fax: Hum Res ■ *Web:* www.mobot.org ■ *E-mail:* rland@admin.mobot.org					
Missouri Historical Society PO Box 11940	Saint Louis	MO	63112	314-746-4599	454-3162
Web: www.livable.com/misshist.htm					
Muny Musical Theater Forest Pk	Saint Louis	MO	63112	314-361-1900	361-0009
Web: www.muny.com					
Museum of Black Inventors 7 S Newstead Ave	Saint Louis	MO	63108	314-533-1333	533-8220
Museum of Contemporary & Religious Art 221 N Grand Blvd Saint Louis University Campus	Saint Louis	MO	63103	314-977-7170	977-2999
Web: www.slu.edu/the_arts					
Museum of Transportation 3015 Barrett Station Rd	Saint Louis	MO	63122	314-965-7998	965-0242
Web: www.thetrainmuseum.org					

Saint Louis — Attractions (Cont'd)

				Phone	Fax
Museum of Western Jesuit Missions 700 Howdershell Rd	Florissant	MO	63031	314-361-5122	758-7182
Old Cathedral Museum 209 Walnut St	Saint Louis	MO	63102	314-231-3250	231-4280
OMNIMAX Theater 5050 Oakland Ave Saint Louis Science Ctr.	Saint Louis	MO	63110	314-289-4400	289-4420
TF: 800-456-7572 ■ *Web:* www.slsc.org/					
Opera Theatre of Saint Louis PO Box 191910	Saint Louis	MO	63119	314-961-0171	961-7463
Web: www.opera-stl.org/ ■ *E-mail:* info@opera-stl.org					
Portfolio Gallery & Educational Center 3514 Delmar Blvd	Saint Louis	MO	63103	314-533-3323	533-3345
Powder Valley Conservation Nature Center 11715 Cragwold Rd.	Saint Louis	MO	63122	314-301-1500	301-1501
Powell Symphony Hall 718 N Grand Blvd	Saint Louis	MO	63103	314-533-2500	286-4142
Web: www.slso.org/new_site/facilities/psh.htm					
Repertory Theatre of Saint Louis 130 Edgar Rd	Saint Louis	MO	63119	314-968-4925	
Saint Louis Art Museum 1 Fine Arts Dr Forest Park	Saint Louis	MO	63110	314-721-0072	721-6172
Web: www.slam.org ■ *E-mail:* infotech@slam.org					
Saint Louis Ballet 10 Kimler Dr	Saint Louis	MO	63043	314-567-4299	567-4299
Saint Louis Black Repertory Co 3610 Grandel Sq.	Saint Louis	MO	63108	314-534-3807	533-3345
Saint Louis Car Museum 1575 Woodson Rd	Saint Louis	MO	63114	314-993-1330	993-1540
Web: www.stlouiscarmuseum.com					
Saint Louis Science Center 5050 Oakland Ave.	Saint Louis	MO	63110	314-289-4400	289-4420
TF: 800-456-7572 ■ *Web:* www.slsc.org ■ *E-mail:* slscweb@slsc.org					
Saint Louis Symphony Orchestra 718 N Grand Blvd.	Saint Louis	MO	63103	314-533-2500	286-4170
Web: www.slso.org					
Saint Louis Union Station 1820 Market St.	Saint Louis	MO	63103	314-421-6655	421-3314
Saint Louis Zoological Park 1 Government Dr	Saint Louis	MO	63110	314-781-0900	647-7969
Web: www.stlzoo.org					
Six Flags Saint Louis I-44 & Allenton Rd	Eureka	MO	63025	636-938-5300	587-3617
Web: www.sixflags.com/stlouis					
Soldiers Memorial Military Museum 1315 Chestnut St	Saint Louis	MO	63103	314-622-4550	622-4237
Soulard Farmer's Market 7th & Lafayette Sts	Saint Louis	MO	63104	314-622-4180	622-4184
Ulysses S Grant National Historic Site 7400 Grant Rd	Saint Louis	MO	63123	314-842-1867	842-1659
Web: www.nps.gov/ulsg/					
Washington University Gallery of Art 1 Brookings Dr.	Saint Louis	MO	63130	314-935-5490	

SPORTS TEAMS & FACILITIES

				Phone	Fax
Busch Memorial Stadium 250 Stadium Plaza	Saint Louis	MO	63102	314-241-3900	425-0640
Web: www.stlcardinals.com/Busch.html					
Fairmount Park 9301 Collinsville Rd	Collinsville	IL	62234	618-345-4300	344-8218
Web: www.fairmountpark.com					
Gateway International Raceway 700 Raceway Blvd.	Madison	IL	62060	618-482-2400	
Kiel Center 1401 Clark Ave	Saint Louis	MO	63103	314-622-5400	622-5410
Web: www.kiel.com					
Saint Louis Blues 1401 Clark Ave Kiel Ctr	Saint Louis	MO	63103	314-622-2583	622-2582
Web: www.stlouisblues.com					
Saint Louis Cardinals 250 Stadium Plaza Busch Memorial Stadium.	Saint Louis	MO	63102	314-421-3060	425-0640
Web: www.stlcardinals.com ■ *E-mail:* cardsmail@icon-stl.net					
Saint Louis Rams 901 N Broadway Trans World Dome	Saint Louis	MO	63101	314-425-8830	770-9261*
**Fax:* PR ■ *Web:* www.nfl.com/rams					
Saint Louis Stampede (football) 1401 Clark Ave Kiel Ctr	Saint Louis	MO	63103	314-589-5899	
Saint Louis Vipers (roller hockey) 1819 Clarkson Rd Suite 301	Chesterfield	MO	63017	636-530-1967	530-7777
Web: www.stlouisvipers.com					
Team Saint Louis 12525 Sportport Rd SportPort Complex	Maryland Heights	MO	63043	314-938-9997	
Trans World Dome at America's Center 701 Convention Plaza	Saint Louis	MO	63101	314-342-5036	342-5040

— Events —

	Phone
African Arts Festival (late May)	314-935-5645
American Indian Society Pow Wow (mid-September)	314-544-5714
An Art Affair (mid-June)	314-576-7100
Annie Malone Parade (mid-May)	314-531-0120
Art & Soul (late May)	314-436-6500
Art Happening (early September)	314-889-0433
Best of Missouri Market (early October)	800-642-8842
Big Muddy Roots & Blues Music Festival (early September)	314-241-5875
Circus Flora (early-mid-May)	314-531-6273
Elvis Birthday Celebration (early January)	314-727-0880
Fair Saint Louis (early July)	314-434-3434
Festival of the Trees (late November)	314-849-4440
Goldenrod Ragtime (early September)	636-946-2020
Grand Festival of Nations (mid-June)	314-773-7733
Grand South Grand House Tour (mid-April)	314-773-4844
Great Apple Jubilee (early September)	314-233-0513
Great Forest Park Balloon Race (mid September)	314-993-2468
Great Saint Louis Golf Show (mid-January)	800-221-1280
Great Saint Louis Kite Festival (mid-April)	636-938-4800
Greater Saint Louis Auto Show (late January-early February)	314-342-5000
Greater Saint Louis Beer Festival (early October)	314-576-7100
Greek Festival (late August-early September)	314-361-6924
Greentree Festival (early-mid-September)	314-822-5855
Historic Shaw Art Fair (early October)	314-771-3101
Holiday Festival of Lights (mid-November)	314-577-7049
Holiday Flower Show (late November)	314-577-5100
International Folkfest (mid-October)	314-773-9090
Japanese Festival (early September)	314-577-5100
Jazz Festivals (June)	314-577-5100
Kwanzaa Holiday Expo (mid-December)	314-367-3440
Laclede's Landing Big Muddy Blues Festival (early September)	314-241-5875
Lafayette Square Victorian Art Festival (early June)	314-772-5724
Laumeier Contemporary Art Fair (early May)	314-821-1209
Lewis & Clark Rendezvous (mid-May)	636-946-7776
Loop in Motion Arts Festival (early October)	314-725-4466
Memorial Day Festival (late May)	314-241-5875
Miller Music Blast (early July)	314-241-5875
Missouri Spring Festival of Art (early April)	314-889-0433
Missouri WineFest (mid-February)	314-576-7100
Moonlight Ramble (mid-August)	314-644-4660
Polish Festival (early September)	314-921-1192
Saint Louis Alive Music Festival (late May-early June)	314-995-4963
Saint Louis Antiques Show (early May)	314-968-7340
Saint Louis Art Fair (early September)	314-863-0278
Saint Louis Blues Heritage Festival (mid-August)	314-644-1551
Saint Louis Boat & Sports Show (early February)	314-567-0020
Saint Louis County Fair & Air Show (early September)	636-530-9386
Saint Louis Earth Day Community Festival (early June)	314-776-4442
Saint Louis International Film Festival (late October-early November)	314-454-0042
Saint Louis National Charity Horse Show (mid-late September)	636-458-7994
Saint Louis Storytelling Festival (early May)	314-516-5036
Saint Louis Strassenfest (early August)	314-849-6322
Saint Patrick's Day Parade & Run (mid-March)	314-421-1800
Six Flags Music Festival (mid-May)	636-938-4800
Soulard Bastille Day Celebration (mid-July)	314-773-6767
Soulard Mardi Gras (early-mid February)	314-421-1023
Spring Home & Garden Show (late February)	314-994-7700
Taste of the Nation Food Festival (late April)	314-863-5500
Taste of Westport Food Festival (early June)	314-576-7100
Tilles Fall Arts & Crafts Fair (mid-September)	636-391-0922
Tilles Spring Arts & Crafts Fair (mid-May)	636-391-0922
Valley of Flower Festival (early May)	314-837-0033
Way of Lights (late November-early January)	314-241-3400
Whitaker Jazz Festival (early June)	314-577-5100
Winter Wonderland (late November-early January)	314-615-7275
World War II Weekend (late April)	314-544-5714

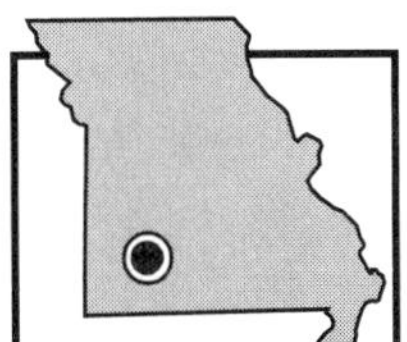

Springfield

Located in the tablelands of the Ozark Mountain Plateau, Springfield, Missouri is within 90 minutes of many Missouri waterways and their abundant stock of crappie, rainbow trout, bluegill, and other fish. The Bass Pro Shops Outdoor World of Springfield is a premier attraction, with mounted wild game, a 30-foot waterfall, indoor boat showroom and firing range, and a 140,000-gallon aquarium. To the east of the city one can visit the home

Springfield (Cont'd)

of the "Little House" series author, Laura Ingalls Wilder. Branson, Missouri, which has earned a reputation as the new Country Music Show Capital, lies south of Springfield. Mel Tillis, Glen Campbell, Roy Clark, and other country music celebrities perform at their own theaters in Branson.

Population	142,898	**Longitude**	93-29-81 W
Area (Land)	67.9 sq mi	**County**	Greene
Area (Water)	0.6 sq mi	**Time Zone**	CST
Elevation	1316 ft	**Area Code/s**	417
Latitude	37-21-53 N		

— Average Temperatures and Precipitation —

TEMPERATURES

	Jan	Feb	Mar	Apr	May	Jun	Jul	Aug	Sep	Oct	Nov	Dec
High	42	46	57	68	76	84	90	89	80	70	57	45
Low	20	25	34	44	53	62	67	65	58	46	36	25

PRECIPITATION

	Jan	Feb	Mar	Apr	May	Jun	Jul	Aug	Sep	Oct	Nov	Dec
Inches	1.8	2.1	3.9	4.2	4.4	5.1	2.9	3.5	4.6	3.6	3.8	3.2

— Important Phone Numbers —

	Phone		*Phone*
AAA	417-882-8040	**Medical Referral**	417-887-1017
American Express Travel	417-866-0477	**Poison Control Center**	800-366-8888
Dental Referral	417-882-4117	**Time/Temp**	417-831-7700
Emergency	911	**Weather**	417-866-1010

— Information Sources —

				Phone	*Fax*
Better Business Bureau Serving Southwest Missouri 205 Park Central E Suite 509 *Web:* www.springfield-mo.bbb.org	Springfield	MO	65806	417-862-4222	869-5544
Greene County 940 N Boonville Ave	Springfield	MO	65802	417-868-4055	868-4170
Springfield Chamber of Commerce 202 S John Q Hammons Pkwy *Web:* www.spfld-mo-chamber.com ■ *E-mail:* spfdcham@spfld-mo-chamber.com	Springfield	MO	65801	417-862-5567	862-1611
Springfield City Hall 840 Boonville Ave *Web:* springfield.missouri.org/gov ■ *E-mail:* city@mail.orion.org	Springfield	MO	65802	417-864-1000	864-1649
Springfield-Greene County Library 397 E Central St *Web:* www.orion.org/library/sgcl/	Springfield	MO	65802	417-874-8150	874-8151
Springfield Mayor 840 Boonville Ave	Springfield	MO	65802	417-864-1651	864-1649
Springfield Missouri Convention & Visitors Bureau 3315 E Battlefield Rd *TF:* 800-678-8767 ■ *Web:* www.springfieldmo.org ■ *E-mail:* cvb@springfieldmo.org	Springfield	MO	65804	417-881-5300	881-2231
Springfield Planning & Development Dept 840 Boonville Ave *Web:* springfield.missouri.org/gov/planning_development ■ *E-mail:* city@ci.springfield.mo.us	Springfield	MO	65802	417-864-1031	864-1030

On-Line Resources

About.com Guide to Springfield/Branson	springfieldmo.about.com
Anthill City Guide Springfield	www.anthill.com/city.asp?city=springfieldmo
Area Guide Springfield	springfieldmo.areaguides.net
Branson Connection	www.bransonconnection.com
BransonNet	www.branson.net
ORION-Ozarks Regional Information Online Network	www.orion.org/
Springfield City Net	www.excite.com/travel/countries/united_states/missouri/springfield
Springfield Community Profile	springfield.missouri.org

— Transportation Services —

AIRPORTS

■ **Springfield-Branson Regional Airport (SGF)**

	Phone
8 miles NW of downtown (approx 20 minutes) Web: www.sgf-branson-airport.com	417-869-0300

Airport Transportation

	Phone
Fisk Limousines $35 fare to downtown	417-862-2900
Yellow Cab $13 fare to downtown	417-862-5511

Commercial Airlines

	Phone		*Phone*
American Eagle	800-433-7300	**TWA Express**	800-221-2000
Atlantic Southeast	800-282-3424	**United**	800-241-6522
Delta	800-221-1212	**United Express**	800-241-6522
Northwest	800-225-2525	**US Airways Express**	800-428-4322
TWA	800-221-2000		

Charter Airlines

	Phone		*Phone*
Pro Flight Air	800-743-9698	**Springfield Aircraft Charter**	800-944-5555

CAR RENTALS

	Phone		*Phone*
Avis	417-865-6226	**Hertz**	417-865-1681
Budget	417-831-2662	**National**	417-865-5311
Dollar	417-862-6090	**Thrifty**	417-866-8777
Enterprise	417-338-2280		

LIMO/TAXI

	Phone		*Phone*
Fisk Limousines	417-862-2900	**Yellow Cab**	417-862-5511

MASS TRANSIT

	Phone
City Bus Service $.75 Base fare	417-831-8782

RAIL/BUS

				Phone
Greyhound/Trailways Bus Station 803 Saint Louis St *TF:* 800-231-2222	Springfield	MO	65806	417-869-2975

— Accommodations —

HOTEL RESERVATION SERVICES

	Phone	*Fax*
Branson Nights Reservations *TF:* 800-329-9999 ■ *Web:* www.branson-nights.com	417-335-6971	335-6025

HOTELS, MOTELS, RESORTS

				Phone	*Fax*
American Inn 3550 E Evergreen St *TF:* 800-905-6343	Springfield	MO	65803	417-831-1080	831-1080
Bass Country Inn 2610 N Glenstone Ave	Springfield	MO	65803	417-866-6671	866-6088
Baymont Inns & Suites 3776 S Glenstone Ave *TF:* 800-301-0200	Springfield	MO	65804	417-889-8188	889-6173
Best Western Coach House Inn 2535 N Glenstone Ave *TF:* 800-528-1234	Springfield	MO	65803	417-862-0701	862-0701
Best Western Deerfield Inn 3343 E Battlefield Rd *TF:* 800-528-1234	Springfield	MO	65804	417-887-2323	887-1242
Best Western Knight's Inn 3215 W Hwy 76 *TF:* 800-528-1234	Branson	MO	65616	417-334-1894	334-3437
Best Western Music Capital Inn 3257 Shepherd of the Hills Expy *TF:* 800-528-1234	Branson	MO	65616	417-334-8378	334-8855
Branson Towers Inn 236 Shepherd of the Hills Expy *TF:* 800-683-1122	Branson	MO	65616	417-336-4500	334-6838

Springfield — Hotels, Motels, Resorts (Cont'd)

	City	State	ZIP	Phone	Fax
Clarion Hotel 3333 S Glenstone Ave *TF:* 800-756-7318	Springfield	MO	65804	417-883-6550	883-5720
Comfort Inn 3330 E Battlefield Rd *TF:* 800-228-5150	Springfield	MO	65804	417-889-6300	889-6565
Comfort Suites 1260 E Independence St *TF:* 800-228-5150	Springfield	MO	65804	417-886-5090	886-6677
Days Inn 2700 N Glenstone Ave *TF:* 800-329-7466	Springfield	MO	65803	417-865-5511	865-5511
Drury Inn & Suites 2715 N Glenstone Ave *TF:* 800-378-7946	Springfield	MO	65803	417-863-8400	863-8400
Econo Lodge 2808 N Kansas Expy *TF:* 800-553-2666	Springfield	MO	65803	417-869-5600	869-3421
Econo Lodge East 2611 N Glenstone Ave *TF:* 800-553-2666	Springfield	MO	65616	417-864-3565	865-0567
Economy Inn 2555 N Glenstone Ave	Springfield	MO	65803	417-864-8459	864-8459
Extended StayAmerica 1333 E Kingsley St *TF:* 800-398-7829	South Springfield	MO	65804	417-823-9100	823-9005
Fairfield Inn by Marriott 1610 E Evergreen St *TF:* 800-228-2800	Springfield	MO	65803	417-869-8800	869-8848
Glenstone Court Motel 2023 N Glenstone Ave	Springfield	MO	65803	417-865-9804	
Grand Ramada Branson 245 N Wildwood Dr *TF:* 800-850-6646	Branson	MO	65616	417-336-6646	337-5535
Guesthouse Inn South 3370 E Battlefield Rd *TF:* 877-570-7378 ■ *Web:* www.guesthouse.net/springsouth.html	Springfield	MO	65804	417-520-6200	520-6600
GuestHouse Suites Plus 1550 E Raynell Pl *TF:* 877-570-7300 ■ *Web:* www.guesthouse.net/springplus.html	Springfield	MO	65804	417-883-7300	883-5779
Hampton Inn East 222 N Ingram Mill Rd *TF:* 800-426-7866	Springfield	MO	65802	417-863-1440	863-2215
Hampton Inn West 3695 W 76 Country Blvd *TF:* 800-426-7866	Branson	MO	65616	417-337-5762	337-8733
Hillbilly Inn 1166 Hwy 76 W *TF:* 800-535-0739	Branson	MO	65616	417-334-3946	334-1179
Holiday Inn North 2720 N Glenstone Ave *TF:* 800-465-4329	Springfield	MO	65803	417-865-8600	862-9415
Holiday Inn University Plaza 333 John Q Hammons Pkwy *TF:* 800-465-4329	Springfield	MO	65806	417-864-7333	831-5893
Interstate Inn 1116 W Norton St *TF:* 800-222-6400	Springfield	MO	65803	417-833-1550	833-4600
Lamplighter Inn 1772 S Glenstone Ave *TF:* 800-749-7275	Springfield	MO	65804	417-882-1113	882-8869
Microtel Inn 3125 N Kentwood Ave *TF:* 800-414-2027	Springfield	MO	65803	417-833-1500	833-1500
Motel 6 3114 N Kentwood Ave *TF:* 800-466-8356	Springfield	MO	65803	417-833-0880	833-5147
Ozark Inn 2601 N Glenstone Ave	Springfield	MO	65803	417-865-6565	865-9008
Pear Tree Inn by Drury 2745 N Glenstone Ave *TF:* 800-282-8733	Springfield	MO	65803	417-869-0001	869-9146
Quality Inn North 3050 N Kentwood St *TF:* 800-225-5288	Springfield	MO	65803	417-833-3108	833-0477
Radisson Hotel Branson 120 S Wildwood Dr *TF:* 888-566-5290	Branson	MO	65616	417-335-5767	335-7979
Ramada Inn 2820 N Glenstone Ave *TF:* 800-707-0326	Springfield	MO	65803	417-869-3900	865-5378
Ramada Limited 3404 E Ridgeview St *TF:* 800-272-6232	Springfield	MO	65804	417-882-2220	881-0002
Rancho Motel 1720 E Kearney St	Springfield	MO	65803	417-862-0535	862-0535
Red Roof Inn 2655 N Glenstone Ave *TF:* 800-843-7663	Springfield	MO	65803	417-831-2100	866-7837
Redwood Inn 3811 W Chestnut Expy	Springfield	MO	65802	417-864-5959	864-7746
Residence Inn 280 S Wildwood Dr *TF:* 800-331-3131 ■ *Web:* www.residenceinn.com/residenceinn/SGFBR	Branson	MO	65616	417-336-4077	336-5837
Rest Haven Court 2000 E Kearney St	Springfield	MO	65803	417-869-9114	
Rock View Resort 1049 Parkview Dr *TF:* 800-742-7625	Hollister	MO	65672	417-334-4678	336-2438
Satellite Motel 2305 N Glenstone Ave	Springfield	MO	65803	417-869-2527	
Shadowbrook Motel 1610 W Hwy 76 *TF:* 800-641-4600	Branson	MO	65615	417-334-4173	
Sheraton Hawthorn Park Hotel 2431 N Glenstone Ave *TF:* 800-223-0092 ■ *Web:* www.springfieldmo.net/sheraton ■ *E-mail:* sheraton@pcis.net	Springfield	MO	65803	417-831-3131	831-9786
Skyline Motel 2120 N Glenstone Ave	Springfield	MO	65803	417-866-4356	866-8480
Sleep Inn 233 E Camino Alto *TF:* 888-753-3760	Springfield	MO	65810	417-886-2464	886-4121
Solar Inn 2355 N Glenstone Ave	Springfield	MO	65803	417-866-6776	863-9347
Super 8 Motel 3022 N Kentwood Ave *TF:* 800-800-8000	Springfield	MO	65803	417-833-9218	833-9218
Walnut Street Inn 900 E Walnut St *TF:* 800-593-6346 ■ *Web:* www.walnutstreetinn.com	Springfield	MO	65806	417-864-6346	864-6184

— Restaurants —

	City	State	ZIP	Phone
Amarillo Mesquite Grill (American) 2020 E Independence St	Springfield	MO	65804	417-883-4440
Bamboo Inn (Chinese) 948 S Glenstone Ave	Springfield	MO	65802	417-869-2506
Bijan's (Seafood) 209 E Walnut St	Springfield	MO	65806	417-831-1480
Cartoon's Oyster Bar & Grill (Seafood) 1614 S Glenstone *Web:* www.cartoonman.com	Springfield	MO	65804	417-882-5752
Cheddar's Casual Cafe (American) 1950 E Primrose Ln	Springfield	MO	65804	417-889-8998
Chinese Chef (Chinese) 3029 S Campbell Ave	Springfield	MO	65810	417-883-4770
Cielito Lindo Mexicano (Mexican) 2953 S National Ave	Springfield	MO	65804	417-886-3320
Clary's American Grill (New American) 3014-A E Sunshine St	Springfield	MO	65804	417-886-1940
Deer Lake Cafe (American) 5544 W Chestnut Expy	Springfield	MO	65802	417-865-3338
Diamond Head (Chinese) 2734 S Campbell Ave	Springfield	MO	65807	417-883-9581
El Chico (Mexican) 2639 S Glenstone St	Springfield	MO	65804	417-886-4768
Gallery Bistro (New American) 221 E Walnut St	Springfield	MO	65806	417-866-0440
Gee's East Wind (Chinese) 2951 E Sunshine St	Springfield	MO	65804	417-883-4567
Hemingway's Blue Water Cafe (American) 1935 S Campbell Ave	Springfield	MO	65807	417-887-3388
Henry's Bar & Grille (American) 3050 N Kentwood	Springfield	MO	65803	417-833-3108
J Parrino's (Italian) 1550-L E Battlefield St	Springfield	MO	65804	417-882-1808
Jade Garden (Chinese) 1128 S Glenstone Ave	Springfield	MO	65804	417-863-0833
Korea House (Korean) 1112 E Saint Louis St	Springfield	MO	65806	417-862-9992
Le Mirabelle (French) 2620 S Glenstone Ave	Springfield	MO	65804	417-883-2550
Mandarin Inn (Chinese) 706 E Battlefield St	Springfield	MO	65807	417-887-8181
McGuffey's (New American) 2101 W Chesterfield Blvd Suite A100	Springfield	MO	65807	417-882-2484
Metropolitan Grill (Italian) 1908 S Glenstone Ave	Springfield	MO	65804	417-889-4951
Mexican Villa West (Mexican) 1100 W Sunshine St	Springfield	MO	65807	417-866-7292
Nakato Japanese Steak House (Japanese) 2615 S Glenstone Ave	Springfield	MO	65804	417-881-7171
Nearly Famous Deli & Pasta House (Italian) 1828 S Kentwood Ave	Springfield	MO	65803	417-883-3403
Ossi Japanese Steakhouse (Japanese) 1410 E Republic Rd	Springfield	MO	65804	417-885-0055
Peppertree The (American) 2720 N Glenstone Ave	Springfield	MO	65803	417-865-8600
Rembrandt's (American) 2431 N Glenstone Ave	Springfield	MO	65803	417-831-3131
Riksha (Chinese) 222 Park Central N	Springfield	MO	65806	417-831-9499
Saint Louis Bread Co (Continental) 1570 E Battlefield Rd Suite E	Springfield	MO	65804	417-889-0070
Schultz & Dooley's (American) 2210 W Chesterfield Blvd	Springfield	MO	65807	417-885-0060
Shady Inn (Steak/Seafood) 524 W Sunshine St	Springfield	MO	65807	417-862-0369
Shanghai Inn (Chinese) 1937 N Glenstone Ave	Springfield	MO	65803	417-865-5111
Silk Road (Chinese) 400 S Glenstone Ave	Springfield	MO	65802	417-869-4403

— Goods and Services —

SHOPPING

	City	State	ZIP	Phone	Fax
Apple Jack's Country Store & Craftmen's Mall 1996 Evangel St	Ozark	MO	65721	417-581-3899	
Bass Country Antique Mall 1832 S Campbell Ave	Springfield	MO	65807	417-869-8255	864-8209
Battlefield Mall 101 Battlefield Mall	Springfield	MO	65804	417-883-7777	883-2641
Chesterfield Village Kansas Expy & James River Fwy	Springfield	MO	65807	417-862-2771	862-4573
Class Act Flea Market 224 E Commercial St	Springfield	MO	65803	417-862-1370	
Grand Village The 2800 W 76 Country Music Blvd *TF:* 800-952-6626 ■ *Web:* www.gvshops.com	Branson	MO	65616	417-336-7280	336-7293
Ozark Antique Mall 200 S 20th St	Ozark	MO	65721	417-581-5233	581-0325
PFI Western Store 2816 S Ingram Mill Rd *TF:* 800-222-4734 ■ *Web:* www.pfiwestern.com ■ *E-mail:* info@pfiwestern.com	Springfield	MO	65804	417-889-2668	889-7204
Traders Market Shopping Gallery 1845 E Sunshine	Springfield	MO	65804	417-889-1145	882-0261

BANKS

	City	State	ZIP	Phone	Fax
Empire Bank 1800 S Glenstone *TF:* 888-231-4637	Springfield	MO	65804	417-881-3100	882-9675

Springfield — Banks (Cont'd)

Name / Address	City	State	ZIP	Phone	Fax
Great Southern Bank FSB 1451 E Battlefield Rd *TF:* 800-749-7113	Springfield	MO	65804	417-887-4400	888-4533
Mercantile Bank of Saint Louis 417 Saint Louis St	Springfield	MO	65806	417-868-4400	868-4408
Metropolitan National Bank 600 S Glenstone Ave	Springfield	MO	65802	417-862-2022	862-6318
UMB Bank 1150 E Battlefield St	Springfield	MO	65807	417-887-5855	887-1808

BUSINESS SERVICES

Name	Phone	Name	Phone
Airborne Express	800-247-2676	**Kinko's**	417-889-1995
BAX Global	800-225-5229	**Mail Boxes Etc**	800-789-4623
DHL Worldwide Express	800-225-5345	**Manpower Temporary Services**	417-886-9300
Express Personnel Services	417-887-5900	**Olsten Staffing Services**	417-889-1100
Federal Express	800-238-5355	**Post Office**	417-864-0117
Interim Personnel	417-881-6200	**UPS**	800-742-5877
Kelly Services	417-883-0830		

— Media —

PUBLICATIONS

Name / Address	City	State	ZIP	Phone	Fax
Springfield Business Journal 313 Park Central W *Web:* www.sbj.net	Springfield	MO	65806	417-831-3238	831-5478
Springfield News Leader‡ PO Box 798 *TF Circ:* 800-695-2005 ■ *Web:* www.ozarksgateway.com/nl.htm	Springfield	MO	65801	417-836-1100	837-1381

‡Daily newspapers

TELEVISION

Name / Address	City	State	ZIP	Phone	Fax
KDEB-TV Ch 27 (Fox) 3000 E Cherry St *Web:* www.fox27.com	Springfield	MO	65802	417-862-2727	831-4209
KOLR-TV Ch 10 (CBS) 2650 E Division St *Web:* www.kolr10.com	Springfield	MO	65803	417-862-1010	862-6439
KOZK-TV Ch 21 (PBS) 821 Washington Ave	Springfield	MO	65802	417-865-2100	863-1599
KSPR-TV Ch 33 (ABC) 1359 Saint Louis St *Web:* www.kspr33.com ■ *E-mail:* admin@kspr33.com	Springfield	MO	65802	417-831-1333	831-4125
KYTV-TV Ch 3 (NBC) PO Box 3500 *Web:* www.ky3.com ■ *E-mail:* ky3news@ky3.com	Springfield	MO	65808	417-268-3000	268-3100

RADIO

Name / Address	City	State	ZIP	Phone	Fax
KADI-FM 99.5 MHz (Rel) 1601 W Sunshine St Suite P *Web:* www.kadi.com	Springfield	MO	65807	417-831-0995	831-4026
KGBX-FM 105.9 MHz (AC) 1856 S Glenstone Ave *Web:* www.kgbx.com	Springfield	MO	65804	417-890-5555	890-5050
KGMY-AM 1400 kHz (Nost) 1856 S Glenstone Ave *Web:* www.mycountry.com	Springfield	MO	65804	417-890-5555	890-5050
KLFJ-AM 1550 kHz (N/T) 610 W College St	Springfield	MO	65806	417-831-1550	
KSMU-FM 91.1 MHz (NPR) Southwest Missouri State University 901 S National Ave *Web:* www.ksmu.org ■ *E-mail:* ksmu@netfocus.net	Springfield	MO	65804	417-836-5878	836-5889
KTOZ-AM 1060 kHz (AAA) 610 W College	Springfield	MO	65806	417-831-1060	831-1231
KTOZ-FM 95.5 MHz (AC) 1856 S Glenstone Ave	Springfield	MO	65804	417-890-5555	890-5050
KTXR-FM 101.3 MHz (B/EZ) 3000 E Chestnut Expy *Web:* www.ktxrfm.com ■ *E-mail:* ktxrfm@ktxrfm.com	Springfield	MO	65802	417-862-3751	869-7675
KWTO-AM 560 kHz (N/T) 3000 E Chestnut Expy	Springfield	MO	65802	417-862-5600	869-7675
KXUS-FM 97.3 MHz (Nost) 1856 S Glenstone Ave	Springfield	MO	65804	417-890-5555	890-5050

— Colleges/Universities —

Name / Address	City	State	ZIP	Phone	Fax
Baptist Bible College 628 E Kearney St *TF:* 800-228-5754 ■ *Web:* www.seebbc.edu ■ *E-mail:* bbc@ncsi.net	Springfield	MO	65803	417-268-6060	268-6694
Berean University 1445 N Boonville Ave *TF:* 800-443-1083 ■ *Web:* www.berean.edu ■ *E-mail:* berean@ag.org	Springfield	MO	65802	417-862-9533	862-5318
Central Bible College 3000 N Grant Ave *TF:* 800-831-4222 ■ *Web:* www.cbcag.edu	Springfield	MO	65803	417-833-2551	833-5141
Drury College 900 N Benton Ave *TF:* 800-922-2274 ■ *Web:* www.drury.edu	Springfield	MO	65802	417-873-7879	873-7529
Evangel University 1111 N Glenstone Ave *TF Admissions:* 800-382-6435 ■ *Web:* www.evangel.edu	Springfield	MO	65802	417-865-2811	865-9599
Southwest Baptist University 1600 University Ave *TF Admissions:* 800-526-5859 ■ *Web:* www.sbuniv.edu ■ *E-mail:* admitme@SBUniv.edu	Bolivar	MO	65613	417-326-5281	326-1514
Southwest Missouri State University 901 S National Ave *TF:* 800-492-7900 ■ *Web:* www.smsu.edu ■ *E-mail:* smsuinfo@vma.smsu.edu	Springfield	MO	65804	417-836-5000	836-6334
Springfield College 1010 W Sunshine *TF:* 888-741-4271 ■ *E-mail:* ccenter@cci.edu	Springfield	MO	65807	417-864-7220	864-5697

— Hospitals —

Name / Address	City	State	ZIP	Phone	Fax
Saint John's Regional Health Center 1235 E Cherokee St **Fax:* Admitting ■ *Web:* www.stjohns.net	Springfield	MO	65804	417-885-2000	885-2288*

— Attractions —

Name / Address	City	State	ZIP	Phone	Fax
76 Music Hall 1945 W 76 Country Music Blvd	Branson	MO	65616	417-335-2484	334-1647
Air & Military Museum 2305 E Kearney St	Springfield	MO	65803	417-864-7997	
Bass Pro Shops 2500 E Kearney St **Fax:* Hum Res ■ *Web:* www.basspro.com	Springfield	MO	65898	417-873-5000	865-9812*
Branson Scenic Railway 206 E Main St *TF:* 800-287-2462	Branson	MO	65616	417-334-6110	336-3909
Children's Choirs of Southwest Missouri 1926 S Glenstone	Springfield	MO	65804	417-885-7880	
Crystal Cave 7225 N Crystal Cave Ln	Springfield	MO	65803	417-833-9599	
Dickerson Park Zoo 3043 N Fort *Web:* www.dickersonparkzoo.org	Springfield	MO	65803	417-833-1570	
Discovery Center 438 Saint Louis St	Springfield	MO	65806	417-862-9910	862-6898
Dixie Stampede Dinner Attraction 1525 W Hwy 76 *TF:* 800-520-5544 ■ *Web:* www.branson.com/branson/dixie/default.html	Branson	MO	65616	417-336-3000	339-4360
Exotic Animal Paradise Rt 1 Box 270	Strafford	MO	65757	417-859-2016	859-4902
Fantastic Caverns 4872 N Farm Rd 125	Springfield	MO	65803	417-833-2010	
Fellows Lake N FM 189 & FM 66	Springfield	MO	65803	417-831-8403	
Frisco Railroad Museum 543 E Commercial St *Web:* www.frisco.org/frisco/frisco.html ■ *E-mail:* slsfmus@aol.com	Springfield	MO	65803	417-866-7573	
George Washington Carver National Monument 5646 Carver Rd *Web:* www.nps.gov/gwca/	Diamond	MO	64840	417-325-4151	325-4231
Grand Palace The 2700 W 76 Country Music Blvd *TF:* 800-884-4536	Branson	MO	65616	417-336-1220	337-5170
Gray/Campbell Farmstead 2400 S Scenic	Springfield	MO	65807	417-862-6293	862-6293
Hammons Juanita K Hall for the Performing Arts 525 Don Q Hammons Pkwy *TF:* 888-476-7849 ■ *Web:* www.hammonshall.smsu.edu	Springfield	MO	65804	417-836-6776	836-6891
History Museum 830 Boonville Ave 3rd Fl *Web:* www.historymuseumsgc.org	Springfield	MO	65802	417-864-1976	864-2019
Medical Museum Health Education Center at the Discovery Center 438 E Saint Louis St	Springfield	MO	65806	417-862-9910	862-6898
Missouri Sports Hall of Fame 3861 E Stan Musial Dr *TF:* 800-498-5678	Springfield	MO	65809	417-889-3100	889-2761
Ozark National Scenic Riverways PO Box 490 *Web:* www.nps.gov/ozar/	Van Buren	MO	63965	573-323-4236	323-4140
Ozarks Discovery IMAX Theater 3562 Shepherd of the Hills Expy *TF:* 800-419-4832 ■ *Web:* members.aol.com/OzarksIMAX/index1.html	Branson	MO	65616	417-335-3533	336-5348

Springfield — Attractions (Cont'd)

				Phone	Fax
Polynesian Princess 1358 Long Creek Rd	Branson	MO	65739	417-337-8366	339-2941
TF: 800-653-6288 ■ *Web:* www.branson.com/branson/princess/princess.htm					
Precious Moments Chapel 4321 Chapel Rd	Carthage	MO	64836	417-359-3010	359-2905
TF: 800-543-7975 ■ *Web:* www.preciousmoments.com					
Ride The Ducks 2320 W Hwy 76	Branson	MO	65616	417-334-3825	334-5382
Shepherd of the Hills Outdoor Theatre 5586 W Hwy 76	Branson	MO	65616	417-334-4191	334-4617
TF: 800-653-6288 ■ *Web:* www.branson.com/branson/shepherd/shepherd.htm					
Showboat Branson Belle 4800 State Hwy 165	Branson	MO	65616	417-336-7171	336-7410
TF: 800-227-8587 ■ *Web:* www.silverdollarcity.com/showboat ■ *E-mail:* tickets@silverdollarcity.com					
Silver Dollar City W Hwy 76	Branson	MO	65616	417-336-7100	
TF: 800-475-9370 ■ *Web:* www.silverdollarcity.com					
Snow Bluff Ski & Fun Area Hwy 13	Brighton	MO	65617	417-376-2201	
Springfield Art Museum 1111 E Brookside Dr	Springfield	MO	65807	417-837-5700	837-5704
Springfield Ballet 311 E Walnut St	Springfield	MO	65806	417-862-1343	864-6577
Springfield Conservation Nature Center 4600 S Chrisman Ave	Springfield	MO	65804	417-888-4237	
Springfield Little Theatre 311 E Walnut	Springfield	MO	65806	417-869-1334	869-4047
Web: www.landerstheatre.org ■ *E-mail:* slt@landerstheatre.org					
Springfield National Cemetery 1702 E Seminole St	Springfield	MO	65804	417-881-9499	
Springfield Regional Opera 311 E Walnut St	Springfield	MO	65806	417-863-1960	863-7416
Springfield Symphony Orchestra 1536 E Division	Springfield	MO	65803	417-864-6683	864-8967
Web: www.orion.org/~symphony					
Stafford Jim Theatre 3440 Hwy 76	Branson	MO	65616	417-335-8080	335-2482
Web: www.jimstafford.com					
Stained Glass Theatre 1700 N Benton Ave	Springfield	MO	65803	417-869-9018	
Stone Hill Winery 601 State Hwy 165	Branson	MO	65616	417-334-1897	334-1942
White Water 3505 W Hwy 76	Branson	MO	65616	417-334-7488	334-7421
Wilder Laura Ingalls-Rose Wilder Lane Museum & Home 3068 Hwy A	Mansfield	MO	65704	417-924-3626	924-8580
Wilson's Creek National Battlefield 6424 W Farm Rd 182	Republic	MO	65738	417-732-2662	732-1167
Web: www.nps.gov/wicr/					

— Events —

	Phone
1860 Lifestyle Exposition (mid-September)	417-862-6293
Artsfest (early May)	417-869-8380
Balloonfest (mid-September)	417-269-5437
Fall Hunting Classic (late August)	417-873-5111
Firefall (early July)	417-864-1049
First Night Springfield (December 31)	417-869-8380
Frisco Days (mid-April)	417-864-7015
Hall of Fame All-Star Game (early July)	417-889-3100
Halloween Spooktacular (late October)	417-833-1570
Nike Ozarks Open (mid-August)	417-886-0408
Ozark Empire Fair (late July-early August)	417-833-2660
Ozark Mountain Christmas Festival of Lights (early November-late December)	417-881-5300
Sheep & Wool Days (early June)	417-881-1659
SMSU Summer Tent Theater (late June-early August)	417-836-5979
Watercolor USA (early June-early August)	417-837-5700

Montana

Population (1999): 882,779 **Area (sq mi): 147,046**

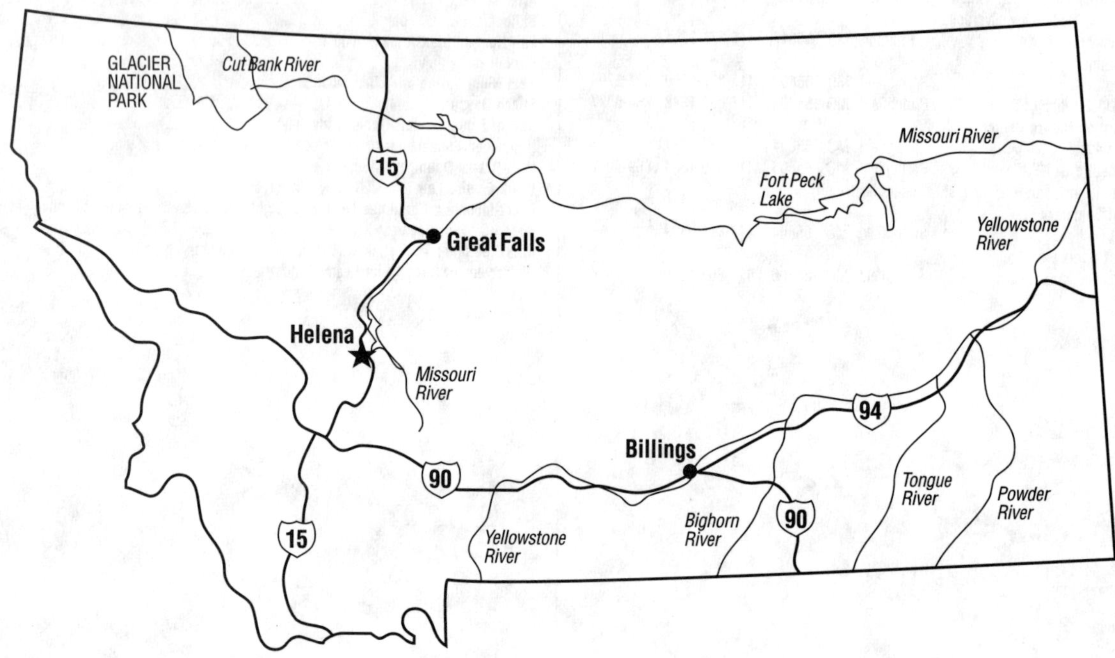

— State Information Sources —

				Phone	Fax
Montana Chamber of Commerce PO Box 1730	Helena	MT	59624	406-442-2405	442-2409
Montana Economic Development Div 1424 9th Ave *Web:* commerce.mt.gov/economic	Helena	MT	59620	406-444-3814	444-1872
Montana Parks Div PO Box 200701 *Web:* travel.mt.gov/eventatt/stpark/stpark.htm	Helena	MT	59620	406-444-3750	444-4952
Montana Promotion Div (Travel Montana) 1424 9th Ave *TF:* 800-847-4868 ■ *Web:* www.visitmt.com	Helena	MT	59620	406-444-2654	444-1800
Montana State Government Information *Web:* www.mt.gov				406-444-2511	
Montana State Library PO Box 201800 *Web:* msl.mt.gov	Helena	MT	59620	406-444-3004	444-5612

ON-LINE RESOURCES

Cybertourist Montana .... www.cybertourist.com/montana.shtml
Destination Northwest: Montana .... www.destinationnw.com/montana
Montana Cities .... dir.yahoo.com/Regional/U_S__States/Montana/Cities
Montana Counties & Regions .... dir.yahoo.com/Regional/U_S__States/Montana/Counties_and_Regions
Montana Cyberzine .... www.montanacyberzine.com
Montana Scenario .... scenariousa.dstylus.com/mt/indexf.htm
Montana Travel & Tourism Guide .... www.travel-library.com/north_america/usa/montana/index.html
MontanaWeb .... search.montanaweb.com
Online Highways Travel Guide to Montana .... www.ohwy.com/mt/homepage.htm
Peaks: An Online Magazine about Montana .... www.aetherserv.com/peaks
Rough Guide Travel Montana travel.roughguides.com/content/1106/index.htm
Travel.org-Montana .... travel.org/montana.html
What's Up Montana! .... www.whatsupmontana.com
Yahoo! Get Local Montana .... dir.yahoo.com/Regional/U_S__States/Montana

— Cities Profiled —

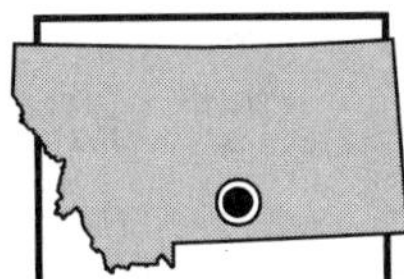

Billings

Billings is considered to be a new city, barely 100 years old. Located in the Yellowstone River Valley, the city is surrounded by 400-foot-high sandstone cliffs (rimrocks) from which seven mountain ranges are visible: Pryor, Big Horn, Bull, Snowy, Crazy, Absaroba, and Beartooth. Beartooth Highway near Billings is one of three Yellowstone National Park entrances located in Montana. The park itself is about 120 miles southwest of Billings. Little Bighorn Battlefield, site of Custer's Last Stand, is just 60 miles from Billings.

Population	91,750	**Longitude**	108-49-60 W
Area (Land)	32.6 sq mi	**County**	Yellowstone
Area (Water)	0.1 sq mi	**Time Zone**	MST
Elevation	3124 ft	**Area Code/s**	406
Latitude	45-77-66 N		

— Average Temperatures and Precipitation —

TEMPERATURES

	Jan	Feb	Mar	Apr	May	Jun	Jul	Aug	Sep	Oct	Nov	Dec
High	32	39	46	57	67	78	87	85	72	61	45	34
Low	14	19	25	34	43	52	58	57	47	38	26	17

PRECIPITATION

	Jan	Feb	Mar	Apr	May	Jun	Jul	Aug	Sep	Oct	Nov	Dec
Inches	0.9	0.6	1.2	1.7	2.6	2.0	0.9	1.0	1.4	1.1	0.8	0.8

— Important Phone Numbers —

	Phone		Phone
AAA	406-248-7738	**Poison Control Center**	800-525-5042
Emergency	911	**Time/Temp**	406-657-1333
HotelDocs	800-468-3537	**Weather**	406-652-1916
Medical Referral	406-238-2500		

— Information Sources —

				Phone	Fax
Billings Area Chamber of Commerce 815 S 27th St. *TF:* 800-735-2635 ■ *Web:* www.wtp.net/bacc	Billings	MT	59107	406-245-4111	245-7333
Billings City Hall PO Box 1178 *Web:* ci.billings.mt.us	Billings	MT	59103	406-657-8200	657-8390
Billings Community Development Dept PO Box 1178 *Web:* ci.billings.mt.us/government/cs	Billings	MT	59103	406-657-8281	657-8252
Billings Convention & Visitors Bureau PO Box 31177 *TF:* 800-735-2635	Billings	MT	59107	406-245-4111	245-7333
Billings Mayor PO Box 1178 *Web:* ci.billings.mt.us/government/mayor.php3	Billings	MT	59103	406-657-8296	657-8390
MetraPark 308 6th Ave N. *TF:* 800-366-8538 ■ *Web:* www.metrapark.com	Billings	MT	59101	406-256-2400	256-2479
Parmly Billings Library 510 N Broadway	Billings	MT	59101	406-657-8257	657-8293
Yellowstone County PO Box 35001 *Web:* www.ystone.mt.gov/	Billings	MT	59107	406-256-2785	256-2736

On-Line Resources

Area Guide Billings	billings.areaguides.net
Big Sky Wire	www.bigskywire.com
Billings CityLink	www.usacitylink.com/citylink/billings/
City Knowledge Billings	www.cityknowledge.com/mt_billings.htm
Excite.com Billings City Guide	www.excite.com/travel/countries/united_states/montana/billings

— Transportation Services —

AIRPORTS

	Phone
■ **Billings Logan International Airport (BIL)** 2 miles NW of downtown (approx 5 minutes) Web: ci.billings.mt.us/government/air	406-657-8495

Airport Transportation

	Phone
Billings Area City Cab $6 fare to downtown	406-252-8700
Yellow Cab $6 fare to downtown	406-245-3033

Commercial Airlines

	Phone		Phone
Big Sky	406-245-9449	**Northwest**	800-225-2525
Delta	800-325-1999	**United**	800-241-6522
Horizon	800-547-9308		

Charter Airlines

	Phone		Phone
Big Sky Airlines	406-245-9449	**Corporate Air Charter**	406-248-1541
Central Airservice	406-538-3767	**Lynch Flying Service Inc**	406-252-0508

CAR RENTALS

	Phone		Phone
Avis	406-252-8007	**Hertz**	406-248-9151
Budget	406-259-4168	**National**	406-252-7626
Dollar	406-259-1147	**Thrifty**	406-259-1025

LIMO/TAXI

	Phone		Phone
A Limo	406-252-2536	**Limo Scene & Carriage Co.**	406-252-1778
Aladdin Limousines	307-672-8812	**Sheridan Transportation Taxi**	307-674-6814
Billings Area City Cab	406-252-8700	**Yellow Cab**	406-245-3033

MASS TRANSIT

	Phone
Billings MET Transit $.75 Base fare	406-657-8218

RAIL/BUS

				Phone
Greyhound Bus Station 2502 1st Ave N *TF:* 800-231-2222	Billings	MT	59101	406-245-5116

— Accommodations —

HOTELS, MOTELS, RESORTS

				Phone	Fax
Airport Metra Inn 403 Main St *TF:* 800-234-6611	Billings	MT	59105	406-245-6611	248-3481
Best Western Billings 5610 S Frontage Rd *TF:* 800-528-1234	Billings	MT	59101	406-248-9800	248-2500
Best Western Ponderosa Inn 2511 1st Ave N. *TF:* 800-628-9081	Billings	MT	59101	406-259-5511	245-8004
Big 5 Motel 2601 4th Ave N. *TF:* 800-283-4678	Billings	MT	59101	406-245-6646	245-9358
Billings Hotel & Convention Center 1223 Mullowney Ln. *TF:* 800-537-7286	Billings	MT	59101	406-248-7151	248-2054
Billings Inn 880 N 29th St. *TF:* 800-231-7782	Billings	MT	59101	406-252-6800	252-6800
C'mon Inn 2020 Overland Ave *TF:* 800-655-1170	Billings	MT	59102	406-655-1100	652-7672
Cherry Tree Inn 823 N Broadway *TF:* 800-237-5882	Billings	MT	59101	406-252-5603	254-0494
Comfort Inn 2030 Overland Ave *TF:* 800-228-5150	Billings	MT	59102	406-652-5200	652-5200
Days Inn 843 Parkway Ln *TF:* 800-329-7466	Billings	MT	59101	406-252-4007	896-1147
Dude Rancher Lodge 415 N 29th St. *TF:* 800-221-3302	Billings	MT	59101	406-259-5561	259-0095
Fairfield Inn by Marriott 2026 Overland Ave *TF:* 800-228-2800 ■ *Web:* fairfieldinn.com/BILMT	Billings	MT	59102	406-652-5330	652-5330

Billings — Hotels, Motels, Resorts (Cont'd)

				Phone	Fax
Hilltop Inn 1116 N 28th St.	Billings	MT	59101	406-245-5000	245-7851
TF: 800-878-9282					
Holiday Inn Grand Montana 5500 Midland Rd	Billings	MT	59101	406-248-7701	248-8954
TF: 800-465-4329					
■ *Web:* www.basshotels.com/holiday-inn/?_franchisee=BILWE					
■ *E-mail:* hi429sales@sagehotel.com					
Howard Johnson 1001 S 27th St	Billings	MT	59101	406-248-4656	248-7268
TF: 800-654-2000					
Juniper Inn 1315 N 27th St	Billings	MT	59101	406-245-4128	245-4128
TF: 800-826-7530					
Kelly Inn 5425 Midland Rd.	Billings	MT	59101	406-252-2700	252-1011
TF: 800-635-3559					
Lewis & Clark Inn 1709 1st Ave N	Billings	MT	59101	406-252-4691	248-3170
TF: 800-821-6741					
Motel 6 5353 Midland Rd	Billings	MT	59101	406-248-7551	245-7032
TF: 800-466-8356					
Quality Inn Homestead 2036 Overland Ave	Billings	MT	59102	406-652-1320	652-1320
TF: 800-228-5151					
Radisson Northern Hotel 19 N 28th St	Billings	MT	59101	406-245-5121	259-9862
TF: 800-333-3333					
Ramada Limited 1345 Mullowney Ln	Billings	MT	59101	406-252-2584	252-2584
TF: 800-272-6232					
Rimrock Inn 1203 N 27th St.	Billings	MT	59101	406-252-7107	252-7107
TF: 800-624-9770					
Rimview Inn 1025 N 27th St	Billings	MT	59101	406-248-2622	248-2622
TF: 800-551-1418					
Sheraton Billings Hotel 27 N 27th St	Billings	MT	59101	406-252-7400	252-2401
TF: 800-588-7666					
Sleep Inn 4904 Southgate Dr	Billings	MT	59101	406-254-0013	254-9878
Super 8 Lodge 5400 Southgate Dr	Billings	MT	59102	406-248-8842	248-8842
TF: 800-800-8000					
Travel West Inn 3311 2nd Ave N	Billings	MT	59101	406-245-6345	245-9882
TF: 888-231-9378					
War Bonnet Inn 2612 Belknap Ave	Billings	MT	59101	406-248-7761	248-7761
TF: 888-242-6023					

— Restaurants —

				Phone
Arapahoe Dining Room (Homestyle) 2612 Belknap Ave	Billings	MT	59101	406-248-7761
Athenian The (Greek) 300 S 24th St West	Billings	MT	59102	406-652-2798
Bruno's (Italian) 1002 1st Ave N	Billings	MT	59105	406-248-4146
Dos Machos (Mexican) 300 S 24th St W	Billings	MT	59102	406-652-2020
George Henry's Restaurant (Continental) 404 N 30th St	Billings	MT	59101	406-245-4570
Golden Belle (Continental) 19 N 28th St.	Billings	MT	59101	406-245-5121
Golden Corral (American) 570 S 24th St West	Billings	MT	59102	406-655-4453
Golden Phoenix Restaurant (Chinese) 279 Swords Ln	Billings	MT	59105	406-256-0319
Granary Restaurant (Steak/Seafood) 1500 Poly Dr.	Billings	MT	59102	406-259-3488
Great Wall (Chinese) 1309 Grand Ave	Billings	MT	59102	406-245-8601
Jade Palace (Chinese) 2021 Overland Ave	Billings	MT	59102	406-656-8888
Jakes (Steak/Seafood) 2701 1st Ave N	Billings	MT	59101	406-259-9375
Juliano's (American) 2912 7th Ave N	Billings	MT	59101	406-248-6400
Kit Kat Cafe (Homestyle) 633 Main St	Billings	MT	59105	406-259-9154
Little Bangkok (Thai/Japanese) 2916 1st Ave N	Billings	MT	59101	406-248-2218
Lucky Diamond (American) 27 N 27th St Sheraton Hotel	Billings	MT	59101	406-252-7400
Main Street Casino (American) 405 Main St.	Billings	MT	59101	406-259-4707
Matthew's Taste of Italy (Italian) 1233 N 27th St	Billings	MT	59101	406-254-8530
Mayflower of China (Chinese) 1720 Grand Ave	Billings	MT	59102	406-245-9566
Muzzle Loader Cafe (American) 4912 Laurel Rd	Billings	MT	59101	406-248-8608
O'Hara's Restaurant (Homestyle) 3222 1st Ave N	Billings	MT	59101	406-259-0388
Poblano (Mexican) 300 S 24th St West	Billings	MT	59102	406-655-0662
Pug Mahon's (American) 3011 1st Ave N	Billings	MT	59101	406-259-4190
Recipes (American) 5500 Midland Rd Holiday Inn	Billings	MT	59101	406-248-7701
Rex The (Steak/Seafood) 2401 Montana Ave.	Billings	MT	59101	406-245-7477
Thai Orchid (Thai) 2926 2nd Ave N	Billings	MT	59101	406-256-2206
Walker's Grill (American) 301 N 27th St	Billings	MT	59101	406-245-9291

— Goods and Services —

SHOPPING

				Phone	Fax
Downtown Billings Shopping District					
2910 3rd Ave N	Billings	MT	59101	406-259-5454	248-6228
Four Seasons Shopping Center 1327 Main St	Billings	MT	59102	406-252-3383	
Rimrock Mall 300 South 24th St W	Billings	MT	59102	406-656-3205	656-9174
West Park Plaza 1603 Grand Ave	Billings	MT	59102	406-252-8858	252-9053

BANKS

				Phone	Fax
First Citizens Bank 2812 1st Ave N.	Billings	MT	59101	406-247-4100	247-4160
First Interstate Bank of Commerce					
401 N 31st St.	Billings	MT	59116	406-255-5000	255-5213*
**Fax:* Hum Res					
Glacier Bank 2209 Central Ave	Billings	MT	59102	406-652-3300	652-6531
Norwest Bank 1325 Main St.	Billings	MT	59105	406-252-6322	245-1284
Norwest Bank Montana NA 175 N 27th St.	Billings	MT	59101	406-657-3400	657-3624
TF: 800-666-8262					
Rocky Mountain Bank 2615 King Ave W	Billings	MT	59102	406-656-3140	652-5923
Security Bank PO Box 2503	Billings	MT	59103	406-238-4800	238-4827
Stockman Bank 2700 King Ave W.	Billings	MT	59102	406-655-2700	655-2727
US Bank NA 303 N Broadway	Billings	MT	59101	406-657-8004	657-8628
Western Security Bank 2929 3rd Ave N.	Billings	MT	59101	406-252-3700	255-5959
Yellowstone Bank Billings 2000 Overland Ave	Billings	MT	59102	406-652-4100	652-4897

BUSINESS SERVICES

Name	Phone	Name	Phone
Airborne Express	800-247-2676	**Manpower Temporary Services**	406-652-9401
BAX Global	800-225-5229	**Olsten Staffing Services**	406-652-7644
DHL Worldwide Express	800-225-5345	**Post Office**	406-657-5700
Federal Express	800-238-5355	**Snelling Personnel Services**	406-652-5267
Kinko's	406-252-6265	**SOS Staffing Service**	406-252-8430
Mail Boxes Etc	800-789-4623	**UPS**	800-742-5877

— Media —

PUBLICATIONS

				Phone	Fax
Billings Gazette‡ PO Box 36300	Billings	MT	59107	406-657-1200	657-1208
TF: 800-543-2505 ■ *Web:* www.bigskywire.com/gazette/					
Billings Times 2919 Montana Ave.	Billings	MT	59101	406-245-4994	

‡*Daily newspapers*

TELEVISION

				Phone	Fax
KHMT-TV Ch 4 (Fox)					
445 South 24th St W Suite 404	Billings	MT	59102	406-652-7366	652-6963
KSVI-TV Ch 6 (ABC) 445 S 24th St W.	Billings	MT	59102	406-652-4743	652-6963
E-mail: ksvi@ksvi.com					
KTVQ-TV Ch 2 (CBS) 3203 3rd Ave N	Billings	MT	59101	406-252-5611	252-9938
Web: www.ktvq.com ■ *E-mail:* q2news@ktvq.com					
KULR-TV Ch 8 (NBC) 2045 Overland Ave.	Billings	MT	59102	406-656-8000	652-8207
Web: www.kulr8.com ■ *E-mail:* kurl8tv@wtp.net					
KUSM-TV Ch 9 (PBS)					
Visual Communications Bldg Rm 172	Bozeman	MT	59717	406-994-3437	994-6545
TF: 800-426-8243 ■ *Web:* www.kusm.montana.edu					

RADIO

Name/Address	City	State	Zip	Phone	Fax
KBLG-AM 910 kHz (N/T) 2075 Central Ave.	Billings	MT	59102	406-652-8400	652-4899
KCTR-FM 102.9 MHz (Ctry)					
27 N 27th St 23rd Fl.	Billings	MT	59103	406-248-7827	252-9577
KEMC-FM 91.7 MHz (NPR) 1500 N 30th St.	Billings	MT	59101	406-657-2941	657-2977
KGHL-AM 790 kHz (Ctry)					
2070 Overland Ave Suite 103	Billings	MT	59102	406-656-1410	656-0110
KIDX-FM 98.5 MHz (Ctry)					
2070 Overland Ave Suite 103	Billings	MT	59102	406-656-1410	656-0110
KMZK-AM 1240 kHz (Rel) PO Box 31038	Billings	MT	59107	406-245-3121	245-0822
KRKX-FM 94.1 MHz (Rock) 2075 Central Ave.	Billings	MT	59102	406-652-8400	652-4899
Web: www.krkx.com					
KYYA-FM 93.3 MHz (AC) 2075 Central Ave	Billings	MT	59102	406-652-8400	652-4899
Web: www.y93.com					

— Colleges/Universities —

Name/Address	City	State	Zip	Phone	Fax
Montana State University Billings					
1500 N 30th St.	Billings	MT	59101	406-657-2011	657-2302
Web: www.msubillings.edu					
Rocky Mountain College 1511 Poly Dr	Billings	MT	59102	406-657-1000	259-9751
TF: 800-877-6259 ■ *Web:* www.rocky.edu					
■ *E-mail:* admissions@rocky.edu					

Billings (Cont'd)

— Hospitals —

				Phone	Fax
Deaconess Medical Center 2800 10th Ave N	Billings	MT	59101	406-657-4000	238-2785
TF: 800-332-7201					
Saint Vincent Hospital & Health Center 1233 N 30th St	Billings	MT	59101	406-657-7000	237-3369*
**Fax:* Admitting ■ *Web:* www.svhhc.org					

— Attractions —

				Phone	Fax
Bair Alberta Theater 2801 3rd Ave N	Billings	MT	59101	406-256-8915	256-5060
Big Splash Waterpark 5720 S Frontage Rd	Billings	MT	59101	406-256-5543	259-8627
Bighorn Canyon National Recreation Area PO Box 7458	Fort Smith	MT	59035	406-666-2412	666-2415
Web: www.nps.gov/bica/					
Billings Studio Theatre 1500 Rimrock Rd	Billings	MT	59102	406-248-1141	248-1576
Billings Symphony Orchestra 201 N Broadway Suite 350	Billings	MT	59101	406-252-3610	252-3353
Web: www.mcn.net/~symphony ■ *E-mail:* symphony@mcn.net					
Little Bighorn Battlefield National Monument PO Box 39	Crow Agency	MT	59022	406-638-2621	638-2623
Web: www.nps.gov/libi/					
Moss Mansion 914 Division St	Billings	MT	59101	406-256-5100	252-0091
Pictograph Cave State Park I-90 Exit 452	Billings	MT	59105	406-247-2940	248-5026
Ralston JK Studio & Gallery 1426 Rimrock Rd	Billings	MT	59102	406-254-0959	
Yegen Peter Jr Yellowstone County Museum 1950 Terminal Cir	Billings	MT	59105	406-256-6811	
Yellowstone Art Museum 401 N 27th St	Billings	MT	59101	406-256-6804	256-6817
Web: yellowstone.artmuseum.org ■ *E-mail:* ccartinfo@artmuseum.org					
Yellowstone National Park PO Box 168	Yellowstone National Park	WY	82190	307-344-7381	344-2323
Web: www.nps.gov/yell/					
Yellowstone Western Heritage Center 2822 Montana Ave	Billings	MT	59101	406-256-6809	256-6850
Web: www.ywhc.org ■ *E-mail:* heritage@ywhc.org					
Zoo Montana 2100 S Shiloh Rd	Billings	MT	59108	406-652-8100	652-9281
Web: www.wtp.net/~zoomont ■ *E-mail:* zoomont@wtp.net					

SPORTS TEAMS & FACILITIES

				Phone	Fax
Billings Bulls (hockey) 308 6th Ave N Metra Park Arena	Billings	MT	59103	406-256-2456	256-2452
Web: www.billingsbulls.com ■ *E-mail:* feedback@billingsbulls.com					
Billings Mustangs (baseball) 901 N 27th St Cobb Field	Billings	MT	59101	406-252-1241	252-2968
Web: www.wtp.net/mustangs/ ■ *E-mail:* mustangs@wtp.net					
MetraPark Arena 308 6th Ave N	Billings	MT	59101	406-256-2400	254-7991
TF: 800-366-8538 ■ *Web:* www.metrapark.com					

— Events —

	Phone
Antique & Collectible Extravaganza (late April & late September)	308-436-8355
Big Sky State Games (late July)	406-254-7426
Billings Home & Garden Show (mid-February)	406-245-0404
Chase Hawks Memorial Rough Stock Invitational Rodeo (mid-December)	406-248-9295
Crow Fair (mid-August)	406-638-2601
Custer's Last Stand Re-enactment (late June)	406-665-1672
Fantasy of Lights (mid-late December)	406-252-9600
Festival of Trees (early November)	406-256-2422
Holiday Festival (mid-December)	406-248-2212
Holiday Parade (late November)	406-259-5454
Laurel Herbstfest (late September)	406-628-8105
Mexican Fiesta (late July-early August)	406-252-0191
MontanaFair (mid-August)	406-256-2400
New Year's Pow Wow (late December)	406-638-2601
Northern International Livestock Expo Pro Rodeo (mid-October)	406-256-2495
Northern International Livestock Expo Stock Show & Sale (early October)	406-256-2495
Northern Rodeo Assn Finals (early February)	406-256-2422
Summerfair (mid-July)	406-256-6804

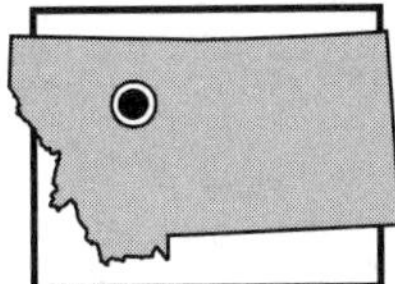

Great Falls

The city of Great Falls is named for the great falls of the Missouri River, discovered by Lewis and Clark in 1805. The city is located in north central Montana, in the portion of the state known as Russell Country. (Russell Country was named for Western artist Charlie Russell, and the C.M. Russell Museum Complex in Great Falls has the most complete collection of his works in the world.) Russell Country includes the 149-mile section of the Missouri River designated as Wild and Scenic, as well as Smith River, which is a favorite for float trips. The area is noted for its excellent fly fishing, especially for trout. Giant Springs State Park, with freshwater springs that bubble at 134,000 gallons per minute, is just five miles east of downtown Great Falls. The park is located between Black Eagle Dam and Falls and Rainbow Dam and Falls Overlook. The River's Edge Trail, which begins in Oddfellows Park in Great Falls, allows hikers to go from the center of the city to the Missouri River (a distance of 5.5 miles), passing Rainbow, Black Eagle, and Crooked Falls along the way.

Population	56,395	**Longitude**	111-18-65 W
Area (Land)	15.4 sq mi	**County**	Cascade
Area (Water)	0.4 sq mi	**Time Zone**	MST
Elevation	3334 ft	**Area Code/s**	406
Latitude	47-50-95 N		

— Average Temperatures and Precipitation —

TEMPERATURES

	Jan	Feb	Mar	Apr	May	Jun	Jul	Aug	Sep	Oct	Nov	Dec
High	31	38	44	55	65	75	83	82	70	59	44	33
Low	12	17	23	32	41	49	53	52	44	36	24	15

PRECIPITATION

	Jan	Feb	Mar	Apr	May	Jun	Jul	Aug	Sep	Oct	Nov	Dec
Inches	0.9	0.6	1.1	1.4	2.5	2.4	1.2	1.5	1.2	0.8	0.7	0.9

— Important Phone Numbers —

	Phone		Phone
AAA	406-727-2900	**Time/Temp**	406-452-8463
Emergency	911	**Weather**	406-453-5469
Poison Control Center	800-525-5042		

— Information Sources —

				Phone	Fax
Cascade County PO Box 2867	Great Falls	MT	59403	406-454-6800	454-6802
Web: www.mcn.net/~cascade ■ *E-mail:* cascade@mcn.net					
Four Seasons Arena 400 3rd St NW	Great Falls	MT	59404	406-727-8900	452-8955
Web: www.city-of-great-falls.com/events/expopark/four_seasons.htm ■ *E-mail:* expopark@city-of-great-falls.com					
Great Falls Area Chamber of Commerce 710 1st Ave N	Great Falls	MT	59401	406-761-4434	761-6129
Web: www.gfa-mtchamber.org					
Great Falls City-County Planning Dept PO Box 5021	Great Falls	MT	59403	406-771-1180	425-6256
Web: www.city-of-great-falls.com/people_offices/planning/index.htm					
Great Falls City Hall PO Box 5021	Great Falls	MT	59403	406-771-1180	727-0005
Web: www.city-of-great-falls.com					
Great Falls Mayor PO Box 5021	Great Falls	MT	59403	406-771-1180	727-0005
Web: www.city-of-great-falls.com/people_offices/boards_commissions/bennett.htm					
Great Falls Public Library 301 2nd Ave N	Great Falls	MT	59401	406-453-0349	453-0181
Web: www.mtgr.mtlib.org/www/library/					

Great Falls — Information Sources (Cont'd)

				Phone	Fax
Russell Country Inc PO Box 3166	Great Falls	MT	59403	800-527-5348	761-5085*

**Fax Area Code:* 406

On-Line Resources

Area Guide Great Falls . . . greatfalls.areaguides.net
Excite.com Great Falls City Guide . . . www.excite.com/travel/countries/united_states/montana/great_falls
OnRoute Destinations: Great Falls Montana . . . www.onroute.com/destinations/montana/greatfalls.html

— Transportation Services —

AIRPORTS

■ **Great Falls International Airport (GTF)**

	Phone
4 miles SW of downtown (approx 20 minutes)	406-727-3404

E-mail: gtfintlairport@mcn.net

Airport Transportation

	Phone
Diamond Cab $8.50 fare to downtown	406-453-3241

Commercial Airlines

	Phone		Phone
Delta	800-221-1212	**Northwest**	800-225-2525
Horizon	800-547-9308		

CAR RENTALS

	Phone		Phone
Avis	406-761-7610	**National**	406-453-4386
Hertz	406-761-6641	**Rent-A-Wreck**	406-761-0722

LIMO/TAXI

	Phone		Phone
Diamond Cab	406-453-3241	**Wright Nite Limo**	406-761-1300

MASS TRANSIT

	Phone
Great Falls Transit District $.50 Base fare	406-727-0382

RAIL/BUS

				Phone
Rim Rock Trailways Bus Station 2800 Terminal Dr Great Falls Airport Ground Level	Great Falls	MT	59404	406-453-1541

— Accommodations —

HOTELS, MOTELS, RESORTS

				Phone	Fax
Alberta Motel 1101 Central Ave W	Great Falls	MT	59404	406-452-3467	
Best Western Heritage Inn 1700 Fox Farm Rd *TF:* 800-548-8256	Great Falls	MT	59404	406-761-1900	761-0136
Best Western Ponderosa Inn 220 Central Ave *TF:* 800-266-3410	Great Falls	MT	59401	406-761-3410	761-3410
Budget Inn 2 Treasure State Dr. *TF:* 800-362-4842	Great Falls	MT	59404	406-453-1602	453-1602
Comfort Inn 1120 9th St S *TF:* 800-228-5150	Great Falls	MT	59405	406-454-2727	454-2727
Crestview Inn 500 13th Ave S *TF:* 800-727-8380	Great Falls	MT	59405	406-727-8380	727-8380
Days Inn Great Falls 101 14th Ave NW *TF:* 800-329-7466	Great Falls	MT	59404	406-727-6565	727-6308
Evergreen Motel 2531 Vaughn Rd	Great Falls	MT	59404	406-452-0312	
Fairfield Inn 1000 9th Ave S *TF:* 800-228-2800 ■ *Web:* fairfieldinn.com/GTFFI	Great Falls	MT	59405	406-454-3000	454-3000
Four Seasons Motel 299 3rd St NW	Great Falls	MT	59404	406-761-1400	
Great Falls Inn 1400 28th St S. *TF:* 800-454-6010	Great Falls	MT	59405	406-453-6000	453-6078
Highwood Village Motel 4009 10th Ave S *TF:* 800-253-8505	Great Falls	MT	59405	406-452-8505	452-2863
Holiday Inn 400 10th Ave S *TF:* 800-465-4329	Great Falls	MT	59405	406-727-7200	727-7200
Old Oak Inn 709 4th Ave N	Great Falls	MT	59401	406-727-5782	
Plaza Inn 1224 10th Ave S. *TF:* 800-354-0868	Great Falls	MT	59405	406-452-9594	
Royal Motel 1300 Central Ave	Great Falls	MT	59401	406-452-9548	
Super 8 Lodge 1214 13th St S *TF:* 800-800-8000	Great Falls	MT	59405	406-727-7600	
Town & Country Motel 2418 10th Ave S	Great Falls	MT	59405	406-452-5643	
TownHouse Inn 1411 10th Ave S *TF:* 800-442-4667	Great Falls	MT	59405	406-761-4600	761-7603
Triple Crown Motor Inn 621 Central Ave	Great Falls	MT	59401	406-727-8300	727-8300
Village Motor Inn 726 10th Ave S. *TF:* 800-354-0868	Great Falls	MT	59405	406-727-7666	727-8750
Wagonwheel Motel 2620 10th Ave S	Great Falls	MT	59405	406-761-1300	
Western Motel 2420 10th Ave S.	Great Falls	MT	59405	406-453-3281	453-3281

— Restaurants —

				Phone
3-D International (International) 1825 Smelter Ave	Black Eagle	MT	59404	406-453-6561
Allie's Place (Homestyle) 600 Central Ave	Great Falls	MT	59401	406-453-5292
Borrie's (Italian) 1800 Smelter Ave	Black Eagle	MT	59414	406-761-0300
Crossroad Cafe (American) 1715 Vaughn Rd.	Great Falls	MT	59404	406-453-7992
Down Under (American) 318 Central Ave	Great Falls	MT	59401	406-727-5172
Eddie's Supper Club (American) 3725 2nd Ave N	Great Falls	MT	59401	406-453-1616
El Comedor (Mexican) 1120 25th St S	Great Falls	MT	59405	406-761-5500
Jakers (Steak/Seafood) 1500 10th Ave S	Great Falls	MT	59405	406-727-1033
La Pastada (Mexican) 1701 9th Ave S	Great Falls	MT	59405	406-452-5804
Little Athens (Greek) 1200 10th Ave S	Great Falls	MT	59405	406-453-1430
Loft Restaurant (American) 4800 10th Ave S	Great Falls	MT	59405	406-727-8988
Maple Garden (Chinese) 5401 9th Ave S	Great Falls	MT	59401	406-727-0310
Mardi Gras Cafe (American) 1700 Fox Farm Rd	Great Falls	MT	59404	406-761-1900
Maria's Mexican Restaurant (Mexican) 2501 10th St S	Great Falls	MT	59405	406-453-5303
Ming's (Chinese) 3212 10th Ave S.	Great Falls	MT	59405	406-727-4153
New Peking (Chinese) 1525 3rd St NW	Great Falls	MT	59404	406-452-2828
Pepper's Grill & Bar (American) 1200 10th Ave S.	Great Falls	MT	59405	406-761-1994
Prime Cut Restaurant (Steak/Seafood) 3219 10th Ave S	Great Falls	MT	59405	406-727-2141
Town House Inn Restaurant (American) 1411 10th Ave S	Great Falls	MT	59405	406-761-4600

— Goods and Services —

SHOPPING

				Phone	Fax
Times Square 525 Central Ave	Great Falls	MT	59401	406-727-3332	
Westgate Mall 1807 3rd St NW	Great Falls	MT	59404	406-761-2464	761-6487

BANKS

				Phone	Fax
First Interstate Bank of Montana 425 1st Ave N	Great Falls	MT	59401	406-454-6200	727-9781
Heritage Bank 120 1st Ave N	Great Falls	MT	59401	406-727-6106	761-5798
Mountain West Bank 12 3rd St NW	Great Falls	MT	59404	406-727-2265	771-7331
Norwest Bank 21 3rd St N	Great Falls	MT	59401	406-454-5400	454-5480

BUSINESS SERVICES

	Phone		Phone
Airborne Express	800-247-2676	**Mail Boxes Etc**	800-789-4623
BAX Global	800-225-5229	**Post Office**	406-771-2160
Central Printing	406-727-4060	**Snelling & Snelling**	406-727-2414
DHL Worldwide Express	800-225-5345	**UPS**	800-742-5877
Express Personnel Services	406-761-3027	**Westside Copy Shop**	406-459-5206
Federal Express	800-238-5355		

Great Falls (Cont'd)

— Media —

PUBLICATIONS

				Phone	Fax
Great Falls Tribune‡ PO Box 5468 *TF:* 800-438-6600	Great Falls	MT	59403	406-761-1268	791-1431

‡*Daily newspapers*

TELEVISION

				Phone	Fax
KFBB-TV Ch 5 (ABC) PO Box 1139 *Web:* www.kfbb.com ■ *E-mail:* kfbb@kfbb.com	Great Falls	MT	59403	406-453-4377	727-9703
KRTV-TV Ch 3 (CBS) PO Box 2989 *Web:* www.krtv.com ■ *E-mail:* krtv@krtv.com	Great Falls	MT	59403	406-453-2433	791-5479
KTGF-TV Ch 16 (NBC) PO Box 1219 *Web:* www.ktgf.com ■ *E-mail:* program@ktgf.com	Great Falls	MT	59403	406-761-8816	454-3484
KUSM-TV Ch 9 (PBS) Visual Communications Bldg Rm 172 *TF:* 800-426-8243 ■ *Web:* www.kusm.montana.edu	Bozeman	MT	59717	406-994-3437	994-6545

RADIO

				Phone	Fax
KAAK-FM 98.9 MHz (AC) 1300 Central Ave W	Great Falls	MT	59404	406-761-2800	452-9467
KEIN-AM 1310 kHz (Ctry) PO Box 1239	Great Falls	MT	59403	406-761-1310	454-3775
KLFM-FM 92.9 MHz (Oldies) 20 3rd St N Suite 231	Great Falls	MT	59401	406-761-7600	761-5511
KMON-AM 560 kHz (Ctry) 20 3rd St N Suite 231	Great Falls	MT	59401	406-761-7600	761-5511
KMON-FM 94.5 MHz (Ctry) 20 3rd St Suite 231	Great Falls	MT	59403	406-761-7600	761-5511
KQDI-AM 1450 kHz (N/T) 1300 Central Ave W	Great Falls	MT	59404	406-761-2800	452-9467
KQDI-FM 106.1 MHz (CR) 1300 Central Ave W	Great Falls	MT	59404	406-761-2800	727-7218
KXGF-AM 1400 kHz (Nost) 1300 Central Ave W	Great Falls	MT	59404	406-727-7211	727-7218

— Colleges/Universities —

				Phone	Fax
Mountain States Baptist College 824 3rd Ave N	Great Falls	MT	59401	406-761-0308	
University of Great Falls 1301 20th St S *Web:* www.ugf.edu	Great Falls	MT	59405	406-761-8210	791-5393

— Hospitals —

				Phone	Fax
Benefis Health Care 1101 26th St S *Web:* www.benefis.org	Great Falls	MT	59405	406-761-1200	455-4587

— Attractions —

				Phone	Fax
Benton Lake National Wildlife Refuge 922 Bootlegger Trail	Great Falls	MT	59404	406-727-7400	727-7432
CM Russell Museum 400 13th St N *Web:* www.cmrussell.org	Great Falls	MT	59401	406-727-8787	727-2402
Gallery Sixteen 608 Central Ave	Great Falls	MT	59401	406-453-6103	
Giant Springs State Park River Rd	Great Falls	MT	59406	406-454-5840	
Glacier National Park PO Box 128 *Web:* www.nps.gov/grba	West Glacier	MT	59936	406-888-7800	888-7808
Great Falls Convention Center & Theatre 2 Park Dr S	Great Falls	MT	59401	406-454-3915	454-3468
Great Falls Symphony Park Dr & Central Ave Civic Center	Great Falls	MT	59401	406-453-4102	453-9779
Malmstrom Air Force Base Museum & Air Park 2nd Ave N	Great Falls	MT	59402	406-731-2705	
Montana River Outfitters Float Trips 923 10th Ave N	Great Falls	MT	59405	406-761-1677	452-3833
Paris Gibson Square Museum of Art 1400 1st Ave N	Great Falls	MT	59401	406-727-8255	727-8256
River's Edge Trail	Great Falls	MT		406-761-4966	
Ulm Pishkun State Park off I-15 at Ulm Exit	Ulm	MT	59485	406-454-5840	

SPORTS TEAMS & FACILITIES

				Phone	Fax
Electric City Speedway Old Haver Hwy	Great Falls	MT	59401	406-727-4884	
Great Falls Dodgers (baseball) 1015 25th St N Legion Pk *Web:* www.mcn.net/~dodgers	Great Falls	MT	59401	406-452-5311	454-0811

— Events —

	Phone
Christmas Stroll (early December)	406-761-4434
CM Russell Auction of Original Western Art (mid-March)	406-761-6453
Cottonwood Festival (early September)	406-452-3462
Ice Breaker Fun Run (late April)	406-771-1265
Lewis & Clark Festival (late June)	406-761-4434
Luminaria Walk on the River Edge Trail (July 16th)	406-761-4434
Montana Agricultural & Industrial Exhibit (mid-January)	406-761-7600
Montana Pro Rodeo Finals (mid-January)	406-761-4434
Montana State Fair (late July-early August)	406-727-1481

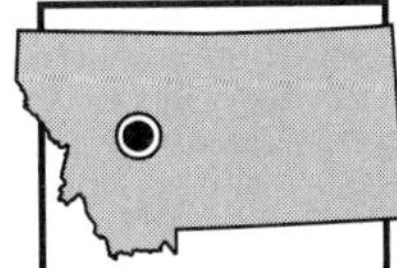

Helena

Situated in the heart of the Rocky Mountains, halfway between Yellowstone and Glacier national parks, Montana's capital city got its start when four goldminers hit paydirt in what's now Last Chance Gulch in downtown Helena. The city is located at the center of a 250-mile area in southwestern Montana that encompasses nearly 70 percent of the state's population. Helena's city limits border the million-acre Helena National Forest, including the southern range of Bob Marshall and Scapegoat wilderness areas. The Great Divide Ski Area and miles of cross-country and snowmobile trails are nearby, and the Missouri River flows near Helena to the east. Numerous reservoirs along the Missouri provide excellent fishing and other recreational opportunities, and the Missouri River plain deposits are also rich in sapphires. In addition, hundreds of bald eagles gather along the Missouri near Helena every November and December to feed on spawning salmon.

Population	28,306	**Longitude**	112-03-53 W
Area (Land)	13.5 sq mi	**County**	Lewis & Clark
Area (Water)	0 sq mi	**Time Zone**	MST
Elevation	4090 ft	**Area Code/s**	406
Latitude	46-59-28 N		

— Average Temperatures and Precipitation —

TEMPERATURES

	Jan	Feb	Mar	Apr	May	Jun	Jul	Aug	Sep	Oct	Nov	Dec
High	30	37	45	56	65	76	85	83	70	59	42	31
Low	10	16	22	31	40	48	53	52	41	32	21	11

PRECIPITATION

	Jan	Feb	Mar	Apr	May	Jun	Jul	Aug	Sep	Oct	Nov	Dec
Inches	0.6	0.4	0.7	1.0	1.8	1.9	1.1	1.3	1.2	0.6	0.5	0.6

Helena (Cont'd)

— Important Phone Numbers —

	Phone		Phone
AAA	406-442-5920	**Time/Temp**	406-442-1730
Emergency	911	**Weather**	406-443-5151
Poison Control Center	800-525-5042		

— Information Sources —

				Phone	Fax
Helena Area Chamber of Commerce 225 Cruse Ave	Helena	MT	59601	406-442-4120	447-1532
TF: 800-743-5362 ■ *Web:* www.helenamt.com					
Helena City Hall 316 N Park Ave	Helena	MT	59623	406-447-8000	447-8460
Web: www.ci.helena.mt.us					
Helena Civic Center 340 Neill Ave	Helena	MT	59601	406-447-8481	447-8480
Helena Mayor 316 N Park Ave	Helena	MT	59623	406-447-8000	447-8460
E-mail: mayor+commission@desktop.org					
Lewis & Clark County PO Box 1721	Helena	MT	59624	406-447-8200	447-8330
Lewis & Clark County Library 120 S Last Chance Gulch	Helena	MT	59601	406-447-1690	447-1687
Web: www.mth.mtlib.org					
Montana Chamber of Commerce PO Box 1730	Helena	MT	59624	406-442-2405	442-2409

On-Line Resources

Anthill City Guide Helena	www.anthill.com/city.asp?city=helena
Area Guide Helena	helena.areaguides.net
Excite.com Helena City Guide	www.excite.com/travel/countries/united_states/montana/helena
Helena CityGuide	cityguide.lycos.com/rockymt/HelenaMT.html
Helena Home Page	www.imageplaza.com/helena/helhome.html
MainTour Helena Vacation & Travel Guide	www.maintour.com/montana/helena.htm
NITC Travelbase City Guide Helena	www.travelbase.com/auto/guides/helena-mt.html

— Transportation Services —

AIRPORTS

	Phone
■ **Helena Regional Airport (HLN)**	
3 miles NE of downtown (approx 10 minutes)	406-442-2821

Airport Transportation

	Phone
Old Trapper Taxi $7.50 fare to downtown	406-449-5525

Commercial Airlines

	Phone		Phone
Delta	406-442-9998	**Horizon**	406-442-0930

Charter Airlines

	Phone		Phone
Executive Air	406-442-2190	**West Air**	406-443-4543

CAR RENTALS

	Phone		Phone
Avis	406-442-4440	**Hertz**	406-449-4167
Enterprise	406-449-3400	**National**	406-442-8620

LIMO/TAXI

	Phone		Phone
Limos of Helena	406-449-9307	**Old Trapper Taxi**	406-449-5525

RAIL/BUS

				Phone
Trailways/Greyhound Bus Terminal 3122 Hwy 12 E	Helena	MT	59601	406-442-5860

— Accommodations —

HOTELS, MOTELS, RESORTS

				Phone	Fax
Aladdin Motor Inns 2101 E 11th Ave	Helena	MT	59601	406-443-2300	442-7057
TF: 800-541-2743					
Barrister Bed & Breakfast 416 N Ewing St	Helena	MT	59601	406-443-7330	442-7964
TF: 800-823-1148					
Best Western Colonial Inn 2301 Colonial Dr	Helena	MT	59601	406-443-2100	442-0301
TF: 800-422-1002					
Boulder Hot Springs Bed & Breakfast 31 Hot Springs Rd	Boulder	MT	59632	406-225-4339	225-4345
Budget Inn Express 524 N Last Chance Gulch	Helena	MT	59601	406-442-0600	443-1700
TF: 800-862-1334					
Comfort Inn 750 Fee St	Helena	MT	59601	406-443-1000	443-1000
TF: 800-228-5150					
Days Inn 2001 Prospect Ave	Helena	MT	59601	406-442-3280	442-3108
TF: 800-329-7466					
Fairmont Hot Springs Resort 1500 Fairmont Rd	Anaconda	MT	59711	406-797-3241	797-3337
TF: 800-332-3272					
Helena Inn 910 N Last Chance Gulch	Helena	MT	59601	406-442-6080	449-4131
Holiday Inn Express 701 Washington St	Helena	MT	59601	406-449-4000	449-4522
TF: 800-465-4329					
Iron Front Hotel 415 N Last Chance Gulch St	Helena	MT	59601	406-443-2400	
Jorgenson's Holiday Hotel 1714 11th Ave	Helena	MT	59601	406-442-1770	449-0155
TF: 800-272-1770 ■ *Web:* www.jorgensonholiday.com					
Knight's Rest Motel 1831 Euclid Ave	Helena	MT	59601	406-442-6384	
TF: 888-442-6384					
Lamplighter Motel 1006 Madison Ave	Helena	MT	59601	406-442-9200	
Motel 6 800 N Oregon St	Helena	MT	59601	406-442-9990	449-7107
TF: 800-466-8356					
Park Plaza Hotel 22 N Last Chance Gulch	Helena	MT	59601	406-443-2200	442-4030
Ramada Copper King Park Hotel 4655 Harrison Ave S	Butte	MT	59701	406-494-6666	494-3274
TF: 800-332-8600					
Red Roof Inn 1998 Euclid Ave	Helena	MT	59601	406-442-0033	
Sanders The Bed & Breakfast 328 N Ewing St	Helena	MT	59601	406-442-3309	
Shilo Inn 2020 Prospect Ave	Helena	MT	59601	406-442-0320	449-4426
TF: 800-222-2244					
Super 8 Motel 2200 11th Ave	Helena	MT	59601	406-443-2450	
TF: 800-800-8000					

— Restaurants —

				Phone
Bert & Ernie's Saloon (American) 361 N Last Chance Gulch St	Helena	MT	59601	406-443-5680
Brewhouse Brew Pub & Grill (American) 939 1/2 Getchell St	Helena	MT	59601	406-457-9390
Carriage House Bistro (European) 234 1/2 Lyndale St	Helena	MT	59601	406-449-6949
Country Harvest (Homestyle) 2000 Prospect Ave	Helena	MT	59601	406-443-7457
Emiliano's (Mexican) 632 Euclid Ave	Helena	MT	59601	406-443-5478
Gilly's (American) 920 E Lyndale	Helena	MT	59601	406-442-6449
House of Wong (Chinese) 2711 N Montana Ave	Helena	MT	59601	406-442-3320
Jorgenson's (Steak/Seafood) 1720 11th Ave	Helena	MT	59601	406-442-6380
Ming's Chinese Kitchen (Chinese) 1306 Euclid Ave	Helena	MT	59601	406-449-2986
On Broadway (Italian) 106 Broadway	Helena	MT	59601	406-443-1929
River Grille (New American) 1225 Custer Ave	Helena	MT	59601	406-442-1075
Rose's Cantina (Mexican) 314 N Last Chance Gulch	Helena	MT	59601	406-442-5221
Staggering Ox (American) 400 Euclid Ave	Helena	MT	59601	406-443-1729
Stonehouse Restaurant (Steak/Seafood) 120 Reeders Alley	Helena	MT	59601	406-449-2552
Tol's Thai Cuisine (Thai) 423 N Last Chance Gulch St	Helena	MT	59601	406-443-6656
Wall Street Cafe (American) 62 N Last Chance Gulch St	Helena	MT	59601	406-443-6215
Windbag The (American) 19 S Last Chance Gulch	Helena	MT	59601	406-443-9669
Yacht Basin Marina (Steak/Seafood) 7035 Canyon Ferry Rd	Helena	MT	59601	406-475-3125
Yat Son (Chinese) 2 S Main St	Helena	MT	59601	406-442-5405

— Goods and Services —

SHOPPING

				Phone
Capital Hill Mall 11th & Prospect	Helena	MT	59601	406-442-0183
Hustad Center 1055 N Rodney St	Helena	MT	59601	406-442-1833
Sears Roebuck & Co 3120 Dredge Dr	Helena	MT	59601	406-442-4212

Helena (Cont'd)

BANKS

				Phone	Fax
American Federal Savings Bank 1400 Prospect Ave	Helena	MT	59604	406-442-3080	457-4035*
*Fax: Cust Svc					
First Bank Helena PO Box 1709	Helena	MT	59624	406-447-5200	449-8923
TF: 800-872-2657					
First Security Bank of Helena 1721 11th Ave.	Helena	MT	59601	406-442-8870	449-7321
Mountain West Bank of Helena NA 1225 Cedar	Helena	MT	59604	406-449-2265	449-4250
Norwest Bank Montana NA 350 N Last Chance Gulch St	Helena	MT	59601	406-447-2000	447-2075
Valley Bank of Helena 3030 N Montana Ave	Helena	MT	59601	406-443-7440	443-7876
Western Security Bank 3171 N Montana Ave	Helena	MT	59602	406-441-3700	443-1783

BUSINESS SERVICES

	Phone		Phone
Airborne Express	800-247-2676	**Mail Boxes Etc**	800-789-4623
BAX Global	800-225-5229	**Post Office**	406-227-5325
DHL Worldwide Express	800-225-5345	**UPS**	800-742-5877
Express Personnel Services	406-442-7501	**Westaff**	406-443-7169
Federal Express	800-238-5355		

— Media —

PUBLICATIONS

				Phone	Fax
Independent-Record‡ PO Box 4249	Helena	MT	59604	406-447-4000	447-4052
Web: www.helenair.com					

‡Daily newspapers

TELEVISION

				Phone	Fax
KFBB-TV Ch 5 (ABC) PO Box 1139	Great Falls	MT	59403	406-453-4377	727-9703
Web: www.kfbb.com ■ *E-mail:* kfbb@kfbb.com					
KTVH-TV Ch 12 (NBC) PO Box 6125	Helena	MT	59604	406-457-1212	442-5106
KUSM-TV Ch 9 (PBS) Visual Communications Bldg Rm 172	Bozeman	MT	59717	406-994-3437	994-6545
TF: 800-426-8243 ■ *Web:* www.kusm.montana.edu					
KWYB-TV Ch 18 (ABC) 505 W Park	Butte	MT	59701	406-782-7185	723-9269
Web: www.abc18-28.com ■ *E-mail:* abc18_28@abc18-28.com					
KXLF-TV Ch 4 (CBS) 1003 S Montana St	Butte	MT	59701	406-782-0444	782-8906

RADIO

				Phone	Fax
KBLL-AM 1240 kHz (N/T) 1400 11th Ave	Helena	MT	59601	406-442-6620	442-6161
KBLL-FM 99.5 MHz (Ctry) 1400 11th Ave	Helena	MT	59601	406-442-6620	442-6161
KHKR-FM 104.1 MHz (Ctry) PO Box 4111	Helena	MT	59604	406-449-4251	442-7356
KMTX-FM 105.3 MHz (AC) PO Box 1183	Helena	MT	59624	406-442-0400	442-0491
KZMT-FM 101.1 MHz (CR) 110 Broadway St	Helena	MT	59601	406-442-4490	442-7356

— Colleges/Universities —

				Phone	Fax
Carroll College 1601 N Benton Ave.	Helena	MT	59625	406-447-4300	447-4533
Web: www.carroll.edu					

— Hospitals —

				Phone	Fax
Saint Peter's Community Hospital 2475 Broadway	Helena	MT	59601	406-442-2480	444-2389
Shodair Hospital 2755 Colonial Dr	Helena	MT	59601	406-444-7500	444-7536

— Attractions —

				Phone	Fax
Big Hole National Battlefield PO Box 237	Wisdom	MT	59761	406-689-3155	689-3151
Web: www.nps.gov/biho/					
Bray Archie Foundation Art Gallery 2915 Country Club Ave	Helena	MT	59602	406-443-3502	443-0934
E-mail: archiebray@archiebray.org					
Frontier Town Hwy 12 & Frontier Town Rd	Helena	MT	59601	406-449-3031	
Gates of the Mountains Wilderness Area Helena National Forest	Helena	MT	59601	406-449-5201	
Gold Collection Museum 350 N Last Chance Gulch	Helena	MT	59601	406-447-2000	
Grand Street Theater 325 N Park Ave	Helena	MT	59624	406-442-4270	447-1573
Grant-Kohrs Ranch National Historic Site PO Box 790	Deer Lodge	MT	59722	406-846-2070	846-3962
Web: www.nps.gov/grko/					
Great Divide Ski Area	Marysville	MT	59640	406-449-3746	
Helena National Forest 2880 Skyway Dr	Helena	MT	59601	406-449-5201	
Helena Symphony PO Box 1073	Helena	MT	59624	406-442-1860	442-0184
Holter Museum of Art 12 E Lawrence St	Helena	MT	59601	406-442-6400	442-2404
Last Chance Tour Train 6th & Roberts Sts	Helena	MT	59601	406-442-4120	
Montana Historical Society Museum 225 N Roberts St	Helena	MT	59620	406-444-2694	444-2696
TF: 800-243-9900 ■ *Web:* www.his.mt.gov/					
Montana Nugget Casino 612 Euclid Ave	Helena	MT	59601	406-442-3544	442-0908
Montana State Capital 1301 6th Ave.	Helena	MT	59620	406-444-4794	
Myrna Loy Center 15 N Ewing	Helena	MT	59601	406-443-0287	443-6620
Old Governor's Mansion 304 N Ewing	Helena	MT	59601	406-444-4794	444-2696
Saint Helena Cathedral Warren & Lawrence Sts	Helena	MT	59601	406-442-5825	
World Museum of Mining & Hell Roarin' Gulch End of W Park St	Butte	MT	59703	406-723-7211	

SPORTS TEAMS & FACILITIES

				Phone	Fax
Helena Brewers (baseball) Kindrick Legion Field	Helena	MT	59601	406-449-7616	449-6979
Web: www.helenabrewers.com ■ *E-mail:* umpire@helenabrewers.com					
Helena Ice Pirates (hockey) 400 Lola St	Helena	MT	59601	406-443-4574	443-4574
Web: www.helenaicepirates.com ■ *E-mail:* helicpir@initco.net					

— Events —

	Phone
Autumn Art & Craft Show (late October)	406-449-4790
Bald Eagle Migration (November-December)	406-442-4120
Downtown Helena Fall Art Walk (late November)	406-447-1535
Festival of Trees (early December)	406-442-7920
Governor's Cup Art & Craft Show (early June)	406-449-4790
Governor's Cup Marathon (early June)	406-444-8261
Governor's Cup Race (early June)	406-447-3414
Helena Railroad Fair (late April)	406-442-4120
Holiday Craft Fair (late November)	406-443-2242
Kaleidoscope Summer Festival (early August)	406-442-0400
Last Chance Stampede & Rodeo (late July)	406-442-1098
Montana Traditional Jazz Festival (late June)	406-449-7969
Oktoberfest/Bullfest (mid-October)	406-442-6449
Race to the Sky (early February)	406-442-4008
Spring Art & Craft Show (mid-March)	406-449-4790

Nebraska

Population (1999): 1,666,028 **Area (sq mi): 77,358**

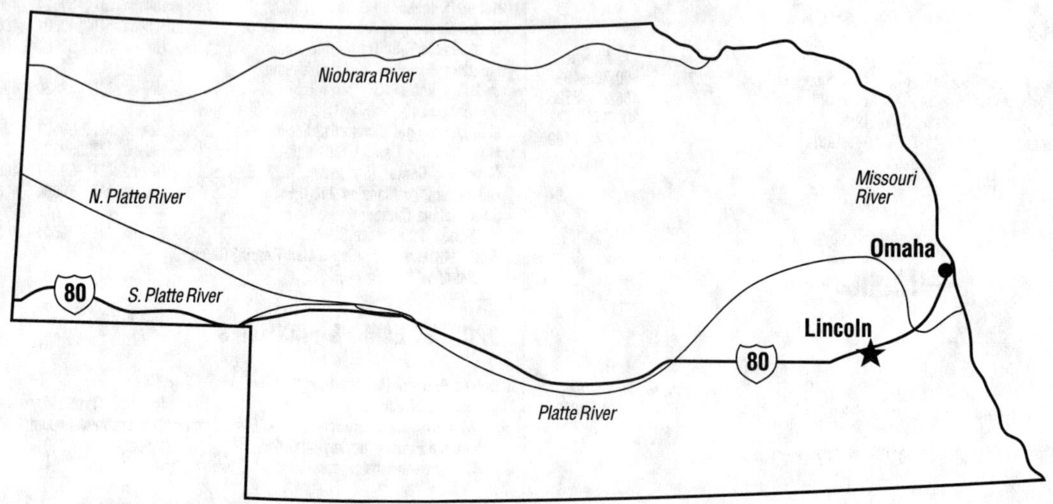

— State Information Sources —

				Phone	Fax
Nebraska Chamber of Commerce & Industry					
PO Box 95128	Lincoln	NE	68509	402-474-4422	474-5681
E-mail: nechamber@sescor.com					
Nebraska Economic Development Dept					
PO Box 94666	Lincoln	NE	68509	402-471-3747	471-3778
TF: 800-426-6505 ■ *Web:* www.ded.state.ne.us					
Nebraska Parks Div PO Box 30370	Lincoln	NE	68503	402-471-5550	471-5528
Web: www.ngpc.state.ne.us/parks					
Nebraska State Government Information				402-471-2311	
Web: www.state.ne.us					
Nebraska State Library					
State Capitol Bldg 3rd Fl S	Lincoln	NE	68509	402-471-3189	471-2197
Web: www.nlc.state.ne.us					
Nebraska Travel & Tourism Div PO Box 98907	Lincoln	NE	68509	402-471-3791	471-3026
TF: 800-228-4307 ■ *Web:* www.visitnebraska.org ■ *E-mail:* tourism@visitnebraska.org					

ON-LINE RESOURCES

Nebraska Cities . . . . dir.yahoo.com/Regional/U_S__States/Nebraska/Cities
Nebraska Counties & Regions . . . . dir.yahoo.com/Regional/U_S__States/Nebraska/Counties_and_Regions
Nebraska Databook . . . . info.ded.state.ne.us/stathand/contents.htm
Nebraska Scenario . . . . scenariousa.dstylus.com/ne/indexf.htm
Nebraska Travel & Tourism Guide . . . www.travel-library.com/north_america/usa/nebraska/index.html
Rough Guide Travel Nebraska travel.roughguides.com/content/1002/index.htm
Rough Guide Travel Nebraska travel.roughguides.com/content/1002/index.htm
Travel.org-Nebraska . . . . travel.org/nebraska.html
Westward to Nebraska . . . . www.westnebraska.com
What's Up Nebraska! . . . . www.whatsupnebraska.com
Yahoo! Get Local Nebraska . . . . dir.yahoo.com/Regional/U_S__States/Nebraska

— Cities Profiled —

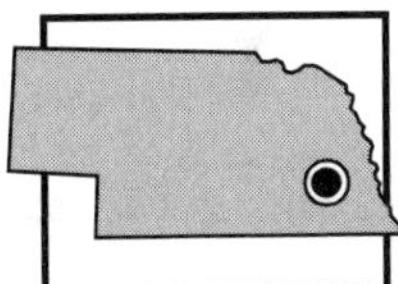

Lincoln

The University of Nebraska is located in the capital city of Lincoln. On its grounds is the University of Nebraska State Museum, also known as "Elephant Hall" due to its large collection of extinct animals that once roamed the Great Plains. The University's Cornhusker football team is consistently ranked as one of the top teams in the country. The city's Pioneers Park and Nature Center has a toboggan run and cross-country ski area, as well as live outdoor animal exhibits of bison, white-tailed deer, and red foxes. Twenty minutes from Lincoln, visitors can hike the natural prairies at Nine-Mile Prairie.

Population	213,088	**Longitude**	96-66-67 W
Area (Land)	63.3 sq mi	**County**	Lancaster
Area (Water)	0.8 sq mi	**Time Zone**	CST
Elevation	1176 ft	**Area Code/s**	402
Latitude	40-80-00 N		

— Average Temperatures and Precipitation —

TEMPERATURES

	Jan	Feb	Mar	Apr	May	Jun	Jul	Aug	Sep	Oct	Nov	Dec
High	32	38	50	64	74	85	90	87	77	67	50	36
Low	10	15	27	39	50	60	66	63	53	41	27	15

PRECIPITATION

	Jan	Feb	Mar	Apr	May	Jun	Jul	Aug	Sep	Oct	Nov	Dec
Inches	0.5	0.7	2.1	2.8	3.9	3.9	3.2	3.4	3.5	2.1	1.3	0.9

— Important Phone Numbers —

	Phone		Phone
AAA	402-474-2229	**Medical Referral**	402-441-8000
American Express Travel	402-291-4131	**Poison Control Center**	803-777-1117
Emergency	911	**Time/Temp**	402-476-9211
HotelDocs	800-468-3537	**Weather**	402-475-6100

— Information Sources —

				Phone	Fax
Better Business Bureau Serving Southern Nebraska 3633 'O' St Suite 1	Lincoln	NE	68510	402-476-8855	476-8221
Web: www.lincoln.bbb.org ■ *E-mail:* info@lincoln.bbb.org					
Lancaster County 555 S 10th St	Lincoln	NE	68508	402-441-7481	441-8728
Web: interlinc.ci.lincoln.ne.us					
Lincoln Chamber of Commerce PO Box 83006	Lincoln	NE	68501	402-436-2350	436-2360
Web: www.lcoc.com					
Lincoln City Hall 555 S 10th St	Lincoln	NE	68508	402-441-7171	441-8325
Web: www.ci.lincoln.ne.us					
Lincoln City Libraries 136 S 14th St	Lincoln	NE	68508	402-441-8500	441-8586
Web: www.ci.lincoln.ne.us/city/library/index.htm ■ *E-mail:* library@rand.lcl.lib.ne.us					
Lincoln Convention & Visitors Bureau 1135 M St Suite 200	Lincoln	NE	68508	402-434-5335	436-2360
TF: 800-423-8212 ■ *Web:* www.lincoln.org/cvb/ ■ *E-mail:* info@lincoln.org					
Lincoln Mayor 555 S 10th St	Lincoln	NE	68508	402-441-7511	441-7120
Web: www.ci.lincoln.ne.us/city/mayor/index.htm					
Lincoln Planning Dept 555 S 10th St Rm 213	Lincoln	NE	68508	402-441-7491	441-6377
Web: www.ci.lincoln.ne.us/city/plan/index.htm ■ *E-mail:* plan@ci.lincoln.ne.us					
Nebraska Travel & Tourism Div PO Box 98907	Lincoln	NE	68509	402-471-3791	471-3026
TF: 800-228-4307 ■ *Web:* www.visitnebraska.org ■ *E-mail:* tourism@visitnebraska.org					
Pershing Auditorium 226 Centennial Mall South	Lincoln	NE	68508	402-441-8744	441-7913

On-Line Resources

Anthill City Guide Lincoln	www.anthill.com/city.asp?city=lincoln
Area Guide Lincoln	lincoln.areaguides.net
City Knowledge Lincoln	www.cityknowledge.com/ne_lincoln.htm
Discover Lincoln	yp.aliant.com/lincoln
Downtown Lincoln Assn	www.downtownlincoln.org/main.html
Excite.com Lincoln City Guide	www.excite.com/travel/countries/united_states/nebraska/lincoln
LincNet	www.lincnet.com
Lincoln Online	lincoln.inetnebr.com
Lincoln Picture Tour	db.4w.com/lincolntour
Lincoln Yellow Pages	yp.aliant.com
Strictly Business Online	www.zaa.com/online/
Surf Lincoln!	www2.lincolnonline.com/lol/IntroLincolnOnline.html

— Transportation Services —

AIRPORTS

	Phone
■ **Lincoln Municipal Airport (LNK)**	
5 miles NW of downtown (approx 15 minutes)	402-474-2770

Airport Transportation

	Phone
Capital Cab $11 fare to downtown	402-477-6074
Husker Cabs $10-12 fare to downtown	402-477-4111

Commercial Airlines

	Phone		Phone
Continental	800-525-0280	**United**	800-241-6522
Northwest	800-225-2525	**United Express**	800-241-6522
TWA	800-221-2000	**US Airways Express**	800-428-4322

Charter Airlines

	Phone		Phone
Capitol Aviation	402-475-5444	**Star Care V**	402-437-3059
Duncan Aviation	402-475-2611		

CAR RENTALS

	Phone		Phone
Avis	402-474-1202	**Hertz**	402-474-4079
Budget	402-474-2800	**National**	402-474-4301

LIMO/TAXI

	Phone		Phone
Ambassador Limousines	402-475-5466	**Husker Cabs**	402-477-4111
Capital Cab	402-477-6074	**Yellow Cab**	402-477-4111
Haymarket Limousine	402-432-0927		

MASS TRANSIT

	Phone
STARTRAN $.85 Base fare	402-476-1234

RAIL/BUS

				Phone
Amtrak Station 201 N 7th St	Lincoln	NE	68508	402-476-1295
TF: 800-872-7245				
Greyhound Bus Station 940 'P' St	Lincoln	NE	68508	402-474-1071
TF: 800-231-2222				

— Accommodations —

HOTELS, MOTELS, RESORTS

				Phone	Fax
Best Western Airport Inn 3200 NW 12th St	Lincoln	NE	68524	402-475-9541	
TF: 800-742-7373					
Cobbler Inn 4808 W 'O' St	Lincoln	NE	68528	402-475-4800	475-4805
TF: 800-777-4808					

Lincoln — Hotels, Motels, Resorts (Cont'd)

	City	State	ZIP	Phone	Fax
Comfort Inn 2940 NW 12th St *TF:* 800-228-5150	Lincoln	NE	68521	402-475-2200	475-2200
Congress Inn Motel 2001 W 'O' St *TF:* 800-477-2393	Lincoln	NE	68528	402-477-4488	477-4086
Cornhusker The 333 S 13th St *TF:* 800-793-7474 ■ *Web:* www.thecornhusker.com/ ■ *E-mail:* reservations@thecornhusker.com	Lincoln	NE	68508	402-474-7474	474-1847
Days Inn 2920 NW 12th St *TF:* 800-329-7466	Lincoln	NE	68521	402-475-3616	475-4356
Econo Lodge 2410 NW 12th St *TF:* 800-553-2666	Lincoln	NE	68521	402-474-1311	474-1311
Fairfield Inn 4221 Industrial Ave *Web:* fairfieldinn.com/LNKFI	Lincoln	NE	68524	402-476-6000	476-6000
GuestHouse Inn 3245 Cornhusker Hwy	Lincoln	NE	68504	402-466-2341	
Hampton Inn Airport 1301 W Bond Cir *TF:* 800-426-7866	Lincoln	NE	68521	402-474-2080	474-3401
Holiday Inn 141 N 9th St *TF:* 800-432-0002	Lincoln	NE	68508	402-475-4011	475-9011
Holiday Inn Express 1133 Belmont *TF:* 800-465-4329	Lincoln	NE	68521	402-435-0200	435-0606
Inn 4 Less 1140 W Cornhusker Hwy	Lincoln	NE	68521	402-475-4511	475-1321
Inn at Lincoln 5250 Cornhusker Hwy	Lincoln	NE	68504	402-464-3171	464-7439
Kings Inn 3510 Cornbusker Hwy	Lincoln	NE	68504	402-466-2324	466-2324
Motel 6 3001 NW 12th St *TF:* 800-466-8356	Lincoln	NE	68521	402-475-3211	475-1632
New World Inn 265 33rd Ave *TF:* 800-433-1492	Columbus	NE	68601	402-564-1492	563-3989
Quality Inn 1101 W Bond St *TF:* 800-228-5151	Lincoln	NE	68521	402-475-4971	475-0606
Residence Inn by Marriott 200 S 68th Pl *TF:* 800-331-3131 ■ *Web:* www.residenceinn.com/LNKNA	Lincoln	NE	68510	402-483-4900	483-4464
Rogers House Bed & Breakfast Inn 2145 B St	Lincoln	NE	68502	402-476-6961	476-6473
Rosewood Inn 2301 NW 12th St	Lincoln	NE	68521	402-475-4400	
Senate Inn 2801 W 'O' St	Lincoln	NE	68528	402-475-4921	
Sleep Inn 3400 NW 12th St *TF:* 800-753-3746	Lincoln	NE	68521	402-475-1550	475-1550
Town House Mini Suites Motel 1744 M St	Lincoln	NE	68508	402-475-3000	475-3000
Travelodge Airport 2901 NW 12th St *TF:* 800-578-7878	Lincoln	NE	68521	402-474-5252	474-5259
Villager Motor Inn 5200 'O' St *TF:* 800-356-4321	Lincoln	NE	68510	402-464-9111	467-0505

— Restaurants —

	City	State	ZIP	Phone
Ali Baba (Greek) 112 N 14th St	Lincoln	NE	68508	402-435-2615
Arturo's (Mexican) 803 Q St	Lincoln	NE	68501	402-475-8226
Billy's (Continental) 1301 H St	Lincoln	NE	68508	402-474-0084
Blue Heron (Continental) 5555 S 48th St	Lincoln	NE	68516	402-421-9555
Bum Steer (Steak) 6440 'O' St	Lincoln	NE	68510	402-467-5110
Crane River Brewpub (American) 200 N 11th St	Lincoln	NE	68508	402-476-7766
El Sitio (Mexican) 17 & Van Dorn Sts	Lincoln	NE	68502	402-476-0414
El Toro (Mexican) 2600 S 48th St	Lincoln	NE	68506	402-488-3939
Forbidden City (Chinese) 5505 'O' St	Lincoln	NE	68510	402-486-3888
Green Gateau (Continental) 330 S 10th St	Lincoln	NE	68508	402-477-0330
Grisanti's (Italian) 6820 'O' St	Lincoln	NE	68510	402-464-8444
Inn Harms Way (Seafood) 201 N 7th St	Lincoln	NE	68501	402-438-3033
Jabrisco (International) 700 P St	Lincoln	NE	68508	402-434-5644
La Paz (Mexican) 321 N Cotner Blvd	Lincoln	NE	68503	402-466-9111
Lazlo's Brewery & Grill (American) 710 'P' St	Lincoln	NE	68508	402-434-5636
Little Saigon (Vietnamese) 940 N 26th St	Lincoln	NE	68503	402-435-4367
Mazatlan (Mexican) 211 N 70th St	Lincoln	NE	68505	402-464-7201
Renaissance The (Continental) 333 S 13th St	Lincoln	NE	68508	402-474-7474
Rock-N-Roll Runza (American) 210 N 14th St	Lincoln	NE	68508	402-474-2030
Steak House The (Steak/Seafood) 3441 Adams St	Lincoln	NE	68504	402-466-2472
Taj Mahal Cuisine of India (Indian) 5500 Old Cheney Rd	Lincoln	NE	68516	402-420-1133
Taste of India (Indian) 1320 'O' St	Lincoln	NE	68508	402-475-1642
Terrace Grille (American) 333 S 13th St	Lincoln	NE	68508	402-479-8292
Thai Garden Restaurant (Thai) 215 N 14th St	Lincoln	NE	68508	402-477-0811
Thai House Restaurant (Thai) 610 N 27th St	Lincoln	NE	68503	402-475-0558
Vincenzo's (Italian) 808 P St	Lincoln	NE	68505	402-435-3889

— Goods and Services —

SHOPPING

	City	State	ZIP	Phone	Fax
East Park Plaza Shopping Center 220 N 66th St	Lincoln	NE	68510	402-467-3703	
Gateway Mall 6100 'O' St	Lincoln	NE	68505	402-464-3196	
Historic Haymarket District downtown-betw 9th & P Sts	Lincoln	NE	68508	402-435-7496	
Meridian Park 70th & 'O' Sts	Lincoln	NE	68510	402-467-6996	441-5805

BANKS

	City	State	ZIP	Phone	Fax
Cornhusker Bank 1101 Cornhusker Hwy	Lincoln	NE	68521	402-434-2265	434-2262
First Federal Lincoln Bank 1235 'N' St	Lincoln	NE	68508	402-475-0521	473-6242
Union Bank & Trust Co 3643 S 48th St *TF:* 800-828-2441 ■ *Web:* www.ubt.com	Lincoln	NE	68506	402-488-0941	483-8156
US Bank NA 233 S 13th St *TF Cust Svc:* 800-869-0423*	Lincoln	NE	68508	402-434-1356	434-1108

BUSINESS SERVICES

	Phone		Phone
Airborne Express	800-247-2676	**Kinko's**	402-420-2679
BAX Global	800-225-5229	**Mail Boxes Etc**	800-789-4623
DHL Worldwide Express	800-225-5345	**Manpower Temporary Services**	402-467-3399
Federal Express	800-238-5355	**Post Office**	800-275-8777
Interim Personnel Services	402-466-1996	**UPS**	800-742-5877
Kelly Services	402-483-4094	**Westaff**	402-465-0060

— Media —

PUBLICATIONS

	City	State	ZIP	Phone	Fax
Lincoln Journal-Star‡ PO Box 81609 *TF:* 800-742-7315 ■ *Web:* www.nebweb.com/ljs ■ *E-mail:* feedback@nebweb.com	Lincoln	NE	68501	402-475-4200	473-7291

‡Daily newspapers

TELEVISION

	City	State	ZIP	Phone	Fax
KETV-TV Ch 7 (ABC) 2665 Douglas St	Omaha	NE	68131	402-345-7777	978-8922
KLKN-TV Ch 8 (ABC) 3240 S 10th St	Lincoln	NE	68502	402-434-8000	436-2236
KOLN-TV Ch 10 (CBS) PO Box 30350	Lincoln	NE	68503	402-467-4321	467-9210
KPTM-TV Ch 42 (Fox) 4625 Farnam St *Web:* www.foxworld.com	Omaha	NE	68132	402-558-4200	554-4279
KUON-TV Ch 12 (PBS) 1800 N 33rd St	Lincoln	NE	68583	402-472-3611	472-1785
WOWT-TV Ch 6 (NBC) 3501 Farnam St *Web:* www.wowt.com	Omaha	NE	68131	402-346-6666	233-7880

RADIO

	City	State	ZIP	Phone	Fax
KFOR-AM 1240 kHz (AC) 6900 Van Dorn St Suite 11 *Web:* www.lincnet.com/kfor/kfor.html	Lincoln	NE	68506	402-483-5100	483-4095
KFRX-FM 102.7 MHz (CHR) 6900 Van Dorn St Suite 11 *Web:* www.lincnet.com/kfrx/kfrx.html	Lincoln	NE	68506	402-483-5100	483-4095
KKNB-FM 104.1 MHz (AC) 4630 Antelope Creek Rd	Lincoln	NE	68506	402-483-1517	483-1579
KRKR-FM 95.1 MHz (CR) 6900 Van Dorn St Suite 11 *Web:* www.lincnet.com/krkr/krkr.html	Lincoln	NE	68506	402-483-5100	483-4095
KUCV-FM 90.9 MHz (NPR) 1800 N 33rd St	Lincoln	NE	68501	402-472-2200	472-2403
KZKX-FM 96.9 MHz (Ctry) 4630 Antelope Creek Rd Suite 200 *Web:* www.kzkx.com	Lincoln	NE	68506	402-488-9601	489-9989

— Colleges/Universities —

	City	State	ZIP	Phone	Fax
Concordia University 800 N Columbia Ave *TF Admissions:* 800-535-5494 ■ *Web:* www.ccsn.edu ■ *E-mail:* info@seward.ccsn.edu	Seward	NE	68434	402-643-3651	643-4073
Doane College 1014 Boswell Ave *TF Admissions:* 800-333-6263 ■ *Web:* www.doane.edu	Crete	NE	68333	402-826-2161	826-8600
Lincoln School of Commerce PO Box 82826	Lincoln	NE	68501	402-474-5315	474-5302
Nebraska Wesleyan University 5000 St Paul Ave *TF Admissions:* 800-541-3818 ■ *Web:* www.nebrwesleyan.edu	Lincoln	NE	68504	402-466-2371	465-2179
Southeast Community College-Lincoln 8800 'O' St *TF:* 800-642-4075 ■ *Web:* www.sccm.cc.ne.us	Lincoln	NE	68520	402-437-2500	437-2404

Lincoln — Colleges/Universities (Cont'd)

				Phone	Fax
Union College 3800 S 48th St	Lincoln	NE	68506	402-488-2331	486-2895
TF: 800-228-4600 ■ *Web:* www.ucollege.edu					
University of Nebraska Lincoln 501 N 14th St	Lincoln	NE	68588	402-472-7211	472-0670
TF Admissions: 800-742-8800 ■ *Web:* www.unl.edu ■ *E-mail:* nuhusker@unl.edu					

— Hospitals —

				Phone	Fax
Bryan LGH Medical Center 2300 S 16th St	Lincoln	NE	68502	402-475-1011	481-5273*
**Fax:* Admitting					
Bryan Memorial Hospital 1600 S 48th St	Lincoln	NE	68506	402-489-0200	483-8306
Web: www.bryan.org					
Saint Elizabeth Regional Medical Center 555 S 70th St	Lincoln	NE	68510	402-489-7181	486-8973*
**Fax:* Admitting					
Veterans Affairs Medical Center 600 S 70th St	Lincoln	NE	68510	402-489-3802	486-7840

— Attractions —

				Phone	Fax
American Historical Society of Germans from Russia 631 D St	Lincoln	NE	68502	402-474-3363	474-7229
Web: www.ahsgr.org ■ *E-mail:* ahsgr@aol.com					
Elder Art Gallery N 50th St & Huntington Ave Wesleyan University Rogers Center for Fine Art	Lincoln	NE	68504	402-465-2230	
Folsom Children's Zoo & Botanical Gardens 1222 S 27th St	Lincoln	NE	68502	402-475-6741	475-6472
Web: www.aza.org/folsom/					
Governor's Mansion 1425 'H' St	Lincoln	NE	68508	402-471-3466	471-2329
Great Plains Art Collection 215 Love Library	Lincoln	NE	68588	402-472-6220	472-2960
Web: www.unl.edu/plains/artcol.html					
Historic Haymarket District downtown-betw 9th & 'P' Sts	Lincoln	NE	68508	402-435-7496	
Homestead National Monument of America Route 3 Box 47	Beatrice	NE	68310	402-223-3514	228-4231
Web: www.nps.gov/home/					
Hyde Memorial Observatory 2740 A St	Lincoln	NE	68502	402-441-7895	441-8706
Web: www.blackstarpress.com/arin/hyde/					
Kennard Thomas P House 1627 H St	Lincoln	NE	68508	402-471-4764	
Lentz Center for Asian Cultures 14th & U Sts 329 Merrill Hall University of Nebraska	Lincoln	NE	68588	402-472-5841	472-8899
Web: www.unl.edu/finearts/lentz.html					
Lied Center for Performing Arts 301 N 12th St	Lincoln	NE	68588	402-472-4700	472-4730
Web: www.unl.edu/lied/					
Lincoln Botanical Garden & Arboretum University of Nebraska 1340 N 17th St	Lincoln	NE	68588	402-472-2679	472-9615
Web: www.unl.edu/unlbga/ ■ *E-mail:* unlbga@cwis.unl.edu					
Lincoln Children's Museum 13th & 'O' Sts	Lincoln	NE	68508	402-477-4000	477-2004
Lincoln Community Playhouse 2500 S 56th St	Lincoln	NE	68506	402-489-7529	489-1035
Lincoln Symphony Orchestra 5225 S 16th St	Lincoln	NE	68512	402-423-2211	423-5220
Mueller Planetarium University of Nebraska Morrill Hall Rm 213	Lincoln	NE	68588	402-472-2641	472-8899
Web: www.spacelaser.com/					
Museum of Nebraska History 131 Centennial Mall N	Lincoln	NE	68508	402-471-4754	471-3314
TF: 800-833-6747 ■ *Web:* www.nebraskahistory.org/sites/mnh/index.htm					
National Museum of Roller Skating 4730 South St	Lincoln	NE	68506	402-483-7551	483-1465
Web: www.rollerskatingmuseum.com					
Nebraska Historical Society 1500 R St	Lincoln	NE	68501	402-471-3270	471-3100
Web: www.nebraskahistory.org ■ *E-mail:* nshs@inetnebr.com					
Nebraska Repertory Theatre 12th & R Sts Howell Theatre	Lincoln	NE	68588	402-472-2073	
Nebraska State Capitol 1445 K St	Lincoln	NE	68509	402-471-0448	
Pioneers Park & Nature Center Van Dorn St & Coddington Ave	Lincoln	NE	68522	402-441-7895	
Sheldon Memorial Art Gallery 12th & R Sts	Lincoln	NE	68588	402-472-2461	472-4258
Web: sheldon.unl.edu/ ■ *E-mail:* feedback@sheldon.unl.edu					
University of Nebraska State Museum 14th & U Sts	Lincoln	NE	68588	402-472-2642	472-8899
Web: www-museum.unl.edu/					
University Place Art Center 2601 N 48th St	Lincoln	NE	68504	402-466-8692	466-3786

SPORTS TEAMS & FACILITIES

				Phone	Fax
Eagle Raceway PO Box 5726	Lincoln	NE	68505	402-420-7223	
Web: www.eagleraceway.com					
Lincoln Stars (hockey) 1800 State Fair Park Dr	Lincoln	NE	68508	402-474-7827	474-7831

— Events —

	Phone
Annual Square and Round Dance Festival (early May)	402-434-5335
Arts in General (mid-November)	402-481-5117
Boat Sport & Travel Show (early February)	402-466-8102
Boo at the Zoo (late October)	402-475-6741
Downtown Performance Series (May-September)	402-434-6900
Gem & Mineral Show (late March)	402-472-7564
Haymarket Farmers Market (May-October)	402-434-6906
Haymarket Heydays (mid-June)	402-434-6906
Holidays in the Haymarket (mid-November-mid-December)	402-434-6900
Home Garden & Leisure Show (mid-March)	402-474-5371
Jazz in June (June)	402-472-2540
July Jamm (late July)	402-434-6900
Lancaster County Fair & Rodeo (late July-early August)	402-441-6545
Lincoln Marathon & Half Marathon (early May)	402-434-5335
Midwest Invitational Tournament (mid-March)	402-434-9217
Nebraska Builders Home & Garden Show (mid-February)	402-423-4225
Nebraska State Fair (late August-early September)	402-474-5371
Shrine Circus (mid-late March)	402-474-6890
Spring Affair (late April)	402-472-2679
Star City Holiday Parade Weekend Festival (early December)	402-441-7391
Taste of Nebraska (mid-April)	402-483-2630
Victorian Holidays Past (December)	402-471-4764
Winter Lights (late November)	402-475-6741

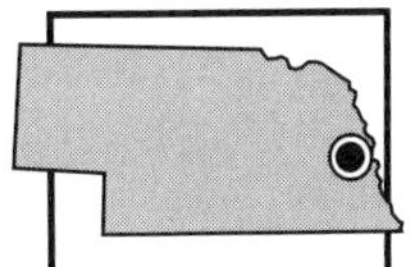

Omaha

Nebraska's largest city, Omaha is perhaps best known as the home of Boys Town. Father Flanagan started Boys Town in 1917 to provide a home for abandoned, neglected, abused, or handicapped children. Today, Boys Town has satellite locations across the U.S. and helps more than 17,000 children each year. Omaha is also site of the Strategic Air Command headquarters (SAC), which has a museum in nearby Bellevue, Nebraska; and is the birthplace of former president Gerald Ford. The Mormon Pioneer Monument commemorates the final resting place of more than 600 Mormon emigrants who died during the winter of 1846-47 while camped in the area that is now Omaha.

Population	371,291	**Longitude**	95-93-75 W
Area (Land)	100.6 sq mi	**County**	Douglas
Area (Water)	3.0 sq mi	**Time Zone**	CST
Elevation	1040 ft	**Area Code/s**	402
Latitude	41-25-86 N		

— Average Temperatures and Precipitation —

TEMPERATURES

	Jan	Feb	Mar	Apr	May	Jun	Jul	Aug	Sep	Oct	Nov	Dec
High	30	35	48	62	73	82	87	84	75	64	48	33
Low	11	17	28	40	52	61	67	64	55	43	30	16

PRECIPITATION

	Jan	Feb	Mar	Apr	May	Jun	Jul	Aug	Sep	Oct	Nov	Dec
Inches	0.7	0.8	2.1	2.7	4.4	3.9	3.3	3.2	3.7	2.4	1.4	0.9

Omaha (Cont'd)

— Important Phone Numbers —

	Phone		Phone
AAA	402-390-1010	Medical Referral	402-393-1415
American Express Travel	402-697-5300	Poison Control Center	402-390-5555
Dental Referral	800-336-8478	Road Conditions	800-906-9069
Emergency	911	Time/Temp	402-342-8463
Events Line	402-444-6800	Weather	402-392-1111
HotelDocs	800-468-3537		

— Information Sources —

				Phone	Fax
Better Business Bureau Serving Northern Nebraska & Southwest Iowa 2237 N 91st Ct *Web:* www.omaha.bbb.org	Omaha	NE	68134	402-391-7612	391-7535
Douglas County 1819 Farnum St. *Web:* www.co.douglas.ne.us	Omaha	NE	68183	402-444-7000	444-5263
Greater Omaha Chamber of Commerce 1301 Harney St. *Web:* www.accessomaha.com ■ *E-mail:* gocc@accessomaha.com	Omaha	NE	68102	402-346-5000	346-7050
Greater Omaha Convention & Visitors Bureau 6800 Mercy Rd Suite 202 *TF:* 800-332-1819 ■ *Web:* www.visitomaha.com ■ *E-mail:* gocvb@aol.com	Omaha	NE	68106	402-444-4660	444-4511
Omaha City Hall 1819 Farnam St *Web:* www.ci.omaha.ne.us	Omaha	NE	68183	402-444-7000	
Omaha Civic Auditorium PO Box 719	Omaha	NE	68101	402-444-4750	444-4739
Omaha Marketing & Business Development Office 1819 Farnam St Rm 304	Omaha	NE	68183	402-444-5546	444-7963
Omaha Mayor 1819 Farnam St Suite 300 *Web:* www.ci.omaha.ne.us/mayor/frame_mayor.htm ■ *E-mail:* mayorswebpage@ci.omaha.ne.us	Omaha	NE	68183	402-444-5000	444-6059
Omaha Public Library 215 S 15th St *Web:* www.omaha.lib.ne.us	Omaha	NE	68102	402-444-4800	444-4504

On-Line Resources

4Omaha.com	www.4omaha.com
Anthill City Guide Omaha	www.anthill.com/city.asp?city=omaha
Area Guide Omaha	omaha.areaguides.net
City Atlas	www.cityatlas.com/
City Knowledge Omaha	www.cityknowledge.com/ne_omaha.htm
DiscoverOmaha.com	www.discoveromaha.com
Excite.com Omaha City Guide	www.excite.com/travel/countries/united_states/nebraska/omaha
Omaha Home Page	omahafreenet.org/
Omaha Internet Site	www.radiks.net/omasite
Omaha Link	www.omaha.org
Omaha Page	www.novia.net/~cmeyers/omaha.html
Surf Omaha	www.surfomaha.com/

— Transportation Services —

AIRPORTS

■ Eppley Airfield (OMA)

	Phone
5 miles NE of downtown (approx 10 minutes)	402-422-6800

Airport Transportation

	Phone
A & B Shuttle $5 fare to downtown	402-331-7558
Taxi $12 fare to downtown	402-339-8294

Commercial Airlines

	Phone		Phone
AirTran	800-247-8726	Midwest Express	800-452-2022
America West	800-235-9292	Northwest	800-225-2525
American	800-433-7300	Southwest	800-435-9792
Continental	402-422-6170	TWA	800-221-2000
Continental Express	800-525-0280	United	800-241-6522
Delta	800-221-1212	US Airways	800-428-4322
Frontier	800-432-1359	US Airways Express	800-428-4322

Charter Airlines

	Phone		Phone
Berry Aviation	800-229-2379	Elliot Beechcraft	402-422-6789
Corporate Aviation Services Inc	918-834-8348	Raytheon Aircraft Charter	800-519-6283
Duncan Aviation	402-475-2611		

CAR RENTALS

	Phone		Phone
Alamo	402-344-0379	Hertz	402-422-6870
Avis	402-422-6480	National	402-422-6565
Budget	402-348-0455	Thrifty	402-345-1040

LIMO/TAXI

	Phone		Phone
Accent Limousine Service	402-592-5003	Old Market Limousine	402-593-7886
Cornhusker Cab	402-734-5556	Safeway Cabs	402-342-7474
Embassy Limousine	402-346-7727	Star Limousine	402-346-5466
Happy Cab	402-339-8294		

MASS TRANSIT

	Phone
MAT $.90 Base fare	402-341-0800

RAIL/BUS

				Phone
Amtrak Station 1003 S 9th St	Omaha	NE	68108	402-342-1501
Greyhound/Trailways Bus Station 1601 Jackson St *TF:* 800-231-2222	Omaha	NE	68102	402-341-1906

— Accommodations —

HOTELS, MOTELS, RESORTS

				Phone	Fax
American Family Inn 1110 Ft Crook Rd S *TF:* 800-253-2865	Bellevue	NE	68005	402-291-0804	292-2162
Baymont Inns & Suites 10760 M St *TF:* 800-301-0200	Omaha	NE	68127	402-592-5200	592-1416
Best Inn 9305 S 145th St. *TF:* 800-835-4045	Omaha	NE	68138	402-895-2555	895-1565
Best Western Central 3650 S 72nd St. *TF:* 800-446-6242	Omaha	NE	68124	402-397-3700	397-8362
Best Western Omaha Inn 4706 S 108th St *TF:* 800-528-1234	Omaha	NE	68137	402-339-7400	339-5155
Best Western Regency West 909 S 107th Ave *TF:* 800-228-9414	Omaha	NE	68114	402-397-8000	397-8000
Clarion Hotel Carlisle 10909 M St *TF:* 800-526-6242	Omaha	NE	68137	402-331-8220	331-8729
Comfort Inn 9595 S 145th St *TF:* 800-228-5150	Omaha	NE	68138	402-896-6300	891-1255
Comfort Inn 2920 S 13th Ct *TF:* 800-228-5150	Omaha	NE	68108	402-342-8000	342-8000
Comfort Inn Hotel & Suites 8736 W Dodge Rd *TF:* 800-228-5150	Omaha	NE	68114	402-343-1000	398-1784
CornHuskers Days Inn Central 7101 Grover St.	Omaha	NE	68106	402-391-5757	393-2432
Days Inn 10560 Sapp Bros Dr *TF:* 800-329-7466	Omaha	NE	68138	402-896-6868	896-6868
Doubletree Guest Suites Hotel 7270 Cedar St *TF:* 800-222-8733 ■ *Web:* www.doubletreehotels.com/DoubleT/Hotel121/137/137Main.htm	Omaha	NE	68124	402-397-5141	397-3266
Doubletree Hotel 1616 Dodge St *TF:* 800-222-8733 ■ *Web:* www.doubletreehotels.com/DoubleT/Hotel141/145/145Main.htm	Omaha	NE	68102	402-346-7600	346-5722
Embassy Suites Downtown 555 S 10th St *TF:* 800-362-2779	Omaha	NE	68102	402-346-9000	346-4236
Hampton Inn 10728 L St *TF:* 800-426-7866	Omaha	NE	68127	402-593-2380	593-0859
Hampton Inn Central 3301 S 72nd St *TF:* 800-426-7866	Omaha	NE	68124	402-391-8129	391-7998
Hampton Inn Westroads Mall 9720 W Dodge Rd *TF:* 800-426-7866	Omaha	NE	68114	402-391-5300	391-8995
Holiday Inn Central 3321 S 72nd St *TF:* 800-465-4329	Omaha	NE	68124	402-393-3950	393-8718
Holiday Inn Express 3001 Chicago St *TF:* 800-465-4329	Omaha	NE	68131	402-345-2222	345-2501
Homewood Suites 7010 Hascall St *TF:* 800-225-5466	Omaha	NE	68106	402-397-7500	397-4281
La Quinta Motor Inn 3330 N 104th Ave *TF:* 800-531-5900	Omaha	NE	68134	402-493-1900	496-0757
Oak Creek Inn 2808 S 72nd St. *TF:* 800-228-9669	Omaha	NE	68124	402-397-7137	397-3492

Omaha — Hotels, Motels, Resorts (Cont'd)

Name / Address	City	State	Zip	Phone	Fax
Omaha Marriott Hotel 10220 Regency Cir	Omaha	NE	68114	402-399-9000	399-0223
TF: 800-228-9290					
Ramada Hotel Central 7007 Grover St	Omaha	NE	68106	402-397-7030	397-8449
TF: 800-228-5299					
Ramada Inn Airport 2002 E Locust St	Omaha	NE	68110	402-342-5100	342-5100
TF: 800-999-1240					
Redick Plaza Hotel 1504 Harney St	Omaha	NE	68102	402-342-1500	342-5317
TF: 888-342-5339					
Residence Inn by Marriott Central 6990 Dodge St	Omaha	NE	68132	402-553-8898	553-8898
TF: 800-331-3131 ■ *Web:* www.residenceinn.com/OMANB					
Savannah Suites 4809 S 107th Ave	Omaha	NE	68127	402-592-8000	592-8000
TF: 800-937-8483					
Sheraton Inn Four Points 4888 S 118th St	Omaha	NE	68137	402-895-1000	896-9247
TF: 800-325-3535					
Sleep Inn 2525 Abbott Dr	Omaha	NE	68110	402-342-2525	342-2525
TF: 800-688-2525					
StudioPLUS 9006 Burt St NW	Omaha	NE	68114	402-343-9000	343-7900
TF: 800-646-8000					
Westin Aquila Hotel 1615 Howard St	Omaha	NE	68102	402-342-2222	342-2569
Wyndham Garden Hotel 11515 Miracle Hills Dr	Omaha	NE	68154	402-496-7500	496-0234
TF: 800-996-3426					

— Restaurants —

Name / Address	City	State	Zip	Phone
Ahmad's Persian (Middle Eastern) 1006 Howard St	Omaha	NE	68102	402-341-9616
Bohemian Cafe (Czechoslovakian) 1406 S 13th St	Omaha	NE	68108	402-342-9838
Brass Grille (Seafood) 1207 Harney St	Omaha	NE	68102	402-342-4010
Breckenridge BBQ & Brewery (Barbecue) 1316 Jones St	Omaha	NE	68102	402-342-4479
Butsy Le Doux's (Cajun/Creole) 1014 Howard St	Omaha	NE	68102	402-346-5100
Cascio's Steak House (Steak) 1622 S 10th St	Omaha	NE	68108	402-345-8313
Chardonnay (French) 10220 Regency Cir	Omaha	NE	68114	402-399-9000
Chu's Chop Suey House (Chinese) 6455 Center St	Omaha	NE	68106	402-553-6454
Di Coppia (Continental) 120 Regency Parkway Dr	Omaha	NE	68114	402-392-2806
Flatiron Cafe (Continental) 1722 Howard St	Omaha	NE	68102	402-344-3040
French Cafe (French) 1017 Howard St	Omaha	NE	68102	402-341-3547
Web: www.frenchcafe.com/				
Gallagher's (Continental) 10730 Pacific St	Omaha	NE	68114	402-393-1421
Gorat's (Steak/Seafood) 49th & Center Sts	Omaha	NE	68106	402-551-3733
Greek Islands (Greek) 3821 Center St	Omaha	NE	68105	402-346-1528
Hector's (Mexican) 3007 S 83rd Plaza	Omaha	NE	68124	402-391-2923
Howard's Charro Cafe (Mexican) 4443 S 13th St	Omaha	NE	68107	402-731-3776
Imperial Palace (Oriental) 11200 Davenport St	Omaha	NE	68154	402-330-3888
Indian Oven (Indian) 1010 Howard St	Omaha	NE	68102	402-342-4856
Jaipur The (Indian) 10922 Elm St	Omaha	NE	68144	402-392-7331
Jim's Rib Haven (Barbecue) 3801 Ames Ave	Omaha	NE	68111	402-451-8061
Johnny's Cafe (Steak) 4702 S 27th St	Omaha	NE	68107	402-731-4774
King Fong's Cafe (Chinese) 315 1/2 S 16th St 2nd Fl	Omaha	NE	68102	402-341-3437
La Fonda de Acebo (Mexican) 2820 S 123rd Ct	Omaha	NE	68144	402-333-8048
La Strada 72 (Italian) 3125 S 72nd St	Omaha	NE	68106	402-397-8389
Le Cafe de Paris (French) 1228 S 6th St	Omaha	NE	68108	402-344-0227
M's Pub (Continental) 422 S 11th St	Omaha	NE	68102	402-342-2550
Maxine's (French) 1616 Dodge St	Omaha	NE	68102	402-346-7600
McFoster's Nautral Kind Cafe (Vegetarian) 302 S 38th St	Omaha	NE	68131	402-345-7477
Old Vienna Cafe (European) 4829 S 24th St	Omaha	NE	68107	402-733-7491
Passport (Steak) 1101 Jackson St	Omaha	NE	68102	402-344-3200
Spanna (European) 721 N 132nd St	Omaha	NE	68154	402-493-7606
Stokes Bar & Grill (Southwest) 646 N 114th St	Omaha	NE	68154	402-498-0804
Tamam (Middle Eastern) 1009 Farnam St	Omaha	NE	68102	402-344-2722
Thai Pepper (Thai) 12775 'Q' St	Omaha	NE	68137	402-895-7788
Trini's Mexican Restaurant (Mexican) 1020 Howard St	Omaha	NE	68102	402-346-8400
Upstream Brewing Co (American) 514 S 11th St	Omaha	NE	68102	402-344-0200
V Mertz Restaurant (Continental) 1022 Howard St	Omaha	NE	68102	402-345-8980
Vivace (Italian) 1108 Howard St	Omaha	NE	68102	402-342-2050
Yoyo Grill (American) 1212 S 119th St	Omaha	NE	68144	402-330-7577

— Goods and Services —

SHOPPING

Name / Address	City	State	Zip	Phone	Fax
Countryside Village Shopping Center 87th & Pacific Sts	Omaha	NE	68114	402-391-2200	391-3084
Crossroads Mall 7400 Dodge St	Omaha	NE	68114	402-397-2343	393-3765
Dillard's 7400 Dodge St	Omaha	NE	68114	402-392-0333	
Market Place Mall 12th & Jackson Sts	Omaha	NE	68102	402-346-4930	
Meadowlark Antique Mall 10700 Sapp Bros Dr	Omaha	NE	68138	402-896-0800	894-9527
Nebraska Crossing Factory Stores 14333 S Hwy 31	Gretna	NE	68028	402-332-4940	
TF: 800-746-7632					
Oak View Mall 144th St & W Center Rd	Omaha	NE	68144	402-330-3332	330-3255
Old Market Harney & Jackson Sts & 10th & 13th Sts	Omaha	NE	68102	402-346-4445	346-4449
Rockbrook Village 108th & W Center Rd	Omaha	NE	68144	402-390-0890	393-7341
Southroads Mall 1001 Fort Crook Rd	Bellevue	NE	68005	402-733-7777	733-3796
Westroads Mall 102nd & W Dodge Rd	Omaha	NE	68114	402-397-2398	397-6701
Younkers Department Store 72nd & Dodge Sts	Omaha	NE	68114	402-399-6638	399-6671

BANKS

Name / Address	City	State	Zip	Phone	Fax
First National Bank of Omaha 1620 Dodge St	Omaha	NE	68102	402-341-0500	636-6033
First Westroads Bank 10855 W Dodge Rd	Omaha	NE	68154	402-330-7200	330-7201
Great Western Bank 6015 NW Radial Hwy	Omaha	NE	68104	402-551-4310	552-1258*
**Fax:* Cust Serv ■ *TF:* 800-952-2039					
US Bank NA 1700 Farnam St	Omaha	NE	68102	402-348-6000	348-2945

BUSINESS SERVICES

Name	Phone	Name	Phone
Express Messenger Systems	402-734-4650	**Manpower Temporary Services**	402-397-5455
Federal Express	800-238-5355	**Olsten Staffing Services**	402-330-5200
Intercity Courier Systems	402-342-7243	**Post Office**	402-348-2861
Kelly Services	402-393-5000	**Snelling Personnel Services**	402-330-0100
Kinko's	402-399-8860	**UPS**	800-742-5877

— Media —

PUBLICATIONS

Name / Address	City	State	Zip	Phone	Fax
Midlands Business Journal PO Box 24245	Omaha	NE	68124	402-330-1760	
Omaha Magazine PO Box 461208	Omaha	NE	68046	402-596-1105	596-0522
Web: www.omahamagazine.com					
Omaha World-Herald‡ 1334 Dodge St	Omaha	NE	68102	402-444-1000	345-0183
TF: 800-284-6397 ■ *Web:* www.omaha.com					

‡Daily newspapers

TELEVISION

Name / Address	City	State	Zip	Phone	Fax
KETV-TV Ch 7 (ABC) 2665 Douglas St	Omaha	NE	68131	402-345-7777	978-8922
KMTV-TV Ch 3 (CBS) 10714 Mockingbird Dr	Omaha	NE	68127	402-592-3333	592-4714
KPTM-TV Ch 42 (Fox) 4625 Farnam St	Omaha	NE	68132	402-558-4200	554-4279
Web: www.foxworld.com					
KXVO-TV Ch 15 (WB) 4625 Farnam St	Omaha	NE	68132	402-554-1500	554-4290
KYNE-TV Ch 26 (PBS) 6001 Dodge St	Omaha	NE	68182	402-554-2516	554-2440
WOWT-TV Ch 6 (NBC) 3501 Farnam St	Omaha	NE	68131	402-346-6666	233-7880
Web: www.wowt.com					

RADIO

Name / Address	City	State	Zip	Phone	Fax
KEFM-FM 96.1 MHz (AC) 105 S 70th St	Omaha	NE	68132	402-558-9696	558-3036
KESY-AM 1420 kHz (AC) 4807 Dodge St	Omaha	NE	68132	402-556-6700	
KEZO-AM 1490 kHz (N/T) 11128 John Galt Blvd Suite 192	Omaha	NE	68137	402-592-5300	592-9434
KEZO-FM 92.3 MHz (Rock) 11128 John Galt Blvd	Omaha	NE	68137	402-592-5300	592-4538
KFAB-AM 1110 kHz (N/T) 5010 Underwood Ave	Omaha	NE	68132	402-556-8000	556-5791
Web: www.kfab.com					
KGOR-FM 99.9 MHz (Oldies) 5010 Underwood Ave	Omaha	NE	68132	402-556-2323	556-8937
Web: www.kgor.com ■ *E-mail:* kgor@kgor.com					
KIOS-FM 91.5 MHz (NPR) 3230 Burt St	Omaha	NE	68131	402-557-2777	557-2559
Web: www.kios.org ■ *E-mail:* kiosinfo@kios.org					
KOIL-AM 1290 kHz (Nost) 1001 Farnam St	Omaha	NE	68102	402-342-2000	342-7041
KQCH-FM 97.7 MHz (Urban) 11128 John Galt Blvd Suite 192	Omaha	NE	68137	402-556-6700	556-9427
KQKQ-FM 98.5 MHz (CHR) 1001 Farnam-on-the-Mall	Omaha	NE	68102	402-342-2000	342-9367
WOW-FM 94.1 MHz (Ctry) 5039 N 72nd St	Omaha	NE	68134	402-573-5900	573-0138
Web: wowradio.com					

— Colleges/Universities —

Name / Address	City	State	Zip	Phone	Fax
Clarkson College 101 S 42nd St	Omaha	NE	68131	402-552-3100	552-6057
TF Admissions: 800-647-5500 ■ *Web:* www.clarksoncollege.edu ■ *E-mail:* admiss@clrkcol.crhsnet.edu					

Omaha — Colleges/Universities (Cont'd)

Name / Address	City	State	Zip	Phone	Fax
College of Saint Mary 1901 S 72nd St	Omaha	NE	68124	402-399-2400	399-2412
TF: 800-926-5534 ■ *Web:* www.csm.edu ■ *E-mail:* enroll@csm.edu					
Creighton University 2500 California Plaza	Omaha	NE	68178	402-280-2700	280-2685
TF Admissions: 800-282-5835 ■ *Web:* www.creighton.edu					
Dana College 2848 College Dr	Blair	NE	68008	402-426-9000	426-7386
Web: www.dana.edu					
Grace University 1311 S 9th St	Omaha	NE	68108	402-449-2800	341-9587
TF Admissions: 800-383-1422 ■ *Web:* www.graceu.edu					
ITT Technical Institute 9814 M St	Omaha	NE	68127	402-331-2900	331-9495
TF: 800-677-9260 ■ *Web:* www.itt-tech.edu					
Metropolitan Community College PO Box 3777	Omaha	NE	68103	402-457-2400	457-2395
TF: 800-228-9553 ■ *Web:* www.mccneb.edu					
Midland Lutheran College 900 N Clarkson St	Fremont	NE	68025	402-721-5480	721-0250
TF: 800-642-8382 ■ *Web:* www.mlc.edu ■ *E-mail:* kahnk@admin.mlc.edu					
Nebraska College of Business 3350 N 90th St	Omaha	NE	68134	402-572-8500	573-1341
TF: 800-642-1456					
Omaha College of Health Careers 225 N 80th St	Omaha	NE	68114	402-392-1300	392-2828
TF: 800-865-8628					
University of Nebraska Omaha 6001 Dodge St	Omaha	NE	68182	402-554-2200	554-3472
TF: 800-858-8648 ■ *Web:* www.unomaha.edu					

— Hospitals —

Name / Address	City	State	Zip	Phone	Fax
Alegent Health Bergen Medical Center 7500 Mercy Rd	Omaha	NE	68124	402-398-6060	398-6920
Alegent Health Immanuel Medical Center 6901 N 72nd St	Omaha	NE	68122	402-572-2121	572-3177
Childrens Hospital 8301 Dodge St	Omaha	NE	68114	402-354-5400	354-5443
Web: www.chsomaha.org					
Immanuel Medical Center 6901 N 72nd St	Omaha	NE	68122	402-572-2121	572-2461
Jennie Edmundson Memorial Hospital 933 E Pierce St	Council Bluffs	IA	51503	712-328-6000	328-6288
Midlands Community Hospital 11111 S 84th St	Papillion	NE	68046	402-593-3000	593-3324
Nebraska Methodist Hospital 8303 Dodge St	Omaha	NE	68114	402-390-4000	354-8735
NHS Clarkson Hospital PO Box 6159	Omaha	NE	68106	402-552-2000	552-2152
NHS University Hospital 985230 Nebraska Medical Ctr	Omaha	NE	68198	402-559-4000	559-5498*
**Fax:* Library ■ *Web:* www.unmc.edu					
Saint Joseph Hospital 601 N 30th St	Omaha	NE	68131	402-449-4000	449-4337
Web: www.tenethealth.com/SaintJoseph					
Veterans Affairs Medical Center 4101 Woolworth Ave	Omaha	NE	68105	402-346-8800	449-0697

— Attractions —

Name / Address	City	State	Zip	Phone	Fax
Aksarben Aquarium 21502 W Hwy 31	Gretna	NE	68028	402-332-3901	332-5853
Belle Riverboat State Recreation Area	Brownville	NE	68321	402-342-3553	
Bemis Center for Contemporary Arts 724 S 12th St	Omaha	NE	68102	402-341-7130	341-9791
Web: www.novia.net/bemis/					
Bluffs Run Casino 2701 23rd Ave	Council Bluffs	IA	51501	712-323-2500	322-9354
TF: 800-238-2946 ■ *Web:* www.bluffsrun.com					
Boys Town 13628 Flanagan Blvd	Boys Town	NE	68010	402-498-1140	498-1194
TF Help Line: 800-448-3000 ■ *Web:* www.ffbh.boystown.org/					
Carter Levi Park 809 Carter Lake & Shore Dr	Omaha	NE	68183	402-444-5900	
Creighton University Mainstage & Studio Theatre 2500 California Plaza	Omaha	NE	68178	402-280-2636	280-2700
Cunningham Glenn Lake 8660 Lake Cunningham Rd	Omaha	NE	68183	402-444-5900	
Dodge NP Memorial Park 11001 John J Pershing Dr	Omaha	NE	68183	402-444-5900	
Doorly Henry Zoo & Aquarium 3701 S 10th St	Omaha	NE	68107	402-733-8401	733-4415
Web: www.omaha.org/oma/zoo.htm					
El Museo Latino 4701 S 25th St	Omaha	NE	68107	402-731-1137	733-7012
Fontenelle Forest Nature Center 1111 Bellevue Blvd N	Bellevue	NE	68005	402-731-3140	731-2403
Fort Atkinson Hwy 75	Fort Calhoun	NE	68023	402-468-5611	
Freedom Park US Naval Museum 2497 Freedom Park Rd	Omaha	NE	68110	402-345-1959	
Fremont/Elkhorn Valley Railroad 1835 N Somers Ave	Fremont	NE	68025	402-727-0615	
General Crook House 5730 N 30th St Bldg 11B	Omaha	NE	68111	402-455-9990	453-9448
Gerald R Ford Birth Site 3212 Woolworth Ave	Omaha	NE	68105	402-444-5900	
Gerald R Ford Conservation Center 1326 S 32nd St	Omaha	NE	68105	402-595-1180	595-1178
Grande Olde Players 2339 N 90th St	Omaha	NE	68114	402-397-5262	
Great Plains Black History Museum 2213 Lake St	Omaha	NE	68111	402-345-2212	345-2256
Heartland of America Park & Fountain 8th & Douglas Sts	Omaha	NE	68102	402-444-7275	
Historic Florence 8502 N 30th St	Omaha	NE	68112	402-453-4462	
Joslyn Art Museum 2200 Dodge St	Omaha	NE	68102	402-342-3300	342-2376
Web: www.joslyn.org ■ *E-mail:* info@joslyn.org					
Kenefick Park 1212 Abbott Dr	Omaha	NE	68110	402-444-5955	
Kountze Mallory Planetarium 67th & Dodge Sts Durham Science Ctr	Omaha	NE	68182	402-554-3722	
Leahy Gene Mall Park 14th & Farnam Sts	Omaha	NE	68102	402-444-5955	
Lewis & Clark National Historic Trail 1709 Jackson St National Park Service	Omaha	NE	68102	402-221-3471	
Lozier IMAX Theatre 3704 S 10th St	Omaha	NE	68107	402-733-8401	
Memorial Park 60th & Underwood Sts	Omaha	NE	68132	402-444-5955	
Mormon Pioneer Monument at Winter Gardens 3215 State St	Omaha	NE	68112	402-453-9372	453-1538
E-mail: mormontrailcenter@juno.com					
Mount Vernon Gardens 13th & Y Sts	Omaha	NE	68107	402-444-5955	444-6838
Neale Woods Nature Center 14323 Edith Marie Ave	Omaha	NE	68112	402-453-5615	453-0724
Nebraska Jewish Historical Museum 333 S 132nd St	Omaha	NE	68154	402-334-6441	334-1330
Old Market Harney & Jackson Sts & 10th & 13th Sts	Omaha	NE	68102	402-346-4445	346-4449
Omaha Botanical Gardens 5th & Cedar Sts	Omaha	NE	68107	402-333-2359	
Omaha Children's Museum 500 S 20th St	Omaha	NE	68102	402-342-6164	342-6165
Web: www.ocm.org/					
Omaha Community Playhouse 6915 Cass St	Omaha	NE	68132	402-553-0800	553-6288
TF: 888-782-4338 ■ *Web:* raptor.omaha.org/ocph					
Omaha Livestock Market 2930 O St	Omaha	NE	68107	402-731-4980	731-5112
TF: 800-228-7301					
Omaha Symphony Orchestra 1605 Howard St	Omaha	NE	68102	402-342-3836	342-3819
Web: www.omahasymphony.org/ ■ *E-mail:* bravo@omahasymphony.org					
Omaha Theater Co for Young People 2001 Farnam St Rose Blumkin Performing Arts Ctr	Omaha	NE	68102	402-345-4849	344-7255
Web: www.otcyp.org					
Opera Omaha 1625 Farnam St Suite 100	Omaha	NE	68102	402-346-0357	346-7323
Orpheum Theatre 409 S 16 St	Omaha	NE	68102	402-444-4750	444-6201
Prospect Hill Cemetery 3202 Parker St	Omaha	NE	68111	402-556-6057	
Strategic Air Command (SAC) Museum 28210 W Park Hwy	Ashland	NE	68003	402-944-3100	944-3160
TF: 800-358-5029 ■ *Web:* www.strategicaircommand.com ■ *E-mail:* staff@strategicaircommand.com					
Western Heritage Museum 801 S 10th St	Omaha	NE	68108	402-444-5071	444-5397

SPORTS TEAMS & FACILITIES

Name / Address	City	State	Zip	Phone	Fax
Aksarben Coliseum/Event Center 6800 Mercy Rd Suite 100	Omaha	NE	68106	402-561-7000	561-7012
TF: 800-228-6001 ■ *E-mail:* office@aksarbenomaha.com					
Omaha Golden Spikes (baseball) 1202 Bert Murphy Ave	Omaha	NE	68107	402-734-2550	734-7166
Omaha Lancers (hockey) 6800 Mercy Rd Aksarben Coliseum	Omaha	NE	68106	402-561-7001	561-7019
Sunset Speedway 8350 N 114th St	Omaha	NE	68142	402-493-5271	493-0181
Web: www.sunsetspeedway.com ■ *E-mail:* mike.zoellner@rocketmail.com					

— Events —

	Phone
Cathedral Flower Festival (late January)	402-558-3100
Jazz on the Green (early July-August)	402-342-3300
NCAA World Series (mid-June)	402-422-1212
Nebraska Shakespeare Festival (mid-June-early July)	402-280-2391
Omaha Boat Sport & Travel Show (late February)	402-393-3339
Omaha Classic (early August)	402-399-1800
Renaissance Faire of the Midlands (early June)	402-345-5401
River City Roundup (late September)	402-554-9602
Septemberfest (early September)	402-346-4800
Shakespeare on the Green (late June-early July)	402-444-4660
Spring Festival-An Arts & Crafts Affair (early April)	402-331-2889
Summer Arts Festival (late June)	402-896-5976
Westfair! (mid-July)	712-323-7722

Nevada

Population (1999): 1,809,253 **Area (sq mi): 110,567**

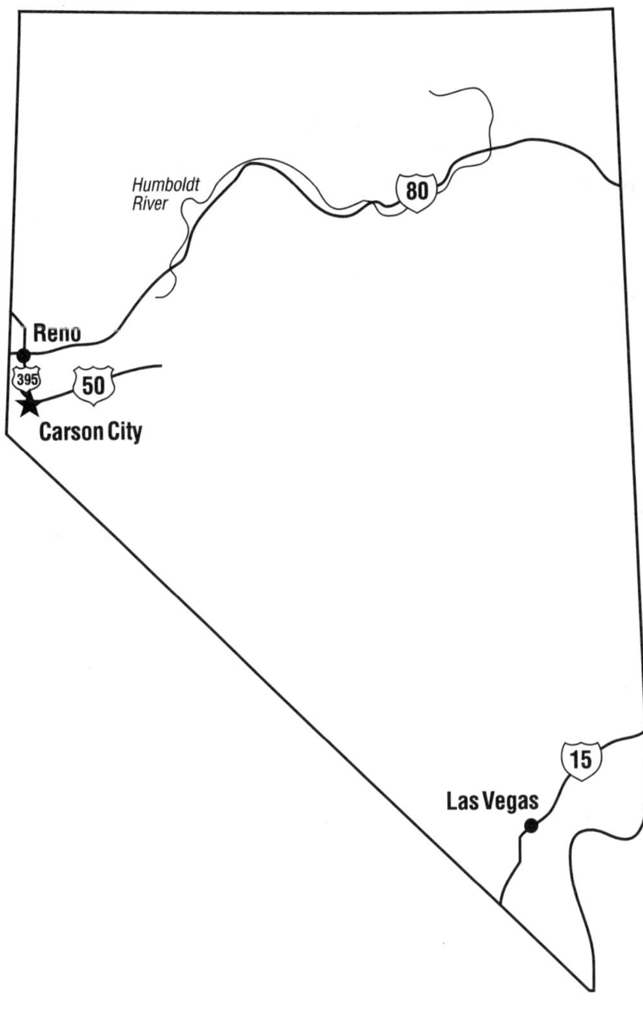

— State Information Sources —

				Phone	Fax
Nevada Economic Development Commission 108 E Proctor St.	Carson City	NV	89701	775-687-4325	687-4450
TF: 800-336-1600 ■ *Web:* www.state.nv.us/businessop/ ■ *E-mail:* bizinfo@bizopp.state.nv.us					
Nevada State Chamber of Commerce 405 Marsh Ave.	Reno	NV	89509	775-686-3030	686-3038
Web: www.reno-sparkschamber.org					
Nevada State Government Information				775-687-5000	
Web: www.state.nv.us					
Nevada State Library & Archives 100 N Stewart St	Carson City	NV	89701	775-684-3360	684-3330
Web: dmla.clan.lib.nv.us/docs/nsla					
Nevada State Parks Dept 1300 S Curry St.	Carson City	NV	89703	775-687-4370	687-4117
Web: www.state.nv.us/stparks ■ *E-mail:* stparks@govmail.state.nv.us					
Nevada Tourism Commission 401 N Carson St.	Carson City	NV	89701	775-687-4322	687-6779
TF: 800-237-0774 ■ *Web:* www.travelnevada.com ■ *E-mail:* ncot@travelnevada.com					

ON-LINE RESOURCES

Cybertourist Nevada	www.cybertourist.com/nevada.shtml
Nevada @ Travel Notes	www.travelnotes.org/NorthAmerica/nevada.htm
Nevada Cities	dir.yahoo.com/Regional/U_S__States/Nevada/Cities
Nevada Counties & Regions	dir.yahoo.com/Regional/U_S__States/Nevada/Counties_and_Regions
Nevada Online Highways	www.nvohwy.com
Nevada Scenario	scenariousa.dstylus.com/nv/indexf.htm
Nevada Travel & Tourism Guide	www.travel-library.com/north_america/usa/nevada/index.html
NevadaNet.com	www.nevadanet.com
Rough Guide Travel Nevada	travel.roughguides.com/content/1279/index.htm
Southwest Passage Nevada	www.swpassage.com
Travel.org-Nevada	travel.org/nevada.html
What's Up Nevada!	www.whatsupnevada.com
Yahoo! Get Local Nevada	dir.yahoo.com/Regional/U_S__States/Nevada

— Cities Profiled —

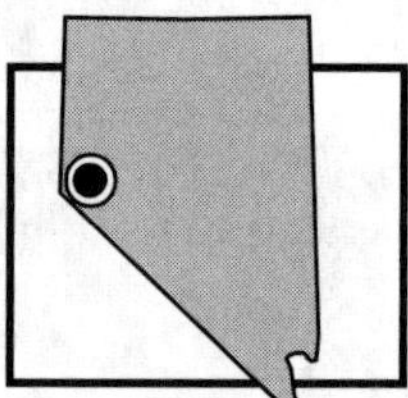

Carson City

Carson City, the capital of the "Silver State," affords an opportunity to revisit the Old West with a walk or drive along the Kit Carson Trail. Popular sights on the Trail include the Historical Homes District, the Nevada Capitol Building, the Governor's Mansion, the Stewart Indian Boarding School Museum, Nevada State Railroad Museum, and the Nevada State Museum, formerly a U.S. Mint, which was completed in 1869 and was built entirely of materials native to Nevada. Today the museum features Indian basketry, a mine, and an extensive Nevada natural history exhibit. Historic Virginia City, site of the Comstock Lode, is just a short drive away.

Population	49,301	**Longitude**	119-74-44 W
Area (Land)	143.5 sq mi	**County**	Independent City
Area (Water)	12.3 sq mi	**Time Zone**	PST
Elevation	4687 ft	**Area Code/s**	775
Latitude	39-15-17 N		

— Average Temperatures and Precipitation —

TEMPERATURES

	Jan	Feb	Mar	Apr	May	Jun	Jul	Aug	Sep	Oct	Nov	Dec
High	47	52	57	63	72	82	90	88	80	70	55	47
Low	21	24	28	32	39	46	50	48	41	32	26	21

PRECIPITATION

	Jan	Feb	Mar	Apr	May	Jun	Jul	Aug	Sep	Oct	Nov	Dec
Inches	1.9	1.6	1.0	0.5	0.6	0.4	0.3	0.3	0.5	0.7	1.4	1.7

— Important Phone Numbers —

	Phone		Phone
AAA	775-883-2470	**Medical Referral**	775-885-2211
Emergency	911	**Poison Control Center**	775-328-4129
Highway Conditions	775-793-1313	**Time**	775-844-1212

— Information Sources —

				Phone	Fax
Better Business Bureau Serving Northern Nevada 991 Bible Way	Reno	NV	89502	775-322-0657	322-8163
Web: www.reno.bbb.org					
Carson City Area Chamber of Commerce 1900 S Carson St Suite 100	Carson City	NV	89701	775-882-1565	882-4179
Web: www.carsoncitychamber.com					
Carson City City Hall 201 N Carson St	Carson City	NV	89701	775-887-2100	887-2286
Web: www.carson-city.nv.us					
Carson City Community Development Dept 2621 Northgate Ln Suite 62	Carson City	NV	89706	775-887-2180	887-2278
Carson City Convention & Visitors Bureau 1900 S Carson St Suite 200	Carson City	NV	89701	775-687-7410	687-7416
TF: 800-638-2321 ■ *Web:* www.carson-city.org					
Carson City (Independent City) 201 N Carson St	Carson City	NV	89701	775-887-2100	887-2286
Carson City Library 900 N Roop St	Carson City	NV	89701	775-887-2247	887-2273
E-mail: cclb@ci.carson-city.nv.us					
Carson City Mayor 201 N Carson St Suite 2	Carson City	NV	89701	775-887-2100	887-2286
E-mail: mayor@ci.carson-city.nv.us					

On-Line Resources

Anthill City Guide Carson City	www.anthill.com/city.asp?city=carsoncity
Area Guide Carson City	carsoncity.areaguides.net
Excite.com Carson City City Guide	www.excite.com/travel/countries/united_states/nevada/carson_city/
NITC Travelbase City Guide Carson City	www.travelbase.com/auto/features/carson_city-nv.html

— Transportation Services —

AIRPORTS

■ **Reno-Tahoe International Airport (RNO)**

	Phone
33 miles N of downtown Carson City (approx 45 minutes)	775-328-6400

Airport Transportation

	Phone
Executive Limousine $55 fare to downtown Carson City	775-882-7776
Yellow Cab $45-50 fare to downtown Carson City	775-355-5555

Commercial Airlines

	Phone		Phone
America West	800-235-9292	**SkyWest**	800-453-9417
American	800-433-7300	**TWA**	800-221-2000
Delta	800-221-1212	**United**	800-241-6522
Northwest	800-225-2525	**United Express**	800-241-6522

Charter Airlines

	Phone		Phone
Berry Aviation	800-229-2379	**Tag Aviation**	800-252-6972

CAR RENTALS

	Phone		Phone
Alamo	775-323-8306	**Enterprise**	775-883-7788
Avis	775-785-2727	**Hertz**	775-785-2554
Budget	775-785-2541	**National**	800-227-7368
Dollar	775-348-2800	**U Save**	775-882-1212

LIMO/TAXI

	Phone		Phone
Bell Luxury Limousine	775-786-3700	**Sierra West Limousine**	775-329-4310
Capitol Cab	775-885-0300	**Yellow Cab**	775-831-8294
Executive Limousine	775-882-7776		

RAIL/BUS

				Phone
Amtrak Station 135 E Commercial Row	Reno	NV	89501	800-872-7245
Greyhound Bus Station 1718 N Carson St	Carson City	NV	89701	775-882-3375
TF: 800-231-2222				

— Accommodations —

HOTELS, MOTELS, RESORTS

				Phone	Fax
Best Value Motel 2731 S Carson St	Carson City	NV	89701	775-882-2007	883-4182
TF: 800-626-1900					
Best Western Carson Station Hotel Casino 900 S Carson St	Carson City	NV	89701	775-883-0900	882-7569
TF: 800-501-2929					
Best Western Trailside Inn 1300 N Carson Dr	Carson City	NV	89701	775-883-7300	885-7506
TF: 800-626-1900					
Camp-N-Town 2438 N Carson St	Carson City	NV	89706	775-883-1123	
Carson City Inn 1930 N Carson St	Carson City	NV	89701	775-882-1785	885-2177
Carson Motor Lodge 1421 N Carson St	Carson City	NV	89701	775-882-3572	
City Center Motel 800 N Carson St	Carson City	NV	89701	775-882-5535	882-6572
TF: 800-338-7760					
Days Inn 3103 N Carson St	Carson City	NV	89706	775-883-3343	887-0446
TF: 800-329-7466					
Desert Hills Motel 1010 S Carson St	Carson City	NV	89701	775-882-1932	882-2864
TF: 800-652-7785 ■ *Web:* www.nevadaconnection.com/deserthillsmotel					
Downtowner Motor Inn 801 N Carson St	Carson City	NV	89701	775-882-1333	883-4873
TF: 888-364-2282					
Frontier Motel 1718 N Carson St	Carson City	NV	89701	775-882-1377	882-9579
Gold Hill Hotel 1540 S Main St	Gold Hill	NV	89440	775-847-0111	847-0575
Hardman House Motor Inn 917 N Carson St	Carson City	NV	89701	775-882-7744	887-0321
TF: 800-626-0793					
Mill House Inn 3251 S Carson St	Carson City	NV	89701	775-882-2715	
Motel 6 2749 S Carson St	Carson City	NV	89701	775-885-7710	885-7671
TF: 800-466-8356					
Nugget Motel 651 N Stewart St	Carson City	NV	89701	775-882-7711	841-5197
TF: 800-948-9111					

Carson City — Hotels, Motels, Resorts (Cont'd)

				Phone	Fax
Ormsby House Hotel 600 S Carson St.	Carson City	NV	89701	775-882-1890	883-8724
TF: 800-662-1890					
Pioneer Motel 907 S Carson St	Carson City	NV	89701	775-882-3046	
TF: 800-882-3046					
Plaza Motel 801 S Carson St	Carson City	NV	89701	775-883-9500	883-3838
Ridge Tahoe The 400 Ridge Club Dr.	Stateline	NV	89449	775-588-3553	588-1551
Web: www.ridge-tahoe.com					
Round House Inn 1400 N Carson St	Carson City	NV	89701	775-882-3446	
Sierra Sage Motel 801 S Carson St	Carson City	NV	89701	775-882-1419	
Sierra Vista Motel 711 Plaza St	Carson City	NV	89701	775-883-9500	883-3838
Silver Queen Inn 201 W Caroline St	Carson City	NV	89703	775-882-5534	
Super 8 Motel 2829 S Carson St	Carson City	NV	89701	775-883-7800	883-0376
TF: 800-800-8000					
Westerner Inn 555 N Stewart St.	Carson City	NV	89701	775-883-6565	882-7801
TF: 800-638-2321					

— Restaurants —

				Phone
Adele's (Continental) 1112 N Carson St	Carson City	NV	89706	775-882-3353
Amimoto Japanese Restaurant (Japanese) 276 Fairview Dr	Carson City	NV	89701	775-883-8127
Bodine's Restaurant & Saloon (American) 5650 S Carson St.	Carson City	NV	89701	775-885-0303
Buffalo Club Grille (American) 2729 N Carson St	Carson City	NV	89706	775-883-8488
Carson Nugget Steak House (Steak/Seafood) 507 N Carson St	Carson City	NV	89701	775-882-1626
China East (Chinese) 1810 Hwy 50 East	Carson City	NV	89701	775-885-6996
China Kitchen (Chinese) 1936 N Carson St.	Carson City	NV	89701	775-887-8888
Dominique's Supper Club (Steak) 600 S Carson St.	Carson City	NV	89701	775-882-1890
East Ocean Restaurant (Chinese) 1214 N Carson St	Carson City	NV	89701	775-883-6668
Garibaldi's (Italian) 301 N Carson St	Carson City	NV	89701	775-884-4574
Genghis Khan Kitchen (Chinese) 260 E Winnie Ln.	Carson City	NV	89706	775-883-7555
Glen Eagles (Steak/Seafood) 3700 N Carson St.	Carson City	NV	89703	775-884-4414
Grandma Hattie's (American) 2811 S Carson St	Carson City	NV	89701	775-882-4900
Heiss' Steak & Seafood House (Steak/Seafood) 107 E Telegraph St.	Carson City	NV	89701	775-882-9012
Los Tres Amigos (Mexican) 1740 S Roop St.	Carson City	NV	89701	775-887-0410
Ming's Chinese Restaurant (Chinese) 202 Fairview Dr.	Carson City	NV	89701	775-841-2888
Panda Kitchen (Chinese) 1986 Hwy 50 East	Carson City	NV	89701	775-882-8128
Pop's Family Restaurant (Barbecue) 224 S Carson St.	Carson City	NV	89701	775-884-4411
Silvana's (Italian) 1301 N Carson St	Carson City	NV	89701	775-883-5100
Stanley's Restaurant (Continental) 4239 N Carson St	Carson City	NV	89706	775-883-7826
Station Grill & Rotisserie (Italian) 1105 S Carson St.	Carson City	NV	89701	775-883-8400
Tequila Dan's Tex Mex (Mexican) 3449 S Carson St.	Carson City	NV	89701	775-885-7475
Thurman's Ranch House (American) 2943 Hwy 50 East	Carson City	NV	89701	775-883-1773
Yamacho (Japanese) 3747 S Carson St	Carson City	NV	89701	775-884-2366

— Goods and Services —

SHOPPING

				Phone	Fax
Carson Mall 1313 S Carson St.	Carson City	NV	89701	775-882-3395	
Frontier Antique Mall 3rd & Currey Sts.	Carson City	NV	89703	775-887-1466	
Meadowood Mall Virginia & McCarren Sts.	Reno	NV	89502	775-827-8450	826-0560
Park Lane Mall 310 E Plumb Ln.	Reno	NV	89502	775-825-7878	825-4375
Silver City Mall 406 Fairview Dr.	Carson City	NV	89701	775-883-3500	

BANKS

				Phone	Fax
Bank of America Nevada 600 E Williams St	Carson City	NV	89701	775-687-7000	387-7026
TF Cust Svc: 800-388-2265*					
Bank of the West 2976 N Carson St	Carson City	NV	89706	775-687-2550	687-2555
California Federal Bank 201 W Telegraph St	Carson City	NV	89701	800-843-2265	882-7515*
**Fax Area Code:* 775 ■ **Fax:* Admin					
First Security Bank of Nevada 901 N Stewart St	Carson City	NV	89701	775-687-2700	687-2710
Nevada State Bank 599 E William St.	Carson City	NV	89701	775-687-1500	687-1519
TF: 800-462-3555					
US Bank of Nevada 1001 N Stewart St	Carson City	NV	89701	775-687-8001	687-8022
TF: 800-872-2657					
Wells Fargo Bank 2424 S Carson St.	Carson City	NV	89701	775-885-1111	885-1101
TF: 800-869-3557					

BUSINESS SERVICES

	Phone		Phone
Airborne Express	800-247-2676	**Mail Boxes Etc**	800-789-4623
BAX Global	800-225-5229	**Post Office**	800-275-8777
DHL Worldwide Express	800-225-5345	**UPS**	800-742-5877
Federal Express	800-238-5355		

— Media —

PUBLICATIONS

				Phone	Fax
Nevada Appeal Carson City Edition‡ PO Box 2288	Carson City	NV	89702	775-882-2111	887-2420
TF: 800-221-8013 ■ *Web:* tahoe.com/appeal					
Nevada Magazine 401 N Carson St.	Carson City	NV	89701	775-687-5416	687-6159
TF: 800-495-3281 ■ *Web:* www.nevadamagazine.com ■ *E-mail:* nevmag@aol.com					
Reno Gazette Journal Carson City Edition‡ 311 N Carson St.	Carson City	NV	89701	775-885-5560	885-5565

‡Daily newspapers

TELEVISION

				Phone	Fax
KAME-TV Ch 21 (UPN) 4920 Brookside Ct	Reno	NV	89502	775-856-2121	856-3915
KNPB-TV Ch 5 (PBS) 1670 N Virginia St	Reno	NV	89503	775-784-4555	784-1438
Web: www.knpb.org					
KOLO-TV Ch 8 (ABC) PO Box 10000	Reno	NV	89510	775-858-8888	858-8877
Web: www.kolotv.com ■ *E-mail:* admin@kolotv.com					
KRNV-TV Ch 4 (NBC) 1790 Vassar St	Reno	NV	89502	775-322-4444	785-1206
Web: www.krnv.com ■ *E-mail:* comments@krnv.com					
KRXI-TV Ch 11 (Fox) 4920 Brookside Ct	Reno	NV	89502	775-856-1100	856-2100
KTVN-TV Ch 2 (CBS) 4925 Energy Way	Reno	NV	89502	775-858-2222	861-4298
Web: www.ktvn.com ■ *E-mail:* ktvn@ktvn.com					

RADIO

				Phone	Fax
KDOT-FM 104.5 MHz (Rock) 2900 Sutro St	Reno	NV	89512	775-329-9261	323-1450
Web: www.kdot.com					
KNIS-FM 91.3 MHz (Rel) 6363 Hwy 50 E	Carson City	NV	89701	775-883-5647	883-5704
TF: 800-541-5647					
KODS-FM 103.7 MHz (Oldies) 255 W Moana Ln Suite 208	Reno	NV	89509	775-829-1964	825-3183
KOZZ-FM 105.7 MHz (CR) 2900 Sutro St	Reno	NV	89512	775-329-9261	323-1450
KPLY-AM 1270 kHz (Sports) 255 W Moana Ln Suite 208	Reno	NV	89509	775-829-1964	825-3183
KPTL-AM 1300 kHz (Oldies) 1960 Idaho St	Carson City	NV	89701	775-884-8000	882-3961
KRNO-FM 106.9 MHz (AC) 255 W Moana Ln Suite 208	Reno	NV	89509	775-829-1964	825-3183
KWNZ-FM 97.3 MHz (CHR) 255 W Moana Ln Suite 208	Reno	NV	89509	775-829-1964	825-3183
Web: www.kwnz.com					
KZZF-FM 102.9 MHz (AC) 1960 Idaho	Carson City	NV	89701	775-884-8000	882-3961

— Colleges/Universities —

				Phone	Fax
Western Nevada Community College 2201 W College Pkwy	Carson City	NV	89703	775-445-3277	887-3141
TF Admissions: 800-748-5690 ■ *Web:* www.wncc.nevada.edu					

— Hospitals —

				Phone	Fax
Carson Tahoe Hospital 775 Fleischmann Way	Carson City	NV	89703	775-882-1361	885-4523*
**Fax:* Admitting					

— Attractions —

				Phone
Bowers Mansion Washoe Valley	Carson City	NV	89704	775-849-0201

Carson City — Attractions (Cont'd)

				Phone	Fax
Brewery Arts Center 449 W King St	Carson City	NV	89703	775-883-1976	883-1922
Web: www.breweryarts.org ■ *E-mail:* bac@powernet.net					
Carson City Chamber Orchestra PO Box 2001	Carson City	NV	89702	775-883-4154	
Carson City Historical District	Carson City	NV		775-687-7410	
Carson Hot Springs 1500 Hot Springs Rd	Carson City	NV	89706	775-885-8844	883-8666
Carson Valley Museum & Cultural Center 1477 Hwy 395	Gardnerville	NV	89410	775-782-2555	
Children's Museum of Northern Nevada 813 N Carson St	Carson City	NV	89701	775-884-2226	884-2179
Web: www.cmnn.org					
Historic Virginia City	Virginia City	NV		775-847-0311	847-0311
Nevada Gambling Museum 50 S 'C' St	Virginia City	NV	89440	775-847-9022	
Nevada State Capitol 101 N Carson St	Carson City	NV	89701	775-687-4811	
Nevada State Library & Archives 100 N Stewart St	Carson City	NV	89701	775-684-3360	684-3330
Web: dmla.clan.lib.nv.us/docs/nsla					
Nevada State Museum 600 N Carson St	Carson City	NV	89701	775-687-4810	687-4168
Web: dmla.clan.lib.nv.us/docs/museums/cc/carson.htm					
Nevada State Railroad Museum 2180 S Carson St	Carson City	NV	89701	775-687-6953	687-8294
Web: www.nsrm-friends.org					
Roberts House Museum 1207 N Carson St	Carson City	NV	89701	775-887-2174	882-3559
Stewart Indian School Museum 5366 Snyder Ave	Carson City	NV	89701	775-882-6929	882-6929
Warren Engine Co No 1 Fire Museum 777 S Stewart St	Carson City	NV	89701	775-887-2210	887-2209
Washoe Lake State Recreation Area 4855 E Lake Blvd	Carson City	NV	89704	775-687-4319	684-8053
Way It Was Museum 113 N 'C' St & Sutton Ave	Virginia City	NV	89440	775-847-0766	
Western Nevada Musical Theater 2201 W College Pkwy Western Nevada Community College	Carson City	NV	89703	775-887-3115	887-3051
Wild West Museum 66 N 'C' St	Virginia City	NV	89440	775-847-0400	

— Events —

	Phone
A Taste of Downtown (late June)	775-883-7654
Beer Tasting & Auction (early November)	775-883-1976
Carson City IRPA Rodeo (early July)	775-577-9427
Carson City Mint/Nevada State Museum Coin Show (mid-September)	775-687-6953
Carson City Rendezvous (early June)	775-687-7410
Carson Valley Days (early June)	775-782-8144
Carson Valley Street Celebration (mid-September)	775-782-8144
Christmas on the Comstock (December)	775-847-0311
Christmas Tree Lighting (early December)	775-882-1565
Cinco de Mayo Chili Cook Off (early May)	775-847-0311
Comstock Historic Preservation Week (mid-May)	775-847-0311
Cowboy Jubilee & Poetry (early March)	775-883-1532
Eagle Valley Muzzleloaders Spring Rendevous (late April)	775-887-1221
Farmers Market (June-August)	775-687-7410
Father's Day Pow Wow/Arts & Crafts Show (mid-June)	775-882-6929
High Desert Jazz Festival (mid-October)	775-883-1976
July 4th Celebration Week (late June-early July)	775-687-4680
Kit Carson Rendezvous & Wagon Train (mid-June)	775-884-3633
Kit Carson Trail Ghost Walk (late October)	775-687-7410
Kit Carson Trail Historic Home Tour (mid-June)	775-687-7410
Kit Carson Trail Walk (late May-late October)	775-687-7410
La Ka L'el Be Pow Wow (late October)	775-265-4191
Lake Tahoe Shakespeare Festival (late July-late August)	800-747-4697
Mother Earth Awakening Pow Wow (mid-March)	775-882-6929
Multi-Cultural Festival (mid-April)	775-887-3060
Nevada Day Celebration (late October)	775-882-2600
Nevada State Railroad Museum's Transportation Fair (early July)	775-687-6953
Outdoor Movie Film Festival (July-August)	775-687-6953
Pony Express Re-ride (mid-June)	775-882-1283
Pops Party Concert (mid-June)	775-882-1565
Robert's House Antique Sale (May-early October)	775-882-1805
Rsvp Spring Fun Fair (late April-early May)	775-687-4680
Run What You Brung Classic Car Show (late June)	775-882-0829
Silver & Snowflake Festival of Lights (November)	775-882-1565
Silver Dollar Car Classic (late July-early August)	775-687-7410
Stewart Indian School Museum Arts & Crafts Festival & Pow Wow (mid-June)	775-882-6929
Victorian Christmas Home Tour (mid-December)	775-882-1805
Virginia City Rodeo (late July)	775-847-0311
Wa She Shudeh Pow Wow (late July)	775-265-4191
Winter Wine & All That Jazz (mid-January)	775-687-7410

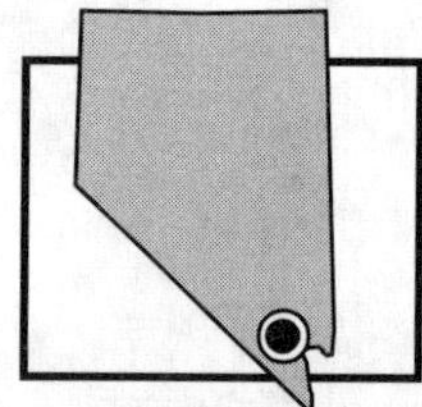

Las Vegas

The Strip in Las Vegas is home to many of the casinos, luxury hotels, nightclubs, and big name entertainers' shows that have made the city famous. While names like Bally's and Caesars Palace are widely recognized, newer and larger hotels have recently gained public attention. The Luxor is a 30-story pyramid hotel and casino with three levels of entertainment; and at Treasure Island visitors are greeted with an authentic pirate battle. Now the world's largest hotel, Las Vegas' MGM Grand has more than 5,000 rooms and a 33-acre theme park. Nearby attractions include Hoover Dam and the Lake Mead National Recreation Area.

Population	404,288	**Longitude**	115-13-64 W
Area (Land)	83.3 sq mi	**County**	Clark
Area (Water)	0.1 sq mi	**Time Zone**	PST
Elevation	2020 ft	**Area Code/s**	702
Latitude	36-17-50 N		

— Average Temperatures and Precipitation —

TEMPERATURES

	Jan	Feb	Mar	Apr	May	Jun	Jul	Aug	Sep	Oct	Nov	Dec
High	57	63	69	78	88	100	106	103	95	82	67	58
Low	34	39	44	51	60	69	76	74	66	54	43	34

PRECIPITATION

	Jan	Feb	Mar	Apr	May	Jun	Jul	Aug	Sep	Oct	Nov	Dec
Inches	0.5	0.5	0.4	0.2	0.3	0.1	0.4	0.5	0.3	0.2	0.3	0.4

— Important Phone Numbers —

	Phone		Phone
AAA	702-870-9171	**HotelDocs**	800-468-3537
American Express Travel	702-876-1410	**Medical Referral**	702-739-9989
Emergency	911	**Poison Control Center**	702-732-4989
Entertainment Line	702-225-5554	**Time/Temp**	702-248-4800
Events Line	702-892-7576	**Travelers Aid**	702-369-4357
Highway Conditions	775-793-1313	**Weather**	702-248-4800

— Information Sources —

				Phone	Fax
Better Business Bureau Serving Southern Nevada 5595 W Spring Mountain Rd	Las Vegas	NV	89146	702-440-3003	320-4560
Web: www.lasvegas.bbb.org ■ *E-mail:* vegasbbb@vegas.infi.net					
Clark County 200 S 3rd St	Las Vegas	NV	89101	702-455-3156	455-4929
Web: www.co.clark.nv.us					
Las Vegas Business Development Office 400 Las Vegas Blvd S	Las Vegas	NV	89101	702-229-6551	385-3128
Web: www.ci.las-vegas.nv.us/obd/default.htm ■ *E-mail:* obd@ci.las-vegas.nv.us					
Las Vegas Chamber of Commerce 3720 Howard Hughes Pkwy	Las Vegas	NV	89109	702-735-1616	735-2170*
**Fax:* PR ■ *Web:* www.lvchamber.com					
Las Vegas City Hall 400 Stewart Ave	Las Vegas	NV	89101	702-229-6011	
Web: www.ci.las-vegas.nv.us/					
Las Vegas-Clark County Library District 833 Las Vegas Blvd N	Las Vegas	NV	89101	702-382-3493	382-1280
Las Vegas Convention & Visitors Authority 3150 Paradise Rd	Las Vegas	NV	89109	702-892-0711	892-2824
TF: 800-332-5333 ■ *Web:* www.lasvegas24hours.com					
Las Vegas Convention Center 3150 Paradise Rd	Las Vegas	NV	89109	702-892-0711	892-2824*
**Fax:* Mktg ■ *TF:* 800-332-5333					
Las Vegas Mayor 400 Stewart Ave	Las Vegas	NV	89101	702-229-6241	385-7960
Web: www.ci.las-vegas.nv.us/mayor.html					

Las Vegas (Cont'd)

On-Line Resources

4LasVegas.com	www.4lasvegas.com
About.com Guide to Las Vegas	lasvegas.about.com/local/southwestus/lasvegas
Access America Las Vegas	lasvegas.accessamer.com
Anthill City Guide Las Vegas	www.anthill.com/city.asp?city=lasvegas
Area Guide Las Vegas	lasvegas.areaguides.net
Best Read Guide Las Vegas	bestreadguide.com/lasvegas
Casino City Casino Directory	www.casinocity.com/
City Knowledge Las Vegas	www.cityknowledge.com/nv_lasvegas.htm
CitySearch Las Vegas	lasvegas.citysearch.com
CityTravelGuide.com Las Vegas	www.citytravelguide.com/las-vegas.htm
DigitalCity Las Vegas	home.digitalcity.com/lasvegas
Excite.com Las Vegas City Guide	www.excite.com/travel/countries/united_states/nevada/las_vegas
Fabulous Las Vegas	www.intermind.net/im/lasvegas.html
Gay Las Vegas	www.gayvegas.com/
Gayot's Guide Restaurant Search Las Vegas	www.perrier.com/restaurants/gayot.asp?area=LSV
HotelGuide Las Vegas	lasvegas.hotelguide.net
In-Vegas.com	www.in-vegas.com/
Info Las Vegas	www.ilv.com
InfoVegas	www.infovegas.com/
Insider Viewpoint of Las Vegas	www.insidervlv.com/
Insiders' Guide to Las Vegas	www.insiders.com/lasvegas/
Las Vegas Entertainment Guide	www.lvindex.com/
Las Vegas Golf Guide	las-vegas-golf.com
Las Vegas Leisure Guide	www.pcap.com/lasvegas.html
Las Vegas Life	www.lasvegaslife.com/
Las Vegas Online Entertainment Guide	www.lvol.com
Las Vegas Weekly	www.lasvegasweekly.com
Lasvegas.com	www.lasvegas.com/
Locals Love Las Vegas	www.localslovelasvegas.com/
MetroGuide Las Vegas	lasvegas.metroguide.net
MetroVille Las Vegas	lasvegas.metroville.com
Night on the Town	www.nightonthetown.com/
NITC Travelbase City Guide Las Vegas	www.travelbase.com/auto/guides/las_vegas-area-nv.html
Online City Guide to Las Vegas	www.olcg.com/nv/lasvegas/index.html
Rough Guide Travel Las Vegas	travel.roughguides.com/content/1280/
Savvy Diner Guide to Las Vegas Restaurants	www.savvydiner.com/lasvegas/
Time Out Las Vegas	www.timeout.com/lasvegas/
Vegas Deluxe	www.vegasdeluxe.com
Vegas Pages	vegaspages.com/
Vegas.com	www.vegas.com/
VegasGuide.com	www.vegasguide.com
Virtual Vegas	www.virtualvegas.com
Virtual Voyages Las Vegas	www.virtualvoyages.com/usa/nv/vegas/vegas.sht
What's On in Las Vegas Magazine	www.whats-on.com/

— Transportation Services —

AIRPORTS

	Phone
■ **McCarran International Airport (LAS)**	
7 miles S of downtown (approx 20 minutes)	702-261-5743
Web: mccarran.com	

Airport Transportation

	Phone
CLS Limo $5 fare to downtown	702-740-4545
Commercial Shuttles Bell Trans $4.75 fare to downtown	702-736-4428
Gray Line Airport Express $5 fare to downtown	702-384-1234
Taxi $15 fare to downtown	702-873-2227

Commercial Airlines

	Phone		Phone
America West	800-235-9292	**Northwest**	800-225-2525
American	800-433-7300	**Scenic**	702-739-1900
Continental	800-525-0280	**Shuttle by United**	800-748-8853
Continental Express	800-525-0280	**SkyWest**	800-453-9417
Delta	800-221-1212	**Southwest**	800-435-9792
Hawaiian	800-367-5320	**TWA**	800-221-2000
Midwest Express	800-452-2022	**United**	800-241-6522
National	888-757-5387	**US Airways**	800-428-4322

Charter Airlines

	Phone		Phone
Air Vegas	702-736-3599	**Helicop-Tours**	702-736-0606
American Trans Air	702-261-3610	**Lake Mead Air**	702-293-9906
Berry Aviation	800-229-2379	**Scenic Airlines**	702-739-1900
Charter Airlines	702-878-2264	**Sun Country**	702-261-3595
Eagle Jet Charter	702-798-7001	**TWC Aviation**	888-892-0035

CAR RENTALS

	Phone		Phone
Alamo	702-733-8886	**Enterprise**	702-795-8842
Avis	702-261-5595	**Hertz**	702-736-4900
Budget	702-736-1212	**National**	702-261-5391
CarTemps USA	702-739-0200	**Sears**	702-736-8006
Dollar	702-739-8408	**Thrifty**	702-896-7600

LIMO/TAXI

	Phone		Phone
Ace Cab Co.	702-736-8383	**On Demand Sedan**	702-876-2222
Bell Trans Limo	702-382-7060	**Presidential Limousine**	702-731-5577
Desert Cab	702-386-9102	**Western Cab**	702-736-8000
Desert Taxi Cab	702-386-9102	**Whittlesea Blue Cab**	702-384-6111
Las Vegas Limousine	702-739-8414	**Yellow/Checker/Star Cab**	702-873-2227

MASS TRANSIT

	Phone
Citizens Area Transit $1.50 Base fare	702-228-7433
Freemont Street Downtown Neighborhood Trolley $.50 Base fare	702-229-6025
Strip The Trolley $1.30 Base fare	702-382-1404

RAIL/BUS

				Phone
Greyhound Bus Station 200 S Main St	Las Vegas	NV	89101	702-384-8009
TF: 800-231-2222				

— Accommodations —

HOTEL RESERVATION SERVICES

	Phone	Fax
Accommodations Express	609-391-2100	525-0111
TF: 800-444-7666 ■ *Web:* www.accommodationsxpress.com ■ *E-mail:* accomexp@acy.digex.net		
Advance Reservations Inn Arizona	480-990-0682	990-3390
TF: 800-456-0682 ■ *Web:* tucson.com/inn ■ *E-mail:* micasa@primenet.com		
Hotel Reservations Network Inc	214-361-7311	361-7299
TF Sales: 800-964-6835 ■ *Web:* www.hoteldiscount.com		
Las Vegas Holidays	702-697-8800	697-8847
TF: 800-926-6836 ■ *Web:* www.lvholidays.com		
Las Vegas Hotel Reservation Services	702-794-2061	
TF: 800-728-4106 ■ *Web:* www.lasvegasreservations.com/		
National Reservation Bureau	702-794-2820	794-3515
TF: 800-831-2754 ■ *E-mail:* hotelrez@nrbinc.com		

HOTELS, MOTELS, RESORTS

				Phone	Fax
Alexis Park Resort 375 E Harmon Ave	Las Vegas	NV	89109	702-796-3300	796-3354
TF: 800-582-2228					
Arizona Charlie's Hotel & Casino 740 S Decatur Blvd	Las Vegas	NV	89107	702-258-5200	258-5196
TF: 800-342-2695					
Bally's Las Vegas Casino & Resort PO Box 93898	Las Vegas	NV	89193	702-739-4111	739-4405
TF: 800-634-3434 ■ *Web:* www.ballyslv.com					
Barbary Coast Hotel & Casino PO Box 19030	Las Vegas	NV	89132	702-737-7111	737-8460*
**Fax:* Hum Res ■ *TF:* 888-227-2279					
Bellagio Hotel & Casino 3600 Las Vegas Blvd S	Las Vegas	NV	89109	702-693-7111	693-8546
TF: 888-987-6667 ■ *Web:* www.bellagiolasvegas.com					
Best Western Mardi Gras Inn 3500 Paradise Rd	Las Vegas	NV	89109	702-731-2020	733-6994
TF: 800-634-6501					
Best Western McCarran Inn 4970 Paradise Rd	Las Vegas	NV	89119	702-798-5530	798-7627
TF: 800-528-1234					
Binion's Horseshoe Hotel & Casino 128 E Fremont St	Las Vegas	NV	89101	702-382-1600	384-1574
TF: 800-237-6537					
Caesars Palace 3570 Las Vegas Blvd S	Las Vegas	NV	89109	702-731-7110	731-6636
TF: 800-634-6661 ■ *Web:* www.caesars.com/palace/default.html					
Circus Circus Hotel & Casino Las Vegas 2880 Las Vegas Blvd S	Las Vegas	NV	89109	702-734-0410	794-3816
TF: 800-634-3450 ■ *Web:* www.circuscircus-lasvegas.com					
Comfort Inn 211 E Flamingo Rd	Las Vegas	NV	89109	702-733-7800	733-7353
TF: 800-221-2222					

Las Vegas — Hotels, Motels, Resorts (Cont'd)

Name / Address	City	State	ZIP	Phone	Fax
Crowne Plaza Hotel 4255 S Paradise Rd *TF:* 800-227-6963	Las Vegas	NV	89109	702-369-4400	369-3770
Excalibur Hotel & Casino 3850 Las Vegas Blvd S *TF:* 800-937-7777 ■ *Web:* www.excalibur-casino.com	Las Vegas	NV	89109	702-597-7777	597-7009
Flamingo Hilton Hotel & Casino 3555 Las Vegas Blvd S *TF:* 800-732-2111	Las Vegas	NV	89109	702-733-3111	733-3528
Four Queens Hotel & Casino 202 E Fremont St *TF:* 800-634-6045 ■ *Web:* www.fourqueens.com	Las Vegas	NV	89101	702-385-4011	387-5133
Four Seasons Hotel Las Vegas 3960 Las Vegas Blvd S *TF:* 877-632-5200	Las Vegas	NV	89119	702-632-5000	632-5195
Gold Coast Hotel & Casino 4000 W Flamingo Rd **Fax:* Sales ■ *TF:* 888-402-6278 ■ *Web:* www.goldcoastcasino.com	Las Vegas	NV	89103	702-367-7111	367-8419*
Golden Nugget Hotel & Casino 129 E Fremont St **Fax:* Sales ■ *TF:* 800-634-3454 ■ *Web:* www.goldennugget.com/	Las Vegas	NV	89101	702-385-7111	386-8248*
Hard Rock Hotel & Casino 4455 Paradise Rd *TF:* 800-473-7625 ■ *Web:* www.hardrockhotel.com	Las Vegas	NV	89109	702-693-5000	693-5010
Harrah's 3475 Las Vegas Blvd S *TF:* 800-427-7247 ■ *Web:* harrahs.lv.com	Las Vegas	NV	89109	702-369-5000	369-6014
Holiday Inn Casino Boardwalk 3750 Las Vegas Blvd S *TF:* 800-635-4581 ■ *Web:* www.hiboardwalk.com	Las Vegas	NV	89109	702-735-2400	730-3166
Howard Johnson Airport 5100 Paradise Rd *TF:* 800-446-4656 ■ *Web:* www.travelbase.com/destinations/las-vegas/howard-johnson ■ *E-mail:* howard-johnson@travelbase.com	Las Vegas	NV	89119	702-798-2777	736-8295
Imperial Palace Hotel & Casino 3535 Las Vegas Blvd S *TF:* 800-634-6441 ■ *Web:* www.imperialpalace.com/	Las Vegas	NV	89109	702-731-3311	735-8328
Key Largo Quality Inn 377 E Flamingo Rd *TF:* 800-634-6617	Las Vegas	NV	89109	702-733-7777	369-6911
Lady Luck Hotel & Casino 206 N 3rd St *TF:* 800-523-9582	Las Vegas	NV	89101	702-477-3000	477-7021
Las Vegas Club Hotel & Casino 18 E Fremont St *TF:* 800-634-6532	Las Vegas	NV	89101	702-385-1664	387-6071
Las Vegas Hilton Hotel & Casino 3000 Paradise Rd *TF:* 800-732-7117 ■ *Web:* www.lv-hilton.com/	Las Vegas	NV	89109	702-732-5111	794-3611
Las Vegas Inn Travelodge 1501 W Sahara Ave *TF:* 800-554-4092	Las Vegas	NV	89102	702-733-0001	733-1571
Laughlin's Don Riverside Resort & Casino 1650 Casino Dr *TF:* 800-227-3849 ■ *Web:* www.riversideresort.com	Laughlin	NV	89029	702-298-2535	298-2231
Luxor Hotel & Casino 3900 Las Vegas Blvd S *TF:* 800-288-1000 ■ *Web:* www.luxor.com	Las Vegas	NV	89119	702-262-4000	262-4404
Main Street Station Hotel 200 N Main St *TF:* 800-465-0711	Las Vegas	NV	89101	702-387-1896	386-4446
Mandalay Bay Resort & Casino 3950 Las Vegas Blvd S *TF:* 877-632-7000 ■ *Web:* www.mandalaybay.com	Las Vegas	NV	89119	702-632-7777	632-7234
Maxim Hotel & Casino 160 E Flamingo Rd *TF:* 800-634-6987 ■ *Web:* www.maximhotel.com ■ *E-mail:* maxim@anv.net	Las Vegas	NV	89109	702-731-4300	735-3252
MGM Grand Hotel & Casino 3799 Las Vegas Blvd S *TF:* 800-929-1111 ■ *Web:* www.mgmgrand.com	Las Vegas	NV	89109	702-891-1111	891-3036
Mirage Resort & Country Club 3400 Las Vegas Blvd S *TF:* 800-627-6667 ■ *Web:* www.themirage.com	Las Vegas	NV	89109	702-791-7111	791-7414
Mirage The 3400 Las Vegas Blvd S *TF:* 800-627-6667 ■ *Web:* www.themirage.com	Las Vegas	NV	89109	702-791-7111	791-7414
Monte Carlo Resort & Casino 3770 Las Vegas Blvd S **Fax:* Sales ■ *TF:* 800-311-8999 ■ *Web:* www.monte-carlo.com	Las Vegas	NV	89109	702-730-7777	730-7275*
Nevada Palace Hotel & Casino 5255 Boulder Hwy *TF:* 800-634-6283	Las Vegas	NV	89122	702-458-8810	458-3361
New York New York Hotel & Casino 3790 Las Vegas Blvd S *TF:* 800-693-6763 ■ *Web:* www.nynyhotelcasino.com	Las Vegas	NV	89109	702-740-6969	740-6700
Palace Station Hotel & Casino 2411 W Sahara Ave *TF:* 800-634-3101 ■ *Web:* www.palacestation.com	Las Vegas	NV	89102	702-367-2411	367-2478
Residence Inn by Marriott 3225 Paradise Rd *TF:* 800-331-3131 ■ *Web:* www.residenceinn.com/LASNV	Las Vegas	NV	89109	702-796-9300	796-9562
Rio Suite Hotel & Casino 3700 W Flamingo Rd *TF:* 888-746-7482 ■ *Web:* www.playrio.com ■ *E-mail:* riorita@playrio.com	Las Vegas	NV	89103	702-252-7777	579-6565
Riviera Hotel & Casino 2901 Las Vegas Blvd S *TF:* 800-634-6753 ■ *Web:* www.theriviera.com	Las Vegas	NV	89109	702-734-5110	794-9663
Saddle West Resort Hotel & Casino 1220 S Hwy 160 *TF:* 800-433-3987 ■ *E-mail:* swsam@saddlewest.com	Pahrump	NV	89048	775-727-5953	727-6749
Sahara Hotel & Casino 2535 Las Vegas Blvd S *TF:* 800-634-6666	Las Vegas	NV	89109	702-737-2111	737-1017
Saint Tropez Hotel 455 E Harmon Ave *TF:* 800-666-5400	Las Vegas	NV	89109	702-369-5400	369-1150
Sam's Town Hotel & Gambling Hall 5111 Boulder Hwy *TF:* 800-634-6371 ■ *Web:* www.samstownlv.com	Las Vegas	NV	89122	702-456-7777	454-8107
Sheraton Desert Inn 3145 Las Vegas Blvd S *TF:* 800-634-6909 ■ *Web:* www.thedesertinn.com	Las Vegas	NV	89109	702-733-4444	733-4774
Showboat Hotel & Casino 2800 Fremont St *TF:* 800-826-2800	Las Vegas	NV	89104	702-385-9123	385-9678
Si Redd's Oasis Resort Hotel Casino PO Box 360 **Fax:* Hum Res ■ *TF:* 800-621-0187 ■ *Web:* www.siredd.com	Mesquite	NV	89024	702-346-5232	346-2984*
Stardust Resort & Casino 3000 Las Vegas Blvd S **Fax:* Resv ■ *TF:* 800-634-6757 ■ *Web:* www.vegasresorts.com/stardust	Las Vegas	NV	89109	702-732-6111	732-6257*
Stratosphere Hotel Casino & Tower 2000 S Las Vegas Blvd *TF:* 800-998-6937 ■ *Web:* www.stratlv.com	Las Vegas	NV	89104	702-380-7777	383-4755
Treasure Island Hotel & Casino 3300 Las Vegas Blvd S *TF:* 800-944-7444 ■ *Web:* www.treasureislandlasvegas.com	Las Vegas	NV	89109	702-894-7111	894-7414
Tropicana Resort & Casino 3801 Las Vegas Blvd S *TF:* 800-634-4000 ■ *Web:* tropicana.lv.com	Las Vegas	NV	89109	702-739-2222	739-3648
Union Plaza Hotel & Casino 1 Main St *TF:* 800-634-6575 ■ *Web:* www.plazahotelcasino.com	Las Vegas	NV	89101	702-386-2110	382-8281
Venetian Resort Hotel & Casino 3355 Las Vegas Blvd S *TF:* 888-283-6423 ■ *Web:* www.venetian.com	Las Vegas	NV	89109	702-733-5000	733-5190
Wild Wild West 3330 W Tropicana Ave *TF:* 800-634-3488	Las Vegas	NV	89103	702-740-0000	736-7106

— Restaurants —

Name / Address	City	State	ZIP	Phone
Andre's (French) 401 S 6th St	Las Vegas	NV	89101	702-385-5016
Aristocrat (French) 850 S Rancho Rd Suite 4	Las Vegas	NV	89106	702-870-1977
Bacchanal (Continental) 3570 Las Vegas Blvd S	Las Vegas	NV	89109	702-731-7525
Bertolini's (Italian) 3750 Las Vegas Blvd S	Las Vegas	NV	89109	702-735-4663
Binion's Ranch Steak House (Steak) 128 E Fremont St	Las Vegas	NV	89101	702-382-1600
Bootlegger Ristorante (Italian) 5025 S Eastern Ave	Las Vegas	NV	89119	702-736-4939
Cafe Nicolle (Continental) 4760 W Sahara Rd	Las Vegas	NV	89102	702-870-7675
Carluccio's Tivoli Gardens (Italian) 1775 E Tropicana Ave	Las Vegas	NV	89119	702-795-3236
Chin's (Chinese) 3200 Las Vegas Blvd S	Las Vegas	NV	89109	702-733-8899
Cipriani (Italian) 2790 E Flamingo Rd	Las Vegas	NV	89121	702-369-6711
Coyote Cafe & Grill (Southwest) 3799 Las Vegas Blvd S	Las Vegas	NV	89109	702-891-7777
El Sombrero Cafe (Mexican) 807 S Main St	Las Vegas	NV	89101	702-382-9234
Emeril's New Orleans Fish House (Seafood) 3799 Las Vegas Blvd	Las Vegas	NV	89109	702-891-7374
Empress Court (Chinese) 3570 Las Vegas Blvd S	Las Vegas	NV	89109	702-731-7888
Ferraro's (Italian) 5900 W Flamingo	Las Vegas	NV	89103	702-364-5300
Fiore Rotisserie & Grill (Italian) 3700 W Flamingo Rd	Las Vegas	NV	89103	702-252-7702
Gandhi India's Cuisine (Indian) 4080 Paradise Rd	Las Vegas	NV	89109	702-734-0094
Garden of the Dragon (Chinese) 3000 Paradise Rd	Las Vegas	NV	89109	702-732-5111
Golden Steer Steak House (Steak) 308 W Sahara Ave	Las Vegas	NV	89102	702-384-4470
Great Moments Room (Continental) 18 E Fremont St	Las Vegas	NV	89101	702-385-1664
Hamada of Japan (Japanese) 598 E Flamingo Rd	Las Vegas	NV	89119	702-733-3005
Hugo's Cellar (American) 202 Fremont St	Las Vegas	NV	89101	702-385-4011
Kiefer's (Continental) 105 E Harmon Ave	Las Vegas	NV	89109	702-739-8000
Le Montrachet (French) 3000 Paradise Rd	Las Vegas	NV	89109	702-732-5111
Lilly Langtree (Cantonese) 129 E Fremont St	Las Vegas	NV	89101	702-385-7111
Marrakech Restaurant (Moroccan) 3900 Paradise Rd	Las Vegas	NV	89109	702-737-5611
Mayflower Cuisinier (Chinese) 4750 W Sahara Ave	Las Vegas	NV	89102	702-870-8432
Michael's (Continental) 3595 Las Vegas Blvd S	Las Vegas	NV	89109	702-737-7111
Monte Carlo (French) 3145 Las Vegas Blvd S *TF:* 800-492-4400	Las Vegas	NV	89102	702-733-4400

Las Vegas — Restaurants (Cont'd)

				Phone
Moongate (Chinese) 3400 Las Vegas Blvd S	Las Vegas	NV	89109	702-791-7223
Napa Restaurant (New American) 3700 W Flamingo Rd	Las Vegas	NV	89103	702-252-7777
Osaka (Japanese) 4205 W Sahara	Las Vegas	NV	89102	702-876-4988
Palace Court (French) 3570 Las Vegas Blvd S	Las Vegas	NV	89109	702-731-7547
Pamplemousse (French) 400 E Sahara	Las Vegas	NV	89104	702-733-2066
Paparazzi (Italian) 115 E Tropicana Ave	Las Vegas	NV	89109	702-739-9000
Philips Supper House (American) 4545 W Sahara	Las Vegas	NV	89102	702-873-5222
Piero's Restaurant (Italian) 355 Convention Center Dr	Las Vegas	NV	89109	702-369-2305
Prime (Steak/Seafood) 3600 Las Vegas Blvd S Bellagio Hotel & Casino	Las Vegas	NV	89109	702-693-7111
Rainforest Cafe (American) 3799 Las Vegas Blvd *Web:* www.rainforestcafe.com	Las Vegas	NV	89109	702-891-8580
Reef The (Seafood) 3000 Paradise Rd	Las Vegas	NV	89109	702-732-5111
Ristorante Italiano (Italian) 2901 Las Vegas Blvd S	Las Vegas	NV	89109	702-734-5110
Sister's Big Sky Restaurant (American) 2000 Las Vegas Blvd S	Las Vegas	NV	89104	702-380-7777
Spago (California) 3500 Las Vegas Blvd S	Las Vegas	NV	89109	702-369-6300
Tillerman (Steak/Seafood) 2245 E Flamingo Rd	Las Vegas	NV	89119	702-731-4036
Venetian (Italian) 3713 W Sahara	Las Vegas	NV	89109	702-876-4190
Wolfgang Puck's Cafe (California) 3799 Las Vegas Blvd S	Las Vegas	NV	89109	702-895-9653
Yolie's Brazilian Steakhouse (Steak) 3900 Paradise Rd	Las Vegas	NV	89109	702-794-0700
Z Tejas Grill (Southwest) 3824 S Paradise Rd	Las Vegas	NV	89109	702-732-1660

— Goods and Services —

SHOPPING

				Phone	Fax
Bally's Shopping Arcade 3645 Las Vegas Blvd S	Las Vegas	NV	89109	702-739-4111	
Belz Factory Outlet World 7400 Las Vegas Blvd S	Las Vegas	NV	89123	702-896-5599	896-4626
Boulevard Mall 3528 S Maryland Pkwy *Web:* www.blvdmall.com ■ *E-mail:* blvdmall@vegas.infi.net	Las Vegas	NV	89109	702-735-8268	732-9197
Fantastic Indoor Swap Meet 1717 S Decatur Blvd	Las Vegas	NV	89102	702-877-0087	877-3102
Fashion Show Mall 3200 Las Vegas Blvd S *Web:* www.thefashionshow.com/	Las Vegas	NV	89109	702-369-8382	369-1613
Forum Shops at Caesars Palace 3500 Las Vegas Blvd S	Las Vegas	NV	89109	702-893-4800	893-3009
Galleria at Sunset 1300 W Sunset Rd	Henderson	NV	89014	702-434-0202	434-0259
Las Vegas Factory Stores 9155 Las Vegas Blvd S Suite 200	Las Vegas	NV	89123	702-897-9090	897-9094
Masquerade Village 3700 W Flamingo Rd Rio Suite Hotel	Las Vegas	NV	89103	702-252-7777	
Meadows Mall 4300 Meadows Ln	Las Vegas	NV	89107	702-878-4849	878-3138

BANKS

				Phone	Fax
American Bankcorp 4335 Industrial Rd	Las Vegas	NV	89103	702-891-8700	891-8787
Bank of America NT & SA 300 S 4th St *TF:* 800-388-2265	Las Vegas	NV	89101	702-386-1000	654-7820
Bank of the West 1771 E Flamingo Rd Suite 213-A	Las Vegas	NV	89119	702-733-2199	733-4967
Bankwest of Nevada 2700 W Sahara Ave	Las Vegas	NV	89102	702-248-4200	362-2026
Business Bank of Nevada 6085 W Twain Ave	Las Vegas	NV	89103	702-220-3302	220-3807
California Federal Bank FSB 103 S Rainbow Blvd	Las Vegas	NV	89128	800-843-2265	
Citibank Nevada 3900 Paradise Rd Suite M	Las Vegas	NV	89109	702-796-7379	796-8239
Colonial Bank 2820 W Charleston Blvd Suite 5	Las Vegas	NV	89102	702-258-9990	870-6313
Community Bank of Nevada 1400 S Rainbow Blvd	Las Vegas	NV	89146	702-878-0700	878-1060
First Republic Bank 6700 W Charleston Blvd	Las Vegas	NV	89146	702-880-3700	880-3600
First Security Bank of Nevada 530 Las Vegas Blvd S	Las Vegas	NV	89101	702-952-7681	952-7685
Nevada State Bank 201 S 4th St *TF Cust Svc:* 800-727-4743*	Las Vegas	NV	89101	702-383-4111	383-4307
Norwest Bank Nevada NA 2283 N Rampart Blvd *TF Cust Svc:* 800-331-1816*	Las Vegas	NV	89128	702-765-2100	765-2110
Pioneer Citizens Bank 8400 W Lake Mead Blvd	Las Vegas	NV	89128	702-242-1279	242-5573
Silver State Bank 170 S Rainbow Blvd	Las Vegas	NV	89128	702-968-8400	968-8415
Sun West Bank 5830 W Flamingo Rd	Las Vegas	NV	89103	702-949-2265	949-2299
US Bank NA 801 E Charleston Blvd *TF Cust Svc:* 800-872-2657*	Las Vegas	NV	89104	702-387-1919	382-9062
Wells Fargo Bank NA 3555 S Jones Blvd	Las Vegas	NV	89103	702-362-7462	362-7671

BUSINESS SERVICES

	Phone		Phone
Accountemps	702-739-9797	**Manpower Temporary Services**	702-893-2626
Courier Express	702-871-8112	**Olsten Staffing Services**	702-247-1711
Federal Express	800-238-5355	**Post Office**	800-275-8777
Kelly Services	702-796-0203	**UCI Distribution Plus**	702-740-5780
Kinko's	702-735-4402	**UPS**	800-742-5877
Legal Wings	702-384-0305	**Westaff Inc**	702-735-4334
Mac's Delivery Service	702-639-0343		

— Media —

PUBLICATIONS

				Phone	Fax
Las Vegas Business Press 3335 Wynn Rd	Las Vegas	NV	89102	702-871-6780	871-3740
Las Vegas Review-Journal‡ PO Box 70 *Web:* www.lvrj.com	Las Vegas	NV	89125	702-383-0211	383-4676
Las Vegas Sun‡ 800 S Valley View Blvd *Web:* www.lasvegassun.com	Las Vegas	NV	89107	702-385-3111	383-7264

‡Daily newspapers

TELEVISION

				Phone	Fax
KBLR-TV Ch 39 (Tele) 5000 W Oakey Suite B-2	Las Vegas	NV	89146	702-258-0039	258-0556
KFBT-TV Ch 33 (Ind) 3830 S Jones Blvd *Web:* pax.net/KFBT ■ *E-mail:* ch33inc@aol.com	Las Vegas	NV	89103	702-783-0033	783-1233
KINC-TV Ch 15 (Uni) 500 Pilot Rd Suite D	Las Vegas	NV	89119	702-434-0015	434-0527
KLAS-TV Ch 8 (CBS) 3228 Channel 8 Dr *Web:* www.klas-tv.com ■ *E-mail:* klas@infi.net	Las Vegas	NV	89109	702-792-8888	734-7437
KLVX-TV Ch 10 (PBS) 4210 Channel 10 Dr *Web:* www.klvx.org	Las Vegas	NV	89119	702-799-1010	799-5586
KTNV-TV Ch 13 (ABC) 3355 S Valley View Blvd *Web:* www.ktnv.com ■ *E-mail:* ktnv13@ktnv.com	Las Vegas	NV	89102	702-876-1313	876-2237
KVBC-TV Ch 3 (NBC) PO Box 44169 *Web:* www.wherenewscomesfirst.com ■ *E-mail:* ch3@kvbc.com	Las Vegas	NV	89116	702-642-3333	657-3152
KVVU-TV Ch 5 (Fox) 25 TV 5 Dr *Web:* www.kvvutv.com	Henderson	NV	89104	702-435-5555	451-4220
KVWB-TV Ch 21 (WB) 3830 S Jones Blvd *Web:* www.wb21.com ■ *E-mail:* info@wb21.com	Las Vegas	NV	89103	702-382-2121	382-1351

RADIO

				Phone	Fax
KBAD-AM 920 kHz (N/T) 4660 S Decatur Blvd	Las Vegas	NV	89103	702-876-1460	876-6685
KBOX-AM 1280 (Span) 953 E Sahara Ave Suite 255	Las Vegas	NV	89104	702-732-1664	732-1937
KCEP-FM 88.1 MHz (NPR) 330 W Washington Ave *Web:* www.kcepfm88.com	Las Vegas	NV	89106	702-648-4218	647-0803
KDWN-AM 720 kHz (N/T) 1 Main St	Las Vegas	NV	89101	702-385-7212	
KENO-AM 1460 kHz (N/T) 4660 S Decatur Blvd	Las Vegas	NV	89103	702-876-1460	876-6685
KFMS-AM 1410 kHz (Ctry) 1130 Desert Inn Rd	Las Vegas	NV	89109	702-732-7753	732-4890
KFMS-FM 101.9 MHz (Ctry) 1130 E Desert Inn Rd	Las Vegas	NV	89109	702-732-7753	792-9018
KISS-FM 103.5 (Alt) 1455 E Tropicana Ave Suite 650	Las Vegas	NV	89119	702-795-1035	798-1738
KJUL-FM 104.3 MHz (Nost) 1455 E Tropicana Ave Suite 440 *Web:* www.kjul.com/ ■ *E-mail:* kjul@kjul.com	Las Vegas	NV	89119	702-248-9100	248-9107
KKLZ-FM 96.3 MHz (CR) 1455 E Tropicana Ave *Web:* www.kklz.com	Las Vegas	NV	89119	702-739-9600	739-0083
KLAV-AM 1230 kHz (N/T) 1810 Weldon Pl *Web:* www.klav1230am.com ■ *E-mail:* klavradio@aol.com	Las Vegas	NV	89104	702-796-1230	796-7433
KLSQ-AM 870 kHz (Span) 6767 W Tropicana Ave Suite 102	Las Vegas	NV	89103	702-367-3322	284-6475
KLUC-FM 98.5 MHz (Rock) 6655 Sahara Ave Suite D208 *Web:* www.kluc.com/ ■ *E-mail:* music@kluc.com	Las Vegas	NV	89146	702-253-9800	889-7398
KMXB-FM 94.1 MHz (AC) 6655 W Sahara Ave Suite C-216	Las Vegas	NV	89102	702-889-5100	257-2936

Las Vegas — Radio (Cont'd)

	City	State	ZIP	Phone	Fax
KMZQ-FM 100.5 MHz (AC) 6655 W Sahara Ave Suite C-216	Las Vegas	NV	89102	702-889-5100	257-2936
KNPR-FM 89.5 MHz (NPR) 1289 S Torrey Pines Dr	Las Vegas	NV	89146	702-258-9895	258-5646
Web: www.knpr.org ■ *E-mail:* info@knpr.org					
KNUU-AM 970 kHz (N/T) 2001 E Flamingo Rd Suite 101	Las Vegas	NV	89119	702-735-8644	735-8184
KOMP-FM 92.3 MHz (Rock) 4660 S Decatur Blvd	Las Vegas	NV	89103	702-876-1460	876-6685
Web: www.komp.com/komp/ ■ *E-mail:* komp@infi.net					
KQOL 93.1 FM (Oldies) 1130 E Desert Inn Rd	Las Vegas	NV	89109	702-732-7753	792-0573
KSNE-FM 106.5 MHz (AC) 1130 E Desert Inn Rd	Las Vegas	NV	89109	702-732-7753	734-1065
KVBC-FM 105.1 MHz (N/T) 1500 Foremaster Ln	Las Vegas	NV	89101	702-657-3105	657-3442
KWNR-FM 95.5 MHz (Ctry) 1130 E Desert Inn Rd	Las Vegas	NV	89109	702-732-7753	733-0433
KXNT-AM 840 kHz (N/T) 6655 W Sahara Ave Suite D-208	Las Vegas	NV	89102	702-364-8400	889-7384
KXPT-FM 97.1 MHz (CR) 4660 S Decatur Blvd	Las Vegas	NV	89103	702-876-1460	876-1886
Web: www.point97.com					
KXTE-FM 107.5 MHz (Alt) 6655 W Sahara Ave Suite C202	Las Vegas	NV	89102	702-257-1075	889-7575
Web: www.xtremeradio.com/					

— Colleges/Universities —

	City	State	ZIP	Phone	Fax
Community College of Southern Nevada Cheyenne Campus 3200 E Cheyenne Ave	North Las Vegas	NV	89030	702-651-4000	643-1474
Web: www.ccsn.nevada.edu					
University of Nevada Las Vegas 4505 S Maryland Pkwy	Las Vegas	NV	89154	702-895-3011	895-1118
TF: 800-334-8658 ■ *Web:* www.unlv.edu ■ *E-mail:* witter@ccmail.nevada.edu					

— Hospitals —

	City	State	ZIP	Phone	Fax
Columbia Sunrise Hospital & Medical Center 3186 S Maryland Pkwy	Las Vegas	NV	89109	702-731-8000	731-8668
Desert Springs Hospital 2075 E Flamingo Rd	Las Vegas	NV	89119	702-733-8800	369-7836
Saint Rose Dominican Hospital 102 E Lake Mead Dr	Henderson	NV	89015	702-564-2622	564-4699
University Medical Center 1800 W Charleston Blvd	Las Vegas	NV	89102	702-383-2000	383-2067
Web: www.umc-cares.org ■ *E-mail:* umcweb@co.clark.nv.us					
Valley Hospital Medical Center 620 Shadow Ln	Las Vegas	NV	89106	702-388-4000	388-4618

— Attractions —

	City	State	ZIP	Phone	Fax
Artemus W Ham Concert Hall 4505 Maryland Pkwy PO Box 455005	Las Vegas	NV	89154	702-895-3535	895-4714
Web: pac.nevada.edu ■ *E-mail:* romito@nevada.edu					
Bonnie Springs Ranch 1 Gunfighter Ln	Las Vegas	NV	89004	702-875-4191	875-4424
Boulder City/Hoover Dam Museum 1305 Arizona St	Boulder City	NV	89005	702-294-1988	294-4380
Caesars Palace Omnimax Theater 3570 Las Vegas Blvd S	Las Vegas	NV	89109	702-731-7900	
Cirque du Soleil Mystère c/o Treasure Island at the Mirage 3300 Las Vegas Blvd S	Las Vegas	NV	89109	702-894-7790	894-7789
Web: www.cirquedusoleil.com/en/piste/mystere/index.html					
Cirque du Soleil 'O' c/o Bellagio Hotel 3600 Las Vegas Blvd S	Las Vegas	NV	89109	702-693-7790	693-7768
Web: www.cirquedusoleil.com/en/piste/o/index.html					
Clark County Heritage Museum 1830 S Boulder Hwy	Henderson	NV	89015	702-455-7955	455-7948
Cranberry World West 1301 American Pacific Dr	Henderson	NV	89014	702-566-7160	566-7159
Ethel M Chocolate Factory 2 Cactus Garden Dr	Henderson	NV	89014	702-458-8864	392-2587*
**Fax Area Code:* 800 ■ *TF:* 800-225-3792 ■ *Web:* www.ethelm.com					
Floyd Lamb State Park 9200 Tule Springs Rd	Las Vegas	NV	89131	702-486-5413	486-5423
Freemont Street Experience Fremont St-betw Main St & Las Vegas Blvd	Las Vegas	NV	89101	702-678-5777	678-5611
TF: 800-249-3559 ■ *Web:* www.pcap.com/frmntexp.htm					
Grand Slam Canyon Adventuredome 2880 Las Vegas Blvd S	Las Vegas	NV	89109	702-734-0410	792-2846
Guinness World of Records Museum 2780 Las Vegas Blvd S	Las Vegas	NV	89109	702-792-3766	792-0530
Hoover Dam Rt 93	Boulder City	NV	89006	702-293-8367	
Web: www.hooverdam.com					
Imperial Palace Auto Collection 3535 Las Vegas Blvd S	Las Vegas	NV	89109	702-731-3311	
International Marshmallow Factory 1180 Marshmallow Ln	Henderson	NV	89014	702-564-3878	564-6382
Lake Mead National Recreation Area 601 Nevada Hwy	Boulder City	NV	89005	702-293-8920	293-8936
Web: www.nps.gov/lame/					
Las Vegas Art Museum 9600 W Sahara Ave	Las Vegas	NV	89117	702-360-8000	360-8080
Web: www.lastplace.com/EXHIBITS/LVAM/index.htm					
Las Vegas Natural History Museum 900 Las Vegas Blvd N	Las Vegas	NV	89101	702-384-3466	384-5343
Web: vegaswebworld.com/lvnathistory					
Lee's Ron World of Clowns 330 Carousel Pkwy	Henderson	NV	89014	702-434-1700	434-4310
Liberace Museum 1775 E Tropicana Ave	Las Vegas	NV	89119	702-798-5595	798-7386
Web: www.liberace.org/museum.html					
Lied Discovery Children's Museum 833 Las Vegas Blvd N	Las Vegas	NV	89101	702-382-3445	382-0592
Lost City Museum of Archeology 721 S Moapa Valley Blvd	Overton	NV	89040	702-397-2193	397-8987
Web: enos.comnett.net/~kolson					
Luxor IMAX Theatre 3900 Las Vegas Blvd S	Las Vegas	NV	89119	702-262-4555	
Magic & Movie Hall of Fame 3555 Las Vegas Blvd S	Las Vegas	NV	89109	702-737-1343	737-3846
MGM Grand Hotel & Casino 3799 Las Vegas Blvd S	Las Vegas	NV	89109	702-891-1111	891-3036
TF: 800-929-1111 ■ *Web:* www.mgmgrand.com					
Nevada Ballet Theatre 1651 Inner Cir	Las Vegas	NV	89134	702-898-6306	804-0364
Web: www.nvballet.com					
Nevada Dance Theater 4505 S Maryland Pkwy Performing Arts Center	Las Vegas	NV	89154	702-895-2787	
Nevada Opera Theatre 4080 Paradise Rd Suite 15	Las Vegas	NV	89109	702-699-9775	699-9831
Nevada State Museum & Historical Society 700 Twin Lakes Dr	Las Vegas	NV	89107	702-486-5205	486-5172
Web: dmla.clan.lib.nv.us/docs/museums/lv/vegas.htm					
Nevada Symphony Orchestra 557 E Sahara Ave	Las Vegas	NV	89104	702-792-4337	
Old Las Vegas Mormon Fort State Historic Park 908 Las Vegas Blvd N	Las Vegas	NV	89158	702-486-3511	
OMNIMAX Theater 3570 Las Vegas Blvd S	Las Vegas	NV	89109	702-731-7901	
Red Rock Canyon National Conservation Area Red Rock Canyon	Las Vegas	NV	89124	702-363-1921	
Reed Whipple Cultural Arts Center 821 Las Vegas Blvd N	Las Vegas	NV	89101	702-229-6211	382-5199
Southern Nevada Zoological Society 1775 N Rancho Dr	Las Vegas	NV	89106	702-648-5955	648-5955
Treasure Island 3300 Las Vegas Blvd S	Las Vegas	NV	89109	702-894-7111	894-7414
Web: www.treasureislandlasvegas.com					
University of Nevada Las Vegas Barrick Museum of Natural History 4505 S Maryland Pkwy	Las Vegas	NV	89154	702-895-3381	895-3094
Web: hrcweb.lv-hrc.nevada.edu					
University of Nevada Las Vegas Performing Arts Center 4505 Maryland Pkwy	Las Vegas	NV	89154	702-895-2787	895-1940
Web: pac.nevada.edu/					
Valley of Fire State Park I-15 N to exit 75	Overton	NV	89040	702-397-2088	
Wet 'n Wild 2601 NW Las Vegas Blvd	Las Vegas	NV	89102	702-734-0088	871-8060
Web: www.wetwild.com					

Las Vegas — Attractions (Cont'd)

				Phone	Fax
World of Coca-Cola Las Vegas 3785 Las Vegas Blvd S *Fax Area Code: 702	Las Vegas	NV	89109	800-720-2653	740-5439*

SPORTS TEAMS & FACILITIES

				Phone	Fax
Las Vegas Speedway Park 7000 Las Vegas Blvd N	Las Vegas	NV	89115	702-644-4444	
Las Vegas Stars (baseball) 850 Las Vegas Blvd N Cashman Field *Web:* www.lasvegasstars.com ■ *E-mail:* jsacc@lasvegasstars.com	Las Vegas	NV	89101	702-386-7200	386-7214
Las Vegas Thunder (hockey) 4505 S Maryland Pkwy Thomas & Mack Ctr	Las Vegas	NV	89154	702-798-7825	798-9464
MGM Grand Garden Arena 3799 Las Vegas Blvd S	Las Vegas	NV	89109	702-891-7800	891-7831
Thomas & Mack Center/Sam Boyd Stadium 4505 S Maryland Pkwy Box 45000 *TF:* 800-406-2566 ■ *Web:* www.thomasandmack.com	Las Vegas	NV	89154	702-895-3761	895-1099

— Events —

	Phone
Big League Weekends (early April)	702-386-7200
Columbus Day Parade (mid-October)	702-892-0711
Comdex Computer Show (mid-November)	781-449-6600
Fremont Street Holiday Festival (late November)	800-249-3559
International Food Festival (May)	702-258-8961
International Mariachi Festival (mid-September)	800-637-1006
Las Vegas Bowl (late December)	702-895-3900
Las Vegas International Marathon & Half-Marathon (February)	702-876-3870
Las Vegas Invitational PGA Golf Tournament (mid-May)	702-242-3000
Las Vegas Jaycees State Fair (early October)	702-457-8832
Las Vegas Mardi Gras (mid-February)	702-678-5777
Las Vegas Senior Classic (late April)	702-242-3000
National Finals Rodeo (early-mid-December)	702-895-3900
Native American Arts Festival (early April)	702-455-7955
Parade of Lights (early December)	702-293-2034
Winston Cup Race (early March)	702-644-4444
World Series of Poker (late April-mid-May)	702-366-7397

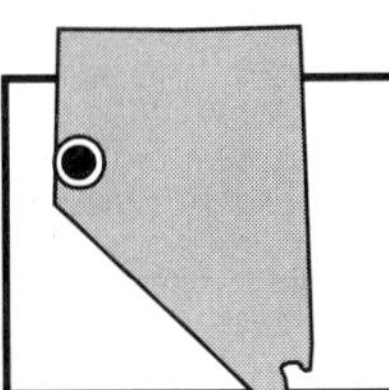

Reno

Since the opening of its first major casinos in 1935, gaming has become a favorite pastime at the many casinos of present-day Reno. "The Biggest Little Town in the World" sits between the slopes of the Sierra and the low eastern hills. Sierra trails provide hikers with a view of mountain forests, meadows, and scenic waterfalls. Southwest of Reno is Lake Tahoe, the largest alpine lake in North America. The Lake lies half in Nevada and half in California, and its size and amazing clarity make it ideal for all types of water sports. During the winter months the Tahoe area is filled with visitors to its world-class alpine resorts.

Population	163,334	**Longitude**	119-81-28 W
Area (Land)	57.5 sq mi	**County**	Washoe
Area (Water)	0.2 sq mi	**Time Zone**	PST
Elevation	4498 ft	**Area Code/s**	775
Latitude	39-52-97 N		

— Average Temperatures and Precipitation —

TEMPERATURES

	Jan	Feb	Mar	Apr	May	Jun	Jul	Aug	Sep	Oct	Nov	Dec
High	45	52	56	64	73	83	92	90	80	69	54	46
Low	21	24	29	33	40	47	51	50	41	33	27	20

PRECIPITATION

	Jan	Feb	Mar	Apr	May	Jun	Jul	Aug	Sep	Oct	Nov	Dec
Inches	1.1	1.0	0.7	0.4	0.7	0.5	0.3	0.3	0.4	0.4	0.9	1.0

— Important Phone Numbers —

	Phone		Phone
AAA	775-826-8800	**Poison Control Center**	775-328-4129
American Express Travel	775-689-7700	**Road Conditions**	775-688-2500
Emergency	911	**Time**	775-844-1212
HotelDocs	800-468-3537	**Weather**	775-793-1300

— Information Sources —

				Phone	Fax
Better Business Bureau Serving Northern Nevada 991 Bible Way *Web:* www.reno.bbb.org	Reno	NV	89502	775-322-0657	322-8163
Nevada State Chamber of Commerce 405 Marsh Ave *Web:* www.reno-sparkschamber.org	Reno	NV	89509	775-686-3030	686-3038
Reno City Hall 490 S Center St *Web:* www.reno.gov	Reno	NV	89501	775-334-2020	334-2097
Reno Community Development Dept PO Box 1900	Reno	NV	89505	775-334-2060	334-2043
Reno Mayor PO Box 1900	Reno	NV	89505	775-334-2001	334-2097
Reno-Sparks Convention & Visitors Authority 4590 S Virginia St. *TF:* 800-443-1482 ■ *Web:* www.playreno.com	Reno	NV	89502	775-827-7600	827-7686
Reno-Sparks Convention Center 4590 S Virginia St.	Reno	NV	89502	775-827-7600	827-7713
Washoe County PO Box 11130	Reno	NV	89520	775-328-3260	328-3582
Washoe County Library PO Box 2151 *Web:* www.washoe.lib.nv.us ■ *E-mail:* jkup@washoe.lib.nv.us	Reno	NV	89505	775-785-4190	785-4609

On-Line Resources

About.com Guide to Reno/Tahoe	renotahoe.about.com
Anthill City Guide Reno	www.anthill.com/city.asp?city=reno
Area Guide Reno	reno.areaguides.net
City Knowledge Reno	www.cityknowledge.com/nv_reno.htm
Excite.com Reno City Guide	www.excite.com/travel/countries/united_states/nevada/reno
HotelGuide Reno/Sparks	hotelguide.net/reno/
Insiders' Guide to Reno & Lake Tahoe	www.insiders.com/reno-tahoe/index.htm
NevadaNet.com	www.nevadanet.com
NITC Travelbase City Guide Reno	www.travelbase.com/auto/guides/reno-area-nv.html
PlayReno.com	www.playreno.com
Reno Nevada	www.renonv.com
Reno Nevada	reno-nevada.com
Reno Pages	www.renopages.com/
Reno Tahoe Territory	www.renotahoe.com
Reno.Net	www.reno.net/
Virtual Voyages Reno	www.virtualvoyages.com/usa/nv/reno/reno.sht

— Transportation Services —

AIRPORTS

	Phone
■ **Reno-Tahoe International Airport (RNO)**	
5 miles SE of downtown (approx 15 minutes) Web: www.renoairport.com	775-328-6400

Airport Transportation

	Phone
Airport Minibus $2.75 fare to downtown	775-786-3700
Reno-Sparks Cab $8-10 fare to downtown	775-333-3333

Reno (Cont'd)

Commercial Airlines

	Phone		Phone
America West	800-235-9292	**SkyWest**	800-453-9417
American	800-433-7300	**Southwest**	800-435-9792
Continental	800-525-0280	**United**	800-241-6522
Delta	800-221-1212	**United Express**	800-241-6522
Northwest	800-225-2525		

Charter Airlines

	Phone		Phone
Berry Aviation	800-229-2379	**Tag Aviation**	800-252-6972
Priester Aviation	847-537-1200		

CAR RENTALS

	Phone		Phone
Alamo	775-323-8306	**Enterprise**	775-329-3773
Avis	775-785-2727	**Hertz**	775-785-2554
Budget	775-785-2541	**Resort**	775-348-1535
Dollar	800-800-4000	**Thrifty**	775-329-0096

LIMO/TAXI

	Phone		Phone
Bell Luxury Limousine	775-786-3700	**Sierra West Limousine**	775-329-4310
Executive Limousine	775-333-3300	**Whittlesea Checker Cab**	775-322-2222
Reno-Sparks Cab	775-333-3333	**Yellow/Deluxe Cab**	775-355-5555

MASS TRANSIT

	Phone
Citifare $1.25 Base fare	775-348-7433

RAIL/BUS

				Phone
Amtrak Station 135 E Commercial Row	Reno	NV	89501	800-872-7245
Greyhound/Trailways Bus Station 155 Stevenson St.	Reno	NV	89503	775-322-2970

— Accommodations —

HOTEL RESERVATION SERVICES

	Phone	Fax
Hotel Reservations Network Inc	214-361-7311	361-7299

TF Sales: 800-964-6835 ■ *Web:* www.hoteldiscount.com

HOTELS, MOTELS, RESORTS

				Phone	Fax
All Suites Executive Inn 205 S Sierra	Reno	NV	89501	775-786-4050	786-5849
TF: 800-648-4545					
Ascuaga's John Nugget Hotel Casino 1100 Nugget Ave	Sparks	NV	89431	775-356-3300	356-4198
TF: 800-843-2427 ■ *Web:* janugget.com					
Atlantis Casino Resort 3800 S Virginia St	Reno	NV	89502	775-825-4700	826-7860
TF: 800-723-6500 ■ *Web:* atlantiscasino.com ■ *E-mail:* mkt@atlantis.reno.nv.us					
Best Inns & Suites 1885 S Virginia St.	Reno	NV	89502	775-329-1001	324-5402
TF: 800-626-1900					
Best Western Airport Plaza Hotel 1981 Terminal Way	Reno	NV	89502	775-348-6370	329-1863
TF: 800-648-3525					
Cal-Neva/Virginian Hotel & Casino Virginia & 2nd Sts	Reno	NV	89505	775-954-4540	785-3299
TF: 877-777-7303					
Circus Circus Hotel & Casino Reno 500 N Sierra St.	Reno	NV	89503	775-329-0711	328-9652
TF: 800-648-5010 ■ *Web:* www.circusreno.com					
Colonial Inn Hotel & Casino Arlington 250 N Arlington	Reno	NV	89501	775-322-3838	323-4588
TF: 800-336-7366					
Colonial Motor Inn 232 West St	Reno	NV	89501	775-786-5038	323-4588
TF: 800-255-7366					
Comstock Hotel & Casino 200 W 2nd St.	Reno	NV	89512	775-329-1880	348-0539
TF: 800-648-4866 ■ *Web:* www.thecomstock.com					
Crest Inn 525 W 4th St	Reno	NV	89503	775-329-0808	
Days Inn 701 E 7th St	Reno	NV	89512	775-786-4070	329-4338
TF: 800-448-4555					
Eldorado Hotel Casino 345 N Virginia St	Reno	NV	89501	775-786-5700	322-7124
TF: 800-648-5966 ■ *Web:* www.eldoradoreno.com/					
Fitzgeralds Casino Hotel 255 N Virginia St	Reno	NV	89504	775-786-3663	786-7180
TF: 800-648-5022 ■ *Web:* www.fitzgeralds.com ■ *E-mail:* info@fitzgeralds.com					
Flamingo Hilton Reno 255 N Sierra St	Reno	NV	89501	775-322-1111	785-7057*
**Fax:* Mktg ■ *TF:* 800-648-4882 ■ *Web:* www.allcasinos.com/flamingoreno/					
Gold Dust West Casino & Motor Lodge 444 Vine St	Reno	NV	89503	775-323-2211	786-2545
TF: 800-438-9378					
Harrah's Casino Hotel Reno 219 N Center St.	Reno	NV	89501	775-786-3232	788-2815
TF: 800-427-7247 ■ *Web:* www.allcasinos.com/harrahs/reno/					
Holiday Inn 1000 E 6th St	Reno	NV	89512	775-786-5151	786-2447
TF: 800-648-4877					
La Quinta Motor Inn 4001 Market St.	Reno	NV	89502	775-348-6100	348-8794
TF: 800-531-5900					
McCarran House 55 E Nugget Ave	Sparks	NV	89431	775-358-6900	359-6065
TF: 800-548-5798					
Motel 6 West 1400 Stardust St	Reno	NV	89503	775-747-7390	747-4527
TF: 800-466-8356					
Peppermill Hotel & Casino 2707 S Virginia St.	Reno	NV	89502	775-826-2121	826-5205
TF: 800-282-2444 ■ *Web:* www.peppermillcasinos.com ■ *E-mail:* hotel@sierra.net					
Pioneer Inn Hotel & Casino 221 S Virginia St	Reno	NV	89501	775-324-7777	323-5343
TF: 800-648-5468					
Ramada Inn Speakeasy Casino 200 E 6th St.	Reno	NV	89501	775-329-7400	329-5934
TF: 888-736-6777					
Reno Hilton by Marriott 2500 E 2nd St.	Reno	NV	89595	775-789-2000	789-1677*
**Fax:* PR ■ *TF:* 800-736-6386 ■ *Web:* www.renohilton.net/					
Residence Inn by Marriott 9845 Gateway Dr	Reno	NV	89511	775-853-8800	853-8805
TF: 800-331-3131 ■ *Web:* residenceinn.com/RNORI					
Seasons Inn 495 West St.	Reno	NV	89503	775-322-6000	324-6434
TF: 800-322-8588					
Showboat Inn 660 N Virginia St	Reno	NV	89501	775-786-4032	786-4032
TF: 800-648-3960					
Silver Legacy Resort & Casino 407 N Virginia St	Reno	NV	89501	775-329-4777	325-7474
TF: 800-687-8733 ■ *Web:* www.silverlegacy.com					
Sundowner Hotel & Casino 450 N Arlington Ave	Reno	NV	89503	775-786-7050	348-6074
TF: 800-648-5490 ■ *Web:* www.sundownercasino.com/					
Super 8 5851 S Virginia St.	Reno	NV	89502	775-825-2940	826-3835
TF: 800-797-7366					
Travelodge 2050 Market St	Reno	NV	89502	775-786-2500	786-3884
TF: 800-648-3800					
Travelodge Downtown 655 W 4th St.	Reno	NV	89503	775-329-3451	329-3454
TF: 800-578-7878					
Vagabond Inn 3131 S Virginia St	Reno	NV	89502	775-825-7134	825-3096
TF: 800-522-1555					
Windsor Inn 60 E Victorian Ave	Sparks	NV	89431	775-356-7770	355-1754
TF: 800-892-3506					

— Restaurants —

				Phone
19th Hole Restaurant (American) 1200 Razor Back Rd.	Reno	NV	89509	775-825-1250
Adele's at the Plaza (American) 425 S Virginia St.	Reno	NV	89509	775-333-6503
Bangkok Cuisine (Thai) 55 Mt Rose St.	Reno	NV	89509	775-322-0299
Bavarian World (German) 595 Valley Rd.	Reno	NV	89512	775-323-7646
Bertha Miranda's (Mexican) 336 Mill St.	Reno	NV	89501	775-786-9697
Bonanza's Cactus Creek Bar & Grille (Southwest) 4720 N Virginia St	Reno	NV	89506	775-323-2724
Brew Brothers Microbrewery (American) 4th & Virginia Sts	Reno	NV	89502	775-786-5700
Bricks (Continental) 1695 S Virginia St.	Reno	NV	89502	775-786-2277
Cafe de Thai (Thai) 3314 S McCarran Blvd	Reno	NV	89502	775-829-8424
Cafe Soleil (American) 4796 Caughlin Pkwy	Reno	NV	89509	775-828-6444
Cantina Los Tres Hombres (Mexican) 7111 S Virginia St.	Reno	NV	89511	775-852-0202
Web: www.cantinalth.com/				
Casablanca Grill (American) 7689 S Virginia St	Reno	NV	89511	775-852-1942
China East Restaurant (Chinese) 1086A S Virginia St	Reno	NV	89502	775-348-7020
Famous Murphy's (American) 3127 S Virginia St.	Reno	NV	89502	775-827-4111
Galena Forest Restaurant (European) 17025 Mt Rose Hwy.	Reno	NV	89511	775-849-2100
Golden Flower (Vietnamese) 205 W 5th St.	Reno	NV	89503	775-323-1628
Ichiban Japanese Steak House (Japanese) 210 N Sierra St	Reno	NV	89501	775-323-5550
La Strada (Italian) 345 N Virginia St	Reno	NV	89501	775-348-9297
Liberty Belle Saloon & Restaurant (American) 4250 S Virginia St	Reno	NV	89502	775-825-1776
Louis' Basque Corner (French) 301 E 4th St.	Reno	NV	89512	775-323-7203
Luciano's (Italian) 719 S Virginia St.	Reno	NV	89501	775-322-7373
Murrieta's Cantina & Restaurant (Mexican) 4385 Neil Rd	Reno	NV	89510	775-827-3585
Pho 777 Vietnamese Restaurant (Vietnamese) 201 E 2nd St	Reno	NV	89501	775-323-7777
Pimparel's La Table Francaise (French) 3065 W 4th St.	Reno	NV	89503	775-323-3200
Rapscallion Seafood House (Seafood) 1555 S Wells	Reno	NV	89502	775-323-1211
Sapna Indian Restaurant (Indian) 3374 Kietzke	Reno	NV	89502	775-829-1537
Web: www.renonv.com/sapna/				

Reno — Restaurants (Cont'd)

				Phone
Seoul Restaurant (Korean) 1999 S Virginia St	Reno	NV	89509	775-829-2115
Super Indian (Indian) 1030 S Virginia St	Reno	NV	89502	775-322-5577
White Orchid (French) 2707 S Virginia St	Reno	NV	89502	775-826-2121

— Goods and Services —

SHOPPING

				Phone	Fax
Meadowood Mall Virginia & McCarren Sts	Reno	NV	89502	775-827-8450	826-0560
Old Town Mall 4001 S Virginia St	Reno	NV	89502	775-823-9666	823-4699
Park Lane Mall 310 E Plumb Ln	Reno	NV	89502	775-825-7878	825-4375
Shopper's Square Mall 277 E Plumb Ln	Reno	NV	89502	775-323-0430	323-6824
Town Center Mall 100 N Sierra St	Reno	NV	89501	775-333-2828	333-2828
Virginia Street Antique Mall 1251 S Virginia St	Reno	NV	89502	775-324-4141	324-7469
E-mail: jose@consumers1st.com					

BANKS

				Phone	Fax
Bank of America 5905 S Virginia St	Reno	NV	89502	775-688-8900	688-8908
Bank of the West 4950 Kietzke Ln	Reno	NV	89509	775-689-2300	689-2333
TF: 800-488-2265					
Heritage Bank of Nevada 1401 S Virginia St	Reno	NV	89502	775-348-1000	348-1022
Pioneer Citizens Bank of Nevada 1 W Liberty	Reno	NV	89505	775-688-7950	688-7963
US Bank 300 S Virginia St	Reno	NV	89501	775-688-6620	348-2730
TF: 800-872-2657					

BUSINESS SERVICES

	Phone
Accustaff Inc	775-322-5004
Airborne Express	800-247-2676
BAX Global	800-225-5229
DHL Worldwide Express	800-225-5345
Federal Express	800-238-5355
Kinko's	775-322-5277
Mail Boxes Etc	800-789-4623
OfficeTeam	775-786-9341
Olsten Staffing Services	775-786-6066
Post Office	775-788-0660
UPS	800-742-5877

— Media —

PUBLICATIONS

				Phone	Fax
Daily Sparks Tribune‡ 1002 C St	Sparks	NV	89431	775-358-8061	359-3837
TF: 800-669-1338					
Reno Gazette Journal‡ PO Box 22000	Reno	NV	89520	775-788-6200	788-6458
TF: 800-648-5048 ■ *Web:* www.rgj.com					

‡Daily newspapers

TELEVISION

				Phone	Fax
KAME-TV Ch 21 (UPN) 4920 Brookside Ct	Reno	NV	89502	775-856-2121	856-3915
KNPB-TV Ch 5 (PBS) 1670 N Virginia St	Reno	NV	89503	775-784-4555	784-1438
Web: www.knpb.org					
KOLO-TV Ch 8 (ABC) PO Box 10000	Reno	NV	89510	775-858-8888	858-8877
Web: www.kolotv.com ■ *E-mail:* admin@kolotv.com					
KREN-TV Ch 27 (WB) 940 Matley Ln Suite 15	Reno	NV	89502	775-333-2727	333-6827
KRNV-TV Ch 4 (NBC) 1790 Vassar St	Reno	NV	89502	775-322-4444	785-1206
Web: www.krnv.com ■ *E-mail:* comments@krnv.com					
KRXI-TV Ch 11 (Fox) 4920 Brookside Ct	Reno	NV	89502	775-856-1100	856-2100
KTVN-TV Ch 2 (CBS) 4925 Energy Way	Reno	NV	89502	775-858-2222	861-4298
Web: www.ktvn.com ■ *E-mail:* ktvn@ktvn.com					

RADIO

				Phone	Fax
KCBN-AM 1230 kHz (Nost) 255 W Moana Ln Suite 208	Reno	NV	89509	775-829-1964	825-3183
TF: 800-896-1669					
KDOT-FM 104.5 MHz (Rock) 2900 Sutro St	Reno	NV	89512	775-329-9261	323-1450
Web: www.kdot.com					
KODS-FM 103.7 MHz (Oldies) 255 W Moana Ln Suite 208	Reno	NV	89509	775-829-1964	825-3183
KOZZ-FM 105.7 MHz (CR) 2900 Sutro St	Reno	NV	89512	775-329-9261	323-1450
KPLY-AM 1270 kHz (Sports) 255 W Moana Ln Suite 208	Reno	NV	89509	775-829-1964	825-3183
KRNO-FM 106.9 MHz (AC) 255 W Moana Ln Suite 208	Reno	NV	89509	775-829-1964	825-3183
KRZQ-FM 100.9 MHz (Alt) 2395 Tampa St	Reno	NV	89512	775-333-0123	333-0101
Web: www.krzq.com					
KTHX-FM 100.1 MHz (AAA) 2395 Tampa St	Reno	NV	89512	775-333-0123	333-0101
KUNR-FM 88.7 MHz (NPR) University of Nevada MS-294	Reno	NV	89557	775-784-1867	784-1381
Web: www.kunr.org/ ■ *E-mail:* kunr@unr.edu					
KWNZ-FM 97.3 MHz (CHR) 255 W Moana Ln Suite 208	Reno	NV	89509	775-829-1964	825-3183
Web: www.kwnz.com					

— Colleges/Universities —

				Phone	Fax
Morrison College 140 Washington St	Reno	NV	89503	775-323-4145	323-8495
Web: www.morrison.edu					
Truckee Meadows Community College 7000 Dandini Blvd	Reno	NV	89512	775-673-7042	673-7028
Web: www.tmcc.edu ■ *E-mail:* costa_lisa@tmcc.edu					
University of Nevada Reno 1664 N Virginia St	Reno	NV	89557	775-784-1110	784-4283
Web: www.unr.edu					

— Hospitals —

				Phone	Fax
Ioannis A Lougaris Veterans Affairs Medical Center 1000 Locust St	Reno	NV	89520	775-786-7200	328-1464
Saint Mary's Regional Medical Center 235 W 6th St	Reno	NV	89520	775-323-2041	789-3958*
**Fax:* Admitting ■ *Web:* www.saintmarysreno.com					
Washoe Medical Center 77 Pringle Way	Reno	NV	89520	775-982-4100	982-4111

— Attractions —

				Phone	Fax
Animal Ark Wildlife Sanctuary & Nature Center 1265 Deerlodge Rd	Reno	NV	89506	775-969-3111	
Fleischmann Planetarium The Space Place University of Nevada	Reno	NV	89557	775-784-4811	784-4822
Web: www.scs.unr.edu/planet/					
Gothic North Theater 3697-A Kings Row	Reno	NV	89503	775-329-7529	
Web: www.gothic-north.org/ ■ *E-mail:* info@gothic-north.org					
Lake Tahoe Nevada State Park 2005 Hwy 28	Incline Village	NV	89450	775-831-0494	831-2514
May Wilbur D Great Basin Adventure Park 1502 Washington St	Reno	NV	89503	775-785-4153	
National Automobile Museum 10 Lake St S	Reno	NV	89501	775-333-9300	333-9309
National Bowling Stadium 300 N Center St	Reno	NV	89501	775-334-2600	334-2606
TF: 800-304-2695 ■ *Web:* bowl.renolaketahoe.com/main.html					
Nevada Historical Society Museum 1650 N Virginia St	Reno	NV	89503	775-688-1190	688-2917
Web: dmla.clan.lib.nv.us/docs/museums/reno/his-soc.htm					
Nevada Museum of Art 160 W Liberty St	Reno	NV	89501	775-329-3333	329-1541
Web: www.nevadaart.org/					
Nevada Opera Assn PO Box 3256	Reno	NV	89505	775-786-4046	786-4063
TF: 800-992-2072					
Ponderosa Ranch 100 Ponderosa Ranch Rd	Incline Village	NV	89451	775-831-0691	831-0113
Web: www.ponderosaranch.com					
Reno Municipal Band PO Box 1900	Reno	NV	89502	775-789-2878	
Web: www.sierrasource.com/RenoMunicipalBand/					
Reno Philharmonic 300 S Wells Ave Suite 5	Reno	NV	89502	775-323-6393	323-6711
Sierra Safari Zoo 10200 N Virginia St	Reno	NV	89506	775-677-1101	677-7874
Truckee River Walk 1st & Arlington Sts	Reno	NV	89501	775-334-2262	
Victorian Square 15th St & Pyramid Way	Sparks	NV	89431	775-353-2291	
Washoe Lake State Recreation Area 4855 E Lake Blvd	Carson City	NV	89704	775-687-4319	684-8053
Wilbur D May Museum & Arboretum/Botanical Gardens 1502 Washington St	Reno	NV	89503	775-785-5961	785-4707
Wild Island 250 Wild Island Ct	Sparks	NV	89434	775-331-9453	359-5942
Web: www.wildisland.com					

Reno (Cont'd)

SPORTS TEAMS & FACILITIES

				Phone	Fax
Nevada Zephyrs (soccer) 1331 E Plumb Ln Wooster High School Stadium	Reno	NV	89502	775-826-7487	826-1508

— Events —

	Phone
Best in the West Rib Cook-off (late August-early September)	775-356-3300
Big Easy (mid-July)	775-332-3333
Celebrate the River (early June)	775-827-7600
Celtic New Year Celebration (mid-October)	775-323-3138
Far West Regional Wheelchair Tennis Championship (mid-June)	775-852-7077
Festival of Trees (early-late December)	775-827-7600
Great Italian Festival (mid-October)	775-786-5700
Great Reno Balloon Race (early September)	775-826-1181
Hometown Farmers Market (mid-June-late August)	775-353-2291
Hot August Nights (early August)	775-356-1956
Lake Tahoe Marathon (mid-October)	530-544-7095
National Championship Air Races (mid-September)	775-972-6663
National Senior Pro Rodeo Finals (early-mid-November)	775-323-8842
Nevada Day Parade (October 31)	800-367-7366
Nevada State Fair (late August)	775-688-5767
Reno Basque Festival (late July)	775-329-1476
Reno Rodeo (mid-June)	775-329-3877
Reno Summer Arts Festival (July)	775-329-1324
Shakespeare at Sand Harbor (August)	775-831-0494
Silver State Marathon (late August)	775-849-0419
Skyfire (July 4)	775-332-3333
Sparks Hometown Christmas (early December)	775-353-2291
Street Vibrations (late September)	775-329-7469
Uptown Downtown Artown Festival (July)	775-334-2536
Virginia City Camel Races (mid-September)	775-847-0311

New Hampshire

Population (1999): 1,201,134 **Area (sq mi): 9,351**

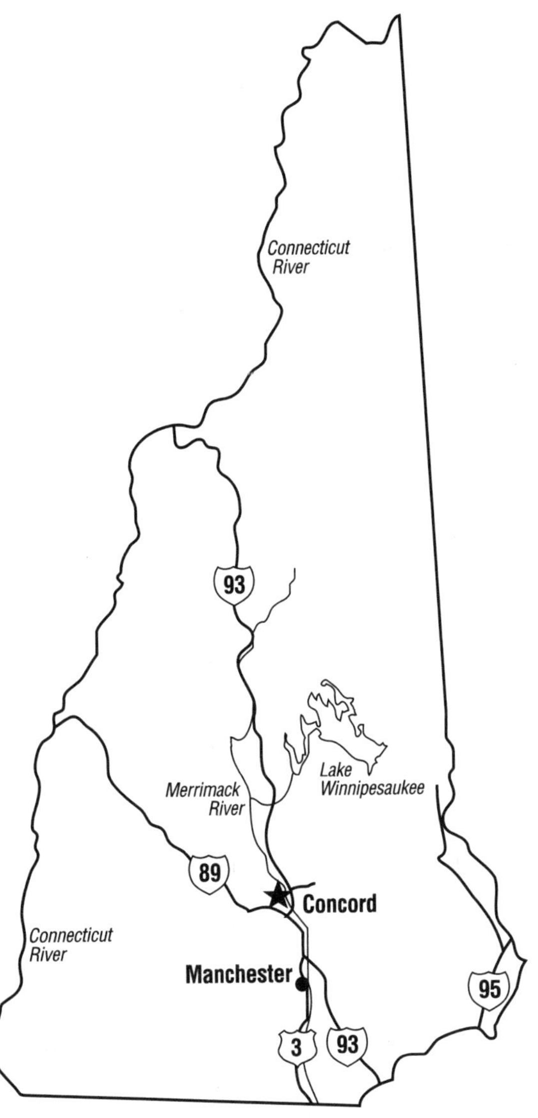

— State Information Sources —

				Phone	Fax
New Hampshire Business & Industry Assn 122 N Main St 3rd Fl. *Web:* www.nhbia.org ■ *E-mail:* ngrbia@aol.com	Concord	NH	03301	603-224-5388	224-2872
New Hampshire Parks & Recreation Div PO Box 1856 *Web:* www.nhparks.state.nh.us	Concord	NH	03302	603-271-3556	271-2629
New Hampshire Resources & Economic Development Dept PO Box 1856 *Web:* www.dred.state.nh.us	Concord	NH	03302	603-271-2412	271-2629
New Hampshire State Government Information *Web:* www.state.nh.us				603-271-1110	
New Hampshire State Library 20 Park St *Web:* www.state.nh.us/nhsl/nhsl.html	Concord	NH	03301	603-271-2144	271-2205
New Hampshire Travel & Tourism Development Office PO Box 1856 *TF:* 800-386-4664 ■ *Web:* www.visitnh.gov ■ *E-mail:* request@visitnh.gov	Concord	NH	03302	603-271-2665	271-6784

ON-LINE RESOURCES

Best Read Guide New Hampshire . . . . . bestreadguide.com/newhampshire
Imbored New Hampshire www.imbored.com/new/rnh01.htm
New Hampshire Accommodations . . . . . www.nettx.com/states/nh.htm
New Hampshire Cities . . . . . dir.yahoo.com/Regional/U_S__States/New_Hampshire/Cities
New Hampshire Counties & Regions . . . . . dir.yahoo.com/Regional/U_S__States/New_Hampshire/Counties_and_Regions
New Hampshire Scenario . . . . . scenariousa.dstylus.com/nh/indexf.htm
New Hampshire Travel & Tourism Guide . . . . . www.travel-library.com/north_america/usa/new_hampshire/index.html
New Hampshire Visitor's Guide . . . . . www.nhweb.com/travel_guide
NewHampshire.com . . . . . www.nh.com
PeekABoo New Hampshire . . . . . www.peekaboo.net/nh
Rough Guide Travel New Hampshire travel.roughguides.com/content/405/index.htm
SeacoastNH.com . . . . . www.seacoastnh.com
Search New Hampshire . . . . . www.newengland.com/nhmap.html
Travel.org-New Hampshire . . . . . travel.org/newhamp.html
What Where When New England . . . . . www.newww.com
Yahoo! Get Local New Hampshire . . . . . dir.yahoo.com/Regional/U_S__States/New_Hampshire

— Cities Profiled —

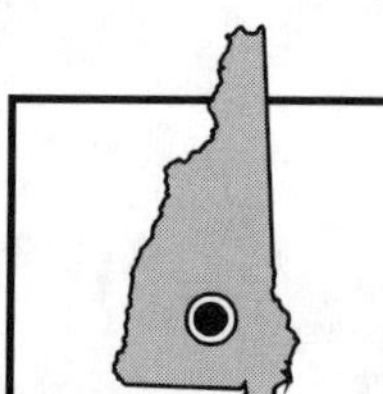

Concord

Situated on the bluffs along the Merrimack River, Concord was first settled by immigrants from Massachusetts in 1725 and became New Hampshire's state capital in 1808. At one time the city was known for its carriage manufacturing, and examples of these Concord coaches are on display today at the Museum of New Hampshire History in Concord. Other major industries in the area include furniture making and granite quarrying - the granite for the U.S. Library of Congress came from the Concord area. A few miles northeast of the city is Canterbury Shaker Village. The Shakers, a religious order, originally settled here in the 1790s, and the Village now serves as a museum of Shaker life where visitors can watch items such as oval boxes, brooms, poplar-ware, and dovetailed totes made in the Shaker tradition. Reproductions of Shaker furniture are available for purchase in the Village gift shop.

Population	37,444	**Longitude**	71-53-81 W
Area (Land)	64.3 sq mi	**County**	Merrimack
Area (Water)	3.2 sq mi	**Time Zone**	EST
Elevation	288 ft	**Area Code/s**	603
Latitude	43-20-81 N		

— Average Temperatures and Precipitation —

TEMPERATURES

	Jan	Feb	Mar	Apr	May	Jun	Jul	Aug	Sep	Oct	Nov	Dec
High	30	33	43	56	69	77	82	80	72	61	47	34
Low	7	10	22	32	41	51	57	55	46	35	27	14

PRECIPITATION

	Jan	Feb	Mar	Apr	May	Jun	Jul	Aug	Sep	Oct	Nov	Dec
Inches	2.5	2.5	2.7	2.9	3.1	3.2	3.2	3.3	2.8	3.2	3.7	3.2

— Important Phone Numbers —

	Phone		*Phone*
AAA	603-228-0301	**Poison Control Center**	800-562-8236
American Express Travel	603-668-7171	**Time/Temp**	603-529-7511
Emergency	911	**Weather**	603-225-5191
HotelDocs	800-468-3537		

— Information Sources —

				Phone	*Fax*
Better Business Bureau Serving New Hampshire 410 S Main St Suite 3 *Web:* www.concord.bbb.org	Concord	NH	03301	603-224-1991	
Concord Chamber of Commerce 244 N Main St *Web:* www.concordnhchamber.com ■ *E-mail:* info@concordnhchamber.com	Concord	NH	03301	603-224-2508	224-8128
Concord City Hall 41 Green St *Web:* www.ci.concord.nh.us/	Concord	NH	03301	603-225-8500	228-2724
Concord Community Development Dept 41 Green St	Concord	NH	03301	603-225-8595	225-8558
Concord Mayor 14 Elm St Box 6116 *Web:* www.ci.concord.nh.us/mayor	Penacook	NH	03303	603-753-4533	753-9324
Concord Public Library 45 Green St *Web:* www.ci.concord.nh.us/quality/library	Concord	NH	03301	603-225-8670	225-8688
Merrimack County 4 Court St Suite 2	Concord	NH	03301	603-228-0331	224-2665
New Hampshire Office of Travel & Tourism PO Box 1856 *TF:* 800-386-4664 ■ *Web:* www.visitnh.gov	Concord	NH	03302	603-271-2343	271-6784

On-Line Resources

Area Guide Concord	concord.areaguides.net
Excite.com Concord City Guide	www.excite.com/travel/countries/united_states/new_hampshire/concord
I-95 Exit Information Guide Concord	www.usastar.com/i95/cityguide/concord.htm

— Transportation Services —

AIRPORTS

■ **Manchester Municipal Airport (MHT)** — *Phone*

15 miles N of downtown Concord (approx 30 minutes) 603-624-6539
Web: www.flymanchester.com ■ *E-mail:* admin@nhms.com

Airport Transportation

	Phone
First Class Transportation $68 fare to downtown Concord	800-252-7754
Queen City Taxi $40 fare to downtown Concord	603-622-0008

Commercial Airlines

	Phone		*Phone*
Continental Express	800-525-0280	**United Express**	800-241-6522
Delta Connection	800-221-1212	**US Airways**	800-428-4322
United	800-241-6522	**US Airways Express**	800-428-4322

CAR RENTALS

	Phone		*Phone*
Avis	603-624-4000	**Budget**	603-668-3166
Avis-Concord	603-225-5652	**Hertz**	603-669-6320

LIMO/TAXI

	Phone		*Phone*
A & P Taxi	603-224-6573	**Checker Cab**	603-228-8197
AA Taxi	603-225-4222	**Concord Cab**	603-225-4222
Central Taxi	603-224-4077	**Starr Limo-Scene Inc**	603-622-5773

MASS TRANSIT

	Phone
Concord Area Transit $.75 Base fare	603-225-1989

RAIL/BUS

				Phone
Concord Trailways Bus Station 30 Stickney Ave	Concord	NH	03301	603-228-3300

— Accommodations —

HOTELS, MOTELS, RESORTS

				Phone	*Fax*
Atwood Maria Inn 71 Hill Rd *Web:* www.atwoodinn.com ■ *E-mail:* info@atwoodinn.com	Franklin	NH	03235	603-934-3666	
Brick Tower Motor Inn 414 S Main St	Concord	NH	03301	603-224-9565	224-6027
Colby Hill Inn The Oaks *TF:* 800-531-0330 ■ *Web:* www.colbyhillinn.com ■ *E-mail:* colbyhillinn@conknet.com	Henniker	NH	03242	603-428-3281	428-9218
Comfort Inn 71 Hall St *TF:* 800-228-5150	Concord	NH	03301	603-226-4100	228-2106
Dame Homestead 205 Horse Corner Rd	Chichester	NH	03234	603-798-5446	
Daniel Webster Motel 188 King St	Boscawen	NH	03303	603-796-2136	796-2703
Days Inn 406 S Main St *TF:* 800-329-7466	Concord	NH	03301	603-224-2511	224-6032
Elmwood Lodge & Motel 200 King St	Boscawen	NH	03303	603-225-2062	
Hampton Inn 515 South St *TF:* 800-426-7866	Bow	NH	03304	603-224-5322	224-4282
Henniker House PO Box 191	Henniker	NH	03242	603-428-3198	
Henniker Motel 5 Craney Pond Rd *TF:* 800-328-5344	Henniker	NH	03242	603-428-3536	
Holiday Inn 172 N Main St *TF:* 800-465-4329	Concord	NH	03301	603-224-9534	224-8266
Inn at Maplewood Farm 447 Center Rd *Web:* www.conknet.com/maplewoodfarm	Hillsboro	NH	03244	603-464-4242	464-5401
Margate Resort 76 Lake St *TF:* 800-627-4283 ■ *Web:* www.themargate.com	Laconia	NH	03246	603-524-5210	528-4485
Meeting House Inn 35 Flanders Rd *Web:* www.conknet.com/meetinghouse ■ *E-mail:* meetinghouse@conknet.com	Henniker	NH	03242	603-428-3228	428-6334

Concord — Hotels, Motels, Resorts (Cont'd)

				Phone	Fax
Misty Harbor Resort Rt 11B	Gilford	NH	03246	603-293-4500	293-4500
Web: www.mistyharbor.net ■ *E-mail:* misty@mistyharbor.net					
Mural House Bed & Breakfast 37 Suncook Valley Rd	Chichester	NH	03234	603-230-9683	
Rosewood Country Inn 67 Pleasant View Rd	Bradford	NH	03221	603-938-5253	938-5253
TF: 800-938-5273 ■ *Web:* www.bbonline.com/nh/rosewood ■ *E-mail:* rosewood@conknet.com					
Snowy Owl Inn Village Rd	Waterville Valley	NH	03215	603-236-8383	236-4890
Tilton Super 8 Motel 7 Tilton Rd	Tilton	NH	03276	603-286-8882	286-8788
TF: 800-800-8000					

— Restaurants —

				Phone
Angelina's Ristorante Italiano (Italian) 11 Depot St.	Concord	NH	03301	603-228-3313
Beefside (American) 106 Manchester St.	Concord	NH	03301	603-228-0208
Caffenio (American) 84 N Main St	Concord	NH	03301	603-229-0020
Cat N' Fiddle (Steak/Seafood) 118 Manchester St	Concord	NH	03301	603-228-8911
Dragon Star Chinese Restaurant (Chinese) 75 S Main St.	Concord	NH	03301	603-226-2423
Grist Mill (American) 520 South St	Bow	NH	03304	603-226-1922
Harry's Steak House (Steak) 61 S Main St	Concord	NH	03301	603-229-0004
Hawaiian Isle II (Polynesian/Chinese) 8 Hall St	Concord	NH	03301	603-228-0194
Hermanos Cocina Mexicana (Mexican) 11 Hills Ave	Concord	NH	03301	603-224-5669
Hong Kong Island (Chinese) 102 Manchester St	Concord	NH	03301	603-228-8833
In a Pinch Cafe (American) 146 Pleasant St	Concord	NH	03301	603-226-2272
Landmark Restaurant (American) 72 Manchester St	Concord	NH	03301	603-224-4101
Lun Hing Restaurant (Chinese) 87 Fisherville Rd	Concord	NH	03301	603-224-1025
Makris Lobster & Steak House (Steak/Seafood) 354 Sheep Davis Rd	Concord	NH	03301	603-225-7665
Man Yee Restaurant (Chinese) 79 South St	Concord	NH	03301	603-226-0001
May King Restaurant (Chinese) 161 Loudon Rd	Concord	NH	03301	603-226-2666
Ocean Tide (Seafood) 53 Storrs St.	Concord	NH	03301	603-229-1955
Olive Garden Restaurant (Italian) 223 Loudon Rd	Concord	NH	03301	603-228-6886
Papa Gino's (Italian) 129 Loudon Rd	Concord	NH	03301	603-225-2011
Pasta House The (Italian) 11 Depot St.	Concord	NH	03301	603-226-4723
Siam Orchid (Thai) 158 N Main St.	Concord	NH	03301	603-228-1529
Skuffy's Family Restaurant (American) 25 Manchester St	Concord	NH	03301	603-224-7164
Szechuan Garden Restaurant (Chinese) 108 Fisherville Rd	Concord	NH	03301	603-226-2650
Tea Garden Restaurant (Chinese) 184 N Main St	Concord	NH	03301	603-228-4420
Tio Juan's Margarita (Mexican) 1 Bicentennial Sq	Concord	NH	03301	603-224-2821
Veano's Italian Kitchen (Italian) 142 Loudon Rd	Concord	NH	03301	603-224-2400
Washington Street Cafe (Middle Eastern) 88 Washington St.	Concord	NH	03301	603-226-2699
Windmill Family Restaurant (American) 72 Loudon Rd	Concord	NH	03301	603-225-0600

— Goods and Services —

SHOPPING

				Phone	Fax
Canterbury Shaker Village 288 Shaker Rd.	Canterbury	NH	03224	603-783-9511	783-9152
Web: www.shakers.org					
LL Bean Factory Store 55 Fort Eddy Rd	Concord	NH	03301	603-225-6575	225-6859
McQuade's 45 N Main St.	Concord	NH	03301	603-228-5451	
Steeplegate Mall 270 Loudon Rd.	Concord	NH	03301	603-224-1523	

BANKS

				Phone	Fax
Bank of New Hampshire PO Box 477	Concord	NH	03302	603-228-5123	228-5124
TF: 800-224-2265					
Citizens Bank 1 Capital Plaza	Concord	NH	03301	603-229-3500	229-3501
Fleet Bank 30 Storrs St.	Concord	NH	03301	800-446-4462	225-4423*
**Fax Area Code:* 603					
Granite Bank 197 Loudon Rd.	Concord	NH	03301	603-226-3600	226-3886

BUSINESS SERVICES

	Phone
Airborne Express	800-247-2676
BAX Global	800-225-5229
DHL Worldwide Express	800-225-5345
Federal Express	800-238-5355
Mail Boxes Etc	800-789-4623
Manpower Temporary Services	603-224-9020
Post Office	603-225-5536
UPS	800-742-5877

— Media —

PUBLICATIONS

				Phone	Fax
Concord Monitor‡ 1 Monitor Dr	Concord	NH	03302	603-224-5301	224-8120
Web: www.concordmonitor.com ■ *E-mail:* primary@www.cmonitor.com					

‡Daily newspapers

TELEVISION

				Phone	Fax
WBZ-TV Ch 4 (CBS) 1170 Soldiers Field Rd	Boston	MA	02134	617-787-7000	254-6383
Web: www.wbz.com					
WCVB-TV Ch 5 (ABC) 5 TV Pl.	Needham	MA	02492	781-449-0400	449-6681
Web: www.wcvb.com ■ *E-mail:* wcvb@aol.com					
WFXT-TV Ch 25 (Fox) 25 Fox Dr.	Dedham	MA	02026	781-326-8825	467-7213
WGBH-TV Ch 2 (PBS) 125 Western Ave.	Boston	MA	02134	617-492-2777	787-0714
Web: www.wgbh.org					
WHDH-TV Ch 7 (NBC) 7 Bulfinch Pl	Boston	MA	02114	617-725-0777	723-6117
Web: www.whdh.com ■ *E-mail:* stationmanagement@whdh.com					

RADIO

				Phone	Fax
WEVO-FM 89.1 MHz (NPR) 207 N Main St	Concord	NH	03301	603-228-8910	224-6052
TF: 800-639-4130 ■ *Web:* www.nhpr.org/					
WJYY-FM 105.5 MHz (AC) 7 Perley St	Concord	NH	03301	603-228-9036	224-7280
Web: www.wjyy.com ■ *E-mail:* club105@wjyy.com					
WKXL-AM 1450 kHz (N/T) 37 Redington Rd.	Concord	NH	03301	603-225-5521	224-6404
WKXL-FM 102.3 MHz (N/T) 37 Redington Rd.	Concord	NH	03301	603-225-5521	224-6404
WNHQ-FM 92.1 MHz (CHR) 7 Perley St.	Concord	NH	03301	603-228-9036	224-7280
WNNH-FM 99.1 MHz (Oldies) 501 South St.	Concord	NH	03304	603-225-1160	225-5938
Web: www.wnnh.com ■ *E-mail:* oldies99@wnnh.com					
WRCI-FM 107.7 MHz (CR) 7 Perley St	Concord	NH	03301	603-478-1077	224-7280

— Colleges/Universities —

				Phone	Fax
New England College 24 Bridge St	Henniker	NH	03242	603-428-2211	428-7230
TF Admissions: 800-521-7642 ■ *Web:* www.nec.edu ■ *E-mail:* admis@nec1.nec.edu					
New Hampshire Technical Institute 11 Institute Dr	Concord	NH	03301	603-271-6484	271-7139*
**Fax:* Admissions ■ *TF:* 800-247-0179 ■ *Web:* www.nhti.net ■ *E-mail:* info@nhti.net					

— Hospitals —

				Phone	Fax
Concord Hospital 250 Pleasant St.	Concord	NH	03301	603-225-2711	228-7020
Web: www.crhc.org					

— Attractions —

				Phone	Fax
Audubon Society of New Hampshire 3 Silk Farm Rd	Concord	NH	03301	603-224-9909	226-0902
Bear Brook State Park Rt 28	Allenstown	NH	03275	603-485-9874	485-9869
Canterbury Shaker Village 288 Shaker Rd.	Canterbury	NH	03224	603-783-9511	783-9152
Web: www.shakers.org					
Capitol Center for the Arts 44 S Main St.	Concord	NH	03301	603-225-1111	224-3408
Web: www.ccanh.com/					
Children's Metamorphosis 217 Rockingham Rd	Londonderry	NH	03053	603-425-2560	
Coach & Eagle Walking Trail	Concord	NH	03301	603-224-2508	
Community Players 435 Josiah Bartlett Rd	Concord	NH	03301	603-225-6078	
Concord Community Music School 23 Wall St	Concord	NH	03301	603-228-1196	226-3151
Discovery Room at Fish & Game Headquarters 2 Hazen Dr.	Concord	NH	03301	603-271-3211	271-1438
Granite State Symphony 57 School St.	Concord	NH	03301	603-226-4776	
Web: gsso.org					
Kimball-Jenkins Estate 266 N Main St	Concord	NH	03301	603-225-3932	225-9288
Web: newww.com/org/kimball-jenkins/index.html					
League Gallery 205 N Main St.	Concord	NH	03301	603-224-3375	225-8452

Concord — Attractions (Cont'd)

				Phone	*Fax*
McAuliffe Christa Planetarium 3 Institute Dr *Web:* www.starhop.com	Concord	NH	03301	603-271-7827	271-7832
McGowen Fine Art 10 Hills Ave	Concord	NH	03301	603-225-2515	225-7791
Mount Kearsarge Indian Museum Kearsarge Mountain Rd *Web:* www.indianmuseum.com ■ *E-mail:* mkim@conknet.com	Warner	NH	03278	603-456-2600	456-3092
Museum of New Hampshire History 6 Eagle Sq *Web:* www.nhhistory.org ■ *E-mail:* nhhsadmin@aol.com	Concord	NH	03301	603-226-3189	228-6308
New Hampshire Historical Society 30 Park St *Web:* www.nhhistory.org	Concord	NH	03301	603-225-3381	224-0463
New Hampshire State House 107 N Main St	Concord	NH	03301	603-271-1110	271-2103
Pierce Manse 14 Penacook St *Web:* newww.com/free/pierce/pierce.html	Concord	NH	03301	603-225-2068	

SPORTS TEAMS & FACILITIES

				Phone	*Fax*
New Hampshire International Speedway 112 Rt 106 N *Web:* www.nhis.com/	Loudon	NH	03301	603-783-4931	
New Hampshire Lady Phantoms (soccer) S Commercial Ave *Web:* www.nhsoccer.com/lphans/default.htm	Manchester	NH	03101	603-578-5588	882-7747

— Events —

	Phone
Canterbury Country Fair (late July)	603-783-9955
Craftsmen's Fair (early August)	603-224-1471
Harvest Moon Festival (October)	603-456-2600
Hopkinton State Fair (late August-early September)	603-746-4191
Motorcycle Week-End Show (mid-June)	603-366-2000
Nevers' 2nd Regiment Band Concerts (late June-mid-July)	603-228-3901
Old Time Fiddling Championship (late August)	603-225-5512
Peanut Carnival (early August)	603-225-8690
Race Fever Street Festival (early July)	603-224-2508
Strawberry Moon Festival (June)	603-224-2508
Summer Market Days (July)	603-224-2508

Manchester

Manchester's beginnings can be traced back to outcroppings of a ledge that formed falls in the Merrimack River. Referred to as "Namoskeag" (place of many fish) by the native Indians, the falls offered outstanding fishing for salmon, shad, and alewife. Today, the Amoskeag Fishways at Amoskeag Dam are busy with activity each May and June when ocean fish return to spawn in the Merrimack River. The Fishway's underwater viewing window allows a view of the fish migration. Manchester is also home to the New Hampshire Symphony Orchestra, New Hampshire Philharmonic Orchestra, Opera League of New Hampshire, and the Palace Theatre, a restored vintage vaudeville and opera house.

Population	102,524	**Longitude**	71-45-53 W
Area (Land)	33.0 sq mi	**County**	Hillsborough
Area (Water)	1.9 sq mi	**Time Zone**	EST
Elevation	225 ft	**Area Code/s**	603
Latitude	42-99-56 N		

— Average Temperatures and Precipitation —

TEMPERATURES

	Jan	Feb	Mar	Apr	May	Jun	Jul	Aug	Sep	Oct	Nov	Dec
High	31	34	42	57	69	78	83	80	72	62	48	35
Low	10	11	22	32	42	52	57	54	47	36	28	15

PRECIPITATION

	Jan	Feb	Mar	Apr	May	Jun	Jul	Aug	Sep	Oct	Nov	Dec
Inches	2.5	2.5	2.7	2.9	3.1	3.2	3.2	3.3	2.8	3.2	3.7	3.2

— Important Phone Numbers —

	Phone		*Phone*
AAA	603-669-0101	**Poison Control Center**	800-562-8236
American Express Travel	603-668-3730	**Time/Temp**	603-529-7511
Dental Referral	603-626-2626	**Weather**	603-225-5191
Emergency	911		

— Information Sources —

				Phone	*Fax*
Better Business Bureau Serving New Hampshire 410 S Main St Suite 3 *Web:* www.concord.bbb.org	Concord	NH	03301	603-224-1991	
Greater Manchester Chamber of Commerce 889 Elm St. *Web:* www.manchester-chamber.org/	Manchester	NH	03101	603-666-6600	626-0910
Hillsborough County 300 Chestnut St Rm 139	Manchester	NH	03101	603-627-5600	627-5603
Manchester City Hall 1 City Hall Plaza. *Web:* ci.manchester.nh.us	Manchester	NH	03101	603-624-6455	624-6481
Manchester City Library 405 Pine St. *Web:* www.manchester.lib.nh.us	Manchester	NH	03104	603-624-6550	624-6559
Manchester Mayor 1 City Hall Plaza *Web:* ci.manchester.nh.us/mayor.htm	Manchester	NH	03101	603-624-6500	624-6576
Manchester Planning Dept 1 City Hall Plaza	Manchester	NH	03101	603-624-6450	624-6529

On-Line Resources

Area Guide Manchester	manchester.areaguides.net
Excite.com Manchester City Guide	www.excite.com/travel/countries/united_states/new_hampshire/manchester

— Transportation Services —

AIRPORTS

	Phone
■ **Manchester Municipal Airport (MHT)** 4 miles S of downtown (approx 10 minutes) Web: www.flymanchester.com	603-624-6556

Airport Transportation

	Phone
Airport Service $13-15 fare to downtown	603-641-4777

Commercial Airlines

	Phone		*Phone*
Continental Express	800-525-0280	**United Express**	800-241-6522
Delta Connection	800-221-1212	**US Airways**	800-428-4322
MetroJet	888-638-7653	**US Airways Express**	800-428-4322
United	800-241-6522		

CAR RENTALS

	Phone		*Phone*
Avis	603-624-4000	**Merchants**	603-666-4559
Budget	603-668-3166	**National**	603-627-2299
Hertz	603-669-6320		

Manchester (Cont'd)

LIMO/TAXI

	Phone
437 Taxi	603-437-8294
City Cab	603-668-3434
First Class Limousine	603-626-5466
Grace Limousine	603-666-0203
Starr Limo-Scene Inc	603-622-5773
Ultimate Limousine	603-622-9877
West Side Taxi	603-669-1212

MASS TRANSIT

	Phone
Manchester Transit Authority $.90 Base fare	603-623-8801

RAIL/BUS

				Phone
Concord Trailways Bus Station 119 Canal St	Manchester	NH	03101	603-668-6133

— Accommodations —

HOTELS, MOTELS, RESORTS

				Phone	Fax
Bedford Village Inn 2 Village Inn Ln *TF:* 800-852-1166	Bedford	NH	03110	603-472-2001	472-2379
Comfort Inn 298 Queen City Ave *TF:* 800-228-5150	Manchester	NH	03102	603-668-2600	668-2600
Courtyard by Marriott 700 Huse Rd *TF:* 888-844-0500 ■ *Web:* courtyard.com/MHTCY	Manchester	NH	03103	603-641-4900	641-0001
Derryfield Bed & Breakfast 1081 Bridge Street Ext.	Manchester	NH	03104	603-627-2082	
Econo Lodge 75 W Hancock St.	Manchester	NH	03102	603-624-0111	623-0268
Fairfield Inn 4 Amherst Rd. *Web:* fairfieldinn.com/MHTFI	Merrimack	NH	03054	603-424-7500	424-7500
Greenfield Inn Rt 31 N Junction 136 *TF:* 800-678-4144	Greenfield	NH	03047	603-547-6327	547-2418
Highlander Inn Airport 2 Highlander Way *TF:* 800-548-9248	Manchester	NH	03103	603-625-6426	625-6426
Holiday Inn 700 Elm St *TF:* 800-465-4329	Manchester	NH	03101	603-625-1000	625-4595
Knights Inn 140 Queen City Ave	Manchester	NH	03103	603-622-6444	
Ramada Inn 21 Front St *TF:* 800-272-6232	Manchester	NH	03102	603-669-2660	669-1135
Residence Inn 246 Daniel Webster Hwy *Web:* www.residenceinn.com/residenceinn/ASHMH	Merrimack	NH	03054	603-424-8100	424-3128
Rice-Hamilton The 123 Pleasant St.	Manchester	NH	03101	603-627-7281	624-2404
Sheraton Four Points Hotel 55 John E Devine Dr *TF:* 800-325-3535	Manchester	NH	03103	603-668-6110	668-0408
Super 8 Motel 2301 Brown Ave *TF:* 800-800-8000	Manchester	NH	03103	603-623-0883	624-9303
Susse Chalet Inn 860 S Porter St *TF:* 800-524-2538 ■ *Web:* www.sussechalet.com/manchester.html	Manchester	NH	03103	603-625-2020	623-7562
Wayfarer Inn 121 S River Rd	Bedford	NH	03110	603-622-3766	625-1126

— Restaurants —

				Phone
Aloha Restaurant (Chinese) 901 Hanover St	Manchester	NH	03104	603-647-2100
Angelo's (Italian) 1037 Hanover St.	Manchester	NH	03104	603-623-9255
Athens Restaurant (Greek) 31 Central St.	Manchester	NH	03101	603-623-9317
Basil's (American) 2 Highlander Way	Manchester	NH	03103	603-625-6426
Bedford Village Inn (American) 2 Village Inn Ln	Bedford	NH	03110	603-472-2001
Belmont Hall & Restaurant (American) 718 Grove St	Manchester	NH	03103	603-625-8540
Billy's Sports Bar & Grill (American) 34 Tarrytown Rd	Manchester	NH	03103	603-625-6294
Brandolini's Restaurant & Pub (Italian) 507 Maple St	Manchester	NH	03104	603-622-1410
Cactus Jacks Southwest Grill (Southwest) 782 S Willow St.	Manchester	NH	03103	603-627-8600
Cafe Pavone (Italian) 75 Arms Park Dr.	Manchester	NH	03101	603-622-5488
Chateau Restaurant (Steak/Seafood) 201 Hanover St.	Manchester	NH	03104	603-627-2677
Chen Yang Li (Chinese) 124 S River Rd.	Bedford	NH	03110	603-641-6922
Chez Vachon (French) 136 Kelley St.	Manchester	NH	03102	603-625-9660
Derryfield Restaurant (American) 625 Mammoth Rd	Manchester	NH	03104	603-623-2880
Fratello's Ristorante Italiano (Italian) 155 Dow St	Manchester	NH	03101	603-624-2022
Heng Won Chinese Restaurant (Chinese) 262 Mammoth Rd	Manchester	NH	03109	603-625-8550
India Palace (Indian) 575 S Willow St	Manchester	NH	03103	603-641-8413
Lakorn Thai Restaurant (Thai) 470 S Main St.	Manchester	NH	03102	603-626-4545
Mansion House Restaurant (American) 331 S Mammoth Rd.	Manchester	NH	03109	603-669-2153
Merrimack Restaurant (American) 786 Elm St	Manchester	NH	03101	603-669-5222
Newick's Seafood Restaurant (Seafood) 696 DW Hwy Old Rt 3	Merrimack	NH	03054	603-429-0262
Nutfield Ale & Steak House (Steak) 55 John E Devine Dr.	Manchester	NH	03103	603-666-3030
On the Rocks (Homestyle) 253 Wilson St.	Manchester	NH	03103	603-626-5866
Richard's Bistro (New American) 36 Lowell St	Manchester	NH	03101	603-644-1180
Salona (Greek) 128 Maple St.	Manchester	NH	03103	603-624-4020
Spanish Corner (American) 135 Cedar St	Manchester	NH	03101	603-668-8780
Stark Mill Brewery & Restaurant (American) 500 Commercial St.	Manchester	NH	03101	603-622-0000
Szechuan House (Chinese) 245 Maple St	Manchester	NH	03103	603-669-8811
Tinker's Seafood (Seafood) 545 DW Hwy Maple Street Mall	Manchester	NH	03104	603-622-4272
Triade's Cafe (American) 521 Wilson St.	Manchester	NH	03103	603-669-0488
Uptown Tavern (American) 1301 Elm St.	Manchester	NH	03104	603-666-0909
Yard Restaurant (American) 1211 S Mammoth Rd	Manchester	NH	03109	603-623-3545

— Goods and Services —

SHOPPING

				Phone	Fax
Bedford Mall 170 S River Rd	Manchester	NH	03110	603-668-0670	
Mall of New Hampshire 1500 S Willow St.	Manchester	NH	03103	603-669-0433	669-5006
Nashua Mall 100 Nashua Mall	Nashua	NH	03063	603-883-3348	421-1896

BANKS

				Phone	Fax
Bank Boston 728 Massabesic St	Manchester	NH	03108	603-625-4644	647-4604
Bank of New Hampshire 300 Franklin St	Manchester	NH	03101	603-624-6600	625-4085
Citizens Bank New Hampshire 875 Elm St. *TF:* 800-922-9999	Manchester	NH	03101	603-634-6000	668-9534
First NH Bank 340 Wilson St	Manchester	NH	03103	603-634-7050	
Fleet Bank 1155 Elm St. **Fax:* Mktg ■ *TF:* 800-462-1400	Manchester	NH	03101	603-647-3700	647-3855*

BUSINESS SERVICES

	Phone
Airborne Express	800-247-2676
BAX Global	800-225-5229
DHL Worldwide Express	800-225-5345
Federal Express	800-238-5355
Kerr Associates	603-647-9422
Mail Boxes Etc	800-789-4623
OfficeTeam	603-641-9233
Post Office	603-644-4111
Tandem	603-647-7777
UPS	800-742-5877

— Media —

PUBLICATIONS

				Phone	Fax
Union Leader‡ PO Box 9555 **Fax:* Edit ■ *Web:* www.theunionleader.com ■ *E-mail:* theul@aol.com	Manchester	NH	03108	603-668-4321	668-0382*

‡Daily newspapers

TELEVISION

				Phone	Fax
WBZ-TV Ch 4 (CBS) 1170 Soldiers Field Rd *Web:* www.wbz.com	Boston	MA	02134	617-787-7000	254-6383
WCVB-TV Ch 5 (ABC) 5 TV Pl. *Web:* www.wcvb.com ■ *E-mail:* wcvb@aol.com	Needham	MA	02492	781-449-0400	449-6681
WFXT-TV Ch 25 (Fox) 25 Fox Dr.	Dedham	MA	02026	781-326-8825	467-7213
WGBH-TV Ch 2 (PBS) 125 Western Ave. *Web:* www.wgbh.org	Boston	MA	02134	617-492-2777	787-0714
WHDH-TV Ch 7 (NBC) 7 Bulfinch Pl *Web:* www.whdh.com ■ *E-mail:* stationmanagement@whdh.com	Boston	MA	02114	617-725-0777	723-6117
WMUR-TV Ch 9 (ABC) 100 S Commercial St *Web:* www.wmur.com ■ *E-mail:* wmur@aol.com	Manchester	NH	03105	603-669-9999	641-9005
WPXB-TV Ch 60 (PAX) 1 Sundial Ave Suite 501 *Web:* www.pax.net/wpxb	Manchester	NH	03103	603-647-6060	644-0060

Manchester (Cont'd)

RADIO

				Phone	Fax
WFEA-AM 1370 kHz (Nost) 500 Commercial St	Manchester	NH	03101	603-669-5777	669-4641
WGIR-AM 610 kHz (N/T) PO Box 610 *E-mail:* info@wgir.com	Manchester	NH	03105	603-625-6915	625-9255
WGIR-FM 101.1 MHz (Rock) PO Box 610 *Web:* www.wgir.com ■ *E-mail:* info@wgir.com	Manchester	NH	03105	603-625-6915	625-9255
WKBR-AM 1250 kHz (Sports) 288 S River Rd	Bedford	NH	03110	603-647-1250	647-1260
WQLL-FM 96.5 MHz (Oldies) 500 N Commercial St	Manchester	NH	03101	603-669-7979	669-4641
WZID-FM 95.7 MHz (AC) 500 Commercial St *Web:* www.wzid.com	Manchester	NH	03101	603-669-5777	669-4641

— Colleges/Universities —

				Phone	Fax
Daniel Webster College 20 University Dr. *TF Admissions:* 800-325-6876 ■ *Web:* www.dwc.edu	Nashua	NH	03063	603-577-6000	577-6001
Franklin Pierce College Nashua Campus 20 Cotton Rd *TF:* 800-325-1090 ■ *Web:* www.fpc.edu	Nashua	NH	03063	603-889-4143	889-3795
Hesser College 3 Sundial Ave *TF Admissions:* 800-526-9231 ■ *Web:* www.hesser.edu ■ *E-mail:* info@hesser.edu	Manchester	NH	03103	603-668-6660	666-4722
New Hampshire College 2500 N River Rd *TF Admissions:* 800-642-4968 ■ *Web:* www.nhc.edu	Manchester	NH	03106	603-668-2211	645-9693
New Hampshire Community Technical College Manchester Campus 1066 Front St *Web:* www.manchester.tec.nh.us ■ *E-mail:* manc-admissions@tec.nh.us	Manchester	NH	03102	603-668-6706	668-5354
Notre Dame College 2321 Elm St *Web:* www.notredame.edu ■ *E-mail:* info@notredame.edu	Manchester	NH	03104	603-669-4298	644-8316
Saint Anselm College 100 St Anselm Dr *TF:* 800-268-5267 ■ *Web:* www.anselm.edu	Manchester	NH	03102	603-669-1030	641-7550
University of New Hampshire Manchester 220 Hackett Hill Rd *Web:* www.unh.edu/unhm/ ■ *E-mail:* unhm@unh.edu	Manchester	NH	03102	603-668-0700	623-2745

— Hospitals —

				Phone	Fax
Catholic Medical Center 100 McGregor St *TF:* 800-437-9666	Manchester	NH	03102	603-668-3545	668-5348
Elliot Hospital 1 Elliot Way	Manchester	NH	03103	603-669-5300	647-4420
Veterans Affairs Medical Center 718 Smyth Rd	Manchester	NH	03104	603-624-4366	626-6583

— Attractions —

				Phone	Fax
American Stage Festival Theater 14 Court St *Web:* www.americanstagefestival.org	Nashua	NH	03060	603-886-7000	889-2336
Amoskeag Fishways Fletcher St *Web:* www.psnh.com/fishways/	Manchester	NH	03101	603-626-3474	644-4386
Budweiser-Clydesdale Hamlet & Anheuser Busch Tour Center 221 Daniel Webster Hwy	Merrimack	NH	03054	603-595-1202	595-1277
Currier Gallery of Art 201 Myrtle Way *Web:* www.currier.org	Manchester	NH	03104	603-669-6144	626-4166
Franco-American Center 52 Concord St	Manchester	NH	03101	603-669-4045	
Lee Lawrence L Scouting Museum 40 Bodwell Rd PO Box 1121	Manchester	NH	03105	603-669-8919	
Manchester Choral Society PO Box 4182 *Web:* www.mcsnh.org ■ *E-mail:* info@mcsnh.org	Manchester	NH	03108	800-639-2928	
Manchester Historic Assn 129 Amherst St *Web:* www.mv.com/org/mha ■ *E-mail:* history@mha.mv.com	Manchester	NH	03101	603-622-7531	622-0822
Nashua Symphony 6 Church St *TF:* 800-639-3101 ■ *Web:* www.newww.com/org/nso	Nashua	NH	03060	603-595-9156	595-1890
New Hampshire Institute of Art 148 Concord St	Manchester	NH	03104	603-623-0313	641-1832
New Hampshire Philharmonic Orchestra 83 Hanover St Palace Theatre *Web:* www.nhpo.com ■ *E-mail:* info@nhpo.com	Manchester	NH	03101	603-647-6476	647-4130
New Hampshire Symphony Orchestra 81 Hanover St Palace Theatre *TF:* 800-639-9320 ■ *Web:* www.nhso.org	Manchester	NH	03101	603-669-3559	623-1195
Opera League of New Hampshire 80 Hanover St Palace Theatre	Manchester	NH	03101	603-429-9887	
Palace Theatre 80 Hanover St	Manchester	NH	03101	603-668-5588	665-9169
Saint Marie's Church 378 Notre Dame Ave	Manchester	NH	03102	603-622-4615	

SPORTS TEAMS & FACILITIES

				Phone	Fax
New Hampshire Phantoms (soccer) S Commercial St *Web:* www.nhphantoms.com ■ *E-mail:* allidee@ix.netcom.com	Manchester	NH	03101	603-578-5588	882-7747

— Events —

	Phone
Downtown Syncopation Summer Concert Series (early July-late August)	603-645-6285
Riverfest (mid-September)	603-666-6600
Winter Craft Festival (late November)	603-224-3375

New Jersey

Population (1999): 8,143,412 **Area (sq mi): 8,722**

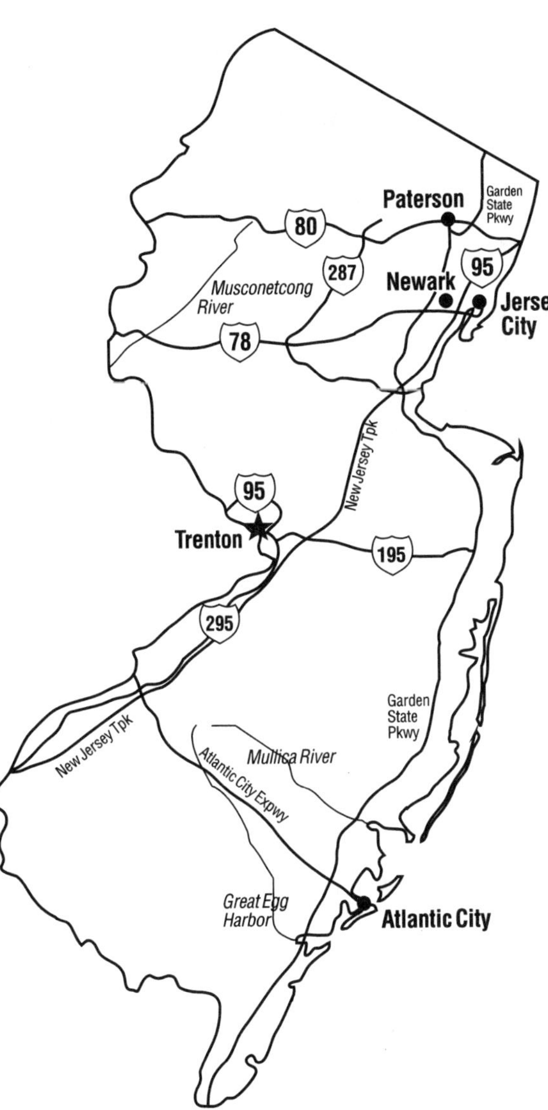

— State Information Sources —

				Phone	Fax
New Jersey Commerce & Economic Development Dept 20 W State St Box 820 ... *Web:* www.state.nj.us/commerce/dcedhome.htm	Trenton	NJ	08625	609-984-2333	777-4097
New Jersey Parks & Forestry Div PO Box 404... *TF:* 800-843-6420 ■ *Web:* www.state.nj.us/dep/forestry/parknj/intro2.htm	Trenton	NJ	08625	609-292-2733	984-0503
New Jersey State Chamber of Commerce 216 W State St. ... *Web:* www.njchamber.com	Trenton	NJ	08608	609-989-7888	989-9696
New Jersey State Government Information ... *Web:* www.state.nj.us ■ *E-mail:* feedback@state.nj.us				609-292-2121	
New Jersey State Library PO Box 520 ... *Web:* www.state.nj.us./statelibrary/njlib.htm	Trenton	NJ	08625	609-292-6200	292-2746
New Jersey Travel & Tourism Div PO Box 820 .. *TF:* 800-847-4865 ■ *Web:* www.visitnj.org	Trenton	NJ	08625	609-292-2470	633-7418

ON-LINE RESOURCES

Go New Jersey ... www.go-newjersey.com
InTheGardenState.com ... www.inthegardenstate.com
Jersey Life ... www.jerseylife.com
JerseyShore-Online ... www.jerseyshore-online.com
New Jersey Cities ... dir.yahoo.com/Regional/U_S__States/New_Jersey/Cities
New Jersey Counties & Regions ... dir.yahoo.com/Regional/U_S__States/New_Jersey/Counties_and_Regions
New Jersey Online ... www.nj.com
New Jersey Scenario ... scenariousa.dstylus.com/nj/indexf.htm
New Jersey Skylands ... www.njskylands.com
New Jersey Travel & Tourism Guide ... www.travel-library.com/north_america/usa/new_jersey/index.html
New Jersey World of Interest ... www.woi.com/nj
Rough Guide Travel New Jersey ... travel.roughguides.com/content/355/index.htm
ShorePoints Jersey Shore Guide ... shorepoints.com
Travel.org-New Jersey ... travel.org/newjerse.html
Virtual New Jersey Shore ... www.virtualnjshore.com
Yahoo! Get Local New Jersey ... dir.yahoo.com/Regional/U_S__States/New_Jersey

— Cities Profiled —

Page

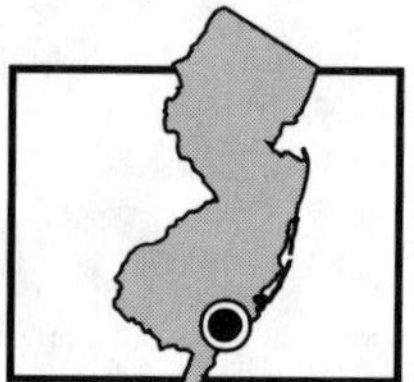

Atlantic City

Atlantic City's world-famous beach is lined by casino hotels that offer gambling, top-name entertainment, and fine dining, along with luxurious accommodations. Equally famous is Atlantic City's Boardwalk, which was built in 1870 and extends four and a half miles along the beach. The Boardwalk offers an uninterrupted view of the beach, as well as shops, arcades, and children's amusements. A rolling chair, which has been a fixture of the Boardwalk since 1887, offers a leisurely ride for casino-hoppers. For history buffs, the nearby town of Smithville combines shopping with history; also nearby is Batsto, which features a Revolutionary Era village and ironworks.

Population 38,063
Area (Land) . . . . . 11.3 sq mi
Area (Water) . . . . . 6.0 sq mi
Elevation . . . . . 8 ft
Latitude . . . . . 39-36-42 N
Longitude . . . . . 74-42-33 W
County . . . . . Atlantic
Time Zone . . . . . EST
Area Code/s 609

— Average Temperatures and Precipitation —

TEMPERATURES

	Jan	Feb	Mar	Apr	May	Jun	Jul	Aug	Sep	Oct	Nov	Dec
High	40	43	52	61	71	80	85	83	77	66	56	45
Low	21	24	31	39	50	59	65	64	56	44	36	26

PRECIPITATION

	Jan	Feb	Mar	Apr	May	Jun	Jul	Aug	Sep	Oct	Nov	Dec
Inches	3.5	3.1	3.6	3.6	3.3	2.6	3.8	4.1	2.9	2.8	3.6	3.3

— Important Phone Numbers —

	Phone
AAA	609-646-6000
Emergency	911
HotelDocs	800-468-3537
Poison Control Center	800-764-7661
Travelers Aid of New Jersey	973-623-5052
Visitors Information Line	888-228-4748

— Information Sources —

				Phone	Fax
Atlantic City City Hall 1301 Bacharach Blvd *Web:* library.atlantic.city.lib.nj.us/ac	Atlantic City	NJ	08401	609-347-5300	347-9476
Atlantic City Convention & Visitors Authority 2314 Pacific Ave *TF:* 800-262-7395 ■ *Web:* www.atlanticcitynj.com ■ *E-mail:* accvaconvdev@worldnet.att.net	Atlantic City	NJ	08401	609-449-7130	345-2200
Atlantic City Convention Center 2001 Kirkman Blvd *Web:* www.atlanticcitynj.com/conventi/convnew.html	Atlantic City	NJ	08401	609-449-2000	449-2090
Atlantic City Mayor 1301 Bacharach Blvd Rm 706	Atlantic City	NJ	08401	609-347-5400	347-5638
Atlantic City Planning & Development Dept 1301 Bacharach Blvd	Atlantic City	NJ	08401	609-347-5404	347-5345
Atlantic City Public Library 1 N Tennessee Ave *Web:* library.atlantic.city.lib.nj.us	Atlantic City	NJ	08401	609-345-2269	348-2547
Atlantic County 5901 Main St *Web:* commlink.atlantic.county.lib.nj.us	Mays Landing	NJ	08330	609-641-7867	625-4738
Better Business Bureau Serving Southern New Jersey 16 Maple Ave *Web:* www.westmont.bbb.org	Westmont	NJ	08108	856-854-8467	854-1130
Greater Atlantic City Chamber of Commerce 1125 Atlantic Ave Suite 105 *Web:* www.vitinc.com/mall/ac ■ *E-mail:* chamber@vitinc.com	Atlantic City	NJ	08401	609-345-5600	345-1666

On-Line Resources

4AtlanticCity.com www.4atlanticcity.com
Area Guide Atlantic City . . . . . atlanticcity.areaguides.net
Atlantic City CityLink . . . . . www.usacitylink.com/citylink/atlantic/
Atlantic City Historical Entertainment Piers . . . . . design.coda.drexel.edu/students/acohen/atlantic_city.html
Atlantic City Insider's Guide . . . . . www.iloveac.com/acinsider
Atlantic City New Jersey . . . . . atlanticcity-newjersey.com
Atlantic City Online . . . . . www.atlantic-city-online.com
City Knowledge Atlantic City . . . . . www.cityknowledge.com/nj_atlantic_city.htm
CityTravelGuide.com Atlantic City . . . . . www.citytravelguide.com/atlantic-city.htm
DigitalCity Atlantic City . . . . . www.digitalcity.com/atlanticcity
Excite.com Atlantic City City Guide . . . . . www.excite.com/travel/countries/united_states/new_jersey/atlantic_city
HotelGuide Atlantic City . . . . . hotelguide.net/atlantic_city/
I Love Atlantic City Online . . . . . www.iloveac.com
Rough Guide Travel Atlantic City travel.roughguides.com/content/362/
Surf & Sun Beach Vacation Guide to Atlantic City . . . . . www.surf-sun.com/nj-atlantic-city-main.htm

— Transportation Services —

AIRPORTS

■ **Atlantic City International Airport (ACY)** — *Phone*

12 miles NW of downtown (approx 20 minutes) 609-645-7895
Web: www.acairport.com ■ *E-mail:* sjtaacy@ix.netcom.com

Airport Transportation

	Phone
Atlantic City Airport Taxi $27 fare to downtown	609-383-1457
Jonathan's Transportation Service $48 fare to downtown	609-344-7535

Commercial Airlines

	Phone
Continental	800-525-0280
Northwest	800-225-2525
Spirit	800-772-7117
US Airways	800-428-4322
US Airways Express	800-428-4322

Charter Airlines

	Phone
MidLantic Jet	609-383-1555

CAR RENTALS

	Phone
Avis	609-383-9356
Budget	609-383-0173
Hertz	800-654-3131
Just 4 Wheels	609-645-8077

LIMO/TAXI

	Phone
Abalon Limousines	609-927-2201
Atlantic City Airport Taxi	609-383-1457
Atlantic Limousines	609-347-0034
Enchantment Limousine	609-266-1600
Jonathan's Limousines	800-524-0488
Mutual Taxi	609-345-6111
Quicker Taxi	609-344-1900

MASS TRANSIT

	Phone
New Jersey Transit $1.40 Base fare	800-582-5946

RAIL/BUS

				Phone
Amtrak Station 1 Atlantic City Expy	Atlantic City	NJ	08401	800-872-7245
Greyhound Bus Station 1901 Atlantic Ave *TF:* 800-231-2222	Atlantic City	NJ	08401	609-345-6617

Atlantic City (Cont'd)

— Accommodations —

HOTEL RESERVATION SERVICES

	Phone	Fax
Accommodations Express	609-391-2100	525-0111
TF: 800-444-7666 ■ *Web:* www.accommodationsxpress.com ■ *E-mail:* accomexp@acy.digex.net		
American International Travel	800-782-9872	897-4007*
**Fax Area Code:* 727 ■ *TF:* 800-681-3965		
Atlantic City Toll-Free Reservations	609-646-7070	646-8655
TF: 800-833-7070 ■ *Web:* www.actollfree.com		
Hotel Reservations Network Inc	214-361-7311	361-7299
TF Sales: 800-964-6835 ■ *Web:* www.hoteldiscount.com		

HOTELS, MOTELS, RESORTS

				Phone	Fax
Airport Inn 500 N Albany Ave	Atlantic City	NJ	08401	609-344-9085	345-4049
TF: 800-292-6384					
Atlantic City Hilton Hotel & Casino Boston & Pacific Ave	Atlantic City	NJ	08401	609-347-7111	340-7128
TF: 800-257-8677 ■ *Web:* www.hilton.com/hotels/ACYAHHH					
Atlantic Palace Suites Hotel 1507 Boardwalk Ave	Atlantic City	NJ	08401	609-344-1200	348-8772
TF: 800-527-8483					
Bally's Park Place Hotel & Casino Park Pl & Boardwalk	Atlantic City	NJ	08401	609-340-2000	340-4713
TF: 800-225-5977 ■ *Web:* www.ballysac.com/parkplace/					
Beachcomber Resort Motel 7900 Dune Dr	Avalon	NJ	08202	609-368-5121	368-3888
TF: 800-462-9703					
Best Western Envoy Inn 1416 Pacific Ave	Atlantic City	NJ	08401	609-344-7116	344-5659
TF: 800-528-1234					
Brunswick Hotel 160 Saint James Pl	Atlantic City	NJ	08401	609-344-8098	
Caesars Atlantic City 2100 Pacific Ave	Atlantic City	NJ	08401	609-348-4411	348-8830
TF: 800-443-0104 ■ *Web:* www.caesars.com/atlantic_city/default.html					
Claridge Casino Hotel Brighton & Park Pl	Atlantic City	NJ	08401	609-340-3400	345-8909
TF: 800-257-8585					
Comfort Inn West 7095 Black Horse Pike	West Atlantic City	NJ	08232	609-645-1818	383-0228
TF: 800-458-1138					
Continental Inn 137 S ML King Jr Blvd	Atlantic City	NJ	08401	609-345-5141	344-4464
TF: 800-634-1706					
Days Inn Boardwalk Boardwalk & Morris Aves	Atlantic City	NJ	08401	609-344-6101	348-5335
TF: 800-329-7466					
Econo Lodge Boardwalk 117 S Kentucky Ave	Atlantic City	NJ	08401	609-344-9093	340-8065
TF: 800-323-6410					
Endicott Hotel 209 S Tennessee Ave	Atlantic City	NJ	08401	609-345-2653	
Flagship Resort 60 N Main Ave	Atlantic City	NJ	08401	609-343-7447	347-9597
TF: 800-647-7890					
Greater Pittsburgh Hotel 142 S Tennessee Ave	Atlantic City	NJ	08401	609-344-6693	
Harrah's Atlantic City Hotel Casino 777 Harrah's Blvd	Atlantic City	NJ	08401	609-441-5000	348-6057
TF: 800-427-7247					
Holiday Inn Boardwalk Chelsea Ave & Boardwalk	Atlantic City	NJ	08401	609-348-2200	348-0168
TF: 800-548-3030 ■ *Web:* www.basshotels.com/holiday-inn/?_franchisee=ACYBW ■ *E-mail:* jtholac@aol.com					
Howard Johnson Tennessee & Pacific Aves	Atlantic City	NJ	08401	609-344-4193	348-1263
TF: 800-341-2279					
Knights Inn 124 S North Carolina Ave	Atlantic City	NJ	08401	609-345-0155	345-4556
TF: 800-843-5644					
Marriott Seaview Resort 401 S New York Rd	Absecon	NJ	08201	609-652-1800	652-2307
TF: 800-228-9290 ■ *Web:* marriotthotels.com/AIYNJ					
Miami Hotel 123 S Kentucky Ave	Atlantic City	NJ	08401	609-344-2077	344-2912
Midtown Bala Motor Inn 1746 Pacific Ave	Atlantic City	NJ	08404	609-348-3031	347-6043
TF: 800-932-0534					
Quality Inn Beach Block S Carolina & Pacific Aves	Atlantic City	NJ	08401	609-345-7070	345-0633
TF: 800-874-5856 ■ *Web:* www.qualityinnatlanticcity.com					
Quarterdeck Inn 351 W 9th St	Ship Bottom	NJ	08008	609-494-3334	494-1706
Ramada Limited 8037 Black Horse Pike	West Atlantic City	NJ	08232	609-646-5220	646-2802
TF: 800-272-6232 ■ *E-mail:* ramadaac@aol.com					
Resorts Casino Hotel 1133 Boardwalk	Atlantic City	NJ	08401	609-344-6000	340-6847*
**Fax:* Cust Svc ■ *TF:* 800-772-9000 ■ *Web:* www.resortsac.com					
Sands Hotel & Casino Indiana & Brighton Pk	Atlantic City	NJ	08401	609-441-4000	441-4180
TF: 800-257-8580 ■ *Web:* www.acsands.com					
Showboat Hotel & Casino 801 Boardwalk	Atlantic City	NJ	08401	609-343-4000	345-2334
TF: 800-621-0200					
Tropicana Casino & Resort Brighton Ave & Boardwalk	Atlantic City	NJ	08401	609-340-4000	343-5211
TF: 800-843-8767 ■ *Web:* www.tropicana.net					
Trump Marina Hotel & Casino Huron Ave & Brigantine Blvd	Atlantic City	NJ	08401	609-441-2000	345-4035*
**Fax:* Hum Res ■ *TF:* 800-777-8477 ■ *Web:* www.trumpmarina.com					
Trump Plaza Mississippi Ave at the Boardwalk	Atlantic City	NJ	08401	609-441-6000	441-7880*
**Fax:* Hum Res ■ *TF:* 800-677-7378					
Trump Taj Mahal Casino Resort 1000 Boardwalk & Virginia Ave	Atlantic City	NJ	08401	609-449-1000	449-5656*
**Fax:* Hum Res ■ *TF:* 800-825-8786 ■ *Web:* www.trumptaj.com ■ *E-mail:* cblock@trumptaj.com					
Trump World's Fair 2500 Boardwalk	Atlantic City	NJ	08401	609-441-6000	441-2603
TF: 800-677-7787					

— Restaurants —

				Phone
12 South (American) 12 S Indiana Ave	Atlantic City	NJ	08401	609-345-1212
Angelo's Fairmount Tavern (Italian) 2300 Fairmount Ave	Atlantic City	NJ	08401	609-344-2439
Angeloni's II (Italian) 2400 Arctic Ave	Atlantic City	NJ	08401	609-344-7875
Black Forest Restaurant (German) 2100 Boardwalk Suite 1	Atlantic City	NJ	08401	609-348-0700
Cancon Restaurant (Mexican) 2503 Pacific Ave	Atlantic City	NJ	08401	609-348-1148
Captain Young's Seafood Emporium (Seafood) Ocean One Mall	Atlantic City	NJ	08401	609-344-2001
Constantino's Restaurant (American) 1100 Pacific Ave	Atlantic City	NJ	08401	609-344-4932
Dock's Oyster House (Seafood) 2405 Atlantic Ave	Atlantic City	NJ	08401	609-345-0092
El Piqueteadero Restaurant (Spanish) 4227 Ventnor Ave	Atlantic City	NJ	08401	609-345-5543
Flying Cloud Cafe (American) 800 N New Hampshire Ave	Atlantic City	NJ	08401	609-345-8222
Girasole Ristorante (Italian) 3108 Pacific Ave	Atlantic City	NJ	08401	609-345-5554
Hard Rock Cafe (American) Boardwalk at Virginia Ave	Atlantic City	NJ	08401	609-441-0007
Hunan Chinese Seafood (Chinese) 2323 Atlantic Ave	Atlantic City	NJ	08401	609-348-5946
Irish Pub & Inn (Irish) 164 St James Pl	Atlantic City	NJ	08401	609-345-9613
Italian Bistro (Italian) 2100 Boardwalk 3rd Fl	Atlantic City	NJ	08401	609-345-8799
Los Amigos (Mexican) 1926 Atlantic Ave	Atlantic City	NJ	08401	609-344-2293
McGettigan's Saloon (Steak/Seafood) 440 N Albany Ave	Atlantic City	NJ	08401	609-344-3030
Old Waterway Inn (Continental) 1660 W Riverside Dr	Atlantic City	NJ	08401	609-347-1793
Planet Hollywood (American) Arkansas Ave & Boardwalk	Atlantic City	NJ	08401	609-347-7827
Rosa's Southern Dining (Southern) 1017 Arctic Ave	Atlantic City	NJ	08401	609-348-8889
Sabatini's (Italian) 2210-14 Pacific Ave	Atlantic City	NJ	08401	609-345-4816
Scannicchio's Restaurant (Italian) 119 S California Ave	Atlantic City	NJ	08401	609-348-6378
Teik Lee Kitchen (Chinese) 325 Atlantic Ave	Atlantic City	NJ	08401	609-348-4880
Tony's Baltimore Grille (American) 2800 Atlantic Ave	Atlantic City	NJ	08401	609-345-5766

— Goods and Services —

SHOPPING

				Phone	Fax
Central Square New Rd & Central Aves	Linwood	NJ	08221	609-926-1000	927-1532
Hamilton Mall 4403 Black Horse Pike	Mays Landing	NJ	08330	609-646-8326	645-7837
Web: www.shophamilton.com ■ *E-mail:* hamilmall@aol.com					
Shops on Ocean One 1 Atlantic Ocean	Atlantic City	NJ	08401	609-347-8086	
Shore Mall Black Horse Pike	Egg Harbor	NJ	08234	609-484-9500	484-9641

BANKS

				Phone	Fax
Cape Savings Bank 1410 Atlantic Ave	Atlantic City	NJ	08401	609-344-9027	345-2379
First Union National Bank 1301 Atlantic Ave	Atlantic City	NJ	08401	800-225-5332	343-7627*
**Fax Area Code:* 609					
Fleet Bank 1300 Atlantic Ave	Atlantic City	NJ	08401	609-344-4483	344-2841
Summit Bank 4201-05 Ventnor Ave	Atlantic City	NJ	08401	609-347-7075	344-6168

Atlantic City (Cont'd)

BUSINESS SERVICES

	Phone		Phone
Airborne Express	800-247-2676	**Mail Boxes Etc**	800-789-4623
BAX Global	800-225-5229	**Post Office**	609-345-4212
DHL Worldwide Express	800-225-5345	**UPS**	800-742-5877
Federal Express	800-238-5355		

— Media —

PUBLICATIONS

	City	State	Zip	Phone	Fax
Atlantic City Magazine 1000 W Washington Ave *TF:* 800-651-8279	Pleasantville	NJ	08232	609-272-7900	272-7910
Press of Atlantic City‡ 11 Devins Ln *Web:* www.pressplus.com	Pleasantville	NJ	08232	609-272-1100	272-7224

‡*Daily newspapers*

TELEVISION

	City	State	Zip	Phone	Fax
WCAU-TV Ch 10 (NBC) 10 Monument Rd *Web:* www.nbc10.com	Bala Cynwyd	PA	19004	610-668-5510	668-3700
WMGM-TV Ch 40 (NBC) 1601 New Rd *Web:* www.wmgmtv.com ■ *E-mail:* wmgmtv@acy.digex.net	Linwood	NJ	08221	609-927-4440	927-7014
WNJT-TV Ch 8 (PBS) PO Box 777	Trenton	NJ	08625	609-777-5000	633-2927
WPVI-TV Ch 6 (ABC) 4100 City Line Ave *Web:* abcnews.go.com/local/wpvi	Philadelphia	PA	19131	215-878-9700	581-4530

RADIO

	City	State	Zip	Phone	Fax
WBNJ-FM 105.5 MHz (AC) 2922 Atlantic Ave Suite 201	Atlantic City	NJ	08401	609-348-4040	348-1303
WFPG-AM 1450 kHz (N/T) 950 Tilton Rd Suite 200 *Web:* www.wfpg.com	Northfield	NJ	08225	609-645-9797	272-9228
WFPG-FM 96.9 MHz (AC) 950 Tilton Rd Suite 200 *Web:* www.literock969.com/ ■ *E-mail:* management@literock969.com	Northfield	NJ	08225	609-645-9797	272-9228
WJSX-FM 102.3 MHz (Jazz) 1825 Murray Ave	Atlantic City	NJ	08401	609-886-0300	348-4442
WMID-AM 1340 kHz (Nost) 1825 Murray Ave	Atlantic City	NJ	08401	609-344-0300	348-4442
WMID-FM 99.3 MHz (NAC) 1825 Murray Ave	Atlantic City	NJ	08401	609-344-0300	348-4442
WZBZ-FM 105.5 MHz (CHR) 2922 Atlantic Ave Suite 201	Atlantic City	NJ	08401	609-348-4040	348-1303

— Colleges/Universities —

	City	State	Zip	Phone	Fax
Atlantic Community College 5100 Black Horse Pike *Web:* www.atlantic.edu ■ *E-mail:* djohnson@nsvm.atlantic.edu	Mays Landing	NJ	08330	609-343-4900	343-4921
Richard Stockton College of New Jersey PO Box 195 *Web:* www.stockton.edu	Pomona	NJ	08240	609-652-4261	748-5541

— Hospitals —

	City	State	Zip	Phone	Fax
Atlantic City Medical Center 1925 Pacific Ave	Atlantic City	NJ	08401	609-344-4081	441-2108

— Attractions —

	City	State	Zip	Phone	Fax
Absecon Lighthouse Pacific & Vermont Aves *Web:* www.virtualac.com/lighthouse/	Atlantic City	NJ	08404	609-449-1360	
Atlantic City Historical Museum Garden Pier *Web:* www.nj.com/acmuseum/	Atlantic City	NJ	08401	609-347-5839	347-5707
Atlantic City Historical Museum and Art Center Boardwalk & New Jersey Ave.	Atlantic City	NJ	08401	609-347-5837	
Atlantic County Historical Society 907 Shore Rd.	Somers Point	NJ	08244	609-927-5218	
Balic Winery Rt 40	Mays Landing	NJ	08330	609-625-2166	
Batsto Historic Village 4110 Nesco Rd Wharton State Forest	Hammonton	NJ	08037	609-561-3262	
Birch Grove Park Burton Ave	Northfield	NJ	08225	609-641-3778	641-8902
Caprice Gallery 777 Harrah's Blvd	Atlantic City	NJ	08401	800-626-7750	
Farley Frank State Marina 600 Huron Ave	Atlantic City	NJ	08401	609-441-8482	340-5093
Forsythe Edwin B Wildlife Refuge Great Creek Rd	Oceanville	NJ	08231	609-652-1665	652-1474
Gardner's Basin 800 New Hampshire Ave	Atlantic City	NJ	08401	609-348-2880	345-4002
Great Egg Harbor National Scenic & Recreational River 109 State Hwy 50 Atlantic County Div of Parks & Recreation *Web:* www.nps.gov/greg/	Mays Landing	NJ	08330	609-645-5960	645-5868
Historic Smithville Rt 9 & New York Rd	Smithville	NJ	08201	609-652-5122	
Lake Lenape Park Park Rd & 13th St *TF:* 800-626-7612	Mays Landing	NJ	08330	609-625-2021	625-7379
Lucy the Elephant 9200 Atlantic Ave	Margate	NJ	08402	609-823-6473	
Marine Mammal Stranding Center 3625 Brigantine Blvd *Web:* www.mmsc.org	Brigantine	NJ	08203	609-266-0538	266-6300
Noyes Museum Lily Lake Rd	Oceanville	NJ	08231	609-652-8848	652-6166
Renault Winery 72 N Bremen Ave.	Egg Harbor City	NJ	08215	609-965-2111	965-1847
Ripley's Believe It or Not! Museum New York Ave & Boardwalk	Atlantic City	NJ	08401	609-347-2001	347-2009
Somers Mansion 1000 Shore Rd	Somers Point	NJ	08723	609-927-2212	
South Jersey Regional Theatre 738 Bay Ave.	Somers Point	NJ	08244	609-653-0553	601-1463
Steel Pier Virginia Ave & Boardwalk	Atlantic City	NJ	08401	609-449-7130	
Stockton Performing Arts Center Jimmie Leeds Rd Richard Stockton College	Pomona	NJ	08240	609-652-9000	748-5523
Story Book Land 6415 Black Horse Pike *Web:* www.storybookland.com	Cardiff	NJ	08234	609-641-7847	646-4533
Wharton State Forest 41 Nesco Batsto	Hammonton	NJ	08037	609-561-3262	
Wheaton Village 1501 Glasstown Rd *TF:* 800-998-4552 ■ *Web:* www.wheatonvillage.org ■ *E-mail:* mail@wheatonvillage.org	Millville	NJ	08332	856-825-6800	825-2410

SPORTS TEAMS & FACILITIES

	City	State	Zip	Phone	Fax
Atlantic City Race Course 4501 Black Horse Pike	Mays Landing	NJ	08330	609-641-2190	645-8309
Atlantic City Seagulls (basketball) 6 W Lancaster Ave *TF:* 888-466-7797 ■ *Web:* www.acconnection.com/ACS-p3.htm	Ardmore	PA	19003	610-642-2900	649-6930
Atlantic City Surf (baseball) 545 N Albany Ave *Web:* www.acsurf.com ■ *E-mail:* surf@acsurf.com	Atlantic City	NJ	08401	609-344-7873	344-7010
South Jersey Barons (soccer) 6th St & Boardwalk Carey Stadium *Web:* sjbarons.com ■ *E-mail:* sjbarons@aol.com	Ocean City	NJ	08226	856-753-7608	753-7351

— Events —

	Phone
American Indian Arts Festival (late May-early October)	609-261-4747
Atlantic City Archery Classic (late April)	609-343-5043
Atlantic City Classic Car Auction (mid-February)	856-768-6900
Atlantic City International Power Boat Show (early February)	609-449-2000
Atlantic City Marathon Festival (mid-October)	609-601-1786
Atlantique City Fall Festival (mid-October)	609-926-1800
Atlantique City Spring Festival (late March)	609-926-1800
Beachfest (mid-June)	609-484-9020
Boardwalk Festival of the Arts Show (mid-June)	609-344-7855
Boardwalk Indian Summer Craft Show (mid-September)	609-347-5837
East Coast International Auto Show (early October)	609-883-5056
Easter Weekend Festival & Parade (mid-April)	609-344-7855
Fall Harvest Grape Stomping Festival (early August-early October)	609-965-2111
Fourth of July Celebration (July 4)	609-347-5427
Grand Christmas Exhibition (November-January)	800-998-4552
Kentucky Avenue Festival (mid-July)	609-348-7100
Latino Festival (early September)	609-345-2772
Miss America Pageant (mid-September)	609-345-7571
Mount Carmel Festival (mid-July)	609-561-0180
New Jersey Fresh Seafood Festival (early June)	609-348-7100

Atlantic City — Events (Cont'd)

	Phone
Ocean City Doll Show (late November)	609-525-9300
Ocean Life Festival (early August)	609-449-7130
Oktoberfest (early October)	609-348-7100
Red White & Blueberry Festival (late June)	609-561-9080
Sail Expo (late January)	609-449-2000
Saint Patrick's Day Parade (mid-March)	609-347-5427
Wheaton Village Craft Show (early October)	800-998-4552
Winter Crafts Show (late February)	609-965-2111

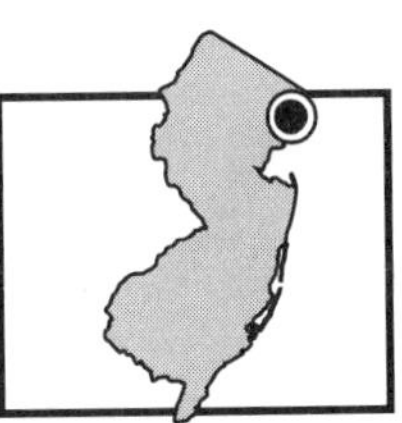

Jersey City

Located just across the Hudson River from New York City, Jersey City is known as "America's Golden Door" because of the vast number of immigrants who settled in the city after entering the U.S. at nearby Ellis Island. Today, a high speed ferry service and a commuter rail system link Jersey City with New York. Over the past decade, the city has undergone major renovations in every area"from its urban appearance to its telecommunications network" and since 1994 30 major companies have either relocated to Jersey City or have built divisions there. The city is expected to be New Jersey's largest by the year 2000.

Population	232,429	**Longitude**	74-03-53 W
Area (Land)	14.9 sq mi	**County**	Hudson
Area (Water)	6.2 sq mi	**Time Zone**	EST
Elevation	83 ft	**Area Code/s**	201
Latitude	40-42-40 N		

— Average Temperatures and Precipitation —

TEMPERATURES

	Jan	Feb	Mar	Apr	May	Jun	Jul	Aug	Sep	Oct	Nov	Dec
High	36	39	47	58	68	77	82	81	74	63	52	40
Low	23	25	33	42	53	62	68	66	59	48	39	28

PRECIPITATION

	Jan	Feb	Mar	Apr	May	Jun	Jul	Aug	Sep	Oct	Nov	Dec
Inches	3.0	2.9	3.7	3.9	4.1	3.5	4.0	3.8	3.7	3.2	4.0	3.7

— Important Phone Numbers —

	Phone		Phone
AAA	201-902-1393	**Medical Referral**	201-795-8358
American Express Travel	201-653-2600	**Poison Control Center**	800-764-7661
Emergency	911	**Travelers Aid of New Jersey**	973-623-5052

— Information Sources —

	City	State	Zip	Phone	Fax
Better Business Bureau Serving Northern New Jersey 400 Lanidex Plaza *Web:* www.parsippany.bbb.org	Parsippany	NJ	07054	973-581-1313	581-7022
Hudson County 583 Newark Ave Brennan Courthouse	Jersey City	NJ	07306	201-795-6112	795-2581
Hudson County Chamber of Commerce 574 Summit Ave Suite 404	Jersey City	NJ	07306	201-653-7400	798-3886
Hudson County Division of Cultural & Heritage Affairs 583 Newark Ave William Brennan Courthouse	Jersey City	NJ	07306	201-459-2070	792-0729
Jersey City City Hall 280 Grove St *Web:* www.cityofjerseycity.com	Jersey City	NJ	07302	201-547-5000	547-4833
Jersey City Economic Development Div 30 Montgomery St *Web:* www.cityofjerseycity.com/docs/hedc.html	Jersey City	NJ	07302	201-547-5070	547-6566
Jersey City Mayor 280 Grove St *Web:* www.cityofjerseycity.com/docs/mayor.htm	Jersey City	NJ	07302	201-547-5200	547-4288
Jersey City Public Library 472 Jersey Ave	Jersey City	NJ	07302	201-547-4500	547-4584

On-Line Resources

Anthill City Guide Jersey City	www.anthill.com/city.asp?city=jerseycity
Area Guide Jersey City	jerseycity.areaguides.net
Excite.com Jersey City City Guide	www.excite.com/travel/countries/united_states/new_jersey/jersey_city

— Transportation Services —

AIRPORTS

■ **Newark International Airport (EWR)**

	Phone
4 miles SW of downtown Jersey City (approx 15 minutes) Web: www.panynj.gov/newarkairport/	973-961-6000

Airport Transportation

	Phone
A-1 Taxi $18 fare to downtown Jersey City	201-222-1200
Alex Limousine Service $41 fare to downtown Jersey City	201-798-0060
Taxi $18 fare to downtown Jersey City	201-432-3333

Commercial Airlines

	Phone		Phone
Air Canada	800-776-3000	**Midway**	800-446-4392
Alitalia	800-223-5730	**Midwest Express**	800-452-2022
America West	800-235-9292	**Northeast Airway**	973-267-2450
American	800-433-7300	**Northwest**	800-225-2525
American Trans Air	800-225-2995	**Pan Am**	800-359-7262
Atlantic Aviation Charter	201-288-7660	**Spirit**	800-772-7117
British Airways	800-247-9297	**TWA**	800-221-2000
Continental	800-525-0280	**United**	800-241-6522
Continental Express	800-525-0280	**United Express**	800-241-6522
Delta	800-221-1212	**US Airways**	800-428-4322
Jet Aviation Business Jets Inc	800-736-8538	**US Airways Express**	800-428-4322
LOT Polish Airlines	800-223-0593	**Virgin Atlantic**	800-862-8621
Lufthansa	800-645-3880		

CAR RENTALS

	Phone		Phone
Avis	973-961-4300	**Hertz**	973-621-2000
Budget	973-961-2990	**Thrifty**	800-367-2277
Dollar	973-824-2002		

LIMO/TAXI

	Phone		Phone
Action Limousine	732-855-0058	**Hudson City Taxi Service**	201-432-3333
City Bergen Taxi	201-333-1700	**Newport Limousine Service**	201-332-7678

MASS TRANSIT

	Phone
New Jersey Transit $1 Base fare	973-491-7000
PATH Trains 1 PATH Plaza	800-234-7284

RAIL/BUS

	City	State	Zip	Phone
Amtrak Station Raymond Plaza W Penn Station *TF:* 800-872-7245	Newark	NJ	07102	973-596-2335
Greyhound/Trailways Bus Station Raymond Plaza W Penn Station	Newark	NJ	07102	800-231-2222

Jersey City (Cont'd)

— Accommodations —

HOTEL RESERVATION SERVICES

	Phone	Fax
American International Travel *Fax Area Code: 727 ■ TF: 800-681-3965	800-782-9872	897-4007*

HOTELS, MOTELS, RESORTS

	City	State	Zip	Phone	Fax
Econo Lodge 750-762 Tonnele Ave	Jersey City	NJ	07307	201-420-9040	
Hudson Regency Motel 360 Tonnele Ave.	Jersey City	NJ	07306	201-792-9500	
Lincoln Inn 13 Lincoln St.	Jersey City	NJ	07307	201-659-8686	659-4143
Quality Inn 180 12th St Holland Tunnel Plaza TF: 800-221-2222	Jersey City	NJ	07310	201-653-0300	659-1963
Skyway Motel 390 Tonnele Ave	Jersey City	NJ	07306	201-795-4700	
Spinning Wheel Motel 459 Tonnele Ave	Jersey City	NJ	07307	201-653-1222	963-8019
Starlite Motel 881 Tonnele Ave	Jersey City	NJ	07307	201-963-3361	

— Restaurants —

	City	State	Zip	Phone
A Taste Of The Caribbean (Caribbean) 800 Communipaw Ave	Jersey City	NJ	07304	201-332-6654
Canton Tea Garden (Chinese) 920 Bergen Ave	Jersey City	NJ	07306	201-653-4728
Casa Dante (Italian) 737 Newark Ave.	Jersey City	NJ	07306	201-795-2750
China Staro (Chinese) 136 Newark Ave.	Jersey City	NJ	07302	201-333-1670
Dominican Restaurant (Spanish) 311 Pacific Ave.	Jersey City	NJ	07304	201-432-9177
Downtown Eddy's Eatery (Italian) 516 Jersey Ave	Jersey City	NJ	07302	201-451-8883
El Sobroso (Puerto Rican) 2 Lincoln St	Jersey City	NJ	07307	201-216-1497
Fortune Chinese Restaurant (Chinese) 352 Palisade Ave	Jersey City	NJ	07302	201-714-9512
Hamilton Park Ale House (International) 708-714 Jersey Ave	Jersey City	NJ	07302	201-659-9111
Ibby's Falafel (Middle Eastern) 303 Grove St	Jersey City	NJ	07302	201-432-2400
JC Winston's (Soul) 292 Barrow St	Jersey City	NJ	07302	201-434-8694
Karina Restaurant (Spanish) 201 Ocean Ave.	Jersey City	NJ	07305	201-413-1963
Komegashi (Japanese) 103 Montgomery St	Jersey City	NJ	07302	201-433-4567
Laico's (Italian) 67 Terhune Ave	Jersey City	NJ	07305	201-434-9853
Lee Hing (Chinese) 457 ML King Jr Dr.	Jersey City	NJ	07304	201-915-9521
Lincoln Inn (Continental) 13 Lincoln St	Jersey City	NJ	07307	201-659-8686
Lisbon Restaurant (Mexican) 256 Warren St.	Jersey City	NJ	07302	201-432-9222
Lucky Chinese Restaurant (Chinese) 735 Grand St	Jersey City	NJ	07304	201-434-3520
Manila Sunset Restaurant (Filipino) 530 Montgomery St	Jersey City	NJ	07302	201-434-7717
Marker's Harborside Grill (Continental) 153 Plaza Two	Jersey City	NJ	07311	201-433-6275
Miss Saigon (Vietnamese) 249 Newark Ave	Jersey City	NJ	07302	201-239-1988
Neptune Cafe (Chinese) 1597 John F Kennedy Blvd.	Jersey City	NJ	07305	201-333-9337
Orange Kitchen (Chinese) 383 Communipaw Ave.	Jersey City	NJ	07304	201-333-1218
Our Place Restaurant (American) 431 Central Ave.	Jersey City	NJ	07307	201-792-1744
Pronto Cena Ristorante (Italian) 87 Sussex St	Jersey City	NJ	07302	201-435-0004
Rasoi Restaurant (Indian) 810 Newark Ave.	Jersey City	NJ	07306	201-222-8850
Sasha Mahal Restaurant (Indian) 824 Newark Ave	Jersey City	NJ	07306	201-963-6672
Siam Cuisine Of Thailand (Thai) 62 Morris St.	Jersey City	NJ	07302	201-433-7034
Tania's Restaurant (Polish) 348 Grove St.	Jersey City	NJ	07302	201-451-6189
Tio Tony (Italian) 90 Newark Ave.	Jersey City	NJ	07302	201-332-0770
Tu Nuevo Restaurant (Puerto Rican) 159 New York Ave.	Jersey City	NJ	07307	201-659-2004

— Goods and Services —

SHOPPING

	City	State	Zip	Phone	Fax
Hudson Mall Rt 440	Jersey City	NJ	07304	201-432-0119	432-4731
Journal Square Kennedy Blvd.	Jersey City	NJ	07306		
Newport Center Mall 30 Mall Dr W.	Jersey City	NJ	07310	201-626-2025	626-2033

BANKS

	City	State	Zip	Phone	Fax
Fleet Bank 10 Exchange Pl 1st Fl	Jersey City	NJ	07302	201-547-7000	547-7840
Hudson City Savings Bank 587 Summit Ave.	Jersey City	NJ	07306	201-653-8950	792-4889
PNC Bank 26 Journal Sq *Fax Area Code: 201	Jersey City	NJ	07306	800-225-2424	368-4680*
Provident Savings Bank 830 Bergen Ave TF: 800-448-7768 ■ Web: www.providentnj.com	Jersey City	NJ	07306	201-333-1000	860-9549
Statewide Savings Bank SLA 70 Sip Ave.	Jersey City	NJ	07306	201-795-7700	795-7721
Summit Bank 186 Newark Ave TF: 800-282-2265	Jersey City	NJ	07302	201-432-4400	432-6836
Trust Co of New Jersey 35 Journal Sq	Jersey City	NJ	07306	201-420-2500	420-0007

BUSINESS SERVICES

	Phone
Adecco Employment Personnel Services	212-682-3438
Airborne Express	800-247-2676
BAX Global	800-225-5229
DHL Worldwide Express	800-225-5345
Federal Express	800-238-5355
Mail Boxes Etc	201-420-6633
Olsten Staffing Services	201-653-8837
Post Office	201-915-7036
UPS	800-742-5877

— Media —

PUBLICATIONS

	City	State	Zip	Phone	Fax
Jersey Journal‡ 30 Journal Sq Web: www.nj.com	Jersey City	NJ	07306	201-653-1000	653-1414
New Jersey Business Magazine 310 Passaic Ave Web: www.njbmagazine.com/ ■ E-mail: njbmag@intac.com	Fairfield	NJ	07004	973-882-5004	882-4648

‡Daily newspapers

TELEVISION

	City	State	Zip	Phone	Fax
WABC-TV Ch 7 (ABC) 7 Lincoln Sq Web: abcnews.go.com/local/wabc	New York	NY	10023	212-456-7777	456-2381
WCBS-TV Ch 2 (CBS) 524 W 57th St Web: www.cbs2ny.com	New York	NY	10019	212-975-4321	975-9387
WNBC-TV Ch 4 (NBC) 30 Rockefeller Plaza Web: www.newschannel4.com ■ E-mail: nbc4ny@nbc.com	New York	NY	10112	212-664-4444	664-2994
WNET-TV Ch 13 (PBS) 450 W 33rd St. Web: www.wnet.org ■ E-mail: webinfo@www.wnet.org	New York	NY	10001	212-560-1313	582-3297
WNYW-TV Ch 5 (Fox) 205 E 67th St.	New York	NY	10021	212-452-5555	249-1182

RADIO

	City	State	Zip	Phone	Fax
WBGO-FM 88.3 MHz (NPR) 54 Park Pl Web: www.wbgo.org	Newark	NJ	07102	973-624-8880	824-8888
WFME-FM 94.7 MHz (Rel) 289 Mount Pleasant Ave TF: 800-543-1495	West Orange	NJ	07052	973-736-3600	736-4832
WKTU-FM 103.5 MHz (CHR) 525 Washington Blvd 16th Fl Web: www.ktu.com	Jersey City	NJ	07310	201-420-3700	420-3770
WNJR-AM 1430 kHz (Misc) 1 Riverfront Plaza Suite 345	Newark	NJ	07102	973-642-8000	642-5208
WPAT-AM 930 kHz (Misc) 449 Broadway 2nd Fl.	New York	NY	10013	212-966-1059	966-9580
WSKQ-FM 97.9 MHz (Span) 26 W 56th St. Web: www.lamega.com ■ E-mail: info@lamega.com	New York	NY	10019	212-541-9200	333-7642

— Colleges/Universities —

	City	State	Zip	Phone	Fax
Hudson County Community College 162 Sip Ave	Jersey City	NJ	07306	201-656-2020	714-2136
New Jersey City University 2039 JFK Blvd. TF Admissions: 888-441-6528 ■ Web: www.njcu.edu	Jersey City	NJ	07305	201-200-2000	200-2044
Saint Peter's College 2641 JFK Blvd. *Fax: Cust Svc ■ Web: www.spc.edu	Jersey City	NJ	07306	201-915-9000	451-0036*

— Hospitals —

	City	State	Zip	Phone	Fax
Christ Hospital 176 Palisade Ave Web: www.christhospital.org	Jersey City	NJ	07306	201-795-8200	795-8796
Jersey City Medical Center 50 Baldwin Ave.	Jersey City	NJ	07304	201-915-2000	915-2002
Saint Francis Hospital 25 McWilliams Pl.	Jersey City	NJ	07302	201-418-1000	418-2011

Jersey City (Cont'd)

— Attractions —

				Phone	Fax
Afro-American Historical Society Museum 1841 Kennedy Blvd	Jersey City	NJ	07305	201-547-5262	547-5392
Central Railroad Terminal Audrey Zapp Dr Liberty State Park	Jersey City	NJ	07304	201-915-3400	915-3413
Jersey City Museum 472 Jersey Ave.	Jersey City	NJ	07302	201-547-4514	
Kodak OMNI Theater 251 Phillip St.	Jersey City	NJ	07305	201-451-0006	451-6383
Liberty Science Center 251 Phillip St *Web:* www.lsc.org	Jersey City	NJ	07305	201-451-0006	451-6383
Liberty State Park Morris Pesin Dr	Jersey City	NJ	07304	201-915-3400	

SPORTS TEAMS & FACILITIES

				Phone	Fax
New Brunswick Brigade (soccer) Joyce Kilmer Ave Memorial Stadium	New Brunswick	NJ	08901	732-517-0278	517-0278
New Brunswick Power (soccer) Joyce Kilmer Ave Memorial Stadium	New Brunswick	NJ	08901	732-517-0278	517-0278
North Jersey Imperials (soccer) Sprague Field Montclair State University Campus *TF:* 888-542-5794 ■ *Web:* www.njimperials.com ■ *E-mail:* info@njimperials.com	Montclair	NJ	07042	201-729-1500	729-1511

— Events —

	Phone
Artists' Studio Tour (early October)	201-547-6969
Cathedral Arts Festival (mid-March)	201-659-2211
Communipaw Commemoratives (mid-May & mid-September)	201-915-3401
Cultural Arts Festival (mid-June)	201-547-5522
Egyptian Festival (mid-September)	201-547-5522
Greek Festival (early September)	201-547-5522
Irish Festival (late September)	201-547-5522
Italian Festival (mid-September)	201-547-5522
Korean Festival (late September)	201-547-5522
New Jersey Ethnic & Diversity Festival (late September)	609-777-0999

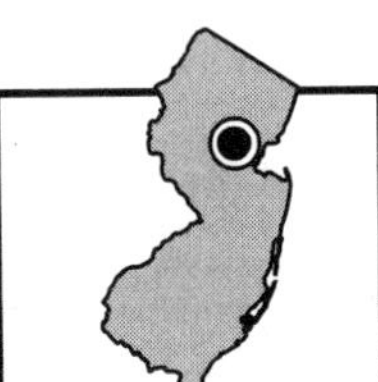

Newark

Originally founded as a Puritan settlement in the 17th Century, Newark is one of the oldest major cities in the U.S. It is noted primarily as a center of industry and commerce, with the largest container ship port and one of the largest airports in the nation. Cultural attractions include the Newark Public Library (founded 1889) and the Newark Museum, which includes a Junior Museum, Fire Museum, Planetarium, Ballantine House (1885), and Lyons Farm Schoolhouse (1784). Notable residents of Newark have included Stephen Crane, Washington Irving, and Jerome Kern.

Population	267,823	**Longitude**	74-17-28 W
Area (Land)	23.8 sq mi	**County**	Essex
Area (Water)	2.2 sq mi	**Time Zone**	EST
Elevation	95 ft	**Area Code/s**	973
Latitude	40-73-56 N		

— Average Temperatures and Precipitation —

TEMPERATURES

	Jan	Feb	Mar	Apr	May	Jun	Jul	Aug	Sep	Oct	Nov	Dec
High	38	41	51	62	72	82	87	85	78	67	55	43
Low	23	25	33	43	53	63	69	67	60	48	39	29

PRECIPITATION

	Jan	Feb	Mar	Apr	May	Jun	Jul	Aug	Sep	Oct	Nov	Dec
Inches	3.4	3.0	3.9	3.8	4.1	3.2	4.5	3.9	3.7	3.1	3.9	3.5

— Important Phone Numbers —

	Phone		Phone
AAA	800-222-4357	**Medical Referral**	973-673-1291
American Express Travel	201-436-5503	**Poison Control Center**	800-764-7661
Emergency	911	**Travelers Aid of New Jersey**	973-623-5052

— Information Sources —

				Phone	Fax
Better Business Bureau Serving Northern New Jersey 400 Lanidex Plaza *Web:* www.parsippany.bbb.org	Parsippany	NJ	07054	973-581-1313	581-7022
Essex County 465 ML King Jr Blvd *Web:* www.localsource.com/essexcty ■ *E-mail:* wcn22@localsource.com	Newark	NJ	07102	973-621-5000	
Meadowlands Exposition Center 355 Plaza Dr *Web:* www.meadowlands-expoctr.com	Secaucus	NJ	07094	201-223-1000	330-1172
Newark City Hall 920 Broad St. *Web:* www.ci.newark.nj.us	Newark	NJ	07102	973-733-8004	733-5352
Newark Development Dept 920 Broad St Rm 218	Newark	NJ	07102	973-733-6575	733-3965
Newark Mayor 920 Broad St City Hall Rm 200. *Web:* www.ci.newark.nj.us/govern/meet.html	Newark	NJ	07102	973-733-6400	733-5325
Newark Public Library 5 Washington St *Web:* www.npl.org	Newark	NJ	07101	973-733-7784	733-5919
Regional Business Partnership 744 Broad St National Newark Bldg 26th Fl *Web:* www.rbp.org ■ *E-mail:* rbp@rbp.org	Newark	NJ	07102	973-522-0099	824-6587

On-Line Resources

Area Guide Newark	newark.areaguides.net
Excite.com Newark City Guide	www.excite.com/travel/countries/united_states/new_jersey/newark
I-95 Exit Information Guide Newark	www.usastar.com/i95/cityguide/newark.htm

— Transportation Services —

AIRPORTS

■ **Newark International Airport (EWR)**

	Phone
3 miles S of downtown (approx 20 minutes) Web: www.panynj.gov/newarkairport	973-961-6000

Airport Transportation

	Phone
A P Personal Limo $23 fare to downtown	973-926-3756
Allaire Limousine $39 fare to downtown	800-255-2473
Green Taxi $11 fare to downtown	973-643-4100

Commercial Airlines

	Phone		Phone
Air Canada	800-776-3000	**Midway**	800-446-4392
Alitalia	800-223-5730	**Midwest Express**	800-452-2022
America West	800-235-9292	**Northwest**	800-225-2525
American	800-433-7300	**Northwest**	800-225-2525
American Trans Air	800-225-2995	**Pan Am**	800-359-7262
British Airways	800-247-9297	**Spirit**	800-772-7117
Continental	800-525-0280	**TWA**	800-221-2000
Continental Express	800-525-0280	**United**	800-241-6522
Czech Airlines	800-223-2365	**United Express**	800-241-6522
Kiwi	800-538-5494	**US Airways**	800-428-4322
LOT Polish Airlines	800-223-0593	**US Airways Express**	800-428-4322
Lufthansa	800-645-3880	**Virgin Atlantic**	800-862-8621

Charter Airlines

	Phone		Phone
Atlantic Aviation Charter	201-288-7660	**Northeast Airway**	973-267-2450
Jet Aviation Business Jets Inc	800-736-8538		

Newark (Cont'd)

CAR RENTALS

	Phone		Phone
Avis	973-961-4300	**Enterprise**	973-242-3400
Budget	973-961-2990	**Hertz**	973-621-2000
Dollar	973-824-2002	**Thrifty**	800-367-2277

LIMO/TAXI

	Phone		Phone
Allaire Limousine	800-255-2473	**Green Taxi**	973-643-4100
Garden State Limousine	800-451-7554	**Olympic Limousine**	800-822-9797
Gemini Limousine	973-578-4901		

MASS TRANSIT

	Phone
New Jersey Transit $1 Base fare	973-491-7000

RAIL/BUS

				Phone
Amtrak Station Raymond Plaza W Penn Station *TF:* 800-872-7245	Newark	NJ	07102	973-596-2335
Greyhound/Trailways Bus Station Raymond Plaza W Penn Station	Newark	NJ	07102	800-231-2222

— Accommodations —

HOTEL RESERVATION SERVICES

	Phone	Fax
American International Travel **Fax Area Code:* 727 ■ *TF:* 800-681-3965	800-782-9872	897-4007*

HOTELS, MOTELS, RESORTS

				Phone	Fax
Best Western Fairfield Executive Inn 216-234 Rt 46 E *TF:* 800-528-1234	Fairfield	NJ	07004	973-575-7700	575-4653
Budget Inn 427 Allen St	Elizabeth	NJ	07202	908-289-8900	
Clarion Hotel & Towers 2055 Lincoln Hwy *TF:* 800-221-2222	Edison	NJ	08817	732-287-3500	287-8190
Courtyard by Marriott Airport 600 Rts 1 & 9 S *TF:* 800-321-2211 ■ *Web:* courtyard.com/EWRCA	Newark	NJ	07114	973-643-8500	648-0662
Days Inn Airport 450 US Rt 1 S *TF:* 800-329-7466	Newark	NJ	07114	973-242-0900	242-8480
Divine Riviera Hotel 169 Clinton Ave	Newark	NJ	07108	973-824-6000	824-8598
Econo Lodge 853 US Hwy 1	Elizabeth	NJ	07201	908-353-1365	353-2927
Grand Summit Hotel 570 Springfield Ave *TF:* 800-346-0773	Summit	NJ	07901	908-273-3000	273-4228
Hamilton Park Conference Center 175 Park Ave *TF:* 800-321-6000 ■ *Web:* www.dolce.com/properties/hamiltonpark ■ *E-mail:* hamiltonpark@dolce.com	Florham Park	NJ	07932	973-377-2424	377-9560
Hampton Inn 1128-38 Spring St *TF:* 800-426-7866	Elizabeth	NJ	07207	908-355-0500	355-4343
Hilton Hotel Airport 1170 Spring St *TF:* 800-445-8667 ■ *Web:* www.hilton.com/hotels/EWRAHHH	Elizabeth	NJ	07201	908-351-3900	351-9556
Hilton Newark Gateway Raymond Blvd 1 Gateway Ctr *TF:* 800-445-8667 ■ *Web:* www.hilton.com/hotels/EWRHGHF	Newark	NJ	07102	973-622-5000	622-2644
Holiday Inn North Airport 160 Frontage Rd *TF:* 800-465-4329	Newark	NJ	07114	973-589-1000	589-2799
Howard Johnson Hotel 20 Frontage Rd *TF:* 800-446-4656	Newark	NJ	07114	973-344-1500	344-3311
Hyatt Regency 2 Albany St *TF:* 800-233-1234 ■ *Web:* www.hyatt.com/usa/new_brunswick/hotels/hotel_ewrrn.html	New Brunswick	NJ	08901	732-873-1234	873-1382
Newark Airport Marriott Hotel Newark International Airport *TF:* 800-228-9290	Newark	NJ	07114	973-623-0006	623-7618
Quality Inn 10 Polito Ave *TF:* 800-468-3588 ■ *Web:* www.qualityinnlyndhurstnj.com	Lyndhurst	NJ	07071	201-933-9800	933-0658
Radisson Hotel & Suites 690 Rt 46 E *TF:* 800-333-3333	Fairfield	NJ	07004	973-227-9200	227-4308
Ramada Inn 248 Haynes Ave *TF:* 800-272-6232	Newark	NJ	07114	973-824-4000	824-2034
Robert Treat House 50 Park Pl *TF:* 800-569-2300	Newark	NJ	07102	973-622-1000	622-6410
Sheraton Hotel Airport 128 Frontage Rd *TF:* 800-627-7158	Newark	NJ	07114	973-690-5500	690-5076
Westin Morristown Hotel 2 Whippany Rd *TF:* 800-221-0241	Morristown	NJ	07960	973-539-7300	984-1036

— Restaurants —

				Phone
Abin's (Italian) 184 Elm St	Newark	NJ	07105	973-589-3349
Anossa Casa (Portuguese) 195 Ferry St	Newark	NJ	07105	973-344-7016
Barbecue Hut (Barbecue) 776 Broad St	Newark	NJ	07102	973-624-7191
Bua Thai Restaurant (Thai) 137 Washington Ave	Belleville	NJ	07109	973-759-7425
Campino Restaurant (Portuguese) 70 Jabez St	Newark	NJ	07105	973-589-4004
Caribbean Palace (Caribbean) 218 Market St	Newark	NJ	07106	973-643-1973
Casa Vasca (Spanish) 141 Elm St	Newark	NJ	07105	973-465-1350
China Sea (Chinese) 136 Elm St	Newark	NJ	07105	973-344-8829
Dugboh Restaurant (African) 259 Halsey St	Newark	NJ	07102	973-622-6729
Europe Restaurant (Portuguese/Spanish) 44 Commerce St	Newark	NJ	07102	973-623-3772
Francine's (American) 144 Washington St	Newark	NJ	07102	973-623-5380
Gold Coast African Restaurant (African) 42 Broadway	Newark	NJ	07104	973-482-7188
Green Street Cafe (Italian) 20 Green St	Newark	NJ	07102	973-642-7373
Heng Sheng Restaurant (Chinese) 58 Green St	Newark	NJ	07102	973-242-3354
Iberia Peninsula Restaurant (Portuguese) 67 Ferry St	Newark	NJ	07105	973-344-5611
Jackson Cafe (Spanish) 108 Jackson St	Newark	NJ	07105	973-465-9155
Kibom Restaurant (Portuguese) 61 Wilson Ave	Newark	NJ	07105	973-491-0405
Little Spain (Spanish) 180 Elm St	Newark	NJ	07105	973-344-3459
Michaelangelo's (Italian) 544 Bloomfield Ave	Newark	NJ	07107	973-485-9057
New Park Restaurant (American) 60 Park Pl	Newark	NJ	07102	973-623-3930
Oscar's Restaurant (International) 51 Academy St	Newark	NJ	07102	973-622-4347
Panda Chinese Restaurant (Chinese) 569 Broad St	Newark	NJ	07102	973-623-2288
Restaurant Oyola (Spanish) 162 Broadway	Newark	NJ	07104	973-485-2811
Seabra's Marisqueria (Seafood) 87 Madison St	Newark	NJ	07105	973-465-1250
Tapajos River Steak House (Steak) 28 Wilson Ave	Newark	NJ	07105	973-491-9196
Taste Delight (Caribbean) 108 Halsey St	Newark	NJ	07102	973-297-1237
Tio Pepe Restaurant (Portugese/Spanish) 118 Stockton St	Newark	NJ	07105	973-344-1927
Wilson Cafe (Portuguese) 147 Wilson Ave	Newark	NJ	07105	973-589-4443
Yoshi Sono Japanese Restaurant (Japanese) 643 Eagle Rock Ave Suite A	West Orange	NJ	07052	973-325-2005

— Goods and Services —

SHOPPING

				Phone	Fax
Hudson Mall Rt 440	Jersey City	NJ	07304	201-432-0119	432-4731
Livingston Mall 112 Eisenhower Pkwy	Livingston	NJ	07039	973-994-9390	
Mall at Short Hills 1200 Morris Tpke	Short Hills	NJ	07078	973-376-7350	376-2976
Newport Center Mall 30 Mall Dr W	Jersey City	NJ	07310	201-626-2025	626-2033
Rockaway Townsquare Mall Rt 80 & Mt Hope Ave	Rockaway	NJ	07866	973-361-4070	361-1561

BANKS

				Phone	Fax
City National Bank of New Jersey 900 Broad St	Newark	NJ	07102	973-624-0865	624-4369
First Union Bank 550 Broad St	Newark	NJ	07102	973-565-3613	565-6992
Fleet Bank 1 Gateway Ctr	Newark	NJ	07102	973-648-8001	504-8515
Independence Community Bank 905 Broad St **Fax:* Hum Res ■ *TF:* 800-371-2625	Newark	NJ	07102	973-624-2300	624-5713*
Penn Federal Savings Bank 36 Ferry St *TF:* 800-722-0351	Newark	NJ	07105	973-589-8616	589-1202
Summit Bank 1 Newark Ctr *TF:* 800-282-2265	Newark	NJ	07102	973-624-3100	624-1446

BUSINESS SERVICES

	Phone		Phone
Airborne Express	800-247-2676	**Mail Boxes Etc**	800-789-4623
BAX Global	800-225-5229	**Post Office**	973-693-5200
DHL Worldwide Express	800-225-5345	**Snelling & Snelling**	973-623-2400
Excorp Temporary Service	973-621-6700	**UPS**	800-742-5877
Federal Express	800-238-5355		

Newark (Cont'd)

— Media —

PUBLICATIONS

Name / Address	City	State	ZIP	Phone	Fax
New Jersey Business Magazine					
310 Passaic Ave	Fairfield	NJ	07004	973-882-5004	882-4648
Web: www.njbmagazine.com/ ■ *E-mail:* njbmag@intac.com					
Star-Ledger‡ 1 Star Ledger Plaza	Newark	NJ	07102	973-877-4141	877-5845
Web: www.nj.com					

‡*Daily newspapers*

TELEVISION

Name / Address	City	State	ZIP	Phone	Fax
WABC-TV Ch 7 (ABC) 7 Lincoln Sq	New York	NY	10023	212-456-7777	456-2381
Web: abcnews.go.com/local/wabc					
WCBS-TV Ch 2 (CBS) 524 W 57th St	New York	NY	10019	212-975-4321	975-9387
Web: www.cbs2ny.com					
WNBC-TV Ch 4 (NBC) 30 Rockefeller Plaza	New York	NY	10112	212-664-4444	664-2994
Web: www.newschannel4.com ■ *E-mail:* nbc4ny@nbc.com					
WNET-TV Ch 13 (PBS) 450 W 33rd St	New York	NY	10001	212-560-1313	582-3297
Web: www.wnet.org ■ *E-mail:* webinfo@www.wnet.org					
WNYW-TV Ch 5 (Fox) 205 E 67th St	New York	NY	10021	212-452-5555	249-1182

RADIO

Name / Address	City	State	ZIP	Phone	Fax
WBGO-FM 88.3 MHz (NPR) 54 Park Pl	Newark	NJ	07102	973-624-8880	824-8888
Web: www.wbgo.org					
WFME-FM 94.7 MHz (Rel)					
289 Mount Pleasant Ave	West Orange	NJ	07052	973-736-3600	736-4832
TF: 800-543-1495					
WMTZ-FM 96.5 MHz (Ctry) PO Box 370	Johnstown	PA	15907	814-535-8554	535-8557
Web: www.mountain96-5.com					
WNJR-AM 1430 kHz (Misc)					
1 Riverfront Plaza Suite 345	Newark	NJ	07102	973-642-8000	642-5208
WPAT-AM 930 kHz (Misc)					
449 Broadway 2nd Fl	New York	NY	10013	212-966-1059	966-9580
WSKQ-FM 97.9 MHz (Span) 26 W 56th St	New York	NY	10019	212-541-9200	333-7642
Web: www.lamega.com ■ *E-mail:* info@lamega.com					

— Colleges/Universities —

Name / Address	City	State	ZIP	Phone	Fax
Bloomfield College 467 Franklin St	Bloomfield	NJ	07003	973-748-9000	743-3998
Web: www.bloomfield.edu					
Caldwell College 9 Ryerson Ave	Caldwell	NJ	07006	973-228-4424	228-3600
TF Admissions: 800-864-9516 ■ *Web:* www.caldwell.edu					
College of Saint Elizabeth 2 Convent Rd	Morristown	NJ	07960	973-290-4000	290-4488
TF Admissions: 800-210-7900 ■ *Web:* www.st-elizabeth.edu					
Drew University 36 Madison Ave	Madison	NJ	07940	973-408-3000	408-3068
Web: www.drew.edu ■ *E-mail:* cwis@www.drew.edu					
Essex County College 303 University Ave	Newark	NJ	07102	973-877-3000	877-3044
Web: www.essex.edu					
Felician College 262 S Main St	Lodi	NJ	07644	973-778-1190	778-4111
Web: www.felician.edu ■ *E-mail:* admissions@inet.felician.edu					
Kean University 1000 Morris Ave	Union	NJ	07083	908-527-2000	351-5187
Web: www.kean.edu					
Montclair State University					
1 Normal Ave	Upper Montclair	NJ	07043	973-655-4000	655-7700
TF: 800-331-9205 ■ *Web:* www.montclair.edu					
New Jersey Institute of Technology					
323 ML King Jr Blvd	Newark	NJ	07102	973-596-3000	596-3461
Web: www.njit.edu					
Rabbinical College of America					
PO Box 1996	Morristown	NJ	07962	973-267-9404	267-5208
Rutgers The State University of New Jersey					
Newark Campus 249 University Ave	Newark	NJ	07102	973-353-1766	353-1440
Web: info.rutgers.edu/newark/rutgers-newark.html					
Seton Hall University					
400 S Orange Ave	South Orange	NJ	07079	973-761-9000	761-9452
Web: www.shu.edu ■ *E-mail:* thehall@lanmail.shu.edu					
Stevens Institute of Technology					
Castle Point on the Hudson	Hoboken	NJ	07030	201-216-5000	216-8348
TF Admissions: 800-458-5323 ■ *Web:* www.stevens-tech.edu ■ *E-mail:* admissions@stevens-tech.edu					

— Hospitals —

Name / Address	City	State	ZIP	Phone	Fax
Columbus Hospital 495 N 13th St	Newark	NJ	07107	973-268-1400	268-1523*
**Fax:* Admitting					
Newark Beth Israel Medical Center					
201 Lyons Ave	Newark	NJ	07112	973-926-7000	923-2886*
**Fax:* Admitting ■ *E-mail:* info@sbhcs.com					
Saint James Hospital of Newark					
155 Jefferson St	Newark	NJ	07105	973-589-1300	425-2861
Web: www.cathedralhealthcare.org/aboutsj.html					
Saint Michael's Medical Center					
268 Dr ML King Jr Blvd	Newark	NJ	07102	973-877-5000	877-2895*
**Fax:* Admissions ■ *Web:* www.cathedralhealthcare.org/aboutsmi.html					

— Attractions —

Name / Address	City	State	ZIP	Phone	Fax
Aljira Center for Contemporary Arts					
2 Washington Pl 4th Fl	Newark	NJ	07102	973-643-6877	643-3594
Ballantine House 49 Washington St	Newark	NJ	07101	973-596-6550	642-0459
Belcher-Ogden Mansion 1046 E Jersey St	Elizabeth	NJ	07210	908-351-2500	355-5519
Boxwood Hall State Historic Site					
1073 E Jersey St	Elizabeth	NJ	07201	973-648-4540	
Branch Brook Park Clifton Ave & Rt 280	Newark	NJ	07014	973-268-3500	
Cathedral Concert Series 89 Ridge St	Newark	NJ	07104	973-484-4600	483-8253
City Without Walls Gallery 1 Gateway Ctr	Newark	NJ	07102	973-622-1188	622-2941
Dreyfuss Planetarium 49 Washington St	Newark	NJ	07101	973-596-6529	642-0459
TF: 800-768-7386 ■ *Web:* rutgers-newark.rutgers.edu/dreyfuss/					
Durand Hedden House 523 Ridgewood Rd	Maplewood	NJ	07040	973-763-7712	
Eagle Rock Reservation					
Eagle Rock & Prospect Aves	West Orange	NJ	07052	973-268-3500	
Elizabeth Playhouse 1100 E Jersey St	Elizabeth	NJ	07201	908-355-0077	
Essex County Courthouse 50 Market St	Newark	NJ	07102	973-693-5701	621-5912
First Baptist Peddie Memorial Church					
Broad & Fulton Sts	Newark	NJ	07102	973-642-2552	
First Presbyterian Church 820 Broad St	Newark	NJ	07102	973-642-0260	
Grace Episcopal Church 950 Broad St	Newark	NJ	07102	973-623-1733	
House of Prayer 407 Broad St	Newark	NJ	07104	973-483-8202	
Montclair Art Museum 3 S Mountain Ave	Montclair	NJ	07042	973-746-5555	746-9118
Web: www.montclair-art.com					
Montclair Historical Society Israel Crane House 110 Orange Rd	Montclair	NJ	07042	973-783-1717	783-9419
Morristown National Historical Park					
Washington Pl	Morristown	NJ	07960	973-539-2085	539-8361
Web: www.nps.gov/morr/					
Mount Pleasant Cemetery 375 Broadway	Newark	NJ	07104	973-483-0288	
New Jersey Historical Society Museum					
52 Park Pl	Newark	NJ	07102	973-596-8500	596-6957
New Jersey Performing Arts Center					
1 Center St	Newark	NJ	07102	973-642-8989	648-6724
TF: 888-466-5722					
New Jersey State Opera 50 Park Pl 10th Fl	Newark	NJ	07102	973-623-5757	623-5761
New Jersey Symphony Orchestra					
2 Central Ave	Newark	NJ	07102	973-624-3713	
Web: www.nj.com/symphony					
Newark Boys Chorus 1016 Broad St	Newark	NJ	07102	973-621-8900	621-7970
Newark City Hall 920 Broad St	Newark	NJ	07102	973-733-8004	733-5352
Newark Museum 49 Washington St	Newark	NJ	07101	973-596-6550	642-0459
TF: 800-768-7386					
Newark Symphony Hall 1030 Broad St	Newark	NJ	07102	973-643-8009	
North Reformed Church 510 Broad St	Newark	NJ	07102	973-623-3198	
Pennsylvania Station Raymond Plaza	Newark	NJ	07015	973-491-8757	
Sacred Heart Cathedral Basilica 89 Ridge St	Newark	NJ	07104	973-484-4600	483-8253
Saint Casimir Roman Polish Catholic Church					
91 Pulaski St	Newark	NJ	07105	973-344-2743	344-5629
Saint James AME Church 588 MLK Jr Blvd	Newark	NJ	07102	973-622-1344	
Saint John's Catholic Church 22 Mulberry St	Newark	NJ	07102	973-623-0822	623-6804
Saint Patrick's Pro-Cathedral					
91 Washington St	Newark	NJ	07102	973-623-0497	623-2030
South Mountain Reservation					
Northfield Ave & Pleasant Valley Way	West Orange	NJ	07052	973-268-3500	
Trinity & Saint Philip's Cathedral					
608 Broad St	Newark	NJ	07102	973-643-0137	622-2235
Washington Park Washington & Broad Sts	Newark	NJ	07102	973-733-6454	

SPORTS TEAMS & FACILITIES

Name / Address	City	State	ZIP	Phone	Fax
New Brunswick Brigade (soccer)					
Joyce Kilmer Ave Memorial Stadium	New Brunswick	NJ	08901	732-517-0278	517-0278
New Brunswick Power (soccer)					
Joyce Kilmer Ave Memorial Stadium	New Brunswick	NJ	08901	732-517-0278	517-0278

Newark (Cont'd)

— Events —

	Phone
Flower & Garden Show (late February-early March)	732-469-4000
Junior Museum Festival (late November)	973-596-6550
Newark Black Film Festival (late June-early August)	973-596-6550
Newark Festival of People (early September)	973-733-8004
Newark Jazz Connection (early December)	973-733-6454

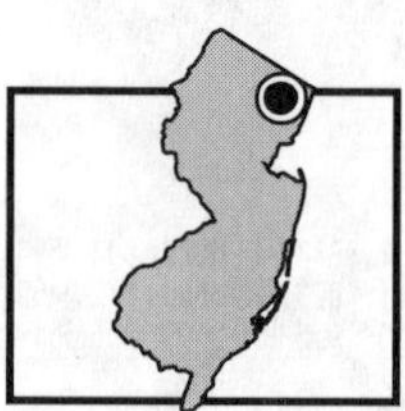

Paterson

Paterson was founded in 1791 as the first planned industrial community in the United States. It was born of Alexander Hamilton's vision of an American nation of "manufactories" drawing upon the water-power potential of the city's Great Falls, the 70-foot-high waterfall that adorns the Passaic River and which remains a popular attraction today. The U.S. silk industry and the Colt revolver can trace their roots to Paterson, along with important innovations in machinery, chemicals, engineering, and urban design. Today the Great Falls historic district and Paterson Museum, which features the world's first submarines, document the city's key role in the industrial revolution. Famed beat writer Jack Kerouac and poet William Carlos Williams are among the literary notables who have immortalized Paterson in their works.

Population	148,212	**Longitude**	74-09-48 W
Area (Land)	8.4 sq mi	**County**	Passaic
Area (Water)	0.3 sq mi	**Time Zone**	EST
Elevation	70 ft	**Area Code/s**	973
Latitude	40-54-52 N		

— Average Temperatures and Precipitation —

TEMPERATURES

	Jan	Feb	Mar	Apr	May	Jun	Jul	Aug	Sep	Oct	Nov	Dec
High	37	40	50	61	72	81	86	84	77	66	54	42
Low	19	21	30	40	50	59	64	63	55	43	35	25

PRECIPITATION

	Jan	Feb	Mar	Apr	May	Jun	Jul	Aug	Sep	Oct	Nov	Dec
Inches	3.5	3.2	4.2	4.4	4.7	4.0	4.5	4.4	4.7	3.9	4.4	4.0

— Important Phone Numbers —

	Phone		Phone
AAA	973-956-2200	**Medical Referral**	973-890-0700
American Express Travel	973-614-0044	**Poison Control Center**	800-764-7661
Dental Referral	973-812-1101	**Travelers Aid of New Jersey**	973-623-5052
Emergency	911	**Weather**	973-267-1093

— Information Sources —

				Phone	Fax
Better Business Bureau Serving Northern New Jersey 400 Lanidex Plaza *Web:* www.parsippany.bbb.org	Parsippany	NJ	07054	973-581-1313	581-7022
Great Falls Historic Landmark District Visitor Center 65 McBride Avenue Ext	Paterson	NJ	07501	973-279-9587	357-0121
Greater Paterson Chamber of Commerce 100 Hamilton Plaza Suite 1201 *Web:* www.greaterpatersoncc.org ■ *E-mail:* gpcc@greaterpatersoncc.org	Paterson	NJ	07505	973-881-7300	881-8233
Passaic County 401 Grand St	Paterson	NJ	07505	973-881-4000	754-1920
Paterson City Hall 155 Market St	Paterson	NJ	07505	973-881-3400	881-7085
Paterson Community Development Dept 125 Ellison St 2nd Fl	Paterson	NJ	07505	973-279-5980	278-2981
Paterson Mayor 155 Market St City Hall	Paterson	NJ	07505	973-881-3380	881-7364
Paterson Public Library 250 Broadway	Paterson	NJ	07501	973-357-3000	881-8338

On-Line Resources

4Paterson.com	www.4paterson.com
Area Guide Paterson	paterson.areaguides.net

— Transportation Services —

AIRPORTS

■ **Newark International Airport (EWR)**

	Phone
15 miles S of downtown Paterson (approx 20 minutes)	973-961-6000

Web: www.panynj.gov/newarkairport/

Airport Transportation

	Phone
Taxi $35 fare to downtown Paterson	973-742-5808
West Paterson Taxi $45 fare to downtown Paterson	973-473-4111

Commercial Airlines

	Phone		Phone
Air Canada	800-776-3000	**Midway**	800-446-4392
Alitalia	800-223-5730	**Midwest Express**	800-452-2022
America West	800-235-9292	**Northwest**	800-225-2525
American	800-433-7300	**Spirit**	800-772-7117
American Trans Air	800-225-2995	**TWA**	800-221-2000
British Airways	800-247-9297	**United**	800-241-6522
Continental	800-525-0280	**United Express**	800-241-6522
Continental Express	800-525-0280	**US Airways**	800-428-4322
Delta	800-221-1212	**US Airways Express**	800-428-4322
LOT Polish Airlines	800-223-0593	**Virgin Atlantic**	800-862-8621
Lufthansa	800-645-3880		

Charter Airlines

	Phone		Phone
Atlantic Aviation Charter	201-288-7660	**Northeast Airway**	973-267-2450
Jet Aviation Business Jets Inc	800-736-8538		

CAR RENTALS

	Phone		Phone
Avis	973-961-4300	**Enterprise**	973-242-3400
Budget	973-961-2990	**Hertz**	973-621-2000
Dollar	973-824-2002	**Thrifty**	800-367-2277

LIMO/TAXI

	Phone		Phone
Allaire Limousine	800-255-2473	**Olympic Limousine**	800-822-9797
Bravo Limousine & Car Service	973-278-2356	**Tri Way Limousine**	973-278-2420
Car Club Inc	973-628-8333	**Vets Taxi Inc**	973-278-1212
Garden State Limousine	800-451-7554	**Wayne Taxi & Limo**	973-742-5808
Gemini Limousine	973-578-4901	**West Paterson Taxi**	973-473-4111
Green Taxi	973-643-4100	**West Way Limousine**	973-256-4040

MASS TRANSIT

	Phone
New Jersey Transit $1 Base fare	973-491-7000

RAIL/BUS

				Phone
Amtrak Station Raymond Plaza W Penn Station *TF:* 800-872-7245	Newark	NJ	07102	973-596-2335
Greyhound/Trailways Bus Station Raymond Plaza W Penn Station	Newark	NJ	07102	800-231-2222

Paterson (Cont'd)

— Accommodations —

HOTEL RESERVATION SERVICES

	Phone	Fax
American International Travel *Fax Area Code: 727 ■ TF: 800-681-3965	800-782-9872	897-4007*

HOTELS, MOTELS, RESORTS

				Phone	Fax
Alexander Hamilton Hotel 55 Church St	Paterson	NJ	07505	973-742-7800	
Clinton Inn Hotel 145 Dean Dr TF: 800-275-4411	Tenafly	NJ	07670	201-871-3200	871-3435
Holiday Inn 334 Rt 46 E Service Rd TF: 800-465-4329	Wayne	NJ	07470	973-256-7000	890-5406
Holiday Inn Totowa 1 Rt 46 TF: 800-465-4329 ■ Web: www.basshotels.com/holiday-inn/?_franchisee=TOTNJ ■ E-mail: crestmotel@aol.com	Totowa	NJ	07512	973-785-9000	785-3031
Hotel Passaic 4 Henry St	Passaic	NJ	07055	973-773-0739	
Howard Johnson 1850 Rt 23 & Ratzer Rd	Wayne	NJ	07470	973-696-8050	696-0682
Howard Johnson 680 Rt 3 W	Clifton	NJ	07014	973-471-3800	471-2128
Radisson Hotel 401 S Van Brunt St TF: 800-333-3333	Englewood	NJ	07631	201-871-2020	871-7116
Radisson Hotel & Suites 690 Rt 46 E TF: 800-333-3333	Fairfield	NJ	07004	973-227-9200	227-4308
Rainbow Motel 411 Broadway	Paterson	NJ	07501	973-684-4455	
Ramada Hotel 265 Rt 3 E TF: 800-272-6232	Clifton	NJ	07014	973-778-6500	778-8724
Regency House Hotel 140 Rt 23 N	Pompton Plains	NJ	07444	973-696-0900	696-0201

— Restaurants —

				Phone
Chappy's Grill (American) 197 E Railway Ave	Paterson	NJ	07503	973-278-0972
Charles Restaurant & Bar (American) 57 Mill St	Paterson	NJ	07501	973-345-3083
Chicken King Barbecue Restaurant (Barbecue) 215 Market St	Paterson	NJ	07505	973-279-0944
China House (Chinese) 178 E 33rd St	Paterson	NJ	07504	973-881-1888
E & V Ristorante (Italian) 320 Chamberlain Ave	Paterson	NJ	07502	973-942-4664
Festejo Restaurant (Latin American) 282 Union Ave	Paterson	NJ	07502	973-956-5877
Griselda's Restaurant (Seafood) 81 Market St	Paterson	NJ	07505	973-225-0331
Hunan Chinese Restaurant (Chinese) 170 Market St	Paterson	NJ	07505	973-881-8898
La Hacienda Restaurant (Mexican) 102 McLean Blvd	Paterson	NJ	07514	973-345-1255
La Trattoria (Italian) 58 Ellison St	Paterson	NJ	07505	973-684-4250
Latin Bar (Mexican) 410 Main St	Paterson	NJ	07501	973-278-3393
Madison Four Diner Restaurant (International) 1212 Madison Ave	Paterson	NJ	07503	973-684-2525
Paterson Seafood Inc (Seafood) 130 Market St	Paterson	NJ	07505	973-279-0087
Piccola Roma Restaurant (Italian) 146 Washington St	Paterson	NJ	07505	973-684-3535
Ramallah Restaurant (Middle Eastern) 1003 Main St	Paterson	NJ	07503	973-345-1901
Salahedin Middle East Restaurant (Middle Eastern) 995 Main St	Paterson	NJ	07503	973-225-0575
Tauruss (Jamacian) 220 Memorial Dr	Paterson	NJ	07505	973-742-4538

— Goods and Services —

SHOPPING

				Phone	Fax
Berdan Shopping Center 1160 Hamburg Tpke	Wayne	NJ	07470	973-694-1343	694-1241
Bergen Mall 2701 Bergen Mall	Paramus	NJ	07652	201-845-4050	
Garden State Plaza 1 Garden State Plaza	Paramus	NJ	07652	201-843-2404	843-1716
Willowbrook Mall 1400 Willowbrook Mall	Wayne	NJ	07470	973-785-1616	785-8632

BANKS

				Phone	Fax
City National Bank of New Jersey 21-2 Mill St	Paterson	NJ	07501	973-279-8700	279-4424
Hudson United Bank 100 Hamilton Plaza	Paterson	NJ	07505	973-742-6000	742-0370
Lakeview Savings Bank 1117 Main St	Paterson	NJ	07503	973-742-3060	742-3505
PNC Bank 129 Market St TF: 800-225-2424	Paterson	NJ	07505	800-762-3955	

BUSINESS SERVICES

	Phone		Phone
Airborne Express	800-247-2676	**Post Office**	973-977-4740
DHL Worldwide Express	800-225-5345	**Uniforce Temporary Services**	973-458-9700
Federal Express	800-238-5355	**UPS**	800-742-5877

— Media —

PUBLICATIONS

				Phone	Fax
New Jersey Business Magazine 310 Passaic Ave Web: www.njbmagazine.com/ ■ E-mail: njbmag@intac.com	Fairfield	NJ	07004	973-882-5004	882-4648
North Jersey Herald & News‡ 988 Main Ave E-mail: njhn@aol.com	Passaic	NJ	07055	973-365-3000	614-0906

‡Daily newspapers

TELEVISION

				Phone	Fax
WABC-TV Ch 7 (ABC) 7 Lincoln Sq Web: abcnews.go.com/local/wabc	New York	NY	10023	212-456-7777	456-2381
WCBS-TV Ch 2 (CBS) 524 W 57th St Web: www.cbs2ny.com	New York	NY	10019	212-975-4321	975-9387
WNBC-TV Ch 4 (NBC) 30 Rockefeller Plaza Web: www.newschannel4.com ■ E-mail: nbc4ny@nbc.com	New York	NY	10112	212-664-4444	664-2994
WNET-TV Ch 13 (PBS) 450 W 33rd St Web: www.wnet.org ■ E-mail: webinfo@www.wnet.org	New York	NY	10001	212-560-1313	582-3297
WNYW-TV Ch 5 (Fox) 205 E 67th St	New York	NY	10021	212-452-5555	249-1182

RADIO

				Phone	Fax
WBGO-FM 88.3 MHz (NPR) 54 Park Pl Web: www.wbgo.org	Newark	NJ	07102	973-624-8880	824-8888
WNJR-AM 1430 kHz (Misc) 1 Riverfront Plaza Suite 345	Newark	NJ	07102	973-642-8000	642-5208
WWRV-AM 1330 KHz (Rel) 419 Broadway	Paterson	NJ	07509	973-881-8700	881-8324

— Colleges/Universities —

				Phone	Fax
Berkeley College of Business 44 Rifle Camp Rd TF: 800-446-5400 ■ Web: www.berkeley.org ■ E-mail: info@berkeley.org	West Paterson	NJ	07424	973-278-5400	278-9141
Passaic County Community College 1 College Blvd Web: www.pccc.cc.nj.us/	Paterson	NJ	07505	973-684-6800	684-5843

— Hospitals —

				Phone	Fax
Barnert Hospital 680 Broadway	Paterson	NJ	07514	973-977-6600	742-6248
Passaic Beth Israel Hospital 70 Parker Ave Web: www.pbih.org	Passaic	NJ	07055	973-365-5000	471-5531
Passaic County Preakness Hospital 40 Valley View Rd	Haledon	NJ	07508	973-904-5000	471-5531
Saint Joseph's Hospital & Medical Center 703 Main St *Fax: Admitting ■ Web: www.sjhmc.org	Paterson	NJ	07503	973-754-2000	754-2208*
Wayne General Hospital 224 Hamburg Tpke	Wayne	NJ	07470	973-942-6900	389-4044

— Attractions —

				Phone	Fax
Garret Mountain Reservation 311 Pennsylvania Ave	Paterson	NJ	07503	973-881-4832	523-8712
Great Falls Historic District 65 McBride Ave Ext	Paterson	NJ	07501	973-279-9587	357-0121
Lambert Castle Museum 3 Valley Rd	Paterson	NJ	07503	973-881-2761	
Paterson Museum 2 Market St Thomas Rogers Bldg	Paterson	NJ	07501	973-881-3874	881-3435

Paterson (Cont'd)

SPORTS TEAMS & FACILITIES

				Phone	Fax
North Jersey Imperials (soccer) Sprague Field Montclair State University Campus	Montclair	NJ	07042	201-729-1500	729-1511

TF: 888-542-5794 ■ *Web:* www.njimperials.com ■ *E-mail:* info@njimperials.com

— Events —

	Phone
Great Falls Festival (Labor Day weekend)	973-523-9201
Jazz It Up Festival (late July)	973-523-9201
Peruvian Festival & Parade (late July)	973-523-9201
Puerto Rican Festival & Parade (late August)	973-523-9201
Wayne Days (mid-June)	973-628-9183

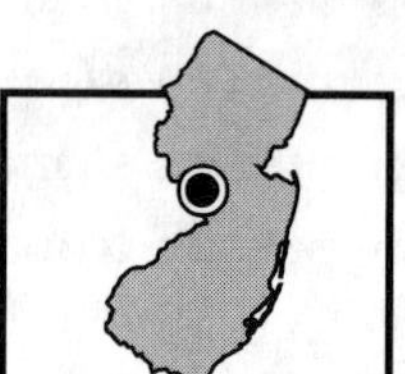

Trenton

The New Jersey State Capitol Complex in Trenton houses not only state government offices but also historical attractions, including the Old Barracks Museum where Washington's troops were quartered after crossing the Delaware and taking the city of Trenton in 1776. The Old Masonic Lodge at the Capitol Complex now houses Trenton's Convention and Visitors Bureau; and the War Memorial, past site of gubernatorial inaugurations and political gatherings, is now a concert hall and theater. Located at the Capitol Complex also are the State House, Museum, and Archives, which illustrate the history of New Jersey through architectecture and exhibits, and the State House Annex and Library. Famous Trenton citizens have included Walter Scott Lenox, creator of Lenox china, and the Roeblings, who designed and built the Brooklyn Bridge.

Population	84,494	**Longitude**	74-74-33 W
Area (Land)	7.7 sq mi	**County**	Mercer
Area (Water)	0.5 sq mi	**Time Zone**	EST
Elevation	54 ft	**Area Code/s**	609
Latitude	40-21-69 N		

— Average Temperatures and Precipitation —

TEMPERATURES

	Jan	Feb	Mar	Apr	May	Jun	Jul	Aug	Sep	Oct	Nov	Dec
High	38	41	52	63	73	82	86	85	78	66	55	43
Low	23	25	33	42	53	62	67	66	59	46	38	28

PRECIPITATION

	Jan	Feb	Mar	Apr	May	Jun	Jul	Aug	Sep	Oct	Nov	Dec
Inches	3.2	2.8	3.5	3.6	3.8	3.7	4.3	3.8	3.4	2.6	3.3	3.4

— Important Phone Numbers —

	Phone		Phone
AAA	609-419-1704	**Poison Control Center**	800-764-7661
Emergency	911	**Travelers Aid of New Jersey**	973-623-5052
HotelDocs	800-468-3537	**Weather**	609-261-6600

— Information Sources —

				Phone	Fax
Better Business Bureau Serving Central New Jersey 1700 Whitehorse-Hamilton Sq Rd Suite D-5	Trenton	NJ	08690	609-588-0808	588-0546
Web: www.trenton.bbb.org					
Mercer County PO Box 8068	Trenton	NJ	08650	609-989-6470	989-1111
Web: www.prodworks.com/trenton/mercer.htm					
Mercer County Chamber of Commerce 214 W State St	Trenton	NJ	08608	609-393-4143	393-1032
Web: www.mercerchamber.org					
Trenton City Hall 319 E State St	Trenton	NJ	08608	609-989-3185	989-3190
Trenton Convention & Visitors Bureau Lafayette & Barrack Sts	Trenton	NJ	08608	609-777-1770	292-3771
Web: www.trentonnj.com ■ *E-mail:* trentoncvb@voicenet.com					
Trenton Downtown Assn 23 E State St	Trenton	NJ	08608	609-393-8998	396-4329
Web: www.trentonnj.com/downtown/default.htm					
Trenton Mayor 319 E State St	Trenton	NJ	06808	609-989-3030	989-3939
Trenton Public Library 120 Academy St	Trenton	NJ	08608	609-392-7188	396-7655
Web: www.trentonlibrary.state.nj.us					

On-Line Resources

Area Guide Trenton	trenton.areaguides.net
City Knowledge Trenton	www.cityknowledge.com/nj_trenton.htm
Excite.com Trenton City Guide	www.excite.com/travel/countries/united_states/new_jersey/trenton
Trenton Home Page	www.prodworks.com/trenton

— Transportation Services —

AIRPORTS

■ **Philadelphia International Airport (PHL)**

	Phone
39 miles W of downtown Trenton (approx 60 minutes)	215-937-6937

Airport Transportation

	Phone
Owen's Taxi & Limo $65 fare to downtown Trenton	609-392-6687

Commercial Airlines

	Phone		Phone
Air Jamaica	800-523-5585	**Mexicana**	800-531-7923
American	800-433-7300	**Midway**	800-446-4392
American Eagle	800-433-7300	**National**	888-757-5387
British Airways	800-247-9297	**Northwest**	800-225-2525
Continental	800-525-0280	**United**	800-241-6522
Continental Express	800-525-0280	**US Airways**	800-428-4322
Delta	800-221-1212	**US Airways Express**	800-428-4322

Charter Airlines

	Phone		Phone
Northeast Aviation Charter Inc	215-677-5592	**Sterling Helicopters**	215-271-2510
Philadelphia Jet Service	800-468-1490	**Wings Charter**	215-646-1800
Ronson Aviation Inc.	609-771-9500		

CAR RENTALS

	Phone		Phone
Alamo	215-492-3960	**Enterprise**	610-521-3700
Avis-Philadelphia	215-492-0900	**Hertz**	215-492-7200
Budget	215-492-9400	**Hertz-Trenton**	609-771-4086
CarTemps USA	215-334-8800	**National**	215-492-2750
Dollar	215-365-2700	**Rent-A-Wreck-Trenton**	609-587-7800

LIMO/TAXI

	Phone		Phone
A-1 Limousine	609-771-0600	**American Limousine**	609-588-5959
Allen's Taxi	609-392-3399	**Yellow Cab**	609-396-8181

MASS TRANSIT

	Phone
NJ Transit $1 Base fare	973-762-5100

RAIL/BUS

				Phone
Amtrak Station 72 S Clinton Ave	Trenton	NJ	08609	800-872-7245

Trenton (Cont'd)

— Accommodations —

HOTEL RESERVATION SERVICES

	Phone	Fax
American International Travel	800-782-9872	897-4007*
**Fax Area Code: 727* ■ *TF:* 800-681-3965		

HOTELS, MOTELS, RESORTS

	City	State	Zip	Phone	Fax
Best Western 2020 Rt 541	Mount Holly	NJ	08060	609-261-3800	267-0958
TF: 800-528-1234 ■ *E-mail:* info@burlington.com					
Best Western Rt 206 & Dunns Mill Rd	Bordentown	NJ	08505	609-298-8000	291-9757
TF: 800-528-1234					
Budget Inn 590 New York Ave	Trenton	NJ	08638	609-599-9300	421-0823
Days Inn 1073 Rt 206 N	Bordentown	NJ	08505	609-298-6100	298-7509
TF: 800-329-7466					
Days Inn 460 Rt 33 E	East Windsor	NJ	08520	609-448-3200	448-8447
TF: 800-329-7466					
Econo Lodge 187 Rt 130	Bordentown	NJ	08505	609-298-5000	298-5009
TF: 800-553-2666					
Freehold Gardens Hotel & Conference Center Rt 537 Gibson Pl	Freehold	NJ	07728	732-780-3870	780-8725
TF: 800-458-8802 ■ *Web:* www.freeholdgardens.com					
Hill Motel 350 S Broad St	Trenton	NJ	08608	609-392-7166	396-7705
Hilton East Brunswick & Towers 3 Tower Ctr Blvd.	East Brunswick	NJ	08816	732-828-2000	828-6958
TF: 800-445-8667 ■ *Web:* www.hilton.com/hotels/EWRBHHH					
Holiday Inn 4355 Rt 1 & Ridge Rd	Princeton	NJ	08540	609-452-2400	452-2494
TF: 800-465-4329					
Hotel Novotel 100 Independence Way	Princeton	NJ	08540	609-520-1200	520-0594
TF: 800-521-6835					
Howard Johnson 2995 Rt 1	Lawrenceville	NJ	08648	609-896-1100	095-1325
Hyatt Regency Princeton 102 Carnegie Center	Princeton	NJ	08540	609-987-1234	987-2584
TF: 800-233-1234 ■ *Web:* www.hyatt.com/usa/princeton/hotels/hotel_princ.html					
Imperial Motel 3312 Rt 206	Bordentown	NJ	08505	609-298-3355	298-4617
Inn at Lambertville Station 11 Bridge St	Lambertville	NJ	08530	609-397-4400	397-9744
TF: 800-524-1091 ■ *Web:* www.lambertvillestation.com/inn.html					
McIntosh Inn US Rt 1	Lawrenceville	NJ	08648	609-896-3700	896-2544
TF: 800-444-2775					
Nassau Inn The 10 Palmer Square	Princeton	NJ	08542	609-921-7500	921-9385
Palmer Inn Best Western 3499 Rt 1 S	Princeton	NJ	08540	609-452-2500	452-1371
TF: 800-688-0500					
Princeton Marriott 201 Village Blvd	Princeton	NJ	08540	609-452-7900	452-1223
TF: 800-228-9290					
Ramada Inn 1083 Rt 206	Bordentown	NJ	08505	609-298-3200	298-8845
TF: 800-272-6232					
Red Roof Inn 3203 Brunswick Pike	Lawrenceville	NJ	08648	609-896-3388	896-4919
TF: 800-843-7663					
Residence Inn by Marriott 4225 Rt 1	Princeton	NJ	08543	732-329-9600	329-8422
TF: 800-331-3131 ■ *Web:* www.residenceinn.com/TTNPR					
Sheraton Bucks County Hotel 400 Oxford Valley Rd	Langhorne	PA	19047	215-547-4100	269-3400
TF: 800-325-3535					
Somerset Marriott Hotel 110 Davidson Ave	Somerset	NJ	08873	732-560-0500	560-0817
TF: 800-228-9290					
Stage Depot Motel 145 Rt 31 N	Pennington	NJ	08534	609-466-2000	466-2622
Town House The Rt 33	Hightstown	NJ	08520	609-448-2400	443-0395
TF: 800-922-0622					
Trent Motel 2006 Brunswick Ave	Lawrenceville	NJ	08648	609-599-9516	394-7681

— Restaurants —

	City	State	Zip	Phone
Amici Milano Restaurant (Italian) 600 Chesnut Ave	Trenton	NJ	08611	609-396-6300
Andros Diner (American) 1781 E State St	Trenton	NJ	08609	609-588-5969
Arctic Restaurant (American) 22 Arctic Pkwy	Trenton	NJ	08638	609-392-6264
Baldassari Regency (Italian) 145 Morris Ave	Trenton	NJ	08611	609-392-2934
Banzai (Japanese) 3690 Quakerbridge Rd	Trenton	NJ	08619	609-587-5454
Blue Danube (European) 538 Adeline St	Trenton	NJ	08621	609-393-6133
Casa Mia (Italian) 273 Morris Ave	Trenton	NJ	08611	609-396-1223
Centre House Pub (American) 499 Centre St	Trenton	NJ	08611	609-599-9558
Chianti's (Italian) 701 Whittaker Ave	Trenton	NJ	08611	609-695-0011
Corner Inn (American) Center & Lalor Sts	Trenton	NJ	08611	609-695-9898
Cricket's (Continental) 1218 S Clinton Ave	Trenton	NJ	08611	609-396-4188
Diamond's (Italian) 132 Kent St	Trenton	NJ	08611	609-393-1000
Web: www.diamonds.inter.net/				
El Mezon Aguadillano (Spanish) 202 Perry St	Trenton	NJ	08618	609-392-8981
Good Times Tavern (American) 160 Ashmore Ave	Trenton	NJ	08611	609-695-5067
Happy Wok Chinese Restaurant (Chinese) 1400 Parkway Ave	Trenton	NJ	08628	609-882-1067
Homestead Inn (American) 800 Kuser Rd	Trenton	NJ	08619	609-890-9851
Joe's Mill Hill Saloon (American) 300 S Broad St	Trenton	NJ	08608	609-394-7222
John Henry's Seafood Restaurant (Seafood) 2 Mifflin St	Trenton	NJ	08611	609-396-3083
La Fontana Ristorante (Italian) 836 Parkway Ave	Trenton	NJ	08618	609-883-0391
Larry Peroni's Waterfront (Steak/Seafood) 1140 River Rd	Trenton	NJ	08628	609-882-0303
Malaga Spanish Restaurant (Spanish) 511 Lalor St	Trenton	NJ	08610	609-396-8878
Marsilio's (Italian) 541 Roebling Ave	Trenton	NJ	08611	609-695-1916
Peking House (Chinese) 1664 Nottingham Way	Trenton	NJ	08619	609-586-6111
River City Cafe (American) 559 Emory Ave	Trenton	NJ	08611	609-394-2900
Rossi's (Continental) 501 Morris Ave	Trenton	NJ	08611	609-394-9089
Soho (American) 142 Mott St	Trenton	NJ	08611	609-695-9028
Something Special to Eat & Drink (American) 18 E Lafayette St	Trenton	NJ	08608	609-392-7313
Towne House Restaurant (American) 39 W State St	Trenton	NJ	08608	609-392-0207

— Goods and Services —

SHOPPING

	City	State	Zip	Phone	Fax
Independence Mall 2465 South Broad St	Hamilton	NJ	08610	609-888-1116	
Palmer Square 47 Hulfish St	Princeton	NJ	08542	609-921-2333	921-3797
TF: 800-644-3489					
Princeton Forrestal Village US 1 & College Rd	Princeton	NJ	08540	609-799-7400	799-0245
Quaker Bridge Mall 150 Quaker Bridge Mall	Lawrenceville	NJ	08648	609-799-8177	275-6523
Web: www.quakerbridgemall.com ■ *E-mail:* info@quakerbridgemall.com					

BANKS

	City	State	Zip	Phone	Fax
First Union Bank 370 Scotch Rd	Pennington	NJ	08628	609-771-5700	530-7267*
**Fax:* Hum Res					
Fleet Bank 200 E State St	Trenton	NJ	08608	609-421-2003	396-9492
Sovereign Bank 33 W State St	Trenton	NJ	08608	609-396-7502	396-5170
Summit Bank 150 W State St	Trenton	NJ	08608	609-695-1100	695-2631

BUSINESS SERVICES

	Phone		Phone
Airborne Express	800-247-2676	**Mail Boxes Etc**	800-789-4623
BAX Global	800-225-5229	**Office Concierge**	609-895-2999
DHL Worldwide Express	800-225-5345	**Post Office**	609-599-4003
Federal Express	800-238-5355	**UPS**	800-742-5877

— Media —

PUBLICATIONS

	City	State	Zip	Phone	Fax
Trenton Times‡ 500 Perry St	Trenton	NJ	08618	609-396-3232	394-2819
Web: www.nj.com					
Trentonian‡ 600 Perry St	Trenton	NJ	08602	609-989-7800	393-6072
Web: www.trentonian.com					

‡Daily newspapers

TELEVISION

	City	State	Zip	Phone	Fax
KYW-TV Ch 3 (CBS) 101 S Independence Mall E	Philadelphia	PA	19106	215-238-4700	238-4783
Web: www.kyw.com					
WABC-TV Ch 7 (ABC) 7 Lincoln Sq	New York	NY	10023	212-456-7777	456-2381
Web: abcnews.go.com/local/wabc					
WCAU-TV Ch 10 (NBC) 10 Monument Rd	Bala Cynwyd	PA	19004	610-668-5510	668-3700
Web: www.nbc10.com					
WCBS-TV Ch 2 (CBS) 524 W 57th St	New York	NY	10019	212-975-4321	975-9387
Web: www.cbs2ny.com					
WNBC-TV Ch 4 (NBC) 30 Rockefeller Plaza	New York	NY	10112	212-664-4444	664-2994
Web: www.newschannel4.com ■ *E-mail:* nbc4ny@nbc.com					
WNJT-TV Ch 52 (PBS) 25 S Stockton St	Trenton	NJ	08611	609-777-5000	633-2927
WNYW-TV Ch 5 (Fox) 205 E 67th St	New York	NY	10021	212-452-5555	249-1182
WPVI-TV Ch 6 (ABC) 4100 City Line Ave	Philadelphia	PA	19131	215-878-9700	581-4530
Web: abcnews.go.com/local/wpvi					

Trenton — Television (Cont'd)

				Phone	Fax
WTXF-TV Ch 29 (Fox) 330 Market St. Web: www.foxphiladelphia.com	Philadelphia	PA	19106	215-925-2929	925-2420

RADIO

				Phone	Fax
WBUD-AM 1260 kHz (N/T) 218 Ewingville Rd.	Trenton	NJ	08638	609-882-4600	883-6684
WKXW-FM 101.5 MHz (N/T) PO Box 5698. *Web:* www.nj1015.com ■ *E-mail:* nj1015@nj1015.com	Trenton	NJ	08638	609-882-4600	883-6684
WNJT-FM 88.1 MHz (NPR) 25 S Stockton St.	Trenton	NJ	08608	609-777-5036	777-5400
WTSR-FM 91.3 MHz (Misc) 2000 Pennington Rd College of New Jersey *Web:* www.tcnj.edu/~wtsr ■ *E-mail:* wtsr@tcnj.edu	Ewing	NJ	08628	609-771-3200	771-3272
WTTM-AM 920 kHz (N/T) 275 Lincoln Hwy	Fairless Hills	PA	19030	215-949-8513	949-9956
WWFM-FM 89.1 MHz (Clas) PO Box B *Web:* www.wwfm.org	Trenton	NJ	08690	609-587-8989	586-4533

— Colleges/Universities —

				Phone	Fax
College of New Jersey PO Box 7718 *Web:* www.trenton.edu	Ewing	NJ	08628	609-771-1855	637-5174
Mercer County Community College PO Box B *Web:* www.mccc.edu	Trenton	NJ	08690	609-586-4800	586-6944
Princeton University 111 W College Bldg. *Web:* www.princeton.edu ■ *E-mail:* Q3436@pucc.princeton.edu	Princeton	NJ	08544	609-258-3000	258-6743
Rider University 2083 Lawrenceville Rd. *TF Admissions:* 800-257-9026 ■ *Web:* www.rider.edu	Lawrenceville	NJ	08648	609-896-5000	895-6645
Thomas Edison State College 101 W State St *Web:* www.tesc.edu ■ *E-mail:* admissions@call.tesc.edu	Trenton	NJ	08608	609-984-1102	984-8447
Westminster Choir College 101 Walnut Ln *Web:* westminster.rider.edu ■ *E-mail:* wccinfo@rider.edu	Princeton	NJ	08540	609-921-7100	921-8829

— Hospitals —

				Phone	Fax
Capital Health System at Mercer PO Box 1658	Trenton	NJ	08618	609-394-4000	394-4032
Fuld Helene Medical Center 750 Brunswick Ave	Trenton	NJ	08638	609-394-6000	394-6687
Medical Center at Princeton 253 Witherspoon St	Princeton	NJ	08540	609-497-4000	497-4977
RWJ University Hospital at Hamilton 1 Hamilton Health Pl	Hamilton	NJ	08690	609-586-7900	584-6429
Saint Francis Medical Center 601 Hamilton Ave **Fax:* Admitting ■ *TF:* 800-225-5249 ■ *Web:* www.healthytimes.com/stfrancis.html	Trenton	NJ	08629	609-599-5000	599-5112*

— Attractions —

				Phone	Fax
Artworks Gallery 19 Everett Alley	Trenton	NJ	08611	609-394-9436	394-9551
Contemporary Victorian Townhouse Museum 176 W State St.	Trenton	NJ	08608	609-392-9727	
Greater Trenton Symphony 28 W State St Suite 202	Trenton	NJ	08608	609-394-1338	394-1394
John Abbott II House 2200 Kuser Rd	Trenton	NJ	08619	609-585-1686	
Mercer County Waterfront Park 1 Thunder Rd	Trenton	NJ	08611	609-394-8326	
Meredith Havens Fire Museum 244 Perry St.	Trenton	NJ	08618	609-989-4038	989-4280
Mill Hill Playhouse Front & Montgomery Sts.	Trenton	NJ	08608	609-989-3038	
New Jersey State House 125 W State St.	Trenton	NJ	08625	609-633-2709	
New Jersey State Museum 205 W State St *Web:* www.state.nj.us/state/museum/musidx.html ■ *E-mail:* feedback@sos.state.nj.us	Trenton	NJ	08625	609-292-6300	599-4098
Old Barracks Museum Barrack St *Web:* www.voicenet.com/~barracks/ ■ *E-mail:* barracks@omni.voicenet.com	Trenton	NJ	08608	609-396-1776	777-4000
Passage Theatre Co Front & Montgomery Sts.	Trenton	NJ	08608	609-392-0766	
Trent William House 15 Market St.	Trenton	NJ	08611	609-989-3027	278-7890
Trenton Battle Monument	Trenton	NJ	08638	609-737-0623	
Trenton City Museum at Ellarslie Mansion Parkside & Stuyvesant Aves *Web:* www.ellarslie.org	Trenton	NJ	08618	609-989-3632	989-3624
War Memorial Theatre W Lafayette St	Trenton	NJ	08625	609-984-8484	777-0581

SPORTS TEAMS & FACILITIES

				Phone	Fax
New Brunswick Brigade (soccer) Joyce Kilmer Ave Memorial Stadium	New Brunswick	NJ	08901	732-517-0278	517-0278
New Brunswick Power (soccer) Joyce Kilmer Ave Memorial Stadium	New Brunswick	NJ	08901	732-517-0278	517-0278
New Jersey Wildcats Old Trenton Rd Mercer County Pk	Trenton	NJ	08690	609-860-2995	860-2995
Trenton Thunder (baseball) 1 Thunder Rd Waterfront Pk *Web:* www.trentonthunder.com	Trenton	NJ	08611	609-394-8326	394-9666

— Events —

	Phone
Crossing The (December 25)	215-493-4076
First Union Classic The (early June)	609-777-1770
Heritage Days (June)	609-777-1770
Super Science Weekend (January)	609-984-0676
Trenton Jazz Festival (late August)	609-777-1770

New Mexico

Population (1999): 1,739,844 **Area (sq mi): 121,598**

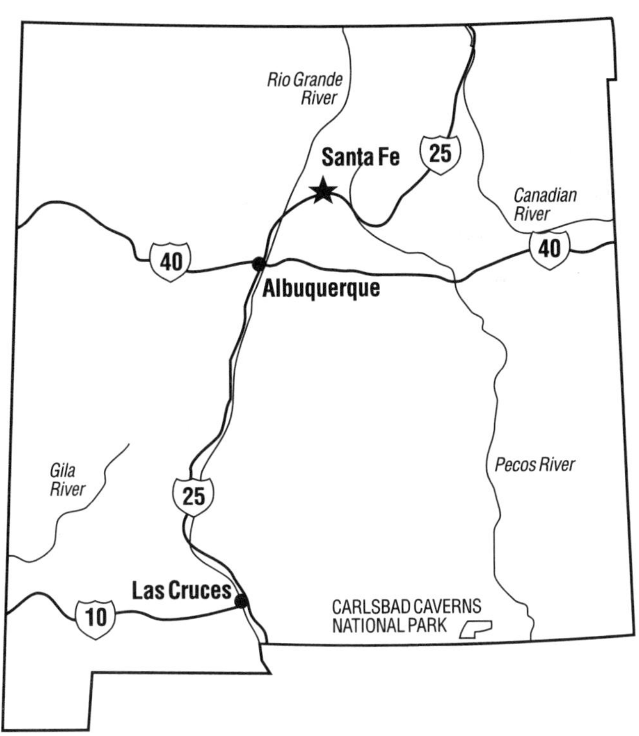

— State Information Sources —

		Phone	Fax
New Mexico Assn of Commerce & Industry PO Box 9706	Albuquerque NM 87119	505-842-0644	842-0734
Web: www.technet.nm.org/aci/ ■ *E-mail:* aci@pop.nm.org			
New Mexico Economic Development Dept PO Box 20003	Santa Fe NM 87504	505-827-0305	827-0328
Web: www.edd.state.nm.us			
New Mexico State Government Information		505-827-9632	
Web: www.state.nm.us ■ *E-mail:* pvigil@isd.state.nm.us			
New Mexico State Parks Div PO Box 1147	Santa Fe NM 87504	505-827-7173	827-1376
TF: 888-667-2757 ■ *Web:* www.emnrd.state.nm.us/nmparks			
New Mexico Tourism Dept 491 Old Santa Fe Trail	Santa Fe NM 87503	505-827-7400	827-7402
TF: 800-545-2040 ■ *Web:* www.newmexico.org ■ *E-mail:* enchantment@newmexico.org			

ON-LINE RESOURCES

Cybertourist New Mexico . . . . www.cybertourist.com/new_mexico.shtml
New Mexico Cities . . . . dir.yahoo.com/Regional/U_S__States/New_Mexico/Cities
New Mexico Counties & Regions . . . . dir.yahoo.com/Regional/U_S__States/New_Mexico/Counties_and_Regions
New Mexico Net . . . . www.bncinc.com/nmnet
New Mexico Online Highways . . . . www.nmohwy.com
New Mexico Restaurant Assn . . . . www.nmrestaurants.org
New Mexico Scenario . . . . scenariousa.dstylus.com/nm/indexf.htm
New Mexico Travel & Tourism Guide . . . . www.travel-library.com/north_america/usa/new_mexico/index.html
Newmexico.net . . . . www.newmexiconet.com
NewMexicom . . . . www.newmexicom.com
Rough Guide Travel New Mexico travel.roughguides.com/content/1140/index.htm
Travel.org-New Mexico . . . . travel.org/newmexi.html
Viva New Mexico . . . . www.viva.com/nm
What's Up New Mexico! . . . . www.whatsupnewmexico.com
Yahoo! Get Local New Mexico . . . . dir.yahoo.com/Regional/U_S__States/New_Mexico

— Cities Profiled —

Page

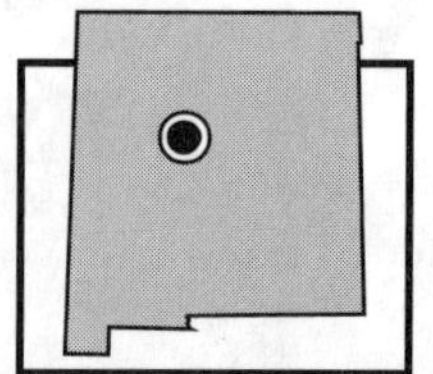

Albuquerque

Albuquerque originated in the part of the present-day city known as Old Town. With more than 150 shops, galleries, and restaurants housed in historic adobe buildings, Old Town is a popular site for visitors to the city. Just north of the Old Town area is the Indian Pueblo Cultural Center, which features arts and crafts from all 19 of New Mexico's pueblos. The Center also houses a restaurant that specializes in Native American-style cooking. On the west side of the city is Petroglyph National Monument, with more than 17,000 ancient images representing the world's largest accessible collection of prehistoric rock art. From downtown Albuquerque one can board the Sandia Peak Aerial Tramway, rising 2.7 miles above deep canyons to the Sandia Peak observation deck, with a panoramic view spanning some 11,000 square miles. Albuquerque is also the site of Sandia National Laboratory, a major U.S. nuclear research, development, and testing facility. Annual events in Albuquerque include the International Balloon Fiesta, which draws 650 hot-air balloons and 1.6 million spectators each October; and the Gathering of Nations Powwow, featuring 5,000 Native American singers and dancers representing more than 300 tribes.

Population	419,311	**Longitude**	106-65-06 W
Area (Land)	132.2 sq mi	**County**	Bernalillo
Area (Water)	0.6 sq mi	**Time Zone**	MST
Elevation	5311 ft	**Area Code/s**	505
Latitude	35-08-44 N		

— Average Temperatures and Precipitation —

TEMPERATURES

	Jan	Feb	Mar	Apr	May	Jun	Jul	Aug	Sep	Oct	Nov	Dec
High	47	54	61	71	80	90	93	89	82	71	57	48
Low	22	26	32	40	49	58	64	63	55	43	31	23

PRECIPITATION

	Jan	Feb	Mar	Apr	May	Jun	Jul	Aug	Sep	Oct	Nov	Dec
Inches	0.4	0.5	0.5	0.5	0.5	0.6	1.4	1.6	1.0	0.9	0.4	0.5

— Important Phone Numbers —

	Phone		Phone
AAA	505-291-6611	**Non-emergency Police**	505-242-2677
American Express Travel	505-332-5900	**Poison Control Center**	505-272-2222
Dental Referral	800-917-6453	**Road Conditions**	800-432-4269
Emergency	911	**Time/Temp**	505-247-1611
Event Information	800-284-2282	**Weather**	505-821-1111
HotelDocs	800-468-3537		

— Information Sources —

				Phone	Fax
Albuquerque City Hall 400 Marquette Ave 1 Civic Plaza	Albuquerque	NM	87102	505-768-2000	768-3019
Web: www.cabq.gov					
Albuquerque Convention & Visitors Bureau 20 First Plaza Suite 601	Albuquerque	NM	87102	505-842-9918	247-9101
TF: 800-284-2282 ■ *Web:* www.abqcvb.org ■ *E-mail:* info@abqcvb.org					
Albuquerque Convention Center PO Box 1293	Albuquerque	NM	87103	505-768-4575	768-3239
Albuquerque Economic Development Board 851 University Blvd SE Suite 203	Albuquerque	NM	87106	505-246-6200	246-6219
TF: 800-451-2933 ■ *Web:* www.abq.org					
Albuquerque Mayor PO Box 1293	Albuquerque	NM	87103	505-768-3000	768-3019
Web: www.cabq.gov/mayor ■ *E-mail:* mayor@cabq.gov					
Albuquerque Planning Dept PO Box 1293	Albuquerque	NM	87103	505-924-3860	924-3339
Web: www.cabq.gov/planning					
Albuquerque Public Library 501 Copper Ave NW	Albuquerque	NM	87102	505-768-5140	768-5191
Web: www.cabq.gov/rgvls/					
Bernalillo County 1 Civic Plaza NW 10th Fl	Albuquerque	NM	87102	505-768-4000	768-4329
Web: www.bernco.gov/					
Better Business Bureau Serving New Mexico 2625 Pennsylvania NE Suite 2050	Albuquerque	NM	87110	505-346-0110	346-0696
TF: 800-873-2224 ■ *Web:* www.bbbnm.com ■ *E-mail:* bureau@bbbnm.com					
Greater Albuquerque Chamber of Commerce PO Box 25100	Albuquerque	NM	87125	505-764-3700	764-3714
Web: www.gacc.org ■ *E-mail:* asutten@gacc.org					
New Mexico Indian Tourism Assn 2401 12th St NW Rm 211	Albuquerque	NM	87104	505-246-1668	246-0344

On-Line Resources

4Albuquerque.com	www.4albuquerque.com
About.com Guide to Albuquerque/Santa Fe	albuquerque.about.com/local/southwestus/albuquerque
Albuquerque CityLink	usacitylink.com/albuquer/
Albuquerque New Mexico	albuquerque-new-mexico.com
Albuquerque On-Line	www.albq-online.com
Albuquerque Santa Fe Web	www.abq-sfe.com
Anthill City Guide Albuquerque	www.anthill.com/city.asp?city=albuquerque
Area Guide Albuquerque	albuquerque.areaguides.net
Boulevards Albuquerque	www.albuquerque.com
City Knowledge Albuquerque	www.cityknowledge.com/nm_albuquerque.htm
DigitalCity Albuquerque	home.digitalcity.com/albuquerque
Excite.com Albuquerque City Guide	www.excite.com/travel/countries/united_states/new_mexico/albuquerque
Great Locations Guidebook Albuquerque	www.nmgl.com
InAlbuquerque.com	www.inalbuquerque.com
Link Jewish Newspaper	www.swcp.com/~thelink/
NITC Travelbase City Guide Albuquerque	www.travelbase.com/auto/guides/albuquerque-area-nm.html
Weekly Alibi	multihome.www.desert.net/alibi/current/

— Transportation Services —

AIRPORTS

■ **Albuquerque International Airport (ABQ)**

	Phone
5 miles SE of downtown (approx 10 minutes)	505-842-4366

Web: www.cabq.gov/airport/

Airport Transportation

	Phone
Checker Airport Express $10 fare to downtown	505-765-1234
ShuttleJack $20 fare to downtown	505-982-4311
Sun Tran Bus Service $.75 fare to downtown	505-843-9200
Taxi $10-12 fare to downtown	505-247-8888

Commercial Airlines

	Phone		Phone
America West	800-235-9292	**Frontier**	800-432-1359
American	800-433-7300	**Mesa**	800-637-2247
Continental	800-525-0280	**Southwest**	505-245-1717
Continental Express	800-525-0280	**TWA**	800-221-2000
Delta	800-221-1212	**United**	800-241-6522

Charter Airlines

	Phone		Phone
Alliance Executive Charter Services	800-232-5387	**Cutter Aviation Service Inc**	505-842-4184
		Mountain Aviation Enterprises	505-842-6660

CAR RENTALS

	Phone		Phone
Advantage	505-247-1066	**Enterprise**	505-764-9100
Alamo	505-842-4057	**Hertz**	505-842-4235
Avis	505-842-4080	**National**	505-842-4222
Budget	505-768-5920	**Rent-A-Wreck**	505-232-7552
Dollar	505-842-4224	**Thrifty**	505-842-8733

Albuquerque (Cont'd)

LIMO/TAXI

	Phone		Phone
Albuquerque Cab	505-883-4888	**Imperial Limousine**	505-298-9944
Checker Cab	505-243-7777	**Yellow Cab**	505-247-8888
Dream Limousine	505-884-6464		

MASS TRANSIT

	Phone
Sun Tran Bus Service $.75 Base fare	505-843-9200
Sun Trolley Transit $.75 Base fare	505-843-9200

RAIL/BUS

				Phone
Albuquerque Amtrak Station 214 1st St SW	Albuquerque	NM	87102	505-842-9650
Greyhound/Trailways Bus Station 300 2nd St SW	Albuquerque	NM	87102	505-243-4435

— Accommodations —

HOTEL RESERVATION SERVICES

	Phone	Fax
Advance Reservations Inn Arizona TF: 800-456-0682 ■ Web: tucson.com/inn ■ E-mail: micasa@primenet.com	480-990-0682	990-3390
New Mexico Central Reservations TF: 800-466-7829 ■ Web: www.nmtravel.com ■ E-mail: reservations@nmtravel.com	505-766-9770	247-8200

HOTELS, MOTELS, RESORTS

				Phone	Fax
Albuquerque Hilton 1901 University Blvd NE TF: 800-274-6835 ■ Web: www.albuquerquehilton.com ■ E-mail: albuquerquehilton@travelbase.com	Albuquerque	NM	87102	505-884-2500	889-9118
Albuquerque Marriott 2101 Louisiana Blvd NE TF: 800-334-2086	Albuquerque	NM	87110	505-881-6800	888-2982
Amberley Suite Hotel 7620 Pan American Fwy NE TF: 800-333-9806 ■ Web: www.amberleysuite.com ■ E-mail: amberleysuitenm@aol.com	Albuquerque	NM	87109	505-823-1300	823-2896
AmeriSuites 6901 Arvada Ave NE TF: 800-833-1516	Albuquerque	NM	87110	505-872-9000	872-3829
AmeriSuites Airport 1400 Sunport Pl SE TF: 800-833-1516	Albuquerque	NM	87106	505-242-9300	242-0998
Angel Fire Resort PO Drawer B TF: 800-633-7463 ■ Web: www.angelfireresort.com	Angel Fire	NM	87710	505-377-6401	377-4200
Barcelona Suites Hotel 900 Louisiana Blvd NE TF: 800-878-9258 ■ Web: www.barsuites.com ■ E-mail: info@barsuites.com	Albuquerque	NM	87110	505-255-5566	266-6644
Baymont Inns & Suites Airport 1511 Gibson SE TF: 877-242-1142	Albuquerque	NM	87108	505-242-1555	242-8801
Best Western Airport Inn 2400 Yale Blvd SE TF: 800-528-1234	Albuquerque	NM	87106	505-242-7022	243-0620
Best Western American Motor Inn 12999 Central Ave NE TF: 800-366-3252	Albuquerque	NM	87123	505-298-7426	298-0212
Best Western Rio Grande Inn 1015 Rio Grande Blvd NW TF: 800-959-4726 ■ Web: www.riograndeinn.com ■ E-mail: bestwestriogrande@travelbase.com	Albuquerque	NM	87104	505-843-9500	843-9238
Best Western Winrock Inn 18 Winrock Ctr TF: 800-866-5252	Albuquerque	NM	87110	505-883-5252	889-3206
ClubHouse Inn 1315 Menaul Blvd NE TF: 800-258-2466	Albuquerque	NM	87107	505-345-0010	344-3911
Comfort Inn Airport 2300 Yale Blvd SE TF: 800-221-2222	Albuquerque	NM	87106	505-243-2244	247-2925
Courtyard by Marriott 1920 Yale Blvd SE TF: 800-321-2211 ■ Web: courtyard.com/ABQCA	Albuquerque	NM	87106	505-843-6600	843-8740
Courtyard by Marriott Journal Center 5151 Journal Ctr Blvd TF: 800-321-2211 ■ Web: courtyard.com/ABQCY	Albuquerque	NM	87109	505-823-1919	823-1918
Crossland Economy Studios 5020 Ellison St NE TF: 800-398-7829 ■ Web: www.extstay.com/loc/nm_albuquerque_northeast_crs.html	Albuquerque	NM	87109	505-343-1100	343-1102
Crowne Plaza Pyramid at Journal Center 5151 San Francisco Rd NE TF: 800-227-6963	Albuquerque	NM	87109	505-821-3333	828-0230
Doubletree Hotel 201 Marquette Ave NW TF: 800-222-8733 ■ Web: www.doubletreehotels.com/DoubleT/Hotel61/68/68Main.htm	Albuquerque	NM	87102	505-247-3344	247-7025
Fairfield Inn by Marriott 2300 Centre SE TF: 800-228-2800 ■ Web: fairfieldinn.com/ABQFA	Albuquerque	NM	87106	505-247-1621	247-9719
Fairfield Inn University Area 1760 Menaul Rd NE TF: 800-228-2800 ■ Web: fairfieldinn.com/ABQFI	Albuquerque	NM	87102	505-889-4000	872-3094
Hampton Inn Airport 2231 Yale Blvd SE TF: 800-246-2288	Albuquerque	NM	87106	505-246-2255	246-2288
Holiday Inn Express 6100 Iliff Rd NW TF: 800-465-4329	Albuquerque	NM	87121	505-836-8600	836-2097
Holiday Inn Midtown 2020 Menaul Blvd NE TF: 800-465-4329	Albuquerque	NM	87107	505-884-2511	884-5720
Howard Johnson Express Inn 7630 Pan American Fwy TF: 800-446-4656	Albuquerque	NM	87109	505-828-1600	856-6446
Hyatt Regency Albuquerque 330 Tijeras Ave NW TF: 800-233-1234 ■ Web: www.hyatt.com/usa/albuquerque/	Albuquerque	NM	87102	505-842-1234	766-6710
La Posada de Albuquerque 125 2nd St NW TF: 800-777-5732	Albuquerque	NM	87102	505-242-9090	242-8664
La Quinta Inn Airport 2116 Yale Blvd SE TF: 800-687-6667	Albuquerque	NM	87106	505-243-5500	247-8288
Plaza Inn 900 Medical Arts NE TF: 800-237-1307 ■ Web: www.plazainnabq.com	Albuquerque	NM	87102	505-243-5693	843-6229
Radisson Hotel & Conference Center 2500 Carlisle Blvd NE TF: 800-333-3333 ■ Web: www.radisson.com/hotels/albuquerquenm_conference/	Albuquerque	NM	87110	505-888-3311	881-7452
Radisson Inn Albuquerque Airport 1901 University Blvd SE TF: 800-333-3333	Albuquerque	NM	87106	505-247-0512	843-7148
Ramada Inn Downtown 717 Central Ave NW TF: 800-272-6232	Albuquerque	NM	87102	505-924-2400	924-2465
Ramada Limited 5601 Alameda Blvd NE TF: 800-272-6232	Albuquerque	NM	87113	505-858-3297	858-3298
Ramada Mountain View 25 Hotel Cir NE TF: 800-435-9843	Albuquerque	NM	87123	505-271-1000	291-9028
Sheraton Albuquerque Uptown Hotel 2600 Louisiana Blvd NE TF: 800-252-7772 ■ Web: www.sheratonuptown.com ■ E-mail: www@sheratonuptown.com	Albuquerque	NM	87110	505-881-0000	881-3736
Sheraton Old Town Hotel 800 Rio Grande Blvd NW TF: 800-237-2133 ■ Web: www.flash.net/~sheraton/	Albuquerque	NM	87104	505-843-6300	842-9863
Sumner Suites 2500 Menaul Blvd NE TF: 800-747-8483	Albuquerque	NM	87107	505-881-0544	881-0380
Travelodge 2120 Menaul Blvd NE TF: 800-444-7378	Albuquerque	NM	87107	505-884-0250	883-0594
Wyndham Albuquerque Hotel at International Sunport 2910 Yale Blvd SE TF: 800-227-1117 ■ Web: www.wynatabq.com	Albuquerque	NM	87106	505-843-7000	843-6307
Wyndham Garden Hotel 6000 Pan American East Fwy NE TF: 800-996-2436	Albuquerque	NM	87109	505-821-9451	858-0239

— Restaurants —

				Phone
66 Diner (American) 1405 Central Ave NE	Albuquerque	NM	87106	505-247-1421
Allie's American Grille (American) 2101 Louisiana Blvd NE	Albuquerque	NM	87110	505-837-6698
Artichoke Cafe (Continental) 424 Central Ave SE Web: www.swcp.com/~webster/artichoke/	Albuquerque	NM	87102	505-243-0200
Assets Grille & SW Brewing Co (California) 6910 Montgomery Blvd NE	Albuquerque	NM	87109	505-889-6400
Barry's Oasis Restaurant (Mediterranean) 5400 San Mateo NE	Albuquerque	NM	87109	505-884-2324
Brio Bar & Grill (Continental) 2500 Carlisle NE	Albuquerque	NM	87110	505-888-3311
Cafe Broadway (Spanish) 606 Broadway SE	Albuquerque	NM	87102	505-842-8973
Casa de Benavidez (Mexican) 8032 4th St NW	Albuquerque	NM	87114	505-898-3311
Casa de Ruiz Church Street Cafe (Southwest) 2111 Church St NW	Albuquerque	NM	87104	505-247-8522

Albuquerque — Restaurants (Cont'd)

				Phone
Conrad's Downtown (American) 125 2nd St	Albuquerque	NM	87102	505-242-9090
Cooperage (Steak/Seafood) 7220 Lomas Blvd NE	Albuquerque	NM	87110	505-255-1657
Customs House (American) 800 Rio Grande Blvd NW	Albuquerque	NM	87104	505-843-6300
Goldmine Cafe (American) 215 Central Ave NW Suite 1D	Albuquerque	NM	87102	505-842-1760
High Finance Restaurant (Steak/Seafood) 40 Tromway Rd NE	Albuquerque	NM	87122	505-243-9742
Il Vicino (Italian) 3403 Central Ave NE	Albuquerque	NM	87106	505-266-7855
Japanese Kitchen (Japanese) 6521 Americas Pkwy NE	Albuquerque	NM	87110	505-884-8937
Kanome (Asian) 3128 Central Ave SE	Albuquerque	NM	87106	505-265-7773
La Crepe Michel (French) 400 San Felipe NW	Albuquerque	NM	87104	505-242-1251
La Posada de Albuquerque (Southwest) 125 2nd St NW	Albuquerque	NM	87102	505-242-9090
Maria Teresa Restaurant (Southwest) 618 Rio Grande Blvd NW	Albuquerque	NM	87104	505-242-3900
Martini Grille (American) 4200 Central Ave SE	Albuquerque	NM	87108	505-255-4111
McGrath's (American) 330 Tijeras NW	Albuquerque	NM	87102	505-842-1234
Monica's El Portal Restaurant (Mexican) 321 Rio Grande Blvd NW	Albuquerque	NM	87104	505-247-9625
Monte Vista Fire Station (New American) 3201 Central Ave NE	Albuquerque	NM	87106	505-255-2424
New Chinatown Restaurant (Chinese) 5001 Central Ave NE	Albuquerque	NM	87108	505-265-8859
Nick's Place (Greek) 111 4th St SW	Albuquerque	NM	87102	505-242-8369
Portobello Restaurant (Italian) 1100 San Mateo NE Suite 50	Albuquerque	NM	87110	505-232-9119
Prairie Star (Continental) 255 Prairie Star Rd	Bernalillo	NM	87004	505-867-3327
Ranchers Club of New Mexico (Steak/Seafood) 1901 University Blvd NE	Albuquerque	NM	87102	505-884-2500
Rancho de Corrales (Mexican) 4895 Corrales Rd	Corrales	NM	87048	505-897-3131
Rio Grande Yacht Club (Steak/Seafood) 2500 Yale Blvd SE *Web:* www.specialtymile.com/riograndeyachtclub/	Albuquerque	NM	87106	505-243-6111
Scalo Northern Italian Grill (Italian) 3500 Central Ave SE	Albuquerque	NM	87106	505-255-8781
Seagull Street Fish Market & Restaurant (Seafood) 5410 Academy Rd NE	Albuquerque	NM	87109	505-821-0020
Smiroll's International Cuisine (Continental) 108 Rio Grande Blvd NW	Albuquerque	NM	87104	505-242-9996
Sweet Mesquite Bar-B-Q (Barbecue) 20 First Plaza Galeria 21	Albuquerque	NM	87102	505-242-2068
Trattoria Trombino (Italian) 5415 Academy NE	Albuquerque	NM	87109	505-821-5974
Vivace (Italian) 3118 Central Ave SE	Albuquerque	NM	87106	505-268-5965
Yanni's Mediterranean Bar & Grill (Mediterranean) 3109 Central Ave NE	Albuquerque	NM	87106	505-268-9250

— Goods and Services —

SHOPPING

				Phone	Fax
Albuquerque's Indoor Mercado 2035 12th St NW	Albuquerque	NM	87104	505-243-8111	243-8419
Classic Century Square Antique Shops 4616 Central Ave SE	Albuquerque	NM	87108	505-265-3161	342-1108
Coronado Center 6600 Menaul St NE	Albuquerque	NM	87110	505-881-4600	881-0145
Cottonwood Mall 10000 Coors Bypass	Albuquerque	NM	87114	505-899-7467	897-6576
First Plaza Galeria 20 First Plaza Suite 510	Albuquerque	NM	87102	505-242-3446	
New Mexico State Fair Open Air Market 300 San Pedro NE *Web:* www.nmstatefair.com ■ *E-mail:* info@nmstatefair.com	Albuquerque	NM	87108	505-265-1791	266-7784
Old Town 323 Romero NW	Albuquerque	NM	87104	505-243-6393	
Western Warehouse 11205 Montgomery Blvd NE *Web:* www.westernwarehouse.com	Albuquerque	NM	87111	505-296-8344	296-0278
Winrock Shopping Center 2100 Louisiana Blvd NE	Albuquerque	NM	87110	505-888-3038	881-6122

BANKS

				Phone	Fax
Bank First 2900 Louisiana Blvd NE Suite 101	Albuquerque	NM	87110	505-872-1536	
Charter Bank 4400 Olsen Rd NE	Albuquerque	NM	81709	505-237-4136	
First Security Bank of New Mexico NA PO Box 1305	Albuquerque	NM	87102	505-765-4000	
First State Bank 5620 Wyoming Blvd NE	Albuquerque	NM	87109	505-241-7631	241-7637
NationsBank 303 Roma Ave NW	Albuquerque	NM	87102	505-765-2211	243-9606
Norwest Bank New Mexico NA 200 Lomas Blvd NW	Albuquerque	NM	87102	505-765-5000	766-6095
Union Savings Bank 1500 Mercantile Ave NE	Albuquerque	NM	87107	505-343-0900	343-1083
Wells Fargo Bank 200 Lomas NW	Albuquerque	NM	87102	800-396-2265	

BUSINESS SERVICES

	Phone
Accountemps	505-884-4557
Adecco Employment Personnel Services	505-888-4545
Federal Express	800-238-5355
Kelly Services	505-883-6873
Kinko's	505-255-9673
Mail Boxes Etc	505-771-8505
Manpower Temporary Services	505-345-6200
Post Office	505-245-9750
Quik-Print Printing	505-881-2927
Staffing Resources	505-889-9500
UPS	800-742-5877
Vince's Delivery Service	505-266-1515

— Media —

PUBLICATIONS

				Phone	Fax
Albuquerque Journal‡ PO Drawer J *TF:* 800-990-5765 ■ *Web:* www.abqjournal.com ■ *E-mail:* journal@abqjournal.com	Albuquerque	NM	87103	505-823-7777	823-3994
New Mexico Business Journal 420 Central Ave SW Suite 104 *Web:* www.nmbiz.com ■ *E-mail:* sierrapg@ix.netcom.com	Albuquerque	NM	87102	505-243-3444	243-4118

‡Daily newspapers

TELEVISION

				Phone	Fax
KASA-TV Ch 2 (Fox) 1377 University Blvd NE *Web:* www.kasa.com	Albuquerque	NM	87102	505-246-2222	242-1355
KASY-TV Ch 50 (UPN) 50 Broadcast Plaza	Albuquerque	NM	87104	505-764-5279	767-9421
KBIM-TV Ch 10 (CBS) 214 N Main St	Roswell	NM	88201	505-622-2120	623-6606
KCHF-TV Ch 11 (Ind) 216 TV E Frontage Rd *TF:* 800-831-9673	Santa Fe	NM	87505	505-473-1111	474-4998
KHFT-TV Ch 29 (UPN) 50 Broadcast Plaza SW	Albuquerque	NM	87104	505-764-5279	767-9421
KLUZ-TV Ch 41 (Uni) 2725 F Broadbent Pkwy	Albuquerque	NM	87107	505-344-5589	344-0891
KNME-TV Ch 5 (PBS) 1130 University Blvd NE *TF:* 800-328-5663 ■ *Web:* www.pbs.org/knme ■ *E-mail:* viewer@knme1.unm.edu	Albuquerque	NM	87102	505-277-2121	277-2191
KOAT-TV Ch 7 (ABC) 3801 Carlisle Blvd NE *E-mail:* news@koat7.com	Albuquerque	NM	87107	505-884-7777	884-6354
KOB-TV Ch 4 (NBC) 4 Broadcast Plaza SW *Web:* www.kobtv.com ■ *E-mail:* opinion@kobtv.com	Albuquerque	NM	87104	505-243-4411	764-2522
KOBF-TV Ch 12 (NBC) 825 W Broadway	Farmington	NM	87401	505-326-1141	327-5196
KOBR-TV Ch 8 (NBC) 124 E 4th St	Roswell	NM	88201	505-625-8888	624-7693
KREZ-TV Ch 6 (CBS) 158 Bodo Dr	Durango	CO	81301	970-259-6666	247-8472
KRQE-TV Ch 13 (CBS) PO Box 1294	Albuquerque	NM	87103	505-243-2285	842-8483

RADIO

				Phone	Fax
KANW-FM 89.1 MHz (NPR) 2020 Coal Ave *Web:* www.kanw.com	Albuquerque	NM	87106	505-242-7848	
KHTL-AM 920 kHz (N/T) 500 4th St NW 5th Fl	Albuquerque	NM	87102	505-767-6700	767-6767
KKOB-AM 770 kHz (N/T) 500 4th St NW	Albuquerque	NM	87102	505-767-6700	767-6767
KKOB-FM 93.3 MHz (AC) 500 4th St NW	Albuquerque	NM	87102	505-767-6700	767-6767
KKSS-FM 97.3 MHz (CHR) 5301 Central NE Suite 1200 *Web:* www.973.com ■ *E-mail:* requests@973.com	Albuquerque	NM	87108	505-265-1431	268-7807
KLSK-FM 104.1 MHz (CR) 2700 San Pedro NE	Albuquerque	NM	87110	505-830-6400	830-6543
KMGA-FM 99.5 MHz (AC) 500 4th St NW 5th Fl	Albuquerque	NM	87102	505-767-6700	767-6767
KNML-AM 1050 kHz (Sports) 500 4th St NW 5th Fl *Web:* www.sportsanimal.nmsource.com ■ *E-mail:* 1050@sportsanimal.com	Albuquerque	NM	87102	505-767-6700	767-6767
KRST-FM 92.3 MHz (Ctry) 500 4th St NW 5th Fl	Albuquerque	NM	87102	505-767-6700	767-6767

Albuquerque — Radio (Cont'd)

Name / Address	City	State	Zip	Phone	Fax
KTBL-FM 103.3 MHz (Ctry) 500 4th St NW	Albuquerque	NM	87102	505-767-6700	767-6767
KUNM-FM 89.9 MHz (NPR) Onate Hall University of New Mexico *Web:* kunm.unm.edu/	Albuquerque	NM	87131	505-277-4806	277-8004
KZRR-FM 94.1 MHz (Rock) 2700 San Pedro NE *Web:* www.swcp.com/kzrr ■ *E-mail:* kzrr@94rock.com	Albuquerque	NM	87110	505-830-6400	830-6543

— Colleges/Universities —

Name / Address	City	State	Zip	Phone	Fax
Albuquerque Technical Vocational Institute 525 Buena Vista SE *Web:* www.tvi.cc.nm.us ■ *E-mail:* melissa@tvi.cc.nm.us	Albuquerque	NM	87106	505-224-3000	224-3237
National American University Albuquerque Campus 1202 Pennsylvania St NE *Web:* www.nationalcollege.edu/campusalb.html	Albuquerque	NM	87110	505-265-7517	265-7542
Nazarene Indian Bible College 2315 Markham Rd SW *TF:* 888-877-6422	Albuquerque	NM	87105	505-877-0240	877-6214
Southwestern Indian Polytechnic Institute PO Box 10146 *TF:* 800-586-7474 ■ *Web:* kafka.sipi.tec.nm.us ■ *E-mail:* jjohnson@kafka.sipi.tec.nm.us	Albuquerque	NM	87184	505-346-2346	346-2343
University of New Mexico University Hill NE *TF:* 800-225-5866 ■ *Web:* www.unm.edu ■ *E-mail:* unmlobos@unm.edu	Albuquerque	NM	87131	505-277-0111	277-6686

— Hospitals —

Name / Address	City	State	Zip	Phone	Fax
Lovelace Medical Center 5400 Gibson Blvd SE *Web:* www.lovelace.com/lhs/lmc.shtml	Albuquerque	NM	87108	505-262-7000	262-7729
Presbyterian Hospital 1100 Central Ave SE	Albuquerque	NM	87106	505-841-1234	841-1153
Presbyterian Kaseman Hospital 8300 Constitution Ave NE	Albuquerque	NM	87110	505-291-2000	291-2983
Saint Joseph West Mesa Hospital 10501 Golf Course Rd	Albuquerque	NM	87114	505-727-2000	727-2121
University Hospital 2211 Lomas Blvd NE *Web:* uhwww.unm.edu	Albuquerque	NM	87106	505-843-2111	272-1827
Veterans Affairs Medical Center 1501 San Pedro SE	Albuquerque	NM	87108	505-265-1711	256-2882

— Attractions —

Name / Address	City	State	Zip	Phone	Fax
Adobe Theater 9813 4th St NW	Albuquerque	NM	87107	505-898-9222	
Albuquerque Aquarium 903 10th St *TF:* 800-764-6200 ■ *Web:* www.cabq.gov/biopark/aquarium	Albuquerque	NM	87102	505-764-6200	848-7192
Albuquerque Biological Park Rio Grande Zoo 903 10th St SW *Web:* www.cabq.gov/biopark/zoo	Albuquerque	NM	87102	505-764-6200	764-6281
Albuquerque Civic Light Opera Assn 4804 Central Ave SE	Albuquerque	NM	87108	505-262-9301	262-9319
Albuquerque Little Theatre 224 San Pasquale SW	Albuquerque	NM	87104	505-242-4750	843-9489
Albuquerque Museum 2000 Mountain Rd NW *Web:* www.collectorsguide.com/ab/m005.html ■ *E-mail:* musjcm@museum.cabq.gov	Albuquerque	NM	87104	505-243-7255	764-6546
American International Rattlesnake Museum 202 San Felipe NW Suite A *Web:* www.rattlesnakes.com ■ *E-mail:* zoomuseum@aol.com	Albuquerque	NM	87104	505-242-6569	242-6569
Archaeology & Material Culture Museum 22 Calvary Rd	Cedar Crest	NM	87008	505-281-2005	
Beach Waterpark 1600 Desert Surf Loop NE	Albuquerque	NM	87107	505-345-6066	344-6759
Casa Rondena Winery 733 Chavez Rd NW	Albuquerque	NM	87107	505-344-5911	343-1823
Chamber Orchestra of Albuquerque 2730 San Pedro NE Suite H *Web:* www.aosys.com/coa/	Albuquerque	NM	87110	505-881-2078	881-2078
Cibola National Forest 2113 Osuna Rd NE Suite A	Albuquerque	NM	87113	505-761-4650	346-2663
Cliff's Amusement Park 4800 Osuna Rd NE *Web:* www.cliffs.net ■ *E-mail:* info@cliffs.net	Albuquerque	NM	87109	505-881-9373	881-7807
Coronado State Monument Hwy 44	Bernalillo	NM	87004	505-867-5351	867-1733
Doll Museum & Shoppe 5201 Constitution Ave NE *TF:* 877-280-3805 ■ *Web:* www.dollmuseumandshoppe.com	Albuquerque	NM	87110	505-255-8555	255-1259
El Malpais National Monument PO Box 939 *Web:* www.nps.gov/elma/	Grants	NM	87020	505-285-4641	285-5661
El Morro National Monument Rt 2 Box 43 *Web:* www.nps.gov/elmo/	Ramah	NM	87321	505-783-4226	783-4689
Ernie Pyle Memorial Library 900 Girard Blvd SE *Web:* www.cabq.gov/rgvls/branch.html	Albuquerque	NM	87106	505-256-2065	256-2069
Explora! Science Center & Children's Museum 800 Rio Grande NW Suite 19 *Web:* www.explora.mus.nm.us ■ *E-mail:* explorainfo@esccma.org	Albuquerque	NM	87104	505-842-1537	842-5915
Fine Arts Center University of New Mexico *Web:* www.unm.edu/~finearts/	Albuquerque	NM	87131	505-277-2111	277-0708
Gruet Winery 8400 Pan American Frwy NE	Albuquerque	NM	87113	505-821-0055	857-0066
Indian Pueblo Cultural Center 2401 12th St NW *Web:* hanksville.phast.umass.edu/defs/independent/PCC/	Albuquerque	NM	87104	505-843-7270	842-6959
Isleta Gaming Palace 11000 Broadway *TF:* 800-460-5686 ■ *Web:* www.isletagamingpalace.com	Albuquerque	NM	87105	505-869-2614	869-0152
KiMo Theater 423 Central Ave NW *Web:* www.cabq.gov/kimo/	Albuquerque	NM	87102	505-848-1370	764-1572
Maxwell Museum of Anthropology University of New Mexico *Web:* www.unm.edu/~maxwell	Albuquerque	NM	87131	505-277-4405	277-1547
National Atomic Museum Kirtland Air Force Base E Wyoming Ave *Web:* www.atomicmuseum.com	Albuquerque	NM	87185	505-284-3243	284-3244
New Mexico Ballet Co PO Box 21518 *Web:* www.mandala.net/nmballet/ ■ *E-mail:* dwestbrk@unm.edu	Albuquerque	NM	87154	505-292-4245	
New Mexico Jazz Workshop 3205 Central Ave NE *Web:* www.flash.net/~nmjw/	Albuquerque	NM	87106	505-255-9798	232-8420
New Mexico Museum of Natural History & Science 1801 Mountain Rd NW *Web:* www.nmmnh-abq.mus.nm.us	Albuquerque	NM	87104	505-841-2800	841-2866
New Mexico Symphony Orchestra PO Box 30208 *TF:* 800-251-6676 ■ *Web:* www.nmso.org	Albuquerque	NM	87190	505-881-9590	881-9456
Old Town 323 Romero NW	Albuquerque	NM	87104	505-243-6393	
Opera Southwest 515 15th St NW	Albuquerque	NM	87105	505-242-5837	242-5837
Petroglyph National Monument 6001 Unser Blvd NW *Web:* www.nps.gov/petr/	Albuquerque	NM	87120	505-899-0205	899-0207
Popejoy Hall University of New Mexico *Web:* www.popejoyhall.com	Albuquerque	NM	87131	505-277-3824	277-7353
Rio Grande Botanic Garden 2601 Central Ave NW *Web:* www.cabq.gov/biopark/garden	Albuquerque	NM	87104	505-764-6200	848-7192
Rio Grande Nature Center State Park 2901 Candelaria Rd NW *Web:* www.unm.edu/~natrcent/	Albuquerque	NM	87107	505-344-7240	344-4505
Salinas Pueblo Missions National Monument PO Box 517 *Web:* www.nps.gov/sapu/	Mountainair	NM	87036	505-847-2585	847-2441
San Felipe Plaza Mountain Rd & San Felipe NW Old Town	Albuquerque	NM	87104	505-244-1094	
Sandia Peak Aerial Tramway 10 Tramway Loop NE *Web:* www.sandiapeak.com	Albuquerque	NM	87122	505-856-7325	856-6490
South Broadway Cultural Center 1025 Broadway SE	Albuquerque	NM	87102	505-848-1320	848-1329
Telephone Pioneer Museum of New Mexico 110 4th St NW *Web:* www.nmculture.org/cgi-bin/showInst.pl?InstID=TPM ■ *E-mail:* lxturne@eni.net	Albuquerque	NM	87102	505-842-2937	
Tinkertown Museum 121 Sandia Crest Rd *Web:* www.tinkertown.com ■ *E-mail:* tinker4u@tinkertown.com	Sandia Park	NM	87047	505-281-5233	286-9335
Turquoise Museum 2107 Central Ave NW *TF:* 800-821-7443	Albuquerque	NM	87104	505-247-8650	247-8765
Turquoise Trail Hwys 536 & 14	Sandia Park	NM	87047	505-281-5233	

Albuquerque — Attractions (Cont'd)

				Phone	Fax
YesterDave's Auto Museum 10601 Montgomery Blvd NE	Albuquerque	NM	87111	505-293-0033	298-5549

SPORTS TEAMS & FACILITIES

				Phone	Fax
Albuquerque Dukes (baseball) 1601 Avenida Cesar Chavez SE *Web:* www.albuquerquedukes.com	Albuquerque	NM	87106	505-243-1791	842-0561
Albuquerque National Dragway 5700 Bobby Foster	Albuquerque	NM	87105	505-873-2684	
Albuquerque Sports Stadium 1601 Avenida Cesar Chavez *E-mail:* kggr90a@prodigy.com	Albuquerque	NM	87106	505-243-1791	842-0561
Downs at Albuquerque Copper & San Pedro NE New Mexico State Fairgrounds *Web:* www.nmracing.com ■ *E-mail:* thedowns@aol.com	Albuquerque	NM	87108	505-266-5555	268-1970
New Mexico Scorpions (hockey) 601 San Pedro NE Tingley Coliseum *TF:* 888-472-6777 ■ *Web:* www.scorpionshockey.com ■ *E-mail:* Scorpion@Scorpionshockey.com	Albuquerque	NM	87108	505-232-7825	232-7829
New Mexico State Fair Racetrack 300 San Pedro NE *Web:* www.nmstatefair.com ■ *E-mail:* info@nmstatefair.com	Albuquerque	NM	87108	505-265-1791	266-7784
Tingley Coliseum 300 San Pedro Dr NE	Albuquerque	NM	87108	505-265-1791	266-7784

— Events —

	Phone
Albuquerque International Balloon Fiesta (early-mid-October)	800-284-2282
American Indian Week (late April)	505-843-7270
Bernalillo Wine Festival (early September)	505-867-3311
Children's Fair (late April)	505-767-6700
Crossroads Winter Championship Series (mid-late January)	505-632-2287
Duke City Marathon (late September)	505-768-3483
Father's Day Multi-Cultural Festival (late June)	505-843-7270
Festival Flamenco Internacional (early-mid-June)	505-344-8695
Fiery Food Show (early March)	505-298-3835
Gathering of Nations Pow Wow (late April)	505-836-2810
Grecian Festival (early October)	505-247-9411
Herb & Wildflower Festival (mid-May)	505-344-7240
Holiday Ole (mid-November)	505-881-0199
Holiday Parade (early December)	505-768-3483
Indian Festival of Living Arts (late March)	505-843-7270
Indian Pueblo Christmas Celebrations (late December)	505-843-7270
International Arabian Horse Show (late October)	800-733-9918
Las Fiestas de San Lorenzo (mid-August)	505-867-3311
Magnifico! Albuquerque Festival of the Arts (mid-May)	505-842-9918
New Mexico Arts & Crafts Fair (late June)	505-884-9043
New Mexico State Fair (mid-late September)	505-265-1791
Rio Grande Arts & Crafts Festival (mid-March)	505-292-7457
Run for the Zoo (early May)	505-764-6200
San Felipe Pueblo Arts & Crafts Show (early October)	505-842-9918
Santa Fe Furniture Expo (early October)	800-299-9886
Southwest Arts Festival (mid-November)	505-875-1748
Summer Festival & Frontier Market (early August)	505-471-2261
Weems Artfest (mid-November)	505-293-6133
Ye Merry Olde Christmas Faire (late November)	505-856-1970
Zia Arts & Crafts Festival (late November)	505-842-9918

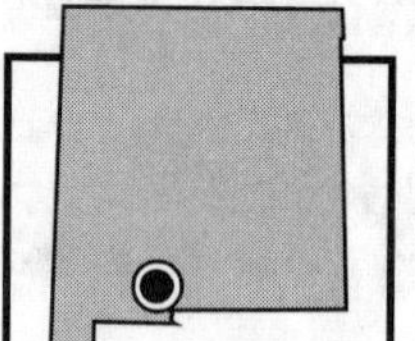

Las Cruces

Las Cruces is located in the Mesilla Valley in south central New Mexico, close to El Paso, Texas and the Rio Grande. The city was originally founded in 1849, and part of the original town site can still be found at the Mesquite Street-Original Townsite Historic District. The Old Mesilla area of Las Cruces was the site of Billy the Kid's trial, sentencing, and escape, and is now a popular attraction featuring shops, restaurants, and cultural events. La Cueva, a natural cave located about 11 miles east of Las Cruces, was first home to ancient Mogollon Indians, then later inhabited by an eccentric Italian nobleman known as the Hermit at La Cueva. Another nearby attraction is Fort Selden State Monument. The fort is the former home of the Buffalo Soldiers, the famous Black Calvary who protected the Mesilla Valley from Indian attacks. Las Cruces is also home to New Mexico State University, which houses the largest contemporary art gallery in south central New Mexico and contains over 1,800 19th Century Mexican retablos. Stahmann Farms, one of the world's largest pecan growers, is also located near Las Cruces.

Population	76,102	**Longitude**	106-55-19 W
Area (Land)	37.5 sq mi	**County**	Doña Ana
Area (Water)	0.1 sq mi	**Time Zone**	MST
Elevation	3896 ft	**Area Code/s**	505
Latitude	32-17-22 N		

— Average Temperatures and Precipitation —

TEMPERATURES

	Jan	Feb	Mar	Apr	May	Jun	Jul	Aug	Sep	Oct	Nov	Dec
High	57	62	69	77	85	94	94	91	86	78	66	58
Low	26	30	36	43	51	60	67	64	58	45	34	27

PRECIPITATION

	Jan	Feb	Mar	Apr	May	Jun	Jul	Aug	Sep	Oct	Nov	Dec
Inches	0.5	0.4	0.2	0.2	0.3	0.7	1.4	2.3	1.4	0.9	0.5	0.7

— Important Phone Numbers —

	Phone		Phone
AAA	505-523-5681	**Medical Referral**	505-841-1777
American Express Travel	505-521-1400	**Poison Control Center**	800-432-6866
Emergency	911		

— Information Sources —

				Phone	Fax
Better Business Bureau Serving New Mexico 2625 Pennsylvania NE Suite 2050 *TF:* 800-873-2224 ■ *Web:* www.bbbnm.com ■ *E-mail:* bureau@bbbnm.com	Albuquerque	NM	87110	505-346-0110	346-0696
Branigan Thomas Memorial Library 200 E Picacho Ave *Web:* library.las-cruces.org	Las Cruces	NM	88001	505-528-4000	528-4030
Doña Ana County 180 W Amador Ave *Web:* chilepepper.co.dona-ana.nm.us	Las Cruces	NM	88001	505-525-6600	647-7224
Las Cruces Chamber of Commerce 760 W Picacho Ave *Web:* lascruces.org/chamber	Las Cruces	NM	88005	505-524-1968	527-5546
Las Cruces City Hall 200 N Church St *Web:* www.las-cruces.org	Las Cruces	NM	88001	505-541-2000	
Las Cruces Convention & Visitors Bureau 211 N Water St *TF:* 800-343-7827 ■ *Web:* www.lascrucescvb.org ■ *E-mail:* cvb@lascruces.org	Las Cruces	NM	88001	505-541-2444	541-2164
Las Cruces Mayor 200 N Church St	Las Cruces	NM	88001	505-541-2067	541-2183
Mesilla Valley Economic Development Alliance 2345 E Nevada St *Web:* www.mveda.com ■ *E-mail:* sites@mveda.com	Las Cruces	NM	88001	505-525-2852	523-5707

On-Line Resources

4LasCruces.com	www.4lascruces.com
City Knowledge Las Cruces	www.cityknowledge.com/nm_lascruces.htm
Excite.com Las Cruces City Guide	www.excite.com/travel/countries/united_states/new_mexico/las_cruces
Las Cruces Citi-Guide	www.citi-guide.com/lascruces/index.htm
Las Cruces CityGuide	cityguide.lycos.com/southwest/LasCrucesNM.html
Las Cruces Information Center	www.zianet.com/snm/ricruces.htm
Lascruces.Org	www.lascruces.org
Mesilla-Valley.Net	arteffects.com/mesilla
NITC Travelbase City Guide Las Cruces	www.travelbase.com/auto/features/las_cruces-nm.html
Online City Guide to Las Cruces	www.olcg.com/nm/lascruces/index.html

Las Cruces (Cont'd)

— Transportation Services —

AIRPORTS

Phone

■ **Las Cruces International Airport (LRU)**

8 miles W of downtown (approx 15 minutes) . . . 505-524-2762

Airport Transportation

Phone

Checker/Yellow Cab $12-15 fare to downtown . . . 505-524-1711

Commercial Airlines

Phone

Mesa Airlines . . . 800-637-2247

Phone

■ **El Paso International Airport (ELP)**

44 miles SE of downtown Las Cruces (approx 50 minutes) . . . 915-772-4271

Airport Transportation

Phone

Checker/Yellow Cab $70 fare to downtown Las Cruces . . . 915-532-2414
El Paso Cab & Shuttle $70-80 fare to downtown Las Cruces . . . 915-772-9906
Las Cruces Shuttle Service $24-30 fare to downtown Las Cruces . . . 505-525-1784

Commercial Airlines

	Phone		Phone
America West	800-235-9292	**Delta**	800-221-1212
American	800-433-7300	**Southwest**	800-435-9792
Continental	800-525-0280		

Charter Airlines

	Phone		Phone
Air Transport Inc	915-772-1448	**Texas Air Charters**	940-898-1200
Rasmark Jet Charter	915-772-4616		

CAR RENTALS

	Phone		Phone
A-One	505-527-4702	**Hertz**	505-521-4807
Alamo-El Paso	800-327-9633	**Hertz-El Paso**	915-772-4255
Avis-El Paso	915-779-2730	**National-El Paso**	915-778-9417
Budget-El Paso	915-778-5287	**Thrifty**	505-524-1510
Dollar-El Paso	915-778-5445	**Thrifty-El Paso**	915-584-6529
Enterprise	505-525-1778		

LIMO/TAXI

	Phone		Phone
Checker/Yellow Cab	505-524-1711	**L&M Limousine**	505-522-5411

MASS TRANSIT

Phone

Las Cruces Transit Dept $.50 Base fare . . . 505-541-2500

RAIL/BUS

Phone

Greyhound Bus Station 490 N Valley Dr . . . Las Cruces NM 88005 505-524-8518
TF: 800-231-2222

— Accommodations —

HOTEL RESERVATION SERVICES

Phone *Fax*

Advance Reservations Inn Arizona . . . 480-990-0682 990-3390
TF: 800-456-0682 ■ *Web:* tucson.com/inn
■ *E-mail:* micasa@primenet.com

HOTELS, MOTELS, RESORTS

Name / Address	City	State	Zip	Phone	Fax
Baymont Inn & Suites 1500 Hickory Dr *TF:* 800-301-0200	Las Cruces	NM	88005	505-523-0100	523-0707
Best Western Mesilla Valley Inn 901 Avenida de Mesilla *TF:* 800-528-1234	Las Cruces	NM	88005	505-524-8603	526-8437
Best Western Mission Inn 1765 S Main St *TF:* 800-390-1440	Las Cruces	NM	88005	505-524-8591	523-4740
Budget Inn 2255 W Picacho Ave	Las Cruces	NM	88005	505-523-0365	
Comfort Inn 2585 S Valley Dr	Las Cruces	NM	88005	505-527-2000	527-0966
Comfort Suites 2101 S Triviz *TF:* 800-228-5150	Las Cruces	NM	88001	505-522-1300	522-1313
Days Inn 2600 S Valley Dr *TF:* 800-329-7466	Las Cruces	NM	88005	505-526-4441	526-1980
Fairfield Inn by Marriott 2101 Summit Ct	Las Cruces	NM	88011	505-522-6840	522-9784
Hampton Inn 755 Avenida de Mesilla *TF:* 888-846-6741 ■ *Web:* www.zianet.com/hampton ■ *E-mail:* hampton@zianet.com	Las Cruces	NM	88005	505-526-8311	527-2015
Hilton 705 S Telshor Blvd *Web:* www.weblifepro.com/lchilton	Las Cruces	NM	88011	505-522-4300	521-4707
Holiday Inn de Las Cruces 201 E University Ave *TF:* 800-465-4329 ■ *Web:* www.holidayinnlc.com ■ *E-mail:* az0426@totacc.com	Las Cruces	NM	88001	505-526-4411	524-0530
Holiday Inn Express 2200 S Valley Dr	Las Cruces	NM	88005	505-527-9947	647-4988
La Quinta Inn 790 Avenida de Mesilla *TF:* 800-531-5900	Las Cruces	NM	88005	505-524-0331	525-8360
Motel 6 235 La Posada Ln *TF:* 800-466-8356	Las Cruces	NM	88001	505-525-1010	525-0139
Plaza Suites 301 E University Ave	Las Cruces	NM	88005	505-525-2083	
Royal Host Motel 2146 W Picacho Ave	Las Cruces	NM	88005	505-524-8536	
Sands Motel 1655 S Main St	Las Cruces	NM	88005	505-524-7791	
Sleep Inn 2121 S Triviz *TF:* 800-753-3746	Las Cruces	NM	88001	505-522-1700	522-1515
Springhill Suites by Marriott 1611 Hickory Loop *TF:* 888-772-8887	Las Cruces	NM	88005	505-541-8887	541-8837
Super 8 Motel 4411 N Main St *TF:* 800-800-8000	Las Cruces	NM	88012	505-382-1490	382-1849
Town House Motel 2205 W Picacho Ave	Las Cruces	NM	88005	505-524-7733	
Villa del Telshor 1955 S Telshor Blvd	Las Cruces	NM	88011	505-522-0804	522-3864
Western Inn Motel 2155 W Picacho Ave	Las Cruces	NM	88005	505-523-5399	

— Restaurants —

Name / Address	City	State	Zip	Phone
Andele (Mexican) 2184 Hwy 28 S	Las Cruces	NM	88005	505-526-9631
Blue Moon (Mexican) 13060 Hwy 85 N	Las Cruces	NM	88005	505-647-9524
Brass Cactus Bistro (Continental) 1800 Avenida de Mesilla Suite B	Las Cruces	NM	88006	505-527-4656
Carillos Cafe (Mexican) 330 S Church St	Las Cruces	NM	88001	505-523-9913
Casa Luna (Italian) 1340 E Lohman Ave	Las Cruces	NM	88001	505-523-0111
Cattle Baron (Steak/Seafood) 790 S Telshor Blvd *Web:* www.cattlebaron.com/las_cruc.htm	Las Cruces	NM	88001	505-522-7533
Chilito's (Mexican) 2405 S Valley Dr	Las Cruces	NM	88005	505-526-4184
Ernesto's (Mexican) 939 N Main St	Las Cruces	NM	88001	505-541-9626
Farley's Bar & Restaurant (American) 3499 Foothills Dr *Web:* www.farleyspub.com	Las Cruces	NM	88011	505-522-0466
Jalisco (Mexican) 301 E Lohman Ave	Las Cruces	NM	88001	505-527-1194
JW Flours (Homestyle) 1030 El Paseo St	Las Cruces	NM	88001	505-526-9588
Lorenzo's (Italian) 741 N Alameda Suite 16	Las Cruces	NM	88005	505-524-2850
Los Compas Cafe (Mexican) 603 S Nevarez	Las Cruces	NM	88001	505-523-1778
Mesilla Valley Kitchen (Homestyle) 2001 E Lohman Suite 103	Las Cruces	NM	88001	505-523-9311
Meson de Mesilla (Continental) 1803 Avenida de Mesilla	Las Cruces	NM	88005	505-525-9212
Nopalito (Mexican) 2605 Missouri Ave	Las Cruces	NM	88011	505-522-0440
O'Ryan's Tavern & Brewery (Irish) 700 S Telshor Blvd	Las Cruces	NM	88001	505-522-8191
Old Town Restaurant (Mexican) 1155 S Valley Dr	Las Cruces	NM	88005	505-523-4586
Purple Sage Restaurant (Native American/Southwest) 4100 Dripping Springs Rd	Las Cruces	NM	88011	505-532-1765
Ranchway (Mexican) 604 N Valley Dr	Las Cruces	NM	88005	505-523-7361
Red Mountain Cafe (American) 1120 Commerce Dr	Las Cruces	NM	88011	505-522-7584
Roberto's (Mexican) 908 E Amador Ave	Las Cruces	NM	88001	505-523-1851
Spanish Kitchen (Mexican) 129 E Madrid Ave	Las Cruces	NM	88001	505-526-4275
Tatsu Restaurant (Japanese) 930 El Paseo St	Las Cruces	NM	88001	505-526-7144
Tony's (Mexican) 125 S Campo St	Las Cruces	NM	88001	505-524-9662
Way Out West Restaurant & Brewing Co (Southwest) 1720 Avenida de Mesilla	Las Cruces	NM	88005	505-541-1969

Las Cruces (Cont'd)

— Goods and Services —

SHOPPING

	City	State	Zip	Phone	Fax
Mesilla Valley Mall 700 Telshor Blvd	Las Cruces	NM	88011	505-522-6022	
Monte Vista Shopping Center 2205 S Main St	Las Cruces	NM	88001	505-526-2281	526-4249

BANKS

	City	State	Zip	Phone	Fax
Bank of the Rio Grande 2535 S Telshor Blvd	Las Cruces	NM	88011	505-525-8960	522-5075
Citizens Bank 2200 Missouri Ave	Las Cruces	NM	88001	505-522-1000	522-1000
Web: www.citizenslc.com					
Community First 201 N Church St	Las Cruces	NM	88001	505-527-6200	527-6250
TF: 800-218-4954					
First Federal Savings Bank 1800 S Telshor Blvd	Las Cruces	NM	88011	505-522-2664	522-5416
TF: 800-432-4412					
First Savings Bank 2804 N Telshor Blvd	Las Cruces	NM	88011	505-521-7931	521-7906
TF: 800-555-6895					
First Security Bank 1375 E Boutz Rd.	Las Cruces	NM	88001	505-526-7350	526-7349
TF: 800-683-5670					
Matrix Capital Bank 3090 N Roadrunner Pkwy	Las Cruces	NM	88011	505-532-9320	532-9317
Norwest Bank 700 N Main St	Las Cruces	NM	88001	505-527-0551	527-0557
TF Cust Svc: 800-396-2265*					
Sierra Bank 225 E Idaho Ave	Las Cruces	NM	88004	505-523-5920	523-5922
White Sands Federal Credit Union 2190 E Lohman Ave	Las Cruces	NM	88001	505-647-4500	524-0173

BUSINESS SERVICES

	Phone
Federal Express	800-238-5355
Kelly Services	505-525-1232
Kinko's	505-522-5758
Mail Boxes Etc	505-523-2820
Manpower Temporary Services	505-522-6028
Post Office	505-524-2841
UPS	800-742-5877

— Media —

PUBLICATIONS

	City	State	Zip	Phone	Fax
Las Cruces Bulletin PO Box 637	Las Cruces	NM	88004	505-524-8061	526-4621*
**Fax:* News Rm ■ *Web:* www.zianet.com/Bulletin ■ *E-mail:* bulletin@zianet.com					
Las Cruces Sun-News‡ 256 W Las Cruces Ave	Las Cruces	NM	88005	505-541-5400	541-5499
TF: 800-745-5851 ■ *Web:* www.newschoice.com/Newspapers/MidStates/LasCruces					
Southern New Mexico Magazine 7440 Arroyo Seco	Las Cruces	NM	88011	505-382-0408	382-0428
Web: www.zianet.com/redsky					

‡*Daily newspapers*

TELEVISION

	City	State	Zip	Phone	Fax
KDBC-TV Ch 4 (CBS) 2201 Wyoming Ave	El Paso	TX	79903	915-532-6551	544-2591
Web: www.kdbc.com					
KFOX-TV Ch 14 (Fox) 6004 N Mesa	El Paso	TX	79912	915-833-8585	833-8717
E-mail: fox14@whc.net					
KKWB-TV Ch 65 (WB) 801 N Oregon St	El Paso	TX	79902	915-833-0065	532-6841
KRWG-TV Ch 22 (PBS) Jordan St Milton Hall Rm 100	Las Cruces	NM	88003	505-646-2222	646-1924
Web: www.nmsu.edu/~krwgtv ■ *E-mail:* viewer@krwg.pbs.org					
KTSM-TV Ch 9 (NBC) 801 N Oregon St	El Paso	TX	79902	915-532-5421	544-0536
Web: www.ktsm.com ■ *E-mail:* ktsmtv@whc.net					
KVIA-TV Ch 7 (ABC) 4140 Rio Bravo St	El Paso	TX	79902	915-532-7777	532-0505
Web: www.kvia.com ■ *E-mail:* feedback@kvia.com					

RADIO

	City	State	Zip	Phone	Fax
KFNA-AM 1060 kHz (Span) 2211 Missouri St Suite 237	El Paso	TX	79903	915-542-2969	542-2958
KGRT-AM 570 kHz (Ctry) 3401 W Picacho St	Las Cruces	NM	88005	505-524-8588	524-8580
KGRT-FM 103.9 MHz (Ctry) 3401 W Picacho St	Las Cruces	NM	88005	505-524-8588	524-8580
E-mail: kgrt@zianet.com					
KHEY-AM 690 kHz (Ctry) 2419 N Piedras St.	El Paso	TX	79930	915-566-9301	566-0928
KMVR-FM 104.9 MHz (AC) 1832 W Amador	Las Cruces	NM	88005	505-526-2496	523-3918
KOBE-AM 1450 kHz (N/T) 1832 W Amador	Las Cruces	NM	88005	505-526-2496	523-3918
KROD-AM 600 kHz (N/T) 4150 Pinnacle St Suite 120	El Paso	TX	79902	915-544-8864	544-9536
KROL-FM 99.5 MHz (Rel) 6900 Commerce St	El Paso	TX	79915	915-779-0016	523-2212*
**Fax Area Code:* 505					
KRWG-FM 90.7 MHz (NPR) PO Box 3000	Las Cruces	NM	88003	505-646-4525	646-1974
Web: www.krwgfm.org/index.htm ■ *E-mail:* krwgfm@nmsu.edu					
KSNM-FM 98.7 MHz (B/EZ) 1355 E California St	Las Cruces	NM	88001	505-525-9298	525-9419
KVLC-FM 101.1 MHz (Oldies) 105 E Idaho Ave Suite B	Las Cruces	NM	88002	505-527-1111	527-1100
Web: www.zianet.com/kvlc ■ *E-mail:* kvlc@zianet.com					
KXDA-FM 103.1 MHz (CR) 1355 E California St	Las Cruces	NM	88001	505-525-9298	525-9419

— Colleges/Universities —

	City	State	Zip	Phone	Fax
Doña Ana Branch Community College Box 30001 Dept 3DA	Las Cruces	NM	88003	505-527-7500	527-7515
TF: 800-903-7503 ■ *Web:* dabcc-www.nmsu.edu					
New Mexico State University PO Box 30001 MSC-3A	Las Cruces	NM	88003	505-646-3121	646-6330
TF: 800-662-6678 ■ *Web:* www.nmsu.edu ■ *E-mail:* admissions@nmsu.edu					

— Hospitals —

	City	State	Zip	Phone	Fax
Memorial Medical Center 2450 S Telshor Blvd	Las Cruces	NM	88011	505-522-8641	521-5050
Mesilla Valley Hospital 3751 Del Rey Blvd	Las Cruces	NM	88012	505-382-3500	382-3071

— Attractions —

	City	State	Zip	Phone	Fax
Bicentennial Log Cabin 671 N Main St	Las Cruces	NM	88001	505-541-2155	
Branigan Cultural Center 500 N Water St	Las Cruces	NM	88001	505-541-2155	
Dripping Springs Recreation Area University Ave.	Las Cruces	NM	88005	505-525-4300	
Fort Selden State Monument 1280 Ft Selden Rd	Radium Springs	NM	88054	505-526-8911	
Historical Lawmen Museum 1725 Marquess St.	Las Cruces	NM	88005	505-525-1911	
La Cueva University Ave	Las Cruces	NM	88005	505-525-4300	
La Viña Winery 4201 Hwy 28.	La Union	NM	88021	505-882-7632	
Las Cruces Chamber Ballet 224 N Campo St.	Las Cruces	NM	88001	505-523-7325	
Las Cruces Community Theater 313 N Downtown Mall	Las Cruces	NM	88001	505-523-1200	525-0015
Web: www.zianet.com/lcct					
Las Cruces Museum of Fine Art & Culture 490 N Water St.	Las Cruces	NM	88001	505-541-2155	
Las Cruces Museum of Natural History 700 Telshor Blvd.	Las Cruces	NM	88001	505-541-2155	
Web: www.nmsu.edu/Museum ■ *E-mail:* mnh@zianet.com					
Las Cruces Symphony New Mexico State University	Las Cruces	NM	88001	505-646-3709	
Leasburg Dam State Park Leasburg State Park Rd.	Radium Springs	NM	88054	505-524-4068	
Log Cabin Museum Lucero & Main Sts.	Las Cruces	NM	88001	505-541-2155	
Mesilla Valley Fine Arts Gallery 1322 Mesilla Valley Mall 700 Telshor Blvd.	Las Cruces	NM	88011	505-522-2933	
Museum of the Horse 841 Hwy 70 W	Ruidoso Downs	NM	88346	505-378-4142	378-4166
New Mexico Farm & Ranch Heritage Museum 4100 Dripping Springs Rd	Las Cruces	NM	88011	505-522-4100	522-4100
New Mexico State University Art Gallery MSC 3572 NMSU PO Box 30001	Las Cruces	NM	88003	505-646-2545	

Las Cruces — Attractions (Cont'd)

				Phone	Fax
New Mexico State University Museum University Ave & Solano St Kent Hall	Las Cruces	NM	88003	505-646-3739	
Our Lady at the Foot of the Cross Shrine Lohman Ave & Water St	Las Cruces	NM	88001	505-541-2444	
Prime Time Amusement Center 706 E Amador Ave	Las Cruces	NM	88001	505-527-8206	527-8206
San Augustin Pass & Aguirre Spring Recreational Area Hwy 70	Las Cruces	NM	88012	505-525-4300	
Space Murals Museum 12450 Hwy 70 E	Las Cruces	NM	88012	505-382-0977	
Volunteer Memorial Sculpture Garden 500 N Water St	Las Cruces	NM	88001	505-541-2155	
Zohn Hershel Theatre New Mexico State University Campus	Las Cruces	NM	88003	505-646-4515	

SPORTS TEAMS & FACILITIES

				Phone	Fax
Ruidoso Downs Racing Inc 1461 Hwy 70 W	Ruidoso Downs	NM	88346	505-378-4431	378-4631
Southern New Mexico Speedway 3530 W Picacho Ave	Las Cruces	NM	88005	505-524-7913	

— Events —

	Phone
Arts Hop (mid-September)	505-523-6403
Baylor Pass Mountain Trail Run (mid-November)	505-524-7824
Burn Lake Triathalon (mid-July)	505-541-2554
Christmas Carols & Luminaries on the Plaza (December 24)	505-524-3262
Christmas in July (mid-July)	505-528-3276
Christmas Lights Guided Night Walk (mid-December)	505-524-8032
Cinco de Mayo Fiesta (early May)	505-524-3262
Dearholt Desert Trail Run (mid-January)	505-524-7824
Diez y Sies de Septembre Fiesta (mid-September)	505-524-3262
Fort Selden Riverwalk (late October)	505-524-8032
Fourth of July Celebration (July 4)	505-528-3149
Frontier Days (mid-late April)	505-526-8911
Great American People Race (late August)	505-544-0469
Gus Macker 3-on-3 Basketball Tournament (April)	505-525-2796
Harvest of Fun (mid-September)	505-528-3276
Independence Day Run (July 4)	505-541-2554
Juneteenth Celebration (mid-late June)	505-524-2906
La Viña Wine Festival (early October)	505-882-7632
Las Cruces International Mariachi Conference (mid-November)	505-523-2681
MVTC Triathalon (mid-April)	505-524-7824
New Mexico Wine & Chile War Festival (late May)	505-646-4543
Nostalgia Club Antique & Collectible Show (mid-September & mid-March)	505-526-8624
Nutcracker Suite (early November)	505-524-8032
Oktoberfest (late September)	505-524-8032
Old Fashion Christmas (mid-December)	505-528-3276
Picacho Street Antique & Collectible Flea Market (late May)	505-526-8624
Renaissance Craftfaire (early November)	505-523-6403
Run Old Mesilla (late March)	505-524-7824
Saint Genevieve's Antique & Craft Show (late November)	505-526-8624
San Juan Fiesta (late June)	505-526-8171
Serra Club Antique & Collectible Show (early June)	505-526-8624
Southern New Mexico State Fair (late September)	505-524-8612
Turkey Trot (late November)	505-524-7824
Whole Enchilada Fiesta (early October)	505-647-1228

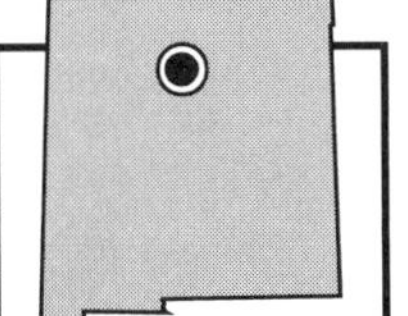

Santa Fe

The architecture of Santa Fe reflects the heritage of its Spanish founders and Pueblo Indian inhabitants. The Pueblo Indian tribes who live in the area today have earned a reputation for their fine jewelry and pottery and feast day dances. The best known among the Pueblo tribes' homes is Taos Pueblo, located 72 miles north of Santa Fe at the base of Taos Mountain. Taos is one of the oldest continuously inhabited communities in the U.S. The heart of Santa Fe is The Plaza, with shops, restaurants, and many art galleries. On the north side of The Plaza is the pueblo-style Palace of the Governors, the oldest public building in the U.S. During the winter, Santa Fe's mountain ranges draw many skiiers to the slopes, and the melting snow of late spring creates higher waters for excellent whitewater rafting.

Population	66,522	**Longitude**	105-95-25 W
Area (Land)	36.6 sq mi	**County**	Santa Fe
Area (Water)	0.1 sq mi	**Time Zone**	MST
Elevation	6989 ft	**Area Code/s**	505
Latitude	35-68-12 N		

— Average Temperatures and Precipitation —

TEMPERATURES

	Jan	Feb	Mar	Apr	May	Jun	Jul	Aug	Sep	Oct	Nov	Dec
High	41	45	52	62	71	81	84	82	77	65	52	43
Low	19	23	27	35	43	52	57	55	49	39	27	21

PRECIPITATION

	Jan	Feb	Mar	Apr	May	Jun	Jul	Aug	Sep	Oct	Nov	Dec
Inches	0.7	0.7	0.7	0.8	1.4	1.4	2.2	2.3	1.4	1.1	0.6	0.7

— Important Phone Numbers —

	Phone		Phone
AAA	505-471-6620	**Poison Control Center**	505-272-2222
Emergency	911	**Time/Temp**	505-473-2211
HotelDocs	800-468-3537	**Weather**	505-988-5151
Medical Referral	505-841-1777		

— Information Sources —

				Phone	Fax
LifeWay Conference Center Glorieta PO Box 8 *Web:* www.lifeway.com/glorieta	Glorieta	NM	87535	505-757-6161	757-6149
New Mexico Indian Tourism Assn 2401 12th St NW Rm 211	Albuquerque	NM	87104	505-246-1668	246-0344
Santa Fe City Hall PO Box 909 *Web:* sfweb.ci.santa-fe.nm.us ■ *E-mail:* cityhall@ci.santa-fe.nm.us	Santa Fe	NM	87504	505-984-6509	984-2409
Santa Fe Convention & Visitors Bureau PO Box 909 *TF:* 800-777-2489 ■ *Web:* www.santafe.org	Santa Fe	NM	87504	505-984-6760	984-6679
Santa Fe County PO Box 276 *Web:* www.co.santa-fe.nm.us	Santa Fe	NM	87504	505-986-6200	995-2740
Santa Fe County Chamber of Commerce 510 N Guadalupe Suite N *Web:* www.santafechamber.com	Santa Fe	NM	87504	505-988-3279	984-2205
Santa Fe Mayor PO Box 909 *Web:* www.ci.santa-fe.nm.us/sfweb/Mayor%20&%20Council.htm ■ *E-mail:* mayor@ci.santa-fe.nm.us	Santa Fe	NM	87504	505-984-6590	984-6695
Santa Fe Planning & Land Use Dept 200 Lincoln Ave	Santa Fe	NM	87501	505-984-6571	984-6829
Santa Fe Public Library 145 Washington Ave *Web:* www.ci.santa-fe.nm.us/sfpl	Santa Fe	NM	87501	505-984-6789	984-6676
Sweeney Convention Center 201 W Marcy St *TF:* 800-777-2489 ■ *Web:* www.santafe.org/destination/sweeney.html ■ *E-mail:* santafe@nets.com	Santa Fe	NM	87501	505-984-6760	984-6679

On-Line Resources

About.com Guide to Albuquerque/Santa Fe	albuquerque.about.com/local/southwestus/albuquerque
Anthill City Guide Santa Fe	www.anthill.com/city.asp?city=santafe
Area Guide Santa Fe	santafe.areaguides.net
City Knowledge Santa Fe	www.cityknowledge.com/nm_santefe.htm
Excite.com Santa Fe City Guide	www.excite.com/travel/countries/united_states/new_mexico/santa_fe
Great Locations Guidebook Santa Fe	www.nmgl.com/santafe_page.htm
Insiders' Guide to Santa Fe	www.insiders.com/santafe/
NITC Travelbase City Guide Santa Fe	www.travelbase.com/auto/guides/santa_fe-area-nm.html

Santa Fe — On-Line Resources (Cont'd)

Performance de Santa Fe	www.performs.com
Rough Guide Travel Santa Fe	travel.roughguides.com/content/1157/
Santa Fe Now	www.santafenow.com
Santa Fe Online	www.sfol.com/sfol/sfol.html

— Transportation Services —

AIRPORTS

■ Santa Fe Municipal Airport (SAF)

	Phone
10 miles SW of downtown (approx 25 minutes)	505-473-7243

Airport Transportation

	Phone
Capital City Cab $20 fare to downtown	505-438-0000

Commercial Airlines

	Phone		Phone
TWA	800-221-2000	**United Express**	505-473-4118

■ Albuquerque International Airport (ABQ)

	Phone
60 miles S of downtown Santa Fe (approx 60 minutes)	505-842-4366

Web: www.cabq.gov/airport/

Airport Transportation

	Phone
Shuttlejack $20 fare to downtown Santa Fe	505-982-4311

Commercial Airlines

	Phone		Phone
America West	800-235-9292	**Mesa**	800-637-2247
American	800-433-7300	**Southwest**	505-245-1717
Continental	800-525-0280	**United**	800-241-6522
Delta	800-221-1212	**US Airways**	800-428-4322

Charter Airlines

	Phone		Phone
Alliance Executive Charter Services	800-232-5387	**Cutter Aviation Service Inc**	505-842-4184
		Mountain Aviation Enterprises	505-842-6660

CAR RENTALS

	Phone		Phone
Advantage	505-247-1066	**Enterprise**	505-764-9100
Alamo	505-842-4057	**Hertz**	505-842-4235
Avis	505-842-4080	**National**	505-842-4222
Avis-Santa Fe	505-982-4361	**Rent-A-Wreck**	505-232-7552
Budget	505-768-5920	**Thrifty**	505-842-8733
Dollar	505-842-4224		

LIMO/TAXI

	Phone		Phone
Capital City Cab	505-438-0000	**Limotion Limousine**	505-820-0816

MASS TRANSIT

	Phone
Santa Fe Trails $.50 Base fare	505-984-6730

RAIL/BUS

				Phone
Amtrak Station CR 33	Lamy	NM	87540	800-872-7245
Greyhound/Trailways Bus Station 858 St Michaels Dr	Santa Fe	NM	87501	505-471-0008

— Accommodations —

HOTEL RESERVATION SERVICES

	Phone	Fax
Advance Reservations Inn Arizona *TF:* 800-456-0682 ■ *Web:* tucson.com/inn ■ *E-mail:* micasa@primenet.com	480-990-0682	990-3390
New Mexico Central Reservations *TF:* 800-466-7829 ■ *Web:* www.nmtravel.com ■ *E-mail:* reservations@nmtravel.com	505-766-9770	247-8200
Santa Fe Central Reservations/Taos Valley Resort Assn **Fax Area Code:* 505 ■ *Web:* www.taoswebb.com/NMResv ■ *E-mail:* res@taoswebb.com	800-776-7669	984-8682*

HOTELS, MOTELS, RESORTS

				Phone	Fax
Alexander's Inn 320 E Marcy St	Santa Fe	NM	87501	505-954-4467	954-4467
Angel Fire Resort PO Drawer B *TF:* 800-633-7463 ■ *Web:* www.angelfireresort.com	Angel Fire	NM	87710	505-377-6401	377-4200
Best Western 3650 Cerillos Rd	Santa Fe	NM	87505	505-438-3822	438-3795
Best Western Lamplighter Motel 2405 Cerillos Rd	Santa Fe	NM	87505	505-471-8000	471-1397
Bishop's Lodge PO Box 2367 *TF:* 800-732-2240 ■ *Web:* www.bishopslodge.com ■ *E-mail:* bishopslodge@nets.com	Santa Fe	NM	87504	505-983-6377	989-8739
Budget Inn 725 Cerillos Rd.	Santa Fe	NM	87501	505-982-5952	984-8879
Cactus Lodge 2864 Cerrillos Rd	Santa Fe	NM	87505	505-471-7699	
Comfort Inn 4312 Cerrillos Rd *TF:* 800-228-5150	Santa Fe	NM	87505	505-474-7330	474-7330
Comfort Suites 1435 Avenida de las Americas *TF:* 800-228-5150	Santa Fe	NM	87505	505-473-9004	438-4627
Days Inn 2900 Cerrillos Rd. *TF:* 800-329-7466	Santa Fe	NM	87505	505-473-4281	424-3297
Doubletree Hotel 3347 Cerillos Rd *TF:* 800-222-8733	Santa Fe	NM	87501	505-473-2800	473-4905
El Rey Inn 1862 Cerillos Rd *TF:* 800-521-1349	Santa Fe	NM	87505	505-982-1931	989-9249
Eldorado Hotel 309 W San Francisco St *TF:* 800-955-4455 ■ *Web:* www.eldoradohotel.com ■ *E-mail:* rez@eldoradohotel.com	Santa Fe	NM	87501	505-988-4455	995-4543
Fairfield Inn by Marriott 4150 Cerrillos Rd *TF:* 800-758-1128 ■ *Web:* fairfieldinn.com/SAFFI	Santa Fe	NM	87505	505-474-4442	474-7569
Fort Marcy Hotel Suites 320 Artist Rd. *TF:* 800-745-9910	Santa Fe	NM	87501	505-982-6636	984-8682
Four Kachinas Inn 512 Webber St *TF:* 800-397-2564 ■ *Web:* www.fourkachinas.com ■ *E-mail:* info@fourkachinas.com	Santa Fe	NM	87501	505-982-2550	989-1323
Garrett's Desert Inn 311 Old Santa Fe Trail *TF:* 800-888-2145	Santa Fe	NM	87501	505-982-1851	989-1647
Hilton of Santa Fe 100 Sandoval St *TF:* 800-336-3676 ■ *Web:* www.hiltonofsantafe.com ■ *E-mail:* relax@hiltonofsantafe.com	Santa Fe	NM	87501	505-988-2811	986-6435
Holiday Inn 4048 Cerillos Rd *TF:* 800-465-4329	Santa Fe	NM	87505	505-473-4646	473-2186
Holiday Inn Express 3470 Cerrillos Rd *TF:* 800-465-4329	Santa Fe	NM	87505	505-474-7570	474-6342
Hotel Loretto 211 Old Santa Fe Trail *TF:* 800-727-5531	Santa Fe	NM	87501	505-988-5531	984-7988
Hotel Saint Francis 210 Don Gaspar Ave. *TF:* 800-529-5700 ■ *Web:* www.hotelstfrancis.com ■ *E-mail:* info@hotelstfrancis.com	Santa Fe	NM	87501	505-983-5700	989-7690
Hotel Santa Fe 1501 Paseo de Peralta. *TF:* 800-825-9876 ■ *Web:* www.hotelsantafe.com ■ *E-mail:* hotelsf@newmexico.com	Santa Fe	NM	87501	505-982-1200	984-2211
Howard Johnson Express 4044 Cerillos Rd *TF:* 800-446-4656	Santa Fe	NM	87505	505-438-8950	471-9129
Inn of the Anasazi 113 Washington Ave *TF:* 800-688-8100 ■ *Web:* www.innoftheanasazi.com	Santa Fe	NM	87501	505-988-3030	988-3277
Inn of the Governors 234 Don Gaspar Ave. *TF:* 800-234-4534 ■ *Web:* www.inn-gov.com ■ *E-mail:* info@inn-gov.com	Santa Fe	NM	87501	505-982-4333	989-9149
Inn on the Alameda 303 E Alameda St *TF:* 800-289-2122 ■ *Web:* www.inn-alameda.com ■ *E-mail:* info@inn-alameda.com	Santa Fe	NM	87501	505-984-2121	986-8325
La Fonda Hotel 100 E San Francisco. *TF:* 800-523-5002 ■ *Web:* www.travelbase.com/destinations/santa-fe/la-fonda ■ *E-mail:* la-fonda@travelbase.com	Santa Fe	NM	87501	505-982-5511	988-2952
La Posada de Santa Fe 330 E Palace Ave *TF:* 800-727-5276	Santa Fe	NM	87501	505-986-0000	982-6850
La Quinta Motor Inn 4298 Cerrillos Rd *TF:* 800-531-5900	Santa Fe	NM	87501	505-471-1142	438-7219
Los Alamos Inn 2201 Trinity Dr *TF:* 800-279-9279	Los Alamos	NM	87544	505-662-7211	

Santa Fe — Hotels, Motels, Resorts (Cont'd)

				Phone	Fax
Luxury Inn 3752 Cerrillos Rd	Santa Fe	NM	87501	505-473-0567	471-9139
TF: 800-647-1346					
Motel 6 3007 Cerrillos Rd	Santa Fe	NM	87505	505-473-1380	473-7784
TF: 800-466-8356					
Quail Ridge Inn PO Box 707	Taos	NM	87571	505-776-2211	776-2949
TF: 800-624-4448					
Quality Inn 3011 Cerrillos Rd	Santa Fe	NM	87505	505-471-1211	438-9535
TF: 800-228-5151					
Radisson Hotel & Suites on the Plaza 125 Washington Ave	Santa Fe	NM	87501	505-988-4900	983-9322
TF: 800-333-3333					
Radisson Hotel Santa Fe 750 N St Francis Dr	Santa Fe	NM	87501	505-982-5591	992-5865
TF: 800-333-3333					
Ramada Limited 3625 Cerrillos Rd	Santa Fe	NM	87501	505-474-3900	474-4440
Rancho Encantado 198 SR 592	Santa Fe	NM	87501	505-982-3537	983-8269
TF: 800-722-9339 ■ *Web:* www.ranchoencantadosantafe.com					
Residence Inn by Marriott 1698 Galisteo St.	Santa Fe	NM	87505	505-988-7300	988-3243
TF: 800-331-3131 ■ *Web:* www.residenceinn.com/SAFNM					
Rio Vista Suites 527 E Alameda	Santa Fe	NM	87501	505-982-6636	984-8682
TF: 800-745-9910					
Steve's Santa Fe Inn 2907 Cerrillos Rd.	Santa Fe	NM	87505	505-471-3000	424-7561
Super 8 Motel 3358 Cerrillos Rd.	Santa Fe	NM	87505	505-471-8811	471-3239
TF: 800-800-8000					
Travelodge Santa Fe Plaza 646 Cerrillos Rd	Santa Fe	NM	87501	505-982-3551	983-8624
TF: 800-578-7878					
Travelodge Santa Fe South 3450 Cerrillos Rd	Santa Fe	NM	87505	505-471-4000	474-4394
TF: 800-578-7878					
Villas de Santa Fe 400 Griffin St	Santa Fe	NM	87501	505-988-3000	988-4700
TF: 800-869-6790 ■ *Web:* www.villasdesantafe.com ■ *E-mail:* villasdesantafe@travelbase.com					

— Restaurants —

				Phone
Bistro 315 (French) 315 Old Santa Fe Trail	Santa Fe	NM	87501	505-986-9190
Blue Corn Grill (Southwest) 133 Water St.	Santa Fe	NM	87501	505-984-1800
Bull Ring (Steak) 150 Washington Ave	Santa Fe	NM	87501	505-983-3328
Cafe Oasis (Natural/Health) 526 Galisteo	Santa Fe	NM	87501	505-983-9599
Cafe Pasqual's (Southwest) 121 Don Gaspar Ave	Santa Fe	NM	87501	505-983-9340
Chopstix (Chinese) 238 N Guadalupe St	Santa Fe	NM	87501	505-820-2126
Cleopatra Cafe (Middle Eastern) 418 Cerrillos Rd	Santa Fe	NM	87501	505-820-7381
Compound The (Continental) 653 Canyon Rd	Santa Fe	NM	87501	505-982-4353
Corn Dance Cafe (Native American) 1501 Paseo de Peralta	Santa Fe	NM	87501	505-982-1200
Cowgirl Hall of Fame BBQ & Western Grill (Barbecue) 319 S Guadalupe St	Santa Fe	NM	87501	505-982-2565
Web: www.santafenow.com/rest/cowgirl/				
Coyote Cafe (Southwest) 132 W Water St.	Santa Fe	NM	87501	505-983-1615
El Farol (Spanish) 808 Canyon Rd	Santa Fe	NM	87501	505-983-9912
El Nido (Steak/Seafood) 591 Bishop's Lodge Rd	Tesuque	NM	87574	505-988-4340
Evangelo's (Mediterranean) 229 Galisteo	Santa Fe	NM	87501	505-820-6526
Fabio's Grill (Italian) 329 W San Francisco St.	Santa Fe	NM	87501	505-984-3080
Garduno's of Santa Fe (Mexican) 130 Lincoln Ave.	Santa Fe	NM	87501	505-983-9797
Geronimo (New American) 724 Canyon Rd	Santa Fe	NM	87501	505-982-1500
Il Piatto (Italian) 95 W Marcy St	Santa Fe	NM	87501	505-984-1091
Il Vicino (Italian) 321 W San Francisco St	Santa Fe	NM	87501	505-986-8700
India House (Indian) 2501 Cerillos Rd	Santa Fe	NM	87505	505-471-2651
India Palace (Indian) 227 Don Gaspar	Santa Fe	NM	87501	505-986-5859
Inn of the Anasazi Dining Room (Southwest) 113 Washington Ave.	Santa Fe	NM	87501	505-988-3236
Jacks (New American) 135 W Palace 3rd Fl	Santa Fe	NM	87501	505-983-7220
La Casa Sena (Southwest) 125 E Palace Ave.	Santa Fe	NM	87501	505-988-9232
La Tertulia (Southwest) 416 Agua Fria St	Santa Fe	NM	87501	505-988-2769
Little Anita's New Mexican Foods (Mexican) 2811 Cerrillos Rd	Santa Fe	NM	87505	505-473-4505
Manana (Southwest) Alameda St & Don Gaspar Ave	Santa Fe	NM	87501	505-982-4333
Maria's New Mexican Kitchen (Southwest) 555 W Cordova Rd.	Santa Fe	NM	87501	505-983-7929
Web: www.sfol.holowww.com/sfol/food/marias/index.html				
Masa Sushi (Japanese/Korean) 927 W Alameda	Santa Fe	NM	87501	505-982-3334
Mu Du Noodles (Pan-Asian) 1494 Cerrillos Rd	Santa Fe	NM	87505	505-983-1411
Old House (Southwest) 309 W San Francisco St	Santa Fe	NM	87501	505-988-4455
Old Mexico Grill (Mexican) 2434 Cerrillos Rd	Santa Fe	NM	87501	505-473-0338
Ore House On the Plaza (Steak/Seafood) 50 Lincoln Ave	Santa Fe	NM	87501	505-983-8687
Palace Restaurant & Saloon (Continental) 142 W Palace Ave	Santa Fe	NM	87501	505-982-9891
Pastability (Italian) 418 Cerrillos Rd.	Santa Fe	NM	87501	505-988-2856
Paul's Restaurant of Santa Fe (International) 72 W Marcy St.	Santa Fe	NM	87501	505-982-8738
Peppers Restaurant & Cantina (Mexican) 2239 Old Pecos Trail	Santa Fe	NM	87505	505-984-2272
Pink Adobe (Continental) 406 Old Santa Fe Trail	Santa Fe	NM	87501	505-983-7712
Web: www.santafenow.com/rest/pinkadobe/				
Pinon Grill (Steak/Seafood) 100 Sandoval St.	Santa Fe	NM	87501	505-986-6400
Plaza Cafe (Greek) 54 Lincoln Ave.	Santa Fe	NM	87501	505-982-1664
Pyramid Cafe (Greek) 505 Cordova Rd	Santa Fe	NM	87501	505-989-1378
Rancho de Chimayo (Southwest) CR 98	Santa Fe	NM	87522	505-351-4444
Ristra (French) 548 Agua Fria St	Santa Fe	NM	87501	505-982-8608
Saigon Cafe (Chinese) 501 W Cordova Rd	Santa Fe	NM	87501	505-988-4951
San Francisco Street Bar & Grill (New American) 114 W San Francisco St	Santa Fe	NM	87501	505-982-2044
Santacafe (New American) 231 Washington Ave	Santa Fe	NM	87501	505-984-1788
Second Street Brewery (English) 1814 2nd St.	Santa Fe	NM	87505	505-982-3030
Web: www.secondstreetbrewery.com/				
Shed The (Southwest) 113 1/2 E Palace Ave	Santa Fe	NM	87501	505-982-9030
Shohko Cafe (Japanese) 321 Johnson St	Santa Fe	NM	87501	505-983-7288
Staab House (Continental) 330 E Palace Ave.	Santa Fe	NM	87501	505-986-0000
Star of Siam (Thai) 2860 Cerillos Rd	Santa Fe	NM	87505	505-438-8644
Tecolote Cafe (Southwest) 1203 Cerrillos Rd.	Santa Fe	NM	87501	505-988-1362
Tiny's (Southwest) 1015 Penn Rd	Santa Fe	NM	87501	505-983-1100
Tortilla Flats (Southwest) 3139 Cerrillos Rd	Santa Fe	NM	87505	505-471-8685
Web: www.santafenow.com/rest/tortilla/				
Vanessie of Santa Fe (Continental) 434 W Water St	Santa Fe	NM	87501	505-982-9966
Whistling Moon Cafe (Mediterranean) 402 N Guadalupe	Santa Fe	NM	87501	505-983-3093
Wolf Canyon Brewing Co (American) 9885 Cerrillos Rd	Santa Fe	NM	87505	505-438-7000
Yin Yang (Chinese) 418 Cerrillos Rd Suite 2	Santa Fe	NM	87501	505-986-9279
Yuri's Cafe (Russian) 227 Don Gaspar Ave	Santa Fe	NM	87501	505-988-1403

— Goods and Services —

SHOPPING

				Phone	Fax
Sanbusco Market Center 500 Montezuma Ave	Santa Fe	NM	87501	505-989-9390	983-0783
Santa Fe Premium Outlets 8380 Cerrillos Rd.	Santa Fe	NM	87505	505-474-4000	474-4173
Web: www.chelseagca.com					
Villa Linda Mall 4250 Cerrillos Rd	Santa Fe	NM	87505	505-473-4253	473-0575
Wind River Trading Co 113 E San Francisco St	Santa Fe	NM	87501	505-989-7062	986-0229

BANKS

				Phone	Fax
Bank of Santa Fe PO Box 2027	Santa Fe	NM	87504	505-984-0500	984-0410
First National Bank of Santa Fe 62 Lincoln Ave	Santa Fe	NM	87501	505-984-7400	984-7405
Sunwest Bank of Santa Fe 1234 St Michael's Dr.	Santa Fe	NM	87501	505-471-1234	473-8669
Wells Fargo Bank PO Box 969	Santa Fe	NM	87504	505-982-3671	982-7490

BUSINESS SERVICES

	Phone		Phone
Accountemps	505-982-3859	**Kinko's**	505-982-6311
Airborne Express	800-247-2676	**Mail Boxes Etc**	800-789-4623
BAX Global	800-225-5229	**OfficeTeam**	505-982-3859
DHL Worldwide Express	800-225-5345	**Pak Mail**	505-989-7380
Federal Express	800-238-5355	**Post Office**	505-988-6351
Group Powell One	505-982-9131	**UPS**	800-742-5877

— Media —

PUBLICATIONS

				Phone	Fax
New Mexico Magazine 495 Old Santa Fe Trail	Santa Fe	NM	87501	505-476-0202	827-6496
TF: 800-898-6639					
Santa Fe New Mexican‡ PO Box 2048	Santa Fe	NM	87504	505-983-3303	986-9147
Web: www.sfnewmexican.com					

‡*Daily newspapers*

TELEVISION

				Phone	Fax
KASA-TV Ch 2 (Fox) 1377 University Blvd NE	Albuquerque	NM	87102	505-246-2222	242-1355
Web: www.kasa.com					

Santa Fe — Television (Cont'd)

				Phone	Fax
KNME-TV Ch 5 (PBS)					
1130 University Blvd NE	Albuquerque	NM	87102	505-277-2121	277-2191
TF: 800-328-5663 ■ *Web:* www.pbs.org/knme					
■ *E-mail:* viewer@knme1.unm.edu					
KOAT-TV Ch 7 (ABC)					
3801 Carlisle Blvd NE	Albuquerque	NM	87107	505-884-7777	884-6354
E-mail: news@koat7.com					
KOB-TV Ch 4 (NBC)					
4 Broadcast Plaza SW	Albuquerque	NM	87104	505-243-4411	764-2522
Web: www.kobtv.com ■ *E-mail:* opinion@kobtv.com					
KRQE-TV Ch 13 (CBS) PO Box 1294	Albuquerque	NM	87103	505-243-2285	842-8483

RADIO

				Phone	Fax
KBAC-FM 98.1 MHz (AAA) 2021 Pinon St	Santa Fe	NM	87505	505-989-3338	989-3881
Web: www.kbac.com					
KBOM-FM 106.7 MHz (Oldies)					
2600-A Camino Entrada	Santa Fe	NM	87505	505-471-1067	473-2667
KIOT-FM 102.5 MHz (CR)					
8009 Marble Ave NE	Albuquerque	NM	87110	505-262-1142	262-9211
TF: 888-262-1025 ■ *Web:* www.arrow1025.com/~arrow/					
■ *E-mail:* arrow@arrow1025.com					
KSFQ-FM 101.1 MHz (Oldies)					
1478 St Francis Dr	Santa Fe	NM	87505	505-954-4500	954-4039
KSWV-AM 810 kHz (Span) 102 Taos St	Santa Fe	NM	87505	505-989-7441	989-7607
KTRC-AM 1400 kHz (Nost)					
2502-C Camino Entrada	Santa Fe	NM	87505	505-471-1067	473-2667
KVSF-AM 1260 kHz (N/T)					
2502 Camino Entrada Suite C	Santa Fe	NM	87505	505-438-8255	473-2667

— Colleges/Universities —

				Phone	Fax
College of Santa Fe 1600 St Michaels Dr	Santa Fe	NM	87505	505-473-6011	473-6127
TF: 800-456-2673 ■ *Web:* www.csf.edu					
Institute of American Indian Arts					
PO Box 20007	Santa Fe	NM	87504	505-988-6487	986-5543
TF Admissions: 800-804-6422 ■ *Web:* www.iaiancad.org					
■ *E-mail:* info@iaiancad.org					
Saint John's College Santa Fe Campus					
1160 Camino Cruz Blanca	Santa Fe	NM	87501	505-982-3691	984-6003
TF Admissions: 800-331-5232*					

— Hospitals —

				Phone	Fax
Lovelace Health Systems					
440 St Michael's Dr.	Santa Fe	NM	87505	505-995-2400	995-2403
Web: www.lovelace.com					
Saint Vincent Hospital 455 St Michael's Dr	Santa Fe	NM	87505	505-983-3361	820-5210
Web: www.stvin.org					

— Attractions —

				Phone	Fax
Archdiocese of Santa Fe Museum					
223 Cathedral Pl	Santa Fe	NM	87501	505-983-3811	992-0341
Aztec Ruins National Monument PO Box 640	Aztec	NM	87410	505-334-6174	334-6372
Web: www.nps.gov/azru/ ■ *E-mail:* azru_interpretation@nps.gov					
Bandelier National Monument					
HCR 1 Box 1 Suite 15	Los Alamos	NM	87544	505-672-3861	672-9607
Web: www.nps.gov/band/					
Bataan Memorial Museum					
1050 Old Pecos Trail	Santa Fe	NM	87501	505-474-1670	
Canyon Road Fine Art 621 Canyon Rd	Santa Fe	NM	87501	505-988-9511	988-9511
Chaco Culture National Historical Park					
PO Box 220	Nageezi	NM	87037	505-786-7014	786-7061
Web: www.nps.gov/chcu/					
Cities of Gold Hwy 285	Santa Fe	NM	87501	505-455-3313	455-7188
TF: 800-455-3313					
Davey Randall Audubon Center					
1800 Upper Canyon Rd	Santa Fe	NM	87501	505-983-4609	983-2355
El Rancho de las Golondrinas Museum					
334 Los Pinos Rd	Santa Fe	NM	87505	505-471-2261	471-5623
E-mail: erdlgolond@aol.com					
Garson Greer Theatre Center					
1600 St Micheal's Dr College of Santa Fe	Santa Fe	NM	87505	505-473-6511	473-6016
Web: www.csf.edu/perfart/pad.html					
Hyde Memorial State Park NM 475	Santa Fe	NM		505-983-7175	983-2783
Institute of American Indian Arts Museum					
108 Cathedral Pl	Santa Fe	NM	87501	505-988-6281	988-6273
Lensic Theatre 211 W San Francisco St	Santa Fe	NM	87501	505-982-0301	
Loretto Chapel 207 Old Santa Fe Trail	Santa Fe	NM	87501	505-982-0092	
Museum of Fine Arts 107 W Palace Ave	Santa Fe	NM	87501	505-827-4455	827-4473
Museum of Indian Arts & Culture					
710 Camino Lejo	Santa Fe	NM	87501	505-827-6344	827-6497
Web: www.miaclab.org					
Museum of International Folk Art					
706 Camino Lejo	Santa Fe	NM	87505	505-827-6350	827-6349
Web: www.moifa.org					
Museum of New Mexico PO Box 2087	Santa Fe	NM	87501	505-827-6451	747-5784*
**Fax Area Code:* 800 ■ *Web:* www.nmculture.org					
Nambe Pueblo State Hwy 503 N to NP101		NM	87501	505-455-2036	
New Mexico Pro Coro 107 W Palace Ave	Santa Fe	NM	87501	505-820-7711	
O'Keeffe Georgia Museum 217 Johnson St	Santa Fe	NM	87501	505-995-0785	995-0786
Web: www.okeeffe-museum.org					
Palace of the Governors 105 W Palace Ave	Santa Fe	NM	87504	505-476-5100	476-5104
Pecos National Historical Park PO Box 418	Pecos	NM	87552	505-757-6414	757-8460
Web: www.nps.gov/peco/					
Picuris Pueblo Hwy 75	Penasco	NM	87553	505-587-1832	
Plan B Evolving Arts 1050 Old Pecos Trail	Santa Fe	NM	87501	505-982-1338	982-9854
Pojoaque Pueblo Hwy 25 N to Pojoaque		NM	87501	505-455-2278	
Saint Francis Cathedral 213 Cathedral Pl	Santa Fe	NM	87501	505-982-5619	989-1952
San Ildefonso Pueblo State Hwy 502		NM	87501	505-455-2273	
San Juan Pueblo State Hwy 84/285 N to Hwy 74		NM	87566	505-852-4400	
San Miguel Mission 401 Old Santa Fe Trail	Santa Fe	NM	87501	505-983-3974	
Sangre de Cristo Chorale PO Box 4462	Santa Fe	NM	87502	505-662-9717	
Santa Clara Pueblo					
State Hwy 84/285 5 miles N of Espanola		NM	87532	505-753-7326	
Santa Fe Children's Museum					
1050 Old Pecos Trail	Santa Fe	NM	87501	505-989-8359	989-7506
Web: www.sfchildmuseum.org ■ *E-mail:* children@trail.com					
Santa Fe Community Orchestra					
107 W Palace Ave	Santa Fe	NM	87501	505-466-4818	
Santa Fe Desert Chorale					
211 Old Santa Fe Trail	Santa Fe	NM	87501	505-988-7505	
Santa Fe Opera					
Hwy 285 Santa Fe Opera House	Santa Fe	NM	87504	505-986-5900	995-3030
Web: www.santafeopera.org					
Santa Fe Performing Arts School & Armory for the Arts 1050 Old Pecos Trail	Santa Fe	NM	87501	505-984-1370	
Santa Fe Playhouse 142 E DeVargas St	Santa Fe	NM	87501	505-988-4262	
Santa Fe Pro Musica					
211 W San Francisco St Lensic Theater	Santa Fe	NM	87501	505-988-4640	984-2501
Santa Fe Ski Area 1210 Luisa St Suite 5	Santa Fe	NM	87505	505-982-4429	
Santa Fe Southern Railway					
410 S Guadalupe	Santa Fe	NM	87501	505-989-8600	983-7620
TF: 888-989-8600 ■ *Web:* www.sfsr.com					
Santa Fe Stages 105 E Marcy St Suite 107	Santa Fe	NM	87501	505-982-6683	
Web: www.santafestages.org ■ *E-mail:* sfstages@ix.netcom.com					
Santa Fe Symphony 1050 Old Pecos Trail	Santa Fe	NM	87505	505-983-3530	982-3888
Web: www.rt66.com/santafe_symph					
Santa Fe Women's Ensemble					
211 Old Santa Fe Trail	Santa Fe	NM	87501	505-983-2137	
Santuario de Guadalupe					
100 S Guadalupe St	Santa Fe	NM	87501	505-988-2027	
School of American Research					
660 E Garcia St	Santa Fe	NM	87501	505-982-3584	989-9809
Shakespeare in Santa Fe					
1160 Camino Cruz Blanca	Santa Fe	NM	87501	505-982-2910	
Site Santa Fe Museum					
1606 Paseo de Peralta	Santa Fe	NM	87501	505-989-1199	989-1188
Web: www.sitesantafe.org ■ *E-mail:* sitesantafe@sitesantafe.org					
Southwest Children's Theatre Productions					
142 E DeVargas St	Santa Fe	NM	87501	505-984-3055	
Taos Pueblo Taos Pueblo Rd	Taos	NM	87571	505-758-1028	758-4604
Tesque Pueblo					
State Hwy 84/285 15 miles N of Santa Fe		NM		505-983-2667	
THEATERWORK 1336 Ruffina Cir	Santa Fe	NM	87505	505-471-1799	
Wadle Galleries Ltd 128 W Palace Ave	Santa Fe	NM	87501	505-983-9219	988-2209
Wheelwright Museum of the American Indian					
PO Box 5153	Santa Fe	NM	87502	505-982-4636	989-7386
TF: 800-607-4636					
White Sands National Monument					
PO Box 1086	Holloman AFB	NM	88330	505-479-6124	479-4333
Web: www.nps.gov/whsa/					

Santa Fe (Cont'd)

— Events —

	Phone
Antique Ethnographic Show (mid-August)	505-992-8929
Antique Indian Art Show & Sale (mid-August)	505-992-8929
Behind Adobe Walls House Tours (late July-mid-August)	505-982-9301
Buffalo Roast (mid-August)	505-827-6474
Eight Northern Indian Pueblos Artists & Craftsmen Show (mid-July)	505-852-4265
Festival de Santa Fe (early September)	505-988-7575
High Country Arts & Crafts Festival (early July)	505-587-2519
Mountain Man Trade Fair (mid-August)	505-476-5100
Nambe Feast Day Celebration (early October)	505-455-2036
Old West Show & Sale (mid-August)	505-992-8929
Picuris Feast Day Celebration (mid-August)	505-984-6760
Pojoaque Feast Day Celebration (early December)	505-455-2278
Pro Musica Holy Week Baroque Festival (late March-early April)	505-988-4640
Rodeo de Santa Fe (mid-July)	505-471-4300
San Ildefonso Feast Day Celebration (late January)	505-455-2273
San Juan Feast Day Celebration (late June)	505-852-4400
Santa Clara Feast Day Celebration (early August)	505-753-7326
Santa Fe Air Show (early-mid-June)	505-471-5111
Santa Fe Bicycle Trek (mid-May)	505-982-1282
Santa Fe Bluegrass & Old Time Music Festival (late August)	505-984-6760
Santa Fe Century Bike Ride (mid-May)	505-982-1282
Santa Fe Chamber Music Festival (mid-July-mid-August)	505-983-2075
Santa Fe Indian Market (late August)	505-983-5220
Santa Fe Trail (September)	505-438-1464
Santa Fe Wine & Chile Fiesta (late September)	505-982-8686
Santa Fe Wine Festival (early July)	505-471-2261
Spring Festival (June)	505-471-2261
Taos Feast Day Celebration (late September)	505-984-6760
Taste of Santa Fe (early May)	505-984-6760
Tesque Feast Day Celebration (early November)	505-983-2667
Traditional Spanish Market (late July)	505-983-4038
Winter Fiesta (late January-early February)	505-983-5615

New York

Population (1999): 18,196,601 **Area (sq mi): 54,471**

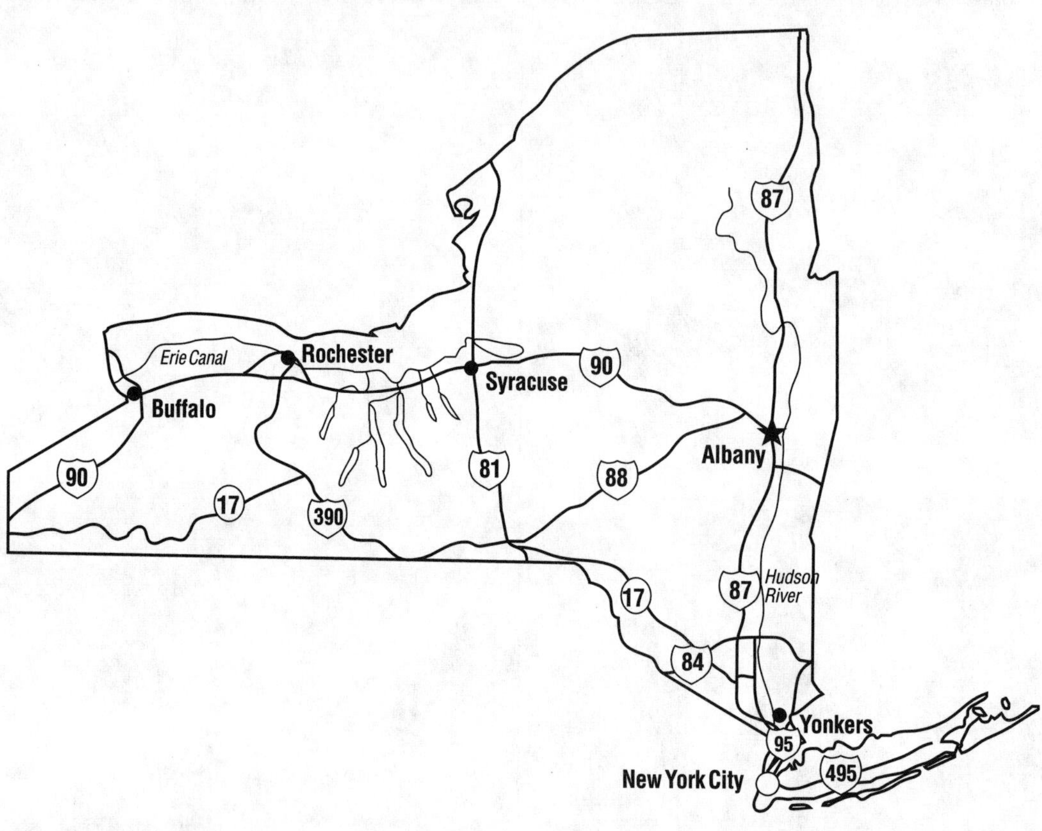

— State Information Sources —

				Phone	Fax
New York Empire State Development Corp 99 Washington Ave 1 Commerce Plaza Rm 900	Albany	NY	12245	518-474-4100	474-1512
Web: www.empire.state.ny.us ■ *E-mail:* esd@nysstf.org					
New York Parks Recreation & Historic Preservation Office 1 Empire State Plaza	Albany	NY	12238	518-474-0456	486-1805
TF: 800-456-2267 ■ *Web:* nysparks.state.ny.us					
New York State Business Council 152 Washington Ave	Albany	NY	12210	518-465-7511	465-4389
TF: 800-358-1202 ■ *Web:* www.bcnys.org ■ *E-mail:* mattison@emi.com					
New York State Government Information				518-474-2121	
Web: www.state.ny.us					
New York State Library Empire State Plaza Cultural Education Ctr	Albany	NY	12230	518-474-5355	474-5786
Web: www.nysl.nysed.gov ■ *E-mail:* nyslweb@unix2.nysed.gov					
New York Tourism Div PO Box 2603	Albany	NY	12220	518-474-4116	486-6416
TF: 800-225-5697 ■ *Web:* iloveny.state.ny.us					

ON-LINE RESOURCES

Central New York . . . . . www.centralnewyork.com
Discover the Finger Lakes . . . . . www.fingerlakes.com
Net Travel Exchange New York . . . . . www.nettx.com/states/ny.html
New York Cities . . . . . dir.yahoo.com/Regional/U_S__States/New_York/Cities
New York Cities By County . . . dir.yahoo.com/Regional/U_S__States/New_York/Counties_and_Regions
New York Scenario . . . . . scenariousa.dstylus.com/ny/indexf.htm
New York State Internet Directory . . . . . www.nysid.com
New York Travel & Tourism Guide . . www.travel-library.com/north_america/usa/new_york/index.html
New York@TownTour.com . . . . . www.towntour.com/newyork_list.htm
Rough Guide Travel New York travel.roughguides.com/content/3/index.htm
RoundTheBend's Upstate New York . . . . . www.roundthebend.com
Travel.org-New York . . . . . travel.org/newyork.html
Upstate New York Travel Guide . . . . . www.upstateguide.com
Welcome to Upstate New York . . . . . www.rawood.com/upstateny
Western New York Travel Guide . . . . . www.westernny.com
Yahoo! Get Local New York . . . . . dir.yahoo.com/Regional/U_S__States/New_York

— Cities Profiled —

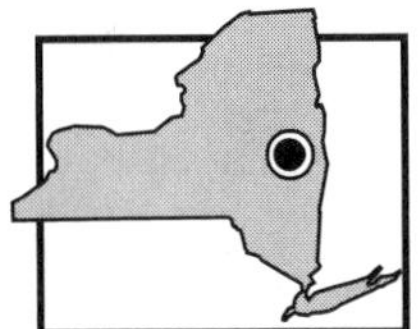

Albany

The capital of New York State is situated on the western bank of the Hudson River. Its location has made it an important transportation center since 1609, when Henry Hudson ended his voyage there. Albany's early settlers were Dutch, Danish, German, Scottish, and Norwegian. Glimpses of their culture and everday life can be seen in area historic homes, museums, and other sites, including the Shaker Heritage Society and the Albany Institute of History and Art, which contains four centuries of Hudson Valley art and history. The heart of Albany is the Empire State Plaza, a half-mile-long, 11-building complex containing the state capitol, a convention center, business and government offices, a performing arts center, and the New York State Museum, which presents exhibits tracing the history of New York State's natural and cultural resources.

Population . . . 94,305
Area (Land) . . . 21.4 sq mi
Area (Water) . . . 0.5 sq mi
Elevation . . . 150 ft
Latitude . . . 42-65-25 N
Longitude . . . 73-75-67 W
County . . . Albany
Time Zone . . . EST
Area Code/s . . . 518

— Average Temperatures and Precipitation —

TEMPERATURES

	Jan	Feb	Mar	Apr	May	Jun	Jul	Aug	Sep	Oct	Nov	Dec
High	30	33	44	58	70	79	84	82	73	62	49	35
Low	11	14	25	35	45	55	60	58	49	39	31	18

PRECIPITATION

	Jan	Feb	Mar	Apr	May	Jun	Jul	Aug	Sep	Oct	Nov	Dec
Inches	2.4	2.3	2.9	3.0	3.4	3.6	3.2	3.5	3.0	2.8	3.2	2.9

— Important Phone Numbers —

	Phone
AAA	518-426-1000
Albany Alive Events Line	518-434-1217
American Express Travel	518-489-7444
Emergency	911
HotelDocs	800-468-3537
Poison Control Center	800-336-6997
Road Conditions	800-847-8929
Travelers Aid	518-463-2124
Weather	518-476-1111

— Information Sources —

				Phone	Fax
Albany City Hall 25 Eagle St *Web:* www.albanyny.org	Albany	NY	12207	518-434-5090	434-5081
Albany-Colonie Regional Chamber of Commerce 107 Washington Ave *Web:* www.ac-chamber.org	Albany	NY	12207	518-434-1214	434-1339
Albany County 112 State St Rm 200 *Web:* www.crisny.org/not-for-profit/lwvac/county1.html	Albany	NY	12207	518-447-7040	447-5589
Albany County Convention & Visitors Bureau 25 Quackenbush Sq *TF:* 800-258-3582 ■ *Web:* www.albany.org ■ *E-mail:* accvb@albany.org	Albany	NY	12207	518-434-1217	434-0887
Albany Economic Development Dept 21 Lodge St	Albany	NY	12207	518-434-2532	434-9846
Albany Mayor 24 Eagle St Rm 102 *E-mail:* mayor@albanyny.org	Albany	NY	12207	518-434-5100	434-5013
Albany Public Library 161 Washington Ave	Albany	NY	12210	518-449-3380	449-3386
Albany Urban Cultural Park Visitors Center 25 Quackenbush Sq	Albany	NY	12207	518-434-0405	
Capital Region Information System of New York 1400 Washington Ave Rm LCSB33 *Web:* www.crisny.org ■ *E-mail:* support@crisny.org	Albany	NY	12222	518-454-5400	442-3672
Downtown Business Improvement District 50 State St.	Albany	NY	12207	518-465-2143	
Empire State Plaza Convention Center Concourse Level Base of EGG. *Web:* www.albany.org/arenas/empire3.html	Albany	NY	12242	518-474-4759	473-2190

On-Line Resources

4Albany.com . . . www.4albany.com
About.com Guide to Albany . . . albany.about.com/local/midlanticus/albany
Albany Online . . . www.albanyonline.com
Anthill City Guide Albany/Troy . . . www.anthill.com/city.asp?city=albanytroy
Area Guide Albany . . . albanyny.areaguides.net
Capital Connections . . . www.capitalconnections.com
Capital Region Community Network . . . www.crisny.org
City Knowledge Albany . . . www.cityknowledge.com/ny_albany.htm
CitySearch Albany . . . albany.citysearch.com
DigitalCity Albany . . . home.digitalcity.com/albany
Excite.com Albany City Guide . . . www.excite.com/travel/countries/united_states/new_york/albany
Metroland . . . www.metland.com

— Transportation Services —

AIRPORTS

■ **Albany International Airport (ALB)**

	Phone
8 miles NW of downtown (approx 15 minutes) Web: www.albanyairport.com/ ■ *E-mail:* info@albanyairport.com	518-242-2200

Airport Transportation

	Phone
Airport Limousine $14 fare to downtown	518-869-2258
Albany Yellow Cab $14 fare to downtown	518-434-2222

Commercial Airlines

	Phone
AirTran	800-247-8726
American	800-433-7300
Continental	800-525-0280
Delta	800-221-1212
Delta Business Express	800-345-3400
Northwest	800-225-2525
TWA	800-221-2000
United	800-241-6522
United Express	800-241-6522
US Airways	800-428-4322
US Airways Express	800-428-4322

Charter Airlines

	Phone
Summit Aviation	800-255-4625

CAR RENTALS

	Phone
Avis	518-869-8404
Budget	518-785-4716
Car Temps USA	518-869-7472
Enterprise	518-453-6222
Hertz	518-783-1081

LIMO/TAXI

	Phone
Advantage Limousine	518-433-0100
Albany Ok Taxi	518-482-5555
Albany Yellow Cab	518-434-2222
Capitaland Taxi	518-453-8888
Checker Cab	518-456-8800
Duffy's Taxi	518-433-8400
National Limousine	518-453-6226
Premiere Limousine	518-459-6123
Today's Limousine	518-452-4242

MASS TRANSIT

	Phone
Capital District Transportation Authority $1 Base fare	518-482-8822

RAIL/BUS

				Phone
Amtrak Station East St *TF:* 800-872-7245	Rensselaer	NY	12144	518-462-5763
Greyhound Bus Station 34 Hamilton St. *TF:* 800-231-2222	Albany	NY	12207	518-427-7060

Albany (Cont'd)

— Accommodations —

HOTELS, MOTELS, RESORTS

				Phone	Fax
Albany Quality Inn 3 Watervliet Ave	Albany	NY	12206	518-438-8431	438-8356
TF: 800-228-5151					
Best Western Albany Inn 200 Wolf Rd	Albany	NY	12205	518-458-1000	458-2807
TF: 800-528-1234					
Best Western Inn 12 Campus Dr Ext	Cobleskill	NY	12043	518-234-4321	234-3869
TF: 800-528-1234					
Canoe Island Lodge Resort PO Box 144	Diamond Point	NY	12824	518-668-5592	668-2012
Century House Inn 997 New Loudon Rd	Latham	NY	12110	518-785-0931	785-3274
TF: 888-674-6873					
Comfort Inn & Business Center 1606 Central Ave	Albany	NY	12205	518-869-5327	456-8971
TF: 800-233-9444					
Comfort Inn Airport 866 Albany-Shaker Rd	Latham	NY	12110	518-783-1216	783-4085
TF: 800-274-9429					
Courtyard by Marriott 1455 Washington Ave	Albany	NY	12206	518-435-1600	435-1616
TF: 800-321-2211 ■ *Web:* courtyard.com/ALBWS					
Courtyard by Marriott 168 Wolf Rd	Albany	NY	12205	518-482-8800	482-0001
TF: 800-321-2211 ■ *Web:* courtyard.com/ALBCA					
Days Inn 16 Wolf Rd	Albany	NY	12205	518-459-3600	459-3677
TF: 800-329-7466					
Desmond The 660 Albany-Shaker Rd	Albany	NY	12211	518-869-8100	869-7659
TF: 800-448-3500 ■ *Web:* www.desmondny.com					
Econo Lodge 1632 Central Ave	Albany	NY	12205	518-456-8811	456-0811
TF: 800-553-2666					
Extended StayAmerica 1395 Washington Ave	Albany	NY	12206	518-446-0680	446-0779
TF: 800-398-7829					
Georgian The 384 Canada St	Lake George	NY	12845	518-668-5401	668-5870
TF: 800-525-3436 ■ *Web:* www.webny.com/georgian/					
Gideon Putnam Hotel & Conference Center 24 Gideon Putnam Rd Saratoga Springs Spa State Pk	Saratoga Springs	NY	12866	518-584-3000	584-1354
TF: 800-732-1560 ■ *Web:* www.gideonputnam.com ■ *E-mail:* generalinfo@gideonputnam.com					
Hampton Inn 10 Ulenski Dr	Albany	NY	12205	518-438-2822	438-2931
TF: 800-426-7866					
Holiday Inn Express 946 New Loudon Rd	Latham	NY	12110	518-783-6161	783-0154
TF: 800-465-4329					
Holiday Inn-Turf on Wolf Road 205 Wolf Rd	Albany	NY	12205	518-458-7250	458-7377
TF: 800-465-4329 ■ *Web:* www.basshotels.com/holiday-inn/?_franchisee=ALBWF ■ *E-mail:* info@holidayinnturf.com					
Howard Johnson Hotel 416 Southern Blvd	Albany	NY	12209	518-462-6555	462-2547
TF: 800-562-7253					
Marriott Hotel Albany 189 Wolf Rd	Albany	NY	12205	518-458-8444	458-7365
TF: 800-228-9290 ■ *Web:* marriotthotels.com/ALBNY					
Omni Albany Hotel 10 Eyck Plaza	Albany	NY	12207	518-462-6611	462-2901
TF: 800-843-6664					
Otesaga Hotel PO Box 311	Cooperstown	NY	13326	607-547-9931	547-9675
TF: 800-348-6222 ■ *Web:* www.otesaga.com					
Pleasantview Gayhead Rd	Freehold	NY	12431	518-634-2523	
Quality Inn Airport 622 Rt 155	Latham	NY	12110	518-785-1414	785-1414
TF: 800-228-5151					
Ramada Inn Albany 1228 Western Ave	Albany	NY	12203	518-489-2981	489-8967
TF: 800-272-6232					
Ramada Inn Downtown 300 Broadway	Albany	NY	12207	518-434-4111	432-5919
TF: 800-863-8351					
Ramada Limited 1630 Central Ave	Albany	NY	12205	518-456-0222	452-1376
TF: 800-272-6232					
Red Carpet Inn 500 Northern Blvd	Albany	NY	12204	518-462-5562	462-5562
TF: 800-251-1962					
Residence Inn by Marriott Albany Airport 1 Residence Inn Dr	Latham	NY	12110	518-783-0600	783-0709
TF: 800-331-3131 ■ *Web:* www.residenceinn.com/ALBTS					
Roaring Brook Ranch PO Box 671	Lake George	NY	12845	518-668-5767	668-4019
TF: 800-882-7665 ■ *Web:* www.adirondack.net/tour/roaring ■ *E-mail:* roaringb@adironack.net					
Super 8 Motel 1579 Central Ave	Albany	NY	12205	518-869-8471	464-4010
TF: 800-800-8000					
Susse Chalet 44 Wolf Rd	Albany	NY	12205	518-459-5670	459-0069
TF: 800-524-2538 ■ *Web:* www.sussechalet.com/albany.html					

— Restaurants —

				Phone
Across the Street Pub (American) 1238 Western Ave	Albany	NY	12203	518-482-9432
Bangkok Thai Restaurant (Thai) 8 Wolf Rd	Albany	NY	12205	518-435-1027
Big House Brewing Co (American) 90 N Pearl St	Albany	NY	12207	518-445-2739
Bugaboo Creek Steak House (Steak) 1 Crossgates Mall Rd	Albany	NY	12203	518-452-2900
Caffe Italia (Italian) 662 Central Ave	Albany	NY	12206	518-459-8029
Chang's (Chinese) 250 Delaware Ave	Albany	NY	12209	518-463-0667
Clayton's Caribbean Restaurant (Caribbean/Spanish) 244 Washington Ave	Albany	NY	12210	518-426-4360
Conway's (Continental) 492 Yates St	Albany	NY	12208	518-489-9999
Cranberry Bog (American) 56 Wolf Rd	Albany	NY	12205	518-459-5110
Web: www.cranbog.com				
Dumpling House (Chinese) 120 Everett Rd	Albany	NY	12205	518-458-7044
El Mariachi (Mexican) 62 Central Ave	Albany	NY	12206	518-465-2568
Figliomeni's (Italian) 1814 Western Ave	Albany	NY	12203	518-456-0686
Jack's Oyster House (Steak/Seafood) 42 State St	Albany	NY	12207	518-465-8854
La Serre (Continental) 14 Green St	Albany	NY	12207	518-463-6056
Madison's End Cafe (American) 1108 Madison Ave	Albany	NY	12208	518-489-8859
Mansion Hill Inn (American) 115 Philip St	Albany	NY	12202	518-465-2038
Web: www.mansionhill.com				
Miyako Japanese Restaurant (Japanese) 192 N Allen St	Albany	NY	12206	518-482-1080
Nicole's Bistro (French) 25 Quackenbush Sq	Albany	NY	12207	518-465-1111
Ogden's (Continental) 42 Howard St	Albany	NY	12207	518-463-6605
Pagliacci's Italian Ristorante (Italian) 44 S Pearl St	Albany	NY	12207	518-465-1001
Scrimshaw The (American) 660 Albany-Shaker Rd	Albany	NY	12211	518-869-8100
Shades of Green (Vegetarian) 187 Lark St	Albany	NY	12210	518-434-1830
Sitar Indian Restaurant (Indian) 1929 Central Ave	Albany	NY	12205	518-456-6670
Taj Mahal Restaurant (Indian) 193 Lark St	Albany	NY	12210	518-426-9000
Thatcher's (Continental) 272 Delaware Ave	Albany	NY	12209	518-465-0115
Yono's (Indonesian) 289 Hamilton St	Albany	NY	12210	518-436-7747
Zia's (Italian) 228 Washington Ave	Albany	NY	12210	518-436-0617

— Goods and Services —

SHOPPING

				Phone	Fax
Colonie Center 1475 Central Ave	Albany	NY	12205	518-459-9020	459-2147
Crossgates Mall 1 Crossgates Mall Rd	Albany	NY	12203	518-869-9565	869-9683
Web: www.crossgatesmall.com					
Lark Street Merchants Assn 301 Lark St	Albany	NY	12210	518-436-7008	
Latham Circle Mall 800 New Loudon Rd	Latham	NY	12110	518-785-6633	785-6647
Latham Factory Stores & More 400 Old Loudon Rd	Latham	NY	12110	413-243-8186	243-0667
Mohawk Mall 440 Balltown Rd	Schenectady	NY	12304	518-374-3521	374-3470
Northway Mall 1440 Central Ave	Albany	NY	12205	518-459-5320	459-4089
Rotterdam Square Mall Campbell Rd	Schenectady	NY	12306	518-374-3713	374-3722
Stuyvesant Plaza 1475 Western Ave	Albany	NY	12203	518-482-8986	482-5190
Web: www.stuyvesantplaza.com					

BANKS

				Phone	Fax
Charter One Bank 10 N Pearl St	Albany	NY	12207	518-432-2200	445-2027*
**Fax:* Hum Res					
Evergreen Bank NA 125 State St	Albany	NY	12207	518-455-9912	426-5710
Fleet Bank 69 State St	Albany	NY	12201	518-447-4000	447-4204
HSBC Bank USA 126 State St	Albany	NY	12207	518-432-2016	432-2036
TF: 800-627-4631					
KeyBank NA Albany District 60 State St	Albany	NY	12207	518-486-8871	487-4286*
**Fax:* Cust Svc ■ *TF:* 800-539-2968					
KeyBank USA NA PO Box 655	Albany	NY	12201	800-872-5553	257-8166*
**Fax Area Code:* 518					

BUSINESS SERVICES

	Phone		Phone
Adecco Staffing Services	518-862-9885	**DHL Worldwide Express**	800-225-5345
Airborne Express	800-247-2676	**Kelly Services**	518-489-6060
Allegra Printing	518-456-6773	**Kinko's**	518-482-9095
BAX Global	800-225-5229	**Mail Boxes Etc**	800-789-4623
Capitaland Courier	518-438-8080	**Manpower Temporary Services**	518-434-8251
CD & L Inc	518-438-6100	**Olsten Staffing Services**	518-862-0500
Corporate Express Delivery Systems	518-274-8000	**Post Office**	518-452-2499
		UPS	800-742-5877

— Media —

PUBLICATIONS

				Phone	Fax
Capital District Business Review PO Box 15081	Albany	NY	12212	518-437-9855	437-0764
Web: www.amcity.com/albany					
Daily Gazette‡ 2345 Maxon Rd Ext	Schenectady	NY	12308	518-374-4141	395-3089*
**Fax:* News Rm ■ *Web:* www.dailygazette.com ■ *E-mail:* gazette@dailygazette.com					

Albany — Publications (Cont'd)

				Phone	Fax
Times Union‡ PO Box 15000	Albany	NY	12212	518-454-5420	454-5628
TF: 800-955-4388 ■ *Web:* www.timesunion.com					

‡Daily newspapers

TELEVISION

				Phone	Fax
WMHQ-TV Ch 45 (PBS) PO Box 17	Schenectady	NY	12301	518-357-1700	357-1709
WMHT-TV Ch 17 (PBS) PO Box 17	Schenectady	NY	12301	518-357-1700	357-1709
TF: 800-477-9648 ■ *Web:* www.wmht.org ■ *E-mail:* reaction@wmht.org					
WNYT-TV Ch 13 (NBC) 15 N Pearl St	Albany	NY	12204	518-436-4791	434-0659
TF: 800-999-9698 ■ *Web:* www.wnyt.com					
WRGB-TV Ch 6 (CBS) PO Box 1400	Schenectady	NY	12301	518-346-6666	346-6249
Web: www.wrgb.com					
WTEN-TV Ch 10 (ABC) 341 Northern Blvd	Albany	NY	12204	518-436-4822	426-4792
Web: www.news10.com					
WXXA-TV Ch 23 (Fox) 28 Corporate Cir	Albany	NY	12203	518-862-2323	862-0930*
**Fax:* News Rm ■ *TF:* 800-999-2882 ■ *Web:* www.fox23tv.com					
WYPX-TV Ch 55 (PAX) 1 Charles Blvd	Guilderland	NY	12084	518-464-0143	464-0633
Web: www.pax.net/WYPX					

RADIO

				Phone	Fax
WAMC-FM 90.3 MHz (NPR) 318 Central Ave	Albany	NY	12206	518-465-5233	432-0991
TF: 800-323-9262 ■ *Web:* www.wamc.org ■ *E-mail:* mail@wamc.org					
WCDB-FM 90.9 MHz (Misc) 1400 Washington Ave SUNY Campus Ctr Suite 316	Albany	NY	12222	518-442-5262	
WFLY-FM 92.3 MHz (CHR) 6 Johnson Rd	Latham	NY	12110	518-786-6600	786-6692
Web: www.fly92.com ■ *E-mail:* wakeupfly@aol.com					
WGNA-FM 107.7 MHz (Ctry) 800 New London Rd Suite 4200	Latham	NY	12110	518-782-1474	782-1486
WQBK-FM 103.9 MHz (Alt) 4 Central Ave	Albany	NY	12210	518-462-5555	462-0784
Web: www.wqbk.com ■ *E-mail:* wqbk@wqbk.com					
WROW-AM 590 kHz (N/T) 6 Johnson Rd	Latham	NY	12110	518-786-6600	786-6692

— Colleges/Universities —

				Phone	Fax
Albany College of Pharmacy 106 New Scotland Ave	Albany	NY	12208	518-445-7200	445-7202
Web: www.panther.acp.edu					
Bryant & Stratton Career College Albany 1259 Central Ave	Albany	NY	12205	518-437-1802	437-1048
Web: www.bryantstratton.edu					
College of Saint Rose 432 Western Ave	Albany	NY	12203	518-454-5111	454-2013
TF: 800-637-8556 ■ *Web:* www.strose.edu					
Maria College 700 New Scotland Ave	Albany	NY	12208	518-438-1368	438-7170
Web: www.mariacollege.org ■ *E-mail:* admissions@mariacollege.org					
Rensselaer Polytechnic Institute 110 8th St	Troy	NY	12180	518-276-6000	276-4072
TF Admissions: 800-448-6562 ■ *Web:* www.rpi.edu ■ *E-mail:* admissions@rpi.edu					
Russell Sage College 45 Ferry St	Troy	NY	12180	518-244-2000	244-6880
TF: 888-837-9724 ■ *Web:* www.sage.edu/html/RSC/Welcome.html ■ *E-mail:* info-request@sage.edu					
Sage Junior College of Albany 140 New Scotland Ave	Albany	NY	12208	518-292-1730	292-1912
TF: 888-837-9724 ■ *Web:* www.sage.edu ■ *E-mail:* info-request@sage.edu					
Siena College 515 Loudon Rd	Loudonville	NY	12211	518-783-2300	783-2436
TF Admissions: 800-457-4362 ■ *Web:* www.siena.edu					
State University of New York Albany 1400 Washington Ave	Albany	NY	12222	518-442-3300	442-5383
TF Admissions: 800-293-7869 ■ *Web:* www.albany.edu					
State University of New York Hudson Valley Community College 80 Vandenburgh Ave	Troy	NY	12180	518-629-4822	629-7542
Web: www.hvcc.edu ■ *E-mail:* postmaster@hvcc.edu					
Union College 807 Union St	Schenectady	NY	12308	518-388-6000	388-6986
Web: www.union.edu					

— Hospitals —

				Phone	Fax
Albany Medical Center 43 New Scotland Ave	Albany	NY	12208	518-262-3125	262-3398
Web: www.amc.edu					
Albany Memorial Hospital 600 Northern Blvd	Albany	NY	12204	518-471-3221	449-4410
Saint Peter's Hospital 315 S Manning Blvd	Albany	NY	12208	518-454-1550	525-1193
Straton Veterans Affairs Medical Center 113 Holland Ave	Albany	NY	12208	518-462-3311	462-0528

— Attractions —

				Phone	Fax
Albany Berkshire Ballet 25 Monroe St	Albany	NY	12210	518-426-0660	426-0671
Web: www.rpi.edu/~ruberd/bb1.html ■ *E-mail:* ruberd@rpi.edu					
Albany Center Galleries 23 Monroe St	Albany	NY	12210	518-462-4775	462-1491
Albany Institute of History & Art 125 Washington Ave	Albany	NY	12210	518-463-4478	462-1522
Web: www.albanyinstitute.org/					
Albany Schenectady League of Arts 19 Clinton Ave	Albany	NY	12207	518-449-5380	449-5404
Albany Symphony Orchestra Inc 19 Clinton Ave	Albany	NY	12207	518-465-4755	465-3711
Web: artsitedesign.com/aso ■ *E-mail:* aso@global2000.net					
Capital Repertory Co 111 N Pearl St Market Street Theater	Albany	NY	12207	518-462-4534	465-0213
Web: www.capitalrep.org/ ■ *E-mail:* capitalrep@global2000.net					
Empire Center at the Egg PO Box 2065	Albany	NY	12220	518-473-1845	473-1848
Web: www.theegg.org/ ■ *E-mail:* info@TheEgg.org					
Empire State Aerosciences Museum 250 Rudy Chase Dr	Glenville	NY	12302	518-377-2191	377-1959
Empire State Plaza Art Collection Empire State Plaza	Albany	NY	12242	518-473-7521	474-0984
Executive Mansion 138 Eagle St	Albany	NY	12202	518-473-7521	
First Church of Albany 110 N Pearl St	Albany	NY	12207	518-463-4449	463-4830
Historic Cherry Hill 53 1/2 S Pearl St	Albany	NY	12202	518-434-4791	434-4806
Hudson Henry Planetarium 25 Quackenbush Sq	Albany	NY	12207	518-434-0405	
Irish American Heritage Museum Rt 145	East Durham	NY	12423	518-634-7497	634-7497
Web: www.irishamericanhermuseum.org ■ *E-mail:* irishmus@crisny.org					
Junior Museum 282 5th Ave	Troy	NY	12182	518-235-2120	235-6836
Web: www.juniormuseum.org					
Martin Van Buren National Historic Site 1013 Old Post Rd	Kinderhook	NY	12106	518-758-9689	758-6986
Web: www.nps.gov/mava/					
National Baseball Hall of Fame & Museum PO Box 590	Cooperstown	NY	13326	607-547-7200	547-2044
Web: www.baseballhalloffame.org ■ *E-mail:* baseball@enews.com					
National Museum of Racing & Hall of Fame 191 Union Ave	Saratoga Springs	NY	12866	518-584-0400	584-4574
TF: 800-562-5394					
New York State Capitol Washington Ave & State St	Albany	NY	12242	518-474-2418	
New York State Museum Madison Ave Cultural Education Ctr Empire State Plaza	Albany	NY	12230	518-474-5877	486-3696
Web: www.nysm.nysed.gov ■ *E-mail:* nysmweb@mail.nysed.gov					
Palace Theatre 19 Clinton Ave	Albany	NY	12207	518-465-3334	427-0151
Park Playhouse The Lakehouse Washington Pk	Albany	NY	12207	518-434-2035	424-5081
Web: home.nycap.rr.com/dmartin1/parkplay/pphone.html					
Proctor's Theatre 432 State St	Schenectady	NY	12305	518-382-3884	346-2468
Web: www.proctors.org					
Saratoga National Historical Park 648 Rt 32	Stillwater	NY	12170	518-664-9821	664-9830
Web: www.nps.gov/sara/					
Schuyler Mansion State Historic Site 32 Catherine St	Albany	NY	12202	518-434-0834	434-3821
Shaker Heritage Society Albany-Shaker Rd 1848 Shaker Meeting House	Albany	NY	12211	518-456-7890	452-7348
Web: www.crisny.org/not-for-profit/shakerwv ■ *E-mail:* shakerwv@crisny.org					
Ten Broeck Mansion 9 Ten Broeck Pl	Albany	NY	12210	518-436-9826	436-1489
Web: www.tenbroeck.org ■ *E-mail:* history@tenbroeck.org					
University Art Museum 1400 Washington Ave Suny Albany	Albany	NY	12222	518-442-4035	442-5075
Web: www.albany.edu/museum					

SPORTS TEAMS & FACILITIES

				Phone	Fax
Albany Diamond Dogs (baseball) Heritage Pk	Albany	NY	12211	518-869-9234	869-5291
Web: www.diamonddogs.com					
Albany Firebirds (football) 51 S Pearl St Pepsi Arena	Albany	NY	12207	518-487-2222	487-2228
Web: www.firebirds.com ■ *E-mail:* firebirds@global2000.net					

Albany — Sports Teams & Facilities (Cont'd)

				Phone	Fax
Albany River Rats (hockey) 51 S Pearl St Pepsi Arena	Albany	NY	12207	518-487-2244	487-2248
Web: www.canoe.ca/AHLAlbany/home.html					
New York Capital District Shockers (soccer) 433 State St	Schenectady	NY	12305	518-382-5104	382-0607
Pepsi Arena 51 S Pearl St	Albany	NY	12207	518-487-2000	487-2020
Web: www.pepsiarena.com					

— Events —

	Phone
Albany American Wine Festival (early February)	518-452-0707
Alive at Five Concert Series (early June-early July)	518-434-1217
Altamont Fair (mid-August)	518-861-6671
Capital District Garden & Flower Show (mid-March)	518-434-1217
Capital District Scottish Games (early September)	518-438-4297
Capital Holiday (late November-late December)	800-258-3582
Capital Springfest (April-May)	800-258-3582
Empire State African American Cultural Festival (early August)	518-473-0559
Fabulous Fourth Festivities (July 4)	518-473-0559
Festival of Trees (late November-early December)	518-463-4478
First Night Albany (December 31)	518-434-1217
Fleet Blues Fest (mid-July)	518-434-1217
Grand Union Food Show (mid-January)	518-473-0559
Great American International Auto Show (early March)	518-452-0584
Great New York State Snow & Travel Expo (early November)	518-383-6183
Great Northeast Home Show (early February)	518-383-6183
House & Garden Tour (mid-June)	518-436-9826
Independence Day Celebration (July 4)	518-473-0559
International Food Festival (mid-late August)	518-434-1217
Italian Festival (early August)	518-456-0292
Lark Street Festival (mid-September)	518-482-2203
Mid-Winter Blues Festival (mid-late January)	518-473-1845
New York in Bloom (mid-February)	518-434-1217
New York State Chocolate Festival (late March)	518-434-1217
Northeast Great Outdoors Show (late March)	518-383-6183
Old Songs Festival of Traditional Music & Dance (late June)	518-765-2815
Riverfront Arts Festival (mid-June)	518-273-0552
Shaker Heritage Society Craft & Harvest Festival (late September)	518-456-7890
Tulip Festival (early May)	518-434-2032
Victorian Spring Ball (late October)	518-583-7224
Waterford/RiverSpark Canalfest (early May)	518-237-7999
Winterfest (late January)	518-584-3255

Buffalo

Located at the eastern end of Lake Erie, New York's second largest city is ringed with 3,000 acres of parks, including the Buffalo Zoological Gardens and the Buffalo and Erie County Naval and Servicemen's Park, the nation's only inland naval park. However, the best-known area attraction is spectacular Niagara Falls, including the view of Goat Island separating the American and Canadian falls. The neighboring Great Lakes create a snow belt that provides top skiing conditions in the Greater Niagara area throughout the winter season. Ice fishing is also popular, and the Erie and Chataqua Lakes are known as some of the best spots for the sport.

Population	300,717	**Longitude**	78-82-36 W
Area (Land)	40.6 sq mi	**County**	Erie
Area (Water)	11.9 sq mi	**Time Zone**	EST
Elevation	600 ft	**Area Code/s**	716
Latitude	42-79-72 N		

— Average Temperatures and Precipitation —

TEMPERATURES

	Jan	Feb	Mar	Apr	May	Jun	Jul	Aug	Sep	Oct	Nov	Dec
High	30	32	42	54	66	75	80	78	71	59	47	35
Low	17	17	26	36	47	57	62	60	53	43	34	23

PRECIPITATION

	Jan	Feb	Mar	Apr	May	Jun	Jul	Aug	Sep	Oct	Nov	Dec
Inches	2.7	2.3	2.7	2.9	3.1	3.6	3.1	4.2	3.5	3.1	3.8	3.7

— Important Phone Numbers —

	Phone		Phone
AAA	716-634-7900	**Poison Control Center**	716-878-7654
American Express Travel	716-856-7373	**Time/Temp**	716-844-1717
Emergency	911	**Travelers Aid**	716-854-8661
HotelDocs	800-468-3537	**Weather**	716-844-4444

— Information Sources —

				Phone	Fax
Better Business Bureau Serving Western New York & the Capital District 741 Delaware Ave	Buffalo	NY	14209	716-881-5222	883-5349
Web: www.buffalo.bbb.org					
Buffalo & Erie County Public Library Lafayette Sq	Buffalo	NY	14203	716-858-8900	858-6211
Web: www.buffalolib.org					
Buffalo City Hall 65 Niagara Sq	Buffalo	NY	14202	716-851-4200	851-4234
Web: www.ci.buffalo.ny.us					
Buffalo Community Development Dept 65 Niagara Sq Rm 920	Buffalo	NY	14202	716-851-5016	854-0172
E-mail: commdev@ci.buffalo.ny.us					
Buffalo Convention Center Convention Center Plaza	Buffalo	NY	14202	716-855-5555	855-3158
TF: 800-995-7570					
Buffalo Free-Net/WNYLRC 4455 Genesee St	Buffalo	NY	14225	716-515-2100	
Web: freenet.buffalo.edu ■ *E-mail:* finamore@ubvms.cc.buffalo.edu					
Buffalo Mayor 65 Niagara Sq Rm 201	Buffalo	NY	14202	716-851-4841	851-4360
Web: www.ci.buffalo.ny.us/mayor/frameset.htm ■ *E-mail:* mayordept@ci.buffalo.ny.us					
Erie County 25 Delaware Ave	Buffalo	NY	14202	716-858-8785	858-6550
Web: www.erie.gov					
Greater Buffalo Convention & Visitors Bureau 617 Main St Suite 400	Buffalo	NY	14203	716-852-0511	852-0131
TF: 800-283-3256 ■ *Web:* www.buffalocvb.org ■ *E-mail:* info@buffalocvb.org					
Greater Buffalo Partnerships 300 Main Pl Tower	Buffalo	NY	14202	716-852-7100	852-2761
Web: www.gbpartnership.org					

On-Line Resources

4Buffalo.com	www.4buffalo.com
About.com Guide to Buffalo/Niagara	buffalo.about.com/local/midlanticus/buffalo
Anthill City Guide Buffalo	www.anthill.com/city.asp?city=buffalo
Area Guide Buffalo	buffalo.areaguides.net
Artvoice.com-Buffalo's Alternative Arts News	www.artvoice.com
Buffalo New York	buffalo-new-york.com
Buffalo Place Inc's Downtown Buffalo	www.dwntwnbuffalo.com
Buffalo Pride Online	www.buffalopride.com/
City Knowledge Buffalo	www.cityknowledge.com/ny_buffalo.htm
DigitalCity Buffalo	home.digitalcity.com/buffalo
Excite.com Buffalo City Guide	www.excite.com/travel/countries/united_states/new_york/buffalo
Online Buffalo	www.onlinebuffalo.com
Online Western New York	www.onlinewny.com/
Virtual Buffalo	www.virtualbuffalo.com/

— Transportation Services —

AIRPORTS

	Phone
■ **Buffalo Niagara International Airport (BUF)** 9 miles E of downtown (approx 35 minutes)	716-630-6000

Buffalo (Cont'd)

Airport Transportation

	Phone
Airport Taxi $20 fare to downtown	716-633-8318
Apex Transportation Services $45 fare to downtown	716-632-4666
NFTA Metrobus $1.25 fare to downtown	716-855-7211

Commercial Airlines

	Phone		Phone
AirTran	800-247-8726	**Northwest**	800-225-2525
American	800-433-7300	**United**	800-241-6522
Continental	716-852-1233	**US Airways**	800-428-4322
Continental Express	800-525-0280		

Charter Airlines

	Phone
Prior Aviation Service Inc	716-633-1000

CAR RENTALS

	Phone		Phone
Alamo	716-631-2044	**Hertz**	716-632-4896
Avis	716-632-1808	**National**	716-632-0203
Budget	716-632-4662	**Thrifty**	716-633-8500
Enterprise	716-884-6666		

LIMO/TAXI

	Phone		Phone
Action Taxi	716-639-0648	**Empire Limousine Service**	716-877-9665
Broadway Cab	716-896-4600	**Kenmore Cab**	716-876-3030
Buffalo Limousine	716-835-4997	**Liberty Cab**	716-877-7111
City Service Taxi of Buffalo	716-852-4000	**Radio Taxi Service**	716-633-4200
Dependable Cab	716-876-5555		

MASS TRANSIT

	Phone
Niagara Frontier Transit Metro System $1.25 Base fare	716-855-7211

RAIL/BUS

				Phone
Exchange Street Amtrak Station 75 Exchange St *TF:* 800-872-7245	Buffalo	NY	14203	716-856-2075
Greyhound/Trailways Bus Station 181 Ellicott St	Buffalo	NY	14203	800-231-2222

— Accommodations —

HOTEL RESERVATION SERVICES

	Phone	Fax
Adventures Bed & Breakfast Reservation Service *TF:* 800-724-1932 ■ *Web:* www.3z.com/bandbres ■ *E-mail:* rj@bandbres.com	716-768-2699	768-9386

HOTELS, MOTELS, RESORTS

				Phone	Fax
Adam's Mark Hotel Buffalo 120 Church St *TF:* 800-444-2326 ■ *Web:* www.adamsmark.com/buffalo2.htm	Buffalo	NY	14202	716-845-5100	845-5377
Best Western Inn Downtown 510 Delaware Ave *TF:* 800-528-1234	Buffalo	NY	14202	716-886-8333	884-3070
Buffalo Campus Lodge 1159 Main St	Buffalo	NY	14209	716-882-3490	886-3570
Buffalo Exit 53 Motor Lodge 475 Dingens St *TF:* 800-437-3744	Buffalo	NY	14206	716-896-2800	896-2828
Buffalo Marriott 1340 Millersport Hwy *TF:* 800-334-4040	Amherst	NY	14221	716-689-6900	689-0483
Buffalo Sheraton Four Points 2040 Walden Ave *TF:* 800-323-3331	Buffalo	NY	14225	716-681-2400	681-8067
Comfort Suites 901 Dick Rd *TF:* 800-228-5150	Buffalo	NY	14225	716-633-6000	633-6858
Days Inn Airport 4345 Genesee St *TF:* 800-329-7466	Buffalo	NY	14225	716-631-0800	631-7589
Econo Lodge 7200 Transit Rd *TF:* 800-932-0291	Williamsville	NY	14221	716-634-1500	634-1500
Fairfield Inn by Marriott 52 Freeman Dr *TF:* 800-228-2800 ■ *Web:* fairfieldinn.com/BUFFI	Williamsville	NY	14221	716-626-1500	626-1500
Fallside Resort 401 Buffalo Ave *TF:* 800-519-9911	Niagara Falls	NY	14303	716-285-2541	285-6108
Garden Place Hotel 6615 Transit Rd *TF:* 800-427-3361	Williamsville	NY	14221	716-635-9000	635-9098
Hampton Inn 10 Flint Rd *TF:* 800-426-7866	Amherst	NY	14226	716-689-4414	689-4382
Hampton Inn Airport 1745 Walden Ave *TF:* 800-426-7866	Buffalo	NY	14225	716-894-8000	894-3554
Heritage House Country Inn 8261 Main St *TF:* 800-283-3899	Williamsville	NY	14221	716-633-4900	633-4900
Holiday Inn Airport 4600 Genesee St. *TF:* 800-465-4329 ■ *Web:* www.harthotels.com/Buffalo_Airport	Cheektowaga	NY	14225	716-634-6969	634-0920
Holiday Inn Buffalo-Amherst NE 1881 Niagara Falls Blvd *TF:* 800-465-4329	Amherst	NY	14228	716-691-8181	691-4965
Holiday Inn Downtown 620 Delaware Ave *TF:* 800-465-4329	Buffalo	NY	14202	716-886-2121	886-7942
Holiday Inn Express 6700 Transit Rd *TF:* 800-465-4329	Williamsville	NY	14221	716-634-7500	634-7502
Holiday Inn Gateway 601 Dingens St *TF:* 800-465-4329	Buffalo	NY	14206	716-896-2900	896-3765
Holiday Inn Grand Island 100 Whitehaven Rd *TF:* 800-465-4329	Grand Island	NY	14072	716-773-1111	773-9386
Homewood Suites 760 Dick Rd *TF:* 800-225-5466	Buffalo	NY	14225	716-685-0700	685-2034
Howard Johnson Lodge 454 Main St. *TF:* 800-282-5261	Niagara Falls	NY	14301	716-285-5261	285-8536
Hyatt Regency Buffalo 2 Fountain Plaza *TF:* 800-233-1234 ■ *Web:* www.hyatt.com/usa/buffalo/hotels/hotel_buffa.html	Buffalo	NY	14202	716-856-1234	852-6157
Lenox Hotel & Suites 140 North St. *TF:* 800-825-3669	Buffalo	NY	14201	716-884-1700	885-8636
Lord Amherst Motor Hotel 5000 Main St. *TF:* 800-544-2200	Amherst	NY	14226	716-839-2200	839-1538
Microtel 50 Freeman Rd *TF:* 800-252-9880	Williamsville	NY	14221	716-633-6200	633-1329
Quality Inn Airport 4217 Genesee St *TF:* 800-228-5151	Cheektowaga	NY	14225	716-633-5500	633-4231
Radisson Hotel & Suites 4243 Genesee St *TF:* 800-333-3333	Buffalo	NY	14225	716-634-2300	632-2387
Radisson Suites Downtown 601 Main St. *TF:* 800-333-3333	Buffalo	NY	14203	716-854-5500	854-4836
Ramada Inn Buffalo Airport 48 Freeman Rd *TF:* 800-272-6232	Williamsville	NY	14221	716-634-2700	634-1644
Red Roof Inn Buffalo Amherst 42 Flint Rd *TF:* 800-843-7663	Amherst	NY	14226	716-689-7474	689-2051
Sleep Inn Buffalo Airport 100 Holtz Rd *TF:* 800-753-3746	Cheektowaga	NY	14225	716-626-4000	626-3370
Sunny Vineyard Motel & Restaurant 3929 Vineyard Dr *TF:* 888-386-5475	Dunkirk	NY	14048	716-366-4400	366-3375
Super 8 Motel 1 Flint Rd *TF:* 800-800-8000	Amherst	NY	14226	716-688-0811	688-2365
University Inn & Conference Center 2401 N Forest Rd	Amherst	NY	14226	716-636-7500	636-8296
Wellesley Inn 4630 Genesee St *TF:* 800-444-8888	Cheektowaga	NY	14225	716-631-8966	631-8977
White Inn 52 E Main St *TF:* 888-373-3664 ■ *Web:* www.whiteinn.com	Fredonia	NY	14063	716-672-2103	672-2107
Williamsville Inn Northeast 5447 Main St	Williamsville	NY	14221	716-634-1111	631-3367

— Restaurants —

				Phone
Ambrosia (Greek) 467 Elmwood Ave	Buffalo	NY	14222	716-881-2196
Anchor Bar & Restaurant (Italian) 1047 Main St	Buffalo	NY	14209	716-886-8920
Asa Ransom House (Continental) 10529 Main St.	Clarence	NY	14031	716-759-2315
Bijou Grille (California) 643 Main St	Buffalo	NY	14203	716-847-1512
Chef's (Italian) 291 Seneca St	Buffalo	NY	14204	716-856-9187
Daffodil's (Steak/Seafood) 930 Maple Rd	Williamsville	NY	14221	716-688-5413
EB Green's (Steak) 2 Fountain Plaza	Buffalo	NY	14202	716-856-1234
Enchante (French) 16 Allen St	Buffalo	NY	14202	716-885-1330
Fajitaville Grille (Tex Mex) 5385 Main St	Buffalo	NY	14222	716-631-0200
Fiddle Heads Restaurant (International) 62 Allen St	Buffalo	NY	14202	716-883-4166
Gigi's Restaurant (American) 257 E Ferry St	Buffalo	NY	14208	716-883-1438
Hourglass (Continental) 981 Kenmore Ave	Kenmore	NY	14217	716-877-8788
Imperial Burrito & Taco Co (Mexican) 1842 Clinton St	Buffalo	NY	14206	716-822-5580
Jacobi's (Italian) 141 Abbott Rd	Buffalo	NY	14220	716-822-2780
Just Pasta (Italian) 307 Bryant St	Buffalo	NY	14222	716-881-1888
King's Wok (Chinese) 3233 Bailey Ave	Buffalo	NY	14215	716-837-1740
Kuni's Sushi (Japanese) 752 Elmwood Ave	Buffalo	NY	14209	716-881-6819

Buffalo — Restaurants (Cont'd)

Name	City	State	ZIP	Phone
Little Talia Trattoria (Italian) 1458 Hertel Ave	Buffalo	NY	14216	716-833-8667
Lone Star Fajita Grill (Tex Mex) 1855 Hertel Ave	Buffalo	NY	14216	716-833-7756
Lord Chumley's (French) 481 Delaware Ave	Buffalo	NY	14202	716-886-2220
Niagara Cafe (Puerto Rican) 525 Niagara St	Buffalo	NY	14201	716-885-2233
Old Red Mill Inn (Steak/Seafood) 8326 Main St	Williamsville	NY	14221	716-633-7878
Oliver's (American) 2095 Delaware Ave	Buffalo	NY	14216	716-877-9662
Rue Franklin (French) 341 Franklin St	Buffalo	NY	14202	716-852-4416
Salvatore's Italian Gardens (Italian) 6461 Transit Rd	Depew	NY	14043	716-683-7990
Sequoia (American) 718 Elmwood Ave	Buffalo	NY	14222	716-882-2219
Taste of India (Indian) 494 Elmwood Ave	Buffalo	NY	14222	716-881-3141

— Goods and Services —

SHOPPING

Name	City	State	ZIP	Phone	Fax
Antique World 10995 Main St *TF:* 800-959-0714	Clarence	NY	14031	716-759-8483	759-6167
Boulevard Mall Niagara Falls Blvd & Maple Rd	Amherst	NY	14226	716-834-8600	836-6127
Eastern Hills Mall 4545 Transit Rd	Williamsville	NY	14221	716-631-5191	631-5127
Main Place Mall 390 Main St.	Buffalo	NY	14202	716-855-1900	855-2487
McKinley Mall Milestrip Rd & McKinley Pkwy	Blasdell	NY	14219	716-824-0462	824-2433
Walden Galleria 1 Walden Galleria	Buffalo	NY	14225	716-681-7600	681-1773

BANKS

Name	City	State	ZIP	Phone	Fax
Charter One Bank 414 Main St. *TF:* 800-457-7272	Buffalo	NY	14202	716-855-2532	855-2536
Chase Manhattan Bank 5 Niagara Sq *TF Cust Svc:* 800-935-9935*	Buffalo	NY	14202	716-852-5280	847-6026
Citibank 2310 Delaware Ave *TF Cust Svc:* 800-934-1609*	Buffalo	NY	14216	716-873-4233	873-4184
Fleet Bank of New York 10 Fountain Plaza *TF:* 800-841-4000	Buffalo	NY	14202	716-847-7200	849-3602
HSBC Bank USA 1 HSBC Ctr **Fax:* Mtkg ■ *E-mail:* custinfo@us.hsbc.com	Buffalo	NY	14203	716-841-2424	841-4746*
KeyBank NA Buffalo District 50 Fountain Plaza **Fax:* Cust Svc	Buffalo	NY	14202	716-847-7743	847-7890*
M & T Bank 788 Tonawanda St	Buffalo	NY	14207	716-873-6300	873-8607
Manufacturers & Traders Trust Co 1 M & T Plaza **Fax:* Hum Res ■ *Web:* www.mandtbank.com	Buffalo	NY	14203	716-842-5789	842-5020*

BUSINESS SERVICES

Name	Phone	Name	Phone
Accountemps	716-833-5322	**Mail Boxes Etc**	716-852-3166
CD & L	716-565-2354	**Manpower Temporary Services**	716-854-4000
Central Copier Service	716-873-9010	**Olsten Staffing Services**	716-685-6322
Federal Express	800-238-5355	**Post Office**	716-846-2432
Kelly Services	716-565-0951	**Town Express**	716-884-0723
Kinko's	716-874-2679	**UPS**	800-742-5877

— Media —

PUBLICATIONS

Name	City	State	ZIP	Phone	Fax
Buffalo News‡ PO Box 100 *Web:* www.buffnews.com	Buffalo	NY	14240	716-849-3434	856-5150
Buffalo Spree Magazine 5678 Main St *Web:* www.buffalospree.com ■ *E-mail:* info@buffalospree.com	Buffalo	NY	14221	716-634-0820	634-4659
Business First 472 Delaware Ave *Web:* www.amcity.com/buffalo	Buffalo	NY	14202	716-882-6200	882-4269

‡Daily newspapers

TELEVISION

Name	City	State	ZIP	Phone	Fax
WGRZ-TV Ch 2 (NBC) 259 Delaware Ave	Buffalo	NY	14202	716-849-2222	849-7602
WIVB-TV Ch 4 (CBS) 2077 Elmwood Ave *Web:* www.wivb.com	Buffalo	NY	14207	716-874-4410	879-4896
WKBW-TV Ch 7 (ABC) 7 Broadcast Plaza **Fax:* News Rm ■ *Web:* www.wkbw.com ■ *E-mail:* wkbwtv@wkbw.com	Buffalo	NY	14202	716-845-6100	856-8784*
WNED-TV Ch 17 (PBS) PO Box 1263 *Web:* www.wned.org	Buffalo	NY	14202	716-845-7000	845-7036
WNGS-TV Ch 67 (UPN) 9279 Dutch Hill Rd *Web:* www.wngstv.com ■ *E-mail:* wngs@wngstv.com	West Valley	NY	14171	716-942-3000	942-3010
WNYO-TV Ch 49 (WB) 699 Hertel Suite 100 *Web:* www.wb49.com	Buffalo	NY	14207	716-875-4949	875-4919
WUTV-TV Ch 29 (Fox) 951 Whitehaven Rd *Web:* www.wutv.com	Grand Island	NY	14072	716-773-7531	773-5753

RADIO

Name	City	State	ZIP	Phone	Fax
WBEN-AM 930 kHz (N/T) 2077 Elmwood Ave **Fax:* News Rm ■ *Web:* www.wben.com ■ *E-mail:* wben@cidcorp.com	Buffalo	NY	14207	716-876-0930	876-1344*
WBFO-FM 88.7 MHz (NPR) 205 Allen Hall *Web:* www.wbfo.buffalo.edu	Buffalo	NY	14214	716-829-2555	829-2277
WBLK-FM 93.7 MHz (Urban) 14 Lafayette Sq Suite 1300 *Web:* www.wblk.com ■ *E-mail:* talk2us@wblk.com	Buffalo	NY	14203	716-852-9393	852-9390
WDCX-FM 99.5 MHz (Rel) 625 Delaware Ave Suite 308	Buffalo	NY	14202	716-883-3010	883-3606
WECK-AM 1230 kHz (Nost) 1200 Rand Bldg Suite 1200	Buffalo	NY	14203	716-852-7444	852-0537
WEDG-FM 103.3 MHz (Alt) 464 Franklin St *Web:* www.wedg.com ■ *E-mail:* edgestu@localnet.com	Buffalo	NY	14202	716-881-4555	884-2931
WGR-AM 550 kHz (N/T) 695 Delaware Ave. *Web:* www.wgr55.com ■ *E-mail:* wgr55@wgr55.com	Buffalo	NY	14209	716-884-5101	885-8255
WGRF-FM 96.9 MHz (CR) 464 Franklin St *Web:* www.wgrf.com ■ *E-mail:* info@wgrf.com	Buffalo	NY	14202	716-881-4555	884-2931
WHTT-AM 1120 kHz (Rel) 425 Franklin St *Web:* www.whtt.com ■ *E-mail:* whtt@whtt.com	Buffalo	NY	14202	716-881-0002	881-0010
WHTT-FM 104.1 MHz (Oldies) 464 Franklin St.	Buffalo	NY	14202	716-881-4555	884-2931
WJYE-FM 96.1 MHz (AC) 1200 Rand Bldg CBS	Buffalo	NY	14203	716-852-7444	852-0537
WKSE-FM 98.5 MHz (CHR) 695 Delaware Ave *Web:* www.kiss985.com	Buffalo	NY	14209	716-884-5101	644-9329
WLCE-FM 92.9 MHz (AC) 14 Lafayette Sq Suite 1300 *Web:* www.aliceradio.com	Buffalo	NY	14202	716-852-9292	852-9290
WMJQ-FM 102.5 MHz (AC) 2077 Elmwood Ave	Buffalo	NY	14207	716-876-0930	875-6201
WNED-AM 970 kHz (NPR) PO Box 1263	Buffalo	NY	14240	716-845-7000	845-7043
WNUC-FM 107.7 MHz (Ctry) 5500 Main St *Web:* www.wnuc.com ■ *E-mail:* station@wnuc.com	Williamsville	NY	14221	716-626-1077	626-1395
WUFO-AM 1080 kHz (Rel) 89 LaSalle Ave	Buffalo	NY	14214	716-834-1080	837-1438
WWKB-AM 1520 kHz (Sports) 695 Delaware Ave	Buffalo	NY	14209	716-884-5101	881-0143
WWWS-AM 1400 kHz (Urban) 2077 Elmwood Ave	Buffalo	NY	14207	716-879-4839	875-6201
WYRK-FM 106.5 MHz (Ctry) 14 Lafayette Sq 1200 Rand Bldg.	Buffalo	NY	14203	716-852-7444	852-5683

— Colleges/Universities —

Name	City	State	ZIP	Phone	Fax
Bryant & Stratton Career College Buffalo 465 Main St	Buffalo	NY	14203	716-884-9120	884-0091
Bryant & Stratton Career College Eastern Hills Campus 200 Bryant & Stratton Way	Williamsville	NY	14221	716-631-0260	631-0273
Bryant & Stratton Career College Lackawanna 1214 Abbott Rd	Lackawanna	NY	14218	716-821-9331	821-9343
Buffalo State College 1300 Elmwood Ave *Web:* www.buffalostate.edu	Buffalo	NY	14222	716-878-4000	878-6100
Canisius College 2001 Main St *TF Admissions:* 800-843-1517 ■ *Web:* gort.canisius.edu	Buffalo	NY	14208	716-883-7000	888-2525
D'Youville College 320 Porter Ave *TF:* 800-777-3921 ■ *Web:* www.dyc.edu ■ *E-mail:* admissions@dyc.edu	Buffalo	NY	14201	716-881-3200	881-7790
Daemen College 4380 Main St. *Web:* www.daemen.edu	Amherst	NY	14226	716-839-3600	839-8516
Erie Community College City Campus 121 Ellicott St. *Web:* www.sunyerie.edu	Buffalo	NY	14203	716-842-2770	851-1129
Erie Community College North Campus 6205 Main St	Williamsville	NY	14221	716-634-0800	851-1429
Hilbert College 5200 S Park Ave *TF Admissions:* 800-649-8003 ■ *Web:* www.hilbert.edu	Hamburg	NY	14075	716-649-7900	649-1152

Buffalo — Colleges/Universities (Cont'd)

				Phone	Fax
Houghton College Seneca Campus 910 Union Rd. *TF:* 800-247-6448	West Seneca	NY	14224	716-674-6363	674-0250
Medaille College 18 Agassiz Cir. *TF:* 800-292-1582	Buffalo	NY	14214	716-884-3281	884-0291
Niagara University *TF Admissions:* 800-462-2111 ■ *Web:* www.niagara.edu	Niagara University	NY	14109	716-285-1212	286-8710
State University of New York Buffalo 3435 Main St *TF Admissions:* 888-822-3648 ■ *Web:* www.buffalo.edu	Buffalo	NY	14214	716-645-2000	645-6411
Trocaire College 360 Choate Ave *Web:* www.trocaire.edu	Buffalo	NY	14220	716-826-1200	826-6107
Villa Maria College of Buffalo 240 Pine Ridge Rd	Buffalo	NY	14225	716-896-0700	896-0705

— Hospitals —

				Phone	Fax
Buffalo General Hospital 100 High St	Buffalo	NY	14203	716-845-5600	859-1530
Children's Hospital 219 Bryant St *Web:* www.chob.edu	Buffalo	NY	14222	716-878-7000	888-3979
Erie County Medical Center 462 Grider St	Buffalo	NY	14215	716-898-3000	898-5178
Kaleida Health/Millard Fillmore Hospital 3 Gates Cir. *Web:* www.mfhs.edu ■ *E-mail:* fsava@mfhs.edu	Buffalo	NY	14209	716-887-4600	887-4379
Kenmore Mercy Hospital 2950 Elmwood Ave	Kenmore	NY	14217	716-879-6100	447-6576
Mercy Hospital 565 Abbott Rd **Fax:* Admitting	Buffalo	NY	14220	716-826-7000	828-2596*
Our Lady of Victory Hospital 55 Melroy	Lackawanna	NY	14218	716-825-8000	827-8635
Saint Joseph Hospital 2605 Harlem Rd	Cheektowaga	NY	14225	716-891-2400	891-2616
Sisters of Charity Hospital of Buffalo 2157 Main St	Buffalo	NY	14214	716-862-2000	862-1019
Veterans Affairs Medical Center 3495 Bailey Ave	Buffalo	NY	14215	716-834-9200	862-3423

— Attractions —

				Phone	Fax
African American Cultural Center 350 Masten Ave	Buffalo	NY	14209	716-884-2013	885-2590
Albright-Knox Art Gallery 1285 Elmwood Ave *Web:* www.albrightknox.org	Buffalo	NY	14222	716-882-8700	882-1958
Alleyway Theatre 1 Curtain Up Alley	Buffalo	NY	14202	716-852-2600	852-2266
Amherst Museum 3755 Tonawanda Creek Rd	Amherst	NY	14228	716-689-1440	689-1409
Anderson Gallery 1 Martha Jackson Pl	Buffalo	NY	14214	716-834-2579	834-7789
Broadway Market 999 Broadway *Web:* www.broadwaymarket.com ■ *E-mail:* manager@broadwaymarket.com	Buffalo	NY	14212	716-893-0705	893-2216
Buffalo & Erie County Botanical Gardens 2655 S Park Ave	Buffalo	NY	14218	716-827-1584	828-0091
Buffalo & Erie County Historical Society 25 Nottingham Ct *Web:* intotem.buffnet.net/bechs/ ■ *E-mail:* bechs@buffnet.net	Buffalo	NY	14216	716-873-9644	873-8754
Buffalo & Erie County Naval & Military Park 1 Naval Park Cove	Buffalo	NY	14202	716-847-1773	847-6405
Buffalo Chamber Music Society Symphony Cir Kleinhans Music Hall	Buffalo	NY	14201	716-838-2383	838-2383
Buffalo Ensemble Theatre 95 N Johnson Pk *Web:* freenet.buffalo.edu/arts/pac/bet/	Buffalo	NY	14201	716-855-2225	
Buffalo Fire Historical Museum 1850 William St	Buffalo	NY	14206	716-892-8400	
Buffalo Inner-City Ballet Co 2495 Main St	Buffalo	NY	14214	716-833-1243	
Buffalo Museum of Science 1020 Humboldt Pkwy *Web:* freenet.buffalo.edu/~bms	Buffalo	NY	14211	716-896-5200	897-6723
Buffalo Philharmonic Orchestra 7170 Symphony Cir. *Web:* www.bpo.org	Buffalo	NY	14201	716-885-0331	885-9372
Buffalo State College Performing Arts Center 1300 Elmwood Ave Rockwell Hall Room 210 *Web:* www.buffalostate.edu/~rockwell/	Buffalo	NY	14222	716-878-3005	878-4234
Buffalo Zoological Gardens 300 Parkside Ave *Web:* www.buffalozoo.org	Buffalo	NY	14214	716-837-3900	837-0738
Burchfield-Penney Art Center 1300 Elmwood Ave Buffalo State College Rockwell Hall	Buffalo	NY	14222	716-878-6011	878-6003
Center for the Arts North Campus University at Buffalo	Buffalo	NY	14260	716-645-2787	645-6973
City Hall Observation Deck 65 Niagara Sq	Buffalo	NY	14202	716-851-5874	851-4791
Cofeld Benjamin & Dr Edgar R Judaic Museum of Temple Beth Zion 805 Delaware Ave	Buffalo	NY	14209	716-886-7150	886-7152
Connecticut Street Armory 184 Connecticut St *Web:* www.dmna.state.ny.us/map/buf-conn.html	Buffalo	NY	14213	716-887-2101	
Delaware Park Parkside Ave, Amherst, Nottingham & Lincoln Pkwy	Buffalo	NY	14214	716-851-5803	
Explore & More-A Children's Museum 430 Main St	East Aurora	NY	14052	716-655-5131	655-5131
Forest Lawn Cemetery & Garden Mausoleums 1411 Delaware Ave *Web:* www.forest-lawn.com ■ *E-mail:* FLC@forest-lawn.com	Buffalo	NY	14209	716-885-1600	881-6482
Hallwalls Contemporary Arts Center 2495 Main St *Web:* darius.pce.net/hallwall	Buffalo	NY	14214	716-835-7362	835-7364
Irish Classical Theatre 625 Main St *Web:* www.irishtheatre.com	Buffalo	NY	14203	716-852-2356	853-0592
Karpeles Manuscript Library 453 Porter Ave *Web:* www.rain.org/~karpeles	Buffalo	NY	14201	716-885-4139	885-4139
Kavinoky Theatre 320 Porter Ave *Web:* www.dyc.edu/Kavinoky	Buffalo	NY	14201	716-881-7668	881-7790
Kleinhans Music Hall Symphony Cir	Buffalo	NY	14201	716-883-3560	883-7430
Millard Fillmore House 24 Shearer Ave	East Aurora	NY	14052	716-652-8875	
Miss Buffalo Boat Trip 79 Marine Dr	Buffalo	NY	14202	716-856-6696	856-8901
New Phoenix Theatre 95 N Johnson Pk	Buffalo	NY	14201	716-855-2225	
Niagara Falls Prospect Park *Web:* www.niagara-info.com	Niagara Falls	NY	14303	716-278-1770	278-1744
Original American Kazoo Co 8703 S Main St *Web:* www.streethockey.com/brimms/kazoo_mus.html	Eden	NY	14057	716-992-3960	992-2728
Paul Robeson Theatre 350 Masten Ave	Buffalo	NY	14209	716-884-2013	885-2590
Pedaling History Bicycle Museum 3943 N Buffalo Rd *Web:* members.aol.com/bicyclemus/bike_museum/PedHist.htm ■ *E-mail:* bicyclemus@aol.com	Orchard Park	NY	14127	716-662-3853	662-4594
Pfeifer Theatre 681 Main St *Web:* www.arts.buffalo.edu	Buffalo	NY	14203	716-846-6461	
QRS Music Rolls Inc 1026 Niagara St *Web:* www.qrsmusic.com	Buffalo	NY	14213	716-885-4600	885-7510
Shea's Performing Arts Center 646 Main St *Web:* www.sheas.org ■ *E-mail:* sheas@buffnet.net	Buffalo	NY	14202	716-847-1410	847-1644
Steel Plant Museum 560 Ridge Rd Lackawanna Public Library	Lackawanna	NY	14218	716-823-0630	827-1997
Studio Arena Theatre 710 Main St *TF:* 800-777-8243 ■ *Web:* www.studioarena.org	Buffalo	NY	14202	716-856-5650	856-3415
Theatre of Youth (TOY) Co 203 Allen St	Buffalo	NY	14201	716-884-4400	887-9761
Theodore Roosevelt Inaugural National Historical Site 641 Delaware Ave Wilcox Mansion *Web:* www.nps.gov/thri/	Buffalo	NY	14202	716-884-0095	884-0330
Tifft Nature Preserve 1200 Fuhrmann Blvd	Buffalo	NY	14203	716-825-6397	823-1492
Ujima Theatre Co 545 Elmwood Ave	Buffalo	NY	14222	716-883-4232	882-4960

SPORTS TEAMS & FACILITIES

				Phone	Fax
Buffalo Bandits (lacrosse) 1 Seymour H Knox III Plaza Marine Midland Arena	Buffalo	NY	14203	716-855-4100	855-4110
Buffalo Bills 1 Bills Dr Ralph Wilson Stadium *Web:* www.buffalobills.com ■ *E-mail:* info@buffalobills.com	Orchard Park	NY	14127	716-649-0015	648-4099
Buffalo Bisons (baseball) 275 Washington St North Americare Pk	Buffalo	NY	14203	716-843-4373	852-6530
Buffalo Blizzard (soccer) 1 Seymour H Knox III Plaza Marine Midland Arena *Web:* www.buffaloblizzard.com	Buffalo	NY	14203	716-855-4100	855-4110
Buffalo Raceway 5600 McKinley Pkwy	Hamburg	NY	14075	716-649-1280	649-0033
Buffalo Sabres 1 Seymour H Knox III Plaza Marine Midland Arena **Fax:* PR ■ *Web:* www.sabres.com	Buffalo	NY	14203	716-855-4100	855-4110*
Buffalo Wings (roller hockey) 49 Illinois St *Web:* www.buffalowings.net ■ *E-mail:* wings@buffnet.net	Buffalo	NY	14203	716-856-0102	856-0214
Holland International Speedway 2 N Main St *Web:* www.hollandspeedway.com ■ *E-mail:* tbennett@hollandspeedway.com	Holland	NY	14080	716-537-2272	537-9749
Marine Midland Arena 1 Seymour Knox Plaza *Web:* www.marinemidlandarena.com	Buffalo	NY	14203	716-855-4100	855-4110

Buffalo (Cont'd)

— Events —

	Phone
Allentown Art Festival (mid-June)	716-881-4269
Antique World Expo (late May & late August)	716-759-8483
Art & Music Festival (late July)	716-924-5848
Blues Festival (late July)	716-855-8800
Buffalo Marathon (early May)	716-837-7223
Canal Fest of the Tonawandas (late July)	716-692-3292
Caribbean Festival (mid-August)	716-881-3266
Dingus Day (early April)	716-852-0511
Erie County Fair & Expo (mid-August)	716-649-3900
Festival of Lights (early November-January)	800-421-5223
First Night Buffalo (December 31)	716-852-0511
Friendship Festival (late June-early July)	716-852-0511
Friendship Tree Lighting (late November)	716-852-0511
Hawk Creek Wildlife Weekend (early August)	716-652-8646
Hellenic Festival (mid-May)	800-283-3256
Ice Castle Extravaganza/Winter Festival (mid-February)	716-357-4569
Italian Festival (mid-July)	716-874-6133
Italian Heritage & Food Festival (mid-July)	716-851-4144
Juneteenth (mid-June)	716-691-8106
Polish American Arts Festival (mid-August)	716-686-3930
Quaker Days (mid-July)	716-662-3366
Saint Patrick's Day Parade (mid-March)	716-825-9535
Shakespeare in Delaware Park (late June-August)	716-876-7430
Shocktober (late October)	716-852-0511
Taste of Buffalo (mid-July)	716-831-9376
Traditional German-American Festival (late August)	716-684-4745
Victorian Christmas Festival (early December)	607-587-9441
Waterfront Festival Summer Concert Series (July-August)	716-884-8865
World Pumpkin Weigh-off (early October)	716-759-2260

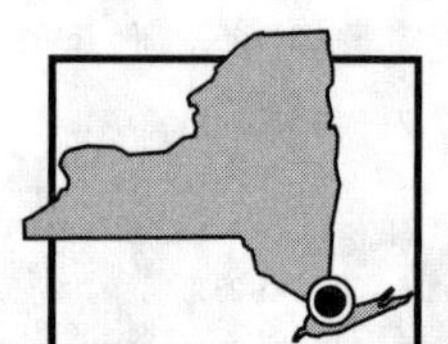

New York

From Wall Street to Coney Island, New York is considered one of the world's largest and most exciting cities. The "Big Apple" is made up of five boroughs - Manhattan, Queens, Brooklyn, Bronx, and Staten Island. Manhattan Island is considered "downtown" and is the site of most of the city's attractions and events. New York's famous skyline includes the twin towers of the World Trade Center and the Empire State Building, which offers an impressive view of the city from its observation deck. Among the city's most popular attractions are the Statue of Liberty, Central Park, and Broadway shows. Other visitor favorites include the New York Public Library, Macy's and Tiffany's, trendy Greenwich Village, SoHo, and Times Square.

Population	7,420,166	**Longitude**	73-59-39 W
Area (Land)	308.9 sq mi	**County**	New York
Area (Water)	159.0 sq mi	**Time Zone**	EST
Elevation	87 ft	**Area Code/s**	212, 718
Latitude	40-45-06 N		

— Average Temperatures and Precipitation —

TEMPERATURES

	Jan	Feb	Mar	Apr	May	Jun	Jul	Aug	Sep	Oct	Nov	Dec
High	37	39	48	59	70	79	84	82	75	64	53	42
Low	26	27	35	44	54	63	69	68	61	51	42	31

PRECIPITATION

	Jan	Feb	Mar	Apr	May	Jun	Jul	Aug	Sep	Oct	Nov	Dec
Inches	3.0	2.9	3.6	3.8	3.8	3.6	4.1	3.8	3.4	3.0	3.8	3.4

— Important Phone Numbers —

	Phone		Phone
AAA	212-586-1166	**Medical Referral**	212-420-4000
American Express Travel	212-687-3700	**New York City Information Hotline**	212-397-8222
Broadway Shows (Information)	212-563-2929	**Poison Control Center**	212-764-7667
Emergency	911	**Travelers Aid**	718-656-4870
HAI Cultural Events Hotline	888-424-4685	**Weather**	631-924-0517
HotelDocs	800-468-3537		

— Information Sources —

				Phone	Fax
Auditorium at Equitable Center 787 7th Ave	New York	NY	10019	212-314-4004	314-4001
Better Business Bureau Serving Metropolitan New York 257 Park Ave S 4th Fl *Web:* www.newyork.bbb.org	New York	NY	10010	212-533-6200	477-4912
Brooklyn Public Library Grand Army Plaza *Web:* www.brooklynpubliclibrary.org	Brooklyn	NY	11238	718-230-2100	783-1770
Fordham Library Center 2556 Bainbridge Ave	Bronx	NY	10458	718-579-4244	579-4264
Grand Prospect Hall 263 Prospect Ave *Web:* www.grandprospect.com	Brooklyn	NY	11215	718-788-0777	788-0404
Jacob K Javits Convention Center 655 W 34th St *Web:* www.javitscenter.com	New York	NY	10001	212-216-2000	216-2588
Manhattan Center Studios 311 W 34th St	New York	NY	10001	212-279-7740	465-2367
New York City Hall Broadway & Murray Sts. *Web:* www.ci.nyc.ny.us	New York	NY	10007	212-788-3000	406-3587
New York City Partnership & Chamber of Commerce 1 Battery Park Plaza *Web:* www.chamber.com ■ *E-mail:* info@chamber.com	New York	NY	10004	212-493-7500	344-3344
New York Convention & Visitors Bureau 810 7th Ave 3rd Fl *TF:* 800-692-8474 ■ *Web:* www.nycvisit.com	New York	NY	10019	212-484-1200	484-1222
New York County 60 Centre St	New York	NY	10007	212-374-8359	
New York Mayor Broadway & Murray Sts City Hall *Web:* www.ci.nyc.ny.us/html/om	New York	NY	10007	212-788-3000	406-3587
New York Public Library 476 5th Ave *Web:* www.nypl.org	New York	NY	10018	212-930-0800	930-0572
Queens Borough Public Library 89-11 Merrick Blvd **Fax:* Hum Res ■ *Web:* www.queens.lib.ny.us	Jamaica	NY	11432	718-990-0700	658-2919*
Saint George Library Center 5 Central Ave	Staten Island	NY	10301	718-442-8560	816-1874

On-Line Resources

4NY.com	www.4ny.com
@New York Newsletter	www.news-ny.com
About.com Guide to New York	nycdowntown.about.com/local/midlanticus/nycdowntown
Access America New York City	www.accessamer.com/newyorkcity/
All New York City Super Resource Guide	www.allny.com/
Alliance for Downtown New York	www.downtownny.com
Anthill City Guide Midtown Manhattan	www.anthill.com/city.asp?city=midtown
Area Guide New York	newyork.areaguides.net
Boulevards New York	www.boulevards.com/cities/newyork.html
Bradmans.com New York	www.bradmans.com/scripts/display_city.cgi?city=240
City Insights New York	www.cityinsights.com/newyork.htm
City Knowledge New York	www.cityknowledge.com/ny_newyork.htm
Cityguide NYC	www.cityguideny.com/
Cityhits New York	www.cityhits.com/newyork/
CitySearch NYC	newyork.citysearch.com
CityTravelGuide.com New York	www.citytravelguide.com/new-york.htm
CuisineNet New York	www.cuisinenet.com/restaurant/new_york/index.shtml
DigitalCity New York	home.digitalcity.com/newyork
Excite.com New York City Guide	www.excite.com/travel/countries/united_states/new_york/new_york
Gayot's Guide Restaurant Search New York	www.perrier.com/restaurants/gayot.asp?area=NYC
GoldenNYC.com	www.goldennyc.com/
Guide to New York's Nightlife	models.com/night
HotelGuide New York	newyork.hotelguide.net
Long Island Home Page	www.webscope.com/li/info.html
Most New York	www.mostnewyork.com
New York City CityWomen	www.citywomen.com/nycwomen.htm
New York City Guide	www.nycguide.net/
New York City Reference	www.panix.com/clay/nyc
New York Graphic City Guide	www.futurecast.com/gcg/newyork.htm
New York Now	nynow.com/
New York Rock Magazine	www.nyrock.com/
New York Subway Finder	www.krusch.com/nysf.html
NewYork.TheLinks.com	newyork.thelinks.com/
NYC Culture Guide & Calendar	www.allianceforarts.org

New York — On-Line Resources (Cont'd)

NYCTourist.com	www.nyctourist.com
Open World City Guides New York City	www.worldexecutive.com/cityguides/new_york/
PaperMag	www.papermag.com/
Rough Guide Travel New York City	travel.roughguides.com/content/4/
Savvy Diner Guide to New York Restaurants	www.savvydiner.com/newyork/
Time Out New York	www.timeout.com/newyork/
Village Alliance	www.villagealliance.org/
Virtual Voyages New York City	www.virtualvoyages.com/usa/ny/nyc/nyc.sht
WeekendEvents.com New York	www.weekendevents.com/NEWYORK/newyork.html
Yahoo! New York	ny.yahoo.com

— Transportation Services —

AIRPORTS

■ John F Kennedy International Airport (JFK)

	Phone
15 miles SE of downtown (approx 60 minutes)	718-244-4444

Web: www.panynj.gov/aviation/jfkframe.HTM

Airport Transportation

	Phone
Carey Airport Express $13 fare to downtown	718-706-9658
Grey Line Air Shuttle $19 fare to downtown	212-315-3006
Taxi $35 fare to downtown	212-666-6666

Commercial Airlines

	Phone		Phone
Aer Lingus	800-474-7424	**Japan**	212-838-4400
Aeroflot	888-686-4949	**KLM**	800-374-7747
Aerolineas Argentinas	212-698-2050	**Korean Air**	800-438-5000
AeroMexico	212-754-2140	**Kuwait Airways**	212-308-5454
Air Afrique	212-586-5908	**LanChile**	718-995-6962
Air Canada	800-776-3000	**LOT Polish Airlines**	800-223-0593
Air China	800-986-1985	**LTU International**	800-888-0200
Air India	212-751-6200	**Lufthansa**	800-645-3880
Air Jamaica	800-523-5585	**Mexicana**	800-531-7923
Air New Zealand	800-262-1234	**Midway**	800-446-4392
Alitalia	800-223-5730	**National**	888-757-5387
All Nippon Airways	800-235-9262	**Northwest**	800-225-2525
ALM-Antillean	800-327-7230	**Olympic Airways**	800-223-1226
America West	800-235-9292	**Pakistan International**	800-221-2552
American	800-433-7300	**Pan Am**	800-359-7262
American Eagle	800-433-7300	**Royal Air Maroc**	212-750-5115
Austrian Airlines	800-843-0002	**Royal Jordanian**	212-949-0050
Avianca	212-399-0800	**Sabena**	516-562-9200
British Airways	800-247-9297	**Saudi Arabian**	800-472-8342
BWIA International	800-538-2942	**Scandinavian**	800-221-2350
Cayman Airways	800-422-9626	**Singapore**	800-742-3333
China Airlines	800-227-5118	**SwissAir**	800-221-4750
Continental	212-319-9494	**TAP Air Portugal**	800-221-7370
Continental Express	800-525-0280	**Tower Air**	800-348-6937
Delta	800-221-1212	**TransBrasil**	800-872-3153
El Al	212-768-9200	**TWA**	800-221-2000
Finnair	718-656-7570	**United**	800-241-6522
First Air	800-945-2990	**US Airways**	800-428-4322
Iberia	800-772-4642	**US Airways Express**	800-428-4322
Icelandair	800-223-5500	**Varig Brazilian**	212-682-3100

Charter Airlines

	Phone		Phone
Atlantic Aviation Charter	201-288-7660	**Northeast Airway**	973-267-2450
Jet Aviation Business Jets Inc	800-736-8538		

■ LaGuardia Airport (LGA)

	Phone
8 miles NE of downtown (approx 45 minutes)	718-476-5000

Airport Transportation

	Phone
Carey Airport Express $10 fare to downtown	718-706-9658
Gray Line Air Shuttle $14 fare to downtown	973-961-5753
Taxi $25 fare to downtown	212-666-6666

Commercial Airlines

	Phone		Phone
AccessAir	877-462-2237	**Midwest Express**	800-452-2022
Air Canada	800-776-3000	**Northwest**	800-225-2525
American	800-433-7300	**Spirit**	800-772-7117
American Eagle	800-433-7300	**TWA**	800-221-2000
Atlantic Coast Airlines	800-241-6522	**United**	800-241-6522
Continental	718-565-1100	**US Airways**	800-428-4322
Delta	800-221-1212	**US Airways Express**	800-428-4322
Midway	800-446-4392		

Charter Airlines

	Phone		Phone
Atlantic Aviation Charter	201-288-7660	**Northeast Airway**	973-267-2450
Jet Aviation Business Jets Inc	800-736-8538		

■ Newark International Airport (EWR)

	Phone
16 miles SW of downtown New York (approx 45 minutes)	973-961-6000

Web: www.panynj.gov/newarkairport/

Airport Transportation

	Phone
Olympia Trails Airport Express $10 fare to Grand Central or Penn Stns	212-964-6233
Taxi $34-38 fare to downtown New York	973-961-6377

Commercial Airlines

	Phone		Phone
Air Canada	800-776-3000	**Martinair Holland**	800-627-8462
Alitalia	800-223-5730	**Midwest Express**	800-452-2022
America West	800-235-9292	**Northwest**	800-225-2525
American	800-433-7300	**Pan Am**	800-359-7262
American Trans Air	800-225-2995	**TWA**	800-221-2000
British Airways	800-247-9297	**United**	800-241-6522
Continental	800-525-0280	**United Express**	800-241-6522
Continental Express	800-525-0280	**US Airways**	800-428-4322
LOT Polish Airlines	800-223-0593	**US Airways Express**	800-428-4322
Lufthansa	800-645-3880	**Virgin Atlantic**	800-862-8621

Charter Airlines

	Phone		Phone
Atlantic Aviation Charter	201-288-7660	**Northeast Airway**	973-267-2450
Jet Aviation Business Jets Inc	800-736-8538		

CAR RENTALS

	Phone		Phone
Avis-La Guardia	718-507-3600	**Hertz-JFK**	718-656-7600
Budget-JFK	718-656-6013	**Hertz-La Guardia**	718-478-5300
Budget-La Guardia	718-639-6400	**Thrifty**	718-721-8500
Dollar-JFK	718-656-2400		

LIMO/TAXI

	Phone		Phone
Absolute Limousine	212-227-6588	**Carmel Taxi**	212-666-6666
Allstate Car & Limousine Svc	212-333-3333	**Crown Limousine**	212-246-2626
American Classic Limousine	212-979-0500	**Elite Limousine**	718-472-2300
American Dream Car & Limo Service	212-426-1010	**Five Star Limousine**	718-821-2600
Bermuda Limousines International	212-249-8400	**Green Taxi**	973-643-4100
Carey Limousine	212-599-1122	**Love Taxi**	718-633-3333
Carmel Car & Limousine	212-666-6666	**Sabra Limousine**	212-777-7171
		Smith Limousine	212-247-0711

MASS TRANSIT

	Phone
New York City Transit Authority Bus/Subway $1.50 Base fare	718-330-1234

RAIL/BUS

				Phone
Amtrak Station 7th Ave & 31st St	New York	NY	10001	800-872-7245
Grand Central Station 89 E 42nd St	New York	NY	10017	212-340-3000
Port Authority Bus Terminal 625 8th Ave	New York	NY	10018	212-564-8484

New York (Cont'd)

— Accommodations —

HOTEL RESERVATION SERVICES

Name	Phone	Fax
Accommodations Express	609-391-2100	525-0111
TF: 800-444-7666 ■ *Web:* www.accommodationsxpress.com ■ *E-mail:* accomexp@acy.digex.net		
Accommodations Plus	718-995-4444	995-6824
TF: 800-733-7666 ■ *Web:* www.accommodationsplus.com		
Central Reservation Service	407-740-6442	740-8222
TF: 800-548-3311 ■ *Web:* www.reservation-services.com ■ *E-mail:* cenresbos@aol.com		
Express Hotel Reservations	303-440-8481	440-0166
TF: 800-356-1123 ■ *Web:* www.express-res.com ■ *E-mail:* info@express-res.com		
Hotel Reservations Network Inc	214-361-7311	361-7299
TF Sales: 800-964-6835 ■ *Web:* www.hoteldiscount.com		
New World Bed & Breakfast	212-675-5600	675-6366
TF: 800-443-3800		
New York By Phone Reservation Service	212-979-9779	
TF: 888-692-2775 ■ *Web:* www.nyctollfree.com		
Quikbook	212-532-1660	532-1556
TF: 800-789-9887 ■ *Web:* www.quikbook.com		
RMC Travel Centre	212-754-6560	754-6571
TF: 800-782-2674		
Room Exchange	212-760-1000	760-1013
TF: 800-846-7000 ■ *Web:* www.hotelrooms.com		
Room Finders USA	504-522-9373	529-1948
TF: 800-473-7829 ■ *Web:* www.roomsusa.com ■ *E-mail:* welcome@roomsusa.com		

HOTELS, MOTELS, RESORTS

Name / Address	City	State	ZIP	Phone	Fax
Algonquin Hotel 59 W 44th St	New York	NY	10036	212-840-6800	944-1419
TF: 800-555-8000					
Amsterdam Court Hotel 226 W 50th St	New York	NY	10019	212-459-1000	265-5070
TF: 800-341-9889					
Barbizon Hotel 140 E 63rd St	New York	NY	10021	212-838-5700	888-4271
TF: 800-223-1020					
Beacon Hotel 2130 Broadway	New York	NY	10023	212-787-1100	724-0839
TF: 800-572-1969 ■ *Web:* www.beaconhotel.com					
Beekman Tower Suite Hotel 3 Mitchell Pl	New York	NY	10017	212-355-7300	753-9366
TF: 800-637-8483					
Best Western Manhattan 17 W 32nd St	New York	NY	10001	212-736-1600	563-4007
TF: 800-567-7720					
Best Western President 234 W 48th St	New York	NY	10036	212-246-8800	265-6227
TF: 800-826-4667					
Best Western Seaport Inn 33 Peck Slip	New York	NY	10023	212-766-6600	766-6615
TF: 800-528-1234					
Broadway Inn 264 W 46th St	New York	NY	10036	212-997-9200	768-2807
TF: 800-826-6300 ■ *Web:* www.broadwayinn.com					
Carlton Arms 160 E 25th St	New York	NY	10010	212-679-0680	
Carlton Hotel on Madison Avenue 22 E 29th St	New York	NY	10016	212-532-4100	889-8683
TF: 800-542-1502					
Carlyle The 35 E 76th St	New York	NY	10021	212-744-1600	717-4682
TF: 800-227-5737					
Cosmopolitan Hotel 95 W Broadway	New York	NY	10007	212-566-1900	566-6909
TF: 888-895-9400 ■ *Web:* www.cosmohotel.com					
Court & The Tuscany 120 E 39th St	New York	NY	10016	212-686-1600	779-7822
TF: 877-946-8357					
Crowne Plaza Manhattan 1605 Broadway	New York	NY	10019	212-977-4000	977-5517*
**Fax:* Sales ■ *TF:* 800-243-6969					
Crowne Plaza United Nations 304 E 42nd St	New York	NY	10017	212-986-8800	986-1758
TF: 800-879-8836					
Days Hotel Midtown 790 8th Ave	New York	NY	10019	212-581-7000	974-0291
TF: 800-572-6232					
Delmonico's Hotel 502 Park Ave	New York	NY	10022	212-355-2500	755-3779
TF: 800-821-3842					
Doral Park Ave Hotel 70 Park Ave	New York	NY	10016	212-687-7050	973-2497
TF: 800-847-4135					
Doubletree Guest Suites 1568 Broadway	New York	NY	10036	212-719-1600	921-5212
TF: 800-325-9033 ■ *Web:* www.doubletreehotels.com/DoubleT/Hotel61/69/69Main.htm					
Dumont Plaza Suite Hotel 150 E 34th St	New York	NY	10016	212-481-7600	889-8856
TF: 800-637-8483					
Four Points Hotel by Sheraton 151-20 Baisley Blvd	Jamaica	NY	11434	718-489-1000	276-8212
TF: 800-325-3535					
Four Seasons Hotel 57 E 57th St	New York	NY	10022	212-758-5700	758-5711
TF: 800-332-3442 ■ *Web:* www.fourseasons.com/locations/NewYork					
Fulton Plaza 106 Fulton St	New York	NY	10038	212-835-8600	748-7913
TF: 888-402-2400					
Gershwin The 7 E 27th St	New York	NY	10016	212-545-8000	684-5546
Web: www.gershwinhotel.com ■ *E-mail:* reservations@gershwinhotel.com					
Gramercy Park Hotel 2 Lexington Ave	New York	NY	10010	212-475-4320	505-0535
TF: 800-221-4083					
Grand Hyatt New York Park Ave at Grand Central	New York	NY	10017	212-883-1234	697-3772
TF: 800-233-1234					
Helmsley Park Lane Hotel 36 Central Pk S	New York	NY	10019	212-371-4000	521-6666
TF: 800-221-4982					
Holiday Inn JFK Airport 144-02 135th Ave	Jamaica	NY	11436	718-659-0200	322-2533
TF: 800-465-4329					
Holiday Inn Manhattan-Downtown/SoHo 138 Lafayette St	New York	NY	10013	212-966-8898	966-3933
TF: 800-465-4329 ■ *Web:* www.basshotels.com/holiday-inn/?_franchisee=NYCDT ■ *E-mail:* holinnsoho@aol.com					
Holiday Inn Midtown 440 W 57th St	New York	NY	10019	212-581-8100	581-7739
TF: 800-231-0405					
Hotel Inter-Continental New York 111 E 48th St	New York	NY	10017	212-755-5900	644-0079
TF: 800-327-0200					
Hotel Nikko-Essex House 160 Central Pk S	New York	NY	10019	212-247-0300	315-1839
TF: 800-645-5687 ■ *Web:* www.essexhouse.com ■ *E-mail:* essex@interport.net					
Hotel Pennsylvania 401 7th Ave	New York	NY	10001	212-736-5000	502-8799
TF: 800-223-8585					
Hotel Plaza Athenee 37 E 64th St	New York	NY	10021	212-734-9100	772-0958
TF: 800-447-8800					
Howard Johnson Plaza Hotel 851 8th Ave	New York	NY	10019	212-581-4100	974-7502
TF: 800-654-2000					
Intercontinental Central Park 112 Central Pk S	New York	NY	10019	212-757-1900	757-9620
TF: 800-327-0200					
JFK Airport Hilton 138-10 135th Ave	Jamaica	NY	11436	718-322-8700	529-0749
TF: 800-445-8667					
Kimberly Suite Hotel 145 E 50th St	New York	NY	10022	212-755-0400	486-6915
TF: 800-683-0400					
Lexington Hotel 511 Lexington Ave	New York	NY	10017	212-755-4400	751-4091
TF: 800-448-4471					
Loews New York Hotel 569 Lexington Ave	New York	NY	10022	212-752-7000	758-6311
TF: 800-836-6471 ■ *Web:* www.loewshotels.com/newyorkhome.html					
Lowell The 28 E 63rd St	New York	NY	10021	212-838-1400	838-9194
TF: 800-221-4444					
Malibu The 2688 Broadway	New York	NY	10025	212-663-0275	678-6842
TF: 800-647-2227 ■ *Web:* www.malibuhotelnyc.com ■ *E-mail:* rooms@malibuhotelnyc.com					
Mark Hotel 25 E 77th St	New York	NY	10021	212-744-4300	744-2749
TF: 800-843-6275					
Marriott East Side 525 Lexington Ave	New York	NY	10017	212-755-4000	751-3440
TF: 800-228-9290 ■ *Web:* marriotthotels.com/NYCEA					
Marriott Financial Center Hotel 85 West St	New York	NY	10006	212-266-6145	385-9174
TF: 800-242-8685 ■ *Web:* marriotthotels.com/NYCWS					
Marriott La Guardia 102-05 Ditmars Blvd	East Elmhurst	NY	11369	718-565-8900	898-4955
TF: 800-228-9290 ■ *Web:* marriotthotels.com/LGAAP					
Marriott World Trade Center Hotel 3 World Trade Ctr	New York	NY	10048	212-938-9100	444-3444
TF: 800-228-9290 ■ *Web:* marriotthotels.com/NYCWT					
Mayflower Hotel on the Park 15 Central Park W	New York	NY	10023	212-265-0060	265-5098
TF: 800-223-4164					
Michelangelo The 152 W 51st St	New York	NY	10019	212-765-1900	541-6604
TF: 800-237-0990					
Millenium Broadway 145 W 44th St	New York	NY	10036	212-768-4400	768-0847
TF: 800-622-5569 ■ *Web:* www.millbdwy.com ■ *E-mail:* mb.sales@mill-cop.com					
Millenium Hilton 55 Church St	New York	NY	10007	212-693-2001	571-2316
TF: 800-752-0014 ■ *Web:* www.hilton.com/hotels/NYCMLHH					
Morgans Hotel 237 Madison Ave	New York	NY	10016	212-686-0300	779-8352
TF: 800-334-3408					
New York Helmsley Hotel 212 E 42nd St	New York	NY	10017	212-490-8900	986-4792
TF: 800-221-4982					
New York Hilton & Towers 1335 Ave of the Americas	New York	NY	10019	212-586-7000	315-1374
TF: 800-445-8667 ■ *Web:* www.hilton.com					
New York Marriott Brooklyn 333 Adams St	Brooklyn	NY	11201	718-246-7000	246-0563
TF: 800-228-9290					
New York Marriott Marquis 1535 Broadway	New York	NY	10036	212-398-1900	704-8930
TF: 800-843-4898					
New York Palace Hotel 455 Madison Ave	New York	NY	10022	212-888-7000	303-6000
TF: 800-697-2522					

New York — Hotels, Motels, Resorts (Cont'd)

Name / Address	City	State	Zip	Phone	Fax
New York Swissotel 440 Park Ave	New York	NY	10022	212-421-0900	371-4190
TF: 800-372-5369					
New Yorker Hotel 481 8th Ave	New York	NY	10001	212-971-0101	563-6136
TF: 800-764-4680					
Novotel New York 226 W 52nd St	New York	NY	10019	212-315-0100	765-5369
TF: 800-221-3185					
Omni Berkshire Place 21 E 52nd St	New York	NY	10022	212-753-5800	754-5018
TF: 800-843-6664					
Paramount Hotel 235 W 46th St	New York	NY	10036	212-764-5500	354-5237
TF: 800-225-7474					
Park Savoy 158 58th St	New York	NY	10019	212-245-5755	765-0668
Parker Meridien Hotel 119 W 56th St	New York	NY	10019	212-245-5000	307-1776
TF: 800-543-4300 ■ *Web:* www.parkermeridien.com					
Peninsula New York 700 5th Ave	New York	NY	10019	212-247-2200	903-3943
TF: 800-262-9467					
■ *Web:* www.peninsula.com/hotels/newyork/newyork.html					
■ *E-mail:* pny@peninsula.com					
Pickwick Arms Hotel 230 E 51st St	New York	NY	10022	212-355-0300	755-5029
TF: 800-742-5945					
Pierre The 2 E 61st St	New York	NY	10021	212-838-8000	940-8109
TF: 800-332-3442					
Plaza Hotel 5th Ave & Central Park S	New York	NY	10019	212-759-3000	759-3167
TF: 800-759-3000 ■ *Web:* www.fairmont.com/newyork.html					
■ *E-mail:* newyork@fairmont.com					
Radisson Hotel JFK Airport 135-30 140th St	Jamaica	NY	11434	718-322-2300	322-6894
TF: 800-333-3333					
Ramada Milford Plaza 270 W 45th St	New York	NY	10036	212-869-3600	944-8357
TF: 800-221-2690					
Ramada Plaza Hotel Van Wyck Expy JFK International Airport Bldg 144	Jamaica	NY	11430	718-995-9000	995-9075
TF: 800-272-6232					
Regal United Nations Plaza Park 1 United Nations Plaza	New York	NY	10017	212-758-1234	702-5051
TF: 800-222-8888					
Regency Hotel 540 Park Ave	New York	NY	10021	212-759-4100	826-5674
TF: 800-233-2356 ■ *Web:* www.loewshotels.com/regencyhome.html					
■ *E-mail:* regency@loewshotels.com					
Rihga Royal Hotel 151 W 54th St	New York	NY	10019	212-307-5000	765-6530
TF: 800-937-5454 ■ *Web:* www.rihga.com					
Ritz Tower 465 Park Ave	New York	NY	10022	212-755-5000	223-6379
Roosevelt Hotel 45 E 45th St	New York	NY	10017	212-661-9600	885-6168
TF: 800-223-0888					
Saint Moritz on the Park 50 Central Pk S	New York	NY	10019	212-752-7760	688-6619
TF: 800-221-4774					
Saint Regis The 2 E 55th St	New York	NY	10022	212-753-4500	787-3447
TF: 800-325-3535					
■ *Web:* www.luxurycollection.com/cgi/t3.cgi/property.taf					
Sheraton Manhattan Hotel 790 7th Ave	New York	NY	10019	212-581-3300	541-9219
TF: 800-325-3535					
Sheraton New York Hotel & Towers 811 7th Ave	New York	NY	10019	212-581-1000	262-4410
TF: 800-223-6550					
Sheraton Russell Hotel 45 Park Ave	New York	NY	10016	212-685-7676	889-3193
TF: 800-223-6550					
Sherry-Netherland Hotel 781 5th Ave	New York	NY	10022	212-355-2800	319-4306
TF: 800-247-4377 ■ *Web:* www.sherrynetherland.com					
Shoreham Hotel 33 W 55th St	New York	NY	10019	212-247-6700	765-9741
TF: 800-533-3347					
SoHo Grand Hotel 310 W Broadway	New York	NY	10013	212-965-3000	965-3200
TF: 800-965-3000					
Southgate Tower Suite Hotel 371 7th Ave	New York	NY	10001	212-563-1800	643-8028
TF: 800-637-8483					
Stanhope The 995 5th Ave	New York	NY	10028	212-288-5800	517-0088
TF: 800-828-1123					
W New York 541 Lexington Ave	New York	NY	10022	212-755-1200	319-8344
TF: 877-946-8357					
Waldorf-Astoria Hotel 301 Park Ave	New York	NY	10022	212-355-3000	872-7272
TF: 800-925-3673 ■ *Web:* www.hilton.com/hotels/NYCWAHH					
Waldorf Towers 100 E 50th St	New York	NY	10022	212-355-3100	872-4799
TF: 800-445-8667					
Warwick Hotel 65 W 54th St	New York	NY	10019	212-247-2700	489-3926*
**Fax:* Sales ■ *TF:* 800-223-4099					
Washington Square Hotel 103 Waverly Pl	New York	NY	10011	212-777-9515	979-8373
TF: 800-222-0418 ■ *Web:* www.wshotel.com					

— Restaurants —

Name / Address	City	State	Zip	Phone
21 Club (American) 21 W 52nd St	New York	NY	10019	212-582-7200
Web: www.21club.com				
Acme Bar & Grill (Southern) 9 Great Jones St	New York	NY	10012	212-420-1934
Alison on Dominick (French) 38 Dominick St	New York	NY	10013	212-727-1188
American Place (American) 565 Lexington St	New York	NY	10016	212-888-5650
Aquagrill (New American) 210 Spring St	New York	NY	10012	212-274-0505
Artusi (Italian) 36 W 52nd St	New York	NY	10019	212-582-6900
Asia de Cuba (Asian/Cuban) 237 Madison Ave	New York	NY	10036	212-726-7755
Aureole (New American) 34 E 61st St	New York	NY	10021	212-319-1660
Web: www.kerrymenu.com/Aureole.htm				
Azure (Mediterranean) 484 Amsterdam Ave	New York	NY	10024	212-721-1000
Balthazar (French) 80 Spring St	New York	NY	10012	212-965-1414
Bambou (Caribbean) 243 E 14th St	New York	NY	10003	212-358-0012
Barbetta (Italian) 321 W 46th St	New York	NY	10036	212-246-9171
Bayamo (Chinese/Latin American) 704 Broadway	New York	NY	10003	212-475-5151
Ben Benson's Steakhouse (Steak) 123 W 52nd St	New York	NY	10019	212-581-8888
Bice (Italian) 7 E 54th St	New York	NY	10022	212-688-1999
Bistro Latino (South American) 1711 Broadway	New York	NY	10019	212-956-1000
Blue Ribbon (New American) 97 Sullivan St	New York	NY	10012	212-274-0404
Boathouse The (American) Park Dr N & 72nd St Central Pk	New York	NY	10028	212-517-2233
Bolo (Spanish) 23 E 22nd St	New York	NY	10010	212-228-2200
Bouley (French) 120 W Broadway	New York	NY	10013	212-608-3852
Brasilia Restaurant (Brazilian) 7 W 45th St	New York	NY	10036	212-869-9200
Bridge Cafe (American) 279 Water St	New York	NY	10038	212-227-3344
Bull & Bear (Steak/Seafood) 301 Park Ave	New York	NY	10022	212-872-4900
Cafe Asean (Pan-Asian) 117 W 10th St	New York	NY	10011	212-633-0348
Cafe Boulud (Continental) 20 E 76th St	New York	NY	10021	212-772-2600
Cafe Con Leche (Cuban) 424 Amsterdam Ave	New York	NY	10024	212-595-7000
Cafe de Bruxelles (French/Belgian) 118 Greenwich Ave	New York	NY	10011	212-206-1830
Cafe des Artistes (French) 1 W 67th St	New York	NY	10023	212-877-3500
Cafe Luxembourg (French) 200 W 70th St	New York	NY	10023	212-873-7411
Cafe Pierre (French) 2 E 61st St	New York	NY	10021	212-940-8185
Campagna (Italian) 24 E 21st St	New York	NY	10010	212-460-0900
Canton (Cantonese) 45 Division St	New York	NY	10002	212-226-4441
Caribe Restaurant (Caribbean) 117 Perry St	New York	NY	10014	212-255-9191
Caroline's on Broadway (American) 1626 Broadway	New York	NY	10019	212-956-0101
Chanterelle (French) 2 Harrison St	New York	NY	10013	212-966-6960
Chez Napoleon (French) 365 W 50th St	New York	NY	10019	212-265-6980
Circa (Mediterranean) 103 2nd Ave	New York	NY	10003	212-777-4120
City Crab & Seafood Co (Seafood) 235 Park Ave S	New York	NY	10003	212-529-3800
Clementine (New American) 1 5th Ave	New York	NY	10003	212-253-0003
Cowgirl Hall of Fame (Tex Mex) 519 Hudson St	New York	NY	10014	212-633-1133
Da Rosina (Italian) 342 W 46th St	New York	NY	10036	212-977-7373
da Umberto (Italian) 107 W 17th St	New York	NY	10011	212-989-0303
Dawat (Indian) 210 E 58th St	New York	NY	10022	212-355-7555
Web: www.kerrymenu.com/Dawat.htm				
Deniz a la Turka (Turkish) 400 E 57th St	New York	NY	10022	212-486-2255
Dish of Salt (Chinese) 133 W 47th St	New York	NY	10036	212-921-4242
Domingo (Spanish) 209 E 49th St	New York	NY	10017	212-826-8269
El Faro (Spanish) 823 Greenwich St	New York	NY	10014	212-929-8210
El Quijote Restaurant (Spanish) 226 W 23rd St	New York	NY	10011	212-929-1855
Emily's (Southern) 1325 5 Ave	New York	NY	10029	212-996-1212
Eros (Greek) 1076 1st Ave	New York	NY	10022	212-223-2322
Felidia (Italian) 243 E 58th St	New York	NY	10022	212-758-1479
Firebird (Russian) 365 W 46th St	New York	NY	10036	212-586-0244
Four Seasons (Continental) 99 E 52nd St	New York	NY	10022	212-754-9494
Gallagher's Steak House (American) 228 W 52nd St	New York	NY	10019	212-245-5336
Golden Unicorn (Chinese) 18 E Broadway	New York	NY	10002	212-941-0911
Gotham Bar & Grill (American) 12 E 12th St	New York	NY	10003	212-620-4020
Gramercy Tavern (American) 42 E 20th St	New York	NY	10003	212-477-0777
Great Jones Cafe (Cajun) 54 Great Jones St	New York	NY	10012	212-674-9304
Greatest Bar on Earth (Continental) 1 World Trade Ctr	New York	NY	10048	212-524-7000
Hangawi (Korean) 12 E 32nd St	New York	NY	10016	212-213-0077
Hard Rock Cafe (American) 221 W 57th St	New York	NY	10019	212-489-6565
Hatsuhana (Japanese) 17 E 48th St	New York	NY	10017	212-355-3345
Haveli (Indian) 100 2nd Ave	New York	NY	10003	212-982-0533
Heartland Brewery (American) 35 Union Sq W	New York	NY	10003	212-645-3400
Web: www.heartlandbrewery.com				
Il Nido (Italian) 251 E 53rd St	New York	NY	10022	212-753-8450
Il Vagabondo (Italian) 351 E 62nd St	New York	NY	10021	212-832-9221
Indochine (Vietnamese/French) 430 Lafayette St	New York	NY	10003	212-505-5111
Iso (Japanese) 175 2nd Ave	New York	NY	10003	212-777-0361
Jean Georges (French) 1 Central Park W	New York	NY	10023	212-299-3900
Joe Allen (American) 326 W 46th St	New York	NY	10036	212-581-6464
Joe's Shanghai (Steak/Seafood) 9 Pell St	New York	NY	10013	212-233-8888
Josephina (American) 1900 Broadway	New York	NY	10023	212-799-1000
Julian's (Italian) 802 9th Ave	New York	NY	10019	212-262-4800
Kin Khao (Thai) 171 Spring St	New York	NY	10012	212-966-3939
La Bella Epoque (French) 827 Broadway	New York	NY	10023	212-254-6436
La Caravelle (French) 33 W 55th St	New York	NY	10019	212-586-4252
La Cote Basque (French) 60 W 55th St	New York	NY	10019	212-688-6525
La Grenouille (French) 3 E 52nd St	New York	NY	10022	212-752-1495
Lanza's (Italian) 168 1st Ave	New York	NY	10009	212-674-7014
Le Bernardin (French) 155 W 51st St	New York	NY	10019	212-489-1515
Le Cirque 2000 (French) 455 Madison Ave	New York	NY	10022	212-303-7788
Le Perigord (French) 405 E 52nd St	New York	NY	10022	212-755-6244
Les Celebrites (French) 155 W 58th St	New York	NY	10019	212-484-5113
Lespinasse (French) 2 E 55th St	New York	NY	10022	212-339-6719
Life Cafe (Vegetarian) 343 E 10th St	New York	NY	10009	212-477-8791

New York — Restaurants (Cont'd)

Name / Address	City	State	Zip	Phone
Little Bangkok Restaurant (Thai) 261 W 54th St	New York	NY	10019	212-333-7229
Little Dove (Continental) 200 E 60th St 2nd Fl	New York	NY	10022	212-861-8080
Lobster Club (Continental) 24 E 80th St	New York	NY	10021	212-249-6500
Lutece (French) 249 E 50th St	New York	NY	10022	212-752-2225
Maloney & Porcelli (American) 37 E 50th St	New York	NY	10022	212-750-2233
Manhattan Cafe (Steak/Seafood) 1161 1st Ave	New York	NY	10021	212-888-6556
Manhattan Ocean Club (Seafood) 57 W 58th St	New York	NY	10019	212-371-7777
Martini's Restaurant & Bar (Italian/Mediterranean) 810 7th Ave	New York	NY	10019	212-767-1717
Maxim's (French) 680 Madison Ave	New York	NY	10021	212-751-5111
Mirezi (Pan-Asian) 59 5th Ave	New York	NY	10003	212-242-9710
Mottsu (Japanese) 285 Mott St	New York	NY	10012	212-343-8017
Mueng Thai (Thai) 23 Pell St	New York	NY	10013	212-406-4259
Negril (Caribbean) 362 W 23rd St	New York	NY	10011	212-807-6411
Nippon (Japanese) 155 E 52nd St	New York	NY	10022	212-355-9020
Odeon (French) 145 W Broadway	New York	NY	10013	212-233-0507
Old Homestead (Steak) 56 9th Ave	New York	NY	10011	212-242-9040
Orso (Italian) 322 W 46th St	New York	NY	10036	212-489-7212
Pad Thai (Thai) 114 8th Ave	New York	NY	10011	212-691-6226
Palio (Italian) 151 W 51st St	New York	NY	10019	212-245-4850
Palm Restaurant (Steak) 837 2nd Ave	New York	NY	10017	212-687-2953
Parioli Romanissimo (Italian) 24 E 81st St	New York	NY	10028	212-288-2391
Park Avenue Cafe (New American) 100 E 63rd St	New York	NY	10021	212-644-1900
Patria (South American) 250 Park Ave S	New York	NY	10003	212-777-6211
Peacock Alley (French) 301 Park Ave	New York	NY	10022	212-872-4895
Periyali (Greek) 35 W 20th St	New York	NY	10011	212-463-7890
Peter Luger Steak House (Steak) 178 Broadway	Brooklyn	NY	11211	718-387-7400
Picholine (French) 35 W 64th St	New York	NY	10023	212-724-8585
Planet Hollywood (American) 140 W 57th St	New York	NY	10019	212-333-7827
Quatorze Bis (French) 323 E 79 St	New York	NY	10021	212-535-1414
Restaurant Daniel (French) 20 E 76th St	New York	NY	10021	212-288-0033
Restaurant Dano (New American) 254 5th Ave	New York	NY	10001	212-725-2922
Ristorante Il Postino (Italian) 337 E 49th St	New York	NY	10017	212-688-0033
River Cafe (New American) 1 Water St	Brooklyn	NY	11201	718-522-5200
Rosa Mexicano (Mexican) 1063 1st Ave	New York	NY	10022	212-753-7407
Russian Samovar (Russian) 256 W 52nd St	New York	NY	10019	212-757-0168
Salaam Bombay (Indian) 319 Greenwich St	New York	NY	10013	212-226-9400
San Domenico NY (Italian) 240 Central Park S	New York	NY	10019	212-265-5959
Serendipity (American) 225 E 60th St	New York	NY	10022	212-838-3531
Shun Lee Palace (Chinese) 155 E 55th St	New York	NY	10022	212-371-8844
Smith & Wollensky (Steak/Seafood) 797 3rd Ave	New York	NY	10022	212-753-1530
Steak Frites (French) 9 E 16th St	New York	NY	10003	212-463-7101
Sylvia's (Southern) 328 Lenox Ave	New York	NY	10027	212-996-0660
Taliesin (New American) 55 Church St	New York	NY	10007	212-693-2001
Tavern on the Green (Continental) W 67th St & Central Pk W	New York	NY	10023	212-873-3200
Tribeca Grill (American) 375 Greenwich St	New York	NY	10013	212-941-3900
Trois Jean (French) 154 E 79th St	New York	NY	10021	212-988-4858
Union Pacific (New American) 111 E 22nd St	New York	NY	10010	212-995-8500
Union Square Cafe (New American) 21 E 16th St	New York	NY	10003	212-243-4020
Veselka (Polish) 144 2nd Ave	New York	NY	10003	212-228-9682
Vong (Thai) 200 E 54th St	New York	NY	10022	212-486-9592
Water Club (Seafood) 500 E 30th St	New York	NY	10016	212-683-3333
Windows on the World (American) 1 World Trade Ctr 107th Fl	New York	NY	10048	212-524-7000
Wollensky's Grill (Steak) 205 E 49th St	New York	NY	10016	212-753-0444
Zen Palate (Vegetarian) 663 9th Ave	New York	NY	10036	212-582-1669

— Goods and Services —

SHOPPING

Name / Address	City	State	Zip	Phone	Fax
Annex Outdoor Antiques Fair & Flea Market 25th St & Avenue of the Americas	New York	NY	10010	212-243-5343	
Barney's 660 Madison Ave	New York	NY	10021	212-826-8900	
Bergdorf Goodman Inc 754 5th Ave	New York	NY	10019	212-753-7300	872-8616
Bloomingdale's 1000 3rd Ave *TF:* 800-950-0047 ■ *Web:* www.bloomingdales.com ■ *E-mail:* comments@bloomingdales.com	New York	NY	10022	212-705-2000	705-2502
Bruckner Boulevard Antique District Bruckner Blvd	Bronx	NY	10454	718-292-3113	
Citicorp Center 53rd St & Lexington Ave	New York	NY	10022	212-559-6758	
FAO Schwarz 767 5th Ave	New York	NY	10153	212-644-9400	
Green Acres Mall 2034 Green Acres Mall	Valley Stream	NY	11581	516-561-7360	561-8370
Historic Orchard Street Shopping District 261 Broome St *TF:* 800-825-8374 ■ *Web:* www.orchardstreet.org	New York	NY	10002	212-226-9010	226-8161
Kings Plaza Shopping Center 5100 Kings Plaza	Brooklyn	NY	11234	718-253-6842	951-8857
Loehmann's 5740 Broadway	Riverdale	NY	10463	718-543-6420	
Lord & Taylor 424 5th Ave **Fax:* Hum Res ■ *Web:* www.mayco.com/may/lt_home.html	New York	NY	10018	212-391-3344	391-3265*
Manhattan Mall 33rd St & Avenue of the Americas	New York	NY	10001	212-465-0500	
Saks Fifth Avenue 611 5th Ave	New York	NY	10022	212-940-4000	940-4849
Tiffany & Co 727 5th Ave *TF Orders:* 800-526-0649 ■ *Web:* www.tiffany.com	New York	NY	10022	212-755-8000	605-4465

BANKS

Name / Address	City	State	Zip	Phone	Fax
Bank Leumi USA 579 5th Ave **Fax Area Code:* 212 ■ *Web:* www.bankleumi.co.il	New York	NY	10017	917-542-2343	599-7579*
Bank of America 1 World Trade Ctr	New York	NY	10048	212-390-2000	390-2560
Chase Manhattan Bank NA 1 Chase Manhattan Plaza	New York	NY	10081	212-552-2222	552-2050
Chinese American Bank 77 Bowery	New York	NY	10002	212-966-3303	966-3396
Citibank NA 399 Park Ave *Web:* www.citibank.com	New York	NY	10043	212-559-7299	559-7373
Excel Bank 400 Park Ave	New York	NY	10017	212-605-6500	605-6560
Fuji Bank & Trust Co 2 World Trade Ctr 79th Fl	New York	NY	10048	212-898-2400	321-9408
Israel Discount Bank of New York 511 5th Ave	New York	NY	10017	212-551-8500	370-9623
Morgan Guaranty Trust Co of New York 60 Wall St	New York	NY	10260	212-483-2323	648-5230
Royal Bank of Canada 1 Liberty Plaza *Web:* www.royalbank.com ■ *E-mail:* feedback@www.royalbank.com	New York	NY	10006	212-428-6200	428-2329
Safra National Bank of New York 546 5th Ave	New York	NY	10036	212-704-5500	704-5527
Sterling National Bank 425 Park Ave	New York	NY	10022	212-935-1440	935-1646

BUSINESS SERVICES

Name	Phone
Accountemps	212-687-7878
Adecco Employment Personnel Services	212-682-3438
Airline Delivery Services Corp	212-687-5145
ARC Trucking & Messenger	212-741-1400
Archer Management Services Inc	212-502-2100
Bullit Courier Services Inc	212-855-5555
Choice Courier Systems Inc	212-370-1414
Columbus Messenger Service	212-989-1200
Corporate Express Delivery Systems	212-802-8800
Federal Express	800-238-5355
Immediate Messenger Service	212-989-5600
Kelly Services	212-949-8545
Kinko's	212-924-0802
Manpower Temporary Services	212-557-9110
Minute Men Messenger Service	212-354-6555
Olsten Staffing Services	212-509-3300
Post Office	212-967-8585
Service Messenger	212-391-1900
Speedmore Delivery Service	212-947-2662
UPS	800-742-5877

— Media —

PUBLICATIONS

Name / Address	City	State	Zip	Phone	Fax
Crain's New York Business 220 E 42nd St *TF:* 800-678-9595 ■ *Web:* www.crainsny.com	New York	NY	10017	212-210-0100	210-0799
Journal of Commerce‡ 2 World Trade Ctr 27th Fl **Fax:* Mktg ■ *TF:* 800-223-0243 ■ *Web:* www.joc.com	New York	NY	10048	212-837-7000	837-7035*
Manhattan 330 W 56th St Suite 3G	New York	NY	10019	212-265-7970	265-8052
New York 444 Madison Ave *TF Circ:* 800-678-0900 ■ *Web:* www.newyorkmag.com	New York	NY	10022	212-508-0700	
New York Observer 54 E 64th St **Fax:* News Rm ■ *Web:* www.observer.com ■ *E-mail:* comments@observer.com	New York	NY	10021	212-755-2400	688-4889*
New York Post‡ 1211 Ave of the Americas *Web:* nypostonline.com	New York	NY	10036	212-930-8000	930-8540
New York Times‡ 229 W 43rd St **Fax:* Sales ■ *Web:* www.nytimes.com	New York	NY	10036	212-556-1234	556-8828*
Our Town Newspaper 242 W 30th St 5th Fl **Fax:* News Rm	New York	NY	10001	212-268-8600	268-0614*
People's Weekly World 239 W 23rd St **Fax:* News Rm ■ *Web:* www.hartford-hwp.com/cp-usa/pww.html ■ *E-mail:* pww@pww.org	New York	NY	10011	212-924-2523	645-5436*
Village Voice 36 Cooper Sq *TF Cust Svc:* 800-875-2997 ■ *Web:* www.villagevoice.com ■ *E-mail:* ads@villagevoice.com	New York	NY	10003	212-475-3300	475-8944
Villager The 80 8th Ave Suite 200 **Fax:* News Rm	New York	NY	10011	212-229-1890	229-2790*
Where New York 475 Park Ave S Suite 2100 *Web:* www.wheremags.com/wheremag.nsf/Cities/NewYork ■ *E-mail:* info@wheremags.com	New York	NY	10016	212-725-8100	725-3412

‡Daily newspapers

New York (Cont'd)

TELEVISION

	City	State	Zip	Phone	Fax
WABC-TV Ch 7 (ABC) 7 Lincoln Sq	New York	NY	10023	212-456-7777	456-2381
Web: abcnews.go.com/local/wabc					
WCBS-TV Ch 2 (CBS) 524 W 57th St	New York	NY	10019	212-975-4321	975-9387
Web: www.cbs2ny.com					
WHSI-TV Ch 67 (Ind) PO Box 609	Central Islip	NY	11722	631-582-6700	582-8337
WLNY-TV Ch 55 (Ind) 270 S Service Rd	Melville	NY	11747	631-777-8855	420-4822
WMBC-TV Ch 63 (Ind) 500 Weldon Rd	Lake Hopatcong	NJ	07849	973-697-0063	697-5515
WNBC-TV Ch 4 (NBC) 30 Rockefeller Plaza	New York	NY	10112	212-664-4444	664-2994
Web: www.newschannel4.com ■ *E-mail:* nbc4ny@nbc.com					
WNET-TV Ch 13 (PBS) 450 W 33rd St	New York	NY	10001	212-560-1313	582-3297
Web: www.wnet.org ■ *E-mail:* webinfo@www.wnet.org					
WNJU-TV Ch 47 (Tele) 47 Industrial Ave	Teterboro	NJ	07608	201-288-5550	288-0129
Web: www.noticiero47.net ■ *E-mail:* redaccion@noticiero47.net					
WNYE-TV Ch 25 (PBS) 112 Tillary St	Brooklyn	NY	11201	718-250-5800	855-8863
Web: www.wnye.nycenet.edu ■ *E-mail:* wnyemail@wnye.pbs.org					
WNYW-TV Ch 5 (Fox) 205 E 67th St	New York	NY	10021	212-452-5555	249-1182
WPIX-TV Ch 11 (WB) 220 E 42nd St	New York	NY	10017	212-949-1100	210-2591
Web: www.wpix.com ■ *E-mail:* wpix11@aol.com					
WPXN-TV Ch 31 (PAX) 1330 Ave of the Americas 32nd Fl	New York	NY	10019	212-757-3100	956-0951
Web: www.pax.net/WPXN					
WRNN-TV Ch 62 (Ind) 721 Broadway	Kingston	NY	12401	914-339-6200	339-6264
Web: www.rnntv.com					
WWOR-TV Ch 9 (UPN) 9 Broadcast Plaza	Secaucus	NJ	07096	201-348-0009	330-3777
Web: www.upn9.com					
WXTV-TV Ch 41 (Uni) 500 Frank W Burr 6th Fl	Teaneck	NJ	07666	201-287-4141	287-9427

RADIO

	City	State	Zip	Phone	Fax
WABC-AM 770 kHz (N/T) 2 Penn Plaza 17th Fl	New York	NY	10121	212-613-3800	947-1340
Web: www.wabcradio.com ■ *E-mail:* postmaster@wabcradio.com					
WALK-FM 97.5 MHz (AC) 66 Colonial Dr	Patchogue	NY	11772	631-475-5200	475-9016
Web: www.walkradio.com ■ *E-mail:* walkie@walkradio.com					
WAXQ-FM 104.3 MHz (CR) 1180 6th Ave 5th Fl	New York	NY	10036	212-575-1043	302-7814
Web: classicq104.amfmi.com					
WBAB-FM 102.3 MHz (Rock) 555 Sunrise Hwy	West Babylon	NY	11704	631-587-1023	587-1282
Web: www.wbab.com ■ *E-mail:* wbab@wbab.com					
WBLI-FM 106.1 MHz (CHR) 3090 Rt 112	Medford	NY	11763	631-732-1061	732-3848
Web: www.wbli.com					
WBLS-FM 107.5 MHz (Urban) 3 Park Ave	New York	NY	10016	212-447-1000	447-5197
Web: www.wbls.com					
WBZO-FM 103.1 MHz (Oldies) 900 Walt Whitman	Melville	NY	11747	631-423-6740	423-6750
Web: www.b103.com ■ *E-mail:* b103@prodigy.com					
WCBS-AM 880 kHz (N/T) 51 W 52nd St	New York	NY	10019	212-975-4321	397-7811
Web: newsradio88.com					
WCBS-FM 101.1 MHz (Oldies) 51 W 52nd St	New York	NY	10019	212-975-4321	975-9123
Web: wcbsfm.com					
WDRE-FM 98.5 MHz (Alt) 1103 Stewart Ave	Garden City	NY	11530	516-222-1103	222-1391
WFUV-FM 90.7 MHz (NPR) Fordham University	Bronx	NY	10458	718-817-4550	817-5595
Web: www.wfuv.org ■ *E-mail:* thefolks@wfuv.org					
WGSM-AM 740 kHz (Nost) 900 Walt Whitman Rd	Melville	NY	11747	631-423-6740	423-6750
WHFM-FM 95.3 MHz (Rock) 33 Flying Point Rd Suite 212	Southampton	NY	11968	631-283-9500	283-9506
WHLI-AM 1100 kHz (Nost) 1055 Franklin Ave	Garden City	NY	11530	516-294-8400	746-0025*
**Fax:* Sales					
WHTZ-FM 100.3 MHz (CHR) 230 Park Ave Suite 605	New York	NY	10169	212-239-2300	239-2308
TF: 800-242-0100 ■ *Web:* www.z100.com ■ *E-mail:* z100radio@aol.com					
WINS-AM 1010 kHz (N/T) 888 7th Ave 10th Fl	New York	NY	10106	212-397-1010	247-7918
WKJY-FM 98.3 MHz (AC) 1055 Franklin Ave	Garden City	NY	11530	516-294-8400	746-0025*
**Fax:* Sales ■ *Web:* www.kjoy.com					
WLIB-AM 1190 kHz (Urban) 3 Park Ave	New York	NY	10016	212-447-1000	447-5193
WLIR-FM 92.7 MHz (Alt) 1103 Stewart Ave	Garden City	NY	11530	516-222-1104	222-1391
Web: www.wlir.com					
WLTW-FM 106.7 MHz (AC) 1515 Broadway 40th Fl	New York	NY	10036	212-258-7000	258-7084
WMJC-FM 94.3 MHz (Ctry) 900 Walt Whitman Rd	Melville	NY	11747	631-423-6740	423-6750
WNEW-FM 102.7 MHz (Rock) 888 7th Ave 9th Fl	New York	NY	10106	212-489-1027	957-9639
Web: www.wnew.com ■ *E-mail:* feedback@wnew.com					
WNYC-AM 820 kHz (NPR) 1 Centre St	New York	NY	10007	212-669-7800	
Web: www.wnyc.org ■ *E-mail:* emailus@wnyc.org					
WNYC-FM 93.9 kHz (NPR) 1 Centre St	New York	NY	10007	212-669-7800	553-0626
WOR-AM 710 kHz (N/T) 1440 Broadway	New York	NY	10018	212-642-4500	921-4204
Web: www.wor710.com					
WPAT-FM 93.1 MHz (Span) 26 W 56th St	New York	NY	10019	212-541-9200	333-7642
WPLJ-FM 95.5 MHz (AC) 2 Penn Plaza 17th Fl	New York	NY	10121	212-613-8900	613-8956
Web: www.plj.com					
WQCD-FM 101.9 MHz (NAC) 395 Hudson St 7th Fl	New York	NY	10014	212-352-1019	929-8559
WQHT-FM 97.1 MHz (Urban) 395 Hudson St 7th Fl	New York	NY	10014	212-229-9797	929-8559
WQXR-FM 96.3 MHz (Clas) 122 5th Ave	New York	NY	10011	212-633-7600	633-7666
Web: www.wqxr.com ■ *E-mail:* wqxr963fm@aol.com					
WRKS-FM 98.7 MHz (Urban) 395 Hudson St 7th Fl	New York	NY	10014	212-242-9870	242-0706
WTJM-FM 105.1 MHz (Oldies) 1120 Ave of the Americas 18th Fl	New York	NY	10036	212-704-1051	398-3299
E-mail: mix105ny@aol.com					
WXRK-FM 92.3 MHz (Alt) 40 W 57th St 14th Fl	New York	NY	10019	212-314-9230	314-9340

— Colleges/Universities —

	City	State	Zip	Phone	Fax
Adelphi University 1 South Ave	Garden City	NY	11530	516-877-3000	877-3039
TF: 800-233-5744 ■ *Web:* www.adelphi.edu					
Albert A List College of Jewish Studies 3080 Broadway	New York	NY	10027	212-678-8832	678-8947
Web: www.jtsa.edu/academic/lc					
American Academy McAllister Institute of Funeral Service 450 W 56th St	New York	NY	10019	212-757-1190	765-5923
American Academy of Dramatic Arts 120 Madison Ave	New York	NY	10016	212-686-9244	545-7934
TF: 800-463-8990 ■ *Web:* www.aada.org ■ *E-mail:* aada@va.pubnix.com					
Audrey Cohen College 75 Varick St	New York	NY	10013	212-343-1234	343-7399
Web: www.audrey-cohen.edu					
Barnard College Columbia University 3009 Broadway	New York	NY	10027	212-854-5262	854-6220
Web: www.barnard.columbia.edu/					
Berkeley College New York 3 E 43rd St	New York	NY	10017	212-986-4343	697-3371
TF: 800-446-5400 ■ *Web:* www.berkeleycollege.edu ■ *E-mail:* nycampus@berkeley.org					
Boricua College 3755 Broadway	New York	NY	10032	212-694-1000	694-1015
Bradford School 8 E 40th St	New York	NY	10016	212-686-9040	686-9171
Bramson ORT College 69-30 Austin St	Forest Hills	NY	11375	718-261-5800	459-6565
City University of New York Bernard M Baruch College 151 E 25th St	New York	NY	10010	212-802-2222	802-2190
Web: www.baruch.cuny.edu ■ *E-mail:* udgbb@cunyvm.cuny.edu					
City University of New York Borough of Manhattan Community College 199 Chambers St Rm S-300	New York	NY	10007	212-346-8105	346-8110
Web: www.bmcc.cuny.edu					
City University of New York City College 138th St & Convent Ave	New York	NY	10031	212-650-7000	650-6417
Web: www.ccny.cuny.edu/					
City University of New York College of Staten Island 2800 Victory Blvd	Staten Island	NY	10314	718-982-2000	982-2500
Web: www.csi.cuny.edu					
City University of New York Herbert H Lehman College 250 Bedford Pk Blvd W	Bronx	NY	10468	718-960-8000	960-8712
Web: www.lehman.cuny.edu					
City University of New York Hostos Community College 500 Grand Concourse	Bronx	NY	10451	718-518-4444	518-6643
Web: www.hostos.cuny.edu					
City University of New York Hunter College 695 Park Ave	New York	NY	10021	212-772-4000	650-3336
Web: www.hunter.cuny.edu/					
City University of New York John Jay College of Criminal Justice 445 W 59th St	New York	NY	10019	212-237-8000	237-8742
Web: www.jjay.cuny.edu/					
City University of New York Kingsborough Community College 2001 Oriental Blvd	Brooklyn	NY	11235	718-368-5000	368-5024
Web: www.kbcc.cuny.edu					
City University of New York LaGuardia Community College 31-10 Thomson Ave	Long Island City	NY	11101	718-482-5000	482-5599
Web: www.lagcc.cuny.edu					

New York — Colleges/Universities (Cont'd)

Phone *Fax*

City University of New York Medgar Evers
College 1650 Bedford Ave.............. Brooklyn NY 11225 718-270-4900 270-6188

City University of New York Queens College
65-30 Kissena Blvd....................Flushing NY 11367 718-997-5000 997-5617
Web: www.qc.edu ■ *E-mail:* admissions@qc.edu

City University of New York Queensborough
Community College 222-05 56th Ave....... Bayside NY 11364 718-631-6262 281-5069

City University of New York York College
94-20 Guy R Brewer Blvd ....Jamaica NY 11451 718-262-2000 262-2601
Web: www.york.cuny.edu ■ *E-mail:* admissions@york.cuny.edu

Cochran School of Nursing 967 N Broadway....Yonkers NY 10701 914-964-4283 964-4971
Web: www.riversidehealth.org/stjohns/html/nursing.html

College of Aeronautics 86-01 23rd Ave....East Elmhurst NY 11369 718-429-6600 779-2231
TF: 800-776-2376 ■ *Web:* www.aero.edu

College of Insurance 101 Murray St.........New York NY 10007 212-962-4111 964-3381
TF: 800-356-5146 ■ *Web:* www.tci.edu

College of Mount Saint Vincent
6301 Riverdale Ave...................Riverdale NY 10471 718-405-3200 549-7945
Web: www.cmsv.edu

College of New Rochelle 29 Castle Pl.....New Rochelle NY 10805 914-632-5300 654-5554*
**Fax:* Admissions ■ *TF:* 800-933-5923 ■ *Web:* www.cnr.edu
■ *E-mail:* cnr2@pppmail.nyser.net

Columbia University
W 116th St & Broadway ....New York NY 10027 212-854-1754 854-2000
Web: www.columbia.edu

Concordia College 171 White Plains Rd ......Bronxville NY 10708 914-337-9300 395-4636
TF Admissions: 800-937-2655 ■ *Web:* www.concordia-ny.edu

Cooper Union College 30 Cooper Sq.........New York NY 10003 212-353-4100 353-4343*
**Fax:* Admissions ■ *Web:* www.cooper.edu

Eugene Lang College 65 W 11th St ....New York NY 10011 212-229-5799 229-5625
Web: www.newschool.edu/academic/lang
■ *E-mail:* lang@newschool.edu

Fashion Institute of Technology
227 W 27th St.......................New York NY 10001 212-217-7675 217-7481
TF Admissions: 800-468-6348 ■ *Web:* www.fitnyc.edu

Fordham University 441 E Fordham Rd......... Bronx NY 10458 718-817-1000 367-9404
TF Admissions: 800-367-3426 ■ *Web:* www.fordham.edu

Hebrew Union College 1 W 4th St ....New York NY 10012 212-674-5300 388-1720
Web: www.huc.edu

Helene Fuld School of Nursing
1879 Madison Ave ....New York NY 10035 212-423-1000 427-2453

Hofstra University 100 Hofstra University.....Hempstead NY 11549 516-463-6700 463-5100
TF: 800-463-7872 ■ *Web:* www.hofstra.edu
■ *E-mail:* hofstra@hofstra.edu

Institute of Design & Construction
141 Willoughby St .... Brooklyn NY 11201 718-855-3661 852-5889

Interboro Institute 450 W 56th St...........New York NY 10019 212-399-0091 765-5772

Iona College 715 North Ave............New Rochelle NY 10801 914-633-2000 633-2096
Web: www.iona.edu

Juilliard School 60 Lincoln Ctr Plaza.........New York NY 10023 212-799-5000 769-6420
Web: www.juilliard.edu

Katharine Gibbs School 200 Park Ave........New York NY 10166 212-867-9300 338-9606
TF: 800-567-3877

Laboratory Institute of Merchandising
12 E 53rd St ....New York NY 10022 212-752-1530 832-6708
TF: 800-677-1323 ■ *E-mail:* limcollege@usa.pipeline.com

Long Island University Brooklyn Campus
University Plaza .... Brooklyn NY 11201 718-488-1000 780-4097
Web: www.brooklyn.liunet.edu/cwis/bklyn/bklyn.html

Manhattan College
4513 Manhattan College Pkwy .... Bronx NY 10471 718-862-8000 862-8019
Web: www.mancol.edu

Manhattan School of Music
601 W 122nd St......................New York NY 10027 212-749-2802 749-5471
Web: www.msmnyc.edu

Mannes College of Music 150 W 85th St .....New York NY 10024 212-580-0210 580-1738
TF: 800-292-3040 ■ *Web:* www.newschool.edu/academic/mannes.htm

Marymount Manhattan College
221 E 71st St........................New York NY 10021 212-517-0400 517-0413
TF Admissions: 800-627-9668 ■ *Web:* marymount.mmm.edu

Mercy College Bronx Campus 50 Antin Pl....... Bronx NY 10462 718-518-7710 518-7879

Molloy College 1000 Hempstead Ave ... Rockville Centre NY 11571 516-678-5000 256-2247
TF: 800-229-1020 ■ *Web:* www.molloy.edu
■ *E-mail:* tufan01@molloy.edu

Monroe College 2501 Jerome Ave .... Bronx NY 10468 718-933-6700 364-3552
TF: 800-556-6676 ■ *Web:* www.monroecoll.edu

New Jersey City University 2039 JFK Blvd....Jersey City NJ 07305 201-200-2000 200-2044
TF Admissions: 888-441-6528 ■ *Web:* www.njcu.edu

New York Career Institute 15 Park Row ......New York NY 10038 212-962-0002 608-8210

New York Institute of Technology New York
City Campus 1855 Broadway...........New York NY 10023 212-261-1500 261-1704
TF Admissions: 800-345-6948*

New York School of Interior Design
170 E 70th St.......................New York NY 10021 212-472-1500 472-1867
TF: 800-336-9743 ■ *Web:* www.nysid.edu
■ *E-mail:* admissions@nysid.edu

New York University 22 Washington Sq N.....New York NY 10011 212-998-4500 995-4902
Web: www.nyu.edu

Pace University 1 Pace Plaza..............New York NY 10038 212-346-1200 346-1040
Web: www.pace.edu

Parsons School of Design 2 W 13th St.......New York NY 10011 212-229-8900 929-2456
TF Admissions: 800-252-0852 ■ *Web:* www.parsons.edu
■ *E-mail:* parsadm@newschool.edu

Phillips Beth Israel School of Nursing
310 E 22nd St 9th Floor ....New York NY 10010 212-614-6108 614-6109

Plaza Business Institute
74-09 37th Ave.................Jackson Heights NY 11372 718-779-1430 779-7423
Web: www.plazacollege.edu ■ *E-mail:* info@plazacollege.edu

Polytechnic University 6 Metrotech Ctr .... Brooklyn NY 11201 718-260-3600 260-3136
Web: www.poly.edu ■ *E-mail:* admub@duke.poly.edu

Pratt Institute 200 Willoughby Ave .... Brooklyn NY 11205 718-636-3600 636-3670*
**Fax:* Admissions ■ *TF Admissions:* 800-331-0834
■ *Web:* www.pratt.edu ■ *E-mail:* info@pratt.edu

Saint Francis College 180 Remsen St......... Brooklyn NY 11201 718-522-2300 522-1274
Web: www.stfranciscollege.edu

Saint John's University 8000 Utopia Pkwy......Jamaica NY 11439 718-969-8000 990-1677*
**Fax:* Admissions ■ *Web:* www.stjohns.edu

Saint John's University Staten Island
Campus 300 Howard Ave............ Staten Island NY 10301 718-447-4343 390-4298

Saint Joseph's College 245 Clinton Ave ...... Brooklyn NY 11205 718-636-6800 636-7245

Saint Peter's College 2641 JFK Blvd.........Jersey City NJ 07306 201-915-9000 451-0036*
**Fax:* Cust Svc ■ *Web:* www.spc.edu

Saint Thomas Aquinas College 125 Rt 340..... Sparkill NY 10976 914-359-9500 359-8136
Web: www.stac.edu

School of Visual Arts 209 E 23rd St.........New York NY 10010 212-592-2000 592-2116
TF Admissions: 800-436-4204 ■ *Web:* www.sva.edu

State University of New York Maritime College
6 Pennyfield Ave Fort Schuyler............. Bronx NY 10465 718-409-7200 409-7465
Web: www.sunymaritime.edu ■ *E-mail:* sunymarit@aol.com

State University of New York Nassau
Community College 1 Education Dr ..... Garden City NY 11530 516-572-7500 572-9743
Web: www.sunynassau.edu ■ *E-mail:* info@sunynassau.edu

Taylor Business Institute 269 W 40th St......New York NY 10018 212-302-4000 302-2624
TF: 800-959-9999

Technical Career Institutes 320 W 31st St ....New York NY 10001 212-594-4000 629-3937
TF: 800-878-8246 ■ *Web:* www.tciedu.com
■ *E-mail:* admissions@tciedu.com

Touro College 27-33 W 23rd St............New York NY 10010 212-463-0400 627-9542
Web: www.touro.edu

US Merchant Marine Academy
Steamboat Rd..................... Kings Point NY 11024 516-773-5000 773-5390
TF Admissions: 800-732-6267 ■ *Web:* www.usmma.edu

Wagner College 1 Campus Rd.......... Staten Island NY 10301 718-390-3411 390-3105*
**Fax:* Admissions ■ *TF Admissions:* 800-221-1010
■ *Web:* www.wagner.edu

Webb Institute Crescent Beach Rd .... Glen Cove NY 11542 516-671-2213 674-9838
Web: www.webb-institute.edu
■ *E-mail:* admissions@webb-institute.edu

Westchester Business Institute
325 Central Ave ....White Plains NY 10606 914-948-4442 948-8216
TF: 800-333-4924 ■ *E-mail:* wbi@ix.netcom.com

Yeshiva University 500 W 185th St ....New York NY 10033 212-960-5400 960-0086
Web: www.yu.edu

— Hospitals —

Phone *Fax*

Bayley Seton Hospital 75 Vanderbilt Ave... Staten Island NY 10304 718-354-6000 354-6011

Bellevue Hospital Center 462 1st Ave........New York NY 10016 212-562-4141 562-4036

Beth Israel Medical Center
1st Ave & 16th St....................New York NY 10003 212-420-2000 420-2881
Web: www.bethisraelny.org/

Beth Israel Medical Center Kings Highway Div
3201 Kings Hwy...................... Brooklyn NY 11234 718-252-3000 252-2233

Beth Israel Medical Center Singer Div
170 East End Ave....................New York NY 10128 212-870-9000 870-9404

Bronx-Lebanon Hospital Center
1276 Fulton Ave...................... Bronx NY 10456 718-590-1800 901-6251

Brookdale Hospital Medical Center
1 Brookdale Plaza..................... Brooklyn NY 11212 718-240-5000 240-5042

Brooklyn Hospital Center 121 DeKalb Ave..... Brooklyn NY 11201 718-250-8000 250-8299*
**Fax:* Admitting

Cabrini Medical Center 227 E 19th St........New York NY 10003 212-995-6000 995-7444*
**Fax:* Hum Res ■ *TF:* 800-222-7464

Catholic Medical Center Mary Immaculate
Hospital 152-11 89th Ave .... Queens NY 11432 718-558-2000 558-2383

New York — Hospitals (Cont'd)

	City	State	ZIP	Phone	Fax
Catholic Medical Center of Brooklyn & Queens 88-25 153rd St	Jamaica	NY	11432	718-558-6900	558-7286
Catholic Medical Center Saint John's Queens Hospital 90-02 Queens Blvd	Elmhurst	NY	11373	718-558-1000	558-1945*
*Fax: Admitting					
Catholic Medical Center Saint Joseph's Hospital 158-40 79th Ave	Flushing	NY	11366	718-558-6200	558-5073
Catholic Medical Center Saint Mary's Hospital of Brooklyn 170 Buffalo Ave	Brooklyn	NY	11213	718-221-3000	221-3181
Coney Island Hospital 2601 Ocean Pkwy	Brooklyn	NY	11235	718-616-3000	616-4439
Flushing Hospital Medical Center 45th Ave at Parsons Blvd	Flushing	NY	11355	718-670-5000	670-4587*
*Fax: Admitting					
Harlem Hospital Center 506 Lenox Ave	New York	NY	10037	212-939-1000	939-1974
Interfaith Medical Center 555 Prospect Pl	Brooklyn	NY	11238	718-935-7000	935-7109
Jacobi Medical Center 1400 Pelham Pkwy S	Bronx	NY	10461	718-918-8141	918-4607
Jamaica Hospital Medical Center 8900 Van Wyck Expy	Jamaica	NY	11418	718-206-6000	657-0545
Web: www.jamaicahospital.org ■ *E-mail:* olepr@aol.com					
Kings County Hospital Center 451 Clarkson Ave	Brooklyn	NY	11203	718-245-3131	245-4494*
*Fax: Admitting					
Kingsbrook Jewish Medical Center 585 Schenectady Ave	Brooklyn	NY	11203	718-604-5000	604-5243
Lenox Hill Hospital 100 E 77th St	New York	NY	10021	212-434-2000	434-3434*
*Fax: Admitting ■ *Web:* www.lenoxhillhospital.org					
Lincoln Medical & Mental Health Center 234 E 149th St	Bronx	NY	10451	718-579-5000	579-5974
Long Island Jewish Medical Center 270-05 76th Ave	New Hyde Park	NY	11040	718-470-7000	470-6724*
*Fax: Admitting ■ *Web:* www.lij.edu					
Lutheran Medical Center 150 55th St	Brooklyn	NY	11220	718-630-7000	630-8228*
*Fax: Admitting					
Maimonides Medical Center 4802 10th Ave	Brooklyn	NY	11219	718-283-6000	283-8553
Web: www.maimonidesmed.org					
Metropolitan Hospital Center 1901 1st Ave	New York	NY	10029	212-423-6262	423-7207*
*Fax: Admitting					
Montefiore Medical Center 111 E 210th St	Bronx	NY	10467	718-920-4321	920-6049*
*Fax: Admitting ■ *Web:* www.montefiore.org					
Mount Sinai Medical Center 100th St & 5th Ave	New York	NY	10029	212-241-6500	348-6583*
*Fax: Hum Res ■ *Web:* www.mountsinai.org					
New York Downtown Hospital 170 William St	New York	NY	10038	212-312-5000	312-5977
E-mail: nydh@poboxes.com					
New York Hospital Medical Center of Queens 56-45 Main St	Flushing	NY	11355	718-670-1021	358-1196
New York Methodist Hospital 506 6th St	Brooklyn	NY	11215	718-780-3000	780-3770
New York Presbyterian Hospital 525 E 68th St	New York	NY	10021	212-746-5454	746-8565*
*Fax: Admitting ■ *Web:* www.nyp.org ■ *E-mail:* publicaffairs@mail.med.cornell.edu					
New York University Medical Center 550 1st Ave	New York	NY	10016	212-263-7300	263-8960*
*Fax: Admitting ■ *Web:* www.med.nyu.edu					
North Central Bronx Hospital 7424 Kossuth Ave	Bronx	NY	10467	718-519-5000	519-4902
North General Hospital 1879 Madison Ave	New York	NY	10035	212-423-4000	423-4204
North Shore University Hospital at Forest Hills 102-01 66th Rd	Forest Hills	NY	11375	718-830-4000	830-4168
Our Lady of Mercy Medical Center 600 E 233rd St	Bronx	NY	10466	718-920-9000	920-9977*
*Fax: Admitting ■ *Web:* www.ourladyofmercy.com					
Our Lady of Mercy Medical Center Florence D'Urso Pavilion 1870 Pelham Park Way S	Bronx	NY	10461	718-430-6000	430-6011*
*Fax: Admissions					
Peninsula Hospital Center 51-15 Beach Channel Dr	Far Rockaway	NY	11691	718-734-2000	945-0993
Queens Hospital Center 82-68 164th St	Jamaica	NY	11432	718-883-3000	883-6156*
*Fax: Admitting					
Saint Barnabas Hospital 4422 3rd Ave	Bronx	NY	10457	718-960-9000	960-3132*
*Fax: Admitting					
Saint Clare's Hospital & Health Center 415 W 51st St	New York	NY	10019	212-586-1500	459-8316*
*Fax: Admitting					
Saint Luke's-Roosevelt Hospital Center 1111 Amsterdam Ave	New York	NY	10025	212-523-4000	523-1981*
*Fax: Admissions ■ *Web:* www.slrhc.org					
Saint Vincent's Hospital & Medical Center of New York 153 W 11th St	New York	NY	10011	212-604-7000	604-2100*
*Fax: Admitting					
Sisters of Charity Medical Center-Saint Vincent's Campus 355 Bard Ave	Staten Island	NY	10310	718-876-1234	876-1322
Web: www.schsi.org					
Staten Island University Hospital 475 Seaview Ave	Staten Island	NY	10305	718-226-9000	226-9093
Web: www.siuh.edu ■ *E-mail:* recruit@siuh.edu					
University Hospital of Brooklyn 450 Clarkson Ave	Brooklyn	NY	11203	718-270-1000	270-1941*
*Fax: Admitting					
Veterans Affairs Medical Center 423 E 23rd St	New York	NY	10010	212-686-7500	951-3375
Victory Memorial Hospital 699 92nd St	Brooklyn	NY	11228	718-567-1234	567-1002

— Attractions —

	City	State	ZIP	Phone	Fax
Alice Austen House Museum & Garden 2 Hylan Blvd	Staten Island	NY	10305	718-816-4506	815-3959
Alvin Ailey American Dance Theater 211 W 61st St 3rd Fl	New York	NY	10023	212-767-0590	767-0625
Web: www.alvinailey.org					
Ambassador Theatre 215 W 49th St	New York	NY	10019	212-239-6200	
TF: 800-432-7250					
American Ballet Theatre 890 Broadway 3rd Fl	New York	NY	10003	212-477-3030	254-5938
Web: www.abt.org					
American Bible Society 1865 Broadway	New York	NY	10023	212-408-1200	408-1512
TF Cust Svc: 800-322-4253 ■ *Web:* www.americanbible.org					
American Composers Orchestra 1775 Broadway Suite 525	New York	NY	10019	212-977-8495	977-8995
Web: www.americancomposers.org ■ *E-mail:* amcomporch@aol.com					
American Craft Museum 40 W 53rd St	New York	NY	10019	212-956-3535	459-0926
Web: www.fieldtrip.com/ny/29563535.htm					
American Indian Dance Theatre 223 E 61 St	New York	NY	10021	212-308-9555	026-0724
American Museum-Hayden Planetarium 79th St & Central Pk W	New York	NY	10024	212-769-5900	769-5007
American Museum of Natural History 175-208 Central Pk W	New York	NY	10024	212-769-5000	769-5199*
*Fax: Hum Res ■ *Web:* www.amnh.org					
American Museum of the Moving Image 3601 35th Ave	Astoria	NY	11106	718-784-4520	784-4681
Web: www.ammi.org					
American Numismatic Society Broadway & 155th St	New York	NY	10032	212-234-3130	234-3381
Web: www.amnumsoc2.org/ ■ *E-mail:* info@amnumsoc.org					
American Symphony Orchestra 850 7th Ave Suite 503	New York	NY	10019	212-581-1365	489-7188
Web: www.americansymphony.org ■ *E-mail:* amsymphony@aol.com					
Americas Society 680 Park Ave	New York	NY	10021	212-249-8950	249-5868
Web: www.americas-society.org					
Avery Fisher Hall W 65th St & Broadway	New York	NY	10023	212-875-5030	875-5027
Web: www.lincolncenter.org					
Ballet Hispanico of New York 167 W 89th St	New York	NY	10024	212-362-6710	362-7809
Barrymore Theatre 243 W 47th St	New York	NY	10036	212-239-6200	
TF: 800-432-7250					
Bartow-Pell Mansion Museum 895 Shore Rd Pelham Bay Pk	Bronx	NY	10464	718-885-1461	885-9164
Web: www.fieldtrip.com/ny/88851461.htm					
Belasco Theatre 111 W 44th St	New York	NY	10036	212-239-6200	
TF: 800-432-7250					
Belvedere Castle 830 5th Ave	New York	NY	10021	212-772-0210	
Booth Theatre 222 W 45th St	New York	NY	10036	212-239-6200	
TF: 800-432-7250					
Broadhurst Theatre 235 W 44th St	New York	NY	10036	212-239-6200	
TF: 800-432-7250					
Broadway Theatre 1681 Broadway	New York	NY	10019	212-239-6200	
TF: 800-432-7250 ■ *Web:* www.broadwaytheater.com/					
Bronx County Historical Society 3309 Bainbridge Ave	Bronx	NY	10467	718-881-8900	881-4827
Web: www.bronxhistoricalsociety.org					
Bronx Museum of the Arts 1040 Grand Concourse	Bronx	NY	10456	718-681-6000	681-6181
Web: www.fieldtrip.com/ny/86816000.htm					
Bronx Zoo Wildlife Conservation Park 2300 Southern Blvd	Bronx	NY	10460	718-220-5100	220-2685*
*Fax: Mktg ■ *Web:* www.wcs.org/zoos/bronxzoo					
Brooklyn Academy of Music 30 Lafayette Ave	Brooklyn	NY	11217	718-636-4111	636-4179
Brooklyn Botanic Garden 1000 Washington Ave	Brooklyn	NY	11225	718-623-7200	857-2430
Web: www.bbg.org					

New York — Attractions (Cont'd)

Phone | Fax

Brooklyn Children's Museum
145 Brooklyn Ave .... Brooklyn NY 11213 718-735-4400 604-7442
Web: www.fieldtrip.com/ny/87354400.htm
Brooklyn Museum of Art 200 Eastern Pkwy .... Brooklyn NY 11238 718-638-5000 638-3731
Web: www.brooklynart.org
Brooklyn Philharmonic Orchestra
1 Hanson Pl Suite 1806................ Brooklyn NY 11243 718-622-5555 622-3774
Brooks Atkinson Theatre 256 W 47th St ......New York NY 10036 212-307-4100
TF: 800-755-4000
Bryant Park 42nd St-betw 5th & 6th Aves .....New York NY 10017 212-983-4142
Carnegie Hall 154 W 57th St..............New York NY 10019 212-247-7800 581-6539
Web: www.carnegiehall.org
Castle Clinton National Monument
Battery Park.........................New York NY 10004 212-344-7220
Web: www.nps.gov/cacl/
Cathedral Church of Saint John the Divine
1047 Amsterdam Ave ....New York NY 10025 212-662-2133
Web: www.stjohndivine.org ■ *E-mail:* stjohns@interport.net
Cathedral Church of Saint John the Divine
1047 Amsterdam Ave ....New York NY 10025 212-316-7540
Web: www.stjohndivine.org ■ *E-mail:* stjohn@interport.net
Central Park 830 5th Ave.................New York NY 10021 212-360-8111 360-1329
Web: www.centralpark.org/
Central Park Wildlife Conservation Center
5th Ave & 64th St....................New York NY 10021 212-861-6030
Web: www.wcs.org/zoos/wildlifecenters/centralpark
Chelsea Piers Sports & Entertainment
Complex W 23rd St & Hudson River.......New York NY 10011 212-336-6666 336-6808
Web: www.chelseapiers.com
Children's Museum of Manhattan
212 W 83rd St......................New York NY 10024 212-721-1223 721-1127
Web: www.cmom.org ■ *E-mail:* mail@cmom.org
Church of the Transfiguration 1 E 29th St.....New York NY 10016 212-684-6770 684-1662
Citicorp Center 53rd St & Lexington Ave......New York NY 10022 212-559-6758
City Center 130 W 56 St.................New York NY 10019 212-247-0430 246-9778
Web: www.citycenter.org
Cloisters Museum Fort Tryon Pk............New York NY 10040 212-923-3700 795-3640
Web: www.fieldtrip.com/ny/29233700.htm
Conservatory Garden
5th Ave & 105th St Central Pk...........New York NY 10029 212-860-1382
Web: www.centralpark.org
Cooper-Hewitt National Design Museum
(Smithsonian Institution) 2 E 91st St......New York NY 10128 212-849-8300 849-8401
Web: www.si.edu/ndm
Cort Theatre 138 W 48th St...............New York NY 10036 212-239-6200
TF: 800-432-7250
Dahesh Museum 601 5th Ave..............New York NY 10017 212-759-0606 759-1235
Web: www.daheshmuseum.org
■ *E-mail:* education@daheshmuseum.org
Dance Theatre of Harlem Inc
466 W 152nd St......................New York NY 10031 212-690-2800 690-8736
E-mail: DnseHarlem@aol.com
Dia Center for the Arts 542 W 22nd St.......New York NY 10011 212-989-5566
Web: www.diacenter.org
Duffy Theatre 1553 Broadway..............New York NY 10036 212-695-3401
Dyckman House 215 Nagle Ave ....New York NY 10034 212-569-7300 304-1642
Empire State Building
350 5th Ave Suite 3210................New York NY 10118 212-736-3100 967-6167
Web: www.esbnyc.com ■ *E-mail:* info@esbnyc.com
Eugene O'Neill Theatre 230 W 49th St.......New York NY 10036 212-239-6200
TF: 800-432-7250
Federal Hall National Memorial 26 Wall St....New York NY 10005 212-825-6888 825-6874
Web: www.nps.gov/feha/
Forbes Magazine Galleries 62 5th Ave ....New York NY 10011 212-206-5548
Ford Center for the Performing Arts
213 W 42nd St.......................New York NY 10036 212-307-4100
TF: 800-755-4000
Frick Collection 1 E 70th St...............New York NY 10021 212-288-0700 628-4417
Gateway National Recreation Area
Headquarters Bldg 69 Floyd Bennett Field ... Brooklyn NY 11234 718-338-3687 338-3560
Web: www.nps.gov/gate/
General Grant National Memorial
Riverside Dr & W 122nd St.............New York NY 10003 212-666-1640 932-9631
Web: www.nps.gov/gegr/
Gershwin Theatre 222 W 51st St ....New York NY 10019 212-307-4100
TF: 800-755-4000
Golden Theatre 252 W 45th St.............New York NY 10036 212-239-6200
Gracie Mansion 88th St & East End Ave ......New York NY 10128 212-570-4751
Guggenheim Museum SoHo 575 Broadway ....New York NY 10012 212-423-3500 360-4340
Web: www.guggenheim.org
Hamilton Grange National Memorial
287 Convent Ave......................New York NY 10031 212-283-5154
Web: www.nps.gov/hagr/

Phone | Fax

Harbor Defense Museum Fort Hamilton....... Brooklyn NY 11252 718-630-4349
Helen Hayes Theatre 240 W 44th St.........New York NY 10036 212-239-6200
TF: 800-432-7250
Historic Richmond Town 441 Clarke Ave ... Staten Island NY 10306 718-351-1611 351-6057
Imperial Theatre 249 W 45th St............New York NY 10036 212-239-6200
TF: 800-432-7250
International Center of Photography
1130 5th Ave ....New York NY 10128 212-860-1777 360-6490
Web: www.icp.org/
Intrepid Sea-Air-Space Museum
W 46th St & 12th Ave Pier 86 ....New York NY 10036 212-245-0072 245-7289
Web: www.intrepid-museum.com
■ *E-mail:* marketing@intrepid-museum.com
Jamaica Bay Wildlife Refuge
Gateway National Recreation Area
Headquarters Bldg 69 Floyd Bennett Field ... Brooklyn NY 11234 718-318-4340 338-3560
Jewish Museum 1109 5th Ave ....New York NY 10128 212-423-3200 423-3232
Web: www.thejewishmuseum.org
Kingsland Homestead 143-35 37th Ave........Flushing NY 11354 718-939-0647 539-9885
Lehman Center for the Performing Arts
250 Bedford Park Blvd W................. Bronx NY 10468 718-960-8232 960-8233
Liberty Street Gallery
225 Liberty St World Financial Ctr.........New York NY 10281 212-945-0505
Lincoln Center for the Performing Arts
70 Lincoln Ctr Plaza ....New York NY 10023 212-875-5223 875-5242
Web: www.lincolncenter.org
Long Island Children's Museum
550 Stewart Ave .... Garden City NY 11530 516-222-0217 222-0225
Web: www.516web.com/museum/licm.htm
Longacre Theatre 220 W 48th St ....New York NY 10036 212-239-6200
TF: 800-432-7250
Lower East Side Tenement Museum
90 Orchard St.......................New York NY 10002 212-431-0233 431-0402
Web: www.wnet.org/archive/tenement/
Lunt-Fontanne Theatre 205 W 46th St ....New York NY 10036 212-307-4100
TF: 800-755-4000
Lyceum Theatre 149 W 45th St ....New York NY 10036 212-239-6200
TF: 800-432-7250
Majestic Theatre 245 W 44th St............New York NY 10036 212-239-6200
TF: 800-432-7250
Manhattan Philharmonic
70 W 36th St Suite 305................New York NY 10018 212-239-0205 563-5587
Web: www.midamerica-music.com/manhattan/home.html
Marchais Jacques Museum of Tibetan Art
338 Lighthouse Ave................ Staten Island NY 10306 718-987-3500 351-0402
Marquis Theatre
211 W 45th ST Marriott Marquis Hotel .....New York NY 10036 212-307-4100
TF: 800-755-4000
Martha Graham Dance Center
440 Lafayette St.....................New York NY 10003 212-832-9166 223-0351
Martin Beck Theatre 302 W 45th St ....New York NY 10036 212-239-6200
TF: 800-432-7250
Medieval Times Dinner & Tournament
720 48th St ....New York NY 10036 212-586-9096
Web: www.medievaltimes.com/NY_realm.htm
Merce Cunningham Dance Co
55 Bethune St ....New York NY 10014 212-255-8240 633-2453
Web: www.merce.org ■ *E-mail:* cdfmerce@delphi.com
Metropolitan Opera Assn Inc Lincoln Ctr......New York NY 10023 212-799-3100 870-7416
Web: www.metopera.org ■ *E-mail:* metinfo@visionfoundry.com
Minskoff Theatre 200 W 45th St............New York NY 10036 212-307-4100
TF: 800-755-4000
Morris-Jumel Museum
65 Jumel Terr at 160th St ....New York NY 10032 212-923-8008 923-8947
Morris Mark Dance Group
225 Lafayette St Suite 504..............New York NY 10012 212-219-3660 219-3960
Web: www.mmdg.org ■ *E-mail:* info@mmdg.org
Museo del Barrio 1230 5th Ave ....New York NY 10029 212-831-7272 831-7927
Web: www.elmuseo.org
Museum for African Art 593 Broadway ....New York NY 10012 212-966-1313 966-1432
Web: www.fieldtrip.com/ny/29661313.htm
Museum of American Financial History
28 Broadway ....New York NY 10004 212-908-4110 908-4601
Web: www.mafh.org
Museum of American Folk Art
555 W 57th St 13th Fl.................New York NY 10019 212-977-7170 977-8134
Web: www.folkartmuse.org ■ *E-mail:* info@folkartmuse.org
Museum of American Illustration
128 E 63rd St.......................New York NY 10021 212-838-2560 838-2561
TF: 800-746-8738 ■ *Web:* www.fieldtrip.com/ny/28382560.htm
Museum of Jewish Heritage
18 1st Pl Battery Park City..............New York NY 10280 212-968-1800 968-1368
Web: www.mjhnyc.org
Museum of Modern Art 11 W 53rd St........New York NY 10019 212-708-9400 333-9691*
**Fax:* PR ■ *Web:* www.moma.org ■ *E-mail:* comments@moma.org

New York — Attractions (Cont'd)

				Phone	Fax
Museum of Television & Radio 25 W 52nd St. *Web:* www.mtr.org	New York	NY	10019	212-621-6600	621-6700
Museum of the American Piano 211 W 58th St *Web:* www.pianomuseum.com ■ *E-mail:* pmuseum@pianomuseum.com	New York	NY	10019	212-246-4646	245-5432
Museum of the City of New York 1220 Fifth Ave *Web:* www.mcny.org ■ *E-mail:* mcny@mcny.org	New York	NY	10029	212-534-1672	534-5974
Music Box Theatre 239 W 45th St *TF:* 800-432-7250	New York	NY	10036	212-239-6200	
Music Hall at Snug Harbor Cultural Center 1000 Richmond Terr	Staten Island	NY	10301	718-448-2500	
National Academy of Design Museum 1083 5th Ave *Web:* www.nationalacademy.org	New York	NY	10128	212-369-4880	360-6795
National Museum of the American Indian (Smithsonian Institution) 1 Bowling Green *TF:* 800-242-6624 ■ *Web:* www.si.edu/nmai	New York	NY	10004	212-514-3700	514-3800
Nederlander Theatre 208 W 41st St *TF:* 800-755-4000	New York	NY	10036	212-307-4100	
Neil Simon Theatre 250 W 52nd St *TF:* 800-755-4000	New York	NY	10019	212-307-4100	
New Amsterdam Theatre 214 W 42nd St *TF:* 800-755-4000	New York	NY	10036	212-307-4100	
New Museum of Contemporary Art 583 Broadway *Web:* www.newmuseum.org/ ■ *E-mail:* newmu@newmuseum.org	New York	NY	10012	212-219-1355	431-5328
New York Aquarium Boardwalk & W 8th St Coney Island *Web:* www.wcs.org/zoos/aquarium	Brooklyn	NY	11224	718-265-3474	265-2660
New York Botanical Garden 200th St & Kazimiroff Blvd. *Web:* www.nybg.org	Bronx	NY	10458	718-817-8700	220-6504
New York Chamber Ensemble 475 Riverside Dr Rm 621	New York	NY	10115	212-870-2439	
New York Chamber Symphony 130 W 56th St Suite 703	New York	NY	10019	212-262-6927	246-3204
New York City Ballet 20 Lincoln Ctr Plaza New York State Theatre 4th Fl *TF:* 800-580-8730 ■ *Web:* www.nycballet.com	New York	NY	10023	212-870-5656	870-4244
New York City Fire Museum 278 Spring St	New York	NY	10013	212-691-1303	924-0430
New York City Opera 20 Lincoln Ctr New York State Theater *Web:* www.nycopera.com	New York	NY	10023	212-870-5600	724-1120
New York Hall of Science 47-01 111th St Flushing Meadows *Web:* www.nyhallsci.org	Corona Park	NY	11368	718-699-0005	699-1341
New York Historical Society 2 W 77th St *Web:* www.nyhistory.org	New York	NY	10024	212-873-3400	874-8706
New York Philharmonic 10 Lincoln Ctr Plaza Avery Fisher Hall **Fax:* Mktg ■ *Web:* www.nyphilharmon.org ■ *E-mail:* nyphil@pegasusnet.com	New York	NY	10023	212-875-5000	875-5717*
New York Pops Orchestra 881 7th Ave Suite 903 *E-mail:* nypops@aol.com	New York	NY	10019	212-765-7677	315-3199
New York Public Library for the Performing Arts 521 W 43rd St. *Web:* www.nypl.org/research/lpa/lpa.html	New York	NY	10036	212-870-1650	870-1794
New York Skyride 350 5th Ave Suite 612 *Web:* www.skyride.com	New York	NY	10118	212-564-2224	564-0652
New York State Theater 63rd St & Columbus Ave	New York	NY	10023	212-870-5570	870-5693
New York Stock Exchange Visitors Center 20 Broad St 3rd Fl	New York	NY	10005	212-656-5162	656-2010
New York Transit Museum Boerum Pl & Schermerhorn St Subway Stn *Web:* www.fieldtrip.com/ny/83303060.htm	Brooklyn	NY	11201	718-243-8601	522-2339
North Wind Undersea Museum 610 City Island Ave	Bronx	NY	10464	718-885-0701	885-1008
Opera Orchestra of New York 239 W 72nd St Suite 2R *Web:* www.oony.org ■ *E-mail:* oony@tiac.net	New York	NY	10023	212-799-1982	721-9170
Orchestra of Saint Luke's 330 W 42nd St 9th Fl *Web:* www.stlukes.cc	New York	NY	10036	212-594-6100	594-3291
Orpheus Chamber Orchestra 490 Riverside Dr *TF:* 800-677-4387	New York	NY	10027	212-896-1700	896-1717
Palace Theatre 1564 Broadway *TF:* 800-755-4000	New York	NY	10036	212-307-4100	
Papp Joseph Public Theater 425 Lafayette St *Web:* www.publictheater.org	New York	NY	10003	212-539-8500	539-8505
Pelham Bay Park Bruckner Blvd & Middletown & Shore Rds.	Bronx	NY	10464	718-430-1890	
Plymouth Theatre 236 W 45th St *TF:* 800-432-7250	New York	NY	10036	212-239-6200	
Poe Edgar Allan Cottage E Kingsbridge Rd Grand Concourse	Bronx	NY	10467	718-881-8900	
Police Academy Museum 25 Broadway 2nd FL *Web:* www.nycpolicemuseum.org	New York	NY	10004	212-301-4440	
Prospect Park Wildlife Center 450 Flatbush Ave *Web:* www.wcs.org/zoos/wildlifecenters/prospectpark	Brooklyn	NY	11225	718-399-7339	399-7337
Queens Botanical Garden 43-50 Main St.	Flushing	NY	11355	718-886-3800	463-0263
Queens County Farm Museum 7350 Little Neck Pkwy Floral Pk *Web:* www.queensfarm.org ■ *E-mail:* queensfarm@citysoftinc.com	Queens	NY	11004	718-347-3276	347-3243
Queens Museum of Art Flushing Meadows Corona Pk. *Web:* www.queensmuse.org	Flushing	NY	11368	718-592-9700	592-5778
Queens Wildlife Center 111th St & 53rd Ave *Web:* www.wcs.org/zoos/wildlifecenters/queens	Flushing Meadows	NY	11368	718-271-7761	
Radio City Music Hall 1260 Ave of the Americas *Web:* www.radiocity.com	New York	NY	10020	212-632-4000	
Richard Rodgers Theatre 226 W 46th St. *TF:* 800-755-4000	New York	NY	10036	212-307-4100	
Riverside Church 121st St & Riverside Dr	New York	NY	10027	212-870-6700	870-6800
Riverside Park 16 W 61st St	New York	NY	10023	212-408-0264	
Rockefeller Center 1230 Ave of the Americas	New York	NY	10020	212-332-6500	
Roundabout Theatre Co 231 W 39th St Suite 1200 *Web:* www.roundabouttheatre.org	New York	NY	10018	212-869-8400	
Royale Theatre 242 W 45th St. *TF:* 800-432-7250	New York	NY	10036	212-239-6200	
Rye Playland Park Playland Pkwy	Rye	NY	10580	914-925-2701	925-2757
Saint James Theatre 246 W 44th St. *TF:* 800-432-7250	New York	NY	10036	212-239-6200	
Saint Patrick's Cathedral 14 E 51st St	New York	NY	10022	212-753-2261	
Saint Paul's Church National Historic Site 897 S Columbus Ave *Web:* www.nps.gov/sapa/	Mount Vernon	NY	10550	914-667-4116	667-3024
Santana Carlota Spanish Dance Co 154 Christopher St Suite 3D.	New York	NY	10014	212-229-9754	229-1085
Shubert Theatre 225 W 44th St *TF:* 800-432-7250	New York	NY	10036	212-239-6200	
Skyscraper Museum 16 Wall St	New York	NY	10005	212-968-1961	766-1324
Smith Abigail Adams Museum & Gardens 421 E 61st St. *Web:* www.fieldtrip.com/ny/28386878.htm	New York	NY	10021	212-838-6878	838-7390
Snug Harbor Cultural Center 1000 Richmond Terr *Web:* community.silive.com/cc/snugharbor	Staten Island	NY	10301	718-448-2500	442-8534
Solomon R Guggenheim Museum 1071 5th Ave *Web:* www.guggenheim.org	New York	NY	10128	212-423-3500	423-3640
Sony IMAX Theatre 1998 Broadway *Web:* www.theatres.sre.sony.com/	New York	NY	10023	212-336-5020	336-5055
Sony Wonder Technology Lab 550 Madison Ave Sony Plaza *Web:* wondertechlab.sony.com	New York	NY	10022	212-833-8100	833-4445
South Street Seaport Market Place 19 Fulton St 2nd Fl *Web:* www.southstseaport.org/	New York	NY	10038	212-732-8257	964-8056
Stardust Theatre 1650 Broadway *TF:* 800-432-7250	New York	NY	10019	212-239-6200	
Staten Island Botanical Garden 1000 Richmond Terr *Web:* www.sibg.org ■ *E-mail:* sibg@erols.com	Staten Island	NY	10301	718-273-8200	442-3645
Staten Island Institute of Arts & Sciences 75 Stuyvesant Pl.	Staten Island	NY	10301	718-727-1135	273-5683
Staten Island Zoo 614 Broadway Staten Island Zoo	Staten Island	NY	10310	718-442-3101	981-8711
Statue of Liberty National Monument & Ellis Island Liberty Island *Web:* www.nps.gov/stli/	New York	NY	10004	212-363-3200	363-8347
Studio Museum in Harlem 144 W 125th St. *Web:* www.studiomuseuminharlem.org	New York	NY	10027	212-864-4500	666-5753

New York — Attractions (Cont'd)

				Phone	*Fax*
Symphony for United Nations 170 West End Ave Suite 27-L	New York	NY	10023	631-723-2251	
Theodore Roosevelt Birthplace National Historic Site 28 E 20th St *Web:* www.nps.gov/thrb/	New York	NY	10003	212-260-1616	677-3587
Top of the World Observation Deck 2 World Trade Ctr Suite 1520	New York	NY	10048	212-323-2340	323-2352
Ukrainian Museum 203 2nd Ave *Web:* brama.com/ukrainian_museum/ ■ *E-mail:* ukrmus@aol.com	New York	NY	10003	212-228-0110	228-1947
United Nations 1st Ave & 42nd St *Web:* www.un.org ■ *E-mail:* ecu@un.org	New York	NY	10017	212-963-1234	371-4360
Van Cortlandt Park Broadway & W 242nd St	Bronx	NY	10463	718-430-1890	
Via Max 37 W 65th St	New York	NY	10023	212-874-6700	877-1146
Virginia Theatre 245 W 52nd St *TF:* 800-432-7250	New York	NY	10019	212-239-6200	
Vivian Beaumont Theatre 150 W 65th St *TF:* 800-432-7250	New York	NY	10023	212-239-6200	
Walter Kerr Theatre 219 W 48th St *TF:* 800-432-7250	New York	NY	10036	212-239-6200	
Wave Hill Garden W 249th St & Independence Ave	Bronx	NY	10471	718-549-3200	
Whitney Museum of American Art 945 Madison Ave *Fax: Library ■ *Web:* www.echonyc.com/~whitney	New York	NY	10021	212-570-3600	570-7729*
Winter Garden Theatre 1634 Broadway *TF:* 800-432-7250	New York	NY	10019	212-239-6200	
World Trade Center 2 World Trade Ctr	New York	NY	10048	212-435-4170	
Yeshiva University Museum 2520 Amsterdam Ave *Web:* www.yu.edu/museum	New York	NY	10033	212-960-5390	960-5406

SPORTS TEAMS & FACILITIES

				Phone	*Fax*
Aqueduct Race Track Rockaway Blvd & 108th St Ozone Pk *Fax: Hum Res ■ *Web:* www.nyracing.com/aqueduct/	Ozone Park	NY	11417	718-641-4700	835-5246*
Belmont Park Race Track 2150 Hempstead Tpke *Web:* www.nyracing.com/belmont/	Elmont	NY	11003	516-488-6000	488-6016
Brooklyn Knights (soccer) 125-08 Flatlands Ave Jefferson Field *Web:* www.brooklynknights.com ■ *E-mail:* knightsocr@aol.com	Brooklyn	NY	11208	718-621-1900	621-1332
Giants Stadium 50 State Hwy 120 *Fax: Hum Res	East Rutherford	NJ	07073	201-935-8500	935-7121*
Long Island Lady Riders (soccer) Evergreen AVe Michael J Tully Jr Stadium *Web:* ladyriders.com ■ *E-mail:* ridersmail@aol.com	New Hyde Park	NY	11753	516-735-2277	735-2288
Long Island Rough Riders (soccer) Charles Lindbergh Blvd Mitchel Athletic Complex *Web:* www.rough-riders.com ■ *E-mail:* info@rough-riders.com	Uniondale	NY	11553	631-756-4625	756-1654
Madison Square Garden 2 Pennsylvania Plaza *Web:* www.thegarden.com	New York	NY	10121	212-465-6000	465-6789
New Jersey Devils Continental Airlines Arena *TF Sales:* 800-653-3845 ■ *Web:* www.newjerseydevils.com	East Rutherford	NJ	07073	201-935-6050	935-2127
New Jersey Nets Continental Airlines Arena *Web:* www.nba.com/nets	East Rutherford	NJ	07073	201-935-3900	
New York CityHawks (football) 196 Trumball St 3rd Fl *Web:* www.ipsnews.com/cityhawks/home.html	Hartford	CT	06103	860-246-7825	240-7618
New York Freedom (soccer) Charles Lindbergh Blvd Mitchel Athletic Complex	Uniondale	NY	11553	631-756-4625	756-1654
New York Giants Giants Stadium *Web:* www.nfl.com/giants	East Rutherford	NJ	07073	201-935-8111	939-4134
New York Islanders Nassau Coliseum	Uniondale	NY	11553	516-794-9300	
New York Jets Giants Stadium *Web:* www.nfl.com/jets	East Rutherford	NJ	07073	201-935-8500	
New York Knicks 2 Penn Plaza Madison Square Garden 14th Fl *Web:* www.nba.com/knicks	New York	NY	10121	212-465-6000	465-6062
New York Liberty (basketball) 2 Penn Plaza 14th Fl *Web:* www.wnba.com/liberty	New York	NY	10121	212-465-6005	465-6250
New York Magic (soccer) 218th St & Broadway Columbia University Stadium	New York	NY	10034	212-447-0932	447-0932
New York Mets 123-01 Roosevelt Ave Shea Stadium *Web:* www.newyorkmets.com	Flushing	NY	11368	718-507-8499	507-6395
New York Rangers 2 Penn Plaza Madison Square Garden *Web:* www.newyorkrangers.com	New York	NY	10121	212-465-6741	465-6494
New York Yankees Yankee Stadium *Web:* www.yankees.com	Bronx	NY	10451	718-293-6000	293-4841
New York/New Jersey MetroStars (soccer) 1 Harmon Plaza 3rd Fl *Web:* www.metrostars.com ■ *E-mail:* kickstuff@aol.com	Secaucus	NJ	07094	201-583-7000	583-7055
Staten Island Vipers (soccer) 1 Campus Rd Wagner Stadium *Web:* www.sivipers.com ■ *E-mail:* sivipers@aol.com	Staten Island	NY	10305	718-447-9000	815-5814
Westchester Flames (soccer) 112 W Boston Post Rd	Mamaroneck	NY	10543	718-626-6767	267-0282
Yankee Stadium 161st St & River Ave *Web:* www.yankees.com	Bronx	NY	10451	718-293-4300	293-8431

— Events —

	Phone
4th of July Concert in Battery Park (July 4)	212-835-2789
5th Avenue Art & Antiques Show (mid-October)	212-249-4865
9th Avenue International Food Festival (mid-May)	212-581-7217
African Film Festival (mid-late April)	718-638-5000
American Crafts Festival (mid-June)	212-875-5000
Art Expo New York (early March & mid-September)	212-216-2000
Bell Atlantic Jazz Festival (early-mid-June)	212-219-3006
Belmont Stakes (early June)	718-641-4700
Big Apple Circus (late October-mid-January)	212-268-2500
Brooklyn Botanical Garden Center Flower Sale (early May)	718-622-4433
Bryant Park Summer Film Festival (mid-June-August)	212-512-5700
Celebrate Brooklyn Festival (July-late August)	718-855-7882
Chinese New Year Celebrations (early-mid-February)	212-431-9740
Chrysanthemum & Bonsai Festival (mid-October)	718-817-8700
Crafts on Columbus (late April-early May)	212-866-2239
Earth Day New York (April 22)	212-922-0048
Empire State Building Holiday Lights (December-early January)	212-736-3100
First Night New York (December 31)	212-818-1777
Gen Art Film Festival (late April-early May)	212-290-0312
Great July 4th Festival (July 4)	212-809-4900
Greenwich Village Halloween Parade (late October)	914-758-5519
JVC Jazz Festival (mid-late June)	212-501-1390
Lincoln Center Family Art Show (mid-December-early January)	212-875-5151
Lincoln Center Festival (early-late July)	212-875-5000
Macy's Fireworks Celebration (July 4)	212-695-4400
Macy's Thanksgiving Day Parade (late November)	212-494-5432
Mostly Mozart Festival (late July-mid-August)	212-875-5030
National Black Fine Art Show (late January)	212-777-5218
New Year's Eve Celebration & Ball Drop in Times Square (December 31)	212-768-1560
New York Film Festival (late September-mid-October)	212-875-5610
New York Lesbian & Gay Film Festival (early-mid-June)	212-254-7228
New York Marathon (early November)	212-860-4455
New York National Boat Show (early-mid-January)	212-984-7070
New York Restaurant & Foodservice Show (late February)	212-216-2000
New York Underground Film Festival (mid-March)	212-925-3440
Outsider Art Fair (late January)	212-777-5218
Passports to Off Broadway Theatres (February-April)	212-768-1818
Paul Winter's Winter Solstice Celebration (mid-December)	212-662-2133
Queens Day Festival (mid-June)	718-886-5069
Radio City Christmas Spectacular (November-January)	212-247-4777
Rockefeller Center Christmas Tree Lighting (early December)	212-332-6500
Saint Patrick's Day Parade (mid-March)	212-484-1222
Seafest (September-June)	212-245-0072
Shakespeare in the Park (late June-late August)	212-539-8500
SummerStage (mid-June-early August)	212-360-2777
US Open Tennis Championships (late August-mid-September)	718-760-6200
Washington Square Music Festival (July)	212-431-1088
Welcome Back to Brooklyn Festival (mid-June)	718-855-7882
Winter Wildlife Holiday Lights (late November-early January)	718-367-1010

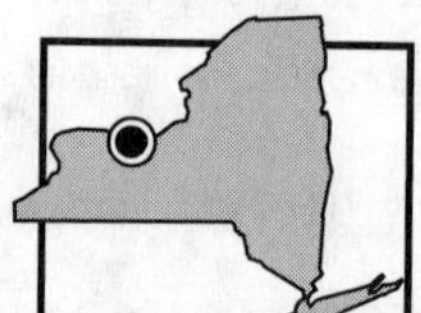

Rochester

Rochester was once home to Susan B. Anthony and to George Eastman. The headquarters of Eastman Kodak Company is now located in the city, and Eastman's former home houses the International Museum of Photography, the world's largest museum of photographic art and technology. South of Rochester is Consensus Lake, part of the Finger

Rochester (Cont'd)

Lakes region. The area extends to Otisco Lake, near Syracuse, and has waterfalls and gorges, as well as vineyards and various local wineries.

Population	216,887	**Longitude**	77-61-58 W
Area (Land)	35.8 sq mi	**County**	Monroe
Area (Water)	1.3 sq mi	**Time Zone**	EST
Elevation	515 ft	**Area Code/s**	716
Latitude	43-15-47 N		

— Average Temperatures and Precipitation —

TEMPERATURES

	Jan	Feb	Mar	Apr	May	Jun	Jul	Aug	Sep	Oct	Nov	Dec
High	31	33	43	56	68	76	81	78	72	61	48	36
Low	16	17	26	36	46	54	60	58	52	42	33	22

PRECIPITATION

	Jan	Feb	Mar	Apr	May	Jun	Jul	Aug	Sep	Oct	Nov	Dec
Inches	2.1	2.1	2.3	2.6	2.7	3.0	2.7	3.4	3.0	2.4	2.9	2.7

— Important Phone Numbers —

	Phone		*Phone*
AAA	716-461-4660	**HotelDocs**	800-468 3537
Emergency	911	**Poison Control Center**	716-275-3232
Events Line	716-546-6810	**Time/Temp**	716-974-1616
Fair Business Council	716-546-6776	**Weather**	716-334-0013

— Information Sources —

				Phone	*Fax*
Better Business Bureau Serving Western New York & the Capital District 741 Delaware Ave	Buffalo	NY	14209	716-881-5222	883-5349
Web: www.buffalo.bbb.org					
Greater Rochester Visitors Assn 126 Andrews St	Rochester	NY	14604	716-546-3070	232-4822
TF: 800-677-7282 ■ *Web:* www.visitrochester.com ■ *E-mail:* grva@visitrochester.com					
International Business Council of Rochester 55 Saint Paul St	Rochester	NY	14604	716-454-2220	263-3679
Web: www.rnychamber.com					
Monroe County 39 W Main St Rm 101	Rochester	NY	14614	716-428-5151	428-5447
Web: www.co.monroe.ny.us ■ *E-mail:* mcplan@servtech.com					
Rochester City Hall 30 Church St	Rochester	NY	14614	716-428-7000	428-6347
Web: www.ci.rochester.ny.us/					
Rochester Economic Development Dept 30 Church St Rm 5A	Rochester	NY	14614	716-428-6808	428-6042
Rochester Mayor 30 Church St Rm 307A	Rochester	NY	14614	716-428-7045	428-6059
Rochester Public Library 115 South Ave	Rochester	NY	14604	716-428-8100	428-8353
Rochester Riverside Convention Center 123 E Main St	Rochester	NY	14604	716-232-7200	232-1510

On-Line Resources

4Rochester.com	www.4rochester.com
@Rochester WWW Guide to Rochester	www.roch.com/sites
About.com Guide to Rochester	rochester.about.com/local/midlanticus/rochester
Anthill City Guide Rochester	www.anthill.com/city.asp?city=rochester
Big Guide	www.thebigguide.com/
City Knowledge Rochester	www.cityknowledge.com/ny_rochester.htm
DigitalCity Rochester	home.digitalcity.com/rochester
FreeTime Magazine	www.freetimemag.com
Freetime Magazine Online	www.freetimemag.com
Gay Rochester Online	www.gayrochester.com/
Genesee Gateway	www.ggw.org/section
Guide to Rochester New York	www.nuwebny.com/rochest.htm
HotelGuide Rochester	hotelguide.net/rochester/
Rochester City Net	www.excite.com/travel/countries/united_states/new_york/rochester
Simply Rochester	www.simplyrochester.com

— Transportation Services —

AIRPORTS

	Phone
■ **Greater Rochester International Airport (ROC)** 4 miles SW of downtown (approx 10 minutes)	716-464-6000

Airport Transportation

	Phone
Regional Transit Service $1.25 fare to downtown	716-288-1700
Taxi $15 fare to downtown	716-232-3232

Commercial Airlines

	Phone		*Phone*
AirTran	800-247-8726	**Northwest**	800-225-2525
American	800-433-7300	**United**	800-241-6522
Continental	800-525-0280	**US Airways**	800-428-4322
Delta	800-221-1212		

Charter Airlines

	Phone		*Phone*
Aerodynamics Inc	248-666-3500	**Tiffany Executive Charter Service**	800-724-7504
Seneca Flight Operations	315-536-4471		

CAR RENTALS

	Phone		*Phone*
Alamo	800-445-5664	**Hertz**	716-328-3700
Avis	716-328-6600	**National**	716-235-5400
Budget	716-436-9310	**Thrifty**	716-235-6200
Dollar	716-235-0772		

LIMO/TAXI

	Phone		*Phone*
Associate Taxi	716-232-3232	**Marketplace Cab Co**	716-647-9970
Cardinal Cab	716-235-7555	**Tiffany Limousine**	716-234-8433

MASS TRANSIT

	Phone
EZ Rider Entertainment Shuttle Free	716-426-3520
Regional Transit Service (RTS) $1.25 Base fare	716-288-1700

RAIL/BUS

				Phone
Greyhound/Trailways Bus Station 187 Midtown Plaza	Rochester	NY	14604	716-232-5121
TF: 800-231-2222				

— Accommodations —

HOTEL RESERVATION SERVICES

	Phone	*Fax*
Adventures Bed & Breakfast Reservation Service	716-768-2699	768-9386
TF: 800-724-1932 ■ *Web:* www.3z.com/bandbres ■ *E-mail:* rj@bandbres.com		

HOTELS, MOTELS, RESORTS

				Phone	*Fax*
428 Mount Vernon 428 Mt Vernon Ave	Rochester	NY	14620	716-271-0792	271-0946
TF: 800-836-3159					
Airport Marriott Hotel 1890 Ridge Rd W	Greece	NY	14615	716-225-6880	225-8167
TF: 800 228-9290					
Avalon Corporate Short Term Apartments Empire Blvd	Rochester	NY	14580	716-671-4421	671-9771
TF: 800-934-9763					
Best Western Diplomat Hotel 1956 Lyll Ave	Rochester	NY	14606	716-254-1000	254-1510
Brookwood Inn 800 Pittsford-Victor Rd	Pittsford	NY	14534	716-248-9000	248-8569
TF: 800-426-9995					
Comfort Inn Central 395 Buell Rd	Rochester	NY	14624	716-436-4400	436-6496
TF: 800-424-6423					
Comfort Inn West 1501 Ridge Rd W	Rochester	NY	14615	716-621-5700	621-8446
TF: 800-228-5150					
Courtyard by Marriott 33 Corporate Woods	Rochester	NY	14623	716-292-1000	292-0905
TF: 800-321-2211 ■ *Web:* courtyard.com/ROCCH					

Rochester — Hotels, Motels, Resorts (Cont'd)

Name / Address	City	State	ZIP	Phone	Fax
Crowne Plaza Rochester Hotel 70 State St	Rochester	NY	14614	716-546-3450	546-8712
TF: 800-243-7760					
Days Inn Downtown 384 East Ave	Rochester	NY	14607	716-325-5010	454-3158
TF: 800-329-7466					
Econo Lodge 940 Jefferson Rd	Henrietta	NY	14623	716-427-2700	427-8504
TF: 800-553-2666					
Extended StayAmerica 600 Center Place Dr	Rochester	NY	14615	716-663-5558	663-5558
TF: 800-398-7829					
Extended StayAmerica 700 Commons Way	Rochester	NY	14623	716-427-7580	427-8849
TF: 800-398-7829					
Fairfield Inn by Marriott Airport 1200 Brooks Ave	Rochester	NY	14624	716-529-5000	529-5011
TF: 800-228-2800 ■ *Web:* fairfieldinn.com/ROCFA					
Fairfield Inn by Marriott South 4695 W Henrietta Rd	Henrietta	NY	14467	716-334-3350	334-2295
TF: 800-228-2800 ■ *Web:* fairfieldinn.com/ROCFI					
Four Points by Sheraton 120 Main St E	Rochester	NY	14604	716-546-6400	546-3908
TF: 888-596-6400					
Geneva on the Lake 1001 Lochland Rd	Geneva	NY	14456	315-789-7190	789-0322
TF: 800-343-6382 ■ *Web:* www.genevaonthelake.com ■ *E-mail:* gotlreso@epix.net					
Hampton Inn 717 E Henrietta Rd	Rochester	NY	14623	716-272-7800	272-1211
TF: 800-426-7866					
Hampton Inn North 500 Center Place Dr	Rochester	NY	14615	716-663-6070	663-9158
TF: 800-426-7866					
Holiday Inn Airport 911 Brooks Ave	Rochester	NY	14624	716-328-6000	328-1012
TF: 800-465-4329 ■ *Web:* www.basshotels.com/holiday-inn/?_franchisee=ROCAP ■ *E-mail:* rochsale@frontiernet.net					
Holiday Inn Rochester South 1111 Jefferson Rd	Rochester	NY	14623	716-475-1510	427-8673
TF: 800-465-4329 ■ *Web:* www.holiday-inn.com/hotels/rochr ■ *E-mail:* holidome@frontiernet.net					
Hyatt Regency 125 E Main St	Rochester	NY	14604	716-546-1234	546-6777
TF: 800-233-1234 ■ *Web:* www.hyatt.com/usa/rochester/hotels/hotel_roche.html					
Inn on the Lake 770 S Main St	Canandaigua	NY	14424	716-394-7800	394-5003
TF: 800-228-2801					
Lodge at Woodcliff 199 Woodcliff Dr	Fairport	NY	14450	716-381-4000	381-2673
TF: 800-365-3065					
Marketplace Inn 800 Jefferson Rd	Rochester	NY	14623	716-475-9190	424-2138
TF: 800-888-8102					
Marriott Thruway Hotel 5257 W Henrietta Rd	Henrietta	NY	14586	716-359-1800	359-1349
TF: 800-228-9290 ■ *Web:* marriotthotels.com/ROCTW					
Microtel 905 Lehigh Station Rd	Henrietta	NY	14467	716-334-3400	334-5042
TF: 800-999-2005					
Oliver Loud's Inn 1474 Marsh Rd	Pittsford	NY	14534	716-248-5200	248-9970
Radisson Inn 175 Jefferson Rd	Rochester	NY	14623	716-475-1910	475-9633
TF: 800-333-3333					
Red Roof Inn 4820 W Henrietta Rd	Henrietta	NY	14467	716-359-1100	359-1121
TF: 800-843-7663					
Residence Inn by Marriott 1300 Jefferson Rd	Rochester	NY	14623	716-272-8850	272-7822
TF: 800-331-3131 ■ *Web:* www.residenceinn.com/ROCNY					
Strathallan Hotel 550 East Ave	Rochester	NY	14607	716-461-5010	461-3387
TF: 800-678-7284 ■ *Web:* www.strathallan.com/					
Wellesley Inn North 1635 W Ridge Rd	Rochester	NY	14615	716-621-2060	621-7102
TF: 800-444-8888					

— Restaurants —

Name / Address	City	State	ZIP	Phone
Acropolis Restaurant (American) 1233 Ridgeway Ave	Rochester	NY	14615	716-254-3627
Bangkok Restaurant (Thai) 155 State St	Rochester	NY	14614	716-325-3517
Barrister's Pub (American) 36 W Main St	Rochester	NY	14614	716-232-2240
Basha (Mediterranean) 798 S Clinton Ave	Rochester	NY	14620	716-256-1370
Beefsteak Mining Co (Steak) 716 Ridge Rd E	Rochester	NY	14621	716-544-8410
Big Apple Cafe (Continental) 682 Park Ave	Rochester	NY	14607	716-271-1039
Brasserie (Continental) 387 E Main St	Rochester	NY	14604	716-232-3350
Web: thebrasserie.com/ ■ *E-mail:* info@thebrasserie.com				
Cartwright Inn (Steak/Seafood) 5691 W Henrietta Rd	West Henrietta	NY	14586	716-334-4444
Cathay Pagoda (Chinese) 488 E Main St	Rochester	NY	14604	716-325-5799
Charlie Brown's (American) 495 N Goodman St	Rochester	NY	14609	716-325-3606
Charlie's Frog Pond (American) 652 Park Ave	Rochester	NY	14607	716-271-1970
City Grill of Rochester (American) 75 Marshall St	Rochester	NY	14607	716-232-1920
Dac Hoa (Thai/Vietnamese) 230 Monroe Ave	Rochester	NY	14607	716-232-6038
Distillery The (American) 1142 Mt Hope Ave	Rochester	NY	14620	716-271-4105
Edwards (Continental) 13 S Fitzhugh St	Rochester	NY	14614	716-423-0140
Web: www.edwardsrestaurant.com/				
EJ's (American) 1890 W Ridge Rd	Greece	NY	14615	716-225-6880
Empire Brewing Co (New American) 300 State St	Rochester	NY	14614	716-454-2337
Web: www.empirebrewco.com				
Gerrys' Rochester Club (Seafood) 120 East Ave	Rochester	NY	14604	716-423-1948
Horizons (American) 199 Woodcliff Dr	Fairport	NY	14450	716-248-4825
India House (Indian) 998 S Clinton Ave	Rochester	NY	14620	716-461-0880
Jeremiah's Tavern (American) 1104 Monroe Ave	Rochester	NY	14620	716-461-1313
Jines Restaurant (American) 658 Park Ave	Rochester	NY	14607	716-461-1280
King & I (Thai) 1475 E Henrietta Rd	Rochester	NY	14623	716-427-8090
Lamplighter Restaurant (Italian) 831 Fetzner Rd	Rochester	NY	14626	716-225-2500
Mamasan (Thai/Vietnamese) 309 University Ave	Rochester	NY	14607	716-262-4580
Mario's Via Abruzzi (Italian) 2740 Monroe Ave	Rochester	NY	14618	716-271-1111
McGillicuty's (American) 17 E Main St	Rochester	NY	14614	716-232-4037
Newport House Restaurant (American) 500 Newport Rd	Rochester	NY	14622	716-467-8480
Old Toad (English) 277 Alexander St	Rochester	NY	14607	716-232-2626
Olive Tree (Greek) 165 Monroe Ave	Rochester	NY	14607	716-454-3510
Palladio (Italian) 125 E Main St	Rochester	NY	14604	716-423-6767
Park 54 (New American) 54 Park Ave	Rochester	NY	14607	716-442-8890
Petals (New American) 5257 W Henrietta Rd	Henrietta	NY	14586	716-359-1800
Phillips European Restaurant (European) 26 Corporate Woods	Rochester	NY	14623	716-272-9910
Portobello Ristorante (Italian) 2171 W Henrietta Rd	Rochester	NY	14623	716-427-0110
Raj Mahal (Indian) 324 Monroe Ave	Rochester	NY	14607	716-546-2315
Remington's (Continental) 425 Merchants Rd	Rochester	NY	14609	716-482-4434
Renaissance Grill (Italian) 2500 East Ave	Rochester	NY	14623	716-383-8170
Richardson's Canal House (New American) 1474 Marsh Rd	Pittsford	NY	14534	716-248-5000
Rio The (Steak/Seafood) 282 Alexander St	Rochester	NY	14607	716-473-2806
Web: www.therio.com/				
Riverview Cafe (American) 70 State St	Rochester	NY	14614	716-546-3450
Rohrbach Brewing Co (German) 315 Gregory St	Rochester	NY	14620	716-244-5680
Rooney's (Continental) 90 Henrietta St	Rochester	NY	14620	716-442-0444
Scotch 'N Sirloin (Steak/Seafood) 3450 Winton Pl	Rochester	NY	14607	716-427-0808
Shannon Pub (Irish) 800 Jefferson Rd	Rochester	NY	14623	716-272-1550
Spring House (American) 3001 Monroe Ave	Rochester	NY	14618	716-586-2300
State Street Sports Bar & Grill (American) 70 State St	Rochester	NY	14614	716-546-3450
Thai Taste (Thai) 1675 Mt Hope Ave	Rochester	NY	14620	716-461-4154
Triphammer Grill (American) 60 Browns Race	Rochester	NY	14614	716-262-2700
Vesuvio (Italian) 58 University Ave	Rochester	NY	14605	716-454-6620
Yangtze (Chinese) 79 State St	Rochester	NY	14614	716-546-3949

— Goods and Services —

SHOPPING

Name / Address	City	State	ZIP	Phone	Fax
Eastview Mall 672 E View Mall	Victor	NY	14564	716-223-3693	425-1809
Irondequoit Mall 285 Irondequoit Mall Dr	Rochester	NY	14622	716-266-4000	467-0189
Mall at Greece Ridge Center 271 Greece Ridge Ctr Dr	Rochester	NY	14626	716-225-1140	227-2525
Marketplace Mall 1 Miracle Mile Dr	Rochester	NY	14623	716-424-6220	427-2745
Midtown Plaza 211 Midtown Plaza	Rochester	NY	14604	716-530-2000	325-2576
Northfield Common 50 State St	Pittsford	NY	14534	716-381-5534	
Park Avenue Shopping District Park Ave-betw Alexander St & Culver Rd	Rochester	NY	14607	716-234-1909	
Rochester Public Market 280 N Union St	Rochester	NY	14609	716-428-6907	
Village Gate Square 274 N Goodman St	Rochester	NY	14607	716-442-9168	
Village of Pittsford 21 N Main St	Pittsford	NY	14534	716-586-4332	586-4597

BANKS

Name / Address	City	State	ZIP	Phone	Fax
Charter One Bank 40 Franklin St	Rochester	NY	14604	716-258-3032	232-2029
TF: 800-458-1190					
Chase Manhattan Bank 2900 Dewey Ave	Rochester	NY	14616	716-935-9935	
Citibank 300 Hylan Dr	Rochester	NY	14623	716-272-0620	272-0418
First National Bank of Rochester 35 State St	Rochester	NY	14614	716-546-3300	258-1655
Fleet National Bank 1 East Ave	Rochester	NY	14638	716-546-9100	546-9207
TF Cust Svc: 800-841-4000*					
Key Bank NA 3420 Monroe Ave	Rochester	NY	14618	716-381-7956	381-4626
TF Cust Svc: 800-539-2968*					
Lyndon Guaranty Bank 3670 Mt Read Blvd	Rochester	NY	14616	716-663-8930	663-4089
M & T Bank 255 East Ave	Rochester	NY	14604	716-258-8400	258-8364
TF Cust Svc: 800-724-2440*					
Upstate Bank 400 Andrews St Suite 210	Rochester	NY	14604	716-454-3450	454-3624

Rochester (Cont'd)

BUSINESS SERVICES

	Phone
Adecco Employment Personnel Services	716-227-9770
Federal Express	800-238-5355
H & H Fast Delivery	716-424-4530
Jet-X Co	716-342-9850
Julmar Secretarial Service	716-227-8930
Kelly Services	716-461-1360
Kinko's	716-240-2679
Post Office	716-272-5839
UPS	800-742-5877

— Media —

PUBLICATIONS

				Phone	Fax
Daily Record‡ PO Box 6	Rochester	NY	14601	716-232-6920	232-2740
Democrat & Chronicle‡ 55 Exchange Blvd	Rochester	NY	14614	716-232-7100	258-2237
TF: 800-473-5274 ■ *Web:* www.rochesterdandc.com					
Rochester Business Journal 55 Saint Paul St	Rochester	NY	14604	716-546-8303	546-3398
Web: www.rbj.net					

‡Daily newspapers

TELEVISION

				Phone	Fax
WHEC-TV Ch 10 (NBC) 191 East Ave	Rochester	NY	14604	716-546-5670	546-5688
Web: www.10nbc.com					
WOKR-TV Ch 13 (ABC) PO Box 20555	Rochester	NY	14602	716-334-8700	334-8719
WROC-TV Ch 8 (CBS) 201 Humboldt St	Rochester	NY	14610	716-288-8400	288-1505
Web: www.wroctv.com ■ *E-mail:* wroc@frontiernet.net					
WUHF-TV Ch 31 (Fox) 360 East Ave	Rochester	NY	14604	716-232-3700	546-4774
Web: www.foxnewsfirst.com					
WXXI-TV Ch 21 (PBS) PO Box 21	Rochester	NY	14601	716-325-7500	258-0338
Web: www.wxxi.org ■ *E-mail:* responses@wxxi.pbs.org					

RADIO

				Phone	Fax
WBBF-FM 98.9 MHz (Oldies) 500 B Forman Bldg Suite 500	Rochester	NY	14604	716-423-2900	423-2947
WBEE-FM 92.5 MHz (Ctry) 500 B Forman Bldg Suite 500	Rochester	NY	14604	716-423-2900	423-2947
Web: www.wbee.com					
WCMF-FM 96.5 MHz (Rock) 1700 Marine Midland Plaza	Rochester	NY	14604	716-399-5700	399-5750
Web: www.96wcmf.com					
WDKX-FM 103.9 MHz (Urban) 683 E Main St	Rochester	NY	14605	716-262-2050	262-2626
Web: www.wdkx.com ■ *E-mail:* wdkx@wdkx.com					
WEZO-AM 950 kHz (Nost) 500 B Forman Bldg Suite 500	Rochester	NY	14604	716-423-2900	423-2947
WHAM-AM 1180 kHz (N/T) 207 Midtown Plaza	Rochester	NY	14604	716-454-4884	454-5081
Web: www.wham1180.com ■ *E-mail:* wham@eznet.net					
WHTK-AM 1280 kHz (Sports) 207 Midtown Plaza	Rochester	NY	14604	716-454-3942	454-5081
WJZR-FM 105.9 MHz (Urban) 1237 E Main St	Rochester	NY	14609	716-288-5020	288-5165
WMAX-FM 107.3 MHz (AAA) 207 Midtown Plaza	Rochester	NY	14604	716-232-8870	262-2334
WNVE-FM 95.1 MHz (Alt) 207 Midtown Plaza	Rochester	NY	14604	716-246-0440	454-5081
WPXY-FM 97.9 MHz (CHR) 1700 HSBC Plaza	Rochester	NY	14604	716-262-2720	399-5750
WQRV-FM 93.3 MHz (CR) 500 B Forman Bldg Midtown Plaza	Rochester	NY	14604	716-423-2900	423-2947
WRMM-FM 101.3 MHz (AC) 1700 Marine Midland Plaza Suite 300	Rochester	NY	14604	716-399-5700	399-5750
TF: 800-840-1013 ■ *Web:* www.warm1013.com ■ *E-mail:* marketing@warm1013.com					
WRUR-FM 88.5 MHz (Misc) PO Box 277356	Rochester	NY	14627	716-275-6400	
WVOR-FM 100.5 MHz (AC) 207 Midtown Plaza	Rochester	NY	14604	716-454-3942	454-5081
E-mail: wvorradio@aol.com					
WXXI-AM 1370 kHz (NPR) PO Box 21	Rochester	NY	14601	716-325-7500	258-0339
Web: www.wxxi.org/ ■ *E-mail:* response@wxxi.pbs.org					
WXXI-FM 91.5 MHz (NPR) PO Box 21	Rochester	NY	14601	716-258-0340	258-0339
Web: www.wxxi.org ■ *E-mail:* responses@wxxi.pbs.org					
WYSY-FM 106.7 MHz (Urban) 207 Midtown Plaza	Rochester	NY	14604	716-454-3942	454-5081
E-mail: wmaxfm@aol.com					
WZNE-FM 94.1 MHz (NAC) 1700 Marine Midland Plaza Suite 300	Rochester	NY	14604	716-399-5700	399-5750
Web: www.thezone941.com ■ *E-mail:* thezone@lsweb.com					

— Colleges/Universities —

				Phone	Fax
Bryant & Stratton Career College Henrietta 1225 Jefferson Rd	Rochester	NY	14623	716-292-5627	292-6015
Bryant & Stratton Career College Rochester 150 Bellwood Dr	Rochester	NY	14606	716-720-0660	720-9226
Nazareth College of Rochester 4245 East Ave	Rochester	NY	14618	716-586-2525	389-2826
TF Admissions: 800-462-3944 ■ *Web:* www.naz.edu					
Roberts Wesleyan College 2301 Westside Dr	Rochester	NY	14624	716-594-6000	594-6371
TF Admissions: 800-777-4792 ■ *Web:* www.roberts.edu ■ *E-mail:* admissions@roberts.edu					
Rochester Institute of Technology 1 Lomb Memorial Dr	Rochester	NY	14623	716-475-2411	475-7424
Web: www.rit.edu ■ *E-mail:* admissions@rit.edu					
Saint John Fisher College 3690 East Ave	Rochester	NY	14618	716-385-8000	385-8129
TF: 800-444-4640 ■ *Web:* www.sjfc.edu ■ *E-mail:* admissions@sjfc.edu					
State University of New York Brockport 350 New Campus Dr	Brockport	NY	14420	716-395-2211	395-5452
TF Admissions: 800-382-8447 ■ *Web:* www.brockport.edu					
State University of New York Geneseo 1 College Cir	Geneseo	NY	14454	716-245-5211	245-5550
Web: www.geneseo.edu					
State University of New York Monroe Community College 1000 E Henrietta Rd	Rochester	NY	14623	716-292-2000	427-2749
Web: www.monroecc.edu					
Talmudical Institution of Upstate New York 769 Park Ave	Rochester	NY	14607	716-473-2810	442-0417
University of Rochester	Rochester	NY	14627	716-275-2121	461-4595
Web: www.rochester.edu ■ *E-mail:* admit@macmail.cc.rochester.edu					

— Hospitals —

				Phone	Fax
Genesee Hospital 224 Alexander St	Rochester	NY	14607	716-263-6000	922-7620
Highland Hospital of Rochester 1000 South Ave	Rochester	NY	14620	716-473-2200	341-8221
Park Ridge Hospital 1555 Long Pond Rd	Rochester	NY	14626	716-723-7000	723-7187*
**Fax:* Admitting ■ *Web:* www.unityhealth.org					
Rochester General Hospital 1425 Portland Ave	Rochester	NY	14621	716-338-4000	339-5836*
**Fax:* Admitting ■ *Web:* www.viahealth.org/rgh					
Strong Memorial Hospital 601 Elmwood Ave University of Rochester Medical Ctr	Rochester	NY	14642	716-275-2100	244-8483*
**Fax:* Admitting ■ *Web:* www.urmc.rochester.edu/URMC					
Unity Health System Saint Mary's Hospital 89 Genesee St	Rochester	NY	14611	716-464-3000	464-0044
Web: www.unityhealth.org					

— Attractions —

				Phone	Fax
Brown's Race Historic District 60 Brown's Race	Rochester	NY	14614	716-325-2030	325-2414
Campbell-Whittlesey House 123 S Fitzhugh St	Rochester	NY	14608	716-546-7028	
Center at High Falls 60 Brown's Race	Rochester	NY	14614	716-325-2030	325-2414
Dryden Theatre at George Eastman House 900 East Ave	Rochester	NY	14607	716-271-4090	271-3970
Web: www.eastman.org					
Eastman Theatre 26 Gibbs St	Rochester	NY	14604	716-274-1110	274-1088
Web: www.rochester.edu/eastman					
Fagan Garth Dance 50 Chestnut St	Rochester	NY	14604	716-454-3260	454-6191
Web: www.loopside.com/fagan/					
Genesee Brewing Co Inc 445 Saint Paul St	Rochester	NY	14605	716-546-1030	546-5011
Genesee Lighthouse at Charlotte 70 Lighthouse St	Rochester	NY	14612	716-621-6179	
Geva Theatre 75 Woodbury Blvd	Rochester	NY	14607	716-232-1363	232-4031
Web: www.gevatheatre.org/					
Hamlin Beach State Park 1 Camp Rd	Hamlin	NY	14464	716-964-2462	

Rochester — Attractions (Cont'd)

				Phone	Fax
International Museum of Photography at George Eastman House 900 East Ave	Rochester	NY	14607	716-271-3361	271-3970
Web: www.eastman.org/ ■ *E-mail:* comments@geh.org					
Memorial Art Gallery of the University of Rochester 500 University Ave.	Rochester	NY	14607	716-473-7720	473-6266
Web: www.rochester.edu/mag/ ■ *E-mail:* maginfo@mag.rochester.edu					
Nazareth College Arts Center 4245 East Ave	Rochester	NY	14618	716-389-2175	389-2182
NTID Performing Arts 52 Lomb Memorial Dr.	Rochester	NY	14623	716-475-6250	475-6787
Opera Theatre of Rochester 100 East Ave	Rochester	NY	14604	716-235-7760	232-5353
Web: www.ggw.org/otr/					
Park Avenue Shopping District Park Ave-betw Alexander St & Culver Rd.	Rochester	NY	14607	716-234-1909	
Pyramid Arts Center 302 N Goodman St	Rochester	NY	14607	716-461-2222	461-2223
Web: www.pyramidarts.org					
Rochester Broadway Theatre League 100 East Ave	Rochester	NY	14604	716-222-5000	325-6742
Rochester Historical Society 485 East Ave	Rochester	NY	14607	716-271-2705	
Rochester Museum & Science Center 657 East Ave	Rochester	NY	14607	716-271-4320	271-5935
Web: www.rmsc.org					
Rochester Philharmonic Orchestra 25 Gibbs St Eastman Theatre	Rochester	NY	14605	716-222-5000	
Web: www.rpo.org/ ■ *E-mail:* webnotes@rpo.org					
Seabreeze Park 4600 Culver Rd	Rochester	NY	14622	716-323-1900	323-2225
Web: www.carousel.org/Seabreeze.html					
Seneca Park Zoo 2222 Saint Paul St.	Rochester	NY	14621	716-266-6846	266-5775
Web: www.senecazoo.com					
Sonnenberg Gardens 151 Charlotte St.	Canandaigua	NY	14424	716-394-4922	394-2192
Web: www.sonnenberg.org/					
Stone-Tolan House 2370 East Ave	Rochester	NY	14610	716-442-4606	
Strasenburgh Planetarium 657 East Ave Rochester Museum & Science Ctr.	Rochester	NY	14607	716-271-4320	271-5935
Web: www.rmsc.org/html/planet/planet.html					
Strong Museum 1 Manhattan Sq.	Rochester	NY	14607	716-263-2700	263-2493
Web: www.strongmuseum.org ■ *E-mail:* strandd@vivanet.com					
Susan B Anthony House 17 Madison St.	Rochester	NY	14608	716-235-6124	235-6212
Web: www.susanbanthonyhouse.org/					
Victorian Doll Museum 4332 Buffalo Rd	North Chili	NY	14514	716-247-0130	
Vietnam Veteran's Memorial 1440 South Ave	Rochester	NY	14620	716-227-7321	
Village of Pittsford 21 N Main St	Pittsford	NY	14534	716-586-4332	586-4597
Woodside Mansion 485 East Ave	Rochester	NY	14607	716-271-2705	

SPORTS TEAMS & FACILITIES

				Phone	Fax
Rochester Americans (hockey) 100 Exchange St Rochester Community War Memorial Auditorium	Rochester	NY	14614	716-454-5335	454-3954
Web: www.amerks.com					
Rochester Knighthawks (lacrosse) 100 Exchange St Rochester Community War Memorial Auditorium	Rochester	NY	14614	716-454-5335	454-3954
Rochester Raging Rhinos (soccer) 333 N Plymouth Ave Frontier Field	Rochester	NY	14608	716-454-5425	454-5453
Web: www.rhinossoccer.com ■ *E-mail:* info@rhinossoccer.com					
Rochester Ravens Library Rd Fauver Stadium	Rochester	NY	14620	716-461-4813	442-9527
Rochester Red Wings (baseball) 333 N Plymouth Ave Frontier Field	Rochester	NY	14608	716-454-1001	454-1056
Web: www.redwingsbaseball.com ■ *E-mail:* redwings@frontiernet.net					

— Events —

	Phone
Celebrate Your Roots at the Market (early October)	716-428-6907
Clothesline Art Festival (mid-September)	716-473-7720
Corn Hill Arts Festival (mid-July)	716-262-3142
Dickens Old Fashioned Christmas Festival (mid-November-late December)	716-392-3456
Festival of Lights (mid-November-early January)	716-394-4922
Flower City Market Days (mid-May-mid-June)	716-428-6907
Ghost Walk (mid-late October)	716-546-7029
Harbor Festival (late June)	716-428-6690
Hilton Apple Fest (early October)	716-392-7773
Historic Hill Cumorah Pageant (early & mid-July)	315-597-6808
Lilac Festival (mid-late May)	716 546-3070
Maplewood Rose Festival (mid-June)	716-428-6690
Monroe County Fair (late July-early August)	716-334-4000
Park Avenue Festival (late July-early August)	716-428-6690
Rochester Air Show (late August)	716-256-4960
Rochester HarborFest (late June)	716-865-3320
Rochester International LPGA Tournament (early-mid-June)	716-427-7040
Rochester River Romance (early October)	716-428-6690
Time Warner MusicFest (mid-July)	716-428-6690
Yuletide in the Country (early-mid-December)	716-538-6822

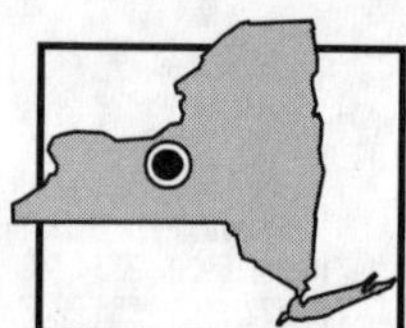

Syracuse

Known as "Crossroads of New York," Syracuse is located in Central New York at the intersection of the state's two major interstate highways. The city's location, along with its air and ground transportation network, have made it a major distribution center in the Northeastern United States. Syracuse is home to a number of colleges and universities, including Syracuse University. Over 40 museums and galleries are located in Syracuse, including the Everson Museum of Art, designed by I.M. Pei. Syracuse hosts a number of special events throughout the year, including a six-week-long Civic Center Summerfest and the Great New York State Fair, the longest running state fair in the country, which runs for 12 days and attracts more than 860,000 visitors to Syracuse each summer.

Population	152,215	**Longitude**	76-08-38 W
Area (Land)	25.1 sq mi	**County**	Onondaga
Area (Water)	0.6 sq mi	**Time Zone**	EST
Elevation	406 ft	**Area Code/s**	315
Latitude	43-02-27 N		

— Average Temperatures and Precipitation —

TEMPERATURES

	Jan	Feb	Mar	Apr	May	Jun	Jul	Aug	Sep	Oct	Nov	Dec
High	31	33	43	56	68	77	82	79	72	60	48	35
Low	14	15	25	36	46	54	59	58	51	41	33	21

PRECIPITATION

	Jan	Feb	Mar	Apr	May	Jun	Jul	Aug	Sep	Oct	Nov	Dec
Inches	2.3	2.2	2.8	3.3	3.3	3.8	3.8	3.5	3.8	3.2	3.7	3.2

— Important Phone Numbers —

	Phone		Phone
AAA	315-451-1115	**Poison Control Center**	315-476-4766
American Express Travel	315-474-3393	**Time/Temp**	315-474-8481
Emergency	911	**Weather**	315-786-9969
Medical Referral	315-424-8118		

— Information Sources —

				Phone	Fax
Greater Syracuse Chamber of Commerce 572 S Salina St.	Syracuse	NY	13202	315-470-1800	471-8545
Web: www.cny.com					
Oncenter Complex 800 S State St.	Syracuse	NY	13202	315-435-8000	435-8112
Web: www.oncenter.org					
Onondaga County 401 Montgomery St	Syracuse	NY	13202	315-435-2226	435-3455
Onondaga County Public Library System 447 S Salina St.	Syracuse	NY	13202	315-435-1800	435-8533
Web: www.cny.com/OCPL/ ■ *E-mail:* anagle@mailbox.syr.edu					

Syracuse — Information Sources (Cont'd)

	City	State	Zip	Phone	Fax
Syracuse City Hall 203 City Hall *Web:* www.syracuse.ny.us	Syracuse	NY	13202	315-448-8005	448-8067
Syracuse Community & Economic Development Dept 233 E Washington St Rm 219 *Web:* www.syracuse.ny.us/syrmayor/development/index.htm ■ *E-mail:* development@www.syracuse.ny.us	Syracuse	NY	13202	315-448-8100	448-8036
Syracuse Convention & Visitors Bureau 572 S Salina St *TF:* 800-234-4797 ■ *Web:* www.syracusecvb.org ■ *E-mail:* cvb@syracusecvb.org	Syracuse	NY	13202	315-470-1910	471-8545
Syracuse Mayor 203 City Hall *Web:* www.syracuse.ny.us/syrmayor/Mayor/home.html	Syracuse	NY	13202	315-448-8005	448-8067

On-Line Resources

4Syracuse.com	www.4syracuse.com
About.com Guide to Syracuse	syracuse.about.com/local/midlanticus/syracuse
Anthill City Guide Syracuse	www.anthill.com/city.asp?city=syracuse
Area Guide Syracuse	syracuse.areaguides.net
City Knowledge Syracuse	www.cityknowledge.com/ny_syracuse.htm
DigitalCity Syracuse	www.digitalcity.com/syracuse
Excite.com Syracuse City Guide	www.excite.com/travel/countries/united_states/new_york/syracuse
NuWeb Guide to Syracuse	nuwebny.com/syracuse.htm
Sybercuse.com	www.sybercuse.com
Syracuse Area Business Directory	www.cny.com/Business/direct.html
Syracuse New Times	newtimes.rway.com

— Transportation Services —

AIRPORTS

■ **Syracuse Hancock International Airport (SYR)**

	Phone
7 miles N of downtown (approx 15 minutes)	315-454-4330

Airport Transportation

	Phone
Taxi $17 fare to downtown	315-471-5151

Commercial Airlines

	Phone		Phone
AirTran	800-247-8726	**Delta Business Express**	800-345-3400
American	800-433-7300	**TWA**	800-221-2000
American Eagle	800-433-7300	**United**	800-241-6522
Continental	800-525-0280	**US Airways**	800-428-4322
Delta	800-221-1212		

Charter Airlines

	Phone		Phone
Great Northern Charter	315-422-1500	**Syracuse Executive Air**	315-455-6617
Kamp Air Aviation	315-363-1980	**United West Airlines Inc**	954-438-9077
Sair Aviation	315-455-7951		

CAR RENTALS

	Phone		Phone
Americar	315-455-2404	**Hertz**	315-455-2496
Avis	315-455-9601	**National**	315-455-7495
Budget	315-458-2017	**Thrifty**	315-455-7012
Enterprise	315-454-3000		

LIMO/TAXI

	Phone		Phone
Ace Taxi	315-471-7133	**Limo USA**	800-451-3011
City Taxi	315-471-3131	**Onondaga Taxi**	315-475-0030
Dependable Taxi	315-475-0030	**Superior Limousine Service**	800-234-7408
Empire International	800-451-5466	**Yellow Cab**	315-471-5151

MASS TRANSIT

	Phone
Centro Bus $1 Base fare	315-442-3400
OnTrack Railroad $1.50 Base fare	800-367-8724

RAIL/BUS

	City	State	Zip	Phone
Amtrak Station 131 P & C Pkwy Suite 2 *TF:* 800-872-7245	Syracuse	NY	13208	315-477-1152
Greyhound Bus Station 130 P & C Pkwy *TF:* 800-231-2222	Syracuse	NY	13210	315-472-4421

— Accommodations —

HOTELS, MOTELS, RESORTS

	City	State	Zip	Phone	Fax
Airflite Motel 110 S Bay Rd	North Syracuse	NY	13212	315-454-4462	
Best Western Syracuse Airport Airport Rd *TF:* 800-528-1234	North Syracuse	NY	13212	315-455-7362	455-6840
Budgetel Inn 4406 S Salina St	Syracuse	NY	13205	315-492-1714	
Carrier Circle Inn 6531 Thompson Rd S	Syracuse	NY	13208	315-437-2711	437-1734
Club Hotel by Doubletree 6701 Buckley Rd *TF:* 888-444-2582	Syracuse	NY	13212	315-457-4000	453-7877
Colgate Inn 1-5 Payne St	Hamilton	NY	13346	315-824-2300	824-4500
Comfort Inn 6491 Thompson Rd *TF:* 800-228-5150	Syracuse	NY	13206	315-437-0222	437-4510
Comfort Inn Fairgrounds 7010 Interstate Island Rd *TF:* 800-638-3247	Syracuse	NY	13209	315-453-0045	453-3689
Courtyard by Marriott 6415 Yorktown Cir *TF:* 800-321-2211 ■ *Web:* courtyard.com/SYRCA	Syracuse	NY	13057	315-432-0300	432-9950
Days Inn 6609 Thompson Rd *TF:* 800-329-7466	Syracuse	NY	13206	315-437-5998	437-5965
Econo Lodge 454 James St *TF:* 800-553-2666	Syracuse	NY	13203	315-425-0015	474-7009
Embassy Suites 6646 Old Collamer Rd *TF:* 800-362-2779	East Syracuse	NY	13057	315-446-3200	437-3302
Extended StayAmerica 6630 Old Collamer Rd *TF:* 800-398-7829	East Syracuse	NY	13057	315-463-1958	463-7966
Fairfield Inn by Marriott 6611 Old Collamer Rd *TF:* 800-228-2800 ■ *Web:* fairfieldinn.com/SYRFI	East Syracuse	NY	13057	315-432-9333	432-9333
Genesee Inn Executive Quarters 1060 E Genesee St *TF:* 800-365-4663	Syracuse	NY	13210	315-476-4212	471-4663
Hampton Inn 6605 Old Collamer Rd *TF:* 800-426-7866	Syracuse	NY	13057	315-463-6443	432-1080
Holiday Inn Convention Center 75 North St *TF:* 800-465-4329 ■ *Web:* www.basshotels.com/holiday-inn/?_franchisee=SYRAU ■ *E-mail:* hisales@localnet.com	Auburn	NY	13021	315-253-4531	252-5843
Holiday Inn Farrell Road 100 Farrell Rd *TF:* 800-465-4329 ■ *Web:* www.basshotels.com/holiday-inn/?_franchisee=SYRWE	Syracuse	NY	13209	315-457-8700	457-2379
Holiday Inn Waterloo/Seneca Falls 2468 Rt 414 *TF:* 800-465-4329 ■ *Web:* www.basshotels.com/holiday-inn/?_franchisee=WSFNY ■ *E-mail:* wsfny@flare.net	Waterloo	NY	13165	315-539-5011	539-8355
John Milton Inn 6578 Thompson Rd *TF:* 800-352-1061	Syracuse	NY	13206	315-463-8555	432-9240
Microtel 6608 Old Collamer Rd *TF:* 800-437-3500	Syracuse	NY	13057	315-437-3500	437-0111
Motel 6 6577 Court Street Rd *TF:* 800-466-8356	Syracuse	NY	13057	315-433-1300	437-2094
Quality Inn North 1308 Buckley Rd *TF:* 800-228-5151	Syracuse	NY	13212	315-451-1212	453-8050
Radisson Hotel Utica Centre 200 Genesee St *TF:* 800-333-3333	Utica	NY	13502	315-797-8010	797-1490
Radisson Plaza Hotel Syracuse 500 S Warren St *TF:* 800-333-3333	Syracuse	NY	13202	315-422-5121	422-3440
Ramada Inn 1305 Buckley Rd *TF:* 800-272-6232	Syracuse	NY	13212	315-457-8670	457-8633
Ramada Limited 6590 Thompson Rd *TF:* 800-272-6232	Syracuse	NY	13206	315-463-0202	463-9270
Red Carpet Inn Airport 2914 Brewerton Rd	North Syracuse	NY	13212	315-454-3266	
Red Roof Inn 6614 N Thompson Rd *TF:* 800-843-7663	Syracuse	NY	13206	315-437-3309	437-7865
Residence Inn by Marriott 9 Gerhard Rd *TF:* 800-331-3131 ■ *Web:* www.residenceinn.com/NYCPL	Plainview	NY	11803	516-433-6200	433-2569
Residence Inn by Marriott 6420 Yorktown Cir *TF:* 800-331-3131 ■ *Web:* www.residenceinn.com/SYRRI	East Syracuse	NY	13057	315-432-4488	432-1042
Sheraton University Hotel & Conference Center 801 University Ave *TF:* 800-395-2105	Syracuse	NY	13210	315-475-3000	475-3311

Syracuse — Hotels, Motels, Resorts (Cont'd)

				Phone	Fax
Super 8 East Syracuse 6620 Old Collamer Rd *TF:* 800-800-8000	East Syracuse	NY	13057	315-432-5612	432-5620
Syracuse Marriott 6301 Rt 298 *TF:* 800-782-9847	East Syracuse	NY	13057	315-432-0200	433-1210
University Tower 701 E Genesee St *TF:* 800-483-7876	Syracuse	NY	13210	315-474-7251	472-2700
Western Ranch Motor Inn Fairgrounds 1255 State Fair Blvd	Syracuse	NY	13209	315-457-9236	457-9236

— Restaurants —

				Phone
Bernardi's Bistro (Continental) 500 S Warren St	Syracuse	NY	13202	315-422-5121
Brick Alley Grille House (Continental) 317 Montgomery St	Syracuse	NY	13202	315-472-3990
Captain Ahab's (Steak/Seafood) 3449 Erie Blvd E	Syracuse	NY	13214	315-446-3272
Casa Di Copani (Italian) 3414 Burnet Ave	Syracuse	NY	13206	315-463-1031
Clark's Ale House (American) 122 W Jefferson St	Syracuse	NY	13202	315-479-9859
Coleman's Authentic Irish Pub (Continental) 100 S Lowell Ave	Syracuse	NY	13204	315-476-1933
Crittela's (Italian) 3705 Brewerton Rd	Syracuse	NY	13210	315-455-1431
Crown Bar & Grill (American) 301 W Fayette St	Syracuse	NY	13202	315-474-0112
Dinosaur Bar-B-Que (Barbecue) 246 W Willow St	Syracuse	NY	13202	315-476-4937
Dry Dock Grill (American) 306 W Division St	Syracuse	NY	13204	315-466-6202
Empire Brewing Co (New American) 120 Walton St *Web:* www.empirebrewco.com	Syracuse	NY	13202	315-475-4400
Faegan's Cafe & Pub (American) 734 S Crouse Ave	Syracuse	NY	13210	315-472-4721
Harvest Grille (American) Rt 298	East Syracuse	NY	13057	315-432-0200
Joey's Restaurant (Italian) 6594 Thompson Rd	Syracuse	NY	13206	315-432-0315
La Bamba (Mexican) 1000 State Fair Blvd	Syracuse	NY	13209	315-488-7302
La Cuisine (French) 441 S Salina St	Syracuse	NY	13202	315-476-4249
Lemon Grass (Thai) 238 W Jefferson St	Syracuse	NY	13202	315-475-1111
Ling Ling (Chinese) 205 E Seneca St	Syracuse	NY	13202	315-682-7731
Maine Lobster Co (Seafood) 500 S Warren St	Syracuse	NY	13202	315-422-5121
Mr Mardi Gras (Barbecue) 107 W Fayette St	Syracuse	NY	13202	315-474-0274
Pascale Wine Bar & Restaurant (American) 204 W Fayette St	Syracuse	NY	13202	315-471-3040
Pastabilities (Italian) 311 S Franklin St	Syracuse	NY	13202	315-474-1153
Pavilion Restaurant (American) 801 University Ave	Syracuse	NY	13210	315-475-3000
Tavern at Ten Sixty (American) 1060 E Genesee St	Syracuse	NY	13210	315-476-9000
To the Moon (Continental) 305 Burnet Ave	Syracuse	NY	13203	315-478-1003
Tower Restaurant (American) 701 E Genesee St	Syracuse	NY	13210	315-479-7000
Welcome Inn (Continental) 501 Tully St	Syracuse	NY	13204	315-478-9489

— Goods and Services —

SHOPPING

				Phone	Fax
Armory Square 247 W Fayette St	Syracuse	NY	13202	315-472-5510	457-5659
Carousel Center 9090 Carousel Center Dr *Web:* www.carouselcenter.com	Syracuse	NY	13290	315-466-7000	466-5405
Fayetteville Mall 5351 N Burdick St	Fayetteville	NY	13066	315-637-5163	637-1336
Galleries of Syracuse The 441 S Salina St	Syracuse	NY	13202	315-475-5351	475-4263
Marshall Square Mall 720 University Ave	Syracuse	NY	13210	315-422-3234	
ShoppingTown Mall 3649 Erie Blvd E	Dewitt	NY	13214	315-446-9160	445-8742

BANKS

				Phone	Fax
Chase Manhattan Bank One Lincoln Ctr	Syracuse	NY	13202	800-935-9935	
First National Bank 120 E Washington St	Syracuse	NY	13202	315-422-5861	422-2368
Fleet Bank of New York One Clinton Sq *TF:* 800-844-4000	Syracuse	NY	13221	315-426-4100	426-4207
HSBC Bank USA 360 S Warren St	Syracuse	NY	13202	315-424-3215	424-2074

BUSINESS SERVICES

	Phone
Airborne Express	800-247-2676
BAX Global	800-225-5229
DHL Worldwide Express	800-225-5345
Federal Express	800-238-5355
Interim Personnel Services	315-461-4212
Kelly Services	315-422-8181
Kinko's	315-455-5507
Mail Boxes Etc	315-488-1222
Manpower Temporary Services	315-457-5000
Olsten Staffing Services	315-422-0273
Post Office	315-472-0817
UPS	800-742-5877

— Media —

PUBLICATIONS

				Phone	Fax
Business Records 208 Townsend St	Syracuse	NY	13203	315-472-6911	422-0040
Central New York Business Journal 231 Walton St	Syracuse	NY	13202	315-472-3104	472-3644
Herald-Journal‡ PO Box 4915 *TF:* 800-765-4569 ■ *Web:* www.syracuse.com	Syracuse	NY	13221	315-470-0011	470-3019
Post-Standard‡ PO Box 4915 *TF:* 800-765-4569 ■ *Web:* www.syracuse.com ■ *E-mail:* linhorst@syracuse.com	Syracuse	NY	13221	315-470-0011	470-3081

‡Daily newspapers

TELEVISION

				Phone	Fax
WCNY-TV Ch 24 (PBS) PO Box 2400 *Web:* www.wcny.org/tv ■ *E-mail:* wcny_online@wcny.pbs.org	Syracuse	NY	13220	315-453-2424	451-8824
WIXT-TV Ch 9 (ABC) 5904 Bridge St *Web:* www.wixt.com ■ *E-mail:* wixt@digitalsherpas.com	East Syracuse	NY	13057	315-446-9999	446-9283
WNYS-TV Ch 43 (UPN) 1000 James St	Syracuse	NY	13203	315-472-6800	471-8889
WSTM-TV Ch 3 (NBC) 1030 James St *E-mail:* wstm@aol.com	Syracuse	NY	13203	315-474-5000	474-5122
WSYT-TV Ch 68 (Fox) 1000 James St *Web:* www.fox68wsyt.com	Syracuse	NY	13203	315-472-6800	471-8889
WTVH-TV Ch 5 (CBS) 980 James St *Web:* www.wtvh.com	Syracuse	NY	13203	315-425-5555	425-0129

RADIO

				Phone	Fax
WAER-FM 88.3 MHz (NPR) 215 University Pl *TF:* 888-918-3688 ■ *Web:* web.syr.edu/~waerfm88/ ■ *E-mail:* waerfm88@mailbox.syr.edu	Syracuse	NY	13244	315-443-4021	443-2148
WAQX-FM 95.7 MHz (Rock) 1064 James St *Web:* www.waqx.com/	Syracuse	NY	13203	315-472-0200	472-1146
WBBS-FM 104.7 MHz (Ctry) 500 Plum St Suite 100 *Web:* www.sybercuse.com/b1047 ■ *E-mail:* b1047@sybercuse.com	Syracuse	NY	13204	315-448-1047	474-7879
WCNY-FM 91.3 MHz (NPR) PO Box 2400 *TF:* 800-451-9269 ■ *Web:* www.wcny.org/classicfm ■ *E-mail:* wcny_online@wcny.pbs.org	Syracuse	NY	13220	315-453-2424	451-8824
WHEN-AM 620 kHz (Sports) 500 Plum St Suite 100 *Web:* www.sybercuse.com/sportsmonster ■ *E-mail:* info@sportsmonster.com	Syracuse	NY	13204	315-472-9797	472-2323
WJPZ-FM 89.1 MHz (CHR) 316 Waverly Ave	Syracuse	NY	13210	315-443-4689	443-4379
WMHR-FM 102.9 MHz (Rel) 4044 Makyes Rd	Syracuse	NY	13215	315-469-5051	
WNTQ-FM 93.1 MHz (CHR) 1064 James St *Web:* www.93q.com ■ *E-mail:* hits93q@aol.com	Syracuse	NY	13203	315-472-0200	478-5625
WSYR-AM 570 kHz (N/T) 500 Plum St *Web:* www.sybercuse.com/wsyr ■ *E-mail:* info@wsyr.com	Syracuse	NY	13204	315-472-9797	472-2323
WYYY-FM 94.5 MHz (AC) 500 Plum St *Web:* www.sybercuse.com/y94fm ■ *E-mail:* y94fm@emi.com	Syracuse	NY	13204	315-472-9797	478-6455

— Colleges/Universities —

				Phone	Fax
Bryant & Stratton Business Institute Syracuse 953 James St	Syracuse	NY	13203	315-472-6603	474-4383
Cazenovia College Sullivan & Nickerson Sts *TF:* 800-654-3210 ■ *Web:* www.cazcollege.edu	Cazenovia	NY	13035	315-655-7000	655-4860
Le Moyne College 1419 Salt Springs Rd *TF Admissions:* 800-333-4733 ■ *Web:* www.lemoyne.edu	Syracuse	NY	13214	315-445-4100	445-4540
State University of New York College of Environmental Science & Forestry 1 Forestry Dr *Web:* www.esf.edu ■ *E-mail:* esfweb@mailbox.syr.edu	Syracuse	NY	13210	315-470-6500	470-6932
State University of New York College of Environmental Science & Forestry-Ranger School 1 Forestry Dr 106 Bray Hall *TF:* 800-777-7373 ■ *Web:* www.esf.edu ■ *E-mail:* esfweb@mailbox.syr.edu	Syracuse	NY	13210	315-470-6600	470-6933
State University of New York Health Science Center 155 Elizabeth Blackwell St *Web:* www.hscsyr.edu	Syracuse	NY	13210	315-464-4570	464-8867
State University of New York Onondaga Community College 4941 Onondaga Rd *Web:* www.sunyocc.edu	Syracuse	NY	13215	315-469-7741	492-9208

Syracuse — Colleges/Universities (Cont'd)

				Phone	Fax
Syracuse University	Syracuse	NY	13244	315-443-1870	443-4226
Web: www.syr.edu					

— Hospitals —

				Phone	Fax
Community-General Hospital of Greater Syracuse 4900 Broad Rd	Syracuse	NY	13215	315-492-5011	492-5329
Crouse Hospital 736 Irving Ave	Syracuse	NY	13210	315-470-7111	470-2851*
**Fax:* Hum Res ■ *Web:* www.crouse.org					
Saint Joseph's Hospital Health Center 301 Prospect Ave	Syracuse	NY	13203	315-448-5111	448-5682*
**Fax:* Admitting ■ *TF:* 888-785-6371 ■ *Web:* www.sjhsyr.org					
University Hospital SUNY Health Center at Syracuse 750 E Adams St	Syracuse	NY	13210	315-464-5540	464-7101
Veterans Affairs Medical Center 800 Irving Ave	Syracuse	NY	13210	315-476-7461	477-4589

— Attractions —

				Phone	Fax
Bristol Omnitheater 500 S Franklin St Museum of Science & Technology	Syracuse	NY	13202	315-425-9068	425-9072
Web: www.most.org/omni_frame.html					
Burnet Park Zoo 1 Conservation Pl	Syracuse	NY	13204	315-435-8511	435-8517
Central New York Regional Farmers & Flea Market 2100 Park St	Syracuse	NY	13208	315-422-8647	422-6897
Erie Canal Museum 318 Erie Blvd E	Syracuse	NY	13202	315-471-0593	471-7220
Web: www.syracuse.com/eriecanal/					
Everson Museum of Art 401 Harrison St	Syracuse	NY	13202	315-474-6064	474-6943
Web: www.everson.org					
Fort Stanwix National Monument 112 E Park St	Rome	NY	13440	315-336-2090	339-3966
Web: www.nps.gov/fost/					
International Boxing Hall of Fame Museum 1 Hall of Fame Dr	Canastota	NY	13032	315-697-7095	697-5356
Web: www.ibhof.com					
Landmark Theater 362 S Salina St	Syracuse	NY	13202	315-475-7980	475-7993
Mulroy John H Civic Center 421 Montgomery St	Syracuse	NY	13202	315-435-8000	435-8272
Museum of Automobile History 321 N Clinton St	Syracuse	NY	13202	315-478-2277	432-8256
Web: www.autolit.com/Museum/index.htm ■ *E-mail:* info@autolit.com					
Museum of Science & Technology 500 S Franklin St	Syracuse	NY	13202	315-425-9068	425-9072
Web: www.most.org					
Onondaga Park 412 Spencer St	Syracuse	NY	13204	315-473-4330	428-8513
Sainte Marie among the Iroquois Living History Museum 1 Onondaga Lake Pkwy	Liverpool	NY	13088	315-453-6767	453-6762
Salt City Center for the Performing Arts 601 S Crouse Ave	Syracuse	NY	13210	315-474-1122	478-5912
Syracuse Opera 411 Montgomery St Suite 60	Syracuse	NY	13202	315-475-5915	475-6319
Syracuse Stage 820 E Genesee St	Syracuse	NY	13210	315-443-3275	443-1408
Web: web.syr.edu/~syrstage					
Syracuse Symphony Orchestra 411 Montgomery St John H Mulroy Civic Ctr	Syracuse	NY	13202	315-424-8200	424-1131
TF: 800-724-3810					
Women's Rights National Historical Park 136 Fall St	Seneca Falls	NY	13148	315-568-2991	568-2141
Web: www.nps.gov/wori/					

SPORTS TEAMS & FACILITIES

				Phone	Fax
Syracuse Crunch (hockey) 800 S State St Onondaga County War Memorial	Syracuse	NY	13202	315-473-4444	473-4449
Web: www.syracusecrunch.com					
Syracuse SkyChiefs (baseball) 1 Tex Simone Dr P & C Stadium	Syracuse	NY	13208	315-474-7833	474-2658
Web: skychiefs.com/skychiefs ■ *E-mail:* baseball@skychiefs.com					

— Events —

	Phone
Arabian Horse Championship (mid-July)	315-487-7711
Autumn in New York Horse Show (late September-early October)	315-487-7711
Downtown Farmer's Market (mid-June-October)	315-422-8284
Empire Appaloosa Show (early August)	315-487-7711
Festival of Centuries (late July)	315-453-6767
Golden Harvest Festival (mid-September)	315-638-2519
Great American Antiquefest (mid-July)	315-451-7275
Great New York State Fair (late August-early September)	315-487-7711
Harvest Happenings (mid-September)	315-435-8511
Holiday Festival of Trees (early December)	315-474-6064
Hot Air Balloon Festival (mid-June)	315-451-7275
International Auto Show Expo (mid-March)	315-487-7711
Lights on the Lake (late November-early January)	315-451-7275
New York Morgan Horse Show (mid-September)	315-487-7711
New York State Rhythm & Blues Fest (mid-July)	315-470-1910
Oktoberfest (mid-September)	315-451-7275
Pops in the Park (July)	315-473-4330
Saint Patrick's Day Parade (mid-March)	315-448-8044
Summerfame (mid-July-mid-August)	315-963-4249
Syracuse Arts and Crafts Festival (mid-July)	315-422-8284
Syracuse International Horse Show (late June)	315-487-7711
Syracuse Jazz Fest (late June)	315-422-8284
Taste of Syracuse (early July)	315-484-1123
Thornden Rose Festival (mid-June)	315-473-4330
Winterfest (mid-February)	315-470-1900
Zoo Boo (late October)	315-435-8511

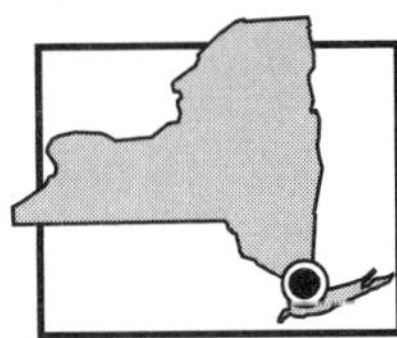

Yonkers

Yonkers is located on the east bank of the Hudson River in Westchester County at the hub of New York City, New Jersey, and Connecticut. This location makes Yonkers an attractive site for business, and it is currently home to more than 10,000 companies. The Hudson River Museum in Yonkers offers visitors a cultural experience that combines art, science, and history, featuring art galleries, the Andrus Space Planetarium, and Glenview, a restored turn-of-the-century mansion. Yonkers Raceway is known both for harness racing and as the site of the annual Westchester County Fair, a 17-day event that attracts more than 300,000 visitors to Yonkers each spring.

Population	190,153	**Longitude**	73-52-03 W
Area (Land)	18.1 sq mi	**County**	Westchester
Area (Water)	2.3 sq mi	**Time Zone**	EST
Elevation	16 ft	**Area Code/s**	914
Latitude	40-56-49 N		

— Average Temperatures and Precipitation —

TEMPERATURES

	Jan	Feb	Mar	Apr	May	Jun	Jul	Aug	Sep	Oct	Nov	Dec
High	37	39	48	59	70	79	84	82	75	64	53	42
Low	26	27	35	44	54	63	69	68	61	51	42	31

PRECIPITATION

	Jan	Feb	Mar	Apr	May	Jun	Jul	Aug	Sep	Oct	Nov	Dec
Inches	3.0	2.9	3.6	3.8	3.8	3.6	4.1	3.8	3.4	3.0	3.8	3.4

— Important Phone Numbers —

	Phone		Phone
AAA	212-586-1166	**Poison Control Center**	800-336-6997
Emergency	911		

Yonkers (Cont'd)

— Information Sources —

				Phone	Fax
Better Business Bureau Serving Metropolitan New York Mid-Hudson Region 30 Glenn St.	White Plains	NY	10603	914-428-1230	428-6030
Web: www.newyork.bbb.org					
Westchester County 110 Dr MLK Jr Blvd	White Plains	NY	10601	914-285-3080	285-3172
Web: www.co.westchester.ny.us					
Yonkers Chamber of Commerce 20 S Broadway Suite 1207	Yonkers	NY	10701	914-963-0332	963-0455
Web: www.yonkerschamber.com ■ *E-mail:* info@yonkerschamber.com					
Yonkers City Hall 40 S Broadway City Hall	Yonkers	NY	10701	914-377-6000	377-6029
Web: www.ci.yonkers.ny.us ■ *E-mail:* cityhall@ci.yonkers.ny.us					
Yonkers Economic Development Office 40 S Broadway Rm 414	Yonkers	NY	10701	914-377-6797	377-6003
Yonkers Mayor 40 S Broadway City Hall	Yonkers	NY	10701	914-377-6300	377-6048
Web: www.ci.yonkers.ny.us/mayor.htm					
Yonkers Public Library 7 Main St	Yonkers	NY	10701	914-337-1500	963-2301
Web: wlsmail.wls.lib.ny.us/libs/yonkers/ypl_home.htm					

On-Line Resources

NITC Travelbase City Guide Yonkers . . . . www.travelbase.com/auto/features/yonkers-ny.html
Online City Guide to Yonkers . . . . www.olcg.com/ny/yonkers/index.html

— Transportation Services —

AIRPORTS

■ John F Kennedy International Airport (JFK)

Phone

20 miles S of downtown Yonkers (approx 40 minutes) 718-244-4444
Web: www.panynj.gov/aviation/jfkframe.HTM

Airport Transportation

Phone

Ambassador Taxi $42 fare to downtown Yonkers 914-969-2800

Commercial Airlines

	Phone		Phone
Aer Lingus	800-474-7424	**KLM**	800-374-7747
Aeroflot	888-686-4949	**Korean Air**	800-438-5000
Aerolineas Argentinas	212-698-2050	**Kuwait Airways**	212-308-5454
AeroMexico	800-237-6639	**LanChile**	718-995-6962
Air Afrique	212-586-5908	**LOT Polish Airlines**	800-223-0593
Air Canada	800-776-3000	**LTU International**	800-888-0200
Air China	800-986-1985	**Lufthansa**	800-645-3880
Air India	212-751-6200	**Martinair Holland**	800-627-8462
Air Jamaica	800-523-5585	**Mexicana**	800-531-7923
Alitalia	800-223-5730	**Midway**	800-446-4392
All Nippon Airways	800-235-9262	**National**	888-757-5387
ALM-Antillean	800-327-7230	**Northwest**	800-225-2525
ALM-Antillean	800-327-7230	**Olympic Airways**	800-223-1226
America West	800-235-9292	**Pakistan International**	800-221-2552
American	800-433-7300	**Pan Am**	800-359-7262
American Eagle	800-433-7300	**Royal Air Maroc**	212-750-5115
Austrian Airlines	800-843-0002	**Royal Jordanian**	212-949-0050
Avianca	212-399-0800	**Sabena**	516-562-9200
British Airways	800-247-9297	**Saudi Arabian**	800-472-8342
BWIA International	800-538-2942	**Scandinavian**	800-221-2350
Cayman Airways	800-422-9626	**Singapore**	800-742-3333
China Airlines	800-227-5118	**SwissAir**	800-221-4750
Continental	212-319-9494	**TAP Air Portugal**	800-221-7370
Continental Express	800-525-0280	**Tower Air**	800-348-6937
Delta	800-221-1212	**TransBrasil**	800-872-3153
El Al	212-768-9200	**TWA**	800-221-2000
Finnair	718-656-7570	**United**	800-241-6522
First Air	800-945-2990	**US Airways**	800-428-4322
Iberia	800-772-4642	**US Airways Express**	800-428-4322
Icelandair	800-223-5500	**Varig Brazilian**	212-682-3100
Japan	212-838-4400		

Charter Airlines

	Phone		Phone
Atlantic Aviation Charter	201-288-7660	**Northeast Airway**	973-267-2450
Jet Aviation Business Jets Inc	800-736-8538		

■ LaGuardia Airport (LGA)

Phone

15 miles S of downtown Yonkers (approx 30 minutes) 718-476-5000

Airport Transportation

Phone

Ambassador Taxi $32 fare to downtown Yonkers 914-969-2800

Commercial Airlines

	Phone		Phone
AccessAir	877-462-2237	**Midwest Express**	800-452-2022
Air Canada	800-776-3000	**Northwest**	800-225-2525
American	800-433-7300	**Spirit**	800-772-7117
American Eagle	800-433-7300	**TWA**	800-221-2000
Atlantic Coast Airlines	800-241-6522	**United**	800-241-6522
Continental	718-565-1100	**US Airways**	800-428-4322
Delta	800-221-1212	**US Airways Express**	800-428-4322
Midway	800-446-4392		

Charter Airlines

	Phone		Phone
Atlantic Aviation Charter	201-288-7660	**Northeast Airway**	973-267-2450
Jet Aviation Business Jets Inc	800-736-8538		

CAR RENTALS

	Phone		Phone
Avis-La Guardia	718-507-3600	**Enterprise**	914-337-1616
Budget-JFK	718-656-6013	**Hertz-JFK**	718-656-7600
Budget-La Guardia	718-639-6400	**Hertz-La Guardia**	718-478-5300
Dollar-JFK	718-656-2400	**Thrifty**	718-721-8500

LIMO/TAXI

	Phone		Phone
Ambassador Taxi	914-969-2800	**Richard's Taxi**	914-965-4770
Capital Executive Limousine	914-968-3363	**Valentine-Ludlow Taxi**	914-968-2800
Eclipse Limousine Service	914-949-8553	**Westchester Car & Limousine**	914-946-4225

MASS TRANSIT

Phone

Bee-Line Bus $1.40 Base fare 914-682-2020

RAIL/BUS

				Phone
Amtrak/Metro-North 2 Dock St & Wells Ave	Yonkers	NY	10701	800-872-7245
Port Authority Bus Terminal 625 8th Ave	New York	NY	10018	212-564-8484

— Accommodations —

HOTELS, MOTELS, RESORTS

				Phone	Fax
Alexander Motel 542 Tarrytown Rd.	White Plains	NY	10607	914-761-5600	328-2163
Apple Motor Inn 775 Saw Mill River Rd.	Ardsley	NY	10502	914-693-2900	693-2996
Ardsley Acres Hotel Court 560 Saw Mill River Rd.	Ardsley	NY	10502	914-693-2700	693-2354
Central Motel Court 441 Central Ave.	White Plains	NY	10606	914-948-8717	948-8718
Courtyard by Marriott 475 White Plains Rd	Tarrytown	NY	10591	914-631-1122	631-1375
TF: 800-321-2211 ■ *Web:* courtyard.com/HPNGR					
Crowne Plaza Hotel 66 Hale Ave.	White Plains	NY	10601	914-682-0050	682-0405
TF: 800-752-4672					
Esplanade Hotel 95 S Broadway	White Plains	NY	10601	914-761-8100	761-5208
TF: 800-247-5322					
Hampton Inn 200 Tarrytown Rd	Elmsford	NY	10523	914-592-5680	592-6727
TF: 800-426-7866 ■ *Web:* www.hamptoninnwhiteplains.com					
Holiday Inn 125 Tuckahoe Rd.	Yonkers	NY	10710	914-476-3800	423-3555
TF: 800-465-4329					
Quality Inn 20 Saw Mill River Rd	Hawthorne	NY	10532	914-592-8600	592-7457
TF: 800-228-5151					
Ramada Inn 1 Ramada Plz.	New Rochelle	NY	10801	914-576-3700	576-5864
TF: 800-272-6232					
Royal Regency Hotel 165 Tuckahoe Rd.	Yonkers	NY	10710	914-476-6200	375-7017
TF: 800-215-3858					
Saw Mill River Motel 25 Valley Ave	Elmsford	NY	10523	914-592-7500	592-6461
Tarrytown Hilton Inn 455 S Broadway	Tarrytown	NY	10591	914-631-5700	631-0075
TF: 800-445-8667					
Trade Winds Motor Court 1141 Yonkers Ave	Yonkers	NY	10704	914-237-0400	
Tuckahoe Motor Inn 307 Tuckahoe Rd	Yonkers	NY	10710	914-793-6300	793-4627
Westchester Marriott Hotel 670 White Plains Rd	Tarrytown	NY	10591	914-631-2200	631-7819
TF: 800-228-9290					
Westchester Residence Inn 5 Barker Ave	White Plains	NY	10601	914-761-7700	761-0136
TF: 800-331-3131					
Yonkers Motor Inn 300 Yonkers Ave	Yonkers	NY	10701	914-476-6600	476-7170

Yonkers (Cont'd)

— Restaurants —

Name	City	State	Zip	Phone
Apollon Restaurant (Greek) 347 1/2 S Broadway	Yonkers	NY	10705	914-423-1922
Baci Pizza & Pasta Inc (Italian) 328 Tuckahoe Rd	Yonkers	NY	10710	914-337-1130
Bene Bene Italian Restaurant (Italian) 2500 Central Park Ave	Yonkers	NY	10710	914-961-3794
Bing Chinese Restaurant (Chinese) 440 S Broadway	Yonkers	NY	10705	914-963-0870
Broadway Seafood Restaurant (Seafood) 397 S Broadway	Yonkers	NY	10705	914-376-2220
Caribbean Pirate (Caribbean) 440 Riverdale Ave	Yonkers	NY	10705	914-423-6607
Casa Filipina (Filipino) 363 S Broadway	Yonkers	NY	10705	914-965-5802
Charlie Browns Steak House (Steak) 1820 Central Park Ave *Web:* www.charliebrowns.com	Yonkers	NY	10710	914-779-7227
Dakota Steakhouse & Saloon (Steak) 2500 Central Park Ave	Yonkers	NY	10710	914-961-3795
East Harbor Seafood Restaurant (Seafood) 1560 Central Park Ave	Yonkers	NY	10710	914-793-2033
Fratta's Italian Village (Italian) 652 Central Park Ave	Yonkers	NY	10704	914-969-9878
Giuliano's (Italian) 1160 Yonkers Ave	Yonkers	NY	10704	914-237-7777
Golden Wok (Chinese) 2250 Central Park Ave	Yonkers	NY	10710	914-779-8438
Heritage Bar & Restaurant (American) 960 Mclean Ave	Yonkers	NY	10704	914-776-7532
Hunan Village Restaurant (Chinese) 1828 Central Park Ave	Yonkers	NY	10710	914-779-2272
Jackie's Bistro (French) 434 White Plains Rd	West Chester	NY	10707	914-337-8447
La Grotta Trattoria (Italian) 861 Midland Ave	Yonkers	NY	10704	914-376-3200
La Pietra Restaurant (Italian) 623 S Broadway	Yonkers	NY	10705	914-969-8738
Morleys Steak & Seafood (Steak/Seafood) 123 Lake Ave	Yonkers	NY	10703	914-969-9336
Parkway Grill (American) 841 Bronx River Rd	Yonkers	NY	10708	914-237-2516
Restaurant Tres Chaves (Portuguese) 44 Orchard St	Yonkers	NY	10703	914-969-9128
Ricky's Clam House (Mediterranean) 1955 Central Park Ave	Yonkers	NY	10710	914-961-8284
Rin Con Cuencano (Spanish) 100 New Main St	Yonkers	NY	10701	914-966-1631
Royal India Palace (Indian) 2223 Central Park Ave	Yonkers	NY	10710	914-961-2620
Royal Thai (Thai) 1109 Central Park Ave	Yonkers	NY	10704	914-472-3607
Sabor Latino Restaurant (Caribbean) 508 S Broadway	Yonkers	NY	10705	914-423-5688
Sprain Lake Restaurant (American) 290 E Grassy Sprain Rd	Yonkers	NY	10710	914-961-8616
Sun Xing Garden (Chinese) 1288 Midland Ave	Yonkers	NY	10704	914-237-8161
Tara Restaurant (Irish) 840 Midland Ave	Yonkers	NY	10704	914-423-1234
Tombolino Restaurant (Continental) 356 Kimball Ave	Yonkers	NY	10704	914-237-1266
Tum Raa Thai Cuisine (Thai) 629 Mclean Ave	Yonkers	NY	10705	914-965-1800
Valentino's Restaurant (Italian) 132 Bronx River Rd	Yonkers	NY	10704	914-776-6731
Wild Cactus Cafe (Mexican) 987 Central Park Ave	Yonkers	NY	10704	914-963-5500

— Goods and Services —

SHOPPING

Name	City	State	Zip	Phone
Cross Country Shopping Center 6K Mall Walk	Yonkers	NY	10704	914-968-9570
Cross Country Square Shopping Center 750 Central Park	Yonkers	NY	10704	914-968-5734

BANKS

Name	City	State	Zip	Phone	Fax
Bank of New York 2195 Central Park Ave	Yonkers	NY	10710	914-779-1770	779-1242
Chase Manhattan Bank 314 S Broadway	Yonkers	NY	10705	914-935-9935	
First Union National Bank 598 Tuckahoe Rd	Yonkers	NY	10710	914-779-4422	779-4456
Fleet Bank 20 S Broadway	Yonkers	NY	10702	914-963-6400	476-4218
HSBC Bank USA 1098 Yonkers Ave	Yonkers	NY	10704	914-237-3332	237-3918
Hudson Valley National Bank 35 E Grassy Sprain Rd	Yonkers	NY	10710	914-961-6100	961-3644
Republic National Bank 2205 Central Park Ave	Yonkers	NY	10710	914-779-5513	779-5642
Yonkers Savings & Loans 1 Manor House Sq	Yonkers	NY	10701	914-968-4500	968-4616

BUSINESS SERVICES

Name	Phone
Airborne Express	800-247-2676
DHL Worldwide Express	800-225-5345
Federal Express	800-238-5355
Mail Boxes Etc	914-237-3100
Olsten Staffing Services	914-423-3220
Post Office	914-378-3600
UPS	800-742-5877

— Media —

PUBLICATIONS

Name	City	State	Zip	Phone	Fax
Journal News‡ 1 Gannett Dr *TF:* 800-942-1010	White Plains	NY	10604	914-694-9300	696-8138

‡*Daily newspapers*

TELEVISION

Name	City	State	Zip	Phone	Fax
WABC-TV Ch 7 (ABC) 7 Lincoln Sq *Web:* abcnews.go.com/local/wabc	New York	NY	10023	212-456-7777	456-2381
WCBS-TV Ch 2 (CBS) 524 W 57th St *Web:* www.cbs2ny.com	New York	NY	10019	212-975-4321	975-9387
WNBC-TV Ch 4 (NBC) 30 Rockefeller Plaza *Web:* www.newschannel4.com ■ *E-mail:* nbc4ny@nbc.com	New York	NY	10112	212-664-4444	664-2994
WNET-TV Ch 13 (PBS) 450 W 33rd St *Web:* www.wnet.org ■ *E-mail:* webinfo@www.wnet.org	New York	NY	10001	212-560-1313	582-3297
WNYW-TV Ch 5 (Fox) 205 E 67th St	New York	NY	10021	212-452-5555	249-1182

— Colleges/Universities —

Name	City	State	Zip	Phone	Fax
Cochran School of Nursing 967 N Broadway *Web:* www.riversidehealth.org/stjohns/html/nursing.html	Yonkers	NY	10701	914-964-4283	964-4971
Westchester Business Institute 325 Central Ave *TF:* 800-333-4924 ■ *E-mail:* wbi@ix.netcom.com	White Plains	NY	10606	914-948-4442	948-8216

— Hospitals —

Name	City	State	Zip	Phone	Fax
Saint Joseph's Medical Center 127 S Broadway	Yonkers	NY	10701	914-378-7000	965-4838
Yonkers General Hospital 2 Park Ave *Web:* www.riversidehealth.org/yonkers/yonkers.html	Yonkers	NY	10703	914-964-7300	964-7311

— Attractions —

Name	City	State	Zip	Phone	Fax
Andreas Space Planetarium 511 Warburton Ave Hudson River Museum of Westchester *Web:* www.hrm.org/Planetarium/planetarium.html	Yonkers	NY	10701	914-963-4550	963-8558
Home of Franklin D Roosevelt National Historic Site 519 Albany Post Rd *Web:* www.nps.gov/hofr/	Hyde Park	NY	12538	914-229-9115	229-0739
Hudson River Museum of Westchester 511 Warburton Ave *Web:* www.hrm.org	Yonkers	NY	10701	914-963-4550	963-8558
Philipse Manor Hall 29 Warburton Ave	Yonkers	NY	10701	914-965-4027	965-6485
Sherwood House 340 Tuckahoe Rd	Yonkers	NY	10710	914-965-0401	965-0401
Untermyer Park 285 Nepperhan Ave	Yonkers	NY	10701	914-377-6450	377-6428
Vanderbilt Mansion National Historic Site 519 Albany Post Rd *Web:* www.nps.gov/vama/	Hyde Park	NY	12538	914-229-9115	229-0739
Yonkers Education & Cultural Arts Center 1109 N Broadway	Yonkers	NY	10701	914-376-8286	376-8288

SPORTS TEAMS & FACILITIES

Name	City	State	Zip	Phone	Fax
Brooklyn Knights (soccer) 125-08 Flatlands Ave Jefferson Field *Web:* www.brooklynknights.com ■ *E-mail:* knightsocr@aol.com	Brooklyn	NY	11208	718-621-1900	621-1332
Long Island Lady Riders (soccer) Evergreen AVe Michael J Tully Jr Stadium *Web:* ladyriders.com ■ *E-mail:* ridersmail@aol.com	New Hyde Park	NY	11753	516-735-2277	735-2288
New York Magic (soccer) 218th St & Broadway Columbia University Stadium	New York	NY	10034	212-447-0932	447-0932
Westchester Flames (soccer) 112 W Boston Post Rd	Mamaroneck	NY	10543	718-626-6767	267-0282
Yonkers Raceway Yonkers & Central Park Aves	Yonkers	NY	10704	914-968-4200	968-4479

— Events —

	Phone
Untermyer Performing Arts Festival (early July-mid-August)	914-377-6442
Westchester County Fair (late May-early June)	914-968-4200
Yonkers Hudson Riverfest (mid-September)	914-377-3378

North Carolina

Population (1999): 7,650,789 **Area (sq mi): 53,821**

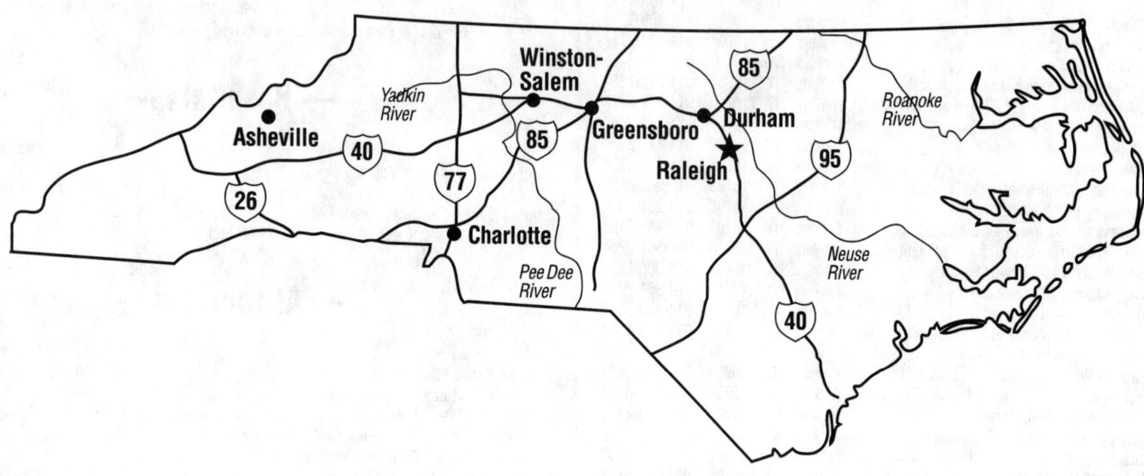

— State Information Sources —

				Phone	*Fax*
North Carolina Citizens for Business & Industry PO Box 2508	Raleigh	NC	27602	919-836-1400	836-1425
Web: www.nccbi.org					
North Carolina Economic Development Div 301 N Wilmington St.	Raleigh	NC	27603	919-733-7978	
North Carolina Parks & Recreation Div PO Box 27687	Raleigh	NC	27699	919-733-4181	715-3085
Web: ils.unc.edu/parkproject/ncparks.html					
North Carolina State Government Information				919-733-1110	
Web: www.state.nc.us ■ *E-mail:* www@sips.state.nc.us					
North Carolina State Library 109 E Jones St	Raleigh	NC	27601	919-733-2570	733-8748
Web: statelibrary.dcr.state.nc.us					
North Carolina Tourism Div 301 N Wilmington St.	Raleigh	NC	27601	919-733-4171	733-8582
TF: 800-847-4862 ■ *Web:* www.visitnc.com					

ON-LINE RESOURCES

Carolina USA .... www.carolinausa.com/carolina/caroncfr.htm
Flatlanders Guide to the Carolina Mountains .... www.carolinamountainguide.com
Go Carolinas .... www.gocarolinas.com
North Carolina Cities .... dir.yahoo.com/Regional/U_S__States/North_Carolina/Cities
North Carolina Coast Host .... www.coasthost-nc.com
North Carolina Counties & Regions .... dir.yahoo.com/Regional/U_S__States/North_Carolina/Counties_and_Regions
North Carolina Encyclopedia .... statelibrary.dcr.state.nc.us/NC/COVER.HTM
North Carolina Guide .... www.ncguide.com/index.htm
North Carolina Scenario .... scenariousa.dstylus.com/nc/indexf.htm
North Carolina Travel & Tourism Guide .... www.travel-library.com/north_america/usa/north_carolina/index.html
Rough Guide Travel North Carolina travel.roughguides.com/content/659/index.htm
Travel.org-North Carolina .... travel.org/n-carol.html
Western North Carolina Guide .... www.wncguide.com
Western North Carolina Guide .... www.wnctoday.net
Yahoo! Get Local North Carolina .... dir.yahoo.com/Regional/U_S__States/North_Carolina

— Cities Profiled —

Asheville

Located in western North Carolina, Asheville is surrounded by the Blue Ridge Mountains, where one can go whitewater rafting, llama trekking, horseback riding, bicycling, rockhounding, or hiking along the mountain trails. The scenic Blue Ridge Parkway winds through the Asheville area and extends from Virginia's Shenandoah National Park to Great Smoky Mountain National Park. The heart of downtown Asheville is Pack Place, which combines arts, culture, science, education, and entertainment in a single location. Not far from Asheville is Black Mountain, the area's antique capital, featuring crafts, antiques, and furniture. The history, culture, and art of the Cherokees can be seen at the 56,000-acre Cherokee Indian Reservation near Asheville.

Population	63,031	**Longitude**	82-55-42 W
Area (Land)	34.9 sq mi	**County**	Buncombe
Area (Water)	0.2 sq mi	**Time Zone**	EST
Elevation	2134 ft	**Area Code/s**	828
Latitude	35-60-08 N		

— Average Temperatures and Precipitation —

TEMPERATURES

	Jan	Feb	Mar	Apr	May	Jun	Jul	Aug	Sep	Oct	Nov	Dec
High	47	50	59	68	75	80	83	82	77	68	59	50
Low	25	28	35	43	51	58	63	62	56	44	36	29

PRECIPITATION

	Jan	Feb	Mar	Apr	May	Jun	Jul	Aug	Sep	Oct	Nov	Dec
Inches	3.3	3.9	4.6	3.4	4.4	4.2	4.5	4.7	3.9	3.6	3.6	3.5

— Important Phone Numbers —

	Phone		Phone
AAA	828-253-5376	**Medical Referral**	828-255-3000
American Express Travel	828-254-0746	**Poison Control Center**	800-848-6946
Emergency	911	**Weather**	828-251-6435

— Information Sources —

				Phone	Fax
Asheville Area Chamber of Commerce 151 Haywood St	Asheville	NC	28801	828-258-6101	254-5583
TF: 800-257-5583 ■ *Web:* www.ashevillechamber.org ■ *E-mail:* asheville@ashevillechamber.org					
Asheville Area Convention & Visitors Bureau PO Box 1010	Asheville	NC	28802	828-258-6102	254-6054
TF: 800-257-1300 ■ *Web:* www.ashevillechamber.org/cvb_top.htm ■ *E-mail:* cvb@ashevillechamber.org					
Asheville-Buncombe Library System 67 Haywood St	Asheville	NC	28801	828-255-5203	255-5213
Web: ils.unc.edu/nclibs/asheville/ablshome.htm					
Asheville City Hall 70 Court Plaza	Asheville	NC	28801	828-259-5601	259-5499
Web: www.ci.asheville.nc.us					
Asheville Civic Center 87 Haywood St	Asheville	NC	28801	828-259-5736	259-5777
Asheville Mayor PO Box 7148	Asheville	NC	28803	828-259-5600	259-5499
Web: www.ci.asheville.nc.us/admin/meetmay.htm					
Asheville Planning & Development Dept PO Box 7148	Asheville	NC	28802	828-259-5830	259-5428
Web: www.ci.asheville.nc.us/planning/menu.htm ■ *E-mail:* planning@cityhallnt.ci.asheville.nc.us					
Better Business Bureau Serving Asheville/Western North Carolina 1200 BB & T Bldg	Asheville	NC	28801	828-253-2392	252-5039
Web: www.asheville.bbb.org					
Buncombe County 1 Oak Plaza	Asheville	NC	28801	828-250-4000	255-5461

On-Line Resources

Area Guide Asheville	asheville.areaguides.net
Asheville Home Page	www.asheville.com
City Knowledge Asheville	www.cityknowledge.com/nc_asheville.htm
CityTravelers.com Guide to Asheville	www.citytravelers.com/asheville.htm
Excite.com Asheville City Guide	www.excite.com/travel/countries/united_states/north_carolina/asheville
NITC Travelbase City Guide Asheville	www.travelbase.com/auto/guides/asheville-area-nc.html
Welcome to Asheville	asheville-nc.com/
Western North Carolina Guide	www.wncguide.com

— Transportation Services —

AIRPORTS

	Phone
■ **Asheville Regional Airport (AVL)**	
12 miles S of downtown (approx 25 minutes)	828-684-2226

Airport Transportation

	Phone
Beaver Lake Cab $19-20 fare to downtown	828-252-1913
Jolly Taxi Co $20-24 fare to downtown	828-253-1411
Yellow Cab $20 fare to downtown	828-253-3311

Commercial Airlines

	Phone		Phone
Atlantic Southeast	800-282-3424	Midway	800-446-4392
Comair	800-354-9822	US Airways	800-428-4322
Delta	800-221-1212	US Airways Express	800-428-4322

Charter Airlines

	Phone		Phone
Asheville Jet Center	828-684-6832	Diamond Ridge Jet	828-687-0091

CAR RENTALS

	Phone		Phone
Avis	828-684-7144	Hertz	828-684-6455
Budget	828-684-2272	National	828-254-7283
Enterprise	828-251-0065	Rent-A-Wreck	828-684-3811

LIMO/TAXI

	Phone		Phone
Beaver Lake Cab	828-252-1913	New Blue Bird Taxi Co	828-258-8331
J & H Cab	828-686-5920	Red Cab Co	828-232-1112
Jolly Taxi Co	828-253-1411	Yellow Cab	828-253-3311

MASS TRANSIT

	Phone
Asheville Transit Authority $.75 Base fare	828-253-5691

RAIL/BUS

				Phone
Greyhound/Trailways Bus Station 2 Tunnel Rd	Asheville	NC	28805	828-253-5353
TF: 800-231-2222				

— Accommodations —

HOTELS, MOTELS, RESORTS

				Phone	Fax
American Court Motel 85 Merrimon Ave	Asheville	NC	28801	828-253-4427	
TF: 800-233-3582					
Applewood Manor Inn 62 Cumberland Cir	Asheville	NC	28801	828-254-2244	254-0899
TF: 800-442-2197 ■ *Web:* www.comscape.com/apple					
Best Inns of America 1435 Tunnel Rd	Asheville	NC	28805	828-298-4000	
TF: 800-237-8466					
Best Western 275 Smokey Pk Hwy	Asheville	NC	28806	828-667-4501	665-6773
TF: 800-528-1234 ■ *Web:* www.bestwesternbiltmore.com					
Best Western Biltmore Hotel 22 Woodfin St	Asheville	NC	28801	828-253-1851	252-9205
TF: 800-528-1234					

Asheville — Hotels, Motels, Resorts (Cont'd)

Name / Address	City	State	ZIP	Phone	Fax
Best Western Hotel 501 Tunnel Rd	Asheville	NC	28805	828-298-5562	298-5002
TF: 800-528-1234					
Blakehouse Inn 150 Royal Pines Dr	Arden	NC	28704	828-681-5227	681-0420
Budget Motel 1 Acton Cir	Asheville	NC	28806	828-665-2100	
Cairn Brae 217 Patton Mountain Rd	Asheville	NC	28804	828-252-9219	
Colby House 230 Pearson Dr	Asheville	NC	28801	828-253-5644	259-9479
TF: 800-982-2118 ■ *Web:* www.colbyhouse.com					
Comfort Inn River Ridge 800 Fairview Rd	Asheville	NC	28803	828-298-9141	298-6629
TF: 800-228-5150					
Comfort Suites 890 Brevard Rd	Asheville	NC	28806	828-665-4000	665-9082
TF: 800-622-4005					
Corner Oak Manor 53 St Dunstans Rd	Asheville	NC	28803	828-253-3525	253-3525
Courtyard by Marriott Asheville 1 Buckstone Pl	Asheville	NC	28805	828-281-0041	281-1069
TF: 800-321-2211 ■ *Web:* courtyard.com/AVLCY					
Days Inn Asheville Airport 183 Underwood Rd	Fletcher	NC	28732	828-684-2281	687-0157
TF: 800-329-7466					
Days Inn Downtown 120 Patton Ave	Asheville	NC	28801	828-254-9661	254-9661
TF: 800-329-7466					
Days Inn East 1500 Tunnel Rd	Asheville	NC	28805	828-298-5140	298-8191
TF: 800-329-7466					
Days Inn North 3 Reynolds Mountain Blvd	Asheville	NC	28804	828-645-9191	645-7180
TF: 800-329-7466					
Econo Lodge 196 Underwood Rd	Fletcher	NC	28732	828-684-1200	687-7861
TF: 800-553-2666					
Extended StayAmerica 6 Kenilworth Knoll	Asheville	NC	28805	828-253-3483	253-3482
TF: 800-398-7829					
Fairfield Inn by Marriott 31 Aiport Pk Dr	Fletcher	NC	28732	828-684-1144	684-3377
TF: 800-228-2800 ■ *Web:* fairfieldinn.com/AVLNC					
Flint Street Inn 116 Flint St	Asheville	NC	28801	828-253-6723	
Forest Manor Inn 866 Hendersonville Rd	Asheville	NC	28803	828-274-3531	274-3036
TF: 800-866-3531					
Grove Park Inn Resort 290 Macon Ave	Asheville	NC	28804	828-252-2711	253-7053
TF: 800-438-5800 ■ *Web:* www.groveparkinn.com ■ *E-mail:* info@groveparkinn.com					
Hampton Inn 1 Rocky Ridge Rd	Asheville	NC	28806	828-667-2022	665-9680
TF: 800-426-7866					
Haywood Park Hotel 1 Battery Park Ave	Asheville	NC	28801	828-252-2522	253-0481
TF: 800-228-2522					
Holiday Inn 1450 Tunnel Rd	Asheville	NC	28805	828-298-5611	299-3308
TF: 800-465-4329					
Holiday Inn 201 Tunnel Rd	Asheville	NC	28805	828-252-4000	258-0359
TF: 800-465-4329					
Holiday Inn Airport 550 Airport Rd	Fletcher	NC	28732	828-684-1213	684-3778
TF: 800-465-4329					
Holiday Inn Express 234 Hendersonville Rd	Asheville	NC	28803	828-274-0101	277-9800
TF: 800-465-4329					
Holiday Inn SunSpree Hotel 1 Holiday Inn Dr	Asheville	NC	28806	828-254-3211	285-2688
TF: 800-733-3211					
Howard Johnson Biltmore 190 Hendersonville Rd	Asheville	NC	28803	828-274-2300	274-2304
TF: 800-446-4656					
Interstate Motel 37 Hiawassee St	Asheville	NC	28801	828-254-0945	285-9398
Mountain Springs Cottages Chalets & Cabins PO Box 6922	Asheville	NC	28816	828-665-1004	667-1581
Web: www.mtnsprings.com ■ *E-mail:* information@mtnsprings.com					
Quality Inn Biltmore 115 Hendersonville Rd	Asheville	NC	28803	828-274-1800	274-5960
TF: 800-228-5151					
Radisson Hotel 1 Thomas Wolfe Plaza	Asheville	NC	28801	828-252-8211	236-9616
TF: 800-333-3333					
Ramada Limited 180 Tunnel Rd	Asheville	NC	28805	828-254-7451	254-3880
TF: 800-272-6232					
Red Roof Inn West 16 Crowell Rd	Asheville	NC	28806	828-667-9803	667-9810
TF: 800-843-7663					
Richmond Hill Inn 87 Richmond Hill Dr	Asheville	NC	28806	828-252-7313	252-8726
TF: 800-545-9238					
Sleep Inn Biltmore 117 Hendersonville Rd	Asheville	NC	28803	828-277-1800	274-7101
TF: 800-753-3746					
Snowbird Mountain Lodge 275 Santeetlah Rd	Robbinsville	NC	28771	828-479-3433	479-3473
TF: 800-941-9290					
Waynesville Country Club Inn 176 Country Club Dr	Waynesville	NC	28786	828-456-3551	456-3555
TF: 800-627-6250					

— Restaurants —

Name / Address	City	State	ZIP	Phone
23 Page (Continental) 1 Battery Park Ave	Asheville	NC	28801	828-252-3685
Apollo Flame Restaurant (American) 485 Hendersonville Rd	Asheville	NC	28803	828-274-3582
Bier Garden (American) 46 Haywood St	Asheville	NC	28801	828-285-0003
Blue Ridge Dining Room (American) 290 Macon Ave	Asheville	NC	28804	828-252-2711
Bosco's Italian Eatery (Italian) 2310 Hendersonville Rd	Arden	NC	28704	828-684-1024
Cafe Max & Rosie's (Vegetarian) 52 N Lexington Ave	Asheville	NC	28801	828-254-5342
Cafe on the Square (Continental) 1 Biltmore Ave Pack Sq	Asheville	NC	28801	828-251-5565
Charlotte Street Grill & Pub (American) 157 Charlotte St	Asheville	NC	28801	828-253-5348
Deerpark Restaurant (American) 1 N Pack Sq Biltmore Estate	Asheville	NC	28801	828-274-6260
El Chapala (Mexican) 868 Merrimon Ave	Asheville	NC	28804	828-258-0899
Flying Frog Cafe (International) 76 Haywood St	Asheville	NC	28801	828-254-9411
Gabrielle's (Continental) 87 Richmond Hill Dr	Asheville	NC	28806	828-252-7313
Greenery The (Continental) 148 Tunnel Rd	Asheville	NC	28805	828-253-2809
Hathaway's (American) 3 Boston Way	Asheville	NC	28803	828-274-1298
Jerusalem Cafe (Middle Eastern) 78 Patton Ave	Asheville	NC	28801	828-254-0255
Laughing Seed Cafe (Vegetarian) 40 Wall St	Asheville	NC	28801	828-252-3445
Magnolia's Raw Bar & Grille (Seafood) 26 Walnut St	Asheville	NC	28801	828-251-5211
Market Place The (American) 20 Wall St	Asheville	NC	28801	828-252-4162
Mountain Smokehouse (Barbecue) 802 Fairview Rd	Asheville	NC	28801	828-298-8121
Pedro's Porch (Mexican) 1 Lodge St	Asheville	NC	28803	828-274-9388
Poseidon Steak & Seafood (Steak/Seafood) 1327 Tunnel Rd	Asheville	NC	28805	828-298-4121
Rio Burrito (Mexican) 11 Broadway	Asheville	NC	28801	828-253-2422
Ristorante da Vincenzo (Italian) 10 N Market St	Asheville	NC	28801	828-254-4698
Sagebrush Steakhouse & Saloon (Steak) 1030 Merrimon Ave	Asheville	NC	28804	828-255-8383
Sunset Terrace at Grove Park Inn (Continental) 290 Macon Ave	Asheville	NC	28804	828-252-2711
Three Brothers Restaurant (American) 183 Haywood St	Asheville	NC	28801	828-253-4971
Tripps (American) 311 College St	Asheville	NC	28801	828-254-9163
Uptown Cafe (International) 22 Battery Park Ave	Asheville	NC	28801	828-253-2158
Westside Grill (American) 1190 Patton Ave	Asheville	NC	28806	828-252-9605
Windmill European Grill (European) 85 Tunnel Rd	Asheville	NC	28805	828-253-5285
Yoshida Steak & Seafood House (Japanese) 4 Regent Park Blvd	Asheville	NC	28806	828-252-5903

— Goods and Services —

SHOPPING

Name / Address	City	State	ZIP	Phone	Fax
Asheville Mall 3 S Tunnel Rd	Asheville	NC	28805	828-298-5080	298-5096
Biltmore Square Mall 800 Brevard Rd	Asheville	NC	28806	828-667-2210	665-1857
Innsbruck Mall 85 Tunnel Rd	Asheville	NC	28805	828-254-0954	254-0965
River Ridge Marketplace 800 Fairview Rd	Asheville	NC	28803	828-298-9785	298-0405
Town & Country Square 175 Weaverville Hwy	Asheville	NC	28804	828-645-7166	645-6726
Western North Carolina Farmer's Market 570 Brevard Rd	Asheville	NC	28806	828-253-1691	252-2025
Westgate Shopping Center 40 Westgate Pkwy	Asheville	NC	28806	828-252-0218	254-7474

BANKS

Name / Address	City	State	ZIP	Phone	Fax
Blue Ridge Savings Bank 20 S Pack Sq	Asheville	NC	28801	828-252-1893	251-1077
Centura Bank 8 O Henry Ave	Asheville	NC	28801	828-252-3600	252-0939
First Citizens Bank 108 Patton Ave	Asheville	NC	28802	828-257-5700	257-5731*
**Fax:* Cust Svc					
First Union National Bank 82 Patton Ave	Asheville	NC	28801	800-275-3862	251-7152*
**Fax Area Code:* 828					
NationsBank of North Carolina NA 68 Patton Ave	Asheville	NC	28801	828-251-8243	251-8203
TF Cust Svc: 800-333-6262*					

BUSINESS SERVICES

Name	Phone
Airborne Express	800-247-2676
BAX Global	800-225-5229
Comforce Staffing Service	828-254-7009
DHL Worldwide Express	800-225-5345
Federal Express	800-238-5355
Kinko's	828-254-0021
Mail Boxes Etc	800-789-4623
Manpower Temporary Services	828-258-0033
Post Office	828-271-6421
UPS	800-742-5877
Westaff Temporary Services	828-254-3898

Asheville (Cont'd)

— Media —

PUBLICATIONS

Name / Address	City	State	Zip	Phone	Fax
Asheville Citizen Times‡ PO Box 2090	Asheville	NC	28802	828-252-5611	251-0585
TF: 800-800-4204 ■ *Web:* www.citizen-times.com ■ *E-mail:* news@citizen-times.com					

‡*Daily newspapers*

TELEVISION

Name / Address	City	State	Zip	Phone	Fax
WASV-TV Ch 62 (WB) 1293 Hendersonville Rd Suite 12	Asheville	NC	28803	828-277-0902	277-5060
WHNS-TV Ch 21 (Fox) 21 Interstate Ct	Greenville	SC	29615	864-288-2100	297-0728
Web: www.whns.com ■ *E-mail:* fox21@whns.com					
WLOS-TV Ch 13 (ABC) 288 Macon Ave	Asheville	NC	28804	828-255-0013	255-4618
Web: www.wlos.com					
WSPA-TV Ch 7 (CBS) PO Box 1717	Spartanburg	SC	29304	864-576-7777	587-5430
Web: www.wspa.com ■ *E-mail:* newschannel7@wspa.com					
WUNC-TV Ch 4 (PBS) PO Box 14900	Research Triangle Park	NC	27709	919-549-7000	549-7201
Web: www.unctv.org ■ *E-mail:* viewer@unctv.org					
WYFF-TV Ch 4 (NBC) PO Box 788	Greenville	SC	29602	864-242-4404	240-5305
Web: www.wyff.com/ ■ *E-mail:* wyff@aol.com					

RADIO

Name / Address	City	State	Zip	Phone	Fax
WCQS-FM 88.1 MHz (NPR) 73 Broadway	Asheville	NC	28801	828-253-6875	253-6700
WISE-AM 1310 kHz (Nost) 90 Lookout Rd	Asheville	NC	28804	828-253-1310	253-5619
E-mail: wiseradio@ioa.com					
WKJV-AM 1380 kHz (Rel) 70 Adams Hill Rd	Asheville	NC	28806	828-252-1380	259-9427
WKSF-FM 99.9 MHz (Ctry) 13 Summerlin Rd	Asheville	NC	28806	828-253-3835	255-7850
WMXF-FM 104.3 Mhz (AC) 1318-B Patton Ave	Asheville	NC	28806	828-281-1049	281-3299
WNCW-FM 88.7 MHz (NPR) PO Box 804	Spindale	NC	28160	828-287-8000	287-8012
Web: www.wncw.org/ ■ *E-mail:* wncw@blueridge.net					
WSKY-AM 1230 kHz (Rel) 40 Westgate Pkwy Suite F	Asheville	NC	28806	828-251-2000	251-2135
WTZQ-AM 1600 kHz (Nost) 90 Lookout Rd	Asheville	NC	28804	828-692-1600	253-5619
WTZY-AM 880 kHz (N/T) 1318-B Patton Ave	Asheville	NC	28806	828-255-1906	281-3299
WWNC-AM 570 kHz (Ctry) 13 Summerlin Rd	Asheville	NC	28806	828-253-3835	255-7850
WZLS-FM 96.5 MHz (Rock) 780 Hendersonville Rd	Asheville	NC	28803	828-277-0011	277-7991

— Colleges/Universities —

Name / Address	City	State	Zip	Phone	Fax
Asheville-Buncombe Technical Community College 340 Victoria Rd	Asheville	NC	28801	828-254-1921	251-6355
Cecils Junior College of Business 1567 Patton Ave	Asheville	NC	28806	828-252-2486	252-8558
Mars Hill College 124 Cascade St	Mars Hill	NC	28754	828-689-1201	689-1478
TF Admissions: 800-543-1514 ■ *Web:* www.mhc.edu ■ *E-mail:* admissions@mhc.edu					
Montreat College 310 Gaither Cir	Montreat	NC	28757	828-669-8011	669-9554
TF Admissions: 800-622-6968 ■ *Web:* www.montreat.edu ■ *E-mail:* admissions@montreat.edu					
University of North Carolina Asheville 1 University Heights	Asheville	NC	28804	828-251-6600	251-6482
Web: www.unca.edu ■ *E-mail:* admissions@unca.edu					
Warren Wilson College PO Box 9000	Asheville	NC	28815	828-298-3325	299-4841
Web: www.warren-wilson.edu					

— Hospitals —

Name / Address	City	State	Zip	Phone	Fax
Memorial Mission Hospital 509 Biltmore Ave	Asheville	NC	28801	828-255-4000	255-4018
Memorial Mission Medical Center 509 Biltmore Ave	Asheville	NC	28801	828-255-4000	255-4018
Saint Joseph's Hospital 428 Biltmore Ave	Asheville	NC	28801	828-255-3100	258-6652*
**Fax:* Admitting					
Veterans Affairs Medical Center 1100 Tunnel Rd	Asheville	NC	28805	828-298-7911	299-2502

— Attractions —

Name / Address	City	State	Zip	Phone	Fax
Antique Car Museum/Grovewood Gallery 111 Grovewood Rd	Asheville	NC	28804	828-253-7651	254-2489
Web: www.grovewood.com/ ■ *E-mail:* grovewood@grovewood.com					
Asheville Art Museum Pack Pl PO Box 1717	Asheville	NC	28802	828-253-3227	257-4503
Asheville Community Theatre 35 E Walnut St	Asheville	NC	28801	828-254-1320	252-4723
Web: www.ashevilletheatre.org ■ *E-mail:* act@ashevilletheatre.org					
Asheville Urban Trail PO Box 7148	Asheville	NC	28802	828-259-5855	259-5832
Biltmore Estate 1 N Pack Sq	Asheville	NC	28801	828-274-6333	274-6396
TF: 800-543-2961 ■ *Web:* www.biltmore.com					
Black Mountain 201 E State St	Black Mountain	NC	28711	828-669-2300	669-1407
Blue Ridge Parkway 400 BB & T Bldg 1 W Pack Sq	Asheville	NC	28801	828-271-4779	271-4313
Web: www.nps.gov/blri/					
Blue Spiral 1 38 Biltmore Ave	Asheville	NC	28801	828-251-0202	251-0884
Botanical Gardens at Asheville 151 WT Weaver Blvd	Asheville	NC	28804	828-252-5190	
Cape Lookout National Seashore 131 Charles St	Harkers Island	NC	28531	252-728-2250	728-2160
Web: www.nps.gov/calo/ ■ *E-mail:* CALO_Administration@nps.gov					
Cherokee Indian Reservation PO Box 460	Cherokee	NC	28719	800-438-1601	
Chimney Rock Park US 74 & 64	Asheville	NC	28720	828-625-9611	625-9610
TF: 800-277-9611 ■ *Web:* www.chimneyrockpark.com/ ■ *E-mail:* visit@chimneyrockpark.com					
Colburn Gem & Mineral Museum PO Box 1617	Asheville	NC	28802	828-254-7162	251-5652
Connemara-Carl Sandburg Home National Historic Site 1928 Little River Rd	Flat Rock	NC	28731	828-693-4178	693-4179
Web: www.nps.gov/carl/					
Downtown Asheville Historic District Downtown Asheville	Asheville	NC		828-251-9973	252-8898
Estes-Winn Memorial Automobile Museum 111 Grovewood Rd	Asheville	NC	28804	828-253-7651	254-2489
Flat Rock Playhouse 2661 Greenville Hwy	Flat Rock	NC	28731	828-693-0731	693-6795
Web: www.flatrockplayhouse.org/ ■ *E-mail:* frp@flatrockplayhouse.org					
Folk Art Center PO Box 9545	Asheville	NC	28815	828-298-7928	298-7962
Web: www.southernhighlandguild.org					
Ghost Town Hwy 19	Maggie Valley	NC	28751	828-926-1140	926-8811
TF: 800-446-7886					
Grandfather Mountain Mile Post 305 US 221 & Blue Ridge Pkwy	Linville	NC	28646	828-733-4337	733-2608
TF: 800-468-7325 ■ *Web:* www.grandfather.com ■ *E-mail:* nature@grandfather.com					
Great Smoky Mountains National Park 107 Park Headquarters Rd	Gatlinburg	TN	37738	865-436-1200	436-1220
Web: www.nps.gov/grsm/					
Health Adventure 2 S Pack Sq	Asheville	NC	28801	828-254-6373	257-4521
Web: www.health-adventure.com/ ■ *E-mail:* info@health-adventure.com					
Linville Caverns US 221	Marion	NC	28752	828-756-4171	
TF: 800-419-0540 ■ *Web:* www.linvillecaverns.com					
North Carolina Arboretum 100 Frederick Law Olmsted Way	Asheville	NC	28806	828-665-2492	665-2371
Pack Place 2 S Pack Sq	Asheville	NC	28801	828-257-4500	251-5652
Web: mainsrv.main.nc.us/packplace/ ■ *E-mail:* packplace@main.nc.us					
Pisgah National Forest NC 280 & US 276	Brevard	NC	28768	828-877-3350	884-7527
Riverside Cemetery 53 Birch St	Asheville	NC	28801	828-258-8480	
Smith McDowell House 283 Victoria Rd	Asheville	NC	28801	828-253-9231	253-5518
Thomas Wolfe Memorial 52 N Market St	Asheville	NC	28801	828-253-8304	252-8171
Web: home.att.net/~WolfeMemorial ■ *E-mail:* wolfememorial@worldnet.att.net					
Vance Birthplace State Historic Site 911 Reems Creek Rd	Weaverville	NC	28787	828-645-6706	
Western North Carolina Agricultural Center 1301 Fanning Bridge Rd	Fletcher	NC	28732	828-687-1414	687-9272
Western North Carolina Farmer's Market 570 Brevard Rd	Asheville	NC	28806	828-253-1691	252-2025
Western North Carolina Nature Center 75 Gashes Creek Rd	Asheville	NC	28805	828-298-5600	298-2644
Wolf Laurel Slopes Rt 3 Box 129	Mars Hill	NC	28754	828-689-4111	689-9819
TF: 800-817-4111 ■ *Web:* www.ioa.com/home/wolflaurel ■ *E-mail:* wolflaurel@ioa.com					
Wortham Diana Theatre 2 S Pack Sq	Asheville	NC	28801	828-257-4530	251-5652
YMI Cultural Center 39 S Market St	Asheville	NC	28801	828-252-4614	257-4539

SPORTS TEAMS & FACILITIES

Name / Address	City	State	Zip	Phone	Fax
Asheville Motor Speedway 219 Amboy Rd	Asheville	NC	28806	828-236-2922	
Asheville Tourists (baseball) 30 Buchanan Pl McCormick Field	Asheville	NC	28801	828-258-0428	258-0320

Asheville (Cont'd)

— Events —

	Phone
Arts & Crafts Antique Conference (mid-February)	800-257-1300
Asheville Christmas Parade (late November)	828-251-4117
Asheville Greek Festival (early October)	828-299-7244
Bele Chere Festival (late July)	828-258-6111
Big Band Dance Weekend (late August)	800-438-5800
Biltmore Estate's Easter Egg Hunt (late March)	800-543-2961
Biltmore Estate's Festival of Flowers (early April-early May)	800-543-2961
Black Mountain Music Festival (late May & mid-October)	828-281-3382
Candlelight Christmas Evenings (early November-early January)	800-543-2961
Christmas at Biltmore Estate (late November-early January)	800-543-2961
Christmas Parade (late November)	828-259-5800
Comedy Classic Weekend (early March)	828-252-2711
Craft Fair of the Southern Highlands (mid-July)	828-298-7928
Days in the Gardens (early May)	828-252-5190
First Night Asheville (December 31)	828-259-5800
Forest Festival Day (early October)	828-877-3130
Fourth of July Celebration (July 4)	828-259-5800
Goombay Festival (late August)	828-252-4614
Great Smoky Mountain Trout Festival (late May)	828-456-3575
Hands On Asheville (early February-late March)	800-280-0005
Happy Trails Week (mid-June)	828-877-3130
High Country Christmas Art & Craft Show (late November)	828-254-0072
Jazz Weekends at the Winery (late September-late October)	800-543-2961
Lake Eden Arts Festival (late May)	828-686-8742
Light Up Your Holidays (late November-late December)	828-259-5800
Michaelmas Fair (late September-late October)	800-543-2961
Mountain Dance & Folk Festival (early August)	828-258-6101
OctoberFest (late September)	800-438-5800
Red White & Blues at the Winery (early July)	800-543-2961
Spring Herb Festival (early May)	828-689-5974
Spring Wildflower & Bird Pilgrimage (early May)	828-251-6444
Thomas Wolfe Festival (early October)	828-253-8304
Very Special Arts Festival (early May)	828-298-7484
Village Art & Craft Fair (early August)	828-274-2831
Winery Al Fresco Jazz Celebration (late May)	800-543-2961
Winter Pastimes: The Arts in America's Largest Home (early February-early May)	800-543-2961
Wonderful Winery Weekend (early September)	800-543-2961

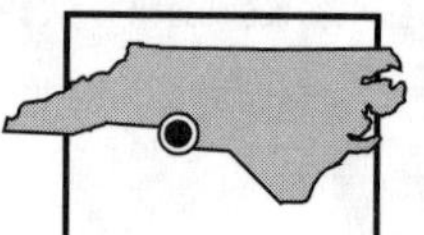

Charlotte

Located between the Carolina beaches and the Great Smoky Mountains, with the spectacular Blue Ridge Mountains several hours to the west, Charlotte is North Carolina's largest city. On the state line between North and South Carolina, just south of Charlotte, is Paramount's Carowinds amusement park. To the southwest of the city is Kings Mountain National Military Park, site of a major battle of the American Revolution. In Charlotte, numerous city parks, as well as nearby lakes, offer recreational activities, and the Charlotte Motor Speedway hosts top racing events.

Population	504,637	**Longitude**	80-84-29 W
Area (Land)	174.3 sq mi	**County**	Mecklenburg
Area (Water)	0.3 sq mi	**Time Zone**	EST
Elevation	700 ft	**Area Code/s**	704
Latitude	35-23-55 N		

— Average Temperatures and Precipitation —

TEMPERATURES

	Jan	Feb	Mar	Apr	May	Jun	Jul	Aug	Sep	Oct	Nov	Dec
High	49	53	62	71	78	86	89	88	82	72	63	52
Low	30	32	39	48	56	66	70	69	63	51	42	33

PRECIPITATION

	Jan	Feb	Mar	Apr	May	Jun	Jul	Aug	Sep	Oct	Nov	Dec
Inches	3.7	3.8	4.4	2.7	3.8	3.4	3.9	3.7	3.5	3.4	3.2	3.5

— Important Phone Numbers —

	Phone		Phone
AAA	704-569-3600	**Medical Referral**	704-376-0847
American Express Travel	704-364-3373	**Poison Control Center**	704-379-5827
Dental Referral	704-376-0847	**Time/Temp**	704-375-6711
Emergency	911	**Traveler's Friend Hotline**	704-536-0001
HotelDocs	800-468-3537	**Travelers Aid**	704-334-7288
Info Net	704-845-4636	**Weather**	704-570-9288

— Information Sources —

				Phone	Fax
Better Business Bureau Serving Southern Piedmont Carolinas 5200 Park Rd Suite 202 *Web:* www.charlotte.bbb.org	Charlotte	NC	28209	704-527-0012	525-7624
Charlotte & Mecklenburg County Public Library 310 N Tryon St *Web:* www.plcmc.lib.nc.us	Charlotte	NC	28202	704-336-2725	336-2002
Charlotte Chamber of Commerce PO Box 32785 *Web:* www.charlottechamber.org	Charlotte	NC	28232	704-378-1300	374-1903
Charlotte City Hall 600 E 4th St Charlotte-Mecklenburg Govt Ctr *Web:* www.ci.charlotte.nc.us	Charlotte	NC	28202	704-336-2241	336-6644
Charlotte Convention & Visitors Bureau 122 E Stonewall St *TF:* 800-722-1994 ■ *Web:* charlottecvb.org	Charlotte	NC	28202	704-334-2282	342-3972
Charlotte Convention Center 501 S College St *TF:* 800-432-7488 ■ *Web:* www.charlotteconventionctr.com	Charlotte	NC	28202	704-339-6000	339-6111
Charlotte Economic Development Dept 600 E 4th St Charlotte-Mecklenburg Govt Ctr 8th Fl *Web:* www.ci.charlotte.nc.us/ciplanning	Charlotte	NC	28202	704-336-3399	336-5123
Charlotte Mayor 600 E 4th St Charlotte-Mecklenburg Govt Ctr *Web:* www.ci.charlotte.nc.us/cimayor	Charlotte	NC	28202	704-336-2241	336-3097
Mecklenburg County 600 E 4th St Charlotte-Mecklenburg Govt Ctr *Web:* www.charmeck.nc.us	Charlotte	NC	28202	704-336-2472	336-5887

On-Line Resources

4Charlotte.com	www.4charlotte.com
About.com Guide to Charlotte	charlotte.about.com
Anthill City Guide Charlotte	www.anthill.com/city.asp?city=charlotte
Area Guide Charlotte	charlotte.areaguides.net
Charlotte CityLink	www.usacitylink.com/citylink/charlotte
Charlotte Just Go	www.justgo.com/charlotte/
Charlotte Net	www.charlottenet.com/
Charlotte Post	www.thepost.mindspring.com/
Charlotte Region	www.charlotteregion.com/
Charlotte Traveler's Friend	www.travelersfriend.com
Charlotte's Web	www.charweb.org/
City Knowledge Charlotte	www.cityknowledge.com/nc_charlotte.htm
CitySearch Charlotte	charlotte.citysearch.com
CityTravelers.com Guide to Charlotte	www.citytravelers.com/charlotte.htm
Creative Loafing Charlotte	www.creativeloafing.com/charlotte/newsstand/current/index.html
DigitalCity Charlotte	home.digitalcity.com/charlotte
Excite.com Charlotte City Guide	www.excite.com/travel/countries/united_states/north_carolina/charlotte
Guest Guide Online	www.guestguideonline.com
Savvy Diner Guide to Charlotte Restaurants	www.savvydiner.com/charlotte/

Charlotte (Cont'd)

— Transportation Services —

AIRPORTS

■ **Charlotte/Douglas International Airport (CLT)**	Phone
7 miles W of downtown (approx 15 minutes)	704-359-4000

Airport Transportation

	Phone
Carolina Airport Express $8 fare to downtown	704-391-1111
Carolina Transportation $8 fare to downtown	704-359-9600
Gold Line Express $8 fare to downtown	704-534-4131
Taxi $14 fare to downtown	704-332-6161

Commercial Airlines

	Phone		Phone
American	800-433-7300	**United**	800-241-6522
Delta	800-221-1212	**US Airways**	800-428-4322
TWA	800-221-2000		

Charter Airlines

	Phone		Phone
Piedmont Aviation Services Inc	800-548-1978	**Southeast Airmotive Corp**	704-359-8403

CAR RENTALS

	Phone		Phone
Alamo	704-359-4360	**Hertz**	704-359-0114
Avis	704-359-4580	**National**	704-359-0215
Budget	704-359-5001	**Payless**	704-359-4640
Dollar	704-359-4700	**Thrifty**	704-394-6588
Enterprise	704-391-0061	**Triangle**	800-643-7368

LIMO/TAXI

	Phone		Phone
Bush Limousine	704-394-0131	**Crown Cab**	704-334-6666
Carolina Classic Limousine	704-525-2393	**Executive Car Service**	704-525-2191
Champagne Transportation	704-398-1007	**Rose Limousine**	704-522-8258
Charlotte Checker Cab	704-333-1111	**Yellow Cab**	704-332-6161

MASS TRANSIT

	Phone
Charlotte Transit System $.80 Base fare	704-336-3366

RAIL/BUS

				Phone
Amtrak Station 1914 N Tryon St *TF:* 800-872-7245	Charlotte	NC	28206	704-376-4416
Greyhound/Trailways Bus Station 601 W Trade St	Charlotte	NC	28202	704-372-0456

— Accommodations —

HOTELS, MOTELS, RESORTS

				Phone	Fax
Adam's Mark Hotel 555 S McDowell St *TF:* 800-444-2326 ■ *Web:* www.adamsmark.com/char.htm	Charlotte	NC	28204	704-372-4100	348-4645
AmeriSuites 7900 Forest Pt Blvd *TF:* 800-833-1516 ■ *Web:* www.amerisuites.com	Charlotte	NC	28273	704-522-8400	522-8489
Ascot Inn 1025 S Tyron St *TF:* 800-333-9417	Charlotte	NC	28203	704-377-3611	377-3611
Best Inn & Suites 219 Archdale Dr *TF:* 800-274-2538	Charlotte	NC	28217	704-527-8500	523-7803
Best Western Airport 2707 Little Rock Rd *TF:* 800-528-1234	Charlotte	NC	28214	704-394-4301	394-1844
Best Western Merchandise Mart 3024 E Independence Blvd *TF:* 800-424-2756	Charlotte	NC	28205	704-358-3755	358-4718
Clarion Hotel 321 W Woodlawn Rd *TF:* 800-252-7466	Charlotte	NC	28217	704-523-1400	529-1448
Comfort Inn 5822 W Park Dr *TF:* 800-228-5150	Charlotte	NC	28217	704-525-2626	525-3372
Country Inn & Suites by Carlson 2541 Little Rock Rd *TF:* 800-456-4000	Charlotte	NC	28214	704-394-2000	394-7467
Courtyard by Marriott 2700 Little Rock Rd *TF:* 800-321-2211 ■ *Web:* courtyard.com/CLTCA	Charlotte	NC	28214	704-319-9900	319-9901
Courtyard by Marriott 800 Arrowood Rd *TF:* 800-321-2211 ■ *Web:* courtyard.com/CLTAW	Charlotte	NC	28217	704-527-5055	525-5848
Days Inn 118 E Woodlawn Rd *TF:* 800-329-7466	Charlotte	NC	28217	704-525-5500	525-9970
Days Inn Central 601 N Tryon St *TF:* 800-325-2525	Charlotte	NC	28208	704-333-4733	329-7466
Doubletree Club Hotel 895 W Trade St *TF:* 800-222-8733 ■ *Web:* www.doubletreehotels.com/DoubleT/Hotel61/70/70Main.htm	Charlotte	NC	28202	704-347-0070	347-0267
Dunhill Hotel 237 N Tryon St *TF:* 800-354-4141	Charlotte	NC	28202	704-332-4141	376-4117
Embassy Suites 4800 S Tryon St *TF:* 800-362-2779	Charlotte	NC	28217	704-527-8400	527-7035
Extended StayAmerica 8211 University Executive Park Dr *TF:* 800-398-7829	Charlotte	NC	28262	704-510-1636	510-1637
Fairfield Inn by Marriott Charlotte Airport 3400 S I-85 Service Rd *TF:* 800-228-2800 ■ *Web:* fairfieldinn.com/CLTAF	Charlotte	NC	28208	704-392-0600	391-1891
Fairfield Inn by Marriott Northeast 5415 N I-85 Service Rd *TF:* 800-228-2800 ■ *Web:* fairfieldinn.com/CLTNE	Charlotte	NC	28262	704-596-2999	596-3329
Four Points by Sheraton 201 S McDowell St *TF:* 800-325-3535	Charlotte	NC	28204	704-372-7550	333-6737
Hampton Inn 440 Griffith Rd *TF:* 800-426-7866	Charlotte	NC	28217	704-525-0747	522-0968
Hampton Inn Airport 3127 Sloan Dr *TF:* 800-426-7866	Charlotte	NC	28208	704-392-1600	392-7952
Hilton at University Place 8629 JM Keynes Dr *Web:* www.hilton.com/hotels/CLTHUHF	Charlotte	NC	28262	704-547-7444	549-9708
Hilton Charlotte & Towers 222 E 3rd St *TF:* 800-445-8667 ■ *Web:* www.hilton.com/hotels/CLTHHHH	Charlotte	NC	28202	704-377-1500	377-4143
Holiday Inn Center City 230 N College St *TF:* 800-465-4329	Charlotte	NC	28202	704-335-5400	376-4921
Holiday Inn Independence 3501 E Independence Blvd *TF:* 800-465-4329	Charlotte	NC	28205	704-537-1010	531-2439
Holiday Inn Salisbury 530 Jake Alexander Blvd S *TF:* 800-465-4329	Salisbury	NC	28147	704-637-3100	637-9152
Holiday Inn Woodlawn 212 Woodlawn Rd *TF:* 800-847-7829	Charlotte	NC	28217	704-525-8350	522-0671
Homestead Village 710 Yorkmont Rd *TF:* 888-782-9473	Charlotte	NC	28217	704-676-0083	676-0211
Homewood Suites Hotel 8340 N Tryon St *TF:* 800-225-5466	Charlotte	NC	28262	704-549-8800	510-0055
Hyatt Charlotte at South Park 5501 Carnegie Blvd *TF:* 800-233-1234 ■ *Web:* www.hyatt.com/usa/charlotte/hotels/hotel_charl.html	Charlotte	NC	28209	704-554-1234	554-8319
La Quinta Inn 3100 S I-85 Service Rd *TF:* 800-531-5900	Charlotte	NC	28208	704-393-5306	394-0550
Manor House Aptel 2800 Selwyn Ave	Charlotte	NC	28209	704-377-2621	
Marriott Executive Park 5700 W Park Dr *TF:* 800-228-9290 ■ *Web:* marriotthotels.com/CLTNC	Charlotte	NC	28217	704-527-9650	527-6918
Marriott Hotel City Center 100 W Trade St *TF:* 800-228-9290 ■ *Web:* marriotthotels.com/CLTCC	Charlotte	NC	28202	704-333-9000	342-3419
Microtel Inn University Place 132 E McCullough Dr *TF:* 800-276-0613	Charlotte	NC	28262	704-549-9900	549-4700
Omni Plaza Hotel 101 S Tryon St *TF:* 800-843-6664	Charlotte	NC	28280	704-377-0400	347-0649
Park Hotel 2200 Rexford Rd *TF:* 800-334-0331 ■ *Web:* www.theparkhotel.com ■ *E-mail:* reserve@theparkhotel.com	Charlotte	NC	28211	704-364-8220	365-4712
Quality Inn & Suites Crown Point 2501 Sardis Rd N *TF:* 800-228-5151	Charlotte	NC	28227	704-845-2810	845-1743
Ramada Inn Charlotte Central 515 Clanton Rd *TF:* 800-272-6232	Charlotte	NC	28217	704-527-3000	527-9476
Ramada Inn East 3000 E Independence Blvd *TF:* 800-532-5376	Charlotte	NC	28205	704-377-1501	342-3978
Ramada Limited 5301 N I-85 *TF:* 800-272-6232	Charlotte	NC	28262	704-596-9390	319-0145
Ramada Limited 1240 I-85 S *TF:* 800-272-6232	Charlotte	NC	28208	704-392-7311	392-4643
Residence Inn by Marriott 5816 Westpark Dr *TF:* 800-331-3131 ■ *Web:* www.residenceinn.com/residenceinn/CLTEP	Charlotte	NC	28217	704-527-8110	521-8282

Charlotte — Hotels, Motels, Resorts (Cont'd)

	City	State	ZIP	Phone	Fax
Sheraton Airport Plaza Hotel					
3315 S I-85 at Billy Graham Pkwy	Charlotte	NC	28208	704-392-1200	393-2207
TF: 800-325-3535					
Southpark Suite Hotel 6300 Morrison Blvd	Charlotte	NC	28211	704-364-2400	362-0203
TF: 800-647-8483 ■ *Web:* www.southparksuites.com					
■ *E-mail:* info@destinationtravel.com					
Sterling Inn 242 E Woodlawn Rd	Charlotte	NC	28217	704-525-5454	525-5637
StudioPLUS 123 E McCullough Dr.	Charlotte	NC	28262	704-510-0108	548-3892
TF: 800-646-8000					
StudioPLUS 5830 Westpark Dr	Charlotte	NC	28217	704-527-1960	529-7482
TF: 800-646-8000					
Summerfield Suites Hotel 4920 S Tryon St.	Charlotte	NC	28217	704-525-2600	521-9932
TF: 800-833-4353					
Super 8 Motel 4930 Sunset Rd	Charlotte	NC	28269	704-598-7710	598-0760
Woodlawn Suites Hotel					
315 E Woodlawn Rd	Charlotte	NC	28217	704-522-0852	522-1634
TF: 800-522-1994					
Wyndham Garden Hotel 2600 Yorkmont Rd.	Charlotte	NC	28208	704-357-9100	357-9159
TF: 800-996-3426					

— Restaurants —

	City	State	ZIP	Phone
300 East (New American) 300 East Blvd.	Charlotte	NC	28203	704-332-6507
Alfiere Restaurant (Mediterranean) 222 E 3rd St.	Charlotte	NC	28202	704-377-1500
Andersons Restaurant (American) 1617 Elizabeth Ave	Charlotte	NC	28204	704-333-3491
Antony's Caribbean Cafe (Caribbean) 145 Brevard Ct	Charlotte	NC	28202	704-339-0303
Atlantic Beer & Ice (American) 330 N Tryon St.	Charlotte	NC	28202	704-339-0566
Baoding Uptown (Chinese) 227 W Trade St Carillon Bldg	Charlotte	NC	28202	704-370-6699
Baoding (Chinese) 4722 Sharon Rd Suite F.	Charlotte	NC	28210	704-552-8899
Bistro 100 (French) College & Trade Sts	Charlotte	NC	28202	704-344-0515
Blue Marlin (Steak/Seafood) 1511 East Blvd.	Charlotte	NC	28203	704-334-3838
Bravo Ristorante (Italian) 555 S McDowell St	Charlotte	NC	28204	704-372-5440
Cajun Queen (Cajun) 1800 E 7th St	Charlotte	NC	28202	704-377-9017
Caty's Grill (American) 101 S Tyron St	Charlotte	NC	28280	704-333-1159
Chin-Tso (Chinese) 1626 East Blvd.	Charlotte	NC	28203	704-358-8188
College Place Restaurant (Southern) 300 S College St.	Charlotte	NC	28282	704-343-9268
Fat Tuesday (Cajun) JM Keynes Dr Suite 355	Charlotte	NC	28262	704-503-3288
Hereford Barn Steakhouse (Steak) 4320 N I-85	Charlotte	NC	28206	704-596-0854
JW's Steakhouse (Steak) 100 W Trade St.	Charlotte	NC	28202	704-333-9000
Kabuto Japanese Steak House (Japanese) 446 Tyvola Rd	Charlotte	NC	28217	704-529-0659
La Biblioteque (French) 1901 Roxborough Rd.	Charlotte	NC	28211	704-365-5000
Lamplighter The (Continental) 1065 E Morehead St.	Charlotte	NC	28204	704-372-5343
Lotus 28 (Chinese)				
20601 Torrance Chapel Rd Southlake Shopping Ctr	Cornelius	NC	28031	704-896-7878
Mama Ricotta's Restaurant (Italian) 8418 Park Rd	Charlotte	NC	28210	704-556-0914
Mangione's (Italian) 1524 East Blvd.	Charlotte	NC	28203	704-334-4417
Marais (French) 1400 E Morehead St.	Charlotte	NC	28204	704-334-8860
Mimosa Grill (New American) 327 S Tryon St	Charlotte	NC	28202	704-343-0700
Monticello The (Continental) 235 N Tryon St	Charlotte	NC	28202	704-342-1193
Morrocrofts (Continental) 2200 Rexford Rd.	Charlotte	NC	28211	704-364-8220
TF: 800-334-0331				
Morton's of Chicago (Steak) 227 W Trade St	Charlotte	NC	28202	704-333-2602
Old Hickory House Restaurant (Barbecue)				
6538 N Tryon St	Charlotte	NC	28213	704-596-8014
Ole Ole (Spanish) 709 S Kings Dr	Charlotte	NC	28204	704-358-1102
Orchard's (American) 895 W Trade St	Charlotte	NC	28202	704-347-0070
Oscar's (American) 3315 S I-85.	Charlotte	NC	28208	704-392-1200
Pastis (French) 2000 South Blvd Suite 300.	Charlotte	NC	28203	704-333-1928
Patou French Bistro (French) 2400 Park Rd	Charlotte	NC	28203	704-376-2233
Porcupine Cafe (American) 1520 East Blvd.	Charlotte	NC	28203	704-376-4010
Restaurant Cibi (French/Italian) 1601 E 7th St	Charlotte	NC	28204	704-344-0844
Restaurant Tokyo (Japanese) 4603 South Blvd	Charlotte	NC	28209	704-527-8787
Ri-Ra (Irish) 208 N Tryon St.	Charlotte	NC	28202	704-333-5554
Shark Finns (Seafood) 6051 Old Pineville Rd.	Charlotte	NC	28217	704-525-3738
Sonoma on Providence (California) 801 Providence Rd	Charlotte	NC	28207	704-377-1333
Southend Brewery & Smokehouse (American)				
2100 South Blvd	Charlotte	NC	28202	704-358-4677
Swing 1000 (Continental) 1000 Central Ave	Charlotte	NC	28203	704-334-4443
Townhouse The (American) 1011 Providence Rd.	Charlotte	NC	28207	704-335-1546
Wellington's (Southern) 201 S McDowell St	Charlotte	NC	28204	704-372-7550
Zydeco (Cajun/Creole) 1400 E Morehead St	Charlotte	NC	28204	704-334-0755

— Goods and Services —

SHOPPING

	City	State	ZIP	Phone	Fax
Cannon Village 200 West Ave	Kannapolis	NC	28081	704-938-3200	932-4188
TF: 800-938-3200 ■ *Web:* www.cannonvillage.com					
Carolina Place Mall					
11025 Carolina Place Pkwy	Pineville	NC	28134	704-543-9300	543-6355
Web: www.shopcarolinaplace.com					
Eastland Mall 5471 Central Ave	Charlotte	NC	28212	704-537-2626	568-0291
Founder's Hall					
100 N Tyron St NationsBank					
Corporate Ctr	Charlotte	NC	28255	704-386-0120	386-1021
Market Place at Mint Hill					
11237 Lawyers Rd	Charlotte	NC	28227	704-545-3117	545-3117
Midtown Square					
401 S Independence Blvd Suite 800	Charlotte	NC	28204	704-377-3467	343-2541
Southpark Shopping Center					
4400 Sharon Rd	Charlotte	NC	28211	704-364-4411	364-4913
TF: 888-364-4411 ■ *Web:* www.southpark.com					
■ *E-mail:* concierge@trammellcrow.com					
Specialty Shops on the Park					
6401 Morrison Blvd.	Charlotte	NC	28211	704-366-9841	

BANKS

	City	State	ZIP	Phone	Fax
Bank of Mecklenburg 2000 Randolph Rd.	Charlotte	NC	28207	704-375-2265	347-5597
BB & T Bank 200 S College St	Charlotte	NC	28202	704-954-1000	954-1206
TF: 800-226-5228					
Central Carolina Bank & Trust Co					
101 S Kings Dr.	Charlotte	NC	28204	704-347-6092	347-6179
TF: 800-422-2226					
First Union-North Carolina					
301 S Tryon St 2 First Union Plaza	Charlotte	NC	28288	704-374-6161	
NationsBank NA (Carolinas) 101 S Tryon St	Charlotte	NC	28255	704-386-5000	386-9928
Web: www.nationsbank.com					
Park Meridian Bank 6826 Morrison Blvd	Charlotte	NC	28211	704-366-7275	366-8165*
*Fax: Cust Svc					
Wachovia Bank NA 6555 Morrison Blvd	Charlotte	NC	28211	704-367-2558	366-5098

BUSINESS SERVICES

	Phone
Corporate Express Delivery Systems	704-358-9971
Creative Temporaries & Personnel	704-529-0111
Federal Express	800-238-5355
Kelly Services	704-364-4790
Kinko's	704-358-8008
Manpower Temporary Services	704-522-9288
Olsten Staffing Services	704-527-6691
Pony Express Courier	704-394-7669
Post Office	704-393-4524
UPS	800-742-5877

— Media —

PUBLICATIONS

	City	State	ZIP	Phone	Fax
Business North Carolina Magazine					
5435 77 Center Dr Suite 50	Charlotte	NC	28217	704-523-6987	523-4211
TF: 800-604-6987					
Charlotte Business Journal					
120 W Morehead St Suite 2250	Charlotte	NC	28202	704-347-2340	937-1102
TF: 800-948-5323 ■ *Web:* www.amcity.com/charlotte					
Charlotte Magazine					
127 W Worthington Ave Suite 208	Charlotte	NC	28203	704-335-7181	335-3739
Charlotte Observer‡ 600 S Tryon St	Charlotte	NC	28202	704-358-5000	358-5036
TF: 800-332-0686 ■ *Web:* www.charlotte.com					
Leader The PO Box 30486	Charlotte	NC	28230	704-331-4842	347-0358*
**Fax:* News Rm ■ *Web:* www.leadernews.com					
■ *E-mail:* editor@leadernews.com					

‡*Daily newspapers*

TELEVISION

	City	State	ZIP	Phone	Fax
WAXN-TV Ch 64 (Ind) 910 Fairview St.	Kannapolis	NC	28083	704-933-9529	932-3880
Web: www.gocarolinas.com/partners/action64					
WBTV-TV Ch 3 (CBS) 1 Julian Price Pl	Charlotte	NC	28208	704-374-3500	374-3885
Web: www.wbtv.com					
WCCB-TV Ch 18 (Fox) 1 Television Pl	Charlotte	NC	28205	704-372-1800	376-3415
Web: www.fox18wccb.com ■ *E-mail:* stationinfo@fox18wccb.com					
WCNC-TV Ch 6 (NBC)					
1001 Wood Ridge Ctr Dr	Charlotte	NC	28217	704-329-3636	357-4975*
**Fax:* Sales ■ *Web:* www.wcnc.com ■ *E-mail:* wcnctv36@aol.com					
WFVT-TV Ch 55 (WB) PO Box 668400	Charlotte	NC	28266	704-398-0046	393-8407
WHKY-TV Ch 14 (Ind) PO Box 1059	Hickory	NC	28603	828-322-5115	322-8256
Web: www.whky.com ■ *E-mail:* whky@whky.com					
WJZY-TV Ch 46 (UPN) 3501 Performance Rd.	Charlotte	NC	28214	704-398-0046	393-8407
Web: www.upn46.com					
WSOC-TV Ch 9 (ABC) 1901 N Tryon St.	Charlotte	NC	28206	704-338-9999	335-4839
Web: www.gocarolinas.com/wsoctv					

Charlotte — Television (Cont'd)

	City	State	Zip	Phone	Fax
WTVI-TV Ch 42 (PBS)					
3242 Commonwealth Ave.	Charlotte	NC	28205	704-372-2442	335-1358
Web: www.wtvi.org					

RADIO

	City	State	Zip	Phone	Fax
WBAV-FM 101.9 MHz (Urban)					
601 S Kings Dr Suite EE	Charlotte	NC	28204	704-786-9111	792-2334
WBT-AM 1110 kHz (N/T) 1 Julian Price Pl	Charlotte	NC	28208	704-374-3500	374-3885
Web: www.wbt.com					
WBT-FM 99.3 MHz (N/T) 1 Julian Price Pl	Charlotte	NC	28208	704-374-3500	374-3885
WCCJ-FM 92.7 MHz (NAC)					
2303 W Moorehead St	Charlotte	NC	28208	704-358-0211	358-3752
Web: www.wccj.com					
WEND-FM 106.5 MHz (Alt)					
801 E Morehead St Suite 200	Charlotte	NC	28202	704-376-1065	334-9525
Web: www.1065.com					
WFAE-FM 90.7 MHz (NPR)					
8801 JM Keynes Dr Suite 91	Charlotte	NC	28262	704-549-9323	547-8851
TF: 800-876-9323 ■ *Web:* www.npr.org/members/WFAE					
WFMX-FM 105.7 MHz (Ctry)					
1117 Radio Rd	Statesville	NC	28677	704-872-6345	873-6921
Web: www.wfmx.com ■ *E-mail:* bbuck@vnet.net					
WFNZ-AM 610 kHz (Sports)					
4015 Stuart Andrew Blvd	Charlotte	NC	28217	704-372-1104	523-4800
Web: www.wfnz.com					
WGFY-AM 1480 kHz (Misc)					
4180 Pompano Rd	Charlotte	NC	28216	704-393-1480	393-5983
WGIV-AM 1600 kHz (Rel) 601 S Kings Dr	Charlotte	NC	28204	704-333-0131	792-2334
WHVN-AM 1240 kHz (Rel) 5732 N Tryon St	Charlotte	NC	28213	704-596-1240	596-6939
WKKT-FM 96.9 MHz (Ctry)					
801 Wood Ridge Center Dr	Charlotte	NC	28217	704-714-9444	332-8805
TF: 800-332-1029					
WLNK-FM 107.9 MHz (AC) 1 Julian Price Pl	Charlotte	NC	28208	704-374-3500	374-3885
WLYT-FM 102.9 MHz (AC)					
801 Wood Ridge Center Dr	Charlotte	NC	27217	704-332-9444	332-8805
TF: 800-332-1029					
WMIT-FM 106.9 MHz (Rel)					
PO Box 159	Black Mountain	NC	28711	828-669-8477	669-6983
WNKS-FM 95.1 MHz (CHR) 137 S Kings Dr	Charlotte	NC	28204	704-331-9510	331-9140
Web: www.kiss951.com/ ■ *E-mail:* kiss951@mindspring.com					
WNMX-FM 106.1 MHz (Nost)					
5732 N Tryon St	Charlotte	NC	28213	704-598-1480	599-1061
Web: www.wmix106.com					
WPEG-FM 97.9 MHz (Urban)					
601 S Kings Dr Suite EE	Charlotte	NC	28204	704-333-0131	792-2334
Web: www.power98fm.com					
WRFX-FM 99.7 MHz (CR)					
801 Wood Ridge Ctr Dr	Charlotte	NC	28217	704-714-9444	332-8805
TF: 800-332-1029 ■ *Web:* wrfx.com					
WSOC-FM 103.7 MHz (Ctry)					
4015 Stuart Andrew Blvd	Charlotte	NC	28217	704-522-1103	523-4800
Web: www.wsocfm.com					
WSSS-FM 104.7 MHz (CR)					
4015 Stuart Andrew Blvd	Charlotte	NC	28217	704-372-1104	523-2444
Web: www.wsss.com					
WWMG-FM 96.1 MHz (Oldies)					
801 E Morehead St Suite 200	Charlotte	NC	28202	704-338-9600	334-9525
WXRC-FM 95.7 MHz (Rock) PO Box 940	Newton	NC	28658	828-322-9472	464-9662
Web: www.957xrc.com					

— Colleges/Universities —

	City	State	Zip	Phone	Fax
Barber-Scotia College 145 Cabarrus Ave W	Concord	NC	28025	704-789-2900	789-2911
TF: 800-610-0778 ■ *Web:* www.barber-scotia.edu					
Belmont Abbey College					
100 Belmont-Mt Holly Rd	Belmont	NC	28012	704-825-6700	825-6670
TF: 888-222-0110 ■ *Web:* www.bac.edu/					
Central Piedmont Community College					
PO Box 35009	Charlotte	NC	28235	704-330-2722	330-5053
Web: www.cpcc.cc.nc.us					
Davidson College PO Box 1719	Davidson	NC	28036	704-892-2000	892-2016
TF: 800-768-0380 ■ *Web:* www.davidson.edu ■ *E-mail:* admission@davidson.edu					
Johnson C Smith University					
100 Beatties Ford Rd	Charlotte	NC	28216	704-378-1000	378-1242
TF Admissions: 800-782-7303 ■ *Web:* www.jcsu.edu					
Lee University 1209 Little Rock Rd	Charlotte	NC	28214	704-394-2307	393-3689
E-mail: ecbc@msn.com					
Queens College 1900 Selwyn Ave	Charlotte	NC	28274	704-337-2200	337-2503
TF Admissions: 800-849-0202 ■ *Web:* www.queens.edu					
University of North Carolina Charlotte					
9201 University City Blvd	Charlotte	NC	28223	704-547-2000	510-6483
Web: www.uncc.edu					
Wingate University PO Box 159	Wingate	NC	28174	704-233-8000	233-8110
TF Admissions: 800-755-5550 ■ *Web:* www.wingate.edu ■ *E-mail:* admit@wingate.edu					

— Hospitals —

	City	State	Zip	Phone	Fax
Anson County Hospital 500 Morven Rd	Wadesboro	NC	28170	704-694-5131	694-3900
Carolinas Medical Center PO Box 32861	Charlotte	NC	28232	704-355-2000	355-5073*
**Fax:* Admitting					
Catawba Memorial Hospital					
810 Fairgrove Church Rd SE	Hickory	NC	28602	828-326-3000	326-3371
Cleveland Regional Medical Center					
201 Grover St	Shelby	NC	28150	704-487-3000	487-3290
Davis Medical Center PO Box 1823	Statesville	NC	28687	704-873-0281	838-7287
Frye Regional Medical Center					
420 N Center St	Hickory	NC	28601	828-322-6070	324-0193
Gaston Memorial Hospital 2525 Court Dr	Gastonia	NC	28054	704-834-2000	834-2500
Iredell Memorial Hospital PO Box 1828	Statesville	NC	28687	704-873-5661	872-7924
Kings Mountain Hospital					
706 W Kings St	Kings Mountain	NC	28086	704-739-3601	739-0800
Lake Norman Regional Medical Center					
PO Box 3250	Mooresville	NC	28117	704-663-1113	660-4049
Lincoln Medical Center PO Box 677	Lincolnton	NC	28093	704-735-3071	735-0584
Mercy Hospital 2001 Vail Ave	Charlotte	NC	28207	704-379-5000	379-6056
Mercy Hospital South 10628 Park Rd	Charlotte	NC	28210	704-543-2000	543-2010
Northeast Medical Center 920 Church St N	Concord	NC	28025	704-783-3000	783-1527
TF: 800-842-6868					
Presbyterian Hospital in Charlotte					
200 Hawthorne Ln	Charlotte	NC	28204	704-384-4000	384-4296
Presbyterian Hospital Matthews					
1500 Matthews Township Pkwy	Matthews	NC	28105	704-384-6570	384-6515
Rowan Regional Medical Center					
612 Mocksville Ave	Salisbury	NC	28144	704-638-1000	638-1288
Stanly Memorial Hospital 301 Yadkin St	Albemarle	NC	28001	704-983-5111	983-3414
Union Regional Medical Center PO Box 5003	Monroe	NC	28111	704-283-3100	296-4175
University Hospital PO Box 560727	Charlotte	NC	28256	704-548-6000	548-6236

— Attractions —

	City	State	Zip	Phone	Fax
Afro-American Cultural Center					
401 N Meyers St	Charlotte	NC	28202	704-374-1565	374-9273
Backing Up Classics Motor Car Museum					
4545 Concord Pkwy S	Harrisburg	NC	28075	704-788-9494	788-9495
TF: 888-736-2519					
Charlotte Botanical Gardens & Sculpture Garden Hwy 49 N University of North Carolina	Charlotte	NC	28223	704-547-2555	547-3128
Charlotte Choral Society 1900 Queens Rd	Charlotte	NC	28207	704-374-1564	372-8733
Charlotte Historic Trolley Museum					
2104 South Blvd	Charlotte	NC	28203	704-375-0850	
Charlotte Museum of History & Hezekiah Alexander Homesite 3500 Shamrock Dr	Charlotte	NC	28215	704-568-1774	566-1817
Charlotte Nature Museum 1658 Sterling Rd	Charlotte	NC	28209	704-372-6261	337-2670
TF: 800-935-0553 ■ *Web:* www.gocarolinas.com/community/groups/nature					
Charlotte Philharmonic Orchestra					
130 N Tryon St Blumenthal Performing Arts Ctr	Charlotte	NC	28202	704-846-2788	847-6043
Web: www.charlottephilharmonic.org/ ■ *E-mail:* CharPhilOr@aol.com					
Charlotte Regional Farmers Market					
1801 Yorkmont Rd	Charlotte	NC	28217	704-357-1269	357-0708
Charlotte Repertory Theatre					
129 W Trade St Suite 401	Charlotte	NC	28202	704-333-8587	333-0224
Web: www.charlotterep.org/					
Charlotte Symphony Orchestra					
201 S College St Suite 110	Charlotte	NC	28244	704-332-0468	332-1963
Web: www.charlottesymphony.org/ ■ *E-mail:* charsym1@aol.com					
Charlotte's Historic Walking Tour					
128 S Tryon St	Charlotte	NC	28202	704-376-1164	
Crowders Mountain State Park					
522 Park Office Ln	Kings Mountain	NC	28086	704-853-5375	853-5391

Charlotte — Attractions (Cont'd)

	City	State	Zip	Phone	Fax
Discovery Place 301 N Tryon St *TF:* 800-935-0553 ■ *Web:* www.discoveryplace.org	Charlotte	NC	28202	704-372-6261	337-2670
Energy Explorium 13339 Hagers Ferry Rd MG03E	Huntersville	NC	28078	704-875-5600	875-5602
Fieldcrest Cannon Textile Museum 200 West Ave	Kannapolis	NC	28081	704-938-3200	932-4188
Freedom Park 2435 Cumberland Ave	Charlotte	NC	28203	704-336-2663	
Hendrick Motorsports Museum 4400 Papa Joe Hendrick Blvd	Harrisburg	NC	28075	704-455-0342	
Historic Latta Plantation 5225 Sample Rd *Web:* www.lattaplantation.org	Huntersville	NC	28078	704-331-2701	
Historic Rosedale 3427 N Tryon St	Charlotte	NC	28206	704-335-0325	335-0384
Kings Mountain National Military Park 2625 Park Rd *Web:* www.nps.gov/kimo/	Blacksburg	SC	29702	864-936-7921	936-9897
McAlpine Creek Greenway & Park 8711 Monroe Rd	Charlotte	NC	28212	704-568-4044	535-5454
McDowell Park 15222 York Rd	Charlotte	NC	28278	704-588-5224	588-5226
Mint Museum of Art 2730 Randolph Rd *Web:* www.mintmuseum.org ■ *E-mail:* comments@mintmuseum.org	Charlotte	NC	28207	704-337-2000	337-2101
Museum of the New South 324 N College St	Charlotte	NC	28202	704-333-1887	333-1896
North Carolina Blumenthal Performing Arts Center 130 N Tryon St Suite 300 *Web:* www.performingartsctr.org/	Charlotte	NC	28202	704-333-4686	376-2289
North Carolina Dance Theatre 800 N College St *Web:* www.ncdance.org/index.html	Charlotte	NC	28206	704-372-0101	375-0260
Observer OMNIMAX Theatre 301 N Tryon St Discovery Pl *TF:* 800-935-0553 ■ *Web:* 24.93.68.194/omniframe.htm	Charlotte	NC	28202	704-372-6261	337-2670
Opera Carolina 345 N College St Suite 409 *Web:* www.operacarolina.com ■ *E-mail:* operacar@charlotte.infi.net	Charlotte	NC	28202	704-332-7177	332-6448
Paramount Carowinds Amusement Park PO Box 410289 *TF:* 800-888-4386 ■ *Web:* www.carowinds.com	Charlotte	NC	28241	704-588-2606	588-5153
Philip Morris USA 2321 Concord Pkwy S	Concord	NC	28027	704-788-5000	788-5099
Polk James K Memorial State Historic Site 308 S Polk St *Web:* www.ah.dcr.state.nc.us/sections/hs/polk/polk.htm ■ *E-mail:* polk1795@aol.com	Pineville	NC	28134	704-889-7145	
Reed Gold Mine State Historic Site 9621 Reed Mine Rd	Stanfield	NC	28163	704-721-4653	721-4657
Reedy Creek Environmental Center 2900 Rocky River Rd	Charlotte	NC	28215	704-598-8857	599-1770
Renaissance Park 1200 W Tyvola Rd	Charlotte	NC	28217	704-523-2862	
Schiele Museum of Natural History & Planetarium 1500 E Garrison Blvd *Web:* www.schielemuseum.org	Gastonia	NC	28054	704-866-6908	866-6041
Spirit Square Center for the Arts 345 N College St	Charlotte	NC	28202	704-348-5750	377-9808
Stowe Daniel Botanical Garden 6400 S New Hope Rd	Belmont	NC	28012	704-825-4490	825-4492
Theatre Charlotte 501 Queens Rd	Charlotte	NC	28207	704-334-9128	347-5216
Vietnam War Memorial Wall 1129 E 3rd St Thompson Pk	Charlotte	NC	28202	704-336-4200	
Wing Haven Garden & Bird Sanctuary 248 Ridgewood Ave	Charlotte	NC	28209	704-331-0664	331-9368

SPORTS TEAMS & FACILITIES

	City	State	Zip	Phone	Fax
Carolina Panthers 800 S Mint St Ericsson Stadium *Web:* www.nfl.com/panthers	Charlotte	NC	28202	704-358-7000	358-7618
Charlotte Checkers (hockey) 2700 E Independence Blvd *Web:* www.gocheckers.com/	Charlotte	NC	28205	704-342-4423	377-4595
Charlotte Coliseum 100 Paul Buck Blvd *Web:* www.charlottecoliseum.com	Charlotte	NC	28217	704-357-4700	357-4757
Charlotte Eagles (soccer) 310 N Kings Dr Memorial Stadium *Web:* www.charlotteeagles.com ■ *E-mail:* charlotteeagles@compuserve.com	Charlotte	NC	28204	704-841-8644	841-8652
Charlotte Hornets 100 Hive Dr *Web:* www.nba.com/hornets	Charlotte	NC	28217	704-357-0252	357-0289
Charlotte Knights (baseball) 2280 Deerfield Dr *Web:* www.aaaknights.com	Fort Mill	SC	29715	803-548-8050	548-8055
Charlotte Motor Speedway Hwy 29 N *Web:* www.charlottemotorspeedway.com	Concord	NC	28026	704-455-3200	455-3237
Charlotte Speed (soccer) 7310 N Kings Dr Charlotte Memorial Stadium	Charlotte	NC	28262	704-721-6415	721-6400
Charlotte Sting (basketball) 3308 Oak Lake Blvd Suite B *Web:* www.wnba.com/sting	Charlotte	NC	28208	704-329-4961	329-4970
Ericsson Stadium 800 S Mint St *Web:* www.cpanthers.com/stadium/index.html	Charlotte	NC	28202	704-358-7000	358-7615
Memorial Stadium 310 N Kings Dr	Charlotte	NC	28204	704-336-8979	
North Carolina Auto Racing Hall of Fame 119 Knob Hill Rd Lakeside Pk *Web:* www.ncarhof.com	Mooresville	NC	28117	704-663-5331	663-6949

— Events —

	Phone
4th Ward Christmas Tour (early December)	704-372-0282
Antiques Spectacular (early June & early November)	704-596-4643
AutoFair 1 (early April)	704-455-3200
Blooming Arts Festival (early May)	704-283-2784
Carolina Renaissance Festival (early October-mid-November)	704-896-5555
Carolina's Carrousel Parade (late November)	800-231-4636
Center CityFest Outdoor Festival (late April)	704-483-6266
Charlotte Festival-New Plays in America Series (early March)	704-372-1000
Charlotte Film & Video Festival (early-mid-May)	704-337-2000
Charlotte International Auto Show (mid-November)	704-364-1078
Charlotte Observer Marathon (early April)	704-358-5425
Charlotte Steeplechase Races (late April)	704-423-3400
Christian Music Festival (late September)	704-588-2600
Coca-Cola 600 (late May)	704-455-3200
Country Christmas Classic Craft and Gift Show (late November)	704-596-4643
Festival in the Park (mid-September)	704-331-2700
Festival of Lights (late November-early January)	704-331-2701
Good Guys Southeastern Rod & Custom Car Show (late October)	704-455-3200
Grandfather Mountain Highland Games (mid-July)	828-733-1333
Great American Antique & Collectible Spectacular (early April & early November)	704-596-4643
Holiday Skylights Tree Lighting Ceremony (early December)	704-378-1335
Home Depot Invitational (late April)	704-846-4699
International Festival (late September)	704-547-2407
July 4th Fireworks (July 4)	704-334-2282
Lake Norman Festival (mid-May)	704-664-3898
LakeFest (mid-September)	704-892-1922
Latta Plantation Holiday Festival (late November)	704-875-2312
Legends Summer Shootout Auto Racing Series (June-August)	704-455-3200
Loch Norman Highland Games (mid-April)	704-875-3113
Mid-Atlantic Boat Show (early February)	704-339-6000
Mint Museum Home & Garden Tour (mid-April)	704-337-2000
Nascar Parade & Speed Street Festival (late May)	704-455-6814
National Balloon Rally & Hot Air Balloon Festival (mid-September)	704-873-2893
North American Karting Championships (mid-October)	704-455-3200
Qualifying Races for Winston No Bull Twin 25s (late May)	704-455-3200
Shrine Bowl of the Carolinas (mid-December)	704-547-1414
Southeastern Origami Festival (late September)	704-375-3692
Southern Christmas Show (mid-late November)	704-376-6594
Southern Farm Show (early February)	704-376-6594
Southern Ideal Home Show (early April)	704-376-6594
Southern Spring Show (late February-early March)	704-376-6594
WBT Skyshow (July 4)	704-374-3500
Winston ARCA Race (late May)	704-455-3200

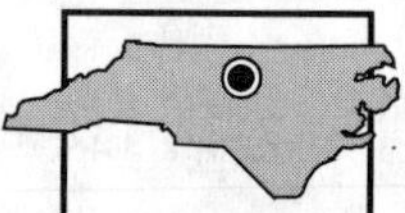

Durham

Known as the "City of Medicine," Durham is home to more than 300 medical and health-related companies and practices, as well as one of the country's finest medical schools, Duke University Medical School. Seventy-five percent of Research Triangle Park, a major center for research and technology and home to major companies such as Glaxo-Wellcome, is located within Durham. The city also offers several attractions for nature lovers, including the Sarah P. Duke Gardens, the Duke University Primate Center, and the North Carolina Museum of Life and Science, which includes a seasonal butterfly house. Historic sites in Durham include the Downtown Durham Historic District, which is listed on the National Register of Historic Places.

Population	153,513	**Longitude**	78-89-89 W
Area (Land)	69.3 sq mi	**County**	Durham
Area (Water)	0.1 sq mi	**Time Zone**	EST
Elevation	394 ft	**Area Code/s**	919
Latitude	35-99-39 N		

Durham (Cont'd)

— Average Temperatures and Precipitation —

TEMPERATURES

	Jan	Feb	Mar	Apr	May	Jun	Jul	Aug	Sep	Oct	Nov	Dec
High	49	52	62	71	79	86	89	88	82	72	63	53
Low	25	27	35	43	53	61	65	64	57	45	36	29

PRECIPITATION

	Jan	Feb	Mar	Apr	May	Jun	Jul	Aug	Sep	Oct	Nov	Dec
Inches	3.9	4.0	4.3	3.3	4.6	4.3	4.3	4.9	3.6	3.6	3.5	3.7

— Important Phone Numbers —

	Phone		Phone
AAA	919-489-3306	**Medical Referral**	800-362-8677
Dental Referral	800-917-6453	**Poison Control Center**	800-848-6946
Durham Bullhorn Information Line	919-688-2855	**Time/Temp**	919-683-9696
Emergency	911	**Weather**	919-515-8225

— Information Sources —

				Phone	Fax
Better Business Bureau Serving Eastern North Carolina 3125 Poplarwood Ct Suite 308	Raleigh	NC	27604	919-688-6143	954-0622
Web: www.raleigh-durham.bbb.org					
Durham City Hall 101 City Hall Plaza	Durham	NC	27701	919-560-4100	
Web: www.ci.durham.nc.us					
Durham Convention & Visitors Bureau 101 E Morgan St	Durham	NC	27701	919-687-0288	683-9555
TF: 800-446-8604 ■ *Web:* dcvb.durham.nc.us/					
Durham County 200 E Main St	Durham	NC	27701	919-560-0000	560-0020
Durham County Library PO Box 3809	Durham	NC	27702	919-560-0220	560-0106
Web: ils.unc.edu/nclibs/durham/dclhome.htm					
Durham Mayor 101 City Hall Plaza	Durham	NC	27701	919-560-4333	560-4801
Durham Planning Dept 101 City Hall Plaza	Durham	NC	27701	919-560-4137	560-4641
Web: www.ci.durham.nc.us/planning/planning.html					
Greater Durham Chamber of Commerce 300 W Morgan St Suite 1400	Durham	NC	27701	919-682-2133	688-8351
Web: www.herald-sun.com/dcc/ ■ *E-mail:* www@herald-sun.com					

On-Line Resources

4RaleighDurham.com	www.4raleighdurham.com
About.com Guide to Raleigh/Durham	raleighdurham.about.com
Anthill City Guide Durham	www.anthill.com/city.asp?city=durham
Area Guide Durham	durham.areaguides.net
City Knowledge Durham	www.cityknowledge.com/nc_durham.htm
CitySearch the Triangle	triangle.citysearch.com
DigitalCity Raleigh/Durham	home.digitalcity.com/raleigh
Excite.com Durham City Guide	www.excite.com/travel/countries/united_states/north_carolina/durham
Guest Guide Online	www.guestguideonline.com
NITC Travelbase City Guide Raleigh-Durham	www.travelbase.com/auto/guides/raleigh-durham-area-nc.html
Welcome to Durham	ncnet.com/ncnw/dur-intr.html

— Transportation Services —

AIRPORTS

■ **Raleigh-Durham International Airport (RDU)**

	Phone
13 miles SE of downtown Durham (approx 15 minutes)	919-840-2100

Web: www.rdu.com/

Airport Transportation

	Phone
Brad's Shuttle $30 fare to downtown Durham	919-493-5890
R & G Airport Shuttle $20 fare to downtown Durham	919-840-0262
TTA Airport Shuttle $1 fare to downtown Durham	919-549-9999
Yellow Cab $22-25 fare to downtown Durham	919-875-1821

Commercial Airlines

	Phone		Phone
Air Canada	800-776-3000	**Midway**	800-446-4392
AirTran	800-247-8726	**Northwest**	800-225-2525
American	919-834-4704	**TWA**	800-221-2000
Continental	800-523-3273	**United**	800-241-6522
Delta	800-221-1212	**US Airways**	800-428-4322
Delta Express	800-325-5205	**US Airways Express**	919-840-4624

Charter Airlines

	Phone		Phone
James Flying Service	800-556-4221	**Piedmont Aviation Services Inc**	800-548-1978
Piedmont Aviation	919-840-2700	**Raleigh Flying Service**	919-840-4400

CAR RENTALS

	Phone		Phone
Alamo	919-840-0132	**Hertz**	919-840-4875
Avis	919-840-4750	**National**	800-227-7368
Budget	919-876-8715	**Thrifty**	919-544-6419
CarTemps USA	919-872-0010	**Triangle**	800-643-7368
Dollar	919-840-4850		

LIMO/TAXI

	Phone		Phone
ABC Cab	919-682-0437	**Elegance Unlimited Limousine**	919-596-8187
Carolina Livery Service	919-544-5828	**Johnny's Taxi**	919-682-8294
Durham & Raleigh Cab	919-688-6121	**National Cab**	919-469-1333
Durham Independent Taxis	919-682-3537	**Rem Taxicab**	919-682-6111

MASS TRANSIT

	Phone
Capital Area Transit $.75 Base fare	919-828-7228
DATA Bus $.75 Base fare	919-683-3282

RAIL/BUS

				Phone
Amtrak Station 400 W Chapel Hill St	Durham	NC	27701	919-956-7932
Greyhound/Trailways Bus Station 820 W Morgan St	Durham	NC	27701	919-687-4800
TF: 800-231-2222				

— Accommodations —

HOTELS, MOTELS, RESORTS

				Phone	Fax
Best Western University Inn PO Box 2118	Chapel Hill	NC	27515	919-932-3000	968-6513
TF: 800-528-1234					
Brookwood Inn 2306 Elba St	Durham	NC	27705	919-286-3111	286-5115
TF: 800-716-6401 ■ *Web:* www.brookwoodinn-duke.com ■ *E-mail:* brookwood@travelbase.com					
Brownestone Inn 2424 Erwin Rd	Durham	NC	27705	919-286-7761	286-1180
TF: 800-367-0293					
Carolina Inn 211 Pittsboro St	Chapel Hill	NC	27516	919-933-2001	962-3400
TF: 800-962-8519					
Comfort Inn University 3508 Mount Moriah Rd	Durham	NC	27707	919-490-4949	419-0535
TF: 800-221-2222					
Courtyard by Marriott 1815 Front St	Durham	NC	27705	919-309-1500	383-8189
TF: 800-321-2211 ■ *Web:* courtyard.com/RDUFS					
Days Inn of Durham 5139 Redwood Rd	Durham	NC	27704	919-688-4338	688-3118
TF: 800-329-7466					
Doubletree Guest Suites 2515 Meridian Pkwy	Durham	NC	27713	919-361-4660	361-2256
TF: 800-222-8733 ■ *Web:* www.doubletreehotels.com/DoubleT/Hotel61/71/71Main.htm					
Duke Towers Residential Suites 807 W Trinity Ave	Durham	NC	27701	919-687-4444	683-1215
Web: www.duketowers.com ■ *E-mail:* duketowers@mindspring.com					
Durham Fairfield Inn 3710 Hillsborough Rd	Durham	NC	27705	919-382-3388	382-3388
TF: 800-228-2800					
Durham Hilton Hotel 3800 Hillsborough Rd	Durham	NC	27705	919-383-8033	383-4287
TF: 800-445-8667					
Econo Tel 2337 Guess Rd	Durham	NC	27705	919-286-7746	286-1855
Extended StayAmerica 3105 Tower Blvd	Durham	NC	27707	919-489-8444	489-8919
TF: 800-398-7829					
Hampton Inn Durham 1816 Hillandale Rd	Durham	NC	27705	919-471-6100	479-7026
TF: 800-426-7866					
Hawthorn Suites Hotel 300 Meredith Dr	Durham	NC	27713	919-361-1234	361-1213
TF: 800-527-1133 ■ *Web:* www.hawthorn.com/reservations/locationdetail.asp?state=TX&facid=1734&pagecode=hdir ■ *E-mail:* hshotel@bellsouth.net					

Durham — Hotels, Motels, Resorts (Cont'd)

	City	State	Zip	Phone	Fax
Holiday Inn 1301 N Fordham Blvd *TF:* 800-465-4329	Chapel Hill	NC	27514	919-929-2171	929-5736
Holiday Inn Airport 4810 New Page Rd *TF:* 800-465-4329	Research Triangle Park	NC	27709	919-941-6000	941-6030
Howard Johnson Inn 1800 Hillandale Rd *TF:* 800-654-2000	Durham	NC	27705	919-477-7381	477-3857
Marriott Hotel 201 Foster St. *TF:* 800-228-9290	Durham	NC	27701	919-683-6664	768-6037
Radisson Governors Inn Hwy 54 at I-40 & Davis Dr. *TF:* 800-333-3333	Research Triangle Park	NC	27709	919-549-8631	547-3510
Ramada Inn 600 Willard St *TF:* 800-272-6232	Durham	NC	27701	919-956-9444	956-5553
Regal University Hotel 2800 Campus Walk *TF:* 800-633-5379	Durham	NC	27705	919-383-8575	383-8495
Residence Inn by Marriott 201 Residence Inn Blvd *TF:* 800-331-3131 ■ *Web:* www.raleighresidenceinn.com/	Durham	NC	27713	919-361-1266	361-1200
Sheraton Chapel Hill 1 Europa Dr. *TF:* 800-325-3535	Chapel Hill	NC	27514	919-968-4900	968-3520
Sheraton Imperial Hotel & Convention Center 4700 Emperor Blvd *TF:* 800-325-3535	Durham	NC	27703	919-941-5050	941-5156
StudioPLUS 2504 NC Hwy 54 E *TF:* 800-646-8000	Research Triangle Park	NC	27713	919-361-1853	572-5072
Washington Duke Inn & Golf Club 3001 Cameron Blvd. *TF:* 800-443-3853 ■ *Web:* www.washingtondukeinn.com ■ *E-mail:* wdi@netmar.com	Durham	NC	27706	919-490-0999	493-0015
Wyndham Garden Hotel 4620 S Miami Blvd *TF:* 800-972-0264	Durham	NC	27703	919-941-6066	941-6363

— Restaurants —

	City	State	Zip	Phone
Anotherthyme (Continental) 109 N Gregson St	Durham	NC	27701	919-682-5225
Bahn's Cuisine (Chinese) 750 9th St	Durham	NC	27705	919-286-5073
Blue Corn Cafe (Latin American) 716-B 9th St	Durham	NC	27705	919-286-9600
Blue Nile (Ethiopian) 2000 Chapel Hill Rd.	Durham	NC	27707	919-490-0462
Brig's at the Park (American) 4900 Hwy 55	Durham	NC	27713	919-544-7473
Bullock's Bar-B-Que (Barbecue) 3330 Quebec Dr.	Durham	NC	27705	919-383-3211
Cafe 201 (American) 201 Foster St	Durham	NC	27701	919-683-6664
Cafe Parizade (Mediterranean) 2200 W Main St	Durham	NC	27705	919-286-9712
Dillard's Bar-B-Que (Barbecue) 3921 Fayetteville St.	Durham	NC	27713	919-544-1587
Down Under Pub (American) 802 W Main St.	Durham	NC	27701	919-682-0039
Fairview Restaurant (American) 3001 Cameron Blvd	Durham	NC	27706	919-490-0999
Fishmonger's (Seafood) 806 W Main St.	Durham	NC	27701	919-682-0128
George's Garage (Seafood) 737 9th St.	Durham	NC	27705	919-286-4131
Hartman's Steak House (American) 1703 E Geer St.	Durham	NC	27704	919-688-7639
International Delights (International) 740 9th St	Durham	NC	27705	919-286-2884
Italian Garden (Italian) 3211 Hillsborough Rd	Durham	NC	27705	919-382-3292
Jamaica Jamaica (Jamaican) 4853 Hwy 55 *Web:* jamaica2.com	Durham	NC	27713	919-544-1532
Kim-Sun Restaurant (Vietnamese) 2425 Guess Rd	Durham	NC	27705	919-416-9009
Kurama Seafood & Steakhouse (Japanese) 3644 Durham Chapel Hill Blvd	Durham	NC	27707	919-489-2669
Le Coco (American) 5277 N Roxboro Rd	Durham	NC	27712	919-477-2282
Magnolia Grill (American) 1002 9th St.	Durham	NC	27705	919-286-3609
Nana's (Southern) 2514 University Dr.	Durham	NC	27707	919-493-8545
Neo-China (Chinese) 4015 University Dr	Durham	NC	27707	919-489-2828
Palace International (African) 117 W Parrish St	Durham	NC	27701	919-687-4922
Papa's Grill (Mediterranean) 1821 Hillandale Rd	Durham	NC	27705	919-383-8502
Pop's Italian Trattoria (Italian) 810 W Peabody St.	Durham	NC	27701	919-956-7677
Saladelia (Lebanese) 4201 University Dr	Durham	NC	27707	919-489-5776
Satisfaction Restaurant (American) 905 W Main St Brightleaf Square	Durham	NC	27701	919-682-7397
Seafood Express (Seafood) 2000 Old Chapel Hill Rd	Durham	NC	27707	919-490-0215
Shanghai Restaurant (Chinese) 3433 Hillsborough Rd	Durham	NC	27705	919-383-7581
Spartacus (Greek) 4139 Durham-Chapel Hill Blvd.	Durham	NC	27707	919-489-2848
Taverna Nikos (Greek) 905 W Main St Brightleaf Square *Web:* www.fuzz.com/nikos/	Durham	NC	27701	919-682-0043
Torero's (Mexican) 800 W Main St.	Durham	NC	27701	919-682-4197
Vinnie's Steakhouse & Tavern (Steak) 4015 University Dr	Durham	NC	27707	919-493-0004
Yamazushi Japanese Restaurant (Japanese) 4711 Hope Valley Rd	Durham	NC	27707	919-493-7748

— Goods and Services —

SHOPPING

	City	State	Zip	Phone	Fax
Northgate Mall 1058 W Club Blvd. *Web:* www.ngatemall.com	Durham	NC	27701	919-286-4400	286-3948
South Square Mall 4001 Chapel Hill Blvd	Durham	NC	27707	919-493-2451	
Willow Park Antique Mall & Galleries 4422 Durham-Chapel Hill Blvd	Durham	NC	27707	919-493-3923	

BANKS

	City	State	Zip	Phone	Fax
Central Carolina Bank & Trust Co 111 Corcoran St	Durham	NC	27701	919-683-7777	683-6881
Centura Bank 8 Park Plaza Research Triangle	Durham	NC	27709	919-990-9115	990-9752
Mechanics and Farmers Bank 116 W Parrish St **Fax:* Cust Svc	Durham	NC	27702	919-683-1521	687-7822*
NationsBank of North Carolina 123 W Main St *TF:* 800-333-6262	Durham	NC	27701	919-956-2200	682-5530
Triangle State Bank 302 W Main St	Durham	NC	27701	919-688-9361	682-2895

BUSINESS SERVICES

	Phone
Adecco Employment Personnel Services	919-572-2662
BAX Global	800-225-5229
DHL Worldwide Express	800-225-5345
Federal Express	800-238-5355
Kinko's	919-405-1800
Office Specialists	919-493-1449
Post Office	919-683-2143
Snelling Personnel Services	919-383-2575
UPS	800-742-5877

— Media —

PUBLICATIONS

	City	State	Zip	Phone	Fax
Herald-Sun‡ PO Box 2092 *TF:* 800-672-0061 ■ *Web:* www.herald-sun.com ■ *E-mail:* www@herald-sun.com	Durham	NC	27702	919-419-6500	419-6889
Triangle Business Journal 1305 Navaho Dr Suite 401 *Web:* www.amcity.com/triangle	Raleigh	NC	27609	919-878-0010	790-6885

‡Daily newspapers

TELEVISION

	City	State	Zip	Phone	Fax
WFPX-TV Ch 62 (PAX) PO Box 62	Lumber Bridge	NC	28357	910-843-3884	843-2873
WKFT-TV Ch 40 (Ind) 230 Donaldson St	Fayetteville	NC	28301	910-323-4040	323-3924
WLFL-TV Ch 22 (WB) 3012 Highwoods Blvd Suite 101 *E-mail:* wlfl22@nando.net	Raleigh	NC	27604	919-872-9535	878-3877
WNCN-TV Ch 17 (NBC) 1205 Front St *Web:* www.nbc17.com	Raleigh	NC	27609	919-836-1717	836-1747
WRAL-TV Ch 5 (CBS) 2619 Western Blvd *Web:* www.wral-tv.com	Raleigh	NC	27606	919-821-8555	821-8541
WRAZ-TV Ch 50 (Fox) 512 S Mangum St *TF:* 800-532-5343 ■ *Web:* www.fox50.com	Durham	NC	27701	919-595-5050	595-5028
WRDC-TV Ch 28 (UPN) 3012 Highwoods Blvd Suite 101	Raleigh	NC	27604	919-872-2854	790-6991
WRPX-TV Ch 47 (PAX) 1507 Oakwood Ave	Raleigh	NC	27610	919-755-2277	755-1702
WTVD-TV Ch 11 (ABC) PO Box 2009	Durham	NC	27702	919-683-1111	687-4373
WUNC-TV Ch 4 (PBS) PO Box 14900 *Web:* www.unctv.org ■ *E-mail:* viewer@unctv.org	Research Triangle Park	NC	27709	919-549-7000	549-7201

RADIO

	City	State	Zip	Phone	Fax
WDCG-FM 105.1 MHz (CHR) 3100 Smoketree Ct Suite 700 *E-mail:* prism@interpath.com	Raleigh	NC	27604	919-871-1051	954-8561
WDNC-AM 620 kHz (N/T) 407 Blackwell St. *Web:* www.wdnc.com	Durham	NC	27701	919-687-6580	688-0180
WFTK-AM 1030 kHz (Rel) 707 Leon St	Durham	NC	27704	919-781-1030	220-0006
WFXK-FM 104.3 MHz (Urban) 8001-101 Creedmoor Rd *Web:* www.foxy107-104.com ■ *E-mail:* info@foxy107-104.com	Raleigh	NC	27613	919-848-9736	844-3947
WKNC-FM 88.1 MHz (Rock) Box 8607 *Web:* wknc.org	Raleigh	NC	27607	919-515-2401	513-2693

Durham — Radio (Cont'd)

				Phone	Fax
WKXU-FM 101.1 MHz (Ctry) PO Box 1119	Burlington	NC	27216	336-584-0126	584-0739
WNCU-FM 90.7 MHz (NPR) PO Box 19875	Durham	NC	27707	919-560-9628	530-7975
Web: www.wncu.com					
WPTF-AM 680 kHz (N/T) 3012 Highwoods Blvd Suite 200	Raleigh	NC	27604	919-876-0674	790-8369
WQDR-FM 94.7 MHz (Ctry) 3012 Highwoods Blvd Suite 200	Raleigh	NC	27604	919-876-0674	790-8893
WQOK-FM 97.5 MHz (Urban) 8001-101 Creedmoor Rd	Raleigh	NC	27613	919-790-1035	863-4862
WRAL-FM 101.5 MHz (AC) PO Box 10100	Raleigh	NC	27605	919-890-6101	890-6146
Web: www.wralfm.com					
WRCQ-FM 103.5 MHz (Rock) 1009 Drayton Rd	Fayetteville	NC	28303	910-860-1401	860-4360
WRDU-FM 106.1 MHz (CR) 3100 Smoketree Ct Suite 700	Raleigh	NC	27604	919-876-1061	876-2929
WRSN-FM 93.9 MHz (AC) 31 Smoketree Ct Suite 700	Raleigh	NC	27604	919-871-1051	954-8561*
**Fax:* News Rm					
WSHA-FM 88.9 MHz (Jazz) 118 E South St	Raleigh	NC	27601	919-546-8430	546-8315
WUNC-FM 91.5 MHz (NPR) University of North Carolina Swain Hall Box 0915	Chapel Hill	NC	27599	919-966-5454	966-5955
Web: wunc.citysearch.com ■ *E-mail:* wunc@unc.edu					
WXDU-FM 88.7 MHz (Alt) PO Box 90869	Durham	NC	27708	919-684-2957	684-3260

— Colleges/Universities —

				Phone	Fax
Duke University 2138 Campus Dr Box 90586	Durham	NC	27708	919-684-3214	681-8941
Web: www.duke.edu ■ *E-mail:* askduke@admissions.duke.edu					
Durham Technical Community College 1637 E Lawson St	Durham	NC	27703	919-686-3300	686-3396
Web: www.dtcc.cc.nc.us					
North Carolina Central University 1801 Fayetteville St	Durham	NC	27707	919-560-6298	530-7625
TF: 877-667-7533 ■ *Web:* www.nccu.edu					

— Hospitals —

				Phone	Fax
Duke University Medical Center PO Box 3708	Durham	NC	27710	919-684-5414	681-8921
Web: www.mc.duke.edu					
Durham Regional Hospital 3643 N Roxboro Rd	Durham	NC	27704	919-470-4000	470-7372*
**Fax:* Admitting					
Veterans Affairs Medical Center 508 Fulton St	Durham	NC	27705	919-286-0411	286-6825

— Attractions —

				Phone	Fax
Bennett Place State Historic Site 4409 Bennett Memorial Rd	Durham	NC	27705	919-383-4345	383-4349
E-mail: bennettplace@mindspring.com					
Downtown Durham Historic District & Brightleaf Square Market St	Durham	NC	27701	919-560-4137	
Duke Homestead State Historic Site & Tobacco Museum 2828 Duke Homestead Rd	Durham	NC	27705	919-477-5498	479-7092
Web: metalab.unc.edu/maggot/dukehome/index.html					
Duke Memorial United Methodist Church 504 W Chapel Hill St	Durham	NC	27701	919-683-3467	682-3349
Duke Sarah P Gardens Anderson St betw Erwin Rd & Campus Dr	Durham	NC	27708	919-684-3698	684-8861
Duke University Chapel Chapel Dr Duke University West Campus	Durham	NC	27706	919-681-1704	
Web: www.chapel.duke.edu/					
Duke University Institute of the Arts Gallery 109 Bivins Bldg	Durham	NC	27708	919-660-3356	684-8906
Web: www.duke.edu/web/dia/					
Duke University Museum of Art N Buchanan St & Trinity Ave	Durham	NC	27701	919-684-5135	681-8624
Web: www.duke.edu/duma/					
Duke University Primate Center 3705 Erwin Rd	Durham	NC	27705	919-489-3364	490-5394
Durham Symphony 120 Morris St	Durham	NC	27702	919-560-2736	
Eno River State Park 6101 Cole Mill Rd	Durham	NC	27705	919-383-1686	382-7378
Funtasia Family Fun Park 4350 Garrett Rd	Durham	NC	27707	919-493-8973	489-5772
Hayti Heritage Center 804 Old Fayetteville St	Durham	NC	27702	919-683-1709	682-5869
Historic Stagville PO Box 71217	Durham	NC	27722	919-620-0120	620-0422
Mangum Hugh Museum of Photography 5101 N Roxboro Rd	Durham	NC	27704	919-471-1623	
North Carolina Central University Art Museum 1801 Fayetteville St	Durham	NC	27705	919-560-6211	
North Carolina Museum of Life & Science 433 Murray Ave	Durham	NC	27704	919-220-5429	220-5575
Web: ils.unc.edu/NCMLS/ncmls.html					
North Carolina Theatre 309 W Morgan St Royall Ctr for the Arts	Durham	NC	27701	919-560-3040	560-3065
Web: www.nctheatre.com					
Patterson's Mill Country Store 5109 Farrington Rd	Chapel Hill	NC	27514	919-493-8149	
Research Triangle Park 2 Hanes Dr	Research Triangle Park	NC	27709	919-549-8181	549-8246
Web: www.rtp.org ■ *E-mail:* parkinfo@rtp.org					
Triangle Opera 309 Morgan St Carolina Theatre	Durham	NC	27701	919-956-7744	956-7788
Web: www.triangleopera.org					
West Point on the Eno City Park 5101 N Roxboro Rd	Durham	NC	27704	919-471-1623	
Wheels Recreation Park 715 N Hoover Rd	Durham	NC	27703	919-598-1944	

— Events —

	Phone
Air Expo (early May)	919-840-2100
American Dance Festival (mid-June-late July)	919-684-6402
Bimbe Festival (late May)	919-560-4355
Brightleaf Music Workshop & Finale (late June-early August)	919-493-0385
Bull Durham Blues Festival (mid-September)	919-683-1709
Centerfest (mid-September)	919-560-2722
CROP Walk (late March)	919-688-3843
Double Take Film Festival (early April)	919-660-3699
Edible Arts Festival of Food & Art (early June)	919-560-2787
Festival for the Eno (early July)	919-477-4549
KwanzaaFest (early January)	919-560-2729
Native American Pow Wow (mid-February)	919-286-3366
North Carolina International Jazz Festival (late January-late April)	919-660-3300
Pine Cone's Old Time Bluegrass Music Festival (early May)	919-990-1900
Summer Festival of Creative Arts (late May-mid-August)	919-684-4741
Triangle Triumph Road Race (late September)	919-990-7938

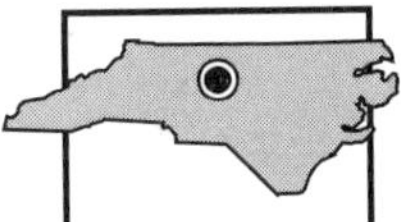

Greensboro

Greensboro is named after General Nathanael Greene, who led one of the most decisive battles of the Revolutionary War. Guilford Courthouse National Military Park, located on Guilford Battleground, remains a popular tourist attraction, and the Greensboro Historical Museum includes displays on Greensboro natives William Sydney Porter (O. Henry) and Dolly Madison. Other attractions in Greensboro include the Blandwood Mansion, home of former North Carolina governor John Motley Morehead; the Colonial Heritage Center at Tannenbaum Park; five art galleries at the Greensboro Cultural Center; the Charlotte Hawkins Brown Memorial State Historic Site, which honors her efforts in African-American education; and the Mattye Reed African Heritage Museum, which houses 3,500 art and craft items from more than 30 African nations, New Guinea, and Haiti. In nearby Jamestown are Castle McCullough; a restored gold refinery; and Mendenhall Plantation, a 19th century Quaker plantation that has a false-bottomed wagon which was used to transport slaves on the Underground Railroad.

Population	197,910	**Longitude**	79-79-22 W
Area (Land)	79.8 sq mi	**County**	Guilford
Area (Water)	1.6 sq mi	**Time Zone**	EST
Elevation	939 ft	**Area Code/s**	336
Latitude	36-07-25 N		

Greensboro (Cont'd)

— Average Temperatures and Precipitation —

TEMPERATURES

	Jan	Feb	Mar	Apr	May	Jun	Jul	Aug	Sep	Oct	Nov	Dec
High	47	51	60	70	77	84	87	86	80	70	61	51
Low	27	29	37	46	55	63	67	66	60	47	39	31

PRECIPITATION

	Jan	Feb	Mar	Apr	May	Jun	Jul	Aug	Sep	Oct	Nov	Dec
Inches	3.2	3.3	3.7	2.8	4.0	3.8	4.5	3.9	3.5	3.5	3.0	3.4

— Important Phone Numbers —

	Phone		Phone
AAA	336-852-0506	Medical Referral	336-832-8000
American Express Travel	336-282-1710	Poison Control Center	336-574-8105
Emergency	911	Weather	336-370-9369

— Information Sources —

				Phone	Fax
Better Business Bureau Serving Central North Carolina 3608 W Friendly Ave *Web:* www.greensboro.bbb.org	Greensboro	NC	27410	336-852-4240	852-7540
Greater Greensboro Merchants Assn 225 Commerce Pl *Web:* www.greensboro.com/gma/	Greensboro	NC	27401	336-378-6350	378-6272
Greensboro Area Chamber of Commerce 342 N Elm St Suite 100 *Web:* www.greensboro.org	Greensboro	NC	27401	336-275-8675	230-1867
Greensboro Area Convention & Visitors Bureau 317 S Greene St *TF:* 800-344-2282 ■ *Web:* www.greensboronc.org ■ *E-mail:* gso@greensboronc.org	Greensboro	NC	27401	336-274-2282	230-1183
Greensboro City Hall 300 W Washington St *Web:* www.ci.greensboro.nc.us	Greensboro	NC	27402	336-373-2000	
Greensboro Cultural Center at Festival Park 200 N Davie St	Greensboro	NC	27401	336-373-2712	373-2659
Greensboro Mayor PO Box 3136 *Web:* www.ci.greensboro.nc.us/newfronts/citycncl.htm	Greensboro	NC	27402	336-373-2396	373-2117
Greensboro Planning Dept PO Box 3136 *Web:* www.ci.greensboro.nc.us/planning	Greensboro	NC	27402	336-373-2144	412-6315
Greensboro Public Library 219 W Church St *Web:* www.greensboro.com/library	Greensboro	NC	27401	336-373-2474	333-6781
Guilford County PO Box 3427 *Web:* www.co.guilford.nc.us/	Greensboro	NC	27402	336-373-3383	333-6833

On-Line Resources

Anthill City Guide Greensboro	www.anthill.com/city.asp?city=greensboro
Area Guide Greensboro	greensboro.areaguides.net
City Knowledge Greensboro	www.cityknowledge.com/nc_greensboro.htm
CityTravelers.com Guide to Greensboro	www.citytravelers.com/greensboro.htm
Depot @ Greensboro.com	www.thedepot.com
Destination Greensboro	www.hickory.nc.us/ncnetworks/grb-intr.html
DigitalCity Greensboro	home.digitalcity.com/greensboro
ESP Magazine	www.espmagazine.com
Excite.com Greensboro City Guide	www.excite.com/travel/countries/united_states/north_carolina/greensboro
Wire The	www.wirecom.com

— Transportation Services —

AIRPORTS

■ **Piedmont Triad International Airport (GSO)**

	Phone
10 miles W of downtown (approx 20 minutes) Web: www.piedmonttriadnc.com/transportation.html	336-665-5600

Airport Transportation

	Phone
Airport Taxi $18 fare to downtown	336-668-0164
United Yellow Cab $18 fare to downtown	336-273-9421

Commercial Airlines

	Phone		Phone
American	800-433-7300	Delta	800-221-1212
American Eagle	800-433-7300	Eastwind	888-327-8946
Atlantic Southeast	800-282-3424	United	800-241-6522
Continental	800-525-0280	US Airways	800-428-4322
Continental Express	800-525-0280		

Charter Airlines

	Phone		Phone
Atlantic Aero	336-668-0411	Piedmont Hawthorne Aviation	336-668-0481
Piedmont Aviation Services Inc	800-548-1978	Richmor Aviation	800-331-6101

CAR RENTALS

	Phone		Phone
Avis	800-331-1212	National	800-227-7368
Budget	336-272-8158	Triangle	336-668-3400
Hertz	336-668-7961		

LIMO/TAXI

	Phone		Phone
A Touch of Class Limousine	336-272-5283	Keck Daniel Taxi	336-275-6337
Blue Bird Taxi	336-272-5112	Piedmont Limousine	336-228-0141
Greensboro Coach Limousines	336-297-1114	United Yellow Cab	336-273-9421

MASS TRANSIT

	Phone
Greensboro Transit Authority $1 Base fare	336-332-6440

RAIL/BUS

				Phone
Amtrak Station 2603 Oakland Ave *TF:* 800-872-7245	Greensboro	NC	27403	336-855-3382
Greyhound Bus Station 501 W Lee St *TF:* 800-231-2222	Greensboro	NC	27406	336-272-8950

— Accommodations —

HOTELS, MOTELS, RESORTS

				Phone	Fax
AmeriSuites 1619 Stanley Rd *TF:* 800-833-1516	Greensboro	NC	27407	336-852-1443	854-9339
Battleground Inn 1517 Westover Terr *TF:* 800-932-4737	Greensboro	NC	27408	336-272-4737	274-6242
Best Inns of America 210 I-40 *TF:* 800-237-8466	Greensboro	NC	27409	336-668-9400	668-9331
Best Western Burlington Inn 770 Huffman Mill Rd *TF:* 800-528-1234	Burlington	NC	27215	336-584-0151	584-3625
Best Western Windsor Suites 2006 Veasley St *TF:* 800-528-1234	Greensboro	NC	27407	336-294-9100	294-9100
Comfort Inn 2001 Veasley St *TF:* 800-228-5150	Greensboro	NC	27407	336-294-6220	294-6220
Comfort Suites Airport 7619 Thorndike Rd *TF:* 800-222-5150	Greensboro	NC	27409	336-882-6666	882-9411
Courtyard by Marriott 4400 W Wendover Ave *TF:* 800-321-2211 ■ *Web:* courtyard.com/GSOWN	Greensboro	NC	27407	336-294-3800	294-9982
Cricket Inn 2914 S Elm St	Greensboro	NC	27406	336-275-9471	272-2556
Days Inn Airport 501 Regional Rd *TF:* 800-329-7466	Greensboro	NC	27409	336-668-0476	665-1777
Days Inn Central 120 Seneca Rd *TF:* 800-329-7466	Greensboro	NC	27406	336-275-9571	275-9571
Days Inn of Greensboro 3304 Isler Ct *TF:* 800-329-7466	Greensboro	NC	27407	336-297-1996	297-1136
Econo Lodge 3303 Isler St *TF:* 800-553-2666	Greensboro	NC	27407	336-852-4080	855-5539
Embassy Suites 204 Centre Port Dr *TF:* 800-362-2779 ■ *Web:* www.embassy-suites.com ■ *E-mail:* embassy_reservation_inquiries@promus.com	Greensboro	NC	27409	336-668-4535	668-3901

Greensboro — Hotels, Motels, Resorts (Cont'd)

				Phone	Fax
Extended StayAmerica 4317 Big Tree Way	Greensboro	NC	27409	336-299-0200	299-2204
TF: 800-398-7829					
Fairfield Inn 2003 Athena Ct	Greensboro	NC	27407	336-294-9922	294-9922
TF: 800-228-2800 ■ *Web:* fairfieldinn.com/GSOHP					
Greensboro Biltmore Hotel 111 W Washington St	Greensboro	NC	27401	336-272-3474	275-2523
TF: 800-332-0303 ■ *Web:* members.aol.com/biltmorenc ■ *E-mail:* biltmorenc@aol.com					
Greensboro High Point Marriott 1 Marriott Dr	Greensboro	NC	27409	336-852-6450	665-6522
TF: 800-228-9290					
Greensboro Hilton 304 N Greene St	Greensboro	NC	27401	336-379-8000	275-2810
TF: 800-533-3944					
Hampton Inn 2004 Veasley St	Greensboro	NC	27407	336-854-8600	854-8741
TF: 800-426-7866					
Holiday Inn Airport 6426 Burnt Poplar Rd	Greensboro	NC	27409	336-668-0421	668-7690
TF: 800-465-4329					
Holiday Inn Four Seasons 3121 High Point Rd	Greensboro	NC	27407	336-292-9161	292-1407
TF: 800-242-6556					
Homestead Lodge 115 E Carteret St	Greensboro	NC	27406	336-272-5834	275-7672
Homewood Suites Hotel 201 Centreport Dr	Greensboro	NC	27409	336-393-0088	393-0070
TF: 800-225-5463					
Howard Johnson Coliseum 3030 High Point Rd	Greensboro	NC	27403	336-294-4920	299-0503
TF: 800-446-4656					
Innkeeper Greensboro 4305 Big Tree Way	Greensboro	NC	27409	336-854-0090	854-4516
TF: 800-466-5337					
Microtel Inn Greensboro 4304 Big Tree Way	Greensboro	NC	27409	336-547-7007	547-0450
TF: 800-956-7007					
Motel 6 Airport 605 S Regional Rd	Greensboro	NC	27409	336-454-6121	454-6120
TF: 800-466-8356					
Park Lane Hotel 3005 High Point Rd	Greensboro	NC	27403	336-294-4565	294-2988
TF: 800-942-6556					
Radisson Hotel 135 S Main St	High Point	NC	27260	336-889-8888	885-2737
TF: 800-333-3333					
Radisson Inn 415 Swing Rd	Greensboro	NC	27409	336-299-7650	854-9146
TF: 800-333-3333					
Ramada Inn & Conference Center 236 S Main St	High Point	NC	27260	336-886-7011	886-5595
TF: 800-272-6232					
Ramada Inn Airport 7067 Albert Pick Rd	Greensboro	NC	27409	336-668-3900	668-7012
TF: 800-272-6232					
Red Roof Inn Airport 615 Regional Rd S	Greensboro	NC	27409	336-271-2636	884-8053
TF: 800-843-7663					
Red Roof Inn Coliseum 2101 W Meadowview Rd	Greensboro	NC	27403	336-852-6560	852-6673
TF: 800-843-7663					
Residence Inn by Marriott 2000 Veasley St	Greensboro	NC	27407	336-294-8600	294-2201
TF: 800-331-3131 ■ *Web:* www.residenceinn.com/GSOVS					
Shoney's Inn & Suites 1103 Lanada Rd	Greensboro	NC	27407	336-297-1055	297-1904
TF: 800-222-2222 ■ *Web:* www.shoneysinn.com/nc1.htm					
StudioPLUS 1705 Stanley Rd	Greensboro	NC	27407	336-547-0405	218-5692
TF: 800-646-8000					
Travelodge 2112 W Meadowview Rd	Greensboro	NC	27403	336-292-2020	852-3476
TF: 800-578-7878					

— Restaurants —

				Phone
Acropolis Restaurant (Greek) 416 N Eugene St	Greensboro	NC	27401	336-273-3306
Anton's Italian Cafe (Italian) 1628 Battleground Ave	Greensboro	NC	27408	336-273-1386
Asahi (Japanese) 4520-B W Market St	Greensboro	NC	27407	336-855-8883
Bangkok Cafe (Thai) 1203-C S Holden Rd	Greensboro	NC	24707	336-855-9370
Cafe Pasta (Italian) 305 State St	Greensboro	NC	27408	336-272-1308
Exchange The (Greek) 338 S Tate St	Greensboro	NC	27403	336-273-2243
Fisher's Grille (American) 608 N Elm St	Greensboro	NC	27401	336-275-8300
Gate City Chop House (American) 106 S Holden Rd	Greensboro	NC	27407	336-294-9977
Green's Supper Club (Steak/Seafood) 4735 US 29 N	Greensboro	NC	27405	336-621-9958
Kyoto Japanese Steak House (Japanese) 1200 S Holden Rd	Greensboro	NC	27407	336-299-1003
Liberty Oak Wine & Cheese (American) 1722 Battleground Ave	Greensboro	NC	27408	336-273-7057
Mahi's Seafood Grill (Seafood) 4721 Lawndale Dr	Greensboro	NC	27455	336-282-8112
Mark's on Westover (American) 1310 Westover Terr	Greensboro	NC	27403	336-273-9090
Mayflower Restaurant (Seafood) 2631 Randleman Rd	Greensboro	NC	27406	336-379-7009
Monterey (Mexican) 3724 Battleground Ave	Greensboro	NC	27410	336-282-5588
Nikita India (Indian) 413 Tate St	Greensboro	NC	27403	336-379-0744
Paisley Pineapple (American) 345 S Elm St	Greensboro	NC	27401	336-279-8488
Park Place (American) 204 Centreport Dr	Greensboro	NC	27409	336-668-4535
Peking Restaurant (Chinese) 106 Westgate Dr	Greensboro	NC	27407	336-218-8555
Revival Grill (American) 5607 W Friendly Ave	Greensboro	NC	27410	336-297-0950
Saigon (Vietnamese) 4205-B High Point Rd	Greensboro	NC	27407	336-294-9286
Salt Marsh Willie's (Steak/Seafood) 1744 Battleground Ave	Greensboro	NC	27408	336-275-6285
Spring Garden Brewing Co (American) 714 Francis King St	Greensboro	NC	27410	336-299-3649
Undercurrant The (European) 600 S Elm St	Greensboro	NC	27406	336-370-1266
Wild Magnolia Cafe (Cajun) 2200 Walker Ave	Greensboro	NC	27403	336-378-0800

— Goods and Services —

SHOPPING

				Phone	Fax
Carolina Circle Mall US 29 N & Cone Blvd	Greensboro	NC	27405	336-621-6610	621-3484
Four Seasons Town Centre 400 Four Seasons Town Centre	Greensboro	NC	27407	336-299-9200	299-9969
E-mail: fourseas@nr.infi.net					
Friendly Center 3110 Kathleen Ave	Greensboro	NC	27408	336-292-2789	292-4297*
**Fax:* Mktg ■ *Web:* www.friendlycenter.com/					
Oak Hollow Mall 921 Eastchester Dr	High Point	NC	27262	336-886-6255	886-6257
Old Downtown Greensborough 447 Arlington St	Greensboro	NC	27406	336-272-6617	
State Street Station 408 1/2 State St	Greensboro	NC	27405	336-275-8586	

BANKS

				Phone	Fax
BB & T Bank 201 W Market St	Greensboro	NC	27401	336-574-5700	574-5731
Central Carolina Bank & Trust Co 3227 Battleground Ave	Greensboro	NC	27408	336-373-5018	282-1705
TF: 800-422-2226					
Centura Bank 2301 Battleground Ave	Greensboro	NC	27408	336-271-5840	271-5850
First Union National Bank 926 E Bessemer Ave	Greensboro	NC	27405	336-574-5800	574-5807
TF Cust Svc: 800-733-3862*					
Mutual Community Savings Bank 100 S Murrow Blvd	Greensboro	NC	27401	336-373-8500	373-1204
NationsBank NA 1616 E Bessemer Ave	Greensboro	NC	27405	336-805-3050	274-8613
TF Cust Svc: 800-333-6262*					
Wachovia Bank NA 1204 Bradford Pkwy	Greensboro	NC	27407	336-856-5200	856-5240
TF Cust Svc: 800-922-4684*					

BUSINESS SERVICES

	Phone
Adecco Employment Personnel Services	336-854-6000
Airborne Express	800-247-2676
BAX Global	336-668-7117
Corporate Express Delivery Systems	336-665-0219
DHL Worldwide Express	800-225-5345
Emery Worldwide	336-668-3613
Express Business Systems	336-854-5606
Federal Express	800-238-5355
KBD Services	336-294-5932
Kelly Services	336-292-4371
Kinko's	336-273-5865
Norrell Temporary Services	336-547-0788
Post Office	336-370-9291

— Media —

PUBLICATIONS

				Phone	Fax
News & Record‡ 200 E Market St	Greensboro	NC	27420	336-373-7000	373-7382
TF: 800-553-6880					
Triad Style 106 S Church St	Greensboro	NC	27401	336-373-7083	373-7323
TF: 800-228-5517 ■ *E-mail:* tstyle@nr.insi.net					

‡*Daily newspapers*

TELEVISION

				Phone	Fax
WBFX-TV Ch 20 (WB) 622G Guilford College Rd	Greensboro	NC	27409	336-547-0020	547-8184
WFMY-TV Ch 2 (CBS) 1615 Phillips Ave	Greensboro	NC	27405	336-379-9369	273-9433
E-mail: fmy2@aol.com					
WGHP-TV Ch 8 (Fox) PO Box HP-8	High Point	NC	27261	336-841-8888	841-5169
Web: www.fox8wghp.com					

Greensboro — Television (Cont'd)

	City	State	ZIP	Phone	Fax
WUNC-TV Ch 4 (PBS) PO Box 14900	Research Triangle Park	NC	27709	919-549-7000	549-7201
Web: www.unctv.org ■ *E-mail:* viewer@unctv.org					
WUNL-TV Ch 26 (PBS) PO Box 14900	Research Triangle Park	NC	27709	919-549-7000	549-7201
WUPN-TV Ch 48 (UPN) 3500 Myer Lee Dr	Winston-Salem	NC	27101	336-274-4848	722-6289
Web: www.wxlv.com/WUPN-48					
WXII-TV Ch 12 (NBC) 700 Coliseum Dr	Winston-Salem	NC	27106	336-721-9944	721-0856
Web: www.wxii.com ■ *E-mail:* newschannel12@wxii.com					

RADIO

	City	State	ZIP	Phone	Fax
WJMH-FM 102.1 MHz (Urban) 7819 National Service Rd Suite 401	Greensboro	NC	27409	336-605-5200	605-5219
WKRR-FM 92.3 MHz (Rock) 192 E Lewis St	Greensboro	NC	27406	336-274-8042	274-1629
Web: www.rock92.com					
WKSI-FM 98.7 MHz (AC) 221 W Meadowview Rd	Greensboro	NC	27406	336-275-9895	275-6236
WKZL-FM 107.5 MHz (AC) 192 E Lewis St	Greensboro	NC	27406	336-274-8042	274-1629*
**Fax:* Sales					
WMQX-FM 93.1 MHz (Oldies) 7819 National Service Rd Suite 401	Greensboro	NC	27409	336-605-5200	605-5221
WNAA-FM 90.1 MHz (Urban) North Carolina A & T State University Price Hall Suite 200	Greensboro	NC	27411	336-334-7936	334-7960
E-mail: whaafm@aurora.ncat.edu					
WPET-AM 950 kHz (Rel) 221 W Meadowview Rd	Greensboro	NC	27406	336-275-9738	275-2090
WQFS-FM 90.9 MHz (Alt) 5800 W Friendly Ave	Greensboro	NC	27410	336-316-2352	
WQMG-AM 1510 kHz (Rel) 7819 National Service Rd	Greensboro	NC	27409	336-605-5200	605-0138
WQMG-FM 97.1 MHz (Urban) 7819 National Service Rd	Greensboro	NC	27409	336-605-5200	605-0138
WUAG-FM 103.1 MHz (Misc) University of North Carolina Taylor Bldg	Greensboro	NC	27402	336-334-5450	334-5168

— Colleges/Universities —

	City	State	ZIP	Phone	Fax
Bennett College 900 E Washington St	Greensboro	NC	27401	336-273-4431	378-0511
TF: 800-413-5323 ■ *Web:* www.bennett.edu ■ *E-mail:* bcinfo@bennett1.bennett.edu					
Elon College PO Box 398	Elon College	NC	27244	336-584-9711	538-3986
Web: www.elon.edu					
Greensboro College 815 W Market St	Greensboro	NC	27401	336-272-7102	378-0154
TF Admissions: 800-346-8226 ■ *Web:* www.gborocollege.edu ■ *E-mail:* admissions@gborocollege.edu					
Guilford College 5800 W Friendly Ave	Greensboro	NC	27410	336-316-2100	316-2954
TF Admissions: 800-992-7759 ■ *Web:* www.guilford.edu					
Guilford Technical Community College PO Box 309	Jamestown	NC	27282	336-334-4822	819-2022
Web: technet.gtcc.cc.nc.us/ ■ *E-mail:* kirklands@gtcc.cc.nc.us					
High Point University 833 Montlieu Ave	High Point	NC	27262	336-841-9000	841-4599
Web: acme.highpoint.edu					
North Carolina A & T State University 1601 E Market St	Greensboro	NC	27411	336-334-7500	334-7478
Web: www.ncat.edu					
University of North Carolina Greensboro PO Box 26166	Greensboro	NC	27402	336-334-5000	334-4180
Web: www.uncg.edu ■ *E-mail:* undergrad_admissions@uncg.edu					

— Hospitals —

	City	State	ZIP	Phone	Fax
High Point Regional Hospital 601 N Elm St	High Point	NC	27262	336-878-6000	878-6130
Moses H Cone Memorial Hospital 1200 N Elm St	Greensboro	NC	27401	336-832-7000	832-8236
Web: www.mosescone.com					
Wesley Long Community Hospital 501 N Elam Ave	Greensboro	NC	27402	336-832-1000	832-0529*
**Fax:* Admitting					
Women's Hospital of Greensboro 801 Green Valley Rd	Greensboro	NC	27408	336-832-6500	274-9408

— Attractions —

	City	State	ZIP	Phone	Fax
Bicentennial Gardens 1105 Hobbs Rd	Greensboro	NC	27408	336-373-2199	299-7940
Blandwood Mansion 447 W Washington St	Greensboro	NC	27401	336-272-5003	
Bog Garden Hobbs Rd & Starmount Farms Dr	Greensboro	NC	27408	336-373-2199	
Broach Theatre 520-C S Elm St	Greensboro	NC	27406	336-378-9300	
Carolina Model Railroaders 300 E Washington St The Depot	Greensboro	NC	27401	336-656-7968	
Carolina Theatre 310 S Greene St	Greensboro	NC	27401	336-333-2600	333-2604
Web: www.carolinatheatre.com ■ *E-mail:* cartheatre@aol.com					
Castle McCulloch 6000 Kersey Valley Rd	Jamestown	NC	27282	336-887-5413	887-5429
Web: www.castlemcculloch.com ■ *E-mail:* castlemcc@juno.com					
Charlotte Hawkins Brown Memorial State Historic Site 6136 Burlington Rd	Sedalia	NC	27342	336-449-4846	449-0176
Web: www.netpath.net/~chb/					
Chinqua-Penn Plantation 2138 Wentworth St	Reidsville	NC	27320	336-349-7069	342-4863
TF: 800-948-0847 ■ *Web:* www.chinquapenn.com/					
Community Theatre of Greensboro 200 N Davie St	Greensboro	NC	27401	336-333-7470	333-2607
Web: www.wirecom.com/ctg/					
Country Park 3902 Nathanael Greene Dr	Greensboro	NC	27455	336-373-2574	545-5342
Emerald Pointe Water Park 3910 S Holden Rd	Greensboro	NC	27406	336-852-9721	852-2391
Fields William House 447 Arlington St	Greensboro	NC	27406	336-272-6617	
Green Hill Center for North Carolina Art 200 N Davie St	Greensboro	NC	27401	336-333-7460	333-2612
Greensboro Arboretum W Wendover Ave & Market St	Greensboro	NC	27403	336-373-2199	
Greensboro Ballet 200 Davie St Greensboro Cultural Ctr	Greensboro	NC	27401	336-333-7480	333-7482
Greensboro Cultural Center at Festival Park 200 N Davie St	Greensboro	NC	27401	336-373-2712	373-2659
Greensboro Historical Museum 130 Summit Ave	Greensboro	NC	27401	336-373-2043	373-2204
Greensboro Opera Co 1834 Pembroke Rd Suite 7	Greensboro	NC	27408	336-273-9472	273-9481
Web: www.greensboro.com/goc					
Greensboro Symphony Orchestra 200 N Davie St Suite 328	Greensboro	NC	27420	336-335-5456	335-5580
Web: www.greensboro.com/gbosymph					
Greensboro War Memorial Auditorium 1921 W Lee St	Greensboro	NC	27403	336-373-7400	373-2170
Guilford College Art Gallery 5800 W Friendly Ave Hege Library	Greensboro	NC	27410	336-316-2438	
Guilford Courthouse National Military Park 2332 New Garden Rd	Greensboro	NC	27410	336-288-1776	282-2296
Web: www.nps.gov/guco/					
Hagan Stone Park 5920 Hagan Stone Park Rd	Greensboro	NC	27313	336-373-2574	674-7410
Hester Park 3615 Deutzia St	Greensboro	NC	27407	336-373-2937	299-2195
Livestock Players Musical Theatre 310 S Greene St Carolina Theatre	Greensboro	NC	27401	336-373-2728	373-2659
Mendenhall Plantation 603 W Main St	Jamestown	NC	27282	336-454-3819	
Natural Science Center 4301 Lawndale Dr	Greensboro	NC	27455	336-288-3769	288-2531
Web: www.greensboro.com/sciencecenter/ ■ *E-mail:* nscg@greensboro.com					
North Carolina Tennis Hall of Fame 3802 Jaycee Park Dr	Greensboro	NC	27455	336-852-8577	852-7334
Web: www.nctennis.com					
North Carolina Zoological Park 4401 Zoo Pkwy	Asheboro	NC	27203	336-879-7000	879-2891
Web: www.nczoo.org					
Old Downtown Greensborough 447 Arlington St	Greensboro	NC	27406	336-272-6617	
Old Mill of Guilford 1340 NC 68 N	Oak Ridge	NC	27310	336-643-4783	
Petty Richard Museum 311 Branson Mill Rd	Randleman	NC	27317	336-495-1143	498-4334
Reed Mattye African Heritage Museum Dudley Bldg A&T State University	Greensboro	NC	27411	336-334-3209	
Tannenbaum Park & Colonial Heritage Center 2200 New Garden Rd	Greensboro	NC	27410	336-545-5315	545-5314
Weatherspoon Art Gallery 1000 Spring Garden & Tate Sts	Greensboro	NC	27402	336-334-5770	334-5907
Web: www.uncg.edu/wag					

Greensboro (Cont'd)

SPORTS TEAMS & FACILITIES

				Phone	Fax
Carolina Dynamo (soccer) 2920 School Pk Rd High Point Athletic Complex	High Point	NC	27265	336-869-1022	869-1190
Web: www.carolinadynamo.com ■ *E-mail:* colleenk@northstate.net					
Carolina Hurricanes (hockey) 1921 W Lee St Greensboro Coliseum Arena	Greensboro	NC	27403	336-852-6170	852-6259
Web: www.caneshockey.com					
Greensboro Bats (baseball) 510 Yanceyville St War Memorial Stadium	Greensboro	NC	27405	336-333-2287	273-7350
Web: www.greensborobats.com					
Greensboro Coliseum 1921 W Lee St	Greensboro	NC	27403	336-373-7400	373-2170
Web: www.greensborocoliseum.com ■ *E-mail:* gsoarena@interpath.com					
Piedmont Spark (soccer) 2920 School Park Rd High Point Athletic Complex	High Point	NC	27265	336-869-1022	869-1190

— Events —

	Phone
African-American Arts Festival (mid-January-mid-March)	336-373-7523
African American Heritage Festival (early June)	336-449-4846
Artists Hang-Up & Put-Down (mid-late January)	336-333-7460
Boo at the Zoo (late October)	800-488-0444
Carolina Blues Festival (mid-May)	336-274-2282
Charlotte Hawkins Brown Gravesite Ceremonies (early June)	336-449-4846
Chili Championship & Rubber Duck Regatta (mid-September)	800-443-4093
City Stage Street Festival (early October)	336-274-2282
Eastern Music Festival (mid-June-late July)	336-333-7450
Eastern Music Festival Wine Tasting (late March)	336-333-7450
Fun Fourth Festival (early July)	336-274-2282
Gatsby Weekend (late August)	336-349-4576
Greater Greensboro Chrysler Classic (mid-April)	336-379-1570
Greensboro Agricultural Fair (mid-late September)	336-373-7400
Greensboro Gun Show (late August)	336-674-9287
GYC Carnival (early May)	336-373-2173
Holiday of Lights (early January)	919-839-2443
Home & Garden Tour (mid-April)	336-292-0057
Ice Cream Festival (mid-July)	336-379-8748
Native American Pow Wow (mid-September)	336-273-8686
Oak Ridge Easter Horse Show (mid-April)	336-643-4151
Pony Baseball Palomino World Series (mid-August)	336-852-8488
Re-Enactment of the Battle of Guilford Courthouse (mid-March)	336-545-5315
Revolutionary War Encampment (early July)	336-545-5315
Rock Festival (mid-August)	336-288-3769
Seafest (mid-February)	336-288-3769
Serendipity Weekend (mid-April)	336-316-2301
State Games of North Carolina (late June)	800-277-8763
Stewfest Weekend (early October)	336-349-4576
Street Rod Safari (mid-April)	800-488-0444
Tannenbaum Park Colonial Fair (early September)	336-545-5315
Tulip Days at Chinqua-Penn Plantation (April)	336-349-4576
US Hot Rod Monster Jam (late January)	336-373-7400

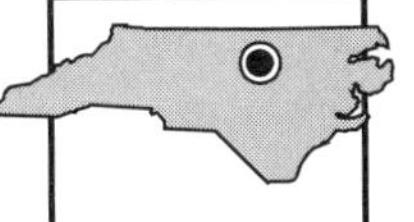

Raleigh

North Carolina's capital city, Raleigh was named for the chivalrous Sir Walter Raleigh. The city was chosen as the capital on a whim of the North Carolina General Assembly that the seat of government should be located within ten miles of Isaac Hunter's tavern. The State Museum of Natural Sciences, as well as the North Carolina Symphony Orchestra, are based in Raleigh. Research Triangle Park, a 6,000-acre scientific research and development center just over ten miles from the city of Raleigh, is home to the U.S. Environmental Protection Agency and more than 50 companies. The Park consolidates the scientific resources of the University of North Carolina in Chapel Hill, Duke University in Durham, and North Carolina State University in Raleigh. The three schools are also prominent basketball rivals of the NCAA's Atlantic Coast Conference.

Population	259,423	**Longitude**	78-63-31 W
Area (Land)	88.1 sq mi	**County**	Wake
Area (Water)	0.7 sq mi	**Time Zone**	EST
Elevation	363 ft	**Area Code/s**	919
Latitude	35-77-38 N		

— Average Temperatures and Precipitation —

TEMPERATURES

	Jan	Feb	Mar	Apr	May	Jun	Jul	Aug	Sep	Oct	Nov	Dec
High	49	53	62	72	79	85	88	87	81	72	63	53
Low	29	31	39	46	55	64	68	68	61	48	40	32

PRECIPITATION

	Jan	Feb	Mar	Apr	May	Jun	Jul	Aug	Sep	Oct	Nov	Dec
Inches	3.5	3.7	3.8	2.6	3.9	3.7	4.0	4.0	3.2	2.9	3.0	3.2

— Important Phone Numbers —

	Phone		Phone
AAA	919-832-0543	**Medical Referral**	800-362-8677
Dental Referral	800-917-6453	**Travelers Aid Society**	919-821-1348
Emergency	911	**Weather**	919-515-8225
HotelDocs	800-468-3537		

— Information Sources —

				Phone	Fax
Better Business Bureau Serving Eastern North Carolina 3125 Poplarwood Ct Suite 308	Raleigh	NC	27604	919-688-6143	954-0622
Web: www.raleigh-durham.bbb.org					
Capital Area Visitor Center 301 N Blount St	Raleigh	NC	27601	919-733-3456	733-1991
Greater Raleigh Chamber of Commerce 800 S Salisbury St	Raleigh	NC	27601	919-664-7000	664-7099
Web: www.raleighchamber.org					
Greater Raleigh Convention & Visitors Bureau 421 Fayetteville St Mall Suite 1505	Raleigh	NC	27601	919-834-5900	831-2887
TF: 800-849-8499 ■ *Web:* www.raleighcvb.org ■ *E-mail:* visit@raleighcvb.org					
Raleigh City Hall PO Box 590	Raleigh	NC	27602	919-890-3000	828-8036
Web: www.raleigh-nc.org					
Raleigh Community Development Dept 310 W Martin St	Raleigh	NC	27602	919-857-4330	857-4359
Web: www.raleigh-nc.org/communitydevelopment					
Raleigh Convention & Conference Center 500 Fayetteville Street Mall	Raleigh	NC	27601	919-831-6011	831-6013
Raleigh Mayor PO Box 590	Raleigh	NC	27602	919-890-3050	890-3058
Wake County PO Box 550	Raleigh	NC	27602	919-856-6160	856-6168
Wake County Public Libraries 4020 Carya Dr	Raleigh	NC	27610	919-250-1200	250-1209
Web: www.co.wake.nc.us/library					

On-Line Resources

4RaleighDurham.com	www.4raleighdurham.com
About.com Guide to Raleigh/Durham	raleighdurham.about.com
Anthill City Guide Raleigh	www.anthill.com/city.asp?city=raleigh
City Knowledge Raleigh	www.cityknowledge.com/nc_raleigh.htm
CitySearch the Triangle	triangle.citysearch.com
DigitalCity Raleigh/Durham	home.digitalcity.com/raleigh
Excite.com Raleigh City Guide	www.excite.com/travel/countries/united_states/north_carolina/raleigh
Guest Guide Online	www.guestguideonline.com
introRaleigh	www.raleigh.acn.net/
NITC Travelbase City Guide Raleigh-Durham	www.travelbase.com/auto/guides/raleigh-durham-area-nc.html
Raleigh CityLink	www.usacitylink.com/citylink/raleigh
Raleigh North Carolina	raleigh-north-carolina.com
Raleigh Online	www.webs4you.com/raleigh
Virtual Raleigh	www.virtualraleigh.com/
Welcome to Raleigh	www.hickory.nc.us/ncnetworks/ral-intr.html

Raleigh (Cont'd)

— Transportation Services —

AIRPORTS

■ Raleigh-Durham International Airport (RDU) — Phone

12 miles NW of downtown Raleigh (approx 15 minutes) 919-840-2100
Web: www.rdu.com

Airport Transportation

	Phone
R & G Airport Shuttle $20 fare to downtown	919-840-0262
Yellow Cab $23 fare to downtown	919-875-1821

Commercial Airlines

	Phone		Phone
Air Canada	800-776-3000	**Midway**	800-446-4392
AirTran	800-247-8726	**Northwest**	800-225-2525
American	919-834-4704	**TWA**	800-221-2000
Continental	800-523-3273	**United**	800-241-6522
Delta	800-221-1212	**US Airways**	800-428-4322
Delta Express	800-325-5205	**US Airways Express**	919-840-4624

Charter Airlines

	Phone		Phone
James Flying Service	800-556-4221	**Raleigh Flying Service**	919-840-4400
Piedmont Aviation Services Inc	800-548-1978		

CAR RENTALS

	Phone		Phone
Budget	919-876-8715	**Hertz**	919-840-4875
Dollar	919-840-4850	**Thrifty**	919-832-9381
Enterprise	919-493-2683	**Triangle**	800-643-7368

LIMO/TAXI

	Phone		Phone
ABC Cab	919-682-0437	**Thorpe's**	919-544-4363
National Cab	919-469-1333	**Yellow Cab**	919-875-1821
R & G Airport Shuttle	919-840-0262		

MASS TRANSIT

	Phone
Capital Area Transit $.75 Base fare	919-828-7228

RAIL/BUS

				Phone
Amtrak Station 320 W Cabarrus St. *TF:* 800-872-7245	Raleigh	NC	27601	919-833-7594
Greyhound/Trailways Bus Station 314 W Jones St. *TF:* 800-231-2222	Raleigh	NC	27603	919-834-8275

— Accommodations —

HOTEL RESERVATION SERVICES

	Phone	Fax
Globe Corporate Stay International *TF:* 800-533-2370	919-851-1511	859-0725

HOTELS, MOTELS, RESORTS

				Phone	Fax
Baymont Inns & Suites 1001 Aerial Center Pkwy *TF:* 800-301-0200	Morrisville	NC	27560	919-481-3600	460-1584
Best Western Cary Inn 1722 Walnut St *TF:* 800-528-1234	Cary	NC	27511	919-481-1200	467-7535
Best Western Hospitality Inn 2800 Brentwood Rd *TF:* 800-528-1234	Raleigh	NC	27604	919-872-8600	872-5273
Brownstone Hotel 1707 Hillsborough St *TF:* 800-237-0772	Raleigh	NC	27605	919-828-0811	834 0904
Candlewood Suites 1020 Buck Jones Rd. *TF:* 800-946-6200	Raleigh	NC	27606	919-468-4222	468-4090
Club Hotel by Doubletree 2815 Capital Blvd. *TF:* 800-222-8733	Raleigh	NC	27604	919-872-7666	872-3915
Country Inn & Suites by Carlson 2715 Capital Blvd *TF:* 800-456-4000	Raleigh	NC	27604	919-872-5000	790-7741
Courtyard by Marriott 102 Edinburgh Dr S. *TF:* 800-321-2211 ■ *Web:* courtyard.com/RDUCA	Cary	NC	27511	919-481-9666	460-0380
Courtyard by Marriott Airport 2001 Hospitality Ct *TF:* 800-321-2211 ■ *Web:* courtyard.com/RDURD	Morrisville	NC	27560	919-467-9444	467-9332
Courtyard by Marriott North 1041 Wake Towne Dr *TF:* 800-321-2211 ■ *Web:* courtyard.com/RDUWF	Raleigh	NC	27609	919-821-3400	821-1209
Crabtree Summit Hotel 3908 Arrow Dr *TF:* 800-521-7521 ■ *Web:* triangle.citysearch.com/E/V/RDUNC/0001/68/66	Raleigh	NC	27612	919-782-6868	881-9340
Days Inn Rocky Mount 6970 Hwy 4 *TF:* 800-329-7466	Battleboro	NC	27809	252-446-0621	977-1059
Econo Lodge Crabtree 5110 Holly Ridge Dr *TF:* 800-446-6900	Raleigh	NC	27612	919-782-3201	782-7995
Embassy Suites 4700 Creedmoor Rd. *TF:* 800-362-2779	Raleigh	NC	27612	919-881-0000	782-7225
Extended StayAmerica 911 Wake Towne Dr. *TF:* 800-398-7829	Raleigh	NC	27609	919-829-7271	829-5746
Extended StayAmerica 1500 Regency Pkwy *TF:* 800-398-7829	Cary	NC	27511	919-854-7715	468-3887
Extended StayAmerica 2700 Slater Rd *TF:* 800-398-7829	Morrisville	NC	27560	919-380-1499	380-1598
Fairfield Inn by Marriott 2641 Appliance Ct *TF:* 800-228-2800 ■ *Web:* fairfieldinn.com/RDUNE	Raleigh	NC	27604	919-856-9800	856-9800
Four Points Hotel 4501 Creedmoor Rd *TF:* 800-325-3535	Raleigh	NC	27612	919-787-7111	783-0024
Hampton Inn 201 Asheville Ave. *TF:* 800-426-7866	Cary	NC	27511	919-859-5559	859-0682
Hampton Inn 1001 Wake Towne Dr. *TF:* 800-426-7866	Raleigh	NC	27609	919-828-1813	834-2672
Hampton Inn Crabtree 6209 Glenwood Ave *TF:* 800-426-7866	Raleigh	NC	27612	919-782-1112	782-9119
Holiday Inn Airport 4810 Page Rd *TF:* 800-465-4329	Research Triangle Park	NC	27709	919-941-6000	941-6030
Holiday Inn State Capitol 320 Hillsborough St *TF:* 800-465-4329	Raleigh	NC	27603	919-832-0501	833-1631
Homestead Village Crabtree 4810 Bluestone Dr	Raleigh	NC	27612	919-510-8551	510-0019
Homewood Suites Cary 100 MacAlyson Ct. *TF:* 800-225-5466	Cary	NC	27511	919-467-4444	467-3074
Homewood Suites Crabtree 5400 Edwards Mill Rd *TF:* 800-225-5466	Raleigh	NC	27612	919-785-1131	781-3119
Howard Johnson Lodge 3120 New Bern Ave *TF:* 800-446-4656	Raleigh	NC	27610	919-231-3000	231-3138
LaQuinta Inn & Suites Cary 191 Crescent Commons *TF:* 800-531-5900	Cary	NC	27511	919-851-2850	851-0728
LaQuinta Inn & Suites Crabtree 2211 Summit Park Ln *TF:* 800-531-5900	Raleigh	NC	27612	919-785-0071	785-0081
Marriott at Research Triangle Park 4700 Guardian Dr *TF:* 800-228-9290 ■ *Web:* marriotthotels.com/RDUCP	Durham	NC	27703	919-941-6200	941-6229
Marriott Raleigh/Crabtree Valley 4500 Marriott Dr. *TF:* 800-228-9290 ■ *Web:* marriotthotels.com/RDUNC	Raleigh	NC	27612	919-781-7000	781-3059
Meredith Village Apartments 2603 Village Ct. *TF:* 800-237-9363	Raleigh	NC	27607	919-781-5088	783-0514
Microtel Inn Raleigh 1209 Plainview Rd *TF:* 888-771-7171	Raleigh	NC	27610	919-231-0002	231-8894
North Raleigh Hilton Inn 3415 Wake Forest Rd *TF:* 800-445-8667	Raleigh	NC	27609	919-872-2323	876-0890
Plantation Inn Resort 6401 Capital Blvd *TF:* 800-521-1932 ■ *Web:* www.plantationinnraleigh.com ■ *E-mail:* plantation-inn@travelbase.com	Raleigh	NC	27616	919-876-1411	790-7093
Quality Suites Hotel 4400 Capital Blvd *TF:* 800-543-5497	Raleigh	NC	27604	919-876-2211	790-1352
Radisson Governors Inn Hwy 54 at I-40 & Davis Dr. *TF:* 800-333-3333	Research Triangle Park	NC	27709	919-549-8631	547-3510
Ramada Inn Crabtree 3920 Arrow Dr *TF:* 800-272-6232	Raleigh	NC	27612	919-782-7525	781-0435
Red Roof Inn 1800 Walnut St. *TF:* 800-843-7663	Cary	NC	27511	919-469-3400	460-9027

Raleigh — Hotels, Motels, Resorts (Cont'd)

				Phone	Fax
Residence Inn by Marriott 1000 Navajo Dr	Raleigh	NC	27609	919-878-6100	876-4117
TF: 800-331-3131 ■ *Web:* www.residenceinn.com/residenceinn/RDURB					
Sheraton Hotel 421 S Salisbury St	Raleigh	NC	27601	919-834-9900	833-1217
TF: 800-325-3535					
Siena Hotel 1505 E Franklin St	Chapel Hill	NC	27514	919-929-4000	968-8527
TF: 800-223-7379					
Sleep Inn Raleigh 2617 Appliance Ct	Raleigh	NC	27604	919-755-6005	755-9007
TF: 800-753-3746					
StudioPLUS 921 Wake Towne Dr	Raleigh	NC	27609	919-546-0879	743-2122
TF: 800-646-8000					
StudioPLUS 600 Weston Pkwy	Cary	NC	27513	919-677-9910	677-2975
TF: 800-646-8000					
Super 8 Motel Hwy 48 & I-95	Battleboro	NC	27809	252-442-8075	
TF: 800-800-8000					
Travelodge 2813 Capital Blvd	Raleigh	NC	27604	919-850-9986	872-2258
TF: 800-578-7878					
Velvet Cloak Inn 1505 Hillsborough St	Raleigh	NC	27605	919-828-0333	828-2656
TF: 800-334-4372					
Wyndham Garden Hotel 4620 S Miami Blvd	Durham	NC	27703	919-941-6066	941-6363
TF: 800-972-0264					

— Restaurants —

				Phone
42nd Street Oyster Bar (Seafood) 508 W Jones St	Raleigh	NC	27603	919-831-2811
Angus Barn (American) 9401 Glenwood Ave	Raleigh	NC	27612	919-781-2444
Ben's Jamaican Restaurant (Jamaican) 8306 Chapel Hill Rd	Cary	NC	27513	919-380-7888
Cappers (New American) 4421 Six Forks Rd	Raleigh	NC	27609	919-787-8963
Casa Carbone Ristorante (Italian)				
6019 Glenwood Ave Suite A	Raleigh	NC	27612	919-781-8750
Charter Room (Continental) 1505 Hillsborough St	Raleigh	NC	27605	919-828-0333
Coyote Cafe (Southwest) 1014 Ryan Rd	Cary	NC	27511	919-469-5253
Dos Tasquitos (Mexican) 5629 Creedmoor Rd	Raleigh	NC	27612	919-787-3373
Farmers Market Restaurant (American)				
1240 Farmers Market Dr	Raleigh	NC	27603	919-833-7973
Fox & Hound (English) 107 Edinburgh St Suite 119	Cary	NC	27511	919-380-0080
Glenwood Grill (Southern) 2929 Essex Cir	Raleigh	NC	27608	919-782-3102
Greenshields Brewery & Pub (English) 214 E Martin St	Raleigh	NC	27601	919-829-0214
Web: www.greenshields.com ■ *E-mail:* info@greenshields.com				
Irregardless Cafe (International) 901 W Morgan St	Raleigh	NC	27603	919-833-8898
Jean Claude's French Cafe (French)				
6112 Falls of Neuse Rd	Raleigh	NC	27609	919-872-6224
Web: www.jeanclaudes.com				
Kanki Japanese House of Steaks (Japanese)				
4500 Old Wake Forest Rd	Raleigh	NC	27609	919-876-4157
Web: www.kanki.com				
Royal India Cuisine (Indian) 3901 Capital Blvd	Raleigh	NC	27604	919-981-0849
Tartines French Restaurant (French) 1110 Navaho Dr	Raleigh	NC	27609	919-790-0091
Thai Gardens (Thai) 1408 Hardimont Rd	Raleigh	NC	27609	919-872-6811
Top of the Tower (American) 320 Hillsborough St	Raleigh	NC	27603	919-832-0501
WickedSmile (New American) 511 W Hargett St	Raleigh	NC	27603	919-828-2223
Winston's Grille (American) 6401 Falls of Neuse Rd	Raleigh	NC	27615	919-790-0700

— Goods and Services —

SHOPPING

				Phone	Fax
Cameron Village 1900 Cameron St	Raleigh	NC	27605	919-821-1350	
Carolina Antique Mall 2050 Clark Ave	Raleigh	NC	27605	919-833-8227	
Cary Town Center 1105 Walnut St	Cary	NC	27511	919-460-1053	
City Market 300/200 Parham St	Raleigh	NC	27601	919-828-4555	
Crabtree Valley Mall 4325 Glenwood Ave	Raleigh	NC	27612	919-787-2506	787-7108
Web: www.crabtree-valley-mall.com					
Crossroads Plaza US 1 & Hwy 64	Cary	NC	27511	919-233-8087	233-6931
Fairgrounds Flea Market 1025 Blue Ridge Rd	Raleigh	NC	27607	919-829-3533	
Magnolia Marketplace 651 Cary Towne Blvd	Cary	NC	27511	919-319-0505	319-1619
North Hills Mall & Plaza 4217 Six Forks Rd	Raleigh	NC	27609	919-787-9042	881-0530
Prime Outlets at Morrisville					
1001 Airport Blvd	Morrisville	NC	27560	919-380-8700	380-8661
State Farmers Market 1201 Agriculture St	Raleigh	NC	27603	919-733-7417	

BANKS

				Phone	Fax
First Citizens Bank & Trust Co					
239 Fayetteville Street Mall	Raleigh	NC	27602	919-755-7000	716-7379*
**Fax:* Cust Svc					
First Union Bank 601 Oberlin Rd	Raleigh	NC	27605	919-881-6324	571-3843
NationsBank 6300 Falls of Neuse Rd	Raleigh	NC	27615	919-829-6690	876-1377*
**Fax:* Cust Svc					
Wachovia Bank NA 227 Fayetteville St	Raleigh	NC	27601	919-755-7872	755-7924*
**Fax:* Cust Svc					

BUSINESS SERVICES

	Phone		Phone
DHL Worldwide Express	800-225-5345	**Post Office**	919-420-5333
Federal Express	800-238-5355	**Staffing Solutions**	919-783-7575
Kinko's	919-832-4533	**Triangle Temporaries**	919-876-0009
Office Specialists	919-848-3444	**UPS**	800-742-5877
Olsten Staffing Services	919-847-9999		

— Media —

PUBLICATIONS

				Phone	Fax
Business Leader					
3801 Wake Forest Rd Suite 102	Raleigh	NC	27609	919-872-7077	872-1590
Web: www.businessleader.com ■ *E-mail:* editor@businessleader.com					
News & Observer‡ 215 S McDowell St	Raleigh	NC	27601	919-829-4500	829-4529
Web: www.news-observer.com ■ *E-mail:* naostaff@nando.com					
Triangle Business Journal					
1305 Navaho Dr Suite 401	Raleigh	NC	27609	919-878-0010	790-6885
Web: www.amcity.com/triangle					

‡Daily newspapers

TELEVISION

				Phone	Fax
WFPX-TV Ch 62 (PAX) PO Box 62	Lumber Bridge	NC	28357	910-843-3884	843-2873
WKFT-TV Ch 40 (Ind) 230 Donaldson St	Fayetteville	NC	28301	910-323-4040	323-3924
WLFL-TV Ch 22 (WB)					
3012 Highwoods Blvd Suite 101	Raleigh	NC	27604	919-872-9535	878-3877
E-mail: wlfl22@nando.net					
WNCN-TV Ch 17 (NBC) 1205 Front St	Raleigh	NC	27609	919-836-1717	836-1747
Web: www.nbc17.com					
WRAL-TV Ch 5 (CBS) 2619 Western Blvd	Raleigh	NC	27606	919-821-8555	821-8541
Web: www.wral-tv.com					
WRAZ-TV Ch 50 (Fox) 512 S Mangum St	Durham	NC	27701	919-595-5050	595-5028
TF: 800-532-5343 ■ *Web:* www.fox50.com					
WRDC-TV Ch 28 (UPN)					
3012 Highwoods Blvd Suite 101	Raleigh	NC	27604	919-872-2854	790-6991
WRPX-TV Ch 47 (PAX) 1507 Oakwood Ave	Raleigh	NC	27610	919-755-2277	755-1702
WTVD-TV Ch 11 (ABC) PO Box 2009	Durham	NC	27702	919-683-1111	687-4373
WUNC-TV Ch 4 (PBS)					
PO Box 14900	Research Triangle Park	NC	27709	919-549-7000	549-7201
Web: www.unctv.org ■ *E-mail:* viewer@unctv.org					

RADIO

				Phone	Fax
WFXC-FM 107.1 MHz (AC)					
8001-101 Creedmoor Rd	Raleigh	NC	27613	919-848-9736	863-4857
TF: 800-467-3699 ■ *Web:* www.foxy107-104.com ■ *E-mail:* info@foxy107-104.com					
WFXK-FM 104.3 MHz (Urban)					
8001-101 Creedmoor Rd	Raleigh	NC	27613	919-848-9736	844-3947
Web: www.foxy107-104.com ■ *E-mail:* info@foxy107-104.com					
WKIX-FM 96.9 MHz (Ctry)					
5706 New Chapel Hill Rd	Raleigh	NC	27607	919-851-2711	859-1482
Web: www.newcountrykix.com					
WKNC-FM 88.1 MHz (Rock) Box 8607	Raleigh	NC	27607	919-515-2401	513-2693
Web: wknc.org					
WKXU-FM 101.1 MHz (Ctry) PO Box 1119	Burlington	NC	27216	336-584-0126	584-0739
WNCU-FM 90.7 MHz (NPR) PO Box 19875	Durham	NC	27707	919-560-9628	530-7975
Web: www.wncu.com					
WNNL-FM 103.9 MHz (Rel)					
8001-101 Creedmoor Rd	Raleigh	NC	27613	919-790-1035	863-4856
WPTF-AM 680 kHz (N/T)					
3012 Highwoods Blvd Suite 200	Raleigh	NC	27604	919-876-0674	790-8369
WQDR-FM 94.7 MHz (Ctry)					
3012 Highwoods Blvd Suite 200	Raleigh	NC	27604	919-876-0674	790-8893
WQOK-FM 97.5 MHz (Urban)					
8001-101 Creedmoor Rd	Raleigh	NC	27613	919-790-1035	863-4862
WRAL-FM 101.5 MHz (AC) PO Box 10100	Raleigh	NC	27605	919-890-6101	890-6146
Web: www.wralfm.com					
WRBZ-AM 850 kHz (N/T)					
5000 Falls of Neuse Rd Suite 308	Raleigh	NC	27609	919-875-9100	875-9080
Web: www.wrbz.com/ ■ *E-mail:* manager@850thebuzz.com					

Raleigh — Radio (Cont'd)

	City	State	ZIP	Phone	Fax
WRCQ-FM 103.5 MHz (Rock) 1009 Drayton Rd	Fayetteville	NC	28303	910-860-1401	860-4360
WRDT-AM 570 kHz (Rel) 649 Maywood Ave	Raleigh	NC	27603	919-833-3874	832-1126
WRDU-FM 106.1 MHz (CR) 3100 Smoketree Ct Suite 700	Raleigh	NC	27604	919-876-1061	876-2929
WSHA-FM 88.9 MHz (Jazz) 118 E South St	Raleigh	NC	27601	919-546-8430	546-8315
WSRC-AM 1410 kHz (Rel) 3202 Guess Rd	Durham	NC	27705	919-477-7999	477-9811
WTRG-FM 100.7 MHz (Oldies) 3100 Smoketree Ct Suite 700	Raleigh	NC	27604	919-876-1007	876-2929
WXDU-FM 88.7 MHz (Alt) PO Box 90869	Durham	NC	27708	919-684-2957	684-3260

— Colleges/Universities —

	City	State	ZIP	Phone	Fax
Durham Technical Community College 1637 E Lawson St	Durham	NC	27703	919-686-3300	686-3396
Web: www.dtcc.cc.nc.us					
Meredith College 3800 Hillsborough St	Raleigh	NC	27607	919-760-8600	760-2348
TF: 800-637-3348 ■ *Web:* www.meredith.edu ■ *E-mail:* admission@meredith.edu					
North Carolina State University 4700 Hillsborough St	Raleigh	NC	27695	919-515-2011	831-3545
Web: www.ncsu.edu ■ *E-mail:* undergrad_admissions@ncsu.edu					
Peace College 15 E Peace St	Raleigh	NC	27604	919-508-2000	508-2326
TF Admissions: 800-732-2347 ■ *Web:* www.peace.edu					
Saint Augustine's College 1315 Oakwood Ave	Raleigh	NC	27610	919-516-4000	516-5805
TF Admissions: 800-948-1126 ■ *Web:* www.st-aug.edu					
Shaw University 118 E South St	Raleigh	NC	27601	919-546-8200	546-8271
TF: 800-214-6683					
University of North Carolina Chapel Hill 2200 Jackson Hall	Chapel Hill	NC	27599	919-962-2211	962-9149
Web: www.unc.edu ■ *E-mail:* uadm@email.unc.edu					
Wake Technical Community College 9101 Fayetteville Rd	Raleigh	NC	27603	919-662-3500	779-3360
Web: wtcc-gw.wake.tec.nc.us					

— Hospitals —

	City	State	ZIP	Phone	Fax
Raleigh Community Hospital 3400 Wake Forest Rd	Raleigh	NC	27609	919-954-3000	954-3900
Rex Healthcare 4420 Lake Boone Trail	Raleigh	NC	27607	919-783-3100	784-7192*
**Fax:* Admitting ■ *Web:* www.rexhealth.com					
Wake Medical Center 3000 New Bern Ave	Raleigh	NC	27610	919-350-8000	350-2847

— Attractions —

	City	State	ZIP	Phone	Fax
African American Cultural Complex 119 Sunnybrook Rd	Raleigh	NC	27610	919-231-0625	
Artspace 201 E Davie St	Raleigh	NC	27601	919-821-2787	821-0383
Web: triangle.citysearch.com/E/V/RDUNC/1000/00/59					
Bond Metro Park 801 High House Rd	Cary	NC	27513	919-469-4100	
Borden Building 820 Clay St	Raleigh	NC	27605	919-831-6430	
Capital City Bicycle Motocross Race Track 516 Dennis Ave Lions Pk	Raleigh	NC	27604	919-890-3285	
Carolina Ballet 2 South St PO Box 37040	Raleigh	NC	27627	919-510-8945	363-7728
Web: www.carolinaballet.com					
Center Stage Cates Ave Talley Student Ctr	Raleigh	NC	27695	919-515-3030	515-1406
Web: www.fis.ncsu.edu/Center_Stage/					
Contemporary Art Museum 336 Fayetteville St Mall 4th Fl	Raleigh	NC	27602	919-836-0088	836-2239
Web: www.camnc.org					
Durant Nature Park 8305 Camp Durant Rd	Raleigh	NC	27614	919-870-2871	
Executive Mansion 200 N Blount St	Raleigh	NC	27601	919-733-3456	
Falls Lake State Recreation Area 13304 Creedmoor Rd	Wake Forest	NC	27587	919-676-1027	773-3499
Haywood Hall House & Gardens 211 New Bern Pl	Raleigh	NC	27601	919-832-8357	
Hemlock Bluffs Nature Preserve 2616 Kildaire Farm Rd	Cary	NC	27511	919-387-5980	
Historic Oak View County Park 4028 Carya Dr	Raleigh	NC	27610	919-250-1013	250-1262
Historic Oakwood 519 Oakwood Ave	Raleigh	NC	27601	919-834-0887	
Historic Trolley Tours 1 Mimosa St Mordecai Historic Pk	Raleigh	NC	27604	919-834-4844	834-7314
Lake Crabtree County Park 1400 Aviation Pkwy	Morrisville	NC	27560	919-460-3390	
Lake Johnson Park 5600 Avent Ferry Rd	Raleigh	NC	27606	919-233-2121	
Lake Wheeler 6404 Lake Wheeler Rd	Raleigh	NC	27603	919-662-5704	
Lane Joel House Museum & Gardens Saint Mary's & W Hargett Sts	Raleigh	NC	27603	919-833-3431	
Laurel Hills Park 3808 Edwards Mill Rd	Raleigh	NC	27612	919-420-2383	
Moorehead Planetarium E Franklin St UNC Chapel Hill Campus Box 3480	Chapel Hill	NC	27599	919-962-1236	962-1238
Web: www.unc.edu/depts/mhplanet/ ■ *E-mail:* mhplanet@unc.edu					
Moores Creek National Battlefield 40 Patriots Hall Dr	Currie	NC	28435	910-283-5591	283-5351
Web: www.nps.gov/mocr/					
Mordecai Ellen Gardens Mimosa St & Wake Forest Rd	Raleigh	NC	27604	919-834-4844	834-7314
E-mail: cappresinc@aol.com					
Mordecai Historic Park 1 Mimosa St	Raleigh	NC	27604	919-834-4844	
National Opera Co PO Box 12800	Raleigh	NC	27605	919-890-6083	890-6279
Web: www.operabase.com/level1/nara.html					
North Carolina Museum of Art 2110 Blue Ridge Rd	Raleigh	NC	27607	919-839-6262	733-8034
Web: ncartmuseum.org					
North Carolina Museum of History 5 E Edenton St	Raleigh	NC	27601	919-715-0200	733-8655
Web: nchistory.dcr.state.nc.us/museums					
North Carolina Railroad Museum New Hill	New Hill	NC	27562	919-362-5416	
North Carolina State Archives 109 E Jones St	Raleigh	NC	27601	919-733-3952	733-1354
Web: www.ah.dcr.state.nc.us					
North Carolina State Capitol 1 E Edenton St	Raleigh	NC	27601	919-733-4993	715-4030
North Carolina State Museum of Natural Sciences 102 N Salisbury St	Raleigh	NC	27603	919-733-7450	733-1573
Web: www.naturalsciences.org					
North Carolina Symphony Orchestra 2 E South St Memorial Auditorium	Raleigh	NC	27601	919-733-2750	733-9920
Web: www.ncsymphony.org					
North Carolina Theatre 1 E South St Memorial Auditorium	Raleigh	NC	27601	919-831-6941	831-6951
Oakwood Cemetery 701 Oakwood Ave	Raleigh	NC	27601	919-832-6077	832-2982
Page-Walker Arts & History Center 119 Ambassador Loop	Cary	NC	27511	919-460-4963	469-4344
Pullen Park 520 Ashe Ave	Raleigh	NC	27606	919-831-6468	
Raleigh City Museum 220 Fayetteville Mall Suite 100	Raleigh	NC	27605	919-832-3775	
Raleigh Contemporary Gallery 323 Blake St	Raleigh	NC	27601	919-828-6500	828-6500
Raleigh Ensemble Players Theatre Co 201 E Davie St	Raleigh	NC	27601	919-832-9607	821-0383
Web: www.realtheatre.org					
Raleigh Little Theatre 301 Pogue St	Raleigh	NC	27607	919-821-4579	821-7961
Web: www.mindspring.com/~rallittletheatre/					
Raleigh Municipal Rose Garden 301 Pogue St	Raleigh	NC	27607	919-821-4579	
Raulston JC Arboretum North Carolina State University 4301 Beryl Rd	Raleigh	NC	27606	919-515-3132	515-7747
Web: arb.ncsu.edu					
Research Triangle Park 2 Hanes Dr	Research Triangle Park	NC	27709	919-549-8181	549-8246
Web: www.rtp.org ■ *E-mail:* parkinfo@rtp.org					
Saint Augustine's College Chapel 1315 Oakwood Ave	Raleigh	NC	27610	919-516-4189	
Sertoma Arts Center 1400 W Millbrook Rd	Raleigh	NC	27612	919-420-2329	
Shelley Lake 1400 W Millbrook Rd Sertoma Park	Raleigh	NC	27612	919-420-2231	
Silver Lake Waterpark 5300 Tyron Rd	Raleigh	NC	27606	919-851-1683	
Spring Hill House 705 Barbours Dr	Raleigh	NC	27603	919-733-5454	
State Farmers Market 1201 Agriculture St	Raleigh	NC	27603	919-733-7417	
State Legislative Building 16 W Jones St	Raleigh	NC	27601	919-733-7928	733-2599
Theatre in the Park 107 Pullen Rd	Raleigh	NC	27607	919-831-6058	831-9475
Web: www.tip.dreamhost.com					
Tucker House 418 N Person St	Raleigh	NC	27601	919-831-6009	
Umstead William B State Park 8801 Glenwood Ave	Raleigh	NC	27612	919-571-4170	
Walnut Creek Amphitheatre 3801 Rock Quarry Rd	Raleigh	NC	27610	919-831-6400	831-6415
Web: www.alltelpavilion.com ■ *E-mail:* info@alltelpavilion.com					

SPORTS TEAMS & FACILITIES

	City	State	ZIP	Phone	Fax
Carolina Mudcats (baseball) 3501 North Carolina Hwy Five County Stadium	Zebulon	NC	27597	919-269-2287	269-4940

Raleigh — Sports Teams & Facilities (Cont'd)

				Phone	Fax
Raleigh Capital Express (soccer) Perry Creek Rd Wral Field	Raleigh	NC	27616	919-781-7259	786-1778
Web: www.raleighexpress.com					
Raleigh Wings (soccer) 7700 Perry Creek Rd Championship Field	Raleigh	NC	27603	919-848-8412	848-4657
Web: www.raleighwings.com ■ *E-mail:* info@raleighwings.com					

— Events —

	Phone
Artsplosure Jazz & Arts Festival (mid-May)	919-832-8699
Bass & Saltwater Fishing Expo (early January)	336-855-0208
Brightleaf Festival (early October)	919-365-6318
Brookhill Steeplechase (early May)	919-510-7915
Capitol's July 4th Celebration (early July)	919-733-4994
Carolian Power & Sailboat Show (mid-February)	336-855-0208
Carolina Christmas Show (mid-late November)	919-831-6011
Carolina Fall Boat Show (early September)	336-855-0208
Celebration of the Outdoors (early May)	919-552-1410
Christmas Celebration on the Mall (early December)	919-733-4994
Civil War Living History (mid-April)	919-733-4994
Farmers Market Festival (early July)	919-733-7417
First Night Raleigh (December 31)	919-832-8699
Great Raleigh Road Race (early May)	919-831-6011
Greater Raleigh Antique Show (early March & mid-November)	919-782-5782
Grecian Festival (mid-September)	919-781-4548
Home & Garden Show (mid-February)	919-831-6011
International Auto Show (late February)	919-831-6011
International Festival (early October)	919-834-5900
Lazy Daze Festival (late August)	919-469-4061
Living Christmas Tree (mid-December)	919-832-2257
Native American Celebration (early November)	919-733-7450
Natural History Halloween (late October)	919-733-7450
Nike Carolina Classic (early May)	919-380-0011
North Carolina Special Olympics Summer Games (mid-May)	800-843-6276
North Carolina State Fair (mid-October)	919-733-2145
North Carolina State Farmers Market Festival (early July)	919-733-7417
Oktoberfest (late September)	919-834-5900
Old Reliable Run (mid-November)	919-829-4843
Raleigh Antiques Extravaganza (mid-January)	336-924-8337
Raleigh Christmas Parade (late November)	919-420-0120
Run for the Roses (mid-February)	919-231-0714
Saint Patrick's Day Parade (mid-March)	919-846-9739
Southern Ideal Home Show (mid-April & late September)	919-851-2911
Tarheel Regatta (early June)	919-662-5704

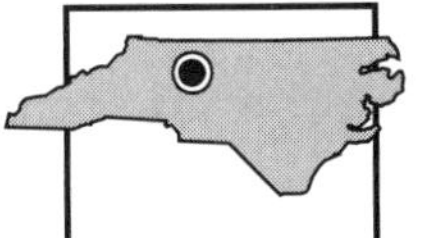

Winston-Salem

Winston-Salem lies in the vast area of rolling hills known as The Piedmont. Both R.J. Reynolds and Stroh Brewery companies offer tours of their facilities in the city. The former country estate of R.J. Reynolds and his wife, Katharine, is now the Reynolda House Museum of American Art. The restored German Moravian town of Old Salem, which dates back to 1766, is a living museum where visitors can watch costumed interpreters re-enact period life or tour among ten exhibit buildings. Tanglewood Park has two top-rated golf courses, plus horseback riding, tennis, camping, and swimming. Winston-Salem is also the home of Wake Forest University.

Population	164,316	**Longitude**	80-24-44 W
Area (Land)	71.1 sq mi	**County**	Forsyth
Area (Water)	0.6 sq mi	**Time Zone**	EST
Elevation	912 ft	**Area Code/s**	336
Latitude	36-09-97 N		

— Average Temperatures and Precipitation —

TEMPERATURES

	Jan	Feb	Mar	Apr	May	Jun	Jul	Aug	Sep	Oct	Nov	Dec
High	47	51	60	70	77	84	87	86	80	70	61	51
Low	27	29	37	46	55	63	67	66	60	47	39	31

PRECIPITATION

	Jan	Feb	Mar	Apr	May	Jun	Jul	Aug	Sep	Oct	Nov	Dec
Inches	3.2	3.3	3.7	2.8	4.0	3.8	4.5	3.9	3.5	3.5	3.0	3.4

— Important Phone Numbers —

	Phone		Phone
AAA	336-774-1200	**Medical Referral**	336-716-2255
Emergency	911	**Poison Control Center**	800-848-6946

— Information Sources —

				Phone	Fax
Benton Convention Center 301 W 5th St	Winston-Salem	NC	27102	336-727-2976	727-2879
Better Business Bureau Serving Northwest North Carolina 500 W 5th St Suite 202	Winston-Salem	NC	27101	336-725-8348	777-3727
Web: www.winstonsalem.bbb.org ■ *E-mail:* wsbbb@ncncbbb.com					
Forsyth County PO Box 20099	Winston-Salem	NC	27120	336-761-2250	761 2018
Web: www.co.forsyth.nc.us					
Forsyth County Public Library 660 W 5th St	Winston-Salem	NC	27101	336-727-2556	727-2549
Web: www.co.forsyth.nc.us/LIBRARY/Fcplhome.htm					
Greater Winston-Salem Chamber of Commerce 601 W 4th St	Winston-Salem	NC	27101	336-725-2361	721-2209
Web: www.winstonsalem.com					
Winston-Salem City Hall 101 N Main St	Winston-Salem	NC	27101	336-727-2123	748-3060
Web: www.ci.winston-salem.nc.us					
Winston-Salem Convention & Visitors Bureau PO Box 1409	Winston-Salem	NC	27102	336-728-4200	728-4220
TF: 800-331-7018 ■ *Web:* www.wscvb.com					
Winston-Salem Mayor PO Box 2511	Winston-Salem	NC	27102	336-727-2058	748-3241
Winston-Salem Planning Board PO Box 2511	Winston-Salem	NC	27102	336-727-2087	748-3163
E-mail: planning@cl.winston-salem.nc.us					

On-Line Resources

Anthill City Guide Winston-Salem	www.anthill.com/city.asp?city=winstonsalem
Area Guide Winston-Salem	winston.areaguides.net
City Knowledge Winston-Salem	www.cityknowledge.com/nc_winstonsalem.htm
CityTravelers.com Guide to Winston-Salem	www.citytravelers.com/winstonsalem.htm
Excite.com Winston-Salem City Guide	www.excite.com/travel/countries/united_states/north_carolina/winston_salem
Welcome to Winston-Salem	www.webpress.net/ncnetworks/ws-intr.html

— Transportation Services —

AIRPORTS

	Phone
■ **Smith Reynolds Airport (INT)**	
2 1/2 miles NE of downtown (approx 5 minutes)	336-767-6361
Web: www.smithreynolds.org	

Airport Transportation

	Phone
Blue Bird Cab $7 fare to downtown	336-722-7121

Commercial Airlines

	Phone
US Airways Express	800-428-4322

Winston-Salem (Cont'd)

Charter Airlines

	Phone
Piedmont Aviation Services Inc	800-548-1978

■ Piedmont Triad International Airport (GSO)

	Phone
27 miles E of downtown Winston-Salem (approx 25 minutes)	336-665-5600

Airport Transportation

	Phone
Airport Express $32 fare to downtown Winston-Salem	800-934-8779

Commercial Airlines

	Phone		Phone
American	800-433-7300	**Continental Express**	800-525-0280
American Eagle	800-433-7300	**Delta**	800-221-1212
Atlantic Southeast	800-282-3424	**United**	800-241-6522
Continental	800-525-0280	**US Airways**	800-428-4322

Charter Airlines

	Phone		Phone
Atlantic Aero	336-668-0411	**Piedmont Hawthorne Aviation**	336-668-0481
Piedmont Aviation Services Inc	800-548-1978	**Richmor Aviation**	800-331-6101

CAR RENTALS

	Phone		Phone
Avis	800-331-1212	**National**	800-227-7368
Budget	336-272-8158	**Triangle**	336-668-3400
Hertz	336-668-7961		

LIMO/TAXI

	Phone		Phone
Blue Bird Cab	336-722-7121	**Ritz Limousine Service**	336-765-4565
Piedmont Executive Transportation	336-723-2179	**Unique Limousine**	336-760-4381
		Willard's Cab	336-725-2227

MASS TRANSIT

	Phone
Winston-Salem Transit Authority $1.00 Base fare	336-727-2000

RAIL/BUS

				Phone
Greyhound/Trailways Bus Station 250 Greyhound Ct *TF:* 800-231-2222	Winston-Salem	NC	27102	336-724-1429

— Accommodations —

HOTELS, MOTELS, RESORTS

				Phone	Fax
Adam's Mark Hotel Winston Plaza 425 N Cherry St *TF:* 800-444-2326 ■ *Web:* www.adamsmark.com/winsalm.htm	Winston-Salem	NC	27101	336-725-3500	721-2240
Brookstown Inn 200 Brookstown Ave. *TF:* 800-845-4262	Winston-Salem	NC	27101	336-725-1120	773-0147
Budget Inn 600 Peters Creek Pkwy	Winston-Salem	NC	27103	336-725-0501	722-1949
Comfort Inn 110 Miller St. *TF:* 800-228-5150	Winston-Salem	NC	27103	336-721-0220	723-2117
Comfort Inn Coliseum 531 Akron Dr *TF:* 800-228-5150	Winston-Salem	NC	27105	336-767-8240	661-9513
Courtyard by Marriott 3111 University Pkwy *TF:* 800-321-2211 ■ *Web:* courtyard.com/INTCY	Winston-Salem	NC	27105	336-727-1277	722-8219
Days Inn 3330 Silas Creek Pkwy. *TF:* 800-329-7466	Winston-Salem	NC	27103	336-760-4770	760-1085
Days Inn North 5218 Germanton Rd *TF:* 800-329-7466	Winston-Salem	NC	27105	336-744-5755	744-5755
Extended StayAmerica 1995 Hampton Inn Ct *TF:* 800-398-7829	Winston-Salem	NC	27103	336-768-0075	768-7225
Hampton Inn 5719 University Pkwy. *TF:* 800-426-7866	Winston-Salem	NC	27105	336-767-9009	661-0448
Hampton Inn 1990 Hampton Inn Ct. *TF:* 800-426-7866	Winston-Salem	NC	27103	336-760-1660	768-9168
Hawthorne Inn & Conference Center 420 High St *TF:* 800-972-3774 ■ *Web:* www.hawthorneinn.com	Winston-Salem	NC	27101	336-777-3000	777-3282
Holiday Inn 5790 University Pkwy. *TF:* 800-553-9595	Winston-Salem	NC	27105	336-767-9595	744-1888
Holiday Inn West 2008 S Hawthorne Rd *TF:* 800-465-4329	Winston-Salem	NC	27103	336-765-6670	659-0436
Innkeeper Motel 2115 Peters Creek Pkwy *TF:* 800-466-5337	Winston-Salem	NC	27127	336-721-0062	721-0062
Kings Inn 5906 University Pkwy	Winston-Salem	NC	27105	336-377-9131	
Motel 6 3810 Patterson Ave *TF:* 800-466-8356	Winston-Salem	NC	27105	336-661-1588	767-8354
Ramada Plaza Coliseum 3050 University Pkwy *TF:* 800-272-6232	Winston-Salem	NC	27105	336-723-2911	777-1003
Residence Inn by Marriott 7835 N Point Blvd. *TF:* 800-331-3131 ■ *Web:* www.marriottwinston-salem.com	Winston-Salem	NC	27106	336-759-0777	759-9671
Salem Inn 127 S Cherry St *TF:* 800-533-8760 ■ *Web:* www.saleminn.com	Winston-Salem	NC	27101	336-725-8561	725-2318
Stratford Inn 160 S Stratford Rd.	Winston-Salem	NC	27104	336-725-7501	725-7501
Tanglewood Park 4201 Clemmons Rd. **Fax:* Hum Res	Clemmons	NC	27012	336-778-6300	778-6322*
Travel Host 4191 N Patterson Ave	Winston-Salem	NC	27105	336-767-1930	767-6394

— Restaurants —

				Phone
Bayberry The (Continental) 420 High St	Winston-Salem	NC	27101	336-777-3000
Bernardin's (Continental) 373 Jonestown Rd.	Winston-Salem	NC	27104	336-768-9365
Bistro 900 (International) 900 S Marshall St.	Winston-Salem	NC	27101	336-721-1336
Cactus Jack's Steakhouse & Saloon (American) 3001 University Pkwy	Winston-Salem	NC	27105	336-721-0055
Cagney's Place (American) 2201 Cloverdale Ave	Winston-Salem	NC	27103	336-724-0940
Darryl's 1880 (Steak) 200 Brookstown Ave	Winston-Salem	NC	27101	336-748-1880
Diamondback Grill (Steak/Seafood) 751 N Avalon Rd	Winston-Salem	NC	27104	336-722-0006
Eddie Romanelli's (Italian/American) 5400 Oleander Dr.	Wilmington	NC	28403	910-799-7000
Elijah's (Continental/Seafood) 2 Ann St	Wilmington	NC	28401	910-343-1448
Gisele Fine Food (American) 226 N Marshall St	Winston-Salem	NC	27101	336-761-0674
Grecian Corner (Greek) 101 Eden Terr	Winston-Salem	NC	27103	336-722-6937
Hawthorne Station (American) 2008 S Hawthorne Rd.	Winston-Salem	NC	27103	336-765-6670
Hieronymus Seafood (Seafood) 5035 Market St	Wilmington	NC	28405	910-392-6318
Ichiban (Japanese) 270 S Stratford Rd.	Winston-Salem	NC	27103	336-725-3050
Jimmy the Greek Kitchen (Greek) 2806 University Pkwy	Winston-Salem	NC	27105	336-722-0184
Kyoto Japanese Steak & Seafood House (Japanese) 585 Bethesda St.	Winston-Salem	NC	27103	336-765-7798
La Carreta (Mexican) 725 Coliseum Dr.	Winston-Salem	NC	27106	336-722-3709
Leon's Cafe (Continental) 924 S Marshall St.	Winston-Salem	NC	27101	336-725-9593
Libby Hill Seafood (Seafood) 2561 Peters Creek Pkwy	Winston-Salem	NC	27127	336-785-3469
Lucky 32 (New American) 109 S. Stratford Rd	Winston-Salem	NC	27103	336-777-0032
Madison Park Cafe (American) 5790 University Pkwy	Winston-Salem	NC	27105	336-767-9595
Mediterraneo (Italian) 3278 Silas Creek Pkwy	Winston-Salem	NC	27103	336-768-0605
Michael's on Fifth (Continental) 848 W 5th St	Winston-Salem	NC	27101	336-777-0000
Midtown Cafe & Dessertery (American) 151 S Stratford Rd.	Winston-Salem	NC	27104	336-724-9800
Morgan's Restaurant (Southern) 3050 University Pkwy	Winston-Salem	NC	27105	336-723-2911
Noble's Grill (California) 380 Knollwood St	Winston-Salem	NC	27103	336-777-8477
Old Salem Tavern (Continental) 736 S Main St.	Winston-Salem	NC	27101	336-748-8585
Oyster Bay Seafood Restaurant (Seafood) 576 Hanes Mall Blvd.	Winston-Salem	NC	27103	336-659-0388
Paul's Fine Italian Dining (Italian) 3443-B Robinhood Rd	Winston-Salem	NC	27106	336-768-2645
Rock-ola Cafe (American) 630 S Stratford Rd.	Winston-Salem	NC	27103	336-765-7627
Royal Thai Restaurant (Thai) 514 S Stratford Rd	Winston-Salem	NC	27103	336-777-1597
Ryan's (Steak/Seafood) 719 Coliseum Dr	Winston-Salem	NC	27106	336-724-6132
Sampan Chinese Restaurant (Chinese) 985 Peters Creek Pkwy	Winston-Salem	NC	27103	336-777-8266
Shuckers (Seafood) 980 Peters Creek Pkwy.	Winston-Salem	NC	27011	336-724-2223
South by Southwest (Southwest) 241 S Marshall St.	Winston-Salem	NC	27101	336-727-0800
Southbound Bistro & Grille (American) 300 S Liberty St.	Winston-Salem	NC	27101	336-723-0322
Staley's Steakhouse (Steak) 2000 Reynolda Rd.	Winston-Salem	NC	27106	336-723-8631
Szechuan Palace (Chinese) 3040 Healy Dr	Winston-Salem	NC	27103	336-768-7123
Trattoria Carolina (Italian) 425 N Cherry St	Winston-Salem	NC	27101	336-725-3500
Vineyards The (Continental) 120 Reynolda Village	Winston-Salem	NC	27106	336-748-0269
Zevely House (Continental) 901 W 4th St.	Winston-Salem	NC	27101	336-725-6666

Winston-Salem (Cont'd)

— Goods and Services —

SHOPPING

Name	Address	City	State	Zip	Phone	Fax
Hanes Mall	3320 Silas Creek Pkwy	Winston-Salem	NC	27103	336-765-8323	
Marketplace Mall	2101 Peters Creek Pkwy	Winston-Salem	NC	27127	336-724-1451	722-7780
Reynolda Village	114 Reynolda Village Suite F	Winston-Salem	NC	27106	336-758-5584	
Stratford Oaks Mini Mall	514 S Stratford Rd	Winston-Salem	NC	27103	336-725-1821	725-6918

BANKS

Name	Address	City	State	Zip	Phone	Fax
BB & T Bank	110 Straford Rd.	Winston-Salem	NC	27104	336-773-1100	773-0114
Central Carolina Bank & Trust Co	2804 Fairlawn Dr	Winston-Salem	NC	27106	336-659-2840	659-2843
Centura Bank	2150 Country Club Rd	Winston-Salem	NC	27113	336-631-5600	631-5603
First Union National Bank	3375 Robinhood Rd	Winston-Salem	NC	27106	336-761-3927	761-3978
Old North State Bank	161 S Stratford Rd	Winston-Salem	NC	27103	336-631-3900	631-3922
Salem Trust Bank	2140 Country Club Rd	Winston-Salem	NC	27104	336-777-1400	723-9102
Wachovia Bank NA	100 N Main St	Winston-Salem	NC	27150	336-770-5000	732-2191

BUSINESS SERVICES

Name	Phone
Accountemps	336-722-0056
Adecco Employment Personnel Services	336-744-5600
Airborne Express	800-247-2676
BAX Global	800-225-5229
DHL Worldwide Express	800-225-5345
Executive Staffing Group	336-765-6200
Federal Express	800-238-5355
Kelly Services	336-759-3700
Kinko's	336-722-6611
Mail Boxes Etc	800-789-4623
Manpower Temporary Services	336-760-6126
OfficeTeam	336-722-3257
Olsten Staffing Services	336-759-9495
Post Office	336-721-6001
UPS	800-742-5877

— Media —

PUBLICATIONS

Name	Address	City	State	Zip	Phone	Fax
Winston-Salem Journal‡	418 N Marshall St. *Web:* w-s-journal.com	Winston-Salem	NC	27101	336-727-7211	727-4071

‡*Daily newspapers*

TELEVISION

Name	Address	City	State	Zip	Phone	Fax
WFMY-TV Ch 2 (CBS)	1615 Phillips Ave *E-mail:* fmy2@aol.com	Greensboro	NC	27405	336-379-9369	273-9433
WGHP-TV Ch 8 (Fox)	PO Box HP-8 *Web:* www.fox8wghp.com	High Point	NC	27261	336-841-8888	841-5169
WGPX-TV Ch 16 (PAX)	1114 N Old Henry Blvd	Greensboro	NC	27405	336-272-9227	272-9298
WUNL-TV Ch 26 (PBS)	PO Box 14900	Research Triangle Park	NC	27709	919-549-7000	549-7201
WXII-TV Ch 12 (NBC)	700 Coliseum Dr *Web:* www.wxii.com ■ *E-mail:* newschannel12@wxii.com	Winston-Salem	NC	27106	336-721-9944	721-0856
WXLV-TV Ch 45 (ABC)	3500 Myer Lee Dr. *Web:* www.wxlv.com	Winston-Salem	NC	27101	336-722-4545	631-9205

RADIO

Name	Address	City	State	Zip	Phone	Fax
WAAA-AM 980 kHz (Urban)	4950 Indiana Ave	Winston-Salem	NC	27106	336-767-0430	767-0433
WBFJ-AM 1550 kHz (Rel)	1249 Trade St *E-mail:* wbjf@netunlimited.net	Winston-Salem	NC	27101	336-721-1560	777-1032
WFDD-FM 88.5 MHz (NPR)	56 Wake Forest Rd	Winston-Salem	NC	27109	336-758-8850	758-5193
WHSL-FM 100.3 MHz (Ctry)	PO Box 5897	High Point	NC	27262	336-727-0995	887-0104
WMAG-FM 99.5 MHz (AC)	PO Box 5897 *Web:* www.wmagradio.com	High Point	NC	27262	336-727-0995	887-0104
WMQX-FM 93.1 MHz (Oldies)	7819 National Service Rd Suite 401	Greensboro	NC	27409	336-605-5200	605-5221
WSJS-AM 600 kHz (N/T)	PO Box 3018	Winston-Salem	NC	27102	336-727-8826	777-3910
WTOB-AM 1380 kHz (N/T)	4405 Providence Ln *Web:* www.wtob.com ■ *E-mail:* wtob@wtob.com	Winston-Salem	NC	27106	336-759-0363	759-0366
WTQR-FM 104.1 MHz (Ctry)	PO Box 3018 *Web:* www.wtqr.com	Winston-Salem	NC	27102	336-727-8826	777-3929
WXRA-FM 94.5 MHz (Alt)	PO Box 3018	Winston-Salem	NC	27102	336-727-8826	777-3929

— Colleges/Universities —

Name	Address	City	State	Zip	Phone	Fax
Forsyth Technical Community College	2100 Silas Creek Pkwy *Web:* www.forsyth.tec.nc.us	Winston-Salem	NC	27103	336-723-0371	761-2399
High Point University	833 Montlieu Ave *Web:* acme.highpoint.edu	High Point	NC	27262	336-841-9000	841-4599
North Carolina School of the Arts	1533 S Main St *Web:* www.ncarts.edu	Winston-Salem	NC	27127	336-770-3399	770-3366
Piedmont Baptist College	716 Franklin St. *Web:* www.pbc.edu ■ *E-mail:* help@pbc.edu	Winston-Salem	NC	27101	336-725-8344	725-5522
Salem College	PO Box 10548 *Web:* www.salem.edu ■ *E-mail:* admissions@salem.edu	Winston-Salem	NC	27108	336-721-2600	721-2832
Wake Forest University	1834 Wake Forest Rd *Web:* www.wfu.edu	Winston-Salem	NC	27106	336-759-5000	758-6074
Winston-Salem State University	601 ML King Jr Dr *TF:* 800-257-4052 ■ *Web:* www.wssu.edu	Winston-Salem	NC	27110	336-750-2000	750-2079

— Hospitals —

Name	Address	City	State	Zip	Phone	Fax
Forsyth Medical Center	3333 Silas Creek Pkwy	Winston-Salem	NC	27103	336-718-5000	718-9258
Wake Forest University Baptist Medical Center	Medical Center Blvd	Winston-Salem	NC	27157	336-716-2011	716-2067

— Attractions —

Name	Address	City	State	Zip	Phone	Fax
Delta Fine Arts Center	1511 E 3rd St	Winston-Salem	NC	27101	336-722-2625	722-9449
Diggs Gallery	Winston-Salem State University	Winston-Salem	NC	27101	336-750-2458	
Historic Bethabara Park	2147 Bethabara Rd	Winston-Salem	NC	27106	336-924-8191	924-0535
Joel Lawrence Veterans Memorial Coliseum	2825 University Pkwy	Winston-Salem	NC	27105	336-725-5635	
Museum of Anthropology	PO Box 7267 Reynolda Stn *Web:* www.wfu.edu/MOA ■ *E-mail:* moa@wfu.edu	Winston-Salem	NC	27109	336-758-5282	758-5116
Museum of Early Southern Decorative Arts	924 S Main St *Web:* store.yahoo.com/oldsalemonline	Winston-Salem	NC	27108	336-721-7360	721-7367
North Carolina Black Repertory Co	610 Coliseum Dr.	Winston-Salem	NC	27106	336-723-2266	723-2223
Old Salem	600 S Main St *TF:* 800-441-5305 ■ *Web:* www.oldsalem.org	Winston-Salem	NC	27101	336-721-7300	721-7335
Piedmont Chamber Singers	845 W 5th St	Winston-Salem	NC	27101	336-722-4022	
Piedmont Craftsmen	1204 Reynolda Rd *Web:* www.piedmontcraftsmen.org ■ *E-mail:* pci@bellsouth.net	Winston-Salem	NC	27104	336-725-1516	722-6038
Piedmont Opera Theatre	405 W 4th St Stephens Ctr *Web:* www.piedmontopera.org ■ *E-mail:* piedop@nr.infi.net	Winston-Salem	NC	27101	336-725-7101	725-7131
Reynolda House Museum of American Art	2250 Reynolda Rd *Web:* www.ols.net/users/rh	Winston-Salem	NC	27106	336-725-5325	721-0991
RJ Reynolds Tobacco Co	PO Box 2959 *Web:* www.rjrt.com	Winston-Salem	NC	27102	336-741-5000	741-4238

Winston-Salem — Attractions (Cont'd)

	City	State	Zip	Phone	Fax
Sawtooth Center for Visual Arts 226 N Marshall St. *Web:* www.sawtooth.org	Winston-Salem	NC	27101	336-723-7395	
Sciworks Science Center & Environmental Park of Forsyth County 400 Hanes-Mill Rd *Web:* www.sciworks.org ■ *E-mail:* info@sciworks.org	Winston-Salem	NC	27105	336-767-6730	661-1777
Southeastern Center for Contemporary Art 750 Marguerite Dr	Winston-Salem	NC	27106	336-725-1904	722-6059
Stevens Center 405 W 4th St.	Winston-Salem	NC	27101	336-723-6320	722-7240
Tanglewood Park 4201 Clemmons Rd. **Fax:* Hum Res	Clemmons	NC	27012	336-778-6300	778-6322*
Tanglewood Park Golf Course 4601 Clemmons Rd.	Clemmons	NC	27012	336-778-6320	766-8991
Vintage Theatre 7 Vintage Ave	Winston-Salem	NC	27127	336-750-0000	
Wake Forest University Fine Arts Gallery Scales Fine Arts Center Bldg Wake Forest University	Winston-Salem	NC	27106	336-758-5000	
Westbend Vineyards 5394 Williams Rd	Lewisville	NC	27023	336-945-5032	
Winston-Salem Piedmont Triad Symphony 610 Coliseum Dr.	Winston-Salem	NC	27106	336-725-1035	725-3924

SPORTS TEAMS & FACILITIES

	City	State	Zip	Phone	Fax
Carolina Dynamo (soccer) 2920 School Pk Rd High Point Athletic Complex. *Web:* www.carolinadynamo.com ■ *E-mail:* colleenk@northstate.net	High Point	NC	27265	336-869-1022	869-1190
Lawrence Joel Veteran Memorial Coliseum 2825 University Pkwy *Web:* www.ljvm.com	Winston-Salem	NC	27105	336-727-2900	727-2922
Piedmont Spark (soccer) 2920 School Park Rd High Point Athletic Complex.	High Point	NC	27265	336-869-1022	869-1190
Winston-Salem Warthogs (baseball) 401 Deacon Blvd Ernie Shore Field *Web:* www.warthogs.com ■ *E-mail:* warthogs@warthogs.com	Winston-Salem	NC	27105	336-759-2233	759-2042

— Events —

	Phone
Candle Tea Christmas Festival (early December)	336-722-6171
Carolina Craftsmen Labor Day Classic (mid-September)	336-274-5550
Christmas Parade (late November)	336-777-3796
Crosby Celebrity Golf Tournament (early June)	336-721-2246
Dixie Classic Fair (early October)	336-727-2236
Fiddle & Bow Festival (September)	336-727-1038
First Night Piedmont (December 31)	336-722-9002
Greek Festival (early May)	336-765-7145
Music at Sunset (late June)	336-725-1035
National Black Theater Festival (early August)	336-723-2266
Old Salem Christmas (mid-December)	800-441-5305
Piedmont Crafts Fair (late November)	336-725-1516
Salem Christmas (late December)	336-721-7300
Tanglewood Festival of Lights (mid-November-mid-January)	336-778-6300
Taste of the Triad (mid-June)	336-727-7393
Vantage Championship Seniors Golf Tournament (early-mid October)	336-721-2246
Winston-Salem Crafts Guild Craft Show (mid-November)	252-727-2976

North Dakota

Population (1999): 633,666 **Area (sq mi): 70,704**

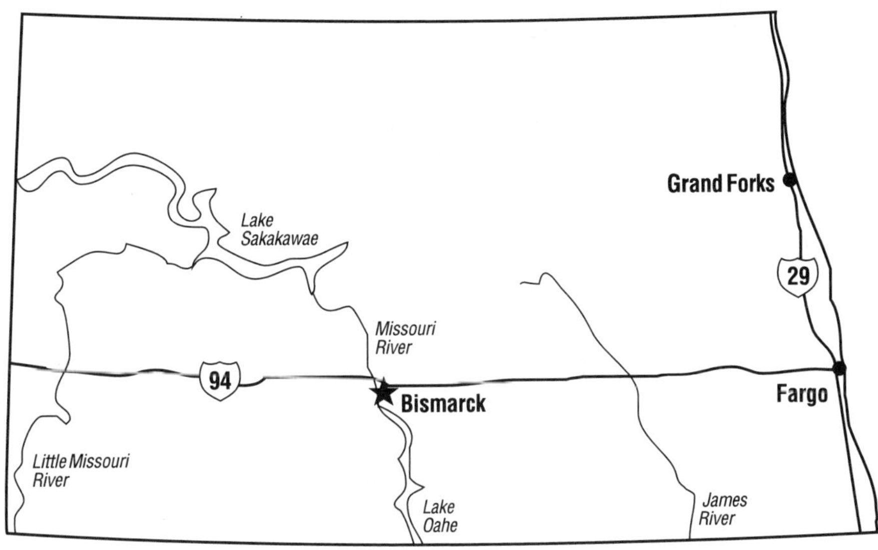

— State Information Sources —

		Phone	Fax
Greater North Dakota Assn PO Box 2639	Bismarck ND 58502	701-222-0929	222-1611
Web: www.gnda.com			
North Dakota Economic Development & Finance Dept 1833 E Bismarck Expy	Bismarck ND 58504	701-328-5300	328-5320
Web: www.growingnd.com ■ *E-mail:* ndedf@ranch.state.nd.us			
North Dakota Parks & Recreation Dept 1835 E Bismarck Expy	Bismarck ND 58504	701-328-5357	328-5363
Web: www.state.nd.us/ndparks ■ *E-mail:* parkrec@pioneer.state.nd.us			
North Dakota State Government Information		701-328-2000	
Web: www.state.nd.us ■ *E-mail:* rutherfo@pioneer.state.nd.us			
North Dakota State Library 604 East Blvd	Bismarck ND 58505	701-328-4622	328-2040
Web: ndsl.lib.state.nd.us			
North Dakota Tourism Dept 604 E Boulevard Ave	Bismarck ND 58505	701-328-2525	328-4878
TF: 800-435-5663 ■ *Web:* www.ndtourism.com			

ON-LINE RESOURCES

Dakotaland . . . . . www.dakotaland.com
DIRT! A Down to Earth Guide to North Dakota . . . . . www.webcom.com/nddirt
North Dakota Cities . . . . . dir.yahoo.com/Regional/U_S__States/North_Dakota/Cities
North Dakota Counties & Regions . . . . . dir.yahoo.com/Regional/U_S__States/North_Dakota/Counties_and_Regions
North Dakota Scenario . . . . . scenariousa.dstylus.com/nd/indexf.htm
North Dakota Travel & Tourism Guide . . . . . www.travel-library.com/north_america/usa/north_dakota/index.html
Rough Guide Travel North Dakota travel.roughguides.com/content/1036/index.htm
Travel.org-North Dakota . . . . . travel.org/n-dak.html
What's Up North Dakota! . . . . . www.whatsupnorthdakota.com
Yahoo! Get Local North Dakota . . . . . dir.yahoo.com/Regional/U_S__States/North_Dakota

— Cities Profiled —

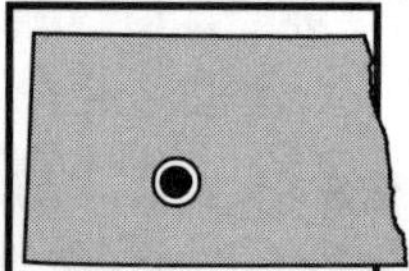

Bismarck

Human occupation of the Bismarck/Mandan area of North Dakota dates back approximately 11,000 years, and Mandan and Hidatsa tribes settled in the area even before Pilgrims arrived at Plymouth. The military activity associated with establishment of the Dakota Territory in 1861 hastened settlement of the area, and development of the railroad led to permanent settlements at Bismarck and Mandan. Bismarck became the Territorial capital in 1883 and state capital in 1889. Exhibits illustrating the many changes in the area over the years can be viewed at the North Dakota Heritage Center on the State Capitol grounds in Bismarck. Other popular historic sites include Knife River Indian Villages National Historic Site, which includes the Hidatsa village that was home to Sakajewea; Fort Abraham Lincoln State Park, the last home of George and Libbie Custer; Double Ditch Indian Village Historic Site; and the Native American arts center at Mandan Depot.

Population 53,514
Area (Land) . . . . . 24.3 sq mi
Area (Water) . . . . . 0.5 sq mi
Elevation . . . . . 1700 ft
Latitude . . . . . 46-82-54 N
Longitude . . . . . 100-78-17 W
County . . . . . Burleigh
Time Zone . . . . . CST
Area Code/s 701

— Average Temperatures and Precipitation —

TEMPERATURES

	Jan	Feb	Mar	Apr	May	Jun	Jul	Aug	Sep	Oct	Nov	Dec
High	20	26	39	55	68	77	84	83	71	59	39	25
Low	-2	5	18	31	42	52	56	54	43	33	18	3

PRECIPITATION

	Jan	Feb	Mar	Apr	May	Jun	Jul	Aug	Sep	Oct	Nov	Dec
Inches	0.5	0.4	0.8	2.7	2.2	2.7	2.1	1.7	1.5	0.9	0.5	0.5

— Important Phone Numbers —

	Phone
AAA	701-223-6660
Emergency	911
HotelDocs	800-468-3537
Poison Control Center	701-234-5575
Weather	701-223-3700

— Information Sources —

				Phone	*Fax*
Bismarck City Hall 221 N 5th St. *Web:* www.bismarck.org	Bismarck	ND	58501	701-222-6471	222-6470
Bismarck Civic Center 601 E Sweet Ave	Bismarck	ND	58504	701-222-6487	222-6599
Bismarck Consumer Protection Div 600 E Boulevard Ave Dept 125 *Web:* expedition.bismarck.ag.state.nd.us/ndag/cpat/cpat.html	Bismarck	ND	58505	701-328-2210	328-3535
Bismarck Mandan Chamber of Commerce 2000 Schafer St *Web:* www.chmbr.org/	Bismarck	ND	58502	701-223-5660	255-6125
Bismarck-Mandan Convention & Visitors Bureau PO Box 2274 *TF:* 800-767-3555 ■ *Web:* www.bismarck-mandancvb.org ■ *E-mail:* visitnd@bismarck-mandancvb.org	Bismarck	ND	58502	701-222-4308	222-0647
Bismarck Mayor PO Box 5503	Bismarck	ND	58506	701-222-6471	222-6470
Bismarck Planning Dept PO Box 5503 *Web:* www.bismarck.org/planning	Bismarck	ND	58506	701-222-6447	222-6450
Bismarck Public Library 515 N 5th St. *Web:* www.bismarck.org/library/web1.htm	Bismarck	ND	58501	701-222-6410	221-6854
Burleigh County PO Box 1055	Bismarck	ND	58502	701-222-6761	222-6689

On-Line Resources

About.com Guide to Bismarck . . . . . bismarck.about.com
Area Guide Bismark . . . . . bismark.areaguides.net
Excite.com Bismarck City Guide . . . . . www.excite.com/travel/countries/united_states/north_dakota/bismarck

— Transportation Services —

AIRPORTS

■ **Bismarck Municipal Airport (BIS)** — *Phone*

3 miles SE of downtown (approx 5 minutes) 701-222-6502
Web: www.bismarckairport.com

Airport Transportation

Taxi 9000 $6 fare to downtown 701-223-9000

Commercial Airlines

	Phone
Frontier	800-432-1359
Northwest	800-225-2525
United	800-241-6522
United Express	800-241-6522

Charter Airlines

	Phone
Capital Aviation	701-223-0260
Executive Air Taxi	701-258-5024

CAR RENTALS

	Phone
Avis	701-255-0707
Enterprise	701-258-2636
Hertz	701-223-3977

LIMO/TAXI

	Phone
Night Life Limousine	701-663-6572
Taxi 9000	701-223-9000
Top Hat Limousines	701-223-9012

RAIL/BUS

				Phone
Greyhound Bus Station 1237 W Divide Ave *TF:* 800-231-2222	Bismarck	ND	58501	701-223-6576

— Accommodations —

HOTELS, MOTELS, RESORTS

				Phone	*Fax*
AmericInn Motel 3235 State St. *TF:* 800-634-3444 ■ *Web:* www.americinn.com/northdakota/bismarck.html	Bismarck	ND	58501	701-250-1000	250-1103
Best Western Seven Seas Motor Inn 2611 Old Red Trail	Mandan	ND	58554	701-663-7401	663-0025
Bismarck Motor Hotel 2301 E Main Ave	Bismarck	ND	58501	701-223-2474	
Comfort Inn 1030 Interstate Ave *TF:* 800-228-5150	Bismarck	ND	58501	701-223-1911	223-6977
Comfort Suites 929 Gateway Ave *TF:* 800-228-5150	Bismarck	ND	58501	701-223-4009	223-9119
Days Inn 1300 E Capitol Ave *TF:* 800-329-7466	Bismarck	ND	58501	701-223-9151	223-9423
Doublewood Best Western 1400 E Interchange Ave *TF:* 800-554-7077	Bismarck	ND	58501	701-258-7000	258-2001
Expressway Inn 200 Bismarck Expy *TF:* 800-456-6388	Bismarck	ND	58504	701-222-2900	222-2900
Expressway Suites 180 E Bismarck Expy *TF:* 888-774-5566	Bismarck	ND	58504	701-222-3311	222-3311
Fairfield Inn Airport 135 Ivy Ave. *TF:* 800-228-2800 ■ *Web:* fairfieldinn.com/BISSO	Bismarck	ND	58504	701-223-9293	223-9293
Fairfield Inn North 1120 Century Ave *TF:* 800-228-2800 ■ *Web:* fairfieldinn.com/BISFI	Bismarck	ND	58501	701-223-9077	223-9077
Fleck House Inn 122 E Thayer Ave	Bismarck	ND	58501	701-255-1450	258-3816
Holiday Inn 605 E Broadway Ave *TF:* 800-465-4329	Bismarck	ND	58501	701-255-6000	223-0400
Hotel Bismarck 1215 W Main *TF:* 800-985-2665	Bismarck	ND	58504	701-223-9600	224-9210

Bismarck — Hotels, Motels, Resorts (Cont'd)

Name / Address	City	State	ZIP	Phone	Fax
Kelly Inn 1800 N 12th St *TF:* 800-635-3559	Bismarck	ND	58501	701-223-8001	223-8001
Motel 6 2433 State St *TF:* 800-466-8356	Bismarck	ND	58501	701-255-6878	223-7534
Nodak Motel 210 N 20th St	Bismarck	ND	58501	701-223-1960	
Radisson Inn Bismarck 800 S 3rd St *TF:* 800-333-3333	Bismarck	ND	58504	701-258-7700	224-8212
Ramada Inn 3808 E Divide Ave *TF:* 800-272-6232	Bismarck	ND	58501	701-221-3030	221-3030
Redwood Motel 1702 E Broadway Ave	Bismarck	ND	58501	701-223-4138	
Select Inn 1505 Interchange Ave. *TF:* 800-641-1000	Bismarck	ND	58501	701-223-8060	
Super 8 Motel 1124 E Capitol Ave *TF:* 800-800-8000	Bismarck	ND	58501	701-255-1314	255-1314

— Restaurants —

Name / Address	City	State	ZIP	Phone
Bistro 1100 (American) 1103 E Front Ave	Bismarck	ND	58504	701-224-8800
Captain Meriwether's (Steak/Seafood) 1700 River Rd	Bismarck	ND	58504	701-224-0455
Casper's East 40 (Continental) 1401 E Interchange Ave	Bismarck	ND	58501	701-258-7222
Drumstick (American) 307 N 3rd St	Bismarck	ND	58501	701-223-8449
Fiesta Villa (Mexican) 411 E Main Ave	Bismarck	ND	58501	701-222-8075
Golden Dragon Restaurant (Chinese) 410 E Main Ave	Bismarck	ND	58501	701-258-0000
Green Earth Cafe (Natural/Health) 208 E Broadway Ave	Bismarck	ND	58501	701-223-8646
Hong Kong Restaurant (Chinese) 1055 E Interstate Ave	Bismarck	ND	58501	701-223-2130
Hunters Club (American) Hwy 1806 Prairie Knights Casino	Fort Yates	ND	58538	701-854-7777
International Restaurant & Stir Fry (Continental) 2240 N 12th St	Bismarck	ND	58501	701-258-6442
Jack's Steakhouse (Steak) 1201 S 12th St	Bismarck	ND	58504	701-221-9120
Little Cottage Cafe (American) 2513 E Main Ave	Bismarck	ND	58501	701-223-4949
Minerva's Restaurant & Bar (American) 1800 N 12th St	Bismarck	ND	58501	701-222-1402
Oasis Restaurant (American) 3938 E Divide Ave	Bismarck	ND	58501	701-222-1568
Paradiso (Mexican) 2620 State St	Bismarck	ND	58501	701-224-1111
Peacock Alley (Gourmet) 5th & Main	Bismarck	ND	58501	701-255-7917
Rice Bowl (Chinese) 609 Main St	Mandan	ND	58554	701-663-1960
River Winds Restaurant (American) 1215 W Main Ave.	Bismarck	ND	58504	701-223-9600
Seasons Cafe (American) 800 S 3rd St	Bismarck	ND	58504	701-258-7700
Sergio's Mexican Bar & Grill (Mexican) 401 E Bismarck Expy	Bismarck	ND	58504	701-223-3422
Walrus The (Italian) Arrowhead Plaza	Bismarck	ND	58502	701-250-0020
Wood House Restaurant (American) 1825 N 13th St	Bismarck	ND	58501	701-255-3654

— Goods and Services —

SHOPPING

Name / Address	City	State	ZIP	Phone	Fax
Gateway Mall I-94 & Hwy 83 N	Bismarck	ND	58501	701-222-8350	
Kirkwood Mall 706 Kirkwood Mall	Bismarck	ND	58504	701-223-3500	255-6126
Third Floor Antique Mall 200 W Main Ave.	Bismarck	ND	58501	701-221-2594	

BANKS

Name / Address	City	State	ZIP	Phone	Fax
Bank of North Dakota 700 E Main Ave. *TF:* 800-472-2166	Bismarck	ND	58501	701-328-5600	328-5632
BNC National Bank 322 E Main St	Bismarck	ND	58501	701-250-3030	250-3028
First Southwest Bank 333 N 4th	Bismarck	ND	58501	701-223-8136	223-1701
Kirkwood Bank & Trust Co 919 S 7th St	Bismarck	ND	58504	701-258-6550	258-7436

BUSINESS SERVICES

Name	Phone
Airborne Express	800-247-2676
ASAP	701-223-2727
BAX Global	800-225-5229
DHL Worldwide Express	800-225-5345
Federal Express	800-238-5355
Mail Boxes Etc	800-789-4623
Office Alternative	701-255-7000
Post Office	701-221-6505
UPS	800-742-5877

— Media —

PUBLICATIONS

Name / Address	City	State	ZIP	Phone	Fax
Bismarck Tribune‡ PO Box 5516 *Web:* www.ndonline.com ■ *E-mail:* bismarcktribune@ndonline.com	Bismarck	ND	58506	701-223-2500	223-2063

‡Daily newspapers

TELEVISION

Name / Address	City	State	ZIP	Phone	Fax
KBME-TV Ch 3 (PBS) 207 N 5th St	Fargo	ND	58108	701-241-6900	239-7650
KBMY-TV Ch 17 (ABC) 919 S 7th St	Bismarck	ND	58504	701-223-1700	258-0886
KFYR-TV Ch 5 (NBC) 200 N 4th St *Web:* www.kfyrtv.com	Bismarck	ND	58501	701-255-5757	255-8244
KXMB-TV Ch 12 (CBS) 1811 N 15th St	Bismarck	ND	58501	701-223-9197	223-3320

RADIO

Name / Address	City	State	ZIP	Phone	Fax
KBMR-AM 1130 kHz (Ctry) PO Box 1233 *Web:* www.kbmr.com ■ *E-mail:* kbmr@gcentral.com	Bismarck	ND	58502	701-255-1234	222-1131
KBYZ-FM 96.5 MHz (CR) 4303 Memorial Hwy	Mandan	ND	58554	701-663-6411	663-8790
KCND-FM 90.5 MHz (NPR) 1814 N 15th St	Bismarck	ND	58501	701-224-1700	224-0555
KLXX-AM 1270 kHz (N/T) 4303 Memorial Hwy	Mandan	ND	58554	701-663-6411	663-8790
KYYY-FM 92.9 MHz (AC) 210 N 4th St	Bismarck	ND	58501	701-224-9393	255-8293

— Colleges/Universities —

Name / Address	City	State	ZIP	Phone	Fax
Bismarck State College 1500 Edwards Ave *TF:* 800-445-5073 ■ *Web:* www.bsc.nodak.edu	Bismarck	ND	58501	701-224-5400	224-5550
University of Mary 7500 University Dr. *Web:* www.umary.edu ■ *E-mail:* marauder@umary.edu	Bismarck	ND	58504	701-255-7500	255-7687

— Hospitals —

Name / Address	City	State	ZIP	Phone	Fax
Medcenter One Health Systems 300 N 7th St **Fax:* Admitting ■ *Web:* www.medcenterone.com	Bismarck	ND	58501	701-323-6000	323-5846*
Saint Alexius Medical Center 900 E Broadway Ave **Fax:* Admitting ■ *Web:* www.saintalexius.org	Bismarck	ND	58501	701-224-7000	530-7127*

— Attractions —

Name / Address	City	State	ZIP	Phone	Fax
Bismarck Art & Galleries Association Visual Arts Center 422 E Front Ave *E-mail:* baga@btigate.com	Bismarck	ND	58504	701-223-5986	223-8960
Bismarck-Mandan Symphony Orchestra Belle Mehus City Auditorium *Web:* www.bisman.com/symphony/	Bismarck	ND	58501	701-258-8345	
Camp Hancock Historic Site 1st & Main	Bismarck	ND	58505	701-328-2666	
Dakota Zoo Sertoma Park Riverside Park Rd	Bismarck	ND	58502	701-223-7543	
Double Ditch Indian Village Historic Site ND 1804 & Site Access Rd	Bismarck	ND	58505	701-328-2666	
Former Governors' Mansion State Historic Site 420 Ave 'B' E	Bismarck	ND	58501	701-328-2666	
Fort Abraham Lincoln Foundation 401 W Main	Mandan	ND	58554	701-663-4758	
Fort Abraham Lincoln State Park 4480 Fort Lincoln Rd.	Mandan	ND	58554	701-663-9571	
Game & Fish Lobby Wildlife Museum 100 N Bismarck Expy	Bismarck	ND	58501	701-328-6300	328-6352
General Sibley Park 5001 S Washington St.	Bismarck	ND	58504	701-222-1844	
Knife River Indian Villages National Historic Site PO Box 9 *Web:* www.nps.gov/knri/	Stanton	ND	58571	701-745-3309	745-3708
Lewis & Clark Riverboat 1700 N River Rd.	Bismarck	ND	58501	701-255-4233	
North Dakota State Capitol 600 East Blvd	Bismarck	ND	58501	701-328-2000	
North Dakota State Railroad Museum 3700 30th Ave NW	Mandan	ND	58554	701-663-9322	
Prairie Knights Casino HC-1 Box 26A	Fort Yates	ND	58538	701-854-7777	854-7785

Bismarck — Attractions (Cont'd)

				Phone	Fax
State Historical Society of North Dakota 612 E Boulevard Ave	Bismarck	ND	58505	701-328-2666	328-3710
Web: www.state.nd.us/hist ■ *E-mail:* histsoc@state.nd.us					
Theodore Roosevelt National Park PO Box 7	Medora	ND	58645	701-623-4466	623-4840
Web: www.nps.gov/thro/					
Ward Earthlodge Village Historic Site Burnt Boat Dr	Bismarck	ND	58505	701-328-2666	

SPORTS TEAMS & FACILITIES

				Phone	Fax
Bismarck Bobcats (hockey) PO Box 1262	Bismarck	ND	58502	701-222-3300	222-3335
Web: www.bismarckbobcats.com ■ *E-mail:* bisbobcats@aol.com					
Dakota Wizards (basketball) 601 E Sweet Ave Civic Center	Bismarck	ND	58504	701-258-2255	255-7967

— Events —

	Phone
Agri-International (mid-February)	701-222-4308
Bismarck Mandan Winter Daze (late January through late February)	701-222-4308
Bismarck Marathon (early September)	701-255-1525
Block Party (early July)	701-223-1958
Capitol A'Fair (early August)	701-223-5986
Capitol Curling Summer Bonspiel (mid-July)	701-222-6455
Crazy Days (late July)	701-223-1958
Custer Christmas (mid-December)	701-663-4758
Fall Craft Show (mid-October)	701-667-3285
Fantasy of Lights Parade (early December)	701-223-1958
Festival of Trees (early November)	701-223-5986
Flickertail Woodcarvers Show (mid-October)	701-222-4308
Folkfest (mid-September)	701-223-1958
Fort Lincoln's Players Theatre (mid-June-late August)	701-663-4758
Frontier Army Days (late June)	701-663-9571
Fur Traders' Rendezvous (mid-August)	701-663-4758
Great American Folkfest (September)	701-223-5660
Great Plains Jazz Festival (mid-August)	701-221-9588
International Indian Arts Exposition (early September)	701-255-3285
Mandan Rodeo Days (early July)	701-663-1136
Missouri River Expo (early June)	701-222-6487
Nu'Eta Corn & Buffalo Festival (August)	701-663-9571
Polkafest (October)	701-222-4308
PRCA Edge of the West (mid-October)	701-222-6489
U-Mary Jazz Festival (late January)	701-255-7500
United Tribes International Pow-Wow (early September)	701-255-3285

Fargo

Fargo is situated on the west bank of the Red River of the North, one of the few rivers in the world that flows north. Directly across the river, on the east bank, is Moorhead, Minnesota. The river area is the site of Riverfront Days, an annual event that features music, sporting events, and other activities on both sides of the water. Bonanzaville, USA in West Fargo is a 15-acre Pioneer Village with antique cars, tractors, and airplanes, as well as Indian artifacts, a church, and bonanza farm homes. More than 30 gaming sites are located in the Fargo-Moorhead area, offering bingo, blackjack, or parimutuel betting.

Population	83,778	**Longitude**	96-80-17 W
Area (Land)	29.8 sq mi	**County**	Cass
Area (Water)	0 sq mi	**Time Zone**	CST
Elevation	900 ft	**Area Code/s**	701
Latitude	46-90-06 N		

— Average Temperatures and Precipitation —

TEMPERATURES

	Jan	Feb	Mar	Apr	May	Jun	Jul	Aug	Sep	Oct	Nov	Dec
High	15	21	35	54	69	77	83	81	69	57	37	20
Low	-4	3	17	32	44	54	59	56	46	35	19	3

PRECIPITATION

	Jan	Feb	Mar	Apr	May	Jun	Jul	Aug	Sep	Oct	Nov	Dec
Inches	0.7	0.5	1.1	1.8	2.5	2.8	2.7	2.4	2.0	1.7	0.7	0.7

— Important Phone Numbers —

	Phone		Phone
AAA	701-282-6222	**Poison Control Center**	701-234-5575
Emergency	911	**Weather**	701-235-2600
Medical Referral	701-280-4500		

— Information Sources —

				Phone	Fax
Bismarck Consumer Protection Div 600 E Boulevard Ave Dept 125	Bismarck	ND	58505	701-328-2210	328-3535
Web: expedition.bismarck.ag.state.nd.us/ndag/cpat/cpat.html					
Cass County PO Box 2806	Fargo	ND	58108	701-241-5601	241-5728
Web: www.co.cass.nd.us					
Chamber of Commerce of Fargo Moorhead 202 1st Ave N	Moorhead	MN	56560	218-233-1100	233-1200
Web: www.fmchamber.com					
Fargo City Hall 200 N 3rd St	Fargo	ND	58102	701-241-1310	241-1526
Web: ci.fargo.nd.us					
Fargo Mayor 200 N 3rd St	Fargo	ND	58102	701-241-1310	241-1526
Fargo-Moorhead Convention & Visitors Bureau 2001 44th St SW	Fargo	ND	58103	701-282-3653	282-4366
TF: 800-235-7654 ■ *Web:* www.fargomoorhead.org					
Fargo Planning & Development Dept 200 3rd St N	Fargo	ND	58102	701-241-1474	241-1526
Web: ci.fargo.nd.us/planning					
Fargo Public Library 102 N 3rd St	Fargo	ND	58102	701-241-1491	241-8581
Web: ci.fargo.nd.us/library					

On-Line Resources

Area Guide Fargo .... fargond.areaguides.net
Excite.com Fargo City Guide ..... www.excite.com/travel/countries/united_states/north_dakota/fargo
FargoWeb Home Page .... www.fargoweb.com

— Transportation Services —

AIRPORTS

■ **Hector International Airport (FAR)**

	Phone
3 miles NW of downtown (approx 10 minutes)	701-241-1501

Web: www.fargoairport.com ■ *E-mail:* email@fargoairport.com

Airport Transportation

	Phone
Yellow Checker Cab $8 fare to downtown	701-235-5535

Commercial Airlines

	Phone		Phone
Frontier	800-432-1359	**United Express**	800-241-6522
Northwest	800-225-2525		

Charter Airlines

	Phone
Aviation Resources	701-237-0123

Fargo (Cont'd)

CAR RENTALS

	Phone		Phone
Avis	701-241-1580	Hertz	701-241-1533
Budget	701-241-1575	National	701-241-1576
Enterprise	701-232-5532		

LIMO/TAXI

	Phone		Phone
Ace of Hearts Limousine	701-282-9366	Yellow Checker Cab	701-235-5535

MASS TRANSIT

	Phone
Metropolitan Area Transit $1 Base fare	701-232-7500

RAIL/BUS

				Phone
Greyhound Bus Station 402 Northern Pacific Ave *TF:* 800-231-2222	Fargo	ND	58102	701-293-1222

— Accommodations —

HOTELS, MOTELS, RESORTS

				Phone	Fax
AmericInn Motel 1423 35th St SW *TF:* 800-634-3444 ■ *Web:* www.americinn.com/northdakota/fargo.html	Fargo	ND	58103	701-234-9946	
Best Western Doublewood Inn 3333 13th Ave S *TF:* 800-433-3235	Fargo	ND	58103	701-235-3333	280-9482
Best Western Kelly Inn 3800 Main Ave *TF:* 800-635-3559	Fargo	ND	58103	701-282-2143	281-0243
C'mon Inn Hotel 4338 20th Ave SW *TF:* 800-334-1570	Fargo	ND	58103	701-277-9944	277-9117
Comfort Inn East 1407 35th St S *TF:* 800-228-5150	Fargo	ND	58103	701-280-9666	280-9666
Comfort Inn West 3825 9th Ave SW *TF:* 800-228-5150	Fargo	ND	58103	701-282-9596	282-9596
Comfort Suites 1415 35th St S *TF:* 800-228-5150	Fargo	ND	58103	701-237-5911	237-5911
Country Suites by Carlson 3316 13th Ave S *TF:* 800-456-4000	Fargo	ND	58103	701-234-0565	234-0565
Days Inn & Suites Airport Dome 1507 19th Ave N *TF:* 800-329-7466	Fargo	ND	58102	701-232-0000	237-4464
Econo Lodge 1401 35th St SW *TF:* 800-553-2666	Fargo	ND	58103	701-232-3412	232-3412
Expressway Inn 1340 S 21st Ave *TF:* 800-437-0044	Fargo	ND	58103	701-235-3141	234-0474
Fairfield Inn by Marriott 3902 9th Ave SW *TF:* 800-228-2800 ■ *Web:* fairfieldinn.com/FARFI	Fargo	ND	58103	701-281-0494	281-0494
Flying J Travel Plaza 3150 39th St SW *TF:* 800-845-1311	Fargo	ND	58104	701-282-8473	277-9951
Hampton Inn 3431 14th Ave SW *TF:* 800-426-7866	Fargo	ND	58103	701-235-5566	235-7382
Holiday Inn 3803 13th Ave S *TF:* 800-465-4329 ■ *Web:* www.basshotels.com/holiday-inn/?_franchisee=FARND ■ *E-mail:* www.farnd@worldnet.att.net	Fargo	ND	58103	701-282-2700	281-1240
Holiday Inn Express 1040 40th St S *TF:* 800-465-4329	Fargo	ND	58103	701-282-2000	282-4721
Kelly Inn 4207 13th Ave SW *TF:* 800-635-3559	Fargo	ND	58103	701-277-8821	277-0208
Motel 6 1202 36th St SW *TF:* 800-466-8356	Fargo	ND	58103	701-232-9251	239-4482
Motel 75 3402 14th Ave S *TF:* 800-828-5962	Fargo	ND	58103	701-232-1321	232-2443
Quality Inn & Suites 301 3rd Ave N *TF:* 888-232-8850	Fargo	ND	58102	701-232-8850	232-8080
Radisson Hotel 201 5th St N *TF:* 800-333-3333	Fargo	ND	58102	701-232-7363	298-9134
Ramada Plaza Suites 1635 42nd St SW *TF:* 800-272-6232	Fargo	ND	58103	701-277-9000	281-7145
Red Roof Inn 901 38th St SW *TF:* 800-843-7663	Fargo	ND	58103	701-282-9100	277-1581
Rodeway Inn 2202 S University Dr	Fargo	ND	58103	701-239-8022	239-4614
Scandia Hotel 717 4th St N *TF:* 800-223-2913	Fargo	ND	58102	701-232-2661	232-3972
Select Inn 1025 38th St SW *TF:* 800-641-1000	Fargo	ND	58103	701-282-6300	282-6308
Sleep Inn 1921 44th St SW *TF:* 800-753-3746	Fargo	ND	58103	701-281-8240	281-2041
Super 8 Motel 3518 Interstate Blvd *TF:* 800-800-8000	Fargo	ND	58103	701-232-9202	232-4543

— Restaurants —

				Phone
Bison Turf (American) 1211 N University Dr	Fargo	ND	58102	701-235-9118
Cafe Aladdin (Greek) 530 6th Ave N	Fargo	ND	58102	701-298-0880
Doublewood Inn Restaurant 3333 (American) 3333 13th Ave S	Fargo	ND	58103	701-235-3333
Embers Restaurant (American) 3838 Main Ave	Fargo	ND	58103	701-282-6330
Fargo Cork (Steak/Seafood) 3301 S University Dr	Fargo	ND	58103	701-237-6790
Full Circle Cafe (American) 69 4th St N	Fargo	ND	58102	701-271-0051
Golden Phoenix (Chinese) 816 30th Ave S	Moorhead	MN	56560	218-236-7089
Grainery The (American) West Acres Shopping Ctr *Web:* www.fm-net.com/grainery	Fargo	ND	58103	701-282-6262
Juano's Mexican Restaurant (Mexican) 402 Broadway	Fargo	ND	58102	701-232-3123
Lone Star Steakhouse & Saloon (Steak) 4328 13th Ave SW	Fargo	ND	58103	701-282-6642
Luigi's (Italian) 613 1st Ave N	Fargo	ND	58102	701-241-4200
Mandarin Restaurant (Chinese) 4228 15th Ave SW	Fargo	ND	58103	701-282-8888
Mexican Village (Mexican) 814 Main Ave *Web:* www.fargoweb.com/mexicanvillage/	Fargo	ND	58103	701-293-0120
My Viet (Vietnamese) 2305 Main Ave	Fargo	ND	58103	701-232-6642
Nine Dragons Restaurant (Chinese) 3228 13th Ave SW	Fargo	ND	58103	701-232-2411
Old Broadway (American) 22 Broadway	Fargo	ND	58102	701-237-6161
Outbound Cafe (American) 114 Broadway	Fargo	ND	58102	701-293-9224
Paradiso Mexican Restaurant (Mexican) 801 38th St SW	Fargo	ND	58103	701-282-5747
Phil Wong's Chinese Restaurant (Chinese) 623 NP Ave *Web:* www.fargoweb.com/philwongs/	Fargo	ND	58102	701-235-6431
Sammiches Restaurant (American) 301 3rd Ave N	Fargo	ND	58102	701-232-8851
Santa Lucia (Italian/Greek) 505 40th St SW	Fargo	ND	58103	701-281-8656
Seasons at Rose Creek (Continental) 1500 Rose Creek Pkwy E	Fargo	ND	58104	701-235-5000
Shang Hai (Chinese) 3051 25th St SW	Fargo	ND	58103	701-280-5818
Speak Easy (Italian) 1001 30th Ave S	Moorhead	MN	56560	218-233-1326
Tree Top Restaurant (Continental) 403 Center Ave	Moorhead	MN	56560	218-233-1393
Upperdeck (American) 2630 S University Dr	Fargo	ND	58103	701-293-0200
Valentino's (Italian) 1443 42nd St SW	Fargo	ND	58103	701-281-0071
Valley Kitchen Restaurant (American) 3601 Main Ave	Fargo	ND	58103	701-237-0731

— Goods and Services —

SHOPPING

				Phone	Fax
Moorhead Center Mall 5th St & Center Ave	Moorhead	MN	56560	218-233-6117	
Northport Shopping Center 25th & Broadway	Fargo	ND	58102	701-235-8240	
West Acres Shopping Center 3902 13th Ave S	Fargo	ND	58103	701-282-2222	282-2229

BANKS

				Phone	Fax
Community First Bank 520 Main Ave	Fargo	ND	58124	701-293-2200	293-2360
Gate City Federal Savings Bank PO Box 2847 *TF:* 800-423-3344	Fargo	ND	58108	701-293-2400	293-2496
Norwest Bank North Dakota NA 406 Main Ave	Fargo	ND	58126	701-293-4200	280-8821
State Bank of Fargo 3100 13th Ave S	Fargo	ND	58103	701-298-1500	298-1509
Union State Bank of Fargo 901 40th St SW	Fargo	ND	58106	701-282-4598	277-1709

BUSINESS SERVICES

	Phone		Phone
Airborne Express	800-247-2676	Kruse Business Services	701-237-0277
BAX Global	800-225-5229	Mail Boxes Etc	800-789-4623
DHL Worldwide Express	800-225-5345	Post Office	701-241-6100
Federal Express	800-238-5355	UPS	800-742-5877

— Media —

PUBLICATIONS

				Phone	Fax
Forum The‡ 101 5th St N *Web:* www.in-forum.com	Fargo	ND	58102	701-235-7311	241-5487

Fargo — Publications (Cont'd)

	City	State	Zip	Phone	Fax
Midweek Eagle PO Box 457	West Fargo	ND	58078	701-282-2443	282-9248
West Fargo Pioneer 322 Sheyenne St	West Fargo	ND	58078	701-282-2443	282-9248

‡Daily newspapers

TELEVISION

	City	State	Zip	Phone	Fax
KFME-TV Ch 13 (PBS) PO Box 3240	Fargo	ND	58108	701-241-6900	239-7650
Web: www.prairiepublic.org ■ *E-mail:* tv@prairiepublic.org					
KVLY-TV Ch 11 (NBC) 1350 21st Ave S	Fargo	ND	58103	701-237-5211	232-0493
Web: www.kvlytv11.com					
KVRR-TV Ch 15 (Fox) PO Box 9115	Fargo	ND	58106	701-277-1515	277-1830
KXJB-TV Ch 4 (CBS) 4302 13th Ave SW	Fargo	ND	58103	701-282-0444	282-9331
Web: www.kx4.com					
WDAY-TV Ch 6 (ABC) 301 S 8th St	Fargo	ND	58103	701-237-6500	241-5358
Web: www.in-forum.com/resources/wday.htm					

RADIO

	City	State	Zip	Phone	Fax
KDSU-FM 91.9 MHz (NPR) North Dakota State University Ceres Hall	Fargo	ND	58105	701-241-6900	231-8899
Web: www.ndsu.nodak.edu/kdsu/ ■ *E-mail:* kdsu@plains.nodak.edu					
KFGO-AM 790 kHz (N/T) 1020 S 25th St	Fargo	ND	58103	701-237-5346	235-4042
Web: www.fargoweb.com/kfgo/ ■ *E-mail:* kfgo@rrnet.com					
KFNW-AM 1200 kHz (Rel) PO Box 6008	Fargo	ND	58108	701-282-5910	282-5781
Web: www.kfnw.org ■ *E-mail:* kfnw@rrnet.com					
KLTA-FM 105.1 MHz (AC) 2501 13th Ave SW Suite 201	Fargo	ND	58103	701-237-4500	235-9082
KPFX-FM 107.9 MHz (CR) 2501 13th Ave SW Suite 201	Fargo	ND	58103	701-237-4500	235-9082
Web: www.kpfx.com/ ■ *E-mail:* cyberfox@kpfx.com					
KQWB-AM 1550 kHz (Nost) 2501 13th Ave SW Suite 201	Fargo	ND	58103	701-237-4500	235-9082
Web: www.q98.com					
KQWB-FM 98.7 MHz (Rock) 301 8th St S	Fargo	ND	58103	701-237-5500	237-5400
WDAY-AM 970 kHz (N/T) 301 S 8th St	Fargo	ND	58103	701-237-6500	241-5373

— Colleges/Universities —

	City	State	Zip	Phone	Fax
Moorhead State University 1104 7th Ave S	Moorhead	MN	56563	218-236-2011	299-5887
TF: 800-593-7246 ■ *Web:* www.moorhead.msus.edu					
North Dakota State University 1301 12th Ave N	Fargo	ND	58105	701-231-8011	231-8802
TF Admissions: 800-488-6378 ■ *Web:* www.ndsu.nodak.edu/index.nojs.shtml					

— Hospitals —

	City	State	Zip	Phone	Fax
Dakota Heartland Health System 1720 S University Dr	Fargo	ND	58103	701-280-4100	280-4136
Web: www.dhhs.com					
MeritCare Health Center 720 4th St N	Fargo	ND	58122	701-234-6000	234-6979
Web: www.meritcare.com/location/center.html					
Veterans Affairs Medical Center 2101 Elm St N	Fargo	ND	58102	701-232-3241	239-3729

— Attractions —

	City	State	Zip	Phone	Fax
Archie's West Art Gallery Hwy 10	Dilworth	MN	56529	218-236-0775	236-0896
Bagg Bonanza Farm PO Box 702	Mooreton	ND	58061	701-274-8989	
Bonanzaville USA 1351 W Main	West Fargo	ND	58078	701-282-2822	282-7606
Web: www.fargocity.com/bonanzaville/home/index.htm					
Chahinkapa Zoo & Prairie Rose Carousel 1004 RJ Hughes Dr	Wahpeton	ND	58075	701-642-2811	642-5053
E-mail: woppark@means.net					
Comstock Historic House 506 8th St S	Moorhead	MN	56560	218-291-4211	
Fargo-Moorhead Civic Opera Co 806 NP Ave	Fargo	ND	58102	701-239-4558	
Fargo-Moorhead Community Theatre 333 4th St S	Fargo	ND	58103	701-235-6778	235-2685
Web: www.fargoweb.com/fmct/					
Fargo-Moorhead Symphony Orchestra PO Box 1753	Fargo	ND	58107	218-233-8397	236-1845
Fargo Theatre 341 Broadway	Fargo	ND	58102	701-235-4152	
Web: www.fargotheatre.org					
Festival Concert Hall North Dakota State University	Fargo	ND	58105	701-231-9564	231-2085
Heritage Hjemkomst Interpretative Center 202 1st Ave N	Moorhead	MN	56560	218-299-5511	
Historic Downtown Fargo downtown	Fargo	ND	58107	701-241-1570	241-8275
Moorhead State University Regional Science Center Moorhead State University 1104 7th Ave S	Moorhead	MN	56563	218-236-2091	299-5864
Red River & Northern Plains Regional Museum 1351 W Main Ave	West Fargo	ND	58078	701-282-2822	282-7606
TF: 800-700-5317 ■ *Web:* www.fargocity.com/bonanzaville/					
Red River Zoological Society 4220 21st Ave S	Fargo	ND	58104	701-277-9240	277-9238
Roger Maris Museum 3902 13th Ave S	Fargo	ND	58103	701-282-2222	
Trollwood Park 36th Ave N	Fargo	ND	58102	701-241-8160	241-8266
Walk of Fame 520 1st Ave N	Fargo	ND	58102	701-241-9026	
Yunker Farm Children's Museum 1201 28th Ave N	Fargo	ND	58102	701-232-6102	232-4605
Web: www.childrensmuseum-yunker.org					

SPORTS TEAMS & FACILITIES

	City	State	Zip	Phone	Fax
Fargo-Moorhead Beez (basketball) 5 1/2 8th St S	Fargo	ND	58103	701-232-4242	232-3715
Web: fmbeez.com ■ *E-mail:* fmbeez@fmbeez.com					
Fargo-Moorhead Ice Sharks (hockey) 807 17th Ave N Fargo Coliseum	Fargo	ND	58102	701-280-0011	280-0791
Web: www.icesharks.com					
Fargo-Moorhead Redhawks (baseball) 1515 15th Ave N	Fargo	ND	58102	701-235-6161	297-9247
TF: 800-303-6161 ■ *Web:* www.fmredhawks.com ■ *E-mail:* redhawks@fmredhawks.com					
Fargodome 1800 N University Dr	Fargo	ND	58102	701-241-9100	237-0987
Web: www.fargodome.com					

— Events —

	Phone
Big Iron Agricultural Expo (mid-September)	701-282-2200
Boat & Marine Show (late January)	701-241-9100
Christmas Bazaar (late August)	701-241-8160
Downtown Fargo Street Fair (mid-July)	701-241-1570
Fargo Farm Show (mid-January)	701-241-9100
Holiday Community Parade (late November)	701-241-1570
Light Up the Night (December 31)	701-241-8160
Merry Prairie Christmas (late November-late December)	800-235-7654
Pioneer Days at Bonanzaville (mid-August)	701-282-2822
Red River Valley Fair (mid-June)	701-282-2200
Red River Valley Home & Garden Show (early March)	701-241-9100
Red River Valley Sportsmen Show (early March)	701-241-9100
Renaissance Festival (mid-April)	701-241-9100
Rib Fest & More (mid-June)	701-241-9100
Riverfront Days (late August)	701-235-2895
Santa's Village at Rheault Farm (late November-late December)	701-241-8160
Scandinavian Hjemkomst Festival (late June)	218-233-8484
Skyway Bazaar (early December)	701-241-1570
Trollwood Park Weekends (early June-late August)	701-241-8160
Valley Fest (early September)	701-282-3653
We Fest (early August)	218-847-1681
Winter Festival (mid-February)	701-241-1350

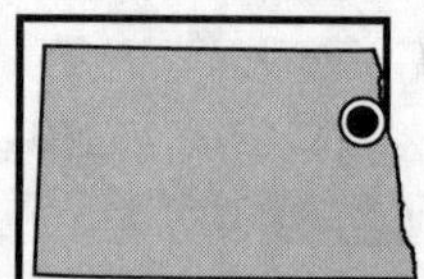

Grand Forks

The Greater Grand Forks area includes the cities of Grand Forks, North Dakota, and East Grand Forks, Minnesota. The two cities are located on either side of the Red River of the North, and river cruises are available on the Dakota Queen Riverboat. Annual events in Grand Forks include the Winterthing and Summerthing festivals. Winterthing is held in February and includes dance, dress, demonstrations, music, storytelling, games, and food

Grand Forks (Cont'd)

from the cultures that make up the Red River Valley. Summerthing is a weekend arts festival held during the months of June and July. Grand Forks is home to the University of North Dakota and is just 14 miles from Grand Forks Air Force Base.

Population ... 50,675
Area (Land) ... 14.4 sq mi
Area (Water) ... 0 sq mi
Elevation ... 834 ft
Latitude ... 47-90-30 N
Longitude ... 97-04-27 W
County ... Grand Forks
Time Zone ... CST
Area Code/s ... 701

— Average Temperatures and Precipitation —

TEMPERATURES

	Jan	Feb	Mar	Apr	May	Jun	Jul	Aug	Sep	Oct	Nov	Dec
High	14	20	33	52	68	76	82	80	68	55	35	19
Low	-5	1	15	31	42	52	57	54	44	34	18	2

PRECIPITATION

	Jan	Feb	Mar	Apr	May	Jun	Jul	Aug	Sep	Oct	Nov	Dec
Inches	0.7	0.5	0.9	1.4	2.1	2.8	2.7	2.4	2.2	1.3	0.7	0.6

— Important Phone Numbers —

	Phone
AAA	701-746-1333
Emergency	911
Poison Control Center	800-732-2200
Road Conditions	701-328-7623
Weather	701-775-7777

— Information Sources —

				Phone	*Fax*
Civic Auditorium 615 1st Ave N	Grand Forks	ND	58203	701-746-2601	746-2532
Grand Forks Chamber of Commerce 202 N 3rd St *E-mail:* gfchambr@gfherald.infi.net	Grand Forks	ND	58203	701-772-7271	772-9238
Grand Forks City Hall 255 N 4th St *Web:* www.grandforksgov.com	Grand Forks	ND	58203	701-746-2607	772-0266
Grand Forks County PO Box 5939	Grand Forks	ND	58206	701-780-8214	
Grand Forks Mayor 255 N 4th St *Web:* www.grandforksgov.com/mayor.htm	Grand Forks	ND	58203	701-746-2607	772-0266
Grand Forks Planning Dept PO Box 5200	Grand Forks	ND	58206	701-746-2660	746-1871
Grand Forks Public Library 2110 Library Cir *Web:* www.grandforksgov.com/library	Grand Forks	ND	58201	701-772-8116	772-1379
Greater Grand Forks Convention & Visitors Bureau 4251 Gateway Dr *TF:* 800-866-4566 ■ *Web:* www.grandforkscvb.org/ ■ *E-mail:* tours@GrandForksCVB.org	Grand Forks	ND	58203	701-746-0444	746-0775

On-Line Resources

Area Guide Grand Forks ... grandforks.areaguides.net
Excite.com Grand Forks City Guide ... www.excite.com/travel/countries/united_states/north_dakota/grand_forks
Welcome to Grand Forks ... www.grandforks.com/

— Transportation Services —

AIRPORTS

■ **Grand Forks International Airport (GFK)**

10 miles NW of downtown (approx 20 minutes) ... 701-795-6981

Airport Transportation

Nodak Cab $25 fare to downtown ... 701-772-3458

Commercial Airlines

Northwest ... 800-225-2525
United Express ... 800-241-6522

Charter Airlines

GFK Flight Support ... 701-772-5504

CAR RENTALS

Avis ... 701-775-0688
Enterprise ... 701-775-3977
Hertz ... 701-746-6426
National ... 701-746-1375
Price King ... 701-775-2509

LIMO/TAXI

Classic Limousine ... 800-246-5612
Emerald Limousine ... 800-567-1601
First Class Limousine ... 701-746-1421
King Limousine ... 701-775-3754
Nodak Cab ... 701-772-3456

MASS TRANSIT

Grand Forks City Bus $1 Base fare ... 701-746-2600

RAIL/BUS

				Phone
Amtrak Station 5555 Demers Ave *TF:* 800-872-7245	Grand Forks	ND	58201	701-775-0484
Greyhound Bus Station 1724 Gateway Dr *TF:* 800-231-2222	Grand Forks	ND	58202	701-775-4781

— Accommodations —

HOTELS, MOTELS, RESORTS

				Phone	*Fax*
AmericInn Motel & Suites 1820 S Columbia Rd *TF:* 800-634-3444 ■ *Web:* www.americinn.com/northdakota/grandforks.html	Grand Forks	ND	58201	701-780-9925	780-2852
Best Western Fabulous Westward Ho Hwy 2 W *TF:* 800-528-1234	Grand Forks	ND	58206	701-775-5341	775-3703
Best Western Town House 710 1st Ave N *TF:* 800-867-9797	Grand Forks	ND	58203	701-746-5411	746-1407
C'mon Inn 3051 32nd Ave S *TF:* 800-255-2323	Grand Forks	ND	58201	701-775-3320	780-8141
Comfort Inn 3251 30th Ave S *TF:* 800-228-5150	Grand Forks	ND	58201	701-775-7503	775-7503
Country Inn & Suites by Carlson 3350 32nd Ave S *TF:* 800-456-4000	Grand Forks	ND	58201	701-775-5000	775-9073
Days Inn 3101 34th St S *TF:* 800-329-7466	Grand Forks	ND	58201	701-775-0060	775-0060
Econo Lodge 900 N 43rd St *TF:* 800-553-2666	Grand Forks	ND	58203	701-746-6666	746-6666
Fairfield Inn 3051 34th St S *TF:* 800-228-2800 ■ *Web:* fairfieldinn.com/GFKGF	Grand Forks	ND	58201	701-775-7910	775-7910
Happy Host Inn 3101 S 17th St *TF:* 800-489-4411	Grand Forks	ND	58201	701-746-4411	746-4755
Holiday Inn 1210 N 43rd St *TF:* 800-465-4329	Grand Forks	ND	58203	701-772-7131	780-9112
North Star Inn 2100 S Washington St	Grand Forks	ND	58201	701-772-8151	
Plainsman Motel 2201 Gateway Dr *TF:* 888-775-8134	Grand Forks	ND	58203	701-775-8134	775-2203
Prairie Inn 1211 47th St N *TF:* 800-571-1115	Grand Forks	ND	58203	701-775-9901	775-9936
Ramada Inn 1205 N 43rd St *TF:* 800-272-6232	Grand Forks	ND	58203	701-775-3951	775-9774
Road King Inn 1015 N 43rd St *TF:* 800-950-0691	Grand Forks	ND	58201	701-775-0691	775-9964
Road King Inn Columbia Mall 3300 30th Ave S *TF:* 800-707-1391	Grand Forks	ND	58201	701-746-1391	746-8586
Rodeway Inn 4001 Gateway Dr *TF:* 800-228-2000	Grand Forks	ND	58203	701-795-9960	795-1953

Grand Forks — Hotels, Motels, Resorts (Cont'd)

Name / Address	City	State	ZIP	Phone	Fax
Select Inn 1000 N 42nd St. *TF:* 800-641-1000	Grand Forks	ND	58203	701-775-0555	775-9967
Super 8 Lodge 1122 N 43rd St. *TF:* 800-800-8000	Grand Forks	ND	58203	701-775-8138	

— Restaurants —

Name / Address	City	State	ZIP	Phone
42nd Street Eatery (American) 425 42nd St N	Grand Forks	ND	58203	701-775-0124
Big Al's Pasta Parlor (Italian) Hwy 2 W	Grand Forks	ND	58203	701-775-5341
Bronze Boot Steakhouse & Lounge (Steak/Seafood) 1804 N Washington St	Grand Forks	ND	58203	701-746-5433
China Garden (Chinese) 2550 32nd Ave S	Grand Forks	ND	58201	701-772-0660
Darcy's Cafe (American) 1400 11th Ave N	Grand Forks	ND	58203	701-775-4050
GF Goodribs (Steak/Seafood) 4223 12th Ave N	Grand Forks	ND	58203	701-746-7115
Grama Butterwick's Restaurant (Homestyle) 1421 S Washington St	Grand Forks	ND	58201	701-772-4764
Hunan Chinese Restaurant (Chinese) 2100 S Columbia Rd.	Grand Forks	ND	58201	701-772-0556
Jeannie's Restaurant (American) 1106 S Washington St	Grand Forks	ND	58201	701-772-6966
John Barley-Corne (American) 2800 S Columbia Rd	Grand Forks	ND	58201	701-775-0501
La Campana Paradiso (Mexican) 905 S Washington St	Grand Forks	ND	58201	701-772-3000
Mexican Village (Mexican) 1218 S Washington St.	Grand Forks	ND	58201	701-775-3653
Muddy Rivers Dining Room (American) 710 1st Ave N	Grand Forks	ND	58203	701-746-5411
Parrot's Cay Tavern (American) 1149 36th Ave S	Grand Forks	ND	58201	701-795-4053
Peartree Restaurant (American) 1210 N 43rd St.	Grand Forks	ND	58201	701-772-7131
Players (Italian) 2120 S Washington St	Grand Forks	ND	58201	701-780-9201
Red Pepper (Mexican) 1011 University Ave.	Grand Forks	ND	58203	701-775-9671
Sanders 1997 (American) 2500 S Washington St.	Grand Forks	ND	58201	701-746-8970
Shangri-La Restaurant (Chinese) 4220 5th Ave N	Grand Forks	ND	58203	701-775-5549
Speedway (American) 805 N 42nd St.	Grand Forks	ND	58203	701-772-8548
Village Inn (American) 2451 S Columbia Rd.	Grand Forks	ND	58201	701-772-7241

— Goods and Services —

SHOPPING

Name / Address	City	State	ZIP	Phone	Fax
City Center Mall Demers Ave & 3rd St	Grand Forks	ND	58201	701-772-3152	
Columbia Mall 2800 S Columbia Rd	Grand Forks	ND	58201	701-746-7383	772-3537
South Forks Plaza & Pavilion 1726 S Washington St.	Grand Forks	ND	58201	701-772-8121	

BANKS

Name / Address	City	State	ZIP	Phone	Fax
Community National Bank 1616 S Washington St. *Web:* www.cnbgf.com	Grand Forks	ND	58201	701-780-7700	780-7709
First American Bank 3100 S Columbia Rd	Grand Forks	ND	58201	701-795-4530	795-4568
First National Bank 2401 Demers Ave W	Grand Forks	ND	58206	701-795-3200	795-3346
US Bank NA 1205 S Columbia Rd *TF:* 800-872-2657	Grand Forks	ND	58201	701-795-6222	795-6215

BUSINESS SERVICES

Name	Phone	Name	Phone
Airborne Express	800-247-2676	**Kelly Services**	701-780-9509
BAX Global	800-225-5229	**Kinko's**	701-780-9708
DHL Worldwide Express	800-225-5345	**Mail Boxes Etc**	701-775-2756
Federal Express	800-238-5355	**Post Office**	701-775-5329

— Media —

PUBLICATIONS

Name / Address	City	State	ZIP	Phone	Fax
Agweek PO Box 6008	Grand Forks	ND	58206	701-780-1230	780-1211
Grand Forks Herald‡ 375 2nd Ave N. *Web:* www.gfherald.com	Grand Forks	ND	58201	701-780-1100	780-1123

‡Daily newspapers

TELEVISION

Name / Address	City	State	ZIP	Phone	Fax
KGFE-TV Ch 2 (PBS) 207 N 5th St	Fargo	ND	58108	701-241-6900	239-7650
KVLY-TV Ch 11 (NBC) 1350 21st Ave S *Web:* www.kvlytv11.com	Fargo	ND	58103	701-237-5211	232-0493
KVRR-TV Ch 15 (Fox) PO Box 9115	Fargo	ND	58106	701-277-1515	277-1830
KXJB-TV Ch 4 (CBS) 4302 13th Ave SW *Web:* www.kx4.com	Fargo	ND	58103	701-282-0444	282-9331
WDAZ-TV Ch 8 (ABC) 2220 S Washington St.	Grand Forks	ND	58208	701-775-2511	746-8565

RADIO

Name / Address	City	State	ZIP	Phone	Fax
KCNN-AM 1590 kHz (N/T) 667 Demers Ave Suite 1003 *TF:* 888-591-8255 ■ *Web:* www.kcnn.com	Grand Forks	ND	58201	701-772-2204	746-0012
KFJM-AM 1370 kHz (Misc) PO Box 8117	Grand Forks	ND	58202	701-777-2577	777-4263
KFJM-FM 90.7 MHz (AAA) PO Box 8117	Grand Forks	ND	58202	701-777-2577	777-4263
KJKJ-FM 107.5 MHz (Rock) PO Box 13598	Grand Forks	ND	58208	701-746-1417	746-1410
KKXL-AM 1440 kHz (Nost) 505 University Ave	Grand Forks	ND	58203	701-746-1417	746-1410
KKXL-FM 92.9 MHz (CHR) PO Box 13598 *Web:* www.xl93.com	Grand Forks	ND	58208	701-746-1417	746-1410
KNOX-FM 94.7 MHz (Ctry) PO Box 13638	Grand Forks	ND	58208	701-775-4611	772-0540
KQHT-FM 96.1 MHz (AC) PO Box 13598	Grand Forks	ND	58208	701-746-1417	746-1410

— Colleges/Universities —

Name / Address	City	State	ZIP	Phone	Fax
University of North Dakota PO Box 7053 *Web:* www.und.nodak.edu ■ *E-mail:* carolyn@badlands.nodak.edu	Grand Forks	ND	58202	701-777-2011	777-2696

— Hospitals —

Name / Address	City	State	ZIP	Phone	Fax
Altru Hospital 1200 S Columbia Rd.	Grand Forks	ND	58201	701-780-5000	780-1631

— Attractions —

Name / Address	City	State	ZIP	Phone	Fax
Bingo Palace 1726 S Washington St.	Grand Forks	ND	58201	701-775-9716	
Center for Aerospace Sciences 4125 University Ave University of North Dakota *Web:* www.aero.und.nodak.edu ■ *E-mail:* www@aero.und.edu	Grand Forks	ND	58202	701-777-2791	777-3016
Fire Hall Theatre 412 2nd Ave N	Grand Forks	ND	58203	701-746-0847	
Fritz Chester Auditorium Yale Dr & University Ave University of North Dakota	Grand Forks	ND	58202	701-777-3076	777-4710
International Peace Garden Rt 1 *Web:* www.peacegarden.com ■ *E-mail:* comments@peacegarden.com	Dunseith	ND	58329	701-263-4390	263-3169
Myra Museum 2405 Belmont Rd. *Web:* gfchs.dakscl.org ■ *E-mail:* lxub80a@prodigy.com	Grand Forks	ND	58201	701-775-2216	
North Dakota Mill PO Box 13078 *TF:* 800-538-7721	Grand Forks	ND	58208	701-795-7000	795-7251
North Dakota Museum of Art Centennial Dr University of North Dakota	Grand Forks	ND	58202	701-777-4195	777-4425
Turtle River State Park Hwy 2 *Web:* www.state.nd.us/ndparks/Parks/Turtle_River/Turtle.htm	Arvilla	ND	58214	701-594-4445	594-2556
University of North Dakota Hughes Fine Arts Center Art Gallery University of North Dakota Campus	Grand Forks	ND	58203	701-777-2257	
University of North Dakota Witmer Art Gallery 2920 5th Ave N.	Grand Forks	ND	58202	701-746-4211	
Walsh County Heritage Village Hwy 17 W.	Grafton	ND	58237	701-352-3280	
Water World Waterslide Park 3651 S Washington St.	Grand Forks	ND	58201	701-746-2795	

SPORTS TEAMS & FACILITIES

Name / Address	City	State	ZIP	Phone
Grand Forks Speedway 2300 Gateway Dr	Grand Forks	ND	58203	701-772-3421

Grand Forks (Cont'd)

— Events —

	Phone
Arts & Crafts Show (early October)	800-866-4566
Catfish Days (mid-August)	800-866-4566
First Night Greater Grand Forks (December 31)	701-746-0444
Forx Fest (late July)	800-866-4566
GGF Fair & Exhibition (mid-July)	800-866-4566
Heritage Days (mid-August)	800-866-4566
Potato Bowl (mid-September)	800-866-4566
Red River Duck Race & Fireworks Display (early July)	800-866-4566
Summerthing (late June & July)	800-866-4566
Time Out Wacippi (early April)	701-746-0444
University of North Dakota Writers' Conference (late March)	701-777-3321
Wacipi/Time Out (mid-April)	701-777-4291

Ohio

Population (1999): 11,256,654 **Area (sq mi): 44,828**

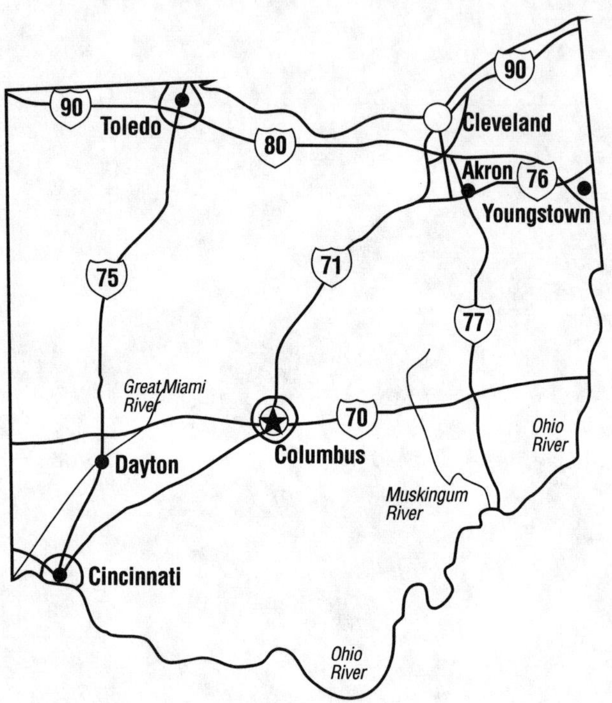

— State Information Sources —

				Phone	Fax
Ohio Chamber of Commerce PO Box 15159 . . . Columbus	OH	43215		614-228-4201	228-6403
TF: 800-622-1893 ■ *Web:* www.ohiochamber.com					
Ohio Development Dept PO Box 1001 . . . . Columbus	OH	43266		614-466-2480	644-5167
Web: www.odod.ohio.gov					
Ohio Parks & Recreation Div					
1952 Belcher Dr Bldg C3 . . . . Columbus	OH	43224		614-265-6561	261-8407
Web: www.dnr.state.oh.us/odnr/parks/					
■ *E-mail:* parkinfo@dnr.state.oh.us					
Ohio State Government Information				614-466-2000	
Web: www.ohio.gov ■ *E-mail:* wwwohio@ohio.gov					
Ohio State Library 65 S Front St Rm 510 . . . . . Columbus	OH	43215		614-644-7061	466-3584
TF: 800-686-1531 ■ *Web:* winslo.state.oh.us					
Ohio Travel & Tourism Div PO Box 1001 . . . . . Columbus	OH	43216		614-466-8844	466-6744
TF: 800-848-1300 ■ *Web:* www.ohiotourism.com					
■ *E-mail:* ohiotourism@odod.ohio.gov					

ON-LINE RESOURCES

CommunityOhio.com . . . . www.communityohio.com
My-Ohio . . . . www.my-ohio.com
Ohio Cities . . . . dir.yahoo.com/Regional/U_S__States/Ohio/Cities
Ohio Counties & Regions . . . . dir.yahoo.com/Regional/U_S__States/Ohio/Counties_and_Regions
Ohio Directory . . . . www.ohio.com
Ohio Travel & Tourism Guide . . . . www.travel-library.com/north_america/usa/ohio/index.html
OhioCities.com . . . . www.ohiocities.com
OhioSites.com . . . . www.ohiosites.net
RickOHIO . . . . www.rickohio.com
Rough Guide Travel Ohio travel.roughguides.com/content/467/index.htm
SitesOnline Ohio . . . . www.sitesonline.com
Travel Ohio Internet Guide . . . . www.travelohio.com
Travel.org-Ohio . . . . travel.org/ohio.html
Virtual Ohio . . . . www.virtual-ohio.com
Yahoo! Get Local Ohio . . . . dir.yahoo.com/Regional/U_S__States/Ohio

— Cities Profiled —

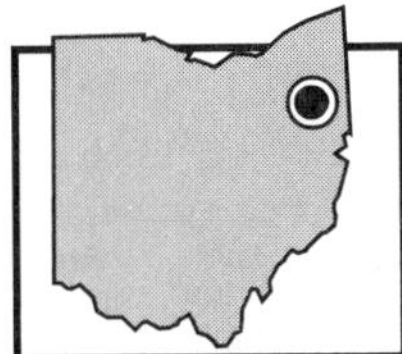

Akron

Akron is located along the Cuyahoga River in Summit County, Ohio. In 1870 Doctor Benjamin Franklin Goodrich organized the first rubber plant in Akron, and the city eventually became known as the "Rubber Capital of the World." Today it is a major center for polymer research and development and remains the home of the top U.S. rubber companies. The Goodyear World of Rubber traces the discovery and growth of rubber making and the history of the rubber industry in Akron. Visitors can also tour Stan Hywet Hall, a 65-room Tudor mansion on 70 acres of landscaped grounds and gardens that was built in the early 1900s for Frank A. Seiberling, co-founder of Goodyear and Seiberling rubber companies. The home of Dr. Bob Smith, co-founder of Alcoholics Anonymous, is also open to the public. Two major sporting events held each year in Akron are the All-American Soap Box Derby and NEC's World Series of Golf. The Pro Football Hall of Fame is a short drive south of Akron in Canton, Ohio; and just north of Akron is the Cuyahoga Valley National Recreation Area, encompassing 33,000 acres along 22 miles of the Cuyahoga River between Akron and Cleveland.

Population	215,712	**Longitude**	81-51-92 W
Area (Land)	62.2 sq mi	**County**	Summit
Area (Water)	0.4 sq mi	**Time Zone**	EST
Elevation	1027 ft	**Area Code/s**	330
Latitude	41-08-14 N		

— Average Temperatures and Precipitation —

TEMPERATURES

	Jan	Feb	Mar	Apr	May	Jun	Jul	Aug	Sep	Oct	Nov	Dec
High	33	36	47	59	70	79	82	80	74	62	50	38
Low	17	19	29	38	48	57	62	60	54	43	34	24

PRECIPITATION

	Jan	Feb	Mar	Apr	May	Jun	Jul	Aug	Sep	Oct	Nov	Dec
Inches	2.1	2.2	3.3	3.2	3.7	3.2	4.1	3.3	3.3	2.4	3.0	3.0

— Important Phone Numbers —

	Phone		Phone
AAA	330-762-0631	**Poison Control Center**	330-379-8562
Akron Info Line	330-376-6660	**Time/Temp**	330-673-9811
American Express Travel	330-836-9577	**Weather**	330-869-8686
Emergency	911		

— Information Sources —

				Phone	Fax
Akron City Hall 166 S High St	Akron	OH	44308	330-375-2121	375-2524
Web: www.ci.akron.oh.us					
Akron Mayor 166 S High St Suite 200	Akron	OH	44308	330-375-2345	375-2468
Akron Planning & Urban Development Dept 166 S High St	Akron	OH	44308	330-375-2770	375-2387
Web: www.ci.akron.oh.us/plud.html					
Akron Regional Development Board 1 Cascade Plaza Suite 800	Akron	OH	44308	330-376-5550	379-3164
TF: 800-621-8001 ■ *Web:* www.ardb.org					
Akron-Summit County Public Library 55 S Main St	Akron	OH	44326	330-643-9000	643-9033
Web: www.ascpl.lib.oh.us/ ■ *E-mail:* ascpl@acorn.net					
Akron/Summit County Convention & Visitors Bureau 77 E Mill St	Akron	OH	44308	330-374-7560	374-7626
TF: 800-245-4254 ■ *Web:* www.visitakron-summit.org					
Better Business Bureau Serving the Akron Area 222 W Market St	Akron	OH	44303	330-253-4590	253-6249
Web: www.akronbbb.org					
Summit County 175 S Main St	Akron	OH	44308	330-643-2500	643-2507

On-Line Resources

Akron Community Online Resource Network	www.acorn.net
Akron Index	www.akr.net
Area Guide Akron	akron.areaguides.net
Excite.com Akron City Guide	www.excite.com/travel/countries/united_states/ohio/akron

— Transportation Services —

AIRPORTS

■ **Akron-Canton Regional Airport (CAK)**

	Phone
13 miles S of downtown (approx 20 minutes)	330-896-2385

Web: www.akroncantonairport.com

Airport Transportation

	Phone
Shuttle One Service $26 fare to downtown	330-494-5800
Thomas Limousine Service $40 fare to downtown	330-753-5001
Yellow Cab $35 fare to downtown	330-456-4343
ZONA Express $28 fare to downtown	330-492-4050

Commercial Airlines

	Phone		Phone
AirTran	800-247-8726	**Northwest**	800-225-2525
American	800-433-7300	**United Express**	800-241-6522
Comair	800-354-9822	**US Airways**	800-428-4322
Continental	800-525-0280		

Charter Airlines

	Phone		Phone
Gordon Air	330-497-1531	**McKinley Air**	800-225-6446

CAR RENTALS

	Phone		Phone
Avis	330-499-4416	**Enterprise**	330-434-2600
Budget	330-499-4111	**Hertz**	330-499-7836
CarTemps USA	330-633-7555	**National**	330-499-8205

LIMO/TAXI

	Phone		Phone
After Six Limousine Service	330-784-0382	**First Choice Limousine**	330-434-7737
American Limousine	330-253-6743	**GI Cab**	330-253-2131
Barberton/Summitt Taxi	330-825-9933	**Pegasus Limousine Service**	330-794-2782
Carrington Coach Limousine Service	330-896-9300	**Thomas Limousine Service**	330-753-5001
Falls Suburban Cab	330-929-3121	**Yellow Cab**	330-253-3141

MASS TRANSIT

	Phone
Metro Regional Transit Authority $1 Base fare	330-762-0341

RAIL/BUS

				Phone
Greyhound/Trailways Bus Station 781 Grant St	Akron	OH	44311	330-434-5171

— Accommodations —

HOTELS, MOTELS, RESORTS

				Phone	Fax
Akron Super 8 79 Rothrock Rd	Akron	OH	44321	330-666-8887	666-8887
TF: 800-800-8000					
Avalon Inn & Resort 9519 E Market St	Warren	OH	44484	330-856-1900	856-2248
TF: 800-828-2566					
Best Western Executive Inn 2677 Gilchrist Rd	Akron	OH	44305	330-794-1050	794-8495
TF: 800-528-1234					
Best Western Inn & Suites 160 Montrose W Ave.	Akron	OH	44321	330-864-7100	668-2926
TF: 800-528-1234					

Akron — Hotels, Motels, Resorts (Cont'd)

				Phone	Fax
Comfort Inn South 2873 S Arlington Rd	Akron	OH	44312	330-645-1100	645-1101
TF: 800-221-5150					
Comfort Inn West 130 Montrose W Ave	Akron	OH	44321	330-666-5050	668-2550
TF: 800-221-2222					
Courtesy Inn 210 W Market St	Akron	OH	44303	330-762-9581	762-1715
Courtyard by Marriott 100 Springside Dr	Akron	OH	44333	330-668-9090	668-9090
TF: 800-321-2211 ■ *Web:* courtyard.com/CAKMT					
Days Inn South 3237 S Arlington Rd	Akron	OH	44312	330-644-1204	644-8426
TF: 800-329-7466					
Extended StayAmerica 185 Montrose W Ave	Akron	OH	44321	330-668-9818	668-9724
TF: 800-398-7829					
Fairfield Inn by Marriott 70 Rothrock Rd	Copley	OH	44321	330-668-2700	668-2700
TF: 800-228-2800 ■ *Web:* fairfieldinn.com/CAKFI					
Four Points Hotel Akron West 3150 W Market St	Akron	OH	44333	330-869-9000	869-8325
TF: 800-325-3535					
Hampton Inn 80 Springside Dr	Akron	OH	44333	330-666-7361	665-7673
TF: 800-426-7866					
Hilton Inn Quaker Square 135 S Broadway St	Akron	OH	44308	330-253-5970	253-2574
Web: www.hilton.com/hotels/CAKQHHF					
Hilton Inn West 3180 W Market St	Akron	OH	44333	330-867-5000	867-1648
TF: 800-445-8667 ■ *Web:* www.hilton.com/hotels/CAKHWHF					
Holiday Inn Akron/Fairlawn 4073 Medina Rd	Akron	OH	44333	330-666-4131	666-7190
TF: 800-465-4329					
Holiday Inn Express South 2940 Chenoweth Rd	Akron	OH	44312	330-644-7126	644-1776
TF: 800-465-4329					
Holiday Inn North Canton 4520 Everhard Rd NW	Canton	OH	44718	330-494-2770	494-6473
TF: 800-465-4329					
Motors Inn Motel 2884 E Waterloo Rd	Akron	OH	44312	330-628-3531	
Radisson Inn Akron/Fairlawn 200 Montrose W Ave	Akron	OH	44321	330-666-9300	668-2270
TF: 800-333-3333					
Ramada Plaza Hotel 20 W Mills St	Akron	OH	44308	330-384-1500	434-5525
Red Roof Inn North 99 Rothrock Rd	Akron	OH	44321	330-666-0566	666-6874
TF: 800-843-7663					
Red Roof Inn South 2939 S Arlington Rd	Akron	OH	44312	330-644-7748	644-6554
TF: 800-843-7663					
Residence Inn by Marriott 120 Montrose W Ave	Akron	OH	44321	330-666-4811	666-8029
TF: 800-331-3131 ■ *Web:* www.residenceinn.com/CAKMR					
Sheraton Suites Hotel 1989 Front St	Cuyahoga Falls	OH	44221	330-929-3000	929-3031
TF: 800-325-3535					
StudioPLUS 170 Montrose W Ave	Akron	OH	44321	330-666-3177	670-6072
TF: 800-656-8000					

— Restaurants —

				Phone
356th Fighter Group (American) 4919 Mt Pleasant Rd	North Canton	OH	44720	330-494-3500
Web: www.starcom2.com/356thFG				
Amber Pub Restaurant (American) 1485 Marion Ave	Akron	OH	44313	330-836-9537
Bangkok Gourmet (Thai) 1283 E Tallmadge Ave	Akron	OH	44310	330-630-9790
Bill Hwang's Restaurant (Chinese) 879 Canton Rd	Akron	OH	44312	330-784-7167
Cafe 115 (American) 115 E Market St	Akron	OH	44308	330-253-4114
Cafe Piscitelli (Italian) 1800 Triplet Blvd	Akron	OH	44312	330-798-1986
Cajun Cafe & Grill (Cajun) 2000 Brittain Rd	Akron	OH	44310	330-630-3744
Diamond Grille (Steak/Seafood) 77 W Market St	Akron	OH	44308	330-253-0041
East Side Cafe (American) 2136 E Market St	Akron	OH	44312	330-733-5005
Gus' Chalet Restaurant (Greek) 938 E Tallmadge Ave	Akron	OH	44310	330-633-2322
Katmandu (American) 1403 E Market St	Akron	OH	44305	330-733-1311
Ken Stewart's Grille (California) 1970 W Market St	Akron	OH	44313	330-867-2555
Lanning's (Steak/Seafood) 826 N Cleveland-Massillon Rd	Akron	OH	44333	330-666-1159
Larry's Main Entrance (Steak) 1964 W Market St	Akron	OH	44313	330-864-8162
Michael Trecaso's (Italian) 780 W Market St	Akron	OH	44303	330-253-7751
New Era Restaurant (Hungarian) 10 Massillon Rd	Akron	OH	44312	330-784-0087
Noisy Oyster (Seafood) 1375 N Portage Path	Akron	OH	44313	330-864-7500
Olde Loyal Oak Tavern (American) 3044 Wadsworth Rd	Norton	OH	44203	330-825-8280
Otani Japanese Restaurant (Japanese) 1684 Merriman Rd	Akron	OH	44313	330-836-1500
Parasson's Italian Restaurant (Italian) 501 N Main St	Akron	OH	44310	330-376-2117
Rizzi's Ristorante (Italian) 3265 W Market St	Fairlawn	OH	44333	330-864-2141
Silver Pheasant The (American) 3085 Graham Rd	Stow	OH	44224	330-678-2116
Sushi Katsu (Japanese) 1446 N Portage Path	Akron	OH	44313	330-867-2334
Ta Chien Chinese Restaurant (Chinese) 1714 Merriman Rd	Akron	OH	44313	330-836-4300
Tangier (Mediterranean) 532 W Market St	Akron	OH	44303	330-376-7171
Thai Gourmet (Thai) 3732 Darrow Rd	Akron	OH	44309	330-688-0880
Vault 328 (American) 328 S Main St	Akron	OH	44308	330-535-5006
Young's (American) 2744 Manchester Rd	Akron	OH	44319	330-745-6116

— Goods and Services —

SHOPPING

				Phone	Fax
Chapel Hill Mall 2000 Brittain Rd	Akron	OH	44310	330-633-7100	633-1503
Fairlawn Town Centre 2855 W Market St	Akron	OH	44333	330-836-9174	836-5139
Orangerie Mall at Akron Centre 76 S Main St	Akron	OH	44308	330-384-9306	384-9134
Quaker Square 135 S Broadway	Akron	OH	44308	330-253-5970	253-2574
Quaker Square Mall 120 E Mill St	Akron	OH	44308	330-253-5970	
Rolling Acres Mall 2400 Romig Rd	Akron	OH	44322	330-753-5045	753-7625
Summit Mall 3265 W Market St	Akron	OH	44333	330-867-1555	867-5852
West Point Market 1711 W Market St	Akron	OH	44313	330-864-2151	869-8666
TF: 800-838-2156 ■ *Web:* www.westpoint-market.com					

BANKS

				Phone	Fax
Bank One Akron NA 50 S Main St	Akron	OH	44309	800-999-5585	972-1772*
**Fax Area Code:* 330					
Charter One Bank FSB 333 S Broadway	Akron	OH	44308	330-762-8491	762-8732
Fifth Third Bank 3750 W Market St Suite Q	Akron	OH	44333	330-665-4710	665-1566
TF Cust Svc: 800-589-5355*					
Firstar Bank 156 S Main St	Akron	OH	44308	330-535-2240	535-2470
FirstMerit Bank NA 106 S Main St	Akron	OH	44308	330-384-8000	253-4476
KeyBank NA Akron District 157 S Main St	Akron	OH	44308	330-379-1446	
National City Bank Northeast 1 Cascade Plaza	Akron	OH	44308	330-375-3842	375-8108
TF: 800-738-3888					

BUSINESS SERVICES

	Phone
Cotter Express Delivery & Courier	330-535-3278
Federal Express	800-238-5355
Golden Touch Secretarial Services	330-376-7672
Interim Personnel Services	330-535-7131
Kinko's	330-376-2679
Olsten Staffing Services	330-922-8367
Post Office	330-996-9905
Special D Rapid Inc.	330-374-0550
Superior Staffing	330-253-8080
UPS	800-742-5877

— Media —

PUBLICATIONS

				Phone	Fax
Akron Beacon Journal‡ 44 E Exchange St	Akron	OH	44328	330-996-3000	376-9235
TF: 800-777-2442 ■ *Web:* www.ohio.com/bj					

‡Daily newspapers

TELEVISION

				Phone	Fax
WEAO-TV Ch 45 (PBS) 1750 Campus Center Dr	Kent	OH	44240	330-677-4549	672-7995
Web: www.ch4549.org ■ *E-mail:* programs@wneo.pbs.org					
WJW-TV Ch 8 (Fox) 5800 S Marginal Rd	Cleveland	OH	44103	216-431-8888	432-4239
E-mail: fox8@en.com					
WKYC-TV Ch 3 (NBC) 1403 E 6th St	Cleveland	OH	44114	216-344-3333	344-3326
E-mail: wkyc@aol.com					
WOIO-TV Ch 19 (CBS) 1717 E 12th St	Cleveland	OH	44114	216-771-1943	436-5460
Web: www.woio.com					
WVPX-TV Ch 23 (PAX) 26650 Renaissance Pkwy Suite E-4	Cleveland	OH	44128	216-831-2367	831-2676
Web: www.pax.net/WVPX					

RADIO

				Phone	Fax
WAKR-AM 1590 kHz (Sports) 9 W Market St	Akron	OH	44313	800-543-1495	864-6799*
**Fax Area Code:* 330					
WAPS-FM 91.3 MHz (Jazz/Alt) 65 Steiner Ave	Akron	OH	44301	330-761-3098	761-3240
Web: www.wapsfm.com					
WCUE-AM 1150 kHz (Rel) 4075 Bellaire Ln	Peninsula	OH	44264	330-920-1150	
TF: 800-543-1495					
WHLO-AM 640 kHz (Rel) 4 Summit Park Dr Suite 150	Independence	OH	44131	216-901-0921	
WKDD-FM 96.5 MHz (Urban) 1867 W Market St	Akron	OH	44313	330-836-4700	836-5321
Web: www.wkdd.com					
WONE-FM 97.5 MHz (Rock) 9 W Market St	Akron	OH	44313	330-869-9800	864-6799
WQMX-FM 94.9 MHz (Ctry) 1795 W Market St	Akron	OH	44313	330-869-9800	865-7889
WTOU-AM 1350 kHz (Urban) 1867 W Market St	Akron	OH	44313	330-836-4700	836-5321
WZIP-FM 88.1 MHz (Urban) 157 University Ave	Akron	OH	44325	330-972-7105	972-5521

Akron (Cont'd)

— Colleges/Universities —

Name / Address	City	State	Zip	Phone	Fax
Kent State University 500 E Main St	Kent	OH	44242	330-672-2121	672-2499
Web: www.kent.edu					
Southern Ohio College Northeast Campus					
2791 Mogadore Rd	Akron	OH	44312	330-733-8766	733-5853
University of Akron 302 Buchtel Common	Akron	OH	44325	330-972-7111	972-7022
TF Admissions: 800-655-4884 ■ *Web:* www.uakron.edu					

— Hospitals —

Name / Address	City	State	Zip	Phone	Fax
Akron City Hospital 525 E Market St	Akron	OH	44309	330-375-3000	375-3050
Akron General Medical Center					
400 Wabash Ave	Akron	OH	44307	330-384-6000	996-2300
TF: 800-221-4601 ■ *Web:* www.agmc.org					
Barberton Citizens Hospital 155 5th St NE	Barberton	OH	44203	330-745-1611	848-7824
Children's Hospital Medical Center of Akron					
1 Perkins Sq	Akron	OH	44308	330-543-1000	543-3008
Cuyahoga Falls General Hospital					
1900 23rd St	Cuyahoga Falls	OH	44223	330-971-7000	971-7155
Medina General Hospital					
1000 E Washington St	Medina	OH	44256	330-725-1000	722-5812
Robinson Memorial Hospital PO Box 1204	Ravenna	OH	44266	330-297-0811	297-2949
Saint Thomas Hospital 444 N Main St	Akron	OH	44310	330-375-3000	375-3445

— Attractions —

Name / Address	City	State	Zip	Phone	Fax
Abell Durbin Arboretum 760 Darrow Rd	Stow	OH	44224	330-688-8238	688-8532
Akron Art Museum 70 E Market St	Akron	OH	44308	330-376-9185	376-1180
Web: www.akronartmuseum.org ■ *E-mail:* mail@akronartmuseum.org					
Akron Civic Theatre 182 S Main St	Akron	OH	44308	330-535-3179	535-9828
Web: www.akroncivic.com					
Akron Symphony Orchestra 17 N Broadway	Akron	OH	44308	330-535-8131	535-7302
Web: www.akronsymphony.org					
Akron Zoological Park 500 Edgewood Ave	Akron	OH	44307	330-375-2525	
Web: www.neo.lrun.com/akzoo/					
Blossom Music Center					
1145 W Steels Corners Rd	Cuyahoga Falls	OH	44223	330-920-8040	920-0968
Web: www.blossommusic.com					
Boston Mills/Brandywine Ski Resort					
7100 Riverview Rd	Peninsula	OH	44264	330-657-2334	657-2660
Web: www.bmbw.com ■ *E-mail:* bmbuski241@aol.com					
Brown John Home 714 Diagonal Rd	Akron	OH	44320	330-535-1120	376-6868
Carousel Dinner Theatre 1275 E Waterloo Rd	Akron	OH	44306	330-724-9855	724-2232
TF: 800-362-4100					
Carriage Trade 8050 Brandywine Rd	Northfield	OH	44067	330-467-9000	468-2845
Coach House Theatre 732 W Exchange St	Akron	OH	44302	330-434-7741	
Cuyahoga Valley National Recreation Area					
15610 Vaughn Rd	Brecksville	OH	44141	440-526-5256	
TF: 800-445-9667 ■ *Web:* www.nps.gov/cuva/					
Cuyahoga Valley Scenic Railroad					
1664 W Main St	Peninsula	OH	44624	330-657-2000	657-2450
TF: 800-468-4070 ■ *Web:* www.cvsr.com					
Dover Lake Water Park					
1150 Highland Rd	Sagamore Hills	OH	44067	330-467-7946	467-1422
TF: 800-372-7946 ■ *Web:* www.doverlake.com					
Dr Bob's Home 855 Ardmore Ave	Akron	OH	44302	330-864-1935	
TF Orders: 800-992-2354 ■ *Web:* www.drbobs.com/					
EJ Thomas Performing Arts Hall					
198 Hill St University of Akron	Akron	OH	44325	330-972-7570	972-6571
FA Seiberling Naturealm 1828 Smith Rd	Akron	OH	44313	330-865-8065	865-8070
Geauga Lake 1060 N Aurora Rd	Aurora	OH	44202	330-562-7131	562-7020
Web: www.sixflags.com/geaugalake					
Goodyear Community Theatre					
1144 E Market St	Akron	OH	44316	330-796-3159	796-2222
Goodyear World of Rubber Museum					
1144 E Market St	Akron	OH	44316	330-796-2121	796-5045
Hale Farm & Village PO Box 296	Bath	OH	44210	330-666-3711	666-9497
Web: www.wrhs.org/sites/hale.htm					
Hower House 60 Fir Hill University of Akron	Akron	OH	44325	330-972-6909	
Hywet Stan Hall & Gardens					
714 N Portage Path	Akron	OH	44303	330-836-5533	836-2680
Web: www.stanhywet.org/					
Inventure Place 221 S Broadway	Akron	OH	44308	330-762-4463	762-6313
TF: 800-968-4332 ■ *Web:* www.invent.org					
Kent State University Museum					
E Main & S Lincoln Sts Rockwell Hall	Kent	OH	44242	330-672-3450	672-3218
Web: www.kent.edu/museum/					
Lockheed Martin Airdock 1210 Massillon Rd	Akron	OH	44306	330-796-2800	
Magical Theatre Co					
565 W Tuscarawas Ave	Barberton	OH	44203	330-848-3708	848-3591
National Inventors Hall of Fame					
221 S Broadway Inventure Place	Akron	OH	44308	330-762-4463	762-6313
Web: www.invent.org ■ *E-mail:* index@invent.org					
Ohio Ballet 354 E Market St	Akron	OH	44325	330-972-7900	972-7902
Web: www.ohioballet.com/					
Perkins Stone Mansion 550 Copley Rd	Akron	OH	44320	330-535-1120	376-6868
Police Museum 217 S High St	Akron	OH	44308	330-375-2390	375-2412
Portage Hills Vineyard 1420 Martin Rd	Suffield	OH	44260	330-628-2668	628-1311
TF: 800-418-6493 ■ *Web:* www.portagehills.com					
Portages Lake State Park 5031 Manchester Rd	Akron	OH	44319	330-644-2220	644-7550
Porthouse Theatre Co					
Kent Rd Kent State University	Kent	OH	44242	330-672-3884	
Web: www.kent.edu/theatre/porthouse/ ■ *E-mail:* porthouse@kent.edu					
Pro Football Hall of Fame					
2121 George Halas Dr NW	Canton	OH	44708	330-456-8207	456-8175
Web: www.profootballhof.com					
Sea World of Ohio 1100 Sea World Dr	Aurora	OH	44202	330-995-2121	995-2115*
**Fax:* Mktg					
■ *Web:* www.seaworld.com/seaworld/sw_ohio/swoframe.html					
Summit County Historical Society					
550 Copley Rd	Akron	OH	44320	330-535-1120	376-6868
Weathervane Community Playhouse					
1301 Weathervane Ln	Akron	OH	44313	330-836-2626	873-2150
Winery at Wolf Creek					
2637 S Cleveland-Massillon Rd	Norton	OH	44203	330-666-9285	665-1445

SPORTS TEAMS & FACILITIES

Name / Address	City	State	Zip	Phone	Fax
Akron Aeros (baseball)					
300 S Main St Canal Pk	Akron	OH	44308	330-253-5151	253-3300
TF: 800-972-3767 ■ *Web:* www.akronaeros.com					
Barberton Speedway 3363 Clarks Mill Rd	Barberton	OH	44203	330-753-8668	
Northfield Park 10705 Northfield Rd	Northfield	OH	44067	330-467-4101	468-2628
Web: www.northfieldpark.com					

— Events —

	Phone
Akron Arts Expo (late July)	330-375-2804
Akron Rib & Music Festival (early July)	330-375-2804
All-American Soap Box Derby (late July)	330-733-8723
Antique & Classic Car Show (mid-June)	330-836-5533
Boo at the Zoo (late October)	330-375-2550
Boston Mills Art Festival (late June-early July)	330-657-2334
Cherry Blossom Festival (mid-May)	330-745-3733
Chickenfest (mid-September)	330-753-8471
Christmas Craft Show (early-mid-December)	330-972-7570
Civil War Reenactment (mid-August)	330-666-3711
Crooked River Fine Arts Festival (late July-early August)	330-971-8137
First Night Akron (December 31)	330-762-9550
Harvest Festival (early October)	330-666-3711
Holiday Lights Celebration (December)	330-375-2550
Holiday Tree Festival (late November)	330-379-8424
Home for the Holidays (December)	330-836-5533
Jazz Festival (mid-June)	330-657-2291
Labor of Love Run (early September)	330-688-9078
Maple Sugaring Days (late February-mid-March)	330-666-3711
May Garden Mart (mid-May)	330-836-5533
Mum Festival (late September)	330-745-3141
Music in the Valley Festival (early July)	330-666-3711
NEC Invitational (August)	330-644-2299
Peninsula Jazz Festival (early April)	330-657-2665
Pro Football Hall of Fame Week (early August)	330-456-8207
Shakespeare at Stan Hywet Hall (mid-July)	330-836-5533
Stitchery Showcase (late March)	330-836-5533
Summit County Fair (late July)	330-633-6200
Twinsburg Twins Days Festival (early August)	330-425-3652
Victorian Holiday Tour (December)	330-972-6909
Witan's Annual French Market (late February)	330-928-7179
Wonderful World of Ohio Mart (early October)	330-836-5533
Yankee Peddler Festival (mid-late September)	800-535-5634

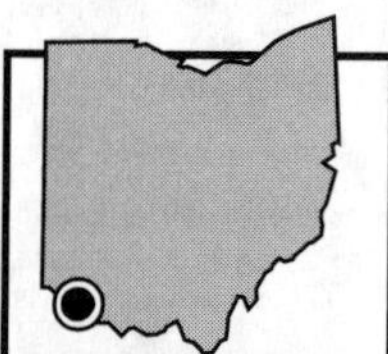

Cincinnati

The riverfront city of Cincinnati serves as the home port of the only remaining overnight paddlewheel boats, and its 'Majestic' is one of the last floating theaters in existence today. Cincinnati's Coliseum and Stadium also occupy the riverfront area. Outdoor attractions in Cincinnati include Sharon Woods Village, an outdoor museum of restored 19th-century buildings, and Mount Airy Forest. The Forest's Garden of the States contains plant life from each of the 50 states. The Roebling Suspension Bridge on the Ohio river (built by John A. Roebling, who later built the Brooklyn Bridge) connects Cincinnati with Kentucky. Just east of the bridge is Covington, Kentucky, which features antebellum homes. The floating entertainment complex, Covington Landing, is located west of the bridge.

Population	336,400	**Longitude**	84-45-69 W
Area (Land)	77.2 sq mi	**County**	Hamilton
Area (Water)	1.6 sq mi	**Time Zone**	EST
Elevation	683 ft	**Area Code/s**	513
Latitude	39-16-19 N		

— Average Temperatures and Precipitation —

TEMPERATURES

	Jan	Feb	Mar	Apr	May	Jun	Jul	Aug	Sep	Oct	Nov	Dec
High	37	42	54	65	75	83	86	85	79	67	54	42
Low	22	25	34	44	54	62	66	64	58	46	37	27

PRECIPITATION

	Jan	Feb	Mar	Apr	May	Jun	Jul	Aug	Sep	Oct	Nov	Dec
Inches	2.6	2.6	4.2	3.8	4.6	3.5	4.0	3.5	3.0	2.9	3.5	3.1

— Important Phone Numbers —

	Phone		Phone
AAA	513-762-3111	**Medical Referral**	513-475-8701
American Express Travel	513-241-1300	**Poison Control Center**	513-558-5111
Dental Referral	800-374-5553	**Time/Temp**	513-721-1700
Dial-the-Arts	513-621-4744	**Travelers Aid**	513-762-5660
Emergency	911	**Visitor Information Line**	800-246-2987
HotelDocs	800-468-3537	**Weather**	513-241-1010

— Information Sources —

				Phone	Fax
Albert B Sabin Cincinnati Convention Center 525 Elm St. *Web:* www.cincycenter.com	Cincinnati	OH	45202	513-352-3750	352-6226
Better Business Bureau Serving Southern Ohio Northern Kentucky & Southeastern Indiana 898 Walnut St 4th Fl. *Web:* www.cincinnati.bbb.org	Cincinnati	OH	45202	513-421-3015	621-0907
Cincinnati & Hamilton County Public Library 800 Vine St *Web:* plch.lib.oh.us	Cincinnati	OH	45202	513-369-6900	369-3123
Cincinnati City Hall 801 Plum St *Web:* www.ci.cincinnati.oh.us	Cincinnati	OH	45202	513-352-3000	352-6284
Cincinnati Economic Development Dept 805 Central Ave 2 Centennial Plaza Suite 710 *Web:* www.cincinnatigov.com/aboutDED/index.html	Cincinnati	OH	45202	513-352-3485	352-6257
Cincinnati Mayor 801 Plum St Rm 150 *E-mail:* roxanne.qualls@cincncl.rcc.org	Cincinnati	OH	45202	513-352-3250	352-5201
Greater Cincinnati Chamber of Commerce 441 Vine St Carew Tower Suite 300 *Web:* www.gccc.com ■ *E-mail:* info@gccc.com	Cincinnati	OH	45202	513-579-3100	579-3102
Greater Cincinnati Convention & Visitors Bureau 300 W 6th St *TF:* 800-246-2987 ■ *Web:* www.cincyusa.com ■ *E-mail:* info@cincyusa.com	Cincinnati	OH	45202	513-621-2142	621-5020
Hamilton County 138 E Court St.	Cincinnati	OH	45202	513-946-4400	946-4444
TriState Online PO Box 54067 *Web:* www.tso.org ■ *E-mail:* sshoe@tso.cin.ix.net	Cincinnati	OH	45254	513-579-1990	

On-Line Resources

4Cincinnati.com	www.4cincinnati.com
About.com Guide to Cincinnati	cincinnati.about.com/local/midwestus/cincinnati
Anthill City Guide Cincinnati	www.anthill.com/city.asp?city=cincinnati
Area Guide Cincinnati	cincinnati.areaguides.net
Best of Cincinnati	www.cinci.com/
Boulevards Cincinnati	www.boulevards.com/cities/cincinnati.html
CinciNet	www.cincinet.com
Cincinnati Atlas Online Guide	www.cincinnatlas.com/
Cincinnati CityBeat	www.citybeat.com
Cincinnati CityLink	www.usacitylink.com/citylink/cincinnati
Cincinnati Home Page	www.cincy.com
Cincinnati.com	www.cincinnati.com
City Knowledge Cincinnati	www.cityknowledge.com/oh_cincinnati.htm
CitySearch Cincinnati	cincinnati.citysearch.com
DigitalCity Cincinnati	home.digitalcity.com/cincinnati
Excite.com Cincinnati City Guide	www.excite.com/travel/countries/united_states/ohio/cincinnati
Insiders' Guide to Greater Cincinnati	www.insiders.com/cincinnati/
NITC Travelbase City Guide Cincinnati	www.travelbase.com/auto/guides/cincinnati-area-oh.html
Rough Guide Travel Cincinnati	travel.roughguides.com/content/476/

— Transportation Services —

AIRPORTS

	Phone
■ **Cincinnati-Northern Kentucky International Airport (CVG)** 13 miles SW of downtown (approx 15 minutes)	606-767-3151

Airport Transportation

	Phone
Community Cab Service $22 fare to downtown	606-727-2900
Yellow Cab $22-25 fare to downtown	513-241-2100

Commercial Airlines

	Phone		Phone
AirTran	800-247-8726	**TWA**	800-221-2000
American	800-433-7300	**United**	800-241-6522
Continental	800-525-0280	**US Airways Express**	800-428-4322
Delta	513-721-7000	**Vanguard**	800-826-4827
Northwest	800-225-2525		

Charter Airlines

	Phone		Phone
Comair Jet Express	606-767-3500	**Sunbird Air Services**	937-322-2711
Executive Jet	513-871-2004		

CAR RENTALS

	Phone		Phone
Alamo	606-746-6400	**Enterprise**	606-371-2330
Avis	606-767-3773	**Hertz**	606-767-3535
Budget	606-283-1166	**National**	606-767-3655
Dollar	606-767-3607	**Thrifty**	606-689-5200

LIMO/TAXI

	Phone		Phone
Air Marvin's Limousine Service	513-369-0065	**Towne Taxi**	513-531-7500
Around the Clock Taxi Cabs	513-542-1450	**Veterans Cabs**	513-531-9300
Carey Limousine	513-531-7321	**Washington Limo**	513-221-0074
Clifton Cab	513-471-2222	**Yellow Cab**	513-241-2100
Skyline Taxi	513-251-7733		

MASS TRANSIT

	Phone
Queen City Metro $.80 Base fare	513-621-4455

Cincinnati (Cont'd)

RAIL/BUS

Phone

Cincinnati Amtrak Station 1301 Western Ave. ... Cincinnati OH 45203 800-872-7245
Greyhound/Trailways Bus Station 1005 Gilbert Ave ... Cincinnati OH 45202 513-352-6012
TF: 800-231-2222

— Accommodations —

HOTEL RESERVATION SERVICES

Phone

Cincinnati Reservations System ... 800-246-2987

HOTELS, MOTELS, RESORTS

Phone Fax

AmeriSuites Blue Ash
11435 Reed Hartman Hwy ... Cincinnati OH 45241 513-489-3666 489-4187
TF: 800-833-1516
AmeriSuites Forest Park
12001 Chase Plaza Dr ... Cincinnati OH 45240 513-825-9035 825-9185
TF: 800-833-1516
Best Western Mariemont Inn
6880 Wooster Pike ... Cincinnati OH 45227 513-271-2100 271-1057
TF: 800-528-1234
Cincinnati Radisson 11320 Chester Rd ... Cincinnati OH 45246 513-772-1720 772-6466
TF: 800-333-3333
Cincinnatian Hotel 601 Vine St. ... Cincinnati OH 45202 513-381-3000 651-0256
TF: 800-942-9000 ■ *Web:* cincinnatianhotel.com
■ *E-mail:* info@cincinnatianhotel.com
Comfort Inn 9011 Fields Ertel Rd ... Cincinnati OH 45249 513-683-9700 683-1284
TF: 800-228-5150
Comfort Inn & Suites 11440 Chester Rd ... Cincinnati OH 45246 513-771-3400 771-3114
TF: 800-228-5150
Crowne Plaza Hotel 15 W 6th St ... Cincinnati OH 45202 513-381-4000 381-5158
TF: 888-279-8260
Days Inn East 4056 Mt Carmel-Tabasco Rd ... Cincinnati OH 45255 513-528-3800 528-5192
TF: 800-451-6009
Doubletree Guest Suites
6300 E Kemper Rd ... Cincinnati OH 45241 513-489-3636 489-8231
TF: 800-222-8733
■ *Web:* www.doubletreehotels.com/DoubleT/Hotel61/72/72Main.htm
Drawbridge Estate Cincinnati
2477 Royal Dr ... Fort Mitchell KY 41017 606-341-2800 341-5644
TF: 800-354-9793
Embassy Suites Hotel Cincinnati Northeast
4554 Lake Forest Dr ... Cincinnati OH 45242 513-733-8900 733-3720
TF: 800-362-2779
Garfield Suites Hotel 2 Garfield Pl ... Cincinnati OH 45202 513-421-3355 421-3729
TF: 800-367-2155
Hampshire House Hotel & Conference Center
30 Tri-County Pkwy ... Cincinnati OH 45246 513-772-5440 772-1611
TF: 800-543-4211
Hilton Commonwealth 7373 Turfway Rd ... Florence KY 41042 606-371-4400 371-3361
TF: 800-445-8667 ■ *Web:* www.hilton.com/hotels/CVGCHHF
Holiday Inn 3855 Hauck Rd ... Cincinnati OH 45241 513-563-8330 563-9679
TF: 800-465-4329
■ *Web:* www.basshotels.com/holiday-inn/?_franchisee=CVGHV
■ *E-mail:* hi275@one.net
Holiday Inn Cincinnati Airport
1717 Airport Exchange Blvd ... Erlanger KY 41018 606-371-2233 371-5002
TF: 800-465-4329
■ *Web:* www.basshotels.com/holiday-inn/?_franchisee=CVGAP
■ *E-mail:* cvgap@internetmci.com
Holiday Inn Downtown 800 W 8th St ... Cincinnati OH 45203 513-241-8660 241-9057
TF: 800-465-4329
Holiday Inn Eastgate Conference Center
4501 Eastgate Blvd ... Cincinnati OH 45245 513-752-4400 753-3178
TF: 800-465-4329
Holiday Inn Express 5589 Kings Mills Rd ... Kings Island OH 45034 513-398-8075 459-1043
TF: 800-227-7100
Howard Johnson North 400 Glensprings Dr ... Cincinnati OH 45246 513-825-3129 825-0467
TF: 800-446-4656
Hyatt Regency Cincinnati 151 W 5th St ... Cincinnati OH 45202 513-579-1234 579-0107
TF: 800-233-1234
■ *Web:* www.hyatt.com/usa/cincinnati/hotels/hotel_cinci.html
Imperial House West 5510 Rybolt Rd ... Cincinnati OH 45248 513-574-6000 574-6566
TF: 800-543-3018
Omni Netherland Plaza 35 W 5th St ... Cincinnati OH 45202 513-421-9100 421-4291
TF: 800-843-6664

Phone Fax

Preston Hotel 2235 Sharon Rd ... Cincinnati OH 45241 513-771-0700 772-0933
TF: 800-308-3663
Quality Inn 1717 Glendale-Milford Rd ... Cincinnati OH 45215 513-771-5252 771-6569
TF: 800-228-5151
Radisson Inn Airport
Cincinnati-Northern Kentucky
International Airport ... Hebron KY 41048 606-371-6166 371-9863
TF: 800-333-3333
Ramada Hotel Central 7965 Reading Rd ... Cincinnati OH 45237 513-821-5110 821-4972
TF: 800-582-7121
Regal Hotel 150 W 5th St ... Cincinnati OH 45202 513-352-2100 352-2148
TF: 800-222-8888
Residence Inn by Marriott
11689 Chester Rd ... Cincinnati OH 45246 513-771-2525 771-3444
TF: 800-331-3131 ■ *Web:* www.residenceinn.com/residenceinn/CVGNN
Sheraton Four Points Hotel
8020 Montgomery Rd ... Cincinnati OH 45236 513-793-4300 793-1413
TF: 800-325-3535
Signature Inn Northeast
8870 Governor's Hill Dr ... Cincinnati OH 45249 513-683-3086 683-3086
TF: 800-822-5252
■ *Web:* www.signature-inns.com/locations/cincinn_ne
■ *E-mail:* feedback@signature-inns.com
Vernon Manor Hotel 400 Oak St ... Cincinnati OH 45219 513-281-3300 281-8933
TF: 800-543-3999
Victoria Inn of Hyde Park 3567 Shaw Ave ... Cincinnati OH 45208 513-321-3567 533-2944
TF: 888-422-4629
Westin Hotel 21 E 5th St ... Cincinnati OH 45202 513-621-7700 852-5670
TF: 800-937-8461
Woodfield Suites 11029 Dowlin Dr ... Sharonville OH 45241 513-771-0300 771-6411
TF: 800-338-0008 ■ *Web:* www.woodfieldsuites.com

— Restaurants —

Phone

Albee The (Mediterranean) 21 E 5th St ... Cincinnati OH 45210 513-621-7700
Ambar (Indian) 350 Ludlow Ave ... Cincinnati OH 45220 513-281-7000
Arloi Dee Restaurant (Thai) 18 E 7th St ... Cincinnati OH 45202 513-421-1304
Barrelhouse Brewing Co (American) 22 E 12th St ... Cincinnati OH 45210 513-421-2337
Boca (New American) 4034 Hamilton Ave ... Cincinnati OH 45223 513-542-2022
Burbank's Real Barbecue (Barbecue) 11167 Dowlin Dr ... Cincinnati OH 45241 513-771-1440
Café Cin-Cin (New American)
25 W 6th St Crowne Plaza Hotel ... Cincinnati OH 45202 513-621-1973
Campanello's Restaurant (Italian) 414 Central Ave ... Cincinnati OH 45202 513-721-9833
Celestial Restaurant (Continental) 1071 Celestial St ... Cincinnati OH 45202 513-241-4455
Chester's Road House (American) 9678 Montgomery Rd ... Cincinnati OH 45241 513-793-8700
Coach & Four Restaurant (New American) 214 Scott St. ... Covington KY 41011 606-431-6700
Dee Felice Cafe (Cajun) 529 Main St ... Covington KY 41011 606-261-2365
Elm Street Grill (American) 150 W 5th St ... Cincinnati OH 45202 513-352-2188
Findlay's (American) 151 W 5th St ... Cincinnati OH 45202 513-579-1234
First Watch (American) 700 Walnut St ... Cincinnati OH 45202 513-721-4744
Golden Lamb (American) 27 S Broadway St ... Lebanon OH 45036 513-932-5065
Grand Finale (Continental) 3 E Sharon Ave ... Cincinnati OH 45246 513-771-5925
House of Hunan (Chinese) 35 E 7th St ... Cincinnati OH 45202 513-721-3600
La Normandie Grill (Steak) 114 E 6th St ... Cincinnati OH 45202 513-721-2761
Le Boxx Cafe (American) 819 Vine St ... Cincinnati OH 45202 513-721-5638
Main Street Brewery (American) 1203 Main St ... Cincinnati OH 45210 513-665-4677
Maisonette (French) 114 E 6th St ... Cincinnati OH 45202 513-721-2260
Mike Fink (Steak/Seafood) Foot of Greenup St ... Covington KY 41011 606-261-4212
Montgomery Inn Boathouse (Barbecue) 925 Eastern Ave ... Cincinnati OH 45202 513-721-7427
Montgomery Inn (Barbecue) 9440 Montgomery Rd ... Cincinnati OH 45242 513-791-3482
Web: www.montgomeryinn.com
Pacific Moon (Pan-Asian) 8300 Market Place Ln ... Cincinnati OH 45242 513-891-0091
Palace The (American) 601 Vine St ... Cincinnati OH 45202 513-381-6006
Petersens Restaurant (American) 1111 Saint Gregory St ... Cincinnati OH 45202 513-651-4777
Plaza 600 (American) 6th & Walnut Sts ... Cincinnati OH 45202 513-721-8600
Precinct The (Steak) 311 Delta Ave ... Cincinnati OH 45226 513-321-5454
Primavista (Italian) 810 Matson Pl ... Cincinnati OH 45204 513-251-6467
Restaurant at the Phoenix (American) 812 Race St ... Cincinnati OH 45202 513-721-8901
Riverview Revolving Restaurant (American)
668 W 5th St ... Covington KY 41011 606-491-1200
Seafood 32 (Seafood) 150 W 5th St ... Cincinnati OH 45202 513-352-2160
Sturkey's (New American) 400 Wyoming Ave ... Cincinnati OH 45215 513-821-9200
Waldo's Cafe (American) 127 W 4th St ... Cincinnati OH 45202 513-651-2233
Waterfront The (Steak/Seafood) 14 Pete Rose Pier ... Covington KY 41011 606-581-1414

— Goods and Services —

SHOPPING

Phone

Convention Place Mall 435 Elm St ... Cincinnati OH 45202 513-421-2089

Cincinnati — Shopping (Cont'd)

Name / Address	City	State	ZIP	Phone	Fax
Eastgate Mall 4601 Eastgate Blvd	Cincinnati	OH	45245	513-752-2290	752-2499
Forest Fair Mall 1047 Forest Fair Dr	Cincinnati	OH	45240	513-671-2929	
Kenwood Towne Center 7875 Montgomery Rd	Cincinnati	OH	45236	513-745-9100	745-9974
Merchants on Main Street Over-the-Rhine Main betw Central Pkwy & Liberty St	Cincinnati	OH	45210	513-241-2690	
Northgate Mall 9501 Colerain Ave	Cincinnati	OH	45251	513-385-5600	385-5603
Saks Fifth Avenue 5th & Race Sts	Cincinnati	OH	45202	513-421-6800	421-6416
Tower Place Mall 28 W 4th St	Cincinnati	OH	45202	513-241-7700	241-7770
Tri-County Mall 11700 Princeton Pike	Cincinnati	OH	45246	513-671-0120	671-2931

BANKS

Name / Address	City	State	ZIP	Phone	Fax
Bank One Cincinnati NA 8044 Montgomery Rd Bank One Towers *TF Cust Svc:* 800-310-1111*	Cincinnati	OH	45236	513-985-5566	985-5703
BenchMark Federal Savings Bank 101 W Central Pkwy	Cincinnati	OH	45202	513-241-0242	684-1044
Centennial Savings Bank 4221 Glenway Ave	Cincinnati	OH	45205	513-921-5505	921-8254
Fifth Third Bank 38 Fountain Sq Plaza **Fax:* Mktg ■ *Web:* www.53.com	Cincinnati	OH	45263	513-579-5300	762-7577*
PNC Bank Ohio NA 201 E 5th St	Cincinnati	OH	45202	513-651-8032	651-8050
Provident Bank 1 E 4th St	Cincinnati	OH	45202	513-579-2036	345-7216
Star Bank NA 425 Walnut St	Cincinnati	OH	45202	513-632-4000	632-5512

BUSINESS SERVICES

Name	Phone	Name	Phone
Action Labor	513-421-5150	**Kinko's**	513-241-3366
CBS Temporary Services	513-651-3600	**Manpower Temporary Services**	513-621-7250
Cincinnati Express	513-721-1900	**Olsten Staffing Services**	513-621-1177
City Dash Delivery Service	513-562-2000	**Post Office**	513-684-5548
Executive Choice	513-489-8883	**Priority Dispatch**	513-791-1300
Federal Express	800-463-3339	**Rapid Delivery Service**	513-733-0500
Kelly Services	513-241-3161	**UPS**	800-742-5877

— Media —

PUBLICATIONS

Name / Address	City	State	ZIP	Phone	Fax
Cincinnati Business Courier 35 E 7th St Suite 700 *Web:* www.amcity.com/cincinnati	Cincinnati	OH	45202	513-621-6665	621-2462
Cincinnati Enquirer‡ 312 Elm St *Web:* enquirer.com	Cincinnati	OH	45202	513-721-2700	768-8340
Cincinnati Magazine 705 Central Ave 1 Centennial Plaza Suite 370 *TF:* 800-837-4800	Cincinnati	OH	45202	513-421-4300	562-2746
Cincinnati Post‡ 125 E Court St *Web:* www.cincypost.com	Cincinnati	OH	45202	513-352-2000	621-3962
Hilltop News-Press 5556 Cheviot Rd **Fax:* News Rm	Cincinnati	OH	45247	513-923-3111	923-1806*
Northwest Press 5556 Cheviot Rd **Fax:* News Rm	Cincinnati	OH	45247	513-923-3111	923-1806*

‡Daily newspapers

TELEVISION

Name / Address	City	State	ZIP	Phone	Fax
WCET-TV Ch 48 (PBS) 1223 Central Pkwy *Web:* www.wcet.org ■ *E-mail:* comments_wcet@wcet.pbs.org	Cincinnati	OH	45214	513-381-4033	381-7520
WCPO-TV Ch 9 (ABC) 500 Central Ave *Web:* www.wcpo.com	Cincinnati	OH	45202	513-721-9900	721-7717
WKRC-TV Ch 12 (CBS) 1906 Highland Ave *Web:* www.wkrc.com	Cincinnati	OH	45219	513-763-5500	421-3820
WLWT-TV Ch 5 (NBC) 140 W 9th St *Web:* www.wlwt.com ■ *E-mail:* mail@wlwt.com	Cincinnati	OH	45202	513-352-5000	352-5073
WSTR-TV Ch 64 (WB) 5177 Fishwick Dr	Cincinnati	OH	45216	513-641 4400	242-2633
WXIX-TV Ch 19 (Fox) 635 W 7th St	Cincinnati	OH	45203	513-421-1919	421-3022

RADIO

Name / Address	City	State	ZIP	Phone	Fax
WAKW-FM 93.3 MHz (Rel) 6275 Collegevue Dr *Web:* www.wakw.com ■ *E-mail:* wakw@eos.net	Cincinnati	OH	45224	513-542-3442	542-9333
WBOB-AM 1160 kHz (Sports) 625 Eden Park Dr Suite 1050 *TF:* 800-561-1160 ■ *Web:* www.1160bob.com	Cincinnati	OH	45202	513-721-1050	562-3060
WCIN-AM 1480 kHz (Oldies) 3540 Reading Rd	Cincinnati	OH	45229	513-281-7180	281-6125
WEBN-FM 102.7 MHz (Rock) 1111 Saint Gregory St *TF:* 800-616-9236 ■ *Web:* www.webn.com ■ *E-mail:* webn@one.net	Cincinnati	OH	45202	513-621-9326	749-3299
WGRR-FM 103.5 MHz (Oldies) 3656 Edwards Rd *Web:* www.wgrr1035.com	Cincinnati	OH	45208	513-321-8900	321-1175
WGUC-FM 90.9 MHz (Clas) 1223 Central Pkwy *Web:* www.wguc.org	Cincinnati	OH	45214	513-241-8282	241-8456
WIZF-FM 100.9 MHz (Urban) 1821 Summit Rd	Cincinnati	OH	45237	513-679-6000	679-6011
WKFS-FM 107.1 MHz (Alt) 1111 Saint Gregory St	Cincinnati	OH	45202	513-621-9326	749-7444
WKRC-AM 550 kHz (N/T) 1111 Saint Gregory St *Web:* www.55krc.com	Cincinnati	OH	45202	513-241-1550	651-2555
WKRQ-FM 101.9 MHz (CHR) 1906 Highland Ave	Cincinnati	OH	45219	513-763-5686	763-5676
WLW-AM 700 kHz (N/T) 1111 Saint Gregory St	Cincinnati	OH	45202	513-241-9597	665-9700
WOFX-FM 92.5 MHz (CR) 1111 Saint Gregory St **Fax:* Sales	Cincinnati	OH	45202	513-621-9326	784-1249*
WRRM-FM 98.5 MHz (AC) 895 Central Ave Suite 900	Cincinnati	OH	45202	513-241-9898	241-6689
WSAI-AM 1530 kHz (Nost) 1111 Saint Gregory St	Cincinnati	OH	45202	513-421-9724	241-0358
WUBE-AM 1230 kHz (Sports) 625 Eden Park Dr Suite 1050 *TF:* 800-561-1160	Cincinnati	OH	45202	513-721-1050	621-2105
WUBE-FM 105.1 MHz (Ctry) 625 Eden Park Dr Suite 1050 **Fax:* Sales	Cincinnati	OH	45202	513-721-1050	621-2105*
WVAE-FM 94.9 MHz (NAC) 895 Central Ave Suite 900	Cincinnati	OH	45202	513-241-9500	241-6689
WVMX-FM 94.1 MHz (AC) 1906 Highland Ave	Cincinnati	OH	45219	513-763-6499	749-6499
WVXU-FM 91.7 MHz (NPR) 3800 Victory Pkwy *Web:* www.xstarnet.com ■ *E-mail:* wvxu@xstarnet.com	Cincinnati	OH	45207	513-731-9898	745-3483
WYGY-FM 96.5 MHz (Ctry) 625 Eden Park Dr Suite 1050	Cincinnati	OH	45202	513-721-1050	721-9949

— Colleges/Universities —

Name / Address	City	State	ZIP	Phone	Fax
Antonelli College 124 E 7th St	Cincinnati	OH	45202	513-241-4338	241-9396
Art Academy of Cincinnati 1125 Saint Gregory St *TF:* 800-323-5692 ■ *Web:* www.artacademy.edu	Cincinnati	OH	45202	513-721-5205	562-8778
Athenaeum of Ohio 6616 Beechmont Ave *Web:* www.mtsm.org ■ *E-mail:* ath@mtsm.org	Cincinnati	OH	45230	513-231-2223	231-3254
Cincinnati Bible College & Seminary 2700 Glenway Ave *TF:* 800-949-4222 ■ *Web:* www.cincybible.edu	Cincinnati	OH	45204	513-244-8100	244-8140
Cincinnati State Technical & Community College 3520 Central Pkwy *Web:* www.cinstate.cc.oh.us/	Cincinnati	OH	45223	513-569-1500	569-1562
Clermont College 4200 Clermont College Dr *Web:* www.clc.uc.edu/	Batavia	OH	45103	513-732-5200	732-5303
College of Mount Saint Joseph 5701 Delhi Rd *Web:* www.msj.edu ■ *E-mail:* mountweb@mail.msj.edu	Cincinnati	OH	45233	513-244-4200	244-4629
Miami University 500 E High St *Web:* www.muohio.edu ■ *E-mail:* admission@muohio.edu	Oxford	OH	45056	513-529-1809	529-1550
Miami University Hamilton Campus 1601 Peck Blvd *Web:* www.ham.muohio.edu ■ *E-mail:* helpdesk@ham.muohio.edu	Hamilton	OH	45011	513-785-3000	785-3145
Northern Kentucky University Nunn Dr *TF:* 800-637-9948 ■ *Web:* www.nku.edu ■ *E-mail:* admitnku@nku.edu	Highland Heights	KY	41099	606-572-5100	572-5566
Raymond Walters College 9555 Plainfield Rd *Web:* www.rwc.uc.edu	Cincinnati	OH	45236	513-745-5600	745-5768

Cincinnati — Colleges/Universities (Cont'd)

Name / Address	City	State	Zip	Phone	Fax
Southern Ohio College 1011 Glendale Milford Rd	Cincinnati	OH	45215	513-771-2424	771-3413
TF: 800-888-1445					
Southwestern College of Business Cincinnati 9910 Princeton-Glendale Rd	Cincinnati	OH	45246	513-874-0432	874-0123
The Union Institute 440 E McMillan St	Cincinnati	OH	45206	513-861-6400	861-0779
TF: 800-486-3116 ■ *Web:* www.tui.edu					
Thomas More College 333 Thomas More Pkwy	Crestview Hills	KY	41017	606-341-5800	344-3345
TF Admissions: 800-825-4557 ■ *Web:* www.thomasmore.edu					
University of Cincinnati PO Box 210091	Cincinnati	OH	45221	513-556-6000	556-1105
Web: www.uc.edu ■ *E-mail:* uc.web.general@uc.edu					
Xavier University 3800 Victory Pkwy	Cincinnati	OH	45207	513-745-3000	745-4319
TF: 800-344-4698 ■ *Web:* www.xu.edu					

— Hospitals —

Name / Address	City	State	Zip	Phone	Fax
Bethesda North Hospital 10500 Montgomery Rd	Cincinnati	OH	45242	513-745-1111	745-1441
Bethesda Oak Hospital 619 Oak St	Cincinnati	OH	45206	513-569-6111	569-4065
Children's Hospital Medical Center 3333 Burnet Ave	Cincinnati	OH	45229	513-636-4200	636-3733
Web: www.cincinnatichildrens.org					
Christ Hospital 2139 Auburn Ave	Cincinnati	OH	45219	513-585-2000	585-3200
TF: 800-527-8919					
Clermont Mercy Hospital 3000 Hospital Dr	Batavia	OH	45103	513-732-8200	732-8537
Deaconess Hospital 311 Straight St	Cincinnati	OH	45219	513-559-2100	475-5251
Fort Hamilton Hospital 630 Eaton Ave	Hamilton	OH	45013	513-867-2000	867-2620
Franciscan Hospital Mount Airy Campus 2446 Kipling Ave	Cincinnati	OH	45239	513-853-5000	853-5910
Franciscan Hospital Western Hills Campus 3131 Queen City Ave	Cincinnati	OH	45238	513-389-5000	389-5469
Good Samaritan Hospital 375 Dixmyth Ave	Cincinnati	OH	45220	513-872-1400	872-3435
Jewish Hospital 4777 E Galbraith Rd	Cincinnati	OH	45236	513-686-3000	686-3003
Mercy Hospital Anderson 7500 State Rd	Cincinnati	OH	45255	513-624-4500	624-4015*
**Fax:* Admitting					
Mercy Hospital Hamilton PO Box 418	Hamilton	OH	45012	513-867-6400	867-6521*
**Fax:* Admitting					
Middletown Regional Hospital 105 McKnight Dr	Middletown	OH	45044	513-424-2111	420-5688*
**Fax:* Admitting ■ *TF:* 800-338-4057					
University of Cincinnati Hospital 234 Goodman St	Cincinnati	OH	45219	513-584-1000	584-3755
Veterans Affairs Medical Center 3200 Vine St	Cincinnati	OH	45220	513-861-3100	475-6464

— Attractions —

Name / Address	City	State	Zip	Phone	Fax
Aronoff Center for the Arts 650 Walnut St	Cincinnati	OH	45202	513-721-3344	977-4150
Web: www.cincinnatiarts.org					
Arts Consortium 1515 Linn St	Cincinnati	OH	45214	513-381-0645	345-3743
Ault Park 3540 Principio at Observatory Ave	Cincinnati	OH	45208	513-321-8439	
Children's Museum of Cincinnati 1301 Western Ave	Cincinnati	OH	45203	513-287-7000	287-7079
TF: 800-733-2077 ■ *Web:* www.cincymuseum.org/cm.htm					
Cincinnati Art Museum 953 Eden Park Dr	Cincinnati	OH	45202	513-721-5204	721-0129
Web: www.cincinnatiartmuseum.com ■ *E-mail:* cincyart@fuse.net					
Cincinnati Ballet 1555 Central Pkwy	Cincinnati	OH	45214	513-621-5219	621-4844
Web: www.cincinnatiballet.com					
Cincinnati Chamber Orchestra 1225 Elm St Memorial Hall	Cincinnati	OH	45210	513-723-1182	723-1182
Web: www.cincinnati.com/cco/Welcome.html					
Cincinnati Fire Museum 315 W Court St	Cincinnati	OH	45202	513-621-5571	621-5571
Web: www.cincinet.com/firemuseum/					
Cincinnati Historical Museum 1301 Western Ave Museum Ctr	Cincinnati	OH	45203	513-287-7020	287-7029
TF: 800-733-2077 ■ *Web:* www.cincymuseum.org/chm.htm					
Cincinnati Museum Center 1301 Western Ave	Cincinnati	OH	45203	513-287-7000	287-7029
TF: 800-733-2077 ■ *Web:* www.cincymuseum.org					
Cincinnati Museum of Natural History & Science 1301 Western Ave Museum Ctr	Cincinnati	OH	45203	513-287-7000	287-7029
TF: 800-733-2077 ■ *Web:* www.cincymuseum.org/mnhs.htm ■ *E-mail:* mnhs@fuse.net					
Cincinnati Music Hall 1243 Elm St	Cincinnati	OH	45210	513-621-1919	744-3345
Web: www.cincinnatiarts.org					
Cincinnati Opera 1241 Elm St Music Hall	Cincinnati	OH	45210	513-241-2742	621-4310
Cincinnati Playhouse in the Park 962 Mt Adams Cir	Cincinnati	OH	45202	513-421-3888	345-2254
Web: www.cincyplay.com ■ *E-mail:* playhous@one.net					
Cincinnati Pops Orchestra 1241 Elm St Music Hall	Cincinnati	OH	45210	513-381-3300	744-3599
Web: www.cincinnatipops.org					
Cincinnati Symphony Orchestra 1241 Elm St Music Hall	Cincinnati	OH	45210	513-621-1919	744-3535
Web: www.cincinnatisymphony.org					
Cincinnati Zoo & Botanical Garden 3400 Vine St	Cincinnati	OH	45220	513-281-4701	559-7790
Web: www.cincyzoo.org ■ *E-mail:* feedback@cincyzoo.org					
Civic Garden Center of Greater Cincinnati 2715 Reading Rd	Cincinnati	OH	45206	513-221-0981	221-0961
Coney Island 6201 Kellogg Ave	Cincinnati	OH	45228	513-232-8230	231-1352
Web: www.coneyislandpark.com					
Contemporary Arts Center 115 E 5th St	Cincinnati	OH	45202	513-721-0390	721-7418
Web: www.spiral.org/					
Contemporary Dance Theatre 1805 Larch Ave	Cincinnati	OH	45224	513-591-1222	591-1222
Downtown Theatre Classics 4 W 4th St Herschede Bldg	Cincinnati	OH	45202	513-621-3822	291-0023
Eden Park Gilbert Ave betw Morris & Elsinore Pl	Cincinnati	OH	45202	513-352-4080	
Emery Theater 1112 Walnut St	Cincinnati	OH	45210	513-721-2741	
Ensemble Theatre of Cincinnati 1127 Vine St	Cincinnati	OH	45210	513-421-3555	562-4104
Fifth Third Bank Broadway Series 650 Walnut St Arnoff Ctr	Cincinnati	OH	45202	513-241-2345	
Findlay Market Elm & Elder Sts	Cincinnati	OH	45202	513-352-6364	352-4839
Fountain Square 5th & Walnut Sts	Cincinnati	OH	45216		
Harriet Beecher Stowe House 2950 Gilbert Ave	Cincinnati	OH	45206	513-632-5120	632-5114
Web: www.ohiohistory.org/places/stowe					
Hudepohl-Schoenling Brewing Co 1599 Central Pkwy	Cincinnati	OH	45214	513-241-4344	357-5217
Web: www.cincys-brewery.com					
Krohn Conservatory 1501 Eden Park Dr	Cincinnati	OH	45202	513-421-5707	421-6007
Lindner Robert D Family Omnimax Theater 1301 Western Ave Museum Ctr	Cincinnati	OH	45203	513-287-7081	287-7002
TF: 800-733-2077 ■ *Web:* www.cincymuseum.org/omni.htm					
Linton Music Series 1223 Central Pkwy	Cincinnati	OH	45214	513-381-6868	241-8456
Meier's Wine Cellars Inc 6955 Plainfield Rd	Silverton	OH	45236	513-891-2900	891-6370
TF: 800-346-2941					
Mount Airy Forest Colerain Ave & W Fork Rd	Cincinnati	OH	45223	513-541-0827	
Mount Airy Forest & Arboretum 5083 Colerain Ave	Cincinnati	OH	45202	513-541-8176	
Old Saint Mary's National Historic Site 123 E 13th St	Cincinnati	OH	45210	513-721-2988	
Paramount's Kings Island PO Box 901	Kings Island	OH	45034	513-754-5700	754-5725
TF: 800-288-0808 ■ *Web:* www.pki.com					
Riverbend Music Center 6295 Kellogg Ave	Cincinnati	OH	45230	513-232-5882	232-7577
Sharon Woods Village 11450 Lebanon Pike	Cincinnati	OH	45241	513-563-9484	563-0914
Taft Museum 316 Pike St	Cincinnati	OH	45202	513-241-0343	241-7762
Web: www.taftmuseum.org					
Taft Theatre 5th & Sycamore Sts	Cincinnati	OH	45202	513-721-8883	721-2864
Web: www.taftevents.com					
William Howard Taft National Historic Site 2038 Auburn Ave	Cincinnati	OH	45219	513-684-3262	684-3627
Web: www.nps.gov/wiho/					

SPORTS TEAMS & FACILITIES

Name / Address	City	State	Zip	Phone	Fax
Cincinnati Bengals 1 Bengals Dr	Cincinnati	OH	45204	513-621-3550	621-3570
Web: www.nfl.com/bengals					
Cincinnati Cyclones (hockey) 100 Broadway	Cincinnati	OH	45202	513-421-7825	421-1210
Web: www.cyclones.fuse.net					
Cincinnati Gardens 2250 Seymour Ave	Cincinnati	OH	45212	513-631-7793	631-2666
Cincinnati Reds Pete Rose Way Cinergy Field	Cincinnati	OH	45202	513-421-4510	
Web: www.cincinnatireds.com					
Cincinnati Riverhawks (soccer) 1018 Town Dr Town & Country Sports Complex	Wilder	KY	41076	513-942-7627	784-0909
Web: www.riverhawks.com ■ *E-mail:* hawks@riverhawks.com					
Cinergy Field 100 Cinergy Field	Cincinnati	OH	45202	513-421-4510	421-7342
River Downs Racetrack 6301 Kellogg Ave	Cincinnati	OH	45230	513-232-8000	232-1412
Turfway Park Racecourse 7500 Turfway Rd	Florence	KY	41042	606-371-0200	647-4730
TF: 800-733-0200 ■ *Web:* www.turfway.com ■ *E-mail:* turfway@turfway.com					

Cincinnati (Cont'd)

— Events —

Event	Phone
All-American Birthday Party (early July)	513-621-2142
Appalachian Festival (early May)	513-232-8230
Boofest (October)	513-287-7000
Celtic Music & Cultural Festival (early September)	513-533-4822
Cincinnati Auto Expo (mid-February)	513-281-0022
Cincinnati Flower Show (late April)	513-872-5194
Cincinnati Heart Mini-Marathon (late March)	513-281-4048
Cincinnati May Festival (mid-May)	513-621-1919
Cincinnati St Patrick Parade (mid-March)	513-251-2222
Coors Light Festival (mid-July)	513-871-3900
Festival of Lights (late November-early January)	513-281-4700
GalleryFurniture.Com Stakes Horseracing (March)	800-733-0200
Gold Star Chili Fest (early August)	513-579-3191
Hamilton County Fair (early-mid-August)	513-761-4224
Harvest Festival (late September)	513-281-4700
Holiday in Lights (late November-late December)	513-287-7103
Jammin' on Main (early May)	513-621-6994
Kids Fest (early June)	513-621-2142
May Festival (late May)	513-381-3300
Oktoberfest Zinzinnati (mid-September)	513-579-3199
Oldiesfest (mid-late June)	513-321-8900
Riverfest (early September)	513-621-6994
Riverfront Stadium Festival (mid-July)	513-871-3900
Spring Floral Show (mid-March-late April)	513-352-4080
Summerfair (early May)	513-531-0050
Tall Stacks (mid-October)	513-744-8820
Taste of Cincinnati (late May)	513-579-3199
Taste of Findlay Market (late October)	513-241-0464

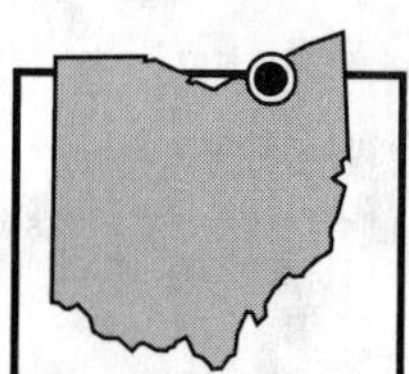

Cleveland

Once known as "The Mistake by the Lake," Cleveland has since developed into a culturally diverse city. The Flats, an area along the Cuyahoga River, is known for its restaurants and nightclubs, while the Inner Harbor area was selected as the site for the new Rock and Roll Hall of Fame. Overlooking The Flats, in Town City Center, is The Avenue, which, along with The Galleria, are the premier shopping venues in the city. Other attractions include the Cleveland Museum of Art, Cleveland Museum of Natural History, and Cleveland Metroparks Zoo. A new baseball park, Jacobs Field, and basketball arena, Gund Arena, were also recently completed. Family amusements not far from Cleveland include Cedar Point amusement park in Sandusky and Sea World in Aurora.

Population	495,817	**Longitude**	81-69-56 W
Area (Land)	77.0 sq mi	**County**	Cuyahoga
Area (Water)	5.1 sq mi	**Time Zone**	EST
Elevation	680 ft	**Area Code/s**	216
Latitude	41-49-94 N		

— Average Temperatures and Precipitation —

TEMPERATURES

	Jan	Feb	Mar	Apr	May	Jun	Jul	Aug	Sep	Oct	Nov	Dec
High	32	35	46	58	69	78	82	81	74	62	50	37
Low	18	19	28	37	47	57	61	60	54	44	35	25

PRECIPITATION

	Jan	Feb	Mar	Apr	May	Jun	Jul	Aug	Sep	Oct	Nov	Dec
Inches	2.0	2.2	2.9	3.1	3.5	3.7	3.5	3.4	3.4	2.5	3.2	3.1

— Important Phone Numbers —

	Phone		Phone
AAA	216-416-1912	**Medical Referral**	216-520-0110
American Express Travel	216-241-4575	**Poison Control Center**	216-231-4455
Dental Referral	216-573-1181	**Road Conditions**	800-394-7623
Emergency	911	**Time**	216-931-1212
HotelDocs	800-468-3537	**Weather**	216-931-1212

— Information Sources —

	City	State	Zip	Phone	Fax
Better Business Bureau Serving Northeast Ohio 2217 E 9th St Suite 200 *Web:* www.cleveland.bbb.org	Cleveland	OH	44115	216-241-7678	861-6365
Cleveland City Hall 601 Lakeside Ave	Cleveland	OH	44114	216-664-2000	664-3837
Cleveland Convention Center 500 Lakeside Ave *TF:* 800-543-2489	Cleveland	OH	44114	216-348-2200	348-2262
Cleveland Economic Development Dept 601 Lakeside Ave Rm 210	Cleveland	OH	44114	216-664-2406	664-3681
Cleveland Free-Net Case Western Reserve University 10900 Euclid Ave *Web:* cnswww.cns.cwru.edu/net/easy/fn/ ■ *E-mail:* xx997@cleveland.freenet.edu	Cleveland	OH	44106	216-368-2982	
Cleveland Mayor 601 Lakeside Ave	Cleveland	OH	44114	216-664-2220	664-2815
Cleveland Public Library 325 Superior Ave E *Web:* www.cpl.org ■ *E-mail:* info@library.cpl.org	Cleveland	OH	44114	216-623-2800	623-7050
Convention & Visitors Bureau of Greater Cleveland 50 Public Sq Tower City Ctr Suite 3100 *TF:* 800-321-1001 ■ *Web:* www.travelcleveland.com/ ■ *E-mail:* cvb@travelcleveland.com	Cleveland	OH	44113	216-621-4110	621-5967
Cuyahoga County 1219 Ontario St.	Cleveland	OH	44114	216-443-7000	
Greater Cleveland Growth Assn 200 Tower City Ctr 50 Public Sq. *TF:* 800-562-7121 ■ *Web:* www.clevelandgrowth.com	Cleveland	OH	44113	216-621-3300	621-6013

On-Line Resources

4Cleveland.com	www.4cleveland.com
About.com Guide to Cleveland	cleveland.about.com/local/midwestus/cleveland
Anthill City Guide Cleveland	www.anthill.com/city.asp?city=cleveland
Area Guide Cleveland	cleveland.areaguides.net
City Knowledge Cleveland	www.cityknowledge.com/oh_cleveland.htm
CitySearch Cleveland	cleveland.citysearch.com
Cleveland	www.clevelandohio.com
Cleveland Central	www.glwc.com/cleveland
Cleveland City Page	cleveland.thelinks.com/
Cleveland Community Information	www.cwru.edu/cleveland.html
Cleveland Free Times	www.freetimes.com
Cleveland Home Page	www.cleveland.oh.us
Cleveland Live	www.cleveland.com/
Cleveland Sites Online	cleveland.sitesonline.com/
Cleveland's Neighborhood Link	little.nhlink.net/nhlink/
Clevescene	www.clevescene.com
DigitalCity Cleveland	home.digitalcity.com/cleveland
Excite.com Cleveland City Guide	www.excite.com/travel/countries/united_states/ohio/cleveland
Flats Net	www.flats.net/
Greater Cleveland Visitors Guide	www.cleve-visitors-guide.com/
NITC Travelbase City Guide Cleveland	www.travelbase.com/auto/guides/cleveland-area-oh.html
Rough Guide Travel Cleveland	travel.roughguides.com/content/468/
Savvy Diner Guide to Cleveland Restaurants	www.savvydiner.com/cleveland/
Sun Newspapers	www.sunnews.com

— Transportation Services —

AIRPORTS

■ **Cleveland Hopkins International Airport (CLE)**	Phone
12 miles SW of downtown (approx 20 minutes)	216-265-6000

Airport Transportation

	Phone
Hopkins Limousine $9 fare to downtown	216-267-8282
Regional Transit Authority (RTA) $1.50 fare to downtown	216-621-9500
Taxi $20-22 fare to downtown	216-623-1550

Cleveland (Cont'd)

Commercial Airlines

	Phone		Phone
Air Canada	800-776-3000	**Northwest**	800-225-2525
American	800-433-7300	**Southwest**	800-435-9792
Continental	800-525-0280	**Spirit**	800-772-7117
Continental Express	800-525-0280	**TWA**	800-221-2000
Delta	800-221-1212	**United**	800-241-6522
MetroJet	888-638-7653	**US Airways**	800-428-4322

Charter Airlines

	Phone		Phone
Chart Air	513-321-3230	**Five K**	216-267-7032
Corporate Wings Inc	216-261-3500		

CAR RENTALS

	Phone		Phone
Avis	216-265-3700	**Hertz**	216-267-8900
Budget	216-433-4433	**National**	216-267-0060
Dollar	216-267-3133	**Thrifty**	216-267-6811

LIMO/TAXI

	Phone		Phone
Ameri Cab	216-881-1111	**Hopkins Limousine**	216-267-8282
American Limousine	216-221-9330	**Yellow Cab**	216-623-1500
Elegant Limousine	440-234-0011		

MASS TRANSIT

	Phone
Regional Transit Authority (RTA) $1.25 Base fare	216-621-9500

RAIL/BUS

	City	State	ZIP	Phone
Amtrak Station 200 Cleveland Memorial Shoreway NE *TF:* 800-872-7245	Cleveland	OH	44114	216-696-5115
Greyhound/Trailways Bus Station 1465 Chester Ave. *TF:* 800-231-2222	Cleveland	OH	44114	216-781-0520

— Accommodations —

HOTEL RESERVATION SERVICES

	Phone	Fax
Hotel Reservations Network Inc *TF Sales:* 800-964-6835 ■ *Web:* www.hoteldiscount.com	214-361-7311	361-7299
Private Lodging Service	216-321-3213	321-8707

HOTELS, MOTELS, RESORTS

	City	State	ZIP	Phone	Fax
Aqua Marine Hotel Resort 216 Miller Rd. *TF:* 800-335-9343	Avon Lake	OH	44012	440-933-2000	930-2659
Baymont Inns 4222 W 150th St *TF:* 800-301-0200	Cleveland	OH	44135	216-251-8500	251-4117
Clarion Hotel 17000 Bagley Rd. *TF:* 800-252-7466	Middleburg Heights	OH	44130	440-243-5200	243-5240
Cleveland Hilton South 6200 Quarry Ln	Independence	OH	44131	216-447-1300	642-9334
Comfort Inn Cleveland Airport 17550 Rosbough Dr	Middleburg Heights	OH	44130	440-234-3131	234-6111
Comfort Inn Downtown 1800 Euclid Ave *TF:* 800-228-5150	Cleveland	OH	44115	216-861-0001	861-0001
Embassy Suites 1701 E 12th St *TF:* 800-362-2779	Cleveland	OH	44114	216-523-8000	523-1698
Embassy Suites Hotel 3775 Park East Dr. *TF:* 800-362-2779	Beachwood	OH	44122	216-765-8066	765-0930
Fairfield Inn by Marriott 16644 Snow Rd *TF:* 800-228-2800 ■ *Web:* fairfieldinn.com/CLEBP	Brook Park	OH	44142	216-676-5200	676-5200
Hampton Inn 25105 Country Club Blvd *TF:* 800-426-7866	North Olmsted	OH	44070	440-734-4477	734-0836
Holiday Inn Airport 4181 W 150th St *TF:* 800-465-4329	Cleveland	OH	44135	216-252-7700	252-3850
Holiday Inn Lakeside 1111 Lakeside Ave. *TF:* 800-465-4329	Cleveland	OH	44114	216-241-5100	241-7437
Holiday Inn Mayfield 780 Beta Dr. *TF:* 800-465-4329	Mayfield Heights	OH	44143	440-461-9200	461-7564
Holiday Inn Strongsville 15471 Royalton Rd *TF:* 800-465-4329	Strongsville	OH	44136	440-238-8800	238-0273
Key Center Marriott Hotel 127 Public Sq. *TF:* 800-228-9290 ■ *Web:* marriotthotels.com/CLESC	Cleveland	OH	44114	216-696-9200	696-0966
Marriott Airport 4277 W 150th St *TF:* 800-228-9290 ■ *Web:* marriotthotels.com/CLEAP	Cleveland	OH	44135	216-252-5333	251-1508
Marriott Hotel East 3663 Park East Dr. *TF:* 800-334-2118 ■ *Web:* marriotthotels.com/CLEEA	Beachwood	OH	44122	216-464-5950	464-6539
Oberlin Inn 7 N Main St. *TF:* 800-376-4173	Oberlin	OH	44074	440-775-1111	775-0676
Omni International Hotel 2065 E 96th St. *TF:* 800-843-6664	Cleveland	OH	44106	216-791-1900	231-3329
Radisson Inn Airport 25070 Country Club Blvd *TF:* 800-333-3333	North Olmsted	OH	44070	440-734-5060	734-5471
Radisson Inn Beachwood 26300 Chagrin Blvd. *TF:* 800-333-3333	Beachwood	OH	44122	216-831-5150	765-1156
Ramada Inn 13930 Brookpark Rd *TF:* 800-272-6232	Cleveland	OH	44135	216-267-5700	267-1609
Renaissance Cleveland Hotel 24 Public Sq *TF:* 800-468-3571	Cleveland	OH	44113	216-696-5600	696-0432
Residence Inn by Marriott Cleveland Airport 17525 Rosbough Dr *TF:* 800-331-3131 ■ *Web:* www.residenceinn.com/CLEOH	Middleburg Heights	OH	44130	440-234-6688	234-3459
Ritz-Carlton Cleveland 1515 W 3rd St. *TF:* 800-241-3333 ■ *Web:* www.ritzcarlton.com/location/NorthAmerica/Cleveland/main.htm	Cleveland	OH	44113	216-623-1300	623-1492
Sawmill Creek Resort 400 Sawmill Creek *TF:* 800-729-6455 ■ *Web:* www.sawmillcreek.com ■ *E-mail:* sawmill@sawmillcreek.com	Huron	OH	44839	419-433-3800	433-2761
Sheraton Airport Hotel 5300 Riverside Dr *TF:* 800-362-2244	Cleveland	OH	44135	216-267-1500	265-3177
Sheraton City Centre Hotel 777 St Clair Ave NE *TF:* 800-321-1090	Cleveland	OH	44114	216-771-7600	566-0736
Travelodge Downtown 3614 Euclid Ave Square Plaza	Cleveland	OH	44115	216-361-8969	
Wyndham Cleveland Hotel at Playhouse Square 1260 Euclid Ave *TF:* 800-996-3426	Cleveland	OH	44115	216-615-7500	621-8659

— Restaurants —

	City	State	ZIP	Phone
Baricelli Inn (European) 2203 Cornell Rd	Cleveland	OH	44106	216-791-6500
Benihana (Japanese) 23611 Chagrin Blvd.	Beachwood	OH	44122	216-464-7575
Bo Loong Restaurant (Chinese) 3922 St Clair Ave	Cleveland	OH	44114	216-391-3113
Brasserie (American) 24 Public Sq.	Cleveland	OH	44113	216-696-5600
City Center Grille (American) 777 St Clair Ave	Cleveland	OH	44114	216-771-7600
Classics (American) 2065 E 96th St.	Cleveland	OH	44106	216-791-1300
David's Restaurant (Steak/Seafood) 127 Public Sq	Cleveland	OH	44114	216-696-9200
Diamondback Brewery (New American) 724 Prospect	Cleveland	OH	44115	216-771-1988
Empress Taytu (Ethiopian) 6125 St Clair Ave.	Cleveland	OH	44103	216-391-9400
Flat Iron Cafe (American) 1114 Center St.	Cleveland	OH	44113	216-696-6968
Garden Restaurant (European) 32045 Detroit Rd	Avon	OH	44011	440-835-5010
Gateway Sports Club (American) 727 Bolivar	Cleveland	OH	44115	216-621-6644
Gene Hickerson's at the Hanna (Steak/Seafood) 1422 Euclid Ave	Cleveland	OH	44115	216-771-1818
Ginza Sushi House (Japanese) 1111 Carnegie Ave.	Cleveland	OH	44105	216-589-8503
Gourmet of China (Chinese) 6901 Rockside Rd.	Independence	OH	44131	216-328-1123
Greek Isles Restaurant (Greek) 500 W St Clair Ave	Cleveland	OH	44113	216-861-1919
Grill Restaurant (American) 1701 E 12th St	Cleveland	OH	44114	216-523-8000
Harry Corvairs (New American) 812 Huron Rd *Web:* www.harrycorvairs.com ■ *E-mail:* harrychef1@aol.com	Cleveland	OH	44115	216-830-2326
Hornblowers (Seafood) 1151 N Marginal Rd	Cleveland	OH	44110	216-363-1151
Hyde Park Steakhouse (Steak/Seafood) 123 Prospect Ave W.	Cleveland	OH	44115	216-344-2444
John Q's Steakhouse (Steak) 55 Public Sq	Cleveland	OH	44113	216-861-0900
Johnny's Bar on Fulton (Italian) 3164 Fulton Rd	Cleveland	OH	44109	216-281-0055
Korea House (Korean) 3700 Superior Ave.	Cleveland	OH	44114	216-431-0462
Lola (New American) 900 Literary Ave	Cleveland	OH	44113	216-771-5652
Lu Cuisine (Chinese) 1228 Euclid Ave	Cleveland	OH	44115	216-241-8488
Luchita's (Mexican) 3456 W 117th St	Cleveland	OH	44111	216-252-1169
Massimo da Milano (Italian) 1400 W 25th St	Cleveland	OH	44113	216-696-2323
Metropolitan Restaurant (New American) 925 Euclid Ave.	Cleveland	OH	44115	216-241-4280
Moxie (American) 3355 Richmond Rd	Beachwood	OH	44122	216-831-5599
Palazzo The (Italian) 10031 Detroit Ave	Cleveland	OH	44102	216-651-3900
Panini's Bar & Grille (Italian) 840 Huron Rd	Cleveland	OH	44115	216-522-1510
Parker's (Continental) 2801 Bridge Ave	Cleveland	OH	44113	216-771-7130
Pete & Dewey's Planet (American) 812 Huron Rd.	Cleveland	OH	44115	216-522-1500
Piccolo Mondo (Italian) 1352 W 6th St	Cleveland	OH	44113	216-241-1300
Pier W (Seafood) 12700 Lake Ave *Web:* www.pierw.com/	Lakewood	OH	44107	216-228-2250

Cleveland — Restaurants (Cont'd)

Name / Address	City	State	ZIP	Phone
Ristorante Giovanni's (Italian) 25550 Chagrin Blvd	Beachwood	OH	44122	216-831-8625
Riverview Room (Continental) 1515 W 3rd St.	Cleveland	OH	44113	216-623-1300
Rock Bottom Brewery (American) 2000 Sycamore	Cleveland	OH	44113	216-623-1555
Sammy's in the Flats (New American) 1400 W 10th St	Cleveland	OH	44113	216-523-5560
Sans Souci (Mediterranean) 24 Public Sq.	Cleveland	OH	44113	216-696-5600
Sergio's in University Circle (International) 1903 Ford Dr	Cleveland	OH	44106	216-231-1234
Shooters on the Water (American) 1148 Main Ave	Cleveland	OH	44113	216-861-6900
Siam Cafe (Asian) 3951 St Clair Ave	Cleveland	OH	44114	216-361-2323
Sweetwater's Cafe Sausalito (Mediterranean) 1301 E 9th St	Cleveland	OH	44114	216-696-2233
Watermark (Seafood) 1250 Old River Rd	Cleveland	OH	44113	216-241-1600
Web: www.watermark-flats.com				
Wilbert's Bar & Grill (Southwest) 1360 W 9th St	Cleveland	OH	44113	216-771-2583

— Goods and Services —

SHOPPING

Name / Address	City	State	ZIP	Phone	Fax
Avenue The at Tower City Center 230 Huron Rd NW	Cleveland	OH	44113	216-771-0033	
Beachcliff Market Square 19300 Detroit Rd	Rocky River	OH	44116	440-333-5074	333-5074
Beachwood Place 26300 Cedar Rd	Beachwood	OH	44122	216-464-9460	464-7939
Flats The downtown Cleveland	Cleveland	OH	44113	216-566-1046	
Web: www.voiceoftheflats.org					
Galleria at Erieview 1301 E 9th St Suite 3333	Cleveland	OH	44114	216-861-4343	
Web: www.shopyourmall.com ■ *E-mail:* galleriaerieview@shopyourmall.com					
Great Lakes Mall 7850 Mentor Ave.	Mentor	OH	44060	440-255-6900	255-0509
Great Northern Mall 4954 Great Northern Mall	North Olmsted	OH	44070	440-734-6300	734-8929
Midway Mall 3343 Midway Mall	Elyria	OH	44035	440-324-6610	
Old Arcade 401 Euclid Ave Suite 800	Cleveland	OH	44114	216-621-8500	861-0877
Parmatown Mall 7899 W Ridgewood Dr	Parma	OH	44129	440-885-5506	884-9330
Randall Park Mall 20801 Miles Rd	Cleveland	OH	44128	216-663-1250	663-8750
Saks Fifth Avenue 26100 Cedar Rd	Beachwood	OH	44122	216-292-5500	292-4791
Severance Town Center 3640 Mayfield Rd	Cleveland	OH	44118	216-381-7323	
Shaker Square 13221 Shaker Sq	Cleveland	OH	44120	216-991-8700	991-8700
Southpark Center 500 Southpark Ctr	Strongsville	OH	44136	440-238-9000	846-8323
Web: www.southparkcenter.com					
Westgate Mall 3211 Westgate Mall	Cleveland	OH	44126	440-333-8336	

BANKS

Name / Address	City	State	ZIP	Phone	Fax
Bank One NA 600 Superior Ave	Cleveland	OH	44114	216-781-4437	781-2238
TF: 800-310-1111					
Charter One Bank FSB 1215 Superior Ave	Cleveland	OH	44114	216-566-5300	566-1465*
**Fax:* Cust Svc ■ *TF:* 800-553-8981 ■ *Web:* www.charterone.com					
Fifth Third Bank 200 Euclid Ave	Cleveland	OH	44114	216-623-2700	241-0262
KeyBank NA 127 Public Sq.	Cleveland	OH	44114	216-689-3000	689-4037*
**Fax:* Mktg ■ *Web:* www.keybank.com ■ *E-mail:* boc_in1@keybank.com					
National City Bank Cleveland 1900 E 9th St.	Cleveland	OH	44114	216-575-2000	420-9512*
**Fax:* Mktg					
Ohio Savings Bank FSB 1801 E 9th St	Cleveland	OH	44114	216-622-4100	622-4417*
**Fax:* Hum Res ■ *TF:* 800-860-2025 ■ *Web:* www.ohiosavings.com					
Third Federal Savings & Loan Assn 7007 Broadway Ave.	Cleveland	OH	44105	216-441-6000	441-6034*
**Fax:* Mktg ■ *TF:* 800-944-7828					

BUSINESS SERVICES

Name	Phone
Bonnie Speed Delivery	216-696-6033
City Express Delivery	216-781-6500
Delivery Service	216-267-8113
Federal Express	800-238-5355
Kelly Services	216-771-2800
Kinko's	216-589-5679
Manpower Temporary Services	216-771-5474
Olsten Staffing Services	216-861-1900
Post Office	216-443-4100
Star Express Delivery Service	216-241-2410
UPS	800-742-5877

— Media —

PUBLICATIONS

Name / Address	City	State	ZIP	Phone	Fax
Cleveland Magazine 1422 Euclid Ave Hanna Bldg Suite 730	Cleveland	OH	44115	216-771-2833	781-6318
Web: www.clevelandmagazine.com					
Crain's Cleveland Business 700 W St Clair Suite 310	Cleveland	OH	44113	216-522-1383	694-4264
TF: 888-909-9111 ■ *Web:* www.crainscleveland.com ■ *E-mail:* cle.crains@mail.multiverse.com					
News Sun 5510 Cloverleaf Pkwy	Cleveland	OH	44125	216-524-0830	524-7792
Web: www.sunnews.com					
Parma Sun Post 5510 Cloverleaf Pkwy	Cleveland	OH	44125	216-524-0830	524-7792
Web: www.sunnews.com					
Plain Dealer‡ 1801 Superior Ave NE	Cleveland	OH	44114	216-999-4800	999-6354
TF: 800-688-4802 ■ *Web:* www.cleveland.com					
Sun Herald 3355 Richmond Rd	Beachwood	OH	44122	216-464-6399	464-8816
Web: www.sunnews.com					
Sun Messenger 3355 Richmond Rd	Beachwood	OH	44122	216-464-6399	464-8816*
**Fax:* News Rm					
Sun Scoop Journal 3355 Richmond Rd	Beachwood	OH	44122	216-464-6399	464-8816
Web: www.sunnews.com					

‡Daily newspapers

TELEVISION

Name / Address	City	State	ZIP	Phone	Fax
WBNX-TV Ch 55 (WB) 2690 State Rd	Cuyahoga Falls	OH	44223	330-922-5500	929-2410
Web: www.wbnx.com					
WEWS-TV Ch 5 (ABC) 3001 Euclid Ave	Cleveland	OH	44115	216-431-5555	431-3666
Web: www.newsnet5.com					
WGGN-TV Ch 52 (Ind) 3809 Maple Ave	Castalia	OH	44824	419-684-5311	684-5378
WJW-TV Ch 8 (Fox) 5800 S Marginal Rd	Cleveland	OH	44103	216-431-8888	432-4239
E-mail: fox8@en.com					
WKYC-TV Ch 3 (NBC) 1403 E 6th St	Cleveland	OH	44114	216-344-3333	344-3326
E-mail: wkyc@aol.com					
WMFD-TV Ch 68 (Ind) 2900 Park Ave W	Mansfield	OH	44906	419-529-5900	529-2319
Web: www.wmfd.com ■ *E-mail:* comments@wmfd.com					
WOIO-TV Ch 19 (CBS) 1717 E 12th St.	Cleveland	OH	44114	216-771-1943	436-5460
Web: www.woio.com					
WUAB-TV Ch 43 (UPN) 1717 E 12th St	Cleveland	OH	44114	216-771-1943	515-7152
WVIZ-TV Ch 25 (PBS) 4300 Brookpark Rd	Cleveland	OH	44134	216-398-2800	749-2560

RADIO

Name / Address	City	State	ZIP	Phone	Fax
WABQ-AM 1540 kHz (Rel) 8000 Euclid Ave	Cleveland	OH	44103	216-231-8005	421-0738
WCLV-FM 95.5 MHz (Clas) 26501 Renaissance Pkwy	Cleveland	OH	44128	216-464-0900	464-2206
Web: www.wclv.com ■ *E-mail:* wclv@wclv.com					
WCPN-FM 90.3 MHz (NPR) Cleveland Public Radio 3100 Chester Ave Suite 300	Cleveland	OH	44114	216-432-3700	432-3681
WDOK-FM 102.1 MHz (AC) 1 Radio Ln	Cleveland	OH	44114	216-696-0123	566-0764
Web: www.wdok.com					
WENZ-FM 107.9 MHz (Alt) 1041 Huron Rd	Cleveland	OH	44115	216-861-0100	696-0385
WERE-AM 1300 kHz (N/T) 1041 Huron Rd	Cleveland	OH	44115	216-861-0100	696-0385
WGAR-FM 99.5 MHz (Ctry) 5005 Rockside Rd Suite 530	Cleveland	OH	44131	216-328-9950	328-9951
WHK-AM 1420 kHz (Rel) 4 Summit Park Dr Suite 150	Independence	OH	44131	216-901-0921	
WJMO-AM 1490 kHz (Oldies) 2510 Saint Clair Ave	Cleveland	OH	44114	216-621-9566	771-4164
WKNR-AM 1220 kHz (Sports) 9446 Broadview Rd	Cleveland	OH	44147	440-838-1220	838-1546
WMJI-FM 105.7 MHz (Oldies) 310 Lakeside Ave 6th Fl.	Cleveland	OH	44113	216-623-1105	696-3299
Web: www.wmji.com					
WMMS-FM 100.7 MHz (Rock) 1660 W 2nd St 200 Skylight Office Tower	Cleveland	OH	44113	216-781-9667	771-1007
Web: www.wmms.com					
WMVX-FM 106.5 MHz (AC) 1468 W 9th St Suite 805	Cleveland	OH	44113	216-696-4444	781-5143
WNCX-FM 98.5 MHz (CR) 1041 Huron Rd	Cleveland	OH	44115	216-861-0100	696-0385
Web: www.wncx.com ■ *E-mail:* wncx@wncx.com					
WNWV-FM 107.3 MHz (NAC) 538 Broad St Suite 400	Elyria	OH	44036	440-322-3761	322-1536
Web: www.wnwv.com ■ *E-mail:* thewave@wnwv.com					
WQAL-FM 104.1 MHz (AC) 1621 Euclid Ave Suite 1800	Cleveland	OH	44115	216-696-6666	348-0104
Web: www.wqal.com ■ *E-mail:* qsales@wqal.com					
WRMR-AM 850 kHz (Nost) 1 Radio Ln	Cleveland	OH	44114	216-696-0123	566-0764
WTAM-AM 1100 kHz (N/T) 1468 W 9th St Suite 805	Cleveland	OH	44113	216-696-4444	781-5143

Cleveland — Radio (Cont'd)

				Phone	Fax
WZAK-FM 93.1 MHz (Urban) 2510 St Clair Ave *Web:* www.wzak.com	Cleveland	OH	44114	216-621-9300	566-8238
WZJM-FM 92.3 MHz (CHR) 2510 St Clair Ave *Web:* www.jammin.com	Cleveland	OH	44114	216-621-9566	771-4164

— Colleges/Universities —

				Phone	Fax
Baldwin-Wallace College 275 Eastland Rd *Web:* www.bw.edu	Berea	OH	44017	440-826-2900	826-3640
Bryant & Stratton Business Institute Parma 12955 Snow Rd *TF:* 800-327-3151	Parma	OH	44130	216-265-3151	265-0325
Bryant & Stratton Career College Willoughby Hills 27557 Chardon Rd	Willoughby Hills	OH	44092	440-944-6800	944-9260
Bryant & Stratton College 1700 E 13th St *Web:* www.bryantstratton.edu	Cleveland	OH	44114	216-771-1700	771-7787
Case Western Reserve University 10900 Euclid Ave *TF Admissions:* 800-967-8898 ■ *Web:* www.cwru.edu ■ *E-mail:* aurora@po.cwru.edu	Cleveland	OH	44106	216-368-2000	368-5111
Cleveland Institute of Art 11141 East Blvd *TF:* 800-223-4700 ■ *Web:* www.cia.edu ■ *E-mail:* info@cia.edu	Cleveland	OH	44106	216-421-7400	421-7438
Cleveland Institute of Electronics 1776 E 17th St *TF:* 800-243-6446 ■ *E-mail:* instruct@cie-uc.edu	Cleveland	OH	44114	216-781-9400	781-0331
Cleveland Institute of Music 11021 East Blvd *Web:* www.cwru.edu/CIM/cimhome.html	Cleveland	OH	44106	216-791-5000	791-1530
Cleveland State University 1983 E 24th St *TF:* 888-278-0440 ■ *Web:* www.csuohio.edu	Cleveland	OH	44115	216-687-2000	687-9210
Cuyahoga Community College Eastern Campus 4250 Richmond Rd *TF:* 800-954-8742 ■ *Web:* www.tri-c.cc.oh.us/east/index.htm	Cleveland	OH	44122	216-987-2024	987-2214
Cuyahoga Community College Metropolitan Campus 2900 Community College Ave *TF:* 800-954-8742 ■ *Web:* www.tri-c.cc.oh.us/metro/index.htm	Cleveland	OH	44115	216-987-4000	696-2567
Cuyahoga Community College Western Campus 11000 Pleasant Valley Rd *TF:* 800-954-8742 ■ *Web:* www.tri-c.cc.oh.us/west/index.htm	Parma	OH	44130	216-987-5154	987-5071
David N Myers College 112 Prospect Ave E *Web:* www.dnmyers.edu	Cleveland	OH	44115	216-696-9000	696-6430
John Carroll University 20700 N Park Blvd *Web:* www.jcu.edu	University Heights	OH	44118	216-397-1886	397-3098
Lake Erie College 391 W Washington St *TF Admissions:* 800-533-4996 ■ *Web:* www.lakeerie.edu	Painesville	OH	44077	440-352-3361	352-3533
Lakeland Community College 7700 Clocktower Dr *TF:* 800-589-8520 ■ *Web:* www.lakeland.cc.oh.us	Kirtland	OH	44094	440-953-7000	953-9710
Notre Dame College of Ohio 4545 College Rd *TF:* 877-632-6446 ■ *Web:* www.ndc.edu	South Euclid	OH	44121	216-381-1680	381-3802
Sawyer College of Business Cleveland 13027 Lorain Ave	Cleveland	OH	44111	216-941-7666	941-1162
Ursuline College 2550 Lander Rd *Web:* www.ursuline.edu/ ■ *E-mail:* dgiaco@en.com	Pepper Pike	OH	44124	440-449-4200	684-6138
Virginia Marti College of Fashion & Art 11724 Detroit Ave *TF:* 800-473-4350	Lakewood	OH	44107	216-221-8584	221-2311
West Side Institute of Technology 9801 Walford Ave	Cleveland	OH	44102	216-651-1656	651-4077

— Hospitals —

				Phone	Fax
Bedford Medical Center 44 Blaine Ave	Bedford	OH	44146	440-439-2000	232-0776
Cleveland Clinic Foundation 9500 Euclid Ave **Fax:* Library ■ *Web:* www.ccf.org	Cleveland	OH	44195	216-444-2200	444-0271*
Deaconess Hospital of Cleveland 4229 Pearl Rd	Cleveland	OH	44109	216-459-6300	459-6746
Fairview General Hospital 18101 Lorain Ave *TF:* 800-323-8434	Cleveland	OH	44111	216-476-7000	476-7017
Lake Hospital System 10 E Washington	Painesville	OH	44077	440-354-2400	354-1994
Lakewood Hospital 14519 Detroit Ave *TF:* 800-521-3955	Lakewood	OH	44107	216-521-4200	529-7161
Lutheran Medical Center 1730 W 25th St	Cleveland	OH	44113	216-696-4300	363-2082
Marymount Hospital 12300 McCracken Rd	Garfield Heights	OH	44125	216-581-0500	587-8212
Meridia Euclid Hospital 18901 Lake Shore Blvd **Fax:* Admitting	Euclid	OH	44119	216-531-9000	692-7488*
Meridia Hillcrest Hospital 6780 Mayfield Rd **Fax:* Admitting	Mayfield Heights	OH	44124	440-449-4500	473-6405*
Meridia Huron Hospital 13951 Terrace Rd **Fax:* Admitting	East Cleveland	OH	44112	216-761-3300	761-3529*
Meridia South Pointe Hospital 4110 Warrensville Ctr Rd **Fax:* Admitting	Warrensville Heights	OH	44122	216-491-6000	491-7193*
MetroHealth Medical Center 2500 MetroHealth Dr **Fax:* Admitting ■ *TF:* 800-554-5251 ■ *Web:* www.metrohealth.org	Cleveland	OH	44109	216-398-6000	778-5226*
Mount Sinai Medical Center 1 Mt Sinai Dr *Web:* www.mtsinai.org ■ *E-mail:* pxa@po.cwru.edu	Cleveland	OH	44106	216-421-4000	421-5111
Saint John West Shore Hospital 29000 Center Ridge Rd	Westlake	OH	44145	440-835-8000	835-6283
Saint Luke's Medical Center 11311 Shaker Blvd *Web:* www.en.com/stlukes	Cleveland	OH	44104	216-368-7000	368-7230
Saint Vincent Charity Hospital 2351 E 22nd St	Cleveland	OH	44115	216-861-6200	363-3333
Southwest General Health Center 18697 Bagley Rd	Middleburg Heights	OH	44130	440-816-8000	816-5348
University Hospitals of Cleveland 11100 Euclid Ave	Cleveland	OH	44106	216-844-1000	844-8118
Veterans Affairs Medical Center 10701 East Blvd	Cleveland	OH	44106	216-791-3800	421-3217

— Attractions —

				Phone	Fax
African American Museum 1765 Crawford Rd	Cleveland	OH	44106	216-791-1700	791-1774
Brecksville Reservation 4101 Fulton Pkwy Cleveland Metroparks	Cleveland	OH	44144	216-351-6300	
Cain Park Theatre Superior & Lee Rds Cain Pk	Cleveland Heights	OH	44118	216-371-3000	
Cedar Point PO Box 5006 **Fax:* Mktg ■ *Web:* www.cedarpoint.com	Sandusky	OH	44871	419-626-0830	627-2200*
Century Village 14653 E Park St	Burton	OH	44021	440-834-4012	
Cleveland Botanical Garden 11030 East Blvd *Web:* www.cbgarden.org ■ *E-mail:* info@cbgarden.org	Cleveland	OH	44106	216-721-1600	721-2056
Cleveland Center for Contemporary Art 8501 Carnegie Ave *Web:* www.artcom.com/museums/nv/af/44106-24.htm	Cleveland	OH	44106	216-421-8671	421-0737
Cleveland Chamber Symphony Drinko Recital Hall Cleveland State University *Web:* www.csuohio.edu/ccs/ ■ *E-mail:* xxrich@grail.csuohio.edu	Cleveland	OH	44115	216-687-9243	687-9279
Cleveland Metroparks Zoo 3900 Wildlife Way *Web:* www.clemetzoo.com ■ *E-mail:* cmzoomkt@interramp.com	Cleveland	OH	44109	216-661-6500	661-3312
Cleveland Museum of Art 11150 East Blvd **Fax:* Mktg ■ *Web:* www.clemusart.com/ ■ *E-mail:* sas6@pocwru.edu	Cleveland	OH	44106	216-421-7340	229-5095*
Cleveland Museum of Natural History 1 Wade Oval Dr University Cir *Web:* www.cmnh.org/ ■ *E-mail:* wwwadmin@cmnh.org	Cleveland	OH	44106	216-231-4600	231-5919
Cleveland Opera 1422 Euclid Ave Suite 1052 *Web:* www.clevelandopera.org ■ *E-mail:* mail@clevelandopera.org	Cleveland	OH	44115	216-575-0903	575-1918
Cleveland Orchestra 11001 Euclid Ave Severance Hall *TF:* 800-686-1141 ■ *Web:* www.clevelandorch.com	Cleveland	OH	44106	216-231-7300	231-0202
Cleveland Public Theatre 6415 Detroit Ave *Web:* www.en.com/cpt/	Cleveland	OH	44102	216-631-2727	631-2575
Cleveland San Jose Ballet 3615 Euclid Ave Suite 1A *Web:* www.csjballet.org	Cleveland	OH	44115	216-426-2500	426-2524
Crawford Auto-Aviation Museum 10825 East Blvd *Web:* www.wrhs.org/sites/auto.htm	Cleveland	OH	44106	216-721-5722	721-0645
Cuyahoga Valley Scenic Railroad 1664 W Main St *TF:* 800-468-4070 ■ *Web:* www.cvsr.com	Peninsula	OH	44624	330-657-2000	657-2450

Cleveland — Attractions (Cont'd)

	City	State	Zip	Phone	Fax
Dittrick Museum of Medical History 11000 Euclid Ave	Cleveland	OH	44106	216-368-3648	368-0165
Web: www.cwru.edu/chsl/hist_div.htm					
Dunham Tavern Museum 6709 Euclid Ave	Cleveland	OH	44103	216-431-1060	
Fairport Harbor Lakefront Park 2 Huntington Beach	Fairport Harbor	OH	44077	440-639-7275	
Flats The downtown Cleveland	Cleveland	OH	44113	216-566-1046	
Web: www.voiceoftheflats.org					
Geauga Lake 1060 N Aurora Rd	Aurora	OH	44202	330-562-7131	562-7020
Web: www.sixflags.com/geaugalake					
Great Lakes Brewing Co 2516 Market St	Cleveland	OH	44113	216-771-4404	771-4466
Great Lakes Science Center 601 Erieside Ave	Cleveland	OH	44114	216-694-2000	696-2140
Web: www.greatscience.com					
Great Lakes Theater Festival 1501 Euclid Ave	Cleveland	OH	44115	216-241-5490	241-6315
Hale Farm & Village PO Box 296	Bath	OH	44210	330-666-3711	666-9497
Web: www.wrhs.org/sites/hale.htm					
Health Museum 8911 Euclid Ave	Cleveland	OH	44106	216-231-5010	231-5129
Web: www.healthmuseum.org/					
Hinckley Reservation 4101 Fulton Pkwy Cleveland Metroparks	Cleveland	OH	44144	216-351-6300	
Holden Arboretum 9500 Sperry Rd	Kirtland	OH	44094	440-256-1110	256-1655
International Women's Air & Space Museum 1501 N Marginal Rd Burke Lakefront Airport Rm 165	Cleveland	OH	44114	216-623-1111	623-1113
Web: www.iwasm.org ■ *E-mail:* iwasm@ecr.net					
James A Garfield National Historic Site 8095 Mentor Ave Lawnfield	Mentor	OH	44060	440-255-8722	255-8545
Web: www.nps.gov/jaga/					
Lake Farmpark 8800 Chardon Rd	Kirtland	OH	44094	440-256-2112	
TF: 800-366-3276 ■ *Web:* www.lakemetroparks.com/					
Lyric Opera Cleveland 11021 East Blvd Cleveland Institute of Music	Cleveland	OH	44106	216-231-2910	231-5502
Mill Stream Run Reservation 4101 Fulton Pkwy Cleveland Metroparks	Cleveland	OH	44144	216-351-6300	
NASA Glenn Research Center 21000 Brookpark Rd MS 8-1	Cleveland	OH	44135	216-433-4000	433-8000
Web: www.grc.nasa.gov					
Old Arcade 401 Euclid Ave Suite 800	Cleveland	OH	44114	216-621-8500	861-0877
OMNIMAX Theater 601 Erieside Ave Great Lakes Science Ctr	Cleveland	OH	44114	216-694-2000	696-2140
Web: www.greatscience.com/omnimax/index.html					
Playhouse Square Center 1501 Euclid Ave Suite 200	Cleveland	OH	44115	216-771-4444	771-0217
TF: 800-888-9941 ■ *Web:* www.playhousesquare.com					
Polka Hall of Fame 291 E 22nd St Shore Cultural Ctr	Euclid	OH	44123	216-261-3263	
Rainbow Children's Museum 10730 Euclid Ave	Cleveland	OH	44106	216-791-7114	791-8838
Rock & Roll Hall of Fame & Museum 1 Key Plaza	Cleveland	OH	44114	216-781-7625	
TF: 800-349-7625 ■ *Web:* www.rockhall.com ■ *E-mail:* visit@rockhall.com					
Rockefeller Park ML King Jr Dr	Cleveland	OH	44108	216-664-3103	
Rocky River Reservation 4101 Fulton Pkwy Cleveland Metroparks	Cleveland	OH	44144	216-351-6300	
Sea World of Ohio 1100 Sea World Dr	Aurora	OH	44202	330-995-2121	995-2115*
**Fax:* Mktg ■ *Web:* www.seaworld.com/seaworld/sw_ohio/swoframe.html					
Severance Hall 11001 Euclid Ave	Cleveland	OH	44106	216-231-7300	231-0202
Shaker Lakes Regional Nature Center 2600 S Park Blvd	Cleveland	OH	44120	216-321-5935	321-1869
Steamship William G Mather Museum 1001 E 9th St Pier	Cleveland	OH	44114	216-574-6262	574-2536
Web: little.nhlink.net/wgm/wgmhome.html					
Trinity Cathedral 2021 E 22nd St	Cleveland	OH	44115	216-771-3630	771-3657
West Side Market 1979 W 25th St	Cleveland	OH	44113	216-781-3663	664-3390
Western Reserve Historical Society 10825 East Blvd	Cleveland	OH	44106	216-721-5722	721-9309
Web: www.wrhs.org/					

SPORTS TEAMS & FACILITIES

	City	State	Zip	Phone	Fax
Cleveland Barons (hockey) 5310 Hauserman	Parma	OH	44130	440-886-0512	886-0512
Cleveland Caps (soccer) 7876 Broadview Rd	Parma	OH	44134	216-901-1277	901-9100
Cleveland Cavaliers 1 Center Ct Gund Arena	Cleveland	OH	44115	216-420-2000	420-2298*
**Fax:* PR ■ *TF:* 800-332-2287 ■ *Web:* www.nba.com/cavs					
Cleveland Crunch (soccer) 34200 Solon Rd 1 Crunch Pl	Solon	OH	44139	440-349-2090	349-0653
Cleveland Eclipse (soccer) Foltz Industrial Pkwy Ehrnfelt Championship Field	Cleveland	OH	441	440-333-0981	835-5405
Cleveland Indians 2401 Ontario St Jacobs Field	Cleveland	OH	44115	216-420-4200	420-4624*
**Fax:* Cust Svc ■ *Web:* www.indians.com					
Cleveland Junior Americans (hockey) 1616 9th Blvd	Lorain	OH	44052	440-246-1075	246-3113
E-mail: jrufo@centuryinter.net					
Cleveland Lions (football) 3290 W 125th St	Cleveland	OH	44111	216-741-2483	661-8953
Cleveland Lumberjacks (hockey) 200 Huron Rd 1 Center Ice	Cleveland	OH	44115	216-420-0000	420-2520
Web: www.jackshockey.com					
Cleveland Rockers (basketball) Gund Arena 1 Center Ct	Cleveland	OH	44115	216-420-2370	420-2101
Web: www.wnba.com/rockers					
Gund Arena 1 Center Ct	Cleveland	OH	44115	216-420-2000	420-2280
TF: 800-332-2287 ■ *Web:* www.gundarena.com					
Jacobs Field 2401 Ontario St	Cleveland	OH	44115	216-420-4200	420-4396
Web: www.indians.com/jacobs/index.html					
Thistledown 21501 Emery Rd	Cleveland	OH	44128	216-662-8600	662-5339
Web: www.debartoloracing.com/tdn					

— Events —

	Phone
500,000 Country Lights (December)	800-366-3276
American & Canadian Sport Travel & Outdoor Show (mid-March)	216-529-1300
American Indian Pow Wow (June 19-20)	216-281-8480
American Legion Holiday Parade (late November)	216-432-4046
Auto Rama (early February)	216-348-2200
Boo at the Zoo (late October)	216-661-6500
Cain Park Arts Festival (early July)	216-371-3000
Cleveland Christmas Connection (mid-November)	440-835-9627
Cleveland Grand Prix (mid-July)	216-781-3500
Cleveland Home & Garden Show (mid-February)	800-600-0307
Cleveland International Film Festival (late March)	216-621-1374
Cleveland National Air Show (late August-early September)	216-781-0747
Cuyahoga County Fair (mid-August)	800-321-1001
CVS-Cleveland Marathon (early May)	800-467-3826
EarthFest (April 22)	216-281-6468
Greater Cleveland Auto Show (late February-early March)	216-676-6000
Hale Farm Harvest Festival (mid-October)	800-589-9703
Haunted Hayrides (mid-October)	800-366-3276
Holiday Lights Festival (early-mid-December)	216-661-6500
Jazzfest (mid-April)	216-987-4400
Johnny Appleseed Festival (mid-September)	440-834-4012
Mid America Sail & Power Boat Show (mid-late January)	216-676-6000
National Home & Garden Show (mid-February)	216-676-6000
Ohio Arts & Crafts Christmas Festival (late October)	440-243-0090
Saint Patrick's Day Parade (mid-March)	216-621-4110
Shaker Apple Festival Weekend (early October)	216-921-1201
Ski Skate & Snowboard Show (early November)	216-676-6000
Tri-C JazzFest (mid-April)	216-987-4400

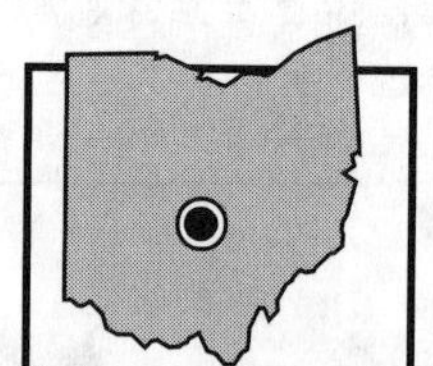

Columbus

Ohio's capital city is also home to one of the largest universities in the country, Ohio State University. OSU is a vital part of the city, and Buckeye football draws over 90,000 fans to its Horseshoe Stadium each year. The state's history is preserved at the Ohio Historical Center and adjacent German Village, a restored district known for its beautifully renovated homes and live music. Columbus' commitment to history is further evidenced at Ohio Village, a recreation of a small 19th century town; and at the Santa Maria, a replica of Christopher Columbus's ship.

Population	670,234	**Longitude**	82-99-89 W
Area (Land)	189.3 sq mi	**County**	Franklin
Area (Water)	2.1 sq mi	**Time Zone**	EST
Elevation	780 ft	**Area Code/s**	614
Latitude	39-96-11 N		

Columbus (Cont'd)

— Average Temperatures and Precipitation —

TEMPERATURES

	Jan	Feb	Mar	Apr	May	Jun	Jul	Aug	Sep	Oct	Nov	Dec
High	34	38	51	62	73	80	84	82	76	65	51	39
Low	19	21	31	40	50	58	63	61	55	43	34	25

PRECIPITATION

	Jan	Feb	Mar	Apr	May	Jun	Jul	Aug	Sep	Oct	Nov	Dec
Inches	2.2	2.2	3.3	3.2	3.9	4.0	4.3	3.7	3.0	2.2	3.2	2.9

— Information Sources —

Phone *Fax*

Better Business Bureau Serving Central Ohio
1335 Dublin Rd Suite 30-A ....Columbus OH 43215 614-486-6336 486-6631
Web: www.columbus-oh.bbb.org
Columbus City Hall 90 W Broad St..........Columbus OH 43215 614-645-8100 645-5880
Web: ci.columbus.oh.us
Columbus Economic Development Div
99 N Front St.......................Columbus OH 43215 614-645-7574 645-7855
Web: td.ci.columbus.oh.us/edps.htm
Columbus Mayor 90 W Broad St Rm 247 .....Columbus OH 43215 614-645-7671 645-8955
Web: ci.columbus.oh.us/mayor.html
Columbus Metropolitan Library
96 S Grant Ave.......................Columbus OH 43215 614-645-2800 645-2870
Web: www.cml.lib.oh.us
Franklin County 369 S High St 3rd Fl ....Columbus OH 43215 614-462-3621 462-4325
Web: www.co.franklin.oh.us/
Greater Columbus Chamber of Commerce
37 N High St.......................Columbus OH 43215 614-221-1321 221-9360
TF: 800-950-1321 ■ *Web:* supersite.rrcol.com/gccc
Greater Columbus Convention & Visitors Bureau 90 N High St..................Columbus OH 43215 614-221-6623 221-5618
TF: 800-354-2657 ■ *Web:* www.columbuscvb.org
■ *E-mail:* 74777.3610@compuserve.com
Greater Columbus Convention Center
400 N High St ....Columbus OH 43215 614-645-5000 221-7239
TF: 800-626-0241 ■ *Web:* www.columbusconventions.com
■ *E-mail:* sales@columbusconventions.com
Greater Columbus Free-Net
1224 Kinnear Rd.....................Columbus OH 43212 614-292-3200 292-7168
Web: www.freenet.columbus.oh.us
■ *E-mail:* sgordon@freenet.columbus.oh.us

On-Line Resources

4Columbus.com www.4columbus.com
About.com Guide to Columbus .... columbusoh.about.com/local/midwestus/columbusoh
Anthill City Guide Columbus .... www.anthill.com/city.asp?city=columbus
Area Guide Columbus .... columbusoh.areaguides.net
Central Ohio Source .... www.sddt.com/~columbus
City Knowledge Columbus .... www.cityknowledge.com/oh_columbus.htm
CitySearch Columbus .... columbus.citysearch.com
Columbus Alive .... www.alivewired.com
Columbus City Net .... www.excite.com/travel/countries/united_states/ohio/columbus
Columbus Home Page .... www.columbus.net/
Columbus Internet Directory users1.ee.net/coldir/
Columbus Pages .... www.columbuspages.com/
Columbus Super Site .... www.columbus.org/
Columbus Webring onart.digitalchainsaw.com/ccw1.htm
ColumbusTour .... www.columbustour.com/
DigitalCity Columbus .... home.digitalcity.com/columbus
Out In Columbus .... www.outincolumbus.com
Savvy Diner Guide to Columbus Restaurants .... www.savvydiner.com/columbus/

— Transportation Services —

AIRPORTS

Phone

■ **Port Columbus International Airport (CMH)**

8 miles NE of downtown (approx 15 minutes).............................614-239-4000
Web: port-columbus.com

Airport Transportation

Phone

Airport Express Shuttle $8.50 fare to downtown............................614-476-3004
Yellow Cab $14 fare to downtown.......................................614-444-4444

Commercial Airlines

	Phone		Phone
Air Canada	800-776-3000	**Delta**	800-221-1212
AirTran	800-247-8726	**Northwest**	800-225-2525
American	800-433-7300	**Southwest**	800-435-9792
Comair	800-354-9822	**TWA**	800-221-2000
Continental	614-224-3152	**United**	800-241-6522
Continental Express	800-525-0280	**US Airways**	800-428-4322

Charter Airlines

	Phone		Phone
Airnet Systems	614-237-9777	**Lane Aviation Corp**	614-237-3747
Helicopters Inc	800-466-2903		

CAR RENTALS

	Phone		Phone
Avis	614-235-3477	**Hertz**	614-239-1084
Budget	614-471-2434	**National**	614-237-0333
CarTemps USA	614-866-8688	**Sears**	800-527-0770
Enterprise	614-235-2500	**Thrifty**	614-237-5800

LIMO/TAXI

	Phone		Phone
Carey Limousine	614-228-5466	**Yellow Cab**	614-444-4444
Northway	614-299-8022		

MASS TRANSIT

Phone

COTA $1.10 Base fare 614-228-1776

RAIL/BUS

Phone

Greyhound/Trailways Bus Station 111 E Town St ....Columbus OH 43215 614-221-2389
TF: 800-231-2222

— Accommodations —

HOTELS, MOTELS, RESORTS

Phone *Fax*

Adam's Mark Columbus 50 N 3rd St.........Columbus OH 43215 614-228-5050 228-2525
TF: 800-444-2326 ■ *Web:* www.adamsmark.com/columbs.htm
Best Western North
888 E Dublin-Granville Rd ....Columbus OH 43229 614-888-8230 888-8223
TF: 800-528-1234
Clarion Hotel 7007 N High St............Worthington OH 43085 614-436-0700 436-1208
TF: 800-252-7466
Comfort Inn North
1213 E Dublin-Granville Rd ....Columbus OH 43229 614-885-4084 885-9280
TF: 800-221-2222
Concourse Hotel & Convention Center
4300 International Gateway ....Columbus OH 43219 614-237-2515 237-6134
TF: 800-541-4574
Courtyard by Marriott 35 W Spring St........Columbus OH 43215 614-228-3200 228-6752
TF: 800-321-2211 ■ *Web:* courtyard.com/CMHCY
Crowne Plaza 33 Nationwide Blvd...........Columbus OH 43215 614-461-4100 461-5828
TF: 800-227-6963
Days Inn Downtown 1559 W Broad St........Columbus OH 43222 614-275-0388 275-4037
TF: 800-325-2525
Doubletree Guest Suites 50 S Front St.......Columbus OH 43215 614-228-4600 228-0297
TF: 800-222-8733
■ *Web:* www.doubletreehotels.com/DoubleT/Hotel61/73/73Main.htm
Embassy Suites Hotel
2700 Corporate Exchange Dr ....Columbus OH 43231 614-890-8600 890-8626
TF: 800-362-2779
Extended StayAmerica 6255 Zumstein Dr .....Columbus OH 43229 614-431-0033 431-0088
TF: 800-398-7829
Fairfield Inn by Marriott
1309 St James Lutheran Ln.............Columbus OH 43228 614-870-2880 870-2927
TF: 800-228-2800 ■ *Web:* fairfieldinn.com/CMHFW
Four Points by Sheraton
2124 S Hamilton Rd ....Columbus OH 43232 614-861-7220 866-9067
TF: 800-797-9865

Columbus — Hotels, Motels, Resorts (Cont'd)

Name / Address	City	State	Zip	Phone	Fax
Holiday Inn City Center 175 E Town St	Columbus	OH	43215	614-221-3281	221-2667
TF: 800-465-4329					
Holiday Inn Columbus Airport 750 Stelzer Rd	Columbus	OH	43219	614-237-6360	237-2978
TF: 800-465-4329					
■ *Web:* www.basshotels.com/holiday-inn/?_franchisee=CMHAP					
Holiday Inn East 4560 Hilton Corporate Dr	Columbus	OH	43232	614-868-1380	863-3210
TF: 800-465-4329					
■ *Web:* www.basshotels.com/holiday-inn/?_franchisee=CMHHC					
■ *E-mail:* hieastcols@aol.com					
Holiday Inn on the Lane 328 W Lane Ave	Columbus	OH	43201	614-294-4848	294-3390
TF: 800-465-4329					
Holiday Inn South 383 E Leffel Ln	Springfield	OH	45505	937-323-8631	323-5389
TF: 800-465-4329					
Holiday Inn Worthington Hotel & Conference Center 175 Hutchinson Ave	Columbus	OH	43235	614-885-3334	846-4353
TF: 800-465-4329					
■ *Web:* www.basshotels.com/templates/franchisee/hi/images/HI.GIF					
■ *E-mail:* cmhwr@internetmci.com					
Hyatt on Capitol Square 75 E State St	Columbus	OH	43215	614-228-1234	469-9664
TF: 800-233-1234					
■ *Web:* www.hyatt.com/usa/columbus/hotels/hotel_capit.html					
Hyatt Regency Columbus 350 N High St	Columbus	OH	43215	614-463-1234	280-3034
TF: 800-233-1234					
■ *Web:* www.hyatt.com/usa/columbus/hotels/hotel_cmhrc.html					
Lenox Inn Rt 256 & I-70 E	Columbus	OH	43068	614-861-7800	759-9059
TF: 800-821-0007					
Marriott Hotel North 6500 Doubletree Ave	Columbus	OH	43229	614-885-1885	885-7222
TF: 800-228-3429 ■ *Web:* marriotthotels.com/CMHNO					
Radisson Hotel & Conference Center Columbus Airport 1375 N Cassady Ave	Columbus	OH	43219	614-475-7551	476-1476
TF: 800-333-3333					
Radisson Hotel Columbus North 4900 Sinclair Rd	Columbus	OH	43229	614-846-0300	847-1022
TF: 800-333-3333					
Ramada University Hotel 3110 Olentangy River Rd	Columbus	OH	43202	614-267-7461	263-5299
TF: 800-272-6232					
Residence Inn by Marriott East 2084 S Hamilton Rd	Columbus	OH	43232	614-864-8844	864-4572
TF: 800-331-3131 ■ *Web:* www.residenceinn.com/CMHHT					
StudioPLUS 2200 Lake Club Dr	Columbus	OH	43232	614-759-1451	863-7755
TF: 800-646-8000					
Westin Great Southern 310 S High St	Columbus	OH	43215	614-228-3800	228-7666
TF: 800-228-3000					
Wyndham Dublin Hotel 600 Metro Pl N	Dublin	OH	43017	614-764-2200	764-1213
TF: 800-996-3426					

— Restaurants —

Name / Address	City	State	Zip	Phone
Alex's Bistro (French) 4681 Reed Rd	Columbus	OH	43220	614-457-8887
Barley's Brewing Co (American) 467 N High St	Columbus	OH	43215	614-228-2537
Benevolence (Vegetarian) 41 W Swan St	Columbus	OH	43215	614-221-9330
Bexley's Monk (New American) 2232 E Main St	Columbus	OH	43209	614-239-6665
Bistro Roti (Italian) 1693 W Lane Ave	Columbus	OH	43221	614-481-7684
Boulevard Grille (Greek) 171 Columbus City Center Dr	Columbus	OH	43215	614-464-2583
Bravo Cucina Italiana (Italian) 3000 Hayden Run Rd	Columbus	OH	43235	614-791-1245
Buckeye Hall of Fame Cafe (American) 1421 Olentangy River Rd	Columbus	OH	43212	614-291-2233
Clarmont The (Steak/Seafood) 684 S High St	Columbus	OH	43215	614-443-1125
Engine House #5 (Seafood) 121 Thurman Ave	Columbus	OH	43206	614-443-4877
Fifty Five on the Blvd (Seafood) 55 Nationwide Blvd	Columbus	OH	43215	614-228-5555
Firdou's Deli & Cafe (Middle Eastern) 1538 N High St	Columbus	OH	43201	614-299-1844
Flatiron Bar & Diner (American) 129 E Nationwide Blvd	Columbus	OH	43215	614-461-0033
Florentine Restaurant (Italian) 907 W Broad St	Columbus	OH	43209	614-228-2262
Frezno Eclectic Kitchen (American) 782 N High St	Columbus	OH	43215	614-298-0031
Gottlieb's Tavern (American) 1027 W 5th Ave	Columbus	OH	43212	614-297-8755
Handke's Cuisine (International) 520 S Front St	Columbus	OH	43215	614-621-2500
Hoster Brewing Co (American) 550 S High St	Columbus	OH	43215	614-228-6066
Hunan Lion (Chinese) 2038 Crown Point Dr	Columbus	OH	43235	614-459-3933
Hyde Park Grille (Steak) 1615 Old Henderson Rd	Columbus	OH	43220	614-442-3310
Japanese Steak House (Japanese) 479 N High St	Columbus	OH	43215	614-228-3030
L'Antibes (French) 772 N High St Suite 106	Columbus	OH	43215	614-291-1666
Lindey's (New American) 169 E Beck St	Columbus	OH	43206	614-228-4343
Market Strand Cafe (Italian) 350 N High St	Columbus	OH	43215	614-463-1234
Martini Ristorante (Italian) 445 N High St	Columbus	OH	43215	614-224-8259
Morton's of Chicago (Steak) 2 Nationwide Plaza Suite 100	Columbus	OH	43215	614-464-4442
Otani (Japanese) 5900 Roche Dr	Columbus	OH	43229	614-431-3333
Out on Main (Continental) 122 E Main St	Columbus	OH	43215	614-224-9510
Refectory (French) 1092 Bethel Rd	Columbus	OH	43220	614-451-9774
Rigsby's Cuisine Volatile (International) 698 N High St	Columbus	OH	43215	614-461-7888
River Club The (American) 679 W Long St	Columbus	OH	43215	614-469-0000
RJ Snappers Bar & Grill (Seafood) 700 N High St	Columbus	OH	43215	614-280-1070
Saigon Palace Restaurant (Vietnamese) 114 N Front St	Columbus	OH	43215	614-464-3325
Sapporo Wind (Japanese) 6188 Cleveland Ave	Columbus	OH	43231	614-895-7575
Schmidt's Sausage Haus (German) 240 E Kossuth St	Columbus	OH	43206	614-444-6808
Strada World Cuisine (International) 106 W Vine St	Columbus	OH	43215	614-228-8244
Theatre Cafe (American) 310 S High St	Columbus	OH	43215	614-228-3800
Tony's Italian Ristorante (Italian) 16 W Beck St	Columbus	OH	43215	614-224-8669
Trattoria Roma (Italian) 1270 Morse Rd	Columbus	OH	43229	614-888-6686
Worthington Inn (American) 649 High St	Worthington	OH	43085	614-885-7700

— Goods and Services —

SHOPPING

Name / Address	City	State	Zip	Phone	Fax
Brice Outlet Mall 5891 Scarborough Blvd	Columbus	OH	43232	614-863-0884	
Columbus City Center 111 S 3rd St	Columbus	OH	43215	614-221-4900	469-5093
Continent The 6076 Busch Blvd Suite 2	Columbus	OH	43229	614-846-0418	846-5599
Eastland Mall 2740B Eastland Mall	Columbus	OH	43232	614-861-3232	861-6279
Greater Columbus Antique Mall 1045 S High St	Columbus	OH	43206	614-443-7858	
Lazarus 141 S High St	Columbus	OH	43215	614-463-2121	463-3217
Marshall Field's 225 S 3rd St	Columbus	OH	43215	614-227-6222	
North Market 59 Spruce St	Columbus	OH	43215	614-463-9664	469-9323
Web: www.northmarket.com/					
Northland Mall 1711 Northland Way	Columbus	OH	43229	614-267-9258	267-3449
Schottenstein 3251 Westerville Rd	Columbus	OH	43224	614-471-4711	471-5031
Westland Mall 4273 Broad St	Columbus	OH	43228	614-272-0012	

BANKS

Name / Address	City	State	Zip	Phone	Fax
Bank One Columbus NA 100 E Broad St	Columbus	OH	43215	614-248-5601	248-6463*
**Fax:* Loans					
Fifth Third Bank of Columbus 21 E State St	Columbus	OH	43215	614-341-2595	341-2516
Firstar Bank 62 E Broad St	Columbus	OH	43215	614-221-2941	222-8775
TF: 800-627-7827					
Huntington National Bank 41 S High St	Columbus	OH	43287	614-480-8300	480-5485
TF: 800-480-2265 ■ *Web:* www.huntington.com					
KeyBank NA Columbus District 88 E Broad St	Columbus	OH	43215	614-460-3400	365-3312
TF Cust Svc: 800-539-2968*					
National City Bank Columbus 155 E Broad St	Columbus	OH	43251	614-463-7100	463-7123*
**Fax:* Hum Res ■ *TF:* 800-738-3888					

BUSINESS SERVICES

Name	Phone
Accountemps	614-221-9300
Columbus Corporate Courier	614-864-9797
Dynamex	614-276-6000
Federal Express	800-238-5355
Kelly Services	614-221-6784
Kinko's	614-294-7485
Local Mail & Freight	614-875-2044
Mail Service	614-878-5854
Manpower Temporary Services	614-275-2300
Olsten Staffing Services	614-228-8114
Post Office	614-469-4223
Premier Couriers	614-221-6433
Priority Dispatch	614-258-8558
UPS	800-742-5877
US Cargo & Courier Service	614-552-2746

— Media —

PUBLICATIONS

Name / Address	City	State	Zip	Phone	Fax
Business First 471 E Broad St Suite 1500	Columbus	OH	43215	614-461-4040	365-2980
Web: www.amcity.com/columbus					
Columbus Dispatch‡ 34 S 3rd St	Columbus	OH	43215	614-461-5000	461-7580
Web: www.dispatch.com ■ *E-mail:* crow@cd.columbus.oh.us					
Columbus Monthly 5255 Sinclair Rd	Columbus	OH	43229	614-888-4567	848-3838
Dublin News PO Box 29912	Columbus	OH	43229	614-785-1212	842-4760*
**Fax:* News Rm ■ *E-mail:* snpnews@cis.compuserve.com					
Dublin Villager PO Box 341890	Columbus	OH	43234	614-841-1781	841-0436*
**Fax:* News Rm ■ *Web:* www.thisweeknews.com					
■ *E-mail:* thisweek@infinet.com					
Eastside Messenger 3378 Sullivant Ave	Columbus	OH	43204	614-272-5422	272-0684*
**Fax:* News Rm					
Eastside This Week PO Box 341890	Columbus	OH	43234	614-841-1781	841-0436*
**Fax:* News Rm					
Ohio Magazine 62 E Broad St 2nd Fl	Columbus	OH	43215	614-461-5083	461-5506
Web: www.ohiomagazine.com/					

‡Daily newspapers

Columbus (Cont'd)

TELEVISION

				Phone	Fax
WBNS-TV Ch 10 (CBS) 770 Twin Rivers Dr	Columbus	OH	43215	614-460-3700	460-2891
Web: www.wbns10tv.com					
WCMH-TV Ch 4 (NBC) 3165 Olentangy River Rd	Columbus	OH	43202	614-263-4444	263-0166
Web: www.wcmh4.com ■ *E-mail:* wcmh4@erinet.com					
WOSU-TV Ch 34 (PBS) 2400 Olentangy River Rd	Columbus	OH	43210	614-292-9678	292-7625
Web: www.wosu.org					
WSFJ-TV Ch 51 (Ind) 10077 Jacksontown Rd SE	Thornville	OH	43076	740-323-0771	323-3242
WSYX-TV Ch 6 (ABC) 1261 Dublin Rd	Columbus	OH	43215	614-481-6666	481-6624
WTTE-TV Ch 28 (Fox) 6130 Sunbury Rd	Westerville	OH	43081	614-895-2800	895-3159
Web: www.wtte.com ■ *E-mail:* viewer@wtte.com					
WWHO-TV Ch 53 (UPN) 1160 Dublin Rd Suite 500	Columbus	OH	43215	614-485-5300	485-5339
Web: www.paramountstations.com/WWHO					

RADIO

				Phone	Fax
WAZU-FM 107.1 MHz (Rock) 2 Nationwide Plaza 10th Fl	Columbus	OH	43215	614-227-9696	461-1059
WBNS-AM 1460 kHz (Sports) 175 S 3rd St	Columbus	OH	43215	614-460-3850	460-3757
Web: www.1460thefan.com					
WBNS-FM 97.1 MHz (Oldies) 175 S 3rd St	Columbus	OH	43215	614-460-3850	460-3757
WBZX-FM 99.7 MHz (Rock) 1458 Dublin Rd	Columbus	OH	43215	614-481-7800	481-8070
Web: www.wbzx.com ■ *E-mail:* theblitz@wbzx.com					
WCBE-FM 90.5 MHz (NPR) 540 Jack Gibbs Blvd	Columbus	OH	43215	614-365-5555	365-5060
Web: wcbe.org/					
WCKX-FM 107.5 MHz (Urban) 1500 W 3rd Ave Suite 300	Columbus	OH	43212	614-487-1444	487 5862
WCOL-FM 92.3 MHz (Ctry) 2 Nationwide Plaza 10th Fl	Columbus	OH	43215	614-821-9265	221-9292
Web: wcol.com ■ *E-mail:* wcol@wcol.com					
WFYI-AM 1230 kHz (N/T) 2 Nationwide Plaza 10th Fl	Columbus	OH	43215	614-821-9265	221-9292
Web: www.wcol.com ■ *E-mail:* 1230wcol@erinet.com					
WHOK-FM 95.5 MHz (Ctry) 2 Nationwide Plaza	Columbus	OH	43215	614-225-9465	677-0116
Web: www.whok.com ■ *E-mail:* whok@whok.com					
WJZA-FM 103.5 MHz (NAC) 655 Metro Pl S Suite 100	Dublin	OH	43017	614-889-1043	717-9200
Web: www.columbusjazz.com					
WLVQ-FM 96.3 MHz (Rock) 2 Nationwide Plaza 10th Fl	Columbus	OH	43215	614-227-9696	461-1059
WMNI-AM 920 kHz (Nost) 1458 Dublin Rd	Columbus	OH	43215	614-481-7800	481-8070
WNCI-FM 97.9 MHz (CHR) 6172 Busch Blvd Suite 2000	Columbus	OH	43215	614-430-9624	847-9593
Web: www.wnci.com					
WOSU-AM 820 kHz (NPR) 2400 Olentangy River Rd	Columbus	OH	43210	614-292-9678	292-0513
Web: www.wosu.org/main/am/news820.htm ■ *E-mail:* wosu@osu.edu					
WSNY-FM 94.7 MHz (AC) 4401 Carriage Hill Ln	Columbus	OH	43220	614-451-2191	821-9595
WTVN-AM 610 kHz (N/T) 1301 Dublin Rd	Columbus	OH	43215	614-486-6101	487-2559
WVKO-AM 1580 kHz (Rel) 4401 Carriage Hill Ln	Columbus	OH	43220	614-451-2191	451-1831
WWCD-FM 101.1 MHz (Alt) 503 S Front St Suite 101	Columbus	OH	43215	614-221-9923	227-0021
WXMG-FM 98.9 MHz (Urban) 1500 W 3rd Ave Suite 300	Columbus	OH	43212	614-487-1444	487-5862
WXST-FM 107.9 MHz (AC) 1 Campus View Blvd Suite 335	Columbus	OH	43235	614-848-3108	433-7108
Web: www.star1079.com ■ *E-mail:* comments@star1079.com					
WZAZ-FM 105.7 MHz (Alt) 6172 Busch Blvd Suite 2000	Columbus	OH	43229	614-848-7625	847-9593
WZJZ-FM 104.3 MHz (NAC) 655 Metro Pl S Suite 100	Dublin	OH	43017	614-889-1043	717-9200
Web: www.columbusjazz.com					

— Colleges/Universities —

				Phone	Fax
Bradford School 6170 Busch Blvd	Columbus	OH	43229	614-846-9410	846-9656
TF: 800-678-7981					
Capital University 2199 E Main St	Columbus	OH	43209	614-236-6011	236-6926
TF Admissions: 800-289-6289 ■ *Web:* www.capital.edu					
Columbus College of Art & Design 107 N 9th St	Columbus	OH	43215	614-224-9101	222-4040
Web: www.ccad.edu ■ *E-mail:* admissions@ccad.edu					
Columbus State Community College 550 E Spring St	Columbus	OH	43215	614-287-2400	287-5117
TF: 800-621-6407 ■ *Web:* www.cscc.edu					
Denison University Main St	Granville	OH	43023	740-587-0810	587-6306
TF: 800-336-4766 ■ *Web:* www.denison.edu ■ *E-mail:* admissions@denison.edu					
DeVRY Institute of Technology 1350 Alum Creek Dr	Columbus	OH	43209	614-253-7291	253-0843
TF: 800-426-2206 ■ *Web:* www.devrycols.edu					
Franklin University 201 S Grant Ave	Columbus	OH	43215	614-341-6237	224-8027
TF: 877-341-6300 ■ *Web:* www.franklin.edu					
Ohio Dominican College 1216 Sunbury Rd	Columbus	OH	43219	614-253-2741	252-0776
TF Admissions: 800-955-6446 ■ *Web:* www.odc.edu					
Ohio State University 1800 Cannon Dr	Columbus	OH	43210	614-292-6446	292-4818
Web: www.osu.edu					
Otterbein College 1 Otterbein College	Westerville	OH	43081	614-890-3000	823-1200
TF: 800-488-8144 ■ *Web:* www.otterbein.edu					

— Hospitals —

				Phone	Fax
Children's Hospital 700 Children's Dr	Columbus	OH	43205	614-722-2000	722-5995
Web: www.childrenshospital.columbus.oh.us					
Doctors Hospital 1087 Dennison Ave	Columbus	OH	43201	614-297-4000	297-4116
Web: www.doctors-10tv.com					
Grant Riverside Methodist Hospitals Grant Campus 111 S Grant Ave	Columbus	OH	43215	614-566-9000	566-8043
Mount Carmel East Hospital 6001 E Broad St	Columbus	OH	43213	614-234-6000	234-6611
Mount Carmel Medical Center 793 W State St	Columbus	OH	43222	614-234-5000	234-1359
Ohio State University Medical Center 450 W 10th Ave	Columbus	OH	43210	614-293-8000	293-3535
Web: www.acs.ohio-state.edu/osu/med-cent.html					
Riverside Hospital 3535 Olentangy River Rd	Columbus	OH	43214	614-566-5000	566-6749
Saint Ann's Hospital 500 S Cleveland Ave	Westerville	OH	43081	614-898-4000	898-8628
University Hospital East 1492 E Broad St	Columbus	OH	43205	614-251-3000	257-3983
TF: 800-863-3000					

— Attractions —

				Phone	Fax
Anheuser-Busch Brewery 700 Schrock Rd	Columbus	OH	43229	614-888-6644	847-6497*
**Fax:* Hum Res					
BalletMet Columbus 322 Mt Vernon Ave	Columbus	OH	43215	614-229-4860	224-3697
Web: www.balletmet.org					
Cloak & Dagger Dinner Theatre 1048 Morse Rd	Columbus	OH	43229	614-523-9347	224-2326
TF: 800-935-4548					
Columbus Light Opera 2199 Naghten St	Columbus	OH	43215	614-461-8101	461-0806
Columbus Museum of Art 480 E Broad St	Columbus	OH	43215	614-221-6801	221-0226
Web: www.columbusart.mus.oh.us ■ *E-mail:* info@columbusart.mus.oh.us					
Columbus Symphony Orchestra 55 E State St	Columbus	OH	43215	614-228-9600	224-7273
Web: www.csobravo.org					
Columbus Zoo 9990 Riverside Dr	Powell	OH	43065	614-645-3400	645-3465
Web: www.colszoo.org					
Contemporary American Theatre Co 77 S High St	Columbus	OH	43215	614-461-0010	461-4917
COSI Center of Science & Industry 280 E Broad St	Columbus	OH	43215	614-228-2674	228-6363
Web: www.cosi.org					
Franklin Park Conservatory & Botanical Garden 1777 E Broad St	Columbus	OH	43203	614-645-8733	645-5921
TF: 800-241-7275 ■ *Web:* www.fpconservatory.org					
German Village 588 S 3rd St	Columbus	OH	43215	614-221-8888	222-4747
Web: www.germanvillage.org					
Griggs Park & Reservoir 2933 Riverside Dr	Columbus	OH	43221	614-645-3300	
Heritage Museum 530 E Town St	Columbus	OH	43215	614-228-6515	228-7809
Hoover Park & Reservoir 7001 Sunbury Rd	Columbus	OH	43081	614-645-3300	
Hopewell Culture National Historical Park 16062 SR-104	Chillicothe	OH	45601	740-774-1125	774-1140
Web: www.nps.gov/hocu/					
Inniswood Metro Gardens 940 Hempstead Rd	Columbus	OH	43081	614-895-6216	895-6352
Jack Nicklaus Museum 5750 Memorial Dr	Dublin	OH	43017	614-792-2353	889-6026

Columbus — Attractions (Cont'd)

				Phone	Fax
Kelton House Museum 586 E Town St	Columbus	OH	43215	614-464-2022	464-3346
King Arts Complex 867 Mt Vernon Ave	Columbus	OH	43203	614-252-5464	252-3807
Motorcycle Heritage Museum 13515 Yarmouth Dr. *TF:* 800-262-5646 ■ *Web:* www.ama-cycle.org/museum/index.html ■ *E-mail:* melissak@ama-cycle.org	Pickerington	OH	43147	614-856-1900	856-1920
Ohio Craft Museum 1665 W 5th Ave	Columbus	OH	43212	614-486-4402	486-7110
Ohio Historical Center 1982 Velma Ave *Web:* www.ohiohistory.org	Columbus	OH	43211	614-297-2300	297-2411
Ohio History of Flight Museum 4275 Sawyer Rd	Columbus	OH	43219	614-231-1300	
Ohio Statehouse Broad & High Sts	Columbus	OH	43215	614-466-2125	
Ohio Theatre 55 E State St *Web:* www.capa.com	Columbus	OH	43215	614-469-1045	461-0429
Ohio Village 1982 Velma Ave	Columbus	OH	43211	614-297-2300	
Ohio Women's Hall of Fame 145 S Front St	Columbus	OH	43215	614-466-4496	466-7912
Olentangy Indian Caverns 1779 Home Rd *Web:* www.olentangyindiancaverns.com ■ *E-mail:* oic@olentangyindiancaverns.com	Delaware	OH	43015	740-548-7917	369-6466
Opera/Columbus 177 Naghten St *Web:* www.operacols.org	Columbus	OH	43215	614-461-8101	461-0806
Palace Theatre 34 W Broad St *Web:* www.capa.com/Palace_Theatre.html ■ *E-mail:* info@capa.com	Columbus	OH	43215	614-469-1332	460-2272
Pimsler Stuart Dance & Theater 27 E Russell St *Web:* innerart.com/SPDT/dance.html ■ *E-mail:* spdanth@aol.com	Columbus	OH	43215	614-461-0132	461-0132
Pro Musica Chamber Orchestra 243 N 5th St Suite 202	Columbus	OH	43215	614-464-0066	464-4141
Roscoe Village 381 Hill St *TF Info:* 800-877-1830 ■ *Web:* www.roscoevillage.com	Coshocton	OH	43812	740-622-9310	623-6555
Saint Joseph Cathedral 212 E Broad St	Columbus	OH	43215	614-224-1295	224-1176
Santa Maria Replica Marconi Blvd & W Broad St Battelle Riverfront Pk *Web:* www.santamaria.org/	Columbus	OH	43215	614-645-8760	645-8748
Shadowbox Cabaret 232 E Spring St *Web:* www.shadowboxcabaret.com/	Columbus	OH	43215	614-224-3374	224-9262
Singing Buckeyes 400 Dublin Ave Suite 250 *Web:* www.harmonize.com/singingbuckeyes/	Columbus	OH	43215	614-221-4480	365-3347
Slate Run Living Historical Farm 1375 SR 674 N.	Canal Winchester	OH	43110	614-833-1880	
Thurber House 77 Jefferson Ave *Web:* www.thurberhouse.org	Columbus	OH	43215	614-464-1032	228-7445
Wexner Center for the Arts 1871 N High St Ohio State University *Web:* www.cgrg.ohio-state.edu/Wexner ■ *E-mail:* wexner@cgrg.ohio-state.edu	Columbus	OH	43210	614-292-0330	292-3369
Whetstone Park 3923 N High St	Columbus	OH	43214	614-645-3217	
Wyandot Lake Adventure Park PO Box 215 *TF:* 800-328-9283	Powell	OH	43065	614-889-9283	766-4753

SPORTS TEAMS & FACILITIES

				Phone	Fax
Beulah Park Race Track 3664 Grant Ave *TF:* 800-433-6905	Grove City	OH	43123	614-871-9600	871-0433
Central Ohio Cows (baseball) 41 S Grant Ave *E-mail:* central.ohio.cows@mailexcite.com	Columbus	OH	43215	614-224-4534	464-4730
Columbus All-Americans (baseball) 50 W Broad St Suite 700	Columbus	OH	43215	614-221-3151	221-8196
Columbus Chill (hockey) 632 E 11th Ave Ohio State Fairgrounds *Web:* www.thechill.com ■ *E-mail:* info@thechill.com	Columbus	OH	43211	614-791-9999	791-9302
Columbus Clippers (baseball) 1155 W Mound St *Web:* www.clippersbaseball.com/ ■ *E-mail:* colsclippers@earthlink.net	Columbus	OH	43223	614-462-5250	462-3271
Columbus Crew (soccer) 2121 Velma Ave *Web:* www.thecrew.com ■ *E-mail:* crew2739@aol.com	Columbus	OH	43211	614-447-2739	447-4109
Columbus Motor Speedway Inc 1845 Williams Rd *Web:* www.columbusspeedway.com ■ *E-mail:* nascar@netwalk.com	Columbus	OH	43207	614-491-1047	491-6010
National Trail Raceway 2650 National Rd SW	Hebron	OH	43025	740-928-5706	928-2922
Ohio Stadium 411 Woody Hayes Dr *Web:* www.ohiostatebuckeyes.com	Columbus	OH	43210	614-292-7572	292-0506
Scioto Downs 6000 S High St *Web:* www.sciotodowns.com	Columbus	OH	43207	614-491-2515	491-4626

— Events —

	Phone
All American Quarter Horse Congress (mid-October)	740-943-2346
Asian Festival (late May)	614-292-0613
Capital Holiday Lights (December)	800-345-4386
Central Ohio Daffodil Society Show (mid-April)	614-645-8733
Columbus Arts Festival (early June)	614-224-2606
Columbus International Festival (early November)	614-228-4010
Columbus International Film & Video Festival (mid-October)	614-841-1666
Columbus Marathon (early November)	614-794-1566
Crusin' on the Riverfront (late July-early August)	614-258-1983
Equine Affaire-The Great American Horse Exposition (early April)	740-845-0085
Fall Festival of Roses (late September)	614-645-8733
First Night Columbus (December 31)	614-481-0020
June Teenth Festival (mid-June)	614-299-4488
Ohio State Fair (early-late August)	614-644-3247
Ohio State Fair Horse Show (late July-late August)	614-644-4035
Oktoberfest (early September)	614-224-4300
PGA Memorial Tournament at Muirfield (late May-early June)	614-889-6700
Red White & Boom (early July)	614-263-4444
Rhythm & Food: A Taste of Columbus (late May)	614-221-6623
Rose Festival (mid-June)	614-645-3379
Saint Patrick's Day Parade (mid-March)	614-645-4375
Wildlight Wonderland (late November-early January)	614-645-3550
Winterfair (early December)	614-486-7119

Dayton

Beginning with Wilbur and Orville Wright, Dayton's history has centered on aviation. The Dayton Aviation National Historical Park, authorized in 1992, preserves the area's aviation heritage associated with the Wright Brothers, their invention and development in aviation, and the life and works of their friend and classmate, the poet Paul Laurence Dunbar. Each July, the world-famous U.S. Air and Trade Show, featuring more than 100 outdoor exhibits, is held in Dayton at Wright-Patterson Air Force Base. At the base also is the United States Air Force Museum, the world's largest military aviation museum, which has more than 200 historic aircraft and missiles.

Population	167,475	**Longitude**	84-73-17 W
Area (Land)	55.0 sq mi	**County**	Montgomery
Area (Water)	0.9 sq mi	**Time Zone**	EST
Elevation	757 ft	**Area Code/s**	937
Latitude	40-19-45 N		

— Average Temperatures and Precipitation —

TEMPERATURES

	Jan	Feb	Mar	Apr	May	Jun	Jul	Aug	Sep	Oct	Nov	Dec
High	34	38	50	62	73	82	85	83	77	65	51	39
Low	18	21	31	41	51	59	63	61	55	44	34	24

PRECIPITATION

	Jan	Feb	Mar	Apr	May	Jun	Jul	Aug	Sep	Oct	Nov	Dec
Inches	2.1	2.2	3.4	3.5	3.9	3.8	3.5	3.2	2.5	2.5	3.1	2.9

— Important Phone Numbers —

	Phone		Phone
AAA	937-224-2888	**Time**	937-499-1212
Emergency	911	**Weather**	937-258-2000
Poison Control Center	937-222-2227		

Dayton (Cont'd)

— Information Sources —

				Phone	Fax
Better Business Bureau Serving Dayton/Miami Valley 40 W 4th St Suite 1250	Dayton	OH	45402	937-222-5825	222-3338
TF: 800-776-5301 ■ *Web:* www.dayton.bbb.org ■ *E-mail:* info@dayton.bbb.org					
Dayton & Montgomery County Public Library 215 E 3rd St	Dayton	OH	45402	937-227-9500	227-9524
Web: www.dayton.lib.oh.us					
Dayton Area Chamber of Commerce 1 Chamber Plaza	Dayton	OH	45402	937-226-1444	226-8254
Web: www.daytonchamber.org					
Dayton City Hall 101 W 3rd St	Dayton	OH	45402	937-443-4000	
Web: www.ci.dayton.oh.us ■ *E-mail:* cityinfo@ci.dayton.oh.us					
Dayton Convention Center 22 E 5th St	Dayton	OH	45402	937-333-4700	333-4711
TF: 800-822-3498					
Dayton Economic Development Dept 101 W 3rd St Rm 430	Dayton	OH	45402	937-443-3634	443-4274
Dayton Mayor 101 W 3rd St	Dayton	OH	45402	937-443-3636	443-4299
Dayton/Montgomery County Convention & Visitors Bureau 1 Chamber Plaza Suite A	Dayton	OH	45402	937-226-8248	226-8294
TF: 800-221-8235 ■ *Web:* www.daytoncvb.com ■ *E-mail:* cvbureau@dnaco.net					
Montgomery County 41 N Perry St	Dayton	OH	45422	937-225-4000	496-7220

On-Line Resources

4Dayton.com	www.4dayton.com
Anthill City Guide Dayton	www.anthill.com/city.asp?city=dayton
Area Guide Dayton	dayton.areaguides.net
City Knowledge Dayton	www.cityknowledge.com/oh_dayton.htm
Dayton Golf Online	www.daytongolf.com/
Dayton Home Page	www.dayton.net/dayton
Excite.com Dayton City Guide	www.excite.com/travel/countries/united_states/ohio/dayton

— Transportation Services —

AIRPORTS

■ Dayton International Airport (DAY)

	Phone
5 miles N of downtown (approx 5 minutes)	937-454-8200

Airport Transportation

	Phone
Airport Taxi $20 fare to downtown	937-228-1155
Checker Cab $20-22 fare to downtown	937-222-4011

Commercial Airlines

	Phone		Phone
AirTran	800-247-8726	**Delta**	800-221-1212
American	800-433-7300	**Northwest**	800-225-2525
Comair	800-354-9822	**TWA**	800-221-2000
Continental Express	800-525-0280	**US Airways**	800-428-4322

Charter Airlines

	Phone		Phone
Aviation Sales	937-898-3927	**Stevens Aviation**	937-454-3400
Helicopters Inc	800-466-2903	**Wright Brothers Aero**	937-890-8900

CAR RENTALS

	Phone		Phone
Alamo	800-327-9633	**Enterprise**	937-228-4555
Avis	937-898-5835	**Hertz**	937-898-5806
Budget	937-898-1396	**National**	937-890-0100
Dollar	937-454-8430		

LIMO/TAXI

	Phone		Phone
Afford-A-Limo	937-236-1481	**Mr Limousine**	937-439-4241
Checker Cab	937-222-4011	**Ohio Limo**	937-592-5466
Cliff Cab Co	937-223-5171	**Southern Hills Limousine**	937-293-9000
Harvest Taxi	937-879-0059	**Thomas Limousine**	937-263-8894
Miami Liberty Cab Co	937-222-2822	**Yellow Cab**	937-228-1155

MASS TRANSIT

	Phone
Miami Valley Regional Transit Authority $1 Base fare	937-226-1144

RAIL/BUS

				Phone
Greyhound/Trailways Bus Station 111 E 5th St	Dayton	OH	45402	937-224-1608
TF: 800-231-2222				

— Accommodations —

HOTELS, MOTELS, RESORTS

				Phone	Fax
Best Western Continental Inn 155 Monarch Ln	Miamisburg	OH	45342	937-866-5500	866-8270
TF: 800-528-1234					
Courtyard by Marriott 100 Prestige Pl	Miamisburg	OH	45342	937-433-3131	433-0285
TF: 800-321-2211 ■ *Web:* courtyard.com/DAYML					
Cross Country Inn 9325 N Main St	Dayton	OH	45415	937-836-8339	836-1772
Crowne Plaza Dayton 33 E 5th St	Dayton	OH	45402	937-224-0800	224-3913
TF: 800-227-6963					
Days Inn Dayton South 3555 Miamisburg-Centerville Rd	Dayton	OH	45449	937-847-8422	847-8862
TF: 800-329-7466					
Days Inn North 7470 Miller Ln	Dayton	OH	45414	937-898-4946	898-0214
TF: 800-329-7466					
Dayton Airport Inn Dayton International Airport	Vandalia	OH	45377	937-898-1000	898-3761
TF: 800-543-7577					
Dayton Lodge 2401 Needmore Rd	Dayton	OH	45414	937-278-5711	278-6048
Dayton Marriott 1414 S Patterson Blvd	Dayton	OH	45409	937-223-1000	223-7853
TF: 800-228-9290					
Dayton North Plaza Inn 3636 N Dixie Dr	Dayton	OH	45414	937-276-6151	275-5603
Doubletree Guest Suites 300 Prestige Pl	Miamisburg	OH	45342	937-436-2400	436-2886
TF: 800-222-8733 ■ *Web:* www.doubletreehotels.com/DoubleT/Hotel61/74/74Main.htm					
Doubletree Hotel Downtown 11 S Ludlow St	Dayton	OH	45402	937-461-4700	461-3440
TF: 800-222-8733					
Fairfield Inn by Marriott 6960 Miller Ln	Dayton	OH	45414	937-898-1120	898-1120
TF: 800-228-2800 ■ *Web:* fairfieldinn.com/DAYFI					
Hampton Inn South 8099 Old Yankee St	Dayton	OH	45458	937-436-3700	436-2995
TF: 800-426-7866					
Holiday Inn Dayton North 2301 Wagoner Ford Rd	Dayton	OH	45414	937-278-4871	278-0146
TF: 800-465-4329					
Holiday Inn Fairborn Hotel & Conference Center 2800 Presidential Dr	Fairborn	OH	45324	937-426-7800	426-1284
TF: 800-465-4329 ■ *Web:* www.basshotels.com/holiday-inn/?_franchisee=FBNPD ■ *E-mail:* fbnpd@cwixmail.com					
Homewood Suites 2750 Presidential Dr	Fairborn	OH	45324	937-429-0600	429-6311
TF: 800-225-4654					
Howard Johnson 7575 Poe Ave	Dayton	OH	45414	937-454-0550	454-5566
TF: 800-446-4656					
Park Inn International Dayton Airport 75 Corporate Center Dr	Vandalia	OH	45377	937-898-8321	898-6334
TF: 800-437-7275					
Ramada Inn North Airport 4079 Little York Rd	Dayton	OH	45414	937-890-9500	890-8525
TF: 800-272-6232					
Red Roof Inn Miamisburg 222 Byers Rd	Miamisburg	OH	45342	937-866-0705	866-0700
TF: 800-843-7663					
Regency Hotel 330 W 1st St	Dayton	OH	45402	937-228-3968	228-3901
StudioPLUS 7851 Lois Cir	Dayton	OH	45459	937-439-2022	436-8273

— Restaurants —

				Phone
Anticoli's (Italian) 3045 Salem Ave	Dayton	OH	45406	937-277-2264
Cafe Boulevard (European) 329 E 5th St	Dayton	OH	45402	937-824-2722
Chins Oriental Cafe (Chinese) 200 S Jefferson St	Dayton	OH	45402	937-461-0111
Coco's 520 Grill (American) 520 E 5th St	Dayton	OH	45402	937-228-2626
Duke's Golden Ox (Steak) 1202 S Main St	Dayton	OH	45409	937-222-6200
Franco's Ristorante Italiano (Italian) 824 E 5th St	Dayton	OH	45402	937-222-0204
L'Auberge (French) 4120 Far Hills Ave	Dayton	OH	45429	937-299-5536
Pacchia (Italian) 410 E 5th St	Dayton	OH	45402	937-443-6223
Parmizzano's (Italian) 1414 S Patterson Blvd	Dayton	OH	45409	937-223-1000
Peasant Stock (Steak/Seafood) 424 E Stroop Rd	Dayton	OH	45429	937-293-3900
Pine Club The (Steak) 1926 Brown St	Dayton	OH	45409	937-228-7463
Star's Restaurant (American) 33 E 5th St	Dayton	OH	45402	937-224-0800
Thomato's (American) 110 N Main St	Dayton	OH	45402	937-228-3333
Welton's (Steak/Seafood) 4614 Wilmington Pike	Dayton	OH	45440	937-293-2233

Dayton (Cont'd)

— Goods and Services —

SHOPPING

			Phone	Fax
Dayton Mall 2700 Miamisburg Centerville Rd	Dayton OH	45459	937-433-9833	433-5289
Elder-Beerman Courthouse Plaza 40 N Ludlow St	Dayton OH	45401	937-224-8000	
Mall at Fairfield Commons 2727 Fairfield Commons	Beavercreek OH	45431	937-427-4300	427-3668
Oregon Historic District	Dayton OH	45402	937-223-0538	
Salem Mall 5200 Salem Ave	Dayton OH	45426	937-854-5000	854-3463
Town & Country Shopping Center Far Hills & Stroop Rd	Dayton OH	45429	937-293-7516	293-5575

BANKS

			Phone	Fax
Bank One NA 40 N Main St Kettering Tower *TF:* 800-333-1049	Dayton OH	45401	937-449-8803	449-2060
Fifth Third Bank 110 N Main St *TF:* 800-972-3030	Dayton OH	45402	937-227-6500	227-6504
Huntington National Bank Courthouse Plaza SW Suite 200	Dayton OH	45402	937-443-5900	443-5914
National City Bank of Dayton 6 N Main St **Fax Area Code:* 888 ■ **Fax:* Cust Svc ■ *TF:* 800-368-0122	Dayton OH	45412	937-226-2000	814-3287*

BUSINESS SERVICES

	Phone		Phone
City to City Courier	937-461-0536	**Post Office**	937-227-1231
Federal Express	800-238-5355	**Priority Dispatch**	937-226-1100
Kelly Services	937-299-2828	**Royal Temporary Services**	937-228-3262
Kinko's	937-228-6200	**Rush Package Delivery**	937-461-8973
Olsten Staffing Services	937-228-3954	**UPS**	800-742-5877

— Media —

PUBLICATIONS

			Phone	Fax
Dayton Daily News‡ 45 S Ludlow St *Web:* www.activedayton.com	Dayton OH	45402	937-225-2000	225-2489
Enon Messenger 1 Herald Sq **Fax:* News Rm	Fairborn OH	45324	937-878-3993	878-8314*

‡*Daily newspapers*

TELEVISION

			Phone	Fax
WDPX-TV Ch 26 (PAX) 2675 Dayton Rd *Web:* www.pax.net/WDPX	Springfield OH	45506	937-323-0026	323-1912
WDTN-TV Ch 2 (ABC) 4595 S Dixie Dr *Web:* wdtn.com ■ *E-mail:* wdtn@erinet.com	Dayton OH	45439	937-293-2101	296-7147
WHIO-TV Ch 7 (CBS) 1414 Wilmington Ave *Web:* www.activedayton.com/whiotv	Dayton OH	45420	937-259-2111	259-2024
WKEF-TV Ch 22 (NBC) 1731 Soldiers Home Rd *Web:* www.nbc22.com ■ *E-mail:* nbc22@erinet.com	Dayton OH	45418	937-263-2662	268-2332
WPTD-TV Ch 16 (PBS) 110 S Jefferson St	Dayton OH	45402	937-220-1600	220-1642
WRGT-TV Ch 45 (Fox) 45 Broadcast Plaza	Dayton OH	45408	937-263-4500	268-5265

RADIO

			Phone	Fax
WCTM-AM 1130 kHz (B/EZ) 320 Woodside Dr	West Alexandria OH	45381	937-456-3200	
WDAO-AM 1210 kHz (Urban) 33 E 2nd St	Dayton OH	45402	937-222-9326	461-6100
WFCJ-FM 93.7 MHz (Rel) PO Box 937 *Web:* www.wfcj.com	Dayton OH	45449	937-866-2471	866-2062
WGTZ-FM 92.9 MHz (CHR) 717 E David Rd *Web:* www.erinet.com/wgtz	Dayton OH	45429	937-294-5858	297-5233
WHIO-AM 1290 kHz (N/T) 1414 Wilmington Ave **Fax:* Sales ■ *Web:* www.activedayton.com/partners/whioam ■ *E-mail:* coxradio@erinet.com	Dayton OH	45420	937-259-2111	259-2168*
WHKO-FM 99.1 MHz (Ctry) 1414 Wilmington Ave	Dayton OH	45420	937-259-2111	259-2168
WING-AM 1410 kHz (N/T) 717 E David Rd	Dayton OH	45429	937-294-5858	297-5233
WING-FM 102.9 MHz (CR) 717 E David Rd	Dayton OH	45429	937-294-5858	297-5233
WLQT-FM 99.9 MHz (AC) 101 Pine St *Web:* www.wlqt.com ■ *E-mail:* lite99@erinet.com	Dayton OH	45402	937-224-1137	224-3667
WMMX-FM 107.7 MHz (AC) 101 Pine St *Web:* www.wmmx.com ■ *E-mail:* wmmx@erinet.com	Dayton OH	45402	937-224-1137	224-3667
WONE-AM 980 kHz (Nost) 101 Pine St *Web:* www.wone.com ■ *E-mail:* wone@erinet.com	Dayton OH	45402	937-224-1137	224-3667
WPFB-FM 105.9 MHz (Ctry) 200 W 2nd St	Dayton OH	45402	513-422-3625	424-9732
WROU-FM 92.1 MHz (Urban) 211 S Main St Fidelity Plaza Suite 1200	Dayton OH	45402	937-222-9768	223-5687
WXEG-FM 103.9 MHz (Alt) 101 Pine St *Web:* www.wxeg.com ■ *E-mail:* thex1039@erinet.com	Dayton OH	45402	937-224-1137	224-3667

— Colleges/Universities —

			Phone	Fax
Antioch College 795 Livermore St *TF Admissions:* 800-543-9436 ■ *Web:* www.antioch-college.edu	Yellow Springs OH	45387	937-767-7331	767-6473
Cedarville College PO Box 601 *TF Admissions:* 800-233-2784 ■ *Web:* www.cedarville.edu	Cedarville OH	45314	937-766-2211	766-7575
Central State University 1400 Brush Row Rd *TF Admissions:* 800-388-2781 ■ *Web:* www.centralstate.edu ■ *E-mail:* info@centralstate.edu	Wilberforce OH	45384	937-376-6011	376-6648
Clark State Community College 570 E Leffel Ln *Web:* www.clark.cc.oh.us	Springfield OH	45505	937-325-0691	328-6133
ITT Technical Institute 3325 Stop Eight Rd *TF:* 800-568-3241 ■ *Web:* www.itt-tech.edu	Dayton OH	45414	937-454-2267	454-2278
Kettering College of Medical Arts 3737 Southern Blvd *TF Admissions:* 800-433-5262 ■ *Web:* www.kcma.edu	Kettering OH	45429	937-296-7201	296-4238
Miami-Jacobs College 400 E 2nd St *Web:* www.miamijacobs.edu ■ *E-mail:* miamijacob@miamijacobs.edu	Dayton OH	45402	937-449-8277	461-3384
Ohio Institute of Photography & Technology 2029 Edgefield Rd *TF:* 800-932-9698 ■ *Web:* www.oipt.com	Dayton OH	45439	937-294-6155	294-2259
RETS Tech Center 555 E Alex Bell Rd *TF:* 800-837-7387	Centerville OH	45459	937-433-3410	435-6516
Sinclair Community College 444 W 3rd St *Web:* www.sinclair.edu	Dayton OH	45402	937-512-2500	512-2393
Southwestern College of Business Dayton 225 W First St	Dayton OH	45402	937-224-0061	224-0065
University of Dayton 300 College Pk *TF Admissions:* 800-837-7433 ■ *Web:* www.udayton.edu ■ *E-mail:* admission@udayton.edu	Dayton OH	45469	937-229-1000	229-4729
Urbana University Dayton Campus 101 W Schantz Ave	Dayton OH	45479	937-298-3973	
Wilberforce University 1055 N Bickett Rd *TF:* 800-367-8568 ■ *Web:* www.wilberforce.edu	Wilberforce OH	45384	937-376-2911	376-4751
Wright State University 3640 Colonel Glenn Hwy **Fax:* Admissions ■ *TF Admissions:* 800-247-1770 ■ *Web:* www.wright.edu ■ *E-mail:* cmdavis@desire.wright.edu	Dayton OH	45435	937-775-3333	775-5795*

— Hospitals —

			Phone	Fax
Children's Medical Center 1 Children's Plaza *Web:* www.cmc-dayton.org	Dayton OH	45404	937-226-8300	226-8326
Clinton Memorial Hospital 610 W Main St	Wilmington OH	45177	937-382-6611	382-6633
Community Hospital 2615 E High St	Springfield OH	45505	937-325-0531	328-9600
Franciscan Medical Center 1 Franciscan Way	Dayton OH	45408	937-229-6000	229-7093
Good Samaritan Hospital & Health Center 2222 Philadelphia Dr	Dayton OH	45406	937-278-2612	276-7617
Grandview Hospital & Medical Center 405 W Grand Ave	Dayton OH	45405	937-226-3200	461-0020
Greene Memorial Hospital 1141 N Monroe Dr	Xenia OH	45385	937-372-8011	376-6983
Kettering Medical Center 3535 Southern Blvd *Web:* www.kmcnetwork.org	Kettering OH	45429	937-298-4331	296-4284
Mercy Medical Center 1343 N Fountain Blvd **Fax:* Admitting	Springfield OH	45501	937-390-5000	390-5527*
Miami Valley Hospital 1 Wyoming St *TF:* 800-544-0630	Dayton OH	45409	937-223-6192	208-2225
Middletown Regional Hospital 105 McKnight Dr **Fax:* Admitting ■ *TF:* 800-338-4057	Middletown OH	45044	513-424-2111	420-5688*

Dayton — Hospitals (Cont'd)

	City	State	ZIP	Phone	Fax
Veterans Affairs Medical Center 4100 W 3rd St	Dayton	OH	45428	937-268-6511	262-2170

— Attractions —

	City	State	ZIP	Phone	Fax
Aullwood Audubon Center & Farm 1000 Aullwood Rd	Dayton	OH	45414	937-890-7360	890-2382
Web: www.audubon.org/local/sanctuary/aullwood/ ■ *E-mail:* aullwood@erinet.com					
Aviation Trail Inc 22 S Williams St	Dayton	OH	45407	937-443-0793	
Carillon Historical Park 100 Carillon Blvd	Dayton	OH	45409	937-293-2841	293-5798
Web: www.classicar.com/MUSEUMS/CARILLON/CARILLON.HTM					
Carriage Hill MetroPark 7800 E Shull Rd Huber Heights	Dayton	OH	45424	937-879-0461	879-8904
Carriage Hills Farm Museum 7800 E Shull Rd	Dayton	OH	45424	937-879-0461	879-8904
Citizens Motorcar Co Packard Museum 420 S Ludlow St	Dayton	OH	45402	937-226-1917	224-1918
Cox Arboretum 6733 Springboro Pike	Dayton	OH	45449	937-434-9005	434-4361
Dayton Art Institute 456 Belmont Pk N	Dayton	OH	454054	937-223-5277	223-3140
Dayton Aviation National Historical Park 22 S Williams St	Dayton	OH	45409	937-225-7705	225-7706
Web: www.nps.gov/daav/					
Dayton Bach Society 300 College Pk	Dayton	OH	45469	937-256-2224	229-3916
E-mail: bach-soc@udayton.edu					
Dayton Ballet 140 N Main St	Dayton	OH	45402	937-449-5060	461-8353
Dayton Contemporary Dance Co 126 N Main St Suite 240	Dayton	OH	45402	937-228-3232	223-6156
Dayton Cultural Center 216 N Main St	Dayton	OH	45402	937-223-2489	223-0795
Dayton Museum of Discovery 2600 DeWeese Pkwy	Dayton	OH	45414	937-275-7431	275-5811
E-mail: damuseum@gte.net					
Dayton Museum of Natural History 2600 DeWeese Pkwy	Dayton	OH	45414	937-275-7431	275-5811
Dayton Opera 125 E 1st St Memorial Hall	Dayton	OH	45402	937-228-0662	228-9612
Dayton Philharmonic Orchestra 125 E 1st St Memorial Hall	Dayton	OH	45402	937-224-3521	223-9189
Dayton Visual Arts Center 40 W 4th St	Dayton	OH	45402	937-224-3822	224-4356
Web: www.sinclair.edu/community/dvac/					
Dunbar Paul Laurence House 219 Paul Laurence Dunbar St	Dayton	OH	45407	937-224-7061	
Eastwood MetroPark Harshman Rd	Dayton	OH	45431	937-426-8521	
Five Rivers MetroParks 1375 E Siebenthaler Ave	Dayton	OH	45414	937-275-7275	278-8849
Web: www.dayton.net/MetroParks/ ■ *E-mail:* metroparks@dayton.net					
Fraze Pavilion for the Performing Arts 695 Lincoln Pk Blvd Lincoln Park Ctr	Kettering	OH	45429	937-296-3300	296-3302
E-mail: fraze@dayton.net					
Germantown MetroPark 6910 Boomershine Rd	Dayton	OH	45327	937-855-7717	
Human Race Theatre Co 126 N Main St	Dayton	OH	45419	937-461-3823	461-7223
E-mail: hrtheatre@aol.com					
IMAX Theatre Springfield Pike US Air Force Museum	Wright-Patterson AFB	OH	45433	937-253-4629	258-3816
Web: www.intecon.com/museum/imax.html					
Kettering-Moraine Museum & Historical Society 35 Moraine Cir S	Dayton	OH	45439	937-299-2722	
Miamisburg Mound State Memorial Mound Ave	Miamisburg	OH	45342	937-866-4532	
National Afro-American Museum & Cultural Center 1350 Brush Row Rd	Wilberforce	OH	45384	937-376-4944	376-2007
Web: www.ohiohistory.org/places/afroam/					
Old Courthouse Museum & Montgomery County Historical Society 7 N Main St	Dayton	OH	45402	937-228-6271	331-7160
Paramount's Kings Island PO Box 901	Kings Island	OH	45034	513-754-5700	754-5725
TF: 800-288-0808 ■ *Web:* www.pki.com					
Patterson Homestead & Gardens 1815 Brown St	Dayton	OH	45409	937-222-9724	
Possum Creek MetroPark 4901 Shank Rd	Dayton	OH	45418	937-268-1312	
Riverbend Arts Center 1301 E Siebenthaler Ave	Dayton	OH	45414	937-278-0655	274-3158
Santa Clara Arts District N Main St & Santa Clara Ave	Dayton	OH	45405	937-278-4900	
Sugarcreek MetroPark Preserve 7636 Wilmington-Dayton Pk	Dayton	OH	45458	937-433-0004	
SunWatch Indian Village Archaeological Park 2301 W River Rd	Dayton	OH	45418	937-268-8199	268-1760
Trapshooting Hall of Fame & Museum 601 W National Rd	Vandalia	OH	45377	937-898-1945	898-5472
US Air Force Museum 1100 Spaatz St Wright-Patterson Air Force Base	Dayton	OH	45433	937-255-3284	255-3910
Web: www.wpafb.af.mil/museum					
Victoria Theatre 138 N Main St	Dayton	OH	45402	937-228-3630	449-5068
Web: www.victoriatheatre.com					
Wegerzyn Horticultural Center & Stillwater Gardens 1301 E Siebenthaler Ave	Dayton	OH	45414	937-277-6545	277-6546
Wright Brothers Cycle Co 22 S Williams St	Dayton	OH	45407	937-225-7705	225-7706

SPORTS TEAMS & FACILITIES

	City	State	ZIP	Phone	Fax
Dayton Bombers (hockey) 3640 Colonel Glen Hwy Nutter Ctr Suite 417	Dayton	OH	45435	937-775-4747	775-4749
TF: 877-523-6684 ■ *Web:* www.bombershockey.com					

— Events —

	Phone
A World A'Fair (mid-May)	937-233-0050
Art in the Park (late May)	937-278-0655
City Folk Festival (mid-June)	937-223-3655
Country Peddler Shows (late February & early June)	937-278-4776
Dayton Art Institute Oktoberfest (early October)	937-223-5277
Dayton Auto Show (mid-March)	937-443-4700
Dayton Black Cultural Festival (early July)	937-224-7100
Dayton Home & Garden Show (late March)	937-443-4700
Dayton Horse Show (late July-early August)	937-461-4740
Dayton Industrial Expo (late October)	937-443-4700
Dayton Sports Fishing Travel & Outdoor Show (mid-January)	937-443-4700
Easter Eggstravaganza (early April)	937-226-8248
Family Fourth of July (July 4)	937-224-1518
Fiesta Latino Americano (mid-June)	937-296-3300
Fly City Music Festival (late August)	937-222-9768
Go 4th Celebration (July 4)	937-296-3281
Grand American World Trapshooting Tournament (mid-August)	937-898-1945
Greek Festival (early September)	937-224-0601
International Festival (late May-early June)	937-443-4700
Jazz at the Bend Jazz Festival (late August)	937-233-2489
MetroParks RiverFest (early October)	937-278-8231
Miami Valley Boat Show (mid-January)	937-278-4776
Montgomery County Fair (early September)	937-224-1619
Ohio Folk Festival (mid-May)	937-293-2841
Oktoberfest (late September)	937-223-5277
SummerFest (late July)	937-268-8199
US Air & Trade Show (late July)	937-898-5901
US Air Force Marathon (mid-September)	937-255-3334
Women in Jazz Festival (late June)	937-461-5300
World Reggae Festival (early September)	937-225-2333

Toledo

Situated at the mouth of the Maumee River on Lake Erie, Toledo serves as one of the largest ports on the Great Lakes. The riverfront area is a popular site for festivals and concerts, and the SS Willis B. Boyer Maritime Museum, a restored freighter representing Toledo's port heritage, is berthed along these shores. The Toledo/Maumee Trolley Tour passes historical sites of the area, including the Wolcott House Museum, which overlooks the Maumee River and serves as the centerpiece of six historical buildings depicting life in the 1800s. Toledo's Historic Old West End is lined with late Victorian houses and is considered one of the nation's richest collections of this architectural style.

Population	312,174	**Longitude**	83-55-53 W
Area (Land)	80.6 sq mi	**County**	Lucas
Area (Water)	3.5 sq mi	**Time Zone**	EST
Elevation	587 ft	**Area Code/s**	419
Latitude	41-66-39 N		

Toledo (Cont'd)

— Average Temperatures and Precipitation —

TEMPERATURES

	Jan	Feb	Mar	Apr	May	Jun	Jul	Aug	Sep	Oct	Nov	Dec
High	30	33	46	59	71	80	83	81	74	62	62	35
Low	15	17	27	36	47	56	61	58	52	40	32	21

PRECIPITATION

	Jan	Feb	Mar	Apr	May	Jun	Jul	Aug	Sep	Oct	Nov	Dec
Inches	1.8	1.7	2.7	3.0	2.9	3.8	3.3	3.3	2.9	2.0	2.8	2.9

— Important Phone Numbers —

	Phone
AAA	419-843-1212
American Express Travel	419-244-3322
Dental Referral	419-474-8611
Emergency	911
Events Line	419-241-1111
Medical Referral	419-251-1000
Poison Control Center	419-383-3897
Time/Temp	419-936-1212
Weather	419-936-1212

— Information Sources —

				Phone	Fax
Better Business Bureau Serving Northwest Ohio & Southeast Michigan 3103 Executive Pkwy Suite 200 *Web:* www.toledobbb.org	Toledo	OH	43606	419-531-3116	578-6001
Greater Toledo Convention & Visitors Bureau 401 Jefferson Ave *TF:* 800-243-4667 ■ *Web:* www.toledocvb.com/ ■ *E-mail:* info@toledocvb.com	Toledo	OH	43604	419-321-6404	255-7731
Lucas County 1 Government Ctr Suite 800	Toledo	OH	43604	419-213-4500	213-4532
SeaGate Convention Centre 401 Jefferson Ave. *TF:* 800-243-4667 ■ *Web:* www.toledo-seagate.com ■ *E-mail:* info@toledo-seagate.com	Toledo	OH	43604	419-255-3300	255-7731
Toledo Area Chamber of Commerce 300 Madison Ave Suite 200 *Web:* www.toledochamber.com ■ *E-mail:* joinus@toledochamber.com	Toledo	OH	43604	419-243-8191	241-8302
Toledo City Hall 1 Government Ctr *Web:* www.ci.toledo.oh.us	Toledo	OH	43604	419-245-1001	
Toledo Economic Development Div 1 Government Ctr Suite 1850 *Web:* www.ci.toledo.oh.us/econ/econ.htm	Toledo	OH	43604	419-245-1286	936-3672
Toledo-Lucas County Public Library 325 N Michigan St *Web:* www.library.toledo.oh.us	Toledo	OH	43624	419-259-5200	255-1334
Toledo Mayor 1 Government Ctr Suite 2200	Toledo	OH	43604	419-245-1001	245-1370

On-Line Resources

About.com Guide to Toledo . . . toledo.about.com/local/midwestus/toledo
Area Guide Toledo . . . toledo.areaguides.net
CitiFest Toledo Events . . . www.citifest.org/
City Knowledge Toledo . . . www.cityknowledge.com/oh_toledo.htm
Excite.com Toledo City Guide . . . www.excite.com/travel/countries/united_states/ohio/toledo
Northwest Ohio Sites Online . . . nwohio.sitesonline.com/nw
Toledo Home Page . . . www.toledolink.com/~matgerke/toledo/toledo.html
Toledo Ohio Local Community & Regional Information . . . toledo.com/community
ToledoGuide . . . www.toledoguide.com
ToledoWeb . . . www.toledo.com/

— Transportation Services —

AIRPORTS

■ **Toledo Express Airport (TOL)**

	Phone
20 miles SW of downtown (approx 35 minutes)	419-865-2351

Airport Transportation

	Phone
Airport Transportation Systems $32 fare to downtown	419-474-0921
Limo $45 fare to downtown	419-531-6344
Taxi $35 fare to downtown	419-243-2537

Commercial Airlines

	Phone
American Eagle	800-433-7300
Continental	800-525-0280
Delta	800-221-1212
Northwest	800-225-2525
United Express	800-241-6522
US Airways	800-428-4322

Charter Airlines

	Phone
Aero Charter Inc	800-535-1445
Bluffton Flying Service Inc	419-358-7045
Grand Aire Express Inc	800-704-7263
National Flight Service	419-865-2311
TOL Aviation Inc	419-866-9375

CAR RENTALS

	Phone
Avis	419-865-5541
Budget	419-865-8825
CarTemps USA	419-867-0100
Enterprise	419-841-9777
Hertz	419-866-3400
National	419-865-5513

LIMO/TAXI

	Phone
Black & White Cabs	419-381-5900
Checker Cab	419-243-2537
Childers Luxury Limousine Service	419-535-7019
Toledo Limousine Service	419-531-3325
White Knight Limousines	419-474-1000

MASS TRANSIT

	Phone
TARTA $.85 Base fare	419-243-7433

RAIL/BUS

				Phone
Central Union Amtrak Station 412 Emerald Ave	Toledo	OH	43602	419-246-0159
Greyhound/Trailways Bus Station 811 Jefferson Ave *TF:* 800-231-2222	Toledo	OH	43624	419-248-4665

— Accommodations —

HOTELS, MOTELS, RESORTS

				Phone	Fax
Best Western Toledo Tower 141 N Summit St *TF:* 800-528-1234	Toledo	OH	43604	419-242-8885	242-1337
Clarion Inn Westgate 3536 Secor Rd *TF:* 800-252-7466	Toledo	OH	43606	419-535-7070	536-4836
Comfort Inn East 2930 Navarre Ave. *TF:* 800-252-7466	Oregon	OH	43616	419-691-8911	691-2107
Comfort Inn South 2426 Oregon Rd *TF:* 800-228-5150	Northwood	OH	43619	419-666-2600	666-0076
Comfort Inn Westgate 3560 Secor Rd *TF:* 800-228-5150	Toledo	OH	43606	419-531-2666	531-4757
Country Inn & Suites 541 W Dussel Dr *TF:* 800-456-4000	Maumee	OH	43537	419-893-8576	893-8576
Courtyard by Marriott 1435 E Mall Dr *TF:* 800-321-2211 ■ *Web:* courtyard.com/TOLCH	Holland	OH	43528	419-866-1001	866-9869
Cross Country Inn 1201 E Mall Dr. *TF:* 800-621-1429	Holland	OH	43528	419-866-6565	866-6608
Crown Inn 1727 W Alexis Rd	Toledo	OH	43613	419-473-1485	473-0364
Days Inn 1821 E Manhattan Blvd *TF:* 800-329-7466	Toledo	OH	43608	419-729-1945	729-2920
Days Inn Toledo Maumee 150 Dussel Dr. *TF:* 800-329-7466	Maumee	OH	43537	419-893-9960	893-9559
Econo Lodge 1800 Miami St. *TF:* 800-553-2666	Toledo	OH	43605	419-666-5120	666-4298
Fairfield Inn Toledo Airport 1401 E Mall Dr. *TF:* 800-228-2800 ■ *Web:* fairfieldinn.com/TOLFA	Holland	OH	43528	419-867-1144	867-1144
Hampton Inn Toledo South 1409 Reynolds Rd *TF:* 800-426-7866	Maumee	OH	43537	419-893-1004	893-4613
Hilton Hotel Toledo 3100 Glendale Ave *TF:* 800-445-8667 ■ *Web:* www.hilton.com/hotels/TOLTHHF	Toledo	OH	43614	419-381-6800	381-0478
Holiday Inn Express 10621 Fremont Pike *TF:* 800-465-4329	Perrysburg	OH	43551	419-874-3101	874-0287

Toledo — Hotels, Motels, Resorts (Cont'd)

	City	State	ZIP	Phone	Fax
Holiday Inn French Quarter 10630 Fremont Pike	Perrysburg	OH	43551	419-874-3111	874-0198
TF: 888-874-2592					
Holiday Inn Toledo West 2340 S Reynolds Rd	Toledo	OH	43614	419-865-1361	865-6177
TF: 800-465-4329 ■ *Web:* www.basshotels.com/holiday-inn/?_franchisee=TOLWE ■ *E-mail:* sls401@macconnect.com					
Howard Johnson South Hanley Rd & I-280	Perrysburg	OH	43551	419-837-5245	837-5245
TF: 800-446-4656					
Knights Inn North 445 E Alexis Rd	Toledo	OH	43612	419-476-0170	476-6111
TF: 800-843-5644					
Knights Inn Toledo West 1520 Holland-Sylvania Rd	Maumee	OH	43537	419-865-1380	865-0344
TF: 800-843-5644					
Maumee Bay Resort 1750 Park Rd 2	Oregon	OH	43618	419-836-1466	836-2438
TF: 800-282-7275					
Radisson Hotel 101 N Summit St	Toledo	OH	43604	419-241-3000	321-2099
TF: 800-333-3333					
Ramada Hotel & Conference Center 2429 S Reynolds Rd	Toledo	OH	43614	419-381-8765	381-0129
TF: 800-323-6708 ■ *Web:* www.toledoramada.com ■ *E-mail:* stay@toledoramada.com					
Red Roof Inn 1214 Corporate Dr	Holland	OH	43528	419-866-5512	866-5886
TF: 800-843-7663					
Red Roof Inn Maumee 1570 S Reynolds Rd	Maumee	OH	43537	419-893-0292	893-8767
TF: 800-843-7663					
Red Roof Inn Toledo Westgate 3530 Executive Pkwy	Toledo	OH	43606	419-536-0118	536-1348
TF: 800-843-7663					
Tharaldson Inn & Suites 521 W Dussel Dr	Maumee	OH	43537	419-897-0865	897-0865
TF: 888-230-5500					
Wyndham Hotel 2 Seagate	Toledo	OH	43604	419-241-1411	241-8161
TF: 800-996-3426					

— Restaurants —

	City	State	ZIP	Phone
American Plaza Cafe (American) 2 Seagate/Summit St	Toledo	OH	43604	419-241-1411
Atrium Cafe (American) 2340 S Reynolds Rd	Toledo	OH	43614	419-865-1361
Barada Restaurant (Lebanese) 3455 W Alexis Rd	Toledo	OH	43623	419-472-7604
Bentley's Bar & Grill (American) 2429 S Reynolds Rd	Toledo	OH	43614	419-381-8765
Carlita's (Italian/Mexican) 4709 Douglas St	Toledo	OH	43613	419-471-1212
Casa di Maria (Italian) 4505 N Summit St	Toledo	OH	43611	419-729-9548
China King Buffet (Chinese) 325 N Superior St	Toledo	OH	43604	419-243-1226
Cousino's Cafe Chez Vin (European) 2022 Woodville Rd	Oregon	OH	43616	419-697-0017
Cousino's Old Navy Bistro (New American) 30 Main St	Toledo	OH	43605	419-697-6289
Web: www.cousinosnavybistro.com				
Cousino's Steak House (Steak/Seafood) 1842 Woodville Rd	Oregon	OH	43616	419-693-0862
Dominic's Italian Restaurant (Italian) 2121 S Reynolds Rd	Toledo	OH	43614	419-381-8822
Eddie B's (Greek) 245 N Summit St	Toledo	OH	43604	419-246-3339
Fifi's (French) 1423 Bernath Pkwy	Toledo	OH	43615	419-866-6777
Fritz & Alfredo's (German/Mexican) 3025 N Summit St	Toledo	OH	43611	419-729-9775
George's City Club (American) 415 1/2 Huron	Toledo	OH	43604	419-248-9139
Georgio's Cafe International (Seafood) 426 N Superior St	Toledo	OH	43604	419-242-2424
Golden Lily (Chinese) 219 N Superior St	Toledo	OH	43604	419-243-2461
Grumpy's (New American) 11 N Michigan	Toledo	OH	43624	419-241-6728
HJ's Prime Cut (Steak/Seafood) 206 New Towne Square Dr	Toledo	OH	43612	419-476-1616
Iris Restaurant (American) 3100 Glendale Ave	Toledo	OH	43614	419-381-6800
J Alexander's (New American) 4315 Talmadge Rd	Toledo	OH	43623	419-474-8620
JD Wesley's Bistro (French) 5333 Monroe St Market Sqare Plaza Suite 23	Toledo	OH	43623	419-841-7594
Joe's Crab Shack (Seafood) 1435 Baronial Plaza	Toledo	OH	43615	419-866-8877
Mancy's (Steak/Seafood) 953 Phillips Ave	Toledo	OH	43612	419-476-4154
Manos Greek Restaurant & Bar (Greek) 1701 Adams St	Toledo	OH	43624	419-244-4479
Matthew's Creative Cuisine (New American) 4400 Heatherdowns Blvd	Toledo	OH	43614	419-382-2559
Maumee Bay Brewing Co (New American) 27 Broadway St	Toledo	OH	43602	419-241-1253
Murphy's Place (Cajun) 151 Water St	Toledo	OH	43604	419-241-7732
Rusty's Jazz Cafe (American) 2202 Tedrow Rd-Jazz Ave	Toledo	OH	43614	419-381-9194
Saba's Charchol House (American) 4031 Talmadge Rd	Toledo	OH	43623	419-475-1111
Smedlap's Smithy (American) 205 Farmsworth Rd	Waterville	OH	43566	419-878-0261
Spaghetti Warehouse (Italian) 42 S Superior St	Toledo	OH	43602	419-255-5038
Summit Street Grill (American) 101 N Summit St	Toledo	OH	43604	419-241-3000
Tony Packo's (Hungarian) 1902 Front St	Toledo	OH	43605	419-691-6054
Web: www.tonypacko.com/				
Ventura's (Mexican) 7742 W Bancroft	Toledo	OH	43617	419-841-7523

— Goods and Services —

SHOPPING

	City	State	ZIP	Phone	Fax
Crafts Mall 27072 Carronade	Perrysburg	OH	43551	419-874-8049	
Franklin Park Mall 5001 Monroe St	Toledo	OH	43623	419-473-3317	473-0199
Lion Store 300 Southwyck Mall Blvd	Toledo	OH	43614	419-865-0593	865-0593
North Towne Square Mall 343 New Towne Square Dr	Toledo	OH	43612	419-476-1771	476-6633
Peddler's Alley 205 Farnsworth Rd	Waterville	OH	43566	419-878-7910	
Southwyck Shopping Center 2040 S Reynolds Rd	Toledo	OH	43614	419-865-7161	865-9503
Toledo Farmers Market 525 Market St	Toledo	OH	43602	419-255-6765	255-6765
Web: www.toledofarmersmarket.org/ ■ *E-mail:* info@toledofarmersmarket.org					
Woodville Mall 3725 Williston Rd	Northwood	OH	43619	419-693-0581	

BANKS

	City	State	ZIP	Phone	Fax
Charter One Bank FSB PO Box 10011	Toledo	OH	43699	419-259-5000	259-5003
TF: 800-458-1190					
Comerica Bank Midwest 3450 W Central Ave Suite 230	Toledo	OH	43606	419-531-5566	531-5256
Fifth Third Bank 3450 W Central Ave Suite 128	Toledo	OH	43606	419-531-0627	531-0630
TF: 800-972-3030					
Fifth Third Bank of Northwestern Ohio NA 606 Madison Ave	Toledo	OH	43604	419-259-7890	259-7624*
**Fax:* Mktg ■ *TF:* 800-972-3030					
Huntington Bank 300 Madison Ave Suite 900	Toledo	OH	43604	419-321-1098	321-1053
Mid American National Bank 519 Madison Ave	Toledo	OH	43604	419-249-3300	249-3375
National City Bank 405 Madison Ave	Toledo	OH	43604	419-259-7700	259-5477*
**Fax:* Cust Svc ■ *TF Cust Svc:* 800-331-8275*					
Standard Federal Bank 300 Madison Ave Suite 100	Toledo	OH	43604	419-249-1081	249-1079
TF: 800-643-9600					

BUSINESS SERVICES

	Phone
Colonial Courier Service	419-891-0922
Federal Express	800-238-5355
Kelly Services	419-292-0555
Kinko's	419-535-5679
Manpower Temporary Services	419-893-4413
Post Office	419-245-6931
Tri-State Expedited Services	419-837-2401
UPS	800-742-5877
US Cargo & Courier Service	419-666-3500

— Media —

PUBLICATIONS

	City	State	ZIP	Phone	Fax
Blade‡ 541 N Superior St	Toledo	OH	43660	419-724-6000	724-6439
TF: 800-232-7253 ■ *Web:* www.toledoblade.com					
Toledo Business Journal 27 Broadway St	Toledo	OH	43602	419-244-8200	244-5773
West Toledo Herald 4444 W Alexis Rd	Toledo	OH	43623	419-475-6000	472-7774*
**Fax:* News Rm					

‡Daily newspapers

TELEVISION

	City	State	ZIP	Phone	Fax
WGTE-TV Ch 30 (PBS) PO Box 30	Toledo	OH	43697	419-243-3091	243-9711
Web: www.wgte.org/TV30.html					
WLMB-TV Ch 40 (Ind) 26693 Eckel Rd PO Box 908	Perrysburg	OH	43552	419-874-8862	874-8867
WNWO-TV Ch 24 (NBC) 300 S Byrne Rd	Toledo	OH	43615	419-535-0024	535-0202
Web: www.nbc24.com					
WTOL-TV Ch 11 (CBS) PO Box 1111	Toledo	OH	43699	419-248-1111	244-7104
Web: www.wtol.com ■ *E-mail:* Toledo11@aol.com					
WTVG-TV Ch 13 (ABC) 4247 Dorr St	Toledo	OH	43607	419-531-1313	534-3898
WUPW-TV Ch 36 (Fox) 4 Sea Gate	Toledo	OH	43604	419-244-3600	244-8842
Web: www.wupw.com					

RADIO

	City	State	ZIP	Phone	Fax
WBUZ-FM 106.5 MHz (Rock) 9900 Airport Hwy	Monclova	OH	43542	419-868-1065	867-3700
Web: www.wbuz.com ■ *E-mail:* wbuz@primenet.com					
WCWA-AM 1230 kHz (Nost) 124 N Summit St Suite 400	Toledo	OH	43604	419-244-8321	244-2483

Toledo — Radio (Cont'd)

	City	State	Zip	Phone	Fax
WGTE-FM 91.3 MHz (NPR) PO Box 30	Toledo	OH	43697	419-243-3091	243-9711
Web: www.wgte.org/FM91.html					
WIOT-FM 104.7 MHz (Rock) 124 N Summit St Suite 400	Toledo	OH	43604	419-244-8321	244-2483
Web: www.wiot.com ■ *E-mail:* wiot@bright.net					
WKKO-FM 99.9 MHz (Ctry) 3225 Arlington Ave	Toledo	OH	43614	419-385-2507	385-2902
WLQR-AM 1470 kHz (Sports) 2965 Pickle Rd.	Oregon	OH	43616	419-691-1470	691-0396
WRQN-FM 93.5 MHz (Oldies) 3225 Arlington Ave	Toledo	OH	43614	419-385-2507	385-2902
WSPD-AM 1370 kHz (N/T) 125 S Superior St.	Toledo	OH	43602	419-244-8321	242-2846
WTOD-AM 1560 kHz (Ctry) 3225 Arlington Ave.	Toledo	OH	43614	419-385-2507	385-2902
WVKS-FM 92.5 MHz (AC) 125 S Superior St.	Toledo	OH	43602	419-244-8321	244-7631
Web: www.925kissfm.com ■ *E-mail:* bigdog@925kissfm.com					

— Colleges/Universities —

	City	State	Zip	Phone	Fax
Bowling Green State University	Bowling Green	OH	43403	419-372-2531	372-6955
Web: www.bgsu.edu ■ *E-mail:* admissions@bgnet.bgsu.edu					
Davis College 4747 Monroe St.	Toledo	OH	43623	419-473-2700	473-2472
TF: 800-477-7021					
Lourdes College 6832 Convent Blvd	Sylvania	OH	43560	419-885-3211	882-3987
TF Admissions: 800-878-3210 ■ *Web:* www.lourdes.edu ■ *E-mail:* srutkows@lourdes.edu					
Owens Community College Toledo 30335 Oregon Rd	Toledo	OH	43699	419-666-0580	661-7734
TF: 800-466-9367 ■ *Web:* www.owens.cc.oh.us					
University of Toledo 2801 W Bancroft St.	Toledo	OH	43606	419-530-2072	530-4504
TF: 800-586-5336 ■ *Web:* www.utoledo.edu					

— Hospitals —

	City	State	Zip	Phone	Fax
Flower Hospital 5200 Harroun Rd.	Sylvania	OH	43560	419-824-1444	882-2342
Medical College of Ohio Hospital 3000 Arlington Ave	Toledo	OH	43614	419-383-4000	383-3850
Web: www.mco.edu					
Riverside Mercy Hospital 1600 N Superior St	Toledo	OH	43604	419-729-6000	729-8119*
**Fax:* Admitting ■ *Web:* www.mercyweb.org/Ref_Desk/facilities/facilities_riverside.html					
Saint Luke's Hospital 5901 Monclova Rd	Maumee	OH	43537	419-893-5911	891-8037*
**Fax:* Admissions					
Saint Vincent Mercy Medical Center 2213 Cherry St.	Toledo	OH	43608	419-321-3232	251-3977*
**Fax:* Admitting ■ *TF:* 800-837-4664 ■ *Web:* www.mercyweb.org/Ref_Desk/facilities/facilities_stvincent.html					
Toledo Hospital & Toledo Children's Hospital 2142 N Cove Blvd	Toledo	OH	43606	419-471-4218	479-6901*
**Fax:* Admitting ■ *Web:* www.promedica.org/hosp/tth.asp					

— Attractions —

	City	State	Zip	Phone	Fax
Cassandra Ballet of Toledo 3157 W Sylvania Ave.	Toledo	OH	43613	419-475-0458	
COSI Center of Science & Industry 1 Discovery Way	Toledo	OH	43604	419-244-2674	255-2674
Web: www.cosi.org					
Fort Meigs St Memorial 29100 W River Rd	Perrysburg	OH	43552	419-874-4121	
TF: 800-686-1545					
Historic Old West End	Toledo	OH	43620	419-321-6404	
TF: 800-243-4667					
Maumee Bay State Park 1400 Park Rd	Oregon	OH	43618	419-836-7758	
Murphy's Lighthouses Inc 2017 W Sylvania Ave.	Toledo	OH	43613	419-244-6444	244-6444
TF: 800-288-0563					
Oak Openings Preserve Metropark 4139 Girdham Rd	Swanton	OH	43558	419-826-6463	
Ohio Theatre The 3114 Lagrange St	Toledo	OH	43608	419-241-6785	241-2151
Pearson Metropark 4600 Starr Ave	Oregon	OH	43616	419-535-3050	535-3053
Queen of the Most Holy Rosary Cathedral 2535 Collingwood Blvd	Toledo	OH	43610	419-244-9575	242-1901
Ritter Planetarium/Brooks Observatory University of Toledo	Toledo	OH	43606	419-530-2650	
Secor Metropark 10000 W Central Ave	Berkey	OH	43504	419-535-3050	
SS Willis B Boyer Maritime Museum 26 Main St International Pk	Toledo	OH	43605	419-936-3070	
Stranahan Theater 4645 Heather Downs Blvd.	Toledo	OH	43614	419-381-8851	381-9525
Swan Creek Preserve Metropark 4659 Airport Hwy	Toledo	OH	43615	419-535-3050	
Toledo Ballet Assn 4645 Heather Downs Blvd Stranahan Theatre	Toledo	OH	43614	419-255-9000	255-4990
Toledo Botanical Garden 5403 Elmer Dr	Toledo	OH	43615	419-936-2986	936-2987
Toledo Firefighters Museum 918 Sylvania Ave.	Toledo	OH	43612	419-478-3473	936-3293
Toledo Jazz Society 406 Adams St	Toledo	OH	43604	419-241-5299	241-4777
Toledo Museum of Art 2445 Monroe St.	Toledo	OH	43620	419-255-8000	255-5638
TF Info: 800-644-6862 ■ *Web:* www.toledomuseum.com					
Toledo Opera 406 Adams St	Toledo	OH	43604	419-255-7464	255-6344
Web: www.toledo-opera.com					
Toledo Repertory Theatre 16 10th St	Toledo	OH	43624	419-243-7335	243-0454
Toledo Sports Arena & Exhibit Hall 1 Main St.	Toledo	OH	43605	419-698-4545	693-3299
Toledo Symphony Orchestra 2 Maritime Plaza	Toledo	OH	43604	419-241-1272	321-6890
TF: 800-348-1253 ■ *Web:* www.toledosymphony.com ■ *E-mail:* tolsymorch@aol.com					
Toledo Zoological Gardens & Museum of Science 2700 Broadway	Toledo	OH	43609	419-385-5721	389-8670
Web: www.toledozoo.org ■ *E-mail:* iwd@iwebd.com					
Village Players 2740 Upton Ave.	Toledo	OH	43606	419-472-6817	
Wildwood Preserve Metropark 5100 W Central Ave Toledo Metroparks	Toledo	OH	43515	419-535-3050	
Wolcott House Museum 1031 River Rd	Maumee	OH	43537	419-893-9602	893-3108

SPORTS TEAMS & FACILITIES

	City	State	Zip	Phone	Fax
Toledo Mud Hens (baseball) 2901 Key St Ned Skeldon Stadium	Maumee	OH	43537	419-893-9483	893-5847
Web: www.mudhens.com/ ■ *E-mail:* mudhens@mudhens.com					
Toledo Raceway Park 5700 Telegraph Rd	Toledo	OH	43612	419-476-7751	476-7979
Toledo Speedway 5639 Benore Rd	Toledo	OH	43612	419-727-1100	727-3300
Toledo Storm (hockey) 1 Main St Toledo Sports Arena	Toledo	OH	43605	419-691-0200	698-8998
Web: www.thestorm.com/ ■ *E-mail:* gostorm999@aol.com					

— Events —

	Phone
Art on the Mall (mid-July)	419-530-2586
Crosby Festival of the Arts (late June)	419-936-2986
First Night Toledo (December 31)	419-241-3777
German-American Festival (late August)	419-321-6404
Homespun Holidays (early-mid-December)	419-535-3050
Irish Heritage Festival (mid-March)	419-321-6404
Jamie Farr LPGA Tournament (late June-early July)	419-882-7153
Kroger Freedom Celebration (early July)	419-243-8024
Lagrange Street Polish Festival (mid-July)	419-255-8406
Lights Before Christmas (early November-late December)	419-385-5721
Lucas County Fair (late July)	419-893-2127
Northwest Ohio Rib-Off (early August)	419-242-9587
Old West End Historic Festival Home Tours (early June)	419-243-1100
Old West End Spring Festival (early June)	419-321-6404
Rallies by the River (early May-late August)	419-243-8024
RiverFest (early September)	419-243-8024
Rock Rhythm n' Blues (late May)	419-243-8024
Rod & Custom Auto-Rama (early March)	419-474-1006
Sunshine Bazaar & Quilt Auction (mid-October)	419-865-0251
Toledo Area Artists Exhibition (early July-early August)	419-255-8000
Warren-Sherman Festival (late July-early August)	419-242-6479

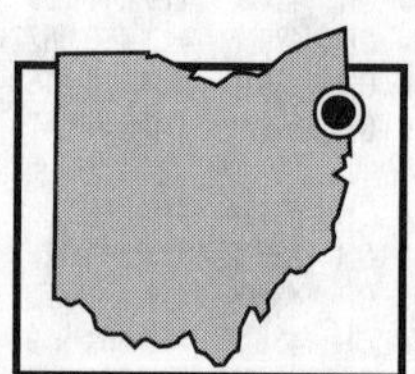

Youngstown

Youngstown is located in northeastern Ohio, in the Mahoning Valley area. One of its principal attractions is the 2,600-acre Mill Creek Park, which houses a number of attractions itself, including two championship golf courses, three lakes, a suspension bridge, and miles of walking and running trails. Lanterman's Mill, a historic landmark as well as a working

Youngstown (Cont'd)

grist mill, can also be found in the park. Another attraction there is Powers Auditorium, which was built by the Warner brothers and was originally named Warner Theatre. (The Warner brothers grew up and began their careers in Youngstown.) The Grand Foyer at Powers Auditorium has a sweeping staircase, imported marble, terrazzo floors, and elaborate chandeliers and mirrors. The War Vet Museum in Youngstown was built in 1809 and houses more than 25,000 American war items, from the Revolutionary War through Operation Desert Storm. Other area museums and historical landmarks include the Butler Institute of American Art, the first structure in the U.S. dedicated to housing works by American artists; the Youngstown Historical Center of Industry and Labor, which features displays that trace the development of the iron and steel industries in the area; and the Austin Log Cabin, which dates back to 1814. The cabin has been authentically restored and is a good example of a frontier homestead.

Population 84,650
Area (Land) . . . . . 33.6 sq mi
Area (Water) . . . . . 0.4 sq mi
Elevation . . . . . 861 ft
Latitude . . . . . 41-05-56 N
Longitude . . . . . 80-38-47 W
County . . . . . Mahoning
Time Zone . . . . . EST
Area Code/s 330

— Average Temperatures and Precipitation —

TEMPERATURES

	Jan	Feb	Mar	Apr	May	Jun	Jul	Aug	Sep	Oct	Nov	Dec
High	31	34	45	58	69	77	81	80	73	61	48	36
Low	16	18	27	37	46	55	59	58	52	42	34	23

PRECIPITATION

	Jan	Feb	Mar	Apr	May	Jun	Jul	Aug	Sep	Oct	Nov	Dec
Inches	2.1	2.0	3.1	3.1	3.5	3.9	4.0	3.3	3.5	2.6	3.1	2.9

— Important Phone Numbers —

	Phone
AAA	330-726-9083
Dental Referral	330-743-7108
Emergency	911
Medical Referral	800-842-9727
Poison Control Center	888-231-4455
Time/Temp	330-394-7070
Weather	216-265-2370

— Information Sources —

	City	State	Zip	Phone	Fax
Better Business Bureau Serving the Youngstown Area PO Box 1495 *Web:* www.youngstown.bbb.org	Youngstown	OH	44501	330-744-3111	744-7336
Mahoning County 120 Market St.	Youngstown	OH	44503	330-740-2104	740-2105
Mahoning Valley Economic Development Corp 4319 Belmont Ave. *Web:* www.mvedc.com	Youngstown	OH	44505	330-759-3668	759-3686
Public Library of Youngstown & Mahoning County 305 Wick Ave *Web:* www.ymc.lib.oh.us	Youngstown	OH	44503	330-744-8636	744-3355
Stambaugh Henry H Auditorium 1000 5th Ave	Youngstown	OH	44504	330-747-5175	747-1981
Youngstown City Hall 26 S Phelps St	Youngstown	OH	44503	330-742-8700	742-8999
Youngstown Mayor 26 S Phelps St	Youngstown	OH	44503	330-742-8701	743-1335
Youngstown Warren Regional Chamber of Commerce 1200 Stambaugh Bldg. *Web:* www.regionalchamber.com ■ *E-mail:* regionalchamber@cboss.com	Youngstown	OH	44503	330-744-2131	746-0330
Youngstown/Mahoning County Convention & Visitors Bureau 100 Federal Plaza E Suite 101 *TF:* 800-447-8201 ■ *Web:* www.youngstowncvb.com	Youngstown	OH	44503	330-747-8200	747-2331

On-Line Resources

4Youngstown.com www.4youngstown.com
About Youngstown . . . . . www.ohiocities.com/welyoung.htm
Area Guide Youngstown . . . . . youngstown.areaguides.net
Excite.com Youngstown City Guide . . . . . www.excite.com/travel/countries/united_states/ohio/youngstown
Heartbeat of Youngstown Businesses . . . . . www.hboy.com
NITC Travelbase City Guide Youngstown . . . . . www.travelbase.com/auto/guides/youngstown-oh.html
Online City Guide to Youngstown . . . . . www.olcg.com/oh/youngstown/index.html
YTown.com . . . . . www.ytown.com

— Transportation Services —

AIRPORTS

■ Youngstown-Warren Regional Airport (YNG)

	Phone
11 miles N of downtown (approx 15 minutes) E-mail: yngwrnair@aol.com	330-856-1537

Airport Transportation

	Phone
Independent Radio Taxi $18 fare to downtown	330-746-8844
Southern Park Limousine $25 fare to downtown	330-726-2800

Commercial Airlines

	Phone
Northwest	800-225-2525
United	800-241-6522
US Airways	800-428-4322

Charter Airlines

	Phone
Levetz Group	800-520-6854

CAR RENTALS

	Phone
American Kar	330-783-1084
Budget	330-726-3838
CarTemps USA	330-652-8878
Enterprise	330-743-2005
Sears	330-726-3833

LIMO/TAXI

	Phone
American Taxicabs	330-788-7763
Fabrication Limousines	330-793-5466
Independent Radio Taxi	330-746-8844
Southern Park Limousine	330-726-2800

MASS TRANSIT

	Phone
WRTA Bus $.85 Base fare	330-744-8431

RAIL/BUS

	City	State	Zip	Phone
Amtrak Station 530 Mahoning Ave	Youngstown	OH	44502	800-872-7245
Greyhound Bus Station 340 Federal Plaza W *TF:* 800-231-2222	Youngstown	OH	44503	330-743-4141

— Accommodations —

HOTELS, MOTELS, RESORTS

	City	State	Zip	Phone	Fax
Best Western Meander Inn 870 N Canfield-Niles Rd.	Youngstown	OH	44515	330-544-2378	544-7926
Boardman Inn 7109 Market St	Boardman	OH	44512	330-758-2315	
Colonial Canfield Motel 7815 Akron-Canfield Rd.	Canfield	OH	44406	330-533-4048	
Comfort Inn North 4055 Belmont Ave *TF:* 800-860-7829	Youngstown	OH	44505	330-759-3180	759-7713
Days Inn South 8392 Market St *TF:* 800-329-7466	Youngstown	OH	44512	330-758-2371	758-2371
Econo Lodge 5431 1/2 76th Dr.	Austintown	OH	44515	330-270-2865	270-2865
El Patio Motel 485 W Main St	Canfield	OH	44406	330-533-3149	
Fairfield Inn by Marriott 7397 Tiffany S *TF:* 800-228-2800	Poland	OH	44514	330-726-5979	726-5979
Hampton Inn South 7395 Tiffany S *TF:* 800-426-7866	Poland	OH	44514	330-758-5191	758-9343

Youngstown — Hotels, Motels, Resorts (Cont'd)

Name / Address	City	State	ZIP	Phone	Fax
Hampton Inn West 880 N Canfield-Niles Rd; *TF:* 800-426-7866	Austintown	OH	44515	330-544-0660	652-7800
Holiday Inn Boardman 7410 South Ave	Boardman	OH	44512	330-726-1611	726-0717
Inn at the Green 500 S Main St	Poland	OH	44514	330-757-4688	
Kings Motel 6965 McCartney Rd	Lowellville	OH	44436	330-536-6273	
Microtel Inns & Suites 7393 South Ave; *TF:* 800-804-8385	Boardman	OH	44512	330-758-1816	758-8117
Motel 6 5431 76th Dr	Austintown	OH	44515	330-793-9305	793-2584
Ramada Inn 4255 Belmont Ave	Youngstown	OH	44505	330-759-7850	759-8147
Red Roof Inn Boardman 1051 Tiffany S	Boardman	OH	44514	330-758-1999	758-8004
Red Roof Inn Youngstown 1051 N Canfield-Niles Rd	Youngstown	OH	44515	330-793-9851	793-7666
Seven Mile Inn 7098 Mahoning Ave	Youngstown	OH	44515	330-799-0938	
Sleep Inn 5555 Interstate Blvd	Austintown	OH	44515	330-544-5555	
Super 8 Motel Austintown 5280 76th Dr; *TF:* 800-800-8000	Austintown	OH	44515	330-793-7788	793-9011
Super 8 Motel Youngstown 4250 Belmont Ave; *TF:* 800-800-8000	Youngstown	OH	44505	330-759-0040	759-0040
Tally Ho-tel 4249 Belmont Ave	Youngstown	OH	44505	330-759-4092	759-4092
Terrace Motel 4972 Market St	Boardman	OH	44512	330-788-5087	
Tower Motel 5235 Market St	Boardman	OH	44512	330-782-8021	
Wagon Wheel Motel 7015 Market St	Boardman	OH	44512	330-758-4551	
Westgate Manor Motel 4493 Mahoning Ave	Austintown	OH	44515	330-792-2351	
Williams Motel 6110 Market St	Boardman	OH	44512	330-758-4556	

— Restaurants —

Name / Address	City	State	ZIP	Phone
Aladdin's Eatery (Mediterranean) 7325 South Ave	Youngstown	OH	44512	330-629-6450
Anthony's on the River (Italian) 15 Oak Hill Ave	Youngstown	OH	44502	330-744-7888
Antone's Italian Café (Italian) 4837 Mahoning Ave	Austintown	OH	44515	330-793-0707
Armadillo's Restaurant (Barbecue) 277 Boardman-Canfield Rd	Boardman	OH	44512	330-758-6250
Belleria Italian Restaurant (Italian) 3187 Center Rd	Youngstown	OH	44514	330-757-9910
Bloomingdale's Point (American) 9835 South Ave	Youngstown	OH	44514	330-549-5445
Blue Light Restaurant & Lounge (American) 3136 Belmont Ave	Youngstown	OH	44505	330-759-8484
Bobby D's Italian Eatery (Italian) 914 E Midlothian Blvd	Youngstown	OH	44502	330-782-1090
Bruno's (Italian) 1984 Boardman-Poland Rd	Boardman	OH	44514	330-757-0840
Café Capri (Italian) 7807 Market St	Boardman	OH	44512	330-726-9900
Café Roma (Italian) 17 N Champion St	Youngstown	OH	44503	330-746-6900
Cancun Restaurant (Mexican) 4055 Belmont Ave	Youngstown	OH	44505	330-759-3301
Casa Ramirez Mexican Restaurant (Mexican) 1578 Mahoning Ave	Youngstown	OH	44509	330-792-9920
Cedar Café (American) 131 W Commerce St	Youngstown	OH	44503	330-743-6560
Checkered Flag Restaurant (American) 6000 Mahoning Ave	Youngstown	OH	44515	330-270-2800
Chrystal's (American) 1931 Belmont Ave	Youngstown	OH	44504	330-743-5381
Das Dutch Haus (American) 14895 South Ave	Columbiana	OH	44408	330-482-2236
Don Pablo's Mexican Kitchen (Mexican) 6651 South Ave	Boardman	OH	44512	330-965-6218
Ezio's Italian Restaurant (Italian) 3032 Center Rd	Poland	OH	44514	330-757-0738
Garland's Bar-B-Que (Barbecue) 520 Belmont Ave	Youngstown	OH	44502	330-746-9461
Golden Hunan Restaurant (Chinese) 3111 Belmont Ave	Youngstown	OH	44505	330-759-7197
Grecian Gourmet (Greek) 1235 Boardman-Canfield Rd	Youngstown	OH	44512	330-758-9692
Jam Bar & Grill (American) 2844 Market St	Youngstown	OH	44507	330-788-5303
Joe's Restaurant (Italian) 2921 Belmont Ave	Youngstown	OH	44505	330-759-8890
La Fiesta Mexican Restaurant (Mexican) 1801 Midland Ave	Youngstown	OH	44509	330-793-3967
La Rocca Pizza & Pasta (Italian) 6505 Clingan Rd	Poland	OH	44514	330-757-1212
Lucianno's Restaurant (Italian) 1732 S Raccoon Rd	Youngstown	OH	44515	330-792-5975
Marino's Restaurant (Italian) 5423 Mahoning Ave	Youngstown	OH	44515	330-799-8326
Mario's Restaurant (Italian) 5162 Youngstown-Poland Rd	Boardman	OH	44514	330-755-0738
Midtowner Restaurant (American) 2104 Hubbard Rd	Youngstown	OH	44505	330-746-9673
Molly's (American) 1309 Salt Springs Rd	Youngstown	OH	44509	330-799-0038
Monaco's (Continental) 5501 Mahoning Ave	Austintown	OH	44515	330-793-3020
Page's Family Restaurant (Homestyle) 1472 Churchill Hubbard Rd	Youngstown	OH	44515	330-759-2789
Paisano's Restaurant (Italian) 5455 Clarkins Dr	Austintown	OH	44515	330-793-4828
Rachel's Steak & Seafood House (Steak/Seafood) 169 S Four-Mile Run Rd	Youngstown	OH	44515	330-799-2800
Riverbend Restaurant (American) 1105 Poland Ave	Youngstown	OH	44502	330-746-3300
Rockne's Pub (American) 1497 Boardman-Canfield Rd; *Web:* www.rocknes.com/BoardmanMap.html	Boardman	OH	44512	330-629-9730
Scacchetti's Italian Steakhouse (Italian) 3781 Mahoning Ave	Austintown	OH	44515	330-799-1316
Scarsella's (Italian) 2846 Market St	Youngstown	OH	44507	330-788-0806
Springfield Grille (American) 7413 Tiffany Rd	Boardman	OH	44514	330-726-0895
Staples Bar-B-Que (Barbecue) 320 Belmont Ave	Youngstown	OH	44502	330-747-7672
Station Square Restaurant (Continental) 4250 Belmont Ave	Youngstown	OH	44505	330-759-8802
Stone Terrace (American) 4255 Belmont Ave	Youngstown	OH	44505	330-759-3887
Tabby's Ribs & Chicken (Barbecue) 1315 Boardman-Canfield Rd	Boardman	OH	44512	330-758-4584
Tip Top Bar & Restaurant (American) 225 Emerald St	Youngstown	OH	44505	330-747-0060
TJ's Restaurant & Lounge (American) 7410 South Ave Holiday Inn	Boardman	OH	44512	330-726-1611
Wang's Restaurant (Chinese) 5423 Mahoning Ave	Youngstown	OH	44515	330-793-8811
West Glen Italian Eatery (Italian) 8600 Glenwood Ave	Boardman	OH	44512	330-758-2388
Winston's Tavern (American) 870 N Canfield-Niles Rd	Austintown	OH	44515	330-544-9333

— Goods and Services —

SHOPPING

Name / Address	City	State	ZIP	Phone	Fax
Austintown Flea Market 5370 Clarkins Dr	Austintown	OH	44515	330-799-1325	
Eastwood Mall 5555 Youngstown-Warren Rd; *Web:* www.eastwoodmall.net	Niles	OH	44446	330-652-6980	544-5929
Hummel Gift Shop 1656 E Garfield Rd; *TF:* 800-354-5438	New Springfield	OH	44443	330-549-3728	549-0879
I-680 Antique Mall 9026 South Ave	Poland	OH	44514	330-726-9261	
Southern Park Mall 7401 Market St	Youngstown	OH	44512	330-758-4511	726-2719
Town 'n Country 13887 Woodworth Rd SR-165	New Springfield	OH	44443	330-549-5740	549-2715
White House Fruit Farm 9249 Youngstown-Salem Rd	Canfield	OH	44406	330-533-4161	

BANKS

Name / Address	City	State	ZIP	Phone	Fax
Bank One NA 4243 Mahoning Ave; *TF:* 800-477-1777	Austintown	OH	44515	330-799-7681	799-3516
Central Federal Savings & Loan 3551 Belmont Ave	Youngstown	OH	44505	330-759-3100	
Charter One Bank FSB 4333 Belmont Ave	Youngstown	OH	44505	330-759-3770	
Farmers National Bank of Canfield 3619 S Meridian Rd	Youngstown	OH	44511	330-793-3971	793-0357
FFY Bank 724 Boardman-Poland Rd; *Web:* www.ffytown.com ■ *E-mail:* ffyinfo@ffytown.com	Youngstown	OH	44512	330-726-3396	758-1356
First Federal Savings & Loan Assn of Warren 5220 Mahoning Ave Suite A	Austintown	OH	44515	330-270-5990	270-2020
First Star Bank 1201 Doral Dr	Youngstown	OH	44514	330-965-4895	
KeyBank NA 100 S Main St	Poland	OH	44514	330-757-1541	757-7954
Mahoning National Bank of Youngstown 23 Federal Plaza	Youngstown	OH	44503	330-742-7000	742-5463
Metropolitan National Bank 1 Federal Plaza W; *TF Cust Svc:* 800-463-8226*	Youngstown	OH	44501	330-747-0292	747-0475
National City Bank 3720 Mahoning Ave	Youngstown	OH	44515	330-742-4103	799-8427
Second National Bank of Warren 60 N Canfield-Niles Rd; *TF:* 800-488-2762	Youngstown	OH	44515	330-799-4411	799-7980
Sky Bank 5961 South Ave	Youngstown	OH	44512	330-758-0531	758-3580

BUSINESS SERVICES

Name	Phone	Name	Phone
Federal Express	800-238-5355	**Mail Boxes Etc**	330-726-7667
Interim Personnel	330-726-8050	**Manpower Temporary Services**	330-758-8308
Kelly Services	330-965-7357	**Post Office**	330-740-8850
Kinko's	330-726-2020	**UPS**	800-742-5877

— Media —

PUBLICATIONS

Name / Address	City	State	ZIP	Phone	Fax
Boardman News 6221 Market St	Youngstown	OH	44512	330-758-2658	758-2658
Boardman Town Crier 100 Debartolo Pl; **Fax:* News Rm	Boardman	OH	44512	330-629-6200	629-6210*
Business Journal The PO Box 714; *TF:* 800-837-6397 ■ *Web:* www.business-journal.com ■ *E-mail:* info@business-journal.com	Youngstown	OH	44501	330-744-5023	744-5838

Youngstown — Publications (Cont'd)

	City	State	ZIP	Phone	Fax
Tribune Chronicle‡ 240 Franklin St SE	Warren	OH	44482	330-841-1600	841-1721
Web: www.tribune-chronicle.com ■ *E-mail:* tribune@cisnet.com					

‡Daily newspapers

TELEVISION

	City	State	ZIP	Phone	Fax
WEAO-TV Ch 45 (PBS) 1750 Campus Center Dr	Kent	OH	44240	330-677-4549	672-7995
Web: www.ch4549.org ■ *E-mail:* programs@wneo.pbs.org					
WFMJ-TV Ch 21 (NBC) 101 W Boardman St	Youngstown	OH	44503	330-744-8611	744-3402
Web: www.wfmj.com					
WKBN-TV Ch 27 (CBS) 3930 Sunset Blvd	Youngstown	OH	44512	330-782-1144	782-3504
Web: www.wkbn.com ■ *E-mail:* program@wkbn.com					
WYFX-TV Ch 62 (Fox) 3930 Sunset Blvd	Youngstown	OH	44512	330-782-1114	782-3504
WYTV-TV Ch 33 (ABC) 3800 Shady Run Rd	Youngstown	OH	44502	330-783-2930	782-8154
Web: www.wytv.com ■ *E-mail:* wytv33@cboss.com					

RADIO

	City	State	ZIP	Phone	Fax
WANR-AM 1570 kHz (Rel) 124 N Park Ave Suite 10	Warren	OH	44481	330-392-3223	
Web: www.am1570.com					
WASN-AM 1330 kHz (N/T) 401 N Blaine Ave	Youngstown	OH	44505	330-746-1330	746-6711
Web: www.wasn.com ■ *E-mail:* talkradio@wasn.com					
WBBG-FM 93.3 MHz (Oldies) 418 Knox St.	Youngstown	OH	44502	330-740-9300	740-9303
E-mail: oldies93@neont.com					
WBBW-AM 1240 kHz (Sports) 4040 Simon Rd	Youngstown	OH	44512	330-783-1000	783-0060
WBTJ-FM 101.9 MHz (CHR) 721 Boardman-Poland Rd Suite 103	Boardman	OH	44512	330-965-0057	707-2413
Web: www.1019thebeat.com					
WBVP-AM 1230 kHz (N/T) 1316 7th Ave	Beaver Falls	PA	15010	724-846-4100	843-7771
WBZY-AM 1200 kHz (Oldies) 1906 Wilmington Rd	New Castle	PA	16105	724-656-1200	656-6397
WDPN-AM 1310 kHz (Nost) 393 Smyth Ave NE	Alliance	OH	44601	330-821-1111	821-0379
WGFT-AM 1500 kHz (Rel) 34 Federal Plaza W 12th Fl.	Youngstown	OH	44503	330-744-5115	744-4020
WGRP-AM 940 kHz (AC) 44 McCracken Rd	Greenville	PA	16125	724-588-8900	588-1043
WHBC-AM 1480 kHz (Misc) 550 Market Ave S	Canton	OH	44702	330-456-7166	456-7199
WHOT-FM 101.1 MHz (CHR) 4040 Simon Rd	Youngstown	OH	44512	330-783-1000	783-0060
Web: www.hot101.com ■ *E-mail:* whot@neont.com					
WKBN-AM 570 kHz (N/T) 721 Boardman-Poland Rd	Youngstown	OH	44513	330-965-0057	965-8277
Web: www.wkbnradio.com					
WKBN-FM 98.9 MHz (AC) 721 Boardman-Poland Rd	Youngstown	OH	44513	330-965-0057	965-8277
Web: www.wkbnradio.com					
WKST-AM 1280 kHz (N/T) 219 Savannah-Gardner Rd	New Castle	PA	16101	724-654-5501	654-3101
WKTX-AM 830 kHz (Oldies) 178 N Mecca St	Cortland	OH	44410	330-638-0830	637-0830
Web: www.wktx.com					
WNCD-FM 106.1 MHz (CR) 5380 W Webb Rd	Austintown	OH	44515	330-652-0106	652-9354
Web: www.cd106.com ■ *E-mail:* thewolf@cd106.com					
WNIO-AM 1390 kHz (AC) 418 Knox St.	Youngstown	OH	44502	330-740-9300	740-9303
WNIO-AM 1540 kHz (Oldies) 5380 W Webb Rd	Austintown	OH	44515	330-652-0106	652-9354
WOHI-AM 1490 kHz (AC) 15655 SR-170	East Liverpool	OH	43920	330-385-1490	385-2339
WPIC-AM 790 kHz (N/T) 2030 Pine Hollow Blvd	Hermitage	PA	16148	724-346-4113	981-4545
Web: www.wpic790.com ■ *E-mail:* hasty@infonline.net					
WQXK-FM 105.1 MHz (Ctry) 465 E State St.	Salem	OH	44460	330-337-9544	337-9977
Web: www.k105country.com ■ *E-mail:* k105@k105country.com					
WRBP-AM 1440 kHz (Urban) 34 Federal Plaza W 12th Fl.	Youngstown	OH	44503	330-744-5115	744-4020
Web: www.am1440.com					
WSOM-AM 600 kHz (Nost) 465 E State St	Salem	OH	44460	330-337-9544	337-9977
WWIZ-FM 103.9 MHz (Ctry) 2030 Pine Hollow Blvd	Hermitage	PA	16148	724-346-4113	981-9050
E-mail: wwiz@pennohio.com					
WYFM-FM 102.9 MHz (CR) 4040 Simon Rd	Youngstown	OH	44512	330-783-1000	783-0060
Web: www.y-103.com ■ *E-mail:* y-103@y-103.com					
WYSU-FM 88.5 MHz (NPR) Youngstown State University 1 University Plaza	Youngstown	OH	44555	330-742-3363	742-1501
Web: www.wysu.org ■ *E-mail:* mscervon@cc.ysu.edu					

— Colleges/Universities —

	City	State	ZIP	Phone	Fax
ITT Technical Institute 1030 N Meridian Rd	Youngstown	OH	44509	330-270-1600	270-8333
TF: 800-832-5001 ■ *Web:* www.itt-tech.edu					
Youngstown State University 1 University Plaza	Youngstown	OH	44555	330-742-3000	742-3154
TF: 800-336-9978 ■ *Web:* www.ysu.edu ■ *E-mail:* ysuinfo@cis.ysu.edu					

— Hospitals —

	City	State	ZIP	Phone	Fax
Forum Health 500 Gypsy Ln.	Youngstown	OH	44501	330-747-0777	740-5670*
**Fax:* Admitting ■ *Web:* www.wrhc.org					
Northside Medical Center 500 Gypsy Ln	Youngstown	OH	44504	330-747-1444	
Saint Elizabeth Health Center 1044 Belmont Ave.	Youngstown	OH	44501	330-746-7211	480-2901*
**Fax:* Admitting					
Youngstown Osteopathic Hospital 1319 Florencedale Ave.	Youngstown	OH	44505	330-744-9200	744-9347*
**Fax:* Admitting ■ *TF:* 800-207-2196					

— Attractions —

	City	State	ZIP	Phone	Fax
Arms Family Museum of Local History 648 Wick Ave.	Youngstown	OH	44502	330-743-2589	743-7210
Austin Log Cabin 3797 S Raccoon Rd.	Austintown	OH	44515	330-799-8051	
Austintown Township Park 82 Old Town Rd	Austintown	OH	44515	330-793-0718	
Ballet Western Reserve 1361 5th Ave.	Youngstown	OH	44505	330-744-1934	
Beecher Ward Planetarium 1 University Plaza Youngstown State University	Youngstown	OH	44555	330-742-3616	742-3121
Boardman Township Park 375 Boardman-Poland Rd	Boardman	OH	44512	330-726-8105	726-4562
Butler Institute of American Art 524 Wick Ave	Youngstown	OH	44502	330-743-1711	743-9567
Web: www.butlerart.com ■ *E-mail:* kp@cisnet.com					
Crandall Park 400 Redondo Rd	Youngstown	OH	44504	330-747-9214	
Fellows Riverside Gardens 123 McKinley Ave	Youngstown	OH	44509	330-740-7116	740-7129
Web: www.cboss.com/millck/frggen.htm ■ *E-mail:* fellows@neont.com					
Ford Nature Education Center 7574 Columbiana-Canfield Dr Box 596	Canfield	OH	44406	330-740-7107	740-7133
Fosterville Park 600 W Indianola Ave	Youngstown	OH	44511	330-788-0257	
Lanterman's Mill & Covered Bridge 980 Canfield Rd	Youngstown	OH	44511	330-740-7115	
Web: www.cboss.com/millck/lantmill.htm					
McDonough Museum of Art 1 University Plaza Youngstown State University Campus	Youngstown	OH	44555	330-742-1400	742-1492
Mill Creek Park 7574 Columbiana-Canfield Rd.	Canfield	OH	44406	330-702-3000	
Web: www.cboss.com/millcreek					
Monday Musical Club 1000 5th Ave Suite 3.	Youngstown	OH	44504	330-743-2717	
Oakland Center for the Arts PO Box 6206	Youngstown	OH	44501	330-746-0404	
Web: www.cboss.com/oakland ■ *E-mail:* oakland@cboss.com					
Powers Edward Auditorium 260 Federal Plaza W	Youngstown	OH	44503	330-744-0264	744-1441
Saint James Meeting House 375 Boardman-Poland Rd	Boardman	OH	44512	330-726-8105	
Strock Stone House 7171 Mahoning Ave	Austintown	OH	44515	330-799-8051	
Vickers Nature Preserve Rt 224	Ellsworth Township	OH	44416	330-702-3000	702-3010
Web: www.cboss.com/millck/vickers.htm					
War Vet Museum 23 E Main St	Canfield	OH	44406	330-533-6311	
Western Reserve Village Canfield Fairgrounds	Canfield	OH	44406	330-747-8200	

Youngstown — Attractions (Cont'd)

				Phone	Fax
White House Fruit Farm 9249 Youngstown-Salem Rd	Canfield	OH	44406	330-533-4161	
Whitehouse Ostrich & Noah's Lost Ark Animal Park 8424 Bedell Rd	Berlin Center	OH	44401	330-584-7835	
Yellow Duck Park 10590 Columbiana-Canfield Rd	Canfield	OH	44406	330-533-3773	
Youngstown Historical Center of Industry & Labor 151 W Wood St.	Youngstown	OH	44503	330-743-5934	743-2999
TF: 800-262-6137 ■ *Web:* www.ohiohistory.org/places/youngst/					
Youngstown Opera Guild 1 University Plaza Kilcawley Ctr	Youngstown	OH	44455	330-759-2327	
Youngstown Playhouse 600 Playhouse Ln	Youngstown	OH	44511	330-782-3402	788-1208
Youngstown Symphony Orchestra 260 Federal Plaza W	Youngstown	OH	44503	330-744-4269	744-1441
Web: www.cboss.com/symphony ■ *E-mail:* symphony@cboss.com					

SPORTS TEAMS & FACILITIES

				Phone
Mahoning Valley Scrappers (baseball) 111 Eastwood Mall Blvd Cafaro Field	Niles	OH	44446	330-505-0000
Web: www.mvscrappers.com				

— Events —

	Phone
American Holiday Fine Arts & Antique Show & Sale (early December)	330-743-1711
Antiques in the Woods (mid-September)	330-457-7202
Arts & Crafts Show (late October)	330-747-8200
Austintown Log Cabin Tours (May-August)	330-792-1129
Austintown's 4th of July (July 4)	330-792-1129
Birthday Bash (late January)	330-792-7620
Canfield Fair (early September)	800-447-8201
Celtic Festival (early April)	330-727-8663
Christmas in the Mill (late November)	330-740-7115
Christmas in the Woods (early-mid-October)	724-728-7084
City Fest (July)	330-747-8200
Community Christmas Tree Lighting Ceremony (late November)	330-792-1129
Easter Egg Hunt (April)	330-726-8105
Easter Seals Drive for Dough Carnival (early June)	330-743-1168
Festival of Lights (late November-early January)	330-533-3773
Ghost Lights of Halloween (October)	330-533-3773
Greater Youngstown Italian Festival (early-mid-July)	330-549-0130
Harvest Festival (mid-September)	330-533-4161
Haunted Hayrides (mid-late October)	330-726-8105
Haunted House & Hayrides (October)	330-792-7620
Holiday of Lights (December)	330-792-7620
Log Cabin Day Arts & Crafts Show (late July)	330-792-1129
Mahoning Valley Kennel Club-Steel Valley Cluster-Dog Show (early August)	330-652-9622
Mahoning Valley Parent Magazine-Family Fun Day (early August)	330-792-7620
Mahoning Valley Rib Cook-Off (late July)	330-792-7620
Maple Syrup Festival (mid-late March)	330-726-8105
Market Day at the Fairgrounds (July)	330-533-4026
Memorial Day Ceremony & Parade (late May)	330-792-1129
Mother's Day Tea Party (mid-May)	330-743-5934
National Midyear Show (early July-late August)	330-743-1711
Octoberfest (late September-early October)	330-726-8105
Pumpkin Carve-Out (mid-late October)	330-726-8105
Shaker Woods Festival (mid-late August)	330-482-0214
Spring into Summer Festival (late June)	330-654-4989
Strock Stone House Tours (May-August)	330-792-1129
Summer Concerts in the Park (June-February)	330-755-7275
Sunfest (late July-early August)	330-740-7106
Thursday Night Music in the Park (June-August)	330-726-8105
Trick or Treat Town (mid-late October)	330-792-7620
Tuesday Concerts in the Park (mid-June-late August)	330-792-1129
Twin Oaks Pioneer Festival (mid-July & late September)	330-538-3097
Walk on Wick Arts & Music Festival (May)	330-747-8200
Wednesday Night Hay Rides & Bonfire (July-August)	330-726-8105
YSU Summer Festival of the Arts (early-mid-July)	330-742-2307
YWCA Women Artists: A Celebration Art Exhibit (mid-May)	330-746-6361

Oklahoma

Population (1999): 3,358,044 **Area (sq mi): 69,903**

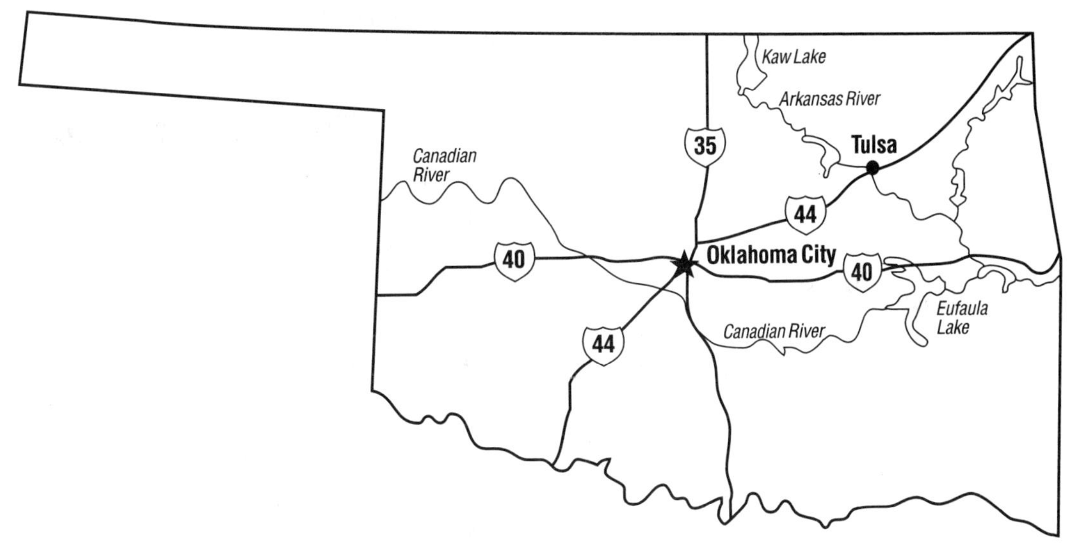

— State Information Sources —

				Phone	Fax
Oklahoma Commerce Dept PO Box 26980 *Web:* www.odoc.state.ok.us	Oklahoma City	OK	73126	405-815-5264	815-5205
Oklahoma Dept of Libraries 200 NE 18th St. *Web:* www.state.ok.us/~odl/	Oklahoma City	OK	73105	405-521-2502	525-7804
Oklahoma Parks Div PO Box 52002 *TF:* 800-654-8240 ■ *Web:* touroklahoma.com	Oklahoma City	OK	73152	405-521-3411	521-2428
Oklahoma State Chamber 330 NE 10th St. *Web:* www.okstatechamber.com ■ *E-mail:* info@okstatechamber.com	Oklahoma City	OK	73104	405-235-3669	235-3670
Oklahoma State Government Information *Web:* www.state.ok.us				405-521-2011	
Oklahoma Tourism & Recreation Dept 15 N Robinson St Suite 801 *TF:* 800-652-6552 ■ *Web:* www.otrd.state.ok.us ■ *E-mail:* info@mail.otrd.state.ok.us	Oklahoma City	OK	73105	405-521-2409	521-3992

ON-LINE RESOURCES

Oklahoma Cities . . . . dir.yahoo.com/Regional/U_S__States/Oklahoma/Cities
Oklahoma Cities By County . . dir.yahoo.com/Regional/U_S__States/Oklahoma/Counties_and_Regions
Oklahoma Scenario . . . . scenariousa.dstylus.com/ok/indexf.htm
Oklahoma Travel & Tourism Guide . . . . www.travel-library.com/north_america/usa/oklahoma/index.html
Oklahoma-Native America . . . . www.travelok.com
Rough Guide Travel Oklahoma travel.roughguides.com/content/958/index.htm
Surfin' Oklahoma . . . . www.surfinok.com/oklahoma.htm
Travel.org-Oklahoma . . . . travel.org/oklahoma.html
Yahoo! Get Local Oklahoma . . . . dir.yahoo.com/Regional/U_S__States/Oklahoma

— Cities Profiled —

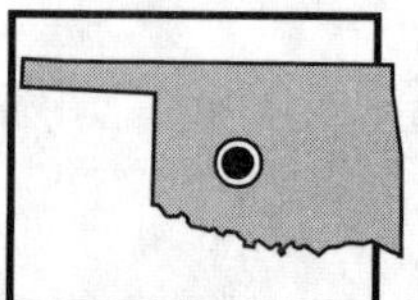

Oklahoma City

On a spring day in 1889, a single cannon shot signaled the start of the Great Land Run and tens of thousands of settlers raced across the boundary line to stake their claim on part of the two million available acres. The "city born in a day," as Oklahoma City was called, is now the capital and largest city in the state, and its Capitol building is the only one in the U.S. with working oil wells on the grounds. Authentic western boots and clothing are hand-made at Stockyards City, site of the Oklahoma National Stockyards, where more than one million head of cattle are auctioned off each year. Other Oklahoma City attractions include the National Cowboy Hall of Fame and Western Heritage Center; and the Kirkpatrick Science and Air Space Museum, with four museums, gardens and greenhouses, and a planetarium.

Population . . . 472,221
Area (Land) . . . 352.3 sq mi
Area (Water) . . . 5.6 sq mi
Elevation . . . 1207 ft
Latitude . . . 35-46-22 N
Longitude . . . 97-52-04 W
County . . . Oklahoma
Time Zone . . . CST
Area Code/s . . . 405

— Average Temperatures and Precipitation —

TEMPERATURES

	Jan	Feb	Mar	Apr	May	Jun	Jul	Aug	Sep	Oct	Nov	Dec
High	47	52	62	72	79	87	93	93	84	74	60	50
Low	25	30	39	49	58	66	71	70	62	50	39	29

PRECIPITATION

	Jan	Feb	Mar	Apr	May	Jun	Jul	Aug	Sep	Oct	Nov	Dec
Inches	1.1	1.6	2.7	2.8	5.2	4.3	2.6	2.6	3.8	3.2	2.0	1.4

— Important Phone Numbers —

	Phone
AAA	405-943-9922
American Express Travel	800-528-4800
Emergency	911
Medical Referral	405-843-5619
Poison Control Center	405-271-5454
Time/Temp	405-599-1234
Travelers Aid	405-232-5507
Weather	405-478-3377

— Information Sources —

				Phone	Fax
Better Business Bureau Serving Central Oklahoma 17 S Dewey Ave *Web:* www.oklahomacity.bbb.org	Oklahoma City	OK	73102	405-239-6081	235-5891
Greater Oklahoma City Chamber of Commerce 123 Park Ave *TF:* 800-616-1114 ■ *Web:* www.okcchamber.com ■ *E-mail:* ccadmin@soonernet.com	Oklahoma City	OK	73102	405-297-8900	297-8916
Metropolitan Library of Oklahoma County 131 Dean A McGee Ave *Web:* www.mls.lib.ok.us	Oklahoma City	OK	73102	405-231-8650	232-5493
Myriad Convention Center 1 Myriad Gardens *TF:* 800-654-3676 ■ *Web:* www.myriadevents.com ■ *E-mail:* gray@myriadevents.com	Oklahoma City	OK	73102	405-232-8871	297-1683
Oklahoma City City Hall 200 N Walker Ave *Web:* www.okc-cityhall.org	Oklahoma City	OK	73102	405-297-2345	297-2570
Oklahoma City Convention & Visitors Bureau 189 W Sheridan St *TF:* 800-225-5652 ■ *Web:* www.okccvb.org ■ *E-mail:* okccvb@okccvb.org	Oklahoma City	OK	73102	405-297-8910	297-8888
Oklahoma City Mayor 200 N Walker Ave *Web:* www.okc-cityhall.org/Mayor-Council/Mayor.html	Oklahoma City	OK	73102	405-297-2424	297-2570
Oklahoma City Planning Dept 420 W Main St 9th Fl *Web:* www.okc-cityhall.org/Planning	Oklahoma City	OK	73102	405-297-2623	297-1631
Oklahoma County 320 Robert S Kerr Ave **Fax:* Library	Oklahoma City	OK	73102	405-270-0082	278-1852*

On-Line Resources

About.com Guide to Oklahoma City . . . oklahomacity.about.com/local/southwestus/oklahomacity
Area Guide Oklahoma City . . . oklahomacity.areaguides.net
City Knowledge Oklahoma City . . . www.cityknowledge.com/ok_oklahomacity.htm
Connect Oklahoma Inc . . . www.connectok.com
DigitalCity Oklahoma City . . . home.digitalcity.com/oklahomacity
Excite.com Oklahoma City City Guide . . . www.excite.com/travel/countries/united_states/oklahoma/oklahoma_city
LDS iAmerica Oklahoma City . . . okc.iamerica.net
Oklahoma City Community Web Site . . . www.oklahomacity.com
Oklahoma City Online . . . okconline.com/

— Transportation Services —

AIRPORTS

■ Will Rogers World Airport (OKC)

	Phone
10 miles SW of downtown (approx 20 minutes)	405-680-3200

Web: www.flyokc.com ■ *E-mail:* carney@ionet.net

Airport Transportation

	Phone
Airport Express $10 fare to downtown	405-681-3311
Taxi $14 fare to downtown	405-737-0040

Commercial Airlines

	Phone
American	800-433-7300
Continental	800-525-0280
Continental Express	800-525-0280
Delta	800-221-1212
Northwest	800-225-2525
Southwest	800-435-9792
TWA	800-221-2000
United	800-241-6522

Charter Airlines

	Phone
Oklahoma Executive Jet	405-218-3920

CAR RENTALS

	Phone
Avis	405-685-7781
Budget	405-681-4977
CarTemps USA	405-842-7557
Dollar	405-681-0151
Hertz	405-681-2341
National	405-685-7726
Thrifty	405-682-5433

LIMO/TAXI

	Phone
ABC Cab	405-232-2402
King Limousine	405-787-9475
Metro Cab	405-659-2569
Regency Limousine	405-722-1312
Royal Coach Limousine	405-685-5466
Yellow Cab	405-232-6161

MASS TRANSIT

	Phone
Metro Transit $1 Base fare	405-235-7433

RAIL/BUS

				Phone
Union Bus Station 427 W Sheridan Ave	Oklahoma City	OK	73102	405-235-6425

— Accommodations —

HOTELS, MOTELS, RESORTS

				Phone	Fax
Best Budget Inn 301 S Council Rd	Oklahoma City	OK	73128	405-495-1232	495-1316
Best Value Inn 4800 S I-35	Oklahoma City	OK	73129	405-670-3815	670-3815

Oklahoma City — Hotels, Motels, Resorts (Cont'd)

Name / Address	City	State	Zip	Phone	Fax
Best Western Saddleback Inn 4300 SW 3rd St *TF:* 800-228-3903	Oklahoma City	OK	73108	405-947-7000	948-7636
Best Western Santa Fe Inn 6101 N Santa Fe Ave *TF:* 800-369-7223	Oklahoma City	OK	73118	405-848-1919	840-1581
Best Western Trade Winds Central 1800 E Reno Ave *TF:* 800-615-2647	Oklahoma City	OK	73117	405-235-4531	235-1861
Biltmore Hotel 401 S Meridian Ave *TF:* 800-522-6620	Oklahoma City	OK	73108	405-947-7681	947-4253
Clarion & Comfort Inn 4345 N Lincoln Blvd *TF:* 800-741-2741	Oklahoma City	OK	73105	405-528-2741	557-1489
Clarion Airport West 737 S Meridian Ave *TF:* 800-252-7466	Oklahoma City	OK	73108	405-942-8511	946-7126
Comfort Inn North 4017 NW 39th Expy *TF:* 800-228-5150	Oklahoma City	OK	73112	405-947-0038	946-7450
Courtesy Inn 6600 Northwest Expy *TF:* 800-444-5133	Oklahoma City	OK	73132	405-722-8694	721-4306
Courtyard by Marriott 4301 Highline Blvd *TF:* 800-321-2211 ■ *Web:* courtyard.com/OKCCA	Oklahoma City	OK	73108	405-946-6500	946-7638
Days Inn Airport Meridian 4712 W I-40 *TF:* 800-329-7466	Oklahoma City	OK	73128	405-947-8721	942-5020
Days Inn Northwest 2801 NW 39th St *TF:* 800-992-3297	Oklahoma City	OK	73112	405-946-0741	942-0181
Days Inn South 2616 S I-35 *TF:* 800-329-7466	Oklahoma City	OK	73129	405-677-0521	672-7347
Embassy Suites 1815 S Meridian Ave *TF:* 800-362-2779	Oklahoma City	OK	73108	405-682-6000	682-9835
Extended StayAmerica 4820 W Reno Ave *TF:* 800-482-1254	Oklahoma City	OK	73127	405-948-4443	948-4434
Governors Suites Hotel 2308 S Meridian *TF:* 888-819-7575	Oklahoma City	OK	73108	405-682-5299	682-3047
Habana Inn 2200 NW 39th Expy *TF:* 800-988-2221	Oklahoma City	OK	73112	405-528-2221	528-0496
Hampton Inn 3022 Northwest Expy *TF:* 800-426-7866	Oklahoma City	OK	73112	405-947-0953	947-7667
Hampton Inn 1905 S Meridian Ave *TF:* 800-426-7866	Oklahoma City	OK	73108	405-682-2080	682-3662
Hilton Inn Northwest 2945 Northwest Expy *TF:* 800-445-8667 ■ *Web:* www.hilton.com/hotels/OKCNWHF	Oklahoma City	OK	73112	405-848-4811	843-4829
Holiday Inn Airport 2101 S Meridian Ave *TF:* 800-622-7666	Oklahoma City	OK	73108	405-685-4000	685-0574
Holiday Inn Express 5405 N Lincoln Blvd *TF:* 800-465-4329	Oklahoma City	OK	73105	405-528-7563	528-0425
Hospitality Inn 3709 NW 39th Expy	Oklahoma City	OK	73112	405-942-7730	948-6238
Howard Johnson Lodge Airport 400 S Meridian Ave *TF:* 800-458-8186	Oklahoma City	OK	73108	405-943-9841	942-1869
Howard Johnson Lodge Central 1629 S Prospect Ave *TF:* 800-446-4656	Oklahoma City	OK	73129	405-677-0551	677-6363
La Quinta Inn Airport 800 S Meridian Ave *TF:* 800-531-5900	Oklahoma City	OK	73108	405-942-0040	942-0638
La Quinta Oklahoma City South 8315 S I-35 *TF:* 800-531-5900	Oklahoma City	OK	73149	405-631-8661	631-1892
Lake Murray Resort 3310 S Lake Murray Dr Box 12A *TF:* 800-654-8240	Ardmore	OK	73401	580-223-6600	223-6154
Lexington Hotel Suites 1200 S Meridian Ave *TF:* 800-537-8483	Oklahoma City	OK	73108	405-943-7800	943-8346
Meridian Hotel 733 S Meridian Ave *TF:* 800-252-7466	Oklahoma City	OK	73108	405-942-8511	946-7126
Oklahoma City Marriott 3233 Northwest Expy *TF:* 800-228-9290	Oklahoma City	OK	73112	405-842-6633	842-3152
Park Inn International 1224 S Meridian Ave *TF:* 800-437-7275	Oklahoma City	OK	73108	405-948-7294	948-7294
Plaza Inn 3200 S Prospect Ave	Oklahoma City	OK	73129	405-672-2341	
Quality Inn 720 S MacArthur Blvd *TF:* 800-257-2393	Oklahoma City	OK	73128	405-943-2393	943-9860
Quality Inn North 12001 N I-35 *TF:* 800-228-5151	Oklahoma City	OK	73131	405-478-0400	478-2774
Ramada Inn Airport South 6800 S I-35 *TF:* 800-228-2828	Oklahoma City	OK	73149	405-631-3321	631-3489
Ramada Limited Airport 2200 S Meridian Ave *TF:* 800-652-3781	Oklahoma City	OK	73108	405-681-9000	681-9000
Residence Inn by Marriott 4361 W Reno Ave *TF:* 800-331-3131 ■ *Web:* www.residenceinn.com/OKCWW	Oklahoma City	OK	73107	405-942-4500	942-7777
Richmond Suites 1600 Richmond Sq *TF:* 800-843-1440	Oklahoma City	OK	73118	405-840-1440	843-4272
Rodeway Inn 4601 SW 3rd St *TF:* 800-949-6748	Oklahoma City	OK	73128	405-947-2400	947-2931
Sheraton Four Points Hotel 6300 E Terminal Dr *TF:* 888-609-3500	Oklahoma City	OK	73159	405-681-3500	682-9090
Southgate Inn 5245 S I-35 *TF:* 800-672-5561	Oklahoma City	OK	73129	405-672-5561	672-2733
StudioPLUS 4811 Northwest Expy *TF:* 800-646-8000	Oklahoma City	OK	73132	405-722-2802	722-2872
Travelers Inn 504 S Meridian Ave	Oklahoma City	OK	73108	405-942-8294	947-3529
Travelodge 820 S MacArthur Blvd *TF:* 800-578-7878	Oklahoma City	OK	73128	405-947-8651	942-6792
Travelodge 3535 NW 39th Expy *TF:* 800-578-7878	Oklahoma City	OK	73112	405-947-2351	948-7752
Travelodge & Fifth Season Hotel 6200 N Robinson Ave *TF:* 800-682-0049	Oklahoma City	OK	73118	405-843-5558	840-3410
Waterford Marriott Hotel 6300 Waterford Blvd *TF:* 800-992-2009	Oklahoma City	OK	73118	405-848-4782	843-9161
Westin Hotel 1 N Broadway *TF:* 800-937-8461	Oklahoma City	OK	73102	405-235-2780	272-0369

— Restaurants —

Name / Address	City	State	Zip	Phone
Abuelo's Mexican Food Embassy (Mexican) 17 E Sheridan St	Oklahoma City	OK	73104	405-235-1422
Ajanta (Indian) 11921 N Pennsylvania Ave	Oklahoma City	OK	73120	405-752-5283
Aloha Garden (Chinese) 2219 SW 74th St	Oklahoma City	OK	73159	405-686-0288
Applewoods Restaurant (American) 4301 SW 3rd St	Oklahoma City	OK	73108	405-947-8484
Bellini's (Italian) 6305 N Waterford Blvd	Oklahoma City	OK	73118	405-848-1065
Billy Balloo's (American) NW Expy & Rockwell	Oklahoma City	OK	73132	405-728-7760
Bricktown Brewery (American) 1 N Oklahoma Ave *Web:* www.bricktownbrewery.com ■ *E-mail:* info@bricktownbrewery.com	Oklahoma City	OK	73104	405-232-2739
Brother Cajun Cuisine (Cajun) 2801 NW 39th	Oklahoma City	OK	73112	405-946-0741
Cattlemans Cafe (Steak) 1309 S Agnew Ave	Oklahoma City	OK	73108	405-236-0416
Cimarron Steak House (Steak) 201 N Meridian Ave	Oklahoma City	OK	73107	405-948-7778
Coach House (French) 6437 Avondale Dr	Oklahoma City	OK	73116	405-842-1000
Crabtown (Seafood) 303 E Sheridan Ave *Web:* www.funfresh.com/crabtown.html	Oklahoma City	OK	73104	405-232-7227
Deep Fork Grill (Steak/Seafood) 5418 N Western Ave	Oklahoma City	OK	73118	405-848-7678
Don Serapio's (Mexican) 11109 N May	Oklahoma City	OK	73120	405-755-1664
Drover's Cafe (American) 2101 S Meridian Ave	Oklahoma City	OK	73108	405-685-4000
Earl's Rib Place (Barbecue) 6816 N Western Ave	Oklahoma City	OK	73116	405-843-9922
Eddy's of Oklahoma City (Steak/Seafood) 4227 N Meridian Ave	Oklahoma City	OK	73112	405-787-2944
Hamilton's Catfish Cabin (Seafood) 6317 N Meridian Ave	Oklahoma City	OK	73112	405-721-7553
Hu-Nan (Chinese) 9211 N 10th Pl	Oklahoma City	OK	73120	405-843-6233
Iguana Lounge (Mexican) 6714 N Western Ave	Oklahoma City	OK	73116	405-840-3474
Innfield The (American) 2616 S I-35	Oklahoma City	OK	73129	405-677-0521
Metro Wine Bar & Bistro (New American) 6418 N Western Ave	Oklahoma City	OK	73116	405-840-9463
Nikz (American) 5900 Mosteller Dr United Founders Tower	Oklahoma City	OK	73112	405-843-7875
OKC Cafe (Continental) 2945 Northwest Expy	Oklahoma City	OK	73112	405-848-4811
Oklahoma County Line (Barbecue) 1226 NE 63rd St	Oklahoma City	OK	73111	405-478-4955
Pearls Oyster Bar (Cajun) 928 NW 63rd *Web:* www.funfresh.com/pearls.html	Oklahoma City	OK	73112	405-848-8008
Pepperoni Grill (Italian) 1001 Penn Square Mall	Oklahoma City	OK	73118	405-848-4660
Rossini's Restaurant (Italian) 6101 N Santa Fe	Oklahoma City	OK	73118	405-848-3248
Royal Bavaria Brewery (German) 3401 S Sooner Rd	Oklahoma City	OK	73160	405-799-7666
Sleepy Hollow (American) 1101 NE 50th St	Oklahoma City	OK	73111	405-424-1614
South by Southwest (American) 1815 S Meridian Ave	Oklahoma City	OK	73108	405-682-6000
TerraLuna Grille (California) 7408 N Western Ave	Oklahoma City	OK	73116	405-879-0009
Trapper's Fishcamp & Grill (Seafood) 4300 W Reno St *Web:* www.funfresh.com/trappers.html	Oklahoma City	OK	73107	405-943-9111

Oklahoma City — Restaurants (Cont'd)

Name / Address	City	State	ZIP	Phone
Varsity Sports Grill (American) 115 E Sheridan St	Oklahoma City	OK	73104	405-235-5525
Waterford (Steak/Seafood) 6300 Waterford Blvd	Oklahoma City	OK	73118	405-848-4782
Zio's Italian Kitchen (Italian) 2035 S Meridian	Oklahoma City	OK	73108	405-680-9999

— Goods and Services —

SHOPPING

Name / Address	City	State	ZIP	Phone	Fax
50 Penn Place 1900 Northwest Expy	Oklahoma City	OK	73118	405-848-7940	848-5921
Bricktown 315 E Sheridan Ave	Oklahoma City	OK	73104	405-236-8666	236-8669
Web: www.bricktown-ok.com/					
Crossroads Mall 7000 Crossroads Blvd	Oklahoma City	OK	73149	405-631-4421	634-1503
Dillard's 7000 Crossroads Blvd.	Oklahoma City	OK	73149	405-634-6569	
Heritage Park Mall 6801 E Reno Ave	Midwest City	OK	73110	405-737-1472	737-5546
Mayfair Village NW 50th & May Ave.	Oklahoma City	OK	73112	405-721-2797	721-5956
Penn Square Mall 1901 Northwest Expy	Oklahoma City	OK	73118	405-842-4424	842-4676
Web: www.shoppenn.com ■ *E-mail:* info@shoppenn.com					
Quail Springs Mall 2501 W Memorial Rd	Oklahoma City	OK	73134	405-755-6530	751-8334
Web: www.quailspringsmall.com					

BANKS

Name / Address	City	State	ZIP	Phone	Fax
BancFirst Corp PO Box 26788	Oklahoma City	OK	73126	405-270-1000	270-1089
Web: www.bancfirst.com					
Bank One Oklahoma City NA 100 N Broadway Ave	Oklahoma City	OK	73102	405-231-6000	
Bankers Bank 5801 N Broadway Parragon Bldg Suite 300	Oklahoma City	OK	73118	405-848-8877	842-4524
TF: 800-522-9220					
NationsBank 211 N Robinson Ave	Oklahoma City	OK	73102	405-230-4000	230-5152*
*Fax: Mktg ■ *TF Cust Svc:* 800-944-0404*					

BUSINESS SERVICES

Name	Phone	Name	Phone
Ala Carte Courier	405-670-2000	**Olsten Staffing Services**	405-525-3456
Federal Express	800-238-5355	**Post Office**	800-275-8777
Kelly Services	405-848-0516	**Sooner Delivery**	405-848-1977
Kinko's	405-528-7955	**UPS**	800-742-5877
Manpower Temporary Services	405-942-5111		

— Media —

PUBLICATIONS

Name / Address	City	State	ZIP	Phone	Fax
Daily Oklahoman‡ PO Box 25125	Oklahoma City	OK	73125	405-475-3311	475-3183
TF: 800-375-6397 ■ *Web:* www.oklahoman.net					
Journal Record Oklahoma City‡ 222 N Robinson St	Oklahoma City	OK	73102	405-235-3100	278-6907
Web: www.journalrecord.com					
Oklahoma Today Magazine 15 N Robinson Ave Colcord Bldg Suite 100	Oklahoma City	OK	73102	405-521-2496	522-4588
TF: 800-777-1793					

‡*Daily newspapers*

TELEVISION

Name / Address	City	State	ZIP	Phone	Fax
KAUT-TV Ch 43 (UPN) 11901 N Eastern Ave	Oklahoma City	OK	73131	405-478-4300	516-4343
KETA-TV Ch 13 (PBS) 7403 N Kelley St	Oklahoma City	OK	73111	405-848-8501	841-9216
Web: www.oeta.onenet.net					
KFOR-TV Ch 4 (NBC) 444 E Britton Rd	Oklahoma City	OK	73114	405-478-1212	478-6337
Web: www.kfor.com ■ *E-mail:* news@kfor.com					
KOCB-TV Ch 34 (WB) 1501 NE 85th St	Oklahoma City	OK	73131	405-478-3434	478-1027
Web: www.kocb.com ■ *E-mail:* kocb@telepath.com					
KOCO-TV Ch 5 (ABC) 1300 E Britton Rd	Oklahoma City	OK	73131	405-478-3000	478-6675
Web: www.ionet.net/koco ■ *E-mail:* koco@ionet.net					
KOKH-TV Ch 25 (Fox) 1228 E Wilshire Blvd	Oklahoma City	OK	73111	405-843-2525	478-4343
Web: www.kokh.com ■ *E-mail:* prgramming@fox25.net					
KOPX-TV Ch 62 (PAX) 1303 Railway Dr	Oklahoma City	OK	73114	405-751-6800	751-6867
Web: www.pax.net/KOPX					
KSBI-TV Ch 52 (Ind) PO Box 26404	Oklahoma City	OK	73126	405-631-7335	631-7367
KWTV-TV Ch 9 (CBS) 7401 N Kelley Ave	Oklahoma City	OK	73111	405-843-6641	841-9989
Web: www.kwtv.com ■ *E-mail:* mailroom@kwtv.com					

RADIO

Name / Address	City	State	ZIP	Phone	Fax
KATT-FM 100.5 MHz (Rock) 4045 NW 64th St Suite 600	Oklahoma City	OK	73116	405-848-0100	848-1915
Web: www.katt.com					
KGOU-FM 106.3 MHz (NPR) 780 Van Vleet Oval	Norman	OK	73019	405-325-3388	325-7129
Web: www.kgou.org/					
KJYO-FM 102.7 MHz (CHR) PO Box 1000	Oklahoma City	OK	73101	405-840-5271	858-1435
KMGL-FM 104.1 MHz (AC) 400 E Britton Rd	Oklahoma City	OK	73114	405-478-5104	478-0448
Web: www.magic104.com ■ *E-mail:* info@magic104.com					
KOMA-FM 92.5 MHz (Oldies) 820 SW 4th St	Moore	OK	73160	405-794-4000	793-0514
KQCV-AM 800 kHz (Rel) 1919 N Broadway	Oklahoma City	OK	73103	405-521-0800	521-1391
KQSR-FM 94.7 MHz (AC) 50 Penn Pl Suite 1000	Oklahoma City	OK	73118	405-840-5271	858-1435
KRXO-FM 107.7 MHz (CR) 400 E Britton Rd	Oklahoma City	OK	73114	405-794-4000	793-0514
KTNT-FM 97.9 MHz (NAC) 4045 NW 64th St Suite 600	Oklahoma City	OK	73116	405-848-0100	843-5288
Web: www.ktnt.com					
KTOK-AM 1000 kHz (N/T) 50 Penn Pl	Oklahoma City	OK	73118	405-840-5271	858-1435
KTST-FM 101.9 MHz (Ctry) 101 NE 28th St	Oklahoma City	OK	73105	405-528-5543	525-3832
Web: www.thetwister.com ■ *E-mail:* twister@thetwister.com					
KXXY-FM 96.1 MHz (Ctry) 101 NE 28th St	Oklahoma City	OK	73105	405-528-5543	524-5823

— Colleges/Universities —

Name / Address	City	State	ZIP	Phone	Fax
Hillsdale Free Will Baptist College PO Box 7208	Moore	OK	73153	405-912-9000	912-9050
E-mail: go-saints@hillsdale.org					
Mid-America Bible College 3500 SW 119th St	Oklahoma City	OK	73170	405-691-3800	692-3165
E-mail: mbcinfo@mabc.edu					
Oklahoma Christian University of Science & Arts 2501 E Memorial Blvd	Edmond	OK	73013	405-425-5000	425-5208
TF Admissions: 800-877-5010 ■ *Web:* www.oc.edu ■ *E-mail:* info@oc.edu					
Oklahoma City Community College 7777 S May Ave	Oklahoma City	OK	73159	405-682-1611	682-7521
Web: www.okc.cc.ok.us					
Oklahoma City University 2501 N Blackwelder Ave	Oklahoma City	OK	73106	405-521-5000	521-5916
TF Admissions: 800-633-7242 ■ *Web:* frodo.okcu.edu ■ *E-mail:* uadmissions@frodo.okcu.edu					
Oklahoma State University Oklahoma City 900 N Portland Ave	Oklahoma City	OK	73107	405-947-4421	945-3277
Web: www.osuokc.edu					
Rose State College 6420 SE 15th St	Midwest City	OK	73110	405-733-7311	736-0309
Web: www.rose.cc.ok.us					
Southern Nazarene University 6729 NW 39th Expy	Bethany	OK	73008	405-789-6400	491-6320
TF Admissions: 800-648-9899 ■ *Web:* www.snu.edu					
Southwestern College of Christian Ministry 7210 NW 39th Expy	Bethany	OK	73008	405-789-7661	495-0078
University of Central Oklahoma 100 N University Dr	Edmond	OK	73034	405-341-2980	341-4964
Web: www.ucok.edu ■ *E-mail:* aix1@ucok.edu					
University of Oklahoma 1000 Asp Ave	Norman	OK	73019	405-325-0311	325-7124
Web: www.ou.edu					
University of Sciences & Arts of Oklahoma PO Box 82345	Chickasha	OK	73018	405-224-3140	522-3176
TF: 800-933-8726 ■ *Web:* www.usao.edu					

Oklahoma City (Cont'd)

— Hospitals —

				Phone	Fax
Columbia Edmond Medical Center 1 S Bryant St	Edmond	OK	73034	405-341-6100	359-5500
Columbia Presbyterian Medical Center 700 NE 13th St	Oklahoma City	OK	73104	405-271-5100	271-6032
Deaconess Hospital 5501 N Portland Ave	Oklahoma City	OK	73112	405-946-5581	604-6153
Hillcrest Health Center 2129 SW 59th St *Web:* www.hillcrest.com	Oklahoma City	OK	73119	405-685-6671	680-2237
Integris Baptist Medical Center 3300 Northwest Expy	Oklahoma City	OK	73112	405-949-3011	949-3573
Integris Southwest Medical Center of Oklahoma 4401 S Western Ave **Fax:* Admitting	Oklahoma City	OK	73109	405-636-7000	636-7881*
Mercy Health Center 4300 W Memorial Rd **Fax:* Admitting	Oklahoma City	OK	73120	405-755-1515	752-3750*
Norman Regional Hospital PO Box 1308	Norman	OK	73070	405-307-1000	307-1304
Saint Anthony Hospital 1000 N Lee St **Fax:* Admitting ■ *TF:* 800-227-6964 ■ *Web:* www.saintsok.com	Oklahoma City	OK	73101	405-272-7000	231-8911*
University Hospitals PO Box 26307	Oklahoma City	OK	73126	405-271-5656	271-3888
Veterans Affairs Medical Center 921 NE 13th St	Oklahoma City	OK	73104	405-270-0501	270-1560

— Attractions —

				Phone	Fax
45th Infantry Division Museum 2145 NE 36th St	Oklahoma City	OK	73111	405-424-5313	424-3748
Ballet Oklahoma 7421 N Classen Blvd *Web:* www.balletoklahoma.com	Oklahoma City	OK	73116	405-843-9898	843-9894
Black Liberated Arts Center 201 Channing Sq	Oklahoma City	OK	73102	405-232-2522	840-0061
Bricktown 315 E Sheridan Ave *Web:* www.bricktown-ok.com/	Oklahoma City	OK	73104	405-236-8666	236-8669
Canterbury Choral Society 428 W California St	Oklahoma City	OK	72102	405-232-7464	232-7465
Carpenter Square Theatre 400 W Main St	Oklahoma City	OK	73101	405-232-6500	232-6502
Chickasaw National Recreation Area PO Box 201 *Web:* www.nps.gov/chic/	Sulphur	OK	73086	580-622-3165	622-6931
City Arts Center 3000 Pershing Blvd *Web:* www.cityartscenter.com ■ *E-mail:* cacoct@ix.netcom.com	Oklahoma City	OK	73107	405-951-0000	951-0003
Earlywine Park 3101 SW 119th St & May Ave	Oklahoma City	OK	73170	405-297-2211	
Enterprise Square USA PO Box 11000 *Web:* www.esusa.org	Oklahoma City	OK	73136	405-425-5030	425-5108
Frontier City Theme Park 11501 Northeast Expy *Web:* www.sixflags.com/frontiercity	Oklahoma City	OK	73131	405-478-2412	478-3104
Governor's Mansion 820 NE 23rd	Oklahoma City	OK	73105	405-521-9211	521-1198
Harn Homestead & 1889er Museum 313 NE 16th St	Oklahoma City	OK	73104	405-235-4058	235-4041
Historic Paseo Artist District NW 30th & Dewey Ave *Web:* www.okclive.com/paseo/	Oklahoma City	OK	73103	405-525-2688	525-3133
International Photography Hall of Fame & Museum 2100 NE 52nd St *E-mail:* info@iphf.org	Oklahoma City	OK	73111	405-424-4055	424-4058
Jewel Box Theatre 3700 N Walker Ave	Oklahoma City	OK	73118	405-521-1786	525-6562
Kirkpatrick Science & Air Space Museum 2100 NE 52nd St *TF:* 800-532-7652 ■ *Web:* www.ionet.net/~omniplex/index.shtml ■ *E-mail:* omniplex@ionet.net	Oklahoma City	OK	73111	405-602-6664	602-3768
Lake Overholser 3201 E Overholser Dr	Oklahoma City	OK	73102	405-297-2211	
Lyric Theatre of Oklahoma 4444 N Classen Blvd Suite 103 *Web:* www.lyrictheatreokc.com	Oklahoma City	OK	73118	405-524-9312	524-9316
Martin Park Nature Center 5000 W Memorial Rd	Oklahoma City	OK	73142	405-755-0676	749-3072
Myriad Botanical Gardens/Crystal Bridge Tropical Conservatory 100 Myriad Gardens *Web:* www.okccvb.org/attractions/myrgard/myrgard.html	Oklahoma City	OK	73102	405-297-3995	297-3620
National Cowboy Hall of Fame & Western Heritage Center 1700 NE 63rd St *Web:* www.cowboyhalloffame.org	Oklahoma City	OK	73111	405-478-2250	478-2046
National Softball Hall of Fame & Museum 2801 NE 50th St *Web:* www.softball.org ■ *E-mail:* info@softball.org	Oklahoma City	OK	73111	405-424-5266	424-3855
Oklahoma City Art Museum at the Fairgrounds 3113 Pershing Blvd *TF:* 800-579-9278 ■ *Web:* www.okcartmuseum.com ■ *E-mail:* info@okcartmuseum.com	Oklahoma City	OK	73107	405-946-4477	946-7671
Oklahoma City Philharmonic 428 W California Ave Suite 210 *Web:* www.okcphilharmonic.org/	Oklahoma City	OK	73102	405-232-7575	232-4353
Oklahoma City Zoo 2101 NE 50th St *Web:* www.okczoo.com	Oklahoma City	OK	73111	405-424-3344	425-0207
Oklahoma Firefighters Museum 2716 NE 50th St *Web:* www.okccvb.org/attractions/firefighters/firemus.htm	Oklahoma City	OK	73111	405-424-3440	424-1032
Oklahoma Heritage Center 201 NW 14th St *Web:* www.telepath.com/oha/weddings.html ■ *E-mail:* oha@telepath.com	Oklahoma City	OK	73103	405-235-4458	235-2714
Oklahoma Opry 404 W Commerce St *E-mail:* scarberry@thor.net	Oklahoma City	OK	73109	405-632-8322	
Oklahoma State Capitol 2300 N Lincoln Blvd	Oklahoma City	OK	73105	405-521-3356	
Omniplex 2100 NE 52nd St *TF:* 800-532-7652 ■ *Web:* www.ionet.net/~omniplex/index.shtml ■ *E-mail:* omniplex@ionet.net	Oklahoma City	OK	73111	405-602-6664	602-3768
Overholser Mansion 405 NW 15th St	Oklahoma City	OK	73103	405-528-8485	
Prairie Dance Theatre 2100 NE 52nd St	Oklahoma City	OK	73111	405-424-2249	
Red Earth Indian Center 2100 NE 52nd St	Oklahoma City	OK	73111	405-427-5228	427-8079
Rogers Will Park 36th St & N Portland Ave	Oklahoma City	OK	73112	405-943-0827	
Stars & Stripes Park 3701 S Lake Hefner Pkwy	Oklahoma City	OK	73102	405-297-2211	
State Fair Park 500 Land Rush St *Web:* www.oklafair.org/	Oklahoma City	OK	73107	405-948-6700	948-6828
State Museum of History 2100 N Lincoln Blvd Wiley Post Historical Bldg *Web:* www.ok-history.mus.ok.us	Oklahoma City	OK	73105	405-521-2491	521-2492
Stockyards & Cowtown 2501 Exchange Ave	Oklahoma City	OK	73108	405-235-8675	236-3277
Trosper Park SE 29th St & Eastern Ave	Oklahoma City	OK	73102	405-297-2211	
White Water Bay 3908 W Reno Ave	Oklahoma City	OK	73107	405-943-9687	947-3714
World Organization of China Painters Museum 2641 NW 10th St *Web:* www.theshop.net/wocporg/ ■ *E-mail:* wocporg@theshop.net	Oklahoma City	OK	73107	405-521-1234	521-1265

SPORTS TEAMS & FACILITIES

				Phone	Fax
Oklahoma City Blazers (hockey) 119 N Robinson Ave Suite 230 *Web:* www.okcblazers.com ■ *E-mail:* info@okcblazers.com	Oklahoma City	OK	73102	405-235-7825	272-9875
Oklahoma RedHawks (baseball) PO Box 75089 *Web:* www.redhawksbaseball.com	Oklahoma City	OK	73147	405-218-1000	218-1001
Remington Park Race Track 1 Remington Pl	Oklahoma City	OK	73111	405-424-1000	425-3297
State Fair Arena 333 Gorden Cooper Blvd *Web:* www.oklafair.org	Oklahoma City	OK	73107	405-948-6700	948-6821
State Fair Speedway 500 Land Rush St *Web:* www.na-motorsports.com/Tracks/StateFair.html	Oklahoma City	OK	73147	405-948-6796	948-6828

— Events —

	Phone
89ers Days PRCA Rodeo (late April)	800-595-7433
Aerospace America International Air Show (early June)	405-685-9546
All-College Basketball Tournament (late December)	800-225-5652
An Affair of the Heart Craft Show (early February & late October)	405-948-6704
Arts Festival Oklahoma (Labor Day weekend)	405-682-7536
Balloon Fest (mid-August)	405-794-4000
Big 12 Baseball Tournament (mid-May)	800-225-5652
Bullnanza (early February)	800-234-3393
Celebration of African-American Heritage (early February)	405-951-0000
Centennial Horse Show (mid-late April)	405-557-9400

Oklahoma City — Events (Cont'd)

	Phone
Cowboy Chuck Wagon Gathering (late May)	405-478-2250
Crystal Lights Holiday Display (late November-late December)	405-297-3995
Festival of the Arts (late April)	405-297-8910
Fourth of July Festival (July 4)	800-225-5652
Grand National Morgan Horse Show (early October)	800-225-5652
Heritage Hills Historic Homes Tour (mid-October)	405-528-8485
Holiday Treefest (late November-early January)	405-602-6664
International Arabian Horse Show (late July)	405-948-6700
International Finals Rodeo (mid-January)	405-235-6540
Lazy E Spring Barrel Futurity (early April)	800-595-7433
National Appaloosa Horse Show (late June-mid-July)	405-297-8938
National Finals Steer Roping (late October)	800-595-7433
National Reining Horse Derby (mid-May)	405-297-8938
Oklahoma City Home & Garden Show (mid-February & late March)	405-948-6704
Oklahoma Farm Show (mid-April)	405-948-6704
Oklahoma State Fair (September-early October)	800-225-5652
Paseo Arts Festival (late May)	405-525-2688
Prairie Circuit Finals Rodeo (mid-November)	800-595-7433
Prix De West Invitational Exhibition & Sale (mid-June)	405-478-2250
Red Earth Native American Cultural Festival (mid-June)	405-427-5228
Sooner State Summer Games (June)	405-235-4222
Southwest Street Rod Nationals (mid-July)	405-948-6700
Sportsfest (early February)	405-235-4222
Spring Fair & Livestock Exposition (late March)	405-948-6704
Spring Festival of the Arts (late April)	405-270-4848
Sunday Twilight Concert Series (June-late August)	405-270-4848
Timed Event Championship of the World (mid-March)	800-595-7433
WinterTales Storytelling Festival (mid-February)	405-270-4848
World Championship Barrel Racing Futurity (mid-December)	405-948-6704
World Championship Quarter Horse Show (mid-November)	800-225-5652

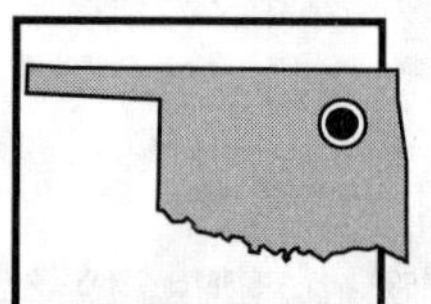

Tulsa

Tulsa's major industry is derived from the gas and oil fields that surround it. The city was built by wealthy oil barons, and its early history is interpreted at the Gilcrease Museum, founded by oilman Thomas Gilcrease, and the Tulsa Historical Museum, which is located in the former Gilcrease residence. Tulsa was also the terminus of the infamous Trail of Tears of the 1830s. Today, the city has the second highest American Indian population in the country, and the annual Tulsa Pow-Wow involves more than 100 tribes. Nearby Tahlequah is home to the Cherokee Nation and includes the Cherokee Heritage Center and the Cherokee National Museum. Other Tulsa area attractions include the Will Rogers Home, Birthplace, and Memorial; Grand Lake O' the Cherokees recreation area; and the Woolaroc Museum and Nature Preserve.

Population	381,393	**Longitude**	95-99-25 W
Area (Land)	172.6 sq mi	**County**	Tulsa
Area (Water)	4.2 sq mi	**Time Zone**	CST
Elevation	750 ft	**Area Code/s**	918
Latitude	36-15-39 N		

— Average Temperatures and Precipitation —

TEMPERATURES

	Jan	Feb	Mar	Apr	May	Jun	Jul	Aug	Sep	Oct	Nov	Dec
High	45	51	62	73	80	88	94	93	84	74	60	49
Low	25	30	39	50	59	68	73	71	63	51	40	29

PRECIPITATION

	Jan	Feb	Mar	Apr	May	Jun	Jul	Aug	Sep	Oct	Nov	Dec
Inches	1.5	2.0	3.5	3.7	5.6	4.4	3.1	3.1	4.7	3.7	3.1	2.2

— Important Phone Numbers —

	Phone		Phone
AAA	918-748-1000	**Poison Control Center**	800-522-4611
American Express Travel	918-743-8856	**Time/Temp**	918-477-1000
Dental Referral	918-451-1017	**Weather**	918-743-3311
Emergency	911		

— Information Sources —

				Phone	Fax
Better Business Bureau Serving Eastern Oklahoma 6711 S Yale Ave Suite 230	Tulsa	OK	74136	918-492-1266	492-1276
Web: www.tulsabbb.org ■ *E-mail:* info@tulsabbb.org					
Metropolitan Tulsa Chamber of Commerce 616 S Boston Ave Suite 100	Tulsa	OK	74119	918-585-1201	585-8016*
**Fax:* Hum Res ■ *Web:* www.tulsachamber.com ■ *E-mail:* mtcc@webzone.net					
Tulsa City-County Library 400 Civic Ctr	Tulsa	OK	74103	918-596-7977	596-7990
Web: www.tulsalibrary.org					
Tulsa City Hall 200 Civic Ctr	Tulsa	OK	74103	918-596-2100	
Web: www.webzone.net/cityoftulsa					
Tulsa Convention & Visitors Bureau 616 S Boston Ave Suite 100	Tulsa	OK	74119	918-585-1201	592-6244
TF: 800-558-3311 ■ *Web:* www.tulsachamber.com/cvb.htm ■ *E-mail:* tcvb@aol.com					
Tulsa Convention Center 100 Civic Ctr	Tulsa	OK	74103	918-596-7177	596-7155
TF: 800-678-7177 ■ *Web:* www.tulsaconvention.com					
Tulsa County 500 S Denver Ave	Tulsa	OK	74103	918-596-5000	596-5819
Tulsa Economic Development Corp 907 S Detroit Suite 1001	Tulsa	OK	74120	918-585-8332	585-2473
Tulsa Mayor 200 Civic Ctr	Tulsa	OK	74103	918-596-7411	596-9010

On-Line Resources

4Tulsa.com	www.4tulsa.com
Anthill City Guide Tulsa	www.anthill.com/city.asp?city=tulsa
Area Guide Tulsa	tulsa.areaguides.net
Art Access	www.webtek.com/arts/
City Knowledge Tulsa	www.cityknowledge.com/ok_tulsa.htm
Excite.com Tulsa City Guide	www.excite.com/travel/countries/united_states/oklahoma/tulsa
LDS iAmerica Tulsa	tulsa.iamerica.net
Tulsa Web	www.tulsaweb.com/
Tulsa.com	www.tulsa.com
Urban Tulsa	www.urbantulsa.com/

— Transportation Services —

AIRPORTS

■ **Tulsa International Airport (TUL)**	Phone
9 miles NE of downtown (approx 10 minutes)	918-838-5000

Airport Transportation

	Phone
Taxi $13 fare to downtown	918-587-6611

Commercial Airlines

	Phone		Phone
American	800-433-7300	**Northwest**	800-225-2525
Continental	918-583-1313	**Southwest**	800-435-9792
Continental Express	800-525-0280	**TWA**	800-221-2000
Delta	800-221-1212	**United**	800-241-6522

Charter Airlines

	Phone		Phone
Allied Helicopter Service	918-425-7558	**Corporate Aviation Services Inc**	918-834-8348
Business Jet Services	888-387-7477		

CAR RENTALS

	Phone		Phone
Alamo	800-327-9633	**Enterprise**	918-583-4880
Avis	918-838-5148	**Hertz**	918-838-1999
Budget	918-836-3761	**National**	918-838-5270
Dollar	918-838-5236	**Thrifty**	918-838-3333

Tulsa (Cont'd)

LIMO/TAXI

Name	Phone
Franklin Limousine Service	918-585-5466
Royal Coachman Limousine	918-437-3975
Yellow/Checker Cab	918-587-6611

MASS TRANSIT

Name	Phone
Metropolitan Tulsa Transit Authority $.75 Base fare	918-585-1195

RAIL/BUS

Name	City	State	Zip	Phone
Greyhound/Trailways Bus Station 317 S Detroit Ave *TF:* 800-231-2222	Tulsa	OK	74120	918-584-4428

— Accommodations —

HOTELS, MOTELS, RESORTS

Name	City	State	Zip	Phone	Fax
Adam's Mark Hotel 100 E 2nd St *TF:* 800-444-2326 ■ *Web:* www.adamsmark.com/tuls.htm	Tulsa	OK	74103	918-582-9000	560-2261
Baymont Inns & Suites 4530 E Skelly Dr *TF:* 800-301-0200	Tulsa	OK	74135	918-488-8777	488-0220
Best Western Airport 222 N Garnett Rd *TF:* 800-438-0780	Tulsa	OK	74116	918-438-0780	438-9296
Best Western Trade Winds Central Inn 3141 E Skelly Dr *TF:* 800-685-4564	Tulsa	OK	74105	918-749-5561	749-6312
Best Western Trade Winds East Inn 3337 E Skelly Dr *TF:* 800-254-7449	Tulsa	OK	74135	918-743-7931	743-4308
Charles Wesley Motor Lodge 302 N Park Dr	Broken Bow	OK	74728	580-584-3303	584-3433
Comfort Inn 4717 S Yale *TF:* 800-228-5160	Tulsa	OK	74135	918-622-6776	622-1809
Comfort Inn Airport 6730 E Archer *TF:* 800-228-5150	Tulsa	OK	74115	918-835-4444	836-3594
Comfort Suites 8338 E 61st St *TF:* 800-221-2222	Tulsa	OK	74133	918-254-0088	254-6820
Country Inn & Suites 1034 N Garnett Rd *TF:* 888-607-5255	Tulsa	OK	74116	918-234-3535	234-2600
Days Inn 8201 E Skelly Dr *TF:* 800-329-7466	Tulsa	OK	74129	918-665-6800	665-7653
Days Inn Airport 1016 N Garnett Rd *TF:* 800-329-7466	Tulsa	OK	74116	918-438-5050	438-8314
Doubletree Hotel at Warren Place 6110 S Yale Ave *TF:* 800-222-8733 ■ *Web:* www.doubletreehotels.com/DoubleT/Hotel61/76/76Main.htm	Tulsa	OK	74136	918-495-1000	495-1944
Doubletree Hotel Downtown 616 W 7th St *TF:* 800-222-8733 ■ *Web:* www.doubletreehotels.com/DoubleT/Hotel61/75/75Main.htm	Tulsa	OK	74127	918-587-8000	587-1642
Econo Lodge Airport 11620 E Skelly Dr *TF:* 800-553-2666	Tulsa	OK	74128	918-437-9200	437-2935
Embassy Suites 3332 S 79th East Ave *TF:* 800-362-2779	Tulsa	OK	74145	918-622-4000	665-2347
Executive Inn 416 W 6th St	Tulsa	OK	74119	918-584-4461	584-4461
Extended StayAmerica 3414 S 79th Ave East *TF:* 800-398-7829	Tulsa	OK	74145	918-664-9494	664-0044
Fairfield Inn 9020 E 71st St *TF:* 800-228-2800 ■ *Web:* fairfieldinn.com/TULFI	Tulsa	OK	74133	918-252-7754	252-7754
GuestHouse Suites Plus 8181 E 41st St *TF:* 800-214-8378 ■ *Web:* www.guesthouse.net/tulsa.html	Tulsa	OK	74145	918-664-7241	622-0314
Hampton Inn 3209 S 79th Ave East *TF:* 800-426-7866	Tulsa	OK	74145	918-663-1000	663-0587
Hawthorn Suites Hotel 3509 S 79th Ave E *TF:* 800-527-1133 ■ *Web:* www.hawthorn.com/reservations/locationdetail.asp?state=OK&facid=246&pagecode=hdir	Tulsa	OK	74145	918-663-3900	664-0548
Holiday Inn 1410 SE Washington Blvd *TF:* 800-465-4329	Bartlesville	OK	74006	918-333-8320	333-8979
Holiday Inn 5000 E Skelly Dr *TF:* 800-836-9635	Tulsa	OK	74135	918-622-7000	664-9353
Holiday Inn East Airport 1010 N Garnett Rd *TF:* 800-465-4329	Tulsa	OK	74116	918-437-7660	438-7538
Howard Johnson Hotel 4724 S Yale *TF:* 800-446-4656	Tulsa	OK	74135	918-496-9300	495-1760
La Quinta Motor Inn Airport 35 N Sheridan Rd *TF:* 800-531-5900	Tulsa	OK	74115	918-836-3931	836-5428
La Quinta Motor Inn South 12525 E 52nd St South *TF:* 800-687-6667	Tulsa	OK	74146	918-254-1626	252-3408
La Quinta Motor Inn Tulsa East 10829 E 41st St South *TF:* 800-531-5900	Tulsa	OK	74146	918-665-0220	664-4810
Lexington Hotel Suites 8525 E 41st St *TF:* 800-927-8483	Tulsa	OK	74145	918-627-0030	627-0587
Marriott Tulsa Southern Hills 1902 E 71st St *TF:* 800-228-9290 ■ *Web:* marriotthotels.com/TULSE	Tulsa	OK	74136	918-493-7000	523-0950
Radisson Inn Airport 2201 N 77th Ave East *TF:* 800-333-3333	Tulsa	OK	74115	918-835-9911	838-2452
Ramada Inn 3131 E 31st St *TF:* 800-272-6232	Tulsa	OK	74105	918-743-9811	743-6499
Ramada Inn 8181 E Skelly Dr *TF:* 888-481-2740	Tulsa	OK	74129	918-663-4541	665-7109
Ramada Inn Downtown Plaza Hotel 17 W 7th St *TF:* 800-585-5101	Tulsa	OK	74119	918-585-5898	585-9388
Shangri-La Resort 57401 E Hwy 125 *TF:* 800-331-4060	Afton	OK	74331	918-257-4204	257-5619
Sheraton Tulsa Hotel 10918 E 41st St *TF:* 800-335-3535	Tulsa	OK	74146	918-627-5000	627-4003
Sheridan Pond Executive Suites 8130 S Lakewood Pl	Tulsa	OK	74137	918-481-6598	492-6644
StudioPLUS 7901 E 31st Ct South *TF:* 800-646-8000	Tulsa	OK	74145	918-660-2890	660-4672
Towers Hotel & Suites 3355 E Skelly Dr	Tulsa	OK	74135	918-744-4263	747-0127
Tulsa Hilton 7900 S Lewis *TF:* 800-444-7263	Tulsa	OK	74136	918-492-5000	492-7256

— Restaurants —

Name	City	State	Zip	Phone
Arizona Mexican Restaurant (Mexican) 2250 E 51st St	Tulsa	OK	74105	918-488-6163
Atlantic Sea Grill (Seafood) 8321 E 61st St Suite A	Tulsa	OK	74133	918-252-7966
Billy Ray's Bar-B-Que & Catfish (Barbecue) 3524 Southwest Blvd	Tulsa	OK	74107	918-445-0972
Bodean Seafood Restaurant (Seafood) 3323 E 51st St	Tulsa	OK	75135	918-743-3861
Bravo (Italian) 100 E 2nd St	Tulsa	OK	74103	918-560-2254
Cajun Boiling Pot of Tulsa (Cajun) 1201 S Memorial Dr	Tulsa	OK	74112	918-838-0155
Casa Bonita (Mexican) 2120 S Sheridan Rd	Tulsa	OK	74129	918-836-6464
Casa Laredo (Mexican) 1411 E 41st St	Tulsa	OK	74105	918-743-3744
Chimi's (Mexican) 1304 E 15th St	Tulsa	OK	74120	918-587-4411
El Paso Bar-B-Que Co (Barbecue) 8161 S Harvard Ave	Tulsa	OK	74137	918-481-1783
Fountains (Continental) 6540 S Lewis Ave	Tulsa	OK	74136	918-749-9916
French Hen The (International) 7143 S Yale Ave	Tulsa	OK	74136	918-492-2596
Fuji (Japanese) 8226 E 71st St	Tulsa	OK	74133	918-250-1821
Green Onion (Continental) 4532 E 51st St	Tulsa	OK	74135	918-481-3338
Hunan China Family Restaurant (Chinese) 3113 S Harvard Ave	Tulsa	OK	74135	918-742-1333
Jamil's (Lebanese) 2833 E 51st St	Tulsa	OK	74105	918-742-9097
Jody's at 2300 Riverside (American) 2300 Riverside Dr	Tulsa	OK	74114	918-582-5639
Joseph's Steakhouse (Steak/Seafood) 4848 S Yale Ave	Tulsa	OK	74135	918-493-5888
Kodiak Bar & Grill (American) 8247 E 71st St	Tulsa	OK	74133	918-250-4196
Monte's American Chop House (Steak/Seafood) 3509 S Peoria Ave	Tulsa	OK	74105	918-744-9463
New Hong Kong Restaurant (Chinese) 2623 E 11th St	Tulsa	OK	74104	918-585-5328
Polo Grill (American) 2038 Utica Sq	Tulsa	OK	74114	918-744-4280
Ri-Le Restaurant (Vietnamese) 3206 S Yale Ave	Tulsa	OK	74135	918-747-3205
Royal Dragon (Chinese) 7837 E 51st St	Tulsa	OK	74145	918-664-2245
S & J Oyster Co (Seafood) 3301 S Peoria Ave	Tulsa	OK	74105	918-744-4440
Spudder The (Steak) 6536 E 50th St	Tulsa	OK	74145	918-665-1416
Taste of China (Chinese) 11360 E 31st St	Tulsa	OK	74146	918-664-2252
Ti Amo (Italian) 8151 E 21st St	Tulsa	OK	74129	918-665-1939
Warren Duck Club (Continental) 6110 S Yale Ave	Tulsa	OK	74136	918-495-1000
Wild Fork (Continental) 1820 Utica Sq *Web:* www.wildfork.com/	Tulsa	OK	74114	918-742-0712

— Goods and Services —

SHOPPING

Name	City	State	Zip	Phone	Fax
Cherry Street District Cherry St-betw Peoria & Harvard Sts	Tulsa	OK	74120	918-587-2566	584-4092
Eastland Mall 14002 E 21st St *TF:* 800-654-3024	Tulsa	OK	74134	918-438-3400	437-6130
Eton Square 61st St & Memorial Dr	Tulsa	OK	74133	918-588-9600	588-9660
Farm The 5321 S Sheridan Rd Suite 27	Tulsa	OK	74145	918-622-3860	622-4675
Tulsa Promenade 4107 S Yale Ave	Tulsa	OK	74135	918-627-9224	663-9385
Utica Square 1579 E 21st St	Tulsa	OK	74114	918-742-5531	747-0766
Woodland Hills Mall 7021 S Memorial Dr	Tulsa	OK	74133	918-250-1449	250-9084

Tulsa (Cont'd)

BANKS

				Phone	Fax
Bank of Oklahoma NA PO Box 2300 *Fax: Cust Svc ■ *TF Cust Svc:* 800-234-6181*	Tulsa	OK	74192	918-588-6000	588-6962*
Bank One Oklahoma NA PO Box 1 *TF:* 800-695-0955	Tulsa	OK	74102	918-586-1000	586-5957
F & M Bank & Trust Co 1330 S Harvard	Tulsa	OK	74112	918-744-1330	743-1134
NationsBank 515 S Boulder Ave *TF:* 800-234-4040	Tulsa	OK	74103	918-591-8444	591-8260

BUSINESS SERVICES

	Phone		Phone
A'La Carte Courier Service	918-834-0050	**Kinko's**	918-584-2774
Accountemps	918-493-5775	**Manpower Temporary Services**	918-492-3131
Darrell's Messenger Service	918-583-8216	**Olsten Staffing Services**	918-496-8700
Federal Express	800-238-5355	**Post Office**	918-599-6800
Kelly Services	918-250-5355	**UPS**	800-742-5877

— Media —

PUBLICATIONS

				Phone	Fax
Tulsa World‡ 315 S Boulder Ave *Web:* www.tulsaworld.com ■ *E-mail:* tulsaworld@fax.webtek.com	Tulsa	OK	74103	918-583-2161	581-8353

‡Daily newspapers

TELEVISION

				Phone	Fax
KETA-TV Ch 13 (PBS) 7403 N Kelley St *Web:* www.oeta.onenet.net	Oklahoma City	OK	73111	405-848-8501	841-9216
KJRH-TV Ch 2 (NBC) 3701 S Peoria Ave *Web:* www.teamtulsa.com	Tulsa	OK	74105	918-743-2222	748-1436
KOKI-TV Ch 23 (Fox) 5416 S Yale Suite 500 *Web:* www.fox23.com ■ *E-mail:* fox23@fox23.com	Tulsa	OK	74135	918-491-0023	491-6650
KOTV-TV Ch 6 (CBS) PO Box 6 *Web:* www.kotv.com/	Tulsa	OK	74101	918-582-6666	581-8616
KTFO-TV Ch 41 (UPN) 5416 S Yale Ave Suite 500 *Web:* www.upn41.com ■ *E-mail:* upn41@upn41.com	Tulsa	OK	74135	918-491-0023	491-6650
KTUL-TV Ch 8 (ABC) PO Box 8 *E-mail:* ktulgmo@ad.com	Tulsa	OK	74101	918-445-8888	445-9316
KWHB-TV Ch 47 (Ind) 8835 S Memorial Dr *Web:* www.kwhb.com	Tulsa	OK	74133	918-254-4701	254-5614

RADIO

				Phone	Fax
KAKC-AM 1300 kHz (N/T) 5801 E 41st St Suite 900	Tulsa	OK	74135	918-664-2810	665-0555
KBEZ-FM 92.9 MHz (AC) 7030 S Yale Ave Suite 711	Tulsa	OK	74136	918-496-9336	495-1850
KCFO-AM 970 kHz (Rel) 3737 S 37th West Ave	Tulsa	OK	74107	918-445-1186	446-7508
KMOD-FM 97.5 MHz (Rock) 5801 E 41st St Suite 900 *Web:* www.kmod.com	Tulsa	OK	74135	918-664-2810	665-0555
KMYZ-FM 104.5 MHz (Alt) 5810 E Skelly Dr Suite 801 *Web:* www.edgeline.com ■ *E-mail:* edgetulsa@aol.com	Tulsa	OK	74135	918-665-3131	663-6622
KRAV-FM 96.5 MHz (AC) 7136 S Yale Ave Suite 500	Tulsa	OK	74136	918-491-9696	493-5385
KRMG-AM 740 kHz (N/T) 7136 S Yale Ave	Tulsa	OK	74136	918-493-7400	493-5321
KTFX-FM 102.3 MHz (Ctry) 8107 E Admiral Pl	Tulsa	OK	74115	918-836-5512	
KVOO-AM 1170 kHz (Ctry) 4590 E 29th St *Web:* www.kvoo.com ■ *E-mail:* info@kvoo.com	Tulsa	OK	74114	918-743-7814	743-7613
KVOO-FM 98.5 MHz (Ctry) 4590 E 29th St *Web:* www.kvoo.com ■ *E-mail:* info@kvoo.com	Tulsa	OK	74114	918-743-7814	743-7613
KWEN-FM 95.5 MHz (Ctry) 7136 S Yale Ave Suite 500	Tulsa	OK	74136	918-493-7400	493-2376
KWGS-FM 89.5 MHz (NPR) 600 S College St *Web:* www.kwgs.org ■ *E-mail:* fm89@kwgs.org	Tulsa	OK	74104	918-631-2577	631-3695

— Colleges/Universities —

				Phone	Fax
Oral Roberts University 7777 S Lewis Ave *TF:* 800-678-8876 ■ *Web:* www.oru.edu	Tulsa	OK	74171	918-495-6161	495-6222
Rogers State University 1701 W Will Rogers Blvd *TF:* 800-256-7511 ■ *Web:* www.rsu.edu ■ *E-mail:* info@rsu.edu	Claremore	OK	74017	918-341-7510	343-7546
Spartan School of Aeronautics PO Box 582833 *TF:* 800-331-1204 ■ *Web:* www.spartan.edu ■ *E-mail:* spartan@mail.webtek.com	Tulsa	OK	74158	918-836-6886	831-5287
Tulsa Community College Metro Campus 909 S Boston Ave *Web:* www.tulsa.cc.ok.us	Tulsa	OK	74119	918-595-7000	595-7347
University of Tulsa 600 S College Ave *TF Admissions:* 800-331-3050 ■ *Web:* www.utulsa.edu ■ *E-mail:* admission@utulsa.edu	Tulsa	OK	74104	918-631-2000	631-5033

— Hospitals —

				Phone	Fax
Children's Medical Center 5300 E Skelly Dr	Tulsa	OK	74153	918-664-6600	628-6306
Columbia Doctors' Hospital 2323 S Harvard Ave *E-mail:* 74467.1121@compuserve.com	Tulsa	OK	74114	918-744-4000	744-5008
Hillcrest Medical Center 1120 S Utica Ave *Web:* www.hillcrest.com	Tulsa	OK	74104	918-579-1000	579-5011
Saint Francis Hospital 6161 S Yale Ave *Fax: Admitting ■ *TF:* 800-888-9599 ■ *Web:* www.saintfrancis.com	Tulsa	OK	74136	918-494-2200	494-6179*
Saint John Medical Center 1923 S Utica Ave *Fax: Admissions ■ *Web:* www.sjmc.org	Tulsa	OK	74104	918-744-2345	744-2398*
Tulsa Regional Medical Center 744 W 9th St	Tulsa	OK	74127	918-587-2561	599-1750

— Attractions —

				Phone	Fax
Arkansas River Historical Society 5350 Cimarron Rd	Catoosa	OK	74015	918-266-2291	266-7678
Cherokee Heritage Center & National Museum Willis Rd PO Box 515 *Web:* www.leftmoon.com/cnhs	Tahlequah	OK	74464	918-456-6007	456-6165
Davis JM Arms & Historical Museum 333 N Lynn Riggs Blvd *Web:* www.state.ok.us/~jmdavis/ ■ *E-mail:* silver@tulsawalk.com	Claremore	OK	74017	918-341-5707	341-5771
Elsing Museum 8555 S Lewis Ave	Tulsa	OK	74136	918-298-3628	
Gilcrease Thomas Institute of American History & Art 1400 Gilcrease Museum Rd *Web:* www.gilcrease.org	Tulsa	OK	74127	918-596-2700	596-2770
Harmon Science Center 5707 E 41st St *Web:* www.sciencecenter.org/	Tulsa	OK	74152	918-622-5000	622-5098
Hogue Alexander Gallery of Art University of Tulsa Phillips Hall	Tulsa	OK	74104	918-631-2202	
Mohawk Park 5701 E 36th St North	Tulsa	OK	74115	918-596-7275	
Oklahoma Jazz Hall of Fame 322 N Greenwood Ave *E-mail:* info@greenwoodcultural.com	Tulsa	OK	74120	918-596-1001	596-1005
Philbrook Museum of Art 2727 S Rockford Rd *TF:* 800-324-7941 ■ *Web:* www.philbrook.org	Tulsa	OK	74114	918-749-7941	743-4230
River Parks 11th St & SW Blvd	Tulsa	OK	74115	918-596-2001	596-2004
Theatre Tulsa 207 N Main St Performing Arts Ctr *Web:* www.theatretulsa.org ■ *E-mail:* theatretul@aol.com	Tulsa	OK	74103	918-587-8402	592-0848
Tulsa Ballet Theatre 4512 S Peoria Ave *Web:* www.webtek.com/tulsaballet/ ■ *E-mail:* tulsaballet@fax.webtek.com	Tulsa	OK	74105	918-749-6030	749-0532
Tulsa Garden Center 2435 S Peoria Ave	Tulsa	OK	74114	918-746-5125	746-5128
Tulsa Opera 101 E 3rd St Tulsa Performing Arts Ctr *TF:* 800-364-7111 ■ *Web:* www.tulsapac.com	Tulsa	OK	74103	918-596-7111	596-7144
Tulsa Performing Arts Center 110 E 2nd St *TF:* 800-364-7122 ■ *Web:* www.tulsapac.com ■ *E-mail:* tulsapac@earthlink.net	Tulsa	OK	74103	918-596-7122	596-7144
Tulsa Philharmonic Orchestra 101 E 3rd St Tulsa Performing Arts Ctr *Web:* www.webtek.com/tulsaphil/ ■ *E-mail:* tulsaphil@mail.webtek.com	Tulsa	OK	74103	918-747-7445	747-7496
Tulsa Zoo 5701 E 36th St North	Tulsa	OK	74115	918-669-6600	669-6260
Will Rogers Memorial 1720 W Will Rogers Blvd *TF:* 800-324-9455 ■ *Web:* www.willrogers.org ■ *E-mail:* wrinfo@willrogers.org	Tulsa	OK	74017	918-341-0719	343-8119

Tulsa — Attractions (Cont'd)

				Phone	Fax
Woolaroc Museum & Nature Preserve RR 3 Box 2100	Bartlesville	OK	74003	918-336-0307	336-0084
Web: www.woolaroc.org/					

SPORTS TEAMS & FACILITIES

				Phone	Fax
Fair Meadows at Tulsa PO Box 4735	Tulsa	OK	74159	918-743-7223	743-8053
Tulsa Drillers (baseball) 4802 E 15th St Drillers Stadium	Tulsa	OK	74112	918-744-5901	747-3267
Tulsa Ice Oilers (hockey) 100 Civic Ctr Tulsa Convention Ctr	Tulsa	OK	74133	918-252-7825	249-0310
Web: www.tulsaoilers.com					
Tulsa Roughnecks (soccer) 12150 E 11th St	Broken Arrow	OK	74012	918-838-9901	838-8071
E-mail: ammskt@aol.com					
Tulsa Speedway 4424 E 66th St North	Tulsa	OK	74117	918-425-7551	425-0646
Web: www.tulspeedway.com					
■ *E-mail:* tulsaspeedway@tulspeedway.com					

— Events —

	Phone
Akdar Shrine Circus (late February-early March)	918-587-6658
Bok Williams Jazz on Greenwood (early August & mid-August)	918-584-3378
Chili Bowl Midget Nationals (early January)	918-838-3777
Chili Cookoff & Bluegrass Festival (early-mid- September)	918-583-2617
Christmas Parade of Lights (early December)	918-583-2617
Gatesway International Balloon Festival (late July-early August)	918-251-2676
Greater Tulsa Antiques Show (mid-March)	918-682-7420
Greater Tulsa Home & Garden Show (mid-March)	918-663-5820
International Auto Show (mid-March)	918-742-2626
Juneteenth on Greenwood Heritage Festival (mid-June)	918-582-1741
Longhorn Rodeo (late January)	918-596-7177
Mayfest (mid-May)	918-582-6435
National Rod & Custom Car Show (late February)	918-257-8073
Oklahoma Scottish Games & Gathering (mid-September)	918-560-0228
Oktoberfest (mid-October)	918-596-2001
Reggaefest/World Peace Festival (late June)	918-596-2001
Summer in the City (mid-July)	918-583-2617
Tulsa Boat Sport & Travel Show (January)	918-744-1113
Tulsa Boom River Celebration & Great American Duck Drop (July 4)	918-596-2001
Tulsa Championship Rodeo (early May)	918-744-1113
Tulsa Charity Horse Show (late April)	918-742-5556
Tulsa County Free Fair (late July)	918-746-3709
Tulsa Easter Pageant (early April)	918-596-5990
Tulsa Indian Art Festival (mid-March)	918-583-2253
Tulsa Morgan Horse Extravaganza (early August)	918-744-1113
Tulsa Nationals Wrestling Tournament (mid-January)	918-366-4411
Tulsa State Fair (late September-early October)	918-744-1113
Tulsa Women's Show (early February)	800-225-4342
TulsaFest (late June)	918-595-7776
Zoolightful (December)	918-560-0228

Oregon

Population (1999): 3,316,154 **Area (sq mi): 98,386**

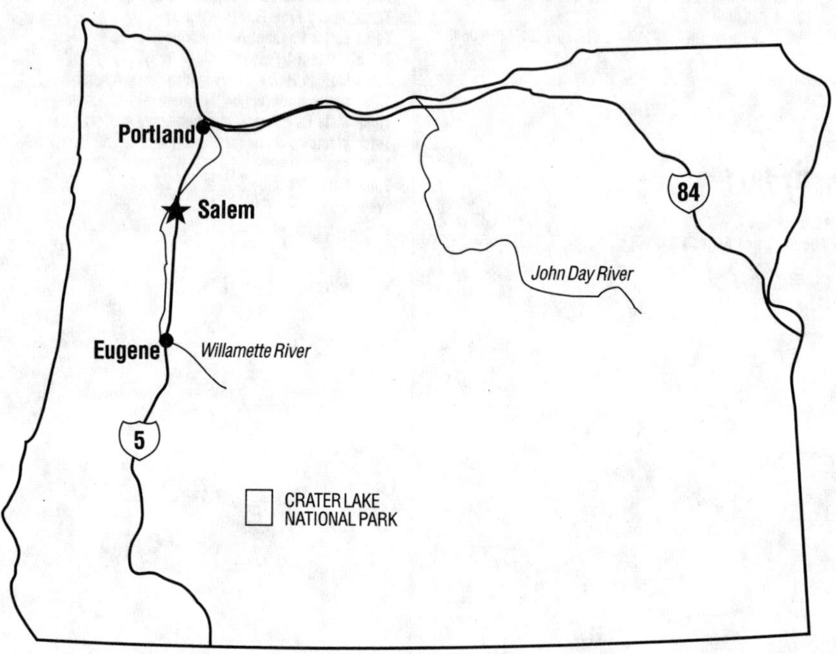

— State Information Sources —

				Phone	Fax
Oregon Economic Development Dept					
775 Summer St NE	Salem	OR	97310	503-986-0123	581-5115
Web: www.econ.state.or.us					
Oregon Parks & Recreation Dept					
1115 Commercial St NE	Salem	OR	97310	503-378-6305	378-6447
TF: 800-452-5687 ■ *Web:* www.prd.state.or.us					
Oregon State Library State Library Bldg	Salem	OR	97310	503-378-4243	588-7119
Web: www.osl.state.or.us/oslhome.html					
Oregon Tourism Commission					
775 Summer St NE	Salem	OR	97310	503-986-0000	986-0001
TF: 800-547-7842 ■ *Web:* www.traveloregon.com					

ON-LINE RESOURCES

Cybertourist Oregon .... www.cybertourist.com/oregon.shtml
Online Highways Travel Guide to Oregon .... www.ohwy.com/or/homepage.htm
Online-Oregon .... www.online-oregon.com
Oregon @ Travel Notes .... www.travelnotes.org/NorthAmerica/oregon.htm
Oregon Cities .... dir.yahoo.com/Regional/U_S__States/Oregon/Cities
Oregon Cities By Counties & Regions .... dir.yahoo.com/Regional/U_S__States/Oregon/Counties_and_Regions
Oregon Scenario .... scenariousa.dstylus.com/or/indexf.htm
Oregon Travel & Tourism Guide .... www.travel-library.com/north_america/usa/oregon/index.html
OregonPages .... oregonpages.com
Rough Guide Travel Oregon travel.roughguides.com/content/1552/index.htm
Travel.org-Oregon .... travel.org/oregon.html
What's Up Oregon! .... www.whatsuporegon.com
WWWelcome to Oregon .... www.el.com/To/Oregon
Yahoo! Get Local Oregon .... dir.yahoo.com/Regional/U_S__States/Oregon

— Cities Profiled —

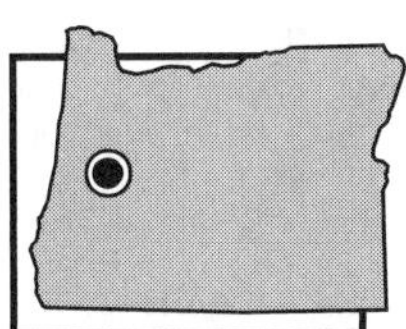

Eugene

Situated at the confluence of the Willamette and McKenzie Rivers, Eugene is surrounded by farmland, forests, and mountains. Three of the city's numerous parks are located along a river bank, and the city's extensive and innovative bike and jogging trails are ranked among the best in the U.S. The many recreational opportunities in the area range from golf to whitewater rafting. Cultural activities include performances by the Eugene Opera, Eugene Symphony, and Eugene Ballet Company, as well as musical and theatrical productions at the Community Center for the Performing Arts. Eugene is also home to the University of Oregon.

Population	128,240	**Longitude**	123-15-97 W
Area (Land)	38.0 sq mi	**County**	Lane
Area (Water)	0.0 sq mi	**Time Zone**	PST
Elevation	419 ft	**Area Code/s**	503
Latitude	44-06-53 N		

— Average Temperatures and Precipitation —

TEMPERATURES

	Jan	Feb	Mar	Apr	May	Jun	Jul	Aug	Sep	Oct	Nov	Dec
High	46	51	56	61	67	74	82	82	76	65	52	46
Low	35	37	39	44	45	50	53	53	49	44	40	36

PRECIPITATION

	Jan	Feb	Mar	Apr	May	Jun	Jul	Aug	Sep	Oct	Nov	Dec
Inches	7.9	5.6	5.5	3.1	2.2	1.4	0.5	1.1	1.7	3.4	8.3	8.6

— Important Phone Numbers —

	Phone		*Phone*
AAA	541-484-0661	**Medical Referral**	541-868-1356
American Express Travel	503-484-1325	**Poison Control Center**	503-494-8968
Dental Referral	541-686-1175	**Weather**	541-484-1200
Emergency	911		

— Information Sources —

				Phone	*Fax*
Better Business Bureau Serving Oregon & Western Washington 333 SW 5th Ave Suite 300 *Web:* www.portland.bbb.org	Portland	OR	97204	503-226-3981	226-8200
Convention & Visitors Assn of Lane County Oregon PO Box 10286 *TF:* 800-547-5445 ■ *Web:* www.cvalco.org ■ *E-mail:* covalco@covalco.org	Eugene	OR	97440	541-484-5307	343-6335
Eugene Chamber of Commerce PO Box 1107 *Web:* www.eugene-commerce.com	Eugene	OR	97440	541-484-1314	484-4942
Eugene City Hall 777 Pearl St *Web:* www.ci.eugene.or.us	Eugene	OR	97401	541-682-5010	682-5414
Eugene Mayor 777 Pearl St Rm 105 *Web:* www.ci.eugene.or.us/council/bios/torrey.htm	Eugene	OR	97401	541-682-5010	682-5414
Eugene Planning & Development Dept 99 W 10th Ave Rm 240 *Web:* www.ci.eugene.or.us/PDD/PDDhome.htm	Eugene	OR	97401	541-682-5443	682-5593
Eugene Public Library 100 W 13th Ave *Web:* www.ci.eugene.or.us/Library	Eugene	OR	97401	541-682-5450	341-5898
Lane County 125 E 8th Ave *Web:* www.co.lane.or.us/	Eugene	OR	97401	541-682-4203	682-3803
Lane County Fair & Convention Center 796 W 13th Ave	Eugene	OR	97402	541-682-4292	682-3614

On-Line Resources

About.com Guide to Eugene	eugene.about.com
Anthill City Guide Eugene	www.anthill.com/city.asp?city=eugene
Area Guide Eugene	eugene.areaguides.net
City Knowledge Eugene	www.cityknowledge.com/or_eugene.htm
Eugene Free Community Network	www.efn.org/
Eugene Weekly	www.eugeneweekly.com
Excite.com Eugene City Guide	www.excite.com/travel/countries/united_states/oregon/eugene
NITC Travelbase City Guide Eugene	www.travelbase.com/auto/guides/eugene-area-or.html
Welcome to Eugene Oregon	www.efn.org/~sgazette/eugenehome.html
Www.el.com to Eugene	www.el.com/To/Eugene

— Transportation Services —

AIRPORTS

■ **Eugene Airport (EUG)**

	Phone
8 miles NW of downtown (approx 15 minutes) Web: www.eugeneairport.com	541-682-5430

Airport Transportation

	Phone
Emerald City Taxi $18 fare to downtown	541-686-2010
United Cab $15 fare to downtown	541-343-9518

Commercial Airlines

	Phone		*Phone*
Horizon	800-547-9308	**United**	800-241-6522
SkyWest	800-453-9417	**United Express**	800-241-6522

Charter Airlines

	Phone		*Phone*
Flightcraft Inc	541-688-9291	**Lawrence Air Service**	541-689-3331
Friendly Air Service	541-461-1605		

CAR RENTALS

	Phone		*Phone*
Avis	541-688-9053	**Hertz**	541-688-9333
Budget	541-688-1229		

LIMO/TAXI

	Phone		*Phone*
Airport-City Taxi	541-689-2621	**United Cab**	541-343-9518
Budget Taxi	541-683-8294	**VIP Limo**	541-683-8131
Eugene/Springfield Taxi	541-746-1234	**VIP Taxi**	541-484-0920
Express Cab	541-341-8444		

MASS TRANSIT

	Phone
Lane Transit District $1.00 Base fare	541-687-5555

RAIL/BUS

				Phone
Eugene Amtrak Station 433 Willamette St	Eugene	OR	97401	541-687-0972
Greyhound Bus Station 987 Pearl St *TF:* 800-231-2222	Eugene	OR	97401	541-344-6265

— Accommodations —

HOTEL RESERVATION SERVICES

	Phone	*Fax*
Eugene Area Bed & Breakfast Assn *TF:* 800-507-1354 ■ *Web:* www.pond.net/~bnbassoc/	541-343-3553	343-0383

HOTELS, MOTELS, RESORTS

				Phone	*Fax*
Best Inn & Suites 3315 Gateway *TF:* 800-626-1900	Springfield	OR	97477	541-746-1314	746-3884
Best Western Entrada Lodge 19221 Century Dr *TF:* 800-528-1234	Bend	OR	97702	541-382-4080	382-4080
Best Western Grand Manor Inn 971 Kruse Way	Springfield	OR	97477	541-726-4769	744-0745

Eugene — Hotels, Motels, Resorts (Cont'd)

				Phone	Fax
Best Western Greentree Inn 1759 Franklin Blvd *TF:* 800-528-1234	Eugene	OR	97403	541-485-2727	686-2094
Best Western New Oregon Motel 1655 Franklin Blvd *TF:* 800-528-1234	Eugene	OR	97403	541-683-3669	484-5556
Best Western Village Green 725 Row River Rd *TF:* 800-343-7666	Cottage Grove	OR	97424	541-942-2491	942-2386
Budget Host Motor Inn 1190 W 6th Ave *TF:* 800-554-9822 ■ *E-mail:* mail@budgethost.com	Eugene	OR	97402	541-342-7273	
Campus Inn 390 E Broadway *TF:* 800-888-6313	Eugene	OR	97401	541-343-3376	
Classic Residence Inn 1140 W 6th Ave	Eugene	OR	97402	541-343-0730	343-0730
Comfort Inn 845 Gateway Blvd *TF:* 800-228-5150	Cottage Grove	OR	97424	541-942-9747	942-8841
Country Squire Inn 33100 Van Duyn Rd	Eugene	OR	97408	541-484-2000	484-2431
Courtesy Inn 345 W 6th Ave	Eugene	OR	97401	541-345-3391	342-6507
Doubletree Hotel Springfield-Eugene 3280 Gateway Rd *TF:* 800-222-8733 ■ *Web:* www.doubletreehotels.com/DoubleT/Hotel141/146/146Main.htm	Springfield	OR	97477	541-726-8181	747-1866
Downtown Motel 361 W 7th Ave *TF:* 800-648-4366	Eugene	OR	97401	541-345-8739	345-3841
Driftwood Shores Resort 88416 1st Ave *TF:* 800-422-5091 ■ *Web:* www.driftwoodshores.com ■ *E-mail:* driftwood@presys.com	Florence	OR	97439	541-997-8263	997-5857
Eugene Motor Lodge 476 E Broadway	Eugene	OR	97401	541-344-5233	344-5233
Executive House Motel 1040 W 6th Ave	Eugene	OR	97402	541-683-4000	
Franklin Inn 1857 Franklin Blvd *TF:* 800-424-5213	Eugene	OR	97403	541-342-4804	342-3114
Gateway Inn 3540 Gateway *TF:* 800-392-3035	Springfield	OR	97477	541-726-1212	746-9504
GuestHouse Inn 1335 Ivy St *TF:* 800-835-5170	Junction City	OR	97448	541-998-6524	998-8932
Hilton Hotel 66 E 6th Ave *TF:* 800-445-8667 ■ *Web:* www.hilton.com/hotels/EUGEHHF	Eugene	OR	97401	541-342-2000	342-6661
Inn of the Seventh Mountain 18575 SW Century Dr *TF:* 800-452-6810	Bend	OR	97702	541-382-8711	382-3517
Manor Motel 599 E Broadway	Eugene	OR	97401	541-345-2331	344-2860
Mount Bachelor Village Resort 19717 Mt Bachelor Dr *TF:* 800-452-9846 ■ *Web:* www.empnet.com/mbvr/ ■ *E-mail:* mbvr@empnet.com	Bend	OR	97702	541-389-5900	388-7820
Phoenix Inn 850 Franklin Blvd *TF:* 800-344-0131	Eugene	OR	97401	541-344-0001	686-1288
Quality Inn & Suites 2121 Franklin Blvd *TF:* 800-456-6487	Eugene	OR	97403	541-342-1243	343-3474
Ramada Inn 225 Coburg Rd *TF:* 800-272-6232	Eugene	OR	97401	541-342-5181	342-5164
Red Lion Inn 205 Coburg Rd *TF:* 800-222-8733	Eugene	OR	97401	541-342-5201	485-2314
Red Lion Inn South 849 NE 3rd St *TF:* 800-733-5466	Bend	OR	97701	541-382-8384	382-9180
Riverhouse Motor Inn 3075 N Hwy 97 *TF:* 800-547-3928	Bend	OR	97701	541-389-3111	389-0870
Rodeway Inn 3480 Hutton St *TF:* 800-363-8471	Springfield	OR	97477	541-746-8471	747-1541
Shilo Inn 3350 Gateway *TF:* 800-222-2244	Springfield	OR	97477	541-747-0332	726-0587
Sixty Six Motel 755 E Broadway	Eugene	OR	97401	541-342-5041	
Timbers Motel 1015 Pearl St *TF:* 800-653-4167	Eugene	OR	97401	541-343-3345	
Travelers Inn 540 E Broadway *TF:* 800-432-5999	Eugene	OR	97401	541-342-1109	343-3438
Travelodge 1859 Franklin Blvd *TF:* 800-444-6383	Eugene	OR	97403	541-342-6383	342-6383
Valley River Inn 1000 Valley River Way *TF:* 800-543-8266 ■ *Web:* www.valleyriverinn.com	Eugene	OR	97401	541-687-0123	683-5121
Village Inn Motel 1875 Mohawk Blvd *TF:* 800-327-6871	Springfield	OR	97477	541-747-4546	747-4452
Western Motel 700 Hwy 99 N	Eugene	OR	97402	541-688-6576	

— Restaurants —

				Phone
Adam's Place (American) 30 E Broadway	Eugene	OR	97401	541-344-6948
Ambrosia Restaurant (Italian) 174 E Broadway	Eugene	OR	97401	541-342-4141
Anatolia's (Indian/Greek) 992 Willamette St	Eugene	OR	97401	541-343-9661
Cafe Soriah (Mediterranean) 384 W 13th Ave	Eugene	OR	97401	541-342-4410
Chanterelle (Continental) 207 E 5th Ave Suite 109	Eugene	OR	97401	541-484-4065
Deb's Family Restaurant (American) 1675 Franklin Blvd	Eugene	OR	97401	541-484-9099
El Torito (Mexican) 1003 Valley River Way	Eugene	OR	97401	541-683-7294
Eugene City Brewery (American) 844 Olive St	Eugene	OR	97401	541-345-8489
Excelsior Cafe (Italian) 754 E 13th	Eugene	OR	97401	541-342-6963
Farmhouse Restaurant (American) 54455 McKenzie River Dr	Blue River	OR	97413	541-822-3715
Fields Restaurant & Brew Pub (American) 1290 Oak St	Eugene	OR	97401	541-341-6599
Ford Grill Cafe (American) 1414 Mohawk Blvd	Springfield	OR	97477	541-726-1129
Garden Terrace (American) 225 Coburg Rd Ramada Inn	Eugene	OR	97401	541-342-5181
Jo Federigo's Cafe & Jazz Bar (Italian) 259 E 5th Ave	Eugene	OR	97401	541-343-8488
LocoMotive Restaurant (Vegetarian) 291 E 5th Ave	Eugene	OR	97401	541-465-4754
Log Cabin Inn (American) 56483 McKenzie Hwy	McKenzie Bridge	OR	97413	541-822-3432
Lyon's Restaurant (American) 1933 Franklin Blvd	Eugene	OR	97401	541-484-4333
Marie Callender's #77 (American) 1300 Valley River Dr *Web:* www.mcpies.com	Eugene	OR	97401	541-484-7111
Mazzi's Restaurant (Italian) 3377 E Amazon Dr	Eugene	OR	97405	541-687-2252
McGrath's Publick Fish House (Seafood) 1036 Valley River Way	Eugene	OR	97401	541-342-6404
Mekala's (Thai) 296 E 5th St	Eugene	OR	97401	541-342-4872
Mona Lizza Ristorante (Italian) 830 Olive St	Eugene	OR	97401	541-345-1072
Nacho's (Mexican) 1190 City View	Eugene	OR	97401	541-485-6595
Oregon Electric Station (American) 27 E 5th Ave	Eugene	OR	97401	541-485-4444
Pacific Grill Restaurant (American) 205 Coburg Rd	Eugene	OR	97401	541-342-5201
Piccolo Eurobistro (Continental) 999 Willamette St	Eugene	OR	97401	541-484-4011
Santa Fe Burrito Co (Mexican) 2621 Willamette St	Eugene	OR	97405	541-683-4209
Shiki Japanese Cuisine (Japanese) 81 Coburg Rd	Eugene	OR	97401	541-343-1936
Sixth Street Grill (Steak/Seafood) 55 W 6th Ave	Eugene	OR	97401	541-485-2961
Steelhead Brewery & Cafe (American) 199 E 5th St	Eugene	OR	97401	541-686-2739
Stuart Anderson's Black Angus Restaurant (Steak) 2123 Franklin Blvd	Eugene	OR	97403	541-686-2020
Surfside Restaurant (American) 88416 1st Ave	Florence	OR	97439	541-997-8263
West Brothers Bar-B-Que (American) 844 Olive St	Eugene	OR	97401	541-345-8489
Wild Duck (American) 169 W 6th Ave	Eugene	OR	97401	541-485-3825
Willie's on 7th Street (American) 388 W 7th St	Eugene	OR	97401	541-485-0601

— Goods and Services —

SHOPPING

				Phone	Fax
Downtown Eugene betw 6th & 11th Sts & Charlton & High Sts	Eugene	OR	97401	541-343-1117	
Fifth Street Public Market 296 E 5th St	Eugene	OR	97401	541-484-0383	686-1220
Gateway Mall 3000 Gateway St	Springfield	OR	97477	541-747-6294	747-5897
Old Town Florence Bay St	Florence	OR	97439	541-997-3128	
Round Tu-it Gift Shop 945 Gateway Blvd	Cottage Grove	OR	97424	541-942-9023	
Valley River Center Valley River Dr & Valley River Way	Eugene	OR	97401	541-683-5513	343-2478

BANKS

				Phone	Fax
Centennial Bank 675 Oak St	Eugene	OR	97401	541-342-3969	342-8126
Liberty Federal Bank 355 Goodpasture Island Rd Suite 200	Eugene	OR	97401	541-681-4800	683-4261
Pacific Continental Bank 111 W 7th Ave	Eugene	OR	97401	541-686-8685	344-2843
Wells Fargo Bank 99 E Broadway *TF:* 800-869-3557 ■ *Web:* www.wellsfargo.com	Eugene	OR	97401	541-465-5623	484-1755

BUSINESS SERVICES

	Phone
Airborne Express	800-247-2676
BAX Global	800-225-5229
DHL Worldwide Express	800-225-5345
Express Personnel Services	541-686-0001
Federal Express	800-238-5355
Kinko's	541-344-3555
Mail Boxes Etc	800-789-4623
Olsten Staffing Services	541-744-2335
Post Office	800-275-8777
UPS	800-742-5877
Westaff	541-687-0113

— Media —

PUBLICATIONS

				Phone	Fax
Register-Guard‡ 3500 Chad Dr. *Web:* www.registerguard.com	Eugene	OR	97408	541-485-1234	683-7631

‡Daily newspapers

Eugene (Cont'd)

TELEVISION

				Phone	Fax
KEVU-TV Ch 25 (UPN) 888 Goodpasture Island Rd	Eugene	OR	97401	541-683-2525	683-8016
KEZI-TV Ch 9 (ABC) PO Box 7009	Eugene	OR	97401	541-485-5611	342-1568
Web: www.kezi.com ■ *E-mail:* kezi@efn.org					
KLSR-TV Ch 34 (Fox) 888 Goodpasture Island Rd	Eugene	OR	97401	541-683-2525	683-8016
KMTR-TV Ch 16 (NBC) 3825 International Ct	Springfield	OR	97477	541-746-1600	747-0866
Web: www.nbc16.com ■ *E-mail:* info@nbc16.com					
KOPB-TV Ch 10 (PBS) 7140 SW Macadam Ave	Portland	OR	97219	503-244-9900	293-1919
Web: www.opb.org/ ■ *E-mail:* kopb@opb.org					
KTVC-TV Ch 36 (PAX) 1 E Broadway	Eugene	OR	97401	541-345-2119	345-9376
Web: www.pax.net/KTVC					
KVAL-TV Ch 13 (CBS) PO Box 1313	Eugene	OR	97440	541-342-4961	342-2635
Web: www.kval.com ■ *E-mail:* kval@rio.com					

RADIO

				Phone	Fax
KDUK-FM 104.7 MHz (CHR) 1345 Olive St	Eugene	OR	97401	541-485-1120	484-5769
KKNU-FM 93.1 MHz (Ctry) 925 Country Club Rd Suite 200	Eugene	OR	97401	541-686-9123	344-9424
KKXO-AM 1450 kHz (Nost) 925 Country Club Rd Suite 200	Eugene	OR	97401	541-484-9400	344-9424
KMGE-FM 94.5 MHz (AC) 925 Country Club Rd Suite 200	Eugene	OR	97401	541-484-9400	344-9424
KODZ-FM 99.1 MHz (Oldies) 1345 Olive St	Eugene	OR	97401	541-485-1120	484-5769
KPNW-AM 1120 kHz (N/T) 1345 Olive St	Eugene	OR	97401	541-485-1120	484-5769
KZEL-FM 96.1 MHz (CR) 2100 W 11th Ave Suite 200	Eugene	OR	97402	541-342-7096	484-6397
Web: www.96kzel.com					

— Colleges/Universities —

				Phone	Fax
Eugene Bible College 2155 Bailey Hill Rd	Eugene	OR	97405	541-485-1780	343-5801
Web: www.ebc.edu					
Gutenberg College 1883 University St	Eugene	OR	97403	541-683-5141	683-6997
Web: www.mckenziestudycenter.org/guten/ ■ *E-mail:* gutenberg@mckenziestudycenter.org					
Lane Community College 4000 E 30th Ave	Eugene	OR	97405	541-747-4501	744-3995
Web: lanecc.edu ■ *E-mail:* lccpurch@class.org					
Northwest Christian College 828 E 11th Ave	Eugene	OR	97401	541-343-1641	684-7323
University of Oregon 1585 E 13th Ave MS 1217	Eugene	OR	97403	541-346-1000	346-5815
TF: 800-232-3825 ■ *Web:* www.uoregon.edu ■ *E-mail:* uoadmit@oregon.uoregon.edu					

— Hospitals —

				Phone	Fax
McKenzie-Willamette Hospital 1460 G St	Springfield	OR	97477	541-726-4400	726-4540
Web: www.mckweb.com					
PeaceHealth Medical Group 1162 Willamette St	Eugene	OR	97401	541-687-6000	687-6050
Sacred Heart Medical Center 1255 Hilyard St	Eugene	OR	97401	541-686-7300	686-8355*
**Fax:* Admitting ■ *TF:* 800-288-7444 ■ *Web:* www.peacehealth.org/Community/owv/WhoWeAreSHMC.htm					

— Attractions —

				Phone	Fax
Actors Cabaret of Eugene 996 Willamette St	Eugene	OR	97401	541-683-4368	
TF: 800-310-4368					
Camp Putt Adventure Golf Park 4006 Franklin Blvd	Eugene	OR	97403	541-741-9828	726-6038
Community Center for the Performing Arts 291 W 8th	Eugene	OR	97401	541-687-2746	
Web: www.efn.org/~wowhall/ ■ *E-mail:* wowhall@efn.org					
Dorris Ranch S 2nd & Doris Sts	Springfield	OR	97477	541-726-2748	
Eugene Ballet Co Hult Ctr for the Performing Arts One Eugene Ctr	Eugene	OR	97401	541-682-5000	687-5745
Web: www.pond.net/~eballet/ ■ *E-mail:* eballet@pond.net					
Eugene Concert Choir 44 W Broadway Suite 301	Eugene	OR	97401	541-485-2278	485-2478
Web: www.efn.org/~ecc/					
Eugene Opera PO Box 11200	Eugene	OR	97440	541-485-3985	683-3783
Web: www.eugeneopera.com ■ *E-mail:* eugeneop@aol.com					
Eugene Symphony 1 Eugene Centre	Eugene	OR	97401	541-687-9487	687-0527
Fifth Street Public Market 296 E 5th St	Eugene	OR	97401	541-484-0383	686-1220
Hinman Vineyards 27012 Briggs Hill Rd	Eugene	OR	97405	541-345-1945	345-6174
Hult Center for the Performing Arts 1 Eugene Ctr	Eugene	OR	97401	541-687-5087	682-5426
Web: www.hultcenter.org					
Lane Arts Council 44 W Broadway Suite 304	Eugene	OR	97401	541-485-2278	485-2478
Web: www.efn.org/~laneartc ■ *E-mail:* lanearts.efn.org					
Lane County Historical Museum 740 W 13 Ave	Eugene	OR	97402	541-687-4242	682-7361
Web: www.hometownonline.com/Historical_Museum/					
Lane ESD Planetarium 2300 Leo Harris Pkwy	Eugene	OR	97401	541-687-7827	
Web: www.efn.org/~esd_plt/ ■ *E-mail:* planetarium@lane.K12.or.us					
LaVelle Vineyards 89697 Sheffler Rd	Elmira	OR	97437	541-935-9406	935-7202
Maude Kerns Art Center 1910 E 15th Ave	Eugene	OR	97403	541-345-1571	345-6248
Web: www.mkartcenter.org ■ *E-mail:* mkac@efn.org					
Orchard Point Park 27060 Clear Lake Rd	Eugene	OR	97402	541-689-4926	461-5865
Oregon Aviation & Space Museum 90377 Boeing Dr	Eugene	OR	97402	541-461-1101	461-1101
Oregon Coast Aquarium 2820 SE Ferry Slip Rd	Newport	OR	97365	541-867-3474	867-6846
Web: www.aquarium.org ■ *E-mail:* akh@aquarium.org					
Oregon Mozart Players 1 Eugene Centre Soreng Theatre - Hult Center for the Performing Arts	Eugene	OR	97401	541-345-6648	345-7849
Sea Lion Caves 91560 Hwy 101	Florence	OR	97439	541-547-3111	547-3545
Web: www.sealioncaves.com ■ *E-mail:* info@sealioncaves.com					
Springfield Museum 590 Main St	Springfield	OR	97477	541-726-2300	726-3689
University of Oregon Museum of Art 1430 Johnson Ln	Eugene	OR	97403	541-346-3027	346-0976
Web: uoma.uoregon.edu/ ■ *E-mail:* info@uoma.uoregon.edu					
University of Oregon Museum of Natural History 1680 E 15th Ave	Eugene	OR	97403	541-346-3024	346-5334
Web: oregon.uoregon.edu/~mnh/					
Willamette Science & Technology Center 2300 Leo Harris Pkwy	Eugene	OR	97401	541-682-7888	484-9027
Web: www.efn.org/~wistec/ ■ *E-mail:* wistec@efn.org					

SPORTS TEAMS & FACILITIES

				Phone	Fax
Eugene Emeralds (baseball) 2077 Willamette St Civic Stadium	Eugene	OR	97405	541-342-5367	342-6089
Web: www.go-ems.com					
Eugene Ice Hawks (hockey) 796 W 13th Ave Lane County Ice Arena	Eugene	OR	97402	541-687-3615	682-7368
Web: www.proaxis.com/~oconnort/icehawks.html					

— Events —

	Phone
Applegate Trail Days (early August)	541-935-1068
Asian Kite Festival (mid-September)	541-687-9600
Bohemia Mining Days (late July)	541-942-8985
Centennial Bank Eugene Celebration (mid-September)	541-681-4108
Christmas Light Parade & Yule Fest (mid-December)	541-998-6154
Christmas Light Up the Valley (December)	541-896-3330
Coburg Antique Fair (early September)	541-688-1181
Coburg Classic Car Show (early August)	541-344-8081
Coburg Golden Years (mid-July)	541-484-5307
Cottage Grove Amateur Rodeo (early July)	541-942-2411
Creswell's Old Fashioned July 4th (July 4)	541-895-5161
Daffodil Drive Day (mid-March)	800-547-5445
Festival of Lights (December)	800-547-5445
Lane County Fair (mid-August)	541-687-4292
Mid-Winter Square Dance Festival (late January)	541-942-7539
Oregon Asian Celebration (mid-February)	541-687-9600
Oregon Bach Festival (late June-early July)	541-346-5669
Oregon Country Fair (mid-July)	541-343-4298
Oregon Dunes Mushers Mail Run (early March)	541-269-1269
Oregon Festival of American Music (early-mid-August)	541-687-6526
Rhododendron Festival & Parade (mid-May)	541-997-3128
Saturday Market (April-November)	541-686-8885
Scandinavian Festival (August)	541-998-6154
Spring Garden Tours (May)	800-726-3657
Ukrainian Celebration (early August)	541-726-7309

Eugene — Events (Cont'd)

	Phone
Whale Watching (November-March)	800-547-5445
Wildflower Festival (mid-May)	541-747-3817

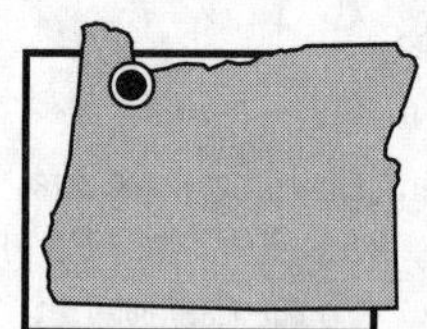

Portland

Located on both sides of the north-flowing Willamette River, Portland, Oregon was named after Portland, Maine, which had been the hometown of one of its early settlers. The city's location and climate are ideal for roses and have earned Portland's nickname as the "City of Roses." The Rose Test Garden in Portland has more than 10,000 rose bushes with some 400 varieties of roses, and a 24-day Festival of Roses is held in Portland every year. Just 50 miles east of the city is Mount Hood National Forest, with facilities for skiing, camping, hiking, fishing, and horseback riding. Along the coast, during the winter and spring, whale watching is a popular pastime. Other points of interest in the Portland area include the Pendleton Woolen Mills, Multnomah Falls, and Crown Point State Park.

Population	503,891	**Longitude**	122-67-50 W
Area (Land)	124.0 sq mi	**County**	Multnomah
Area (Water)	9.7 sq mi	**Time Zone**	PST
Elevation	77 ft	**Area Code/s**	503
Latitude	45-52-36 N		

— Average Temperatures and Precipitation —

TEMPERATURES

	Jan	Feb	Mar	Apr	May	Jun	Jul	Aug	Sep	Oct	Nov	Dec
High	45	51	56	61	67	74	80	80	75	64	53	46
Low	34	36	39	41	47	53	57	57	52	45	40	35

PRECIPITATION

	Jan	Feb	Mar	Apr	May	Jun	Jul	Aug	Sep	Oct	Nov	Dec
Inches	5.4	3.9	3.6	2.4	2.1	1.5	0.6	1.1	1.8	2.7	5.3	6.1

— Important Phone Numbers —

	Phone		Phone
AAA	503-222-6734	**Medical Referral**	503-335-3500
American Express Travel	503-226-2961	**Poison Control Center**	503-494-8968
Emergency	911	**Rose Quarter Event Hotline**	503-321-3211
HotelDocs	800-468-3537	**Weather**	503-243-7575

— Information Sources —

	City	State	Zip	Phone	Fax
Better Business Bureau Serving Oregon & Western Washington 333 SW 5th Ave Suite 300 *Web:* www.portland.bbb.org	Portland	OR	97204	503-226-3981	226-8200
Multnomah County 1021 SW 4th Ave Rm 236 *Web:* www.multnomah.lib.or.us	Portland	OR	97204	503-248-3511	306-5773
Multnomah County Library 801 SW 10th St. *Web:* www.multnomah.lib.or.us/lib	Portland	OR	97205	503-248-5123	248-5226
Oregon Convention Center 777 NE ML King Jr Blvd *TF:* 800-791-2250 ■ *Web:* www.oregoncc.org	Portland	OR	97232	503-235-7575	235-7417
Portland City Hall 1221 SW 4th Ave *Web:* www.ci.portland.or.us	Portland	OR	97204	503-823-4000	
Portland Development Commission 1900 SW 4th Ave Suite 100 *Web:* www.portlanddev.org	Portland	OR	97201	503-823-3200	823-3368
Portland Mayor 1221 SW 4th Ave Rm 340 *Web:* www.ci.portland.or.us/mayor ■ *E-mail:* mayorkatz@ci.portland.or.us	Portland	OR	97204	503-823-4120	823-3588
Portland Metropolitan Chamber of Commerce 221 NW 2nd Ave *Web:* pdxchamber.org	Portland	OR	97209	503-228-9411	228-5126
Portland Oregon Visitors Assn 26 SW Salmon St 3 World Trade Ctr. *TF:* 800-962-3700 ■ *Web:* www.pova.com	Portland	OR	97204	503-275-9750	275-9774

On-Line Resources

4Portland.com	www.4portland.com
About.com Guide to Portland	portlandor.about.com/local/pacnwus/portlandor
Anthill City Guide Portland	www.anthill.com/city.asp?city=portland
Area Guide Portland	portlandor.areaguides.net
Boulevards Portland	www.boulevards.com/portland-or/
City Knowledge Portland	www.cityknowledge.com/or_portland.htm
CitySearch Portland	katu.citysearch.com
CuisineNet Portland	www.cuisinenet.com/restaurant/portland/index.shtml
DigitalCity Portland	home.digitalcity.com/portland
Insiders' Guide to Portland	www.insiders.com/portland/
Portland City Net	www.excite.com/travel/countries/united_states/oregon/portland
Portland Essential Links	www.el.com/To/Portland/Links/
Portland Low-Budget Guide	www.hevanet.com/chezxx/low-rent/
Portland Oregon	www.ohwy.com/or/p/portland.htm
Portland Practical Guide	www.teleport.com/~repmail/pdxprat.html
Portland.TheLinks.com	portland.thelinks.com/
Rough Guide Travel Portland	travel.roughguides.com/content/1553/
Savvy Diner Guide to Portland Restaurants	www.savvydiner.com/portland/
Welcome to Portland	www.el.com/To/Portland
Willamette Week	www.wweek.com

— Transportation Services —

AIRPORTS

■ **Portland International Airport (PDX)**	Phone
20 miles NE of downtown (approx 20 minutes) Web: www.portlandairportpdx.com	503-460-4040

Airport Transportation

	Phone
Gray Line Express Service $12 fare to downtown	503-285-9845
Taxi $22 fare to downtown	503-227-1212
Tri-Met $1.10 fare to downtown	503-238-7433

Commercial Airlines

	Phone		Phone
Alaska	800-426-0333	**Shuttle by United**	800-748-8853
America West	800-235-9292	**Southwest**	800-435-9792
American	800-433-7300	**TWA**	800-221-2000
Continental	503-224-4560	**United**	800-241-6522
Delta	800-221-1212	**US Airways**	800-428-4322
Northwest	800-225-2525		

Charter Airlines

	Phone		Phone
Aero Air Inc	503-640-3711	**Flightcraft**	503-331-4244

CAR RENTALS

	Phone		Phone
Alamo	503-252-7039	**Enterprise**	503-252-6834
Avis	503-249-4950	**Hertz**	503-249-8216
Budget	503-249-6500	**National**	503-249-4900
Crown Auto Rental	503-230-1103	**Thrifty**	503-254-6563
Dollar	503-249-4792		

Portland (Cont'd)

LIMO/TAXI

	Phone		Phone
Broadway Cab	503-227-1234	**Portland Limousine**	503-235-2221
Classic Chauffeur	503-238-8880	**Portland Taxi Co**	503-256-5400
New Rose City Cab	503-282-7707	**Prestige Limousine**	503-282-5009
Pacific Executive	503-234-2400	**Radio Cab**	503-227-1212

MASS TRANSIT

	Phone
MAX Light Rail Line $1.10 Base fare	503-238-7433
Tri-Met $1.10 Base fare	503-238-7433

RAIL/BUS

				Phone
Greyhound Bus Station 550 NW 6th Ave *TF:* 800-231-2222	Portland	OR	97209	503-243-2357
Portland Amtrak Station 800 NW 6th Ave	Portland	OR	97209	503-273-4871

— Accommodations —

HOTEL RESERVATION SERVICES

	Phone	Fax
Pacific Reservation Service *TF:* 800-684-2932 ■ *Web:* www.seattlebedandbreakfast.com/ ■ *E-mail:* pacificb@nwlink.com	206-439-7677	431-0932

HOTELS, MOTELS, RESORTS

				Phone	Fax
5th Avenue Suites Hotel 506 SW Washington St *TF:* 800-711-2971 ■ *Web:* 135.145.16.183/5thavenuesuites.com ■ *E-mail:* sales@5thavenuesuites.com	Portland	OR	97204	503-222-0001	222-0004
Benson Hotel 309 SW Broadway *TF:* 800-426-0670 ■ *Web:* www.westcoasthotels.com/benson ■ *E-mail:* reservations@bensonhotel.com	Portland	OR	97205	503-228-2000	226-4603
Best Western Hallmark Inn 3500 NE Cornell Rd *TF:* 800-336-3797	Hillsboro	OR	97124	503-648-3500	640-2789
Best Western Hood River Inn 1108 E Marina Way *TF:* 800-828-7873	Hood River	OR	97031	541-386-2200	386-8905
Best Western Inn Convention Center 420 NE Holladay St *TF:* 800-528-1234	Portland	OR	97232	503-233-6331	233-2677
Best Western Pony Soldier Motor Inn 9901 NE Sandy Blvd *TF:* 800-634-7669	Portland	OR	97220	503-256-1504	256-5928
Best Western Rose Garden Hotel 10 N Weidler St *TF:* 800-528-1234	Portland	OR	97227	503-287-9900	287-3500
Clarion Hotel Airport 6233 NE 78th Ct *TF:* 800-994-7878	Portland	OR	97218	503-251-2000	253-9306
Comfort Inn Convention Center 431 NE Multnomah St *TF:* 800-228-5150	Portland	OR	97232	503-233-7933	233-6921
Courtyard by Marriott 8500 SW Nimbus Ave *Web:* courtyard.com/PDXCY	Beaverton	OR	97008	503-641-3200	641-1287
Courtyard by Marriott Portland Airport 11550 NE Airport Way *TF:* 800-321-2211 ■ *Web:* courtyard.com/PDXCA	Portland	OR	97220	503-252-3200	252-8921
Crowne Plaza 14811 Kruse Oaks Blvd *TF:* 800-465-4329	Lake Oswego	OR	97035	503-624-8400	684-8234
Days Inn City Center 1414 SW 6th Ave *TF:* 800-899-0248	Portland	OR	97201	503-221-1611	226-0447
Doubletree Hotel Columbia 1401 N Hayden Island Dr *TF:* 800-222-8733 ■ *Web:* www.doubletreehotels.com/DoubleT/Hotel141/151/151Main.htm	Portland	OR	97217	503-283-2111	283-4718
Doubletree Hotel Lloyd Center 1000 NE Multnomah St *TF:* 800-222-8733 ■ *Web:* www.doubletreehotels.com/DoubleT/Hotel141/143/143Main.htm	Portland	OR	97232	503-281-6111	284-8553
Doubletree Portland Downtown 310 SW Lincoln St *TF:* 800-222-8733 ■ *Web:* www.doubletreehotels.com/DoubleT/Hotel141/144/144Main.htm	Portland	OR	97201	503-221-0450	225-4303
Econo Lodge Airport 9520 NE Sandy Blvd *TF:* 800-553-2666	Portland	OR	97220	503-252-6666	257-4848
Embassy Suites at the Multnomah Hotel Downtown 319 SW Pine St *TF:* 800-362-2779	Portland	OR	97204	503-279-9000	497-9051
Embassy Suites Hotel & Conference Center 9000 SW Washington Square Rd *TF:* 800-362-2779	Tigard	OR	97223	503-644-4000	641-4654
Four Points by Sheraton 50 SW Morrison St *TF:* 800-899-0247 ■ *Web:* www.fourpointsportland.com	Portland	OR	97204	503-221-0711	274-0312
Gearhart By the Sea PO Box 2700 *TF:* 800-547-0115 ■ *Web:* www.ohwy.com/or/g/gearhbts.htm	Gearhart	OR	97138	503-738-8331	738-0881
Governor Hotel 611 SW 10th Ave *TF:* 800-554-3456	Portland	OR	97205	503-224-3400	241-2122
Greenwood Inn 10700 SW Allen Blvd *TF:* 800-289-1300	Beaverton	OR	97005	503-643-7444	626-4553
Hallmark Resort PO Box 547 *TF:* 800-345-5676	Cannon Beach	OR	97110	503-436-1566	436-0324
Hampton Inn Portland Airport 8633 NE Airport Way *TF:* 800-426-7866	Portland	OR	97220	503-288-2423	288-2620
Heathman Hotel 1001 SW Broadway *TF:* 800-551-0011 ■ *Web:* www.slh.com/slh/pages/m/manmexe.html	Portland	OR	97205	503-241-4100	790-7110
Hilton Hotel 921 SW 6th Ave *TF:* 800-445-8667 ■ *Web:* www.hilton.com/hotels/PDXPHHH	Portland	OR	97204	503-226-1611	220-2565
Holiday Inn Airport 8439 NE Columbia Blvd *TF:* 800-465-4329	Portland	OR	97220	503-256-5000	257-4742
Holiday Inn Downtown 1021 NE Grand Ave *TF:* 800-465-4329	Portland	OR	97232	503-235-2100	235-0396
Holiday Inn Express Portland Airport 11938 NE Airport Way *TF:* 800-465-4329	Portland	OR	97220	503-251-9991	251-9992
Hotel Vintage Plaza 422 SW Broadway *TF:* 800-243-0555 ■ *Web:* www.holog.com/vintage/	Portland	OR	97205	503-228-1212	228-3598
Howard Johnson 7101 NE 82nd Ave *TF:* 800-446-4656	Portland	OR	97220	503-255-6722	254-3370
Imperial Hotel 400 SW Broadway *TF:* 800-452-2323	Portland	OR	97205	503-228-7221	223-4551
Mallory Hotel 729 SW 15th Ave *TF:* 800-228-8657	Portland	OR	97205	503-223-6311	223-0522
Mark Spencer Hotel 409 SW 11th Ave *TF:* 800-548-3934 ■ *Web:* www.markspencer.com/	Portland	OR	97205	503-224-3293	223-7848
Monarch Hotel & Conference Center 12566 SE 93rd Ave *TF:* 800-492-8700	Clackamas	OR	97015	503-652-1515	652-7509
Oxford Suites 12226 N Jantzen Dr *TF:* 800-548-7848	Portland	OR	97217	503-283-3030	735-1661
Portland Marriott 1401 SW Naito Pkwy *TF:* 800-228-9290	Portland	OR	97201	503-226-7600	221-1789
Portland White House 1914 NE 22nd Ave *TF:* 800-272-7131 ■ *Web:* www.portlandswhitehouse.com ■ *E-mail:* portlandwhitehouse@travelbase.com	Portland	OR	97212	503-287-7131	249-1641
Quality Inn Portland Airport 8247 NE Sandy Blvd *TF:* 800-246-4649	Portland	OR	97220	503-256-4111	254-1507
Ramada Inn Portland Airport 6221 NE 82nd Ave *TF:* 800-272-6232	Portland	OR	97220	503-255-6511	255-8417
Ramada Plaza 1441 NE 2nd Ave *TF:* 800-272-6232	Portland	OR	97232	503-233-2401	238-7016
Residence Inn by Marriott 1710 NE Multnomah St *TF:* 800-331-3131 ■ *Web:* www.residenceinn.com/PDXLC	Portland	OR	97232	503-288-1400	288-0241
Residence Inn by Marriott Portland South 15200 SW Bangy Rd *TF:* 800-331-3131 ■ *Web:* www.residenceinn.com/PDXLO	Lake Oswego	OR	97035	503-684-2603	620-6712
Riverplace Hotel 1510 SW Harbor Way *TF:* 800-227-1333 ■ *Web:* www.riverplacehotel.com ■ *E-mail:* sales@riverplacehotel.com	Portland	OR	97201	503-228-3233	295-6161
Sheraton Portland Airport Hotel 8235 NE Airport Way *TF:* 800-325-3535	Portland	OR	97220	503-281-2500	249-7602
Shilo Inn Suites Hotel Airport 11707 NE Airport Way *TF:* 800-222-2244	Portland	OR	97220	503-252-7500	254-0794
Shilo Inn West 9900 SW Canyon Rd *TF:* 800-222-2244	Portland	OR	97225	503-297-2551	297-7708
Silver Cloud Inn 2426 NW Vaughn St *TF:* 800-205-6939	Portland	OR	97210	503-242-2400	242-1770
Surfsand Resort PO Box 219 *TF:* 800-547-6100	Cannon Beach	OR	97110	503-436-2274	436-9116
US Suites 10220 SW Nimbus St *TF:* 800-877-8483	Portland	OR	97223	503-952-7700	620-8593

Portland (Cont'd)

— Restaurants —

				Phone
Alessandro's (Italian) 301 SW Morrison St	Portland	OR	97204	503-222-3900
Alexander's Restaurant (Continental) 921 SW 6th Ave	Portland	OR	97204	503-220-2687
Alexis Restaurant (Greek) 215 W Burnside St	Portland	OR	97209	503-224-8577
Atwater's Restaurant & Bar (Northwest) 111 SW 5th Ave 30th Fl	Portland	OR	97204	503-275-3600
August Moon (Chinese) 405 NW 23rd Ave	Portland	OR	97210	503-248-9040
Basta's Trattoria (Italian) 410 NW 21st Ave	Portland	OR	97209	503-274-1572
Big Red's (Southwest) 5515 SW Canyon Ct	Portland	OR	97221	503-297-5568
Brasserie Montmartre (French) 626 SW Park Ave	Portland	OR	97205	503-224-5552
Bush Garden Restaurant (Japanese) 900 SW Morrison St	Portland	OR	97205	503-226-7181
Cafe des Amis (French) 1987 NW Kearney St	Portland	OR	97209	503-295-6487
Cafe Sol (Spanish) 620 SW 9th Ave	Portland	OR	97205	503-243-2181
Caprial's Bistro (American) 7015 SE Milwaukee Ave	Portland	OR	97202	503-236-6457
Casablanca (Moroccan) 2221 SE Hawthorne	Portland	OR	97214	503-233-4400
Chameleon Restaurant & Bar (International) 2000 NE 40th Ave	Portland	OR	97212	503-460-2682
Chart House (American) 5700 SW Terwilliger Blvd	Portland	OR	97201	503-246-6963
Cisco & Pancho's (Mexican) 107 NW 5th Ave	Portland	OR	97209	503-223-5048
Couch Street Fish House (Seafood) 105 NW 3rd Ave	Portland	OR	97209	503-223-6173
Cozze (Italian) 1205 SE Morrison St	Portland	OR	97214	503-232-3275
Dan & Louis Oyster Bar (Seafood) 208 SW Ankeny St	Portland	OR	97204	503-227-5906
Esparza's Tex-Mex Cafe (Mexican) 2725 SE Ankeny St	Portland	OR	97214	503-234-7909
Esplanade at RiverPlace (American) 1510 SW Harbor Way	Portland	OR	97201	503-228-3233
Genoa (Italian) 2832 SE Belmont St	Portland	OR	97214	503-238-1464
Greek Cusina (Greek) 404 SW Washington St	Portland	OR	97204	503-224-2288
Heathman Restaurant (New American) 1001 SW Broadway	Portland	OR	97205	503-241-4100
Huber's Cafe (American) 411 SW 3rd Ave	Portland	OR	97204	503-228-5686
Jake's Famous Crawfish (Seafood) 401 SW 12th Ave	Portland	OR	97205	503-226-1419
Jake's Grill (Steak) 611 SW 10th St	Portland	OR	97205	503-220-1850
Kelly's Olympian Co (American) 426 SW Washington St	Portland	OR	97204	503-228-3669
Kojo of Japan (Japanese) 12000 SE 82nd Ave Suite D219	Portland	OR	97266	503-652-8066
L'Auberge (French) 2601 NW Vaughn St	Portland	OR	97210	503-223-3302
La Catalana (Spanish) 2821 SE Stark St	Portland	OR	97214	503-232-0948
Le Bistro Montage (Cajun/Creole) 301 SE Morrison St	Portland	OR	97214	503-234-1324
London Grill (Continental) 309 SW Broadway	Portland	OR	97205	503-295-4110
Marco Polo Garden (Chinese) 19 NW 5th	Portland	OR	97209	503-222-1090
Marrakesh (Moroccan) 1201 NW 21st Ave	Portland	OR	97209	503-248-9442
Maxi's Restaurant Lloyd Center (Continental) 1000 NE Multnomah St	Portland	OR	97232	503-281-6111
McCalls Waterfront Cafe (American) 1020 SW Front Ave	Portland	OR	97204	503-248-9710
Oba! (Latin American) 555 NW 12th Ave	Portland	OR	97209	503-228-6161
Ohm (American) 31 NW 1st Ave	Portland	OR	97209	503-224-3147
Old Market Pub & Brewery (American) 6959 SW Garden Home Rd	Portland	OR	97223	503-244-0450
Opus Too (American) 33 NW 2nd Ave	Portland	OR	97209	503-222-6077
Paley's Place (New American) 1204 NW 21st Ave	Portland	OR	97209	503-243-2403
Papa Haydn (New American) 701 NW 23rd Ave	Portland	OR	97210	503-228-7317
Pazzo Ristorante (Italian) 627 SW Washington St	Portland	OR	97205	503-228-1515
Plainfield's Mayur (Indian) 852 SW 21st *Web:* www.plainfields.com/	Portland	OR	97205	503-223-2995
Red Star Tavern & Roast House (New American) 503 SW Alder St	Portland	OR	97205	503-222-0005
Republic Cafe (Chinese) 222 NW 4th Ave	Portland	OR	97209	503-226-4388
Rheinlander German Restaurant (German) 5035 NE Sandy Blvd	Portland	OR	97213	503-288-5503
Ringside The (Steak/Seafood) 2165 W Burnside St	Portland	OR	97210	503-223-1513
Rock Bottom Brewery (American) 206 SW Morrison St	Portland	OR	97204	503-796-2739
Rustica Italian Caffe (Italian) 1700 NE Broadway	Portland	OR	97232	503-288-0990
Saigon Kitchen (Vietnamese) 835 NE Broadway	Portland	OR	97232	503-281-3669
Salty's on the Columbia (Seafood) 3839 NE Marine Dr	Portland	OR	97211	503-288-4444
Stanford's (Steak/Seafood) 913 Lloyd Ctr	Portland	OR	97232	503-335-0811
Trianon (European) 9225 SW Allen Blvd	Portland	OR	97223	503-245-2775
Typhoon! (Thai) 400 SW Broadway Imperial Hotel	Portland	OR	97205	503-224-8285
Wildwood Restaurant & Bar (Northwest) 1221 NW 21st Ave	Portland	OR	97209	503-248-9663
Winterborne (Seafood) 3520 NE 42nd Ave	Portland	OR	97213	503-249-8486
Yen Ha (Vietnamese) 6820 NE Sandy Blvd	Portland	OR	97213	503-287-3698
Zefiro (Mediterranean) 500 NW 21st Ave	Portland	OR	97209	503-226-3394

— Goods and Services —

SHOPPING

Name	City	State	Zip	Phone	Fax
Clackamas Town Center 12000 SE 82nd Ave **Fax:* Cust Svc ■ *Web:* www.clackamastowncenter.com	Portland	OR	97266	503-653-6913	653-7357*
Galleria 921 SW Morrison St	Portland	OR	97205	503-228-2748	
Hawthorne Boulevard Hawthorne Blvd betw 12th & 51st	Portland	OR	97293	503-774-2832	788-0412
Lloyd Center 2201 Lloyd Ctr	Portland	OR	97232	503-282-2511	280-9407
Meier & Frank Department Stores 621 SW 5th Ave *TF Orders:* 800-452-6323 ■ *Web:* www.mayco.com/mf/mf_home.html	Portland	OR	97204	503-223-0512	241-5783
Multnomah Village SW 35th Ave & Capitol Hwy	Portland	OR	97219	503-245-4014	
Nordstrom 701 SW Broadway	Portland	OR	97205	503-224-6666	299-2822
Pendleton Woolen Mills Inc PO Box 3030 *TF:* 800-760-4844 ■ *Web:* www.pendleton-usa.com ■ *E-mail:* wool@pendleton-usa.com	Portland	OR	97208	503-226-4801	535-5599
Pioneer Place 888 SW 5th Ave Suite 410	Portland	OR	97204	503-228-5800	228-5864
Portland Saturday Market 1st & Front Sts under Burnside Bridge	Portland	OR	97209	503-222-6072	222-0254
Portland Skidmore Fountain Market 120 SW Ankeny	Portland	OR	97204	503-228-2392	228-0576
Powell's City of Books 1005 W Burnside St **Fax Area Code:* 503 ■ *Web:* www.powells.com ■ *E-mail:* help@powells.com	Portland	OR	97209	800-878-7323	227-4631*
Stars Antique Mall 7027 SE Milwaukee Ave	Portland	OR	97202	503-239-0346	
Washington Square Shopping Center 9585 SW Washington Square Rd	Tigard	OR	97223	503-639-8860	620-5612
Water Tower at Johns Landing 5331 SW Macadam Ave	Portland	OR	97201	503-228-9431	228-9473

BANKS

Name	City	State	Zip	Phone	Fax
American State Bank 2737 NE M L King Jr Blvd	Portland	OR	97212	503-282-2216	282-5751
Bank of America Oregon 121 SW Morrison St Suite 170	Portland	OR	97204	503-275-2222	275-0903
KeyBank NA Oregon District 1222 SW 6th Ave Suite 200 *TF:* 800-539-2968	Portland	OR	97204	503-790-7690	790-7693
Northern Bank of Commerce 1001 SW 5th Ave Suite 250	Portland	OR	97204	503-222-9164	222-0501
US Bank NA 321 SW 6th Ave	Portland	OR	97204	503-275-5122	275-4193

BUSINESS SERVICES

Name	Phone
Accountemps	503-222-9778
Barrett Business Services Inc	503-220-0988
Corporate Express Delivery Systems	503-228-4444
Express Personnel Services	503-224-5500
Federal Express	800-238-5355
Kelly Services	503-230-2210
Kinko's	503-223-2056
Manpower Temporary Services	503-226-6281
Olsten Staffing Services	503-224-6878
Post Office	800-275-8777
Pronto Messenger	503-239-7666
UPS	800-742-5877

— Media —

PUBLICATIONS

Name	City	State	Zip	Phone	Fax
Business Journal PO Box 14490 *Web:* www.amcity.com/portland	Portland	OR	97293	503-274-8733	227-2650
Daily Journal of Commerce‡ PO Box 10127 *Web:* www.djc-or.com ■ *E-mail:* subscriptions@djc-or.com	Portland	OR	97296	503-226-1311	224-7140
Oregonian‡ 1320 SW Broadway *TF:* 800-826-0376 ■ *Web:* www.oregonlive.com	Portland	OR	97201	503-221-8100	227-5306

‡Daily newspapers

TELEVISION

Name	City	State	Zip	Phone	Fax
KATU-TV Ch 2 (ABC) 2153 NE Sandy Blvd *Web:* local.katu.citysearch.com	Portland	OR	97232	503-231-4222	231-4263
KGW-TV Ch 8 (NBC) 1501 SW Jefferson St *Web:* www.kgw.com	Portland	OR	97201	503-226-5000	226-4448
KOIN-TV Ch 6 (CBS) 222 SW Columbia St *Web:* www.koin.com ■ *E-mail:* koin06a@prodigy.com	Portland	OR	97201	503-464-0600	464-0717
KOPB-TV Ch 10 (PBS) 7140 SW Macadam Ave *Web:* www.opb.org/ ■ *E-mail:* kopb@opb.org	Portland	OR	97219	503-244-9900	293-1919
KPDX-TV Ch 49 (Fox) 910 NE ML King Jr Blvd *Web:* www.kpdx.com	Portland	OR	97232	503-239-4949	239-6184
KPTV-TV Ch 12 (UPN) 211 SE Caruthers St *Web:* www.kptv.com	Portland	OR	97214	503-230-1200	230-1065
KPXG-TV Ch 22 (PAX) 54 SW Yamhill *Web:* www.pax.net/KPXG	Portland	OR	97204	503-222-2221	222-3732

Portland — Television (Cont'd)

				Phone	Fax
KWBP-TV Ch 32 (WB) 10255 SW Arctic Dr	Beaverton	OR	97005	503-644-3232	626-3576

RADIO

				Phone	Fax
KBBT-FM 107.5 kHz (AC) 2040 SW 1st Ave	Portland	OR	97201	503-222-1011	222-2047
TF: 800-567-1075 ■ *Web:* www.thebeat.com					
KBPS-FM 89.9 MHz (Clas) 515 NE 15th Ave	Portland	OR	97232	503-916-5828	916-2642
Web: www.kbps.org					
KEWS-AM 620 kHz (N/T) 4949 SW Macadam Ave	Portland	OR	97201	503-225-1190	227-5873
KEX-AM 1190 kHz (N/T) 4949 SW Macadam Ave	Portland	OR	97201	503-225-1190	224-3216
Web: www.1190kex.com					
KFXX-AM 910 kHz (Sports) 0700 SW Bancroft St	Portland	OR	97201	503-223-1441	223-6909
Web: www.kfxx.com ■ *E-mail:* kfxx@kfxx.com					
KGON-FM 92.3 MHz (CR) 4614 SW Kelly Ave	Portland	OR	97201	503-223-1441	223-6909
Web: www.kgon.com					
KINK-FM 102.9 MHz (AAA) 1501 SW Jefferson St	Portland	OR	97201	503-226-5080	226-4578
Web: www.kinkfm102.com ■ *E-mail:* kinkfm102@kinkfm102.com					
KKCW-FM 103.3 MHz (AC) 5005 SW Macadam Ave	Portland	OR	97201	503-222-5103	222-0030
Web: www.k103.com					
KKJZ-FM 106.7 MHz (NAC) 222 SW Columbia Ave Suite 350	Portland	OR	97201	503-223-0300	497-2333
Web: www.kkjz.com					
KKRZ-FM 100.3 MHz (CHR) 4949 SW Macadam Ave	Portland	OR	97201	503-226-0100	295-9281
Web: www.z100portland.com ■ *E-mail:* hlg@z100portland.com					
KKSN-AM 1520 kHz (Nost) 888 SW 5th Ave Suite 790	Portland	OR	97204	503-226-9791	243-3299
KKSN-FM 97.1 MHz (Oldies) 888 SW 5th Ave Suite 790	Portland	OR	97204	503-226-9791	243-3299
Web: www.kisnfm.com					
KNRK-FM 94.7 MHz (Alt) 0700 SW Bankroft	Portland	OR	97201	503-223-1441	223-6909
Web: www.knrk.com					
KOPB-FM 91.5 MHz (NPR) 7140 SW Macadam Ave	Portland	OR	97219	503-293-1905	293-1919
KPDQ-FM 93.7 MHz (Rel) 5110 SE Stark St	Portland	OR	97215	503-231-7800	238-7202
Web: www.kpdq.com					
KRSK-FM 105.1 MHz (AC) 888 SW 5th Ave Suite 790	Portland	OR	97204	503-223-0105	224-3070
Web: www.rosie105.com					
KUFO-FM 101.1 MHz (Rock) 2040 SW 1st Ave	Portland	OR	97201	503-222-1011	222-2047
Web: www.kufo.com					
KUPL-FM 98.7 MHz (Ctry) 222 SW Columbia Ave Suite 350	Portland	OR	97221	503-223-0300	497-2336
KWJJ-FM 99.5 MHz (Ctry) 2000 SW 1st Ave Suite 300	Portland	OR	97201	503-228-4393	227-3938
Web: www.kwjj.com					
KXL-AM 750 kHz (N/T) 0234 SW Bancroft St	Portland	OR	97201	503-243-7595	417-7660*
**Fax:* Sales ■ *Web:* www.kxl.com					
KXL-FM 95.5 MHz (AC) 0234 SW Bancroft St	Portland	OR	97201	503-243-7595	417-7660*
**Fax:* Sales					

— Colleges/Universities —

				Phone	Fax
Art Institute of Portland 2000 SW 5th Ave	Portland	OR	97201	503-228-6528	525-8331
TF: 888-228-6528					
Cascade College 9101 E Burnside St	Portland	OR	97216	503-255-7060	257-1222
TF: 800-550-7678 ■ *Web:* www.cascade.edu					
Clackamas Community College 19600 S Molalla Ave	Oregon City	OR	97045	503-657-8400	650-6654
Web: www.clackamas.cc.or.us					
Concordia University 2811 NE Holman St	Portland	OR	97211	503-288-9371	280-8531
TF Admissions: 800-321-9371 ■ *Web:* www.cu-portland.edu ■ *E-mail:* cu-admissions@cu-portland.edu					
George Fox University 414 N Meridian St	Newberg	OR	97132	503-538-8383	538-7234
TF Admissions: 800-765-4369 ■ *Web:* www.georgefox.edu					
ITT Technical Institute 6035 NE 78th Ct	Portland	OR	97218	503-255-6500	255-6135
TF: 800-234-5488 ■ *Web:* www.itt-tech.edu					
Lewis & Clark College 0615 SW Palatine Hill Rd	Portland	OR	97219	503-244-6161	768-7055
Web: www.lclark.edu					
Mount Hood Community College 26000 SE Stark St	Gresham	OR	97030	503-667-6422	491-7388
Web: www.mhcc.cc.or.us					
Oregon Health Sciences University 3181 SW Sam Jackson Pk Rd	Portland	OR	97201	503-494-8311	494-4812*
**Fax:* Admitting ■ *Web:* www.ohsu.edu					
Pacific Northwest College of Art 1241 NW Johnson St	Portland	OR	97209	503-226-4391	226-3587
Web: www.pnca.edu					
Pacific University 2043 College Way	Forest Grove	OR	97116	503-357-6151	359-2975
TF: 800-635-0561 ■ *Web:* www.pacificu.edu					
Portland Community College Sylvania 12000 SW 49th Ave	Portland	OR	97219	503-244-6111	977-4740
Web: www.pcc.edu					
Portland State University PO Box 751	Portland	OR	97207	503-725-3000	725-5525
TF Admissions: 800-547-8887 ■ *Web:* www.pdx.edu ■ *E-mail:* askadm@osa.pdx.edu					
Reed College 3203 SE Woodstock Blvd	Portland	OR	97202	503-771-1112	777-7553
TF Admissions: 800-547-4750 ■ *Web:* www.reed.edu ■ *E-mail:* admission@reed.edu					
University of Portland 5000 N Willamette Blvd	Portland	OR	97203	503-943-7911	943-7315
TF: 800-227-4568 ■ *Web:* www.uofport.edu ■ *E-mail:* info@uofport.edu					
Warner Pacific College 2219 SE 68th Ave	Portland	OR	97215	503-775-4366	517-1352
TF Admissions: 800-582-7885 ■ *Web:* www.warnerpacific.edu ■ *E-mail:* admiss@warnerpacific.edu					

— Hospitals —

				Phone	Fax
Adventist Medical Center 10123 SE Market St	Portland	OR	97216	503-257-2500	261-6638
Kaiser Permanente Medical Center 10180 SE Sunnyside Rd	Clackamas	OR	97015	503-652-2880	813-2000*
**Fax Area Code:* 800					
Legacy Emanuel Hospital & Health Center 2801 N Gantenbein Ave	Portland	OR	97227	503-413-2200	413-2756
Legacy Good Samaritan Hospital 1015 NW 22nd Ave	Portland	OR	97210	503-229-7711	413-8016*
**Fax:* Library					
Legacy Meridian Park Hospital 19300 SW 65th Ave	Tualatin	OR	97062	503-692-1212	692-2478*
**Fax:* Admitting					
Legacy Mount Hood Medical Center 24800 SE Stark	Gresham	OR	97030	503-667-1122	674-1608
Oregon Health Sciences University 3181 SW Sam Jackson Pk Rd	Portland	OR	97201	503-494-8311	494-4812*
**Fax:* Admitting ■ *Web:* www.ohsu.edu					
Providence Medical Center 4805 NE Glisan St	Portland	OR	97213	503-215-1111	215-6349*
**Fax:* Admitting					
Providence Saint Vincent Medical Center 9205 SW Barnes Rd	Portland	OR	97225	503-297-4411	216-4141*
**Fax:* Admitting ■ *Web:* www.providence.org					
Tuality Community Hospital 3395 SE 8th Ave	Hillsboro	OR	97123	503-681-1111	681-1608
Veterans Affairs Medical Center 3710 US Veterans Hospital Rd	Portland	OR	97201	503-220-8262	273-5319
Willamette Falls Hospital 1500 Division St	Oregon City	OR	97045	503-656-1631	650-6807
Woodland Park Hospital 10300 NE Hancock St	Portland	OR	97220	503-257-5500	257-5672

— Attractions —

				Phone	Fax
American Advertising Museum 5035 SE 24th Ave	Portland	OR	97202	503-226-0000	238-6674
Web: www.admuseum.org/					
Artists Repertory Theatre 1516 SW Alder St	Portland	OR	97205	503-241-9807	241-8268
Web: www.artistsrep.org/					
Berry Botanic Garden 1505 SW Summerville Ave	Portland	OR	97219	503-636-4112	636-7496
Web: www.berrybot.org ■ *E-mail:* bbg@agora.rdrop.com					
Blitz-Weinhard Brewing Co 1133 W Burnside St	Portland	OR	97209	503-222-4351	229-4689
BridgePort Brewing Co 1318 NW Northrup St	Portland	OR	97209	503-241-7179	241-0625
Web: www.firkin.com ■ *E-mail:* brewmaster@firkin.com					
Chamber Music Northwest 522 SW 5th Ave Suite 725	Portland	OR	97204	503-223-3202	294-1690
Web: www.teleport.com/~cmnw/ ■ *E-mail:* info@cmnw.org					

Portland — Attractions (Cont'd)

Name / Address	City	State	Zip	Phone	Fax
Columbia River Gorge Information 405 Port Way Ave	Hood River	OR	97031	541-386-2000	386-2057
Crown Point State Park PO Box 204	Corbett	OR	97019	503-695-2230	695-2250
First Avenue Gallery 205 SW 1st	Portland	OR	97204	503-222-3850	222-1475
Forest Park Newberry Rd betw NW Skyline & Saint Helens Rd	Portland	OR	97210	503-823-2223	
Fort Vancouver National Historic Site 612 E Reserve St	Vancouver	WA	98661	360-696-7655	696-7657
TF: 800-832-3599 ■ *Web:* www.nps.gov/fova/					
Grotto The Sandy Blvd & NE 85th Ave	Portland	OR	97220	503-254-7371	254-7948
Web: www.thegrotto.org ■ *E-mail:* grottog1@tdeport.com					
International Rose Test Garden 400 SW Kingston Dr	Portland	OR	97201	503-823-3636	
Japanese Garden PO Box 3847	Portland	OR	97208	503-223-4070	223-8303
Lloyd Center 2201 Lloyd Ctr	Portland	OR	97232	503-282-2511	280-9407
McMenamins Breweries Inc 1624 NW Glisan St	Portland	OR	97209	503-223-0109	294-0837
Web: www.mcmenamins.com/Brewing					
Mount Hood National Forest 16400 Champion Way	Sandy	OR	97055	503-668-1700	
Multnomah Village SW 35th Ave & Capitol Hwy	Portland	OR	97219	503-245-4014	
Musical Theatre Co 531 SE 14th Ave	Portland	OR	97214	503-224-8730	224-5123
Web: www.rdrop.com/~mluce/tmc.html					
Oaks Amusement Park SE Spokane St	Portland	OR	97202	503-233-5777	236-9143
Web: www.oakspark.com					
OMNIMAX Theater 1945 SE Water Ave	Portland	OR	97214	503-797-4640	797-4500
Web: www.omsi.edu/explore/omnimax/					
Oregon Ballet Theater 1120 SW 10th Ave	Portland	OR	97205	503-227-0977	227-4186
TF: 888-922-5538 ■ *Web:* www.obt.org					
Oregon City Trolley 1726 Washington St	Oregon City	OR	97045	503-657-0891	657-7892
TF: 800-424-3002					
Oregon Historical Society 1200 SW Park Ave	Portland	OR	97205	503-222-1741	221-2035
Web: www.ohs.org ■ *E-mail:* orhist@ohs.org					
Oregon Maritime Center & Museum 113 SW Naito Pkwy	Portland	OR	97204	503-224-7724	224-7767
Web: www.teleport.com/~omcm/index.shtml ■ *E-mail:* omcm@teleport.com					
Oregon Military Museum 10101 SE Clackamas Rd Bldg 6101	Clackamas	OR	97015	503-557-5336	557-5202
Oregon Museum of Science & Industry 1945 SE Water Ave	Portland	OR	97214	503-797-4000	797-4500
Web: www.omsi.edu					
Oregon Symphony Orchestra 921 SW Washington St Suite 200	Portland	OR	97205	503-228-4294	228-4150
TF: 800-228-7343 ■ *Web:* www.orsymphony.org					
Oregon Zoo 4001 SW Canyon Rd	Portland	OR	97221	503-226-1561	226-6836
Web: www.zooregon.org ■ *E-mail:* hartlinej@metro.dst.or.us					
Photographic Image Gallery 240 SW 1st Ave	Portland	OR	97204	503-224-3543	224-3607
Pioneer Courthouse Square 701 SW 6th Ave	Portland	OR	97204	503-223-1613	222-7425
Pittock Mansion 3229 NW Pittock Dr	Portland	OR	97210	503-823-3624	823-3619
Portland Art Museum 1219 SW Park Ave	Portland	OR	97205	503-226-2811	226-4842
Web: www.pam.org ■ *E-mail:* paminfo@pam.org					
Portland Audubon Society 5151 NW Cornell Rd	Portland	OR	97210	503-292-6855	292-1021
Portland Brewers Guild 510 NW 3rd Ave	Portland	OR	97209	503-295-1862	226-4895
TF: 800-440-2537					
Portland Brewing Co 2730 NW 31st Ave	Portland	OR	97210	503-226-7623	226-2702
TF: 800-356-2017 ■ *Web:* portlandbrew.com					
Portland Center for the Performing Arts 1111 SW Broadway	Portland	OR	97205	503-248-4335	274-7490
Web: www.pcpa.com					
Portland Center Stage 1111 SW Broadway	Portland	OR	97205	503-274-6588	228-7058
Portland Childen's Museum 3037 SW 2nd Ave	Portland	OR	97201	503-823-2227	823-3667
Web: www.parks.ci.portland.or.us/parks					
Portland Institute for Contemporary Art 720 SW Washington St Suite 700	Portland	OR	97205	503-242-1419	243-1167
Web: www.pica.org/					
Portland Opera Assn 1515 SW Morrison St	Portland	OR	97205	503-241-1401	241-4212
Portland Saturday Market 1st & Front Sts under Burnside Bridge	Portland	OR	97209	503-222-6072	222-0254
Portland Skidmore Fountain Market 120 SW Ankeny	Portland	OR	97204	503-228-2392	228-0576
Powell Butte Nature Park SE 162nd & Powell Blvd	Portland	OR	97204	503-823-2223	
Powell's City of Books 1005 W Burnside St	Portland	OR	97209	800-878-7323	227-4631*
**Fax Area Code:* 503 ■ *Web:* www.powells.com ■ *E-mail:* help@powells.com					
Rogue Ales Co 2320 OSU Dr	Newport	OR	97365	541-867-3660	867-3260
TF: 800-489-5482 ■ *Web:* www.rogueales.com ■ *E-mail:* roguedawg@rogueales.com					
Washington Park SW Park Pl-Hwy 26	Portland	OR	97204	503-823-2223	
Water Tower at Johns Landing 5331 SW Macadam Ave	Portland	OR	97201	503-228-9431	228-9473
Widmer Brothers Brewing Co 929 N Russell St	Portland	OR	97227	503-281-2437	281-1496
Web: www.widmer.com					
Willamette Shore Trolley 311 N State St	Lake Oswego	OR	97034	503-222-2226	
World Forestry Center 4033 SW Canyon Rd	Portland	OR	97221	503-228-1367	
Web: www.teleport.com/~wfc/					

SPORTS TEAMS & FACILITIES

Name / Address	City	State	Zip	Phone	Fax
Multnomah Greyhound Park PO Box 9	Fairview	OR	97024	503-667-7700	667-4852
TF: 800-888-7576 ■ *Web:* www.ez2winmgp.com/ ■ *E-mail:* mgp@ez2winmgp.com					
Portland Civic Stadium 1844 SW Morrison St	Portland	OR	97205	503-248-4345	221-3983
Portland Forest Dragons (football) 9400 SW Beaverton-Hillsdale Hwy Suite 101	Beaverton	OR	97005	503-292-8253	292-8498
Portland International Raceway 1940 N Victory Blvd	Portland	OR	97217	503-823-7223	823-5896
Web: www.indytrax.com/pir ■ *E-mail:* indytrax@teleport.com					
Portland Meadows Horse Track 1001 N Schmeer Rd	Portland	OR	97217	503-285-9144	286-9763
TF: 800-944-3127 ■ *Web:* www.portlandmeadows.com ■ *E-mail:* tnpm@portlandmeadows.com					
Portland Pythons (soccer) 1 Center Ct Rose Garden	Portland	OR	97227	503-684-5425	639-8084
Web: www.portlandpythons.com					
Portland Rockies (baseball) 1844 SW Morrison St Civic Stadium	Portland	OR	97205	503-223-2837	223-2948
Web: www.portlandrockies.com					
Portland Trail Blazers 1 Center Ct Suite 200	Portland	OR	97227	503-234-9291	736-2187
Web: www.nba.com/blazers					
Portland Winter Hawks (hockey) 1 Center Ct Memorial Coliseum	Portland	OR	97208	503-238-6366	238-7629
Web: www.winterhawks.com ■ *E-mail:* hawks@teleport.com					
Rose Garden 1 Center Ct	Portland	OR	97227	503-797-9617	736-2191
Web: www.rosequarter.com					

— Events —

	Phone
America's Largest Christmas Bazaar (late November-early December)	503-736-5200
Bite-A Taste of Portland (mid-August)	503-248-0600
Christmas at the Pittock Mansion (late November-late December)	503-823-3624
Cinco de Mayo Celebration (early May)	503-222-9807
Clark County Fair (early-mid-August)	360-737-6180
Evening Concerts at the Zoo (mid-June-mid-August)	503-226-1561
Festa Italiana (late August)	503-771-0310
Festival of Lights at the Grotto (late November-late December)	503-254-7371
Greek Festival (early October)	503-234-0468
Homowo Festival of African Arts (mid-August)	503-288-3025
International Film Festival (mid-February-early March)	503-221-1156
Mount Hood Jazz Festival (early August)	503-232-3000
Oregon Brewers Festival (late July)	503-778-5917
Oregon State Fair (late August-early September)	503-378-3247
Portland Creative Conference (mid-September)	503-234-1641
Portland Marathon (late September)	503-226-1111
Portland Rose Festival (early June)	503-227-2681
Portland Scottish Highland Games (mid-July)	503-293-8501
Rose Festival Airshow (late June)	503-227-2681
Seafood & Wine Festival (late February)	800-262-7844
Seven Up Winter Wonderland Celebration of Lights (late November-early January)	503-232-3000
Starlight Parade (early June)	503-227-2681
Tulip Festival (late April)	503-228-5108
Washington County Fair & Rodeo (early August)	503-648-1416
Waterfront Blues Festival (early July)	503-973-3378
Zoolights (December)	503-226-1561

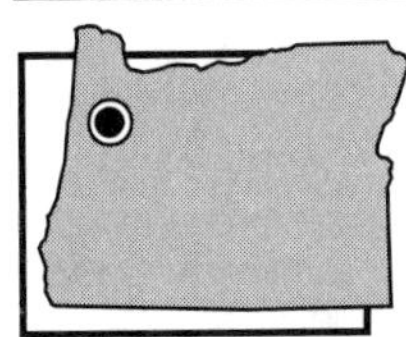

Salem

Among the cities that occupy the hills of Oregon's wine country is Salem. Salem area wineries feature a variety of special events, plus tasting and tours for visitors. Salem and its neighboring towns are also known for beautiful iris gardens, including Cooleys and Schreiner's Iris Gardens. Twenty-six miles east of Salem is Silver Falls State Park, with ten spectacular waterfalls ranging in height from 27 to 178 feet and accessible to hikers. Salem is also home to Willamette University, the oldest college in the West.

Population	126,702	**Longitude**	123-01-77 W
Area (Land)	36.9 sq mi	**County**	Marion
Area (Water)	0.4 sq mi	**Time Zone**	PST
Elevation	154 ft	**Area Code/s**	503
Latitude	44-98-46 N		

— Average Temperatures and Precipitation —

TEMPERATURES

	Jan	Feb	Mar	Apr	May	Jun	Jul	Aug	Sep	Oct	Nov	Dec
High	46	52	56	60	67	75	82	82	76	64	52	46
Low	33	34	36	38	42	48	51	51	47	41	38	34

PRECIPITATION

	Jan	Feb	Mar	Apr	May	Jun	Jul	Aug	Sep	Oct	Nov	Dec
Inches	5.9	4.5	4.2	2.4	1.9	1.3	0.6	0.8	1.6	3.0	6.3	6.9

— Important Phone Numbers —

	Phone		*Phone*
AAA	503-581-1608	**Time**	503-363-7600
American Express Travel	503-378-0084	**Weather**	503-363-4131
Emergency	911		

— Information Sources —

				Phone	*Fax*
Better Business Bureau Serving Oregon & Western Washington 333 SW 5th Ave Suite 300	Portland	OR	97204	503-226-3981	226-8200
Web: www.portland.bbb.org					
Marion County 100 High St NE Rm 1331	Salem	OR	97301	503-588-5225	373-4408
Web: www.open.org/~marion					
Oregon State Fair & Expo Center 2330 17th St NE	Salem	OR	97303	503-378-3247	373-1788
Salem Area Chamber of Commerce 1110 Commercial St NE	Salem	OR	97301	503-581-1466	581-0972
Web: www.salemchamber.org					
Salem City Hall 555 Liberty St SE	Salem	OR	97301	503-588-6161	588-6354
Web: www.ci.salem.or.us					
Salem Community Development Dept 555 Liberty St SE Rm 305	Salem	OR	97301	503-588-6173	588-6005
Web: www.open.org/~scdev					
Salem Convention & Visitors Assn 1313 Mill St SE	Salem	OR	97301	503-581-4325	581-4540
TF: 800-874-7012 ■ *Web:* www.scva.org ■ *E-mail:* service@scva.org					
Salem Mayor 555 Liberty St SE Rm 220	Salem	OR	97301	503-588-6159	588-6354
Web: www.open.org/~scouncil/mayor.html ■ *E-mail:* mswaim@open.org					
Salem Public Library 585 Liberty St SE	Salem	OR	97309	503-588-6060	588-6055
Web: www.open.org/~library ■ *E-mail:* library@open.org					

On-Line Resources

Anthill City Guide Salem	www.anthill.com/city.asp?city=salem
City Knowledge Salem	www.cityknowledge.com/or_salem.htm
Excite.com Salem City Guide	www.excite.com/travel/countries/united_states/oregon/salem
Salem OnLine	www.oregonlink.com/
Salem (OR) Home Page	www.open.org/~salem
Www.el.com to Salem Oregon	www.el.com/To/Salem

— Transportation Services —

AIRPORTS

■ **Portland International Airport (PDX)**

	Phone
47 miles N of downtown Salem (approx 75 minutes)	503-460-4234
Web: www.portlandairportpdx.com	

Airport Transportation

	Phone
HUT Airport Shuttle $22 fare to downtown Salem	503-363-8059

Commercial Airlines

	Phone		*Phone*
Alaska	800-426-0333	**Northwest**	800-225-2525
America West	800-235-9292	**TWA**	800-221-2000
American	800-433-7300	**United**	800-241-6522
Continental	503-224-4560	**US Airways**	800-428-4322
Delta	800-221-1212		

Charter Airlines

	Phone
Flightcraft	503-331-4244

CAR RENTALS

	Phone		*Phone*
Alamo	503-252-7039	**Enterprise**	503-252-6834
Avis	503-249-4950	**Hertz**	503 249-8216
Budget	503-249-6500	**Hertz-Salem**	503-581-4466
Budget-Salem	503-362-0041	**National**	503-249-4900
Dollar	503-249-4792	**Thrifty**	503-254-6563

LIMO/TAXI

	Phone		*Phone*
Five Star Limousine	503-585-8533	**Yellow Cab**	503-362-2411

MASS TRANSIT

	Phone
Cherriots Transit $.75 Base fare	503-588-2877

RAIL/BUS

				Phone
Amtrak Station 500 13th St SE	Salem	OR	97301	503-588-1551
Greyhound/Trailways Bus Station 450 Church St NE	Salem	OR	97301	503-362-2428

— Accommodations —

HOTELS, MOTELS, RESORTS

				Phone	*Fax*
Best Western Mill Creek Inn 3125 Ryan Dr SE	Salem	OR	97301	503-585-3332	375-9618
TF: 800-346-9659					
Best Western New Kings Inn 1600 Motor Ct NE	Salem	OR	97301	503-581-1559	364-4272
TF: 800-528-1234					
Best Western Pacific Highway Inn 4646 Portland Rd NE	Salem	OR	97305	503-390-3200	393-7989
Best Western Vineyard Inn 2035 S Hwy 99 West	McMinnville	OR	97128	503-472-4900	434-9157
City Center Motel 510 Liberty St SE	Salem	OR	97301	503-364-0121	581-0554
TF: 800-289-0121					
Comfort Suites 630 Hawthorne SE	Salem	OR	97301	503-585-9705	585-9761
TF: 800-228-5150					
Cozzzy Inn 1875 Fisher Rd NE	Salem	OR	97305	503-588-5423	391-4781
Embarcadero Resort Hotel & Marina 1000 SE Bay Blvd	Newport	OR	97365	541-265-8521	265-7844
TF: 800-547-4779 ■ *Web:* www.embarcadero-resort.com ■ *E-mail:* information@embarcadero-resort.com					
Holiday Inn 3019 N Coast Hwy	Newport	OR	97365	541-265-9411	265-8773
TF: 800-547-3310					

Salem — Hotels, Motels, Resorts (Cont'd)

				Phone	Fax
Holiday Lodge 1400 Hawthorne Ave	Salem	OR	97301	503-585-2323	585-2153
Inn at Otter Crest PO Box 50	Otter Rock	OR	97369	541-765-2111	765-2047
TF: 800-452-2101					
Inn at Spanish Head 4009 SW Hwy 101	Lincoln City	OR	97367	541-996-2161	996-4089
TF: 800-452-8127					
Lincoln Shores Motel 136 NE Hwy 101	Lincoln City	OR	97367	541-994-8155	994-5581
TF: 800-423-6240					
Motel 6 North 1401 Hawthorne Ave NE	Salem	OR	97301	503-371-8024	371-7691
TF: 800-466-8356					
Oregon Capitol Inn 745 Commercial St SE	Salem	OR	97301	503-363-2451	
Phoenix Inn 4370 Commercial St SE	Salem	OR	97302	503-588-9220	585-3616
TF: 800-445-4498					
Phoenix Inn 1590 Weston Ct NE	Salem	OR	97301	503-581-7004	362-3587
TF: 888-239-9593					
Quality Inn Hotel & Convention Center 3301 Market St NE	Salem	OR	97301	503-370-7888	370-6305
TF: 800-248-6273					
Ramada Inn 200 Commercial St SE	Salem	OR	97301	503-363-4123	363-8993
TF: 800-272-6232					
Ramada Inn 1550 NW 9th St	Corvallis	OR	97330	541-753-9151	758-7089
TF: 800-272-6232					
Rodeway Inn 3195 Portland Rd NE	Salem	OR	97303	503-585-2900	585-3522
TF: 800-228-2000					
Safari Motor Inn 345 N Hwy 99 West	McMinnville	OR	97128	503-472-5187	434-6380
TF: 800-321-5543					
Salem Inn 1775 Freeway Ct NE	Salem	OR	97303	503-588-0515	588-1426
TF: 888-305-0515					
Shanico Inn 1113 NW 9th St	Corvallis	OR	97330	541-754-7474	754-2437
TF: 800-432-1233					
Shilo Inn 1880 NW 6th St	Grants Pass	OR	97526	541-479-8391	474-7344
TF: 800-222-2244					
Shilo Inn Suites 3304 Market St	Salem	OR	97301	503-581-4001	399-9385
TF: 800-222-2244					
Stone Lion Inn 4692 Lancaster Dr NE	Salem	OR	97305	503-463-6374	
TF: 888-673-3465					
Surftides Beach Resort 2945 NW Jetty Ave	Lincoln City	OR	97367	541-994-2191	994-2727
TF: 800-452-2159					
Tiki Lodge 3705 Market St NE	Salem	OR	97301	503-581-4441	581-4442
TF: 800-438-8458					
Travelers Inn Motel 3230 Portland Rd NE	Salem	OR	97303	503-581-2444	364-9860
Westin Salishan Lodge PO Box 118	Gleneden Beach	OR	97388	541-764-2371	764-3681
TF: 800-452-2300					

— Restaurants —

				Phone
A Taste of Thai (Thai) 3405 Commercial St SE	Salem	OR	97302	503-363-9010
Alessandro's Park Plaza (Italian) 325 High St SE	Salem	OR	97301	503-370-9951
Arbor Cafe (Continental) 380 High St NE	Salem	OR	97301	503-588-2353
Change of Seasons (Continental) 300 Liberty St SE	Salem	OR	97301	503-365-9722
Da Vinci (Italian) 180 High St	Salem	OR	97301	503-399-1413
Heritage Tree Restaurant (Homestyle) 574 Cottage St NE	Salem	OR	97301	503-399-7075
Kwan's Cuisine (Cantonese) 835 Commercial St SE	Salem	OR	97302	503-362-7711
Kyoto Japanese Steak & Seafood House (Japanese) 1610 Lancaster Dr NE	Salem	OR	97301	503-363-3552
La Margarita Co (Mexican) 545 Ferry St SE	Salem	OR	97301	503-362-8861
Macedonia (Greek) 189 Liberty St NE	Salem	OR	97301	503-316-9997
McGrath's Fish House (Seafood) 350 Chemeketa St NE	Salem	OR	97301	503-362-0736
Newport Bay Restaurant (American) 1717 Freeway Ct NE	Salem	OR	97303	503-315-7100
Nona Rozelli's (Italian) 1311 Edgewater NW	Salem	OR	97304	503-391-1010
Old Europe Inn (European) 1395 Liberty St	Salem	OR	97302	503-588-3639
Paprikas Hungarian Restaurant (Hungarian) 1696 Capitol St NE	Salem	OR	97303	503-370-8992
Pointe The (American) 195 Commercial St NE	Salem	OR	97301	503-585-5588
Porter's Pub (American) 4820 River Rd N	Salem	OR	97303	503-393-3269
Ram Big Horn Brewery (American) 515 12th St SE	Salem	OR	97301	503-363-1904
Richard's Restaurant (American) 1486 Hawthorne NE	Salem	OR	97301	503-581-9313
S'ghetti's (Italian) 695 Orchard Heights Rd NW	Salem	OR	97304	503-378-1780
Village Inn Restaurant (American) 3310 Market St NE	Salem	OR	97301	503-378-0100
West Gate Cafe (American) 605 Wallace Rd NW	Salem	OR	97304	503-362-9588

— Goods and Services —

SHOPPING

				Phone	Fax
Lancaster Mall 831 Lancaster Dr NE	Salem	OR	97301	503-585-1338	362-7297
Mission Mill Village 1313 Mill St SE	Salem	OR	97301	503-585-7012	
Salem Centre 401 Center St NE Suite 172	Salem	OR	97301	503-364-0495	364-1284

BANKS

				Phone	Fax
Bank of Salem 1995 Commercial St SE	Salem	OR	97302	503-585-5290	585-7368
First Security Bank of Oregon 580 State St NE	Salem	OR	97301	800-574-4200	
Wells Fargo Bank 280 Liberty St NE	Salem	OR	97301	503-399-3541	399-3584
TF: 800-869-3557 ■ *Web:* www.wellsfargo.com					
West Coast Bank 301 Church St NE	Salem	OR	97301	503-399-2900	399-2996

BUSINESS SERVICES

	Phone		Phone
Airborne Express	800-247-2676	**Mail Boxes Etc**	800-789-4623
BAX Global	800-225-5229	**Norrell Temporary Services**	503-371-3635
DHL Worldwide Express	800-225-5345	**Post Office**	800-275-8777
Express Personnel Services	503-399-1200	**Selectemp**	503-581-1748
Federal Express	800-238-5355	**UPS**	800-742-5877
Kinko's	503-375-6340		

— Media —

PUBLICATIONS

				Phone	Fax
Statesman Journal‡ 280 Church St NE	Salem	OR	97301	503-399-6611	399-6706
TF: 800-452-2511 ■ *Web:* www.statesmanjournal.com ■ *E-mail:* online@statesmanjournal.com					

‡Daily newspapers

TELEVISION

				Phone	Fax
KATU-TV Ch 2 (ABC) 2153 NE Sandy Blvd	Portland	OR	97232	503-231-4222	231-4263
Web: local.katu.citysearch.com					
KGW-TV Ch 8 (NBC) 1501 SW Jefferson St	Portland	OR	97201	503-226-5000	226-4448
Web: www.kgw.com					
KOIN-TV Ch 6 (CBS) 222 SW Columbia St	Portland	OR	97201	503-464-0600	464-0717
Web: www.koin.com ■ *E-mail:* koin06a@prodigy.com					
KOPB-TV Ch 10 (PBS) 7140 SW Macadam Ave	Portland	OR	97219	503-244-9900	293-1919
Web: www.opb.org/ ■ *E-mail:* kopb@opb.org					
KPDX-TV Ch 49 (Fox) 910 NE ML King Jr Blvd	Portland	OR	97232	503-239-4949	239-6184
Web: www.kpdx.com					

RADIO

				Phone	Fax
KBZY-AM 1490 kHz (AC) PO Box 14900	Salem	OR	97309	503-362-1490	362-6545
Web: www.kbzy.com ■ *E-mail:* kzby@cyberis.net					
KCCS-AM 1220 kHz (Rel) 1850 45th Ave NE	Salem	OR	97305	503-364-1000	364-1022
Web: www.kccs.org					
KWBY-AM 940 kHz (Span) PO Box 158	Woodburn	OR	97071	503-981-9400	981-3561
Web: www.radio-fiesta.com					
KYKN-AM 1430 kHz (N/T) PO Box 1430	Salem	OR	97308	503-390-3014	390-3728
Web: www.kykn.com					

— Colleges/Universities —

				Phone	Fax
Chemeketa Community College PO Box 14007	Salem	OR	97309	503-399-5006	399-3918
Web: www.chemek.cc.or.us ■ *E-mail:* postmaster@chemek.cc.or.us					
Linfield College 900 S Baker St	McMinnville	OR	97128	503-434-2200	434-2472
TF: 800-640-2287 ■ *Web:* www.linfield.edu					
Western Baptist College 5000 Deer Pk Dr SE	Salem	OR	97301	503-581-8600	585-4316
TF: 800-845-3005 ■ *Web:* www.wbc.edu					
Western Oregon University 345 Monmouth Ave N	Monmouth	OR	97361	503-838-8000	838-8067
Web: www.wosc.osshe.edu					
Willamette University 900 State St	Salem	OR	97301	503-370-6303	375-5363
TF: 877-542-2787 ■ *Web:* www.willamette.edu ■ *E-mail:* undergrad-admission@willamette.edu					

— Hospitals —

				Phone	Fax
Salem Hospital PO Box 14001	Salem	OR	97309	503-370-5200	375-4846
Web: www.salemhospital.org ■ *E-mail:* cr@salemhospital.org					

Salem (Cont'd)

— Attractions —

				Phone	Fax
Brunk House 5705 Salem-Dallas Hwy NW	Salem	OR	97304	503-371-8586	
Bush Barn Art Center 600 Mission St SE	Salem	OR	97302	503-581-2228	
Bush House Museum 600 Mission St SE	Salem	OR	97302	503-363-4714	
Champoeg State Park 8239 Champoeg Rd NE	Saint Paul	OR	97137	503-678-1251	
Chemeketa Community College Planetarium 4000 Lancaster Dr NE	Salem	OR	97305	503-399-5161	
Cooley's Gardens 11553 Silverton Rd NE	Silverton	OR	97381	503-873-5463	873-5812
Web: www.cooleysgardens.com ■ *E-mail:* cooleyiris@aol.com					
Deepwood Estate 1116 Mission St SE	Salem	OR	97302	503-363-1825	
Enchanted Forest 8462 Enchanted Way SE	Turner	OR	97392	503-371-4242	
Fort Clatsop National Memorial Route 3 Box 604-FC	Astoria	OR	97103	503-861-2471	861-2585
Web: www.nps.gov/focl/					
Gilbert House Children's Museum 116 Marion St NE	Salem	OR	97301	503-371-3631	316-3485
Web: www.acgilbert.org ■ *E-mail:* e-mail: explore@teleport.com					
Historic Downtown Salem 350 Commercial St NE	Salem	OR	97301	503-371-4000	
Historic Elsinore Theatre 170 High St SE	Salem	OR	97301	503-375-3574	375-0284
Web: www.wvi.com/~stage ■ *E-mail:* stage@wvi.com					
Honeywood Winery 1350 Hines St SE	Salem	OR	97302	503-362-4111	
Jensen Paul Arctic Museum 590 W Church St	Monmouth	OR	97361	503-838-8468	838-8289
E-mail: macem@wou.edu/wou/offices.html					
Marion County Historical Society Museum 260 12th St SE	Salem	OR	97301	503-364-2128	
Mission Mill Village 1313 Mill St SE	Salem	OR	97301	503-585-7012	
Mount Angel Abbey 1 Abbey Dr	Mount Angel	OR	97373	503-845-3066	
Oregon Coast Aquarium 2820 SE Ferry Slip Rd	Newport	OR	97365	541-867-3474	867-6846
Web: www.aquarium.org ■ *E-mail:* akh@aquarium.org					
Oregon State Capitol 900 Court St	Salem	OR	97310	503-986-1388	986-1131
Pentacle Theater 324 52nd Ave NW	Salem	OR	97304	503-364-7121	362-6393
Web: www.oregonlink.com/pentacle_theater/index.html					
Redhawk Winery 2995 Michigan City Ave NW	Salem	OR	97304	503-362-1596	589-9189
Saint Innocent Winery 1360 Tandem Ave NE	Salem	OR	97303	503-378-1526	378-1041
Web: www.stinnocentwine.com					
Salem Chamber Orchestra Smith Auditorium Willamette University	Salem	OR	97308	503-375-5483	
Schreiner's Iris Gardens 3625 Quinaby Rd NE	Salem	OR	97303	503-393-3232	393-5590
Web: www.oregonlink.com/iris/index.html					
Silver Falls State Park 20024 Silver Falls Hwy SE	Sublimity	OR	97385	503-873-8681	
Thrill-Ville USA 8372 Enchanted Way SE	Turner	OR	97392	503-363-4095	
Western Antique Powerland 3995 Brooklake Rd NE	Salem	OR	97303	503-393-2424	
Willamette Mission State Park 10991 Wheatland Rd NE	Gervais	OR	97026	503-393-1172	393-8863
Willamette Valley Vineyards 8800 Enchanted Way SE	Turner	OR	97392	503-588-9463	588-8894
TF Sales: 800-344-9463 ■ *Web:* www.wvv.com ■ *E-mail:* information@wvv.com					
Witness Tree Winery 7111 Spring Valley Rd NW	West Salem	OR	97304	503-585-7874	
Woolen Mill Museum 1313 Mill St SE	Salem	OR	97301	503-585-7012	588-9902

SPORTS TEAMS & FACILITIES

				Phone	Fax
Cascade Surge (soccer) Mission & Winter Sts McCulloch Stadium	Salem	OR	97308	503-362-7308	371-3639
Web: www.cascadesurge.com ■ *E-mail:* surgerks@open.org					
Salem-Keizer Volcanoes (baseball) 6700 Field of Dreams Way Volcanoes Stadium	Keizer	OR	97307	503-390-2225	390-2227
Web: www.volcanoesbaseball.com ■ *E-mail:* probasebal@aol.com					
Willamette Valley Firebirds (soccer) 175 SW Twin Oaks Cir	Corvallis	OR	97333	541-757-0776	753-4187

— Events —

	Phone
Bite of Salem (late July)	503-581-4325
Celebrate Oregon Wine & Food Festival (mid-February)	503-581-0540
Civil War Reenactment (early July)	503-393-1172
Destruction Derby & Fireworks (early July)	503-581-4325
Festival of Lights Parade (mid-December)	800-874-7012
Great Northwest Train Show (early October)	503-378-3247
Holidays at the Capitol (December)	503-581-4325
Keizer Iris Festival (early May)	503-393-9111
Marion County Fair (early-mid-July)	503-581-1466
Mission Mill Museum Classic Car Show (late September)	503-585-7012
Oregon AG Fest (late April)	503-581-4325
Oregon State Fair (late August-early September)	503-378-3247
Quilt Show & Hand Weavers Sale (early October)	503-581-4325
Salem Art Fair & Festival (mid-July)	503-581-2228
Salem Belly Dance Festival (early August)	503-378-7875
Salem Collectors' Market (September-July)	503-393-1261
Salem Music on the Green (August)	503-581-4325
Salem Rodeo Days (mid-May)	503-371-6040
Sheep to Shawl (early June)	503-581-4325
Summer in the City Festival (late July)	503-581-4325
West Salem Waterfront Parade (late July)	503-581-4325

Pennsylvania

Population (1999): 11,994,016 **Area (sq mi): 46,058**

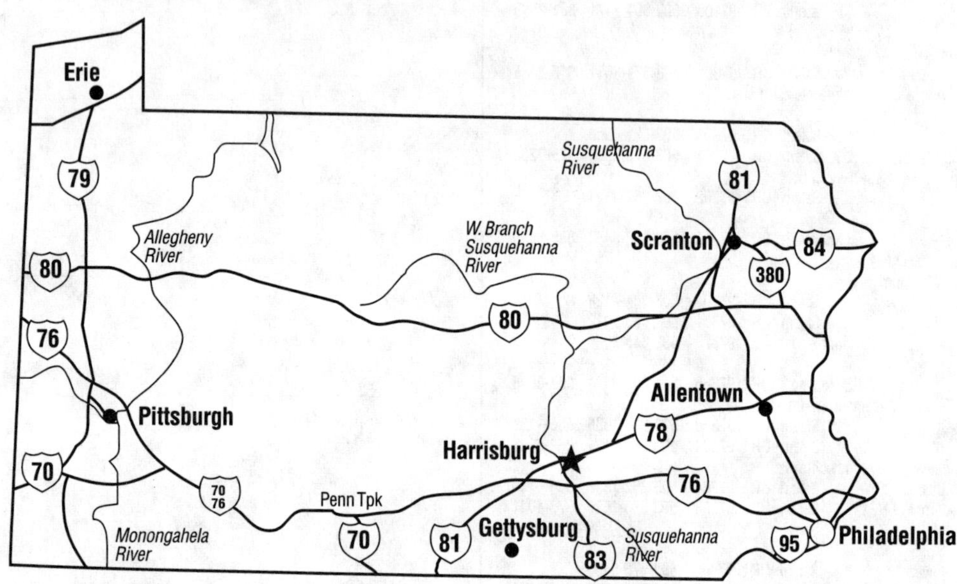

— State Information Sources —

		Phone	Fax
Pennsylvania Chamber of Business & Industry			
417 Walnut St . . . . Harrisburg PA 17101		717-255-3252	255-3298
TF: 800-225-7224 ■ *Web:* www.pachamber.org			
Pennsylvania Commonwealth Library			
PO Box 1601 . . . . Harrisburg PA 17105		717-787-2646	772-3265
Web: www1.huji.ac.il/www_lib1/us407.html			
Pennsylvania Community & Economic Development Dept			
433 Forum Bldg . . . . Harrisburg PA 17120		717-787-3003	234-4560
Web: www.state.pa.us/PA_Exec/Commerce			
Pennsylvania State Government Information		717-787-2121	
Web: www.state.pa.us			
Pennsylvania State Parks Bureau			
PO Box 8551 . . . . Harrisburg PA 17105		717-787-6640	787-8817
TF: 888-727-2757 ■ *Web:* www.dcnr.state.pa.us/stateparks/spintro.htm			
Pennsylvania Travel & Tourism Office			
Forum Bldg Room 404 . . . . Harrisburg PA 17120		717-787-5453	787-0687
TF: 800-847-4872 ■ *Web:* www.dced.state.pa.us/visit			
■ *E-mail:* dcedtravel@dced.state.pa.us			

ON-LINE RESOURCES

Daily Orbit Pennsylvania . . . . www.dailyorbit.com/pennsylvania
Pennsylvania Cities . . . . dir.yahoo.com/Regional/U_S__States/Pennsylvania/Cities
Pennsylvania Counties & Regions . . . . dir.yahoo.com/Regional/U_S__States/Pennsylvania/Counties_and_Regions
Pennsylvania Outdoor Recreation & Information Guide . . . . www.parec.com
Pennsylvania Scenario . . . . scenariousa.dstylus.com/pa/indexf.htm
Pennsylvania Travel & Tourism Guide . . . . www.travel-library.com/north_america/usa/pennsylvania/index.html
Pennsylvania Visitors Network . . . . www.pavisnet.com
Pennsylvania.com . . . . www.pennsylvania.com
Rough Guide Travel Pennsylvania travel.roughguides.com/content/331/index.htm
Travel.org-Pennsylvania . . . . .travel.org/pennsyl.html
Yahoo! Get Local Pennsylvania . . . . dir.yahoo.com/Regional/U_S__States/Pennsylvania

— Cities Profiled —

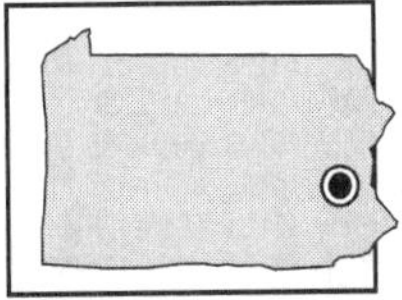

Allentown

Located in Pennsylvania's Lehigh Valley region, Allentown was founded in 1792 and takes its name from William Allen, a Colonial chief justice, merchant, and the second-largest landholder in Pennsylvania. When the British seized control of Philadelphia during the American Revolution in 1777, patriots brought the Liberty Bell to Allentown by cart and hid it for a year under the floor in Zion's Reformed United Church of Christ. Today, that hideaway on Hamilton Mall, the Liberty Bell Shrine, is a major tourist attraction. Other cultural and historical attractions in the area include the Allentown Art Museum; Lehigh County Museum, which features exhibits of the area's original Indian inhabitants, the Lennni-Lenape; Haines Mill Museum, an operating grist mill built in 1760 and restored in 1909; and Trout Hall, Allentown's oldest home. Mayfair Festival of the Arts, a week-long celebration of theater, dance, music, and visual arts, is held each May in Allentown's Cedar Beach Park; and the Great Allentown Fair, one of the nation's top 50 fairs, is held each August.

Population	100,757	**Longitude**	75-28-39 W
Area (Land)	17.7 sq mi	**County**	Lehigh
Area (Water)	0.2 sq mi	**Time Zone**	EST
Elevation	387 ft	**Area Code/s**	610
Latitude	40-35-46 N		

— Average Temperatures and Precipitation —

TEMPERATURES

	Jan	Feb	Mar	Apr	May	Jun	Jul	Aug	Sep	Oct	Nov	Dec
High	34	38	49	60	71	80	85	82	75	64	52	39
Low	19	21	30	39	49	59	64	62	54	43	34	24

PRECIPITATION

	Jan	Feb	Mar	Apr	May	Jun	Jul	Aug	Sep	Oct	Nov	Dec
Inches	3.2	3.0	3.3	3.5	4.2	3.8	4.1	4.3	3.9	2.9	3.9	3.5

— Important Phone Numbers —

	Phone		*Phone*
AAA	610-434-5141	**Medical Referral**	610-402-2273
American Express Travel	610-265-7450	**Poison Control Center**	800-722-7112
Emergency	911	**Time/Temp/Weather**	610-797-5900

— Information Sources —

				Phone	*Fax*
Allentown City Hall 435 Hamilton St.	Allentown	PA	18101	610-437-7511	437-8730
Allentown Community Development 435 Hamilton St Suite 325	Allentown	PA	18101	610-437-7761	437-8781
Allentown Downtown Improvement District Authority 805 Hamilton Mall	Allentown	PA	18101	610-776-7117	776-4117
Allentown Fairgrounds' Agricultural Hall 302 N 17th St	Allentown	PA	18104	610-437-6020	433-4005
Allentown-Lehigh County Chamber of Commerce 462 Walnut St *Web:* www.lehighcountychamber.org	Allentown	PA	18102	610-437-9661	437-4907
Allentown Mayor 435 Hamilton St.	Allentown	PA	18101	610-437-7546	437-8730
Allentown Public Library 1210 W Hamilton St *Web:* www.allentownpl.org	Allentown	PA	18102	610-820-2400	820-0640
Lehigh County 455 W Hamilton St *Web:* www.pavisnet.com/lehigh	Allentown	PA	18101	610-782-3000	820-3093
Lehigh Valley Convention & Visitors Bureau 2200 Ave A *TF:* 800-747-0561 ■ *Web:* lehighvalleypa.org	Bethlehem	PA	18017	610-882-9200	882-0343

On-Line Resources

4Allentown.com	www.4allentown.com
City Knowledge Allentown	www.cityknowledge.com/pa_allentown.htm
Excite.com Allentown City Guide	www.excite.com/travel/countries/united_states/pennsylvania/allentown
Lehigh Valley Town Square	townsquare.ot.com
Region Online Lehigh Valley	www.regiononline.com

— Transportation Services —

AIRPORTS

■ **Lehigh Valley International Airport (ABE)**

	Phone
4 miles NE of downtown(approx 10 minutes) Web: www.lvia.org	610-266-6000

Airport Transportation

	Phone
J & J Ground Transport $35 fare to downtown	800-726-5466
Lehigh Valley Airport Limo $10-15 fare to downtown	800-292-6380

Commercial Airlines

	Phone		*Phone*
Air Canada	800-776-3000	**Northwest**	800-225-2525
AirTran	800-247-8726	**United**	800-241-6522
Continental	800-525-0280	**US Airways**	800-428-4322
Delta	800-221-1212		

Charter Airlines

	Phone		*Phone*
Piedmont Aviation Services Inc	800-548-1978	**Summit Aviation**	800-255-4625

CAR RENTALS

	Phone		*Phone*
Budget	610-391-1300	**Hertz**	610-264-4571
Enterprise	610-266-6460	**National**	610-264-5535
Express	610-782-0850	**Sears**	610-366-1060

LIMO/TAXI

	Phone		*Phone*
ABE Limo	610-821-9303	**J & J Ground Transport**	800-726-5466
Elite Limousine	610-435-1441	**Lehigh Valley Airport Limo**	800-292-6380
First Class Limousine	610-791-3330	**Quick Service Taxi**	610-434-8132

MASS TRANSIT

	Phone
LANTA Bus $1.35 Base fare	610-776-7433

— Accommodations —

HOTELS, MOTELS, RESORTS

				Phone	*Fax*
Allentown Comfort Inn 7625 Imperial Way *TF:* 800-228-5150	Allentown	PA	18106	610-391-0344	391-0974
Allentown Hilton 904 Hamilton St. *TF:* 800-999-7784	Allentown	PA	18101	610-433-2221	433-6455
Allenwood Motel 1058 Hausman Rd	Allentown	PA	18104	610-395-3707	
Americus Center 549 Hamilton St.	Allentown	PA	18101	610-434-6100	434-6828
Best Western 185 S 3rd St *TF:* 800-882-0113	Easton	PA	18042	610-253-9131	252-5145
Budget Inn 731 Hausman Rd	Allentown	PA	18104	610-395-3377	
Comfort Suites 3712 Hamilton Blvd. *TF:* 800-228-5150	Allentown	PA	18103	610-437-9100	437-0221
Comfort Suites Bethlehem 120 W 3rd St. *TF:* 800-228-5140	Bethlehem	PA	10815	610-882-9700	882-4389
Courtyard by Marriott 2160 Motel Dr. *TF:* 800-321-2211 ■ *Web:* courtyard.com/ABECY	Bethlehem	PA	18018	610-317-6200	317-2606

Allentown — Hotels, Motels, Resorts (Cont'd)

Name	City	State	Zip	Phone	Fax
Days Inn & Conference Center 1151 Bulldog Dr *TF:* 888-395-5200	Allentown	PA	18104	610-395-3731	395-9899
Days Inn Lehigh Street 2622 Lehigh St *TF:* 800-329-7466	Allentown	PA	18103	610-797-1234	797-3452
Econo Lodge of Allentown 2115 Downyflake Ln *TF:* 800-553-2666	Allentown	PA	18103	610-797-2200	797-2818
Fairfield by Marriott 2140 Motel Dr *TF:* 800-228-2800	Bethlehem	PA	18018	610-867-8681	758-9000
Fernwood Resort & Country Club Rt 209 *TF:* 800-233-8103	Bushkill	PA	18324	570-588-9500	588-6680
Hampton Inn 7471 Keebler Way *TF:* 800-486-7866	Allentown	PA	18106	610-391-1500	391-0386
Holiday Inn Bethlehem Rts 512 & 22 *TF:* 800-222-8512	Bethlehem	PA	18020	610-866-5800	867-9120
Holiday Inn Conference Center I-78 & Rt 100 S **Fax:* Sales ■ *TF:* 800-465-4329	Lehigh Valley	PA	18031	610-391-1000	391-1346*
Holiday Inn Express Allentown Rt 22 *TF:* 800-465-4329	Allentown	PA	18104	610-435-7880	432-2555
Holiday Inn Express Hotel & Suites 3620 Hamilton Blvd *TF:* 800-465-4329	Allentown	PA	18103	610-437-9255	437-9541
Howard Johnson Inn & Suites 3220 Hamilton Blvd *TF:* 800-446-4656	Allentown	PA	18103	610-439-4000	439-8947
Lehigh Motor Inn 5828 Memorial Rd	Allentown	PA	18104	610-395-3331	395-5302
McIntosh Inn 1701 Catasaqua Rd *TF:* 800-444-2775	Allentown	PA	18103	610-264-7531	264-5474
Microtel Allentown 1880 Steel Stone Rd *TF:* 888-771-7171	Allentown	PA	18103	610-266-9070	266-0377
Ramada Inn 1500 MacArthur Rd *TF:* 800-272-6232	Whitehall	PA	18052	610-439-1037	770-1425
Red Roof Inn 1846 Catasauqua Rd *TF:* 800-883-7663	Allentown	PA	18103	610-264-5404	264-7618
Residence Inn by Marriott 2180 Motel Dr *TF:* 800-331-3131 ■ *Web:* residenceinn.com/ABERI	Bethlehem	PA	18018	610-317-2662	317-2663
Sheraton Inn Jetport 3400 Airport Rd *TF:* 800-325-3535 ■ *Web:* www.sheratonjetport.com ■ *E-mail:* info@sheratonjetport.com	Allentown	PA	18103	610-266-1000	266-1888
Travelodge 321 3rd St *TF:* 800-578-7878	Coopersburg	PA	18036	610-282-1212	282-1052

— Restaurants —

Name	City	State	Zip	Phone
Akatsuki Japanese Restaurant (Japanese) 2653 MacArthur Rd *Web:* www.acclaimed.com/sushi/index.html	Allentown	PA	18102	610-264-5881
Aladdin (Middle Eastern) 651 Union Blvd	Allentown	PA	18103	610-437-4243
Ambassador Restaurant (American) 3750 Hamilton Blvd	Allentown	PA	18103	610-432-2025
Amigo Mio Cafe (Mexican) 545 Cleveland St	Allentown	PA	18103	610-776-2026
Appennino Ristorante (Italian) 3079 Willow St	Allentown	PA	18104	610-799-2727
Attilio's Restaurant (Italian) Cedar Crest Plaza Shopping Ctr	Allentown	PA	18104	610-395-7006
Bay Leaf (International) 935 Hamilton Blvd	Allentown	PA	18101	610-433-4211
Beirut (Middle Eastern) 651 Union Blvd	Allentown	PA	18103	610-437-4023
Brass Rail Restaurant (Italian) 1137 Hamilton St	Allentown	PA	18103	610-434-9383
Captain's Table (American) 2720 S Pike Ave	Allentown	PA	18103	610-797-3127
Casa Bianca (Italian) 3104 Hamilton Blvd	Allentown	PA	18103	610-432-2770
Century Cafe (American) 546 N 7th St	Allentown	PA	18102	610-821-0545
China House (Chinese) 4783 Tilghman St	Allentown	PA	18104	610-395-1855
Damascus Restaurant (Middle Eastern) 449 N 2nd St	Allentown	PA	18102	610-432-2036
Federal Grill (American) 536 Hamilton St *Web:* www.federalgrill.com	Allentown	PA	18102	610-776-7600
Foo Joy (Chinese) 3245 Hamilton Blvd	Allentown	PA	18103	610-432-1800
Gregory's (American) 2201 Schoenersville Rd	Allentown	PA	18103	610-264-9301
Hoffbrau Haus (American) 1027 E Hamilton St	Allentown	PA	18103	610-432-2620
House of Chen (Chinese) 732 Hamilton Mall	Allentown	PA	18101	610-439-1330
Kern's Restaurant (American) 2101 W Liberty St	Allentown	PA	18104	610-432-7553
King George Inn (International) Cedar Crest & Hamilton Blvds	Allentown	PA	18103	610-435-1723
La Cucina (Italian) 4558 Crackersport Rd	Allentown	PA	18104	610-481-9600
Lobaido's Cafe (Italian) 442 N 8th St	Allentown	PA	18102	610-820-7570
Mexicana Grille (Mexican) 407 N 7th St	Allentown	PA	18102	610-776-6376
O'Hara's Pub & Restaurant (American) 3712 Hamilton Blvd	Allentown	PA	18103	610-437-9400
Pho Vung Tau (Vietnamese) 1500 Union Blvd	Allentown	PA	18103	610-433-3405
Pip's (Steak/Seafood) 904 Hamilton Mall	Allentown	PA	18102	610-433-1820
Ritz Barbecue (Barbecue) 17th & Chew Sts	Allentown	PA	18104	610-432-0952
Robata Of Tokyo (Japanese) 39 S 9th St	Allentown	PA	18102	610-821-6900
Spice of Life (Continental) 1259 S Cedar Crest Blvd	Allentown	PA	18103	610-821-8081
Star of India (Indian) 229 W Hamilton St	Allentown	PA	18101	610-820-0625
Sunset Grille (Tex Mex) 6751 Ruppsville Rd	Allentown	PA	18103	610-395-9622
Villa Romana (Italian) 1908 Walbert Ave	Allentown	PA	18104	610-437-8877
Villa Rosa (Italian) 3 American Pkwy	Allentown	PA	18101	610-435-5111
Washington Grille (American) 929 W Washington St	Allentown	PA	18102	610-432-0300
Youell's Oyster House (Seafood) 23rd & Walnut Sts	Allentown	PA	18104	610-439-1203

— Goods and Services —

SHOPPING

Name	City	State	Zip	Phone	Fax
Barns The 4186 Easton Ave *Web:* www.christmasbarn.com	Bethlehem	PA	18020	610-861-0477	861-5986
Hamilton Mall Shopping District 805 Hamilton Mall	Allentown	PA	18101	610-776-7117	
Lehigh Valley Mall 250 Lehigh Valley Mall	Whitehall	PA	18052	610-264-5511	264-5957

BANKS

Name	City	State	Zip	Phone	Fax
First Union National Bank 702 Hamilton Mall *TF:* 800-225-5332	Allentown	PA	18101	610-821-7452	821-7484
Firstrust Bank 701 Hamilton Mall	Allentown	PA	18101	610-437-3701	434-4030
PNC Bank NA 730 W Emmaus Ave	Allentown	PA	18103	610-797-2860	797-4566
Summit Bank 15th & Allen Sts	Allentown	PA	18102	610-776-6788	776-6712

BUSINESS SERVICES

Name	Phone
Adecco Employment Personnel Services	610-398-6619
Allied Personnel Services	610-821-0220
BAX Global	800-225-5229
DHL Worldwide Express	800-225-5345
Federal Express	800-238-5355
Interim Personnel	610-432-7500
Kelly Services	610-776-2310
Manpower Temporary Services	610-395-8900
Post Office	610-266-5300
Sir Speedy Printing	610-264-5660
UPS	800-742-5877

— Media —

PUBLICATIONS

Name	City	State	Zip	Phone	Fax
Bethlehem Star 531 Main St **Fax:* News Rm	Bethlehem	PA	18018	610-867-5000	866-1771*
Eastern Pennsylvania Business Journal 65 E Elizabeth Ave Suite 700 *TF:* 800-328-1026	Bethlehem	PA	18018	610-807-9619	807-9612
Express-Times‡ 30 N 4th St *TF:* 800-360-3601 ■ *Web:* www.express-times.com ■ *E-mail:* staff@express-times.com	Easton	PA	18044	610-258-7171	258-7130
Lehigh Valley Magazine 910 13th Ave	Bethlehem	PA	18018	610-691-8833	861-9924
Morning Call‡ PO Box 1260 *TF:* 800-666-5492 ■ *Web:* www.mcall.com	Allentown	PA	18105	610-820-6500	820-6693

‡Daily newspapers

TELEVISION

Name	City	State	Zip	Phone	Fax
KYW-TV Ch 3 (CBS) 101 S Independence Mall E *Web:* www.kyw.com	Philadelphia	PA	19106	215-238-4700	238-4783
WCAU-TV Ch 10 (NBC) 10 Monument Rd *Web:* www.nbc10.com	Bala Cynwyd	PA	19004	610-668-5510	668-3700
WFMZ-TV Ch 69 (Ind) 300 E Rock Rd *Web:* www.wfmz.com/	Allentown	PA	18103	610-797-4530	791-3000
WLVT-TV Ch 39 (PBS) 123 Sesame St *Web:* www.lehighvalleypbs.org	Bethlehem	PA	18015	610-867-4677	867-3544
WNYW-TV Ch 5 (Fox) 205 E 67th St	New York	NY	10021	212-452-5555	249-1182
WPVI-TV Ch 6 (ABC) 4100 City Line Ave *Web:* abcnews.go.com/local/wpvi	Philadelphia	PA	19131	215-878-9700	581-4530

RADIO

Name	City	State	Zip	Phone	Fax
WAEB-AM 790 kHz (N/T) PO Box 9876	Allentown	PA	18105	610-434-1742	434-3808
WAEB-FM 104.1 MHz (AC) 1541 Alta Dr 4th Fl *Web:* www.b104.com	Whitehall	PA	18052	610-434-1742	434-6288

Allentown — Radio (Cont'd)

				Phone	Fax
WDIY-FM 88.1 MHz (NPR) 301 Broadway	Bethlehem	PA	18015	610-694-8100	954-9474
Web: www.wdiyfm.org ■ *E-mail:* fm881@wdiyfm.org					
WEST-AM 1400 kHz (Nost) 436 Northampton St	Easton	PA	18042	610-250-9557	250-9675
WGPA-AM 1100 kHz (Oldies) 528 N New St	Bethlehem	PA	18018	610-866-8074	866-9381
WHOL-AM 1600 kHz (Misc) 1125 Colorado St	Allentown	PA	18103	610-434-4801	
WLEV-FM 100.7 MHz (AC) 2158 Ave C	Bethlehem	PA	18017	610-266-7600	231-0400
WODE-FM 99.9 MHz (Oldies) 107 W Paxinosa Rd	Easton	PA	18040	610-258-6155	253-3384
WTKZ-AM 1320 kHz (Sports) 961 Marcon Blvd Suite 400	Allentown	PA	18103	610-264-4040	266-6464
Web: www.wtkz.com ■ *E-mail:* info@wtkz.com					
WZZO-FM 95.1 MHz (Rock) 1541 Alta Dr Suite 400	Whitehall	PA	18052	610-821-9559	434-6288

— Colleges/Universities —

				Phone	Fax
Allentown Business School 1501 Lehigh St	Allentown	PA	18103	610-791-5100	791-7810
Web: www.chooseabs.com ■ *E-mail:* absinfo@allentownbusinesssch.com					
Allentown College of Saint Francis DeSales 2755 Station Ave	Center Valley	PA	18034	610-282-1100	282-2254*
**Fax:* Admissions ■ *TF Admissions:* 800-228-5114 ■ *Web:* www.allencol.edu ■ *E-mail:* finley@www.allencol.edu					
Cedar Crest College 100 College Dr	Allentown	PA	18104	610-437-4471	606-4647*
**Fax:* Admissions ■ *TF:* 800-360-1222 ■ *Web:* www.cedarcrest.edu ■ *E-mail:* cccadmis@ccdarcrest.edu					
Lafayette College 118 Markle Hall	Easton	PA	18042	610-330-5000	330-5355
Web: www.lafayette.edu ■ *E-mail:* faccipop@lafayette.edu					
Lehigh Carbon Community College 4525 Education Pk Dr	Schnecksville	PA	18078	610-799-2121	799-1159*
**Fax:* Library ■ *Web:* www.lccc.edu					
Lehigh University 27 Memorial Dr W	Bethlehem	PA	18015	610-758-3000	758-4361
Web: www.lehigh.edu					
Lincoln Technical Institute 5151 Tilghman St	Allentown	PA	18104	610-398-5301	395-2706
Web: www.lincolntech.com					
Moravian College 1200 Main St	Bethlehem	PA	18018	610-861-1300	861-1577*
**Fax:* Library ■ *Web:* www.moravian.edu					
Muhlenberg College 2400 W Chew St	Allentown	PA	18104	610-821-3100	821-3234
Web: www.muhlberg.edu ■ *E-mail:* admissions@hal.muhlberg.edu					
Northampton Community College 3835 Green Pond Rd	Bethlehem	PA	18020	610-861-5500	861-4560
Web: www.nrhm.cc.pa.us					
Pennsylvania State University Lehigh Valley Campus 8380 Mohr Ln	Fogelsville	PA	18051	610-285-5000	285-5220
Web: www.lv.psu.edu					
Welder Training & Testing Institute 1144 N Graham St	Allentown	PA	18103	610-820-9551	820-0271
TF: 800-223-9884					

— Hospitals —

				Phone	Fax
Easton Hospital 250 S 21st St	Easton	PA	18042	610-250-4000	250-4877
TF: 800-532-1313 ■ *Web:* www.eastonhospital.org					
Lehigh Valley Hospital 17th & Chew PO Box 689	Allentown	PA	18105	610-402-8000	402-9696*
**Fax:* Admitting ■ *Web:* www.lvh.com ■ *E-mail:* 402care@lvhhn.org					
Muhlenberg Hospital Center 2545 Schoenersville Rd	Bethlehem	PA	18017	610-861-2200	861-7747
Sacred Heart Hospital 421 Chew St	Allentown	PA	18102	610-776-4500	776-4559
Saint Luke's Hospital 801 Ostrum St	Bethlehem	PA	18015	610-954-4000	954-4149*
**Fax:* Admitting					

— Attractions —

				Phone	Fax
Allentown Art Museum 5th & Court Sts	Allentown	PA	18105	610-432-4333	434-7409
Web: www.lvartspage.org/artmseum.htm					
Allentown Symphony Orchestra 23 N 6th St	Allentown	PA	18101	610-432-7961	432-6009
Web: www.allentownsymphony.org ■ *E-mail:* info@allentownsymphony.org					
Baker Center for the Arts 2400 Chew St Muhlenberg College	Allentown	PA	18104	610-821-3333	821-3633
Ballet Guild of the Lehigh Valley 556 Main St	Bethlehem	PA	18018	610-865-0353	865-2698
Web: www.bglv.org ■ *E-mail:* ythballet@aol.com					
Bear Creek Ski & Recreation Area 101 Doe Mountain Ln	Macungie	PA	18062	610-682-7100	682-7110
TF: 800-475-4363					
Blue Mountain Ski Area 1660 Blue Mountain Dr	Palmerton	PA	18071	610-826-7700	826-7723
Web: www.skibluemt.com ■ *E-mail:* information@skibluemt.com					
Buchman Frank House 117 N 11th St	Allentown	PA	18105	610-435-4664	435-9812
Burnside Plantation 1461 Schoenersville Rd	Bethlehem	PA	18016	610-868-5044	868-5044
Bushkill Park 2100 Bushkill Park Dr	Easton	PA	18040	610-258-6941	258-6004
Web: www.bushkillpark.com ■ *E-mail:* party@bushkillpark.com					
Cedar Crest Stage Co 100 College Dr	Allentown	PA	18104	610-437-4471	606-4654
Civic Theatre 527 N 19th St	Allentown	PA	18104	610-432-8943	432-7381
Web: www.civictheatre.com					
Colonial Industrial Quarter 459 Old York Rd	Bethlehem	PA	18016	610-882-0450	882-0460
Crayola Factory 30 Centre Sq Two Rivers Landing	Easton	PA	18042	610-515-8000	559-6690
Web: www.crayola.com/fact_index.html					
Crystal Cave Park Crystal Cave Rd	Kutztown	PA	19530	610-683-6765	
Delaware National Scenic River Delaware Water Gap National Recreation Area	Bushkill	PA	18324	570-588-2435	588-2780
Web: www.nps.gov/dela/					
Delaware Water Gap National Recreation Area	Bushkill	PA	18324	570-588-2435	588-2780
Web: www.nps.gov/dewa/					
Discovery Center of Science & Technology 511 E 3rd St	Bethlehem	PA	18015	610-865-5010	865-5010
Web: www.discovery-center.org/					
Dorney Park & Wildwater Kingdom 3830 Dorney Park Rd	Allentown	PA	18104	610-395-3724	391-7685*
**Fax:* Mktg ■ *TF Sales:* 800-551-5656 ■ *Web:* www.dorneypark.com					
Dutch Springs 4733 Hanoverville Rd	Bethlehem	PA	18017	610-759-2270	759-9441
Web: www.dutchsprings.com ■ *E-mail:* dutchspr@epix.net					
Fairgrounds Farmers Market 17th & Chew Sts	Allentown	PA	18104	610-432-8425	427-0891
Haines Mill Museum 3600 Haines Mill Rd	Allentown	PA	18104	610-435-4664	
Holland Raymond E Art Collection 111 N 4th St	Allentown	PA	18102	610-821-0111	821-9070
Kemerer Museum of Decorative Arts 427 N New St	Bethlehem	PA	18016	610-868-6868	882-0460
Web: www.historicbethlehem.org/decor.htm					
Lehigh County Historical Society Hamilton & 5th St	Allentown	PA	18101	610-435-4664	435-9812
Lehigh County Museum 501 Hamilton St Old Courthouse	Allentown	PA	18101	610-435-4664	435-9812
Web: www.voicenet.com/~lchs					
Lehigh Valley Chamber Orchestra PO Box 20641	Allentown	PA	18002	610-266-8555	266-8525
Web: www.lvco.org ■ *E-mail:* lvco@fast.net					
Lenni Lenape Historical Society 2825 Fish Hatchery Rd	Allentown	PA	18103	610-797-2121	797-2801
Web: www.lenape.org ■ *E-mail:* lenape@comcat.com					
Liberty Bell Shrine 622 Hamilton Mall	Allentown	PA	18101	610-435-4232	
Lost River Caverns 726 Durham St	Hellertown	PA	18055	610-838-8767	838-2961
Malcolm W Gross Memorial Rose Garden 2700 Parkway Blvd	Allentown	PA	18104	610-437-7628	437-7685
Moore Hugh Historical Park & National Canal Museum 30 Centre Sq	Easton	PA	18042	610-515-8000	
Web: canals.org ■ *E-mail:* ncm@canals.org					
Museum of Indian Culture 2825 Fish Hatchery Rd	Allentown	PA	18103	610-797-2121	797-2801
Web: www.lenape.org/aboutmuseum.html					
Pennsylvania Sinfonia Orchestra 1524 Linden St	Allentown	PA	18102	610-434-7811	434-7811
Queen City Nursery Fish Hatchery Rd	Allentown	PA	18103	610-437-7656	
Repertory Dance Theatre 1402 Linden St	Allentown	PA	18102	610-433-1680	967-2826
Trout Hall 414 Walnut St	Allentown	PA	18101	610-435-4664	435-9812

SPORTS TEAMS & FACILITIES

				Phone	Fax
Allentown Ambassadors (baseball) 1511-25 Hamilton St	Allentown	PA	18102	610-437-6800	437-6804
Web: www.ambassadorbaseball.com					
Lehigh Valley Steam (soccer) PO Box 4000	Easton	PA	18043	610-250-2273	250-6552
Web: www.steamsoccer.com					

Allentown — Sports Teams & Facilities (Cont'd)

				Phone	Fax
Nazareth Speedway Hwy 191	Nazareth	PA	18064	610-759-8800	759-9055
TF: 888-629-7223					
Parkette National Gymnastic Team 401 ML King Jr Dr	Allentown	PA	18102	610-433-0011	433-8948

— Events —

	Phone
Allentown Tree Lighting Ceremony (late November)	610-776-7117
Antique Show (late October)	610-433-7541
Apparitions of Allentown: A Walk of Historic Haunts (late October)	610-435-4664
Bach Choir of Bethlehem Christmas Concert (early December)	610-866-4382
Boo at the Zoo (late October)	610-799-4171
Celtic Classic Highland Games & Festival (late September)	610-868-9599
Cement Belt Free Fair (mid-June)	610-262-9750
Christkindlmarkt (late November-mid-December)	610-861-0678
Das Awkscht Fescht (early August)	610-967-2317
Elvis Birthday Bash (mid-January)	610-252-3132
Fall Foliage Festival (October)	610-799-4171
German Festival (late June-early July)	800-963-8824
Great Allentown Fair (late August-early September)	610-433-7541
Harvest Festival (mid-October)	610-868-5044
Lehigh Valley Air Show (mid-October)	610-231-5229
Lights in the Parkway (late November-mid-January)	610-437-7616
Mayfair Festival of the Arts (late May)	610-437-6900
Mule & Viking Art & Craft Show (early October)	610-821-3305
Musikfest (mid-August)	610-861-0678
Pennsylvania Shakespeare Festival (mid-June-mid-July)	610-282-3192
Riverside Art Festival (mid-September)	610-250-6710
Spring Corn Festival (early March)	610-797-2121
Time of Thanksgiving (mid-November)	610-797-2121
Wheels of Time Rod & Custom Jamboree (mid-August)	610-865-4114

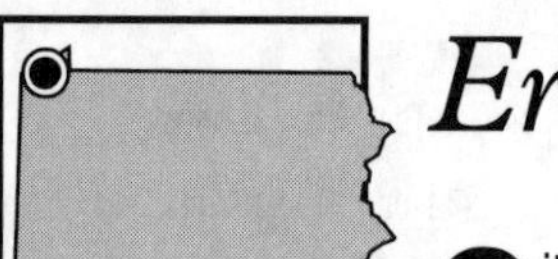

Erie

Situated on the shores of Lake Erie, the city of Erie is the third largest in Pennsylvania. Its deepwater port (five miles long and two miles wide) is considered to be the most accessible natural harbor on the Great Lakes, and the city is steeped in maritime history. The area was the site of the War of 1812's Battle of Lake Erie, in which Commander Oliver Hazard Perry defeated the British fleet. Perry's relief flagship, the US Brig Niagara, has been reconstructed and is moored on Erie's bayfront. The entire bayfront is the site of a major development that will include a maritime museum, a new county library, a hotel, and shops. Most of the city's numerous historical attractions, dating from the early 19th century, are located in the heart of downtown Erie. Next to the city is Presque Isle State Park, a 3,200-acre sandy peninsula that juts seven miles into Lake Erie and is a popular destination for tourists.

Population	102,640	**Longitude**	80-08-53 W
Area (Land)	22.0 sq mi	**County**	Erie
Area (Water)	6.0 sq mi	**Time Zone**	EST
Elevation	650 ft	**Area Code/s**	814
Latitude	42-12-92 N		

— Average Temperatures and Precipitation —

TEMPERATURES

	Jan	Feb	Mar	Apr	May	Jun	Jul	Aug	Sep	Oct	Nov	Dec
High	33	34	44	55	66	75	80	79	72	61	49	38
Low	18	18	28	38	48	58	63	62	56	46	37	25

PRECIPITATION

	Jan	Feb	Mar	Apr	May	Jun	Jul	Aug	Sep	Oct	Nov	Dec
Inches	2.2	2.3	3.0	3.2	3.4	4.1	3.4	4.1	4.4	3.8	4.0	3.6

— Important Phone Numbers —

	Phone		Phone
AAA	814-454-0123	**Poison Control Center**	412-681-6669
Arts Council Hotline	814-452-2000	**Weather**	216-265-2370
Emergency	911		

— Information Sources —

				Phone	Fax
Better Business Bureau Serving Western Pennsylvania 300 6th Ave Suite 100-UL	Pittsburgh	PA	15222	412-456-2700	456-2739
Web: www.pittsburgh.bbb.org					
Blasco Raymond M Memorial Library 160 E Front St	Erie	PA	16507	814-451-6900	451-6907
Web: www.ecls.lib.pa.us ■ *E-mail:* erielib@velocity.net					
Erie Area Chamber of Commerce 109 Boston Store Pl	Erie	PA	16501	814-454-7191	459-0241
Web: www.erie.net/~chamber/corner.html ■ *E-mail:* erie-chamber@erie.net					
Erie Area Convention & Visitors Bureau 101 Boston Store Pl	Erie	PA	16501	814-454-7191	459-0241
Web: www.erie.net/~chamber/tourist.html ■ *E-mail:* Erie-Tourism@erie.net					
Erie City Hall 626 State St	Erie	PA	16501	814-870-1234	870-1386
Erie County 140 W 6th St	Erie	PA	16501	814-451-6000	451-6350
Erie Mayor 626 State St	Erie	PA	16501	814-870-1201	870-1208
Tullio Louis J Convention Center 809 French St	Erie	PA	16501	814-452-4857	455-9931
Web: www.erieciviccenter.com/arena.htm					

On-Line Resources

Access Erie	www.accesserie.com
Anthill City Guide Erie	www.anthill.com/city.asp?city=erie
Area Guide Erie	erie.areaguides.net
City Knowledge Erie	www.cityknowledge.com/pa_erie.htm
Excite.com Erie City Guide	www.excite.com/travel/countries/united_states/pennsylvania/erie

— Transportation Services —

AIRPORTS

■ **Erie International Airport (ERI)**	Phone
6 miles SW of downtown (approx 15 minutes)	814-833-4258

Airport Transportation

	Phone
Erie Metropolitan Transit Authority $1.10 fare to downtown	814-459-4287

Commercial Airlines

	Phone		Phone
Delta	800-221-1212	**United**	800-241-6522
Northwest	800-225-2525	**United Express**	800-241-6522
Northwest Airlink	814-833-3030	**US Airways**	800-428-4322
TWA Express	800-221-2000	**US Airways Express**	800-428-4322

Charter Airlines

	Phone
Erie Aviation	814-833-1188

CAR RENTALS

	Phone		Phone
Avis	814-833-9879	**Enterprise**	814-864-6899
Budget	814-838-4502	**Hertz**	814-838-9691
CarTemps USA	814-868-3677	**New Car Rental**	814-833-3500

Erie (Cont'd)

LIMO/TAXI

	Phone		Phone
Area Taxi	814-725-3677	Executive Limousine	814-833-8330
Classic Limo	814-456-8614	Rupp Limousine	814-452-2025
Executive Limousine	814-833-3500	Yellow Cab	814-455-4441

MASS TRANSIT

	Phone
Erie Metropolitan Transit Authority $1.10 Base fare	814-452-3515

RAIL/BUS

				Phone
Amtrak Station 14th & Peach Sts Union Depot *TF:* 800-872-7245	Erie	PA	16501	800-872-7245
Greyhound/Trailways Bus Station 5759 Peach St	Erie	PA	16509	814-864-5949

— Accommodations —

HOTELS, MOTELS, RESORTS

				Phone	Fax
Avalon Hotel 16 W 10th St *TF:* 800-822-5011	Erie	PA	16501	814-459-2220	459-2322
Bel Aire Hotel 2800 W 8th St *TF:* 800-888-8781 ■ *Web:* www.bel-airehotel.com	Erie	PA	16505	814-833-1116	838-3242
Best Western Presque Isle Country Inn 6467 Sterrettania Rd *TF:* 800-528-1234	Fairview	PA	16415	814-838-7647	838-7647
Capri Motel 2540 W 8th St	Erie	PA	16505	814-838-2081	
Comfort Inn 8051 Peach St *TF:* 800-221-2222	Erie	PA	16509	814-866-6666	864-1367
Cross Creek Resort RD 3 Box 152	Titusville	PA	16354	814-827-9611	827-2062
Days Inn 7415 Schultz Rd *TF:* 800-329-7466	Erie	PA	16509	814-868-8521	866-8073
Days Inn Conference Center Meadville 18360 Conneaut Lake Rd *TF:* 800-329-7466	Meadville	PA	16335	814-337-4264	337-7304
Econo Lodge 8050 Peach St *TF:* 800-553-2666	Erie	PA	16509	814-866-5544	864-6218
Erie Downtown Inn 205 W 10th St	Erie	PA	16501	814-456-6251	455-8500
Glass House Inn 3202 W 26th St *TF:* 800-956-7222	Erie	PA	16506	814-833-7751	833-4222
Hampton Inn 3041 W 12th St	Erie	PA	16505	814-835-4200	835-5212
Holiday Inn Downtown 18 W 18th St *TF:* 800-465-4329	Erie	PA	16501	814-456-2961	456-7067
Lakeview-on-the-Lake Motel 8696 E Lake Rd	Erie	PA	16511	814-899-6948	
Microtel 8100 Peach St *TF:* 800-975-4400	Erie	PA	16509	814-864-1010	866-6661
Motel 6 7875 Peach St *TF:* 800-466-8356	Erie	PA	16509	814-864-4811	868-1277
Quality Inn & Suites 8040 Perry Hwy *TF:* 800-228-5151	Erie	PA	16509	814-864-4911	864-3743
Ramada Inn Rt 6 N *TF:* 800-272-6232	Edinboro	PA	16412	814-734-5650	734-7532
Ramada Inn 6101 Wattsburg Rd *TF:* 800-272-6232	Erie	PA	16509	814-825-3100	825-0857
Red Carpet Inn 7455 Schultz Rd	Erie	PA	16509	814-868-0879	866-5974
Red Roof Inn 7865 Perry Hwy *TF:* 800-843-7663	Erie	PA	16509	814-868-5246	868-5450
Residence Inn by Marriott 8061 Peach St *TF:* 800-331-3131 ■ *Web:* www.residenceinn.com/ERIRI	Erie	PA	16509	814-864-2500	864-0688
Riverside Inn 1 Fountain Ave	Cambridge Springs	PA	16403	814-398-4645	
Riviera Motel 3101 W Lake Rd	Erie	PA	16505	814-838-1997	833-0723
Scott's Beachcomber Inn 2930 W 6th St	Erie	PA	16505	814-838-1961	
Vernondale Motel 5422 W Lake Rd	Erie	PA	16505	814-838-2372	

— Restaurants —

				Phone
Barbato's (Italian) 1707 State St	Erie	PA	16501	814-459-2158
Calamari's (Seafood) 1317 State St	Erie	PA	16501	814-459-4276
China Garden Restaurant (Chinese) 6801 Peach St	Erie	PA	16509	814-868-2695
Colony Pub & Grille (American) 2670 W 8th St	Erie	PA	16505	814-838-2162
Eduardo's (American) 3979 W Ridge Rd	Erie	PA	16506	814-838-9827
Hibachi Japanese Steak House (Japanese) 3000 W 12th St	Erie	PA	16505	814-838-2495
Hoss's Steak & Sea House (Steak/Seafood) 3302 W 26th St	Erie	PA	16506	814-838-6718
Marketplace Grill (American) 319 State St	Erie	PA	16507	814-455-7272
Panos Restaurant (Homestyle) 1504 W 38th St	Erie	PA	16508	814-866-0517
Pio's Italian Restaurant (Italian) 815 East Ave	Erie	PA	16503	814-456-8866
Porters (American) 121 W 14th St	Erie	PA	16501	814-452-2787
Pufferbelly (Steak/Seafood) 414 French St	Erie	PA	16507	814-454-1557
Shaggy Dog (American) 414 W 8th St	Erie	PA	16502	814-454-6821
Smuggler's Wharf (Steak/Seafood) 3 State St	Erie	PA	16507	814-459-4273
Spinner McGee's Steak House (Steak) 4940 Peach St	Erie	PA	16509	814-866-7746
Sullivan's Pub & Eatery (American) 301 French St	Erie	PA	16507	814-452-3446
Valerio's (Italian) 3205 Pittsburgh Ave	Erie	PA	16509	814-833-2959
Waterfront Seafood & Steakhouse (Steak/Seafood) 4 State St	Erie	PA	16509	814-456-8642

— Goods and Services —

SHOPPING

				Phone	Fax
Mill Creek Mall 654 Mill Creek Mall	Erie	PA	16565	814-868-9000	864-1193
Village West Plaza 3330 W 26th St	Erie	PA	16506	814-838-9762	838-7743

BANKS

				Phone	Fax
Marquette Savings Bank 920 Peach St	Erie	PA	16501	814-455-4481	453-5345
Mellon Bank 1128 State St	Erie	PA	16501	814-453-7400	453-7208
Northwest Savings Bank 401 State St	Erie	PA	16501	814-454-1275	455-4381
PNC Bank 901 State St **Fax:* Cust Svc	Erie	PA	16501	814-871-9316	871-9456*
Sky Bank 831 State St	Erie	PA	16501	814-453-6002	456-2226

BUSINESS SERVICES

	Phone		Phone
Airborne Express	800-247-2676	Mail Boxes Etc	800-789-4623
BAX Global	800-225-5229	Manpower Temporary Services	814-453-7901
DHL Worldwide Express	800-225-5345	Olsten Staffing Services	814-452-6555
Executive Secretarial Services	814-459-5667	Post Office	814-898-7300
Federal Express	800-238-5355	UPS	800-742-5877
Kinko's	814-866-5679		

— Media —

PUBLICATIONS

				Phone	Fax
Erie Daily Times‡ 205 W 12th St *TF:* 800-352-0043 ■ *Web:* www.goerie.com	Erie	PA	16534	814-870-1600	870-1808
Erie Weekender‡ 205 W 12th St	Erie	PA	16534	814-870-1600	870-1808
Morning News‡ 205 W 12th St *TF:* 800-352-0043 ■ *Web:* www.goerie.com	Erie	PA	16534	814-870-1600	870-1808
Times Leader‡ 15 N Main St *Web:* www.leader.net	Wilkes-Barre	PA	18711	570-829-7100	829-5537

‡Daily newspapers

TELEVISION

				Phone	Fax
WFXP-TV Ch 66 (Fox) 8455 Peach St	Erie	PA	16509	814-864-2400	864-5393
WICU-TV Ch 12 (NBC) 3514 State St	Erie	PA	16508	814-454-5201	455-0703
WJET-TV Ch 24 (ABC) 8455 Peach St *Web:* www.wjet-tv24.com/ ■ *E-mail:* wjet@erie.net	Erie	PA	16509	814-864-2400	864-1704
WQLN-TV Ch 54 (PBS) 8425 Peach St *Web:* www.wqln.org	Erie	PA	16509	814-864-3001	864-4077
WSEE-TV Ch 35 (CBS) 1220 Peach St	Erie	PA	16501	814-455-7575	459-3500

RADIO

				Phone	Fax
WFLP-AM 1330 kHz (N/T) 2953 W 12th St *Web:* www.flagship1330.com ■ *E-mail:* flagship@erie.net	Erie	PA	16505	814-835-5000	835-8395
WJET-FM 102.3 MHz (Alt) 4216 Sterrettania Rd *Web:* www.jet102.com	Erie	PA	16506	814-836-8000	836-8336
WLKK-AM 1400 kHz (N/T) 18 W 9th St *Web:* www.wlkk.com ■ *E-mail:* wlkk@erie.net	Erie	PA	16501	814-456-7034	456-0292
WQLN-FM 91.3 Mhz (NPR) 8425 Peach St *Web:* www.wqln.org/ ■ *E-mail:* wqln@wqln.org	Erie	PA	16509	814-864-3001	864-4077
WRIE-AM 1260 kHz (Nost) 471 Robison Rd	Erie	PA	16509	814-868-5355	868-1876
WXKC-FM 99.9 MHz (AC) 471 Robison Rd	Erie	PA	16509	814-868-5355	868-1876

Erie (Cont'd)

— Colleges/Universities —

	City	State	ZIP	Phone	Fax
Behrend College 5091 Station Rd	Erie	PA	16563	814-898-6000	898-6461
Web: www.pserie.psu.edu					
Edinboro University of Pennsylvania	Edinboro	PA	16444	814-732-2000	734-2420
TF Admissions: 800-626-2203 ■ *Web:* www.edinboro.edu ■ *E-mail:* postmaster@edinboro.edu					
Erie Business Center Main 246 W 9th St	Erie	PA	16501	814-456-7504	456-4882
TF: 800-352-3743 ■ *Web:* www.eriebc.com					
Gannon University 109 University Sq	Erie	PA	16541	814-871-7000	871-5803
TF: 800-426-6668 ■ *Web:* www.gannon.edu					
Mercyhurst College 501 E 38th St	Erie	PA	16546	814-824-2000	824-2071
TF: 800-825-1926 ■ *Web:* eden.mercy.edu ■ *E-mail:* admug@paradise.mercy.edu					

— Hospitals —

	City	State	ZIP	Phone	Fax
Hamot Medical Center 201 State St	Erie	PA	16550	814-877-6000	877-6104
Web: www.hamot.org					
Metro Health Center 252 W 11th St	Erie	PA	16501	814-870-3400	870-3511
Web: www.ncinter.net/~metro ■ *E-mail:* metro@ncinter.net					
Millcreek Community Hospital 5515 Peach St	Erie	PA	16509	814-864-4031	868-8249
Saint Vincent Health Center 232 W 25th St	Erie	PA	16544	814-452-5000	451-8026*
**Fax:* Admitting ■ *Web:* www.svhs.org ■ *E-mail:* mail@svhs.org					
Veterans Affairs Medical Center 135 E 38th St	Erie	PA	16504	814-868-8661	868-6224

— Attractions —

	City	State	ZIP	Phone	Fax
Asbury Nature Center 4105 Asbury Rd	Erie	PA	16506	814-835-5356	835-5653
Cashiers House 417 State St	Erie	PA	16501	814-454-1813	
Commodore Perry Chorus 3520 Perry St	Erie	PA	16510	814-456-7464	
Web: moose.erie.net/~doctag/cpc.htm					
Dafmark Dance Academy 510 State St	Erie	PA	16501	814-454-3993	
Discovery Square betw 4th & 5th Sts	Erie	PA	16501	814-452-1942	452-1744
Erie Art Museum 411 State St	Erie	PA	16501	814-459-5477	452-1744
Web: www.erie.net/~erieartm/ ■ *E-mail:* erieartm@erie.net					
Erie Chamber Orchestra PO Box 437 Gannon University	Erie	PA	16541	814-871-7755	838-0966
Web: www.erie.net/~eco ■ *E-mail:* wright002@mail1.gannon.edu					
Erie Civic Ballet Co 3830 Liberty St	Erie	PA	16509	814-864-1580	
Erie Civic Center 809 French St	Erie	PA	16501	814-452-4857	455-9931
Erie Historical Museum & Planetarium 356 W 6th St	Erie	PA	16507	814-871-5790	879-0988
Erie History Center 417-421 State St	Erie	PA	16501	814-454-1813	452-1744
Erie Philharmonic Orchestra 801 State St Warner Theatre	Erie	PA	16501	814-455-1375	455-1377
Web: www.eriephil.org ■ *E-mail:* info@eriephil.org					
Erie Playhouse 13 W 10th St	Erie	PA	16501	814-454-2851	454-0601
Erie Zoo 423 W 38th St	Erie	PA	16508	814-864-4091	
ExpERIEnce Children's Museum 420 French St	Erie	PA	16507	814-453-3743	459-9735
Family First Sports Park 8155 Oliver Rd	Erie	PA	16509	814-866-5425	866-8066
Web: www.thesportspark.com					
Firefighters Historical Museum 428 Chestnut St Old Station House 4	Erie	PA	16507	814-456-5969	
Heritage Wine Cellar 12162 E Main Rd	North East	PA	16428	814-725-8015	725-8654
Web: www.heritagewine.com					
Lake Shore Railway Museum 31 Wall St	North East	PA	16428	814-825-2724	
Mazza Vineyards & Winery 11815 E Lake Rd	North East	PA	16428	814-725-8695	725-3948
Peek 'n Peak Resort 1405 Olde Rd	Clymer	NY	14724	716-355-4141	355-4542
Web: www.pknpk.com ■ *E-mail:* pk-n-pk@travelbase.com					
Penn Shore Vineyards & Winery 10225 E Lake Rd	North East	PA	16428	814-725-8688	
Presque Isle State Park PO Box 8510	Erie	PA	16505	814-833-7424	
Union City Historical Museum 11 S Main St	Union City	PA	16348	814-438-7573	
US Brig Niagara 150 E Front St	Erie	PA	16507	814-452-2744	455-6760
Web: www.ncinter.net/~niagara ■ *E-mail:* niagara@ncinter.net					
Waldameer Park & Water World 220 Peninsula Dr	Erie	PA	16505	814-838-3591	
Web: www.waldameer.com ■ *E-mail:* info@waldameer.com					
Warner Theatre 811 State St	Erie	PA	16501	814-452-4857	455-9931
Web: www.erieciviccenter.com/warner.htm ■ *E-mail:* eccjen@erie.net					

SPORTS TEAMS & FACILITIES

	City	State	ZIP	Phone	Fax
Erie Otters (hockey) 809 French St Erie Civic Ctr	Erie	PA	16501	814-455-7779	455-0911
Web: www.ottershockey.com ■ *E-mail:* puck@ottershockey.com					
Erie SeaWolves (baseball) 110 E 10th St Jerry Uht Park	Erie	PA	16501	814-456-1300	456-7520
Web: www.seawolves.com ■ *E-mail:* seawolves@erie.net					

— Events —

	Phone
4th of July Fireworks (July 4)	814-838-3591
American Folkways Festival (late June & early September)	814-385-6040
Cherry Festival (early July)	814-725-4262
Erie County Fair (late August-early September)	814-739-2232
Erie Summer Festival of the Arts (late June)	814-871-7493
Erie Zoo Parade (mid-May)	814-864-4091
First Night Erie (December 31)	814-877-7097
Greek Festival (mid-July)	814-838-8808
Harborfest (mid-July)	814-899-9173
Heritage Wine Fest (late September)	814-725-8015
Maple Syrup Festival (mid-March)	814-835-5356
Professional Bowlers Tour (late March-early April)	814-899-9855
Saint Patrick's Day Parade (mid-March)	814-454-7191
Spring Highland Festival (early May)	814-836-1955
We Love Erie Days (mid-August)	814-454-7191
Wild Rib Cookoff & Music Festival (early June)	814-833-7343
Wine Country Harvest Festival (late September)	814-725-4262
ZooBoo (mid-late October)	814-864-4091
ZooLumination (mid-late December)	814-864-4091

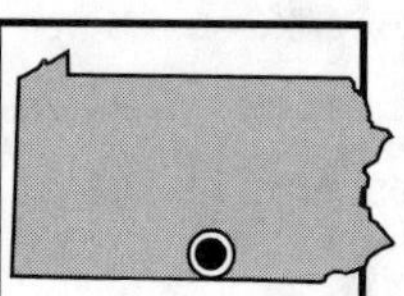

Gettysburg

The Battle of Gettysburg was the turning point of the Civil War and the bloodiest battle of American history, with over 51,000 casualties in three days of fighting in 1863. More men actually fought and more men died on the Gettysburg Battlefield than in any other battle before or since on North American soil. The Gettysburg National Cemetery was dedicated by President Abraham Lincoln in his historic Gettysburg Address just four months later. Today, the 5,700-acre Gettysburg National Military Park is the largest battlefield shrine in America, with more than 1,000 monuments and cannon along 40 miles. A 360-degree view of the Battlefield can be seen from two decks at the Gettysburg National Tower. Among the many museums in the area that house Civil War artifacts are the house that was General Robert E. Lee's headquarters, where he made plans for the Battle of Gettysburg; and the National Civil War Wax Museum, which includes more than 200 life-sized figures in 30 scenes. Located also at Gettysburg is the Eisenhower National Historic Site, which was the home and farm of General Dwight D. Eisenhower and his wife Mamie. The Eisenhowers are featured also at the Hall of Presidents, where the U.S. Presidents and their wives are reproduced in wax. Some of the events held in Gettysburg each year to celebrate its history include the Gettysburg Civil War Heritage Days, two Civil War Battle Re-enactments, and the Eisenhower World War II weekend encampment.

Population	7,376	**Longitude**	77-14-04 W
Area (Land)	1.6 sq mi	**County**	Adams
Area (Water)	0.0 sq mi	**Time Zone**	EST
Elevation	520 ft	**Area Code/s**	717
Latitude	39-49-48 N		

Gettysburg (Cont'd)

— Average Temperatures and Precipitation —

TEMPERATURES

	Jan	Feb	Mar	Apr	May	Jun	Jul	Aug	Sep	Oct	Nov	Dec
High	38	41	51	63	74	82	86	85	78	66	55	43
Low	20	22	31	40	50	59	64	62	54	43	35	25

PRECIPITATION

	Jan	Feb	Mar	Apr	May	Jun	Jul	Aug	Sep	Oct	Nov	Dec
Inches	3.0	2.7	3.2	3.4	3.8	3.5	3.1	3.3	3.6	3.1	3.2	3.2

— Important Phone Numbers —

	Phone
AAA	717-334-1155
Emergency	911
Medical Referral	717-334-4646
Poison Control Center	800-521-6110
Time/Temp	717-337-1234
Weather	717-264-1144

— Information Sources —

	City	State	Zip	Phone	Fax
Adams County 111-117 Baltimore St	Gettysburg	PA	17325	717-334-6781	334-2091
Adams County Economic Development 261 S Franklin St	Gettysburg	PA	17325	717-334-0042	
Adams County Public Library 140 Baltimore St	Gettysburg	PA	17325	717-334-5716	334-7992
Better Business Bureau Serving Eastern Pennsylvania 1608 Walnut St Suite 600 *Web:* www.easternpa.bbb.org	Philadelphia	PA	19103	215-985-9313	893-9312
Gettysburg-Adams County Area Chamber of Commerce 18 Carlisle St Suite 203 *Web:* www.visitgettysburg.com/chamberofcommerce ■ *E-mail:* gacac@cvn.net	Gettysburg	PA	17325	717-334-8151	334-3368
Gettysburg Borough Hall 59 E High St	Gettysburg	PA	17325	717-334-1160	
Gettysburg Convention & Visitors Bureau 35 Carlisle St *Web:* www.gettysburg.com	Gettysburg	PA	17325	717-334-6274	334-1166
Gettysburg Mayor 59 E High St	Gettysburg	PA	17325	717-334-1160	

On-Line Resources

Area Guide Gettysburg .... gettysburg.areaguides.net
City Knowledge Gettysburg .... www.cityknowledge.com/pa_gettysburg.htm
Excite.com Gettysburg City Guide .... www.excite.com/travel/countries/united_states/pennsylvania/gettysburg
Gettysburg Marketplace .... www.gettysburgmarketplace.com
NITC Travelbase City Guide Gettysburg .... www.travelbase.com/auto/guides/gettysburg-pa.html
Online City Guide to Gettysburg .... www.olcg.com/pa/gettysburg/index.html

— Transportation Services —

AIRPORTS

■ **Harrisburg International Airport (MDT)**

43 miles NE of downtown (approx 55 minutes) .... *Phone* 717-948-3987

Airport Transportation

	Phone
Gettysburg Tour Center Airport Shuttle $51 fare to downtown Gettysburg	717-334-6296
Yellow Cab $65 fare to downtown Gettysburg	717-337-9099

Commercial Airlines

	Phone
Allegheny	717-944-8700
American	800-433-7300
American Eagle	800-433-7300
Continental	800-525-0280
Continental Express	800-525-0280
Delta	800-221-1212
Delta Connection	800-221-1212
Northwest	800-225-2525
TWA	800-221-2000
TWA Express	800-221-2000
United	800-241-6522
United Express	800-241-6522
US Airways	800-428-4322
US Airways Express	800-428-4322

Charter Airlines

	Phone
Harrisburg Jet Center	717-774-0145

CAR RENTALS

	Phone
Enterprise	717-337-9000

LIMO/TAXI

	Phone
Yellow Cab	717-337-9099

— Accommodations —

HOTELS, MOTELS, RESORTS

	City	State	Zip	Phone	Fax
Baladerry Inn 40 Hospital Rd *Web:* www.baladerryinn.com ■ *E-mail:* baladerry@mail.wideopen.net	Gettysburg	PA	17325	717-337-1342	
Battlefield Motel 2075 Old Harrisburg Rd	Gettysburg	PA	17325	717-334-6867	
Beechmont Inn 315 Broadway *TF:* 800-553-7009	Hanover	PA	17331	717-632-3013	
Best Inn 301 Steinwehr Ave *TF:* 800-237-8466	Gettysburg	PA	17325	717-334-1188	334-1188
Best Western Gettysburg Hotel 1 Lincoln Sq *TF:* 800-528-1234	Gettysburg	PA	17325	717-337-2000	337-2075
Blue Sky Motel 2585 Biglerville Rd *TF:* 800-745-8194 ■ *E-mail:* info@blueskymotel.com	Gettysburg	PA	17325	717-677-7736	
Brafferton Inn 44 York St *Web:* www.gettysburg.com/gcvb/braffinn.htm	Gettysburg	PA	17325	717-337-3423	
Brickhouse Inn 452 Baltimore St *TF:* 800-864-3464 ■ *Web:* www.brickhouseinn.com ■ *E-mail:* stay@brickhouseinn.com	Gettysburg	PA	17325	717-338-9337	
Budget Host Three Crowns Motor Lodge 205 Steinwehr Ave	Gettysburg	PA	17325	717-334-3168	
Carroll Valley Golf Resort 121 Sanders Rd *TF:* 800-548-8504 ■ *Web:* www.carrollvalley.com ■ *E-mail:* golf@carrollvalley.com	Fairfield	PA	17320	717-642-8211	642-5529
Cashtown Inn 1797 1325 Old Rt 30 *TF:* 800-367-1797 ■ *Web:* www.cashtowninn.com ■ *E-mail:* cashtowninn@mail.cvn.net	Cashtown	PA	17310	717-334-9722	334-1442
College Motel 345 Carlisle St *TF:* 800-367-6731	Gettysburg	PA	17325	717-334-6731	
Colonial Motel 157 Carlisle St *TF:* 800-336-3126	Gettysburg	PA	17325	717-334-3126	
Colton Motel 232 Steinwehr Ave *TF:* 800-262-0317	Gettysburg	PA	17325	717-334-5514	
Comfort Inn Gettysburg 871 York Rd *TF:* 800-228-5150	Gettysburg	PA	17325	717-337-2400	334-0831
Cozy Country Inn 103 Frederick Rd *Web:* www.cozyvillage.com ■ *E-mail:* cozyville@aol.com	Thurmont	MD	21788	301-271-4301	
Days Inn Gettysburg 865 York Rd *TF:* 800-329-7466	Gettysburg	PA	17325	717-334-0030	337-1002
Doubleday Inn 104 Doubleday Ave	Gettysburg	PA	17325	717-334-9119	
Econo Lodge 945 Baltimore Pike *TF:* 800-334-6912	Gettysburg	PA	17325	717-334-6715	334-6580
Eisenhower Inn & Conference Center 2634 Emmitsburg Rd *TF:* 800-776-8349 ■ *Web:* www.eisenhower.com	Gettysburg	PA	17325	717-334-8121	334-6066
Farnsworth House Inn 401 Baltimore St *Web:* www.gettysburgaddress.com/HTMLS/farn.B&B.html ■ *E-mail:* farnhaus@mail.cvn.net	Gettysburg	PA	17325	717-334-8838	334-5862
Flaherty House 104 Lincolnway W *TF:* 800-217-0618	New Oxford	PA	17350	717-624-9494	
Gaslight Inn 33 E Middle St *Web:* www.thegaslightinn.com ■ *E-mail:* info@thegaslightinn.com	Gettysburg	PA	17325	717-337-9100	
Gettysburg Inn 1980 Biglerville Rd	Gettysburg	PA	17325	717-334-2263	
Hampton Inn 1280 York Rd	Gettysburg	PA	17325	717-338-9121	
Heritage Motor Lodge 64 Steinwehr Ave	Gettysburg	PA	17325	717-334-9281	
Herr Tavern & Publick House 900 Chambersburg Rd *TF:* 800-362-9849 ■ *Web:* www.herrtavern.com ■ *E-mail:* herrtav@mail.cvn.net	Gettysburg	PA	17325	717-334-4332	334-3332
Holiday Inn Battlefield 516 Baltimore St	Gettysburg	PA	17325	717-334-6211	334-7183
Holiday Inn Express 869 York Rd	Gettysburg	PA	17325	717-337-1400	337-0159
Home Sweet Home Motel 593 Steinwehr Ave *TF:* 800-440-3916	Gettysburg	PA	17325	717-334-3916	
James Gettys Hotel 27 Chambersburg St *Web:* www.jamesgettyshotel.com ■ *E-mail:* jghotel@mail.cvn.net	Gettysburg	PA	17325	717-337-1334	334-2103
Keystone Inn 231 Hanover St	Gettysburg	PA	17325	717-337-3888	

Gettysburg — Hotels, Motels, Resorts (Cont'd)

				Phone	Fax
Lincolnway East Motel 983 York Rd	Gettysburg	PA	17325	717-334-4208	
North Ridge Motel 1950 Biglerville Rd. *TF:* 800-550-2392	Gettysburg	PA	17325	717-334-8100	
Quality Inn 380 Steinwehr Ave *TF:* 800-228-5151	Gettysburg	PA	17325	717-334-1103	334-1103
Quality Inn Gettysburg Motor Lodge 380 Steinwehr Ave	Gettysburg	PA	17325	717-334-1106	
Quality Inn Larson's 401 Buford Ave. *TF:* 800-221-2222 ■ *Web:* www.thegettysburgaddress.com	Gettysburg	PA	17325	717-334-3141	334-1813
Red Carpet Inn 2450 Emmitsburg Rd *TF:* 800-336-1345	Gettysburg	PA	17325	717-334-1345	334-1345
Ski Liberty Hotel 78 Country Club Rd *Web:* www.skiliberty.com ■ *E-mail:* skiliberty@skiliberty.com	Carroll Valley	PA	17320	717-642-8288	742-6228
South Ridge Motel 3180 Emmitsburg Rd.	Gettysburg	PA	17325	717-334-5284	
Stonehurst Inn 9436 Waynesboro Rd *TF:* 800-497-8458	Emmitsburg	MD	21727	301-447-2880	447-3521
Western Inn 2520 Emmitsburg Rd	Gettysburg	PA	17325	717-334-1339	

— Restaurants —

				Phone
Altland House (American) PO Box 448	Abbotstown	PA	17301	717-259-9535
Avenue Restaurant (Continental) 21 Steinwehr Ave	Gettysburg	PA	17325	717-334-3235
Barker House Inn 10 Lincoln Way W *TF:* 888-546-1520	New Oxford	PA	17350	717-624-9066
Blue Parrot Bistro (American) 35 Chambersburg St.	Gettysburg	PA	17325	717-337-3739
Buckley's Pub (Irish) 44 Steinwehr Ave.	Gettysburg	PA	17325	717-334-2333
Carriage House Inn (Steak/Seafood) 200 S Seton Ave *Web:* www.carriagehouseinn.net ■ *E-mail:* chouseinn@aol.com	Emmitsburg	MD	21727	301-447-2366
Cashtown Inn Restaurant (American) 1325 Old Rt 30 *TF:* 800-367-1797	Gettysburg	PA	17310	717-334-9722
Centuries on the Square (Continental) 1 Lincoln Sq Best Western Gettysburg Hotel	Gettysburg	PA	17325	717-337-2000
Dobbin House Tavern (American) 89 Steinwehr Ave *Web:* www.dobbinhouse.com ■ *E-mail:* info@dobbinhouse.com	Gettysburg	PA	17325	717-334-2100
Eastside Lounge & Restaurant (American) 1063-A York Rd	Gettysburg	PA	17325	717-337-0118
Farnsworth House Inn (Continental) 401 Baltimore St	Gettysburg	PA	17325	717-334-8838
General Pickett's Buffet Restaurant (Homestyle) 571 Steinwehr Ave	Gettysburg	PA	17325	717-334-7580
Gettysburg Family Restaurant (Homestyle) 1275 York Rd	Gettysburg	PA	17325	717-337-2700
Gettysburg Pub & Brewery (American) 248 Hunterstown Rd. *Web:* www.gettysbrew.com ■ *E-mail:* info@gettysbrew.com	Gettysburg	PA	17325	717-337-1001
Gina's Place (American) 16 E Hanover St.	Bonneville	PA	17325	717-337-2697
Gingerbread Man (American) 217 Steinwehr Ave.	Gettysburg	PA	17325	717-334-1100
Herr Tavern (American) 900 Chambersburg Rd	Gettysburg	PA	17325	717-334-4332
Hickory Bridge Farm (Homestyle) 96 Hickory Bridge Rd. *TF:* 800-642-1766	Gettysburg	PA	17325	717-642-5261
Hoss's Steak & Sea House (Steak/Seafood) 1140 York Rd	Gettysburg	PA	17325	717-337-2961
JD's Grill (American) 401 Buford Ave.	Gettysburg	PA	17325	717-334-2200
La Bella Italia (Italian) 402 York St.	Gettysburg	PA	17325	717-334-1978
Lupita's Mexican Restaurant (Mexican) 51 West St.	Gettysburg	PA	17325	717-337-9575
Mamma Ventura Restaurant (Italian) 13 Chambersburg St.	Gettysburg	PA	17325	717-334-5548
Plaza Restaurant (Greek) 2-8 Baltimore St	Gettysburg	PA	17325	717-334-1999
Richards Restaurant (American) 2634 Emmitsburg Rd Eisenhower Inn & Conference Ctr	Gettysburg	PA	17325	717-334-8121
Stonehenge Restaurant (American) 985 Baltimore Pike	Gettysburg	PA	17325	717-334-9227

— Goods and Services —

SHOPPING

				Phone	Fax
Habitat 1 Steinwehr Ave. *Web:* www.tbhabitat.com	Gettysburg	PA	17325	717-334-1218	338-9573
Horse Soldier Antique Store 777 Baltimore St. *Web:* www.horsesoldier.com ■ *E-mail:* info@horsesoldier.com	Gettysburg	PA	17325	717-334-0347	334-5016
House of Bender 1 Baltimore St	Gettysburg	PA	17325	717-334-4315	334-0625
Koony's Barn Antiques 1295 Frederick Pike *TF:* 800-754-8091 ■ *Web:* www.koonysbarn.com ■ *E-mail:* shop@koonysbarn.com	Littlestown	PA	17340	717-359-7411	
Quilt Patch Village Shoppes 1897 Hanover Pike	Littlestown	PA	17340	717-359-4121	

BANKS

				Phone	Fax
Adams County National Bank 675 Old Harrisburg Rd	Gettysburg	PA	17325	717-334-3161	334-8670
Bank of Hanover & Trust Co 6 York St *TF Cust Svc:* 800-788-2201*	Gettysburg	PA	17325	717-337-9011	337-9417
Farmers & Mechanics National Bank 545 W Middle St.	Gettysburg	PA	17325	717-337-3699	337-0117
Keystone Financial Bank NA 105 Chambersburg St	Gettysburg	PA	17325	717-337-1525	337-1505
PNC Bank NA 245 Breckenridge St	Gettysburg	PA	17325	717-334-4382	334-3185
Sovereign Bank 29 N Washington St.	Gettysburg	PA	17325	717-334-6238	334-0667
Unitas Bank 1275 York Rd Suite 9	Gettysburg	PA	17325	717-337-2233	337-2234

BUSINESS SERVICES

	Phone
Adecco Employment Services	717-337-0060
Central Pack & Ship	717-337-0137
Copy Store	717-337-0709
Post Office	717-337-3781
Westminster Professional Associates	717-337-3424

— Media —

PUBLICATIONS

				Phone	Fax
Gettysburg Times‡ PO Box 3669 *Web:* www.gburgtimes.com ■ *E-mail:* times@cvn.net	Gettysburg	PA	17325	717-334-1131	334-4243

‡*Daily newspapers*

TELEVISION

				Phone	Fax
WGAL-TV Ch 8 (NBC) PO Box 7127 *Web:* www.wgal.com ■ *E-mail:* services@wgal.com	Lancaster	PA	17604	717-393-5851	393-9484
WGCB-TV Ch 49 (Ind) PO Box 88	Red Lion	PA	17356	717-246-1681	244-9316
WHP-TV Ch 21 (CBS) 3300 N 6th St. *Web:* www.whptv.com	Harrisburg	PA	17110	717-238-2100	238-4903
WHTM-TV Ch 27 (ABC) PO Box 5860 *Web:* www.whtm.com/	Harrisburg	PA	17110	717-236-2727	236-1263
WITF-TV Ch 33 (PBS) 1982 Locust Ln. *TF:* 800-366-9483 ■ *Web:* www.witf.org ■ *E-mail:* witf@witf.org	Harrisburg	PA	17109	717-236-6000	236-4628
WLYH-TV Ch 15 (UPN) 3300 N 6th St. *Web:* www.upn15.com	Harrisburg	PA	17110	717-238-2100	238-4903
WPMT-TV Ch 43 (Fox) 2005 S Queen St *Web:* www.fox43.com ■ *E-mail:* publicaffairs@mail.fox43.com	York	PA	17403	717-843-0043	843-9741

RADIO

				Phone	Fax
WAYZ-FM 101.5 MHz (Ctry) 10960 John Wayne Dr. *TF:* 800-758-0838 ■ *Web:* www.wayz.com ■ *E-mail:* info@wayz.com	Greencastle	PA	17225	717-597-9200	597-9210
WCHA-AM 800 kHz (Ctry) 25 Pencraft Ave	Chambersburg	PA	17201	717-264-7121	263-9649
WFRE-FM 99.9 MHz (Ctry) 5966 Grove Hill Rd	Frederick	MD	21703	301-663-4181	682-8018
WGET-AM 1320 kHz (AC) 1560 Fairfield Rd	Gettysburg	PA	17325	717-334-3101	334-5822
WGRX-FM 100.7 MHz (Ctry) 11350 McCormick Rd Executive Plaza 3 Suite 701	Hunt Valley	MD	21031	410-771-8484	771-1616
WGTY-FM 107.7 FM (Ctry) 1560 Fairfield Rd *Web:* www.wgty.com ■ *E-mail:* music@wgty.com	Gettysburg	PA	17325	717-334-3101	334-5822
WHVR-AM 1280 kHz (AC) Radio Rd	Hanover	PA	17331	717-637-3831	637-9006
WHYL-AM 960 kHz (Oldies) 1703 Walnut Bottom Rd *E-mail:* whyl@pa.net	Carlisle	PA	17013	717-249-1717	258-4638
WIKZ-FM 95.1 MHz (AC) 25 Pencraft Ave *Web:* www.mix95.com ■ *E-mail:* mix95@cvn.net	Chambersburg	PA	17201	717-264-7121	263-9649
WIOO-AM 1000 kHz (Ctry) 180 York Rd	Carlisle	PA	17013	717-243-1200	243-1277
WJEJ-AM 1240 kHz (AC) 1135 Haven Rd.	Hagerstown	MD	21742	301-739-2325	797-7408
WSBA-AM 910 kHz (N/T) 5989 Susquehanna Plaza Dr. *Web:* www.wsba910.com ■ *E-mail:* wsba910@blazenet.net	York	PA	17406	717-764-1155	252-4708
WSHP-AM 1480 kHz (B/EZ) PO Box E	Shippensburg	PA	17257	717-532-5118	532-6344
WTHU-AM 1450 kHz (B/EZ) 10 Radio Ln	Thurmont	MD	21788	301-271-2188	

Gettysburg — Radio (Cont'd)

				Phone	Fax
WTTR-AM 1470 kHz (Oldies)					
101 WTTR Ln.	Westminster	MD	21158	410-848-5511	876-5095
Web: www.wttr.com ■ *E-mail:* info@wttr.com					
WWII-AM 720 kHz (Rel) 8 W Main St	Shiremanstown	PA	17011	717-731-9944	731-4002
E-mail: therock@igateway.com					
WWMD-FM 104.7 MHz (B/EZ)					
1135 Haven Rd.	Hagerstown	MD	21742	301-739-2325	797-7408
WYCR-FM 98.5 MHz (CHR) Radio Rd	Hanover	PA	17331	717-637-3831	637-9006
WZBT-FM 91.1 MHz (Alt)					
Box 435 Gettysburg College	Gettysburg	PA	17325	717-337-6315	337-6314
Web: www.gettysburg.edu/~wzbt ■ *E-mail:* wzbt@gettysburg.edu					

— Colleges/Universities —

				Phone	Fax
Gettysburg College 300 Carlisle St	Gettysburg	PA	17325	717-337-6000	337-6145
TF Admissions: 800-431-0803 ■ *Web:* www.gettysburg.edu ■ *E-mail:* admiss@gettysburg.edu					
Harrisburg Area Community College					
705 Old Harrisburg Rd	Gettysburg	PA	17325	717-337-3855	337-3015

— Hospitals —

				Phone	Fax
Gettysburg Hospital 147 Gettys St	Gettysburg	PA	17325	717-334-2121	337-4314

— Attractions —

				Phone	Fax
Adams County Historical Society					
PO Box 4325	Gettysburg	PA	17325	717-334-4723	
Adams County Winery 251 Peach Tree Rd.	Orrtanna	PA	17353	717-334-4631	334-4026
Battle Theatre 571 Steinwehr Ave.	Gettysburg	PA	17325	717-334-6100	
Caledonia State Park					
40 Rocky Mountain Rd	Fayetteville	PA	17222	717-352-2161	352-7026
TF: 888-727-2757 ■ *Web:* www.dcnr.state.pa.us/stateparks/parks/caledonia.htm					
Codorus State Park					
1066 Blooming Grove Rd Rt 216	Hanover	PA	17331	717-637-2816	
TF: 888-727-2757 ■ *Web:* www.dcnr.state.pa.us/stateparks/parks/codorus.htm					
Conflict Theatre 213 Steinwehr Ave	Gettysburg	PA	17325	717-334-8003	
Eisenhower National Historic Site					
97 Taneytown Rd	Gettysburg	PA	17325	717-334-1124	334-1891
Web: www.nps.gov/eise/					
Farnsworth House Ghost Stories & Candlelight Ghost Walks					
401 Baltimore St.	Gettysburg	PA	17325	717-334-8838	
Farnsworth House Tour & Garret Museum					
401 Baltimore St.	Gettysburg	PA	17325	717-334-8838	
Farnsworth Military Gallery					
415 Baltimore St.	Gettysburg	PA	17325	717-334-8838	
General Lee's Headquarters Museum					
401 Buford Ave.	Gettysburg	PA	17325	717-334-3141	
Gettysburg Battlefield Bus Tours					
778 Baltimore St.	Gettysburg	PA	17325	717-334-6296	
Web: www.gettysburgtours.com					
Gettysburg Miniature Battlefield Diorama					
610 Taneytown Rd Artillery Ridge Camping Resort	Gettysburg	PA	17325	717-334-6408	
Gettysburg National Military Park					
97 Taneytown Rd	Gettysburg	PA	17325	717-334-1124	334-1891
Web: www.nps.gov/gett/					
Gettysburg National Tower					
999 Baltimore Pike	Gettysburg	PA	17325	717-334-6754	
Web: www.gettysburgtower.com ■ *E-mail:* gbtower@cvn.net					
Gettysburg Scenic Railway					
106 N Washington	Gettysburg	PA	17325	717-334-6932	
TF: 888-948-7246 ■ *Web:* www.gettysburgrail.com ■ *E-mail:* gbry@innernet.net					
Ghosts of Gettysburg Candlelight Walking Tours 271 Baltimore St	Gettysburg	PA	17325	717-337-0445	
Hall of Presidents & First Ladies					
789 Baltimore St.	Gettysburg	PA	17325	717-334-5717	
Historic Battlefield Bus Tours					
55 Steinwehr Ave	Gettysburg	PA	17325	717-334-8000	
Historic Round Barn & Farm Market					
298 Cashtown Rd	Biglerville	PA	17307	717-334-1984	
Inkwell Autograph Gallery					
777 Baltimore St.	Gettysburg	PA	17325	717-337-2220	337-2221
Web: www.inkwellgallery.com ■ *E-mail:* inkwellgallery@yahoo.com					
Jennie Wade House 528 Baltimore St.	Gettysburg	PA	17325	717-334-4100	
Land of Little Horses 125 Glenwood Dr.	Gettysburg	PA	17325	717-334-7259	
Web: www.landoflittlehorses.com ■ *E-mail:* lilhorse@cvn.net					
Lincoln Train Museum Steinwehr Ave	Gettysburg	PA	17325	717-334-5678	
Magic Town 49 Steinwehr Ave	Gettysburg	PA	17325	717-337-0442	
TF: 800-878-4276 ■ *Web:* users.desupernet.com/magictown ■ *E-mail:* joycemagic@cvn.net					
Mont Alto State Park					
40 Rocky Mountain Rd	Fayetteville	PA	17222	717-352-2161	352-7026
TF: 888-727-2757 ■ *Web:* www.dcnr.state.pa.us/stateparks/parks/alto.htm					
National Civil War Wax Museum					
297 Steinwehr Ave	Gettysburg	PA	17325	717-334-6245	334-9686
Web: www.gettysburggiftcenter.com/wax.htm ■ *E-mail:* shop@gettysburggiftcenter.com					
Pine Grove Furnace State Park					
1100 Pine Grove Rd	Gardners	PA	17324	717-486-7174	
TF: 888-727-2757 ■ *Web:* www.dcnr.state.pa.us/stateparks/parks/pine.htm					
Schriver House Museum 309 Baltimore St.	Gettysburg	PA	17325	717-337-2800	
Seton Shrine Center 331 S Seton Ave.	Emmitsburg	MD	21727	301-447-6606	447-6038
Web: www.setonshrine.org ■ *E-mail:* setonshrine@fwp.net					
Ski Liberty Ski Area Box SKI	Carroll Valley	PA	17320	717-642-8282	
Web: www.skiliberty.com ■ *E-mail:* skiliberty@skiliberty.com					
Soldier's National Museum					
777 Baltimore St.	Gettysburg	PA	17325	717-334-4890	
State Museum of Pennsylvania					
3rd & North Sts	Harrisburg	PA	17108	717-787-4980	783-4558
Web: www.statemuseumpa.org					

— Events —

	Phone
Adams County Heritage Festival (late September)	717-334-0752
Adams County Historic Properties Tour (mid-June)	717-334-8188
Anniversary of Lincoln's Gettysburg Address (November 19)	717-334-6274
Apple Blossom Festival (early May)	717-334-6274
Civil War Battle Reenactments (early July & late September)	717-338-1525
East Berlin Colonial Day (mid-September)	717-259-0822
Eisenhower World War II Weekend (mid-late September)	717-338-9114
Fairfield Pippenfest (late September)	717-642-5640
Gettysburg Brass Band Festival (mid-late June)	717-334-6274
Gettysburg Civil War Book Fair (late June)	717-334-6274
Gettysburg Civil War Collectors Show (late June)	717-334-6274
Gettysburg Civil War Heritage Days (late June-early July)	717-334-6274
Gettysburg Fall Bluegrass Festival (late August-early September)	717-642-8749
Gettysburg Fall Outdoor Antique Show (late September)	717-334-6274
Gettysburg Firemen's Festival (early July)	717-334-6274
Gettysburg Spring Bluegrass Festival (mid-May)	717-642-8749
Gettysburg Spring Outdoor Antique Show (early-mid-May)	717-334-6274
Gettysburg Square-Dance Round-Up (late May)	717-528-4442
Gettysburg Yuletide Festival (late November-mid-December)	717-334-6274
History Meets the Arts (mid-late April)	717-334-8151
International Gift Festival (mid-November)	717-334-6274
Littlestown Good Ole Days Festival (mid-late August)	717-334-6274
Mason-Dixon Civil War Collector's Show (late June)	717-334-6274
Memorial Day Parade & Ceremonies (late May)	717-334-6274
National Apple Harvest Festival (early October)	717-677-9413
New Oxford Flea Market & Antique Show (mid-late June)	717-334-6274
Remembrance Day (mid-November)	717-334-6274
South Mountain Fair (late August)	717-334-6274
Sunday in the Park Concert Series (early June-mid-late August)	717-334-2028

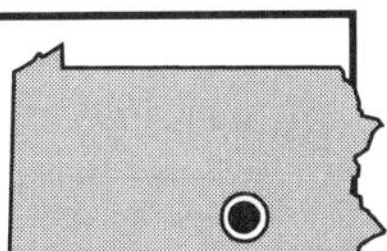

Harrisburg

The central area of Harrisburg, referred to as Center City, includes the Central Business District, the Capitol District, and the Riverfront District. Among the sights in the Capitol District are the Capitol Building itself, an Italian Renaissance building with a dome styled after Rome's Saint Peter's Basilica and a staircase modeled after Paris's Grand Opera House;

Harrisburg (Cont'd)

and the Downtown Harrisburg Historic District, which is just one of seven National Historic Districts in Harrisburg. In the Riverfront District, four historic bridges span the Susquehanna River at Harrisburg. This area also includes City Island, a major center for outdoor recreational activities with 63 acres of parkland; and Riverfront Park, a five-mile-long resort that lines the eastern bank of the Susquehanna.

Population	49,502	**Longitude**	76-88-47 W
Area (Land)	8.1 sq mi	**County**	Dauphin
Area (Water)	3.3 sq mi	**Time Zone**	EST
Elevation	320 ft	**Area Code/s**	717
Latitude	40-27-36 N		

— Average Temperatures and Precipitation —

TEMPERATURES

	Jan	Feb	Mar	Apr	May	Jun	Jul	Aug	Sep	Oct	Nov	Dec
High	36	39	50	62	73	81	86	84	76	65	53	41
Low	21	23	32	41	51	61	66	64	57	45	36	27

PRECIPITATION

	Jan	Feb	Mar	Apr	May	Jun	Jul	Aug	Sep	Oct	Nov	Dec
Inches	2.8	2.9	3.3	3.2	4.3	3.9	3.6	3.3	3.5	2.9	3.5	3.2

— Important Phone Numbers —

	Phone		*Phone*
AAA	717-236-4021	**HotelDocs**	800-468-3537
American Express Travel	717-233-5641	**Medical Referral**	800-243-1455
Dental Referral	800-917-6453	**Poison Control Center**	800-521-6110
Emergency	911	**Time/Temp**	717-534-2121

— Information Sources —

				Phone	*Fax*
Better Business Bureau Serving Eastern Pennsylvania 1608 Walnut St Suite 600 *Web:* www.easternpa.bbb.org	Philadelphia	PA	19103	215-985-9313	893-9312
Better Business Bureau Serving Lancaster 29 E King St Suite 322 *Web:* www.easternpa.bbb.org	Lancaster	PA	17602	717-291-1151	291-3241
Capital Region Chamber of Commerce 3211 N Front St Suite 201 *Web:* www.hbgchamber.com	Harrisburg	PA	17110	717-232-4099	232-5184
Dauphin County PO Box 1295	Harrisburg	PA	17108	717-255-2810	257-1604
Dauphin County Library System 101 Walnut St *Web:* dcls.org	Harrisburg	PA	17101	717-234-4961	234-7479
Farm Show Complex 2301 N Cameron St	Harrisburg	PA	17110	717-787-5373	783-8710
Harrisburg City Hall 10 N 2nd St	Harrisburg	PA	17101	717-255-3011	
Harrisburg-Hershey-Carlisle Tourism & Convention Bureau 25 N Front St *TF:* 800-995-0969 ■ *Web:* www.visithhc.com/	Harrisburg	PA	17101	717-231-7788	231-7790
Harrisburg Mayor 10 N 2nd St Suite 202	Harrisburg	PA	17101	717-255-3040	255-3036
Harrisburg Planning Dept 10 N 2nd St Suite 206	Harrisburg	PA	17101	717-255-6424	255-6421
Pennsylvania Travel & Tourism Office Forum Bldg Room 404 *TF:* 800-847-4872 ■ *Web:* www.dced.state.pa.us/visit ■ *E-mail:* dcedtravel@dced.state.pa.us	Harrisburg	PA	17120	717-787-5453	787-0687

On-Line Resources

Anthill City Guide Harrisburg	www.anthill.com/city.asp?city=harrisburg
Area Guide Harrisburg	harrisburgpa.areaguides.net
City Knowledge Harrisburg	www.cityknowledge.com/pa_harrisburg.htm
DigitalCity Harrisburg	www.digitalcity.com/harrisburg
Excite.com Harrisburg City Guide	www.excite.com/travel/countries/united_states/pennsylvania/harrisburg
Harrisburg Online	www.teem.com/hburg
Harrisburg.com	www.harrisburg.com/

— Transportation Services —

AIRPORTS

	Phone
■ **Harrisburg International Airport (MDT)** 10 miles SE of downtown (approx 15 minutes)	717-948-3987

Airport Transportation

	Phone
Airport Limousine $18 fare to downtown	717-737-3943
Yellow Cab $12-16 fare to downtown	717-238-7252

Commercial Airlines

	Phone		*Phone*
Allegheny	717-944-8700	**Northwest**	800-225-2525
American	800-433-7300	**TWA**	800-221-2000
American Eagle	800-433-7300	**TWA Express**	800-221-2000
Continental	800-525-0280	**United**	800-241-6522
Continental Express	800-525-0280	**United Express**	800-241-6522
Delta	800-221-1212	**US Airways**	800-428-4322
Delta Connection	800-221-1212	**US Airways Express**	800-428-4322

Charter Airlines

	Phone
Harrisburg Jet Center	717-774-0145

CAR RENTALS

	Phone		*Phone*
Alamo	800-327-9633	**Enterprise**	717-564-9444
Avis	717-944-4401	**Hertz**	717-944-4080
Budget	717-944-4019	**Thrifty**	717-948-5710

LIMO/TAXI

	Phone		*Phone*
Airport Limousine	717-737-3943	**Superior Limo**	717-564-3174
Harrisburg Corporate Limo	717-697-4400	**Villa Limo**	717-774-5202
Penn-Harris Taxi	717-238-7377	**Yellow Cab**	717-238-7252

MASS TRANSIT

	Phone
Capital Area Transit $1.35 Base fare	717-238-8304

RAIL/BUS

				Phone
Amtrak Station 4th & Chestnut Sts *TF:* 800-872-7245	Harrisburg	PA	17101	717-232-3331
Greyhound/Trailways Bus Station 4th & Chestnut Sts	Harrisburg	PA	17101	717-232-4251

— Accommodations —

HOTELS, MOTELS, RESORTS

				Phone	*Fax*
Alva Hotel 19 S 4th St	Harrisburg	PA	17111	717-238-7553	
Baymont Inns & Suites 990 Eisenhower Blvd *TF:* 800-301-0200	Harrisburg	PA	17111	717-939-8000	939-0500
Baymont Inns & Suites 200 N Mountain Rd *TF:* 800-301-0200	Harrisburg	PA	17112	717-540-9339	540-9486
Best Western Eden Resort Inn & Conference Center 222 Eden Rd *TF:* 800-528-1234	Lancaster	PA	17601	717-569-6444	569-4208
Best Western Hotel 300 N Mountain Rd *TF:* 800-528-1234	Harrisburg	PA	17112	717-652-7180	541-8991
Best Western Inn of the Butterfly 1245 Harrisburg Pike	Carlisle	PA	17013	717-243-5411	243-0778
Comfort Inn 4021 Union Deposit Rd *TF:* 800-228-5150	Harrisburg	PA	17109	717-561-8100	561-1357
Days Inn 3919 N Front St *TF:* 800-329-7466	Harrisburg	PA	17110	717-233-3100	233-6415

Harrisburg — Hotels, Motels, Resorts (Cont'd)

				Phone	Fax
Doubletree Club Hotel 815 S Eisenhower Blvd TF: 800-528-1234	Middletown	PA	17057	717-939-1600	939-8763
Eagle Hotel 1361 N Mountain Rd	Harrisburg	PA	17112	717-545-2839	
Econo Lodge 495 Eisenhower Blvd TF: 800-553-2666	Harrisburg	PA	17111	717-561-1885	561-1888
Eisenhower Inn & Conference Center 2634 Emmitsburg Rd TF: 800-776-8349 ■ Web: www.eisenhower.com	Gettysburg	PA	17325	717-334-8121	334-6066
Fairfield Inn by Marriott 175 Beacon Hill Blvd TF: 800-228-2800 ■ Web: fairfieldinn.com/HARFI	New Cumberland	PA	17070	717-774-6200	774-6200
Fairview Inn 1350 Eisenhower Blvd	Harrisburg	PA	17111	717-939-9531	
Friendly Inn 8004 Allentown Blvd	Harrisburg	PA	17112	717-652-2634	
Hampton Inn 4230 Union Deposit Rd TF: 800-426-7866	Harrisburg	PA	17111	717-545-9595	545-6907
Harrisburg Holiday Inn Pennsylvania Tpke Exit 18 & I-83 TF: 800-465-4329	New Cumberland	PA	17070	717-774-2721	774-2485
Hershey Country Club 1000 E Derry Rd TF: 800-900-4653	Hershey	PA	17033	717-533-2360	533-2752
Hershey Lodge & Convention Center PO Box 446 TF: 800-533-3131	Hershey	PA	17033	717-533-3311	533-9642
Hilton Harrisburg & Towers 1 N 2nd St TF: 800-445-8667 ■ Web: www.hilton.com/hotels/MDTHHHF	Harrisburg	PA	17101	717-233-6000	233-6271
Holiday Inn 334 Arsenal Rd TF: 800-465-4329	York	PA	17402	717-845-5671	845-1898
Holiday Inn East 4751 Lindle Rd TF: 800-637-4817	Harrisburg	PA	17111	717-939-7841	939-9317
Holiday Inn Express Riverfront 525 S Front St TF: 800-465-4329	Harrisburg	PA	17104	717-233-1611	238-2172
Holiday Inn Harrisburg West 5401 Carlisle Pike TF: 800-772-7829	Mechanicsburg	PA	17055	717-697-0321	697-5917
Holiday Inn Holidome 2000 Loucks Rd TF: 800-465-4329	York	PA	17404	717-846-9500	764-5038
Hotel Hale 216 Market St	Millersburg	PA	17061	717-692-8177	
Hotel Hershey Hotel Rd TF: 800-533-3131	Hershey	PA	17033	717-533-2171	534-8887
Howard Johnson 473 Eisenhower Blvd TF: 800-446-4656 ■ Web: www.hersheyhotels.com ■ E-mail: hjharris@microserve.net	Harrisburg	PA	17111	717-564-4730	564-4840
Lancaster Host Resort 2300 Lincoln Hwy E TF: 800-233-0121	Lancaster	PA	17602	717-299-5500	295-5112
Lantern Lodge Motor Inn 411 N College St TF: 800-262-5564	Myerstown	PA	17067	717-866-6536	
Marriott Hotel 4650 Lindle Rd TF: 800-228-9290 ■ Web: marriotthotels.com/HARPA	Harrisburg	PA	17111	717-564-5511	564-6173
McIntosh Inn 130 Limekiln Rd TF: 800-444-2775	New Cumberland	PA	17070	717-774-8888	774-7717
Quality Inn 380 Steinwehr Ave TF: 800-228-5151	Gettysburg	PA	17325	717-334-1103	334-1103
Quality Inn Larson's 401 Buford Ave TF: 800-221-2222 ■ Web: www.thegettysburgaddress.com	Gettysburg	PA	17325	717-334-3141	334-1813
Radisson Penn Harris Hotel & Convention Center 1150 Camp Hill Bypass TF: 800-333-3333	Camp Hill	PA	17011	717-763-7117	763-4518
Ramada Inn on Market Square 23 S 2nd St TF: 800-272-6232	Harrisburg	PA	17101	717-234-5021	234-2347
Red Roof Inn 400 Corporate Cir TF: 800-843-7663	Harrisburg	PA	17110	717-657-1445	657-2775
Residence Inn by Marriott 4480 Lewis Rd TF: 800-331-3131 ■ Web: www.residenceinn.com/HARHB	Harrisburg	PA	17111	717-561-1900	561-8617
Sheraton Inn East 800 E Park Dr TF: 800-325-3535	Harrisburg	PA	17111	717-561-2800	561-8398
Sleep Inn 7930 Linglestown Rd TF: 800-753-3746	Harrisburg	PA	17112	717-540-9100	671-8514
Super 8 Motel 4131 Executive Park Dr TF: 800-800-8000	Harrisburg	PA	17111	717-564-7790	564-0730
Travelodge 110 Limekiln Rd TF: 800-578-7878	New Cumberland	PA	17070	717-774-1100	774-0634
Willow Valley Resort & Conference Center 2416 Willow Street Pike TF: 800-444-1714 ■ Web: www.willowvalley.com ■ E-mail: info@willowval.com	Lancaster	PA	17602	717-464-2711	464-4784
Wyndham Garden Hotel 765 Eisenhower Blvd TF: 800-253-0238	Harrisburg	PA	17111	717-558-9500	558-8956

— Restaurants —

				Phone
2nd Street Cafe (American) 23 S 2nd St	Harrisburg	PA	17101	717-234-5021
Alfred's Victorian Restaurant (Italian) 38 N Union St	Middletown	PA	17057	717-944-5373
Appalachian Brewing Co (American) 50 N Cameron St	Harrisburg	PA	17101	717-221-1080
Arches The (American) 4125 N Front St	Harrisburg	PA	17110	717-233-5472
Dewey's Dry Dock & Deli (American) 37 N 2nd St	Harrisburg	PA	17101	717-233-3700
Dodge City USA (Steak) 1037 Paxton St	Harrisburg	PA	17104	717-236-2719
Double Jacks (American) 1313 N 2nd St	Harrisburg	PA	17102	717-233-5095
Felicita (Continental) 2201 Fishing Creek Valley Rd	Harrisburg	PA	17112	717-599-5301
Fuji Do Restaurant (Japanese) 2800 Paxton St	Harrisburg	PA	17111	717-561-1380
Gabriella (Italian) 3907 Jonestown Rd	Harrisburg	PA	17109	717-540-0040
Golden Sheaf (Continental) 1 N 2nd St	Harrisburg	PA	17101	717-237-6400
Great Wall (Chinese) 2905 N 7th St	Harrisburg	PA	17110	717-233-1500
Harris House Tavern (American) 3951 Union Deposit Rd	Harrisburg	PA	17109	717-564-4270
Kiwi's Bar & Grill (American) 1257 Derry St	Harrisburg	PA	17104	717-238-6611
Little Saigon Restaurant (Vietnamese) 2800 Paxton St	Harrisburg	PA	17111	717-561-1117
Mama's (Italian) 305 Market St	Harrisburg	PA	17101	717-232-4171
Manada Hill Inn (American) 128 N Hershey Rd	Harrisburg	PA	17112	717-652-0400
Nick's 1014 Cafe (American) 1014 N 3rd St	Harrisburg	PA	17102	717-238-8844
Olga's (American) 800 E Park Dr	Harrisburg	PA	17111	717-561-2800
Passage to India (Indian) 525 S Front St	Harrisburg	PA	17104	717-233-1202
Paxtang Grill (American) 3323 Derry St	Harrisburg	PA	17111	717-564-2738
Pizza Delight (Italian) 5840 Derry St	Harrisburg	PA	17111	717-564-5100
Platt's Seafood (Seafood) 3407 Derry St	Harrisburg	PA	17111	717-558-8152
Raspberries (International) 1 N 2nd St	Harrisburg	PA	17101	717-237-6419
Royal Thai Restaurant (Thai) 1917 Paxton St	Harrisburg	PA	17104	717-236-2931
Salvatore's (Italian) 955 Eisenhower Blvd	Harrisburg	PA	17111	717-939-1898
Scott's Grille (American) 212 Locust St	Harrisburg	PA	17101	717-234-7599
Seasons (American) 4751 Lindle Rd	Harrisburg	PA	17111	717-939-7841
Tom's Place Restaurant (Homestyle) 19 S 3rd St	Harrisburg	PA	17101	717-233-0871
Wharf The (Seafood) 6852 Derry St	Harrisburg	PA	17111	717-564-9920
Zembie's Restaurant (American) 226 N 2nd St	Harrisburg	PA	17101	717-232-5020
Zephyr Express (California) 400 N 2nd St	Harrisburg	PA	17101	717-257-1328

— Goods and Services —

SHOPPING

				Phone	Fax
Factory Stores at Hershey 40 Outlet Sq	Hershey	PA	17033	717-520-1236	520-1345
Harrisburg East Mall I-83 & Paxton St	Harrisburg	PA	17111	717-564-0980	561-8225
Kline Village Flea Market 146 Kline Plaza	Harrisburg	PA	17104	717-238-7788	
Strawberry Square 11 N 3rd St	Harrisburg	PA	17101	717-236-5061	
Uptown Plaza 2903-2971 N 7th St	Harrisburg	PA	17110	717-232-5682	

BANKS

				Phone	Fax
Allfirst Bank 213 Market St TF: 800-269-8463	Harrisburg	PA	17101	717-255-2121	237-6853
First Union Bank 30 N 3rd TF: 800-231-1291	Harrisburg	PA	17101	717-234-2860	234-2731
Harris Savings Bank PO Box 1711 TF: 800-232-6995 ■ Web: www.harrissavingsbank.com	Harrisburg	PA	17105	717-236-4041	231-2950
Mellon Bank 10 S 2nd St	Harrisburg	PA	17108	717-231-7465	231-5852
PNC Bank 2 N 2nd St	Harrisburg	PA	17101	717-232-5626	232-9427

BUSINESS SERVICES

	Phone
Airborne Express	800-247-2676
BAX Global	800-225-5229
Capital Area Temporary Service	717-761-0133
DHL Worldwide Express	800-225-5345
Federal Express	800-238-5355
Kelly Services	717-652-4041
Kinko's	717-541-5679
Mail Boxes Etc	800-789-4623
Manpower Temporary Services	717-540-6000
Post Office	717-257-2100
UPS	800-742-5877

— Media —

PUBLICATIONS

				Phone	Fax
Mode Magazine PO Box 5566 Web: www.modemagazine.com/ ■ E-mail: feedback@modemagazine.com	Harrisburg	PA	17110	717-234-6633	236-0886
Patriot-News The‡ PO Box 2265 *Fax: Edit ■ TF: 800-692-7207	Harrisburg	PA	17105	717-255-8100	255-8456*

‡*Daily newspapers*

Harrisburg (Cont'd)

TELEVISION

				Phone	Fax
WGAL-TV Ch 8 (NBC) PO Box 7127	Lancaster	PA	17604	717-393-5851	393-9484
Web: www.wgal.com ■ *E-mail:* services@wgal.com					
WGCB-TV Ch 49 (Ind) PO Box 88	Red Lion	PA	17356	717-246-1681	244-9316
WHP-TV Ch 21 (CBS) 3300 N 6th St	Harrisburg	PA	17110	717-238-2100	238-4903
Web: www.whptv.com					
WHTM-TV Ch 27 (ABC) PO Box 5860	Harrisburg	PA	17110	717-236-2727	236-1263
Web: www.whtm.com/					
WITF-TV Ch 33 (PBS) 1982 Locust Ln	Harrisburg	PA	17109	717-236-6000	236-4628
TF: 800-366-9483 ■ *Web:* www.witf.org ■ *E-mail:* witf@witf.org					
WLYH-TV Ch 15 (UPN) 3300 N 6th St	Harrisburg	PA	17110	717-238-2100	238-4903
Web: www.upn15.com					
WPMT-TV Ch 43 (Fox) 2005 S Queen St	York	PA	17403	717-843-0043	843-9741
Web: www.fox43.com ■ *E-mail:* publicaffairs@mail.fox43.com					

RADIO

				Phone	Fax
KOOL-AM 1460 kHz (N/T) PO Box 6477	Harrisburg	PA	17112	717-540-8800	233-0503
WHP-AM 580 kHz (N/T) 600 Corporate Cir	Harrisburg	PA	17110	717-540-8800	540-9268
WITF-FM 89.5 MHz (NPR) 1982 Locust Ln	Harrisburg	PA	17109	717-236-6000	236-4628
Web: www.witf.org/fm.html					
WKBO-AM 1230 kHz (Oldies) PO Box 6477	Harrisburg	PA	17112	717-540-8800	540-9268
WNNK-FM 104.1 MHz (CHR) PO Box 104	Harrisburg	PA	17108	717-238-1041	238-1454
Web: wink104.com ■ *E-mail:* wink@wink104.com					
WRBT-FM 94.9 MHz (Ctry) PO Box 6477	Harrisburg	PA	17112	717-540-8800	540-8814
WRVV-FM 97.3 MHz (AC) PO Box 6477	Harrisburg	PA	17110	717-540-8800	540-9268
WWKL-FM 99.3 MHz (Oldies) PO Box 6477	Harrisburg	PA	17112	717-540-8800	540-8814
Web: www.kool993.com					

— Colleges/Universities —

				Phone	Fax
Dickinson College PO Box 1773	Carlisle	PA	17013	717-245-1231	245-1442
TF: 800-644-1773 ■ *Web:* www.dickinson.edu ■ *E-mail:* postmaster@dickinson.edu					
Dixon University Center 2986 N 2nd St	Harrisburg	PA	17110	717-720-4080	720-7259
Elizabethtown College 1 Alpha Dr	Elizabethtown	PA	17022	717-361-1000	361-1365
Web: www.etown.edu					
Lebanon Valley College 101 N College Ave	Annville	PA	17003	717-867-6100	867-6124
TF Admissions: 800-445-6181 ■ *Web:* www.lvc.edu					
Messiah College	Grantham	PA	17027	717-766-2511	691-6025
TF: 800-233-4220 ■ *Web:* www.messiah.edu					
Pennsylvania State University Harrisburg 777 W Harrisburg Pike	Middletown	PA	17057	717-948-6000	948-6325
TF Admissions: 800-222-2056 ■ *Web:* www.hbg.psu.edu ■ *E-mail:* www@www.hbg.psu.edu					
Thompson Institute 5650 Derry St	Harrisburg	PA	17111	717-564-4112	564-3779
TF: 800-272-4632 ■ *Web:* www.thompsoninstitute.org ■ *E-mail:* admissions@thompsoninstitute.org					

— Hospitals —

				Phone	Fax
Carlisle Hospital 246 Parker St	Carlisle	PA	17013	717-249-1212	249-0770
Harrisburg Hospital 111 S Front St	Harrisburg	PA	17101	717-782-3131	782-5911
Holy Spirit Hospital 503 N 21st St	Camp Hill	PA	17011	717-763-2100	763-2183
Pennsylvania State University Hospital Milton S Hershey Medical Center PO Box 850	Hershey	PA	17033	717-531-8521	531-4707
Web: www.hmc.psu.edu					
Pinnacle Health Hospital at Community General PO Box 3000	Harrisburg	PA	17105	717-652-3000	231-8635*
**Fax:* Hum Res					

— Attractions —

				Phone	Fax
Art Association of Harrisburg 21 N Front St	Harrisburg	PA	17101	717-236-1432	236-6631
Web: www.nimage.com/aah/					
City Island Railroad 10 N 2nd St	Harrisburg	PA	17103	717-232-2332	
Eisenhower National Historic Site 97 Taneytown Rd	Gettysburg	PA	17325	717-334-1124	334-1891
Web: www.nps.gov/eise/					
Fire Museum of Greater Harrisburg 1820 N 4th St	Harrisburg	PA	17102	717-232-8915	232-8916
Fort Hunter Mansion 5300 N Front St	Harrisburg	PA	17110	717-599-5751	
Fort Hunter Park 5000 N Front St	Harrisburg	PA	17110	717-599-5751	
Gettysburg National Military Park 97 Taneytown Rd	Gettysburg	PA	17325	717-334-1124	334-1891
Web: www.nps.gov/gett/					
Harris John Mansion 219 S Front St	Harrisburg	PA	17104	717-233-3462	
Harrisburg Opera Assn 301 Market St	Harrisburg	PA	17101	717-236-7372	236-8146
Web: www.hbg-opera.org					
Harrisburg Symphony Orchestra 800 Corporate Circle Suite 101	Harrisburg	PA	17100	717-545-5527	545-6501
Web: www.harrisburgsymphony.org					
Hersheypark 100 W Hersheypark Dr	Hershey	PA	17033	717-534-3900	534-3165*
**Fax:* Mktg ■ *TF:* 800-437-7439 ■ *Web:* www.hersheypark.com ■ *E-mail:* prpark@800hershey.com					
Historic Harrisburg District 1230 N 3rd St	Harrisburg	PA	17102	717-233-4646	
Indian Echo Caverns 368 Middletown Rd	Hummelstown	PA	17036	717-566-8131	
Pennsylvania Historical & Museum Commission PO Box 1026	Harrisburg	PA	17108	717-787-2891	783-1073
Web: www.phmc.state.pa.us					
Pennsylvania State Capitol 3rd & State Sts	Harrisburg	PA	17120	717-787-2121	
Pride of Susquehanna Riverboat Market Street Bridge City Island	Harrisburg	PA	17108	717-234-6500	
Riverfront Park	Harrisburg	PA		717-255-3020	
State Museum of Pennsylvania 3rd & North Sts	Harrisburg	PA	17108	717-787-4980	783-4558
Web: www.statemuseumpa.org					
Sunday Flea Market	Harrisburg	PA		717-545-5901	
Theatre Harrisburg 513 Hurlock St	Harrisburg	PA	17110	717-232-5501	232-5912
Web: www.harrisburgstage.com					
ZooAmerica North American Wildlife Park 100 W Hershey Park Dr	Hershey	PA	17033	717-534-3860	

SPORTS TEAMS & FACILITIES

				Phone	Fax
Harrisburg Heat (soccer) Maclay & Cameron Sts	Harrisburg	PA	17106	717-652-4328	
Web: www.heatsoccer.com					
Harrisburg Senators (baseball) PO Box 15757	Harrisburg	PA	17105	717-231-4444	
Web: www.senatorsbaseball.com ■ *E-mail:* hbgsenator@aol.com					
Hershey Bears (hockey) PO Box 866	Hershey	PA	17033	717-534-3380	534-3383
Hershey Wildcats (soccer) 100 W Hersheypark Dr	Hershey	PA	17033	717-534-8900	534-8945
Penn National Thoroughbred Race Course PO Box 32	Grantville	PA	17028	717-469-2211	469-2910
Web: www.pennnational.com ■ *E-mail:* pnrc@pennnational.com					

— Events —

	Phone
City Island Flower & Craft Festival (mid-September)	717-234-6500
Harrisburg Arts Festival (late May)	717-238-5180
Harrisburg Holiday Parade (mid-November)	717-255-3020
Harrisburg Independence Weekend Festival (early July)	717-255-3020
Kipona Festival (early September)	717-255-3020
Pennsylvania National Arts & Crafts Show (late March)	717-796-0531
Susquehanna River Celebration (early June)	717-255-3020
Zembo Shrine Circus (early April)	717-238-8107

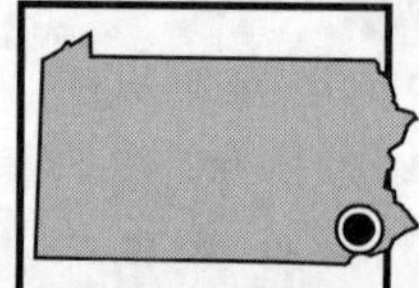

Philadelphia

Founded by William Penn in 1682, Philadelphia is sometimes referred to as the "Cradle of the Nation." The city's Waterfront and Independence National Historic Park includes Independence Hall, where the Declaration of Independence and the Constitution were signed; Independence Square, where the Declaration of Independence was first read aloud; the Liberty Bell Pavilion, where the famous symbol of liberty is kept; and Congress Hall, where the U.S. Congress met when Philadelphia was the nation's capital.

Philadelphia (Cont'd)

Located here also is Carpenter's Hall, where the First Continental Congress met in 1774, and Christ Church, where many of the founding fathers worshipped; many are buried in the Christ Church Burial Ground. Other area attractions include the houses where Thomas Jefferson drafted the Declaration of Independence and Betsy Ross sewed the first American flag; and the U.S. Mint. Less than an hour away is Valley Forge National Historical Park.

Population	1,436,287	**Longitude**	75-16-42 W
Area (Land)	135.1 sq mi	**County**	Philadelphia
Area (Water)	7.5 sq mi	**Time Zone**	EST
Elevation	40 ft	**Area Code/s**	215
Latitude	39-95-22 N		

— Average Temperatures and Precipitation —

TEMPERATURES

	Jan	Feb	Mar	Apr	May	Jun	Jul	Aug	Sep	Oct	Nov	Dec
High	38	41	52	63	73	82	86	85	78	66	55	43
Low	23	24	33	42	53	62	67	66	59	46	38	28

PRECIPITATION

	Jan	Feb	Mar	Apr	May	Jun	Jul	Aug	Sep	Oct	Nov	Dec
Inches	3.2	2.8	3.5	3.6	3.8	3.7	4.3	3.8	3.4	2.6	3.3	3.4

— Important Phone Numbers —

	Phone		Phone
AAA	215-864-5000	**Medical Referral**	215-563-5343
Airport Medical Emergencies	215-937-3111	**Poison Control Center**	215-386-2100
American Express Travel	215-592-9211	**Time**	610-846-1212
Dental Referral	800-917-6453	**Travelers Aid Society**	215-523-7580
Emergency	911	**Weather**	610-936-1212
HotelDocs	800-468-3537		

— Information Sources —

				Phone	Fax
Better Business Bureau Serving Eastern Pennsylvania 1608 Walnut St Suite 600 *Web:* www.easternpa.bbb.org	Philadelphia	PA	19103	215-985-9313	893-9312
Greater Philadelphia Chamber of Commerce 200 S Broad St Suite 700 *Web:* www.gpcc.com	Philadelphia	PA	19102	215-545-1234	970-3600
Pennsylvania Convention Center 1101 Arch St *TF:* 800-428-9000 ■ *Web:* www.paconvention.com	Philadelphia	PA	19107	215-418-4700	418-4747
Philadelphia City Hall *Web:* www.phila.gov	Philadelphia	PA	19107	215-686-1776	
Philadelphia City Planning Commission 1515 Arch St 13th Fl *Web:* www.libertynet.org/philplan ■ *E-mail:* philplan@libertynet.org	Philadelphia	PA	19102	215-683-4615	683-4630
Philadelphia Convention & Visitors Bureau 1515 Market St Suite 2020 *TF:* 800-537-7676 ■ *Web:* www.libertynet.org/phila-visitor ■ *E-mail:* tourism@libertynet.org	Philadelphia	PA	19102	215-636-3300	636-3327
Philadelphia County City Hall	Philadelphia	PA	19107	215-686-1776	
Philadelphia Free Library 1901 Vine St. *Web:* www.library.phila.gov	Philadelphia	PA	19103	215-686-5320	563-3628
Philadelphia Mayor 215 City Hall	Philadelphia	PA	19107	215-686-2181	686-2180

On-Line Resources

4Philadelphia.com	www.4philadelphia.com
About.com Guide to Philadelphia	philadelphia.about.com/local/midlanticus/philadelphia
Access America Philadelphia	www.accessamer.com/philadelphia/
Anthill City Guide Philadelphia	www.anthill.com/city.asp?city=philadelphia
Area Guide Philadelphia	philadelphia.areaguides.net
Boulevards Philadelphia	www.philadelphia.com
Bradmans.com Philadelphia	www.bradmans.com/scripts/display_city.cgi?city=241
City Knowledge Philadelphia	www.cityknowledge.com/pa_philadelphia.htm
CitySearch Philadelphia	philadelphia.citysearch.com
CityTravelGuide.com Philadelphia	www.citytravelguide.com/philadelphia.htm
CuisineNet Philadelphia	www.cuisinenet.com/restaurant/philadelphia/
DigitalCity Philadelphia	www.digitalcity.com/philadelphia/
Essential Guide to Philadelphia	www.ego.net/us/pa/phl/index.htm
Excite.com Philadelphia City Guide	www.excite.com/travel/countries/united_states/pennsylvania/philadelphia
InPhiladelphia.com	www.inphiladelphia.com
Philadelphia City Pages	philadelphia.thelinks.com/
Philadelphia City Paper	www.citypaper.net
Philadelphia CityWomen	www.citywomen.com/philwomen.htm
Philadelphia Interactive	www.nealcomm.com/pi/index.htm
Philadelphia Liberty Net	www.libertynet.org
Philadelphia Night Life	www.phillynightlife.com
Philadelphia Online	www.philly.com
Philadelphia's Center City District	www.centercityphila.org/
Philanet.com	philanet.com/
Philly Web	www.phillyweb.com/
Phillyfriend.com	www.phillyfriend.com
Rough Guide Travel Philadelphia	travel.roughguides.com/content/332/
Savvy Diner Guide to Philadelphia Restaurants	www.savvydiner.com/philadelphia/
Time Out Philadelphia	www.timeout.com/philadelphia/
Virtual Philly	www.virtualphilly.com/

— Transportation Services —

AIRPORTS

	Phone
■ **Philadelphia International Airport (PHL)** 7 miles SW of downtown (approx 30 minutes) Web: www.phl.org	215-937-6937

Airport Transportation

	Phone
Airport Express $12 fare to downtown	215-331-1130
SEPTA Airport Rail Line $10 fare to downtown	215-580-7800
Taxi $20 fare to downtown	215-829-4222
Transline Limousine $30 fare to downtown	215-535-4040

Commercial Airlines

	Phone		Phone
Air Jamaica	800-523-5585	**Mexicana**	800-531-7923
American	800-433-7300	**Midway**	800-446-4392
American Eagle	800-433-7300	**National**	888-757-5387
British Airways	800-247-9297	**Northwest**	800-225-2525
Continental	800-525-0280	**United**	800-241-6522
Continental Express	800-525-0280	**US Airways**	800-428-4322
Delta	800-221-1212	**US Airways Express**	800-428-4322

Charter Airlines

	Phone		Phone
Northeast Aviation Charter Inc	215-677-5592	**Sterling Helicopters**	215-271-2510
Philadelphia Jet Service	800-468-1490	**Wings Charter**	215-646-1800

CAR RENTALS

	Phone		Phone
Alamo	215-492-3960	**Dollar**	215-365-2700
Avis-Philadelphia	215-492-0900	**Enterprise**	610-521-3700
Budget	215-492-9400	**Hertz**	215-492-7200
CarTemps USA	215-334-8800	**National**	215-492-2750

LIMO/TAXI

	Phone		Phone
Ali Baba Limousine	215-842-0328	**Olde City Taxi Coach**	215-247-7678
Bell Taxi	215-425-7000	**Quaker City Cab**	215-728-8000
Carey Limousine	215-492-8402	**Transline Limousine**	215-535-4040
Dav El Limousines	215-334-7900	**USA Limousine**	800-872-6070
London Limousine	800-834-0708	**Yellow Cab**	215-829-4222

MASS TRANSIT

	Phone
Philly Phlash $1.50 Base fare	215-474-5274
Port Authority Transit $.75 Base fare	215-922-4600
RiverLink Ferry Service $5 Base fare	215-925-5465
SEPTA $1.60 Base fare	215-580-7800

Philadelphia (Cont'd)

RAIL/BUS

				Phone
30th Street Amtrak Station 30th & Market Sts	Philadelphia	PA	19104	800-872-7245
Greyhound Bus Station 1001 Filbert St *TF:* 800-231-2222	Philadelphia	PA	19107	215-931-4027

— Accommodations —

HOTEL RESERVATION SERVICES

	Phone	Fax
Accommodations Express *TF:* 800-444-7666 ■ *Web:* www.accommodationsxpress.com ■ *E-mail:* accomexp@acy.digex.net	609-391-2100	525-0111
Accommodations Plus *TF:* 800-733-7666 ■ *Web:* www.accommodationsplus.com	718-995-4444	995-6824
AmeriRoom-Philadelphia Hotel Reservation Bureau **Fax Area Code:* 609 ■ *Web:* www.ameriroom.com ■ *E-mail:* vhs@ameriroom.com	800-888-5825	645-1147*
Association of Bed & Breakfasts in Philadelphia *TF:* 800-344-0123 ■ *E-mail:* pa@bnbassociation.com	610-783-7838	783-7787
Bed & Breakfast of Philadelphia *TF:* 800-448-3619 ■ *Web:* www.bnbphiladelphia.com/ ■ *E-mail:* bnb@bnbphiladelphia.com	610-687-3565	995-9524
Global Reservations Inc **Fax Area Code:* 623	480-596-5156	707-6223*
Hotel Reservations Network Inc *TF Sales:* 800-964-6835 ■ *Web:* www.hoteldiscount.com	214-361-7311	361-7299
Quikbook *TF:* 800-789-9887 ■ *Web:* www.quikbook.com	212-532-1660	532-1556
RMC Travel Centre *TF:* 800-782-2674	212-754-6560	754-6571

HOTELS, MOTELS, RESORTS

				Phone	Fax
Adam's Mark Hotel City Line Ave & Monument Rd **Fax:* Sales ■ *TF:* 800-444-2326 ■ *Web:* www.adamsmark.com/philad.htm	Philadelphia	PA	19131	215-581-5000	581-5069*
Best Western Center City Hotel 501 N 22nd St *TF:* 800-528-1234	Philadelphia	PA	19130	215-568-8300	557-0259
Best Western Independence Park Inn 235 Chestnut St *TF:* 800-528-1234	Philadelphia	PA	19106	215-922-4443	922-4487
Chestnut Hill Hotel 8229 Germantown Ave *TF:* 800-628-9744 ■ *Web:* www.chestnuthillhotel.com ■ *E-mail:* chhotel@chestnuthillhotel.com	Philadelphia	PA	19118	215-242-5905	242-8778
Clarion Suites Convention Center 1010 Race St *TF:* 800-252-7466	Philadelphia	PA	19107	215-922-1730	922-6258
Comfort Inn Downtown 100 N Columbus Blvd *TF:* 800-228-5150	Philadelphia	PA	19106	215-627-7900	238-0809
Comfort Inn Philadelphia Airport 53 Industrial Hwy *TF:* 800-228-5150	Essington	PA	19029	610-521-9800	521-4847
Courtyard by Marriott 8900 Bartram Ave *TF:* 800-321-2211 ■ *Web:* courtyard.com/PHLAT	Philadelphia	PA	19153	215-365-2200	365-6905
Desmond Great Valley 1 Liberty Blvd *TF:* 800-575-1776 ■ *Web:* www.desmondgv.com ■ *E-mail:* info@desmondgv.com a	Malvern	PA	19355	610-296-9800	889-9869
Doubletree Hotel Philadelphia Broad & Locust Sts *TF:* 800-222-8733 ■ *Web:* www.doubletreehotels.com/DoubleT/Hotel61/79/79Main.htm	Philadelphia	PA	19107	215-893-1600	893-1663
Embassy Suites Center City 1776 Ben Franklin Pkwy *TF:* 800-362-2779	Philadelphia	PA	19103	215-561-1776	561-5930
Embassy Suites Philadelphia Airport 9000 Bartram Ave *TF:* 800-362-2779	Philadelphia	PA	19153	215-365-4500	365-3195
Extended StayAmerica 9000 Tinicum Blvd *TF:* 800-398-7829	Philadelphia	PA	19153	215-492-6766	492-6765
Four Seasons Hotel 1 Logan Sq *TF:* 800-332-3442 ■ *Web:* www.fourseasons.com/locations/Philadelphia	Philadelphia	PA	19103	215-963-1500	963-9506
Hampton Inn 530 W Dekalb Pike *TF:* 800-426-7866	King of Prussia	PA	19406	610-962-8111	962-5494
Holiday Inn City Centre 1800 Market St *TF:* 800-465-4329	Philadelphia	PA	19103	215-561-7500	561-4484
Holiday Inn City Line 4100 Presidential Blvd *TF:* 800-465-4329 ■ *Web:* www.basshotels.com/holiday-inn/?_franchisee=PHLCI	Philadelphia	PA	19131	215-477-0200	473-5510
Holiday Inn Express Midtown 1305 Walnut St *TF:* 800-465-4329	Philadelphia	PA	19107	215-735-9300	732-2682
Holiday Inn Independence Mall 400 Arch St *TF:* 800-465-4329 ■ *Web:* www.basshotels.com/holiday-inn/?_franchisee=PHLIM	Philadelphia	PA	19106	215-923-8660	923-4633
Holiday Inn Stadium 900 Packer Ave *TF:* 800-424-0291 ■ *Web:* www.basshotels.com/holiday-inn/?_franchisee=PHLPS ■ *E-mail:* histadium1@aol.com	Philadelphia	PA	19148	215-755-9500	462-6947
KormanSuites Hotel 2001 Hamilton St *TF:* 888-456-7626	Philadelphia	PA	19130	215-569-7000	569-1422
Latham Hotel Center City 135 S 17th St *TF:* 800-528-4261	Philadelphia	PA	19103	215-563-7474	568-0110
Omni Hotel at Independence Park 401 Chestnut St *TF:* 800-843-6664	Philadelphia	PA	19106	215-925-0000	925-1263
Park Hyatt Philadelphia at the Bellevue 1415 Chancellor Ct **Fax:* Sales ■ *TF:* 800-233-1234	Philadelphia	PA	19102	215-893-1776	893-9868*
Penn Tower Hotel 34th & Civic Cntr Blvd *TF:* 800-356-7366 ■ *Web:* www.upenn.edu/penntower	Philadelphia	PA	19104	215-387-8333	386-8306
Penn's View Hotel 14 N Front St *TF:* 800-331-7634 ■ *Web:* www.pennsviewhotel.com	Philadelphia	PA	19106	215-922-7600	922-7642
Philadelphia Airport Hilton 4509 Island Ave *TF:* 800-445-8667	Philadelphia	PA	19153	215-365-4150	365-3002
Philadelphia Marriott 1201 Market St *TF:* 800-228-9290	Philadelphia	PA	19107	215-625-2900	625-6000
Radisson Hotel Philadelphia Airport 500 Stevens Dr *TF:* 800-333-3333	Philadelphia	PA	19113	610-521-5900	521-4362
Radnor Hotel 591 E Lancaster Ave *TF:* 800-537-3000	Saint Davids	PA	19087	610-688-5800	341-3299
Rittenhouse Hotel 210 W Rittenhouse Sq *TF:* 800-635-1042 ■ *Web:* www.rittenhousehotel.com/	Philadelphia	PA	19103	215-546-9000	732-3364
Saint Regis Hotel 17 S Chestnut St	Philadelphia	PA	19103	215-563-1600	
Sheraton Philadelphia Airport 4101 Island Ave *TF:* 800-325-3535	Philadelphia	PA	19153	215-492-0400	365-6035
Sheraton Society Hill Hotel 1 Dock St *TF:* 800-325-3535	Philadelphia	PA	19106	215-238-6000	922-2709
Sheraton University City Hotel 36th & Chestnut Sts *TF:* 800-325-3535	Philadelphia	PA	19104	215-387-8000	387-7920
Shippen Way Inn 418 Bainbridge St *TF:* 800-245-4873	Philadelphia	PA	19147	215-627-7266	627-7781
Warwick Hotel Downtown 1701 Locust St *TF:* 800-523-4210	Philadelphia	PA	19103	215-735-6000	790-7766
Westin Suites 4101 Island Ave *TF:* 800-937-8461	Philadelphia	PA	19153	215-365-6600	492-8471
Wyndham Franklin Plaza Hotel 2 Franklin Plaza *TF:* 800-996-3426	Philadelphia	PA	19103	215-448-2000	448-2864

— Restaurants —

				Phone
Abilene (Southwest) 429 South St	Philadelphia	PA	19147	215-922-2583
Arroyo Grille (Southwest) 1 Leverington St	Philadelphia	PA	19127	215-487-1400
Bistro Romano (Italian) 120 Lombard St	Philadelphia	PA	19147	215-925-8880
Bistro St Tropez (French) 2400 Market St 4th Fl	Philadelphia	PA	19103	215-569-9269
Blt's Cobblefish (Seafood) 443 Shurs Ln	Philadelphia	PA	19128	215-483-5478
Bonaparte Restaurant (New American) Broad & Spruce Sts	Philadelphia	PA	19107	215-893-9100
Bookbinders Seafood House (Seafood) 215 S 15th St	Philadelphia	PA	19102	215-545-1137
Brasserie Perrier (French) 1619 Walnut St	Philadelphia	PA	19103	215-568-3000
Caribou Cafe (French) 1126 Walnut St	Philadelphia	PA	19107	215-625-9535
Cent'Anni Ristorante (Italian) 770 S 7th St	Philadelphia	PA	19147	215-925-5558
Ciboulette (French) 200 S Broad St	Philadelphia	PA	19102	215-790-1210
Circa (American) 1518 Walnut St	Philadelphia	PA	19102	215-545-6800
City Tavern (American) 138 S 2nd St	Philadelphia	PA	19106	215-413-1443
Cutters (New American) 2005 Market St	Philadelphia	PA	19103	215-851-6262
Cuvee Notre Dame (Belgian) 1701 Green St	Philadelphia	PA	19130	215-765-2777
Deux Cheminees (French) 1221 Locust St	Philadelphia	PA	19107	215-790-0200
Dickens Inn (Continental) 421 S 2nd St	Philadelphia	PA	19147	215-928-9307
DiLullo's Centro (Italian) 1407 Locust St	Philadelphia	PA	19102	215-546-2000

Philadelphia — Restaurants (Cont'd)

				Phone
Dinardo's Famous Crabs (Seafood) 312 Race St	Philadelphia	PA	19106	215-925-5115
Dmitri's (Mediterranean) 795 S 3rd St	Philadelphia	PA	19147	215-625-0556
Dock Street Brewery (French) 2 Logan Sq	Philadelphia	PA	19103	215-496-0413
Downey's (American) 526 S Front St	Philadelphia	PA	19147	215-629-0525
Dr Watson's Pub (American) 216 S 11th St	Philadelphia	PA	19107	215-922-3427
Fork (New American) 306 Market St	Philadelphia	PA	19106	215-625-9425
Founders Dining Room (French) 1415 Chancellor Ct	Philadelphia	PA	19102	215-790-2814
Fountain Restaurant (French) 1 Logan Sq	Philadelphia	PA	19103	215-963-1500
Friday Saturday Sunday (Continental) 261 S 21st St	Philadelphia	PA	19103	215-546-4232
Web: www.libertynet.org/frisatsun/				
Garden The (Continental) 1617 Spruce St	Philadelphia	PA	19103	215-546-4455
Girasole Ristorante (Italian) 1305 Locust St	Philadelphia	PA	19107	215-985-4659
Grasshopper (French) 4427 Main St	Philadelphia	PA	19127	215-483-1888
Happy Rooster (French) 118 S 16th St	Philadelphia	PA	19102	215-563-1481
Harry's Bar & Grill (Continental) 22 S 18th St	Philadelphia	PA	19103	215-561-5757
Hikaru (Japanese) 607 S 2nd St	Philadelphia	PA	19147	215-627-7110
Ho Sai Gai (Chinese) 131 Cherry St	Philadelphia	PA	19106	215-925-8384
Il Portico (Italian) 1519 Walnut St	Philadelphia	PA	19102	215-587-7000
Imperial Inn (Chinese) 142 N 10th St	Philadelphia	PA	19107	215-627-5588
Irish Pub (American) 1123 Walnut St	Philadelphia	PA	19107	215-925-3311
Jake's (New American) 4365 Main St	Philadelphia	PA	19127	215-483-0444
Jim's Steaks (Steak) 400 South St	Philadelphia	PA	19147	215-928-1911
Joseph Poon (Chinese) 1002 Arch St	Philadelphia	PA	19107	215-928-9333
La Famiglia (Italian) 8 S Front St	Philadelphia	PA	19106	215-922-2803
La Terrasse (French) 3432 Sansom St	Philadelphia	PA	19104	215-386-5000
Le Bec-Fin (French) 1523 Walnut St	Philadelphia	PA	19102	215-567-1000
Web: www.lebecfin.com ■ *E-mail:* info@lebecfin.com				
Le Champignon (Asian) 122 Lombard St	Philadelphia	PA	19147	215-922-2515
Leneghan's Tavern (American) 704 Chestnut St	Philadelphia	PA	19106	215-592-9533
Locust Rendezvous (American) 1415 Locust St	Philadelphia	PA	19102	215-985-1163
London Grill (New American) 2301 Fairmount Ave	Philadelphia	PA	19130	215-978-4545
MaMa Yolanda's (Italian) 746 S 8th St	Philadelphia	PA	19147	215-592-0195
Marrakesh (Moroccan) 517 S Leithgow St	Philadelphia	PA	19147	215-925-5929
McGillin's Ole Ale House (American) 1310 Drury St	Philadelphia	PA	19107	215-735-5562
Melrose Diner (American) 1501 Snyder Ave	Philadelphia	PA	19145	215-467-6644
Monk's Cafe (Belgian) 264 S 16th St	Philadelphia	PA	19102	215-545-7005
Monte Carlo Living Room (Italian) 150 South St	Philadelphia	PA	19147	215-925-2220
MontSerrat American Bistro (American) 623 South St	Philadelphia	PA	19147	215-627-4224
Moonstruck (Italian) 7955 Oxford Ave	Philadelphia	PA	19111	215-725-6000
Moshulu (Continental) 735 S Columbus Blvd Pier 34	Philadelphia	PA	19147	215-923-2500
New Delhi Indian Restaurant (Indian) 4004 Chestnut St	Philadelphia	PA	19104	215-386-1941
Opus 251 (New American) 251 S 18th St	Philadelphia	PA	19103	215-735-6787
Palm Restaurant (Continental) 200 S Broad St	Philadelphia	PA	19102	215-546-7256
Passerelle (Mediterranean) 175 King of Prussia Rd	Radnor	PA	19087	610-293-9411
Peacock on the Parkway (Mediterranean) 1700 Ben Franklin Pkwy	Philadelphia	PA	19102	215-569-8888
Philippe Chin (French/Asian) 1614 Locust St	Philadelphia	PA	19103	215-735-7551
Pompeii (Italian) 121 S Broad St	Philadelphia	PA	19107	215-772-9238
Provence (French) 379 Lancaster Ave	Haverford	PA	19041	610-896-0400
Rembrandt's (New American) 741 N 23rd St	Philadelphia	PA	19130	215-763-2228
Restaurant School (American) 4207 Walnut St	Philadelphia	PA	19104	215-222-4200
Rococo (American) 123 Chestnut St	Philadelphia	PA	19106	215-629-1100
Roscoe's Kodiak Cafe (Seafood) 4425 Main St	Philadelphia	PA	19127	215-483-7108
Saloon (Italian) 750 S 7th St	Philadelphia	PA	19147	215-627-1811
Sansom Street Oyster House (Seafood) 1516 Sansom St	Philadelphia	PA	19102	215-567-7683
Serrano (International) 20 S 2nd St	Philadelphia	PA	19106	215-928-0770
Sonoma (Italian) 4411 Main St	Philadelphia	PA	19127	215-483-9400
South Street Souvlaki (Greek) 509 South St	Philadelphia	PA	19147	215-925-3026
Striped Bass (Seafood) 1500 Walnut St	Philadelphia	PA	19102	215-732-4444
Susanna Foo (Chinese) 1512 Walnut St	Philadelphia	PA	19102	215-545-2666
Swann Lounge & Cafe (American) 1 Logan Sq	Philadelphia	PA	19103	215-963-1500
Tai Lake Restaurant (Chinese) 134 N 10th St	Philadelphia	PA	19107	215-922-0698
Tree Top (New American) 210 W Rittenhouse Sq	Philadelphia	PA	19103	215-790-2534
US Hotel Bar & Grill (American) 4439 Main St	Philadelphia	PA	19127	215-483-9222
Vega Grill (Latin American) 4141 Main St	Philadelphia	PA	19127	215-487-9600
Warmdaddy's (Southern) 4 S Front St	Philadelphia	PA	19106	215-627-2500
Warsaw Cafe (Polish) 306 S 16th St	Philadelphia	PA	19102	215-546-0204
White Dog Cafe (New American) 3420 Sansom St	Philadelphia	PA	19104	215-386-9224
Wichita Steak & Brew (New American) 22 S 3rd St	Philadelphia	PA	19106	215-627-4825
Zanzibar Blue (Continental) 200 S Broad St	Philadelphia	PA	19102	215-732-5200
Zocalo (Mexican) 3600 Lancaster Ave	Philadelphia	PA	19104	215-895-0139

— Goods and Services —

SHOPPING

				Phone	Fax
Chestnut Hill Shopping District 7900-8700 Germantown Ave	Philadelphia	PA	19118	215-247-6696	247-5680
Court & Plaza at King of Prussia 160 N Gulph Rd	King of Prussia	PA	19406	610-265-5727	
Franklin Mills 1455 Franklin Mills Cir	Philadelphia	PA	19114	215-632-1500	632-7888
TF: 800-336-6255 ■ *Web:* www.franklin-mills-mall.com					
Gallery at Market East 9th & Market Sts	Philadelphia	PA	19107	215-925-7162	440-0116
Jewelers' Row Sansom St-betw 9th & 7th	Philadelphia	PA	19107	215-636-1666	
King of Prussia Plaza 1600 N Gulf Rd	King of Prussia	PA	19406	610-768-6420	265-1640
Web: www.shopking.com					
Oxford Valley Mall 2300 E Lincoln Hwy	Langhorne	PA	19047	215-752-0222	752-2869
Web: www.oxfordvalleymall.com ■ *E-mail:* info@oxfordvalleymall.com					
Rittenhouse Row 1830 Rittenhouse Sq	Philadelphia	PA	19103	215-735-4899	
Roosevelt Mall 2329 Cottman Ave	Philadelphia	PA	19149	215-331-2000	331-5771
Shops at Liberty Place 1625 Chestnut St	Philadelphia	PA	19103	215-851-9055	851-9154
Shops at The Bellevue Broad & Walnut Sts	Philadelphia	PA	19102	215-875-8350	
South Street Antiques Market 615 S 6th St	Philadelphia	PA	19147	215-592-0256	
South Street Shopping District South St betw Front & 8th Sts	Philadelphia	PA	19147	215-636-1666	

BANKS

				Phone	Fax
Beneficial Savings Bank 1200 Chestnut St	Philadelphia	PA	19107	215-864-6000	864-6018
TF: 888-784-8490 ■ *Web:* www.beneficialsavings.com ■ *E-mail:* bsb@libertynet.org					
First Bank of Philadelphia 1424 Walnut St	Philadelphia	PA	19102	215-790-9000	790-5208*
**Fax:* Cust Svc					
Firstrust Bank 1931 Cottman Ave	Philadelphia	PA	19111	215-722-2000	725-1614
TF: 800-220-2265					
PNC Bank Broad & Chestnut Sts	Philadelphia	PA	19102	215-585-5178	
United Bank of Philadelphia 714 Market St	Philadelphia	PA	19106	215-829-2265	829-2269

BUSINESS SERVICES

	Phone		Phone
Accountemps	215-568-4580	**Olsten Staffing Services**	215-568-7795
Federal Express	800-463-3339	**Philadelphia Express Courier**	215-627-6700
Kangaroo Couriers	215-561-5132	**Post Office**	215-895-8000
Kelly Services	215-564-3110	**Quick Courier Service**	610-825-2603
Kinko's	215-473-0500	**Rapid Delivery Service**	215-496-9600
Manpower Temporary Services	215-568-4050	**UPS**	800-742-5877

— Media —

PUBLICATIONS

				Phone	Fax
Germantown Courier PO Box 18971	Philadelphia	PA	19119	215-248-7580	848-9160*
**Fax:* News Rm					
Leader The 2385 W Cheltenham Ave Suite 182	Philadelphia	PA	19150	215-885-4111	885-0226*
**Fax:* News Rm					
Mount Airy Times Express 7169 Germantown Ave	Philadelphia	PA	19119	215-248-7580	248-7587
Philadelphia Business Journal 400 Market St Suite 300	Philadelphia	PA	19106	215-238-1450	238-1466
Web: www.amcity.com/philadelphia/index.html ■ *E-mail:* philadelphia@amcity.com.					
Philadelphia Daily News‡ PO Box 7788	Philadelphia	PA	19101	215-854-2000	854-5910
Web: www.phillynews.com/pdn ■ *E-mail:* dailynews.opinion@phillynews.com					
Philadelphia Inquirer‡ PO Box 8263	Philadelphia	PA	19101	215-854-2000	854-5099
Web: www.phillynews.com/inq ■ *E-mail:* Inquirer.opinion@phillynews.com					
Philadelphia Magazine 1818 Market St	Philadelphia	PA	19103	215-564-7700	656-3500
TF: 800-777-1003 ■ *Web:* www.phillymag.com ■ *E-mail:* mail@phillymag.com					
Review The 6220 Ridge Ave	Philadelphia	PA	19128	215-483-7300	483-2073
Web: www.ausinc.com/ing					
Where Philadelphia Magazine 301 S 19th St Suite 1-C	Philadelphia	PA	19103	215-893-5100	893-5105

‡*Daily newspapers*

Philadelphia (Cont'd)

TELEVISION

				Phone	Fax
KYW-TV Ch 3 (CBS) 101 S Independence Mall E ... *Web:* www.kyw.com	Philadelphia	PA	19106	215-238-4700	238-4783
WCAU-TV Ch 10 (NBC) 10 Monument Rd ... *Web:* www.nbc10.com	Bala Cynwyd	PA	19004	610-668-5510	668-3700
WGTW-TV Ch 48 (Ind) 3900 Main St.	Philadelphia	PA	19127	215-930-0482	930-0496
WHYY-TV Ch 12 (PBS) 150 N 6th St. ... *Web:* whyy.org ■ *E-mail:* talkback@whyy.org	Philadelphia	PA	19106	215-351-1200	351-0398
WMGM-TV Ch 40 (NBC) 1601 New Rd ... *Web:* www.wmgmtv.com ■ *E-mail:* wmgmtv@acy.digex.net	Linwood	NJ	08221	609-927-4440	927-7014
WPHL-TV Ch 17 (WB) 5001 Wynnefield Ave. ... **Fax:* Sales ■ *Web:* www.wb17.com ■ *E-mail:* wb17philly@aol.com	Philadelphia	PA	19131	215-878-1700	879-3665*
WPPX-TV Ch 61 (PAX) 520 N Columbus Blvd ... *Web:* www.pax.net/wppx	Philadelphia	PA	19123	215-923-2661	923-2677
WPSG-TV Ch 57 (UPN) 420 N 20th St. ... *Web:* www.paramountstations.com/WPSG ■ *E-mail:* upn57@paramount.com	Philadelphia	PA	19130	215-563-5757	563-5786
WPVI-TV Ch 6 (ABC) 4100 City Line Ave ... *Web:* abcnews.go.com/local/wpvi	Philadelphia	PA	19131	215-878-9700	581-4530
WTVE-TV Ch 51 (Tele) 1729 N 11th St	Reading	PA	19604	610-921-9181	921-9139
WTXF-TV Ch 29 (Fox) 330 Market St. ... *Web:* www.foxphiladelphia.com	Philadelphia	PA	19106	215-925-2929	925-2420
WWAC-TV Ch 53 (Ind) 19 S New York Ave.	Atlantic City	NJ	08401	609-344-5030	347-4758

RADIO

				Phone	Fax
KYW-AM 1060 kHz (N/T) 101 S Independence Mall E	Philadelphia	PA	19106	215-238-4700	238-4657
WBEB-FM 101.1 MHz (AC) 10 Presidential Blvd. ... *Web:* www.b101radio.com	Bala Cynwyd	PA	19004	610-667-8400	667-6795
WDAS-AM 1480 kHz (Rel) 23 W City Line Ave.	Bala Cynwyd	PA	19004	610-617-8500	617-2576
WDAS-FM 105.3 MHz (Urban) 23 W City Line Ave	Bala Cynwyd	PA	19004	610-617-8500	617-2576
WHAT-AM 1340 kHz (N/T) 2471 N 54th St Suite 220	Philadelphia	PA	19131	215-581-5161	581-5185
WHYY-FM 90.9 MHz (NPR) 150 N 6th St ... *Web:* www.whyy.org/91FM/index.html	Philadelphia	PA	19106	215-351-9200	627-1867
WIOQ-FM 102.1 MHz (CHR) 1 Bala Plaza Suite 243 ... *Web:* q102philly.amfmi.com ■ *E-mail:* wmq102@q102philly.com	Bala Cynwyd	PA	19004	610-667-8100	668-4657
WIP-AM 610 kHz (Sports) 441 N 5th St.	Philadelphia	PA	19123	215-922-5000	922-2364
WJJZ-FM 106.1 MHz (NAC) 440 Domino Ln.	Philadelphia	PA	19128	215-508-1200	508-4466
WMGK-FM 102.9 MHz (CR) 1 Bala Plaza Suite 339 ... *Web:* www.wmgk.com ■ *E-mail:* programdirector@wmgk.com	Bala Cynwyd	PA	19004	610-667-8500	664-9610
WMMR-FM 93.3 MHz (Rock) 1 Bala Plaza Suite 424 ... *Web:* www.wmmr.com	Bala Cynwyd	PA	19004	610-771-0933	771-9610
WOGL-FM 98.1 MHz (Oldies) 10 Monument Rd	Bala Cynwyd	PA	19004	610-668-5900	668-5977
WPEN-AM 950 kHz (Nost) 1 Bala Plaza Suite 339 ... *Web:* www.wpen.com	Bala Cynwyd	PA	19004	610-667-8500	664-9610
WPHI-FM 103.9 MHz (Urban) 100 Old York Rd.	Jenkintown	PA	19046	215-884-9400	884-2608
WPHT-AM 1210 kHz (N/T) 10 Monument Rd ... **Fax:* Sales	Bala Cynwyd	PA	19004	610-668-5800	668-5888*
WPLY-FM 100.3 MHz (Alt) 1003 Baltimore Pike ... *Web:* www.y100.com	Media	PA	19063	610-565-8900	565-6024
WPST-FM 97.5 MHz (CHR) 619 Alexander Rd 3rd Fl ... *Web:* www.wpst.com	Princeton	NJ	08540	609-419-0300	419-0143
WUSL-FM 98.9 MHz (Urban) 440 Domino Ln.	Philadelphia	PA	19128	215-483-8900	483-5930
WWDB-FM 96.5 MHz (N/T) 166 E Levering Mill Rd	Bala Cynwyd	PA	19004	610-668-4400	668-4468
WXTU-FM 92.5 MHz (Ctry) 555 City Line Ave Suite 330 ... *Web:* www.wxtu.com ■ *E-mail:* comments@wxtu.com	Bala Cynwyd	PA	19004	610-667-9000	667-5978
WXXM-FM 95.7 MHz (AC) 8200 Ridge Ave	Philadelphia	PA	19128	215-482-6000	482-3777
WYSP-FM 94.1 MHz (Rock) 101 S Independence Mall E	Philadelphia	PA	19106	215-625-9460	625-6555
WYXR-FM 104.5 MHz (AC) 1 Bala Plaza Suite 243 W.	Bala Cynwyd	PA	19004	610-668-0750	668-8253

— Colleges/Universities —

				Phone	Fax
American College 270 S Bryn Mawr Ave ... *Web:* www.amercoll.edu	Bryn Mawr	PA	19010	610-526-1000	526-1310
Antonelli Institute 300 Montgomery Ave ... *TF:* 800-722-7871 ■ *Web:* www.antonelli.org ■ *E-mail:* admissions@antonelli.org	Erdenheim	PA	19038	215-836-2222	836-2794
Art Institute of Philadelphia 1622 Chestnut St ... *TF:* 800-275-2474 ■ *Web:* www.aii.edu	Philadelphia	PA	19103	215-567-7080	246-3339
Beaver College 450 S Easton Rd ... *TF:* 888-232-8373 ■ *Web:* www.beaver.edu	Glenside	PA	19038	215-572-2900	572-4049
Berean Institute 1901 W Girard Ave	Philadelphia	PA	19130	215-763-4833	236-6011
Bryn Athyn College of the New Church PO Box 717 ... *Web:* www.newchurch.org	Bryn Athyn	PA	19009	215-938-2543	938-2658
Bryn Mawr College 101 N Merion Ave. ... *Web:* www.brynmawr.edu ■ *E-mail:* agiardin@brynmawr.edu	Bryn Mawr	PA	19010	610-526-5000	526-7471
Cabrini College 610 King of Prussia Rd ... *TF Admissions:* 800-848-1003 ■ *Web:* www.cabrini.edu ■ *E-mail:* admit@cabrini.edu	Radnor	PA	19087	610-902-8100	902-8508
Chestnut Hill College 9601 Germantown Ave ... *TF Admissions:* 800-248-0052 ■ *Web:* www.chc.edu	Philadelphia	PA	19118	215-248-7000	248-7082
Cheyney University of Pennsylvania ... *TF Admissions:* 800-243-9639 ■ *Web:* www.cheyney.edu	Cheyney	PA	19319	610-399-2000	399-2099
CHI Institute 2641 Westchester Pike	Broomall	PA	19008	610-353-7630	359-1370
Community College of Philadelphia 1700 Spring Garden St ... *Web:* www.ccp.cc.pa.us	Philadelphia	PA	19130	215-751-8000	751-8001
Curtis Institute of Music 1726 Locust St ... *Web:* www.curtis.edu	Philadelphia	PA	19103	215-893-5252	893-9065
Delaware County Community College 901 S Media Line Rd. ... **Fax:* Library ■ *Web:* www.dccc.edu	Media	PA	19063	610-359-5000	359-5343*
Drexel University 3141 Chestnut St ... *TF Admissions:* 800-237-3935 ■ *Web:* www.drexel.edu ■ *E-mail:* admissions@post.drexel.edu	Philadelphia	PA	19104	215-895-2000	895-5939
Eastern College 1300 Eagle Rd. ... *Web:* www.eastern.edu ■ *E-mail:* ugadm@eastern.edu	Saint Davids	PA	19087	610-341-5800	341-1723
Gwynedd-Mercy College PO Box 901 ... *TF Admissions:* 800-342-5462 ■ *Web:* www.gmc.edu	Gwynedd Valley	PA	19437	215-646-7300	641-5556
Hahnemann University of the Health Sciences 245 N 15th St ... *Web:* www.mcphu.edu	Philadelphia	PA	19102	215-762-8288	762-6194
Harcum College 750 Montgomery Ave ... *TF:* 800-345-2600 ■ *Web:* www.harcum.edu ■ *E-mail:* enroll@harcum.edu	Bryn Mawr	PA	19010	610-525-4100	526-6147
Haverford College 370 W Lancaster Ave ... *Web:* www.haverford.edu	Haverford	PA	19041	610-896-1000	896-1224
Holy Family College Grant & Frankford Aves ... *Web:* www.hfc.edu	Philadelphia	PA	19114	215-637-7700	281-1022
Hussian School of Art 1118 Market St. ... *Web:* www.hussianart.edu	Philadelphia	PA	19107	215-981-0900	864-9115
Immaculata College 1145 King Rd ... *TF Admissions:* 888-777-2780 ■ *Web:* www.immaculata.edu	Immaculata	PA	19345	610-647-4400	251-1668
La Salle University 1900 W Olney Ave ... *Web:* www.lasalle.edu ■ *E-mail:* webadmin@lasalle.edu	Philadelphia	PA	19141	215-951-1000	951-1656
Lincoln Technical Institute 9191 Torresdale Ave	Philadelphia	PA	19136	215-335-0800	335-1443
Manor Junior College 700 Fox Chase Rd. ... *Web:* manor.edu	Jenkintown	PA	19046	215-885-2360	576-6564
Montgomery County Community College Central Campus 340 DeKalb Pike ... *Web:* www.mc3.edu	Blue Bell	PA	19422	215-641-6300	641-6516
Moore College of Art & Design 20th & Race Sts ... *TF:* 800-523-2025 ■ *Web:* www.moore.edu	Philadelphia	PA	19103	215-568-4515	568-8017
Peirce College 1420 Pine St ... *TF:* 888-467-3472 ■ *Web:* www.peirce.edu/index.html ■ *E-mail:* peirce@libertynet.org	Philadelphia	PA	19102	215-545-6400	546-5996
Pennco Tech 3815 Otter St ... *TF:* 800-579-9399 ■ *Web:* www.penncotech.com ■ *E-mail:* admissions@penncotech.com	Bristol	PA	19007	215-824-3200	785-1945
Pennsylvania Institute of Technology 800 Manchester Ave ... *TF:* 800-422-0025 ■ *Web:* www.pit.edu ■ *E-mail:* info@pit.edu	Media	PA	19063	610-565-7900	892-1510
Pennsylvania State University Abington Campus 1600 Woodland Rd. ... *Web:* www.abington.psu.edu	Abington	PA	19001	215-881-7300	881-7317

Philadelphia — Colleges/Universities (Cont'd)

Name / Address	City	State	ZIP	Phone	Fax
Philadelphia College of Bible 200 Manor Ave *TF Admissions:* 800-366-0049 ■ *Web:* www.pcb.edu	Langhorne	PA	19047	215-752-5800	702-4248
Philadelphia College of Textiles & Science 4201 Henry Ave *TF:* 800-951-7287 ■ *Web:* www.philacol.edu ■ *E-mail:* admissions@philacol.edu	Philadelphia	PA	19144	215-951-2700	951-2907
Rosemont College 1400 Montgomery Ave *TF:* 800-331-0708 ■ *Web:* www.rosemont.edu	Rosemont	PA	19010	610-527-0200	527-0341
Rutgers The State University of New Jersey Camden Campus 311 N 5th St *Web:* camden-www.rutgers.edu ■ *E-mail:* camden@asb-ugadm.rutgers.edu	Camden	NJ	08102	856-225-1766	225-6495
Saint Joseph's University 5600 City Ave *Web:* www.sju.edu	Philadelphia	PA	19131	610-660-1000	660-1314
Swarthmore College 500 College Ave *TF:* 800-667-3110 ■ *Web:* www.swarthmore.edu	Swarthmore	PA	19081	610-328-8000	328-8673
Temple University Broad St & Montgomery Ave *Web:* www.temple.edu	Philadelphia	PA	19122	215-204-7000	204-5694
Thomas Jefferson University 1025 Walnut St *TF Admissions:* 800-247-6933 ■ *Web:* www.tju.edu	Philadelphia	PA	19107	215-955-6000	503-7241
University of Pennsylvania 3451 Walnut St *Web:* www.upenn.edu ■ *E-mail:* regist@pobox.upenn.edu	Philadelphia	PA	19104	215-898-5000	898-5000
University of the Arts 320 S Broad St *TF:* 800-616-2787 ■ *Web:* www.uarts.edu ■ *E-mail:* emuarts@netaxs.com	Philadelphia	PA	19102	215-717-6000	717-6045
University of the Sciences 600 S 43rd St *Web:* www.pcps.edu	Philadelphia	PA	19104	215-596-8800	895-1100
Valley Forge Military Academy & College 1001 Eagle Rd *TF Admissions:* 800-234-8362 ■ *Web:* www.vfmac.edu	Wayne	PA	19087	610-989-1200	688-1545
Villanova University 800 Lancaster Ave *TF:* 800-338-7927 ■ *Web:* www.villanova.edu	Villanova	PA	19085	610-519-4500	519-6450
Widener University 1 University Pl **Fax:* Admissions ■ *Web:* www.widener.edu	Chester	PA	19013	610-499-4000	499-4676*
Williamson Free School of Mechanical Trades 106 S New Middletown Rd *Web:* www.libertynet.org/wiltech ■ *E-mail:* wiltech@libertynet.org	Media	PA	19063	610-566-1776	566-6502

— Hospitals —

Name / Address	City	State	ZIP	Phone	Fax
Albert Einstein Medical Center 5501 Old York Rd *Web:* www.einstein.edu/aehn/aemed_center.html	Philadelphia	PA	19141	215-456-7010	456-6199
Alegany Parkview Hospital 1331 E Wyoming Ave	Philadelphia	PA	19124	215-537-7400	537-7680
Chestnut Hill Hospital 8835 Germantown Ave	Philadelphia	PA	19118	215-248-8200	248-8053
Children's Hospital of Philadelphia 34th St & Civic Ctr Blvd **Fax:* Admitting ■ *Web:* www.chop.edu	Philadelphia	PA	19104	215-590-1000	590-1413*
City Avenue Hospital 4150 City Avenue	Philadelphia	PA	19131	215-871-1000	871-2526
Episcopal Hospital 100 E Lehigh Ave	Philadelphia	PA	19125	215-427-7000	426-6966
Frankford Hospital of the City of Philadelphia Knights & Red Lion Rds **Fax:* Library	Philadelphia	PA	19114	215-612-4000	612-4942*
Graduate Hospital 1800 Lombard St	Philadelphia	PA	19146	215-893-2000	893-7205
Hahnemann University Hospital Center City Broad & Vine Sts	Philadelphia	PA	19102	215-762-7000	762-3895
Hospital Health System University of Pennsylvania 3400 Spruce St *Web:* www.med.upenn.edu/	Philadelphia	PA	19104	215-662-4000	662-2599
Jeanes Hospital 7600 Central Ave *Web:* www.jeanes.com ■ *E-mail:* mpomrink@becnet.com	Philadelphia	PA	19111	215-728-2000	728-2118
Methodist Hospital 2301 S Broad St **Fax:* Admitting	Philadelphia	PA	19148	215-952-9000	952-9933*
Nazareth Hospital 2601 Holme Ave **Fax:* Admitting	Philadelphia	PA	19152	215-335-6000	335-7620*
Neumann Medical Center 1741 Frankford Ave	Philadelphia	PA	19125	215-291-2000	291-2028
North Philadelphia Health Systems Saint Joseph Hospital 16th St & Girard Ave	Philadelphia	PA	19130	215-787-9000	787-9558
Northeastern Hospital of Philadelphia 2301 E Allegheny Ave	Philadelphia	PA	19134	215-291-3000	291-3611
Pennsylvania Hospital 800 Spruce St **Fax:* Admitting ■ *Web:* www.pahosp.com	Philadelphia	PA	19107	215-829-3000	829-6363*
Presbyterian Medical Center of Philadelphia 39th & Market Sts	Philadelphia	PA	19104	215-662-8000	662-9850
Roxborough Memorial Hospital 5800 Ridge Ave	Philadelphia	PA	19128	215-483-9900	487-4274
Saint Agnes Medical Center 1900 S Broad St	Philadelphia	PA	19145	215-339-4100	339-0482
Saint Christopher's Hospital for Children Erie Ave & Front St	Philadelphia	PA	19134	215-427-5000	427-4444
Shriners Hospitals for Children Philadelphia Unit 3551 N Broad St *TF:* 800-281-4050 ■ *Web:* www.shrinershq.org/Hospitals/Directry/philadelphia.html	Philadelphia	PA	19140	215-430-4000	430-4079
Temple University Hospital 3401 N Broad St *Web:* www.health.temple.edu/tuh ■ *E-mail:* tuhs@blue.vm.temple.edu	Philadelphia	PA	19140	215-707-2000	707-3261
Thomas Jefferson University Hospital 111 S 11th St *Web:* www.jeffersonhealth.org/tjuh	Philadelphia	PA	19107	215-955-6000	955-5207
Veterans Affairs Medical Center University & Woodland Aves	Philadelphia	PA	19104	215-823-5800	823-6054

— Attractions —

Name / Address	City	State	ZIP	Phone	Fax
Academy of Natural Sciences Museum 1900 Benjamin Franklin Pkwy *Web:* www.acnatsci.org/	Philadelphia	PA	19103	215-299-1000	299-1028
African-American Museum in Philadelphia 701 Arch St *Web:* www.aampmuseum.org	Philadelphia	PA	19106	215-574-0380	574-3110
American Swedish Historical Museum 1900 Pattison Ave *Web:* www.libertynet.org/~ashm/ ■ *E-mail:* ashm@libertynet.org	Philadelphia	PA	19145	215-389-1776	389-7701
Arch Street Meeting House 320 Arch St	Philadelphia	PA	19106	215-627-2667	
Arden Theatre Co 40 N 2nd St *Web:* www.libertynet.org/arden ■ *E-mail:* ardenthco@aol.com	Philadelphia	PA	19106	215-922-8900	922-7011
Athenaeum The of Philadelphia 219 S 6th St *Web:* www.libertynet.org/athena/ ■ *E-mail:* athena@libertynet.org	Philadelphia	PA	19106	215-925-2688	925-3755
AVA Opera Theatre 1920 Spruce St	Philadelphia	PA	19103	215-735-1685	732-2189
Balch Institute for Ethnic Studies 18 S 7th St *Web:* www.libertynet.org/balch/ ■ *E-mail:* balchlib@balchinstitute.org	Philadelphia	PA	19106	215-925-8090	925-8195
Barnes Foundation Museum & Arboretum 300 N Latch's Ln *Web:* www.thebarnes.org	Merion	PA	19066	610-667-0290	664-4026
Betsy Ross House 239 Arch St *Web:* www.libertynet.org/iha/betsy/	Philadelphia	PA	19106	215-627-5343	627-0591
Blockbuster-Sony Waterfront Music Centre 1 Harbour Blvd *Web:* www.ecentre.com	Camden	NJ	08103	856-365-1300	365-1062
Blue Cross River Rink at Penn's Landing 121 N Columbus Blvd	Philadelphia	PA	19106	215-925-7465	923-3782
Carpenter's Hall 320 Chestnut St	Philadelphia	PA	19106	215-925-0167	925-3880
Christ Church in Philadelphia 20 N American St	Philadelphia	PA	19106	215-922-1695	922-3578
Civil War Library & Museum 1805 Pine St *Web:* www.libertynet.org/~cwlm/library.html	Philadelphia	PA	19103	215-735-8196	735-3812
Congregation Mikveh Israel 44 N 4th St	Philadelphia	PA	19106	215-922-5446	922-1550
Dorney Park & Wildwater Kingdom 3830 Dorney Park Rd **Fax:* Mktg ■ *TF Sales:* 800-551-5656 ■ *Web:* www.dorneypark.com	Allentown	PA	18104	610-395-3724	391-7685*
Eastern State Penitentiary Historic Site 22nd St & Fairmount Ave *Web:* www.easternstate.com ■ *E-mail:* e-state@libertynet.org	Philadelphia	PA	19130	215-236-3300	
Edgar Allan Poe National Historic Site 532 N 7th St *Web:* www.nps.gov/edal/	Philadelphia	PA	19123	215-597-8780	
Elfreth's Alley Museum 126 Elfreth's Alley	Philadelphia	PA	19106	215-574-0560	922-7869
Fairmount Park Benjamin Franklin Pkwy	Philadelphia	PA	19131	215-686-1776	
Fireman's Hall 147 N 2nd St	Philadelphia	PA	19106	215-923-1438	
Fleisher Art Memorial 719 Catherine St	Philadelphia	PA	19147	215-922-3456	
Franklin Court 313 Walnut St	Philadelphia	PA	19106	215-597-2761	
Franklin Institute Science Museum 222 N 20th St *Web:* www.fi.edu	Philadelphia	PA	19103	215-448-1200	448-1235
Germantown Historical Society 5501 Germantown Ave	Philadelphia	PA	19144	215-844-0514	844-2831
Girard Stephen Collection 2101 S College Ave Founder's Hall	Philadelphia	PA	19121	215-787-2602	787-2725
Historic Bartram's Garden 54th St & Lindbergh Blvd	Philadelphia	PA	19143	215-729-5281	729-1047

Philadelphia — Attractions (Cont'd)

				Phone	Fax
Historic New Hope 1 W Mechanic St.	New Hope	PA	18938	215-862-5030	862-5245
Web: www.newhopepa.com					
Historic Olde Saint Augustine's Church 243 N Lawrence St	Philadelphia	PA	19106	215-627-1838	
Historic Saint George's United Methodist Church 235 N 4th St	Philadelphia	PA	19106	215-925-7788	
Historical Society of Pennsylvania 1300 Locust St.	Philadelphia	PA	19107	215-732-6201	732-2680
Web: www.libertynet.org/~pahist/ ■ *E-mail:* hsppr@aol.com					
Hopewell Furnace National Historic Site 2 Mark Bird Ln	Elverson	PA	19520	610-582-8773	582-2768
Web: www.nps.gov/hofu/					
Independence Brewing Co 1000 E Comly St.	Philadelphia	PA	19149	215-537-2337	537-4677
Independence Hall & Congress Hall Chestnut St betw 5th & 6th Sts	Philadelphia	PA	19106	215-597-8974	
Web: www.nps.gov/inde/					
Independence National Historical Park 313 Walnut St	Philadelphia	PA	19106	215-597-8787	597-1548
Web: www.nps.gov/inde/					
Independence Seaport Museum 211 S Columbus Blvd	Philadelphia	PA	19106	215-925-5439	925-6713
Web: www.libertynet.org/seaport/ ■ *E-mail:* seaport@libertynet.org					
Institute of Contemporary Art 118 S 36th St University of Pennsylvania.	Philadelphia	PA	19104	215-898-7108	898-5050
Web: www.upenn.edu/ica/ ■ *E-mail:* icaup@pobox.upenn.edu					
Italian Market 9th St betw Christian & Washington Sts	Philadelphia	PA	19147	215-922-5557	
Japanese House & Garden West Fairmount Pk	Philadelphia	PA	19103	215-878-5097	
Web: www.libertynet.org/~jhg/ ■ *E-mail:* JHG@libertynet.org					
Kent Atwater Museum-History Museum of Philadelphia 15 S 7th St.	Philadelphia	PA	19106	215-922-3031	922-0708
Web: www.philadelphiahistory.org					
Liberty Bell Pavilion Market & 5th Sts	Philadelphia	PA	19106	215-597-8975	
Longwood Gardens 1001 Longwood Rd.	Kennett Square	PA	19348	610-388-1000	388-2183
TF: 800-737-5500 ■ *Web:* www.longwoodgardens.com/					
Mann Center for the Performing Arts 123 S Broad St Suite 1930	Philadelphia	PA	19109	215-546-7900	546-9524
Web: www.manncenter.org					
Mario Lanza Museum 416 Queen St Settlement Music School	Philadelphia	PA	19147	215-468-3623	468-1903
Merriam Theater 250 S Broad St	Philadelphia	PA	19102	215-732-5997	732-1396
Morris Arboretum of the University of Pennsylvania 100 Northwestern Ave	Philadelphia	PA	19118	215-247-5882	248-4439
Mummers Museum 1100 S 2nd St	Philadelphia	PA	19147	215-336-3050	389-5630
Web: members.zdial.com/~gbanks/mummers/mummersmuseum.html ■ *E-mail:* mummersmus@aol.com					
National Museum of American Jewish History 55 N 5th St.	Philadelphia	PA	19106	215-923-3811	923-0763
Web: www.nmajh.org ■ *E-mail:* nmajh@nmajh.org					
National Shrine of Saint John Neumann 1019 N 5th St	Philadelphia	PA	19123	215-627-3080	
New Jersey State Aquarium 1 Riverside Dr	Camden	NJ	08103	856-365-3300	365-3311
Web: www.njaquarium.org					
Old City Gallery & Cultural District 303 Cherry St.	Philadelphia	PA	19106	215-238-9576	
Opera Co of Philadelphia Broad & Locust Sts Academy of Music	Philadelphia	PA	19102	215-928-2110	928-2112
Web: www.operaphilly.com ■ *E-mail:* tix@operaphilly.com					
Painted Bride Art Center 230 Vine St	Philadelphia	PA	19106	215-925-9914	925-7402
Penn's Landing Columbus Blvd & Chestnut St Great Plaza.	Philadelphia	PA	19106	215-923-8181	923-2801
Web: www.pennslandingcorp.com/					
Pennsylvania Academy of the Fine Arts Museum 118 N Broad St.	Philadelphia	PA	19102	215-972-7600	567-2429
Web: www.pafa.org/museum					
Pennsylvania Ballet 1101 S Broad St	Philadelphia	PA	19147	215-551-7000	551-7224
Web: www.paballet.org ■ *E-mail:* info@paballet.org					
Philadelphia Academy of Music Broad & Locust Sts.	Philadelphia	PA	19102	215-893-1935	893-1933
TF: 800-457-8354 ■ *Web:* www.philorch.org					
Philadelphia Chamber Music Society 135 S 18th St.	Philadelphia	PA	19103	215-569-8587	569-9497
Web: www.pcmsnet.org ■ *E-mail:* mail@pcmsnet.org					
Philadelphia Dance Co 9 N Preston St	Philadelphia	PA	19104	215-387-8200	387-8203
Philadelphia Museum of Art 26th & Benjamin Franklin Pkwy	Philadelphia	PA	19130	215-763-8100	236-4465
Web: www.philamuseum.org/					
Philadelphia Orchestra 1420 Locust St Suite 400	Philadelphia	PA	19102	215-893-1900	893-1948
Web: www.philorch.org/					
Philadelphia Zoological Garden 3400 W Girard Ave	Philadelphia	PA	19104	215-243-1100	243-5385
Web: www.phillyzoo.org					
Philadelphia's Vietnam Veterans Memorial Delaware & Spruce Sts	Philadelphia	PA	19104	215-535-0643	
Web: razeinnovations.com/memorial1/					
Physick House 321 S 4th St.	Philadelphia	PA	19106	215-925-7866	
Please Touch Museum 210 N 21st St	Philadelphia	PA	19103	215-963-0666	963-0424
Web: www.libertynet.org/pleastch ■ *E-mail:* pleastch@libertynet.org					
Polish American Cultural Center Museum 308 Walnut St	Philadelphia	PA	19106	215-922-1700	922-1518
Web: www.polishamericancenter.org ■ *E-mail:* mail@polishamericancenter.org					
Powel House 244 S 3rd St.	Philadelphia	PA	19106	215-627-0364	
Presbyterian Historical Society 425 Lombard St	Philadelphia	PA	19147	215-627-1852	627-0509
Pretzel Museum 211 N 3rd St	Philadelphia	PA	19106	215-413-3010	
Web: www.libertynet.org/iha/tour/_pretzel.html					
Quaker Information Center 1501 Cherry St.	Philadelphia	PA	19102	215-241-7024	567-2096
Reading Terminal Market 12th & Arch Sts	Philadelphia	PA	19107	215-922-2317	922-2040
Rodin Museum 26nd & Benjamin Franklin Pkwy	Philadelphia	PA	19130	215-763-8100	236-4465
Web: www.rodinmuseum.org/					
Rosenbach Museum & Library 2010 DeLancey Pl.	Philadelphia	PA	19103	215-732-1600	545-7529
Web: www.rosenbach.org					
Society Hill Walnut, S 5th, Lombard & S 2nd Sts	Philadelphia	PA	19106		
Society Hill Playhouse 507 S 8th St.	Philadelphia	PA	19147	215-923-0210	
Stenton Museum 4601 N 18th St	Philadelphia	PA	19140	215-329-7312	329-7312
Thaddeus Kosciuszko National Memorial 313 Walnut St Independence National Historical Pk.	Philadelphia	PA	19106	215-597-7120	597-1003
Web: www.nps.gov/thko/					
Tuttleman Omniverse Theater 222 N 20th St	Philadelphia	PA	19103	215-448-1200	
Web: www.fi.edu/tfi/info/omnivers.html ■ *E-mail:* webteam@www.fi.edu					
University of Pennsylvania Museum of Archaeology & Anthropology 33rd & Spruce Sts.	Philadelphia	PA	19104	215-898-4000	898-0657
Web: www.upenn.edu/museum					
US Mint 5th & Arch Sts.	Philadelphia	PA	19106	215-408-0114	408-2700
Web: www.usmint.gov/					
Valley Forge National Historical Park PO Box 953	Valley Forge	PA	19482	610-783-1011	783-1088
Web: www.nps.gov/vafo/					
Wagner Free Institute of Science 1700 W Montgomery Ave	Philadelphia	PA	19121	215-763-6529	763-1299
Walnut Street Theatre 825 Walnut St	Philadelphia	PA	19107	215-574-3550	574-3598
Web: www.wstonline.org					
Wilma Theater Broad & Spruce Sts	Philadelphia	PA	19107	215-546-7824	893-0895
Web: www.libertynet.org/wilma/					
Woodlands The 4000 Woodland Ave.	Philadelphia	PA	19104	215-386-2181	386-2431

SPORTS TEAMS & FACILITIES

				Phone	Fax
First Union Center Broad St & Pattison Ave	Philadelphia	PA	19148	215-336-3600	389-9579
Philadelphia 76ers 3601 S Broad St First Union Ctr	Philadelphia	PA	19148	215-339-7676	
Web: www.nba.com/sixers/					
Philadelphia Eagles 3501 S Broad St Veterans Stadium	Philadelphia	PA	19148	215-463-2500	339-5464
Web: www.eaglesnet.com					
Philadelphia Flyers 3601 S Broad St First Union Ctr	Philadelphia	PA	19148	215-465-4500	389-9403
Web: www.philadelphiaflyers.com					
Philadelphia Kixx (soccer) 3601 S Broad St First Union Ctr	Philadelphia	PA	19148	215-952-5499	952-5488
TF: 888-888-5499 ■ *Web:* kixxonline.com ■ *E-mail:* kixxsoccer@aol.com					
Philadelphia Phantoms (hockey) 3601 S Broad St First Union Ctr	Philadelphia	PA	19148	215-465-4522	952-5245
Philadelphia Phillies 3501 S Broad St Veterans Stadium	Philadelphia	PA	19148	215-463-1000	463-9434
Web: www.phillies.com ■ *E-mail:* phans@phillies.com					
Philadelphia Wings (lacrosse) 3601 S Broad St First Union Ctr	Philadelphia	PA	19148	215-389-9464	389-9506

Philadelphia — Sports Teams & Facilities (Cont'd)

				Phone	Fax
Veterans Stadium 3501 S Broad St.	Philadelphia	PA	19148	215-685-1500	463-9878

— Events —

	Phone
Advanta Tennis Championships for Women (mid-November)	610-828-5777
Bach Festival of Philadelphia (September-March)	215-247-2224
Black Writer's Festival (mid-February)	215-732-5207
Book & Cook Fair (mid-March)	215-636-1666
Chestnut Hill Garden Festival Blooms (late April-early May)	215-248-8504
Chocolate Festival (mid-February)	215-925-7465
Devon Horse Show & Country Fair (late May-early June)	610-964-0550
Festival of Fountains (late May-early September)	610-388-1000
First Union US Pro Championship The (mid-June)	215-973-3580
Flower & Garden Festival (early May)	215-794-4000
Historic Houses in Flower (late April)	215-763-8100
Jam Festival (late May)	215-629-3237
Jam on the River (late May)	215-636-1666
Junior Jazz Weekend (mid-February)	215-963-0667
Manayunk Arts Fest (late June)	215-482-9565
Maple Syrup Festival (late March)	215-922-2317
Mardi Gras JAMboree (late February)	215-925-7465
Market Street East Holiday Festival (late December)	215-625-4962
Midsommarfest (early June)	215-389-1776
Mummers Parade (January 1)	215-686-3622
Odunde African Street Festival & Marketplace (mid-June)	215-732-8508
PECO Energy Jazz Festival (mid-February)	215-636-1666
Penn Relays (mid-April)	215-898-6128
Pennsylvania Fair (mid-May)	215-639-9000
Philadelphia Boat Show (mid-January)	610-449-9910
Philadelphia Festival of World Cinema (late April-early May)	215-569-9700
Philadelphia Flower Show (early March)	215-418-4700
Philadelphia International Film Festival (mid-late July)	215-879-8209
Philadelphia Museum of Art Craft Show (late October-early November)	215-684-7930
Philadelphia Open House Tours (late April-mid-May)	215-928-1188
Purim Festival (early March)	215-923-3811
Renninger Antique (late February)	610-337-4000
Rittenhouse Square Fine Arts Annual (early June)	877-689-4112
Springside School Antiques Show (mid-April)	215-247-7200
US Hot Rod Grand Slam Monster Jam (mid-February)	215-336-3600
Welcome America (late June-early July)	215-636-1666
Yo Philadelphia Festival (early September)	215-636-1666

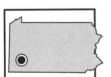

Pittsburgh

Fort Pitt, later renamed Pittsburgh, was built at the point where the Allegheny and Monongahela rivers meet to form the great Ohio River. These waterways inspired the name for Three Rivers Stadium (home of the Pittsburgh Steelers and Pittsburgh Pirates), located across the Allegheny from downtown on the North Side. The Andy Warhol Museum and Carnegie Science Center are also located in this part of town. Across the Monongahela from downtown are the shops and restaurants of Station Square; further down the river is the South Side, which blends coffee houses, jazz clubs, ethnic neighborhoods, and antique dealers. East of downtown Pittsburgh, in the neighborhood of Oakland, are many of the region's largest hospitals, the University of Pittsburgh and Carnegie-Mellon University, and the Carnegie Museums of Art and Natural History. A ride to the top of Mount Washington on either the Duquesne or the Monongahela Incline affords a spectacular view of the entire city.

Population	340,520	**Longitude**	79-86-87 W
Area (Land)	55.6 sq mi	**County**	Allegheny
Area (Water)	2.7 sq mi	**Time Zone**	EST
Elevation	770 ft	**Area Code/s**	412, 724
Latitude	40-36-31 N		

— Average Temperatures and Precipitation —

TEMPERATURES

	Jan	Feb	Mar	Apr	May	Jun	Jul	Aug	Sep	Oct	Nov	Dec
High	34	37	49	60	71	79	83	81	74	63	50	39
Low	19	20	30	39	48	57	62	60	54	42	34	24

PRECIPITATION

	Jan	Feb	Mar	Apr	May	Jun	Jul	Aug	Sep	Oct	Nov	Dec
Inches	2.5	2.4	3.4	3.2	3.6	3.7	3.8	3.2	3.0	2.4	2.9	2.9

— Important Phone Numbers —

	Phone		Phone
AAA	412-363-5100	**Medical Referral**	412-321-5030
American Express Travel	412-391-3202	**Poison Control Center**	412-681-6669
Dental Referral	800-917-6453	**Time/Temp**	412-391-9500
Emergency	911	**Travelers Aid**	412-281-5474
Events Line	800-366-0093	**Weather**	412-936-1212
HotelDocs	800-468-3537		

— Information Sources —

				Phone	Fax
Allegheny County 436 Grant St Rm 101 County Courthouse *Web:* info.co.allegheny.pa.us	Pittsburgh	PA	15219	412-350-5300	350-4360
Better Business Bureau Serving Western Pennsylvania 300 6th Ave Suite 100-UL *Web:* www.pittsburgh.bbb.org	Pittsburgh	PA	15222	412-456-2700	456-2739
Carnegie Library of Pittsburgh 4400 Forbes Ave *Web:* www.clpgh.org	Pittsburgh	PA	15213	412-622-3116	622-6278
Greater Pittsburgh Chamber of Commerce 425 6th Ave *Web:* www.pittsburghchamber.com ■ *E-mail:* info@pittsburghchamber.com	Pittsburgh	PA	15219	412-392-4500	392-4520
Greater Pittsburgh Convention & Visitors Bureau 425 6th Ave 30th Fl *TF:* 800-359-0758 ■ *Web:* www.pittsburgh-cvb.org ■ *E-mail:* info@gpcvb.org	Pittsburgh	PA	15219	412-281-7711	644-5512
Lawrence David L Convention Center 1001 Penn Ave *TF:* 800-222-5200 ■ *Web:* www.pgh-conventionctr.com	Pittsburgh	PA	15222	412-565-6000	565-6008
Pittsburgh City Hall 414 Grant St *Web:* www.city.pittsburgh.pa.us	Pittsburgh	PA	15219	412-255-2621	255-2821
Pittsburgh Mayor 414 Grant St Rm 512 *Web:* www.city.pittsburgh.pa.us/mayor	Pittsburgh	PA	15219	412-255-2626	255-2687
Pittsburgh Planning Dept 200 Ross St Robin Civic Bldg 4th fl *Web:* www.city.pittsburgh.pa.us/cp/	Pittsburgh	PA	15219	412-255-2201	255-2838

On-Line Resources

4Pittsburgh.com	www.4pittsburgh.com
About.com Guide to Pittsburgh	pittsburgh.about.com/local/midlanticus/pittsburgh
Access America Pittsburgh	www.accessamer.com/pittsburgh/
Anthill City Guide Pittsburgh	www.anthill.com/city.asp?city=pittsburgh
Area Guide Pittsburgh	pittsburgh.areaguides.net
Boulevards Pittsburgh	www.boulevards.com/cities/pittsburgh.html
City Knowledge Pittsburgh	www.cityknowledge.com/pa_pittsburgh.htm
CitySearch Pittsburgh	pittsburgh.citysearch.com
Cyburgh Pittsburgh	www.cyburgh.com/
DigitalCity Pittsburgh	home.digitalcity.com/pittsburgh
Excite.com Pittsburgh City Guide	www.excite.com/travel/countries/united_states/pennsylvania/pittsburgh
Greater Pittsburgh Museum Council	huntbot.andrew.cmu.edu/GPMC/GPghMusCouncil.html
In Pittsburgh Newsweekly	www.inpgh.com
Marbles E-Zine	www.sgi.net/marbles
OnTv: Pittsburgh's Community Webstation	www.ontv.com/
Pittsburgh City Pages	pittsburgh.thelinks.com
Pittsburgh City Paper	www.pghcitypaper.com
Pittsburgh Guide	www.pghguide.com/
Pittsburgh Travel Aid	www.nb.net/~tsalacri/pghtrav.html
Pittsburgh's South Side	betatesters.com/penn/sahside
Pittsburgh.Net	www.pittsburgh.net
Practical Pittsburgher	www.cs.cmu.edu/practical.html

Pittsburgh — On-Line Resources (Cont'd)

Real Pittsburgh.com .... www.realpittsburgh.com
Telerama's Virtual Tour of Pittsburgh .... web.lm.com/pittsburgh.html
Three Rivers Free-Net .... trfn.pgh.pa.us/

— Transportation Services —

AIRPORTS

■ Greater Pittsburgh International Airport (PIT)

	Phone
18 miles W of downtown (approx 25 minutes)	412-472-3525

Airport Transportation

	Phone
Airlines Transportation Co $12 fare to downtown	412-471-8900
Taxi $28 fare to downtown	412-665-8100

Commercial Airlines

	Phone		Phone
American	800-433-7300	**TWA**	800-221-2000
British Airways	800-247-9297	**United**	800-241-6522
Continental	412-391-6910	**US Airways**	800-428-4322
Delta	800-221-1212	**US Airways Express**	800-428-4322
Northwest	800-225-2525		

Charter Airlines

	Phone		Phone
Beaver Aviation Service Inc	724-843-8600	**Corporate Jets Inc**	412-466-2500
Corporate Air Inc	412-469-6800	**Superior Aviation**	800-882-7751

CAR RENTALS

	Phone		Phone
Alamo	412-472-5060	**Dollar**	412-472-5100
Avis	412-472-5200	**Enterprise**	800-325-8007
Budget	412-472-5252	**Hertz**	412-472-5955
CarTemps USA	412-264-0990	**National**	412-472-5094

LIMO/TAXI

	Phone		Phone
Absolute Limousine	412-429-8123	**People's Cab**	412-681-3131
Allegheny Limousines	412-731-8671	**Riemer's Limousine**	412-661-6054
Carey Limousine	412-731-8671	**Yellow Cab**	412-665-8100

MASS TRANSIT

	Phone
Port Authority Transit $1.25 Base fare	412-442-2000
T Light Rail Transit $1.25 Base fare	412-442-2000

RAIL/BUS

				Phone
Greyhound/Trailways Bus Station 11th & Liberty Aves *TF:* 800-231-2222	Pittsburgh	PA	15222	412-392-6513
Pittsburgh Amtrak Station 1100 Liberty Ave	Pittsburgh	PA	15222	800-872-7245

— Accommodations —

HOTELS, MOTELS, RESORTS

				Phone	Fax
Best Western 3401 Blvd of the Allies *TF:* 800-528-1234	Pittsburgh	PA	15213	412-683-6100	682-6115
Best Western Parkway Center Inn 875 Greentree Rd *TF:* 800-528-1234	Pittsburgh	PA	15220	412-922-7070	922-4949
Clarion Royce Hotel Airport 1160 Thorn Run Rd Ext. *TF:* 800-627-6373	Coraopolis	PA	15108	412-262-2400	264-9373
Courtyard by Marriott Airport 450 Cherrington Pkwy *TF:* 800-321-2211 ■ *Web:* courtyard.com/PITCA	Coraopolis	PA	15108	412-264-5000	264-7979
Doubletree Hotel 1000 Penn Ave *TF:* 800-222-8733 ■ *Web:* www.doubletreehotels.com/DoubleT/Hotel61/80/80Main.htm	Pittsburgh	PA	15222	412-281-3700	227-4500
Embassy Suites Airport 550 Cherrington Pkwy *TF:* 800-362-2779	Coraopolis	PA	15108	412-269-9070	262-4119
Greentree Hampton Inn 555 Trumbull Dr. *TF:* 800-426-7866	Pittsburgh	PA	15205	412-922-0100	921-7631
Greentree Holiday Inn 401 Holiday Dr. *TF:* 800-465-4329 ■ *Web:* www.basshotels.com/holiday-inn/?_franchisee=PITGT ■ *E-mail:* gmgtr@lodgian.com	Pittsburgh	PA	15220	412-922-8100	922-6511
Hampton Inn Oakland 3315 Hamlet St. *TF:* 800-426-7866	Pittsburgh	PA	15213	412-681-1000	681-3022
Hawthorn Suites Hotel 700 Mansfield Ave *TF:* 800-527-1133 ■ *Web:* www.hawthorn.com/reservations/locationdetail.asp?state=PA&facid=243&pagecode=hdir	Pittsburgh	PA	15205	412-279-6300	279-4993
Holiday Inn Allegheny Valley-RIDC Park 180 Gamma Dr. *TF:* 800-465-4329 ■ *Web:* www.basshotels.com/holiday-inn/?_franchisee=PITAV ■ *E-mail:* astark@sgi.net	Pittsburgh	PA	15238	412-963-0600	963-7852
Holiday Inn McKnight Road 4859 McKnight Rd *TF:* 800-465-4329	Pittsburgh	PA	15237	412-366-5200	366-5682
Holiday Inn Meadowlands 340 Race Track Rd *TF:* 800-465-4329	Washington	PA	15301	724-222-6200	228-1977
Holiday Inn Pittsburgh Airport 1406 Beers School Rd. *TF:* 800-333-4835 ■ *Web:* www.basshotels.com/holiday-inn/?_franchisee=PITIA	Coraopolis	PA	15108	412-262-3600	262-6221
Holiday Inn South 164 Fort Couch Rd *TF:* 800-465-4329 ■ *Web:* www.basshotels.com/holiday-inn/?_franchisee=PITSO ■ *E-mail:* www.holiday@sgi.net	Pittsburgh	PA	15241	412-833-5300	831-8539
Holiday Inn University Center 100 Lytton Ave. *TF:* 800-465-4329	Pittsburgh	PA	15213	412-682-6200	682-5745
La Quinta Motor Inn Airport 1433 Beers School Rd. *TF:* 800-531-5900	Coraopolis	PA	15108	412-269-0400	269-9258
Marriott City Center 112 Washington Pl *TF:* 888-456-6600 ■ *Web:* marriotthotels.com/PITDT	Pittsburgh	PA	15219	412-471-4000	281-4797
Marriott Hotel Pittsburgh Airport 777 Aten Rd. *TF:* 800-328-9297 ■ *Web:* marriotthotels.com/PITAP	Coraopolis	PA	15108	412-788-8800	788-0743
Motel 6 1170 Thorn Run Rd. *TF:* 800-466-8356	Coraopolis	PA	15108	412-269-0990	269-0462
Mountain View Inn 1001 Village Dr. *TF:* 800-537-8709	Greensburg	PA	15601	724-834-5300	834-5304
Pittsburgh Clubhouse Inn 5311 Campbells Run Rd *TF:* 800-258-2466	Pittsburgh	PA	15205	412-788-8400	788-2577
Pittsburgh Green Tree Marriott 101 Marriott Dr. *TF:* 800-525-5902	Pittsburgh	PA	15205	412-922-8400	922-8981
Pittsburgh Hilton 600 Commonwealth Pl Gateway Ctr. *TF:* 800-445-8667	Pittsburgh	PA	15222	412-391-4600	594-5161
Pittsburgh Plaza Hotel 1500 Beers School Rd. *TF:* 800-542-8111	Moon Township	PA	15108	412-264-7900	262-3229
Priory The 614 Pressley St.	Pittsburgh	PA	15212	412-231-3338	231-4838
Radisson Hotel 101 Mall Blvd *TF:* 800-333-3333	Monroeville	PA	15146	412-373-7300	373-1549
Ramada Inn 699 Rodi Rd *TF:* 800-272-6232	Pittsburgh	PA	15235	412-244-1600	829-2334
Ramada Plaza Suites 1 Bigelow Sq *TF:* 800-225-5858 ■ *Web:* www.ibp.com/pit/rps/ ■ *E-mail:* rampitdt@aol.com	Pittsburgh	PA	15219	412-281-5800	281-8467
Red Roof Inn 6404 Steubenville Pike	Pittsburgh	PA	15205	412-787-7870	787-8392
Sheraton Hotel Station Square 7 Station Square Dr. *TF:* 800-255-7488 ■ *E-mail:* sheraton@stargate.net	Pittsburgh	PA	15219	412-261-2000	261-2932
Westin William Penn Hotel 530 William Penn Pl *TF:* 800-228-3000	Pittsburgh	PA	15219	412-281-7100	553-5252

— Restaurants —

				Phone
Ali Baba (Middle Eastern) 404 S Craig St. *Web:* www.ibp.com/pitt/ali-baba/	Pittsburgh	PA	15213	412-682-2829

Pittsburgh — Restaurants (Cont'd)

				Phone
Baum Vivant (International) 5102 Baum Blvd	Pittsburgh	PA	15224	412-682-2620
Benihana (Japanese) 2100 Greentree Rd	Pittsburgh	PA	15220	412-276-2100
Buffalo Blues (American) 216 S Highland Ave	Pittsburgh	PA	15206	412-362-5837
Cafe Amante (Italian) 5th Avenue Pl	Pittsburgh	PA	15222	412-391-1226
Carlton Restaurant (American) 500 Grant St 1 Mellon Bank Ctr	Pittsburgh	PA	15219	412-391-4099
Carmassi's Tuscany Grill (Italian) 711 Penn Ave	Pittsburgh	PA	15222	412-281-6644
Casbah (Mediterranean) 229 S Highland Ave	Pittsburgh	PA	15206	412-661-5656
Cheese Cellar (American) 1 Station Sq	Pittsburgh	PA	15219	412-471-3355
Chiodo's Tavern (American) 107 W 8th Ave	Homestead	PA	15120	412-461-3113
Clark Bar & Grill (American) 503 Martindale St	Pittsburgh	PA	15212	412-231-5720
Cliffside (Continental) 1208 Grandview Ave	Pittsburgh	PA	15211	412-431-6996
Colony The (American) Greentree & Cochran Rds	Pittsburgh	PA	15220	412-561-2060
Common Plea Restaurant (Italian) 310 Ross St	Pittsburgh	PA	15219	412-281-5140
Crawford Grill (Southern) 2141 Wylie Ave	Pittsburgh	PA	15219	412-471-1565
Froggy's (American) 100 Market St	Pittsburgh	PA	15222	412-471-3764
Ginza (Korean) 239 Atwood St	Pittsburgh	PA	15213	412-682-9226
Grand Concourse (Continental) 1 Station Sq	Pittsburgh	PA	15219	412-261-1717
Grandview Saloon (American) 1212 Grandview Ave	Pittsburgh	PA	15211	412-431-1400
Gullifty's (American) 1922 Murray Ave	Pittsburgh	PA	15217	412-521-8222
Hana Japanese Restaurant (Japanese) 1 Graeme St Market Sq	Pittsburgh	PA	15222	412-471-9988
Hyeholde (New American) 190 Hyeholde Dr	Coraopolis	PA	15108	412-264-3116
Kaya (Caribbean) 2000 Smallman St	Pittsburgh	PA	15222	412-261-6565
La Feria (Peruvian) 5527 Walnut St	Pittsburgh	PA	15232	412-682-4501
La Scala Ristorante (Italian) 144 6th St	Pittsburgh	PA	15222	412-434-6244
Le Mont (French) 1114 Grandview Ave *Web:* www.le-mont.com/	Pittsburgh	PA	15211	412-431-3100
Le Pommier (French) 2104 E Carson St	Pittsburgh	PA	15203	412-431-1901
Lemongrass (Thai) 5846 Forbes Ave	Pittsburgh	PA	15217	412-521-0728
Louis Tambellini's Restaurant (Seafood) 860 Saw Mill Run Blvd	Pittsburgh	PA	15226	412-481-1118
Mad Mex (Mexican) 370 Atwood St	Pittsburgh	PA	15213	412-681-5656
Mullaney's Harp & Fiddle (Irish) 24th St & Penn Ave	Pittsburgh	PA	15222	412-642-6622
Pasta Piatto (Italian) 736 Bellefonte St	Pittsburgh	PA	15232	412-621-5547
Penn Brewery (German) 800 Vinial St	Pittsburgh	PA	15212	412-237-9402
Piccolo Mondo (Italian) 661 Anderson Dr Bldg 7	Pittsburgh	PA	15220	412-922-0920
Pittsburgh Steak Co (Steak) 1924 E Carson St	Pittsburgh	PA	15203	412-381-5505
Poli's (Seafood) 2607 Murray Ave	Pittsburgh	PA	15217	412-521-6400
Primanti Brothers (American) 48 18th St	Pittsburgh	PA	15222	412-263-2142
Rico's (Italian) 1 Rico Ln	Pittsburgh	PA	15237	412-931-0556
Road to Karakash (International) 320 Atwood St	Pittsburgh	PA	15213	412-687-0533
Roland's Seafood Grill (Seafood) 1904 Penn Ave	Pittsburgh	PA	15222	412-261-3401
Siena on the Water (American) 1366 Old Freeport Rd	Pittsburgh	PA	15238	412-963-8881
Southwest Bistro (Southwest) 129 6th St	Pittsburgh	PA	15229	412-261-8866
Star of India (Indian) 412 S Craig St	Pittsburgh	PA	15213	412-681-5700
Steelhead Grill (Seafood) 112 Washington Pl	Pittsburgh	PA	15219	412-394-3474
Top of the Triangle (American) 600 Grant St	Pittsburgh	PA	15219	412-471-4100
Valhalla Restaurant & Brewery (Creole) 1150 Smallman St	Pittsburgh	PA	15222	412-434-1440
Vermont Flatbread Co (New American) 2701 Penn Ave	Pittsburgh	PA	15222	412-434-1220
Waterfall Terrace (Continental) 7 Station Square Dr	Pittsburgh	PA	15219	412-261-2000

— Goods and Services —

SHOPPING

				Phone	Fax
Arcade Shops at Fifth Avenue Place 120 5th Ave	Pittsburgh	PA	15222	412-456-7800	456-7810
Century III Mall 3075 Clairton Rd	West Mifflin	PA	15123	412-653-1220	655-0202
East Carson Street Shopping District E Carson St betw 8th & 25th Sts	Pittsburgh	PA	15203	412-481-0651	481-2624
Kaufmann's 400 5th Ave **Fax:* Cust Svc ■ *Web:* www.mayco.com/may/kf_home.html	Pittsburgh	PA	15219	412-232-2000	232-2141*
Monroeville Mall 200 Mall Blvd	Monroeville	PA	15146	412-243-8511	372-0205
North Hills Village 4801 McKnight Rd	Pittsburgh	PA	15237	412-366-2250	366-5418
Ross Park Mall 1000 Ross Park Mall Dr	Pittsburgh	PA	15237	412-369-4400	369-4408
Saks Fifth Avenue 513 Smithfield St	Pittsburgh	PA	15222	412-263-4800	263-4880
Shops of One Oxford Centre 301 Grant St	Pittsburgh	PA	15219	412-391-5300	391-5309
Station Square Station Sq Dr *Web:* www.stationsquare.com/	Pittsburgh	PA	15219	412-261-2811	261-2825
Westmoreland Mall Rt 30 E	Greensburg	PA	15601	724-836-5025	836-4825

BANKS

				Phone	Fax
Dollar Bank FSB PO Box 765 *Web:* www.dollarbank.com ■ *E-mail:* customerservice@dollarbank.com	Pittsburgh	PA	15230	412-261-4900	261-8535
Great American Federal Savings & Loan Assn 4750 Clairton Blvd **Fax:* Mktg	Pittsburgh	PA	15236	412-882-9800	882-5866*
Mellon Bank NA 500 Grant St 1 Mellon Bank Ctr **Fax:* Cust Svc ■ *TF:* 800-635-5662 ■ *Web:* www.mellon.com	Pittsburgh	PA	15258	412-234-5000	236-4491*
National City Bank of Pennsylvania 300 4th Ave **Fax:* Cust Svc	Pittsburgh	PA	15278	412-644-8111	644-8781*
PNC Bank NA 249 5th Ave 1 PNC Plaza *TF:* 888-762-2265 ■ *Web:* www.pncbank.com	Pittsburgh	PA	15222	412-762-2000	762-5798

BUSINESS SERVICES

	Phone
Accountemps	412-471-5946
Courier Express	412-481-7300
Federal Express	800-238-5355
Kelly Services	412-391-3222
Kinko's	412-687-2752
Manpower Temporary Services	412-434-6507
Olsten Staffing Services	412-261-7200
Post Office	412-359-7500
UPS	800-742-5877

— Media —

PUBLICATIONS

				Phone	Fax
Pittsburgh Business Times 2313 E Carson St Suite 200 *Web:* www.amcity.com/pittsburgh/	Pittsburgh	PA	15203	412-481-6397	481-9956
Pittsburgh Magazine 4802 5th Ave *TF Sales:* 800-495-7323*	Pittsburgh	PA	15213	412-622-6440	622-7066
Pittsburgh Post-Gazette‡ 34 Blvd of the Allies *Web:* www.post-gazette.com	Pittsburgh	PA	15222	412-263-1100	391-8452
Pittsburgh Tribune-Review‡ 503 Martindale St 503 DL Clark Bldg **Fax Area Code:* 724 ■ *TF:* 800-433-3045 ■ *Web:* triblive.com	Pittsburgh	PA	15212	412-321-6460	320-7965*

‡Daily newspapers

TELEVISION

				Phone	Fax
KDKA-TV Ch 2 (CBS) 1 Gateway Ctr *Web:* www.kdka.com	Pittsburgh	PA	15222	412-575-2200	575-2871
WCWB-TV Ch 22 (WB) 3474 Wm Penn Hwy	Pittsburgh	PA	15235	412-829-9788	829-0313
WPGH-TV Ch 53 (Fox) 750 Ivory Ave	Pittsburgh	PA	15214	412-931-5300	931-8029
WPXI-TV Ch 11 (NBC) 11 Television Hill *Web:* www.realpittsburgh.com/partners/wpxi	Pittsburgh	PA	15214	412-237-1100	327-4900
WQED-TV Ch 13 (PBS) 4802 5th Ave *Web:* www.wqed.org	Pittsburgh	PA	15213	412-622-1300	622-6413
WTAE-TV Ch 4 (ABC) 400 Ardmore Blvd *Web:* www.wtaetv.com	Pittsburgh	PA	15221	412-242-4300	244-4628

RADIO

				Phone	Fax
KDKA-AM 1020 kHz (N/T) 1 Gateway Ctr **Fax:* Sales ■ *Web:* www.kdkaradio.com	Pittsburgh	PA	15222	412-575-2200	575-2424*
KQV-AM 1410 kHz (N/T) 650 Smithfield St Centre City Towers *Web:* www.kqv.com ■ *E-mail:* kqvradio@trib.infi.net	Pittsburgh	PA	15222	412-562-5900	562-5903
WAMO-FM 106.7 MHz (Urban) 960 Penn Ave Suite 200	Pittsburgh	PA	15222	412-471-2181	391-3559
WASP-FM 94.9 MHz (Ctry) National City Bank Bldg 7th Fl	Uniontown	PA	15401	724-938-9277	439-9265
WBZZ-FM 93.7 MHz (CHR) 651 Holiday Dr Foster Plaza 2nd Fl	Pittsburgh	PA	15220	412-920-9400	920-9449
WDSY-FM 107.9 MHz (Ctry) 651 Holiday Dr Foster Plaza 2nd Fl	Pittsburgh	PA	15220	412-920-9400	920-9449
WDUQ-FM 90.5 MHz (NPR) Duquesne University *Web:* www.wduq.org ■ *E-mail:* info@wduq.org	Pittsburgh	PA	15282	412-396-6030	396-5601
WDVE-FM 102.5 MHz (Rock) 200 Fleet St *Web:* www.dve.com	Pittsburgh	PA	15220	412-937-1441	937-0323
WJAS-AM 1320 kHz (Nost) 900 Parish St 3rd Fl	Pittsburgh	PA	15220	412-875-4800	875-9570
WJJJ-FM 104.7 MHz (NAC) 200 Fleet St Suite 300	Pittsburgh	PA	15220	412-937-1441	937-9239
WLTJ-FM 92.9 MHz (AC) 7 Parkway Ctr Suite 780 *Web:* www.wltj.com/ ■ *E-mail:* info@wltj.net	Pittsburgh	PA	15220	412-922-9290	928-9290
WMIX-FM 96.1 MHz (AC) 200 Fleet St	Pittsburgh	PA	15220	412-937-1441	937-9239

Pittsburgh — Radio (Cont'd)

	City	State	Zip	Phone	Fax
WORD-FM 101.5 MHz (Rel) 7 Parkway Ctr Suite 625 *Web:* www.wordwpit.com	Pittsburgh	PA	15220	412-937-1500	937-1576
WQED-FM 89.3 MHz (NPR) 4802 5th Ave *Web:* www.wqed.org/fm/index.html ■ *E-mail:* radio@wqed.org	Pittsburgh	PA	15213	412-622-1436	622-7073
WRRK-FM 96.9 MHz (CR) 7 Parkway Ctr Suite 780 *Web:* www.rrk.com ■ *E-mail:* quinn@sgi.net	Pittsburgh	PA	15220	412-922-9290	928-9290
WSHH-FM 99.7 MHz (AC) 900 Parish St 3rd Fl *Web:* www.wshh.com	Pittsburgh	PA	15220	412-875-9500	875-9970
WTAE-AM 1250 kHz (Sports) 400 Ardmore Blvd *Web:* www.wtaeradio.com	Pittsburgh	PA	15221	412-731-0996	244-4596
WWSW-AM 970 kHz (Oldies) 1 Allegheny Sq Suite 800 *Web:* www.realpittsburgh.com/partners/3ws	Pittsburgh	PA	15212	412-323-5300	323-5313
WWSW-FM 94.5 MHz (Oldies) 1 Allegheny Sq Suite 800	Pittsburgh	PA	15212	412-323-5300	323-5313
WXDX-FM 105.9 MHz (Alt) 200 Fleet St *Web:* www.wxdx.com	Pittsburgh	PA	15220	412-937-1441	937-9239
WYEP-FM 91.3 MHz (NPR) 2313 E Carson St *Web:* www.wyep.org ■ *E-mail:* info@wyep.org	Pittsburgh	PA	15203	412-381-9131	381-9126
WZPT-FM 100.7 MHz (Oldies) 651 Holiday Dr Foster Plaza 2nd Fl	Pittsburgh	PA	15220	412-920-9400	920-9449

— Colleges/Universities —

	City	State	Zip	Phone	Fax
Art Institute of Pittsburgh 526 Penn Ave *TF:* 800-275-2470 ■ *Web:* www.aii.edu	Pittsburgh	PA	15222	412-263-6600	263-6667
Carlow College 3333 5th Ave *TF Admissions:* 800-333-2275 ■ *Web:* www.carlow.edu ■ *E-mail:* ehof@carlow.edu	Pittsburgh	PA	15213	412-578-6000	578-6668
Carnegie Mellon University 5000 Forbes Ave Warner Hall *Web:* www.cmu.edu ■ *E-mail:* undergraduate-admissions+@CMU.edu	Pittsburgh	PA	15213	412-268-2000	268-7838
Chatham College Woodland Rd *TF Admissions:* 800-837-1290 ■ *Web:* www.chatham.edu	Pittsburgh	PA	15232	412-365-1100	365-1609
Community College of Allegheny County Allegheny Campus 808 Ridge Ave *Web:* www.ccac.edu	Pittsburgh	PA	15212	412-237-2525	237-4581
Community College of Allegheny County Boyce Campus 595 Beatty Rd *Web:* www.ccac.edu	Monroeville	PA	15146	724-327-1327	325-6859
Community College of Allegheny County North Campus 8701 Perry Hwy	Pittsburgh	PA	15237	412-366-7000	369-3635
Dean Institute of Technology 1501 W Liberty Ave. *E-mail:* deantech@earthlink.net	Pittsburgh	PA	15226	412-531-4433	531-4435
Duff's Business Institute 110 9th St *TF:* 888-279-3314	Pittsburgh	PA	15222	412-261-4520	261-4546
Duquesne University 600 Forbes Ave *TF Admissions:* 800-456-0590 ■ *Web:* www.duq.edu ■ *E-mail:* mclaughc@duq2.cc.duq.edu	Pittsburgh	PA	15282	412-396-6000	396-5644
Geneva College 3200 College Ave. *TF:* 800-847-8255 ■ *Web:* www.geneva.edu	Beaver Falls	PA	15010	724-846-5100	847-6776
ICM School of Business 10 Wood St *TF:* 800-441-5222 ■ *Web:* www.icmschool.com	Pittsburgh	PA	15222	412-261-2647	261-0998
La Roche College 9000 Babcock Blvd **Fax:* Library ■ *Web:* www.laroche.edu	Pittsburgh	PA	15237	412-367-9300	536-1062*
Penn Technical Institute 110 9th St	Pittsburgh	PA	15222	412-232-3547	355-7904
Pennsylvania State University Beaver Campus 100 University Dr *Web:* www.br.psu.edu	Monaca	PA	15061	724-773-3500	773-3658
Pennsylvania State University Delaware County Campus 25 Yearsley Mill Rd *Web:* www.de.psu.edu	Media	PA	19063	610-892-1350	892-1357
Pennsylvania State University McKeesport Campus 4000 University Dr *Web:* www.mk.psu.edu	McKeesport	PA	15132	412-675-9000	675-9056
Pennsylvania State University New Kensington Campus 3550 7th Street Rd Rt 780 *Web:* www.nk.psu.edu	Upper Burrell	PA	15068	724-334-6000	334-6111
Pittsburgh Institute of Aeronautics PO Box 10897 *TF:* 800-444-1440 ■ *Web:* www.piainfo.org ■ *E-mail:* admissions@piainfo.org	Pittsburgh	PA	15236	412-462-9011	466-0513
Pittsburgh Institute of Mortuary Science Inc 5808 Baum Blvd *TF:* 800-933-5808 ■ *Web:* www.p-i-m-s.com ■ *E-mail:* pims5805@aol.com	Pittsburgh	PA	15206	412-362-8500	362-1684
Pittsburgh Technical Institute 635 Smithfield St *E-mail:* pti@fujinet	Pittsburgh	PA	15222	412-471-1011	232-3945
Point Park College 201 Wood St *Web:* www.ppc.edu	Pittsburgh	PA	15222	412-391-4100	391-1980
Robert Morris College 881 Narrows Run Rd. *TF:* 800-762-0097 ■ *Web:* www.robert-morris.edu	Moon Township	PA	15108	412-262-8200	299-2425
Slippery Rock University *TF Admissions:* 800-929-4778 ■ *Web:* www.sru.edu ■ *E-mail:* dms@sruvm.sru.edu	Slippery Rock	PA	16057	724-738-9000	738-2913
Triangle Tech Inc 1940 Perrysville Ave *TF:* 800-874-8324	Pittsburgh	PA	15214	412-359-1000	359-1012
University of Pittsburgh 4200 5th Ave **Fax:* Admissions ■ *Web:* www.pitt.edu ■ *E-mail:* hrpitt+@pitt.edu	Pittsburgh	PA	15260	412-624-4141	648-8815*

— Hospitals —

	City	State	Zip	Phone	Fax
Allegheny General Hospital 320 E North Ave *Web:* www.allhealth.edu	Pittsburgh	PA	15212	412-359-3131	359-4108
Allegheny Valley Hospital 1301 Carlisle St	Natrona Heights	PA	15065	724-224-5100	226-7490
Braddock Medical Center 400 Holland Ave	Braddock	PA	15104	412-636-5000	636-5398
Butler Memorial Hospital 911 E Brady St	Butler	PA	16001	724-283-6666	284-4645
Canonsburg General Hospital 100 Medical Blvd	Canonsburg	PA	15317	724-745-6100	873-5876
Children's Hospital of Pittsburgh 3705 5th Ave *Web:* www.chp.edu	Pittsburgh	PA	15213	412-692-5325	692-8509
Citizens General Hospital 651 4th Ave	New Kensington	PA	15068	724-337-3541	337-3541
Forbes Regional Hospital 2570 Haymaker Rd	Monroeville	PA	15146	412-858-2000	858-2088
Jeannette District Memorial Hospital 600 Jefferson Ave	Jeannette	PA	15644	724-527-3551	527-9430
Jefferson Hospital Coal Valley Rd	Pittsburgh	PA	15236	412-469-5000	469-7174
Latrobe Area Hospital 121 W 2nd Ave **Fax:* Admitting ■ *Web:* www.lah.com	Latrobe	PA	15650	724-537-1000	532-6073*
McKeesport Hospital 1500 5th Ave	McKeesport	PA	15132	412-664-2000	664-2309
Medical Center The 1000 Dutch Ridge Rd	Beaver	PA	15009	724-728-7000	728-5322
Mercy Hospital of Pittsburgh 1400 Locust St **Fax:* Admitting ■ *Web:* www.mercylink.org	Pittsburgh	PA	15219	412-232-8111	232-7380*
Mercy Providence Hospital 1004 Arch St **Fax:* Admitting	Pittsburgh	PA	15212	412-323-5600	323-5646*
Monongahela Valley Hospital 1163 Country Club Rd **Fax:* Admitting	Monongahela	PA	15063	724-258-1000	258-1925*
Monsour Medical Center 70 Lincoln Way E	Jeannette	PA	15644	724-527-1511	523-4234
Ohio Valley General Hospital 25 Heckel Rd	McKees Rocks	PA	15136	412-777-6161	777-6806
Saint Clair Hospital 1000 Bower Hill Rd **Fax:* Admissions	Pittsburgh	PA	15243	412-561-4900	572-6580*
Saint Francis Central Hospital 1200 Centre Ave	Pittsburgh	PA	15219	412-562-3000	261-5575
Saint Francis Medical Center 400 45th St *Web:* www.sfhs.edu/sfmc ■ *E-mail:* leff+@pitt.edu	Pittsburgh	PA	15201	412-622-4343	622-4858
University of Pittsburgh Medical Center 200 Lothrop St **Fax:* Hum Res ■ *Web:* www.upmc.edu	Pittsburgh	PA	15213	412-648-6000	647-4801*
University of Pittsburgh Medical Center Beaver Valley 2500 Hospital Dr *Web:* www.upmc.edu/BeaverValley/default.htm	Aliquippa	PA	15001	724-857-1212	857-1298
University of Pittsburgh Medical Center Shadyside 5230 Centre Ave **Fax:* Admitting ■ *Web:* www.upmc.edu/SHADYSIDE	Pittsburgh	PA	15232	412-623-2121	683-7539*
University of Pittsburgh Medical Center South Side 2000 Mary St	Pittsburgh	PA	15203	412-488-5550	488-5748
UPMC Passavant Hospital 9100 Babcock Blvd **Fax:* Admitting ■ *Web:* www.upmc.edu/Passavant/default.htm	Pittsburgh	PA	15237	412-367-6700	367-5498*
UPMC Saint Margaret 815 Freeport Rd *Web:* www.upmc.edu/StMargaret	Pittsburgh	PA	15215	412-784-4000	784-4008
Veterans Affairs Medical Center 325 New Castle Rd	Butler	PA	16001	724-287-4781	477-5007
Veterans Affairs Medical Center 7180 Highland Dr	Pittsburgh	PA	15206	412-365-4900	365-5105
Washington Hospital 155 Wilson Ave	Washington	PA	15301	724-225-7000	222-7316

Pittsburgh — Hospitals (Cont'd)

	City	State	Zip	Phone	Fax
Western Pennsylvania Hospital 4800 Friendship Ave *Web:* www.westpennhospital.com	Pittsburgh	PA	15224	412-578-5000	578-4321
Westmoreland Regional Hospital 532 W Pittsburgh St **Fax:* Mail Rm ■ *Web:* www.westmoreland.org ■ *E-mail:* pr@westmoreland.org	Greensburg	PA	15601	724-832-4000	830-8573*

— Attractions —

	City	State	Zip	Phone	Fax
Allegheny Portage Railroad National Historic Site 110 Federal Park Rd *Web:* www.nps.gov/alpo ■ *E-mail:* alpo_visitor_center@nps.gov	Gallitzin	PA	16641	814-886-6150	886-6117
American Wind Symphony Orchestra PO Box 1824	Pittsburgh	PA	15230	724-934-8334	742-2897
Andy Warhol Museum 117 Sandusky St *Web:* www.warhol.org ■ *E-mail:* warhol@alphaclp.clpgh.org	Pittsburgh	PA	15212	412-237-8300	237-8340
Benedum Center for the Performing Arts 719 Liberty Ave	Pittsburgh	PA	15222	412-456-6666	456-2694
Carnegie Library 4400 Forbes Ave *Web:* www.clpgh.org/clp/	Pittsburgh	PA	15213	412-622-3131	622-6278
Carnegie Museum of Art 4400 Forbes Ave. *Web:* www.cmoa.org	Pittsburgh	PA	15213	412-622-3131	622-6258
Carnegie Museum of Natural History 4400 Forbes Ave. *Web:* www.clpgh.org/cmnh	Pittsburgh	PA	15213	412-622-3131	622-6258
Carnegie Music Hall 4400 Forbes Ave.	Pittsburgh	PA	15213	412-622-3360	688-8664
Carnegie Science Center 1 Allegheny Ave *Web:* www.csc.clpgh.org	Pittsburgh	PA	15212	412-237-3400	237-3375
Cathedral of Learning's Nationality Rooms 4200 5th Ave University of Pittsburgh *Web:* www.pitt.edu/~bdobler/rooms/countries/natrooms.html	Pittsburgh	PA	15260	412-624-6000	624-4214
Civic Light Opera 719 Liberty Ave Benedum Ctr *Web:* www.pittsburghclo.org ■ *E-mail:* mail@pittsburghclo.org	Pittsburgh	PA	15222	412-263-2560	281-5339
Dance Alloy 5530 Penn Ave *E-mail:* alloy@telerama.im.com	Pittsburgh	PA	15206	412-363-4321	363-4320
Duquesne Incline 1220 Grandview Ave	Pittsburgh	PA	15211	412-381-1665	
Fallingwater PO Box R	Mill Run	PA	15464	724-329-8501	329-0553
Fort Necessity National Battlefield 1 Washington Pkwy. *Web:* www.nps.gov/fone	Farmington	PA	15437	724-329-5512	329-8682
Fort Pitt Museum 101 Commonwealth Pl.	Pittsburgh	PA	15222	412-281-9284	281-1417
Foster Stephen C Memorial Forbes Ave University of Pittsburgh *E-mail:* dlr@pitt.edu	Pittsburgh	PA	15260	412-624-4100	624-7447
Frick Art & Historical Center 7227 Reynolds St *E-mail:* videoweb@usaor.net	Pittsburgh	PA	15208	412-371-0600	371-6140
Frick Park S Braddock & Forbes Aves	Pittsburgh	PA	15221	412-241-7190	
Friendship Hill National Historic Site Rd 1 box 149-A *Web:* www.nps.gov/frhi/	Point Marion	PA	15474	724-725-9190	725-1999
Heinz Hall for the Performing Arts 600 Penn Ave. *Web:* www.pittsburghsymphony.org/pghsymph.nsf/web/heinz.html	Pittsburgh	PA	15222	412-392-4800	392-4910
Heinz Memorial Chapel 5th & Bellefield Aves University of Pittsburgh	Pittsburgh	PA	15260	412-624-4157	624-4155
Highland Park Stanton, Bunker Hill & Highland Ave	Pittsburgh	PA	15206	412-255-2539	
Johnstown Flood National Memorial 733 Lake Rd. *Web:* www.nps.gov/jofl/	Saint Michael	PA	15951	814-495-4643	495-7181
Kennywood Park 4800 Kennywood Blvd *Web:* www.kennywood.com	West Mifflin	PA	15122	412-461-0500	464-0719
Mattress Factory 500 Sampsonia Way *Web:* www.mattress.org/ ■ *E-mail:* info@mattress.org	Pittsburgh	PA	15212	412-231-3169	322-2231
Monongahela Incline W Carson & Smithfield Sts	Pittsburgh	PA	15233	412-442-2000	
National Aviary in Pittsburgh Allegheny Commons West *TF:* 800-972-2473 ■ *Web:* www.aviary.org ■ *E-mail:* ntlaviary@aol.com	Pittsburgh	PA	15212	412-323-7234	321-4364
Old Economy Village 14th & Church Sts *Web:* www.beavercounty.net/oldeconomy	Ambridge	PA	15003	724-266-4500	266-7506
Phipps Conservatory 1 Schenley Pk *Web:* trfn.clpgh.org/phipps ■ *E-mail:* phipps@trfn.clpgh.org	Pittsburgh	PA	15213	412-622-6915	622-7363
Pittsburgh Ballet Theatre 2900 Liberty Ave. *Web:* artsnet.heinz.cmu.edu/pbt	Pittsburgh	PA	15201	412-281-0360	281-9901
Pittsburgh Brewing Co 3340 Liberty Ave *Web:* www.pittsburghbrewingco.com ■ *E-mail:* info@pittsburghbrewingco.com	Pittsburgh	PA	15201	412-682-7400	692-1189
Pittsburgh Center for the Arts 6300 5th Ave	Pittsburgh	PA	15232	412-361-0873	361-8338
Pittsburgh Chamber Music Society 4400 Forbes Ave Carnegie Music Hall *Web:* trfn.clpgh.org/pcms/ ■ *E-mail:* pcms@trfn.clpgh.org	Pittsburgh	PA	15213	412-624-4129	
Pittsburgh Children's Museum 10 Childrens Way *Web:* www.pittsburghkids.org ■ *E-mail:* info@pittsburghkids.org	Pittsburgh	PA	15212	412-322-5059	322-4932
Pittsburgh Civic Light Opera 719 Liberty Ave	Pittsburgh	PA	15222	412-281-3973	281-5339
Pittsburgh Opera 801 Penn Ave *Web:* www.contrib.andrew.cmu.edu/usr/dma4 ■ *E-mail:* paopera@aol.com	Pittsburgh	PA	15222	412-281-0912	281-4324
Pittsburgh Public Theater 6 Allegheny Sq *Web:* www.ppt.org/ ■ *E-mail:* pittpublic@aol.com	Pittsburgh	PA	15212	412-321-9800	323-8550
Pittsburgh Symphony Orchestra 600 Penn Ave. *Web:* www.pittsburghsymphony.org	Pittsburgh	PA	15222	412-392-4800	392-3311
Pittsburgh Zoo 1 Wild Pl *TF:* 888-744-3378 ■ *Web:* zoo.pgh.pa.us	Pittsburgh	PA	15206	412-665-3639	665-3661
PPG Wintergarden Stanwix St & 4th Ave.	Pittsburgh	PA	15222	412-434-1900	434-1901
Rangos Omnimax Theater 1 Allegheny Ave Carnegie Science Ctr *Web:* www.carnegiesciencecenter.org/family_omnimax.html	Pittsburgh	PA	15212	412-237-3400	237-3375
River City Brass Band PO Box 6436 *Web:* www.rcbb.com	Pittsburgh	PA	15212	412-322-7222	322-6821
Riverview Park Riverview Ave	Pittsburgh	PA	15214	412-255-2539	
Schenley Park Schenley Dr	Pittsburgh	PA	15213	412-255-2539	
Senator John Heinz Pittsburgh Regional History Center 1212 Smallman St.	Pittsburgh	PA	15222	412-454-6000	454-6028
Silver Eye Center for Photography 1015 E Carson St	Pittsburgh	PA	15203	412-431-1810	431-5777
Soldiers & Sailors Memorial Hall 4141 5th Ave	Pittsburgh	PA	15213	412-621-4253	683-9339
Station Square Station Sq Dr *Web:* www.stationsquare.com/	Pittsburgh	PA	15219	412-261-2811	261-2825
Trinity Cathedral 328 6th Ave.	Pittsburgh	PA	15222	412-232-6404	232-6408

SPORTS TEAMS & FACILITIES

	City	State	Zip	Phone	Fax
Ladbroke at The Meadows Race Track Rd *Web:* www.latm.com	Meadow Lands	PA	15347	724-225-9300	225-9556
Mellon Arena 66 Mario Lemieux Pl. *Web:* www.civicarena.com	Pittsburgh	PA	15219	412-642-1800	642-1925
Pittsburgh Penguins 66 Mario Lemieux Pl Mellon Arena **Fax:* Cust Svc ■ *Web:* www.pittsburghpenguins.com	Pittsburgh	PA	15219	412-642-1300	642-1316*
Pittsburgh Pirates 600 Stadium Cir Three Rivers Stadium *Web:* www.pirateball.com ■ *E-mail:* talkback@pirates.usa.com	Pittsburgh	PA	15212	412-321-2827	323-1724
Pittsburgh Riverhounds (soccer) Church Rd Bethel Pk Stadium *Web:* riverhounds.com ■ *E-mail:* cheasley@riverhounds.com	Pittsburgh	PA	15203	412-381-4625	
Pittsburgh Steelers 300 Stadium Cir Three Rivers Stadium *Web:* steelershome.com	Pittsburgh	PA	15212	412-323-1200	323-1393
Three Rivers Stadium 400 Stadium Cir *Web:* www.3riversstadium.com	Pittsburgh	PA	15212	412-321-0650	321-1436

— Events —

	Phone
Celebration of Lights-Hartwood (November-January)	800-366-0093
First Night Pittsburgh (December 31)	888-744-3378
Greater Pittsburgh Renaissance Festival (late June)	412-281-7711
Head of the Ohio Regatta (early October)	412-232-7506
Juneteenth Celebration (mid-June)	412-281-7711
Maple Sugar Fest (late March)	412-422-6558
Mellon Jazz Festival (mid-late June)	800-366-0093
Penn's Colony Festival & Marketplace (mid-late September)	412-487-6922
Pittsburgh Children's Festival (mid-May)	412-321-5520
Pittsburgh Folk Festival (late May)	800-366-0093
Pittsburgh International Lesbian & Gay Film Festival (mid-October)	412-232-3277
Pittsburgh Irish Festival (mid-September)	412-661-1221
Pittsburgh Three Rivers Regatta (early August)	412-338-8765
Pittsburgh Vintage Grand Prix (mid-July)	800-366-0093
Pittsburgh Zoo Holiday Lights Festival (December-early January)	412-665-3639

Pittsburgh — Events (Cont'd)

	Phone
Saint Patrick's Day Parade (mid-March)	412-621-0600
Science & Engineering Fair (mid-March)	412-237-1821
Shadyside Summer Arts & Jazz Festival (early August)	412-681-2809
Southside Summer Street Spectacular (mid-July)	412-481-0651
Sparkle Season (late November-early January)	412-566-4190
Spring Flower Show (late March-mid-April)	412-622-6915
Station Square Festival (early June)	412-621-7223
Summerfest (mid-August)	412-562-9900
Three Rivers Arts Festival (early-mid-June)	412-281-8723
Three Rivers Film Festival (early-mid-November)	412-681-5449
UPMC Pittsburgh City Marathon (early May)	412-647-7866
US Beer & Music Festival (late June)	412-562-9900
Westmoreland Arts & Heritage Festival (early July)	724-834-7474
Winter Flower Show (late November-early January)	412-622-6915
Winterfest (early February)	814-352-7777
WTAE-TV4 Summerfest (late June)	412-462-6666

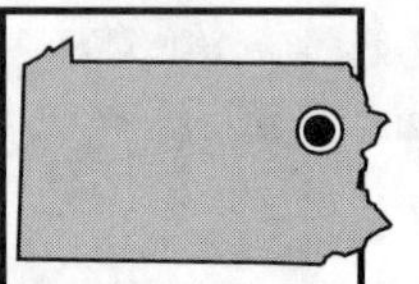

Scranton

Scranton lies in a valley where the Pocono and Endless Mountains meet. The city's industrial heritage is exhibited at three area attractions: the Steamtown National Historic Site, a collection of authentic locomotives and cars located in downtown Scranton; the Lackawanna County Coal Mine Tour, which takes visitors to a restored mine 300 feet underground; and the Pennsylvania Anthracite Heritage Museum (one of four anthracite museums in the area), which explores the history of the people who settled and worked in the anthracite region. The Steamtown National Historic Site also features steam-powered rail excursions through the countryside.

Population	74,683	**Longitude**	75-66-28 W
Area (Land)	25.2 sq mi	**County**	Lackawanna
Area (Water)	0.2 sq mi	**Time Zone**	EST
Elevation	754 ft	**Area Code/s**	570
Latitude	41-40-89 N		

— Average Temperatures and Precipitation —

TEMPERATURES

	Jan	Feb	Mar	Apr	May	Jun	Jul	Aug	Sep	Oct	Nov	Dec
High	32	35	46	58	69	78	82	80	72	61	49	37
Low	18	19	28	38	48	57	62	60	53	42	34	23

PRECIPITATION

	Jan	Feb	Mar	Apr	May	Jun	Jul	Aug	Sep	Oct	Nov	Dec
Inches	2.1	2.2	2.6	3.0	3.7	4.0	3.8	3.3	3.3	2.8	3.1	2.5

— Important Phone Numbers —

	Phone		Phone
AAA	570-348-2511	**Medical Referral**	570-344-3616
Dental Referral	570-344-9080	**Poison Control Center**	800-521-6110
Emergency	911		

— Information Sources —

				Phone	Fax
Better Business Bureau Serving Northeastern & Central Pennsylvania PO Box 993	Scranton	PA	18501	570-342-9129	342-1282
Web: www.nepa.bbb.org ■ *E-mail:* info@nepa.bbb.org					
Greater Scranton Chamber of Commerce 222 Mulberry St	Scranton	PA	18503	570-342-7711	347-6262
TF: 800-722-5289 ■ *Web:* www.scrantonchamber.com					
Lackawanna County 200 N Washington Ave.	Scranton	PA	18503	570-963-6723	
Scranton City Hall 340 N Washington Ave.	Scranton	PA	18503	570-348-4113	348-4207
Scranton Cultural Center 420 N Washington Ave	Scranton	PA	18503	570-346-7369	346-7365
Scranton Economic & Community Development Dept 340 N Washington Ave	Scranton	PA	18503	570-348-4216	348-4123
Scranton Mayor 340 N Washington Ave.	Scranton	PA	18503	570-348-4100	348-4251
Scranton Public Library 500 Vine St	Scranton	PA	18509	570-348-3000	961-3041
Web: www.albright.org					

On-Line Resources

About.com Guide to Wilkes-Barre/Scranton	wilkesbarre.about.com
City Knowledge Scranton	www.cityknowledge.com/pa_scranton.htm
Excite.com Scranton City Guide	www.excite.com/travel/countries/united_states/pennsylvania/scranton
Scranton: A Step Back in Time	www.microserve.net/~magicusa/scranton.html
Scranton Tourist Fun Guide	www.microserve.net/~magicusa/index.html#funguide

— Transportation Services —

AIRPORTS

	Phone
■ **Wilkes-Barre/Scranton International Airport (AVP)**	
7 miles SW of downtown (approx 20 minutes)	570-346-0672
Web: www.flyavp.com ■ *E-mail:* airport@epix.net	

Airport Transportation

	Phone
A-1 Limousine $40 fare to downtown	570-586-6599
Airport Limo & Taxi $17 fare to downtown	570-457-8109

Commercial Airlines

	Phone		Phone
Continental Express	800-525-0280	**United Express**	800-241-6522
Delta	800-221-1212	**US Airways**	800-428-4322
TWA Express	800-221-2000		

CAR RENTALS

	Phone		Phone
Budget	570-457-5661	**Thrifty**	570-883-1010
Hertz	570-655-1452		

LIMO/TAXI

	Phone		Phone
A-1 Limousine	570-586-6599	**McCarthy Cab**	570-342-3131
Elegance Limousine	570-343-9717	**Northeastern Transit**	570-347-8877
Luxury Limousine	570-823-5233		

MASS TRANSIT

	Phone
COLTS $1.25 Base fare	570-346-2061

RAIL/BUS

				Phone
Martz/Trailways Bus Station 23 Lackawanna Ave	Scranton	PA	18503	570-346-7113

— Accommodations —

HOTELS, MOTELS, RESORTS

				Phone	Fax
Best Western East Mountain Inn 2400 East End Blvd	Wilkes-Barre	PA	18702	570-822-1011	822-6072
TF: 800-528-1234					

Scranton — Hotels, Motels, Resorts (Cont'd)

Name/Address	City	State	Zip	Phone	Fax
Clarion Hotel 300 Meadow Ave	Scranton	PA	18505	570-344-9811	344-7799
Courtyard by Marriott 16 Glenmaura National Blvd — *TF:* 800-321-2211 ■ *Web:* courtyard.com/SCRCY	Moosic	PA	18507	570-969-2100	969-2110
Days Inn 811 Northern Blvd — *TF:* 800-329-7466	Clarks Summit	PA	18411	570-586-9100	586-9111
Days Inn Dunmore 1226 O'Neill Hwy — *TF:* 800-329-7466	Dunmore	PA	18512	570-348-6101	348-5064
Days Inn Moosic 4130-40 Birney Ave — *TF:* 800-724-3866	Moosic	PA	18507	570-457-6713	457-4479
Econo Lodge 1175 Kane St — *TF:* 800-553-2666	Scranton	PA	18505	570-348-1000	348-0683
Econo Lodge Dunmore 1027 O'Neill Hwy — *TF:* 800-553-2666	Dunmore	PA	18512	570-346-8782	346-7825
Hampton Inn 22 Montage Mountain Rd — *TF:* 800-426-7866	Scranton	PA	18507	570-342-7002	342-7012
Hampton Inn Wilkes-Barre 1063 Hwy 315 — *TF:* 800-426-7866	Wilkes-Barre	PA	18702	570-825-3838	825-8775
Holiday Inn Express 30 Concorde Dr — *TF:* 800-465-4329	Pittston	PA	18641	570-654-3300	883-7301
Holiday Inn Scranton East 200 Tigue St — *TF:* 800-465-4329	Dunmore	PA	18512	570-343-4771	343-5171
Howard Johnson Mulberry St & Franklin Ave	Scranton	PA	18503	570-346-7061	347-4667
Howard Johnson Plaza Hotel Wilkes-Barre/Scranton Hwy — *TF:* 800-446-4656	Pittston	PA	18640	570-654-3301	883-0288
Inn at Nichols Village 1101 Northern Blvd — *TF:* 800-642-2215 ■ *Web:* www.nicholsvillage.com ■ *E-mail:* nichols@epix.net	Clarks Summit	PA	18411	570-587-1135	586-7140
Quality Hotel 1946 Scranton Carbondale Hwy — *TF:* 800-228-5151	Scranton	PA	18508	570-383-9979	383-1756
Radisson Lackawanna Station Hotel 700 Lackawanna Ave — *TF:* 800-347-6888	Scranton	PA	18503	570-342-8300	342-0380
Ramada Hotel on the Square 20 Public Sq — *TF:* 800-272-6232	Wilkes-Barre	PA	18701	570-824-7100	823-5599
Ramada Inn Clarks Summit 820 Northern Blvd — *TF:* 800-272-6232	Clarks Summit	PA	18411	570-586-2730	587-0740
Shadowbrook Resort 615 SR 6 E — *TF:* 800-955-0295 ■ *Web:* www.shadowbrookresort.com ■ *E-mail:* shadowb@epix.net	Tunkhannock	PA	18657	570-836-2151	836-5655
Summit Inn 649 Northern Blvd	Clarks Summit	PA	18411	570-586-1211	586-7928
Victoria Inn Hwy 315 — *TF:* 800-937-4667	Pittston	PA	18640	570-655-1234	655-2267
West Side Hotel 129 S Main Ave	Scranton	PA	18504	570-961-1978	

— Restaurants —

				Phone
Aegean Restaurant (Greek) 134 N Main Ave	Scranton	PA	18504	570-342-2800
Angela Bistocchi's Restaurant (Italian) 1120 Wheeler Ave	Scranton	PA	18510	570-961-9112
Carmen's (Italian) 700 Lackawanna Ave	Scranton	PA	18503	570-342-8300
Casa De Mama (Italian) 1829 Bundy St	Scranton	PA	18508	570-961-2202
China Town (Chinese) 503 Linden St	Scranton	PA	18503	570-961-0467
Cooper's Seafood House (Seafood) 701 N Washington Ave	Scranton	PA	18509	570-346-6883
Cooper's Waterfront (Seafood) 304 Kennedy Blvd	Pittston	PA	18640	570-654-6883
Dougherty Restaurant (American) 1243 Capouse Ave	Scranton	PA	18509	570-346-8488
Farley's Eatery & Pub (American) 300 Adams Ave	Scranton	PA	18503	570-346-3000
Foliage (Chinese) 118 N Main Ave	Scranton	PA	18504	570-347-1071
Great Wall Chinese Restaurant (Chinese) 1400 Monroe Ave	Scranton	PA	18509	570-969-1544
House of China (Chinese) 1137 Moosic St	Scranton	PA	18505	570-343-8118
Jack's Draft House (American) 802 Prescott Ave	Scranton	PA	18510	570-346-3494
Jad's Place (American) Rt 315	Pittston Township	PA	18640	570-655-1234
Keystone Restaurant (American) 130 N Main Ave	Scranton	PA	18504	570-342-0509
La Cucina (Italian) 1946 Scranton Carbondale Hwy	Dickson City	PA	18519	570-383-9979
Marco Giovanni's (Italian) 1146 S Main Ave	Scranton	PA	18504	570-963-1084
Nana's Pasta House (Italian) 1223 Springbrook Ave	Moosic	PA	18507	570-457-9612
Pat McMullens Restaurant (American) 219 E Market St	Scranton	PA	18509	570-342-3486
Robata Japanese Seafood & Steak House (Japanese) 244 Adams Ave	Scranton	PA	18503	570-961-3675
Ryah House (American) 1101 Northern Blvd	Clarks Summit	PA	18411	570-587-4124
Smith's Restaurant (American) 1402 Cedar Ave	Scranton	PA	18509	570-961-9192
Sojourner (American) 1101 Northern Blvd	Clarks Summit	PA	18411	570-587-1135

— Goods and Services —

SHOPPING

Name/Address	City	State	Zip	Phone	Fax
Carriage Barn 1550 Fairview Rd — *Web:* www.carriagebarnantiques.com ■ *E-mail:* cbarnant@epix.net	Clarks Summit	PA	18411	570-587-5405	586-0712
Mall at Steamtown 300 The Mall at Steamtown	Scranton	PA	18503	570-343-3400	941-8623
Scranton Marketplace 710 Capouse Ave	Scranton	PA	18509	570-346-8777	
Viewmont Mall Rt 6 & Scranton-Carbondale Hwy — *Web:* www.crownam.com/viewpage.htm	Scranton	PA	18508	570-346-9165	346-6832

BANKS

Name/Address	City	State	Zip	Phone	Fax
Mellon Bank 400 Spruce St — *TF:* 800-245-4920	Scranton	PA	18503	570-343-9691	344-5267
Penn Security Bank & Trust Co 150 N Washington Ave — *TF:* 800-327-0394	Scranton	PA	18503	570-346-7741	961-3768
Pioneer American Bank NA 611 Luzerne St	West Scranton	PA	18504	570-343-5915	343-2710

BUSINESS SERVICES

Name	Phone	Name	Phone
Airborne Express	800-247-2676	**Mail Boxes Etc**	800-789-4623
BAX Global	800-225-5229	**Manpower Temporary Services**	570-347-3317
DHL Worldwide Express	800-225-5345	**Olsten Staffing Services**	570-344-3220
Federal Express	800-238-5355	**Post Office**	570-969-5120
Kelly Services	570-346-7406	**UPS**	800-742-5877

— Media —

PUBLICATIONS

Name/Address	City	State	Zip	Phone	Fax
Scranton Times-Tribune‡ PO Box 3311 — *TF:* 800-228-4637 ■ *Web:* www.scrantontimes.com ■ *E-mail:* newsroom@scrantontimes.com	Scranton	PA	18505	570-348-9100	348-9135
Times Tribune‡ PO Box 3311 — *Web:* www.scrantontimes.com	Scranton	PA	18505	570-348-9100	348-9135

‡Daily newspapers

TELEVISION

Name/Address	City	State	Zip	Phone	Fax
WBRE-TV Ch 28 (NBC) 62 S Franklin St — *Web:* www.wbre.com ■ *E-mail:* wbre@brigadoon.com	Wilkes-Barre	PA	18701	570-823-2828	829-0440
WILF-TV Ch 53 (Fox) 916 Oak St	Scranton	PA	18508	570-347-9653	347-3141
WNEP-TV Ch 16 (ABC) 16 Montage Mountain Rd — *Web:* www.wnep.com ■ *E-mail:* wneptv@aol.com	Moosic	PA	18507	570-346-7474	347-0359
WOLF-TV Ch 56 (Fox) 916 Oak St — *Web:* www.fox56tv.com	Scranton	PA	18508	570-347-9653	347-3141
WVIA-TV Ch 44 (PBS) 70 Old Boston Rd — *Web:* www.wvia.org/tv/tv.html	Pittston	PA	18640	570-344-1244	655-1180
WWLF-TV Ch 56 (Fox) 916 Oak St	Scranton	PA	18508	570-347-9653	347-3141
WYOU-TV Ch 22 (CBS) 415 Lackawanna Ave — *Web:* www.wyou.com	Scranton	PA	18503	570-961-2222	344-4484

RADIO

Name/Address	City	State	Zip	Phone	Fax
WEJL-AM 630 kHz (Nost) 149 Penn Ave	Scranton	PA	18503	570-346-6555	346-6038
WEZX-FM 106.9 MHz (CR) 149 Penn Ave — *Web:* www.rock107.com	Scranton	PA	18503	570-346-6555	346-6038
WEZX-FM 106.9 MHz (Rock) 149 Penn Ave	Scranton	PA	18503	570-961-1842	346-6038
WHLM-FM 106.5 MHz (AC) 107 W Main St — *Web:* www.whlm.com ■ *E-mail:* mix106@whlm.com	Bloomsburg	PA	17815	570-784-5500	784-1004
WICK-AM 1400 kHz (Oldies) 1049 N Sekol Rd — *Web:* wick-am.com	Scranton	PA	18504	570-344-1221	344-0996
WJMW-AM 550 kHz (Misc) 107 W Main St	Bloomsburg	PA	17815	570-784-5500	784-1004
WKRZ-FM 98.5 MHz (CHR) 305 Hwy 315 — *Web:* www.wkrz.com ■ *E-mail:* feedback@wkrz.com	Pittston	PA	18640	570-883-9850	883-9851
WVMW-FM 91.5 MHz (Alt) 2300 Adams Ave Marywood College	Scranton	PA	18509	570-348-6202	961-4769
WWDL-FM 104.9 MHz (AC) 1049 N Sekol Rd — *Web:* www.wwdl.com ■ *E-mail:* comments@wwdl.com	Scranton	PA	18504	570-344-1221	344-0996

Scranton (Cont'd)

— Colleges/Universities —

				Phone	Fax
College Misericordia 301 Lake St.	Dallas	PA	18612	570-674-6400	675-2441
TF Admissions: 800-852-7675 ■ *Web:* www.miseri.edu ■ *E-mail:* admiss@miseri.edu					
ICS Learning Systems 925 Oak St	Scranton	PA	18515	570-342-7701	343-3620
TF Cust Svc: 800-233-0259 ■ *Web:* www.icslearn.com ■ *E-mail:* info@icslearn.com					
Johnson Technical Institute 3427 N Main Ave	Scranton	PA	18508	570-342-6404	348-2181
TF: 800-293-9675 ■ *Web:* www.jti.org ■ *E-mail:* johntech@jti.org					
Keystone College 1 College Green	La Plume	PA	18440	570-945-5141	945-7916
TF: 800-824-2764 ■ *Web:* www.keystone.edu					
King's College 133 N River St	Wilkes-Barre	PA	18711	570-208-5900	208-9049
TF Admissions: 800-955-5777 ■ *Web:* www.kings.edu					
Lackawanna Junior College 501 Vine St	Scranton	PA	18509	570-961-7810	961-7843
TF: 877-346-3552 ■ *Web:* members.aol.com/grifflew/ljc					
Marywood University 2300 Adams Ave	Scranton	PA	18509	570-348-6211	961-4763
Web: www.marywood.edu					
Pennsylvania State University Worthington Scranton 120 Ridge View Dr	Dunmore	PA	18512	570-963-2500	963-2535
Web: www.sn.psu.edu					
University of Scranton Linden & Monroe Aves St Thomas Hall 3rd Fl	Scranton	PA	18510	570-941-7400	941-6369
Web: www.uofs.edu ■ *E-mail:* admissions@uofs.edu					
Wilkes University PO Box 111	Wilkes-Barre	PA	18766	570-824-4651	408-4904
TF Admissions: 800-945-5378 ■ *Web:* www.wilkes.edu					

— Hospitals —

				Phone	Fax
Community Medical Center 1822 Mulberry St	Scranton	PA	18510	570-969-8000	969-8951
Marian Community Hospital 100 Lincoln Ave	Carbondale	PA	18407	570-282-2100	282-7177
Mercy Hospital of Scranton 746 Jefferson Ave	Scranton	PA	18501	570-348-7100	348-7639*
**Fax:* Admitting					
Moses Taylor Hospital 700 Quincy Ave	Scranton	PA	18510	570-340-2100	969-2629
Web: www.mth.org					

— Attractions —

				Phone	Fax
Anthracite People c/o Pennsylvania Anthracite Heritage Museum Bald Mountain Rd RR #1	Scranton	PA	18504	570-963-4804	963-4194
Ashland Pioneer Tunnel & Coal Mine 19th & Oak Sts.	Ashland	PA	17921	570-875-3850	875-3301
Ballet Theatre of Scranton 310 Penn Ave	Scranton	PA	18503	570-347-2867	
Broadway Theatre of Northeast Pennsylvania 108 N Washington Ave Suite 802	Scranton	PA	18501	570-342-7784	
Claws 'n' Paws Wild Animal Park Rt 590	Lake Ariel	PA	18436	570-698-6154	698-2957
Web: www.microserve.net/~magicusa/clawspaws.html					
Everhart Museum 1901 Mulberry St	Scranton	PA	18510	570-346-7186	346-0652
Web: www.northeastweb.com/everhart					
Holocaust Museum & Resource Center 601 Jefferson Ave.	Scranton	PA	18510	570-961-2300	346-6147
Web: www.ncx.com/wwi/hmrc/ ■ *E-mail:* jaytov@mail.microserve.net					
Houdini Museum 1433 N Main Ave.	Scranton	PA	18508	570-342-5555	
Web: www.houdini.org					
Lackawanna County Coal Mine Bald Mountain Rd	Scranton	PA	18504	570-963-6463	963-6701
Lahey Family Fun Park 500 Morgan Hwy	Clarks Summit	PA	18411	570-586-5699	586-7109
Montage Mountain Ski Area 1000 Montage Mountain Rd.	Scranton	PA	18505	570-969-7669	963-6621
TF: 800-468-7669 ■ *Web:* www.skimontage.com ■ *E-mail:* montage@sunlink.net					
Music Box Dinner Playhouse 196 Hughes St	Swoyersville	PA	18704	570-283-2195	
Web: members.aol.com/oreoking/musicbox.htm					
Northeastern Pennsylvania Philharmonic 957 Broadcast Ctr	Avoca	PA	18641	570-457-8301	457-5901
TF: 800-836-3413					
Pennsylvania Anthracite Heritage Museum RR1 Bald Mountain Rd	Scranton	PA	18504	570-963-4804	963-4194
Providence Playhouse 1256 Providence Rd	Scranton	PA	18508	570-342-9707	
Saint Ann's Monastery 1230 Saint Ann St	Scranton	PA	18504	570-347-5691	347-9387
Scranton Cultural Center 420 N Washington Ave	Scranton	PA	18503	570-346-7369	346-7365
Scranton Iron Furnace 159 Cedar Ave	Scranton	PA	18505	570-963-3208	
Scranton Public Theatre PO Box 1451	Scranton	PA	18501	570-344-3656	
Slocum Hollow Family Fun Park 3200 N Main Ave	Scranton	PA	18508	570-346-4386	
Steamtown National Historic Site 150 S Washington Ave	Scranton	PA	18503	570-340-5200	340-5265
Web: www.nps.gov/stea/					
Upper Delaware Scenic & Recreational River PO Box 2428	Beach Lake	PA	18405	570-685-4871	685-4874
Web: www.nps.gov/upde/ ■ *E-mail:* upde_interpretation@nps.gov					

SPORTS TEAMS & FACILITIES

				Phone	Fax
Pocono Downs 1280 Hwy 315	Wilkes-Barre	PA	18702	570-825-6681	823-9407
Scranton/Wilkes-Barre Red Barons (baseball) Lackawanna Stadium	Scranton	PA	18505	570-963-6556	963-6564

— Events —

	Phone
Armed Forces Airshow (early May)	570-824-1879
Artisan's Marketplace (late November)	570-586-8191
Jazz Fest at Cherry Blossom Time (early May)	570-823-3165
La Festa Italiana (early September)	800-229-3526
Moscow Country Fair (mid-August)	570-842-7252
Pennsylvania National Arts & Crafts Show (mid-March)	717-796-0531
Saint Patrick's Day Parade (mid-March)	570-348-3412
Spring Carnival (mid-March)	570-679-2611
Wings Over Montage (early September)	570-969-7669

Rhode Island

Population (1999): 990,819 **Area (sq mi): 1,545**

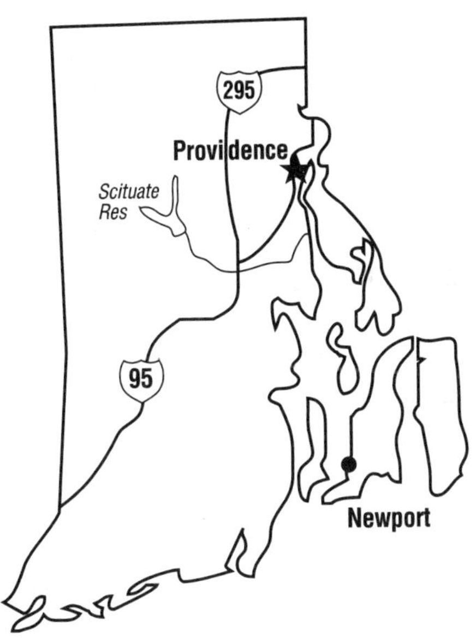

— State Information Sources —

				Phone	Fax
Rhode Island Economic Development Corp 1 W Exchange St ... *Web:* www.riedc.com ■ *E-mail:* riedc@riedc.com	Providence	RI	02903	401-222-2601	222-2102
Rhode Island Office of Library & Information Services 1 Capitol Hill ... *Web:* www.dsls.state.ri.us	Providence	RI	02908	401-222-2726	222-4195
Rhode Island Parks & Recreation Div 2321 Hartford Ave ... *Web:* www.riparks.com	Johnston	RI	02919	401-222-2632	934-0610
Rhode Island State Government Information ... *Web:* www.state.ri.us ■ *E-mail:* comments@sec.state.ri.us				401-222-2000	
Rhode Island Tourism Div 1 West Exchange St ... *TF:* 800-556-2484 ■ *Web:* visitrhodeisland.com	Providence	RI	02903	401-222-2601	222-2102

ON-LINE RESOURCES

Block Island Tourism Council ... www.block-island.com
Imbored Rhode Island ... www.imbored.com/new/rri01.htm
Net Travel Rhode Island ... www.nettx.com/states/ri.htm
PeekABoo Rhode Island ... www.peekaboo.net/ri
Rhode Island Cities ... dir.yahoo.com/Regional/U_S__States/Rhode_Island/Cities
Rhode Island Counties & Regions ... dir.yahoo.com/Regional/U_S__States/Rhode_Island/Counties_and_Regions
Rhode Island Family Guide ... www.rifamilyguide.com
Rhode Island Scenario ... scenariousa.dstylus.com/ri/indexf.htm
Rhode Island Travel & Tourism Guide ... www.travel-library.com/north_america/usa/rhode_island/index.html
RITourism.com ... www.ritourism.com/
Rough Guide Travel Rhode Island ... travel.roughguides.com/content/390/index.htm
Search Rhode Island ... www.newengland.com/rimap.html
Travel.org-Rhode Island ... travel.org/rhode.html
Visit RI ... www.visitri.com
Welcome to Rhode Island ... www.guidetori.com
Yahoo! Get Local Rhode Island ... dir.yahoo.com/Regional/U_S__States/Rhode_Island

— Cities Profiled —

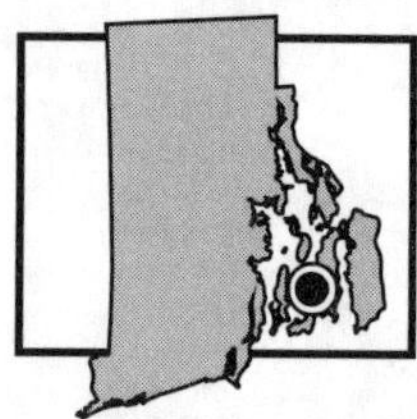

Newport

Founded in 1639, the island community of Newport became known as a summer playground for the wealthy, particularly southern plantation owners and industrial giants, during the 1800s. Many of the elaborate mansions and villas (built as "summer cottages') of that period are now open for tours, including Newport's most magnificent mansion, The Breakers, which was built for Cornelius Vanderbilt in 1895. The Astors' Beechwood Mansion is now a living history museum, with the 1890s lifestyle re-enacted daily by the Beechwood Theatre Company; and Belcourt Castle, designed in the style of Louis XIII's Hunting Lodge at Versailles, includes more than 2,000 art treasures. Newport also has more than 300 17th and 18th century Colonial structures, many of which are open to the public. Other Newport attractions include the International Tennis Hall of Fame; White Horse Tavern (1673), the oldest in the country and still in operation; Hammersmith Farm, summer home of the Auchincloss family and "Summer White House" for the Kennedys; Saint Mary's Church, the oldest Catholic parish in the state, which is also a National Shrine and the site where JFK was married; and Touro Synagogue (1763), the oldest Jewish house of worship in the U.S., and the historic Jewish cemetery near it. In addition, Ocean Drive and Cliff Walk provide spectacular views of shoreline, beaches, and harbors.

Population	24,279	**Longitude**	71-30-35 W
Area (Land)	7.9 sq mi	**County**	Newport
Area (Water)	3.5 sq mi	**Time Zone**	EST
Elevation	96 ft	**Area Code/s**	401
Latitude	41-49-69 N		

— Average Temperatures and Precipitation —

TEMPERATURES

	Jan	Feb	Mar	Apr	May	Jun	Jul	Aug	Sep	Oct	Nov	Dec
High	38	39	46	55	64	73	78	78	72	63	53	43
Low	23	24	30	38	47	57	63	63	57	47	38	28

PRECIPITATION

	Jan	Feb	Mar	Apr	May	Jun	Jul	Aug	Sep	Oct	Nov	Dec
Inches	3.8	3.6	4.1	4.2	3.7	3.1	2.9	3.3	3.5	3.5	4.7	4.4

— Important Phone Numbers —

	Phone		Phone
AAA	401-841-5000	**Poison Control Center**	401-444-5727
American Express Travel	401-274-2900	**Travelers Aid of Rhode Island**	401-521-2255
Emergency	911	**Weather**	401-848-0028

— Information Sources —

				Phone	Fax
Better Business Bureau Serving Rhode Island 120 Lavan St	Warwick	RI	02888	401-785-1212	785-3061
Web: www.rhodeisland.bbb.org					
Newport City Hall 43 Broadway	Newport	RI	02840	401-846-9600	848-5750
Web: www.cityofnewport.com/ ■ *E-mail:* newport@wsii.com					
Newport County 45 Washington Sq	Newport	RI	02840	401-841-8330	
Newport County Chamber of Commerce 45 Valley Rd.	Middletown	RI	02842	401-847-1600	849-5848
Web: www.newportchamber.com					
Newport County Convention & Visitors Bureau 23 America's Cup Ave	Newport	RI	02840	401-849-8048	849-0291
TF: 800-326-6030 ■ *Web:* www.gonewport.com					
Newport Marina & Event Center 4 Commercial Wharf	Newport	RI	02840	401-846-1600	847-7754
Newport Mayor 43 Broadway	Newport	RI	02840	401-846-9600	848-5750
Newport Planning Zoning & Development Dept 43 Broadway	Newport	RI	02840	401-846-9600	848-5750
Web: www.cityofnewport.com/nwplan.html					
Newport Public Library 300 Spring St.	Newport	RI	02840	401-847-8720	842-0841
Rhode Island Tourism Div 1 West Exchange St	Providence	RI	02903	401-222-2601	222-2102
TF: 800-556-2484 ■ *Web:* visitrhodeisland.com					

On-Line Resources

Area Guide Newport	newportri.areaguides.net
Best Read Guide Newport	www.newportri.com/
Excite.com Newport City Guide	www.excite.com/travel/countries/united_states/rhode_island/newport
Guide to Antique Shops in Newport	www.drawrm.com/dealers.htm
Guide to Newport	www.mswebpros.com
Newport Online	www.newportonline.com
Newport Rhode Island	www.bbsnet.com/Newport/newport.html
Newport RI On-line Guide	members.aol.com/newporters
NITC Travelbase City Guide Newport	www.travelbase.com/auto/guides/newport-area-ri.html
Rough Guide Travel Newport	travel.roughguides.com/content/392/
Surf & Sun Beach Vacation Guide to Newport	www.surf-sun.com/ri-newport-main.htm
Visit Newport	www.visitnewport.com

— Transportation Services —

AIRPORTS

■ Theodore Francis Green State Airport (PVD)

	Phone
27 miles NW of downtown Newport (approx 45 minutes)	401-737-4000
Web: www.pvd-ri.com	

Airport Transportation

	Phone
Cozy Cab Shuttle Service $15 fare to downtown Newport	401-846-2500
Yellow Cab $65 fare to downtown Newport	401-846-1500

Commercial Airlines

	Phone		Phone
American	800-433-7300	**Northwest**	800-225-2525
Continental	800-525-0280	**United**	800-241-6522
Continental Express	800-525-0280	**US Airways**	800-428-4322
Delta	800-221-1212		

Charter Airlines

	Phone		Phone
Corporate Air Charter	401-732-0782	**Richmor Aviation Inc**	800-359-2299
Jet America Corp	401-737-3674		

CAR RENTALS

	Phone		Phone
Avis	401-736-7500	**Hertz-Newport**	401-846-1645
Budget	401-739-8900	**National**	401-737-4800
CarTemps USA	401-738-5910	**Thrifty**	401-732-2000
Hertz	401-738-7500	**Thrifty-Newport**	401-846-4371

LIMO/TAXI

	Phone		Phone
Cozy Cab	401-846-2500	**Rainbow Cab**	401-849-1333
Cozy Limousine	401-846-2500	**Yellow Cab**	401-846-1500

MASS TRANSIT

	Phone
RIPTA $1.25 Base fare	401-847-0209

RAIL/BUS

				Phone
Bonanza Bus Station 23 America's Cup Ave	Newport	RI	02840	401-521-6700

Newport (Cont'd)

— Accommodations —

HOTEL RESERVATION SERVICES

Name	Phone	Fax
Bed & Breakfast Newport Ltd	401-846-5408	846-1828
TF: 800-800-8765 ■ *Web:* www.bbnewport.com		
■ *E-mail:* bbnewport@ids.net		
Newport Reservations	401-842-0102	842-0104
TF: 800-842-0102		
■ *Web:* www.aqua.net/lodging/newportres/newportres.html		
■ *E-mail:* newpresvn@edgenet.net		
Taylor-Made Reservations	401-848-0300	848-0301
TF: 800-848-8848 ■ *Web:* www.enjoy-newport.com		

HOTELS, MOTELS, RESORTS

Name	City	State	Zip	Phone	Fax
Admiral Benbow Inn 8 Fair St	Newport	RI	02840	401-848-8000	848-8006
TF: 800-343-2863 ■ *Web:* www.admiralsinns.com					
Best Western Mainstay Inn 151 Admiral Kalbfus Rd	Newport	RI	02840	401-849-9880	849-4391
TF: 800-528-1234					
Castle Hill Inn & Resort 590 Ocean Dr	Newport	RI	02840	401-849-3800	849-3838
TF: 888-466-1355 ■ *Web:* www.castlehillinn.com					
■ *E-mail:* castlehill@edgenet.net					
Cliffside Inn 2 Seaview Ave	Newport	RI	02840	401-847-1811	848-5850
TF: 800-845-1811 ■ *Web:* www.cliffsideinn.com					
■ *E-mail:* cliff@wsll.com					
Courtyard by Marriott 9 Commerce Dr	Newport	RI	02840	401 849-8000	849-8313
TF: 800-321-2211 ■ *Web:* courtyard.com/PVDMD					
Doubletree Islander Hotel 1 Goat Island	Newport	RI	02840	401-849-2600	846-7210
TF: 800-222-8733 ■ *Web:* www.newportislander.doubletreehotels.com					
Harbor Base Pineapple Inn 372 Coddington Hwy	Newport	RI	02840	401-847-2600	847-5230
Web: www.newportri.com/users/pineapple					
Harborside Inn Christie's Landing	Newport	RI	02840	401-846-6600	849-3023
TF: 800-427-9444 ■ *Web:* www.historicinnsofnewport.com/hion.htm					
■ *E-mail:* vacation@theharborside.com					
Hotel Viking 1 Bellevue Ave	Newport	RI	02840	401-847-3300	849-0749*
**Fax:* Sales ■ *TF:* 800-556-7126 ■ *Web:* www.hotelviking.com					
Howard Johnson Lodge 351 W Main Rd	Middletown	RI	02842	401-849-2000	849-6047
TF: 800-446-4656					
Inn at Newport Beach Memorial Blvd	Newport	RI	02840	401-846-0310	847-2621
TF: 800-786-0310					
Inn on Long Wharf 5 Washington St	Newport	RI	02840	401-847-7800	846-3888
TF: 800-225-3522					
Inn on the Harbor 359 Thames St	Newport	RI	02840	401-849-6789	846-3888
TF: 800-225-3522					
Marriott Newport 25 America's Cup Ave	Newport	RI	02840	401-849-1000	849-3422
TF: 800-458-3066 ■ *Web:* marriotthotels.com/PVDLW					
Mill Street Inn 75 Mill St	Newport	RI	02840	401-849-9500	848-5131
TF: 800-392-1316 ■ *Web:* www.millstreetinn.com					
■ *E-mail:* millstreet@travelbase.com					
Motel 6 249 JT Connell Hwy	Newport	RI	02840	401-848-0600	848-9966
TF: 800-466-8356					
Newport Bay Club & Hotel 337 Thames St	Newport	RI	02840	401-849-8600	846-6857
Web: www.newportbayclub.com/					
Newport Gateway Hotel 31 W Main Rd	Middletown	RI	02842	401-847-2735	847-5434
TF: 800-427-9444 ■ *Web:* www.historicinnsofnewport.com/gatway.htm					
■ *E-mail:* gateway@historicinnsofnewport.com					
Newport Harbor Hotel & Marina 49 America's Cup Ave	Newport	RI	02840	401-847-9000	849-6380
TF: 800-955-2558 ■ *Web:* www.nhhm.com					
■ *E-mail:* individualsales@nhhm.com					
Newport Ramada Inn 936 W Main Rd	Middletown	RI	02842	401-846-7600	849-6919
TF: 800-846-8322					
Oceancliff Hotel & Resort 65 Ridge Rd	Newport	RI	02840	401-841-8868	849-3927
Royal Plaza Hotel 425 E Main Rd	Newport	RI	02842	401-846-3555	846-3666
TF: 800-825-7072 ■ *Web:* www.royalplazahotel.com					
■ *E-mail:* royalplaza@travelbase.com					
Sanford-Covell Villa Marina 72 Washington St	Newport	RI	02840	401-847-0206	
SeaView Inn 240 Aquidneck Ave	Newport	RI	02840	401-846-5000	848-0873
TF: 800-495-2046					
Susse Chalet Navy Hotel 1290 Perry Rd	Newport	RI	02841	401-841-0800	841-0937
TF: 800-524-2538					
Travelodge 1185 W Main Rd	Middletown	RI	02842	401-849-4700	848-7704
Vanderbilt Hall Hotel 41 Mary St	Newport	RI	02840	401-846-6200	846-0701
TF: 888-826-4255 ■ *Web:* www.vanderbilthall.com					
Wellington Resort 551 Thames St	Newport	RI	02840	401-849-1770	847-6250

— Restaurants —

Name	City	State	Zip	Phone
Atlantic Beach Club (American) 55 Purgatory Rd	Middletown	RI	02842	401-847-3059
Batik Garden (Chinese) 11 E Main Rd	Middletown	RI	02842	401-848-0663
Black Pearl (Steak/Seafood) W Pelham St	Newport	RI	02840	401-846-5264
Brick Alley Pub & Restaurant (American) 140 Thames St	Newport	RI	02840	401-849-6334
Web: www.brickalley.com				
Cafe Zelda (American) 528 Lower Thames St	Newport	RI	02840	401-849-4002
Canfield House (Steak/Seafood) 5 Memorial Blvd	Newport	RI	02840	401-847-0416
Charlie's Good Egg (Homestyle) 12 Broadway	Newport	RI	02840	401-849-7817
Chart House Restaurant (Steak/Seafood) 22 Bowen's Wharf	Newport	RI	02840	401-849-7555
Christie's of Newport (Steak/Seafood) 351 Thames St	Newport	RI	02840	401-847-5400
Dave's On Thames (American) 509 Thames St	Newport	RI	02840	401-846-4411
Dry Dock Seafood (Seafood) 448 Thames St	Newport	RI	02840	401-847-3974
East Side Mario's (Italian) 593 W Main Rd	Middletown	RI	02840	401-841-0700
Griswold's Tavern (American) 103 Bellevue Ave	Newport	RI	02840	401-846-4660
Hisae's Japanese Restaurant (Japanese) 21 Valley Rd	Portsmouth	RI	02842	401-848-6262
Jake & Ella's (American) 636 Thames St	Newport	RI	02840	401-846-7700
JW Sea Grill (Steak/Seafood) 25 America Cup Ave	Newport	RI	02840	401-849-7788
La Forge Casino (American) 186 Bellevue Ave	Newport	RI	02840	401-847-0418
La Petite Auberge (French) 19 Charles St	Newport	RI	02840	401-849-6669
Long Wharf Steak House (American) Washington St & Long Wharf	Newport	RI	02840	401-847-7800
Mamma Luisa (Italian) 673 Thames St	Newport	RI	02840	401-848-5257
Moorings The (Seafood) Sayer's Wharf	Newport	RI	02840	401-846-2260
Web: www.mooringrestaurant.com				
Mudville Pub (American) 8 Marlboro St	Newport	RI	02840	401-849-1408
Music Hall Cafe (Southwest) 250 Thames St	Newport	RI	02840	401-848-2330
Newport Blues Cafe (American) 286 Thames St	Newport	RI	02840	401-841-5510
Ocean Breeze Cafe (American) 580 Thames St	Newport	RI	02840	401-849-1750
Pezzulli's Cafe (Italian) 136 Thames St	Newport	RI	02840	401-846-5830
Red Parrot (Caribbean) 348 Thames St	Newport	RI	02840	401-847-3140
Rhumb Line Restaurant (American) 62 Bridge St	Newport	RI	02840	401-849-6950
Sardella's (Italian) 30 Memorial Blvd W	Newport	RI	02840	401-849-6312
Web: www.sardellas.com				
Sea Fare's American Cafe (American) Brick Market Pl	Newport	RI	02840	401-849-9188
West Deck (Gourmet) 1 Waitcs Wharf	Newport	RI	02840	401-847-3610
White Horse Tavern (Continental) Marlborough & Farewel Sts	Newport	RI	02840	401-849-3600
Web: www.whitehorsetavern.com				
Windward Restaurant (Seafood) 1 Goat Island	Newport	RI	02840	401-849-2600

— Goods and Services —

SHOPPING

Name	City	State	Zip	Phone	Fax
Aquidneck Centre 99 E Main Rd	Middletown	RI	02842	401-849-6800	849-7863
Bannister's Wharf W Pelham St Bannister's Wharf	Newport	RI	02840	401-846-4500	849-8750
Web: www.bannisterswharf.com					
Bellevue Gardens Shopping Center Bellevue Ave	Newport	RI	02840		
Fall River Factory Outlet District Rt 24 N & 195	Fall River	RI	02721	800-424-5519	677-4956*
**Fax Area Code:* 508					
Newport Mall 199 Connell Hwy	Newport	RI	02840		
Shops at Brick Marketplace Thames St & America's Cup Ave	Newport	RI	02840	401-849-8048	

BANKS

Name	City	State	Zip	Phone	Fax
Bank of Newport 10 Washington Sq	Newport	RI	02840	401-846-3400	847-8850
TF: 800-234-8586 ■ *Web:* www.bankofnewport.com					
■ *E-mail:* intouch@bankofnewport.com					
Citizens Bank 8 Washington Sq	Newport	RI	02840	401-847-4411	
Fleet National Bank 181 Bellevue Ave	Newport	RI	02840	401-845-2610	849-6399
TF: 800-841-4000					
Newport Federal Savings Bank 100 Bellevue Ave	Newport	RI	02840	401-847-5500	848-5910

BUSINESS SERVICES

Name	Phone	Name	Phone
Airborne Express	800-247-2676	**Kinko's**	401-848-0580
BAX Global	800-225-5229	**Mail Boxes Etc**	800-789-4623
DHL Worldwide Express	800-225-5345	**Post Office**	401-846-0444
Federal Express	800-238-5355	**UPS**	800-742-5877

Newport (Cont'd)

— Media —

PUBLICATIONS

				Phone	Fax
Newport Daily News‡ 101 Malbone Rd	Newport	RI	02840	401-849-3300	849-3306
Newport Mercury 101 Malbone Rd	Newport	RI	02840	401-849-3300	849-3306
Newport This Week 38 Bellevue Ave	Newport	RI	02840	401-847-7766	846-4974
Web: www.newportthisweek.com/					

‡*Daily newspapers*

TELEVISION

				Phone	Fax
WJAR-TV Ch 10 (NBC) 23 Kenney Dr	Cranston	RI	02920	401-455-9100	455-9140
Web: www.nbc10wjar.com ■ *E-mail:* mail.box10@nbc.com					
WLNE-TV Ch 6 (ABC) 10 Orms St	Providence	RI	02904	401-453-8000	453-8092
Web: www.abc6.com					
WPRI-TV Ch 12 (CBS) 25 Catamore Blvd	East Providence	RI	02914	401-438-7200	431-1012
Web: www.wpri.com ■ *E-mail:* wpri@wpri.com					
WSBE-TV Ch 36 (PBS) 50 Park Ln	Providence	RI	02907	401-222-3636	222-3407
Web: www.wsbe.org					

RADIO

				Phone	Fax
WADK-AM 1540 kHz (N/T) PO Box 367	Newport	RI	02840	401-846-1540	846-1598
Web: www.wadk.com					
WCTK-FM 98.1 MHz (Ctry) 75 Oxford St	Providence	RI	02905	401-467-4366	941-2983
WPRO-AM 630 kHz (N/T) 1502 Wampanoag Trail	East Providence	RI	02915	401-433-4200	433-5967
WPRO-FM 92.3 MHz (CHR) 1502 Wampanoag Trail	East Providence	RI	02915	401-433-4200	433-5967
WRKO-AM 680 kHz (N/T) 116 Huntington Ave	Boston	MA	02116	617-236-6800	236-6890
Web: www.wrko.com					
WSNE-FM 93.3 MHz (AC) 100 Boyd Ave	East Providence	RI	02914	401-438-9300	434-4243
Web: www.wsne.com/					
WWRX-FM 103.7 MHz (CR) 75 Oxford St	Providence	RI	02905	401-781-9979	781-9329
Web: www.wrx.com					

— Colleges/Universities —

				Phone	Fax
Salve Regina University 100 Ochre Point Ave	Newport	RI	02840	401-847-6650	848-2823
Web: www.salve.edu					
University of Rhode Island	Kingston	RI	02881	401-874-1000	874-5523
Web: www.uri.edu					

— Hospitals —

				Phone	Fax
Newport Hospital 11 Friendship St	Newport	RI	02840	401-846-6400	845-1088
Web: www.lifespan.org/about/newport					
South County Hospital 100 Kenyon Ave	Wakefield	RI	02879	401-782-8000	783-6330
Web: www.schospital.com ■ *E-mail:* info@schospital.com					

— Attractions —

				Phone	Fax
Artillery Co of Newport Military Museum 23 Clarke St	Newport	RI	02840	401-846-8488	
Astors' Beechwood Mansion 580 Bellevue Ave	Newport	RI	02840	401-846-3772	849-6998
Web: www.astors-beechwood.com					
Bannister's Wharf W Pelham St Bannister's Wharf	Newport	RI	02840	401-846-4500	849-8750
Web: www.bannisterswharf.com					
Belcourt Castle 657 Bellevue Ave	Newport	RI	02840	401-846-0669	846-5345
Breakers Stable & Carriage House Bateman & Coggeshall Ave	Newport	RI	02840	401-847-1000	847-1361
Web: www.newportmansions.org/html/bsch.html					
Breakers The Ochre Point Ave	Newport	RI	02840	401-847-1000	847-1361
Web: www.newportmansions.org/html/breakers.html					
Brenton Point State Park Ocean Dr	Newport	RI	02840	401-847-2400	841-9821
Chateau-Sur-Mer Bellevue Ave	Newport	RI	02840	401-847-1000	847-1361
Web: www.newportmansions.org/html/csm.html					
Edward King House 35 King St	Newport	RI	02840	401-846-7426	846-5308
Elms The Bellevue Ave	Newport	RI	02840	401-847-1000	847-1361
Web: www.newportmansions.org/html/elms.html					
Fort Adams State Park Harrison Ave	Newport	RI	02840	401-847-2400	841-9821
Web: www.moonbase.com/davemann/ftadams/					
Green Animals Cory's Ln	Portsmouth	RI	02871	401-847-1000	847-1361
Web: www.newportmansions.org/html/animals.html					
Hammersmith Farm Ocean Dr	Newport	RI	02840	401-846-7346	849-4973
Web: www.hammersmithfarm.com					
Hunter House 54 Washington St	Newport	RI	02840	401-847-1000	847-1361
Web: www.newportmansions.org/html/hunter.html					
International Tennis Hall of Fame & Museum 194 Bellevue Ave	Newport	RI	02840	401-849-3990	849-8780
Web: www.tennisfame.org ■ *E-mail:* ithf@aol.com					
King Roger Gallery of Fine Art 21 Bowen's Wharf	Newport	RI	02840	401-847-4359	846-4096
Web: www.rkingfinearts.com ■ *E-mail:* rking@rkingfinearts.com					
Kingscote 424 Bellevue Ave	Newport	RI	02840	401-847-1000	847-1361
Web: www.newportmansions.org/html/kingscote.html					
Marble House Bellevue Ave	Newport	RI	02840	401-847-1000	847-1361
Web: www.newportmansions.org/html/marble.html					
Museum of Newport History at the Brick Market 127 Thames St	Newport	RI	02840	401-841-8770	846-1853
Web: www.newporthistorical.com					
Museum of Yachting Fort Adams State Pk	Newport	RI	02840	401-847-1018	847-8320
Web: www.moy.org					
Naval War College Museum Coasters Harbor Island	Newport	RI	02841	401-841-4052	841-7689
Web: www.visitnewport.com/buspages/navy					
Newport Art Museum 76 Bellevue Ave	Newport	RI	02840	401-848-8200	848-8205
Newport Casino 194 Bellevue Ave	Newport	RI	02840	401-849-3990	849-8780
Newport Historical Society 575 Thames St	Newport	RI	02840	401-846-0813	846-1853
Norman Bird Sanctuary 583 Third Beach Rd	Middletown	RI	02840	401-846-2577	846-2772
Web: www.normanbirdsanctuary.org ■ *E-mail:* info@normanbirdsanctuary.org					
Prescott Farm 2009 W Main Rd	Middletown	RI	02842	401-847-6230	
Redwood Library & Athenaeum 50 Bellevue Ave	Newport	RI	02840	401-847-0292	841-5680
Web: www.redwood1747.org					
Rose Island Lighthouse 365 Thames St	Newport	RI	02840	401-847-4242	847-7262
Web: www.roseislandlighthouse.org					
Rosecliff Bellevue Ave	Newport	RI	02840	401-847-1000	847-1361
Web: www.newportmansions.org/html/rosecliff.html					
Saint Mary's Church 12 William St	Newport	RI	02840	401-847-0475	
Sakonnet Vineyards 162 W Main Rd	Little Compton	RI	02837	401-635-8486	635-2101
TF: 800-919-4637 ■ *Web:* www.sakonnetwine.com ■ *E-mail:* sakonnetri@aol.com					
Thames Science Center 77 Long Wharf	Newport	RI	02840	401-849-6966	
Web: www.thamesscience.org					
Touro Synagogue National Historic Site 85 Touro St	Newport	RI	02840	401-847-4794	847-8121
Web: www.tourosynagogue.org					
Wanton-Lyman-Hazard House 17 Broadway	Newport	RI	02840	401-846-0813	846-1853
White Horse Tavern 26 Marlborough St	Newport	RI	02840	401-849-3600	849-7317
Whitehorne Samuel House 416 Thames St	Newport	RI	02840	401-849-7300	849-0125

SPORTS TEAMS & FACILITIES

				Phone	Fax
Newport Grand Jai Alai 150 Admiral Kalbfus Rd	Newport	RI	02840	401-849-5000	846-0290
Web: newportgrand.com					
Rhode Island Rays 44 Border Dr	Wakefield	RI	02879	401-789-7477	782-1652

— Events —

	Phone
Ben & Jerry's Newport Folk Festival (early August)	401-847-3700
Black Ships Festival (mid-July)	401-846-2720
Bowen's Wharf Waterfront Seafood Festival (mid-October)	401-849-2243
Christmas in Newport (December)	401-849-6454
Christmas Tree Lighting (early December)	401-849-2243
Classic Yacht Regatta (early September)	401-847-1018
Craft Fair (late November)	401-847-3213
Fiesta Italiana (early October)	401-849-8048
Great Chowder Cook-off (early-mid-June)	401-846-1600
Harvest Fair (early October)	401-846-2577
Home for the Holidays Craft & Gift Expo (mid-October)	401-846-1600
July 3rd Clambake (July 3)	401-847-1441

Newport — Events (Cont'd)

	Phone
Newport Flower Show (mid-July)	401-847-1000
Newport International Boat Show (mid-September)	401-846-1115
Newport International Polo Series (early June-mid-September)	401-847-7090
Newport Irish Heritage Month (March)	401-845-9123
Newport Jazz Festival (early August)	401-847-3700
Newport Music Festival (early July)	401-846-1133
Newport Winter Festival (mid-late February)	401-847-7666
Octoberfest (early October)	401-846-1600
Secret Garden Tour (mid-June)	401-847-0514
Small Boat Regatta (mid-July)	401-847-1018
Taste of Newport (mid-November)	401-849-2300
Taste of Rhode Island (late September)	401-846-1600
Victorian Christmas Feast (mid-December)	401-846-3772
We Rose for Rose Regatta (mid-September)	401-847-4242

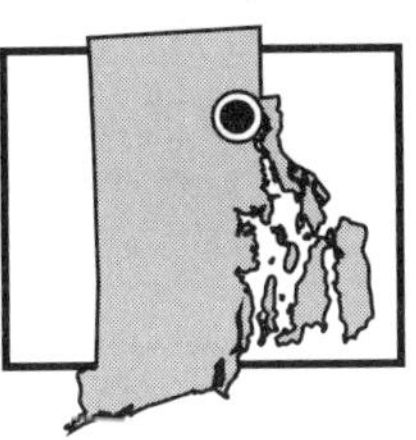

Providence

Rhode Island's capital was founded by Roger Williams in 1635 as a haven for religious dissenters and free thinkers. Today, several attractions in Providence are situated along the Roger Williams Heritage Trail, including Colonial homes along Benefit Street (also called the "Mile of History'), prestigious Brown University, Rhode Island School of Design Museum of Art, the State Capitol (an important architectural landmark), and Roger Williams Park, which has its own planetarium, zoo, and natural history museum. Visitors can also enjoy outdoor concerts at the Park's Benedict Temple to Music. Shopping along the Trail is available at The Arcade, the country's oldest indoor shopping center.

Population	150,890	**Longitude**	71-41-33 W
Area (Land)	18.5 sq mi	**County**	Providence
Area (Water)	2.1 sq mi	**Time Zone**	EST
Elevation	24 ft	**Area Code/s**	401
Latitude	41-82-39 N		

— Average Temperatures and Precipitation —

TEMPERATURES

	Jan	Feb	Mar	Apr	May	Jun	Jul	Aug	Sep	Oct	Nov	Dec
High	37	38	46	57	67	77	82	81	74	64	53	41
Low	19	21	29	38	47	57	63	62	54	43	35	24

PRECIPITATION

	Jan	Feb	Mar	Apr	May	Jun	Jul	Aug	Sep	Oct	Nov	Dec
Inches	3.9	3.6	4.1	4.1	3.8	3.3	3.2	3.6	3.5	3.7	4.4	4.4

— Important Phone Numbers —

	Phone		Phone
AAA	401-272-7100	**Poison Control Center**	401-444-5727
American Express Travel	401-274-2900	**Travelers Aid of Rhode Island**	401-521-2255
Emergency	911	**Weather**	401-277-7777
Medical Referral	401-456-4636		

— Information Sources —

				Phone	Fax
Better Business Bureau Serving Rhode Island 120 Lavan St *Web:* www.rhodeisland.bbb.org	Warwick	RI	02888	401-785-1212	785-3061
Greater Providence Chamber of Commerce 30 Exchange Terr *Web:* www.provchamber.com	Providence	RI	02903	401-521-5000	751-2434
Providence City Hall 25 Dorrance St. *Web:* www.providenceri.com	Providence	RI	02903	401-421-7740	
Providence Civic Center 1 LaSalle Sq *Web:* www.provcc.com	Providence	RI	02903	401-331-0700	751-6792
Providence County 1 Dorrance Plaza	Providence	RI	02903	401-458-5200	222-3462
Providence Mayor 25 Dorrance St *Web:* www.providenceri.com/home.html	Providence	RI	02903	401-421-7740	274-8240
Providence Planning & Development Dept 400 Westminster St. *Web:* www.providenceri.com/planning/index.html ■ *E-mail:* planning@ids.net	Providence	RI	02903	401-351-4300	351-9533
Providence Public Library 225 Washington St	Providence	RI	02903	401-455-8000	455-8080
Providence Warwick Convention & Visitors Bureau 1 W Exchange St. *TF:* 800-233-1636 ■ *Web:* www.providencecvb.com/ ■ *E-mail:* provcvb1@wsii.com	Providence	RI	02903	401-274-1636	351-2090
Rhode Island Convention Center 1 Sabin St *Web:* www.guidetori.com	Providence	RI	02903	401-458-6000	458-6500
Rhode Island Economic Development Corp 1 W Exchange St *Web:* www.riedc.com ■ *E-mail:* riedc@riedc.com	Providence	RI	02903	401-222-2601	222-2102
Rhode Island Tourism Div 1 West Exchange St *TF:* 800-556-2484 ■ *Web:* visitrhodeisland.com	Providence	RI	02903	401-222-2601	222-2102

On-Line Resources

4Providence.com	www.4providence.com
Area Guide Providence	providence.areaguides.net
City Knowledge Providence	www.cityknowledge.com/ri_providence.htm
DigitalCity Providence	home.digitalcity.com/providence
Excite.com Providence City Guide	www.excite.com/travel/countries/united_states/rhode_island/providence
Federal Hill Gazette	www.fedhillgazette.com/
I-95 Exit Information Guide Providence	www.usastar.com/i95/cityguide/providence.htm
Providence CityLink	usacitylink.com/providen/
Rough Guide Travel Providence	travel.roughguides.com/content/391/

— Transportation Services —

AIRPORTS

■ **Theodore Francis Green State Airport (PVD)**

	Phone
7 miles S of downtown Providence (approx 15 minutes)	401-737-4000

Airport Transportation

	Phone
Airport Taxi $21 fare to downtown Providence	401-737-2868
Airport Van Shuttle $9 fare to downtown Providence	401-736-1900

Commercial Airlines

	Phone		Phone
AirTran	800-247-8726	**MetroJet**	888-638-7653
American	800-433-7300	**Northwest**	800-225-2525
Continental	800-525-0280	**Southwest**	800-435-9792
Continental Express	800-525-0280	**United**	800-241-6522
Delta	800-221-1212	**US Airways**	800-428-4322

Charter Airlines

	Phone		Phone
Corporate Air Charter	401-732-0782	**Jet America Corp**	401-737-3674
Executive Airlines	631-537-1010	**Richmor Aviation Inc**	800-359-2299

Providence (Cont'd)

CAR RENTALS

	Phone		Phone
Avis	401-736-7500	**Enterprise-Providence**	401-438-8550
Avis-Providence	401-521-7900	**Hertz**	401-738-7500
Budget	401-739-8900	**National**	401-737-4800
CarTemps USA	401-738-5910	**Thrifty**	401-732-2000

LIMO/TAXI

	Phone		Phone
Best Taxi	401-781-0706	**Prestige Limousine**	401-732-8600

MASS TRANSIT

	Phone
Rhode Island Public Transit $1.25 Base fare	401-781-9400

RAIL/BUS

				Phone
Amtrak Station 100 Gaspee St *TF:* 800-872-7245	Providence	RI	02903	401-727-7388
Bonanza Bus Station 1 Bonanza Way	Providence	RI	02904	401-751-8800

— Accommodations —

HOTELS, MOTELS, RESORTS

				Phone	Fax
Comfort Inn 2 George St *TF:* 800-221-2222	Pawtucket	RI	02860	401-723-6700	726-6380
Comfort Inn Airport 1940 Post Rd. *TF:* 800-228-5150	Warwick	RI	02886	401-732-0470	732-4247
Days Hotel on the Harbor 220 India St *TF:* 800-329-7466	Providence	RI	02903	401-272-5577	272-5577
Days Inn 101 New London Ave. *TF:* 800-329-7466	Cranston	RI	02920	401-942-4200	943-8807
Holiday Inn Downtown 21 Atwells Ave. *TF:* 800-465-4329	Providence	RI	02903	401-831-3900	751-0007
Marriott Hotel 1 Orms St. *TF:* 800-228-9290 ■ *Web:* marriotthotels.com/PVDRI	Providence	RI	02904	401-272-2400	273-2686
Motel 6 20 Jefferson Blvd *TF:* 800-466-8356	Warwick	RI	02888	401-467-9800	467-6780
Providence Biltmore Hotel Kennedy Plaza *TF:* 800-294-7709 ■ *Web:* www.grandheritage.com/Hotels/Namerican/Provbilt/provbiltindex.html	Providence	RI	02903	401-421-0700	455-3050
Radisson Airport Hotel 2081 Post Rd *TF:* 800-333-3333	Warwick	RI	02886	401-739-3000	732-9309
Residence Inn by Marriott 500 Kilvert St. *TF:* 800-331-3131 ■ *Web:* www.residenceinn.com/PVDPR	Warwick	RI	02886	401-737-7100	739-2909
Sheraton Providence Airport Hotel 1850 Post Rd. *TF:* 800-325-3535	Warwick	RI	02886	401-738-4000	738-8206
State House Inn 43 Jewett St.	Providence	RI	02908	401-785-1235	351-4261
Susse Chalet 36 Jefferson Blvd *TF:* 800-258-1980 ■ *Web:* www.sussechalet.com/warwick.html	Warwick	RI	02888	401-941-6600	785-1260
Westin Hotel 1 W Exchange St. *TF:* 800-228-3000	Providence	RI	02903	401-598-8000	598-8200

— Restaurants —

				Phone
3 Steeple Street (New American) 125 Canal St.	Providence	RI	02903	401-272-3620
Adesso (California) 161 Cushing St	Providence	RI	02906	401-521-0770
Al Forno (Italian) 577 S Main St	Providence	RI	02903	401-273-9760
AS220 Cafe (American) 115 Empire St.	Providence	RI	02903	401-861-9190
Atomic Grill (New American) 99 Chestnut St.	Providence	RI	02903	401-621-8888
Barnsider's Mile & Quarter (Steak/Seafood) 375 S Main St	Providence	RI	02903	401-351-7300
Blake's Tavern (American) 122 Washington St	Providence	RI	02903	401-274-1230
Blue Grotto (Italian) 210 Atwells Ave	Providence	RI	02903	401-272-9030
Cactus Bar & Grille (Southwest) 370 Richmond St	Providence	RI	02903	401-421-3300
Cafe Nuovo (New American) 1 Citizens Plaza	Providence	RI	02903	401-421-2525
Camille's (Italian) 71 Bradford St	Providence	RI	02903	401-751-4812
Capital Grille (American) 1 Cookson Pl	Providence	RI	02903	401-521-5600
Capriccio (Italian) 2 Pine St	Providence	RI	02903	401-421-1320
Cassarino's Restaurant (Italian) 177 Atwells Ave.	Providence	RI	02903	401-751-3333
CAV (Mediterranean) 14 Imperial Pl.	Providence	RI	02903	401-751-9164
Davio's at the Biltmore (Italian) Kennedy Plaza.	Providence	RI	02903	401-421-0700
Federal Reserve (American) Westminster & Dorrance Sts	Providence	RI	02903	401-621-5700
Finnegan's Wake (Irish) 395-397 Westminster Pl	Providence	RI	02903	401-751-0290
Gatehouse The (New American) 4 Richmond Sq	Providence	RI	02906	401-521-9229
Grappa (Mediterranean) 525 S Water St.	Providence	RI	02903	401-454-1611
Hemenway's Seafood Grille (Seafood) S Main St Providence Washington Plaza	Providence	RI	02903	401-351-8570
India (Indian) 123 Dorrance St.	Providence	RI	02903	401-278-2000
Intermezzo (Italian) 220 Weybosset St	Providence	RI	02903	401-331-5100
L'Epicureo Ristorante (Italian) 238 Atwells Ave	Providence	RI	02903	401-454-8431
Leon's on the West Side (California) 166 Broadway	Providence	RI	02903	401-273-1055
Montana (Tex Mex) 272 Thayer St	Providence	RI	02906	401-273-7427
New Japan Restaurant (Japanese) 145 Washington St.	Providence	RI	02903	401-351-0300
New Rivers Restaurant (New American) 7 Steeple St	Providence	RI	02903	401-751-0350
O'Cha Cafe (Thai) 221 Wickenden St	Providence	RI	02903	401-421-4699
Ocean Express (Seafood) 800 Allens Ave	Providence	RI	02905	401-461-3434
Pakarang (Thai) 303 S Main St	Providence	RI	02903	401-453-3660
Parkside Rotisserie & Bar (Mediterranean) 76 S Main St.	Providence	RI	02903	401-331-0003
Pizzico (Italian) 762 Hope St.	Providence	RI	02906	401-421-4114
Pot Au Feu (French) 44 Custom House St.	Providence	RI	02905	401-273-8953
Raphael Bar-Ristro (Italian) 1 Cookson Pl	Providence	RI	02909	401-421-4646
Rue De L'Espoir (Continental) 99 Hope St	Providence	RI	02906	401-751-8890
Siam Square (Thai) 1050 Willett Ave	Riverside	RI	02915	401-433-0123
Tokyo Restaurant (Japanese) 388 Wickenden St	Providence	RI	02903	401-331-5330
Trinity Brewhouse (American) 186 Fountain St	Providence	RI	02903	401-453-2337
Union Station Brewery (Continental) 36 Exchange Terr	Providence	RI	02903	401-274-2739
Walter's La Locanda del Cocchio (Italian) 265 Atwells Ave	Providence	RI	02903	401-273-2652
Yun Nan (Chinese) 316 Smith St.	Providence	RI	02908	401-351-9311
Z Bar & Grill (American) 244 Wickenden St	Providence	RI	02910	401-831-1566

— Goods and Services —

SHOPPING

				Phone	Fax
Ann & Hope Inc 1 Ann & Hope Way	Cumberland	RI	02864	401-722-1000	725-7190
Arcade The 65 Weybosset St	Providence	RI	02903	401-598-1199	
Catalog Fashion Outlet 1689 Post Rd	Warwick	RI	02888	401-738-5145	
Garden City Center 100 Midway Rd	Providence	RI	02920	401-942-2800	
Providence Place Mall 1 Providence Pl. *Web:* www.oso.com/partners/ppm	Providence	RI	02903	401-270-1000	270-1001
Rhode Island Mall 191 Rhode Island Mall	Warwick	RI	02886	401-828-7651	
Warwick Mall 400 Baldhill Rd	Warwick	RI	02886	401-739-7500	732-6052
Wayland Square Medway & Waterman St	Providence	RI	02903	401-751-1177	

BANKS

				Phone	Fax
Bank of Rhode Island 870 Westminster St. *TF Cust Svc:* 800-922-9999*	Providence	RI	02903	401-456-7000	456-7278
Bank Rhode Island 195 Taunton Ave.	East Providence	RI	02914	401-435-8700	435-8710
Citizens Bank of Rhode Island 1 Citizens Plaza. *TF Cust Svc:* 800-922-9999*	Providence	RI	02903	401-456-7000	455-5715
First Bank & Trust Co 180 Washington St **Fax:* Cust Svc	Providence	RI	02903	401-421-3600	861-6221*
Fleet National Bank 111 Westminster St. **Fax:* Cust Svc ■ *TF:* 800-445-4542 ■ *Web:* www.fleet.com	Providence	RI	02903	401-278-6000	278-6523*
Union Bank 1565 Mineral Spring Ave	North Providence	RI	02904	401-353-8910	353-8938

BUSINESS SERVICES

	Phone		Phone
AAA Courier & Messenger Service	401-751-2500	**Interim Personnel Services**	401-431-5600
Airborne Express	800-247-2676	**Kinko's**	401-273-2830
Arrow Messenger	401-831-5252	**Mail Boxes Etc**	800-789-4623
BAX Global	800-225-5229	**Mr Messenger**	401-461-2240
DHL Worldwide Express	800-225-5345	**Post Office**	401-276-6800
Eastway Delivery Service	401-463-3200	**Secretarial Concepts**	401-245-3535
Federal Express	800-238-5355	**Todays Temporary**	401-823-7100
Initial Staffing Services	401-421-0488	**UPS**	800-742-5877

— Media —

PUBLICATIONS

				Phone	Fax
Providence Business News 300 Richmond St Suite 202 *Web:* www.pbn.com ■ *E-mail:* editor@pbn.com	Providence	RI	02903	401-273-2201	274-0270

Providence — Publications (Cont'd)

	City	State	Zip	Phone	Fax
Providence Journal-Bulletin‡ 75 Fountain St *Web:* www.projo.com	Providence	RI	02902	401-277-7000	277-7346
Rhode Island Monthly 280 Kinsley Ave *Web:* www.rimonthly.com/	Providence	RI	02903	401-421-2552	831-5624

‡Daily newspapers

TELEVISION

	City	State	Zip	Phone	Fax
WJAR-TV Ch 10 (NBC) 23 Kenney Dr *Web:* www.nbc10wjar.com ■ *E-mail:* mail.box10@nbc.com	Cranston	RI	02920	401-455-9100	455-9140
WLNE-TV Ch 6 (ABC) 10 Orms St *Web:* www.abc6.com	Providence	RI	02904	401-453-8000	453-8092
WLWC-TV Ch 28 (WB) 10 Dorrance St Suite 805	Providence	RI	02903	401-351-8828	351-0222
WNAC-TV Ch 64 (Fox) 25 Catamore Blvd *Web:* www.fox64.com ■ *E-mail:* fox64@fox64.com	East Providence	RI	02914	401-438-7200	431-1012
WPRI-TV Ch 12 (CBS) 25 Catamore Blvd *Web:* www.wpri.com ■ *E-mail:* wpri@wpri.com	East Providence	RI	02914	401-438-7200	431-1012
WPXQ-TV Ch 69 (PAX) 1 Richmond Sq *Web:* www.pax.net/WPXQ	Providence	RI	02906	401-453-6969	453-6901
WSBE-TV Ch 36 (PBS) 50 Park Ln *Web:* www.wsbe.org	Providence	RI	02907	401-222-3636	222-3407

RADIO

	City	State	Zip	Phone	Fax
WAKX-FM 102.7 MHz (CHR) 1110 Central Ave	Pawtucket	RI	02861	401-723-1063	725-8609
WALE-AM 990 kHz (N/T) 1185 N Main St	Providence	RI	02904	401-521-0990	521-5077
WBRU-FM 95.5 MHz (Alt) 88 Benevolent St *Web:* www.wbru.com	Providence	RI	02906	401-272-9550	272-9278
WBSM-AM 1420 kHz (N/T) 22 Sconticut Neck Rd	Fairhaven	MA	02719	508-993-1767	999-1420
WDOM-FM 91.3 MHz (Urban) Providence College River Ave	Providence	RI	02918	401-865-2460	
WFHN-FM 107.1 MHz (CHR) 22 Sconticut Neck Rd	Fairhaven	MA	02719	508-993-1767	999-1420
WHJJ-AM 920 kHz (N/T) 115 Eastern Ave	East Providence	RI	02915	401-438-6110	438-3520
WHJY-FM 94.1 MHz (Rock) 115 Eastern Ave *Web:* www.whjy.com	East Providence	RI	02915	401-438-6110	438-3520
WHKK-FM 100.3 MHz (CR) 1502 Wampanoag Trail **Fax Area Code:* 317 ■ *E-mail:* bgwotb1003@aol.com	East Providence	RI	02915	401-433-4200	433-1183*
WLKW-AM 550 kHz (Nost) 1110 Central Ave	Pawtucket	RI	02861	401-723-1063	725-8609
WPRO-AM 630 kHz (N/T) 1502 Wampanoag Trail	East Providence	RI	02915	401-433-4200	433-5967
WPRO-FM 92.3 MHz (CHR) 1502 Wampanoag Trail	East Providence	RI	02915	401-433-4200	433-5967
WSNE-FM 93.3 MHz (AC) 100 Boyd Ave *Web:* www.wsne.com/	East Providence	RI	02914	401-438-9300	434-4243
WWBB-FM 101.5 MHz (Oldies) 75 Oxford St 3rd Fl *Web:* www.b101.com ■ *E-mail:* oldiesb101@aol.com	Providence	RI	02905	401-781-9979	781-9329
WWKX-FM 106.3 MHz (CHR) 1110 Central Ave	Pawtucket	RI	02861	401-723-1063	725-8609
WWLI-FM 105.1 MHz (AC) 1502 Wampanoag Trail *Web:* www.lite105.com	East Providence	RI	02915	401-433-4200	433-1183
WWRX-FM 103.7 MHz (CR) 75 Oxford St *Web:* www.wrx.com	Providence	RI	02905	401-781-9979	781-9329
WXEX-FM 99.7 MHz (Alt) 1502 Wampanoag Trail *E-mail:* lzevon@amaltd.com	East Providence	RI	02915	401-433-4200	433-1183

— Colleges/Universities —

	City	State	Zip	Phone	Fax
Brown University *Web:* www.brown.edu ■ *E-mail:* Admission_Undergraduate@Brown.Edu	Providence	RI	02912	401-863-1000	863-9300
Bryant College 1150 Douglas Pike *TF Admissions:* 800-622-7001 ■ *Web:* www.bryant.edu ■ *E-mail:* postmaster@research1.bryant.edu	Smithfield	RI	02917	401-232-6000	232-6741
Community College of Rhode Island Flanagan Campus 1762 Louisquissett Pike *Web:* www.ccri.cc.ri.us	Lincoln	RI	02865	401-333-7000	333-7111
Community College of Rhode Island Knight Campus 400 East Ave	Warwick	RI	02886	401-825-1000	825-2394
Johnson & Wales University 8 Abbott Park Pl *TF:* 800-342-5598 ■ *Web:* www.jwu.edu	Providence	RI	02903	401-598-1000	598-2948
New England Institute of Technology 2500 Post Rd *TF:* 800-736-7744 ■ *Web:* www.neit.edu	Warwick	RI	02886	401-467-7744	738-5122
Providence College River Ave **Fax:* Admissions ■ *TF:* 800-721-6444 ■ *Web:* www.providence.edu	Providence	RI	02918	401-865-1000	865-2826*
Rhode Island College 600 Mt Pleasant Ave *Web:* www.ric.edu ■ *E-mail:* admissions@grog.ric.edu	Providence	RI	02908	401-456-8000	456-8817
Rhode Island School of Design 2 College St *Web:* www.risd.edu ■ *E-mail:* admissions@risd.edu	Providence	RI	02903	401-454-6100	454-6309
Roger Williams University 1 Old Ferry Rd *Web:* www.rwu.edu	Bristol	RI	02809	401-253-1040	254-3557

— Hospitals —

	City	State	Zip	Phone	Fax
Emma Pendleton Bradley Hospital 1011 Veterans Memorial Pkwy	East Providence	RI	02915	401-432-1000	432-1500
Memorial Hospital of Rhode Island 111 Brewster St	Pawtucket	RI	02860	401-729-2000	722-0198
Miriam Hospital 164 Summit Ave **Fax:* Admitting ■ *Web:* www.lifespan.org/about/miriam	Providence	RI	02906	401-793-2500	331-6496*
Rhode Island Hospital 593 Eddy St **Fax:* Admitting ■ *Web:* www.lifespan.org/about/ri	Providence	RI	02903	401-444-4000	444-5139*
Roger Williams Medical Center 825 Chalkstone Ave *Web:* www.rwmc.com ■ *E-mail:* rwmc@aol.com	Providence	RI	02908	401-456-2000	456-2282
Saint Joseph Health Services of Rhode Island 200 High Service Ave *Web:* www.saintjosephri.com	North Providence	RI	02904	401-456-3000	456-3652
Veterans Affairs Medical Center 830 Chalkstone Ave	Providence	RI	02908	401-457-3042	457-3370

— Attractions —

	City	State	Zip	Phone	Fax
Aldrich House-Museum of Rhode Island History 110 Benevolent St	Providence	RI	02906	401-331-8575	351-0127
Arcade The 65 Weybosset St	Providence	RI	02903	401-598-1199	
AS220 Center for Arts 115 Empire St *Web:* www.as220.org	Providence	RI	02903	401-831-9327	454-7445
Banner Trail Trolley Tour 10 Nate Whipple Hwy	Cumberland	RI	02864	401-658-3400	
Bayard Ewing Building 231 S Main St	Providence	RI	02903	401-454-6280	454-6299
Bell David Winton Gallery 64 College St	Providence	RI	02912	401-863-2932	863-9323
Brown AnnMary Memorial 21 Brown St	Providence	RI	02912	401-863-1994	
Brown John House 52 Power St	Providence	RI	02906	401-331-8575	751-2307
Cathedral of Saint John 271 N Main St	Providence	RI	02903	401-331-4622	831-8425
Cathedral of Saints Peter & Paul 30 Fenner St Cathedral Sq	Providence	RI	02903	401-331-2434	331-2435
Culinary Archives & Museum at Johnson & Wales University 315 Harborside Blvd	Providence	RI	02905	401-598-2805	598-2807
Festival Ballet 5 Hennessey Ave	North Providence	RI	02911	401-353-1129	353-8853
First Baptist Church in America 75 N Main St	Providence	RI	02903	401-454-3418	421-4095
Governor Henry Lippitt House Museum 199 Hope St	Providence	RI	02906	401-453-0688	453-8221
Governor Stephen Hopkins House 15 Hopkins St	Providence	RI	02903	401-421-0694	
Groundwerx Dance Theater 95 Empire St *Web:* www.as220.org/groundwerx ■ *E-mail:* groundwerx@as220.org	Providence	RI	02903	401-454-4564	454-4564
Haffenreffer Museum of Anthropology 300 Tower St *Web:* www.brown.edu/Facilities/Haffenreffer	Bristol	RI	02809	401-253-8388	253-1198
Hay John Library 20 Prospect St Brown University	Providence	RI	02912	401-863-2146	
La Gondola River Tours 1 Citizens Plaza	Providence	RI	02903	401-421-8877	
Nature's Best Dairy 2032 Plainfield Pike	Cranston	RI	02921	401-946-1122	946-9960

Providence — Attractions (Cont'd)

				Phone	Fax
Old State House 150 Benefit St	Providence	RI	02903	401-222-2678	
Pendleton House 224 Benefit St	Providence	RI	02903	401-454-6500	454-6556
Perishable Theatre 95 Empire St *Web:* www.as220.org/perishable/	Providence	RI	02903	401-331-2695	331-7811
Providence Athenaeum 251 Benefit St. *Web:* www.providenceathenaeum.org/	Providence	RI	02903	401-421-6970	421-2860
Providence Children's Museum 100 South St *Web:* www.childrenmuseum.org ■ *E-mail:* provcm@childrenmuseum.org	Providence	RI	02903	401-273-5437	273-1004
Providence Jewelry Museum 1 Spectacle St	Providence	RI	02910	401-781-3100	
Providence Performing Arts Center 220 Weybosset St. *Web:* www.ppacri.org/	Providence	RI	02903	401-421-2787	421-5767
Providence Preservation Society 21 Meeting St Shakespeare's Head	Providence	RI	02903	401-831-7440	831-8583
Rhode Island Black Heritage Society 202 Washington St.	Providence	RI	02903	401-751-3490	751-0040
Rhode Island Historical Society 110 Benevolent St. *Web:* www.rihs.org/	Providence	RI	02906	401-331-8575	751-7930
Rhode Island Philharmonic Orchestra 222 Richmond St Suite 112 *Web:* www.ri-philharmonic.org	Providence	RI	02903	401-831-3123	831-4577
Rhode Island School of Design Museum of Art 224 Benefit St.	Providence	RI	02903	401-454-6501	454-6556
Rhode Island School of Design Woods-Gerry Gallery 62 Prospect St	Providence	RI	02903	401-454-6141	454-6608
Rhode Island State Archives 337 Westminster St.	Providence	RI	02903	401-222-2353	222-3199
Rhode Island State Capitol 82 Smith St *Web:* www.state.ri.us ■ *E-mail:* comments@sec.state.ri.us	Providence	RI	02903	401-222-2357	222-1356
Roger Williams National Memorial 282 N Main St *Web:* www.nps.gov/rowi/	Providence	RI	02903	401-521-7266	521-7239
Roger Williams Park Museum of Natural History Roger Williams Pk *Web:* www.osfn.org/museum	Providence	RI	02905	401-785-9450	461-5146
Roger Williams Park Zoo 1000 Elmwood Ave *Web:* users.ids.net/~rwpz/	Providence	RI	02905	401-785-3510	941-3988
Sandra Feinstein-Gamm Theatre 31 Elbow St *Web:* www.sfgt.org	Providence	RI	02903	401-831-2919	
Sloop Providence War Ship India Point Pk	Providence	RI	02903	401-274-7447	
Trinity Repertory Co 201 Washington St *Web:* www.trinityrep.com/	Providence	RI	02903	401-351-4242	
Warwick Museum 3259 Post Rd.	Warwick	RI	02886	401-737-0010	
Waterplace Park American Express Way & Memorial Blvd	Providence	RI	02903	401-274-1636	
Wayland Square Medway & Waterman St	Providence	RI	02903	401-751-1177	

SPORTS TEAMS & FACILITIES

				Phone	Fax
Pawtucket Red Sox (baseball) 1 Columbus Ave McCoy Stadium *Web:* www.pawsox.com ■ *E-mail:* pawsox@worldnet.att.net	Pawtucket	RI	02860	401-724-7300	724-2140
Providence Bruins (hockey) 1 LaSalle Sq Providence Civic Ctr *Web:* www.canoe.ca/AHLProvidence/	Providence	RI	02903	401-273-5000	273-5004
Rhode Island Stingrays (soccer) 201 Mercer St Pierce Memorial Stadium *Web:* www.stingraysoccer.com ■ *E-mail:* info@stingraysoccer.com	East Providence	RI	02914	401-351-8455	351-4818

— Events —

	Phone
Festival of Historic Houses (mid-June)	401-831-7440
First Night Providence (December 31)	401-521-1166
Gaspee Days Arts & Crafts Festival (late May)	401-461-9068
Heritage Day Festival (mid-September)	401-222-2669
Holiday Tours in Historic Providence (mid-December)	401-831-8587
Latin Christmas Carol Celebration (early December)	401-863-2123
Providence Auto Show (mid-January)	401-274-1636
Providence Boat Show (late January)	401-458-6000
Providence Walking Tours (early July-late September)	401-831-7440
Providence Waterfront Festival (mid-September)	401-785-9450
Rhode Island Spring Flower & Garden Show (mid-February)	401-458-6000
Water Fire Providence (mid-May-late December)	401-331-3624

South Carolina

Population (1999): 3,885,736 **Area (sq mi): 32,008**

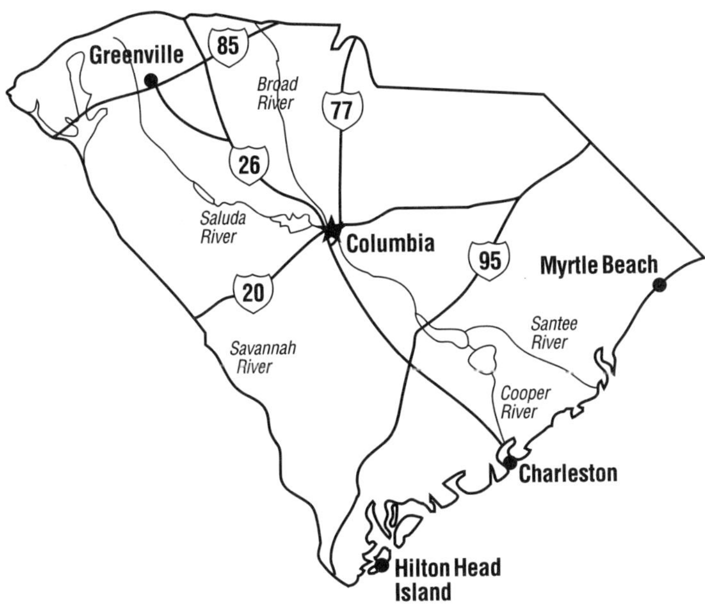

— State Information Sources —

				Phone	Fax
South Carolina Chamber of Commerce 1201 Main St AT & T Bldg Suite 1810 ..... *Web:* www.sccc.org	Columbia	SC	29201	803-799-4601	779-6043
South Carolina Commerce Dept PO Box 927 ... *Web:* www.state.sc.us/commerce/ ■ *E-mail:* msligh@commerce.state.sc.us	Columbia	SC	29202	803-737-0400	737-0418
South Carolina Parks Recreation & Tourism Dept 1205 Pendleton St Suite 110 .... *Web:* www.travelsc.com/thingstodo/stateparks/home.html	Columbia	SC	29201	803-734-0122	734-1019
South Carolina State Government Information .... *Web:* www.state.sc.us/ ■ *E-mail:* smccand@oir.state.sc.us				803-734-1000	
South Carolina State Library PO Box 11469 ... *Web:* www.state.sc.us/scsl	Columbia	SC	29211	803-734-8666	734-8676
South Carolina Tourism Div 1205 Pendleton St .... *TF:* 800-346-3634 ■ *Web:* www.travelsc.com	Columbia	SC	29201	803-734-0122	734-0133

ON-LINE RESOURCES

Carolina USA .... www.carolinausa.com/carolina/caroscfr.htm
Go Carolinas .... www.gocarolinas.com
Kiawah Island .... www.kiawahisland.com/home.html
Rough Guide Travel South Carolina travel.roughguides.com/content/695/index.htm
South Carolina Cities .... dir.yahoo.com/Regional/U_S__States/South_Carolina/Cities
South Carolina Counties & Regions .... dir.yahoo.com/Regional/U_S__States/South_Carolina/Counties_and_Regions
South Carolina Directory .... www.scad.com
South Carolina Information Highway .... www.sciway.net
South Carolina Scenario .... scenariousa.dstylus.com/sc/indexf.htm
South Carolina Travel & Tourism Guide .... www.travel-library.com/north_america/usa/south_carolina/index.html
Travel South Carolina .... www.travelsc.com
Travel South Carolina .... www.travelsc.com
Travel.org-South Carolina .... travel.org/s-carol.html
Yahoo! Get Local South Carolina .... dir.yahoo.com/Regional/U_S__States/South_Carolina

— Cities Profiled —

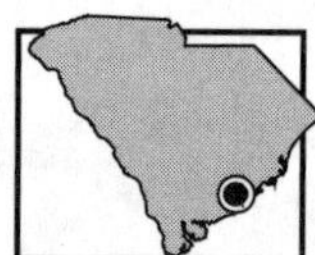

Charleston

The historic area in Charleston features house museums and buildings where people actually live and work, as well as a wide range of other museums and historical churches. Among these is The Charleston Museum, which is America's oldest. The historic area also includes the Market area and Waterfront Park, with a view of Charleston Harbor. Water tours of the harbor include stops at Fort Sumter, where the Civil War began, and the U.S. Naval Base. Popular resorts in the Charleston area include Kiawah Island, noted for its award-winning golf courses, and Isle of Palms.

Population 87,044
Area (Land) . . . . . 43.2 sq mi
Area (Water) . . . . . 8.4 sq mi
Elevation . . . . . 118 ft
Latitude . . . . . 32-77-85 N
Longitude . . . . . 79-93-55 W
County . . . . . Charleston
Time Zone . . . . . EST
Area Code/s 843

— Average Temperatures and Precipitation —

TEMPERATURES

	Jan	Feb	Mar	Apr	May	Jun	Jul	Aug	Sep	Oct	Nov	Dec
High	58	61	67	76	83	88	90	89	85	77	70	62
Low	38	40	48	54	63	69	73	72	68	56	47	41

PRECIPITATION

	Jan	Feb	Mar	Apr	May	Jun	Jul	Aug	Sep	Oct	Nov	Dec
Inches	3.5	3.3	4.3	2.7	4.0	6.4	6.8	7.2	4.7	2.9	2.5	3.2

— Important Phone Numbers —

	Phone
AAA	843-766-2394
Dental Referral	800-327-2598
Emergency	911
HotelDocs	800-468-3537
Medical Referral	843-577-3613
Poison Control Center	803-777-1117
Time	843-572-8463
Weather	843-744-3207

— Information Sources —

				Phone	*Fax*
Better Business Bureau Serving Central South Carolina & the Charleston Area PO Box 8326 *Web:* www.columbia.bbb.org	Columbia	SC	29202	803-254-2525	779-3117
Charleston Area Convention & Visitors Bureau PO Box 975 *TF:* 800-868-8118 ■ *Web:* www.charlestoncvb.com ■ *E-mail:* mail@charlestoncvb.com	Charleston	SC	29402	843-853-8000	853-0444
Charleston City Hall 80 Broad St *Web:* www.charleston.net/charlestoncity	Charleston	SC	29401	843-577-6970	720-3959
Charleston County 2 Courthouse Sq *Web:* www.charlestoncounty.org ■ *E-mail:* publicinfo@charlestoncounty.org	Charleston	SC	29401	843-723-6772	724-0654
Charleston County Library System 68 Calhoun St *Web:* www.ccpl.org	Charleston	SC	29403	843-805-6801	727-6752
Charleston Mayor 80 Broad St	Charleston	SC	29401	843-577-6970	720-3827
Charleston Metro Chamber of Commerce 81 Mary St. *Web:* chamber.charleston.net ■ *E-mail:* chambercomm@charleston.net	Charleston	SC	29402	843-577-2510	723-4853
Charleston Planning & Urban Development Dept 75 Calhoun St. *Web:* www.charleston.net/charlestoncity/planning.html ■ *E-mail:* chasplanning@charleston.net	Charleston	SC	29401	843-724-3765	724-3772

On-Line Resources

4Charleston.com www.4charleston.com
About.com Guide to Charleston . . . . . charleston.about.com
Area Guide Charleston . . . . . charlestonsc.areaguides.net
Best Read Guide Charleston . . . . . bestreadguide.com/charleston/
Charleston City Net . . . . . www.excite.com/travel/countries/united_states/south_carolina/charleston
Charleston Connections . . . . . www.aesir.com/Charleston
Charleston Internet Directory . . . . . www.cityofcharleston.com
Charleston Navi-Gator . . . . . www.navi-gator.com/charleston
Charleston Net . . . . . www.charleston.net
Charleston Online . . . . . www.charleston-online.com
Charleston Traveler Online . . . . . www.charlestontraveler.com
Charleston's Finest . . . . . www.charlestonsfinest.com
City Knowledge Charleston . . . . . www.cityknowledge.com/sc_charleston.htm
CityTravelers.com Guide to Charleston . . . . . www.citytravelers.com/charleston.htm
Essential Guide to Charleston . . . . . www.ego.net/us/sc/chs/
InCharleston.com . . . . . www.incharleston.com/
Insiders' Guide to Charleston . . . . . www.insiders.com/charleston-sc/index.htm
Insiders' Guide to Charleston . . . . . www.insiders.com/charleston-sc/
NITC Travelbase City Guide Charleston . . . . . www.travelbase.com/auto/guides/charleston-area-sc.html
Open World City Guides Charleston . . . . . www.worldexecutive.com/cityguides/charleston/
Streets of Charleston . . . . . www.streetsofcharleston.com
Surf & Sun Beach Vacation Guide to Charleston . . . . . www.surf-sun.com/sc-charleston-main.htm
Tour Charleston . . . . . tourcharleston.com/

— Transportation Services —

AIRPORTS

	Phone
■ **Charleston International Airport (CHS)**	
13 miles NW of downtown (approx 20 minutes) Web: www.callsouthcarolina.com/aeronautics/chs.htm	843-767-1100

Airport Transportation

	Phone
Airport Limousine $18 fare to downtown	800-750-1311
Yellow Cab $20 fare to downtown	843-577-6565

Commercial Airlines

	Phone
Continental	800-525-0280
Continental Express	800-525-0280
Delta	800-221-1212
United	800-241-6522
United Express	800-241-6522
US Airways	800-428-4322
US Airways Express	800-428-4322

CAR RENTALS

	Phone
Alamo	843-767-4417
Avis	843-767-7030
Budget	843-760-9025
Enterprise	843-556-7889
Hertz	843-767-4554
Thrifty	843-552-7531
U-Save Auto	843-767-9822

LIMO/TAXI

	Phone
Airport Limousine	800-750-1311
Checker Taxi	843-747-9200
Express Cab Co.	843-577-8816
Jennings Limo	843-853-9726
Lowcountry Limousine Service	843-760-6060
Metro Limo Taxi	843-729-2231
Safety Cab Co.	843-722-4066
Williams Taxi	843-744-2294
Yellow Cab	843-577-6565

MASS TRANSIT

	Phone
Downtown Area Shuttle $.75 Base fare	843-724-7420
SCE&G City Bus $.75 Base fare	843-747-0922

RAIL/BUS

				Phone
Amtrak Station 4565 Gaynor Ave *TF:* 800-872-7245	Charleston	SC	29405	843-744-8264

Charleston (Cont'd)

— Accommodations —

HOTEL RESERVATION SERVICES

Phone *Fax*

Historic Charleston Bed & Breakfast Reservations Service 800-743-3583 722-9589*
Fax Area Code: 843 ■ *TF:* 800-743-3583
■ *Web:* www.charleston.net/com/bed&breakfast

HOTELS, MOTELS, RESORTS

Phone *Fax*

1837 Bed & Breakfast 126 Wentworth St . . . . Charleston SC 29401 843-723-7166
Anchorage Inn 26 Vendue Range . . . . Charleston SC 29401 843-723-8300 723-9543
TF: 800-421-2952
Ansonborough Inn 21 Hasell St. . . . . Charleston SC 29401 843-723-1655 577-6888
TF: 800-522-2073
Best Western Inn 1540 Savannah Hwy . . . . . . Charleston SC 29407 843-571-6100 766-6261
TF: 800-528-1234
Best Western Northwoods
7401 Northwoods Blvd . . . . Charleston SC 29406 843-572-2200 863-8316
TF: 800-528-1234
Charleston Place 130 Market St . . . . Charleston SC 29401 843-722-4900 722-0728
TF: 800-611-5545 ■ *Web:* www.charleston-place.com
Comfort Inn 144 Bee St . . . . Charleston SC 29401 843-577-2224 577-9001
TF: 800-228-5150
Comfort Inn Airport 5055 N Arco Ln . . . .North Charleston SC 29418 843-554-6485 566-9466
TF: 800-228-5150
Courtyard by Marriott 35 Lockwood Dr . . . . . . Charleston SC 29401 843-722-7229 722-2880
TF: 800-321-2211 ■ *Web:* courtyard.com/CHSCY
Days Inn 261 Johnnie Dodds Blvd. . . . . . .Mount Pleasant SC 29464 843-881-1800 881-3769
TF: 800-329-7466
Days Inn Airport 2998 W Montague Ave . . . . . Charleston SC 29418 843-747-4101 566 0378
TF: 800-329-7466
Days Inn Historic District 155 Meeting St . . . . Charleston SC 29401 843-722-8411 723-5361
TF: 800-329-7466
Doubletree Hotel 181 Church St. . . . . Charleston SC 29401 843-577-2644 577-2697
TF: 800-222-8733
Elliott House Inn 78 Queen St . . . . Charleston SC 29401 843-723-1855 722-1567
TF: 800-729-1855
Embassy Suites 337 Meeting St . . . . Charleston SC 29403 843-723-6900 723-6938
TF: 800-362-2779
Fairfield Inn 7415 Northside Dr . . . . Charleston SC 29420 843-572-6677 764-3790
TF: 800-228-2800 ■ *Web:* fairfieldinn.com/CHSFI
Francis Marion Hotel 387 King St. . . . . Charleston SC 29403 843-722-0600 723-4633
TF: 800-433-3733
Hampton Inn 11 Ashley Pointe Dr. . . . . Charleston SC 29407 843-556-5200 571-5499
TF: 800-426-7866
Hampton Inn Airport 4701 Saul White Blvd . . . Charleston SC 29418 843-554-7154 566-9299
TF: 800-426-7866
Hampton Inn Historic District
345 Meeting St. . . . . Charleston SC 29403 843-723-4000 722-3725
TF: 800-426-7866
Hilton Hotel Charleston
4770 Goer Dr. . . . . .North Charleston SC 29406 843-747-1900 744-2530
TF: 800-445-8667 ■ *Web:* www.hilton.com/hotels/CHSCHHF
Holiday Inn Airport 6099 Fain St. . . . . . .North Charleston SC 29406 843-744-1621 744-0942
TF: 800-465-4329
Holiday Inn Riverview 301 Savannah Hwy. . . . Charleston SC 29407 843-556-7100 556-6176
TF: 800-465-4329
Howard Johnson 250 Spring St . . . . Charleston SC 29403 843-722-4000 723-2573
TF: 800-446-4656
Howard Johnson Inn 3640 Dorchester Rd . . . . Charleston SC 29405 843-554-4140 554-4148
TF: 800-446-4656
Indigo Inn 1 Maiden Ln . . . . Charleston SC 29401 843-577-5900 577-0378
TF: 800-845-7639 ■ *Web:* www.aesir.com/indigoinn
■ *E-mail:* IndigoInn@aesir.com
John Rutledge House Inn 116 Broad St. . . . . . Charleston SC 29401 843-723-7999 720-2615
TF: 800-476-9741
■ *Web:* www.aesir.com/CharmingInns/JohnRutledge.html
Kiawah Island Resort
12 Kiawah Beach Dr . . . . .Kiawah Island SC 29455 843-768-2121 768-9339
TF: 800-654-2924
Kings Courtyard Inn 198 King St. . . . . Charleston SC 29401 843-723-7000 720-2608
TF: 800-845-6119 ■ *Web:* www.charminginns.com
Knights Inn 2355 Aviation Ave . . . . Charleston SC 29406 843-744-4900 745-0668
TF: 800-843-5644
La Quinta 2499 La Quinta Ln . . . . Charleston SC 29420 843-797-8181 569-1608
TF: 800-531-5900
Meeting Street Inn 173 Meeting St. . . . . Charleston SC 29401 843-723-1882 577-0851
TF: 800-842-8022
Mills House Hotel 115 Meeting St . . . . Charleston SC 29401 843-577-2400 722-0623
TF: 800-874-9600

Phone *Fax*

Motel 6 2058 Savannah Hwy . . . . Charleston SC 29407 843-556-5144 556-2241
TF: 800-466-8356
Planters Inn 112 N Market St. . . . . Charleston SC 29401 843-722-2345 577-2125
TF: 800-845-7082 ■ *Web:* www.plantersinn.com
Quality Suites 5225 N Arco Ln. . . . . Charleston SC 29418 843-747-7300 747-6324
TF: 800-228-5151
Radisson Inn Airport 5991 Rivers Ave. . . . . . . Charleston SC 29406 843-744-2501
TF: 800-333-3333
Ramada Inn Coliseum
2934 W Montague Ave . . . . .North Charleston SC 29418 843-744-8281 744-6230
TF: 800-272-6232
Residence Inn by Marriott
7645 Northwoods Blvd . . . . .North Charleston SC 29406 843-572-5757 797-8529
TF: 800-331-3131 ■ *Web:* www.residenceinn.com/CHSNW
Royal Inn 3668 Dorchester Rd . . . . Charleston SC 29405 843-747-0961 747-3230
Sheraton Charleston Hotel
170 Lockwood Dr . . . . Charleston SC 29403 843-723-3000 720-0844
TF: 800-325-3535
Siesta Motor Lodge 4044 Rivers Ave . . . . Charleston SC 29405 843-747-3659
Stayover Lodge 2070 McMillan Ave . . . .North Charleston SC 29405 843-554-1600 529-1208
StudioPLUS 7641 Northwoods Blvd. . . . . Charleston SC 29406 843-553-0036 824-9092
TF: 800-646-8000
Super 8 Motel 4620 Dorchester Rd. . . . . Charleston SC 29405 843-747-7500 745-9594
TF: 800-800-8000
Town & Country Inn 2008 Savannah Hwy . . . . Charleston SC 29407 843-571-1000 766-9444
TF: 800-334-6660
Wild Dunes Resort 5757 Palm Blvd . . . . . . Isle of Palms SC 29451 843-886-6000 886-2916
TF: 800-845-8880 ■ *Web:* www.wilddunes.com
■ *E-mail:* reservations@wilddunes.com

— Restaurants —

Phone

82 Queen (Steak/Seafood) 82 Queen St . . . . Charleston SC 29401 843-723-7591
Anson's (Seafood) 12 Anson St . . . . Charleston SC 29401 843-577-0551
AW Shuck's (Seafood) 70 State St. . . . . Charleston SC 29401 843-723-1151
Web: www.charleston.net/com/awshucks/
Barbadoes Room The (Continental) 115 Meeting St. . . . . . Charleston SC 29401 843-577-2400
TF: 800-874-9600
Bessinger's Barbecue (Barbecue) 1602 Savannah Hwy . . . Charleston SC 29407 843-556-1354
Bocci's (Italian) 158 Church St . . . . Charleston SC 29401 843-720-2121
Web: www.charleston.net/com/boccis/
Carolina's (International) 10 Exchange St. . . . . Charleston SC 29401 843-724-3800
Celia's Porta Via (Italian) 49 Archdale St . . . . Charleston SC 29401 843-722-9003
Web: www2.discovernet.com/rest/celias/
■ *E-mail:* celia@discovernet.com
Charleston Crab House (Seafood) 145 Wappoo Creek Dr . . Charleston SC 29412 843-795-1963
Charleston Grill (Continental) 224 King St . . . . Charleston SC 29401 843-577-4522
Elliott's on the Square (American) 387 King St. . . . . Charleston SC 29403 843-724-8888
Emperors Garden (Chinese) 874 Orleans Rd . . . . Charleston SC 29407 843-556-7212
Fulton Five (Italian) 5 Fulton St. Charleston SC 29401 843-853-5555
Garibaldi (Italian) 49 S Market St . . . . Charleston SC 29401 843-723-7153
Web: www.cityofcharleston.com/garibaldi.htm
Gaulart & Maliclet (French) 98 Broad St . . . . Charleston SC 29401 843-577-9797
Horse & Cart Cafe (American) 347 King St. . . . . Charleston SC 29401 843-722-0797
Hyman's (Seafood) 215 Meeting St . . . . Charleston SC 29401 843-723-6000
Web: www.scad.com/hymans/
Library at Vendue (Continental) 23 Vendue Range. . . . . . . Charleston SC 29401 843-723-0485
Louis's Restaurant & Bar (Southern)
200 Meeting St Suite 8 . . . . Charleston SC 29401 843-853-2550
Magnolias (Southern) 185 E Bay St . . . . Charleston SC 29401 843-577-7771
McCrady's (Continental) 2 Unity Alley. . . . . Charleston SC 29401 843-577-0025
New Great Wall (Chinese) 34 George St. . . . . Charleston SC 29401 843-722-8834
Noisy Oyster (Seafood) 7571 Rivers Ave. . . . . .North Charleston SC 29406 843-824-1000
Peninsula Grill (Continental)
112 N Market St Planters Inn Historic Hotel . . . . Charleston SC 29401 843-723-0700
Poogan's Porch (Seafood) 72 Queen St . . . . Charleston SC 29401 843-577-2337
Saracen Restaurant (Continental) 141 E Bay St. . . . . Charleston SC 29401 843-723-6242
Sermet's (Mediterranean) 276 King St. . . . . Charleston SC 29401 843-853-7775
Slightly North of Broad (Continental) 192 E Bay St . . . . . . Charleston SC 29401 843-723-3424
Sonoma Cafe & Winebar (California) 304 King St. . . . . . . Charleston SC 29401 843-853-3222
Southend Brewery Smokehouse (Continental)
161 E Bay St . . . . Charleston SC 29401 843-722-0722
Tokyo Japanese Steak House (Japanese)
6185 Rivers Ave. . . . . .North Charleston SC 29406 843-572-1518
Zebo Restaurant & Brewery (American) 275 King St . . . . . Charleston SC 29401 843-577-7600

— Goods and Services —

SHOPPING

Phone *Fax*

Citadel Mall 2070 Sam Rittenberg Blvd . . . . . . Charleston SC 29407 843-766-8511
Northwoods Mall
2150 Northwoods Blvd . . . . .North Charleston SC 29406 843-797-3060 797-8363

Charleston — Shopping (Cont'd)

	City	State	ZIP	Phone
Shops at Charleston Place 130 Market St Charleston Place Hotel	Charleston	SC	29401	843-722-4900

BANKS

	City	State	ZIP	Phone	Fax
Anchor Bank 276 E Bay St	Charleston	SC	29401	843-577-4600	723-7296
Bank of South Carolina 256 Meeting St.	Charleston	SC	29402	843-724-1500	723-1473
First Citizens Bank & Trust 182 Meeting St.	Charleston	SC	29401	843-577-4560	722-5823
NationsBank 200 Meeting St *TF:* 800-333-6262	Charleston	SC	29401	843-723-6819	723-6850

BUSINESS SERVICES

	Phone		Phone
AccuStaff Inc.	843-745-9324	**Kinko's**	843-723-5130
Adecco Employment Personnel Services	843-571-3113	**Mail Boxes Etc**	843-763-6894
Airborne Express	800-247-2676	**Manpower Temporary Services**	843-554-0285
BAX Global	800-225-5229	**Post Office**	843-760-5421
DHL Worldwide Express	800-225-5345	**Sullivan's Staffing**	843-744-0404
Federal Express	800-238-5355	**UPS**	800-742-5877

— Media —

PUBLICATIONS

	City	State	ZIP	Phone	Fax
Post & Courier‡ 134 Columbus St *Web:* www.charleston.net ■ *E-mail:* seima@postandcourier.com	Charleston	SC	29403	843-577-7111	937-5579

‡Daily newspapers

TELEVISION

	City	State	ZIP	Phone	Fax
WCBD-TV Ch 2 (NBC) 210 W Coleman Blvd.	Mount Pleasant	SC	29464	843-884-2222	881-3410
WCIV-TV Ch 4 (ABC) PO Box 22165 **Fax:* News Rm ■ *Web:* www.wciv.com ■ *E-mail:* newsroom@wciv.com	Charleston	SC	29413	843-881-4444	849-2519*
WCSC-TV Ch 5 (CBS) 2126 Charlie Hull Blvd. *Web:* www.wcsc5.com	Charleston	SC	29414	843-577-6397	402-5744
WITV-TV Ch 7 (PBS) PO Box 11000	Columbia	SC	29201	803-737-3200	737-3476
WTAT-TV Ch 24 (Fox) 4301 Arco Ln.	Charleston	SC	29418	843-744-2424	554-9649

RADIO

	City	State	ZIP	Phone	Fax
WAVF-FM 96.1 MHz (Rock) 1964 Ashley River Rd *Web:* www.96wave.net ■ *E-mail:* comments@96wave.net	Charleston	SC	29407	843-852-9003	852-9041
WMGL-FM 101.7 MHz (Urban) 2045 Spaulding Dr *Web:* www.charlestonradio.com/magic	Charleston	SC	29418	843-308-9300	308-9590
WPAL-FM 100.9 mHz (Urban) 1717 Wappoo Rd	Charleston	SC	29407	843-763-6330	769-4857
WQSC-AM 1340 kHz (Sports) 4995 LaCross Rd Suite 2200	North Charleston	SC	29418	843-566-0074	566-0806
WSSX-FM 95.1 MHz (AC) 1 Orange Grove Rd.	Charleston	SC	29407	843-556-5660	763-0304
WSUY-FM 96.9 MHz (NAC) 1 Orange Grove Rd.	Charleston	SC	29407	843-556-5660	763-0304
WTMA-AM 1250 kHz (N/T) 1 Orange Grove Rd.	Charleston	SC	29407	843-556-5660	763-0304
WYBB-FM 98.1 MHz (CR) 59 Windermere Blvd *Web:* www.98rock.net ■ *E-mail:* 98rock@awod.com	Charleston	SC	29407	843-769-4799	769-4797

— Colleges/Universities —

	City	State	ZIP	Phone	Fax
Charleston Southern University PO Box 118087 *TF:* 800-947-7474 ■ *Web:* www.csuniv.edu	Charleston	SC	29423	843-863-7000	863-8074
Citadel The 171 Moultrie Ave *Web:* www.citadel.edu	Charleston	SC	29409	843-953-5000	953-7036
College of Charleston 66 George St *Web:* www.cofc.edu ■ *E-mail:* admissions@cofc.edu	Charleston	SC	29424	843-953-5507	953-6322
Medical University of South Carolina 171 Ashley Ave. *Web:* www.musc.edu	Charleston	SC	29425	843-792-2300	792-0392
Nielsen Electronics Institute 1275 Barracks Rd *TF:* 800-821-9430 ■ *E-mail:* nielei@aol.com	North Charleston	SC	29405	843-747-7080	308-2403
Trident Technical College PO Box 118067 *Web:* www.trident.tec.sc.us	Charleston	SC	29423	843-574-6111	574-6483

— Hospitals —

	City	State	ZIP	Phone	Fax
Bon Secours Saint Francis Xavier Hospital 2095 Henry Tecklenburg Dr	Charleston	SC	29414	843-402-1000	402-1808
Charleston Memorial Hospital 326 Calhoun St.	Charleston	SC	29401	843-577-0600	953-8728
Charleston Naval Hospital 3600 Rivers Ave	North Charleston	SC	29405	843-743-7000	743-7256
Columbia Summerville Medical Center 295 Midland Pkwy	Summerville	SC	29485	843-875-3993	832-5104
Columbia Trident Regional Medical Center 9330 Medical Plaza Dr.	Charleston	SC	29406	843-797-7000	797-4086
East Cooper Regional Medical Center 1200 Johnnie Dodds Blvd *Web:* www.tenethealth.com/EastCooper	Mount Pleasant	SC	29464	843-881-0100	881-4396
Johnson Ralph H Veterans Affairs Medical Center 109 Bee St *TF:* 888-878-6884	Charleston	SC	29401	843-577-5011	853-9167
Medical University of South Carolina 171 Ashley Ave. *Web:* www.musc.edu	Charleston	SC	29425	843-792-2300	792-0392
MUSC Medical Center of Medical University of South Carolina 171 Ashley Ave	Charleston	SC	29425	843-792-2300	792-6682
Roper Hospital 316 Calhoun St **Fax:* Admitting	Charleston	SC	29401	843-724-2000	724-2360*
Roper Hospital North 2750 Speissegger Dr.	North Charleston	SC	29405	843-744-2110	745-1797

— Attractions —

	City	State	ZIP	Phone	Fax
Aiken-Rhett House 48 Elizabeth St	Charleston	SC	29423	843-723-1159	
Audubon Swamp Garden 3550 Ashley River Rd Magnolia Plantation & Gardens.	Charleston	SC	29414	843-571-1266	571-5346
Avery Research Center for African-American History & Culture 125 Bull St *Web:* www.coax.net/people/lwf/avery.htm ■ *E-mail:* netmgr@coax.net	Charleston	SC	29424	843-953-7609	953-7607
Best Friend Museum 31 Ann St	Charleston	SC	29403	843-973-7269	720-3999
Boone Hall Plantation 1235 Longpoint Rd.	Charleston	SC	29464	843-884-4371	881-3642
Calhoun Mansion 16 Meeting St.	Charleston	SC	29401	843-722-8205	
Cape Romain National Wildlife Refuge 5801 Hwy 17 N *Web:* southeast.fws.gov/wildlife/nwrcrm.html	Awendaw	SC	29429	843-928-3264	928-3803
Charles Pinckney National Historic Site 1254 Long Point Rd *Web:* www.nps.gov/chpi/	Mount Pleasant	SC	29464	843-881-5516	881-7070
Charles Towne Landing 1500 Old Towne Rd	Charleston	SC	29407	843-852-4200	852-4205
Charleston Ballet Theatre 477 King St *Web:* www.charlestonballet.com ■ *E-mail:* tdominey@charlestonballet.com	Charleston	SC	29403	843-723-7334	723-9099
Charleston Museum 360 Meeting St *Web:* www.charlestonmuseum.com	Charleston	SC	29403	843-722-2996	722-1784
Charleston Stage Co 133 Church St Suite 7.	Charleston	SC	29401	843-577-5967	577-5422
Charleston Symphony Orchestra 14 George St *Web:* www.charlestonsymphony.com ■ *E-mail:* info@charlestonsymphony.com	Charleston	SC	29401	843-723-7528	722-3463
Charleston Visitor Center 375 Meeting St	Charleston	SC	29402	843-853-8000	
Circular Congregation Church 150 Meeting St.	Charleston	SC	29401	843-577-6400	
Citadel Museum & Archives 171 Moultrie St The Citadel	Charleston	SC	29409	843-953-6846	953-5190
City Marina 17 Lockwood Blvd.	Charleston	SC	29401	843-723-5098	853-1840

Charleston — Attractions (Cont'd)

	City	State	ZIP	Phone	Fax
College of Charleston Saint Philip & George Sts	Charleston	SC	29401	843-953-5507	
Confederate Museum 34 Pitt St	Charleston	SC	29401	843-723-1541	
Congregation Beth Elohim 90 Hasell St	Charleston	SC	29401	843-723-1090	723-0537
Cypress Gardens 3030 Cypress Gardens Rd	Moncks Corner	SC	29461	843-553-0515	569-0644
Dock Street Theatre 135 Church St	Charleston	SC	29401	843-965-4032	720-3967
Drayton Hall 3380 Ashley River Rd	Charleston	SC	29414	843-766-0188	766-0878
Web: www.draytonhall.org					
Edmondston-Alston House 21 E Battery	Charleston	SC	29401	843-722-7171	
Emanuel African Methodist Episcopal Church 110 Calhoun St	Charleston	SC	29401	843-722-2561	
First Baptist Church 48 Meeting St	Charleston	SC	29401	843-722-3896	720-2175
First (Scots) Presbyterian Church 53 Meeting St	Charleston	SC	29401	843-722-8882	722-8538
Footlight Players 20 Queen St	Charleston	SC	29401	843-722-7521	
Fort Sumter National Monument 1214 Middle St	Sullivans Island	SC	29482	843-883-3123	883-3910
Web: www.nps.gov/fosu/					
French Protestant (Huguenot) Church 136 Church St	Charleston	SC	29401	843-722-4385	
Gibbes Museum of Art 135 Meeting St	Charleston	SC	29401	843-722-2706	720-1682
Web: www.gibbes.com					
Hall Gallery at City Hall 80 Broad St	Charleston	SC	29402	843-724-3799	
Heyward-Washington House 87 Church St	Charleston	SC	29401	843-722-0354	
Karpeles Manuscript Library Museum 68 Spring St	Charleston	SC	29403	843-853-4651	853-4651
Web: www.rain.org/~karpeles/chr.html					
Magnolia Plantation & Gardens 3550 Ashley River Rd	Charleston	SC	29414	843-571-1266	571-5346
TF: 800-367-3517 ■ *Web:* www.magnoliaplantation.net ■ *E-mail:* magnolia@internetx.net					
Middleton Place 4300 Ashley River Rd	Charleston	SC	29414	843-556-6020	766-4460
Web: www2.middletonplace.org					
Museum on the Common 217 Lucas St	Mount Pleasant	SC	29464	843-849-9000	
Nathaniel Russell House 51 Meeting St	Charleston	SC	29401	843-724-8481	
Old Bethel Methodist Church 222 Calhoun St	Charleston	SC	29401	843-722-3470	
Old Exchange & Provost Dungeon 122 E Bay St	Charleston	SC	29401	843-727-2165	727-2163
Web: www.ccpl.org/ccl/exchange.html					
Old Powder Magazine 79 Cumberland St	Charleston	SC	29401	843-805-6730	
Palmetto Islands County Park 444 Needlerush Pkwy	Mount Pleasant	SC	29464	843-884-0832	884-0254
Patriots Point Naval & Maritime Museum Charleston Harbor	Mount Pleasant	SC	29464	843-884-2727	881-4232
TF: 800-248-3508 ■ *Web:* www.state.sc.us/patpt/					
Postal Museum Meeting & Broad Sts	Charleston	SC	29401	843-853-8000	
Rainbow Row 99-101 E Bay St	Charleston	SC	29401		
Saint Andrews Parish Church 2604 Ashley River Rd	Charleston	SC	29401	843-766-1541	
Saint John's Lutheran Church Clifford & Archdale Sts	Charleston	SC	29401	843-723-2426	577-2543
Saint Mary's Roman Catholic Church 89 Hasell St	Charleston	SC	29401	843-722-7696	577-5036
Saint Michael's Episcopal Church Meeting & Broad Sts	Charleston	SC	29401	843-723-0603	724-7578
Shem Creek Maritime Museum 510 Mill St	Mount Pleasant	SC	29464	843-849-9000	884-5020
South Carolina Aquarium 57 Hasell St	Charleston	SC	29401	843-720-1990	720-3861
Web: www.scaquarium.org ■ *E-mail:* seaquarium@awod.com					
Washington Square Meeting & Broad Sts	Charleston	SC	29401	843-853-8000	
White Point Gardens 2 Murray Blvd	Charleston	SC	29401	843-724-7321	

SPORTS TEAMS & FACILITIES

	City	State	ZIP	Phone	Fax
Charleston Battery (soccer) 2000 Daniel Island Rd Blackbaud Stadium	Daniel Island	SC	29492	843-740-7787	740-5415
Web: www.charlestonbattery.com					
Charleston Riverdogs (baseball) 360 Fishburne St	Charleston	SC	29403	843-577-3647	723-2641
Web: www.awod.com/riverdogs ■ *E-mail:* dogrus@riverdogs.com					
North Charleston Coliseum & Convention Center 5001 Coliseum Dr	North Charleston	SC	29418	843-529-5050	529-5010
South Carolina Stingrays (hockey) 3107 Firestone Rd	North Charleston	SC	29418	843-744-2248	744-2898
Web: www.stingrayshockey.com					

— Events —

	Phone
Battle of Secessionville (early November)	843-795-3049
Big Kahuna Tournament (September)	843-588-3474
Blues Festival (early-mid February)	843-762-9125
Carolina Day (late June)	843-883-3123
Charleston Antiques Show (mid-June)	843-849-1949
Charleston Cup (early November)	843-766-6208
Charleston Garden Festival (early October)	843-722-7526
Charleston Maritime Harborfest (mid-April)	843-577-8878
Christmas in Charleston (December)	843-853-8000
Fall Candlelight Tours of Homes & Gardens (late September-early October)	843-722-4630
Festival of Houses & Gardens (March-April)	843-723-1623
Festival on the Fourth (July 4)	843-556-5660
Flowertown Festival (late March)	843-871-9622
Folly River Float Frenzy & Fish Fry (mid-August)	843-588-6663
Holiday Festival of Lights (mid-November-early January)	843-853-8000
Low Country Cajun Festival (early-mid-April)	843-762-2172
Low Country Oyster Festival (mid-January)	843-577-4030
LowCountry Blues Bash (early-mid-February)	800-868-8118
Moja Arts Festival (late September-early October)	843-724-7305
Plantation Christmas at Middleton Place (December)	843-556-6020
Plantation Days (November)	843-556-6020
Scottish Games & Highland Gathering (September)	843-884-4371
Southeastern Wildlife Exposition (February)	800-221-5273
Spoleto Festival USA (late May-early June)	843-722-2764
Summer Classic Horse Show (July)	843-768-2500
Taste of Charleston (October)	843-577-4030
This Magic Moment (late June)	843-853-8000
Visitor Value Days (late November-February)	800-868-8118
World Grits Festival (mid-April)	843-563-2150

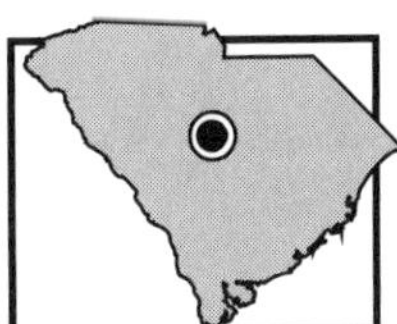

Columbia

The capital of the state and home of the University of South Carolina, Columbia has one of the top zoological parks in the U.S., Riverbanks Zoo, with more than 2,000 animals. Lake Murray is a popular outdoor recreation area for residents and visitors alike, with more than 540 miles of shoreline. Among the many antebellum historic homes and churches in Columbia is the First Baptist Church where the first secession convention opened in 1860. The State Capitol Building was still under construction when the city was burned by Union soldiers during the Civil War, and bronze stars have been placed on the building to indicate the marks left by General Sherman's cannons. Another historic site in Columbia is the cottage built by Cecilia Mann, a black slave who bought her freedom and walked to Columbia. Not far from the city is Fort Jackson (named for Andrew Jackson), the U.S. Army's largest initial entry training center.

Population	112,773	**Longitude**	81-03-53 W
Area (Land)	117.1 sq mi	**County**	Richland
Area (Water)	1.9 sq mi	**Time Zone**	EST
Elevation	213 ft	**Area Code/s**	803
Latitude	33-99-89 N		

— Average Temperatures and Precipitation —

TEMPERATURES

	Jan	Feb	Mar	Apr	May	Jun	Jul	Aug	Sep	Oct	Nov	Dec
High	55	59	68	77	84	89	92	90	85	76	68	59
Low	22	34	42	49	58	66	70	69	69	50	42	35

PRECIPITATION

	Jan	Feb	Mar	Apr	May	Jun	Jul	Aug	Sep	Oct	Nov	Dec
Inches	4.4	4.1	4.8	3.3	3.7	4.8	5.5	6.1	3.7	3.0	2.9	3.6

Columbia (Cont'd)

— Important Phone Numbers —

	Phone		Phone
AAA	803-798-9205	**Poison Control Center**	803-777-1117
Emergency	911	**Time/Temp**	803-714-9900
HotelDocs	800-468-3537	**Travelers Aid Society**	803-343-7071
Medical Referral	803-765-1498	**Weather**	803-822-8135

— Information Sources —

	City	State	Zip	Phone	Fax
Better Business Bureau Serving Central South Carolina & the Charleston Area PO Box 8326 *Web:* www.columbia.bbb.org	Columbia	SC	29202	803-254-2525	779-3117
Columbia City Hall PO Box 147 *Web:* www.columbiasc.net/city/city1aa.htm	Columbia	SC	29217	803-733-8200	343-8719
Columbia Community Development Dept 1225 Laurel St	Columbia	SC	29217	803-733-8315	988-8014
Columbia Mayor PO Box 147 *Web:* www.columbiasc.net/city/city1ab.htm	Columbia	SC	29217	803-733-8221	733-8633
Columbia Metropolitan Convention & Visitors Bureau PO Box 15 *TF:* 800-264-4884 ■ *Web:* www.columbiasc.net ■ *E-mail:* visit@columbiasc.net	Columbia	SC	29202	803-254-0479	799-6529
Greater Columbia Chamber of Commerce PO Box 1360 *Web:* www.gcbn.com	Columbia	SC	29202	803-733-1110	733-1149
Richland County PO Box 192 *Web:* www.richlanddata.com	Columbia	SC	29202	803-748-4600	748-4644
Richland County Public Library 1431 Assembly St. *Web:* www.richland.lib.sc.us	Columbia	SC	29201	803-799-9084	929-3438

On-Line Resources

About.com Guide to Columbia	columbiasc.about.com
Anthill City Guide Columbia	www.anthill.com/city.asp?city=columbia
Area Guide Columbia	columbiasc.areaguides.net
City Knowledge Columbia	www.cityknowledge.com/sc_columbia.htm
CityTravelers.com Guide to Columbia	www.citytravelers.com/columbia.htm
Columbia A to Z	www.columbiasouthcarolina.com/
Columbia Directory	www.scad.com/columbia/
Columbia Free Times	www.free-times.com/
Columbia Home Page	www.columbiasc.net/
Columbia Mapped Out	www.gamecock.sc.edu/mapped_out/colamap.html
Columbia Metropolitan Magazine	www.columbiametro.com/
Excite.com Columbia City Guide	www.excite.com/travel/countries/united_states/south_carolina/columbia
Five Points Online	www.scfivepoints.com

— Transportation Services —

AIRPORTS

■ **Columbia Metropolitan Airport (CAE)**

	Phone
7 miles SW of downtown (approx 20 minutes) Web: www.ricommunity.com/ri/Columbia_airport.asp	803-822-5010

Airport Transportation

	Phone
AAA Airport Shuttle $15 fare to downtown	803-796-3626
AAA Taxi $12-14 fare to downtown	803-791-7282

Commercial Airlines

	Phone		Phone
American	800-433-7300	**United**	800-241-6522
American Eagle	800-433-7300	**United Express**	800-241-6522
Comair	800-354-9822	**US Airways**	800-428-4322
Delta	800-221-1212		

Charter Airlines

	Phone		Phone
Bank Air	803-822-8832	**Midlands Aviation**	803-771-7915
Eagle Aviation	803-822-5555		

CAR RENTALS

	Phone		Phone
Alamo	800-445-5664	**Enterprise**	803-750-9764
Avis	803-822-5100	**Hertz**	803-822-8341
Budget	803-822-8346		

LIMO/TAXI

	Phone		Phone
AAA Taxi	803-791-7282	**Dream Ride Limousine**	803-786-9904
Affordable Limo	803-771-8062	**Fantasy Limousine**	803-796-0820
Ard's Lexington Cab	803-791-5767	**Gamecock Cab**	803-796-7700
Blue Ribbon Cab	803-754-8163	**McDaniel Cab**	803-730-3546
Checker-Yellow Cab	803-799-3311	**Royal Limousine**	803-790-5466
Columbia Limousine	803-699-1015	**Shuttleways of Columbia**	803-783-0265
Courtesy Limousine	803-749-4377		

MASS TRANSIT

	Phone
SCE & G City Bus $.75 Base fare	803-748-3019

RAIL/BUS

	City	State	Zip	Phone
Amtrak Station 850 Pulaski St *TF:* 800-872-7245	Columbia	SC	29201	800-252-8246
Greyhound Bus Station 2015 Gervais St *TF:* 800-231-2222	Columbia	SC	29204	803-256-6465

— Accommodations —

HOTELS, MOTELS, RESORTS

	City	State	Zip	Phone	Fax
Adam's Mark Hotel 1200 Hampton St *TF:* 800-444-2326 ■ *Web:* www.adamsmark.com/columba.htm	Columbia	SC	29201	803-771-7000	254-8307
AmeriSuites 7525 Two Notch Rd *TF:* 800-833-1516	Columbia	SC	29223	803-736-6666	788-6011
Baymont Inns & Suites 1538 Horseshoe Dr *TF:* 800-301-0200	Columbia	SC	29223	803-736-6400	788-7875
Best Inn Conference Center I-20 & Broad River Rd. *TF:* 800-237-8466	Columbia	SC	29210	803-772-0270	798-0467
Best Western Riverside Inn 111 Knox Abbott Dr *TF:* 800-528-1234	Cayce	SC	29033	803-939-4688	926-5547
Clarion Town House 1615 Gervais St *TF:* 800-277-8711	Columbia	SC	29201	803-771-8711	252-9347
Claussen's Inn 2003 Green St *TF:* 800-622-3382	Columbia	SC	29205	803-765-0440	799-7924
Comfort Inn Rt 7700 Two Notch Rd *TF:* 800-228-5150	Columbia	SC	29223	803-788-5544	788-5544
Comfort Inn Airport 110 Branch Rd. *TF:* 800-228-5150	West Columbia	SC	29169	803-796-0044	796-0044
Comfort Inn Capital City 2025 Main St *TF:* 800-228-5150	Columbia	SC	29201	803-252-6321	254-9941
Courtyard by Marriott 347 Zimalcrest Dr *TF:* 800-321-2211 ■ *Web:* courtyard.com/CAENW	Columbia	SC	29210	803-731-2300	772-6965
Days Inn Columbia 133 Plumbers Rd *TF:* 800-325-2525	Columbia	SC	29203	803-754-4408	786-2821
Days Inn Northeast 7128 Parklane Rd. *TF:* 800-329-7466	Columbia	SC	29223	803-736-0000	736-9328
Days Inn Southeast 7300 Garners Ferry Rd *TF:* 800-329-7466	Columbia	SC	29209	803-783-5500	776-1391
Econo Lodge 494 Piney Grove Rd. *TF:* 800-553-2666	Columbia	SC	29210	803-731-4060	798-6612
Embassy Suites Hotel 200 Stoneridge Dr. *TF:* 800-362-2779	Columbia	SC	29210	803-252-8700	256-8749
Executive Inn 1107 Harbor Dr	West Columbia	SC	29169	803-796-4934	796-4934
Extended StayAmerica 5430 Forest Dr *TF:* 800-398-7829	Columbia	SC	29206	803-782-2025	782-1449
Extended StayAmerica 450 Gracern Rd *TF:* 800-398-7829	Columbia	SC	29210	803-251-7878	252-7596
Fairfield Inn by Marriott 8104 Two Notch Rd *TF:* 800-228-2800 ■ *Web:* fairfieldinn.com/CAEFI	Columbia	SC	29223	803-736-0822	699-6058
Fairground Plaza Hotel 621 S Assembly St *TF:* 800-220-2752	Columbia	SC	29201	803-252-2000	779-0026

Columbia — Hotels, Motels, Resorts (Cont'd)

	City	State	ZIP	Phone	Fax
Governors House Hotel 1301 Main St *TF:* 800-800-0835	Columbia	SC	29201	803-779-7790	779-7856
Hampton Inn Southeast 7333 Garners Ferry Rd *TF:* 800-426-7866	Columbia	SC	29209	803-783-5410	783-8102
HoJo Inn 200 Zimalcrest Dr *TF:* 800-446-4656	Columbia	SC	29210	803-772-7200	772-6484
Holiday Inn Camden PO Box 96 *TF:* 800-465-4329	Lugoff	SC	29078	803-438-9441	438-5784
Holiday Inn Coliseum 630 Assembly St *TF:* 800-465-4329	Columbia	SC	29201	803-799-7800	252-5909
Holiday Inn Columbia Airport 500 Chris Dr *TF:* 800-465-4329	West Columbia	SC	29169	803-794-9440	794-9449
Holiday Inn Express 7251 Garners Ferry Rd *TF:* 800-465-4329	Columbia	SC	29209	803-695-1111	695-0008
Holiday Inn Northeast 7510 Two Notch Rd *TF:* 800-465-4329	Columbia	SC	29223	803-736-3000	736-6399
Knights Inn Airport 1987 Airport Blvd *TF:* 800-843-5644	Cayce	SC	29033	803-794-0222	794-7798
La Quinta 1335 Garner Ln *TF:* 800-531-5900	Columbia	SC	29210	803-798-9590	731-5574
Masters Economy Inn 613 Knox Abbott Dr *TF:* 800-633-3434	Cayce	SC	29033	803-796-4300	796-2743
Ramada Hotel 8105 Two Notch Rd *TF:* 800-272-6232	Columbia	SC	29223	803-736-5600	736-1241
Red Roof Inn 10 Berryhill Rd *TF:* 800-843-7663	Columbia	SC	29210	803-798-9220	798-9065
Royal Inn 1323 Garner Ln	Columbia	SC	29210	803-750-5060	750-5060
Sheraton Hotel & Conference Center 2100 Bush River Rd *TF:* 800-325-3535 ■ *Web:* www.columbiasouthcarolina.com/sheraton/	Columbia	SC	29210	803-731-0300	731-2839
StudioPLUS 180 Stoneridge Dr *TF:* 800-646-8000	Columbia	SC	29210	803-771-0303	212-1652
Super 8 Motel 2516 Augusta Hwy *TF:* 800-800-8000	West Columbia	SC	29169	803-796-4833	796-4833
Travelodge 2210 Bush River Rd *TF:* 800-578-7878	Columbia	SC	29210	803-798-9665	798-9665
Travelodge Northeast 1539 Horseshoe Dr *TF:* 800-578-7878	Columbia	SC	29223	803-736-1600	736-1600
Villagers Lodge 827 Bush River Rd *TF:* 800-328-7829	Columbia	SC	29210	803-772-9672	551-2303
Whitney Hotel 700 Woodrow St *TF:* 800-637-4008	Columbia	SC	29205	803-252-0845	771-0495

— Restaurants —

	City	State	ZIP	Phone
Andrew's (Continental) 2100 Bush River Rd	Columbia	SC	29210	803-731-0300
Birds On A Wire (Southern) 2631 Devine St *Web:* www.birdsonawire.com	Columbia	SC	29205	803-254-2035
Blue Marlin (Seafood) 1200 Lincoln St	Columbia	SC	29201	803-799-3838
California Dreaming (American) 401 South Main St	Columbia	SC	29201	803-254-6767
Cellars Restaurant (New American) 108 Columbia NE Dr Suite G	Columbia	SC	29223	803-736-8665
Dianne's (Italian) 2400 Devine St	Columbia	SC	29205	803-254-3535
Finlay's (American) 1200 Hampton St	Columbia	SC	29201	803-771-7000
Garibaldi's (Italian) 2013 Green St	Columbia	SC	29205	803-771-8888
Garrett's Grille & Grog (American) 715 Harden St	Columbia	SC	29205	803-256-7733
Grecian Gardens (Greek) 2312 Sunset Blvd W	Columbia	SC	29169	803-794-7552
Hampton Street Vineyard (American) 1207 Hampton St	Columbia	SC	29201	803-252-0850
Hennessy's Restaurant and Lounge (New American) 1649 Main St *Web:* www.colasc.com/hennessy/	Columbia	SC	29201	803-799-8280
Key West Bar & Grill (Steak/Seafood) 1736 Bush River Rd	Columbia	SC	29210	803-772-0000
Maurice's Piggie Park (Barbecue) 1600 Charleston Hwy	West Columbia	SC	29169	803-791-5887
Motor Supply Co Bistro (American) 920 Gervais St	Columbia	SC	29201	803-256-6687
Mr Friendly's New Southern Cafe (Southern) 2001 Greene St Suite A *Web:* www.mrfriendlys.com/	Columbia	SC	29205	803-254-7828
Villa Tronco (Italian) 1213 Blanding St *Web:* www.colasc.com/villa_tronco/	Columbia	SC	29201	803-256-7677
Yamato Steak House of Japan (Japanese) 736M St Andrews Rd	Columbia	SC	29210	803-798-7542
Yesterday's (American) 2030 Devine St *Web:* www.yesterdayssc.com	Columbia	SC	29205	803-799-0196
Zorba's (Greek) 6169 St Andrews Rd	Columbia	SC	29212	803-772-4617

— Goods and Services —

SHOPPING

	City	State	ZIP	Phone	Fax
Columbia Mall 7201 Two Notch Rd	Columbia	SC	29223	803-788-4676	
Columbiana Centre Mall 100 Columbiana Cir	Columbia	SC	29212	803-732-6255	
Dutch Square Center Broad River at Bush River Rd	Columbia	SC	29210	803-772-3864	
Market Pointe Mall 300-13 Outlet Pointe Blvd	Columbia	SC	29210	803-798-8520	798-8520
Old Mill Antique Mall 310 State St	West Columbia	SC	29169	803-796-4229	
Old Towne Antique Mall 2956 Broad River Rd	Columbia	SC	29210	803-772-9335	
Richland Fashion Mall 3400 Forest Dr	Columbia	SC	29204	803-738-2995	
Thieves Antique Flea Market 502 Gadsden St	Columbia	SC	29201	803-254-4997	

BANKS

	City	State	ZIP	Phone	Fax
Bank of America 1901 Main St	Columbia	SC	29201	803-255-7555	255-7550
Branch Banking & Trust Co of South Carolina 1901 Assembly St *TF:* 800-421-9899	Columbia	SC	29202	803-251-3301	251-3549
Carolina First Bank 102 S Main St *TF:* 800-951-2699	Columbia	SC	29601	864-239-6400	255-4782
First Citizens Bank & Trust Co 1230 Main St **Fax:* Hum Res	Columbia	SC	29201	803-771-8700	733-3480*
Wachovia Bank NA 1426 Main St *TF:* 800-922-7750	Columbia	SC	29226	803-765-3945	765-3949

BUSINESS SERVICES

	Phone		Phone
Airborne Express	800-247-2676	**Kelly Services**	803-798-0765
BAX Global	800-225-5229	**Kinko's**	803-799-3807
DHL Worldwide Express	800-225-5345	**Mail Boxes Etc**	800-789-4623
Federal Express	800-238-5355	**Post Office**	803-926-6000
Gallman Personnel Services	803-772-8046	**UPS**	800-742-5877

— Media —

PUBLICATIONS

	City	State	ZIP	Phone	Fax
State The‡ PO Box 1333 *Web:* www.thestate.com ■ *E-mail:* cyberst@cyberstate.infi.net	Columbia	SC	29202	803-771-6161	771-8430

‡Daily newspapers

TELEVISION

	City	State	ZIP	Phone	Fax
WACH-TV Ch 57 (Fox) 1400 Pickens St	Columbia	SC	29201	803-252-5757	212-7270
WIS-TV Ch 10 (NBC) 1111 Bull St **Fax:* News Rm ■ *Web:* www.wistv.com ■ *E-mail:* wis-tv10@aol.com	Columbia	SC	29201	803-758-1218	758-1278*
WLTX-TV Ch 19 (CBS) 6027 Devine St	Columbia	SC	29209	803-776-3600	776-1791
WOLO-TV Ch 25 (ABC) 5807 Shakespeare Rd *Web:* www.wolo.com ■ *E-mail:* info@wolo.com	Columbia	SC	29223	803-754-7525	754-6147
WQHB-TV Ch 63 (PAX) PO Box 160 *Web:* www.pax.net/WQHB	Sumter	SC	29151	803-775-2817	775-4486

RADIO

	City	State	ZIP	Phone	Fax
WARQ-FM 93.5 MHz (Rock) PO Box 9127 *Web:* www.warq.com ■ *E-mail:* rock935@aol.com	Columbia	SC	29290	803-695-8680	695-8605
WCOS-AM 1400 kHz (Sports) 56 Radio Ln *Web:* www.allsportstalk.com	Columbia	SC	29210	803-772-5600	798-5255
WLTR-FM 91.3 MHz (NPR) 1101 George Rogers Blvd	Columbia	SC	29201	803-737-3420	737-3552
WLTY-FM 96.7 MHz (AC) PO Box 748	Columbia	SC	29202	803-254-0967	779-7572
WMFX-FM 102.3 MHz (Ctry) 1900 Pineview Rd	Columbia	SC	29209	803-742-9639	695-8605
WNOK-FM 104.7 MHz (CHR) 1300 Pickens St *Web:* www.wnok.com	Columbia	SC	29201	803-771-0105	799-4367
WOIC-AM 1230 kHz (Rel) 1900 Pineview Rd	Columbia	SC	29209	803-776-1013	695-8605
WQXL-AM 1470 kHz (Rel) PO Box 3277 *E-mail:* wqxl@aol.com	Columbia	SC	29230	803-779-7911	252-2158

Columbia — Radio (Cont'd)

Phone Fax

WTCB-FM 106.7 MHz (AC) PO Box 5106...... Columbia SC 29250 803-796-7600 796-9291
WVOC-AM 560 kHz (N/T) PO Box 21567...... Columbia SC 29221 803-772-5600 798-5255
Web: www.wvoc.com ■ *E-mail:* mail@wvoc.com
WWDM-FM 101.3 MHz (Urban)
PO Box 9127...................... Columbia SC 29290 803-776-1013 695-8605
Web: www.thebigdm.com

— Colleges/Universities —

Phone Fax

Allen University 1530 Harden St........... Columbia SC 29204 803-254-4165 376-5709
Benedict College 1600 Harden St........... Columbia SC 29204 803-256-4220 253-5167
TF: 800-868-6598
Columbia College
1301 Columbia College Dr............. Columbia SC 29203 803-786-3012 786-3674
Columbia International University
7435 Monticello Rd.................. Columbia SC 29230 803-754-4100 786-4209
TF: 800-777-2227 ■ *Web:* www.gospelcom.net/ciu/
■ *E-mail:* publicrelations@ciu.edu
Columbia Junior College of Business
3810 Main St...................... Columbia SC 29203 803-799-9082 799-9038
Midlands Technical College PO Box 2408..... Columbia SC 29202 803-738-1400 738-7784
Web: www.mid.tec.sc.us
Morris College 100 W College St............ Sumter SC 29150 803-775-9371 773-3687
TF: 800-778-1345 ■ *Web:* www.morris.edu
University of South Carolina............. Columbia SC 29208 803-777-7000 777-0101
TF Admissions: 800-922-9755 ■ *Web:* www.sc.edu
■ *E-mail:* admissions-ugrad@sc.edu

— Hospitals —

Phone Fax

Baptist Medical Center 1330 Taylor St....... Columbia SC 29220 803-771-5010 771-5462
Web: www.bmcc-sc.com
Lexington Medical Center
2720 Sunset Blvd................West Columbia SC 29169 803-791-2000 791-2483*
**Fax:* Admitting ■ *Web:* www.lexmed.com
Palmetto Richland Memorial Hospital
5 Richland Medical Pk................... Columbia SC 29203 803-434-7000 434-6892*
**Fax:* Admitting ■ *Web:* www.rmh.edu ■ *E-mail:* info@rmh.edu
Providence Hospital 2435 Forest Dr......... Columbia SC 29204 803-256-5300 256-5358*
**Fax:* Admitting ■ *Web:* www.columbiaprovidence.com
William Jennings Bryan Dorn Veterans
Hospital 6439 Garners Ferry Rd.......... Columbia SC 29209 803-776-4000 695-6799*
**Fax:* Mail Rm

— Attractions —

Phone Fax

Ashland Park St Andrews Rd & I-26......... Columbia SC 29210 803-256-9000
Carolina Ballet 914 Pulaski St............ Columbia SC 29201 803-771-6303 771-2625
Carolina Coliseum 701 Assembly St......... Columbia SC 29201 803-777-5113 777-5114
Cayce Historical Museum 1800 12th St........ Cayce SC 29033 803-796-9020 796-9072
Columbia City Ballet 1128 Taylor St......... Columbia SC 29201 803-799-7605 779-7928
TF: 800-899-7408 ■ *Web:* www.columbiacityballet.com
■ *E-mail:* email@columbiacityballet.com
Columbia Fire Department Museum
1800 Laurel St...................... Columbia SC 29201 803-733-8350 733-8311
Columbia Marionette Theatre 401 Laurel St ... Columbia SC 29201 803-252-7366
Web: www.scescape.com/marionette/
Columbia Museum of Art PO Box 2068....... Columbia SC 29202 803-799-2810 343-2150
Web: www.colmusart.org ■ *E-mail:* ktucker@colmusart.org
Columbia Riverfront Park & Historic Canal
Laurel St.......................... Columbia SC 29201 803-733-8331
Confederate Relic Room & Museum
920 Sumter St...................... Columbia SC 29201 803-898-8095 898-8099
Web: www.state.sc.us/crr
Congaree Swamp National Monument
200 Caroline Sims Rd.................. Hopkins SC 29061 803-776-4396 783-4241
Web: www.nps.gov/cosw/
Dreher Island State Park
3677 State Park Rd.................. Prosperity SC 29127 803-364-3530 364-0756
Finlay Park 930 Laurel St................ Columbia SC 29201 803-733-8331
First Baptist Church 1306 Hampton St....... Columbia SC 29201 803-256-4251

Phone Fax

Fort Jackson Museum 2179 Sumter St.....Fort Jackson SC 29207 803-751-7419 751-4435
Francis Marion-Sumter National Forest
4931 Broad River Rd................. Columbia SC 29212 803-561-4000 561-4004
Web: www.fs.fed.us/r8/fms
Governor's Mansion & Green
800 Richland St..................... Columbia SC 29201 803-737-1710 737-3860
Hampton-Preston Mansion & Garden
1615 Blanding St.................... Columbia SC 29201 803-252-1770
Keenan Ensor House 801 Wildwood Ave...... Columbia SC 29203 803-733-8510
Koger Center for the Arts 1051 Greene St..... Columbia SC 29201 803-777-7500 777-9774
Lake Murray Tourism & Recreation
Association 2184 N Lake Dr............. Columbia SC 29212 803-781-5940 781-6197
Web: www.lakemurraycountry.com/
Longstreet Theatre Greene & Sumter Sts...... Columbia SC 29201 803-777-2551 777-6669
Mann-Simons Cottage 1403 Richland St...... Columbia SC 29201 803-252-7742
Memorial Park Washington St............. Columbia SC 29201 803-733-8331
Mills Robert House 1618 Blanding St........ Columbia SC 29201 803-252-7742
Nickelodeon Theatre of the Columbia Film
Society 937 Main St.................. Columbia SC 29201 803-254-8234 254-0299
Web: www.nickelodeon.org
Riverbanks Zoological Park
500 Wildlife Pkwy................... Columbia SC 29210 803-779-8717 253-6381
Web: www.riverbanks.org
Seibels House 1601 Richland St........... Columbia SC 29201 803-252-7742 929-7695
Sesquicentennial State Park
9564 Two Notch Rd.................. Columbia SC 29223 803-788-2706 788-2706
South Carolina Criminal Justice Hall of Fame
5400 Broad River Rd................. Columbia SC 29210 803-896-8199 896-8067
South Carolina Philharmonic Orchestra
1237 Gadsden St Suite 102............. Columbia SC 29201 803-771-7937 771-0268
Web: www.scphilharmonic.com ■ *E-mail:* music@scphilharmonic.com
South Carolina State Capitol Sumter St...... Columbia SC 29201 803-734-2430
South Carolina State Museum
301 Gervais St..................... Columbia SC 29201 803-898-4921 898-4969
Web: www.museum.state.sc.us
Southeastern Regional Opera
914 Pulaski St..................... Columbia SC 29201 803-771-6303 771-2625
State Farmers Market 1001 Bluff Rd......... Columbia SC 29201 803-737-4664 737-4667
Town Theatre 10125 Sumter St............ Columbia SC 29201 803-799-2510
Web: www.scescape.com/towntheatre/
Trustus Theatre 520 Lady St............. Columbia SC 29201 803-254-9732 771-9153
Web: www.scescape.com/trustus/
University of South Carolina McKissick
Museum Pendleton & Bull Sts........... Columbia SC 29208 803-777-7251 777-2829
Woodrow Wilson's Boyhood Home
1705 Hampton St.................... Columbia SC 29201 803-252-7742 929-7695
Workshop Theatre 1136 Bull St............ Columbia SC 29201 803-799-4876 799-4876
Web: www.scescape.com/workshop/

SPORTS TEAMS & FACILITIES

Phone Fax

Capital City Bombers (baseball)
301 S Assembly St Capital City Stadium.... Columbia SC 29201 803-254-4487 256-4338

— Events —

Phone

Carolina Classic Home & Garden Show (mid-March)........803-256-6238
Carolina Marathon (late February)........803-929-1996
Christmas Candlelight Tours (early December)........803-252-7742
Christmas Traditions (early December)........803-779-8717
Columbia International Festival (early April)........803-799-3452
Congaree Western Weekend Festival & Rodeo (mid-September)........803-755-2512
Greek Bake Sale (early March)........803-252-6758
Greek Festival (late September)........803-252-6758
Jubilee Festival of Heritage (mid-August)........803-252-7742
Labor Day Festival (early September)........803-345-1100
Lexinton County Peach Festival (early July)........803-254-0479
Lights Before Christmas at the Zoo (December)........803-779-8717
Main Street Jazz (late May)........803-254-0479
Mayfest (early May)........803-254-0479
NatureFest (late April)........803-776-4396
Riverfest Celebration (mid-April)........803-254-0479
Saint Patrick's Day Festival (mid-March)........803-738-1499
South Carolina Oyster Festival (mid-March)........803-695-0676
South Carolina State Fair (early October)........803-254-0479
Spring Things Art & Craft Show (mid-March)........803-772-3336
Vista After Five Spring Concerts (early April-late May)........803-256-7501
Vista Lights (mid-November)........803-254-0479

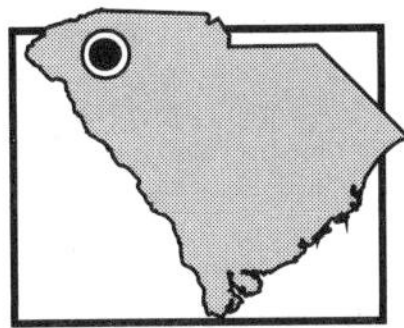

Greenville

Greenville is located in the northwest corner of South Carolina, with the Blue Ridge chain of the Appalachian Mountains just minutes from the heart of the city. This part of the state was occupied by Cherokee Indians until 1777. During the antebellum period, the city of Greenville was primarily a resort for low-country planters, but after the Reconstruction its textile industry flourished. In addition to the many scenic points of interest in and around the city, the 250 acres of the Clemson University Botanical Gardens include wildflower, fern, and bog gardens containing hundreds of species native to South Carolina. The Sacred Art Museum at Bob Jones University in Greenville features religious art dating from the 13th century, including works by Rembrandt, Rubens, Titian, and Van Dyck; and the area of the city known as Little Stores of West End is a unique shopping village of specialty stores.

Population . . . 56,436
Area (Land) . . . 25.1 sq mi
Area (Water) . . . 0.1 sq mi
Elevation . . . 966 ft
Latitude . . . 34-84-81 N
Longitude . . . 82-40-64 W
County . . . Greenville
Time Zone . . . EST
Area Code/s . . . 864

— Average Temperatures and Precipitation —

TEMPERATURES

	Jan	Feb	Mar	Apr	May	Jun	Jul	Aug	Sep	Oct	Nov	Dec
High	50	54	64	72	79	86	88	87	81	72	63	53
Low	30	32	40	48	56	64	68	67	61	49	41	33

PRECIPITATION

	Jan	Feb	Mar	Apr	May	Jun	Jul	Aug	Sep	Oct	Nov	Dec
Inches	4.1	4.4	5.4	3.9	4.4	4.8	4.6	4.0	4.0	4.0	3.7	4.1

— Important Phone Numbers —

	Phone
AAA	864-240-3010
American Express Travel	864-292-9970
Emergency	911
HotelDocs	800-468-3537
Poison Control Center	803-777-1117
Time/Temp	864-233-3000
Weather	864-233-3000

— Information Sources —

	City	State	Zip	Phone	Fax
Better Business Bureau Serving Central South Carolina & the Charleston Area PO Box 8326 *Web:* www.columbia.bbb.org	Columbia	SC	29202	803-254-2525	779-3117
Greater Greenville Chamber of Commerce 24 Cleveland St. **Fax:* PR	Greenville	SC	29601	864-242-1050	282-8509*
Greater Greenville Convention & Visitors Bureau 206 S Main St. *TF:* 800-717-0023 ■ *Web:* www.greatergreenville.com	Greenville	SC	29601	864-421-0000	421-0005
Greenville City Hall PO Box 2207 *Web:* www.greatergreenville.com	Greenville	SC	29602	864-467-4500	467-5725
Greenville County 305 E North St Courthouse Suite 224	Greenville	SC	29601	864-467-8551	467-8540
Greenville County Library 300 College St *Web:* www.greenvillelibrary.org	Greenville	SC	29601	864-242-5000	235-8375
Greenville Economic Development Div PO Box 2207	Greenville	SC	29602	864-467-4401	467-5744
Greenville Mayor PO Box 2207	Greenville	SC	29602	864-467-4590	467-5725
Palmetto Exposition Center PO Box 5823 *Web:* www.palmettoexpo.com	Greenville	SC	29606	864-233-2562	233-0619

On-Line Resources

4Greenville.com . . . www.4greenville.com
About.com Guide to Greenville . . . greenville.about.com
Anthill City Guide Greenville . . . www.anthill.com/city.asp?city=greenville
Area Guide Greenville . . . greenvillesc.areaguides.net
City Knowledge Greenville . . . www.cityknowledge.com/sc_greenville.htm
CityTravelers.com Guide to Greenville . . . www.citytravelers.com/gsp.htm
Creative Loafing Online Greenville . . . www.creativeloafing.com/greenville/newsstand/current/
Excite.com Greenville City Guide . . . www.excite.com/travel/countries/united_states/south_carolina/greenville
Greenville Directory . . . www.scad.com/greenvil
GreenvilleNet . . . www.greenvillenet.com/

— Transportation Services —

AIRPORTS

■ **Greenville-Spartanburg Airport (GSP)**

	Phone
12 miles NE of downtown (approx 25 minutes)	864-877-7426

Airport Transportation

	Phone
Airport Taxi $20 fare to downtown	864-879-2315

Commercial Airlines

	Phone
AirTran	800-247-8726
American	800-433-7300
Continental	800-525-0280
Continental Express	800-525-0280
Delta	800-221-1212
Delta Connection	800-221-1212
Northwest	800-225-2525
US Airways	800-428-4322
US Airways Express	800-428-4322

Charter Airlines

	Phone
Greenville Jet Center	864-235-6383
Stevens Aviation	800-359-7838

CAR RENTALS

	Phone
Avis	864-877-6458
Budget	864-879-2134
Enterprise	864-233-8182
Hertz	864-877-4261
National	864-877-6446
Thrifty	864-877-7799

LIMO/TAXI

	Phone
Diamond Cab	864-235-1713
Expressions Limo	864-233-6891
Royal Crest Limousine	864-879-2862
Upstate Limousine	864-233-7776
Yellow Cab	864-232-5322

MASS TRANSIT

	Phone
Greenville Transit Authority $1 Base fare	864-467-5000

RAIL/BUS

	City	State	Zip	Phone
Amtrak Station 1120 W Washington St *TF:* 800-872-7245	Greenville	SC	29601	864-255-4221
Greyhound Bus Station 100 W McBee Ave *TF:* 800-231-2222	Greenville	SC	29601	864-235-3513

— Accommodations —

HOTEL RESERVATION SERVICES

	Phone	Fax
Greenville Area Central Reservations *TF:* 800-351-7180	864-233-0461	421-0005

Greenville (Cont'd)

HOTELS, MOTELS, RESORTS

Name / Address	City	State	ZIP	Phone	Fax
AmeriSuites 40 W Orchard Park Dr. *TF:* 800-833-1516	Greenville	SC	29615	864-232-3000	271-4388
Comfort Inn 412 Mauldin Rd *TF:* 800-228-5150	Greenville	SC	29605	864-277-6730	672-6739
Comfort Inn Executive Center 540 N Pleasantburg Dr *TF:* 800-228-5150	Greenville	SC	29607	864-271-0060	242-4096
Courtyard by Marriott 70 Orchard Pk Dr *TF:* 800-321-2211 ■ *Web:* courtyard.com/GSPCH	Greenville	SC	29615	864-234-0300	234-0296
Crowne Plaza 851 Congaree Rd *TF:* 800-227-6963	Greenville	SC	29607	864-297-6300	234-0747
Days Inn 3905 Augusta Rd. *TF:* 800-329-7466	Greenville	SC	29605	864-277-4010	672-4012
Days Inn 831 Congaree Rd. *TF:* 800-329-7466	Greenville	SC	29607	864-288-6221	288-2778
Embassy Suites 670 Verdae Blvd *TF:* 800-362-2779	Greenville	SC	29607	864-676-9090	676-0669
Extended StayAmerica 3715 Pelham Rd *TF:* 800-398-7829	Greenville	SC	29615	864-213-9698	213-9836
Fairfield Inn 60 Roper Mountain Rd *TF:* 800-228-2800 ■ *Web:* fairfieldinn.com/GSPGT	Greenville	SC	29607	864-297-9996	297-9965
Greenville Hilton & Towers 45 W Orchard Park Dr. *TF:* 800-445-8667	Greenville	SC	29615	864-232-4747	235-6248
Guest House Suites Plus 48 McPrice Ct *TF:* 800-214-8378	Greenville	SC	29615	864-297-0099	288-8203
Hampton Inn 246 Congaree Rd. *TF:* 800-426-7866	Greenville	SC	29607	864-288-1200	288-5667
Hampton Inn Airport 47 Fisherman Ln. *TF:* 800-426-7866	Greenville	SC	29615	864-288-3500	234-0728
Holiday Inn Express 5009 Pelham Rd *TF:* 800-465-4329	Greenville	SC	29615	864-297-5353	676-1167
Holiday Inn I-85 4295 Augusta Rd *TF:* 800-465-4329	Greenville	SC	29605	864-277-8921	299-6066
Howard Johnson Lodge & Suites 2756 Laurens Rd *TF:* 800-446-4656	Greenville	SC	29607	864-288-6900	288-5935
Hyatt Regency Greenville 220 N Main St *TF:* 800-233-1234 ■ *Web:* www.hyatt.com/usa/greenville/hotels/hotel_gsprg.html	Greenville	SC	29601	864-235-1234	232-7584
La Quinta 31 Old Country Rd *TF:* 800-687-6667	Greenville	SC	29607	864-297-3500	458-9818
MainStay Suites 2671 Dry Pocket Rd *TF:* 800-660-6246	Greer	SC	29650	864-987-5566	675-0305
Marriott Hotel Airport 1 Parkway E. *TF:* 800-441-1737 ■ *Web:* marriotthotels.com/GSPAP	Greenville	SC	29615	864-297-0300	281-0801
Microtel Inn Greenville 20 Interstate Court *TF:* 888-297-7866	Greenville	SC	29615	864-297-7866	297-7883
Motel 6 224 Bruce Rd *TF:* 800-466-8356	Greenville	SC	29605	864-277-8630	299-1239
Pettigru Place 302 Pettigru St	Greenville	SC	29601	864-242-4529	
Quality Hotel & Conference Center 7136 Asheville Hwy. *TF:* 800-221-2222	Spartanburg	SC	29303	864-503-0780	
Quality Inn 50 Orchard Park Dr *TF:* 800-525-8250	Greenville	SC	29615	864-297-9000	297-8292
Ramada Hotel & Convention Center 1001 S Church St. *TF:* 800-272-6232	Greenville	SC	29601	864-678-7800	678-7801
Ramada Inn South 1314 S Pleasantburg Dr *TF:* 800-272-6232	Greenville	SC	29605	864-277-3734	
Red Roof Inn 2801 Laurens Rd *TF:* 800-843-7663	Greenville	SC	29615	864-297-4458	297-9800
StudioPLUS 530 Woods Lake Rd *TF:* 800-646-8000	Greenville	SC	29607	864-288-4300	234-0054
Super 8 Motel 27 S Pleasantburg Dr. *TF:* 800-800-8000	Greenville	SC	29607	864-232-3339	672-3344
Travelodge 755 Wade Hampton Blvd. *TF:* 800-578-7878	Greenville	SC	29609	864-233-5393	233-6014
Wingate Inn 33 Beacon Dr.	Greenville	SC	29615	864-281-1281	281-0406

— Restaurants —

Name / Address	City	State	ZIP	Phone
Addy's Dutch Cafe & Restaurant (Dutch) 17 E Coffee St.	Greenville	SC	29601	864-232-2339
Anita's (Mexican) 101 Alice Ave.	Simpsonville	SC	29681	864-963-3855
Austin's (Steak) 1 Parkway E.	Greenville	SC	29615	864-297-0300
Big River Grille & Brewing Works (American) 211 E Broad St	Greenville	SC	29601	864-370-1118
Bistro Europa (American) 219 N Main St	Greenville	SC	29601	864-467-9975
Blockhouse Restaurant & Oyster Bar (Steak/Seafood) 1619 Augusta Rd	Greenville	SC	29605	864-232-4280
Blue Ridge Brewing Co (American) 217 N Main St	Greenville	SC	29601	864-232-4677
California Dreaming Restaurant & Bar (Continental) 40 Beacon Dr.	Greenville	SC	29615	864-234-9000
Corona Mexican Restaurant (Mexican) 2112 Wade Hampton Blvd.	Greenville	SC	29615	864-292-3719
Cottage Cuisine at the Peace Center (Continental) 101 W Broad St	Greenville	SC	29601	864-467-3020
Dragon Den (Chinese) 420 N Pleasantburg Dr.	Greenville	SC	29607	864-242-1777
Farmhuse Grill (French) 301 Haywood Rd	Greenville	SC	29607	864-234-0443
Handlebar The (American) 400 Mills Ave *Web:* www.skydance.com/handlebar/ ■ *E-mail:* thehandlebar@juno.com	Greenville	SC	29605	864-233-6173
McGuffey's (American) 711 Congaree Rd	Greenville	SC	29607	864-288-3116
Nippon Center Yagoto (Japanese) 500 Congaree Rd	Greenville	SC	29607	864-288-8471
Occasionally Blues (Southern) 1 Augusta St.	Greenville	SC	29601	864-242-6000
Open Hearth (Steak/Seafood) 2801 Wade Hampton Blvd	Taylors	SC	29687	864-244-2665
Peppino's (Italian) 219-C W Antrim Dr.	Greenville	SC	29607	864-271-4860
Peter David's Fine Dining (Continental) 921 Grove Rd.	Greenville	SC	29605	864-242-0404
Provencia (Mediterranean) 220 N Main St	Greenville	SC	29601	864-235-1234
Rene's Fishmarket (Seafood) 301 Haywood Rd.	Greenville	SC	29607	864-297-3456
Seven Oaks (Continental) 104 Broadus Ave	Greenville	SC	29601	864-232-1895
Soby's (Southern) 207 S Main St.	Greenville	SC	29601	864-232-7007
Sophisticated Palate (Continental) 34 S Main St.	Greenville	SC	29601	864-235-4202
Stax Brolier Room Tavern (American) 233 N Main St	Greenville	SC	29601	864-271-1400
Stax's Original (American) 1704 Poinsett Hwy	Greenville	SC	29609	864-232-2133
Tipton's Restaurant (American) 1001 S Church St.	Greenville	SC	29601	864-232-7666
Trio Brick Oven Cafe (Italian) 22 N Main St	Greenville	SC	29601	864-467-1000
Vercitti (Italian) 45 W Orchard Park Dr.	Greenville	SC	29615	864-232-4747
Vince's (American) 1 E Antrim Dr	Greenville	SC	29607	864-233-1621

— Goods and Services —

SHOPPING

Name / Address	City	State	ZIP	Phone	Fax
Augusta Commons 2222 Augusta St.	Greenville	SC	29605	864-232-5669	
Foothills Factory Stores I-26 & New Cut Rd.	Spartanburg	SC	29301	864-574-8587	
Greenville Mall 1025 Woodruff Rd.	Greenville	SC	29607	864-297-8800	281-0359
Haywood Mall 700 Haywood Rd.	Greenville	SC	29607	864-288-0511	297-6018
Little Stores of West End 315 Augusta St	Greenville	SC	29601	864-467-1770	
McAlister Square 225 S Pleasantburg Dr.	Greenville	SC	29607	864-232-6204	

BANKS

Name / Address	City	State	ZIP	Phone	Fax
American Federal Bank FSB 300 E McBee Ave *TF:* 888-232-9980	Greenville	SC	29601	864-255-7000	255-7504
Bank of America 7 N Laurens St.	Greenville	SC	29601	864-271-5600	
Carolina First Bank 102 S Main St.	Greenville	SC	29601	864-255-7900	239-6401
First Citizens Bank & Trust 75 Beattie Pl 2 Insignia Financial Plaza	Greenville	SC	29601	864-255-3700	
First Union National Bank PO Box 1329	Greenville	SC	29602	864-255-8000	255-8306
Regions Bank PO Box 17308	Greenville	SC	29606	864-233-7989	235-6636

BUSINESS SERVICES

Name	Phone	Name	Phone
Airborne Express	800-247-2676	**Mail Boxes Etc**	864-292-3880
BAX Global	864-879-8500	**Post Office**	864-282-8401
Federal Express	800-238-5355	**Tate's Temporary Service**	864-235-2875
Kelly Services	864-292-2888	**UPS**	800-742-5877
Kinko's	864-627-8646		

— Media —

PUBLICATIONS

Name / Address	City	State	ZIP	Phone	Fax
Greenville Magazine 213 E Broad St. *Web:* www.greenvillemagazine.com ■ *E-mail:* gmag@greenvillemagazine.com	Greenville	SC	29601	864-271-1105	271-1165
Greenville News‡ PO Box 1688 *TF:* 800-274-7879 ■ *Web:* greenvilleonline.com ■ *E-mail:* newsletters@greenville.infi.net	Greenville	SC	29602	864-298-4100	298-4395

‡Daily newspapers

Greenville (Cont'd)

TELEVISION

	City	State	ZIP	Phone	Fax
WASV-TV Ch 62 (WB) 1293 Hendersonville Rd Suite 12	Asheville	NC	28803	828-277-0902	277-5060
WFBC-TV Ch 40 (Ind) 288 Macon Ave	Asheville	NC	28804	828-255-0013	255-4612
TF: 800-288-8813 ■ *Web:* www.wfbc.com ■ *E-mail:* contact@wfbc.com					
WGGS-TV Ch 16 (Ind) 3409 Rutherford Rd	Taylors	SC	29687	864-244-1616	292-8481
TF: 800-849-3683					
WHNS-TV Ch 21 (Fox) 21 Interstate Ct	Greenville	SC	29615	864-288-2100	297-0728
Web: www.whns.com ■ *E-mail:* fox21@whns.com					
WNEG-TV Ch 32 (CBS) 100 Boulevard	Toccoa	GA	30577	706-886-0032	886-7033
Web: www.toccoa.net/hosted/ch32/ch32.htm ■ *E-mail:* wnegtv@bellsouth.net					
WRET-TV Ch 49 (PBS) PO Box 4069	Spartanburg	SC	29305	864-503-9371	503-3615
Web: www.wret.org					
WRLK-TV Ch 35 (PBS) 1101 George Rogers Blvd	Columbia	SC	29201	803-737-3200	737-3526
WSPA-TV Ch 7 (CBS) PO Box 1717	Spartanburg	SC	29304	864-576-7777	587-5430
Web: www.wspa.com ■ *E-mail:* newschannel7@wspa.com					
WYFF-TV Ch 4 (NBC) PO Box 788	Greenville	SC	29602	864-242-4404	240-5305
Web: www.wyff.com/ ■ *E-mail:* wyff@aol.com					

RADIO

	City	State	ZIP	Phone	Fax
WESC-FM 92.5 MHz (Ctry) 223 W Stone Ave	Greenville	SC	29609	864-242-4660	271-5029
WFBC-FM 93.7 MHz (CHR) 501 Rutherford St	Greenville	SC	29609	864-271-9200	241-4387*
**Fax:* Sales					
WGVL-AM 1440 kHz (Ctry) 7 N Laurens St Suite 700	Greenville	SC	29601	864-242-1005	271-3830
WJMZ FM 107.3 MHz (Urban) 220 N Main St Suite 402	Greenville	SC	29602	864-235-1073	370-3403
Web: www.wjmz.com					
WMUU-AM 1260 kHz (Rel) 920 Wade Hampton Blvd	Greenville	SC	29609	864-242-6240	370-3829
Web: www.bju.edu/wmuu ■ *E-mail:* wmuu@bju.edu					
WMUU-FM 94.5 MHz (B/EZ) 920 Wade Hampton Blvd	Greenville	SC	29609	864-242-6240	370-3829
Web: www.bju.edu/wmuu ■ *E-mail:* wmuu@bju.edu					
WMYI-FM 102.5 MHz (AC) 7 N Laurens St Suite 700	Greenville	SC	29601	864-235-1025	242-1025
WROQ-FM 101.1 MHz (CR) 7 N Laurens St Suite 700	Greenville	SC	29601	864-242-0101	298-0067
Web: www.wroq.com					
WTPT-FM 93.3 MHz (Rock) 223 W Stone Ave	Greenville	SC	29609	864-242-4660	271-5029
Web: www.93planet.com					

— Colleges/Universities —

	City	State	ZIP	Phone	Fax
Bob Jones University 1700 Wade Hampton Blvd	Greenville	SC	29614	864-242-5100	271-1302
Web: www.bju.edu					
Clemson University 105 Sikes Hall	Clemson	SC	29634	864-656-3311	656-2464
Web: www.clemson.edu ■ *E-mail:* mikeh@clemson.edu					
Furman University 3300 Poinsett Hwy	Greenville	SC	29613	864-294-2000	294-3127
Web: www.furman.edu					
Greenville Technical College PO Box 5616	Greenville	SC	29606	864-250-8000	250-8534
Web: www.greenvilletech.com					
North Greenville College PO Box 1892	Tigerville	SC	29688	864-977-7000	977-7021
TF: 800-468-6642 ■ *Web:* www.ngc.edu ■ *E-mail:* admissions@ngc.edu					
Southern Wesleyan College PO Box 1020	Central	SC	29630	864-644-5000	644-5900
TF Admissions: 800-282-8798 ■ *Web:* www.swu.edu ■ *E-mail:* admissions@swu.edu					

— Hospitals —

	City	State	ZIP	Phone	Fax
Baptist Medical Center Easley 200 Fleetwood Dr	Easley	SC	29640	864-855-7200	855-7521
Greenville Memorial Hospital 701 Grove Rd	Greenville	SC	29605	864-455-7000	455-8434
Saint Francis Hospital 1 St Francis Dr	Greenville	SC	29601	864-255-1000	255-1034*
**Fax:* Admitting					
Shriners Hospitals for Children Greenville Unit 950 W Faris Rd	Greenville	SC	29605	864-271-3444	271-4471
Web: www.shrinershq.org/Hospitals/Directory/greenville.html					

— Attractions —

	City	State	ZIP	Phone	Fax
16th South Carolina Volunteers Museum of the Confederate History 15 Boyce Ave	Greenville	SC	29601	864-421-9039	
Bob Jones University Artist Series & Univeristy Classic Players 1700 Wade Hampton Blvd	Greenville	SC	29614	864-242-5100	242-3923
Bob Jones University Collection of Sacred Art Bob Jones University 1700 Wade Hampton Blvd	Greenville	SC	29614	864-242-5100	233-9829
Center Stage-South Carolina! 501 River St	Greenville	SC	29601	864-233-6733	233-3901
Christ Episcopal Church 10 N Church St	Greenville	SC	29601	864-271-8773	
Cleveland Park Downtown Greenville-betw Stone Ave & Washington St	Greenville	SC	29601	864-467-4355	467-5735
TF: 800-849-4339					
Cowpens National Battlefield 4001 Chesnee Hwy	Gaffney	SC	29341	864-461-2828	461-7795
Web: www.nps.gov/cowp/					
Downtown Baptist Church 101 W McBee Ave	Greenville	SC	29601	864-235-5746	
First Presbyterian Church 200 W Washington St	Greenville	SC	29601	864-235-0496	
Fort Hill-The John C Calhoun House Fort Hill St	Clemson	SC	29634	864-656-2475	
Furman University Theatre 3300 Poinsett Hwy	Greenville	SC	29613	864-294-2125	
Gassaway Mansion 106 Dupont Dr	Greenville	SC	29607	864-271-0188	
Greenville Ballet 100 S Main St Peace Center for the Performing Arts	Greenville	SC	29601	864-235-6456	235-8146
Greenville County Historical Society 211 E Washington St	Greenville	SC	29601	864-233-4103	
Greenville County Museum of Art 420 College St	Greenville	SC	29601	864-271-7570	271-7579
Web: www.greenvillemuseum.org					
Greenville Little Theatre 444 College St	Greenville	SC	29601	864-233-6238	233-6237
Greenville Symphony Orchestra PO Box 10002	Greenville	SC	29603	864-232-0344	467-3113
Greenville Zoo 150 Cleveland Pk Dr	Greenville	SC	29601	864-467-4300	467-4314
Web: www.greenvillezoo.org					
Historic Greenville Foundation 123 W Broad St	Greenville	SC	29601	864-467-3100	467-3133
Historic Reedy River Falls Park Corner of S Main St & Camperdown Way	Greenville	SC	29601	864-467-4355	467-6662
Kilgore-Lewis House 560 N Academy St	Greenville	SC	29601	864-232-3020	
Little Stores of West End 315 Augusta St	Greenville	SC	29601	864-467-1770	
Ninety Six National Historic Site 1103 Hwy 248 S	Ninety Six	SC	29666	864-543-4068	543-2058
Web: www.nps.gov/nisi/					
Nippon Cultural Center 500 Congaree Rd	Greenville	SC	29607	864-288-8471	288-8018
Paris Mountain State Park 2401 State Park Rd	Greenville	SC	29609	864-244-5565	244-5565
Peace Center for the Performing Arts 101 W Broad St	Greenville	SC	29601	864-467-3030	467-3040
Reedy River Falls Historic Park 123 W Broad St	Greenville	SC	29601	864-987-5572	
Roper Mountain Science Center 402 Roper Mountain Rd	Greenville	SC	29615	864-281-1188	458-7034
Web: www.ropermountain.org					
Scuffletown USA 603 Scuffletown Rd	Simpsonville	SC	29681	864-967-2276	967-4499
Shoeless Joe Jackson Memorial Park 406 West Ave	Greenville	SC	29611	864-288-6470	
South Carolina Botanical Garden 102 Garden Trail Clemson University	Clemson	SC	29634	864-656-3405	
South Carolina Children's Theatre 106 Augusta St	Greenville	SC	29601	864-235-2885	235-0208
Thompson Gallery 3300 Poinsett Hwy Furman University	Greenville	SC	29613	864-294-2074	
Warehouse Theatre 3700 Augusta St	Greenville	SC	29601	864-235-6948	235-6729
Wesley John United Methodist Church 101 E Court St	Greenville	SC	29601	864-232-6903	
Whitehall Plantation 310 Earle St	Greenville	SC	29609	864-987-5572	
Wild Water Ltd Rafting Trips PO Box 309	Long Creek	SC	29658	864-647-9587	647-5361
TF: 800-451-9972					

Greenville (Cont'd)

SPORTS TEAMS & FACILITIES

				Phone	Fax
Bi-Lo Center Arena 650 N Academy St	Greenville	SC	29601	864-241-3800	241-3872
Greenville Braves (baseball) 1 Braves Ave Greenville Municipal Stadium *Web:* www.gbraves.com	Greenville	SC	29607	864-299-3456	277-7369
South Carolina Shamrocks (soccer) 601 Arlington Ave Shamrock Stadium	Greer	SC	29650	864-585-5009	585-0083

— Events —

	Phone
Antiques Extravaganza (mid-August)	864-233-2562
Art in the Park (mid-September)	864-467-6627
Aunt Het Festival (early October)	864-862-2586
Back to Nature Festival (mid-October)	864-288-6470
Boat RV & Sport Show (early February)	864-233-2562
Boo in the Zoo Festival (late October)	864-467-4300
Christmas Light Show (late November-late December)	864-421-0000
Country Corn Festival (mid-July)	864-834-0704
Fall for Greenville-A Taste of Our Town (mid-October)	864-370-1795
First Night Greenville (December 31)	864-467-5780
Freedom Weekend Aloft Balloon Race (Memorial Day weekend)	864-232-3700
Halloween Spooktacular (late October)	864-288-6470
Holiday Fair & Crafts Show (early December)	864-233-2562
Main Street Jazz (early April-early-October)	864-467-5780
Michelin Cycling Classic (mid-October)	864-467-6627
Music on the Mountain (June-August)	864-288-6470
River Place Festival (early May)	864-467-5780
Thursday Night Downtown Alive (April-September)	864-467-8089

Hilton Head Island

Hilton Head Island is located off the southernmost point of South Carolina in a 42-square-mile area called the Lowcountry. The island is warmed year-round by the Gulf Stream and has a subtropical climate that has helped make it a major tourist destination. The area has more than 40 championship golf courses that are open to the public, as well as more than 300 tennis courts. The MCI Classic ' The Heritage of Golf and the Family Circle Cup women's tennis championship held in the spring mark the beginning of the tourist season on Hilton Head Island each year. Another major event is the Native Islander Gullah Celebration. The Gullah people were some of the Lowcountry's first residents, and this month-long series of events celebrates their contributions to the island's culture and heritage. A variety of other festivals are held throughout the year as well, including SpringFest, Winefest, ChocolateFest, and even WingFest. (However, seafood dishes, including shrimp, blue crabs, and oysters, are the island's specialty ' the seafood boil is to the Lowcountry what the clambake is to Cape Cod.) Hilton Head considers itself a leader in environmental consciousness and has three major nature preserves and 12 miles of beaches where trained naturalists can point out some of the island's native plants and animals. Spartina grass is the one species that can withstand the salinity of the salt marsh and can be seen throughout the island. The Coastal Discovery Museum provides visitors with the opportunity to study both the nature and history of the island.

Population	30,377	**Longitude**	80-41-51 W
Area (Land)	42.0 sq mi	**County**	Beaufort
Area (Water)	13.5 sq mi	**Time Zone**	EST
Elevation	19 ft	**Area Code/s**	843
Latitude	32-12-28 N		

— Average Temperatures and Precipitation —

TEMPERATURES

	Jan	Feb	Mar	Apr	May	Jun	Jul	Aug	Sep	Oct	Nov	Dec
High	60	63	70	76	83	87	90	89	85	78	70	63
Low	38	40	47	54	62	69	72	72	68	57	48	40

PRECIPITATION

	Jan	Feb	Mar	Apr	May	Jun	Jul	Aug	Sep	Oct	Nov	Dec
Inches	3.7	3.5	3.9	3.0	3.6	5.3	6.2	8.9	5.1	0.6	2.4	3.2

— Important Phone Numbers —

	Phone		Phone
AAA	912-352-8222	**Medical Referral**	800-577-2243
Dental Referral	800-327-2598	**Poison Control Center**	803-777-1117
Emergency	911	**Travelers Aid Society**	803-343-7071
HotelDocs	800-468-3537	**Weather**	843-686-6397

— Information Sources —

				Phone	Fax
Beaufort County 100 Ribaut Rd *Web:* www.co.beaufort.sc.us/default.htm	Beaufort	SC	29902	843-525-7100	522-8362
Beaufort County Economic Development Board 100 Ribaut Rd *Web:* www.co.beaufort.sc.us/econo/default.htm ■ *E-mail:* johnw@mail.co.beaufort.sc.us	Beaufort	SC	29902	843-470-2611	470-2610
Better Business Bureau Serving Southeast Georgia & Southeast South Carolina 6606 Abercorn St Suite 108C *Web:* www.savannah.bbb.org	Savannah	GA	31405	912-354-7521	354-5068
Hilton Head Island Chamber of Commerce 1 Chamber Dr *TF:* 800-523-3373 ■ *Web:* www.hiltonheadisland.org ■ *E-mail:* info@hiltonheadisland.org	Hilton Head Island	SC	29928	843-785-3673	785-7110
Hilton Head Island Mayor 1 Town Center Ct *Web:* www.ci.hilton-head-island.sc.us	Hilton Head Island	SC	29928	843-341-4600	842-7728
Hilton Head Island Town Hall 1 Town Center Ct *Web:* www.ci.hilton-head-island.sc.us	Hilton Head Island	SC	29928	843-341-4600	842-7728
Hilton Head Island Visitors & Convention Bureau PO Box 5647 *TF:* 800-523-3373 ■ *Web:* www.hiltonheadisland.org	Hilton Head Island	SC	29938	843-785-3673	785-7110
Hilton Head Library 11 Beach City Rd	Hilton Head Island	SC	29926	843-785-3266	342-9220

On-Line Resources

Best Read Guide Hilton Head	bestreadguide.com/hiltonhead
City Knowledge Hilton Head Island	www.cityknowledge.com/sc_hiltonhead.htm
Dining Guide	www.conciergediningguide.com/
Hilton Head CityLink	www.usacitylink.com/citylink/sc/hilton-head
Hilton Head Connection	www.aesir.com/HiltonHead/Welcome.html
Hilton Head Island	www.hhisland.com/
Hilton Head Navi-gator	www.navi-gator.com/hiltonhead/
Hilton Head USA	www.hiltonhead-usa.com/
NITC Travelbase City Guide Hilton Head	www.travelbase.com/auto/guides/hilton_head-area-sc.html
Online City Guide to Hilton Head	www.olcg.com/sc/hiltonhead/index.html
Surf & Sun Beach Vacation Guide to Hilton Head Island	www.surf-sun.com/sc-hilton-main.htm
This is Hilton Head	www.this-is-hiltonhead.com/

— Transportation Services —

AIRPORTS

■ **Hilton Head Island Airport (HXD)**

	Phone
7 miles NE of downtown (approx 15 minutes)	843-689-5400

E-mail: adminhxd@hartgray.com

Airport Transportation

	Phone
Ferguson Transportation Limo $15 fare to downtown	843-681-5883
Low Country Taxi & Limo $18 fare to downtown	843-681-8294
Yellow Taxi Cab $15 fare to downtown	843-686-6666

Hilton Head Island (Cont'd)

Commercial Airlines

	Phone
US Airways	800-428-4322

Charter Airlines

	Phone
Corporate America Aviation Inc	800-521-8585

■ Savannah International Airport (SAV)

55 miles SW of downtown Hilton Head Island (approx 60 minutes) 912-964-0514
Web: www.savapt.com ■ *E-mail:* info@savannahairport.com

Airport Transportation

	Phone
AAA Adam Cab Inc $45 fare to downtown Hilton Head	912-927-7466
Southside Taxi Service $60 fare to downtown Hilton Head Island	912-239-9900

Commercial Airlines

	Phone
AirTran	800-247-8726
Continental	800-525-0280
Delta	800-221-1212
United	800-241-6522
US Airways	800-428-4322

Charter Airlines

	Phone
Air Savannah	912-964-5655
Corporate America Aviation Inc	800-521-8585
Savannah Aviation	912-964-1022
Signature Flight Support	912-964-1557

CAR RENTALS

	Phone
Alamo-Savannah	912-964-7364
Avis	843-681-4216
Avis-Savannah	912-964-1781
Budget	843-689-4040
Budget-Savannah	912-966-1771
Enterprise	843-689-9919
Enterprise-Savannah	912-355-6622
Hertz	843-681-7604
Hertz-Savannah	912-964-9595
National	843-681-7368
Sears-Savannah	912-966-1676
Thrifty-Savannah	912-966-2277

LIMO/TAXI

	Phone
AAA Adam Cab Inc	912-927-7466
Carlin Cab	843-785-4854
Checker Cab	843-842-8294
Ferguson Transportation Limo	843-681-5883
Hilton Head Taxi & Limousine	843-785-8294
Low Country Taxi & Limo	843-681-8294
Southside Taxi Service	912-239-9900
Yellow Taxi Cab	843-686-6666

— Accommodations —

HOTEL RESERVATION SERVICES

	Phone	Fax
Vacation Co. *TF:* 800-845-7018 ■ *Web:* www.vacationcompany.com/ ■ *E-mail:* info@vacationcompany.com	843-686-6100	686-3255
Vacations on Hilton Head *TF:* 800-732-7671 ■ *Web:* www.800beachme.com ■ *E-mail:* hhvr@800beachme.com	843-686-3500	686-3701

HOTELS, MOTELS, RESORTS

	City	State	Zip	Phone	Fax
Adventure Inn Beach & Golf Club 41 S Forest Beach Dr *TF:* 800-845-9500	Hilton Head Island	SC	29928	843-785-5151	785-7806
Best Western 40 Waterside Dr *TF:* 888-813-2560	Hilton Head Island	SC	29928	843-842-8888	842-5948
Comfort Inn & Suites 2 Tanglewood Dr *TF:* 800-228-5150	Hilton Head Island	SC	29928	843-842-6662	842-6664
Crowne Plaza Resort 130 Shipyard Dr *TF:* 800-334-1881	Hilton Head Island	SC	29928	843-842-2400	785-8463
Disney Hilton Head Island Resort 22 Harborside Ln *TF:* 800-453-4911 ■ *Web:* disney.go.com/DisneyVacationClub/HiltonHeadIsland/index.html	Hilton Head Island	SC	29928	843-341-4000	341-4151
Fairfield Inn by Marriott 9 Marina Side Dr *TF:* 800-833-6334	Hilton Head Island	SC	29928	843-842-4800	842-4800
Four Points Sheraton Hotel 36 S Forest Beach Dr *TF:* 800-535-3248	Hilton Head Island	SC	29938	843-842-3100	785-6928
Hampton Inn 1 Dillon Rd *Web:* www.hampton-inn.net ■ *E-mail:* mhobson@hampton-inn.net	Hilton Head Island	SC	29926	843-681-7900	681-4330
Harbour Town Golf Links at Seapines Resort 11 Lighthouse Ln *TF:* 800-955-8337 ■ *Web:* www.seapines.com/golf.html	Hilton Head Island	SC	29928	843-363-4485	363-4501
Harbour Town Resort & Yacht Club 149 Lighthouse Rd *TF:* 800-541-7375	Hilton Head Island	SC	29928	843-671-1400	671-0422
Hilton Head Island Beach & Tennis Resort 40 Folly Field Rd *TF:* 800-475-2631	Hilton Head Island	SC	29928	843-842-4402	842-3323
Hilton Oceanfront Resort 23 Ocean Ln *TF:* 800-845-8001 ■ *Web:* www.hilton.com/hotels/HHHHBHF	Hilton Head Island	SC	29928	843-842-8000	341-8033
Hyatt Regency 1 Hyatt Cir *TF:* 800-233-1234 ■ *Web:* www.hyatt.com/usa/hilton_head_island/hotels/hotel_hhhhh.html	Hilton Head Island	SC	29928	843-785-1234	842-4695
Main Street Inn 2200 Main St *TF:* 800-471-3001	Hilton Head Island	SC	29926	843-681-3001	681-5541
Motel 6 830 William Hilton Pkwy *TF:* 800-466-8356	Hilton Head Island	SC	29928	843-785-2700	842-9543
Plantation Inn 200 Museum St *TF:* 800-995-3928	Hilton Head Island	SC	29926	843-681-3655	681-3655
Player's Club Resort 35 De Allyon Ave *TF:* 800-497-7529	Hilton Head Island	SC	29928	843-785-8000	785-9185
Red Roof Inn 5 Regency Pkwy *TF:* 800-843-7663	Hilton Head Island	SC	29928	843-686-6808	842-3352
Residence Inn by Marriott 12 Park Ln *TF:* 800-331-3131	Hilton Head Island	SC	29928	843-686-5700	686-3952
Sea Pines Resort 32 Greenwood Dr *TF:* 800-732-7463	Hilton Head Island	SC	29928	843-785-3333	842-1475
South Beach Marina Inn 232 South Sea Pines Dr	Hilton Head Island	SC	29928	843-671-6498	671-7495
Villamare 27-C Coligny Plaza *TF:* 800-845-6802	Hilton Head Island	SC	29928	843-842-6212	785-2147
Westin Resort at Hilton Head 2 Grasslawn Ave *TF:* 800-228-3000	Hilton Head Island	SC	29928	843-681-4000	681-1087

— Restaurants —

	City	State	Zip	Phone
Abe's Native Shrimp House (Seafood) 650 Hwy 278	Hilton Head Island	SC	29928	843-785-3675
Alexander's Seafood Restaurant (Steak/Seafood) 76 Queens Folly Rd *Web:* www.hiltonheaddlc.com/alexande.htm	Hilton Head Island	SC	29928	843-785-4999
Alligator Grille (Seafood) 1 N Forest Beach Dr Suite 16	Hilton Head Island	SC	29928	843-842-4888
Amigos Cafe y Cantina (Mexican) 70 Pope Ave.	Hilton Head Island	SC	29928	843-785-8226
Anna's Beachside Cafe (Mediterranean) 110 Beach Market	Hilton Head Island	SC	29928	843-842-8797
Antonio's Restaurant (Italian) 1000 William Hilton Pkwy Village at Wexford Suite G-2 *Web:* www.celebrationusa.com	Hilton Head Island	SC	29928	843-842-5505
Bella Italia Bistro (Italian) 95 Matthews Dr Suite 813	Hilton Head Island	SC	29926	843-689-5560
Big Bamboo Cafe (American) B2 Avocet St.	Hilton Head Island	SC	29928	843-686-3443
Boathouse Grill (Seafood) 145 Squire Pope Rd	Hilton Head Island	SC	29926	843-681-3663
Brellas Cafe (American) 130 Shipyard Dr	Hilton Head Island	SC	29928	843-842-2400
Brian's (New American) Main Street Village	Hilton Head Island	SC	29928	843-681-6001
Brick Oven Cafe (American) 33 Office Park Rd Park Plaza Shopping Ctr	Hilton Head Island	SC	29928	843-686-2233
Cafe at Wexford (French) Village at Wexford Bldg J Suite 6 *Web:* www.hiltonheadisland.com/cafeatwexford.htm	Hilton Head Island	SC	29928	843-686-5969
Cafe Europa (Continental) 160 Lighthouse Rd	Hilton Head Island	SC	29928	843-671-3399
Captain John's Galley (Seafood) 232 S Sea Pines Dr	Hilton Head Island	SC	29928	843-671-5199
Cattails Restaurant (Seafood) 302 Moss Creek Village Dr	Hilton Head Island	SC	29926	843-837-7000
Charleston's (Southern) 8 New Orleans Rd	Hilton Head Island	SC	29928	843-785-5008
Charlie's L'Etoile Verte (Seafood) 1000 Plantation Ctr.	Hilton Head Island	SC	29928	843-785-9277
Chart House Restaurant (Steak/Seafood) 106 Helmsman Way	Hilton Head Island	SC	29928	843-785-9666
CQ's Restaurant (French) 170 Lighthouse Ln Harbour Town *Web:* www.celebrationusa.com	Hilton Head Island	SC	29928	843-671-2779

Hilton Head Island — Restaurants (Cont'd)

Name / Address	City	State	Zip	Phone
Crabby Nick's Seafood House (Seafood) 2 Regency Pkwy	Hilton Head Island	SC	29928	843-842-2425
Crazy Crab (Seafood) 149 Lighthouse Rd	Hilton Head Island	SC	29928	843-363-2722
Damon's (Barbecue) Village at Wexford Bldg B Suite 6	Hilton Head Island	SC	29928	843-785-6677
Di Vino Fine Italian Cuisine (Italian) 5 Northridge Plaza	Hilton Head Island	SC	29926	843-681-7700
Express Wok (Chinese) 55 Mathews Dr Suite 150	Hilton Head Island	SC	29926	843-689-8168
Fazio Grill (American) 2 Carnoustie Rd	Hilton Head Island	SC	29928	843-785-1291
Fishtales Bar & Grill (Steak/Seafood) 2 Tanglewood Dr	Hilton Head Island	SC	29928	843-785-8253
Fitzgerald's (Steak/Seafood) 41 S Forest Beach Blvd	Hilton Head Island	SC	29928	843-785-5151
Flannery's Downtown (American) 27 Archer Rd	Hilton Head Island	SC	29928	843-686-3388
Fratello's (Italian) 811 William Hilton Pkwy	Hilton Head Island	SC	29928	843-785-6620
Gaslight (French) 29 Park Plaza	Hilton Head Island	SC	29928	843-785-5814
Giovanna's (Italian) 214 Park Plaza	Hilton Head Island	SC	29928	843-842-7255
Giuseppi's (Italian) 32 Shelter Cove Ln Suite B	Hilton Head Island	SC	29928	843-785-4144
Grouper's & Co (Seafood) 1 S Forest Beach Dr	Hilton Head Island	SC	29928	843-785-5126
Harbourmaster Restaurant (Continental) 1 Shelter Cove Ln	Hilton Head Island	SC	29928	843-785-3030
Harbourside Cafe (American) 149 Lighthouse Rd	Hilton Head Island	SC	29928	843-671-0403
Harold's Beachside Grill (American) 641 US Hwy 278	Hilton Head Island	SC	29928	843-842-9292
Hemingway's (New American) 1 Hyatt Cir Hyatt Regency Hotel	Hilton Head Island	SC	29928	843-785-1234
Henry's Seafood House (Seafood) 7-B Greenwood Dr Suite 1	Hilton Head Island	SC	29928	843-686-2299
Hofbrauhaus Restaurant (German) 8 Pope Ave	Hilton Head Island	SC	29928	843-785-3663
Hudson's (Seafood) 1 Hudsons Rd	Hilton Head Island	SC	29926	843-681-2772
Island Restaurant (Greek) 890 William Hilton Pkwy Suite 1	Hilton Head Island	SC	29928	843-686-6664
It's Greek to Me Inc (Greek) 1 New Orleans Rd Suite G	Hilton Head Island	SC	29928	843-341-3556
Juleps Restaurant (Seafood) 14 Greenwood Dr *Web:* www.hiltonheaddlc.com/juleps.htm	Hilton Head Island	SC	29928	843-842-5857
Just Pasta (Italian) 1 Coligny Plaza	Hilton Head Island	SC	29928	843-686-3900
Kingfisher (Seafood) 18 Harborside Ln Shelter Cove Harbour	Hilton Head Island	SC	29928	843-785-4442
Kurama Japanese Restaurant (Japanese) 9 Palmetto Bay Rd	Hilton Head Island	SC	29928	843-785-4955
Little Venice (Italian) Hwy 278 & Shelter Cove Rd Shelter Cove Marina	Hilton Head Island	SC	29928	843-785-3300
Makoto Japanese Seafood (Japanese) 39 New Orleans Rd	Hilton Head Island	SC	29928	843-785-7199
Mi Tierra Mexican Restaurant (Mexican) 160 William Hilton Pkwy Suite 6	Hilton Head Island	SC	29926	843-342-3409
Pepper Beach Grill (American) 1034 US Hwy 278	Hilton Head Island	SC	29928	843-785-5299
Quarterdeck (Steak/Seafood) 149 Lighthouse Rd	Hilton Head Island	SC	29928	843-671-2222
Reilley's (Irish) 7D Greenwood Dr	Hilton Head Island	SC	29928	843-842-4414
Remy's Restaurant (Steak/Seafood) 28 Arrow Rd	Hilton Head Island	SC	29928	843-842-3800
Rendez-Vous Cafe (French) 14 Greenwood Dr	Hilton Head Island	SC	29928	843-785-5070
Robert's Restaurant (American) 5 Robert Trent Jones Ln	Hilton Head Island	SC	29928	843-785-1165
San Miguel's Mexican Cafe (Mexican) Shelter Cove Harbor Bldg 3	Hilton Head Island	SC	29928	843-842-4555
Spartina Grill (New American) 70 Marshland Rd	Hilton Head Island	SC	29926	843-689-2433
Starfire Contemporary Bistro (New American) 37 New Orleans Rd	Hilton Head Island	SC	29928	843-785-3434
Stellini Italian Restaurant (Italian) 15 Pope Ave Executive Park	Hilton Head Island	SC	29928	843-785-7006
Tapas Restaurant (International) 11 Northridge Plaza *Web:* www.tapasrestaurant.com/ ■ *E-mail:* thetapas@aol.com	Hilton Head Island	SC	29926	843-681-8590

— Goods and Services —

SHOPPING

Name / Address	City	State	Zip	Phone	Fax
Coligny Plaza Coligny Plaza Shopping Center Bldg K-8	Hilton Head Island	SC	29928	843-842-6050	686-3270
Hilton Head Factory Stores I 1270 Fording Island Rd (Hwy 278) *TF:* 888-746-7333 ■ *Web:* www.shophiltonhead.com ■ *E-mail:* info@shophiltonhead.com	Bluffton	SC	29910	843-837-4339	837-4141
Hilton Head Factory Stores II 1414 Fording Island Rd (Hwy 278) *TF:* 888-746-7333 ■ *Web:* www.shophiltonhead.com ■ *E-mail:* info@shophiltonhead.com	Bluffton	SC	29910	843-837-4339	837-4141
Main Street Village 200 Main St Suite 201-B	Hilton Head Island	SC	29926	843-681-5500	681-5583
Mall at Shelter Cove 24 Shelter Cove Ln Box 326	Hilton Head Island	SC	29928	843-686-3090	686-5581
Pineland Station 430 William Hilton Pkwy	Hilton Head Island	SC	29928	843-681-8907	689-3368
Shoppes on the Parkway 890 William Hilton Pkwy	Hilton Head Island	SC	29928	843-686-6233	686-5064
Swan House Antiques Gallery 88 Arrow Rd	Hilton Head Island	SC	29928	843-785-7926	

BANKS

Name / Address	City	State	Zip	Phone	Fax
Anchor Bank 62 New Orleans Rd	Hilton Head	SC	29928	843-785-4848	341-4535
Atlantic Savings Bank FSB Village at Wexford Suite F-4	Hilton Head	SC	29928	843-686-9600	686-9683
Carolina First Bank 401 William Hilton Pkwy *TF:* 800-892-2655 ■ *Web:* www.carolinafirst.com	Hilton Head Island	SC	29926	843-689-6414	681-4261
First Union National Bank 4 Pope Ave *TF:* 800-275-3862	Hilton Head Island	SC	29928	843-686-5100	842-9522
Liberty Savings Bank FSB 4 Southwood Park Dr	Hilton Head Island	SC	29926	843-689-2343	689-9905
Lighthouse Community Bank 2 Greenwood Dr *TF:* 888-686-5505	Hilton Head Island	SC	29928	843-341-2100	341-2121
National Bank of South Carolina 430 William Hilton Pkwy	Hilton Head Island	SC	29926	843-681-2800	681-2801
NationsBank 59 Pope Ave	Hilton Head Island	SC	29928	843-686-1456	686-1422
Regions Bank 77 Pope Ave	Hilton Head Island	SC	29928	843-785-4249	842-5626
Wachovia Bank NA 1 Sea Pines Cir	Hilton Head Island	SC	29928	843-686-9343	686-9363

BUSINESS SERVICES

Name	Phone
Adecco Employment Personnel Services	843-785-7373
Business Center Plus	843-842-6992
Curry Printing & Copy Center	843-681-3410
Mail Boxes Etc	843-689-6507
Post Office	843-681-3548
Smith Personnel Inc	843-785-4604
Sneakers Courier Service	843-785-5777
STAT Courier Service	843-785-6520
Tempo Personnel Service	843-681-9066
UPS	800-742-5877

— Media —

PUBLICATIONS

Name / Address	City	State	Zip	Phone	Fax
Hilton Head Monthly 5 Office Park Rd Suite 205	Hilton Head Island	SC	29928	843-842-6988	842-5743
Hilton Head News 1316 Fording Island Rd	Bluffton	SC	29910	843-785-5255	837-5266
Island Packet‡ PO Box 5727 *Web:* www.islandpacket.com ■ *E-mail:* info@islandpacket.com	Hilton Head Island	SC	29938	843-785-4293	706-3070

‡*Daily newspapers*

TELEVISION

Name / Address	City	State	Zip	Phone	Fax
WHHI-TV Ch 3 (Ind) 103 Courtyard Bldg	Hilton Head Island	SC	29928	843-785-4545	
WJCL-TV Ch 22 (ABC) 10001 Abercorn Ext	Savannah	GA	31406	912-925-0022	921-2235
WJWJ-TV Ch 6 (PBS) 430 William Hilton Pkwy Suite 205	Hilton Head Island	SC	29926	843-681-5449	
WSAV-TV Ch 3 (NBC) 1430 E Victory Dr *Web:* www.wsav.com ■ *E-mail:* wsav@ix.netcom.com	Savannah	GA	31404	912-651-0300	651-0304
WTGS-TV Ch 28 (Fox) 10001 Abercorn St	Savannah	GA	31420	912-925-2287	921-2235
WTOC-TV Ch 11 (CBS) PO Box 8086 *Web:* www.wtoctv.com ■ *E-mail:* wtoctv@sava.gulfnet.com	Savannah	GA	31412	912-234-1111	232-4945

RADIO

Name / Address	City	State	Zip	Phone	Fax
WFXH-AM 1130 kHz (Sports) 1 St Augustine Pl	Hilton Head Island	SC	29928	843-785-9569	842-3369
WFXH-FM 106.1 MHz (CR) 1 St Augustine Pl	Hilton Head Island	SC	29928	843-785-9569	842-3369

Hilton Head Island — Radio (Cont'd)

				Phone	Fax
WGCO-FM 98.3 & 103.1 MHz (Oldies) 401 Mall Blvd Suite 201F	Savannah	GA	31406	912-351-9830	352-4821
WGZO-FM 98.3 MHz (Oldies) 1 St Augustine Pl	Hilton Head Island	SC	29928	843-785-9569	842-3369
WGZR-FM 104.9 MHz (Ctry) 1 St Augustine Pl	Hilton Head Island	SC	29928	843-785-9569	842-3369
WHBZ-FM 99.7 MHz (Oldies) 37 New Orleans Rd	Hilton Head Island	SC	29928	843-686-6877	686-5983
WIXV-FM 95.5 MHz (Rock) 1 Riverview Rd	Savannah	GA	31410	912-897-1529	897-4047
Web: www.rockofsavannah.com					
WLOW-FM 107.9 MHz (AC) 1 St Augustine Pl	Hilton Head Island	SC	29928	843-785-9569	842-3369
WVVE-FM 106.9 MHz (AC) 1 St Augustine Pl	Hilton Head Island	SC	29928	843-785-9569	
WWVV-FM 106.9 MHz (AC) 1 St Augustine Pl	Hilton Head Island	SC	29928	843-785-3001	842-3369

— Colleges/Universities —

				Phone	Fax
Technical College of the Low Country 921 Ribaut Rd	Beaufort	SC	29901	843-525-8324	525-8208
TF: 800-768-8252 ■ *Web:* www.tcl-tec-sc-us.org					
University of South Carolina Hilton Head Island 1 College Center Dr	Hilton Head Island	SC	29928	843-785-3995	785-7730

— Hospitals —

				Phone	Fax
Hilton Head Medical Center 25 Hospital Center Blvd	Hilton Head Island	SC	29926	843-681-6122	689-8211*
**Fax:* Admitting ■ *Web:* www.tenethealth.com/HiltonHead/hs/					

— Attractions —

				Phone	Fax
Brothers Amusements 78-D Arrow Rd	Hilton Head Island	SC	29928	843-785-7270	785-8460
TF: 800-794-8049					
Coastal Discovery Museum 100 William Hilton Pkwy	Hilton Head Island	SC	29926	843-689-6767	689-6769
Web: www.hhisland.com/hiltonhead/museum.html ■ *E-mail:* hhimuseum@hargray.com					
Endangered Arts Ltd 841 William Hilton Pkwy South Island Sq Unit B	Hilton Head Island	SC	29928	843-785-5075	341-5075
Web: www.hiltonheadisland.com/endanger.htm ■ *E-mail:* wylandhhi@aol.com					
John Stobart Gallery 149 Lighthouse Rd	Hilton Head Island	SC	29928	843-671-2739	671-2789
TF: 800-435-8992 ■ *Web:* www.hiltonheadisland.com/stobart.htm ■ *E-mail:* stobart@icglink.com					
Newhall Audubon Preserve Palmetto Bay Rd	Hilton Head Island	SC	29928	843-785-5775	
Pinckney Island National Wildlife Preserve Hwy 278	Hilton Head Island	SC	29928	912-652-4415	
Self Family Arts Center 14 Shelter Cove Ln	Hilton Head Island	SC	29928	843-686-3945	842-7877

— Events —

	Phone
Antique Show (late June & early November)	843-686-3090
Art & Flower Show (late April)	843-785-3673
Arts & Crafts Show (late May & mid-October)	843-686-3090
Banana Open Mixed Doubles (mid-July)	843-785-6613
Banana Open Singles (mid-August)	843-785-6613
Chili Cook-off (early October)	843-785-7738
Ghost Stories (late October)	843-363-4530
Golf Fair (mid-April)	843-785-1136
HarbourFest (mid-June-late August)	843-785-1106
Hilton Head Island Celebrity Golf Tournament (early September)	843-842-7711
Hilton Head Playhouse Series (September-May)	843-686-3945
July 4th Celebration (July 4)	843-785-3673
MCI Classic (mid-April)	800-234-1107
Taste of the Season (mid-November)	843-785-3673
Thanksgiving Hayride (late November)	843-363-4530
Week of Champions (early-mid-June)	843-757-2150

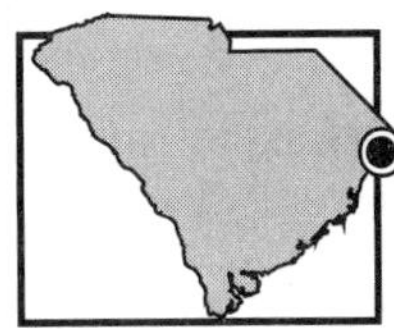

Myrtle Beach

Visited by 12 million adults and children each year, Myrtle Beach is hailed as one of the top vacation spots in the nation. The Grand Strand, a 60-mile stretch of beach, encompasses all varieties of dining, shopping, and attractions. Popular recreational activities in the area include fishing, tennis, and golf—and the city boasts more than 90 courses. Myrtle Beach is also popularly known as the "miniature golf course capital of the world", with more than 40 courses in the area.. The city also features plantations, centuries-old churches, and Brookgreen Gardens, the world's largest outdoor sculpture gardens. Another major attraction is the Carolina Opry, a theater featuring music, magic, and more. The city also holds a number of events each year, the most popular being the Grand Strand Fishing Rodeo, a Myrtle Beach traditon since 1954.

Population	25,284	**Longitude**	78-53-32 W
Area (Land)	15.5 sq mi	**County**	Horry
Area (Water)	0.0 sq mi	**Time Zone**	EST
Elevation	30 ft	**Area Code/s**	843
Latitude	33-41-56 N		

— Average Temperatures and Precipitation —

TEMPERATURES

	Jan	Feb	Mar	Apr	May	Jun	Jul	Aug	Sep	Oct	Nov	Dec
High	58	62	70	78	84	89	92	90	85	77	70	61
Low	35	38	45	51	59	66	70	70	65	53	45	38

PRECIPITATION

	Jan	Feb	Mar	Apr	May	Jun	Jul	Aug	Sep	Oct	Nov	Dec
Inches	3.7	3.8	4.1	2.8	3.8	5.2	6.0	6.2	4.4	3.4	2.8	3.3

— Important Phone Numbers —

	Phone		Phone
AAA	843-692-9601	**Poison Control Center**	800-922-1117
Emergency	911	**Time/Temp**	843-293-6600
HotelDocs	800-468-3537	**Weather**	843-293-6600
Medical Referral	843-716-7000		

— Information Sources —

				Phone	Fax
Better Business Bureau Serving Coastal North & South Carolina 1601 N Oak St Suite 101	Myrtle Beach	SC	29577	843-626-6881	626-7455
Web: www.mb.bbb.org ■ *E-mail:* mrtlebcb@gte.net					
Center for Economic Development PO Box 261954	Conway	SC	29528	843-349-2686	349-2455
Horry County PO Box 677	Conway	SC	29528	843-248-1200	248-1341
Myrtle Beach Area Chamber of Commerce 1200 N Oak St	Myrtle Beach	SC	29578	843-626-7444	626-0009
TF: 800-356-3016 ■ *Web:* www.mbchamber.com					

Myrtle Beach — Information Sources (Cont'd)

				Phone	Fax
Myrtle Beach Area Convention Bureau 1200 N Oak St	Myrtle Beach	SC	29577	843-626-7444	448-3010
TF: 800-488-8998 ■ *Web:* www.myrtlebeach-info.com					
Myrtle Beach Chapin Memorial Library 400 14th Ave N	Myrtle Beach	SC	29577	843-918-1275	918-1288
Web: 165.166.112.103/library.html					
Myrtle Beach City Hall 937 Broadway	Myrtle Beach	SC	29577	843-918-1000	918-1028
Web: www.cityofmyrtlebeach.com					
Myrtle Beach Convention Center 2101 N Oak St	Myrtle Beach	SC	29577	843-918-1225	444-6408
TF: 800-537-1690 ■ *Web:* www.myrtlebeachconvcntr.com					
Myrtle Beach Mayor 937 Broadway	Myrtle Beach	SC	29577	843-918-1000	918-1028
Web: www.cityofmyrtlebeach.com					

On-Line Resources

4MyrtleBeach.com www.4myrtlebeach.com
Access America Myrtle Beach .... www.accessamer.com/myrtlebeach/
AllAboutMyrtleBeach.com .... www.allaboutmyrtlebeach.com
Area Guide Myrtle Beach .... myrtlebeach.areaguides.net
Beach Access @ thegrandstrand.com .... www.thegrandstrand.com
City Knowledge Myrtle Beach .... www.cityknowledge.com/sc_myrtlebeach.htm
Discover Myrtle Beach .... www.discovermyrtlebeach.com
Excite.com Myrtle Beach City Guide .... www.excite.com/travel/countries/united_states/south_carolina/myrtle_beach
Insiders' Guide to Myrtle Beach .... www.insiders.com/myrtle-beach/
MetroDine Myrtle Beach .... www.metrodine.com/myrtlebeach
Myrtle Beach Access .... www.myrtlebeachaccess.com
Myrtle Beach CityLink .... usacitylink.com/citylink/sc/myrtle-beach/
Myrtle Beach Connection www3.aesir.com/MyrtleBeach/welcome.html
Myrtle Beach Directory .... www.scad.com/myrtleb
Myrtle Beach Golf.com .... www.myrtlebeachgolf.com
Myrtle Beach Live .... www.myrtlebeachlive.com
Myrtle Beach Navi-gator .... www.navi-gator.com/mb
Myrtle Online .... city-info.com/main.html
NITC Travelbase City Guide Myrtle Beach .... www.travelbase.com/auto/guides/myrtle_beach-area-sc.html
Online City Guide to Myrtle Beach .... www.olcg.com/sc/myrtlebeach/index.html
Sunny Day Guide Grand Strand .... www.sunnydayguides.com/gs/
Surf & Sun Beach Vacation Guide to Myrtle Beach .... www.surf-sun.com/sc-myrtle-main.htm
Travel Myrtle Beach .... www.travelmyrtlebeach.com

— Transportation Services —

AIRPORTS

■ **Myrtle Beach International Airport (MYR)**

	Phone
2 miles S of downtown (approx 15 minutes)	843-448-1589

Airport Transportation

	Phone
Carolina Cab $7 fare to downtown	843-626-2050
Coastal Cabs $8 fare to downtown	843-448-4444
Executive Coach Services $7 fare to downtown	843-448-4047

Commercial Airlines

	Phone		Phone
Air Canada	800-776-3000	**Spirit**	800-772-7117
Atlantic Southeast	800-282-3424	**US Airways**	800-428-4322
Comair	800-354-9822		

Charter Airlines

	Phone
Corporate America Aviation Inc	800-521-8585

CAR RENTALS

	Phone		Phone
Alamo	800-327-9633	**Enterprise**	843-626-4277
Avis	843-448-1751	**Hertz**	843-448-8235
Budget	843-626-4770	**National**	843-626-3687
Dollar	843-626-2277	**Thrifty**	843-626-6527

LIMO/TAXI

	Phone		Phone
Absolute Limo & Bus	843-272-1182	**Executive Coach Services**	843-448-4047
American Cab	843-444-2970	**Midnight Express Limos**	843-236-7910
Carolina Cab	843-626-2050	**Midnite Express**	843-626-6369
Coastal Cabs	843-448-4444	**National Transportation/VIP Limo**	800-659-7053
Coker's Cab	843-448-4170	**Ritz Limousines**	843-497-7288

MASS TRANSIT

	Phone
CRPTA Bus $.75 Base fare	843-248-7277

RAIL/BUS

				Phone
Greyhound Bus Station 511 7th Ave N	Myrtle Beach	SC	29577	843-448-2472
TF: 800-231-2222				

— Accommodations —

HOTEL RESERVATION SERVICES

	Phone	Fax
Hotels @ Nevada Room Reservation Services	800-449-4701	
Web: www.biznet.mb.ca		
Myrtle Beach Reservation Service	843-626-7477	
TF: 800-626-7477 ■ *Web:* www.mbhospitality.com		
Room Finders USA	504-522-9373	529-1948
TF: 800-473-7829 ■ *Web:* www.roomsusa.com ■ *E-mail:* welcome@roomsusa.com		
USA Hotels	252-331-1555	331-2021
TF: 800-872-4683 ■ *Web:* www.1800usahotels.com ■ *E-mail:* info@1800usahotels.com		

HOTELS, MOTELS, RESORTS

				Phone	Fax
Anderson Inn 2600 N Ocean Blvd	Myrtle Beach	SC	29577	843-448-1535	
TF: 800-437-7376 ■ *Web:* www.hotelroom.com/scarolina/mbanderson.html					
Beach Colony Resort 5308 N Ocean Blvd	Myrtle Beach	SC	29577	843-449-4010	449-2810
TF: 800-222-2414 ■ *Web:* www.beachcolony.com ■ *E-mail:* bhcolony@sccoast.net					
Beach Dunes 1807 S Ocean Blvd	Myrtle Beach	SC	29577	843-626-3653	946-6443
Best Western 1525 S Ocean Blvd	North Myrtle Beach	SC	29577	843-272-6101	
TF: 800-588-3570					
Beverly Motel 703 N Ocean Blvd	Myrtle Beach	SC	29577	843-448-9496	
TF: 800-843-0415 ■ *Web:* www.beverlymotel.com					
Bluewater Resort 2001 S Ocean Blvd	Myrtle Beach	SC	29577	843-626-8345	448-2310
TF: 800-845-6994 ■ *Web:* www.bluewaterresort.com ■ *E-mail:* bluewatr@sccoast.net					
Breakers Resort 2006 N Ocean Blvd	Myrtle Beach	SC	29577	843-626-5000	626-5001
TF: 800-845-0688 ■ *Web:* www.breakers.com					
Breakers Resort North Tower PO Box 485	Myrtle Beach	SC	29578	843-444-4440	626-5001
TF: 800-845-0688					
Brustman House 400 25th Ave S	Myrtle Beach	SC	29577	843-448-7699	626-2478
Budget Inn 504 N Ocean Blvd	Myrtle Beach	SC	29577	843-448-1671	
TF: 800-968-1671					
Caravelle Resort Hotel & Villas 6900 N Ocean Blvd	Myrtle Beach	SC	29572	843-918-8000	449-0643
TF: 800-845-0893 ■ *Web:* www.thecaravelle.com					
Caribbean Resort & Villas 3000 N Ocean Blvd	Myrtle Beach	SC	29577	843-448-7181	448-3224
TF: 800-845-0883					
Cherry Tree Inn 5400 N Ocean Blvd	Myrtle Beach	SC	29577	843-449-6425	449-6424
Comfort Inn 1755 Hwy 17 N	North Myrtle Beach	SC	29582	843-249-2490	280-5494
TF: 800-494-4489					
Compass Cove Ocean Resort 2311 S Ocean Blvd	Myrtle Beach	SC	29577	843-448-8373	448-5444
TF: 800-228-9894 ■ *Web:* www.compasscove.com					
Coral Beach Resort Hotel & Suites 1105 S Ocean Blvd	Myrtle Beach	SC	29577	843-448-8421	626-0156
TF: 800-843-2684 ■ *Web:* www.coral-beach.com					
Court Capri Hotel 2610 N Ocean Blvd	Myrtle Beach	SC	29577	843-448-6119	626-9259
TF: 800-533-1388 ■ *Web:* www.courtcapri.com ■ *E-mail:* ctcapri@sccoast.net					
David's Landing 2708 S Ocean Blvd	Myrtle Beach	SC	29577	843-448-8488	
TF: 800-561-3504					
Days Inn 2104 N Ocean Blvd	Myrtle Beach	SC	29577	843-448-1776	
TF: 800-448-8541					
Days Inn 205 77th Ave N	Myrtle Beach	SC	29572	843-449-7431	
TF: 800-845-0656					

Myrtle Beach — Hotels, Motels, Resorts (Cont'd)

				Phone	Fax
Days Inn 601 S Ocean Blvd *TF:* 800-521-7333	Myrtle Beach	SC	29577	843-448-1491	
Dunes Village Resort 5200 N Ocean Blvd *TF:* 800-648-3539	Myrtle Beach	SC	29577	843-449-5275	449-2107
Fairfield Inn by Marriott 1350 Paradise Cir	Myrtle Beach	SC	29577	843-444-8097	444-8394
Firebird Motor Inn 2007 S Ocean Blvd *TF:* 800-852-7032 ■ *Web:* www.firebirdinn.com ■ *E-mail:* firebird@firebirdinn.com	Myrtle Beach	SC	29577	843-448-7032	448-9281
Four Seasons Beach Resort 5801 N Ocean Blvd *TF:* 800-277-8562	Myrtle Beach	SC	29577	843-449-6441	
Foxfire Motor Inn 1403 S Ocean Blvd *TF:* 800-826-2779 ■ *E-mail:* foxfire@worldnet.att.net	Myrtle Beach	SC	29575	843-448-1636	
Hampton Inn 1140 Celebrity Cir *TF:* 888-916-2001	Myrtle Beach	SC	29577	843-916-0600	
Holiday Inn Resort Hotel 1200 N Ocean Blvd *TF:* 800-874-7401 ■ *Web:* www.holidayinnresort.com ■ *E-mail:* hiresort@sccoast.net	Myrtle Beach	SC	29577	843-913-5805	
Indigo Inn 2209 S Ocean Blvd *TF:* 800-448-1631 ■ *Web:* www.indigoinnmyrtlebeach.com	Myrtle Beach	SC	29577	843-448-5101	
Island Green Golf Villas 455 Sunnehanna Dr. *Web:* www.aboveparvacations.com	Myrtle Beach	SC	29575	843-650-1115	650-6446
Jonathan Harbour Hotel 2611 S Ocean Blvd *TF:* 800-448-1948 ■ *Web:* www.jhoceanfront.com	Myrtle Beach	SC	29577	843-448-1948	445-1624
La Quinta Inn 1561 21st Ave N *TF:* 800-687-6667	Myrtle Beach	SC	29577	843-916-8801	916-8701
Meridian Plaza Resort 2310 N Ocean Blvd *TF:* 800-323-3011	Myrtle Beach	SC	29577	843-626-4734	448-4569
Myrtle Beach Martinique Resort Hotel 7100 N Ocean Blvd *TF:* 800-542-0048 ■ *Web:* www.mbmartinique.com/mart	Myrtle Beach	SC	29577	843-449-4441	497-3041
Myrtle Beach Resort 5905 S Kings Hwy *TF:* 800-845-0629 ■ *Web:* www.myrtle-beach-resort.com	Myrtle Beach	SC	29575	843-238-1559	238-2424
Mystic Sea Resort 2105 S Ocean Blvd	Myrtle Beach	SC	29578	843-448-8466	626-2024
Ocean Dunes/Sand Dunes Resort & Villas 201 74th Ave N *TF:* 800-845-6701	Myrtle Beach	SC	29578	843-449-7441	449-0558
Ocean Forest Villa Resort 5601 N Ocean Blvd *TF:* 800-845-0347	Myrtle Beach	SC	29577	843-449-9661	449-9207
Ocean Park Resort 1905 S Ocean Blvd *TF:* 800-624-8539	Myrtle Beach	SC	29578	843-448-1915	626-2966
Palms The 2500 N Ocean Blvd *TF:* 800-528-0451	Myrtle Beach	SC	29578	843-626-8334	448-1950
Patricia Grand Resort 2710 N Ocean Blvd *TF:* 800-255-4763 ■ *Web:* www.patricia.com	Myrtle Beach	SC	29577	843-448-8453	448-3080
Poindexter Golf Resort 1702 N Ocean Blvd *TF:* 800-248-0003	Myrtle Beach	SC	29577	843-448-8327	448-0043
Red Roof Inn 2801 S Kings Hwy *TF:* 800-868-1990	Myrtle Beach	SC	29577	843-626-4444	626-0753
Reef Resort 2101 S Ocean Blvd *TF:* 800-845-1212	Myrtle Beach	SC	29577	843-448-1765	448-3288
Sea Crest Resort 803 S Ocean Blvd *TF:* 800-845-1112 ■ *Web:* www.seacrestresort.com	Myrtle Beach	SC	29577	843-913-5800	913-5801
Sea Mist Resort 1200 S Ocean Blvd *TF:* 800-732-6478 ■ *Web:* www.seamist.com ■ *E-mail:* seamist@sccoast.net	Myrtle Beach	SC	29577	843-448-1551	448-5858
Sportsman Motor Inn 1405 S Ocean Blvd *TF:* 800-334-5547 ■ *Web:* www.hads.net/sportsmanmotorinn	Myrtle Beach	SC	29578	843-448-4311	
Strand Central Station 1957 10th Ave N *TF:* 888-544-7266 ■ *E-mail:* strandcs@aol.com	Myrtle Beach	SC	29577	843-444-5600	448-4100
Tropical Seas 2807 S Ocean Blvd *TF:* 800-438-5015 ■ *Web:* www.tropicalseashotel.com	Myrtle Beach	SC	29577	843-448-1171	448-0253
Tropical Winds Hotel 705 S Ocean Blvd *TF:* 800-843-3466	Myrtle Beach	SC	29578	843-448-4304	
Waterside Inn 2000 N Ocean Blvd *TF:* 800-248-8286 ■ *Web:* www.watersideinn.com	Myrtle Beach	SC	29577	843-448-5935	448-3577
Wyndham Myrtle Beach Resort 10000 Beach Club Dr *TF:* 800-248-9228	Myrtle Beach	SC	29572	843-449-5000	497-0168
Yachtsman Resort Hotel 1400 N Ocean Blvd *TF:* 800-868-8886 ■ *Web:* www.yachtsmanhotel.com ■ *E-mail:* yachtsmn@sccoast.net	Myrtle Beach	SC	29577	843-448-1441	626-6261

— Restaurants —

				Phone
Angelo's (Italian) 2011 S Kings Hwy	Myrtle Beach	SC	29577	843-626-2800
Benito's Restaurante (Italian) 1310 Celebrity Cir Broadway at the Beach	Myrtle Beach	SC	29577	843-444-0006
Carolina Roadhouse (Steak/Seafood) 4617 N Kings Hwy	Myrtle Beach	SC	29577	843-497-9911
Chesapeake House (Seafood) 9918 N Kings Hwy	Myrtle Beach	SC	29572	843-449-3231
Crab House (Seafood) 1313 Celebrity Cir Broadway at the Beach	Myrtle Beach	SC	29577	843-444-2717
Daruma Japanese Restaurant (Japanese) 960 Lake Arrowhead Rd	Myrtle Beach	SC	29572	843-497-6038
Flamingo Grill (Steak/Seafood) 7100 N Kings Hwy	Myrtle Beach	SC	29572	843-449-5388
Four Seasons Restaurant (Continental) 10600 N Kings Hwy	Myrtle Beach	SC	29572	843-272-9621
Giovanni's Italian Gourmet (Italian) 504 27th Ave N Suite H	Myrtle Beach	SC	29577	843-626-8995
Golden Gate Restaurant (Chinese) 1201 N Kings Hwy	Myrtle Beach	SC	29577	843-448-9367
Grecian Corner I (Greek) 9606 N Kings Hwy	Myrtle Beach	SC	29572	843-449-9234
Gullyfield Restaurant (Steak/Seafood) 9916 N Kings Hwy	Myrtle Beach	SC	29572	843-449-3111
Horst Gasthaus (German) 802 37th Ave S.	North Myrtle Beach	SC	29582	843-272-3351
Key West Grill (Seafood) 1214 Celebrity Cir	Myrtle Beach	SC	29577	843-444-3663
Latif's Bakery & Cafe (Continental) 503 61st Ave N.	Myrtle Beach	SC	29577	843-449-1716
Mario's Italian Restaurant (Italian) 2500 N Kings Hwy	Myrtle Beach	SC	29577	843-626-0139
Martin's Restaurant (American) 7300 N Ocean Blvd	Myrtle Beach	SC	29572	843-449-1368
Miyabi (Japanese) 9732 N Kings Hwy	Myrtle Beach	SC	29572	843-449-9294
Nakato Japanese Steak House (Japanese) 9912 Hwy 17 N	Myrtle Beach	SC	29577	843-449-3344
Pier 14 Restaurant & Lounge (Steak/Seafood) 1304 N Ocean Blvd.	Myrtle Beach	SC	29577	843-448-4314
Planet Hollywood (American) 2915 Hollywood Dr	Myrtle Beach	SC	29577	843-916-0411
Ramando's Italian Ristorante (Italian) 2001 N Kings Hwy	Myrtle Beach	SC	29577	843-626-7060
Roma Restaurant (Italian) 5815 N Kings Hwy	Myrtle Beach	SC	29577	843-449-9359
Rossi's (Italian) 9636 N Kings Hwy	Myrtle Beach	SC	29577	843-449-0481
Sir John's Restaurant (Seafood) 411 N Kings Hwy	Myrtle Beach	SC	29577	843-626-7896
Sun Wah Restaurant (Chinese) 2711 Beaver Run Blvd	Surfside Beach	SC	29575	843-215-4525
Villa Mare (Italian) 7819 N Kings Hwy	Myrtle Beach	SC	29577	843-449-8654
Yamato Steak House of Japan (Japanese) 1213 Celebrity Cir Suite R-5 *Web:* www.yamato-inc.com	Myrtle Beach	SC	29577	843-448-1959

— Goods and Services —

SHOPPING

				Phone	Fax
Barefoot Landing 4898 Hwy 17 S. *TF:* 800-272-2320 ■ *Web:* www.bflanding.com	Myrtle Beach	SC	29582	843-272-8349	272-1052
Briarcliffe Mall 10177 N Kings Hwy **Fax:* Mktg ■ *E-mail:* peox@colonialprop.com	Myrtle Beach	SC	29572	843-272-4040	272-4090*
Broadway at the Beach 1325 Celebrity Cir *TF:* 800-386-4662 ■ *Web:* www.broadwayatthebeach.com	Myrtle Beach	SC	29577	843-444-3200	444-3222
Inlet Square Mall 10125 Hwy 17 Bypass	Murells Inlet	SC	29576	843-651-6990	651-7670
Myrtle Beach Antiques Mall 1014 Hwy 501 *E-mail:* oldthings@earthlink.net	Myrtle Beach	SC	29577	843-448-4762	
Myrtle Beach Factory Outlet 3001 N Kings Hwy	Myrtle Beach	SC	29577	843-626-9344	626-9524
Myrtle Beach Factory Stores 4635 Factory Stores Blvd. *Web:* www.shopmyrtlebeach.com ■ *E-mail:* info@shopmyrtlebeach.com	Myrtle Beach	SC	29579	843-236-5100	
Myrtle Square Mall 2501 N Kings Hwy	Myrtle Beach	SC	29577	843-448-2513	626-3595
North Myrtle Beach Swap Lot & Flea Market 100 Hwy 17 N	North Myrtle Beach	SC	29582	843-249-4701	

BANKS

				Phone	Fax
Anchor Bank 2002 Oak St	Myrtle Beach	SC	29577	843-448-1411	946-3169
Beach First National Bank 1550 N Oak St	Myrtle Beach	SC	29577	843-626-2265	916-7818
Carolina First Bank 2003 Oak St.	Myrtle Beach	SC	29577	843-448-9458	626-1726
Coastal FSB 2619 N Oak St *TF:* 800-613-8179	Myrtle Beach	SC	29577	843-448-5151	626-0410
Conway National Bank 9726 Hwy 17 N.	Myrtle Beach	SC	29572	843-449-3373	449-9967
First Citizens Bank & Trust Co 7400 N Kings Hwy	Myrtle Beach	SC	29572	843-449-9687	497-2580
First Union National Bank 2110 Oak St.	Myrtle Beach	SC	29577	843-448-2688	448-6447

Myrtle Beach — Banks (Cont'd)

				Phone	Fax
National Bank of South Carolina 2411 Oak St.	Myrtle Beach	SC	29577	843-626-1800	626-1807
NationsBank NA 2501 Oak St.	Myrtle Beach	SC	29577	843-946-2100	946-3211
Wachovia Bank NA 1200 N Kings Hwy	Myrtle Beach	SC	29578	843-626-5681	
TF: 800-922-4684 ■ *Web:* www.wachovia.com					

BUSINESS SERVICES

	Phone
DHL Worldwide Express	800-225-5345
Eastern Personnel Services	843-626-7620
Federal Express	800-238-5355
Grand Strand Personnel	843-293-7470
Interim Personnel	843-449-6727
Kelly Services	843-626-4403
Kinko's	843-626-5592
Mail Boxes Etc	843-626-2626
Mega Force Temporaries	843-449-7305
Palmetto Temporary Services	843-449-8544
Post Office	843-626-9533
Staff Mark	843-293-0074
UPS	800-742-5877

— Media —

PUBLICATIONS

				Phone	Fax
Myrtle Beach Herald 2105-B Farlow St	Myrtle Beach	SC	29577	843-626-3131	448-4860
E-mail: mbherald@aol.com					
Strand Magazine 1357 21st Ave N Suite 102	Myrtle Beach	SC	29577	843-626-8911	626-6452
Web: city-info.com/strand.html					
Sun News‡ PO Box 406	Myrtle Beach	SC	29578	843-626-8555	626-0356
TF: 800-568-1800 ■ *Web:* www.myrtlebeachaccess.com					

‡*Daily newspapers*

TELEVISION

				Phone	Fax
WBTW-TV Ch 13 (CBS) 101 McDonald Ct	Myrtle Beach	SC	29577	843-293-1301	293-7701
Web: www.wbtw.com					
WFXB-TV Ch 43 (Fox) 3364 Huger St	Myrtle Beach	SC	29577	843-828-4300	828-4343
Web: www.wfxb.com ■ *E-mail:* listen43@wfxb.com					
WIS-TV Ch 10 (NBC) 1111 Bull St.	Columbia	SC	29201	803-758-1218	758-1278*
**Fax:* News Rm ■ *Web:* www.wistv.com ■ *E-mail:* wis-tv10@aol.com					
WPDE-TV Ch 15 (ABC) 2411 Oak St Suite 206	Myrtle Beach	SC	29577	843-448-9733	626-2504
TF: 800-698-9733 ■ *Web:* www.wpdetv15.com					
WRJA-TV Ch 27 (PBS) 18 N Harvin St.	Sumter	SC	29150	803-773-5546	775-1059
WWMB-TV Ch 21 (UPN) 2411 N Oak St Suite 206	Myrtle Beach	SC	29577	843-448-9733	626-2504

RADIO

				Phone	Fax
WAVE-FM 104.1 MHz (CR) 1571 Trade St	Myrtle Beach	SC	29577	843-448-1041	626-4896
Web: www.wave104.com ■ *E-mail:* wave104@sccoast.net					
WDAI-FM 98.5 MHz (Urban) 11640 Hwy 17 Byp	Murrells Inlet	SC	29576	843-651-7869	651-3197
WGTR-FM 107.9 MHz (Ctry) 4841 Hwy 17 Bypass S	Myrtle Beach	SC	29577	843-293-0107	293-1717
WJYR-FM 92.1 MHz (B/EZ) 1116 Ocala St.	Myrtle Beach	SC	29577	843-448-4739	626-2508
WKZQ-AM 1450 kHz (Sports) 1116 Ocala St.	Myrtle Beach	SC	29577	843-448-4739	626-2508
WKZQ-FM 101.7 MHz (Rock) 1116 Ocala St.	Myrtle Beach	SC	29577	843-448-4739	626-2508
WNMB-FM 105.9 MHz (AC) 429 Pine Ave	North Myrtle Beach	SC	29582	843-249-3441	249-7823
Web: www.b1059.net ■ *E-mail:* staff@b1059.net					
WRNN-FM 94.5 MHz (N/T) 1571 Trade St	Myrtle Beach	SC	29577	843-448-1041	626-5988
WSYN-FM 106.5 MHz (Oldies) 11640 Hwy 17 Byp	Murrells Inlet	SC	29576	843-651-1065	651-3197
WVCO-FM 94.9 MHz (Nost) 1114 3rd Ave S	Myrtle Beach	SC	29577	843-445-9491	445-9490
WWSK-FM 107.1 MHz (CR) 4841 Hwy 17	Myrtle Beach	SC	29577	843-293-0107	293-1717
WYAK-FM 103.1 MHz (Ctry) 1571 Trade St	Myrtle Beach	SC	29577	843-651-7936	651-6840
Web: www.wyak.com					
WYAV-FM 104.1 MHz (CR) 1571 Trade St	Myrtle Beach	SC	29577	843-448-1041	626-5988

— Colleges/Universities —

				Phone	Fax
Cathedral Bible College 803 Howard Pkwy	Myrtle Beach	SC	29577	843-477-1448	477-1627
Coastal Carolina University PO Box 261954	Conway	SC	29528	843-349-2026	349-2127
TF Admissions: 800-277-7000 ■ *Web:* www.coastal.edu ■ *E-mail:* admissions@coastal.edu					
Horry-Georgetown Technical College 743 Hemlock Ave	Myrtle Beach	SC	29577	843-477-0808	477-0775
Web: www.hor.tec.sc.us					
Webster University 4589 Oleander Dr	Myrtle Beach	SC	29577	843-497-3677	497-9268

— Hospitals —

				Phone	Fax
Conway Hospital 300 Singleton Ridge Rd	Conway	SC	29526	843-347-7111	347-8056*
**Fax:* Personnel					
Grand Strand Regional Medical Ctr 809 82nd Pkwy.	Myrtle Beach	SC	29572	843-692-1000	692-1109
TF: 800-222-1859					

— Attractions —

				Phone	Fax
Alabama Theatre 4750 Hwy 17 S	North Myrtle Beach	SC	29582	843-272-1111	272-7748
TF: 800-342-2262 ■ *Web:* www.alabama-theatre.com ■ *E-mail:* alabamathr@aol.com					
Alligator Adventure 4604 Hwy 17 S Barefoot Landing	North Myrtle Beach	SC	29598	843-361-0789	361-0742
Art Museum 3100 S Ocean Blvd	Myrtle Beach	SC	29578	843-238-2510	238-2910
Barefoot Landing 4898 Hwy 17 S	Myrtle Beach	SC	29582	843-272-8349	272-1052
TF: 800-272-2320 ■ *Web:* www.bflanding.com					
Broadway at the Beach 1325 Celebrity Cir	Myrtle Beach	SC	29577	843-444-3200	444-3222
TF: 800-386-4662 ■ *Web:* www.broadwayatthebeach.com					
Brookgreen Gardens 1931 Brookgreen Gardens Dr	Murrells Inlet	SC	29576	843-237-4218	237-1014
Carolina Opry 8901 Hwy 17 N Suite A	Myrtle Beach	SC	29577	843-238-8888	913-1442
TF: 800-843-6779 ■ *Web:* www.cgp.net					
Children's Museum of South Carolina 2501 N Kings Hwy	Myrtle Beach	SC	29578	843-946-9469	946-7011
Web: www.bearweb.com/cmsckids					
Civil War Collection 4857 Hwy 17 Bypass S	Myrtle Beach	SC	29577	843-293-4344	
Dixie Stampede Dinner Theater 8901-B Hwy 17 Business	Myrtle Beach	SC	29577	843-497-6615	497-6767
Web: www.dixiestampede.com					
Family Kingdom Amusement Park 301 S Ocean Blvd	Myrtle Beach	SC	29577	843-916-8378	448-4548
Web: www.seamist.com/familyking/fkhome.htm					
Family Kingdom Water Park 301 S Ocean Blvd	Myrtle Beach	SC	29577	843-916-0400	448-4548
Web: www.seamist.com/familyking/wphome.htm					
Fine Arts Gallery Ltd 4515 Hwy 17 Bypass S	Myrtle Beach	SC	29577	843-293-5152	
Great American Riverboat Company 4898 Hwy 17 S Barefoot Landing	North Myrtle Beach	SC	29582	843-236-1700	
TF: 800-685-6601					
Haunted House Mayhem Manor 204 9th Ave N	Myrtle Beach	SC	29577	843-626-4413	
Horry County Museum 428 Main St	Conway	SC	29526	843-248-1542	248-1854
E-mail: hcmuseum@sccoast.net					
Howard Gallery 532 W Broadway St	Myrtle Beach	SC	29577	843-626-3118	
IMAX Discovery Theater 1195 Celebrity Cir	Myrtle Beach	SC	29577	843-448-4629	444-3350
TF: 800-380-4629 ■ *Web:* www.myrtlebeachimax.com ■ *E-mail:* imax2@earthlink.net					
Legends in Concert 301 Hwy 17 S	Surfside Beach	SC	29575	843-477-5678	
Maze Mania 3013 Hwy 17	Murrells Inlet	SC	29576	843-651-1641	
Medieval Times Dinner & Tournament 2904 Fantasy Way	Myrtle Beach	SC	29579	843-236-8080	236-2611
TF: 800-436-4386 ■ *Web:* www.medievaltimes.com/SC_realm.htm ■ *E-mail:* myrtlebeach@medievaltimes.com					
Motion Master Theater 917 N Ocean Blvd	Myrtle Beach	SC	29577	843-626-0069	626-2168
Myrtle Beach Grand Prix 3900 Hwy 17 S.	Myrtle Beach	SC	29582	843-272-6010	361-7870
Web: www.mbgrandprix.com					

Myrtle Beach — Attractions (Cont'd)

				Phone	Fax
Myrtle Beach Pavilion Amusement Park 812 N Ocean Blvd	Myrtle Beach	SC	29577	843-448-6456	448-0711
Web: www.navi-gator.com/mb/entertan					
Myrtle Beach State Park 4401 S Kings Hwy	Myrtle Beach	SC	29575	843-238-5325	
Myrtle Beach Wax Museum 1000 N Ocean Blvd	Myrtle Beach	SC	29577	843-448-9921	626-7132
Myrtle Waves Water Park 3000 10th Ave N Ext	Myrtle Beach	SC	29577	843-448-1026	626-3719
TF: 800-524-9283 ■ *Web:* www.myrtlewaves.com					
Palace Theater 1420 Celebrity Cir Broadway at the Beach	Myrtle Beach	SC	29577	843-448-9224	626-9659
TF: 800-905-4228 ■ *Web:* www.broadwayatthebeach.com/entertainment/palace.htm					
Riemer Gallery 7721 N Kings Hwy	Myrtle Beach	SC	29577	843-449-2991	
Ripley's Aquarium 1110 Celebrity Cir Broadway at the Beach	Myrtle Beach	SC	29577	843-916-0888	916-0752
TF: 800-734-8888 ■ *Web:* www.ripleysaquarium.com					
Ripley's Believe It or Not! Museum 901 N Ocean Blvd	Myrtle Beach	SC	29577	843-448-2331	626-2168
Savoy Theater 2924 Fantasy Way	Myrtle Beach	SC	29577	843-236-2200	
Waccatee Zoo 8500 Enterprise Rd	Myrtle Beach	SC	29575	843-650-8500	

SPORTS TEAMS & FACILITIES

				Phone	Fax
Myrtle Beach Pelicans (baseball) 2411 Oak St Suite 308	Myrtle Beach	SC	29577	843-918-6000	946-6273
Web: www.myrtlebeachpelicans.com					
Myrtle Beach Sea Dawgs (soccer) Oak St & 33rd Ave N Doug Shaw Memorial Stadium	Myrtle Beach	SC	29577	843-236-7767	236-1971
E-mail: seadawgs@seadawgs.com					
Myrtle Beach Speedway 3456 Sea Mountain Hwy	Little River	SC	29566	843-236-0500	236-0525

— Events —

	Phone
Art in the Park (early May)	843-249-4937
Blessing of the Inlet (early May)	843-651-5099
Blue Crab Arts & Crafts Festival (mid-May)	843-249-6604
Canadian American Days Festival (mid-late March)	843-626-7444
Carolina Craftsman Summer Classic (early August)	843-918-1225
Carolina Women's Show (mid-March)	800-610-7469
Dickens Christmas Show & Festival (mid-November)	843-448-9483
Doll Show & Sale (mid-March)	843-248-5643
DuPont World Amateur Handicap (late August-early September)	843-477-8833
Frantic Atlantic Big Bucks Bonanza (early-mid-October)	843-249-7881
Frantic Atlantic Spring King Classic (mid-late May & mid-late September)	843-249-7881
Georgetown Plantation Tours (late March)	843-546-4358
Grand Strand Fishing Rodeo (early April-late October)	843-626-7444
Grand Strand Passion Play (late March)	843-448-3155
Great American Shootout Soccer Tournament (mid-late October)	843-449-9622
Harley Davidson Biker Rally (mid-May)	843-651-5555
Holiday Celebration (early November-late January)	843-626-7444
Home Improvement Expo (early-mid-October)	843-347-7311
Intracoastal Christmas Regatta (late November)	843-280-6354
Mark Sloan Golf Tournament (early September)	843-626-3638
Murrells Inlet Fourth of July Boat Parade (July 4)	843-651-5675
Myrtle Beach Greek Festival (late September)	843-448-3773
Myrtle Beach Marathon (late February)	843-293-7223
Oktoberfest (early October)	843-918-1242
Pier King Mackerel Tournament (early June & mid-September)	843-626-7444
Rivertown Music Festival (early May)	843-444-5614
Saint Patrick's Day Festival (mid-March)	843-361-0038
SOS Spring Safari (mid-late April)	888-767-3113
South Carolina State Bluegrass Festival (late November)	843-918-1226
Spring Arts & Crafts Show (mid-March)	843-448-2513
Spring Games Kite Festival (early-mid-April)	843-448-7261
Sun Fun Festival (early June)	843-626-7444
Taste of Broadway Spring Festival (early-mid-April)	843-444-3200
Taste of the Town (late October-early November)	843-448-6062
Treasures by the Sea (early November-mid-February)	800-356-3016

South Dakota

Population (1999): 733,133 **Area (sq mi): 77,121**

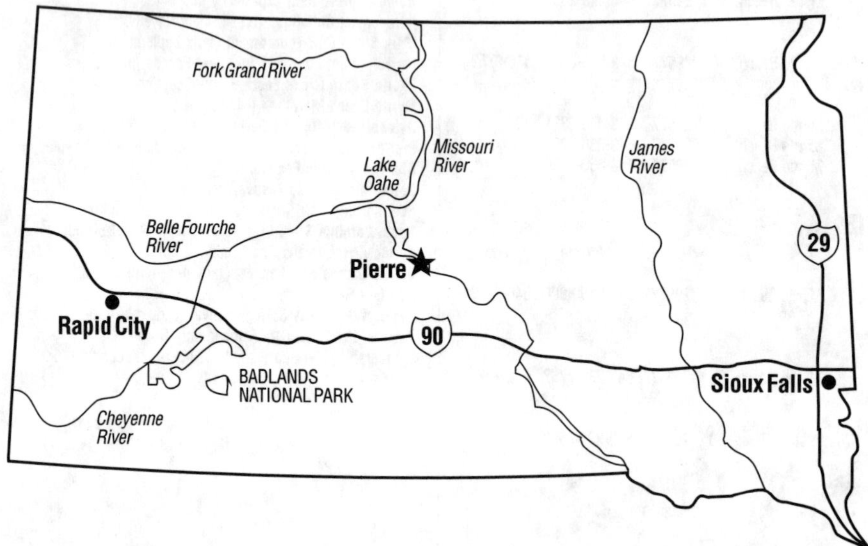

— State Information Sources —

				Phone	Fax
South Dakota Chamber of Commerce & Industry					
PO Box 190	Pierre	SD	57501	605-224-6161	224-7198
E-mail: icasdghd@iw.net					
South Dakota Economic Development Office					
711 E Wells Ave	Pierre	SD	57501	605-773-5032	773-3256
Web: www.state.sd.us/goed/index.htm ■ *E-mail:* goedinfo@goed.state.sd.us					
South Dakota Parks & Recreation Div					
523 E Capitol Ave	Pierre	SD	57501	605-773-3391	773-6245
TF: 800-710-2267 ■ *Web:* www.state.sd.us/state/executive/tourism/sdparks ■ *E-mail:* scottc@gfp.state.sd.us					
South Dakota State Government Information				605-773-3011	
Web: www.state.sd.us					
South Dakota State Library 800 Governors Dr	Pierre	SD	57501	605-773-3131	773-4950
TF: 800-423-6665 ■ *Web:* www.state.sd.us/state/executive/deca/st_lib/st_lib.htm					
South Dakota Tourism Dept 711 E Wells Ave	Pierre	SD	57501	605-773-3301	773-3256
TF: 800-732-5682 ■ *Web:* www.state.sd.us/state/executive/tourism/ ■ *E-mail:* sdinfo@goed.state.sd.us					

ON-LINE RESOURCES

About South Dakota . . . . . www.state.sd.us/state/executive/deca/st_lib/abtsdk.htm
Dakotaland . . . . . www.dakotaland.com
Rough Guide Travel South Dakota travel.roughguides.com/content/1012
South Dakota Cities . . . . . dir.yahoo.com/Regional/U_S__States/South_Dakota/Cities
South Dakota Counties & Regions . . . . . dir.yahoo.com/Regional/U_S__States/South_Dakota/Counties_and_Regions
South Dakota Scenario . . . . . scenariousa.dstylus.com/sd/indexf.htm
South Dakota Travel & Tourism Guide . . . . . www.travel-library.com/north_america/usa/south_dakota/index.html
Travel.org-South Dakota . . . . . travel.org/s-dak.html
What's Up South Dakota! . . . . . www.whatsupsouthdakota.com
Yahoo! Get Local South Dakota . . . . . dir.yahoo.com/Regional/U_S__States/South_Dakota

— Cities Profiled —

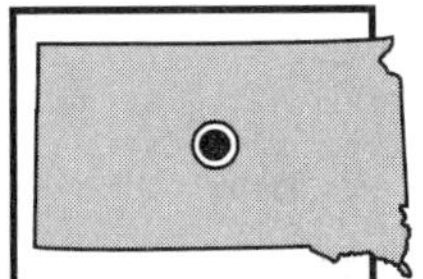

Pierre

Pierre's Capitol Lake, situated on the east State Capitol grounds, never freezes and serves as a winter haven for Canada geese, mallards, and other migratory waterfowl. The city's Flaming Fountain is fed by an artesian well with a gas content so high it can be lit; the fountain glows perpetually as a memorial to veterans. Pierre's Lake Oahe stretches from Pierre to Bismarck and is famous for its walleye fishing. Its public hunting grounds provide both big game and waterfowl. Visitors to LaFramboise Island in Pierre can walk eight miles of nature trails or partake in seasonal bow and arrow hunting.

Population	13,267	**Longitude**	100-33-49 W
Area (Land)	13.0 sq mi	**County**	Hughes
Area (Water)	0 sq mi	**Time Zone**	CST
Elevation	1484 ft	**Area Code/s**	605
Latitude	44-36-86 N		

— Average Temperatures and Precipitation —

TEMPERATURES

	Jan	Feb	Mar	Apr	May	Jun	Jul	Aug	Sep	Oct	Nov	Dec
High	27	33	44	59	71	82	90	88	76	63	45	31
Low	7	12	23	35	46	56	62	60	49	37	24	11

PRECIPITATION

	Jan	Feb	Mar	Apr	May	Jun	Jul	Aug	Sep	Oct	Nov	Dec
Inches	0.4	0.5	1.1	2.1	2.9	3.5	2.6	1.7	1.6	1.2	0.5	0.6

— Important Phone Numbers —

	Phone		Phone
AAA	605-224-0422	**Emergency**	911
Consumer Protection	605-773-4400	**Poison Control Center**	800-764-7661

— Information Sources —

				Phone	Fax
Hughes County PO Box 1112	Pierre	SD	57501	605-773-3713	
Pierre Area Chamber of Commerce PO Box 548	Pierre	SD	57501	605-224-7361	224-6485
TF: 800-962-2034 ■ *Web:* www.pierre.org ■ *E-mail:* chamber@sd.cybernex.net					
Pierre City Hall 222 E Dakota Ave	Pierre	SD	57501	605-773-7407	773-7406
Pierre Convention & Visitors Bureau PO Box 548	Pierre	SD	57501	605-224-7361	224-6485
TF: 800-962-2034 ■ *Web:* www.pierre.org/cvb.htm					
Pierre Economic Development Corp 800 W Dakota	Pierre	SD	57501	605-224-6610	224-6485
Pierre Mayor 222 E Dakota	Pierre	SD	57501	605-773-7407	773-7406
RE Rawlins Municipal Library 1000 E Church St	Pierre	SD	57501	605-773-7421	773-7423
Web: www.dakotariver.com/rawlins					
RiverCentre Convention Center 920 W Sioux Ave	Pierre	SD	57501	605-224-6877	224-1042
Web: www.rivercentre.org ■ *E-mail:* rivercentre@riverdentre.org					
South Dakota Tourism Dept 711 E Wells Ave	Pierre	SD	57501	605-773-3301	773-3256
TF: 800-732-5682 ■ *Web:* www.state.sd.us/state/executive/tourism/ ■ *E-mail:* sdinfo@goed.state.sd.us					

On-Line Resources

Area Guide Pierre .... pierre.areaguides.net
Excite.com Pierre City Guide .... www.excite.com/travel/countries/united_states/south_dakota/pierre

— Transportation Services —

AIRPORTS

■ **Pierre Municipal Airport (PIR)** — *Phone*
5 miles E of downtown (approx 15 minutes) 605-773-7447

Airport Transportation

Capital City Taxi $7.25 fare to downtown 605-223-2919

Commercial Airlines

	Phone		Phone
Northwest	800-225-2525	**United Express**	800-241-6522
United	800-241-6522		

Charter Airlines

	Phone
Capital Air Carrier	605-224-9000

CAR RENTALS

	Phone		Phone
Avis	605-224-2911	**Budget**	605-224-8099

LIMO/TAXI

	Phone		Phone
Capital City Taxi	605-223-2919	**Forell Limo**	605-224-0073
Classic Limo	605-224-0303		

RAIL/BUS

				Phone
Jack Rabbit Bus Station 621 W Sioux Ave	Pierre	SD	57501	605-224-7651

— Accommodations —

HOTELS, MOTELS, RESORTS

				Phone	Fax
Best Western Kings Inn 220 S Pierre St	Pierre	SD	57501	605-224-5951	224-5301
TF: 800-232-1112					
Best Western Ramkota Inn 920 W Sioux Ave.	Pierre	SD	57501	605-224-6877	224-1042
TF: 800-528-1234					
Capitol Inn 815 Wells Ave	Pierre	SD	57501	605-224-6387	224-8083
TF: 800-658-3055					
Comfort Inn 410 W Sioux Ave	Pierre	SD	57501	605-224-0377	224-0377
TF: 800-228-5150					
Days Inn 520 W Sioux Ave.	Pierre	SD	57501	605-224-0411	224-0411
TF: 800-329-7466					
Fawn Motel 818 N Euclid Ave.	Pierre	SD	57501	605-224-5885	
Fort Pierre Motel 211 S 1st St Hwy 83 S	Fort Pierre	SD	57532	605-223-3111	
TF: 800-286-0895					
Governor's Inn 700 W Sioux Ave	Pierre	SD	57501	605-224-4200	
TF: 800-341-8000					
Iron Horse Inn 205 W Pleasant Dr	Pierre	SD	57501	605-224-5981	224-7125
Kelley Inn 713 W Sioux Ave.	Pierre	SD	57501	605-224-4140	224-8284
TF: 800-635-3559					
Oahe Lodge 19602 Lake Pl	Pierre	SD	57501	605-224-9340	224-0242
Spring Creek Resort 16 miles N on Hwy 1804	Pierre	SD	57501	605-224-8336	945-1074
State Motel 640 N Euclid	Pierre	SD	57501	605-224-5896	224-1815
TF: 800-283-4678					
Terrace Motel 231 N Euclid Ave	Pierre	SD	57501	605-224-7797	

— Restaurants —

				Phone
Cactus Jack's (American) 108 N Garfield Ave	Pierre	SD	57501	605-224-1020
Chicadilly Country Restaurant (American) 808 W Sioux Ave.	Pierre	SD	57501	605-224-7183
Happy Chef Restaurant (American) 314 W Sioux Ave	Pierre	SD	57501	605-224-0352
Jake's Good Time Place (Steak) E Hwy 34 & Truck By Pass	Pierre	SD	57501	605-945-0485
Longbranch Saloon (American) 351 S Pierre St.	Pierre	SD	57501	605-224-6166
Oahe Lodge (American) 19602 Lake Pl.	Pierre	SD	57501	605-224-9340
Outpost Lodge (Steak/Seafood) 28229 Cow Creek Rd	Pierre	SD	57501	605-264-5450
Ruby's Roost (American) 807 Ft Chouteau Rd.	Pierre	SD	57532	605-223-2525
Saint Charles Restaurant (Steak/Seafood) 207 E Capitol	Pierre	SD	57501	605-224-7690
Shenanigans Sports Pub (American) 602 W Sioux Ave	Pierre	SD	57501	605-224-5657

Pierre — Restaurants (Cont'd)

				Phone
Smokee's Bbq (Barbecue) 1415 E Wells Ave	Pierre	SD	57501	605-224-7427
Spring Creek Resort (American) 16 miles N on Hwy 1804	Pierre	SD	57501	605-224-8336
Wonderful House (Chinese) 317 S Pierre St	Pierre	SD	57501	605-224-0495

— Goods and Services —

SHOPPING

				Phone	Fax
Pierre Mall 1615 N Harrison	Pierre	SD	57501	605-224-6331	224-6720

BANKS

				Phone	Fax
American State Bank 700 E Sioux Ave	Pierre	SD	57501	605-224-9233	224-1872
BankWest Inc 420 S Pierre St *TF:* 800-253-0362	Pierre	SD	57501	605-224-7391	224-7393
First National Bank 125 W Sioux Ave	Pierre	SD	57501	605-945-3900	945-3914
Norwest Bank 333 E Sioux Ave	Pierre	SD	57501	605-224-6460	224-1530

BUSINESS SERVICES

	Phone		Phone
Airborne Express	800-247-2676	**Mail Boxes Etc**	800-789-4623
BAX Global	800-225-5229	**Post Office**	605-224-2912
DHL Worldwide Express	800-225-5345	**UPS**	800-742-5877
Federal Express	800-238-5355		

— Media —

PUBLICATIONS

				Phone	Fax
Capital Journal‡ PO Box 878	Pierre	SD	57501	605-224-7301	224-9210

Web: www.capjournal.com ■ *E-mail:* capjournal@capjournal.com

‡Daily newspapers

TELEVISION

				Phone	Fax
KDLT-TV Ch 46 (NBC) 3600 S Westport Ave *Web:* www.kdlt.com	Sioux Falls	SD	57106	605-361-5555	361-3982
KPLO-TV Ch 6 (CBS) 501 S Phillips Ave	Sioux Falls	SD	57104	605-336-1100	336-0202
KPRY-TV Ch 4 (ABC) 300 N Dakota Ave Suite 100	Sioux Falls	SD	57104	605-336-1300	336-7936
KTSD-TV Ch 10 (PBS) Dakota & Cherry Sts Telecom Bldg	Vermillion	SD	57069	605-677-5861	677-5010
KTTW-TV Ch 17 (Fox) 2817 W 11th St	Sioux Falls	SD	57104	605-338-0017	338-7173

RADIO

				Phone	Fax
KCCR-AM 1240 kHz (AC) 106 W Capitol Ave	Pierre	SD	57501	605-224-1240	224-0095
KELO-AM 1320 kHz (Oldies) 500 S Phillips Ave. *Web:* www.keloam.com ■ *E-mail:* keloam@mmi.net	Sioux Falls	SD	57104	605-331-5350	336-0415
KELO-FM 92.5 MHz (AC) 500 S Phillips Ave. *Web:* www.kelofm.com ■ *E-mail:* kelofm@mmi.net	Sioux Falls	SD	57104	605-331-5350	336-0415
KGFX-AM 1060 kHz (Ctry) 214 W Pleasant Dr	Pierre	SD	57501	605-224-8686	224-8984
KGFX-FM 92.7 MHz (AC) 214 W Pleasant Dr	Pierre	SD	57501	605-224-8686	224-8984
KLXS-FM 95.3 MHz (Oldies) 106 W Capitol Ave.	Pierre	SD	57501	605-224-0095	224-0095
KMLO-FM 100.7 MHz (Ctry) 214 W Pleasant Dr	Pierre	SD	57501	605-224-8686	224-8984
KPLO-FM 94.5 MHz (Ctry) 214 W Pleasant Dr	Pierre	SD	57501	605-224-8686	224-8984

— Hospitals —

				Phone	Fax
Saint Mary's Hospital 800 E Dakota Ave **Fax:* Library	Pierre	SD	57501	605-224-3100	224-8339*

— Attractions —

				Phone	Fax
Farm Island Recreation Area 4 miles E off SD 34	Pierre	SD	57501	605-224-5605	
Fighting Stallions Memorial State Capitol Grounds	Pierre	SD	57501	605-773-3765	
Golden Buffalo Casino 321 Sitting Bull Ln	Lower Brule	SD	57548	605-473-5577	473-9270
Hilger's Gulch Park & Governor's Grove Church St.	Pierre	SD	57501	605-224-7361	
Houck's Buffalo Ranch Hwy 1806	Pierre	SD	57501	605-567-3624	567-3625
LaFramboise Island LaFramboise Cswy	Pierre	SD	57501	605-224-5862	
Museum of South Dakota State Historical Society 900 Governors Dr Cultural Heritage Ctr	Pierre	SD	57501	605-773-3458	773-6041
Oahe Dam & Reservoir 6 miles N on Hwy 1804	Pierre	SD	57501	605-224-5862	
Pierre Native Plant Arboretum Izaak Walton Rd	Pierre	SD	57501	605-773-3594	773-4003
South Dakota Discovery Center & Aquarium 805 W Sioux Ave	Pierre	SD	57501	605-224-8295	224-2865
South Dakota National Guard Museum 301 E Dakota	Pierre	SD	57501	605-224-9991	773-5382
South Dakota State Capitol Capitol Ave E	Pierre	SD	57501	605-773-3765	773-3887
West Bend Recreation Area 26 miles E off SD 34	Pierre	SD	57501	605-875-3220	

— Events —

	Phone
August Jamboree & Old West Shoot-out (late August)	605-223-3154
Capital Christmas Trees Display (late November-late December)	605-773-3765
Casey Tibbs Match of Champions Bronc Riding Event (early June)	605-223-2449
Dakota Blast (mid-June)	605-223-3154
Downtown Pierre Crazy Days (late July)	605-224-7825
Fall Arts & Crafts Show (late September)	605-224-7754
Farm Home & Sports Show (mid-March)	605-224-1240
Fort Pierre Horse Races (mid April-early May)	605-223-2178
Fourth of July Rodeo (July 4)	605-224-7361
Goosefest (late September)	605-224-7361
Gun Show (February)	605-224-1371
Infisherman's Pro/AM Walleye Tournament (late June)	605-224-7361
Shrine Circus (mid-June)	605-224-7361
South Dakota State Fair (late August-early September)	605-353-7340
Sturgis Motorcycle Rally & Races (mid-August)	605-347-6570
Volksmarch at Crazy Horse (early June)	605-673-4681

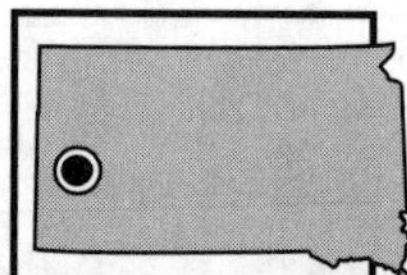

Rapid City

Centrally located in the foothills of the Black Hills, Rapid City serves as a gateway to some of the country's most famous national park areas. A short drive away one can see Badlands National Park (244,000 acres of spires, canyons, and buttes), Mount Rushmore, Devils Tower National Monument in northeastern Wyoming, and Jewel Cave National Monument, the second longest cave in the U.S. Jewel Cave and Mount Rushmore are located in Black Hills National Forest, the area featured in the movie "Dances With Wolves." The Black Hills Passion Play, held in Spearfish, is one of America's longest-running stage productions.

Population	57,513	**Longitude**	103-28-03 W
Area (Land)	35.3 sq mi	**County**	Pennington
Area (Water)	0.1 sq mi	**Time Zone**	MST
Elevation	3247 ft	**Area Code/s**	605
Latitude	44-06-58 N		

Rapid City (Cont'd)

— Average Temperatures and Precipitation —

TEMPERATURES

	Jan	Feb	Mar	Apr	May	Jun	Jul	Aug	Sep	Oct	Nov	Dec
High	34	38	46	58	68	78	86	85	74	63	47	36
Low	11	15	22	32	42	52	58	56	46	35	23	13

PRECIPITATION

	Jan	Feb	Mar	Apr	May	Jun	Jul	Aug	Sep	Oct	Nov	Dec
Inches	0.4	0.5	1.0	1.9	2.7	3.1	2.0	1.7	1.2	1.1	0.6	0.5

— Important Phone Numbers —

	Phone
AAA	605-342-8482
Emergency	911
Medical Referral	605-341-8107
Poison Control Center	800-952-0123
Weather	605-341-7531

— Information Sources —

				Phone	Fax
Pennington County 315 Saint Joseph St	Rapid City	SD	57701	605-394-2171	394-6833
Rapid City Area Chamber of Commerce PO Box 747	Rapid City	SD	57709	605-343-1744	343-6550

Web: www.rapidcitycvb.com ■ *E-mail:* tourist@rapidcitycvb.com

Rapid City City Hall 300 6th St	Rapid City	SD	57701	605-394-4110	

Web: ci.rapid-city.sd.us

Rapid City Convention & Visitors Bureau PO Box 747	Rapid City	SD	57709	605-343-1744	348-9217

TF: 800-487-3223 ■ *Web:* www.rapidcitycvb.com/
■ *E-mail:* tourist@rapidcitycvb.com

Rapid City Mayor 300 6th St	Rapid City	SD	57701	605-394-4110	394-6793

Web: ci.rapid-city.sd.us/citygovt/mayor/mayor.htm
■ *E-mail:* mayor@ci.rapid-city.sd.us

Rapid City Planning Dept 300 6th St	Rapid City	SD	57701	605-394-4120	394-6636

Web: ci.rapid-city.sd.us/citygovt/planning/planning.htm

Rapid City Public Library 610 Quincy St	Rapid City	SD	57701	605-394-4171	394-6626

Web: www.sdln.net/libs/rcp

Rushmore Plaza Civic Center 444 Mount Rushmore Rd N	Rapid City	SD	57701	605-394-4115	394-4119

Web: www.gotmine.com ■ *E-mail:* civicctr@rapidnet.com

On-Line Resources

Area Guide Rapid City	rapidcity.areaguides.net
Black Hills Information Web	rapidweb.com/
BlackHills Online	www.blackhills.com
Excite.com Rapid City City Guide	www.excite.com/travel/countries/united_states/south_dakota/rapid_city

— Transportation Services —

AIRPORTS

■ Rapid City Regional Airport (RAP)

	Phone
9 miles SE of downtown (approx 20 minutes)	605-394-4195

Web: www.rapairport.org ■ *E-mail:* rap@rapidnet.com

Airport Transportation

	Phone
Airport Express Limo $10 fare to downtown	605-399-9999
Airport Express Shuttle $10 fare to downtown	605-399-9999

Commercial Airlines

	Phone
Continental	800-525-0280
Delta	800-221-1212
Northwest	800-225-2525
United	800-241-6522
United Express	800-241-6522

Charter Airlines

	Phone
Superior Aviation	800-882-7751
Westjet Air Center Inc	605-393-2500

CAR RENTALS

	Phone
Avis	605-393-0740
Budget	605-393-0488
Dollar	605-342-7071
Enterprise	605-399-9939
Hertz	605-393-0160
Thrifty	605-393-0663

LIMO/TAXI

	Phone
Airport Express Limo	605-399-9999
City Cab	605-341-4141
Diamond Limousine	605-787-6796
Rapid Taxi	605-348-8080

MASS TRANSIT

	Phone
Rapid Ride $1 Base fare	605-394-6631

— Accommodations —

HOTELS, MOTELS, RESORTS

				Phone	Fax
Alpine Motel 209 E North St	Rapid City	SD	57701	605-342-3701	
AmericInn Motel & Suites 1632 Rapp St.	Rapid City	SD	57701	605-343-8424	343-2200
TF: 800-634-3444					
■ *Web:* www.americinn.com/southdakota/rapidcity.html					
Avanti Motel 102 N Maple Ave	Rapid City	SD	57701	605-348-1112	348-1112
TF: 800-658-5464					
Bavarian Inn PO Box 152	Custer	SD	57730	605-673-2802	673-4777
TF: 800-657-4312					
Bel Air Budget Host Inn 2101 Mt Rushmore Rd	Rapid City	SD	57701	605-343-5126	343-5126
TF: 800-456-3431					
Best Western Golden Spike Inn 106 Main St.	Hill City	SD	57745	605-574-2577	574-4719
Best Western Town 'N Country Motel 2505 Mt Rushmore Rd	Rapid City	SD	57701	605-343-5383	343-9670
TF: 800-528-1234					
Big Sky Motel 4080 Tower Rd	Rapid City	SD	57701	605-348-3200	
Blue Bell Lodge & Resort Hwy 87 Custer State Pk.	Custer	SD	57730	605-255-4531	255-4407
TF: 800-658-3530					
Budget Inn Motel 610 E North St	Rapid City	SD	57701	605-342-8594	
Castle Inn 15 E North St	Rapid City	SD	57701	605-348-4120	348-1112
TF: 800-658-5464					
Classic Inn 125 Main St.	Rapid City	SD	57701	605-343-5501	343-4313
Comfort Inn 1550 N La Crosse St	Rapid City	SD	57701	605-348-2221	348-3110
TF: 800-228-5150					
Days Inn 1570 Rapp St	Rapid City	SD	57701	605-348-8410	348-3392
TF: 800-329-7466					
Days Inn 1901 W Main St	Rapid City	SD	57709	605-343-6040	343-0314
Econo Lodge 625 E Disk Dr	Rapid City	SD	57701	605-342-6400	394-9539
TF: 800-214-1971					
Fair Value Inn 1607 N Lacrosse St	Rapid City	SD	57701	605-342-8118	342-8118
TF: 800-954-8118					
Family Inns Of America 3737 Sturgis Rd	Rapid City	SD	57702	605-342-2892	342-2892
TF: 800-349-2892					
Foothills Inn 1625 N La Crosse St	Rapid City	SD	57701	605-348-5640	348-0073
TF: 800-348-5640					
Holiday Inn Express 750 Cathedral Dr	Rapid City	SD	57701	605-341-9300	341-9333
TF: 800-465-4329					
Holiday Inn Hotel & Convention Center Northern Black Hills PO Box 399	Spearfish	SD	57783	605-642-4683	642-0203
TF: 800-999-3541					
■ *Web:* www.basshotels.com/holiday-inn/?_franchisee=BLKNO					
Holiday Inn Rushmore Plaza 505 N 5th St	Rapid City	SD	57701	605-348-4000	348-9777
TF: 800-465-4329					
■ *Web:* www.basshotels.com/holiday-inn/?_franchisee=RAPCC					
Hotel Alex Johnson The 523 6th St	Rapid City	SD	57701	605-342-1210	342-1210
TF: 800-888-2539 ■ *Web:* www.alexjohnson.com					
■ *E-mail:* Info@AlexJohnson.com					
Lamplighter Inn 27 Saint Joseph St	Rapid City	SD	57701	605-342-3385	343-7809
TF: 800-775-5267					
Motel 6 620 Latrobe Ave	Rapid City	SD	57701	605-343-3687	343-7566
TF: 800-466-8356					
Quality Inn 1902 N Lacrosse St	Rapid City	SD	57701	605-342-3322	342-9005
TF: 800-228-5151					
Radisson Hotel Rapid City 445 Mt Rushmore Rd	Rapid City	SD	57701	605-348-8300	348-3833
TF: 800-333-3333 ■ *Web:* www.radissonrapidcity.com					
■ *E-mail:* radisson@rapidcity.com					

Rapid City — Hotels, Motels, Resorts (Cont'd)

				Phone	Fax
Ram Kota Inn 2211 La Crosse St	Rapid City	SD	57701	605-343-8550	343-9107
Ramada Inn 1721 La Crosse St *TF:* 800-272-6232	Rapid City	SD	57701	605-342-1300	342-0663
Rodeway Inn 2208 Mt Rushmore Rd *TF:* 800-228-2000	Rapid City	SD	57701	605-355-0500	355-9811
Rushmore Inn Travelodge 5410 Mount Rushmore Rd *TF:* 800-698-1676	Rapid City	SD	57701	605-343-4700	343-6678
Super 8 Motel 2124 La Crosse St *TF:* 800-800-8000	Rapid City	SD	57701	605-348-8070	348-0833
Triple R Ranch PO Box 124 *TF:* 888-777-2624 ■ *Web:* www.rrrranch.com ■ *E-mail:* rrr@guestranches.com	Keystone	SD	57751	605-666-4605	

— Restaurants —

				Phone
American Pie Bistro (New American) 710 Saint Joseph St	Rapid City	SD	57701	605-343-3773
Art's Smoke House Barbecue (Barbecue) 1109 W Omaha St	Rapid City	SD	57702	605-355-9490
Asian Cafe (Asian) 208 E North St	Rapid City	SD	57701	605-399-1579
Botticelli Italian Restaurant (Italian) 523 Main St	Rapid City	SD	57701	605-348-0089
Cajun Cafe (Cajun) 2200 N Maple Ave	Rapid City	SD	57701	605-388-9687
Carini Italian Food (Italian) 324 Saint Joseph St	Rapid City	SD	57701	605-348-3704
Casa del Rey (Mexican) 1902 Mt Rushmore Rd	Rapid City	SD	57701	605-348-5679
Colonial House (American) 2501 Mt Rushmore Rd	Rapid City	SD	57701	605-342-4640
Firehouse Brewing Co (American) 610 Main St	Rapid City	SD	57701	605-348-1915
Gigglebees (American) 937 E North St	Rapid City	SD	57701	605-399-1494
Golden Phoenix (Chinese) 2421 W Main St	Rapid City	SD	57702	605-348-4195
Harold's Prime Rib (Steak/Seafood) 318 East Blvd	Rapid City	SD	57701	605-343-1927
Hearthstone Cafe (American) 807 Columbus St	Rapid City	SD	57701	605-341-4529
Imperial Restaurant (Chinese) 702 E North St	Rapid City	SD	57701	605-394-8888
Landmark Restaurant (American) 523 6th St	Rapid City	SD	57701	605-342-1210
Monterey Jack's Mexican Restaurant (Mexican) 1009 Mt Rushmore Rd	Rapid City	SD	57701	605-394-8877
Parkway Restaurant (Homestyle) 312 East Blvd N	Rapid City	SD	57701	605-342-9640
Piesano's Pacchia (Italian) 3618 Canyon Lake Dr	Rapid City	SD	57701	605-341-6941
Remington's (American) 603 Omaha St	Rapid City	SD	57701	605-348-4160
Saigon (Asian) 221 E North St	Rapid City	SD	57701	605-348-8523
Tiffany Grille (American) 505 N 5th St	Rapid City	SD	57701	605-348-4000
Valley Sports Bar & Grill (American) 1865 S Valley Dr	Rapid City	SD	57701	605-343-2528
Windmill Restaurant (American) 2783 Deadwood Ave	Rapid City	SD	57702	605-342-9456

— Goods and Services —

SHOPPING

				Phone
Rushmore Mall 2200 N Maple Ave	Rapid City	SD	57701	605-341-5880

BANKS

				Phone	Fax
American State Bank of Rapid City 632 Main St *TF:* 800-363-7698 ■ *Web:* www.americanstate.com ■ *E-mail:* ams@rapidnet.com	Rapid City	SD	57702	605-348-3322	348-0012
First Western Federal Savings Bank 402 Main St	Rapid City	SD	57701	605-341-1203	341-5267
Norwest Bank 825 Saint Joseph St *TF:* 800-321-4141	Rapid City	SD	57701	605-394-3800	394-3947
Rushmore State Bank 14 Saint Joseph St	Rapid City	SD	57701	605-343-9230	343-8418
US Bank NA 701 Saint Joseph St *TF:* 800-872-2657	Rapid City	SD	57701	800-872-2657	

BUSINESS SERVICES

	Phone		Phone
Airborne Express	800-247-2676	**Manpower Temporary Services**	605-341-0100
BAX Global	800-225-5229	**Olsten Staffing Services**	605-348-8010
DHL Worldwide Express	800-225-5345	**Post Office**	605-394-8604
Federal Express	800-238-5355	**UPS**	800-742-5877
Kelly Services	605-341-5054	**Westaff**	605-343-4775
Mail Boxes Etc	800-789-4623		

— Media —

PUBLICATIONS

				Phone	Fax
Rapid City Journal‡ 507 Main St *TF:* 800-843-2300	Rapid City	SD	57701	605-394-8300	394-8463

‡Daily newspapers

TELEVISION

				Phone	Fax
KBHE-TV Ch 9 (PBS) Dakota & Cherry Sts Telecom Bldg *TF:* 800-456-0766 ■ *Web:* www.sdpb.org	Vermillion	SD	57069	605-677-5861	677-5010
KCLO-TV Ch 15 (CBS) 2497 W Chicago St	Rapid City	SD	57702	605-341-1500	348-5518
KEVN-TV Ch 7 (Fox) 2000 Skyline Dr *Web:* fox7.blackhills.com/ ■ *E-mail:* fox7tv@blackhills.com	Rapid City	SD	57709	605-394-7777	348-9128
KNBN-TV Ch 27 (NBC) 2424 South Plaza Dr	Rapid City	SD	57702	605-355-0024	355-9274
KOTA-TV Ch 3 (ABC) 518 Saint Joseph St *Web:* www.kotatv.com ■ *E-mail:* kotanews@rapidnet.com	Rapid City	SD	57701	605-342-2000	342-7305

RADIO

				Phone	Fax
KFXS-FM 100.3 MHz (CR) PO Box 8205	Rapid City	SD	57709	605-348-1100	348-8121
KIMM-AM 1150 kHz (Ctry) PO Box 8205	Rapid City	SD	57709	605-348-1100	348-8121
KKLS-AM 920 kHz (Oldies) PO Box 460	Rapid City	SD	57709	605-343-6161	343-9012
KLMP-FM 97.9 MHz (Rel) PO Box 168	Rapid City	SD	57709	605-342-6822	342-0854
KOTA-AM 1380 kHz (N/T) 518 Saint Joseph St	Rapid City	SD	57701	605-342-2000	342-7305
KTEQ-FM 91.3 MHz (Misc) 501 E Saint Joseph St	Rapid City	SD	57701	605-394-2231	

— Colleges/Universities —

				Phone	Fax
Black Hills State University 1200 University St *TF Admissions:* 800-255-2478 ■ *Web:* www.bhsu.edu	Spearfish	SD	57799	605-642-6011	642-6254
National American University 321 Kansas City St *TF:* 800-843-8892 ■ *Web:* www.nationalcollege.edu/campusrapid.html	Rapid City	SD	57701	605-394-4800	394-4871
South Dakota School of Mines & Technology 501 E Saint Joseph St *TF Admissions:* 800-544-8162 ■ *Web:* www.sdsmt.edu	Rapid City	SD	57701	605-394-2511	394-6131

— Hospitals —

				Phone	Fax
Children's Care Hospital 2800 Jackson Blvd	Rapid City	SD	57702	605-342-4412	342-4211
Rapid City Indian Hospital 3200 Canyon Lake Dr	Rapid City	SD	57702	605-355-2500	355-2504
Rapid City Regional Hospital 353 Fairmont Blvd *Web:* www.rcrh.org ■ *E-mail:* pr-marketing@rcrh.org	Rapid City	SD	57701	605-341-1000	341-8053

— Attractions —

				Phone	Fax
Adams Memorial Museum 54 Sherman St	Deadwood	SD	57732	605-578-1714	
Badlands National Park PO Box 6 *Web:* www.nps.gov/badl/	Interior	SD	57750	605-433-5361	433-5404
Bear Country USA 13820 S Hwy 16 *Web:* www.bearcountryusa.com ■ *E-mail:* pabear@bearcountryusa.com	Rapid City	SD	57702	605-343-2290	341-3206
Black Hill Institute of Geological Research 217 Main St	Hill City	SD	57745	605-574-4289	574-2518
Black Hills Caverns 2600 Cavern Rd *TF:* 800-837-9358 ■ *Web:* www.blackhillscaverns.com ■ *E-mail:* info@blackhillscaverns.com	Rapid City	SD	57702	605-343-0542	
Black Hills Community Theatre 713 7th St	Rapid City	SD	57701	605-394-1786	
Black Hills Maze & Amusements 6400 S Hwy 16	Rapid City	SD	57701	605-343-5439	
Black Hills National Forest Hwy 385 N *Web:* www.fs.fed.us/r2/blackhills	Custer	SD	57730	605-673-2251	673-5567
Black Hills Reptile Gardens Inc S Hwy 16	Rapid City	SD	57701	605-342-5873	342-6249

Rapid City — Attractions (Cont'd)

	City	State	ZIP	Phone	Fax
Booth DC Historic Fish Hatchery 423 Hatchery Cir.	Spearfish	SD	57783	605-642-7730	
Broken Boot Gold Mine Hwy 14A	Deadwood	SD	57732	605-578-9997	
Circle B Ranch Chuckwagon Suppers & Western Music Show 22735 Hwy 385	Rapid City	SD	57702	605-348-7358	348-2340
Web: blackhills-info.com/circleb/index.htm					
Cosmos of the Black Hills 3616 W Main St	Rapid City	SD	57702	605-343-9802	
Web: www.rapidweb.com/cosmos/index2.htm					
Custer County 1881 Courthouse Museum 411 Mt Rushmore Rd	Custer	SD	57730	605-673-2443	673-2443
Dahl Arts Center 713 7th St	Rapid City	SD	57701	605-394-4101	394-6121
Deadwood Livery 601 Main St	Deadwood	SD	57732	605-578-2095	578-2037
TF: 800-847-2522					
Deadwood Stage Lines Hwy 14-A	Deadwood	SD	57732	605-578-3830	
Devils Tower National Monument Hwy 110 Bldg 170	Devils Tower	WY	82714	307-467-5283	467-5350
Web: www.nps.gov/deto/					
Flintstone Bedrock City Hwys 16 & 385	Custer	SD	57730	605-673-4079	
Flying T Chuckwagon Supper & Show 8971 Hwy 16 S	Rapid City	SD	57701	605-342-1905	342-9596
Fort Hays Chuckwagon Suppers 2255 Moon Meadows Rd	Rapid City	SD	57702	605-394-9653	394-0197
Fort Meade Museum Sheridan St Bldg 55	Fort Meade	SD	57741	605-347-9822	
Ghosts of Deadwood Gulch Wax Museum 12 Lee St	Deadwood	SD	57732	605-578-3583	
Gulches of Fun Hwy 85 S	Deadwood	SD	57732	605-578-3386	
Heritage Village 1 Village Ave	Crazy Horse	SD	57730	605-673-4761	673-4775
Jewel Cave National Monument RR 1 Box 60AA	Custer	SD	57730	605-673-2288	673-3294
Web: www.nps.gov/jeca/					
Journey Museum 222 New York St	Rapid City	SD	57701	605-394-6923	394-6940
Web: www.journeymuseum.org ■ *E-mail:* journey@journeymuseum.org					
Matthews Opera House 614 Main St	Spearfish	SD	57783	605-642-7973	
Minnilusa Pioneer Museum 222 New York St	Rapid City	SD	57701	605-394-6099	394-6940
Web: www.journeymuseum.com/pioneer.html ■ *E-mail:* journey@journeymuseum.org					
Mount Rushmore Aerial Tramway 203 Cemetery Rd	Keystone	SD	57751	605-666-4478	
Mount Rushmore National Memorial Hwy 244	Keystone	SD	57751	605-574-2523	574-2307
Web: www.nps.gov/moru/					
Mountain Music Show Mt Rushmore Rd	Custer	SD	57730	605-673-2405	673-3114
Museum of Geology 501 E Saint Joseph St South Dakota School of Mines & Technology	Rapid City	SD	57701	605-394-2467	394-6131
TF: 800-544-8162 ■ *Web:* www.sdsmt.edu/services/museum ■ *E-mail:* cherbel@silver.sdsmt.edu					
National Museum of Wood Carving Hwy 16 W	Custer	SD	57730	605-673-4404	673-3843
Ranch Amusement Park 6303 S Hwy 16	Rapid City	SD	57701	605-342-3321	342-3321
Rushmore Cave 13622 Hwy 40	Keystone	SD	57751	605-255-4384	
Rushmore Waterslide Park 1715 S Hwy 16	Rapid City	SD	57701	605-348-8962	348-8962
Sitting Bull Crystal Caverns Hwy 16	Rapid City	SD	57701	605-342-2777	
South Dakota Air & Space Museum 2890 Davis Dr	Ellsworth AFB	SD	57706	605-385-5188	385-6295
Stavkirk Chapel Chapel Lane Dr	Rapid City	SD	57702	605-342-8281	
Wades Gold Mill 12401 Deerfield Rd	Hill City	SD	57745	605-574-2680	
Wind Cave National Park Hwy 385	Hot Springs	SD	57747	605-745-4600	745-4207
Web: www.nps.gov/wica/					
Windmill Energy Station I-90 & Deadwood Ave	Rapid City	SD	57709	605-348-7070	348-3438

SPORTS TEAMS & FACILITIES

	City	State	ZIP	Phone	Fax
Black Hills Gold (basketball) 444 Mt Rushmore Rd N Civic Ctr	Rapid City	SD	57701	605-343-9591	343-9643
Web: www.blackhillsbasketball.com ■ *E-mail:* contact@blackhillsbasketball.com					

— Events —

	Phone
Badlands Circuit Finals Rodeo (late October)	605-394-4115
Black Hills Heritage Festival (late June-early July)	605-341-5714
Black Hills Jazz & Blues Festival (late July)	605-394-4101
Black Hills Passion Play (early June-early September)	800-487-3223
Black Hills Pow Wow (early October)	605-341-0925
Black Hills Stock Show & Rodeo (late January-early February)	605-355-3861
Blue Grass Festival (late June)	605-394-4101
Central States Fair (mid-late August)	605-355-3861
Custer State Park Buffalo Roundup (early October)	605-255-4515
Days of '76 (late July-early August)	800-999-1876
Home & Industry Show (late March)	800-487-3223
Mount Rushmore International Marathon (mid-October)	605-348-7866
Spearfish Festival in the Park (July)	800-487-3223

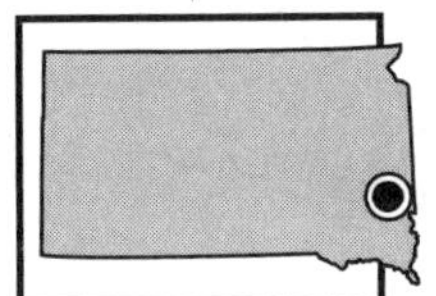

Sioux Falls

The city known today as Sioux Falls was abandoned in 1862 due to Indian uprisings. Three years later Fort Dakota was established in the area, and by 1870 settlers returned to reclaim the town. The city was named for the triple waterfalls of Big Sioux River, and today there are three areas from which Big Sioux River Falls may be viewed. Downtown Sioux Falls is home to the Great Plains Zoo and Delbridge Museum of Natural History, and replicas of Michelangelo's David and Moses are among the city's many public sculptures. Ten miles northeast of downtown is the Earth Resources Observation System (EROS) Data Center, a program of the U.S. Department of the Interior. EROS houses millions of frames of satellite and aircraft photographs of the earth.

Population	116,762	**Longitude**	96-70-00 W
Area (Land)	43.3 sq mi	**County**	Minnehana
Area (Water)	0 sq mi	**Time Zone**	CST
Elevation	1442 ft	**Area Code/s**	605
Latitude	43-55-00 N		

— Average Temperatures and Precipitation —

TEMPERATURES

	Jan	Feb	Mar	Apr	May	Jun	Jul	Aug	Sep	Oct	Nov	Dec
High	24	30	42	59	71	81	86	83	73	61	43	28
Low	3	10	23	35	46	56	62	59	49	36	23	9

PRECIPITATION

	Jan	Feb	Mar	Apr	May	Jun	Jul	Aug	Sep	Oct	Nov	Dec
Inches	0.5	0.6	1.6	2.5	3.0	3.4	2.7	2.9	3.0	1.8	1.1	0.7

— Important Phone Numbers —

	Phone		Phone
AAA	605-336-3690	**Time/Temp**	605-361-5050
Emergency	911	**Weather**	605-330-4444
Poison Control Center	800-352-2222		

— Information Sources —

	City	State	ZIP	Phone	Fax
Minnehaha County 415 N Dakota Ave	Sioux Falls	SD	57104	605-367-4206	367-8314
Sioux Falls Area Chamber of Commerce 200 N Phillips Ave Suite 102	Sioux Falls	SD	57104	605-336-1620	336-6499
Web: www.siouxfalls.org					
Sioux Falls Arena 1201 West Ave N	Sioux Falls	SD	57104	605-367-7288	338-1463
Sioux Falls City Hall 224 W 9th St	Sioux Falls	SD	57104	605-367-7200	367-8490
Web: www.sioux-falls.org					
Sioux Falls Community Development Dept 224 W 9th St	Sioux Falls	SD	57104	605-367-7125	367-8798
Web: www.sioux-falls.org/traditional/city_departments/community_development					
Sioux Falls Convention & Visitors Bureau 200 N Phillips Ave Suite 102	Sioux Falls	SD	57104	605-336-1620	336-6499
TF: 800-333-2072 ■ *Web:* www.siouxfalls.org/					

Sioux Falls — Information Sources (Cont'd)

	City	State	ZIP	Phone	Fax
Sioux Falls Development Foundation Inc 200 N Phillips Ave Suite 101 *TF:* 800-658-3373	Sioux Falls	SD	57104	605-339-0103	339-0055
Sioux Falls Mayor 224 W 9th St.	Sioux Falls	SD	57104	605-367-7200	367-8490
Sioux Falls Siouxland Libraries 201 N Main Ave *Web:* www.siouxland.lib.sd.us	Sioux Falls	SD	57104	605-367-7081	367-4312

On-Line Resources

Area Guide Sioux Falls .... siouxfalls.areaguides.net
Excite.com Sioux Falls City Guide .... www.excite.com/travel/countries/united_states/south_dakota/sioux_falls

— Transportation Services —

AIRPORTS

■ **Sioux Falls Regional Airport (FSD)**

Phone

3 miles NW of downtown (approx 10 minutes) 605-336-0762
Web: www.sfairport.com ■ *E-mail:* info@sfairport.com

Airport Transportation

	Phone
Airport Taxi $6 fare to downtown	605-336-1500
Yellow Cab $6 fare to downtown	605-336-1616

Commercial Airlines

	Phone		Phone
Northwest	800-225-2525	**United Express**	800-241-6522
TWA	800-221-2000		

Charter Airlines

	Phone		Phone
Business Aviation	605-336-7791	**Superior Aviation**	800-882-7751
Helicopter Flight Inc	800-452-3884		

CAR RENTALS

	Phone		Phone
Avis	605-336-1184	**Five Star Rental**	605-336-3515
Budget	605-334-4211	**Hertz**	605-336-8790
Enterprise	605-338-1900	**National**	605-332-8111

LIMO/TAXI

	Phone		Phone
Diamond Dynasty Limousine	605-336-7433	**Royal Limousine**	605-332-7952
Metro Taxi	605-332-1234	**Yellow Cab**	605-336-1616

MASS TRANSIT

	Phone
Sioux Falls Transit $1 Base fare	605-367-7183

RAIL/BUS

	City	State	ZIP	Phone
Greyhound Bus Station 301 N Dakota Ave *TF:* 800-231-2222	Sioux Falls	SD	57104	605-336-0885

— Accommodations —

HOTELS, MOTELS, RESORTS

	City	State	ZIP	Phone	Fax
Albert House Hotel 333 N Phillips Ave	Sioux Falls	SD	57104	605-336-1680	
AmericInn Motel 3508 S Gateway Blvd *TF:* 800-634-3444 ■ *Web:* www.americinn.com/southdakota/siouxfalls.html	Sioux Falls	SD	57106	605-361-3538	
Arena Motel 2401 W Russell St *TF:* 800-204-1470	Sioux Falls	SD	57104	605-336-1470	373-0693
Baymont Inns & Suites 3200 Meadow Ave. *TF:* 800-301-0200	Sioux Falls	SD	57106	605-362-0835	362-0836
Best Western Empire Towers 4100 W Shirley Pl. *TF:* 800-528-1234	Sioux Falls	SD	57106	605-361-3118	361-3118
Best Western Ramkota Inn 2400 N Louise Ave *TF:* 800-528-1234	Sioux Falls	SD	57107	605-336-0650	336-1687
Best Western Staurolite Inn 2515 E 6th St *TF:* 800-528-1234	Brookings	SD	57006	605-692-9421	692-9421
Brimark Inn 3200 W Russell St *TF:* 800-658-4508	Sioux Falls	SD	57107	605-332-2000	332-2000
Brookings Inn 2500 E 6th St *TF:* 877-831-5162	Brookings	SD	57006	605-692-9471	692-5807
Budget Host Inn 2620 E 10th St *TF:* 888-336-1550	Sioux Falls	SD	57103	605-336-1550	338-4752
Center Inn 900 E 20th St *TF:* 800-456-0074	Sioux Falls	SD	57105	605-334-9002	
Comfort Inn 3216 S Carolyn Ave *TF:* 800-228-5150	Sioux Falls	SD	57106	605-361-2822	361-2822
Comfort Inn North 5100 N Cliff Ave. *TF:* 800-228-5150 ■ *Web:* www.comfortinn.com/hotel/sd011	Sioux Falls	SD	57104	605-331-4490	331-4490
Comfort Suites 3208 Carolyn Ave *TF:* 800-228-5150	Sioux Falls	SD	57106	605-362-9711	362-9711
Country Inn & Suites 200 E 8th St *TF:* 800-456-4000	Sioux Falls	SD	57102	605-373-0153	373-0153
Days Inn Empire 3401 Gateway Blvd *TF:* 800-329-7466	Sioux Falls	SD	57106	605-361-9240	361-5419
Days Inn North 5001 N Cliff Ave *TF:* 800-329-7466	Sioux Falls	SD	57104	605-331-5959	331-5959
Empire Inn 4208 W 41st St *TF:* 800-341-8000	Sioux Falls	SD	57106	605-361-2345	361-2345
Exel Inn 1300 W Russell St *TF:* 800-356-8013	Sioux Falls	SD	57104	605-331-5800	331-4074
Fairfield Inn by Marriott 4501 W Empire Pl. *TF:* 800-228-2800 ■ *Web:* fairfieldinn.com/FSDSF	Sioux Falls	SD	57106	605-361-2211	361-2211
Holiday Inn City Centre 100 W 8th St. *TF:* 800-465-4329	Sioux Falls	SD	57104	605-339-2000	339-3724
Kelly Inn Sioux Falls 3101 W Russell St. *TF:* 800-635-3559	Sioux Falls	SD	57107	605-338-6242	338-5453
Microtel Inn 2901 S Carolyn Ave *TF:* 888-771-7171	Sioux Falls	SD	57106	605-361-7484	361-7884
Motel 6 3009 W Russell St *TF:* 800-466-8356	Sioux Falls	SD	57107	605-336-7800	330-9273
Oaks Hotel 3300 W Russell St *TF:* 800-326-4656	Sioux Falls	SD	57101	605-336-9000	336-9000
Radisson Encore Inn 4300 Empire Pl *TF:* 800-333-3333	Sioux Falls	SD	57106	605-361-6684	362-0916
Ramada Inn 1301 W Russell St *TF:* 800-272-6232	Sioux Falls	SD	57104	605-336-1020	336-3030
Ramada Limited 407 S Lyons Ave *TF:* 800-272-6232	Sioux Falls	SD	57106	605-330-0000	330-0402
Residence Inn by Marriott 4509 W Empire Pl. *TF:* 800-331-3131 ■ *Web:* www.residenceinn.com/FSDRI	Sioux Falls	SD	57103	605-361-2202	361-2202
Select Inn 3500 S Gateway Blvd *TF:* 800-641-1000 ■ *Web:* www.selectinn.com	Sioux Falls	SD	57106	605-361-1864	361-9287
Sleep Inn 1500 N Kiwanis Ave *TF:* 800-753-3746	Sioux Falls	SD	57104	605-339-3992	339-3992
Super 8 Motel 4100 W 41st St. *TF:* 800-800-8000	Sioux Falls	SD	57106	605-361-9719	361-9719
Super 8 Motel North Cliff 4808 N Cliff Ave *TF:* 800-800-8000	Sioux Falls	SD	57104	605-339-9212	333-0447
Valley Inn 1000 S Grange Ave	Sioux Falls	SD	57105	605-335-3040	335-0073

— Restaurants —

	City	State	ZIP	Phone
Baxter's Cafe (American) 4001 E 10th St	Sioux Falls	SD	57103	605-331-3615
Block & Barrel Bar & Grill (American) 1301 W Russell St	Sioux Falls	SD	57104	605-336-1020
Cherry Creek Grill (American) 3104 E 26th St.	Sioux Falls	SD	57103	605-336-2333
Doc & Eddy's (American) 3501 W 41st St	Sioux Falls	SD	57116	605-361-8700
Dorchester The (American) 2400 N Louise Ave	Sioux Falls	SD	57107	605-336-0650
French Quarter (Cajun) 3915 S Hawthorne Ave	Sioux Falls	SD	57105	605-334-8838
Minerva's (Steak/Seafood) 301 S Phillips Ave	Sioux Falls	SD	57104	605-334-0386
Park Place Cafe & Terrace (American) 100 W 8th St	Sioux Falls	SD	57104	605-339-2000
Sanchez Taquitos (Mexican) 332 S Phillips Ave.	Sioux Falls	SD	57104	605-336-5040
Sioux Falls Brewing Company (American) 431 N Phillips Ave *Web:* www.sfbrewco.com	Sioux Falls	SD	57104	605-332-4847
Soon's Jade Garden (Chinese) 3312 S Holly Ave.	Sioux Falls	SD	57105	605-334-1911
Spezia (Italian) 1716 S Western Ave	Sioux Falls	SD	57105	605-334-7491
Theo's Restaurant (American) 601 W 33rd St.	Sioux Falls	SD	57105	605-338-6801

Sioux Falls — Restaurants (Cont'd)

				Phone
Upper Cut (American) 2819 E 10th St	Sioux Falls	SD	57103	605-336-0900
Valentino's (Italian) 2000 W 41st St	Sioux Falls	SD	57105	605-339-9900

— Goods and Services —

SHOPPING

				Phone	Fax
Empire Mall 4001 W 41st St	Sioux Falls	SD	57106	605-361-3300	361-5411
Main Street Sioux Falls 230 S Phillips Ave Suite 110	Sioux Falls	SD	57104	605-338-4009	338-8816
Western Mall 2101 W 41st St	Sioux Falls	SD	57105	605-336-6920	336-5651
E-mail: www.western.mall@ideasign.com					

BANKS

				Phone	Fax
BankFirst 2600 W 49th St	Sioux Falls	SD	57105	605-361-2111	361-2690
Web: www.bankfirstcorp.com ■ *E-mail:* customer.service@bankfirstcorp.com					
Citibank NA 701 E 60th St N	Sioux Falls	SD	57117	605-331-2626	331-1185*
**Fax:* Hum Res ■ *TF:* 800-843-0777					
CorTrust Bank 1801 S Marion Rd	Sioux Falls	SD	57106	605-361-8356	361-9237
Dacotah Bank 1707 S Marion Rd	Sioux Falls	SD	57106	605-361-5636	362-1331
Dakota State Bank PO Box 85307	Sioux Falls	SD	57118	605-338-7255	334-0788
Dial Bank 3201 N 4th Ave	Sioux Falls	SD	57104	605-336-3933	433-9491*
**Fax Area Code:* 800					
F & M Bank 1901 41st St	Sioux Falls	SD	57105	605-334-2548	339-8862
First National Bank of Sioux Falls PO Box 5186	Sioux Falls	SD	57117	605-335-5100	335-5191*
**Fax:* Mail Rm					
First Premier Bank 601 S Minnesota Ave	Sioux Falls	SD	57104	605-357-3000	357-3185
First Savings Bank 2301 E 10th St	Sioux Falls	SD	57103	605-373-9840	373-9731
Founders Trust National Bank 418 S Minnesota Ave	Sioux Falls	SD	57104	605-333-9828	333-9843
Home Federal Savings Bank 225 S Main Ave	Sioux Falls	SD	57104	605-333-7620	333-7621
Norwest Bank South Dakota NA 101 N Phillips Ave	Sioux Falls	SD	57101	605-575-7300	575-4984*
**Fax:* Hum Res ■ *TF:* 800-321-4141					
US Bank NA 141 N Main Ave	Sioux Falls	SD	57104	605-339-8941	
TF: 800-872-2657					

BUSINESS SERVICES

	Phone		Phone
Airborne Express	800-247-2676	**Kinko's**	605-333-0750
BAX Global	800-225-5229	**Mail Boxes Etc**	800-789-4623
DHL Worldwide Express	800-225-5345	**Post Office**	605-357-5000
Federal Express	800-238-5355	**UPS**	800-742-5877

— Media —

PUBLICATIONS

				Phone	Fax
Argus Leader‡ 200 S Minnesota Ave	Sioux Falls	SD	57104	605-331-2200	331-2294
Web: www.argusleader.com					

‡Daily newspapers

TELEVISION

				Phone	Fax
KDLT-TV Ch 46 (NBC) 3600 S Westport Ave	Sioux Falls	SD	57106	605-361-5555	361-3982
Web: www.kdlt.com					
KELO-TV Ch 11 (CBS) 501 S Phillips Ave	Sioux Falls	SD	57104	605-336-1100	336-0202*
**Fax:* News Rm ■ *Web:* www.kelotv.com ■ *E-mail:* kelotv@dakotaconnect.com					
KSFY-TV Ch 13 (ABC) 300 N Dakota Ave Suite 100	Sioux Falls	SD	57104	605-336-1300	336-7936
Web: www.ksfy.com ■ *E-mail:* ksfy@ksfy.com					
KTTW-TV Ch 17 (Fox) 2817 W 11th St	Sioux Falls	SD	57104	605-338-0017	338-7173
KUSD-TV Ch 2 (PBS) Dakota & Cherry Sts Telecom Bldg	Vermillion	SD	57069	605-677-5861	677-5010
TF: 800-456-0766 ■ *Web:* www.sdpb.org					

RADIO

				Phone	Fax
KBHE-FM 89.3 MHz (NPR) PO Box 5000	Vermillion	SD	57069	605-677-5861	677-5010
Web: www.sdpb.org					
KCSD-FM 90.9 MHz (NPR) 1101 W 22nd St	Sioux Falls	SD	57105	605-331-6690	331-6692
KELO-AM 1320 kHz (Oldies) 500 S Phillips Ave	Sioux Falls	SD	57104	605-331-5350	336-0415
Web: www.keloam.com ■ *E-mail:* keloam@mmi.net					
KELO-FM 92.5 MHz (AC) 500 S Phillips Ave	Sioux Falls	SD	57104	605-331-5350	336-0415
Web: www.kelofm.com ■ *E-mail:* kelofm@mmi.net					
KESD-FM 88.3 MHz (NPR) PO Box 5000	Vermillion	SD	57069	605-677-5861	677-5010
Web: www.sdpb.org					
KKLS-FM 104.7 MHz (CHR) 3205 S Meadow Ave	Sioux Falls	SD	57106	605-361-6550	361-5410
KNWC-AM 1270 kHz (Rel) 26908 Marion Rd	Sioux Falls	SD	57108	605-339-1270	339-1271
TF: 888-569-5692 ■ *Web:* www.knwc.org ■ *E-mail:* knwc@knwc.org					
KRSD-FM 88.1 MHz (Clas) Augustana College Box 737	Sioux Falls	SD	57197	605-335-6666	335-1259
TF: 800-228-7123					
KSFS-AM 1520 kHz (Sports) 305 W 14th St	Sioux Falls	SD	57104	605-335-8800	335-8428
Web: www.ksfs.com ■ *E-mail:* thezone@dakotaconnect.com					
KSOO-AM 1140 kHz (N/T) 2600 S Spring Ave	Sioux Falls	SD	57105	605-339-1140	339-2735
Web: www.ksoo.com					
KTSD-FM 91.1 MHz (NPR) PO Box 5000	Vermillion	SD	57069	605-677-5861	677-5010
Web: www.sdpb.org					
KTWB-FM 101.9 MHz (Ctry) 500 S Phillips Ave	Sioux Falls	SD	57104	605-331-5350	336-0415
Web: www.ktwb.com					
KXRB-AM 1000 kHz (Ctry) 3205 S Meadow Ave	Sioux Falls	SD	57106	605-361-6550	361-5410
Web: www.kxrb.com					

— Colleges/Universities —

				Phone	Fax
Augustana College 2001 S Summit Ave	Sioux Falls	SD	57197	605-336-0770	336-5518
Web: www.augie.edu ■ *E-mail:* info@inst.augie.edu					
Kilian Community College 224 N Phillips Ave	Sioux Falls	SD	57104	605-336-1711	336-2606
TF: 800-888-1147 ■ *Web:* kcc.cc.sd.us					
National American University Sioux Falls Campus 2801 S Kiwanis Ave Suite 100	Sioux Falls	SD	57105	605-334-5430	334-1575
Web: www.nationalcollege.edu/campusfalls.html					
University of Sioux Falls 1101 W 22nd St	Sioux Falls	SD	57105	605-331-5000	331-6615
TF Admissions: 800-888-1047 ■ *Web:* www.thecoo.edu					

— Hospitals —

				Phone	Fax
Avera McKennan Hospital 800 E 21st St	Sioux Falls	SD	57105	605-322-8000	322-7822
Web: www.mckennan.org					
Royal C Johnson Veterans Memorial Hospital PO Box 5046	Sioux Falls	SD	57117	605-336-3230	333-6878
Sioux Valley Hospital 1100 S Euclid Ave	Sioux Falls	SD	57117	605-333-1000	333-7201*
**Fax:* Admitting ■ *Web:* www.siouxvalley.org ■ *E-mail:* info@siouxvalley.org					

— Attractions —

				Phone	Fax
Buffalo Ridge Old West Ghost Town I-90 5 miles W of Sioux Falls	Sioux Falls	SD	57115	605-528-3931	
Catfish Bay 5500 N Show Pl	Sioux Falls	SD	57104	605-339-0911	
Center for Western Studies 29th St & S Summit Ave Augustana College	Sioux Falls	SD	57197	605-336-4007	336-4999
Civic Fine Arts Center 235 W 10th St	Sioux Falls	SD	57104	605-336-1167	332-2615
Delbridge Museum of Natural History 805 S Kiwanis Ave	Sioux Falls	SD	57104	605-367-7003	367-8340
Falls Park McClellan St & 3rd Ave	Sioux Falls	SD	57109	605-367-7060	
Great Plains Zoo 805 S Kiwanis Ave	Sioux Falls	SD	57104	605-367-7059	367-8340
Main Street Sioux Falls 230 S Phillips Ave Suite 110	Sioux Falls	SD	57104	605-338-4009	338-8816

Sioux Falls — Attractions (Cont'd)

	City	State	ZIP	Phone	Fax
Multi-Cultural Center of Sioux Falls 515 N Main Ave	Sioux Falls	SD	57104	605-367-7400	367-7404
Northern Plains Tribal Arts Gallery 1000 N West Ave Suite 230 *TF:* 800-658-4797	Sioux Falls	SD	57104	605-334-4060	334-8415
Old Courthouse Museum 200 W 6th St	Sioux Falls	SD	57104	605-367-4210	367-6004
Palisades State Park 25495 485th Ave	Garretson	SD	57030	605-594-3824	
Performance Car Museum 3505 S Phillips Ave *Web:* www.performancecarmuseum.com	Sioux Falls	SD	57105	605-338-4884	357-9640
Pettigrew Home & Museum 131 N Duluth Ave	Sioux Falls	SD	57104	605-367-7097	331-0467
Rehfeld's Galleries 210 S Phillips Ave	Sioux Falls	SD	57104	605-336-9737	336-2631
Savage Art Gallery & Museum 3301 E 26th St *TF:* 888-781-4304 ■ *Web:* www.savageartgallery.com	Sioux Falls	SD	57103	605-332-7551	332-7551
Sioux Empire Medical Museum 1100 S Euclid Ave	Sioux Falls	SD	57117	605-333-6397	333-1577
South Dakota Symphony Orchestra Washington Pavilion of Arts & Science	Sioux Falls	SD	57104	605-335-7933	335-1958
Statue of Moses 30th St & Grange Ave	Sioux Falls	SD	57105	605-336-5417	
Thunder Road Family Fun Park 401 N Kiwanis Ave *TF:* 888-943-7623	Sioux Falls	SD	57104	605-334-4181	978-1831
USGS AEROS Data Center Mundt Federal Bldg **Fax:* Cust Svc ■ *TF Cust Svc:* 800-252-4547 ■ *Web:* edcwww.cr.usgs.gov ■ *E-mail:* edcweb@edcwww.cr.usgs.gov	Sioux Falls	SD	57198	605-594-6511	594-6589*
USS South Dakota Battleship Memorial 12th St & Kiwanis Ave	Sioux Falls	SD	57102	605-367-7060	
Wild Water West 26767 466th Ave	Sioux Falls	SD	57106	605-339-2837	361-3173

SPORTS TEAMS & FACILITIES

	City	State	ZIP	Phone	Fax
Huset's Speedway Hwy 11 *Web:* www.husets-speedway.com	Brandon	SD	57005	605-582-3536	582-6082
Sioux Falls Arena 1201 West Ave N	Sioux Falls	SD	57104	605-367-7288	338-1463
Sioux Falls Canaries (baseball) West Ave N Sioux Falls Stadium *Web:* canaries.iw.net	Sioux Falls	SD	57104	605-333-0179	333-0139
Sioux Falls Skyforce (basketball) 1201 West Ave N Sioux Falls Arena *Web:* skyforce.iw.net ■ *E-mail:* skyforce@iw.net	Sioux Falls	SD	57102	605-332-0605	332-2305

— Events —

	Phone
Almost Forgotten Crafts (late April)	605-367-4210
Artists of the Plains Art Show & Sale (mid-February)	605-336-4007
Augustana Jazz Festival (early March)	605-336-4049
Festival of Choirs (early April)	605-367-7957
Northern Plains Tribal Art Show & Market (late September)	605-334-4060
Northern Prairie Storytelling Festival (early June)	605-331-6622
Sidewalk Arts Festival (early September)	605-336-1167
Sioux Empire Fair (early-mid-August)	605-367-7178
Sioux Empire Farm Show (late January)	605-373-2016
University of Sioux Falls Cougar Days (early October)	605-331-5000
Viking Days (early October)	605-336-5521
Winter Fest (late January)	605-338-4009

Tennessee

Population (1999): 5,483,535 **Area (sq mi): 42,146**

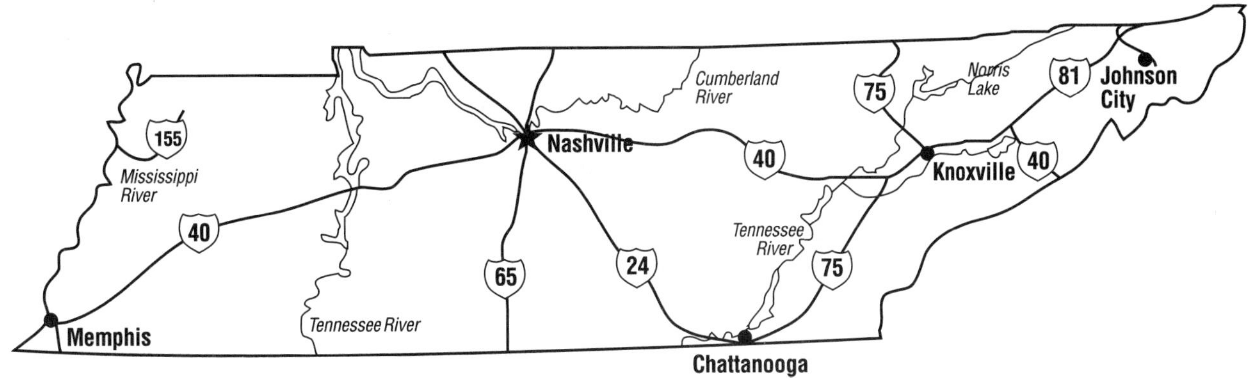

— State Information Sources —

				Phone	Fax
Tennessee Assn of Business 611 Commerce St Suite 3030 *Web:* www.tennbiz.org	Nashville	TN	37203	615-256-5141	256-6726
Tennessee Economic & Community Development Dept 320 6th Ave N *Web:* www.state.tn.us/ecd/	Nashville	TN	37243	615-741-1888	741-7306
Tennessee State Government Information *Web:* www.state.tn.us				615-741-3011	
Tennessee State Library & Archives 403 7th Ave N *Web:* www.state.tn.us/sos/statelib/tslahome.htm ■ *E-mail:* referenc@mail.state.tn.us	Nashville	TN	37243	615-741-2764	741-6471
Tennessee State Parks Bureau 401 Church St L&C Tower 7th Fl *TF:* 888-867-2757 ■ *Web:* www.tnstateparks.com	Nashville	TN	37243	615-532-0001	532-0732
Tennessee Tourist Development Dept 320 6th Ave Rachel Jackson Bldg 5th Fl *TF:* 800-836-6200 ■ *Web:* www.state.tn.us/tourdev ■ *E-mail:* tourdev@www.state.tn.us	Nashville	TN	37243	615-741-8299	741-7225

ON-LINE RESOURCES

Best Read Guide Smoky Mountains . . . . . bestreadguide.com/smokymtns
Go Tennessee . . . . . www.gotennessee.com
InTennessee.com . . . . . www.intennessee.com
Rough Guide Travel Tennessee travel.roughguides.com/content/746/index.htm
Smoky Mountain Information . . . . . www.smoky.net
Tennessee Cities . . . . . dir.yahoo.com/Regional/U_S__States/Tennessee/Cities
Tennessee Cities By County . . . . . dir.yahoo.com/Regional/U_S__States/Tennessee/Counties_and_Regions
Tennessee Scenario . . . . . scenariousa.dstylus.com/tn/indexf.htm
Tennessee Travel & Tourism Guide . . . . . www.travel-library.com/north_america/usa/tennessee/index.html
Tennessee Web . . . . . www.tennweb.com
Travel.org-Tennessee . . . . . travel.org/tennesse.html
Welcome to Smoky Mountain Land . . . . . www.smokymountainland.com
Yahoo! Get Local Tennessee . . . . . dir.yahoo.com/Regional/U_S__States/Tennessee

— Cities Profiled —

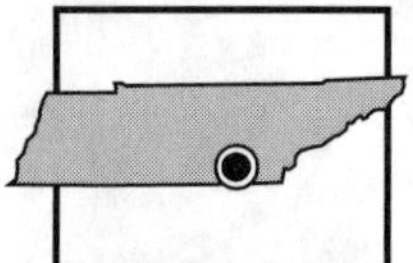

Chattanooga

The name Chattanooga comes from the Creek word meaning "rock coming to a point," which was used to describe Lookout Mountain. The city is situated at the base of the mountain, along the Tennessee River, and is the geographic center of the seven-state region served by the Tennessee Valley Authority. All seven states can be seen from Rock City Gardens (named for its unusual rock formations), which is just one of several attractions on Lookout Mountain. Others include Ruby Falls, a 145-foot underground waterfall in a cavern in the heart of the mountain; the Incline Railway, which offers rides up and down the mountain and has a 72.7 percent grade near the top; and Point Park, located on the mountain's crest overlooking Chattanooga. In the city itself, in the center of Ross's Landing Park and Plaza, is the Tennessee Aquarium, the world's first freshwater aquarium. Ross's Landing was the trading center from which the city of Chattanooga evolved. By the time of the Civil War the city had become an important railroad center, and the old railroad terminal is now part of the Chattanooga Choo Choo/Holiday Inn Complex, which also includes restaurants, shops, sleeping rooms in railroad cars, a convention center, a trolley, gardens, and a largest-of-its-kind model railroad exhibit.

Population	147,790	**Longitude**	85-23-86 W
Area (Land)	118.4 sq mi	**County**	Hamilton
Area (Water)	7.9 sq mi	**Time Zone**	EST
Elevation	685 ft	**Area Code/s**	423
Latitude	34-99-72 N		

— Average Temperatures and Precipitation —

TEMPERATURES

	Jan	Feb	Mar	Apr	May	Jun	Jul	Aug	Sep	Oct	Nov	Dec
High	47	52	62	71	79	86	89	88	82	72	61	51
Low	28	31	39	47	55	64	68	68	63	49	40	31

PRECIPITATION

	Jan	Feb	Mar	Apr	May	Jun	Jul	Aug	Sep	Oct	Nov	Dec
Inches	4.9	4.8	6.0	4.3	4.4	3.5	4.9	3.5	4.2	3.2	4.6	5.2

— Important Phone Numbers —

	Phone		Phone
AAA	423-490-2000	**HotelDocs**	800-468-3537
American Express Travel	423-266-1893	**Poison Control Center**	803-777-1117
ARTSline	423-756-2787	**Time/Temp**	423-265-1411
Emergency	911		

— Information Sources —

				Phone	Fax
Better Business Bureau Serving Southeast Tennessee & Northwest Georgia 1010 Market St Suite 200	Chattanooga	TN	37402	423-266-6144	267-1924
Web: www.chattanooga.bbb.org ■ *E-mail:* tngabbb@gte.net					
Chattanooga Area Chamber of Commerce 1001 Market St.	Chattanooga	TN	37402	423-756-2121	267-7242
Web: www.chattanooga.net/chamber ■ *E-mail:* info@chamber.chattanooga.net					
Chattanooga Area Convention & Visitors Bureau 2 Broad St	Chattanooga	TN	37402	423-756-8687	265-1630
TF: 800-322-3344 ■ *Web:* www.chattanooga.net/cvb ■ *E-mail:* cvb@chattanooga.net					
Chattanooga City Hall 100 E 11th St Suite 100	Chattanooga	TN	37402	423-757-5152	757-0005
Web: www.chattanooga.gov					
Chattanooga Downtown Partnership 850 Market St Miller Plaza 2nd Fl	Chattanooga	TN	37402	423-265-0771	265-6952
Chattanooga-Hamilton County Bicentennial Library 1001 Broad St.	Chattanooga	TN	37402	423-757-5310	
Web: www.lib.chattanooga.gov ■ *E-mail:* library@lib.chattanooga.gov					
Chattanooga Mayor 100 E 11th St	Chattanooga	TN	37402	423-757-5152	757-0005
Web: www.chattanooga.gov/mayor ■ *E-mail:* mayor@mail.chattanooga.gov					
Chattanooga Regional Planning Agency 100 City Hall Annex Suite 200	Chattanooga	TN	37402	423-757-5216	757-5532
Web: www.chcrpa.org					
East Ridge Convention Center 1417 N Mack Smith Rd	Chattanooga	TN	37412	423-899-6370	899-5849
Hamilton County County Courthouse Rm 201	Chattanooga	TN	37402	423-209-6500	209-6501

On-Line Resources

Anthill City Guide Chattanooga	www.anthill.com/city.asp?city=chattanooga
Area Guide Chattanooga	chattanooga.areaguides.net
Chattanooga CityLink	www.usacitylink.com/citylink/chatt/
Chattanooga Directory	www.vic.com/~smokyweb/chatt/
Chattanooga.TheLinks.com	chattanooga.thelinks.com/
City Knowledge Chattanooga	www.cityknowledge.com/tn_chattanooga.htm
Excite.com Chattanooga City Guide	www.excite.com/travel/countries/united_states/tennessee/chattanooga
Guest Guide Online	www.guestguideonline.com
SurfNChattanooga	www.surfnchattanooga.com
Virtual Chattanooga	www.chattanooga.net/

— Transportation Services —

AIRPORTS

■ **Chattanooga Metropolitan Airport (CHA)**

	Phone
8 miles E of downtown (approx 20 minutes)	423-855-2200
Web: www.chattairport.com	

Airport Transportation

	Phone
Checker Cab $12 fare to downtown	423-624-1410

Commercial Airlines

	Phone		Phone
Atlantic Southeast	800-282-3424	**Northwest**	800-225-2525
Comair	800-354-9822	**US Airways**	800-428-4322
Delta Connection	800-221-1212	**US Airways Express**	800-428-4322

CAR RENTALS

	Phone		Phone
Avis	423-855-2232	**Hertz**	423-855-8131
Budget	423-855-2224	**National**	423-855-2229
Enterprise	423-894-0707	**Rent-A-Wreck**	423-899-3127
Express	423-855-2277		

LIMO/TAXI

	Phone		Phone
Aaero Limousine	423-490-0208	**Nino's Limousine**	423-624-1495
Bell Limo	423-867-1515	**Redbird Cab Co.**	423-756-0008
Checker Cab	423-624-1410	**Turner Limousine**	423-622-3173
East Ridge Cab Co	423-899-2289	**United Cab**	423-622-5114
Mercury Cab	423-624-1084		

MASS TRANSIT

	Phone
CARTA $1.00 Base fare	423-629-1473
Downtown Electric Shuttle Free	423-629-1411

RAIL/BUS

				Phone
Greyhound Bus Station 960 Airport Rd	Chattanooga	TN	37402	423-892-1277
TF: 800-231-2222				

Chattanooga (Cont'd)

— Accommodations —

HOTELS, MOTELS, RESORTS

				Phone	Fax
Adams Hilborne Hotel 801 Vine St	Chattanooga	TN	37403	423-265-5000	265-5555
TF: 888-446-6569					
Best Western Heritage Inn 7641 Lee Hwy	Chattanooga	TN	37421	423-899-3311	899-4259
TF: 800-441-8034					
Best Western Royal Inn 3644 Cummings Hwy	Chattanooga	TN	37419	423-821-6840	821-6840
Britcan Inns 6510 Ringgold Rd	Chattanooga	TN	37412	423-894-0911	894-0920
Clarion Hotel Chattanooga 407 Chestnut St	Chattanooga	TN	37402	423-756-5150	265-8708
TF: 800-252-7466 ■ *Web:* www.chattanoogaclarion.com ■ *E-mail:* clarion@cdc.net					
Comfort Suites 7324 Shallowford Rd	Chattanooga	TN	37421	423-892-1500	892-0111
TF: 800-228-5150					
Country Suites by Carlson 7051 McCutcheon Rd	Chattanooga	TN	37421	423-899-2300	899-2282
TF: 800-456-4000					
Courtyard by Marriott 2210 Bams Dr.	Chattanooga	TN	37421	423-499-4400	499-2642
TF: 800-321-2211 ■ *Web:* courtyard.com/CHACH					
Days Inn 7725 Lee Hwy	Chattanooga	TN	37421	423-899-2288	899-2288
TF: 800-329-7466					
Days Inn & Suites 101 E 20th St	Chattanooga	TN	37408	423-267-9761	267-5410
TF: 800-325-2525					
Econo Lodge 7421 Bonny Oaks Dr	Chattanooga	TN	37421	423-499-9550	499-8715
TF: 800-553-2666					
Extended StayAmerica 6240 Airpark Dr	Chattanooga	TN	37421	423-892-1315	892-6871
TF: 800-398-7829					
Fairfield Inn 2350 Shallowford Village Dr.	Chattanooga	TN	37421	423-499-3800	
TF: 800-228-2800 ■ *Web:* fairfieldinn.com/CHAFI/					
Hampton Inn 7013 Shallowford Rd	Chattanooga	TN	37421	423-855-0095	894-7600
TF: 800-426-7866					
Holiday Inn 2345 Shallowford Village Dr	Chattanooga	TN	37421	423-855-2898	499-8771
TF: 800-842-8396					
Holiday Inn Chattanooga Choo Choo 1400 Market St.	Chattanooga	TN	37402	423-266-5000	265-4635
TF: 800-872-2529 ■ *Web:* www.choochoo.com ■ *E-mail:* frontdesk@choochoo.com					
Kings Lodge 2400 Westside Dr.	Chattanooga	TN	37404	423-698-8944	698-8949
TF: 800-251-7702					
Knights Inn 2100 Market St	Chattanooga	TN	37408	423-265-0551	265-7946
TF: 800-843-5644					
La Quinta Motor Inn 7015 Shallowford Rd.	Chattanooga	TN	37421	423-855-0011	499-5409
TF: 800-687-6667					
Marriott Chattanooga 2 Carter Plaza	Chattanooga	TN	37402	423-756-0002	266-2254
TF: 800-841-1674 ■ *Web:* marriotthotels.com/CHADT					
McElhattan's Owl Hill 617 Scenic Hwy	Chattanooga	TN	37409	423-821-2040	
Microtel Inn 2440 Williams St	Chattanooga	TN	37408	423-265-7300	265-1140
TF: 888-771-7171					
Motel 6 7707 Lee Hwy.	Chattanooga	TN	37421	423-892-7707	899-3818
TF: 800-466-8356					
Quality Inn 2000 E 23rd St	Chattanooga	TN	37404	423-622-8353	622-0931
TF: 800-221-2222					
Radisson Read House Hotel & Suites 827 Broad St	Chattanooga	TN	37402	423-266-4121	267-6447
TF: 800-333-3333					
Ramada Limited 2361 Shallowford Village Dr.	Chattanooga	TN	37421	423-855-2090	
TF: 800-272-6232					
Ramada Stadium Inn 100 W 21st St.	Chattanooga	TN	37408	423-265-3151	265-3532
TF: 800-828-4656					
Red Roof Inn 7014 Shallowford Rd.	Chattanooga	TN	37421	423-899-0143	899-8384
TF: 800-843-7663					
Shoney's Inn 5505 Brainerd Rd	Chattanooga	TN	37411	423-894-2040	894-0464
TF: 800-222-2222 ■ *Web:* www.shoneysinn.com/tn1.htm					
Sleep Inn 2351 Shallowford Village Dr.	Chattanooga	TN	37421	423-894-5333	894-9813
TF: 800-753-3746					
Super 8 Motel 20 Birmingham Rd.	Chattanooga	TN	37419	423-821-8880	821-8880

— Restaurants —

				Phone
212 Market Restaurant (International) 212 N Market St.	Chattanooga	TN	37402	423-265-1212
Acropolis The (Continental) 2213 Hamilton Place Blvd	Hamilton Place	TN	37421	423-899-5341
Adams Hilborne Restaurant (Southern) 801 Vine St.	Chattanooga	TN	37403	423-265-5000
Back Inn Cafe (Italian) 412 E 2nd Ave	Chattanooga	TN	37403	423-265-5033
Big River Grille & Brewing Works (American) 222 Broad St	Chattanooga	TN	37402	423-267-2739
Boiled Frog (Cajun) 1269 Market St.	Chattanooga	TN	37402	423-756-3764
Brass Register (American) 618 Georgia Ave	Chattanooga	TN	37402	423-265-2175
Cafe Canoe (Seafood) 1011 Riverside Dr	Chattanooga	TN	37406	423-622-4432
Chatt's Restaurant & Lounge (Continental) 100 W 21st St	Chattanooga	TN	37408	423-265-3151
Chef's Underground (Caribbean) 720 Walnut St	Chattanooga	TN	37402	423-266-3142
Country Place Restaurant (American) 7320 Shallowford Rd	Chattanooga	TN	37421	423-855-1392
David's Restaurant & Lounge (American) 422 Vine St.	Chattanooga	TN	37403	423-267-6418
Durty Nelly's Irish Pub (American) 109 N Market St	Chattanooga	TN	37405	423-265-9970
El Meson Mexican Restaurante (Mexican) 2204 Hamilton Place Blvd	Hamilton Place	TN	37421	423-894-8726
Greyfriar's (American) 406B Broad St	Chattanooga	TN	37402	423-267-0376
La Dolce Vita (Italian) 850 Market St.	Chattanooga	TN	37402	423-267-7141
Loft The (Continental) 328 Cherokee Blvd	Chattanooga	TN	37405	423-266-3061
Madelyne's Tavern (Southwest) 827 Broad St.	Chattanooga	TN	37402	423-266-4121
Mandarin Garden (Chinese) 5450 Hwy 153.	Hixson	TN	37343	423-877-8899
Mount Vernon (Southern) 1707 A Cummings Hwy	Chattanooga	TN	37409	423-266-6591
Nikki's Forties Restaurant (American) 899 Cherokee Blvd	Chattanooga	TN	37405	423-265-9015
Porker's BBQ (Barbecue) 1251 Market St	Chattanooga	TN	37402	423-267-2726
Rib & Loin (Barbecue) 5946 Brainerd Rd	Chattanooga	TN	37411	423-499-6465
Rocky Top Grill (American) 200 Market St	Chattanooga	TN	37402	423-265-7313
Southern Belle Riverboat (Continental) Ross's Landing & Chestnut St	Chattanooga	TN	37402	423-266-4488
Southside Grill (Continental) 1400 Cowart St	Chattanooga	TN	37408	423-266-9211
Web: www.southsidegrill.com				
Station House (American) 1400 Market St	Chattanooga	TN	37402	423-266-5000
Steaks At The Green Room (Steak) 827 Broad St	Chattanooga	TN	37402	423-266-4121
Terrace The (American) 2 Carter Plaza	Chattanooga	TN	37402	423-756-0002
Thai Food of Chattanooga (Thai) 340 Market St	Chattanooga	TN	37402	423-267-4433

— Goods and Services —

SHOPPING

				Phone	Fax
Eastgate Town Center 5600 Brainerd Rd	Chattanooga	TN	37411	423-894-9199	
Hamilton Place 2100 Hamilton Place Blvd	Chattanooga	TN	37421	423-894-7177	892-0765
Northgate Mall 5000 Hixson Pike	Chattanooga	TN	37415	423-870-9521	
Warehouse Row Factory Shops 1110 Market St.	Chattanooga	TN	37402	423-267-1111	267-1129

BANKS

				Phone	Fax
AmSouth Bank of Tennessee 601 Market St	Chattanooga	TN	37402	423-756-4600	752-1557
First American 801 Broad St	Chattanooga	TN	37401	423-755-6000	755-6051
First Tennessee Bank NA 701 Market St	Chattanooga	TN	37402	423-757-4034	757-4021
Volunteer Bank & Trust Co 728 Broad St	Chattanooga	TN	37402	423-265-5001	265-0609

BUSINESS SERVICES

	Phone		Phone
Airborne Express	800-247-2676	**Kinko's**	423-899-3550
BAX Global	800-225-5229	**Mail Boxes Etc**	800-789-4623
DHL Worldwide Express	800-225-5345	**Post Office**	423-499-8231
Federal Express	800-238-5355	**UPS**	800-742-5877
Interim Personnel Services	423-499-8899		

— Media —

PUBLICATIONS

				Phone	Fax
Chattanooga Times‡ PO Box 1447	Chattanooga	TN	37402	423-756-1234	757-6383
Web: www.chattimes.com ■ *E-mail:* pneely@chattimes.mindspring.com					

‡*Daily newspapers*

TELEVISION

				Phone	Fax
WDEF-TV Ch 12 (CBS) 3300 Broad St	Chattanooga	TN	37408	423-785-1200	785-1273
Web: www.wdef.com ■ *E-mail:* news@wdef.com					

Chattanooga — Television (Cont'd)

				Phone	Fax
WDSI-TV Ch 61 (Fox) 1101 E Main St. *Web:* www.fox61tv.com ■ *E-mail:* wdsi@fox61tv.com	Chattanooga	TN	37408	423-265-0061	242-1010
WFLI-TV Ch 53 (UPN) 6024 Shallowford Rd Suite 100	Chattanooga	TN	37421	423-893-9553	893-9853
WRCB-TV Ch 3 (NBC) 900 Whitehall Rd **Fax:* News Rm ■ *E-mail:* news@wrcbtv.com	Chattanooga	TN	37405	423-267-5412	756-3148*
WTCI-TV Ch 45 (PBS) 4411 Amnicola Hwy *Web:* www.wtci-tv45.com	Chattanooga	TN	37406	423-629-0045	698-8557
WTVC-TV Ch 9 (ABC) PO Box 1150 *Web:* www.newschannel9.com	Chattanooga	TN	37401	423-757-7320	757-7401

RADIO

				Phone	Fax
WDEF-AM 1370 kHz (N/T) 2615 S Broad St	Chattanooga	TN	37408	423-321-6200	321-6220
WDEF-FM 92.3 MHz (AC) 2615 S Broad St	Chattanooga	TN	37408	423-321-6200	321-6220
WDOD-FM 96.5 MHz (Rock) 2615 Broad St	Chattanooga	TN	37408	423-321-6200	321-6270
WGOW-AM 1150 kHz (N/T) 821 Pineville Rd *Web:* www.wgow.com ■ *E-mail:* wgow@chattanooga.net	Chattanooga	TN	37405	423-756-6141	266-3629
WGOW-FM 102.3 MHz (N/T) 821 Pineville Rd *Web:* www.wgow.com ■ *E-mail:* wgow@chattanooga.net	Chattanooga	TN	37405	423-756-6141	266-3629
WJTT-FM 94.3 MHz (Urban) 409 Chestnut St Suite A154 *Web:* power94.com	Chattanooga	TN	37402	423-265-9494	266-2335
WMBW-FM 88.9 MHz (Rel) PO Box 73026 *Web:* wmbw.mbn.org ■ *E-mail:* wmbw@moody.edu	Chattanooga	TN	37407	423-629-8900	629-0021
WNOO-AM 1260 kHz (Rel) 1108 Hendricks St	Chattanooga	TN	37406	423-698-8617	629-0244
WSKZ-FM 106.5 MHz (Rock) 821 Pineville Rd *Web:* www.wskz.com ■ *E-mail:* kz106@chattanooga.net	Chattanooga	TN	37405	423-756-6141	266-3629
WUTC-FM 88.1 MHz (NPR) 615 McCallie Ave Detp 1151	Chattanooga	TN	37403	423-755-4790	755-4174

— Colleges/Universities —

				Phone	Fax
Chattanooga State Technical Community College 4501 Amnicola Hwy *Web:* cstcc.chattanooga.net ■ *E-mail:* joe@cstcc.chattanooga.net	Chattanooga	TN	37406	423-697-4400	697-4709
Covenant College 14049 Scenic Hwy *Web:* www.covenant.edu ■ *E-mail:* conference@covenant.edu	Lookout Mountain	GA	30750	706-820-1560	820-0893
Lee University PO Box 3450 *TF:* 800-533-9930 ■ *Web:* www.leeuniversity.edu	Cleveland	TN	37320	423-614-8000	614-8016
Southern Adventist University PO Box 370 *TF Admissions:* 800-768-8437 ■ *Web:* www.southern.edu ■ *E-mail:* pr@southern.edu	Collegedale	TN	37315	423-238-2111	238-3001
Tennessee Temple University 1815 Union Ave *TF:* 800-553-4050	Chattanooga	TN	37404	423-493-4100	493-4497
University of Tennessee Chattanooga 615 McCallie Ave *TF:* 800-882-6627 ■ *Web:* www.utc.edu	Chattanooga	TN	37403	423-755-4662	755-4157

— Hospitals —

				Phone	Fax
Columbia East Ridge Hospital 941 Spring Creek Rd *Web:* www.columbiachat.com/east/default.html	East Ridge	TN	37412	423-894-7870	855-3648
Columbia Parkridge Medical Center 2333 McCallie Ave **Fax:* Admitting	Chattanooga	TN	37404	423-698-6061	493-1558*
Erlanger Medical Center 975 E 3rd St. **Fax:* Mktg ■ *Web:* www.erlanger.org	Chattanooga	TN	37403	423-778-7000	778-8068*
Memorial Hospital 2525 Desales Ave *Web:* www.memorial.org	Chattanooga	TN	37404	423-495-2525	495-7726

— Attractions —

				Phone	Fax
Backstage Playhouse Dinner Theater 3264 Brainerd Rd *Web:* www.cdc.net/~keng144/ ■ *E-mail:* keng144@cdc.net	Chattanooga	TN	37411	423-629-1565	629-7543
Ballet Tennessee 3202 Kelly's Ferry Rd.	Chattanooga	TN	37419	423-821-2055	821-2156
Battles for Chattanooga Museum 1110 E Brow Rd	Chattanooga	TN	37350	423-821-2812	
Bessie Smith Performance Hall 200 ML King Blvd	Chattanooga	TN	37403	423-757-0020	
Chattanooga African-American Museum 200 E ML King Blvd	Chattanooga	TN	37401	423-267-1076	267-1076
Chattanooga National Cemetery 1200 Bailey Ave *Web:* www.cem.va.gov/listcem.htm	Chattanooga	TN	37404	423-855-6590	855-6597
Chattanooga Nature Center 400 Garden Rd *Web:* www.cdc.net/~nature	Chattanooga	TN	37419	423-821-1160	821-1702
Chattanooga Regional History Museum 400 Chestnut St	Chattanooga	TN	37402	423-265-3247	266-9280
Chattanooga Symphony & Opera Assn 630 Chestnut St *Web:* www.chattanoogasymphony.org ■ *E-mail:* csoa@chattanooga.net	Chattanooga	TN	37402	423-267-8583	265-6520
Chattanooga Theatre Centre 400 River St. *Web:* www.theatrecentre.com	Chattanooga	TN	37405	423-267-8534	267-8617
Chickamauga & Chattanooga National Military Park PO Box 2128 **Fax Area Code:* 423 ■ *Web:* www.nps.gov/chch/	Fort Oglethorpe	GA	30742	706-866-9241	752-5215*
Creative Discovery Museum 4th & Chestnut Sts *Web:* www.cdmfun.org	Chattanooga	TN	37402	423-756-2738	267-9344
Flea Market-East Ridge 6725 Ringgold Rd.	Chattanooga	TN	37412	423-894-3960	
Georgia Winery 447 High Point Dr	Chickamauga	GA	30707	706-937-2177	931-2851
Houston Museum of Decorative Arts 201 High St *Web:* www.chattanooga.net/houston ■ *E-mail:* houston@chattanooga.net	Chattanooga	TN	37403	423-267-7176	756-2156
Hunter Museum of American Art 10 Bluff View St *Web:* www.huntermuseum.org/ ■ *E-mail:* info@huntermuseum.org	Chattanooga	TN	37403	423-267-0968	267-9844
IMAX 3D Theater 201 Chestnut St *TF:* 800-262-0695 ■ *Web:* www.tennis.org/IMAX/imax.html	Chattanooga	TN	37401	423-266-4629	756-1849
International Towing & Recovery Hall of Fame & Museum 401 Broad St	Chattanooga	TN	37402	423-267-3132	267-3132
Lake Winnepesaukah Amusement Park 1115 Lakeview Dr	Rossville	GA	30741	706-866-5681	858-0497
Lookout Mountain Battlefield 1116 E Brow Rd	Lookout Mountain	TN	37350	423-821-7786	821-7788
Lookout Mountain Incline Railway 827 E Brow Rd	Lookout Mountain	TN	37350	423-821-4224	821-9444
Lost Sea 140 Lost Sea Rd	Sweetwater	TN	37874	423-337-6616	337-0803
Messianic Museum 1928 Hamill Rd *TF:* 888-876-8150	Hixson	TN	37343	423-876-8150	876-8156
National Knife Museum 7201 Shallowford Rd. *TF:* 800-548-3907	Chattanooga	TN	37421	423-892-5007	899-9456
National Medal of Honor Museum of Military History PO Box 11467 *Web:* www.smoky.com/medalofhonor	Chattanooga	TN	37401	423-267-1737	266-7771
Raccoon Mountain Caverns 319 W Hills Dr	Chattanooga	TN	37419	423-821-9403	
River Gallery Sculpture Garden 400 E 2nd St *TF:* 800-374-2923	Chattanooga	TN	37403	423-267-7353	265-5944
Rock City Gardens 1400 Patten Rd *Web:* www.seerockcity.com/home.html ■ *E-mail:* info@seerockcity.com	Lookout Mountain	GA	30750	706-820-2531	820-2533
Ruby Falls-Lookout Mountain Caverns 1720 S Scenic Hwy *Web:* www.rubyfalls.com/	Chattanooga	TN	37409	423-821-2544	821-6705
Southern Belle 201 Riverfront Pkwy Pier 2 *TF:* 800-766-2784	Chattanooga	TN	37402	423-266-4488	265-9447
Tennessee Aquarium 201 Chestnut St. *TF:* 800-262-0695 ■ *Web:* www.tennis.org	Chattanooga	TN	37401	423-265-0695	267-3561
Tennessee Valley Railroad 4119 Cromwell Rd *Web:* www.tvrail.com	Chattanooga	TN	37421	423-894-8028	894-8029

Chattanooga — Attractions (Cont'd)

				Phone	Fax
Tivoli Theatre 709 Broad St	Chattanooga	TN	37402	423-757-5050	757-5326
Warner Park Zoo 1254 E 3rd St	Chattanooga	TN	37404	423-697-9722	697-1331
Web: zoo.chattanooga.org					

SPORTS TEAMS & FACILITIES

				Phone	Fax
Chattanooga Lookouts (baseball) 1130 E 3rd St Historic Engel Stadium	Chattanooga	TN	37403	423-267-2208	267-4258
Web: www.lookouts.com ■ *E-mail:* lookouts@cyfx.com					

— Events —

	Phone
Chattanooga Traditional Jazz Festival (early May)	423-266-0944
Dixieland Excursions (April-November)	423-894-8028
Downtown Partnership Nightfall Concerts (late May-late September)	423-265-0771
Enchanted Garden of Lights (mid-November-early January)	423-756-8687
Fall Color Cruise & Folk Festival (late October)	423-892-0223
Hamilton County Fair (late September)	423-756-8687
Houston Museum's Antiques Show & Sale (late February)	423-267-7176
Longhorn World Championship Rodeo (early March)	423-266-6627
Pat Boone Celebrity Spectacular (mid-May)	423-842-5757
Praters Mill Country Fair (May & October)	423-756-8687
River Roast (mid-May)	423-266-7070
Riverbend Festival (late June)	423-265-4112
Taste of Chattanooga (early February)	423-265-4397
Wildflower Festival (early April)	423-821-1160

Johnson City

Located in northeastern Tennessee, Johnson City and the surrounding area contains more than half of the Cherokee National Forest as well as one of the two springs in the world that are known to flow at regular intervals. The Davy Crockett Birthplace State Park is also located near Johnson City, along the Nolichucky River in Limestone, and contains a replica of the log cabin where Crockett was born in 1786. Other area attractions include the Tipton-Haynes Historic Site, which houses the 18th Century restored home that was originally built by Colonel John Tipton and later inhabited by Confederate Senator Landon C. Haynes, as well as a museum, a natural limestone cave, and natural trails; and the Rocky Mount Museum, located in nearby Piney Flats, which was the first headquarters of the Southwest Territory and stands today as the oldest original territorial capital in the U.S. Pioneering musicians began the country music recording industry in nearby Bristol, helping to start the careers of such stars as Mom and Pop Stoneman, the Carter Family, Jimmie Rodgers, and Tennessee Ernie Ford. Another nearby city, Greeneville, is home to the Andrew Johnson National Historic Site, which includes his two homes and the National Cemetery where he is buried. The President Andrew Johnson Museum and Library is located at Tusculum College, also in Greeneville, which was founded in 1794 and is the oldest college west of the Allegheny Mountains. Another attration in Greeneville is the Dickson-Williams Mansion, which served as headquarters for both Union and Confederate armies during the Civil War and was known as the "Showplace of East Tennessee."

Population	57,079	**Longitude**	82-22-15 W
Area (Land)	29.4 sq mi	**County**	Washington
Area (Water)	0.1 sq mi	**Time Zone**	EST
Elevation	1635 ft	**Area Code/s**	423
Latitude	36-19-52 N		

— Average Temperatures and Precipitation —

TEMPERATURES

	Jan	Feb	Mar	Apr	May	Jun	Jul	Aug	Sep	Oct	Nov	Dec
High	46	51	62	71	79	85	87	86	81	71	60	50
Low	26	29	37	44	53	61	65	64	58	46	38	30

PRECIPITATION

	Jan	Feb	Mar	Apr	May	Jun	Jul	Aug	Sep	Oct	Nov	Dec
Inches	3.7	3.7	3.9	3.5	4.0	3.7	4.7	3.7	3.3	2.9	3.2	3.5

— Important Phone Numbers —

	Phone		Phone
AAA	423-928-7671	**Poison Control Center**	615-936-2034
Emergency	911	**Time/Temp**	423-929-9191
Johnson City Infoline	423-926-4636	**Weather**	423-586-3771
Medical Referral	423-926-1111		

— Information Sources —

				Phone	Fax
Better Business Bureau Serving Greater East Tennessee PO Box 10327	Knoxville	TN	37939	865-522-2552	637-8042
Web: www.knoxville.bbb.org					
Freedom Hall Civic Center Liberty Bell Blvd	Johnson City	TN	37604	423-461-4855	461-4867
Web: www.freedomhall-tn.com					
Johnson City City Hall 601 E Main St	Johnson City	TN	37601	423-434-6000	434-6087
Web: www.johnsoncitytn.com					
Johnson City Convention & Visitors Bureau 603 E Market St	Johnson City	TN	37601	423-461-8000	926-7360
TF: 800-852-3392					
Johnson City Economic & Development Board 603 E Market St	Johnson City	TN	37601	423-975-2380	975-2388
Web: www.jcedb.org					
Johnson City Mayor 601 E Main St	Johnson City	TN	37605	423-434-6000	434-6087
Johnson City Public Library 100 W Millard St	Johnson City	TN	37604	423-434-4450	434-4469
Web: www.jcpl.net					
Johnson City/Jonesborough/Washington County Chamber of Commerce 603 E Market St	Johnson City	TN	37605	423-461-8000	461-8047
TF: 800-852-3392 ■ *Web:* www.johnsoncitytn.com/chamber					
Washington County PO Box 218	Jonesborough	TN	37659	423-753-1621	753-4716

On-Line Resources

Excite.com Johnson City City Guide	www.excite.com/travel/countries/united_states/tennessee/johnson_city
Johnson City Community	leonhumphrey.com/Community/demographics.htm
Johnson City Star Online	www.starhq.com
Loafer Online Magazine	loafernet.com
NITC Travelbase City Guide Johnson City	www.travelbase.com/auto/features/johnson_city-tn.html

— Transportation Services —

AIRPORTS

	Phone
■ **Tri-Cities Regional Airport (TRI)**	
25 miles N of downtown (approx 35 minutes)	423-325-6000
Web: www.triflight.com	

Airport Transportation

	Phone
WW Cab Co $22 fare to downtown Johnson City	423-929-8316

Commercial Airlines

	Phone		Phone
Atlantic Southeast	800-282-3424	**United Express**	800-241-6522
Comair	800-354-9822	**US Airways**	800-428-4322
Delta Connection	800-221-1212		

Johnson City (Cont'd)

Charter Airlines

Name	Phone
Edwards & Assoc	423-538-5111

CAR RENTALS

Name	Phone	Name	Phone
Cherokee	423-282-6855	Hertz	423-928-9081
Enterprise	423-282-6169	Ron's	423-283-4000

LIMO/TAXI

Name	Phone	Name	Phone
Posh Limousine	423-282-5466	WW Cab Co	423-929-8316

MASS TRANSIT

Name	Phone
Johnson City Transit System $.60 Base fare	423-929-7119

RAIL/BUS

Name	City	State	Zip	Phone
Greyhound Bus Station 137 W Market St *TF:* 800-231-2222	Johnson City	TN	37604	423-926-6181

— Accommodations —

HOTEL RESERVATION SERVICES

Name	Phone	Fax
Reservations USA *TF:* 800-251-4444 ■ *Web:* www.reservationsusa.com ■ *E-mail:* reserve@lodging4u.com	865-453-1000	453-7484

HOTELS, MOTELS, RESORTS

Name	City	State	Zip	Phone	Fax
11-E Motel 3500 W Market St	Johnson City	TN	37601	423-928-2131	
Best Southern Motel 2606 N Roan St *TF:* 888-283-7208	Johnson City	TN	37601	423-282-4011	282-4011
Capri Motel 3008 W Market St	Johnson City	TN	37604	423-926-2952	
Comfort Inn 1900 S Roan St *TF:* 800-228-5150	Johnson City	TN	37601	423-928-9600	928-0046
Comfort Suites 3118 Browns Mill Rd. *TF:* 800-228-5150	Johnson City	TN	37604	423-610-0010	610-0153
Days Inn 2312 Browns Mill Rd *TF:* 800-329-7466	Johnson City	TN	37604	423-282-2211	282-6111
Fairfield Inn by Marriott 207 E Mountcastle Dr *TF:* 800-228-2800	Johnson City	TN	37601	423-282-3335	282-3335
Fox Motel 3406 W Market St	Johnson City	TN	37604	423-928-0267	
Garden Plaza Hotel 211 Mockingbird Ln *TF:* 800-342-7336	Johnson City	TN	37604	423-929-2000	929-1783
Hampton Inn 508 N State of Franklin Rd	Johnson City	TN	37604	423-929-8000	929-3336
Holiday Inn 101 W Springbrook Dr *TF:* 800-465-4329	Johnson City	TN	37604	423-282-4611	283-4869
Jam 'n Jelly Inn 1310 Indian Ridge Rd *Web:* www.jamnjellyinn.com ■ *E-mail:* jjkidner@preferred.com	Johnson City	TN	37604	423-929-0039	929-9026
Johnson Inn 2700 W Market St	Johnson City	TN	37604	423-926-8145	929-0989
Ramada Inn 2406 N Roan St *TF:* 800-272-6232	Johnson City	TN	37601	423-282-2161	282-2488
Red Roof Inn 210 Broyles Dr *TF:* 800-843-7663	Johnson City	TN	37601	423-282-3040	283-0673
Sleep Inn 925 W Oakland Ave *TF:* 800-627-5337	Johnson City	TN	37604	423-915-0081	915-0029
Super 8 Motel 108 Wesley St. *TF:* 800-800-8000	Johnson City	TN	37601	423-282-8818	282-8818
Villager Lodge 2316 Browns Mill Rd.	Johnson City	TN	37604	423-282-3737	

— Restaurants —

Name	City	State	Zip	Phone
Alta Cucina (Italian) 1200 N Roan St	Johnson City	TN	37601	423-928-2092
Amigo Mexican Restaurant (Mexican) 1705 W Market St	Johnson City	TN	37604	423-975-0252
Bailey's Sports Grill (American) 2102 N Roan St	Johnson City	TN	37601	423-929-1370
Bello Vita (Italian) 2927 N Roan St	Johnson City	TN	37601	423-282-8600
Bombay Club (Indian) 2103 Mountcastle Dr	Johnson City	TN	37604	423-952-0033
Café Pacific (New American) 1033 W Oakland Ave	Johnson City	TN	37604	423-610-0117
Chen's (Chinese) 3102 Bristol Hwy	Johnson City	TN	37601	423-915-0080
China Garden (Chinese) 3008 Bristol Hwy	Johnson City	TN	37601	423-282-8332
Cottage The (American) 705 W Market St.	Johnson City	TN	37604	423-928-9753
Dixie Barbecue Co (Barbecue) 3301 N Roan St.	Johnson City	TN	37601	423-283-7447
El Matador (Mexican) 2904 Bristol Hwy	Johnson City	TN	37601	423-282-8111
Fifi's (Mediterranean) 803 W Walnut St	Johnson City	TN	37604	423-232-1717
Firehouse Restaurant (Barbecue) 627 W Walnut St *Web:* www.thefirehouse.com ■ *E-mail:* info@thefirehouse.com	Johnson City	TN	37604	423-929-7377
Galloways Restaurant (American) 807 N Roan St	Johnson City	TN	37601	423-926-1166
Gatsby's Café & Saloon (American) 227 E Main St	Johnson City	TN	37604	423-928-2295
Ginza Japanese Steakhouse (Japanese) 1805 N Roan St	Johnson City	TN	37601	423-232-1289
Harbor House Seafood (Seafood) 2510 N Roan St.	Johnson City	TN	37601	423-282-5122
Horseshoe Restaurant & Lounge (American) 908 W Market St	Johnson City	TN	37604	423-928-8992
House of Ribs (Barbecue) 3100 Kingsport Hwy	Johnson City	TN	37601	423-282-8077
Kokomo's (American) 3122 E Oakland Ave	Johnson City	TN	37601	423-282-1444
Logan's Roadhouse (American) 3112 Browns Mill Rd	Johnson City	TN	37604	423-915-1122
Makato's Japanese Steakhouse (Japanese) 3021 Oakland Ave.	Johnson City	TN	37601	423-282-4441
Misaki Seafood & Steak House of Japan (Japanese) 3104 Bristol Hwy	Johnson City	TN	37601	423-282-5451
Moto Japanese Restaurant (Japanese) 2607 N Roan St	Johnson City	TN	37601	423-282-6686
Parson's Table (American) 102 W Woodrow Ave.	Johnson City	TN	37601	423-753-8002
Peerless Steak House (Steak/Seafood) 2531 N Roan St	Johnson City	TN	37601	423-282-2351
Red Pig Bar-B-Q (Barbecue) 2201 Ferguson Rd	Johnson City	TN	37604	423-282-6585
Sevier Café (American) 111 McClure St	Johnson City	TN	37604	423-928-9737
Sophisticated Otter Brewery & Restaurant (American) 400 Ashe St.	Johnson City	TN	37604	423-928-1705
Taps Restaurant & Pub (American) 2708 N Roan St	Johnson City	TN	37601	423-282-1194

— Goods and Services —

SHOPPING

Name	City	State	Zip	Phone	Fax
Factory Stores of America 354 Shadowtown Rd *TF:* 800-746-7872	Blountville	TN	37617	423-323-4419	323-3056
Fort Henry Mall 2101 Fort Henry Dr	Kingsport	TN	37664	423-246-3871	246-1664
Mall at Johnson City 2011 N Roan St.	Johnson City	TN	37601	423-282-5312	282-0819
Market Street Center 1221 Indian Ridge Rd	Johnson City	TN	37604	423-929-2766	

BANKS

Name	City	State	Zip	Phone	Fax
Bank of America 2105 N Roan St.	Johnson City	TN	37601	423-461-8115	282-9043
Bank of Tennessee 112 Mountcastle Dr.	Johnson City	TN	37601	423-282-9500	854-5263
Carter County Bank 601 Elk Ave	Elizabethton	TN	37643	423-543-2131	
Elizabethton Federal Savings Bank 304 Sunset Dr	Johnson City	TN	37604	423-952-2560	282-1924
First American National Bank 1408 W State of Franklin Rd	Johnson City	TN	37604	423-282-7664	929-8735
First Bank & Trust 1185 N State of Franklin Rd	Johnson City	TN	37604	423-975-9900	915-0694
First Tennessee Bank NA 2710 S Roan St	Johnson City	TN	37601	423-461-1333	926-1156
People's Community Bank 300 Sunset Dr	Johnson City	TN	37604	423-915-2200	915-2247
State of Franklin Savings Bank 1907 N Roan St *Web:* www.stateoffranklin.com ■ *E-mail:* info@sofb.com	Johnson City	TN	37601	423-926-3300	232-4449
SunTrust Bank 207 Mockingbird Ln. *TF:* 877-578-2265	Johnson City	TN	37604	423-461-1000	461-1125
Tri-City Bank & Trust Co 112 Sunset Dr	Johnson City	TN	37604	423-283-7837	
Washington County Bank 3111 Browns Mill Rd.	Johnson City	TN	37604	423-854-4600	854-4605

BUSINESS SERVICES

Name	Phone	Name	Phone
Adecco Employment Service	423-926-2444	Manpower Temporary Services	423-282-4190
Copy Max	423-854-8729	Olsten Staffing Services	423-282-9675
Federal Express	800-238-5355	Pip Printing	423-928-6183
Interim Personnel	423-283-0607	Post Office	423-232-5800
Kelly Services	423-282-5550	Snelling Personnel Services	423-968-9111
Kinko's	423-283-9503	UPS	800-742-5877
Mail Boxes Etc	423-283-9333		

Johnson City (Cont'd)

— Media —

PUBLICATIONS

	City	State	ZIP	Phone	Fax
Elizabethton Star‡ PO Box 1960	Elizabethton	TN	37644	423-928-4151	542-2004
Web: www.starhq.com					
Johnson City Press‡ PO Box 1717	Johnson City	TN	37605	423-929-3111	929-7484
Tri Cities Business Journal PO Box 643	Blountville	TN	37617	423-323-7111	323-1479
Web: www.bjournal.com					

‡Daily newspapers

TELEVISION

	City	State	ZIP	Phone	Fax
WAPK-TV Ch 30 (UPN) 222 Commerce St	Kingsport	TN	37660	423-246-9578	246-1863
Web: www.wkpttv.com					
WEMT-TV Ch 39 (Fox) 3206 Hanover Rd	Johnson City	TN	37604	423-283-3900	283-4938
Web: fox39.xtc.net ■ *E-mail:* fox39@fox39.xtn.net					
WJHL-TV Ch 11 (CBS) 338 E Main St	Johnson City	TN	37601	423-926-2151	434-4537
Web: www.wjhl.com					
WKPT-TV Ch 19 (ABC) 222 Commerce St	Kingsport	TN	37660	423-246-9578	246-1863
Web: www.wkpttv.com ■ *E-mail:* sales@wkpttv.com					

RADIO

	City	State	ZIP	Phone	Fax
WBCV-AM 1550 kHz (Rel) 26 1/2 6th St	Bristol	TN	37620	423-968-5221	968-7711
Web: www.vol-business.net/wbcv/main.html ■ *E-mail:* wbcv@aol.com					
WBEJ-AM 1240 kHz (Ctry) 626 1/2 E Elk Ave	Elizabethton	TN	37643	423-542-2184	542-2185
WCQR-FM 88.3 MHz (Rel) PO Box 8039	Gray	TN	37615	423-477-5676	477-7060
Web: www.preferred.com/wcqr ■ *E-mail:* wcqr@preferred.com					
WEMB-AM 1420 kHz (Misc) 101 Riverview Rd	Erwin	TN	37650	423-743-6123	743-6124*
**Fax:* Sales ■ *Web:* www.wemb.com					
WETB-AM 790 kHz (Rel) 231 Brandonwood Dr	Johnson City	TN	37602	423-928-7131	928-8392
WETS-FM 89.5 MHz (NPR) PO Box 70630 East Tennessee State University	Johnson City	TN	37614	423-439-6440	439-6449
Web: www.wets.org ■ *E-mail:* wets@naws.com					
WGOC-AM 640 kHz (Ctry) 640 Radio Way	Blountville	TN	37617	423-323-0640	323-1864
Web: www.wgoc.com ■ *E-mail:* wgoc@mounet.com					
WGRV-AM 1340 kHz (Ctry) 1004 Arnold Rd	Greeneville	TN	37743	423-638-4147	638-1979
Web: www.greeneville.com/wgrv ■ *E-mail:* wgrv@greeneville.com					
WIKQ-FM 94.9 MHz (Ctry) 1004 Arnold Rd	Greeneville	TN	37743	423-638-4147	638-1979
Web: www.greeneville.com/wikq					
WJCW-AM 910 kHz (N/T) 162 Freehill Rd	Gray	TN	37615	423-477-1000	477-4747
WKIN-AM 1320 kHz (Sports) 162 Freehill Rd	Gray	TN	37615	423-477-1000	477-4747
WKOS-FM 104.9 MHz (Oldies) 162 Freehill Rd.	Gray	TN	37615	423-477-1010	477-1013
WKPT-AM 1400 kHz (Nost) 222 Commerce St	Kinsport	TN	37660	423-246-9578	247-9826
Web: www.wkptam.com ■ *E-mail:* wkpt-am@tricon.net					
WKTP-AM 1590 kHz (Misc) 222 Commerce St	Kingsport	TN	37660	423-246-9578	247-9836
WOPI-AM 1490 kHz (Ctry) 288 Delaney St	Bristol	TN	37620	423-764-5131	247-9836
Web: www.wopi.com ■ *E-mail:* wkpt-am@tricon.net					
WQUT-FM 101.5 MHz (CR) 162 Freehill Rd	Gray	TN	37615	423-477-1000	477-1013
WSMG-AM 1450 kHz (Ctry) 942 Snapps Ferry Rd.	Greeneville	TN	37745	423-638-3188	638-3180
WTFM-FM 98.5 MHz (AC) 222 Commerce St	Kingsport	TN	37660	423-246-9578	247-9836
Web: www.wtfm.com ■ *E-mail:* comments@wtfm.com					
WXIS-FM 103.9 MHz (CHR) 101 Riverview Rd	Erwin	TN	37650	423-743-6123	743-6124*
**Fax:* Sales ■ *Web:* www.x104.com ■ *E-mail:* info@sevensgw.com					

— Colleges/Universities —

	City	State	ZIP	Phone	Fax
East Tennessee State University 801 University Pkwy	Johnson City	TN	37614	423-929-4112	439-7630
TF Admissions: 800-462-3878 ■ *Web:* www.etsu.edu					
Graham Bible College PO Box 1630	Bristol	VA	24203	423-968-4201	968-4266
Web: www.3wave.com/gbc ■ *E-mail:* gbc@3wave.com					
King College 1350 King College Rd.	Bristol	TN	37620	423-968-1187	968-4456
TF Admissions: 800-362-0014*					
Milligan College PO Box 210	Milligan College	TN	37682	423-929-0116	871-2147
TF Admissions: 800-682-3648 ■ *Web:* www.milligan.edu					
National Business College Bristol 300 A Piedmont Ave	Bristol	VA	24201	540-669-5333	669-4793
Northeast State Technical Community College PO Box 696	Elizabethton	TN	37644	423-547-8450	547-8451
Web: www.nstcc.cc.tn.us ■ *E-mail:* infomaster@nstcc.cc.tn.us					
Tusculum College 60 Shiloh Rd Hwy 107	Greeneville	TN	37743	423-636-7300	638-7166
TF: 800-729-0256 ■ *Web:* www.tusculum.edu ■ *E-mail:* admissions@tusculum.edu					
Virginia Intermont College 1013 Moore St	Bristol	VA	24201	540-669-6101	466-7855
TF: 800-451-1842 ■ *Web:* www.vic.edu					

— Hospitals —

	City	State	ZIP	Phone	Fax
Columbia North Side Hospital PO Box 4900CRS	Johnson City	TN	37602	423-282-4111	854-5638
James H Quillens Veterans Affairs Medical Center PO Box 4000	Mountain Home	TN	37684	423-926-1171	461-7972
Johnson City Medical Center Hospital 400 N State of Franklin Rd.	Johnson City	TN	37604	423-431-6111	431-6236*
**Fax:* Admitting ■ *TF:* 800-888-5551 ■ *Web:* www.jcmc.com					
Johnson City Specialty Hospital 203 E Watauga Ave	Johnson City	TN	37601	423-926-1111	926-8785
Web: www.jcspecialty.com					

— Attractions —

	City	State	ZIP	Phone	Fax
Bays Mountain Planetarium 853 Bays Mountain Park Rd	Kingsport	TN	37660	423-229-9447	224-2589
Web: home.naxs.com/baysmtn/planetdept					
Blue Ridge Parkway 400 BB & T Bldg 1 W Pack Sq	Asheville	NC	28801	828-271-4779	271-4313
Web: www.nps.gov/blri/					
Buffalo Mountain Park High Ridge Rd	Johnson City	TN	37605	423-283-5815	
Cherokee National Forest 2800 N Ocoee St	Cleveland	TN	37312	423-476-9700	339-8652
Web: www.gorp.com/gorp/resource/US_National_Forest/tn_chero.HTM					
Countryside Vineyards Winery 658 Henry Harr Rd	Blountville	TN	37617	423-323-1660	323-1660
Doak House Museum 690 Erwin Hwy	Greeneville	TN	37745	423-636-8554	638-7166
Web: www.tusculum.edu/museum/doak.html ■ *E-mail:* clucas@tusculum.edu					
Great Smoky Mountains National Park 107 Park Headquarters Rd	Gatlinburg	TN	37738	865-436-1200	436-1220
Web: www.nps.gov/grsm/					
Hands On! Regional Museum 315 E Main St	Johnson City	TN	37601	423-434-4263	928-6915
Web: www.handsonmuseum.org					
Historic Jonesborough Visitors Center & Museum 117 Boone St	Jonesborough	TN	37659	423-753-1010	753-1020
Johnson City Area Arts Council 214 E Main St	Johnson City	TN	37604	423-928-8229	928-4511
Web: www.arts.org ■ *E-mail:* jcarts@mounet.com					
Johnson City Community Theater 600 E Maple St.	Johnson City	TN	37605	423-926-2542	
Johnson City Symphony Orchestra 1 Blowers Blvd Seeger Chapel	Milligan College	TN	37682	423-926-8742	926-8979
Jonesborough-Washington County History Museum 117 Boone St	Jonesborough	TN	37659	423-753-1015	753-1020
Reece Carroll Museum PO Box 70660	Johnson City	TN	37614	423-439-4392	439-4283
Web: cass.etsu.edu/museum ■ *E-mail:* cass@tusculum.edu					
Rocky Mount Museum 200 Hyder Hill Rd.	Piney Flats	TN	37686	423-538-7396	538-1086
Steadman Harry V Mountain Heritage Farmstead Museum 853 Bays Mountain Park Rd	Kingsport	TN	37660	423-229-9361	224-2589
Tipton-Haynes Historic Site 2620 S Roan St	Johnson City	TN	37605	423-926-3631	
Web: www.tipton-haynes.org ■ *E-mail:* information@tipton-haynes.org					
Wetlands Water Park 1521 Persimmon Ridge Rd	Jonesborough	TN	37659	423-753-1550	
Winged Deer Park 242 Carroll Creek Rd	Johnson City	TN	37601	423-283-5815	

SPORTS TEAMS & FACILITIES

	City	State	ZIP	Phone	Fax
Bristol International Raceway PO Box 3966	Bristol	TN	37625	423-764-1161	764-1646
Web: www.bristolmotorspeedway.com					
Johnson City Cardinals (baseball) 111 Legion St Howard Johnson Field	Johnson City	TN	37601	423-461-4866	461-4864
Web: www.freeyellow.com:8080/members2/jccardinals ■ *E-mail:* jccardinals@worldnet.att.net					

Johnson City — Sports Teams & Facilities (Cont'd)

				Phone	Fax
Kingsport Mets (baseball) 800 Granby Rd Hunter Wright Stadium ..... *Web:* www.kmets.com	Kingsport	TN	37662	423-378-3744	392-8538

— Events —

	Phone
Appalachian Fair (late August)	423-477-3211
Archie Campbell Homecoming Day (early September)	423-235-5216
Bristol Racefest (late August)	423-989-4850
Candlelight Tour (early December)	423-538-7396
Canjoe Festival (late July-early August)	800-606-4833
Children's Christmas Event (mid-December)	423-753-1010
Christmas at President Andrew Johnson Homestead (mid-December)	423-638-3551
Christmas at the Carter Mansion (mid-December)	423-543-5808
Christmas Craft Show & Sale (late November)	423-753-1010
Christmas Crafts Show (mid-November)	423-543-5808
Christmas Garrison at Fort Watauga (mid-late December)	423-543-5808
Christmas in the Country Craft Show & Sale (early December)	423-288-6071
Cranberry Festival (early October)	423-739-5455
Davy Crockett Celebration (mid-August)	423-257-4655
Downtown Kingsport Arts & Crafts Festival (September 11 & 12)	423-246-6550
Fall Folks Arts Festival (late September)	423-288-6071
Fantasy in Lights (mid-November-early January)	423-764-1161
Farm Fest (mid-late July)	423-288-6071
Fireworks in the Park (July 4)	423-727-5800
Folklife Festival (mid-July)	423-239-6786
Fort Watauga Knap-In (mid-September)	423-543-5808
Fourth of July Fireworks (July 4)	423-245-2856
Fun Fest (mid-late July)	423-392-8809
Halloween Haunts & Happenings (late October)	423-753-1550
Halloween Skating Party (late Otober)	423-461-4851
Harvest Hoedown (early October)	423-323-5686
Heritage Days (mid-October)	423-272-1961
Jericho Shrine Circus (late October)	423-323-1982
Mountainfest Arts & Crafts Show (late October)	423-652-2674
National Storytelling Festival (early October)	423-753-2171
Old Butler Days (mid-August)	423-768-2432
Old Time Fiddlers & Bluegrass Festival (mid-September)	423-247-9181
Overmountain Victory Trail March & Celebration (late September)	423-543-5808
Pepsi Independence Day Celebration (July 4)	423-928-9211
Quiltfest (early August)	423-753-1010
Riverfront Festival (September)	423-345-2213
Roan Mountain Fall Naturalists Rally (early-mid-September)	423-772-0190
Roan Mountain State Park's Fall Festival (mid-September)	423-772-0190
Roan Mountain State Park's Independence Day Activities (early July)	423-772-0190
Spirits of the Harvest (mid-October)	888-538-1791
Spooktacular Halloween Party (late October)	423-434-4263
Spring Garden Fair (late April)	423-288-6071
Stories From the Pumpkin Patch (late October)	423-926-3631
Thanksgiving Garrison at Fort Watauga (late November)	423-543-5808
Times of the Tiptons (mid-September)	423-926-3631
Unicoi County Apple Festival (early October)	423-743-3000
Unity Day Festival (early August)	423-461-8830
Visions of Christmas Candlelight Tour (mid-December)	423-926-3631
Witches Wynd (late October)	423-288-6071
Yule Log Ceremony (early December)	423-288-6071

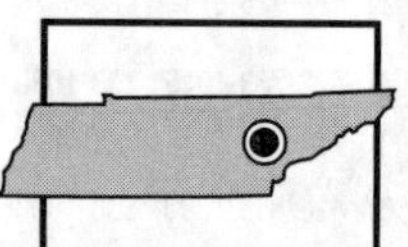

Knoxville

Knoxville is surrounded by seven of the "Great Lakes of the South" created by the hydroelectric dams of the Tennessee Valley Authority, which has its headquarters here. Host of the 1982 World's Fair, Knoxville is also the home of the University of Tennessee's main campus. In addition to numerous historic homes and sites that chronicle the city's revolutionary and civil war history, the East Tennessee Discovery Center and the Knoxville Zoo are popular attractions. Other attractions in the area include Dolly Parton's Dollywood in Pigeon Forge and the mountain resort town of Gatlinburg, located at the north entrance to Great Smoky Mountains National Park.

Population	165,540	**Longitude**	83-92-08 W
Area (Land)	77.2 sq mi	**County**	Knox
Area (Water)	1.7 sq mi	**Time Zone**	EST
Elevation	889 ft	**Area Code/s**	865
Latitude	35-96-06 N		

— Average Temperatures and Precipitation —

TEMPERATURES

	Jan	Feb	Mar	Apr	May	Jun	Jul	Aug	Sep	Oct	Nov	Dec
High	46	51	61	70	78	85	87	87	81	71	60	50
Low	26	29	37	45	53	62	66	65	59	46	38	30

PRECIPITATION

	Jan	Feb	Mar	Apr	May	Jun	Jul	Aug	Sep	Oct	Nov	Dec
Inches	4.2	4.1	5.1	3.7	4.1	4.0	4.7	3.1	3.1	2.8	3.8	4.5

— Important Phone Numbers —

	Phone		Phone
AAA	865-637-1910	**Poison Control Center**	865-544-9400
Emergency	911	**Time/Temp**	865-521-6300
Knoxvoice Events Line	865-525-9900	**Visitors Information**	865-523-7263
Medical Referral	865-673-3678	**Weather**	865-521-6300

— Information Sources —

				Phone	Fax
Better Business Bureau Serving Greater East Tennessee PO Box 10327 *Web:* www.knoxville.bbb.org	Knoxville	TN	37939	865-522-2552	637-8042
Knox County PO Box 1566	Knoxville	TN	37901	865-215-2000	215-3655
Knox County Public Library System 500 W Church Ave	Knoxville	TN	37902	865-544-5750	544-5708
Knoxville Area Chamber Partnership 601 W Summit Hill Suite 300 *Web:* www.knoxville.org	Knoxville	TN	37902	865-637-4550	523-2071
Knoxville City Hall 400 Main St *Web:* www.ci.knoxville.tn.us	Knoxville	TN	37902	865-215-2000	
Knoxville Convention & Visitors Bureau 601 W Summit Hill Dr Suite 200B *TF:* 800-727-8045 ■ *Web:* www.knoxville.org ■ *E-mail:* tourism@knoxville.org	Knoxville	TN	37902	865-523-7263	673-4400
Knoxville Convention Exhibition Center PO Box 2603	Knoxville	TN	37901	865-544-5371	544-5376
Knoxville Mayor PO Box 1631 *Web:* www.ci.knoxville.tn.us/mayor/mayorhome.htm	Knoxville	TN	37901	865-215-2040	215-2085
Knoxville Metropolitan Planning Commission 400 Main St Suite 403 City-County Bldg *Web:* www.ci.knoxville.tn.us/departments/mpc.htm	Knoxville	TN	37902	865-215-2500	215-2068

On-Line Resources

4Knoxville.com	www.4knoxville.com
About Knoxville	www.knoxvilletennessee.com
About.com Guide to Knoxville	knoxville.about.com/local/southeastus/knoxville
Anthill City Guide Knoxville	www.anthill.com/city.asp?city=knoxville
Area Guide Knoxville	knoxville.areaguides.net
DiningGuide Fort Lauderdale	fort.lauderdale.diningguide.net
Excite.com Knoxville City Guide	www.excite.com/travel/countries/united_states/tennessee/knoxville
KnoxFirst	www.knoxfirst.com/
Knoxville Directory	www.vic.com/~smokyweb/knox/
Knoxville-TN.com	www.knoxville-tn.com/
Knoxville Tourist Bureau	www.goknox.com/
KORRnet	www.korrnet.org/
Kvine Online Knoxville	www.kvine.com/
Metro Pulse	www.metropulse.com

— Transportation Services —

AIRPORTS

	Phone
■ **McGhee Tyson Airport (TYS)**	
13 miles S of downtown (approx 35 minutes) Web: www.tys.org ■ *E-mail:* trevisga@www.tys.org	865-970-2773

Airport Transportation

	Phone
AAA Airport Service $17 fare to downtown	865-531-1930
ABC Airport Taxi $17 fare to downtown	865-970-4545

Knoxville (Cont'd)

Commercial Airlines

	Phone		Phone
AirTran	800-247-8726	**TWA Express**	800-221-2000
American Eagle	800-433-7300	**United**	800-241-6522
Delta	800-221-1212	**United Express**	800-241-6522
Delta Connection	800-221-1212	**US Airways**	800-428-4322
Northwest	800-225-2525	**US Airways Express**	800-428-4322

Charter Airlines

	Phone
Richmor Aviation	800-331-6101

CAR RENTALS

	Phone		Phone
Alamo	865-681-3966	**Hertz**	865-970-3010
Avis	865-970-2985	**Thrifty**	865-525-7300
Budget	865-694-3401		

LIMO/TAXI

	Phone		Phone
AAA Taxi	865-531-1930	**National**	800-227-7368
Chariots of Hire	865-522-8108	**Yellow Cab**	865-523-5151

MASS TRANSIT

	Phone
KAT $1 Base fare	865-546-3752

RAIL/BUS

				Phone
Greyhound Bus Station 100 Magnolia Ave NE *TF:* 800-231-2222	Knoxville	TN	37917	865-522-5144

— Accommodations —

HOTEL RESERVATION SERVICES

	Phone	Fax
Reservations USA *TF:* 800-251-4444 ■ *Web:* www.reservationsusa.com ■ *E-mail:* reserve@lodging4u.com	865-453-1000	453-7484

HOTELS, MOTELS, RESORTS

				Phone	Fax
Baymont Inns & Suites 11341 Campbell Lake Dr *TF:* 800-301-0200	Knoxville	TN	37922	865-671-1010	675-5039
Best Western Hotel 118 Merchants Dr *TF:* 800-826-4360	Knoxville	TN	37912	865-688-3141	687-4645
Best Western Hotel West 500 Lovell Rd **Fax Area Code:* 800	Knoxville	TN	37932	865-675-7666	528-1234*
Best Western Luxbury Inn 420 N Peters Rd *TF:* 800-528-1234	Knoxville	TN	37922	865-539-0058	539-4887
Brookside Resort 463 E Parkway *TF:* 800-251-9597	Gatlinburg	TN	37738	865-436-5611	436-0039
Budget Inn 323 Cedarbluff Rd	Knoxville	TN	37923	865-693-7330	693-7383
Comfort Hotel 7737 Kingston Pike *TF:* 800-228-5150	Knoxville	TN	37919	865-690-0034	690-8173
Comfort Inn 5334 Central Avenue Pike *TF:* 800-228-5150	Knoxville	TN	37912	865-688-1010	687-4235
Comfort Inn East 7424 Strawberry Plains Pk	Knoxville	TN	37924	865-932-1217	932-1856
Comfort Suites 811 N Campbell Station Rd *TF:* 800-228-5150	Knoxville	TN	37922	865-675-7585	675-4442
Country Inn & Suites by Carlson 7525 Crosswood Blvd *TF:* 800-456-4000	Knoxville	TN	37914	865-546-5700	546-8830
Courtyard by Marriott Knoxville 216 Langely Pl *Web:* courtyard.com/TYSCY	Knoxville	TN	37922	865-539-0600	539-4488
Days Inn Campus 1706 W Cumberland Ave *TF:* 800-329-7466	Knoxville	TN	37916	865-521-5000	540-3866
Days Inn Convention Center 5335 Central Ave Pike *TF:* 800-695-7065	Knoxville	TN	37912	865-688-9110	687-8706
Days Inn East 5423 Asheville Hwy	Knoxville	TN	37914	865-637-3511	971-4445
Days Inn Glenstone Lodge 504 Airport Rd *TF:* 800-362-9522	Gatlinburg	TN	37738	865-436-9361	436-6951
Days Inn West 326 Lovell Rd NW *TF:* 800-329-7466	Knoxville	TN	37922	865-966-5801	966-1755
Econo Lodge North 5505 Merchant Center Blvd	Knoxville	TN	37912	865-687-5680	687-5680
Executive Inn 3400 Chapman Hwy	Knoxville	TN	37920	865-577-4451	577-4451
Extended StayAmerica 214 Langley Pl. *TF:* 800-398-7829	Knoxville	TN	37922	865-769-0822	769-0821
Fairfield Inn by Marriott 1551 Cracker Barrel Ln *Web:* fairfieldinn.com/TYSKE	Knoxville	TN	37914	865-971-4033	971-6846
Family Inns of America 2450 Airport Hwy *TF:* 800-352-8383	Alcoa	TN	37701	865-970-2006	970-9261
Hampton Inn Airport 148 International Ave. *TF:* 800-426-7866	Alcoa	TN	37701	865-983-1101	984-0110
Hampton Inn East 814 Brakebill Rd *TF:* 800-426-7866	Knoxville	TN	37914	865-525-3511	525-3546
Hampton Inn North 119 Cedar Ln *TF:* 800-426-7866	Knoxville	TN	37912	865-689-1011	689-7917
Hampton Inn West 9128 Executive Park Dr *TF:* 800-426-7866	Knoxville	TN	37923	865-693-1101	531-1183
Hilton Inn Knoxville Airport 2001 Alcoa Hwy **Fax:* Resv ■ *TF:* 800-445-8667 ■ *Web:* www.hilton.com/hotels/KNXAHHF	Alcoa	TN	37701	865-970-4300	984-7080*
Holiday Inn 520 Airport Rd *TF:* 800-435-9201	Gatlinburg	TN	37738	865-436-9201	436-7974
Holiday Inn Cedar Bluff 304 Cedar Bluff Rd *TF:* 800-465-4329	Knoxville	TN	37923	865-693-1011	694-0253
Holiday Inn Central 1315 Kirby Rd *TF:* 800-854-8315	Knoxville	TN	37909	865-584-3911	588-0920
Holiday Inn Express 7520 Primetime Rd	Knoxville	TN	37849	865-938-3800	938-4660
Holiday Inn Select Downtown 525 Henley St *TF:* 800-465-4329	Knoxville	TN	37902	865-522-2800	523-0738
Hyatt Regency Knoxville 500 Hill Ave SE *TF:* 800-233-1234 ■ *Web:* www.hyatt.com/pages/t/tysrka.html	Knoxville	TN	37915	865-637-1234	637-1193
Jellico Motel PO Box 177 *TF:* 800-251-9498	Jellico	TN	37762	423-784-7211	784-6784
Knoxville Hilton 501 W Church Ave *TF:* 800-445-8667	Knoxville	TN	37902	865-523-2300	525-6532
La Quinta 5634 Merchant Center Blvd *TF:* 800-687-6667	Knoxville	TN	37912	865-687-8989	687-9351
La Quinta Motor Inn 258 N Peters Rd *TF:* 800-687-6667	Knoxville	TN	37923	865-690-9777	531-8304
Microtel Knoxville 309 N Peters Rd	Knoxville	TN	37922	865-531-8041	539-1792
Motel 6 402 Lovell Rd *TF:* 800-466-8356	Knoxville	TN	37922	865-675-7200	671-3339
Nation's Best 8167 Kingston Pike	Knoxville	TN	37919	865-693-1811	693-6505
Park Vista Hotel 705 Cherokee Orchard Rd *TF:* 800-421-7275 ■ *Web:* www.parkvista.com	Gatlinburg	TN	37738	865-436-9211	436-5141
Pine Trace Inn 2306 Airport Hwy *TF:* 877-977-7228	Alcoa	TN	37701	865-970-3140	380-9783
Quality Inn 6712 Central Avenue Pike *TF:* 800-272-6700	Knoxville	TN	37912	865-689-6600	689-9896
Radisson Hotel Summit Hill 401 Summitt Hill Dr *TF:* 800-333-3333	Knoxville	TN	37902	865-522-2600	523-7200
Ramada Inn 756 Parkway St *TF:* 800-933-8678	Gatlinburg	TN	37738	865-436-7881	430-3029
Ramada Inn Airport 2962 US Hwy 129 *TF:* 800-272-6232	Alcoa	TN	37701	865-970-3060	977-8951
Ramada Suites Limited 5317 Pratt Rd	Knoxville	TN	37912	865-687-9922	687-1032
Red Roof Inn North 5640 Merchants Center Blvd *TF:* 800-843-7663	Knoxville	TN	37912	865-689-7100	689-7974
Scottish Inn 9340 Park West Blvd	Knoxville	TN	37923	865-693-6061	693-0702
Signature Inn Cedar Bluff 209 Market Place Ln *TF:* 800-822-5252 ■ *Web:* www.signature-inns.com/locations/knoxville ■ *E-mail:* feedback@signature-inns.com	Knoxville	TN	37922	865-531-7444	531-7444
Sleep Inn 5460 Central Avenue Pike *TF:* 800-424-6423	Knoxville	TN	37912	865-688-7300	688-7300
Sleep Inn 214 Prosperity Dr	Knoxville	TN	37922	865-531-5900	531-5904
Smoky Shadows Motel 4215 Parkway *TF:* 800-282-2121	Pigeon Forge	TN	37863	865-453-7155	453-0308
StudioPLUS 1700 Winston Rd	Knoxville	TN	37919	865-694-4178	539-3278
Suburban Lodge 109 S Gallaher View Rd *TF:* 800-951-7829	Knoxville	TN	37919	865-670-1976	769-1522
Super 8 11748 Snyder Rd W *TF:* 800-800-8000	Knoxville	TN	37922	865-675-5566	966-2028
Travelodge 608 Lovell Rd *TF:* 800-578-7878	Knoxville	TN	37932	865-966-6781	966-4401
Wyndham Garden Hotel 208 Market Place Ln *TF:* 800-996-3426	Knoxville	TN	37922	865-531-1900	531-8807

Knoxville (Cont'd)

— Restaurants —

Name	Address	City	State	ZIP	Phone
Alex's Havana Cafe (Cuban)	5123 Homberg Dr	Knoxville	TN	37919	865-588-8681
Bayou Bay Seafood House (Seafood)	7117 Chapman Hwy	Knoxville	TN	37920	865-573-7936
Butcher Shop (American)	801 W Jackson Ave	Knoxville	TN	37902	865-637-0204
Capuccino's (Italian)	7316 Kingston Pike	Knoxville	TN	37919	865-673-3422
Charlie Peppers (American)	716 20th St	Knoxville	TN	37916	865-524-8669
Chesapeake's (Seafood)	500 Henley St	Knoxville	TN	37902	865-673-3433
Chop House (Steak)	9700 Kingston Pk	Knoxville	TN	37923	865-531-2467
Copper Cellar (American)	1807 Cumberland Ave	Knoxville	TN	37916	865-673-3411
Corky's Ribs & BBQ (Barbecue)	260 N Peters Rd	Knoxville	TN	37923	865-690-3137
Darryl's 1879 Restaurant (American)	6604 Kingston Pike	Knoxville	TN	37919	865-584-1879
Great Southern Brewing Co (American)	424 S Gay St	Knoxville	TN	37902	865-523-0750
Hawkeye's (American)	1717 White Ave	Knoxville	TN	37916	865-524-5326
Italian Market & Grill (Italian)	9648 Kingston Pike *Web:* www.italianmarketandgrill.com/	Knoxville	TN	37922	865-690-2600
Louis Inn (Italian)	4626 Broadway	Knoxville	TN	37918	865-687-8111
Mandarin House (Chinese)	8111 Gleason Rd	Knoxville	TN	37919	865-694-0340
Michael's (Continental)	7049 Kingston Pk	Knoxville	TN	37919	865-588-2455
Monterrey Mexican Grill (Mexican)	11151 Kingston Pike	Knoxville	TN	37927	865-671-3119
New Mexicali Rose Restaurant (Mexican)	6418 Papermill Dr	Knoxville	TN	37919	865-588-9191
Orangery The (Continental)	5412 Kingston Pk	Knoxville	TN	37919	865-588-2964
Patrick Sullivan's (American)	100 N Central St	Knoxville	TN	37902	865-637-4255
Rafferty's (American)	8906 Kingston Pike	Knoxville	TN	37923	865-539-1323
Regas (American)	318 N Gay St	Knoxville	TN	37902	865-637-9805
Romano's Macaroni Grill (Italian)	7723 Kingston Pike	Knoxville	TN	37923	865-691-0809
Savelli's (Italian)	3055 Sutherland Ave	Knoxville	TN	37919	865-521-9085
Shrimp Shack Restaurant (Seafood)	8027 Kingston Pk	Knoxville	TN	37919	865-539-1700
Sullivan's Fine Food (American)	137 S Central St	Knoxville	TN	37902	865-522-4511
Tomato Head (American)	12 Market Sq	Knoxville	TN	37902	865-637-4067
Ye Olde Steak House (Steak/Seafood)	6838 Chapman Hwy	Knoxville	TN	37920	865-577-9328

— Goods and Services —

SHOPPING

Name	Address	City	State	ZIP	Phone	Fax
Bearden Antique Mall	310 Mohican St	Knoxville	TN	37919	865-584-1521	
Homespun Craft & Antique Mall	11523 Kingston Pk	Knoxville	TN	37922	865-671-3444	671-0301
Knoxville Center	3000-A Mall Rd N	Knoxville	TN	37924	865-544-1500	
Pigeon Forge Factory Mall	2850 Parkway	Pigeon Forge	TN	37864	865-428-2828	
West Town Mall	7600 Kingston Pike	Knoxville	TN	37919	865-693-0292	531-0503

BANKS

Name	Address	City	State	ZIP	Phone	Fax
First Tennessee Bank	800 S Gay St	Knoxville	TN	37929	865-971-2114	971-2025
Home Federal Bank of Tennessee FSB	515 Market St	Knoxville	TN	37902	865-546-0330	541-6962
NationsBank	9375 Kingston Pike	Knoxville	TN	37922	865-541-6130	694-5009
SunTrust Bank	700 E Hill Ave	Knoxville	TN	37915	865-544-2250	524-5956

BUSINESS SERVICES

Name	Phone
Airborne Express	800-247-2676
ASAP Courier	865-539-4674
BAX Global	800-225-5229
DHL Worldwide Express	800-225-5345
Express Courier	865-983-4050
Federal Express	800-238-5355
Interim Personnel Services	865-588-9095
Kelly Services	865-691-5552
Kinko's	865-523-8213
Mail Boxes Etc	800-789-4623
Olsten Staffing Services	865-583-0013
Post Office	865-558-4528
Priority Courier	865-970-3606
RPS Inc	800-762-3725
UPS	800-742-5877

— Media —

PUBLICATIONS

Name	Address	City	State	ZIP	Phone	Fax
Knoxville News-Sentinel‡	208 W Church Ave *TF:* 800-237-5821 ■ *Web:* www.knoxnews.com	Knoxville	TN	37902	865-523-3131	521-8124
Press Enterprise	11863 Kingston Pike **Fax:* News Rm ■ *E-mail:* pressent@aol.com	Knoxville	TN	37922	865-675-6397	675-1675*

‡*Daily newspapers*

TELEVISION

Name	Address	City	State	ZIP	Phone	Fax
WATE-TV Ch 6 (ABC)	1306 Broadway NE *Web:* www.wate.com ■ *E-mail:* coverage@wate.com	Knoxville	TN	37917	865-637-6666	525-4091
WBIR-TV Ch 10 (NBC)	1513 Hutchinson Ave	Knoxville	TN	37917	865-637-1010	637-6380
WSJK-TV Ch 2 (PBS)	1611 E Magnolia	Knoxville	TN	37917	865-595-0220	595-0300
WTNZ-TV Ch 43 (Fox)	9000 Executive Pk Dr Bldg D Suite 300 *Web:* www.wtnzfox43.com ■ *E-mail:* programming@wtnzfox43.com	Knoxville	TN	37923	865-693-4343	691-6904
WVLT-TV Ch 8 (CBS)	6516 Papermill Dr *Web:* www.volunteertv.com	Knoxville	TN	37950	865-450-8888	584-1978

RADIO

Name	Address	City	State	ZIP	Phone	Fax
WHJM-AM 1180 kHz (Rel)	802 S Central Ave	Knoxville	TN	37902	865-546-4653	637-7133
WIMZ-FM 103.5 MHz (CR)	1100 Sharps Ridge Rd	Knoxville	TN	37917	865-525-6000	525-2000
WITA-AM 1490 kHz (Rel)	7212 Kingston Pike	Knoxville	TN	37919	865-588-2974	
WIVK-FM 107.7 MHz (Ctry)	4711 Kingston Pike	Knoxville	TN	37939	865-588-6511	588-3725
WJXB-FM 97.5 MHz (AC)	1100 Sharps Ridge Rd *Web:* www.b975.com/	Knoxville	TN	37917	865-525-6000	525-2000
WMYU-FM 102.1 MHz (Oldies)	8419 Kingston Pike	Knoxville	TN	37919	865-693-1020	693-8493
WNFZ-FM 94.3 MHz (Alt)	1100 Sharps Rd	Knoxville	TN	37919	865-525-6000	525-2000
WNOX-FM 99.1 MHz (N/T)	4711 Old Kingston Pike	Knoxville	TN	37919	865-558-9900	558-4218
WOKI-FM 100.3 MHz (CR)	4711 Old Kingston Pike	Knoxville	TN	37919	865-588-6511	558-4218
WUOT-FM 91.9 MHz (NPR)	209 Communications Bldg *Web:* sunsite.utk.edu/wuot	Knoxville	TN	37996	865-974-5375	974-3941

— Colleges/Universities —

Name	Address	City	State	ZIP	Phone	Fax
Carson-Newman College	1646 S Russell Ave *TF:* 800-678-9061 ■ *Web:* www.cn.edu	Jefferson City	TN	37760	865-475-9061	471-3502
ITT Technical Institute	10208 Technology Dr *TF:* 800-671-2801 ■ *Web:* www.itt-tech.edu	Knoxville	TN	37932	865-671-2800	671-2811
Johnson Bible College	7900 Johnson Dr *TF Admissions:* 800-827-2122 ■ *Web:* www.jbc.edu ■ *E-mail:* jbc@jbc.edu	Knoxville	TN	37998	865-573-4517	579-2337
Knoxville College	901 College St *TF Admissions:* 800-743-5669 ■ *Web:* falcon.nest.kxcol.edu	Knoxville	TN	37921	865-524-6500	524-6686
Maryville College	502 E Lamar Alexander Pkwy *TF:* 800-597-2687 ■ *Web:* www.maryvillecollege.edu	Maryville	TN	37804	865-981-8000	981-8005
Pellissippi State Technical Community College	10915 Hardin Valley Rd *TF:* 800-548-6925 ■ *Web:* www.pstcc.cc.tn.us	Knoxville	TN	37933	865-694-6400	539-7217
Tennessee Institute of Electronics	3203 Tazewell Pike	Knoxville	TN	37918	865-688-9422	688-2419
University of Tennessee	*TF:* 800-221-8657 ■ *Web:* www.utk.edu	Knoxville	TN	37996	865-974-1000	974-6435
Walters State Community College	500 S Davy Crockett Pkwy *TF:* 800-225-4770 ■ *Web:* www.wscc.cc.tn.us	Morristown	TN	37813	423-585-2600	585-2631

— Hospitals —

Name	Address	City	State	ZIP	Phone	Fax
Baptist Hospital of East Tennessee	137 Blount Ave	Knoxville	TN	37918	865-632-5011	549-2807
East Tennessee Children's Hospital	PO Box 15010 *Web:* www.etch.com ■ *E-mail:* care@etch.com	Knoxville	TN	37901	865-546-7711	541-8343
Fort Sanders-Parkwest Medical Center	9352 Park West Blvd **Fax:* Admitting	Knoxville	TN	37923	865-693-5151	531-4420*

Knoxville — Hospitals (Cont'd)

				Phone	Fax
Fort Sanders Regional Medical Center 1901 Clinch Ave SW	Knoxville	TN	37916	865-541-1111	541-1262
Saint Mary's Medical Center 900 E Oak Hill Ave	Knoxville	TN	37917	865-545-8000	545-6732
Web: www.mercy.com/stmarys/index.htm					
University of Tennessee Medical Center 1924 Alcoa Hwy	Knoxville	TN	37920	865-544-9000	544-9429
Web: www.utmck.edu/library					

— Attractions —

				Phone	Fax
American Museum of Science & Energy 300 S Tulane Ave	Oak Ridge	TN	37830	865-576-3200	576-6024
Web: www.korrnet.org/amse/ ■ *E-mail:* info@amse.org					
Andrew Johnson National Historic Site PO Box 1088	Greeneville	TN	37744	423-638-3551	638-9194
Web: www.nps.gov/anjo/					
Armstrong-Lockett House 2728 Kingston Pike	Knoxville	TN	37919	865-637-3163	
Beck Cultural Exchange Center 1927 Dandridge Ave	Knoxville	TN	37915	865-524-8461	524-8462
Big South Fork National River & Recreation Area 4564 Leatherwood Rd	Oneida	TN	37841	423-569-9778	569-5505
Web: www.nps.gov/biso/					
Bijou Theatre 803 S Gay St	Knoxville	TN	37902	865-522-0832	522-0238
Blount Mansion 200 W Hill Ave	Knoxville	TN	37901	865-525-2375	546-5315
Web: www.korrnet.org/blount96/ ■ *E-mail:* blount96@korrnet.org					
Brown Clarence Theatre 1714 Andy Holt Blvd	Knoxville	TN	37996	865-974-5161	
Carousel Theatre 1714 Andy Holt Blvd	Knoxville	TN	37996	865-974-5161	
Children's Museum of Oak Ridge 461 W Outer Dr	Oak Ridge	TN	37830	865-482-1074	481-4889
Web: newsite.com/cmor/					
Chilhowee Park 3301 E Magnolia Ave	Knoxville	TN	37914	865-637-5840	637-7914
City Ballet Inc 803 S Gay St	Knoxville	TN	37902	865-544-0495	522-3043
Web: www.knoxballet.org					
Confederate Memorial Hall 3148 Kingston Pike	Knoxville	TN	37919	865-522-2371	
Cumberland Gap National Historical Park PO Box 1848	Middlesboro	KY	40965	606-248-2817	248-7276
Web: www.nps.gov/cuga/					
Dollywood Inc 1020 Dollywood Ln	Pigeon Forge	TN	37863	865-428-9400	428-9494*
**Fax:* Mktg ■ *Web:* www.dollywood.com					
East Tennessee Discovery Center 516 N Beaman St Chilhowee Pk	Knoxville	TN	37914	865-594-1494	594-1469
Web: web.utk.edu/~loganj/etdc					
East Tennessee Historical Society Museum 600 Market St	Knoxville	TN	37901	865-544-4262	544-4319
Web: www.east-tennessee-history.org/museum/mushome.htm					
Ewing Gallery of Art & Architecture 1715 Volunteer Blvd	Knoxville	TN	37996	865-974-3200	
E-mail: spangler@utk.edu					
Farragut Folklife Museum 11408 Municipal Center Dr	Farragut	TN	37922	865-966-7057	675-2096
Web: www.farragut.tn.us/arts.html					
Great Smoky Mountains National Park 107 Park Headquarters Rd	Gatlinburg	TN	37738	865-436-1200	436-1220
Web: www.nps.gov/grsm/					
Ijams Nature Center 2915 Island Home Ave	Knoxville	TN	37917	865-577-4717	577-1683
Web: www.ijams.org ■ *E-mail:* ijams@nxs.net					
Knox County Old Gray Cemetery 543 N Broadway	Knoxville	TN	37901	865-522-1424	
Knox County Regional Farmers' Market 4700 New Harvest Ln	Knoxville	TN	37918	865-524-3276	522-4833
Knoxville Ballet 500 E Church Ave Civic Auditorium	Knoxville	TN	37902	865-544-0495	
Knoxville Museum of Art 1050 World Fair Park Dr	Knoxville	TN	37916	865-525-6101	546-3635
Web: www.knoxart.org ■ *E-mail:* kma@esper.com					
Knoxville Opera Co 612 E Depot Ave	Knoxville	TN	37917	865-523-8712	524-7384
Knoxville Symphony Orchestra PO Box 360	Knoxville	TN	37901	865-523-1178	546-3766
Knoxville Zoo 3333 Woodbine Ave	Knoxville	TN	37914	865-637-5331	637-1943
Web: www.knoxville-zoo.org					
Laurel Theatre & Jubilee Center 16th St & Laurel Ave	Knoxville	TN	37916	865-522-5851	
Web: www.korrnet.org/jca ■ *E-mail:* jubilee@korrnet.org					
Lost Sea 140 Lost Sea Rd	Sweetwater	TN	37874	423-337-6616	337-0803
Mabry-Hazen House 1176 Dandridge Ave	Knoxville	TN	37915	865-522-8661	
Marble Springs 1220 W Governor John Sevier Hwy	Knoxville	TN	37920	865-573-5508	
McClung Frank H Museum 1327 Circle Park Dr University of Tennessee	Knoxville	TN	37996	865-974-2144	974-3827
Web: mcclungmuseum.utk.edu/ ■ *E-mail:* museum@utkux.utcc.utk.edu					
Museum of Appalachia PO Box 1189	Norris	TN	37828	865-494-7680	494-8957
Obed Wild & Scenic River 208 N Maiden St	Wartburg	TN	37887	423-346-6294	346-3362
Web: www.nps.gov/obed/					
Old City District Jackson Ave E & Central St S	Knoxville	TN	37915		
Ramsey House 2614 Thorngrove Pike	Knoxville	TN	37914	865-546-0745	
South's Finest Chocolate Factory 1060 World's Fair Park Dr World's Fair Park	Knoxville	TN	37916	865-522-2049	522-0874
Star of Knoxville Riverboat 300 Neyland Dr	Knoxville	TN	37902	865-522-4630	522-5941
Sunsphere 810 W Clinch Ave	Knoxville	TN	37902	865-523-4228	
Tennessee Children's Dance Ensemble 4216 Sutherland Ave	Knoxville	TN	37919	865-588-8842	
Tennessee Riverboat Company 300 Neyland Dr Volunteer Landing	Knoxville	TN	37902	865-525-7827	522-5941
TF: 800-509-2628 ■ *Web:* www.tnriverboat.com ■ *E-mail:* capt@tnriverboat.com					
Tennessee Stage Company 1060 World's Fair Park Dr	Knoxville	TN	37916	865-546-4280	
Tennessee Theater 604 S Gay St	Knoxville	TN	37902	865-522-1174	637-2141
University of Tennessee Music Hall 1741 Volunteer Blvd	Knoxville	TN	37996	865-974-3241	974-1941
Victorian Houses 11th St & Laurel Ave	Knoxville	TN	37916	865-525-7619	
White James Fort 205 E Hill Ave	Knoxville	TN	37915	865-525-6514	525-6514

SPORTS TEAMS & FACILITIES

				Phone	Fax
Knoxville Smokies (baseball) 633 Jesamine St Bill Meyer Stadium	Knoxville	TN	37917	865-637-9494	523-9913
Web: www.smokiesbaseball.com ■ *E-mail:* info@smokiesbaseball.com					

— Events —

	Phone
Artfest (early September-late October)	865-523-7543
Boomsday (early September)	865-693-1020
Christmas in the City (late November-late December)	865-215-4248
Dogwood Arts Festival (early-mid-April)	865-637-4561
Fantasy of Trees (late November)	865-541-8385
Foothills Craft Guild Fall Show & Sale (mid-November)	865-483-6400
Fourth of July Celebration & Anvil Shoot (early July)	865-494-7680
International Jubilee Festival (late May)	865-522-5851
Knoxville Boat Show (early March)	865-588-1233
Knoxville Western Film Caravan (late April)	865-522-2600
Kuumba Festival (early July)	865-525-0961
Ragin' Cajun Cookout (late May)	865-558-9040
Smoky Mountain Marathon (late February)	865-588-7465
Statehood Day Celebration (early June)	865-525-2375
Tennessee Fall Homecoming (early October)	865-494-7680
Tennessee Valley Fair (mid-September)	865-637-5840

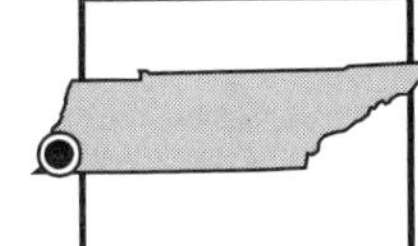

Memphis

Memphis received its name from General James Winchester, who was inspired by the Nile-like Mississippi River to name the area for the Egyptian city of Memphis, and today the banks of the Mississippi are home to a 32-story sports/entertainment/music complex called The Pyramid. Between Riverside Drive and Danny Thomas Boulevard is Memphis' Beale Street, the "Birthplace of the Blues," where W.C. Handy first wrote Blues music of the Mississippi Delta. But Memphis is perhaps best known as the city where Elvis Presley began his musical career. Thousands of visitors come to visit his home, Graceland, and the city remembers "The King" every August with memorial celebrations.

Population	603,507	**Longitude**	90-03-13 W
Area (Land)	256.0 sq mi	**County**	Shelby
Area (Water)	15.1 sq mi	**Time Zone**	CST
Elevation	254 ft	**Area Code/s**	901
Latitude	35-08-46 N		

Memphis (Cont'd)

— Average Temperatures and Precipitation —

TEMPERATURES

	Jan	Feb	Mar	Apr	May	Jun	Jul	Aug	Sep	Oct	Nov	Dec
High	49	54	63	73	81	89	92	91	84	74	62	53
Low	31	35	43	52	61	69	73	71	65	52	43	35

PRECIPITATION

	Jan	Feb	Mar	Apr	May	Jun	Jul	Aug	Sep	Oct	Nov	Dec
Inches	3.7	4.4	5.4	5.5	5.0	3.6	3.8	3.4	3.5	3.0	5.1	5.7

— Important Phone Numbers —

	Phone		Phone
AAA	901-761-5371	**Medical Referral**	901-362-8677
American Express Travel	901-291-1400	**Poison Control Center**	901-528-6048
Emergency	911	**Time/Temp**	901-526-5261
Events Line	901-753-5847	**Travelers Aid**	901-525-5466
HotelDocs	800-468-3537	**Weather**	901-544-0399

— Information Sources —

				Phone	Fax
Better Business Bureau Serving West Tennessee North Mississippi & Eastern Arkansas PO Box 17036	Memphis	TN	38187	901-759-1300	757-2997
Web: www.memphis.bbb.org ■ *E-mail:* info@bbbmidsouth.org					
Memphis Area Chamber of Commerce PO Box 224	Memphis	TN	38101	901-543-3500	543-3510
Web: www.memphischamber.com					
Memphis Center City Commission 114 N Main St Crump Bldg	Memphis	TN	38103	901-575-0540	575-0541
Web: www.downtownmemphis.com					
Memphis City Hall 125 N Main St	Memphis	TN	38103	901-576-6500	
Web: www.ci.memphis.tn.us					
Memphis Convention & Visitors Bureau 47 Union Ave	Memphis	TN	38103	901-543-5300	543-5350
TF: 800-873-6282 ■ *Web:* www.memphistravel.com					
Memphis Cook Convention Center 255 N Main St	Memphis	TN	38103	901-576-1200	576-1212
TF: 800-726-0915 ■ *Web:* www.memphisconvention.com					
Memphis Mayor 125 N Main St Suite 700	Memphis	TN	38103	901-576-6000	576-6012
Web: www.ci.memphis.tn.us/divisions/executive.cfm					
Memphis Planning & Development Dept 125 N Main St	Memphis	TN	38103	901-576-7197	576-7188
Web: www.ci.memphis.tn.us/divisions/planning.cfm					
Memphis-Shelby County Public Library & Information Center 1850 Peabody Ave	Memphis	TN	38104	901-725-8855	725-8883
Web: www.memphislibrary.lib.tn.us					
Memphis Visitors Information Center 119 N Riverside Dr	Memphis	TN	38103	901-543-5333	543-5335
Shelby County 160 N Main St Suite 619	Memphis	TN	38103	901-545-4301	576-4283
Web: www.co.shelby.tn.us					

On-Line Resources

4Memphis.com	www.4memphis.com
Area Guide Memphis	memphis.areaguides.net
Boulevards Memphis	www.memphis.com
City Knowledge Memphis	www.cityknowledge.com/tn_memphis.htm
DigitalCity Memphis	home.digitalcity.com/memphis
Downtown Memphis	www.downtownmemphis.com/
Excite.com Memphis City Guide	www.excite.com/travel/countries/united_states/tennessee/memphis
IntroMemphis	www.intromemphis.com
LocalPaper@Memphis	www.localpaper.com/
Memphis Community Network	www.memphis.acn.net/
Memphis Connection	www.memphisconnection.com/
Memphis Flyer	www.memphisflyer.com
Memphis Guide	www.memphisguide.com/
MemphisNet	www.memphisnet.com/
Mid-South Citizen Site	www.lunaweb.com/index.htm
Rough Guide Travel Memphis	travel.roughguides.com/content/747/
Search Memphis	www.searchmemphis.com/

— Transportation Services —

AIRPORTS

■ **Memphis International Airport (MEM)**

	Phone
10 miles SE of downtown (approx 20 minutes)	901-922-8000
Web: www.mscaa.com	

Airport Transportation

	Phone
MATA $1.20 fare to downtown	901-274-6282
Taxi $20-22 fare to downtown	901-577-7777

Commercial Airlines

	Phone		Phone
American	800-433-7300	**TWA**	800-221-2000
Delta	800-221-1212	**United**	800-241-6522
KLM	800-374-7747	**US Airways**	800-428-4322
Northwest	800-225-2525		

Charter Airlines

	Phone
Richards Aviation	901-332-7239

CAR RENTALS

	Phone		Phone
Alamo	901-332-8412	**Enterprise**	901-345-8588
Avis	901-345-2847	**Hertz**	901-345-5680
Budget	901-332-2222	**National**	901-345-0070
Dollar	901-345-3890	**Thrifty**	901-345-0170

LIMO/TAXI

	Phone		Phone
Amore Limousine	901-362-7000	**Tennessee Limousine Service**	901-452-6207
City Wide Cab	901-324-4202	**Yellow & Checker Cab**	901-577-7777
Memphis Executive Limousine	901-396-7733		

MASS TRANSIT

	Phone
Main Street Trolley $.50 Base fare	901-274-6282
MATA $1.10 Base fare	901-274-6282

RAIL/BUS

				Phone
Greyhound Bus Station 203 Union Ave	Memphis	TN	38105	901-523-9253
TF: 800-231-2222				
Memphis Amtrak Station 545 S Main St	Memphis	TN	38103	901-526-0052

— Accommodations —

HOTELS, MOTELS, RESORTS

				Phone	Fax
Adam's Mark Hotel 939 Ridge Lake Blvd	Memphis	TN	38120	901-684-6664	762-7411
TF: 800-444-2326 ■ *Web:* www.adamsmark.com/memph.htm					
AmeriSuites Cordova 7905 Giacosa Pl.	Memphis	TN	38133	901-371-0010	371-9988
TF: 800-833-1516					
AmeriSuites Primacy Parkway 1220 Primacy Pkwy.	Memphis	TN	38119	901-680-9700	681-0102
TF: 800-833-1516					
Benchmark Hotel 164 Union Ave	Memphis	TN	38103	901-527-4100	525-1747
Comfort Inn 2889 Old Austin Peay Hwy	Memphis	TN	38128	901-386-0033	386-0036
TF: 800-228-5150					
Comfort Inn 1963 US Hwy 45 Bypass	Jackson	TN	38305	901-668-4100	664-6940
TF: 800-850-1131					
Comfort Inn Downtown 100 N Front St	Memphis	TN	38103	901-526-0583	525-7512
TF: 800-228-5150					
Courtyard by Marriott 6015 Park Ave	Memphis	TN	38119	901-761-0330	682-8422
TF: 800-321-2211 ■ *Web:* courtyard.com/MEMPA					
Days Inn 340 W Illinois Ave	Memphis	TN	38106	901-948-9005	946-5716
TF: 800-329-7466					
Days Inn Graceland 3839 Elvis Presley Blvd	Memphis	TN	38116	901-346-5500	345-7452
TF: 800-329-7466					
Elvis Presley Heartbreak Hotel 3677 Elvis Presley Blvd	Memphis	TN	38116	901-332-1000	332-2107
TF: 877-777-0606					

Memphis — Hotels, Motels, Resorts (Cont'd)

	City	State	ZIP	Phone	Fax
Elvis Presley's Memphis (American) 126 Beale St.	Memphis	TN	38103	901-527-6900	
Web: www.epmemphis.com					
Embassy Suites Memphis 1022 S Shady Grove Rd	Memphis	TN	38120	901-684-1777	685-8185
TF: 800-362-2779					
Extended StayAmerica 5885 Shelby Oaks Dr.	Memphis	TN	38134	901-386-0026	386-5198
TF: 800-398-7829					
Four Points Hotel by Sheraton 2240 Democrat Rd	Memphis	TN	38132	901-332-1130	398-5206
TF: 800-325-3535					
French Quarter Suites Hotel 2144 Madison Ave	Memphis	TN	38104	901-728-4000	278-1262
TF: 800-843-0353					
Hampton Inn Airport 2979 Millbranch Rd.	Memphis	TN	38116	901-396-2200	396-7034
TF: 800-426-7866					
Hampton Inn Medical Center 1180 Union Ave	Memphis	TN	38104	901-276-1175	276-4261
TF: 800-426-7866					
Hilton Hotel East 5069 Sanderlin Ave	Memphis	TN	38117	901-767-6666	767-5428
TF: 800-445-8667 ■ *Web:* www.hilton.com/hotels/MEMEHHF					
Holiday Inn Hotel 160 Union Ave	Memphis	TN	38103	901-525-5491	529-8950
TF: 888-300-5491					
Holiday Inn Midtown Medical Center 1837 Union Ave	Memphis	TN	38104	901-278-4100	272-3810
TF: 800-465-4329					
Holiday Inn Mount Moriah 2490 Mt Moriah Rd.	Memphis	TN	38115	901-362-8010	368-0452
TF: 800-477-5519					
Howard Johnson Airport 1441 E Brooks Rd	Memphis	TN	38116	901-398-9211	398-7258
TF: 800-446-4656					
La Quinta Inn Airport 2745 Airways Blvd	Memphis	TN	38132	901-396-1000	332-5720
TF: 800-531-5900					
Marriott Downtown 250 N Main St	Memphis	TN	38103	901-527-7300	526-1561
TF: 888-557-8740					
Marriott Hotel Memphis 2625 Thousand Oaks Blvd	Memphis	TN	38118	901-362-6200	360-8836
TF: 800-228-9290 ■ *Web:* marriotthotels.com/MEMTN					
Peabody Hotel 149 Union Ave	Memphis	TN	38103	901-529-4000	529-3600
TF: 800-732-2639 ■ *Web:* www.peabodymemphis.com					
Radisson Hotel Memphis 185 Union Ave.	Memphis	TN	38103	901-528-1800	526-3226
TF: 800-333-3333					
Radisson Inn 2411 Winchester Rd	Memphis	TN	38116	901-332-2370	398-4085
TF: 800-365-2370					
Ramada Inn Airport 1471 E Brooks Rd	Memphis	TN	38116	901-332-3500	346-0017
TF: 800-228-2828					
Residence Inn by Marriott Memphis East 6141 Poplar Pike	Memphis	TN	38119	901-685-9595	685-1636
TF: 800-331-3131 ■ *Web:* www.residenceinn.com/MEMPP					
Ridgeway Inn 5679 Poplar Ave.	Memphis	TN	38119	901-766-4000	763-1857
TF: 800-822-3360					
Sleep Inn 40 N Front St Court Sq	Memphis	TN	38104	901-522-9700	522-9710
TF: 800-627-5337					
Studio 6 4300 American Way	Memphis	TN	38118	901-366-9333	366-7835
TF: 800-214-8378					
Wilson World Hotel & Suites 2715 Cherry Rd	Memphis	TN	38118	901-366-0000	366-6361
TF: 800-945-7667					

— Restaurants —

	City	State	ZIP	Phone
Alfred's (American) 197 Beale St	Memphis	TN	38103	901-525-3711
Anderton's Seafood Restaurant & Oyster Bar (Seafood) 1901 Madison Ave	Memphis	TN	38104	901-726-4010
Automatic Slim's Tonga Club (Southwest/Caribbean) 83 S 2nd St.	Memphis	TN	38103	901-525-7948
BB King's Blues Club & Restaurant (Southern) 143 Beale St	Memphis	TN	38103	901-524-5464
Blues City Cafe (Steak) 138 Beale St	Memphis	TN	38103	901-526-3637
Buckley's Downtown Fine Filet Grill (American) 117 Union Ave.	Memphis	TN	38103	901-578-9001
Butcher Shop (Steak) 101 S Front St	Memphis	TN	38103	901-521-0856
Chez Philippe (French) 149 Union Ave	Memphis	TN	38103	901-529-4188
Cupboard Too (Homestyle) 149 Madison Ave	Memphis	TN	38103	901-527-9111
Dux (New American) 149 Union Ave Rd	Memphis	TN	38103	901-529-4199
Elliott's Restaurant (American) 16 S 2nd St	Memphis	TN	38103	901-525-4895
Grisanti (Italian) 1022 Shady Grove	Memphis	TN	38120	901-761-9462
Web: www.frankgrisanti-embassy.com/				
Hard Rock Cafe (American) 315 Beale St	Memphis	TN	38103	901-529-0007
King's Palace Cafe (Cajun) 162 Beale St	Memphis	TN	38103	901-521-1851
Kudzu's (American) 603 Monroe St	Memphis	TN	38103	901-525-4924
La Tourelle (French) 2146 Monroe Ave.	Memphis	TN	38104	901-726-5771
Landry's (Seafood) 263 Wagner Pl.	Memphis	TN	38103	901-526-1966
Le Chardonnay (Continental) 2100-5 Overton Sq.	Memphis	TN	38104	901-725-1375
Web: www.lechardonnay.com/				
Mallards (American) 149 Union Ave.	Memphis	TN	38103	901-529-4000
Marmalade (Southern) 153 E Calhoun Ave	Memphis	TN	38103	901-522-8800
North End (American) 346 N Main St.	Memphis	TN	38103	901-526-0319
Owen Brennan's Restaurant (Cajun/Creole) 6150 Poplar Ave.	Memphis	TN	38119	901-761-0990
Paulette's (Continental) 2110 Madison Ave.	Memphis	TN	38104	901-726-5128
Pier The (Steak/Seafood) 100 Wagner Pl	Memphis	TN	38103	901-526-7381
Public Eye (Barbecue) 17 S Cooper St	Memphis	TN	38104	901-726-4040
Rendezvous (Barbecue) 52 S 2nd St	Memphis	TN	38103	901-523-2746
Rum Boogie Cafe (American) 182 Beale St.	Memphis	TN	38103	901-528-0150
Silky O'Sullivan's (American) 183 Beale St.	Memphis	TN	38103	901-522-9596
Sleep Out Louies (Seafood) 88 Union Ave	Memphis	TN	38103	901-527-5337
TJ Mulligan's (American) 362 N Main St	Memphis	TN	38103	901-523-1453

— Goods and Services —

SHOPPING

	City	State	ZIP	Phone	Fax
Chickasaw Oaks Plaza 3092 Poplar Ave	Memphis	TN	38111	901-766-4208	
Dillard's 4430 American Way	Memphis	TN	38118	901-363-0063	
Goldsmith's 4545 Poplar Ave	Memphis	TN	38117	901-766-4199	529-4522
Hickory Ridge Mall 6075 Winchester Rd	Memphis	TN	38115	901-795-8844	363-8471
Laurelwood Shopping Center Poplar Ave & Perkins Rd	Memphis	TN	38117	901-794-6022	
Mall of Memphis Perkins Rd & American Way	Memphis	TN	38118	901-362-9315	
Oak Court Mall Poplar Ave & Perkins Rd	Memphis	TN	38117	901-682-8928	
Raleigh Springs Mall 3384 Austin Peay Hwy.	Memphis	TN	38128	901-388-4300	388-6970
Regalia The Poplar Ave & Ridgeway	Memphis	TN	38119	901-767-0100	
Shops of Saddle Creek Poplar Ave & W Farmington Blvd	Germantown	TN	38138	901-761-2571	761-5325
Southland Mall Elvis Presley Blvd & Shelby Dr	Memphis	TN	38116	901-346-1210	398-3501
Whitehaven Plaza Elvis Presley Blvd & Raines Rd.	Memphis	TN	38116	901-458-8922	458-7668
Wolfchase Galleria 2760 N Germantown Pkwy.	Memphis	TN	38133	901-381-2769	388-5542

BANKS

	City	State	ZIP	Phone	Fax
First Tennessee Bank NA 165 Madison Ave.	Memphis	TN	38103	901-523-4444	523-4145*
**Fax:* Mktg ■ *TF:* 800-999-0110					
National Bank of Commerce 1 Commerce Sq	Memphis	TN	38150	901-523-3434	523-3310
Web: www.nbcbank.com ■ *E-mail:* nbc@wspice.com					
NationsBank 200 Madison Ave	Memphis	TN	38103	901-529-6005	529-6057
Regions Bank 5384 Poplar Ave.	Memphis	TN	38119	901-766-2700	766-2856
TF: 800-690-5857					
Union Planters National Bank 6200 Poplar Ave	Memphis	TN	38122	901-580-6000	

BUSINESS SERVICES

	Phone
Ablest Temporary Services	901-398-7853
Above Average Express	901-763-3306
Emery Worldwide	901-396-5536
Federal Express	800-463-3339
Kelly Services	901-375-4252
Kinko's	901-327-2679
Manpower Temporary Services	901-576-8282
Olsten Staffing Services	901-761-1060
Post Office	901-521-2140
UPS	800-742-5877
VIP Express	901-396-1801

— Media —

PUBLICATIONS

	City	State	ZIP	Phone	Fax
Commercial Appeal‡ 495 Union Ave.	Memphis	TN	38103	901-529-2345	529-2522
TF: 800-444-6397 ■ *Web:* www.gomemphis.com					

Memphis — Publications (Cont'd)

				Phone	Fax
Memphis Business Journal					
88 Union Ave Suite 102	Memphis	TN	38103	901-523-1000	526-5240
Memphis Magazine 460 Tennessee St.	Memphis	TN	38103	901-521-9000	521-0129
E-mail: memflyer@aol.com					

‡*Daily newspapers*

TELEVISION

				Phone	Fax
WBUY-TV Ch 40 (TBN) PO Box 38421	Memphis	TN	38183	901-521-9289	521-9989
WHBQ-TV Ch 13 (Fox) 485 S Highland St	Memphis	TN	38111	901-320-1313	320-1366
Web: www.fox13whbq.com ■ *E-mail:* news@fox13whbq.com					
WKNO-TV Ch 10 (PBS) 900 Getwell Rd	Memphis	TN	38111	901-458-2521	325-6505
Web: www.wkno.org ■ *E-mail:* wknopi@wkno.org					
WLMT-TV Ch 30 (UPN) 2701 Union Ave Ext.	Memphis	TN	38112	901-323-2430	452-1820
Web: www.upn30memphis.com					
WMC-TV Ch 5 (NBC) 1960 Union Ave	Memphis	TN	38104	901-726-0555	278-7633
Web: www.wmcstations.com/wmctv					
WPTY-TV Ch 24 (ABC) 2701 Union Ave	Memphis	TN	38112	901-323-2430	452-1820
Web: www.abc24.com ■ *E-mail:* newsdesk@abc24.com					
WREG-TV Ch 3 (CBS) 803 Channel Three Dr	Memphis	TN	38103	901-543-2333	543-2167
Web: www.wreg.com ■ *E-mail:* wreg@wreg.com					

RADIO

				Phone	Fax
KJMS-FM 101.1 MHz (Urban)					
112 Union Ave	Memphis	TN	38103	901-527-0101	529-9557
Web: www.smooth101.com					
KWAM-AM 990 khz (Rel) 112 Union Ave	Memphis	TN	38103	901-527-5926	527-1393
Web: www.am990.com					
KXHT-FM 107.1 MHz (Urban)					
6080 Mt Moriah Blvd.	Memphis	TN	38115	901-375-9324	795-4454
WBBP-AM 1480 kHz (Rel) 250 E Raines Rd.	Memphis	TN	38109	901-278-7878	344-0038
WCRV-AM 640 kHz (Rel)					
555 Perkins Rd Ext Suite 201	Memphis	TN	38117	901-763-4640	763-4920*
**Fax:* Sales					
WDIA-AM 1070 kHz (AC) 112 Union Ave	Memphis	TN	38103	901-529-4300	529-9557
Web: www.am1070wdia.com ■ *E-mail:* promo@am1070wdia.com					
WEGR-FM 102.7 MHz (CR)					
203 Beale St Suite 200	Memphis	TN	38103	901-578-1103	525-8054
Web: www.rock103.com					
WGKX-FM 105.9 MHz (Ctry)					
965 Ridgelake Blvd Suite 102	Memphis	TN	38120	901-682-1106	767-9531
Web: www.wgkx.com ■ *E-mail:* news@wgkx.com					
WHBQ-AM 560 kHz (Sports)					
6080 Mt Moriah Blvd.	Memphis	TN	38115	901-375-9324	795-4454
Web: www.sports56whbq.com					
WHRK-FM 97.1 MHz (Urban) 112 Union Ave	Memphis	TN	38103	901-529-4397	527-3455
WJCE-AM 680 kHz (Urban)					
5904 Ridgeway Ctr Pkwy	Memphis	TN	38120	901-767-0104	767-0582
WKNO-FM 91.1 MHz (NPR) 900 Getwell Rd.	Memphis	TN	38111	901-325-6544	325-6506
Web: www.wknofm.org ■ *E-mail:* wknofm@aol.com					
WLOK-AM 1340 kHz (Rel) 363 S 2nd St	Memphis	TN	38103	901-527-9565	528-0335
WMC-AM 790 kHz (N/T) 1960 Union Ave	Memphis	TN	38104	901-726-0555	722-5643
Web: www.wmcstations.com/am790/ ■ *E-mail:* talk@wmcstations.com					
WMC-FM 100 MHz (AC) 1960 Union Ave	Memphis	TN	38104	901-726-0555	272-9186*
**Fax:* Sales ■ *Web:* www.wmcstations.com/fm100/ ■ *E-mail:* info@wmcstations.com					
WMFS-FM 92.9 MHz (Rock)					
1632 Sycamore View	Memphis	TN	38134	901-383-9637	373-1478
Web: www.wmfs.com					
WOGY-FM 94.1 MHz (Ctry)					
5904 Ridgeway Ctr Pkwy	Memphis	TN	38120	901-683-9400	682-2804
Web: www.froggy94.com ■ *E-mail:* froggy94@accessus.net					
WOWW-AM 1430 kHz (N/T) 6080 Mt Moriah	Memphis	TN	38115	901-375-9324	795-4454
WPLX-AM 1170 kHz (B/EZ)					
6655 Poplar Ave Suite 200	Germantown	TN	38138	901-751-1513	751-1501
WREC-AM 600 kHz (N/T)					
203 Beale St Suite 200	Memphis	TN	38103	901-578-1160	525-8054
WRVR-FM 104.5 MHz (AC)					
5904 Ridgeway Center Pkwy	Memphis	TN	38120	901-767-0104	767-0582
Web: www.wrvr.com ■ *E-mail:* river104@wrvr.com					
WRXQ-FM 95.7 MHz (Alt)					
203 Beale St Suite 200	Memphis	TN	38103	901-578-1100	578-1132
Web: www.96x.com ■ *E-mail:* wrxq96x@aol.com					
WSRR-FM 98.1 MHz (Rock)					
965 Ridgelake Blvd Suite 102	Memphis	TN	38120	901-680-9898	680-0482

— Colleges/Universities —

				Phone	Fax
Christian Brothers University					
650 East Pkwy S.	Memphis	TN	38104	901-321-3000	321-3494
TF Admissions: 800-288-7576 ■ *Web:* www.cbu.edu ■ *E-mail:* admissions@bucs.cbu.edu					
Crichton College PO Box 757830	Memphis	TN	38175	901-367-9800	367-3866
TF: 800-960-9777					
LeMoyne-Owen College 807 Walker Ave	Memphis	TN	38126	901-774-9090	942-6272
TF: 800-737-7778 ■ *Web:* www.mecca.org/LOC/page/LOC.html					
Memphis College of Art Overton Park					
1930 Poplar Ave	Memphis	TN	38107	901-726-4085	272-6830
TF: 800-727-1088 ■ *Web:* www.mca.edu					
Rhodes College 2000 North Pkwy.	Memphis	TN	38112	901-843-3000	843-3719
TF Admissions: 800-844-5969 ■ *Web:* www.rhodes.edu ■ *E-mail:* adminfo@rhodes.edu					
Rust College 150 E Rust Ave	Holly Springs	MS	38635	662-252-4661	252-6107
Shelby State Community College					
PO Box 40568	Memphis	TN	38174	901-333-5000	333-5920
State Technical Institute Memphis					
5983 Macon Cove	Memphis	TN	38134	901-383-4100	383-4503
TF: 888-832-4937 ■ *Web:* www.stim.tec.tn.us ■ *E-mail:* postmaster@stim.tec.tn.us					
Tri-State Baptist College 6001 Goodman Rd	Walls	MS	38680	662-781-7777	781-7777
University of Memphis	Memphis	TN	38152	901-678-2040	678-3053
TF Admissions: 800-669-2678 ■ *Web:* www.memphis.edu					
University of Tennessee Memphis					
800 Madison Ave	Memphis	TN	38163	901-448-5000	448-7772
Web: www.utmem.edu					

— Hospitals —

				Phone	Fax
Baptist Memorial Hospital East Memphis					
6019 Walnut Grove Rd	Memphis	TN	38120	901-226-5000	226-5618
Baptist Memorial Hospital Medical Center					
899 Madison Ave	Memphis	TN	38146	901-227-2727	227-5650
Delta Medical Center 3000 Getwell Rd	Memphis	TN	38118	901-369-8500	369-8503
Le Bonheur Children's Medical Center					
50 N Dunlap Ave.	Memphis	TN	38103	901-572-3000	572-4586
Methodist Germantown Hospital					
7691 Poplar Ave	Germantown	TN	38138	901-754-6418	757-6669
Methodist Hospital Central 1265 Union Ave.	Memphis	TN	38104	901-726-7000	726-7339*
**Fax:* Admitting					
Methodist Hospital North					
3960 New Covington Pike	Memphis	TN	38128	901-384-5200	384-5582*
**Fax:* Admitting					
Methodist Hospital South 1300 Wesley Dr.	Memphis	TN	38116	901-346-3700	346-3766
Regional Medical Center at Memphis					
877 Jefferson Ave.	Memphis	TN	38103	901-545-7100	545-7674*
**Fax:* Admitting ■ *Web:* www.the-med.com					
Saint Francis Hospital 5959 Park Ave	Memphis	TN	38119	901-765-1000	765-1799*
**Fax:* Admitting ■ *Web:* www.tenethealth.com/SaintFrancis					
Saint Jude Children's Research Hospital					
332 N Lauderdale St	Memphis	TN	38105	901-495-3300	525-2720
Web: www.stjude.org ■ *E-mail:* info@stjude.org					
University of Tennessee Bowld Hospital					
951 Court Ave	Memphis	TN	38103	901-448-4108	448-4054
Veterans Affairs Medical Center					
1030 Jefferson Ave	Memphis	TN	38104	901-523-8990	577-7251

— Attractions —

				Phone	Fax
Art Museum of the University of Memphis					
3750 Norriswood Ave Communication & Fine Arts Bldg.	Memphis	TN	38152	901-678-2224	678-5118
Web: www.people.memphis.edu/~artmuseum/amhome.html					
Ballet Memphis PO Box 3675	Cordova	TN	38088	901-737-7457	737-7037
Web: www.balletmemphis.org					
Beale Street Historic District					
downtown Memphis	Memphis	TN	38103	901-543-5333	
Web: www.bealestreet.com ■ *E-mail:* bluesmaster@bealestreet.com					
Burkle Estate Museum 826 N 2nd St	Memphis	TN	38107	901-527-3427	527-8784
Center for Southern Folklore 209 Beale St.	Memphis	TN	38103	901-525-3655	525-3945
Children's Museum of Memphis					
2525 Central Ave	Memphis	TN	38104	901-458-2678	458-4033
Web: www.cmom.com/ ■ *E-mail:* children@cmom.com					
Chucalissa Indian Village					
1987 Indian Village Dr.	Memphis	TN	38109	901-785-3160	785-0519
Web: www.people.memphis.edu/~chucalissa/					

Memphis — Attractions (Cont'd)

				Phone	Fax
Circuit Playhouse 1705 Poplar Ave	Memphis	TN	38104	901-726-4656	272-7530
Clough-Hanson Gallery Rhodes College 2000 North Pkwy	Memphis	TN	38112	901-843-3442	
Cooper Young Entertainment District S Cooper St & Young Ave	Memphis	TN	38104	901-272-1459	272-1455
Crystal Shrine Grotto 5668 Poplar Ave Memorial Park Cemetary	Memphis	TN	38119	901-767-8930	763-2442
Davies Manor House 9336 Davies Plantation Rd	Memphis	TN	38133	901-386-0715	
Dixon Gallery & Gardens 4339 Park Ave	Memphis	TN	38117	901-761-5250	682-0943
Web: www.dixon.org/ ■ *E-mail:* info@dixon.org					
Fire Museum of Memphis 118 Adams Ave	Memphis	TN	38103	901-320-5650	529-8422
Web: www.firemuseum.com ■ *E-mail:* gwitt@memphisonline.com					
Fuller State Recreation Park 1500 Mitchell Rd	Memphis	TN	38109	901-543-7581	785-8485
Germantown Performing Arts Centre 1801 Exeter Rd	Germantown	TN	38138	901-751-7500	751-7514
E-mail: info@gpacweb.com					
Graceland (Elvis Presley Mansion) 3734 Elvis Presley Blvd	Memphis	TN	38116	901-332-3322	344-3131
TF: 800-238-2000 ■ *Web:* www.elvis-presley.com/ ■ *E-mail:* graceland@memphisonline.com					
Haley Alex House Museum 200 S Church St	Memphis	TN	38041	901-738-2240	738-2585
Historic Elmwood Cemetery 824 S Dudley St	Memphis	TN	38104	901-774-3212	774-0085
Hunt-Phelan Home 533 Beale St	Memphis	TN	38103	901-525-8225	542-5042
TF: 800-350-9009 ■ *Web:* www.hunt-phelan.com					
King Martin Luther Riverside Park Riverside & Pkwy	Memphis	TN	38112	901-454-5200	
Libertyland 940 Early Maxwell Blvd	Memphis	TN	38104	901-274-1776	274-8804
Web: www.libertyland.com ■ *E-mail:* llweb@libertyland.com					
Lichterman Nature Center 1680 Lynfield Rd	Memphis	TN	38119	901-767-7322	682-3050
Web: www.memphismuseums.org/nature.htm ■ *E-mail:* more_info@memphismuseums.org					
Lindenwood Concerts 2400 Union Ave	Memphis	TN	38112	901-458-1652	458-0145
Web: www.lroom.org					
Magevney House 198 Adams Ave	Memphis	TN	38103	901-526-4464	526-8666
Web: www.memphismuseums.org/magevney.htm ■ *E-mail:* more-info@memphismuseums.org					
Main Street Trolley 547 N Main St	Memphis	TN	38105	901-577-2640	577-2660
Mallory Neely House 652 Adams Ave	Memphis	TN	38105	901-523-1484	526-8666
Web: www.memphismuseums.org/mallory.htm ■ *E-mail:* more_info@memphismuseums.org					
Mason Temple Church of God in Christ 938 Mason St	Memphis	TN	38126	901-578-3830	578-3859
McKellar Park Airways at Holmes Rd	Memphis	TN	38116	901-454-5200	
Meeman Shelby State Park Rt 3 PO Box SF1	Millington	TN	38053	901-876-5215	873-3217
Memphis Belle B-17 Bomber 125 N Front St Mud Island	Memphis	TN	38103	901-576-7241	
TF: 800-507-6507 ■ *Web:* www.memphisbelle.com/ ■ *E-mail:* belle@memphisbelle.com					
Memphis Botanic Garden 750 Cherry Rd	Memphis	TN	38117	901-685-1566	682-1561
Memphis Brooks Museum of Art 1934 Poplar Ave Overton Pk	Memphis	TN	38104	901-544-6200	725-4071
Web: www.brooksmuseum.org					
Memphis Music Hall of Fame 97 S 2nd St	Memphis	TN	38103	901-525-4007	525-0162
Memphis Pink Palace Museum & Planetarium 3050 Central Ave	Memphis	TN	38111	901-320-6320	320-6391
Web: www.memphismuseums.org ■ *E-mail:* more_info@memphismuseums.org					
Memphis Queen River Excursions 45 S Riverside Dr	Memphis	TN	38103	901-527-5694	524-5757
TF: 800-221-6197 ■ *Web:* www.memphisqueen.com/ ■ *E-mail:* mqueen@memphisqueen.com					
Memphis Symphony Orchestra 3100 Walnut Grove Rd Suite 501	Memphis	TN	38111	901-324-3627	324-3698
Web: www.memphissymphony.org					
Memphis Transportation Museum 125 N Rowlett St	Collierville	TN	38017	901-683-2266	
Memphis Zoo & Aquarium 2000 Galloway St	Memphis	TN	38112	901-726-4787	725-9305
Web: www.memphiszoo.org ■ *E-mail:* jheizer@memphiszoo.org					
Mississippi River Museum 125 N Front St	Memphis	TN	38103	901-576-7230	576-6666
TF: 800-507-6507 ■ *Web:* www.mudisland.com/museum.html					
Mud Island 125 N Front St	Memphis	TN	38103	901-576-7241	576-6666
TF: 800-507-6507 ■ *Web:* www.mudisland.com					
National Civil Rights Museum 450 Mulberry St	Memphis	TN	38103	901-521-9699	521-9740
Web: www.mecca.org/~crights					
National Ornamental Metal Museum 374 Metal Museum Dr	Memphis	TN	38106	901-774-6380	774-6382
Opera Memphis University of Memphis Campus Box 526331	Memphis	TN	38152	901-678-2706	678-3506
Web: gray.music.rhodes.edu/operahtmls/opera.html					
Orpheum Theatre PO Box 3370	Memphis	TN	38173	901-525-7800	526-0829
Web: www.orpheum-memphis.com					
Overton Park 2080 Poplar Ave	Memphis	TN	38104	901-454-5200	
Overton Square Entertainment District Madison & Cooper Sts	Memphis	TN	38104	901-278-6300	278-0145
Playhouse on the Square 51 S Cooper St	Memphis	TN	38104	901-726-4656	272-7530
Pyramid Arena 1 Auction Ave	Memphis	TN	38105	901-521-9675	528-0153
Web: www.pyramidarena.com					
Rainbow Works 387 S Main St	Memphis	TN	38103	901-521-0400	521-8310
TF: 800-873-4604					
Saint Mary's Catholic Church & Grotto of Lourdes 155 Market St	Memphis	TN	38105	901-522-9420	
Shelby Farms 7171 Mullins Station Rd Shelby Park	Memphis	TN	38134	901-382-4250	
Sun Studio 706 Union Ave	Memphis	TN	38103	901-521-0664	
Web: www.sunstudio.com/ ■ *E-mail:* sun@wspice.com					
Theatre Memphis 630 Perkins Ext	Memphis	TN	38117	901-682-8601	763-4096
Union Planters IMAX Theater 3050 Central Ave Pink Palace Museum	Memphis	TN	38111	901-320-6320	320-6391
Web: www.memphismuseums.org/imax.htm ■ *E-mail:* more_info@memphismuseums.org					
WC Handy Museum 352 Beale St	Memphis	TN	38103	901-522-1556	527-8784
Wonders: The Memphis International Cultural Series 1 Auction Ave The Pyramid	Memphis	TN	38103	901-576-1231	576-1280
TF: 800-263-6744 ■ *Web:* www.wonders.org ■ *E-mail:* peruinfo@wonders.org					
Woodruff Fontaine House 680 Adams Ave	Memphis	TN	38105	901-526-1469	526-4531

SPORTS TEAMS & FACILITIES

				Phone	Fax
Liberty Bowl Memorial Stadium 335 S Hollywood St	Memphis	TN	38104	901-729-4344	276-2756
Memphis International Motorsports Park 5500 Taylor Forge Dr	Millington	TN	38053	901-358-7223	358-7274
Memphis Riverkings (hockey) 996 Early Maxwell Blvd Mid-South Coliseum	Memphis	TN	38104	901-278-9009	274-3209
TF: 888-748-3754 ■ *Web:* www.riverkings.com					
Mid-South Coliseum 996 Early Maxwell Blvd	Memphis	TN	38104	901-274-3982	276-8653
Web: www.midsouthcoliseum.com					
Southland Greyhound Park 1550 Ingram Blvd	West Memphis	AR	72301	870-735-3670	732-8335
TF: 800-467-6182 ■ *Web:* www.southlandgreyhound.com					
Tennessee Titans Adelphia Coliseum 1 Titans Way	Nashville	TN	37213	888-313-8326	
Web: www.nfl.com/titans					

— Events —

	Phone
Africa in April Cultural Awareness Festival (mid-April)	901-947-2133
Arts in the Park (mid-October)	901-761-1278
Beale Street Music Festival (early May)	901-525-4611
Beale Street New Year's Eve Celebration (December 31)	901-526-0110
Carnival Memphis (early-mid-June)	901-278-0243
Choctaw Indian Cultural Festival (early August)	901-785-3160
Christmas at Graceland (late November-early January)	800-238-2000
Dr Martin Luther King Jr Celebration/March (January)	901-525-2458
Ducks Unlimited Great Outdoors Festival (early June)	901-523-8463
Elvis Presley International Tribute Week (early-mid-August)	901-332-3322
First Tennessee Memphis Marathon (early December)	800-893-7223
Germantown Charity Horse Show (early June)	901-754-7443
Information Open House (early April)	901-383-4116
Juneteenth Freedom Festival (mid-June)	901-385-4943
Liberty Bowl (late December)	901-795-7700
Memphis Boat Show (mid-January)	901-684-6211
Memphis Christmas Parade (early December)	901-575-0540
Memphis Cotton Makers Jubilee (early May)	901-774-1118
Memphis in May International Festival (May)	901-525-4611
Memphis Italian Festival (early June)	901-767-6949
Memphis Music & Heritage Festival (early September)	901-525-3655
Mid-South Fair (late September-early October)	901-274-8800
Native American Days (late October)	901-785-3160
New Year's Eve Festival (December 31)	901-526-0110
Pink Palace Crafts Fair (early October)	901-320-6320
Southern Heritage Classic (early September)	901-398-6655
Spring Festival (mid-April)	901-526-0110
Spring Music Festival (mid-April)	901-526-0110
Spring's Best Plant Sale (mid-April)	901-685-1566
Zydeco Festival (mid-February)	901-526-0110

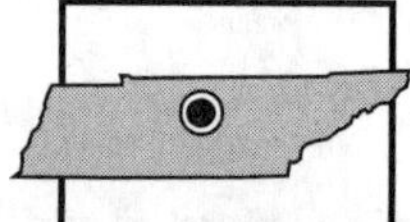

Nashville

The name Nashville is synonymous with country music - Opryland theme park's Grand Ole Opry House has launched some of the most famous names in the industry and is the broadcast site for the nation's oldest continuous radio show. Nashville is also the only city in the country with a cable television network that uses the city's name - The Nashville Network. The city is also home to Andrew Jackson's estate, The Hermitage. Its 660 acres include a museum and formal gardens, and the burial place of Jackson and his wife, Rachel. The Parthenon in Nashville's Centennial Park is a reproduction of the original Greek structure and contains regional and national art collections, as well as a 42-foot statue of the goddess Athena.

Population	510,274	**Longitude**	86-78-44 W
Area (Land)	473.3 sq mi	**County**	Davidson
Area (Water)	23.7 sq mi	**Time Zone**	CST
Elevation	440 ft	**Area Code/s**	615
Latitude	36-16-58 N		

— Average Temperatures and Precipitation —

TEMPERATURES

	Jan	Feb	Mar	Apr	May	Jun	Jul	Aug	Sep	Oct	Nov	Dec
High	46	51	61	71	79	87	90	88	83	73	60	50
Low	27	30	39	48	57	65	69	68	61	48	40	31

PRECIPITATION

	Jan	Feb	Mar	Apr	May	Jun	Jul	Aug	Sep	Oct	Nov	Dec
Inches	3.6	3.8	4.9	4.4	4.9	3.6	4.0	3.5	3.5	2.6	4.1	4.6

— Important Phone Numbers —

	Phone		Phone
AAA	615-333-4840	**Poison Control Center**	615-936-2034
American Express Travel	615-385-3535	**Time/Temp**	615-259-2222
Emergency	911	**Travelers Aid**	615-780-9472
HotelDocs	800-468-3537	**Weather**	615-244-9393
Information Line	615-244-9393		

— Information Sources —

				Phone	Fax
Better Business Bureau Serving Middle Tennessee PO Box 198436 *Web:* www.middletennessee.bbb.org ■ *E-mail:* bbbnash@aol.com	Nashville	TN	37219	615-242-4222	250-4245
Davidson County 205 Metro Courthouse *Web:* www.nashville.org/index.html	Nashville	TN	37201	615-862-6770	862-6774
Nashville Chamber of Commerce 161 4th Ave N *TF:* 800-657-6910 ■ *Web:* www.nashvillechamber.com ■ *E-mail:* musiccity@nashville.com	Nashville	TN	37219	615-259-4755	256-3074
Nashville City Hall 102 Metro Courthouse *Web:* www.nashville.org	Nashville	TN	37201	615-862-5000	862-6784
Nashville Convention & Visitors Bureau 161 4th Ave N *TF:* 800-657-6910 ■ *Web:* www.nashvillecvb.com	Nashville	TN	37219	615-259-4730	244-6278
Nashville Convention Center 601 Commerce St **Fax:* Mktg	Nashville	TN	37203	615-742-2000	742-2014*
Nashville Economic Development Office 117 Union St *Web:* www.nashville.org/ecdev	Nashville	TN	37201	615-862-6026	862-6025
Nashville Mayor 107 Metro Courthouse *Web:* www.nashville.org/mayor ■ *E-mail:* mayor@nashville.org	Nashville	TN	37201	615-862-6000	862-6040
Nashville Tourist Information Center 501 Broadway St	Nashville	TN	37203	615-259-4747	259-4747
West Ben Public Library 225 Polk Ave	Nashville	TN	37203	615-862-5800	880-2605

On-Line Resources

4Nashville.com	www.4nashville.com
About.com Guide to Nashville	nashville.about.com/local/southeastus/nashville
Area Guide Nashville	nashville.areaguides.net
Best Read Guide Nashville	bestreadguide.com/nashville/
Boulevards Nashville	www.boulevards.com/cities/nashville.html
City Knowledge Nashville	www.cityknowledge.com/tn_nashville.htm
CitySearch Nashville	nashville.citysearch.com
Country.Com	www.country.com
DigitalCity Nashville	home.digitalcity.com/nashville
Excite.com Nashville City Guide	www.excite.com/travel/countries/united_states/tennessee/nashville
Insiders' Guide to Nashville	www.insiders.com/nashville/
Jackson-Crockett's Nashville Guide	www.hermitage.com/nashville.html
Nashville Best Read Guide	bestreadguide.com/nashville
Nashville City Pages	nashville.thelinks.com/
Nashville Directory	www.nashvilledirectory.com/
Nashville Net	www.nashville.net
Nashville Scene	www.nashscene.com
Nashville.Net	www.nashville.net/
Nashvillenet.com	www.nashvillenet.com/
NITC Travelbase City Guide Nashville	www.travelbase.com/auto/guides/nashville-area-tn.html
Rough Guide Travel Nashville	travel.roughguides.com/content/758/
WeekendEvents.com Nashville	www.weekendevents.com/misccity/nashville/nashville.htm

— Transportation Services —

AIRPORTS

■ **Nashville International Airport (BNA)**	Phone
8 miles SE of downtown (approx 20 minutes) Web: www.nashintl.com	615-275-1600

Airport Transportation

	Phone
Allied Cab $16-18 fare to downtown	615-244-7433
Gray Line Downtown Airport Express $9 fare to downtown	615-275-1180
MTA Bus $1.40 fare to downtown	615-862-5950

Commercial Airlines

	Phone		Phone
AirTran	800-247-8726	**Southwest**	800-435-9792
American	800-433-7300	**TWA**	800-221-2000
American Eagle	800-433-7300	**United**	800-241-6522
Delta	800-221-1212	**US Airways**	800-428-4322
Northwest	800-225-2525		

Charter Airlines

	Phone		Phone
Alliance Executive Charter Services	800-232-5387	**Aviation Assoc**	615-889-3100
		Corporate Air Fleet Inc	615-350-8400

CAR RENTALS

	Phone		Phone
Alamo	615-367-1844	**Enterprise**	615-872-7722
Atlas	615-865-3995	**Hertz**	615-361-3131
Budget	615-366-0800	**National**	615-361-7467
Dollar	615-275-1005	**Thrifty**	615-275-4257

LIMO/TAXI

	Phone		Phone
American Rivergate Taxi	615-865-4100	**Country Music Limousine**	615-226-9692
Black Tie Limousines	615-254-1254	**Music City Taxi**	615-262-0451
Capitol Limousines	615-248-6522	**Music Row Limousine**	615-242-4866
Carey Limousine	615-360-8700	**Nashville Cab**	615-242-7070
Celebrity Limousines	615-316-9999	**Opryland River Taxis**	615-889-6611
Checker Cab	615-256-7000	**Yellow Cab**	615-256-0101

MASS TRANSIT

	Phone
Metropolitan Transit Authority $1.40 Base fare	615-862-5950
Nashville Trolley $1 Base fare	615-862-5950

RAIL/BUS

				Phone
Greyhound Bus Station 200 8th Ave S	Nashville	TN	37203	800-231-2222

Nashville (Cont'd)

— Accommodations —

HOTEL RESERVATION SERVICES

Phone | Fax

Hotel Reservations Network Inc 214-361-7311 361-7299
TF Sales: 800-964-6835 ■ *Web:* www.hoteldiscount.com
Quikbook 212-532-1660 532-1556
TF: 800-789-9887 ■ *Web:* www.quikbook.com
Reservations USA 865-453-1000 453-7484
TF: 800-251-4444 ■ *Web:* www.reservationsusa.com
■ *E-mail:* reserve@lodging4u.com

HOTELS, MOTELS, RESORTS

Phone | Fax

AmeriSuites 220 Rudy's Cir . . . . . Nashville TN 37214 615-872-0422 872-9283
TF: 800-833-1516
Best Suites of America 2521 Elm Hill Pike . . . . . Nashville TN 37214 615-391-3919 391-5995
TF: 800-237-8466
Best Western Metro Inn 99 Spring St . . . . . Nashville TN 37207 615-259-9160 244-5871
TF: 800-528-1234
Best Western Music City Inn
13010 Old Hickory Blvd . . . . . Nashville TN 37013 615-641-7721 641-6263
TF: 800-237-8124
Best Western Suites 201 Music City Cir . . . . . Nashville TN 37214 615-902-9940 902-9950
TF: 800-528-1234
Clarion Hotel 733 Briley Pkwy . . . . . Nashville TN 37217 615-361-5900 367-0339
TF: 888-881-7666
ClubHouse Inn & Conference Center
920 Broadway & 10th Ave . . . . . Nashville TN 37203 615-244-0150 244-0445
TF: 800-258-2466
■ *Web:* www.nashville.citysearch.com/E/V/NASTN/0000/89/38/
ClubHouse Inn Airport 2435 Atrium Way . . . . . Nashville TN 37214 615-883-0500 889-4827
TF: 800-258-2466 ■ *E-mail:* info@clubhouseinn.com
Courtyard by Marriott 2508 Elm Hill Pike . . . . . Nashville TN 37214 615-883-9500 883-0172
TF: 800-321-2211 ■ *Web:* courtyard.com/BNACA
Courtyard by Marriott Brentwood
103 E Park Dr . . . . . Brentwood TN 37027 615-371-9200 371-0832
TF: 800-321-2211 ■ *Web:* courtyard.com/BNABR
Crossland Economy Studios
1210 Murfreesboro Rd . . . . . Nashville TN 37217 615-366-0559 366-0493
TF: 800-398-7829
■ *Web:* www.extstay.com/loc/tn_nashville_airport_crs.html
Crowne Plaza Nashville 623 Union St . . . . . Nashville TN 37219 615-259-2000 742-6056
TF: 800-227-6963
Days Inn Airport 1 International Plaza . . . . . Nashville TN 37217 615-361-7666 399-0283
TF: 800-329-7466
Days Inn Downtown Convention Ctr
711 Union St . . . . . Nashville TN 37219 615-242-4311 242-1654
TF: 800-627-3297
Doubletree Guest Suites 2424 Atrium Way . . . . . Nashville TN 37214 615-889-8889 883-7779
TF: 800-222-8733
■ *Web:* www.doubletreehotels.com/DoubleT/Hotel81/83/83Main.htm
Doubletree Hotel 315 4th Ave N . . . . . Nashville TN 37219 615-244-8200 747-4894
TF: 800-222-8733
■ *Web:* www.doubletreehotels.com/DoubleT/Hotel81/84/84Main.htm
Econo Lodge Southeast 97 Wallace Rd . . . . . Nashville TN 37211 615-833-6860 315-8076
TF: 800-553-2666
Embassy Suites Hotel 10 Century Blvd . . . . . Nashville TN 37214 615-871-0033 883-9245
TF: 800-362-2779
Extended StayAmerica 2525 Elm Hill Pike . . . . . Nashville TN 37214 615-883-7667 883-0583
TF: 800-398-7829
Extended StayAmerica 9020 Church St E . . . . . Brentwood TN 37027 615-377-7847 377-6631
TF: 800-398-7829
Fairfield Inn Opryland 211 Music City Cir . . . . . Nashville TN 37214 615-872-8939 872-7230
TF: 800-228-2800 ■ *Web:* fairfieldinn.com/BNAOP
Family Inns of America
3430 Percy Priest Dr . . . . . Nashville TN 37214 615-889-5090 883-6786
TF: 800-457-2299
Guesthouse Inn & Suites 1909 Hayes St . . . . . Nashville TN 37203 615-329-1000 329-1000
TF: 800-777-4904 ■ *Web:* www.guesthouse.net/nashville.html
Hampton Inn & Suites Nashville Airport
583 Donelson Pike . . . . . Nashville TN 37214 615-885-4242 885-6726
TF: 800-426-7866
Heartbreak Hotel 10 Interstate Dr . . . . . Nashville TN 37213 615-244-6050
Hermitage Nashville All Suite Hotel
231 6th Ave N . . . . . Nashville TN 37219 615-244-3121 254-6909
TF: 800-251-1908
Hilton Suites Brentwood
9000 Overlook Blvd . . . . . Brentwood TN 37027 615-370-0111 370-0272
TF: 800-445-8667 ■ *Web:* www.hilton.com/hotels/BNABWHS

Phone | Fax

Holiday Inn Brentwood
760 Old Hickory Blvd . . . . . Brentwood TN 37027 615-373-2600 377-3893
TF: 800-465-4329
Holiday Inn Express Airport 1111 Airport Ctr . . . Nashville TN 37214 615-883-1366 889-6867
TF: 800-465-4329
Holiday Inn Express Southeast Airport
981 Murfreesboro Rd . . . . . Nashville TN 37217 615-367-9150 361-4865
TF: 800-465-4329
■ *Web:* www.basshotels.com/hiexpress/?_franchisee=BNASE
■ *E-mail:* gmnvl@lodgian.com
Holiday Inn Select Opryland/Airport
2200 Elm Hill Pike . . . . . Nashville TN 37214 615-883-9770 391-4521
TF: 800-633-4427
■ *Web:* www.basshotels.com/holiday-inn/?_franchisee=BNAOP
■ *E-mail:* his-nashville@bristolhotels.com
Holiday Inn Select Vanderbilt
2613 West End Ave . . . . . Nashville TN 37203 615-327-4707 327-8034
TF: 800-465-4329
Inn at Opryland 2401 Music Valley Dr . . . . . Nashville TN 37214 615-889-0800 883-1230
La Quinta Inn Nashville Airport
2345 Atrium Way . . . . . Nashville TN 37214 615-885-3000 889-9131
TF: 800-531-5900
Loews Vanderbilt Plaza Hotel
2100 W End Ave . . . . . Nashville TN 37203 615-320-1700 320-5019
TF: 800-336-3335 ■ *Web:* www.loewshotels.com/vanderbilthome.html
Marriott Hotel 600 Marriott Dr . . . . . Nashville TN 37214 615-889-9300 889-9315
TF: 800-228-9290 ■ *Web:* marriotthotels.com/BNATN
Opryland Hotel 2800 Opryland Dr . . . . . Nashville TN 37214 615-889-1000 871-7741
Web: www.oprylandhotel.com
Quality Inn Airport 821 Murfreesboro Rd . . . . . Nashville TN 37217 615-399-0017 399-0017
TF: 800-228-5151
Ramada Inn Airport 709 Spence Ln . . . . . Nashville TN 37217 615-361-0102 361-4765
TF: 800-228-2828
Ramada Inn North 1412 Brick Church Pike . . . . Nashville TN 37207 615-226-3230 262-7611
TF: 800-544-6385
Regal Maxwell House
2025 Metro Center Blvd . . . . . Nashville TN 37228 615-259-4343 313-1327
TF: 800-222-8888
Renaissance Nashville Hotel
611 Commerce St . . . . . Nashville TN 37203 615-255-8400 255-8202
TF: 800-327-6618
Residence Inn by Marriott
2300 Elm Hill Pike . . . . . Nashville TN 37214 615-889-8600 871-4970
TF: 800-331-3131 ■ *Web:* www.residenceinn.com/BNABN
Sheraton Music City Hotel
777 McGavok Pike . . . . . Nashville TN 37214 615-885-2200 231-1134
TF: 800-325-3535 ■ *Web:* www.tenn.com/sheraton
StudioPLUS 2511 Elm Hill Pike . . . . . Nashville TN 37214 615-871-9669 231-6063
TF: 800-646-8000
Union Station Hotel 1001 Broadway . . . . . Nashville TN 37203 615-726-1001 248-3554
TF: 800-996-3426
■ *Web:* www.grandheritage.com/htmlcode/hus_unionst.html
Villager Lodge 727 Briley Pkwy . . . . . Nashville TN 37217 615-367-9202 367-9202
Wilson Inn 600 Ermac Dr . . . . . Nashville TN 37214 615-889-4466 889-0484
TF: 800-945-7667
Wyndham Garden Hotel Nashville Airport
1112 Airport Center Dr . . . . . Nashville TN 37214 615-889-9090 885-1564
TF: 800-996-3426

— Restaurants —

Phone

Amerigo (Italian) 1920 West End Ave . . . . . Nashville TN 37203 615-320-1740
Antonios' of Nashville (Italian) 7097 Old Harding Rd . . . . . Nashville TN 37221 615-646-9166
Arthur's (Continental) 1001 Broadway . . . . . Nashville TN 37203 615-255-1494
Belle Meade Brasserie (New American) 101 Page Rd . . . . . Nashville TN 37205 615-356-5450
Big River Grille & Brewing Works (American)
111 Broadway . . . . . Nashville TN 37201 615-251-4677
Blackstone Restaurant & Brewery (American)
1918 West End Ave . . . . . Nashville TN 37203 615-327-9969
Blue Moon Waterfront Cafe (American)
525 Basswood Ave . . . . . Nashville TN 37209 615-352-5892
Bluebird Cafe (American) 4104 Hillsboro Rd . . . . . Nashville TN 37215 615-383-1461
Web: www.bluebirdcafe.com/
Bourbon Street Blues & Boogie Bar (Cajun)
220 Printer's Alley . . . . . Nashville TN 37201 615-242-5837
Broadway Dinner Train (American) 108 1st Ave S . . . . . Nashville TN 37201 615-254-8000
TF: 800-274-8010
Cafe 123 (Southern) 123 12th Ave N . . . . . Nashville TN 37203 615-255-2233
Caffe Milano (Italian) 174 3rd Ave N . . . . . Nashville TN 37201 615-255-0253
Capital Grill (American) 231 6th Ave N . . . . . Nashville TN 37219 615-244-3121
Cock of the Walk (Seafood) 2624 Music Valley Dr . . . . . Nashville TN 37214 615-889-1930
Crab House (Seafood) 123 2nd Ave S . . . . . Nashville TN 37201 615-242-2722
F Scott's (American) 2210 Crestmoor Rd . . . . . Nashville TN 37215 615-269-5861
Faison's (Cajun/Creole) 2000 Belcourt Ave . . . . . Nashville TN 37212 615-298-2112

Nashville — Restaurants (Cont'd)

Name / Address	City	State	Zip	Phone
Finezza Trattoria (Italian) 5404 Harding Rd	Nashville	TN	37205	615-356-9398
Gerst Haus (German) 228 Woodland St	Nashville	TN	37213	615-256-9760
Goten Japanese Steak & Sushi Bar (Japanese) 110 21st Ave S	Nashville	TN	37203	615-321-4537
Granite Falls (New American) 2000 Broadway	Nashville	TN	37203	615-327-9250
Hard Rock Cafe (American) 100 Broadway	Nashville	TN	37201	615-742-9900
Ichiban (Japanese) 109 2nd Ave N.	Nashville	TN	39201	615-254-7185
Jimmy Kelly's (Steak) 217 Louise Ave	Nashville	TN	37203	615-329-4349
La Paz Restaurante Cantina (Mexican) 3808 Cleghorn Ave	Nashville	TN	37215	615-383-5200
Loveless Restaurant (Southern) 8400 Hwy 100	Nashville	TN	37221	615-646-9700
Mario's (Italian) 2005 Broadway	Nashville	TN	37203	615-327-3232
Market Street Brewery & Public House (American) 134 2nd Ave N.	Nashville	TN	37201	615-259-9611
Merchants The (American) 401 Broadway	Nashville	TN	37203	615-254-1892
Mere Bulles (Continental) 152 2nd Ave N.	Nashville	TN	37201	615-256-1946
Midtown Cafe (American) 102 19th Ave S	Nashville	TN	37203	615-320-7176
Morton's of Chicago (Steak) 618 Church St	Nashville	TN	37219	615-259-4558
Mulligan's Pub (Irish) 117 2nd Ave N	Nashville	TN	37201	615-242-8010
New Orleans Manor (Seafood) 1400 Murfreesboro Rd	Nashville	TN	37217	615-367-2777
Planet Hollywood (New American) 322 Broadway	Nashville	TN	37201	615-313-7827
Radio Cafe (American) 1313 Woodland St	Nashville	TN	37206	615-262-1766
Rio Bravo Cantina (Tex Mex) 3015 West End Ave	Nashville	TN	37203	615-329-1745
Ruth's Chris Steak House (Steak) 2100 West End Ave	Nashville	TN	37203	615-320-0163
Seanachie Irish Pub (Irish) 327 Broadway	Nashville	TN	37201	615-726-2006
Shadowbrook (Southern) 5397 Rawlings Rd	Joelton	TN	37080	615-876-0700
South Street (American) 907 20th Ave S	Nashville	TN	37203	615-320-5555
Sperry's (Steak/Seafood) 5109 Harding Rd	Nashville	TN	37205	615-353-0809
Stock Yard (Steak/Seafood) 901 2nd Ave N	Nashville	TN	37201	615-255-6464
Sunset Grill (New American) 2001-A Belcourt Ave. *Web:* www.sunsetgrill.com/	Nashville	TN	37212	615-386-3663
Valentino's (Italian) 1907 West End Ave.	Nashville	TN	37203	615-327-0148
Wild Boar The (French) 2014 Broadway	Nashville	TN	37203	615-329-1313
Wildhorse Saloon (American) 120 2nd Ave N	Nashville	TN	37201	615-251-1000
Zola (Mediterranean) 3001 West End Ave.	Nashville	TN	37203	615-320-7778

— Goods and Services —

SHOPPING

Name / Address	City	State	Zip	Phone	Fax
100 Oaks Mall 719 Thompson Ln.	Nashville	TN	37204	615-383-6002	383-1050
Bellevue Center 7620 Hwy 70 S.	Nashville	TN	37221	615-646-8690	
CoolSprings Galleria 1800 Galleria Blvd *Web:* www.thediscovery.org	Brentwood	TN	37067	615-771-2128	771-2127
Dillard's 2126 Abbott Martin Rd.	Nashville	TN	37215	615-297-0971	
Factory Stores of America 2434 Music Valley Dr *Web:* www.factorystores.com/	Nashville	TN	37214	615-885-5140	
Green Hills Antique Mall 4108 Hillsboro Rd	Nashville	TN	37215	615-383-3893	383-4886
Harding Mall 4050 Nolensville Rd.	Nashville	TN	37211	615-833-6327	333-6890
Mall at Green Hills 2126 Abbott Martin Rd	Nashville	TN	37215	615-298-5478	
Nashville Arcade 4th Ave N & 5th Ave N.	Nashville	TN	37219	615-255-1034	
Rivergate Mall 1000 Two Mile Pkwy Suite 1	Goodlettsville	TN	37072	615-859-3456	851-9656

BANKS

Name / Address	City	State	Zip	Phone	Fax
First American National Bank 300 Union St First American Ctr **Fax:* Mktg	Nashville	TN	37237	615-748-2000	748-2905*
First Union National Bank 150 4th Ave N	Nashville	TN	37219	615-251-9200	251-9323
Nashville Bank of Commerce 221 4th Ave N	Nashville	TN	37219	615-871-7000	871-7011
NationsBank of Tennessee NA 1 NationsBank Plaza	Nashville	TN	37239	615-749-3333	749-4290
SunTrust Bank Nashville NA PO Box 305110	Nashville	TN	37230	615-748-4000	748-5071

BUSINESS SERVICES

Name	Phone
AA Dispatch	615-329-4297
Accelerated Courier	615-367-0949
Federal Express	800-238-5355
Kelly Services	615-367-1960
Kinko's	615-244-1000
Manpower Temporary Services	615-327-9922
Olsten Staffing Services	615-872-9600
Post Office	615-885-1005
UPS	800-742-5877

— Media —

PUBLICATIONS

Name / Address	City	State	Zip	Phone	Fax
Nashville Business Journal 222 2nd Ave N Suite 610 *Web:* www.nashbiz.com/	Nashville	TN	37202	615-248-2222	248-6246
Tennessean‡ 1100 Broadway *TF:* 800-342-8237 ■ *Web:* www.tennessean.com	Nashville	TN	37203	615-259-8800	259-8093

‡Daily newspapers

TELEVISION

Name / Address	City	State	Zip	Phone	Fax
WDCN-TV Ch 8 (PBS) 161 Rains Ave *Web:* www.wdcn.org	Nashville	TN	37203	615-259-9325	248-6120
WKRN-TV Ch 2 (ABC) 441 Murfreesboro Rd *Web:* www.wkrn.com/ ■ *E-mail:* wkrntv@edge.ercnet.com	Nashville	TN	37210	615-259-2200	248-7329
WNAB-TV Ch 58 (WB) 3201 Dickerson Pike	Nashville	TN	37207	615-650-5858	650-5859
WNPX-TV Ch 28 (PAX) 209 10th Ave S Suite 349 *Web:* www.pax.net/wnpx	Nashville	TN	37203	615-726-2828	726-2854
WSMV-TV Ch 4 (NBC) 5700 Knob Rd *Web:* www.wsmv.com	Nashville	TN	37209	615-353-4444	353-2343
WTVF-TV Ch 5 (CBS) 474 James Robertson Pkwy *Web:* www.newschannel5.com	Nashville	TN	37219	615-244-5000	244-9883
WUXP-TV Ch 30 (UPN) 631 Mainstream Dr	Nashville	TN	37228	615-259-5630	259-3962
WZTV-TV Ch 17 (Fox) 631 Mainstream Dr *Web:* local.fox17.citysearch.com	Nashville	TN	37228	615-244-1717	259-3962

RADIO

Name / Address	City	State	Zip	Phone	Fax
WAMB-AM 1160 kHz (Nost) 1617 Lebanon Rd	Nashville	TN	37210	615-889-1960	
WGFX-FM 104.5 MHz (Oldies) 506 2nd Ave S *Web:* www.arrow1045.com	Nashville	TN	37210	615-244-9533	259-1271
WJXA-FM 92.9 MHz (AC) 504 Rosedale Ave	Nashville	TN	37211	615-259-9696	259-4594
WJZC-FM 101.1 MHz (NAC) 10 Music Cir E.	Nashville	TN	37203	615-256-0555	242-4826
WKDF-FM 103.3 MHz (Alt) PO Box 101604 *Web:* www.103kdf.com	Nashville	TN	37224	615-244-9533	259-1271
WLAC-AM 1510 kHz (N/T) 10 Music Cir E *Web:* www.wlac.com ■ *E-mail:* 1510@wlac.com	Nashville	TN	37203	615-256-0555	242-4826
WMDB-AM 880 kHz (Urban) 3051 Stokers Ln.	Nashville	TN	37218	615-255-2876	
WNRQ-FM 105.9 MHz (CR) 10 Music Cir E	Nashville	TN	37203	615-256-0555	242-4826
WPLN-FM 90.3 MHz (NPR) 630 Mainstream Dr *Web:* www.wpln.org	Nashville	TN	37228	615-760-2903	760-2904
WQQK-FM 92.1 MHz (Urban) 50 Music Sq W Suite 901	Nashville	TN	37203	615-321-1067	321-5771
WQZQ-FM 102.5 MHz (CHR) 1824 Murfreesboro Rd	Nashville	TN	37217	615-399-1029	399-1023
WRLG-FM 94.1 MHz (AAA) 401 Church St 30th Fl *Web:* wrlg.com	Nashville	TN	37219	615-242-5600	242-9877
WRLT-FM 100.1 MHz (AAA) 401 Church St L & C Tower 30th Fl *Web:* www.wrlt.com ■ *E-mail:* comments@wrlt.com	Nashville	TN	37219	615-242-5600	242-9877
WRMX-FM 96.3 MHz (Oldies) 504 Rosedale Ave	Nashville	TN	37211	615-259-9696	259-4594
WRVW-FM 107.5 MHz (CHR) 55 Music Sq W *Web:* www.1075theriver.com	Nashville	TN	37203	615-664-2400	664-2457
WSIX-FM 97.9 MHz (Ctry) 55 Music Sq W *Web:* www.wsix.com	Nashville	TN	37203	615-664-2400	664-2457
WSM-AM 650 kHz (Ctry) 2644 McGavock Pike	Nashville	TN	37214	615-889-6595	871-5982
WSM-FM 95.5 MHz (Ctry) 2644 McGavock Pike	Nashville	TN	37214	615-889-6595	871-5982
WVOL-AM 1470 kHz (Urban) 50 Music Sq W Suite 901	Nashville	TN	37203	615-321-1067	321-5771
WWTN-FM 99.7 MHz (N/T) 107 Music City Cir Suite 203	Nashville	TN	37214	615-885-9986	885-9900
WYYB-FM 93.7 MHz (Misc) 401 Church St 30th Fl	Nashville	TN	37219	615-242-5600	242-9877
WZPC-FM 102.9 MHz (Ctry) 1824 Murfreesboro Rd	Nashville	TN	37217	615-399-1029	399-1023

Nashville (Cont'd)

— Colleges/Universities —

Name / Address	City	State	Zip	Phone	Fax
Aquinas College 4210 Harding Rd	Nashville	TN	37205	615-297-7545	297-7970
Web: www.aquinas-tn.edu					
Belmont University 1900 Belmont Blvd	Nashville	TN	37212	615-460-6000	460-5434
TF: 800-563-6765 ■ *Web:* www.belmont.edu ■ *E-mail:* Warren@Belmont.Edu					
Cumberland University 1 Cumberland Sq.	Lebanon	TN	37087	615-444-2562	444-2569
Web: www.cumberland.edu					
David Lipscomb University 3901 Granny White Pike	Nashville	TN	37204	615-269-1000	269-1804
TF: 800-333-4358 ■ *Web:* www.dlu.edu					
Draughons Junior College PO Box 17386	Nashville	TN	37217	615-361-7555	367-2736
Fisk University 1000 17th Ave N.	Nashville	TN	37208	615-329-8500	329-8715
TF Admissions: 800-443-3474 ■ *Web:* www.fisk.edu ■ *E-mail:* gwash@dubois.fisk.edu					
Free Will Baptist Bible College 3606 W End Ave.	Nashville	TN	37205	615-383-1340	269-6028
TF: 800-763-9222 ■ *Web:* www.fwbbc.edu					
ITT Technical Institute 441 Donelson Pike	Nashville	TN	37214	615-889-8700	872-7209
TF: 800-331-8386 ■ *Web:* www.itt-tech.edu					
John A Gupton College 1616 Church St	Nashville	TN	37203	615-327-3927	321-4518
Web: www.guptoncollege.com					
Nashville State Technical Institute 120 White Bridge Rd	Nashville	TN	37209	615-353-3333	353-3243
Web: www.nsti.tec.tn.us					
O'More College of Design 423 S Margin St.	Franklin	TN	37064	615-794-4254	790-1662
Web: www.omorecollege.edu					
Tennessee State University 3500 John A Merritt Blvd.	Nashville	TN	37209	615-963-5000	963-2929
Web: www.tnstate.edu					
Trevecca Nazarene University 333 Murfreesboro Rd	Nashville	TN	37210	615-248-1200	248-7406
TF: 888-210-4868 ■ *Web:* www.trevecca.edu					
Vanderbilt University 2305 West End Ave	Nashville	TN	37203	615-322-7311	343-7765
TF Admissions: 800-288-0432 ■ *Web:* www.vanderbilt.edu ■ *E-mail:* admissions@vanderbilt.edu					

— Hospitals —

Name / Address	City	State	Zip	Phone	Fax
Baptist Hospital 2000 Church St.	Nashville	TN	37236	615-329-5555	340-4606
Web: www.baptist-hosp.org ■ *E-mail:* info@email.baptist-hosp.org					
Centennial Medical Center 2300 Patterson St.	Nashville	TN	37203	615-342-1000	342-1045
TF: 800-251-8200					
Columbia Nashville Memorial Hospital 612 W Due West Ave	Madison	TN	37115	615-865-3511	865-3131
Columbia Southern Hills Medical Center 391 Wallace Rd	Nashville	TN	37211	615-781-4000	781-4113
Metropolitan Nashville General Hospital 1818 Albion St	Nashville	TN	37208	615-341-4000	341-4617*
**Fax:* Admitting					
Saint Thomas Health Services 4220 Harding Rd	Nashville	TN	37205	615-222-2111	222-6223*
**Fax:* Admitting ■ *Web:* www.saintthomas.org					
Tennessee Christian Medical Center 500 Hospital Dr	Madison	TN	37115	615-865-2373	860-6311
Vanderbilt University Medical Center 1211 22nd Ave S	Nashville	TN	37232	615-322-5000	343-5555
TF: 800-288-7777 ■ *Web:* www.mc.vanderbilt.edu					
Veterans Affairs Medical Center 1310 24th Ave S.	Nashville	TN	37212	615-327-4751	321-6350

— Attractions —

Name / Address	City	State	Zip	Phone	Fax
328 Performance Hall 328 4th Ave S	Nashville	TN	37201	615-259-3288	
Belle Meade Plantation 5025 Harding Rd	Nashville	TN	37205	615-356-0501	356-2336
TF Info: 800-270-3991*					
Belmont Mansion 1900 Belmont Blvd	Nashville	TN	37212	615-460-5459	460-5688
Bicentennial Mall State Park 598 James Robertson Pkwy	Nashville	TN	37243	615-741-5280	532-2683
Carnton Plantation 1345 Carnton Ln	Franklin	TN	37064	615-794-0903	794-6563
Carter House 1140 Columbia Ave	Franklin	TN	37064	615-791-1861	794-1327
Centennial Park West End betw 25th & 28th Aves	Nashville	TN	37201	615-862-8431	
Chaffin's Barn Dinner Theatre 8204 Hwy 100	Nashville	TN	37221	615-646-9977	662-5439
Web: www.dinnertheatre.com					
Cheekwood-Tennessee Botanical Gardens & Museum of Art 1200 Forrest Park Dr	Nashville	TN	37205	615-356-8000	353-2156
Web: www.cheekwood.org					
Country Music Hall of Fame & Museum 4 Music Sq E	Nashville	TN	37203	615-256-1639	255-2245
Web: www.country.com/hof/hof-f.html					
Cumberland Caverns 1437 Cumberland Caverns Rd	McMinnville	TN	37110	931-668-4396	668-5382
Cumberland Science Museum 800 Fort Negley Blvd	Nashville	TN	37203	615-862-5160	401-5086
Web: www.csmisfun.com					
Darkhorse Theater 4610 Charlotte Ave	Nashville	TN	37209	615-297-7113	665-3336
Web: www.darkhorsetheater.com ■ *E-mail:* info@darkhorsetheater.com					
Farris Oscar Agricultural Museum Hogan & Marchant Rds	South Nashville	TN	37204	615-837-5197	837-5194
Fort Donelson National Battlefield PO Box 434	Dover	TN	37058	931-232-5706	232-6331
Web: www.nps.gov/fodo/					
General Jackson Showboat 2802 Opryland Dr	Nashville	TN	37214	615-889-6611	871-5772
Grand Ole Opry 2808 Opryland Dr	Nashville	TN	37214	615-889-3060	871-6166
Web: www.grandoleopry.com					
Grand Ole Opry Museum 2802 Opryland Dr	Nashville	TN	37214	615-889-6611	871-5772
Hartzler-Towner Multicultural Museum 1008 19th Ave S.	Nashville	TN	37212	615-340-7500	340-7463
Hermitage The: Home of Andrew Jackson 4580 Rachel's Ln	Hermitage	TN	37076	615-889-2941	889-9289
Web: www.thehermitage.com ■ *E-mail:* info@thehermitage.com					
Historic Rock Castle 139 Rock Castle Ln.	Hendersonville	TN	37075	615-824-0502	824-0502
Historic Travellers Rest 636 Farrell Pkwy	Nashville	TN	37220	615-832-8197	832-8169
Museum of Beverage Containers & Advertising 1055 Ridgecrest Dr	Millersville	TN	37072	615-859-5236	859-5238
Web: www.gono.com/cc/museum.htm ■ *E-mail:* info@nostalgiaville.com					
Music City Queen Opryland USA Riverfront Pk	Nashville	TN	37203	615-889-6611	
Music Valley Car Museum 2611 McGavock Pike	Nashville	TN	37214	615-885-7400	
Music Valley Wax Museum of the Stars 2515 McGavock Pike	Nashville	TN	37214	615-883-3612	
Nashville Ballet 2976 Sidco Dr	Nashville	TN	37204	615-244-7233	242-1741
Nashville Network The (TNN) 2806 Opryland Dr	Nashville	TN	37214	615-883-7000	457-9660*
**Fax:* Hum Res					
Nashville Opera 3628 Trousdale Dr Suite D	Nashville	TN	37204	615-832-5242	832-5243
Nashville Symphony 209 10th Ave S Suite 448	Nashville	TN	37203	615-255-5600	255-5656
Web: www.nashvillesymphony.com					
Nashville Toy Museum 2613-B McGavock Pike	Nashville	TN	37214	615-883-8870	391-0556
Nashville Zoo 3777 Nolensville Rd	Nashville	TN	37211	615-833-1534	333-0728
Web: www.nashvillezoo.org					
Parthenon The West End Ave & 25th Ave N Centennial Pk	Nashville	TN	37201	615-862-8431	880-2265
Web: www.parthenon.org ■ *E-mail:* info@parthenon.org					
Radnor Lake State Natural Area 1160 Otter Creek Rd	Nashville	TN	37220	615-373-3467	373-7893
Ryman Auditorium 116 5th Ave N.	Nashville	TN	37219	615-254-1445	251-1026
Shiloh National Military Park 1055 Pittsburg Landing Rd	Shiloh	TN	38376	901-689-5275	689-5450
Web: www.nps.gov/shil/					
Stones River National Battlefield 3501 Old Nashville Hwy.	Murfreesboro	TN	37129	615-893-9501	893-9508
Web: www.nps.gov/stri/					
Tennessee Dance Theatre 625-A 7th Ave S.	Nashville	TN	37203	615-248-3262	256-3576
Tennessee Fox Trot Carousel Riverfront Park	Nashville	TN	37203	615-254-7020	
Tennessee Performing Arts Center 505 Deaderick St	Nashville	TN	37219	615-782-4000	782-4001
Web: www.tpac.org					
Tennessee Repertory Theatre 427 Chestnut St	Nashville	TN	37203	615-244-4878	244-1232
Web: therep.hammock.com/ ■ *E-mail:* therep@hammock.com					
Tennessee State Capitol Charlotte Ave	Nashville	TN	37243	615-741-1621	532-9711
Tennessee State Museum 505 Deaderick St	Nashville	TN	37243	615-741-2692	741-7231
TF: 800-407-4324					
Texas Troubadour Theatre 2416 Music Valley Dr	Nashville	TN	37214	615-885-0028	316-9269
Web: www.etrs.net/theatre.htm					

Nashville — Attractions (Cont'd)

				Phone	Fax
Travellers Rest Plantation House & Grounds 636 Farrell Pkwy	Nashville	TN	37220	615-832-8197	832-8169
Upper Room Chapel & Museum 1908 Grand Ave	Nashville	TN	37212	615-340-7207	340-7293
Van Vechten Gallery Jackson St & DB Todd Blvd Fisk University	Nashville	TN	37208	615-329-8720	329-8544
Vanderbilt University Fine Arts Gallery 23rd & West End Aves	Nashville	TN	37203	615-322-0605	343-1382
Web: www.vanderbilt.edu/ans/finearts/gallery.html					
Warner Edwin Park 50 Vaughn Rd	Nashville	TN	37201	615-862-8400	
Warner Percy Park 2500 Old Hickory Blvd	Nashville	TN	37201	615-862-8400	
Willie Nelson & Friends Showcase Museum 2613A McGavock Pike	Nashville	TN	37214	615-885-1515	885-0733
You're the Star Recording Studio 172 2nd Ave N	Nashville	TN	37201	615-742-9942	

SPORTS TEAMS & FACILITIES

				Phone	Fax
Gaylord Entertainment Center 501 Broadway	Nashville	TN	37203	615-770-2000	770-2010
Web: www.nashvillearena.com ■ *E-mail:* info@nashvillearena.com					
Music City Raceway 3302 Ivy Point Rd	Goodlettsville	TN	37072	615-876-0981	264-0362
Web: www.musiccityraceway.com ■ *E-mail:* racersrick@msn.com					
Nashville Kats (football) 5th & Broadway Nashville Arena	Nashville	TN	37201	615-254-5287	843-5206
Web: www.katsfan.com ■ *E-mail:* editor@katsfan.com					
Nashville Municipal Auditorium 417 4th Ave N	Nashville	TN	37201	615-862-6390	862-6394
Web: www.nashville.org/ma ■ *E-mail:* munaud@nashville.org					
Nashville Sounds (baseball) 534 Chestnut St Herschel Greer Stadium	Nashville	TN	37203	615-242-4371	256-5684
Web: www.nashsounds.com					
Nashville Speedway USA Wedgewood Ave & Nolensville Rd	Nashville	TN	37203	615-726-1818	726-0691
Web: www.nashvillespeedway.com					
Tennessee Rhythm (soccer) 1314 Columbia Ave Battle Ground Stadium	Franklin	TN	37064	615-591-9545	591-2130
E-mail: tennesseefc@aol.com					

— Events —

	Phone
A Country Christmas (early November-late December)	615-871-6169
African Street Festival (mid-September)	615-299-0412
American Artisan Festival (mid-June)	615-298-4691
Americana Sampler Craft Folk Art & Antique Show (early August)	615-227-2080
Antiques & Garden Show of Nashville (mid-February)	615-352-1282
Balloon Classic (mid-June)	615-329-7807
Belle Meade Fall Fest (mid-September)	615-356-0501
Boo at the Zoo (mid-late October)	615-371-8462
Chet Atkins' Musician Days (late June)	615-256-9596
Colonial Fair Day (early May)	615-859-7979
Dancin' in the District (early May-late July)	615-256-9596
Fan Fair (mid-June)	615-862-8980
Franklin Jazz Festival (early September)	615-790-7094
Grand Ole Opry Birthday Celebration (mid-October)	615-889-6611
Heart of Country Antiques Show (mid-February)	615-883-2211
Historic Edgefield Tour of Homes (mid-May)	615-226-3340
Independence Day Celebration (July 4)	615-862-8400
International Country Music Fan Fair (mid-June)	615-889-7503
Iroquois Steeplechase (early May)	615-322-7450
Italian Street Fair (early September)	615-255-5600
Longhorn World Championship Rodeo (mid-November)	800-357-6336
Main Street Festival (late April)	615-791-9924
Music City Hog Jam (early October)	615-259-4700
NAIA Pow Wow (mid-October)	615-726-0806
Nashville Boat & Sport Show (early January)	615-742-2000
Nashville Lawn & Garden Show (early March)	615-352-3863
Nashville's Country Holidays (early November-late December)	615-259-4700
Oktoberfest (early October)	615-256-2729
Southern Gospel Music Fest (mid-late April)	888-326-3378
TACA Fall Crafts Fair (late September)	615-665-0502
Tennessee Crafts Fair (early May)	615-665-0502
Tennessee Renaissance Festival (May)	615-259-4747
Tennessee State Fair (early-mid-September)	615-862-8980
Tennessee Walking Horse National Celebration (late August-early September)	931-684-5915
Tin Pan South (mid-April)	615-251-3472
Wildflower Fair (early April)	615-353-2148

Texas

Population (1999): 20,044,141 **Area (sq mi): 268,601**

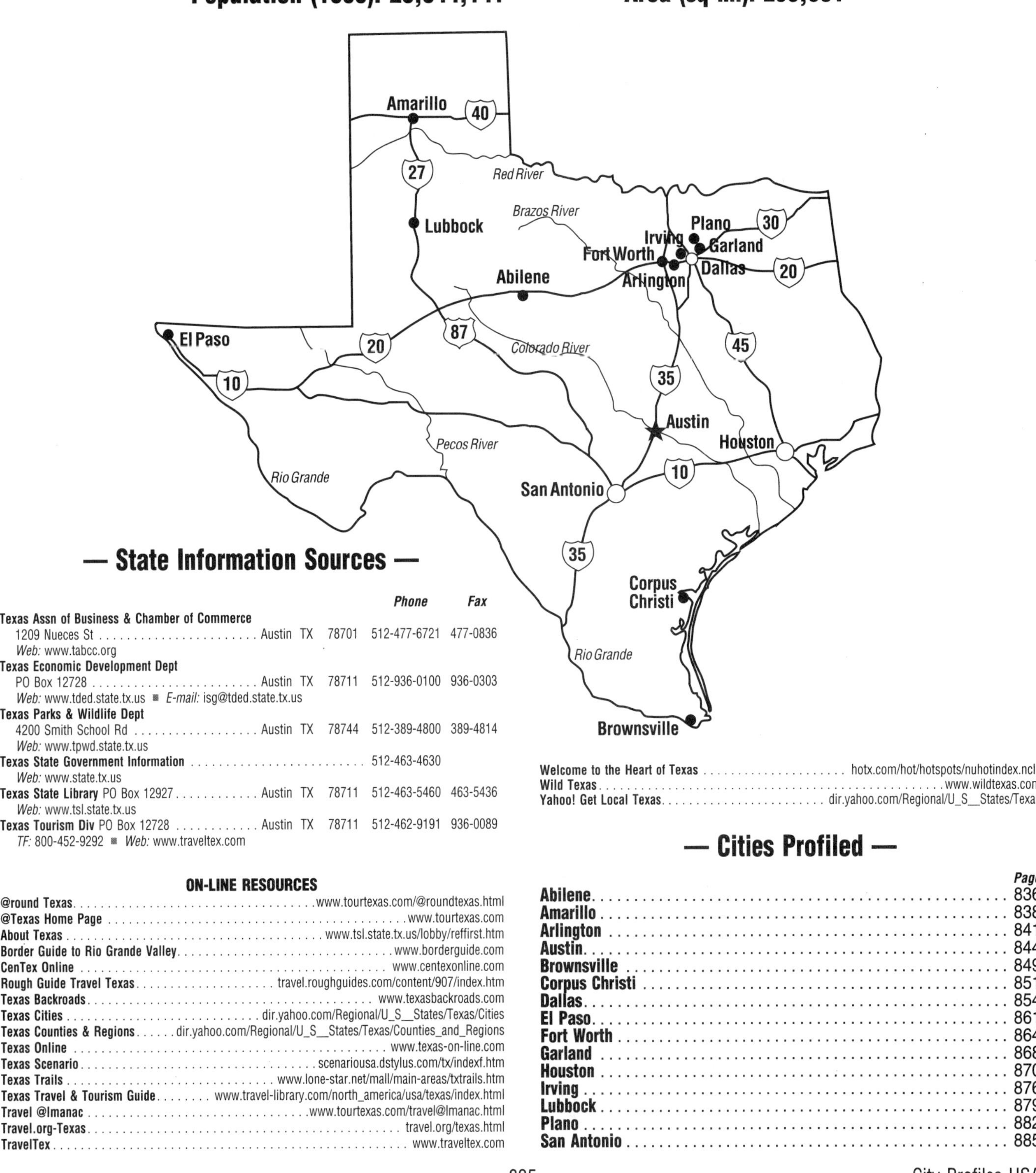

— State Information Sources —

			Phone	Fax
Texas Assn of Business & Chamber of Commerce 1209 Nueces St *Web:* www.tabcc.org	Austin TX	78701	512-477-6721	477-0836
Texas Economic Development Dept PO Box 12728 *Web:* www.tded.state.tx.us ■ *E-mail:* isg@tded.state.tx.us	Austin TX	78711	512-936-0100	936-0303
Texas Parks & Wildlife Dept 4200 Smith School Rd *Web:* www.tpwd.state.tx.us	Austin TX	78744	512-389-4800	389-4814
Texas State Government Information *Web:* www.state.tx.us			512-463-4630	
Texas State Library PO Box 12927 *Web:* www.tsl.state.tx.us	Austin TX	78711	512-463-5460	463-5436
Texas Tourism Div PO Box 12728 *TF:* 800-452-9292 ■ *Web:* www.traveltex.com	Austin TX	78711	512-462-9191	936-0089

ON-LINE RESOURCES

@round Texas . . . . www.tourtexas.com/@roundtexas.html
@Texas Home Page . . . . www.tourtexas.com
About Texas . . . . www.tsl.state.tx.us/lobby/reffirst.htm
Border Guide to Rio Grande Valley . . . . www.borderguide.com
CenTex Online . . . . www.centexonline.com
Rough Guide Travel Texas travel.roughguides.com/content/907/index.htm
Texas Backroads . . . . www.texasbackroads.com
Texas Cities . . . . dir.yahoo.com/Regional/U_S__States/Texas/Cities
Texas Counties & Regions . . . . dir.yahoo.com/Regional/U_S__States/Texas/Counties_and_Regions
Texas Online . . . . www.texas-on-line.com
Texas Scenario . . . . scenariousa.dstylus.com/tx/indexf.htm
Texas Trails . . . . www.lone-star.net/mall/main-areas/txtrails.htm
Texas Travel & Tourism Guide . . . . www.travel-library.com/north_america/usa/texas/index.html
Travel @lmanac . . . . www.tourtexas.com/travel@lmanac.html
Travel.org-Texas . . . . travel.org/texas.html
TravelTex . . . . www.traveltex.com
Welcome to the Heart of Texas . . . . hotx.com/hot/hotspots/nuhotindex.nclk
Wild Texas . . . . www.wildtexas.com
Yahoo! Get Local Texas . . . . dir.yahoo.com/Regional/U_S__States/Texas

— Cities Profiled —

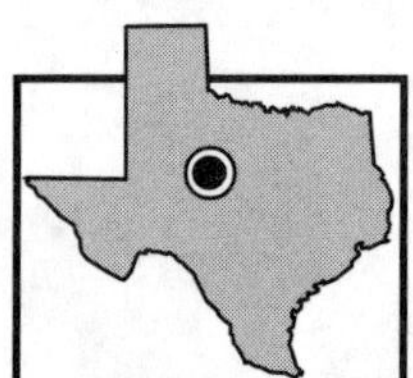

Abilene

Located in the central part of the state, the city of Abilene, Texas is named after another town known for its western heritage, Abilene, Kansas. First settled in 1881 by buffalo hunters, much of Abilene remains the same: ranches worked by cowboys still surround the city, and cowboys still rope and brand. Two of Abilene's biggest events are the Western Heritage Classic in May and the West Texas Fair and Rodeo in September. Smaller events, such as the frequent cowboy rodeos, also celebrate this important way of life. Though much of Abilene is still rural, the area does offer some big-city indulgences, such as theaters, art galleries, museums, a zoo, a symphony orchestra, and a ballet company. The Old Jail Art Center in nearby Albany has Pablo Picasso's works on paper, a Henry Moore sculpture and an Alexander Calder mobile, and is listed in John Dilani's "100 Best Small Art Towns in America." Abilene is also home to Dyess Air Force Base and the Linear Air Park, where visitors can view aircraft spanning 60 years, from World War II to Operation Desert Storm.

Population	111,799	**Longitude**	99-40-55 W
Area (Land)	91.4 sq mi	**County**	Taylor
Area (Water)	1.6 sq mi	**Time Zone**	CST
Elevation	1790 ft	**Area Code/s**	915
Latitude	32-24-41 N		

— Average Temperatures and Precipitation —

TEMPERATURES

	Jan	Feb	Mar	Apr	May	Jun	Jul	Aug	Sep	Oct	Nov	Dec
High	55	60	69	78	84	91	95	95	87	78	66	57
Low	31	35	43	53	61	69	73	72	65	55	43	34

PRECIPITATION

	Jan	Feb	Mar	Apr	May	Jun	Jul	Aug	Sep	Oct	Nov	Dec
Inches	1.0	1.2	1.4	1.9	3.0	2.9	2.1	2.8	3.2	2.5	1.5	1.0

— Important Phone Numbers —

	Phone		Phone
AAA	214-528-7481	**Medical Referral**	800-424-3627
Dental Referral	800-424-3627	**Poison Control Center**	800-764-7661
Emergency	911	**Time/Temp**	915-672-2881

— Information Sources —

				Phone	Fax
Abilene Chamber of Commerce PO Box 2281	Abilene	TX	79601	915-677-7241	677-0622
Web: www.abilene.com/chamber ■ *E-mail:* chamber@abiline.com					
Abilene City Hall 555 Walnut St	Abilene	TX	79601	915-676-6202	
Web: www.abilenetx.com ■ *E-mail:* abilene@camalott.com					
Abilene Civic Center 1100 N 6th St	Abilene	TX	79601	915-676-6211	676-6343
Abilene Convention & Visitors Bureau 1101 N 1st St	Abilene	TX	79601	915-676-2556	676-1630
TF: 800-727-7704 ■ *Web:* www.abilene.com/visitors ■ *E-mail:* visitors@abilene.com					
Abilene Mayor 555 Walnut St	Abilene	TX	79601	915-676-6205	676-6229
Web: www.abilenetx.com/mayor.htm ■ *E-mail:* abilene@camalott.com					
Abilene Public Library 202 Cedar St	Abilene	TX	79601	915-677-2474	
Web: www.abilenetx.com/apl					
Better Business Bureau Serving the Abilene Area 3300 S 14th St Suite 307	Abilene	TX	79605	915-691-1533	691-0309
Web: www.abilene.bbb.org					
Development Corp of Abilene Inc 555 Walnut St Suite 107	Abilene	TX	79601	915-676-6390	676-6377
Expo Center of Taylor County 1700 Hwy 36	Abilene	TX	79602	915-677-4376	677-0709
Taylor County 300 Oak St	Abilene	TX	79602	915-674-1380	674-1279

On-Line Resources

4Abilene.com	www.4abilene.com
Abilene Online	www.abilene.com
Area Guide Abilene	abilene.areaguides.net
City Knowledge Abilene	www.cityknowledge.com/tx_abilene.htm
Excite.com Abilene City Guide	www.excite.com/travel/countries/united_states/texas/abilene
NITC Travelbase City Guide Abilene	www.travelbase.com/auto/guides/abilene-tx.html
Online City Guide to Abilene	www.olcg.com/tx/abilene/index.html
Onroute Destinations Abilene	www.onroute.com/destinations/texas/abilene.html
PlacesToStay Abilene	www.placestostay.com/destination/usa/texas/abilene/dest.asp
Welcome to Abilene	www.texnews.com/abilene/index.html

— Transportation Services —

AIRPORTS

	Phone
■ **Abilene Regional Airport (ABI)**	
3 miles SE of downtown (approx 10 minutes)	915-676-6367

Airport Transportation

	Phone
A-1 Yellow Checker Cab $11 fare to downtown	915-677-2446
Classic Cab $11 fare to downtown	915-677-8294
Yellow Cab $11 fare to downtown	915-677-4334

Commercial Airlines

	Phone
American Eagle	800-433-7300

Charter Airlines

	Phone
Abilene Aero Inc	915-677-2601

CAR RENTALS

	Phone		Phone
Avis	915-677-9240	**Hertz**	915-673-6774
Budget	915-677-7777	**National**	915-673-2553
Dollar	915-672-2281		

LIMO/TAXI

	Phone		Phone
A-1 Yellow Checker Cab	915-677-2446	**Yellow Cab**	915-677-4334
Classic Cab	915-677-8294		

MASS TRANSIT

	Phone
Abilene Transit System $.75 Base fare	915-676-6287
CityLink Downtown Trolley free	915-676-6287

RAIL/BUS

				Phone
Greyhound Bus Station 535 Cedar St	Abilene	TX	79601	915-677-8127
TF: 800-531-5332				

— Accommodations —

HOTELS, MOTELS, RESORTS

				Phone	Fax
Alamo Motel 2957 S 1st St	Abilene	TX	79605	915-676-7149	
Antilley Inn 6550 Hwy 83	Abilene	TX	79602	915-695-3330	695-9872
TF: 800-959-1001					
Best Western 3950 Ridgemont Dr	Abilene	TX	79606	915-695-1262	695-2593
TF: 800-346-1574					
Budget Host Colonial Inn 3210 Pine St	Abilene	TX	79601	915-677-2683	677-8211
TF: 888-672-5293					
Century Lodge 3509 S 1st St	Abilene	TX	79605	915-677-8557	
Clarion Hotel & Conference Center 5403 S 1st St	Abilene	TX	79605	915-695-2150	698-6742
TF: 800-252-7466					

Abilene — Hotels, Motels, Resorts (Cont'd)

				Phone	Fax
Comfort Inn & Suites 1758 I-20 E	Abilene	TX	79601	915-676-0203	676-0203
TF: 800-228-5150					
Courtyard by Marriott 4350 Ridgemont Dr	Abilene	TX	79606	915-695-9600	695-0250
TF: 800-321-2211					
D&L Motel 358 S 11th St	Abilene	TX	79602	915-672-0044	
Days Inn 1702 I-20 E	Abilene	TX	79601	915-672-6433	676-9312
TF: 800-375-6433					
Econo Lodge 1633 W Stamford St	Abilene	TX	79601	915-673-5424	673-0412
Embassy Suites 4250 Ridgemont Dr	Abilene	TX	79606	915-698-1234	698-2771
TF: 800-632-2779					
Fairfield Inn by Marriott 3902 Turner Plaza	Abilene	TX	79606	915-695-2448	695-2448
TF: 800-228-2800					
Hampton Inn 3917 Ridgemont Dr	Abilene	TX	79606	915-695-0044	695-4192
TF: 800-426-7866					
Holiday Inn Express 1625 Hwy 351	Abilene	TX	79601	915-673-5271	673-8240
TF: 800-588-0072					
La Quinta Inn 3501 Westlake Rd	Abilene	TX	79601	915-676-1676	672-8323
TF: 800-531-5900					
Lamplighter Motel 3153 S 1st St	Abilene	TX	79605	915-673-4251	673-4251
Motel 6 4951 W Stamford St	Abilene	TX	79603	915-672-8462	672-3118
TF: 800-466-8356					
Ponca Motel 3101 S 1st St	Abilene	TX	79605	915-673-9682	
Quality Inn 505 W Pine St	Abilene	TX	79601	915-676-0222	676-0513
TF: 800-588-0222					
Ramada Inn 3450 S Clack St	Abilene	TX	79606	915-695-7700	698-0546
TF: 800-676-7262					
Rodeway Inn 1650 I-20 E	Abilene	TX	79601	915-677-2200	677-0472
TF: 800-228-2000					
Royal Inn 5695 S 1st St	Abilene	TX	79605	915-692-3022	692-3137
TF: 800-588-4386 ■ *E-mail:* royalabi@aol.com					
Super 8 Motel 1525 I-20 E	Abilene	TX	79601	915-673-5251	673-5314
TF: 800-800-8000					
Tower Motel 3417 S 1st St	Abilene	TX	79605	915-672-7849	672-6597
Travel Inn 2202 I-20	Abilene	TX	79603	915-677-2463	676-0750
Travelodge 840 Hwy 80 E	Abilene	TX	79601	915-677-8100	677-8147
TF: 800-880-7666					
Western Motel 3201 S 1st St	Abilene	TX	79605	915-672-7858	676-8412

— Restaurants —

				Phone
Abuelo's (Mexican) 4782 S 14th St	Abilene	TX	79605	915-692-4776
Alfredo's Mexican Food (Mexican) 2849 S 14th St	Abilene	TX	79605	915-698-0104
Betty Rose's (Barbecue) 2402 S 7th St	Abilene	TX	79606	915-673-5809
Borderlands (Mexican) 1150 E S 11th St	Abilene	TX	79605	915-677-1925
Cahoots (Seafood) 301 S 11th St	Abilene	TX	79605	915-672-6540
Casa Herrera (Mexican) 4109 Ridgemont Dr	Abilene	TX	79606	915-692-7065
Catfish Corner (Seafood) 780 S Treadaway Blvd	Abilene	TX	79602	915-672-3620
China Garden (Chinese) 2525 S 14th St	Abilene	TX	79605	915-692-3872
China King (Chinese) 4621 S 14th St	Abilene	TX	79605	915-695-6888
Clyde's Turnerhill House (Barbecue)				
1881 N Treadaway Blvd	Abilene	TX	79601	915-672-5811
Cotton Patch Cafe (Homestyle) 3302 S Clack St	Abilene	TX	79606	915-691-0509
Cypress Street Station (American) 158 Cypress St	Abilene	TX	79601	915-676-3463
Dos Amigos (Mexican) 3650 N 6th St	Abilene	TX	79603	915-672-2992
Eckos Restaurant (Chinese) 2701 S 1st St	Abilene	TX	79605	915-672-3792
El Fenix Cafe (Mexican) 3241 S 1st St	Abilene	TX	79605	915-677-3996
Farolito Restaurant (Mexican) 209 Cottonwood St	Abilene	TX	79601	915-672-0002
Fuji Japanese Steak House (Japanese) 3110 S 27th St	Abilene	TX	79605	915-695-9233
Harlow's Smokehouse (Barbecue) 2002 N Clack St	Abilene	TX	79603	915-672-2132
Harold's (Barbecue) 1305 Walnut St	Abilene	TX	79601	915-672-4451
Harvest Moon (Chinese) 1149 N 10th St	Abilene	TX	79601	915-676-0066
Hitchin Post Restaurant (Homestyle)				
2534 S Treadaway Blvd	Abilene	TX	79602	915-690-0087
Joe Allen's Pit Bar-B-Que (Barbecue)				
1233 S Treadaway Blvd	Abilene	TX	79602	915-672-6082
La Rancherita (Mexican) 3413 Ambler Ave	Abilene	TX	79603	915-672-5100
Monterrey Restaurant (Mexican) 3310 N 10th St	Abilene	TX	79603	915-673-1722
Outpost (American) 3126 S Clack St	Abilene	TX	79606	915-692-3595
Oxford Street Restaurant (Continental) 1882 S Clack St	Abilene	TX	79605	915-695-1770
Railhead Grill (Continental) 901 N 1st St	Abilene	TX	79601	915-672-7004
Remingtons (American)				
4250 Ridgemont Dr Embassy Suites	Abilene	TX	79606	915-698-1234
Spano's (Italian) 4534 Buffalo Gap Rd	Abilene	TX	79606	915-698-3704
Square's (Barbecue) 210 N Leggett Dr	Abilene	TX	79603	915-672-6752
Texas Roadhouse (Steak) 1381 S Danville Rd	Abilene	TX	79605	915-690-0145
Tonala Restaurant (Mexican) 1525 Pine St	Abilene	TX	79601	915-670-9214
Towne Crier Steak House (Steak) 818 Hwy 80 E	Abilene	TX	79601	915-673-4551
Zapata's (Mexican) 3114 S Clack St	Abilene	TX	79606	915-691-9218
Zentner's Daughter Steakhouse (Steak) 4358 Sayles Blvd	Abilene	TX	79605	915-695-4290

— Goods and Services —

SHOPPING

				Phone	Fax
Mall of Abilene 4310 Buffalo Gap Rd	Abilene	TX	79606	915-698-4351	698-4171

BANKS

				Phone	Fax
American State Bank 402 Cypress St	Abilene	TX	79601	915-673-8374	794-1120
Bank of America 500 Chestnut St	Abilene	TX	79602	915-675-7500	675-7598
TF Cust Svc: 800-247-6262*					
Bank One 3444 N 1st St	Abilene	TX	79603	915-674-3800	676-1130
TF: 800-695-1111					
First American Bank 3800 S Clack St	Abilene	TX	79606	915-695-2940	695-4339
TF: 800-725-1901					
First National Bank of Abilene 400 Pine St	Abilene	TX	79601	915-627-7000	627-7197*
**Fax:* Cust Svc ■ *TF:* 800-588-7000 ■ *Web:* www.fnbabilene.com ■ *E-mail:* fnbacsrv@ffin.com					
First State Bank 547 Chestnut St	Abilene	TX	79602	915-672-2902	672-2968
TF: 888-663-2902					
United Bank & Trust Co 4702 S 14th St	Abilene	TX	79605	915-695-0527	676-3868

BUSINESS SERVICES

	Phone
Abilene Quick Print & Copy Center	915-673-2700
Allied Parcel & Post	915-672-8443
Federal Express	800-238-5355
Interim Personnel	915-695-2999
Kelly Services	915-695-4110
Kinko's	915-698-3300
Mail Boxes Etc	915-692-9643
Manpower Temporary Services	915-677-2065
Post Office	915-673-6485
Snelling Personnel Services	915-695-4840
UPS	800-742-5877

— Media —

PUBLICATIONS

				Phone	Fax
Abilene Reporter-News‡ PO Box 30	Abilene	TX	79604	915-673-4271	670-5242
TF: 800-588-6397 ■ *Web:* texnews.com ■ *E-mail:* abinews@aol.com					

‡Daily newspapers

TELEVISION

				Phone	Fax
KIDY-TV Ch 6 (Fox) 406 S Irving St	San Angelo	TX	76903	915-655-6006	655-8461
KRBC-TV Ch 9 (NBC) 4510 S 14th St	Abilene	TX	79605	915-692-4242	692-8265
E-mail: krbc@abilene.com					
KTAB-TV Ch 32 (CBS) 5401 S 14th St	Abilene	TX	79606	915-695-2777	695-9922
Web: www.ktabtv.com ■ *E-mail:* sales@ktabtv.com					
KTXS-TV Ch 12 (ABC) 4420 N Clack St	Abilene	TX	79603	915-677-2281	676-9231
Web: www.ktxs.com ■ *E-mail:* star12@ktxs.com					

RADIO

				Phone	Fax
KACU-FM 89.7 MHz (NPR) 1600 Campus Ct	Abilene	TX	79699	915-674-2441	674-2417
Web: www.kacu.org ■ *E-mail:* info@kacu.org					
KBBA-AM 1280 (Span) 3911 S 1st St	Abilene	TX	79603	915-677-7225	676-3851
KBCY-FM 99.7 MHz (Ctry) 2525 S Danville Dr	Abilene	TX	79605	915-793-9700	692-1576
KCDD-FM 103.7 MHz (CHR)					
2525 S Danville Dr	Abilene	TX	79605	915-793-9700	692-1576
KEAN-FM 105.1 MHz (Ctry) 3911 S 1st St	Abilene	TX	79605	915-676-7711	676-3851
Web: www.keanradio.com ■ *E-mail:* kean@keanradio.com					
KEYJ-FM 107.9 MHz (Rock) 3911 S 1st St	Abilene	TX	79603	915-677-7225	676-3851
KGMM-AM 1280 kHz (Ctry) 3911 S 1st St	Abilene	TX	79605	915-676-7711	676-3851
Web: keanradio.com/1280am.html ■ *E-mail:* kean@keanradio.com					
KGNZ-FM 88.1 MHz (Rel) 542 Butternut St	Abilene	TX	79602	915-673-3045	672-7938
KHXS-FM 102.7 MHz (CR) 2525 S Danville Dr	Abilene	TX	79608	915-793-9700	692-1576
KHYF-FM 100.7 MHz (AC) 3911 S 1st St	Abilene	TX	79603	915-677-7225	676-3851
KKHR-FM 106.3 MHz (Span)					
3301 S 14th St Suite A-10	Abilene	TX	79605	915-695-9898	695-9968
Web: camalott.com/~star98 ■ *E-mail:* star98@camalott.com					
KMPC-AM 1560 kHz (B/EZ) 1749 N 2nd St	Abilene	TX	79603	915-673-1455	
KULL-FM 92.5 MHz (Oldies) 3911 S 1st St	Abilene	TX	79605	915-676-7711	676-3851
KWKC-AM 1340 kHz (N/T) 1749 N 2nd St	Abilene	TX	79603	915-673-1455	673-3485

Abilene (Cont'd)

— Colleges/Universities —

				Phone	Fax
Abilene Christian University PO Box ACU29000	Abilene	TX	79699	915-674-2000	674-2130
TF: 800-460-6228 ■ *Web:* www.acu.edu ■ *E-mail:* townsend@admissions.acu.edu					
Cisco Junior College 841 N Judge Ely Blvd	Abilene	TX	79601	915-673-4567	673-4575
Web: www.cisco.cc.tx.us/led/abilenehome.html					
Hardin-Simmons University 2200 Hickory St	Abilene	TX	79698	915-670-1000	671-1527
TF Admissions: 800-562-2692 ■ *Web:* www.hsutx.edu/ ■ *E-mail:* media@hsutx.edu					
McMurry University S 14 St & Sayles Blvd	Abilene	TX	79697	915-793-3800	691-6599
TF Admissions: 800-460-2392 ■ *Web:* www.mcm.acu.edu					
Texas State Technical College Abilene Campus 650 Hwy 80 E	Abilene	TX	79601	915-672-7091	672-7091
Web: www.sweetwater.tstc.edu/abilene/index.html ■ *E-mail:* ymelende@abadmin.tstc.edu					

— Hospitals —

				Phone	Fax
Abilene Regional Medical Center 6250 S Hwy 83-84	Abilene	TX	79606	915-695-9900	695-0670
Web: www.abilene.com/armc					

— Attractions —

				Phone	Fax
Abilene Ballet Theatre 1265 N 2nd St.	Abilene	TX	79601	915-675-0303	
Abilene Community Theatre 801 S Mockingbird Ln.	Abilene	TX	79605	915-673-6271	
Abilene Opera Association PO Box 6611	Abilene	TX	79608	915-928-6049	676-1541
Abilene Philharmonic Orchestra 402 Cypress St Suite 130	Abilene	TX	79601	915-677-6710	677-1299
TF: 800-460-0610 ■ *Web:* www.abilene.com/philharmonic ■ *E-mail:* philharmonic@abilene.com					
Abilene Repertory Theatre 801 S Mockingbird Ln.	Abilene	TX	79605	915-672-9991	
Abilene State Park 150 Park Rd 32	Tuscola	TX	79562	915-572-3204	572-3008
Web: www.tpwd.state.tx.us/park/abilene/abilene.htm ■ *E-mail:* webcomments@tpwd.state.tx.us					
Abilene Zoological Gardens 2070 Zoo Ln	Abilene	TX	79602	915-676-6085	676-6084
Web: www.abilenetx.com/zoo					
ACU Theatre 1600 Campus Ct Abilene Christian University	Abilene	TX	79699	915-674-2739	674-6887
Web: www.acu.edu/academics/theatre					
Artwalk Historic Downtown	Abilene	TX	79601	915-677-8389	
Buffalo Gap Historic Village 133 William St	Buffalo Gap	TX	79508	915-572-3365	698-7910
Web: www.abilene.com/art/bgap					
Center for Contemporary Arts 220 Cypress St	Abilene	TX	79601	915-677-8389	677-1847
Web: www.abilene.com/art/cca ■ *E-mail:* cca@abilene.com					
Dyess Air Force Base	Dyess AFB	TX	79607	915-696-3113	696-2866
Web: www.dyess.af.mil/public					
Expo Center of Taylor County 1700 Hwy 36	Abilene	TX	79602	915-677-4376	677-0709
Grace Cultural Museum 102 Cypress St	Abilene	TX	79601	915-673-4587	675-5993
Web: www.abilene.com/grace ■ *E-mail:* moa@abilene.com					
Linear Air Park Dyess Air Force Base	West Abilene	TX	79607	915-696-3113	
Paramount Theatre 352 Cypress St.	Abilene	TX	79601	915-676-9620	676-0642
Ryan Little Theatre S 14th St & Sayles Blvd McMurry University Ryan Fine Arts Bldg	Abilene	TX	79605	915-793-3889	793-4662
Van Ellis Theatre 2200 Hickory Hardin-Simmons University	Abilene	TX	79698	915-670-1405	677-8351

SPORTS TEAMS & FACILITIES

				Phone	Fax
Abilene Aviators (hockey) Century Plaza 1 Suite 103	Abilene	TX	79606	915-695-4625	695-2110
Web: www.aviatorshockey.com ■ *E-mail:* aviators@aviatorshockey.com					
Abilene Speedway 6825 W Hwy 80	Abilene	TX	79605	915-692-8800	
Web: www.geocities.com/MotorCity/Shop/2750/ABISPEEDWAY.html ■ *E-mail:* g3301@aol.com					

— Events —

	Phone
Abilene Kennel Club All-Breed Dog Show (late January)	915-676-2556
Abilene Shoot-out (early October)	915-698-2176
Altrusa Antique Show (mid-September)	915-676-6211
American Country Peddler Arts & Crafts Show (late July-early August)	915-676-6211
Arts & Crafts Festival (mid-June)	915-676-6211
Big Country Appreciation Day (August-November)	915-696-5609
Big Country Cat Fanciers Show (late January)	915-676-6211
Big Country Cutting Horse Assn Show (late May)	915-677-4376
Big Country Quarter Horse Assn Spring Show (late April)	915-677-4376
Biggest Little Arts & Crafts Show (mid-August & late September))	915-676-6211
Celebrate Abilene (late March-mid-April)	915-676-3775
Celebration Park Display (mid-November-early January)	915-691-1034
Central Texas Gem & Mineral Show (mid-April)	915-676-6211
Chili Super Bowl (early September)	915-675-8412
Christmas Carousel (early November)	915-676-6211
Christmas in November (mid-November)	915-676-6211
City Sidewalks Tree Lighting (late November)	915-676-6211
Coors Original Team Roping (early May)	915-677-4376
Cowboy Christmas Ball (mid-December)	915-823-3259
Cowboys Heritage Texas Team Roping (late May)	915-677-4376
Crossroads Gun & Knife Show (late February & late July & early December)	915-676-6211
Fort Griffin Fandangle (mid-late June)	915-762-3838
Hot Air Balloon Festival (late September)	915-675-8041
KEAN Big Bass Bonanza (mid-late May)	915-676-7711
Key City Amateur Radio Ham Fest (early May)	915-672-8889
KTXS Festival of Fun (late August)	915-677-2281
KTXS Parade of Lights (late November-early December)	915-677-2281
Police Athletic Federation Annual Games (late June)	915-676-6523
Southwest Regional Fly-In (mid-October)	915-676-2556
Stars Over Abilene Quilt Show (late May)	915-676-6211
Sunburn Grand Prix (late May)	915-698-2176
Supercar Show (mid-June)	915-676-6211
Texas Amateur Quarter Horse Assn State Championship Show (late April)	915-677-4376
Texas Firefighters Olympics (mid-late July)	915-676-6433
Texas Gun & Knife Show (mid-January & mid-May)	915-676-6211
Texas State 4-H Horse Show (mid-late July)	915-677-4376
Travis Boat Show (late June)	915-676-6211
West Texas Fair & Rodeo (mid-September)	915-677-4376
West Texas Renaissance Faire (early October)	915-672-3010
Western Heritage Classic (early May)	915-677-4376
Western Heritage Classic Fashion Show (early April)	915-672-3051
Western Heritage Classic Parade (early May)	915-677-4376
World's Largest Barbecue (mid-April)	915-677-7241

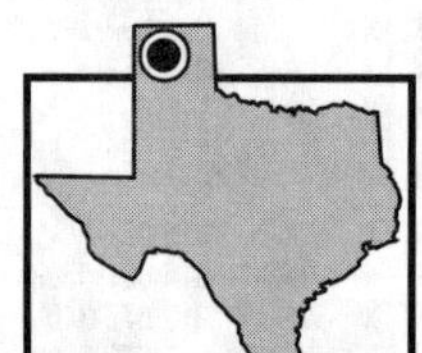

Amarillo

Located in the Texas Panhandle, Amarillo, which means "yellow" in Spanish, was named after the color of the subsoil in Amarillo Creek. Agriculture (primarily cattle and wheat) has played a major role in Amarillo's economic development since the city's early history. The Amarillo Civic Center hosts the annual Farm and Ranch Show, which has been named one of the top five agricultural trade shows in the United States. The city is also home to the world's largest natural gas development and provides pipelines to many American cities. Top attractions include Amarillo Zoo and Amarillo Museum of Art. In addition, Palo Duro Canyon State Park, the country's second largest canyon, is just a few miles from the city. Nearby also is Cadillac Ranch, where visitors can see ten Cadillacs buried nose-down in a field.

Population	171,207	**Longitude**	101-47-57 W
Area (Land)	88.0 sq mi	**County**	Potter, Randall
Area (Water)	0.4 sq mi	**Time Zone**	CST
Elevation	3,676 ft	**Area Code/s**	806
Latitude	35-13-13 N		

Amarillo (Cont'd)

— Average Temperatures and Precipitation —

TEMPERATURES

	Jan	Feb	Mar	Apr	May	Jun	Jul	Aug	Sep	Oct	Nov	Dec
High	49	53	62	72	79	88	92	89	82	73	60	50
Low	21	26	33	42	52	61	66	64	56	45	32	24

PRECIPITATION

	Jan	Feb	Mar	Apr	May	Jun	Jul	Aug	Sep	Oct	Nov	Dec
Inches	0.5	0.6	1.0	1.0	2.5	3.7	2.6	3.2	2.0	1.4	0.7	0.4

— Important Phone Numbers —

	Phone		*Phone*
AAA	806-354-8288	**Poison Control Center**	800-764-7661
Emergency	911	**Time/Temp**	806-372-2611
Highway Conditions	800-452-9292	**Weather**	806-358-7755
HotelDocs	800-468-3537		

— Information Sources —

				Phone	*Fax*
Amarillo Chamber of Commerce 1000 S Polk St	Amarillo	TX	79101	806-373-7800	373-3909
Web: www.amarillo-cvb.org					
Amarillo City Hall 509 E 7th St	Amarillo	TX	79101	806-378-3014	378-9394
Web: www.ci.amarillo.tx.us ■ *E-mail:* planning@ci.amarillo.tx.us					
Amarillo Civic Center 401 S Buchanan St	Amarillo	TX	79101	806-378-4297	378-4234
Web: www.civicamarillo.com					
Amarillo Community Development Dept PO Box 1971	Amarillo	TX	79105	806-378-3023	378-9389
Amarillo Convention & Visitor Council PO Box 9480	Amarillo	TX	79105	806-374-1497	373-3909
TF: 800-692-1338 ■ *Web:* www.amarillo-cvb.org					
Amarillo Economic Development Corp 600 S Tyler St Suite1503	Amarillo	TX	79101	806-379-6411	371-0112
TF: 800-333-7892 ■ *Web:* www.amarillo-tx.com/ ■ *E-mail:* aedc@arn.net					
Amarillo Mayor 509 E 7th St	Amarillo	TX	79101	806-378-3010	378-9394
Web: www.ci.amarillo.tx.us/city_officials.htm					
Amarillo Public Library 413 E 4th Ave	Amarillo	TX	79101	806-378-3054	378-9327
Web: www.ci.amarillo.tx.us/library/mainpage2.html					
Better Business Bureau Serving the Texas Panhandle PO Box 1905	Amarillo	TX	79105	806-379-6222	379-8206
Web: www.amarillo.bbb.org ■ *E-mail:* info@amarillo.bbb.org					
Potter County PO Box 9638	Amarillo	TX	79105	806-379-2275	379-2296

On-Line Resources

City Knowledge Amarillo	www.cityknowledge.com/tx_amarilo.htm
Excite.com Amarillo City Guide	www.excite.com/travel/countries/united_states/texas/amarillo
Internet Amarillo	www.amarillo.searchtexas.com/
Texas Panhandle Pages	www.searchtexas.com/panhandle

— Transportation Services —

AIRPORTS

■ Amarillo International Airport (AMA)

	Phone
9 miles E of downtown (approx 20 minutes)	806-335-1671

Airport Transportation

	Phone
AAA Taxi Service $14-16 fare to downtown	806-379-9395
Amarillo Cab Co $12-13 fare to downtown	806-371-8294

Commercial Airlines

	Phone		*Phone*
American	806-335-7000	**Northwest**	800-225-2525
American Eagle	806-335-7000	**Southwest**	800-435-9792

CAR RENTALS

	Phone		*Phone*
Alamo	800-327-9633	**CarTemps USA**	806-358-7577
Avis	806-335-2313	**Enterprise**	806-353-9227
Budget	806-355-3324	**Hertz**	806-335-2331

LIMO/TAXI

	Phone		*Phone*
AAA Taxi Service	806-379-9395	**Bob's Taxi Service**	806-373-1171
ABC Taxi Service	806-379-9393	**Limo USA**	800-451-3011
Amarillo Cab Co	806-371-8294	**Yellow Checker Cab**	806-374-8444

MASS TRANSIT

	Phone
City Transit $.75 Base fare	806-378-3094

RAIL/BUS

				Phone
Greyhound Bus Station 700 S Tyler St	Amarillo	TX	79101	806-374-5371
TF: 800-231-2222				

— Accommodations —

HOTELS, MOTELS, RESORTS

				Phone	*Fax*
Ambassador Hotel 3100 I-40 W	Amarillo	TX	79102	806-358-6161	358-9869
TF: 800-817-0521					
American Motor Inn 4541 Canyon Dr	Amarillo	TX	79110	806-355-5611	352-4076
Best Western Amarillo Inn 1610 Coulter Dr	Amarillo	TX	79106	806-358-7861	352-7287
TF: 800-528-1234					
Best Western Inn 4600 I-40 E	Amarillo	TX	79103	806-372-1885	372-5384
TF: 800-528-1234					
Big Texan Hotel 7700 E I-40	Amarillo	TX	79103	806-372-5000	371-0099
TF: 800-657-7177					
Civic Center Inn 715 S Fillmore St	Amarillo	TX	79101	806-376-4603	
Comfort Inn 2100 S Coulter Dr	Amarillo	TX	79106	806-358-6141	358-3916
TF: 800-228-5150					
Comfort Inn Airport 1515 I-40 E	Amarillo	TX	79102	806-376-9993	373-5343
TF: 800-228-5150					
Comfort Suites 2103 Lakeview Dr	Amarillo	TX	79109	806-352-8300	359-3616
TF: 888-373-8400					
Days Inn 2102 Coulter Dr	Amarillo	TX	79106	806-359-9393	359-9450
TF: 800-329-7466					
Days Inn 1701 I-40 E	Amarillo	TX	79102	806-379-6255	379-8204
TF: 800-329-7466					
Econo Lodge 2915 I-40 E	Amarillo	TX	79104	806-372-8101	374-5221
TF: 800-228-5160					
Fairfield Inn 6600 I-40 W	Amarillo	TX	79106	806-351-0172	351-0172
TF: 800-228-2800 ■ *Web:* fairfieldinn.com/AMAFI					
Georgia Street Inn 2801 I-40 W	Amarillo	TX	79109	806-355-9171	355-0691
Hampton Inn 1700 I-40 E	Amarillo	TX	79103	806-372-1425	379-8807
TF: 800-426-7866					
Hillcrest Motel 3017 E Amarillo Blvd	Amarillo	TX	79107	806-383-6931	
Holiday Inn 1911 I-40 E	Amarillo	TX	79102	806-372-8741	372-7045
TF: 800-465-4329					
Holiday Inn Express 3411 I-40 W	Amarillo	TX	79109	806-356-6800	356-0401
TF: 800-465-4329					
HomeGate Studios & Suites 6800 I-40 W	Amarillo	TX	79106	806-358-7943	358-8475
La Quinta Inn Airport 1708 I-40 E	Amarillo	TX	79103	806-373-7486	372-4100
TF: 800-531-5900					
La Quinta Inn West 2108 Coulter St	Amarillo	TX	79106	806-352-6311	359-3179
TF: 800-531-5900					
Motel 6 2032 Paramount Blvd	Amarillo	TX	79109	806-355-6554	355-5317
TF: 800-466-8356					
Quality Inn 1803 S Lakeside Dr	Amarillo	TX	79120	806-335-1561	335-1808
TF: 800-228-5151					
Radisson Inn Airport 7909 I-40 E	Amarillo	TX	79118	806-373-3303	373-3353
TF: 800-333-3333					
Ramada Inn East 2501 I-40 E	Amarillo	TX	79104	806-379-6555	372-7355
TF: 800-272-6232					
Ramada Inn West 6801 I-40 W	Amarillo	TX	79106	806-358-7881	358-1726
TF: 800-858-2223					
Red Roof Inn 1620 E I-40	Amarillo	TX	79103	806-374-2020	374-7140
TF: 800-843-7663					

Amarillo — Hotels, Motels, Resorts (Cont'd)

				Phone	Fax
Residence Inn by Marriott 6700 I-40 W	Amarillo	TX	79106	806-354-2978	354-2978
TF: 800-331-3131 ■ *Web:* www.residenceinn.com/residenceinn/AMARI					
Super 8 Motel 8701 E I-40	Amarillo	TX	79118	806-335-2836	335-2836
TF: 800-800-8000					
Townhouse Motel 112 W Amarillo Blvd	Amarillo	TX	79107	806-376-6737	372-6691
Travelodge East 3205 I-40 E	Amarillo	TX	79104	806-372-8171	372-2815
TF: 800-578-7878					
Travelodge West 2035 Paramount Blvd	Amarillo	TX	79109	806-353-3541	353-0201
TF: 800-578-7878					

— Restaurants —

				Phone
Abuelo's (Mexican) 3501 W 45th Ave	Amarillo	TX	79109	806-354-8294
Bangkok Restaurant (Thai) 5901 E Amarillo Blvd	Amarillo	TX	79107	806-383-9008
Beans & Things Bar-be-que (Barbecue) 1700 E Amarillo Blvd Suite A	Amarillo	TX	79107	806-373-7383
Big Texan Steak Ranch (Steak) 7701 I-40 E	Amarillo	TX	79120	806-372-7000
TF: 800-657-7177				
Buns Over Texas (American) 3320 Bell St	Amarillo	TX	79106	806-358-6808
Catfish Shack & Seafood Grill (Seafood) 3301 Olsen Blvd	Amarillo	TX	79109	806-358-3812
Cattle Call (Barbecue) 7701 I-40 W	Amarillo	TX	79160	806-353-1227
Coyote Bluff Cafe (American) 2417 S Grand St	Amarillo	TX	79103	806-373-4640
Doodles (American) 3701-B Olsen Blvd	Amarillo	TX	79109	806-355-0064
El Chico (Mexican) 2909 I-40 W	Amarillo	TX	79109	806-356-7186
English Field House (American) 10609 American Dr	Amarillo	TX	79111	806-335-2996
Fenderz Bar & Grill (American) 3605 Olsen Blvd	Amarillo	TX	79109	806-358-6767
Georgia Street Grill (American) 2509 S Georgia St	Amarillo	TX	79109	806-355-4000
Hickory Stick Barbecue (Barbecue) 501 S McMasters St	Amarillo	TX	79106	806-373-3322
Hummer's Sports Cafe (American) 2600 Paramount Blvd	Amarillo	TX	79109	806-353-0723
Italian Delight (Italian) 2710 W 10th Ave	Amarillo	TX	79102	806-372-5444
Kabuki Japanese Steakhouse (Japanese) 3319 I-40 W	Amarillo	TX	79109	806-358-7799
La Frontera (Mexican) 1401 S Arthur St	Amarillo	TX	79102	806-372-4593
Lone Star Bar & Grill (American) Washington St & Old Claude Hwy	Amarillo	TX	79118	806-622-9827
Ming Palace Restaurant (Chinese) 4925 S Western St	Amarillo	TX	79109	806-353-3691
My Thai (Thai) 2029 Coulter Dr	Amarillo	TX	79106	806-355-9541
OHMS Gallery Cafe (International) 619 S Tyler St	Amarillo	TX	79101	806-373-3233
Oyster Bar (Seafood) 4150 Paramount Blvd	Amarillo	TX	79109	806-354-9110
Pizza Planet (Italian) 2400 Paramount Blvd	Amarillo	TX	79109	806-353-6666
Ribs & Blues (Barbecue) 2917 W 6th Ave	Amarillo	TX	79106	806-372-7427
Ruby Tequila's (Mexican) 2108 Paramount Blvd	Amarillo	TX	79109	806-358-7829
Santa Fe (Mexican) 3333 Coulter Dr	Amarillo	TX	79106	806-358-8333

— Goods and Services —

SHOPPING

				Phone	Fax
Route 66 District 6th St betw Georgia & Western	Amarillo	TX	79106	806-374-0459	
Western Plaza Shopping Center 2201 S Western St	Amarillo	TX	79109	806-355-8216	352-8158
Westgate Mall 7701 W I-40 Suite 140	Amarillo	TX	79160	806-358-7221	353-5424
Web: westgatemalltx.com					
Wolflin Square & Village 1901 S Georgia St	Amarillo	TX	79109	806-355-6131	

BANKS

				Phone	Fax
Amarillo National Bank 410 S Taylor St Plaza One	Amarillo	TX	79105	806-378-8000	373-7505*
**Fax:* Cust Svc ■ *Web:* www.anb.com					
Bank of America 701 S Taylor St	Amarillo	TX	79101	806-378-1400	378-1514
Bank One 600 S Tyler St	Amarillo	TX	79101	806-378-3100	378-3221*
**Fax:* Cust Svc					
First State Bank 3501 Soncy Rd Suite 1	Amarillo	TX	79121	806-354-2265	354-2407
Western National Bank 4241 W 45th St	Amarillo	TX	79109	806-355-9641	353-3269

BUSINESS SERVICES

	Phone
Airborne Express	800-247-2676
DHL Worldwide Express	800-225-5345
Express Pack N Ship	806-354-2282
Federal Express	800-238-5355
Interim Personnel Services	806-359-1111
Kelly Services	806-355-9696
Kinko's	806-359-9684
Mail Boxes Etc	806-352-2600
Manpower Temporary Services	806-358-6221
Post Office	806-468-2148
UPS	800-742-5877

— Media —

PUBLICATIONS

				Phone	Fax
Amarillo Daily News‡ PO Box 2091	Amarillo	TX	79166	806-376-4488	373-0810
Web: www.amarillonet.com					
Amarillo Globe Times‡ PO Box 2091	Amarillo	TX	79166	806-376-4488	373-0810
Web: www.amarillonet.com					

‡Daily newspapers

TELEVISION

				Phone	Fax
KACV-TV Ch 2 (PBS) PO Box 447	Amarillo	TX	79178	806-371-5230	371-5258
Web: kacvtv.org					
KAMR-TV Ch 4 (NBC) 2000 N Polk St	Amarillo	TX	79107	806-383-3321	381-2943
Web: www.kamr.com ■ *E-mail:* kamr@arn.net					
KCIT-TV Ch 14 (Fox) 1015 S Fillmore St	Amarillo	TX	79101	806-374-1414	371-0408
KCPN-TV Ch 65 (UPN) 1015 S Filmore St	Amarillo	TX	79101	806-374-1414	371-0408
KFDA-TV Ch 10 (CBS) 7900 Broadway	Amarillo	TX	79108	806-383-1010	381-9859
Web: www.newschannel10.com ■ *E-mail:* 10assign@arn.net					
KVII-TV Ch 7 (ABC) 1 Broadcast Ctr	Amarillo	TX	79101	806-373-1787	371-7329
Web: www.kvii.com					

RADIO

				Phone	Fax
KACV-FM 89.9 MHz (Misc) PO Box 447	Amarillo	TX	79178	806-371-5222	371-5258
Web: kacvfm.org ■ *E-mail:* kacvfm90@actx.edu					
KARX-FM 95.7 MHz (CR) 301 S Polk St Suite 100	Amarillo	TX	79101	806-342-5200	342-5202
KATP-FM 101.9 MHz (Ctry) 5406 Winners Cir	Amarillo	TX	79110	806-359-5999	359-0136
KBZD-FM 99.7 MHz (Rock) 5200 Amarillo Blvd E	Amarillo	TX	79107	806-372-6543	379-7339
KGNC-AM 710 kHz (N/T) PO Box 710	Amarillo	TX	79189	806-355-9801	354-9450
Web: www.kgnc.com					
KGNC-FM 97.9 Mhz (Ctry) PO Box 710	Amarillo	TX	79189	806-355-9801	354-9450
Web: www.kgnc.com/FM/fm_main.htm ■ *E-mail:* kgnc@kgnc.com					
KNSY-FM 98.7 MHz (CR) 1703 Avondale St	Amarillo	TX	79106	806-355-9777	355-5832
KPUR-FM 107.1 MHz (Oldies) 301 S Polk St Suite 100	Amarillo	TX	79106	806-342-5200	342-5202
KQFX-FM 104.3 MHz (Span) 3639 B Wolflin Ave	Amarillo	TX	79102	806-355-1044	352-6525
KQIZ-FM 93.1 MHz (CHR) 301 S Polk St Suite 100	Amarillo	TX	79101	806-342-5200	342-5200
KZRK-FM 107.9 MHz (Rock) 301 S Polk St Suite 100	Amarillo	TX	79101	806-342-5200	342-5200

— Colleges/Universities —

				Phone	Fax
Amarillo College PO Box 447	Amarillo	TX	79178	806-371-5000	371-5066
TF: 800-996-6707 ■ *Web:* www.actx.edu					

— Hospitals —

				Phone	Fax
Baptist-Saint Anthony's Hospital 1600 Wallace Blvd	Amarillo	TX	79106	806-212-2000	212-2932*
**Fax:* Admitting ■ *Web:* www.bsahs.com					
Northwest Texas Hospital PO Box 1110	Amarillo	TX	79175	806-354-1000	354-1122
Web: www.nwths.com					
Saint Anthony's Baptist Health System 1600 Wallace Blvd	Amarillo	TX	79106	806-356-2000	356-2919
Veterans Affairs Medical Center 6010 Amarillo Blvd W	Amarillo	TX	79106	806-355-9703	354-7869

— Attractions —

				Phone	Fax
Alibates Flint Quarries National Monument PO Box 1460	Fritch	TX	79036	806-857-3151	857-2319
Web: www.nps.gov/alfl/					
Amarillo Botanical Gardens 1400 Streit Dr	Amarillo	TX	79106	806-352-6513	352-6227
Amarillo Livestock Auction 100 S Manhattan	Amarillo	TX	79104	806-373-7464	376-1765
Web: www.amarillo-cvb.org/cattle.html					

Amarillo — Attractions (Cont'd)

	City	State	ZIP	Phone	Fax
Amarillo Museum of Art 2200 S Van Buren St. *Web:* www.amarilloart.org ■ *E-mail:* amoa@arn.net	Amarillo	TX	79109	806-371-5050	373-9235
Amarillo Opera Amarillo Civic Center Auditorium	Amarillo	TX	79101	806-372-7464	372-7465
Amarillo Symphony 1000 Polk St *Web:* www.actx.edu/~symphony ■ *E-mail:* symphony@dns.genesis.net	Amarillo	TX	79101	806-376-8782	376-7127
Amarillo Zoo Hwy 287 N Thompson Pk.	Amarillo	TX	79107	806-381-7911	
American Quarter Horse Heritage Center & Museum 2601 I-40 E	Amarillo	TX	79104	806-376-5181	376-1005
Cadillac Ranch I-40 W to Arnot Exit	Amarillo	TX			
English Field Air & Space Museum 2014 English Rd	Amarillo	TX	79108	806-335-1812	335-1993
Farley's Cal Boys Ranch PO Box 1890 *TF:* 800-373-6600 ■ *Web:* www.calfarleysboysranch.org	Amarillo	TX	79174	806-372-2341	372-6638
Harrington Don Discovery Center 1200 Streit Dr *TF:* 800-784-9548 ■ *Web:* www.searchtexas.com/discovery/	Amarillo	TX	79106	806-355-9547	355-5703
Lake Meredith Recreation Area PO Box 1460 *Web:* www.nps.gov/lamr/	Fritch	TX	79036	806-857-3151	857-2319
Lone Star Ballet 1000 S Polk St.	Amarillo	TX	79101	806-372-2463	372-3131
Palo Duro Canyon State Park Rt 2 *Web:* www.amintech.com/amarillo/paloduro/ ■ *E-mail:* pdc@amaonline.com	Canyon	TX	79015	806-488-2227	
Panhandle-Plains Historical Museum 2401 4th Ave *Web:* www.wtamu.edu/museum ■ *E-mail:* museum@wtamu.edu	Canyon	TX	79015	806-651-2244	651-2250
Route 66 District 6th St betw Georgia & Western	Amarillo	TX	79106	806-374-0459	
Wonderland Amusement Park 2601 Dumas Dr *Web:* www.amarillo-cvb.org/wonder.html	Amarillo	TX	79107	806-383-4712	383-8737

SPORTS TEAMS & FACILITIES

	City	State	ZIP	Phone	Fax
Amarillo Dillas (baseball) Potter County Memorial Stadium	Amarillo	TX	79105	806-342-3455	374-2269
Amarillo Rattlers (hockey) 1422 S Tyler St Suite 100 *Web:* www.amarillorattlers.com/ ■ *E-mail:* rattlers@arn.net	Amarillo	TX	79101	806-374-7825	374-7835

— Events —

	Phone
Amarillo Farm & Ranch Show (early December)	806-378-4297
Best of Texas Festival (late March)	806-374-0802
Boys Ranch Rodeo (Labor Day weekend)	806-372-2341
Circus Gatti (late February)	806-378-4297
Coors Ranch Rodeo (early-mid June)	806-376-7767
FunFest (late May)	806-374-0802
High Plains Book Festival (early October)	806-651-2231
Mel Phillips' Outdoor World Sportsman's Show (late January)	806-378-4297
Octoberfest (early September)	806-373-7800
Panhandle Boat Sport & Travel Show (early February)	806-383-4408
Range Riders Rodeo (early July)	806-355-2212
Super Bull Tour (late January)	806-378-3096
Texas Musical Drama (early June-late August)	806-655-2181
Tri-State Fair (mid-September)	806-376-7767
WRCA World Championship Ranch Rodeo (mid-November)	806-374-9722

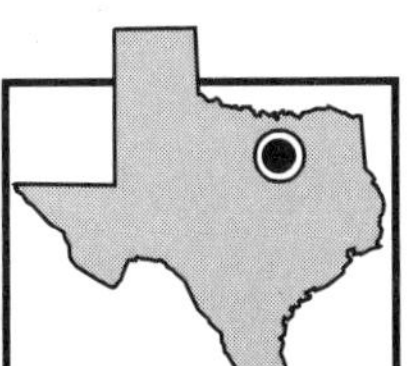

Arlington

Founded in 1876 as a midpoint stop between Dallas and Fort Worth along the Texas & Pacific Railroad, Arlington is currently the number one tourist destination in Texas. The city's main tourist attraction is Six Flags Over Texas, a major theme park that features special events throughout the year. The Ballpark at Arlington is the home field of the Texas Rangers, drawing large numbers of sports fans to the city each season. The city's Air Combat School allows visitors to experience piloting a jet fighter using flight simulators.

Population	306,497	**Longitude**	97-07-39 W
Area (Land)	93.0 sq mi	**County**	Tarrant
Area (Water)	3.2 sq mi	**Time Zone**	CST
Elevation	616 ft	**Area Code/s**	817
Latitude	32-41-40 N		

— Average Temperatures and Precipitation —

TEMPERATURES

	Jan	Feb	Mar	Apr	May	Jun	Jul	Aug	Sep	Oct	Nov	Dec
High	53	58	67	76	82	90	95	95	88	78	66	57
Low	30	35	43	53	61	68	72	72	65	54	44	34

PRECIPITATION

	Jan	Feb	Mar	Apr	May	Jun	Jul	Aug	Sep	Oct	Nov	Dec
Inches	1.9	2.5	3.1	3.6	5.2	3.2	2.5	2.0	4.0	3.5	2.4	2.0

— Important Phone Numbers —

	Phone		Phone
AAA	817-370-2503	**Medical Referral**	817-548-6500
American Express Travel	817-738-5441	**Poison Control Center**	800-764-7661
Dental Referral	800-917-6453	**Time/Temp**	817-277-4000
Emergency	911	**Weather**	817-787-1111
Highway Conditions	800-452-9292		

— Information Sources —

	City	State	ZIP	Phone	Fax
Arlington Chamber 316 W Main St *TF:* 800-834-3928 ■ *Web:* www.chamber.arlingtontx.com	Arlington	TX	76010	817-275-2613	261-7535
Arlington City Hall 101 W Abrams *Web:* www.ci.arlington.tx.us/cityhal.html	Arlington	TX	76010	817-275-3271	459-6199
Arlington Community Center 2800 S Center St	Arlington	TX	76014	817-465-6661	465-6663
Arlington Convention & Visitors Bureau 1905 E Randol Mill Rd Suite 650 *TF:* 800-433-5374 ■ *Web:* www.acvb.org ■ *E-mail:* visitinfo@acvb.org	Arlington	TX	76011	817-265-7721	265-5640
Arlington Convention Center 1200 Ballpark Way *Web:* www.ci.arlington.tx.us/aconvctr/	Arlington	TX	76011	817-459-5000	459-5091
Arlington Mayor 101 W Abram St. *Web:* www.ci.arlington.tx.us/odom.html	Arlington	TX	76010	817-459-6122	459-6120
Arlington Planning & Development Dept 101 W Abrams *Web:* www.ci.arlington.tx.us/planning/index.html ■ *E-mail:* arlplan1@ci.arlington.tx.us	Arlington	TX	76010	817-459-6650	459-6671
Arlington Public Library 101 E Abram St. *Web:* www.pub-lib.ci.arlington.tx.us	Arlington	TX	76010	817-459-6900	459-6902
Better Business Bureau Serving the Fort Worth Area 1612 Summit Ave Suite 260 *Web:* www.fortworth.bbb.org	Fort Worth	TX	76102	817-332-7585	882-0566
Tarrant County 100 W Weatherford St. *Web:* www.tarrantcounty.com	Fort Worth	TX	76196	817-884-1195	
Visitor Information Center 1905 E Randol Mill Rd *TF:* 800-342-4305	Arlington	TX	76011	817-461-3888	461-6689

On-Line Resources

Area Guide Arlington	arlingtontx.areaguides.net
Arlington City Net	www.excite.com/travel/countries/united_states/texas/arlington
City Knowledge Arlington	www.cityknowledge.com/tx_arlington.htm

Arlington (Cont'd)

— Transportation Services —

AIRPORTS

	Phone
■ **Dallas-Fort Worth International Airport (DFW)**	
8 miles N of downtown Arlington (approx 15 minutes)	972-574-8888

Airport Transportation

	Phone
Discount Shuttle $12-20 fare to downtown Arlington	817-267-5150
SuperShuttle $10-15 fare to downtown Arlington	800-258-3826
Yellow Cab $20-25 fare to downtown Arlington	817-534-5555

Commercial Airlines

	Phone		Phone
American	800-433-7300	**Midwest Express**	800-452-2022
American Eagle	800-433-7300	**National**	888-757-5387
Aspen Mountain Air Inc	972-641-7337	**Northwest**	800-225-2525
British Airways	800-247-9297	**Southwest**	972-263-1717
Continental	800-525-0280	**Thai**	800-426-5204
Delta	214-630-3200	**TWA**	800-221-2000
El Al	800-223-6700	**United**	800-241-6522
Lufthansa	800-645-3880	**US Airways**	800-428-4322
Mesa	800-637-2247	**Vanguard**	800-826-4827
Mexicana	800-531-7923		

Charter Airlines

	Phone		Phone
Alpha Aviation	214-352-4801	**Million Air**	800-248-1602
Miami Air International	305-871-3300	**Sun Country**	800-359-5786

CAR RENTALS

	Phone		Phone
Avis	972-574-4130	**Enterprise**	817-589-0471
Budget	817-329-2277	**Hertz**	972-453-0370
Dollar	972-929-8888		

LIMO/TAXI

	Phone		Phone
Carey Limousine	817-338-1012	**Yellow & Checker Cab**	817-469-1111
VIP Limousine	972-490-6305		

RAIL/BUS

				Phone
Amtrak Station 1501 Jones St	Fort Worth	TX	76102	817-332-2931
Greyhound/Trailways Bus Station 2075 E Division St *TF:* 800-231-2222*	Arlington	TX	76011	817-461-5337

— Accommodations —

HOTEL RESERVATION SERVICES

	Phone	Fax
USA Hotels *TF:* 800-872-4683 ■ *Web:* www.1800usahotels.com ■ *E-mail:* info@1800usahotels.com	252-331-1555	331-2021

HOTELS, MOTELS, RESORTS

				Phone	Fax
Abram Inn 3020 E Abram St	Arlington	TX	76011	817-652-0176	
AmeriSuites Arlington 2380 E Road to Six Flags *TF:* 800-833-1516	Arlington	TX	76011	817-649-7676	649-7753
Ballpark Inn 903 N Collins St	Arlington	TX	76011	817-261-3621	274-7420
Baymont Inns 2401 Diplomacy Dr *TF:* 800-301-0200	Arlington	TX	76011	817-633-2400	633-3500
Best Western Cooper Inn & Suites 4024 Melear Dr *TF:* 800-528-1234	Arlington	TX	76015	817-784-9490	557-4450
Best Western Great Southwest Inn 3501 E Division St *TF:* 800-528-1234	Arlington	TX	76011	817-640-7722	640-9043
Comfort Inn 1601 E Division St *TF:* 800-472-9258	Arlington	TX	76011	817-261-2300	861-8679
Country Suites by Carlson 1075 Wet 'n Wild Way *TF:* 800-456-4000	Arlington	TX	76011	817-261-8900	274-0343
Courtyard by Marriott 1500 Nolan Ryan Expy *TF:* 800-321-2211 ■ *Web:* courtyard.com/DALAL	Arlington	TX	76011	817-277-2774	277-3103
Days Inn Ballpark Arlington 910 N Collins St *TF:* 800-325-2525	Arlington	TX	76011	817-261-8444	860-8326
Days Inn Six Flags 1195 N Watson Rd *TF:* 800-329-7466	Arlington	TX	76011	817-649-8881	649-8881
Economy Inn 314 N Collins St	Arlington	TX	76011	817-548-9977	265-2409
Fairfield Inn by Marriott 2500 E Lamar Blvd *TF:* 800-228-2800 ■ *Web:* fairfieldinn.com/DFWAR	Arlington	TX	76006	817-649-5800	649-5800
Fiesta Motor Inn 1000 E Division St *TF:* 800-842-9084	Arlington	TX	76011	817-459-2171	
Hampton Inn 121 E I-20 *TF:* 800-426-7866	Arlington	TX	76018	817-467-3535	467-5570
Hawthorn Suites Hotel 2401 Brookhollow Plaza Dr *TF:* 800-527-1133	Arlington	TX	76006	817-640-1188	640-1188
Hilton Hotel Arlington 2401 E Lamar Blvd *TF:* 800-445-8667 ■ *Web:* www.hilton.com/hotels/ARLAHHF	Arlington	TX	76006	817-640-3322	633-1430
Holiday Inn Arlington 1507 N Watson Rd *TF:* 800-465-4329	Arlington	TX	76006	817-640-7712	640-3174
Holiday Inn Express 2451 E Randol Mill Rd *TF:* 800-465-4329	Arlington	TX	76011	817-640-5454	652-0763
Homestead Village North 1221 N Watson Rd *TF:* 888-782-9473	Arlington	TX	76006	817-633-7588	633-2778
Homestead Village South 1980 Pleasant Ridge Rd	Arlington	TX	76015	817-465-8500	465-8552
Howard Johnson 117 S Watson Rd *TF:* 800-446-4656	Arlington	TX	76010	817-633-4000	633-4931
Inn Towne Lodge 1181 N Watson Rd *TF:* 800-441-1651	Arlington	TX	76011	817-649-0993	649-0738
Kings Inn Motel 1717 E Division St	Arlington	TX	76011	817-277-6311	277-6311
La Quinta Inn & Conference Center 825 N Watson Rd *TF:* 800-531-5900	Arlington	TX	76011	817-640-4142	649-7864
Lexington Hotel Suites 700 E Lamar Blvd *TF:* 800-927-8483	Arlington	TX	76011	817-265-7711	861-9633
Lexington Suites Arlington 1607 N Watson Rd *TF:* 800-640-4445	Arlington	TX	76006	817-640-4444	640-4494
Marriott Arlington 1500 Convention Ctr Dr *TF:* 800-228-9290 ■ *Web:* marriotthotels.com/DFWSO	Arlington	TX	76011	817-261-8200	548-2873
Motel 6 2626 E Randol Mill Rd *TF:* 800-466-8356	Arlington	TX	76011	817-649-0147	649-7130
Park Inn Limited 703 Benge Dr *TF:* 800-437-7275	Arlington	TX	76013	817-860-2323	795-5228
Radisson Suites Hotel 700 Ave H E *TF:* 800-333-3333	Arlington	TX	76011	817-640-0440	649-2480
Ramada Limited 2001 E Copeland Rd *TF:* 800-272-6232	Arlington	TX	76011	817-461-1122	860-5832
Residence Inn 1050 Brookhollow Plaza Dr *TF:* 800-331-3131 ■ *Web:* www.residenceinn.com/residenceinn/DALAR	Arlington	TX	76006	817-649-7300	649-7600
Sleep Inn 750 Six Flags Dr *TF:* 888-753-3762	Arlington	TX	76011	817-649-1010	649-8811
StudioPLUS 2420 E Lamar Blvd *TF:* 800-646-8000	Arlington	TX	76006	817-649-0021	649-2281
Travelodge 1175 N Watson Rd *TF:* 800-578-7878	Arlington	TX	76011	817-640-9139	640-0397
Value Inn 820 N Watson Rd *TF:* 800-935-8466	Arlington	TX	76011	817-640-5151	640-5151

— Restaurants —

				Phone
Al's Hamburgers (American) 1001 NE Green Oaks Blvd	Arlington	TX	76006	817-275-8918
Arc-En-Ciel (Chinese) 2208 New York Ave	Arlington	TX	76010	817-469-9999
Arlington Steak House (Steak) 1724 W Division St	Arlington	TX	76012	817-275-7881
Big Horn Brewery (American) 700 Six Flags Dr	Arlington	TX	76010	817-640-8553
Birraporetti's (Italian) 668 Lincoln Square Ctr	Arlington	TX	76011	817-265-0555
Bobby Valentine's Sports Gallery (American) 4301 S Bowen Rd	Arlington	TX	76016	817-467-9922
Bodacious Bar-B-Q (Barbecue) 1206 E Division St	Arlington	TX	76011	817-860-4248
Cacharel (French) 2221 E Lamar Blvd Suite 910	Arlington	TX	76006	817-640-9981
Cafe Acapulco (Mexican) 4001 SW Green Oaks	Arlington	TX	76016	817-483-4171
Cafe de France (French) 322 Lincoln Sq	Arlington	TX	76011	817-261-1777
Candlelite Inn Restaurant (Steak) 1202 E Division St	Arlington	TX	76011	817-275-9613
Catfish Sam's Barge (Seafood) 2735 W Division St	Arlington	TX	76012	817-275-9631

Arlington — Restaurants (Cont'd)

Name / Address	City	State	ZIP	Phone
China Pearl Restaurant (Chinese) 4101 Green Oaks Blvd W	Arlington	TX	76016	817-483-1255
Colter's BBQ & Grill (Barbecue) 1322 N Collins St	Arlington	TX	76011	817-261-1444
Conrad's (American) 2401 E Lamar	Arlington	TX	76006	817-640-3322
Country Kitchen (American) 1409 N Collins St.	Arlington	TX	76011	817-261-5663
Cozymels (Mexican) 1300 E Copeland Rd	Arlington	TX	76011	817-469-9595
Cracker Barrel (American) 4300 S Bowen Rd	Arlington	TX	76016	817-465-9583
Fox & Hound Sport Tavern (American) 1001 NE Green Oaks Blvd	Arlington	TX	76006	817-277-3591
Friday's Front Row Sports Grill (American) 1000 Ballpark Way	Arlington	TX	76011	817-265-5192
Gaylen's Bar-B-Q (Barbecue) 826 N Collins St	Arlington	TX	76011	817-277-1945
Green Oaks Chinese Cafe (Chinese) 101 NE Green Oaks	Arlington	TX	76006	817-860-8338
Hunan Garden Restaurant (Chinese) 2801 Galleria Dr	Arlington	TX	76011	817-640-5515
Jason's Deli (American) 780 Road to Six Flags W.	Arlington	TX	76012	817-860-2888
Joe's Crab Shack (Seafood) 1520 Nolan Ryan Expy	Arlington	TX	76011	817-261-4696
Kracker Seafood (Seafood) 816 N Collins St	Arlington	TX	76010	817-261-5798
La Madeleine (French) 2101 N Collins St	Arlington	TX	76011	817-459-1326
Levi Seafood Restaurant (Seafood) 1010 E Pioneer Pkwy	Arlington	TX	76010	817-274-2828
Lone Star Oyster Bar (Seafood) 780 E Road to Six Flags Suite 258	Arlington	TX	76011	817-469-6616
Mandolins (American) 700 H Ave E	Arlington	TX	76011	817-640-0440
Mariano's (Mexican) 2614 Majesty Dr	Arlington	TX	76011	817-640-5118
Moni's Pasta & Pizza (Italian) 1730 W Randol Mill Rd Suite 100	Arlington	TX	76012	817-860-6664
Owen's Family Restaurant (American) 839 N Watson Rd	Arlington	TX	76011	817-640-8027
Pappadeaux Seafood Restaurant (Seafood) 1304 E Copeland Rd	Arlington	TX	76011	817-543-0545
Peking Garden Restaurant (Chinese) 1208 S Bowen Rd	Arlington	TX	76013	817-274-8284
Piccolo Mondo (Italian) 829 E Lamar Blvd	Arlington	TX	76011	817-265-9174
Portofino Ristorante (Italian) 226 Lincoln Sq	Arlington	TX	76011	817-861-8300
Rocco's Pasta (Italian) 780 Road to Six Flags Suite 780	Arlington	TX	76011	817-265-8897
Royal Cathay (Chinese) 740 Lincoln Sq	Arlington	TX	76011	817-860-2662
Shogun Japanese Steak & Seafood House (Japanese) 851 NE Green Oaks Blvd	Arlington	TX	76006	817-261-1636
Shusmi East Indian Restaurant (Indian) 859 NE Green Oaks Blvd	Arlington	TX	76006	817-461-4525
Spices Thai Cuisine (Thai) 3701 S Cooper St Suite 131	Arlington	TX	76015	817-784-0799
Spring Creek Barbecue (Barbecue) 3608 S Cooper St	Arlington	TX	76015	817-465-0553
Star India (Indian) 703 West Park Row	Arlington	TX	76013	817-265-9020
Taste of India (Indian) 520 W Park Row	Arlington	TX	76010	817-795-6714
Terrace Bistro (American) 1500 Convention Center Dr	Arlington	TX	76011	817-261-8200
Texas Land & Cattle Co (Steak) 2009 E Copeland Rd	Arlington	TX	76011	817-461-1500
Tia's Tex Mex (Mexican) 1301 N Collins St	Arlington	TX	76011	817-469-1013
Tippin's Restaurant (American) 3321 S Cooper St	Arlington	TX	76015	817-467-7437
Trail Dust Steakhouse (Steak) 2300 E Lamar Blvd	Arlington	TX	76006	817-640-6411

— Goods and Services —

SHOPPING

Name / Address	City	State	ZIP	Phone	Fax
Antique Marketplace of Arlington 3500 S Cooper St	Arlington	TX	76015	817-467-7030	468-7719
Coomers Craft Mall 2805 W Park Row Dr	Arlington	TX	76013	817-795-4433	
Cooper Street Craft Mall 1701 S Cooper St	Arlington	TX	76010	817-261-3184	861-4470
Festival Marketplace Mall 2900 Pioneer Pkwy	Arlington	TX	76010	817-213-1000	213-1010
Lincoln Square Hwy 157 & I-30	Arlington	TX	76011	817-265-5233	265-0982
Parks at Arlington 3811 S Cooper St Suite 2206	Arlington	TX	76015	817-467-0200	468-5356
Six Flags Mall 2911 E Division St	Arlington	TX	76011	817-640-1641	649-1825

BANKS

Name / Address	City	State	ZIP	Phone	Fax
Arlington National Bank 5901 S Cooper St	Arlington	TX	76017	817-468-3222	472-9577
Bank of America 1206 S Bowen Rd *TF:* 800-247-6262	Arlington	TX	76013	817-276-6800	276-6817
Bank of America Texas 925 N Collins St *TF:* 800-247-6262	Arlington	TX	76010	817-261-1013	261-1012
Bank One 1301 S Bowen Rd	Arlington	TX	76013	817-548-3000	548-3074
Bank United of Texas 1400 S Bowen Rd	Arlington	TX	76013	817-261-3111	261-3166
Colonial Savings 1605 S Bowen Rd	Arlington	TX	76013	817-860-7331	548-1875
Comerica Bank Texas 4200 S Cooper St	Arlington	TX	76015	817-339-6201	339-6237
First International Bank 2206 S Collins St	Arlington	TX	76010	817-261-5585	261-5575
First Savings Bank 301 S Center St Suite 120	Arlington	TX	76010	817-861-3633	861-9282
First State Bank of Texas 1889 Brown Blvd	Arlington	TX	76006	817-608-2400	608-2407
Frost National Bank 1881 N Ballpark Way	Arlington	TX	76006	817-377-6580	377-6589
Guaranty Federal Bank 100 E Abram St	Arlington	TX	76010	817-275-3258	460-3891
Northwest National Bank of Arlington 610 W Randol Mill Rd	Arlington	TX	76011	817-860-2061	261-7668
Norwest Bank 201 E Abram St *TF:* 800-224-7334	Arlington	TX	76010	817-347-8600	347-8647
Southtrust Bank 1521 N Cooper St Suite 100	Arlington	TX	76011	817-277-6565	277-0058
Wells Fargo Bank Little Rd & I-Hwy 20 *TF:* 800-869-3557	Arlington	TX	76017	817-478-9271	478-9465

BUSINESS SERVICES

Name	Phone
DHL Worldwide Express	800-225-5345
Federal Express	800-238-5355
Interim Personnel Services	817-335-6333
Kelly Services	817-649-0043
Kinko's	817-543-0833
Manpower Temporary Services	817-277-7522
Olsten Staffing Services	817-265-6695
Post Office	800-222-1811
UPS	800-742-5877

— Media —

PUBLICATIONS

Name / Address	City	State	ZIP	Phone	Fax
Arlington Morning News‡ 1112 Copeland Rd Suite 400	Arlington	TX	76011	817-461-6397	436-4140

‡Daily newspapers

TELEVISION

Name / Address	City	State	ZIP	Phone	Fax
KDAF-TV Ch 33 (WB) 8001 John Carpenter Fwy *Web:* www.wb33.com	Dallas	TX	75247	214-640-3300	252-3379
KDFW-TV Ch 4 (Fox) 400 N Griffin St	Dallas	TX	75202	214-720-4444	720-3263
KDTN-TV Ch 2 (PBS) 3000 Harry Hines Blvd	Dallas	TX	75201	214-871-1390	754-0635
KERA-TV Ch 13 (PBS) 3000 Harry Hines Blvd *Web:* www.kera.org	Dallas	TX	75201	214-871-1390	740-9369
KTVT-TV Ch 11 (CBS) 5233 Bridge St *Web:* www.ktvt.com	Fort Worth	TX	76103	817-451-1111	496-7739
KTXA-TV Ch 21 (UPN) 301 N Market Suite 700 *Web:* www.paramountstations.com/KTXA	Dallas	TX	75202	214-743-2100	743-2121
KXAS-TV Ch 5 (NBC) 3900 Barnett St *Web:* www.kxas.com	Fort Worth	TX	76103	817-429-5555	654-6325
WFAA-TV Ch 8 (ABC) 606 Young St Communications Ctr *Web:* www.wfaa.com	Dallas	TX	75202	214-748-9631	977-6585

RADIO

Name / Address	City	State	ZIP	Phone	Fax
KBFB-FM 97.9 MHz (AC) 4131 N Central Expy Suite 1200 *Web:* www.kbfb.com ■ *E-mail:* kbfb@kbfb.com	Dallas	TX	75204	214-528-5500	528-0747
KCBI-FM 90.9 MHz (Rel) PO Box 619000	Dallas	TX	75261	817-792-3800	277-9929
KDMX-FM 102.9 MHz (AC) 14001 N Dallas Pkwy Suite 1210	Dallas	TX	75240	972-991-1029	448-1029
KEGL-FM 97.1 MHz (Rock) 14001 N Dallas Pkwy Suite 1210 *Web:* www.kegl.com	Dallas	TX	75240	972-869-9700	263-9710
KERA-FM 90.1 MHz (NPR) 3000 Harry Hines Blvd. *Web:* www.kera.org/ ■ *E-mail:* kerafm@metronet.com	Dallas	TX	75201	214-871-1390	740-9369
KFJZ-AM 870 kHz (Span) 2214 E 4th St	Fort Worth	TX	76102	817-336-7175	338-1205
KKDA-AM 730 kHz (Oldies) PO Box 530860	Grand Prairie	TX	75053	972-263-9911	558-0010
KLTY-FM 94.1 MHz (Rel) 7700 Carpenter Fwy *Web:* www.klty.com ■ *E-mail:* klty@onramp.net	Dallas	TX	75247	214-630-9400	630-0060
KLUV-FM 98.7 MHz (Oldies) 4131 N Central Expy Suite 700 *Web:* www.kluv.com ■ *E-mail:* kluv@ix.netcom.com	Dallas	TX	75204	214-526-9870	443-1570
KPLX-FM 99.5 MHz (Ctry) 3500 Maple Ave Suite 1600	Dallas	TX	75219	214-526-2400	520-4343
KRLD-AM 1080 kHz (N/T) 1080 Ballpark Way *Web:* www.krld.com	Arlington	TX	76011	817-543-5400	543-5572
KSCS-FM 96.3 MHz (Ctry) 2221 E Lamar Blvd Suite 400 *Web:* www.kscs.com	Arlington	TX	76006	817-640-1963	654-9227
KTNO-AM 1440 kHz (Rel) 3105 Arkansas Ln	Arlington	TX	76016	817-469-1540	261-2137
KTXQ-FM 102.1 MHz (Oldies) 4131 N Central Expy Suite 1200 *Web:* www.ktxq.com	Dallas	TX	75204	214-528-5500	528-0747
KYNG-FM 105.3 MHz (Ctry) 12201 Merit Dr Suite 930 *Web:* www.young-country.com	Dallas	TX	75251	972-716-7800	716-7835

Arlington — Radio (Cont'd)

	Phone	Fax
WBAP-AM 820 kHz (N/T) 2221 E Lamar Blvd Suite 400 ... Arlington TX 76006 *Web:* www.wbap.com	817-640-1963	654-9227

— Colleges/Universities —

	Phone	Fax
Arlington Baptist College 3001 W Division St ... Arlington TX 76012	817-461-8741	274-1138
ITT Technical Institute 551 Ryan Plaza Dr ... Arlington TX 76011 *Web:* www.itttech.edu	817-794-5100	275-8446
Tarrant County Junior College Southeast Campus 2100 TCJC Pkwy ... Arlington TX 76018 *Web:* www.tcjc.cc.tx.us/se_campusindx.html	817-515-3100	515-3182
University of Texas Arlington 701 S Nedderman Dr ... Arlington TX 76019 *TF Admissions:* 800-687-2882 ■ *Web:* www.uta.edu	817-272-2011	272-3435

— Hospitals —

	Phone	Fax
Arlington Memorial Hospital 800 W Randol Mill Rd ... Arlington TX 76012	817-548-6100	548-6357
Medical Center Arlington 3301 Matlock Rd ... Arlington TX 76015	817-465-3241	472-4878

— Attractions —

	Phone	Fax
Air Combat School 921 Six Flags Dr Suite 117 ... Arlington TX 76011	817-640-1886	
American Airlines CR Smith Museum 4601 Hwy 360 at FAA Rd ... Fort Worth TX 76155	817-967-1560	967-5737
Antique Sewing Machine Museum 804 W Abram St ... Arlington TX 76013	817-275-0971	
Arlington Museum of Art 201 W Main St ... Arlington TX 76010	817-275-4600	860-4800
Arlington Skatium 5515 S Cooper St ... Arlington TX 76017	817-784-6222	784-6481
Ballpark in Arlington 1000 Ballpark Way ... Arlington TX 76011	817-273-5222	273-5174
Creative Arts Theatre 1100 W Randol Mill Rd ... Arlington TX 76012 *Web:* www.creativearts.org ■ *E-mail:* cats@azone.net	817-861-2287	274-0793
Fielder House Museum 1616 W Abram St ... Arlington TX 76013	817-460-4001	460-1315
Hurricane Harbor 1800 E Lamar Blvd ... Arlington TX 76006	817-265-3356	265-9892
Johnnie High's Country Music Revue 224 N Center St ... Arlington TX 76011 **Fax Area Code:* 817	800-540-5127	460-3913*
Johnson Plantation Cemetery & Log Cabins 512 W Arkansas Ln ... Arlington TX 76014 **Fax Area Code:* 817	800-433-5374	460-1315*
Lake Arlington 6300 W Arkansas La ... Arlington TX 76016	817-451-6860	451-4688
Legends of the Game Baseball Museum 1000 Ballpark Way ... Arlington TX 76011	817-273-5023	273-5093
Mill Randol Park 1901 W Randol Mill Rd ... Arlington TX 76012	817-459-5473	
Palace of Wax & Ripley's Believe It or Not! 601 E Safari Pkwy ... Grand Prairie TX 75050 *Web:* www.tourtexas.com/ripleys ■ *E-mail:* lowcpm@onramp.net	972-263-2391	263-5954
River Legacy Living Science Center 703 NW Green Oaks Blvd ... Arlington TX 76006 *Web:* www.riverlegacy.com ■ *E-mail:* rlegacy@arlington.net	817-860-6752	860-1595
Six Flags Over Texas 2201 Road to Six Flags ... Arlington TX 76011 *Web:* www.sixflags.com/texas	817-640-8900	530-6040
Sports Legacy Art Gallery 1000 Ballpark Way Suite 122 ... Arlington TX 76011 *TF:* 800-659-9631	817-461-1994	460-6068
Stovall Park 2800 W Sublett Rd ... Arlington TX 76017	817-459-5473	
Theatre Arlington 305 W Main St ... Arlington TX 76010 *Web:* www.theatrearlington.org ■ *E-mail:* theatrearlington@theatrearlington.org	817-275-7661	275-3370
Traders Village 2602 Mayfield Rd ... Grand Prairie TX 75052 *Web:* www.tradersvillage.com/gp1.html	972-647-2331	647-8585
Vandergriff Park 2801 Matlock Rd ... Arlington TX 76015	817-459-5473	
Veterans Park 3600 W Arkansas Ln ... Arlington TX 76016	817-459-5473	

SPORTS TEAMS & FACILITIES

	Phone	Fax
Ballpark in Arlington 1000 Ballpark Way Suite 400 ... Arlington TX 76011 *Web:* www.texasrangers.com/99site/pages/ballpark/index.html	817-273-5222	273-5264
Texas Rangers 1000 Ballpark Way Ballpark at Arlington ... Arlington TX 76011 *TF:* 888-968-3927 ■ *Web:* www.texasrangers.com	817-273-5100	273-5174
Texas Toros (soccer) Freeman St Old Panther Stadium ... Duncanville TX 75116 *E-mail:* txtoros@airmail.com	214-891-7059	891-8117

— Events —

	Phone
Auto Swap Meet (early June)	972-647-2331
Cardboard Boat Regatta (mid-April)	817-860-6752
Celebration of Lights (early-December)	817-459-6122
Country at Heart Art & Craft Show (early August)	817-459-5000
Fourth of July Celebration (July 4)	817-459-6100
International Week (late March-early April)	817-272-2355
National Championship Indian Pow Wow (early September)	972-647-2331
Neil Sperry's All Garden Show (late February-early March)	817-459-5000
Semana de Cultura (early April)	817-272-2099
Taste of Arlington (mid-September)	817-459-5000
Texas Indian Market (late March)	817-459-5000
Texas Scottish Festival & Games (early June)	817-654-2293
Yacht Club Regatta (early May)	817-275-8074
Young Country Christmas Fireworks to Music (late November)	214-855-1881

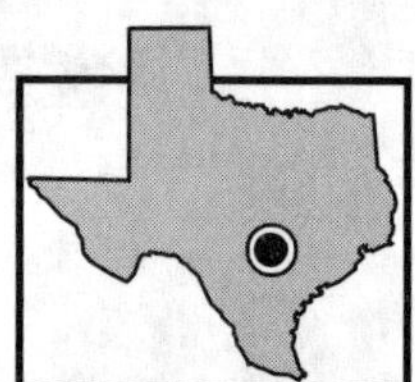

Austin

Nicknamed the "live music capital of the world," Austin's musical heritage includes Stevie Ray Vaughn, Janis Joplin, Willie Nelson, Jerry Jeff Walker, and The Fabulous Thunderbirds. The center of the music district is Old Pecan Street (Sixth Street), a nine-block historic area with restaurants, clubs, and shops. Annual musical events feature every style of music, from rock to jazz, and free lakeside concerts are held at Auditorium Shores year round. From April to October, 1.5 million bats make their own music at dusk as they emerge en masse from under the Congress Avenue Bridge.

Population	552,434	**Longitude**	97-74-28 W
Area (Land)	213.7 sq mi	**County**	Travis
Area (Water)	6.9 sq mi	**Time Zone**	CST
Elevation	501 ft	**Area Code/s**	512
Latitude	30-26-69 N		

— Average Temperatures and Precipitation —

TEMPERATURES

	Jan	Feb	Mar	Apr	May	Jun	Jul	Aug	Sep	Oct	Nov	Dec
High	59	63	72	79	85	91	95	96	91	82	72	62
Low	39	42	51	60	67	72	74	74	70	60	50	41

PRECIPITATION

	Jan	Feb	Mar	Apr	May	Jun	Jul	Aug	Sep	Oct	Nov	Dec
Inches	1.7	2.2	1.9	2.6	4.8	3.7	2.0	2.1	3.3	3.4	2.4	1.9

— Important Phone Numbers —

	Phone		Phone
AAA	512-335-5222	**HotelDocs**	800-468-3537
American Express Travel	512-452-8166	**Poison Control Center**	800-764-7661
Emergency	911	**Time/Temp**	512-973-3555
Highway Conditions	800-452-9292	**Weather**	512-451-2424

Austin (Cont'd)

— Information Sources —

				Phone	Fax
Austin City Hall PO Box 1088 *Web:* www.ci.austin.tx.us	Austin	TX	78767	512-499-2000	499-2832
Austin Convention & Visitors Bureau 201 E 2nd St *TF:* 800-926-2282 ■ *Web:* www.austin360.com/acvb	Austin	TX	78701	512-474-5171	404-4383
Austin Convention Center 500 E Cesar Chavez St *Web:* www.convention.ci.austin.tx.us	Austin	TX	78701	512-476-5461	404-4416
Austin Mayor PO Box 1088	Austin	TX	78767	512-499-2250	499-2337
Austin Planning & Development Dept PO Box 1088 *Web:* www.ci.austin.tx.us/planning	Austin	TX	78767	512-499-2613	499-2269
Austin Public Library PO Box 2287 *Web:* www.ci.austin.tx.us/library ■ *E-mail:* aplmail@library.ci.austin.tx.us	Austin	TX	78768	512-499-7300	499-7403
Better Business Bureau Serving Central Texas 2101 S IH 35 Suite 302 *Web:* www.centraltx.bbb.org	Austin	TX	78741	512-445-2911	445-2096
Greater Austin Chamber of Commerce PO Box 1967 *Web:* www.austin-chamber.org	Austin	TX	78767	512-478-9383	478-6389
Travis County PO Box 1748 *Web:* www.co.travis.tx.us	Austin	TX	78767	512-473-9188	473-9075

On-Line Resources

4Austin.com	www.4austin.com
About.com Guide to Austin	austin.about.com/local/southwestus/austin
Anthill City Guide Austin	www.anthill.com/city.asp?city=austin
Area Guide Austin	austin.areaguides.net
Arrive @ Austin	www.arrive-at.com/austin/
Austin Axis	www.awpi.com/AustinAxis
Austin Chronicle	www.auschron.com
Austin City Limits	www.pbs.org/klru/austin
Austin CityGuide	www.austincityguide.com
Austin Metro Entertainment	www.austinmetro.com
Austin Music Web	www.ddg.com/AMW/
Austin Relocation Center	www.io.com/house/tour.html
Austin Virtual Restaurant Mall	www.virtual-restaurants.com
Austin Web Page	www.austinwebpage.com
Austin.Data.Net	austin.data.net/
Boulevards Austin	www.boulevards.com/austin/
Capitol City Arts & Entertainment Magazine	www.capitol-city.com/
City Knowledge Austin	www.cityknowledge.com/tx_austin.htm
CitySearch Austin	austin.citysearch.com
DigitalCity Austin	home.digitalcity.com/austin
Excite.com Austin City Guide	www.excite.com/travel/countries/united_states/texas/austin
HotelGuide Austin	hotelguide.net/austin/
Insiders' Guide to Austin	www.insiders.com/austin/
LDS iAmerica Austin	austin.iamerica.net
Metropolitan Austin Interactive Network	www.main.org
NITC Travelbase City Guide Austin	www.travelbase.com/auto/guides/austin-area-tx.html
Onroute Destinations Austin	www.onroute.com/destinations/texas/austin.html
Virtual Voyages Austin	www.virtualvoyages.com/usa/tx/austin/austin.sht
Yahoo! Austin	austin.yahoo.com

— Transportation Services —

AIRPORTS

■ Robert Mueller Municipal Airport (AUS)

	Phone
4 miles NE of downtown (approx 15 minutes)	512-472-5439

Web: www.ci.austin.tx.us/airport

Airport Transportation

	Phone
Capitol Metropolitan Transit Authority $.50 fare to downtown	512-474-1200
Taxi $8 fare to downtown	512-472-1111

Commercial Airlines

	Phone		Phone
AeroMexico	800-237-6639	**Delta**	800-221-1212
America West	800-235-9292	**Northwest**	800-225-2525
American	800-433-7300	**Southwest**	512-476-6354
Continental	512-477-6716	**TWA**	800-221-2000
Continental Express	800-525-0280	**United**	800-241-6522

Charter Airlines

	Phone		Phone
Austin Jet	830-598-1010	**Berry Aviation**	800-229-2379

CAR RENTALS

	Phone		Phone
Alamo	512-474-2922	**Hertz**	512-478-9321
Avis	512-476-6137	**National**	512-476-6189
Budget	512-478-9945	**Thrifty**	512-474-2985
Dollar	512-322-9881		

LIMO/TAXI

	Phone		Phone
Ace Taxi	512-244-1133	**Austin Cab**	512-478-2222
American/Yellow/Checker Cab	512-472-1111	**Carey Limousine**	512-328-2600
Austin Area Limousine	512-386-8600	**Roy's Taxi**	512-482-0000

MASS TRANSIT

	Phone
Capitol Metropolitan Transit Authority $.50 Base fare	512-474-1200

RAIL/BUS

				Phone
Austin Amtrak Station 250 N Lamar Blvd	Austin	TX	78703	512-476-5684
Greyhound/Trailways Bus Station 916 E Koenig Ln	Austin	TX	78751	800-231-2222

— Accommodations —

HOTELS, MOTELS, RESORTS

				Phone	Fax
Barton Creek Conference Resort 8212 Barton Club Dr *TF:* 800-336-6158 ■ *Web:* www.bartoncreek.com	Austin	TX	78735	512-329-4000	329-4597
Best Western 7928 Gessner Dr. *TF:* 800-468-3708	Austin	TX	78753	512-339-7311	339-3687
Best Western Seville Plaza Inn 4323 S IH-35 *TF:* 800-528-1234	Austin	TX	78744	512-447-5511	443-8055
Budget Inn 9106 N IH-35 *TF:* 800-446-4656	Austin	TX	78753	512-837-7900	837-7964
Clarion Inn & Suites Conference Center 2200 S IH-35 *TF:* 800-434-7378	Austin	TX	78704	512-444-0561	444-7254
Comfort Inn 700 Delmar Ave *TF:* 800-228-5150	Austin	TX	78752	512-302-5576	302-5576
Courtyard by Marriott 5660 N IH-35 *TF:* 800-321-2211 ■ *Web:* courtyard.com/AUSCY	Austin	TX	78751	512-458-2340	458-8525
Days Inn North 820 E Anderson Ln *TF:* 800-329-7466	Austin	TX	78752	512-835-4311	835-1740
Days Inn University 3105 N IH-35 *TF:* 800-725-7666	Austin	TX	78722	512-478-1631	478-1631
Doubletree Guest Suites 303 W 15th St *TF:* 800-222-8733 ■ *Web:* www.doubletreehotels.com/DoubleT/Hotel81/85/85Main.htm	Austin	TX	78701	512-478-7000	478-5103
Doubletree Hotel 6505 N IH-35 *TF:* 800-222-8733 ■ *Web:* www.doubletreehotels.com/DoubleT/Hotel81/86/86Main.htm	Austin	TX	78752	512-454-3737	454-6915
Driskill Hotel 604 Brazos St. *TF:* 800-252-9367 ■ *Web:* www.driskillhotel.com	Austin	TX	78701	512-474-5911	474-2214
Drury Inn Highland Mall 919 E Koenig Ln *TF:* 800-378-7946	Austin	TX	78751	512-454-1144	454-1144
Drury Inn North 6711 N IH-35 *TF:* 800-378-7946	Austin	TX	78752	512-467-9500	467-9500
Econo Lodge 6201 Hwy 290 E *TF:* 800-553-2666	Austin	TX	78723	512-458-4759	458-4759
Embassy Suites Downtown 300 S Congress Ave *TF:* 800-362-2779	Austin	TX	78704	512-469-9000	480-9164
Embassy Suites North 5901 N IH-35 *TF:* 800-362-2779	Austin	TX	78723	512-454-8004	454-9047
Fairfield Inn by Marriott 959 Reinli St. *TF:* 800-228-2800 ■ *Web:* fairfieldinn.com/AUSFI	Austin	TX	78751	512-302-5550	454-8270
Four Seasons 98 San Jacinto Blvd *TF:* 800-332-3442 ■ *Web:* www.fourseasons.com/locations/Austin	Austin	TX	78701	512-478-4500	478-3117
Georgian Suites 8005 Georgian Dr *Web:* www.walji.com/georgian ■ *E-mail:* travelodge@walji.com	Austin	TX	78753	512-837-3379	837-3579
Habitat Suites 500 Highland Mall Blvd. *TF:* 800-535-4663 ■ *Web:* habitatsuites.com	Austin	TX	78752	512-467-6000	467-6000
Hampton Inn 7619 N IH-35 *TF:* 800-426-7866	Austin	TX	78752	512-452-3300	452-3124

Austin — Hotels, Motels, Resorts (Cont'd)

				Phone	Fax
Hawthorn Suites Austin Central					
935 La Posada Dr	Austin	TX	78752	512-459-3335	467-9736
TF: 800-527-1133 ■ *E-mail:* suite@onr.com					
Hawthorn Suites Northwest 8888 Tallwood Dr	Austin	TX	78759	512-343-0008	343-6532
TF: 800-527-1133					
Hawthorn Suites South 4020 S IH-35	Austin	TX	78704	512-440-7722	440-4815
TF: 800-527-1133					
Hilton Hotel & Towers					
6000 Middle Fiskville Rd	Austin	TX	78752	512-451-5757	467-7644
TF: 800-347-0330 ■ *Web:* www.hilton.com/hotels/AUSHIHF					
Holiday Inn Airport 6911 N IH-35	Austin	TX	78752	512-459-4251	459-9274
TF: 800-465-4329 ■ *Web:* www.holidayinnaustin.com					
■ *E-mail:* holiday-austin@travelbase.com					
Holiday Inn Express 7622 N IH-35	Austin	TX	78752	512-467-1701	451-0966
TF: 800-465-4329					
Holiday Inn Northwest Plaza					
8901 Business Pk Dr	Austin	TX	78759	512-343-0888	343-6891
TF: 800-465-4329					
■ *Web:* www.basshotels.com/holiday-inn/?_franchisee=AUSNW					
Holiday Inn South 3401 S IH-35	Austin	TX	78741	512-448-2444	448-4999
TF: 800-465-4329					
■ *Web:* www.basshotels.com/holiday-inn/?_franchisee=AUSSO					
■ *E-mail:* gmaus@lodgian.com					
Holiday Inn Townlake 20 N IH-35	Austin	TX	78701	512-472-8211	472-4636
TF: 800-465-4329					
Hyatt Regency Austin 208 Barton Springs Rd	Austin	TX	78704	512-477-1234	480-2069
TF: 800-233-1234					
■ *Web:* www.hyatt.com/usa/austin/hotels/hotel_ausra.html					
La Quinta Motor Inn 1603 E Oltorf St	Austin	TX	78741	512-447-6661	447-1744
TF: 800-687-6667					
La Quinta Motor Inn Ben White 4200 S IH-35	Austin	TX	78745	512-443-1774	447-1555
TF: 800-687-6667					
La Quinta Motor Inn Highland Mall					
5812 N IH-35	Austin	TX	78751	512-459-4381	452-3917
TF: 800-687-6667					
La Quinta Motor Inn North 7100 N IH-35	Austin	TX	78752	512-452-9401	452-0856
TF: 800-687-6667					
Lago Vista Resort 1918 American Dr	Austin	TX	78645	512-267-1161	267-1164
TF: 800-288-1882 ■ *Web:* www.lagovista.com					
Lake Austin Spa Resort 1705 S Quinlan Pk Rd	Austin	TX	78732	512-266-2444	266-1572
TF: 800-847-5637 ■ *Web:* www.lakeaustin.com					
■ *E-mail:* info@lakeaustin.com					
Lakeway Inn 101 Lakeway Dr	Austin	TX	78734	512-261-6600	261-7311
TF: 800-525-3929 ■ *Web:* www.lakewayinn.com/					
Marriott at the Capitol 701 E 11th St	Austin	TX	78701	512-478-1111	478-3700
TF: 800-228-9290 ■ *Web:* marriotthotels.com/AUSDT					
Motel 6 Austin Airport 5330 N IH-35	Austin	TX	78751	512-467-9111	206-0573
TF: 800-466-8356					
Northpark Executive Suite Hotel					
7685 Northcross Dr	Austin	TX	78757	512-452-9391	459-4433
TF: 800-851-9111					
Omni Hotel 4140 Governors Row	Austin	TX	78744	512-448-2222	383-2729*
**Fax:* Sales ■ *TF:* 800-843-6664					
Omni Hotel 700 San Jacinto Blvd	Austin	TX	78701	512-476-3700	397-4888
TF: 800-843-6664 ■ *E-mail:* omniaus@realtime.net					
Quality Inn Airport 909 E Koenig Ln	Austin	TX	78751	512-452-4200	374-0652
TF: 800-228-5151					
Radisson Hotel Austin 111 Cesar Chavez St	Austin	TX	78701	512-478-9611	473-8399
TF: 800-333-3333					
Ramada Inn South 1212 W Ben White Blvd	Austin	TX	78704	512-447-0151	441-2051
TF: 800-272-6232					
Ramada Limited Airport 5526 N IH-35	Austin	TX	78751	512-451-7001	451-3028
TF: 800-228-2828					
Red Lion Hotel 6121 N IH-35	Austin	TX	78752	512-323-5466	453-1945
TF: 800-733-5466					
Red Roof Inn 8210 N IH-35	Austin	TX	78753	512-835-2200	339-9043
TF: 800-843-7663					
Renaissance Austin Hotel					
9721 Arboretum Blvd	Austin	TX	78759	512-343-2626	346-7953
TF: 800-228-9290					
Sheraton Four Points Hotel 7800 N IH-35	Austin	TX	78753	512-836-8520	837-0897
TF: 800-325-3535					
StudioPLUS 6300 Hwy 290 E	Austin	TX	78723	512-452-0880	452-7730
TF: 800-646-8000					
Sumner Suites 7522 N IH-35	Austin	TX	78752	512-323-2121	323-5118
TF: 800-747-8483					
Super 8 Inn & Suites 8128 N IH-35	Austin	TX	78753	512-339-1300	339-0820
TF: 800-800-8000					

— Restaurants —

				Phone
Ararat (Middle Eastern) 111 E North Loop	Austin	TX	78751	512-419-1692
Austin Club (Continental) 110 E 9th St	Austin	TX	78701	512-477-9496
Basil's (Italian) 900 W 10th St	Austin	TX	78703	512-477-5576
Bitter End Bistro & Brewery (American) 311 Colorado St	Austin	TX	78701	512-478-2337
Brio Vista (Southwest) 9400 B Arboretum Blvd	Austin	TX	78769	512-342-2642
Cafe at the Four Seasons (American) 98 San Jacinto Blvd	Austin	TX	78701	512-478-4500
Cafe Josie (Seafood) 1200-B W 6th St	Austin	TX	78703	512-322-9226
Calabash (Caribbean) 2015 Manor Rd	Austin	TX	78722	512-478-4857
Carmelo's Italian Restaurant (Italian) 504 E 5th St	Austin	TX	78701	512-477-7497
Chez Nous (French) 510 Neches St	Austin	TX	78701	512-473-2413
Chuy's Hula Hut (Mexican/Polynesian)				
3825 Lake Austin Blvd	Austin	TX	78703	512-476-4852
Cisco's (Mexican) 1511 E 6th St	Austin	TX	78702	512-478-2420
City Grill (Steak/Seafood) 401 Sabine St	Austin	TX	78701	512-479-0817
County Line (Barbecue) 6500 W Bee Caves Rd	Austin	TX	78746	512-327-1742
Dog & Duck Pub (English) 406 W 17th St	Austin	TX	78701	512-479-0598
Eastside Cafe (American) 2113 Manor Rd	Austin	TX	78722	512-476-5858
Emerald Cafe (Irish) 13614 Hwy 71 W	Austin	TX	78734	512-263-2147
Fado's Irish Pub (Irish) 214 W 4th St	Austin	TX	78701	512-457-0172
Fonda San Miguel (Mexican) 2330 W North Loop Blvd	Austin	TX	78756	512-459-4121
Gilligan's Seafood (Caribbean) 407 Colorado St	Austin	TX	78701	512-474-7474
Granite Cafe (New American) 2905 San Gabriel St	Austin	TX	78705	512-472-6483
Green Pastures (Continental) 811 W Live Oak	Austin	TX	78704	512-444-4747
Guero's (Mexican) 1412 S Congress Ave	Austin	TX	78704	512-447-7688
Hunan Lion (Chinese) 4006 S Lamar Blvd	Austin	TX	78704	512-447-3388
Iron Cactus (Southwest) 606 Trinity St	Austin	TX	78701	512-472-9240
Iron Works Barbecue (Barbecue) 100 Red River St	Austin	TX	78701	512-478-4855
Jazz Restaurant (Cajun/Creole) 214 E 6th St	Austin	TX	78701	512-479-0474
Web: www.jazzkitchen.com				
Jean Lucs French Bistro (French) 705 Colorado St	Austin	TX	78701	512-494-0033
Jeffery's Restaurant (American) 1204 W Lynn St	Austin	TX	78703	512-477-5584
Kyoto Japanese Restaurant (Japanese)				
315 Congress Ave Suite 200	Austin	TX	78701	512-482-9010
Las Manitas (Mexican) 211 Congress Ave	Austin	TX	78701	512-472-9357
Louie's 106 (Mediterranean) 106 E 6th St	Austin	TX	78701	512-476-2010
Mars (International) 1610 San Antonio St	Austin	TX	78701	512-472-3901
Mesa Hills Cafe (Continental) 3435 Greystone Dr	Austin	TX	78731	512-345-7423
Mezzaluna (Italian) 310 Colorado St	Austin	TX	78701	512-472-6770
Miguel's La Bodega (Mexican) 415 Colorado St	Austin	TX	78701	512-472-2369
Oasis The (American) 6550 Comanche Trail	Austin	TX	78732	512-266-2442
Osaka Restaurant (Japanese)				
13492 Research Blvd Suite 160	Austin	TX	78701	512-918-8012
Paos Mandarin House (Chinese) 800 Brazos St Suite 3100	Austin	TX	78701	512-482-8100
Salt Lick (Barbecue) FM 1826	Driftwood	TX	78619	512-858-4959
Satay (Malaysian) 3202 W Anderson Ln	Austin	TX	78757	512-467-6731
Scholz Garten (German) 1607 San Jacinto Blvd	Austin	TX	78701	512-474-1958
Shoreline Grill (Seafood) 98 San Jacinto Blvd	Austin	TX	78701	512-477-3300
Web: www.shorelinegrill.com				
Stubb's Bar-B-Q (Barbecue) 801 Red River St	Austin	TX	78701	512-480-8341
Taj Palace (Indian) 6700 Middle Fiskville Rd	Austin	TX	78752	512-452-9959
Texas Chili Parlor (Tex Mex) 1409 Lavaca St	Austin	TX	78701	512-472-2828
Thai Kitchen (Thai) 803-A E William Cannon Dr	Austin	TX	78745	512-445-4844
Thai Passion (Thai) 620 Congress Ave	Austin	TX	78701	512-472-1244
Threadgill's (American) 6416 N Lamar Blvd	Austin	TX	78752	512-451-5440
Web: www.threadgills.com/				
Trattoria Grande (Italian) 9721 Arboretum Blvd	Austin	TX	78759	512-343-2626
Waterloo Brewing Co (Southwest) 401 Guadalupe St	Austin	TX	78701	512-477-1836
West Lynn Cafe (Vegetarian) 1110 W Lynn St	Austin	TX	78703	512-482-0950
Zoot (New American) 509 Hearn St	Austin	TX	78703	512-477-6535

— Goods and Services —

SHOPPING

				Phone	Fax
23rd Street Renaissance Market					
23rd & Guadaloupe Sts	Austin	TX	78705	512-474-5171	
Arboretum The 10000 Research Blvd	Austin	TX	78759	512-338-4437	338-9252
Barton Creek Square Mall					
2901 S Capital of Texas Hwy	Austin	TX	78746	512-327-7040	328-0923
Beall's 2415 S Congress Ave	Austin	TX	78704	512-444-4711	
Dillard's 2901 Capital of Texas Hwy	Austin	TX	78746	512-327-6100	347-3462
Drag The Guadaloupe St-betw 21st & 25th Sts	Austin	TX	78705	512-474-5171	
Highland Mall 6001 Airport Blvd	Austin	TX	78752	512-451-2920	
Lakeline Mall 11200 Lakeline Mall Dr	Cedar Park	TX	78613	512-257-7467	257-0522
Northcross Mall 2525 W Anderson Ln	Austin	TX	78757	512-451-7466	451-2330
Scarbroughs 4001 N Lamar	Austin	TX	78756	512-452-4220	452-6608

BANKS

				Phone	Fax
American Bank of Commerce 816 Colorado St	Austin	TX	78701	512-473-2446	391-5550
TF: 888-793-1973 ■ *Web:* www.theabcbank.com					
Bank of America					
600 Congress Ave Suite G260	Austin	TX	78701	512-427-3200	427-3201
TF: 800-730-6000 ■ *Web:* www.bankamerica.com					

Austin — Banks (Cont'd)

Name / Address	City	State	ZIP	Phone	Fax
Bank One Texas 221 W 6th St	Austin	TX	78701	512-479-5400	479-5820
TF Cust Svc: 800-695-1111*					
Chase Bank of Texas 700 Lavaca	Austin	TX	78701	512-479-2444	479-2021
Web: www.chase.com					
Comerica Bank 804 Congress Ave Suite 100	Austin	TX	78701	512-206-6100	427-7104
TF: 800-925-2160					
Compass Bank 321 W 6th St	Austin	TX	78701	512-476-2836	421-5762
TF: 800-239-4357 ■ *Web:* www.compassweb.com					
First American Bank Texas					
2110 Boca Raton Dr	Austin	TX	78747	512-280-0001	280-0005
Frost National Bank 816 Congress Ave	Austin	TX	78701	512-473-4343	473-4750
TF: 800-562-3732					
Guaranty Federal Bank FSB 301 Congress Ave	Austin	TX	78701	512-434-1000	320-1262
NationsBank of Texas NA 501 Congress Ave	Austin	TX	78701	512-397-2200	397-3164*
**Fax:* Cust Svc ■ *TF:* 800-247-6262 ■ *Web:* www.nationsbank.com					
Norwest Bank 111 Congress Ave	Austin	TX	78701	512-344-7000	756-6755
TF: 800-224-7334 ■ *Web:* www.norwest.com					

BUSINESS SERVICES

Name	Phone	Name	Phone
Affordable Business Couriers	512-461-1453	**Kelly Services**	512-343-7006
AlphaGraphics Printshops	512-478-8981	**Kinko's**	512-452-3600
America's Skilled Personnel	512-462-1112	**Manpower Temporary Services**	512-343-2141
Corporate Express Delivery Systems	512-339-5050	**Olsten Staffing Services**	512-345-3327
Federal Express	800-238-5355	**Pony Express Courier**	512-339-2884
Ginny's Printing & Copying	512-477-9827	**Post Office**	800-725-2161
Hospitality Personnel	512-480-9191	**UPS**	800-742-5877

— Media —

PUBLICATIONS

Name / Address	City	State	ZIP	Phone	Fax
Austin American-Statesman‡ PO Box 670	Austin	TX	78767	512-445-3500	445-3679
Web: www.austin360.com ■ *E-mail:* help360@cimedia.com					
Austin Business Journal					
111 Congress Ave Suite 750	Austin	TX	78701	512-494-2500	494-2525*
**Fax:* Edit ■ *Web:* www.amcity.com/austin					
Texas Monthly PO Box 1569	Austin	TX	78767	512-320-6900	476-9007
TF: 800-759-2000 ■ *Web:* www.texasmonthly.com					

‡*Daily newspapers*

TELEVISION

Name / Address	City	State	ZIP	Phone	Fax
KEYE-TV Ch 42 (CBS) 10700 Metric Blvd	Austin	TX	78758	512-835-0042	837-6753
Web: www.k-eyetv.com ■ *E-mail:* upah@k-eyetv.com					
KLRU-TV Ch 18 (PBS) 2504-B Whitis Ave	Austin	TX	78705	512-471-4811	475-9090
Web: www.klru.org ■ *E-mail:* info@www.klru.org					
KNVA-TV Ch 54 (WB) 908 W ML King Blvd	Austin	TX	78701	512-478-5400	476-1520
Web: www.knva.com ■ *E-mail:* prog54@knva.com					
KTBC-TV Ch 7 (Fox) 119 E 10th St	Austin	TX	78701	512-476-7777	495-7060
Web: www.fox7.com ■ *E-mail:* news@fox7.com					
KVUE-TV Ch 24 (ABC) PO Box 9927	Austin	TX	78766	512-459-6521	459-6538
Web: www.kvue.com					
KXAN-TV Ch 36 (NBC) 908 W ML King Jr Blvd	Austin	TX	78701	512-476-3636	469-0630
Web: www.kxan.com ■ *E-mail:* news36@kxan.com					

RADIO

Name / Address	City	State	ZIP	Phone	Fax
KAJZ-FM 93.3 MHz (Ctry) 8309 N IH-35	Austin	TX	78753	512-832-4000	832-1579
Web: www.kjazz.com					
KAMX-FM 94.7 MHz (Alt)					
4301 Westbank Dr Bldg B Suite 350	Austin	TX	78746	512-327-9595	329-6257
Web: www.mix947.com ■ *E-mail:* mornings@mix947.com					
KASE-FM 100.7 MHz (Ctry) PO Box 380	Austin	TX	78767	512-390-5273	495-1329
TF: 800-950-5273 ■ *Web:* www.kase101.com					
KELG-AM 1440 kHz (Span)					
7524 N Lamar Ave Suite 200	Austin	TX	78752	512-453-1491	453-6809
KEYI-FM 103.5 MHz (Oldies)					
811 Barton Springs Rd Suite 100	Austin	TX	78704	512-474-9233	397-1400
Web: www.oldies103austin.com					
KFON-AM 1490 kHz (Sports)					
811 Barton Springs Rd Suite 100	Austin	TX	78704	512-474-9233	397-1400
KGSR-FM 107.1 MHz (AAA) 8309 N IH 35	Austin	TX	78753	512-832-4000	832-1579
KHFI-FM 96.7 MHz (CHR)					
811 Barton Springs Rd Suite 100	Austin	TX	78704	512-474-9233	397-1410
Web: www.khfi.com					
KIXL-AM 970 kHz (N/T)					
11615 Angus Rd Suite 120B	Austin	TX	78759	512-372-9700	372-9088
KJCE-AM 1370 kHz (Urban)					
4301 Westbank Dr Bldg B Suite 350	Austin	TX	78746	512-327-9595	329-6257
Web: www.kjuice.com					
KJFK-FM 98.9 (N/T)					
12710 Research Blvd Suite 390	Austin	TX	78759	512-331-9191	331-9933
Web: 989kjfk.com					
KKMJ-FM 95.5 MHz (AC)					
4301 Westbank Dr Bldg B Suite 350	Austin	TX	78746	512-327-9595	329-6257
Web: www.majic.com					
KLBJ-AM 590 kHz (N/T) 8309 N IH-35	Austin	TX	78753	512-832-4000	832-1579
Web: www.lbj.com/am/news.html ■ *E-mail:* klbj590@lbj.com					
KLBJ-FM 93.7 MHz (Rock) 8309 N IH-35	Austin	TX	78753	512-832-4000	832-1579
Web: www.lbj.com/fm					
KMFA-FM 89.5 MHz (Clas)					
3001 N Lamar Blvd Suite 100	Austin	TX	78705	512-476-5632	474-7463
Web: www.kmfa.org ■ *E-mail:* classical@kmfa.org					
KPEZ-FM 102.3 MHz (CR)					
811 Barton Springs Rd Suite 967	Austin	TX	78704	512-474-9233	397-1410
Web: www.z102austin.com					
KROX-FM 101.5 MHz (Rock) 8309 N IH 35	Austin	TX	78753	512-832-4000	832-1579
Web: www.krox.com					
KUT-FM 90.5 MHz (NPR)					
University of Texas Communications Bldg B	Austin	TX	78712	512-471-1631	471-3700
Web: www.kut.org					
KVET-AM 1300 kHz (Sports) PO Box 380	Austin	TX	78767	512-495-1300	495-9423
KVET-FM 98.1 MHz (Ctry) PO Box 380	Austin	TX	78767	512-495-1300	495-9423

— Colleges/Universities —

Name / Address	City	State	ZIP	Phone	Fax
Austin Community College					
5930 Middle Fiskville Rd	Austin	TX	78752	512-223-7000	483-7665
Web: www.austin.cc.tx.us					
Concordia University at Austin 3400 IH-35 N	Austin	TX	78705	512-452-7661	459-8517
TF Admissions: 800-865-4282 ■ *Web:* www.concordia.edu					
Huston-Tillotson College 900 Chicon St	Austin	TX	78702	512-505-3000	505-3190
Institute for Christian Studies					
1909 University Ave	Austin	TX	78705	512-476-2772	476-3919
Web: www.io.com/~ics/					
ITT Technical Institute					
6330 Hwy 290 E Suite 150	Austin	TX	78723	512-467-6800	467-6677
TF: 800-431-0677 ■ *Web:* www.itt-tech.edu					
Saint Edward's University					
3001 S Congress Ave	Austin	TX	78704	512-448-8500	464-8877
Web: www.stedwards.edu ■ *E-mail:* sheryls@admin.stedwards.edu					
Southwest Texas State University					
601 University Dr	San Marcos	TX	78666	512-245-2111	245-8044
TF Admissions: 800-782-7653 ■ *Web:* www.swt.edu ■ *E-mail:* fy01@swt.edu					
Southwestern University PO Box 770	Georgetown	TX	78627	512-863-6511	863-9601
TF Admissions: 800-252-3166 ■ *Web:* www.southwestern.edu					
University of Texas Austin Main Bldg Rm 1	Austin	TX	78712	512-471-3434	475-7478
Web: www.utexas.edu ■ *E-mail:* admit@utxdp.dp.utexas.edu					

— Hospitals —

Name / Address	City	State	ZIP	Phone	Fax
Austin Diagnostic Medical Center					
12221 N Mopac Expy	Austin	TX	78758	512-901-1000	901-1995
Web: www.adclinic.com					
Brackenridge Hospital 601 E 15th St	Austin	TX	78701	512-324-7000	324-7779
Central Texas Medical Center					
1301 Wonder World Dr	San Marcos	TX	78666	512-353-8979	753-3598
Saint David's Hospital 919 E 32nd St	Austin	TX	78705	512-476-7111	370-4432
Saint Davis Round Rock Medical Center					
2400 Round Rock Ave	Round Rock	TX	78681	512-341-1000	341-4882
Seton Medical Center 1201 W 38th St	Austin	TX	78705	512-324-1000	324-1141
Web: www.goodhealth.com					
South Austin Hospital 901 W Ben White Blvd	Austin	TX	78704	512-447-2211	416-6222

— Attractions —

Name / Address	City	State	ZIP	Phone	Fax
Austin Chamber Music Center					
4930 Burnet Rd Suite 203	Austin	TX	78756	512-454-7562	454-0029
Web: www.austinchambermusic.org ■ *E-mail:* info@austinchambermusic.org					
Austin Children's Museum 201 Colorado St	Austin	TX	78701	512-472-2494	472-2795
Web: www.austinkids.org					

Austin — Attractions (Cont'd)

	City	State	Zip	Phone	Fax
Austin Civic Orchestra PO Box 27132	Austin	TX	78755	512-926-8596	926-8596
Austin History Center 810 Guadalupe	Austin	TX	78701	512-499-7480	499-7483
Web: www.ci.austin.tx.us/library/lbahc.htm					
Austin Lyric Opera PO Box 984	Austin	TX	78767	512-472-5927	472-4143
TF Box Office: 800-316-7372 ■ *Web:* www.austinlyricopera.org					
Austin Museum of Art Laguna Gloria 3809 W 35th St	Austin	TX	78763	512-458-8191	454-9408
Web: www.amoa.org ■ *E-mail:* info@amoa.org					
Austin Music Hall 208 Nueces St	Austin	TX	78701	512-495-9962	263-4194
Austin Nature & Science Center 301 Nature Ctr Dr	Austin	TX	78746	512-327-8181	327-8745
Web: www.ci.austin.tx.us/nature-science					
Austin Shakespeare Festival PO Box 683	Austin	TX	78767	512-454-2273	
Web: members.aol.com/asf/ ■ *E-mail:* asf@aol.com					
Austin Symphony Orchestra 1101 Red River	Austin	TX	78701	512-476-6064	476-6242
Web: www.austinsymphony.org					
Austin Theatre for Youth PO Box 26794	Austin	TX	78755	512-459-7144	459-7451
Web: www.onr.com/user/aty ■ *E-mail:* aty@aol.com					
Austin Zoo 10807 Rawhide Trail	Austin	TX	78736	512-288-1490	288-3972
TF: 800-291-1490 ■ *Web:* www.austinzoo.com ■ *E-mail:* austinzu@aol.com					
Ballet Austin 3002 Guadalupe	Austin	TX	78705	512-476-9051	472-3073
Web: www.balletaustin.org					
Barton Springs Pool 2201 Barton Springs Rd Zilker Pk	Austin	TX	78746	512-476-9044	
Celis Brewery PO Box 141636	Austin	TX	78714	512-835-0884	835-0130
Web: www.celis.com ■ *E-mail:* celis@celis.com					
Center for Women & Their Work 1710 Lavaca St	Austin	TX	78701	512-477-1064	477-1090
Crowe's Nest Farms 10300 Taylor Ln	Manor	TX	78653	512-272-4418	272-8313
Dougherty Arts Center 1110 Barton Springs Rd	Austin	TX	78704	512-397-1468	397-1475
French Legation Museum 802 San Marcos St	Austin	TX	78702	512-472-8180	472-9457
Web: www.french-legation.mus.tx.us ■ *E-mail:* dubois@french-ligation.mus.tx.us					
George Washington Carver Museum & Cultural Art Center 1165 Angelina St	Austin	TX	78702	512-472-4809	708-1639
Governor's Mansion 1010 Colorado St	Austin	TX	78701	512-463-5518	
Helm Fine Arts Center 2900 Bunny Run	Austin	TX	78746	512-329-0964	327-1311
Hill Country Flyer Steam Train PO Box 1632	Austin	TX	78767	512-477-8468	477-8633
Web: www.main.org/flyer					
Inner Space Caverns 4200 S IH-35	Georgetown	TX	78627	512-863-5545	863-8159
Web: www.innerspace.com					
Jack S Blanton Museum of Art 23rd & San Jacinto Sts University of Texas at Austin	Austin	TX	78712	512-471-7324	471-7023
Web: www.utexas.edu/cofa/hag ■ *E-mail:* hag@www.utexas.edu					
Jourdan-Bachman Pioneer Farm 11418 Sprinkle Cut Off	Austin	TX	78754	512-837-1215	837-4503
E-mail: jbfarmer@eden.com					
Lady Bird Johnson Wildflower Center 4801 LaCrosse Ave	Austin	TX	78739	512-292-4200	292-4627
Web: www.wildflower.org/					
Lake Walter E Long Metropolitan Park Blue Bluff Rd	Austin	TX	78768	512-926-5230	
Lone Star Riverboat PO Box 160608	Austin	TX	78716	512-327-1388	329-0677
Long Emma Metropolitan Park 1706 City Park Rd	Austin	TX	78767	512-346-1831	
Lyndon B Johnson Library & Museum 2313 Red River St	Austin	TX	78705	512-916-5137	916-5171
Web: www.lbjlib.utexas.edu ■ *E-mail:* library@johnson.nara.gov					
Lyndon B Johnson National Historical Park PO Box 329	Johnson City	TX	78636	830-868-7128	868-7863
Web: www.nps.gov/lyjo/					
McKinney Falls State Park 5808 McKinney Falls Pkwy	Austin	TX	78744	512-243-1643	243-0536
Mexic-Arte Museum 419 Congress Ave	Austin	TX	78701	512-480-9373	480-8626
Web: www.main.org/mexic-arte/ ■ *E-mail:* mexicart@onr.org					
Mt Bonnell 3800 Mt Bonnell Dr	Austin	TX	78731	512-499-6700	
Neill-Cochran House 2310 San Gabriel St	Austin	TX	78705	512-478-2335	478-1865
Ney Elisabet Museum 304 E 44th St	Austin	TX	78751	512-458-2255	453-0638
O Henry Home & Museum 409 E 5th St	Austin	TX	78701	512-472-1903	472-7102
Web: www.ci.austin.tx.us/parks/ohenry.htm					
Old German Free School Building 507 E 10th St	Austin	TX	78701	512-482-0927	482-8809
Web: www.main.org/germantxn/					
Old Pecan Street Historical District E 6th St & Congress Ave	Austin	TX	78701	512-476-4946	
Paramount Theatre 713 Congress Ave	Austin	TX	78701	512-472-5411	472-5824
Web: camalott.com/~paramnt/index.html					
Planet Theatre 2307 Manor Rd	Austin	TX	78722	512-478-5282	
Web: www.hyperweb.com/planett/					
Republic of Texas Museum 510 E Anderson Ln	Austin	TX	78752	512-339-1997	339-1998
Symphony Square 1101 Red River	Austin	TX	78701	512-476-6064	476-6242
TF: 888-462-3787					
Texas Memorial Museum 2400 Trinity St	Austin	TX	78705	512-471-1604	471-4794
Web: www.utexas.edu/depts/tmm/					
Texas Military Forces Museum 2200 W 35th St Camp Mabry	Austin	TX	78703	512-465-5659	706-6750
Web: www.kwanah.com/txmilmus/					
Texas State Capitol Bldg 1100 Congress Ave	Austin	TX	78701	512-463-0063	
Town Lake Metropolitan Park Tom Miller Dam	Austin	TX	78767	512-499-6700	
Umlauf Museum & Sculpture Garden 605 Robert E Lee Rd	Austin	TX	78704	512-445-5582	445-5583
Web: www.io.com/~tam/umlauf/					
University of Texas Performing Arts Center E 23rd & E Campus Dr	Austin	TX	78705	512-471-1444	471-3636
TF: 800-687-6010 ■ *Web:* www.utpac.org					
Wild Basin Wilderness Preserve 805 N Capital of Texas Hwy	Austin	TX	78746	512-327-7622	328-5632
Web: www.wildbasin.org ■ *E-mail:* hike@wildbasin.org					
Wonder World 1000 Prospect	San Marcos	TX	78666	512-392-3760	754-0373
TF: 800-782-7653 ■ *Web:* www.wonderworldpark.com					
Zachary Scott Theatre Center 1510 Toomey Rd	Austin	TX	78704	512-476-0594	476-0314
Web: www.zachscott.com/					
Zilker Botanical Gardens 2220 Barton Springs Rd	Austin	TX	78746	512-477-8672	481-8253
Web: www.zilker-garden.org					
Zilker Hillside Theatre 2201 Barton Springs Rd Zilker Pk	Austin	TX	78704	512-479-9491	
Zilker Metropolitan Park 2105 Andrew Zilker Dr	Austin	TX	78746	512-472-4914	
Zilker Park 2100 Barton Springs Rd	Austin	TX	78746	512-476-9044	

SPORTS TEAMS & FACILITIES

	City	State	Zip	Phone	Fax
Austin Ice Bats (hockey) 7311 Decker Ln	Austin	TX	78724	512-927-7825	927-7828
Web: www.icebats.com ■ *E-mail:* icebats@texas.net					
Austin Lady Lone Stars (soccer) 5446 Hwy 290 W Suite 105	Austin	TX	78735	512-892-7477	892-7402
Austin Lone Stars (soccer) 5446 Hwy 290 W Suite 105	Austin	TX	78735	512-892-7477	892-7402
Web: www.austinlonestars.com/ ■ *E-mail:* lonestars@jump.net					
Manor Downs 101 Hill Ln	Manor	TX	78653	512-272-5581	272-4403
Travis County Exposition & Heritage Center 7311 Decker Ln	Austin	TX	78724	512-473-9200	928-9953

— Events —

	Phone
Armadillo Christmas Bazaar (mid-late December)	512-447-1605
Austin Boat & Fishing Show (mid-January)	512-494-1128
Austin Chronicle Hot Sauce Festival (late August)	512-454-5766
Austin Collectors Exposition (late June)	512-454-9882
Austin Founders Trail Ride (early-mid-March)	512-477-4711
Austin Heart of Film Festival (October)	512-478-4795
Austin Home & Garden Show (mid-January)	512-476-5461
Austin International Poetry Festival (early April)	512-346-8717
Austin Jazz & Arts Festival (early September)	512-477-9438
Austin Rugby Tournament (early April)	512-926-9017
Austin Theatre Week (mid-April)	512-499-8388
Austin/Travis County Livestock Show & Rodeo (mid-March)	512-467-9811
Ben Hur Shrine Circus (early October)	512-327-3810
Bob Marley Festival (early April)	512-312-0435
Canterbury Faire (late September)	512-327-7622
Cinco de Mayo Celebration (May 5)	512-499-6720
Diez y Seis de Septiembre (September 16)	512-476-3868
Fiesta Laguna Gloria (mid-May)	512-458-6073
Freedom Festival & Fireworks (July 4)	800-926-2282
FronteraFest (late January)	512-499-8497
Frontier Days (mid-July)	512-255-5805
Halloween on Sixth Street (October 31)	512-476-8876
Heritage Homes Tour (early May)	512-474-5198
Jerry Jeff Walker's Birthday Celebration (late March)	512-477-0036
Juneteenth Freedom Festival (mid-June)	512-472-6838
Louisiana Swamp Romp (late April)	512-441-9015
New Texas Festival (early June)	512-476-5775
Oktoberfest (mid-October)	512-479-0598
Old Pecan Street Festival (early May & late September)	512-441-9015
Pioneer Farm Fall Festival (mid-September)	512-837-1215
Pow Wow & American Indian Heritage Festival (early November)	512-414-3849
Republic of Texas Chilympiad (late September)	512-478-0098
South By Southwest Music Festival (mid-March)	512-467-7979
Spamarama (early May)	512-834-1960

Austin — Events (Cont'd)

	Phone
Texas Independence Day Celebration (early March)	512-477-1836
Texas Wildlife Exposition (early October)	512-389-4472
Travis County Livestock Show & PRCA Rodeo (mid-March)	512-467-9811
Victorian Christmas on Sixth Street (late November)	512-441-9015
Volunteer Firemen's BBQ Extravaganza (mid-September)	512-282-3600
Western Days (late July)	512-285-4515
Wildflower Days Festival (late March & late May)	512-292-4200
Women in Jazz Concert Series (early June)	512-258-6947
Wooden Boat Show (late May)	512-288-5359
Zilker Fall Jazz Festival (early September)	512-440-1414
Zilker Garden Festival (early May)	512-477-8672
Zilker Kite Festival (early March)	512-478-0098

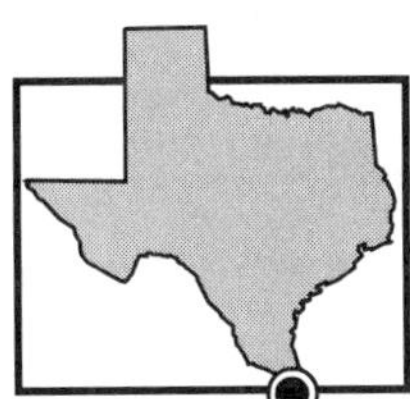

Brownsville

Brownsville is the southernmost city in the continental U.S, separated from Matamoros, Mexico by the Rio Grande River. To celebrate its unique relationship with Mexico, the city hosts Charro Days each February, which is Brownsville's version of Mardi Gras and includes carnivals, parades, dances, and cultural events. South Padre Island, noted for its beaches and watersports, is only 20 minutes away. Brownsville is also home to one of the top ten zoos in the country, the Gladys Porter Zoo, a unique, cageless zoo. The 3,400-acre Palo Alto Battlefield National Historic Site in Brownsville is the site of the first battle of the Mexican-American War, and the Historic Fort Brown Area, the oldest permanent U.S. Army post on the Rio Grande, is also located in Brownsville. The 1850 home of Charles Stillman, the founder of Brownsville, is on display as the Stillman House Museum. The University of Texas at Brownsville, the nation's first community university, is also located in the city.

Population	137,883	**Longitude**	97-28-55 W
Area (Land)	27.9 sq mi	**County**	Cameron
Area (Water)	0.9 sq mi	**Time Zone**	CST
Elevation	19 ft	**Area Code/s**	956
Latitude	25-55-30 N		

— Average Temperatures and Precipitation —

TEMPERATURES

	Jan	Feb	Mar	Apr	May	Jun	Jul	Aug	Sep	Oct	Nov	Dec
High	69	72	78	84	88	91	93	94	90	85	78	72
Low	50	53	59	67	72	75	76	75	73	66	59	52

PRECIPITATION

	Jan	Feb	Mar	Apr	May	Jun	Jul	Aug	Sep	Oct	Nov	Dec
Inches	1.6	1.1	0.5	1.6	2.9	2.7	1.9	2.8	6.0	2.8	1.5	1.3

— Important Phone Numbers —

	Phone		Phone
AAA	800-222-4357	**Medical Referral**	956-542-5433
American Express Travel	956-546-6112	**Poison Control Center**	800-764-7661
Emergency	911	**Time/Temp**	956-546-2481
Highway Conditions	800-452-9292	**Weather**	956-546-5378

— Information Sources —

				Phone	Fax
Better Business Bureau Serving South Texas PO Box 69 *Web:* www.weslaco.bbb.org	Weslaco	TX	78599	956-968-3678	968-7638
Brownsville Chamber of Commerce 1600 E Elizabeth St *Web:* www.brownsvillechamber.com ■ *E-mail:* info@brownsvillechamber.com	Brownsville	TX	78520	956-542-4341	504-3348
Brownsville City Hall 12th St & Market Sq *Web:* www.ci.brownsville.tx.us	Brownsville	TX	78520	956-548-6000	548-6060
Brownsville Convention & Visitors Bureau PO Box 4697 *TF:* 800-626-2639 ■ *Web:* www.brownsville.org ■ *E-mail:* visitors@brownsville.org	Brownsville	TX	78523	956-546-3721	546-3972
Brownsville Economic Development Council 1205 North Expy *TF:* 800-552-5352 ■ *Web:* www.bedc.com ■ *E-mail:* broedc@aol.com	Brownsville	TX	78520	956-541-1183	546-3938
Brownsville Mayor 12th St & Market Sq *Web:* www.ci.brownsville.tx.us/cm ■ *E-mail:* sylviap@ci.brownsville.tx.us	Brownsville	TX	78520	956-548-6007	548-6010
Brownsville Public Library 2600 Central Blvd *Web:* www.brownsville.lib.tx.us ■ *E-mail:* info@brownsville.lib.tx.us	Brownsville	TX	78520	956-548-1055	548-0684
Cameron County PO Box 2178	Brownsville	TX	78522	956-544-0815	550-7287
International Convention Center 4434 E 14th St	Brownsville	TX	78521	956-546-8878	
Jacob Brown Civic Center 600 International Blvd	Brownsville	TX	78520	956-982-1820	982-1358
South Padre Island Convention & Visitors Bureau 600 Padre Blvd *TF:* 800-767-2373 ■ *Web:* www.sopadre.com ■ *E-mail:* cvb@sopadre.com	South Padre Island	TX	78597	956-761-6433	761-9462
South Padre Island Convention Centre 7355 Padre Blvd *TF:* 800-657-2373 ■ *E-mail:* convctr@sopadre.com	South Padre Island	TX	78597	956-761-3005	761-3024

On-Line Resources

4Brownsville.com	www.4brownsville.com
Excite.com Brownsville City Guide	www.excite.com/travel/countries/united_states/texas/brownsville
NITC Travelbase Guide Brownsville	www.travelbase.com/auto/guides/brownsville-tx.html
Online City Guide to Brownsville	www.onlinecityguide.com/tx/brownsville

— Transportation Services —

AIRPORTS

■ **Brownsville-South Padre Island International Airport (BRO)**

	Phone
4 miles E of downtown (approx 10 minutes) Web: www.ci.brownsville.tx.us/airport	956-542-4373

Airport Transportation

	Phone
ABC Taxi $10 fare to downtown	956-504-9222
Balli Taxi $10-12 fare to downtown	956-548-1111
Checker Taxi Cab $8 fare to downtown	956-542-9694
Garden Taxi $7-8 fare to downtown	956-542-9924
Red Top Taxi $10 fare to downtown	956-544-4450

Commercial Airlines

	Phone
Continental	800-525-0280

CAR RENTALS

	Phone		Phone
Advantage	956-350-3718	**Enterprise**	956-548-2224
Avis	956-541-9271	**Hertz**	956-542-7466
Budget	956-546-5119		

Brownsville (Cont'd)

LIMO/TAXI

Name	Phone	Name	Phone
ABC Taxi	956-504-9222	**GC Taxi**	956-541-1669
American Taxi	956-541-0959	**Grayline Limousine**	956-761-4343
Balli Taxi	956-548-1111	**Imperial Taxi**	956-542-1800
Checker Taxi Cab	956-542-9694	**International Taxi**	956-548-0111
City Taxi	956-544-3030	**Lerma Taxi**	956-542-2983
Fiesta Taxi Cabs	956-504-2490	**Red Top Taxi**	956-544-4450
Garden Taxi	956-542-9924	**Surftran Limousine**	956-761-1641

MASS TRANSIT

Name	Phone
Brownsville Urban System $.75 Base fare	956-548-6050

RAIL/BUS

Name	City	State	Zip	Phone
Greyhound/Valley Transit Bus Station 1134 E St Charles Ave	Brownsville	TX	78520	956-546-2264
Union Pacific Railroad Co 600 E Fronton St	Brownsville	TX	78520	956-548-2420

— Accommodations —

HOTELS, MOTELS, RESORTS

Name	City	State	Zip	Phone	Fax
Bahia Mar Resort & Conference Center 6300 Padre Blvd. *TF:* 800-997-2373	South Padre Island	TX	78597	956-761-1343	761-6287
Best Western Rose Garden Inn & Suites 845 North Expy. *TF:* 800-528-1234	Brownsville	TX	78520	956-546-5501	546-6474
Brown Pelican Inn 207 W Aries St. *Web:* www.brownpelican.com ■ *E-mail:* inkeeper@brownpelican.com	South Padre Island	TX	78597	956-761-2722	
Cameron Motor Hotel 912 E Washington Ave	Brownsville	TX	78520	956-542-3551	
Citrus Motel 2054 Central Blvd	Brownsville	TX	78520	956-550-9077	
Colonial Hotel 1147 E Levee St *TF:* 800-644-9176	Brownsville	TX	78520	956-541-9176	541-9160
Comfort Inn 825 North Expy	Brownsville	TX	78520	956-504-3331	546-0379
Days Inn 715 N Frontage Rd *TF:* 800-329-7466	Brownsville	TX	78520	956-541-2201	541-6011
Flamingo Motel 1741 Central Blvd	Brownsville	TX	78520	956-546-2478	
Four Points by Sheraton 3777 North Exwy *TF:* 800-325-3535	Brownsville	TX	78520	956-547-1500	547-1550
Holiday Inn Fort Brown Resort 1900 E Elizabeth St. *TF:* 800-465-4329	Brownsville	TX	78520	956-546-2201	546-0756
Motel 6 2255 North Exwy	Brownsville	TX	78520	956-546-4699	546-8982
Plaza Square Motor Lodge 2255 Central Blvd	Brownsville	TX	78520	956-546-5104	
Ramada Limited 1900 E Elizabeth St. *TF:* 800-272-6232	Brownsville	TX	78520	956-541-2921	541-2695
Rancho Viejo Resort & Country Club 1 Rancho Viejo Dr. *TF:* 800-531-7400	Rancho Viejo	TX	78575	956-350-4000	350-9681
Red Roof Inn 2377 North Exwy *TF:* 800-843-7663	Brownsville	TX	78520	956-504-2300	504-2303
Sands Motel 2834 Central Blvd.	Brownsville	TX	78520	956-542-4362	
Super 8 Motel 55 Sam Perl Blvd. *TF:* 800-800-8000	Brownsville	TX	78520	956-546-0381	541-5313
Tropical Motel 811 Central Blvd	Brownsville	TX	78520	956-542-7162	504-0659

— Restaurants —

Name	City	State	Zip	Phone
802 Cafe (American) 3535 Coffeeport Rd	Brownsville	TX	78521	956-542-9517
Antonio's (Mexican) 1800 North Expy.	Brownsville	TX	78520	956-542-6504
Bigo's Bar & Grill (American) 2005 Southmost Rd	Brownsville	TX	78521	956-982-4467
Chilitos Restaurant (Mexican) 230 Security Dr	Brownsville	TX	78521	956-541-1668
Cobblehead's Bar & Grill (American) 3154 Central Blvd.	Brownsville	TX	78520	956-546-6224
D-D Cafe (Mexican) 927 E Saint Francis St	Brownsville	TX	78520	956-542-9015
Danny's Restaurant (Mexican) 55 Sam Perl Blvd.	Brownsville	TX	78520	956-541-4535
El Pato Restaurant (Mexican) 1631 Price Rd.	Brownsville	TX	78520	956-541-0241
El Torito Restaurant (Mexican) 625 North Exwy	Brownsville	TX	78520	956-541-4426
Elias Cafe (Mexican) 1104 E 14th St	Brownsville	TX	78520	956-548-2931
Elva's Restaurant (Mexican) 1775 Central Blvd	Brownsville	TX	78520	956-504-3371
Estrella Mexican Plate (Mexican) 114 E Elizabeth St	Brownsville	TX	78520	956-546-1504
Frank's Round Up (Mexican) 946 W Price Rd	Brownsville	TX	78520	956-542-9429
Friend's Family Restaurant (Homestyle) 7102 E 14th St	Brownsville	TX	78521	956-831-3201
Garden Terrace Restaurant (American) 1900 E Elizabeth St Holiday Inn Fort Brown Resort	Brownsville	TX	78520	956-546-2201
Gil's Cafe (Mexican) 735 International Blvd.	Brownsville	TX	78520	956-541-8786
Ho's Garden (Chinese) 1552 Palm Blvd Palm Village Shopping Ctr	Brownsville	TX	78520	956-544-3009
Isabella's Restaurant (Mexican) 1156 Market Sq.	Brownsville	TX	78520	956-542-4782
Janitzio Restaurant (Mexican) 1042 E Adams St.	Brownsville	TX	78520	956-541-2559
JR's Restaurant (Mexican) 5250 Paredes Line Rd	Brownsville	TX	78520	956-546-7417
Juan O'Leary's (American) 2134 Central Blvd	Brownsville	TX	78520	956-541-3200
La Fonda Chiquita (Mexican) 1435 Southmost Rd.	Brownsville	TX	78521	956-504-5258
La Fragata Oyster Restaurant (Seafood) 814 E 14th St	Brownsville	TX	78520	956-542-1715
Las Brasas (Mexican) 2040 Central Blvd.	Brownsville	TX	78520	956-542-9372
Los Camperos (Mexican) 1400 International Blvd.	Brownsville	TX	78520	956-546-8172
Los Mismos Restaurant (Mexican) 1701 Price Rd	Brownsville	TX	78521	956-542-5995
Los Paisanos (Mexican) 3302 Coffeeport Rd.	Brownsville	TX	78521	956-504-1777
Lotus Court Restaurant (Chinese) 1774 E Price Rd	Brownsville	TX	78520	956-542-5712
Maria's (Mexican) 1124 Central Blvd	Brownsville	TX	78520	956-542-9819
Mi Mexico Lindo (Mexican) 3955 Business Hwy 77 W.	Brownsville	TX	78520	956-504-2002
Mi Ranchito Cafe (Mexican) 220 Palm Blvd	Brownsville	TX	78520	956-504-9196
Mi Tierra Restaurant (Mexican) 1104 E 7th St	Brownsville	TX	78520	956-541-9236
Mr Bull's (Mexican) 644 Palm Blvd	Brownsville	TX	78520	956-541-7777
Oasis Cafe (Mexican) 1417 E Adams St	Brownsville	TX	78520	956-548-1216
Palm Court Restaurant (American) 2200 Boca Chica Blvd	Brownsville	TX	78521	956-542-3575
Peso Bill's Mexican Restaurant (Steak) 2635 Boca Chica Blvd	Brownsville	TX	78520	956-546-0939
Rafael's Coney Island (American) 605 E 14th St.	Brownsville	TX	78520	956-546-9518
Rancho Alegre Cafe (Mexican) 3224 E 14th St	Brownsville	TX	78521	956-504-3104
Sylvia's Restaurant (Mexican) 1843 Southmost Rd	Brownsville	TX	78521	956-542-9220
Taqueria Martinez (Mexican) 804 E 14th St	Brownsville	TX	78520	956-542-9265
Taqueria Siberia (Mexican) 2915 International Blvd.	Brownsville	TX	78521	956-542-9357
Tia Ines (Mexican) 16 Palm Village	Brownsville	TX	78520	956-541-6997
Tidewater Bar-B-Que (Barbecue) 4999 N Frontage Rd	Brownsville	TX	78520	956-350-5199
Tony's Taquito Express (Mexican) 2207 E Price Rd	Brownsville	TX	78521	956-542-6552
Valley International Country (American) Country Club Rd.	Brownsville	TX	78520	956-546-5331
Vermillion The (American) 115 Paredes Line Rd	Brownsville	TX	78520	956-542-9893

— Goods and Services —

SHOPPING

Name	City	State	Zip	Phone	Fax
Amigoland Mall 301 Mexico Blvd	Brownsville	TX	78520	956-546-3788	
Palm Village Shopping Center 21 Palm Village.	Brownsville	TX	78520	956-542-7733	
Sunrise Mall 2370 North Exwy	Brownsville	TX	78526	956-541-5302	546-0251

BANKS

Name	City	State	Zip	Phone	Fax
Chase Texas 1034 E Levee St	Brownsville	TX	78520	956-548-6968	548-6929
Coastal Banc 3302 Boca Chica Blvd *TF Cust Svc:* 888-393-3434*	Brownsville	TX	78521	956-546-4528	541-0997
First National Bank 701 E Levee St.	Brownsville	TX	78520	956-986-7000	986-7045
International Bank of Commerce 630 E Elizabeth St.	Brownsville	TX	78520	956-542-8060	547-1006
Norwest Bank 3310 Boca Chica Blvd.	Brownsville	TX	78521	956-504-2265	504-2619
Texas State Bank 629 E Elizabeth St.	Brownsville	TX	78520	956-546-4503	547-3808

BUSINESS SERVICES

Name	Phone	Name	Phone
Austin Personnel Services	956-544-6229	**Manpower Temporary Services**	956-544-7153
Federal Express	800-238-5355	**Post Office**	956-546-2411
Kelly Services	956-412-1156	**Quik Print**	956-548-1301
Mail Boxes Etc	956-542-0513	**UPS**	800-742-5877

— Media —

PUBLICATIONS

Name	City	State	Zip	Phone	Fax
Brownsville Herald‡ PO Box 351 **Fax:* Edit ■ *Web:* www.brownsvilleherald.com ■ *E-mail:* herald@hiline.net	Brownsville	TX	78520	956-542-4301	542-0840*

Brownsville — Publications (Cont'd)

				Phone	Fax
El Bravo‡ 1144 Lincoln St	Brownsville	TX	78520	956-542-5800	452-6023
Rio Grande Valley Business Journal 1300 Wild Rose Ln	Brownsville	TX	78520	956-546-5113	546-0903*
Fax: Sales ■ *E-mail:* bsales@rgvbusiness.hiline.net					

‡*Daily newspapers*

TELEVISION

				Phone	Fax
KGBT-TV Ch 4 (CBS) 9201 W Exwy 83	Harlingen	TX	78552	956-421-4444	421-3699
Web: www.kgbttv.com					
KNVO-TV Ch 48 (Uni) 801 N Jackson Rd	McAllen	TX	78501	956-687-4848	687-7784
Web: www.knvo.com ■ *E-mail:* feedback@knvo.com					
KRGV-TV Ch 5 (ABC) 900 East Expy	Weslaco	TX	78596	956-968-5555	973-5016
Web: www.krgv.com ■ *E-mail:* sales@krgv.com					
KVEO-TV Ch 23 (NBC) 394 North Expy	Brownsville	TX	78521	956-544-2323	544-4636
Web: www.kveo.com ■ *E-mail:* kvesales@hiline.net					

RADIO

				Phone	Fax
KBNR-FM 88.3 MHz (Rel) 216 W Elizabeth	Brownsville	TX	78520	956-542-6933	542-0523
KBOR-AM 1600 kHz (Span) 1050 McIntosh St	Brownsville	TX	78521	956-544-1600	542-4109
KFRQ-FM 94.5 MHz (Rock) 901 E Pike Blvd	Weslaco	TX	78596	956-968-1548	968-1643
KGBT-FM 98.5 MHz (Span) 200 S 10th St Suite 600	McAllen	TX	78501	956-631-5499	631-0090
Web: www.kgbt.com ■ *E-mail:* sales@kgbt.com					
KIWW-FM 96.1 MHz (Span) 200 S 10th St Suite 600	McAllen	TX	78501	956-631-5499	631-0090
Web: www.kiww.com ■ *E-mail:* info@kiww.com					
KKPS-FM 99.5 MHz (Span) 901 E Pike Blvd	Weslaco	TX	78596	956-968-1548	968-1643
KRGE-AM 1290 kHz (Rel) PO Box 1290	Weslaco	TX	78599	956-968-7777	968-5143
KTEX-FM 100.3 MHz (Ctry) 3301 S Expy 83	Harlingen	TX	78550	956-423-5068	
Web: www.ktex.net ■ *E-mail:* ktexx@aol.com					
KTJN-FM 106.3 MHz (Span) 1050 McIntosh St	Brownsville	TX	78521	956-544-1600	542-4109
KTJX-FM 105.5 MHz (Span) 1050 McIntosh St	Brownsville	TX	78523	956-544-1600	544-0311

— Colleges/Universities —

				Phone	Fax
South Texas Vocational Technical Institute 2255 N Coria St	Brownsville	TX	78520	956-546-0353	546-0914
Web: www.hiline.net/~stvtm ■ *E-mail:* stvtw@hiline.net					
Texas Southmost College 80 Fort Brown St	Brownsville	TX	78520	956-544-8200	544-8832
TF: 800-850-0160 ■ *Web:* www.utb.edu					
University of Texas Brownsville 80 Fort Brown St	Brownsville	TX	78520	956-544-8200	544-8832
TF Admissions: 800-850-0160 ■ *Web:* www.utb.edu					

— Hospitals —

				Phone	Fax
Brownsville Medical Center 1040 W Jefferson St	Brownsville	TX	78520	956-544-1400	541-0747*
**Fax:* Admitting					
Valley Regional Medical Center 100-A Alton Gloor Blvd	Brownsville	TX	78521	956-350-9611	350-7117

— Attractions —

				Phone	Fax
Antonio Gonzales Park 34 Tony Gonzalez Dr	Brownsville	TX	78521	956-542-2064	
Bentsen-Rio Grande State Park PO Box 988	Mission	TX	78572	956-585-1107	585-3448
TF: 800-792-1112 ■ *Web:* www.hiline.net/~bentsen					
Bro-Mat 'Old Mexico' Tours 300 E 6th St	Los Fresnos	TX	78566	956-233-1900	
Brownsville Art League Gallery 230 Neale Dr	Brownsville	TX	78520	956-542-0941	
Confederate Air Force Museum Rio Grande Valley Wing 955 S Minnesota Brownsville Airport	Brownsville	TX	78521	956-541-8585	
Dean Porter Park 501 E Ringgold St	Brownsville	TX	78520	956-542-2064	982-1049
Edelstein Park E 12th & Polk Sts	Brownsville	TX	78520	956-542-2064	982-1049
Garfield Park E 16th & Garfield Sts	Brownsville	TX	78520	956-542-2064	982-1049
Historic Brownsville Museum 641 E Madison St	Brownsville	TX	78520	956-548-1313	548-1391
Historic Brownsville Trolley Tours 650 FM-802 Convention & Visitors Bureau	Brownsville	TX	78520	956-546-3721	
Laguna Atascosa National Wildlife Refuge Hwy 106 & Buena Vista Rd	Brownsville	TX	78520	956-748-3608	748-3609
Lightner Camille Playhouse 1 Dean Porter Dr	Brownsville	TX	78520	956-542-8900	542-0567
Web: www.camilleplayhouse.vt1.com					
Number One Fun Amusement Center 2370 North Expy Sunrise Mall	Brownsville	TX	78526	956-546-3050	
Palo Alto Battlefield National Historic Site 1623 Central Blvd	Brownsville	TX	78520	956-541-2785	541-6356
Web: www.nps.gov/paal/					
Port of Brownsville 1000 Foust Rd	Brownsville	TX	78521	956-831-4592	831-5006
Porter Gladys Zoo 500 Ringgold St	Brownsville	TX	78520	956-546-7187	541-4940
Web: www.gpz.org					
Sabal Palm Grove Sanctuary Sabal Palm Rd & FM-1419	Brownsville	TX	78523	956-541-8034	504-0543
Web: www.audubon.org/local/sanctuary/sabal					
Santa Ana National Wildlife Refuge FM-907 & Hwy 281	Alamo	TX	78516	956-787-3079	
Web: southwest.fws.gov/refuges/texas/santana.html					
Smith Marion Hendrick Outdoor Ampitheater South Bldg University of Texas at Brownsville Campus	Brownsville	TX	78520	956-544-8200	
Stillman House & Museum 1305 E Washington St	Brownsville	TX	78520	956-542-3929	541-5524
Web: brownsville.org/museum.html					
Super Splash Adventure Water Park 1616 S Raul Longonia Rd	Edinburg	TX	78539	956-318-3286	316-1877
Web: www.supersplashadventure.com					
Washington Plaza Park E 7th & Madison Sts	Brownsville	TX	78520	956-542-2064	982-1049
Whaling Wall Mural 7355 Padre Blvd Convention Centre	South Padre Island	TX	78597	956-761-3005	

— Events —

	Phone
Beachcomber's Art Show (late July)	956-423-6707
Birdathon (mid-May)	956-541-8034
Boo at the Zoo (late October)	956-546-7187
Brownsville Appreciation Day at the Zoo (mid-September)	956-546-7187
Brownsville Art League International Art Show (early March)	956-542-0941
Brownsville Art League International Student Art Show (late April-early May)	956-542-0941
Charro Days Festival (late February)	956-542-4245
Christmas Parade (early December)	956-542-4341
Christmas Tree Lighting Ceremony (late November)	956-546-3721
CineSol Latino Film Festival (early June)	956-428-8983
Confederate Air Force Fiesta (early March)	956-541-8585
Fall Faculty Art Exhibition (October-November)	956-544-8247
Feast with the Beast (mid-May)	956-546-7187
Fly-Ins (October-March)	956-748-2112
Friday Night Fireworks Over the Bay (late May-early September)	956-761-3000
Memorial Day Fireworks over the Bay (late May)	956-761-3000
Rio Grande Valley Arts & Crafts Expo (early November)	956-542-0941
Semana Santa (Holy Week) (late March-early April)	956-761-6433
Shrimp on the Barbie Cook-Off (May)	956-761-2831
Sombrero Festival (late February)	956-542-4341
South Padre Island Bikefest (mid-October)	956-761-3000
South Padre Island Easter Egg Hunt (early April)	956-761-6433
South Padre Island Fireworks Extravaganza (July 4)	956-761-3000
Spring Faculty Art Exhibition (early February-early March)	956-544-8247
Zoofari Fundraiser (early October)	956-546-7187

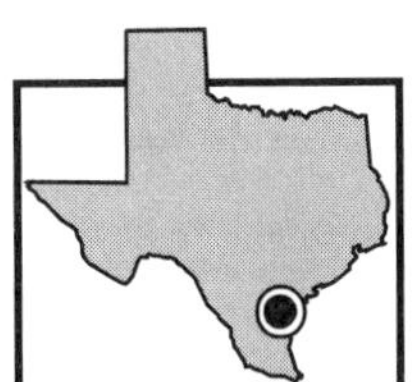

Corpus Christi

Located on the Texas coast, halfway between Houston and the U.S.-Mexico border, Corpus Christi sits on a bay surrounded by tropical islands, combining Texas traditions with the beaches and fishing of a Gulf resort. Port Aransas, a village on the tip of Mustang Island, is known for its

Corpus Christi (Cont'd)

great deep-sea fishing, and Conn Brown Harbor in Aransas Pass has the largest shrimping fleet on the Texas Coast. One can also go horseback riding on the beach at Mustang Island, or relax on the beaches at Padre Island National Seashore. In the city itself, popular sites include the Texas State Aquarium, which focuses exclusively on marine life of the Gulf of Mexico and Caribbean; the USS Lexington Museum-On-The Bay; and the lifesize replicas of the Pinta, Nina, and Santa Maria docked in the Port of Corpus Christi.

Population 281,453
Area (Land) .... 134.4 sq mi
Area (Water) .... 274.9 sq mi
Elevation .... 35 ft
Latitude .... 27-22-64 N
Longitude .... 97-96-15 W
County .... Nueces
Time Zone .... CST
Area Code/s 361

— Average Temperatures and Precipitation —

TEMPERATURES

	Jan	Feb	Mar	Apr	May	Jun	Jul	Aug	Sep	Oct	Nov	Dec
High	65	69	76	82	86	90	93	93	90	84	76	68
Low	45	48	55	63	70	73	75	75	72	64	56	48

PRECIPITATION

	Jan	Feb	Mar	Apr	May	Jun	Jul	Aug	Sep	Oct	Nov	Dec
Inches	1.7	2.0	0.9	1.7	3.3	3.4	2.4	3.3	5.5	3.0	1.6	1.3

— Important Phone Numbers —

	Phone		Phone
AAA	800-222-4357	**HotelDocs**	800-468-3537
Emergency	911	**Poison Control Center**	800-764-7661
Highway Conditions	800-452-9292	**Weather**	361-289-1861

— Information Sources —

				Phone	Fax
Better Business Bureau Serving the Coastal Bend of Texas 4301 Ocean Dr	Corpus Christi	TX	78412	361-852-4949	852-4990
Web: www.caller.com/bbb					
Corpus Christi City Hall PO Box 9277	Corpus Christi	TX	78469	361-880-3000	
Web: www.ci.corpus-christi.tx.us					
Corpus Christi Convention & Visitors Bureau 1201 N Shoreline Blvd	Corpus Christi	TX	78401	361-881-1888	887-9023
TF: 800-766-2322 ■ *Web:* www.corpuschristi-tx-cvb.org ■ *E-mail:* tmorales@cctexas.org					
Corpus Christi Mayor PO Box 9277	Corpus Christi	TX	78469	361-880-3100	880-3103
Corpus Christi Planning Dept PO Box 9277	Corpus Christi	TX	78469	361-880-3560	880-3590
Web: www.ci.corpus-christi.tx.us/services/planning					
Corpus Christi Public Libraries 805 Comanche St	Corpus Christi	TX	78401	361-880-7000	880-7005
Web: www.library.ci.corpus-christi.tx.us ■ *E-mail:* library@ccpl.ci.corpus-christi.tx.us					
Corpus Christi Tourist Information Center PO Box 260185	Corpus Christi	TX	78426	361-241-1464	241-6312
Greater Corpus Christi Business Alliance 1201 N Shoreline Blvd.	Corpus Christi	TX	78401	361-881-1888	883-5027
TF: 800-678-6232 ■ *Web:* www.cctexas.org					
Nueces County PO Box 2627	Corpus Christi	TX	78403	361-888-0580	888-0329

On-Line Resources

Area Guide Corpus Christi .... corpuschristi.areaguides.net
City Knowledge Corpus Christi .... www.cityknowledge.com/tx_corpuschristi.htm
Corpus Christi.com .... www.corpuschristi.com
Corpus Quest .... www.corpusquest.com
Excite.com Corpus Christi City Guide .... www.excite.com/travel/countries/united_states/texas/corpus_christi/
NITC Travelbase City Guide Corpus Christi .... www.travelbase.com/auto/guides/corpus_christi-area-tx.html

— Transportation Services —

AIRPORTS

■ **Corpus Christi International Airport (CRP)** — Phone
15 miles SW of downtown (approx 20 minutes) 361-289-0171

Airport Transportation

City Yellow Cab $13 fare to downtown 361-881-8294

Commercial Airlines

	Phone		Phone
American	800-433-7300	**Continental Express**	800-525-0280
American Eagle	800-433-7300	**Delta Connection**	800-221-1212
Continental	800-525-0280	**Southwest**	800-435-9792

CAR RENTALS

	Phone		Phone
Avis	361-289-0073	**Hertz**	361-289-0777
Budget	361-289-0434	**Thrifty**	361-289-0041
Dollar	361-289-2886		

LIMO/TAXI

	Phone		Phone
City Yellow Cab	361-881-8294	**Star Cab**	361-884-9451
Liberty Taxi	361-882-7654	**United Taxi**	361-852-5555
Limos Unlimited	361-884-5466	**Yellow Checker Cab**	361-884-3211

MASS TRANSIT

	Phone
B Ride Bus $.50 Base fare	361-289-2600
RTA Trolley $.50 base fare	361-289-2600
RTA Water Taxi $1 Base fare	361-289-2600

RAIL/BUS

Greyhound/Trailways Bus Station 702 N Chaparral St .. Corpus Christi TX 78401 — Phone 361-882-2516

— Accommodations —

HOTELS, MOTELS, RESORTS

				Phone	Fax
Bayfront Inn 601 N Shoreline Blvd	Corpus Christi	TX	78401	361-883-7271	883-2052
TF: 800-456-2293					
Best Western Corpus Christi Inn 2838 S Padre Island Dr	Corpus Christi	TX	78415	361-854-0005	854-2642
TF: 800-445-9463					
Best Western Sandy Shores Beach Hotel 3200 Surfside Blvd	Corpus Christi	TX	78402	361-883-7456	883-1437
TF: 800-528-1234					
Christy Estates Suites 3942 Holly Rd	Corpus Christi	TX	78415	361-854-1091	854-4766
TF: 800-784-8376					
Embassy Suites Hotel 4337 S Padre Island Dr	Corpus Christi	TX	78411	361-853-7899	851-1310
TF: 800-362-2779					
Hampton Inn Airport 5501 I-37 & McBride Ln	Corpus Christi	TX	78408	361-289-5861	299-1718
TF: 800-426-7866					
Holiday Inn Emerald Beach 1102 S Shoreline Blvd	Corpus Christi	TX	78401	361-883-5731	883-9079
TF: 800-465-4329					
Holiday Inn Gulf Beach Resort 15202 Windward Dr	Corpus Christi	TX	78418	361-949-8041	949-9139
TF: 800-465-4329					
Island House Condos 15340 Leeward Dr	Corpus Christi	TX	78418	361-949-8166	949-8904
TF: 800-333-8806					
Koronado Motel 3615 Timon St	Corpus Christi	TX	78402	361-883-4411	
TF: 800-883-0424					

Corpus Christi — Hotels, Motels, Resorts (Cont'd)

				Phone	Fax
La Quinta North 5155 IH-37 North	Corpus Christi	TX	78408	361-888-5721	888-5401
TF: 800-531-5900					
La Quinta South 6225 S Padre Island Dr	Corpus Christi	TX	78412	361-991-5730	993-1578
TF: 800-531-5900					
Omni Bayfront Hotel 900 N Shoreline Blvd.	Corpus Christi	TX	78401	361-887-1600	887-6715
TF: 800-843-6664					
Omni Marina Hotel 707 N Shoreline Blvd.	Corpus Christi	TX	78401	361-882-1700	882-3113
TF: 800-843-6664					
Ramada Hotel Bayfront 601 N Water St.	Corpus Christi	TX	78401	361-882-8100	888-6540
TF: 800-272-6232					
Residence Inn by Marriott 5229 Blanche Moore Dr.	Corpus Christi	TX	78411	361-985-1113	985-1113
TF: 800-331-3131 ■ *Web:* www.residenceinn.com/residenceinn/CRPRI					
Sea Shell Inn Motel 202 Kleberg	Corpus Christi	TX	78402	361-888-5391	
The Holiday Inn Corpus Christi Padre Island Drive (Airport Area) 5549 Leopard St.	Corpus Christi	TX	78408	361-289-5100	289-6209
TF: 800-465-4329 ■ *Web:* www.basshotels.com/holiday-inn/?_franchisee=CRPAP ■ *E-mail:* gm535@swbell.net					
Travelodge Hotel Shoreline 300 N Shoreline Blvd.	Corpus Christi	TX	78401	361-883-5111	883-7702
TF: 800-883-5119					
Villa del Sol 3938 Surfside Blvd.	Corpus Christi	TX	78402	361-883-9748	883-7537
TF: 800-242-3291 ■ *Web:* www.villa-delsol.com ■ *E-mail:* info@villa-delsol.com					

— Restaurants —

				Phone
Acapulco Restaurant (Mexican) 1133 Airline Rd	Corpus Christi	TX	78412	361-994-7274
Ancient Mariner (Steak/Seafood) 4366 S Alameda St.	Corpus Christi	TX	78412	361-992-7371
Bayou Grill (Cajun) 3741 S Alameda	Corpus Christi	TX	78411	361-854-8626
Bee's Bar-b-que (Barbecue) 4301 S Alameda St	Corpus Christi	TX	78412	361-991-3364
Black Diamond Oyster Bar (Seafood) 7202 S Padre Island Dr.	Corpus Christi	TX	78412	361-992-2432
Charco's (American) 4902A S Staples	Corpus Christi	TX	78411	361-991-1522
County Line (American) 6102 Ocean Dr	Corpus Christi	TX	78412	361-991-7427
Crawdaddy's (Cajun) 414 Starr St	Corpus Christi	TX	78401	361-883-5432
Edelweiss Cafe & Restaurant (German) 1209 Airline Rd	Corpus Christi	TX	78412	361-993-1901
El Chico Restaurant (Mexican) 5201 S Padre Island Dr.	Corpus Christi	TX	78411	361-992-1947
Executive Surf Club (American) 309 N Water St	Corpus Christi	TX	78401	361-884-7873
Frank's Spaghetti House (Italian) 2724 Leopard St	Corpus Christi	TX	78408	361-882-0075
Golden Pacific Restaurant (Asian) 8225 S Padre Island Dr.	Corpus Christi	TX	78412	361-992-1136
Happy Buddha (Chinese) 3602 Leopard St	Corpus Christi	TX	78408	361-882-2747
Hofbrau Steaks & Bar (American) 1214 N Chaparral St.	Corpus Christi	TX	78401	361-881-8722
Hua T'ai (Chinese) 149 S Alameda St.	Corpus Christi	TX	78404	361-857-8788
Landry's (Seafood) 600 N Shoreline Blvd	Corpus Christi	TX	78401	361-882-6666
Lo Differente (Mexican) 8081 Leopard St.	Corpus Christi	TX	78409	361-289-2624
Mandarin Inn (Chinese) 4455 S Padre Island Dr	Corpus Christi	TX	78411	361-852-8983
Old Mexico Restaurant (Mexican) 3329 Leopard St.	Corpus Christi	TX	78408	361-883-6461
Rosita's (Mexican) 2319 Morgan St.	Corpus Christi	TX	78405	361-883-8363
U & I Restaurant (American) 309 S Water St	Corpus Christi	TX	78401	361-883-3492
Vernon's (Barbecue) 1030 3rd St.	Corpus Christi	TX	78404	361-884-6552
Water Street Seafood Co (Seafood) 309 N Water St	Corpus Christi	TX	78401	361-882-8683

— Goods and Services —

SHOPPING

				Phone	Fax
Crossroads Shopping Village 5830 McArdle St.	Corpus Christi	TX	78412	361-991-4950	991-9453
Lamar Park Shopping Center 3817 S Alameda St.	Corpus Christi	TX	78411	361-854-8885	854-5889
Padre Island Park Co 20420 Park Rd 22 Malaquite Beach.	Corpus Christi	TX	78418	361-949-9368	949-9368
Padre-Staples Mall 5488 S Padre Island Dr.	Corpus Christi	TX	78411	361-991-3755	993-5631
Sunrise Mall 5858 S Padre Island Dr	Corpus Christi	TX	78412	361-993-2900	
Water Street Market 309 N Water St.	Corpus Christi	TX	78401	361-881-9322	881-9208

BANKS

				Phone	Fax
American National Bank 5120 S Padre Island Dr.	Corpus Christi	TX	78411	361-992-9900	991-0084
Frost Bank 2402 Leopard St.	Corpus Christi	TX	78403	361-844-1128	844-1134
TF: 800-513-7678					
International Bank of Commerce 221 S Shoreline Blvd.	Corpus Christi	TX	78401	361-888-4000	888-5243
Norwest Bank PO Box 4666	Corpus Christi	TX	78469	361-884-3051	886-6592
TF: 800-772-2228					
Pacific Southwest Bank FSB 800 N Shoreline Blvd South Tower Suite 200	Corpus Christi	TX	78401	361-889-7700	889-7816
TF: 800-933-7224					

BUSINESS SERVICES

	Phone		Phone
Airborne Express	800-247-2676	**Kinko's**	361-857-5795
BAX Global	800-225-5229	**Mail Boxes Etc**	800-789-4623
DHL Worldwide Express	800-225-5345	**Post Office**	800-275-8777
Federal Express	800-238-5355	**UPS**	800-742-5877

— Media —

PUBLICATIONS

				Phone	Fax
Caller-Times‡ 820 N Lower Broadway	Corpus Christi	TX	78401	361-884-2011	886-3732
TF: 800-827-2011 ■ *Web:* www.caller.com					
South Texas Informer & Business Journal 4455 S Padre Island Dr Suite 101	Corpus Christi	TX	78411	361-857-6332	857-6337

‡Daily newspapers

TELEVISION

				Phone	Fax
KAJA-TV Ch 68 (Tele) 409 S Staples	Corpus Christi	TX	78401	361-886-6101	886-6116
KDF-TV Ch 47 (Fox) 409 S Staples	Corpus Christi	TX	78401	361-886-6101	886-6116
KEDT-TV Ch 16 (PBS) 4455 S Padre Island Dr Suite 38	Corpus Christi	TX	78411	361-855-2213	855-3877
TF: 800-307-5338 ■ *Web:* www.esc2.net/kedt/KEDT.htm ■ *E-mail:* mail@kedt.pbs.org					
KIII-TV Ch 3 (ABC) PO Box 6669	Corpus Christi	TX	78466	361-854-4733	851-1541
KORO-TV Ch 28 (Uni) 102 N Mesquite	Corpus Christi	TX	78401	361-883-2823	883-2931
KRIS-TV Ch 6 (NBC) 409 S Staples St.	Corpus Christi	TX	78401	361-886-6100	886-6666
Web: www.kristv.com/ ■ *E-mail:* kris@trip.net					
KZTV-TV Ch 10 (CBS) 301 Artesian St.	Corpus Christi	TX	78401	361-883-7070	884-8111

RADIO

				Phone	Fax
KEDT-FM 90.3 MHz (NPR) 4455 S Padre Island Dr Suite 38	Corpus Christi	TX	78411	361-855-2213	855-3877
TF: 800-850-5717 ■ *Web:* www.kedt.org					
KEYS-AM 1440 kHz (N/T) PO Box 9757	Corpus Christi	TX	78469	361-882-7411	882-9767
KFTX-FM 97.5 MHz (Ctry) 1520 S Port Ave	Corpus Christi	TX	78405	361-883-5987	883-3648
KLTG-FM 96.5 MHz (CHR) PO Box 898	Corpus Christi	TX	78403	361-883-1600	888-5685
KLUX-FM 89.5 MHz (B/EZ) 1200 Lantana St	Corpus Christi	TX	78407	361-289-2487	289-1420
KOUL-FM 103.7 MHz (Ctry) 1300 Antelope St	Corpus Christi	TX	78401	361-883-1600	888-5685
KZFM-FM 95.5 MHz (CHR) PO Box 9757	Corpus Christi	TX	78469	361-882-7411	882-9767

— Colleges/Universities —

				Phone	Fax
Del Mar College East Campus 101 Baldwin Blvd	Corpus Christi	TX	78404	361-698-1200	698-1182*
**Fax:* Library ■ *TF Admissions:* 800-652-3357 ■ *Web:* www.delmar.edu					
Texas A & M University Corpus Christi 6300 Ocean Dr	Corpus Christi	TX	78412	361-991-6810	994-5887
TF: 800-482-6822 ■ *Web:* www.tamucc.edu					

Corpus Christi (Cont'd)

— Hospitals —

Name / Address	City	State	Zip	Phone	Fax
Christus Spohn Hospital Kleberg PO Box 1197	Kingsville	TX	78363	361-595-1661	595-5005
Christus Spohn Hospital-Shoreline 600 Elizabeth St **Fax: Admitting*	Corpus Christi	TX	78404	361-881-3000	881-3738*
Christus Spohn Memorial Hospital 2606 Hospital Blvd	Corpus Christi	TX	78405	361-902-4000	902-4968
Columbia Alice Physicians & Surgeons Hospital 300 E 3rd St	Alice	TX	78332	361-664-4376	664-4021
Columbia Doctors Regional Medical Center 3315 S Alameda St.	Corpus Christi	TX	78411	361-857-1501	857-5960
Corpus Christi Medical Center 7101 S Padre Island Dr	Corpus Christi	TX	78412	361-985-1200	985-3670
Driscoll Children's Hospital PO Box 6530	Corpus Christi	TX	78466	361-694-5000	694-5317

— Attractions —

Name / Address	City	State	Zip	Phone	Fax
Aransas National Wildlife Refuge PO Box 100	Austwell	TX	77950	361-286-3559	286-3722
Art Center of Corpus Christi 100 Shoreline Dr.	Corpus Christi	TX	78401	361-884-6406	884-8836
Asian Cultures Museum 1809 N Chaparral St	Corpus Christi	TX	78401	361-882-2641	882-5718
Bayfront Plaza Convention Center 1901 N Shoreline Blvd.	Corpus Christi	TX	78401	361-883-8543	883-0788
Captain Clark's Flagship People's Street T-Head Corpus Christi Marina	Corpus Christi	TX	78401	361-884-8306	
Conner John E Museum 821 W Santa Gertrudis St	Kingsville	TX	78363	361-593-2810	593-2112
Corpus Christi Ballet 1621 N Mesquite St *Web:* www.tamu.edu/ccballet/	Corpus Christi	TX	78401	361-882-4588	881-9291
Corpus Christi Botanical Gardens 8545 S Staples St	Corpus Christi	TX	78413	361-852-2100	852-7875
Corpus Christi Museum of Science & History 1900 N Chaparral St	Corpus Christi	TX	78401	361-883-2862	884-7392
Corpus Christi Symphony 1901 N Shoreline Blvd Selena Auditorium *TF:* 877-286-6683	Corpus Christi	TX	78401	361-882-4091	882-4132
Corpus Christi Zoo County Rd 33	Corpus Christi	TX	78403	361-814-8000	
French-Galvan House 1581 N Chaparral St	Corpus Christi	TX	78401	361-883-0639	883-0676
Fulton Mansion 317 Fulton Beach Rd	Rockport	TX	78382	361-729-0386	729-6581
Grande-Grossman House 1517 N Chaparral St	Corpus Christi	TX	78401	361-887-0868	887-9773
Gugenheim House 1601 N Chaparral St.	Corpus Christi	TX	78401	361-887-1601	887-1602
Harbor Playhouse 1 Bayfront Pk. *Web:* www.harborplayhouse.com/ ■ *E-mail:* boxoffic@harborplayhouse.com	Corpus Christi	TX	78401	361-888-7469	888-4779
Henrietta Memorial Center 405 N 6th St.	Kingsville	TX	78363	361-595-1881	592-3247
Heritage Park 1581 N Chaparral St.	Corpus Christi	TX	78401	361-883-0639	883-0676
International Kite Museum 3200 Surfside	Corpus Christi	TX	78403	361-883-7456	883-1437
Jalufka-Govatos House 1513 N Chaparral St	Corpus Christi	TX	78401	361-882-9226	
King Ranch Hwy 141 W *Web:* www.king-ranch.com	Kingsville	TX	78363	361-592-8055	595-1344
Littles-Martin House 1519 N Chaparral St	Corpus Christi	TX	78401	361-883-0639	
McCampbell House 1501 N Chaparral St	Corpus Christi	TX	78401	361-883-0639	
Mustang Island State Park Hwy 361	Port Aransas	TX	78373	361-749-5246	749-6455
Padre Island National Seashore PO Box 181300 *Web:* www.nps.gov/pais/	Corpus Christi	TX	78480	361-949-8173	949-8023
Palo Alto Battlefield National Historic Site 1623 Central Blvd *Web:* www.nps.gov/paal/	Brownsville	TX	78520	956-541-2785	541-6356
Port Aransas Park 321 Beach Rd Mustang Island	Port Aransas	TX	78412	361-749-6117	
Port of Corpus Christi 222 Power St. *TF:* 800-580-7110 ■ *Web:* www.portofcorpuschristi.com	Corpus Christi	TX	78401	361-882-5633	882-7110
Rockport Center for the Arts 902 Navigation Cir	Rockport	TX	78382	361-729-5519	729-3551
Ships of Christopher Columbus 1900 N Chaparral St	Corpus Christi	TX	78401	361-883-2862	884-7392
Sidbury House 1606 N Chaparral St	Corpus Christi	TX	78401	361-883-0639	
South Texas Institute for the Arts 1902 N Shoreline Blvd. *Web:* www.stia.org ■ *E-mail:* stiaweb@falcon.tamucc.edu	Corpus Christi	TX	78401	361-980-3500	980-3520
Texas Maritime Museum 1202 Navigation Cir.	Rockport	TX	78382	361-729-1271	729-9938
Texas State Aquarium 2710 N Shoreline Blvd. *Web:* www.txstateaq.org ■ *E-mail:* tsa@davlin.net	Corpus Christi	TX	78402	361-881-1200	881-1257
USS Lexington Museum on the Bay 2914 N Shoreline Blvd.	Corpus Christi	TX	78402	361-888-4873	883-8361
Xeriscape Learning Center & Design Garden 1900 N Chaparral St	Corpus Christi	TX	78401	361-883-2862	884-7392

SPORTS TEAMS & FACILITIES

Name / Address	City	State	Zip	Phone	Fax
Corpus Christi Greyhound Race Track 5302 Leopard St.	Corpus Christi	TX	78408	361-289-9333	289-4307
Corpus Christi Speedway SR-358 & SR-44	Corpus Christi	TX	78405	512-289-8847	

— Events —

	Phone
Annual Christmas Tree Forest (December)	361-980-3500
Artfest (mid-April)	361-884-6406
Bayfest (mid-September)	361-887-0868
Beach to Bay Marathon (mid-May)	361-225-3338
Buccaneer Days & Rodeo (mid-April-early May)	361-882-3242
Corpus Christi Maritime Festival (May)	361-883-5011
Deep Sea Roundup (early July)	361-749-5919
Harbor Lights (December)	361-985-1555
La Feria De Las Flores (early August)	361-883-8543
Oysterfest (early March)	361-729-2388
Rockport Art Festival (early July)	361-729-6445
Rockport Seafair (mid-October)	361-729-3312
Shrimporee (September)	361-758-2750
South Texas Ranching Heritage Festival (February)	361-595-3712
Texas Jazz Festival (mid-October)	361-883-4500
US Open Windsurfing Regatta (late May)	361-985-1555

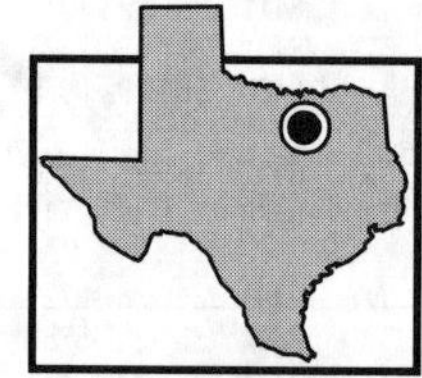

Dallas

Home to 22 Fortune 500 companies, the largest urban arts district in America, and hundreds of tourist attractions in the city and surrounding area, Dallas is a major center for business, culture, and entertainment. The downtown area of Dallas includes Dealey Plaza and the former Texas School Book Depository from which Lee Harvey Oswald fired the shots that took the life of President John F. Kennedy in 1963. The Sixth Floor Museum, located on the sixth floor of the Depository, now includes an exhibit that chronicles JFK's life. Located also in the downtown area is the West End MarketPlace, a popular restaurant and entertainment center; and just east of there is Deep Ellum, an area of trendy art galleries, restaurants, and clubs. The upscale area of North Dallas is known for its shopping. With four professional sports teams—the Dallas Cowboys (football), the Texas Rangers (baseball), the Dallas Mavericks (basketball), and the Dallas Stars (hockey)—the Dallas area is also popular among sports enthusiasts.

Population	1,075,894	**Longitude**	96-81-00 W
Area (Land)	327 sq mi	**County**	Dallas
Area (Water)	19.7 sq mi	**Time Zone**	CST
Elevation	463 ft	**Area Code/s**	214, 972
Latitude	32-78-00 N		

Dallas (Cont'd)

— Average Temperatures and Precipitation —

TEMPERATURES

	Jan	Feb	Mar	Apr	May	Jun	Jul	Aug	Sep	Oct	Nov	Dec
High	55	60	69	77	84	91	96	96	88	78	67	58
Low	35	39	47	56	64	72	76	76	68	57	47	38

PRECIPITATION

	Jan	Feb	Mar	Apr	May	Jun	Jul	Aug	Sep	Oct	Nov	Dec
Inches	1.8	2.3	3.2	3.9	5.0	3.5	2.4	2.3	3.6	3.9	2.4	1.9

— Important Phone Numbers —

	Phone
AAA	214-526-7911
American Express Travel	214-363-0214
Dallas Artsline	214-522-2659
Dental Referral	214-526-3435
Emergency	911
Highway Conditions	800-452-9292
HotelDocs	800-468-3537
Medical Referral	214-320-7750
Poison Control Center	800-764-7661
Special Events Hotline	214-746-6679
Travelers Aid	972-574-4420
Weather	214-787-1111

— Information Sources —

				Phone	Fax
Better Business Bureau Serving Metropolitan Dallas & Northeast Texas 2001 Bryan St Suite 850 *Web:* www.dallas.bbb.org	Dallas	TX	75201	214-220-2000	740-0321
Dallas City Hall 1500 Marilla St *Web:* www.ci.dallas.tx.us/	Dallas	TX	75201	214-670-3011	670-3946
Dallas Convention & Visitors Bureau 1201 Elm St Suite 2000 *TF:* 800-232-5527 ■ *Web:* www.dallascvb.com	Dallas	TX	75270	214-571-1000	571-1008
Dallas Convention Center 650 S Griffin St *TF:* 877-850-2100	Dallas	TX	75202	214-939-2700	939-2795
Dallas County 411 Elm St	Dallas	TX	75202	214-653-7361	653-7057
Dallas Mayor 1500 Marilla St Rm 5E-N *Web:* www.ci.dallas.tx.us/html/mayor_and_city_council.html	Dallas	TX	75201	214-670-0773	670-0646
Dallas Planning & Development Dept 1500 Marilla St Rm 5D-N *Web:* www.ci.dallas.tx.us/html/planning___development.html	Dallas	TX	75201	214-670-4127	670-5755
Greater Dallas Chamber of Commerce 1201 Elm St Suite 2000 *Web:* www.gdc.org	Dallas	TX	75270	214-746-6600	746-6799
Jonsson J Eric Public Library 1515 Young St *Web:* www.lib.ci.dallas.tx.us/home.htm	Dallas	TX	75201	214-670-1400	670-7839

On-Line Resources

4Dallas.com . . . www.4dallas.com
About.com Guide to Dallas . . . dallas.about.com/local/southwestus/dallas
Access America Dallas . . . www.accessamer.com/dallas/
Anthill City Guide Dallas/Fort Worth . . . www.anthill.com/city.asp?city=dallas
Area Guide Dallas . . . dallas.areaguides.net
Boulevards Dallas . . . www.dallas.com
Bradmans.com Dallas . . . www.bradmans.com/scripts/display_city.cgi?city=234
City Knowledge Dallas . . . www.cityknowledge.com/tx_dallas.htm
Cityhits Dallas . . . www.cityhits.com/dallas/
CuisineNet Dallas . . . www.menusonline.com/cities/dallas/locmain.shtml
Dallas CityWomen . . . www.citywomen.com/dalwomen.htm
Dallas Entertainment Guide . . . www.wn.com/dallas
Dallas Fort Worth City Pages . . . dallas.thelinks.com/
Dallas Fort Worth Metroplex Directory . . . www.flash.net/~dfwmet/
Dallas-Fort Worth Texas . . . www.dallas-fort-worth.com
Dallas Gay/Lesbian Guide . . . www.cyberramp.net/~woofbyte/dfw_home.htm
Dallas Information . . . www.dallas.org/
Dallas Observer . . . www.dallasobserver.com
Dallas Virtual Jewish Community . . . www.dvjc.org
Dallas/Fort Worth Area Web . . . www.dfwareaweb.com/
DigitalCity Dallas-Fort Worth . . . home.digitalcity.com/dallas
Excite.com Dallas City Guide . . . www.excite.com/travel/countries/united_states/texas/dallas
GuideLive: Arts & Entertainment in Dallas & Fort Worth . . . www.guidelive.com
Hometown Dallas . . . www.hometowndallas.com
HotelGuide Dallas/Fort Worth . . . hotelguide.net/dfw/
LDS iAmerica Dallas . . . dallas.iamerica.net
MetroGuide Dallas/Fort Worth . . . metroguide.net/dfw/
NITC Travelbase City Guide Dallas-Fort Worth . . . www.travelbase.com/auto/guides/dallas_ft_worth-area-tx.html
Open World City Guides Dallas . . . www.worldexecutive.com/cityguides/dallas/
Preservation Dallas . . . www.preservationdallas.org/
Rough Guide Travel Dallas . . . travel.roughguides.com/content/938/
Savvy Diner Guide to Dallas Restaurants . . . www.savvydiner.com/dallas/
Virtual Voyages Dallas-Fort Worth . . . www.virtualvoyages.com/usa/tx/dfw/dfw.sht
Yahoo! Dallas/Fort Worth . . . dfw.yahoo.com
YourDallas.com . . . www.yourdallas.com/

— Transportation Services —

AIRPORTS

■ **Dallas-Fort Worth International Airport (DFW)**

	Phone
16 miles NW of downtown Dallas (approx 30 minutes) Web: www.dfwairport.com	972-574-8888

Airport Transportation

	Phone
Discount Shuttle $11 fare to downtown Dallas	817-267-5150
Taxi $32-34 fare to downtown Dallas	214-426-6262
Taxi Dallas $30 fare to downtown Dallas	214-821-8294

Commercial Airlines

	Phone
AeroMexico	972-751-1484
AirTran	800-247-8726
American	800-433-7300
American Eagle	800-433-7300
Aspen Mountain Air Inc	972-641-7337
British Airways	800-247-9297
Continental	972-263-0523
Continental Express	800-525-0280
Delta	214-630-3200
El Al	800-223-6700
Lufthansa	800-645-3880
Mesa	800-637-2247
Mexicana	800-531-7923
Midwest Express	800-452-2022
National	888-757-5387
Northwest	800-225-2525
Southwest	972-263-1717
Spirit	800-772-7117
Thai	800-426-5204
TWA	800-221-2000
United	800-241-6522
US Airways	800-428-4322
Vanguard	800-826-4827

Charter Airlines

	Phone
Alpha Aviation	214-352-4801
Miami Air International	305-871-3300
Million Air	800-248-1602
Sun Country	800-359-5786

■ **Love Field (DAL)**

	Phone
6 miles NW of downtown (approx 15 minutes)	214-670-6080

Airport Transportation

	Phone
Discount Shuttle $11 fare to downtown Dallas	817-267-5150
SuperShuttle $11 fare to downtown Dallas	817-329-2025

Commercial Airlines

	Phone
Continental	800-525-0280
Southwest	972-263-1717

Charter Airlines

	Phone
Aerodynamics Inc	214-352-2376
All-Star Helicopters Inc	972-250-9907
Alliance Executive Charter Services	800-232-5387
American Business Charter Inc	972-732-7344
American Jet International Corp	888-435-9254
Business Jet Services	888-387-7477
Corporate Aviation Services Inc	918-834-8348
Helicopters Inc	800-466-2903
Jet Aviation	214-351-6571
Raytheon Aircraft Charter	800-519-6283
Regal Aviation	877-359-6520
Rivair Flying Service Inc	918-299-1234
Stebbins Jet Center	903-643-2601
Texas Air Charters	940-898-1200
TXI Aviation Inc	972-647-7365
Zebra Air Inc	214-358-7200

CAR RENTALS

	Phone
Ace	972-329-0647
Advantage	214-350-8961
Alamo	972-621-0236
Avis	972-574-4130
Budget	817-329-2277
Dollar	972-929-8888
Enterprise	972-986-0193
Hertz	972-453-0370
National	972-574-3400
Thrifty	972-621-1234

Dallas (Cont'd)

LIMO/TAXI

	Phone
Allied Taxi	214-819-9999
Carey Limousine	214-638-4828
Checker Cab	214-841-0000
Cowboy Cab	214-428-0202
Dallas Limousine	972-910-9090
Five Star Limousine	972-234-5466
Republic Taxi	214-902-7077
Taxi Dallas	214-821-8294
Terminal Taxi	214-350-4445
Texas Limousines	214-426-1111
VIP Limousine	817-481-3060
Wynne Transportation	972-481-1234
Yellow Cab	214-426-6262

MASS TRANSIT

	Phone
DART $1 Base fare	214-979-1111

RAIL/BUS

				Phone
Dallas Union Amtrak Station 400 S Houston St.	Dallas	TX	75202	214-653-1101
Greyhound Bus Station 205 S Lamar St *TF:* 800-231-2222	Dallas	TX	75202	214-655-7082

— Accommodations —

HOTEL RESERVATION SERVICES

	Phone	Fax
Hotel Reservations Network Inc *TF Sales:* 800-964-6835 ■ *Web:* www.hoteldiscount.com	214-361-7311	361-7299
Quikbook *TF:* 800-789-9887 ■ *Web:* www.quikbook.com	212-532-1660	532-1556
USA Hotels *TF:* 800-872-4683 ■ *Web:* www.1800usahotels.com ■ *E-mail:* info@1800usahotels.com	252-331-1555	331-2021

HOTELS, MOTELS, RESORTS

				Phone	Fax
Adam's Mark Hotel 400 N Olive St *TF:* 800-444-2326 ■ *Web:* www.adamsmark.com/dallas/index.htm	Dallas	TX	75201	214-922-8000	969-7650
Adolphus Hotel 1321 Commerce St. *TF:* 800-221-9083	Dallas	TX	75202	214-742-8200	651-3588
Best Western Market Center Hotel 2023 Market Center Blvd *TF:* 800-275-7419	Dallas	TX	75207	214-741-9000	741-6100
Best Western Preston Suites 6104 LBJ Fwy *TF:* 800-524-7038	Dallas	TX	75240	972-458-2626	385-8331
Clarion Hotel 1981 N Central Expy *TF:* 800-285-3434	Richardson	TX	75080	972-644-4000	644-0135
Clarion Suites 2363 Stemmons Trail *TF:* 800-252-7466	Dallas	TX	75220	214-350-2300	350-5144
Courtyard by Marriott 2383 Stemmons Trail *TF:* 800-321-2211 ■ *Web:* courtyard.com/DALSM	Dallas	TX	75220	214-352-7676	352-4914
Courtyard by Marriott 2930 Forest Ln *TF:* 800-321-2211 ■ *Web:* courtyard.com/DALNW	Dallas	TX	75234	972-620-8000	620-9267
Courtyard by Marriott Las Colinas 1151 W Walnut Hill Ln *TF:* 800-321-2211 ■ *Web:* courtyard.com/DALLA	Irving	TX	75038	972-550-8100	550-0764
Courtyard by Marriott Market Center 2150 Market Ctr Blvd *TF:* 800-321-2211 ■ *Web:* courtyard.com/DALCH	Dallas	TX	75207	214-653-1166	653-1892
Courtyard by Marriott Northpark 10325 N Central Expy *TF:* 800-321-2211 ■ *Web:* courtyard.com/DALCC	Dallas	TX	75231	214-739-2500	739-6450
Crescent Court Hotel 400 Crescent Ct *TF:* 800-654-6541	Dallas	TX	75201	214-871-3200	871-3272
Crowne Plaza Market Center 7050 Stemmons Fwy *TF:* 800-227-6963	Dallas	TX	75247	214-630-8500	630-9486
Crowne Plaza Suites 7800 Alpha Rd *TF:* 800-227-6963 ■ *Web:* www.basshotels.com/crowneplaza/?_franchisee=DALTX ■ *E-mail:* cps-dallas@bristolhotels.com	Dallas	TX	75240	972-233-7600	701-8618
Dallas Grand Hotel 1914 Commerce St. *TF:* 800-421-0011 ■ *Web:* www.dallasgrandhotel.com	Dallas	TX	75201	214-747-7000	749-0231
DFW Hilton Executive Conference Center 1800 Hwy 26 E. *Fax: Sales ■ *TF:* 800-645-1019	Grapevine	TX	76051	817-481-8444	481-3146*
Doubletree Hotel 8250 N Central Expy *TF:* 800-222-8733 ■ *Web:* www.doubletreehotels.com/DoubleT/Hotel81/88/88Main.htm	Dallas	TX	75206	214-691-8700	706-0187
Doubletree Hotel at Lincoln Centre 5410 LBJ Fwy *TF:* 800-222-8733 ■ *Web:* www.dallaslc.doubletreehotels.com	Dallas	TX	75240	972-934-8400	701-5244
Drury Inn Airport 4210 W Airport Fwy *TF:* 800-325-8300 ■ *Web:* www.druryinns.com/room/reservation/dallas_1.htm	Irving	TX	75062	972-986-1200	986-1200
Drury Inn North 2421 Walnut Hill Ln *TF:* 800-378-7946	Dallas	TX	75229	972-484-3330	484-3330
Embassy Suites 4650 W Airport Fwy *TF:* 800-362-2779	Irving	TX	75062	972-790-0093	790-4768
Embassy Suites Love Field 3880 W Northwest Hwy *TF:* 800-362-2779	Dallas	TX	75220	214-357-4500	357-0683
Embassy Suites Market Center 2727 Stemmons Fwy *TF:* 800-362-2779	Dallas	TX	75207	214-630-5332	630-3446
Embassy Suites Park Central 13131 N Central Expy *TF:* 800-362-2779	Dallas	TX	75243	972-234-3300	437-4247
Fairfield Inn 1575 Regal Row *TF:* 800-228-2800 ■ *Web:* fairfieldinn.com/DALFS	Dallas	TX	75247	214-638-6100	905-1963
Fairfield Inn by Marriott 2110 Market Ctr Blvd *TF:* 800-228-2800 ■ *Web:* fairfieldinn.com/DALMC	Dallas	TX	75207	214-760-8800	760-1659
Fairmont Hotel 1717 N Akard St. *TF:* 800-527-4727 ■ *Web:* www.fairmont.com/Hotels/Index_D.html ■ *E-mail:* dallas@fairmont.com	Dallas	TX	75201	214-720-2020	871-0673
Four Seasons Resort & Club 4150 N MacArthur Blvd *TF:* 800-332-3442 ■ *Web:* www.fourseasons.com/locations/Dallas	Irving	TX	75038	972-717-0700	717-2550
Guest Lodge at Cooper Aerobic Center Clinic 12230 Preston Rd *TF:* 800-444-5187 ■ *Web:* www.cooperaerobics.com	Dallas	TX	75230	972-239-7223	386-5415
Hampton Inn Garland 12670 E Northwest Hwy *TF:* 800-426-7866	Dallas	TX	75228	972-613-5000	613-4535
Harvey Hotel 7815 LBJ Fwy *TF:* 800-922-9222	Dallas	TX	75251	972-960-7000	788-4227
Harvey Hotel DFW Airport 4545 W John Carpenter Fwy *TF:* 800-922-9222	Irving	TX	75063	972-929-4500	929-0733
Hawthorn Suites Market Center 7900 Brookriver Dr *TF:* 800-527-1133	Dallas	TX	75247	214-688-1010	638-5215
Hilton Dallas Parkway 4801 LBJ Fwy *TF:* 800-345-6565	Dallas	TX	75244	972-661-3600	661-1060
Hiltop Hotel 5600 N Central Expy	Dallas	TX	75206	214-826-9434	821-1748
Holiday Inn 1515 N Beckley Rd *TF:* 800-465-4329	DeSoto	TX	75115	972-224-9100	228-8238
Holiday Inn Airport North 4441 W Hwy 114 *TF:* 800-465-4329	Irving	TX	75063	972-929-8181	929-8233
Holiday Inn Aristocrat Hotel 1933 Main St. *TF:* 800-465-4329 ■ *Web:* www.basshotels.com/holiday-inn/?_franchisee=DALAR	Dallas	TX	75201	214-741-7700	939-3639
Holiday Inn Express 8510 E RL Thornton Fwy *TF:* 800-465-4329	Dallas	TX	75228	214-328-8500	328-9701
Holiday Inn Market Center 1955 Market Center Blvd *TF:* 800-465-4329	Dallas	TX	75207	214-747-9551	747-0600
Holiday Inn Select Dallas Central 10650 N Central Expy *TF:* 800-465-4329 ■ *Web:* www.basshotels.com/holiday-inn/?_franchisee=DALDC ■ *E-mail:* hbassler@hisdc.com	Dallas	TX	75231	214-373-6000	373-1037
Holiday Inn Select Dallas/Fort Worth Airport South 4440 W Airport Fwy *TF:* 800-465-4329 ■ *Web:* www.basshotels.com/holiday-inn/?_franchisee=DFWSO ■ *E-mail:* john_thackray@meristar.com	Irving	TX	75062	972-399-1010	790-8545
Holiday Inn Select LBJ Northeast 11350 LBJ Fwy *TF:* 800-346-0660	Dallas	TX	75238	214-341-5400	553-9349
Holiday Inn Select North Dallas 2645 LBJ Fwy *TF:* 800-465-4329 ■ *Web:* www.basshotels.com/holiday-inn/?_franchisee=DALGW	Dallas	TX	75234	972-243-3363	484-7082
Homestead Village 2395 Stemmons Trail *TF:* 888-782-9478	Dallas	TX	75220	214-904-1400	904-1500
Homewood Suites Las Colinas 4300 Wingren Dr *TF:* 800-225-5466	Irving	TX	75039	972-556-0665	401-3765
Hotel Intercontinental Dallas 15201 Dallas Pkwy *TF:* 800-327-0200 ■ *Web:* www.interconti.com/usa/dallas/hotel_dalic.html ■ *E-mail:* ihcdallas@interconti.com	Dallas	TX	75248	972-386-6000	991-6937
Hotel St-Germain 2516 Maple Ave *TF:* 800-683-2516 ■ *Web:* lonestar.texas.net/~hotelsg/	Dallas	TX	75201	214-871-2516	871-0740

Dallas — Hotels, Motels, Resorts (Cont'd)

				Phone	Fax
Hyatt Regency 300 Reunion Blvd *TF:* 800-233-1234 ■ *Web:* www.hyatt.com/usa/dallas/hotels/hotel_dfwrd.html	Dallas	TX	75207	214-651-1234	742-8126
La Quinta Motor Inn 1625 Regal Row *TF:* 800-531-5900	Dallas	TX	75247	214-630-5701	634-2315
La Quinta Motor Inn Northpark 10001 N Central Expy *TF:* 800-531-5900	Dallas	TX	75231	214-361-8200	691-0482
La Quinta Motor Inn Richardson 13685 N Central Expy *TF:* 800-531-5900	Dallas	TX	75243	972-234-1016	234-0682
Le Meridien Dallas Hotel 650 N Pearl St *TF:* 800-543-4300 ■ *Web:* www.lemeridien-hotels.com	Dallas	TX	75201	214-979-9000	953-1931
Lexington Hotel Suites 4150 Independence Dr *TF:* 800-927-8483	Dallas	TX	75237	972-298-7014	709-1680
Mansion on Turtle Creek 2821 Turtle Creek Blvd *TF:* 800-527-5432 ■ *Web:* www.rosewood-hotels.com/mansion.htm	Dallas	TX	75219	214-559-2100	528-4187
Marriott Hotel Airport 8440 Freeport Pkwy *TF:* 800-228-9290 ■ *Web:* marriotthotels.com/DFWAP	Irving	TX	75063	972-929-8800	929-6501
Marriott Quorum 14901 Dallas Pkwy *TF:* 800-228-9290 ■ *Web:* marriotthotels.com/DALQC	Dallas	TX	75240	972-661-2800	934-1731
Melrose Hotel 3015 Oak Lawn Ave *TF:* 800-635-7673	Dallas	TX	75219	214-521-5151	521-2470
Omni Dallas Park West 1590 LBJ Fwy *TF:* 800-843-6664	Dallas	TX	75234	972-869-4300	869-3295
Omni Mandalay Hotel 221 E Las Colinas Blvd *TF:* 800-843-6664	Irving	TX	75039	972-556-0800	556-0729
Omni Richardson Hotel 701 E Campbell Rd *TF:* 800-843-6664	Richardson	TX	75081	972-231-9600	907-2578
Paramount Hotel 302 S Houston *TF:* 800-767-1664	Dallas	TX	75202	214-761-9090	761-0740
Radisson Hotel 1893 W Mockingbird Ln *TF:* 800-333-3333	Dallas	TX	75235	214-634-8850	630-8134
Radisson Hotel & Suites 2330 W Northwest Hwy *TF:* 800-333-3333	Dallas	TX	75220	214-351-4477	351-4499
Radisson Hotel Central 6060 N Central Expy *TF:* 800-333-3333	Dallas	TX	75206	214-750-6060	750-5959
Ramada Inn & Suites 4110 W Airport Fwy *TF:* 800-272-6232	Irving	TX	75062	972-790-2262	986-7620
Ramada Limited Park Cities Inn 6101 Hillcrest *TF:* 800-272-6232	Dallas	TX	75205	214-521-0330	521-0336
Ramada Market Center 1055 Regal Row *TF:* 800-441-3318	Dallas	TX	75247	214-634-8550	634-8418
Ramada Plaza Hotel Dallas Convention Center 1011 S Akard St *TF:* 800-527-7606	Dallas	TX	75215	214-421-1083	428-6827
Renaissance Dallas Hotel 2222 N Stemmons Fwy *TF:* 800-468-3571	Dallas	TX	75207	214-631-2222	905-3814
Renaissance Hotel 4099 Valley View Ln *TF:* 800-468-3571	Dallas	TX	75244	972-385-9000	788-1174
Residence Inn by Marriott 10333 N Central Expy *TF:* 800-331-3131 ■ *Web:* www.residenceinn.com/DALCE	Dallas	TX	75231	214-750-8220	750-8244
Residence Inn by Marriott Las Colinas 950 Walnut Hill Ln *TF:* 800-331-3131 ■ *Web:* www.residenceinn.com/DALLS	Irving	TX	75038	972-580-7773	550-8824
Residence Inn by Marriott Market Center 6950 N Stemmons Fwy *TF:* 800-331-3131 ■ *Web:* www.residenceinn.com/DALMK	Dallas	TX	75247	214-631-2472	634-9645
Residence Inn by Marriott North Central 13636 Goldmark Dr *TF:* 800-331-3131 ■ *Web:* www.residenceinn.com/DALRN	Dallas	TX	75240	972-669-0478	644-2632
Sheraton Dallas Brookhollow 1241 W Mockingbird Ln *TF:* 800-325-3535	Dallas	TX	75247	214-630-7000	638-6943
Sheraton Grand Hotel 4440 W John Carpenter Fwy *TF:* 800-325-3535	Irving	TX	75063	972-929-8400	929-4885
Sheraton Park Central 7750 LBJ Fwy *TF:* 800-325-3535	Dallas	TX	75251	972-233-4421	701-8351
Sheraton Suites Market Center 2101 Stemmons Fwy *TF:* 888-325-3535	Dallas	TX	75207	214-747-3000	742-5713
Stoneleigh Hotel 2927 Maple Ave *TF:* 800-255-9299 ■ *Web:* www.stoneleighhotel.com	Dallas	TX	75201	214-871-7111	871-9379
StudioPLUS 2979 N Stemmons Fwy *TF:* 800-646-8000	Dallas	TX	75247	214-630-0154	630-0197
Sumner Suites Dallas Galleria 5229 Spring Valley Rd *TF:* 800-747-8483	Dallas	TX	75240	972-716-2001	716-4054
Terra Cotta Inn 6101 LBJ Fwy *TF:* 800-533-3591	Dallas	TX	75240	972-387-2525	387-3784
Travel Inn 4500 Harry Hines Blvd	Dallas	TX	75219	214-522-6650	526-0049
Westin Hotel Galleria Dallas 13340 Dallas Pkwy *TF:* 800-228-3000	Dallas	TX	75240	972-934-9494	851-2869
Westin Park Central Hotel & Towers 12720 Merit Dr *TF:* 800-937-8461	Dallas	TX	75251	972-385-3000	991-4557
Wilson World Hotel & Suites Market Center Dallas 2325 N Stemmons Fwy *TF:* 800-945-7667	Dallas	TX	75207	214-630-3330	689-0420
Wyndham Anatole Hotel 2201 Stemmons Fwy *TF:* 800-996-3426	Dallas	TX	75207	214-748-1200	761-7520
Wyndham Garden Hotel Las Colinas 110 W John Carpenter Fwy *TF:* 800-996-3426	Irving	TX	75039	972-650-1600	541-0501
Wyndham Garden Market Center 2015 Market Center Blvd *TF:* 800-996-3426	Dallas	TX	75207	214-741-7481	747-6191

— Restaurants —

				Phone
650 North (New American) 650 N Pearl St	Dallas	TX	75201	214-855-1708
Adelmo's (Mediterranean) 4537 Cole Ave	Dallas	TX	75205	214-559-0325
Amici Signature (Italian) 1022 S Broadway St	Carrollton	TX	75506	972-245-3191
Antares (American) 300 Reunion Blvd	Dallas	TX	75207	214-712-7145
Anzu (Pan-Asian) 4620 McKinney Ave	Dallas	TX	75205	214-526-7398
AquaKnox (International) 3214 Knox Ave	Dallas	TX	75205	214-219-2782
August Moon (Chinese) 15030 Preston Rd *Web:* august moon.com/	Dallas	TX	75240	972-385-7227
Baby Doe's (Steak/Seafood) 3305 Harry Hines Blvd	Dallas	TX	75201	214-871-7310
Beau Nash (New American) 400 Crescent Ct	Dallas	TX	75201	214-871-3240
Blind Lemon Restaurant (American) 2805 Main St	Dallas	TX	75226	214-939-0202
Blue Goose Cantina (Tex Mex) 2905 Greenville Ave	Dallas	TX	75206	214-823-8339
Bombay Cricket Club (Indian) 2508 Maple Ave	Dallas	TX	75201	214-871-1333
Cacharel (French) 2221 E Lamar Blvd Suite 910	Arlington	TX	76006	817-640-9981
Cafe Capri (Continental) 15107 Addison Rd	Dallas	TX	75248	972-960-8686
Cafe Esplanade (Southwest) 300 Reunion Blvd	Dallas	TX	75207	214-712-7148
Cafe on the Green (New American) 4150 N MacArthur Blvd	Irving	TX	75038	972-717-0700
Cafe Pacific (Seafood) 24 Highland Park Village	Dallas	TX	75205	214-526-1170
Chez Gerard (French) 4444 McKinney	Dallas	TX	75205	214-522-6865
City Cafe (American) 5757 W Lovers Ln	Dallas	TX	75209	214-351-2233
Dakota's (American) 600 N Akard St	Dallas	TX	75201	214-740-4001
Deep Ellum Cafe (New American) 2706 Elm St	Dallas	TX	75226	214-741-9012
Deep Sushi (Japanese) 2624 Elm St	Dallas	TX	75226	214-651-1177
Del Frisco's Double Eagle Steak House (Steak) 5251 Spring Valley	Dallas	TX	75240	972-490-9000
Dick's Last Resort (American) 1701 N Market St Suite 110	Dallas	TX	75202	214-747-0001
French Room (French) 1321 Commerce St	Dallas	TX	75202	214-742-8200
Gloria's (Mexican) 4140 Lemmon Ave	Dallas	TX	75219	214-521-7576
Hard Rock Cafe (American) 2601 McKinney Ave	Dallas	TX	75204	214-855-0007
Hoffbrau Steaks (Steak) 3205 Knox St *Web:* www.dallassites.com/hoffbrau/	Dallas	TX	75205	214-559-2680
India Palace Restaurant (Indian) 12817 Preston Rd	Dallas	TX	75230	972-392-0190
Javier's Gourmet Mexicano (Mexican) 4912 Cole Ave	Dallas	TX	75205	214-521-4211
Jennivine (Continental) 3604 McKinney Ave	Dallas	TX	75205	214-528-6010
Korea House Restaurant (Korean) 2598 Royal Ln	Dallas	TX	75229	972-243-0434
L'Ancestral (French) 4514 Travis St	Dallas	TX	75205	214-528-1081
La Trattoria Lombardi (Italian) 2916 N Hall St	Dallas	TX	75204	214-954-0803
Lavendou (French) 19009 Preston Rd	Dallas	TX	75252	972-248-1911
Le Castel (French) 2023 Market Center Blvd	Dallas	TX	75207	214-741-9000
Lombardi's (Italian) 311 N Market St	Dallas	TX	75202	214-747-0322
Lone Star Oyster Bar (Seafood) 3707 Greenville	Dallas	TX	75206	214-827-3013
Lulu's Bait Shack (Cajun/Creole) 2621 McKinney Ave	Dallas	TX	75204	214-969-1927
Mansion on Turtle Creek (Southwest) 2821 Turtle Creek Blvd	Dallas	TX	75219	214-559-2100
Margaux's (Cajun) 2404 Cedar Springs	Dallas	TX	75205	214-740-1985
May Dragon (Chinese) 4848 Beltline Rd	Dallas	TX	75240	972-392-9998
Mediterraneo (Mediterranean) 18111 Preston Rd Suite 120	Dallas	TX	75252	972-447-0066
Mercado Juarez (Mexican) 1901 W Northwest Hwy	Dallas	TX	75220	972-556-0796
Nana Grill (New American) 2201 Stemmons Fwy	Dallas	TX	75207	214-761-7479
Nero's (Italian) 2104 Greenville Ave	Dallas	TX	75206	214-826-6376
Newport's Seafood (Seafood) 703 McKinney Ave	Dallas	TX	75202	214-954-0220
Old San Francisco Steakhouse (Steak) 10965 Composite Dr	Dallas	TX	75220	214-357-0484
Old Warsaw (Continental) 2610 Maple Ave	Dallas	TX	75201	214-528-0032
Palm The Restaurant (Steak/Seafood) 701 Ross Ave	Dallas	TX	75202	214-698-0470
Palomino Euro Bistro (Mediterranean) 500 Crescent Ct	Dallas	TX	75201	214-999-1222
Pappadeaux Seafood Kitchen (Cajun/Creole) 3520 Oak Lawn	Dallas	TX	75219	214-521-4700
Pierre's by the Lake (Continental) 3430 Shorecrest Dr	Dallas	TX	75235	214-358-2379
Planet Hollywood (American) 603 Munger Ave Suite 105	Dallas	TX	75202	214-749-7827

Dallas — Restaurants (Cont'd)

Name / Address	City	State	ZIP	Phone
Prego Pasta House (Italian) 4930 Greenville Ave	Dallas	TX	75206	214-363-9204
Primo's (Mexican) 3309 McKinney Ave	Dallas	TX	75204	214-220-0510
Pyramid Room (French) 1717 N Akard St	Dallas	TX	75201	214-720-5249
Queen of Sheba (Ethopian) 3527 McKinney	Dallas	TX	75204	214-521-0491
Rainforest Cafe (American) 300 Grapevine Mills Pkwy	Grapevine	TX	76051	972-539-5001
Web: www.rainforestcafe.com				
Rancho Martinez (Tex Mex) 6332 La Vista Dr	Dallas	TX	75214	214-823-5517
Riviera (French) 7709 Inwood Rd	Dallas	TX	75209	214-351-0094
Royal Tokyo (Japanese) 7525 Greenville Ave	Dallas	TX	75231	214-368-3304
Ruggeri's Ristorante (Italian) 2911 Routh St	Dallas	TX	75201	214-871-7377
Ruth's Chris Steak House (Steak) 5922 Cedar Springs Rd	Dallas	TX	75235	214-902-8080
Saint Martin's (Steak/Seafood) 8350 N Central Expy Suite M-1000	Dallas	TX	75206	214-361-8833
Sevy's Grill (Southwest) 8201 Preston Rd	Dallas	TX	75225	214-265-7389
Sipango (Italian) 4513 Travis St	Dallas	TX	75205	214-522-2411
Sonny Bryan's Smoke House (Barbecue) 2202 Inwood Rd	Dallas	TX	75235	214-357-7120
Web: www.sonnybryans.com				
Star Canyon (New American) 3102 Oak Lawn Ave Suite 144	Dallas	TX	75219	214-520-7827
Table Five (New American) 400 Decorative Center	Dallas	TX	75207	214-698-3001
Trail Dust Steak House (Steak) 10841 Composite Dr	Dallas	TX	75220	214-357-3862
Web: www.traildust.com				
Truluck's (Steak/Seafood) 2401 McKinney Ave	Dallas	TX	75201	214-220-2401

— Goods and Services —

SHOPPING

Name / Address	City	State	ZIP	Phone	Fax
Collin Creek Mall 811 N Central Expy	Plano	TX	75075	972-422-1070	881-1642
Web: www.collincreekmall.com					
Deep Ellum 2932 Main St Suite 101	Dallas	TX	75226	214-748-4332	741-4567
Web: www.deepellumtx.com/					
Galleria The 13350 Dallas Pkwy	Dallas	TX	75240	972-702-7100	702-7172
Grapevine Mills 3000 Grapevine Mills Pkwy	Grapevine	TX	76051	972-724-4904	724-4920
Web: www.grapevinemills.com					
Highland Park Village Preston Rd & Mockingbird Ln	Dallas	TX	75205	214-559-2740	521-4326
Web: www.hpvillage.com					
Inwood Trade Center 1300 Inwood Rd	Dallas	TX	75247	214-521-4777	559-9795
Love Field Antique Mall 6500 Cedar Springs	Dallas	TX	75235	214-357-6500	358-2188
McKinney Avenue Antique Market 2710 McKinney Ave	Dallas	TX	75204	214-871-9803	871-2463
Neiman Marcus 1618 Main St	Dallas	TX	75201	214-741-6911	573-6136
TF Orders: 800-825-8000 ■ *Web:* www.neimanmarcus.com					
Northpark Center 8687 N Central Expy	Dallas	TX	75231	214-363-7441	
Plaza of the Americas 700 N Pearl	Dallas	TX	75201	214-720-8000	969-1081
Quadrangle The 2828 Routh St	Dallas	TX	75201	214-871-0878	871-1136
Richardson Square Mall 501 S Plano Rd	Richardson	TX	75081	972-783-0117	470-9087
Saks Fifth Avenue 13250 Dallas Pkwy	Dallas	TX	75240	972-458-7000	458-7679
Southwest Center Mall 3662 W Camp Wisdom Rd	Dallas	TX	75237	972-296-1491	296-4220
Valley View Center Mall Preston Rd & LBJ Fwy	Dallas	TX	75240	972-661-2425	239-1344
Vista Ridge Mall 2401 S Stemmons Fwy	Lewisville	TX	75067	972-315-0015	315-3725
West End MarketPlace 603 Munger Ave	Dallas	TX	75202	214-748-4801	748-4803

BANKS

Name / Address	City	State	ZIP	Phone	Fax
Bank of America 901 Main St	Dallas	TX	75202	214-508-6262	978-1354*
**Fax:* Cust Svc ■ *TF Cust Svc:* 800-247-6262*					
Bank One Texas NA 1717 Main St	Dallas	TX	75201	214-290-2000	290-3696
TF: 800-695-1111					
Chase Bank of Texas 2200 Ross Ave	Dallas	TX	75201	214-922-2300	965-3767*
**Fax:* Cust Svc ■ *TF:* 800-882-7230					
Comerica Bank-Texas 1919 Woodall Rogers Frwy	Dallas	TX	75201	214-953-1268	871-0313
Guaranty Federal Bank FSB 8333 Douglas Ave	Dallas	TX	75225	214-360-3360	369-1004
Web: www.gfbank.com					
NationsBank of Texas NA 1401 Elm St	Dallas	TX	75202	214-508-7799	978-1805*
**Fax:* Hum Res					
Provident Bank 13760 Noel St Suite 100	Dallas	TX	75240	972-458-0500	448-8480
Wells Fargo Bank 1445 Ross Ave	Dallas	TX	75202	214-740-0099	953-0238

BUSINESS SERVICES

Name	Phone	Name	Phone
Accountemps	972-644-5252	**One Hour Delivery Service**	972-444-2900
Dunhill Staffing	817-282-8367	**Post Office**	214-760-4489
Federal Express	800-463-3339	**Suite Images**	972-991-8880
Kelly Services	214-373-6736	**United Messengers**	214-871-1515
Kinko's	214-696-9863	**UPS**	800-742-5877
Manpower Temporary Services	214-363-5325	**US Courier**	214-358-0872
Olsten Staffing Services	214-979-0099	**Wingtip Couriers**	972-222-0222

— Media —

PUBLICATIONS

Name / Address	City	State	ZIP	Phone	Fax
D Magazine 1700 Commerce 18th Fl	Dallas	TX	75201	214-939-3636	748-4153*
**Fax:* Edit ■ *Web:* www.dmagazine.com ■ *E-mail:* feedback@dmagazine.com					
Dallas Business Journal 10670 N Central Expy Suite 710	Dallas	TX	75231	214-696-5959	361-4045*
**Fax:* Edit ■ *Web:* www.amcity.com/dallas					
Dallas Morning News‡ PO Box 655237	Dallas	TX	75265	214-977-8222	977-8319
Web: www.dallasnews.com ■ *E-mail:* tdmned@cityview.com					
Northside People 6116 N Central Expy Suite 230	Dallas	TX	75206	214-739-2244	363-6948
Web: www.peoplenewspapers.com ■ *E-mail:* people@peoplenewspapers.com					

‡*Daily newspapers*

TELEVISION

Name / Address	City	State	ZIP	Phone	Fax
KDAF-TV Ch 33 (WB) 8001 John Carpenter Fwy	Dallas	TX	75247	214-640-3300	252-3379
Web: www.wb33.com					
KDFI-TV Ch 27 (Ind) 400 N Griffin St	Dallas	TX	75202	214-637-2727	720-3355
KDFW-TV Ch 4 (Fox) 400 N Griffin St	Dallas	TX	75202	214-720-4444	720-3263
KERA-TV Ch 13 (PBS) 3000 Harry Hines Blvd	Dallas	TX	75201	214-871-1390	740-9369
Web: www.kera.org					
KFWD-TV Ch 52 (Tele) 3000 W Story Rd	Irving	TX	75038	972-255-5200	258-1770
KLDT-TV Ch 55 (Ind) 2450 Rockbrook Dr	Lewisville	TX	75067	972-316-2115	316-1112
KMPX-TV Ch 29 (Ind) PO Box 612066	Dallas	TX	75261	817-571-1229	571-7458
KPXD-TV Ch 68 (PAX) 800 W Airport Fwy Suite 750	Irving	TX	75062	972-438-6868	579-3045
Web: www.pax.net/KPXD					
KTVT-TV Ch 11 (CBS) 5233 Bridge St	Fort Worth	TX	76103	817-451-1111	496-7739
Web: www.ktvt.com					
KTXA-TV Ch 21 (UPN) 301 N Market Suite 700	Dallas	TX	75202	214-743-2100	743-2121
Web: www.paramountstations.com/KTXA					
KUVN-TV Ch 23 (Uni) 2323 Bryan St Suite 1900	Dallas	TX	75201	214-758-2300	758-2324
TF: 800-494-5886 ■ *Web:* www.univision.net/stations/kuvn.htm					
KXAS-TV Ch 5 (NBC) 3900 Barnett St	Fort Worth	TX	76103	817-429-5555	654-6325
Web: www.kxas.com					
KXTX-TV Ch 39 (Ind) 3900 Harry Hines Blvd	Dallas	TX	75219	214-521-3900	523-5946
TF: 800-465-5989 ■ *Web:* www.kxtx.com					
WFAA-TV Ch 8 (ABC) 606 Young St Communications Ctr	Dallas	TX	75202	214-748-9631	977-6585
Web: www.wfaa.com					

RADIO

Name / Address	City	State	ZIP	Phone	Fax
KBFB-FM 97.9 MHz (AC) 4131 N Central Expy Suite 1200	Dallas	TX	75204	214-528-5500	528-0747
Web: www.kbfb.com ■ *E-mail:* kbfb@kbfb.com					
KDGE-FM 94.5 MHz (Alt) 15851 N Dallas Pkwy Suite 1200	Addison	TX	75001	972-770-7777	770-7747
Web: www.kdge.com					
KDMM-AM 1150 (Rel) 7700 Carpenter Fwy 1st Fl	Dallas	TX	75247	214-630-9400	630-0060
KDMX-FM 102.9 MHz (AC) 14001 N Dallas Pkwy Suite 1210	Dallas	TX	75240	972-991-1029	448-1029
KDXX-AM 1480 kHz (Span) 7700 Carpenter Fwy	Dallas	TX	75427	214-630-8531	920-2507
KEGL-FM 97.1 MHz (Rock) 14001 N Dallas Pkwy Suite 1210	Dallas	TX	75240	972-869-9700	263-9710
Web: www.kegl.com					
KERA-FM 90.1 MHz (NPR) 3000 Harry Hines Blvd	Dallas	TX	75201	214-871-1390	740-9369
Web: www.kera.org/ ■ *E-mail:* kerafm@metronet.com					
KESS-AM 1270 kHz (Span) 7700 Carpenter Fwy	Dallas	TX	75247	214-630-8531	920-2507
KHKS-FM 106.1 MHz (CHR) 8235 Douglas Ave Suite 300	Dallas	TX	75225	214-891-3400	692-9844
Web: www.1061kissfm.com					
KICI-FM 107.9 MHz (Span) 7700 Carpenter Fwy	Dallas	TX	75247	214-630-8531	920-2507

Dallas — Radio (Cont'd)

	City	State	Zip	Phone	Fax
KKDA-AM 730 kHz (Oldies) PO Box 530860	Grand Prairie	TX	75053	972-263-9911	558-0010
KKDA-FM 104.5 MHz (Urban) PO Box 860	Grand Prairie	TX	75053	972-263-9911	558-0010
KKZN-FM 93.3 MHz (AAA) 3500 Maple Ave Suite 1310 — *Web:* www.933thezone.com	Dallas	TX	75219	214-526-7400	787-1946
KLIF-AM 570 kHz (N/T) 3500 Maple Ave Suite 1600 — *Web:* www.klif.com	Dallas	TX	75219	214-526-2400	520-4343
KLTY-FM 94.1 MHz (Rel) 7700 Carpenter Fwy — *Web:* www.klty.com ■ *E-mail:* klty@onramp.net	Dallas	TX	75247	214-630-9400	630-0060
KLUV-AM 1190 kHz (Oldies) 4131 N Central Expy Suite 700	Dallas	TX	75204	214-526-9870	443-1570
KLUV-FM 98.7 MHz (Oldies) 4131 N Central Expy Suite 700 — *Web:* www.kluv.com ■ *E-mail:* kluv@ix.netcom.com	Dallas	TX	75204	214-526-9870	443-1570
KOAI-FM 107.5 MHz (NAC) 7901 Carpenter Fwy	Dallas	TX	75247	214-630-3011	688-7760
KPLX-FM 99.5 MHz (Ctry) 3500 Maple Ave Suite 1600	Dallas	TX	75219	214-526-2400	520-4343
KRBV-FM 100.3 MHz (Urban) 7901 John Carpenter Fwy	Dallas	TX	75247	214-630-3011	688-7760
KRLD-AM 1080 kHz (N/T) 1080 Ballpark Way — *Web:* www.krld.com	Arlington	TX	76011	817-543-5400	543-5572
KRNB-FM 105.7 MHz (AC) 621 NW 6th St	Grand Prairie	TX	75050	972-263-9911	558-0010
KRVA-AM 1600 kHz (Span) 5307 E Mockingbird Ln Suite 500	Dallas	TX	75206	214-887-9107	841-4215
KRVA-FM 106.9 MHz (Span) 5307 E Mockingbird Ln Suite 500	Dallas	TX	75206	214-887-9107	841-4215
KSCS-FM 96.3 MHz (Ctry) 2221 E Lamar Blvd Suite 400 — *Web:* www.kscs.com	Arlington	TX	76006	817-640-1963	654-9227
KTCK-AM 1310 kHz (N/T) 3500 Maple Ave Suite 1310 — *Web:* www.theticket.com	Dallas	TX	75219	214-526-7400	525-2525
KTXQ-FM 102.1 MHz (Oldies) 4131 N Central Expy Suite 1200 — *Web:* www.ktxq.com	Dallas	TX	75204	214-528-5500	528-0747
KVIL-FM 103.7 MHz (AC) 9400 N Central Expy Suite 1600 — *Web:* www.kvil.com	Dallas	TX	75231	214-691-1037	891-7975
KVTT-FM 91.7 MHz (Rel) 11061 Shady Tr	Dallas	TX	75229	214-351-6655	351-6809
KYNG-FM 105.3 MHz (Ctry) 12201 Merit Dr Suite 930 — *Web:* www.young-country.com	Dallas	TX	75251	972-716-7800	716-7835
KZMP-AM 1540 kHz (Span) 5307 E Mockingbird Ln Suite 500	Dallas	TX	75206	214-887-9107	841-4215
KZMP-FM 101.7 MHz (Span) 5307 E Mockingbird Ln Suite 500	Dallas	TX	75206	214-887-9107	841-4215
KZPS-FM 92.5 MHz (CR) 15851 Dallas Pkwy Suite 1200 — *Web:* www.kzps.com ■ *E-mail:* balberts@iadfw.net	Addison	TX	75001	972-770-7777	770-7747
WBAP-AM 820 kHz (N/T) 2221 E Lamar Blvd Suite 400 — *Web:* www.wbap.com	Arlington	TX	76006	817-640-1963	654-9227
WRR-FM 101.1 MHz (Clas) PO Box 159001 — *Web:* www.wrr101.com	Dallas	TX	75315	214-670-8888	670-8394

— Colleges/Universities —

	City	State	Zip	Phone	Fax
Amber University 1700 Eastgate Dr. — *Web:* www.amberu.edu	Garland	TX	75041	972-279-6511	279-9773
Arlington Baptist College 3001 W Division St.	Arlington	TX	76012	817-461-8741	274-1138
Art Institute of Dallas 8080 Park Ln — *TF:* 800-275-4243 ■ *Web:* www.aid.aii.edu	Dallas	TX	75231	214-692-8080	692-6541
Brookhaven College 3939 Valley View Ln — *Web:* www.dcccd.edu/bhc/bhc-home.htm	Farmers Branch	TX	75244	972-860-4700	860-4886
Cedar Valley College 3030 N Dallas Ave — *Web:* www.dcccd.edu/cvc/cvc.htm	Lancaster	TX	75134	972-860-8200	372-8207
Collin County Community College Central Park Campus PO Box 8001 — *Web:* www.ccccd.edu	McKinney	TX	75070	972-548-6790	548-6702
Dallas Baptist University 3000 Mountain Creek Pkwy — *TF Admissions:* 800-460-1328 ■ *Web:* www.dbu.edu ■ *E-mail:* info@dbu.edu	Dallas	TX	75211	214-331-8311	333-5447
Dallas Christian College 2700 Christian Pkwy — *TF:* 800-688-1029 ■ *Web:* www.dallas.edu	Dallas	TX	75234	972-241-3371	241-8021
Dallas County Community College District System 701 Elm St. — *Web:* www.dcccd.edu	Dallas	TX	75202	214-860-2125	860-2009
DeVRY Institute of Technology 4800 Regent Blvd — *TF:* 800-633-3879 ■ *Web:* www.dal.devry.edu ■ *E-mail:* admissions@dal.devry.edu	Irving	TX	75063	972-929-6777	929-6778
Eastfield College 3737 Motley Dr — *Web:* www.efc.dcccd.edu	Mesquite	TX	75150	972-860-7002	860-8306
El Centro College Main & Lamar — *Web:* www.ecc.dcccd.edu/	Dallas	TX	75202	214-860-2037	860-2233
Independent Baptist College 5101 Western Center Blvd	Fort Worth	TX	76137	817-514-6364	281-8257
ITT Technical Institute 2101 Water View Pkwy — *TF:* 888-488-5761 ■ *Web:* www.itt-tech.edu	Richardson	TX	75080	972-690-9100	690-0853
Mountain View College 4849 W Illinois Ave. — *Web:* www.mvc.dcccd.edu	Dallas	TX	75211	214-860-8600	860-8570
North Lake College 5001 N MacArthur Blvd. — *Web:* www.dcccd.edu/nlc/nlchp.htm	Irving	TX	75038	972-273-3000	273-3014
Northwood University Texas Campus 1114 W FM 1382 — *TF:* 800-927-9663 ■ *Web:* www.northwood.edu ■ *E-mail:* info@northwood.edu	Cedar Hill	TX	75106	972-291-1541	291-3824
Paul Quinn College 3837 Simpson Stuart Rd.	Dallas	TX	75241	214-376-1000	302-3613
Richland College 12800 Abrams Rd — *Web:* www.rlc.dcccd.edu	Dallas	TX	75243	972-238-6100	238-6346
Southern Methodist University 6425 Boaz Ln. — *TF Admissions:* 800-323-0672 ■ *Web:* www.smu.edu	Dallas	TX	75275	214-768-2000	768-2507
Southwestern Adventist University 100 W Hillcrest Dr — *TF:* 800-433-2240 ■ *Web:* www.swac.edu ■ *E-mail:* illingworth@swac.edu	Keene	TX	76059	817-645-3921	556-4744
Southwestern Assemblies of God University 1200 Sycamore St — *TF:* 888-937-7248 ■ *Web:* www.sagu.edu ■ *E-mail:* info@sagu.edu	Waxahachie	TX	75165	972-937-4010	923-0006
Southwestern Christian College PO Box 10 — *TF:* 800-925-9357	Terrell	TX	75160	972-524-3341	563-7133
Texas Woman's University PO Box 425589 — *Web:* www.twu.edu	Denton	TX	76204	940-898-2000	898-2767
University of Dallas 1845 E Northgate Dr — *TF:* 800-628-6999 ■ *Web:* acad.udallas.edu	Irving	TX	75062	972-721-5000	721-5017
University of North Texas PO Box 311277 — *Web:* www.unt.edu ■ *E-mail:* undergrad@abn.unt.edu	Denton	TX	76203	940-565-2000	565-2408
University of Texas Arlington 701 S Nedderman Dr. — *TF Admissions:* 800-687-2882 ■ *Web:* www.uta.edu	Arlington	TX	76019	817-272-2011	272-3435
University of Texas Dallas PO Box 830688 — *Web:* www.utdallas.edu	Richardson	TX	75083	972-883-2111	883-6803
Wade College 2300 Stemmons Fwy — *TF:* 800-624-4850	Dallas	TX	75258	214-637-3530	637-0827

— Hospitals —

	City	State	Zip	Phone	Fax
Baylor Medical Center at Ellis 1405 W Jefferson St — *TF:* 800-422-9657	Waxahachie	TX	75165	972-923-7000	938-1657
Baylor Medical Center at Garland 2300 Marie Curie Blvd — *Web:* www.baylorhealth.com/garland/index.htm	Garland	TX	75042	972-487-5000	487-5005
Baylor Medical Center at Irving 1901 N MacArthur Blvd	Irving	TX	75061	972-579-8100	579-5290
Baylor Richardson Medical Center 401 W Campbell Rd — *Web:* www.bhcs.com/Richardson	Richardson	TX	75080	972-231-1441	498-4883
Baylor University Medical Center 3500 Gaston Ave — *TF:* 800-422-9567	Dallas	TX	75246	214-820-0111	
Charlton Methodist Hospital 3500 W Wheatland Rd.	Dallas	TX	75237	214-947-7777	947-7525
Children's Medical Center of Dallas 1935 Motor St — *Web:* www.childrens.com	Dallas	TX	75235	214-640-2000	456-2197
Columbia Hospital Lewisville 500 W Main	Lewisville	TX	75057	972-420-1000	420-1073
Columbia Medical Center 4405 N I-35	Denton	TX	76207	940-566-4000	382-4864
Columbia Medical Center 4500 Medical Ctr Dr	McKinney	TX	75069	972-547-8000	547-8008
Columbia Medical Center of Plano 3901 W 15th St	Plano	TX	75075	972-596-6800	519-1295

Dallas — Hospitals (Cont'd)

Name / Address	City	State	Zip	Phone	Fax
Dallas-Fort Worth Medical Center					
2709 Hospital Blvd	Grand Prairie	TX	75051	972-641-5000	660-9589
Web: www.dfwmedicalcenter.com					
Dallas Southwest Medical Center					
2929 S Hampton Rd	Dallas	TX	75224	214-330-4611	330-0199
Denton Community Hospital					
207 N Bonnie Brae	Denton	TX	76201	940-898-7000	898-7071
Doctors Hospital of Dallas 9440 Poppy Dr	Dallas	TX	75218	214-324-6100	324-0612
Web: www.tenethealth.com/DoctorsDallas					
Garland Community Hospital					
2696 W Walnut St	Garland	TX	75042	972-276-7116	494-6913
Lake Pointe Medical Center PO Box 1550	Rowlett	TX	75030	972-412-2273	412-3276
Medical Center of Lancaster					
2600 W Pleasant Run Rd	Lancaster	TX	75146	972-223-9600	230-2966
Medical Center of Mesquite					
1011 N Galloway Ave	Mesquite	TX	75149	214-320-7000	289-9468*
**Fax Area Code:* 972					
Medical City Dallas 7777 Forest Ln	Dallas	TX	75230	972-661-7000	566-6248
Mesquite Community Hospital					
3500 Interstate 30	Mesquite	TX	75150	972-698-3300	698-2580
Methodist Medical Center PO Box 655999	Dallas	TX	75265	214-947-8181	947-3403*
**Fax:* Admitting					
Parkland Memorial Hospital					
5201 Harry Hines Blvd.	Dallas	TX	75235	214-590-8000	590-8096
Web: www.swmed.edu/home_pages/parkland/					
Presbyterian Hospital of Dallas					
8200 Walnut Hill Ln	Dallas	TX	75231	214-345-6789	345-2350*
**Fax:* Library					
Presbyterian Hospital of Kaufman					
PO Box 310	Kaufman	TX	75142	214-345-8463	932-5425*
**Fax Area Code:* 972					
Presbyterian Hospital of Plano					
6200 W Parker Rd	Plano	TX	75093	972-608-8000	608-8111
RHD Memorial Medical Center					
7 Medical Pkwy	Farmers Branch	TX	75234	972-247-1000	888-7090
Web: www.tenethealth.com/RHDMemorial					
Saint Paul Medical Center					
5909 Harry Hines Blvd.	Dallas	TX	75235	214-879-1000	879-6694
Texas Scottish Rite Hospital for Children					
2222 Wellborn St	Dallas	TX	75219	214-521-3168	559-7612
Tri-City Hospital 7525 Scyene Rd	Dallas	TX	75227	214-381-7171	275-1239
Trinity Medical Center 4343 N Josey Ln	Carrollton	TX	75010	972-492-1010	394-4783
Web: www.tenethealth.com/Trinity					
Veterans Affairs Medical Center					
4500 S Lancaster Rd.	Dallas	TX	75216	214-857-1141	857-1171
Zale Lipshy University Hospital					
5151 Harry Hines Blvd.	Dallas	TX	75235	214-590-3000	590-3465*
**Fax:* Admitting					

— Attractions —

Name / Address	City	State	Zip	Phone	Fax
African American Museum					
3536 Grand Ave Fair Pk.	Dallas	TX	75210	214-565-9026	421-8204
Age of Steam Railroad Museum					
1105 Washington St Fair Pk.	Dallas	TX	75315	214-428-0101	426-1937
Web: www.startext.net/homes/railroad/musmain.htm					
Bachman Lake Park 2750 Bachman Dr	Dallas	TX	75220	214-670-6266	670-6271
Bath House Cultural Center 521 E Lawther Dr	Dallas	TX	75218	214-670-8749	670-8751
Biblical Arts Center 7500 Park Ln.	Dallas	TX	75225	214-691-4661	691-4752
Web: www.biblicalarts.org					
Cavanaugh Flight Museum					
4572 Claire Chennault Addison Airport	Addison	TX	75001	972-380-8800	248-0907
Web: www.cavanaughflightmuseum.com					
Conspiracy Museum 110 S Market	Dallas	TX	75202	214-741-3040	741-9339
Conte de Loyo Flamenco Theatre					
3630 Harry Hines Blvd.	Dallas	TX	75219	214-521-0222	559-4643
Web: www.flash.net/~flamenco ■ *E-mail:* flamenco@flash.net					
Dallas Aquarium					
1st Ave & ML King Blvd Fair Pk	Dallas	TX	75226	214-670-8443	670-8452
E-mail: dallasaq@airmail.net					
Dallas Arboretum & Botanical Garden					
8617 Garland Rd.	Dallas	TX	75218	214-327-8263	324-9801
Dallas Black Dance Theatre 2627 Flora St.	Dallas	TX	75201	214-871-2376	871-2842
TF: 888-222-3238 ■ *Web:* www.dbdt.com ■ *E-mail:* dbdt@gte.net					
Dallas Farmers Market 1010 S Pearl Expy.	Dallas	TX	75201	214-939-2808	
Dallas Firefighters Museum 3801 Parry Ave	Dallas	TX	75226	214-821-1500	
Dallas Horticulture Center					
3601 ML King Blvd Fair Pk	Dallas	TX	75315	214-428-7476	428-5338
Dallas Memorial Center for Holocaust Studies					
7900 Northaven Rd.	Dallas	TX	75230	214-750-4654	750-4672
Dallas Museum of Art 1717 N Harwood St	Dallas	TX	75201	214-922-1200	954-0174
Web: www.dm-art.org					
Dallas Museum of Natural History					
PO Box 150349	Dallas	TX	75315	214-421-3466	428-4356
Web: www.dallasdino.org					
Dallas Nature Center					
7171 Mountain Creek Pkwy	Dallas	TX	75249	972-296-1955	
Dallas Opera 3102 Oak Lawn Ave Suite 450	Dallas	TX	75219	214-443-1043	443-1060
Web: www.dallasopera.org					
Dallas Science Place 1318 2nd Ave	Dallas	TX	75210	214-428-5555	428-2033
Web: www.scienceplace.org					
Dallas Symphony Orchestra					
2301 Flora St Suite 300	Dallas	TX	75201	214-692-0203	
Web: www.dalsym.com					
Dallas Visual Art Center 2917 Swiss	Dallas	TX	75204	214-821-2522	821-9103
Dallas Zoo 650 S RL Thornton Fwy	Dallas	TX	75203	214-670-6826	670-7450
Web: www.dallas-zoo.org					
Deep Ellum 2932 Main St Suite 101	Dallas	TX	75226	214-748-4332	741-4567
Web: www.deepellumtx.com/					
Fair Park Dallas 1300 Robert B Cullum Blvd	Dallas	TX	75210	214-670-8400	670-8907
Hall of State 3939 Grand Ave Fair Pk	Dallas	TX	75226	214-421-4500	421-7500
Web: www.dallashistory.org/					
International Museum of Cultures					
7500 W Camp Wisdom Rd.	Dallas	TX	75236	972-708-7406	708-7341
Web: www.sil.org/imc/ ■ *E-mail:* imc_museum@sil.org					
Kiest Park 3080 S Hampton Rd	Dallas	TX	75224	214-670-1918	
Majestic Theatre 1925 Elm St	Dallas	TX	75201	214-880-0137	880-0097
Malibu SpeedZone 11130 Malibu Dr.	Dallas	TX	75229	972-247-7223	243-3170
Web: www.speedzone.com/dallas/dallas.html					
Martinez Anita N Ballet Folklorico					
4422 Live Oak	Dallas	TX	75204	214-828-0181	828-0101
Web: www.anmbf.org					
Meadows Museum					
Owen Fine Arts Ctr Southern Methodist University	Dallas	TX	75275	214-768-2516	768-1688
Web: www.smu.edu/meadows/museum					
Medieval Times Dinner & Tournament					
2021 N Stemmons Fwy	Dallas	TX	75207	214-761-1800	761-1805
TF: 800-229-9900 ■ *Web:* www.medievaltimes.com/TX_realm.htm ■ *E-mail:* dallas@medievaltimes.com					
Morton H Meyerson Symphony Center					
2301 Flora St Suite 100	Dallas	TX	75201	214-670-3600	670-4334
Museum of the Americas 1717 N Harwood St	Dallas	TX	75201	214-922-1200	954-0174
Music Hall at Fair Park 909 1st Ave	Dallas	TX	75210	214-565-1116	565-0071
Web: www.dallassummermusicals.org/theatre-music-hall.htm					
NASCAR Silicon Motor Speedway					
13350 Dallas Pkwy Suite 3800	Dallas	TX	75240	972-490-7223	490-4240
Old City Park 1717 Gano St	Dallas	TX	75215	214-421-5141	428-6351
Six Flags Over Texas					
2201 Road to Six Flags	Arlington	TX	76011	817-640-8900	530-6040
Web: www.sixflags.com/texas					
Sixth Floor Museum 411 Elm St Dealey Plaza	Dallas	TX	75202	214-747-6660	747-6662
TF: 888-485-4854 ■ *Web:* www.jfk.org ■ *E-mail:* jfk@jfk.org					
Skyline Ranch 1801 E Wheatland	Dallas	TX	75241	972-224-8055	224-7004
Southfork Ranch 3700 Hogge Rd	Parker	TX	75002	972-442-7800	442-5259
TF: 800-989-7800 ■ *Web:* www.southforkranch.com					
TI Founders IMAX Theater					
1318 2nd Ave Fair Pk	Dallas	TX	75210	214-428-5555	428-4310
Web: www.scienceplace.org/imaxhome.htm					
TILT Adventure Motion Theater					
603 Munger Ave West End Marketplace	Dallas	TX	75202	214-720-7276	
West End MarketPlace 603 Munger Ave	Dallas	TX	75202	214-748-4801	748-4803
White Rock Lake Park 8300 Garland Rd	Dallas	TX	75238	214-670-8895	
Wilson Block Historic District					
2922 Block of Swiss Ave	Dallas	TX	75204	214-821-3290	821-3573
Web: www.preservationdallas.org/wilson.html					

SPORTS TEAMS & FACILITIES

Name / Address	City	State	Zip	Phone	Fax
Cotton Bowl 3750 Midway Dr	Dallas	TX	75215	214-939-2222	939-2224
Dallas Burn (soccer) 2602 McKinney Suite 200	Dallas	TX	75204	214-979-0303	979-1118
Web: www.burnsoccer.com ■ *E-mail:* theburnone@aol.com					
Dallas Convention Center 650 S Griffin St.	Dallas	TX	75202	214-939-2750	939-2795
Web: www.dallascc.com					
Dallas Cowboys					
2401 E Airport Fwy Texas Stadium	Irving	TX	75062	972-785-5000	556-9304
Web: www.dallascowboys.com					
Dallas Mavericks 777 Sports St Reunion Arena	Dallas	TX	75207	214-748-1810	741-6731
TF: 800-634-6287 ■ *Web:* www.nba.com/mavericks					
Dallas Sidekicks (soccer)					
777 Sports St Reunion Arena	Dallas	TX	75207	214-653-0200	741-6731
Dallas Stars 777 Sports St Reunion Arena	Dallas	TX	75207	214-939-2770	939-2872
Web: www.dallasstarshockey.com					
Lone Star Park at Grand Prairie					
1000 Lone Star Pkwy	Grand Prairie	TX	75050	972-263-7223	237-5109
Web: www.lonestarpark.com					

Dallas — Sports Teams & Facilities (Cont'd)

				Phone	Fax
North Texas Heat (soccer) 2001 Kelley Blvd Polk Football Stadium	Carrollton	TX	75006	972-492-7863	242-3600
E-mail: cdemarco@ntxsoccer.org					
Reunion Arena 777 Sports St	Dallas	TX	75207	214-939-2770	939-2872
Texas Motorplex 7500 W Hwy 287	Ennis	TX	75119	972-878-2641	878-1848
Web: www.texasmotorplex.com					
Texas Rangers 1000 Ballpark Way Ballpark at Arlington	Arlington	TX	76011	817-273-5100	273-5174
TF: 888-968-3927 ■ *Web:* www.texasrangers.com					
Texas Toros (soccer) Freeman St Old Panther Stadium	Duncanville	TX	75116	214-891-7059	891-8117
E-mail: txtoros@airmail.com					

— Events —

	Phone
American Indian Art Festival & Market (September-November)	214-891-9640
Cotton Bowl (January 1)	214-634-7525
Dallas Air Show (mid-September)	214-350-1651
Dallas Artfest (late May)	214-361-2011
Dallas Blooms (March-early April)	214-327-8263
Dallas Boat Show (late January-early February)	972-714-0177
Dallas Home & Garden Show (early March)	800-654-1480
Dallas Morning News Dance Festival (late August-early September)	214-953-1977
Dallas Summer Musicals (June-October)	214-421-0662
Dallas Video Festival (late March)	214-999-8999
Golden Gloves Tournament (mid-February)	214-670-8400
Greek Food Festival (late September)	972-991-1166
Kidfilm Festival (mid-January)	214-821-3456
Mesquite Rodeo (April-September)	972-285-8777
Montage (mid-September)	214-361-2011
North Texas Irish Festival (early March)	214-821-4174
Oasis Fireworks to Music (early July)	214-855-1881
Plano Balloon Festival (mid-September)	972-867-7566
Saint Patrick's Day Parade (mid-March)	972-991-6677
Shakespeare Festival of Dallas (mid-June-late July)	214-559-2778
State Fair of Texas (late September-mid-October)	214-565-9931
Taste of Dallas (mid-July)	214-741-7180
USA Film Festival (late April)	214-821-6300
Waxahachie Scarborough Renaissance Fair (April-June)	972-938-1888
White Rock Marathon (early December)	214-528-2962

El Paso

El Paso is a shortened version of El Paso del Rio del Norte (the Pass Through the River of the North), the name given to the city by conquistador Don Juan Onate more than four centuries ago. A wholly Mexican town throughout the Texas Revolution, El Paso surrendered to U.S. forces fighting the Mexican War in 1846. In that same year, a military post that was later to be named Fort Bliss was established there. (Today the fort is the largest air defense center in the western world.) In 1848, the city was divided between present-day Ciudad Juarez (El Paso's sister city across the Rio Grande in Mexico) and what was to become El Paso proper. The Chamizal Treaty of 1963 shifted this border, returning 700 acres to Mexico, and the Chamizal National Memorial in El Paso commemorates the settlement of this land dispute between the U.S. and Mexico. The city is also home to Ysleta Mission, the oldest mission in Texas.

Population	615,032	**Longitude**	106-60-50 W
Area (Land)	254.4 sq mi	**County**	El Paso
Area (Water)	1.5 sq mi	**Time Zone**	MST
Elevation	3700 ft	**Area Code/s**	915
Latitude	31-97-54 N		

— Average Temperatures and Precipitation —

TEMPERATURES

	Jan	Feb	Mar	Apr	May	Jun	Jul	Aug	Sep	Oct	Nov	Dec
High	56	62	70	79	87	97	96	94	87	78	66	58
Low	29	34	40	48	57	64	68	67	62	50	38	31

PRECIPITATION

	Jan	Feb	Mar	Apr	May	Jun	Jul	Aug	Sep	Oct	Nov	Dec
Inches	0.4	0.4	0.3	0.2	0.3	0.7	1.5	1.6	1.7	0.8	0.4	0.6

— Important Phone Numbers —

	Phone		Phone
AAA	915-778-9521	**Medical Referral**	800-327-9107
American Express Travel	915-532-8900	**Poison Control Center**	800-764-7661
Emergency	911	**Time/Temp**	915-532-9911
Highway Conditions	800-452-9292	**Weather**	915-562-4040

— Information Sources —

				Phone	Fax
Better Business Bureau Serving the El Paso Area 221 N Kansas St Suite 1101	El Paso	TX	79901	915-577-0191	577-0209
Web: www.elpaso.bbb.org					
El Paso City Hall 2 Civic Center Plaza	El Paso	TX	79901	915-541-4000	541-4501
Web: www.ci.el-paso.tx.us					
El Paso Convention & Performing Arts Center 1 Civic Center Plaza	El Paso	TX	79901	915-534-0600	534-0686
TF: 800-351-6024					
El Paso Convention & Visitors Bureau 1 Civic Center Plaza	El Paso	TX	79901	915-534-0696	534-0687
TF: 800-351-6024 ■ *Web:* www.elpasocvb.com ■ *E-mail:* elpasotx@huntel.com					
El Paso County 500 E San Antonio Ave	El Paso	TX	79901	915-546-2000	
El Paso Economic Development Dept 2 Civic Center Plaza	El Paso	TX	79901	915-533-4284	541-1316
Web: www.ci.el-paso.tx.us/EcoDev/anormal5.htm					
El Paso Mayor 2 Civic Center Plaza	El Paso	TX	79901	915-541-4015	541-4501
E-mail: mayor@ci.el-paso.tx.us					
El Paso Public Library 501 N Oregon St	El Paso	TX	79901	915-543-5401	543-5410
Web: rgfn.epcc.edu/users/eplib					
Greater El Paso Chamber of Commerce 10 Civic Ctr Plaza	El Paso	TX	79901	915-534-0500	534-0513
Web: www.elpaso.org					

On-Line Resources

4ElPaso.com	www.4elpaso.com
Anthill City Guide El Paso	www.anthill.com/city.asp?city=elpaso
Area Guide El Paso	elpaso.areaguides.net
City Knowledge El Paso	www.cityknowledge.com/tx_elpaso.htm
Ciudad Juarez-El Paso	www.mexguide.net/juarez/
El Paso Citi-Guide	www.citi-guide.com
El Paso Home Page	www.elpasotx.com/
El Paso Info Page	www.elpasoinfo.com
El Paso Scene Online	www.epscene.com/
El Paso Texas.com	www.elpasotexas.com/
El Paso Webtree	www.webtree.com
Excite.com El Paso City Guide	www.excite.com/travel/countries/united_states/texas/el_paso
GuestLife El Paso	www.guestlife.com/elpaso/
Road Runner El Paso	www.elp.rr.com/around_town/
Virtual El Paso	www.virtualelpaso.com/

— Transportation Services —

AIRPORTS

	Phone
■ **El Paso International Airport (ELP)**	
8 miles NE of downtown (approx 15 minutes)	915-772-4271

Airport Transportation

	Phone
Checker Cab $15 fare to downtown	915-532-2626
Taxi $15 fare to downtown	915-533-3433

El Paso (Cont'd)

Commercial Airlines

	Phone		Phone
America West	800-235-9292	**Delta**	800-221-1212
American	800-433-7300	**Southwest**	800-435-9792
Continental	800-525-0280		

Charter Airlines

	Phone		Phone
Aero Exec	915-772-3273	**Rasmark Jet Charter**	915-772-4616
Air Transport Inc	915-772-1448	**Texas Air Charters**	940-898-1200

CAR RENTALS

	Phone		Phone
Alamo	800-327-9633	**Hertz**	915-772-4255
Avis	915-779-2730	**National**	915-778-9417
Budget	915-778-5287	**Thrifty**	915-584-6529
Dollar	915-778-5445		

LIMO/TAXI

	Phone		Phone
Advanced Limousine	915-591-8100	**Premier Limousine**	915-594-4422
Border Cab	915-533-4245	**Presidential Limousine**	915-594-1446
Checker Cab	915-532-2626	**Sun City Cab**	915-544-2211
City Lights Limousine	915-590-5944	**Superior Limousine**	915-775-3923
Diamond Cab	915-544-4464	**Texas Cab Co**	915-562-0022
El Paso Cab Co	915-771-7791	**United Independent Cab**	915-590-8294
Night Life Limousine	915-594-0842	**Yellow Cab**	915-533-3433

MASS TRANSIT

	Phone
Sun Metro $1 Base fare	915-533-3333

RAIL/BUS

				Phone
El Paso Amtrak Station/Union Depot 700 San Francisco Ave.	El Paso	TX	79901	915-545-2248
Greyhound/Trailways Bus Station 200 W San Antonio St *TF:* 800-231-2222	El Paso	TX	79901	915-532-2365

— Accommodations —

HOTELS, MOTELS, RESORTS

				Phone	Fax
Americana Inn 14387 Gateway Blvd W	El Paso	TX	79927	915-852-3025	
Baymont Inns & Suites 7944 Gateway Blvd E. *TF:* 800-301-0200	El Paso	TX	79915	915-591-3300	591-3700
Best Western Airport Inn 7144 Gateway Blvd E. *TF:* 800-295-7276	El Paso	TX	79915	915-779-7700	772-1920
Camino Real El Paso 101 S El Paso St. *TF:* 800-769-4300 ■ *Web:* www.caminoreal.com/elpaso/	El Paso	TX	79901	915-534-3000	534-3024
Chase Suites Hotel 6791 Montana Ave *TF:* 800-331-3131	El Paso	TX	79925	915-772-8000	772-7254
Cliff Inn 1600 Cliff Dr *TF:* 800-333-2543	El Paso	TX	79902	915-533-6700	544-2127
Comfort Inn 900 N Yarbrough. *TF:* 800-228-5150	El Paso	TX	79915	915-594-9111	590-4364
Econo Lodge 6363 Montana Ave. *TF:* 800-553-2666	El Paso	TX	79925	915-778-3311	778-1097
El Paso Airport Hilton 2027 Airway Blvd *TF:* 800-742-7248 ■ *Web:* www.hilton.com/hotels/ELPHIHF/index.html	El Paso	TX	79925	915-778-4241	772-6871
El Paso Marriott 1600 Airway Blvd *TF:* 800-228-9290 ■ *Web:* www.marriott.com/marriott/tx-177.htm	El Paso	TX	79925	915-779-3300	772-0915
Embassy Suites 6100 Gateway Blvd E *TF:* 800-362-2779	El Paso	TX	79905	915-779-6222	779-8846
Extended StayAmerica 6580 Montana Ave. *TF:* 800-398-7829	El Paso	TX	79925	915-772-5754	772-5714
Gardner Hotel 311 E Franklin Ave.	El Paso	TX	79901	915-532-3661	532-0302
Hampton Inn Suites 6635 Gateway Blvd W *TF:* 800-436-7866	El Paso	TX	79925	915-771-6644	771-6368
Holiday Inn Airport 6655 Gateway Blvd W. *TF:* 800-465-4329 ■ *Web:* www.holidayinnairport.com	El Paso	TX	79925	915-778-6411	778-6517
Holiday Inn Sunland Park 900 Sunland Park Dr. *TF:* 800-465-4329	El Paso	TX	79922	915-833-2900	833-6338
HomeGate Studios & Suites 8250 Gateway Blvd E. *TF:* 888-456-4283	El Paso	TX	79907	915-591-9600	591-3263
Howard Johnson Lodge 8887 Gateway Blvd W *TF:* 800-446-4656	El Paso	TX	79925	915-591-9471	591-5602
La Hacienda Airport Inn 6400 Montana Dr. *TF:* 800-772-4231	El Paso	TX	79925	915-772-4231	779-2918
La Quinta Inn 9125 Gateway Blvd W. *TF:* 800-687-6667	El Paso	TX	79925	915-593-8400	599-1268
La Quinta Motor Inn El Paso Airport 6140 Gateway Blvd E. *TF:* 800-531-5900	El Paso	TX	79905	915-778-9321	779-1505
Motel 6 4800 Gateway Blvd E. *TF:* 800-466-8356	El Paso	TX	79905	915-533-7521	544-4904
Quality Inn Airport 6201 Gateway Blvd W *TF:* 800-228-5151 ■ *Web:* www.elpasoquality.com	El Paso	TX	79925	915-778-6611	779-2270
Radisson Inn Suites Airport 1770 Airway Blvd *TF:* 800-333-3333	El Paso	TX	79925	915-772-3333	779-3323
Ramada Inn 500 Executive Center Blvd *TF:* 800-272-6232	El Paso	TX	79902	915-532-8981	577-9997
Sumner Suites 6030 Gateway Blvd E. *TF:* 800-743-8483	El Paso	TX	79905	915-771-0022	771-0599
Sunset Heights Inn 717 W Yandell Ave *TF:* 800-767-8513	El Paso	TX	79902	915-544-1743	544-5119
Travelers Inn West 7815 N Mesa St. *TF:* 800-633-8300	El Paso	TX	79923	915-833-1666	833-1006
Travelodge El Paso City Center 409 E Missouri Ave. *TF:* 800-578-7878	El Paso	TX	79901	915-544-3333	533-4109

— Restaurants —

				Phone
Avila's Mexican Food (Mexican) 6232 N Mesa St	El Paso	TX	79912	915-584-3621
Bella Napoli (Italian) 6331 N Mesa St	El Paso	TX	79912	915-584-3321
Big Fisherman (Seafood) 9052 Dyer St	El Paso	TX	79904	915-751-1700
Bill Park's Bar-B-Q (Barbecue) 3130 Gateway Blvd E.	El Paso	TX	79905	915-542-0960
Bistro The (Continental) 7500 N Mesa St Suite 212	El Paso	TX	79912	915-584-5757
Cafe Central (Continental) 109 N Oregon St *Web:* www.cafecentral.com	El Paso	TX	79901	915-545-2233
Carlos & Mickey's (Mexican) 1310 Magruder	El Paso	TX	79925	915-778-3323
Cattle Baron (Steak) 1700 Airway Blvd	El Paso	TX	79925	915-779-6633
Cattleman's Steakhouse (Steak) Indian Cliff's Ranch *Web:* www.cattlemanssteakhouse.com	Fabens	TX	79838	915-544-3200
Delhi Palace Cuisine of India (Indian) 1160 Airway Blvd	El Paso	TX	79925	915-772-9334
Dome The (International) 101 S El Paso St.	El Paso	TX	79901	915-534-3010
El Rancho Escondido (Mexican) 14261 Montana Ave Suite A.	El Paso	TX	79938	915-857-1184
Forti's Mexican Elder (Mexican) 321 Chelsea St	El Paso	TX	79905	915-772-0066
Great American Land & Cattle Co (Steak) 7600 Alabama St *Web:* www.grtamerican.com/	El Paso	TX	79904	915-751-5300
Gunther's Edelweiss (German) 11055 Gateway Blvd W	El Paso	TX	79935	915-592-1084
Japanese Kitchen (Japanese) 4024 N Mesa St	El Paso	TX	79902	915-533-4267
Jaxon's Restaurant & Brewing Co (American) 1135 Airway Blvd	El Paso	TX	79925	915-778-9696
Jaxon's (Southwest) 4799 N Mesa St. *Web:* www.jaxons.com	El Paso	TX	79912	915-544-1188
Magnim's (Continental) 2027 Airway Blvd.	El Paso	TX	79925	915-778-4241
Mountain View Grill (American) 1600 Airway Blvd.	El Paso	TX	79925	915-774-6916
Pelican's (Steak/Seafood) 130 Shadow Mountain	El Paso	TX	79912	915-581-1392
Rib Hut (Barbecue) 2612 N Mesa St.	El Paso	TX	79902	915-532-7427
San Francisco Grill (American) 127-A Pioneer Plaza	El Paso	TX	79901	915-545-1386
Seafarer Seafood (Seafood) 1711 Lee Trevino Dr	El Paso	TX	79936	915-593-8388
Seafood Galley (Seafood) 1130 Geronimo	El Paso	TX	79925	915-778-8388
Senor Juan's Griggs (Mexican) 9007 Montana Ave	El Paso	TX	79925	915-598-3451
Shogun Steakhouse (Japanese) 1201 Airway Blvd.	El Paso	TX	79925	915-775-1282
Sioux Street (Steak) 1610 Sioux Dr	El Paso	TX	79925	915-772-1800
Sorrento Restaurant (Italian) 5325 Dyer St.	El Paso	TX	79904	915-565-3937
Stateline Restaurant (American) 1222 Sunland Park Dr. *Web:* www.airribs.com/	El Paso	TX	79922	915-581-3371
Three Continents Restaurant (International) 1600 Cliff Dr	El Paso	TX	79902	915-533-6700
Uncle Bao's (Chinese) 9515 Gateway Blvd W	El Paso	TX	79925	915-592-1101
Wings (Mexican) 122 S Old Pueblo Rd.	El Paso	TX	79907	915-859-3916

— Goods and Services —

SHOPPING

				Phone	Fax
Bassett Center 6101 Gateway Blvd W Suite M36	El Paso	TX	79925	915-772-7479	778-9603
Cielo Vista Mall 8401 Gateway Blvd W.	El Paso	TX	79925	915-779-7070	772-4926
Sunland Park Mall 750 Sunland Park Dr	El Paso	TX	79912	915-833-5595	584-0040

El Paso — Shopping (Cont'd)

				Phone
Trevino Mall 1323 Lee Trevino Dr.	El Paso	TX	79936	915-591-0333

BANKS

				Phone	Fax
Bank of the West 500 N Mesa St	El Paso	TX	79901	915-532-1000	747-1025
Chase Bank of Texas 201 E Main Dr.	El Paso	TX	79901	915-546-6500	
NationsBank 416 N Stanton St	El Paso	TX	79901	915-577-2415	577-2020
Norwest Bank 221 N Kansas St	El Paso	TX	79901	915-532-9922	546-4806

BUSINESS SERVICES

	Phone		Phone
Accountemps	915-593-6699	**Kinko's**	915-592-1190
Airborne Express	800-247-2676	**Manpower Temporary Services**	915-592-6196
BAX Global	800-225-5229	**Olsten Staffing Services**	915-592-5400
DHL Worldwide Express	800-225-5345	**Post Office**	915-780-7500
Federal Express	800-238-5355	**Rush Delivery**	915-581-2340
Kelly Services	915-772-8811	**UPS**	800-742-5877

— Media —

PUBLICATIONS

				Phone	Fax
El Paso Times‡ 300 N Campbell St Times Plaza *TF:* 800-351-6007	El Paso	TX	79901	915-546-6100	546-6415

‡*Daily newspapers*

TELEVISION

				Phone	Fax
KCOS-TV Ch 13 (PBS) Education Bldg Rm 105 *Web:* www.kcostv.org	El Paso	TX	79902	915-747-6500	747-6605
KDBC-TV Ch 4 (CBS) 2201 Wyoming Ave *Web:* www.kdbc.com	El Paso	TX	79903	915-532-6551	544-2591
KFOX-TV Ch 14 (Fox) 6004 N Mesa *E-mail:* fox14@whc.net	El Paso	TX	79912	915-833-8585	833-8717
KINT-TV Ch 26 (Uni) 5426 N Mesa *Web:* www.kint.com ■ *E-mail:* feedback@kint.com	El Paso	TX	79912	915-581-1126	581-1393
KKWB-TV Ch 65 (WB) 801 N Oregon St	El Paso	TX	79902	915-833-0065	532-6841
KMAZ-TV Ch 48 (Tele) 10033 Carnegie	El Paso	TX	79925	915-591-9595	591-9896
KTSM-TV Ch 9 (NBC) 801 N Oregon St *Web:* www.ktsm.com ■ *E-mail:* ktsmtv@whc.net	El Paso	TX	79902	915-532-5421	544-0536
KVIA-TV Ch 7 (ABC) 4140 Rio Bravo St *Web:* www.kvia.com ■ *E-mail:* feedback@kvia.com	El Paso	TX	79902	915-532-7777	532-0505

RADIO

				Phone	Fax
KAMA-AM 750 kHz (Span) 2211 E Missouri Ave Suite S-300	El Paso	TX	79903	915-544-9797	544-1247
KAMZ-FM 93.1 MHz (AC) 4150 Pinnacle St Suite 120	El Paso	TX	79902	915-544-7600	532-0947
KHEY-AM 690 kHz (Ctry) 2419 N Piedras St.	El Paso	TX	79930	915-566-9301	566-0928
KHEY-FM 96.3 MHz (Ctry) 2419 N Piedras St	El Paso	TX	79930	915-566-9301	566-0928
KLAQ-FM 95.5 MHz (Rock) 4150 Pinnacle St Suite 120	El Paso	TX	79902	915-544-8864	544-9536
KPRR-FM 102.1 MHz (CHR) 2419 N Piedras St. *Web:* www.kprr.com	El Paso	TX	79930	915-566-9301	566-0928
KROD-AM 600 kHz (N/T) 4150 Pinnacle St Suite 120	El Paso	TX	79902	915-544-8864	544-9536
KTEP-FM 88.5 MHz (NPR) 500 W University Ave Cotton Memorial Bldg Rm 203 *E-mail:* ktep@utep.edu	El Paso	TX	79968	915-747-5152	747-5641
KTSM-FM 99.9 MHz (AC) 801 N Oregon St *Web:* www.ktsmradio.com	El Paso	TX	79902	915-880-9909	544-5658

— Colleges/Universities —

				Phone	Fax
El Paso Community College Valle Verde Campus PO Box 20500 *Web:* www.epcc.edu ■ *E-mail:* postmaster@laguna.epcc.edu	El Paso	TX	79998	915-831-2000	831-2161
New Mexico State University PO Box 30001 MSC-3A *TF:* 800-662-6678 ■ *Web:* www.nmsu.edu ■ *E-mail:* admissions@nmsu.edu	Las Cruces	NM	88003	505-646-3121	646-6330
University of Texas El Paso 500 W University Ave *Web:* www.utep.edu	El Paso	TX	79968	915-747-5000	747-5848

— Hospitals —

				Phone	Fax
Columbia Medical Center East 10301 Gateway W.	El Paso	TX	79925	915-595-9000	595-7224
Columbia Medical Center West 1801 N Oregon St.	El Paso	TX	79902	915-521-1200	544-5203
Providence Memorial Hospital 2001 N Oregon St.	El Paso	TX	79902	915-577-6011	577-6109
RE Thomason General Hospital 4815 Alameda Ave	El Paso	TX	79905	915-544-1200	521-7612
Sierra Medical Center 1625 Medical Center Dr.	El Paso	TX	79902	915-747-4000	747-2138

— Attractions —

				Phone	Fax
Americana Museum 5 Civic Center Plaza	El Paso	TX	79901	915-542-0394	
Amistad National Recreation Area HCR 3 Box 5J *Web:* www.nps.gov/amis/	Del Rio	TX	78840	830-775-7491	775-7299
Ascarate Park 6900 Delta Dr	El Paso	TX	79905	915-772-5605	
Big Bend National Park PO Box 129 *Web:* www.nps.gov/bibe/	Big Bend National Park	TX	79834	915-477-2251	477-2357
Border Jumper Trolley 1 Civic Center Plaza *TF:* 800-259-6284	El Paso	TX	79901	915-544-0062	544-0002
Chamizal National Memorial 800 S San Marcial St *Web:* www.nps.gov/cham	El Paso	TX	79905	915-534-6668	532-7240
El Paso Centennial Museum University & Wiggins University of Texas *Web:* www.utep.edu/museum ■ *E-mail:* museum@mail.utep.edu	El Paso	TX	79968	915-747-5565	747-5411
El Paso Holocaust Museum & Study Center 401 Wallenberg Dr *Web:* www.huntel.com/~ht2/holocst.html	El Paso	TX	79912	915-833-5656	833-9523
El Paso Museum of Art 1 Art Festival Plaza	El Paso	TX	79901	915-532-1707	532-1010
El Paso Museum of History 12901 Gateway Blvd W	El Paso	TX	79927	915-858-1928	858-4591
El Paso Pro-Musica 6557 N Mesa St. *Web:* cs.utep.edu/elpaso/promusica.html	El Paso	TX	79913	915-833-9400	833-9425
El Paso Symphony Orchestra PO Box 180 *Web:* www.epso.org	El Paso	TX	79942	915-532-3776	533-8162
El Paso Zoo 4001 E Paisano St	El Paso	TX	79905	915-544-1928	
Fort Bliss Air Defense/Artillery Museum Pleasanton Rd Fort Bliss Bldg 5000	El Paso	TX	79916	915-568-5412	568-6941
Fort Davis National Historic Site PO Box 1456 *Web:* www.nps.gov/foda/	Fort Davis	TX	79734	915-426-3224	426-3122
Franklin Mountain State Park Transmountain Rd.	El Paso	TX		915-566-6441	566-6468
Guadalupe Mountains National Park HC 60 Box 400 *Web:* www.nps.gov/gumo/	Salt Flat	TX	79847	915-828-3251	828-3269
Hueco Tanks State Historical Park 6900 Hueco Tanks Rd #1 *Web:* www.tpwd.state.tx.us/park/hueco/hueco.htm	El Paso	TX	79936	915-857-1135	857-3628
Indian Cliffs Ranch I-10 & Fabens Exit	Fabens	TX	79838	915-544-3200	
Insights Science Museum 505 N Santa Fe *Web:* nasa.utep.edu/insights ■ *E-mail:* insights@dzn.com	El Paso	TX	79901	915-542-2990	532-7416
Magoffin Homestead 1120 Magoffin Ave	El Paso	TX	79901	915-533-5147	544-4398
McKelligon Canyon 3 McKelligon Rd.	El Paso	TX	79930	915-565-6900	
Rio Grande Wild & Scenic River PO Box 129 *Web:* www.nps.gov/rigr	Big Bend National Park	TX	79834	915-477-2251	477-2357
San Elizario Presidio of El Paso 1556 San Elizario Rd.	El Paso	TX	79849	915-851-2333	
Skyline Park 5050 Yvette Ave.	El Paso	TX	79924	915-541-4331	
Socorro Mission 328 S Nevarez St	El Paso	TX	79927	915-859-7718	
Speaking Rock Casino & Entertainment Center 122 S Old Pueblo Rd.	El Paso	TX	79907	915-860-7777	860-7745
Tigua Indian Reservation 119 S Old Pueblo Rd.	El Paso	TX	79907	915-859-7913	859-2988

El Paso — Attractions (Cont'd)

				Phone	Fax
US Border Patrol National Museum 4315 Transmountain Rd. *Web:* www.borderpatrolmuseum.org	El Paso	TX	79924	915-759-6060	759-0992
Western Playland Amusement Park 6900 Delta St	El Paso	TX	79905	915-772-3953	778-9821
Wet 'N' Wild Waterworld I-10 & Anthony Exit 0 *E-mail:* wetwild@1eagle1.com	Anthony	TX	79821	915-886-2222	886-2341
Wilderness Park Museum 4301 Woodrow Bean St.	El Paso	TX	79924	915-755-4332	759-6824
Ysleta Mission 131 S Zaragosa Rd	El Paso	TX	79907	915-859-9848	

SPORTS TEAMS & FACILITIES

				Phone	Fax
El Paso Buzzards (hockey) 4100 E Paisano Dr El Paso County Coliseum *Web:* www.buzzards.com	El Paso	TX	79905	915-534-7825	534-7876
El Paso Diablos (baseball) 9700 Gateway Blvd N *Web:* www.diablos.com/	El Paso	TX	79924	915-755-2000	757-0671
El Paso Patriots (soccer) 6941 Industrial Ave *Web:* www.elpaso-patriots.com/ ■ *E-mail:* Info@patriout.usisl.com	El Paso	TX	79915	915-771-6620	778-8802
Juarez Mexico Race Track 240 Thundergbird Dr Suite C	El Paso	TX	79912	915-775-0555	
Sun Bowl 2800 Sun Bowl Dr	El Paso	TX	79902	915-747-5000	747-5162
Sunland Park Race Track 1200 Futurity Dr *Web:* www.nmracing.com/sun.htm ■ *E-mail:* lucky@nmracing.com	Sunland Park	NM	88063	505-589-1131	589-1518

— Events —

	Phone
A Christmas Fair (mid-November)	915-584-3511
Amigo Airsho (mid-October)	915-545-2865
Border Folk Festival (mid-October)	915-532-7273
El Paso Chamber Music Festival (early January)	915-833-9400
Fiesta de las Flores (Labor Day weekend)	915-542-3464
First Thanksgiving Festival (late April)	915-534-0677
International Balloon Festival (Memorial Day weekend)	915-886-2222
International Mariachi Festival (late June)	915-566-4066
Kermezaar Arts & Crafts Show (mid-October)	915-584-5685
Shakespeare on the Rocks Festival (early September)	915-565-6900
Siglo de Oro Drama Festival (early March)	915-532-7273
Southwestern International Livestock Show & Rodeo (early-mid-February)	915-534-4229
Sun Carnival Football Classic (late December)	915-533-4416
Tour of Lights (mid-late December)	915-544-0062
Viva El Paso! (June-August)	915-565-6900

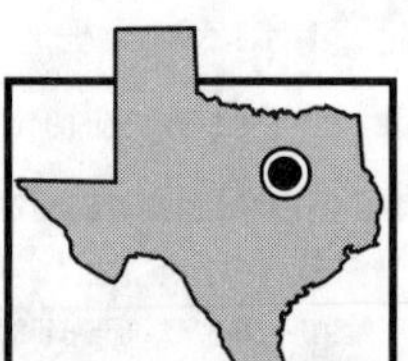

Fort Worth

Fort Worth is located just 34 miles from its sister city, Dallas. The area's cattle and cowboy history can be seen in the Stockyards Historic District of Fort Worth, which is also the home of Billy Bob's Texas, "the world's largest honky-tonk"—so large, in fact, that live bullriding is a featured event. The city is also home to the Cattleman's Museum, which features multimedia shows and life-size dioramas. Each winter the city hosts the Southwestern Exposition & Livestock Show and Rodeo, which draws nearly one million visitors annually. Other attractions in Fort Worth include the Fort Worth Botanical Garden, the Fort Worth Zoo, and the Amon Carter Museum, which features works by American artists, including the famous Southwestern artist, Georgia O'Keefe.

Population	491,801	**Longitude**	97-32-06 W
Area (Land)	277.3 sq mi	**County**	Tarrant
Area (Water)	6.4 sq mi	**Time Zone**	CST
Elevation	670 ft	**Area Code/s**	817
Latitude	32-72-53 N		

— Average Temperatures and Precipitation —

TEMPERATURES

	Jan	Feb	Mar	Apr	May	Jun	Jul	Aug	Sep	Oct	Nov	Dec
High	54	59	68	76	83	92	97	96	88	79	67	58
Low	33	37	46	55	63	70	74	74	67	56	45	36

PRECIPITATION

	Jan	Feb	Mar	Apr	May	Jun	Jul	Aug	Sep	Oct	Nov	Dec
Inches	1.8	2.2	2.8	3.5	4.9	3.0	2.3	2.2	3.4	3.5	2.3	1.8

— Important Phone Numbers —

	Phone		Phone
AAA	817-370-2503	**Medical Referral**	817-732-2825
American Express Travel	817-738-5441	**Poison Control Center**	800-764-7661
Emergency	911	**Travelers Aid**	972-574-4420
Events Hotline	817-332-2000	**Weather**	214-787-1111
Highway Conditions	800-452-9292		

— Information Sources —

				Phone	Fax
Better Business Bureau Serving the Fort Worth Area 1612 Summit Ave Suite 260 *Web:* www.fortworth.bbb.org	Fort Worth	TX	76102	817-332-7585	882-0566
Fort Worth Chamber of Commerce 777 Taylor St Suite 900 *Web:* www.fortworthcoc.org	Fort Worth	TX	76102	817-336-2491	877-4034
Fort Worth City Hall 1000 Throckmorton St. *Web:* ci.fort-worth.tx.us	Fort Worth	TX	76102	817-871-8900	
Fort Worth Convention & Visitors Bureau 415 Throckmorton St *TF:* 800-433-5747 ■ *Web:* www.fortworth.com	Fort Worth	TX	76102	817-336-8791	336-3282
Fort Worth Economic Development Dept 1000 Throckmorton St 3rd Fl	Fort Worth	TX	76102	817-871-6192	871-6134
Fort Worth Mayor 1000 Throckmorton St 3rd Fl *Web:* ci.fort-worth.tx.us/fortworth/council ■ *E-mail:* mayor@ci.fort-worth.tx.us	Fort Worth	TX	76102	817-871-6110	871-6187
Fort Worth Public Library 300 Taylor St *Web:* 198.215.16.8:443/fortworth/fwpl	Fort Worth	TX	76102	817-871-7701	871-7734
Fort Worth/Tarrant County Convention Center 1111 Houston St *Web:* www.fortworth.com/fwtccc.htm ■ *E-mail:* jaesea@onramp.net	Fort Worth	TX	76102	817-884-2222	212-2756
Tarrant County 100 W Weatherford St. *Web:* www.tarrantcounty.com	Fort Worth	TX	76196	817-884-1195	

On-Line Resources

Anthill City Guide Dallas/Fort Worth	www.anthill.com/city.asp?city=dallas
City Knowledge Fort Worth	www.cityknowledge.com/tx_fortworth.htm
Dallas Fort Worth City Pages	dallas.thelinks.com/
Dallas Fort Worth Metroplex Directory	www.flash.net/~dfwmet/
Dallas-Fort Worth Texas	www.dallas-fort-worth.com
Dallas/Fort Worth Area Web	www.dfwareaweb.com/
Excite.com Fort Worth City Guide	www.excite.com/travel/countries/united_states/texas/fort_worth
Fort Worth CyberRodeo	www.cyberrodeo.com/fortworth
GuideLive: Arts & Entertainment in Dallas & Fort Worth	www.guidelive.com
HotelGuide Dallas/Fort Worth	hotelguide.net/dfw/
Intro Fort Worth	www.introfortworth.com/
IntroFortWorth	www.fortworth.acn.net/
MetroGuide Dallas/Fort Worth	metroguide.net/dfw/
NITC Travelbase City Guide Dallas-Fort Worth	www.travelbase.com/auto/guides/dallas_ft_worth-area-tx.html
Virtual Voyages Dallas-Fort Worth	www.virtualvoyages.com/usa/tx/dfw/dfw.sht
Yahoo! Dallas/Fort Worth	dfw.yahoo.com

Fort Worth (Cont'd)

— Transportation Services —

AIRPORTS

■ **Dallas-Fort Worth International Airport (DFW)**

	Phone
20 miles NE of downtown Forth Worth (approx 35 minutes)	972-574-8888

Web: www.dfwairport.com

Airport Transportation

	Phone
Airporter Express Bus $8 fare to downtown Fort Worth	817-334-0092
SuperShuttle $12-15 fare to downtown Fort Worth	817-329-2001
Taxi $30 fare to downtown Fort Worth	817-534-5555

Commercial Airlines

	Phone		Phone
AeroMexico	972-751-1484	**Mesa**	800-637-2247
AirTran	800-247-8726	**Mexicana**	800-531-7923
American	800-433-7300	**Midwest Express**	800-452-2022
American Eagle	800-433-7300	**National**	888-757-5387
Aspen Mountain Air Inc	972-641-7337	**Northwest**	800-225-2525
British Airways	800-247-9297	**Southwest**	972-263-1717
Continental	972-263-0523	**Spirit**	800-772-7117
Continental Express	800-525-0280	**TWA**	800-221-2000
Delta	214-630-3200	**United**	800-241-6522
El Al	800-223-6700	**US Airways**	800-428-4322
Lufthansa	800-645-3880	**Vanguard**	800-826-4827

Charter Airlines

	Phone		Phone
Alpha Aviation	214-352-4801	**Million Air**	800-248-1602
Miami Air International	305-871-3300	**Sun Country**	800-359-5786

CAR RENTALS

	Phone		Phone
Advantage	817-560-8222	**Dollar**	972-929-8888
Alamo	972-263-2752	**Enterprise**	817-589-0471
Avis	817-335-3211	**Hertz**	817-429-8541
Budget	817-329-2277	**Thrifty**	817-263-4519

LIMO/TAXI

	Phone		Phone
Fort Worth Limousine	817-870-9783	**Wynne Transportation**	214-361-6125
Silver West Limousine	817-870-1333	**Yellow & Checker Cab**	817-534-7777

MASS TRANSIT

	Phone
The 'T'-Fort Worth $.80 Base fare	817-215-8600

RAIL/BUS

				Phone
Amtrak Station 1501 Jones St	Fort Worth	TX	76102	817-332-2931
Greyhound/Trailways Bus Station 901 Commerce St	Fort Worth	TX	76102	817-429-3089
TF: 800-231-2222				

— Accommodations —

HOTEL RESERVATION SERVICES

	Phone	Fax
USA Hotels	252-331-1555	331-2021

TF: 800-872-4683 ■ *Web:* www.1800usahotels.com
■ *E-mail:* info@1800usahotels.com

HOTELS, MOTELS, RESORTS

				Phone	Fax
Best Western West Branch Inn 7301 West Frwy	Fort Worth	TX	76116	817-244-7444	244-7902
TF: 888-474-9566					
Care-A-Lot Inn 1111 W Lancaster	Fort Worth	TX	76102	817-338-0215	338-2539
TF: 800-952-3011					
Clarion Hotel 600 Commerce St	Fort Worth	TX	76102	817-332-6900	877-5440
TF: 800-252-7466					
Comfort Inn 4850 North Frwy	Fort Worth	TX	76137	817-834-8001	834-3159
TF: 800-228-5150					
Comfort Inn 2425 Scott Ave	Fort Worth	TX	76103	817-535-2591	531-1373
TF: 800-228-5150					
Courtyard by Marriott 3150 Riverfront Dr.	Fort Worth	TX	76107	817-335-1300	336-6926
TF: 800-321-2211 ■ *Web:* courtyard.com/DFWCH					
Delux Inn 4451 South Fwy	Fort Worth	TX	76115	817-924-5011	923-4120
Executive Inn 3800 Hwy 377 S	Fort Worth	TX	76116	817-560-2831	560-2831
Green Oaks Hotel 6901 West Fwy	Fort Worth	TX	76116	817-738-7311	377-1308
TF: 800-433-2174					
Hampton Inn 2700 Cherry Ln	Fort Worth	TX	76116	817-560-4180	560-8032
TF: 800-426-7866					
Holiday Inn Central 2000 Beach St	Fort Worth	TX	76103	817-534-4801	536-5384
TF: 800-465-4329					
Holiday Inn Fort Worth North Hotel & Conference Center 2540 Meacham Blvd	Fort Worth	TX	76106	817-625-9911	625-5132
TF: 800-465-4329 ■ *Web:* www.basshotels.com/holiday-inn/?_franchisee=FTWND ■ *E-mail:* ftwnd@internetmci.com					
Hyatt Regency DFW Airport International Pkwy.	DFW Airport	TX	75261	972-453-1234	456-8668
TF: 800-233-1234 ■ *Web:* www.hyatt.com/usa/dallas/hotels/hotel_dfwap.html					
Park Central Hotel 1010 Houston St	Fort Worth	TX	76102	817-336-2011	336-0623
TF: 800-848-7275 ■ *Web:* www.parkcentralhotel.com					
Radisson Plaza Hotel 815 Main St	Fort Worth	TX	76102	817-870-2100	882-1300
TF: 800-333-3333					
Ramada Inn Midtown 1401 S University Dr.	Fort Worth	TX	76107	817-336-9311	877-3023
TF: 800-272-6232					
Ramada Plaza Downtown 1701 Commerce St	Fort Worth	TX	76102	817-335-7000	335-3333
TF: 800-228-2828					
Residence Inn by Marriott Fort Worth 1701 S University Dr	Fort Worth	TX	76107	817-870-1011	877-5500
TF: 800-331-3131 ■ *Web:* www.residenceinn.com/DFWRP					
Stockyards Hotel 109 E Exchange Ave	Fort Worth	TX	76106	817-625-6427	624-2571
TF: 800-423-8471					
Travelodge 4201 South Fwy	Fort Worth	TX	76115	817-923-8281	926-8756
TF: 800-578-7878					
Travelodge Suites 8401 I-30 W	Fort Worth	TX	76116	817-560-0060	244-3047
TF: 800-840-7951					
Worthington Hotel 200 Main St	Fort Worth	TX	76102	817-870-1000	338-9176
TF: 800-433-5677 ■ *Web:* www.worthingtonhotel.com/					

— Restaurants —

				Phone
Angelo's BBQ (Barbecue) 2533 White Settlement Rd	Fort Worth	TX	76107	817-332-0357
Billy Miner's Saloon (American) 150 W 3rd St	Fort Worth	TX	76112	817-877-3301
Web: cyberrodeo.com/billyminers/				
Bistro Louise (Mediterranean) 2900 S Hulen St	Fort Worth	TX	76109	817-922-9244
Byblos (Lebanese) 1406 N Main St	Fort Worth	TX	76106	817-625-9667
Cactus Bar & Grill (Southwest) 815 Main St	Fort Worth	TX	76102	817-870-2100
Cactus Flower Cafe (American) 509 University Dr	Fort Worth	TX	76107	817-332-9552
Cafe Texas (American) 815 Main St	Fort Worth	TX	76102	817-870-2100
Cattlemen's Steak House (Steak) 2458 N Main St	Fort Worth	TX	76106	817-624-3945
China Jade (Chinese) 114 Main St	Fort Worth	TX	76102	817-336-6242
Dos Gringos (Mexican) 1015 University Dr	Fort Worth	TX	76107	817-338-9393
El Rancho Grande Restaurante (Mexican) 1400 N Main St	Fort Worth	TX	76106	817-624-9206
Forest Park Cafe (Mediterranean) 2418 Forest Park Blvd.	Fort Worth	TX	76110	817-921-4567
H3 Ranch (Steak) 109 E Exchange Ave Stockyards Hotel	Fort Worth	TX	76106	817-624-1246
J & J Oyster Bar (Seafood) 612 University Dr	Fort Worth	TX	76107	817-335-2756
Joe T Garcia's (Mexican) 2201 N Commerce St	Fort Worth	TX	76106	817-626-4356
La Piazza (Italian) 1600 S University Dr	Fort Worth	TX	76107	817-334-0000
Le Saint Emilion (French) 3617 W 7th St	Fort Worth	TX	76107	817-737-2781
Web: www.lesaint-emilion.com ■ *E-mail:* rrenchrest@aol.com				
Lone Star Oyster Bar (Seafood) 4750 Bryant Irvin Rd Cityview Ctr.	Fort Worth	TX	76132	817-370-0030
Los Vaqueros (Mexican) 2629 N Main St	Fort Worth	TX	76106	817-624-1511
Maharaja Restaurant (Indian) 6308 Hulen Bend Blvd	Fort Worth	TX	76132	817-263-7156
Michael's (New American) 3413 W 7th St	Fort Worth	TX	76107	817-877-3413
Paris Coffee Shop (American) 704 W Magnolia Ave	Fort Worth	TX	76104	817-335-2041
Pour House Sports Grill (American) 209 W 5th St	Fort Worth	TX	76102	817-335-2575
Railhead Smokehouse (Barbecue) 2900 Montgomery	Fort Worth	TX	76107	817-738-9808
Razzoo's Cajun Cafe (Cajun/Creole) 318 Main St	Fort Worth	TX	76102	817-429-7009
Reflections (New American) 200 Main St	Fort Worth	TX	76102	817-870-1000
Risckys Bar-B-Q (Barbecue) 300 N Main St	Fort Worth	TX	76102	817-877-3306
Web: www.risckys.com				
Rodeo Steakhouse (Steak/Seafood) 1309 Calhoun St	Fort Worth	TX	76102	817-332-1288
Web: cyberrodeo.com/rodeosteakhouse/				

Fort Worth — Restaurants (Cont'd)

				Phone
Sardines Ristorante Italiano (Italian) 3410 Camp Bowie Blvd	Fort Worth	TX	76107	817-332-9937
Star Cafe (Steak) 111 W Exchange Ave	Fort Worth	TX	76106	817-624-8701
Tai-Pan Restaurant (Chinese) 3020 W 7th St	Fort Worth	TX	76107	817-335-6027
Water Street Seafood Company (Seafood) 1540 S University Dr	Fort Worth	TX	76107	817-877-3474
White Elephant Saloon (Southwest) 106 E Exchange Ave	Fort Worth	TX	76106	817-624-1887

— Goods and Services —

SHOPPING

				Phone	Fax
Fort Worth Outlet Square 150 Throckmorton St *Web:* www.fwoutletsquare.com	Fort Worth	TX	76102	817-390-3720	415-0284
Fort Worth Town Center 4200 South Fwy Suite 100	Fort Worth	TX	76115	817-927-8459	927-1833
Hulen Mall 4800 S Hulen St	Fort Worth	TX	76132	817-294-1200	370-0932
Montgomery Street Antique Mall 2601 Montgomery St	Fort Worth	TX	76107	817-735-9685	735-9379
Neiman Marcus 2100 Green Oaks Rd *Web:* www.neimanmarcus.com	Fort Worth	TX	76116	817-738-3581	732-0920
North East Mall 1101 Melbourne Rd Suite 1000	Hurst	TX	76053	817-284-3427	595-4471
North Hills Mall 7624 Grapevine Hwy	North Richland Hills	TX	76180	817-589-2236	284-9730
Richland Point Mall 5201 Rufe Snow Dr	Fort Worth	TX	76180	817-281-7283	428-6611
Ridgmar Mall 2060 Green Oaks Rd	Fort Worth	TX	76116	817-731-0856	763-5146
Stripling & Cox 6370 Camp Bowie Blvd	Fort Worth	TX	76116	817-738-7361	377-5305
Sundance Square 505 Main St Suite 500 *Web:* www.sundancesquare.com/	Fort Worth	TX	76102	817-390-7777	339-7216

BANKS

				Phone	Fax
Bank of America 811 Lamar St *TF:* 800-730-6000	Fort Worth	TX	76102	817-332-4152	
Bank One Texas 500 Throckmorton St *TF:* 800-695-1111	Fort Worth	TX	76102	817-884-4000	884-4907
Bank United 343 Throckmorton St *TF:* 800-366-7378	Fort Worth	TX	76102	817-336-1666	336-1340
Frost Bank 777 Main St **Fax:* Loans ■ *TF:* 800-513-7678	Fort Worth	TX	76102	817-731-0101	731-9123*
NationsBank of Texas 500 W 7th St *TF:* 800-333-6262	Fort Worth	TX	76102	817-390-6161	390-6958
Norwest Bank 100 Main St	Fort Worth	TX	76102	817-870-8200	870-8282

BUSINESS SERVICES

	Phone
Corporate Express Delivery Systems	972-538-3675
Express 60-Minutes Delivery Services Inc	817-336-5333
Interim Personnel Services	817-335-6333
Kelly Services	817-332-7807
Kinko's	817-737-8021
Manpower Temporary Services	817-926-4600
Olsten Staffing Services	817-336-9401
Post Office	800-275-8777
Quick Way Courier	817-568-2988
UPS	800-742-5877

— Media —

PUBLICATIONS

				Phone	Fax
Business Press 314 Main St Suite 300 *Web:* www.dfwbusinesspress.com	Fort Worth	TX	76102	817-336-8300	332-3038
Fort Worth Star-Telegram‡ PO Box 1870 *Web:* www.star-telegram.com	Fort Worth	TX	76101	817-390-7400	390-7789

‡Daily newspapers

TELEVISION

				Phone	Fax
KDAF-TV Ch 33 (WB) 8001 John Carpenter Fwy *Web:* www.wb33.com	Dallas	TX	75247	214-640-3300	252-3379
KDFI-TV Ch 27 (Ind) 400 N Griffin St	Dallas	TX	75202	214-637-2727	720-3355
KDFW-TV Ch 4 (Fox) 400 N Griffin St	Dallas	TX	75202	214-720-4444	720-3263
KERA-TV Ch 13 (PBS) 3000 Harry Hines Blvd *Web:* www.kera.org	Dallas	TX	75201	214-871-1390	740-9369
KFWD-TV Ch 52 (Tele) 3000 W Story Rd	Irving	TX	75038	972-255-5200	258-1770
KLDT-TV Ch 55 (Ind) 2450 Rockbrook Dr	Lewisville	TX	75067	972-316-2115	316-1112
KMPX-TV Ch 29 (Ind) PO Box 612066	Dallas	TX	75261	817-571-1229	571-7458
KPXD-TV Ch 68 (PAX) 800 W Airport Fwy Suite 750 *Web:* www.pax.net/KPXD	Irving	TX	75062	972-438-6868	579-3045
KTVT-TV Ch 11 (CBS) 5233 Bridge St *Web:* www.ktvt.com	Fort Worth	TX	76103	817-451-1111	496-7739
KTXA-TV Ch 21 (UPN) 301 N Market Suite 700 *Web:* www.paramountstations.com/KTXA	Dallas	TX	75202	214-743-2100	743-2121
KUVN-TV Ch 23 (Uni) 2323 Bryan St Suite 1900 *TF:* 800-494-5886 ■ *Web:* www.univision.net/stations/kuvn.htm	Dallas	TX	75201	214-758-2300	758-2324
KXAS-TV Ch 5 (NBC) 3900 Barnett St *Web:* www.kxas.com	Fort Worth	TX	76103	817-429-5555	654-6325
KXTX-TV Ch 39 (Ind) 3900 Harry Hines Blvd *TF:* 800-465-5989 ■ *Web:* www.kxtx.com	Dallas	TX	75219	214-521-3900	523-5946
WFAA-TV Ch 8 (ABC) 606 Young St Communications Ctr *Web:* www.wfaa.com	Dallas	TX	75202	214-748-9631	977-6585

RADIO

				Phone	Fax
KBFB-FM 97.9 MHz (AC) 4131 N Central Expy Suite 1200 *Web:* www.kbfb.com ■ *E-mail:* kbfb@kbfb.com	Dallas	TX	75204	214-528-5500	528-0747
KDMX-FM 102.9 MHz (AC) 14001 N Dallas Pkwy Suite 1210	Dallas	TX	75240	972-991-1029	448-1029
KERA-FM 90.1 MHz (NPR) 3000 Harry Hines Blvd *Web:* www.kera.org/ ■ *E-mail:* kerafm@metronet.com	Dallas	TX	75201	214-871-1390	740-9369
KESS-AM 1270 kHz (Span) 7700 Carpenter Fwy	Dallas	TX	75247	214-630-8531	920-2507
KFJZ-AM 870 kHz (Span) 2214 E 4th St	Fort Worth	TX	76102	817-336-7175	338-1205
KICI-FM 107.9 MHz (Span) 7700 Carpenter Fwy	Dallas	TX	75247	214-630-8531	920-2507
KKDA-FM 104.5 MHz (Urban) PO Box 860	Grand Prairie	TX	75053	972-263-9911	558-0010
KKZN-FM 93.3 MHz (AAA) 3500 Maple Ave Suite 1310 *Web:* www.933thezone.com	Dallas	TX	75219	214-526-7400	787-1946
KLTY-FM 94.1 MHz (Rel) 7700 Carpenter Fwy *Web:* www.klty.com ■ *E-mail:* klty@onramp.net	Dallas	TX	75247	214-630-9400	630-0060
KLUV-FM 98.7 MHz (Oldies) 4131 N Central Expy Suite 700 *Web:* www.kluv.com ■ *E-mail:* kluv@ix.netcom.com	Dallas	TX	75204	214-526-9870	443-1570
KPLX-FM 99.5 MHz (Ctry) 3500 Maple Ave Suite 1600	Dallas	TX	75219	214-526-2400	520-4343
KRBV-FM 100.3 MHz (Urban) 7901 John Carpenter Fwy	Dallas	TX	75247	214-630-3011	688-7760
KRNB-FM 105.7 MHz (AC) 621 NW 6th St	Grand Prairie	TX	75050	972-263-9911	558-0010
KTXQ-FM 102.1 MHz (Oldies) 4131 N Central Expy Suite 1200 *Web:* www.ktxq.com	Dallas	TX	75204	214-528-5500	528-0747
KVIL-FM 103.7 MHz (AC) 9400 N Central Expy Suite 1600 *Web:* www.kvil.com	Dallas	TX	75231	214-691-1037	891-7975
KYNG-FM 105.3 MHz (Ctry) 12201 Merit Dr Suite 930 *Web:* www.young-country.com	Dallas	TX	75251	972-716-7800	716-7835

— Colleges/Universities —

				Phone	Fax
ITT Technical Institute 551 Ryan Plaza Dr *Web:* www.itttech.edu	Arlington	TX	76011	817-794-5100	275-8446
Tarrant County Junior College 1500 Houston St *Web:* www.tcjc.cc.tx.us	Fort Worth	TX	76102	817-515-5293	515-5278
Tarrant County Junior College Southeast Campus 2100 TCJC Pkwy *Web:* www.tcjc.cc.tx.us/se_campusindx.html	Arlington	TX	76018	817-515-3100	515-3182
Texas Christian University TCU Box 297013 *TF Admissions:* 800-828-3764 ■ *Web:* www.tcu.edu ■ *E-mail:* admwww@tcuavm.is.tcu.edu	Fort Worth	TX	76129	817-921-7000	257-7268
Texas Wesleyan University 1201 Wesleyan St *TF Admissions:* 800-580-8980 ■ *Web:* www.txwesleyan.edu ■ *E-mail:* info@txwesleyan.edu	Fort Worth	TX	76105	817-531-4444	531-4231

Fort Worth (Cont'd)

— Hospitals —

Name / Address	City	State	ZIP	Phone	Fax
All Saints Episcopal Hospital of Fort Worth 1400 8th Ave *Web:* www.allsaints.com	Fort Worth	TX	76104	817-926-2544	927-6226
Arlington Memorial Hospital 800 W Randol Mill Rd	Arlington	TX	76012	817-548-6100	548-6357
Baylor Medical Center at Grapevine 1650 W College St	Grapevine	TX	76051	817-488-7546	481-2962
Columbia North Hills Hospital 4401 Booth Calloway Rd	Fort Worth	TX	76180	817-284-1431	284-4817
Cook Children's Medical Center 801 7th Ave *Web:* www.cookchildrens.org	Fort Worth	TX	76104	817-885-4000	885-4229
Harris Methodist Fort Worth 1301 Pennsylvania Ave	Fort Worth	TX	76104	817-882-2000	882-2149
Harris Methodist-HEB 1600 Hospital Pkwy	Bedford	TX	76022	817-685-4000	685-4895
Harris Methodist Southwest 6100 Harris Pkwy	Fort Worth	TX	76132	817-346-5050	882-3169
Huguley Memorial Medical Center 11801 S Fwy	Fort Worth	TX	76134	817-293-9110	568-3269
Medical Center Arlington 3301 Matlock Rd	Arlington	TX	76015	817-465-3241	472-4878
Osteopathic Medical Center of Texas 1000 Montgomery St. *Web:* www.ohst.com ■ *E-mail:* ohst@ohst.com	Fort Worth	TX	76107	817-731-4311	735-6442
Plaza Medical Center 900 8th Ave	Fort Worth	TX	76104	817-336-2100	347-5769

— Attractions —

Name / Address	City	State	ZIP	Phone	Fax
Amon Carter Museum 500 Commerce St. *Web:* www.cartermuseum.org/	Fort Worth	TX	76102	817-738-1933	377-8523
Bass Performance Hall 4th & Calhoun Sts. *Web:* www.basshall.com	Fort Worth	TX	76102	817-212-4200	810-9294
Billy Bob's Texas 2520 Rodeo Plaza	Fort Worth	TX	76106	817-624-7117	626-2340
Cattleman's Museum 1301 W 7th St.	Fort Worth	TX	76102	817-332-7064	332-8523
Circle Theatre 230 W 4th St *Web:* home.swbell.net/circleth/	Fort Worth	TX	76102	817-877-3040	877-3536
Cowtown Coliseum 121 E Exchange Ave *TF:* 888-269-8696 ■ *Web:* www.cowtowncoliseum.com	Fort Worth	TX	76106	817-625-1025	625-1148
Eddleman-McFarland House Museum 1110 Penn St	Fort Worth	TX	76102	817-332-5875	332-5877
Fort Worth Ballet 6845 Green Oaks Rd	Fort Worth	TX	76116	817-763-0207	763-0624
Fort Worth Botanic Garden 3220 Botanic Garden Blvd	Fort Worth	TX	76107	817-871-7686	871-7638
Fort Worth Museum of Science & History 1501 Montgomery St. *TF:* 888-255-9300 ■ *Web:* www.fwmuseum.org ■ *E-mail:* fwmsh1@metronet.com	Fort Worth	TX	76107	817-732-1631	732-7635
Fort Worth Nature Center & Refuge 9601 Fossil Ridge Rd	Fort Worth	TX	76135	817-237-1111	237-0653
Fort Worth Opera 3505 W Lancaster *Web:* www.startext.net/interact/fwopera.htm ■ *E-mail:* fwopera@startext.net	Fort Worth	TX	76107	817-731-0833	731-0835
Fort Worth Symphony Orchestra 4th & Calhoun Sts Bass Performance Hall *Web:* www.fwsymphony.org/ ■ *E-mail:* ticks@fwsymphony.org	Fort Worth	TX	76102	817-665-6000	665-6100
Fort Worth Water Gardens 1502 Commerce St	Fort Worth	TX	76102	817-871-7698	871-5724
Fort Worth Zoological Park 1989 Colonial Pkwy. *Web:* www.fortworthzoo.com	Fort Worth	TX	76110	817-871-7000	871-7012
Gateway Park 750 N Beach	Fort Worth	TX	76137	817-871-7275	
Imagisphere Children's Museum 7624 Grapevine Hwy Suite 716 *Web:* www.imagisphere.org/ ■ *E-mail:* imaginc@imagisphere.com	North Richland Hills	TX	76180	817-589-9000	
Jubilee Theatre 506 Main St *Web:* www.jubileetheatre.org	Fort Worth	TX	76102	817-338-4411	338-4206
Kimbell Art Museum 3333 Camp Bowie Blvd *Web:* www.kimbellart.org	Fort Worth	TX	76107	817-332-8451	877-1264
Log Cabin Village 2100 Log Cabin Village Ln	Fort Worth	TX	76109	817-926-5881	922-0504
Modern Art Museum of Fort Worth 1309 Montgomery St. *Web:* www.mamfw.org	Fort Worth	TX	76107	817-738-9215	735-1161
National Cowgirl Museum & Hall of Fame 111 W 4th St Suite 300 *TF:* 800-476-3263 ■ *Web:* www.cowgirl.net/	Fort Worth	TX	76102	817-336-4475	336-2470
Noble Planetarium 1501 Montgomery St Museum of Science & History *TF:* 888-255-9300 ■ *Web:* www.fwmuseum.org/tnoble.html	Fort Worth	TX	76107	817-732-1631	732-7635
Omni Theater 1501 Montgomery St Museum of Science & History *TF:* 888-255-9300 ■ *Web:* www.fwmuseum.org/tomni.html	Fort Worth	TX	76107	817-732-1631	732-7635
Pate Museum of Transportation Hwy 377 S of Fort Worth **Fax Area Code:* 800 ■ *Web:* www.classicar.com/MUSEUMS/PATE/PATE.HTM	Cresson	TX	76035	817-396-4305	827-0711*
Richarson Sid Collection of Western Art 309 Main St *Web:* www.sidrmuseum.org ■ *E-mail:* sidrmus@txcc.net	Fort Worth	TX	76102	817-332-6554	332-8671
Six Flags Over Texas 2201 Road to Six Flags *Web:* www.sixflags.com/texas	Arlington	TX	76011	817-640-8900	530-6040
Stockyards Museum 131 E Exchange Ave	Fort Worth	TX	76106	817-625-5087	625-5083
Stockyards National Historic District 130 E Exchange St	Fort Worth	TX	76106	817-624-4741	625-9744
Sundance Square 505 Main St Suite 500 *Web:* www.sundancesquare.com/	Fort Worth	TX	76102	817-390-7777	339-7216
Tandy Charles D Archaeological Museum 2001 W Seminary Dr.	Fort Worth	TX	76115	817-923-1921	921-8765
Tarrant County Courthouse 100 W Weatherford St.	Fort Worth	TX	76196	817-884-1111	884-1702
Thistle Hill 1509 Pennsylvania Ave	Fort Worth	TX	76104	817-336-1212	335-5338
Traders Village 2602 Mayfield Rd. *Web:* www.tradersvillage.com/gp1.html	Grand Prairie	TX	75052	972-647-2331	647-8585
Trinity Park 2401 N University Dr	Fort Worth	TX	76107	817-871-7275	
Vintage Flying Museum 505 NW 38th St Hanger 33 S Meacham Field *Web:* www.startext.net/homes/vfm/ ■ *E-mail:* vfm@startext.net	Fort Worth	TX	76106	817-624-1935	
Will Rogers Memorial Center 3401 W Lancaster Ave.	Fort Worth	TX	76107	817-871-8150	871-8170

SPORTS TEAMS & FACILITIES

Name / Address	City	State	ZIP	Phone	Fax
Fort Worth Brahmas (hockey) 1314 Lake St Suite 200 *Web:* www.brahmas.com ■ *E-mail:* info@brahmas.com	Fort Worth	TX	76102	817-336-4423	336-3334
Fort Worth Fire (hockey) 508 Main St. *Web:* www.fwfire.com	Fort Worth	TX	76102	817-336-1992	336-1997
Lone Star Park at Grand Prairie 1000 Lone Star Pkwy *Web:* www.lonestarpark.com	Grand Prairie	TX	75050	972-263-7223	237-5109
Texas Motor Speedway 3601 Hwy 114	Fort Worth	TX	76247	817-215-8500	491-3749

— Events —

	Phone
Cowtown Goes Green (mid-March)	800-433-5747
Fort Worth Chisholm Trail Round-Up (mid-June)	817-625-7005
Fort Worth Fourth (July 4)	800-433-5747
Fort Worth International Air Show (early October)	817-870-1515
Fort Worth RetroFest (mid-September-mid-November)	817-924-0492
Juneteenth Celebration (mid-June)	800-433-5747
Last Great Gunfight (early February)	800-433-5747
Main Street Fort Worth Arts Festival (mid-April)	817-336-2787
Mayfest (late April-early May)	800-433-5747
Oasis Fireworks to Music (early July)	214-855-1881
Oktoberfest (early October)	800-433-5747
Parade of Lights (late November-late December)	800-433-5747
Pioneer Days (mid-September)	800-433-5747
Red Steagall Cowboy Gathering (late October)	800-433-5747
Shakespeare In the Park (June-July)	800-433-5747
Southwestern Exposition & Livestock Show (late January-early February)	817-877-2400
Stockyards Championship Rodeo (early August-late November)	800-433-5747

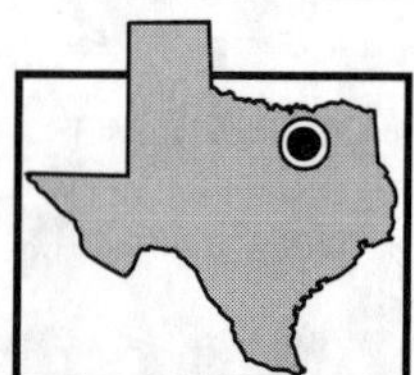

Garland

Founded in 1891 with the combining of the towns of Embree and Duck Creek, Garland developed from a small farming community to become the ninth largest city in Texas. Located within the Dallas/Fort Worth Metroplex, Garland's business environment has helped it to establish a strong industrial base of more than 4100 businesses, with major operations in electronics, metal fabrication, paints and chemicals, and food processing. The Garland Center for the Performing Arts is home to a symphony orchestra, a civic theater, and summer musicals. Visitors to Heritage Park will find the Garland Landmark Museum, located in a restored, 1901-vintage Sante Fe Railroad Depot, and two 19th century prairie homes, the Pace House and the Lyles House.

Population 190,055
Area (Land) . . . . . 57.32 sq mi
Area (Water) . . . . . 0.0 sq mi
Elevation . . . . . 595 ft
Latitude . . . . . 32-54-34 N
Longitude . . . . . 96-37-48 W
County . . . . . Collin, Dallas, Rockwall
Time Zone . . . . . CST
Area Code/s 214, 972

— Average Temperatures and Precipitation —

TEMPERATURES

	Jan	Feb	Mar	Apr	May	Jun	Jul	Aug	Sep	Oct	Nov	Dec
High	54	59	68	76	83	92	97	96	88	79	67	58
Low	33	37	46	55	63	70	74	74	67	56	45	36

PRECIPITATION

	Jan	Feb	Mar	Apr	May	Jun	Jul	Aug	Sep	Oct	Nov	Dec
Inches	1.8	2.2	2.8	3.5	4.9	3.0	2.3	2.2	3.4	3.5	2.3	1.8

— Important Phone Numbers —

	Phone
AAA	214-526-7911
American Express Travel	972-424-7554
Emergency	911
Highway Conditions	800-452-9292
Poison Control Center	800-764-7661
Time/Temp	214-844-6611
Weather	214-787-1111

— Information Sources —

				Phone	Fax
Better Business Bureau Serving Metropolitan Dallas & Northeast Texas 2001 Bryan St Suite 850	Dallas	TX	75201	214-220-2000	740-0321
Web: www.dallas.bbb.org					
Dallas County 411 Elm St	Dallas	TX	75202	214-653-7361	653-7057
Garland Chamber of Commerce 914 S Garland Ave	Garland	TX	75040	972-272-7551	276-9261
Web: www.garlandchamber.org					
■ *E-mail:* information@garlandchamber.com					
Garland City Hall 200 N 5th St	Garland	TX	75040	972-205-2000	205-2504
Web: www.ci.garland.tx.us					
Garland Convention & Visitors Bureau 200 N 4th St	Garland	TX	75046	972-205-2749	205-2504
Garland Mayor 200 N 5th St	Garland	TX	75040	972-205-2400	205-2504
Garland Planning Dept PO Box 469002	Garland	TX	75046	972-205-2445	205-2474
Web: www.ci.garland.tx.us/cogplan.htm					
Nicholson Memorial Library System 625 Austin St	Garland	TX	75040	972-205-2543	205-2523

On-Line Resources

Area Guide Garland . . . . . garland.areaguides.net
City Knowledge Garland . . . . . www.cityknowledge.com/tx_garland.htm
Excite.com Garland City Guide . . . . . www.excite.com/travel/countries/united_states/texas/garland

— Transportation Services —

AIRPORTS

■ Dallas Love Field (DAL)

	Phone
17 miles W of downtown Garland (approx 45 minutes)	214-670-6080

Airport Transportation

	Phone
Discount Shuttle $26-$30 fare to downtown Garland	817-267-5150
SuperShuttle $20 fare to downtown Garland	817-329-2025
Taxi $25 fare to downtown Garland	214-426-6262

Commercial Airlines

	Phone
Southwest	972-263-1717

Charter Airlines

	Phone
Aerodynamics Inc	214-352-2376
All-Star Helicopters Inc	972-250-9907
Alliance Executive Charter Services	800-232-5387
American Business Charter Inc.	972-732-7344
American Jet International Corp	888-435-9254
Business Jet Services	888-387-7477
Corporate Aviation Services Inc	918-834-8348
Helicopters Inc	800-466-2903
Jet Aviation	214-351-6571
Raytheon Aircraft Charter	800-519-6283
Regal Aviation	877-359-6520
Rivair Flying Service Inc	918-299-1234
Stebbins Jet Center	903-643-2601
Texas Air Charters	940-898-1200
TXI Aviation Inc.	972-647-7365
Zebra Air Inc.	214-358-7200

■ Dallas-Fort Worth International Airport (DFW)

	Phone
25 miles W of downtown Garland (approx 45 minutes)	972-574-8888

Airport Transportation

	Phone
Discount Shuttle $24-32 fare to downtown Garland	817-267-5150
SuperShuttle $30 fare to downtown Garland	817-329-2025
Taxi $37 fare to downtown Garland	214-426-6262

Commercial Airlines

	Phone
American	800-433-7300
American Eagle	800-433-7300
Aspen Mountain Air Inc	972-641-7337
British Airways	800-247-9297
Continental	972-263-0523
Continental Express	800-525-0280
Delta	800-221-1212
El Al	800-223-6700
Lufthansa	800-645-3880
Mesa	800-637-2247
Mexicana	800-531-7923
Midwest Express	800-452-2022
National	888-757-5387
Northwest	800-225-2525
Southwest	972-263-1717
Thai	800-426-5204
TWA	800-221-2000
United	800-241-6522
US Airways	800-428-4322
Vanguard	800-826-4827

Charter Airlines

	Phone
Alpha Aviation	214-352-4801
Miami Air International	305-871-3300
Million Air	800-248-1602
Sun Country	800-359-5786

CAR RENTALS

	Phone
Avis	972-574-4130
Budget	817-329-8700
Dollar	972-929-8888
Enterprise	972-986-0193
Hertz	972-453-0370
National	972-574-3400
Thrifty	972-621-1234

LIMO/TAXI

	Phone
Ambiance Limousine	214-343-4046
Carey Limousine	214-638-4828
Taxi & Limo Service	972-278-0077
Terminal Taxi	214-350-4445
Yellow Cab	214-426-6262

Garland (Cont'd)

MASS TRANSIT

	Phone
DART $1 Base fare	214-979-1111

RAIL/BUS

				Phone
Dallas Union Amtrak Station 400 S Houston St.	Dallas	TX	75202	214-653-1101
Greyhound Bus Station 4125 Broadway Blvd *TF:* 800-231-2222	Garland	TX	75043	972-276-5663

— Accommodations —

HOTELS, MOTELS, RESORTS

				Phone	Fax
Best Western Inn 1635 E I-30 *TF:* 800-528-1234	Garland	TX	75043	972-303-1601	303-1466
Comfort Inn 3536 W Kingsley Rd *TF:* 800-228-5150	Garland	TX	75041	214-340-3501	348-4617
Courtyard by Marriott 1000 S Sherman St. *TF:* 800-321-2211 ■ *Web:* courtyard.com/DALNE	Richardson	TX	75081	972-235-5000	235-3423
Delux Inn 3635 Leon Rd	Garland	TX	75041	972-864-1802	
Delux Inn 2306 S Jupiter Rd	Garland	TX	75041	972-271-4487	
Hampton Inn 1577 Gateway Blvd *TF:* 800-426-7866	Richardson	TX	75080	972-234-5400	234-8942
Hampton Inn Garland 12670 E Northwest Hwy. *TF:* 800-426-7866	Dallas	TX	75228	972-613-5000	613-4535
Hawthorn Suites Hotel 250 Municipal Dr. *TF:* 800-527-1133	Richardson	TX	75080	972-669-1000	437-4146
Holiday Inn Select Richardson 1655 N Central Expy *TF:* 800-465-4329 ■ *Web:* www.basshotels.com/holiday-inn/?_franchisee=DALRS ■ *E-mail:* hisdalrs@aol.com	Richardson	TX	75080	972-238-1900	644-7728
Jupiter Inn 2417 Executive Dr.	Garland	TX	75041	972-271-9700	
La Quinta Inn 12721 I-635 *TF:* 800-687-6667	Garland	TX	75041	972-271-7581	271-1388
Motel 6 436 W I-30 *TF:* 800-466-8356	Garland	TX	75043	972-226-7140	226-2416
Omni Richardson Hotel 701 E Campbell Rd *TF:* 800-843-6664	Richardson	TX	75081	972-231-9600	907-2578
Red Roof Inn 13700 Lyndon B Johnson Fwy *TF:* 800-833-8751	Garland	TX	75041	972-686-0202	686-8836
Sleep Inn 2458 N Central Expy	Richardson	TX	75080	972-470-9440	470-0996
Travelers Inn 2413 S Garland Ave.	Garland	TX	75041	972-278-3921	

— Restaurants —

				Phone
A Taste of Italy (Italian) 200 Walnut Village Shopping Center	Garland	TX	75042	972-276-8913
Aztec Tortillas (Mexican) 4119 Forest Ln	Garland	TX	75042	972-272-0959
Beef House (Steak) 3110 Saturn Rd Suite 103	Garland	TX	75041	972-278-2833
Catfish King (Seafood) 430 E I-30	Garland	TX	75043	972-226-1701
China Star (Chinese) 2425 W Walnut St.	Garland	TX	75042	972-487-8311
Colter's Bar-B-Q & Grill (Barbecue) 2015 Northwest Hwy	Garland	TX	75041	972-278-2106
Egg Roll Cafe (Chinese) 4002 N Jupiter Rd	Garland	TX	75044	972-530-2102
General Pao Chinese Restaurant (Chinese) 1311 Plaza Dr	Garland	TX	75041	972-686-8691
Mama Rugi's (Italian) 4040 S Shiloh Rd	Garland	TX	75041	972-278-6669
Marshall's Barbeque (Barbecue) 510 Walnut Cir W	Garland	TX	75040	972-272-8766
My-tho (Vietnamese) 4413 W Walnut St.	Garland	TX	75042	972-494-3963
New China (Chinese) 5010 N Jupiter Rd.	Garland	TX	75044	972-414-0880
On The Border Cafe (Mexican) 1350 Northwest Hwy	Garland	TX	75041	972-686-7867
Pastuer (Vietnamese) 3465 W Walnut St	Garland	TX	75042	972-276-7625
Plaza Del Sol (Mexican) 3125 S 1st St	Garland	TX	75041	972-840-8041
Rancho La Sandia (Mexican) 999 W Centerville Rd	Garland	TX	75041	972-613-2294
Rick's Smoke House Barbecue (Barbecue) 1417 Jupiter Rd	Garland	TX	75042	972-276-4353
Saigon Kitchen (Vietnamese) 801 N Jupiter Rd.	Garland	TX	75042	972-276-2214
Soulman's Barbeque (Barbecue) 3414 Broadway Blvd	Garland	TX	75043	972-271-6885
Taqueria Cholula (Mexican) 1902 S 1st St	Garland	TX	75040	972-840-8584
Uncle Wing Chinese Restaurant (Chinese) 107 N 1st St	Garland	TX	75040	972-272-2775
Vetoni's Italian Restaurant (Italian) 3420 Broadway Blvd	Garland	TX	75043	972-278-7707
Victor's Taqueria (Mexican) 2441 W Walnut St.	Garland	TX	75042	972-205-0870
Walnut Cafe (Homestyle) 3415 W Walnut St.	Garland	TX	75042	972-276-7633
Whataburger Restaurant (American) 1506 Buckingham Rd.	Garland	TX	75042	972-276-6900
Young Shing Restaurant (Chinese) 3701 W Walnut St.	Garland	TX	75042	972-487-1188

— Goods and Services —

SHOPPING

				Phone	Fax
Big Town Mall 800 Big Town Shopping Center	Mesquite	TX	75149	214-327-4541	320-2713
Town East Mall 2063 Town East Mall	Mesquite	TX	75150	972-270-4431	

BANKS

				Phone	Fax
Bank of America 700 W Ave 'A'	Garland	TX	75040	972-494-7500	494-7520
Bank One Texas 111 S Garland Ave	Garland	TX	75040	972-276-2265	276-7407
Bank United of Texas 3300 Broadway Blvd	Garland	TX	75043	972-271-4611	271-4613
Security Bank 2720 Belt Line Rd.	Garland	TX	75044	972-530-2265	530-7612
United Central Bank 4555 W Walnut St.	Garland	TX	75042	972-487-1505	276-3972

BUSINESS SERVICES

	Phone		Phone
DHL Worldwide Express	800-225-5345	**Manpower Temporary Services**	972-840-6022
Federal Express	800-238-5355	**Post Office**	972-272-5541
Mail Post Co.	972-278-7688	**UPS**	800-742-5877

— Media —

PUBLICATIONS

				Phone	Fax
Dallas Morning News‡ PO Box 655237 *Web:* www.dallasnews.com ■ *E-mail:* tdmned@cityview.com	Dallas	TX	75265	214-977-8222	977-8319

‡Daily newspapers

TELEVISION

				Phone	Fax
KDAF-TV Ch 33 (WB) 8001 John Carpenter Fwy *Web:* www.wb33.com	Dallas	TX	75247	214-640-3300	252-3379
KDFW-TV Ch 4 (Fox) 400 N Griffin St	Dallas	TX	75202	214-720-4444	720-3263
KERA-TV Ch 13 (PBS) 3000 Harry Hines Blvd *Web:* www.kera.org	Dallas	TX	75201	214-871-1390	740-9369
KTVT-TV Ch 11 (CBS) 5233 Bridge St *Web:* www.ktvt.com	Fort Worth	TX	76103	817-451-1111	496-7739
KTXA-TV Ch 21 (UPN) 301 N Market Suite 700 *Web:* www.paramountstations.com/KTXA	Dallas	TX	75202	214-743-2100	743-2121
KXAS-TV Ch 5 (NBC) 3900 Barnett St *Web:* www.kxas.com	Fort Worth	TX	76103	817-429-5555	654-6325
WFAA-TV Ch 8 (ABC) 606 Young St Communications Ctr *Web:* www.wfaa.com	Dallas	TX	75202	214-748-9631	977-6585

RADIO

				Phone
KEGG-AM 1560 KHz (N/T) PO Box 497931	Garland	TX	75049	972-645-7351

— Colleges/Universities —

				Phone	Fax
Amber University 1700 Eastgate Dr. *Web:* www.amberu.edu	Garland	TX	75041	972-279-6511	279-9773
Eastfield College 3737 Motley Dr *Web:* www.efc.dcccd.edu	Mesquite	TX	75150	972-860-7002	860-8306

— Hospitals —

				Phone	Fax
Baylor Medical Center at Garland 2300 Marie Curie Blvd. *Web:* www.baylorhealth.com/garland/index.htm	Garland	TX	75042	972-487-5000	487-5005
Doctors Hospital of Dallas 9440 Poppy Dr *Web:* www.tenethealth.com/DoctorsDallas	Dallas	TX	75218	214-324-6100	324-0612
Garland Community Hospital 2696 W Walnut St	Garland	TX	75042	972-276-7116	494-6913
Mesquite Community Hospital 3500 Interstate 30.	Mesquite	TX	75150	972-698-3300	698-2580

Garland (Cont'd)

— Attractions —

				Phone	Fax
Garland Civic Theatre 108 N 6th Stt	Garland	TX	75040	972-485-8884	487-2159
Garland Landmark Museum 200 Museum Plaza Dr	Garland	TX	75040	972-205-2749	
Garland Performing Arts Center PO Box 469002	Garland	TX	75046	972-205-2780	205-2775
Garland Symphony Orchestra 1919 S Shiloh St Suite 101 *E-mail:* garlandsymphony@juno.com	Garland	TX	75042	972-926-0611	926-0811
Lake Ray Hubbard 9501 Lakeview Pkwy	Rockwall	TX	75088	972-412-0101	
Lyles House 200 Museum Plaza Dr	Garland	TX	75040	972-205-2749	
Pace House 200 Museum Plaza Dr	Garland	TX	75040	972-205-2780	

SPORTS TEAMS & FACILITIES

				Phone	Fax
North Texas Heat (soccer) 2001 Kelley Blvd Polk Football Stadium *E-mail:* cdemarco@ntxsoccer.org	Carrollton	TX	75006	972-492-7863	242-3600

— Events —

	Phone
Autumn Fest (late October)	972-205-2749
Christmas Tree Lighting (December)	972-205-2749
Garland Summer Musicals (June-July)	972-205-2790
It's a Gas Vintage Car Show (mid-October)	972-205-2749
Labor Day Jubilee (late August-early September)	972-276-9366
Star Spangled 4th (July 4)	972-205-2749
State Fair of Texas (late September-mid-October)	214-565-9931
Trick or Treat Trot (late October)	972-205-2749

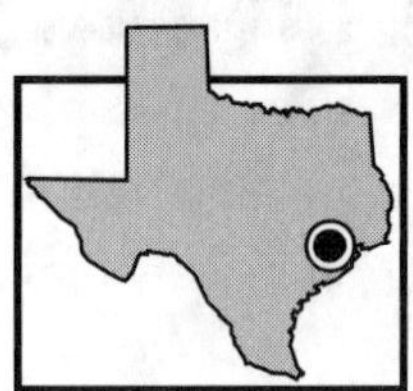

Houston

Houston is home to Texas Medical Center, the largest medical center in the world. The complex covers 670 acres and comprises 40 non-profit institutions and more than 100 permanent buildings. The Center's Texas Heart Institute is known for its excellence in research and medical training. Near downtown Houston is 401-acre Hermann Park, which includes the Houston Zoological Park and Japanese Friendship Gardens, riding trails, the Museum of Natural Science, and the Mecom Rockwell Fountain, one of the city's most beautiful structures. Houston's Western heritage is celebrated every February at the Houston Livestock Show and Rodeo. The event is held at the Astrodome and lasts 17 days. Approximately 25 miles southeast of Houston is Space Center Houston, which includes NASA's Johnson Space Center.

Population	1,786,691	**Longitude**	95-36-31 W
Area (Land)	527.1 sq mi	**County**	Harris
Area (Water)	21.8 sq mi	**Time Zone**	CST
Elevation	55 ft	**Area Code/s**	281, 713, 832
Latitude	29-76-31 N		

— Average Temperatures and Precipitation —

TEMPERATURES

	Jan	Feb	Mar	Apr	May	Jun	Jul	Aug	Sep	Oct	Nov	Dec
High	61	65	71	78	85	90	90	93	93	88	81	72
Low	40	43	50	58	64	64	71	72	72	68	58	50

PRECIPITATION

	Jan	Feb	Mar	Apr	May	Jun	Jul	Aug	Sep	Oct	Nov	Dec
Inches	3.3	3.0	2.9	3.2	5.2	5.0	3.6	3.5	4.9	4.3	3.8	3.5

— Important Phone Numbers —

	Phone		Phone
AAA	713-524-1851	**Medical Referral**	713-794-6000
American Express Travel	713-658-1114	**Poison Control Center**	800-764-7661
Dental Referral	713-961-4337	**Time/Temp**	713-529-4444
Emergency	911	**Travelers Aid**	713-526-8300
Highway Conditions	800-452-9292	**Weather**	713-529-4444
HotelDocs	800-468-3537		

— Information Sources —

				Phone	Fax
Better Business Bureau Serving Houston 5225 Katy Fwy Suite 500 *Web:* www.bbbhou.org ■ *E-mail:* bbbinfo@bbbhou.org	Houston	TX	77007	713-868-9500	867-4947
Brown George R Convention Center 1001 Avenida de Las Americas *TF:* 800-427-4697	Houston	TX	77010	713-853-8001	853-8090
Greater Houston Convention & Visitors Bureau 901 Bagby St *TF:* 800-446-8786 ■ *Web:* www.houston-guide.com/	Houston	TX	77002	713-437-5200	227-6336
Greater Houston Partnership 1200 Smith St Suite 700 *Web:* www.houston.org	Houston	TX	77002	713-844-3600	844-0200
Harris County 1001 Preston St *Web:* www.co.harris.tx.us	Houston	TX	77002	713-755-5000	
Houston City Hall 901 Bagby St *Web:* www.ci.houston.tx.us	Houston	TX	77002	713-247-1000	247-3439
Houston Mayor 901 Bagby St 3rd Fl *Web:* www.ci.houston.tx.us/citygovt/mayor ■ *E-mail:* mayor@ci.houston.tx.us	Houston	TX	77002	713-247-2200	247-2355
Houston Planning & Development Dept PO Box 1562 *Web:* www.ci.houston.tx.us/departme/planning/index.html	Houston	TX	77251	713-837-7701	837-7921
Houston Public Library 500 McKinney St. *Web:* www.hpl.lib.tx.us	Houston	TX	77002	713-236-1313	

On-Line Resources

4Houston.com	www.2houston.com
About.com Guide to Houston	houston.about.com/local/southwestus/houston
Annual Guide for the Arts	www.guide4arts.com/tx/
Anthill City Guide Houston	www.anthill.com/city.asp?city=houston
Area Guide Houston	houston.areaguides.net
Around Houston Index & Directory	aroundhouston.com/
Bradmans.com Houston	www.bradmans.com/scripts/display_city.cgi?city=236
City Knowledge Houston	www.cityknowledge.com/tx_houston.htm
CitySearch Houston	houston.citysearch.com
CuisineNet Houston	www.menusonline.com/cities/houston/locmain.shtml
DigitalCity Houston	home.digitalcity.com/houston
Excite.com Houston City Guide	www.excite.com/travel/countries/united_states/texas/houston
Gay Web Resource Guide to Houston	www.houstongayweb.com/
HotelGuide Houston	hotelguide.net/houston/
Houston City Pages	houston.thelinks.com/
Houston Eats	www.webside.com/eats
Houston Interactive Map & Guide	www.houstonet.com/
HoustonSites	www.houstonsites.com
LDS iAmerica Houston	houston.iamerica.net
NITC Travelbase City Guide Houston	www.travelbase.com/auto/guides/houston-area-tx.html
Rough Guide Travel Houston	travel.roughguides.com/content/909/
Texas On-Line	www.texas-on-line.com/graphic/houston.htm
Virtual Voyages Houston	www.virtualvoyages.com/usa/tx/houston/houston.sht

— Transportation Services —

AIRPORTS

	Phone
■ **Bush Intercontinental Airport (IAH)** 22 miles N of downtown (approx 60 minutes)	281-233-3000

Houston (Cont'd)

Airport Transportation

	Phone
Airport Express $16 fare to downtown	713-523-8888
Express Shuttle $17 fare to downtown	713-523-8888
Sam's Charter Limousine Services $67.25 fare to downtown	713-780-7077

Commercial Airlines

	Phone		Phone
AeroMexico	713-939-0077	**KLM**	800-374-7747
America West	800-235-9292	**Lufthansa**	800-645-3880
American	800-433-7300	**Northwest**	800-225-2525
British Airways	800-247-9297	**Southwest**	800-435-9792
Cayman Airways	800-422-9626	**TACA International**	713-665-1595
Continental	800-525-0280	**TWA**	800-221-2000
Continental Express	800-525-0280	**United**	800-241-6522
Delta	800-221-1212	**US Airways**	800-428-4322

■ William P Hobby Airport (HOU)

	Phone
8 miles SE of downtown (approx 25 minutes)	713-640-3000

Airport Transportation

	Phone
Metropolitan Transit $1 fare to downtown	713-635-4000
Taxi $25 fare to downtown	713-225-2666

Commercial Airlines

	Phone		Phone
American	800-433-7300	**Southwest**	800-435-9792
Continental	800-525-0280	**TWA**	800-221-2000
Continental Express	800-525-0280	**United**	800-241-6522
Northwest	800-225-2525		

Charter Airlines

	Phone		Phone
American Jet International Corp	888-435-9254	**Million Air**	713-641-6666
Atlantic Aviation	713-644-6431	**Raytheon Aircraft Charter**	800-519-6283
Corporate Aviation Services Inc	918-834-8348		

CAR RENTALS

	Phone		Phone
Alamo	713-944-8220	**Hertz**	713-941-6821
Alamo-Intercon	281-590-5100	**Hertz-Intercon**	281-443-0800
Avis-Intercon	281-443-5800	**National**	281-443-8850
Budget	713-944-1888	**Thrifty**	713-947-9125
Dollar	713-850-0080	**Thrifty-Intercon**	281-442-5000
Dollar-Intercon	281-449-0538		

LIMO/TAXI

	Phone		Phone
Clear Lake Limousine	281-482-9777	**United Cab**	713-699-0000
Fiesta Cab	713-236-9400	**VIP Limousine**	713-522-0861
Liberty Cab	713-695-6700	**Yellow Cab**	713-236-1111
Square Deal Cab	713-659-5105		

MASS TRANSIT

	Phone
Metropolitan Transit $1 Base fare	713-635-4000

RAIL/BUS

				Phone
Greyhound/Trailways Bus Station 2121 Main St *TF:* 800-231-2222	Houston	TX	77002	713-759-6565
Houston Amtrak Station 902 Washington Ave	Houston	TX	77002	713-224-1577

— Accommodations —

HOTEL RESERVATION SERVICES

	Phone	Fax
Hotel Reservations Network Inc *TF Sales:* 800-964-6835 ■ *Web:* www.hoteldiscount.com	214-361-7311	361-7299

HOTELS, MOTELS, RESORTS

				Phone	Fax
Adam's Mark Hotel 2900 Briarpark Dr. *TF:* 800-444-2326 ■ *Web:* www.adamsmark.com/houstn.htm	Houston	TX	77042	713-978-7400	735-2727
Allen Park Inn 2121 Allen Pkwy *TF:* 800-231-6310	Houston	TX	77019	713-521-9321	521-9321
AmeriSuites 300 Ronan Park Pl *TF:* 800-833-1516	Houston	TX	77060	281-820-6060	820-6464
Braeswood Hotel & Convention Center 2100 S Braeswood Blvd. *TF:* 800-722-1368	Houston	TX	77030	713-797-9000	799-8362
Clarion Inn 500 N Sam Houston Pkwy. *TF:* 800-252-7466	Houston	TX	77060	281-931-0101	931-3523
Columbia Lakes Resort & Conference Center 188 Freeman Blvd. *TF:* 800-231-1030	West Columbia	TX	77486	409-345-5151	345-3069
Comfort Suites Galleria Area 6221 Richmond Ave *TF:* 800-228-5150	Houston	TX	77057	713-787-0004	787-0004
Courtyard by Marriott Brookhollow 2504 North Loop W *TF:* 800-321-2211 ■ *Web:* courtyard.com/HOUCY	Houston	TX	77092	713-688-7711	688-3561
Crowne Plaza 2222 West Loop S *TF:* 800-465-4329	Houston	TX	77027	713-961-7272	961-3327
Crowne Plaza 6701 S Main St *TF:* 800-227-6963	Houston	TX	77030	713-797-1110	797-1034
Days Inn Astrodome 8500 Kirby Dr. *TF:* 800-325-2525	Houston	TX	77054	713-796-8383	795-8453
Doubletree Guest Suites Galleria West 5353 Westheimer Rd. *TF:* 800-222-8733 ■ *Web:* www.doubletreehotels.com/DoubleT/Hotel81/91/91Main.htm	Houston	TX	77056	713-961-9000	877-8835
Doubletree Hotel 400 Dallas St. *TF:* 800-222-8733 ■ *Web:* www.doubletreehotels.com/DoubleT/Hotel81/92/92Main.htm	Houston	TX	77002	713-759-0202	752-2734
Doubletree Hotel 2001 Post Oak Blvd *TF:* 800-222-8733 ■ *Web:* www.doubletreehotels.com/DoubleT/Hotel81/94/94Main.htm	Houston	TX	77056	713-961-9300	623-6685
Econo Lodge Medical Center 7905 S Main St *TF:* 800-553-2666	Houston	TX	77025	713-667-8200	665-6679
Embassy Suites Hotel 9090 Southwest Fwy. *TF:* 800-553-3417	Houston	TX	77074	713-995-0123	779-0703
Flagship Hotel Over the Gulf 2501 Seawall Blvd. *TF:* 800-392-6542 ■ *Web:* www.galveston.com/accom/flagship ■ *E-mail:* flagship@galveston.com	Galveston	TX	77550	409-762-9000	762-1619
Four Seasons Hotel 1300 Lamar St *TF:* 800-332-3442 ■ *Web:* www.fourseasons.com/locations/Houston	Houston	TX	77010	713-650-1300	652-6220
Hampton Inn Intercontinental 502 N Sam Houston Pkwy. *TF:* 800-426-7866	Houston	TX	77060	281-820-2101	820-9652
Harbor House 28 Pier 21 *TF:* 800-874-3721 ■ *Web:* www.harborhousepier21.com ■ *E-mail:* hhouse@galveston.com	Galveston	TX	77550	409-763-3321	765-6421
Harvey Suites Houston Medical Center 6800 Main St. *TF:* 800-922-9222	Houston	TX	77030	713-528-7744	528-6983
Hilton Hotel Hobby Airport 8181 Airport Blvd. *TF:* 800-445-8667 ■ *Web:* www.hilton.com/hotels/HOUHAHF	Houston	TX	77061	713-645-3000	645-2251
Hilton Southwest 6780 Southwest Fwy *TF:* 800-445-8667	Houston	TX	77074	713-977-7911	974-5808
Holiday Inn Hotel & Suites 7787 Katy Fwy *TF:* 800-822-8373	Houston	TX	77024	713-682-1611	682-8400
Holiday Inn Intercontinental Airport 15222 JFK Blvd *TF:* 800-465-4329	Houston	TX	77032	281-449-2311	442-6833
Holiday Inn Northwest 14996 Northwest Fwy. *TF:* 800-465-4329 ■ *Web:* www.basshotels.com/holiday-inn/?_franchisee=HOUNW ■ *E-mail:* gmhi290@pahmanagement.com	Houston	TX	77040	713-939-9955	937-8121
Holiday Inn Select 14703 Park Row *TF:* 800-465-4329	Houston	TX	77079	281-558-5580	496-4150
Holiday Inn Southwest 11160 Southwest Fwy *TF:* 800-465-4329	Houston	TX	77031	281-530-1400	530-2191
Hotel Galvez 2024 Seawall Blvd *TF:* 800-996-3426	Galveston	TX	77550	409-765-7721	765-5780
Hotel Sofitel 425 N Sam Houston Pkwy E *TF:* 800-763-4835	Houston	TX	77060	281-445-9000	445-9826
Houstonian Hotel & Conference Center 111 N Post Oak Ln *TF:* 800-231-2759 ■ *Web:* www.houstonian.com	Houston	TX	77024	713-680-2626	680-2992
Howard Johnson Central 4225 North Fwy *TF:* 800-446-4656	Houston	TX	77022	713-695-6011	697-6404

Houston — Hotels, Motels, Resorts (Cont'd)

Phone *Fax*

Howard Johnson Hotel Plaza Suites
702 N Sam Houston Pkwy . . . . Houston TX 77060 281-999-9942 591-1215
TF: 800-446-4656
Hyatt Regency Houston 1200 Louisiana St. . . . . . Houston TX 77002 713-654-1234 951-0934
TF: 800-233-1234
■ *Web:* www.hyatt.com/usa/houston/hotels/hotel_hourh.html
Hyatt Regency Houston Airport
15747 JFK Blvd . . . . Houston TX 77032 281-987-1234 590-8461
TF: 800-233-1234
■ *Web:* www.hyatt.com/usa/houston/hotels/hotel_houap.html
JW Marriott Hotel Houston
5150 Westheimer Rd. . . . . Houston TX 77056 713-961-1500 961-5045
TF: 800-228-9290
La Colombe D'Or Inn 3410 Montrose Blvd. . . . . . Houston TX 77006 713-524-7999 524-8923
Web: www.lacolombedorhouston.com
La Quinta Motor Inn Beltway
10552 Southwest Fwy . . . . Houston TX 77074 713-270-9559 270-0219
TF: 800-531-5900
La Quinta Motor Inn Hobby Airport
9902 Gulf Fwy . . . . Houston TX 77034 713-941-0900 946-1987
TF: 800-531-5900
La Quinta Motor Inn Intercontinental Airport
6 North Belt E . . . . Houston TX 77060 281-447-6888 847-3921
TF: 800-531-5900
Lancaster Hotel 701 Texas St. . . . . Houston TX 77002 713-228-9500 223-4528
TF: 800-231-0336 ■ *Web:* www.lancaster.com
Lexington Hotel Suites 16410 I-45 N . . . . Houston TX 77090 281-821-1000 821-1420
TF: 800-537-8483
Luxury Collection of Houston
1919 Briar Oaks Ln. . . . . Houston TX 77027 713-840-7600 840-8036
TF: 800-325-3589
Marriott Hotel Houston Medical Center
6580 Fannin St. . . . . Houston TX 77030 713-796-0080 770-8100
TF: 800-228-9290 ■ *Web:* marriotthotels.com/HOUMC
Marriott Hotel Intercontinental Airport
18700 JFK Blvd . . . . Houston TX 77032 281-443-2310 443-5294
TF: 800-228-9290 ■ *Web:* marriotthotels.com/IAHAP
Marriott North/Greenspoint
255 N Sam Houston Pkwy. . . . . Houston TX 77060 281-875-4000 875-6208
TF: 800-228-9290 ■ *Web:* marriotthotels.com/HOUGP
Marriott West Loop 1750 West Loop S . . . . Houston TX 77027 713-960-0111 624-1560
TF: 800-613-3982 ■ *Web:* marriotthotels.com/HOUWL
Marriott Westside 13210 Katy Fwy . . . . Houston TX 77079 281-558-8338 558-4028
TF: 800-228-9290 ■ *Web:* marriotthotels.com/HOUWS
Nassau Bay Hilton & Marina 3000 NASA Rd . . . . Houston TX 77058 281-333-9300 333-3750
TF: 800-634-4320
Omni Hotel 4 Riverway Dr . . . . Houston TX 77056 713-871-8181 871-0719
TF: 800-843-6664
Park Plaza Warwick Hotel 5701 Main St . . . . . . Houston TX 77005 713-526-1991 639-4545
TF: 800-670-7275
Plaza Hilton 6633 Travis St . . . . Houston TX 77030 713-313-4000 313-4660
TF: 800-445-8667
Quality Inn Bush Intercontinental Airport
6115 Will Clayton Pkwy. . . . . Humble TX 77338 281-446-9131 446-2251
TF: 800-228-5151
Quality Inn Nasa 904 E Nasa Rd 1 . . . . Houston TX 77058 281-333-3737 333-8354
TF: 800-228-5151
Raddison Hotel Astrodome Convention Center
8686 Kirby Dr. . . . . Houston TX 77054 713-748-3221 795-8492
TF: 800-627-6461
Radisson Hotel & Conference Center
9100 Gulf Fwy . . . . Houston TX 77017 713-943-7979 943-2160
TF: 800-333-3333
Radisson Suite Hotel Astrodome
1400 Old Spanish Trail . . . . Houston TX 77054 713-796-1000 796-8055
TF: 800-333-3333
Radisson Suite Hotel Houston West
10655 Katy Fwy . . . . Houston TX 77024 713-461-6000 467-2357
TF: 800-333-3333
Ramada Inn 1301 Nasa Rd . . . . Houston TX 77058 281-488-0220 488-1759
TF: 800-272-6232
Ramada Inn Hobby Airport 8611 Airport Blvd . . . Houston TX 77061 713-947-0000 944-0357
TF: 800-272-6232
Red Lion Hotel 2525 West Loop S . . . . Houston TX 77027 713-961-3000 297-4395
TF: 800-733-5466
Red Roof Inn Hobby Airport
9005 Airport Blvd . . . . Houston TX 77061 713-943-3300 943-1370
TF: 800-843-7663
Renaissance Houston Hotel
6 E Greenway Plaza. Houston TX 77046 713-629-1200 629-4702
TF: 800-228-9290

Phone *Fax*

Residence Inn by Marriott Astrodome
7710 S Main St . . . . Houston TX 77030 713-660-7993 660-8019
TF: 800-331-3131 ■ *Web:* www.residenceinn.com/HOUAS
Sheraton Houston Brook Hollow
3000 North Loop W . . . . Houston TX 77092 713-688-0100 688-9224
TF: 800-325-3535
Sheraton North Houston 15700 JFK Blvd . . . . Houston TX 77032 281-442-5100 987-9130
TF: 800-325-3535
Sleep Inn Intercontinental Airport
15675 JFK Blvd . . . . Houston TX 77032 281-442-7770 442-6699
TF: 800-753-3746
StudioPLUS 1303 La Concha Ln . . . . Houston TX 77054 713-790-9753 790-9743
TF: 800-646-8000
StudioPLUS 5454 Hollister St . . . . Houston TX 77040 713-895-0965 895-0532
TF: 800-646-8000
Sumner Suites Houston Hobby
7922 Moseley Rd . . . . Houston TX 77061 713-943-1713 943-1813
TF: 800-747-8483
The Woodlands Conference Center Resort & Country Club 2301 N
Millbend Dr . . . . The Woodlands TX 77380 281-367-1100 364-6275
TF: 800-433-2624 ■ *Web:* www.thewoodlands.com
Victorian Condo Hotel & Conference Ctr
6300 Seawall Blvd. Galveston TX 77551 409-740-3555 744-3801
TF: 800-231-6363 ■ *Web:* www.galveston.com/victorian
Waterwood National Resort & Country Club
1 Waterwood Pkwy . . . . Huntsville TX 77340 409-891-5211 891-5011
TF: 800-441-5211 ■ *Web:* www.tonti.com/wedgewood.html
Westchase Hilton & Towers
9999 Westheimer Rd. . . . . Houston TX 77042 713-974-1000 974-6866
TF: 800-445-8667
Westin Galleria Plaza Hotel
5060 W Alabama St . . . . Houston TX 77056 713-960-8100 960-6553
TF: 800-228-3000
Westin Oaks 5011 Westheimer Rd . . . . Houston TX 77056 713-960-8100 960-6554
TF: 800-228-3000
Wyndham Greenspoint Hotel
12400 Greenspoint Dr . . . . Houston TX 77060 281-875-2222 875-1652
TF: 800-996-3426

— Restaurants —

Phone

Americas (International) 1800 Post Oak Blvd The Pavilion . . . Houston TX 77056 713-961-1492
Annemarie's Old Heidelberg (German)
1810 Fountain View . . . . Houston TX 77057 713-781-3581
Anthony's (Continental) 4007 Westheimer Rd . . . . Houston TX 77027 713-961-0552
Arcodoro (Italian) 5000 Westheimer Rd Suite 120 . . . . Houston TX 77056 713-621-6888
Athens Bar & Grill (Greek) 8037 Clinton Dr . . . . Houston TX 77029 713-675-1644
Billy Blue's Bar & Grill (Barbecue) 6025 Richmond Ave . . . . Houston TX 77057 713-266-9294
Boulevard Bistro (Continental) 4319 Montrose Blvd . . . . Houston TX 77006 713-524-6922
Brennan's of Houston (Southwest/Creole) 3300 Smith St . . . . Houston TX 77006 713-522-9711
Brownstone The (Continental) 2736 Virginia St . . . . Houston TX 77098 713-520-5666
Cafe Annie (Southwest) 1728 Post Oak Blvd . . . . Houston TX 77056 713-840-1111
Cafe Noche (Mexican/Southwest) 2409 Montrose Blvd . . . . . . Houston TX 77006 713-529-2409
Cafe Pappadeaux (Cajun) 2410 Richmond St . . . . Houston TX 77006 713-527-9137
Cafe Royal (French) 425 N Sam Houston Pkwy E . . . . Houston TX 77060 281-445-9000
Chianti Cucina Rustica (Italian) 1515 S Post Oak Ln . . . . Houston TX 77056 713-840-0303
Churrasco's (South American) 2055 Westheimer Rd . . . . Houston TX 77098 713-527-8300
Clive's (Steak/Seafood) 517 Louisiana St . . . . Houston TX 77002 713-224-4438
Web: www.clives.com
Confederate House (Steak/Seafood) 2925 Weslayan St . . . . . Houston TX 77027 713-622-1936
Damian's Cucina Italiana (Italian) 3011 Smith St . . . . Houston TX 77006 713-522-0439
Del Frisco's Steakhouse (Steak) 14641 Gladebrook Dr. . . . . . Houston TX 77068 281-893-3339
DeVille (American) 1300 Lamar St. Houston TX 77010 713-650-1300
Dimassi's (Middle Eastern) 5064 Richmond Ave . . . . Houston TX 77056 713-439-7481
Dining Room (Continental) 1919 Briar Oaks Ln . . . . Houston TX 77027 713-840-7600
Dong Ting (Chinese) 611 Stuart St. Houston TX 77006 713-527-0005
Dover's (Southwest) 400 Dallas St. Houston TX 77002 713-759-6042
Goode Co Texas Barbecue (Barbecue) 5109 Kirby Dr . . . . . . Houston TX 77098 713-522-2530
Hard Rock Cafe (American) 2801 Kirby Dr . . . . Houston TX 77098 713-520-1134
Houston Brewery (Creole/Southwest) 6224 Richmond Ave . . . Houston TX 77057 713-953-0101
Kaneyama (Japanese) 9527 Westheimer St. . . . . Houston TX 77063 713-784-5168
Kim Son (Vietnamese) 2001 Jefferson . . . . Houston TX 77003 713-222-2461
King Fish Market (Seafood) 6356 Richmond Ave. . . . . Houston TX 77057 713-974-3474
La Colombe D'Or (French) 3410 Montrose Blvd. . . . . Houston TX 77006 713-524-7999
La Griglia (Italian) 2002 W Gray St . . . . Houston TX 77019 713-526-4700
La Reserve (Continental) 4 Riverway Dr . . . . Houston TX 77056 713-871-8177
La Tour D'Argent (French) 2011 Ella Blvd . . . . Houston TX 77008 713-864-9864
Lancaster Grille (International) 701 Texas St . . . . Houston TX 77002 713-228-9502
Luther's Bar-B-Q (Barbecue) 1100 Smith St . . . . Houston TX 77002 713-759-0018
Magnolia Bar & Grill (Cajun) 6000 Richmond Ave. . . . . Houston TX 77057 713-781-6207
Web: www.magnolia-grill.com/
Mai Thai (Thai) 3819 Kirby Dr. . . . . Houston TX 77098 713-522-6707
Maxim's (Continental) 3755 Richmond Ave. . . . . Houston TX 77046 713-877-8899

Houston — Restaurants (Cont'd)

	City	State	Zip	Phone
McGonigel's Mucky Duck (Irish) 2425 Norfolk St.	Houston	TX	77098	713-528-5999
Ninfa's (Mexican) 2704 Navigation Blvd	Houston	TX	77003	713-228-1175
Pappas Brothers Steakhouse (Steak) 5839 Westheimer Rd.	Houston	TX	77057	713-917-0090
Post Oak Grill (American) 1415 S Post Oak Ln	Houston	TX	77056	713-993-9966
Richmond Arms Pub (English) 5920 Richmond Ave	Houston	TX	77057	713-784-7722
Riviera Grill (Mediterranean) 10655 Katy Fwy.	Houston	TX	77024	713-974-4445
Rivoli (Continental) 5636 Richmond Ave.	Houston	TX	77057	713-789-1900
Rotisserie for Beef & Bird (Continental) 2200 Wilcrest Dr	Houston	TX	77042	713-977-9524
Ruggles Grill (American) 903 Westheimer Rd	Houston	TX	77006	713-524-3839
Ruth's Chris Steak House (Steak) 6213 Richmond Ave	Houston	TX	77057	713-789-2333
Sabroso Grill (South American) 5510 Morningside St Suite 100	Houston	TX	77098	713-942-9900
Thai Pepper (Thai) 2049 W Alabama St	Houston	TX	77098	713-520-8225
Tony Mandola's Gulf Coast Kitchen (Cajun/Creole) 1962 W Gray St.	Houston	TX	77109	713-528-3474
Vietnam Coast (Vietnamese) 2910 Hillcroft St.	Houston	TX	77057	713-266-0884

— Goods and Services —

SHOPPING

	City	State	Zip	Phone	Fax
Almeda Mall 12200 Gulf Fwy	Houston	TX	77075	713-944-1010	944-5948
Centre at Post Oak 5000 Westheimer St	Houston	TX	77056	713-866-6923	
Conroe Outlet Center 1111 League Line Rd	Conroe	TX	77303	409-756-0999	
Deerbrook Mall 20131 Hwy 59 N	Humble	TX	77338	281-446-5300	446-1921
First Colony Mall 16535 Southwest Fwy Suite 1	Sugar Land	TX	77479	281-265-6123	265-6124
Foley's 1110 Main St	Houston	TX	77002	713-405-7035	651-6698
TF: 800-527-7147 ■ *Web:* www.mayco.com/may/fo_home.html					
Galleria The 5075 Westheimer Rd	Houston	TX	77056	713-621-1907	
Greenspoint Mall 208 Greenspoint Mall	Houston	TX	77060	281-875-4201	873-7144
Gulfgate Mall 7100 Gulf Fwy	Houston	TX	77087	713-643-5777	
Highland Village Shopping Center 3900 & 4000 block of Westheimer	Houston	TX	77027	713-850-3100	850-3190
Memorial City Mall 900 S Gessner Rd Suite 303	Houston	TX	77024	713-464-8640	464-7845
Meyerland Plaza Shopping Center 4700 Beechnut St	Houston	TX	77096	713-664-1166	
Northline Shopping Center 4400 North Fwy	Houston	TX	77022	713-692-6131	692-7543
Northwest Mall 9800 Hempstead Rd	Houston	TX	77092	713-681-1303	681-4362
Old Town Spring Spring Cypress Rd	Spring	TX	77373	281-353-9310	288-6674
TF: 800-653-8696 ■ *Web:* www.oldtownspringtx.com ■ *E-mail:* otspl@oldtownspringtx.com					
Park Shops 1200 McKinney Houston Ctr	Houston	TX	77010	713-759-1442	
Web: www.houstoncenter.com					
Pavilion The on Post Oak 1800 Post Oak Blvd Suite 240	Houston	TX	77056	713-622-7979	622-6843
River Oaks Antiques Center 2030 Westheimer Rd.	Houston	TX	77098	713-520-8238	
River Oaks Shopping Center 1964 W Gray St	Houston	TX	77019	713-866-6936	
Sharpstown Center 7500 Bellaire Blvd	Houston	TX	77036	713-777-1111	777-7924
Town & Country Center 800 W Sam Houston Pkwy N	Houston	TX	77024	713-468-1565	468-0328
Upper Kirby District 3015 Richmond Ave Suite 200	Houston	TX	77098	713-524-8000	524-2786
Web: www.upperkirby.com					
West Oaks Mall 1000 West Oaks Mall	Houston	TX	77082	281-531-1332	531-1579
Westwood Mall 9700 Bissonnet	Houston	TX	77036	713-777-8282	988-9781
Willowbrook Mall 2000 Willowbrook Mall	Houston	TX	77070	281-890-8000	890-3109

BANKS

	City	State	Zip	Phone	Fax
American Bank 1600 Smith St Suite 300	Houston	TX	77002	713-951-7100	951-7172
Web: www.americanbk.com ■ *E-mail:* info@americanbk.com					
Bank of Houston 5115 S Main St	Houston	TX	77002	713-529-4881	529-9131
Central Bank of Houston 55 Waugh Dr	Houston	TX	77007	713-868-5577	868-3317*
**Fax:* Cust Svc					
Chase Bank of Texas 712 Main St	Houston	TX	77002	713-216-4865	216-2269*
**Fax:* Cust Svc ■ *TF:* 800-392-3936					
NationsBank of Texas 700 Louisiana St.	Houston	TX	77002	713-247-6000	247-6161*
**Fax:* Cust Svc ■ *TF:* 800-247-6262					
Southwest Bank of Texas NA 4400 Post Oak Pkwy	Houston	TX	77027	713-235-8800	235-8816
TF: 800-287-0301					
Wells Fargo Bank 1000 Louisiana St.	Houston	TX	77002	800-411-4932	739-1035*
**Fax Area Code:* 713					

BUSINESS SERVICES

	Phone
Accountemps	713-623-8367
Central Delivery Service	281-931-4700
Dispatch Management Systems	713-613-9100
Federal Express	800-463-3339
Houston Delivery Service	713-655-0555
Kelly Services	713-972-1151
Kinko's	713-521-9465
Mail Boxes Etc	713-626-2920
Manpower Temporary Services	713-228-3131
Olsten Staffing Services	713-626-0199
Post Office	713-227-1474
Pro Staff Personnel Services	713-623-8822
RHDC International	713-863-8080
Runners Group	713-939-0900
Texas Executive Courier	713-863-0055
UPS	800-742-5877

— Media —

PUBLICATIONS

	City	State	Zip	Phone	Fax
Houston Business Journal 1001 West Loop S Suite 650	Houston	TX	77027	713-688-8811	968-8025*
**Fax:* Edit ■ *Web:* www.amcity.com/houston ■ *E-mail:* houston@amcity.com					
Houston Chronicle‡ 801 Texas Ave	Houston	TX	77002	713-220-7171	220-6806
TF: 800-735-3800 ■ *Web:* www.chron.com ■ *E-mail:* hci@chron.com					
Houston Forward Times PO Box 2962	Houston	TX	77001	713-526-4727	526-3170*
**Fax:* News Rm ■ *Web:* www.forwardtimes.com ■ *E-mail:* forwardt@flash.net					
Houston LifeStyle Magazine 10707 Corporate Dr Suite 170	Stafford	TX	77477	281-240-2445	240-5079
Leader The PO Box 924487	Houston	TX	77292	713-686-8494	686-0970*
**Fax:* News Rm					

‡Daily newspapers

TELEVISION

	City	State	Zip	Phone	Fax
KHOU-TV Ch 11 (CBS) 1945 Allen Pkwy	Houston	TX	77019	713-526-1111	520-7763
Web: www.khou.com ■ *E-mail:* 11listens@khou.com					
KHTV-TV Ch 39 (WB) 7700 Westpark Dr	Houston	TX	77063	713-781-3939	781-3441
Web: www.khtv.com					
KNWS-TV Ch 51 (Ind) 8440 Westpark Dr.	Houston	TX	77063	713-974-5151	975-6397
TF: 800-974-6397					
KPRC-TV Ch 2 (NBC) PO Box 2222	Houston	TX	77252	713-222-2222	771-4930
Web: www.kprc.com ■ *E-mail:* news2@kprc.com					
KPXB-TV Ch 49 (PAX) 256 N Sam Houston Pkwy E Suite 49	Houston	TX	77060	281-820-4900	820-4840
KRIV-TV Ch 26 (Fox) 4261 Southwest Fwy.	Houston	TX	77027	713-479-2600	479-2859
KTBU-TV Ch 55 (Ind) 7026 Old Katy Rd Suite 201	Houston	TX	77024	713-864-0455	864-1993
KTMD-TV Ch 48 (Tele) 3903 Stoney Brook St	Houston	TX	77063	713-974-4848	974-5875
Web: www.ktmd.com ■ *E-mail:* t48gm@ktmd.com					
KTRK-TV Ch 13 (ABC) 3310 Bissonnet St	Houston	TX	77005	713-666-0713	664-0013
Web: www.ktrk.com ■ *E-mail:* ktrktv@aol.com					
KTXH-TV Ch 20 (UPN) 8950 Kirby Dr	Houston	TX	77054	713-661-2020	665-3909
Web: www.paramountstations.com/KTXH					
KUHT-TV Ch 8 (PBS) 4513 Cullen Blvd	Houston	TX	77004	713-748-8888	749-8216
Web: www.kuht.uh.edu ■ *E-mail:* postmaster@kuht.uh.edu					
KXLN-TV Ch 45 (Uni) 9440 Kirby Dr	Houston	TX	77054	713-662-4545	668-9057

RADIO

	City	State	Zip	Phone	Fax
KBME-AM 790 kHz (Nost) 510 Lovett Blvd.	Houston	TX	77006	713-526-5874	630-3666
KBXX-FM 97.9 MHz (CHR) 24 Greenway Plaza Suite 1508	Houston	TX	77046	713-623-2108	623-0344
Web: www.kbxx.com					
KENR-AM 1070 kHz (Rel) 6161 Savoy St Suite 1200	Houston	TX	77036	713-260-3600	260-3628
KHMX-FM 96.5 MHz (AC) 1990 Post Oak Blvd Suite 2300	Houston	TX	77056	713-790-0965	297-0300
Web: www.khmx.com ■ *E-mail:* mix965@khmx.com					
KIKK-FM 95.7 MHz (Ctry) 24 Greenway Plaza Suite 1900	Houston	TX	77046	713-881-5100	881-5999
Web: www.youngcountry957.com					
KILT-AM 610 kHz (Sports) 24 Greenway Plaza Suite 1900	Houston	TX	77046	713-881-5100	881-5199
Web: www.star610kilt.com					
KILT-FM 100.3 MHz (Ctry) 24 Greenway Plaza Suite 1900	Houston	TX	77046	713-881-5100	881-5199
Web: www.kilt.com ■ *E-mail:* kilt@kilt.com					
KKBQ-FM 92.9 MHz (Ctry) 3050 Post Oak Blvd Suite 1250	Houston	TX	77056	713-961-0093	963-1293
Web: www.kkbq.com					
KKHT-FM 106.9 MHz (Rel) 6161 Savoy St Suite 1200	Houston	TX	77036	713-260-3600	260-3628
Web: www.kkht.com/ ■ *E-mail:* kkht@kkht.com					

Houston — Radio (Cont'd)

Phone *Fax*

KKRW-FM 93.7 MHz (CR)
350 Post Oak Blvd 12th Fl . . . . .Houston TX 77056 713-830-8000 830-8099
Web: www.kkrw.com
KLAT-AM 1010 kHz (N/T)
1415 North Loop W Suite 400 . . . . .Houston TX 77008 713-868-4344 407-1400
KLDE-FM 94.5 MHz (Oldies)
5353 W Alabama St Suite 410 . . . . .Houston TX 77056 713-622-5533 963-0590
KLOL-FM 101.1 MHz (Rock) 510 Lovett Blvd . . . .Houston TX 77006 713-526-6855 630-3555
Web: www.klol.com ■ *E-mail:* klol@klol.com
KLTN-FM 93.3 MHz (Span)
1415 North Loop W Suite 400 . . . . .Houston TX 77008 713-868-4344 407-1400
KLTO-FM 104.9 MHz (Span)
1415 North Loop W Suite 400 . . . . .Houston TX 77008 713-868-4344 407-1400
KMJQ-FM 102.1 MHz (Urban)
24 Greenway Plaza Suite 1508 . . . . .Houston TX 77046 713-623-2108 623-0106
Web: www.kmjq.com
KODA-FM 99.1 MHz (AC)
3050 Post Oak Blvd 12th Fl . . . . .Houston TX 77056 713-830-8000 830-8099
Web: www.sunny99.com
KOVE-FM 100.7 MHz (Span)
1415 North Loop West Suite 400 . . . . .Houston TX 77008 713-407-1415 407-1400
KPRC-AM 950 kHz (N/T)
11767 Katy Fwy Suite 1170 . . . . .Houston TX 77079 281-588-4800 588-4820
KQQK-FM 106.5 MHz (Span)
1980 Post Oak Blvd Suite 1500 . . . . .Houston TX 77056 713-993-8000 993-8003
KRBE-FM 104.1 MHz (CHR)
9801 Westheimer Rd Suite 700 . . . . .Houston TX 77042 713-266-1000 954-2344
Web: www.krbe.com ■ *E-mail:* mailbox@krbe.com
KSEV-AM 700 kHz (N/T)
11767 Katy Fwy Suite 1170 . . . . .Houston TX 77079 281-588-4800 588-4820
KTBZ-FM 107.5 MHz (Rock)
3050 Post Oak Blvd Suite 1100 . . . . .Houston TX 77056 713-968-1000 968-1070
Web: www.thebuzz.com ■ *E-mail:* thebuzz@thebuzz.com
KTRH-AM 740 kHz (N/T) PO Box 1520 . . . . .Houston TX 77251 713-526-5874 630-3666
Web: www.ktrh.com
KUHF-FM 88.7 MHz (NPR)
3801 Cullen Blvd Communications Bldg
Suite 101 . . . . .Houston TX 77004 713-743-0887 743-0868
Web: www.uh.edu/campus/kuhf ■ *E-mail:* gsmith@uh.edu
KVPU-FM 91.3 MHz (NPR) PO Box 156. . . . . Prairie View TX 77446 409-857-4511 857-2309
KXTJ-FM 107.9 MHz (Span)
1980 Post Oak Blvd Suite 1500 . . . . .Houston TX 77056 713-993-8000 965-0108

— Colleges/Universities —

Phone *Fax*

Alvin Community College 3110 Mustang Rd . . . . . . Alvin TX 77511 281-331-6111 388-4929
Web: www.alvin.cc.tx.us ■ *E-mail:* admiss@flipper.alvin.cc.tx.us
Art Institute of Houston 1900 Yorktown. . . . . . . .Houston TX 77056 713-623-2040 966-2700
TF: 800-275-4244 ■ *Web:* www.aih.aii.edu
College of the Mainland 1200 Amburn Rd. . . . Texas City TX 77591 409-938-1211 938-3126
Web: www.mainland.cc.tx.us
Galveston College 4015 Ave Q. . . . . .Galveston TX 77550 409-763-6551 762-0667
Web: www.gc.edu ■ *E-mail:* psanger@tusk.gc.edu
Houston Baptist University 7502 Fondren Rd. . . .Houston TX 77074 281-649-3000 649-3217
Web: www.hbu.edu
Houston Community College (System)
PO Box 7849 . . . . .Houston TX 77270 713-869-5021 863-0529
Web: www.hccs.cc.tx.us ■ *E-mail:* postmaster@hccs.cc.tx.us
ITT Technical Institute
15621 Blue Ash Dr Suite 160. . . . . .Houston TX 77090 281-873-0512 873-0518
TF: 800-879-6486 ■ *Web:* www.itt-tech.edu
Kingwood College 20000 Kingwood Dr . . . . . . .Kingwood TX 77339 281-312-1600 312-1477
TF: 800-883-7939 ■ *Web:* kcweb.nhmccd.edu
Lee College 200 Lee Dr. . . . . .Baytown TX 77522 281-427-5611 425-6831
Web: www.lee.edu ■ *E-mail:* clightfo@lee.edu
North Harris Montgomery Community College
District 250 North Sam Houston Pkwy E. . . . .Houston TX 77060 281-260-3500 260-3513
Web: www.nhmccd.cc.tx.us
Rice University PO Box 1892. . . . . .Houston TX 77251 713-527-8101 737-5646
Web: www.rice.edu ■ *E-mail:* admi@rice.edu
San Jacinto College North 5800 Uvalde Rd . . . . .Houston TX 77049 281-458-4050 459-7125
Web: www.sjcd.cc.tx.us/overview/north.htm
San Jacinto College South
13735 Beamer Rd. .Houston TX 77089 281-922-3431 922-3485
Web: www.sjcd.cc.tx.us/overview/south.htm
Texas Southern University 3100 Cleburne St . . . .Houston TX 77004 713-313-7011 527-7318
Web: www.tsu.edu
Tomball College 30555 Tomball Pkwy. . . . . Tomball TX 77375 281-351-3300 351-3384
Web: wwwtc.nhmccd.edu

Phone *Fax*

University of Houston 4800 Calhoun Rd . . . . . . .Houston TX 77004 713-743-1000 743-9633
Web: www.uh.edu ■ *E-mail:* admissions@uh.edu
University of Houston Clear Lake
2700 Bay Area Blvd. .Houston TX 77058 281-283-7600 283-2530
Web: www.cl.uh.edu
University of Saint Thomas
3800 Montrose Blvd .Houston TX 77006 713-522-7911 525-3558
TF: 800-856-8565 ■ *Web:* basil.stthom.edu
■ *E-mail:* postmaster@basil.stthom.edu
University of Texas Health Science Center at
Houston 7000 Fannin St . . . . .Houston TX 77225 713-500-4472 500-3805
Web: www.uth.tmc.edu ■ *E-mail:* cwis@oac.hsc.uth.tmc.edu

— Hospitals —

Phone *Fax*

Bayou City Medical Center
1213 Hermann Dr. . . . . .Houston TX 77004 713-623-2500 522-6723
Columbia Bellaire Medical Center
5314 Dashwood St .Houston TX 77081 713-512-1200 512-1407
Web: www.columbiahouston.net/bellaire.html
Columbia East Houston Medical Center
13111 East Fwy . . . . .Houston TX 77015 713-393-2000 393-2714
Columbia Kingwood Medical Center
22999 US Hwy 59. .Kingwood TX 77339 281-359-7500 348-1310
Web: www.columbiahouston.net/kingwood.html
Columbia Rosewood Medical Center
9200 Westheimer Rd. . . . . .Houston TX 77063 713-780-7900 782-3207
Web: www.columbiahouston.net/rose.html
Cypress Fairbanks Medical Center
10655 Steepletop Dr . . . . .Houston TX 77065 281-890-4285 890-5341
Diagnostic Center Hospital 6447 Main St . . . . . .Houston TX 77030 713-790-0790 796-6587
Doctors Hospital Parkway 233 W Parker Rd . . . .Houston TX 77076 713-697-2831 699-6408
Hermann Hospital 6411 Fannin St . . . . .Houston TX 77030 713-704-4000 704-5872
Web: www.mhhs.org/locations/mher/mher.html
Houston Northwest Medical Center
710 FM 1960 W . . . . .Houston TX 77090 281-440-1000 440-2666
Web: www.reddingmedicalcenter.com/HoustonNorthwest/yh
Memorial City Medical Center
920 Frostwood Dr. .Houston TX 77024 713-932-3000 827-4096
Web: www.mhcs.org/locations/mhmc/mhmc.html
Memorial Hospital Southwest
7600 Beechnut St . . . . .Houston TX 77074 713-776-5000 776-5652
Web: www.mhcs.org/locations/mhsw/mhsw.html
North Houston Medical Center
7333 North Fwy . . . . .Houston TX 77076 713-692-3014
Saint Joseph Hospital 1919 La Branch St . . . . . .Houston TX 77002 713-757-1000 657-7123
Saint Luke's Episcopal Hospital
6720 Bertner . . . . .Houston TX 77032 713-791-2011 794-6182
Web: www.sleh.com
Spring Branch Medical Center
8850 Long Pt St. . . . . .Houston TX 77055 713-467-6555 722-3771
Web: www.columbiahouston.net/spring.html
Texas Children's Hospital 6621 Fannin . . . . .Houston TX 77030 713-770-1000 770-1005
Web: www.texaschildrenshospital.org
Veterans Affairs Medical Center
2002 Holcombe Blvd . . . . .Houston TX 77030 713-791-1414 794-7218
West Houston Medical Center
12141 Richmond Ave . . . . .Houston TX 77082 281-558-3444 558-7169
Web: www.columbiahouston.net/westhous.html

— Attractions —

Phone *Fax*

AD Players 2710 W Alabama St . . . . .Houston TX 77098 713-526-2721 439-0905*
**Fax:* Hum Res
Aerial Theater at Bayou Place
520 Texas Ave . . . . .Houston TX 77002 713-230-1666
Web: webadv.chron.com/display/a/aerialtheater/index.html
Alley Theatre 615 Texas Ave . . . . .Houston TX 77002 713-228-9341 222-6542
TF: 800-259-2553 ■ *Web:* www.alleytheatre.com/
American Cowboy Museum 11822 Almeda St . . .Houston TX 77045 713-433-4441 433-4441
Armand Bayou Nature Center
8500 Bay Area Blvd. . . . . .Houston TX 77258 281-474-2551 474-2552
Astrodome 8400 Kirby Dr. . . . . .Houston TX 77054 713-799-9500 799-9718
Web: www.astros.com/dome.htm
Baker Burke Planetarium
1 Hermann Circle Dr . . . . .Houston TX 77030 713-639-4600 523-4125
Web: www.hmns.org/hmns/planetarium.html
Battleship Texas SHS 3527 Battleground Rd . . . .La Porte TX 77571 281-479-2411 479-4197
Bayou Bend Museum 1 Westcott St . . . . .Houston TX 77007 713-639-7750 639-7770

Houston — Attractions (Cont'd)

	City	State	ZIP	Phone	Fax
Big Thicket National Preserve 3785 Milam St	Beaumont	TX	77701	409-839-2689	839-2599
Web: www.nps.gov/bith/					
Castle Park 1105 W Loop North	Houston	TX	77055	713-688-5273	680-0603
Children's Museum of Houston 1500 Binz St	Houston	TX	77004	713-522-1138	522-5747
Web: www.cmhouston.org ■ *E-mail:* childrensmuseum@cmhouston.org					
Contemporary Arts Museum 5216 Montrose Blvd	Houston	TX	77006	713-284-8250	284-8275
Web: www.camh.org/					
Cullen Park 19008 Saums Rd	Houston	TX	77023	713-845-1111	
Da Camera of Houston 1427 Branard	Houston	TX	77006	713-524-7601	524-4148
Web: www.dacamera.com					
Ensemble Theatre 3535 Main St	Houston	TX	77002	713-520-0055	520-1269
Forbidden Gardens 23500 Franz Rd	Katy	TX	77493	281-347-8000	347-8080
Fort Dend Museum 500 Houston St	Richmond	TX	77469	281-342-6478	342-2439
George Ranch Historical Park 10215 FM 762	Richmond	TX	77469	281-545-9212	343-9316
Web: www.georgeranch.org/					
Hermann Park 6000 Fannin St	Houston	TX	77004	713-845-1000	
Holocaust Museum Houston 5401 Caroline St	Houston	TX	77004	713-942-8000	942-7953
Web: www.hmh.org/					
Houston Arboretum & Nature Center 4501 Woodway	Houston	TX	77024	713-681-8433	681-1191
Web: www.neosoft.com/~arbor					
Houston Ballet 1921 W Bell St	Houston	TX	77019	713-523-6300	523-4038
Web: www.neosoft.com/~ballet					
Houston Fire Museum 2403 Milam St	Houston	TX	77006	713-524-2526	520-7566
Web: www.houstonfiremuseum.org					
Houston Grand Opera Assn 510 Preston Suite 500	Houston	TX	77002	713-546-0200	247-0906
TF: 800-626-7372 ■ *Web:* www.hgo.com					
Houston Museum of Natural Science 1 Hermann Circle Dr Hermann Pk	Houston	TX	77030	713-639-4600	639-4761
Web: www.hmns.org					
Houston Symphony Orchestra 615 Louisiana St Suite 102	Houston	TX	77002	713-224-4240	222-7024
Web: www.housym.org ■ *E-mail:* hso@iwi.net					
Houston Zoological Gardens 1513 N MacGregor	Houston	TX	77030	713-284-1300	284-1329
Web: www.houstonzoo.org					
IMAX 3D Theater 1 Hope Blvd Moody Gardens	Galveston	TX	77551	409-744-4673	744-1631
TF: 800-582-4673					
Johnson Space Center 1601 Nasa Rd 1	Houston	TX	77058	281-244-2100	283-7724
TF: 800-972-0369 ■ *Web:* www.spacecenter.org					
Jones Jesse H Hall for the Performing Arts 615 Louisiana St	Houston	TX	77002	713-227-3974	228-9629
Jung CG Educational Center of Houston 5200 Montrose Blvd	Houston	TX	77006	713-524-8253	524-8096
Web: www.cgjunghouston.org					
Lawndale Art & Performance Center 4912 Main St	Houston	TX	77002	713-528-5858	528-4140
Web: www.neosoft.com/~lawndale/ ■ *E-mail:* lawndale@neosoft.com					
Lone Star Flight Museum 2002 Terminal Dr	Galveston	TX	77554	409-740-7722	740-7612
Web: www.lsfm.org					
Memorial Park Loop 610 at Memorial Dr	Houston	TX	77024	713-845-1111	
Menil The Collection Museum 1515 Sul Ross St	Houston	TX	77006	713-525-9400	525-9444
Web: www.menil.org/					
Miller Outdoor Theatre PO Box 1562	Houston	TX	77251	713-284-8351	
Moody Gardens 1 Hope Blvd	Galveston	TX	77554	409-744-4673	744-1631
TF: 800-582-4673 ■ *Web:* www.moodygardens.com/					
Museum of Fine Arts 1001 Bissonnet St	Houston	TX	77265	713-639-7300	639-7399
Web: www.mfah.org					
Museum of Health & Medical Science 1515 Herman Dr	Houston	TX	77004	713-521-1515	526-1434
Web: www.mhms.org ■ *E-mail:* lblanch@mhms.org					
National Museum of Funeral History 415 Barren Springs Dr	Houston	TX	77090	281-876-3063	876-4403
Web: www.nmfh.org					
Old Town Spring Spring Cypress Rd	Spring	TX	77373	281-353-9310	288-6674
TF: 800-653-8696 ■ *Web:* www.oldtownspringtx.com ■ *E-mail:* otspl@oldtownspringtx.com					
Port of Houston PO Box 2562	Houston	TX	77252	713-670-2400	670-2429
TF Cust Svc: 800-688-3625 ■ *Web:* www.portofhouston.com					
Rice University Art Gallery 6100 S Main Rice University	Houston	TX	77005	713-527-6069	285-5980
Web: www.ruf.rice.edu/~ruag/					
Richmond Avenue Entertainment District 5600-6500 Block of Richmond Ave	Houston	TX	77257	713-974-4686	
Sam Houston Park 1100 Bagby St	Houston	TX	77002	713-655-1912	655-7527
San Jacinto Battleground 3523 Hwy 134	La Porte	TX	77571	281-479-2431	479-5618
Six Flags WaterWorld 9001 Kirby Dr	Houston	TX	77054	713-799-8404	799-1491
Spring Historical Museum 403 Main St Old Town Spring	Spring	TX	77373	281-651-0055	
Stages Repertory Theatre 3201 Allen Pkwy Suite 101	Houston	TX	77019	713-527-8243	527-8669
Theatre Under the Stars 2600 Southwest Fwy Suite 600	Houston	TX	77098	713-558-2600	558-2650
TF: 800-678-5440 ■ *Web:* www.tuts.com/					
Traders Village Flea Market 7979 N Eldridge Rd	Houston	TX	77041	281-890-5500	
Upper Kirby District 3015 Richmond Ave Suite 200	Houston	TX	77098	713-524-8000	524-2786
Web: www.upperkirby.com					
Wortham IMAX Theatre 1 Hermann Cir Dr Houston Museum of Natural Science	Houston	TX	77030	713-639-4629	523-4125
Web: www.hmns.org					
Wortham Theater Center 510 Preston St	Houston	TX	77002	713-237-1439	237-9313

SPORTS TEAMS & FACILITIES

	City	State	ZIP	Phone	Fax
Battleground Speedway I-10 & Exit 787	Highlands	TX	77562	713-946-7223	
TF: 800-722-3464					
Compaq Center 10 E Greenway Plaza	Houston	TX	77046	713-843-3900	843-3986
Gulf Greyhound Park 1000 FM 2004	La Marque	TX	77568	800-275-2946	
Web: www.gulfgreyhound.com					
Houston Aeros (hockey) 3100 Wilcrest Suite 260	Houston	TX	77042	713-974-7825	361-7900
Web: www.aeros.com ■ *E-mail:* wwwaeros@aeros.com					
Houston Astros 8400 Kirby Dr The Astrodome	Houston	TX	77054	713-799-9555	799-9562
Web: www.astros.com ■ *E-mail:* twinspin@astros.com					
Houston Comets (basketball) 10 Greenway Plaza Compaq Ctr	Houston	TX	77046	713-627-9622	963-7315
Web: www.wnba.com/comets					
Houston Hotshots (soccer) 8400 Kirby Dr The Astrodome	Houston	TX	77054	713-468-5100	799-9743
Web: www.houstonhotshots.com ■ *E-mail:* hotshots@neosoft.com					
Houston Hurricanes (soccer) 13755 Main St Butler Stadium	Houston	TX	77035	281-647-6285	859-8839
Web: www.hurricanesprosoccer.com ■ *E-mail:* info@hurricanesprosoccer.com					
Houston Raceway Park 2525 FM 565	Baytown	TX	77522	281-383-2666	383-3777
Web: www.houstonraceway.com ■ *E-mail:* feedback@houstonraceway.com					
Houston Rockets 2 Greenway Plaza Suite 400	Houston	TX	77046	713-627-3865	963-7315
Web: www.nba.com/rockets					
Houston Speedway Mt Houston Rd & SR-8	The Woodlands	TX	77387	281-458-1972	458-2052
Houston Thunderbears (football) 10 Greenway Plaza Compaq Ctr	Houston	TX	77046	713-513-9622	963-7315
Web: www.thunderbears.com					
Sam Houston Race Park 7575 North Sam Houston Pkwy W	Houston	TX	77064	281-807-8700	807-8777
Web: www.shrp.com/					

— Events —

Event	Phone
Asian-American Festival (mid-October)	713-861-8270
Bayou City Art Festival (late March & mid-October)	713-521-0133
Christmas Candlelight Tours (early December)	713-655-1912
Cinco de Mayo Festival (May 5)	713-437-5200
Fall Motor Fest (early November)	281-890-5500
Festa Italiana (mid-October)	713-524-4222
Fotofest (early March-early April)	713-529-9140
Freedom Festival (July 4)	713-621-8600
Greek Festival (early October)	713-526-5377
Hot Air Balloon Festival (late August)	281-488-7676
Houston International Boat Sport & Travel Show (mid-January)	713-526-6361
Houston International Festival (late April)	713-654-8808
Houston International Jazz Festival (early August)	713-839-7000
Houston Livestock Show & Rodeo (mid-February-early March)	713-791-9000
Houston Methodist Hospital Marathon (mid-January)	713-957-3453
International Quilt Festival (late October-early November)	713-781-6864
Juneteenth Celebration (mid-June)	713-437-5200
Moody Gardens Red White & Boom/Palm Beach (late May)	409-744-4673
Oktoberfest (early October)	281-890-5500
Texas Crawfish Festival (mid-late May)	281-353-9310
Texas Renaissance Festival (early October-mid-November)	800-458-3435
Texian Market Days (late October)	281-343-0218
Thanksgiving Day Parade (late November)	713-654-8808

Houston — Events (Cont'd)

	Phone
Uptown Tree Lighting Ceremony (late November)	713-621-2011
Wings Over Houston Airshow (mid-October)	713-644-1018
World Championship Bar-B-Que Contest (mid-February)	713-791-9000
Worldfest Houston International Film Festival (early-mid-April)	713-965-9955

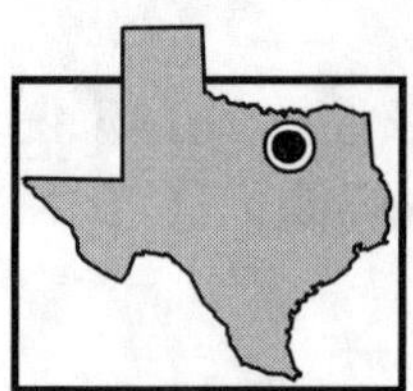

Irving

Irving is located in the heart of the Dallas-Fort Worth "Metroplex." Major companies based in Irving include Kimberly-Clark and Caltex Petroleum; Exxon and GTE are among those that have divisions there. Dallas Stadium, home of the NFL's World Champion Dallas Cowboys, and StarCenter Ice Arena, home of the NHL's Dallas Stars, are both located in Irving. Las Colinas, the city's European-style business-residential-entertainment area, contains the world's largest equestrian sculpture, Mustangs of Las Colinas, as well as a movie studio that offers tours, a world-class equestrian center, and many shops and restaurants. The Mandalay Canal Walk at Las Colinas allows visitors to stroll down cobblestone walkways beside the canal or explore the area in mahogany water taxis.

Population	178,253	**Longitude**	96-58-09 W
Area (Land)	67.6 sq mi	**County**	Dallas
Area (Water)	0.4 sq mi	**Time Zone**	CST
Elevation	675 ft	**Area Code/s**	214, 972
Latitude	32-51-27 N		

— Average Temperatures and Precipitation —

TEMPERATURES

	Jan	Feb	Mar	Apr	May	Jun	Jul	Aug	Sep	Oct	Nov	Dec
High	54	59	68	76	83	92	97	96	88	79	67	58
Low	33	37	46	55	63	70	74	74	67	56	45	36

PRECIPITATION

	Jan	Feb	Mar	Apr	May	Jun	Jul	Aug	Sep	Oct	Nov	Dec
Inches	1.8	2.2	2.8	3.5	4.9	3.0	2.3	2.2	3.4	3.5	2.3	1.8

— Important Phone Numbers —

	Phone		Phone
AAA	214-526-7911	**Medical Referral**	972-579-8100
American Express Travel	972-556-0253	**Poison Control Center**	800-764-7661
Dental Referral	214-526-3435	**Time/Temp**	214-844-6611
Emergency	911	**Weather**	214-787-1111
Highway Conditions	800-452-9292		

— Information Sources —

				Phone	Fax
Better Business Bureau Serving Metropolitan Dallas & Northeast Texas 2001 Bryan St Suite 850 *Web:* www.dallas.bbb.org	Dallas	TX	75201	214-220-2000	740-0321
Dallas County 411 Elm St	Dallas	TX	75202	214-653-7361	653-7057
Greater Irving Chamber of Commerce 3333 N MacArthur Blvd Suite 100 *Web:* www.irving.net/chamber	Irving	TX	75062	972-252-8484	252-6710
Irving City Hall 825 W Irving Blvd *Web:* www.ci.irving.tx.us	Irving	TX	75060	972-721-2600	721-2384
Irving Community Development Dept 825 W Irving Blvd 2nd Fl *Web:* www.ci.irving.tx.us/CommDev	Irving	TX	75060	972-721-2424	721-2422
Irving Convention & Visitors Bureau 3333 N MacArthur Blvd Suite 200 *TF:* 800-247-8464 ■ *Web:* www.irvingtexas.com ■ *E-mail:* magast@airmail.net	Irving	TX	75062	972-252-7476	257-3153
Irving Mayor PO Box 152288 *Web:* www.ci.irving.tx.us/CityCouncil	Irving	TX	75015	972-721-2410	721-2384
Irving Public Library System 801 W Irving Blvd *Web:* www.irving.lib.tx.us ■ *E-mail:* support@irving.lib.tx.us	Irving	TX	75060	972-721-2606	721-2463

On-Line Resources

About.com Guide to Irving	irving.about.com/local/southwestus/irving
Area Guide Irving	irving.areaguides.net
Excite.com Irving City Guide	www.excite.com/travel/countries/united_states/texas/irving
Irving Net	www.irving.net/

— Transportation Services —

AIRPORTS

■ **Dallas-Fort Worth International Airport (DFW)**

	Phone
5 miles NW of downtown Irving (approx 15 minutes)	972-574-8888

Airport Transportation

	Phone
Allied Taxi $20 fare to downtown Irving	214-819-9999
Discount Shuttle $11 fare to downtown Irving	817-267-5150
SuperShuttle $15 fare to downtown Irving	817-329-2025
Terminal Choice Cabs $15-20 fare to downtown Irving	972-222-2000

Commercial Airlines

	Phone		Phone
American	800-433-7300	**Midwest Express**	800-452-2022
American Eagle	800-433-7300	**National**	888-757-5387
Aspen Mountain Air Inc	972-641-7337	**Northwest**	800-225-2525
British Airways	800-247-9297	**Southwest**	972-263-1717
Continental	972-263-0523	**Thai**	800-426-5204
Delta	214-630-3200	**TWA**	800-221-2000
El Al	800-223-6700	**United**	800-241-6522
Lufthansa	800-645-3880	**US Airways**	800-428-4322
Mesa	800-637-2247	**Vanguard**	800-826-4827
Mexicana	800-531-7923		

Charter Airlines

	Phone		Phone
Alpha Aviation	214-352-4801	**Million Air**	800-248-1602
Miami Air International	305-871-3300	**Sun Country**	800-359-5786

■ **Dallas Love Field (DAL)**

	Phone
10 miles NE of downtown Irving (approx 15 minutes)	214-670-6080

Airport Transportation

	Phone
Discount Shuttle $15 fare to downtown Irving	817-267-5150
SuperShuttle $15 fare to downtown Irving	817-329-2025
Terminal Choice Cabs $15-20 fare to downtown Irving	972-222-2000

Commercial Airlines

	Phone		Phone
Continental	800-525-0280	**Southwest**	972-263-1717

Charter Airlines

	Phone		Phone
Aerodynamics Inc	214-352-2376	**Jet Aviation**	214-351-6571
All-Star Helicopters Inc	972-250-9907	**Raytheon Aircraft Charter**	800-519-6283
Alliance Executive Charter Services	800-232-5387	**Regal Aviation**	877-359-6520
		Rivair Flying Service Inc	918-299-1234
American Business Charter Inc	972-732-7344	**Stebbins Jet Center**	903-643-2601
American Jet International Corp	888-435-9254	**Texas Air Charters**	940-898-1200
Business Jet Services	888-387-7477	**TXI Aviation Inc**	972-647-7365
Corporate Aviation Services Inc	918-834-8348	**Zebra Air Inc**	214-358-7200
Helicopters Inc	800-466-2903		

Irving (Cont'd)

CAR RENTALS

	Phone		Phone
Alamo	800-327-9633	**Enterprise**	972-986-1890
Avis	800-831-2847	**Hertz**	800-654-3131
Budget	800-527-0700	**National**	800-227-7368
Capps	972-929-0003	**Thrifty**	972-621-1234
Dollar	800-800-4000		

LIMO/TAXI

	Phone		Phone
Airport Sedan Service	972-721-0073	**Luxury Sedans Unlimited**	972-436-5657
Allied Taxi	214-819-9999	**Terminal Choice Cabs**	972-222-2000
Executive Taxi Service	972-554-1212		

MASS TRANSIT

	Phone
DART $1 Base fare	214-979-1111

RAIL/BUS

				Phone
Dallas Union Amtrak Station 400 S Houston St.	Dallas	TX	75202	214-653-1101
Greyhound/Trailways Bus Station 969 E Irving Blvd *TF:* 800-231-2222	Irving	TX	75060	972-254-8412

— Accommodations —

HOTEL RESERVATION SERVICES

	Phone	Fax
USA Hotels *TF:* 800-872-4683 ■ *Web:* www.1800usahotels.com ■ *E-mail:* info@1800usahotels.com	252-331-1555	331-2021

HOTELS, MOTELS, RESORTS

				Phone	Fax
AmeriSuites 4235 W Airport Fwy *TF:* 800-833-1516	Irving	TX	75062	972-659-1272	570-0676
Atrium Suites Inn 215 E Airport Fwy	Irving	TX	75062	972-255-5500	255-5500
Budget Inn 1205 Loop 12 S	Irving	TX	75060	972-721-1025	445-1664
Comfort Inn Airport 4940 W Airport Fwy *TF:* 800-228-5150	Irving	TX	75062	972-790-7979	790-0031
Comfort Inn-DFW Airport 8205 Esters Blvd *TF:* 800-228-5150	Irving	TX	75063	972-929-0066	929-5083
Country Suites by Carlson 4100 W John Carpenter Fwy *TF:* 800-456-4000	Irving	TX	75063	972-929-4008	929-4224
Courtyard by Marriott Dallas-Fort Worth 4949 Regent Blvd *TF:* 800-321-2211 ■ *Web:* courtyard.com/DFWCY	Irving	TX	75063	972-929-4004	929-4207
Courtyard by Marriott Las Colinas 1151 W Walnut Hill Ln *TF:* 800-321-2211 ■ *Web:* courtyard.com/DALLA	Irving	TX	75038	972-550-8100	550-0764
Days Inn DFW Airport 4325 W John Carpenter Fwy *TF:* 800-329-7466	Irving	TX	75063	972-621-8277	929-4932
Days Inn Texas Stadium 2200 E Airport Fwy *TF:* 800-325-2525	Irving	TX	75062	972-438-6666	579-4902
Delux Inn 1400 E Airport Fwy	Irving	TX	75062	972-579-8990	721-0174
Delux Suites 1409 N Loop 12	Irving	TX	75061	972-554-5051	554-5051
Drury Inn Airport 4210 W Airport Fwy *TF:* 800-325-8300 ■ *Web:* www.druryinns.com/room/reservation/dallas_1.htm	Irving	TX	75062	972-986-1200	986-1200
Embassy Suites 4650 W Airport Fwy *TF:* 800-362-2779	Irving	TX	75062	972-790-0093	790-4768
Fairfield Inn by Marriott 4800 W John Carpenter Fwy *TF:* 800-228-2800 ■ *Web:* fairfieldinn.com/DALFL	Irving	TX	75063	972-929-7257	
Four Seasons Resort & Club 4150 N MacArthur Blvd *TF:* 800-332-3442 ■ *Web:* www.fourseasons.com/locations/Dallas	Irving	TX	75038	972-717-0700	717-2550
Hampton Inn Dallas-Fort Worth South 4340 W Airport Fwy *TF:* 800-462-7866	Irving	TX	75062	972-986-3606	986-6852
Hampton Inn Las Colinas 820 Walnut Hill Ln. *TF:* 800-426-7866	Irving	TX	75038	972-753-1232	550-0300
Harvey Hotel DFW Airport 4545 W John Carpenter Fwy *TF:* 800-922-9222	Irving	TX	75063	972-929-4500	929-0733
Harvey Suites Hotel 4550 W John Carpenter Fwy *TF:* 800-922-9222	Irving	TX	75063	972-929-4499	929-0733
Hilton Garden Inn 7516 Las Colinas Blvd. *TF:* 800-445-8667 ■ *Web:* www.hilton.com/hotels/DFWLCGI	Irving	TX	75063	972-444-8434	831-9311
Holiday Inn Airport North 4441 W Hwy 114 *TF:* 800-465-4329	Irving	TX	75063	972-929-8181	929-8233
Holiday Inn Select Dallas/Fort Worth Airport South 4440 W Airport Fwy *TF:* 800-465-4329 ■ *Web:* www.basshotels.com/holiday-inn/?_franchisee=DFWSO ■ *E-mail:* john_thackray@meristar.com	Irving	TX	75062	972-399-1010	790-8545
Homegate Hotel 3950 W Airport Fwy *TF:* 888-456-4283	Irving	TX	75062	972-790-1950	790-4750
Homestead Village 5315 Carnaby *TF:* 888-782-9473	Irving	TX	75038	972-756-0458	756-0553
Homewood Suites Las Colinas 4300 Wingren Dr *TF:* 800-225-5466	Irving	TX	75039	972-556-0665	401-3765
Howard Johnson 120 W Airport Fwy *TF:* 800-446-4656	Irving	TX	75062	972-579-8911	721-1846
Irving Inn Suites 909 W Airport Fwy	Irving	TX	75062	972-255-7108	255-4827
La Quinta Inn 4105 W Airport Fwy *TF:* 800-687-6667	Irving	TX	75062	972-252-6546	570-4225
La Quinta Inn & Suites 4850 Carpenter Fwy *TF:* 800-687-6667	Irving	TX	75063	972-915-4022	915-6960
Las Colinas Comfort Suites 1223 Greenway *TF:* 800-228-5150	Irving	TX	75038	972-518-0606	518-0722
Motel 6 510 Loop 12 S *TF:* 800-466-8356	Irving	TX	75060	972-438-4227	554-0048
Omni Mandalay Hotel 221 E Las Colinas Blvd *TF:* 800-843-6664	Irving	TX	75039	972-556-0800	556-0729
Ramada Inn & Suites 4110 W Airport Fwy *TF:* 800-272-6232	Irving	TX	75062	972-790-2262	986-7620
Red Roof Inn-DFW Airport North 8150 Esters Blvd. *TF:* 800-843-7663	Irving	TX	75063	972-929-0020	929-6664
Red Roof Inn-DFW Airport South 2611 W Airport Fwy *TF:* 800-843-7663	Irving	TX	75062	972-570-7500	594-1693
Residence Inn by Marriott Las Colinas 950 Walnut Hill Ln *TF:* 800-331-3131 ■ *Web:* www.residenceinn.com/DALLS	Irving	TX	75038	972-580-7773	550-8824
Sheraton Grand Hotel 4440 W John Carpenter Fwy *TF:* 800-325-3535	Irving	TX	75063	972-929-8400	929-4885
Suites Inn 1701 W Airport Fwy	Irving	TX	75062	972-255-1133	255-1133
Summerfield Suites 5901 N MacArthur Blvd *TF:* 800-833-4353	Irving	TX	75039	972-831-0909	506-0011
Super 8 Motel 4245 W Airport Fwy *TF:* 800-800-8000	Irving	TX	75062	972-257-1810	257-1932
Travelodge 110 W Airport Fwy	Irving	TX	75062	972-438-2000	438-5707
Wilson World Hotel 4600 W Airport Fwy *TF:* 800-945-7667	Irving	TX	75062	972-513-0800	513-0106
Wingate Inn 850 W Walnut Hill Ln *TF:* 800-228-1000	Irving	TX	75038	972-751-1031	465-0111
Wyndham Garden Hotel Las Colinas 110 W John Carpenter Fwy *TF:* 800-996-3426	Irving	TX	75039	972-650-1600	541-0501

— Restaurants —

				Phone
Ashley's (American) 4440 W Carpenter Fwy	Irving	TX	75063	972-929-8400
Benton's (American) 4545 W Carpenter Fwy	Irving	TX	75063	972-929-4500
Bruno's (Italian) 9462 N MacArthur Blvd.	Irving	TX	75063	972-556-2465
Cafe Cipriani (Italian) 220 E Las Colinas Blvd	Irving	TX	75039	972-869-0713
Cafe D'or (American) 221 E Las Colinas Blvd	Irving	TX	75039	972-556-0800
Capistrano's (Italian) 4650 W Airport Fwy	Irving	TX	75062	972-513-0116
China Terrace (Chinese) 5435 N MacArthur Blvd	Irving	TX	75038	972-550-1113
Colter's Bar-B-Q (Barbecue) 2605 W Airport Fwy	Irving	TX	75062	972-258-2422
Cowboy's Sports Cafe (American) 9454 N MacArthur Blvd	Irving	TX	75063	972-401-3939
Don Pablo's (Mexican) 3911 W Airport Fwy	Irving	TX	75062	972-252-0070
Empress of China (Chinese) 2648 N Belt Line Rd	Irving	TX	75062	972-252-7677
Good Eats Cafe (American) 3516 W Airport Fwy	Irving	TX	75062	972-313-0803
Hanasho (Japanese) 2938 N Belt Line Rd	Irving	TX	75062	972-258-0250
Humperdink's (Steak/Seafood) 4959 N O'Connor Blvd	Irving	TX	75062	972-717-5515
I Fratelli (Italian) 1105 N Coker St.	Irving	TX	75062	972-570-0400
Italian Garden Gourmet (Italian) 2301 N O'Connor Rd	Irving	TX	75062	972-594-8585
Jinbeh (Japanese) 301 E Las Colinas Blvd	Irving	TX	75039	972-869-4011
JoJo's Bakery Restaurant (American) 1118 W Airport Fwy	Irving	TX	75062	972-253-7611
LePeep Grill of Las Colinas (American) 4835 N O'Connor Rd.	Irving	TX	75062	972-717-0422

Irving — Restaurants (Cont'd)

	City	State	Zip	Phone
Mustang Cafe (American) 5205 N O'Connor Blvd Suite 105	Irving	TX	75039	972-869-9942
On the Border Cafe (Mexican) 2400 N Belt Line Rd	Irving	TX	75062	972-570-5032
Pancho's (Mexican) 3425 Grande Blvd	Irving	TX	75062	972-258-6522
Rice Boxx (Chinese) 7750 N MacArthur Blvd	Irving	TX	75063	972-506-7423
Sonny Bryan's Smoke House (Barbecue) 4030 N MacArthur Blvd Suite 222	Irving	TX	75038	972-650-9564
Southern Receipe (Homestyle) 2101 W Rochelle St.	Irving	TX	75062	972-252-2003
Spirit Grill (American) 4030 N MacArthur Blvd Suite 112	Irving	TX	75062	972-717-7575
Spring Creek Barbecue (Barbecue) 3514 W Airport Fwy	Irving	TX	75062	972-313-0987
Texas Bar & Grill (Tex Mex) 220 E Las Colinas Blvd Suite 260	Irving	TX	75039	972-869-2007
Tommy's Bar-B-Que (Barbecue) 2840 Irving Blvd	Irving	TX	75061	972-986-0559
Veranda Greek Cafe (Greek) 5433 N MacArthur Blvd	Irving	TX	75038	972-518-0939
Via Real Restaurant (Mexican) 4020 N MacArthur Blvd	Irving	TX	75038	972-255-0064
Won Ton Restaurant (Chinese) 2427 W Airport Fwy	Irving	TX	75062	972-258-8663

— Goods and Services —

SHOPPING

	City	State	Zip	Phone	Fax
Coomers Mall 900 W Airport Fwy	Irving	TX	75062	972-554-1882	
Irving Mall 3880 Irving Mall	Irving	TX	75062	972-255-0571	570-7310
Plymouth Park Shopping Center Irving Blvd at Story Rd	Irving	TX	75061	972-790-3996	790-8285

BANKS

	City	State	Zip	Phone	Fax
Bank of America Texas NA 2520 W Irving Blvd *TF:* 800-247-6262	Irving	TX	75061	972-986-3900	986-3965
Bank of the West 2111 W Airport Fwy *Web:* www.bnkwest.com ■ *E-mail:* info@bnkwest.com	Irving	TX	75062	972-256-4290	570-1703
Chase Bank of Texas 111 E Irving Blvd *TF Cust Svc:* 800-235-8522*	Irving	TX	75060	972-253-2234	253-2299
Comerica-Texas/Irving Branch 301 W Irving Blvd **Fax Area Code:* 972	Irving	TX	75060	800-925-2160	259-1412*
Compass Bank-Las Colinas 4925 N O'Connor Rd	Irving	TX	75062	972-705-4500	705-4510
First Bank Texas 2101 Gateway Dr *TF:* 800-760-2265	Irving	TX	75038	972-550-1234	550-0893
Guaranty Federal Bank 650 N MacArthur Blvd	Irving	TX	75061	972-259-2226	259-2622
Independent National Bank 3636 W Northgate Dr	Irving	TX	75062	972-257-1818	252-1473
State Bank of Texas 313 W Irving Blvd *TF:* 800-860-1887 ■ *Web:* www.statebnk.com ■ *E-mail:* statebnk@statebnk.com	Irving	TX	75060	972-253-2000	253-3300
Texas Independent Bank 350 Phelps Ct Suite 200 *TF:* 800-288-4842 ■ *Web:* www.tibsite.com	Irving	TX	75038	972-650-6000	541-2211
Wells Fargo Bank 800 W Airport Rd Fwy *TF:* 800-869-3557	Irving	TX	75062	972-579-7911	721-0298

BUSINESS SERVICES

	Phone
Adecco Employment Personnel Services	972-550-1594
BAX Global	972-453-0722
DHL Worldwide Express	800-225-5345
Federal Express	800-238-5355
Interim Personnel Services	972-570-4676
Kelly Services	972-751-0345
Kinko's	972-570-5110
Mail Boxes Etc	972-650-1185
Manpower Temporary Services	972-893-2950
Olsten Staffing Services	972-751-0332
Post Office	800-275-8777
Snelling Personnel Services	972-258-5973
UPS	800-742-5877

— Media —

PUBLICATIONS

	City	State	Zip	Phone	Fax
Dallas Morning News‡ PO Box 655237 *Web:* www.dallasnews.com ■ *E-mail:* tdmned@cityview.com	Dallas	TX	75265	214-977-8222	977-8319
Fort Worth Star-Telegram‡ PO Box 1870 *Web:* www.star-telegram.com	Fort Worth	TX	76101	817-390-7400	390-7789
Irving News 1000 Ave 'H' E	Arlington	TX	76011	817-695-0500	695-0318

‡*Daily newspapers*

TELEVISION

	City	State	Zip	Phone	Fax
KDAF-TV Ch 33 (WB) 8001 John Carpenter Fwy *Web:* www.wb33.com	Dallas	TX	75247	214-640-3300	252-3379
KDFW-TV Ch 4 (Fox) 400 N Griffin St	Dallas	TX	75202	214-720-4444	720-3263
KPXD-TV Ch 68 (PAX) 800 W Airport Fwy Suite 750 *Web:* www.pax.net/KPXD	Irving	TX	75062	972-438-6868	579-3045
KTVT-TV Ch 11 (CBS) 5233 Bridge St *Web:* www.ktvt.com	Fort Worth	TX	76103	817-451-1111	496-7739
KTXA-TV Ch 21 (UPN) 301 N Market Suite 700 *Web:* www.paramountstations.com/KTXA	Dallas	TX	75202	214-743-2100	743-2121
KXAS-TV Ch 5 (NBC) 3900 Barnett St *Web:* www.kxas.com	Fort Worth	TX	76103	817-429-5555	654-6325
WFAA-TV Ch 8 (ABC) 606 Young St Communications Ctr *Web:* www.wfaa.com	Dallas	TX	75202	214-748-9631	977-6585

RADIO

	City	State	Zip	Phone	Fax
KBFB-FM 97.9 MHz (AC) 4131 N Central Expy Suite 1200 *Web:* www.kbfb.com ■ *E-mail:* kbfb@kbfb.com	Dallas	TX	75204	214-528-5500	528-0747
KDMX-FM 102.9 MHz (AC) 14001 N Dallas Pkwy Suite 1210	Dallas	TX	75240	972-991-1029	448-1029
KERA-FM 90.1 MHz (NPR) 3000 Harry Hines Blvd. *Web:* www.kera.org/ ■ *E-mail:* kerafm@metronet.com	Dallas	TX	75201	214-871-1390	740-9369
KHVN-AM 970 kHz (Rel) 7901 John Carpenter Fwy	Dallas	TX	75247	214-630-3011	905-5052
KPLX-FM 99.5 MHz (Ctry) 3500 Maple Ave Suite 1600	Dallas	TX	75219	214-526-2400	520-4343
KRBV-FM 100.3 MHz (Urban) 7901 John Carpenter Fwy	Dallas	TX	75247	214-630-3011	688-7760
KTXQ-FM 102.1 MHz (Oldies) 4131 N Central Expy Suite 1200 *Web:* www.ktxq.com	Dallas	TX	75204	214-528-5500	528-0747
KVIL-FM 103.7 MHz (AC) 9400 N Central Expy Suite 1600 *Web:* www.kvil.com	Dallas	TX	75231	214-691-1037	891-7975
KWRD-FM 94.9 MHz (Rel) 545 E John Carpenter Fwy Suite 450	Irving	TX	75062	972-402-9673	869-4975
KYNG-FM 105.3 MHz (Ctry) 12201 Merit Dr Suite 930 *Web:* www.young-country.com	Dallas	TX	75251	972-716-7800	716-7835

— Colleges/Universities —

	City	State	Zip	Phone	Fax
DeVRY Institute of Technology 4800 Regent Blvd *TF:* 800-633-3879 ■ *Web:* www.dal.devry.edu ■ *E-mail:* admissions@dal.devry.edu	Irving	TX	75063	972-929-6777	929-6778
North Lake College 5001 N MacArthur Blvd *Web:* www.dcccd.edu/nlc/nlchp.htm	Irving	TX	75038	972-273-3000	273-3014
University of Dallas 1845 E Northgate Dr *TF:* 800-628-6999 ■ *Web:* acad.udallas.edu	Irving	TX	75062	972-721-5000	721-5017

— Hospitals —

	City	State	Zip	Phone	Fax
Baylor Medical Center at Irving 1901 N MacArthur Blvd	Irving	TX	75061	972-579-8100	579-5290
Parkland Memorial Hospital 5201 Harry Hines Blvd. *Web:* www.swmed.edu/home_pages/parkland/	Dallas	TX	75235	214-590-8000	590-8096
Saint Jude Children's Hospital 4324 North Belt Line Rd *Web:* www.stjude.org	Irving	TX	75038	972-594-8080	594-1026
Saint Paul Medical Center 5909 Harry Hines Blvd.	Dallas	TX	75235	214-879-1000	879-6694

Irving (Cont'd)

— Attractions —

				Phone	Fax
Carpenter Performance Hall 3333 N MacArthur Blvd *Web:* www.irving.net/iac/	Irving	TX	75062	972-252-2787	570-4962
Dallas Communications Complex 6311 N O'Connor Rd	Irving	TX	75039	972-869-7600	869-7657
Dr Pepper Bottling Co of Texas 2304 Century Ctr Blvd *Web:* www.drpep.com	Irving	TX	75062	972-579-1024	721-8147
Dupree Theater 3333 N MacArthur Blvd *Web:* www.irving.net/iac	Irving	TX	75062	972-252-2787	570-4962
Heritage House 303 S O'Connor Rd	Irving	TX	75060	972-438-5775	
Irving Arts Center 3333 N MacArthur Blvd *Web:* www.irving.net/iac	Irving	TX	75062	972-252-7558	570-4962
Irving Symphony Orchestra 3333 N MacArthur Blvd Carpenter Performance Hall	Irving	TX	75062	972-831-8818	831-8817
Las Colinas Equestrian Center 600 Royal Ln	Irving	TX	75039	972-869-0600	
Las Colinas Symphony Orchestra 1300 Walnut Hill Irving Art Center	Irving	TX	75014	972-580-1566	550-7954
Las Colinas Water Taxi 202 Mandalay Canal	Irving	TX	75062	972-869-4321	
Movie Studio at Las Colinas 6301 N O'Connor Blvd	Irving	TX	75039	972-869-3456	869-7756

SPORTS TEAMS & FACILITIES

				Phone	Fax
Dallas Cowboys 2401 E Airport Fwy Texas Stadium *Web:* www.dallascowboys.com	Irving	TX	75062	972-785-5000	556-9304
Dallas Stars 777 Sports St Reunion Arena *Web:* www.dallasstarshockey.com	Dallas	TX	75207	214-939-2770	939-2872
Texas Stadium 2401 E Airport Fwy *Web:* www.dallascowboys.com/stadium/facts	Irving	TX	75062	972-785-4000	785-4709
Texas Toros (soccer) Freeman St Old Panther Stadium *E-mail:* txtoros@airmail.com	Duncanville	TX	75116	214-891-7059	891-8117

— Events —

	Phone
A Ghostly Affair (late October)	972-790-8505
Annual Main Event (late October)	972-259-1249
Bedford Blues Festival & Arts Fair (early September)	214-855-1881
Canalfest & Boat Parade (early June)	972-556-0625
Christmas Parade & Santa in the Park (mid-December)	972-259-7881
Cinco de Mayo Festival (early May)	972-721-2501
Fourth of July Pops Concert & Fireworks (July 4)	972-831-8818
Independence Day Parade & Old-Fashioned Picnic (July 4)	972-721-2501
Irving Heritage Festival (mid-June)	972-721-2424
Irving Open Tennis Tournament (late July-early August)	972-252-7476
Las Colinas Fall Horse Show (early October)	972-869-0600
Las Colinas Horse Trials (late September)	972-869-0600
Motocross (April)	972-438-7676
North Texas Hunter/Jumper Show (October)	972-869-0600
Taste of Irving (early August)	972-579-4390

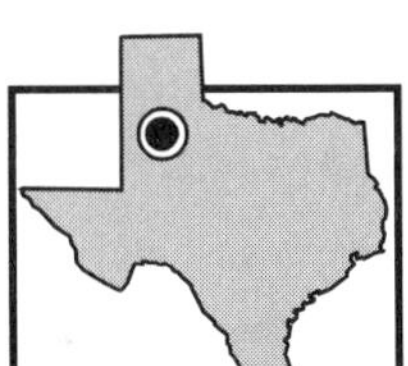

Lubbock

A bronze statue of Buddy Holly marks Lubbock as the singer's birthplace. Near the statue, "Walk of Fame" bronze plaques honor other West Texans who have made significant contributions in the entertainment industry. The city is also proud of its Western heritage, as evidenced at the Ranching Heritage Center and the National Cowboy Symposium and Celebration. The Center recounts the history of ranching in the West at restored ranch structures adjacent to the Museum of Texas Tech University. Held each September, the Symposium features cowboy poets, musicians, storytellers, and cook-offs. At Lubbock Lake Landmark State Historical Park, the remains of extinct animals and ancient cultures have been unearthed.

Population	190,974	**Longitude**	101-50-33 W
Area (Land)	104.1 sq mi	**County**	Lubbock
Area (Water)	0.1 sq mi	**Time Zone**	CST
Elevation	3241 ft	**Area Code/s**	806
Latitude	33-35-05 N		

— Average Temperatures and Precipitation —

TEMPERATURES

	Jan	Feb	Mar	Apr	May	Jun	Jul	Aug	Sep	Oct	Nov	Dec
High	53	58	66	75	83	90	92	90	83	75	63	54
Low	25	29	36	47	56	64	68	66	59	48	37	27

PRECIPITATION

	Jan	Feb	Mar	Apr	May	Jun	Jul	Aug	Sep	Oct	Nov	Dec
Inches	0.4	0.7	0.9	1.0	2.4	2.8	2.4	2.5	2.6	1.9	0.8	0.5

— Important Phone Numbers —

	Phone		Phone
AAA	800-222-4357	**HotelDocs**	800-468-3537
Dental Referral	806-762-4006	**Poison Control Center**	800-764-7661
Emergency	911	**Time/Temp**	806-763-2222
Highway Conditions	800-452-9292	**Weather**	806-745-1058

— Information Sources —

				Phone	Fax
Better Business Bureau Serving the South Plains of Texas 916 Main St Suite 800 *Web:* www.lubbock.bbb.org ■ *E-mail:* info@bbbsouthplains.org	Lubbock	TX	79401	806-763-0459	744-9748
Lubbock Chamber of Commerce 1301 Broadway Suite 101 *TF:* 800-321-5822 ■ *Web:* lubbock.org	Lubbock	TX	79408	806-761-7000	761-7010
Lubbock City-County Library 1306 9th St. *Web:* library.ci.lubbock.tx.us	Lubbock	TX	79401	806-775-2835	775-2827
Lubbock City Hall PO Box 2000 *Web:* www.ci.lubbock.tx.us ■ *E-mail:* comment@lub550.ci.lubbock.tx.us	Lubbock	TX	79457	806-775-3000	
Lubbock Convention & Tourism Bureau PO Box 561 *TF:* 800-692-4035 ■ *Web:* www.lubbocklegends.com/ ■ *E-mail:* lubbock@nts-online.net	Lubbock	TX	79408	806-747-5232	747-1419
Lubbock County PO Box 10536	Lubbock	TX	79408	806-775-1043	775-1660
Lubbock Mayor PO Box 2000	Lubbock	TX	79457	806-775-2009	775-3335
Lubbock Memorial Civic Center 1501 6th St *Web:* interoz.com/lubbock/cc.htm	Lubbock	TX	79401	806-775-2243	775-3240
Lubbock Planning Dept PO Box 2000 *Web:* planning.ci.lubbock.tx.us	Lubbock	TX	79457	806-775-2102	775-2100

On-Line Resources

Anthill City Guide Lubbock	www.anthill.com/city.asp?city=lubbock
Area Guide Lubbock	lubbock.areaguides.net
City Knowledge Lubbock	www.cityknowledge.com/tx_lubbock.htm
Excite.com Lubbock City Guide	www.excite.com/travel/countries/united_states/texas/lubbock
Lubbock Hospitality	www.lubbockhospitality.com
Lubbock Magazine	interoz.com/lubbock/lubmag/index.htm

— Transportation Services —

AIRPORTS

■ **Lubbock International Airport (LBB)**

	Phone
6 miles N of downtown (approx 10 minutes) Web: www.flylia.com/ ■ *E-mail:* info@flylia.com	806-775-2035

Airport Transportation

	Phone
Royal Limo $8 fare to downtown	806-795-3888
Yellow Cab $10 fare to downtown	806-765-7777

Lubbock (Cont'd)

Commercial Airlines

	Phone		Phone
American	800-433-7300	Delta Connection	800-221-1212
American Eagle	800-433-7300	Southwest	800-435-9792
Continental Express	800-525-0280	United Express	800-241-6522
Delta	800-221-1212		

Charter Airlines

	Phone
Aerocare	800-627-2376

CAR RENTALS

	Phone		Phone
Advantage	806-744-8566	Hertz	806-762-0222
Avis	806-763-5433	National	800-227-7368
Budget	806-763-6471	Trusty	806-744-5080
Enterprise	806-765-0622		

LIMO/TAXI

	Phone		Phone
City Cab	806-765-7474	White Knights Limousine	806-799-3366
Royal Cab	806-892-2332	Yellow Cab	806-765-7777
Royal Coach Towne Car	806-795-3888		

MASS TRANSIT

	Phone
Citibus $1.00 Base fare	806-762-0111

RAIL/BUS

				Phone
Greyhound Bus Station 1313 13th St TF: 800-231-2222	Lubbock	TX	79401	806-765-6641

— Accommodations —

HOTELS, MOTELS, RESORTS

				Phone	Fax
Apple Inn 310 Ave Q TF: 800-524-3788	Lubbock	TX	79415	806-763-2861	747-1020
Ashmore Inn & Suites 4019 S Loop 289 TF: 800-785-0061	Lubbock	TX	79423	806-785-0060	785-6001
Barcelona Court 5215 S Loop 289 TF: 800-222-1122	Lubbock	TX	79424	806-794-5353	798-3630
Best Western Lubbock Regency 6624 I-27 TF: 800-588-5677	Lubbock	TX	79404	806-745-2208	745-1265
Carriage House 910 E Slaton Hwy	Lubbock	TX	79404	806-745-4500	745-4599
Circus Inn 150 Slaton Rd	Lubbock	TX	79404	806-745-2515	745-2249
Comfort Suites 5113 S Loop 289 TF: 800-228-5150	Lubbock	TX	79424	806-798-0002	798-0035
Country Inn 4105 19th St	Lubbock	TX	79410	806-795-5271	795-5271
Courtyard by Marriott 4011 S Loop 289 TF: 800-321-2211 ■ Web: courtyard.com/LBBCY	Lubbock	TX	79423	806-795-1633	795-1633
Days Inn 6025 Ave A	Lubbock	TX	79404	806-745-5111	
Days Inn University 2401 4th St TF: 800-325-2525	Lubbock	TX	79415	806-747-7111	747-9749
Fairfield Inn 4007 S Loop 289 TF: 800-228-2800 ■ Web: fairfieldinn.com/LBBFI	Lubbock	TX	79423	806-795-1288	795-1288
GuestHouse Inn 3815 21st St TF: 800-284-1838	Lubbock	TX	79410	806-791-0433	
Hampton Inn 4003 S Loop 289 TF: 800-426-7866	Lubbock	TX	79423	806-795-1080	795-1376
Holiday Inn Civic Center 801 Ave Q TF: 800-465-4329	Lubbock	TX	79401	806-763-1200	763-2656
Holiday Inn Lubbock Plaza 3201 S Loop 289 TF: 800-465-4329	Lubbock	TX	79423	806-797-3241	793-1203
Howard Johnson 4801 Ave Q TF: 800-446-4656	Lubbock	TX	79412	806-747-1671	747-4265
Koko Inn 5201 Ave Q TF: 800-782-3254	Lubbock	TX	79412	806-747-2591	747-2591
La Quinta Motor Inn 601 Ave Q TF: 800-531-5900	Lubbock	TX	79401	806-763-9441	747-9325
La Quinta Motor Inn Lubbock 4115 Brownfield Hwy TF: 800-531-5900	Lubbock	TX	79407	806-792-0065	792-0178
Lubbock Inn 3901 19th St TF: 800-545-8226	Lubbock	TX	79410	806-792-5181	792-1319
Motel 6 909 66th St TF: 800-466-8356	Lubbock	TX	79412	806-745-5541	748-0889
Residence Inn by Marriott 2551 S Loop 289 TF: 800-331-3131 ■ Web: www.residenceinn.com/LBBSL	Lubbock	TX	79423	806-745-1963	748-1183
Sheraton Four Points Hotel 505 Ave Q TF: 800-325-3535	Lubbock	TX	79401	806-747-0171	747-9243
Super 8 Motel 501 Ave Q TF: 800-800-8000	Lubbock	TX	79401	806-762-8726	762-8726
Townhouse Inn 4401 Ave Q	Lubbock	TX	79412	806-747-1677	749-0824
Villa Inn 5401 Ave Q TF: 800-448-0073	Lubbock	TX	79412	806-747-3525	

— Restaurants —

				Phone
50 Yard Line Steakhouse (Steak/Seafood) 2549 Loop 289 S	Lubbock	TX	79423	806-745-3991
82nd Street Cafe (American) 3416 82nd St	Lubbock	TX	79423	806-792-9497
Abuelo's Mexican Restaurante & Cantina (Mexican) 4401 82nd St	Lubbock	TX	79414	806-794-1762
Casa Olé Restaurant & Cantina (Mexican) 4413 S Loop 289	Lubbock	TX	79424	806-793-9351
Cattle Baron (Steak/Seafood) 8201 Quaker	Lubbock	TX	79424	806-798-7033
Chao Thai Restaurant (Thai) 3004 34th St	Lubbock	TX	79410	806-795-1148
Chez Suzette (French/Italian) 4423 50th St	Lubbock	TX	79423	806-795-6796
China Star (Chinese) 1919 50th St	Lubbock	TX	79412	806-749-2100
Copper Caboose (Tex Mex) 4th & Boston Ave	Lubbock	TX	79415	806-744-0183
Cricket Grill & Draft House (American) 2412 Broadway	Lubbock	TX	79401	806-744-4677
Delhi Palace (Indian) 5401 Aberdeen Ave	Lubbock	TX	79414	806-799-6772
Don Pablo's (Tex Mex) 4625 50th St	Lubbock	TX	79414	806-793-7204
Gardski's (American) 2009 Broadway St	Lubbock	TX	79401	806-744-2391
Grapevine Cafe & Wine Bar (International) 2407 19th St Suite B	Lubbock	TX	79401	806-744-8246
Hub City Brewery (American) 1807 Buddy Holly Ave Web: interoz.com/lubbock/brew.htm	Lubbock	TX	79415	806-747-1535
Jazz Restaurant (Cajun/Creole) 3703 19th Suite C Web: www.jazzkitchen.com	Lubbock	TX	79410	806-799-2124
Josie's Restaurant (Mexican) 212 University Ave	Lubbock	TX	79415	806-747-8546
Montelongo's (Mexican) 3021 Clovis Rd	Lubbock	TX	79415	806-762-3068
Old Town Cafe (American) 2402 Ave J	Lubbock	TX	79405	806-762-4768
Orlando's (Italian) 2402 Ave 'Q'	Lubbock	TX	79405	806-747-5998
Otto's (American) 4301 Brownfield Hwy	Lubbock	TX	79407	806-795-2569
Rendezvous Restaurant (American) 701 East 50th St	Lubbock	TX	79404	806-744-7777
Ronnie's Restaurant (Continental) 5206 82nd St	Lubbock	TX	79424	806-798-0276
Shogun Japanese Steak & Seafood House (Japanese) 4520 50th St	Lubbock	TX	79414	806-797-6044
Skyview's Restaurant (Continental) 1901 University Ave	Lubbock	TX	79410	806-744-7462
Spanky's (American) 811 University Ave Web: www.spankyslubbock.com	Lubbock	TX	79401	806-744-5677
Stubb's Bar-B-Q (Barbecue) 620 19th St Web: interoz.com/lubbock/stubsmen.htm	Lubbock	TX	79401	806-747-4777
Taqueria Jalisco (Mexican) 2211 Ave Q	Lubbock	TX	79405	806-763-7605
Texas Cafe & Bar (Barbecue) 3604 50th St	Lubbock	TX	79413	806-792-8544

— Goods and Services —

SHOPPING

				Phone	Fax
Antique Mall of Lubbock 7907 W 19th St	Lubbock	TX	79407	806-796-2166	796-2164
Cactus Alley 2610 Salem Ave	Lubbock	TX	79410	806-796-0178	
Kingsgate Shopping Center 8201 Quaker Ave	Lubbock	TX	79424	806-745-9718	
South Plains Mall 6002 Slide Rd	Lubbock	TX	79414	806-792-4653	799-2331

BANKS

				Phone	Fax
American Bank of Commerce 50th St & Memphis Ave	Lubbock	TX	79413	806-793-2265	795-9643
City Bank 5211 Brownfield Hwy	Lubbock	TX	79408	806-792-7101	791-5331
First United Bank 5802 4th St	Lubbock	TX	79416	806-797-6500	799-2915
Lubbock National Bank 4811 50th St	Lubbock	TX	79414	806-792-1000	792-0976

Lubbock (Cont'd)

BUSINESS SERVICES

	Phone
Airborne Express	800-247-2676
BAX Global	800-225-5229
DHL Worldwide Express	800-225-5345
Federal Express	800-238-5355
Kinko's	806-791-1224
Mail Boxes Etc	806-794-0056
Manpower Temporary Services	806-793-2408
Post Office	806-762-7844
Secretarial Consultants	806-785-0088
Temporary Help Service	806-744-5600
UPS	800-742-5877

— Media —

PUBLICATIONS

				Phone	Fax
Lubbock Avalanche-Journal‡ PO Box 491 *Web:* www.lubbockonline.com	Lubbock	TX	79408	806-762-8844	744-9603
Lubbock Magazine 1716 Ave H *TF:* 800-484-9268 ■ *Web:* interoz.com/lubbock/lubmag/index.htm	Lubbock	TX	79401	806-747-4020	

‡*Daily newspapers*

TELEVISION

				Phone	Fax
KAMC-TV Ch 28 (ABC) PO Box 3790 **Fax:* Sales ■ *Web:* www.kamc28.com ■ *E-mail:* kamc28@hub.ofthe.net	Lubbock	TX	79452	806-745-2828	748-1080*
KCBD-TV Ch 11 (NBC) 5600 Ave A *Web:* www.kcbd.com	Lubbock	TX	79404	806-744-1414	749-1111
KJTV-TV Ch 34 (Fox) PO Box 3757	Lubbock	TX	79452	806-745-3434	748-1949
KLBK-TV Ch 13 (CBS) 7403 University Ave *Web:* www.klbk.com ■ *E-mail:* klbk@interoz.com	Lubbock	TX	79423	806 745-2345	748-2250
KTXT-TV Ch 5 (PBS) Texas Tech Univ Box 42161	Lubbock	TX	79409	806-742-2209	742-1274

RADIO

				Phone	Fax
KCRM-FM 99.5 MHz (CR) PO Box 53120	Lubbock	TX	79424	806-798-7078	798-7052
KFMX-FM 94.5 MHz (Rock) PO Box 53120	Lubbock	TX	79453	806-798-7078	798-7052
KFYO-AM 790 kHz (N/T) PO Box 53120 *Web:* www.kfyo.com	Lubbock	TX	79453	806-794-7979	794-1660
KKAM-AM 1340 kHz (Sports) PO Box 53120	Lubbock	TX	79453	806-798-7078	798-7052
KKCL-FM 98.1 (Oldies) PO Box 53120 *Web:* www.hub.ofthe.net/98Kool/ ■ *E-mail:* 98kool@hub.ofthe.net	Lubbock	TX	79453	806-798-9880	763-5922
KLFB-AM 1420 kHz (Span) 2700 Marshall St	Lubbock	TX	79415	806-765-8114	763-0428
KLLL-FM 96.3 MHz (Ctry) 33 Briercroft Office Park *Web:* www.klll.com/ ■ *E-mail:* info@klll.com	Lubbock	TX	79412	806-762-3000	770-5363
KMMX-FM 100.3 MHz (AC) 33 Briercroft Office Park	Lubbock	TX	79412	806-762-3000	762-8419
KOHM-FM 89.1 MHz (NPR) PO Box 43082 *E-mail:* kohm@ttu.edu	Lubbock	TX	79409	806-742-3100	742-3906
KRFE-AM 580 kHz (B/EZ) 6602 ML King Blvd	Lubbock	TX	79404	806-745-5800	745-1088

— Colleges/Universities —

				Phone	Fax
Lubbock Christian University 5601 19th St *TF:* 800-933-7601 ■ *Web:* www.lcu.edu ■ *E-mail:* library@mail.lcu.edu	Lubbock	TX	79407	806-796-8800	796-8917
South Plains College Lubbock Campus 1302 Main St *Web:* www.spc.cc.tx.us	Lubbock	TX	79401	806-747-0576	765-2775
Texas Tech University PO Box 45015 *Web:* www.texastech.edu	Lubbock	TX	79409	806-742-2011	742-0355

— Hosptials —

				Phone	Fax
Covenenant Medical Ctr 3615 19th St **Fax:* Admitting	Lubbock	TX	79410	806-725-1011	723-7188*
Saint Mary of the Plains Hospital 4000 24th St	Lubbock	TX	79410	806-796-6000	791-6166
University Medical Center PO Box 5980	Lubbock	TX	79408	806-743-3111	743-1946

— Attractions —

				Phone	Fax
Ballet Lubbock 5015 University Ave	Lubbock	TX	79413	806-785-3090	
Buddy Holly Statue & Walk of Fame 8th St & Q Ave	Lubbock	TX	79401		
Buffalo Springs Lake Rt 10	Lubbock	TX	79404	806-747-3353	747-3714
Cactus Theater 1812 Buddy Holly Ave	Lubbock	TX	79401	806-747-7047	747-5671
Cap-Rock Winery Rt 6 Box 713K	Lubbock	TX	79423	806-863-2704	863-2712
Depot District 19th St & Buddy Holly Ave *Web:* interoz.com/lubbock/depodist.htm	Lubbock	TX	79408	806-747-7047	
Godbold Cultural Center 2601 19th St.	Lubbock	TX	79410	806-741-1953	763-6362
Heritage Farm S of Shallowater on FM 179	Shallowater	TX	79363	806-832-4294	
House Bronze Fine Arts Foundry 6830 66th St	Lubbock	TX	79424	806-794-3571	798-2519
Joyland Amusement Park IH-27 & Forest St Mackenzie State Park	Lubbock	TX	79408	806-763-2719	741-1552
Llano Estacado Winery E of US 87 S on FM 1585 *Web:* www.winery.com/winery-bin/wine-inv?15+0 ■ *E-mail:* llano@winery.com	Lubbock	TX	79404	806-745-2258	748-1674
Lubbock Fine Arts Center 2600 Ave P *Web:* interoz.com/lubbock/FINEART.htm	Lubbock	TX	79405	806-767-2686	767-0732
Lubbock Lake Landmark State Historical Park N Loop 289 & US 84 *Web:* interoz.com/lubbock/landmark.htm	Lubbock	TX	79415	806-765-0737	763-1968
Lubbock Memorial Arboretum 4111 University Ave	Lubbock	TX	79413	806-797-4520	
Lubbock Symphony Orchestra 1500 Broadway Ave Suite 1117 *Web:* interoz.com/lubbock/lso1.HTM	Lubbock	TX	79401	806-762-1688	762-1824
Mackenzie State Park 4th St & IH-27	Lubbock	TX	79408	806-767-2687	
Moody Planetarium 4th St & Indiana Ave Museum of Texas Tech University *Web:* www.ttu.edu/~museum	Lubbock	TX	79409	806-742-2432	742-1136
Museum of Texas Tech University 4th St & Indiana Ave *Web:* www.ttu.edu/~museum/ ■ *E-mail:* mxgfe@ttacs.ttu.edu	Lubbock	TX	79409	806-742-2442	742-1136
National Ranching Heritage Center 3121 4th St *Web:* interoz.com/lubbock/ranch.htm	Lubbock	TX	79409	806-742-0498	742-0616
Omnimax & Science Spectrum 2579 S Loop 289 Suite 250 *Web:* www.sciencespectrum.com	Lubbock	TX	79423	806-745-6299	745-1115
Texas Water Rampage Spur 327 & Brownfield Hwy *Web:* bikini.net/rampage.htm	Lubbock	TX	79452	806-796-0701	799-5701
Vietnam Archives Texas Tech University Library MS 1041 *Web:* www.ttu.edu/~vietnam/archive.htm ■ *E-mail:* livna@ttacs.ttu.edu	Lubbock	TX	79409	806-742-9010	742-0496
Yellowhouse Canyon Lakes NW Loop 289 & Canyon Lake Rd	Lubbock	TX	79415	806-767-2660	762-0954

SPORTS TEAMS & FACILITIES

				Phone	Fax
Lubbock Municipal Auditorium/Coliseum 2720 Drive of Champions *Web:* www.lmcc.ci.lubbock.tx.us	Lubbock	TX	79409	806-775-2243	775-3240
West Texas Speedway FM-1585 & Tahoka Hwy	Lubbock	TX	79423	806-745-1066	863-2188

— Events —

	Phone
4th on Broadway (July 4)	806-747-5232
ABC Rodeo (early April)	806-747-5232
Buddy Holly Music Festival (early September)	806-749-2929
Cork & Fork Affair (early-April)	806-749-2212
Farmer Stockman Show (early October)	806-747-7134
Fiesta del Llano (mid-September)	806-762-5059
Garden & Arts Fiesta (mid-September)	806-767-3724
Grape Crush (August)	806-745-2258
High Noon Concert Series (June-August)	806-747-5232
Lights on Broadway (early-December)	806-747-5232
Lubbock Arts Festival (mid-April)	806-744-2787
National Cowboy Symposium & Celebration (early September)	806-795-2455
Panhandle South Plains Fair (late September-early October)	806-763-2833
Performing Arts Festival (mid-September)	806-792-5251
Texas Tech Intercollegiate Rodeo (mid-October)	806-742-3351
West Texas Native American Association Pow Wow (late March)	806-792-0757

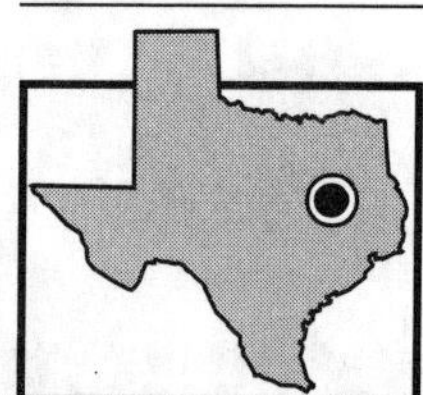

Plano

The city of Plano, Texas, is located just north of Dallas and is home to the Southfork Ranch, which was the setting for the television show Dallas. Visitor attractions at the Southfork Ranch include a western store, museum, and restaurant, as well as a "Dallas Legends" exhibit that features exciting moments from the TV show. Other attractions in the Plano area include the Heritage Farmstead Museum, an 1891 Victorian farmhouse listed on the National Register of Historic Places that depicts farm life on the Blackland Prairie; and the Interurban Museum, which is actually one of the original electric railway cars from the Texas Electric Railway that ran between Denison and Waco. The Historic Old Downtown area in Plano has more than 40 unique shops, including tea rooms and an antique mall. Plano's biggest annual event is the Plano Hot Air Balloon Festival, which is held each year in September.

Population	219,486	**Longitude**	96-44-34 W
Area (Land)	66.2 sq mi	**County**	Collin, Denton
Area (Water)	0.0 sq mi	**Time Zone**	CST
Elevation	674 ft	**Area Code/s**	972
Latitude	33-02-47 N		

— Average Temperatures and Precipitation —

TEMPERATURES

	Jan	Feb	Mar	Apr	May	Jun	Jul	Aug	Sep	Oct	Nov	Dec
High	55	60	69	77	84	91	96	96	88	78	67	58
Low	35	39	47	56	64	72	76	76	68	57	47	38

PRECIPITATION

	Jan	Feb	Mar	Apr	May	Jun	Jul	Aug	Sep	Oct	Nov	Dec
Inches	1.8	2.3	3.2	3.9	5.0	3.5	2.4	2.3	3.6	3.9	2.4	1.9

— Important Phone Numbers —

	Phone		Phone
AAA	972-661-3300	**HotelDocs**	800-468-3537
American Express Travel	972-424-7554	**Medical Referral**	972-612-7273
Dental Referral	214-526-3435	**Poison Control Center**	800-764-7661
Emergency	911	**Weather**	214-787-1111
Highway Conditions	800-452-9292		

— Information Sources —

				Phone	Fax
Better Business Bureau Serving Metropolitan Dallas & Northeast Texas 2001 Bryan St Suite 850 *Web:* www.dallas.bbb.org	Dallas	TX	75201	214-220-2000	740-0321
Collin County 200 S McDonald St Suite 120	McKinney	TX	75069	972-548-4100	
Plano Centre 2000 E Springcreek Pkwy *Web:* www.planocentre.com ■ *E-mail:* jims@gwmail.plano.gov	Plano	TX	75074	972-422-0296	424-0002
Plano Chamber of Commerce PO Drawer 940287 *Web:* www.planocc.org ■ *E-mail:* info@planocc.org	Plano	TX	75094	972-424-7547	422-5182
Plano City Hall 1520 Ave K *Web:* www.ci.plano.tx.us	Plano	TX	75086	972-941-7000	423-9587
Plano Convention & Visitors Bureau 2000 E Spring Creek Pkwy *TF:* 800-817-5266 ■ *Web:* www.planocvb.com	Plano	TX	75074	972-422-0296	424-0002
Plano Economic Development Board 4800 Preston Park Blvd Suite A-100 *Web:* www.planotexas.org	Plano	TX	75093	972-985-3700	985-3703
Plano Mayor 1520 Ave K *E-mail:* mayor@plano.net	Plano	TX	75086	972-941-7107	423-9587
Plano Public Library System 2501 Coit Rd *Web:* www.ci.plano.tx.us/library/	Plano	TX	75075	972-964-4250	964-4256

On-Line Resources

4Plano.com	www.4plano.com
Excite.com Plano City Guide	www.excite.com/travel/countries/united_states/texas/plano
NITC Travelbase City Guide Plano	www.travelbase.com/auto/features/plano-tx.html
Online City Guide to Plano	www.onlinecityguide.com/tx/plano
Plano Community Information Network	www.cinco.net/plano
Plano Town Square	www.town2.com

— Transportation Services —

AIRPORTS

■ **Dallas-Fort Worth International Airport (DFW)**

	Phone
28 miles SW of downtown Plano (approx 35 minutes)	972-574-8888

Airport Transportation

	Phone
Discount Shuttle $24 fare to downtown Plano	817-267-5150
Executive Transportation $40 fare to downtown Plano	972-365-6455
Legacy Airport Transportation $55 fare to downtown Plano	972-527-5300
Super Shuttle $24 fare to downtown Plano	817-329-2000

Commercial Airlines

	Phone		Phone
AeroMexico	972-751-1484	**Mesa**	800-637-2247
AirTran	800-247-8726	**Mexicana**	800-531-7923
American	800-433-7300	**Midwest Express**	800-452-2022
American Eagle	800-433-7300	**Northwest**	800-225-2525
Aspen Mountain Air Inc	972-641-7337	**Southwest**	972-263-1717
British Airways	800-247-9297	**Spirit**	800-772-7117
Continental	972-263-0523	**Thai**	800-426-5204
Continental Express	800-525-0280	**TWA**	800-221-2000
Delta	214-630-3200	**United**	800-241-6522
El Al	800-223-6700	**US Airways**	800-428-4322
Lufthansa	800-645-3880	**Vanguard**	800-826-4827

Charter Airlines

	Phone		Phone
Alpha Aviation	214-352-4801	**Sun Country**	800-359-5786
Miami Air International	305-871-3300		

■ **Dallas Love Field (DAL)**

	Phone
18 miles SW of downtown Plano (approx 25 minutes)	214-670-6080

Airport Transportation

	Phone
Discount Shuttle $25 fare to downtown Plano	817-267-5150
Executive Transportation $35 fare to downtown Plano	972-365-6455
Legacy Airport Transportation $35 fare to downtown Plano	972-527-5300
Super Shuttle $22 fare to downtown Plano	817-329-2000

Commercial Airlines

	Phone		Phone
American	800-433-7300	**Southwest**	800-435-9792
Continental	800-525-0280		

Charter Airlines

	Phone		Phone
Aerodynamics Inc	214-352-2376	**Jet Aviation**	214-351-6571
All-Star Helicopters Inc	972-250-9907	**Raytheon Aircraft Charter**	800-519-6283
Alliance Executive Charter Services	800-232-5387	**Regal Aviation**	877-359-6520
American Business Charter Inc	972-732-7344	**Rivair Flying Service Inc**	918-299-1234
American Jet International Corp	888-435-9254	**Stebbins Jet Center**	903-643-2601
Business Jet Services	888-387-7477	**Texas Air Charters**	940-898-1200
Corporate Aviation Services Inc	918-834-8348	**TXI Aviation Inc**	972-647-7365
Helicopters Inc	800-466-2903	**Zebra Air Inc**	214-358-7200

Plano (Cont'd)

CAR RENTALS

	Phone		Phone
Advantage-Dallas	214-350-8961	**Enterprise-Dallas**	972-986-0193
Alamo-Dallas	972-621-0236	**Hertz-Dallas**	972-453-0370
Avis-Dallas	972-574-4130	**National-Dallas**	972-574-3400
Budget	972-424-7293	**Premier**	972-612-7070
Budget-Dallas	817-329-2277	**Rent-A-Bargain**	972-423-1389
Dollar-Dallas	972-929-8888	**Rent-A-Wreck**	972-881-8142
Enterprise	972-516-0097	**Thrifty-Dallas**	972-621-1234

LIMO/TAXI

	Phone		Phone
AAA Cab	972-208-1500	**First Impression Limousines**	214-351-0610
Alante Limousines	972-475-8080	**Plano Car Co**	972-424-9093
All-American Taxi	972-404-1001	**Plano-Richardson Taxi**	972-234-0404
Carey Limousine	800-524-3837	**Yellow Cab**	214-426-6262
Dino Limousines	972-263-2200		

MASS TRANSIT

	Phone
DART $1 Base fare	214-979-1111

RAIL/BUS

				Phone
Greyhound Bus Station 400 N Greeneville Ave *TF:* 800-231-2222	Richardson	TX	75081	972-424-4211

— Accommodations —

HOTELS, MOTELS, RESORTS

				Phone	Fax
AmeriSuites 3100 Dallas Pkwy *TF:* 800-833-1516	Plano	TX	75093	972-378-3997	378-3887
Best Western Park Suites 640 Park Blvd E *TF:* 800-528-1234	Plano	TX	75074	972-578-2243	578-0563
Candlewood Suites 4701 Legacy Dr *TF:* 800-946-6200	Plano	TX	75024	972-618-5446	618-4581
Comfort Inn Plano 621 Central Pkwy E *TF:* 800-228-5150	Plano	TX	75074	972-424-5568	881-7265
Courtyard by Marriott 4901 W Plano Pkwy *TF:* 800-321-2211	Plano	TX	75093	972-867-8000	596-4009
Courtyard by Marriott Legacy Park 6840 N Dallas Pkwy *TF:* 800-321-2211	Plano	TX	75024	972-403-0802	378-9245
Fairfield Inn 4712 W Plano Pkwy *TF:* 800-228-2800	Plano	TX	75093	972-519-0303	519-0303
Hampton Inn Plano 4901 Old Shepard Pl. *TF:* 800-426-7866	Plano	TX	75093	972-519-1000	519-1001
Harvey Hotel Plano 1600 N Central Expy. *TF:* 800-922-2222	Plano	TX	75074	972-578-8555	578-9720
Holiday Inn Express 5021 W Plano Pkwy. *TF:* 800-627-5337	Plano	TX	75093	972-733-4700	733-4558
Holiday Inn Plano 700 E Central Pkwy	Plano	TX	75074	972-881-1881	422-2184
Homewood Suites 4705 Old Shepard Pl *TF:* 800-225-5466	Plano	TX	75093	972-758-8800	758-8801
La Quinta Inn & Suites 4800 W Plano Pkwy *TF:* 800-531-5900	Plano	TX	75093	972-599-0700	599-1361
La Quinta Inn Plano 1820 N Central Expy *TF:* 800-531-5900	Plano	TX	75074	972-423-1300	423-6593
MainStay Suites 4709 W Plano Pkwy *TF:* 800-660-6246	Plano	TX	75093	972-596-9966	596-9967
Motel 6 Plano 2550 N Central Expy	Plano	TX	75074	972-578-1626	423-6994
Red Roof Inn 301 Ruisseau Dr *TF:* 800-843-7663	Plano	TX	75023	972-881-8191	881-0722
Residence Inn by Marriott 5001 Whitestone Ln *TF:* 800-331-3131	Plano	TX	75024	972-473-6761	473-6628
Sleep Inn Plano 4801 W Plano Pkwy *TF:* 800-627-5337	Plano	TX	75093	972-867-1111	612-6753
StudioPLUS 4636 W Plano Pkwy	Plano	TX	75093	972-398-0135	398-0136
Super 8 Plano 1704 N Central Expy *TF:* 800-800-8000	Plano	TX	75074	972-423-8300	881-7744
Wellesley Inns & Suites 2900 Dallas Pkwy	Plano	TX	75093	972-378-9978	378-9979

— Restaurants —

				Phone
Akbar Restaurant (Indian) 301 W Parker Rd	Plano	TX	75023	972-423-3007
August Moon (Chinese) 2300 N Central Expy. *Web:* www.august-moon.com	Plano	TX	75074	972-881-0071
Austin Avenue Sports Grill (American) 935 W Parker Rd Suite 410	Plano	TX	75023	972-422-8003
Bar-B-Que Barn (Barbecue) 2129 W Parker Rd	Plano	TX	75023	972-867-5550
Bavarian Grill (German) 221 W Parker Rd	Plano	TX	75023	972-881-0705
Big Easy The (Cajun) 1915 N Central Expy	Plano	TX	75075	972-424-5261
Campisi's (Italian) 3115 W Parker Rd Suite 400	Plano	TX	75023	972-612-1177
Colter's (Barbecue) 921 N Central Expy	Plano	TX	75075	972-424-0696
Covino's (Italian) 3265 Independence Pkwy.	Plano	TX	75075	972-519-0345
Cozymel's (Mexican) 5021 W Park Blvd	Plano	TX	75093	972-964-2809
Darbar Pakistani & Indian Grill (Indian) 935 W Parker Rd Suite 404	Plano	TX	75023	972-424-4972
Dickey's Barbeque (Barbecue) 1211 E 14th St	Plano	TX	75074	972-423-9960
Fishmonger's Seafood (Seafood) 1915 N Central Expy.	Plano	TX	75074	972-423-3699
Greek Isles Tavern & Restaurant (Greek) 3309 N Central Expy.	Plano	TX	75074	972-423-7778
Hoffbrau Steaks (Steak/Seafood) 3310 N Central Expy.	Plano	TX	75074	972-423-4475
Hutchins BBQ (Barbecue) 1301 N Tennessee St.	McKinney	TX	75069	972-548-2629
Jalapeno's (Mexican) 3115 W Parker Rd	Plano	TX	75023	972-612-3800
Joe's Crab Shack (Seafood) 3320 N Central Expy	Plano	TX	75074	972-423-2800
Kirby's Steakhouse (Steak) 3408 Preston Rd	Plano	TX	75093	972-867-2122
Kosta's Cafe (Greek) 4621 W Park Blvd	Plano	TX	75093	972-596-8424
La Madeleine (French) 5000 W Park Blvd.	Plano	TX	75093	972-407-1878
Ming Garden (Chinese) 2205 N Central Expy.	Plano	TX	75075	972-516-0770
New Café de France (French) 2205 N Central Expy	Plano	TX	75075	972-423-2323
Ocean Seafood & Grill (Seafood) 3115 Parker Rd	Plano	TX	75023	972-758-1232
On the Border (Mexican) 1505 Central Expy	Plano	TX	75075	972-881-2257
Paesano's (Italian) 508 E 14th St	Plano	TX	75074	972-578-2727
Picasso's (Italian) 3948 Legacy Dr.	Plano	TX	75023	972-618-4143
Plano Tortilla Factory (Mexican) 1009 E 18th St.	Plano	TX	75074	972-423-6980
Portofino Italian Restaurant (Italian) 1301 Custer Rd Suite 360	Plano	TX	75075	972-578-0746
Pranzo Italian Grill (Italian) 2301 N Central Expy	Plano	TX	75075	972-633-9200
Red Hot & Blue (Barbecue) 5017 W Plano Pkwy.	Plano	TX	75093	972-248-3866
Sea Grill (Seafood) 2205 N Central Expy *Web:* www.seagrill.com	Plano	TX	75075	972-509-5542
Taqueria El Torito (Mexican) 717 18th St.	Plano	TX	75074	972-424-6411
Tia's (Tex-Mex) 941 N Central Expy	Plano	TX	75075	972-881-9119
Veladi Ranch Steak House (Steak) 901 W Plano Pkwy.	Plano	TX	75075	972-424-7807
Vincent's (Seafood) 2432 Preston Rd	Plano	TX	75093	972-612-6208
Wienerschnitzel (American) 1301 Coit Rd.	Plano	TX	75075	972-596-9764

— Goods and Services —

SHOPPING

				Phone	Fax
Collin Creek Mall 811 N Central Expy *Web:* www.collincreekmall.com	Plano	TX	75075	972-422-1070	881-1642
Galleria The 13350 Dallas Pkwy.	Dallas	TX	75240	972-702-7100	702-7172
Grapevine Mills 3000 Grapevine Mills Pkwy. *Web:* www.grapevinemills.com	Grapevine	TX	76051	972-724-4904	724-4920
McKinney's Historic Downtown Square E Louisiana St	McKinney	TX	75069	972-542-0163	
Northpark Center 8687 N Central Expy	Dallas	TX	75231	214-363-7441	
Plano Market Square Mall 1717 E Spring Creek Pkwy.	Plano	TX	75074	972-578-1591	
Plaza of the Americas 700 N Pearl	Dallas	TX	75201	214-720-8000	969-1081
Town East Mall 2063 Town East Mall	Mesquite	TX	75150	972-270-2363	
Valley View Center Mall Preston Rd & LBJ Fwy	Dallas	TX	75240	972-661-2425	239-1344
West End MarketPlace 603 Munger Ave	Dallas	TX	75202	214-748-4801	748-4803

BANKS

				Phone	Fax
Bank of America Texas NA 2015 Coit Rd	Plano	TX	75075	972-985-9668	612-2299
Bank One Texas NA 2000 W 15th St.	Plano	TX	75075	972-423-6560	
Bank United 2850 W Parker Rd	Plano	TX	75075	972-867-2941	985-0826
Chase Bank of Texas NA 1517 Preston Rd	Plano	TX	75093	972-738-5400	
Comerica Bank Texas 3310 Premier Rd **Fax Area Code:* 972	Plano	TX	75023	214-630-3030	424-3879*
Compass Bank 1420 Independence Pkwy.	Plano	TX	75093	972-705-4400	
First Independent National Bank 8901 Independence Pkwy.	Plano	TX	75025	972-377-7380	377-3052
First International Bank 1912 Ave K Suite 100	Plano	TX	75074	972-578-7777	422-7144
Inwood National Bank 930 W Parker Rd Suite 500	Plano	TX	75075	214-358-5281	
Legacy Bank of Texas 1105 W 15th St	Plano	TX	75075	972-461-1300	461-4812

Plano — Banks (Cont'd)

Name / Address	City	State	ZIP	Phone	Fax
Mercantile Bank & Trust FSB 4901 W Park Blvd Suite 521	Plano	TX	75093	972-801-1600	
North Dallas Bank & Trust Co 3900 Preston Rd	Plano	TX	75093	972-387-1300	964-1875
Washington Mutual Bank 3041 W Parker Rd	Plano	TX	75023	972-985-7939	
Wells Fargo Bank Texas NA 660 N Central Expy	Plano	TX	75074	972-422-7500	422-7538

BUSINESS SERVICES

Name	Phone	Name	Phone
Airborne Express	800-247-2676	**Mail Boxes Etc**	972-491-7047
Express Personnel Services	972-422-6992	**Post Office**	800-275-8777
Federal Express	800-238-5355	**Staffmark**	972-422-4646
Insty Prints	972-424-4902	**UPS**	800-742-5877
Kelly Services	972-423-4205	**Westaff**	972-422-7250
Kwik Kopy Printing	972-985-8840		

— Media —

PUBLICATIONS

Name / Address	City	State	ZIP	Phone	Fax
Inside Collin County Business Journal 2121 W Spring Creek Suite 202 *Web:* www.insidetxbiz.com	Plano	TX	75023	972-612-2425	612-9329
Plano Profile 1101 E Plano Pkwy Suite G *Web:* www.planoprofile.com ■ *E-mail:* advertising@planoprofile.com	Plano	TX	75074	972-578-7505	
Plano Star Courier‡ 801 E Plano Pkwy *Web:* www.planostar.com ■ *E-mail:* stareditor@aol.com	Plano	TX	75074	972-424-6565	881-9495

‡*Daily newspapers*

TELEVISION

Name / Address	City	State	ZIP	Phone	Fax
KDAF-TV Ch 33 (WB) 8001 John Carpenter Fwy *Web:* www.wb33.com	Dallas	TX	75247	214-640-3300	252-3379
KDFW-TV Ch 4 (Fox) 400 N Griffin St	Dallas	TX	75202	214-720-4444	720-3263
KERA-TV Ch 13 (PBS) 3000 Harry Hines Blvd *Web:* www.kera.org	Dallas	TX	75201	214-871-1390	740-9369
KPXD-TV Ch 68 (PAX) 800 W Airport Fwy Suite 750 *Web:* www.pax.net/KPXD	Irving	TX	75062	972-438-6868	579-3045
KTVT-TV Ch 11 (CBS) 5233 Bridge St *Web:* www.ktvt.com	Fort Worth	TX	76103	817-451-1111	496-7739
KTXA-TV Ch 21 (UPN) 301 N Market Suite 700 *Web:* www.paramountstations.com/KTXA	Dallas	TX	75202	214-743-2100	743-2121
KXAS-TV Ch 5 (NBC) 3900 Barnett St *Web:* www.kxas.com	Fort Worth	TX	76103	817-429-5555	654-6325
WFAA-TV Ch 8 (ABC) 606 Young St Communications Ctr *Web:* www.wfaa.com	Dallas	TX	75202	214-748-9631	977-6585

RADIO

Name / Address	City	State	ZIP	Phone	Fax
KBFB-FM 97.9 MHz (AC) 4131 N Central Expy Suite 1200 *Web:* www.kbfb.com ■ *E-mail:* kbfb@kbfb.com	Dallas	TX	75204	214-528-5500	528-0747
KCBI-FM 90.9 MHz (Rel) PO Box 619000	Dallas	TX	75261	817-792-3800	277-9929
KDGE-FM 94.5 MHz (Alt) 15851 N Dallas Pkwy Suite 1200 *Web:* www.kdge.com	Addison	TX	75001	972-770-7777	770-7747
KDMM-AM 1150 (Rel) 7700 Carpenter Fwy 1st Fl	Dallas	TX	75247	214-630-9400	630-0060
KDMX-FM 102.9 MHz (AC) 14001 N Dallas Pkwy Suite 1210	Dallas	TX	75240	972-991-1029	448-1029
KDXX-AM 1480 kHz (Span) 7700 Carpenter Fwy	Dallas	TX	75427	214-630-8531	920-2507
KEGL-FM 97.1 MHz (Rock) 14001 N Dallas Pkwy Suite 1210 *Web:* www.kegl.com	Dallas	TX	75240	972-869-9700	263-9710
KERA-FM 90.1 MHz (NPR) 3000 Harry Hines Blvd *Web:* www.kera.org/ ■ *E-mail:* kerafm@metronet.com	Dallas	TX	75201	214-871-1390	740-9369
KESS-AM 1270 kHz (Span) 7700 Carpenter Fwy	Dallas	TX	75247	214-630-8531	920-2507
KHKS-FM 106.1 MHz (CHR) 8235 Douglas Ave Suite 300 *Web:* www.1061kissfm.com	Dallas	TX	75225	214-891-3400	692-9844
KKDA-AM 730 kHz (Oldies) PO Box 530860	Grand Prairie	TX	75053	972-263-9911	558-0010
KKDA-FM 104.5 MHz (Urban) PO Box 860	Grand Prairie	TX	75053	972-263-9911	558-0010
KLIF-AM 570 kHz (N/T) 3500 Maple Ave Suite 1600 *Web:* www.klif.com	Dallas	TX	75219	214-526-2400	520-4343
KLTY-FM 94.1 MHz (Rel) 7700 Carpenter Fwy *Web:* www.klty.com ■ *E-mail:* klty@onramp.net	Dallas	TX	75247	214-630-9400	630-0060
KLUV-AM 1190 kHz (Oldies) 4131 N Central Expy Suite 700	Dallas	TX	75204	214-526-9870	443-1570
KLUV-FM 98.7 MHz (Oldies) 4131 N Central Expy Suite 700 *Web:* www.kluv.com ■ *E-mail:* kluv@ix.netcom.com	Dallas	TX	75204	214-526-9870	443-1570
KOAI-FM 107.5 MHz (NAC) 7901 Carpenter Fwy	Dallas	TX	75247	214-630-3011	688-7760
KPLX-FM 99.5 MHz (Ctry) 3500 Maple Ave Suite 1600	Dallas	TX	75219	214-526-2400	520-4343
KRBV-FM 100.3 MHz (Urban) 7901 John Carpenter Fwy	Dallas	TX	75247	214-630-3011	688-7760
KRLD-AM 1080 kHz (N/T) 1080 Ballpark Way *Web:* www.krld.com	Arlington	TX	76011	817-543-5400	543-5572
KRVA-AM 1600 kHz (Span) 5307 E Mockingbird Ln Suite 500	Dallas	TX	75206	214-887-9107	841-4215
KRVA-FM 106.9 MHz (Span) 5307 E Mockingbird Ln Suite 500	Dallas	TX	75206	214-887-9107	841-4215
KSCS-FM 96.3 MHz (Ctry) 2221 E Lamar Blvd Suite 400 *Web:* www.kscs.com	Arlington	TX	76006	817-640-1963	654-9227
KSKY-AM 660 kHz (Rel) 4144 N Central Expy Suite 266 *Web:* www.ksky.com ■ *E-mail:* kskyradio@ksky.com	Dallas	TX	75204	214-827-5759	827-7983
KTCK-AM 1310 kHz (N/T) 3500 Maple Ave Suite 1310 *Web:* www.theticket.com	Dallas	TX	75219	214-526-7400	525-2525
KTNO-AM 1440 kHz (Rel) 3105 Arkansas Ln	Arlington	TX	76016	817-469-1540	261-2137
KTXQ-FM 102.1 MHz (Oldies) 4131 N Central Expy Suite 1200 *Web:* www.ktxq.com	Dallas	TX	75204	214-528-5500	528-0747
KVIL-FM 103.7 MHz (AC) 9400 N Central Expy Suite 1600 *Web:* www.kvil.com	Dallas	TX	75231	214-691-1037	891-7975
KVTT-FM 91.7 MHz (Rel) 11061 Shady Tr	Dallas	TX	75229	214-351-6655	351-6809
KWRD-FM 94.9 MHz (Rel) 545 E John Carpenter Fwy Suite 450	Irving	TX	75062	972-402-9673	869-4975
KYNG-FM 105.3 MHz (Ctry) 12201 Merit Dr Suite 930 *Web:* www.young-country.com	Dallas	TX	75251	972-716-7800	716-7835
KZMP-AM 1540 kHz (Span) 5307 E Mockingbird Ln Suite 500	Dallas	TX	75206	214-887-9107	841-4215
KZMP-FM 101.7 MHz (Span) 5307 E Mockingbird Ln Suite 500	Dallas	TX	75206	214-887-9107	841-4215
KZPS-FM 92.5 MHz (CR) 15851 Dallas Pkwy Suite 1200 *Web:* www.kzps.com ■ *E-mail:* balberts@iadfw.net	Addison	TX	75001	972-770-7777	770-7747
WRR-FM 101.1 MHz (Clas) PO Box 159001 *Web:* www.wrr101.com	Dallas	TX	75315	214-670-8888	670-8394

— Colleges/Universities —

Name / Address	City	State	ZIP	Phone	Fax
Collin County Community College Spring Creek Campus 2800 E Spring Creek Pkwy	Plano	TX	75074	972-881-5790	881-5636

— Hospitals —

Name / Address	City	State	ZIP	Phone	Fax
Columbia Medical Center of Plano 3901 W 15th St	Plano	TX	75075	972-596-6800	519-1295
Presbyterian Hospital of Plano 6200 W Parker Rd	Plano	TX	75093	972-608-8000	608-8111

— Attractions —

Name / Address	City	State	ZIP	Phone	Fax
Cavanaugh Flight Museum 4572 Claire Chennault Addison Airport *Web:* www.cavanaughflightmuseum.com	Addison	TX	75001	972-380-8800	248-0907
Dallas Arboretum & Botanical Garden 8617 Garland Rd	Dallas	TX	75218	214-327-8263	324-9801

Plano — Attractions (Cont'd)

				Phone	Fax
Dallas Zoo 650 S RL Thornton Fwy *Web:* www.dallas-zoo.org	Dallas	TX	75203	214-670-6826	670-7450
Heard Natural Science Museum & Wildlife Sanctuary 1 Nature Pl *Web:* www.heardmuseum.org ■ *E-mail:* heardmuseum@texoma.net	McKinney	TX	75069	972-562-5566	548-9119
Heritage Farmstead Museum 1900 W 15th St	Plano	TX	75075	972-424-7874	
Ice Bound Entertainment Center 4020 W Plano Pkwy	Plano	TX	75093	972-758-7528	
Interurban Railway Station Museum 901 E 15th St *Web:* www.ci.plano.tx.us/parks/facilhtm9.htm	Plano	TX	75074	972-941-7250	
Malibu SpeedZone 11130 Malibu Dr *Web:* www.speedzone.com/dallas/dallas.html	Dallas	TX	75229	972-247-7223	243-3170
Medieval Times Dinner & Tournament 2021 N Stemmons Fwy *TF:* 800-229-9900 ■ *Web:* www.medievaltimes.com/TX_realm.htm ■ *E-mail:* dallas@medievaltimes.com	Dallas	TX	75207	214-761-1800	761-1805
Mountasia Family Fun Center 2400 Premier Dr	Plano	TX	75075	972-424-9940	
NASCAR Silicon Motor Speedway 13350 Dallas Pkwy Suite 3800	Dallas	TX	75240	972-490-7223	490-4240
Palace of Wax & Ripley's Believe It or Not! 601 E Safari Pkwy *Web:* www.tourtexas.com/ripleys ■ *E-mail:* lowcpm@onramp.net	Grand Prairie	TX	75050	972-263-2391	263-5954
Plano ArtCentre Theatre 1028 E 15th Pl	Plano	TX	75074	972-422-7460	578-7072
Plano Repertory Theatre 1028 E 15th Pl Plano ArtCentre *Web:* www.intur.net/prt ■ *E-mail:* planorep@intur.net	Plano	TX	75074	972-422-7460	578-7072
Plano Symphony Orchestra 850 Lexington Dr Fellowship Bible Church *Web:* www.planosymphony.org ■ *E-mail:* info@planosymphony.org	Plano	TX	75075	972-473-7262	473-4639
Six Flags Over Texas 2201 Road to Six Flags *Web:* www.sixflags.com/texas	Arlington	TX	76011	817-640-8900	530-6040
Sixth Floor Museum 411 Elm St Dealey Plaza *TF:* 888-485-4854 ■ *Web:* www.jfk.org ■ *E-mail:* jfk@jfk.org	Dallas	TX	75202	214-747-6660	747-6662
Southfork Ranch 3700 Hogge Rd *TF:* 800-989-7800 ■ *Web:* www.southforkranch.com	Parker	TX	75002	972-442-7800	442-5259
TILT Adventure Motion Theater 603 Munger Ave West End Marketplace	Dallas	TX	75202	214-720-7276	
West End MarketPlace 603 Munger Ave	Dallas	TX	75202	214-748-4801	748-4803

SPORTS TEAMS & FACILITIES

				Phone	Fax
Cotton Bowl 3750 Midway Dr	Dallas	TX	75215	214-939-2222	939-2224
Dallas Burn 2602 McKinney Suite 200 *Web:* www.burnsoccer.com ■ *E-mail:* theburnone@aol.com	Dallas	TX	75204	214-979-0303	979-1118
Dallas Cowboys 2401 E Airport Fwy Texas Stadium *Web:* www.dallascowboys.com	Irving	TX	75062	972-785-5000	556-9304
Dallas Mavericks 777 Sports St Reunion Arena *TF:* 800-634-6287 ■ *Web:* www.nba.com/mavericks	Dallas	TX	75207	214-748-1810	741-6731
Dallas Sidekicks (soccer) 777 Sports St Reunion Arena	Dallas	TX	75207	214-653-0200	741-6731
Dallas Stars 777 Sports St Reunion Arena *Web:* www.dallasstarshockey.com	Dallas	TX	75207	214-939-2770	939-2872
Lone Star Park at Grand Prairie 1000 Lone Star Pkwy *Web:* www.lonestarpark.com	Grand Prairie	TX	75050	972-263-7223	237-5109
North Texas Heat (soccer) 2001 Kelley Blvd Polk Football Stadium *E-mail:* cdemarco@ntxsoccer.org	Carrollton	TX	75006	972-492-7863	242-3600
Texas Motor Speedway 3601 Hwy 114	Fort Worth	TX	76247	817-215-8500	491-3749
Texas Rangers 1000 Ballpark Way Ballpark at Arlington *TF:* 888-968-3927 ■ *Web:* www.texasrangers.com	Arlington	TX	76011	817-273-5100	273-5174

— Events —

	Phone
Back to Grandma's Attic Craft Show (January-April)	800-783-4526
Boo at the Zoo (late October)	214-670-5656
Christmas Crafts Fair (late November)	972-941-7250
Christmas in Old Downtown Plano (early December)	972-941-7250
City of Plano Martin Luther King Celebration (mid-January)	972-422-0296
Collin County Community College Jazz Festival (late March)	972-881-5790
Columbus Day Weekend Sidewalk Sale (mid-October)	972-578-1591
Cotton Jubilee (mid-October)	903-455-1510
Cottonwood Art Festival (early October & early May)	972-231-4798
Country at Heart Craft Show (March-December)	800-783-4526
Dallas Video Festival (late March)	214-999-8999
Data Music Festival (mid-December)	214-987-3282
Dickens of a Christmas (November)	888-649-8499
Greek Food Festival (late September)	972-991-1166
Halloween at the Wax Museum (early-late October)	972-263-2391
HarvestFest (late September)	888-649-8499
Martin Luther King Jr Celebration & Parade (mid-January)	972-941-7174
Mesquite Rodeo (April-September)	972-285-8777
North Texas Irish Festival (early March)	214-821-4174
Plano Balloon Festival (mid-September)	972-867-7566
Scarborough Faire Renaissance Festival (mid-April-early June)	972-938-3247
State Fair of Texas (late September-mid-October)	214-565-9931
Taste of Plano (late February)	972-519-8262
Very Special Arts Festival (late February)	972-941-7272
Waxahachie Scarborough Renaissance Fair (April-June)	972-938-1888

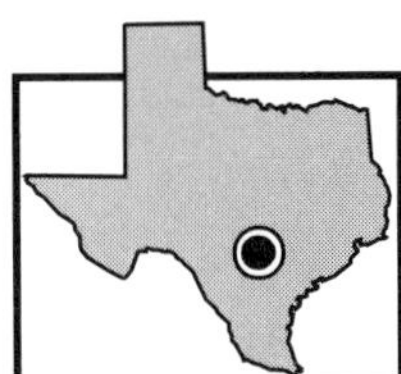

San Antonio

For 12 days in 1836, volunteers at the Alamo in San Antonio fought against the forces of Mexican General Santa Anna. The 13th day the siege ended with 189 dead and a victory for the Mexican forces. This defeat inspired citizens to "Remember the Alamo" and eventually win Texas independence. Today, a tour along the Texas Star Trail begins and ends at the Alamo, where guns and other artifacts that belonged to heroes like Davy Crockett and Jim Bowie are on display. Along the 2.6-mile Texas Star Trail one can also see some 80 other historic sites and landmarks. Near the Trail, too, is San Antonio's River Walk. Built a full story below street level, River Walk's restaurants, hotels, and bars sit on scenic stone pathways on both banks of the San Antonio River. River Walk's nightly celebration, Fiesta Noche del Rio, features dancers, trumpets, and flamenco guitarists. Southeast of River Walk, not far from the Alamo, is HemisFair Park, the onetime site of a world exposition and still home to the Tower of the Americas, a 750-foot structure that was once the symbol of Hemisfair, and the Institute of Texan Cultures. South of downtown San Antonio, visitors can pick up the Mission Trail, which connects four of the beautiful stone missions built along the San Antonio River.

Population	1,114,130	**Longitude**	98-52-57 W
Area (Land)	333.0 sq mi	**County**	Bexar
Area (Water)	4.5 sq mi	**Time Zone**	CST
Elevation	701 ft	**Area Code/s**	210
Latitude	29-46-41 N		

— Average Temperatures and Precipitation —

TEMPERATURES

	Jan	Feb	Mar	Apr	May	Jun	Jul	Aug	Sep	Oct	Nov	Dec
High	61	66	74	80	85	92	95	95	89	82	72	64
Low	38	41	50	58	66	73	75	75	69	59	49	41

PRECIPITATION

	Jan	Feb	Mar	Apr	May	Jun	Jul	Aug	Sep	Oct	Nov	Dec
Inches	1.7	1.8	1.5	2.5	4.2	3.8	2.2	2.5	3.4	3.2	2.6	1.5

— Important Phone Numbers —

	Phone		Phone
AAA	210-736-4691	**HotelDocs**	800-468-3537
American Express Travel	210-828-4809	**Medical Referral**	210-734-6691
Dental Referral	210-699-9529	**Poison Control Center**	800-764-7661
Emergency	911	**Time/Temp**	210-226-3232
Highway Conditions	800-452-9292	**Weather**	210-225-0404

San Antonio (Cont'd)

— Information Sources —

				Phone	Fax
Alamodome 100 Montana St	San Antonio	TX	78203	210-207-3663	207-3646
TF: 800-884-3663 ■ *Web:* www.alamodome.com					
Better Business Bureau Serving the South Central Area 1800 NE Loop 410 Suite 400	San Antonio	TX	78217	210-828-9441	828-3101
Web: www.sanantonio.bbb.org					
Bexar County 100 Dolorosa St	San Antonio	TX	78205	210-335-2011	335-2926
Gonzalez Henry B Convention Center 200 E Market St	San Antonio	TX	78205	210-207-8500	223-1495
Web: www.ci.sat.tx.us/convfac/					
Greater San Antonio Chamber of Commerce 602 E Commerce St	San Antonio	TX	78205	210-229-2100	229-1600
Web: www.sachamber.org					
San Antonio City Hall 100 Military Plaza 2nd Fl	San Antonio	TX	78205	210-207-7040	207-7027
Web: www.ci.sat.tx.us					
San Antonio Convention & Visitors Bureau PO Box 2277	San Antonio	TX	78298	210-207-6700	207-6782
TF: 800-447-3372 ■ *Web:* www.sanantoniocvb.com/ ■ *E-mail:* sacvb@ci.sat.tx.us					
San Antonio Economic Development Dept 100 Military Plaza City Hall 4th Fl	San Antonio	TX	78205	210-207-8080	207-8151
Web: www.ci.sat.tx.us/edd/index.htm					
San Antonio Mayor PO Box 839966	San Antonio	TX	78283	210-207-7060	207-4077
Web: www.ci.sat.tx.us/mayor/index.htm ■ *E-mail:* mayor@ci.sat.tx.us					
San Antonio Public Library 600 Soledad St	San Antonio	TX	78205	210-207-2500	207-2556
Web: www.sat.lib.tx.us/					

On-Line Resources

4SanAntonio.com	www.4sanantonio.com
About.com Guide to San Antonio	sanantonio.about.com/local/southwestus/sanantonio
Alamo City Guide	www.alamocity.com
Anthill City Guide San Antonio	www.anthill.com/city.asp?city=sanantonio
Area Guide San Antonio	sanantonio.areaguides.net
Arrive @ San Antonio	www.arrive-at.com/sanantonio/
Boulevards San Antonio	www.sanantonio.com
Cain's San Antonio Page	www.cains.com/sa
City Knowledge San Antonio	www.cityknowledge.com/tx_sanantonio.htm
CitySearch San Antonio	sanantonio.citysearch.com
DigitalCity San Antonio	home.digitalcity.com/sanantonio
Everything San Antonio	www.esanantonio.com/
Excite.com San Antonio City Guide	www.excite.com/travel/countries/united_states/texas/san_antonio
Heart of San Antonio	heartofsanantonio.com
HotelGuide San Antonio	hotelguide.net/san_antonio/
LDS iAmerica San Antonio	san-antonio.iamerica.net
NITC Travelbase City Guide San Antonio	www.travelbase.com/auto/guides/san_antonio-area-tx.html
No Place But Texas	www.noplacebuttexas.com
Open World City Guides San Antonio	www.worldexecutive.com/cityguides/san_antonio/
San Antonio Food & Leisure	food-leisure.com/
San Antonio Marketplace	samarketplace.com
SanAntonio.TheLinks.com	sanantonio.thelinks.com/
South Texas Outdoor Recreation Pages	wildtexas.com/
Virtual City San Antonio	www.txdirect.net/vcity-sa
Virtual Voyages San Antonio	www.virtualvoyages.com/usa/tx/san_anto/san_anto.sht

— Transportation Services —

AIRPORTS

■ San Antonio International Airport (SAT)

	Phone
8 miles N of downtown (approx 20 minutes)	210-207-3411

Web: www.ci.sat.tx.us/aviation/index.htm

Airport Transportation

	Phone
Downtown Cab $15 fare to downtown	210-222-2222
Star Shuttle $6 fare to downtown	210-366-3183
Taxi $14 fare to downtown	210-226-4242
VIA Metropolitan Transit $.75 fare to downtown	210-362-2020

Commercial Airlines

	Phone		Phone
Aeroliteral	210-828-7180	**Mexicana**	800-531-7921
AirTran	800-247-8726	**Northwest**	800-225-2525
American	800-433-7300	**Southwest**	210-617-1221
Continental	210-828-8381	**TWA**	800-221-2000
Continental Express	800-525-0280	**United**	800-241-6522
Delta	800-221-1212		

Charter Airlines

	Phone
Million Air	800-248-1602

CAR RENTALS

	Phone		Phone
Alamo	210-828-7967	**Enterprise**	210-341-5309
Avis	210-826-6332	**Hertz**	210-841-8800
Budget	210-828-8888	**National**	210-824-7544
Dollar	210-524-3250	**Thrifty**	210-341-4677

LIMO/TAXI

	Phone		Phone
Aladdin's Limousine	210-436-1178	**Elegant Limousines**	210-225-5466
Arrow Limousine	210-491-9555	**Metro Cab**	210-222-2222
Carey Limousine	210-525-0007	**River City Limo**	210-824-2275
Checker Cab	210-222-2151	**Texas Star Limousines**	210-222-2223
Concert Limousine	210-735-1934	**Yellow Cab**	210-226-4242
Downtown Cab	210-222-2222	**Yellow Checker Cab**	210-227-8294

MASS TRANSIT

	Phone
VIA Metropolitan Transit $.75 Base fare	210-362-2020

RAIL/BUS

				Phone
Greyhound/Trailways Bus Station 500 N Saint Mary's St	San Antonio	TX	78205	210-270-5824

— Accommodations —

HOTEL RESERVATION SERVICES

	Phone	Fax
Hotel Reservations Network Inc	214-361-7311	361-7299
TF Sales: 800-964-6835 ■ *Web:* www.hoteldiscount.com		

HOTELS, MOTELS, RESORTS

				Phone	Fax
Adam's Mark River Walk 111 E Pecan	San Antonio	TX	78205	210-354-2800	354-2700
TF: 800-444-2326 ■ *Web:* www.adamsmark.com/sanant.htm					
Alamo Travelodge 405 Broadway	San Antonio	TX	78205	210-222-1000	229-9744
TF: 800-578-7878					
AmeriSuites 7615 Jones Maltsberger	San Antonio	TX	78216	210-930-2333	930-2336
TF: 800-833-1516					
AmeriSuites Northwest 4325 Amerisuites Dr	San Antonio	TX	78230	210-561-0099	561-0513
TF: 800-833-1516					
Best Western Continental Inn 9735 I-35 N	San Antonio	TX	78223	210-655-3510	655-0778
TF: 800-451-3510					
Best Western Hotel 7401 Wurzbach Rd	San Antonio	TX	78229	210-614-9900	614-2105
TF: 800-468-3507					
Best Western Lackland Inn & Suites 6815 Hwy 90 W	San Antonio	TX	78227	210-675-9690	670-9471
TF: 800-528-1234					
Camberley Gunter Hotel 205 E Houston St	San Antonio	TX	78205	210-227-3241	227-9305
TF: 800-555-8000 ■ *Web:* www.camberleyhotels.com/gunter.htm					
Club Hotel by Doubletree 1111 NE Loop 410	San Antonio	TX	78209	210-828-9031	828-3066
TF: 800-222-8733					
Comfort Inn Airport 2635 NE Loop 410	San Antonio	TX	78217	210-653-9110	653-8615
TF: 800-424-6423					
Comfort Inn Six Flags 6755 N FM 1604 West	San Antonio	TX	78256	210-696-4766	696-4766
TF: 800-228-5150					
Comfort Suites Airport 14202 US Hwy 281 N	San Antonio	TX	78232	210-494-9000	494-7200
TF: 888-727-8483					

San Antonio — Hotels, Motels, Resorts (Cont'd)

				Phone	Fax
Courtyard by Marriott 600 S Santa Rosa *TF:* 800-321-2211 ■ *Web:* courtyard.com/SATCD	San Antonio	TX	78204	210-229-9449	229-1853
Courtyard by Marriott 8585 Marriott Dr *TF:* 800-321-2211 ■ *Web:* courtyard.com/SATMC	San Antonio	TX	78229	210-614-7100	614-7110
Courtyard by Marriott Airport 8615 Broadway St *TF:* 800-321-2211 ■ *Web:* courtyard.com/SATCA	San Antonio	TX	78217	210-828-7200	828-9003
Doubletree Club Hotel 37 NE Loop 410 *TF:* 800-535-1980	San Antonio	TX	78216	210-366-2424	341-0410
Drury Inn & Suites 95 NE Loop 410 *TF:* 800-436-3310	San Antonio	TX	78216	210-308-8100	341-6758
Embassy Suites Airport 10110 US Hwy 281 N *TF:* 800-362-2779	San Antonio	TX	78216	210-525-9999	525-0626
Embassy Suites Northwest 7750 Briaridge *TF:* 800-362-2779	San Antonio	TX	78230	210-340-5421	340-1843
Executive Guest House 12828 Hwy 281 N *TF:* 800-362-8700	San Antonio	TX	78216	210-494-7600	545-4314
Fairfield Inn by Marriott Airport 88 NE Loop 410 *TF:* 800-228-2800 ■ *Web:* fairfieldinn.com/SATFA	San Antonio	TX	78216	210-530-9899	530-0394
Fairfield Inn by Marriott Market Square 620 S Santa Rosa *TF:* 800-228-2800 ■ *Web:* fairfieldinn.com/SATFI	San Antonio	TX	78204	210-299-1000	299-1030
Fairmount Hotel 401 S Alamo St *TF:* 800-642-3363	San Antonio	TX	78205	210-224-8800	224-2767
Four Points by Sheraton 110 Lexington Ave *TF:* 800-288-3927	San Antonio	TX	78205	210-223-9461	223-9267
Hampton Inn 11010 W IH-10 *TF:* 800-426-7866	San Antonio	TX	78230	210-561-9058	690-5566
Hampton Inn Airport 8818 Jones Maltsberger *TF:* 800-426-7866	San Antonio	TX	78216	210-366-1800	342-9694
Hampton Inn River Walk 414 Bowie *TF:* 800-426-7866	San Antonio	TX	78205	210-225-8500	225-8526
Hawthorn Suites Hotel 2383 NE Loop 410 *TF:* 800-314-3424	San Antonio	TX	78217	210-599-4204	599-0356
Hawthorn Suites Hotel 4041 Bluemel Rd *TF:* 800-527-1133	San Antonio	TX	78240	210-561-9660	561-9663
Hilton Airport & Conference Center 611 NW Loop 410 *TF:* 800-445-8667 ■ *Web:* www.hilton.com/hotels/SATAPHF	San Antonio	TX	78216	210-340-6060	377-4674
Hilton Palacio del Rio 200 S Alamo St *TF:* 800-445-8667 ■ *Web:* www.hilton.com/hotels/SATPDHH	San Antonio	TX	78205	210-222-1400	226-4123
Holiday Inn Airport Select 77 NE Loop 410 *TF:* 800-465-4329	San Antonio	TX	78216	210-349-9900	349-4660
Holiday Inn Crockett Hotel 320 Bonham *TF:* 800-292-1050	San Antonio	TX	78205	210-225-6500	225-6251
Holiday Inn Express Airport 91 NE Loop 410 *TF:* 800-465-4329	San Antonio	TX	78216	210-308-6700	308-6700
Holiday Inn Market Square 318 W Durango *TF:* 800-465-4329 ■ *Web:* www.basshotels.com/holiday-inn/?_franchisee=SATAL ■ *E-mail:* hi-sanantonio@bristolhotels.com	San Antonio	TX	78204	210-225-3211	225-1125
Holiday Inn River Walk 217 N Saint Mary's St *TF:* 800-465-4329 ■ *Web:* www.basshotels.com/holiday-inn/?_franchisee=SATRW	San Antonio	TX	78205	210-224-2500	223-1302
Home Gate Studios & Suites 10950 Laureate Dr *TF:* 888-246-6301	San Antonio	TX	78249	210-691-1103	691-2180
Homestead Village 10802 IH-10 W *TF:* 800-782-9473	San Antonio	TX	78230	210-691-0121	691-1617
Homestead Village Airport 1015 Central Pkwy S *TF:* 888-782-9473	San Antonio	TX	78232	210-491-9009	491-9033
Homewood Suites Hotel 4323 Spectrum One *TF:* 800-225-5466	San Antonio	TX	78230	210-696-5400	696-8899
Hyatt Regency Hill Country Resort 9800 Hyatt Resort Dr *TF:* 800-233-1234 ■ *Web:* www.hyatt.com/usa/san_antonio/hotels/hotel_sanhc.html	San Antonio	TX	78251	210-647-1234	681-9681
Hyatt Regency San Antonio 123 Losoya St *TF:* 800-233-1234 ■ *Web:* www.hyatt.com/usa/san_antonio/hotels/hotel_satrs.html	San Antonio	TX	78205	210-222-1234	227-4925
Inn of the Hills River Resort 1001 Junction Hwy	Kerrville	TX	78028	830-895-5000	895-6020
La Mansion del Rio Hotel 112 College St *TF:* 800-292-7300 ■ *Web:* www.lamansion.com	San Antonio	TX	78205	210-225-2581	226-0389
La Quinta Convention Center 1001 E Commerce St *TF:* 800-531-5900	San Antonio	TX	78205	210-222-9181	228-9816
La Quinta Motor Inn Market Square 900 Dolorosa St *TF:* 800-687-6667	San Antonio	TX	78207	210-271-0001	228-0663
Marriott Rivercenter Hotel 101 Bowie St *TF:* 800-648-4462 ■ *Web:* marriotthotels.com/SATRC	San Antonio	TX	78205	210-223-1000	223-6239
Marriott Riverwalk Hotel 889 E Market St *TF:* 800-228-9290 ■ *Web:* marriotthotels.com/SATDT	San Antonio	TX	78205	210-224-4555	224-2754
Menger Hotel 204 Alamo Plaza *TF:* 800-345-9285 ■ *Web:* mengerhotel.com/ ■ *E-mail:* menger@ipsa.net	San Antonio	TX	78205	210-223-4361	228-0022
Newcombe John Tennis Ranch 325 Mission Valley Rd *TF:* 800-444-6204 ■ *Web:* www.newktennis.com ■ *E-mail:* newktennis@aol.com	New Braunfels	TX	78132	830-625-9105	625-2004
Omni Hotel 9821 Colonnade Blvd *TF:* 800-843-6664	San Antonio	TX	78230	210-691-8888	691-1128
Plaza San Antonio Hotel 555 S Alamo St *TF:* 800-727-3239 ■ *Web:* www.plazasa.com/	San Antonio	TX	78205	210-229-1000	229-1418
Quality Inn 6023 I-10 W *TF:* 800-228-5151	San Antonio	TX	78201	210-736-1900	737-0981
Radisson Market Square 502 W Durango *TF:* 800-333-3333	San Antonio	TX	78207	210-224-7155	224-9130
Red Roof Inn 1011 E Houston *TF:* 800-843-7663	San Antonio	TX	78205	210-229-9973	229-9985
Red Roof Inn 6861 Hwy 90 W *TF:* 800-843-7663	San Antonio	TX	78227	210-675-4120	670-1890
Residence Inn Alamo Plaza 425 Bonham St *TF:* 800-331-3131 ■ *Web:* www.residenceinn.com/residenceinn/SATRW	San Antonio	TX	78205	210-212-5555	212-5554
Residence Inn Market Square 628 S Santa Rosa *TF:* 800-331-3131 ■ *Web:* www.residenceinn.com/residenceinn/SATRI	San Antonio	TX	78204	210-231-6000	231-6001
Riverhill Country Club 100 River Hill Club Ln	Kerrville	TX	78028	830-896-1400	896-3331
Saint Anthony Hotel A Wyndham Grand Heritage 300 E Travis St *TF:* 800-996-3426 ■ *Web:* www.stanthonyhotel.com ■ *E-mail:* stanthonyhotel@travelbase.com	San Antonio	TX	78205	210-227-4392	227-0915
Seven Oaks Resort & Conference Center 1400 Austin Hwy **Fax Area Code:* 210 ■ *E-mail:* oaksevenresort@aol.com	San Antonio	TX	78209	800-346-5866	822-3451*
Sierra Royale All Suite Hotel 6300 Rue Marielyne St *TF:* 800-289-2444 ■ *Web:* www.sierra-royale.com/	San Antonio	TX	78238	210-647-0041	647-4442
Sumner Suites River Walk 601 S St Mary's *TF:* 800-747-8483	San Antonio	TX	78205	210-227-6854	227-1247
Tapatio Springs Resort & Conference Center PO Box 550 *TF:* 800-999-3299	Boerne	TX	78006	830-537-4611	537-4611
Travelodge Suites 4934 NW Loop 410 *TF:* 800-267-3605	San Antonio	TX	78229	210-680-3351	680-5182

— Restaurants —

				Phone
Aldo's Ristorante Italiano (Italian) 8539 Fredericksburg Rd	San Antonio	TX	78229	210-696-2536
Anaqua (Southwest) 555 S Alamo St	San Antonio	TX	78205	210-229-1000
Bananas (American) 2003 San Pedro Ave	San Antonio	TX	78212	210-226-2627
Blanco Cafe (Mexican) 1720 Blanco Rd	San Antonio	TX	78212	210-732-6480
Boudro's On The Riverwalk (Steak/Seafood) 421 E Commerce St *Web:* www.boudros.com/	San Antonio	TX	78205	210-224-8484
Casbeer's Center Bar & Grill (American) 1719 Blanco Rd	San Antonio	TX	78212	210-732-3511
Cascabel (Southwest) 37 NE Loop 410	San Antonio	TX	78216	210-321-4860
Crumpet's Restaurant (Continental) 3920 Harry Wurzbach St	San Antonio	TX	78209	210-821-5454
El Mirador (Mexican) 722 Saint Mary's St	San Antonio	TX	78210	210-225-9444
EZ's (American) 6498 N New Brunfels St	San Antonio	TX	78209	210-828-1111
Fig Tree (Continental) 515 Villita St	San Antonio	TX	78205	210-224-1976
Grey Moss Inn (American) 19010 Scenic Loop Rd	Grey Forest	TX	78028	210-695-8301

San Antonio — Restaurants (Cont'd)

				Phone
L'Etoile (French) 6106 Broadway St	San Antonio	TX	78209	210-826-4551
La Fogata (Mexican) 2427 Vance Jackson Rd *Web:* www.lafogata.com/	San Antonio	TX	78213	210-340-1337
Liberty Bar (International) 328 E Josephine St	San Antonio	TX	78205	210-227-1187
Little Rhein Steakhouse (Steak) 231 S Alamo St	San Antonio	TX	78205	210-225-2111
Mi Tierra Cafe & Bakery (Tex Mex) 218 Produce Row	San Antonio	TX	78207	210-225-1262
Morton's of Chicago (Steak) 300 Crockett St	San Antonio	TX	78205	210-228-0700
Old San Francisco Steak House (Steak/Seafood) 10223 Sahara St	San Antonio	TX	78216	210-342-2321
Paesano's (Italian) 555 E Basse Rd	San Antonio	TX	78209	210-828-5191
Polo's (Continental) 401 S Alamo St	San Antonio	TX	78205	210-224-8800
Restaurant BIGA (American) 206 E Locust St *Web:* www.biga.com/index.html	San Antonio	TX	78212	210-225-0722
Rio Rio Cantina (Mexican) 421 E Commerce St	San Antonio	TX	78210	210-226-8462
Romano's Macaroni Grill (Italian) 24116 IH-10 W	San Antonio	TX	78257	210-698-0003
Rosario's (Mexican) 1014 S Alamo	San Antonio	TX	78210	210-223-1806
Ruth's Chris Steak House (Steak) 7720 Jones Maltsberger Rd	San Antonio	TX	78216	210-821-5051
Silo (New American) 1133 Austin Hwy	San Antonio	TX	78209	210-824-8686
Yolanda's Uptown Cafe (Mexican) 615 Fredricksburg Rd	San Antonio	TX	78201	210-732-2633

— Goods and Services —

SHOPPING

				Phone	Fax
Crossroads of San Antonio 4522 Fredericksburg Rd *TF:* 888-301-0148	San Antonio	TX	78201	210-735-9137	732-5205
Ingram Park Mall 6301 NW Loop 410	San Antonio	TX	78238	210-523-1228	681-4614
La Villita 418 Villita St *Web:* hotx.com/sa/lavillita/	San Antonio	TX	78205	210-207-8610	207-4390
North Star Mall 2000 North Star Mall	San Antonio	TX	78216	210-342-2325	342-7023
Rivercenter Mall 849 E Commerce St	San Antonio	TX	78205	210-225-0000	224-7294
Windsor Park Mall 7900 IH-35 N	San Antonio	TX	78218	210-654-9084	654-4850

BANKS

				Phone	Fax
Bank of America 3500 San Pedro Ave	San Antonio	TX	78212	210-828-7988	826-4854
Broadway National Bank 1177 NE Loop 410	San Antonio	TX	78209	210-283-6500	283-6527
Citizens State Bank 1300 W Hildebrand Ave	San Antonio	TX	78201	210-785-2300	785-2301
First National Bank 750 E Mulberry Ave **Fax:* Hum Res	San Antonio	TX	78212	210-733-3388	733-6560*
Frost National Bank 100 W Houston St **Fax:* Mktg ■ *TF:* 800-562-6732 ■ *Web:* www.frostbank.com ■ *E-mail:* frostbank@frostbank.com	San Antonio	TX	78205	210-220-4011	220-4673*
Guaranty Federal Bank 1100 NE Loop 410 1st Fl	San Antonio	TX	78209	210-829-3779	804-0851
International Bank of Commerce 2201 NW Military Hwy	San Antonio	TX	78213	210-366-0617	366-2341
Norwest Bank Texas NA 40 NE Loop 410 *TF:* 800-224-7334	San Antonio	TX	78216	210-856-5000	856-0834

BUSINESS SERVICES

	Phone		Phone
Bexar Delivery Service	210-650-3110	**Kinko's**	210-732-4952
Consolidated Parcel Service	210-654-4547	**Manpower Temporary Services**	210-734-7300
Federal Express	800-238-5355	**Olsten Staffing Services**	210-349-9911
Flash Delivery Service	210-646-9944	**Post Office**	800-725-2161
Kelly Services	210-680-1000	**UPS**	800-742-5877

— Media —

PUBLICATIONS

				Phone	Fax
North San Antonio Recorder-Times 17400 Judson Rd *Web:* www.primetimenewspapers.com/recorder/northsid.htm	San Antonio	TX	78247	210-453-3300	453-3300
San Antonio Business Journal 8200 IH-10 W Suite 300 *Web:* www.amcity.com/sanantonio	San Antonio	TX	78230	210-341-3202	341-3031
San Antonio Express-News‡ Ave 'E' & 3rd St *TF:* 800-555-1551 ■ *Web:* www.express-news.net	San Antonio	TX	78205	210-225-7411	250-3105

‡Daily newspapers

TELEVISION

				Phone	Fax
KABB-TV Ch 29 (Fox) 4335 NW Loop 410 *Web:* www.kabb.com ■ *E-mail:* kabbtv@kabb.com	San Antonio	TX	78229	210-366-1129	377-4758
KENS-TV Ch 5 (CBS) 5400 Fredericksburg Rd	San Antonio	TX	78229	210-366-5000	377-0740
KLRN-TV Ch 9 (PBS) 501 Broadway St *Web:* www.klrn.org	San Antonio	TX	78215	210-270-9000	270-9078
KMOL-TV Ch 4 (NBC) 1031 Navarro St *Web:* www.kmol.com ■ *E-mail:* kmol@kmol.com	San Antonio	TX	78205	210-226-4444	224-9898
KRRT-TV Ch 35 (WB) 4335 NW Loop 410 *Web:* www.krrt.com ■ *E-mail:* krrt@krrt.com	San Antonio	TX	78229	210-366-1129	442-6333
KSAT-TV Ch 12 (ABC) 1408 N Saint Mary's St	San Antonio	TX	78215	210-351-1200	351-1310
KVDA-TV Ch 60 (Tele) 6234 San Pedro Ave *Web:* www.kvda.com	San Antonio	TX	78216	210-340-8860	341-2051
KWEX-TV Ch 41 (Uni) 411 E Durango Blvd	San Antonio	TX	78204	210-227-4141	226-0131

RADIO

				Phone	Fax
KAJA-FM 97.3 MHz (Ctry) 6222 NW IH-10 *Web:* www.kj97.com/	San Antonio	TX	78201	210-736-9700	735-8811
KCJZ-FM 106.7 MHz (NAC) 8122 Datapoint Dr Suite 500 *Web:* www.kcjz.com	San Antonio	TX	78229	210-615-5400	615-5300
KCOR-AM 1350 kHz (Span) 1777 NE Loop 410 Suite 400	San Antonio	TX	78217	210-829-1075	804-7820
KCYY-FM 100.3 MHz (Ctry) 8122 Datapoint Dr Suite 500 *Web:* www.y100fm.com	San Antonio	TX	78229	210-615-5400	615-5300
KISS-FM 99.5 MHz (Rock) 8930 Four Winds Dr Suite 500 *Web:* www.kissrocks.com	San Antonio	TX	78239	210-646-0105	871-6116
KKYX-AM 680 kHz (Ctry) 8122 Datapoint Dr Suite 500 *Web:* www.kkyx.com	San Antonio	TX	78229	210-615-5400	615-5300
KLEY-FM 94.1 MHz (Span) 7800 I-10 W Suite 330	San Antonio	TX	78230	210-340-1234	340-1775
KLUP-AM 930 kHz (Nost) 8930 Four Winds Dr Suite 500 *Web:* www.klup.com	San Antonio	TX	78239	210-646-0105	871-6116
KONO-AM 860 kHz (Oldies) 7800 I-10 W Suite 330 *Web:* www.kono.com	San Antonio	TX	78230	210-340-0800	340-3118
KONO-FM 101.1 MHz (Oldies) 8122 Datapoint Dr Suite 500	San Antonio	TX	78229	210-615-5400	615-5300
KQXT-FM 101.9 MHz (AC) 6222 NW IH-10 *Web:* www.kq102.com	San Antonio	TX	78201	210-736-9700	736-9776
KROM-FM 92.9 MHz (Span) 1777 NE Loop 410 Suite 400	San Antonio	TX	78217	210-829-1075	804-7820
KSAH-AM 720 mHz (Span) 1777 NE Loop 410 Suite 803	San Antonio	TX	78217	210-820-3503	820-3428
KSJL-FM 92.5 MHz (Urban) 6222 NW IH 10 *Web:* www.ksjl.com ■ *E-mail:* jockbox@ksjl.com	San Antonio	TX	78201	210-736-9700	735-8811
KSMG-FM 105.3 MHz (AC) 8930 Four Winds Dr Suite 500 *Web:* www.magic105.com	San Antonio	TX	78239	210-646-0105	871-6116
KSTX-FM 89.1 MHz (NPR) 8401 Data Point Dr Suite 800 *Web:* www.tpr.org ■ *E-mail:* kstx@tpr.org	San Antonio	TX	78229	210-614-8977	614-8983
KTFM-FM 102.7 MHz (CHR) 4050 Eisenhauer Rd *Web:* www.ktfm.com ■ *E-mail:* janitor@ktfm.com	San Antonio	TX	78218	210-599-5500	599-5588
KTSA-AM 550 kHz (N/T) 4050 Eisenhauer Rd *Web:* www.ktsa.com	San Antonio	TX	78218	210-599-5500	599-5588
KXTN-AM 1310 kHz (N/T) 1777 NE Loop 410 Suite 400	San Antonio	TX	78217	210-829-1075	804-7820
KXTN-FM 107.5 MHz (Span) 1777 NE Loop 410 Suite 400	San Antonio	TX	78217	210-829-1075	804-7820
KZEP-FM 104.5 MHz (CR) 427 E 9th St *Web:* www.kzep.com	San Antonio	TX	78215	210-226-6444	225-5736
WOAI-AM 1200 kHz (N/T) 6222 NW IH-10 *Web:* www.woai.com ■ *E-mail:* woai@texas.net	San Antonio	TX	78201	210-736-9700	436-9748

San Antonio (Cont'd)

— Colleges/Universities —

Name / Address	City	State	ZIP	Phone	Fax
Alamo Community College District					
811 W Houston St	San Antonio	TX	78207	210-220-1500	220-1584*
Fax: Acctg ■ *Web:* www.accd.edu					
ITT Technical Institute					
5700 Northwest Pkwy	San Antonio	TX	78249	210-694-4612	694-4651
TF: 800-880-0570 ■ *Web:* www.itt-tech.edu					
Our Lady of the Lake University					
411 SW 24th St	San Antonio	TX	78207	210-434-6711	431-4036
TF: 800-436-6558 ■ *Web:* www.ollusa.edu					
■ *E-mail:* hamid@lake.ollusa.edu					
Palo Alto College 1400 W Villaret	San Antonio	TX	78224	210-921-5000	921-5310
Web: accd.edu/pac/pacmain/pachp.htm ■ *E-mail:* pacinfo@accd.edu					
Saint Mary's University					
1 Camino Santa Maria St	San Antonio	TX	78228	210-436-3327	431-6742
Web: www.stmarytx.edu					
Saint Philip's College 1801 ML King Dr	San Antonio	TX	78203	210-531-3200	531-3235
Web: www.accd.edu/spc/					
San Antonio College					
1300 San Pedro Ave	San Antonio	TX	78212	210-733-2000	733-2579
Web: www.accd.edu/sac/					
Texas Lutheran University 1000 W Court St	Seguin	TX	78155	830-372-8000	372-8096
Web: www.txlutheran.edu ■ *E-mail:* admissions@txlutheran.edu					
Trinity University 715 Stadium Dr	San Antonio	TX	78212	210-999-7011	999-8164
TF Admissions: 800-874-6489 ■ *Web:* www.trinity.edu					
■ *E-mail:* admissions@trinity.edu					
University of Texas San Antonio					
6900 North Loop 1604 W	San Antonio	TX	78249	210-458-4011	458-4571
Web: www.utsa.edu					
University of the Incarnate Word					
4301 Broadway St	San Antonio	TX	78209	210-829-6000	829-3921
Web: www.uiw.edu					

— Hospitals —

Name / Address	City	State	ZIP	Phone	Fax
Audie L Murphy Memorial Veterans					
Hospital 7400 Merton Minter Blvd	San Antonio	TX	78284	210-617-5300	617-5195
Baptist Medical Center 111 Dallas St	San Antonio	TX	78205	210-297-7000	297-0701
Christus Santa Rosa Children's Hospital					
519 W Houston	San Antonio	TX	78207	210-704-2011	704-2015
Web: www.santarosahealth.org/9SRchildrenhospital.html					
Christus Santa Rosa Health Care					
519 W Houston	San Antonio	TX	78207	210-704-2011	704-2015
Web: www.santarosahealth.org					
Christus Santa Rosa Health Center					
Northwest 2827 Babcock Rd	San Antonio	TX	78229	210-705-6300	705-6170*
*Fax: Admitting					
Methodist Specialty & Transplant Hospital					
8026 Floyd Curl Dr	San Antonio	TX	78229	210-692-8110	692-8303
Web: www.mhshealth.com/facilities/sacomm/index.html					
Metropolitan Methodist Hospital					
1310 McCullough Ave	San Antonio	TX	78212	210-208-2200	208-2657*
*Fax: Admitting ■ *Web:* www.mhshealth.com/facilities/metro					
Nix Health Care System 414 Navarro St	San Antonio	TX	78205	210-271-1800	271-2023
Northeast Baptist Hospital					
8811 Village Dr	San Antonio	TX	78217	210-297-2000	297-0264
Northeast Methodist Hospital					
12412 Judson Rd	San Antonio	TX	78233	210-650-4949	590-3535
Web: www.mhshealth.com/facilities/nemeth					
Saint Luke's Baptist Hospital					
7930 Floyd Curl Dr	San Antonio	TX	78229	210-297-5000	297-0501
Southeast Baptist Hospital					
4214 E Southcross	San Antonio	TX	78222	210-297-3000	297-0312
Southwest General Hospital					
7400 Barlite Blvd	San Antonio	TX	78224	210-921-2000	921-3501
Southwest Texas Methodist Hospital					
7700 Floyd Curl Dr	San Antonio	TX	78229	210-575-4000	575-4950*
*Fax: Admitting					
■ *Web:* www.mhshealth.com/facilities/methodist/index.html					
University Health System					
4502 Medical Dr	San Antonio	TX	78229	210-358-4000	358-4090

— Attractions —

Name / Address	City	State	ZIP	Phone	Fax
Alamo The 300 Alamo Plaza	San Antonio	TX	78205	210-225-1391	229-1343
Web: www.thealamo.org ■ *E-mail:* curator@swbell.net					
Arneson River Theatre					
418 Villita St La Villita	San Antonio	TX	78205	210-207-8610	207-4390
Blue Star Arts Complex 116 Blue Star	San Antonio	TX	78204	210-227-6960	229-9412
Brackenridge Park 950 E Hildebrand	San Antonio	TX	78212	210-207-3000	207-3045
Carver Community Cultural Center					
226 N Hackberry	San Antonio	TX	78202	210-207-7211	207-4412
Cascade Caverns Park					
226 Cascade Caverns Rd	Boerne	TX	78015	830-755-8080	
Cowboy Museum & Gallery					
209 Alamo Plaza	San Antonio	TX	78205	210-229-1257	223-3711
Fort Sam Houston Museum &					
National Historic Landmark					
1207 Stanley Rd	Fort Sam Houston	TX	78234	210-221-1886	221-1311
Friedrich Emilie & Albert Park					
21480 Milsa	San Antonio	TX	78283	210-207-8480	
Guadalupe Cultural Arts Center					
1300 Guadalupe St	San Antonio	TX	78207	210-271-3151	271-3480
Web: www.guadalupeculturalarts.org ■ *E-mail:* guadarts@aol.com					
Institute of Texan Cultures					
801 S Bowie HemisFair Pk	San Antonio	TX	78205	210-458-2300	458-2205
Web: www.texancultures.utsa.edu/					
Jose Antonio Navarro State Historic Site					
228 S Laredo St	San Antonio	TX	78207	210-226-4801	
Josephine Theatre 339 W Josephine St	San Antonio	TX	78212	210-734-4646	734-0077
King William Historic District					
1032 S Alamo	San Antonio	TX	78210	210-227-8786	227-8030
La Villita 418 Villita St	San Antonio	TX	78205	210-207-8610	207-4390
Web: hotx.com/sa/lavillita/					
Lila Cockrell Theatre 200 E Market St	San Antonio	TX	78205	210-207-8500	223-1495
Web: www.ci.sat.tx.us/convfac/lila.htm					
Lone Star Brewing Co Inc					
600 Lone Star Blvd	San Antonio	TX	78204	210-226-8301	270-9430
Lonestar Buckhorn Museum					
318 E Houston St	San Antonio	TX	78205	210-247-4000	247-4020
Web: www.buckhornmuseum.com/					
Majestic Theatre 208 E Houston St	San Antonio	TX	78205	210-226-5700	226-3377
Web: www.themajestic.com/theatre.htm					
Marion Koogler McNay Art Museum					
6000 N New Braunfels Ave	San Antonio	TX	78209	210-824-5368	824-0218
Web: www.mcnayart.org					
Mission San Jose 701 E Pyron Ave	San Antonio	TX	78214	210-922-0543	
Natural Bridge Caverns					
26495 Natural Bridge Caverns Rd	San Antonio	TX	78266	210-651-6101	438-7432*
*Fax Area Code: 830 ■ *Web:* www.naturalbridgetexas.com/caverns/					
Natural Bridge Wildlife Ranch					
26515 Natural Bridge Caverns Rd	San Antonio	TX	78266	830-438-7400	438-3494
Nelson A Rockefeller Center for Latin					
American Art 200 W Jones Ave	San Antonio	TX	78215	210-978-8100	978-8134
Pabst Brewing Co 312 Pearl Pkwy	San Antonio	TX	78215	210-226-0231	226-2512
Web: www.pabst.com					
Pioneer Museum 3805 Broadway St	San Antonio	TX	78209	210-822-9011	666-5607
Plaza Theatre of Wax 301 Alamo Plaza	San Antonio	TX	78205	210-224-9299	224-1516
Web: www.tourtexas.com/ripleys/plazatheatreofwax.html					
Ripley's Believe It or Not! Museum					
301 Alamo Plaza	San Antonio	TX	78205	210-224-9299	224-1516
Web: www.tourtexas.com/ripleys/plazatheatreofwax.html					
River Walk Downtown San Antonio	San Antonio	TX	78205	210-207-8480	
Rivercenter IMAX					
849 E Commerce St Rivercenter Mall	San Antonio	TX	78205	210-225-4629	354-4629*
*Fax Area Code: 800 ■ *Web:* www.imax-sa.com					
■ *E-mail:* IMAX@imax-sa.com					
San Antonio Botanical Gardens					
555 Funston Pl	San Antonio	TX	78209	210-207-3250	207-3274
Web: www.sabot.org					
San Antonio Children's Museum					
305 E Houston St	San Antonio	TX	78205	210-212-4453	242-1313
San Antonio Missions National Historic					
Park 2202 Roosevelt Ave	San Antonio	TX	78210	210-534-8833	534-1106
Web: www.nps.gov/saan/					
San Antonio Museum of Art					
200 W Jones Ave	San Antonio	TX	78215	210-978-8100	978-8134
Web: www.samuseum.org/					
San Antonio Symphony Orchestra					
222 E Houston Majestic Bldg					
Suite 200	San Antonio	TX	78205	210-554-1000	554-1008
Web: www.sasymphony.org/ ■ *E-mail:* sasympho@swbell.net					
San Antonio Zoological Gardens &					
Aquarium 3903 N Saint Mary's St	San Antonio	TX	78212	210-734-7184	734-7291
Web: www.sazoo-aq.org/ ■ *E-mail:* sazoo@sazoo-aq.org					
San Pedro Playhouse					
San Pedro Pk & Ashby	San Antonio	TX	78212	210-733-7258	734-2651
Sea World of Texas 10500 Sea World Dr	San Antonio	TX	78251	210-523-3000	523-3199*
*Fax: Mktg ■ *TF:* 800-722-2762					
■ *Web:* www.seaworld.com/seaworld/sw_texas/swtframe.html					
Six Flags Fiesta Texas 17000 IH-10 W	San Antonio	TX	78257	210-697-5000	697-5415
TF: 800-473-4378 ■ *Web:* www.sixflags.com/sanantonio					

San Antonio — Attractions (Cont'd)

				Phone	*Fax*
Spanish Governor's Palace 105 Military Plaza	San Antonio	TX	78205	210-224-0601	
Splashtown 3600 I-35 N *Web:* www.splashtownsa.com	San Antonio	TX	78219	210-227-1100	225-7946
Tower of the Americas 600 HemisFair Pkwy	San Antonio	TX	78205	210-207-8615	
Witte Museum 3801 Broadway St *Web:* www.wittemuseum.org	San Antonio	TX	78209	210-357-1900	357-1882
WW McAllister Park 13102 Jones-Maltsberger	San Antonio	TX	78283	210-207-8480	

SPORTS TEAMS & FACILITIES

				Phone	*Fax*
Freeman Coliseum 3201 E Houston St *Web:* www.freeman-coliseum.com	San Antonio	TX	78219	210-226-1177	226-5081
San Antonio Iguanas (hockey) 3201 E Houston Freeman Coliseum *Web:* www.sa-iguanas.com	Houston	TX	78219	210-527-0009	670-0001
San Antonio Missions (baseball) Hwy 90 & Calleghan Rd Nelson Wolff Stadium *Web:* www.samissions.com	San Antonio	TX	78227	210-675-7275	670-0001
San Antonio Speedway 14901 S Hwy 16	San Antonio	TX	78264	210-628-1499	
San Antonio Spurs 100 Montana St Alamodome **Fax:* PR ■ *Web:* www.nba.com/spurs	San Antonio	TX	78203	210-554-7787	554-7701*

— Events —

	Phone
Alamo Bowl (December 30)	210-226-2695
Alamo Irish Festival (mid-March)	210-344-4317
Artesanos del Pueblo (mid-November)	210-922-3218
Carnaval del Rio (early February)	210-227-4262
Celebrate San Antonio (December 31)	210-207-8480
Clogger's Showcase (early May)	210-492-8700
Encanto en la Mision (mid-June-late July)	210-822-2453
Festival de Animales (late April)	210-734-7184
Festival of the Armed Forces Air Show (late May)	210-207-6700
Fiesta Arts Fair (mid-April)	210-224-1848
Fiesta De Las Luminarias (December)	210-227-4262
Fiesta del Mercado (mid-late April)	210-207-8600
Fiesta Gardenfest (late April)	210-222-1521
Fiesta Mariachi Festival (late April)	210-227-4262
Fiesta San Antonio (mid-April)	210-227-5191
Fiestas Patrias (mid-September)	210-207-8600
Floating Christmas Pageant (early-mid-December)	210-225-0000
Freedom Fest (early July)	210-207-8600
Great Country River Festival (mid-January)	210-227-4262
Haymarket Festival (early October)	210-207-8600
Home & Garden Show (February & September)	210-207-3663
JazzsAlive (late September)	210-207-8480
Juneteenth Festival (mid-June)	210-533-4383
Latino Laugh Festival (early June)	800-447-3372
Lighting Ceremony & Riverwalk Holiday Parade (late November-early January)	210-227-4262
Lowrider Custom Car & Truck Festival (early April)	210-432-1896
Mission San Jose Spring Festival (mid-April)	210-922-0543
Musica San Antonio: A Festival Celebration (early June)	210-434-6711
National Skeet Shooting Association Showcase (mid-May)	210-688-3371
National Sporting Clays Championship (mid-September)	210-688-3371
Oktoberfest San Antonio (early-mid-October)	210-222-1521
Remembering the Alamo Living History Weekend (early March)	210-650-3343
Return of the Chili Queens (late May)	210-207-8600
River Walk Arts & Crafts Fair (mid-December)	210-229-2104
River Walk Holiday Festival (late November-late December)	210-227-4262
River Walk Mud Festival & Mud Parade (mid-January)	210-227-4262
Saint Patrick's River Dyeing (mid-March)	210-497-8435
Saint Patrick's Street Parade (mid-March)	210-497-8435
San Antonio CineFestival (early June)	210-271-3151
San Antonio Conjunto Shootout (mid-July)	210-246-9626
San Antonio Marathon (early November)	210-732-1332
San Antonio Stock Show & Rodeo (early-mid-February)	210-225-5851
Spring Break Out Extreme (mid-March)	210-697-5050
Starving Artists Show (early April)	210-226-3593
Taste of New Orleans (mid-April)	210-637-8328
Tejano Conjunto Festival (mid-May)	210-271-3151
Tejano Music Awards Fanfair & Festival (early March)	210-222-8862
Texas Folklife Festival (early August)	210-458-2300
Viva Botanica (mid-April)	210-207-3255
Westin Texas Open at La Cantera (late September)	210-341-0823
Wurstfest (late October-early November)	800-221-4369
Zoo Boo (October 31)	210-734-7184

Utah

Population (1999): 2,129,836 **Area (sq mi): 84,904**

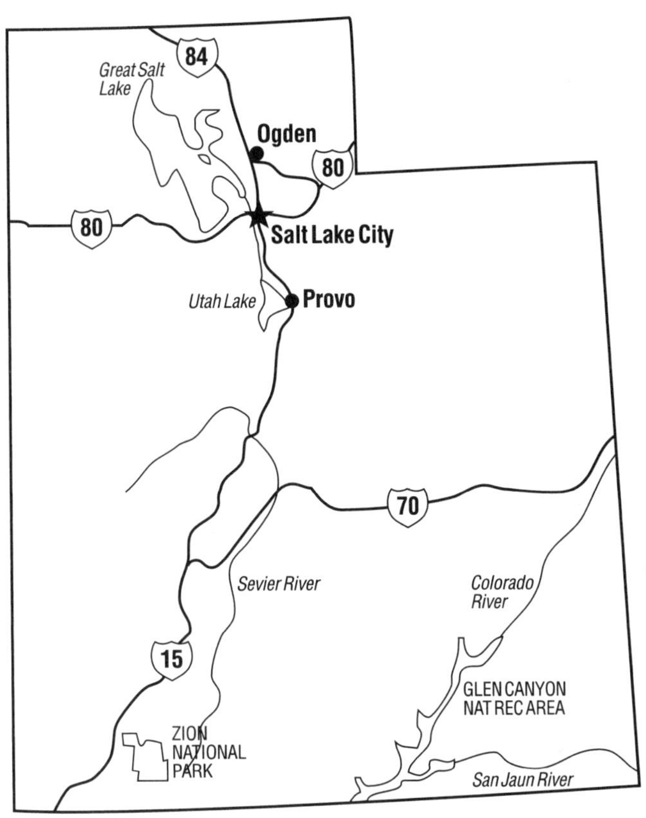

— State Information Sources —

				Phone	Fax
Utah Community & Economic Development Dept					
324 S State St Suite 500	Salt Lake City	UT	84111	801-538-8700	538-8888
Web: www.dced.state.ut.us					
Utah Parks & Recreation Div					
PO Box 146001	Salt Lake City	UT	84114	801-538-7220	538-7378
Web: www.nr.state.ut.us/parks/utahstpk.htm					
Utah State Government Information				801-538-3000	
Web: www.state.ut.us					
Utah State Library					
2150 S 300 West Suite 16	Salt Lake City	UT	84115	801-468-6777	468-6767
Web: www.state.lib.ut.us					
Utah Travel Council					
300 N State St Council Hall Capitol Hill	Salt Lake City	UT	84114	801-538-1030	538-1399
TF: 800-200-1160 ■ *Web:* www.utah.com					

ON-LINE RESOURCES

Cybertourist Utah	www.cybertourist.com/utah.shtml
Discover Utah	www.infowest.com/Utah
Rough Guide Travel Utah	travel.roughguides.com/content/1240/index.htm
Search Utah	searchutah.com
Travel.org-Utah	travel.org/utah.html
Utah @ Travel Notes	www.travelnotes.org/NorthAmerica/utah.htm
Utah Adventures	www.utahadventure.com
Utah Cities	dir.yahoo.com/Regional/U_S__States/Utah/Cities
Utah Counties & Regions	dir.yahoo.com/Regional/U_S__States/Utah/Counties_and_Regions
Utah Online	www.utah.com
Utah Online Highways	www.utohwy.com
Utah Pages	utahpages.com
Utah Recreation	www.utahrec.com
Utah Scenario	scenariousa.dstylus.com/ut/indexf.htm
Utah Travel & Tourism Guide	www.travel-library.com/north_america/usa/utah/index.html
Web Utah	www.webutah.com
What's Up Utah!	www.whatsuputah.com
Yahoo! Get Local Utah	dir.yahoo.com/Regional/U_S__States/Utah

— Cities Profiled —

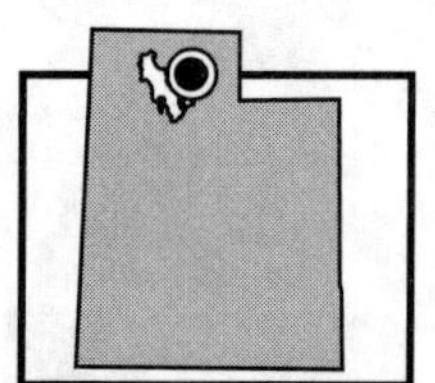

Ogden

Ogden, Utah is just 35 miles north of Salt Lake City, in Weber County, with the Wasatch Mountains to the east of the city and the Great Salt Lake to the west. Major employers in the area include Thiokol Corporation, which has its headquarters in Ogden, and Hill Air Force Base, which abuts Weber County to the south. In addition to three ski resorts - Powder Mountain, Snowbasin, and Nordic Valley - Ogden has excellent areas for snowmobiling, tubing, and cross-country skiing. Most waters in the area are open year-round for fishing, and good trout fishing is available right in downtown Ogden. The fall color route up Ogden Canyon to Monte Cristo Park is considered one of the finest displays in Utah.

Population	66,507	**Longitude**	111-97-31 W
Area (Land)	26.1 sq mi	**County**	Weber
Area (Water)	0 sq mi	**Time Zone**	MST
Elevation	4299 ft	**Area Code/s**	801
Latitude	41-22-31 N		

— Average Temperatures and Precipitation —

TEMPERATURES

	Jan	Feb	Mar	Apr	May	Jun	Jul	Aug	Sep	Oct	Nov	Dec
High	38	45	53	63	73	84	92	90	80	67	51	39
Low	20	25	31	39	47	56	63	61	52	41	31	22

PRECIPITATION

	Jan	Feb	Mar	Apr	May	Jun	Jul	Aug	Sep	Oct	Nov	Dec
Inches	2.0	1.9	2.3	2.6	2.5	1.6	0.8	1.0	1.7	1.9	2.1	2.1

— Important Phone Numbers —

	Phone		Phone
AAA	801-476-1666	**Poison Control Center**	800-456-7707
Emergency	911	**Road Conditions**	800-492-2400
Medical Referral	801-479-2920	**Time/Temp**	801-621-8463

— Information Sources —

				Phone	Fax
Better Business Bureau Serving Utah 5673 S Redwood Rd	Salt Lake City	UT	84123	801-892-6009	892-6002
Web: www.saltlakecity.bbb.org					
Chamber Ogden/Weber 2393 Washington Blvd.	Ogden	UT	84401	801-621-8300	392-7609
TF: 800-255-8824 ■ *Web:* www.chamberogdenweber.org					
David Eccles Conference Center 2415 Washington Blvd.	Ogden	UT	84401	801-395-3200	395-3201
TF: 800-237-2690 ■ *Web:* www.oecenter.com					
Golden Spike Arena Events Center 1000 N 1200 West	Ogden	UT	84404	801-399-8544	392-1995
TF: 800-442-7362					
Ogden City Hall 2484 Washington Blvd	Ogden	UT	84401	801-629-8150	629-8154
Web: www.ogdencity.com					
Ogden Community Development Dept 2484 Washington Blvd.	Ogden	UT	84401	801-629-8901	629-8902
Web: www.ogdencity.com/commdev					
Ogden Mayor 2484 Washington Blvd Suite 300	Ogden	UT	84401	801-629-8100	629-8154
Web: www.ogdencity.com/admin/mayor/mayorpg.stm					
Ogden/Weber Convention & Visitors Bureau 2501 Wall Ave Union Stn.	Ogden	UT	84401	801-627-8288	399-0783
TF: 800-255-8824 ■ *Web:* www.ogdencvb.org/ ■ *E-mail:* info@ogdencvb.org					
Weber County 2380 Washington Blvd	Ogden	UT	84401	801-399-8610	399-8314
Web: www.co.weber.ut.us ■ *E-mail:* services@co.weber.ut.us					
Weber County Library 2464 Jefferson Ave	Ogden	UT	84401	801-627-6913	399-8519
Web: www.weberpl.lib.ut.us					

On-Line Resources

City Knowledge Ogden	www.cityknowledge.com/ut_ogden.htm
Excite.com Ogden City Guide	www.excite.com/travel/countries/united_states/utah/ogden
Ogden Page	www.ogden-ut.com

— Transportation Services —

AIRPORTS

■ **Ogden-Hinckley Airport (OGD)** — *Phone*

1 mile SW of downtown (approx 5 minutes) 801-629-8251
Web: www.ogdencity.com/pubworks/airport/airport.stm

Airport Transportation

	Phone
Yellow Cab $12 fare to downtown	801-394-9411

Charter Airlines

	Phone		Phone
Ogden Air Service	801-394-3400	**Spectrasonics Aviation**	801-392-7533

■ **Salt Lake City International Airport (SLC)** — *Phone*

34 miles S of downtown Ogden (approx 45 minutes) 801-575-2400

Airport Transportation

	Phone
Express Shuttle $23 fare to downtown Ogden	801-485-4100

Commercial Airlines

	Phone		Phone
America West	800-235-9292	**Northwest**	800-225-2525
American	800-433-7300	**SkyWest**	800-453-9417
Continental	800-525-0280	**TWA**	800-221-2000
Delta	800-221-1212	**United**	800-241-6522

Charter Airlines

	Phone		Phone
Barken International	801-539-7700	**D & D Aviation**	800-532-0991

CAR RENTALS

	Phone		Phone
Advantage	801-531-1199	**Dollar**	801-575-2580
Alamo	801-575-2211	**Enterprise-Ogden**	801-399-5555
All American-Ogden	801-394-3828	**Hertz**	801-575-2683
Avis	801-575-2847	**Hertz-Ogden**	801-621-6500
Avis-Ogden	801-394-5984	**National**	801-575-2277
Budget	801-575-2821	**Thrifty**	801-595-6677
CarTemps USA	801-264-9929		

LIMO/TAXI

	Phone		Phone
Airport Limousine	801-485-1400	**Ute Cab**	801-359-7788
Classic Limousine	801-774-6027	**Yellow Cab**	801-394-9411
Legend Limousine	801-296-0233		

MASS TRANSIT

	Phone
Utah Transit Authority $1 Base fare	801-287-4636

RAIL/BUS

				Phone
Greyhound Bus Station 2501 Grant Ave	Ogden	UT	84401	801-394-5573
TF: 800-231-2222				

Ogden (Cont'd)

— Accommodations —

HOTELS, MOTELS, RESORTS

Name / Address	City	State	Zip	Phone	Fax
Best Rest The 1206 W 21st St	Ogden	UT	84401	801-393-8644	399-0954
TF: 800-343-8644					
Best Western High Country Inn 1335 W 1200 South	Ogden	UT	84404	801-394-9474	392-6589
TF: 800-528-1234					
Big Z Motel 1123 W 2100 South	Ogden	UT	84401	801-394-6632	
Circle R Motel 5223 S 1900 West	Roy	UT	84405	801-773-7432	
Colonial Motel 1269 Washington Blvd.	Ogden	UT	84404	801-399-5851	
Comfort Suites 1150 W 2150 S	Ogden	UT	84401	801-621-2545	627-4782
TF: 800-629-8444					
Holiday Inn 3306 Washington Blvd	Ogden	UT	84401	801-399-5671	621-0321
TF: 800-999-6841					
Jackson Fork Inn 7345 E 900 South	Huntsville	UT	84317	801-745-0051	
TF: 800-255-0672					
Millstream Motel 1450 Washington Blvd	Ogden	UT	84404	801-394-9425	
Motel 6 1455 Washington Blvd.	Ogden	UT	84401	801-627-4560	392-1878
TF: 800-466-8356					
Ogden Lodge 2110 Washington Blvd.	Ogden	UT	84401	801-394-4563	394-4568
TF: 800-578-7878					
Ogden Marriott 247 24th St	Ogden	UT	84401	801-627-1190	394-6312
TF: 800-421-7599					
Radisson Suite Hotel 2510 Washington Blvd	Ogden	UT	84401	801-627-1900	394-5342
TF: 800-333-3333					
Sleep Inn 1155 S 1700 West	Ogden	UT	84404	801-731-6500	
TF: 800-753-3746					
Super 8 Motel 1508 W 2100 South	Ogden	UT	84401	801-731-7100	731-2627
TF: 800-800-8000					
Western Colony Inn 234 24th St	Ogden	UT	84401	801-627-1332	392-0600

— Restaurants —

Name / Address	City	State	Zip	Phone
Allies American Grill (American) 247 24th St	Ogden	UT	84401	801-627-1190
Angelo's (Italian) 130 25th St	Ogden	UT	84401	801-629-0911
Athenian Souvlaki (Greek) 252 25th St	Ogden	UT	84401	801-621-4911
Bamboo Noodle Parlor (Japanese) 2426 Grant Ave	Ogden	UT	84401	801-394-6091
Bavarian Chalet (German) 4387 Harrison Blvd	Ogden	UT	84403	801-479-7561
Branding Iron Restaurant (American) 1310 Wall Ave	Ogden	UT	84401	801-621-5535
Cajun Skillet (Cajun) 2550 Washington Blvd	Ogden	UT	84401	801-393-7702
Chaparro's Fine Mexican Food (Mexican) 3981 Wall Ave	Ogden	UT	84405	801-392-7777
Delights of Ogden (American) 258 25th St	Ogden	UT	84401	801-394-1111
El Matador (Mexican) 2564 Ogden Ave	Ogden	UT	84401	801-393-3151
El Rancho Mexicali (Mexican) 924 Washington Blvd	Ogden	UT	84404	801-393-7227
Fiesta Mexicana (Mexican) 236 24th St	Ogden	UT	84404	801-394-3310
Gray Cliff Lodge (American) 508 Ogden Canyon	Ogden	UT	84401	801-392-6775
Greenery Restaurant (American) 1875 Valley Dr	Ogden	UT	84401	801-392-1777
Jackson Fork Inn (Steak/Seafood) 7345 E 900 South	Huntsville	UT	84317	801-745-0051
La Cabana (Mexican) 2263 Grant Ave Ogden City Plaza	Ogden	UT	84401	801-392-3535
La Ferrovia Ristorante (Italian) 234 25th St	Ogden	UT	84401	801-394-8628
Mansion House Restaurant (American) 2350 Adams Ave	Ogden	UT	84401	801-392-2225
Pantheon Cafe (Greek) 1045 N Washington Blvd	Ogden	UT	84404	801-782-5303
Prairie Schooner Restaurant (Steak/Seafood) 445 Park Blvd	Ogden	UT	84404	801-621-5511
Star Noodle Parlor (Chinese) 225 25th St.	Ogden	UT	84401	801-394-6331
Timber Mine (Steak/Seafood) 1701 Park Blvd	Ogden	UT	84401	801-393-2155
Union Grill (American) 2501 Wall Ave	Ogden	UT	84401	801-621-2830
Western Sunrise Cafe (American) 1071 W 27th St	Ogden	UT	84403	801-392-6603

— Goods and Services —

SHOPPING

Name / Address	City	State	Zip	Phone	Fax
Downtown Ogden 2404 Washington Blvd	Ogden	UT	84401	801-394-6634	394-6647
Newgate Mall 36th St & Wall Ave	Ogden	UT	84405	801-621-1161	
Ogden City Mall 24th St & Washington Blvd	Ogden	UT	84401	801-399-1314	
Ogden's Historic 25th St Wall & Grant Aves	Ogden	UT	84401		

BANKS

Name / Address	City	State	Zip	Phone	Fax
Bank of Utah 2605 Washington Blvd	Ogden	UT	84401	801-625-3500	625-3520
First Security Bank 2404 Washington Blvd.	Ogden	UT	84402	801-626-9500	626-9612
Washington Mutual Bank 4185 Harrison Blvd.	Ogden	UT	84403	801-626-2258	626-2225

BUSINESS SERVICES

Name	Phone	Name	Phone
Airborne Express	800-247-2676	**Kinko's**	801-393-0120
Altres Labor Services	801-625-0607	**Mail Boxes Etc**	800-789-4623
BAX Global	800-225-5229	**Manpower Temporary Services**	801-621-5228
DHL Worldwide Express	800-225-5345	**Post Office**	800-275-8777
Federal Express	800-238-5355	**UPS**	800-742-5877

— Media —

PUBLICATIONS

Name / Address	City	State	Zip	Phone	Fax
Standard-Examiner‡ 455 23rd St	Ogden	UT	84401	801-625-4200	625-4508
TF: 800-234-5505 ■ *Web:* www.standard.net					

‡Daily newspapers

TELEVISION

Name / Address	City	State	Zip	Phone	Fax
KSL-TV Ch 5 (NBC) PO Box 1160	Salt Lake City	UT	84110	801-575-5555	575-5560
Web: www.ksl.com/TV/ ■ *E-mail:* eyewitness@ksl.com					
KSTU-TV Ch 13 (Fox) 5020 W Amelia Earhart Dr	Salt Lake City	UT	84116	801-532-1300	537-5335
Web: www.fox13.com					
KTVX-TV Ch 4 (ABC) 1760 Fremont Dr	Salt Lake City	UT	84104	801-975-4444	975-4442
Web: www.4utah.com ■ *E-mail:* news@4utah.com					
KUED-TV Ch 7 (PBS) 101 Wasatch Dr	Salt Lake City	UT	84112	801-581-7777	585-5096
Web: eddy.media.utah.edu/					
KUTV-TV Ch 2 (CBS) 2185 S 3600 West	West Valley City	UT	84119	801-973-3000	973-3349
Web: www.kutv.com					
KUWB-TV Ch 30 (WB) 6135 S Stratler Ave.	Murray	UT	84107	801-281-0330	281-4503

RADIO

Name / Address	City	State	Zip	Phone	Fax
KALL-AM 910 kHz (N/T) 2801 S Decker Lake Dr	West Valley City	UT	84119	801-575-5255	908-1499
Web: www.kall910.com					
KANN-AM 1120 kHz (Rel) PO Box 3880	Syracuse	UT	84409	801-776-0249	
KBZN-FM 97.9 MHz (NAC) 257 E 200 South Suite 400	Salt Lake City	UT	84111	801-670-9079	364-8068
Web: www.kbzn.com ■ *E-mail:* breeze@kbzn.com					
KCPX-FM 105.7 MHz (Oldies) 4001 S 700 East Suite 800	Salt Lake City	UT	84107	801-262-9797	262-9772
E-mail: mountain@xmission.com					
KDYL-AM 1280 kHz (Nost) 57 W South Temple Suite 700	Salt Lake City	UT	84101	801-524-2600	521-9234
KENZ-FM 107.5 MHz (AAA) 434 Bearcat Dr	Salt Lake City	UT	84115	801-485-6700	487-5369
Web: www.1075.com					
KFAN-AM 1320 kHz (Sports) 434 Bearcat Dr	Salt Lake City	UT	84115	801-485-6700	487-5369
Web: www.1320kfan.com ■ *E-mail:* info@1320kfan.com					
KLO-AM 1430 kHz (Nost) 4155 Harrison Blvd Suite 206	Ogden	UT	84403	801-627-1430	627-0317
KNRS-AM 570 kHz (N/T) 2801 S Decker Lake Dr	Salt Lake City	UT	84119	801-908-1300	908-1459
KOSY-FM 106.5 (Nost) 4001 S 700 East Suite 800	Salt Lake City	UT	84107	801-262-9797	262-9772
KRAR-FM 106.9 MHz (Rock) 4455 S 5500 West	Hooper	UT	84315	801-731-9000	731-9666
KSFI-FM 100.3 MHz (AC) 57 W South Temple Suite 700	Salt Lake City	UT	84101	801-524-2600	521-9234
Web: www.fm100.com ■ *E-mail:* info@fm100.com					
KSOP-AM 1370 kHz (Ctry) 1285 W 2320 South	Salt Lake City	UT	84119	801-972-1043	974-0868
KSOS-AM 800 kHz (Oldies) 4455 S 5500 West	Hooper	UT	84315	801-731-9000	731-9666
Web: www.ksos.com ■ *E-mail:* ksos@ksos.com					
KUBL-FM 93.3 MHz (Ctry) 434 Bearcat Dr	Salt Lake City	UT	84115	801-485-6700	487-5369
Web: www.xmission.com/~bull ■ *E-mail:* bull@xmission.com					
KUER-FM 90.1 MHz (NPR) 101 S Wasatch Dr.	Salt Lake City	UT	84112	801-581-6625	
E-mail: fm90@media.utah.edu					
KURR-FM 99.5 MHz (Rock) 2801 S Decker Lake Dr	West Valley City	UT	84119	801-908-1300	908-1499
Web: www.rock99.com					
KWCR-FM 88.1 MHz (CHR) 2188 University Cir	Ogden	UT	84408	801-626-6450	626-6935

Ogden — Radio (Cont'd)

				Phone	Fax
KXRK-FM 96.3 MHz (Alt) 165 S West Temple 2nd Fl. *Web:* www.x96.com	Salt Lake City	UT	84101	801-521-9696	364-1811

— Colleges/Universities —

				Phone	Fax
Stevens Henager College 2168 Washington Blvd. *TF:* 800-371-7791 ■ *Web:* www.stevenshenager.com	Ogden	UT	84401	801-394-7791	393-1748
Weber State University 3750 Harrison Blvd *Web:* www.weber.edu	Ogden	UT	84408	801-626-6000	626-6747

— Hospitals —

				Phone	Fax
Columbia Ogden Regional Medical Center 5475 S 500 East *Web:* www.cormc.com	Ogden	UT	84405	801-479-2111	479-2091
McKay-Dee Hospital Center 3939 Harrison Blvd	Ogden	UT	84409	801-627-2800	625-2032

— Attractions —

				Phone	Fax
Bear River Migratory Bird Refuge Forest St 16 miles W of Brigham City	Brigham City	UT	84302	435-723-5887	
Browning Firearms Museum 2501 Wall Ave Union Stn *Web:* www.ogden-ut.com/attractions/UnionStation02.html	Ogden	UT	84401	801-393-9882	629-8555
Browning-Kimball Car Collection 25th St & Wall Ave Union Stn	Ogden	UT	84401	801-629-8444	
Collett Art Gallery 2001 University Cir Weber State University	Ogden	UT	84408	801-626-6420	626-6976
Daughters of the Utah Pioneers Museum 2148 Grant Ave.	Ogden	UT	84401	801-393-4460	
Downtown Ogden 2404 Washington Blvd	Ogden	UT	84401	801-394-6634	394-6647
Eccles Community Art Center 2580 Jefferson Ave	Ogden	UT	84401	801-392-6935	392-5295
Eccles George S Dinosaur Park 1544 E Park Blvd	Ogden	UT	84401	801-393-3466	399-0895
Eccles Spencer S & Hope F Railroad Center 25th St & Wall Ave Union Stn	Ogden	UT	84401	801-629-8444	
Fort Buenaventura State Park/Historic Site 2450 A Ave	Ogden	UT	84401	801-621-4808	392-2431
Golden Spike National Historic Site PO Box 897 *Web:* www.nps.gov/gosp/	Brigham City	UT	84302	435-471-2209	471-2341
Hill Aerospace Museum 7961 Wardleigh Rd Bldg 1955 *Web:* www.hill.af.mil/	Hill AFB	UT	84056	801-777-6818	
Layton/Ott Planetarium Weber State University Lind Lecture Hall 2nd Fl *Web:* www.physics.weber.edu	Ogden	UT	84408	801-626-6855	
Lorin Farr Park Canyon Rd & Gramercy Ave	Ogden	UT	84401	801-629-8284	
Millstream Car Museum 1450 Washington Blvd.	Ogden	UT	84404	801-394-9425	392-9145
Museum of Natural History Weber State University Lind Lecture Hall	Ogden	UT	84408	801-626-6653	
Natural History Museum 2501 Wall Ave Union Stn	Ogden	UT	84401	801-629-8444	
Nordic Valley Ski Resort 3567 Nordic Valley Way	Eden	UT	84310	801-392-0900	
Ogden Canyon SR 39	Ogden	UT	84404	801-627-8288	
Ogden Eccles Conference Center 2415 Washington Blvd. *TF:* 800-337-2690	Ogden	UT	84401	801-395-3200	395-3201
Ogden Nature Center 966 W 12th St.	Ogden	UT	84404	801-621-7595	621-1867
Ogden Symphony Ballet 2415 Washington Blvd Ogden Egyptian Theatre *Web:* www.symphonyballet.org	Ogden	UT	84401	801-399-9214	612-0757
Powder Mountain Ski Resort PO Box 450	Eden	UT	84310	801-745-3772	745-3619
Powell Myra Gallery 2501 Wall Ave Union Stn.	Ogden	UT	84401	801-629-8444	
Roy Historical Museum 5550 S 1700 West	Roy	UT	84067	801-776-3626	
Saint Joseph's Catholic Church 514 24th St	Ogden	UT	84401	801-399-5627	399-5918
Shooting Star Saloon 7350 E 200 South	Huntsville	UT	84317	801-745-2002	
Snowbasin Ski Resort Hwy 226 17 miles E of Ogden	Huntsville	UT	84317	801-399-1135	
Terrace Plaza Playhouse 99 E 4700 South	Ogden	UT	84405	801-393-0070	
Treehouse Children's Museum 24th St & Washington Blvd Ogden City Mall *Web:* www.relia.net/~treehouse/ ■ *E-mail:* treehouse@relia.net	Ogden	UT	84401	801-394-9663	393-6820
Two-Bit Street Trolley 2501 Wall Ave **Fax Area Code:* 801	Ogden	UT	84401	800-255-8824	399-0783*
Union Station 2501 Wall Ave *Web:* www.ogden-ut.com/attractions/UnionStation.html	Ogden	UT	84401	801-629-8444	
Utah Musical Theatre 3401 University Cir Weber State University	Ogden	UT	84408	801-626-8500	626-6811
Utah State Railroad Museum 2501 Wall Ave Union Stn	Ogden	UT	84401	801-629-8444	625-4299
Wattis-Dumke Model Railroad Museum 2500 Wall Ave Union Stn	Ogden	UT	84401	801-629-8444	625-4299
Willard Bay State Park I-15 15 miles N of Ogden *TF:* 800-322-3770	Ogden	UT	84340	435-734-9494	734-2659

SPORTS TEAMS & FACILITIES

				Phone
Ogden Raptors (baseball) 2330 Lincoln Ave Lindquist Field *Web:* www.ogden-raptors.com	Ogden	UT	84401	801-393-2400

— Events —

	Phone
A Taste of Ogden (early June)	801-394-6634
Christmas Village (December)	801-629-8284
Festival of the American West (early August)	435-797-1143
First Night Ogden (December 31)	801-394-6634
Gem & Mineral Show (mid-March)	801-629-8444
Jazz Concert (early April)	801-626-8500
Ogden Christmas Parade (late November)	801-629-8242
Ogden Greek Festival (late September)	801-399-2231
Ogden Heritage Street Festival (mid-July)	801-629-8242
Ogden Pioneer Days Rodeo & Celebration (July)	801-629-8214
Solstice Celebration (mid-June)	801-621-7595
Storytelling Festival (mid-November)	801-626-8500
Weber County Fair (late July-August)	801-399-8711
Wildwoods Bash (mid-September)	801-621-7595

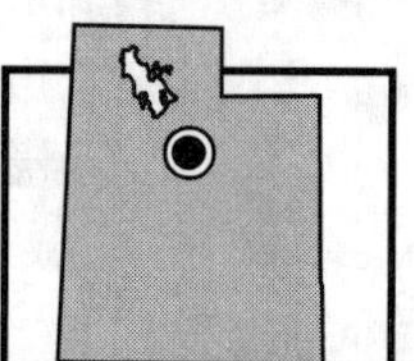

Provo

Scenic drives provide the best opportunity to view the attractions of Provo and the Utah County area. The Provo Canyon Byway winds through Provo Canyon all the way to Heber Valley. At the west end of Provo Canyon, Squaw Peak Trail offers views of the Utah Valley and a high-altitude mountain bike trek across the front of the Wasatch Mountains. Accessible also from the Byway are the Bridal Veil Falls and Skytram. The steepest passenger tram in the world, the Skytram provides aerial views of the double cataract falls, which drop 607 feet. At the top of Provo Canyon is Deer Creek Reservoir, a popular site for fishing, boating, and waterskiing. The Provo Canyon Byway continues past another scenic drive known as the Alpine Look Scenic Backway. The Backway is 24 miles long and accesses Timpanogos Cave National Monument, Mount Timpanogos hiking trails, and Robert Redford's Sundance Resort. Provo's Brigham Young University, with an enrollment of 27,000 students, is one of the largest private universities in the world.

Population	110,419	**Longitude**	111-64-79 W
Area (Land)	38.6 sq mi	**County**	Utah
Area (Water)	2.1 sq mi	**Time Zone**	MST
Elevation	4549 ft	**Area Code/s**	801
Latitude	40-24-88 N		

Provo (Cont'd)

— Average Temperatures and Precipitation —

TEMPERATURES

	Jan	Feb	Mar	Apr	May	Jun	Jul	Aug	Sep	Oct	Nov	Dec
High	36	44	52	61	72	83	92	89	79	66	51	38
Low	19	25	31	38	46	55	64	62	51	40	31	22

PRECIPITATION

	Jan	Feb	Mar	Apr	May	Jun	Jul	Aug	Sep	Oct	Nov	Dec
Inches	1.1	1.2	1.9	2.1	1.8	0.9	0.8	0.9	1.3	1.4	1.3	1.4

— Important Phone Numbers —

	Phone
AAA	801-225-4801
Emergency	911
Medical Referral	800-515-2220
Poison Control Center	800-456-7707
Road Conditions	801-964-6000
Time/Temp	801-373-9120
Weather	801-975-4499

— Information Sources —

	City	State	Zip	Phone	Fax
Better Business Bureau Serving Utah 5673 S Redwood Rd *Web:* www.saltlakecity.bbb.org	Salt Lake City	UT	84123	801-892-6009	892-6002
Mountainland Travel Region Office 586 E 800 North *Web:* www.mountainland.org	Orem	UT	84097	801-229-3800	229-3801
Provo City Hall 351 W Center St. *Web:* www.provo.org	Provo	UT	84601	801-852-6000	
Provo Economic Development Dept PO Box 1849 *Web:* www.provo.org/econdev	Provo	UT	84603	801-852-6161	375-1469
Provo Mayor 351 W Center St *Web:* www.provo.org/mayor ■ *E-mail:* provo.lbilling@state.ut.us	Provo	UT	84601	801-852-6100	852-6107
Provo Public Library 425 W Center St. *Web:* www.provo.lib.ut.us	Provo	UT	84601	801-852-6650	852-6670
Provo/Orem Chamber of Commerce 51 S University Ave Suite 215 *Web:* www.thechamber.org	Provo	UT	84601	801-379-2555	379-2557
Utah County PO Box 1847 *Web:* www.co.utah.ut.us	Provo	UT	84603	801-429-1000	429-1033
Utah County Convention & Visitors Bureau 51 S University Ave Suite 111 *TF:* 800-222-8824	Provo	UT	84601	801-370-8393	370-8050

On-Line Resources

Anthill City Guide Provo/Orem .... www.anthill.com/city.asp?city=provoorem
City Knowledge Provo .... www.cityknowledge.com/ut_provo.htm
Excite.com Provo City Guide .... www.excite.com/travel/countries/united_states/utah/provo

— Transportation Services —

AIRPORTS

	Phone
■ **Salt Lake City International Airport (SLC)** 50 miles N of downtown Provo (approx 80 minutes)	801-575-2400

Airport Transportation

	Phone
Cinderella's Airport Shuttle $25-35 fare to downtown Provo	801-373-7141
Express Shuttle $23 fare to downtown Provo	801-375-5533

Commercial Airlines

	Phone
America West	800-235-9292
American	800-433-1790
Continental	801-359-9800
Delta	801-532-7123
Northwest	800-225-2525
SkyWest	800-453-9417
TWA	800-221-2000
United	800-241-6522

Charter Airlines

	Phone
Barken International	801-539-7700
D & D Aviation	800-532-0991

CAR RENTALS

	Phone
Advantage	801-531-1199
Alamo	801-575-2211
Avis	801-575-2847
Budget	801-575-2821
Budget-Provo	801-377-9313
CarTemps USA	801-264-9929
Dollar	801-575-2580
Enterprise	801-534-1622
Hertz	801-575-2683
National	801-575-2277
Thrifty	801-595-6677

LIMO/TAXI

	Phone
Diamond Limousine	801-263-9606
Sterling Limousine	801-224-2724
Yellow Cab	801-377-7070

MASS TRANSIT

	Phone
Utah Transit Authority $1.00 Base fare	801-375-4636

— Accommodations —

HOTELS, MOTELS, RESORTS

	City	State	Zip	Phone	Fax
Best Value Western Inn 40 W 300 South *TF:* 800-500-5003	Provo	UT	84601	801-373-0660	373-5182
Best Western Columbian 70 E 300 South *TF:* 800-321-0055	Provo	UT	84601	801-373-8973	373-8973
Best Western Cotton Tree Inn 2230 N University Pkwy *TF:* 800-528-1234	Provo	UT	84604	801-373-7044	375-5240
Best Western Landmark Inn 6560 N Landmark Dr *TF:* 800-548-8824	Park City	UT	84060	435-649-7300	649-1760
City Center Motel 150 W 300 South	Provo	UT	84601	801-373-8489	
Comfort Inn 1555 N Canyon Rd *TF:* 800-228-5150	Provo	UT	84604	801-374-6020	374-0015
Courtyard by Marriott 1600 N Freedom Blvd *TF:* 800-321-2211 ■ *Web:* courtyard.com/SLCPR	Provo	UT	84604	801-373-2222	374-2207
Days Inn 1675 N 200 West *TF:* 800-329-7466	Provo	UT	84604	801-375-8600	374-6654
Econo Lodge 1625 W Center St *TF:* 800-553-2666	Provo	UT	84601	801-373-0099	370-0210
Fairfield Inn by Marriott 1515 S University Ave *TF:* 800-228-2800 ■ *Web:* fairfieldinn.com/SLCPV	Provo	UT	84601	801-377-9500	377-9591
Hampton Inn 1511 S 40 East *TF:* 800-426-7866	Provo	UT	84601	801-377-6396	377-2797
Holiday Inn 1460 S University Ave *TF:* 800-465-4329	Provo	UT	84601	801-374-9750	377-1615
Horne's Howard Johnson Hotel 1292 S University Ave *TF:* 800-326-0025	Provo	UT	84601	801-374-2500	373-1146
Hotel Roberts 192 S University Ave	Provo	UT	84601	801-373-3400	
Lodge at Mountain Village 1415 Lowell Ave *TF:* 800-754-2002	Park City	UT	84060	435-649-0800	649-1464
Motel 6 1600 S University Ave *TF:* 800-466-8356	Provo	UT	84601	801-375-5064	374-0266
National 9 Colony Inn 1380 S University Ave *TF:* 800-524-9999	Provo	UT	84601	801-374-6800	374-8603
Olympia Park Hotel & Convention Center 1895 Sidewinder Dr *TF:* 800-234-9003 ■ *Web:* www.parkcityutah.com	Park City	UT	84060	435-649-2900	649-4852
Prospector Square Hotel & Conference Center PO Box 1698 *TF:* 800-453-3812 ■ *Web:* www.thelodgingcompany.com	Park City	UT	84060	435-649-7100	649-8377
Provo Marriott 101 W 100 North *TF:* 800-777-7144	Provo	UT	84601	801-377-4700	377-4708
Residence Inn by Marriott 252 W 2230 North *TF:* 800-331-3131 ■ *Web:* residenceinn.com/SLCPO	Provo	UT	84601	801-374-1000	374-1090
Silver King Hotel 1485 Empire Ave *TF:* 800-331-8652	Park City	UT	84060	435-649-5500	649-6647
Sleep Inn 1505 S 40 East *TF:* 800-753-3746	Provo	UT	84601	801-377-6597	377-6597
Sundance Cottages RR 3 Box A1 *TF:* 800-892-1600	Sundance	UT	84604	801-225-4107	226-1937
Super 8 Motel 1288 S University Ave *TF:* 800-800-8000	Provo	UT	84601	801-375-8766	377-7569
Travelodge 124 S University Ave *TF:* 800-578-7878	Provo	UT	84601	801-373-1974	

Provo — Hotels, Motels, Resorts (Cont'd)

Name	City	State	Zip	Phone	Fax
Uptown Motel 469 W Center St	Provo	UT	84601	801-373-8248	
Yarrow Hotel 1800 Park Ave *TF:* 800-327-2332	Park City	UT	84060	435-649-7000	645-7007

— Restaurants —

Name	City	State	Zip	Phone
Allie's American Grill (American) 101 W 100 North	Provo	UT	84601	801-377-4700
Bamboo Hut (Hawaiian) 845 S 200 Freedom St.	Provo	UT	84601	801-375-6842
Bombay House (Indian) 463 N University Ave	Provo	UT	84601	801-373-6677
Brick Oven (Italian) 111 E 800 North	Provo	UT	84606	801-374-8800
Cafe Thanh (Chinese) 278 W Center St	Provo	UT	84601	801-373-8373
China Lily (Chinese) 98 W Center St	Provo	UT	84601	801-371-8888
Demae Japanese Restaurant (Japanese) 82 W Center St.	Provo	UT	84601	801-374-0306
El Azteca (Mexican) 746 E 820 North	Provo	UT	84606	801-373-9312
El Salvador Restaurant (Salvadorian) 332 W Center St	Provo	UT	84601	801-377-9411
Four Winds Restaurant (Chinese) 250 W Center St	Provo	UT	84601	801-374-9323
La Dolce Vita (Italian) 61 N 100 East	Provo	UT	84606	801-373-8482
Le Bistro at Bon Losee (French) 2230 N University Pkwy	Provo	UT	84604	801-375-8585
Los Hermanos (Mexican) 16 W Center St	Provo	UT	84601	801-375-5732
Magelby's (American) 1675 N 200 West	Provo	UT	84604	801-374-6249
Many Lands (German/Japanese) 1145 N 500 West	Provo	UT	84604	801-375-3789
Osaka Japanese Restaurant (Japanese) 46 W Center St	Provo	UT	84601	801-373-1060
Peppercorn Grill (American) 3301 N University Ave	Provo	UT	84604	801-373-1161
Ruby River Steakhouse (American) 1454 S University Ave	Provo	UT	84601	801-371-0648
Steak House The (Steak/Seafood) 1488 S State	Orem	UT	84057	801-221-1222
Sundance Tree Room (American) Sundance Canyon	Provo	UT	84604	801-225-4107
Taiwan Cafe (Chinese) 2250 N University Pkwy.	Provo	UT	84604	801-373-0389
Tepanyaki Japanese Steak House (Japanese) 1240 N State St	Provo	UT	84604	801-374-0633

— Goods and Services —

SHOPPING

Name	City	State	Zip	Phone
Provo Town Square 51 S University Ave	Provo	UT	84601	801-379-2555
University Mall 1229 S State St	Orem	UT	84058	801-224-0694

BANKS

Name	City	State	Zip	Phone	Fax
Bonneville Bank 1675 N 200 West	Provo	UT	84604	801-374-9500	377-1036
Central Bank 75 N University Ave	Provo	UT	84603	801-375-1000	377-7637
Far West Bank 201 E Center St	Provo	UT	84606	801-342-6000	377-3351
Wells Fargo Bank 66 E 1650 North	Provo	UT	84604	801-375-1929	377-6578
Zions First National Bank 1060 N University Ave	Provo	UT	84604	801-375-9995	370-4124

BUSINESS SERVICES

Name	Phone	Name	Phone
Airborne Express	800-247-2676	**Kinko's**	801-377-1791
BAX Global	800-225-5229	**Mail Boxes Etc**	800-789-4623
DHL Worldwide Express	800-225-5345	**Post Office**	800-275-8777
Federal Express	800-238-5355	**Skill Staff**	801-426-4948
Intermountain Staffing Resources	801-374-8000	**UPS**	800-742-5877
Kelly Services	801-373-1616		

— Media —

PUBLICATIONS

Name	City	State	Zip	Phone	Fax
Daily Herald‡ PO Box 717 *Web:* www.daily-herald.com	Provo	UT	84603	801-373-5050	373-5489

‡*Daily newspapers*

TELEVISION

Name	City	State	Zip	Phone	Fax
KBYU-TV Ch 11 (PBS) 2000 Ironton Blvd Brigham Young University *Web:* www.kbyu.org/tv ■ *E-mail:* kbyu@byu.edu	Provo	UT	84606	801-378-8450	378-8478
KSL-TV Ch 5 (NBC) PO Box 1160 *Web:* www.ksl.com/TV/ ■ *E-mail:* eyewitness@ksl.com	Salt Lake City	UT	84110	801-575-5555	575-5560
KSTU-TV Ch 13 (Fox) 5020 W Amelia Earhart Dr *Web:* www.fox13.com	Salt Lake City	UT	84116	801-532-1300	537-5335
KTVX-TV Ch 4 (ABC) 1760 Fremont Dr *Web:* www.4utah.com ■ *E-mail:* news@4utah.com	Salt Lake City	UT	84104	801-975-4444	975-4442
KUTV-TV Ch 2 (CBS) 2185 S 3600 West *Web:* www.kutv.com	West Valley City	UT	84119	801-973-3000	973-3349

RADIO

Name	City	State	Zip	Phone	Fax
KALL-AM 910 kHz (N/T) 2801 S Decker Lake Dr *Web:* www.kall910.com	West Valley City	UT	84119	801-575-5255	908-1499
KBEE-FM 98.7 MHz (AC) 434 Bearcat Dr *Web:* www.b987.com ■ *E-mail:* pdirector@b987.com	Salt Lake City	UT	84115	801-485-6700	487-5369
KBER-FM 101.1 MHz (Rock) 434 Bearcat Dr *Web:* www.kber.com	Salt Lake City	UT	84115	801-485-6700	487-5369
KEYY-AM 1450 kHz (Rel) 307 S 1600 West *Web:* www.keyy.com ■ *E-mail:* mail@keyy.com	Provo	UT	84601	801-374-5210	374-2910
KISN-FM 97.1 MHz (AC) 4001 S 700 East Suite 800	Salt Lake City	UT	84107	801-262-9797	262-9772
KNRS-AM 570 kHz (N/T) 2801 S Decker Lake Dr	Salt Lake City	UT	84119	801-908-1300	908-1459
KOSY-FM 106.5 (Nost) 4001 S 700 East Suite 800	Salt Lake City	UT	84107	801-262-9797	262-9772
KRAR-FM 106.9 MHz (Rock) 4455 S 5500 West	Hooper	UT	84315	801-731-9000	731-9666
KUBL-FM 93.3 MHz (Ctry) 434 Bearcat Dr *Web:* www.xmission.com/~bull ■ *E-mail:* bull@xmission.com	Salt Lake City	UT	84115	801-485-6700	487-5369
KZHT-FM 94.9 MHz (CHR) 2801 S Decker Lake Dr *Web:* www.949zht.com	Salt Lake City	UT	84119	801-908-1300	908-1449

— Colleges/Universities —

Name	City	State	Zip	Phone	Fax
Brigham Young University Administration Bldg A153 ASB *Web:* www.byu.edu ■ *E-mail:* admissions@byu.edu	Provo	UT	84602	801-378-1211	378-4264
Utah Valley State College 800 W University Pkwy *Web:* www.uvsc.edu ■ *E-mail:* info@www.uvsc.edu	Orem	UT	84058	801-222-8000	225-4677

— Hospitals —

Name	City	State	Zip	Phone	Fax
Utah Valley Regional Medical Center 1034 N 500 West	Provo	UT	84604	801-373-7850	371-7780

— Attractions —

Name	City	State	Zip	Phone	Fax
Brigham Young University Earth Science Museum 1683 N Canyon Rd *Web:* cpms.byu.edu/ESM	Provo	UT	84602	801-378-3680	378-7911
Brigham Young University Museum of Arts North Campus Dr *Web:* www.byu.edu/moa	Provo	UT	84602	801-378-8200	378-8222
Brigham Young University Museum of Peoples & Cultures 700 N 100 East	Provo	UT	84602	801-378-6112	378-7123
Crandall Historical Printing Museum 275 E Center St	Provo	UT	84606	801-377-7777	374-3333
Fort Utah 200 N Geneva Rd	Provo	UT	84601	801-379-6600	
Hale Family Theater 225 W 400 North *Web:* www.haletheater.com ■ *E-mail:* hcto@inet-1.com	Orem	UT	84057	801-226-8600	852-3189
Hall of Fame Museum of National Awards Vehicles 407 W 100 South	Provo	UT	84601	801-373-3040	
Heber Valley Historic Railroad 450 S 600 West	Provo	UT	84032	435-654-5601	
Historic County Court House 51 S University Ave.	Provo	UT	84606	801-370-8393	

Provo — Attractions (Cont'd)

				Phone	Fax
McCurdy Historical Doll Museum 246 N 100 East	Provo	UT	84606	801-377-9935	
Monte L Bean Life Science Museum 290 Monte L Bean Museum Bldg	Provo	UT	84602	801-378-5051	378-3733
Northpark Museum 500 W 600 North	Provo	UT	84601	801-377-7078	
Provo Canyon N Hwy 189	Provo	UT	84604	801-370-8393	
Provo Historic Buildings (Tour)	Provo	UT	84606	801-370-8393	
Provo Theatre Co 105 E 100 North	Provo	UT	84606	801-379-0600	
Seven Peaks Water Park 1330 E 300 North. *Web:* www.sevenpeaks.com	Provo	UT	84606	801-373-8777	373-8791
Springville Museum of Art 126 E 400 South. *Web:* www.shs.nebo.edu/museum/museum.html	Springville	UT	84663	801-489-2727	489-2739
Sundance Ski Resort North Fork Provo Canyon. *TF:* 800-892-1600 ■ *Web:* www.sundance.net	Provo	UT	84604	801-225-4107	
Timpanogos Cave National Monument RR 3 Box 200. *Web:* www.nps.gov/tica/	American Fork	UT	84003	801-756-5239	756-5661
Trafalga Family Fun Center 168 S 1200 West	Orem	UT	84058	801-224-6000	
Uinta National Forest 88 W 100 North	Provo	UT	84601	801-342-5200	342-5144
Utah Lake State Park 4400 W Center	Provo	UT	84601	801-375-0731	373-4215
Utah Valley Symphony 50 S University Ave Provo LDS Tabernacle	Provo	UT	84601	801-377-6995	
Valley Center Playhouse 780 N 200 East	Lindon	UT	84042	801-785-1186	

— Events —

	Phone
Alpine Days (mid-August)	801-756-6347
America's Freedom Festival (mid-June-early July)	801-370-8019
Highland Fling (early August)	801-370-8393
Lehi Roundup (late June)	801-370-8393
Park City Art Festival (early August)	435-649-8882
Pioneer Day Celebrations (mid-July)	800-541-4955
Santaquin Cherry Days (late July-early August)	801-370-8393
Spanish Fork Fiesta Days (late July)	801-370-8393
Springville Art City Days (mid-June)	801-370-8393
Sundance Institute Film Festival (late January)	801-328-3456
Swiss Days (late August)	435-654-3666
Torchlight Parade (late December)	435-649-8111
World Dance & Music Folkfest (early July)	801-489-2726

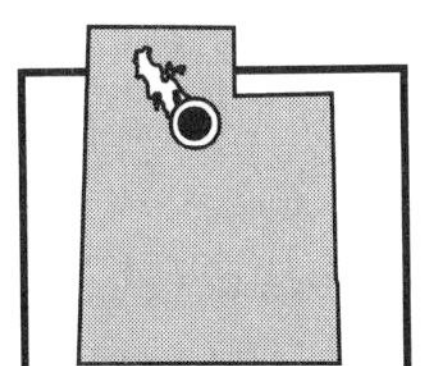

Salt Lake City

Temple Square serves as the center for the Mormon religion in Salt Lake City. Both the Mormon Tabernacle, home of the world-famous Mormon Tabernacle Choir, and the beautiful Temple are located in the Square. At Pioneer Trail State Park, located at the mouth of Emigration Canyon where Mormon pioneers first entered the valley, is the Old Deseret Pioneer Village, a living museum that depicts pioneer life in the area. Of the many ski resorts in the Salt Lake City area, six are located in Wasatch-Cache National Forest. Among these is Snowbird in the Wasatch Mountains, with a 3,100-foot drop and a 125-passenger tram that provides mountaintop views of the area. Park City, located 29 miles east of Salt Lake City, is home to the U.S. Ski Team. (Park City is considered Utah's best ski destination and only bona fide resort town.) West of downtown Salt Lake City is the Great Salt Lake. Many different species of birds choose the lakeshore and neighboring wetlands for their nesting grounds.

Population	174,348	**Longitude**	111-89-03 W
Area (Land)	109.0 sq mi	**County**	Salt Lake
Area (Water)	1.3 sq mi	**Time Zone**	MST
Elevation	4266 ft	**Area Code/s**	801
Latitude	40-76-08 N		

— Average Temperatures and Precipitation —

TEMPERATURES

	Jan	Feb	Mar	Apr	May	Jun	Jul	Aug	Sep	Oct	Nov	Dec
High	36	44	52	61	72	83	92	89	79	66	51	38
Low	19	25	31	38	46	55	64	62	51	40	31	22

PRECIPITATION

	Jan	Feb	Mar	Apr	May	Jun	Jul	Aug	Sep	Oct	Nov	Dec
Inches	1.1	1.2	1.9	2.1	1.8	0.9	0.8	0.9	1.3	1.4	1.3	1.4

— Important Phone Numbers —

	Phone		Phone
AAA	801-364-5615	**Road Conditions**	801-964-6000
American Express Travel	801-328-9733	**Time/Temp**	801-467-8463
Emergency	911	**Travelers Aid**	801-359-4142
Medical Referral	801-355-7477	**Weather**	801-975-4499
Poison Control Center	801-581-2151		

— Information Sources —

				Phone	Fax
Better Business Bureau Serving Utah 5673 S Redwood Rd. *Web:* www.saltlakecity.bbb.org	Salt Lake City	UT	84123	801-892-6009	892-6002
Salt Lake City Area Chamber of Commerce 175 E 400 South Suite 600. *Web:* www.slachamber.com	Salt Lake City	UT	84111	801-364-3631	328-5098
Salt Lake City City Hall 451 S State St. *Web:* www.ci.slc.ut.us	Salt Lake City	UT	84111	801-535-6333	535-7634
Salt Lake City Community & Economic Development Office 451 S State St Rm 404	Salt Lake City	UT	84111	801-535-7777	535-6005
Salt Lake City Mayor 451 S State St Rm 306. *Web:* www.ci.slc.ut.us/government/mayor	Salt Lake City	UT	84111	801-535-7704	535-6331
Salt Lake City Public Library 209 E 500 South. *Web:* www.slcpl.lib.ut.us	Salt Lake City	UT	84111	801-524-8200	524-8297
Salt Lake Convention & Visitors Bureau 90 S West Temple. *TF:* 800-541-4955 ■ *Web:* www.visitsaltlake.com ■ *E-mail:* slcvb@saltlake.org	Salt Lake City	UT	84101	801-521-2822	534-4927
Salt Lake County 2001 S State St Suite S2200. *Web:* www.co.slc.ut.us	Salt Lake City	UT	84190	801-468-3000	468-3440
Salt Palace Convention Center 100 S West Temple. *Web:* www.saltpalace.com	Salt Lake City	UT	84101	801-534-4777	534-6383

On-Line Resources

4SaltLakeCity.com	www.4saltlakecity.com
About.com Guide to Salt Lake City	saltlakecity.about.com/local/mountainus/saltlakecity
Anthill City Guide Salt Lake City	www.anthill.com/city.asp?city=saltlake
Area Guide Salt Lake City	saltlakecity.areaguides.net
City Knowledge Salt Lake City	www.cityknowledge.com/ut_salt_lake_city.htm
CitySearch Salt Lake City	utah.citysearch.com
DigitalCity Salt Lake City	home.digitalcity.com/saltlakecity
Downtown Alliance	www.downtownslc.org/
Excite.com Salt Lake City City Guide	www.excite.com/travel/countries/united_states/utah/salt_lake_city
Insiders' Guide to Salt Lake City	www.insiders.com/saltlake/index.htm
NITC Travelbase City Guide Salt Lake City	www.travelbase.com/auto/guides/salt_lake_city-area-ut.html
Rough Guide Travel Salt Lake City	travel.roughguides.com/content/1268/
Travel West Salt Lake City Guide	www.travelwest.net/cities/saltlake/
Utah Valley Online	www.uvol.com/

Salt Lake City (Cont'd)

— Transportation Services —

AIRPORTS

■ **Salt Lake City International Airport (SLC)**

	Phone
7 miles W of downtown (approx 12 minutes)	801-575-2400

Web: www.ci.slc.ut.us/services/airport

Airport Transportation

	Phone
Rocky Mountain Super Express $14 fare to downtown	801-566-6400
Salt Lake Shuttle $15 fare to downtown	801-266-8775
Yellow Cab $13 fare to downtown	801-521-2100

Commercial Airlines

	Phone		Phone
America West	800-235-9292	**SkyWest**	800-453-9417
American	800-433-1790	**Southwest**	800-435-9792
Continental	801-359-9800	**TWA**	800-221-2000
Delta	801-532-7123	**United**	800-241-6522
Northwest	800-225-2525	**Vanguard**	800-826-4827

Charter Airlines

	Phone		Phone
Barken International	801-539-7700	**D & D Aviation**	800-532-0991

CAR RENTALS

	Phone		Phone
Advantage	801-531-1199	**Dollar**	801-575-2580
Alamo	801-575-2211	**Enterprise**	801-534-1622
Avis	801-575-2847	**Hertz**	801-575-2683
Budget	801-575-2821	**National**	801-575-2277
CarTemps USA	801-264-9929	**Thrifty**	801-595-6677

LIMO/TAXI

	Phone		Phone
Airport Limousine	801-485-1400	**Ute Cab**	801-359-7788
City Cab	801-363-5550	**Yellow Cab**	801-521-2100
Legend Limousine	801-296-0233		

MASS TRANSIT

	Phone
UTA Trolley $1 Base fare	801-287-4636
Utah Transit Authority $1 Base fare	801-287-4636

RAIL/BUS

				Phone
Amtrak Station 340 South 600 W. *TF:* 800-872-7245	Salt Lake City	UT	84101	801-322-3510
Greyhound Bus Station 160 W South Temple *TF:* 800-231-2222	Salt Lake City	UT	84101	801-355-9581

— Accommodations —

HOTEL RESERVATION SERVICES

	Phone	Fax
Advance Reservations Inn Arizona *TF:* 800-456-0682 ■ *Web:* tucson.com/inn ■ *E-mail:* micasa@primenet.com	480-990-0682	990-3390
Hotel Reservations Network Inc *TF Sales:* 800-964-6835 ■ *Web:* www.hoteldiscount.com	214-361-7311	361-7299
Reservations Center *TF:* 800-255-6451 ■ *Web:* www.rescenter.com ■ *E-mail:* resnet@rescenter.com	435-649-1592	649-1593
Salt Lake Reservations *Web:* www.visitsaltlake.com/reservations	877-752-4386	

HOTELS, MOTELS, RESORTS

				Phone	Fax
Airport Inn Suites 2333 W North Temple *TF:* 800-835-9755	Salt Lake City	UT	84116	801-539-0438	539-8852
Best Western Cotton Tree Inn 1030 N 400 East *TF:* 800-662-6886	Salt Lake City	UT	84054	801-292-7666	292-9664
Best Western Olympus Hotel 161 W 600 South *TF:* 800-426-0722	Salt Lake City	UT	84101	801-521-7373	524-0354
Best Western Plaza 122 W South Temple *TF:* 800-366-3684	Salt Lake City	UT	84101	801-521-0130	322-5057
Brigham Street Inn 1135 E South Temple *TF:* 800-417-4461	Salt Lake City	UT	84102	801-364-4461	521-3201
Broadway Tower Executive Suites 230 E Broadway	Salt Lake City	UT	84111	801-534-1222	359-3624
Comfort Inn Airport 200 N Admiral Byrd Rd *TF:* 800-535-8742	Salt Lake City	UT	84116	801-537-7444	532-4721
Courtyard by Marriott Downtown 130 W 400 South *TF:* 800-321-2211 ■ *Web:* courtyard.com/SLCCY	Salt Lake City	UT	84101	801-531-6000	531-1273
Crystal Inn Downtown 230 W 500 South *TF:* 800-366-4466	Salt Lake City	UT	84101	801-328-4466	328-4072
Days Inn Airport 1900 W North Temple *TF:* 800-329-7466	Salt Lake City	UT	84116	801-539-8538	595-1041
Deer Valley Lodging 1375 Deer Valley Dr S. *TF:* 800-453-3833 ■ *Web:* www.deervalley.com	Park City	UT	84060	435-649-4040	645-8419
Doubletree Hotel Salt Lake 255 S West Temple *TF:* 800-222-8733 ■ *Web:* www.doubletreehotels.com/DoubleT/Hotel121/125/125Main.htm	Salt Lake City	UT	84101	801-328-2000	532-1953
Econo Lodge 715 W North Temple *TF:* 877-233-2666	Salt Lake City	UT	84116	801-363-0062	359-3926
Embassy Suites Hotel 110 W 600 South *TF:* 800-362-2779	Salt Lake City	UT	84101	801-359-7800	359-3753
Fairfield Inn by Marriott Airport 230 N Admiral Byrd Rd *TF:* 800-228-2800 ■ *Web:* fairfieldinn.com/SLCFA	Salt Lake City	UT	84116	801-355-3331	355-3360
Goldener Hirsch Inn 7570 Royal St E *TF:* 800-252-3373 ■ *Web:* www.goldenerhirschinn.com ■ *E-mail:* escape@goldenerhirschInn.com	Park City	UT	84060	435-649-7770	649-7901
Hampton Inn Downtown 425 S 300 West *TF:* 800-426-7866	Salt Lake City	UT	84101	801-741-1110	741-1171
Hilton Hotel Airport 5151 Wiley Post Way *TF:* 800-999-3736 ■ *Web:* www.hilton.com/hotels/SLCAHHF	Salt Lake City	UT	84116	801-539-1515	539-1113
Holiday Inn 5575 W Amelia Earhart Dr *TF:* 800-522-5575	Salt Lake City	UT	84116	801-537-7020	537-7701
Holiday Inn Airport 1659 W North Temple St *TF:* 800-465-4329	Salt Lake City	UT	84116	801-533-9000	364-0614
Holiday Inn Downtown 999 S Main St *TF:* 800-465-4329	Salt Lake City	UT	84111	801-359-8600	359-7186
Holiday Inn Express 2080 W North Temple *TF:* 800-465-4329	Salt Lake City	UT	84116	801-355-0088	355-0099
Inn at Temple Square 71 W South Temple *TF:* 800-843-4668 ■ *Web:* www.theinn.com/	Salt Lake City	UT	84101	801-531-1000	536-7272
La Europa Royale 1135 E Vine St *TF:* 800-523-8767	Salt Lake City	UT	84121	801-263-7999	263-8090
La Quinta Inn & Suites 4905 W Wiley Post Way *TF:* 800-687-6667	Salt Lake City	UT	84116	801-366-4444	366-5555
Little America Hotel & Towers 500 S Main St *TF:* 800-453-9450	Salt Lake City	UT	84101	801-363-6781	596-5911
Peery Hotel 110 W 300 South *TF:* 800-331-0073	Salt Lake City	UT	84101	801-521-4300	575-5014
Quality Inn 154 W 600 South *TF:* 800-521-9997	Salt Lake City	UT	84101	801-521-2930	355-0733
Quality Inn Midvalley 4465 S Century Dr *TF:* 800-228-5151	Salt Lake City	UT	84123	801-268-2533	266-6206
Radisson Hotel Airport 2177 W North Temple *TF:* 800-333-3333	Salt Lake City	UT	84116	801-364-5800	364-5823
Ramada Inn 2455 S State St *TF:* 800-272-6232	Salt Lake City	UT	84115	801-486-2400	485-5300

Salt Lake City — Hotels, Motels, Resorts (Cont'd)

	City	State	ZIP	*Phone*	*Fax*
Residence Inn by Marriott					
285 W Broadway	Salt Lake City	UT	84101	801-355-3300	355-0440
TF: 800-331-3131 ■ *Web:* residenceinn.com/SLCRI					
Residence Inn by Marriott					
765 E 400 South	Salt Lake City	UT	84102	801-532-5511	532-0416
TF: 800-331-3131					
Reston Hotel 5335 College Dr	Murray	UT	84123	801-264-1054	264-1054
TF: 800-231-9710					
Royal Executive Inn 121 N 300 West	Salt Lake City	UT	84103	801-521-3450	521-3452
TF: 800-541-7639					
Salt Lake City Hilton Hotel					
150 W 500 South	Salt Lake City	UT	84101	801-532-3344	531-0705
TF: 800-421-7602					
Salt Lake City Marriott Hotel					
75 S West Temple	Salt Lake City	UT	84101	801-531-0800	532-4127
TF: 800-228-9290					
Shadow Ridge Resort Hotel & Conference					
Center 50 Shadow Ridge Rd	Park City	UT	84060	435-649-4300	649-5951
TF: 800-451-3031					
Shilo Inn 206 S West Temple	Salt Lake City	UT	84101	801-521-9500	359-6527
TF: 800-222-2244					
Sky Harbor Executive Suites					
1876 W North Temple	Salt Lake City	UT	84116	801-539-8420	539-8007
TF: 800-677-8483					
Snowbird Ski & Summer Resort					
PO Box 929000	Snowbird	UT	84092	801-742-2222	947-8227
TF: 800-453-3000 ■ *Web:* www.snowbird.com					
Stein Eriksen Lodge 7700 Stein Way	Park City	UT	84060	435-649-3700	649-5825
TF: 800-453-1302 ■ *Web:* www.steinlodge.com					
■ *E-mail:* info@steinlodge.com					
Travelodge Temple Square					
144 W North Temple	Salt Lake City	UT	84103	801-533-8200	596-0332
TF: 800-578-7878					
University Park Hotel 480 Wakara Way	Salt Lake City	UT	84108	801-581-1000	584-3321
TF: 800-637-4390					
Wyndham Hotel 215 W South Temple	Salt Lake City	UT	84101	801-531-7500	328-1289
TF: 800-996-3426					

— Restaurants —

	City	State	ZIP	*Phone*
Absolute (European) 52 W 200 South	Salt Lake City	UT	84101	801-359-0899
American Grill (Continental) 4835 Highland Dr	Salt Lake City	UT	84117	801-277-7082
Archibald's (American) 1100 W 7800 South	West Jordan	UT	84088	801-566-6940
Baba Afghan Restaurant (Afghan) 55 E 400 South	Salt Lake City	UT	84111	801-596-0786
Bangkok Thai (Thai) 1400 S Foothill Dr	Salt Lake City	UT	84108	801-582-8424
Web: www.vii.com/~bangkok/				
Benihana of Tokyo (Japanese) 165 S West Temple	Salt Lake City	UT	84101	801-322-2421
Cabana Club (Steak/Seafood) 31 E 400 South	Salt Lake City	UT	84111	801-359-6271
Cafe Molise (Italian) 55 W 100 South	Salt Lake City	UT	84101	801-364-8833
Cafe Pierpont (Mexican) 122 W Pierpont Ave	Salt Lake City	UT	84101	801-364-1222
Cafe Trang (Chinese) 818 S Main St	Salt Lake City	UT	84101	801-539-1638
Capitol Cafe (California) 52 W 200 South	Salt Lake City	UT	84101	801-532-7000
Carriage Court Restaurant (American)				
71 W South Temple	Salt Lake City	UT	84101	801-536-7200
Cedars of Lebanon (Middle Eastern)				
152 E 200 South	Salt Lake City	UT	84111	801-364-4096
Desert Edge Brewery (American) 273 Trolley Sq	Salt Lake City	UT	84102	801-521-8917
DoDo Restaurant (International) 680 S 900 East	Salt Lake City	UT	84102	801-328-9348
Glitretind (American) 7700 Stein Way Stein Eriksen Lodge	Park City	UT	84060	435-645-6455
JW Steak House (Steak) 75 S West Temple	Salt Lake City	UT	84101	801-531-0800
La Caille at Quail Run (French) 9565 Wasatch Blvd	Salt Lake City	UT	84092	801-942-1751
Lamb's Restaurant (American) 169 S Main St	Salt Lake City	UT	84111	801-364-7166
Le Parisien (French/Italian) 417 S 300 East	Salt Lake City	UT	84111	801-364-5223
Market Street Broiler (Steak/Seafood)				
260 S 1300 East	Salt Lake City	UT	84102	801-583-8808
Market Street Grill (Steak/Seafood) 48 Market St	Salt Lake City	UT	84101	801-322-4668
Metropolitan (New American) 173 W Broadway	Salt Lake City	UT	84101	801-364-3472
Mikado (Japanese) 67 W 100 South	Salt Lake City	UT	84101	801-328-0929
Millcreek Inn (Continental) Millcreek Canyon	Salt Lake City	UT	84109	801-278-7927
Mullboon's 13th Floor (Steak/Seafood)				
161 W 600 South	Salt Lake City	UT	84101	801-530-1313
New Yorker (Continental) 60 Market St	Salt Lake City	UT	84101	801-363-0166
Oasis Cafe (Vegetarian) 151 S 500 East	Salt Lake City	UT	84102	801-322-0404
Ocean's (Seafood) 4760 S 900 East	Salt Lake City	UT	84117	801-261-0115
Oyster Bar (Seafood) 54 Market St	Salt Lake City	UT	84101	801-531-6044
Pagoda Restaurant (Japanese) 26 'E' St	Salt Lake City	UT	84103	801-355-8155
Pomodoro (Italian) 2440 E Fort Union Blvd	Salt Lake City	UT	84121	801-944-1895
Rio Grande Cafe (Mexican) 455 W 300 South	Salt Lake City	UT	84101	801-364-3302
Squatter's Pub Brewery (American) 147 W Broadway	Salt Lake City	UT	84101	801-363-2739
Star of India (Indian) 177 E 200 South	Salt Lake City	UT	84111	801-363-7555
Taj India (Indian) 73 E 400 South	Salt Lake City	UT	84111	801-596-8727

— Goods and Services —

SHOPPING

	City	State	ZIP	*Phone*	*Fax*
Cottonwood Mall 4835 S Highland Dr	Salt Lake City	UT	84117	801-278-0416	278-1575
Crossroads Plaza 50 S Main St	Salt Lake City	UT	84144	801-531-1799	532-4345
Web: www.crossroadsplaza.com					
Factory Stores at Park City					
6699 N Landmark Dr	Park City	UT	84098	435-645-7078	645-7098
TF: 888-746-7333					
Foothill Village					
1400 Foothill Dr Suite 46	Salt Lake City	UT	84108	801-582-3646	582-2803
Gardner Village 1100 W 7800 South	West Jordan	UT	84088	801-566-8903	566-5390
Web: www.gardnervillage.com					
Mormon Handicraft					
36 S State St Suite 220	Salt Lake City	UT	84111	801-355-2141	
Salt Lake Antiques Mall					
4791 S State St	Salt Lake City	UT	84107	801-322-1275	
South Towne Center 10450 S State St	Sandy	UT	84070	801-572-1516	571-3927
Trolley Square 367 Trolley Sq	Salt Lake City	UT	84102	801-521-9877	521-1777
Valley Fair Mall 3601 Constitution Blvd	Salt Lake City	UT	84119	801-969-6211	969-6233
ZCMI Center Mall 36 S State St	Salt Lake City	UT	84111	801-321-8743	

BANKS

	City	State	ZIP	*Phone*	*Fax*
Bank One Utah NA 185 S State St	Salt Lake City	UT	84111	801-481-5014	481-5009
TF: 800-877-0608					
First Security Bank of Utah NA					
1985 E 7000 South	Salt Lake City	UT	84121	801-246-6600	
KeyBank NA Salt Lake City District					
50 S Main St Suite 132	Salt Lake City	UT	84144	801-535-1000	535-1129
TF: 800-658-5399					
Zions First National Bank 1 S Main St	Salt Lake City	UT	84111	801-524-4711	524-4772
Web: www.zionsbank.com ■ *E-mail:* info@zionsbank.com					

BUSINESS SERVICES

	Phone
All Seasons Staffing Services	801-484-5227
Federal Express	800-238-5355
Handle With Care Packaging	801-364-7225
Intermountain Staffing Resources	801-467-6500
Kelly Services	801-972-8645
Kinko's	801-533-9444
Manpower Temporary Services	801-364-6561
Post Office	800-275-8777
SOS Temporary Services	801-485-5252
Target Mailing	801-973-7557
Unishippers Assn	801-487-0600
UPS	800-742-5877

— Media —

PUBLICATIONS

	City	State	ZIP	*Phone*	*Fax*
Deseret News‡ PO Box 1257	Salt Lake City	UT	84110	801-237-2800	237-2121
Web: www.desnews.com ■ *E-mail:* cservice@desnews.com					
Enterprise 136 S Main St Suite 721	Salt Lake City	UT	84101	801-533-0556	533-0684
Salt Lake City Weekly 60 W 400 South	Salt Lake City	UT	84101	801-575-7003	575-8011
Web: www.avenews.com/index_cw.html					
Salt Lake Tribune‡ 143 S Main St	Salt Lake City	UT	84111	801-237-2800	521-9418
Web: www.sltrib.com ■ *E-mail:* the.editors@sltrib.com					
Utah Business 85 E Fort Union Blvd	Midvale	UT	84047	801-568-0114	568-0812
Web: www.utahbusiness.com ■ *E-mail:* bpittman@uy801.homestar.net					

‡Daily newspapers

TELEVISION

	City	State	ZIP	*Phone*	*Fax*
KJZZ-TV Ch 14 (UPN)					
5181 Amelia Earhart Dr	Salt Lake City	UT	84116	801-537-1414	238-6415*
**Fax:* Sales ■ *Web:* www.kjzz.com					
KSL-TV Ch 5 (NBC) PO Box 1160	Salt Lake City	UT	84110	801-575-5555	575-5560
Web: www.ksl.com/TV/ ■ *E-mail:* eyewitness@ksl.com					
KSTU-TV Ch 13 (Fox)					
5020 W Amelia Earhart Dr	Salt Lake City	UT	84116	801-532-1300	537-5335
Web: www.fox13.com					
KTVX-TV Ch 4 (ABC) 1760 Fremont Dr	Salt Lake City	UT	84104	801-975-4444	975-4442
Web: www.4utah.com ■ *E-mail:* news@4utah.com					
KUED-TV Ch 7 (PBS) 101 Wasatch Dr	Salt Lake City	UT	84112	801-581-7777	585-5096
Web: eddy.media.utah.edu/					
KUTV-TV Ch 2 (CBS)					
2185 S 3600 West	West Valley City	UT	84119	801-973-3000	973-3349
Web: www.kutv.com					

Salt Lake City (Cont'd)

RADIO

				Phone	Fax
KALL-AM 910 kHz (N/T) 2801 S Decker Lake Dr *Web:* www.kall910.com	West Valley City	UT	84119	801-575-5255	908-1499
KBEE-FM 98.7 MHz (AC) 434 Bearcat Dr *Web:* www.b987.com ■ *E-mail:* pdirector@b987.com	Salt Lake City	UT	84115	801-485-6700	487-5369
KBER-FM 101.1 MHz (Rock) 434 Bearcat Dr *Web:* www.kber.com	Salt Lake City	UT	84115	801-485-6700	487-5369
KBZN-FM 97.9 MHz (NAC) 257 E 200 South Suite 400 *Web:* www.kbzn.com ■ *E-mail:* breeze@kbzn.com	Salt Lake City	UT	84111	801-670-9079	364-8068
KCPW-FM 88.3 MHz (NPR) 445 Marsac Ave *E-mail:* kcpw@ditell.com	Park City	UT	84060	435-649-9004	645-9063
KCPX-FM 105.7 MHz (Oldies) 4001 S 700 East Suite 800 *E-mail:* mountain@xmission.com	Salt Lake City	UT	84107	801-262-9797	262-9772
KDYL-AM 1280 kHz (Nost) 57 W South Temple Suite 700	Salt Lake City	UT	84101	801-524-2600	521-9234
KENZ-FM 107.5 MHz (AAA) 434 Bearcat Dr *Web:* www.1075.com	Salt Lake City	UT	84115	801-485-6700	487-5369
KFAN-AM 1320 kHz (Sports) 434 Bearcat Dr *Web:* www.1320kfan.com ■ *E-mail:* info@1320kfan.com	Salt Lake City	UT	84115	801-485-6700	487-5369
KISN-FM 97.1 MHz (AC) 4001 S 700 East Suite 800	Salt Lake City	UT	84107	801-262-9797	262-9772
KKAT-FM 101.9 MHz (Ctry) 2801 S Decker Lake Dr *Web:* www.kkat.com	West Valley City	UT	84119	801-908-1300	908-1459
KNRS-AM 570 kHz (N/T) 2801 S Decker Lake Dr	Salt Lake City	UT	84119	801-908-1300	908-1459
KODJ-FM 94.1 MHz (Oldies) 2801 S Decker Lake Dr *Web:* www.oldies941.com	West Valley City	UT	84119	801-575-5255	908-1499
KOSY-FM 106.5 (Nost) 4001 S 700 East Suite 800	Salt Lake City	UT	84107	801-262-9797	262-9772
KPCW-FM 91.9 MHz (NPR) PO Box 1372	Park City	UT	84060	435-649-9004	
KQMB-FM 102.7 MHz (AC) 57 W South Temple Suite 700 *Web:* www.star1027.com	Salt Lake City	UT	84101	801-524-2600	521-9234
KRAR-FM 106.9 MHz (Rock) 4455 S 5500 West	Hooper	UT	84315	801-731-9000	731-9666
KRSP-FM 103.5 MHz (CR) 57 W South Temple Suite 700 *Web:* www.arrow1035.com	Salt Lake City	UT	84101	801-524-2600	521-9234
KSFI-FM 100.3 MHz (AC) 57 W South Temple Suite 700 *Web:* www.fm100.com ■ *E-mail:* info@fm100.com	Salt Lake City	UT	84101	801-524-2600	521-9234
KSL-AM 1160 kHz (N/T) PO Box 1160 *Web:* www.ksl.com/radio/ ■ *E-mail:* talk@ksl.com	Salt Lake City	UT	84110	801-575-7600	575-7625
KSOP-AM 1370 kHz (Ctry) 1285 W 2320 South	Salt Lake City	UT	84119	801-972-1043	974-0868
KSOP-FM 104.3 MHz (Ctry) PO Box 25548 *Web:* www.ksopcountry.com ■ *E-mail:* ksop@ksopcountry.com	Salt Lake City	UT	84125	801-972-1043	974-0868
KUBL-FM 93.3 MHz (Ctry) 434 Bearcat Dr *Web:* www.xmission.com/~bull ■ *E-mail:* bull@xmission.com	Salt Lake City	UT	84115	801-485-6700	487-5369
KUER-FM 90.1 MHz (NPR) 101 S Wasatch Dr *E-mail:* fm90@media.utah.edu	Salt Lake City	UT	84112	801-581-6625	
KURR-FM 99.5 MHz (Rock) 2801 S Decker Lake Dr *Web:* www.rock99.com	West Valley City	UT	84119	801-908-1300	908-1499
KXRK-FM 96.3 MHz (Alt) 165 S West Temple 2nd Fl *Web:* www.x96.com	Salt Lake City	UT	84101	801-521-9696	364-1811
KZHT-FM 94.9 MHz (CHR) 2801 S Decker Lake Dr *Web:* www.949zht.com	Salt Lake City	UT	84119	801-908-1300	908-1449

— Colleges/Universities —

				Phone	Fax
ITT Technical Institute 920 W Levoy Dr *TF:* 800-365-2136 ■ *Web:* www.itt-tech.edu	Murray	UT	84123	801-263-3313	263-3497
Latter Day Saints Business College 411 E South Temple St *TF:* 800-999-5767 ■ *Web:* www.ldsbc.edu	Salt Lake City	UT	84111	801-524-8100	524-1900
Salt Lake Community College 4600 S Redwood Rd *Web:* www.slcc.edu ■ *E-mail:* herdsc@slcc.edu	Salt Lake City	UT	84130	801-957-4111	957-4958
Stevens Henager College 2168 Washington Blvd. *TF:* 800-371-7791 ■ *Web:* www.stevenshenager.com	Ogden	UT	84401	801-394-7791	393-1748
University of Utah 201 S 1460 E *Web:* www.utah.edu	Salt Lake City	UT	84112	801-581-7200	581-7880
Utah State University 1600 Old Main Hill *Web:* www.usu.edu ■ *E-mail:* hscr@cc.usu.edu	Logan	UT	84322	435-797-1000	797-4077
Westminster College of Salt Lake City 1840 S 1300 East *TF:* 800-748-4753 ■ *Web:* www.wcslc.edu ■ *E-mail:* admispub@wcslc.edu	Salt Lake City	UT	84105	801-484-7651	484-3252

— Hospitals —

				Phone	Fax
Alta View Hospital 9660 S 1300 East	Sandy	UT	84094	801-501-2600	576-2789
Columbia Lakeview Hospital 630 E Medical Dr *Web:* www.columbia-utah.com/lv.html	Bountiful	UT	84010	801-292-6231	299-2534
Columbia Saint Mark's Hospital 1200 E 3900 South **Fax:* Admitting ■ *Web:* www.stmarkshospital.com	Salt Lake City	UT	84124	801-268-7111	270-3341*
Cottonwood Hospital Medical Center 5770 S 300 East	Murray	UT	84107	801-262-3461	269-2272
Davis Hospital & Medical Center 1600 W Antelope Dr	Layton	UT	84041	801-825-9561	774-7045
LDS Hospital 8th Ave & C St **Fax:* Admitting	Salt Lake City	UT	84143	801-321-1100	408-5133*
Pioneer Valley Hospital 3460 S Pioneer Pkwy	West Valley City	UT	84120	801-964-3100	964-3247
Primary Children's Medical Center 100 N Medical Dr	Salt Lake City	UT	84113	801-588-2000	588-2435
Salt Lake Regional Hospital 1050 E South Temple St	Salt Lake City	UT	84102	801-350-4111	350-4522
University of Utah Hospital & Clinics 50 N Medical Dr *Web:* www.med.utah.edu	Salt Lake City	UT	84132	801-581-2121	585-5280
Veterans Affairs Medical Center 500 S Foothill Dr	Salt Lake City	UT	84148	801-582-1565	584-1289

— Attractions —

				Phone	Fax
Aperture Gallery 307 W 200 South Suite 1004 *TF:* 800-777-2076 ■ *Web:* www.tssphoto.com/art.html	Salt Lake City	UT	84101	801-363-9700	363-9707
Ballet West 50 W 200 South *Web:* www.balletwest.org/	Salt Lake City	UT	84101	801-323-6901	359-3504
Beehive House 67 E South Temple St	Salt Lake City	UT	84111	801-240-2671	
Capitol Theatre 50 W 200 S. *TF:* 888-451-2787 ■ *Web:* www.arttix.org/capitol_theatre.htm	Salt Lake City	UT	84101	801-323-6800	538-2272
Cathedral Church of St Mark 231 E 100 South	Salt Lake City	UT	84111	801-322-3400	322-3410
Catholic Cathedral of the Madeleine 331 E South Temple St	Salt Lake City	UT	84111	801-328-8941	364-6504
Chase Home Museum of Utah Folk Art 600 E 1300 South	Salt Lake City	UT	84105	801-533-5760	
Children's Museum of Utah 840 N 300 West *Web:* www.childmuseum.org	Salt Lake City	UT	84103	801-328-3383	328-3384
Delta Center 301 W South Temple St **Fax:* PR	Salt Lake City	UT	84101	801-325-2000	325-2578*
Family History Library 35 N West Temple St	Salt Lake City	UT	84150	801-240-2331	240-5551
Foothill Village 1400 Foothill Dr Suite 46	Salt Lake City	UT	84108	801-582-3646	582-2803
Fort Douglas Military Museum 32 Potter St Fort Douglas	Salt Lake City	UT	84113	801-581-1710	581-9846
Gallivan Utah Center Plaza 36 E 200 South	Salt Lake City	UT	84111	801-532-0459	521-8329
Goblin Valley State Park PO Box 637 *TF:* 800-322-3770	Green River	UT	84525	435-564-3633	
Governor's Mansion 603 E South Temple	Salt Lake City	UT	84102	801-538-1005	538-1970
Great Salt Lake Exit 104 off I-80	Salt Lake City	UT	84404	801-250-1822	

Salt Lake City — Attractions (Cont'd)

Name / Address	City	State	ZIP	Phone	Fax
Hale Centre Theater 3333 S Decker Lake Dr	West Valley City	UT	84119	801-984-9000	984-9009
Web: www.halecentretheatre.com/ ■ *E-mail:* feedback@halecentretheatre.com					
Hansen Planetarium 15 S State St	Salt Lake City	UT	84111	801-538-2104	531-4948
Web: www.utah.edu/Planetarium/					
Hogle Zoological Gardens 2600 Sunnyside Ave	Salt Lake City	UT	84108	801-582-1631	584-1770
Web: www.hoglezoo.org					
Holy Trinity Greek Orthodox Church 279 S 300 West	Salt Lake City	UT	84101	801-328-9681	328-9688
International Peace Garden 1000 S 900 West Jordan Park	Salt Lake City	UT	84104	801-972-7800	972-7847
Lagoon & Pioneer Village 375 N Hwy 91	Farmington	UT	84025	801-451-8000	451-8015
TF: 800-748-5246 ■ *Web:* www.lagoonpark.com					
Latter Day Saints Church Office Building Observation Deck 50 E North Temple St	Salt Lake City	UT	84150	801-240-3789	
Liberty Park 589 E 1300 South	Salt Lake City	UT	84105	801-972-7800	972-7847
Maurice Abravanel Hall 123 W South Temple	Salt Lake City	UT	84101	801-533-6407	533-4268
Mormon Tabernacle Temple Sq	Salt Lake City	UT	84150	801-240-3221	240-2033
Museum of Church History & Art 45 N West Temple St	Salt Lake City	UT	84150	801-240-3310	240-5342
Natural Bridges National Monument PO Box 1	Lake Powell	UT	84533	435-692-1234	692-1111
Web: www.nps.gov/nabr/ ■ *E-mail:* nabr_interpretation@nps.gov					
Off Broadway Theatre 272 S Main St	Salt Lake City	UT	84101	801-355-4628	
Old Deseret Village 2601 Sunnyside Ave	Salt Lake City	UT	84108	801-584-8392	
Phillips Gallery 444 E 200 South	Salt Lake City	UT	84111	801-364-8284	364-8293
Pioneer Memorial Museum 300 N Main St	Salt Lake City	UT	84103	801-538-1050	538-1119
Raging Waters 1700 S 1200 West	Salt Lake City	UT	84104	801-972-3300	974-9686
TF: 800-333-3333					
Red Butte Gardens & Arboretum 300 Wakara Way University of Utah	Salt Lake City	UT	84108	801-581-5322	581-4990
Repertory Dance Theatre 138 W 300 South	Salt Lake City	UT	84101	801-534-1000	534-1110
Web: www.xmission.com/~rdt					
Rio Grande Depot 300 S Rio Grande St.	Salt Lake City	UT	84101	801-533-3500	
Ririe-Woodbury Dance Co 50 W 200 South	Salt Lake City	UT	84101	801-323-6801	359-3504
Web: www.ririewoodbury.com ■ *E-mail:* dance@ririewoodbury.com					
Rockport State Park 9040 N Hwy 302	Peoa	UT	84061	435-336-2241	336-2248
TF: 800-322-3770					
Salt Lake Art Center 20 S West Temple	Salt Lake City	UT	84101	801-328-4201	322-4323
Salt Lake Community College Grand Theatre 1575 S State St	Salt Lake City	UT	84115	801-957-3322	957-3300
Salt Lake County Performing Arts Center 50 W 200 S	Salt Lake City	UT	84101	801-323-6800	538-2272
Salt Lake Opera Theatre 48 W Broadway Suite 405	Salt Lake City	UT	84100	801-328-2065	
Smith Joseph Memorial Building 15 E South Temple St	Salt Lake City	UT	84111	801-240-1266	
Social Hall Heritage Museum 55 S State St	Salt Lake City	UT	84103	801-321-8745	
Sports Park 8695 S Sandy Pkwy	Sandy	UT	84070	801-562-4444	562-5063
Temple Square 50 E North Temple St	Salt Lake City	UT	84150	801-240-2534	240-1471
TF: 800-453-3860					
This is the Place State Park 2601 Sunnyside Ave	Salt Lake City	UT	84108	801-584-8391	
Timpanogos Cave National Monument RR 3 Box 200	American Fork	UT	84003	801-756-5239	756-5661
Web: www.nps.gov/tica/					
Tivoli Gallery 255 S State St	Salt Lake City	UT	84111	801-521-6288	
Tracy Aviary 589 E 1300 South	Salt Lake City	UT	84105	801-596-8500	596-7325
Trolley Square 367 Trolley Sq	Salt Lake City	UT	84102	801-521-9877	521-1777
Utah Fun Dome 4998 S 360 West	Murray	UT	84123	801-263-8769	265-3869
Utah Museum of Fine Arts 1530 E 370 S University of Utah	Salt Lake City	UT	84112	801-581-7332	585-5198
Web: www.utah.edu/umfa/					
Utah Museum of Natural History 1390 E Presidents Cir University of Utah	Salt Lake City	UT	84112	801-581-6928	585-3684
Web: raven.umnh.utah.edu/					
Utah Opera Co 50 W 200 South	Salt Lake City	UT	84101	801-736-6868	736-6815
Web: www.utahopera.org					
Utah State Capitol 350 N Main St.	Salt Lake City	UT	84114	801-538-3000	
Utah Symphony Orchestra 123 W South Temple St	Salt Lake City	UT	84101	801-533-5626	521-6634
Web: www.utahsymphony.org ■ *E-mail:* utsymph@aros.net					
Wall Enos A Mansion 411 E South Temple Latter Day Saints Business College	Salt Lake City	UT	84111	801-524-8100	524-1900
TF: 800-999-5767					
Wasatch Brewery 1763 S 300 West	Salt Lake City	UT	84115	801-466-8855	484-6665
Wasatch-Cache National Forest 125 S State St	Salt Lake City	UT	84138	801-524-3900	
Wheeler Historic Farm 6351 S 900 East	Salt Lake City	UT	84121	801-264-2241	264-2213

SPORTS TEAMS & FACILITIES

Name / Address	City	State	ZIP	Phone	Fax
Salt Lake Buzz (baseball) 13th S & West Temple St Franklin Quest Field	Salt Lake City	UT	84115	801-485-3800	485-6818
Utah Grizzlies (hockey) 3200 S Decker Lake Dr	Salt Lake City	UT	84119	801-988-8000	988-7000
Web: www.utahgrizz.com					
Utah Jazz 301 W South Temple St Delta Center	Salt Lake City	UT	84101	801-355-3865	
TF: 800-358-7328 ■ *Web:* www.nba.com/jazz					
Utah Starzz (basketball) 301 W South Temple St Delta Ctr.	Salt Lake City	UT	84101	801-325-2584	325-2578
Web: www.wnba.com/starzz					

— Events —

	Phone
Bison Roundup (late October)	801-773-2941
Candlelight Christmas (mid-December)	801-584-8391
Christmas Lights at Temple Square (late November-late December)	801-240-1000
Cinco de Mayo (early May)	801-355-2521
Days of '47 Celebration (mid-late July)	801-521-2822
Days of '47 Pioneer Parade (late July)	801-521-2822
Days of '47 World Championship Rodeo (mid-late July)	801-521-2822
Deseret News Marathon (late July)	801-468-2560
Dickens Festival (late November-early December)	801-538-8440
Festival of Lights (early November-early January)	801-264-2241
Festival of the American West (late July-early August)	800-225-3378
Festival of Trees (early December)	801-588-3677
First Night New Years Eve Celebration (December 31)	801-359-5118
Hispanic Dance (mid-September)	801-534-4777
Home & Garden Show (early-mid-March)	801-534-4777
Living Traditions Festival (mid-May)	801-596-5000
Madeleine Festival of Arts & Humanities (late May)	801-328-8941
Memorial Day & Spring Celebration (late May)	801-584-8391
Mormon Miracle Pageant (late June)	435-835-3000
Nouveau Beaujolais Festival (late November)	435-645-6640
Oktoberfest (early October)	801-532-0459
Peach Days (early September)	435-723-3931
Railroader's Festival (early August)	435-471-2209
Scottish Celebration & Blessing of the Clans (late October)	801-363-3889
Snowbird's Winterfest (early December)	801-742-2222
Sundance Institute Film Festival (late January)	801-328-3456
US Freestyle Championships (early March)	801-742-2222
Utah Arts Festival (late June)	801-322-2428
Utah Auto Show (late January)	801-534-4777
Utah Boat & Fishing Show (mid-February)	801-534-4777
Utah State Fair (mid-September)	801-538-8440
Utah's Days of '47 (mid-late July)	801-538-1050

Vermont

Population (1999): 593,740 **Area (sq mi): 9,615**

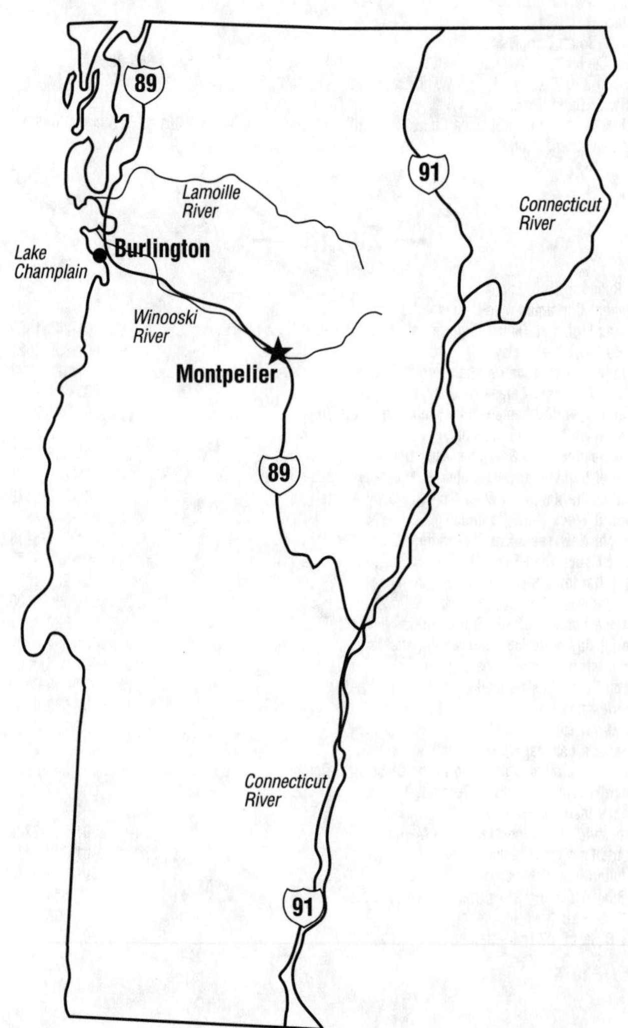

— State Information Sources —

				Phone	Fax
Vermont Chamber of Commerce PO Box 37 . . Montpelier	VT	05601	802-223-3443	229-4581
Web: www.vtchamber.com				
Vermont Dept of Libraries 109 State St. . . . . . Montpelier	VT	05609	802-828-3261	828-2199
Web: dol.state.vt.us				
Vermont Economic Development Dept				
National Life Bldg Drawer 20 . . . . Montpelier	VT	05620	802-828-3080	828-3258
Web: www.state.vt.us/dca/economic/developm.htm				
Vermont Forests Parks & Recreation Dept				
103 S Main St Bldg 10S . . . . Waterbury	VT	05671	802-241-3655	244-1481
Web: www.state.vt.us/anr/fpr				
Vermont State Government Information			802-828-1110	
Web: www.state.vt.us				
Vermont Tourism & Marketing Dept				
6 Baldwin St. . . . . Montpelier	VT	05602	802-828-3236	828-3233
TF: 800-837-6668 ■ *Web:* www.travel-vermont.com				

ON-LINE RESOURCES

Discover Vermont . . . . discover-vermont.com
Imbored Vermont www.imbored.com/new/rvt01.htm
Net Travel Vermont . . . . www.nettx.com/states/vt.htm
PeekABoo Vermont . . . . www.peekaboo.net/vt
Rough Guide Travel Vermont travel.roughguides.com/content/424/index.htm
Search Vermont . . . . www.newengland.com/vtmap.html
Southern Vermont Guide . . . . www.southvermont.com
This is Vermont . . . . www.thisisvermont.com
Travel.org-Vermont . . . . travel.org/vermont.html
Vermont Cities . . . . dir.yahoo.com/Regional/U_S__States/Vermont/Cities
Vermont Counties & Regions . . . . dir.yahoo.com/Regional/U_S__States/Vermont/Counties_and_Regions
Vermont Living . . . . www.vtliving.com
Vermont Scenario . . . . scenariousa.dstylus.com/vt/indexf.htm
Vermont Travel & Tourism Guide . . . . www.travel-library.com/north_america/usa/vermont/index.html
Vermont.com . . . . www.vermont.com
VermontGuides.com . . . . www.vermontguides.com
Virtual Vermont . . . . www.virtualvermont.com
Welcome to Rural Vermont . . . . www.ruralvermont.com
Yahoo! Get Local Vermont . . . . dir.yahoo.com/Regional/U_S__States/Vermont

— Cities Profiled —

Page

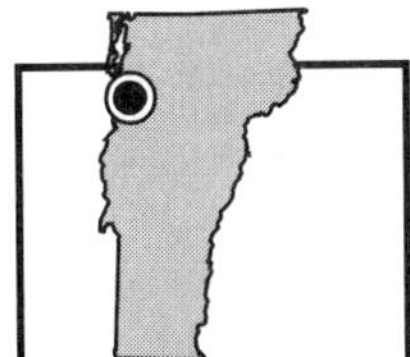

Burlington

Situated along the eastern shore of Lake Champlain, with the Green Mountains to the east and the Adirondacks across the lake to the west, Vermont's largest city offers not only panoramic scenery, but also a wide range of water- and mountain-oriented events and activities. Five New England ski resorts are within an hour's drive of Burlington, and the area is also home to the Taproot Morgan Horse Farm and the Lake Champlain Maritime Museum.

Population 38,453
Area (Land) . . . . 10.5 sq mi
Area (Water) . . . . 4.9 sq mi
Elevation . . . . 113 ft
Latitude . . . . 44-48-50 N
Longitude . . . . 73-22-09 W
County . . . . Chittenden
Time Zone . . . . EST
Area Code/s 802

— Average Temperatures and Precipitation —

TEMPERATURES

	Jan	Feb	Mar	Apr	May	Jun	Jul	Aug	Sep	Oct	Nov	Dec
High	25	28	39	54	67	76	81	78	69	57	44	30
Low	8	9	22	34	45	55	60	58	49	39	30	16

PRECIPITATION

	Jan	Feb	Mar	Apr	May	Jun	Jul	Aug	Sep	Oct	Nov	Dec
Inches	1.8	1.6	2.2	2.8	3.1	3.5	3.7	4.1	3.3	2.9	3.1	2.4

— Important Phone Numbers —

	Phone
AAA	802-863-1323
American Express Travel	802-878-5326
Dental Referral	802-864-0115
Emergency	911
Poison Control Center	877-658-3456
Weather	802-862-2475

— Information Sources —

				Phone	Fax
Burlington City Hall Main & Church Sts Rm 20	Burlington	VT	05401	802-865-7272	865-7024
Web: www.ci.burlington.vt.us					
Burlington Convention & Visitors Bureau 60 Main St Suite 100	Burlington	VT	05401	802-863-3489	863-1538
Web: www.vermont.org ■ *E-mail:* vermont@vermont.org					
Burlington Mayor City Hall Rm 34	Burlington	VT	05401	802-865-7272	865-7024
Web: www.burlingtonvt.together.com/mayor/mayor.htm ■ *E-mail:* clavelle@vbimail.champlain.edu					
Burlington Memorial Auditorium 250 Main St	Burlington	VT	05401	802-864-6044	863-4322
Burlington Planning & Zoning Dept 135 Church St	Burlington	VT	05401	802-865-7188	865-7195
Web: homepages.together.net/~burlgis					
Chittenden County PO Box 187	Burlington	VT	05402	802-863-3467	
Fletcher Free Public Library 235 College St	Burlington	VT	05401	802-863-3403	865-7227
Lake Champlain Regional Chamber of Commerce 60 Main St Suite 100	Burlington	VT	05401	802-863-3489	863-1538
TF: 877-686-5253 ■ *Web:* www.vermont.org					

On-Line Resources

About.com Guide to Burlington . . . . burlingtonvt.about.com
Area Guide Burlington . . . . burlington.areaguides.net
BurlingtonVermont.com . . . . www.burlingtonvt.com/
City Knowledge Burlington . . . . www.cityknowledge.com/vt_burlington.htm
Excite.com Burlington City Guide . . . . www.excite.com/travel/countries/united_states/vermont/burlington
Rough Guide Travel Burlington travel.roughguides.com/content/438/
Welcome to Burlington Vermont . . . . discover-vermont.com/burlington/welcome.htm

— Transportation Services —

AIRPORTS

	Phone
■ **Burlington International Airport (BTV)** 3 miles E of downtown (approx 10 minutes)	802-863-2874

Airport Transportation

	Phone
Anywhere Taxi $8.50 fare to downtown	802-658-5131
B & B Taxi $7.50 fare to downtown	802-862-3300
Checker Cab $7.50 fare to downtown	802-864-7474

Commercial Airlines

	Phone
Continental Express	800-525-0280
Delta Connection	800-221-1212
United	800-241-6522
United Express	800-241-6522
US Airways	800-428-4322
US Airways Express	800-428-4322

Charter Airlines

	Phone
Valley Air Services	802-863-3626

CAR RENTALS

	Phone
Avis	802-864-0411
Budget	802-658-1211
Hertz	802-864-7409
Thrifty	802-863-5500

LIMO/TAXI

	Phone
Anywhere Taxi	802-658-5131
B & B Taxi	802-862-3300
Checker Cab	802-864-7474
Chittenden Taxi	802-862-6446
Green Mountain Limousine Service	800-698-4100
Limos For Less	802-865-8005
Yellow Cab	802-864-7411

MASS TRANSIT

	Phone
Chittenden County Transit Authority $1 Base fare	802-864-0211

RAIL/BUS

				Phone
Amtrak Station 29 Railroad Ave	Essex Junction	VT	05452	802-879-7298
TF: 800-872-7245				
Vermont Transit Bus Station 345 Pine St	Burlington	VT	05401	802-864-6811

— Accommodations —

HOTELS, MOTELS, RESORTS

				Phone	Fax
Anchorage Inn 108 Dorset St	South Burlington	VT	05403	802-863-7000	
Basin Harbor Club Basin Harbor Rd	Vergennes	VT	05491	802-475-2311	475-6545
Web: www.basinharbor.com ■ *E-mail:* res@basinharbor.com					
Best Western 1076 Williston Rd	South Burlington	VT	05403	802-863-1125	658-1296
TF: 800-371-1125					
Colonial Motor Inn 462 Shelburne Rd	Burlington	VT	05401	802-862-5754	860-0998
Comfort Inn 1285 Williston Rd	South Burlington	VT	05403	802-865-3400	865-3400
TF: 800-228-5150					
Days Inn Colchester 23 College Pkwy	Colchester	VT	05446	802-655-0900	655-6851
TF: 800-336-1445					
Ethan Allen Motel 1611 Williston Rd	South Burlington	VT	05403	802-863-4573	
Fairfield Inn by Marriott 15 S Park Dr	Colchester	VT	05446	802-655-1400	655-1400
TF: 800-228-2800 ■ *Web:* fairfieldinn.com/BTVFI					
Hampton Inn 8 Mountain View Dr	Colchester	VT	05446	802-655-6177	655-4962
TF: 800-426-7866					
Holiday Inn Burlington 1068 Williston Rd	South Burlington	VT	05403	802-863-6363	863-3061
TF: 800-799-6363 ■ *Web:* www.basshotels.com/holiday-inn/?_franchisee=BTVVT ■ *E-mail:* holiday@together.net					

Burlington — Hotels, Motels, Resorts (Cont'd)

Name	City	State	Zip	Phone	Fax
Holiday Inn Express 1712 Shelburne Rd *TF:* 800-874-1554	South Burlington	VT	05403	802-860-1112	860-1112
Howard Johnson Hotel & Suites 1720 Shelburne Rd *TF:* 800-874-1554	South Burlington	VT	05403	802-860-6000	864-9919
Howard Johnson Inn 1 Dorset St *TF:* 800-808-4656	South Burlington	VT	05403	802-863-5541	862-2755
Marble Island Resort PO Box 646	Colchester	VT	05446	802-864-6800	864-7047
Radisson Hotel Burlington 60 Battery St *TF:* 800-333-3333	Burlington	VT	05401	802-658-6500	658-4659
Ramada Inn & Conference Center 1117 Williston Rd *TF:* 800-272-6232	South Burlington	VT	05403	802-658-0250	660-7516
Residence Inn by Marriott 35 Hurricane Ln *TF:* 800-331-3131 ■ *Web:* www.residenceinn.com/BTVBU	Williston	VT	05495	802-878-2001	878-0025
Sheraton Hotel & Conference Center 870 Williston Rd *TF:* 800-325-3535	South Burlington	VT	05403	802-865-6600	865-6670
Smugglers' Notch Resort 4323 Vermont Rt 108 S *TF:* 800-451-8752 ■ *Web:* www.smuggs.com ■ *E-mail:* smuggs@smuggs.com	Smugglers' Notch	VT	05464	802-644-8851	644-1230
Stowe Mountain Resort 5781 Mountain Rd *TF:* 800-253-4754 ■ *Web:* www.hyperski.com/vermont/stowe_sm.html ■ *E-mail:* stosales@sover.net	Stowe	VT	05672	802-253-3000	253-3659
Stoweflake Inn & Resort 1746 Mountain Rd *TF:* 800-253-2232	Stowe	VT	05672	802-253-7355	253-4419
Super 8 Motel 1016 Shelburne Rd *TF:* 800-800-8000	South Burlington	VT	05403	802-862-6421	862-8009
Susse Chalet Inn 590 St George Rd *TF:* 800-524-2538 ■ *Web:* www.sussechalet.com/williston.html	Williston	VT	05495	802-879-8999	879-2735
Town & Country Motel 490 Shelburne Rd	South Burlington	VT	05401	802-862-5786	
Travelodge 2572 Shelburne Rd *TF:* 800-578-7878	Shelburne	VT	05482	802-985-8037	985-8200

— Restaurants —

Name	City	State	Zip	Phone
Amigos (Mexican) 1900 Shelburne Rd	Shelburne	VT	05482	802-985-8226
Bourbon Street Grill (Cajun) 213 College St	Burlington	VT	05401	802-865-2800
Buono Appetito (Italian) 3182 Shelburne Rd	Shelburne	VT	05482	802-985-2232
Cafe Espresso (Italian) Rt 2A	Williston	VT	05495	802-879-3100
Cafe Shelburne (French) Rt 7	Shelburne	VT	05482	802-985-3939
Carbur's (Continental) 115 Saint Paul St	Burlington	VT	05401	802-862-4106
Chef Leus House (Chinese) 3761 Shelburne Rd	Shelburne	VT	05482	802-985-5258
Chequers (American) Rt 2	Richmond	VT	05477	802-434-2870
Coyote's Tex-Mex Cafe (Tex Mex) 161 Church St	Burlington	VT	05401	802-865-3632
Dockside (Seafood) 209 Battery St	Burlington	VT	05401	802-864-5266
Five Spice Cafe (Pan-Asian) 175 Church St	Burlington	VT	05401	802-864-4045
Halvorson's Upstreet Cafe (American) 16 Church St	Burlington	VT	05401	802-658-0278
Hunan Chinese Restaurant (Chinese) 126 College St	Burlington	VT	05401	802-863-1023
Ice House Restaurant (American) 171 Battery St	Burlington	VT	05401	802-864-1800
India House Restaurant (Indian) 207 Colchester Ave	Burlington	VT	05401	802-862-7800
Isabel's on the Waterfront (American) 112 Lake St	Burlington	VT	05401	802-865-2522
Leunig's Bistro (American) 113 Church St	Burlington	VT	05401	802-862-5306
Mexicali Authentic Mexican Grill (Mexican) 299 Williston Rd Tafts Corner Shopping Ctr	Williston	VT	05495	802-879-9492
Oak Street Cafe (American) 60 Battery St	Burlington	VT	05401	802-658-6500
Orchid (Chinese) 5 Corporate Way	Burlington	VT	05403	802-658-3626
Pacific Rim Cafe (Pan-Asian) 111 Saint Paul St	Burlington	VT	05401	802-651-3000
Parlima (Thai) 185 Pearl St	Burlington	VT	05401	802-864-7917
Peking Duck House (Chinese) 79 W Canal St	Winooski	VT	05404	802-655-7474
Perry's (Seafood) 1080 Shelburne Rd	South Burlington	VT	05403	802-862-1300
Rusty Scuffer (Steak/Seafood) 148 Church St	Burlington	VT	05401	802-864-9451
Sakura (Japanese) 2 Church St	Burlington	VT	05401	802-863-1988
Shanty on the Shore (Seafood) 181 Battery St	Burlington	VT	05401	802-864-0238
Sweetwaters (American) 120 Church St	Burlington	VT	05401	802-864-9800
Tortilla Flat (Mexican) 317 Riverside Ave	Burlington	VT	05401	802-864-4874
Trattoria Delia (Italian) 152 Saint Paul St	Burlington	VT	05401	802-864-5253
Vermont Pub & Brewery of Burlington (American) 144 College St	Burlington	VT	05401	802-865-0500
Windjammer (Steak/Seafood) 1076 Williston Rd	South Burlington	VT	05403	802-862-6585

— Goods and Services —

SHOPPING

Name	City	State	Zip	Phone	Fax
Bennington Potters North 127 College St	Burlington	VT	05401	802-863-2221	
Burlington Square Mall 5 Burlington Sq	Burlington	VT	05401	802-658-2545	658-0181
Church Street Marketplace 135 Church St	Burlington	VT	05401	802-863-1648	865-7252
University Mall 155 Dorset St	South Burlington	VT	05403	802-863-1066	863-5836

BANKS

Name	City	State	Zip	Phone	Fax
Chittenden Bank PO Box 820 **Fax:* Mktg ■ *TF:* 800-752-0006 ■ *Web:* www.chittenden.com ■ *E-mail:* info@chittenden.com	Burlington	VT	05402	802-658-4000	660-1319*
Howard Bank NA 111 Main St	Burlington	VT	05401	802-658-1010	863-2442
KeyBank NA Vermont District 149 Bank St *TF Cust Svc:* 800-642-5154*	Burlington	VT	05401	802-658-1810	658-5566
Merchants Bank 275 Kennedy Dr *Web:* www.mnbank.com ■ *E-mail:* mnb@bnt.com	South Burlington	VT	05403	802-658-3400	865-1975
Vermont National Bank 150 Bank St	Burlington	VT	05401	802-863-8900	863-8914

BUSINESS SERVICES

Name	Phone	Name	Phone
Airborne Express	800-247-2676	**Manpower Temporary Services**	802-862-5747
BAX Global	800-225-5229	**Norell Staffing Services**	802-864-5900
DHL Worldwide Express	800-225-5345	**Olsten Staffing Services**	802-658-9111
Federal Express	800-238-5355	**Post Office**	802-863-6033
Kinko's	802-658-2561	**UPS**	800-742-5877
Mail Boxes Etc	800-789-4623	**Westaff**	802-862-6500

— Media —

PUBLICATIONS

Name	City	State	Zip	Phone	Fax
Burlington Free Press‡ 191 College St *TF:* 800-872-6414 ■ *Web:* www.burlingtonfreepress.com	Burlington	VT	05401	802-863-3441	660-1802

‡*Daily newspapers*

TELEVISION

Name	City	State	Zip	Phone	Fax
WBVT-TV Ch 39 (WB) 29 Church St Suite 9 *Web:* www.wbvt.com ■ *E-mail:* other@wbvt.com	Burlington	VT	05401	802-660-0036	660-2701
WCAX-TV Ch 3 (CBS) 30 Joy Dr *Web:* www.wcax.com	South Burlington	VT	05403	802-658-6300	652-6399
WETK-TV Ch 33 (PBS) 88 Ethan Allen Ave *Web:* www.vermontpublictv.org	Colchester	VT	05446	802-655-4800	655-6593
WFFF-TV Ch 44 (Fox) 1233 Shelburne Rd Lakewood Commons Suite 200	South Burlington	VT	05403	802-660-9333	660-8673
WPTZ-TV Ch 5 (NBC) 5 Television Dr *Web:* www.wptz.com	Plattsburgh	NY	12901	518-561-5555	561-5940
WVNY-TV Ch 22 (ABC) 530 Shelburne Rd	Burlington	VT	05401	802-658-8022	863-2422

RADIO

Name	City	State	Zip	Phone	Fax
WEZF-FM 92.9 MHz (AC) 1500 Hegeman Ave	Colchester	VT	05446	802-655-0093	655-0478
WJOY-AM 1230 kHz (Nost) PO Box 4489 *E-mail:* wjoy@hall.com	Burlington	VT	05403	802-658-1230	862-0786
WKDR-AM 1390 kHz (N/T) 1 Main St *TF:* 800-286-9537 ■ *Web:* www.mainstreetvermont.com/wkdr1.htm ■ *E-mail:* wkdr@together.net	Winooski	VT	05404	802-655-6753	655-4284
WOKO-FM 98.9 MHz (Ctry) PO Box 4489 *E-mail:* woko@hallradio.com	Burlington	VT	05406	802-658-1230	862-0786
WRUV-FM 90.1 MHz (Misc) University of Vermont	Burlington	VT	05405	802-656-0796	656-2281

— Colleges/Universities —

Name	City	State	Zip	Phone	Fax
Burlington College 95 North Ave *TF Admissions:* 800-862-9616 ■ *Web:* www.burlcol.edu	Burlington	VT	05401	802-862-9616	658-0071
Saint Michael's College Winooski Pk *TF Admissions:* 800-762-8000 ■ *Web:* waldo.smcvt.edu	Colchester	VT	05439	802-654-2000	654-2591
Trinity College of Vermont 208 Colchester Ave *TF:* 888-277-5975 ■ *Web:* www.trinityvt.edu	Burlington	VT	05401	802-658-0337	658-5446
University of Vermont 85 S Prospect St *Web:* www.uvm.edu ■ *E-mail:* admissions@uvm.edu	Burlington	VT	05405	802-656-3131	656-8611

Burlington (Cont'd)

— Hospitals —

				Phone	Fax
Fletcher Allen Health Care 111 Colchester Ave *Web:* www.fahc.org	Burlington	VT	05401	802-656-2345	656-5677

— Attractions —

				Phone	Fax
Ben & Jerry's Rt 100 N *Web:* www.benjerry.com	Waterbury	VT	05676	802-244-5641	882-1249
Burklyn Ballet Theatre Johnson State College PO Box 302	Johnson	VT	05656	802-862-6466	
Colburn Francis Gallery University of Vermont Williams Hall	Burlington	VT	05405	802-656-2014	656-2064
Ethan Allen Homestead 1 Ethan Allen Homestead	Burlington	VT	05401	802-865-4556	
Fleming Robert Hull Museum 61 Colchester Ave University of Vermont	Burlington	VT	05405	802-656-0750	656-8059
Flynn Theatre for the Performing Arts 153 Main St	Burlington	VT	05401	802-863-5966	863-8776
Green Mountain Audubon Nature Center 255 Sherman Hollow Rd	Huntington	VT	05462	802-434-3068	434-4686
Lake Champlain Basin Science Center 1 College St *Web:* www.uvm.edu/~lcbsc	Burlington	VT	05401	802-864-1848	864-6832
Lake Champlain Maritime Museum 4472 Basin Harbor Rd *Web:* www.lcmm.org ■ *E-mail:* lcmm@sover.net	Vergennes	VT	05491	802-475-2022	
National Museum of the Morgan Horse PO Box 700	Shelburne	VT	05482	802-985-8665	985-5242
Rokeby Museum 4334 Rt 7	Ferrisburg	VT	05456	802-877-3406	
Shelburne Farms Rt 7	Shelburne	VT	05482	802-985-8442	
Shelburne Museum 5555 Shelburne Rd *Web:* www.burnemuseum.org	Shelburne	VT	05482	802-985-3346	985-2331
Spirit of Ethan Allen Cruise College St Burlington Boathouse	Burlington	VT	05401	802-862-9685	
Taproot Morgan Horse Farm Shelburne/Hinesburg Rd	Hinesburg	VT	05461	802-482-2168	
Theatre Factory Inc 6 Chestnut Ln Suite 1 *Web:* homepages.together.net/~theatre/ ■ *E-mail:* theatre@together.net	Colchester	VT	05446	802-872-2738	
Vermont Symphony Orchestra 2 Church St *Web:* www.vso.org	Burlington	VT	05401	802-864-5741	864-5109
Vermont Teddy Bear Co Inc 6655 Shelburne Rd *TF:* 800-829-2327 ■ *Web:* www.vtbear.com	Shelburne	VT	05482	802-985-3001	985-1104
Vermont Wildflower Farm Rt 7	Charlotte	VT	05445	802-425-3500	

SPORTS TEAMS & FACILITIES

				Phone	Fax
Vermont Expos (baseball) Champlain Mill Box 4 *Web:* www.vermontexpos.com	Winooski	VT	05404	802-655-4200	655-5660
Vermont Voltage (soccer) 3 Liberty St	Montpelier	VT	05602	802-229-6233	229-6442

— Events —

	Phone
Burlington Winter Festival (mid-February)	802-864-0123
Champlain Valley Fair (late August-early September)	802-878-5545
Champlain Valley Folk Festival (early August)	800-769-9176
Church Street Marketplace Holiday Season (late November-late December)	802-863-1648
Colchester Holiday Show (early December)	802-878-7559
Discover Jazz Festival (mid-June)	802-863-7992
Essex Fall Craft Show (late October)	802-878-4786
Fall Harvest Festival (mid-September)	802-879-5226
First Night Burlington (December 31)	802-863-6005
Green Mountain Festival of Trees (late November)	802-656-5100
International Craft Fair & Cultural Expo (early December)	802-863-6713
Latino Festival (early August)	802-864-0123
Marketfest (mid-September)	802-863-1648
Stowe Winter Carnival (late January-early February)	802-253-7321
Stoweflake Hot Air Balloon Festival (mid-July)	802-253-7321
Vermont Brewers Festival (mid-July)	802-244-6828
Vermont City Marathon & Marathon Relay (late May)	802-863-8412
Vermont International Film Festival (late October)	802-660-2600
Vermont Mozart Festival (mid-July-mid-August)	802-862-7352

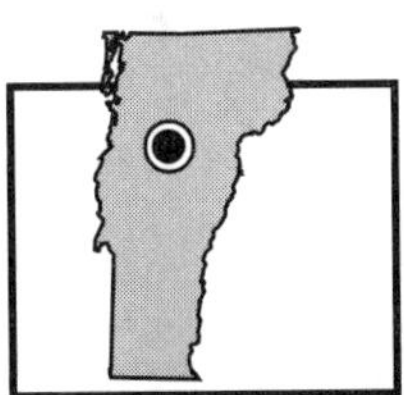

Montpelier

The Vermont State House is set against a wooded hillside in downtown Montpelier, the nation's smallest state capital. A statue of the Vermont folk hero Ethan Allen stands at the Capitol's front doors. Just blocks from the Capitol are the picnic areas and nature trails of Hubbard Park. Hubbard Tower is the city's highest point and affords a view of the entire countryside. The fall foliage and Sugarbush and Mad River Glen ski resorts draw tourists to Montpelier and surrounding Central Vermont cities. Many backroads tours of the area begin in Montpelier and wind around Central Vermont, showing the sugaring process, rural farms, covered bridges, or the Green Mountains.

Population	7,734	**Longitude**	72-57-58 W
Area (Land)	10.3 sq mi	**County**	Washington
Area (Water)	0 sq mi	**Time Zone**	EST
Elevation	525 ft	**Area Code/s**	802
Latitude	44-26-00 N		

— Average Temperatures and Precipitation —

TEMPERATURES

	Jan	Feb	Mar	Apr	May	Jun	Jul	Aug	Sep	Oct	Nov	Dec
High	25	27	37	51	65	73	78	75	67	56	42	29
Low	6	8	19	31	42	51	56	54	46	36	27	13

PRECIPITATION

	Jan	Feb	Mar	Apr	May	Jun	Jul	Aug	Sep	Oct	Nov	Dec
Inches	2.2	2.1	2.3	2.4	3.2	3.5	3.1	3.8	2.9	2.8	3.2	2.8

— Important Phone Numbers —

	Phone		Phone
AAA	802-223-5291	**Medical Referral**	802-223-7898
American Express Travel	802-229-0055	**Poison Control Center**	802-658-3456
Dental Referral	802-864-0115	**Weather**	802-655-2322
Emergency	911		

— Information Sources —

				Phone	Fax
Central Vermont Chamber of Commerce PO Box 336 *Web:* www.central-vt.com/chamber/index.html ■ *E-mail:* cvchamber@aol.com	Barre	VT	05641	802-229-5711	229-5713
Kellogg-Hubbard Library 135 Main St *Web:* www.state.vt.us/libraries/m761 ■ *E-mail:* kellogg_hubb@dol.state.vt.us	Montpelier	VT	05602	802-223-3338	223-3338
Montpelier City Hall 39 Main St *Web:* montpelier-vt.org	Montpelier	VT	05602	802-223-9502	223-9519
Montpelier Mayor 39 Main St	Montpelier	VT	05602	802-223-9502	223-9519
Montpelier Planning & Development Dept 39 Main St *Web:* montpelier-vt.org/montpelier/htm/citydepts_planning_dev.shtml	Montpelier	VT	05602	802-223-9506	223-9524
Washington County PO Box 426	Montpelier	VT	05602	802-828-2091	

Montpelier (Cont'd)

On-Line Resources

Area Guide Montpelier ....montpelier.areaguides.net
Excite.com Montpelier
City Guide .... www.excite.com/travel/countries/united_states/vermont/montpelier
Montpelier Vermont Home Page.......... www.discover-vermont.com/Montpelier/Montpelier.htm

— Transportation Services —

AIRPORTS

■ **Burlington International Airport (BTV)** — *Phone*

35 miles NW of downtown Montpelier (approx 45 minutes) 802-863-2874

Airport Transportation

	Phone
Benways Taxi $55 fare to downtown Montpelier	802-862-1010
Pierce's Taxi $65 fare to downtown Montpelier	802-888-4025

Commercial Airlines

	Phone		*Phone*
Continental Express	800-525-0280	**United Express**	800-241-6522
Delta Connection	800-221-1212	**US Airways**	800-428-4322
Northwest	800-225-2525	**US Airways Express**	800-428-4322
United	800-241-6522		

Charter Airlines

	Phone		*Phone*
Northern Airways	800-245-0087	**Valley Air Services**	802-863-3626

CAR RENTALS

	Phone		*Phone*
Avis	802-864-0411	**Hertz**	802-864-7409
Avis-Montpelier	802-864-0411	**Thrifty**	802-863-5500
Budget	802-658-1211		

LIMO/TAXI

	Phone		*Phone*
Benways Taxi	802-862-1010	**Pierce's Taxi**	802-888-4025
Limo Service by Jules	802-476-8658	**Richard's Limo**	802-888-3176

MASS TRANSIT

	Phone
Wheels Transportation $1.25 Base fare	802-223-2882

RAIL/BUS

				Phone
Amtrak Station Montpelier Junction Rd *TF:* 800-872-7245	Montpelier	VT	05602	800-872-7245
Vermont Transit Bus Station 1 Taylor St	Montpelier	VT	05602	802-223-7112

— Accommodations —

HOTELS, MOTELS, RESORTS

				Phone	*Fax*
Betsy's Bed & Breakfast 74 E State St *Web:* www.central-vt.com/web/betsybb ■ *E-mail:* betsybb@together.net	Montpelier	VT	05602	802-229-0466	229-5412
Bridges Resort & Racquet Club Sugarbush Access Rd *TF:* 800-453-2922 ■ *Web:* www.thebridges.com ■ *E-mail:* bridgesresort@madriver.com	Warren	VT	05674	802-583-2922	583-1018
Budget Inn 573 N Main St	Barre	VT	05641	802-479-3333	479-0529
Capitol Plaza Hotel 100 State St. *TF:* 800-274-5252	Montpelier	VT	05602	802-223-5252	229-5427
Comfort Inn 213 Paine Tpke N *TF:* 800-228-5150	Berlin	VT	05602	802-229-2222	229-2222
Days Inn 173 S Main St. *TF:* 800-329-7466	Barre	VT	05641	802-476-6678	476-6678
Doyles Guest House 35 School St	Montpelier	VT	05602	802-223-3535	
Econo Lodge 101 Northfield St *TF:* 800-553-2666	Montpelier	VT	05602	802-223-5258	223-0716
Golden Eagle Resort 511 Mountain Rd *TF:* 800-626-1010 ■ *Web:* www.stoweinfo.com/saa/golden_eagle/ ■ *E-mail:* stoweagle@aol.com	Stowe	VT	05672	802-253-4811	253-2561
Hollow Inn 278 S Main St *TF:* 800-998-9444	Barre	VT	05641	802-479-9313	476-5242
Inn at Montpelier 147 Main St	Montpelier	VT	05602	802-223-2727	223-0722
La Gue Inn 394 Fisher Rd *Web:* www.lagueinc.com/lagueinn.htm	Berlin	VT	05602	802-229-5766	229-5766
Montpelier Guest Home 22 North St.	Montpelier	VT	05602	802-229-0878	229-0878
Ramada Inn Holiday Inn Dr *TF:* 800-272-6232	White River Junction	VT	05001	802-295-3000	295-3774
Sugarbush Resort & Inn RR 1 Box 350 *TF:* 800-537-8427 ■ *Web:* www.sugarbush.com ■ *E-mail:* info@sugarbush.com	Warren	VT	05673	802-583-6130	583-3209
Topnotch At Stowe Resort & Spa PO Box 1458 *TF:* 800-451-8686 ■ *Web:* www.topnotch-resort.com	Stowe	VT	05672	802-253-8585	253-9263
Trapp Family Lodge 700 Trapp Hill Rd *TF:* 800-826-7000 ■ *Web:* www.trappfamily.com ■ *E-mail:* info@trappfamily.com	Stowe	VT	05672	802-253-8511	253-5740
Twin City Motel 1537 US Rt 302-Berlin	Barre	VT	05641	802-476-3104	476-3105
Vermonter Motel 509 Montpelier Rd	Barre	VT	05641	802-476-8541	

— Restaurants —

				Phone
About Thyme Cafe (Vegetarian) 40 State St	Montpelier	VT	05602	802-223-0427
China Star Chinese Restaurant (Chinese) 15 Main St	Montpelier	VT	05602	802-223-0808
Del's Pizza & Pasta House (Italian) 248 N Main St	Barre	VT	05641	802-476-6684
Horn of the Moon Cafe (Vegetarian) 8 Langdon St	Montpelier	VT	05602	802-223-2895
House of Tang (Chinese) 114 River St	Montpelier	VT	05602	802-223-6020
Julio's Restaurant (Tex Mex) 44 Main St	Montpelier	VT	05602	802-229-9348
La Pizzaria (Italian) 23 Berlin St	Montpelier	VT	05602	802-229-5122
Lobster Pot (Steak/Seafood) 1028 US Rt 302	Barre	VT	05641	802-476-9900
Main Street Grill & Bar (Continental) 118 Main St	Montpelier	VT	05602	802-223-3188
McGillicuddy's Irish Pub (American) 14 Langdon St	Montpelier	VT	05602	802-223-2721
Sambel's Restaurant (American) Main St	Northfield Falls	VT	05664	802-223-6776
Sarducci's (Italian) 3 Main St	Montpelier	VT	05602	802-223-0229
Soup'N Greens Restaurant (Steak/Seafood) 321 N Main St	Barre	VT	05641	802-479-9862
Steak House Restaurant (Steak) 354 Barre-Montpelier Rd	Berlin	VT	05641	802-479-9181
Suzanna's Restaurant (American) Airport Rd	Berlin	VT	05602	802-229-5766
Thrush Tavern (American) 107 State St	Montpelier	VT	05602	802-223-2030

— Goods and Services —

SHOPPING

				Phone
Berlin Mall 282 Berlin Mall Rd	Berlin	VT	05602	802-229-4151
Sears Roebuck & Co 1598 US Rt 302-Berlin	Barre	VT	05641	802-479-2541

BANKS

				Phone	*Fax*
Howard Bank 90 Main St	Montpelier	VT	05602	802-223-5203	223-0518
Northfield Savings Bank 100 State St *TF:* 800-672-2274	Montpelier	VT	05602	802-223-3488	229-2165
Vermont National Bank 7 Main St	Montpelier	VT	05602	802-223-9545	223-9538

BUSINESS SERVICES

	Phone		*Phone*
Airborne Express	800-247-2676	**Kelly Services**	802-229-5082
BAX Global	800-225-5229	**Mail Boxes Etc**	800-789-4623
DHL Worldwide Express	800-225-5345	**Post Office**	802-229-1718
Federal Express	800-238-5355	**UPS**	800-742-5877

— Media —

PUBLICATIONS

				Phone	*Fax*
Times-Argus‡ 112 Main St. *Web:* www.timesargus.com	Montpelier	VT	05602	802-223-3191	229-2046

Montpelier — Publications (Cont'd)

				Phone	Fax
Vermont Life 6 Baldwin St	Montpelier	VT	05602	802-828-3241	828-3366
TF: 800-284-3243 ■ *Web:* www.vtlife.com					

‡*Daily newspapers*

TELEVISION

				Phone	Fax
WETK-TV Ch 33 (PBS) 88 Ethan Allen Ave	Colchester	VT	05446	802-655-4800	655-6593
Web: www.vermontpublictv.org					
WNNE-TV Ch 31 (NBC) 203 Dewitt Dr	White River Junction	VT	05001	802-295-3100	295-9056*
**Fax:* News Rm ■ *TF:* 800-996-6388 ■ *Web:* www.wnne.com ■ *E-mail:* info@wnne.com					
WVNY-TV Ch 22 (ABC) 530 Shelburne Rd	Burlington	VT	05401	802-658-8022	863-2422

RADIO

				Phone	Fax
WCVT-FM 101.7 MHz (Clas) PO Box 3536	Stowe	VT	05672	802-244-1764	244-1771
TF: 800-498-4877 ■ *E-mail:* wcvt@classicvermont.com					
WDEV-AM 550 kHz (AC) 9 Stowe St	Waterbury	VT	05676	802-244-7321	244-1771
TF: 800-639-9338					
WNCS-FM 104.7 MHz (AAA) PO Box 551	Montpelier	VT	05601	802-223-2396	223-1520
Web: pointfm.com/wncs/htm/home.shtml					
WORK-FM 107.1 MHz (CHR) 41 Jacques St.	Barre	VT	05641	802-476-4168	479-5893
Web: www.workradio.com					
WSKI-AM 1240 kHz (Oldies) PO Box 487	Montpelier	VT	05601	802-223-5275	223-1520
WSNO-AM 1450 kHz (N/T) 41 Jacques St	Barre	VT	05641	802-476-4168	479-5893

— Colleges/Universities —

				Phone	Fax
Goddard College 123 Pitkin Rd	Plainfield	VT	05667	802-454-8311	454-8017
TF Admissions: 800-468-4888 ■ *Web:* www.goddard.edu ■ *E-mail:* ellenc@earth.goddard.edu					
New England Culinary Institute 250 Main St	Montpelier	VT	05602	802-223-6324	223-0634
TF: 877-223-6324 ■ *Web:* www.neculinary.com					
Norwich University 158 Harmon Dr.	Northfield	VT	05663	802-485-2000	485-2032
TF: 800-468-6679 ■ *Web:* www.norwich.edu					
Vermont College of Norwich University 36 College St	Montpelier	VT	05602	802-828-8500	828-8855
TF Admissions: 800-336-6794 ■ *Web:* www.norwich.edu/vermontcollege ■ *E-mail:* vcadmis@norwich.edu					

— Hospitals —

				Phone	Fax
Central Vermont Medical Center Fisher Rd	Berlin	VT	05602	802-371-4100	371-4402
Mountain View Physicians Center 195 Hospital Loop Suite 3	Berlin	VT	05602	802-223-6196	229-6137
Vermont State Hospital 103 S Main St	Waterbury	VT	05671	802-241-1000	241-3001

— Attractions —

				Phone	Fax
Barre Opera House 6 N Main St	Barre	VT	05641	802-476-8188	476-5648
Web: www.geocities.com/Broadway/4339					
Ben & Jerry's Rt 100 N	Waterbury	VT	05676	802-244-5641	882-1249
Web: www.benjerry.com					
Bragg Farm Sugar House Rt 14 N	East Montpelier	VT	05651	802-223-5757	
TF: 800-376-5757 ■ *Web:* www.central-vt.com/web/bragg					
Chimney Point State Historic Site Rt 74 & Hwy 125	Vergennes	VT	05491	802-759-2412	759-2547
Cold Hollow Cider Mill Rt 100 Waterbury Ctr	Waterbury	VT	05677	802-244-8771	244-7212
TF: 800-327-7537 ■ *Web:* www.coldhollow.com					
Danforth's Sugarhouse US Rt 2	East Montpelier	VT	05651	802-229-9536	229-1527
TF: 800-887-9536					
Lost Nation Theater 39 Main St	Montpelier	VT	05602	802-229-0492	
Web: www.lostnationtheater.org					
Morse Farm County Rd 1168	Montpelier	VT	05602	802-223-2740	223-7450
TF: 800-242-2740 ■ *Web:* www.morsefarm.com ■ *E-mail:* maple@morsefarm.com					
President Chester A Arthur Birthplace Chester Arthur Rd	Fairfield	VT	05455	802-828-3051	828-3206
Rock of Ages Tourist Center 773 Graniteville Rd	Graniteville	VT	05654	802-476-3115	476-3110
Web: www.rockofages.com/visitor.htm ■ *E-mail:* visitor@rockofages.com					
TW Wood Gallery & Art Center 36 College St	Montpelier	VT	05602	802-828-8743	828-8855
Vermont Historical Society Museum 109 State St Pavilion Bldg	Montpelier	VT	05609	802-828-2291	828-3638
Web: www.state.vt.us/vhs ■ *E-mail:* vhs@vhs.state.vt.us					
Vermont State House 115 State St	Montpelier	VT	05602	802-828-2228	828-2424
TF: 800-322-5616 ■ *Web:* www.leg.state.vt.us					

SPORTS TEAMS & FACILITIES

				Phone	Fax
Vermont Voltage (soccer) 3 Liberty St	Montpelier	VT	05602	802-229-6233	229-6442

— Events —

	Phone
Barre Art Show (late September)	802-476-7513
Barre Tones Barber Shop Musical (late September)	802-229-7623
Lawn Fest (mid-September & early October)	802-244-8089
New England Bach Festival (early-mid-October)	802-257-4523
Old Time Fiddler's Contest (late September)	802-476-0256
Vermont Farm Show (late January)	802-828-2433

Virginia

Population (1999): 6,872,912 **Area (sq mi): 42,777**

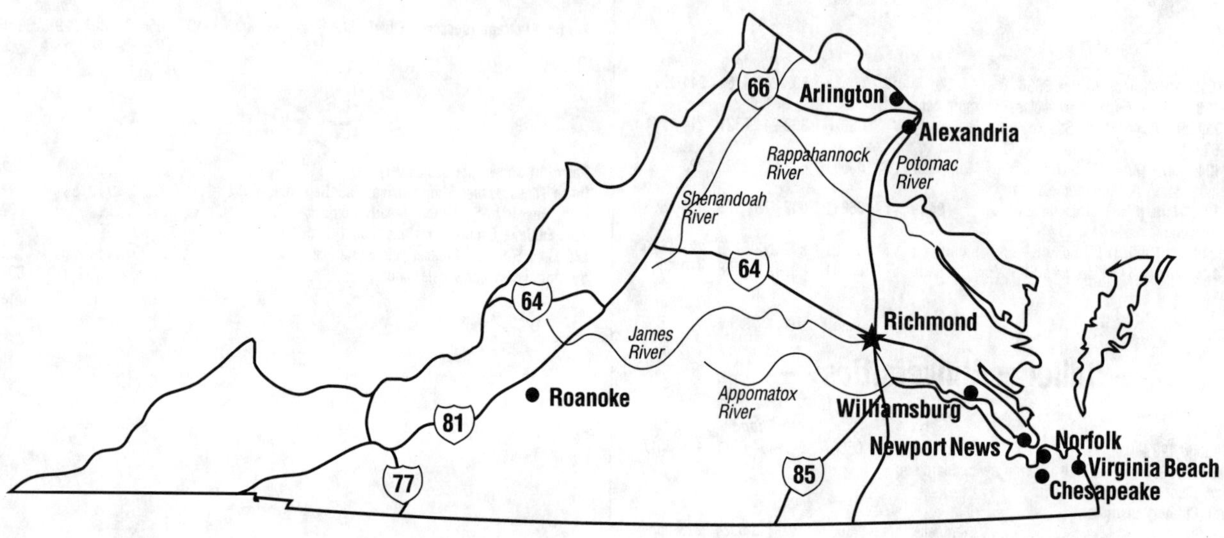

— State Information Sources —

				Phone	Fax
Virginia Chamber of Commerce 9 S 5th St . . .	Richmond	VA	23219	804-644-1607	783-0903
TF: 800-477-7682 ■ *Web:* www.vachamber.com					
Virginia Economic Development Dept 901 E Byrd St.	Richmond	VA	23219	804-371-8100	371-8112
Web: www2.yesvirginia.org					
Virginia Library 800 E Broad St	Richmond	VA	23219	804-692-3500	692-3594
Web: leo.vsla.edu					
Virginia State Government Information				804-786-0000	
Web: www.state.va.us ■ *E-mail:* aphaup.dit@state.va.us					
Virginia State Parks Div 203 Governor St Suite 302.	Richmond	VA	23219	804-786-1712	371-2072
TF: 800-933-7275 ■ *Web:* www.state.va.us/~dcr/parks/parkindx.htm					
Virginia Tourism Div 901 E Byrd St	Richmond	VA	23219	804-786-4484	786-1919
TF: 800-847-4882 ■ *Web:* www.virginia.org					

ON-LINE RESOURCES

Daily Orbit Virginia . . . . www.dailyorbit.com/virginia
Eastern Shore of Virginia Directory. . . . . www.easternshorevirginia.com
Rough Guide Travel Virginia travel.roughguides.com/content/587/index.htm
Travel.org-Virginia . . . . travel.org/virginia.html
Virginia Cities. . . . . dir.yahoo.com/Regional/U_S__States/Virginia/Cities
Virginia Counties & Regions . . . dir.yahoo.com/Regional/U_S__States/Virginia/Counties_and_Regions
Virginia Scenario . . . . scenariousa.dstylus.com/va/indexf.htm
Virginia Travel & Tourism Guide . . . . . www.travel-library.com/north_america/usa/virginia/index.html
Virginia Waterfront . . . . www.thevirginiawaterfront.com
Yahoo! Get Local Virginia . . . . dir.yahoo.com/Regional/U_S__States/Virginia

— Cities Profiled —

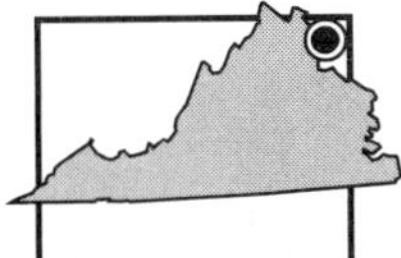

Alexandria

Alexandria is located in northern Virginia, just minutes from Arlington, VA and Washington, DC. It is one of America's most historic cities (about one-quarter of the town's 15 square miles has been designated as a national or local historic district), celebrating its 250th birthday in 1999. The founder of Alexandria was John Carlyle, and the Carlyle House and Historic Park today provide a unique example of 18th Century architecture. The city's most famous resident was George Washington, whose home, the Mount Vernon Estate and Gardens, is open to the public year-round. Washington attended services at Christ Church, and his pew remains there today; and he attended the last public celebration of his birthday at Gadsby's Tavern, which is now a museum. Alexandria was also the boyhood home of Robert E. Lee, and the Lee-Fendall House, which was built by a Lee descendant in 1875, contains many Lee furnishings, family records, and inventories. During the Civil War, Alexandria served as a supply and hospital center for the Union, and Alexandria National Cemetery, established in 1862, contains more than 3,500 graves of Civil War soldiers. The African-American Heritage Park commemorates the men and women of Alexandria's past; and the once-segregated library has become the Alexandria Black History Resource Center.

Population	118,300	**Longitude**	77-05-10 W
Area (Land)	15.3 sq mi	**County**	Independent City
Area (Water)	0.1 sq mi	**Time Zone**	EST
Elevation	30 ft	**Area Code/s**	703
Latitude	38-49-16 N		

— Average Temperatures and Precipitation —

TEMPERATURES

	Jan	Feb	Mar	Apr	May	Jun	Jul	Aug	Sep	Oct	Nov	Dec
High	43	47	58	68	77	86	89	87	81	71	59	47
Low	23	25	34	42	52	60	66	64	57	44	36	28

PRECIPITATION

	Jan	Feb	Mar	Apr	May	Jun	Jul	Aug	Sep	Oct	Nov	Dec
Inches	2.6	2.5	2.8	2.9	3.7	3.2	3.1	3.2	3.3	3.1	3.1	2.7

— Important Phone Numbers —

	Phone		*Phone*
AAA	703-549-1080	**Poison Control Center**	202-625-3333
American Express Travel	703-768-6020	**Special Events Hotline**	800-388-9119
Emergency	911	**Virginia Highway Conditions**	800-367-7623
HotelDocs	800-468-3537	**Weather**	202-936-1212
Medical Referral	703-204-3344		

— Information Sources —

				Phone	*Fax*
Alexandria Chamber of Commerce 801 N Fairfax St Suite 402 *Web:* www.alexchamber.com	Alexandria	VA	22314	703-549-1000	739-3805
Alexandria City Hall 301 King St *Web:* ci.alexandria.va.us	Alexandria	VA	22314	703-838-4000	838-6433
Alexandria Convention & Visitors Bureau 221 King St *TF:* 800-388-9119 ■ *Web:* www.funside.com ■ *E-mail:* acva@funside.com	Alexandria	VA	22314	703-838-4200	838-4683
Alexandria Economic Development Partnership Inc 1055 N Fairfax St Suite 204 *Web:* ci.alexandria.va.us/aedp ■ *E-mail:* alexecon@erols.com	Alexandria	VA	22314	703-739-3820	739-1384
Alexandria (Independent City) 301 King St Suite 2300 *Web:* ci.alexandria.va.us ■ *E-mail:* alexcity@capaccess.org	Alexandria	VA	22314	703-838-4000	838-6433
Alexandria Library 717 Queen St *Web:* www.alexandria.lib.va.us	Alexandria	VA	22314	703-838-4555	838-4524
Alexandria Mayor 301 King St City Hall *Web:* ci.alexandria.va.us/amacc/amacc.htm	Alexandria	VA	22314	703-838-4500	838-6433
Better Business Bureau Serving Metropolitan Washington 1411 K St NW 10th Fl. *Web:* www.dc.bbb.org ■ *E-mail:* sales@dc.bbb.org	Washington	DC	20005	202-393-8000	393-1198

On-Line Resources

4Alexandria.com	www.4alexandria.com
ALEX Electronic Alexandria Community	www.alex.org
Alexandria City Guide	alexandriacity.com
Anthill City Guide Alexandria	www.anthill.com/city.asp?city=alexandriawood
Area Guide Alexandria	alexandriava.areaguides.net
Excite.com Alexandria City Guide	www.excite.com/travel/countries/united_states/virginia/alexandria
I-95 Exit Information Guide Northern Virginia	www.usastar.com/i95/cityguide/nova.htm
NITC Travelbase City Guide Alexandria	www.travelbase.com/auto/guides/alexandria-va.html
Online City Guide to Alexandria	www.olcg.com/va/alexandria/index.html
PlacesToStay Alexandria	pts.placestostay.com/destination/usa/virginia/alexandria/dest.asp

— Transportation Services —

AIRPORTS

■ **Ronald Reagan Washington National Airport (DCA)**

	Phone
7 miles NE of downtown Alexandria (approx 10 minutes) Web: www.mwaa.com/National/index.html	703-417-8000

Airport Transportation

	Phone
Diamond Executive Transportation $25 fare to downtown Alexandria	703-549-6266
Metro Airport Shuttle $16 fare to downtown Alexandria	703-313-5005
Metrorail $1.10 fare to downtown Alexandria	202-637-7000
Supershuttle $10 fare to downtown Alexandria	800-258-3826
Yellow Cab $9 fare to downtown Alexandria	703-549-2500

Commercial Airlines

	Phone		*Phone*
Air Canada	800-776-3000	**Midwest Express**	800-452-2022
America West	800-235-9292	**Northwest**	800-225-2525
American	800-433-7300	**TWA**	800-221-2000
Continental	800-525-0280	**United**	800-241-6522
Delta	800-221-1212	**US Airways**	800-428-4322
Midway	800-446-4392		

Charter Airlines

	Phone
Pelican Air	703-820-3907

CAR RENTALS

	Phone		*Phone*
Bargain	703-317-0673	**Prestige**	703-418-7660
Enterprise	703-549-6434	**Thrifty**	703-684-2054
Premier	703-823-8383	**Total**	703-549-4493

LIMO/TAXI

	Phone		*Phone*
Alexandria VIP Cab	703-549-6900	**Majestic Limousine**	703-461-3700
Diamond Cab	703-549-6200	**White Top Cab**	703-644-4500
King Cab Co	703-549-3530	**Yellow Cab**	703-549-2500

MASS TRANSIT

	Phone
Metrorail/Metrobus $1.10 Base fare	202-637-7000

RAIL/BUS

				Phone
Amtrak Station 110 Callahan Dr Union Station	Alexandria	VA	22314	800-872-7245
Virginia Railway Express 110 Callahan Dr Union Station *TF:* 800-743-3873	Alexandria	VA	22314	703-684-0400

Alexandria (Cont'd)

— Accommodations —

HOTEL RESERVATION SERVICES

	Phone	Fax
Alexandria & Arlington Bed & Breakfast Network	703-549-3415	549-3411
TF: 888-549-3415 ■ *Web:* www.aabbn.com		
■ *E-mail:* aabbn@juno.com		
Alexandria Hotel Assn	800-296-1000	838-4683*
**Fax Area Code:* 703		
Princely Bed & Breakfast Reservation Service	800-470-5588	

HOTELS, MOTELS, RESORTS

				Phone	Fax
Alexandria Suites Hotel					
420 N Van Dorn St	Alexandria	VA	22304	703-370-1000	751-1467
TF: 800-368-3339 ■ *Web:* www.alexandriasuites.com					
■ *E-mail:* alexandriasuites@erols.com					
Best Western Inn 8751 Richmond Hwy	Alexandria	VA	22309	703-360-1300	799-7713
TF: 800-528-1234					
Best Western Old Colony Inn 615 1st St	Alexandria	VA	22314	703-739-2222	549-2568
TF: 800-528-1234					
Comfort Inn Alexandria					
5716 S Van Dorn St	Alexandria	VA	22310	703-922-9200	922-0132
Comfort Inn Landmark 6254 Duke St	Alexandria	VA	22312	703-642-3422	642-1354
TF: 800-229-5150					
Comfort Inn Mount Vernon					
7212 Richmond Hwy	Alexandria	VA	22306	703-765-9000	765-2325
TF: 800-433-2546					
Courtyard by Marriott					
2700 Eisenhower Ave	Alexandria	VA	22314	703-329-2323	329-6853
TF: 800-321-2211					
Days Inn 6100 Richmond Hwy	Alexandria	VA	22303	703-329-0500	329-0747
TF: 800-329-7466					
Days Inn Alexandria 110 S Bragg St	Alexandria	VA	22312	703-354-4950	642-2873
TF: 800-241-7382					
Doubletree Guest Suites					
100 S Reynolds St	Alexandria	VA	22304	703-370-9600	370-0467
TF: 800-222-8733					
■ *Web:* www.doubletreehotels.com/DoubleT/Hotel81/97/97Main.htm					
Econo Lodge Mount Vernon					
8849 Richmond Hwy	Alexandria	VA	22309	703-780-0300	780-0842
Embassy Suites Alexandria					
1900 Diagonal Rd	Alexandria	VA	22314	703-684-5900	684-1403
TF: 800-362-2779					
Executive Club Suites 610 Bashford Ln	Alexandria	VA	22314	703-739-2582	548-0266
TF: 800-535-2582					
Hampton Inn 4800 Leesburg Pike	Alexandria	VA	22302	703-671-4800	671-2442
TF: 800-426-7866					
Hampton Inn Alexandria Old Town					
5821 Richmond Hwy	Alexandria	VA	22303	703-329-1400	329-1424
TF: 800-426-7866					
Holiday Inn Eisenhower Metro Center					
2460 Eisenhower Ave	Alexandria	VA	22314	703-960-3400	329-0953
TF: 800-465-4329					
Holiday Inn Hotel & Suites 625 1st St	Alexandria	VA	22304	703-548-6300	548-8032
TF: 800-465-4329					
Holiday Inn Select 480 King St	Alexandria	VA	22314	703-549-6080	684-6508
TF: 800-368-5047 ■ *E-mail:* othismtg@erols.com					
Home-Style Inn 6461 Edsall Rd	Alexandria	VA	22312	703-354-4400	354-8359
Homewood Suites 4850 Leesburg Pike	Alexandria	VA	22302	703-671-6500	671-9322
Howard Johnson Hotel					
2650 Jefferson Davis Hwy	Arlington	VA	22202	703-684-7200	684-3217
TF: 800-446-4656					
Morrison House 116 S Alfred St	Alexandria	VA	22314	703-838-8000	684-6283
TF: 800-367-0800 ■ *Web:* www.morrisonhouse.com					
Radisson Plaza Hotel 5000 Seminary Rd	Alexandria	VA	22311	703-845-1010	845-7662
TF: 800-333-3333					
Ramada Plaza Hotel Old Town					
901 N Fairfax St	Alexandria	VA	22314	703-683-6000	683-7597
TF: 800-272-6232					
Ramada Plaza Pentagon					
4641 Kenmore Ave	Alexandria	VA	22304	703-751-4510	751-9170
TF: 800-272-6232					
Red Roof Inn 5975 Richmond Hwy	Alexandria	VA	22303	703-960-5200	960-5209
TF: 800-843-7663					
Sheraton Suites Alexandria					
801 N Saint Asaph St	Alexandria	VA	22314	703-836-4700	548-4514
TF: 800-325-3535					

— Restaurants —

				Phone
Afghan Restaurant (Afghan) 2700 Jefferson Davis Hwy	Alexandria	VA	22301	703-548-0022
Akasaka Japanese Restaurant (Japanese)				
514-C S Van Dorn St	Alexandria	VA	22304	703-751-3133
Annette's BBQ Heaven (Barbecue) 279 S Van Dorn St	Alexandria	VA	22304	703-823-5393
Atlantis Restaurant (Greek) 3672 King St	Alexandria	VA	22302	703-671-0250
Austin Grill (American) 801 King St	Alexandria	VA	22314	703-684-8969
Web: www.austingrill.com/rest/alex.htm				
Bilbo Baggins Restaurant (American) 208 Queen St	Alexandria	VA	22314	703-683-0300
Web: www.bilbobaggins.net				
Blue Point Grill (Seafood) 600 Franklin St	Alexandria	VA	22314	703-739-0404
Bombay Curry Co (Indian) 3110 Mt Vernon Ave	Alexandria	VA	22305	703-836-6363
Bullfeathers (American) 112 King St	Alexandria	VA	22314	703-836-8088
Café Calliope (American) 1755 Duke St	Alexandria	VA	22314	703-838-9601
Cajun Bangkok (Thai) 907 King St	Alexandria	VA	22314	703-836-0038
Cajun Gourmet (Cajun) 5801 Duke St	Alexandria	VA	22304	703-658-0918
Captain John's Seafood Co (Seafood)				
7405 Richmond Hwy	Alexandria	VA	22306	703-660-9203
Web: www.captain-johns-seafood.com				
■ *E-mail:* captainjohns@erols.com				
Captain White's Crab House (Seafood)				
7305 Richmond Hwy	Alexandria	VA	22306	703-765-7900
Casa Fiesta Restaurant (Mexican)				
6241 Little River Tpke	Alexandria	VA	22312	703-354-7229
Casablanca (Moroccan) 1504 King St	Alexandria	VA	22314	703-549-6464
Chadwicks Old Town (Continental) 203 Strand St	Alexandria	VA	22314	703-836-4442
Chart House Restaurant (Steak/Seafood) 1 Cameron St	Alexandria	VA	22314	703-684-5080
Web: www.chart-house.com/Locations/alexandria/index.htm				
■ *E-mail:* alexandria@chart-house.com				
Chef Huang's Restaurant (Chinese) 8638 Richmond Hwy	Alexandria	VA	22309	703-360-0600
Chequers Restaurant (Continental)				
901 N Fairfax St Ramada Plaza Hotel Old Town	Alexandria	VA	22314	703-683-6000
Chez Andree Restaurant (French) 10 E Glebe Rd	Alexandria	VA	22305	703-836-1404
Chintana Thai Restaurant (Thai) 1019 King St	Alexandria	VA	22314	703-519-3710
Clydes Restaurant (American) 1700 N Beauregard St	Alexandria	VA	22311	703-820-8300
Dancing Peppers Cantina (Mexican) 1120 King St	Alexandria	VA	22314	703-299-9915
Dave & Chung's (Chinese) 362 S Pickett St	Alexandria	VA	22304	703-461-6688
Dishes of India (Indian) 1510 Belleview Blvd	Alexandria	VA	22307	703-660-6085
Ecco Café (Italian) 220 N Lee St	Alexandria	VA	22314	703-684-0321
Web: www.eccocafe.com				
Edgardo's Restaurant (Italian) 281 S Van Dorn St	Alexandria	VA	22304	703-751-6700
Edoya Restaurant (Japanese) 2301 Jefferson Davis Hwy	Alexandria	VA	22301	703-418-2345
Elysium (Continental) 116 S Alfred St Morrison House	Alexandria	VA	22314	703-838-8000
Ernie's Original Crab House (Seafood) 1623 Fern St	Alexandria	VA	22302	703-836-1623
Fish Market (Seafood) 105 King St	Alexandria	VA	22314	703-836-5676
Web: www.fishmarketoldtown.com ■ *E-mail:* fishmkt@pop.dn.net				
Gadsby's Tavern (American) 138 N Royal St	Alexandria	VA	22314	703-548-1288
Gan Mee Oak Restaurant (Korean)				
6531 Little River Tpke	Alexandria	VA	22312	703-658-0505
Geno's Restaurant (Italian) 1300 King St	Alexandria	VA	22314	703-549-1796
Georgio's (Italian) 3015 Mt Vernon Ave	Alexandria	VA	22305	703-549-6440
Geranio Ristorante (Italian) 722 King St	Alexandria	VA	22314	703-548-0088
Hard Times Café (American) 1404 King St	Alexandria	VA	22314	703-683-5340
Il Porto Ristorante (Italian) 121 King St	Alexandria	VA	22314	703-836-8833
Web: www.ilporto.com				
Ireland's Own (Irish) 132 N Royal St	Alexandria	VA	22314	703-549-4535
Joe Theismann's Restaurant (American)				
1800 Diagonal Rd	Alexandria	VA	22314	703-739-0777
King Pepper Restaurant (Southwest) 808 King St	Alexandria	VA	22314	703-683-5124
Kyoto Restaurant (Japanese) 6027 Richmond Hwy	Alexandria	VA	22303	703-329-1334
Land & Sea Grill (Steak/Seafood) 6141 Franconia Rd	Alexandria	VA	22310	703-922-9832
Laporta's Restaurant (Italian) 1600 Duke St	Alexandria	VA	22314	703-683-6313
Las Tapas Restaurant (Spanish) 710 King St	Alexandria	VA	22314	703-836-4000
Le Gaulois Café (French) 1106 King St	Alexandria	VA	22314	703-739-9494
Le Refuge Restaurant (French) 127 N Washington St	Alexandria	VA	22314	703-548-4661
Mango Mike's (Caribbean) 4111 Duke St	Alexandria	VA	22314	703-823-1166
Web: www.mangomikes.com				
Midori Restaurant (Japanese) 9108 Richmond Hwy	Alexandria	VA	22309	703-799-9381
Mike's Restaurant (Italian) 8368 Richmond Hwy	Alexandria	VA	22309	703-780-5966
Monroe's American Trattoria (American)				
1603 Commonwealth Ave	Alexandria	VA	22301	703-548-5792
Murphy's Grand Irish Pub (Irish) 713 King St	Alexandria	VA	22314	703-548-1717
Web: www.murphyspub.com ■ *E-mail:* murphys@moon.jic.com				
Owen Thai Restaurant (Thai) 1743 King St	Alexandria	VA	22314	703-684-5977
Papa George's House of Pasta (Italian)				
7554 Telegraph Rd	Alexandria	VA	22315	703-922-8878
Paradiso Ristorante Italiano (Italian) 6124 Franconia Rd	Alexandria	VA	22310	703-922-6222
Pasta Peasant (Italian) 1024 Cameron St	Alexandria	VA	22314	703-519-8755
Pines of Florence (Italian) 4603 Duke St	Alexandria	VA	22304	703-370-6383
Pita House Family Restaurant (Lebanese)				
407 Cameron St	Alexandria	VA	22314	703-684-9194
Polo Grill (New American) 7784 Gunston Plaza Dr	Lorton	VA	22079	703-550-0002
Potowmack Landing Restaurant (Seafood) 1 Marina Dr	Alexandria	VA	22314	703-548-0001
Web: www.guestservices.com/potowmack				
Romeo & Juliet Ristorante (Italian)				
7622 Richmond Hwy	Alexandria	VA	22306	703-721-0050

Alexandria — Restaurants (Cont'd)

Name / Address	City	State	Zip	Phone
Sampam Café (Oriental) 6116 Franconia Rd	Alexandria	VA	22310	703-971-5404
Santa Fe East (Southwest) 110 S Pitt St.	Alexandria	VA	22314	703-548-6900
Web: www.santa-fe-east.com				
Seaport Inn (Seafood) 6 King St	Alexandria	VA	22314	703-549-2341
Web: www.alexandriacity.com/TheSeaportInn.htm ■ *E-mail:* seaportinn@earthlink.com				
Shiro Japanese Steak House (Japanese) 5860 Kingstowne Ctr	Alexandria	VA	22315	703-313-9000
Stardust Restaurant (American) 608 Montgomery St	Alexandria	VA	22314	703-548-9864
Web: www.stardustrestaurant.com ■ *E-mail:* star-dust@stardustrestaurant.com				
Sushi Town (Japanese) 6303 Little River Tpke	Alexandria	VA	22312	703-914-8877
Taverna Cretekou (Greek) 818 King St	Alexandria	VA	22314	703-548-8688
Tempo Restaurant (French/Italian) 4231 Duke St	Alexandria	VA	22304	703-370-7900
Thai Hut Restaurant (Thai) 408 S Van Dorn St	Alexandria	VA	22304	703-823-5357
Thai Lemon Grass Restaurant (Thai) 506 S Van Dorn St	Alexandria	VA	22304	703-751-4627
Thai Old Town Restaurant (Thai) 300 King St	Alexandria	VA	22314	703-684-6503
Tokyo Japanese Steak House (Japanese) 66 Canal Ctr Plaza	Alexandria	VA	22314	703-683-8878
Traditions Restaurant (Continental) 625 1st St Holiday Inn	Alexandria	VA	22304	703-548-6300
Trattoria Da Franco (Italian) 305 S Washington St	Alexandria	VA	22314	703-548-9338
Union Street Public House (American) 121 S Union St	Alexandria	VA	22314	703-548-1785
Via Veneto Restaurant (Italian) 1309 Shenandoah Rd	Alexandria	VA	22308	703-765-6661
Villa D'Este Restaurant (Italian) 818 N Saint Asaph St.	Alexandria	VA	22314	703-549-9477
Village Wharf Restaurant (Seafood) 7966 Fort Hunt Rd	Alexandria	VA	22308	703-765-0661
Virginia Beverage Co Brewery & Restaurant (American) 607 King St.	Alexandria	VA	22314	703-684-5397
Warehouse Bar & Grill (American) 214 King St	Alexandria	VA	22314	703-683-6868
Web: warehousebarandgrill.com				
Waterfront Café (American) 209 Madison St.	Alexandria	VA	22314	703-836-6161
Wharf The (Seafood) 119 King St	Alexandria	VA	22314	703-836-2836
Web: www.wharfrestaurant.com				

— Goods and Services —

SHOPPING

Name / Address	City	State	Zip	Phone	Fax
Christmas Attic Inc 125 S Union St.	Alexandria	VA	22314	703-548-2829	684-7064
TF: 800-881-0084 ■ *Web:* www.christmasattic.com					
House in the Country 107 N Fairfax St	Alexandria	VA	22314	703-548-4267	548-1008
TF: 800-771-8427					
Landmark Mall 5801 Duke St.	Alexandria	VA	22314	703-941-2582	941-2590
Potomac Mills Value Outlet Mall 2700 Potomac Mills Cir	Prince William	VA	22192	703-490-5948	
TF: 800-826-4557 ■ *Web:* www.potomacmills.com					
Thieves Market Antiques Mall 8101 Richmond Hwy	Alexandria	VA	22309	703-360-4200	360-5002
Web: www.thievesmarketantiques.com ■ *E-mail:* tmantiques@thievesmarketantiques.com					

BANKS

Name / Address	City	State	Zip	Phone	Fax
Branch Banking & Trust 1421 Prince St	Alexandria	VA	22314	703-684-6700	683-8397
Burke & Herbert Bank & Trust 100 S Fairfax St	Alexandria	VA	22314	703-549-6600	548-5759
Chevy Chase Bank 500 S Washington St.	Alexandria	VA	22314	703-838-2891	838-3656
TF Cust Svc: 800-807-5880*					
Crestar Bank 515 King St.	Alexandria	VA	22314	703-838-3302	838-3363
F & M Bank 1717 King St	Alexandria	VA	22314	703-549-8262	549-6946
First Union National Bank 330 N Washington St	Alexandria	VA	22306	703-739-3400	739-4834
First Virginia Bank 6618 Richmond Hwy	Alexandria	VA	22306	703-241-3435	660-2383
NationsBank 2747 Duke St.	Alexandria	VA	22314	703-461-6050	461-6054
Riggs National Bank 1700 Diagonal Rd	Alexandria	VA	22314	703-518-2433	683-5232
Virginia Commerce Bank 1414 Prince St.	Alexandria	VA	22314	703-739-3242	683-0412
Wachovia Bank NA 3624 King St	Alexandria	VA	22302	703-671-7523	824-0594

BUSINESS SERVICES

Name	Phone	Name	Phone
Alexandria Copy Center	703-765-1367	**Mail Boxes Etc**	703-683-8441
Core Personnel	703-519-0900	**Olsten Staffing Services**	703-548-5050
Federal Express	800-238-5355	**Pip Printing**	703-683-3886
Kelly Services	703-739-2250	**Post Office**	703-549-4201
Kinko's	703-739-0783	**UPS**	800-742-5877

— Media —

PUBLICATIONS

Name / Address	City	State	Zip	Phone	Fax
Alexandria Gazette Packet 1610 King St	Alexandria	VA	22314	703-838-0302	549-9655
Alexandria Journal‡ 6408 Edsall Rd	Alexandria	VA	22312	703-560-4000	846-8366*
**Fax:* Edit ■ *TF:* 800-531-1223 ■ *Web:* www.jrnl.com					
Country Plus Magazine 6933 Westhampton Dr.	Alexandria	VA	22307	703-765-8838	
Historic Alexandria Quarterly PO Box 178	Alexandria	VA	22313	703-838-4554	838-6451
Web: ci.alexandria.va.us/oha/oha-main/oha-quarterly.html					
Times-Dispatch Alexandria Bureau 108 S Columbus St Suite 201	Alexandria	VA	22314	703-548-8758	
Washington Post Alexandria/Arlington Bureau 526 King St	Alexandria	VA	22314	703-518-3000	

‡*Daily newspapers*

TELEVISION

Name / Address	City	State	Zip	Phone	Fax
WBDC-TV Ch 50 (WB) 2121 Wisconsin Ave NW Suite 350	Washington	DC	20007	202-965-5050	965-0050
WETA-TV Ch 26 (PBS) 3620 S 27th St	Arlington	VA	22206	703-998-2600	998-3401
Web: www.weta.org ■ *E-mail:* info@weta.com					
WJLA-TV Ch 7 (ABC) 3007 Tilden St NW	Washington	DC	20008	202-364-7777	364-7734
Web: www.abc7dc.com					
WRC-TV Ch 4 (NBC) 4001 Nebraska Ave NW	Washington	DC	20016	202-885-4000	885-4104
Web: www.nbc4dc.com					
WTTG-TV Ch 5 (Fox) 5151 Wisconsin Ave NW	Washington	DC	20016	202-244-5151	244-1745
WUSA-TV Ch 9 (CBS) 4100 Wisconsin Ave NW	Washington	DC	20016	202-895-5999	966-7948
Web: www.wusatv9.com ■ *E-mail:* 9news@wusatv.com					

RADIO

Name / Address	City	State	Zip	Phone	Fax
WABS-AM 780 kHz (Rel) 5545 Lee Hwy	Arlington	VA	22207	703-534-2000	534-3330
WAMU-FM 88.5 MHz (NPR) American University	Washington	DC	20016	202-885-1200	885-1269*
**Fax:* News Rm ■ *Web:* www.wamu.org ■ *E-mail:* feedback@wamu.org					
WARW-FM 94.7 MHz (CR) 5912 Hubbard Dr	Rockville	MD	20852	301-984-6000	468-2490
Web: www.classicrock947.com					
WASH-FM 97.1 MHz (AC) 1801 Rockville Pike	Rockville	MD	20852	301-984-9710	255-4344
Web: www.washfm.com					
WAVA-FM 105.1 MHz (Rel) 1901 N Moore St Suite 200	Arlington	VA	22209	703-807-2266	807-2248
WBIG-FM 100.3 MHz (Oldies) 1801 Rockville Pike 6th Fl	Rockville	MD	20852	301-468-1800	770-0236
WBIS-AM 1190 kHz (N/T) 1081 Bay Ridge Rd	Annapolis	MD	21403	410-269-0700	269-0692
WCTN-AM 950 kHz (Rel) 7825 Tuckerman Ln Suite 211	Potomac	MD	20854	301-299-7026	299-5301
Web: www.wctn.net ■ *E-mail:* wctn@wctn.net					
WETA-FM 90.9 MHz (NPR) 2775 S Quincy St	Arlington	VA	22206	703-998-2790	824-7288
Web: www.weta.org/weta/fm ■ *E-mail:* radio@weta.com					
WFAX-AM 1220 kHz (Rel) 161-B Hillwood Ave	Falls Church	VA	22046	703-532-1220	533-7572
Web: www.wfaxam.com ■ *E-mail:* wfax@erols.com					
WFSI-FM 107.9 MHz (Rel) 918 Chesapeake Ave	Annapolis	MD	21403	410-268-6200	
Web: www.wfsiradio.com					
WGMS-FM 103.5 MHz (Clas) 3400 Idaho Ave NW	Washington	DC	20016	202-895-5000	895-4168
WGTS-FM 91.9 MHz (Rel) 7600 Flower Ave	Takoma Park	MD	20912	301-891-4200	270-9191
Web: www.wgts.org ■ *E-mail:* wgts@wgts.org					
WHFS-FM 99.1 MHz (Alt) 8201 Corporate Dr Suite 550	Landover	MD	20785	301-306-0991	731-0431
Web: www.whfs.com					
WHUR-FM 96.3 MHz (Urban) 529 Bryant St NW	Washington	DC	20059	202-806-3500	806-3522
WILC-AM 900 kHz (Span) PO Box 42	Laurel	MD	20725	301-419-2122	419-2409
WJFK-AM 1300 kHz (N/T) 1 W Pennsylvania Ave Suite 850	Baltimore	MD	21204	410-823-1570	821-5482
WJFK-FM 106.7 MHz (N/T) 10800 Main St	Fairfax	VA	22030	703-691-1900	352-0111
WJZW-FM 105.9 MHz (NAC) 4400 Jenifer St NW	Washington	DC	20015	202-895-2300	686-3064
WKYS-FM 93.9 MHz (Urban) 5900 Princess Garden Pkwy Suite 800	Lanham	MD	20706	301-306-1111	306-9609
WMAL-AM 630 kHz (N/T) 4400 Jenifer St NW	Washington	DC	20015	202-686-3100	686-3061

Alexandria — Radio (Cont'd)

				Phone	Fax
WMET-AM 1150 kHz (N/T)					
8945 N Westland Dr Suite 302	Gaithersburg	MD	20877	301-921-0093	
WMMJ-FM 102.3 MHz (Urban)					
5900 Princess Garden Pkwy Suite 800	Lanham	MD	20706	301-306-1111	306-9609
WMZQ-FM 98.7 MHz (Ctry)					
1801 Rockville Pike 6th Fl	Rockville	MD	20852	301-231-8231	984-4895
WNAV-AM 1430 kHz (AC) PO Box 829	Annapolis	MD	21404	410-263-1430	268-5360
Web: www.wnav.com					
WOL-AM 1450 kHz (N/T)					
5900 Princess Garden Pkwy	Lanham	MD	20706	301-306-1111	306-9609
WPGC-AM 1580 kHz (Rel)					
6301 Ivy Ln Suite 800	Greenbelt	MD	20770	301-441-3500	345-9505
WPGC-FM 95.5 MHz (CHR)					
6301 Ivy Ln Suite 800	Greenbelt	MD	20770	301-441-3500	345-9505
WRQX-FM 107.3 MHz (AC)					
4400 Jenifer St NW	Washington	DC	20015	202-686-3100	686-3091*
**Fax:* New Rm					
WTEM-AM 980 kHz (Sports)					
11300 Rockville Pike Suite 707	Rockville	MD	20852	301-231-7798	881-8030
Web: www.wtem.com ■ *E-mail:* tcastle@erols.com					
WTOP-AM 1500 kHz (N/T)					
3400 Idaho Ave NW	Washington	DC	20016	202-895-5000	895-5140
WWDC-FM 101.1 MHz (Rock)					
8750 Brookville Rd	Silver Spring	MD	20910	301-587-7100	587-5267
Web: www.dc101.com					
WWRC-AM 570 kHz (N/T)					
8750 Brookville Rd	Silver Spring	MD	20910	301-587-4900	587-8086
WWZZ-FM 104.1 MHz (CHR)					
2000 15th St N Suite 200	Arlington	VA	22201	703-522-1041	526-0250
Web: www.thez.com					
WYCB-AM 1340 kHz (Rel)					
5900 Princess Garden Pkwy Suite 800	Lanham	MD	20706	301-306-1111	306-9609

— Colleges/Universities —

				Phone	Fax
Florida Institute of Technology					
4875 Eisenhower Ave Suite 200	Alexandria	VA	22304	703-751-1060	751-4592
Web: www.segs.fit.edu					
Northern Virginia Community College					
Alexandria Campus 3001 N Beauregard St	Alexandria	VA	22311	703-845-6200	845-6046
Web: www.nv.cc.va.us/alexandria/					
Strayer University Alexandria Campus					
2730 Eisenhower Ave	Alexandria	VA	22314	703-329-9100	329-9602

— Hospitals —

				Phone	Fax
Alexandria Hospital 4320 Seminary Rd	Alexandria	VA	22304	703-504-3000	504-3700
Mount Vernon Hospital 2501 Parker's Ln.	Alexandria	VA	22306	703-664-7000	664-7235

— Attractions —

				Phone	Fax
Alexandria African-American Heritage Park					
Holland Ln betw Duke St & Eisenhower Ave	Alexandria	VA	22314	703-838-4356	
Web: ci.alexandria.va.us/oha/bhrc/bh-heritage-park.html					
Alexandria Archaeology Museum					
105 N Union St Rm 327	Alexandria	VA	22314	703-838-4399	838-6491
Web: ci.alexandria.va.us/oha/archaeology					
■ *E-mail:* archaeology@ci.alexandria.va.us					
Alexandria Ballet					
201 Prince St Athenaeum	Alexandria	VA	22314	703-548-0035	768-7471
Alexandria Chorale Society					
101 Callahan Dr George Washington National Memorial Auditorium	Alexandria	VA	22314	703-548-4734	
Alexandria Harmonizers PO Box 11274	Alexandria	VA	22312	703-836-0969	
Web: www.harmonizers.org					
Alexandria National Cemetery					
1450 Wilkes St	Alexandria	VA	22314	540-825-0027	
Alexandria Seaport Foundation's Seaport Center Alexandria Waterfront	Alexandria	VA	22314	703-549-7078	
Web: www.capaccess.org/snt/alexsea/ ■ *E-mail:* asfhqs@aol.com					
Alexandria Symphony Orchestra					
1900 N Beauregard St Suite 14	Alexandria	VA	22311	703-845-8005	845-8007
Web: www.alexsym.org ■ *E-mail:* nseeger@alexsym.org					
American Historical Society at River Farm					
7931 E Boulevard Dr	Alexandria	VA	22308	703-768-5700	
Web: www.ahs.org/nonmembers/riverfarm.htm					
Arlington National Cemetery					
Arlington Cemetery	Arlington	VA	22211	703-697-2131	697-4967
Web: www.mdw.army.mil/cemetery.htm					
Arts Afire Glass Gallery 112 N Royal St	Alexandria	VA	22314	703-838-9785	838-9787
Web: www.artsafire.com ■ *E-mail:* artsafire@bellatlantic.net					
Birchmere Music Hall					
3701 Mt Vernon Ave	Alexandria	VA	22314	703-549-7500	
Web: www.birchmere.com ■ *E-mail:* birch@birchmere.com					
Black History Resource Center					
638 N Alfred St	Alexandria	VA	22314	703-838-4356	706-3999
Web: ci.alexandria.va.us/oha/bhrc					
■ *E-mail:* black.history@ci.alexandria.va. us					
Cameron Run Regional Park					
4001 Eisenhower Ave	Alexandria	VA	22314	703-960-0767	
Web: www.nvrpa.org/cameron.html					
Carlyle House Museum & Historic Park					
121 N Fairfax St	Alexandria	VA	22314	703-549-2997	549-5738
Chinquapin Park 3210 King St	Alexandria	VA	22314	703-838-4343	
Christ Church 118 N Washington St	Alexandria	VA	22314	703-549-1450	
Confederate Statue Appomattox					
Prince & S Washington Sts	Alexandria	VA	22314		
Dandy Restaurant Cruise Ship 0 Prince St.	Alexandria	VA	22314	703-683-6076	
Web: www.dandydinnerboat.com ■ *E-mail:* dandy1@erols.com					
Farmer's Market 301 King St Market Sq	Alexandria	VA	22314	800-388-9119	
Fort Ward Museum & Historic Site					
4301 W Braddock Rd	Alexandria	VA	22304	703-838-4848	671-7350
Web: ci.alexandria.va.us/oha/fortward					
■ *E-mail:* fort.ward@ci.alexandria.va.us					
Frank Lloyd Wright's Pope-Leighey House					
9000 Richmond Hwy Woodlawn Plantation	Alexandria	VA	22309	703-780-3264	780-8509
Friendship Fire House Museum					
107 S Alfred St.	Alexandria	VA	22314	703-838-3891	
Web: ci.alexandria.va.us/oha/friendship					
■ *E-mail:* friendship@ci.alexandria.va.us					
Gadsby's Tavern Museum 134 N Royal St.	Alexandria	VA	22314	703-838-4242	838-4270
Web: ci.alexandria.va.us/oha/gadsby					
■ *E-mail:* gadsbys.tavern@ci.alexandria.va.us					
George Washington Birthplace National Monument RR 1 Box 717	Washington's Birthplace	VA	22443	804-224-1732	224-2142
Web: www.nps.gov/gewa/					
George Washington Masonic National Memorial 101 Callahan Dr.	Alexandria	VA	22301	703-683-2007	519-9270
Web: www.gwmemorial.org					
George Washington's Mount Vernon Estate & Gardens					
George Washington Memorial Pkwy	Mount Vernon	VA	22121	703-780-2000	799-8698
Web: www.mountvernon.org					
Gunston Hall Plantation					
10709 Gunston Rd	Mason Neck	VA	22079	703-550-9220	550-9480
Web: gunstonhall.org ■ *E-mail:* historic@gunstonhall.org					
Jones Point Park 1 S Lee St	Alexandria	VA	22314	703-838-4343	
Lee-Fendall House 614 Oronoco St	Alexandria	VA	22314	703-548-1789	
Little Theatre of Alexandria 600 Wolfe St	Alexandria	VA	22314	703-683-5778	683-1378
Lloyd House 220 N Washington St	Alexandria	VA	22314	703-838-4577	
Lyceum History Museum					
201 S Washington St	Alexandria	VA	22314	703-838-4994	838-4997
Web: ci.alexandria.va.us/oha/lyceum					
■ *E-mail:* lyceum@ci.alexandria.va.us					
Marine Corps Memorial					
Rt 50 & George Washington Memorial Pkwy	Arlington	VA	22211	703-289-2510	289-2598
MetroStage PO Box 329	Alexandria	VA	22313	703-548-9044	548-9089
Mount Vernon Chamber Orchestra Assn					
201 S Washington St Lyceum	Alexandria	VA	22314	703-799-8229	360-7391
Mount Vernon Forest Trail	Alexandria	VA	22314	703-780-2000	
Newseum 1101 Wilson Blvd	Arlington	VA	22209	703-284-3725	284-3777
TF: 800-639-7386 ■ *Web:* www.newseum.org					
Oceans of Wildlife Fine Art Gallery					
201 King St	Alexandria	VA	22314	703-739-3202	
Web: www.alexandriacity.com/art/wyland.htm					
Old Presbyterian Meeting House					
321 S Fairfax St	Alexandria	VA	22314	703-549-6670	
Old Warsaw Galleries 319 Cameron St	Alexandria	VA	22314	703-548-9188	
Oronoco Bay Park Union & Madison Sts	Alexandria	VA	22314	703-838-4343	
Potomac Heritage National Scenic Trail	Alexandria	VA	22314	703-838-4200	
Prince Royal Gallery 204 S Royal St.	Alexandria	VA	22314	703-548-5151	
Web: look.net/princeroyal ■ *E-mail:* princeroyal@look.net					

Alexandria — Attractions (Cont'd)

				Phone	Fax
Robert E Lee Boyhood Home 607 Oronoco St	Alexandria	VA	22314	703-548-8454	
Stabler-Leadbeater Apothecary Museum 107 S Fairfax St *Web:* www.apothecary.org	Alexandria	VA	22314	703-836-3713	
Torpedo Factory Art Center 105 N Union St. *Web:* www.torpedofactory.org	Alexandria	VA	22314	703-838-4565	549-6877
West End Dinner Theatre 4615 Duke St *Web:* www.wedt.com ■ *E-mail:* wedt@wedt.com	Alexandria	VA	22304	703-370-2500	
Woodlawn Plantation 9000 Richmond Hwy	Alexandria	VA	22314	703-780-4000	780-8509

SPORTS TEAMS & FACILITIES

				Phone	Fax
Northern Virginia Royals PO Box 1447	Centerville	VA	20120	703-492-9944	492-9944

— Events —

	Phone
18th Century Grand Ball (mid-April)	703-838-4242
18th Century Masquerade Ball (October)	703-838-4242
African-American Festival (late July)	703-838-4844
Alexandria Archaeology Super Weekend (early October)	703-838-4399
Alexandria Arts Safari (early October)	800-388-9119
Alexandria Holiday Tree Lighting Ceremony (late November)	800-388-9119
Alexandria Red Cross Waterfront Festival (mid-June)	703-549-8300
Annual Needlework Exhibition (March)	703-780-4000
Annual Tour of Historic Alexandria Homes (late September)	800-388-9119
Antiques in Alexandria (mid-March)	703-549-5922
Braddock Day (early April)	703-549-2997
Campagna Center's Designer Tour of Homes (early December)	703-549-0111
Campagna Center's Scottish Christmas Walk Weekend (early December)	703-549-0111
Carlyle Housewarming (early August)	703-549-2997
Christmas in Camp Open House (mid-December)	703-838-4848
Christmas with the Presidents (late November-late December)	703-780-4000
Civil War Reunion Day (mid-June)	703-838-4848
Civil War Symposium (mid-May)	703-838-4848
Crafts Fair (mid-September)	703-780-2000
Deutche Marque Concours d'Elegance Car Exhibition (early May)	703-780-4000
Earth Day (April 22)	703-838-4844
First Night Alexandria (December 31)	800-388-9119
Friendship Fire House Festival (early August)	703-838-4399
Full Harvest Family Days (late October)	703-780-2000
George Washington Birthday Celebration Weekend (mid-February)	703-549-7662
George Washington Birthday Night Ball (February)	703-838-4242
George Washington Celebration Parade (mid-February)	703-549-7662
Hard Times Chili Cook-Off (late September)	800-388-9119
Historic Alexandria Antiques Show & Sale (late November)	800-388-9119
Historic Alexandria Candlelight Tours (mid-December)	703-838-4242
Historic Alexandria Hauntings Family-Friendly Trick or Treat (late October)	703-838-4242
Historic Garden Tour of Alexandria (mid-late April)	804-644-7776
History Walking Tours (April-October)	703-838-4200
Independence Day Celebration (July 4)	703-780-2000
Irish Festival (mid-August)	703-838-4844
Italian Festival (mid-September)	703-838-4844
Juneteenth Commemoration (mid-late June)	703-838-4356
Lee Birthday Celebrations (mid-January)	703-548-8454
Memorial Day Jazz Festival (late May)	703-838-4844
Mount Vernon by Candlelight Weekends (late november-mid-December)	703-780-2000
Mount Vernon's Wine Tasting & Sunset Tour (mid-May)	703-799-8604
Native American Indian Festival (late August)	703-838-4844
Saint Patrick's Day Celebration & Parade (early March)	703-549-4535
Scottish Heritage Festival (early October)	703-838-4844
Tavern Day (early August)	703-838-4242
USA & Alexandria Birthday Celebration (early-mid-July)	703-838-4343
Virginia Scottish Games & Festival (late July)	703-912-1943

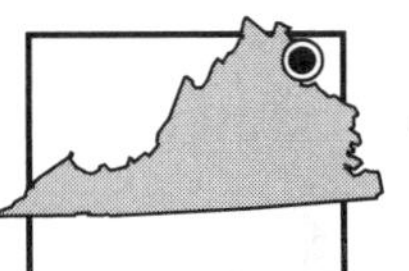

Arlington

Arlington, known as "Neighbor to the Nation's Capital," is located just across the Potomac River from Washington, DC. Arlington National Cemetery, the final resting place of nearly 240,000 American heroes, includes the grave sites of John F. Kennedy and Robert F. Kennedy, the Eternal Flame, and the Tomb of the Unknowns. Other national monuments and memorials in Arlington include the U.S. Marine Corps Memorial, Iwo Jima; and Arlington House, the Robert E. Lee Memorial. The headquarters of the United States Department of Defense, the Pentagon, is also located in Arlington.

Population	177,275	**Longitude**	77-10-19 W
Area (Land)	25.9 sq mi	**County**	Arlington
Area (Water)	0.1 sq mi	**Time Zone**	EST
Elevation	200 ft	**Area Code/s**	703
Latitude	38-87-87 N		

— Average Temperatures and Precipitation —

TEMPERATURES

	Jan	Feb	Mar	Apr	May	Jun	Jul	Aug	Sep	Oct	Nov	Dec
High	42	46	57	67	76	85	89	87	80	69	58	47
Low	27	29	38	46	57	67	71	70	63	50	41	32

PRECIPITATION

	Jan	Feb	Mar	Apr	May	Jun	Jul	Aug	Sep	Oct	Nov	Dec
Inches	2.7	2.7	3.2	2.7	3.7	3.4	3.8	3.9	3.3	3.0	3.1	3.1

— Important Phone Numbers —

	Phone		Phone
AAA	703-549-1080	**Events Line**	703-228-6966
American Express Travel	703-415-5400	**Medical Referral**	800-265-8624
Dental Referral	703-642-5297	**Poison Control Center**	202-625-3333
Emergency	911		

— Information Sources —

				Phone	Fax
Arlington Chamber of Commerce 2009 N 14th St Suite 111 *Web:* www.arlingtonchamber.com	Arlington	VA	22201	703-525-2400	522-5273
Arlington Convention & Visitors Service 2100 Clarendon Blvd *Web:* www.co.arlington.va.us/acvs ■ *E-mail:* acvs@us.net	Arlington	VA	22201	703-228-3988	228-3667
Arlington County 2100 Clarendon Blvd 1 Courthouse Plaza Suite 302 *Web:* www.co.arlington.va.us ■ *E-mail:* arlicnty@capaccess.org	Arlington	VA	22201	703-228-3120	
Arlington Economic Development Dept 2100 Clarendon Blvd Rm 700 *Web:* www.co.arlington.va.us/ded/ded.htm ■ *E-mail:* oed@co.arlington.va.us	Arlington	VA	22201	703-228-0808	228-3574
Arlington Libraries Dept 1015 N Quincy St *Web:* www.co.arlington.va.us/lib/	Arlington	VA	22201	703-228-5990	228-7720
Arlington Visitors Center 735 S 18th St *TF:* 800-677-6267	Arlington	VA	22202	703-228-5720	892-9469
Better Business Bureau Serving Metropolitan Washington 1411 K St NW 10th Fl. *Web:* www.dc.bbb.org ■ *E-mail:* sales@dc.bbb.org	Washington	DC	20005	202-393-8000	393-1198

On-Line Resources

Area Guide Arlington	arlingtonva.areaguides.net
Arlington City Net	www.excite.com/travel/countries/united_states/virginia/arlington
I-95 Exit Information Guide Northern Virginia	www.usastar.com/i95/cityguide/nova.htm

— Transportation Services —

AIRPORTS

■ **Ronald Reagan Washington National Airport (DCA)**

	Phone
3 miles E of downtown Arlington (approx 10 minutes) Web: www.mwaa.com/National/index.html	703-417-8000

Arlington (Cont'd)

Airport Transportation

	Phone
Metrorail $1.10 fare to downtown	202-637-7000
Taxi $10 fare to downtown	703-527-2222
Washington Flyer $16 fare to downtown	703-685-1400

Commercial Airlines

	Phone		Phone
AccessAir	877-462-2237	**Midway**	800-446-4392
America West	800-235-9292	**Midwest Express**	800-452-2022
American	800-433-7300	**Northwest**	800-225-2525
Continental Express	800-525-0280	**TWA**	800-221-2000
Delta	800-221-1212	**United**	800-241-6522
Delta Business Express	800-345-3400	**US Airways**	800-428-4322

Charter Airlines

	Phone		Phone
Capital Helicopters	703-417-2150	**Martinair Inc**	877-419-5400

CAR RENTALS

	Phone		Phone
Alamo	800-327-9633	**Enterprise**	703-243-5404
Avis	800-331-1212	**Hertz**	800-654-3131
Budget-National	703-920-3360	**Thrifty**	703-658-2200
Dollar-National	703-519-8700		

LIMO/TAXI

	Phone		Phone
Arlington Limousine	703-241-0400	**Red Top Cab**	703-522-3333
Blue Top Cab	703-243-8294	**United Limousine Service**	703-525-4844
Carey Limousine	703-892-2000	**Yellow Cab**	703-527-2222

MASS TRANSIT

	Phone
Metrorail/Metrobus $1.10 Base fare	202-637-7000

RAIL/BUS

	City	State	Zip	Phone
Amtrak Station 50 Massachusetts Ave NE Union Station TF: 800-872-7245	Washington	DC	20002	202-906-3193
Greyhound Bus Station 1005 NE 1st St TF: 800-231-2222	Washington	DC	20002	202-289-5154

— Accommodations —

HOTEL RESERVATION SERVICES

	Phone	Fax
Accommodations Express *TF:* 800-444-7666 ■ *Web:* www.accommodationsxpress.com ■ *E-mail:* accomexp@acy.digex.net	609-391-2100	525-0111
Alexandria & Arlington Bed & Breakfast Network *TF:* 888-549-3415 ■ *Web:* www.aabbn.com ■ *E-mail:* aabbn@juno.com	703-549-3415	549-3411

HOTELS, MOTELS, RESORTS

	City	State	Zip	Phone	Fax
Americana Motel 1400 Jefferson Davis Hwy *TF:* 800-548-6261	Arlington	VA	22202	703-979-3772	979-3772
Arlington Hilton 950 N Stafford St *TF:* 800-445-8667	Arlington	VA	22203	703-528-6000	528-4386
Best Western Fairfax City 3535 Chain Bridge Rd *TF:* 800-465-4329	Fairfax	VA	22030	703-591-5500	591-7483
Best Western Key Bridge 1850 N Ft Myers Dr *TF:* 800-528-1234	Arlington	VA	22209	703-522-0400	524-5275
Best Western Old Colony Inn 615 1st St *TF:* 800-528-1234	Alexandria	VA	22314	703-739-2222	549-2568
Best Western Rosslyn Westpark 1900 N Ft Myer Dr *TF:* 800-368-3408	Arlington	VA	22209	703-527-4814	522-8864
Comfort Inn Ballston 1211 N Glebe Rd *TF:* 800-228-5150	Arlington	VA	22201	703-247-3399	524-8739
Courtyard by Marriott 1533 Clarendon Blvd *TF:* 800-321-2211	Arlington	VA	22209	703-528-2222	528-1027
Courtyard by Marriott Crystal City 2899 Jefferson Davis Hwy *TF:* 800-321-2211 ■ *Web:* courtyard.com/WASCT	Arlington	VA	22202	703-549-3434	549-7440
Crystal City Marriott 1999 Jefferson Davis Hwy *TF:* 800-228-9290	Arlington	VA	22202	703-413-5500	413-0192
Days Inn 2201 Arlington Blvd *TF:* 800-329-7466	Arlington	VA	22201	703-525-0300	525-5671
Days Inn Crystal City 2000 Jefferson Davis Hwy *TF:* 800-329-7466	Arlington	VA	22202	703-920-8600	920-2840
Doubletree Guest Suites 100 S Reynolds St *TF:* 800-222-8733 ■ *Web:* www.doubletreehotels.com/DoubleT/Hotel81/97/97Main.htm	Alexandria	VA	22304	703-370-9600	370-0467
Doubletree Hotel 300 Army-Navy Dr *TF:* 800-222-8733 ■ *Web:* www.doubletreehotels.com/DoubleT/Hotel81/98/98Main.htm	Arlington	VA	22202	703-416-4100	416-4126
Econo Lodge 6800 Lee Hwy *TF:* 800-785-6343	Arlington	VA	22213	703-538-5300	538-2110
Econo Lodge 2485 S Glebe Rd *TF:* 800-553-2666	Arlington	VA	22206	703-979-4100	979-6120
Embassy Suites Crystal City 1300 Jefferson Davis Hwy *TF:* 800-362-2779	Arlington	VA	22202	703-979-9799	920-5947
Embassy Suites Hotel Tysons Corner 8517 Leesburg Pike *TF:* 800-362-2779	Vienna	VA	22182	703-883-0707	883-0694
Executive Club Suites 108 S Court House Rd *TF:* 800-535-2582	Arlington	VA	22204	703-522-2582	486-2694
Highlander Motel 3336 Wilson Blvd *TF:* 800-786-4301	Arlington	VA	22201	703-524-4300	525-8321
Holiday Inn Washington National Airport 1489 Jefferson Davis Hwy *TF:* 800-465-4329 ■ *Web:* www.basshotels.com/holiday-inn/?_franchisee=WASNA ■ *E-mail:* weadbrock@bfsaulco.com	Arlington	VA	22202	703-416-1600	416-1615
Hotel Strasburg 213 S Holliday St *TF:* 800-348-8327	Strasburg	VA	22657	540-465-9191	465-4788
Howard Johnson Hotel 2650 Jefferson Davis Hwy *TF:* 800-446-4656	Arlington	VA	22202	703-684-7200	684-3217
Hyatt Arlington Washington Key Bridge 1325 Wilson Blvd *TF:* 800-233-1234 ■ *Web:* www.hyatt.com/usa/arlington/hotels/hotel_wasar.html	Arlington	VA	22209	703-525-1234	875-3393
Hyatt Regency Crystal City 2799 Jefferson Davis Hwy *TF:* 800-223-1234 ■ *Web:* www.hyatt.com/usa/arlington/hotels/hotel_wasrc.html	Arlington	VA	22202	703-418-1234	418-1289
Hyatt Regency Reston 1800 Presidents St *TF:* 800-233-1234 ■ *Web:* www.hyatt.com/usa/reston/hotels/hotel_resto.html	Reston	VA	20190	703-709-1234	709-2291
Inn at Little Washington Middle & Main Sts	Washington	VA	22747	540-675-3800	675-3100
Key Bridge Marriott 1401 Lee Hwy *TF:* 800-228-9290	Arlington	VA	22209	703-524-6400	524-8964
Lansdowne Resort 44050 Woodridge Pkwy *TF:* 800-541-4801	Leesburg	VA	20176	703-729-8400	729-4111
Marriott Crystal Gateway Hotel 1700 Jefferson Davis Hwy *TF:* 800-228-9290 ■ *Web:* marriotthotels.com/WASGW	Arlington	VA	22202	703-920-3230	271-5212
Morrison House 116 S Alfred St *TF:* 800-367-0800 ■ *Web:* www.morrisonhouse.com	Alexandria	VA	22314	703-838-8000	684-6283
Quality Hotel 1200 N Courthouse Rd	Arlington	VA	22201	703-524-4000	524-1046
Quality Inn East 603 Millwood Ave *TF:* 800-228-5151	Winchester	VA	22601	540-667-2250	667-0850
Quality Inn Iwo Jima 1501 Arlington Blvd *TF:* 800-221-2222	Arlington	VA	22209	703-524-5000	522-5484
Radisson Plaza Hotel 5000 Seminary Rd *TF:* 800-333-3333	Alexandria	VA	22311	703-845-1010	845-7662
Residence Inn 550 Army Navy Dr *TF:* 800-321-2121 ■ *Web:* www.residenceinn.com/residenceinn/WASPT	Arlington	VA	22202	703-413-6630	418-1751
Ritz-Carlton Pentagon City 1250 S Hayes St *TF:* 800-241-3333 ■ *Web:* www.ritzcarlton.com/location/NorthAmerica/PentagonCity/main.htm	Arlington	VA	22202	703-415-5000	415-5061
Sheraton Crystal City 1800 Jefferson Davis Hwy *TF:* 800-862-7666	Arlington	VA	22202	703-486-1111	920-5827
Sheraton Inn & Conference Center 2801 Plank Rd *TF:* 800-682-1049	Fredericksburg	VA	22404	540-786-8321	786-3957

Arlington — Hotels, Motels, Resorts (Cont'd)

Name	City	State	Zip	Phone	Fax
Sheraton National Hotel 900 S Orme St *TF:* 800-325-3535	Arlington	VA	22204	703-521-1900	521-0332
Sheraton Premiere 8661 Leesburg Pike *TF:* 800-572-7666	Vienna	VA	22182	703-448-1234	893-8193
Sheraton Reston Hotel 11810 Sunrise Valley Dr *TF:* 800-325-3535	Reston	VA	20191	703-620-9000	860-1594
Smith Corporate Living 2345 Crystal Dr	Arlington	VA	22202	703-920-8500	769-5621
Travelodge 3030 Columbia Pike *TF:* 800-578-7878	Arlington	VA	22204	703-521-5570	271-0081
Virginian Suites 1500 Arlington Blvd *TF:* 800-275-2866	Arlington	VA	22209	703-522-9600	525-4462

— Restaurants —

Name	City	State	Zip	Phone
Aegean Taverna (Greek) 2950 Clarendon Blvd	Arlington	VA	22201	703-841-9494
Aryana Cafe (American) 2201 Arlington Blvd	Arlington	VA	22201	703-528-3730
Bangkok Siam Restaurant (Thai) 307 N Glebe Rd	Arlington	VA	22203	703-524-0711
Blancas (Mexican) 3902 Wilson Blvd	Arlington	VA	22203	703-807-0126
Bombay Curry House (Indian) 2529 Wilson Blvd	Arlington	VA	22201	703-528-0849
Cajun Gourmet (Cajun) 4238 Wilson Blvd	Arlington	VA	22203	703-527-5286
Caribbean Grill (Caribbean) 5183 Lee Hwy	Arlington	VA	22207	703-241-8947
Cha Cha Seafood & Pasta (American) 509 S 23rd St	Arlington	VA	22202	703-979-7676
Clarendon Grill (New American) 1101 N Highland St *Web:* www.cgrill.com ■ *E-mail:* cgrill@mindspring.com	Arlington	VA	22201	703-524-7455
Dan & Brad's (Steak/Seafood) 950 N Stafford St *Web:* www.danandbrads.com	Arlington	VA	22203	703-812-5114
Edoya Japanese Steak House (Japanese) 2301 Jefferson Davis Hwy	Arlington	VA	22202	703-418-2344
El Sabroso (Latin American) 5104 Wilson Blvd	Arlington	VA	22205	703-522-4074
Fuji Restaurant (Japanese) 77 N Glebe Rd	Arlington	VA	22203	703-524-3666
Gatwick's (American) 2000 Jefferson Davis Hwy	Arlington	VA	22202	703-920-8600
Hudson Grill (American) 1227 N Hudson St	Arlington	VA	22201	703-243-4800
Hunan Place (Chinese) 1812 N Moore St	Arlington	VA	22209	703-528-8188
Jay's Saloon & Grill (American) 3114 10th St N	Arlington	VA	22201	703-527-3093
Kabob Place (Middle Eastern) 2315 S Eads St	Arlington	VA	22202	703-486-3535
Kabul Caravan (Afghan) 1725 Wilson Blvd	Arlington	VA	22209	703-522-8394
Mediterraneo Restaurant (Mediterranean) 3520 Lee Hwy	Arlington	VA	22207	703-527-7276
Oak Street Cafe (American) 1501 Wilson Blvd	Arlington	VA	22209	703-528-6886
Oreste Italian Cafe (Italian) 1813 N Lynn St	Arlington	VA	22209	703-522-4455
Pettibon's American Grill & Bar (American) 1911 N Ft Meyer Dr *Web:* www.petitbons.com	Arlington	VA	22209	703-527-7501
Rainforest Cafe (American) 7928 L Tysons Corner Ctr *Web:* www.rainforestcafe.com	McLean	VA	22102	703-821-1900
Red Hot & Blue (Barbecue) 1600 Wilson Blvd	Arlington	VA	22209	703-276-7427
Rhodeside Grill (New American) 1836 Wilson Blvd *Web:* arlingtoncounty.com/dining/rhodeside.htm ■ *E-mail:* rhodesidegrill@sprynet.com	Arlington	VA	22201	703-243-0145
Rocklands Washington Barbeque (Barbecue) 4000 Fairfax Dr	Arlington	VA	22203	703-528-9663
Sagebrush Grill (Southwest) 1345 N Court House Rd	Arlington	VA	22201	703-524-1432
Santa Fe Cafe (Tex Mex) 1500 Wilson Blvd	Arlington	VA	22209	703-276-0361
Tequilla's Restaurant (Mexican) 6019 Wilson Blvd	Arlington	VA	22205	703-241-1127
Terrace The (American) 1700 Jefferson Davis Hwy	Arlington	VA	22202	703-920-3230
Thai Square (Thai) 3217 Columbia Pike	Arlington	VA	22204	703-685-7040
Tom Sarris' Orleans House (Steak/Seafood) 1213 Wilson Blvd	Arlington	VA	22209	703-524-2929
Via Cucina (Italian) 2345 Crystal Dr	Arlington	VA	22202	703-418-1001
View The (Steak/Seafood) 1401 Lee Hwy	Arlington	VA	22209	703-243-1745
Village Bistro (Continental) 1723 Wilson Blvd	Arlington	VA	22209	703-522-0284
Whitey's Restaurant (American) 2761 Washington Blvd	Arlington	VA	22201	703-525-9825

— Goods and Services —

SHOPPING

Name	City	State	Zip	Phone	Fax
Ballston Common 4238 Wilson Blvd *Web:* www.ballston-common.com	Arlington	VA	22203	703-243-8088	525-4247
Fair Oaks Shopping Center 11750 Fair Oaks	Fairfax	VA	22033	703-359-8300	273-0547
Fashion Centre at Pentagon City 1100 S Hayes St	Arlington	VA	22202	703-415-2400	415-2175
Strawbridge's 685 N Glebe Rd *Web:* www.mayco.com/may/st_home.html	Arlington	VA	22203	703-558-1200	524-2985
Tysons Corner Center 1961 Chain Bridge Rd Suite 105 *TF:* 888-289-7667 ■ *Web:* www.shoptysons.com	McLean	VA	22102	703-893-9400	847-3089
Village At Shirlington 2700 S Quincy St	Arlington	VA	22206	703-379-0007	

BANKS

Name	City	State	Zip	Phone	Fax
Bank of Northern Virginia 1010 North Glebe Rd	Arlington	VA	22201	703-243-3900	243-6826
Crestar Bank 1550 Wilson Blvd *TF:* 800-273-7827	Arlington	VA	22209	703-838-3140	838-3158
TeleBanc Financial Corp 1111 N Highland St *TF Cust Svc:* 888-989-4422 ■ *Web:* www.telebankonline.com	Arlington	VA	22201	703-247-3700	247-5455
United Bank 3801 Wilson Blvd	Arlington	VA	22203	703-841-8700	841-9237
Virginia Commerce Bank 5350 Lee Hwy	Arlington	VA	22207	703-534-0700	534-1782
Wachovia Bank 2026 Wilson Blvd	Arlington	VA	22201	703-684-2663	524-1632

BUSINESS SERVICES

Name	Phone	Name	Phone
BAX Global	800-225-5229	**Mail Boxes Etc**	703-358-9500
DHL Worldwide Express	800-225-5345	**Manpower Temporary Services**	703-243-5225
Federal Express	800-238-5355	**Post Office**	703-525-4838
Kelly Services	703-739-2250	**UPS**	800-742-5877
Kinko's	703-525-9224		

— Media —

PUBLICATIONS

Name	City	State	Zip	Phone	Fax
Arlington Courier 1600 Scotts Crossing Rd *E-mail:* emily@arlcourier.com	McLean	VA	22102	703-821-5050	917-0991
Arlington Journal‡ 6408 Edsall Rd *Web:* www.jrnl.com ■ *E-mail:* exp@aol.com	Alexandria	VA	22312	703-560-4000	846-8366
Washington Business Journal 1555 Wilson Blvd Suite 400 *Web:* www.amcity.com/washington	Arlington	VA	22209	703-875-2200	875-2231

‡Daily newspapers

TELEVISION

Name	City	State	Zip	Phone	Fax
WBDC-TV Ch 50 (WB) 2121 Wisconsin Ave NW Suite 350	Washington	DC	20007	202-965-5050	965-0050
WETA-TV Ch 26 (PBS) 3620 S 27th St *Web:* www.weta.org ■ *E-mail:* info@weta.com	Arlington	VA	22206	703-998-2600	998-3401
WJLA-TV Ch 7 (ABC) 3007 Tilden St NW *Web:* www.abc7dc.com	Washington	DC	20008	202-364-7777	364-7734
WRC-TV Ch 4 (NBC) 4001 Nebraska Ave NW *Web:* www.nbc4dc.com	Washington	DC	20016	202-885-4000	885-4104
WTTG-TV Ch 5 (Fox) 5151 Wisconsin Ave NW	Washington	DC	20016	202-244-5151	244-1745
WUSA-TV Ch 9 (CBS) 4100 Wisconsin Ave NW *Web:* www.wusatv9.com ■ *E-mail:* 9news@wusatv.com	Washington	DC	20016	202-895-5999	966-7948

RADIO

Name	City	State	Zip	Phone	Fax
WABS-AM 780 kHz (Rel) 5545 Lee Hwy	Arlington	VA	22207	703-534-2000	534-3330
WAVA-FM 105.1 MHz (Rel) 1901 N Moore St Suite 200	Arlington	VA	22209	703-807-2266	807-2248
WETA-FM 90.9 MHz (NPR) 2775 S Quincy St *Web:* www.weta.org/weta/fm ■ *E-mail:* radio@weta.com	Arlington	VA	22206	703-998-2790	824-7288
WKYS-FM 93.9 MHz (Urban) 5900 Princess Garden Pkwy Suite 800	Lanham	MD	20706	301-306-1111	306-9609
WMAL-AM 630 kHz (N/T) 4400 Jenifer St NW	Washington	DC	20015	202-686-3100	686-3061
WMZQ-FM 98.7 MHz (Ctry) 1801 Rockville Pike 6th Fl	Rockville	MD	20852	301-231-8231	984-4895
WRQX-FM 107.3 MHz (AC) 4400 Jenifer St NW **Fax:* New Rm	Washington	DC	20015	202-686-3100	686-3091*
WTOP-AM 1500 kHz (N/T) 3400 Idaho Ave NW	Washington	DC	20016	202-895-5000	895-5140

Arlington (Cont'd)

— Colleges/Universities —

	City	State	Zip	Phone	Fax
Marymount University 2807 N Glebe Rd	Arlington	VA	22207	703-522-5600	522-0349
TF Admissions: 800-548-7638 ■ *Web:* www.marymount.edu ■ *E-mail:* admissions@marymount.edu					

— Hospitals —

	City	State	Zip	Phone	Fax
Arlington Hospital 1701 N George Mason Dr	Arlington	VA	22205	703-558-5000	558-6553*
**Fax:* Hum Res ■ *Web:* www.arlhosp.org					
National Hospital Medical Center 2455 Army Navy Dr.	Arlington	VA	22206	703-920-6700	553-2484
Vencor Hospital of Arlington 601 S Carlin Springs Rd	Arlington	VA	22204	703-671-1200	578-2281

— Attractions —

	City	State	Zip	Phone	Fax
Arlington Arts Center 3550 Wilson Blvd.	Arlington	VA	22201	703-524-1494	527-4050
E-mail: artscenter@erols.com					
Arlington Historical Museum 1805 S Arlington Ridge Rd	Arlington	VA	22202	703-892-4204	
Arlington House-Robert E Lee Memorial George Washington Memorial Pkwy Turkey Run Pk	McLean	VA	22101	703-557-0613	235-9063
Web: www.nps.gov/arho/					
Arlington National Cemetery Arlington Cemetery	Arlington	VA	22211	703-697-2131	697-4967
Web: www.mdw.army.mil/cemetery.htm					
Arlington Symphony 6600 Little Falls Rd	Arlington	VA	22213	703-528-1817	528-1911
Bon Air Park 850 N Lexington St	Arlington	VA	22205	703-228-4747	
Clark Street Playhouse 601 S Clark St	Arlington	VA	22202	703-418-4808	
Drug Enforcement Administration Museum & Visitors Center 700 Army Navy Dr	Arlington	VA	22202	202-307-3463	
Ellipse Arts Center 4350 N Fairfax Dr	Arlington	VA	22203	703-358-7710	516-4468
E-mail: ellipse@erols.com					
George Mason Center for the Arts George Mason University	Fairfax	VA	22030	703-993-8888	
George Washington Birthplace National Monument RR 1 Box 717	Washington's Birthplace	VA	22443	804-224-1732	224-2142
Web: www.nps.gov/gewa/					
George Washington Memorial Parkway Turkey Run Pk	McLean	VA	22101	703-285-2598	285-2398
Web: www.nps.gov/gwmp/					
Grey House Potters 5509 Wilson Blvd	Arlington	VA	22205	703-522-7738	
Gulf Branch Nature Center 3608 N Military Rd	Arlington	VA	22207	703-228-3403	351-9437
Long Branch Nature Center 625 S Carlin Springs Rd	Arlington	VA	22204	703-228-6535	845-2654
Lyndon Baines Johnson Memorial Grove on the Potomac George Washington Memorial Pkwy Turkey Run Pk	McLean	VA	22101	703-285-2598	285-2398
Web: www.nps.gov/lyba/					
Manassas National Battlefield Park 6511 Sudley Rd	Manassas	VA	20109	703-361-1339	
Web: www.nps.gov/mana/					
Marine Corps Memorial Rt 50 & George Washington Memorial Pkwy	Arlington	VA	22211	703-289-2510	289-2598
National Firearms Museum 11250 Waples Mill Rd	Fairfax	VA	22030	703-267-1600	267-3913
Web: www.nrahq.org/shooting/museum					
Netherlands Carillon Turkey Run Park	Arlington	VA	22101	703-289-2500	
Newseum 1101 Wilson Blvd	Arlington	VA	22209	703-284-3725	284-3777
TF: 800-639-7386 ■ *Web:* www.newseum.org					
Old Guard Museum Sheridan Ave Fort Myer Bldg 249	Arlington	VA	22211	703-696-6670	696-4256
Opera Theatre of Northern Virginia 125 S Old Glebe Rd Thomas Jefferson Theatre	Arlington	VA	22205	703-528-1433	812-5039
Pentagon The	Arlington	VA	20301	703-695-1776	
Web: www.defenselink.mil/pubs/pentagon					
Potomac Overlook Regional Park 2845 N Marcey Rd	Arlington	VA	22207	703-528-5406	528-0750
Prince William Forest Park 18100 Park Headquarters Rd	Triangle	VA	22172	703-221-7181	221-4322
Web: www.nps.gov/prwi/					
Richmond National Battlefield Park 3215 E Broad St	Richmond	VA	23223	804-226-1981	771-8522
Web: www.nps.gov/rich/					
Shenandoah National Park 3655 US Hwy 211E	Luray	VA	22835	540-999-2243	999-3679
Web: www.nps.gov/shen/					
Signature Theatre 3806 S Four Mile Run Dr	Arlington	VA	22206	703-820-9771	820-7790
Sully Plantation 3601 Sully Rd	Chantilly	VA	20151	703-437-1794	787-3314
Theodore Roosevelt Island George Washington Pkwy Turkey Run Park	McLean	VA	22101	703-289-2530	289-2598
Web: www.nps.gov/this/					
Thomas Jefferson Theatre 125 S Old Glebe Rd	Arlington	VA	22204	703-228-6960	358-6968
US Marine Corps Memorial-Iwo Jima Rt 50 & Arlington National Cemetery	Arlington	VA	22211	703-228-4747	
Wolf Trap Farm Park for the Performing Arts 1624-A Trap Rd	Vienna	VA	22182	703-255-1868	
Web: www.nps.gov/wotr/					
Women in Military Service for America Memorial Arlington National Cemetery	Arlington	VA	22211	800-472-5883	931-4208*
**Fax Area Code:* 703					

SPORTS TEAMS & FACILITIES

	City	State	Zip	Phone	Fax
Northern Virginia Royals PO Box 1447	Centerville	VA	20120	703-492-9944	492-9944

— Events —

	Phone
Arlington County Fair (mid-August)	703-228-6400
Arlington Farmers Market (mid-April-mid-December)	703-228-6400
Bringing in Christmas (December)	703-557-0613
Candlelight Tours & Concerts (mid-December)	703-437-1794
Crossroads Village Antique Car Show (late July)	810-736-7100
Crystal City Water Park (late May-late Sept)	703-413-0789
Fairfax Fair (mid-June)	703-324-3247
General & Mrs Lee's Wedding Anniversary (June 30)	703-557-0613
Herndon Festival (early June)	703-435-6868
International Children's Festival (mid-September)	703-642-0862
Joy To The World Holiday/Grand Illumination (late November-early January)	703-528-3527
Labor Day Jazz Celebration (early September)	703-435-6868
Light Up Rosslyn (late November-early December)	703-522-6628
Marine Corps Sunset Parades (late May-mid-August)	202-433-4173
Northern Virginia Christmas Market (mid-November)	757-486-0220
Rosslyn Jazz Festival (mid-September)	703-522-6628
Saint Patricks Day Celebration (March 17)	703-557-0613
Taste of Arlington (mid-May)	703-486-0626
Theodore Roosevelt's Birthday Celebration (late October)	703-289-2553
Veterans Day Ceremonies (November 11)	202-619-7222
Wolf Trap Summer Season (late May-mid-September)	703-255-1868

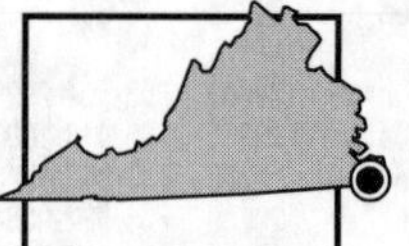

Chesapeake

With over 30 miles of waterways, Chesapeake has more miles of deep water canals than any other city in the United States. The Dismal Swamp Canal is the oldest manmade canal in the country that is still in use, and the Great Dismal Swamp National Wildlife Refuge is home to many species of birds, black bears, bobcats, foxes, and white-tailed deer. Both agriculture and commerce are important parts of the city's economic base, as depicted in Chesapeake's city seal, which shows a farmer shaking hands with a businessman.

Population	199,564	**Longitude**	76-30-88 W
Area (Land)	340.7 sq mi	**County**	Independent City
Area (Water)	10.2 sq mi	**Time Zone**	EST
Elevation	12 ft	**Area Code/s**	757
Latitude	36-67-88 N		

Chesapeake (Cont'd)

— Average Temperatures and Precipitation —

TEMPERATURES

	Jan	Feb	Mar	Apr	May	Jun	Jul	Aug	Sep	Oct	Nov	Dec
High	48	51	60	69	77	84	88	86	80	70	62	52
Low	29	37	38	46	56	64	68	67	61	50	41	33

PRECIPITATION

	Jan	Feb	Mar	Apr	May	Jun	Jul	Aug	Sep	Oct	Nov	Dec
Inches	3.9	3.7	4.1	3.0	3.8	4.3	4.8	5.2	4.5	3.2	2.9	3.4

— Important Phone Numbers —

	Phone
AAA	757-547-9741
American Express Travel	800-528-4800
Emergency	911
Medical Referral	757-547-8121
Poison Control Center	800-552-6337
Time	757-622-9311
Weather	757-666-1212

— Information Sources —

				Phone	Fax
Better Business Bureau Serving Greater Hampton Roads 586 Virginian Dr	Norfolk	VA	23505	757-531-1300	531-1388

Web: www.hamptonroadsbbb.org ■ *E-mail:* info@hamptonroadsbbb.org

				Phone	Fax
Chesapeake City Hall 306 Cedar Rd	Chesapeake	VA	23322	757-382-6241	382-8749

Web: www.chesapeake.va.us/quick-govt.html ■ *E-mail:* pubcomm@city.chesapeake.va.us

				Phone	Fax
Chesapeake Conference Center 900 Greenbrier Cir	Chesapeake	VA	23320	757-382-2500	382-2525

Web: www.chesapeakeconference.com ■ *E-mail:* chesconf@confctr.city.chesapeake.va.us

				Phone	Fax
Chesapeake Economic Development Dept 501 Independence Pkwy Suite 200	Chesapeake	VA	23320	757-382-8040	382-8050

TF: 888-224-3782 ■ *Web:* www.chesapeake.va.us/economic/econindex.html ■ *E-mail:* call_us@econdev.city.chesapeake.va.us

				Phone	Fax
Chesapeake (Independent City) PO Box 15225	Chesapeake	VA	23328	757-382-6151	382-6678

Web: www.chesapeake.va.us

				Phone	Fax
Chesapeake Mayor PO Box 15225	Chesapeake	VA	23328	757-382-6462	382-6678
Chesapeake Public Communications Dept 306 Cedar Rd	Chesapeake	VA	23322	757-382-6241	382-8538

Web: www.chesapeake.va.us ■ *E-mail:* pubcomm@city.chesapeake.va.us

				Phone	Fax
Chesapeake Public Library 298 Cedar Rd	Chesapeake	VA	23322	757-382-6576	382-8567

Web: www.chesapeake.lib.va.us

				Phone	Fax
Hampton Roads Chamber of Commerce 420 Bank St	Norfolk	VA	23501	757-622-2312	622-5563

Web: www.hrccva.com ■ *E-mail:* info@hrccva.com

On-Line Resources

Area Guide Chesapeake	chesapeake.areaguides.net
Excite.com Chesapeake City Guide	www.excite.com/travel/countries/united_states/virginia/chesapeake
Guide to Hampton Roads	www.abel-info.com/regguide/
Insiders' Guide to Virginia's Chesapeake	www.insiders.com/chesapeake-va/

— Transportation Services —

AIRPORTS

■ Norfolk International Airport (ORF)

	Phone
18 miles NW of downtown Chesapeake(approx 30 minutes)	757-857-3351

Web: www.norfolkairport.com ■ *E-mail:* airport@infi.net

Airport Transportation

	Phone
Airport Shuttle $20 fare to downtown Chesapeake	757-857-1231
Blue & White Taxi $20 fare to downtown Chesapeake	757-548-3273

Commercial Airlines

	Phone
American	800-433-7300
American Eagle	800-433-7300
Continental	800-525-0280
Continental Express	800-525-0280
Delta	800-221-1212
Northwest	800-225-2525
TWA	800-221-2000
United	800-241-6522
US Airways	800-428-4322

Charter Airlines

	Phone
Air Charter of Virginia	757-488-1687
Berry Aviation	800-229-2379
Horizon Aviation of Virginia	757-421-9000
Mercury Flight Center	757-488-1687
Piedmont Aviation	757-857-3309

CAR RENTALS

	Phone
Avis	800-331-1212
Budget	757-855-1038
Dollar	757-857-0500
Enterprise	757-853-7700
Hertz	757-857-1261
National	757-857-5385

LIMO/TAXI

	Phone
Black & White Cabs	757-489-7725
Brown & White Taxi	757-366-9288
Cardinal Taxi	757-543-1300
Carey VIP & Celebrity Limousines Inc	757-853-5466
Executive Shuttle Service	757-547-9606
Norfolk Checker Taxi	757-855-3333
Yellow Cab	757-622-3232

MASS TRANSIT

	Phone
Tidewater Regional Transit $1.50 Base fare	757-640-6300

RAIL/BUS

				Phone
Greyhound Bus Station 701 Monticello Ave	Norfolk	VA	23510	757-625-2608

TF: 800-231-2222

— Accommodations —

HOTELS, MOTELS, RESORTS

				Phone	Fax
Best Western Patrick Henry Inn 249 York St	Williamsburg	VA	23187	757-229-9540	220-1273
TF: 800-446-9228					
Budget Lodge 3009 S Military Hwy	Chesapeake	VA	23323	757-487-8888	
Chamberlin Hotel 2 Fenwick Rd	Hampton	VA	23651	757-723-6511	722-5088
TF: 800-582-8975					
Comfort Inn 4433 S Military Hwy	Chesapeake	VA	23321	757-488-7900	488-6152
TF: 800-228-5150					
Comfort Inn & Suites 1420 Richmond Rd	Williamsburg	VA	23185	757-229-2981	229-8179
TF: 800-444-4678					
Comfort Suites 1550 Crossways Blvd	Chesapeake	VA	23320	757-420-1600	420-0099
TF: 800-428-0562					
Days Inn 1433 N Battlefield Blvd	Chesapeake	VA	23320	757-547-9262	547-4334
TF: 800-329-7466					
Days Inn 921 W Atlantic St	Emporia	VA	23847	804-634-9481	348-0746
TF: 800-329-7466					
Econo Lodge Chesapeake 3244 Western Branch Blvd	Chesapeake	VA	23321	757-484-6143	483-2353
TF: 800-553-2666					
Extended StayAmerica 1540 Crossways Blvd	Chesapeake	VA	23320	757-424-8600	424-4446
TF: 800-398-7829					
Fairfield Inn 1560 Crossways Blvd	Chesapeake	VA	23320	757-420-1300	366-0608
TF: 800-228-2800 ■ *Web:* fairfieldinn.com/ORFFC					
Hampton Inn 701A Woodlake Dr	Chesapeake	VA	23320	757-420-1550	424-7414
TF: 800-426-7866					
Holiday Inn Chesapeake 725 Woodlake Dr	Chesapeake	VA	23320	757-523-1500	523-0683
TF: 800-465-4329					
Holiday Inn Patriot 3032 Richmond Rd	Williamsburg	VA	23185	757-565-2600	564-9738
TF: 800-446-6001					
Kingsmill Resort & Conference Center 1010 Kingsmill Rd	Williamsburg	VA	23185	757-253-1703	253-8246
TF: 800-832-5665 ■ *Web:* www.kingsmill.com					
Marriott Hotel & Conference Center 50 Kingsmill Rd	Williamsburg	VA	23185	757-220-2500	253-0541*
**Fax:* Sales ■ *TF:* 800-228-9290 ■ *Web:* marriotthotels.com/PHFCW					

Chesapeake — Hotels, Motels, Resorts (Cont'd)

Name / Address	City	State	ZIP	Phone	Fax
Motel 6 701 Woodlake Dr	Chesapeake	VA	23320	757-420-2976	366-9915
TF: 800-466-8356					
Open 24 Lodge 3265 S Military Hwy	Chesapeake	VA	23323	757-487-2516	
Quality Inn Lord Paget 901 Capitol Landing Rd	Williamsburg	VA	23185	757-229-4444	220-9314
TF: 800-537-2438					
Radisson Fort Magruder Hotel & Conference Center 6945 Pocahontas Trail	Williamsburg	VA	23185	757-220-2250	321-6982
TF: 800-333-3333 ■ *Web:* www.radissonftmagruder.com ■ *E-mail:* hotelsales@earthlink.net					
Ramada Inn Central Williamsburg 5351 Richmond Rd	Williamsburg	VA	23188	757-565-2000	565-4652
TF: 800-446-9200 ■ *Web:* www.williamsburg-ramada.com					
Red Roof Inn 724 Woodlake Dr	Chesapeake	VA	23320	757-523-0123	523-4763
TF: 800-843-7663					
Sunset Manor Motel 3345 S Military Hwy	Chesapeake	VA	23323	757-487-2564	487-1610
Super 8 Motel 100 Red Cedar Ct	Chesapeake	VA	23320	757-547-8880	547-8880
TF: 800-800-8000					
Wellesley Inn 1750 Sara Dr	Chesapeake	VA	23320	757-366-0100	366-0396
TF: 800-444-8888					
Williamsburg Hospitality House 415 Richmond Rd	Williamsburg	VA	23185	757-229-4020	220-1560
TF: 800-932-9192 ■ *Web:* www.williamsburghosphouse.com ■ *E-mail:* reservations@williamsburghosphouse.com					
Williamsburg Lodge 310 S England St	Williamsburg	VA	23185	757-229-1000	220-7799
TF: 800-447-8679					

— Restaurants —

Name / Address	City	State	ZIP	Phone
3 Amigos (Mexican) 200 N Battlefield Blvd	Chesapeake	VA	23320	757-548-4105
Andrea's Italian Restaurant (Italian) 138 S Battlefield Blvd	Chesapeake	VA	23320	757-482-4600
Beijing Chinese Restaurant (Chinese) 1725 Parkview Dr	Chesapeake	VA	23320	757-523-5566
Caras (New American) 123 N Battlefield Blvd	Chesapeake	VA	23320	757-548-0006
Cheer's Unlimited Cafe & Tavern (American) 1405 Greenbrier Pkwy Greenbrier Mall	Chesapeake	VA	23320	757-424-4665
Chesapeake Bay Crab House (Seafood) 2592 Campostella Rd	Chesapeake	VA	23324	757-543-7009
Cooker Bar & Grille (American) 628 Jarman Rd	Chesapeake	VA	23352	757-424-7800
Court House Cafe (American) 350 S Battlefield Blvd.	Chesapeake	VA	23320	757-482-7077
Dragon China (Chinese) 701 Butterfield Blvd	Chesapeake	VA	23320	757-547-5084
El Rancho Grande (Mexican) 1320 S Military Hwy	Chesapeake	VA	23320	757-366-5128
Four Brothers Steak House (Steak) 3268 S Military Hwy	Chesapeake	VA	23323	757-487-6562
Frank's II Italian Restaurant (Italian) 200 N Battlefield Blvd	Chesapeake	VA	23320	757-548-4243
Golden Corral Steak House (Steak) 101 Volvo Pkwy	Chesapeake	VA	23320	757-549-2819
Ho-Ho Chinese Restaurant (Chinese) 202 S Battlefield Blvd	Chesapeake	VA	23320	757-482-2242
Jade Garden Restaurant (Chinese) 1200 Battlefield Blvd N	Chesapeake	VA	23320	757-436-1010
Key West Restaurant (Seafood) 725 Woodlake Dr	Chesapeake	VA	23320	757-523-1212
Kyoto Japanese Steak & Seafood House (Japanese) 1412 Greenbrier Pkwy Suite 129	Chesapeake	VA	23320	757-420-0950
Locks Pointe (Seafood) 136 N Battlefield Blvd	Chesapeake	VA	23320	757-547-9618
Mr. Pig's Bar-B-Q (Barbecue) 445 N Battlefield Blvd	Chesapeake	VA	23320	757-547-5171
Osaka Restaurant (Japanese) 3115 Western Branch Blvd	Chesapeake	VA	23321	757-686-8544
Oysterette Restaurant (Seafood) 3916 Portsmouth Blvd	Chesapeake	VA	23321	757-465-2156
Pargo's Restaurant (American) 1436 Greenbrier Pkwy	Chesapeake	VA	23320	757-420-1900
Pastavita (Italian) 445 Battlefield Blvd	Chesapeake	VA	23320	757-548-4892
Rio Bravo Cantina (Mexican) 4105 Chesapeake Square Blvd	Chesapeake	VA	23321	757-488-7316
Ryan's (American) 1508 Sam's Circle	Chesapeake	VA	23320	757-547-5502
S & W Crab House (Seafood) 3206 Bainbridge Blvd.	Chesapeake	VA	23324	757-545-2904
Stonebridge Restaurant Pub (American) 2449 Taylor Rd	Chesapeake	VA	23321	757-488-9488
Szechuan Inn (Chinese) 3916 Portsmouth Blvd	Chesapeake	VA	23321	757-488-4421
Taboo (American) 1036 Volvo Pkwy Suite 7	Chesapeake	VA	23320	757-548-1996

— Goods and Services —

SHOPPING

Name / Address	City	State	ZIP	Phone	Fax
Chesapeake Square Mall 4200 Portsmouth Blvd	Chesapeake	VA	23321	757-488-9636	465-5590
Greenbrier Mall 1401 Greenbrier Pkwy	Chesapeake	VA	23320	757-424-7300	420-8048
Tower Mall 4040 Victory Blvd	Portsmouth	VA	23701	757-488-4453	465-5889

BANKS

Name / Address	City	State	ZIP	Phone	Fax
Bank of Hampton Roads 201 Volvo Pkwy	Chesapeake	VA	23320	757-436-1000	436-3148
TF: 800-474-2265 ■ *Web:* www.bankofhamptonroads.com					
Bank of Tidewater 821 N Battlefield Blvd	Chesapeake	VA	23320	757-422-0000	436-3820
Branch Banking & Trust Co 3133 Western Branch Blvd	Chesapeake	VA	23321	757-398-8015	686-8271
CENIT Bank FSB 675 N Battlefield Blvd	Chesapeake	VA	23320	757-446-6601	547-8649
First Virginia Bank of Tidewater 239 S Battlefield Blvd	Chesapeake	VA	23322	757-628-6936	
TF: 800-382-4115					
Wachovia Bank 1428 Greenbrier Pkwy	Chesapeake	VA	23320	757-413-6670	523-0012
TF: 800-922-4684					

BUSINESS SERVICES

Name	Phone	Name	Phone
Aarow Temporary Services	757-487-8650	**Manpower Temporary Services**	757-420-2782
DHL Worldwide Express	800-225-5345	**Pak Mail**	757-436-0499
Federal Express	800-463-3339	**Post Office**	757-547-2144
Mail Works	757-436-3486	**UPS**	800-742-5877

— Media —

PUBLICATIONS

Name / Address	City	State	ZIP	Phone	Fax
Chesapeake Bay Magazine 1819 Bay Ridge Ave Suite 158	Annapolis	MD	21403	410-263-2662	267-6924
TF: 800-584-5066					
Daily Press‡ 7505 Warwick Blvd	Newport News	VA	23607	757-247-4600	245-8618

‡*Daily newspapers*

TELEVISION

Name / Address	City	State	ZIP	Phone	Fax
WAVY-TV Ch 10 (NBC) 300 Wavy St	Portsmouth	VA	23704	757-393-1010	397-8279
Web: www.wavy.com ■ *E-mail:* wavy10p@infi.net					
WHRO-TV Ch 15 (PBS) 5200 Hampton Blvd.	Norfolk	VA	23508	757-889-9400	489-0007
Web: www.whro-pbs.org ■ *E-mail:* info@whro.org					
WTKR-TV Ch 3 (CBS) PO Box 300	Norfolk	VA	23501	757-446-1000	446-1376
Web: www.wtkr.com					
WTVZ-TV Ch 33 (WB) 900 Granby St	Norfolk	VA	23510	757-622-3333	623-1541
WVEC-TV Ch 13 (ABC) 613 Woodis Ave	Norfolk	VA	23510	757-625-1313	628-5855
Web: wvec.com					

RADIO

Name / Address	City	State	ZIP	Phone	Fax
WAFX-FM 106.9 MHz (CR) 870 Greenbrier Cir Suite 399	Chesapeake	VA	23320	757-366-9900	366-0022
WCMS-AM 1050 kHz (Ctry) 900 Commonwealth Pl.	Virginia Beach	VA	23464	757-424-1050	424-3479
WCMS-FM 100.5 MHz (Ctry) 900 Commonwealth Pl.	Virginia Beach	VA	23464	757-424-1050	424-3479
WFOG-FM 92.9 MHz (AC) 236 Clearfield Ave Suite 206	Virginia Beach	VA	23462	757-497-2000	473-1100
WHRO-FM 90.3 MHz (Clas) 5200 Hampton Blvd.	Norfolk	VA	23508	757-889-9400	489-0007
WKOC-FM 93.7 MHz (AAA) 999 Waterside Dr Dominion Tower Suite 500	Norfolk	VA	23510	757-640-8500	640-8557
WNOR-AM 1230 kHz (Rock) 870 Greenbrier Cir Suite 399	Chesapeake	VA	23320	757-366-9900	366-0022
E-mail: wnor99a@aol.com					
WNOR-FM 98.7 MHz (Rock) 870 Greenbrier Cir Suite 399	Chesapeake	VA	23320	757-366-9900	366-0022
Web: www.fm99.com ■ *E-mail:* gm@fm99.com					
WOWI-FM 102.9 MHz (Urban) 1003 Norfolk Sq	Norfolk	VA	23502	757-466-0009	466-7043

— Colleges/Universities —

Name / Address	City	State	ZIP	Phone	Fax
Tidewater Community College Chesapeake Campus 1428 Cedar Rd.	Chesapeake	VA	23322	757-822-5100	822-5122
Web: www.tc.cc.va.us					

Chesapeake (Cont'd)

— Hospitals —

				Phone	Fax
Chesapeake General Hospital 736 Battlefield Blvd N	Chesapeake	VA	23327	757-482-6100	482-6184

Web: www.chesgh.org ■ *E-mail:* cgh@chesgh.org

— Attractions —

				Phone	Fax
Chesapeake Fine Arts Commission PO Box 15225	Chesapeake	VA	23328	757-382-6411	382-8418
Chesapeake Planetarium Shea Dr.	Chesapeake	VA	23320	757-547-0153	547-0279
Chrysler Museum of Art 245 W Olney Rd (*Web:* www.chrysler.org)	Norfolk	VA	23510	757-664-6200	664-6201
Great Dismal Swamp National Wildlife Refuge Washington Ditch (*E-mail:* R5RW_GDSNWR@mail.fws.gov)	Suffolk	VA	23439	757-986-3705	
Norfolk Botanical Gardens 6700 Azalea Garden Rd (*Web:* sites.community.org/nbg)	Norfolk	VA	23518	757-441-5830	853-8294
Northwest River Park 1733 Indian Creek Rd	Chesapeake	VA	23322	757-421-7151	
Virginia Marine Science Museum 717 General Booth Blvd (*Web:* www.va-beach.com/va-marine-science-museum/ ■ *E-mail:* vmsm@infi.net)	Virginia Beach	VA	23451	757-425-3474	437-4976

— Events —

	Phone
Annual 4th In the Park (July)	757-543-5721
Bark in the Park (mid-October)	757-382-6411
Battle of Great Bridge Reenactment (early December)	757-382-6411
Beef Fest (mid-September)	757-487-6122
Chesapeake Eggstravaganza (late March)	757-382-8466
Chesapeake Holiday Wonderland (late November-early December)	757-482-6241
Chesapeake Jubilee (mid-May)	757-482-4848
Civil War Days (early September)	757-382-6591
Great American Food Fest (early October)	757-382-6159
Hampton Roads Highland Games (late June)	757-481-2165
Harborfest (early June)	757-441-2345
Holiday Tree Lighting (early December)	757-382-6241
Indian River Craft Show (mid-November)	757-382-8464
Kwanzaa Celebrations (late December)	757-382-6411
Labor Day Celebration (early September)	757-382-6411
Scottish Festival (late June)	757-481-2165
Sheep to Shawl (mid-April)	757-382-6591
Stardust Ball (late May)	757-382-2330

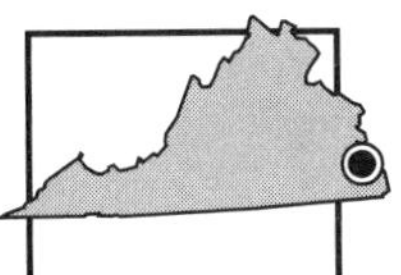

Newport News

Located on the Virginia Peninsula in the southeastern part of the state, Newport News has been a leader in the shipbuilding industry since the turn of the century. During World War I Newport News manufactured vessels for the U.S. Navy, and today the Navy's aircraft carriers and nuclear powered submarines are built in the city. Newport News is also home to the largest private shipyard in the world, Newport News Shipbuilding. Historical sites in Newport News include a number of Civil War sites, the Virginia War Museum, and the Victory Arch through which U.S. troops marched to celebrate the Allied victory following World War I.

Population	178,615	**Longitude**	76-51-42 W
Area (Land)	68.3 sq mi	**County**	Independent City
Area (Water)	50.7 sq mi	**Time Zone**	EST
Elevation	25 ft	**Area Code/s**	757
Latitude	37-07-59 N		

— Average Temperatures and Precipitation —

TEMPERATURES

	Jan	Feb	Mar	Apr	May	Jun	Jul	Aug	Sep	Oct	Nov	Dec
High	48	51	61	70	78	85	88	87	81	71	63	52
Low	27	29	36	44	54	62	67	66	60	48	39	31

PRECIPITATION

	Jan	Feb	Mar	Apr	May	Jun	Jul	Aug	Sep	Oct	Nov	Dec
Inches	3.8	3.5	4.2	3.0	4.5	4.0	5.0	4.7	4.3	3.2	3.5	3.4

— Important Phone Numbers —

	Phone		Phone
AAA	757-826-1061	**Poison Control Center**	800-552-6337
American Express Travel	800-528-4800	**Time**	757-229-1140
Emergency	911	**Weather**	757-877-1221
Medical Referral	757-889-3627		

— Information Sources —

				Phone	Fax
Better Business Bureau Serving Greater Hampton Roads 586 Virginian Dr (*Web:* www.hamptonroadsbbb.org ■ *E-mail:* info@hamptonroadsbbb.org)	Norfolk	VA	23505	757-531-1300	531-1388
Newport News Development Div 2400 Washington Ave	Newport News	VA	23607	757-926-8428	926-3504
Newport News (Independent City) 2400 Washington Ave	Newport News	VA	23607	757-926-8411	926-3503
Newport News Mayor 2400 Washington Ave (*Web:* www.newport-news.va.us)	Newport News	VA	23607	757-926-8403	926-3546
Newport News Public Library 110 Main St (*Web:* www.newport-news.va.us/library)	Newport News	VA	23601	757-591-4858	591-7425
Newport News Tourism Development Office 2400 Washington Ave 7th Fl. (*TF:* 888-493-7386 ■ *Web:* www.newport-news.org)	Newport News	VA	23607	757-926-3561	926-6901
Virginia Peninsula Chamber of Commerce PO Box 7269 (*TF:* 800-556-1822 ■ *Web:* www.vpcc.org)	Hampton	VA	23666	757-766-2000	865-0339

On-Line Resources

Excite.com Newport News City Guide .... www.excite.com/travel/countries/united_states/virginia/newport_news

— Transportation Services —

AIRPORTS

■ **Newport News/Williamsburg International Airport (PHF)**

	Phone
12 miles NW of downtown (approx 20 minutes)	757-877-0221

Web: www.phf-airport.org

Airport Transportation

	Phone
Associated Shuttle $14 fare to downtown	757-887-3412
Taxi $17 fare to downtown	757-245-7777
Williamsburg Shuttle $15 fare to downtown	757-877-0279

Commercial Airlines

	Phone		Phone
United Express	800-241-6522	**US Airways Express**	800-428-4322

Charter Airlines

	Phone		Phone
Flight International	757-886-5755	**Rick Aviation Inc**	757-874-5727

Newport News (Cont'd)

CAR RENTALS

	Phone		Phone
Alamo	800-327-9633	**Hertz**	757-877-9229
Avis	757-877-0291	**National**	757-877-6486
Budget	800-874-5794	**Thrifty**	757-877-5700
Enterprise	757-873-3003		

LIMO/TAXI

	Phone		Phone
Carey VIP & Celebrity Limousine	757-875-0979	**Langley Yellow Cab**	757-723-3316
Celebrity & VIP Limousines	757-875-5466	**Williamsburg Limo & Shuttle**	757-877-0279
Hop's Taxi	757-245-3005	**Yellow Cab**	757-245-7777
Independent Cabs	757-245-8378		

MASS TRANSIT

	Phone
Hampton Roads Transit $1.50 Base fare	757-222-6100

RAIL/BUS

				Phone
Amtrak Station 9304 Warwick Blvd.	Newport News	VA	23601	800-872-7245
Greyhound Bus Station 2 W Pembroke Ave. *TF:* 800-231-2222	Newport News	VA	23605	757-722-9861

— Accommodations —

HOTELS, MOTELS, RESORTS

				Phone	Fax
Capri Country Inn 12880 Jefferson Ave *TF:* 877-622-9901 ■ *Web:* www.hotelroom.com/capri	Newport News	VA	23608	757-877-7000	872-7303
Comfort Inn 12330 Jefferson Ave *TF:* 800-368-2477	Newport News	VA	23602	757-249-0200	249-4736
Days Inn Newport News 14747 Warwick Blvd *TF:* 800-329-7466	Newport News	VA	23602	757-874-0201	874-0201
Days Inn Oyster Point 11829 Fishing Point Dr *TF:* 800-873-2369	Newport News	VA	23606	757-873-6700	873-3755
Econo Lodge Oyster Point 11845 Jefferson Ave *TF:* 800-424-4777	Newport News	VA	23606	757-599-3237	599-0413
Econo Lodge Warwick 15237 Warwick Blvd *TF:* 800-424-4777	Newport News	VA	23608	757-874-9244	872-6883
Extended StayAmerica 11708 Jefferson Ave *TF:* 800-398-7829	Newport News	VA	23606	757-873-2266	873-8891
Hampton Inn & Suites 12251 Jefferson Ave *TF:* 800-426-7866	Newport News	VA	23602	757-249-0001	249-3911
Host Inn 985 J Clyde Morris Blvd	Newport News	VA	23601	757-599-3303	591-0405
Kiln Creek Golf & Country Club 1003 Brick Kiln Blvd	Newport News	VA	23602	757-874-2600	988-3237
Motel 6 797 J Clyde Morris Blvd. *TF:* 800-466-8356	Newport News	VA	23601	757-595-6336	595-8124
Mulberry Inn 16890 Warwick Blvd *TF:* 800-223-0404	Newport News	VA	23603	757-887-3000	887-3665
Omni Hotel 1000 Omni Blvd. *TF:* 800-843-6664	Newport News	VA	23606	757-873-6664	873-1732
Ramada Inn & Conference Center 950 J Clyde Morris Blvd *TF:* 800-272-6232	Newport News	VA	23601	757-599-4460	599-4336
Relax Inn 12340 Warwick Blvd *TF:* 800-596-4521	Newport News	VA	23606	757-599-6035	596-0482
StudioPLUS 12359 Hornsby Ln. *TF:* 800-398-7829	Newport News	VA	23602	757-882-8847	882-8378
Travelodge 13700 Warwick Blvd. *TF:* 800-578-7878	Newport News	VA	23602	757-874-4100	898-4765

— Restaurants —

				Phone
Atlanta Beer Garden (American) 12644 Jefferson Ave.	Newport News	VA	23602	757-988-1669
Bodine's Hickory Smoked Bar-B-Que (Barbecue) 754 J Clyde Morris Blvd	Newport News	VA	23601	757-596-7427
Bon Appetit (French) 11710-A Jefferson Ave.	Newport News	VA	23606	757-873-0644
Carmelia's Homestyle Italian Cuisine (Italian) 14501-A Warwick Blvd	Newport News	VA	23608	757-874-8421
Chao Praya Restaurant (Chinese) 12300 Jefferson Ave.	Newport News	VA	23602	757-249-8872
Chatfield's Grille (American) 950 J Clyde Morris Blvd	Newport News	VA	23601	757-599-4460
Chris' Steak House (Greek) 3506 Washington Ave.	Newport News	VA	23607	757-380-1380
Das Waldcafe (German) 12529 Warwick Blvd	Newport News	VA	23602	757-930-1781
Deer Run Grille (American) 901 Clubhouse Way	Newport News	VA	23608	757-886-1500
Dry Dock Restaurant (American) 3510 Washington Ave.	Newport News	VA	23607	757-380-1854
Eatery The (American) 2600 Washington Ave	Newport News	VA	23607	757-245-3365
Egg Roll King (Chinese) 605 J Clyde Morris Blvd	Newport News	VA	23601	757-596-7177
Heartbreak Cafe (American) 100 Newmarket Sq	Newport News	VA	23605	757-245-3313
Herman's Harbor House (Seafood) 663 Deep Creek Rd.	Newport News	VA	23606	757-930-1000
Hong Kong (Chinese) 865 Newport Square	Newport News	VA	23602	757-599-5858
Japan Samurai (Japanese) 12233 Jefferson Ave	Newport News	VA	23602	757-249-4400
Kappo Nara (Japanese) 550-A Oyster Point Rd	Newport News	VA	23602	757-249-5395
Kyung Sung Korean Restaurant (Korean) 13748 Warwick Blvd.	Newport News	VA	23602	757-877-2797
Luiji's Italian Restaurant (Italian) 15400 Warwick Blvd.	Newport News	VA	23602	757-874-6078
Mai Vietnamese Restaurant (Vietnamese) 14346 Warwick Blvd.	Newport News	VA	23602	757-874-2700
Mitty's Italian Ristorante (Italian) 1000 Omni Blvd	Newport News	VA	23606	757-873-6664
Mulberry Inn (Seafood) 16890 Warwick Blvd.	Newport News	VA	23602	757-887-3000
Port Arthur (Chinese) 11137 Warwick Blvd	Newport News	VA	23601	757-599-6474
Real Bread Co Bistro (American) 11861 Canon Blvd Suite C.	Newport News	VA	23606	757-873-2466
RJ's Restaurant & Sports Pub (American) 12743 Jefferson Ave.	Newport News	VA	23602	757-874-4246
Rocky Mount Bar-b-q House (Barbecue) 10113 Jefferson Ave.	Newport News	VA	23605	757-596-0243
Sammy's Grille (American) 11719 Jefferson Ave.	Newport News	VA	23606	757-595-6671
So Ya Japenese Restaurant (Japanese) 12715 Warwick Blvd Suite J	Newport News	VA	23606	757-930-0156

— Goods and Services —

SHOPPING

				Phone	Fax
Historic Hilton Village 10000 Block of Warwick Blvd.	Newport News	VA	23602	757-596-5630	
Newmarket Center 110 Newmarket Fair	Newport News	VA	23605	757-838-9500	825-0243
Patrick Henry Mall 12300 Jefferson Ave	Newport News	VA	23602	757-249-4305	249-2730

BANKS

				Phone	Fax
Bank of America 608 J Clyde Morris Blvd *TF Cust Svc:* 800-880-5454*	Newport News	VA	23601	757-591-5200	591-5202
BB & T Bank 12301 Warwick Blvd	Newport News	VA	23606	757-873-6031	873-7853
Crestar Bank 12227 Jefferson Ave	Newport News	VA	23602	757-873-7853	873-7859
Harbor Bank 11001 Warwick Blvd.	Newport News	VA	23601	757-591-7000	591-8936
Old Point National Bank 11134 Warwick Blvd	Newport News	VA	23602	757-728-1293	596-0652
Wachovia Bank 956 J Clyde Morris Blvd *TF:* 800-922-4684	Newport News	VA	23601	757-591-4200	420-9316

BUSINESS SERVICES

	Phone		Phone
AccuStaff Inc.	757-249-0059	**Mail Boxes Etc**	757-874-0322
Airborne Express	800-247-2676	**Manpower Temporary Services**	757-873-2260
BAX Global	800-225-5229	**Olsten Staffing Services**	757-881-9760
DHL Worldwide Express	800-225-5345	**Post Office**	757-247-5241
Federal Express	800-238-5355	**UPS**	800-742-5877
Kelly Services	757-873-8739		

— Media —

PUBLICATIONS

				Phone	Fax
Daily Press‡ 7505 Warwick Blvd	Newport News	VA	23607	757-247-4600	245-8618

‡*Daily newspapers*

Newport News (Cont'd)

TELEVISION

				Phone	Fax
WAVY-TV Ch 10 (NBC) 300 Wavy St. *Web:* www.wavy.com ■ *E-mail:* wavy10p@infi.net	Portsmouth	VA	23704	757-393-1010	397-8279
WHRO-TV Ch 15 (PBS) 5200 Hampton Blvd. *Web:* www.whro-pbs.org ■ *E-mail:* info@whro.org	Norfolk	VA	23508	757-889-9400	489-0007
WTKR-TV Ch 3 (CBS) PO Box 300 *Web:* www.wtkr.com	Norfolk	VA	23501	757-446-1000	446-1376
WTVZ-TV Ch 33 (WB) 900 Granby St	Norfolk	VA	23510	757-622-3333	623-1541
WVEC-TV Ch 13 (ABC) 613 Woodis Ave *Web:* wvec.com	Norfolk	VA	23510	757-625-1313	628-5855

RADIO

				Phone	Fax
WAFX-FM 106.9 MHz (CR) 870 Greenbrier Cir Suite 399	Chesapeake	VA	23320	757-366-9900	366-0022
WCMS-AM 1050 kHz (Ctry) 900 Commonwealth Pl.	Virginia Beach	VA	23464	757-424-1050	424-3479
WCMS-FM 100.5 MHz (Ctry) 900 Commonwealth Pl.	Virginia Beach	VA	23464	757-424-1050	424-3479
WFOG-FM 92.9 MHz (AC) 236 Clearfield Ave Suite 206	Virginia Beach	VA	23462	757-497-2000	473-1100
WGH-FM 97.3 MHz (Ctry) 5589 Greenwich Rd Suite 200 *Web:* www.eagle97.com	Virginia Beach	VA	23462	757-671-1000	671-1010
WHRO-FM 90.3 MHz (Clas) 5200 Hampton Blvd.	Norfolk	VA	23508	757-889-9400	489-0007
WKOC-FM 93.7 MHz (AAA) 999 Waterside Dr Dominion Tower Suite 500	Norfolk	VA	23510	757-640-8500	640-8557
WNIS-AM 790 kHz (N/T) 999 Waterside Dr Dominion Tower Suite 500 *Web:* wnis.exis.net ■ *E-mail:* wnis@exis.net	Norfolk	VA	23510	757-640-8500	622-6397
WNOR-AM 1230 kHz (Rock) 870 Greenbrier Cir Suite 399 *E-mail:* wnor99a@aol.com	Chesapeake	VA	23320	757-366-9900	366-0022
WPCE-AM 1400 kHz (Rel) 645 Church St Suite 400	Norfolk	VA	23510	757-622-4600	624-6515
WTAR-AM 850 kHz (N/T) 999 Waterside Dr 500 Dominion Tower *Web:* wtar.exis.net	Norfolk	VA	23510	757-640-8500	640-8552

— Colleges/Universities —

				Phone	Fax
Christopher Newport University 1 University Pl *TF:* 800-333-4268 ■ *Web:* www.cnu.edu ■ *E-mail:* admit@cnu.edu	Newport News	VA	23606	757-594-7000	594-7333

— Hospitals —

				Phone	Fax
Mary Immaculate Hospital 2 Bernardine Dr *Web:* www.mihospital.com	Newport News	VA	23602	757-886-6600	886-6751
Riverside Regional Medical Center 500 J Clyde Morris Blvd *Web:* www.riverside-online.com/rrmc.htm	Newport News	VA	23601	757-594-2000	594-4495

— Attractions —

				Phone	Fax
Jones Matthew House Taylor & Harrison Rds Fort Eustis	Newport News	VA	23604	757-898-5090	
Lee Hall Mansion 163 Yorktown Rd *Web:* www.leehall.org	Newport News	VA	23603	757-888-3371	
Mariners' Museum 100 Museum Dr *Web:* www.mariner.org ■ *E-mail:* info@mariner.org	Newport News	VA	23606	757-596-2222	591-7310
Newport News Park 13564 Jefferson Ave	Newport News	VA	23603	757-888-3333	
Newsome House and Cultural Center 2803 Oak Ave	Newport News	VA	23607	757-247-2380	928-6754
Peninsula Community Theatre PO Box 11056	Newport News	VA	23601	757-595-5728	
Peninsula Fine Arts Center 101 Museum Dr *E-mail:* pfac@whro.org	Newport News	VA	23606	757-596-8175	596-0807
Saint Luke's Historic Church 14477 Benns Church Blvd	Smithfield	VA	23430	757-357-3367	
US Army Transportation Museum Bldg 300 Besson Hall *Web:* www.eustis.army.mil/dptmsec/museum.htm ■ *E-mail:* atzfptm@eustis.army.mil	Fort Eustis	VA	23604	757-878-1182	878-5656
Victory Arch West Ave & 25th St	Newport News	VA	23607		
Virginia Living Museum 524 J Clyde Morris Blvd *Web:* www.valivingmuseum.org	Newport News	VA	23601	757-595-1900	599-4897
Virginia War Museum 9285 Warwick Blvd	Newport News	VA	23607	757-247-8523	247-8627

SPORTS TEAMS & FACILITIES

				Phone	Fax
Langley Speedway 3165 N Armstead Ave	Hampton	VA	23666	757-865-1100	865-1147

— Events —

	Phone
A Newsome House Christmas (December)	757-247-2360
Annual Civil War Re-enactment (late April)	757-887-1862
Artful Giving & Home for the Holidays (mid-November-early January)	757-596-8175
Celebration in Lights (late November-early January)	757-926-8451
Christmas in the Field Civil War Re-enactment (mid-December)	757-887-1862
Ella Fitzgerald Music Festival (late April)	757-594-8752
Fall Festival (early October)	888-493-7386
Hampton Bay Days Festival (mid-September)	757-727-6122
Jubilee on the James (mid-June)	757-926-8451
King-Lincoln Music Festival (late August)	757-926-8451
October Oyster Roast (mid-October)	888-493-7386
Peninsula Fine Arts Center Juried Exhibition (late August-early November)	757-596-8175
Star of Wonder (late November-early January)	757-595-1900
Stars in the Sky (July 4)	757-926-8451
Wildlife Arts Festival (late January)	757-595-1900
Yuletides at the Mariners Museum (late December)	757-596-2222

Norfolk

Norfolk's harbor, rivers, and the Chesapeake Bay make it the center of the Virginia Waterfront. These waters are the site of Norfolk Naval Base, the largest naval installation in the world and home port to more than 100 ships. The Waterside Marketplace overlooks the Elizabeth River, where one can see a daily parade of Navy vessels, sailboats, and tugboats. The downtown Norfolk waterfront is also home to NAUTICUS, the National Maritime Center, which features multimedia shows, virtual reality experiences, ship tours, laser shows, and other activities. Spanning 17.6 miles across the water is the Chesapeake Bay Bridge-Tunnel, touted as one of the "Seven Wonders of the Modern World."

Population	215,215	**Longitude**	76-27-84 W
Area (Land)	53.8 sq mi	**County**	Independent City
Area (Water)	42.5 sq mi	**Time Zone**	EST
Elevation	12 ft	**Area Code/s**	757
Latitude	36-85-10 N		

— Average Temperatures and Precipitation —

TEMPERATURES

	Jan	Feb	Mar	Apr	May	Jun	Jul	Aug	Sep	Oct	Nov	Dec
High	47	50	58	67	75	83	86	85	80	70	61	52
Low	31	32	39	47	57	65	70	69	64	53	44	35

Norfolk (Cont'd)

PRECIPITATION

	Jan	Feb	Mar	Apr	May	Jun	Jul	Aug	Sep	Oct	Nov	Dec
Inches	3.8	3.5	3.7	3.1	3.8	3.8	5.1	4.8	3.9	3.2	2.9	3.2

— Important Phone Numbers —

	Phone
AAA	757-622-5634
American Express Travel	757-622-6692
Dental Referral	757-491-4626
Emergency	911
Medical Referral	800-736-8272
Poison Control Center	800-552-6337
Time	757-622-9311
Travelers Aid	757-622-7017
Weather	757-666-1212

— Information Sources —

				Phone	Fax
Better Business Bureau Serving Greater Hampton Roads 586 Virginian Dr *Web:* www.hamptonroadsbbb.org ■ *E-mail:* info@hamptonroadsbbb.org	Norfolk	VA	23505	757-531-1300	531-1388
Hampton Roads Chamber of Commerce 420 Bank St *Web:* www.hrccva.com ■ *E-mail:* info@hrccva.com	Norfolk	VA	23501	757-622-2312	622-5563
Norfolk City Hall 810 Union St *Web:* www.norfolk.va.us	Norfolk	VA	23510	757-664-4000	664-4006
Norfolk City Planning & Codes Administration Dept 810 Union St 5th fl *Web:* www.norfolk.va.us/codes/index.html	Norfolk	VA	23510	757-664-4752	664-4748
Norfolk (Independent City) 1101 City Hall Bldg *Web:* www.city.norfolk.va.us	Norfolk	VA	23510	757-664-4242	664-4239
Norfolk Mayor 810 Union St Rm 1109	Norfolk	VA	23510	757-664-4679	441-2909
Norfolk Public Library 301 E City Hall Ave *Web:* www.npl.lib.va.us	Norfolk	VA	23510	757-664-7323	664-7320
Norfolk Scope Cultural & Convention Center 201 E Brambleton Ave *Web:* www.norfolkscope.com	Norfolk	VA	23501	757-664-6464	664-6990

On-Line Resources

4Norfolk.com	www.4norfolk.com
Anthill City Guide Norfolk	www.anthill.com/city.asp?city=norfolk
Area Guide Norfolk	norfolk.areaguides.net
City Knowledge Norfolk	www.cityknowledge.com/va_norfolk.htm
Excite.com Norfolk City Guide	www.excite.com/travel/countries/united_states/virginia/norfolk
Festevents	www.festeventsva.org
Insiders' Guide to Virginia's Chesapeake	www.insiders.com/chesapeake-va/
Norfolk CityLink	www.usacitylink.com/citylink/norfolk
Norfolk Visitors' Guide	www.vgnet.com/norfolk/
Surf & Sun Beach Vacation Guide to Norfolk	www.surf-sun.com/va-norfolk-main.htm

— Transportation Services —

AIRPORTS

■ Norfolk International Airport (ORF)

	Phone
8 miles NE of downtown (approx 15 minutes) Web: www.norfolkairport.com	757-857-3351

Airport Transportation

	Phone
Airport Shuttle $13 fare to downtown	757-857-1231
Taxi $17-20 fare to downtown	757-622-3232

Commercial Airlines

	Phone
AirTran	800-247-8726
American	800-433-7300
American Eagle	800-433-7300
Continental	800-525-0280
Continental Express	800-525-0280
Delta	800-221-1212
Northwest	800-225-2525
TWA	800-221-2000
United	800-241-6522
US Airways	800-428-4322

Charter Airlines

	Phone
Berry Aviation	800-229-2379
Piedmont Aviation	757-857-3309

CAR RENTALS

	Phone
Alamo	800-327-9633
Avis	800-331-1212
Budget	757-855-8035
Dollar	757-857-0500
Enterprise	757-853-7700
Hertz	757-857-1261
National	757-857-5385
Thrifty	757-855-5900

LIMO/TAXI

	Phone
Black & White Cabs	757-489-7725
Carey VIP & Celebrity Limousines Inc	757-853-5466
Green & White Checker Cabs	757-855-6611
LPR Limousines Unlimited	757-858-1234
Norfolk Checker Taxi	757-855-3333
Park Avenue Limousine	757-461-1331
Yellow Cab	757-622-3232

MASS TRANSIT

	Phone
Tidewater Regional Transit $1.50 Base fare	757-640-6300

RAIL/BUS

				Phone
Greyhound Bus Station 701 Monticello Ave *TF:* 800-231-2222	Norfolk	VA	23510	757-625-2608

— Accommodations —

HOTELS, MOTELS, RESORTS

				Phone	Fax
Best Western Center Inn 235 N Military Hwy *TF:* 800-237-5517	Norfolk	VA	23502	757-461-6600	466-9093
Budget Lodge 1001 N Military Hwy *TF:* 800-251-1952	Norfolk	VA	23502	757-461-4391	459-2285
Clarion The 700 Monticello Ave	Norfolk	VA	23510	757-627-5555	533-9651
Comfort Inn Airport 6360 Newtown Rd *TF:* 800-221-2222	Norfolk	VA	23502	757-461-1081	461-4390
Comfort Inn Naval Base 8051 Hampton Blvd *TF:* 800-228-5150	Norfolk	VA	23505	757-451-0000	451-8394
Courtyard by Marriott Norfolk 5700 Greenwich Rd *TF:* 800-321-2211 ■ *Web:* courtyard.com/ORFVB	Virginia Beach	VA	23462	757-490-2002	490-0169
Days Inn 1918 Coliseum Dr *TF:* 800-329-7466	Hampton	VA	23666	757-826-4810	827-6503
Days Inn Airport 5708 Northampton Blvd *TF:* 800-329-7466	Virginia Beach	VA	23455	757-460-2205	363-8089
Days Inn Marina 1631 Bayville St *TF:* 800-329-7466	Norfolk	VA	23503	757-583-4521	583-9544
Days Inn Norfolk Military Circle 5701 Chambers St *TF:* 800-329-7466	Norfolk	VA	23502	757-461-0100	461-5883
Doubletree Club Hotel 880 N Military Hwy Suite 35 *TF:* 800-933-9600 ■ *Web:* www.doubletreehotels.com/DoubleT/Hotel81/99/99Main.htm	Norfolk	VA	23502	757-461-9192	461-8290
Econo Lodge 9601 4th View St *TF:* 800-553-2666	Norfolk	VA	23503	757-480-9611	480-1307
Econo Lodge 1111 E Ocean View Ave *TF:* 800-360-3529	Norfolk	VA	23503	757-480-1111	480-1111
Hampton Inn Airport 1450 N Military Hwy *TF:* 800-426-7866	Norfolk	VA	23502	757-466-7474	466-0117
Hampton Inn Norfolk Naval Base 8501 Hampton Blvd *TF:* 800-426-7866	Norfolk	VA	23505	757-489-1000	489-4509
Holiday Inn Conference Center 1815 W Mercury Blvd *TF:* 800-842-9370	Hampton	VA	23666	757-838-0200	838-4964
Holiday Inn Portsmouth Waterfront 8 Crawford Pkwy *TF:* 800-465-4269	Portsmouth	VA	23704	757-393-2573	393-2573
Holiday Sands Motel 1330 E Ocean View Ave *TF:* 800-525-5156	Norfolk	VA	23503	757-583-2621	587-7540
James Madison Hotel 345 Granby St *TF:* 888-402-6682	Norfolk	VA	23510	757-622-6682	623-5949
Marriott Hotel Waterside 235 E Main St *TF:* 800-228-9290 ■ *Web:* marriotthotels.com/ORFWS	Norfolk	VA	23510	757-627-4200	628-6466
Norfolk Airport Hilton 1500 N Military Hwy *TF:* 800-422-7474	Norfolk	VA	23502	757-466-8000	466-8802

Norfolk — Hotels, Motels, Resorts (Cont'd)

				Phone	Fax
Quality Inn 1010 W Ocean View Ave *TF:* 800-688-8761	Norfolk	VA	23503	757-587-8761	
Quality Inn Lake Wright Resort & Convention Center 6280 Northampton Blvd *TF:* 800-228-5157 ■ *Web:* www.lakewrighthotel.com	Norfolk	VA	23502	757-461-6251	461-5925
Quality Inn Suites 1809 W Mercury Blvd *TF:* 800-228-5151	Hampton	VA	23666	757-838-5011	838-7349
Ramada Limited 719 E Ocean View Ave *TF:* 800-272-6232	Norfolk	VA	23503	757-583-5211	588-6327
Ramada Limited Norfolk 515 N Military Hwy *TF:* 800-272-6232	Norfolk	VA	23502	757-461-1880	461-4216
Relax Inn 315 E Ocean View Ave	Norfolk	VA	23503	757-480-2350	
Rodeway Inn 7969 Shore Dr *TF:* 800-228-2000	Norfolk	VA	23503	757-588-3600	588-3600
Sheraton Norfolk Waterside 777 Waterside Dr *TF:* 800-325-3535	Norfolk	VA	23510	757-622-6664	625-8271
Tides Inn 7950 Shore Dr *TF:* 800-284-3035	Norfolk	VA	23518	757-587-8781	480-6071
Travelers Inn 800 E Ocean View Ave *TF:* 800-799-2335	Norfolk	VA	23503	757-583-2335	583-2035
Welcome Inn 8901 Hampton Blvd *TF:* 800-780-6289	Norfolk	VA	23505	757-489-0801	489-3086

— Restaurants —

				Phone
219 Restaurant (International) 219 Granby St	Norfolk	VA	23510	757-627-2896
Anthony's (Mediterranean) 2502 Colley Ave	Norfolk	VA	23517	757-622-7411
Antiquities (Continental) 1500 N Military Hwy	Norfolk	VA	23502	757-466-8000
Banque (American) 1849 E Little Creek Rd	Norfolk	VA	23518	757-480-3600
Bienville Grill (Cajun/Creole) 723 W 21st St	Norfolk	VA	23517	757-625-5427
Blue Crab Bar & Grille (Seafood) 4521 Pretty Lake Ave	Norfolk	VA	23518	757-362-8000
Bobbywood (New American) 7515 Granby St	Norfolk	VA	23509	757-440-7515
Cafe Europa (Continental) 319 High St	Portsmouth	VA	23704	757-399-6652
Cafe Rosso (Italian) 123 W 21st St	Norfolk	VA	23517	757-627-2078
Chances Restaurant (American) 6425 Tidewater Dr	Norfolk	VA	23509	757-853-2214
Dockside Restaurant & Pub (American) 7856 Hampton Blvd	Norfolk	VA	23505	757-489-2210
Downtowner Restaurant (American) 209 Granby St	Norfolk	VA	23510	757-627-9469
Fellini's (Italian) 3910 Colley Ave	Norfolk	VA	23508	757-625-3000
Freemason Abbey (American) 209 W Freemason St	Norfolk	VA	23510	757-622-3966
German Pantry (German) 5329 Virginia Beach Blvd	Norfolk	VA	23502	757-461-5100
Grate Steak The (Steak) 235 N Military Hwy	Norfolk	VA	23502	757-461-5501
Harbor Inn Restaurant (Seafood) 1009 Sunset Dr	Norfolk	VA	23503	757-588-9687
Hummingbird Caribbean (Caribbean) 1000 Park Ave Suite A	Norfolk	VA	23504	757-623-4032
India Restaurant (Indian) 5760 Northampton Blvd	Norfolk	VA	23455	757-460-2100
Kevin's Pub (American) 700 Monticello Ave	Norfolk	VA	23510	757-627-5555
La Galleria Ristorante (Italian) 120 College Pl	Norfolk	VA	23510	757-623-3939
Loaves & Fishes by Dail (American) 2100 Colonial Ave	Norfolk	VA	23517	757-627-8794
Magnolia Steak (Steak) Colley Ave & Princess Anne Rd	Norfolk	VA	23517	757-625-0400
Mario's (Italian) 611 Airline Blvd	Portsmouth	VA	23707	757-399-8970
Maude's House (American) 313 W Bute St	Norfolk	VA	23510	757-622-4990
Max The (American) 1421 Colley Ave	Norfolk	VA	23517	757-625-0259
Monastery The (Continental) 443 Granby St	Norfolk	VA	23510	757-625-8193
Nawab (Indian) 888 N Military Hwy	Norfolk	VA	23504	757-455-8080
Orapax Inn (Greek) 1300 Redgate Ave	Norfolk	VA	23507	757-627-8041
Painted Lady (Steak/Seafood) 112 E 17th St	Norfolk	VA	23517	757-623-8872
Sandbar Restaurant (American) 2939 E Ocean View Ave	Norfolk	VA	23518	757-583-9942
Scale O' De Whale (Seafood) 3515 Shipwright St	Portsmouth	VA	23703	757-483-2772
Ship's Cabin (Seafood) 4110 E Ocean View Ave	Norfolk	VA	23518	757-362-4659
Spaghetti Warehouse (Italian) 1900 Monticello Ave	Norfolk	VA	23517	757-622-0151
Spirit of Norfolk (American) 100 W Plume St	Norfolk	VA	23510	757-627-7771
Szechuan Garden (Chinese) 123 W Charlotte St	Norfolk	VA	23510	757-627-6130
Tabouli (Middle Eastern) 4140 Granby St	Norfolk	VA	23504	757-627-1143
Thailand Cuisine (Thai) 333 Waterside Dr	Norfolk	VA	23510	757-627-5986
Todd Jurich's Bistro (New American) 210 York St	Norfolk	VA	23510	757-622-3210
Wild Monkey (New American) 1603 Colley Ave	Norfolk	VA	23517	757-627-6462

— Goods and Services —

SHOPPING

				Phone	Fax
Altschul's 427 Granby St	Norfolk	VA	23510	757-622-2317	622-5514
Ghent Colley Ave & 21st St	Norfolk	VA	23517	757-664-6620	
Janaf Shopping Center 5900 E Virginia Beach Blvd	Norfolk	VA	23502	757-461-4954	459-2229
Military Circle Mall 880 N Military Hwy	Norfolk	VA	23502	757-461-1940	
Ocean View Shopping Center 179 W Ocean View Ave	Norfolk	VA	23503	757-627-8611	
Waterside The 333 Waterside Dr	Norfolk	VA	23510	757-627-3300	627-3981

BANKS

				Phone	Fax
Bank of the Commonwealth 403 Boush St	Norfolk	VA	23510	757-446-6900	446-6929
CENIT Bank FSB 225 W Olney Rd	Norfolk	VA	23510	757-446-6600	446-6643
First Union National Bank 999 Waterside Dr	Norfolk	VA	23510	757-628-0458	
First Virginia Bank Tidewater PO Box 3097	Norfolk	VA	23514	757-628-6600	628-6619
Heritage Bank & Trust 841 N Military Hwy *TF:* 800-790-6691	Norfolk	VA	23502	757-523-2672	523-2677

BUSINESS SERVICES

	Phone
B & C Courier Services	757-518-8147
Central Delivery Service	757-460-0875
Corporate Express Delivery Systems	757-461-8830
Federal Express	800-238-5355
Kinko's	757-461-7136
Manpower Temporary Services	757-627-1106
Metro Courier	757-625-1311
Norrell Temporary Services	757-436-3633
Post Office	757-629-2198
UPS	800-742-5877

— Media —

PUBLICATIONS

				Phone	Fax
Virginia Business Magazine 411 E Franklin St Suite 105 *Web:* virginiabusiness.com	Richmond	VA	23219	804-649-6999	649-6311
Virginian-Pilot‡ PO Box 449 *TF:* 800-446-2004 ■ *Web:* www.pilotonline.com ■ *E-mail:* pilot@infi.net	Norfolk	VA	23501	757-446-2000	446-2414

‡Daily newspapers

TELEVISION

				Phone	Fax
WAVY-TV Ch 10 (NBC) 300 Wavy St *Web:* www.wavy.com ■ *E-mail:* wavy10p@infi.net	Portsmouth	VA	23704	757-393-1010	397-8279
WGNT-TV Ch 27 (UPN) 1318 Spratley St *Web:* www.paramountstations.com/WGNT ■ *E-mail:* upn27@paramount.com	Portsmouth	VA	23704	757-393-2501	399-3303
WHRO-TV Ch 15 (PBS) 5200 Hampton Blvd *Web:* www.whro-pbs.org ■ *E-mail:* info@whro.org	Norfolk	VA	23508	757-889-9400	489-0007
WPXV-TV Ch 49 (PAX) 230 Clearfield Ave Suite 104 *Web:* www.pax.net/WPXV	Virginia Beach	VA	23462	757-490-1249	499-1679
WTKR-TV Ch 3 (CBS) PO Box 300 *Web:* www.wtkr.com	Norfolk	VA	23501	757-446-1000	446-1376
WTVZ-TV Ch 33 (WB) 900 Granby St	Norfolk	VA	23510	757-622-3333	623-1541
WVBT-TV Ch 43 (Fox) 243 Wavy St *Web:* www.wvbt.com	Portsmouth	VA	23704	757-393-4343	393-7615
WVEC-TV Ch 13 (ABC) 613 Woodis Ave *Web:* wvec.com	Norfolk	VA	23510	757-625-1313	628-5855

RADIO

				Phone	Fax
WAFX-FM 106.9 MHz (CR) 870 Greenbrier Cir Suite 399	Chesapeake	VA	23320	757-366-9900	366-0022
WCMS-AM 1050 kHz (Ctry) 900 Commonwealth Pl	Virginia Beach	VA	23464	757-424-1050	424-3479
WCMS-FM 100.5 MHz (Ctry) 900 Commonwealth Pl	Virginia Beach	VA	23464	757-424-1050	424-3479
WFOG-FM 92.9 MHz (AC) 236 Clearfield Ave Suite 206	Virginia Beach	VA	23462	757-497-2000	473-1100
WGPL-AM 1350 kHz (Rel) 645 Church St Suite 400	Norfolk	VA	23510	757-622-4600	624-6515
WHRO-FM 90.3 MHz (Clas) 5200 Hampton Blvd	Norfolk	VA	23508	757-889-9400	489-0007
WHRV-FM 89.5 MHz (NPR) 5200 Hampton Blvd	Norfolk	VA	23508	757-889-9400	489-0007
WJCD-FM 105.3 MHz (NAC) 1003 Norfolk Sq *Web:* wjcd.com ■ *E-mail:* cd105.3@wjcd.com	Norfolk	VA	23502	757-466-0009	466-1155
WKOC-FM 93.7 MHz (AAA) 999 Waterside Dr Dominion Tower Suite 500	Norfolk	VA	23510	757-640-8500	640-8557

Norfolk — Radio (Cont'd)

				Phone	Fax
WNIS-AM 790 kHz (N/T) 999 Waterside Dr Dominion Tower Suite 500 *Web:* wnis.exis.net ■ *E-mail:* wnis@exis.net	Norfolk	VA	23510	757-640-8500	622-6397
WNOR-AM 1230 kHz (Rock) 870 Greenbrier Cir Suite 399 *E-mail:* wnor99a@aol.com	Chesapeake	VA	23320	757-366-9900	366-0022
WNOR-FM 98.7 MHz (Rock) 870 Greenbrier Cir Suite 399 *Web:* www.fm99.com ■ *E-mail:* gm@fm99.com	Chesapeake	VA	23320	757-366-9900	366-0022
WNSB-FM 91.1 MHz (NPR) 2401 Corprew Ave. *E-mail:* wnsb@vger.nsu.edu	Norfolk	VA	23504	757-823-9672	823-2385
WOWI-FM 102.9 MHz (Urban) 1003 Norfolk Sq	Norfolk	VA	23502	757-466-0009	466-7043
WPCE-AM 1400 kHz (Rel) 645 Church St Suite 400	Norfolk	VA	23510	757-622-4600	624-6515
WPTE-FM 94.9 MHz (AC) 236 Clearfield Ave Suite 206 *Web:* www.pointradio.com	Virginia Beach	VA	23462	757-497-2000	473-1100
WROX-FM 96.1 MHz (Alt) 999 Waterside Dr Dominion Tower Suite 500	Norfolk	VA	23510	757-640-8500	640-8552
WSVV-FM 92.1 MHz (CHR) 1003 Norfolk Sq	Norfolk	VA	23502	757-466-0009	466-7043
WSVY-FM 107.7 MHz (Urban) 1003 Norfolk Sq	Norfolk	VA	23502	757-466-0009	466-0082
WXEZ-FM 94.1 MHz (B/EZ) 4026 George Washington Hwy *Web:* www.ez94.com	Yorktown	VA	23692	757-898-9494	898-9401

— Colleges/Universities —

				Phone	Fax
Bryant & Stratton Career College Virginia Beach 301 Center Pt Dr. *Web:* www.bryantstratton.edu	Virginia Beach	VA	23462	757-499-7900	499-9977
Christopher Newport University 1 University Pl *TF:* 800-333-4268 ■ *Web:* www.cnu.edu ■ *E-mail:* admit@cnu.edu	Newport News	VA	23606	757-594-7000	594-7333
College of William & Mary PO Box 8795 *Web:* www.wm.edu ■ *E-mail:* ccharr@facstaff.wm.edu	Williamsburg	VA	23187	757-221-4000	221-1242
Hampton University *TF Admissions:* 800-624-3328 ■ *Web:* www.hamptonu.edu	Hampton	VA	23668	757-727-5000	727-5998
ITT Technical Institute 863 Glenrock Rd *TF:* 800-253-8324 ■ *Web:* www.itt-tech.edu	Norfolk	VA	23502	757-466-1260	466-7630
Norfolk State University 700 Park Ave. *Web:* www.nsu.edu	Norfolk	VA	23504	757-683-8396	823-2078
Old Dominion University Hampton Blvd. *TF Admissions:* 800-348-7926 ■ *Web:* web.odu.edu ■ *E-mail:* aos100s@shawnee.oa.odu.edu	Norfolk	VA	23529	757-683-3000	683-3255
Thomas Nelson Community College 99 Thomas Nelson Dr *Web:* www.tncc.cc.va.us	Hampton	VA	23666	757-825-2700	825-2763
Tidewater Community College Chesapeake Campus 1428 Cedar Rd. *Web:* www.tc.cc.va.us	Chesapeake	VA	23322	757-822-5100	822-5122
Tidewater Community College Portsmouth Campus 7000 College Dr. *Web:* www.tc.cc.va.us	Portsmouth	VA	23703	757-822-2124	686-5173
Tidewater Community College Virginia Beach Campus 1700 College Crescent *Web:* www.tc.cc.va.us/campuses/vabeach.htm	Virginia Beach	VA	23456	757-822-7100	427-7041
Virginia Wesleyan College 1584 Wesleyan Dr *TF Admissions:* 800-737-8684 ■ *Web:* www.vwc.edu	Norfolk	VA	23502	757-455-3200	461-5238

— Hospitals —

				Phone	Fax
Bon Secours Maryview Medical Center 3636 High St **Fax:* Admitting	Portsmouth	VA	23707	757-398-2200	397-2446*
Chesapeake General Hospital 736 Battlefield Blvd N *Web:* www.chesgh.org ■ *E-mail:* cgh@chesgh.org	Chesapeake	VA	23327	757-482-6100	482-6184
Children's Hospital of the King's Daughters 601 Children's Ln *Web:* www.chkd.org	Norfolk	VA	23507	757-668-7000	668-8050
DePaul Medical Center 150 Kingsley Ln **Fax:* Admitting	Norfolk	VA	23505	757-489-5000	489-3509*
Sentara Leigh Hospital 830 Kempsville Rd *Web:* www.sentara.com/hospitals/sentara_leigh.html	Norfolk	VA	23502	757-466-6000	466-6765
Sentara Norfolk General Hospital 600 Gresham Dr *Web:* www.sentara.com/hospitals/sentara_norfolk.html	Norfolk	VA	23507	757-668-3000	668-2256
Sentara Virginia Beach General Hospital 1060 First Colonial Rd *TF:* 800-736-8272 ■ *Web:* www.sentara.com/hospitals/virginiabeach.html	Virginia Beach	VA	23454	757-395-8000	395-6106

— Attractions —

				Phone	Fax
Arts Center of the Portsmouth Museums 420 High St	Portsmouth	VA	23704	757-393-8543	393-5228
Chesapeake Bay Bridge-Tunnel PO Box 111	Cape Charles	VA	23310	757-331-2960	
Children's Museum of Virginia 221 High St	Portsmouth	VA	23704	757-393-8393	393-5228
Chrysler Hall 215 Saint Pauls Blvd	Norfolk	VA	23510	757-664-6464	664-6690
Chrysler Museum of Art 245 W Olney Rd *Web:* www.chrysler.org	Norfolk	VA	23510	757-664-6200	664-6201
Colonial National Historical Park Colonial Pkwy & Rt 238 *Web:* www.nps.gov/colo/	Yorktown	VA	23690	757-898-3400	898-3400
d'Art Center 125 College Pl *Web:* sites.communitylink.org/dArt	Norfolk	VA	23510	757-625-4211	
Fort Norfolk 810 Front St.	Norfolk	VA	23508	757-625-1720	
General Douglas MacArthur Memorial MacArthur Sq *Web:* sites.communitylink.org/mac/ ■ *E-mail:* macmem@norfolk.infi.net	Norfolk	VA	23510	757-441-2965	441-5389
Generic Theater 912 W 21st St *Web:* www.generictheater.org ■ *E-mail:* generic@whro.net	Norfolk	VA	23517	757-441-2160	441-2729
Hermitage Foundation Museum 7637 N Shore Rd	Norfolk	VA	23505	757-423-2052	423-1604
Hill House 221 North St	Portsmouth	VA	23704	757-393-0241	
Hunter House Victorian Museum 240 W Freemason St.	Norfolk	VA	23510	757-623-9814	
Hurrah Players 935 Woodrow Ave	Norfolk	VA	23517	757-627-5437	623-7418
IMAX Theater 600 Settlers Landing Rd *Web:* www.vasc.org/imax.html	Hampton	VA	23669	757-727-0800	727-0898
Lancaster Train & Toy Museum 5661 Shoulder Hill Rd	Suffolk	VA	23435	757-484-4224	484-1475
Lightship Museum Water St & London Blvd	Portsmouth	VA	23704	757-393-8741	
Little Theatre of Norfolk 801 Claremont Ave	Norfolk	VA	23507	757-627-8551	
Myers Moses House 331 Bank St	Norfolk	VA	23510	757-664-6200	441-2329
NAUTICUS The National Maritime Center 1 Waterside Dr *Web:* www.nauticus.org	Norfolk	VA	23510	757-664-1000	623-1287
Norfolk Botanical Gardens 6700 Azalea Garden Rd *Web:* sites.community.org/nbg	Norfolk	VA	23518	757-441-5830	853-8294
Norfolk Chamber Consort Hampton Blvd Chandler Recital Hall	Norfolk	VA	23529	757-440-1803	440-1964
Norfolk Naval Air Station 9420 3rd Ave.	Norfolk	VA	23511	757-444-8047	
Portsmouth Naval Shipyard Museum PO Box 248	Portsmouth	VA	23705	757-393-8591	393-5244
Riddick's Folly 510 N Main St	Suffolk	VA	23434	757-934-1390	
Saint Pauls Church 201 St Paul's Blvd	Norfolk	VA	23510	757-627-4353	
Spirit of Norfolk Cruises 100 W Plume St Suite 106 *Web:* www.spiritcruises.com/norfolk/location.asp	Norfolk	VA	23510	757-625-1463	625-1321
Suffolk Museum 118 Bosley Ave.	Suffolk	VA	23434	757-925-6311	538-0833
Virginia Air & Space Center/Hampton Roads History Center 600 Settlers Landing Rd. *Web:* www.vasc.org	Hampton	VA	23669	757-727-0800	727-0898
Virginia Ballet Theater 134 W Olney Rd	Norfolk	VA	23510	757-622-4822	622-7904
Virginia Stage Co Monticello & Tazewell Sts *Web:* www.vastage.com ■ *E-mail:* boxoffice@vastage.com	Norfolk	VA	23514	757-627-6988	628-5958
Virginia Symphony PO Box 26 *Web:* www.windborne.com/wbpi/VASymphony/	Norfolk	VA	23501	757-623-2310	627-6546
Virginia Zoological Park 3500 Granby St. *Web:* sites.communitylink.org/vazoo/ ■ *E-mail:* vazoo@whro.org	Norfolk	VA	23504	757-441-2706	
Waterside The 333 Waterside Dr	Norfolk	VA	23510	757-627-3300	627-3981
Willoughby-Baylor House 601 E Freemason St.	Norfolk	VA	23510	757-664-6296	

SPORTS TEAMS & FACILITIES

				Phone	Fax
Hampton Coliseum 1000 Coliseum Dr. *Web:* www.hampton.va.us/coliseum	Hampton	VA	23666	757-838-5650	838-2595

Norfolk — Sports Teams & Facilities (Cont'd)

				Phone	*Fax*
Hampton Roads Admirals (hockey) 201 E Brambleton Ave Scope Arena	Norfolk	VA	23510	757-640-1212	
Hampton Roads Mariners (soccer) 2181 Landstown Rd Virginia Beach Sportsplex	Virginia Beach	VA	23456	757-430-8873	430-8803
Norfolk Scope 201 E Brambleton Ave Scope Arena *Web:* www.norfolkscope.com	Norfolk	VA	23501	757-664-6464	664-6990
Norfolk Tides (baseball) 150 Park Ave Harbor Pk *Web:* www.gohamptonroads.com/partners/tides	Norfolk	VA	23510	757-622-2222	624-9090

— Events —

	Phone
A Fare for the Arts (late August)	757-393-5327
AFR'AM Fest (late May)	757-456-1743
Art Explosure (early May)	757-622-4262
Bayou Boogaloo & Cajun Food Festival (late June)	757-441-2345
Cock Island Race (late June-early July)	757-393-9933
Concerts at the Point (May-June)	757-441-2345
Crawford Bay Crew Classic (late March)	757-393-9933
Downtown Doo Dah Parade (early April)	757-441-2345
Elizabeth River Run (early May)	757-421-2602
First Night Norfolk (December 31)	757-441-2345
Garden of Lights Holiday Festival (late November-early January)	757-441-5830
Great American Picnic (July 4)	757-441-2345
Greek Festival (early May)	757-440-0500
Harborfest (early June)	757-441-2345
Holidays in the City (late November-late December)	757-441-2345
Holly Festival (mid-late November)	757-668-7098
International Azalea Festival-Norfolk (mid-April)	757-622-2312
Ocean View Beach Festival (mid-May)	757-583-0000
Peanut Festival (mid-October)	757-539-6751
Reggae on the River (mid-September)	757-441-2345
Seawall Festival (early June)	757-393-5327
Stockley Gardens Art Festival (mid-May)	757-625-6161
Town Point Air Show & 4th of July Celebration-Norfolk (early July)	757-441-2345
Town Point Jazz & Blues Festival (mid-May)	757-441-2345
Town Point Virginia Wine Festival (mid-October)	757-441-2345
Virginia Children's Festival (mid-September)	757-441-2345

Richmond

The historic city of Richmond played key roles both in the American Revolution and the Civil War. Thomas Jefferson designed the State Capitol Building in Richmond, which was built in 1785, and it was here that Aaron Burr was tried for treason, the Articles of Secession were ratified, Robert E. Lee became commander of the Virginia Army, and the Confederate Congress held its meetings. Patrick Henry's "Give me liberty..." speech was given in Richmond's Church Hill Historic District, which is also the site of the Edgar Allen Poe Museum. Richmond's other historic sites include the home of former Supreme Court Justice John Marshall; the Confederate Museum; and the White House of the Confederacy, where Jefferson Davis lived during the years that Richmond was capital of the Confederacy.

Population	194,173	**Longitude**	77-46-06 W
Area (Land)	60.1 sq mi	**County**	Independent City
Area (Water)	2.5 sq mi	**Time Zone**	EST
Elevation	150 ft	**Area Code/s**	804
Latitude	37-55-36 N		

— Average Temperatures and Precipitation —

TEMPERATURES

	Jan	Feb	Mar	Apr	May	Jun	Jul	Aug	Sep	Oct	Nov	Dec
High	46	49	60	70	78	85	88	87	81	71	61	50
Low	26	28	36	45	54	63	68	66	59	47	38	30

PRECIPITATION

	Jan	Feb	Mar	Apr	May	Jun	Jul	Aug	Sep	Oct	Nov	Dec
Inches	3.2	3.2	3.6	3.0	3.8	3.6	5.0	4.4	3.3	3.5	3.2	3.3

— Important Phone Numbers —

	Phone		*Phone*
AAA	804-285-8912	**Poison Control Center**	804-828-9123
American Express Travel	804-740-2030	**Time/Temp**	804-844-3711
Emergency	911	**Travelers Aid**	804-643-0279
Medical Referral	804-643-6631	**Weather**	804-348-9382

— Information Sources —

				Phone	*Fax*
Better Business Bureau Serving Central Virginia 701 E Franklin St Suite 712 *Web:* www.richmond.bbb.org ■ *E-mail:* bbbcenva@richmond.infi.net	Richmond	VA	23219	804-648-0016	648-3115
Central Virginia Chamber of Commerce 2318 Goodes Bridge Rd	Richmond	VA	23224	804-745-6000	745-6695
Greater Richmond Chamber of Commerce PO Box 12280 *Web:* www.grcc.com ■ *E-mail:* chamber@grcc.com	Richmond	VA	23241	804-648-1234	780-0344
Metropolitan Richmond Convention & Visitors Bureau 550 E Marshall St *TF:* 800-370-9004	Richmond	VA	23219	804-782-2777	780-2577
Richmond Center 400 E Marshall St	Richmond	VA	23219	804-783-7300	225-0508
Richmond City Hall 900 E Broad St *Web:* www.ci.richmond.va.us	Richmond	VA	23219	804-780-7000	
Richmond Economic Development Office 900 E Broad St Rm 305 *Web:* www.ci.richmond.va.us/econdev	Richmond	VA	23219	804-780-5633	780-6793
Richmond (Independent City) 900 E Broad St Rm 201	Richmond	VA	23219	804-780-7970	780-7987
Richmond Mayor 900 E Broad St Suite 201	Richmond	VA	23219	804-780-7977	698-3027
Richmond Public Library 101 E Franklin St	Richmond	VA	23219	804-780-4256	780-8685

On-Line Resources

4Richmond.com	www.4richmond.com
About.com Guide to Richmond	richmond.about.com/local/southeastus/richmond
Anthill City Guide Richmond	www.anthill.com/city.asp?city=richmondva
Area Guide Richmond	richmond.areaguides.net
City Knowledge Richmond	www.cityknowledge.com/va_richmond.htm
CitySearch Richmond	richmond.citysearch.com
DigitalCity Richmond	home.digitalcity.com/richmond
Essential Guide to Richmond	www.ego.net/us/va/ric
Excite.com Richmond City Guide	www.excite.com/travel/countries/united_states/virginia/richmond
Guest Guide Online	www.guestguideonline.com
Guide to Historic Richmond	freenet.vcu.edu/tourism/histrich/histrich.html
InRichmond.com	www.inrichmond.com
Insiders' Guide to Richmond	www.insiders.com/richmond-va/
Metro-Web Richmond	www.metro-web.com
Richmond Online	www.richmond-online.com/directory/
Style Weekly Online	www.styleweekly.com
Virtual Richmond	virtual-richmond.com/

— Transportation Services —

AIRPORTS

■ **Richmond International Airport (RIC)**	*Phone*
5 miles E of downtown (approx 15 minutes) Web: www.flyrichmond.com	804-226-3052

Airport Transportation

	Phone
Airport Limousine Service $13.50 fare to downtown	804-222-7222
Taxi $16-18 fare to downtown	804-222-7300

Richmond (Cont'd)

Commercial Airlines

	Phone		Phone
American	800-433-7300	**TWA**	800-221-2000
American Eagle	800-433-7300	**United**	800-241-6522
Continental Express	800-525-0280	**United Express**	800-241-6522
Delta	800-221-1212	**US Airways**	800-428-4322
Northwest	800-225-2525	**US Airways Express**	800-428-4322

Charter Airlines

	Phone		Phone
Aero Industries Inc	804-222-7211	**Martinair Inc**	804-222-7401
Berry Aviation	800-229-2379		

CAR RENTALS

	Phone		Phone
Alamo	800-462-5266	**Enterprise**	804-222-2700
Avis	804-222-2562	**Hertz**	804-222-7228
Budget	804-222-5310	**Thrifty**	804-222-7022
CarTemps USA	804-560-3747		

LIMO/TAXI

	Phone		Phone
Carey Limousine	757-220-5466	**Veterans Cab**	804-329-3333
Formal Transportation	804-273-0800	**Yellow Cab**	804-222-7300
Town & Country Taxi	804-271-2211		

MASS TRANSIT

	Phone
Greater Richmond Transit $1.25 Base fare	804-358-4782

RAIL/BUS

				Phone
Amtrak Station 7519 Staples Mill Rd *TF:* 800-872-7245	Richmond	VA	23228	804-553-2903
Greyhound/Trailways Bus Station 2910 North Blvd *TF:* 800-231-2222	Richmond	VA	23230	804-254-5910

— Accommodations —

HOTELS, MOTELS, RESORTS

				Phone	Fax
AmeriSuites 4100 Cox Rd *TF:* 800-833-1516	Glen Allen	VA	23060	804-747-9644	346-9320
AmeriSuites 201 Arboretum Pl *TF:* 800-833-1516	Richmond	VA	23236	804-560-1566	560-1703
Berkeley Hotel 1200 E Cary St	Richmond	VA	23219	804-780-1300	343-1885
Best Western Governor's Inn 9826 Midlothian Tpke	Richmond	VA	23235	804-323-0007	272-0759
Best Western Hanover House 10296 Sliding Hill Rd	Ashland	VA	23005	804-550-2805	550-3843
Brandermill Inn 13550 Harbour Pointe Pkwy *TF:* 800-554-0130 ■ *Web:* www.brandermillinn.com	Midlothian	VA	23112	804-739-8871	739-8463
Comfort Inn Corporate Gateway 8710 Midlothian Tpke	Richmond	VA	23235	804-320-8900	320-0403
Comfort Inn Executive Center 7201 W Broad St *TF:* 800-221-2222	Richmond	VA	23294	804-672-1108	755-1625
Comfort Inn Midtown Conference Center 3200 W Broad St *TF:* 800-866-0553	Richmond	VA	23230	804-359-4061	359-3189
Commonwealth Park Suites Hotel 901 Bank St *TF:* 888-343-7301	Richmond	VA	23219	804-343-7300	343-1025
Courtyard by Marriott Richmond West 6400 W Broad St *TF:* 800-228-2100 ■ *Web:* courtyard.com/RICWE	Richmond	VA	23229	804-282-1881	288-2934
Crowne Plaza 555 E Canal St *TF:* 800-227-6963	Richmond	VA	23219	804-788-0900	788-0791
Days Inn 2100 Dickens Rd *TF:* 800-329-7466	Richmond	VA	23230	804-282-3300	288-2145
Days Inn 6346 Midlothian Tpke *TF:* 800-329-7466	Richmond	VA	23225	804-276-6450	674-4243
Days Inn 1600 Robin Hood Rd *TF:* 800-325-2525	Richmond	VA	23220	804-353-1287	355-2659
Days Inn Airport 5500 Williamsburg Rd *TF:* 800-329-7466	Sandston	VA	23150	804-222-2041	226-1311
Days Inn Chesterfield 1301 Huguenot Rd *TF:* 800-329-7466	Midlothian	VA	23113	804-794-4999	794-1028
Diamond Lodge & Suites 1501 Robin Hood Rd. *TF:* 888-666-9191	Richmond	VA	23220	804-353-0116	355-6555
Econo Lodge Airport 5408 Williamsburg Rd *TF:* 800-553-2666	Sandston	VA	23150	804-222-1020	222-1020
Embassy Suites Commerce Center 2925 Emerywood Pkwy *TF:* 800-362-2779	Richmond	VA	23294	804-672-8585	672-3749
Executive Inn 5215 W Broad St	Richmond	VA	23230	804-288-4011	288-2163
Extended StayAmerica 6811 Paragon Pl *TF:* 800-398-7829	Richmond	VA	23230	804-285-2065	285-2064
Fairfield Inn 7300 W Broad St *TF:* 800-228-2800 ■ *Web:* fairfieldinn.com/RICRW	Richmond	VA	23294	804-672-8621	755-7155
Hampton Inn Airport 5300 Airport Square Ln *TF:* 800-426-7866	Sandston	VA	23150	804-222-8200	222-4915
Hampton Inn Richmond West 10800 W Broad St *TF:* 800-426-7866	Glen Allen	VA	23060	804-747-7777	747-7069
Hilton Airport 5501 Eubank Rd *TF:* 800-445-8667 ■ *Web:* www.hilton.com/hotels/RICAHHF	Sandston	VA	23150	804-226-6400	226-1269
Holiday Inn Airport 5203 Williamsburg Rd *TF:* 800-465-4329	Sandston	VA	23150	804-222-6450	226-4305
Holiday Inn Central 3207 North Blvd *TF:* 800-465-4329	Richmond	VA	23230	804-359-9441	359-3207
Holiday Inn Crossroads 2000 Staples Mill Rd *TF:* 800-465-4329	Richmond	VA	23230	804-359-6061	359-3177
Holiday Inn Executive Conference Center 1021 Koger Center Blvd *TF:* 800-465-4329	Richmond	VA	23235	804-379-3800	379-2763
Holiday Inn Southeast 4303 Commerce Rd *TF:* 800-465-4329	Richmond	VA	23234	804-275-7891	275-2901
Hyatt Richmond 6624 W Broad St *TF:* 800-233-1234 ■ *Web:* www.hyatt.com/usa/richmond/hotels/hotel_ricrm.html	Richmond	VA	23230	804-285-1234	288-3961
Inn at Richmond 7007 W Broad St *TF:* 800-428-2586	Richmond	VA	23294	804-672-7007	672-3251
Jefferson Hotel Franklin & Adams Sts *TF:* 800-424-8014 ■ *Web:* www.jefferson-hotel.com/	Richmond	VA	23220	804-788-8000	225-0334
La Quinta Motor Inn 6910 Midlothian Tpke *TF:* 800-531-5900	Richmond	VA	23225	804-745-7100	276-6660
Legacy Inn Airport 5252 Airport Square Ln	Sandston	VA	23150	804-226-4519	222-0641
Linden Row Inn 100 E Franklin St. *TF:* 800-348-7424	Richmond	VA	23219	804-783-7000	648-7504
Marriott Hotel 500 E Broad St *TF:* 800-228-9290 ■ *Web:* marriotthotels.com/RICDT	Richmond	VA	23219	804-643-3400	788-1230
Motel 6 5704 Williamsburg Rd *TF:* 800-466-8356	Sandston	VA	23150	804-222-7600	222-4153
Mr Patrick Henry's Inn 2300-02 E Broad St. *TF:* 800-932-2654	Richmond	VA	23223	804-644-1322	
Omni Richmond Hotel 100 S 12th St *TF:* 800-843-6664	Richmond	VA	23219	804-344-7000	648-6704
Quality Inn 8008 W Broad St *TF:* 800-228-5151	Richmond	VA	23229	804-346-0000	346-4547
Radisson Historic Hotel 301 W Franklin St *TF:* 800-333-3333	Richmond	VA	23220	804-644-9871	344-4380
Ramada Inn South 2126 Willis Rd *TF:* 800-272-6232	Richmond	VA	23237	804-271-1281	271-3315
Ramada Inn West 1500 E Ridge Rd *TF:* 800-272-6232	Richmond	VA	23229	804-285-9061	288-0104
Ramada Limited 5221 Brook Rd. *TF:* 800-637-3297	Richmond	VA	23227	804-266-7603	261-1829
Red Roof Inn 4350 Commerce Rd. *TF:* 800-843-7663	Richmond	VA	23234	804-271-7240	271-7245
Residence Inn by Marriott 2121 Dickens Rd *TF:* 800-331-3131 ■ *Web:* www.residenceinn.com/RICWW	Richmond	VA	23230	804-285-8200	285-2530
Richmond Hotel & Conference Center 6531 W Broad St *TF:* 800-987-8170	Richmond	VA	23230	804-285-9951	282-5642
Sheraton Park South 9901 Midlothian Tpke *TF:* 800-525-9538	Richmond	VA	23235	804-323-1144	320-5255
Sleep Inn 2321 Willis Rd *TF:* 800-753-3746	Richmond	VA	23237	804-275-8800	275-0949
Wyndham Gardens Hotel Richmond Airport 4700 S Laburnum Ave *TF:* 800-996-3426	Richmond	VA	23231	804-226-4300	226-6516

Richmond (Cont'd)

— Restaurants —

Name	City	State	Zip	Phone
Allies American Grill (American) 500 E Broad St	Richmond	VA	23219	804-643-3400
Amici (Italian) 3343 W Cary St	Richmond	VA	23221	804-353-4700
Azzurro (Italian) 6221 River Rd	Richmond	VA	23229	804-282-1509
Buckhead's (Steak/Seafood) 8510 Patterson Ave	Richmond	VA	23229	804-750-2000
Chopstix (Vietnamese) 3129 W Cary St	Richmond	VA	23221	804-358-7027
Crab Louie's Seafood Tavern (Seafood) Sycamore Square Shopping Village	Midlothian	VA	23113	804-275-2722
Dena's (Greek/Italian) 11314 Midlothian Tpk	Richmond	VA	23235	804-794-9551
Dining Room at the Berkeley (American) 1200 E Cary St	Richmond	VA	23219	804-780-1300
du Jour (International) 5806 Grove Ave	Richmond	VA	23226	804-285-1301
Franco's Ristorante (Italian) 9031 W Broad St	Richmond	VA	23294	804-270-9124
Frog & the Redneck (American) 1423 E Cary St *Web:* www.frogandredneck.com/	Richmond	VA	23219	804-648-3764
Full Kee (Chinese) 6400 Horespen Rd	Richmond	VA	23226	804-673-2233
Grafiti Grille (Continental) 403B Ridge Rd	Richmond	VA	23229	804-288-0633
Greek Islands (Greek) 10902 Hull St Rd	Midlothian	VA	23112	804-674-9199
Half Way House (Continental) 10301 Jefferson Davis Hwy	Richmond	VA	23237	804-275-1760
Hana Zushi (Japanese) 1309 E Cary St	Richmond	VA	23219	804-225-8801
Hard Shell The (Seafood) 1411 E Cary St *Web:* www.thehardshell.com/	Richmond	VA	23219	804-643-2333
Havana '59 (Cuban) 16 N 17th St	Richmond	VA	23219	804-649-2822
Helen's (American) 2527 W Main St	Richmond	VA	23220	804-358-4370
India House (Indian) 2313 Westwood Ave	Richmond	VA	23230	804-355-8378
India K'Raja (Indian) 9051-5 W Broad St	Richmond	VA	23294	804-965-6345
Indochine (Vietnamese/French) 2923 W Cary St	Richmond	VA	23221	804-353-5799
Julian's (Italian) 2617 W Broad St	Richmond	VA	23220	804-359-0605
Kabuto Steak House (Japanese) 8025 W Broad St	Richmond	VA	23294	804-747-9573
L'Italia (Italian) 10610 Patterson Ave	Richmond	VA	23233	804-740-1165
La Petite France (French) 4415 W Broad St	Richmond	VA	23230	804-353-8729
La Siesta (Mexican) 9900 Midlothian Tpke	Richmond	VA	23235	804-272-7333
Lemaire (Southern) Franklin & Adams Sts	Richmond	VA	23220	804-788-8000
Mamma 'Zu (Italian) 501 S Pine St	Richmond	VA	23220	804-788-4205
Mekong (Vietnamese) 6004 W Broad St	Richmond	VA	23230	804-288-8929
Millie's Diner (American) 2603 E Main St	Richmond	VA	23223	804-643-5512
Mr Patrick Henry's Inn (Continental) 2300 E Broad St	Richmond	VA	23223	804-644-1322
Peking Restaurant (Chinese) 5710 Grove Ave	Richmond	VA	23226	804-288-8371
Saigon (Vietnamese) 903 W Grace St	Richmond	VA	23220	804-355-6633
Saito's (Japanese) 611 E Laburnum Ave	Richmond	VA	23222	804-329-9765
Sam Miller's Warehouse (Seafood) 1210 E Cary St	Richmond	VA	23219	804-643-1301
Seasons (International) 13124 Midlothian Tpk	Richmond	VA	23113	804-379-0444
Skilligalee (Seafood) 5416 Glenside Dr	Richmond	VA	23228	804-672-6200
Strawberry Street Cafe (American) 421 N Strawberry St	Richmond	VA	23220	804-353-6860
Tex-Mex Cafe (Tex Mex) 3511 Courthouse Rd	Richmond	VA	23236	804-745-6440
Thai Diner (Thai) Westland Shopping Ctr	Richmond	VA	23294	804-270-2699
Thai Room The (Thai) 103 E Cary St	Richmond	VA	23219	804-644-2328
Tobacco Co (American) 1201 E Cary St	Richmond	VA	23219	804-782-9431
Track The (Seafood) 2915 W Cary St	Richmond	VA	23221	804-359-4781
Venice Restaurant (Italian) 3556 W Cary St	Richmond	VA	23221	804-353-2725
Winnie's Caribbean Restaurant (Caribbean) 200 E Main St	Richmond	VA	23219	804-649-4974
Zeus Gallery Cafe (Continental) 201 N Belmont Ave	Richmond	VA	23221	804-359-3219

— Goods and Services —

SHOPPING

Name	City	State	Zip	Phone	Fax
6th Street Marketplace 550 E Broad St	Richmond	VA	23219	804-648-6600	788-0454
17th Street Market 17th & Cary Sts Shockoe Slip area	Richmond	VA	23219		
Antique Village 10203 Chamberlayne Rd	Mechanicsville	VA	23116	804-746-8914	
Carytown Cary & Boulevard Sts	Richmond	VA	23220		
Chesterfield Towne Center 11500 Midlothian Tpke **Fax:* Cust Svc	Richmond	VA	23235	804-794-4660	379-7661*
Cloverleaf Mall 7201 Midlothian Tpke	Richmond	VA	23225	804-276-8650	276-7965
Fairfield Commons 4869 Nine Mile Rd	Richmond	VA	23223	804-222-4167	226-2510
Regency Square Mall 1420 Parham Rd	Richmond	VA	23229	804-740-7467	741-4763
Shockoe Slip E Cary St	Richmond	VA	23219		
Sycamore Square Shopping Village Midlothian Tpke	Midlothian	VA	23113	804-320-7600	330-8924

BANKS

Name	City	State	Zip	Phone	Fax
Crestar Bank PO Box 26665 *Web:* www.crestar.com ■ *E-mail:* netbanker@crestar.com	Richmond	VA	23261	804-782-5000	782-5566
F & M Bank 9401 W Broad St	Richmond	VA	23294	804-346-8080	346-8723
F & M Bank of Richmond 5756 Hopkins Rd	Richmond	VA	23234	804-271-5000	271-4367
First Union Bank 800 E Main St *TF:* 800-275-3862	Richmond	VA	23219	804-771-7008	698-5472
First Union National Bank 901 E Cary St	Richmond	VA	23219	804-788-9600	788-9673
First Virginia Bank Colonial 700 E Main St *TF:* 800-382-4115	Richmond	VA	23219	804-697-5200	697-5261
NationsBank 111 E Main St	Richmond	VA	23219	804-788-2251	788-3688
Wachovia Bank NA 1021 E Cary St	Richmond	VA	23219	804-697-6710	697-6717

BUSINESS SERVICES

Name	Phone
Airborne Express	800-247-2676
Corporate Express Delivery Systems	804-798-2518
Express Mail	804-775-6148
Federal Express	800-238-5355
Judith Fox Temporaries	804-285-8686
Kelly Services	804-648-6526
Kinko's	804-355-0061
Manpower Temporary Services	804-780-1800
Olsten Staffing Services	804-226-3550
Photo Transit	804-321-6515
Post Office	804-775-6231
UPS	800-742-5877

— Media —

PUBLICATIONS

Name	City	State	Zip	Phone	Fax
Richmond Times-Dispatch‡ 333 E Franklin St *Web:* www.gateway-va.com/pages/tdmain.htm	Richmond	VA	23219	804-649-6000	775-8059
Virginia Business Magazine 411 E Franklin St Suite 105 *Web:* virginiabusiness.com	Richmond	VA	23219	804-649-6999	649-6311

‡Daily newspapers

TELEVISION

Name	City	State	Zip	Phone	Fax
WCVE-TV Ch 23 (PBS) 23 Sesame St *Web:* www.wcve.org/TV23-Frame1.HTM	Richmond	VA	23235	804-320-1301	320-8729
WRIC-TV Ch 8 (ABC) 301 Arboretum Pl *Web:* www.wric.com	Richmond	VA	23236	804-330-8888	330-8883
WRLH-TV Ch 35 (Fox) 1925 Westmoreland St *Web:* www.fox35.com ■ *E-mail:* fox35@fox35.com	Richmond	VA	23230	804-358-3535	358-1495
WTVR-TV Ch 6 (CBS) 3301 W Broad St *Web:* www.newschannel6.com	Richmond	VA	23230	804-254-3600	254-3697
WUPV-TV Ch 65 (UPN) 4120 E Parham Rd	Richmond	VA	23228	804-672-6565	672-6571
WWBT-TV Ch 12 (NBC) 5710 Midlothian Tpke *Web:* www.nbc12.com	Richmond	VA	23225	804-230-1212	230-2793

RADIO

Name	City	State	Zip	Phone	Fax
WCVE-FM 88.9 MHz (NPR) 23 Sesame St	Richmond	VA	23235	804-320-1301	320-8729
WLEE-AM 1320 kHz (Oldies) 812 Moorefield Pk Dr Suite 300	Richmond	VA	23236	804-330-5700	327-9616
WRCL-FM 106.5 MHz (Oldies) 812 Moorefield Park Dr Suite 300	Richmond	VA	23236	804-330-5700	330-4079
WRNL-AM 910 kHz (Sports) 200 N 22nd St *Web:* www.wrnl.com ■ *E-mail:* sports@wrnl.com	Richmond	VA	23223	804-780-3400	780-3427
WRVA-AM 1140 kHz (N/T) 200 N 22nd St *Web:* www.wrva.com	Richmond	VA	23223	804-780-3400	780-3427
WRVQ-FM 94.5 MHz (CHR) 3245 Basie Rd *Web:* www.wrvq94.com ■ *E-mail:* qmail@wrvq94.com	Richmond	VA	23228	804-576-3200	576-3222
WRXL-FM 102.1 MHz (Rock) 3245 Basie Rd *Web:* www.wrxl.com	Richmond	VA	23228	804-756-6400	756-6444
WTVR-AM 1380 kHz (Nost) 3314 Cutshaw Ave	Richmond	VA	23230	804-355-3217	355-8682
WTVR-FM 98.1 MHz (AC) 3314 Cutshaw Ave *Web:* www.lite98.com ■ *E-mail:* comments@lite98.com	Richmond	VA	23230	804-355-3217	355-8682
WXGI-AM 950 kHz (Ctry) 701 German School RD	Richmond	VA	23225	804-233-7666	233-7681

— Colleges/Universities —

Name	City	State	Zip	Phone	Fax
Bryant & Stratton Career College Richmond 8141 Hull St Rd	Richmond	VA	23235	804-745-2444	745-6884

Richmond — Colleges/Universities (Cont'd)

	City	State	Zip	Phone	Fax
J Sargeant Reynolds Community College PO Box 85622	Richmond	VA	23285	804-371-3000	371-3650
Web: www.jsr.cc.va.us					
Randolph-Macon College PO Box 5005	Ashland	VA	23005	804-798-8372	752-4707
Web: www.rmc.edu					
University of Richmond	Richmond	VA	23173	804-289-8000	287-6003
TF: 800-700-1662 ■ *Web:* www.urich.edu					
Virginia Commonwealth University 907 Floyd Ave	Richmond	VA	23284	804-828-0100	828-1899
TF Admissions: 800-841-3638 ■ *Web:* www.vcu.edu ■ *E-mail:* vcuinfo@vcu.edu					
Virginia State University 1 Haydens Dr	Petersburg	VA	23806	804-524-5000	524-5055
TF Admissions: 800-871-7611 ■ *Web:* www.vsu.edu/ ■ *E-mail:* vsuadmin@vsu.edu					
Virginia Union University 1500 N Lombardy St	Richmond	VA	23220	804-257-5600	257-5818
TF: 800-368-3227 ■ *Web:* www.vuu.edu					

— Hospitals —

	City	State	Zip	Phone	Fax
Bon Secours Saint Mary's Hospital 5801 Bremo Rd	Richmond	VA	23226	804-285-2011	673-2230*
**Fax:* Admitting					
Bon Secours Stuart Circle 413 Stuart Circle	Richmond	VA	23220	804-358-7051	354-1286
Capitol Medical Center 701 W Grace St	Richmond	VA	23220	804-775-4100	775-2557
Children's Medical Center PO Box 980646	Richmond	VA	23298	804-828-9602	828-6455
TF: 800-828-1120					
Columbia Retreat Hospital 2621 Grove Ave	Richmond	VA	23220	804-254-5100	254-5187
HCA Chippenham Medical Center 7101 Jahnke Rd	Richmond	VA	23225	804-320-3911	323-8049
HealthSouth Medical Center 7700 E Parham Rd	Richmond	VA	23294	804-747-5600	527-5840
Web: www.healthsouth-richmond.com ■ *E-mail:* hlthsth@healthsouth-richmond.com					
Henrico Doctor's Hospital 1602 Skipwith Rd	Richmond	VA	23229	804-289-4500	287-4329
Hunter Holmes McGuire Veterans Affairs Medical Center 1201 Broad Rock Blvd	Richmond	VA	23249	804-675-5000	675-5585
Johnston-Willis Hospital 1401 Johnston Willis Dr	Richmond	VA	23235	804-330-2000	330-2158
Medical College of Virginia Hospitals Virginia Commonwealth University PO Box 980510	Richmond	VA	23298	804-828-4682	828-0170
Memorial Regional Medical Center 8260 Atlee Rd	Mechanicsville	VA	23116	804-764-6000	764-6420
Richmond Community Hospital 1500 N 28th St	Richmond	VA	23223	804-225-1700	649-3311
Southside Regional Medical Center 801 S Adams St	Petersburg	VA	23803	804-862-5000	862-5566

— Attractions —

	City	State	Zip	Phone	Fax
Agecroft Hall 4305 Sulgrave Rd	Richmond	VA	23221	804-353-4241	353-2151
American Historical Foundation Museum 1142 W Grace St	Richmond	VA	23220	804-353-1812	359-4895
TF: 800-368-8080					
Anderson Gallery Virginia Commonwealth University 907 1/2 W Franklin St	Richmond	VA	23284	804-828-1522	828-8585
Annabel Lee 4400 E Main St Intermediate Terminal	Richmond	VA	23223	804-644-5700	644-5760
TF: 800-752-7093 ■ *Web:* www.annabellee.com					
Appomattox Court House National Historical Park PO Box 218	Appomattox	VA	24522	804-352-8987	352-8330
Web: www.nps.gov/apco/					
Barksdale Theatre 1601 Willow Lawn Dr Suite 301E	Richmond	VA	23230	804-282-2620	288-6470
E-mail: barksdalev@aol.com					
Beth Ahabah Museum & Archives 1109 W Franklin St	Richmond	VA	23220	804-353-2668	358-3451
Black History Museum & Cultural Center of Virginia 00 Clay St	Richmond	VA	23219	804-780-9093	780-9107
Web: members.spree.com/education/bhmv					
Capitol Square 9th & Grace Sts	Richmond	VA	23219	804-698-1788	
Carpenter Center for the Performing Arts 600 E Grace St	Richmond	VA	23219	804-225-9000	649-7402
Web: www.chp2001.com/carpentercenter/index.html					
Chesterfield Museum 10011 Iron Bridge Rd	Chesterfield	VA	23832	804-748-1026	777-9643
Church Hill Historic District E Broad & E Main Sts	Richmond	VA	23223		
City Hall Observation Deck 900 E Broad St	Richmond	VA	23219	804-780-5990	780-6629
Ethyl IMAX Dome & Planetarium 2500 W Broad St	Richmond	VA	23220	804-367-6552	367-9348
TF: 800-659-1727 ■ *Web:* www.smv.org/ethyl/index.html					
Fan The & Monument Ave Monument Ave & Blvd	Richmond	VA			
Federal Reserve Bank of Richmond 701 E Byrd St	Richmond	VA	23219	804-697-8000	697-8490*
**Fax:* Hum Res ■ *Web:* www.rich.frb.org					
Fredericksburg & Spotsylvania National Military Park 120 Chatham Ln	Fredericksburg	VA	22405	540-371-0802	371-1907
Web: www.nps.gov/frsp/					
Governor's Mansion Capitol Sq	Richmond	VA	23219	804-371-2642	
Hollywood Cemetery Albemarle & Cherry Sts	Richmond	VA	23220	804-648-8501	644-7345
Landmark Theater 6 N Laurel St	Richmond	VA	23220	804-780-4213	280-6101
Lewis Ginter Botanical Garden 1800 Lakeside Ave	Richmond	VA	23228	804-262-9887	262-9934
Marshall John House 818 E Marshall St	Richmond	VA	23219	804-648-7998	
Maymont 1700 Hampton St	Richmond	VA	23220	804-358-7166	358-9994
Web: www.maymont.org					
Meadow Farm Museum 3400 Mountain Rd General Sheppard Crump Memorial Pk	Glen Allen	VA	23060	804-501-5520	501-5284
Web: www.co.henrico.va.us/rec/kmfarm.htm ■ *E-mail:* henrec@co.henrico.va.us					
Museum of the Confederacy 1201 E Clay St	Richmond	VA	23219	804-649-1861	644-7150
Web: www.moc.org ■ *E-mail:* info@moc.org					
Old Dominion Railway Museum 102 Hull St	Richmond	VA	23224	804-233-6237	
Paramount's Kings Dominion 16000 Theme Pkwy	Doswell	VA	23047	804-876-5000	876-5864
Web: www.pkd4fun.com					
Petersburg National Battlefield 1539 Hickory Hill Rd	Petersburg	VA	23803	804-732-3531	732-0835
Web: www.nps.gov/pete/					
Pocahontas State Park 10301 State Park Rd 4m S of US 10 & VA 655	Chesterfield	VA	23838	804-796-4255	
Poe Edgar Allan Museum 1914-16 E Main St	Richmond	VA	23223	804-648-5523	648-8729
TF: 888-213-2763 ■ *Web:* www.poemuseum.org/ ■ *E-mail:* peomuseum@erols.com					
Richmond Ballet 614 N Lombardy St	Richmond	VA	23220	804-359-0906	355-4640
Richmond Children's Museum 740 Navy Hill Dr	Richmond	VA	23219	804-788-4949	643-5436
Richmond National Battlefield Park 3215 E Broad St	Richmond	VA	23223	804-226-1981	771-8522
Web: www.nps.gov/rich/					
Richmond Philharmonic 922 Park Ave VCU Performing Arts Ctr	Richmond	VA	23284	804-673-4001	673-4010
Web: www.bznet.com/philharmonic/					
Richmond Symphony 6th & Grace Sts	Richmond	VA	23220	804-788-1212	788-1541
Web: www.richmondsymphony.com					
Saint John's Church 2401 E Broad St	Richmond	VA	23223	804-648-5015	
Science Museum of Virginia 2500 W Broad St	Richmond	VA	23220	804-367-6552	367-9348
TF: 800-659-1727 ■ *Web:* www.smv.org					
Sherwood Forest Plantation 14501 John Tyler Memorial Hwy	Charles City	VA	23030	804-829-5377	829-2947
Web: www.sherwoodforest.org ■ *E-mail:* ktyler1@aol.com					
Shockoe Bottom Arts Center 2001 E Grace St	Richmond	VA	23223	804-643-7959	
Theatre IV 114 W Broad St	Richmond	VA	23220	804-344-8040	643-2671
TheatreVirginia 2800 Grove Ave	Richmond	VA	23221	804-353-6161	353-8799
TF: 877-353-6161 ■ *Web:* www.theatreva.com ■ *E-mail:* tva@erols.com					
Three Lakes Nature Center & Aquarium 400 Sausiluta Dr	Richmond	VA	23227	804-261-8230	266-6938
Tuckahoe Plantation 12601 River Rd	Richmond	VA	23233	804-784-5736	784-5736
Valentine Museum 1015 E Clay St	Richmond	VA	23219	804-649-0711	643-3510
Web: www.valentinemuseum.com/					
Virginia Aviation Museum 5701 Huntsman Rd Richmond International Airport	Sandston	VA	23250	804-236-3622	
Virginia Fire & Police Museum 200 W Marshall St	Richmond	VA	23220	804-644-1849	644-1850
E-mail: trobinso@worldnet.att.net					

Richmond — Attractions (Cont'd)

				Phone	Fax
Virginia Historical Society 428 N Boulevard *Web:* www.vahistorical.org	Richmond	VA	23220	804-358-4901	355-2399
Virginia House 4301 Sulgrave Rd	Richmond	VA	23221	804-353-4251	354-8247
Virginia Museum of Fine Arts 2800 Grove Ave *Web:* www.vmfa.state.va.us	Richmond	VA	23221	804-367-0844	367-9393
Virginia Opera 600 E Grace St Carpenter Center for the Performing Arts	Richmond	VA	23219	804-644-8168	644-0415
Virginia State Capitol 9th & Grace Sts	Richmond	VA	23219	804-698-1788	
Walker Maggie L National Historic Site 600 N 2nd St *Web:* www.nps.gov/malw/	Richmond	VA	23219	804-771-2017	771-2226
Wilton House Museum 215 S Wilton Rd	Richmond	VA	23226	804-282-5936	288-9805

SPORTS TEAMS & FACILITIES

				Phone	Fax
Richmond Braves (baseball) 3001 North Blvd The Diamond *Web:* www.rbraves.com ■ *E-mail:* rbraves@i2020.net	Richmond	VA	23230	804-359-4444	359-0731
Richmond Coliseum 601 E Leigh St *Web:* www.richmondcoliseum.org	Richmond	VA	23219	804-780-4970	780-4606
Richmond International Raceway 602 E Laburnum Ave *Web:* www.rir.com	Richmond	VA	23222	804-345-7223	321-3833
Richmond Kickers (soccer) McCloy & Douglas Dale Sts University of Richmond Stadium *Web:* www.richmondkickers.com/ ■ *E-mail:* rkickrs@aol.com	Richmond	VA	23220	804-644-5425	359-5037
Richmond Renegades (hockey) 601 E Leigh St Richmond Coliseum *Web:* www.renegades.com/	Richmond	VA	23219	804-643-7865	649-0651
Southside Speedway 12800 Genito Rd *Web:* www.southsidespeedway.com ■ *E-mail:* racing@southsidespeedway.com	Midlothian	VA	23113	804-763-3567	

— Events —

	Phone
2nd Street Festival (early October)	804-643-2826
Agribusiness Food Festival (early August)	804-228-3200
Arts in the Park (early May)	804-353-8198
Azalea Festival Parade (mid-April)	804-233-2093
Camptown Races (early May)	804-752-6678
Capital City Kwanzaa Festival (late December)	804-782-2777
Crestar Richmond Marathon (mid-November)	804-285-9495
Dogwood Dell Festival of the Arts (mid-June-mid-August)	804-780-6091
Easter on Parade (late April)	804-643-2826
Festival 1893 (mid-October)	804-358-7166
Gardenfest of Lights (early-late December)	804-782-2777
Great Southern Weapons Fair (late November)	804-228-3200
Harvest Festival at Meadow Farm (mid-October)	804-501-5523
Historic Garden Week (mid-late April)	804-644-7776
James River Parade of Lights (November)	804-748-1567
James River Wine Festival (early May)	804-359-4645
Rainbow of Arts (September)	804-748-1130
Second Street Festival (early October)	804-782-2777
State Fair of Virginia (late September-early October)	804-228-3200
Strawberry Hill Races (early-mid-April)	804-228-3200
The Big Gig (mid-July)	804-643-2826
Ykrop's Target Family Jubilee (early June)	804-782-2777

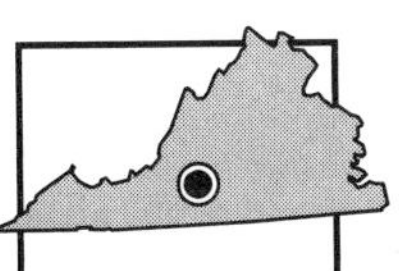

Roanoke

The railroad hub city of Roanoke is located in western Virginia. Hiking is excellent along the 28 miles of the Appalachian Trail that cut through the Roanoke Valley, and the city's portion of the Blue Ridge Parkway offers scenic views and camping areas. Roanoke's Mill Mountain features its own theatre, a zoological park atop its peak, and the World's Largest Man-Made Star, a 100-foot star erected in 1949, with an observation deck that overlooks the Roanoke Valley. Both Roanoke and nearby Salem offer many places for antiques shopping.

Population	93,749	**Longitude**	79-94-17 W
Area (Land)	42.9 sq mi	**County**	Independent City
Area (Water)	0 sq mi	**Time Zone**	EST
Elevation	948 ft	**Area Code/s**	540
Latitude	37-27-08 N		

— Average Temperatures and Precipitation —

TEMPERATURES

	Jan	Feb	Mar	Apr	May	Jun	Jul	Aug	Sep	Oct	Nov	Dec
High	44	47	58	67	76	83	86	85	79	68	58	48
Low	25	27	36	44	53	60	65	64	57	45	37	29

PRECIPITATION

	Jan	Feb	Mar	Apr	May	Jun	Jul	Aug	Sep	Oct	Nov	Dec
Inches	2.6	3.0	3.5	3.3	4.0	3.2	3.9	4.2	3.5	3.9	3.2	3.0

— Important Phone Numbers —

	Phone		Phone
AAA	540-344-0943	**Time/Temp**	540-342-9011
Emergency	911	**Travelers Aid**	540-344-1948
Poison Control Center	800-451-1428	**Weather**	540-982-2303
Road Conditions	800-367-7623		

— Information Sources —

				Phone	Fax
Better Business Bureau Serving Western Virginia 31 W Campbell Ave *Web:* www.roanoke.bbb.org	Roanoke	VA	24011	540-342-3455	345-2289
Roanoke City Hall 215 Church Ave SW *Web:* www.ci.roanoke.va	Roanoke	VA	24011	540-853-2000	853-3145
Roanoke Civic Center 710 Williamson Rd *Web:* www.roanokeciviccenter.com/ ■ *E-mail:* cityweb@ci.roanoke.va.us	Roanoke	VA	24016	540-981-1201	853-6583
Roanoke (Independent City) 215 Church Ave SW *Web:* www.ci.roanoke.va.us ■ *E-mail:* cityweb@ci.roanoke.va.us	Roanoke	VA	24011	540-853-2542	853-1145
Roanoke Mayor 215 Church Ave SW	Roanoke	VA	24011	540-853-2444	853-1145
Roanoke Public Library System 706 S Jefferson St *Web:* www.ci.roanoke.va.us/depts/library ■ *E-mail:* library@ci.roanoke.va.us	Roanoke	VA	24016	540-853-2475	853-1781
Roanoke Valley Convention & Visitors Bureau 114 Market St *TF:* 800-635-5535 ■ *Web:* www.visitroanokeva.com/ ■ *E-mail:* info@visitroanokeva.com	Roanoke	VA	24011	540-342-6025	342-7119
Salem Civic Center 1001 Roanoke Blvd.	Salem	VA	24153	540-375-3004	375-4011
Salem/Roanoke County Chamber of Commerce PO Box 832 *Web:* www.roanokeva.com/travel/salem.html ■ *E-mail:* ttd@roanokeva.com	Salem	VA	24153	540-387-0267	387-4110

On-Line Resources

Area Guide Roanoke	roanoke.areaguides.net
City Knowledge Roanoke	www.cityknowledge.com/va_roanoke.htm
DigitalCity Roanoke	www.digitalcity.com/roanoke
Excite.com Roanoke City Guide	www.excite.com/travel/countries/united_states/virginia/roanoke/

— Transportation Services —

AIRPORTS

■ Roanoke Regional Airport (ROA)

	Phone
4 miles NW of downtown (approx 15 minutes) Web: www.roanokeairport.com	540-362-1999

Roanoke (Cont'd)

Airport Transportation

	Phone
Liberty Cab $8-10 fare to downtown	540-344-1776
Roanoke Airport Limo $12 fare to downtown	540-345-7710

Commercial Airlines

	Phone		Phone
Delta Connection	800-221-1212	**US Airways**	800-428-4322
Northwest	800-225-2525	**US Airways Express**	800-428-4322
United Express	800-241-6522		

Charter Airlines

	Phone		Phone
Executive Air	540-362-9728	**Piedmont Aviation**	540-563-4401
Greenbrier Valley Aviation	800-624-6075	**Saker Flying Service**	540-362-5331
Hillman Aviation	540-366-5033		

CAR RENTALS

	Phone		Phone
Avis	540-366-2436	**Four Star**	540-562-2126
Budget	540-362-1654	**Hertz**	540-366-3421
Dollar	540-563-8055	**National**	800-227-7368
Enterprise	800-325-8007		

LIMO/TAXI

	Phone		Phone
Cartier Limousine	540-982-5466	**Salem Taxi**	540-389-8131
Liberty Cab	540-344-1776	**Yellow Cab**	540-345-7711
Prestige Limousine	540-342-8049		

MASS TRANSIT

	Phone
Valley Metro $1.25 Base fare	540-982-2222

RAIL/BUS

				Phone
Greyhound Bus Station 26 Salem Ave SW *TF:* 800-231-2222	Roanoke	VA	24011	540-343-7885

— Accommodations —

HOTELS, MOTELS, RESORTS

				Phone	Fax
AmeriSuites 5040 Valley View Blvd *TF:* 800-833-1516	Roanoke	VA	24012	540-366-4700	366-1157
Best Western Coachman Inn 235 Roanoke Rd *TF:* 800-628-1958	Daleville	VA	24083	540-992-1234	992-2227
Best Western Inn Valley View 5050 Valley View Dr *TF:* 800-362-2410	Roanoke	VA	24012	540-362-2400	362-2400
Clarion Hotel 2727 Ferndale Dr. *TF:* 800-252-7466	Roanoke	VA	24017	540-362-4500	362-4506
Colony House 3560 Franklin Rd SW	Roanoke	VA	24014	540-345-0411	345-0411
Country Inn & Suites 7860 Plantation Rd. *TF:* 800-456-4000	Roanoke	VA	24019	540-366-5678	366-8214
Days Inn Airport 8118 Plantation Rd *TF:* 800-329-7466	Roanoke	VA	24019	540-366-0341	366-3935
Days Inn Civic Center 535 Orange Ave *TF:* 800-329-7466	Roanoke	VA	24016	540-342-4551	343-3547
Econo Lodge Downtown 308 Orange Ave NW *TF:* 800-553-2666	Roanoke	VA	24016	540-343-2413	343-2413
Extended StayAmerica 2775 Ferndale Dr NW *TF:* 800-398-7829	Roanoke	VA	24017	540-366-3216	366-3207
Hampton Inn Airport 6621 Thirlane Rd NW *TF:* 800-426-7866	Roanoke	VA	24019	540-265-2600	366-2091
Hampton Inn Tanglewood 3816 Franklin Rd SW *TF:* 800-426-7866	Roanoke	VA	24014	540-989-4000	989-0250
Holiday Inn Airport 6626 Thirlane Rd NW *TF:* 800-465-4329	Roanoke	VA	24019	540-366-8861	366-1637
Holiday Inn Express 815 Gainsboro Rd	Roanoke	VA	24016	540-982-0100	345-4551
Holiday Inn Hotel Tanglewood 4468 Starkey Rd SW *TF:* 800-465-4329 ■ *Web:* www.basshotels.com/holiday-inn/?_franchisee=ROATW ■ *E-mail:* hitang1@aol.com	Roanoke	VA	24014	540-774-4400	774-1195
Hotel Roanoke & Conference Center 110 Shenandoah Ave *TF:* 800-222-8733	Roanoke	VA	24016	540-985-5900	853-8290
Howard Johnson Airport 3695 Thirlane Rd NW *TF:* 800-446-4656	Roanoke	VA	24019	540-563-0229	362-9202
Howard Johnson Express 320 Kimball Ave NE *TF:* 800-446-4656	Roanoke	VA	24016	540-344-0981	344-4680
Jefferson Lodge 616 S Jefferson St *TF:* 800-950-2580	Roanoke	VA	24011	540-342-2951	342-2951
Knight's Inn 7120 Williamson Rd	Roanoke	VA	24019	540-366-7681	366-6025
Marriott Hotel Airport 2801 Hershberger Rd NW *TF:* 800-228-9290	Roanoke	VA	24017	540-563-9300	366-5846
Patrick Henry Hotel 617 S Jefferson St *TF:* 800-303-0988 ■ *Web:* www.patrickhenryroanoke.com	Roanoke	VA	24011	540-345-8811	342-9908
Quality Inn Civic Center 501 Orange Ave *TF:* 800-228-5151	Roanoke	VA	24016	540-342-8961	342-3813
Ramada Inn 1927 Franklin Rd *TF:* 800-272-6232	Roanoke	VA	24014	540-343-0121	342-2048
Ramada Limited 6520 Thirlane Rd	Roanoke	VA	24019	540-563-2871	362-5653
Rodeway Inn 526 Orange Ave NE *TF:* 800-424-4777	Roanoke	VA	24016	540-981-9341	345-8477
Showtimers Theater 2067 McVitty Rd	Roanoke	VA	24018	540-774-2660	
Sleep Inn Tanglewood 4045 Electric Rd *TF:* 800-628-1929	Roanoke	VA	24014	540-772-1500	
Super 8 Motel 6616 Thirlane Rd NW *TF:* 800-800-8000	Roanoke	VA	24019	540-563-8888	563-8888

— Restaurants —

				Phone
309 First Street (American) 309 Market St	Roanoke	VA	24011	540-343-0179
Alexander's (American) 105 S Jefferson St	Roanoke	VA	24011	540-982-6983
Arzu (Italian/French) 213 Williamson Rd	Roanoke	VA	24011	540-982-7160
Awful Arthur's (Seafood) 108 Campbell Ave SE *Web:* www.awfularthurs.com	Roanoke	VA	24011	540-344-2997
Billy's Ritz (American) 102 Salem Ave	Roanoke	VA	24011	540-342-3937
Buck Mountain Grille (New American) 220 S Franklin Rd	Roanoke	VA	24014	540-776-1830
Carlos Brazilian International Cuisine (Brazilian) 312 Market St SE	Roanoke	VA	24011	540-345-7661
Charcoal Steak House (Steak) 5225 Williamson Rd	Roanoke	VA	24019	540-366-3710
Confeddy's Restaurant & Bar (American) 24 E Campbell Ave	Roanoke	VA	24011	540-343-9746
Corned Beef & Company (American) 107 Jefferson St	Roanoke	VA	24011	540-342-3354
Eden's Way (Vegetarian) 104 Church Ave	Roanoke	VA	24011	540-344-3336
El Rodeo (Mexican) 4301 Brambleton Ave SW	Roanoke	VA	24015	540-772-2927
Hunter's Grille (American) 617 Jefferson St	Roanoke	VA	24011	540-342-7552
Kim's Seafood (Seafood) 32 Market Sq	Roanoke	VA	24011	540-343-0516
Landing The (Continental) 773 Ashmead Rd	Moneta	VA	24121	540-721-3028
Legends (International) 305 1st St.	Roanoke	VA	24011	540-342-4887
Library The (French) 3117 Franklin Rd SW	Roanoke	VA	24014	540-985-0811
Luigi's (Italian) 3301 Brambleton Ave SW	Roanoke	VA	24015	540-989-6277
Mac & Maggie's (Barbecue) Tanglewood Mall	Roanoke	VA	24014	540-774-7427
Macado's (American) 120 Church Ave	Roanoke	VA	24011	540-342-7231
Montano's (Italian/Latin) 3733 Franklin Rd SW *Web:* www.montanos.com	Roanoke	VA	24015	540-344-8960
Mount Olive Bar & Grill (Middle Eastern) 303 S Jefferson St	Roanoke	VA	24011	540-344-5509
Nawab Indian Cuisine (Indian) 118A Campbell Ave	Roanoke	VA	24011	540-345-5150
Pargo's (American) 4330 Franklin Rd SW	Roanoke	VA	24014	540-989-3189
Pine Room (American) 110 Shenanhoah Ave.	Roanoke	VA	24016	540-985-5900
Ragazzi's (Italian) 3843 Electric Rd	Roanoke	VA	24018	540-989-9022
Red Coyote Mexican Grill (Mexican) 32 Market Sq	Roanoke	VA	24011	540-345-2180
Regency Room (American) 110 Shenandoah Ave.	Roanoke	VA	24016	540-985-5900
Roanoker The (Homestyle) 2522 Colonial Ave	Roanoke	VA	24015	540-344-7746
Saigon (Vietnamese/Thai) 32 Market Sq.	Roanoke	VA	24011	540-345-5593
Sunnybrook Inn Restaurant (American) 7342 Plantation Rd	Hollins	VA	24019	540-366-4555
Szechuan (Chinese) 5207 Bernard Dr	Roanoke	VA	24018	540-989-7947
Texas Tavern (American) 114 Church Ave	Roanoke	VA	24011	540-342-4825
Three Li'l Pigs Barbeque (Barbecue) 32 Market Sq	Roanoke	VA	24011	540-345-7447
Ye Olde English Inn (Steak) 6063 Bent Mountain Rd	Roanoke	VA	24018	540-774-2670
Zorba (Greek) 32 Market Sq	Roanoke	VA	24011	540-342-4107

Roanoke (Cont'd)

— Goods and Services —

SHOPPING

				Phone	Fax
Crossroads Mall 5002 Airport Rd	Roanoke	VA	24012	540-366-4270	366-5791
Historic Farmers Market 310 1st St	Roanoke	VA	24011	540-342-2028	
Roanoke Antique Mall 2302 Orange Ave NE	Roanoke	VA	24012	540-344-0264	345-7211
Tanglewood Mall 4420 Electric Rd	Roanoke	VA	24014	540-989-4388	
Towers Shopping Center Brandon & Colonial Aves	Roanoke	VA	24015	540-982-6791	
Valley View Mall 4802 Valley View Blvd	Roanoke	VA	24012	540-563-4400	366-8742

TF: 800-321-1711 ■ *Web:* www.valleyviewmall.com ■ *E-mail:* email@valleyviewmall.com

BANKS

				Phone	Fax
Bank of America 302 S Jefferson St	Roanoke	VA	24011	540-265-3110	265-3158
First Citizens Bank 110 Church Ave	Roanoke	VA	24011	540-985-3334	985-3221
First Union National Bank 201 S Jefferson St	Roanoke	VA	24011	540-563-7000	561-5955*
First Virginia Bank Southwest 601 S Jefferson St	Roanoke	VA	24011	540-561-8746	561-8688

*Fax: Hum Res (First Union National Bank)

BUSINESS SERVICES

	Phone		Phone
Airborne Express	800-247-2676	**Kinko's**	540-344-5000
BAX Global	800-225-5229	**Mail Boxes Etc**	540-772-7300
DHL Worldwide Express	800-225-5345	**Olsten Staffing Services**	540-774-2101
Federal Express	800-238-5355	**Post Office**	540-985-8713
Kelly Services	540-774-8300	**UPS**	800-742-5877

— Media —

PUBLICATIONS

				Phone	Fax
Blue Ridge Business Journal 821 Franklin Rd SW	Roanoke	VA	24016	540-985-0143	343-7845
Roanoke Times‡ PO Box 2491	Roanoke	VA	24010	540-981-3100	981-3346
Roanoker Magazine 3424 Brambleton Ave SW	Roanoke	VA	24018	540-989-6138	989-7603

Blue Ridge Business Journal — *TF:* 800-283-0274 ■ *Web:* bizjournal.com ■ *E-mail:* brbj@rev.net

Roanoke Times — *TF:* 800-346-1234 ■ *Web:* www.roanoke.com ■ *E-mail:* roatimes@infi.net

Roanoker Magazine — *Web:* www.theroanoker.com ■ *E-mail:* comments@theroanoker.com

‡Daily newspapers

TELEVISION

				Phone	Fax
WBRA-TV Ch 15 (PBS) 1215 McNeil Dr *Web:* www.wbra.org	Roanoke	VA	24015	540-344-0991	344-2148
WDBJ-TV Ch 7 (CBS) 2001 Colonial Ave *Web:* www.wdbj7.com ■ *E-mail:* news@wdbj7.com	Roanoke	VA	24015	540-344-7000	344-5097
WFXR-TV Ch 27 (Fox) 2618 Colonial Ave SW *Web:* www.fox2127.com	Roanoke	VA	24015	540-344-2127	345-1912
WPXR-TV Ch 38 (PAX) 210 1st St SW Suite 110 *Web:* www.pax.net/WPXR	Roanoke	VA	24011	540-857-0038	345-8568
WSET-TV Ch 13 (ABC) 2320 Langhorne Rd *Web:* www.wset.com ■ *E-mail:* wset@wset.com	Lynchburg	VA	24501	540-981-1313	981-0467
WSLS-TV Ch 10 (NBC) PO Box 10 *Web:* www.newschannelten.com	Roanoke	VA	24022	540-981-9110	343-2059

RADIO

				Phone	Fax
WFIR-AM 960 kHz (N/T) 3509 Hounds Chase Ln SW *Web:* www.wfir960.com	Roanoke	VA	24014	540-345-1511	342-2270
WJLM-FM 93.5 MHz (Ctry) 3807 Brandon Ave Suite 2350	Roanoke	VA	24018	540-725-1220	725-1245
WPVR-FM 94.9 MHz (CR) 3509 Hounds Chase Ln SW *Web:* www.arrow949.com	Roanoke	VA	24014	540-345-1511	342-2270
WRIS-AM 1410 kHz (Rel) 219 Luckett St NW	Roanoke	VA	24017	540-342-1410	342-5952
WROV-FM 96.3 MHz (Rock) 3807 Brandon Ave Suite 2350 *Web:* www.96-3rov.com	Roanoke	VA	24018	540-725-1220	725-1245
WSLC-AM 610 kHz (Ctry) 1002 Newman Dr	Salem	VA	24153	540-387-0234	389-0837
WSLQ-FM 99.1 MHz (AC) 1002 Newman Dr	Salem	VA	24153	540-387-0234	389-0837
WVTF-FM 89.1 MHz (NPR) 4235 Electric Rd SW Suite 105	Roanoke	VA	24014	540-989-8900	776-2727
WXLK-FM 92.3 MHz (CHR) 3934 Electric Rd SW *Web:* www.k92radio.com	Roanoke	VA	24018	540-774-9200	774-5667

— Colleges/Universities —

				Phone	Fax
Community Hospital of Roanoke Valley-College of Health Sciences PO Box 13186 *TF:* 888-985-8483 ■ *Web:* www.chs.edu	Roanoke	VA	24031	540-985-8481	985-9773
Ferrum College PO Box 1000 *TF Admissions:* 800-868-9797 ■ *Web:* www.ferrum.edu ■ *E-mail:* admissions@ferrum.edu	Ferrum	VA	24088	540-365-2121	365-4266
Hollins University 7916 Williamson Rd *TF:* 800-456-9595 ■ *Web:* www.hollins.edu	Roanoke	VA	24020	540-362-6000	362-6642
National Business College Salem PO Box 6400 *TF:* 800-664-1886	Roanoke	VA	24017	540-986-1800	986-1344
Radford University Norwood St & Rt 11 *TF Admissions:* 800-890-4265 ■ *Web:* www.runet.edu ■ *E-mail:* pwhite@runet.edu	Radford	VA	24142	540-831-5000	831-5138
Roanoke College 221 College Ln *TF Admissions:* 800-388-2276 ■ *Web:* www.roanoke.edu ■ *E-mail:* admissions@acc.Roanoke.edu	Salem	VA	24153	540-375-2500	375-2267
Virginia Tech 104 Burruss Hall *Web:* www.vt.edu ■ *E-mail:* vtadmiss@vt.edu	Blacksburg	VA	24061	540-231-6000	231-3242
Virginia Western Community College PO Box 14007 *Web:* www.vw.cc.va.us ■ *E-mail:* info@vw.cc.va.us	Roanoke	VA	24038	540-857-7231	857-7544

— Hospitals —

				Phone	Fax
Carilion Roanoke Memorial Hospital PO Box 13367 **Fax:* Admitting ■ *Web:* www.carilion.com/hospitals/crmh.html	Roanoke	VA	24033	540-981-7000	985-4954*
Community Hospital of Roanoke Valley PO Box 12946	Roanoke	VA	24029	540-985-8000	985-0475

— Attractions —

				Phone	Fax
Art Museum of Western Virginia 1 Market Sq 2nd Fl *Web:* www.artmuseumroanoke.org ■ *E-mail:* info@artmuseumroanoke.org	Roanoke	VA	24011	540-342-5760	342-5798
Arts Council of the Blue Ridge 20 E Church Ave *Web:* www.theartscouncil.org ■ *E-mail:* artscncl@aol.com	Roanoke	VA	24011	540-342-5790	342-5720
Booker T Washington National Monument 12130 Booker T Washington Hwy *Web:* www.nps.gov/bowa/	Hardy	VA	24101	540-721-2094	721-8311
Center in the Square 1 Market Sq *Web:* www.cits.org ■ *E-mail:* cits@cits.org	Roanoke	VA	24011	540-342-5700	224-1238
Chateau Morrisette Winery RR 1 Box 766 *Web:* www.chateaumorrisette.com	Meadows of Dan	VA	24120	540-593-2865	593-2868
Dixie Caverns & Pottery 5753 W Main St	Salem	VA	24153	540-380-2085	
Harrison Museum of African-American Culture 523 Harrison Ave NW	Roanoke	VA	24016	540-345-4818	
Historic Farmers Market 310 1st St	Roanoke	VA	24011	540-342-2028	
Hopkins Planetarium 1 Market Sq	Roanoke	VA	24011	540-342-5710	
Jefferson National Forest 5162 Valley Pointe Pkwy *TF:* 888-265-0019	Roanoke	VA	24019	540-265-5100	
Mill Mountain Theatre 1 Market Sq *Web:* www.millmountain.org ■ *E-mail:* mmtmail@millmountain.org	Roanoke	VA	24011	540-342-5740	342-5745
Mill Mountain Zoological Park Mill Mountain Pk. *Web:* www.mmzoo.org	Roanoke	VA	24014	540-343-3241	343-8111

Roanoke — Attractions (Cont'd)

				Phone	Fax
Opera Roanoke PO Box 1014	Roanoke	VA	24005	540-982-2742	982-3601
Roanoke Symphony & Choral Society 541 Luck Ave Suite 200	Roanoke	VA	24016	540-343-6221	343-0065
Web: rso.com ■ *E-mail:* music@rso.com					
Roanoke Valley History Museum 1 Market Sq Square Bldg 3rd Fl	Roanoke	VA	24011	540-342-5770	224-1256
E-mail: history@roanoke.infi.net					
Salem Museum 801 E Main St	Salem	VA	24153	540-389-6760	
Science Museum of Western Virginia 1 Market Sq	Roanoke	VA	24011	540-342-5710	224-1240
To the Rescue Museum 4428 Electric Rd Tanglewood Mall	Roanoke	VA	24014	540-776-0364	776-0653
Web: naemt.org/ttrescue					
Virginia Museum of Transportation 303 Norfolk Ave SW	Roanoke	VA	24016	540-342-5670	342-6898
Web: www.vmt.org/					
Virginia's Explore Park 3900 Rutrough Rd	Roanoke	VA	24014	540-427-1800	427-1880
Web: www.explorepark.com					

SPORTS TEAMS & FACILITIES

				Phone	Fax
Roanoke Civic Center 710 Williamson Rd	Roanoke	VA	24016	540-853-2241	853-2748
Web: www.roanokeciviccenter.com					
Roanoke Express (hockey) 4504 Starkey Rd Suite 208	Roanoke	VA	24014	540-989-4625	
Web: www.roanokeexpress.com/					
Roanoke Wrath (soccer) Reserve Ave Victory Stadium	Roanoke	VA	24014	540-344-8565	344-8451
Web: www.roanokewrath.com ■ *E-mail:* sholt65581@aol.com					
Salem Avalanche (baseball) Salem Memorial Stadium 10004 Texas St	Roanoke	VA	24153	540-389-3333	
E-mail: avalanch@roanoke.infi.net					

— Events —

	Phone
Commonwealth Games of Virginia (mid-July)	800-635-5535
Dickens of a Christmas (early-mid-December)	540-342-2028
Festival of Lights Parade (early December)	540-981-2889
First Night Roanoke (December 31)	540-342-2640
Greening of the Market (late November)	540-342-2028
Henry Street Heritage Festival (mid-late September)	800-635-5535
Life on Wagon Road (mid-October)	540-427-1800
Local Colors (mid-April)	800-635-5535
Native American Heritage Festival & PowWow (early October)	540-342-6025
Olde Salem Days (mid-September)	540-772-8871
Railfair & Model Mania (early May)	540-342-5670
Roanoke Christmas Parade (early December)	540-853-2889
Roanoke Festival in the Park (late May-early June)	540-342-6025
Roanoke Jazz & Blues Festival (mid-September)	540-981-2889
Saint Patrick's Day Parade (mid-March)	800-635-5535
Salem Fair & Exposition (early July)	540-342-6025
Strawberry Festival (late April-early May)	800-635-5535
Vinton Dogwood Festival (late April)	800-635-5535
Vinton Old-Time Bluegrass Festival (mid-August)	540-345-8548
Virginia Mountain Peach Festival (early August)	540-342-2028
Virginia State Championship Chili Cookoff (early May)	540-342-2028
Zoo Boo (late October)	540-343-3241

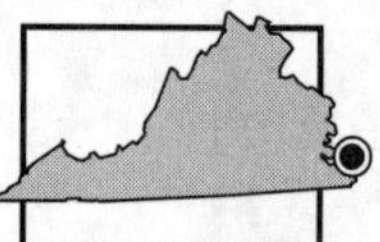

Virginia Beach

Located adjacent to Norfolk in the Hampton Roads region of southeastern Virginia, Virginia Beach is the state's most populous city. Unisys and Lillian Vernon have divisions there, and two major cable television networks, the Christian Broadcasting Network and the Family Channel, are based in Virginia Beach. The city's 26 miles of beaches along the Atlantic Ocean and Chesapeake Bay make Virginia Beach a popular resort area. In addition to the many beachfront hotels and attractions, the city is also home to Virginia's most visited state park, Seashore State Park, which offers a variety of outdoor recreational opportunities. Back Bay National Wildlife Refuge, home to sea turtles, white-tailed deer, and many species of birds, is also located in Virginia Beach.

Population	432,380	**Longitude**	75-98-12 W
Area (Land)	248.3 sq mi	**County**	Independent City
Area (Water)	58.3 sq mi	**Time Zone**	EST
Elevation	12 ft	**Area Code/s**	757
Latitude	36-85-97 N		

— Average Temperatures and Precipitation —

TEMPERATURES

	Jan	Feb	Mar	Apr	May	Jun	Jul	Aug	Sep	Oct	Nov	Dec
High	49	50	57	68	76	84	87	85	80	70	61	51
Low	32	33	39	48	57	66	70	69	64	53	43	34

PRECIPITATION

	Jan	Feb	Mar	Apr	May	Jun	Jul	Aug	Sep	Oct	Nov	Dec
Inches	3.8	3.5	3.7	3.1	3.8	3.8	5.1	4.8	3.9	3.2	2.9	3.2

— Important Phone Numbers —

	Phone		Phone
AAA	757-340-7271	**Special Events**	757-437-4800
American Express Travel	757-499-2333	**Time**	757-622-9311
Emergency	911	**Weather**	757-666-1212

— Information Sources —

				Phone	Fax
Hampton Roads Chamber of Commerce 420 Bank St	Norfolk	VA	23501	757-622-2312	622-5563
Web: www.hrccva.com ■ *E-mail:* info@hrccva.com					
Virginia Beach Central Library 4100 Virginia Beach Blvd	Virginia Beach	VA	23452	757-431-3001	431-3018
Web: www.virginia-beach.va.us/services/library ■ *E-mail:* central@city.virginia-beach.va.us					
Virginia Beach City Hall Municipal Ctr Bldg 22	Virginia Beach	VA	23456	757-427-4111	
Web: www.virginia-beach.va.us/cityhall					
Virginia Beach Convention And Visitor Bureau 2101 Parks Ave Suite 500	Virginia Beach	VA	23451	757-437-4700	437-4747
TF: 800-700-7702 ■ *Web:* www.vbfun.com					
Virginia Beach Economic Development Dept 1 Columbus Ctr Suite 300	Virginia Beach	VA	23462	757-437-6464	499-9894
TF: 800-989-4567 ■ *Web:* www.virginia-beach.va.us/dept/econdev ■ *E-mail:* ecdev@city.virginia-beach.va.us					
Virginia Beach (Independent City) 2401 Courthouse Dr Municipal Ctr Bldg 1	Virginia Beach	VA	23456	757-427-4242	427-4135
Web: www.virginia-beach.va.us					
Virginia Beach Mayor 2401 Courthouse Dr Municipal Ctr	Virginia Beach	VA	23456	757-427-4581	426-5699
Virginia Beach Pavilion Convention Center 1000 19th St	Virginia Beach	VA	23451	757-437-7600	422-8860
Web: www.vabeach.com/pavilion/ ■ *E-mail:* pavilion@vabeach.com					
Virginia Beach Visitors Information Center 2100 Parks Ave	Virginia Beach	VA	23451	757-437-4888	437-4918
TF: 800-446-8038 ■ *Web:* www.city.virginia-beach.va.us ■ *E-mail:* webvb@city.virginia.va.us					

On-Line Resources

Area Guide Virginia Beach	virginiabeach.areaguides.net
City Knowledge Virginia Beach	www.cityknowledge.com/va_virginia_beach.htm
DigitalCity Hampton Roads	hamptonroads.digitalcity.com
Essential Guide to Virginia Beach	www.ego.net/us/va/vb/index.htm
Excite.com Virginia Beach City Guide	www.excite.com/travel/countries/united_states/virginia/virginia_beach
NITC Travelbase City Guide Virginia Beach	www.travelbase.com/auto/guides/virginia_beach-area-va.html
Sunny Day Guide Virginia Beach	www.sunnydayguides.com/vb/
Surf & Sun Beach Vacation Guide to Virginia Beach	www.surf-sun.com/va-virginia-beach-main.htm

Virginia Beach — On-Line Resources (Cont'd)

Virginia Beach . . . . emporium.turnpike.net/~ntravel/vabeach/fun.htm
Virginia Beach Net . . . . www.vabeach.com/
Virginia Beach Visitor's Guide . . . . www.vgnet.com/VirginiaBeach/index_r.html

— Transportation Services —

AIRPORTS

■ Norfolk International Airport (ORF)

	Phone
18 miles W of downtown Virginia Beach (approx 30 minutes)	757-857-3351

Web: www.norfolkairport.com ■ *E-mail:* airport@infi.net

Airport Transportation

	Phone
Airport Shuttle $17.50 fare to downtown Virginia Beach	757-857-1231

Commercial Airlines

	Phone		Phone
American	800-433-7300	**Northwest**	800-225-2525
American Eagle	800-433-7300	**TWA**	800-221-2000
Continental	800-525-0280	**United**	800-241-6522
Continental Express	800-525-0280	**US Airways**	800-428-4322
Delta	800-221-1212		

Charter Airlines

	Phone		Phone
Berry Aviation	800-229-2379	**Piedmont Aviation**	757-857-3309

CAR RENTALS

	Phone		Phone
Alamo	800-327-9633	**Enterprise**	757-671-7700
Budget	757-855-1038		

LIMO/TAXI

	Phone		Phone
Beach Taxi	757-486-6585	**Green & White Checker Cabs**	757-855-6611
Black & White Cabs	757-489-7725	**Taxi**	757-460-0605
Carey VIP & Celebrity Limousines Inc	757-853-5466	**Yellow Cab**	757-460-0607

MASS TRANSIT

	Phone
Tidewater Regional Transit $1.50 Base fare	757-640-6300

RAIL/BUS

				Phone
Greyhound Bus Station 1017 Laskin Rd	Virginia Beach	VA	23451	757-422-2998

TF: 800-231-2222

— Accommodations —

HOTELS, MOTELS, RESORTS

				Phone	Fax
Alamar Resort Motel 311 16th St. *TF:* 800-346-5681	Virginia Beach	VA	23451	757-428-7582	
Barclay Towers 809 Atlantic Ave. *TF:* 800-344-4473 ■ *Web:* www.thebalsams.com	Virginia Beach	VA	23451	757-491-2700	428-3790
Belvedere Resort Motel 36th St & Atlantic Ave. *TF:* 800-425-0612	Virginia Beach	VA	23451	757-425-0612	425-1397
Best Western Inn 5718 Northampton Blvd.	Virginia Beach	VA	23455	757-363-2500	460-3770
Best Western Oceanfront 1101 Atlantic Ave *TF:* 800-631-5000	Virginia Beach	VA	23451	757-422-5000	425-2356
Breakers Resort Inn 16th St & Oceanfront *TF:* 800-237-7532	Virginia Beach	VA	23451	757-428-1821	422-9602
Cavalier Hotel 42nd St & Oceanfront *TF:* 800-446-8199	Virginia Beach	VA	23451	757-425-8555	425-0629
Clarion Hotel 4453 Bonney Rd *TF:* 800-252-7466	Virginia Beach	VA	23462	757-473-1700	552-0477
Clarion Resort & Conference Center 501 Atlantic Ave *TF:* 800-345-3186	Virginia Beach	VA	23451	757-422-3186	491-3379
Colonial Inn 2809 Atlantic Ave *TF:* 800-344-3342	Virginia Beach	VA	23451	757-428-5370	422-5902
Comfort Inn 2800 Pacific Ave *TF:* 800-441-0684	Virginia Beach	VA	23451	757-428-2203	422-6043
Comfort Inn Little Creek 5189 Shore Dr	Virginia Beach	VA	23455	757-460-5566	460-5571
Comfort Inn Oceanfront 2015 Atlantic Ave	Virginia Beach	VA	23451	757-425-8200	425-6521
Courtyard by Marriott Norfolk 5700 Greenwich Rd. *TF:* 800-321-2211 ■ *Web:* courtyard.com/ORFVB	Virginia Beach	VA	23462	757-490-2002	490-0169
Days Inn Airport 5708 Northampton Blvd. *TF:* 800-329-7466	Virginia Beach	VA	23455	757-460-2205	363-8089
Days Inn Oceanfront 3107 Atlantic Ave *TF:* 800-292-3297	Virginia Beach	VA	23451	757-428-7233	491-1936
Dolphin Inn 1705 Atlantic Ave *TF:* 800-365-3467	Virginia Beach	VA	23451	757-491-1420	425-8390
Doubletree Hotel 1900 Pavilion Dr *TF:* 800-222-8733	Virginia Beach	VA	23451	757-422-8900	425-8460
Econo Lodge 5819 Northampton Blvd *TF:* 800-421-2325	Virginia Beach	VA	23455	757-460-1000	464-3210
Econo Lodge 2109 Atlantic Ave. *TF:* 800-999-3630	Virginia Beach	VA	23451	757-428-2403	422-2530
Econo Lodge on the Ocean 2707 Atlantic Ave *TF:* 800-228-3970	Virginia Beach	VA	23451	757-428-3970	422-1851
Executive Inn 717 S Military Hwy *TF:* 800-678-3466	Virginia Beach	VA	23464	757-420-2120	523-2516
Extended StayAmerica 4548 Bonney Rd. *TF:* 800-398-7829	Virginia Beach	VA	23462	757-473-9200	473-8851
Fairfield Inn 4760 Euclid Rd. *TF:* 800-228-2800 ■ *Web:* fairfieldinn.com/ORFFI	Virginia Beach	VA	23462	757-499-1935	499-1935
Founders Inn & Conference Center 5641 Indian River Rd *TF:* 800-926-4466 ■ *Web:* www.foundersinn.com/	Virginia Beach	VA	23464	757-424-5511	366-0613
Four Sails Resort Hotel 3301 Atlantic Ave *TF:* 800-227-4213 ■ *Web:* www.foursails.com ■ *E-mail:* 4sails@foursails.com	Virginia Beach	VA	23451	757-491-8100	491-0573
Hampton Inn 5793 Greenwich Rd *TF:* 800-426-7866	Virginia Beach	VA	23462	757-490-9800	490-3573
Hilton Virginia Beach Oceanfront 8th St & Atlantic Ave. *TF:* 800-445-8667 ■ *Web:* www.hilton.com/hotels/VBVHIHF	Virginia Beach	VA	23451	757-428-8935	425-2769
Holiday Inn Executive Center Hotel 5655 Greenwich Rd. *TF:* 800-465-4329 ■ *Web:* www.basshotels.com/holiday-inn/?_franchisee=ORFGR ■ *E-mail:* hiexec@erols.com	Virginia Beach	VA	23462	757-499-4400	473-0517
Holiday Inn Oceanside 2101 Atlantic Ave *TF:* 800-882-3224 ■ *Web:* www.vabeach.com/oceanside ■ *E-mail:* oceanside@va-beach.com	Virginia Beach	VA	23451	757-491-1500	491-1945
Holiday Inn on the Ocean 3900 Atlantic Ave *TF:* 800-942-3224	Virginia Beach	VA	23451	757-428-1711	425-5742
La Quinta Inn 192 Newtown Rd *TF:* 800-687-6667	Virginia Beach	VA	23462	757-497-6620	456-9780
Ocean Key Resort 4242 Atlantic Ave *TF:* 800-955-9300	Virginia Beach	VA	23451	757-425-2200	491-7751
Ocean Sand Resort 2207 Atlantic Ave *TF:* 800-874-8661	Virginia Beach	VA	23451	757-428-5141	422-8436
Quality Inn Pavilion 716 21st St. *TF:* 800-228-5151	Virginia Beach	VA	23451	757-422-3617	428-7434
Ramada Inn Airport 5725 Northampton Blvd.	Virginia Beach	VA	23455	757-464-9351	363-8569
Ramada Plaza Resort 57th St & Ocean Front. *TF:* 800-365-3032	Virginia Beach	VA	23451	757-428-7025	428-2921
Rodeway Inn 5745 Northampton Blvd *TF:* 877-460-6700	Virginia Beach	VA	23455	757-460-3414	460-1262
Sea Gull Motel on the Beach 2613 Atlantic Ave *TF:* 800-426-4855 ■ *Web:* www.seagullmotel.com ■ *E-mail:* info@seagullmotel.com	Virginia Beach	VA	23451	757-425-5711	425-5710
Sheraton Oceanfront Hotel 36th St & Atlantic Ave. *TF:* 800-521-5635	Virginia Beach	VA	23451	757-425-9000	428-5352

Virginia Beach — Hotels, Motels, Resorts (Cont'd)

				Phone	Fax
Stargate Oceanfront Suites 1909 Atlantic Ave *TF:* 800-372-4900	Virginia Beach	VA	23451	757-425-0650	425-8898
Station One Hotel 2321 Atlantic Ave *TF:* 800-435-2424	Virginia Beach	VA	23451	757-491-2400	491-8204
Surfside Inn 13th & Atlantic Ave *TF:* 800-437-2497	Virginia Beach	VA	23451	757-428-1183	428-2243
Thunderbird Motor Lodge 35th St & Ocean Front Ave *TF:* 800-633-6669	Virginia Beach	VA	23451	757-428-3024	428-9077
Tradewinds Resort Hotel 1601 Atlantic Ave *TF:* 888-399-4637	Virginia Beach	VA	23451	757-491-8334	491-8586
Tropicana Resort Hotel 1719 Atlantic Ave *TF:* 800-451-5161	Virginia Beach	VA	23451	757-425-5511	422-3597
Virginia Beach Resort Hotel & Conference Center 2800 Shore Dr *TF:* 800-468-2722	Virginia Beach	VA	23451	757-481-9000	496-7429

— Restaurants —

				Phone
22nd Street Raw Bar & Grill (Seafood) 202 22nd St	Virginia Beach	VA	23451	757-491-2222
Abbey Road (American) 203 22nd St	Virginia Beach	VA	23451	757-425-6330
Aberdeen Barn (American) 5805 Northampton Blvd	Norfolk	VA	23508	757-464-1580
Alexander's on the Bay (Continental) 4536 Ocean View Ave	Virginia Beach	VA	23455	757-464-4999
Baja Restaurant (American) 3701 S Sandpiper Rd	Virginia Beach	VA	23456	757-426-7748
Beach Bully (Barbecue) 601 19th St.	Virginia Beach	VA	23451	757-422-4222
Bella Monte Cafe (International) 1201 Laskin Rd Suite 100	Virginia Beach	VA	23451	757-425-6290
Blue Pete's Restaurant (Seafood/Steak) 1400 Muddy Creek Rd *Web:* www.bluepetes.com	Virginia Beach	VA	23456	757-426-2005
Boulevard Cafe (Greek/Italian) 2935 Virginia Beach Blvd.	Virginia Beach	VA	23452	757-463-1311
Brewer's East Inn (American) 2484 N Landing Rd	Virginia Beach	VA	23456	757-427-5880
Captain George's Seafood (Seafood) 2272 Old Pungo Ferry Rd	Virginia Beach	VA	23457	757-721-3463
Chick's Beach Cafe (American) 4600 Lookout Rd	Virginia Beach	VA	23455	757-460-2580
Ciola's (Italian) 1889 Virginia Beach Blvd	Virginia Beach	VA	23455	757-428-9601
Coastal Grill (Seafood) 1427 N Great Neck Rd	Virginia Beach	VA	23454	757-496-3348
Coyote Cafe Cantina (Southwest) 972A Laskin Rd	Virginia Beach	VA	23451	757-425-8705
Croc's Restaurant (Caribbean) 620 Cypress Ave	Virginia Beach	VA	23451	757-428-5444
Desperado's (American) 315 17th St	Virginia Beach	VA	23451	757-425-5566
Five 01 City Grill (American) 501 N Birdneck Rd	Virginia Beach	VA	23451	757-425-7195
Foon's (Chinese) 4365 Shore Dr	Virginia Beach	VA	23455	757-460-1985
Forbidden City (Chinese) 3644 Virginia Beach Blvd	Virginia Beach	VA	23452	757-486-8823
Ginza (Japanese) 3972 Holland Rd.	Virginia Beach	VA	23462	757-431-8000
Harpoon Larry's (Seafood) 216 24th St	Virginia Beach	VA	23451	757-422-6000
Havana Restaurant (New American) 1423 N Great Neck Rd	Virginia Beach	VA	23454	757-496-3333
Henry's Seafood (Seafood) 3319 Shore Dr	Virginia Beach	VA	23451	757-481-7300
Hunt Room (Seafood/Steak) 42nd St & Oceanfront	Virginia Beach	VA	23451	757-425-8555
Il Giardino (Italian) 910 Atlantic Ave *Web:* www.ilgiardino.com	Virginia Beach	VA	23451	757-422-6464
La Caravelle (French/Vietnamese) 1040 Laskin Rd	Virginia Beach	VA	23451	757-428-2477
Le Chambord (French) 324 N Greatneck Rd	Virginia Beach	VA	23454	757-498-1234
Lighthouse The (Steak/Seafood) 1st St & Atlantic Ave	Virginia Beach	VA	23451	757-428-7974
Little Feets Cafe (American) 2613 Atlantic Ave	Virginia Beach	VA	23451	757-425-1133
Lynnhaven Fish House (Seafood) 2350 Starfish Rd	Virginia Beach	VA	23451	757-481-0003
Mary's Country Kitchen (American) 616 Virginia Beach Blvd	Virginia Beach	VA	23451	757-428-1355
Pungo Grill (Steak/Seafood) 1785 Princess Anne Rd	Virginia Beach	VA	23456	757-426-6655
Raven The (American) 1200 Atlantic Ave *Web:* www.theraven.com/	Virginia Beach	VA	23451	757-425-9556
Sage's (American) 1658 Pleasure House Rd	Virginia Beach	VA	23455	757-460-1691
San Antonio Sam's Ice House Cafe (Southwest) 604 Norfolk Ave	Virginia Beach	VA	23451	757-491-0263
Silverado (American) 501 Atlantic Ave	Virginia Beach	VA	23451	757-491-4700
Tandom's Pine Tree Inn (Continental) 2932 Virginia Beach Blvd.	Virginia Beach	VA	23452	757-340-3661
Tautog's (Seafood) 205 23rd St.	Virginia Beach	VA	23451	757-422-0081
Tokyo Inn (Japanese) 371 Independence Blvd	Virginia Beach	VA	23462	757-499-4448
Tradewinds (American) 2800 Shore Dr.	Virginia Beach	VA	23451	757-481-9000
Waterman's Grill (American) 415 Atlantic Ave.	Virginia Beach	VA	23451	757-428-3644

— Goods and Services —

SHOPPING

				Phone	Fax
La Promenade 1860 Laskin Rd	Virginia Beach	VA	23454	757-422-8839	
Lynnhaven Mall 701 S Lynnhaven Pkwy	Virginia Beach	VA	23452	757-340-9340	463-8150
Pembroke Mall Suite 201 4582 Pembroke Mall *Web:* www.pembrokemall.com ■ *E-mail:* pembmll@infi.net	Virginia Beach	VA	23462	757-497-6255	671-8546
Uptons 5254 Providence Rd	Virginia Beach	VA	23464	757-474-1315	

BANKS

				Phone	Fax
BB & T Bank 3450 Pacific Ave	Virginia Beach	VA	23451	757-437-3782	422-6089
Branch Banking & Trust 944 Independence Blvd	Virginia Beach	VA	23455	757-318-6180	318-6190
CENIT Bank 641 Lynnhaven Pkwy	Virginia Beach	VA	23452	757-486-8600	486-0897
Centura Bank 2101 Parks Ave Suite 400 **Fax:* Mktg	Virginia Beach	VA	23451	757-491-2667	491-1169*
Crestar Bank 711 First Colonial Rd *TF:* 800-273-7827	Virginia Beach	VA	23451	757-858-3309	858-3135
First Union Bank 5293 Princess Anne Rd *TF Cust Svc:* 800-275-3862*	Virginia Beach	VA	23462	757-490-9807	499-4002
First Union National Bank 4287 Holland Rd *TF Cust Svc:* 800-275-3862*	Virginia Beach	VA	23452	757-467-6365	495-9011
First Virginia Bank of Tidewater 969 Chimney Hill	Virginia Beach	VA	23452	757-628-6903	
NationsBank 745 Lynnhaven Pkwy **Fax:* Cust Svc	Virginia Beach	VA	23452	757-498-6013	498-6018*
Resource Bank 3720 Virginia Beach Blvd	Virginia Beach	VA	23452	757-463-2265	431-2441
Wachovia Bank 1612 Independence Blvd **Fax:* Cust Svc ■ *TF Cust Svc:* 800-825-8667*	Virginia Beach	VA	23455	757-363-3600	363-9829*

BUSINESS SERVICES

	Phone
Ace Courier	757-486-2016
Adecco Employment Personnel Services	757-499-0688
BAX Global	800-225-5229
DHL Worldwide Express	800-225-5345
Federal Express	800-238-5355
Kinko's	757-340-8999
Olsten Staffing Services	757-490-0904
Post Office	757-340-6227
UPS	800-742-5877

— Media —

PUBLICATIONS

				Phone	Fax
Virginian-Pilot‡ PO Box 449 *TF:* 800-446-2004 ■ *Web:* www.pilotonline.com ■ *E-mail:* pilot@infi.net	Norfolk	VA	23501	757-446-2000	446-2414

‡Daily newspapers

TELEVISION

				Phone	Fax
WAVY-TV Ch 10 (NBC) 300 Wavy St *Web:* www.wavy.com ■ *E-mail:* wavy10p@infi.net	Portsmouth	VA	23704	757-393-1010	397-8279
WHRO-TV Ch 15 (PBS) 5200 Hampton Blvd *Web:* www.whro-pbs.org ■ *E-mail:* info@whro.org	Norfolk	VA	23508	757-889-9400	489-0007
WPXV-TV Ch 49 (PAX) 230 Clearfield Ave Suite 104 *Web:* www.pax.net/WPXV	Virginia Beach	VA	23462	757-490-1249	499-1679
WTKR-TV Ch 3 (CBS) PO Box 300 *Web:* www.wtkr.com	Norfolk	VA	23501	757-446-1000	446-1376
WTVZ-TV Ch 33 (WB) 900 Granby St	Norfolk	VA	23510	757-622-3333	623-1541
WVEC-TV Ch 13 (ABC) 613 Woodis Ave *Web:* wvec.com	Norfolk	VA	23510	757-625-1313	628-5855

RADIO

				Phone	Fax
WCMS-AM 1050 kHz (Ctry) 900 Commonwealth Pl.	Virginia Beach	VA	23464	757-424-1050	424-3479
WCMS-FM 100.5 MHz (Ctry) 900 Commonwealth Pl.	Virginia Beach	VA	23464	757-424-1050	424-3479

Virginia Beach — Radio (Cont'd)

	City	State	ZIP	Phone	Fax
WFOG-FM 92.9 MHz (AC) 236 Clearfield Ave Suite 206	Virginia Beach	VA	23462	757-497-2000	473-1100
WGH-AM 1310 kHz (Sports) 5589 Greenwich Rd Suite 200	Virginia Beach	VA	23462	757-671-1000	671-1010
WGH-FM 97.3 MHz (Ctry) 5589 Greenwich Rd Suite 200 *Web:* www.eagle97.com	Virginia Beach	VA	23462	757-671-1000	671-1010
WGPL-AM 1350 kHz (Rel) 645 Church St Suite 400	Norfolk	VA	23510	757-622-4600	624-6515
WHRO-FM 90.3 MHz (Clas) 5200 Hampton Blvd.	Norfolk	VA	23508	757-889-9400	489-0007
WNVZ-FM 104.5 MHz (CHR) 236 Clearfield Ave Suite 206 **Fax:* Sales ■ *Web:* www.z104.com	Virginia Beach	VA	23462	757-497-2000	456-5458*
WOWI-FM 102.9 MHz (Urban) 1003 Norfolk Sq	Norfolk	VA	23502	757-466-0009	466-7043
WROX-FM 96.1 MHz (Alt) 999 Waterside Dr Dominion Tower Suite 500	Norfolk	VA	23510	757-640-8500	640-8552
WSVV-FM 92.1 MHz (CHR) 1003 Norfolk Sq	Norfolk	VA	23502	757-466-0009	466-7043
WSVY-FM 107.7 MHz (Urban) 1003 Norfolk Sq	Norfolk	VA	23502	757-466-0009	466-0082
WTAR-AM 850 kHz (N/T) 999 Waterside Dr 500 Dominion Tower *Web:* wtar.exis.net	Norfolk	VA	23510	757-640-8500	640-8552
WVKL-FM 95.7 MHz (Oldies) 5589 Greenwich Rd Suite 200 *Web:* www.kool957.com	Virginia Beach	VA	23462	757-671-1000	671-1010
WWDE-FM 101.3 MHz (AC) 236 Clearfield Ave Suite 206	Virginia Beach	VA	23462	757-497-2000	456-5458
WXEZ-FM 94.1 MHz (B/EZ) 4026 George Washington Hwy *Web:* www.ez94.com	Yorktown	VA	23692	757-898-9494	898-9401

— Colleges/Universities —

	City	State	ZIP	Phone	Fax
Tabernacle Baptist Bible College & Theological Seminary 717 N Whitehurst Landing Rd	Virginia Beach	VA	23464	757-420-5476	424-3014
Tidewater Community College Virginia Beach Campus 1700 College Crescent *Web:* www.tc.cc.va.us/campuses/vabeach.htm	Virginia Beach	VA	23456	757-822-7100	427-7041

— Hospitals —

	City	State	ZIP	Phone	Fax
Chesapeake General Hospital 736 Battlefield Blvd N *Web:* www.chesgh.org ■ *E-mail:* cgh@chesgh.org	Chesapeake	VA	23327	757-482-6100	482-6184
Sentara Bayside Hospital 800 Independence Blvd *Web:* www.sentara.com/hospitals/sentara_bayside.html	Virginia Beach	VA	23455	757-363-6100	363-6650
Sentara Leigh Hospital 830 Kempsville Rd *Web:* www.sentara.com/hospitals/sentara_leigh.html	Norfolk	VA	23502	757-466-6000	466-6765
Sentara Virginia Beach General Hospital 1060 First Colonial Rd *TF:* 800-736-8272 ■ *Web:* www.sentara.com/hospitals/virginiabeach.html	Virginia Beach	VA	23454	757-395-8000	395-6106

— Attractions —

	City	State	ZIP	Phone	Fax
Atlantic Wildfowl Heritage Museum 1113 Atlantic Ave *Web:* www.pilot.infi.net/~raven/wildfowl.html ■ *E-mail:* wmuseum@aol.com	Virginia Beach	VA	23451	757-437-8432	437-9055
Back Bay National Wildlife Refuge 4005 Sandpiper Rd	Virginia Beach	VA	23456	757-721-2412	721-6141
Christian Broadcasting Network 977 Centerville Tpke	Virginia Beach	VA	23463	757-579-7000	
Contemporary Art Center of Virginia 2200 Parks Ave *Web:* www.cacv.org	Virginia Beach	VA	23451	757-425-0000	425-8186
Discovery Cruises 600 Laskin Rd	Virginia Beach	VA	23451	757-422-2900	491-9007
False Cape State Park 4001 Sandpiper Rd	Virginia Beach	VA	23456	757-426-7128	426-0055
Fort Story N Atlantic Ave	Virginia Beach	VA	23459	757-422-7164	422-7750
IMAX Theater 717 General Booth Blvd Virginia Marine Science Museum	Virginia Beach	VA	23451	757-437-4949	437-4976
Land Francis House 3131 Virginia Beach Blvd	Virginia Beach	VA	23452	757-431-4000	
Little Theater of Virginia Beach 24th St & Barberton Dr	Virginia Beach	VA	23451	757-428-9233	
Lynnhaven House 4401 Wishart Rd.	Virginia Beach	VA	23455	757-460-1688	
Lynnhaven Seafood Marina & Dockside Restaurant 3311 Shore Dr.	Virginia Beach	VA	23451	757-481-7211	481-1533
Mount Trashmore Park 300 Edwin Dr	Virginia Beach	VA	23462	757-497-2157	473-5187
Naval Amphibious Base Little Creek 2600 Tarawa Ctr Suite 112.	Norfolk	VA	23512	757-462-7923	462-3144
Old Cape Henry Lighthouse N Atlantic Ave Fort Story	Virginia Beach	VA	23459	757-422-9421	
Old Coast Guard Station 24th St & Oceanfront *Web:* www.vabeach.com/old_coast/index.html ■ *E-mail:* Old_Coast@Va-Beach.com	Virginia Beach	VA	23451	757-422-1587	491-8609
Princess Anne Park 3475 Princess Anne Rd	Virginia Beach	VA	23456	757-563-1100	
Seashore State Park & Natural Area 2500 Shore Dr *TF:* 800-933-7275	Virginia Beach	VA	23451	757-412-2300	412-2315
Thoroughgood Adam House 1636 Parish Rd.	Virginia Beach	VA	23455	757-460-0007	
Time Machine 1606 Atlantic Ave.	Virginia Beach	VA	23451	757-491-6876	
Virginia Beach Farmer's Market 3640 Dam Neck Rd.	Virginia Beach	VA	23456	757-427-4395	427-4364
Virginia Marine Science Museum 717 General Booth Blvd. *Web:* www.va-beach.com/va-marine-science-museum/ ■ *E mail:* vmsm@infi.net	Virginia Beach	VA	23451	757-425-3474	437-4976
Virginia Sports Hall of Fame 420 High St	Portsmouth	VA	23704	757-393-8031	393-5228
Wild Water Rapids 849 General Booth Blvd.	Virginia Beach	VA	23451	757-422-0718	422-8984

SPORTS TEAMS & FACILITIES

	City	State	ZIP	Phone	Fax
Hampton Coliseum 1000 Coliseum Dr. *Web:* www.hampton.va.us/coliseum	Hampton	VA	23666	757-838-5650	838-2595
Hampton Roads Admirals (hockey) 201 E Brambleton Ave Scope Arena	Norfolk	VA	23510	757-640-1212	
Hampton Roads Mariners (soccer) 2181 Landstown Rd Virginia Beach Sportsplex	Virginia Beach	VA	23456	757-430-8873	430-8803
Hampton Roads Piranhas (soccer) 2181 Landstown Rd Virginia Beach Sportsplex	Virginia Beach	VA	23456	757-405-6022	431-3259
Norfolk Tides (baseball) 150 Park Ave Harbor Pk *Web:* www.gohamptonroads.com/partners/tides	Norfolk	VA	23510	757-622-2222	624-9090

— Events —

	Phone
American Music Festival (early September)	757-437-4800
Bayou Boogaloo & Cajun Food Festival (late June)	757-441-2345
Beach Music Weekend (mid-May)	757-491-7866
Big Band Weekend (late May)	757-491-7866
Blues at the Beach (early September)	757-491-7866
Boardwalk Art Show (mid-June)	757-425-0000
Boardwalk Exotic Auto Expo (mid-October)	757-491-7866
Cinco de Mayo (early May)	757-491-7866
Cinco de Mayo Celebration (early May)	757-491-7866
Elvis is Everywhere Festival (early June)	800-446-8038
Holiday Lights at the Beach (late November-early January)	757-491-7866
Men's Pro-Am Volleyball Tournament (mid-August)	757-437-4882
Mid-Atlantic Sports & Boat Show (mid-February)	757-934-7504
Mid-Atlantic Wildfowl Festival (early March)	757-437-8432
Neptune Festival & Air Show (late September)	757-498-0215
October Brewfest (late October)	757-463-1940
Pungo Strawberry Festival (late May)	757-721-6001
Shamrock Sportsfest Marathon (mid-March)	757-481-5090
ShowDeo (early September)	757-427-6020
Virginia Beach East Coast Surfing Championships (late August)	800-861-7873
Virginia International Waterfront Arts Festival (early April-early May)	757-664-6492
Whale Watching (late December-early March)	757-437-4949

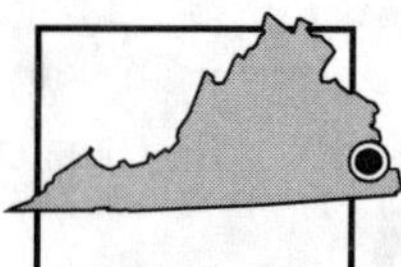

Williamsburg

Williamsburg, named after England's King William III, was the colonial capital from 1699 until 1780. The 18th Century community has been restored on a 173-acre site, with more than 500 public buildings and homes, costumed historical interpreters, and greens and gardens. Carter's Grove, in Williamsburg, includes a partially reconstructed 17th Century English settlement, an 18th Century slave quarters, and the Winthrop Rockefeller Archaeological Museum. Williamsburg is also the home of the College of William and Mary (charterd in 1693), which contains the oldest American academic building still in use. The city is located near the midpoint of the 23-mile scenic Colonial Drive Parkway, which connects Jamestown and Yorktown to form the "Historic Triangle." From Jamestown, the birthplace of English colonial America (1607), to Yorktown, site of the last major battle of the American Revolution (1781), 174 years of English colonial America are preserved and interpreted in this historic area.

Population 11,971
Area (Land) . . . . . 8.6 sq mi
Area (Water) . . . . . 0.1 sq mi
Elevation . . . . . 86 ft
Latitude . . . . . 37-16-12 N
Longitude . . . . . 76-42-25 W
County . . . . . Independent City
Time Zone . . . . . EST
Area Code/s 757

— Average Temperatures and Precipitation —

TEMPERATURES

	Jan	Feb	Mar	Apr	May	Jun	Jul	Aug	Sep	Oct	Nov	Dec
High	48	51	61	70	78	85	88	87	81	71	63	52
Low	27	29	36	44	54	62	67	66	60	48	39	31

PRECIPITATION

	Jan	Feb	Mar	Apr	May	Jun	Jul	Aug	Sep	Oct	Nov	Dec
Inches	3.8	3.5	4.2	3.0	4.5	4.0	5.0	4.7	4.3	3.2	3.5	3.4

— Important Phone Numbers —

	Phone
AAA	757-564-7711
Emergency	911
HotelDocs	800-468-3537
Medical Referral	757-229-4636
Poison Control Center	800-552-6337
Time	757-229-1140
Virginia Highway Conditions	800-367-7623
Weather	757-877-1221

— Information Sources —

				Phone	Fax
Better Business Bureau Serving Greater Hampton Roads 586 Virginian Dr	Norfolk	VA	23505	757-531-1300	531-1388

Web: www.hamptonroadsbbb.org
■ *E-mail:* info@hamptonroadsbbb.org

				Phone	Fax
Colonial Williamsburg Foundation PO Box 1776	Williamsburg	VA	23187	757-229-1000	220-7259*

**Fax:* Hum Res ■ *Web:* www.colonialwilliamsburg.org
■ *E-mail:* cwres@cwf.org

				Phone	Fax
Williamsburg Area Chamber of Commerce 201 Penniman Rd	Williamsburg	VA	23185	757-229-6511	229-2047

TF: 800-368-6511 ■ *Web:* www.williamsburgcc.com

				Phone	Fax
Williamsburg Area Convention & Visitors Bureau 201 Penniman Rd	Williamsburg	VA	23185	757-253-0192	229-2047

TF: 800-368-6511 ■ *Web:* www.visitwilliamsburg.com
■ *E-mail:* wacvb@VisitWilliamsburg.com

				Phone	Fax
Williamsburg City Hall 401 Lafayette St	Williamsburg	VA	23185	757-220-6100	220-6107

Web: www.ci.williamsburg.va.us ■ *E-mail:* info@ci.williamsburg.va.us

				Phone	Fax
Williamsburg City Hall 401 Lafayette St	Williamsburg	VA	23185	757-220-6100	220-6107

Web: www.ci.williamsburg.va.us ■ *E-mail:* info@ci.williamsburg.va.us

				Phone	Fax
Williamsburg City Manager 401 Lafayette St	Williamsburg	VA	23185	757-220-6100	220-6107
Williamsburg Economic Development 401 Lafayette St	Williamsburg	VA	23185	757-220-6100	
Williamsburg Regional Library 515 Scotland St	Williamsburg	VA	23185	757-259-4050	259-4079

Web: www.wrl.org

On-Line Resources

4Williamsburg.com www.4williamsburg.com
Access America Williamsburg . . . . . www.accessamer.com/williamsburg/
Area Guide Williamsburg . . . . . williamsburg.areaguides.net
City Knowledge Williamsburg . . . . . www.cityknowledge.com/va_williamsburg.htm
Excite.com Williamsburg City Guide . . . . . www.excite.com/travel/countries/united_states/virginia/williamsburg
Insiders' Guide to Williamsburg . . . . . www.insiders.com/williamsburg/
It's Williamsburg Guide to Williamsburg . . . . . www.wmbg.org
NITC Travelbase City Guide Williamsburg . . . www.travelbase.com/auto/features/williamsburg-va.html
Online City Guide to Williamsburg . . . . . www.olcg.com/va/williamsburg/main.html
Sunny Day Guide Colonial Williamsburg . . . . . www.sunnydayguides.com/cg/default.htm
Visions of Williamsburg Business Directory . . . . . williamsburg-virginia.com
Welcome to Colonial Williamsburg . . . . . www.history.org/welcome.html
Williamsburg Online . . . . . www.williamsburg.com
Williamsburg-Virginia.com . . . . . www.williamsburg-virginia.com

— Transportation Services —

AIRPORTS

■ **Newport News/Williamsburg International Airport (PHF)**

	Phone
20 miles SE of downtown Williamsburg (approx 30 minutes)	757-877-0221

Web: www.phf-airport.org

Airport Transportation

	Phone
Williamsburg Limo & Shuttle $15 fare to downtown	757-877-0279

Commercial Airlines

	Phone
AirTran	800-247-8726
United Express	800-241-6522
US Airways Express	800-428-4322

Charter Airlines

	Phone
Flight International	757-886-5755
Rick Aviation Inc	757-874-5727

CAR RENTALS

	Phone
Alamo	800-327-9633
Avis	757-877-0291
Budget	800-874-5794
Enterprise	757-873-3003
Hertz	757-877-9229
National	757-877-6486
Thrifty	757-877-5700

LIMO/TAXI

	Phone
Carey Limousine	757-220-5466
Williamsburg Limo & Shuttle	757-877-0279

MASS TRANSIT

	Phone
Relax & Ride Visitors Shuttle $1 Base fare	757-220-1621

RAIL/BUS

				Phone
Amtrak Station 468 N Boundary St	Williamsburg	VA	23185	757-229-8750

TF: 800-872-7245

				Phone
Greyhound Bus Station 468 N Boundary St	Williamsburg	VA	23185	757-229-1460

TF: 800-231-2222

Williamsburg (Cont'd)

— Accommodations —

HOTEL RESERVATION SERVICES

Phone *Fax*

Colonial Williamsburg Reservation Center 757-253-2277 565-8797
TF: 800-447-8679 ■ *Web:* www.history.org

Reservations USA 865-453-1000 453-7484
TF: 800-251-4444 ■ *Web:* www.reservationsusa.com
■ *E-mail:* reserve@lodging4u.com

Williamsburg Room Reservations 757-220-3330 220-3136
TF: 800-999-4485 ■ *Web:* www.williamsburghotel.com
■ *E-mail:* whma@williamsburghotel.com

HOTELS, MOTELS, RESORTS

Phone *Fax*

Anderson's Corner Motel 8550 Richmond Rd Toano VA 23168 757-566-0807

Bassett Motel 800 York St Williamsburg VA 23185 757-229-5175

Best Western Colonial Capitol Inn
111 Penniman Rd Williamsburg VA 23187 757-253-1222 229-9264
TF: 800-446-9228

Best Western Patrick Henry Inn
249 York St Williamsburg VA 23187 757-229-9540 220-1273
TF: 800-446-9228

Best Western Williamsburg
Rt 60 E & 199 Overpass Williamsburg VA 23187 757-229-3003 229-9239
TF: 800-446-9228

Budget Host Governor Spottswood Motel
1508 Richmond Rd Williamsburg VA 23185 757-229-6444 253-2410
TF: 800-368-1244

Capitol Motel 924 Capitol Landing Rd Williamsburg VA 23185 757-229-5215
TF: 800-368-8383

Captain John Smith Inn
2225 Richmond Rd Williamsburg VA 23185 757-220-0710 220-1166
TF: 800-933-6788

Colonial America Hotel
6483 Richmond Rd Williamsburg VA 23188 757-565-1000 565-8627
TF: 800-922-9277

Colonial Motel 1452 Richmond Rd Williamsburg VA 23185 757-229-3621
TF: 800-232-1452 ■ *Web:* www.wmbg.com/colonial
■ *E-mail:* colonial@wmbg.com

Comfort Inn & Suites
1420 Richmond Rd Williamsburg VA 23185 757-229-2981 229-8179
TF: 800-444-4678

Comfort Inn Central 2007 Richmond Rd Williamsburg VA 23185 757-220-3888
TF: 800-346-5247

Comfort Inn King George Historic
706 Bypass Rd Williamsburg VA 23185 757-229-9230 253-1654
Web: www.comfortinnhistoric.com

Comfort Inn Outlet Center
5611 Richmond Rd Williamsburg VA 23188 757-565-1100 565-1443
TF: 800-964-1774

Commonwealth Inn 1233 Richmond Rd Williamsburg VA 23185 757-253-1087
TF: 800-344-0046

Days Inn Downtown 902 Richmond Rd Williamsburg VA 23185 757-229-5060 220-9153
TF: 800-329-7466

Days Inn East Williamsburg
201 Water Country Pkwy Williamsburg VA 23185 757-253-6444 253-0986
TF: 800-635-5366

Days Inn Pottery 6488 Richmond Rd Lightfoot VA 23188 757-565-0090 565-3545

Days Inn West Williamsburg
5437 Richmond Rd Williamsburg VA 23188 757-565-2700 565-3700

Econo Lodge Central
1900 Richmond Rd Williamsburg VA 23185 757-229-6600 229-6600
TF: 800-828-5353

Econo Lodge Colonial 216 Parkway Dr Williamsburg VA 23185 757-253-6450 229-2888
TF: 800-296-7829 ■ *Web:* www.econolodge-colonial.com
■ *E-mail:* econolodge-colonial@travelbase.com

Embassy Suites Williamsburg
3006 Mooretown Rd Williamsburg VA 23185 757-229-6800 220-3486
TF: 800-333-0924

Family Inns of America 5413 Airport Rd Williamsburg VA 23188 757-565-1900 565-1900
TF: 800-521-3377

Four Points Hotel by Sheraton
351 York St Williamsburg VA 23185 757-229-4100 229-0176
TF: 800-962-4743 ■ *Web:* sheraton-fourpoints.com

Governor's Inn 506 N Henry St Williamsburg VA 23185 757-229-1000 221-8797

Phone *Fax*

Hampton Inn & Suites Historic Area
1880 Richmond Rd Williamsburg VA 23185 757-229-4900
TF: 800-346-3055

Hampton Inn Historic Area 505 York St Williamsburg VA 23185 757-220-3100 229-2447
TF: 800-444-4678

Hampton Inn Williamsburg Center
201 Bypass Rd Williamsburg VA 23185 757-220-0880 229-7175
TF: 800-444-4678

Heritage Inn 1324 Richmond Rd Williamsburg VA 23185 757-229-6220 229-2774
TF: 800-782-3800
■ *Web:* www.travelbase.com/destinations/williamsburg/heritage/index.html
■ *E-mail:* heritage@travelbase.com

Holiday Inn 1776 725 Bypass Rd Williamsburg VA 23185 757-220-1776 220-3124
TF: 800-446-2848

Holiday Inn Downtown & Holidome
814 Capitol Landing Rd Williamsburg VA 23185 757-229-0200 220-1642
TF: 800-368-0200

Holiday Inn Express Historic Area
119 Bypass Rd Williamsburg VA 23185 757-253-1663 220-9117
TF: 800-283-1663

Holiday Inn Patriot 3032 Richmond Rd Williamsburg VA 23185 757-565-2600 564-9738
TF: 800-446-6001

Homewood Suites Hotel 601 Bypass Rd Williamsburg VA 23185 757-259-1199
TF: 888-892-9900

Howard Johnson Hotel Historic Area
7135 Pocahontas Tr Williamsburg VA 23185 757-229-6900 220-3211
TF: 800-841-9100 ■ *Web:* www.hojohst.com
■ *E-mail:* hojohst@hojohst.com

King William Inn
824 Capitol Landing Rd Williamsburg VA 23185 757-229-4933 229-9686
TF: 800-446-1041 ■ *Web:* www2.cybernex.net/~patelkar/king_will
■ *E-mail:* hotelkw@hotmail.com

Kingsmill Resort & Conference Center
1010 Kingsmill Rd Williamsburg VA 23185 757-253-1703 253-8246
TF: 800-832-5665 ■ *Web:* www.kingsmill.com

Marriott Hotel & Conference Center
50 Kingsmill Rd Williamsburg VA 23185 757-220-2500 253-0541*
**Fax:* Sales ■ *TF:* 800-228-9290 ■ *Web:* marriotthotels.com/PHFCW

Marriott Manor Club 101 St Andrews Dr Williamsburg VA 23188 757-258-1120 258-5705

Princess Anne The 1350 Richmond Rd Williamsburg VA 23185 757-229-2455 229-0122
TF: 800-552-5571

Quality Inn at Kingsmill
480 McLaws Cir Williamsburg VA 23185 757-220-1100 220-1100
TF: 800-296-4667

Quality Inn Colony 309 Page St Williamsburg VA 23187 757-229-1855 229-3470

Quality Inn Historic Area
1402 Richmond Rd Williamsburg VA 23185 757-220-2367 220-3527
TF: 800-444-4678

Quality Inn Lord Paget
901 Capitol Landing Rd Williamsburg VA 23185 757-229-4444 220-9314
TF: 800-537-2438

Quality Inn Outlet Mall
6493 Richmond Rd Williamsburg VA 23188 757-565-1111 564-3033
TF: 800-524-1443
■ *Web:* www.travelbase.com/destinations/williamsburg/quality/index.html

Quality Suites 1406 Richmond Rd Williamsburg VA 23185 757-220-9304 220-1823
TF: 800-444-4678 ■ *Web:* www.quality-suites.com
■ *E-mail:* info@qswilliamsburg.com

Quarterpath Inn 620 York St Williamsburg VA 23185 757-220-0960 220-1531
TF: 800-446-9222 ■ *Web:* www.hotelroom.com/virginia/wmquar.html

Radisson Fort Magruder Hotel & Conference Center
6945 Pocahontas Trail Williamsburg VA 23185 757-220-2250 321-6982
TF: 800-333-3333 ■ *Web:* www.radissonftmagruder.com
■ *E-mail:* hotelsales@earthlink.net

Ramada Inn Central Williamsburg
5351 Richmond Rd Williamsburg VA 23188 757-565-2000 565-4652
TF: 800-446-9200 ■ *Web:* www.williamsburg-ramada.com

Ramada Inn Historic Area
500 Merrimac Tr Williamsburg VA 23185 757-220-1410 259-4662
TF: 800-666-8888

Rochambeau Motel
929 Capitol Landing Rd Williamsburg VA 23185 757-229-2851
TF: 800-368-1055

Rodeway Inn 7224 Merrimac Tr Williamsburg VA 23185 757-229-0400 258-3989

Super 8 Motel 304 2nd St Williamsburg VA 23185 757-229-0500
TF: 800-336-0500

Travelodge Historic Area
120 Bypass Rd Williamsburg VA 23185 757-229-2000 220-2826
TF: 800-544-7774

White Lion Motel
912 Capitol Landing Rd Williamsburg VA 23185 757-229-3931
TF: 800-368-1055

Williamsburg Center Hotel
600 Bypass Rd Williamsburg VA 23185 757-220-2800 220-8986
TF: 800-492-2855

Williamsburg — Hotels, Motels, Resorts (Cont'd)

Phone *Fax*

Williamsburg Hospitality House
415 Richmond Rd . . . . . Williamsburg VA 23185 757-229-4020 220-1560
TF: 800-932-9192 ■ *Web:* www.williamsburghosphouse.com
■ *E-mail:* reservations@williamsburghosphouse.com

Williamsburg Inn 136 E Francis St . . . . . Williamsburg VA 23185 757-229-1000 220-7096
TF: 800-447-8679 ■ *Web:* www.history.org/tours/hotel_will_inn.html
■ *E-mail:* cwres@cwf.org

Williamsburg Lodge 310 S England St . . . . Williamsburg VA 23185 757-229-1000 220-7799
TF: 800-447-8679

Williamsburg Travel Inn
1800 Richmond Rd . . . . . Williamsburg VA 23185 757-229-2781 229-2544

— Restaurants —

Phone

Aberdeen Barn (Steak/Seafood) 1601 Richmond Rd . . . Williamsburg VA 23185 757-229-6661
Beethoven's Inn (American) 467 Merrimac Tr . . . . . Williamsburg VA 23185 757-229-7069
Berret's Seafood Restaurant & Raw Bar (Seafood)
199 S Boundary St . . . . . Williamsburg VA 23185 757-253-1847
Candle Factory Restaurant (American)
7521 Richmond Rd Williamsburg Candle Factory . . . . Williamsburg VA 23188 757-564-0803
Captain George's Seafood Buffet (Seafood)
5363 Richmond Rd . . . . . Williamsburg VA 23188 757-565-2323
Carmela's Basta Pasta (Italian) 207 Bypass Rd . . . . . Williamsburg VA 23185 757-253-6544
Cary Street Bistro & Tavern (American)
500 Jamestown Rd . . . . . Williamsburg VA 23185 757-229-2297
CB Wood Grill (American) 6678 Richmond Rd . . . . . Williamsburg VA 23188 757-565-2800
Christiana Campbell's Tavern (American) Waller St . . . . Williamsburg VA 23185 757-229-2141
Christopher's Tavern (American)
415 Richmond Rd Williamsburg Hospitality House . . . Williamsburg VA 23185 757-229-4020
Fez Restaurant (Moroccan)
Rt 60 E Festival Market Place . . . . . Williamsburg VA 23185 757-220-8880
Fireside Steak House (Steak/Seafood)
1995 Richmond Rd . . . . . Williamsburg VA 23185 757-229-3310
Giuseppe's Italian Cafe (Italian) 5601 Richmond Rd . . . Williamsburg VA 23188 757-565-1977
Hayashi Pastels Japanese Restaurant (Japanese)
5601 Richmond Rd . . . . . Williamsburg VA 23188 757-253-0282
Jefferson Restaurant (American) 1453 Richmond Rd . . . Williamsburg VA 23185 757-229-2296
Josiah Chowning's Tavern (American)
Duke of Gloucester St Market Sq . . . . . Williamsburg VA 23185 757-229-2141
King's Arms Tavern (American) Duke of Gloucester St . . Williamsburg VA 23185 757-229-2141
La Tolteca Mexican Restaurant (Mexican)
135 2nd St . . . . . Williamsburg VA 23185 757-259-0598
Library Tavern (American) 1330 Richmond Rd . . . . . Williamsburg VA 23185 757-229-1012
Marino's Italian Cuisine (Italian) 1338 Richmond Rd . . Williamsburg VA 23185 757-253-1844
Milano's Italian Restaurant (Italian)
1635 Richmond Rd . . . . . Williamsburg VA 23185 757-220-2527
Nawab Indian Cuisine (Indian)
204 Monticello Ave Monticello Shopping Ctr . . . . . Williamsburg VA 23185 757-565-3200
Old Chickahominy House (Southern)
1211 Jamestown Rd . . . . . Williamsburg VA 23185 757-229-4689
Papillon Bistro (Steak/Seafood)
415 Richmond Rd Williamsburg Hospitality House . . . Williamsburg VA 23185 757-229-4020
Pierce's Pitt Bar-B-Que (Barbecue)
477 E Rochambeau Dr . . . . . Williamsburg VA 23185 757-565-2955
Prime Rib House (Continental) 1433 Richmond Rd . . . . Williamsburg VA 23185 757-229-6823
Sal's Piccolo Forno (Italian) 835 Capitol Landing Rd . . . Williamsburg VA 23185 757-221-0443
Sal's Restaurant by Victor (Italian)
1242 Richmond Rd . . . . . Williamsburg VA 23185 757-220-2641
Seafare The (Seafood) 1632 Richmond Rd . . . . . Williamsburg VA 23185 757-229-0099
Seasons Restaurant (Steak/Seafood)
110 S Henry St Merchants Sq . . . . . Williamsburg VA 23185 757-259-0018
Second Street Restaurant & Tavern (American)
140 2nd St . . . . . Williamsburg VA 23185 757-220-2286
Web: www.secondst.com ■ *E-mail:* 2ndst@secondst.com
Shields Tavern (American) Duke of Gloucester St . . . . . Williamsburg VA 23185 757-229-2141
Sportsman's Grille (American)
240 McLaws Cir Marketplace Shopping Ctr . . . . . Williamsburg VA 23185 757-221-8002
That Seafood Place (Steak/Seafood)
1647 Richmond Rd . . . . . Williamsburg VA 23185 757-220-3011
Trellis Restaurant (American)
403 Duke of Gloucester St . . . . . Williamsburg VA 23185 757-229-8610
Whaling Co The (Steak/Seafood) 494 McLaws Cir . . . . . Williamsburg VA 23185 757-229-0275
Whitehall Restaurant (European) 1325 Jamestown Rd . . Williamsburg VA 23185 757-229-4677
Web: www.thewhitehall.com ■ *E-mail:* info@thewhitehall.com
Yorkshire Steak & Seafood Restaurant (Steak/Seafood)
700 York St . . . . . Williamsburg VA 23185 757-229-9790
Web: www.yorkshire-wmbg.com ■ *E-mail:* yorkshire@ontheline.com

— Goods and Services —

SHOPPING

Phone *Fax*

Lenox Factory Outlet
3032-2 Richmond Rd . . . . . Williamsburg VA 23185 757-565-0800
Merchants Square
Duke of Gloucester St . . . . . Williamsburg VA 23185 757-220-7354
Nike Factory Store
5707-6 Richmond Rd Prime Outlets
at Williamsburg . . . . . Williamsburg VA 23188 757-565-2963
Prime Outlets at Williamsburg
5715-62A Richmond Rd . . . . . Williamsburg VA 23188 757-565-0702 565-0369
Web: www.primeoutlets.com/Williamsburg/index.html
Williamsburg Antique Mall
500 Lightfoot Rd . . . . . Williamsburg VA 23188 757-565-3422
Williamsburg Outlet Mall
6401 Richmond Rd . . . . . Williamsburg VA 23188 757-565-3378
TF: 888-746-7333 ■ *Web:* www.charter-oak.com/williamsburg
Williamsburg Pottery Factory Rt 60 W . . . . . Lightfoot VA 23090 757-564-3326 564-8241
TF: 800-768-8379

BANKS

Phone *Fax*

Bank of America 1801 Richmond Rd . . . . . Williamsburg VA 23185 757-259-5481 259-5483
Bank of Williamsburg
5251 John Tyler Hwy Suite 52 . . . . . Williamsburg VA 23185 757-229-5448
Centura Bank 4541 John Tyler Hwy . . . . . Williamsburg VA 23185 757-259-1981
Citizens & Farmers Bank
4780 Longhill Rd . . . . . Williamsburg VA 23188 757-565-0593 565-4584
Crestar Bank
401 W Duke of Gloucester St . . . . . Williamsburg VA 23185 757-253-9200
First Virginia Bank Commonwealth
300 2nd St . . . . . Williamsburg VA 23185 757-229-4191 565-5897
Old Point National Bank
5273 John Tyler Hwy . . . . . Williamsburg VA 23185 757-221-0155 221-0354
Peninsula Trust Bank Inc
1031 Richmond Rd . . . . . Williamsburg VA 23185 757-220-1252 220-0420
Wachovia Bank NA 1006 Richmond Rd . . . . Williamsburg VA 23185 757-220-6200 220-2538

BUSINESS SERVICES

	Phone		Phone
Affordable Temporary Service	757-229-4008	**More than Mail**	757-220-9430
Airborne Express	800-247-2676	**Post Office**	757-229-4668
Federal Express	800-238-5355	**Pro Temps Temporary Service**	757-220-0022
Kinko's	757-253-5676	**UPS**	800-742-5877

— Media —

PUBLICATIONS

Phone *Fax*

Daily Press‡ 7505 Warwick Blvd . . . . . Newport News VA 23607 757-247-4600 245-8618
Virginia Gazette 216 Ironbound Rd . . . . . Williamsburg VA 23188 757-220-1736 220-1665*
**Fax:* News Rm
Williamsburg Great Entertainer Magazine
1915 Pocahontas Tr Suite F-10 . . . . . Williamsburg VA 23185 757-229-8508 220-3136

‡*Daily newspapers*

TELEVISION

Phone *Fax*

WCVE-TV Ch 23 (PBS) 23 Sesame St . . . . . Richmond VA 23235 804-320-1301 320-8729
Web: www.wcve.org/TV23-Frame1.HTM
WHRO-TV Ch 15 (PBS) 5200 Hampton Blvd . . . . . Norfolk VA 23508 757-889-9400 489-0007
Web: www.whro-pbs.org ■ *E-mail:* info@whro.org
WRIC-TV Ch 8 (ABC) 301 Arboretum Pl . . . . . Richmond VA 23236 804-330-8888 330-8883
Web: www.wric.com
WRLH-TV Ch 35 (Fox)
1925 Westmoreland St . . . . . Richmond VA 23230 804-358-3535 358-1495
Web: www.fox35.com ■ *E-mail:* fox35@fox35.com
WTVR-TV Ch 6 (CBS) 3301 W Broad St . . . . . Richmond VA 23230 804-254-3600 254-3697
Web: www.newschannel6.com
WUPV-TV Ch 65 (UPN) 4120 E Parham Rd . . . Richmond VA 23228 804-672-6565 672-6571
WVBT-TV Ch 43 (Fox) 243 Wavy St . . . . . Portsmouth VA 23704 757-393-4343 393-7615
Web: www.wvbt.com
WWBT-TV Ch 12 (NBC)
5710 Midlothian Tpke . . . . . Richmond VA 23225 804-230-1212 230-2793
Web: www.nbc12.com

Williamsburg (Cont'd)

RADIO

Phone Fax

WBYM-AM 1490 kHz (Ctry)
2845 N Armistead Ave. . . . . Hampton VA 23666 757-766-9262 766-7439
E-mail: wbym@arronet.com
WCPK-AM 1600 kHz (Rel) 2202 Joilliff Rd. . . Chesapeake VA 23321 757-488-1010
WCWM-FM 90.7 MHz (Misc)
Campus Ctr College of William
& Mary . . . . Williamsburg VA 23185 757-221-3287 221-3451
WGH-AM 1310 kHz (Sports)
5589 Greenwich Rd Suite 200 . . . . .Virginia Beach VA 23462 757-671-1000 671-1010
WGH-FM 97.3 MHz (Ctry)
5589 Greenwich Rd Suite 200 . . . . .Virginia Beach VA 23462 757-671-1000 671-1010
Web: www.eagle97.com
WGPL-AM 1350 kHz (Rel)
645 Church St Suite 400 . . . . Norfolk VA 23510 757-622-4600 624-6515
WKGM-AM 940 kHz (Rel)
13379 Great Spring Rd . . . . .Smithfield VA 23430 757-357-9546 365-0412
WNIS-AM 790 kHz (N/T)
999 Waterside Dr Dominion Tower
Suite 500. . . . . Norfolk VA 23510 757-640-8500 622-6397
Web: wnis.exis.net ■ *E-mail:* wnis@exis.net
WNVZ-FM 104.5 MHz (CHR)
236 Clearfield Ave Suite 206 . . . . .Virginia Beach VA 23462 757-497-2000 456-5458*
**Fax:* Sales ■ *Web:* www.z104.com
WPTG-FM 107.9 MHz (Ctry)
207 Parkway Dr . . . . Williamsburg VA 23185 757-565-1079 565-2250
WRVA-AM 1140 kHz (N/T) 200 N 22nd St . . . . Richmond VA 23223 804-780-3400 780-3427
Web: www.wrva.com
WTAR-AM 850 kHz (N/T)
999 Waterside Dr 500 Dominion Tower . . . . . . Norfolk VA 23510 757-640-8500 640-8552
Web: wtar.exis.net
WXEZ-FM 94.1 MHz (B/EZ)
4026 George Washington Hwy . . . . Yorktown VA 23692 757-898-9494 898-9401
Web: www.ez94.com
WXGM-AM 1420 kHz (AC)
6267 Professional Dr. . . . . Gloucester VA 23061 804-693-9946 693-2182
WXGM-FM 99.1 MHz (AC)
6267 Professional Dr. . . . . Gloucester VA 23061 804-693-9946 693-2182
Web: www.xtra99.com ■ *E-mail:* office@xtra99.com
WYCS-FM 91.5 MHz (Rel) PO Box 1007 . . . . . . Yorktown VA 23692 757-886-7490

— Colleges/Universities —

Phone Fax

College of William & Mary
PO Box 8795 . . . . Williamsburg VA 23187 757-221-4000 221-1242
Web: www.wm.edu ■ *E-mail:* ccharr@facstaff.wm.edu

— Hospitals —

Phone Fax

Williamsburg Community Hospital
301 Monticello Ave . . . . Williamsburg VA 23185 757-259-6000 259-6327

— Attractions —

Phone Fax

America's Railroads
1915 Pocahontas Tr Village Shops
at Kingsmill . . . . Williamsburg VA 23185 757-220-8725
Berkeley Plantation
12602 Harrison Landing Rd . . . . Charles City VA 23030 804-829-6018
Busch Gardens 1 Busch Gardens Blvd. . . . . Williamsburg VA 23187 757-253-3350 253-3399
TF: 800-772-8886
■ *Web:* www.buschgardens.com/buschgardens/bg_williamsburg/frame.html
Carter's Grove
8797 Pocahontas Tr
Colonial Williamsburg . . . . Williamsburg VA 23187 800-447-8679
Colonial National Historical Park
Colonial Pkwy & Rt 238. . . . . Yorktown VA 23690 757-898-3400 898-3400
Web: www.nps.gov/colo/
Colonial Parkway Scenic Drive
Colonial Pkwy. . . . . Williamburg VA 23185 757-898-3400

Phone Fax

Colonial Williamsburg Visitor's Center
Giftshop 100 Visitor Center Dr . . . . Williamsburg VA 23185 757-229-1000 565-8965
TF: 800-447-8679
Destination Williamsburg Walking Tours
501 Prince George St . . . . Williamsburg VA 23185 757-229-7193
Web: www.destinationwbg.com ■ *E-mail:* info@destinationwbg.com
DeWitt Wallace Gallery 325 Francis St . . . . Williamsburg VA 23187 757-220-7724
Evelynton Plantation
6701 John Tyler Memorial Hwy . . . . Charles City VA 23030 804-829-5075
TF: 800-473-5075
Ghosts of Williamsburg Candlelight Tour
5715 Richmond Rd Williamsburg
Attraction Ctr . . . . Williamsburg VA 23185 757-565-4821
TF: 877-624-4678
Haunted Dinner Theatre
5363 Richmond Rd. . . . . Williamsburg VA 23188 888-426-3746
Web: www.wmbgdinnertheater.com
Jamestown Island Explorer Nature Cruise
Jamestown Rd Jamestown
Yacht Basin . . . . Williamsburg VA 23185 757-259-0400
Jamestown Settlement
Rt 31 S & Colonial Pkwy . . . . Williamsburg VA 23185 757-253-4838
Web: www.historyisfun.org/jyf1/js.html
Jamestown Visitor Center
Colonial National Historic Pk PO Box 210 . . . Yorktown VA 23690 757-898-3400
Lee Hall Mansion 163 Yorktown Rd . . . . . Newport News VA 23603 757-888-3371
Web: www.leehall.org
Mariners' Museum 100 Museum Dr . . . . . Newport News VA 23606 757-596-2222 591-7310
Web: www.mariner.org ■ *E-mail:* info@mariner.org
Muscarelle Museum of Art
PO Box 8795 . . . . Williamsburg VA 23187 757-221-2700 221-2711
Web: www.wm.edu/muscarelle
Music Theatre of Williamsburg
7575 Richmond Rd. . . . . Williamsburg VA 23188 757-564-0200 229-7130
TF: 888-687-4220 ■ *Web:* www.musictheatre.com
■ *E-mail:* info@musictheatre.com
Mystery Dinner Playhouse
5351 Richmond Rd Ramada Inn
Central Williamsburg . . . . Williamsburg VA 23188 888-471-4802
Web: www.mysterydinner.com/williamsburg.htm
■ *E-mail:* info@mysterydinner.com
Rockefeller Abby Aldrich Folk Art Center
307 S England St . . . . Williamsburg VA 23185 757-229-1000 565-8915
Rockefeller Winthrop Archaeology
Museum 8797 Pocahontas Tr
Carter's Grove. Williamsburg VA 23187 757-229-1000
Rosie Rumpe's Regal Dumpe Dinner
Theatre 1402 Richmond Rd Quality
Inn Historic . . . . Williamsburg VA 23185 757-565-4443
Web: www.rosierumpes.com ■ *E-mail:* iact@aol.com
Sherwood Forest Plantation
14501 John Tyler Memorial Hwy . . . . Charles City VA 23030 804-829-5377 829-2947
Web: www.sherwoodforest.org ■ *E-mail:* ktyler1@aol.com
Student Dinner Theatre
5363 Richmond Rd. . . . . Williamsburg VA 23188 888-426-3746
US Army Transportation Museum
Bldg 300 Besson Hall . . . . Fort Eustis VA 23604 757-878-1182 878-5656
Web: www.eustis.army.mil/dptmsec/museum.htm
■ *E-mail:* atzfptm@eustis.army.mil
Virginia Living Museum
524 J Clyde Morris Blvd . . . . Newport News VA 23601 757-595-1900 599-4897
Web: www.valivingmuseum.org
Water Country USA
176 Water Country Pkwy . . . . Williamsburg VA 23185 757-229-9300 220-2816
TF: 800-343-7946
■ *Web:* www.4adventure.com/waterparks/watercountry/frame.html
Williamsburg Players 200 Hubbard Ln . . . . Williamsburg VA 23185 757-229-0431
Williamsburg Soap & Candle Co Candle
Factory Outlet 7521 Richmond Rd . . . . . Williamsburg VA 23188 757-564-3354 564-8453
TF Orders: 800-367-9722 ■ *Web:* www.wmbg.com/candles
■ *E-mail:* candles@wmbg.com
Williamsburg Winery Ltd
5800 Wessex Hundred. . . . . Williamsburg VA 23185 757-229-0999 229-0911
Web: www.williamsburgwineryltd.com ■ *E-mail:* wine@wmbgwine.com
Yorktown Battlefield
Colonial National Historical Pk PO
Box 210. . . . . Yorktown VA 23690 757-898-3400
Yorktown Victory Center
Old Rt 238 & Colonial Pkwy. . . . . Yorktown VA 23690 757-253-4838
Web: www.historyisfun.org/jyf1/yvc.html

— Events —

Phone

A Colonial Christmas (late November-late December) 757-253-4838

Williamsburg — Events (Cont'd)

	Phone
Annual Garden Symposium (late March)	800-603-0948
Berkeley Plantation's Colonial Christmas (mid-December)	804-829-6018
Civil War Encampment (late July-early August)	804-829-5075
Civil War Weekend (late May)	757-898-3400
Feast & the Fury Living History Weekend (mid-October)	804-829-5121
Fife Fiddle & Fun (late April)	757-253-4838
First Assembly Day (late July)	757-898-3400
Grand Illuminaton The (early December)	800-447-8679
Historic Garden Week (mid-late April)	804-644-7776
Independence Day Celebration (July 4)	757-890-3300
Jamestown Founding Weekend (mid-May)	757-898-3400
Jamestown Landing Day (May 13)	757-253-4838
Lighted Boat Parade (early December)	757-898-5060
Michelob Championship at Kingsmill (early October)	757-253-3985
President Tyler's Birthday Celebration (March 29)	804-829-5377
Revolutionary War Weekend (late April)	757-898-3400
Virginia's First Thanksgiving Festival (early November)	804-829-6018
Williamsburg Area Christmas Parade (early December)	757-229-6511
Williamsburg Folk Art Show (mid-April)	717-337-3060
Williamsburg Independence Day (July 4)	800-447-8678
Williamsburg's First Night Celebration (December 31)	757-258-0015
Winter & Wine Festival (early December)	757-229-0999
Yorktown Day Celebration (mid-late October)	757-890-3300
Yorktown Holiday Tree Lighting (early December)	757-890-3300
Yorktown Victory Celebration (late October)	757-253-4838

Washington

Population (1999): 5,756,361 **Area (sq mi): 71,302**

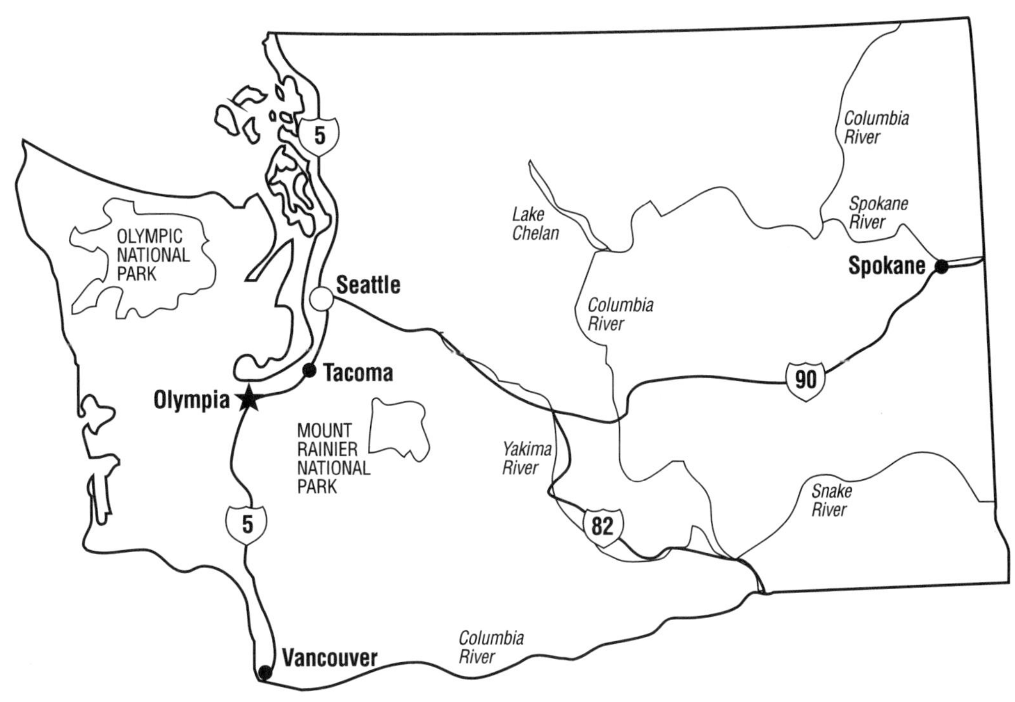

— State Information Sources —

	Phone	Fax
Association of Washington Business PO Box 658 . . . Olympia WA 98507	360-943-1600	943-5811
TF: 800-521-9325 ■ *Web:* www.awb.org ■ *E-mail:* members@awb.org		
Washington Community Trade & Economic Development Dept 906 Columbia St SW . . . Olympia WA 98504	360-753-2200	586-3582
Web: www.wa.gov/cted		
Washington State Government Information . . .	360-753-5000	
Web: access.wa.gov		
Washington State Library PO Box 42460 . . . Olympia WA 98504	360-753-5592	586-7575
Web: www.wa.gov/wsl		
Washington State Parks & Recreation Commission PO Box 42650 . . . Olympia WA 98504	360-902-8500	753-1594
TF: 800-233-0321 ■ *Web:* www.parks.wa.gov		
Washington Tourism Div PO Box 42500 . . . Olympia WA 98504	360-753-5600	753-4470
TF: 800-544-1800 ■ *Web:* www.tourism.wa.gov		

ON-LINE RESOURCES

Cascade Loop Scenic Highway Guide . . . www.cascadeloop.com
Cybertourist Washington . . . www.cybertourist.com/washington.shtml
Destination Northwest: Washington . . . www.destinationnw.com/washington
EasternWashington.com . . . www.easternwashington.com
Olympic Peninsula Travel Assn . . . www.waypt.com/opta
Online Highways Travel Guide to Washington . . . www.ohwy.com/wa/homepage.htm
Rough Guide Travel Washington . . . travel.roughguides.com/content/1508/index.htm
Travel in Washington . . . www.travel-in-wa.com
Travel.org-Washington . . . travel.org/washing.html
Washington Cities . . . dir.yahoo.com/Regional/U_S__States/Washington/Cities
Washington Counties & Regions . . . dir.yahoo.com/Regional/U_S__States/Washington/Counties_and_Regions
Washington Place Names Database . . . www.tpl.lib.wa.us/v2/nwroom/wanames.htm
Washington Scenario . . . scenariousa.dstylus.com/wa/indexf.htm
Washington State @ Travel Notes . . . www.travelnotes.org/NorthAmerica/washington.htm
Washington State Internet Maps . . . www.wamaps.com
Washington Travel & Tourism Guide . . . www.travel-library.com/north_america/usa/washington/index.html
WesternWashington.com . . . www.westernwashington.com
What's Up Washington! . . . www.whatsupwashington.com
Yahoo! Get Local Washington . . . dir.yahoo.com/Regional/U_S__States/Washington

— Cities Profiled —

Page

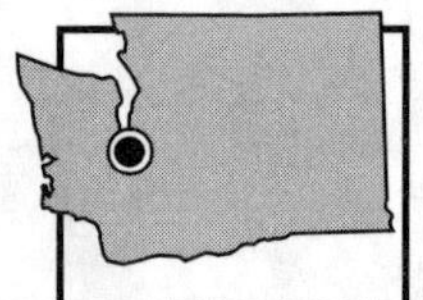

Olympia

Olympia, Washington's capital, is situated at the southern end of Puget Sound, with Seattle to the north and Mt. Saint Helens to the south, and serves as a gateway to the Olympic Peninsula and the beaches of the Pacific Ocean. The Olympic Mountains from which the city derives its name rise across the water west of the city, with Mt. Ranier and the Cascades to the east. The tower at Percival Landing Park in Olympia provides a view that spans from the Capitol dome to the Olympic Mountains. The tower is situated on a one-and-a-half-mile-long public boardwalk that wraps around a tiny harbor and provides a link to the Olympia Farmers Market. Nisqually National Wildlife Refuge and nearby Wolf Haven provide homes to a variety of wildlife. Wolf Haven is a sanctuary for abandoned or displaced captive-born wolves and currently houses 40 wolves. Nisqually residents include owls, ducks, salmon, and small mammals, and the Refuge's mixed conifer forests on bluffs above the delta serve as perches for bald eagle and osprey and as a nesting site for blue herons.

Population	39,188	**Longitude**	122-93-91 W
Area (Land)	16.1 sq mi	**County**	Thurston
Area (Water)	1.8 sq mi	**Time Zone**	PST
Elevation	100 ft	**Area Code/s**	360
Latitude	47-02-70 N		

— Average Temperatures and Precipitation —

TEMPERATURES

	Jan	Feb	Mar	Apr	May	Jun	Jul	Aug	Sep	Oct	Nov	Dec
High	44	50	54	59	65	71	77	77	71	61	50	44
Low	32	33	34	36	41	46	49	50	45	39	35	32

PRECIPITATION

	Jan	Feb	Mar	Apr	May	Jun	Jul	Aug	Sep	Oct	Nov	Dec
Inches	8.0	5.8	5.0	3.3	2.1	1.6	0.8	1.3	2.3	4.3	8.1	8.1

— Important Phone Numbers —

	Phone		*Phone*
AAA	360-357-5561	**Medical Referral**	360-352-1417
Dental Referral	800-917-6453	**Poison Control Center**	800-732-6985
Emergency	911	**Weather**	360-357-6453

— Information Sources —

				Phone	*Fax*
Better Business Bureau Serving Oregon & Western Washington 4800 S 188th St Suite 222 *Web:* www.seatac.bbb.org	SeaTac	WA	98188	206-431-2222	431-2211
Olympia City Hall PO Box 1967 *Web:* www.olywa.net/isd/olympia.htm	Olympia	WA	98507	360-753-8447	753-8165
Olympia Mayor PO Box 1967	Olympia	WA	98507	360-753-8450	709-2791
Olympia/Thurston County Chamber of Commerce PO Box 1427 *Web:* www.olympiachamber.com ■ *E-mail:* info@olympiachamber.com	Olympia	WA	98507	360-357-3362	357-3376
State Capital Visitor Center 14th & Capitol Way	Olympia	WA	98504	360-586-3460	586-4636
Thurston County 2000 Lakeridge Dr SW Bldg 2 *Web:* www.halcyon.com/thurston/ ■ *E-mail:* comment@co.thurston.wa.us	Olympia	WA	98502	360-786-5430	754-4060
Timberland Regional Library 415 Airdustrial Way SW *Web:* www.timberland.lib.wa.us	Olympia	WA	98501	360-943-5001	586-6838

On-Line Resources

Anthill City Guide Olympia	www.anthill.com/city.asp?city=olympia
Area Guide Olympia	olympia.areaguides.net
City Knowledge Olympia	www.cityknowledge.com/wa_olympia.htm
Excite.com Olympia City Guide	www.excite.com/travel/countries/united_states/washington/olympia
Olympia Online	www.olympiaonline.com
Online Highways Travel Guide to Olympia	www.ohwy.com/wa/o/olympia.htm
Welcome to Olympia Washington	www.city-olympia.com/

— Transportation Services —

AIRPORTS

■ **Seattle-Tacoma International Airport (SEA)**

	Phone
45 miles NW of downtown Olympia (approx 60 minutes)	206-431-4444

Airport Transportation

	Phone
Capital Aeroporter $22 fare to downtown Olympia	360-754-7113
Centralia Sea-Tac Airport Shuttle $24 fare to downtown Olympia	800-773-9490

Commercial Airlines

	Phone		*Phone*
Aeroflot	888-686-4949	**Kenmore Air Harbor**	800-543-9595
Alaska	206-433-3100	**Northwest**	800-225-2525
America West	206-433-5704	**Scandinavian**	800-221-2350
American	800-433-7300	**Shuttle by United**	800-748-8853
British Airways	800-247-9297	**TWA**	800-221-2000
Continental	206-624-1740	**United**	800-241-6522
Harbor	800-359-3220	**United Express**	800-241-6522
Horizon	800-547-9308	**US Airways**	800-428-4322

Charter Airlines

	Phone		*Phone*
Flightcraft	206-764-6100	**Galvin Flying Service**	206-763-0350

CAR RENTALS

	Phone		*Phone*
Alamo	206-433-0182	**Hertz**	206-433-5275
Avis	206-433-5231	**National**	206-433-5501
Budget	206-682-2277	**Thrifty**	206-246-7565
Dollar	206-433-5825		

LIMO/TAXI

	Phone		*Phone*
Alexis Limousine	360-491-4728	**DC Cab Co**	360-786-5226
Bayview Limousine	253-474-6300	**Red Top Taxi**	360-357-3700
Capital City Taxi	360-357-4949		

MASS TRANSIT

	Phone
Capitol Shuttle free	360-786-1881
Intercity Transit $.60 Base fare	360-786-1881

RAIL/BUS

				Phone
Amtrak Station 6600 Yelm Hwy SE	Lacey	WA	98513	360-923-4602
Greyhound Bus Station 107 E 7th St *TF:* 800-231-2222	Olympia	WA	98501	360-357-5541

— Accommodations —

HOTELS, MOTELS, RESORTS

				Phone	*Fax*
Bailey Motor Inn 3333 Martin Way E	Olympia	WA	98506	360-491-7515	
Best Western Aladdin Motor Inn 900 Capitol Way S *TF:* 800-317-7771	Olympia	WA	98501	360-352-7200	352-0846
Best Western Tumwater Inn 5188 Capitol Blvd *TF:* 800-528-1234	Tumwater	WA	98501	360-956-1235	956-1235
Carriage Inn Motel 1211 Quince St SE	Olympia	WA	98501	360-943-4710	943-0804

Olympia — Hotels, Motels, Resorts (Cont'd)

Name / Address	City	State	Zip	Phone	Fax
Cavanaugh's 2300 Evergreen Park Dr SW *TF:* 800-325-4000	Olympia	WA	98502	360-943-4000	357-6604
Comfort Inn 4700 Park Center Ave NE *TF:* 800-228-5150	Lacey	WA	98516	360-456-6300	456-7423
Days Inn 120 College St SE *TF:* 800-282-7028	Olympia	WA	98503	360-493-1991	493-1991
Golden Gavel Motor Hotel 909 Capitol Way S	Olympia	WA	98501	360-352-8533	
Harbinger Inn Bed & Breakfast 1136 East Bay Dr NE	Olympia	WA	98506	360-754-0389	
Holiday Inn Express 4704 Park Center Ave NE *TF:* 800-465-4329	Olympia	WA	98516	360-412-1200	412-1100
Holly Motel 2816 Martin Way E	Olympia	WA	98506	360-943-3000	
Lee Street Suites 348 Lee St SW	Olympia	WA	98501	360-943-8391	943-8428
Motel 6 400 Lee St SW *TF:* 800-466-8356	Tumwater	WA	98501	360-754-7320	705-0655
Prairie Motel 700 Prairie Park Ln	Yelm	WA	98597	360-458-8300	458-8301
Ramada Inn Governor House Hotel 621 S Capitol Way *TF:* 800-272-6232	Olympia	WA	98501	360-352-7700	943-9349
Ranch Motel 8819 Martin Way E	Olympia	WA	98516	360-491-5410	
Salmon Shores Resort 5446 Black Lake Blvd SW	Olympia	WA	98512	360-357-8618	956-9116
Shalimar Suites 5895 Capitol Blvd S	Olympia	WA	98501	360-943-8391	943-8428
Super 8 Motel 4615 Martin Way SE	Lacey	WA	98503	360-459-8888	438-0179
Tyee Hotel 500 Tyee Dr SW *TF:* 800-386-8933	Tumwater	WA	98512	360-352-0511	943-6448

— Restaurants —

Name / Address	City	State	Zip	Phone
Apollo's (Italian) 2010 Harrison Ave NW	Olympia	WA	98502	360-754-7444
Budd Bay Cafe (Seafood) 525 N Columbia St *Web:* www.olywa.net/bbaycafe/	Olympia	WA	98501	360-357-6963
Capitale Espresso Grill (International) 609 Capitol Way S	Olympia	WA	98501	360-352-8007
Casa Mia (Italian) 716 Plum St S	Olympia	WA	98501	360-352-0440
El Sarape (Mexican) 4043 Martin Way E	Olympia	WA	98506	360-459-5525
Emperor's Palace (Chinese) 400 Cooper Point Rd SW	Olympia	WA	98502	360-352-0777
Falls Terrace (American) 106 S Deschutes Way	Tumwater	WA	98501	360-943-7830
Far East Restaurant (Asian) 6327 Capitol Blvd S	Olympia	WA	98501	360-534-0306
Fishbowl Brew Pub & Cafe (Mexican) 515 Jefferson St SE	Olympia	WA	98501	360-943-3650
Fuji Teriyaki (Japanese) 214 4th Ave W	Olympia	WA	98501	360-352-0306
Gardner's Seafood & Pasta (Italian) 111 Thurston Ave NW	Olympia	WA	98501	360-786-8466
Genoas on the Bay (Steak/Seafood) 1525 N Washington St	Olympia	WA	98507	360-943-7770
Keg The (Steak/Seafood) 625 Blacklake Blvd	Olympia	WA	98502	360-754-4434
King Solomon's Reef (American) 212 E 4th Ave	Olympia	WA	98501	360-357-5552
La Petit Maison (French) 101 Division St	Olympia	WA	98502	360-943-8812
Little Saigon Cuisine (Vietnamese) 237 Division St NW	Olympia	WA	98502	360-943-8013
Oyster House (Seafood) 320 4th Ave W	Olympia	WA	98502	360-753-7000
Parker House (Steak) 900 Capitol Way S	Olympia	WA	98501	360-754-9409
Peppers South Of The Border (Mexican) 422 Legion Way SE	Olympia	WA	98501	360-943-1111
Pipers Lady (Irish) 200 4th Ave W	Olympia	WA	98501	360-943-5575
Saigon Rendez-vous (Vietnamese) 117 5th Ave SW	Olympia	WA	98501	360-352-1989
Sampan Restaurant (Chinese) 922 Hensley St NE	Olympia	WA	98516	360-456-0826
Santosh (Indian) 116 4th Ave W	Olympia	WA	98501	360-943-3442
Thai Pavillion (Thai) 303 4th Ave E	Olympia	WA	98501	360-943-9093
Trinacria Ristorante (Italian) 113 Capitol Way N	Olympia	WA	98501	360-352-8892
Urban Onion (Vegetarian) 116 Legion Way SE	Olympia	WA	98501	360-943-9242

— Goods and Services —

SHOPPING

Name / Address	City	State	Zip	Phone
Capital Mall 324 Capital Mall Dr	West Olympia	WA	98502	360-754-8017
Centralia Square 201 S Pearl St	Centralia	WA	98531	360-736-6406
South Sound Center Mall 691 Sleater Kinney Rd SE Suite 100	Lacey	WA	98503	360-491-6850

BANKS

Name / Address	City	State	Zip	Phone	Fax
Continental Savings Bank 720 Lilly Rd	Olympia	WA	98501	360-438-4200	438-1106
Heritage Bank FSB 201 W 5th Ave	Olympia	WA	98501	360-943-1500	943-8046
KeyBank NA 3611 Martin Way E	Olympia	WA	98506	360-753-8533	753-8536
West Coast Bank 2850 Harrison Ave NW *TF:* 800-847-4983	Olympia	WA	98502	360-754-2400	956-0866

BUSINESS SERVICES

Name	Phone	Name	Phone
Airborne Express	800-247-2676	**Kinko's**	360-459-3680
BAX Global	800-225-5229	**Mail Boxes Etc**	800-789-4623
DHL Worldwide Express	800-225-5345	**Post Office**	800-275-8777
Federal Express	800-238-5355	**UPS**	800-742-5877
Kelly Services	360-493-0160		

— Media —

PUBLICATIONS

Name / Address	City	State	Zip	Phone	Fax
Olympian The‡ PO Box 407 *Web:* www.theolympian.com	Olympia	WA	98507	360-754-5400	357-0202
South Sound Business Examiner 204 N Quince St Suite 200	Olympia	WA	98506	360-956-3133	956-3135

‡Daily newspapers

TELEVISION

Name / Address	City	State	Zip	Phone	Fax
KCPQ-TV Ch 13 (Fox) 1813 Westlake Ave N *Web:* www.kcpq.com ■ *E-mail:* reception@kcpq.com	Seattle	WA	98109	206-674-1313	674-1777
KCTS-TV Ch 9 (PBS) 401 Mercer St *Web:* www.kcts.org ■ *E-mail:* viewer@kcts.org	Seattle	WA	98109	206-728-6463	443-6691
KING-TV Ch 5 (NBC) 333 Dexter Ave N *Web:* www.king5.com ■ *E-mail:* kingtv@king5.com	Seattle	WA	98109	206-448-5555	448-4525
KIRO-TV Ch 7 (CBS) 2807 3rd Ave *Web:* www.kirotv.com ■ *E-mail:* kironews7@kiro-tv.com	Seattle	WA	98121	206-728-7777	441-4840
KOMO-TV Ch 4 (ABC) 100 4th Ave N *Web:* www.komotv.com	Seattle	WA	98109	206-443-4000	443-3422
KSTW-TV Ch 11 (UPN) PO Box 11411 *Web:* www.paramountstations.com/KSTW ■ *E-mail:* kstw98d@prodigy.com	Tacoma	WA	98411	253-572-5789	272-7581

RADIO

Name / Address	City	State	Zip	Phone	Fax
KGY-AM 1240 kHz (AC) 1240 NE Washington St *Web:* www.kgyradio.com ■ *E-mail:* kgyeng@kgyradio.com	Olympia	WA	98501	360-943-1240	352-1222
KGY-FM 96.9 kHz (Ctry) 1240 NE Washington St *Web:* www.kgyradio.com ■ *E-mail:* kgyeng@kgyradio.com	Olympia	WA	98501	360-943-1240	352-1222
KXXO-FM 96.1 MHz (AC) 119 N Washington St	Olympia	WA	98501	360-943-9937	352-3643

— Colleges/Universities —

Name / Address	City	State	Zip	Phone	Fax
Evergreen State College 2700 Evergreen Pkwy NW *Web:* www.evergreen.edu	Olympia	WA	98505	360-866-6000	866-6680
South Puget Sound Community College 2011 Mottman Rd SW *Web:* www.spscc.ctc.edu	Olympia	WA	98512	360-754-7711	664-4336

— Hospitals —

Name / Address	City	State	Zip	Phone	Fax
Columbia Capital Medical Center 3900 Capital Mall Dr SW	Olympia	WA	98502	360-754-5858	956-2574
Providence Saint Peter Hospital 413 NE Lilly Rd *TF:* 888-492-9480	Olympia	WA	98506	360-491-9480	493-7089

— Attractions —

Name / Address	City	State	Zip	Phone	Fax
Bigelow House 918 Glass Ave	Olympia	WA	98506	360-753-1215	
Executive Mansion 14th Ave & Capitol Way Capitol Campus	Olympia	WA	98504	360-586-8687	
Hands On Children's Museum 106 11th Ave SW *Web:* www.wln.com/~deltapac/hocm.html	Olympia	WA	98501	360-956-0818	754-8626
Japanese Garden 1010 Plum St SE	Olympia	WA	98501	360-753-8380	

Olympia — Attractions (Cont'd)

				Phone	Fax
Little Creek Casino W 91 Hwy 108	Shelton	WA	98584	360-427-7711	427-7868
TF: 800-667-7711					
Miller Brewing Co Custer Way & Schmidt Pl	Tumwater	WA	98501	360-754-5177	754-5252
Millersylvania State Park 12245 Tilley Rd S	Olympia	WA	98502	360-753-1519	
Nisqually National Wildlife Refuge 100 Brown Farm Rd	Olympia	WA	98516	360-753-9467	534-9302
Nisqually Reach Nature Center 4949 D'Milluhr Rd NE	Olympia	WA	98516	360-459-0387	
Olympia Farmers Market 7010 N Capitol Way	Olympia	WA	98501	360-352-9096	
Web: www.farmers-market.org/					
Olympia Film Society 416 Washington St SE	Olympia	WA	98501	360-754-6670	943-9100
Web: www.olywa.net/ofs ■ *E-mail:* ofs@olywa.net					
Olympia Little Theatre 1925 Miller Ave NE	Olympia	WA	98506	360-786-9484	
Web: www.orcalink.com/~olt/					
Olympia Symphony Orchestra 512 Washington St SE Washington Ctr for the Performing Arts	Olympia	WA	98501	360-753-0074	753-4735
Rainbow Falls State Park 4008 State Hwy 6	Chehalis	WA	98532	360-291-3767	
TF: 800-233-0321					
Tenino Depot Museum 339 West Park South Thurston County Historical Society	Tenino	WA	98589	360-264-4321	
Tolmie State Park 8 miles NE of Olympia Johnson Pt	Olympia	WA	98512	360-456-6464	
TF: 800-233-0321					
Tumwater Falls Park Deschutes St	Tumwater	WA	98502	360-943-2550	
Washington Center for the Performing Arts 512 Washington St SE	Olympia	WA	98501	360-753-8586	754-1177
Web: www.washingtoncenter.com ■ *E-mail:* info@washingtoncenter.com					
Washington State Capital Museum 211 W 21st Ave	Olympia	WA	98501	360-753-2580	586-8322
Washington State Capitol PO Box 41034	Olympia	WA	98504	360-586-8687	664-9647
Wolf Haven International 3111 Offut Lake Rd	Tenino	WA	98589	360-264-4695	264-4639
Web: www.wolfhaven.org ■ *E-mail:* wolfhvn@aol.com					

— Events —

	Phone
Capital Food & Wine Festival (late March)	360-438-4366
Capital Lakefair (mid-July)	360-586-3460
Greater Olympia Dixieland Jazz Festival (early July)	360-754-8129
Harbor Days (September)	360-352-4557
Music in the Park (July-August)	360-357-8948
Olympia Film Festival (mid-late October)	360-754-6670
Oregon Trail Days (late July)	360-264-5075
Parade of Lighted Ships (early December)	360-357-6767
Shakespeare Festival (late May-August)	360-943-9492
Super Saturday (June)	360-866-6000
Thurston County Fair (late July-early August)	360-786-5453
Winterfest in Historic Tenino (early December)	360-264-5855
Wooden Boat Festival (mid-May)	360-943-5404
Yelm Prairie Days (mid-July)	360-458-3492

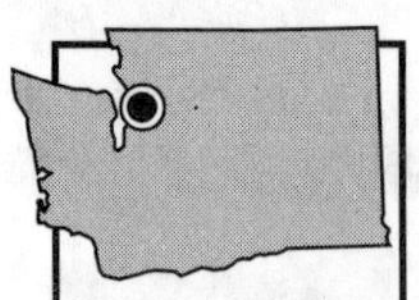

Seattle

Surrounded by the Cascade and Olympic mountain ranges, Puget Sound, and Lake Washington, Seattle offers spectacular views and a variety of attractions for residents and visitors alike. Seattle Center, one of the city's main attractions, is an urban park with outdoor stages and the Pacific Science Center. The Seattle Center is also the site of the Seattle Arts Festival, Bumbershoot, which is ranked among the top festivals nationwide. The Space Needle towers above Seattle Center and is visible from almost any part of the downtown area. Underground tours of Pioneer Square, the birthplace of Seattle, lead below the streets and provide a glimpse of Seattle prior to the great fire of 1889. The Kingdome and Klondike Gold Rush National Historic Park are also located in Pioneer Square. Seattle's Pike Place Market, one of the last remaining farmer's markets in the country, is situated along the waterfront of Elliott Bay.

Population	536,978	**Longitude**	122-33-08 W
Area (Land)	83.9 sq mi	**County**	King
Area (Water)	58.7 sq mi	**Time Zone**	PST
Elevation	125 ft	**Area Code/s**	206
Latitude	47-60-64 N		

— Average Temperatures and Precipitation —

TEMPERATURES

	Jan	Feb	Mar	Apr	May	Jun	Jul	Aug	Sep	Oct	Nov	Dec
High	46	51	54	58	64	70	74	74	69	60	52	46
Low	36	38	40	43	48	54	57	57	53	47	41	37

PRECIPITATION

	Jan	Feb	Mar	Apr	May	Jun	Jul	Aug	Sep	Oct	Nov	Dec
Inches	5.4	4.0	3.8	2.6	2.0	1.8	0.9	1.3	2.0	3.3	5.5	6.0

— Important Phone Numbers —

	Phone		Phone
AAA	206-448-5353	**Poison Control Center**	206-526-2121
American Express Travel	206-441-8622	**Time/Temp**	206-361-8463
Emergency	911	**Travelers Aid**	206-461-3888
HotelDocs	800-468-3537	**Weather**	206-464-2000
Medical Referral	206-622-9933		

— Information Sources —

				Phone	Fax
Better Business Bureau Serving Oregon & Western Washington 4800 S 188th St Suite 222	SeaTac	WA	98188	206-431-2222	431-2211
Web: www.seatac.bbb.org					
Greater Seattle Chamber of Commerce 1301 5th Ave Suite 2400	Seattle	WA	98101	206-389-7200	389-7288
Web: www.seattlechamber.com					
King County 516 3rd Ave Rm 400	Seattle	WA	98104	206-296-4040	296-0194
Web: www.metrokc.gov					
Seattle City Hall 600 4th Ave	Seattle	WA	98104	206-386-1234	
Web: www.ci.seattle.wa.us					
Seattle Community Network PO Box 85539	Seattle	WA	98145	206-365-4528	362-1495
Web: www.scn.org ■ *E-mail:* help@scn.org					
Seattle-King County Convention & Visitors Bureau 520 Pike St Suite 1300	Seattle	WA	98101	206-461-5840	461-5855
TF: 800-535-7071 ■ *Web:* www.seeseattle.org/home/skccvb.htm					
Seattle Mayor 600 4th Ave 12th Fl	Seattle	WA	98104	206-684-4000	684-5360
Web: www.ci.seattle.wa.us/seattle/mayor					
Seattle Planning Dept 600 4th Ave Rm 300	Seattle	WA	98104	206-684-8080	233-0085
Web: www.ci.seattle.wa.us/planning					
Seattle Public Library 1000 4th Ave	Seattle	WA	98104	206-386-4100	386-4119
Web: www.spl.lib.wa.us					
Washington State Convention & Trade Center 800 Convention Pl	Seattle	WA	98101	206-694-5000	694-5399
Web: www.wsctc.com ■ *E-mail:* waconv@halcyon.com					

On-Line Resources

4Seattle.com	www.4seattle.com
About.com Guide to Seattle/Tacoma	seattle.about.com/local/pacnwus/seattle
All Seattle	www.allcitynet.com/seattle
Anthill City Guide Seattle	www.anthill.com/city.asp?city=seattle
Area Guide Seattle	seattle.areaguides.net
Art Guide Northwest	www.artguidenw.com
Boulevards Seattle	www.seattle.com
Bradmans.com Seattle	www.bradmans.com/scripts/display_city.cgi?city=243
City Knowledge Seattle	www.cityknowledge.com/wa_seattle.htm
Cityhits Seattle	www.cityhits.com/seattle/
CitySearch Seattle	seattle.citysearch.com
CuisineNet Seattle	www.cuisinenet.com/restaurant/seattle/index.shtml

Seattle — On-Line Resources (Cont'd)

DigitalCity Seattle .... www.digitalcity.com/seattle
Excite.com Seattle City Guide .... www.excite.com/travel/countries/united_states/washington/seattle
Greater Seattle InfoGuide .... www.seattleinfoguide.com/
NITC Travelbase City Guide Seattle .... www.travelbase.com/auto/guides/seattle-area-wa.html
Rough Guide Travel Seattle travel.roughguides.com/content/4604/
Savvy Diner Guide to Seattle Restaurants .... www.savvydiner.com/seattle/
Seattle .... sensemedia.net/seattle
Seattle CityWomen .... www.citywomen.com/seatwomen.htm
Seattle Home Page .... www.seattle.net/SeattleHome.html
Seattle Web .... www.seattleweb.com/
Seattle.Bizhost.com .... seattle.bizhost.com/
Seattle.TheLinks.com .... seattle.thelinks.com/
SeattleSquare.com .... www.seattlesquare.com/
Virtual Voyages Seattle .... www.virtualvoyages.com/usa/wa/seattle/seattle.sht
Yahoo! Seattle .... seattle.yahoo.com

— Transportation Services —

AIRPORTS

Phone

■ **Seattle-Tacoma International Airport (SEA)**

10 miles S of downtown (approx 20 minutes) 206-431-4444
Web: www.seatac.org

Airport Transportation

	Phone
Gray Line Airport Express $7.50 fare to downtown	206-626-6088
Shuttle Express $18 fare to downtown	206-622-1424

Commercial Airlines

	Phone		*Phone*
Aeroflot	888-686-4949	**Kenmore Air Harbor**	800-543-9595
Alaska	206-433-3100	**Northwest**	800-225-2525
America West	206-433-5704	**Scandinavian**	800-221-2350
American	800-433-7300	**Shuttle by United**	800-748-8853
American Trans Air	800-225-2995	**Southwest**	800-435-9792
British Airways	800-247-9297	**Thai**	800-426-5204
Continental	206-624-1740	**TWA**	800-221-2000
Delta	800-221-1212	**United**	800-241-6522
Harbor	800-359-3220	**United Express**	800-241-6522
Horizon	800-547-9308	**US Airways**	800-428-4322
Japan	800-525-3663	**Vanguard**	800-826-4827

Charter Airlines

	Phone		*Phone*
Crossings Aviation Inc	253-851-2381	**Galvin Flying Service**	206-763-0350
Flightcraft	206-764-6100	**Snohomish Flying Service Inc**	360-568-1541

CAR RENTALS

	Phone		*Phone*
Advantage	206-824-0161	**Enterprise**	206-382-1051
Avis	206-433-5231	**Hertz**	206-433-5275
Budget	206-682-2277	**National**	206-433-5501
Dollar	206-433-5825	**Thrifty**	206-246-7565

LIMO/TAXI

	Phone		*Phone*
British Motorcoach	206-622-0444	**Star Limousine**	206-363-7827
Checker Deluxe Cab	206-622-1234	**Washington Limousine**	206-523-8000
Far West Cab	206-622-1717	**Yellow Cab**	206-622-6500
Graytop Cab	206-782-8294		

MASS TRANSIT

	Phone
Metropolitan Transit $1.25 Base fare	206-553-3000
Washington State Ferry System fare varies with destination	206-464-6400

RAIL/BUS

Phone

Greyhound Bus Station 811 Stewart St .... Seattle WA 98101 206-628-5526
TF: 800-231-2222
King Street Amtrak Station 3035 S Jackson St .... Seattle WA 98104 206-382-4125

— Accommodations —

HOTEL RESERVATION SERVICES

Phone *Fax*

Bed & Breakfast Association of Seattle 206-547-1020
TF: 800-348-5630 ■ *Web:* www.seattlebandbs.com
California Reservations 415-252-1107 252-1483
TF: 800-576-0003 ■ *Web:* www.cal-res.com
Executive Inn Express 206-223-9300 233-0241
TF: 800-906-6226
Executive Residence Inc 206-329-8000 382-0511
TF: 800-428-3867 ■ *Web:* www.halcyon.com/execres/execres
■ *E-mail:* execres@halcyon.com
Hotel Reservations Network Inc 214-361-7311 361-7299
TF Sales: 800-964-6835 ■ *Web:* www.hoteldiscount.com
Pacific Reservation Service 206-439-7677 431-0932
TF: 800-684-2932 ■ *Web:* www.seattlebedandbreakfast.com/
■ *E-mail:* pacificb@nwlink.com
Quikbook 212-532-1660 532-1556
TF: 800-789-9887 ■ *Web:* www.quikbook.com
Seattle Super Saver 206-461-5800 461-5855
TF: 800-535-7071 ■ *Web:* www.seeseattle.org/hotels/superhm.htm

HOTELS, MOTELS, RESORTS

Phone *Fax*

Airport Hilton 17620 Pacific Hwy S .... Seattle WA 98188 206-244-4800 248-4499
TF: 800-445-8667
Airport Plaza Hotel 18601 Pacific Hwy S .... Seattle WA 98188 206-433-0400 241-2222
TF: 877-433-0400
Alderbrook Resort Golf & Conference Center
7101 E SR 106 .... Union WA 98592 360-898-2200 898-4610
TF: 800-622-9370
Alexis Hotel 1007 1st Ave .... Seattle WA 98104 206-624-4844 621-9009
TF: 800-426-7033 ■ *Web:* 135.145.16.183/alexishotel.com
Bellevue Hilton Inn 100 112th Ave NE .... Bellevue WA 98004 425-455-3330 451-2473
TF: 800-235-4458
Best Western Airport Executel
20717 International Blvd .... Seattle WA 98198 206-878-3300 824-9000
TF: 800-648-3311
Best Western Tulalip Inn
6128 33rd Ave NE .... Marysville WA 98271 360-659-4488 659-5688
TF: 800-481-4804
Bestwestern Pioneer Square Hotel
77 Yesler Way .... Seattle WA 98104 206-340-1234 467-0707
TF: 800-800-5514 ■ *Web:* www.pioneersquare.com
■ *E-mail:* info@pioneersquare.com
Cavanaugh's Inn on Fifth Avenue
1415 5th Ave .... Seattle WA 98101 206-971-8000 971-8100
Claremont Hotel 2000 4th Ave .... Seattle WA 98121 206-448-8600 441-7140
TF: 800-448-8601
■ *Web:* www.travelbase.com/destinations/seattle/claremont/
■ *E-mail:* claremont@travelbase.com
Clarion Hotel SeaTac Airport 3000 S 176th St .... Seattle WA 98188 206-242-0200 242-1998
TF: 800-252-7466
Coachman Inn 32959 SR Hwy 20 .... Oak Harbor WA 98277 360-675-0727 675-1419
TF: 800-635-0043
College Inn 4000 University Way NE .... Seattle WA 98105 206-633-4441 547-1335
Crowne Plaza Seattle 1113 6th Ave .... Seattle WA 98101 206-464-1980 340-1617
TF: 800-521-2762
Days Inn Town Center 2205 7th Ave .... Seattle WA 98121 206-448-3434 441-6976
TF: 800-225-7169
Doubletree Hotel 818 112th Ave NE .... Bellevue WA 98004 425-455-1515 454-3964
TF: 800-222-8733
■ *Web:* www.doubletreehotels.com/DoubleT/Hotel141/147/147Main.htm
Doubletree Hotel Seattle Airport
18740 International Blvd .... Seattle WA 98188 206-246-8600 431-8687
TF: 800-222-8733
■ *Web:* www.doubletreehotels.com/DoubleT/Hotel161/163/163Main.htm
Doubletree Inn Southcenter 205 Strander Blvd .... Seattle WA 98188 206-246-8220 575-4749
TF: 800-222-8733
■ *Web:* www.doubletreehotels.com/DoubleT/Hotel100/102/102Main.htm
Doubletree Suites Hotel
16500 Southcenter Pkwy .... Seattle WA 98188 206-575-8220 575-4743
TF: 800-222-8733
■ *Web:* www.doubletreehotels.com/DoubleT/Hotel100/103/103Main.htm
Edgewater Inn 2411 Alaskan Way .... Seattle WA 98121 206-728-7000 441-4119
TF: 800-624-0670 ■ *Web:* www.noblehousehotels.com/edgewater
■ *E-mail:* 75173.2654@compuserve.com
Four Seasons Olympic Hotel 411 University St .... Seattle WA 98101 206-621-1700 682-9633
TF: 800-223-8772 ■ *Web:* www.fourseasons.com/locations/Seattle
Gaslight Inn 1727 15th Ave .... Seattle WA 98122 206-325-3654 328-4803
Hampton Inn & Suites 700 5th Ave N .... Seattle WA 98109 206-282-7700 282-0899
TF: 800-426-7866
Hampton Inn Seattle Airport
19445 International Blvd .... Seattle WA 98188 206-878-1700 824-0720

Seattle — Hotels, Motels, Resorts (Cont'd)

Name / Address	City	State	ZIP	Phone	Fax
Hilton Hotel 1301 6th Ave	Seattle	WA	98101	206-624-0500	682-9029
TF: 800-426-0535 ■ *Web:* www.hilton.com/hotels/SEASHHF					
Holiday Inn 1801 12th Ave NW	Issaquah	WA	98027	425-392-6421	391-4650
TF: 800-465-4329					
■ *Web:* www.basshotels.com/holiday-inn/?_franchisee=SEAIQ					
■ *E-mail:* hiissaquah@aol.com					
Holiday Inn Express SeaTac Airport					
19631 International Blvd	Seattle	WA	98188	206-824-3200	824-3232
TF: 888-824-3200					
Holiday Inn Hotel & Conference Center					
101 128th St SE	Everett	WA	98208	425-337-2900	337-0707
TF: 800-465-4329					
■ *Web:* www.basshotels.com/holiday-inn/?_franchisee=EVEWA					
■ *E-mail:* bob@wiredweb.com					
Holiday Inn Seattle-Tacoma Airport					
17338 International Blvd	Seattle	WA	98188	206-248-1000	242-7089
TF: 800-465-4329					
■ *Web:* www.basshotels.com/holiday-inn/?_franchisee=SEAIA					
■ *E-mail:* hiseatac@seanet.com					
Hotel Monaco Seattle 1101 4th Ave	Seattle	WA	98101	206-621-1770	621-7779
TF: 800-945-2240					
Howard Johnson 2500 Aurora Ave N	Seattle	WA	98109	206-284-1900	283-5298
TF: 877-284-1900					
Hyatt Regency Bellevue					
900 Bellevue Way NE	Bellevue	WA	98004	425-462-1234	646-7567
TF: 800-233-1234					
■ *Web:* www.hyatt.com/usa/bellevue/hotels/hotel_belle.html					
Inn at the Market 86 Pine St	Seattle	WA	98101	206-443-3600	448-0631
TF: 800-446-4484 ■ *Web:* www.innatthemarket.com					
■ *E-mail:* info@innatthemarket.com					
Madison Renaissance Hotel 515 Madison St	Seattle	WA	98104	206-583-0300	622-8635
TF: 800-278-4159					
Marriott Hotel Sea-Tac Airport					
3201 S 176th St	Seattle	WA	98188	206-241-2000	248-0789
TF: 800-643-5479 ■ *Web:* marriotthotels.com/SEAWA					
Mayflower Park Hotel 405 Olive Way	Seattle	WA	98101	206-623-8700	382-6997
TF: 800-426-5100					
Meany Tower Hotel 4507 Brooklyn Ave NE	Seattle	WA	98105	206-634-2000	547-6029
TF: 800-899-0251 ■ *Web:* www.meany.com/					
Pacific Plaza Hotel 400 Spring St	Seattle	WA	98104	206-623-3900	623-2059
TF: 800-426-1165 ■ *Web:* www.pacificplazahotel.com					
Paramount Hotel 724 Pine St	Seattle	WA	98101	206-292-9500	292-8610
TF: 800-426-0670 ■ *Web:* www.westcoasthotels.com/paramount/					
Quality Inn City Center 2224 8th Ave	Seattle	WA	98121	206-624-6820	467-6926
Radisson Hotel Airport 17001 Pacific Hwy S	Seattle	WA	98188	206-244-6000	246-6835
TF: 800-333-3333					
Ramada Inn Downtown 2200 5th Ave	Seattle	WA	98121	206-441-9785	448-0924
TF: 800-272-6232					
Residence Inn by Marriott Seattle Downtown					
800 Fairview Ave N	Seattle	WA	98109	206-624-6000	223-8160
TF: 800-331-3131 ■ *Web:* www.residenceinn.com/SEALU					
Residence Inn by Marriott Seattle South					
16201 W Valley Hwy	Seattle	WA	98188	425-226-5500	271-5023
TF: 800-331-3131 ■ *Web:* residenceinn.com/SEASO					
Roosevelt Hotel 1531 7th Ave	Seattle	WA	98101	206-621-1200	233-0335
TF: 800-426-0670 ■ *Web:* www.westcoasthotels.com/washington.html					
Seattle Inn 225 Aurora Ave N	Seattle	WA	98109	206-728-7666	728-6108
TF: 800-255-7932					
Sheraton Seattle Hotel & Towers					
1400 6th Ave	Seattle	WA	98101	206-621-9000	621-8441
TF: 800-204-6100					
Sixth Avenue Inn 2000 6th Ave	Seattle	WA	98121	206-441-8300	441-9903
TF: 800-648-6440					
Sorrento Hotel 900 Madison St	Seattle	WA	98104	206-622-6400	343-6155
TF: 800-426-1265 ■ *Web:* www.hotelsorrento.com/					
Summerfield Suites 1011 Pike St	Seattle	WA	98101	206-682-8282	682-5315
TF: 800-833-4353					
Travelodge by the Space Needle					
200 6th Ave N	Seattle	WA	98109	206-441-7878	448-4825
Travelodge Seattle City Center 2213 8th Ave	Seattle	WA	98121	206-624-6300	233-0185
TF: 800-578-7878					
Warwick Hotel 401 Lenora St	Seattle	WA	98121	206-443-4300	448-1662
TF: 800-426-9280 ■ *Web:* www.warwickhotel.com/					
■ *E-mail:* warwick@travelbase.com					
WestCoast Camlin Hotel 1619 9th Ave	Seattle	WA	98101	206-682-0100	682-7415
TF: 800-426-0670					
Westin Seattle Hotel 1900 5th Ave	Seattle	WA	98101	206-728-1000	728-2259
TF: 800-228-3000					
Woodmark Hotel 1200 Carillon Point	Kirkland	WA	98033	425-822-3700	822-3699
TF: 800-822-3700 ■ *Web:* www.thewoodmark.com					
■ *E-mail:* mail@thewoodmark.com					

— Restaurants —

Name / Address	City	State	ZIP	Phone
13 Coins (Continental) 125 Boren Ave N	Seattle	WA	98109	206-682-2513
Adriatica (Mediterranean) 1107 Dexter Ave N	Seattle	WA	98109	206-285-5000
Al Boccalino (Italian) 1 Yesler Way	Seattle	WA	98104	206-622-7688
Andaluca (Mediterranean) 405 Olive Way	Seattle	WA	98101	206-382-6999
Andiamo (Italian) 1400 6th Ave	Seattle	WA	98101	206-389-5769
Anthony's Pier 66 (Seafood) 2201 Alaskan Way	Seattle	WA	98121	206-448-6688
Asgard (Continental) 6th Ave & University St 29th Fl	Seattle	WA	98111	206-467-2667
Assaggio Ristorante (Italian) 2010 4th Ave	Seattle	WA	98121	206-441-1399
Avenue One (French) 1921 1st Ave	Seattle	WA	98122	206-441-6139
Belltown Pub (American) 2322 1st Ave	Seattle	WA	98121	206-728-4311
Blowfish Asian Cafe (Asian) 722 Pine St	Seattle	WA	98101	206-467-7777
Bruno's (Mexican/Italian) 1417 3rd Ave	Seattle	WA	98101	206-622-3180
Cafe Nola (Italian) 101 Winslow Way	Seattle	WA	98110	206-842-3822
Cafe Septieme (International) 214 Broadway E	Seattle	WA	98102	206-860-8858
Campagne (French) 86 Pine St	Seattle	WA	98101	206-728-2800
Canlis Restaurant (Steak/Seafood) 2576 Aurora Ave N	Seattle	WA	98109	206-283-3313
Web: www.canlis.com/				
Chez Shea (American) 94 Pike St	Seattle	WA	98101	206-467-9990
Web: www.chezshea.com				
Chutneys (Indian) 519 1st Ave N	Seattle	WA	98109	206-284-6799
Cloud Room (American) 1619 9th Ave	Seattle	WA	98101	206-682-0100
Crab Pot (Seafood) 1301 Alaskan Way	Seattle	WA	98101	206-624-1890
Crepe de Paris (French) 1333 5th Ave	Seattle	WA	98101	206-623-4111
Cutters Bayhouse (American) 2001 Western Ave	Seattle	WA	98121	206-448-4884
Dahlia Lounge (American) 1904 4th Ave	Seattle	WA	98101	206-682-4142
Web: www.tomdouglas.com/				
Elliott's (Seafood) Pier 56 Puget Sound	Seattle	WA	98101	206-623-4340
Etta's Restaurant (Seafood) 2020 Western Ave	Seattle	WA	98121	206-443-6000
Fountain Court (American) 22 103rd Ave NE	Bellevue	WA	98004	425-451-0426
Fuller's (Northwest) 1400 6th Ave	Seattle	WA	98101	206-447-5544
FX McRory's Steak Chop & Oyster House (American)				
419 Occidental St S	Seattle	WA	98104	206-623-4800
Georgian Room (American) 411 University St	Seattle	WA	98101	206-621-7889
Gravity Bar (Vegetarian) 415 Broadway E	Seattle	WA	98102	206-325-7186
Herbfarm (New American) 32804 Issaquah-Fall City Rd	Fall City	WA	98024	206-784-2222
Hillside Bar & Grill (American) 17121 Bothell Way NE	Bothell	WA	98011	425-485-7600
Hunt Club The (American) 900 Madison St	Seattle	WA	98104	206-622-6400
Il Terrazzo Carmine (Italian) 411 1st Ave S	Seattle	WA	98104	206-467-7797
Ivar's Acres of Clams (Seafood) Pier 54	Seattle	WA	98104	206-624-6852
Web: www.ivarsrestaurants.com/				
Jitter Bug (American) 2114 N 45th St	Seattle	WA	98103	206-547-6313
Kaspar's by the Bay (American) 19 W Harrison St	Seattle	WA	98121	206-298-0123
Kells (Irish) 1916 Post Alley	Seattle	WA	98101	206-728-1916
Web: www.kellsirish.com				
Latitude 47 (Seafood) 1232 N Westlake Ave	Seattle	WA	98109	206-284-1047
LeoMelina (Italian) 96 Union St	Seattle	WA	98101	206-623-3783
Mama's Mexican Kitchen (Mexican) 2234 2nd Ave	Seattle	WA	98121	206-728-6262
McCormick & Schmick's (Seafood) 1103 1st Ave	Seattle	WA	98101	206-623-5500
Metropolitan Grill (Steak) 820 2nd Ave	Seattle	WA	98104	206-624-3287
Nikko (Japanese) 1900 5th Ave Westin Hotel	Seattle	WA	98101	206-322-4641
Pabla Indian Cuisine (Indian) 1516 2nd Ave	Seattle	WA	98101	206-623-2868
Palace Kitchen (European) 2030 5th Ave	Seattle	WA	98121	206-448-2001
Palomino Euro Bistro (Mediterranean) 1420 5th Ave	Seattle	WA	98101	206-623-1300
Pescatore (Seafood) 5300 34th Ave NW	Seattle	WA	98107	206-784-1733
Pike Street Cafe (American) 1400 6th Ave	Seattle	WA	98101	206-447-1987
Place Pigalle (International) 81 Pike St	Seattle	WA	98101	206-624-1756
Planet Hollywood (American) 1500 6th Ave Suite 200	Seattle	WA	98101	206-287-0001
Prego's (Italian) 515 Madison St	Seattle	WA	98104	206-583-0300
Ray's Boathouse (Seafood) 6049 Seaview Ave NW	Seattle	WA	98107	206-789-3770
Web: www.rays.com				
Reiner's (European) 1106 8th Ave	Seattle	WA	98101	206-624-2222
Roma on Post (Thai) 83 Spring St	Seattle	WA	98104	206-340-9047
Rover's (French) 2808 E Madison St	Seattle	WA	98112	206-325-7442
Web: www.rovers-seattle.com/				
Roy's Seattle (European) 1900 5th Ave Westin Seattle Hotel	Seattle	WA	98101	206-728-1000
Saleh al Lago (Italian) 6804 East Green Lake Way N	Seattle	WA	98115	206-524-4044
Sazerac (Southern) 1101 4th Ave	Seattle	WA	98101	206-624-7755
Sea Garden Restaurant (Chinese) 509 7th Ave S	Seattle	WA	98104	206-623-2100
Shamiana (Indian/Pakistani) 10724 NE 68th St	Kirkland	WA	98033	425-827-4902
Shilla Restaurant (Japanese/Korean) 2300 8th Ave	Seattle	WA	98121	206-623-9996
Space Needle Restaurant (American) 5th & Broad Sts	Seattle	WA	98109	206-443-2100
Web: spaceneedle.com/restaurants/space_rest.htm				
■ *E-mail:* spaceneedle@digital-sherpas.com				
Swingside Cafe (Italian) 4212 Fremont Ave N	Seattle	WA	98103	206-633-4057
Szmania's (Northwest) 3321 W McGraw St	Seattle	WA	98199	206-284-7305
Theoz Restaurant (New American) 1523 6th Ave	Seattle	WA	98101	206-749-9660
Union Square Grill (Steak/Seafood) 621 Union St	Seattle	WA	98101	206-224-4321
Von's Grand City Cafe (American) 619 Pine St	Seattle	WA	98101	206-621-8667
Wild Ginger Asian Restaurant (Asian) 1400 Western Ave	Seattle	WA	98101	206-623-4450
Wild Hare (American) 2220 Queen Anne Ave N	Seattle	WA	98109	206-285-3360
Zasu Restaurant (Northwest) 608 1st Ave	Seattle	WA	98104	206-682-1200

Seattle (Cont'd)

— Goods and Services —

SHOPPING

				Phone	Fax
Antiques at Pikes Place 92 Stewart St	Seattle	WA	98101	206-441-9643	448-9588
Bay Pavilion 1301 Alaskan Way	Seattle	WA	98101	206-623-8600	343-9173
Bellevue Square 302 Bellevue Sq	Bellevue	WA	98004	425-454-2431	455-3631
Bon Marche Inc 1601 3rd Ave	Seattle	WA	98181	206-506-6000	506-6007
TF: 800-552-7288 ■ *Web:* www.federated-fds.com/divisions/bon1.html					
City Centre 1420 5th Ave	Seattle	WA	98101	206-223-8999	624-8884
Downtown Seattle Pine S to University Sts & 1st-7th Sts	Seattle	WA	98101	206-461-5840	
Nordstrom Inc 1616 6th Ave Suite 500	Seattle	WA	98101	206-364-8800	628-1795
Web: www.nordstrom.com					
Northgate Mall 555 Northgate Mall	Seattle	WA	98125	206-362-4777	361-8760
Pike Place Market 1st Ave & Pike St	Seattle	WA	98101	206-682-7453	625-0646
Pioneer Square Antique Mall 602 1st Ave	Seattle	WA	98104	206-624-1164	
Prime Outlets at Burlington 448 Fashion Way	Burlington	WA	98233	360-757-3549	
Rainier Square 4th & 5th Aves-betw Union & University Sts	Seattle	WA	98101	206-623-0340	
SeaTac Mall 1928 S SeaTac Mall	Federal Way	WA	98003	253-839-6151	946-1413
Southcenter Mall 633 Southcenter Mall	Seattle	WA	98188	206-246-7400	244-8607
Supermall of the Great Northwest 1101 SuperMall Way	Auburn	WA	98001	253-833-9500	833-9006
TF: 800-729-8258					
University Village 2673 NW University Village Suite 7	Seattle	WA	98105	206-523-0622	525-3859
Westlake Center 400 Pine St	Seattle	WA	98101	206-287-0762	467-1603

BANKS

				Phone	Fax
KeyBank NA Seattle District 815 2nd Ave	Seattle	WA	98104	206-447-5730	447-5760
TF: 800-539-8189					
Seafirst Bank 701 5th Ave	Seattle	WA	98104	206-358-3000	358-6091
US Bank NA 1420 5th Ave	Seattle	WA	98101	206-344-3690	344-4555
West One Bank Washington 1301 5th Ave	Seattle	WA	98101	800-872-2657	585-5735*
**Fax Area Code:* 206					

BUSINESS SERVICES

	Phone
ABC Legal Messengers	206-623-8771
American Messenger Services	206-431-9657
Bucky's Courier	206-448-9280
Dependable Messenger Service	206-728-4066
Elliott Bay Messenger	206-340-9525
ENA Couriers	206-624-3200
Federal Express	800-463-3339
Fleetfoot Messenger Service	206-728-7700
General Employment	425-251-5006
Kelly Services	206-382-7171
Kinko's	206-545-7218
Mail Boxes Etc	206-682-0998
Manpower Temporary Services	206-583-0880
Olsten Staffing Services	206-441-2962
Post Office	800-275-8777
UPS	800-742-5877

— Media —

PUBLICATIONS

				Phone	Fax
Beacon Hill News/South District Journal 2314 3rd Ave	Seattle	WA	98121	206-461-1300	
Capitol Hill Times 2314 3rd Ave	Seattle	WA	98121	206-461-1300	
Web: www.seamedia.com					
Puget Sound Business Journal 720 3rd Ave Suite 800	Seattle	WA	98104	206-583-0701	447-8510
Web: www.amcity.com/seattle ■ *E-mail:* seattle@amcity.com.					
Seattle Post-Intelligencer‡ 101 Elliott Ave W	Seattle	WA	98119	206-448-8000	448-8166
Web: www.seattle-pi.com					
Seattle Times‡ PO Box 70	Seattle	WA	98111	206-464-2111	464-2261
Web: www.seattletimes.com ■ *E-mail:* opinion@seatimes.com					
West Seattle Herald 3500 SW Alaska St	Seattle	WA	98126	206-932-0300	937-1223*
**Fax:* News Rm ■ *Web:* www.westseattleherald.com ■ *E-mail:* wsherald@wolfenet.com					
Where Seattle Magazine 113 1st Ave N	Seattle	WA	98109	206-378-1300	378-0023
E-mail: wheresea@aol.com					

‡Daily newspapers

TELEVISION

				Phone	Fax
KCPQ-TV Ch 13 (Fox) 1813 Westlake Ave N	Seattle	WA	98109	206-674-1313	674-1777
Web: www.kcpq.com ■ *E-mail:* reception@kcpq.com					
KCTS-TV Ch 9 (PBS) 401 Mercer St	Seattle	WA	98109	206-728-6463	443-6691
Web: www.kcts.org ■ *E-mail:* viewer@kcts.org					
KING-TV Ch 5 (NBC) 333 Dexter Ave N	Seattle	WA	98109	206-448-5555	448-4525
Web: www.king5.com ■ *E-mail:* kingtv@king5.com					
KIRO-TV Ch 7 (CBS) 2807 3rd Ave	Seattle	WA	98121	206-728-7777	441-4840
Web: www.kirotv.com ■ *E-mail:* kironews7@kiro-tv.com					
KOMO-TV Ch 4 (ABC) 100 4th Ave N	Seattle	WA	98109	206-443-4000	443-3422
Web: www.komotv.com					
KONG-TV Ch 16 (Ind) 333 Dexter Ave N	Seattle	WA	98109	206-448-3166	448-3167
Web: www.kongtv.com					
KSTW-TV Ch 11 (UPN) PO Box 11411	Tacoma	WA	98411	253-572-5789	272-7581
Web: www.paramountstations.com/KSTW ■ *E-mail:* kstw98d@prodigy.com					
KTZZ-TV Ch 22 (WB) 945 Dexter Ave N	Seattle	WA	98109	206-282-2202	281-0207
KVOS-TV Ch 12 (Ind) 1151 Ellis St	Bellingham	WA	98225	360-671-1212	647-0824
TF: 800-488-5867					
KWPX-TV Ch 33 (PAX) 18000 International Blvd Suite 513	SeaTac	WA	98104	206-439-0333	246-5940
Web: www.pax.net/KWPX					

RADIO

				Phone	Fax
KBSG-AM 1210 kHz (Oldies) 1730 Minor Ave 20th Fl	Seattle	WA	98101	206-343-9700	623-7677
KBSG-FM 97.3 MHz (Oldies) 1730 Minor Ave 20th Fl	Seattle	WA	98101	206-343-9700	623-7677
Web: www.kbsg.com ■ *E-mail:* suggestionbox@kbsg.com					
KCMS-FM 105.3 MHz (Rel) 19303 Fremont Ave N	Seattle	WA	98133	206-546-7350	546-7372
KING-FM 98.1 MHz (Clas) 333 Dexter Ave N Suite 400	Seattle	WA	98109	206-448-3981	448-0928
Web: www.king.org					
KIRO-AM 710 kHz (N/T) 1820 E Lake Ave East	Seattle	WA	98102	206-726-7000	726-5446
Web: www.kiro710.com					
KIRO-FM 100.7 MHz (N/T) 1820 E Lake Ave East	Seattle	WA	98102	206-726-7000	726-5446
KISW-FM 99.9 MHz (CR) 1100 Olive Way Suite 1650	Seattle	WA	98101	206-285-7625	282-7018
Web: www.kisw.com					
KIXI-AM 880 kHz (Nost) 3650 131st Ave SE Suite 550	Bellevue	WA	98006	425-373-5545	373-5507
Web: www.kixi.com ■ *E-mail:* am880kixi@aol.com					
KJR-AM 950 kHz (Sports) 190 Queen Anne Ave N Suite 100	Seattle	WA	98109	206-285-2295	286-2376
Web: www.sportsradio950.com					
KJR-FM 95.7 MHz (Oldies) 190 Queen Anne Ave N Suite 100	Seattle	WA	98109	206-285-2295	286-2376
Web: www.kjrfm.com					
KLSY-FM 92.5 MHz (AC) 3650 131st Ave SE Suite 550	Bellevue	WA	98006	425-454-1540	455-8849
KMPS-FM 94.1 MHz (Ctry) 1000 Dexter Ave N Suite 100	Seattle	WA	98109	206-805-0941	805-0907
Web: www.kmps.com					
KMTT-FM 103.7 MHz (AAA) 1100 Olive Way Suite 1650	Seattle	WA	98101	206-233-1037	233-8979
Web: www.kmtt.com ■ *E-mail:* mountain@kmtt.com					
KNDD-FM 107.7 MHz (Alt) 1100 Olive Way Suite 1550	Seattle	WA	98101	206-622-3251	682-8349
Web: www.kndd.com					
KNWX-AM 770 kHz (N/T) 1820 E Lake Ave East	Seattle	WA	98102	206-726-7000	726-5446
KOMO-AM 1000 kHz (N/T) 1809 7th Ave Suite 200	Seattle	WA	98101	206-223-5700	516-3110
Web: www.komo-am.com ■ *E-mail:* comments@komoradio.com					
KPLZ-FM 101.5 MHz (AC) 1809 7th Ave Suite 200	Seattle	WA	98101	206-223-5703	292-1015
Web: www.kplz.com					
KRPM-AM 1090 kHz (CHR) 1000 Dexter Ave N Suite 100	Seattle	WA	98109	206-805-1061	805-0907
KRWM-FM 106.9 MHz (AC) 3650 131st Ave SE Suite 550	Bellevue	WA	98006	425-373-5545	373-5507
KUBE-FM 93.3 MHz (CHR) 190 Queen Anne Ave N Suite 100	Seattle	WA	98109	206-285-2295	286-2376
Web: www.kube93.com					
KUOW-FM 94.9 MHz (NPR) University of Washington Comm Bldg Rm 325 Box 353750	Seattle	WA	98195	206-543-2710	543-2720
Web: www.kuow.washington.edu/kuow.html ■ *E-mail:* kuow@u.washington.edu					
KVI-AM 570 kHz (N/T) 1809 7th Ave Suite 200	Seattle	WA	98101	206-223-5700	516-3194
Web: www.570kvi.com					
KWJZ-FM 98.9 MHz (NAC) 3650 131st Ave SE Suite 550	Bellevue	WA	98006	425-373-5536	373-5548
Web: www.kwjz.com ■ *E-mail:* jazz@connectexpress.com					

Seattle — Radio (Cont'd)

Name / Address	City	State	Zip	Phone	Fax
KYCW-FM 96.5 MHz (Ctry) 3131 Elliott Ave Suite 750	Seattle	WA	98121	206-216-0965	286-2139
Web: www.kycw.com					
KZOK-FM 102.5 MHz (CR) 113 Dexter Ave N	Seattle	WA	98109	206-443-1025	727-2299
Web: www.kzok.com ■ *E-mail:* comments@kzok.com					

— Colleges/Universities —

Name / Address	City	State	Zip	Phone	Fax
Antioch University 2326 6th Ave	Seattle	WA	98121	206-441-5352	441-3307
Web: www.seattleantioch.edu					
Art Institute of Seattle 2323 Elliott Ave	Seattle	WA	98121	206-448-0900	448-2501
TF: 800-275-2471 ■ *Web:* www.ais.edu ■ *E-mail:* admissions@ais.edu					
Bellevue Community College 3000 Landerholm Cir SE House 2	Bellevue	WA	98007	425-641-2222	603-4065
Web: www.bcc.ctc.edu					
City University of Bellevue 335 116th Ave SE	Bellevue	WA	98004	425-637-1010	450-4611
TF: 800-426-5596 ■ *Web:* www.cityu.edu					
Cornish College of the Arts 710 E Roy St	Seattle	WA	98102	206-323-1400	720-1011
TF: 800-726-2787 ■ *Web:* www.cornish.edu ■ *E-mail:* adm@cornish.edu					
Edmonds Community College 20000 68th Ave W	Lynnwood	WA	98036	425-640-1500	640-1159
Web: www.edcc.edu					
Everett Community College 801 Wetmore Ave	Everett	WA	98201	425-388-9100	388-9129
Web: www.evcc.ctc.edu					
Green River Community College 12401 SE 320th St	Auburn	WA	98092	253-833-9111	288-3454
Web: www.greenriver.ctc.edu ■ *E-mail:* jramsey@grcc.ctc.edu					
Henry Cogswell College 2802 Wetmore Ave Suite 100	Everett	WA	98201	425-258-3351	257-0405
Web: www.henrycogswell.edu					
ITT Technical Institute 12720 Gateway Dr Suite 100	Seattle	WA	98168	206-244-3300	246-7635
TF: 800-422-2029 ■ *Web:* www.itt-tech.edu					
North Seattle Community College 9600 College Way N	Seattle	WA	98103	206-527-3600	527-3635
Web: nsccux.sccd.ctc.edu/ ■ *E-mail:* nsccinfo@nsccgate.sccd.ctc.edu					
Northwest College of the Assemblies of God 5520 108th Ave NE	Kirkland	WA	98033	425-822-8266	827-0148
TF: 800-669-3781 ■ *Web:* www.nwcollege.edu ■ *E-mail:* admissions@ncag.edu					
Puget Sound Christian College 410 4th Ave N	Edmonds	WA	98020	425-775-8686	775-8688
Web: members.aa.net/~bluvase/pscchome.html					
Seattle Bible College 2363 NW 80th St	Seattle	WA	98117	206-784-1888	784-2187
E-mail: seattle_bc@msn.com					
Seattle Central Community College 1701 Broadway	Seattle	WA	98122	206-587-3800	344-4390
Web: edison.sccd.ctc.edu ■ *E-mail:* info@seaccc.sccd.ctc.edu					
Seattle Community College District VI 1500 Harvard Ave	Seattle	WA	98122	206-587-4155	587-3883
Web: seaccd.sccd.ctc.edu					
Seattle Pacific University 3307 3rd Ave W	Seattle	WA	98119	206-281-2000	281-2669
Web: www.spu.edu					
Seattle University 900 Broadway	Seattle	WA	98122	206-296-6000	296-5656
Web: www.seattleu.edu					
Shoreline Community College 16101 Greenwood Ave N	Shoreline	WA	98133	206-546-4101	546-5835
Web: oscar.ctc.edu/shoreline/					
South Seattle Community College 6000 16th Ave SW	Seattle	WA	98106	206-764-5300	764-7947
Web: www.sccd.ctc.edu/south					
University of Washington	Seattle	WA	98195	206-543-2100	685-3655
Web: www.washington.edu ■ *E-mail:* help@cac.washington.edu					
Western Washington University 516 High St	Bellingham	WA	98225	360-650-3000	650-7369
Web: www.wwu.edu					

— Hospitals —

Name / Address	City	State	Zip	Phone	Fax
Auburn Regional Medical Center 202 N Division St Plaza 1	Auburn	WA	98001	253-833-7711	939-2376
Web: www.armcuhs.com					
Children's Hospital & Regional Medical Center PO Box 5371	Seattle	WA	98105	206-526-2000	527-3879*
**Fax:* Admitting ■ *Web:* www.chmc.org ■ *E-mail:* info@chmc.org					
Eastside Hospital 2700 152nd Ave NE	Redmond	WA	98052	425-883-5151	883-5638
Evergreen Hospital Medical Center 12040 NE 128th St	Kirkland	WA	98034	425-899-1000	899-2624
Group Health Cooperative Central Hospital 201 16th Ave E	Seattle	WA	98112	206-326-3000	326-3436
Harborview Medical Center 325 9th Ave	Seattle	WA	98104	206-223-3000	731-8699
Web: www.washington.edu/medical/hmc					
Harrison Memorial Hospital 2520 Cherry Ave	Bremerton	WA	98310	360-377-3911	792-6527
Web: www.harrisonhospital.org					
Highline Community Hospital 16251 Sylvester Rd SW	Burien	WA	98166	206-244-9970	246-5862
Web: www.hchnet.org					
Northwest Hospital 1550 N 115th St	Seattle	WA	98133	206-368-1700	368-1291
Web: www.nwhospital.org					
Overlake Hospital Medical Center 1035 116th Ave NE	Bellevue	WA	98004	425-688-5000	688-5650*
**Fax:* Admitting ■ *Web:* www.overlakehospital.org					
Providence General Medical Center Colby Campus PO Box 1147	Everett	WA	98206	425-261-2000	261-4051
Web: www.providence.org/everett/pgmc.htm					
Providence General Medical Center Pacific Campus PO Box 1067	Everett	WA	98206	425-258-7123	261-4051
Web: www.providence.org/everett/ppc.htm					
Providence Seattle Medical Center 500 17th Ave	Seattle	WA	98122	206-320-2000	320-3152*
**Fax:* Admitting ■ *Web:* www.providence.org/pugetsound					
Saint Francis Community Hospital 34515 9th Ave S	Federal Way	WA	98003	253-838-9700	952-7988
Stevens Memorial Hospital 21601 76th Ave W	Edmonds	WA	98026	425-640-4000	640-4010
Swedish Medical Center 747 Broadway	Seattle	WA	98122	206-386-6000	386-2277
Swedish Medical Center/Bullard 5300 Tallman Ave NW	Seattle	WA	98107	206-782-2700	781-6195
Web: www.swedish.org					
University of Washington Medical Center Seattle 1959 NE Pacific Ave	Seattle	WA	98195	206-548-3300	598-6963
Web: www.washington.edu/medical					
Valley Medical Center 400 S 43rd St	Renton	WA	98055	425-228-3450	656-4202
TF: 800-540-1814 ■ *Web:* www.valleymed.org ■ *E-mail:* valley@cnw.com					
Veterans Affairs Puget Sound Medical Center 1660 S Columbian Way	Seattle	WA	98108	206-762-1010	764-2224
Virginia Mason Medical Center 925 Seneca St	Seattle	WA	98111	206-624-1144	223-6976
Web: www.vmmc.org					

— Attractions —

Name / Address	City	State	Zip	Phone	Fax
5th Avenue Theater 1308 5th Ave	Seattle	WA	98101	206-625-0235	292-9610
A Contemporary Theatre 700 Union St	Seattle	WA	98101	206-292-7660	292-7670
Bay Pavilion 1301 Alaskan Way	Seattle	WA	98101	206-623-8600	343-9173
Bellevue Art Museum 301 Bellevue Sq	Bellevue	WA	98004	425-454-3322	637-1799
Web: www.bellevueart.org ■ *E-mail:* bam@bellevueart.org					
Burke Museum of Natural History & Culture NE 45th St & 17th Ave NE University of Washington	Seattle	WA	98195	206-543-7907	685-3039
Web: www.washington.edu/burkemuseum ■ *E-mail:* recept@u.washington.edu					
Burke Thomas Memorial Washington State Museum University of Washington	Seattle	WA	98195	206-543-5590	685-3039
Web: www.washington.edu/burkemuseum					
Center for Wooden Boats 1010 Valley St	Seattle	WA	98109	206-382-2628	382-2699
Children's Museum 305 Harrison St	Seattle	WA	98109	206-441-1768	448-0910
Web: www.thechildrensmuseum.org ■ *E-mail:* tcm@thechildrensmuseum.org					
Chittenden Hiram M Locks 3015 NW 54th St	Seattle	WA	98107	206-783-7001	782-3192
Civic Light Opera 34th Ave NE & 110th St Jane Addams Theatre	Seattle	WA	98125	206-363-2809	363-0702
Dash Point State Park 5700 SW Dash Point Rd	Federal Way	WA	98023	253-661-4955	838-2777
TF: 800-452-5687					
Daybreak Star Arts Center PO Box 99100	Seattle	WA	98119	206-285-4425	282-3640
Discovery Park 3801 W Government Way	Seattle	WA	98199	206-386-4236	684-0195
Downtown Seattle Pine S to University Sts & 1st-7th Sts	Seattle	WA	98101	206-461-5840	
Fireworks Fine Crafts Gallery 210 1st Ave S	Seattle	WA	98104	206-682-8707	467-6366
TF: 800-505-8882 ■ *Web:* www.fireworksgallery.net					

Seattle — Attractions (Cont'd)

	Phone	Fax
Frye Charles & Emma Art Museum 704 Terry Ave. . . . Seattle WA 98104	206-622-9250	223-1707
Web: fryeart.org ■ *E-mail:* fryeart@aol.com		
Fun Forest Amusement Park 305 Harrison St . . . . Seattle WA 98109	206-728-1585	441-9897
Green Lake Park 7201 E Green Lake Dr North . . . . Seattle WA 98109	206-684-4075	
Henry Art Gallery University of Washington Box 351410. . . . Seattle WA 98195	206-543-2281	685-3123
Web: www.henryart.org ■ *E-mail:* hartg@u.washington.edu		
Herbfarm The 32804 Issaquah-Fall City Rd . . . . Fall City WA 98024	206-784-2222	789-2279
Web: www.theherbfarm.com ■ *E-mail:* HerbOrder@aol.com		
IMAX Theater 200 2nd Ave N. . . . Seattle WA 98109	206-443-2001	
Web: www.pacsci.org/public/imax/theater		
Intiman Theatre 201 Mercer St Seattle Ctr. . . . Seattle WA 98109	206-269-1900	269-1928
Klondike Gold Rush National Historical Park 117 S Main St . . . . Seattle WA 98104	206-553-7220	553-0614
Web: www.nps.gov/klgo ■ *E-mail:* klse_ranger_activities@nps.gov		
Lake Chelan National Recreation Area 2105 SR-20 . . . . Sedro Woolley WA 98284	360-856-5700	856-1934
Web: www.nps.gov/lach/		
Museum of Flight 9404 East Marginal Way S. . . . Seattle WA 98108	206-764-5700	764-5707
Web: www.museumofflight.org		
Museum of History & Industry 2700 24th Ave E. . . . Seattle WA 98112	206-324-1125	324-1346
Web: www.historymuse-nw.org		
North Cascades National Park 2105 SR-20 . . . . Sedro-Woolley WA 98284	360-856-5700	856-1934
Web: www.nps.gov/noca ■ *E-mail:* noca_interpretation@nps.gov		
Northwest Railway Museum PO Box 459. . . . Snoqualmie WA 98065	425-888-0373	888-9311
Web: www.trainmuseum.org ■ *E-mail:* visitorservices@trainmuseum.org		
Northwest Trek Wildlife Park 11610 Trek Dr E. . . . Eatonville WA 98328	360-832-6117	832-6118
Web: www.nwtrek.org		
Ocheami Afrikan Dance Co PO Box 31635. . . . Seattle WA 98103	206-329-8876	
Olympic National Park 600 E Park Ave . . . . Port Angeles WA 98362	360-452-4501	452-0335*
**Fax:* Mail Rm ■ *Web:* www.nps.gov/olym/		
Omnidome Film Experience Pier 59 Waterfront Pk . . . . Seattle WA 98101	206-622-1868	
Pacific Northwest Ballet 301 Mercer St. . . . Seattle WA 98109	206-441-9411	441-2440
Web: www.pnb.org		
Pacific Science Center 200 2nd Ave N . . . . Seattle WA 98109	206-443-2001	443-3631
Web: www.pacsci.org		
Pike Place Market 1st Ave & Pike St . . . . Seattle WA 98101	206-682-7453	625-0646
Pioneer Square PO Box 4333. . . . Seattle WA 98104	206-622-6235	
E-mail: psbia@pioneersquare.org		
Pyramid Breweries Inc 91 S Royal Brougham Way . . . . Seattle WA 98134	206-682-8322	682-8420
Web: www.pyramidbrew.com		
Redhook Ale Brewery & Trolleyman Pub 3400 Phinney Ave N . . . . Seattle WA 98103	206-548-8000	548-1305
Web: www.redhook.com/		
Redhook Ale Brewery Inc 3400 Phinney Ave N. . . . Seattle WA 98103	206-548-8000	548-1305
Web: www.redhook.com ■ *E-mail:* redhook@redhook.com		
Ross Lake National Recreation Area 2105 SR-20 . . . . Sedro Woolley WA 98284	360-856-5700	856-1934
Web: www.nps.gov/rola/		
Seattle Aquarium 1483 Alaskan Way Waterfront Pk Pier 59. . . . Seattle WA 98101	206-386-4300	386-4328
Web: www.seattleaquarium.org		
Seattle Art Museum 100 University St. . . . Seattle WA 98101	206-625-8900	654-3135
Web: www.seattleartmuseum.org		
Seattle Asian Art Museum 1400 E Prospect St Volunteer Pk . . . . Seattle WA 98112	206-654-3206	654-3191
Web: www.seattleartmuseum.org		
Seattle Center 305 Harrison St. . . . Seattle WA 98109	206-684-7200	684-7342
Web: www.seattlecenter.com		
Seattle Imax Dome Theatre Pier 59 Waterfront Pk . . . . Seattle WA 98101	206-622-1869	622-5837
Seattle Opera PO Box 9248 . . . . Seattle WA 98109	206-389-7600	389-7651
Web: www.seattleopera.org ■ *E-mail:* webfeedback@seattleopera.org		
Seattle Repertory Theatre 155 Mercer St . . . . Seattle WA 98109	206-443-2210	443-2379
Web: www.seattlerep.org/		
Seattle Symphony Orchestra 200 University St Benaroya Hall . . . . Seattle WA 98109	206-215-4747	
Web: www.seattlesymphony.org		
Seattle Youth Symphony Orchestra 11065 5th Ave NE. . . . Seattle WA 98125	206-362-2300	361-9254
Web: www.syso.org		
Seward Park 5898 Lake Washington Blvd S. . . . Seattle WA 98109	206-684-4075	
Space Needle 219 4th Ave N. . . . Seattle WA 98109	206-443-9700	441-7415
Web: spaceneedle.com ■ *E-mail:* reservation@spaceneedle.com		
Tillicum Village 2200 6th Ave Suite 804 . . . . Seattle WA 98121	206-443-1244	443-4723
TF: 800-426-1205 ■ *Web:* www.tillicumvillage.com ■ *E-mail:* mail@tillicumvillage.com		
Unexpected Productions 1428 Post Alley Market Theater . . . . Seattle WA 98101	206-587-2414	587-2413
Web: www.web1.com/up/		
Volunteer Park 1400 E Prospect St. . . . Seattle WA 98112	206-461-5800	684-4304
Westlake Center 400 Pine St . . . . Seattle WA 98101	206-287-0762	467-1603
Wing Luke Asian Museum 407 7th Ave S . . . . Seattle WA 98104	206-623-5124	623-4559
Web: www.wingluke.org		
Woodland Park Zoological Gardens 5500 Phinney Ave N . . . . Seattle WA 98103	206-684-4800	684-4854
Web: www.zoo.org		

SPORTS TEAMS & FACILITIES

	Phone	Fax
Emerald Downs 2300 Emerald Downs Dr. . . . Auburn WA 98001	253-288-7000	288-7710
TF: 888-931-8400 ■ *Web:* www.emdowns.com		
Key Arena 305 Harrison St Seattle Ctr. . . . Seattle WA 98109	206-684-7202	684-7343
Safeco Field 1250 1st Ave. . . . Seattle WA 98134	206-346-4000	346-4300
Web: www.safeco.com/safecofield/default.asp		
Seattle Bigfoot 6303 NE 181st St Suite 201. . . . Seattle WA 98155	206-522-5626	522-1446
E-mail: billhur@johnlscott.com		
Seattle International Raceway 31001 144th Ave SE . . . . Kent WA 98042	253-631-1550	630-0888
Seattle Mariners 1250 1st Ave Safeco Field. . . . Seattle WA 98134	206-346-4000	346-4300
Web: www.mariners.org		
Seattle Seahawks 11220 NE 53rd St. . . . Kirkland WA 98033	425-827-9777	827-9008
Web: www.seahawks.com		
Seattle Sounders (soccer) 406 N Logan Ave Memorial Stadium. . . . Renton WA 98055	206-622-3415	643-3515*
**Fax Area Code:* 425 ■ *TF:* 800-796-5425 ■ *Web:* www.seattlesounders.com/		
Seattle SuperSonics Key Arena. . . . Seattle WA 98109	206-281-5800	
Web: www.nba.com/sonics		
Seattle Thunderbirds (hockey) Key Arena Seattle Ctr. . . . Seattle WA 98109	425-869-7825	497-0812
Web: www.seattleinsider.com/sports/hockey/seattle-thunderbirds.html		

— Events —

	Phone
AT & T Summer Nights at the Pier (late June-late August)	206-281-8111
Bite of Seattle (July)	206-232-2982
Bubble Festival (mid-August)	206-443-2001
Bumbershoot Festival (early September)	206-684-7200
Cherry Blossom & Japanese Cultural Festival (mid-April)	206-684-7200
Chinese New Year's Celebration (January)	206-382-1197
Cinco de Mayo Celebration (early May)	206-706-7776
Eatonville Arts Festival (late July-early August)	360-832-4000
Family Fourth at Lake Union (July 4)	206-281-8111
Festival Sundiata (mid-February)	206-684-7200
Fiesta Patrias (mid-September)	206-706-7776
Fourth of Jul-Ivars at the Waterfront (July 4)	206-587-6500
Hmong New Year's Celebration (early November)	206-684-7284
Holiday Parade of Boats Cruise (December)	206-674-3500
Imagination Celebration (early April)	206-684-7200
Indian Pow Wow (late July)	206-285-4425
Northwest Flower & Garden Show (early February)	800-229-6311
Northwest Folklife Festival (late May)	206-684-7300
Pioneer Square Fire Festival (early June)	206-622-6235
Salmon Days Festival (October)	425-392-0661
Seafair Summer Festival (early July-early August)	206-728-0123
Seattle Fringe Festival (mid-March)	206-526-1959
Seattle International Boat Show (mid-January)	206-634-0911
Seattle International Film Festival (mid-May-early June)	206-464-5830
Seattle Marathon (late November)	253-552-1702
University District Street Fair (mid-May)	206-632-9084
Winterfest (late November-early January)	206-684-7200

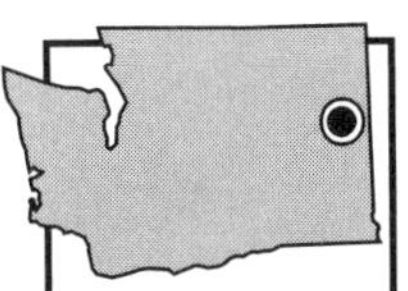

Spokane

Spokane began as a sawmill powered by the Spokane Falls. The city was the only point where railroads could cross the Rockies and reach the Columbia Basin, and this factor, and, later, the gold fields of Idaho, contributed to the city's growth. One can now view the Falls and Spokane

Spokane (Cont'd)

River at Riverfront Park, a premier attraction in Spokane that includes the Flour Mill, a unique complex of restaurants, boutiques, and galleries. The newest attraction in Spokane, and still under construction, is the Spokane River Centennial Trail, which begins at the confluence of the Spokane and Little Spokane Rivers and ends at the Washington/Idaho border. The Trail also connects with the Idaho Centennial Trail. Mount Spokane State Park is known for its skiing both on Mount Kit Carson and on Mount Spokane. Three states and two Canadian provinces are visible from the top of Mount Spokane: Washington, Idaho, Montana, Alberta, and British Columbia.

Population 184,058
Area (Land) .... 55.9 sq mi
Area (Water) .... 0.7 sq mi
Elevation .... 1898 ft
Latitude .... 47-66-56 N
Longitude .... 117-43-35 W
County .... Spokane
Time Zone .... PST
Area Code/s 509

— Average Temperatures and Precipitation —

TEMPERATURES

	Jan	Feb	Mar	Apr	May	Jun	Jul	Aug	Sep	Oct	Nov	Dec
High	33	41	48	57	66	75	83	83	72	59	41	34
Low	21	26	30	35	42	49	54	54	46	36	29	22

PRECIPITATION

	Jan	Feb	Mar	Apr	May	Jun	Jul	Aug	Sep	Oct	Nov	Dec
Inches	2.0	1.5	1.5	1.2	1.4	1.3	0.7	0.7	0.7	1.0	2.2	2.4

— Important Phone Numbers —

	Phone
AAA	509-358-6900
Emergency	911
HotelDocs	800-468-3537
Poison Control Center	206-526-2121
Time	509-458-8800
Weather	509-624-8905

— Information Sources —

Phone *Fax*

Better Business Bureau Serving the Inland Northwest 508 W 6th Ave Suite 401 .... Spokane WA 99204 509-455-4200 838-1079
Web: www.spokane.bbb.org ■ *E-mail:* info@spokane.bbb.org
Spokane Area Chamber of Commerce
PO Box 2147 .... Spokane WA 99210 509-624-1393 747-0077
Web: www.spokane.org/chamber/ ■ *E-mail:* chamber@spokane.org
Spokane Center W 334 Spokane Falls Blvd .... Spokane WA 99201 509-353-6500 353-6511
Web: www.spokane-areacvb.org/spokanecenter
Spokane City Hall 808 W Spokane Falls Blvd .... Spokane WA 99201 509-625-6250 625-6217
Web: www.spokanecity.org
Spokane Community Development Dept
808 W Spokane Falls Blvd .... Spokane WA 99201 509-625-6325 625-6315
Spokane Convention & Visitors Bureau
801 W Riverside Ave Suite 301 .... Spokane WA 99201 509-624-1341 623-1297
TF: 800-248-3230 ■ *Web:* www.spokane-areacvb.org
Spokane County 1116 W Broadway Ave .... Spokane WA 99260 509-456-2265 456-2274
Web: www.spokanecounty.org/
Spokane Mayor 808 W Spokane Falls Blvd .... Spokane WA 99201 509-625-6250 625-6217
Web: www.spokanecity.org/mayor ■ *E-mail:* jtalbott@spokanecity.org
Spokane Public Library 906 W Main Ave .... Spokane WA 99201 509-444-5336 444-5366
Web: splnet.spokpl.lib.wa.us

On-Line Resources

About.com Guide to Spokane .... spokane.about.com
Anthill City Guide Spokane .... www.anthill.com/city.asp?city=spokane
Area Guide Spokane .... spokane.areaguides.net
City Knowledge Spokane .... www.cityknowledge.com/wa_spokane.htm
Excite.com Spokane City Guide .... www.excite.com/travel/countries/united_states/washington/spokane
Spokane.net .... www.spokane.net

— Transportation Services —

AIRPORTS

■ Spokane International Airport (GEG) *Phone*

6 miles SW of downtown (approx 15 minutes) 509-624-3218
Web: www.spokane.org/sia

Airport Transportation

United Taxi $15 fare to downtown 509-535-6151

Commercial Airlines

	Phone
Delta	800-221-1212
Horizon	800-547-9308
Northwest	800-225-2525
Southwest	800-435-9792
United	800-241-6522
United Express	800-241-6522

Charter Airlines

Spokane Airways 509-747-2017

CAR RENTALS

	Phone
Avis	509-747-8081
Budget	800-345-6655
Dollar	509-458-2619
Enterprise	509-458-3340
Hertz	509-747-3101
Thrifty	509-924-9111
U-Save Auto	509-535-0156

LIMO/TAXI

	Phone
American Limousine	509-328-5466
Australian Limousine	509-924-9232
Budget Taxi	509-326-8294
Classic Limo	509-924-4194
Lilac City Cab	509-838-9800
Spokane Cab	509-535-2535
United Taxi	509-535-6151
Valley Cab	509-535-7007

MASS TRANSIT

Spokane Transit Authority $.75 Base fare 509-328-7433

RAIL/BUS

Spokane Amtrak Station W 221 1st Ave .... Spokane WA 99204 509-624-5144
Trailways Bus Station W 221 1st Ave .... Spokane WA 99201 509-838-5262

— Accommodations —

HOTELS, MOTELS, RESORTS

Phone *Fax*

Apple Tree Inn 9508 N Division .... Spokane WA 99218 509-466-3020 467-4377
TF: 800-323-5796 ■ *Web:* www.appletreeinnmotel.com/
Best Inn 6309 E Broadway Ave .... Spokane WA 99212 509-535-7185 533-5450
TF: 800-237-8466
Best Western Peppertree Airport Inn
3711 S Geiger .... Spokane WA 99224 509-624-4655 838-6416
TF: 800-799-3933
Best Western Pheasant Hill
12415 E Mission Ave .... Spokane WA 99216 509-926-7432 892-1914
TF: 888-297-1555
Best Western Thunderbird Inn
120 W 3rd Ave .... Spokane WA 99204 509-747-2011 747-9170
TF: 800-578-2473
Best Western Trade Winds North
3033 N Division St .... Spokane WA 99207 509-326-5500 328-1357
TF: 800-621-8593
Cavanaugh's Inn 110 E 4th Ave .... Spokane WA 99202 509-838-6101 624-0733
TF: 800-325-4000
Cavanaugh's Inn at the Park
303 W North River Dr .... Spokane WA 99201 509-326-8000 325-7329
TF: 800-843-4667
Cavanaugh's Ridpath Hotel
515 W Sprague Ave .... Spokane WA 99204 509-838-2711 747-6970
TF: 800-325-4000
Cavanaugh's River Inn N 700 Division St .... Spokane WA 99202 509-326-5577 326-1120
TF: 800-325-4000

Spokane — Hotels, Motels, Resorts (Cont'd)

				Phone	Fax
Comfort Inn North 7111 N Division *TF:* 800-228-5150	Spokane	WA	99208	509-467-7111	468-7512
Courtyard by Marriott 401 N Riverpoint Blvd *TF:* 800-321-2211 ■ *Web:* courtyard.com/GEGCH	Spokane	WA	99202	509-456-7600	456-0969
Days Inn Spokane Airport 4212 W Sunset Blvd *TF:* 800-318-2611	Spokane	WA	99224	509-747-2021	747-5950
Doubletree Hotel Spokane City Center 322 N Spokane Falls Ct *TF:* 800-222-8733 ■ *Web:* www.doubletreehotels.com/DoubleT/Hotel141/152/152Main.htm	Spokane	WA	99201	509-455-9600	455-6285
Doubletree Hotel Spokane Valley N 1100 Sullivan Rd *TF:* 800-222-8733 ■ *Web:* www.doubletreehotels.com/DoubleT/Hotel141/153/153Main.htm	Veradale	WA	99037	509-924-9000	922-4965
Fairfield Inn 311 N Riverpoint Blvd *TF:* 800-228-2800 ■ *Web:* fairfieldinn.com/GEGFI	Spokane	WA	99202	509-747-9131	747-9131
Hampton Inn 2010 S Assembly Rd *TF:* 800-426-7866	Spokane	WA	99224	509-747-1100	747-8722
Holiday Inn Express 801 N Division St *TF:* 800-465-4329	Spokane	WA	99202	509-328-8505	325-9842
Howard Johnson Inn 211 S Division *TF:* 800-888-6630	Spokane	WA	99202	509-838-6630	624-2147
Kempis Executive Suites 326 W 6th Ave *TF:* 888-236-4321	Spokane	WA	99204	509-747-4321	747-4301
Motel 6 1919 N Hutchinson Rd *TF:* 800-466-8356	Spokane	WA	99212	509-926-5399	928-5974
Quality Inn Oakwood 7919 N Division St *TF:* 888-535-4900	Spokane	WA	99208	509-467-4900	467-4933
Quality Inn-Valley Suites 8923 E Mission Ave *TF:* 800-777-7355	Spokane	WA	99212	509-928-5218	928-5211
Ramada Inn Airport Spokane International Airport *TF:* 800-272-6232	Spokane	WA	99219	509-838-5211	838-1074
Red Top Motel 7217 E Trent Ave	Spokane	WA	99212	509-926-5728	922-5528
Resident Court 1203 W 5th Ave	Spokane	WA	99204	509-624-4142	838-6114
Shilo Inn Spokane 923 E 3rd Ave *TF:* 800-222-2244	Spokane	WA	99202	509-535-9000	535-5740
Spokane House 4301 W Sunset Hwy	Spokane	WA	99204	509-838-1471	838-1705
Spokane Valley Super 8 2020 N Argonne Rd *TF:* 800-800-8000	Spokane	WA	99212	509-928-4888	928-4888
Super 8 11102 W Westbow Rd *TF:* 800-800-8000	Spokane	WA	99204	509-838-8800	624-3157
Towne Centre Motor Inn 901 W 1st Ave *TF:* 800-247-1041	Spokane	WA	99204	509-747-1041	624-6674
Trade Winds Downtown Motel 907 W 3rd Ave *TF:* 800-586-5397	Spokane	WA	99204	509-838-2091	838-2094
Travelodge 33 W Spokane Falls Blvd *TF:* 800-578-7878	Spokane	WA	99201	509-623-9727	623-9737
Wolff Lodging 9514 E Montgomery Rd Suite 20 *TF:* 800-528-9519 ■ *Web:* www.awolff.com	Spokane	WA	99206	509-444-1690	924-4902

— Restaurants —

				Phone
Ankeny's Restaurant (Mediterranean) 515 W Sprague Ave	Spokane	WA	99204	509-838-2711
Arizona Steakhouse (Steak) 333 W Spokane Falls Blvd	Spokane	WA	99206	509-455-8206
Azteca (Mexican) 200 W Spokane Falls Blvd	Spokane	WA	99206	509-456-0350
Bayou Brewing Co (American) 1003 E Trent	Spokane	WA	99202	509-484-4818
Bong's Restaurant (Chinese) 3004 N Monroe	Spokane	WA	99205	509-327-3770
Calgary Steak House (Steak/Seafood) 3040 E Sprague Ave	Spokane	WA	99202	509-535-7502
Cannon St Grill (Continental) 144 Cannon St	Spokane	WA	99204	509-456-8660
Cathay Inn (Chinese) 3714 N Division	Spokane	WA	99205	509-326-2226
Chapter XI (Steak/Seafood) 105 E Mission St	Spokane	WA	99218	509-326-0466
Charley's Grill & Spirits (American) 801 N Monroe	Spokane	WA	99201	509-328-8911
Chic-A-Ria (Steak/Seafood) 1812 W Francis Ave	Spokane	WA	99205	509-326-2214
Cl Shenanigan's (Steak/Seafood) 332 N Spokane Falls Ct	Spokane	WA	99201	509-455-6690
Clinkerdagger (American) 621 W Mallon Ave	Spokane	WA	99201	509-328-5965
Conley's Place (American) 12622 E Sprague Ave	Spokane	WA	99216	509-924-5411
Cucina!Cucina! (Italian) 707 W Main Ave	Spokane	WA	99201	509-838-3388
Dewey Cheatam & Howe (Steak/Seafood) 3022 N Division St	Spokane	WA	99207	509-326-7741
Finnerty's Red Lion BBQ (Barbecue) 126 N Division	Spokane	WA	99202	509-624-1934
Fort Spokane Brewery (American) 401 W Spokane Falls Blvd	Spokane	WA	99201	509-838-3809
Fugazzi Cafe (American) 1 N Post St	Spokane	WA	99201	509-624-1133
Glover Mansion (Continental) 321 W 8th Ave	Spokane	WA	99204	509-459-0000
Hobarts Restaurant (American) 110 E 4th Ave	Spokane	WA	99202	509-838-6101
Ichi Shogun Restaurant (Japanese) 821 E 3rd Ave	Spokane	WA	99202	509-534-7777
Luigi's (Italian) 245 Main St	Spokane	WA	99201	509-624-5226
Luna (American) 5620 S Perry St	Spokane	WA	99223	509-448-2383
Marrakesh (Continental) 2008 Northwest Blvd	Spokane	WA	99205	509-328-9733
Milford's Fish House (Steak/Seafood) 719 N Monroe St	Spokane	WA	99201	509-326-7251
Mizuna (Vegetarian) 214 N Howard	Spokane	WA	99201	509-747-2004
Mustard Seed (Japanese) 245 W Spokane Falls Blvd	Spokane	WA	99201	509-747-2689
Niko's (Greek) 321 S Dishman-Mica Rd	Spokane	WA	99206	509-928-9590
O'Doherty's Irish Grill (Irish) 525 W Spokane Falls Blvd	Spokane	WA	99201	509-747-0322
Onions Inc (American) 7522 N Division St	Spokane	WA	99208	509-482-6100
Patsy Clark's Mansion (Continental) 2208 W 2nd Ave	Spokane	WA	99204	509-838-8300
Rancho Chico (Mexican) 128 W 3rd Ave	Spokane	WA	99202	509-456-4806
Ripples on the River (American) 700 N Division	Spokane	WA	99201	509-326-5577
Rock City (Italian) 505 W Riverside	Spokane	WA	99201	509-455-4400
Sierra Mirage Restaurant (American) 4212 W Sunset Blvd	Spokane	WA	99224	509-747-2021
Someplace Else Restaurant & Pub (Continental) 518 W Sprague	Spokane	WA	99201	509-747-3946
Spencer's (Steak) 322 N Spokane Falls Ct	Spokane	WA	99201	509-455-9600
Sportsman Cafe (American) 6410 N Market St	Spokane	WA	99207	509-467-6388
Suki Yaki Inn (Japanese) 119 N Bernard	Spokane	WA	99201	509-624-0022
Thadeus T Thudpucker's (American) 43 W Riverside	Spokane	WA	99201	509-747-5577
Tomato Street North (Italian) 6220 N Division St	Spokane	WA	99207	509-484-4500
Windows of the Seasons (French) 303 W Northriver Dr	Spokane	WA	99201	509-328-9526

— Goods and Services —

SHOPPING

				Phone	Fax
Crescent Court 700 W Main Ave *Web:* www.rosewood-hotels.com/crescent.htm	Spokane	WA	99201	509-459-6111	325-7324
Flour Mill 621 W Mallon Ave	Spokane	WA	99201	509-459-6100	325-7324
Monroe Street Bridge Antique Market 604 N Monroe St	Spokane	WA	99201	509-327-6398	325-9545
Northtown Mall 4750 N Division St	Spokane	WA	99207	509-482-0178	483-0360
RiverPark Square 221 N Wall St Suite 212	Spokane	WA	99201	509-838-7970	623-1715
Shadle Shopping Center 2501 W Wellesley Ave	Spokane	WA	99205	509-838-8500	838-3099
Spokane Antique Mall 12 W Sprague	Spokane	WA	99204	509-747-1466	
Spokane Market Place Ruby St & Desmet Ave	Spokane	WA	99207	509-456-0100	
University City Mall Sprague Ave & University Rd	Spokane	WA	99206	509-927-0470	

BANKS

				Phone	Fax
Inland Northwest Bank 421 W Riverside Ave Suite 113	Spokane	WA	99201	509-456-8888	623-1787
Seattle-First National Bank 601 W Riverside Ave	Spokane	WA	99210	509-353-1445	353-1455
US Bank of Washington NA 428 W Riverside Ave *TF:* 800-872-2657	Spokane	WA	99201	509-353-5025	353-5032
Washington Trust Bank 717 W Sprague Ave	Spokane	WA	99204	509-353-4122	353-6962
Wells Fargo Bank 524 W Riverside Ave *TF:* 800-869-3557 ■ *Web:* www.wellsfargo.com	Spokane	WA	99201	509-455-5773	455-5718

BUSINESS SERVICES

	Phone
Adecco Employment Personnel Services	509-926-2133
Airborne Express	800-247-2676
BAX Global	509-534-4318
DHL Worldwide Express	800-225-5345
Express Personnel Services	509-747-6011
Federal Express	800-238-5355
Kelly Services	509-327-3637
Kinko's	509-484-0601
Mail Boxes Etc	800-789-4623
Post Office	800-275-8777
UPS	800-742-5877

— Media —

PUBLICATIONS

				Phone	Fax
Journal of Business 112 E 1st Ave *Web:* www.spokanejournal.com ■ *E-mail:* journal@spokanejournal.com	Spokane	WA	99202	509-456-5257	456-0624
Spokesman Review‡ PO Box 2160 *TF:* 800-338-8801 ■ *Web:* www.virtuallynw.com ■ *E-mail:* editor@spokesman.com	Spokane	WA	99201	509-459-5000	459-5482

‡*Daily newspapers*

Spokane (Cont'd)

TELEVISION

	City	State	Zip	Phone	Fax
KAYU-TV Ch 28 (Fox) PO Box 30028	Spokane	WA	99223	509-448-2828	448-3815
KHQ-TV Ch 6 (NBC) PO Box 8088	Spokane	WA	99203	509-448-6000	448-4644
Web: www.msnbc.com/local/KHQ/default.asp					
KREM-TV Ch 2 (CBS) 4103 S Regal St	Spokane	WA	99223	509-448-2000	448-6397
Web: www.krem.com					
KSKN-TV Ch 22 (UPN) PO Box 30699	Spokane	WA	99223	509-742-3563	443-9100
KSPS-TV Ch 7 (PBS) 3911 S Regal St	Spokane	WA	99223	509-353-5777	354-7757
Web: www.ksps.org/					
KXLY-TV Ch 4 (ABC) 500 W Boone Ave	Spokane	WA	99201	509-324-4000	327-3932
Web: www.kxly.com ■ *E-mail:* kxly@iea.com					

RADIO

	City	State	Zip	Phone	Fax
KAEP-FM 105.7 MHz (Alt) PO Box 30013	Spokane	WA	99223	509-448-1000	448-7015
Web: www.1057thepeak.com					
KAQQ-AM 590 kHz (Nost) 300 E 3rd Ave	Spokane	WA	99202	509-459-9800	459-9850
Web: www.q59.com					
KDRK-FM 93.7 MHz (Ctry) E 1601 57th Ave	Spokane	WA	99223	509-448-1000	448-7015
Web: www.catcountry94.com					
KEYF-FM 101.1 MHz (Oldies) S 6019 Crestline St	Spokane	WA	99223	509-441-3322	448-6523
Web: www.oldies1011.com					
KGA-AM 1510 kHz (N/T) PO Box 30013	Spokane	WA	99223	509-448-1000	448-7015
Web: www.1510kga.com ■ *E-mail:* 1510kga@iea.com					
KISC-FM 98.1 MHz (AC) 300 E 3rd Ave	Spokane	WA	99202	509-459-9800	459-9850
Web: www.98kiss.com					
KKZX-FM 98.9 MHz (CR) 5106 S Palouse Hwy	Spokane	WA	99223	509-448-9900	448-4043
KPBX-FM 91.1 MHz (NPR) N 2319 Monroe St	Spokane	WA	99205	509-328-5729	328-5764
Web: www.kpbx.org ■ *E-mail:* kpbx@kpbx.org					
KXLY-AM 920 kHz (N/T) 500 W Boone Ave	Spokane	WA	99201	509-328-6292	325-0676
Web: www.kxly920.com					

— Colleges/Universities —

	City	State	Zip	Phone	Fax
Eastern Washington University 526 5th St MS 148	Cheney	WA	99004	509-359-6200	359-4330
TF Admissions: 888-740-1914 ■ *Web:* www.ewu.edu ■ *E-mail:* admissions@ewu.edu					
Gonzaga University E 502 Boone Ave	Spokane	WA	99258	509-328-4220	323-5780
TF Admissions: 800-986-9585 ■ *Web:* www.gonzaga.edu					
ITT Technical Institute N 1050 Argonne Rd	Spokane	WA	99212	509-926-2900	926-2908
TF: 800-777-8324 ■ *Web:* www.itt-tech.edu					
Spokane Community College 1810 N Greene St	Spokane	WA	99217	509-533-7000	533-8839
TF Admissions: 800-248-5644 ■ *Web:* www.scc.spokane.cc.wa.us ■ *E-mail:* sccinfo@scc.spokane.cc.wa.us					
Spokane Falls Community College 3410 W Fort George Wright Dr	Spokane	WA	99224	509-533-3500	533-3237
Web: www.sfcc.spokane.cc.wa.us					
Washington State University Spokane 601 W 1st Ave	Spokane	WA	99201	509-358-7500	358-7505
Web: www.spokane.wsu.edu ■ *E-mail:* brazier@wsu.edu					
Whitworth College 300 W Hawthorne Rd	Spokane	WA	99251	509-777-1000	777-3758
TF: 800-533-4668 ■ *Web:* whitworth.edu					

— Hospitals —

	City	State	Zip	Phone	Fax
Deaconess Medical Center Spokane 800 W 5th St	Spokane	WA	99204	509-458-5800	473-7286
Holy Family Hospital 5633 N Lidgerwood St	Spokane	WA	99207	509-482-0111	482-2481
Web: www.holy-family.org					
Sacred Heart Medical Center 101 W 8th Ave	Spokane	WA	99204	509-455-3131	474-4773*
**Fax:* Admitting ■ *Web:* www.shmc.org					
Valley Hospital & Medical Center 12606 E Mission Ave	Spokane	WA	99216	509-924-6650	922-5421
Veterans Affairs Medical Center 4815 N Assembly St	Spokane	WA	99205	509-328-4521	325-7909

— Attractions —

	City	State	Zip	Phone	Fax
Arbor Crest Winery 4705 N Fruit Hill Rd	Spokane	WA	99217	509-927-9894	927-0574
Bing Crosby Memorabilia Room at Gonzaga University 502 E Boone Ave	Spokane	WA	99258	509-328-4220	324-5718
Carr's One of a Kind in the World Museum 5225 N Freya St	Spokane	WA	99207	509-489-8859	489-8859
TF: 800-350-6469					
Cat Tales Endangered Species Conservation Park 17020 N Newport Hwy	Mead	WA	99021	509-238-4126	
Web: www.cattales.org					
Caterina Winery 905 N Washington	Spokane	WA	99201	509-328-5069	325-7324
Web: www.caterina.com					
Chase Gallery 808 W Spokane Falls Blvd	Spokane	WA	99201	509-625-6050	625-6777
Children's Museum of Spokane 110 N Post St	Spokane	WA	99201	509-624-5437	624-6453
Web: www.vpds.wsu.edu/cmos/ ■ *E-mail:* cmspokane@aol.com					
Corbin Art Center 507 W 7th Ave	Spokane	WA	99204	509-625-6677	
Coulee Dam National Recreation Area 1008 Crest Dr	Coulee Dam	WA	99116	509-633-9441	633-9332
Web: www.nps.gov/laro					
Douglas Gallery 120 N Wall	Spokane	WA	99201	509-624-4179	624-4170
Fairchild Air Force Base Heritage Museum 100 E Bong St	Fairchild AFB	WA	99011	509-247-2100	247-4110
Finch John A Arboretum 809 N Washington City Pk Maintenance	Spokane	WA	99201	509-625-6655	
Interplayers Ensemble S 174 Howard	Spokane	WA	99201	509-455-7529	624-5902
Web: www.interplayers.com					
Jundt Art Museum 202 E Cataldo Ave Gonzaga University	Spokane	WA	99258	509-328-4220	323-5525
Knipprath Cellars 6634 E Commere Ave	Spokane	WA	99212	509-534-5121	
Latah Creek Wine Cellars 13030 E Indiana	Spokane	WA	99216	509-926-0164	926-0710
Manito Park S Grand & 18th St	Spokane	WA	99203	509-625-6622	625-6958
Metropolitan Performing Arts Center 901 W Sprague Ave	Spokane	WA	99201	509-455-6500	835-2778
TF: 800-541-0828 ■ *Web:* www.metmtg.com/themet					
Mount Spokane State Park N 26107 Mt Spokane Dr	Mead	WA	99201	509-238-4258	
Resort at Mount Spokane 24817 N Mount Spokane Park Dr	Spokane	WA	99021	509-238-9114	238-4243
Riverfront Park 507 Howard St	Spokane	WA	99201	509-625-6600	625-6630
Riverfront Park IMAX Theatre 507 N Howard St	Spokane	WA	99201	509-625-6746	625-6630
Saint John's Cathedral 127 E 12th Ave	Spokane	WA	99202	509-838-4277	
Spokane Civic Theatre 1020 N Howard St	Spokane	WA	99205	509-325-1413	325-9287
TF: 800-446-9576					
Spokane Market Place Ruby St & Desmet Ave	Spokane	WA	99207	509-456-0100	
Spokane Symphony 334 W Spokane Falls Blvd Spokane Opera House	Spokane	WA	99201	509-624-1200	326-3921
Turnbull National Wildlife Refuge 26010 S Smith Rd	Cheney	WA	99004	509-235-4723	235-4703
Uptown Opera 901 W Sprague Ave Metropolitan Performing Arts Ctr	Spokane	WA	99204	509-533-1150	
Web: www.spokaneopera.com					
Valley Repertory Theatre 12212 1/2 E Sprague Ave	Spokane	WA	99206	509-927-6878	
Worden Winery 7217 W 45th St	Spokane	WA	99224	509-455-7835	838-4723
E-mail: wordenwines@msn.com					

SPORTS TEAMS & FACILITIES

	City	State	Zip	Phone	Fax
Playfair Race Course Altamont & Main	Spokane	WA	99202	509-534-0505	534-0101
Spokane Arena 720 Mallon Ave W	Spokane	WA	99201	509-324-7000	324-7050
Web: www.spokanearena.com					
Spokane Chiefs (hockey) 701 W Mallon Ave Spokane Veterans Memorial Arena	Spokane	WA	99201	509-328-0450	
Web: www.spokanechiefs.com/ ■ *E-mail:* spokanechiefs@worldnet.att.net					
Spokane Indians (baseball) I-90 Interstate Fairgrounds	Spokane	WA	99202	509-535-2922	534-5368
Spokane Raceway Park N 101 Hayford Rd	Spokane	WA	99224	509-244-3663	244-2472
Spokane Shadow W 4918 Everett Joe Albi Stadium	Spokane	WA	99205	509-326-4625	326-0636
Web: www.spokaneshadow.com ■ *E-mail:* robbinsjb@aol.com					

— Events —

	Phone
AHRA World Finals Drag Racing (late July)	509-244-3663

Spokane — Events (Cont'd)

	Phone
ArtFest (early June)	509-456-3931
Arts & Crafts Christmas Show & Sale (mid-November)	509-924-0588
Bloomsday Race (early May)	509-838-1579
Bloomsday Trade Show (early May)	509-838-1579
Cathedral & the Arts Music Series (October-March)	509-838-4277
Cherry Pickers Trot & Pit Spit (mid-July)	509-238-6970
Christmas Arts & Crafts Sale (mid-November)	509-924-0588
Christmas Candlelight Concert (mid-December)	800-325-7328
Christmas Tree Elegance (late November-early December)	509-326-3136
Green Bluff Apple Festival (late September-late October)	509-238-4709
Homefest (mid-October)	509-838-8755
Inland Craft Warnings (early October)	509-328-7240
Mozart on a Summer's Eve (late July)	509-326-4942
Northwest Bach Festival (late January-early February)	509-326-4942
Pig-Out in the Park (early September)	509-921-2205
Saint Patricks Day Parade (mid-March)	509-747-3230
Shrine Circus (late March)	509-624-1341
Spokane Hoop Fest (late June)	509-747-3230
Spokane Interstate Fair (early-mid-September)	509-747-3230
Spokane Lilac Festival (mid-May)	509-747-3230

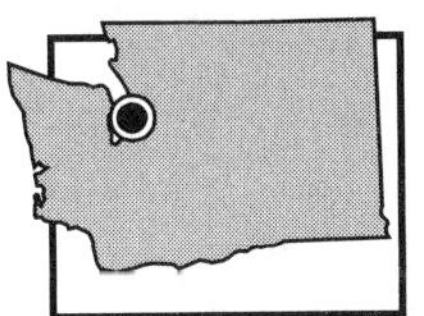

Tacoma

Approximately 30 minutes from Seattle is the city of Tacoma, Washington's "City of Destiny." Tacoma's location on Puget Sound's Commencement Bay has helped it to become one of the country's major trade centers, earning it the title "Gateway to the Pacific Rim." Point Defiance Park in Tacoma is 700 forested acres of a peninsula and bluff which juts into Puget Sound and includes a zoo and aquarium. Mount Rainier, located 74 miles southeast of Tacoma, can be seen from almost any vantage point in the city. Tacoma is home to the world's largest wood-domed structure, Tacoma Dome Arena and Exhibition Center, which is the site of concerts, conventions, trade shows, and other events.

Population	178,814	**Longitude**	122-44-31 W
Area (Land)	48.0 sq mi	**County**	Pierce
Area (Water)	12.5 sq mi	**Time Zone**	PST
Elevation	250 ft	**Area Code/s**	253
Latitude	47-25-31 N		

— Average Temperatures and Precipitation —

TEMPERATURES

	Jan	Feb	Mar	Apr	May	Jun	Jul	Aug	Sep	Oct	Nov	Dec
High	45	50	53	57	64	70	75	75	69	60	51	45
Low	35	37	39	41	46	52	55	56	52	46	40	36

PRECIPITATION

	Jan	Feb	Mar	Apr	May	Jun	Jul	Aug	Sep	Oct	Nov	Dec
Inches	5.4	4.0	3.5	2.3	1.7	1.5	0.8	1.1	1.9	3.2	5.8	5.9

— Important Phone Numbers —

	Phone		Phone
AAA	206-448-5353	**Poison Control Center**	800-732-6985
American Express Travel	206-441-8622	**Time/Temp**	206-361-8463
Emergency	911	**Weather**	206-464-2000
Medical Referral	206-622-9933		

— Information Sources —

	City	State	Zip	Phone	Fax
Better Business Bureau Serving Oregon & Western Washington 4800 S 188th St Suite 222 *Web:* www.seatac.bbb.org	SeaTac	WA	98188	206-431-2222	431-2211
Pierce County 930 Tacoma Ave S *Web:* www.co.pierce.wa.us	Tacoma	WA	98402	253-798-3495	798-3428
Tacoma City Hall 747 Market St *Web:* www.ci.tacoma.wa.us ■ *E-mail:* webmgr@ci.tacoma.wa.us	Tacoma	WA	98402	253-591-5000	591-5300
Tacoma Convention Center 1320 Broadway Plaza	Tacoma	WA	98402	253-572-3200	591-4105
Tacoma Dome Arena & Exhibition Hall 2727 E D St **Fax:* Mktg ■ *Web:* www.ci.tacoma.wa.us/tdome	Tacoma	WA	98421	253-272-3663	593-7620*
Tacoma Economic Development Dept 747 Market St Suite 900 *Web:* www.ci.tacoma.wa.us/ed	Tacoma	WA	98402	253-591-5206	591-2002
Tacoma Mayor 747 Market St Suite 1200	Tacoma	WA	98402	253-591-5100	591-5123
Tacoma-Pierce County Chamber of Commerce 950 Pacific Ave Suite 300 *Web:* www.tpchamber.org	Tacoma	WA	98402	253-627-2175	597-7305
Tacoma-Pierce County Visitor & Convention Bureau 1001 Pacific Ave Suite 400 *TF:* 800-272-2662 ■ *Web:* www.tpctourism.org ■ *E-mail:* info@tpctourism.org	Tacoma	WA	98402	253-627-2836	627-8783
Tacoma Public Library 1102 Tacoma Ave S *Web:* www.tpl.lib.wa.us	Tacoma	WA	98402	253-591-5666	591-5470

On-Line Resources

About.com Guide to Seattle/Tacoma	seattle.about.com/local/pacnwus/seattle
All Tacoma	www.alltacoma.com
Anthill City Guide Tacoma	www.anthill.com/city.asp?city=tacoma
Area Guide Tacoma	tacoma.areaguides.net
City Knowledge Tacoma	www.cityknowledge.com/wa_tacoma.htm
Dining Northwest Tacoma	www.diningnw.com
Excite.com Tacoma City Guide	www.excite.com/travel/countries/united_states/washington/tacoma
Table in Seattle Dining Guide	www.atable.com
Tacoma Net	www.tacoma.net/

— Transportation Services —

AIRPORTS

■ **Seattle-Tacoma International Airport (SEA)**	Phone
18 miles NE of downtown Tacoma (approx 30 minutes)	206-431-4444

Airport Transportation

	Phone
Capital Aeroporter $18 fare to downtown Tacoma	253-927-6179
Shuttle Express $25 fare to downtown Tacoma	206-622-1424
Taxi $45 fare to downtown Tacoma	253-531-7489

Commercial Airlines

	Phone		Phone
Aeroflot	888-686-4949	**Kenmore Air Harbor**	800-543-9595
Alaska	206-433-3100	**Northwest**	800-225-2525
America West	206-433-5704	**Scandinavian**	800-221-2350
American	800-433-7300	**Shuttle by United**	800-748-8853
American Trans Air	800-225-2995	**Southwest**	800-435-9792
British Airways	800-247-9297	**Thai**	800-426-5204
Continental	206-624-1740	**TWA**	800-221-2000
Delta	800-221-1212	**United**	800-241-6522
Harbor	800-359-3220	**United Express**	800-241-6522
Horizon	800-547-9308	**US Airways**	800-428-4322
Japan	800-525-3663		

Charter Airlines

	Phone		Phone
Crossings Aviation Inc	253-851-2381	**Galvin Flying Service**	206-763-0350
Flightcraft	206-764-6100	**Snohomish Flying Service Inc**	360-568-1541

CAR RENTALS

	Phone		Phone
Alamo	206-433-0182	**Hertz**	253-922-6688
Budget	253-383-4944	**Thrifty**	253-535-1122
Dollar	206-433-5825	**U-Save Auto**	253-475-1050

Tacoma (Cont'd)

LIMO/TAXI

	Phone		Phone
Checker Deluxe Cab	206-622-1234	**Soundview Limousine**	253-851-8687
Pierce Taxi	253-582-3455	**Washington Limousine**	206-523-8000

MASS TRANSIT

	Phone
Pierce County Transit $1 Base fare	253-581-8000

RAIL/BUS

				Phone
Greyhound Bus Station 811 Stewart St *TF:* 800-231-2222	Seattle	WA	98101	206-628-5526
King Street Amtrak Station 3035 S Jackson St	Seattle	WA	98104	206-382-4125

— Accommodations —

HOTEL RESERVATION SERVICES

	Phone	Fax
Greater Tacoma Bed & Breakfast Reservation Service *TF:* 800-406-4088 ■ *Web:* www.tacoma-inns.org ■ *E-mail:* reservations@tacoma-inns.org	253-752-8175	759-4025

HOTELS, MOTELS, RESORTS

				Phone	Fax
Best Western Executive Inn & Convention Center 5700 Pacific Hwy E. *TF:* 800-938-8500	Tacoma	WA	98424	253-922-0080	922-6439
Best Western Lakewood Motor Inn 6125 Motor Ave SW *TF:* 800-528-1234	Tacoma	WA	98499	253-584-2212	588-5546
Best Western Park Plaza 620 S Hill Park Dr *TF:* 800-528-1234	Puyallup	WA	98373	253-848-1500	848-1511
Best Western Tacoma Inn 8726 S Hosmer St *TF:* 800-528-1234 ■ *Web:* www.bwtacomainn.com/ ■ *E-mail:* reservations@bwtacomainn.com	Tacoma	WA	98444	253-535-2880	537-8379
Best Western Wesley Inn Gig Harbor 6575 Kimball Dr *TF:* 800-462-0002	Gig Harbor	WA	98335	253-858-9690	858-9893
Comfort Inn Tacoma 5601 Pacific Hwy E. *TF:* 800-228-5150	Tacoma	WA	98424	253-926-2301	922-1179
Days Inn 6802 Tacoma Mall Blvd *TF:* 800-329-7466	Tacoma	WA	98409	253-475-5900	475-3540
Extended StayAmerica 2120 S 48th St *TF:* 800-398-7829	Tacoma	WA	98409	253-475-6565	475-6562
Howard Johnson 1521 D St NE *TF:* 800-446-4656	Auburn	WA	98002	253-939-5950	735-4197
Howard Johnson Lodge 8702 S Hosmer St	Tacoma	WA	98444	253-535-3100	537-6497
La Quinta Motor Inn 1425 E 27th St *TF:* 800-531-5900	Tacoma	WA	98421	253-383-0146	627-3280
Quality Inn 9920 S Tacoma Way *TF:* 800-600-9751	Tacoma	WA	98499	253-588-5241	581-0652
Ramada Inn 2611 E 'E' St *TF:* 800-755-1547	Tacoma	WA	98421	253-572-7272	572-9664
Ramada Limited 3501 Pacific Hwy E. *TF:* 800-272-6232	Fife	WA	98424	253-926-1000	926-3009
Royal Coachman Inn 5805 Pacific Hwy E *TF:* 800-422-3051 ■ *Web:* www.royalcoachmaninn.com/ ■ *E-mail:* service@royalcoachmaninn.com	Tacoma	WA	98424	253-922-2500	922-6443
Sheraton Tacoma Hotel 1320 Broadway Plaza *TF:* 800-845-9466	Tacoma	WA	98402	253-572-3200	591-4105
Sherwood Inn 8402 S Hosmer St *TF:* 800-362-4296	Tacoma	WA	98444	253-535-2800	535-2777
Shilo Inn 7414 S Hosmer St.	Tacoma	WA	98408	253-475-4020	475-1236

— Restaurants —

				Phone
Ale House Pub & Eatery (American) 2122 Mildred W	Tacoma	WA	98466	253-565-9367
Atezzo's (Italian) 1320 Broadway Plaza	Tacoma	WA	98402	253-572-3200
Azteca (Mexican) 4801 Tacoma Mall Blvd	Tacoma	WA	98409	253-472-0246
Broadway Grill (Northwest) 1320 Broadway Plaza	Tacoma	WA	98402	253-591-4151
Cafe 322 (American) 322 Tacoma Ave S.	Tacoma	WA	98402	253-272-3081
Cl Shenanigans (Steak/Seafood) 3017 Ruston Way	Tacoma	WA	98402	253-752-8811
Cliff House (Steak/Seafood) 6300 Marine View Dr	Tacoma	WA	98422	253-927-0400
Cucina Cucina Italian Cafe (Italian) 4201 S Steele St	Tacoma	WA	98409	253-475-6000
El Toro (Mexican) 204 N Kay St.	Tacoma	WA	98403	253-627-5010
Haiku Gardens (Japanese) 9530 Bridgeport Way SW.	Tacoma	WA	98499	253-582-2779
Harbor Lights (Steak/Seafood) 2761 Ruston Way	Tacoma	WA	98402	253-752-8600
Harmon Brewing Company (American) 1938 Pacific Ave	Tacoma	WA	98402	253-383-2739
Johnny's Dock (Steak/Seafood) 1900 E 'D' St	Tacoma	WA	98445	253-627-3186
Kabuki Japanese Restaurant (Japanese) 2919 S 38th St Suite B	Tacoma	WA	98409	253-474-1650
Lobster Shop South (Steak/Seafood) 4015 Ruston Way	Tacoma	WA	98402	253-759-2165
Luciano's Waterfront Italian (Italian) 3327 Ruston Way	Tacoma	WA	98402	253-756-5611
Mandarin on Broadway (Chinese) 1128 Broadway Plaza	Tacoma	WA	98402	253-627-3400
Marsan's (Northwest) 2611 E 'E' St	Tacoma	WA	98421	253-572-7272
Moctezuma's Tacoma (Mexican) 4102 S 56th St.	Tacoma	WA	98409	253-474-5593
Old Spaghetti Factory (Italian) 1735 Jefferson Ave S	Tacoma	WA	98402	253-383-2214
Porter's Place (Barbecue) 3579 Portland Ave E	Tacoma	WA	98404	253-472-6595
Ravenous Restaurant (Northwest) 785 Broadway	Tacoma	WA	98402	253-572-6374
Roof-n-Doof's New Orleans Cafe (Cajun/Creole) 754 Pacific Ave	Tacoma	WA	98402	253-572-5113
Southern Kitchen (Southern) 1716 6th Ave	Tacoma	WA	98405	253-627-4282
Spar Tavern in Old Town (American) 2121 N 30th St	Tacoma	WA	98403	253-627-8215
Stanley & Seafort's (Seafood) 115 E 34th St	Tacoma	WA	98404	253-473-7300
Steamers Seafood Cafe (Seafood) 8802 6th Ave	Tacoma	WA	98465	253-565-4532
Tacoma Bar & Grill (American) 625 Commerce St.	Tacoma	WA	98402	253-572-4861
Trattoria Grazie (Italian) 2301 N 30th St	Tacoma	WA	98403	253-627-0231

— Goods and Services —

SHOPPING

				Phone	Fax
Freighthouse Square 25th & E 'D' Sts.	Tacoma	WA	98421	253-305-0678	627-0270
Lakewood Mall 10509 Gravelly Lake Dr SW.	Tacoma	WA	98499	253-984-6100	584-7476
South Hill Mall 3500 S Meridian.	Puyallup	WA	98373	253-840-2828	848-6836
Tacoma Mall 4502 S Steele St	Tacoma	WA	98409	253-475-4565	472-3413

BANKS

				Phone	Fax
Columbia Bank 1102 Broadway Plaza **Fax:* Hum Res	Tacoma	WA	98402	253-305-1900	272-7103*
Heritage Bank 5448 S Tacoma Way	Tacoma	WA	98409	253-472-3333	472-7573
KeyBank NA Tacoma District 1119 Pacific Ave. *TF:* 800-539-8189	Tacoma	WA	98411	253-305-7750	305-7951
US Bank of Washington NA 6723 S 19th St. *TF Cust Svc:* 800-872-2657*	Tacoma	WA	98466	253-566-3990	566-3993
Washington Mutual Bank 6916 19th St W. *TF Cust Svc:* 800-756-8000*	Tacoma	WA	98466	253-305-5390	305-5396
Westside Community Bank 4922 Bridgeport Way W.	Tacoma	WA	98467	253-565-9737	565-9705

BUSINESS SERVICES

	Phone		Phone
Airborne Express	800-247-2676	**Manpower Temporary Services**	253-473-5023
DHL Worldwide Express	800-225-5345	**Minuteman Press**	253-383-4377
Federal Express	800-238-5355	**Parker Services**	253-272-0979
General Employment	425-251-5006	**Post Office**	800-275-8777
Kinko's	253-582-1995	**UPS**	800-742-5877

— Media —

PUBLICATIONS

				Phone	Fax
Business Examiner 1517 S Fawcett Ave Suite 350 *TF:* 800-540-8322 ■ *Web:* www.businessexaminer.com	Tacoma	WA	98402	253-404-0891	404-0892
News Tribune‡ PO Box 11000 *TF:* 800-388-8742 ■ *Web:* www.tribnet.com	Tacoma	WA	98411	253-597-8511	597-8274

‡Daily newspapers

TELEVISION

				Phone	Fax
KBTC-TV Ch 28 (PBS) 1101 S Yakima Ave.	Tacoma	WA	98405	253-596-1528	596-1623
KCPQ-TV Ch 13 (Fox) 1813 Westlake Ave N. *Web:* www.kcpq.com ■ *E-mail:* reception@kcpq.com	Seattle	WA	98109	206-674-1313	674-1777
KCTS-TV Ch 9 (PBS) 401 Mercer St *Web:* www.kcts.org ■ *E-mail:* viewer@kcts.org	Seattle	WA	98109	206-728-6463	443-6691

Tacoma — Television (Cont'd)

				Phone	Fax
KING-TV Ch 5 (NBC) 333 Dexter Ave N *Web:* www.king5.com ■ *E-mail:* kingtv@king5.com	Seattle	WA	98109	206-448-5555	448-4525
KIRO-TV Ch 7 (CBS) 2807 3rd Ave *Web:* www.kirotv.com ■ *E-mail:* kironews7@kiro-tv.com	Seattle	WA	98121	206-728-7777	441-4840
KOMO-TV Ch 4 (ABC) 100 4th Ave N *Web:* www.komotv.com	Seattle	WA	98109	206-443-4000	443-3422
KSTW-TV Ch 11 (UPN) PO Box 11411 *Web:* www.paramountstations.com/KSTW ■ *E-mail:* kstw98d@prodigy.com	Tacoma	WA	98411	253-572-5789	272-7581
KTZZ-TV Ch 22 (WB) 945 Dexter Ave N	Seattle	WA	98109	206-282-2202	281-0207
KVOS-TV Ch 12 (Ind) 1151 Ellis St *TF:* 800-488-5867	Bellingham	WA	98225	360-671-1212	647-0824
KWPX-TV Ch 33 (PAX) 18000 International Blvd Suite 513 *Web:* www.pax.net/KWPX	SeaTac	WA	98104	206-439-0333	246-5940

RADIO

				Phone	Fax
KBSG-AM 1210 kHz (Oldies) 1730 Minor Ave 20th Fl	Seattle	WA	98101	206-343-9700	623-7677
KBSG-FM 97.3 MHz (Oldies) 1730 Minor Ave 20th Fl *Web:* www.kbsg.com ■ *E-mail:* suggestionbox@kbsg.com	Seattle	WA	98101	206-343-9700	623-7677
KHHO-AM 850 kHz (N/T) 950 Pacific Ave Suite 1200	Tacoma	WA	98402	253-383-8850	572-7850
KING-FM 98.1 MHz (Clas) 333 Dexter Ave N Suite 400 *Web:* www.king.org	Seattle	WA	98109	206-448-3981	448-0928
KIRO-AM 710 kHz (N/T) 1820 E Lake Ave East *Web:* www.kiro710.com	Seattle	WA	98102	206-726-7000	726-5446
KISW FM 99.9 MHz (CR) 1100 Olive Way Suite 1650 *Web:* www.kisw.com	Seattle	WA	98101	206-285-7625	282-7018
KIXI-AM 880 kHz (Nost) 3650 131st Ave SE Suite 550 *Web:* www.kixi.com ■ *E-mail:* am880kixi@aol.com	Bellevue	WA	98006	425-373-5545	373-5507
KLSY-FM 92.5 MHz (AC) 3650 131st Ave SE Suite 550	Bellevue	WA	98006	425-454-1540	455-8849
KMPS-FM 94.1 MHz (Ctry) 1000 Dexter Ave N Suite 100 *Web:* www.kmps.com	Seattle	WA	98109	206-805-0941	805-0907
KNDD-FM 107.7 MHz (Alt) 1100 Olive Way Suite 1550 *Web:* www.kndd.com	Seattle	WA	98101	206-622-3251	682-8349
KOMO-AM 1000 kHz (N/T) 1809 7th Ave Suite 200 *Web:* www.komo-am.com ■ *E-mail:* comments@komoradio.com	Seattle	WA	98101	206-223-5700	516-3110
KPLU-FM 88.5 MHz (NPR) Pacific Lutheran University *TF:* 800-677-5758 ■ *Web:* www.kplu.org ■ *E-mail:* kplu@plu.edu	Tacoma	WA	98447	253-535-7758	535-8332
KPLZ-FM 101.5 MHz (AC) 1809 7th Ave Suite 200 *Web:* www.kplz.com	Seattle	WA	98101	206-223-5703	292-1015
KUBE-FM 93.3 MHz (CHR) 190 Queen Anne Ave N Suite 100 *Web:* www.kube93.com	Seattle	WA	98109	206-285-2295	286-2376
KWJZ-FM 98.9 MHz (NAC) 3650 131st Ave SE Suite 550 *Web:* www.kwjz.com ■ *E-mail:* jazz@connectexpress.com	Bellevue	WA	98006	425-373-5536	373-5548

— Colleges/Universities —

				Phone	Fax
Pacific Lutheran University 12180 Park Ave S *Web:* www.plu.edu	Tacoma	WA	98447	253-531-6900	536-5136
Pierce College 9401 Farwest Dr SW *Web:* www.pierce.ctc.edu ■ *E-mail:* info@pierce.ctc.edu	Lakewood	WA	98498	253-964-6500	964-6427
South Puget Sound Community College 2011 Mottman Rd SW *Web:* www.spscc.ctc.edu	Olympia	WA	98512	360-754-7711	664-4336
Tacoma Community College 6501 S 19th St *Web:* www.tacoma.ctc.edu	Tacoma	WA	98466	253-566-5000	566-6011
University of Puget Sound 1500 N Warner St *TF Admissions:* 800-396-7191 ■ *Web:* www.ups.edu	Tacoma	WA	98416	253-879-3100	879-3500
University of Washington Tacoma 1900 Commerce St *TF:* 800-736-7750 ■ *Web:* www-uwt.u.washington.edu	Tacoma	WA	98402	253-692-4400	692-4414

— Hospitals —

				Phone	Fax
Good Samaritan Community Healthcare PO Box 1247	Puyallup	WA	98371	253-848-6661	845-5966
Madigan Army Medical Center 9040 Jackson Ave	Tacoma	WA	98431	253-968-1110	968-1633
Mary Bridge Children's Hospital & Health Center 315 MLK Way *Web:* www.multicare.com/marybridge/index.html ■ *E-mail:* information@multicare.com	Tacoma	WA	98405	253-552-1400	552-1180
Puget Sound Hospital 215 S 36th St	Tacoma	WA	98408	253-474-0561	756-2450
Saint Joseph Medical Center 1717 S 'J' St **Fax:* Admitting	Tacoma	WA	98405	253-627-4101	591-6609*
Tacoma General Hospital PO Box 5299	Tacoma	WA	98405	253-552-1000	552-1180
Veterans Affairs Puget Sound Health Care Systems American Lake Div 9600 Veterans Dr SW	Tacoma	WA	98493	253-582-8440	589-4017
Western State Hospital 9601 Steilacoom Blvd SW	Tacoma	WA	98498	253-582-8900	756-2879

— Attractions —

				Phone	Fax
Broadway Center for the Performing Arts 901 Broadway	Tacoma	WA	98402	253-591-5890	591-2013
Camp 6 Logging Exhibit Museum 5400 N Pearl St Point Defiance Pk	Tacoma	WA	98407	253-752-0047	
Children's Museum of Tacoma 936 Broadway *E-mail:* cmtstaff@shl.uswest.net	Tacoma	WA	98402	253-627-6031	627-2436
Commencement Bay Maritime Center 705 Dock St	Tacoma	WA	98402	253-272-2750	
Emerald Queen Casino 2102 Alexander Ave *Web:* www.emeraldqueen.com	Tacoma	WA	98421	253-594-7777	272-6725
Enchanted Parks Amusement Complex 36201 Enchanted Pkwy S	Federal Way	WA	98003	253-925-8001	925-1332
Fort Lewis Military Museum Fort Lewis Bldg 4320	Fort Lewis	WA	98433	253-967-7206	967-0837
Karpeles Manuscript Library Museum 407 S G St *Web:* www.rain.org/~karpeles/taq.html ■ *E-mail:* kmuseumtaz@aol.com	Tacoma	WA	98405	253-383-2575	572-6044
Lakewold Gardens 12317 Gravelly Lake Dr SW	Lakewood	WA	98499	253-584-4106	584-3021
McCord Air Museum McChord Air Force Base PO Box 4205	Tacoma	WA	98438	253-984-2485	984-5113
Mount Rainier National Park Tahoma Woods Star Route *Web:* www.nps.gov/mora/	Ashford	WA	98304	360-569-2211	569-2170
Northwest Trek Wildlife Park 11610 Trek Dr E *Web:* www.nwtrek.org	Eatonville	WA	98328	360-832-6117	832-6118
Old Town District N 30th St	Tacoma	WA	98403	253-627-8215	
Pacific Rim Bonsai Collection 33663 Weyerhaeuser Way S *TF:* 800-525-5440 ■ *Web:* www.weyerhaeuser.com/bonsai/ ■ *E-mail:* contactus@wdni.com	Federal Way	WA	98003	253-924-3153	
Pantages Theater 901 Broadway	Tacoma	WA	98402	253-591-5890	591-2013
Point Defiance Park 5400 N Pearl St	Tacoma	WA	98407	253-305-1000	
Point Defiance Zoo & Aquarium 5400 N Pearl St *Web:* www.pdza.org/	Tacoma	WA	98407	253-591-5337	591-5448
Port of Tacoma PO Box 1837 *Web:* www.portoftacoma.com	Tacoma	WA	98401	253-383-5841	593-4534
Puget Sound Music Society 825 Center St	Tacoma	WA	98409	253-383-2674	383-1709
Rialto Theater 9th St-betw Market & Broadway	Tacoma	WA	98402	253-591-5890	
Ruston Way Waterfront 3427 Ruston Way	Tacoma	WA	98402	253-591-2046	
Shanaman Sports Museum of Tacoma 2727 E D St Tacoma Dome	Tacoma	WA	98421	253-272-3663	
Sprinker Recreation Center 14824 S C St	Tacoma	WA	98444	253-798-4000	798-4024
Steilacoom Historical Museum 112 Main St	Steilacoom	WA	98388	253-584-4133	
Steilacoom Tribal Cultural Museum 1515 Lafayette St	Steilacoom	WA	98388	253-584-6308	584-0224
Tacoma Actors Guild 915 Broadway 6th Fl	Tacoma	WA	98402	253-272-2145	
Tacoma Art Museum 1123 Pacific Ave *Web:* www.tamart.org/ ■ *E-mail:* info@tamart.org	Tacoma	WA	98402	253-272-4258	627-1898
Tacoma Dome Arena & Exhibition Hall 2727 E D St **Fax:* Mktg ■ *Web:* www.ci.tacoma.wa.us/tdome	Tacoma	WA	98421	253-272-3663	593-7620*
Tacoma Little Theatre 210 N 'I' St *Web:* webforce.nwrain.com/tlthome/ ■ *E-mail:* tlt@nwrain.com	Tacoma	WA	98403	253-272-2281	272-3972

Tacoma — Attractions (Cont'd)

				Phone	Fax
Tacoma Master Chorale 7116 6th Ave Tacoma Musical Playhouse	Tacoma	WA	98406	253-565-6867	
Tacoma Musical Playhouse 7116 6th Ave *Web:* www.tmp.org	Tacoma	WA	98406	253-565-6867	
Tacoma Philharmonic 901 Broadway Pantages Theater	Tacoma	WA	98402	253-591-5894	
Tacoma Symphony 727 Commerce St Suite 210 *TF:* 888-274-1376	Tacoma	WA	98402	253-272-7264	272-1676
Tacoma's Landmark Convention Center & Temple Theatre 47 Saint Helens Ave	Tacoma	WA	98402	253-272-2042	272-3793
Union Station 1717 Pacific Ave	Tacoma	WA	98402	253-593-6792	
Washington State History Museum 1911 Pacific Ave *TF:* 888-238-4373 ■ *Web:* www.wshs.org/text/mus_hist.htm ■ *E-mail:* slile@wshs.wa.gov	Tacoma	WA	98402	253-272-3500	272-9518
WW Seymour Botanical Conservatory 316 S 'G' St Wright Pk	Tacoma	WA	98405	253-591-5330	

SPORTS TEAMS & FACILITIES

				Phone	Fax
Cheney Stadium 2502 S Tyler St *E-mail:* tacomapcl@aol.com	Tacoma	WA	98405	253-752-7707	752-7135
Emerald Downs 2300 Emerald Downs Dr. *TF:* 888-931-8400 ■ *Web:* www.emdowns.com	Auburn	WA	98001	253-288-7000	288-7710
Tacoma Rainiers (baseball) 2502 S Tyler St Cheney Stadium	Tacoma	WA	98405	253-752-7707	752-7135

— Events —

	Phone
Art a La Carte (early July)	253-627-2836
Art Ala Carte-Tacoma (early July)	253-305-1036
Civil War Encampment & Battle Demonstration (late May)	800-260-5997
Daffodil Festival Grand Floral Parade (mid-April)	253-627-6176
Ethnic Fest (late July)	253-798-7590
Fantasylights (late November-early January)	253-627-2836
Festival of Trees (early December)	253-552-1368
First Night Tacoma (December 31)	253-798-7205
Floral Daffodil Marine Regatta (mid-April)	253-752-3555
Fort Nisqually Brigade Encampment (early August)	253-591-5339
Freedom Fair (early July)	253-761-9433
Gardens of Tacoma Tour (late June)	253-474-0400
Gig Harbor Peninsula on Parade (early June)	253-851-6865
Holiday Parade & Tree Lighting (early December)	253-627-2175
Isia Spring Fever Skating Competition (mid-April)	253-798-4000
Junior Daffodil Parade (mid-April)	253-756-9020
Mardi Gras at Freighthouse Square (early February)	253-305-0678
Maritime Fest (mid-September)	253-383-2429
Meeker Days Hoedown & Blue Grass Festival (mid-June)	253-840-2631
Norwegian Heritage Festival (mid-May)	206-242-5289
Puyallup Spring Fair (mid-April)	253-841-5045
Scandinavian Days Festival (early October)	253-845-5446
Seafirst Freedom Fair & Fireworks Spectacular (July 4)	253-761-9433
Sprint PCS Taste of Tacoma (early July)	206-232-2982
Tacoma Farmers Market (June-September)	253-272-7077
Tacoma Old Town Blues Festival (mid-July)	253-627-1290
Tacoma Third Thursday Artwalk (early January-late December)	253-591-5341
Thursday Night Concerts in the Park (early July-late August)	253-581-1076
Western Washington Fair (early September)	253-841-5045
WIAA Spring Fest (late May)	425-746-7102
Wintergrass Bluegrass Festival (late February)	253-926-4164
Zoolights (late December-early January)	253-591-5337

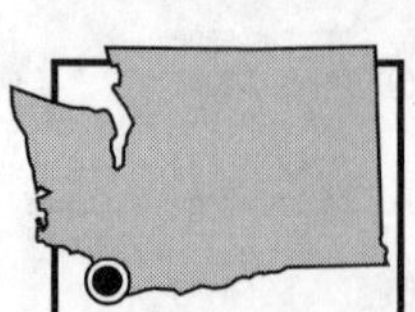

Vancouver

Vancouver is located in southwest Washington on the north bank of the Columbia River, directly across from Portland, OR. The city is noted for being the oldest non-Native American community in the Northwest, and one of its attractions, Fort Vancouver National Historic Site, is the oldest non-Native American settlement in the Northwest. The fort was the headquarters for the Hudson's Bay Company from 1825 to 1849, and it was the fur trading capital of the West Coast until 1860. The stockade and nine buildings have been reconstructed in their original locations, and each year the fort hosts Fort Vancouver Days in June, the Fort Vancouver Fourth of July Celebration in July, and the Brigade Encampment, also in July. Another historic attraction is the Officers Row National Historic District, which once served as residential housing for soldiers, officers, and their families who were stationed at the Vancouver Barracks and today is a four-block neighborhood of 21 restored 19th Century homes, including the homes of Generals George C. Marshall, O.O. Howard, and Ulysses S. Grant. Another area attraction, simply known as The Old Apple Tree, was planted in 1826 and is the oldest apple tree in the entire Northwest. Pearson Field, one of the oldest continuously operating airfields in the U.S. (and the site of the landing of history's first non-stop, transpolar flight), houses the Jack Murdock Aviation Center as well as the Pearson Air Museum.

Population	73,526	**Longitude**	122-38-35 W
Area (Land)	14.1 sq mi	**County**	Clark
Area (Water)	1.3 sq mi	**Time Zone**	PST
Elevation	210 ft	**Area Code/s**	360
Latitude	45-38-03 N		

— Average Temperatures and Precipitation —

TEMPERATURES

	Jan	Feb	Mar	Apr	May	Jun	Jul	Aug	Sep	Oct	Nov	Dec
High	45	50	55	59	66	72	77	78	73	63	52	45
Low	31	34	36	39	44	49	52	52	47	41	37	33

PRECIPITATION

	Jan	Feb	Mar	Apr	May	Jun	Jul	Aug	Sep	Oct	Nov	Dec
Inches	6.1	4.5	4.0	2.8	2.4	1.6	0.8	1.2	2.0	3.1	5.9	6.8

— Important Phone Numbers —

	Phone		Phone
AAA	360-696-4081	**Emergency**	911
American Express Travel	360-573-4320	**Poison Control Center**	800-732-6985

— Information Sources —

				Phone	Fax
Better Business Bureau Serving Oregon & Western Washington 4800 S 188th St Suite 222 *Web:* www.seatac.bbb.org	SeaTac	WA	98188	206-431-2222	431-2211
Clark County PO Box 5000 *Web:* www.crab.wa.gov/clark	Vancouver	WA	98666	360-699-2292	
Columbia River Economic Development Council 100 E Columbia Way *Web:* www.credc.org ■ *E-mail:* info@credc.org	Vancouver	WA	98661	360-694-5006	694-9927
Fort Vancouver Regional Library 1007 E Mill Plain Blvd *TF:* 800-750-9876 ■ *Web:* www.fvrl.org	Vancouver	WA	98663	360-695-1561	693-2681
Greater Vancouver Chamber of Commerce 404 E 15th St Suite 11 *Web:* www.vancouverusa.com	Vancouver	WA	98663	360-694-2588	693-8279
Vancouver City Hall 210 E 13th St *Web:* www.ci.vancouver.wa.us	Vancouver	WA	98668	360-696-8121	696-8049
Vancouver Mayor 210 E 13th St *Web:* www.ci.vancouver.wa.us ■ *E-mail:* mayor@ci.vancouver.wa.us	Vancouver	WA	98668	360-696-8211	696-8049

On-Line Resources

Cascade Link	www.cascadelink.org
City Knowledge Vancouver	www.cityknowledge.com/wa_vancouver.htm
Excite.com Vancouver City Guide	www.excite.com/travel/countries/united_states/washington/vancouver
NITC Travelbase City Guide Vancouver	www.travelbase.com/auto/features/vancouver-wa.html
Online City Guide to Vancouver	www.onlinecityguide.com/wa/vancouver
Southwest Washington Community Network	www.swwcn.org
Vancouver Network	www.vanusa.net
Vancouver USA Metro Area	www.mkt-place.com/market/vanusa/vanintro.html

Vancouver (Cont'd)

— Transportation Services —

AIRPORTS

■ Portland International Airport (PDX)

	Phone
8 miles SE of downtown Vancouver (approx 15 minutes)	503-460-4234

Web: www.portlandairportpdx.com

Airport Transportation

	Phone
Airport Executive Car Services Inc $36 fare to downtown Vancouver	360-735-0039
Cloud 9 Airport Shuttle Service $17 fare to downtown Vancouver	360-891-0844

Commercial Airlines

	Phone		Phone
Alaska	800-426-0333	**Hawaiian**	800-367-5320
America West	800-235-9292	**Horizon**	800-547-9308
American	800-433-7300	**Northwest**	800-225-2525
Continental	800-525-0280	**SkyWest**	800-453-9417
Delta	800-221-1212	**Southwest**	800-435-9792
Delta Connection	800-221-1212	**TWA**	800-221-2000
Frontier	800-432-1359	**United**	800-241-6522
Harbor	800-359-3220	**United Express**	800-241-6522

Charter Airlines

	Phone
C & C Aviation Inc	503-760-6969

CAR RENTALS

	Phone		Phone
Budget	360-574-5331	**Sears**	360-574-6671
Enterprise	360-576-9999		

LIMO/TAXI

	Phone		Phone
Vancouver Cab Co	360-693-1234	**Yellow Cab Co**	360-693-3333

MASS TRANSIT

	Phone
C-Tran $.60 Base fare	360-695-0123

RAIL/BUS

				Phone
Amtrak Station 1301 W 11th St *TF:* 800-872-7245	Vancouver	WA	98660	360-694-7307
Greyhound Bus Station 613 Main St *TF:* 800-231-2222	Vancouver	WA	98660	360-696-0186

— Accommodations —

HOTELS, MOTELS, RESORTS

				Phone	Fax
Best Inn & Suites 221 NE Chkalov Dr *TF:* 800-426-5110	Vancouver	WA	98684	360-256-7044	256-1231
Best Western Inn of Vancouver 11506 NE 3rd St *TF:* 888-254-3900	Vancouver	WA	98684	360-254-4000	254-8741
Camas Hotel 405 NE 4th Ave	Camas	WA	98607	360-834-5722	
Comfort Inn 13207 NE 20th Ave *TF:* 800-228-5150	Vancouver	WA	98686	360-574-6000	573-3746
Comfort Suites at Vancouver Mall 4714 NE 94th Ave	Vancouver	WA	98662	360-253-3100	253-7998
Courtyard by Marriott 470 McLaws Cir *TF:* 800-321-2211	Williamsburg	VA	23185	757-221-0700	221-0741
Days Inn Historic Area 331 Bypass Rd *TF:* 800-759-1166	Williamsburg	VA	23185	757-253-1166	221-0637
Doubletree Hotel at the Quay 100 Columbia St *TF:* 800-222-8733 ■ *Web:* www.doubletreehotels.com/DoubleT/Hotel161/176/176Main.htm	Vancouver	WA	98660	360-694-8341	694-2023
Extended StayAmerica 300 NE 115th Ave	Vancouver	WA	98684	360-604-8530	604-8541
Ferryman's Inn 7901 NE 6th Ave	Vancouver	WA	98665	360-574-2151	574-9644
Fort Motel 500 E 13th St	Vancouver	WA	98660	360-694-3327	737-3951
Guest House Motel 11504 NE 2nd St	Vancouver	WA	98684	360-254-4511	254-7274
Heathman Lodge 7801 NE Greenwood Dr *Web:* www.heathmanlodge.com	Vancouver	WA	98662	360-254-3100	254-6100
Holiday Inn Express 9107 NE Vancouver Mall Dr	Vancouver	WA	98662	360-253-5000	253-3137
Homewood Suites 701 SE Columbia Shores Blvd	Vancouver	WA	98661	360-750-1100	750-4899
Kays Motel 6700 NE Hwy 99	Vancouver	WA	98665	360-693-4221	
Phoenix Inn 12712 SE 2nd Cir	Vancouver	WA	98684	360-891-9777	891-8866
Quality Inn 7001 NE Hwy 99	Vancouver	WA	98665	360-696-0516	693-8343
Rama Inn 544 6th St	Washougal	WA	98671	360-835-8591	835-0240
Residence Inn by Marriott 8005 NE Parkway Dr	Vancouver	WA	98662	360-253-4800	256-4758
Salmon Creek Motel 11901 NE Hwy 99	Vancouver	WA	96868	360-573-0751	573-8567
Shilo Inn 401 E 13th St	Vancouver	WA	98660	360-696-0411	750-0933
Shilo Inn Hazel Dell 13206 Hwy 99	Vancouver	WA	98686	360-573-0511	573-0396
Sleep Inn 9201 NE Vancouver Mall Dr	Vancouver	WA	98662	360-254-0900	253-9343
Sunnyside Motel 12200 NE Hwy 99	Vancouver	WA	98686	360-573-4141	
Value Motel 708 NE 78th St	Vancouver	WA	98665	360-574-2345	576-0329
Vancouver Lodge 601 Broadway St	Vancouver	WA	98660	360-693-3668	735-0817
Vintage Inn 310 W 11th St *TF:* 888-693-6635 ■ *Web:* www.vintage-inn.com ■ *E-mail:* info@vintage-inn.com	Vancouver	WA	98660	360-693-6635	

— Restaurants —

				Phone
Andale Mexican Restaurant (Mexican) 16200 SE McGillivray Blvd	Vancouver	WA	98683	360-944-1413
Belltower Brewhouse (American) 707 SE 164th Ave	Vancouver	WA	98684	360-944-7800
Bill's Chicken & Steak House (Steak) 2200 St Johns Blvd	Vancouver	WA	98661	360-695-1591
Buster's Texas-Style Barbecue (Barbecue) 1118 NE 78th St	Vancouver	WA	98665	360-546-2439
Café Augustino's (Italian) 1109 Washington St	Vancouver	WA	98660	360-750-1272
Carol's Corner Café (American) 7800 NE St Johns Blvd	Vancouver	WA	98665	360-573-6357
Carrows Restaurant (American) 2903 NE Andresen Rd	Vancouver	WA	98661	360-892-6488
Casa Grande Restaurant (Mexican) 2014 Main St	Vancouver	WA	98660	360-694-7031
Chart House Restaurant (Steak/Seafood) 101 SE Columbia Way	Vancouver	WA	98661	360-693-9211
Christine's Restaurant (American) 2626 E Evergreen Blvd	Vancouver	WA	98661	360-694-1750
Clancy's (Seafood) 9901 NE 7th Ave	Vancouver	WA	98685	360-573-3474
Edelweiss Restaurant & Lounge (German) 8800 NE Hwy 99	Vancouver	WA	98665	360-574-4051
El Charrito Mexican Restaurant (Mexican) 516 SE Chkalov Dr	Vancouver	WA	98683	360-892-1676
El Tapatio (Mexican) 6202 NE Hwy 99	Vancouver	WA	98665	360-693-2443
Hazel Dell Brewpub (American) 8513 NE Hwy 99	Vancouver	WA	98665	360-576-0996
Hidden House Restaurant (American) 100 W 13th St	Vancouver	WA	98660	360-696-2847
Holland Restaurant (Homestyle) 1708 Main St	Vancouver	WA	98660	360-694-7842
Lindo Mexico (Mexican) 316 SE 123rd Ave	Vancouver	WA	98683	360-883-5555
Little Italy's Trattoria (Italian) 901 Washington St	Vancouver	WA	98660	360-737-2363
McMenamins on the Columbia (American) 1801 SE Columbia River Dr	Vancouver	WA	98661	360-699-1521
Saigon Restaurant (Vietnamese) 3021 NE 72nd Dr	Vancouver	WA	98661	360-944-8338
Sakura of Tokyo (Japanese) 8010 NE Hwy 99	Vancouver	WA	98665	360-573-3883
Salcido's Mexican Restaurant (Mexican) 14415 SE Mill Plain Blvd	Vancouver	WA	98684	360-256-2427
Salmon Creek Brewery & Pub (American) 108 W Evergreen Blvd	Vancouver	WA	98660	360-993-1827
Skipper's Seafood 'n Chowder (Seafood) 5207 E Mill Plain Blvd	Vancouver	WA	98661	360-694-0481
Sukhothai Restaurant (Thai) 611 Main St	Vancouver	WA	98660	360-906-8541
Thai Little Home (Thai) 3214 E Fourth Plain Blvd	Vancouver	WA	98661	360-693-4061
Thai Orchid (Thai) 1004 Washington St	Vancouver	WA	98660	360-695-7786
Thai Place Cuisine (Thai) 212 NE 164th Ave	Vancouver	WA	98684	360-882-7349
Timber Lanes Restaurant (American) 2306 NE Andresen Rd	Vancouver	WA	98661	360-695-2501
Uncle Joe's Pasta & Deli House (Italian) 615 SE Chkalov Dr	Vancouver	WA	98683	360-260-9846
Vietnam Garden (Vietnamese) 2904 E Fourth Plain Blvd	Vancouver	WA	98661	360-735-1032

— Goods and Services —

SHOPPING

				Phone
Pendleton Woolen Mill & Outlet Store 2 17th St *TF:* 800-568-2480	Washougal	WA	98671	360-835-1118

Vancouver — Shopping (Cont'd)

	City	State	ZIP	Phone	Fax
Vancouver Mall 8700 NE Vancouver Mall Dr	Vancouver	WA	98662	360-892-6255	892-0124

BANKS

	City	State	ZIP	Phone	Fax
Bank of America NA 805 Broadway St.	Vancouver	WA	98660	360-696-5664	696-5682
Bank of Clark County 1400 Washington St Suite 200 *Web:* www.bankofclarkcounty.com ■ *E-mail:* info@bankofclarkcounty.com	Vancouver	WA	98660	360-993-2265	
Centennial Bank 600 NE 99th St.	Vancouver	WA	98665	360-573-4010	696-5035
Continental Savings Bank 2100 SE 164th Ave Suite F-104	Vancouver	WA	98683	360-253-6166	253-9390
First Independent Bank 1220 Main St. *Web:* www.firstindy.com	Vancouver	WA	98668	360-699-4242	699-4347
Riverview Community Bank 7735 NE Hwy 99.	Vancouver	WA	98665	360-574-2084	576-0488
Sterling Savings Bank 14610 SE Mill Plain Blvd	Vancouver	WA	98684	360-892-4911	892-5147
Today's Bank 915 MacArthur Blvd	Vancouver	WA	98661	360-258-6329	258-3441
US Bank NA 13001 NE Hwy 99.	Vancouver	WA	98686	360-574-5077	573-5328
Washington Federal Savings & Loan Assn 13411 SE Mill Plain Blvd Suite A-1	Vancouver	WA	98684	360-944-6003	944-5573
Washington Mutual Bank 3205 NE 52nd St *TF:* 800-452-8315	Vancouver	WA	98663	360-750-3040	693-3253
Wells Fargo Bank 1800 Main St. *TF Cust Svc:* 800-688-9100*	Vancouver	WA	98660	360-695-7218	750-0394
West Coast Bank 801 Main St	Vancouver	WA	98660	360-695-3439	693-5667

BUSINESS SERVICES

	Phone
Express Personnel Services	360-696-3600
Interim Personnel	360-254-1163
Kelly Services	360-699-5337
Kinko's	360-694-8584
Kwik Kopy Printing	360-891-6666
Mail Boxes Etc	360-896-4916
Manpower Temporary Services	360-253-7131
Olsten Staffing Services	360-885-2515
Post Office	800-275-8777

— Media —

PUBLICATIONS

	City	State	ZIP	Phone	Fax
Columbian‡ PO Box 180 *TF:* 800-743-3391 ■ *Web:* www.columbian.com	Vancouver	WA	98666	360-694-3391	699-6033
Vancouver Business Journal 2525 E Fourth Plain Blvd *Web:* www.vbjusa.com ■ *E-mail:* editorial@vbjusa.com	Vancouver	WA	98661	360-695-2442	695-3056

‡Daily newspapers

TELEVISION

	City	State	ZIP	Phone	Fax
KATU-TV Ch 2 (ABC) 2153 NE Sandy Blvd *Web:* local.katu.citysearch.com	Portland	OR	97232	503-231-4222	231-4263
KGW-TV Ch 8 (NBC) 1501 SW Jefferson St *Web:* www.kgw.com	Portland	OR	97201	503-226-5000	226-4448
KOIN-TV Ch 6 (CBS) 222 SW Columbia St. *Web:* www.koin.com ■ *E-mail:* koin06a@prodigy.com	Portland	OR	97201	503-464-0600	464-0717
KOPB-TV Ch 10 (PBS) 7140 SW Macadam Ave. *Web:* www.opb.org/ ■ *E-mail:* kopb@opb.org	Portland	OR	97219	503-244-9900	293-1919
KPDX-TV Ch 49 (Fox) 910 NE ML King Jr Blvd *Web:* www.kpdx.com	Portland	OR	97232	503-239-4949	239-6184
KPTV-TV Ch 12 (UPN) 211 SE Caruthers St *Web:* www.kptv.com	Portland	OR	97214	503-230-1200	230-1065

RADIO

	City	State	ZIP	Phone	Fax
KBBT-FM 107.5 kHz (AC) 2040 SW 1st Ave *TF:* 800-567-1075 ■ *Web:* www.thebeat.com	Portland	OR	97201	503-222-1011	222-2047
KBMS-AM 1480 kHz (Urban) 601 Main St Suite 600	Vancouver	WA	98660	360-699-1881	
KBNP-AM 1410 kHz (Misc) 278 SW Arthur St *Web:* www.kbnp.com ■ *E-mail:* kbnp@kbnp.com	Portland	OR	97201	503-223-6769	
KBOO-FM 90.7 MHz (Misc) 20 SE 8th Ave. *Web:* www.kboo.org ■ *E-mail:* general@kboo.org	Portland	OR	97214	503-231-8032	231-7145
KBPS-FM 89.9 MHz (Clas) 515 NE 15th Ave *Web:* www.kbps.org	Portland	OR	97232	503-916-5828	916-2642
KBVM-FM 88.3 MHz (Rel) 5000 N Willamette Blvd Suite 44	Portland	OR	97203	503-285-5200	
KEWS-AM 620 kHz (N/T) 4949 SW Macadam Ave.	Portland	OR	97201	503-225-1190	227-5873
KEX-AM 1190 kHz (N/T) 4949 SW Macadam Ave. *Web:* www.1190kex.com	Portland	OR	97201	503-225-1190	224-3216
KFXX-AM 910 kHz (Sports) 0700 SW Bancroft St. *Web:* www.kfxx.com ■ *E-mail:* kfxx@kfxx.com	Portland	OR	97201	503-223-1441	223-6909
KGON-FM 92.3 MHz (CR) 4614 SW Kelly Ave *Web:* www.kgon.com	Portland	OR	97201	503-223-1441	223-6909
KINK-FM 102.9 MHz (AAA) 1501 SW Jefferson St *Web:* www.kinkfm102.com ■ *E-mail:* kinkfm102@kinkfm102.com	Portland	OR	97201	503-226-5080	226-4578
KKCW-FM 103.3 MHz (AC) 5005 SW Macadam Ave. *Web:* www.k103.com	Portland	OR	97201	503-222-5103	222-0030
KKGT-AM 1150 kHz (N/T) 15240 SE 82nd Dr *Web:* www.greattalk1150am.com	Clackamas	OR	97015	503-222-1150	722-9111
KKJZ-FM 106.7 MHz (NAC) 222 SW Columbia Ave Suite 350 *Web:* www.kkjz.com	Portland	OR	97201	503-223-0300	497-2333
KKRZ-FM 100.3 MHz (CHR) 4949 SW Macadam Ave. *Web:* www.z100portland.com ■ *E-mail:* hlg@z100portland.com	Portland	OR	97201	503-226-0100	295-9281
KKSN-AM 1520 kHz (Nost) 888 SW 5th Ave Suite 790	Portland	OR	97204	503-226-9791	243-3299
KKSN-FM 97.1 MHz (Oldies) 888 SW 5th Ave Suite 790 *Web:* www.kisnfm.com	Portland	OR	97204	503-226-9791	243-3299
KNRK-FM 94.7 MHz (Alt) 0700 SW Bankroft *Web:* www.knrk.com	Portland	OR	97201	503-223-1441	223-6909
KOPB-FM 91.5 MHz (NPR) 7140 SW Macadam Ave.	Portland	OR	97219	503-293-1905	293-1919
KPDQ-FM 93.7 MHz (Rel) 5110 SE Stark St *Web:* www.kpdq.com	Portland	OR	97215	503-231-7800	238-7202
KUFO-FM 101.1 MHz (Rock) 2040 SW 1st Ave *Web:* www.kufo.com	Portland	OR	97201	503-222-1011	222-2047
KUPL-FM 98.7 MHz (Ctry) 222 SW Columbia Ave Suite 350	Portland	OR	97221	503-223-0300	497-2336
KVAN-AM 1550 kHz (N/T) 7710 NE Vancouver Mall Dr *Web:* www.kvan.com ■ *E-mail:* feedback@kvan.com	Vancouver	WA	98662	360-944-1550	944-6679
KWJJ-FM 99.5 MHz (Ctry) 2000 SW 1st Ave Suite 300 *Web:* www.kwjj.com	Portland	OR	97201	503-228-4393	227-3938
KXL-AM 750 kHz (N/T) 0234 SW Bancroft St **Fax:* Sales ■ *Web:* www.kxl.com	Portland	OR	97201	503-243-7595	417-7660*

— Colleges/Universities —

	City	State	ZIP	Phone	Fax
Clark College 1800 E McLoughlin Blvd *Web:* www.clark.edu ■ *E-mail:* grotsd@ooi.clark.edu	Vancouver	WA	98663	360-694-6521	992-2876
Washington State University Vancouver 14204 NE Salmon Creek Ave *Web:* www.vancouver.wsu.edu ■ *E-mail:* admissions@vancouver.wsu.edu	Vancouver	WA	98686	360-546-9779	546-9030

— Hospitals —

	City	State	ZIP	Phone	Fax
Southwest Washington Medical Center PO Box 1600 **Fax:* Admitting ■ *Web:* www.swmedctr.com ■ *E-mail:* marketing@swmedctr.com	Vancouver	WA	98668	360-256-2000	256-3035*

— Attractions —

	City	State	ZIP	Phone
Altman Gallery 210 W Evergreen Blvd	Vancouver	WA	98660	360-695-9298

Vancouver — Attractions (Cont'd)

				Phone	Fax
Battle Ground Lake State Park 18002 NE 249th St	Battle Ground	WA	98604	360-687-4621	
TF: 800-233-0321					
Cedar Creek Grist Mill & Covered Bridge Grist Mill Rd.	Woodland	WA	98674	360-225-8532	
Clark County Historical Museum 1511 Main St	Vancouver	WA	98660	360-695-4681	
Covington House 4201 Main St	Vancouver	WA	98663	360-695-6750	
Downtown Vancouver Assn 609 Main St	Vancouver	WA	98660	360-693-2978	
Fort Vancouver National Historic Site 612 E Reserve St	Vancouver	WA	98661	360-696-7655	696-7657
TF: 800-832-3599 ■ *Web:* www.nps.gov/fova/					
Frenchman's Bar Regional Park 9612 NW Lower River Rd	Vancouver	WA	98660	360-735-8839	
General Howard House 750 Andresen St.	Vancouver	WA	98661	360-992-1820	
Gifford Pinchot National Forest 10600 NE 51st St	Vancouver	WA	98682	360-891-5001	891-5045
Web: www.fs.fed.us/gpnf/					
Grant House Folk Art Center 1101 Officers Row	Vancouver	WA	98661	360-694-5252	
Great Western Malting Co PO Box 1529	Vancouver	WA	98668	360-693-3661	696-8354
Kaiser Henry J Shipyard Memorial & Interpretive Center Columbia Way Marine Pk	Vancouver	WA	98661	360-696-8173	696-8009
Leverich Park E 39th & M Sts	Vancouver	WA	98660	360-696-8171	
Lewisville County Park 26411 NE Lewisville Hwy.	Vancouver	WA		360-696-8171	
Marshall House & Gift Shop 1301 Officers Row	Vancouver	WA	98661	360-693-3103	
Mount Saint Helens National Volcanic Monument Headquarters 42218 NE Yale Bridge Rd.	Amboy	WA	98601	360-247-3900	247 3001
Web: www.fs.fed.us/gpnf/mshnvm					
North Clark Historical Museum 399th St & Hwy 503 United Brethren Church	Amboy	WA	98601	360-263-4429	
Parkersville National Historic Site 24 S 'A' St.	Washougal	WA	98671	360-834-4792	
Pearson Air Museum 1115 E 5th St	Vancouver	WA	98661	360-694-7026	694-0824
Web: www.pearsonairmuseum.org ■ *E-mail:* pearson@pacifier.com					
Pendleton Woolen Mill & Outlet Store 2 17th St.	Washougal	WA	98671	360-835-1118	
TF: 800-568-2480					
Pomeroy Living History Farm 20902 NE Lucia Falls Rd	Yacolt	WA	98675	360-686-3537	
Port of Vancouver 3103 Lower River Rd	Vancouver	WA	98660	360-693-3611	735-1565
Web: www.portvanusa.com ■ *E-mail:* povinfo@portvanusa.com					
Ridgefield National Wildlife Refuge 301 N 3rd Ave	Ridgefield	WA	98642	360-887-4106	
Rocket City Neon Advertising Museum 1554 NE 3rd Ave	Camas	WA	98607	360-834-6366	
Web: www.rocketcityneon.com ■ *E-mail:* david@rocketcityneon.com					
Royal Durst Theater 3101 Main St	Vancouver	WA	98663	360-737-4284	696-5227
Salishan Vineyards 35011 N Fork Ave.	LaCenter	WA	98629	360-263-2713	
Salmon Creek Regional Park 1112 NE 117th St.	Vancouver	WA	98685	360-735-8839	
Steigerwald Lake National Wildlife Refuge 36062 SR-14	Stevenson	WA	98648	509-427-5208	
Tears of Joy Puppet Theatre 601 Main St Suite 403.	Vancouver	WA	98660	360-695-0477	695-0438
Two Rivers Heritage Museum 001 16th St	Washougal	WA	98671	360-835-8742	
Vancouver Lake Park 6801 NW Lower River Rd	Vancouver	WA	98660	360-696-8171	
Vancouver Symphony Orchestra 3101 Main St Vancouver School of the Arts	Vancouver	WA	98660	360-735-7278	
Water Resources Education Center 4600 SE Columbia Way	Vancouver	WA	98668	360-696-8478	
Web: www.ci.vancouver.wa.us/watercenter					
Wendel Museum of Animal Conservation 8303 SE Evergreen Hwy.	Vancouver	WA	98664	360-694-8651	254-3698

SPORTS TEAMS & FACILITIES

				Phone	Fax
Portland International Raceway 1940 N Victory Blvd	Portland	OR	97217	503-823-7223	823-5896
Web: www.indytrax.com/pir ■ *E-mail:* indytrax@teleport.com					
Vancouver Indoor Sports Arena 3315 NE 112th Ave	Vancouver	WA	98682	360-254-8453	

— Events —

	Phone
Amboy Territorial Days Celebration (early-mid-July)	360-686-3383
An Olde-Fashioned Fourth (early July)	360-686-3537
Antique Aircraft Fly-In (early July)	360-694-7026
Camas Days (late July)	360-834-2472
Candlelight Tour (mid-September)	360-696-7655
Christmas at Fort Vancouver (mid-December)	360-696-7655
Clark County Rural Heritage Fair (mid-July)	360-687-4554
Earth Action Day (mid-April)	360-696-8478
Fort James Health & Safety Fair (early May)	360-834-3021
Fort Vancouver Brigade Encampment (mid-July)	360-696-7655
Fort Vancouver Days Celebration (early-mid-July)	360-696-8171
Fort Vancouver Fourth of July Celebration (July 4)	360-693-5481
Founders Day (late August)	360-696-7655
Harvest Days Celebration (mid-July)	360-687-1510
Hazel Dell Parade of Bands (mid-May)	360-576-1195
Herb Festival (mid-May)	360-686-3537
Home & Garden Idea Fair (late April)	360-992-3231
International Discovery Walk Festival (late April)	360-892-6758
LaCenter Summer Our Days Festival (late July)	360-263-7168
Mount Tum Tum Native American Indian Encampment (early July)	360-247-5235
Our Days Festival (late July)	360-263-8850
Queen Victoria's Birthday (late May)	360-696-7655
River Rhythms & Chili Cook-Off (early-mid-July)	360-696-8171
Rose Show (late June)	360-693-6822
Seafarer's International Festival (late July)	360-694-9300
Spring Castles Programs (early March-early June)	360-992-1821
Spring Dance (late May)	360-694-7026
Sturgeon Festival (late May)	360-696-8478
Vancouver Farmers Market Saturdays (April-October)	360-737-8298

West Virginia

Population (1999): 1,806,928 **Area (sq mi): 24,231**

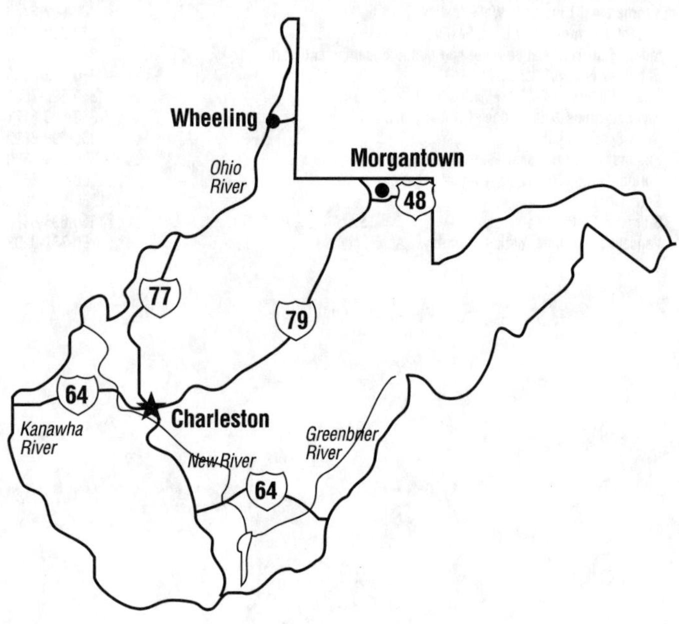

— State Information Sources —

				Phone	Fax
West Virginia Chamber of Commerce					
PO Box 2789	Charleston	WV	25330	304-342-1115	342-1130
Web: www.wvchamber.com					
West Virginia Development Office					
1900 Kanawah Blvd E Bldg 6 Rm 525B	Charleston	WV	25305	304-558-2234	558-1189
Web: www.wvdo.org ■ *E-mail:* wvdo@wvdo.org					
West Virginia Library Commission					
1900 Kanawha Blvd E	Charleston	WV	25305	304-558-2041	558-2044
Web: www.wvlc.wvnet.edu					
West Virginia Parks & Recreation					
State Capit0l Complex Bldg 3 Rm 714	Charleston	WV	25305	304-558-2764	558-0077
TF: 800-225-5982 ■ *Web:* wvweb.com/www/wv_parks.html					
West Virginia State Government Information				304-558-3456	
Web: www.state.wv.us					
West Virginia Tourism Div					
2101 Washington St E	Charleston	WV	25305	304-558-2200	558-2279
TF: 800-225-5982 ■ *Web:* www.state.wv.us/tourism ■ *E-mail:* research@tourism.state.wv.us					

ON-LINE RESOURCES

Discover the Eastern Panhandle of West Virginia . . . . wvweb.com/www/discover/index.html
Rough Guide Travel West Virginia travel.roughguides.com/content/616/index.htm
Travel.org-West Virginia . . . . travel.org/westvirg.html
Visit Southern West Virginia . . . . www.visitwv.com
West Virginia Cities . . . . dir.yahoo.com/Regional/U_S__States/West_Virginia/Cities
West Virginia Counties & Regions . . . . dir.yahoo.com/Regional/U_S__States/West_Virginia/Counties_and_Regions
West Virginia Online . . . . www.wvonline.com
West Virginia Online . . . . www.westvirginia.com
West Virginia Online Web Directory . . . . www.wvstate.com
West Virginia Scenario . . . . scenariousa.dstylus.com/wv/indexf.htm
West Virginia Travel & Tourism Guide . . . . .www.travel-library.com/north_america/usa/west_virginia/index.html
West Virginia Web . . . . wvweb.com
Yahoo! Get Local West Virginia . . . . .dir.yahoo.com/Regional/U_S__States/West_Virginia

— Cities Profiled —

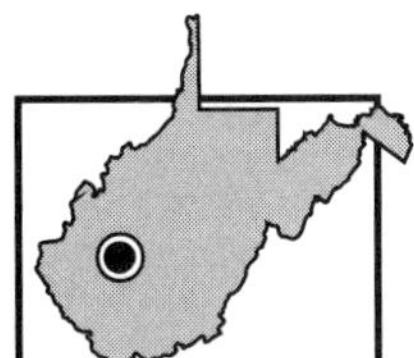

Charleston

Downtown Charleston features restored turn-of-the-century architecture, as well as the Charleston Town Center, an indoor shopping center with more than 160 stores, Picnic Place, and a three-story waterfall in its atrium. Guided tours of the State Capitol Building in Charleston, designed by architect Cass Gilbert (designer of the U.S. Supreme Court Building), are available year-round. Day trips in the area include whitewater rafting on the New River Gorge or Gauley River. New River Gorge Bridge is a man-made wonder, and the Gorge itself has been called the "Grand Canyon of the East." The Kanawha River, on which Charleston is situated, is a site for sternwheeler excursions as well as the annual Sternwheel Regatta, an 11-day event that ends on Labor Day. Not far from Charleston is the Blenko Glass Company, with a factory outlet area, stained glass exhibits, a museum with historical glass displays, and an observation deck that allows visitors to see inside the plant and to view the various steps involved in handcrafting glass.

Population 55,056
Area (Land) . . . . . . 29.5 sq mi
Area (Water) . . . . . . 1.1 sq mi
Elevation . . . . . . 601 ft
Latitude . . . . . . 38-35-35 N
Longitude . . . . . . 81-63-87 W
County . . . . . . Kanawha
Time Zone . . . . . . EST
Area Code/s 304

— Average Temperatures and Precipitation —

TEMPERATURES

	Jan	Feb	Mar	Apr	May	Jun	Jul	Aug	Sep	Oct	Nov	Dec
High	41	45	57	67	76	83	86	84	79	68	57	46
Low	23	26	35	43	52	60	64	63	57	44	36	28

PRECIPITATION

	Jan	Feb	Mar	Apr	May	Jun	Jul	Aug	Sep	Oct	Nov	Dec
Inches	2.9	3.0	3.6	3.3	3.9	3.6	5.0	4.0	3.2	2.9	3.6	3.4

— Important Phone Numbers —

	Phone
AAA	304-925-4937
Emergency	911
Events Line	304-345-5555
HotelDocs	800-468-3537
Poison Control Center	800-642-3625
Time/Temp	304-344-5111
Weather	304-345-2121

— Information Sources —

				Phone	Fax
Charleston City Hall PO Box 2749	Charleston	WV	25330	304-348-8000	348-8157
Charleston Civic Center & Coliseum 200 Civic Center Dr	Charleston	WV	25301	304-345-1500	357-7432
Charleston Convention & Visitors Bureau 200 Civic Center Dr	Charleston	WV	25301	304-344-5075	344-1241
TF: 800-733-5469 ■ *Web:* www.charlestonwv.com					
Charleston Economic & Community Development PO Box 2749	Charleston	WV	25330	304-348-8035	348-0704
Charleston Mayor PO Box 2749	Charleston	WV	25330	304-348-8174	348-8034
Charleston Regional Chamber of Commerce 106 Capitol St Suite 100	Charleston	WV	25301	304-345-0770	345-0776
Web: www.charleywestchamber.org					
Kanawha County PO Box 3226	Charleston	WV	25332	304-357-0130	357-0585
Kanawha County Public Library 123 Capital St	Charleston	WV	25301	304-343-4646	348-6530
Web: kanawha.lib.wv.us/					

On-Line Resources

About.com Guide to Charleston . . . . . . charlestonwv.about.com
Area Guide Charleston . . . . . . charlestonwv.areaguides.net
Charleston City Net . . . . . . www.excite.com/travel/countries/united_states/west_virginia/charleston
City Knowledge Charleston . . . . . . www.cityknowledge.com/wv_charleston.htm

— Transportation Services —

AIRPORTS

■ **Yeager Airport (CRW)**

	Phone
4 miles NE of downtown (approx 10 minutes)	304-345-0661

Web: www.yeagerairport.com ■ *E-mail:* fly@yeagerairport.com

Airport Transportation

	Phone
C & H Taxi $10 fare to downtown	304-344-4902

Commercial Airlines

	Phone
Comair	304-342-6548
Northwest Airlink	304-346-8617
United Express	304-343-4731
US Airways	304-342-3823

Charter Airlines

	Phone
Executive Air Terminal	304-343-8818

CAR RENTALS

	Phone
Avis	304-343-9453
Budget	304-343-4381
Hertz	304-346-0573
National	304-344-2563

LIMO/TAXI

	Phone
Executive Limousine	800-660-0824
Gary's Taxi	304-727-9342
Mountaineer Limousine	304-343-1505

MASS TRANSIT

	Phone
Kanawha Rapid Transit $.75 Base fare	304-343-7586
The Trolley $.50 Base fare	304-343-7586

RAIL/BUS

				Phone
Amtrak Station 350 MacCorkle Ave SE	Charleston	WV	25314	304-342-6766
TF: 800-872-7245				
Greyhound/Trailways Bus Station 300 Reynolds Ave	Charleston	WV	25301	304-357-0056

— Accommodations —

HOTELS, MOTELS, RESORTS

				Phone	Fax
Brass Pineapple Bed & Breakfast 1611 Virginia St E	Charleston	WV	25311	304-344-0748	
TF: 800-216-2123					
Comfort Inn 102 Racer Dr	Cross Lanes	WV	25313	304-776-8070	776-6460
TF: 800-228-5150					
Cutlip's Motor Inn 1607 Bigley Ave	Charleston	WV	25302	304-345-3500	
Embassy Suites 300 Court St	Charleston	WV	25301	304-347-8700	347-8737
TF: 888-983-6227					
Hampton Inn 1 Virginia St W	Charleston	WV	25302	304-343-9300	342-9393
TF: 800-426-7866					
Historic Charleston Bed & Breakfast 110 Elizabeth St	Charleston	WV	25311	304-345-8156	
TF: 800-225-5982					
Holiday Inn I-77 & Hwy 50	Parkersburg	WV	26101	304-485-6200	485-6261
TF: 800-465-4329					
Holiday Inn Charleston House 600 Kanawha Blvd E	Charleston	WV	25301	304-344-4092	345-4847
TF: 800-465-4329					
Holiday Inn Civic Center 100 Civic Center Dr	Charleston	WV	25304	304-345-0600	343-1322
TF: 800-465-4329					
Ivy Terrace Motel 5311 MacCorkle Ave SE	Charleston	WV	25304	304-925-4736	

Charleston — Hotels, Motels, Resorts (Cont'd)

Name / Address	City	State	Zip	Phone	Fax
Jefferson Motel 6204 MacCorkle Ave SW	Saint Albans	WV	25177	304-768-5242	
Kanawha City Motor Lodge 3103 MacCorkle Ave SE	Charleston	WV	25304	304-344-2461	345-1419
Knights Inn Charleston East 6401 MacCorkle Ave SE *TF:* 800-843-5644	Charleston	WV	25304	304-925-0451	925-4703
Marriott Hotel 200 Lee St E *TF:* 800-228-9290 ■ *Web:* marriotthotels.com/CRWWV	Charleston	WV	25301	304-345-6500	353-3722
Motel 6 330 Goff Mountain Rd *TF:* 800-466-8356	Cross Lanes	WV	25313	304-776-5911	776-7450
Ramada Inn 2nd Ave & B St *TF:* 800-272-6232	South Charleston	WV	25309	304-744-4641	744-4525
Red Roof Inn 6305 MacCorkle Ave SE *TF:* 800-843-7663	Charleston	WV	25304	304-925-6953	925-8111
Super 8 Motel Dunbar 911 Dunbar Ave *TF:* 800-800-8000	Dunbar	WV	25064	304-768-6888	
Travelodge 1007 Dunbar Ave *TF:* 800-578-7878	Dunbar	WV	25064	304-768-1000	768-2705

— Restaurants —

Name / Address	City	State	Zip	Phone
Allie's Restaurant (American) 200 Lee St E	Charleston	WV	25301	304-345-6500
Cagney's Old Place (American) 400 Court St	Charleston	WV	25301	304-345-3463
Chesapeake Crabhouse Grill (Seafood) 600 Kanawha Blvd E	Charleston	WV	25301	304-344-4092
Fifth Quarter (Steak/Seafood) 201 Clendenin St	Charleston	WV	25304	304-345-2726
Hibachi Japanese Steak House (Japanese) 741 W Washington St	Charleston	WV	25302	304-342-7616
Humphrey's Pine Room (American) 1600 Bigley Ave	Charleston	WV	25302	304-342-8234
Joe Fazio's (Italian) 1008 Bulett St	Charleston	WV	25301	304-344-3071
Joey's (Barbecue) 241 Capitol St	Charleston	WV	25301	304-343-8004
Laury's (Continental) 350 MacCorkle Ave SE	Charleston	WV	25314	304-343-0055
Sassy's (American) 100 Civic Center Dr	Charleston	WV	25301	304-345-0600
Southern Kitchen (Homestyle) MacCorkle Avenue at 53rd St	Charleston	WV	25304	304-925-3154
Tarragon (Continental) 200 Lee St E	Charleston	WV	25301	304-353-3636
Tidewater Grill (Seafood) 1060 Charleston Town Ctr	Charleston	WV	25389	304-345-2620
Wellington's (French) 1 Dairy Rd	Poca	WV	25159	304-755-8219
Wren's Nest (American) Coal River Rd	Saint Albans	WV	25177	304-727-3224

— Goods and Services —

SHOPPING

Name / Address	City	State	Zip	Phone	Fax
Charleston Town Center 3000 Charleston Town Ctr	Charleston	WV	25389	304-345-9525	
Charleston's Downtown District	Charleston	WV		304-345-1738	
Hale Street Antique Mall 213 Hale St	Charleston	WV	25301	304-345-6040	
Kanawha Mall 163 Kanawha Mall	Charleston	WV	25387	304-925-4921	925-4923

BANKS

Name / Address	City	State	Zip	Phone	Fax
Bank One 707 Virginia St	Charleston	WV	25301	304-348-4411	348-6966
Capital State Bank 2402 Mountaineer Blvd	Charleston	WV	25309	304-746-4600	746-4626
City National Bank of Charleston PO Box 4168 *TF:* 877-203-8700	Charleston	WV	25364	304-926-3300	925-8073
Huntington National Bank 1 Huntington Sq *TF:* 800-480-2265	Charleston	WV	25301	304-348-5000	348-7159
One Valley Bank NA 1 Valley Sq **Fax:* Hum Res ■ *TF Cust Svc:* 800-428-9665*	Charleston	WV	25301	304-348-7000	353-1720*
United National Bank 500 Virginia St E **Fax:* Cust Svc	Charleston	WV	25301	304-348-8400	348-8448*

BUSINESS SERVICES

Name	Phone	Name	Phone
Airborne Express	800-247-2676	**Kinko's**	304-343-1400
BAX Global	800-225-5229	**Post Office**	304-746-5000
DHL Worldwide Express	800-225-5345	**Snelling Personnel Services**	304-925-1818
Federal Express	800-238-5355	**UPS**	800-742-5877
Kelly Services	304-345-4840		

— Media —

PUBLICATIONS

Name / Address	City	State	Zip	Phone	Fax
Charleston Daily Mail‡ 1001 Virginia St E *TF:* 800-982-6397 ■ *Web:* www.dailymail.com ■ *E-mail:* dmnews@dailymail.com	Charleston	WV	25301	304-348-5140	348-4847
Charleston Gazette‡ 1001 Virginia St E *TF:* 800-982-6397 ■ *Web:* www.wvgazette.com ■ *E-mail:* gazette@wvgazette.com	Charleston	WV	25301	304-348-5140	348-1233

‡*Daily newspapers*

TELEVISION

Name / Address	City	State	Zip	Phone	Fax
WCHS-TV Ch 8 (ABC) 1301 Piedmont Rd *Web:* www.wchstv.com ■ *E-mail:* info@wchstv.com	Charleston	WV	25301	304-346-5358	346-4765
WOWK-TV Ch 13 (CBS) PO Box 13 *TF:* 800-234-9695 ■ *Web:* www.wowktv.com ■ *E-mail:* wowk@wowktv.com	Huntington	WV	25706	304-525-1313	523-0545
WPBY-TV Ch 33 (PBS) PO Box 7366 *Web:* web.marshall.edu/wpby ■ *E-mail:* tv33mail@wpby.pbs.org	Huntington	WV	25776	304-696-6630	696-4343
WSAZ-TV Ch 3 (NBC) PO Box 2115 *Web:* www.wsaz.com ■ *E-mail:* newschannel3@wsaz.com	Huntington	WV	25721	304-697-4780	697-4325
WVAH-TV Ch 11 (Fox) 11 Broadcast Plaza *Web:* www.wvah.com ■ *E-mail:* info@wvah.com	Hurricane	WV	25526	304-757-0011	757-7533

RADIO

Name / Address	City	State	Zip	Phone	Fax
WBES-FM 94.5 MHz (AC) 817 Suncrest Pl	Charleston	WV	25303	304-345-9237	342-3118
WCHS-AM 580 kHz (N/T) 1111 Virginia St E *Web:* www.58wchs.com ■ *E-mail:* wchs@58wchs.com	Charleston	WV	25301	304-342-8131	344-4745
WKAZ-FM 107.3 MHz (Oldies) 1111 Virginia St E *E-mail:* wkaz1073@aol.com	Charleston	WV	25301	304-342-8131	344-4745
WKLC-FM 105.1 MHz (Rock) 100 Kanawha Terr *Web:* www.wklc.com ■ *E-mail:* rock105@newwave.net	Saint Albans	WV	25177	304-722-3308	727-1300
WKWS-FM 96.1 MHz (Ctry) 1111 Virginia St E *Web:* www.wkws.com	Charleston	WV	25301	304-342-8131	344-4745
WQBE-FM 97.5 MHz (Ctry) 4250 W Washington St *E-mail:* wqbe@citynet.net	Charleston	WV	25313	304-744-9691	744-8562
WVAF-FM 99.9 MHz (CHR) 1111 Virginia St E *Web:* www.wvaf.com	Charleston	WV	25301	304-342-8131	344-4745
WVNP-FM 89.9 MHz (N/T) 600 Capitol St *Web:* www.wvpubrad.org	Charleston	WV	25301	304-558-3000	558-4034
WVPN-FM 88.5 MHz (NPR) 600 Capital St *E-mail:* wvtubrad@wtcwvnet.edu	Charleston	WV	25301	304-558-3000	558-4034
WVSR-FM 102.7 MHz (CHR) 817 Suncrest Pl	Charleston	WV	25303	304-342-3136	342-3118

— Colleges/Universities —

Name / Address	City	State	Zip	Phone	Fax
University of Charleston 2300 MacCorkle Ave SE *TF Admissions:* 800-995-4682 ■ *Web:* www.uchaswv.edu	Charleston	WV	25304	304-357-4800	357-4715
West Virginia Career College Charleston 1000 Virginia St E	Charleston	WV	25301	304-345-2820	345-1425
West Virginia State College Barron Dr *Web:* www.wvsc.edu	Institute	WV	25112	304-766-3000	766-5182
West Virginia University Institute of Technology 405 Fayette Pike *TF:* 888-554-8324 ■ *Web:* wvit.wvnet.edu ■ *E-mail:* wvutech@wvit.wvnet.edu	Montgomery	WV	25136	304-442-3071	442-3097

— Hospitals —

Name / Address	City	State	Zip	Phone	Fax
Charleston Area Medical Center 501 Morris St **Fax:* Admitting	Charleston	WV	25301	304-348-6037	348-7615*
Columbia Saint Francis Hospital 333 Laidley St *Web:* www.stfrancishospital.com ■ *E-mail:* mail@stfrancishospital.com	Charleston	WV	25301	304-347-6500	347-6885

Charleston — Hospitals (Cont'd)

				Phone	Fax
Thomas Memorial Hospital 4605 MacCorkle Ave SW	South Charleston	WV	25309	304-766-3600	766-3477

— Attractions —

				Phone	Fax
Blenko Glass Co Inc PO Box 67	Milton	WV	25541	304-743-9081	743-0547
Web: www.blenkoglass.com ■ *E-mail:* blenko@usa.net					
Bluestone National Scenic River PO Box 246	Glen Jean	WV	25846	304-465-0508	465-0591
Web: www.nps.gov/blue/					
Capitol Center 123 Summers St	Charleston	WV	25301	304-342-6522	344-5546
Cato Park 200 Bakers Ln	Charleston	WV	25302	304-348-6860	
Charleston Ballet 822 Virginia St E	Charleston	WV	25301	304-342-6541	345-1134
E-mail: chballet@newwave.net					
Charleston Community Music Assn PO Box 8008	South Charleston	WV	25303	304-744-1400	
Web: www.cmawva.org ■ *E-mail:* dlbush.st.albans@worldnet.att.net					
Charleston Light Opera Guild 200 Civic Center Dr Charleston Little Theater	Charleston	WV	25301	304-346-1885	
Charleston's Downtown District	Charleston	WV		304-345-1738	
Craik Patton House US Rt 60 E	Charleston	WV	25311	304-925-5341	
Daniel Boone Park Kanawha Blvd	Charleston	WV	25301	304-347-1803	
Denny PA Sternwheeler US Rt 60 Daniel Boone Park	Charleston	WV	25302	304-348-0709	
East End Historical District	Charleston	WV	23505	304-344-3879	
Gauley River National Recreation Area PO Box 246	Glen Jean	WV	25846	304-465-0508	465-0591
Web: www.nps.gov/gari/					
Governor's Mansion Kanawha Blvd E Capitol Complex	Charleston	WV	25305	304-558-3456	
Hawks Nest State Park PO Box 857	Ansted	WV	25812	304-658-5212	658-4549
TF: 800-221-1982 ■ *Web:* wvweb.com/www/hawks_nest.html					
Kanawha State Forest Rt 2 Box 285	Charleston	WV	25314	304-558-3500	
Mountain River Tours PO Box 88	Hico	WV	25854	800-822-1386	
Mountain Stage 600 Capitol St	Charleston	WV	25301	304-558-3000	
New River Gorge National River 104 Main St	Glen Jean	WV	25846	304-465-0508	465-0591
Web: www.nps.gov/neri/ ■ *E-mail:* neri_interpretation@nps.gov					
Saint John's Episcopal Church 1105 Quarrier St	Charleston	WV	25301	304-346-0359	
Sunrise Museum 746 Myrtle Rd	Charleston	WV	25314	304-344-8035	344-8038
Watoga State Park Hwy 219	Marlinton	WV	24954	800-225-5982	
West Virginia State Capitol 1800-1900 Kanawha Blvd E	Charleston	WV	25305	304-558-3456	
West Virginia State Museum 1900 Kanawha Blvd E Capitol Complex	Charleston	WV	25305	304-558-0220	558-2779
Web: www.wvlc.wvnet.edu/culture/collect.html					
West Virginia Symphony Orchestra Municipal Auditorium	Charleston	WV	25328	304-342-0151	342-0152
Web: www.wvsymphony.org					

SPORTS TEAMS & FACILITIES

				Phone	Fax
Charleston Alley Cats (baseball) 3403 MacCorkle Ave SE Watt Powell Baseball Pk	Charleston	WV	25304	304-925-8222	344-0083
Tri-State Greyhound Park 1 Greyhound Dr	Cross Lanes	WV	25313	304-776-1000	776-1239

— Events —

	Phone
A Taste of Charleston (mid-October)	843-577-4030
Black Bear 40k Bicycle Race (late June)	304-558-3500
Capital City Arts & Crafts Show (mid-November)	304-345-1500
Kanawha County Majorette Festival (mid-September)	304-348-6169
Mound Arts & Crafts Festival (mid-September)	800-238-9488
Mountain Heritage Arts & Crafts Festival (mid-June & late September)	304-725-2055
Multifest (early August)	304-342-4600
Native American PowWow (mid-May)	800-238-9488
Octoberfest (mid-October)	800-238-9488
Rhododendron Art & Craft Show (early June)	304-744-4323
Sternwheel Regatta (late August)	304-348-6419
Vandalia Gathering (late May)	304-558-0220
West Virginia Dance Festival (late May)	304-558-0220
West Virginia Day Celebration (mid-June)	304-345-1738
West Virginia International Film Festival (early May)	304-342-7100
Winter Wonderland (November-December)	304-348-6419

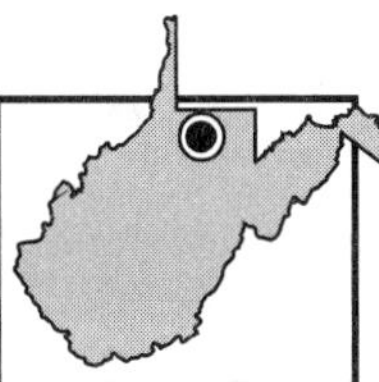

Morgantown

Morgantown, home of West Virginia University, is situated among the wooded mountains of northern West Virginia. The oldest stone house in Monongalia County is in Morgantown - built in 1795, The Old Stone House has been a tavern, pottery, tannery, tailor shop, and dwelling house, and presently houses crafts and other gift items. The Gentile Glass Co. in Morgantown features hand-cut lead crystal, tableware, handmade paperweights, art glass, and antique reproductions, while the LG Lamp Co. has hand-decorated candy jars, vases, and Victorian and early American lamps. Dent's Run Covered Bridge in Morgantown is the only remaining covered bridge in the county and is still in use today. Coopers Rock State Forest near Morgantown is a popular site for rock climbing and rappelling, and the Cheat River, which is uncontrolled by dams, has some of the best white water in the country. Camping, boating, fishing, and other activities are also available on the Monongahela River near Morgantown.

Population	26,751	**Longitude**	79-95-61 W
Area (Land)	7.7 sq mi	**County**	Monongalia
Area (Water)	0.3 sq mi	**Time Zone**	EST
Elevation	892 ft	**Area Code/s**	304
Latitude	39-62-94 N		

— Average Temperatures and Precipitation —

TEMPERATURES

	Jan	Feb	Mar	Apr	May	Jun	Jul	Aug	Sep	Oct	Nov	Dec
High	37	41	53	63	73	80	83	82	76	65	53	42
Low	21	23	32	41	50	58	63	61	55	44	36	26

PRECIPITATION

	Jan	Feb	Mar	Apr	May	Jun	Jul	Aug	Sep	Oct	Nov	Dec
Inches	2.5	2.5	3.8	3.5	4.0	4.0	4.3	4.0	3.5	2.8	3.3	3.2

— Important Phone Numbers —

	Phone		Phone
AAA	304-983-6480	**Poison Control Center**	800-642-3625
Emergency	911	**Time/Temp**	304-296-1212
Events Line	800-458-7373	**Weather**	304-296-1212

— Information Sources —

				Phone	Fax
Greater Morgantown Convention & Visitors Bureau 709 Beechurst Ave	Morgantown	WV	26505	304-292-5081	291-1354
TF: 800-458-7373 ■ *Web:* www.mgtn.com ■ *E-mail:* cvb@mgtn.com					
Monongalia County 243 High St	Morgantown	WV	26505	304-291-7230	291-7233
Morgantown Area Chamber of Commerce PO Box 658	Morgantown	WV	26507	304-292-3311	296-6619
Web: www.mgnchamber.org					
Morgantown City Hall 389 Spruce St	Morgantown	WV	26505	304-284-7439	284-7430
Web: www.morgantown.com					
Morgantown Mayor 389 Spruce St	Morgantown	WV	26505	304-284-7439	284-7430

Morgantown — Information Sources (Cont'd)

	Phone	Fax
Morgantown Public Library 373 Spruce St . . . . Morgantown WV 26505 *Web:* clark.lib.wv.us/morg/morg.html	304-291-7425	291-7437

On-Line Resources

All About Morgantown . . . . www.literati.com/morgantown
Area Guide Morgantown . . . . morgantown.areaguides.net
City Knowledge Morgantown . . . . www.cityknowledge.com/wv_morgantown.htm
Excite.com Morgantown City Guide . . . . www.excite.com/travel/countries/united_states/west_virginia/morgantown
Virtual Morgantown . . . . www.dmssoft.com/mrgntwn

— Transportation Services —

AIRPORTS

■ Morgantown Municipal Airport (MGW)

	Phone
3 miles E of downtown (approx 5 minutes)	304-291-7461

Airport Transportation

	Phone
Yellow Cab $4.50 fare to downtown	304-292-7441

Commercial Airlines

	Phone
US Airways Express	304-291-3311

Charter Airlines

	Phone
Aero Services	304-296-2359

■ Pittsburgh International Airport (PIT)

	Phone
75 miles NW of downtown Morgantown (approx 2 hours)	412-472-3525

Airport Transportation

	Phone
Airport Limousine $78 fare to downtown Morgantown	800-326-2907
Morgantown Limousine $50-65 fare to downtown Morgantown	800-245-8354

Commercial Airlines

	Phone		Phone
British Airways	800-247-9297	**TWA**	800-221-2000
Continental	412-391-6910	**United**	800-241-6522
Delta	800-221-1212	**US Airways**	800-428-4322
Northwest	800-225-2525	**US Airways Express**	800-428-4322

Charter Airlines

	Phone		Phone
Beaver Aviation Service Inc	724-843-8600	**Corporate Jets Inc**	412-466-2500
Corporate Air Inc	412-469-6800		

CAR RENTALS

	Phone		Phone
Alamo	412-472-5060	**Dollar**	412-472-5100
Avis	412-472-5200	**Enterprise**	800-325-8007
Avis-Morgantown	304-291-5867	**Enterprise-Morgantown**	304-292-2333
Budget	412-472-5252	**Hertz**	412-472-5955
Budget-Morgantown	304-292-1646	**Hertz-Morgantown**	304-296-2331
CarTemps USA	412-264-0990	**National**	412-472-5094

LIMO/TAXI

	Phone		Phone
Morgantown Limousine	304-598-3890	**Yellow Cab**	304-292-7441

MASS TRANSIT

	Phone
Morgantown Bus System $.75 Base fare	304-291-7467
West Virginia University Personal Rapid Transit $.50 Base fare	304-293-5011

— Accommodations —

HOTELS, MOTELS, RESORTS

				Phone	Fax
Canaan Valley Resort HC 70 Box 330 *TF:* 800-622-4121 ■ *Web:* www.canaanresort.com	Davis	WV	26260	304-866-4121	866-2172
Comfort Inn 225 Comfort Inn Dr *TF:* 800-228-5150	Morgantown	WV	26505	304-296-9364	296-0469
Days Inn of Morgantown 366 Boyers Ave *TF:* 800-329-7466	Star City	WV	26505	304-598-2120	598-3272
Econo Lodge Coliseum 3506 Monongahela Blvd *TF:* 800-553-2666	Morgantown	WV	26505	304-599-8181	599-8181
Econo Lodge Morgantown 15 Commerce Dr *TF:* 800-553-2666	Morgantown	WV	26502	304-296-8774	296-8774
Euro-Suites Hotel 501 Chestnut Ridge Rd *TF:* 800-678-4837	Morgantown	WV	26505	304-598-1000	599-2736
Friendship Inn 452 Country Club Dr *TF:* 800-424-4777	Morgantown	WV	26505	304-599-4850	599-4866
Hampton Inn 1053 Van Voorhis Rd *TF:* 800-426-7866	Morgantown	WV	26505	304-599-1200	598-7331
Holiday Inn Morgantown 1400 Saratoga Ave *TF:* 800-465-4329 ■ *Web:* www.basshotels.com/holiday-inn/?_franchisee=MGWWV ■ *E-mail:* dwarchola@lodgian.com	Morgantown	WV	26505	304-599-1680	598-0989
Hotel Morgan 127 High St	Morgantown	WV	26505	304-292-8401	292-8200
Lakeview Scanticon Resort & Conference Center 1 Lakeview Dr *TF:* 800-624-8300 ■ *Web:* www.lakeviewresort.com ■ *E-mail:* lakeview@lakeviewresort.com	Morgantown	WV	26508	304-594-1111	594-9472
Ramada Inn PO Box 1242 *TF:* 800-272-6232	Morgantown	WV	26505	304-296-3431	296-3431

— Restaurants —

				Phone
AJ's on the Fairway (Italian) 2506 Cranberry Sq	Morgantown	WV	26505	304-594-3700
Ali Baba Restaurant (Middle Eastern) 345 High St	Morgantown	WV	26505	304-292-4701
Asian Garden Restaurant (Malaysian) 3109-D University Ave	Morgantown	WV	26505	304-599-1888
Back Bay (Seafood) 1869 Mileground Rd	Morgantown	WV	26505	304-296-3027
BW-3 Grill & Pub (American) 268 High St	Morgantown	WV	26505	304-292-2999
Cafe Of India (Indian) 210 Fayette St	Morgantown	WV	26505	304-292-0770
Casa De Amici (Italian) 485 High St	Morgantown	WV	26505	304-292-4400
Colasante's (Italian) 416 Fairmont Rd	Westover	WV	26505	304-296-7689
Flame Steak House (Steak/Seafood) 76 High St	Morgantown	WV	26505	304-296-2976
Foosheen Chinese Restaurant (Chinese) 450 Beechurst Ave	Morgantown	WV	26505	304-296-6999
Gibbie's Pub (American) 368 High St.	Morgantown	WV	26505	304-296-4427
Glasshouse Grille (American) 709 Beechurst Ave	Morgantown	WV	20605	304-296-8460
Hibachi Japanese Steak House (Japanese) 3091 University Ave	Morgantown	WV	26505	304-598-7140
La Casa Mexican Grill (Mexican) 156 Clay St.	Morgantown	WV	26505	304-292-6701
Maxwell's (Vegetarian) 1 Wall St.	Morgantown	WV	26505	304-292-0982
Mountain People's Kitchen (Vegetarian) 1400 University Ave	Morgantown	WV	26505	304-291-6131
Pargo's (American) 334 Patterson Dr	Morgantown	WV	26505	304-598-0700
Reflections On The Lake (American) 1 Lakeview Dr.	Morgantown	WV	26505	304-594-1111
Tiberio's (Italian) Rt 857 N	Morgantown	WV	26505	304-594-0832
Weng's Garden (Chinese) 247 Beechurst Ave	Morgantown	WV	26505	304-292-8885
West Virginia Brewing Company (American) 1291 University Ave *Web:* www.dmssoft.com/wvb/	Morgantown	WV	26505	304-296-2739
Wings Ole (Mexican) 1125 University Ave.	Morgantown	WV	26505	304-296-4486
Yama Japanese Restaurant (Japanese) 387 1/2 High St	Morgantown	WV	26505	304-291-2456

— Goods and Services —

SHOPPING

				Phone	Fax
Gentile Glass Co Inc 425 Industrial Ave	Star City	WV	26505	304-599-2750	
Historic Downtown Morgantown downtown	Morgantown	WV		304-292-0168	
LG Lamp Co 408 Boyers Ave *E-mail:* lglamp@wvonline.com	Star City	WV	26505	304-598-7558	598-7561
Morgantown Mall 9500 Mall Rd	Morgantown	WV	26505	304-983-6255	983-6204

Morgantown — Shopping (Cont'd)

				Phone	Fax
Mountaineer Mall 5000 Greenbag Rd	Morgantown	WV	26501	304-296-0096	296-1526
Riverfront Antique & Flea Market 1389 University Ave	Morgantown	WV	26505	304-292-9230	
Seneca Center 709 Beechurst Ave	Morgantown	WV	26505	304-292-5081	

BANKS

				Phone	Fax
Bruceton Bank 169 Fairchance Rd	Morgantown	WV	26505	304-594-2210	
Citizens Bank of Morgantown Inc 265 High St	Morgantown	WV	26505	304-292-8411	292-1637
Huntington National Bank 201 High St	Morgantown	WV	26505	304-291-7700	291-7724*
**Fax:* Hum Res ■ *TF:* 800-480-2265 ■ *Web:* www.huntington.com					
One Valley Bank 496 High St	Morgantown	WV	26505	304-285-2378	285-2411*
**Fax:* Cust Svc ■ *TF:* 800-543-6727					
United National Bank 176 Holland Ave	Westover	WV	26502	304-296-8351	284-0298
Wesbanco of Fairmont 344 High St	Morgantown	WV	26505	304-284-2400	284-2404
TF: 888-664-5400					

BUSINESS SERVICES

	Phone		Phone
Airborne Express	800-247-2676	**Mail Boxes Etc**	304-599-0001
BAX Global	800-225-5229	**Olsten Staffing Services**	304-292-7378
Custom Pack & Ship	304-292-7225	**Post Office**	304-291-1035
DHL Worldwide Express	800-225-5345	**Presort Plus Inc**	304-363-1194
Federal Express	800-238-5355	**UPS**	800-742-5877

— Media —

PUBLICATIONS

				Phone	Fax
Daily Athenaeum‡ 284 Prospect St	Morgantown	WV	26506	304-293-2540	293-6857
Web: www.da.wvu.edu ■ *E-mail:* arts.entertainment@da.wvu.edu					
Dominion Post‡ 1251 Earl L Core Rd	Morgantown	WV	26505	304-292-6301	291-2326
TF: 800-654-4676 ■ *Web:* www.dominionpost.com/ ■ *E-mail:* postpage@dominionpost.com					

‡*Daily newspapers*

TELEVISION

				Phone	Fax
KDKA-TV Ch 2 (CBS) 1 Gateway Ctr	Pittsburgh	PA	15222	412-575-2200	575-2871
Web: www.kdka.com					
WNPB-TV Ch 24 (PBS) 191 Scott Ave	Morgantown	WV	26505	304-293-6511	293-2642
TF: 800-227-9672					
WPGH-TV Ch 53 (Fox) 750 Ivory Ave	Pittsburgh	PA	15214	412-931-5300	931-8029
WPXI-TV Ch 11 (NBC) 11 Television Hill	Pittsburgh	PA	15214	412-237-1100	327-4900
Web: www.realpittsburgh.com/partners/wpxi					
WTAE-TV Ch 4 (ABC) 400 Ardmore Blvd	Pittsburgh	PA	15221	412-242-4300	244-4628
Web: www.wtaetv.com					

RADIO

				Phone	Fax
WAJR-AM 1440 kHz (N/T) 1251 Earl L Core Rd	Morgantown	WV	26505	304-296-0029	296-3876
Web: www.wajr.com					
WCLG-AM 1300 kHz (Oldies) PO Box 885	Morgantown	WV	26507	304-292-2222	292-2224
WCLG-FM 100.1 MHz (CR) PO Box 885	Morgantown	WV	26507	304-292-2222	292-2224
Web: www.wclg.com ■ *E-mail:* wclgfm@mail.wclg.com					
WVAQ-FM 101.9 MHz (CHR) 1251 Earl L Core Rd	Morgantown	WV	26505	304-296-0029	296-3876
Web: www.wvaq.com ■ *E-mail:* wvaq@juno.com					
WWVU-FM 91.7 MHz (Misc) PO Box 6446	Morgantown	WV	26506	304-293-3329	293-7363
Web: www.wvu.edu/~u92/					
WZST-FM 100.9 MHz (AC) 7011 Grand Central Station Dr	Morgantown	WV	26505	304-292-1101	292-1101
Web: www.wvstar.com					

— Colleges/Universities —

				Phone	Fax
Fairmont State College 1201 Locust Ave	Fairmont	WV	26554	304-367-4000	366-4870
TF: 800-641-5678 ■ *Web:* www.fairmont.wvnet.edu					
West Virginia Career College Morgantown 148 Willey St	Morgantown	WV	26505	304-296-8282	296-5612
TF: 800-786-0479					
West Virginia University PO Box 6009	Morgantown	WV	26506	304-293-0111	293-8991
TF: 800-344-9881 ■ *Web:* www.wvu.edu					

— Hospitals —

				Phone	Fax
Monongalia General Hospital 1200 JD Anderson Dr	Morgantown	WV	26505	304-598-1200	599-8382

— Attractions —

				Phone	Fax
Appalachian Gallery 44 High St	Morgantown	WV	26505	304-296-0163	
Art Attic 316 High St	Morgantown	WV	26505	304-292-7785	
Chestnut Ridge Park Rt 1	Bruceton Mills	WV	26525	304-594-1773	594-1711
Comer Museum West Virginia University Mineral Resource Bldg	Morgantown	WV	26506	304-293-5695	293-6751
Cook-Hayman Pharmacy Museum West Virginia University Health Sciences Bldg N	Morgantown	WV	26506	304-293-1468	
Cooper's Rock State Forest RR 1 Box 270	Bruceton Mills	WV	26525	304-594-1561	594-9024
Core Arboretum West Virginia University Dept of Biology PO Box 6507	Morgantown	WV	26506	304-293-5201	293-6363
Easton Roller Mill Easton Mill Rd	Morgantown	WV	26506	304-599-0833	
Forks of Cheat Winery Stewart Town Rd	Morgantown	WV	26505	304-599-8660	
GARO 111 Walnut St	Morgantown	WV	26505	304-291-5299	291-3470
TF: 800-247-8015					
Gentile Glass Co Inc 425 Industrial Ave	Star City	WV	26505	304-599-2750	
Historic Downtown Morgantown downtown	Morgantown	WV		304-292-0168	
Main Street Morgantown 389 Spruce St	Morgantown	WV	26505	304-292-0168	284-7518
Web: www.dmssoft.com/mainst/					
Mason Dixon Historical Park SR-39	Core	WV	26529	304-879-5500	
Monongalia Arts Center 107 High St	Morgantown	WV	26505	304-292-3325	
Web: www.homestead.com/monarts ■ *E-mail:* mon_arts_center@hotmail.com					
Old Stone House 313 Chestnut St	Morgantown	WV	26505	304-296-7825	
Pricketts Fort State Park Rt 3 Box 407	Fairmont	WV	26554	304-363-3030	363-3857
West Virginia Public Theatre 453 Oakland St	Morgantown	WV	26506	304-598-0144	598-0145
West Virginia University Creative Arts Center West Virginia University	Morgantown	WV	26506	304-293-4841	293-3550

— Events —

	Phone
4th of July Celebration & Parade (July 4)	304-292-0062
18th Century Rendezvous (mid-June & late October)	304-363-3030
Black Heritage Festival (early September)	304-622-4256
Christmas at Pricketts Fort (late November-early December)	304-363-3030
Concerts in the Park (June-late August)	304-296-8356
Courthouse Square Noontime Concerts (June-October)	304-291-7257
Dunkard Valley Frontier Festival (late August)	304-879-5500
Fall Eighteenth Century Rendezvous (late October)	304-292-5081
Fall Frolic (mid-October)	800-524-4043
Fall Home Show (mid-September)	304-983-6255
Gospel Music Concert (early December)	304-363-3030
Grand National Championship (mid-November)	800-848-2263
Haunted Hayride (October)	304-296-0150
Holiday Open House (mid-November)	304-296-7825
Mason-Dixon Festival (mid-September)	304-594-1104
Mill Day (late September)	304-599-1575
Monongalia County Fair (early-mid-August)	304-291-7201
Mountaineer Balloon Festival (early October)	304-296-8356
Mountaineer Week (early November)	304-293-2702
Mountaineer Week Craft Show (mid-November)	304-293-2702
Old Fashioned Brass Band Concert (July 4)	304-363-3030
Three Centuries of American Farm Life Exhibit (early June-early July)	304-363-3030

Morgantown — Events (Cont'd)

	Phone
Traditional Appalachian Mountain Music (late May)	304-363-3030
Wine & Jazz Festival (late September)	304-292-5081

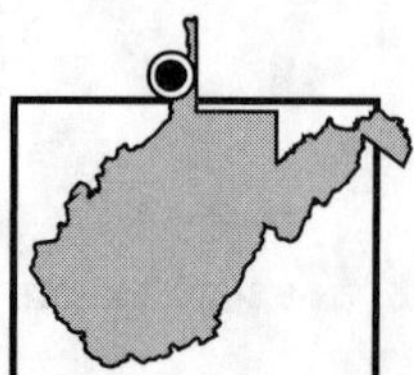

Wheeling

The city of Wheeling's Oglebay is recognized as the nation's model municipal park. Oglebay is the former estate of Wheeling industrialist Colonel Earl W. Oglebay, who willed the grounds to the city in 1926. Today Oglebay is a resort-park that encompasses 1,500 acres and features golf and tennis facilities, stables, a nature center, children's zoo, and lodge. The winter brings more that one million visitors to see the Oglebay Festival of Lights and Wheeling's City of Lights. The festivals' highlights include animated displays, lighted cityscapes and countrysides, and outstanding holiday light parades.

Population	32,541	**Longitude**	80-69-67 W
Area (Land)	13.6 sq mi	**County**	Ohio
Area (Water)	1.9 sq mi	**Time Zone**	EST
Elevation	672 ft	**Area Code/s**	304
Latitude	40-06-76 N		

— Average Temperatures and Precipitation —

TEMPERATURES

	Jan	Feb	Mar	Apr	May	Jun	Jul	Aug	Sep	Oct	Nov	Dec
High	34	37	49	60	71	79	83	81	74	63	50	39
Low	19	20	30	39	48	57	62	60	54	42	34	24

PRECIPITATION

	Jan	Feb	Mar	Apr	May	Jun	Jul	Aug	Sep	Oct	Nov	Dec
Inches	2.5	2.4	3.4	3.2	3.6	3.7	3.8	3.2	3.0	2.4	2.9	2.9

— Important Phone Numbers —

	Phone		Phone
AAA	304-233-1810	**Emergency**	911
Consumer Protection Agency	304-558-8986	**Poison Control Center**	800-642-3625

— Information Sources —

				Phone	Fax
Ohio County 205 City County Bldg	Wheeling	WV	26003	304-234-3656	234-3829
Ohio County Public Library 52 16th St	Wheeling	WV	26003	304-232-0244	232-6848

Web: 129.71.122.114/main/index.htm
■ *E-mail:* ocplweb@weirton.lib.wv.us

Wheeling Area Chamber of Commerce 1310 Market St.	Wheeling	WV	26003	304-233-2575	233-1320
Wheeling City Hall 1500 Chaplaine St.	Wheeling	WV	26003	304-234-3694	234-3605
Wheeling Civic Center 2 14th St	Wheeling	WV	26003	304-233-7000	233-7001

Web: www.wheelingciviccenter.com ■ *E-mail:* wcc@hgo.net

Wheeling Convention & Visitors Bureau 1401 Main St.	Wheeling	WV	26003	304-233-7709	233-1470

TF: 800-828-3097 ■ *Web:* www.wheelingcvb.com

Wheeling Mayor 1500 Chapline St	Wheeling	WV	26003	304-234-3604	234-3605

On-Line Resources

Area Guide Wheeling	wheelingwv.areaguides.net
Excite.com Wheeling City Guide	www.excite.com/travel/countries/united_states/west_virginia/wheeling
Welcome to Wheeling	wheelingwv.com

— Transportation Services —

AIRPORTS

■ **Wheeling-Ohio County Airport (HLG)**

	Phone
10 miles N of downtown (approx 20 minutes)	304-234-3865

Airport Transportation

	Phone
Yellow Cab $19 fare to downtown	304-232-1313

■ **Greater Pittsburgh International Airport (PIT)**

	Phone
50 miles NE of downtown Wheeling (approx 60 minutes)	412-472-3525

Airport Transportation

	Phone
Airport Limo Service $46 fare to downtown Wheeling	304-232-1175

Commercial Airlines

	Phone		Phone
American	800-433-7300	**TWA**	800-221-2000
British Airways	800-247-9297	**United**	800-241-6522
Continental	412-391-6910	**US Airways**	800-428-4322
Delta	800-221-1212	**US Airways Express**	800-428-4322

Charter Airlines

	Phone		Phone
Beaver Aviation Service Inc	724-843-8600	**Corporate Jets Inc**	412-466-2500
Corporate Air Inc	412-469-6800		

CAR RENTALS

	Phone		Phone
Alamo	412-472-5060	**Dollar**	412-472-5100
Avis	412-472-5200	**Enterprise**	800-325-8007
Budget	412-472-5252	**Hertz**	412-472-5955
Budget	304-232-3621	**National**	412-472-5094
CarTemps USA	412-264-0990		

LIMO/TAXI

	Phone		Phone
Mountaineer Limousine	304-343-1505	**Yellow Cab**	304-232-1313

MASS TRANSIT

	Phone
Ohio Valley Regional Transit Authority $.80 Base fare	304-232-2190

RAIL/BUS

				Phone
Greyhound/Trailways Bus Station 1405 Main St	Wheeling	WV	26003	304-232-1500

— Accommodations —

HOTELS, MOTELS, RESORTS

				Phone	Fax
Best Western Inn 949 Main St *TF:* 800-528-1234	Wheeling	WV	26003	304-233-8500	
Days Inn East I-70 & Dallas Pike *TF:* 800-329-7466	Triadelphia	WV	26059	304-547-0610	547-9029
Hampton Inn 795 National Rd. *TF:* 800-426-7866	Wheeling	WV	26003	304-233-0440	233-2198
Hampton Inn 51130 National Rd *TF:* 800-426-7866	Saint Clairsville	OH	43950	740-695-3961	695-0739
Holiday Inn Express Dallas Pike Exit 11 *TF:* 800-465-4329 ■ *Web:* www.basshotels.com/hiexpress/?_franchisee=WHLTD	Wheeling	WV	26003	304-547-1380	547-9270
Knights Inn 51260 National Rd	Saint Clairsville	OH	43950	740-695-5038	695-3014

Wheeling — Hotels, Motels, Resorts (Cont'd)

Name / Address	City	State	Zip	Phone	Fax
McLure House Hotel & Conference Center 1200 Market St. *TF:* 800-862-5873	Wheeling	WV	26003	304-232-0300	233-1653
Oglebay's Wilson Lodge Rt 88 N Oglebay Pk *TF:* 800-624-6988 ■ *Web:* www.oglebay-resort.com	Wheeling	WV	26003	304-243-4000	243-4070
Red Roof Inn 68301 Red Roof Ln. *TF:* 800-843-7663	Saint Clairsville	OH	43950	740-695-4057	695-6956

— Restaurants —

Name / Address	City	State	Zip	Phone
Abbeys (American) 145 Zane St.	Wheeling	WV	26003	304-233-0729
Bella Via (Italian) 1 Burkham Ct	Wheeling	WV	26003	304-242-8181
Boots Texas Roadhouse (Steak) 836 National Rd.	Wheeling	WV	26003	304-233-9259
Bridge Tavern & Grill (American) 950 Main St	Wheeling	WV	26003	304-232-1900
Bugsy's (American) 19 11th St	Wheeling	WV	26003	304-233-4864
Coleman's Fish Market (Seafood) 2226 Centre Market	Wheeling	WV	26003	304-232-8510
Ernie's Cork & Bottle (Continental) 39 12th St	Wheeling	WV	26003	304-232-4400
Figaretti's Restaurant (Italian) 1035 Mt De Chantal Rd	Wheeling	WV	26003	304-243-5625
Golden Chopsticks (Chinese) 329 N York St	Wheeling	WV	26003	304-232-2888
Keg Und Kraut (German) 167 16th St.	Wheeling	WV	26003	304-232-5654
Panda Chinese Kitchen (Chinese) 1133 Market St.	Wheeling	WV	26003	304-232-7572
Riverside Restaurant (American) 949 Main St.	Wheeling	WV	26003	304-233-8507
Sesame Cafe (Asian) 1010 Main St	Wheeling	WV	26003	304-232-2937
Silver Chopsticks (Chinese) 2135 National Rd.	Elm Grove	WV	26003	304-242-5858
Stratford Springs (American) 355 Oglebay Dr	Wheeling	WV	26003	304-233-5100
TJ's Sports Garden Restaurant (American) 808 National Rd. *Web:* www.hgo.net/~tjs/	Wheeling	WV	26003	304-232-9555

— Goods and Services —

SHOPPING

Name / Address	City	State	Zip	Phone	Fax
Centre Market Market St	Wheeling	WV	26003	304-234-3878	232-4459
Ohio Valley Mall 67800 Mall Rd.	Saint Clairsville	OH	43950	740-695-4526	695-4451
Stratford Springs Shoppes 355 Oglebay Dr	Wheeling	WV	26003	304-233-5100	
Washington Mall 301 Oak Spring Rd	Washington	PA	15301	724-222-7390	222-4706

BANKS

Name / Address	City	State	Zip	Phone	Fax
Bank One NA 1114 Market St.	Wheeling	WV	26003	304-234-4100	232-3560
Progressive Bank 1701 Warwood Ave.	Wheeling	WV	26003	304-277-1100	277-4705
United National Bank 21 12th St *TF:* 877-334-4646	Wheeling	WV	26003	304-233-1100	233-3913
WesBanco Bank Wheeling 1 Bank Plaza	Wheeling	WV	26003	304-234-9000	232-3795
Wheeling National Bank 1145 Market St.	Wheeling	WV	26003	304-232-0110	233-0258

BUSINESS SERVICES

Name	Phone
Airborne Express	800-247-2676
BAX Global	800-225-5229
DHL Worldwide Express	800-225-5345
Federal Express	800-238-5355
Kelly Services	304-243-0230
Mail Boxes Etc	800-789-4623
Manpower Temporary Services	304-232-0028
Post Office	304-232-4270
UPS	800-742-5877

— Media —

PUBLICATIONS

Name / Address	City	State	Zip	Phone	Fax
Intelligencer The‡ 1500 Main St. *TF:* 800-852-5475 ■ *Web:* www.oweb.com/intelligencer/	Wheeling	WV	26003	304-233-0100	232-1399
Wheeling News-Register‡ 1500 Main St. **Fax:* Edit ■ *Web:* www.news-register.net	Wheeling	WV	26003	304-233-0100	232-5718*

‡Daily newspapers

TELEVISION

Name / Address	City	State	Zip	Phone	Fax
WPGH-TV Ch 53 (Fox) 750 Ivory Ave	Pittsburgh	PA	15214	412-931-5300	931-8029
WQED-TV Ch 13 (PBS) 4802 5th Ave *Web:* www.wqed.org	Pittsburgh	PA	15213	412-622-1300	622-6413
WTAE-TV Ch 4 (ABC) 400 Ardmore Blvd *Web:* www.wtaetv.com	Pittsburgh	PA	15221	412-242-4300	244-4628
WTOV-TV Ch 9 (NBC) PO Box 9999 *Web:* www.wtov.com	Steubenville	OH	43952	740-282-0911	282-0439
WTRF-TV Ch 7 (CBS) 96 16th St *Web:* www.wtrf.com	Wheeling	WV	26003	304-232-7777	233-5822

RADIO

Name / Address	City	State	Zip	Phone	Fax
WBBD-AM 1400 kHz (Nost) 1015 Main St	Wheeling	WV	26003	304-232-1170	234-0067
WEGW-FM 107.5 kHz (Rock) 1015 Main St *Web:* www.wegw.com	Wheeling	WV	26003	304-232-1170	234-0067
WKWK-FM 97.3 MHz (AC) 1015 Main St.	Wheeling	WV	26003	304-232-1170	234-0036
WOVK-FM 98.7 MHz (Ctry) 1015 Main St *Web:* www.wovk.com	Wheeling	WV	26003	304-232-1170	234-0067
WRKY-FM 103.5 MHz (Ctry) 320 Market St *Web:* www.wrky.com ■ *E-mail:* wrky@weir.net	Steubenville	OH	43952	740-283-4747	283-3655
WSTV-AM 1340 kHz (N/T) PO Box 1340	Steubenville	OH	43952	740-283-4747	283-3655
WWVA-AM 1170 kHz (N/T) 1015 Main St *Web:* www.wwva.com	Wheeling	WV	26003	304-232-1170	234-0067
WZNW-FM 105.5 MHz (AC) 1015 Main St. *Web:* www.wznw.com	Wheeling	WV	26003	304-232-1170	234-0036

— Colleges/Universities —

Name / Address	City	State	Zip	Phone	Fax
Bethany College Main St. *TF:* 800-922-7611 ■ *Web:* info.bethany.wvnet.edu	Bethany	WV	26032	304-829-7000	829-7108
Ohio University Eastern Campus 45425 National Rd W *TF:* 800-648-3331 ■ *Web:* www.eastern.ohiou.edu	Saint Clairsville	OH	43950	740-695-1720	695-7079
West Liberty State College PO Box 295 *TF:* 800-732-6204 ■ *Web:* www.wlsc.wvnet.edu	West Liberty	WV	26074	304-336-5000	336-8403
West Virginia Northern Community College 1704 Market St. *Web:* www.northern.wvnet.edu	Wheeling	WV	26003	304-233-5900	232-0965
Wheeling Jesuit University 316 Washington Ave *TF:* 800-624-6992 ■ *Web:* www.wju.edu	Wheeling	WV	26003	304-243-2000	243-2243

— Hospitals —

Name / Address	City	State	Zip	Phone	Fax
Ohio Valley Medical Center 2000 Eoff St **Fax:* Admitting ■ *Web:* www.wvha.com/web/ovmc/ovmc.htm	Wheeling	WV	26003	304-234-0123	234-8229*
Wheeling Hospital 1 Medical Pk.	Wheeling	WV	26003	304-243-3000	243-3060

— Attractions —

Name / Address	City	State	Zip	Phone	Fax
Artisan Center 1400 Main St Heritage Sq.	Wheeling	WV	26003	304-232-1810	
Capitol Music Hall/Jamboree USA 1015 Main St. *TF:* 800-624-5456 ■ *Web:* www.jamboreeusa.com/ ■ *E-mail:* jamboree@hgo.net	Wheeling	WV	26003	304-234-0050	234-0067
Centre Market Market St	Wheeling	WV	26003	304-234-3878	232-4459
Challenger Learning Center 316 Washington Ave Wheeling Jesuit University *Web:* www.wju.edu/clc	Wheeling	WV	26003	304-243-4325	243-2497
Eckhart House 810 Main St Old Town	Wheeling	WV	26003	304-232-5439	232-5439
Good Zoo Rt 88 N Oglebay Pk *TF:* 800-624-6988 ■ *Web:* www.oglebay-resort.com/goodzoo	Wheeling	WV	26003	304-243-4030	243-4110
Grand Vue Park Rd 4 Box 16A	Moundsville	WV	26041	304-845-9810	845-9811
Grave Creek Mound State Park 801 Jefferson Ave	Moundsville	WV	26041	304-843-4128	843-4131
Kruger Street Toy & Train Museum 144 Kruger St. *Web:* www.toyandtrain.com	Wheeling	WV	26003	304-242-8133	242-1925

Wheeling — Attractions (Cont'd)

				Phone	Fax
Oglebay Institute's AB Brooks Nature Center Oglebay Pk.	Wheeling	WV	26003	304-242-6855	243-4203
TF: 800-624-6988 ■ *Web:* www.hgo.net/~inspire/nature.html ■ *E-mail:* inspire@hgo.net					
Oglebay Institute's Mansion & Glass Museums The Burton Center Oglebay Pk	Wheeling	WV	26003	304-242-7272	242-4203
TF: 800-624-6988 ■ *Web:* www.hgo.net/~inspire/museums.html ■ *E-mail:* inspire@hgo.net					
Oglebay Institute's Stifel Fine Arts Center 1330 National Rd	Wheeling	WV	26003	304-242-7700	242-7747
TF: 800-624-6988 ■ *Web:* www.hgo.net/~inspire/arts.html ■ *E-mail:* inspire@hgo.net					
Oglebay Institute's Towngate Theatre 2118 Market St.	Wheeling	WV	26003	304-233-4257	233-4257
Web: www.hgo.net/~inspire/theatre.html ■ *E-mail:* inspire@hgo.net					
Pike Island Locks and Dam Rt 1 Box 33	Wheeling	WV	26003	304-277-2240	277-4566
Point Overlook Museum 989 Grandview St	Wheeling	WV	26003	304-232-3010	
Stratford Springs Shoppes 355 Oglebay Dr	Wheeling	WV	26003	304-233-5100	
Victoria Vaudeville Theater Market St.	Wheeling	WV	26003	304-233-7464	
TF: 800-525-7464					
Victorian Homes Tours	Wheeling	WV	26003	304-233-1600	
West Virginia Independence Hall 1528 Market St.	Wheeling	WV	26003	304-238-1300	
West Virginia Penitentiary Tours 818 Jefferson Ave	Moundsville	WV	26041	304-845-6200	843-4148
Wheeling Suspension Bridge 10th & Main Sts	Wheeling	WV	26003		
Wheeling Symphony Orchestra 1025 Main St Capitol Music Hall	Wheeling	WV	26003	304-232-6192	232-6192
Web: www.wso.weir.net/					

SPORTS TEAMS & FACILITIES

				Phone	Fax
Wheeling Downs 1 S Stone St	Wheeling	WV	26003	304-232-5050	232-4802
Wheeling Nailers (hockey) 1144 Market St Suite 202	Wheeling	WV	26003	304-234-4625	233-4846
Web: www.wheelingnailers.com					

— Events —

	Phone
African-American Jubilee (late June)	304-233-7709
American Heritage Glass & Craft Festival (early August)	304-233-7709
Big Boy Classic 20K Run (late May)	304-242-7322
Car Show & Swap Meet (late August)	888-645-3229
City of Lights (early November-mid-January)	304-233-2575
Dungeon of Horrors (mid-late October)	304-843-1993
Fall Horse Show (mid-September)	304-243-4042
Fantasy in Lights Parade (mid-November)	304-233-2575
Independence Day Symphony & Fireworks (July 4)	304-233-7709
Jamboree in the Hills (mid-July)	800-624-5456
New Years Eve Celebration (December 31)	304-232-5050
Oglebayfest (early October)	304-243-4000
Upper Ohio Valley Italian Festival (July)	304-233-1090
West Virginia Day Celebration (late June)	304-233-7709
Wheeling Celtic Celebration (early March)	304-232-3087
Winter Festival of Lights (early November-early January)	304-233-7709

Wisconsin

Population (1999): 5,250,446 **Area (sq mi): 65,499**

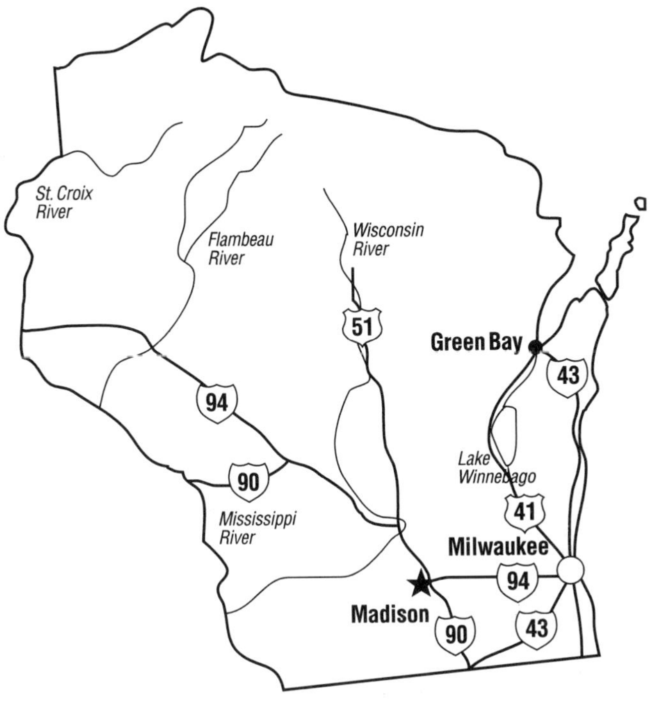

— State Information Sources —

				Phone	Fax
Wisconsin Dept of Public Instruction Library Services Div PO Box 7841	Madison	WI	53707	608-267-9219	267-1052
Web: www.dpi.state.wi.us/					
Wisconsin Economic Development Div PO Box 7970	Madison	WI	53707	608-266-0770	267-0436
Wisconsin Manufacturers & Commerce PO Box 352	Madison	WI	53701	608-258-3400	258-3413
Web: www.wmc.org ■ *E-mail:* wmc@wmc.org					
Wisconsin Parks & Recreation Bureau PO Box 7921	Madison	WI	53707	608-266-2181	267-7474
Web: www.dnr.state.wi.us/org/land/parks/					
Wisconsin State Government Information				608-266-2211	
Web: www.state.wi.us ■ *E-mail:* wisc-web@badger.state.wi.us					
Wisconsin Tourism Dept 201 W Washington Ave 2nd Fl	Madison	WI	53707	608-266-7621	266-3403
TF: 800-432-8747 ■ *Web:* www.state.wi.us/agencies/tourism ■ *E-mail:* tourinfo@tourism.state.wi.us					

ON-LINE RESOURCES

Northern Wisconsin Online	www.northern-wisconsin.com
Northern Wisconsin Tourism Travel & Outdoors Information Network	northernwisconsin.com
Rough Guide Travel Wisconsin	travel.roughguides.com/content/525/index.htm
Travel.org-Wisconsin	travel.org/wisconsi.html
Welcome to Wisconsin	www.wistravel.com
Wisconsin Cities	dir.yahoo.com/Regional/U_S__States/Wisconsin/Cities
Wisconsin Counties & Regions	dir.yahoo.com/Regional/U_S__States/Wisconsin/Counties_and_Regions
Wisconsin Online	www.wisconline.com
Wisconsin Pages	infomad.com/wisconsin
Wisconsin Scenario	scenariousa.dstylus.com/wi/indexf.htm
Wisconsin Travel & Tourism Guide	www.travel-library.com/north_america/usa/wisconsin/index.html
Wisconsin.com	www.wisconsin.com
Yahoo! Get Local Wisconsin	dir.yahoo.com/Regional/U_S__States/Wisconsin

— Cities Profiled —

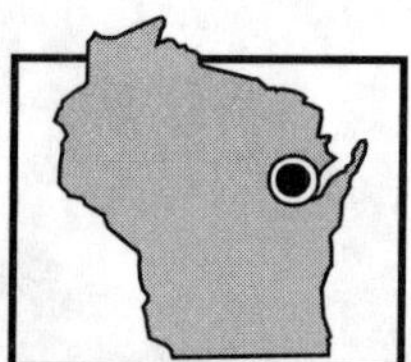

Green Bay

Located in northeast Wisconsin, Green Bay is situated on a Lake Michigan bay from which the city takes its name. This location has made Green Bay one of the busiest ports on the Great Lakes and an important center of both trucking and railroad activity. The National Railroad Museum in Green Bay preserves and exhibits 75 pieces of rolling stock and has a model train display with over a mile of track. Green Bay is also well known for its professional football team, the Green Bay Packers. The Green Bay Packer Hall of Fame traces the team's history from 1919 to the present, including those years when it was coached by Vince Lombardi and won five NFL championships.

Population 97,789
Area (Land) . . . . 43.8 sq mi
Area (Water) . . . . 10.5 sq mi
Elevation . . . . 594 ft
Latitude . . . . 44-48-48 N
Longitude . . . . 88-01-88 W
County . . . . Brown
Time Zone . . . . CST
Area Code/s 920

— Average Temperatures and Precipitation —

TEMPERATURES

	Jan	Feb	Mar	Apr	May	Jun	Jul	Aug	Sep	Oct	Nov	Dec
High	23	27	39	54	67	76	81	78	69	57	42	28
Low	6	10	21	34	44	54	59	57	49	39	27	13

PRECIPITATION

	Jan	Feb	Mar	Apr	May	Jun	Jul	Aug	Sep	Oct	Nov	Dec
Inches	1.2	1.0	2.1	2.4	2.8	3.4	3.1	3.5	3.5	2.2	2.2	1.5

— Important Phone Numbers —

	Phone
AAA	920-436-7860
Emergency	911
Events Line	920-494-1111
Poison Control Center	414-266-2222
Weather	920-494-2363

— Information Sources —

				Phone	Fax
Better Business Bureau Serving Wisconsin PO Box 2190 *Web:* www.wisconsin.bbb.org ■ *E-mail:* bbbwi@execpc.com	Milwaukee	WI	53201	414-273-1600	224-0881
Brown County PO Box 23600	Green Bay	WI	54305	920-448-4016	448-4498
Brown County Expo Centre 1901 S Oneida St	Green Bay	WI	54304	920-494-3401	494-6868
Brown County Library 515 Pine St *Web:* www.gbonline.com/org/bcl	Green Bay	WI	54301	920-448-4400	448-4388
Green Bay Area Chamber of Commerce 400 S Washington St *Web:* www.titletown.org	Green Bay	WI	54301	920-437-8704	437-1024
Green Bay Area Visitor & Convention Bureau PO Box 10596 *TF:* 800-236-3976 ■ *Web:* www.greenbaywi.com ■ *E-mail:* tourism@dct.com	Green Bay	WI	54307	920-494-9507	494-9229
Green Bay City Hall 100 N Jefferson St.	Green Bay	WI	54301	920-448-3010	448-3016
Green Bay Mayor 100 N Jefferson St Rm 200	Green Bay	WI	54301	920-448-3005	448-3081
Green Bay Planning Dept 100 N Jefferson St Rm 608	Green Bay	WI	54301	920-448-3400	448-3426

On-Line Resources

Area Guide Green Bay . . . . greenbay.areaguides.net
City Knowledge Green Bay . . . . www.cityknowledge.com/wi_greenbay.htm
Excite.com Green Bay City Guide . . . . www.excite.com/travel/countries/united_states/wisconsin/green_bay
Green Bay Home Page . . . . www.greenbay.com
Green Bay Online . . . . www.gbonline.com/index.phtml

— Transportation Services —

AIRPORTS

	Phone
■ **Austin Straubel International Airport (GRB)** 8 miles SW of downtown (approx 15 minutes)	920-498-4800

Airport Transportation

	Phone
Bay City Cab $11 fare to downtown	920-432-3456
Green Bay Taxi $10-15 fare to downtown	920-435-6985

Commercial Airlines

	Phone
American Eagle	800-433-7300
Chicago Express	800-435-9282
Midwest Express	800-452-2022
Northwest	800-225-2525
United Express	800-241-6522

Charter Airlines

	Phone
Maxair	920-498-8188

CAR RENTALS

	Phone
Avis	920-498-4900
Budget	920-498-4855
Hertz	920-498-6400
National	920-498-4884

LIMO/TAXI

	Phone
A-1 Taxi	920-430-7777
Astro Taxi	920-499-9119
Bay City Cab	920-432-3456
Escort Limousine	920-430-1467
Green Bay Taxi	920-435-6985
Presidential Limousine	920-468-7738
Titletown Cab	920-432-5151

MASS TRANSIT

	Phone
Green Bay Transit $1.00 Base fare	920-448-3450

RAIL/BUS

				Phone
Greyhound Bus Station 800 Cedar St *TF:* 800-231-2222	Green Bay	WI	54301	920-432-4883

— Accommodations —

HOTELS, MOTELS, RESORTS

				Phone	Fax
Alpine The PO Box 200 *Web:* www.alpineresort.com	Egg Harbor	WI	54209	920-868-3000	
AmericInn Motel 2032 Velp Ave *TF:* 800-634-3444 ■ *Web:* www.americinn.com/wisconsin/greenbay.html	Green Bay	WI	54303	920-434-9790	434-8790
Amerihost Inn Green Bay 2911 Voyager Drive *TF:* 800-434-5800 ■ *Web:* www.amerihostinn.com/137-main.html ■ *E-mail:* 137@amerihostinn.com	Green Bay	WI	54311	920-406-8200	406-8130
Arena Motel 871 Lombardi Ave	Green Bay	WI	54304	920-494-5636	494-5932
Baymont Inns & Suites 2840 S Oneida St *TF:* 800-301-0200	Green Bay	WI	53404	920-494-7887	494-3370
Best Western Midway Hotel 780 Packer Dr *TF:* 800-528-1234	Green Bay	WI	54304	920-499-3161	499-9401
Best Western Suites 2815 Ramada Way *TF:* 800-999-4268	Green Bay	WI	54304	920-494-8790	494-8749
Best Western Washington Street Inn 321 S Washington St *TF:* 800-252-2952	Green Bay	WI	54301	920-437-8771	437-3839

Green Bay — Hotels, Motels, Resorts (Cont'd)

				Phone	Fax
Comfort Inn 2841 Ramada Way	Green Bay	WI	54304	920-498-2060	498-2060
TF: 800-228-5150					
Comfort Suites 1951 Bond St.	Green Bay	WI	54303	920-499-7449	499-0322
TF: 800-228-5150					
Days Inn 406 N Washington St.	Green Bay	WI	54301	920-435-4484	435-3120
TF: 800-329-7466					
Days Inn West 1978 Holmgren Way	Green Bay	WI	54304	920-498-8088	498-8492
TF: 800-329-7466					
Exel Inn 2870 Ramada Way	Green Bay	WI	54304	920-499-3599	498-4055
TF: 800-356-8013					
Fairfield Inn 2850 S Oneida	Green Bay	WI	54304	920-497-1010	497-3098
TF: 800-228-2800 ■ *Web:* fairfieldinn.com/GRBFI					
Fox Valley Inn 2000 Holly Rd.	Neenah	WI	54956	920-734-9872	
Hampton Inn 2840 Ramada Way.	Green Bay	WI	54304	920-498-9200	498-3376
TF: 800-426-7866					
Holiday Inn Airport 2580 S Ashland Ave	Green Bay	WI	54304	920-499-5121	499-6777
TF: 800-465-4329					
Holiday Inn City Centre Downtown 200 Main St.	Green Bay	WI	54301	920-437-5900	437-1199
TF: 800-465-4329 ■ *Web:* www.holidayinngb.com ■ *E-mail:* info@holidayinngb.com					
Mariner Motel 2222 Riverside Dr	Green Bay	WI	54301	920-437-7107	437-2877
Motel 6 1614 Shawano Ave	Green Bay	WI	54303	920-494-6730	494-0474
TF: 800-466-8356					
Pioneer Inn & Marina 1000 Pioneer Dr.	Oshkosh	WI	54901	920-233-1980	426-2115
TF: 800-683-1980					
Priced Rite Suites 2327 Universiy Ave	Green Bay	WI	54302	920-469-2130	
Radisson Inn Green Bay 2040 Airport Dr.	Green Bay	WI	54313	920-494-7300	494-9599
TF: 800-333-3333					
Ramada Inn 2750 Ramada Way	Green Bay	WI	54304	920-499-0631	499-5476
TF: 800-272-6232					
Regency Suites 333 Main St	Green Bay	WI	54301	920-432-4555	432-0700
TF: 800-236-3330 ■ *Web:* www.regencygb.com					
Residence Inn by Marriott 335 W Saint Joseph St	Green Bay	WI	54301	920-435-2222	435-4068
TF: 800-331-3131 ■ *Web:* www.residenceinn.com/GRBWI					
Roadstar Inn 1941 True Ln	Green Bay	WI	54304	920-497-2666	497-4754
TF: 800-445-4667					
Settle Inn Airport 2620 S Packerland Dr	Green Bay	WI	54313	920-499-1900	499-1973
TF: 800-688-9052					
Super 8 Motel 2868 S Oneida St	Green Bay	WI	54304	920-494-2042	494-6959
TF: 800-800-8000					
Valley Motel 116 N Military Ave	Green Bay	WI	54303	920-494-3455	
Villager Inn 119 North Monroe Ave.	Green Bay	WI	54301	920-437-0525	437-6232
TF: 800-328-7829					

— Restaurants —

				Phone
Annie's American Cafe (American) 411 S Military Ave	Green Bay	WI	54303	920-494-4585
Backgammon Pub & Restaurant (American) 2920 Ramada Way	Green Bay	WI	54304	920-336-0335
Brewbaker's Pub (American) 209 N Washington St	Green Bay	WI	54301	920-435-2739
Brogan's (American) 2750 Ramada Way	Green Bay	WI	54304	920-499-0631
Chanterelles (French) 2638 Bay Settlement Rd	Green Bay	WI	54311	920-469-3200
Charley's Steakery (Steak) 205 Bay Park Sq	Green Bay	WI	54304	920-498-3069
Chili John's Restaurant (Mexican) 519 S Military Ave	Green Bay	WI	54303	920-494-4624
Country Inn & Suites by Carlson 2945 Allied St.	Green Bay	WI	54304	920-336-6600
TF: 800-456-4000				
Dasa's Czech Inn (Czechoslovakian) 1434 N Irwin Ave.	Green Bay	WI	54302	920-432-3941
Dragonwyck (Chinese) 1992 Holgren Way	Green Bay	WI	54304	920-498-9801
Eve's Supper Club (American) 2020 Riverside Dr	Green Bay	WI	54301	920-435-1571
Farr's Grove (Seafood) 2443 Shawano Ave	Green Bay	WI	54313	920-494-9956
Gasachapala (Mexican) 2035 University Ave	Green Bay	WI	54302	920-433-0402
La Bonne Femme (French) 1244 Main St	Green Bay	WI	54301	920-432-2897
Lee's Cantonese (Chinese) 2245 University Ave	Green Bay	WI	54302	920-468-9500
Lorelei Inn (German) 1412 S Webster Ave	Green Bay	WI	54301	920-432-5921
Los Banditos (Mexican) 1258 Main St	Green Bay	WI	54302	920-432-6460
New China (Chinese) 1923 S Webster Ave	Green Bay	WI	54301	920-431-0386
Prime Quarter Steak House (Steak) 2610 S Oneida St	Green Bay	WI	54304	920-498-8701
River's Bend (American) 792 N Riverview Dr	Howard	WI	54303	920-434-1383
Rock Garden (American) 1951 Bond St	Green Bay	WI	54303	920-497-4701
Seigo's Japanese Steak House (Japanese) 2148 University Ave	Green Bay	WI	54302	920-465-8400
Sharkey's (American) 2475 W Mason St.	Green Bay	WI	54303	920-494-6800
Smokin Joe's Southern Grill (Southern) 333 Main St.	Green Bay	WI	54301	920-432-4555
TF: 800-236-3330				
Timber Lodge Steakhouse (Steak) 2476 S Oneida St	Green Bay	WI	54304	920-498-1005
Titletown Brewing Co (American) 200 Dousman St	Green Bay	WI	54303	920-437-2337
Viands (Greek) 418 S Military Ave	Green Bay	WI	54303	920-497-9646
Victoria's (Italian) 2610 Bay Settlement Rd.	Green Bay	WI	54311	920-468-8070
Wellington Restaurant (Continental) 1060 Hansen Rd	Green Bay	WI	54304	920-499-2000
Willie Wood Inn (Steak/Seafood) 2607 Nicolet Dr	Green Bay	WI	54311	920-468-1086

— Goods and Services —

SHOPPING

				Phone	Fax
Bay Park Square Mall Oneida St.	Green Bay	WI	54304	920-499-2277	499-4804
East Town Mall 2350 E Mason St.	Green Bay	WI	54302	920-468-8500	468-8889
Fox River Mall 4301 W Wisconsin Ave	Appleton	WI	54913	920-739-4100	739-8210
Port Plaza Mall A-1175 Port Plaza Mall	Green Bay	WI	54301	920-432-0641	432-1099
Vickery Village 1749 Riverside Dr.	Suamico	WI	54173	920-434-0614	

BANKS

				Phone	Fax
Associated Bank Green Bay NA 200 N Adams St.	Green Bay	WI	54301	920-433-3200	433-3060
Bank One Green Bay PO Box 19029	Green Bay	WI	54307	920-437-0421	436-2524
TF: 800-947-1111					
Firstar Bank Green Bay PO Box 23089	Green Bay	WI	54305	920-432-0321	436-5528
M & I Bank Northeast 310 W Walnut St	Green Bay	WI	54306	920-436-1800	436-1938
TF: 888-464-5463					

BUSINESS SERVICES

	Phone
Airborne Express	800-247-2676
BAX Global	800-225-5229
Clark Business Service	920-499-3150
DHL Worldwide Express	800-225-5345
Federal Express	800-238-5355
Kelly Services	920-497-1300
Kinko's	920-496-2679
Mail Boxes Etc	800-789-4623
Manpower Temporary Services	920-498-2400
Post Office	920-498-3999
UPS	800-742-5877

— Media —

PUBLICATIONS

				Phone	Fax
Green Bay News-Chronicle‡ 133 S Monroe St	Green Bay	WI	54301	920-432-2941	432-8581
Web: www.greenbaynewschron.com					
Green Bay Press-Gazette‡ PO Box 19430	Green Bay	WI	54307	920-435-4411	431-8379
TF: 800-289-8221 ■ *Web:* www.greenbaypressgazette.com ■ *E-mail:* pgonline@netnet.net					

‡Daily newspapers

TELEVISION

				Phone	Fax
WBAY-TV Ch 2 (ABC) 115 S Jefferson St.	Green Bay	WI	54301	920-432-3331	432-1190
Web: www.wbay.com ■ *E-mail:* wbay2@netnet.net					
WFRV-TV Ch 5 (CBS) 1181 E Mason St.	Green Bay	WI	54301	920-437-5411	437-4576
Web: www.wfrv.com ■ *E-mail:* wfrv@dct.com					
WGBA-TV Ch 26 (NBC) 1391 North Rd	Green Bay	WI	54313	920-494-2626	494-7071*
**Fax:* Sales ■ *Web:* www.wgba.com					
WLUK-TV Ch 11 (Fox) 787 Lombardi Ave	Green Bay	WI	54307	920-494-8711	494-8782
Web: www.wluk.com					
WPNE-TV Ch 38 (PBS) 821 University Ave.	Madison	WI	53706	608-263-2121	263-9763
Web: www.wpt.org					

RADIO

				Phone	Fax
WDUZ-AM 1400 kHz (Sports) PO Box 310	Green Bay	WI	54305	920-468-4100	468-0250
WHID FM 88.1 MHz (N/T) 2420 Nicolet Dr.	Green Bay	WI	54311	920-465-2444	465-2517
WIXX-FM 101.1 MHz (CHR) PO Box 23333	Green Bay	WI	54305	920-435-3771	455-1155
WNFL-AM 1440 kHz (N/T) PO Box 23333	Green Bay	WI	54305	920-435-3771	455-1155
WQLH-FM 98.5 MHz (AC) PO Box 310	Green Bay	WI	54305	920-468-4100	468-0250

— Colleges/Universities —

				Phone	Fax
Bellin College of Nursing PO Box 23400	Green Bay	WI	54305	920-433-3560	433-7416
Lawrence University PO Box 599	Appleton	WI	54912	920-832-7000	832-6782
Web: www.lawrence.edu ■ *E-mail:* helpdesk@lawrence.edu					

Green Bay — Colleges/Universities (Cont'd)

				Phone	Fax
Saint Norbert College 100 Grant St	De Pere	WI	54115	920-337-3181	403-4088
TF Admissions: 800-236-4878 ■ *Web:* www.snc.edu ■ *E-mail:* weslcs@sncad.snc.edu					
Silver Lake College 2406 S Alverno Rd.	Manitowoc	WI	54220	920-684-6691	684-7082
TF: 800-236-4752 ■ *Web:* www.sl.edu/slc.html					
University of Wisconsin Green Bay 2420 Nicolet Dr	Green Bay	WI	54311	920-465-2000	465-5754
Web: www.uwgb.edu ■ *E-mail:* UWGB@uwgb.edu					

— Hospitals —

				Phone	Fax
Bellin Memorial Hospital PO Box 23400	Green Bay	WI	54305	920-433-3500	433-7405
Saint Mary's Medical Center 1726 Shawano Ave	Green Bay	WI	54303	920-498-4200	498-1861
Saint Vincent Hospital 835 S Van Buren St	Green Bay	WI	54301	920-433-0111	431-3273*
**Fax:* Admitting					

— Attractions —

				Phone	Fax
Barkhausen Waterfowl Preserve 2024 Lakeview Dr	Suamico	WI	54173	920-448-4466	
Bay Beach Amusement Park 1313 Bay Beach Dr	Green Bay	WI	54302	920-448-3365	448-3393
Bay Beach Wildlife Sanctuary 1660 E Shore Dr	Green Bay	WI	54302	920-391-3671	
Great Explorations Children's Museum 320 N Adams St Port Plaza Mall	Green Bay	WI	54301	920-432-4397	432-4566
Web: www.gbonline.com/org/child_museum					
Green Bay Botanical Garden 2600 Larson Rd	Green Bay	WI	54303	920-490-9457	490-9461
Green Bay Community Theatre 122 N Chestnut Ave	Green Bay	WI	54303	920-435-6300	
E-mail: gbct@netnet.net					
Green Bay Packers Hall of Fame 855 Lombardi Ave.	Green Bay	WI	54307	920-499-4281	405-5564
TF: 888-442-7225 ■ *Web:* www.packerhalloffame.com ■ *E-mail:* packhof@dct.com					
Green Bay Symphony Orchestra Inc PO Box 222	Green Bay	WI	54305	920-435-3465	435-1427
Web: www.gbsymphony.org					
Hazelwood Historic Home Museum 1008 S Monroe Ave	Green Bay	WI	54301	920-437-1840	437-1840
Heritage Hill Living History Museum 2640 S Webster	Green Bay	WI	54301	920-448-5150	448-5147
Web: www.netnet.net/heritagehill/					
National Railroad Museum 2285 S Broadway	Green Bay	WI	54304	920-437-7623	437-1291
Web: www.nationalrrmuseum.org					
Neville Public Museum of Brown County 210 Museum Pl	Green Bay	WI	54303	920-448-4460	448-4458
Web: www.gbonline.com/org/neville/					
New Zoo 4418 Reforestation Rd	Suamico	WI	54313	920-448-4466	
Oneida Bingo & Casino 2020-2100 Airport Dr	Oneida	WI	54313	920-494-4500	496-3745
TF: 800-238-4263					
Oneida Nation Museum PO Box 365	Oneida	WI	54155	920-869-2768	869-2959
Pamiro Opera Co 2420 Nicolet Dr UWGB Weidner Ctr	Green Bay	WI	54311	920-437-8331	437-8352
Web: www.pamiro.org					
Weidner Center for the Performing Arts 2420 Nicolet Dr University of Wisconsin at Green Bay	Green Bay	WI	54311	920-465-2726	465-2921
TF: 800-328-8587 ■ *Web:* www.uwgb.edu/~weidner ■ *E-mail:* weidner@uwgb.edu					
White Pillars Museum 403 N Broadway	De Pere	WI	54115	920-336-3877	

SPORTS TEAMS & FACILITIES

				Phone	Fax
Green Bay Gamblers (hockey) 1901 S Oneida St Brown County Expo Centre	Green Bay	WI	54304	920-497-5001	494-6868
Green Bay Packers 1265 Lombardi Ave Lambeau Field	Green Bay	WI	54304	920-496-5719	496-5738
Web: www.nfl.com/packers					
Lambeau Field 1265 Lombardi Ave.	Green Bay	WI	54304	920-496-5700	496-5738
Web: www.packers.com/lambeau					
Wisconsin Timber Rattlers (baseball) 2400 N Casaloma Dr Fox Cities Stadium	Appleton	WI	54915	920-733-4152	733-8032
Web: www.mwlguide.com/links/rattlers.html					

— Events —

	Phone
Arti Gras (early February)	920-494-9507
Artstreet (late August)	920-435-2787
Bayfest (June)	920-465-2145
Brown County Fair (late July)	920-336-6123
Celebrate Americafest (July 4)	920-494-9507
De Pere Celebration (late May)	920-433-7767
Garden Walk (mid-July)	920-490-9457
Holiday Parade (late November)	920-494-9507
Oneida Indian Pow Wow & Festival of Performing Arts (July)	920-869-1600
Pulaski Polka Days (late July)	920-822-3869

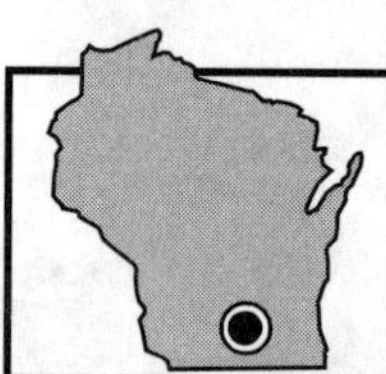

Madison

The center of the city of Madison lies on an eight-block-wide isthmus between Lakes Mendota and Monona. Much of the city's activity is focused around the lakes, where one can rent canoes, fish year round, and hike, roller skate, or bike on numerous paths. State Street, with its array of boutiques, galleries, coffee houses, and ethnic restaurants, links the State Capitol to the University of Wisconsin campus. This prominent Big Ten University has the acclaimed Elvehjem Museum of Art and the University Arboretum, with more than 1,200 acres of natural plant and animal communities. Just west of Madison is Blue Mound State Park. The Park's lookout tower, located along the nearly 40-mile Military Ridge Trail, affords a perfect view of the area's rolling hills. Little Norway, a restored 1856 Norwegian homestead, is also west of the city.

Population	209,306	**Longitude**	89-22-55 W
Area (Land)	57.8 sq mi	**County**	Dane
Area (Water)	16.0 sq mi	**Time Zone**	CST
Elevation	863 ft	**Area Code/s**	608
Latitude	43-04-23 N		

— Average Temperatures and Precipitation —

TEMPERATURES

	Jan	Feb	Mar	Apr	May	Jun	Jul	Aug	Sep	Oct	Nov	Dec
High	25	30	42	57	69	78	82	79	72	60	44	30
Low	7	11	23	34	44	54	60	57	48	38	27	14

PRECIPITATION

	Jan	Feb	Mar	Apr	May	Jun	Jul	Aug	Sep	Oct	Nov	Dec
Inches	1.1	1.1	2.2	2.9	3.1	3.7	3.4	4.0	3.4	2.2	2.1	1.8

— Important Phone Numbers —

	Phone		Phone
AAA	800-236-1300	**Poison Control Center**	608-262-3702
Emergency	911	**Time/Temp**	608-255-1234
HotelDocs	800-468-3537	**Weather**	608-936-1212

Madison (Cont'd)

— Information Sources —

			Phone	Fax
Better Business Bureau Serving Wisconsin PO Box 2190	Milwaukee WI	53201	414-273-1600	224-0881
Web: www.wisconsin.bbb.org ■ *E-mail:* bbbwi@execpc.com				
Dane County 210 ML King Jr Blvd Rm 112	Madison WI	53709	608-266-4121	
Web: www.co.dane.wi.us				
Dane County Exposition Center 1919 Expo Way	Madison WI	53713	608-267-3976	267-0146
Greater Madison Chamber of Commerce 615 E Washington Ave	Madison WI	53703	608-256-8348	256-0333
Web: www.greatermadisonchamber.com				
Greater Madison Convention & Visitors Bureau 615 E Washington Ave	Madison WI	53703	608-255-2537	258-4950
TF: 800-373-6376 ■ *Web:* www.visitmadison.com ■ *E-mail:* gmcvb@visitmadison.com				
Madison City Hall 210 ML King Jr Blvd.	Madison WI	53709	608-266-4611	
Web: www.ci.madison.wi.us/				
Madison Civic Center 211 State St	Madison WI	53703	608-266-6550	266-4864
Web: www.madcivic.org ■ *E-mail:* civiccenter@ci.madison.wi.us				
Madison Community & Economic Development Unit PO Box 2983	Madison WI	53701	608-266-4222	267-8739
Madison Mayor 210 ML King Jr Blvd Rm 403	Madison WI	53709	608-266-4611	267-8671
Web: www.ci.madison.wi.us/mayor/mayor.html ■ *E-mail:* mayor@ci.madison.wi.us				
Madison Public Library 201 W Mifflin St	Madison WI	53703	608-266-6300	266-4338
Web: www.scls.lib.wi.us/madison				
Monona Terrace Community & Convention Center 1 John Nolan Dr	Madison WI	53703	608-261-4000	261-4049
Web: mononaterrace.visitmadison.com				

On-Line Resources

4Madison.com	www.4madison.com
About.com Guide to Madison	madison.about.com/local/midwestus/madison
All-Info Madison	www.all-info.com/
Anthill City Guide Madison	www.anthill.com/city.asp?city=madison
Area Guide Madison	madison.areaguides.net
Boulevards Madison	www.boulevards.com/cities/madison.html
City Knowledge Madison	www.cityknowledge.com/wi_madison.htm
Excite.com Madison City Guide	www.excite.com/travel/countries/united_states/wisconsin/madison
Insiders' Guide to Madison	www.insiders.com/madison/
Insiders' Guide to Madison	www.insiders.com/madison/index.htm
Madison Business Internet Guide	www.abcon.com/ablinks.html
Madison Online	www.netphoria.com/mol/
Madison's Online Magazine	www.link-here.com
Madison.com	www.madison.com
Surf Madison	www.mabb.com/

— Transportation Services —

AIRPORTS

■ Dane County Regional Airport (MSN)

	Phone
5 miles NE of downtown (approx 15 minutes)	608-246-3380

Web: www.co.dane.wi.us/airport

Airport Transportation

	Phone
Madison Taxi $10-13 fare to downtown	608-258-7458
Union Cab $12 fare to downtown	608-242-2000

Commercial Airlines

	Phone		Phone
American	800-433-7300	**Northwest**	800-225-2525
Comair	800-354-9822	**TWA**	800-221-2000
Midwest Express	800-452-2022	**United**	800-241-6522

Charter Airlines

	Phone
Wisconsin Aviation	608-249-2189

CAR RENTALS

	Phone		Phone
Avis	608-242-0600	**Enterprise**	608-833-2220
Budget	608-249-5544	**Hertz**	608-241-3803
Campus Car	608-251-1717	**National**	608-249-1614

LIMO/TAXI

	Phone		Phone
Badger Cab	608-256-5566	**Madison Taxi**	608-258-7458
Classic Limo	800-300-7595	**Union Cab**	608-242-2000

MASS TRANSIT

	Phone
Madison Metro Transit $1.25 Base fare	608-266-4466

RAIL/BUS

			Phone
Greyhound Bus Station 2 S Bedford St	Madison WI	53703	608-257-3050
TF: 800-231-2222			

— Accommodations —

HOTELS, MOTELS, RESORTS

			Phone	Fax
Baymont Inns & Suites 8102 Excelsior Dr	Madison WI	53717	608-831-7711	831-1942
TF: 800-301-0200				
Best Western Inn on the Park Hotel 22 S Carroll St	Madison WI	53703	608-257-8811	257-5995
TF: 800-279-8811				
Best Western Inntowner 2424 University Ave	Madison WI	53705	608-233-8778	233-1325
TF: 800-528-1234 ■ *Web:* www.inntowner.com/				
Best Western West Towne Suites 650 Grand Canyon Dr	Madison WI	53719	608-833-4200	833-5614
TF: 800-528-1234				
Chula Vista Resort 4031 N River Rd	Wisconsin Dells WI	53965	608-254-8366	254-7653
TF: 800-388-4782 ■ *Web:* www.wisdells.com/chula				
College Park Towers 502 N Frances St	Madison WI	53703	608-257-0701	257-3078
TF: 800-458-1876				
Comfort Inn 4822 E Washington Ave	Madison WI	53704	608-244-6265	244-1293
TF: 800-221-2222				
Comfort Suites 1253 John Q Hammons Dr	Madison WI	53717	608-836-3033	836-0949
TF: 800-228-5150				
Concourse Hotel & Governors Club 1 W Dayton St	Madison WI	53703	608-257-6000	257-5280
TF: 800-356-8293 ■ *Web:* www.concoursehotel.com ■ *E-mail:* slsnctr@madison.tds.net				
Days Inn Madison 4402 E Broadway	Madison WI	53716	608-223-1800	223-1374
TF: 800-329-7466				
East Towne Suites 4801 Annamark Dr.	Madison WI	53704	608-244-2020	244-3434
TF: 800-950-1919 ■ *Web:* www.globaldialog.com/~easttown/				
Edgewater Hotel 666 Wisconsin Ave	Madison WI	53703	608-256-9071	256-0910
TF: 800-922-5512 ■ *Web:* www.gowisconsin.com/edgewater/				
Expo Inn 910 Ann St	Madison WI	53713	608-251-6555	251-6242
TF: 888-448-1414				
Fairfield Inn by Marriott 4765 Hayes Rd	Madison WI	53704	608-249-5300	240-9335
TF: 800-228-2800 ■ *Web:* fairfieldinn.com/MSNFI				
Hampton Inn West 516 Grand Canyon Dr	Madison WI	53719	608-833-3511	833-7140
TF: 800-426-7866				
Holiday Inn 722 John Nolen Dr	Madison WI	53713	608-255-7400	255-3152
TF: 800-465-4329				
Howard Johnson Plaza Hotel 525 W Johnson St	Madison WI	53703	608-251-5511	251-4824
TF: 800-446-4656				
Ivy Inn Hotel 2355 University Ave	Madison WI	53705	608-233-9717	233-2660
TF: 877-489-4661				
Madison Hampton Inn East 4820 Hayes Rd	Madison WI	53704	608-244-9400	244-7177
TF: 800-426-7866				
Madison Radisson Inn 517 Grand Canyon Dr	Madison WI	53719	608-833-0100	833-6543
TF: 800-333-3333 ■ *Web:* www.radisson.com/hotels/madisonwi/				
Mansion Hill Inn 424 N Pinckney St	Madison WI	53703	608-255-3999	255-2217
TF: 800-798-9070 ■ *Web:* www.mansionhillinn.com				
Merrill Springs Inn 5101 University Ave	Madison WI	53705	608-233-5357	233-1399
Microtel Inn & Suites 2139 E Springs Dr	Madison WI	53704	608-242-9000	242-8700
TF: 888-258-1283				
Quality Inn South 4916 E Broadway	Madison WI	53716	608-222-5501	222-0859
TF: 800-228-5151				
Ramada Inn 3431 Milton Ave	Janesville WI	53545	608-756-2341	756-4183
TF: 800-272-6232				
Red Roof Inn 4830 Hayes Rd	Madison WI	53704	608-241-1787	241-7034
TF: 800-843-7663				

Madison — Hotels, Motels, Resorts (Cont'd)

				Phone	Fax
Residence Inn 501 D'Onofrio Dr	Madison	WI	53719	608-833-8333	833-2693
TF: 800-331-3131 ■ *Web:* www.residenceinn.com/residenceinn/MSNWI					
Select Inn of Madison 4845 Hayes Rd	Madison	WI	53704	608-249-1815	249-1815
TF: 800-641-1000					
Sheraton Madison Hotel 706 John Nolen Dr	Madison	WI	53713	608-251-2300	251-1189
TF: 800-325-3535					
Voyageur Inn PO Box 608	Reedsburg	WI	53959	608-524-6431	524-6431
TF: 800-362-5483 ■ *Web:* www.voyageurinn.com					
Wingate Inn 3510 Mill Pond Rd	Madison	WI	53704	608-224-1500	224-0586
TF: 800-510-3510 ■ *Web:* www.wingate-madison.com					

— Restaurants —

				Phone
Admiralty Room (Continental) 666 Wisconsin Ave	Madison	WI	53703	608-256-9071
Angelic Brewing Company (American) 322 W Johnson St	Madison	WI	53703	608-257-2707
Web: www.angelicbrewing.com/				
Bahn Thai Restaurant (Thai) 944 Williamson St	Madison	WI	53703	608-256-0202
Beijing Restaurant (Chinese) 40 University Sq	Madison	WI	53715	608-257-8388
Big Mama & Uncle Fats' Barbeque & Blues (Barbecue) 6824 Odana Rd	Madison	WI	53719	608-829-2683
Bistro at the Madison Concourse (Continental) 1 W Dayton St	Madison	WI	53703	608-257-6000
Blue Marlin (Seafood) 101 N Hamilton St	Madison	WI	53703	608-255-2255
Cafe Monmartre (French) 127 E Mifflin St	Madison	WI	53703	608-255-5900
Caspian Cafe (Persian) 17 University Sq	Madison	WI	53715	608-259-9009
Chautara (Tibetan) 334 State St	Madison	WI	53703	608-251-3626
Coyote Capers (International) 1201 Williamson St	Madison	WI	53703	608-251-1313
Dardanelles (Mediterranean) 1851 Monroe St	Madison	WI	53711	608-256-8804
Delaney's Charcoal Steaks (Steak) 449 Grand Canyon Dr	Madison	WI	53719	608-833-7337
Dry Bean Saloon & Smokehouse (American) 5264 Verona Rd	Madison	WI	53711	608-274-2326
Essen Haus (German) 514 E Wilson St	Madison	WI	53703	608-255-4674
Great Dane Pub & Brewing Co (American) 123 E Doty St	Madison	WI	53703	608-284-0000
Heartland Grill (American) 706 John Nolen Dr	Madison	WI	53713	608-251-2300
Himal Chuli (Indian) 318 State St	Madison	WI	53703	608-251-9225
Horn of Africa (Ethiopian) 117 E Mifflin St	Madison	WI	53703	608-255-2077
Imperial Garden (Chinese) 4214 E Washington Ave	Madison	WI	53714	608-249-0466
Ivy Inn Restaurant (American) 2355 University Ave	Madison	WI	53705	608-233-9717
Jolly Bob's (Caribbean) 1210 Williamson St	Madison	WI	53703	608-251-3902
Kabul (Afghan/Mediterranean) 541 State St	Madison	WI	53703	608-256-6322
Kosta's Restaurant (Greek) 117 State St	Madison	WI	53703	608-255-6671
L'Etoile (New American) 25 N Pinckney St	Madison	WI	53703	608-251-0500
La Bamba (Mexican) 449 State St	Madison	WI	53703	608-257-1511
La Paella (Spanish) 2784 S Fish Hatchery Rd	Madison	WI	53711	608-273-2666
Web: www.lapaella.com/				
Mariner's Inn (Steak/Seafood) 5339 Lighthouse Bay Dr	Madison	WI	53704	608-244-8418
Noodles & Company (American) 232 State St	Madison	WI	53703	608-257-6393
Opera House Restaurant (New American) 117 ML King Jr Blvd	Madison	WI	53703	608-284-8466
Ovens of Brittany (Continental) 3244 University Ave	Madison	WI	53705	608-231-6858
Paisan's (Italian) 800 University Square Mall	Madison	WI	53703	608-257-3832
Pedro's Mexican Restaurante (Mexican) 3555 E Washington Ave	Madison	WI	53704	608-241-8110
Porta Bella (Italian) 425 N Frances St	Madison	WI	53703	608-256-3186
Quivey's Grove (American) 6261 Nesbitt Rd	Madison	WI	53719	608-273-4900
Restaurant Magnus (Continental) 120 E Wilson St	Madison	WI	53703	608-258-8787
Saz The (Turkish/Mexican) 558 State St	Madison	WI	53703	608-256-1917
Smoky's Club (Steak) 3005 University Ave	Madison	WI	53705	608-233-2120
State Street Brats (American) 603 State St	Madison	WI	53703	608-255-5544
Taqueria Gila Monster (Mexican) 106 King St	Madison	WI	53703	608-255-6425
Taste of India (Indian) 6713 Odana Rd	Madison	WI	53719	608-833-3113
Tiffany Grille (American) 1313 John Q Hammons Dr	Madison	WI	53562	608-831-2000
Ton-Ton Restaurant (Japanese) 122 State St	Madison	WI	53703	608-251-2171
Wasabi Japanese Restaurant (Japanese) 449 State St	Madison	WI	53703	608-255-5020
Zorba's (Greek) 315 State St	Madison	WI	53703	608-255-8870

— Goods and Services —

SHOPPING

				Phone	Fax
Antiques Mall of Madison 4748 Cottage Grove Rd	Madison	WI	53716	608-222-2049	222-2261
East Towne Mall E Washington & Zeier Rds	Madison	WI	53704	608-244-1501	244-8306
Hilldale Mall 702 N Midvale Mall	Madison	WI	53705	608-238-6640	238-7338
Lands' End Outlet 209 Junction Rd	Madison	WI	53717	608-833-3343	833-3491
State Street District State & Gorham Sts	Madison	WI	53703	608-255-2537	
Web: www.state-st.com/					
West Towne Mall 66 West Towne Way	Madison	WI	53719	608-833-6330	833-5878

BANKS

				Phone	Fax
Bank One Madison 1965 Atwood Ave	Madison	WI	53704	608-246-2333	246-2326
TF: 800-947-1111					
Bankers' Bank 7700 Mineral Point Rd	Madison	WI	53717	608-833-5550	829-5590
Web: www.bankersbankusa.com					
Firstar Bank Madison 1 S Pinckney St on the Square	Madison	WI	53703	608-252-4000	252-7609*
**Fax:* Mktg ■ *TF:* 800-236-1947					
M & I Bank of Southern Wisconsin 1 W Main St	Madison	WI	53703	608-252-5800	252-5880
TF Cust Svc: 888-464-5463 ■ *Web:* www.mibank.com					

BUSINESS SERVICES

	Phone
Adtec Staffing Services	608-231-3210
Airborne Express	800-247-2676
DHL Worldwide Express	800-225-5345
Dunham Express	608-242-1000
Express Mail	608-246-1247
Federal Express	800-238-5355
Kelly Services	608-238-3055
Kinko's	608-255-2679
Manpower Temporary Services	608-233-5244
Matt's Express Inc	608-249-9977
Post Office	608-246-1249
Professional Temporaries Inc	608-257-2775
TNT Express Delivery	608-249-2988

— Media —

PUBLICATIONS

				Phone	Fax
Capital Times‡ 1901 Fish Hatchery Rd	Madison	WI	53713	608-252-6400	252-6445
Web: www.thecapitaltimes.com ■ *E-mail:* tctvoice@captimes.madison.com					
In Business Magazine 2718 Dryden Dr	Madison	WI	53704	608-246-3599	246-3597
Wisconsin State Journal‡ 1901 Fish Hatchery Rd	Madison	WI	53713	608-252-6100	252-6119
Web: www.madison.com/wsj/					
Wisconsin Trails PO Box 5650	Madison	WI	53705	608-231-2444	231-1557
TF: 800-236-8088 ■ *Web:* www.wistrails.com/magazine.html ■ *E-mail:* info@wistrails.com					

‡Daily newspapers

TELEVISION

				Phone	Fax
WHA-TV Ch 21 (PBS) 821 University Ave	Madison	WI	53706	608-263-2121	263-9763
Web: www.wpt.org					
WISC-TV Ch 3 (CBS) PO Box 44965	Madison	WI	53744	608-271-4321	271-0800
Web: www.wisctv.com ■ *E-mail:* talkback@wisctv.com					
WKOW-TV Ch 27 (ABC) 5727 Tokay Blvd	Madison	WI	53719	608-274-1234	274-9514
Web: www.wkowtv.com ■ *E-mail:* 27listens@wkowtv.com					
WMSN-TV Ch 47 (Fox) 7847 Big Sky Dr	Madison	WI	53719	608-833-0047	833-5055
WMTV-Ch 15 (NBC) 615 Forward Dr	Madison	WI	53711	608-274-1515	271-5194

RADIO

				Phone	Fax
WERN-FM 88.7 MHz (NPR) 821 University Ave	Madison	WI	53706	608-264-9600	264-9622
Web: www.wpr.org					
WHA-AM 970 kHz (NPR) 821 University Ave	Madison	WI	53706	608-263-3970	263-9763
Web: www.wpr.org					
WHLA-FM 90.3 MHz (N/T) 821 University Ave	Madison	WI	53706	608-263-3970	
WIBA-FM 101.5 MHz (CR) PO Box 99	Madison	WI	53701	608-274-5450	274-5521
WJJO-FM 94.1 MHz (Rock) 2740 Ski Ln	Madison	WI	53713	608-273-1000	271-8182
Web: www.wjjo.com/					
WMGN-FM 98.1 MHz (AC) 2740 Ski Ln	Madison	WI	53713	608-273-1000	271-8182
Web: www.magic98.com					
WMLI-FM 96.3 MHz (AC) 2651 Fish Hatchery Rd	Madison	WI	53711	608-274-1070	274-5521
E-mail: lite@madcity.com					
WTSO-AM 1070 kHz (N/T) 2651 S Fish Hatchery Rd	Madison	WI	53711	608-274-1070	274-5521
WWQM-FM 106.3 MHz (Ctry) 2740 Ski Ln	Madison	WI	53713	608-271-6611	271-0400
Web: www.q106.com					

Madison (Cont'd)

— Colleges/Universities —

	City	State	ZIP	Phone	Fax
Edgewood College 855 Woodrow St *TF:* 800-444-4861 ■ *Web:* www.edgewood.edu	Madison	WI	53711	608-257-4861	663-3291
Herzing College of Technology 1227 N Sherman Ave *TF:* 800-582-1227 ■ *Web:* www.herzing.edu/madison/home.htm ■ *E-mail:* mailbag@msn.herzing.edu	Madison	WI	53704	608-249-6611	249-8593
Madison Area Technical College 3550 Anderson St *Web:* www.madison.tec.wi.us	Madison	WI	53704	608-246-6100	246-6880
University of Wisconsin Colleges 780 Regent St *Web:* www.uwc.edu	Madison	WI	53708	608-262-1783	262-7872
University of Wisconsin Madison 716 Langdon St *Web:* wiscinfo.wisc.edu ■ *E-mail:* on.wisconsin@mail.admin.wisc.edu	Madison	WI	53706	608-262-1234	262-1429

— Hospitals —

	City	State	ZIP	Phone	Fax
Meriter Hospital 202 S Park St **Fax:* Admitting ■ *Web:* www.meriter.com/meriter/mhs/index.htm	Madison	WI	53715	608-267-6000	267-6419*
Saint Mary's Hospital Medical Center 707 S Mills St **Fax:* Admitting ■ *Web:* www.stmarysmadison.com	Madison	WI	53715	608-251-6100	258-6273*
University of Wisconsin Hospital & Clinics 600 Highland Ave *Web:* www.medicine.wisc.edu	Madison	WI	53792	608-263-6400	263-9830
William S Middleton Memorial Veterans Hospital 2500 Overlook Terr	Madison	WI	53705	608-256-1901	262-7095

— Attractions —

	City	State	ZIP	Phone	Fax
American Players Theater 5950 Golf Course Rd *Web:* www.americanplayers.org	Spring Green	WI	53588	608-588-7401	588-7085
Barrymore Theatre 2090 Atwood Ave	Madison	WI	53704	608-241-8633	241-8861
Blue Mound State Park 4350 Mounds Park Rd *Web:* www.dnr.state.wi.us	Blue Mounds	WI	53517	608-437-5711	
Broom Street Theatre 1119 Williamson St *Web:* www.geocities.com/~broomstreet	Madison	WI	53703	608-244-8338	
Cave of the Mounds 2975 Cave of the Mounds Rd	Blue Mounds	WI	53517	608-437-3038	437-4181
Elvehjem Museum of Art 800 University Ave University of Wisconsin *Web:* www.uwpd.wisc.edu/elvehjem.htm	Madison	WI	53706	608-263-2246	263-8188
Governor Nelson State Park 5140 County Hwy M	Waunakee	WI	53597	608-831-3005	
House on the Rock 5754 Hwy 23 *Web:* www.thehouseontherock.com	Spring Green	WI	53588	608-935-3639	935-9472
Lake Kegonsa State Park 2405 Door Creek Rd	Stoughton	WI	53589	608-873-9695	873-0674
Little Norway 3576 Hwy JG N *Web:* www.littlenorway.com	Blue Mounds	WI	53517	608-437-8211	437-7827
Madison Art Center 211 State St *Web:* members.aol.com/MadArtCtr ■ *E-mail:* mac@itis.com	Madison	WI	53703	608-257-0158	257-5722
Madison Children's Museum 100 State St *Web:* www.link-here.com/mcm/ ■ *E-mail:* mcm@terracom.net	Madison	WI	53703	608-256-6445	256-3226
Madison Opera 211 State St Oscar Mayer Theatre	Madison	WI	53703	608-238-8085	233-3431
Madison Repertory Theater 211 State St Isthmus Playhouse *Web:* www.madstage.com	Madison	WI	53703	608-256-0029	256-7433
Madison Symphony Orchestra 211 N Carroll St *Web:* www.madisonsymphony.org	Madison	WI	53703	608-257-3734	258-2315
Olbrich Botanical Gardens 3330 Atwood Ave *Web:* www.olbrich.org/	Madison	WI	53704	608-246-4551	246-4719
Oscar Mayer Theater 211 State St Madison Civic Ctr	Madison	WI	53703	608-266-9055	261-9975
State Historical Museum of Wisconsin 30 N Carroll St *Web:* www.shsw.wisc.edu/museum	Madison	WI	53703	608-264-6555	264-6575
State Street District State & Gorham Sts *Web:* www.state-st.com/	Madison	WI	53703	608-255-2537	
Swiss Historical Village 612 7th Ave	New Glarus	WI	53574	608-527-2317	
Taliesin Hwy 23 & Hwy C *Web:* www.taliesinpreservation.org	Spring Green	WI	53588	608-588-7900	588-7514
University of Wisconsin Arboretum 1207 Seminole Hwy	Madison	WI	53711	608-263-7888	262-5209
Vilas Henry Park Zoo 702 S Randall Ave *Web:* www.vilaszoo.com ■ *E-mail:* zoo@abcon.com	Madison	WI	53715	608-266-4732	266-5923
Wisconsin Chamber Orchestra 22 N Carroll St Suite 104	Madison	WI	53703	608-257-0638	257-0611
Wisconsin Dance Ensemble 6320 Monona Dr Suite 319	Madison	WI	53716	608-222-5552	222-5662
Wisconsin Dells 701 Superior St *TF:* 800-223-3557 ■ *Web:* www.dells.com/index-a.html	Wisconsin Dells	WI	53965	608-254-8088	254-4293
Wisconsin State Capitol Capitol Sq	Madison	WI	53702	608-266-0382	
Wisconsin Union Art Collection & Theater Galleries 800 Langdon St Room 507 *Web:* www.wisc.edu/union ■ *E-mail:* union@macc.wisc.edu	Madison	WI	53706	608-262-5969	262-8862
Wisconsin Union Theater 800 Langdon St *Web:* www.wisc.edu/union/mu/muarts/wut/wut.html	Madison	WI	53706	608-262-2201	
Wisconsin Veterans Museum 30 W Mifflin St *Web:* badger.state.wi.us/agencies/dva/museum/wvmmain.html	Madison	WI	53703	608-264-6086	

SPORTS TEAMS & FACILITIES

	City	State	ZIP	Phone	Fax
Madison Black Wolf (baseball) 2920 N Sherman Ave Warner Pk *Web:* www.madwolf.com ■ *E-mail:* madwolf@madwall.com	Madison	WI	53704	608-244-5666	244-6996

— Events —

	Phone
Art Fair off the Square (mid-July)	608-798-4811
Audubon Art Fair (early May)	608-255-2473
Badger State Summer Games (mid-late June)	608-226-4780
Capital City Jazz Festival (late April)	608-877-4171
Capitol Christmas Pageant (early December)	608-849-9529
Concerts in the Gardens (June-August)	608-246-4551
Concerts on the Square (late June-late July)	608-257-0638
Cows on the Concourse (early June)	608-221-8698
Crazy Legs Run (late April)	608-263-7894
Dane County Fair (mid-July)	608-224-6455
Dane County Farmers' Market (late April-early November)	920-563-5037
Executive Residence Christmas Tours (December)	608-266-3554
Executive Residence Public Tours (April-August)	608-266-3554
Fall Festival (mid-October)	608-437-5914
Firstar Eve (December 31)	608-255-2537
Garden Expo (mid-February)	608-262-5255
Halloween at the Zoo (late October)	608-266-4732
Heroes Madison Marathon (late May)	608-256-9922
Holiday Art Fair (late November)	608-257-0158
Holiday Fantasy of Lights (late November-early January)	608-222-7630
Holiday Flower & Train Show (December)	608-246-4718
Hometown USA Festival (mid-June)	608-831-5696
International Children's Film Festival (March)	608-266-9055
International Holiday Festival (mid-November)	608-266-6550
Isthmus Jazz Festival (early October)	608-266-6550
Jingle Bell Run (mid-December)	608-221-9800
June Jam (early June)	608-276-6606
Kwanzaa Holiday Marketplace (late November)	608-255-9600
Madison Folk Music Festival (early May)	608-836-8422
Maxwell Street Days (mid-July)	608-266-6033
Midwest Horse Fair (mid-April)	608-267-3976
Mount Horeb Art Fair (mid-July)	608-437-5914
National Mustard Day (early August)	608-437-3986
Paddle & Portage (late July)	608-255-1008
Rhapsody in Bloom (mid-June)	608-246-4550
Rhythm & Booms (early July)	800-951-2264
Spring Flower Show (mid-March)	608-246-4550
Summer Concerts in the Gardens (early June-mid-August)	608-246-4551
Taste of Madison (early September)	800-373-6376
Triangle Ethnic Fest (mid-August)	800-373-6376
Tuesday Noon Concerts (June-September)	608-266-0382
Umbrella Daze (mid-July)	608-423-3780
Wednesday Farmers' Market (May-late October)	920-563-5037
Willy Street Fair (mid-September)	608-256-3527
Winter Art Festival (mid-November)	608-798-4811
Winter Concerts in the Gardens (January-March)	608-246-4551
Wisconsin Quarter Horse Show (mid-late August)	608-267-3976
World Dairy Expo (late September-early October)	608-224-6455
Zor Shrine Circus (mid-February)	608-274-2260

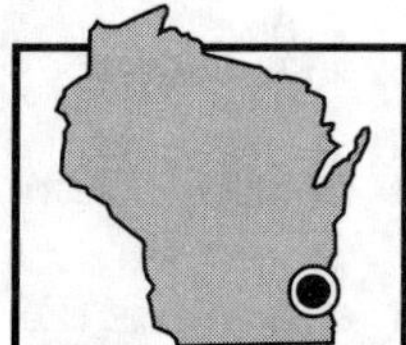

Milwaukee

Milwaukee's many breweries have earned it a reputation as the "beer capital" of the nation, and visitors to the city can tour the facilities of Pabst, Miller, or Schlitz brewing companies. Milwaukee is notorious for its harsh winters, but the Mitchell Park Horticultural Conservatory is a haven from the cold. It houses three domes - tropical, arid, and show - which feature seasonal shows and year-round exhibits. Spring and summer are the best times of year for a visit to the Milwaukee County Zoo or a drive along Lake Michigan. Milwaukee is also home to Marquette University.

Population . . . 578,364
Area (Land) . . . 96.0 sq mi
Area (Water) . . . 0.8 sq mi
Elevation . . . 634 ft
Latitude . . . 43-03-89 N
Longitude . . . 87-90-64 W
County . . . Milwaukee
Time Zone . . . CST
Area Code/s . . . 414

— Average Temperatures and Precipitation —

TEMPERATURES

	Jan	Feb	Mar	Apr	May	Jun	Jul	Aug	Sep	Oct	Nov	Dec
High	27	32	43	57	70	80	84	82	74	61	47	33
Low	12	16	27	37	47	57	63	61	54	43	32	19

PRECIPITATION

	Jan	Feb	Mar	Apr	May	Jun	Jul	Aug	Sep	Oct	Nov	Dec
Inches	1.6	1.5	2.7	3.5	2.8	3.2	3.5	3.5	3.4	2.4	2.5	2.3

— Important Phone Numbers —

	Phone
AAA	262-796-8960
American Express Travel	414-332-3157
Dental Referral	800-503-3682
Emergency	911
Greater Milwaukee Events	800-554-1448
HotelDocs	800-468-3537
Medical Referral	262-544-2745
Poison Control Center	414-266-2222
Time	414-844-1414
Travelers Aid	414-449-4777
Weather	414-936-1212

— Information Sources —

				Phone	*Fax*
Better Business Bureau Serving Wisconsin PO Box 2190	Milwaukee	WI	53201	414-273-1600	224-0881

Web: www.wisconsin.bbb.org ■ *E-mail:* bbbwi@execpc.com

Greater Milwaukee Convention & Visitors Bureau 510 W Kilbourn Ave	Milwaukee	WI	53203	414-273-3950	273-5596

TF: 800-231-0903 ■ *Web:* www.milwaukee.org

Metropolitan Milwaukee Assn of Commerce 756 N Milwaukee St	Milwaukee	WI	53202	414-287-4100	271-7753
Midwest Express Center 400 W Wisconsin Ave	Milwaukee	WI	53203	414-908-6000	908-6010

Web: www.wcd.org/site/home/fac/mid_exp_cen/main.html

Milwaukee City Hall 200 E Wells St	Milwaukee	WI	53202	414-286-2150	286-3245

Web: www.ci.mil.wi.us

Milwaukee County 901 N 9th St	Milwaukee	WI	53233	414-278-4067	
Milwaukee Economic Development Div 809 N Broadway	Milwaukee	WI	53202	414-286-5840	286-5778

Web: www.dcd.mpw.net

Milwaukee Mayor 200 E Wells St City Hall Rm 201	Milwaukee	WI	53202	414-286-2200	286-3191

Web: www.ci.mil.wi.us/mayor/mayor.htm ■ *E-mail:* mayor@ci.mil.wi.us

Milwaukee Public Library 814 W Wisconsin Ave	Milwaukee	WI	53233	414-286-3000	286-2137

Web: www.mpl.org

On-Line Resources

4Milwaukee.com . . . www.2milwaukee.com
About.com Guide to Milwaukee . . . milwaukee.about.com/local/midwestus/milwaukee
Boulevards Milwaukee . . . www.milwaukee.com
City Knowledge Milwaukee . . . www.cityknowledge.com/wi_milwaukee.htm
DigitalCity Milwaukee . . . home.digitalcity.com/milwaukee
Excite.com Milwaukee City Guide . . . www.excite.com/travel/countries/united_states/wisconsin/milwaukee
Explore Milwaukee . . . www.exploremilwaukee.com
Milwaukee Footlights Performing Arts Guide . . . www.footlights.com
Milwaukee Home Page . . . www.execpc.com/~trilux
Milwaukee.TheLinks.com . . . milwaukee.thelinks.com/
NITC Travelbase City Guide Milwaukee . . . www.travelbase.com/auto/guides/milwaukee-area-wi.html
Rough Guide Travel Milwaukee . . . travel.roughguides.com/content/526/

— Transportation Services —

AIRPORTS

■ **General Mitchell International Airport (MKE)**

11 miles S of downtown (approx 15 minutes) . . . *Phone* 414-747-5300
Web: www.mitchellairport.com ■ *E-mail:* info@mitchellairport.com

Airport Transportation

	Phone
Milwaukee Airport Car Service $8.50 fare to downtown	414-769-2450
Milwaukee County Transit System $1.35 fare to downtown	414-344-4550
Taxi $16 fare to downtown	414-271-1800

Commercial Airlines

	Phone
American	800-433-7300
American Eagle	800-433-7300
Comair	800-354-9822
Continental	414-342-3099
Continental Express	800-525-0280
Delta	800-221-1212
Midwest Express	800-452-2022
Northwest	800-225-2525
TWA	800-221-2000
United	800-241-6522
US Airways	800-428-4322

Charter Airlines

	Phone
Grand Air	414-461-3222
Scott Air Charter	414-744-1300
Wisconsin Aviation Inc	920-261-4567

CAR RENTALS

	Phone
Alamo	414-481-6600
Avis	414-744-2266
Budget	414-541-8750
Enterprise	414-257-4499
Hertz	414-747-5200
National	414-483-9800
Thrifty	414-483-5870

LIMO/TAXI

	Phone
Carey Limousine	414-482-9950
City Veteran Taxicab	414-291-8080
Corporate Limousine	414-483-0003
Limousine Services	414-769-9100
Limousines Inc	414-671-5466
Midwest Limo Coaches	414-529-0606
Yellow Cab	414-271-1800

MASS TRANSIT

	Phone
Milwaukee County Transit System $1.35 Base fare	414-344-4550

RAIL/BUS

				Phone
Greyhound/Trailways Bus Station 606 N James Lovell St	Milwaukee	WI	53233	414-272-2259

TF: 800-231-2222

Milwaukee Amtrak Station 433 W St Paul Ave	Milwaukee	WI	53203	414-271-0840

TF: 800-872-7245

— Accommodations —

HOTELS, MOTELS, RESORTS

				Phone	*Fax*
Ambassador Hotel 2308 W Wisconsin Ave	Milwaukee	WI	53233	414-342-8400	931-0279

Milwaukee — Hotels, Motels, Resorts (Cont'd)

	City	State	ZIP	Phone	Fax
Astor Hotel 924 E Juneau Ave	Milwaukee	WI	53202	414-271-4220	271-6370
TF: 800-558-0200 ■ *Web:* www.theastorhotel.com ■ *E-mail:* info@theastorhotel.com					
Best Western N 88 West 14776 Main St	Menomonee Falls	WI	53051	262-255-1700	255-2305
TF: 800-528-1234					
Best Western Midway Motor Lodge Airport 5105 S Howell Ave	Milwaukee	WI	53207	414-769-2100	769-0064
TF: 800-528-1234					
Country Inn Hotel & Conference Center 2810 Golf Rd	Waukesha	WI	53072	262-547-0201	547-0207
TF: 800-247-6640 ■ *Web:* www.countryinn.com/countryinn					
Embassy Suites Hotel Milwaukee West 1200 S Moorland Rd	Brookfield	WI	53008	262-782-2900	796-9159
TF: 800-362-2779					
Excel Inn West 115 N Mayfair Rd	Milwaukee	WI	53226	414-257-0140	475-7875
TF: 800-367-3935					
Four Points by Sheraton 4747 S Howell Ave	Milwaukee	WI	53207	414-481-8000	481-8065
TF: 800-325-3535					
Grand Geneva Resort & Spa 7036 Grand Geneva Way	Lake Geneva	WI	53147	262-248-8811	249-4763
TF: 800-558-3417 ■ *Web:* www.grandgeneva.com					
Hampton Inn Milwaukee Airport 1200 W College Ave	Milwaukee	WI	53221	414-762-4240	762-9810
TF: 800-426-7866					
Holiday Inn 2417 W Bluemound Rd	Waukesha	WI	53186	262-786-0460	786-1599
TF: 800-465-4329					
Holiday Inn City Centre 611 W Wisconsin Ave	Milwaukee	WI	53203	414-273-2950	273-7662
TF: 800-465-4329					
Hospitality Inn 4400 S 27th St	Milwaukee	WI	53221	414-282 8800	
TF: 800-825-8466 ■ *Web:* www.hospitalityinn.com					
Hotel Wisconsin 720 N Old World 3rd St	Milwaukee	WI	53203	414-271-4900	271-9998
Hyatt Regency Milwaukee 333 W Kilbourn Ave	Milwaukee	WI	53203	414-276-1234	276-6338
TF: 800-233-1234 ■ *Web:* www.hyatt.com/usa/milwaukee/hotels/hotel_mkerm.html					
Interlaken Resort & Country Spa W 4240 SR-50	Lake Geneva	WI	53147	262-248-9121	245-5016
TF: 800-225-5558					
Knickerbocker on the Lake 1028 E Juneau Ave	Milwaukee	WI	53202	414-276-8500	276-3668
Lake Lawn Lodge 2400 E Geneva St	Delavan	WI	53115	262-728-5511	728-2347
TF: 800-338-5253					
Manchester Hotel & Suites East 7065 N Port Washington Rd	Glendale	WI	53217	414-351-6960	351-5194
TF: 800-723-8280					
Manchester Suites Airport 200 W Grange Ave	Milwaukee	WI	53207	414-744-3600	744-4188
TF: 800-723-8280					
Marriott Hotel Racine 7111 Washington Ave	Racine	WI	53406	262-886-6100	886-1048
TF: 800-228-9290 ■ *Web:* marriotthotels.com/MKERW					
Milwaukee Hilton Hotel 509 W Wisconsin Ave	Milwaukee	WI	53203	414-271-7250	271-1039
TF: 800-445-8667					
Milwaukee River Hilton Inn 4700 N Port Washington Rd	Milwaukee	WI	53212	414-962-6040	962-6166
TF: 800-445-8667					
Olympia Resort & Spa 1350 Royale Mile Rd	Oconomowoc	WI	53066	262-567-0311	567-5934
TF: 800-558-9573 ■ *Web:* www.olympiaresort.com					
Park East Hotel 916 E State St	Milwaukee	WI	53202	414-276-8800	765-1919
TF: 800-328-7275 ■ *Web:* www.parkeasthotel.com					
Pfister Hotel 424 E Wisconsin Ave	Milwaukee	WI	53202	414-273-8222	273-5025
TF: 800-558-8222 ■ *Web:* www.pfister-hotel.com					
Plaza Hotel & Apartments 1007 N Cass St	Milwaukee	WI	53202	414-276-2101	276-0404
TF: 800-340-9590					
Radisson Inn 2303 N Mayfair Rd	Wauwatosa	WI	53226	414-257-3400	257-0900
TF: 800-333-3333					
Ramada Inn Airport South 6401 S 13th St.	Milwaukee	WI	53221	414-764-5300	764-6815
TF: 800-272-6232					
Ramada Inn Downtown 633 W Michigan St	Milwaukee	WI	53203	414-272-8410	272-4651
TF: 800-272-6232					
Residence Inn by Marriott 7275 N Port Washington Rd	Glendale	WI	53217	414-352-0070	352-3743
TF: 800-331-3131 ■ *Web:* residenceinn.com/MKEGL					
Sheraton Inn Milwaukee North 8900 N Kildeer Ct	Brown Deer	WI	53209	414-355-8585	355-3566
TF: 800-325-3535					
Sheraton Milwaukee Brookfield 375 S Moorland Rd	Brookfield	WI	53005	262-786-1100	786-5210
TF: 800-325-3535					
Westwood Hotel 201 N Mayfair Rd	Milwaukee	WI	53226	414-771-4400	771-4517
TF: 800-531-3965					
Woodfield Suites 5423 N Port Washington Rd	Glendale	WI	53217	414-962-6767	962-8811
TF: 800-338-0008					
Wyndham Milwaukee Center 139 E Kilbourn Ave	Milwaukee	WI	53202	414-276-8686	276-8007
TF: 800-996-3426					

— Restaurants —

	City	State	ZIP	Phone
African Hut (African) 1107 N Old World Third St	Milwaukee	WI	53203	414-765-1110
Aladdin (Middle Eastern) 800 N Plankinton Ave	Milwaukee	WI	53203	414-271-9870
Amann's Beach Club Bar & Pub (American) 20770 S Denoon Rd	Muskego	WI	53150	262-895-3550
Astor Street (American) 924 E Juneau Ave	Milwaukee	WI	53202	414-278-8660
Balkanian New Star Maric (Serbian) 901 Milwaukee Ave	Milwaukee	WI	53172	414-762-6397
Bartolotta's Lake Park Bistro (French) 3133 E Newberry	Milwaukee	WI	53211	414-962-6300
Bavarian Wurst Haus (German) 8310 W Appleton Ave	Milwaukee	WI	53218	414-464-0060
Boder's on-the-River (American) 11919 N River Rd	Mequon	WI	53092	262-242-0335
Boulevard Inn (Continental) 925 E Wells St	Milwaukee	WI	53202	414-765-1166
Web: www.boulevardinn.com/				
Buca Little Italy (Italian) 1233 N Van Buren St	Milwaukee	WI	53202	414-224-8672
Cafe at the Pfister (American) 424 E Wisconsin Ave	Milwaukee	WI	53202	414-273-8222
China Palace (Chinese) 4511 N Oakland Ave	Milwaukee	WI	53211	414-332-2024
County Clare (Irish) 1234 N Astor St	Milwaukee	WI	53202	414-272-5273
Crawdaddy's (Cajun/Creole) 6414 W Greenfield Ave	Milwaukee	WI	53214	414-778-2228
Don Quijote (Spanish) 2624 N Downer Ave	Milwaukee	WI	53211	414-967-1322
Eddie Martini's (Steak/Seafood) 8612 Watertown Plank Rd	Milwaukee	WI	53213	414-771-6680
Egan's on Water (Seafood) 1000 N Water St	Milwaukee	WI	53202	414-271-6900
Elsa's on the Park (American) 833 N Jefferson St	Milwaukee	WI	53202	414-765-0615
English Room (American) 424 E Wisconsin Ave	Milwaukee	WI	53202	414-273-8222
Fox & Hounds (American) 1298 Friess Lake Rd	Hubertus	WI	53033	262-628-1111
Gallery The (American) 6331 S 13th St	Milwaukee	WI	53221	414-764-1500
Giovanni's Restaurant (Italian) 1683 N Van Buren St	Milwaukee	WI	53202	414-291-5600
Grenadier's (Continental) 747 N Broadway	Milwaukee	WI	53202	414-276-0747
Hector's (Mexican) 7118 W State St	Milwaukee	WI	53213	414-258-5600
Historic Turner Restaurant (American) 1034 N 4th St	Milwaukee	WI	53203	414-276-4844
John Ernst Restaurant (German) 600 E Ogden Ave	Milwaukee	WI	53202	414-273-1878
Karl Ratzsch's Old World Restaurant (German) 320 E Mason St	Milwaukee	WI	53202	414-276-2720
King & I (Thai) 823 N 2nd St	Milwaukee	WI	53203	414-276-4181
Knick The (International) 1030 E Juneau Ave	Milwaukee	WI	53202	414-272-0011
La Casita Mexican Cafe (Mexican) 2014 N Farwell Ave	Milwaukee	WI	53211	414-277-1177
La Fuente (Mexican) 625 S 5th St	Milwaukee	WI	53204	414-271-8595
Louise's Trattoria (Italian) 801 N Jefferson St	Milwaukee	WI	53202	414-273-4224
Mader's German Restaurant (German) 1037 N Old World 3rd St	Milwaukee	WI	53203	414-271-3377
Old Town (European) 522 W Lincoln Ave	Milwaukee	WI	53207	414-672-0206
Osteria del Mondo (Italian) 1028 E Juneau Ave	Milwaukee	WI	53202	414-291-3770
Pandl's Inn Bayside (American) 8825 N Lake Dr	Milwaukee	WI	53217	414-352-7300
Pieces of Eight (Steak/Seafood) 550 N Harbor Dr	Milwaukee	WI	53202	414-271-0597
Red Rock Cafe (Seafood) 4022 N Oakland Ave	Milwaukee	WI	53211	414-962-4545
River Lane Inn (Seafood) 4313 W River Ln	Brown Deer	WI	53223	414-354-1995
Rock Bottom Restaurant (American) 740 N Plankinton Ave	Milwaukee	WI	53203	414-276-3030
Sanford (New American) 1547 N Jackson St	Milwaukee	WI	53202	414-276-9608
Saz's (American) 5539 W State St	Milwaukee	WI	53208	414-453-2410
Toy's Chinatown (Chinese) 830 N 3rd St	Milwaukee	WI	53203	414-271-5166
Water Street Brewery (American) 1101 N Water St	Milwaukee	WI	53202	414-272-1195
Weissgerber's Third Street Pier (Steak/Seafood) 1110 N Old World 3rd St	Milwaukee	WI	53203	414-272-0330
West Bank Cafe (Vietnamese) 732 E Burleigh St	Milwaukee	WI	53212	414-562-5555
Zydeco's (Cajun/Creole) 8222 W Forest Home Ave	Greenfield	WI	53220	414-427-9270

— Goods and Services —

SHOPPING

	City	State	ZIP	Phone	Fax
Bayshore Mall 5900 N Port Washington Rd	Milwaukee	WI	53217	414-332-8136	
Boston Store 331 W Wisconsin Ave	Milwaukee	WI	53203	414-347-4141	347-5337
East Town 770 N Jefferson St	Milwaukee	WI	53202	414-271-1416	271-6401
Grand Avenue Mall 275 W Wisconsin Ave	Milwaukee	WI	53203	414-224-0384	224-0849
Historic Third Ward 219 N Milwaukee St	Milwaukee	WI	53202	414-273-1173	273-2205
Web: www.milwaukee-htw.org					
Mayfair Mall 2500 N Mayfair Rd	Milwaukee	WI	53226	414-771-1300	
Northridge Mall 7700 W Brown Deer Rd	Milwaukee	WI	53223	414-354-2900	354-0951

Milwaukee — Shopping (Cont'd)

Phone Fax

Northridge Shopping Center
7700 W Brown Deer Rd. . . . . Milwaukee WI 53223 414-354-1804 354-0951
Old World Third Street
Wisconsin Ave & 3rd St . . . . Milwaukee WI 53203 414-273-3950
Regency Mall 5538 Durand Ave . . . . Racine WI 53406 262-554-7979 554-7477
Southridge Mall 5300 S 76th St. . . . . Greendale WI 53129 414-421-1102 421-0492

BANKS

Phone Fax

Bank One Milwaukee NA
111 E Wisconsin Ave. . . . . Milwaukee WI 53202 414-765-3000 765-0553*
**Fax:* Mktg ■ *TF Cust Svc:* 800-947-1111*
Firstar Bank Milwaukee NA
777 E Wisconsin Ave. . . . . Milwaukee WI 53202 414-765-4321 287-3439
M & I Marshall & Ilsley Bank
770 N Water St. . . . . Milwaukee WI 53202 414-765-7700 765-7436
Mutual Savings Bank
4949 W Brown Deer Rd. . . . . Milwaukee WI 53223 414-354-1500 362-6197*
**Fax:* Loans

BUSINESS SERVICES

	Phone		Phone
Action Express	262-549-3300	**Kinko's**	414-344-3506
Bonded Messenger Service	414-933-4500	**Manpower Temporary Services**	414-272-8500
City Veterans Package Delivery	414-291-8081	**Olsten Staffing Services**	414-278-7900
Federal Express	800-238-5355	**Post Office**	414-270-2000
Kelly Services	414-258-0444	**UPS**	800-742-5877

— Media —

PUBLICATIONS

Phone Fax

Business Journal of Milwaukee
600 W Virginia St Suite 500. . . . . Milwaukee WI 53204 414-278-7788 278-7028
Web: www.amcity.com/milwaukee/ ■ *E-mail:* milwaukee@amcity.com
Exclusively Yours Magazine
740 N Plankinton Ave Suite 500 . . . . Milwaukee WI 53203 414-271-4270 271-0383
Milwaukee Courier PO Box 06279 . . . . Milwaukee WI 53206 414-449-4860 449-4872*
**Fax:* News Rm
Milwaukee Journal Sentinel‡
333 W State St. Milwaukee WI 53203 414-224-2000 224-2047
Web: www.jsonline.com
Milwaukee Magazine 417 E Chicago St. . . . . . Milwaukee WI 53202 414-273-1101 273-0016
TF: 800-662-4818 ■ *Web:* www.milwaukeemagazine.com
■ *E-mail:* milmag@qgraph.com
Shepherd Express Metro 413 N 2nd St . . . . . . Milwaukee WI 53203 414-276-2222 276-3312*
**Fax:* News Rm ■ *E-mail:* ctyed@aol.com

‡Daily newspapers

TELEVISION

Phone Fax

WCGV-TV Ch 24 (UPN) 4041 N 35th St. . . . . . Milwaukee WI 53216 414-874-1824 874-1899
WDJT-TV Ch 58 (CBS)
509 W Wisconsin Ave Suite 2500. . . . . Milwaukee WI 53203 414-777-5800 777-5802
Web: www.cbs58.com ■ *E-mail:* news@cbs58.com
WISN-TV Ch 12 (ABC) 759 N 19th St . . . . Milwaukee WI 53233 414-342-8812 342-7505
Web: www.wisn.com ■ *E-mail:* news@wisn.com
WITI-TV Ch 6 (Fox) 9001 N Green Bay Rd. . . . Milwaukee WI 53217 414-355-6666 362-2141
Web: www.fox6news.com
WJJA-TV Ch 49 (Ind) 4311 E Oakwood Rd. . . . Oak Creek WI 53154 414-764-4953 764-5190
WMVS-TV Ch 10 (PBS) 1036 N 8th St. . . . . . . Milwaukee WI 53233 414-271-1036 297-7536
Web: www.mptv.org
WMVT-TV Ch 36 (PBS) 1036 N 8th St. . . . . . . Milwaukee WI 53233 414-271-1036 297-7536
WPXE-TV Ch 55 (PAX)
700 W Virginia St Suite 650. . . . . Kenosha WI 53204 414-278-5500 278-5501
TF: 800-585-7676 ■ *Web:* www.pax.net/wpxe
WTMJ-TV Ch 4 (NBC) 720 E Capitol Dr . . . . . . Milwaukee WI 53212 414-332-9611 967-5378
Web: www.touchtmj4.com
WVCY-TV Ch 30 (Ind)
3434 W Kilbourn Ave . . . . Milwaukee WI 53208 414-935-3000 935-3015
Web: www.vcyamerica.org/wvcytv30.html
■ *E-mail:* tv30@vcyamerica.org
WVTV-TV Ch 18 (WB) 4041 N 35th St. . . . . . . Milwaukee WI 53216 414-874-1824 874-1899

RADIO

Phone Fax

WAUK-AM 1510 kHz (Sports)
1801 Coral Dr. . . . . Waukesha WI 53186 262-544-6800 544-1705
WEZY-FM 92.1 MHz (B/EZ) 4201 Victory Ave. . . . . Racine WI 53405 262-634-3311 634-6515
WFMR-FM 98.3 MHz (Clas)
W 172 N 7348 Shady Ln . . . . Menomonee Falls WI 53051 262-250-0983 255-3909
Web: www.wfmr.com ■ *E-mail:* feedback@wfmr.com
WHAD-FM 90.7 MHz (NPR)
111 E Kilbourn Ave Suite 1650. . . . . Milwaukee WI 53202 414-227-2040 227-2043
Web: www.wpr.org ■ *E-mail:* whad@execpc.com
WISN-AM 1130 kHz (N/T) 759 N 19th St . . . . . Milwaukee WI 53233 414-342-1111 342-4734
WJYI-AM 1340 kHz (Rel)
5407 W McKinley Ave . . . . Milwaukee WI 53208 414-454-0900 978-9001
WJZI-FM 93.3 MHz (NAC)
2979 N Mayfair Rd Suite 593. . . . . Milwaukee WI 53222 414-778-1933 771-3036
WKKV-FM 100.7 MHz (Urban)
PO Box 20920 . . . . Milwaukee WI 53220 414-321-1007 546-9654
Web: www.v100.com ■ *E-mail:* info@v100.com
WKLH-FM 96.5 MHz (CR)
5407 W McKinley Ave . . . . Milwaukee WI 53208 414-454-0900 978-9001
WKTI-FM 94.5 MHz (AC) 720 E Capitol Dr. . . . Milwaukee WI 53212 414-332-9611 967-5266
Web: www.wkti.com ■ *E-mail:* info@wkti.com
WLTQ-FM 97.3 MHz (AC) 759 N 19th St . . . . . Milwaukee WI 53233 414-342-1111 342-4734
WLUM-FM 102.1 MHz (Rock)
2979 N Mayfair Rd . . . . Milwaukee WI 53222 414-771-1021 771-3036
Web: www.newrock.com
WLZR-FM 102.9 MHz (Rock)
5407 W McKinley Ave . . . . Milwaukee WI 53208 414-454-0900 978-9001
Web: www.lazer103.com
WMCS-AM 1290 kHz (Urban)
4222 W Capitol Dr . . . . Milwaukee WI 53216 414-444-1290 444-1409
WMIL-FM 106.1 MHz (Ctry)
12100 W Howard Ave . . . . Greenfield WI 53228 414-545-8900 546-9657
E-mail: fm106@execpc.com
WMYX-FM 99.1 MHz (AC)
11800 W Grange Ave . . . . Hales Corners WI 53130 414-529-1250 529-2122
WNOV-AM 860 kHz (Urban)
3815 N Teutonia Ave. . . . . Milwaukee WI 53206 414-449-9668 449-9945
WOKY-AM 920 kHz (Nost)
12100 W Howard Ave . . . . Greenfield WI 53228 414-545-5920 546-9657
WPNT-FM 106.9 MHz (NAC)
5407 W McKinley Ave . . . . Milwaukee WI 53208 414-454-0800 454-0877
Web: www.wpnt.com
WTMJ-AM 620 kHz (N/T) 720 E Capitol Dr. . . . Milwaukee WI 53212 414-332-9611 967-5298
WUWM-FM 89.7 MHz (NPR) PO Box 413 . . . . Milwaukee WI 53201 414-229-4664 229-5749
Web: www.uwm.edu/WUWM
WXSS-FM 103.7 MHz (CHR)
11800 W Grange Ave . . . . Hales Corners WI 53130 414-529-1250 529-2122
WZTR-FM 95.7 MHz (Oldies)
520 W Capitol Dr . . . . Milwaukee WI 53212 414-964-8300 964-9740

— Colleges/Universities —

Phone Fax

Alverno College 3400 S 43rd St. . . . . Milwaukee WI 53234 414-382-6100 382-6354
TF Admissions: 800-933-3401 ■ *Web:* www.alverno.edu
■ *E-mail:* alvadmsh@execpc.com
Bryant & Stratton Career College
1300 N Jackson St . . . . Milwaukee WI 53202 414-276-5200 276-3930
Cardinal Stritch University
6801 N Yates Rd . . . . Milwaukee WI 53217 414-410-4000 410-4239
TF Admissions: 800-347-8822 ■ *Web:* www.stritch.edu
Carroll College 100 N East Ave . . . . Waukesha WI 53186 262-547-1211 524-7139
TF: 800-227-7655 ■ *Web:* www.cc.edu
Carthage College 2001 Alford Pk Dr. . . . . Kenosha WI 53140 262-551-8500 551-5762
TF Admissions: 800-351-4058 ■ *Web:* www.carthage.edu
Columbia College of Nursing
2121 E Newport Ave . . . . Milwaukee WI 53211 414-961-3530 961-4121
Web: www.ccon.edu
Concordia University Wisconsin
12800 N Lake Shore Dr. . . . . Mequon WI 53097 262-243-5700 243-4545
Web: www.cuw.edu
ITT Technical Institute 6300 W Layton Ave . . . . Greenfield WI 53220 414-282-9494 282-9698
Web: www.itt-tech.edu
Marquette University
1442 W Wisconsin Ave . . . . Milwaukee WI 53233 414-288-7700 288-3764
Web: www.mu.edu
Milwaukee Area Technical College
700 W State St. . . . . Milwaukee WI 53233 414-297-6600 297-7990
Web: www.milwaukee.tec.wi.us
Milwaukee Institute of Art & Design
273 E Erie St . . . . Milwaukee WI 53202 414-276-7889 291-8077
TF: 888-749-6423 ■ *Web:* www.miad.edu

Milwaukee — Colleges/Universities (Cont'd)

				Phone	Fax
Milwaukee School of Engineering 1025 N Broadway St	Milwaukee	WI	53202	414-277-7300	277-7475
TF: 800-332-6763 ■ *Web:* www.msoe.edu ■ *E-mail:* explore@msoe.edu					
Mount Mary College 2900 N Menomonee River Pkwy	Milwaukee	WI	53222	414-258-4810	256-0180
TF Admissions: 800-321-6265 ■ *Web:* www.mtmary.edu ■ *E-mail:* mktg@mtmary.edu					
University of Wisconsin Colleges Waukesha County 1500 University Dr	Waukesha	WI	53188	262-521-5210	521-5491
Web: www.uwc.edu/waukesha/ ■ *E-mail:* uwwak@uwc.edu					
University of Wisconsin Milwaukee PO Box 749	Milwaukee	WI	53201	414-229-1122	229-6940
Web: www.uwm.edu ■ *E-mail:* dgm@bfs.uwm.edu					
Wisconsin Lutheran College 8800 W Bluemound Rd	Milwaukee	WI	53226	414-443-8800	443-8514
TF: 888-947-5884 ■ *Web:* www.wlc.edu ■ *E-mail:* admissions@wlc.edu					

— Hospitals —

				Phone	Fax
All Saints Health Care 3801 Spring St	Racine	WI	53405	262-636-4011	636-4540
Children's Hospital of Wisconsin PO Box 1997	Milwaukee	WI	53201	414-266-2000	266-2179
Web: www.chw.org					
Columbia Hospital 2025 E Newport Ave	Milwaukee	WI	53211	414-961-3300	961-8712
Web: www.columbia-stmarys.com/html/columbia.shtml					
Community Memorial Hospital PO Box 408	Menomonee Falls	WI	53052	262-251-1000	253-7169
Elmbrook Memorial Hospital 19333 W North Ave	Brookfield	WI	53045	262-785-2000	785-2444
Web: www.covhealth.org/affiliat/elmbr.html					
Froedtert Memorial Lutheran Hospital 9200 W Wisconsin Ave	Milwaukee	WI	53226	414-259-3000	259-8910
Web: www.froedtert.com					
Kenosha Hospital & Medical Center 6308 8th Ave	Kenosha	WI	53143	262-656-2011	656-2124
Lakeland Medical Center PO Box 1002	Elkhorn	WI	53121	262-741-2000	741-2482
Web: www.aurorahealthcare.org/facilities/sites/0008/0008.htm					
Memorial Hospital 252 McHenry St	Burlington	WI	53105	262-763-2411	763-0309
Memorial Hospital of Oconomowoc 791 Summit Ave	Oconomowoc	WI	53066	262-569-9400	569-0904
Northwest General Hospital 5310 W Capitol Dr	Milwaukee	WI	53216	414-447-8543	447-8589
Saint Catherine's Hospital 3556 7th Ave	Kenosha	WI	53140	262-656-3011	656-3804
Saint Francis Hospital 3237 S 16th St	Milwaukee	WI	53215	414-647-5000	647-5565
Web: www.covhealth.org/affiliat/sfh.html					
Saint Joseph's Community Hospital 551 S Silverbrook Dr	West Bend	WI	53095	262-334-5533	334-8575*
**Fax:* Hum Res					
Saint Joseph's Hospital 5000 W Chambers St	Milwaukee	WI	53210	414-447-2000	447-2768*
**Fax:* Admitting ■ *Web:* www.covhealth.org/affiliat/sjh.html					
Saint Luke's Hospital 1320 Wisconsin Ave	Racine	WI	53403	262-636-2011	636-2494
Saint Luke's Medical Center 2900 W Oklahoma Ave	Milwaukee	WI	53215	414-649-6000	649-5562*
**Fax:* Admitting ■ *Web:* www.aurorahealthcare.org/facilities/sites/0001/0001.htm					
Saint Luke's South Hospital 5900 S Lake Dr	Cudahy	WI	53110	414-769-9000	489-4013
Saint Mary's Hospital 2323 N Lake Dr	Milwaukee	WI	53211	414-291-1000	291-1048
Web: www.columbia-stmarys.com/html/stmarysmil.shtml					
Saint Mary's Hospital Ozaukee 1311 N Port Washington Rd	Mequon	WI	53097	262-243-7300	243-7416
Web: www.columbia-stmarys.com/html/stmarysoz.shtml					
Saint Michael Hospital 2400 W Villard Ave	Milwaukee	WI	53209	414-527-8000	527-8461
Web: www.covhealth.org/affiliat/smh.html					
Sinai Samaritan Medical Center 945 N 12th St	Milwaukee	WI	53201	414-219-2000	219-6735
TF: 888-414-7762 ■ *Web:* www.aurorahealthcare.org/facilities/sites/0012/0012.htm					
Veterans Affairs Medical Center 5000 W National Ave	Milwaukee	WI	53295	414-384-2000	382-5319
Waukesha Memorial Hospital 725 American Ave	Waukesha	WI	53188	262-928-1000	928-4995*
**Fax:* Admitting ■ *TF:* 800-326-2011					
West Allis Memorial Hospital 8901 W Lincoln Ave	West Allis	WI	53227	414-328-6000	328-8515*
**Fax:* Admitting ■ *Web:* www.aurorahealthcare.org/facilities/sites/0006/0006.htm					

— Attractions —

				Phone	Fax
Boerner Botanical Gardens 5879 S 92nd St	Hales Corners	WI	53130	414-425-1130	425-8679
Web: www.uwm.edu/Dept/Biology/Boerner/ ■ *E-mail:* schuck@csd.uwm.edu					
Brinn Betty Children's Museum 929 E Wisconsin Ave	Milwaukee	WI	53202	414-291-0888	291-0906
Web: www.bbcmkids.org ■ *E-mail:* kiplade@execpc.com					
Brown Deer Park 7835 N Green Bay Rd	Milwaukee	WI	53209	414-352-7502	
Charles Allis Art Museum 1801 N Prospect Ave	Milwaukee	WI	53202	414-278-8295	278-0335
City Ballet Theatre 3908 W Capitol Dr	Milwaukee	WI	53216	414-445-3006	578-1588
E-mail: cbt@pitnet.net					
Discovery World Museum of Science Economics & Technology 712 W Wells St	Milwaukee	WI	53233	414-765-9966	765-0311
Web: www.braintools.org					
East Town 770 N Jefferson St	Milwaukee	WI	53202	414-271-1416	271-6401
First Stage Milwaukee 929 N Water St Marcus Ctr	Milwaukee	WI	53202	414-273-2314	273-5595
Florentine Opera of Milwaukee 735 N Water St Suite 1315	Milwaukee	WI	53202	414-291-5700	291-5706
Greene Memorial Museum 3209 N Maryland Ave Lapham Hall UWM Campus	Milwaukee	WI	53211	414-229-4561	229-5452
Haggerty Patrick & Beatrice Museum of Art 13th & Clybourn Sts Marquette University	Milwaukee	WI	53223	414-288-7290	288-5415
Web: www.marquette.edu/haggerty/ ■ *E-mail:* haggertym@vms.csd.mu.edu					
Historic Third Ward 219 N Milwaukee St	Milwaukee	WI	53202	414-273-1173	273-2205
Web: www.milwaukee-htw.org					
Humphrey IMAX Dome Theater 710 W Wells St	Milwaukee	WI	53201	414-319-4629	
Web: www.humphreyimax.com ■ *E-mail:* hamilton@humphreyimax.com					
International Clown Hall of Fame Inc 161 W Wisconsin Ave	Milwaukee	WI	53203	414-319-0848	319-1070
Joan of Arc Chapel Marquette Univ Alumni Memorial Union Rm 236	Milwaukee	WI	53201	414-288-7039	
Kettle Moraine Scenic Steam Train Hwy 83	North Lake	WI	53064	262-782-8074	
Kilbourntown House 4400 N Estabrook Dr Estabrook Pk	Milwaukee	WI	53211	414-273-8288	
Web: www.milwaukeecountyhistsoc.org					
Lakefront Brewery 1872 N Commerce St	Milwaukee	WI	53212	414-372-8800	372-4400
Lincoln Park 1000 W Hampton Ave	Milwaukee	WI	53209	414-332-1350	
Marcus Center for the Performing Arts 929 N Water St	Milwaukee	WI	53202	414-273-7206	273-5480
Web: www.milwaukeearts.org					
Miller Brewing Co 3939 W Highland Blvd	Milwaukee	WI	53208	414-931-2000	931-3735
Web: www.millerbrewing.com					
Milwaukee Art Museum 750 N Lincoln Memorial Dr	Milwaukee	WI	53202	414-224-3200	271-7588
Web: www.mam.org/ ■ *E-mail:* asktheartist@mam.org					
Milwaukee Ballet 929 N Waters St Marcus Ctr for the Performing Arts	Milwaukee	WI	53202	414-643-7677	649-4066
Web: www.milwaukeeballet.org					
Milwaukee Chamber Theatre 158 N Broadway Broadway Theatre Ctr	Milwaukee	WI	53202	414-276-8842	277-4477
Web: www.chamber-theatre.com					
Milwaukee County Historical Society 910 N Old World 3rd St	Milwaukee	WI	53203	414-273-8288	273-3268
Milwaukee County Sports Complex 6000 W Ryan Rd	Franklin	WI	53132	414-421-9733	421-6353
Milwaukee County War Memorial 750 N Lincoln Memorial Dr Rm 315	Milwaukee	WI	53202	414-273-5533	273-2455
Milwaukee County Zoo 10001 W Bluemound Rd	Milwaukee	WI	53226	414-256-5433	256-5410
Web: www.execpc.com/~cwzoo					
Milwaukee Public Museum 800 W Wells St	Milwaukee	WI	53233	414-278-2700	278-6100
Web: www.mpm.edu					
Milwaukee Repertory Theater 108 E Wells St	Milwaukee	WI	53202	414-224-9490	224-9097
Web: www.milwaukeerep.com/mrt.htm					
Milwaukee Symphony Orchestra 330 E Kilbourn Ave Suite 900	Milwaukee	WI	53202	414-291-6010	291-7610
Web: www.milwaukeesymphony.org					
Mitchell Gallery of Flight 5300 S Howell Ave Mitchell International Airport	Milwaukee	WI	53207	414-747-5300	747-4525

Milwaukee — Attractions (Cont'd)

Name / Address	City	State	Zip	Phone	Fax
Mitchell Park Conservatory 524 S Layton Blvd	Milwaukee	WI	53215	414-649-9830	649-8616
Web: www.uwm.edu/Dept/Biology/domes ■ *E-mail:* schuck@csd.uwm.edu					
Old Mill District 210 S Water St.	Watertown	WI	53094	920-262-2348	262-2382
Old World Third Street Wisconsin Ave & 3rd St	Milwaukee	WI	53203	414-273-3950	
Old World Wisconsin S 103 West 37890 Hwy 67	Eagle	WI	53119	262-594-6300	594-6342
Web: www.pressenter.com/org/oldwrld ■ *E-mail:* owwvisit@idcnet.com					
Pabst Mansion 2000 W Wisconsin Ave	Milwaukee	WI	53233	414-931-0808	931-1005
Pabst Theater 144 E Wells St.	Milwaukee	WI	53202	414-286-3665	286-2154
Potawatomi Bingo Casino 1721 W Canal St.	Milwaukee	WI	53233	414-645-6888	645-6866
Web: www.paysbig.com					
Present Music 1840 N Farwell Ave	Milwaukee	WI	53202	414-271-0711	271-7998
Riveredge Nature Center 4438 W Hawthorne Dr Box 375	Newburg	WI	53060	262-375-2715	375-2714
Saint Joan of Arc Chapel 14th St & Wisconsin Ave.	Milwaukee	WI	53233	414-288-6873	288-3696
Web: www.marquette.edu/campus/joanarc.html					
Saint Josaphat Basilica 6th St & Lincoln Ave.	Milwaukee	WI	53215	414-645-5623	385-3270
Schlitz Audubon Center 1111 E Brown Deer Rd	Milwaukee	WI	53217	414-352-2880	352-6091
Skylight Opera Theatre 158 N Broadway	Milwaukee	WI	53202	414-291-7811	291-7815
Web: www.skylightopera.com					
Sprecher Brewing Company 701 W Glendale Ave	Glendale	WI	53209	414-964-2739	964-2462
Web: www.sprecherbrewery.com					
Villa Terrace Decorative Arts Museum 2220 N Terrace Ave.	Milwaukee	WI	53202	414-271-3656	271-3986
Wehr Nature Center 9701 W College Ave.	Franklin	WI	53132	414-425-8550	425-6992
Whitnall Park 5879 S 92nd St	Hales Corners	WI	53130	414-257-6100	
Wisconsin Black Historical Museum Society 2620 W Center St.	Milwaukee	WI	53206	414-372-7677	372-4888
Wisconsin Conservatory of Music 1845 N Fairwell Ave Suite 200	Milwaukee	WI	53202	414-276-5760	276-6076
Web: www.wcmusic.org					
Wisconsin Maritime Museum 75 Maritime Dr.	Manitowoc	WI	54220	920-684-0218	684-0219
Wisconsin's Ethnic Settlement Trail 5900 N Port Washington Rd	Milwaukee	WI	53217	414-961-2110	961-2110

SPORTS TEAMS & FACILITIES

Name / Address	City	State	Zip	Phone	Fax
Bradley Center 1001 N 4th St	Milwaukee	WI	53203	414-227-0400	227-0497
Dairyland Greyhound Park 5522 104th Ave	Kenosha	WI	53144	262-657-8200	657-8231
TF: 800-233-3357 ■ *Web:* www.dairylandgreyhoundpark.com ■ *E-mail:* dgpsimul@execpc.com					
Great Lakes Dragway 18411 1st St.	Union Grove	WI	53182	262-878-3783	878-4462
TF: 888-324-7683					
Green Bay Packers 1265 Lombardi Ave Lambeau Field	Green Bay	WI	54304	920-496-5719	496-5738
Web: www.nfl.com/packers					
Milwaukee Admirals (hockey) 1001 N 4th St Bradley Ctr	Milwaukee	WI	53203	414-227-0550	227-0568
TF: 800-927-6630 ■ *Web:* www.milwaukeeadmirals.com ■ *E-mail:* comments@milwaukeeadmirals.com					
Milwaukee Auditorium 575 W Kilbourne Ave.	Milwaukee	WI	53203	414-908-6000	908-6010
Web: www.wcd.org/site/home/fac/are/main.html					
Milwaukee Brewers PO Box 3099	Milwaukee	WI	53201	414-933-9000	
Web: www.milwaukeebrewers.com					
Milwaukee Bucks 1001 N 4th St.	Milwaukee	WI	53203	414-227-0500	227-0543
Web: www.nba.com/bucks					
Milwaukee County Stadium 201 S 46th St.	Milwaukee	WI	53214	414-933-4114	933-7111
TF: 800-933-7890 ■ *Web:* www.milwaukeebrewers.com					
Milwaukee Mile 7722 W Greenfield Ave	West Allis	WI	53214	414-453-8277	453-9920
Web: www.milmile.com ■ *E-mail:* feedback@milmile.com					
Milwaukee Mustangs (football) 1001 N 4th St Bradley Ctr	Milwaukee	WI	53203	414-272-1555	272-3891
Web: www.milwaukeemustangs.com ■ *E-mail:* mustangsmail@milwaukeemustangs.com					
Milwaukee Rampage (soccer) 7101 W Good Hope Rd Uihlein Soccer Pk	Milwaukee	WI	53223	414-358-2655	358-2618
Web: www.milwaukeerampage.com ■ *E-mail:* bear@milwaukeerampage.com					
Milwaukee Wave (soccer) 10201 N Port Washington Rd Suite 200	Mequon	WI	53092	262-241-7500	241-7506
Wilmot Speedway Kenosha County Fairgrounds	Wilmot	WI	53192	847-395-0500	395-0363

— Events —

	Phone
African World Festival (early August)	414-372-4567
Bastille Days (mid-July)	414-271-1416
Bavarian Volksfest (late June)	414-462-9147
Christmas in the Country (early December)	262-377-9620
Christmas in the Ward (early December)	414-273-1173
Cinco de Mayo Festival (early May)	414-671-5700
Festa Italiana (mid-July)	920-232-2192
Firstar Eve Celebration (December 31)	414-765-6500
Gen Con Game Fair (early August)	800-529-3976
German Fest (late July)	414-464-9444
Grape Lakes Food & Wine Festival (mid-May)	414-224-3850
Great Circus Parade Week (mid-July)	414-273-7877
Greater Milwaukee Auto Show (late February-early March)	414-908-6000
Greater Milwaukee Open (early-mid-July)	414-365-4466
Harvest Fair (late September)	414-266-7000
Holiday Craft & Gift Show (late November)	414-321-2100
Holiday Folk Fair (mid-November)	414-225-6225
Indian Summer Festival (mid-September)	414-774-7119
International Arts Festival (February)	414-273-3950
Irish Feast (mid-August)	414-476-3378
Jazz in the Park (early June-late August)	414-271-1416
Juneteenth Day (mid-June)	414-372-3770
Lakefront Festival of the Arts (mid-June)	414-224-3283
Mexican Fiesta (mid-late August)	414-383-7066
Milwaukee a la Carte (mid-August)	414-771-3040
Milwaukee Boat Show (mid-February)	414-908-6000
Milwaukee Christmas Parade (mid-November)	414-273-3950
Milwaukee Highland Games (early June)	262-796-0807
Milwaukee Journal Sentinel Rose Festival (mid-June)	414-273-3950
Oktoberfest (September)	414-964-4221
Polish Fest (late June)	414-529-2140
Rainbow Summer (early June-late August)	414-273-7206
RiverSplash (early June)	414-286-8436
Senior Fest (early June)	414-647-6040
Shermanfest-Milwaukee's Premier Blues Festival (mid-June)	414-444-9813
South Shore Water Frolics (mid-July)	414-224-2753
Spring Craft & Gift Show (early March)	414-321-2100
Strawberry Festival (late June)	800-827-8020
Summerfest (late June-early July)	800-837-3378
TosaFest (mid-September)	414-476-5300
US International Snow Sculpting Competition (late January)	414-476-5573
Wisconsin State Fair (early August)	800-231-0903

Wyoming

Population (1999): 479,602 **Area (sq mi): 97,818**

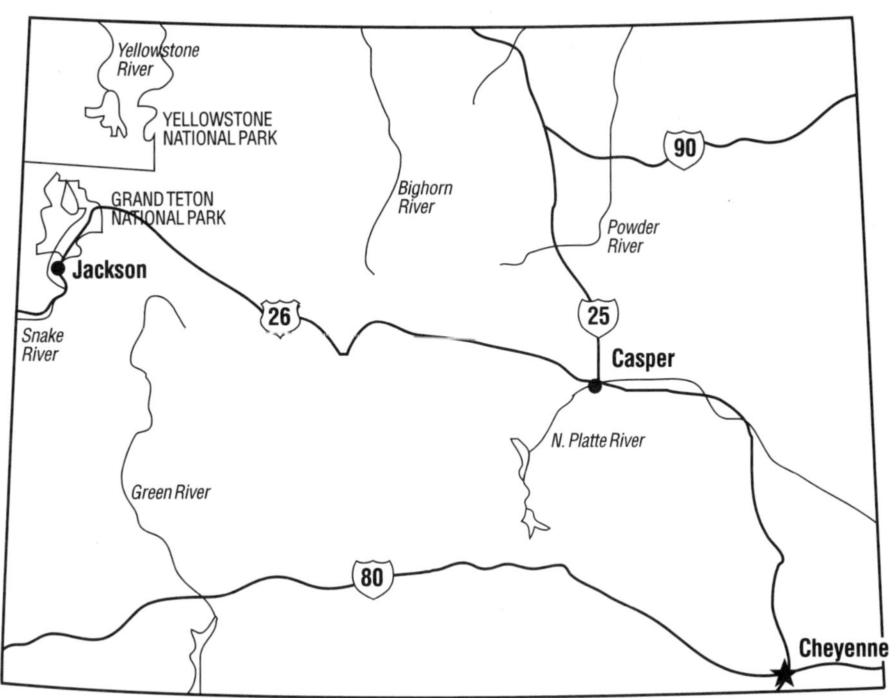

— State Information Sources —

				Phone	Fax
Wyoming Economic & Community Development Div					
122 W 25th St 1st Fl E	Cheyenne	WY	82002	307-777-7284	777-5840
Web: commerce.state.wy.us/decd					
Wyoming State Government Information				307-777-7220	
Web: www.state.wy.us/state/government/government.html					
Wyoming State Library 2301 Capitol Ave.	Cheyenne	WY	82002	307-777-7281	777-6289
Web: www-wsl.state.wy.us					
Wyoming State Parks & Historical Sites Div					
1E Herschler Bldg 122 W 25th St	Cheyenne	WY	82002	307-777-6323	777-6472
Web: commerce.state.wy.us/sphs					
Wyoming Tourism Div I-25 & College Dr.	Cheyenne	WY	82002	307-777-7777	777-2877
TF: 800-225-5996 ■ *Web:* www.wyomingtourism.org ■ *E-mail:* tourism@missc.state.wy.us					

ON-LINE RESOURCES

Cybertourist Wyoming . . . . . www.cybertourist.com/wyoming.shtml
Destination Northwest: Wyoming . . . . . www.destinationnw.com/wyoming
Mountain Country Visitors's Guide . . . . . www.jacksonholenet.com/mountainctry
Rough Guide Travel Wyoming travel.roughguides.com/content/1073/index.htm
Travel.org-Wyoming . . . . . travel.org/wyoming.html
Virtual Tour of Wyoming . . . . . www.state.wy.us/state/virtual_map/wyoming_map.html
What's Up Wyoming! . . . . . www.whatsupwyoming.com
Wyoming Cities . . . . . dir.yahoo.com/Regional/U_S__States/Wyoming/Cities
Wyoming Companion . . . . . www.wyomingcompanion.com
Wyoming Counties & Regions . . . . . dir.yahoo.com/Regional/U_S__States/Wyoming/Counties_and_Regions
Wyoming Scenario . . . . . scenariousa.dstylus.com/wy/indexf.htm
Wyoming Tourism . . . . . www.state.wy.us/state/tourism/tourism.html
Wyoming Travel & Tourism Guide . . . . . www.travel-library.com/north_america/usa/wyoming/index.html
Wyoming's Wind River Country . . . . . www.wind-river.org
Yahoo! Get Local Wyoming . . . . . dir.yahoo.com/Regional/U_S__States/Wyoming

— Cities Profiled —

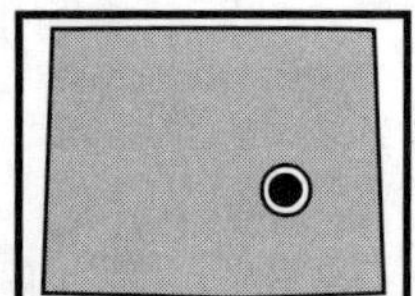

Casper

Located on the banks of the Platte River, Casper was the point of convergence for all the major westward trails during the 1800s. Today (in dry weather) visitors can follow off-highway trails near Casper to the foothills of the Big Horn Mountains, Butch Cassidy's "Hole in the Wall," or Hell's Half-Acre. Over 75 percent of the world's Pronghorn antelope live within 150 miles of Casper, and Mule deer, fox, Sage grouse, and elk are also plentiful in and around the city. The area is a popular destination for game hunting and for fishing, especially trout fishing.

Population	48,283	**Longitude**	106-32-13 W
Area (Land)	20.6 sq mi	**County**	Natrona
Area (Water)	0.3 sq mi	**Time Zone**	MST
Elevation	5140 ft	**Area Code/s**	307
Latitude	42-85-07 N		

— Average Temperatures and Precipitation —

TEMPERATURES

	Jan	Feb	Mar	Apr	May	Jun	Jul	Aug	Sep	Oct	Nov	Dec
High	33	37	45	56	67	79	88	86	74	61	44	34
Low	12	16	22	30	38	47	54	52	42	32	22	14

PRECIPITATION

	Jan	Feb	Mar	Apr	May	Jun	Jul	Aug	Sep	Oct	Nov	Dec
Inches	0.6	0.6	1.0	1.6	2.1	1.5	1.3	0.7	0.9	1.0	0.8	0.7

— Important Phone Numbers —

	Phone		*Phone*
AAA	307-634-8861	**Poison Control Center**	803-777-1117
American Express Travel	307-265-9020	**Road Conditions**	307-772-0824
Emergency	911	**Weather**	307-234-4804
Medical Referral	307-577-2190		

— Information Sources —

				Phone	*Fax*
Better Business Bureau Serving the Mountain States 1730 S College Ave Suite 303	Fort Collins	CO	80525	970-484-1348	221-1239
Web: www.rockymtn.bbb.org ■ *E-mail:* info@rockymtn.bbb.org					
Casper Area Chamber of Commerce 500 N Center St	Casper	WY	82602	307-234-5311	265-2643
TF: 800-852-1889 ■ *Web:* www.casperets.com ■ *E-mail:* cacc@trib.com					
Casper Area Convention & Visitors Bureau PO Box 399	Casper	WY	82602	307-234-5362	265-2643
TF: 800-852-1889 ■ *Web:* www.trib.com/ADS/CASPER/ ■ *E-mail:* visitor@trib.com					
Casper City Hall 200 N David	Casper	WY	82601	307-235-8400	235-8313
Casper Events Center 1 Events Dr	Casper	WY	82601	307-235-8441	235-8445
TF: 800-442-2256					
Casper Mayor 200 N David St	Casper	WY	82601	307-235-8224	235-8313
Casper Planning & Community Development Dept 200 N David	Casper	WY	82601	307-235-8400	235-7575
Natrona County PO Box 863	Casper	WY	82602	307-235-9210	235-9367
Natrona County Public Library 307 E 2nd St	Casper	WY	82601	307-237-4935	266-3734

On-Line Resources

Area Guide Casper	casper.areaguides.net
Casper Electronic Town Square	www.casperets.com/index.htm
Casper Wyoming	www.trib.com/CASPER
Excite.com Casper City Guide	www.excite.com/travel/countries/united_states/wyoming/casper

— Transportation Services —

AIRPORTS

■ **Natrona County International Airport (CPR)**

	Phone
8 miles NW of downtown (approx 20 minutes)	307-472-6688

E-mail: arptmgr@trib.com

Airport Transportation

	Phone
RC Cab $13 fare to downtown	307-235-5203

Commercial Airlines

	Phone		*Phone*
SkyWest	800-453-9417	**United Express**	800-241-6522

Charter Airlines

	Phone
Casper Air Service Inc	307-472-3400

CAR RENTALS

	Phone		*Phone*
Around Town	307-265-5667	**Enterprise**	307-234-8122
Avis	307-237-2634	**Hertz**	307-265-1355
Budget	307-266-1122		

LIMO/TAXI

	Phone
RC Cab	307-235-5203

— Accommodations —

HOTELS, MOTELS, RESORTS

				Phone	*Fax*
All American Inn 5755 CY Ave	Casper	WY	82604	307-235-6688	234-0125
Best Western Hotel East 2325 E Yellowstone Hwy	Casper	WY	82609	307-234-3541	266-5850
TF: 800-675-4242					
Comfort Inn 480 Lathrop Rd	Evansville	WY	82636	307-235-3038	235-3038
TF: 800-228-5150					
Days Inn 301 E 'E' St	Casper	WY	82601	307-234-1159	265-0829
TF: 800-325-2525					
First Interstate Inn 20 SE Wyoming Blvd	Casper	WY	82609	307-234-9125	234-9128
TF: 800-462-4667					
Hampton Inn 400 W F St	Casper	WY	82601	307-235-6668	235-2027
TF: 800-426-7866					
Holiday Inn Casper 300 W F St	Casper	WY	82601	307-235-2531	473-3100
TF: 800-465-4329					
Kelly Inn 821 N Poplar St	Casper	WY	82601	307-266-2400	266-1146
TF: 800-635-3559					
Motel 6 1150 Wilkins Cir	Casper	WY	82601	307-234-3903	234-8359
TF: 800-466-8356					
National 9 Inn Showboat Hotel 100 W F St	Casper	WY	82601	307-235-2711	235-2711
TF: 800-524-9999					
Parkway Plaza Hotel 123 W 'E' St	Casper	WY	82601	307-235-5713	235-8068
TF: 800-270-7829					
Radisson Hotel Casper 800 N Poplar St	Casper	WY	82601	307-266-6000	473-1010
TF: 800-333-3333					
Royal Inn 440 E A St	Casper	WY	82601	307-234-3501	234-7340
Shilo Inn Casper 739 Luker Ln	Evansville	WY	82636	307-237-1335	577-7429
TF: 800-222-2244					
Super 8 Lodge 3838 CY Ave	Casper	WY	82604	307-266-3480	266-3480
TF: 800-800-8000					
Westridge Motel 955 CY Ave	Casper	WY	82601	307-234-8911	234-8917
TF: 800-356-6268					

— Restaurants —

				Phone
Armor's Restaurant (Continental) 3422 S Energy Ln	Casper	WY	82604	307-235-3000
Bosco's (Italian) 847 E 'A' St	Casper	WY	82601	307-265-9658
Bum Steer Steak House (Steak) 739 N Center St	Casper	WY	82601	307-234-4531
Cafe Jose's (Mexican) 1600 2nd St	Casper	WY	82601	307-235-6599
Chef's Coop (Homestyle) 1040 N Center	Casper	WY	82601	307-237-1132
China Buffet (Chinese) 4005 Cy Ave	Casper	WY	82604	307-237-8911

Casper — Restaurants (Cont'd)

	City	State	ZIP	Phone
Chinese Garden (Chinese) 1937 E 2nd St	Casper	WY	82601	307-234-8138
Dorn's Fireside (American) 1745 CY Ave	Casper	WY	82604	307-235-6831
Duke's Old Fashioned Steakhouse (Steak/Seafood) 739 Luker Ln	Evansville	WY	82636	307-237-1335
Goose Egg Inn (American) 10580 Goose Egg Rd	Casper	WY	82604	307-473-8838
Karen & Jim's Restaurant (American/Greek) 915 CY Ave	Casper	WY	82601	307-473-2309
Lanai Restaurant (American) 201 E 2nd St	Casper	WY	82601	307-237-7516
Maxies Bar & Grill (American) 2740 E 3rd St	Casper	WY	82609	307-234-5386
Ming House (Chinese) 233 E 2nd St	Casper	WY	82601	307-265-1838
New Moon Cafe (Chinese) 832 Cy Ave	Casper	WY	82601	307-234-2915
Sedar's Colonial Restaurant (American) 4370 S Poplar St	Casper	WY	82601	307-234-6839
South Sea Chinese Restaurant (Chinese) 2025 E 2nd St	Casper	WY	82609	307-237-4777
Szechwan (Chinese) 1151 Cy Ave	Casper	WY	82604	307-265-8881
Village Inn (American) 350 SE Wyoming Blvd	Casper	WY	82609	307-234-1485

— Goods and Services —

SHOPPING

	City	State	ZIP	Phone	Fax
Eastridge Mall 601 SE Wyoming Blvd	Casper	WY	82609	307-265-9392	472-5708
Sunrise Shopping Center 4000 S Poplar St	Casper	WY	82601	307-234-5886	

BANKS

	City	State	ZIP	Phone	Fax
American National Bank 201 E 2nd St Suite 25	Casper	WY	82601	307-234-5300	234-0446
Community First Bank 300 S Wolcott St	Casper	WY	82601	307-577-3000	577-3250
First Interstate Bank of Wyoming NA 104 S Wolcott St *TF:* 800-843-4652	Casper	WY	82601	307-235-4201	235-4350
Hilltop National Bank 300 Country Club Rd	Casper	WY	82609	307-265-2740	577-3485
Norwest Bank Wyoming NA 234 E 1st St **Fax:* Hum Res	Casper	WY	82601	307-266-1100	235-7626*

BUSINESS SERVICES

	Phone
Airborne Express	800-247-2676
BAX Global	800-225-5229
DHL Worldwide Express	800-225-5345
Federal Express	800-238-5355
Mail Boxes Etc	800-789-4623
Manpower Temporary Services	307-237-2523
Olsten Staffing Services	307-237-3283
Post Office	800-275-8777
UPS	800-742-5877

— Media —

PUBLICATIONS

	City	State	ZIP	Phone	Fax
Star-Tribune‡ PO Box 80 *Web:* www.trib.com	Casper	WY	82602	307-266-0500	266-0568

‡Daily newspapers

TELEVISION

	City	State	ZIP	Phone	Fax
KCWC-TV Ch 4 (PBS) 2660 Peck Ave	Riverton	WY	82501	307-856-6944	856-3893
KFNB-TV Ch 20 (ABC) 1856 Skyview Dr	Casper	WY	82601	307-577-5923	577-5928
KGWC-TV Ch 14 (CBS) 2500 CY Ave	Casper	WY	82604	307-234-1111	234-2835
KLWY-TV Ch 27 (Fox) 1856 Skyview Dr	Casper	WY	82601	307-577-5923	577-5928
KTWO-TV Ch 2 (NBC) 4200 E 2nd St **Fax:* News Rm	Casper	WY	82609	307-237-3711	237-3713*

RADIO

	City	State	ZIP	Phone	Fax
KCSP-FM 90.3 MHz (Rel) 1400 Kati Ln	Casper	WY	82601	307-265-5414	
KMGW-FM 94.5 MHz (AC) 150 N Nichols	Casper	WY	82601	307-266-5252	235-9143
KQLT-FM 103.7 MHz (Ctry) PO Box 2515	Casper	WY	82602	307-265-1984	473-7461
KTWO-AM 1030 kHz (Ctry) 150 N Nichols Ave	Casper	WY	82601	307-266-5252	235-9143
KUYO-AM 830 kHz (Rel) PO Box 50607	Casper	WY	82605	307-577-5896	
KVOC-AM 1230 kHz (Nost) 218 N Wolcott St	Casper	WY	82601	307-265-1984	473-7461
KWYY-FM 95.5 MHz (Ctry) 251 W 1st St	Casper	WY	82601	307-235-7000	237-5836

— Colleges/Universities —

	City	State	ZIP	Phone	Fax
Casper College 125 College Dr *TF:* 800-442-2963 ■ *Web:* www.cc.whecn.edu	Casper	WY	82601	307-268-2110	268-2611

— Hospitals —

	City	State	ZIP	Phone	Fax
Wyoming Medical Center 1233 E 2nd St *Web:* www.wmcnet.org	Casper	WY	82601	307-577-7201	237-1703

— Attractions —

	City	State	ZIP	Phone	Fax
Casper Chamber Music Society PO Box 40051 *Web:* members.aol.com/wycasper/ccms/index.html ■ *E-mail:* rbTurner@aol.com	Casper	WY	82604	307-268-2531	
Casper Mountain Nature Trails Casper Mountain	Casper	WY	82601	307-235-9311	
Casper Planetarium 904 N Poplar St	Casper	WY	82601	307-577-0310	
Casper Speedway 2201 East Rd	Casper	WY	82601	307-472-7223	472-7223
Dr Spokes Cyclery 240 S Center St	Casper	WY	82601	307-265-7740	265-7740
Edness Kimball Wilkins State Park 8700 E US Hwy 20-26	Evansville	WY	82636	307-577-5150	577-5150
Fort Caspar Museum & Historic Site 4001 Fort Caspar Rd	Casper	WY	82604	307-235-8462	235-8464
Fort Laramie National Historic Site HCR 72 Box 389 *Web:* www.nps.gov/fola/	Fort Laramie	WY	82212	307-837-2221	837-2120
Hogadon Ski Area 1800 East K Casper Mountain	Casper	WY	82601	307-235-8499	235-8498
National Historic Trails Center 500 N Center St	Casper	WY	82601	307-265-8030	265-2643
Nicolaysen Art Museum 400 E Collins Dr	Casper	WY	82601	307-235-5247	235-0923
Stage III Community Theatre 4080 S Poplar St	Casper	WY	82601	307-234-0946	
Werner Wildlife Museum 405 E 15th St	Casper	WY	82601	307-235-2108	
Wyoming Symphony Orchestra PO Box 667 *Web:* www.coffey.com/~wso/index.html	Casper	WY	82602	307-266-1478	266-4522

SPORTS TEAMS & FACILITIES

	City	State	ZIP	Phone	Fax
Central Wyoming Fairgrounds 1700 Fairgrounds Rd	Casper	WY	82604	307-235-5775	266-4224

— Events —

	Phone
Bear Trap Summer Festival (late July)	307-235-9325
Central Wyoming Fair & Rodeo (mid-July)	800-852-1889
Central Wyoming Home & Garden Show (late March)	307-577-3030
Christmas Parade (late November)	800-852-1889
Christmas with the Frontier Soldiers (early December)	307-235-8462
Classicfest (late June-early July)	307-235-8441
Cowboy Shootout (late December)	307-235-8441
Cowboy State Games Winter Sports Festival (early February)	307-577-1125
Cowboy State Summer Games (early-June)	307-577-1125
Mountain Man Rendezvous & Primitive Skills Contest (late June)	307-235-8462
Platte Bridge Cavalry Encampment (early August)	307-235-8462
PRCA Night Rodeo (mid-July)	307-235-5775
PRCA Season Finale Rodeo (late October-early November)	307-235-8441
Wyoming Outdoors Sports Show (early April)	307-577-3030
Wyoming Ski & Winter Sports Show (mid-November)	307-235-8441

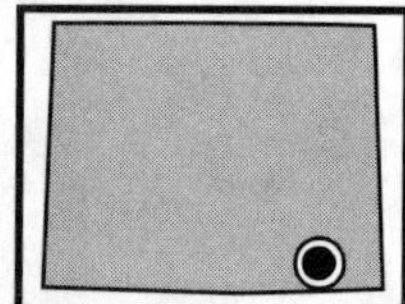

Cheyenne

Wyoming's capital is home to Cheyenne Frontier Days, the world's largest outdoor rodeo. The Cheyenne Frontier Days Old West Museum includes a major collection of Western wagons, and enactments of Old West gunfights are held in downtown Cheyenne during the summer. The city itself has more than 1,400 acres of developed parkland, and within a short drive to the west are Medicine Bow National Forest, Crystal and Granite reservoirs, and the Snowy Range Ski Area. East of the city is the Wyoming Hereford Ranch; tours of the ranch are available but must be arranged in advance. Cheyenne is also the site of the F.E. Warren Air Force Base and Heritage Museum.

Population 53,640
Area (Land) .... 18.8 sq mi
Area (Water) .... 0.1 sq mi
Elevation .... 6098 ft
Latitude .... 41-13-33 N
Longitude .... 104-81-67 W
County .... Laramie
Time Zone .... MST
Area Code/s 307

— Average Temperatures and Precipitation —

TEMPERATURES

	Jan	Feb	Mar	Apr	May	Jun	Jul	Aug	Sep	Oct	Nov	Dec
High	38	41	45	55	65	74	82	80	71	60	47	39
Low	15	18	22	30	39	48	55	53	44	34	24	17

PRECIPITATION

	Jan	Feb	Mar	Apr	May	Jun	Jul	Aug	Sep	Oct	Nov	Dec
Inches	0.4	0.4	1.0	1.4	2.4	2.1	2.1	1.7	1.3	0.7	0.5	0.4

— Important Phone Numbers —

	Phone
AAA	307-634-8861
American Express Travel	307-635-7616
Emergency	911
Poison Control Center	803-777-1117
Weather	307-635-9901

— Information Sources —

				Phone	Fax
Better Business Bureau Serving the Mountain States 1730 S College Ave Suite 303	Fort Collins	CO	80525	970-484-1348	221-1239
Web: www.rockymtn.bbb.org ■ *E-mail:* info@rockymtn.bbb.org					
Cheyenne Area Convention & Visitors Bureau 309 W Lincolnway	Cheyenne	WY	82003	307-778-3133	778-3190
TF: 800-426-5009 ■ *Web:* www.cheyenne.org ■ *E-mail:* info@cheyenne.org					
Cheyenne City Hall 2101 O'Neil Ave	Cheyenne	WY	82001	307-637-6200	637-6454
Cheyenne Civic Center 2101 O'Neil Ave.	Cheyenne	WY	82001	307-637-6363	637-6365
Cheyenne Mayor 2101 O'Neil Ave.	Cheyenne	WY	82001	307-637-6300	637-6378
Cheyenne Planning Dept 2101 O'Neil Ave	Cheyenne	WY	82001	307-637-6286	637-6454
Greater Cheyenne Chamber of Commerce 301 W 16th St	Cheyenne	WY	82001	307-638-3388	778-1450
Web: www.cheyennechamber.org ■ *E-mail:* info@cheyennechamber.org					
Laramie County PO Box 608	Cheyenne	WY	82003	307-633-4264	633-4240
Laramie County Public Library 2800 Central Ave	Cheyenne	WY	82001	307-634-3561	634-2082

On-Line Resources

All About Wyoming .... www.trib.com/WYOMING/
Cheyenne Community Connection .... www.wyoinfo.com
Cheyenne Home Page .... www.lcc.whecn.edu/scc/Cheyenne/
Cheyenne Web .... www.cheyenneweb.com/
City Knowledge Cheyenne .... www.cityknowledge.com/wy_cheyenne.htm
Excite.com Cheyenne City Guide .... www.excite.com/travel/countries/united_states/wyoming/cheyenne

— Transportation Services —

AIRPORTS

■ **Cheyenne Municipal Airport (CYS)** — Phone
1 mile N of downtown (approx 5 minutes) 307-634-7071
Web: www.cheyenneairport.com ■ *E-mail:* cheyair@cheyenneairport.com

Airport Transportation

	Phone
TLC Yellow Cab $5 fare to downtown	307-635-5555

Commercial Airlines

	Phone
United Express	307-635-6623

Charter Airlines

	Phone
Sky Harbor Air Service Inc	307-634-4417

CAR RENTALS

	Phone
Affordable	307-634-5666
Avis	307-632-9371
Dollar	307-632-2422
Enterprise	307-632-1907
Hertz	307-634-2131

LIMO/TAXI

	Phone
TLC Yellow Cab	307-635-5555
Yellow Cab	307-638-3333

MASS TRANSIT

	Phone
Cheyenne Transit $1 Base fare	307-637-6253

RAIL/BUS

				Phone
Amtrak Station 120 N Greeley Hwy.	Cheyenne	WY	82001	307-635-1327
Bus Line Transportation Services 222 Demming Rd	Cheyenne	WY	82007	307-634-7744

— Accommodations —

HOTELS, MOTELS, RESORTS

				Phone	Fax
Atlas Motel 1524 W Lincolnway	Cheyenne	WY	82001	307-632-9214	
Best Western Fosters Country Inn 1561 Snowy Range Rd	Laramie	WY	82070	307-742-8371	742-0884
Best Western Hitching Post Inn 1700 W Lincolnway	Cheyenne	WY	82001	307-638-3301	778-7194
TF: 800-221-0125					
Cheyenne Motel 1601 E Lincolnway	Cheyenne	WY	82001	307-632-5505	
Comfort Inn 2245 Etchepare Dr.	Cheyenne	WY	82007	307-638-7202	635-8560
TF: 800-777-7218					
Days Inn 2360 W Lincolnway	Cheyenne	WY	82001	307-778-8877	778-8697
TF: 800-329-7466					
Drummond's Ranch Bed & Breakfast 399 Happy Jack Rd.	Cheyenne	WY	82007	307-634-6042	634-6042
Web: www.cruising-america.com/drummond.html ■ *E-mail:* adrummond@juno.com					
Econo Lodge 2512 W Lincolnway	Cheyenne	WY	82001	307-632-7556	635-9141
Fairfield Inn 1415 Stillwater Ave.	Cheyenne	WY	82001	307-637-4070	637-4070
TF: 800-228-2800 ■ *Web:* fairfieldinn.com/CYSFI					
Guest Ranch Motel 1100 W Lincolnway	Cheyenne	WY	82001	307-634-2137	
Holiday Inn 2313 Soldier Springs Rd.	Laramie	WY	82070	307-742-6611	745-8371
TF: 800-465-4329					
Holiday Inn 204 W Fox Farm Rd.	Cheyenne	WY	82007	307-638-4466	638-3677
TF: 800-465-4329					
Home Ranch Motel 2414 E Lincolnway	Cheyenne	WY	82001	307-634-3575	634-3575
La Quinta Motor Inn 2410 W Lincolnway	Cheyenne	WY	82009	307-632-7117	638-7807
TF: 800-531-5900					

Cheyenne — Hotels, Motels, Resorts (Cont'd)

Name / Address	City	State	ZIP	Phone	Fax
Lincoln Court 1720 W Lincolnway	Cheyenne	WY	82001	307-638-3302	638-7921
TF: 800-221-0125					
Little America Hotel 2800 W Lincolnway	Cheyenne	WY	82001	307-775-8400	775-8425
TF: 800-445-6945					
Luxury Inn 1805 Westland Rd.	Cheyenne	WY	82001	307-638-2550	778-8113
Motel 6 1735 Westland Rd.	Cheyenne	WY	82001	307-635-6806	638-3017
TF: 800-466-8356					
Plains Hotel 1600 Central Ave	Cheyenne	WY	82001	307-638-3311	
Porch Swing Bed & Breakfast 712 E 20th St.	Cheyenne	WY	82001	307-778-7182	778-7182
Web: www.cruising-america.com/porch.html ■ *E-mail:* porchswing@juno.com					
Quality Hotel 5401 Walker Rd	Cheyenne	WY	82009	307-632-8901	634-8839
TF: 800-228-5151					
Rainsford Inn 219 E 18th St.	Cheyenne	WY	82001	307-638-2337	
Rodeo Inn 3839 E Lincolnway	Cheyenne	WY	82001	307-634-2171	637-5626
TF: 800-843-5644					
Sands Motel 1000 W Lincolnway	Cheyenne	WY	82001	307-634-7771	
Super 8 Motel 1900 W Lincolnway	Cheyenne	WY	82001	307-635-8741	
TF: 800-800-8000					
Windy Hills Guest House 393 Happy Jack Rd.	Cheyenne	WY	82007	307-632-6423	637-2824
Web: www.windyhillswyo.com					

— Restaurants —

Name / Address	City	State	ZIP	Phone
Albany The (American) 1506 Capitol Ave	Cheyenne	WY	82007	307-638-3507
Armadillo (Mexican) 3617 E Lincolnway	Cheyenne	WY	82001	307-778-0822
Avanti's (Italian) 4620 Grandview Ave	Cheyenne	WY	82009	307-634 3432
Blazer's All American Barbeque (Barbecue) 3713 E Lincolnway	Cheyenne	WY	82001	307-778-8801
Carriage Court (Continental) 1700 W Lincolnway	Cheyenne	WY	82001	307-638-3301
Casa de Trujillo (Mexican) 122 W 6th St	Cheyenne	WY	82007	307-635-1227
Dynasty Cafe (Chinese) 600 W 19th St.	Cheyenne	WY	82001	307-632-4888
Estevan's Cafe (Mexican) 1820 Ridge Rd	Cheyenne	WY	82001	307-632-6828
Golden Corral Steak House (Steak) 2612 E Lincolnway	Cheyenne	WY	82001	307-632-8257
Han River Cafe (Chinese) 5225 Yellowstone Rd	Cheyenne	WY	82009	307-632-2449
Lexie's (New American) 216 E 17th St.	Cheyenne	WY	82001	307-638-8712
Los Amigos (Mexican) 620 Central Ave.	Cheyenne	WY	82007	307-638-8591
Owl Inn Restaurant (American) 3919 Central Ave	Cheyenne	WY	82001	307-638-8578
Poor Richards (Continental) 2233 E Lincolnway	Cheyenne	WY	82001	307-635-5114
Renzios Greek Food (Greek) 1400 Dell Range Blvd	Cheyenne	WY	82009	307-637-5411
Senator's Restaurant (American) 51 I-25 Service Rd E	Cheyenne	WY	82007	307-634-4171
Twin Dragons (Chinese) 1809 Carey Ave	Cheyenne	WY	82001	307-637-6622
Victorian Rose (American) 1600 Central Ave.	Cheyenne	WY	82001	307-637-8701

— Goods and Services —

SHOPPING

Name / Address	City	State	ZIP	Phone	Fax
Frontier Mall 1400 Dell Range Blvd	Cheyenne	WY	82009	307-638-2290	632-1705
Web: www.frontiermall.com					
Sierra Trading Post 5025 Campstool Rd	Cheyenne	WY	82007	307-775-8050	775-8088

BANKS

Name / Address	City	State	ZIP	Phone	Fax
American National Bank of Cheyenne 1912 Capitol Ave.	Cheyenne	WY	82001	307-634-2121	778-5326*
**Fax:* Cust Svc					
Equality State Bank 401 W 19th St.	Cheyenne	WY	82001	307-635-1101	632-3566
Security First Bank 2501 E Lincolnway	Cheyenne	WY	82001	307-775-6501	775-6519
US Bank 2020 Carey Ave	Cheyenne	WY	82001	307-778-1650	778-1639
TF: 800-846-4646					
Wyoming Bank & Trust 120 W Carlson	Cheyenne	WY	82009	307-632-7733	635-0595
Web: www.wyomingbank.com ■ *E-mail:* info@wyomingbank.com					

BUSINESS SERVICES

Name	Phone
Airborne Express	800-247-2676
BAX Global	800-225-5229
DHL Worldwide Express	800-225-5345
Express Personnel Services	307-632-0567
Federal Express	800-238-5355
Kinko's	307-635-3441
Mail Boxes Etc	800-789-4623
Manpower Temporary Services	307-634-5909
Olsten Staffing Services	307-632-4476
Post Office	800-275-8777
UPS	800-742-5877

— Media —

PUBLICATIONS

Name / Address	City	State	ZIP	Phone	Fax
Wyoming Tribune-Eagle‡ 702 W Lincolnway	Cheyenne	WY	82001	307-634-3361	638-7330
Web: www.wyomingnews.com					

‡Daily newspapers

TELEVISION

Name / Address	City	State	ZIP	Phone	Fax
KCWC-TV Ch 4 (PBS) 2660 Peck Ave	Riverton	WY	82501	307-856-6944	856-3893
KGWN-TV Ch 5 (CBS) 2923 E Lincolnway	Cheyenne	WY	82001	307-634-7755	638-0182
Web: www.cbs5.com ■ *E-mail:* cbs5@sisna.com					
KKTU-TV Ch 33 (NBC) 612 W 17th St	Cheyenne	WY	82001	307-632-2662	632-8556
Web: www.msnbc.com/local/KKTU/ ■ *E-mail:* k2cybernews@2tv.com					

RADIO

Name / Address	City	State	ZIP	Phone	Fax
KFBC-AM 1240 kHz (CHR) 1806 Capitol Ave	Cheyenne	WY	82001	307-634-4462	632-8586
KGAB-AM 650 kHz (N/T) 1912 Capitol Ave Suite 300	Cheyenne	WY	82001	307-632-4400	632-1818
KJJL-AM 1370 kHz (Nost) 110 E 17th St Suite 205	Cheyenne	WY	82001	307-635-8787	635-8788
KLEN-FM 106.3 MHz (AC) 1912 Capitol Ave Suite 300	Cheyenne	WY	82001	307-637-5555	632-1818
KMUS-FM 101.9 MHz (Ctry) 1513 Carey Ave	Cheyenne	WY	82001	307-637-8844	632-4845
KOLZ-FM 100.7 MHz (Ctry) 1912 Capitol Ave Suite 300	Cheyenne	WY	82001	307-632-4400	632-1818
KQLT-FM 103.7 MHz (Ctry) PO Box 2515	Casper	WY	82602	307-265-1984	473-7461
KRAE-AM 1480 kHz (Oldies) PO Box 189	Cheyenne	WY	82003	307-635-9100	638-8922
KTWO-AM 1030 kHz (Ctry) 150 N Nichols Ave	Casper	WY	82601	307 266 5252	235-9143
KUWR-FM 91.9 MHz (NPR) PO Box 3984	Laramie	WY	82071	307-766-4240	766-6184
Web: www.uwyo.edu/wpr ■ *E-mail:* wpr@uwyo.edu					
KZCY-FM 104.9 MHz (Alt) PO Box 189	Cheyenne	WY	82003	307-635-9100	638-8922

— Colleges/Universities —

Name / Address	City	State	ZIP	Phone	Fax
Laramie County Community College 1400 E College Dr.	Cheyenne	WY	82007	307-778-5222	778-1399*
**Fax:* Library ■ *TF:* 800-522-2993 ■ *Web:* www.lcc.whecn.edu					
University of Wyoming PO Box 3435	Laramie	WY	82071	307-766-1121	766-4042
TF: 800-342-5996 ■ *Web:* www.uwyo.edu ■ *E-mail:* fromkin@uwyo.edu					

— Hospitals —

Name / Address	City	State	ZIP	Phone	Fax
United Medical Center 214 E 23rd St	Cheyenne	WY	82001	307-634-2273	633-7715

— Attractions —

Name / Address	City	State	ZIP	Phone	Fax
Atlas Theatre 211 W Lincolnway	Cheyenne	WY	82001	307-638-6543	
Cheyenne Botanic Gardens 710 S Lions Park Dr	Cheyenne	WY	82001	307-637-6458	637-6453
Web: botanic.org ■ *E-mail:* info@botanic.org					
Cheyenne Frontier Days Old West Museum 4610 N Carey Ave	Cheyenne	WY	82001	307-778-7290	778-7288
TF: 800-778-7290 ■ *Web:* www.state.wy.us/state/images/qtvr/museum.html					
Cheyenne Little Theatre 2706 E Pershing Blvd	Cheyenne	WY	82001	307-638-6543	638-6430
Cheyenne Symphony Orchestra 1902 Thomes Ave Suite 203	Cheyenne	WY	82001	307-778-8561	
Gowdy Curt State Park 1319 Hynds Lodge Rd.	Cheyenne	WY	82009	307-632-7946	632-7946
Historic Governors' Mansion 300 E 21st St.	Cheyenne	WY	82001	307-777-7878	
Holiday Park 17th St & Morrie Ave.	Cheyenne	WY	82001	307-637-6423	
Lions Park Carey & 8th Aves	Cheyenne	WY	82001	307-637-6423	638-4304
Medicine Bow National Forest 2468 Jackson St.	Laramie	WY	82070	307-745-2300	745-2398

Cheyenne — Attractions (Cont'd)

Name / Address	City	State	Zip	Phone	Fax
Snowy Range Ski Area 6416 Mountain Mist Ct *TF:* 800-462-7669	Laramie	WY	82070	307-745-5750	745-4718
Terry Bison Ranch 51 I-25 Service Rd E *TF:* 800-319-4171	Cheyenne	WY	82007	307-634-4171	634-9746
Vedauwoo Recreation Area 2468 Jackson St Medicine Bow National Forest	Laramie	WY	82070	307-745-2300	745-2398
Warren FE Heritage Museum 7405 Marne Loop Warren AFB Bldg 210 *Web:* www.pawnee.com/fewmuseum/	Cheyenne	WY	82005	307-773-2980	773-2791
Wyoming Arts Council Gallery 2320 Capitol Ave. *Web:* commerce.state.wy.us/CR/Arts/ ■ *E-mail:* wyoarts@tmn.com	Cheyenne	WY	82002	307-777-7742	777-5499
Wyoming Game & Fish Visitors Center 5400 Bishop Blvd *Web:* gf.state.wy.us	Cheyenne	WY	82006	307-777-4554	777-4610
Wyoming Hereford Ranch 1600 Hereford Ranch Rd Box 868	Cheyenne	WY	82003	307-634-1905	
Wyoming State Museum 2301 Central Ave *Web:* commerce.state.wy.us/cr/wsm/index.htm	Cheyenne	WY	82002	307-777-7013	777-5375

SPORTS TEAMS & FACILITIES

Name / Address	City	State	Zip	Phone
Big Country Speedway US Hwy 85	Cheyenne	WY	82007	307-632-2107

— Events —

	Phone
Cheyenne Christmas Parade Craft Show & Concert (Thanksgiving weekend)	307-638-0151
Cheyenne Farmer's Market (early August-early October)	307-635-9291
Cheyenne Frontier Days (late July)	307-778-7200
Cheyenne Frontier Days Western Art Show & Sale (late July)	307-778-7290
Cheyenne Gunslinger Gunfights (early June-late July)	307-778-3133
Cheyenne Motorsports Shootout (late June)	307-778-3133
Cheyenne Street Railway (mid-May-September)	307-778-3133
Cheyenne Western Film Festival (mid-September)	307-635-4646
Laramie County Fair (early August)	307-778-3133
Old Fashioned Melodrama (early July-mid-August)	307-638-6543
Outdoor Arts & Crafts Festival (early August)	307-777-7022
Silver Bells in the City (late November)	517-372-4636
Superday (late June)	307-637-6423
Tumbleweed Buckle Series Rodeo (June-August)	307-634-4171
Wyoming Open Golf Tournament (mid-July)	307-637-6418

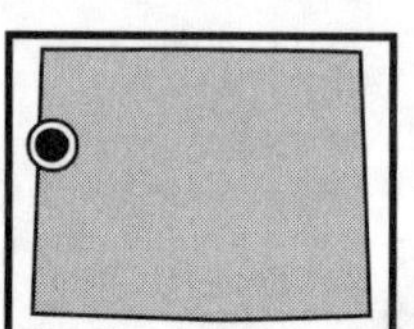

Jackson

The town of Jackson is located near the resort area of Jackson Hole, which is a high mountain valley located in the northwestern corner of Wyoming and is part of the largest intact ecosystem in the lower 48 states. It is surrounded by the Bridger-Teton National Forest, which encompasses nearly 3.5 million acres, and Grand Teton National Park, which offers not only spectacular scenery but also some of the best wildlife viewing in the U.S. Tours that are available in the area offer glimpses of bears, coyotes, bison, elk, antelope, and other area wildlife. Yellowstone National Park is less than an hour away from Jackson Hole, and the 25,000-acre National Elk Refuge, which was created in the town of Jackson in 1912, is the only U.S. Fish and Wildlife Service refuge devoted primarily to elk management. The National Museum of Wildlife Art overlooks the National Elk Refuge and is one of the few American art museums with a focus on wildlife, housing nearly 2,300 works of art. Among the many activites available in the Jackson Hole area are hiking, mountain biking, skiing, horseback riding, and whitewater rafting. In addition, several popular events are held in the area each year, including Old West Days, held on Memorial Day weekend to celebrate the town's heritage; the Grand Teton Music Festival, which takes place in July; and the Jackson Hole Fall Arts Festival, which is held each September.

Population	5,817	**Longitude**	110-45-49 W
Area (Land)	2.0 sq mi	**County**	Teton
Area (Water)	0.0 sq mi	**Time Zone**	MST
Elevation	6230 ft	**Area Code/s**	307
Latitude	43-28-26 N		

— Important Phone Numbers —

	Phone		Phone
AAA	800-391-4222	**Jackson Hole Teton Village Information Line**	307-733-2291
American Express Travel	307-733-2310	**Poison Control Center**	800-955-9119
Emergency	911		
Grand Targhee Snow Conditions	800-827-4433		

— Important Phone Numbers —

	Phone		Phone
AAA	800-391-4222	**Jackson Hole Teton Village Information Line**	307-733-2291
American Express Travel	307-733-2310	**Poison Control Center**	800-955-9119
Emergency	911		
Grand Targhee Snow Conditions	800-827-4433		

— Information Sources —

Name / Address	City	State	Zip	Phone	Fax
Better Business Bureau Serving the Mountain States 1730 S College Ave Suite 303 *Web:* www.rockymtn.bbb.org ■ *E-mail:* info@rockymtn.bbb.org	Fort Collins	CO	80525	970-484-1348	221-1239
Jackson Hole Chamber of Commerce PO Box 550 *Web:* www.jacksonholechamber.com ■ *E-mail:* info@jacksonholechamber.com	Jackson	WY	83001	307-733-3316	733-5585
Jackson Mayor 150 E Pearl Ave	Jackson	WY	83001	307-733-3932	
Jackson Town Hall 150 E Pearl Ave *Web:* www.ci.jackson.wy.us	Jackson	WY	83001	307-733-3932	
Teton County PO Box 1727 *Web:* www.jacksonwy.com/info/jhpg.htm	Jackson	WY	83001	307-733-4430	739-8681
Teton County Public Library 125 Virginian Ln *Web:* will.state.wy.us/teton/home/ ■ *E-mail:* tetnref@wyld.state.wy.us	Jackson	WY	83001	307-733-2164	733-4568

On-Line Resources

Area Guide Jackson Hole	areaguide.net/ag/FP/c1/JAK/
Excite.com Jackson (WY) City Guide	www.excite.com/travel/countries/united_states/wyoming/jackson
Jackson Hole Net Magazine	www.jacksonholenet.com
Jackson Hole Online Travel Guide	www.jackson-hole.com
NITC Travelbase City Guide Jackson	www.travelbase.com/auto/features/jackson-wy.html
Online City Guide to Jackson Hole	www.olcg.com/wy/jacksonhole/index.html

— Transportation Services —

AIRPORTS

■ Jackson Hole Airport (JAC)

	Phone
10 miles N of downtown (approx 15 minutes)	307-733-7682

Airport Transportation

	Phone
All Star Transportation Service $18 fare to downtown	307-733-2888
Alltrans Inc $12 fare to downtown	307-733-3135
Buckboard Cab $18 fare to downtown	307-733-7372
Cowboy Cab/Shuttle Taxi $18 fare to downtown	307-733-2728

Commercial Airlines

	Phone		Phone
American	800-433-7300	**SkyWest**	800-453-9417
Delta	800-221-1212	**United**	800-241-6522
Mesa	800-637-2247	**United Express**	800-241-6522

Jackson (Cont'd)

Charter Airlines

	Phone		Phone
Corporate America Aviation Inc	800-521-8585	**Jackson Hole Aviation**	307-733-4767

CAR RENTALS

	Phone		Phone
Alamo	307-733-0671	**Eagle**	307-739-9999
Aspen	307-733-9224	**Hertz**	307-733-2272
Avis	307-733-3422	**Rent-A-Wreck**	307-733-5014
Budget	307-733-2206	**Thrifty**	307-739-9300

LIMO/TAXI

	Phone		Phone
Buckboard Cab	307-733-7372	**Cowboy Cab/Shuttle Taxi**	307-733-2728

MASS TRANSIT

	Phone
START Bus $.50 Base fare	307-733-4521

— Accommodations —

HOTEL RESERVATION SERVICES

	Phone	Fax
Jackson Hole Central Reservations *TF:* 800-443-6931 ■ *Web:* www.jacksonholeresort.com ■ *E-mail:* info@jacksonholeresort.com	307-733-4005	733-1286
Jackson Hole Resort Reservations LLC *TF:* 800-329-9205 ■ *Web:* www.jacksonholeres.com ■ *E-mail:* reservations@jacksonholeres.com	307-733-6331	733-4728
Premier Lodging Reservations *TF:* 800-322-5766 ■ *Web:* www.jhlodging.com ■ *E-mail:* info@jhlodging.com	307-733-0353	733-3487
Reservations Center *TF:* 800-255-6451 ■ *Web:* www.rescenter.com ■ *E-mail:* resnet@rescenter.com	435-649-1592	649-1593

HOTELS, MOTELS, RESORTS

	City	State	Zip	Phone	Fax
Alpenhof Lodge PO Box 288 *TF:* 800-732-3244 ■ *Web:* www.alpenhoflodge.com ■ *E-mail:* gm@alpenhoflodge.com	Teton Village	WY	83025	307-733-3242	739-1516
Angler's Inn 265 N Millward St. *TF:* 800-867-4667 ■ *Web:* anglersinn.net ■ *E-mail:* anglersinn@wyoming.com	Jackson	WY	83001	307-733-3682	733-8662
Antler Motel 43 W Pearl St *TF:* 800-522-2406 ■ *Web:* townsquareinns.com/antler.shtml ■ *E-mail:* antlerjh@aol.com	Jackson	WY	83001	307-733-2535	733-4158
Anvil Motel 215 N Cache St. *TF:* 800-234-4507 ■ *Web:* www.anvilmotel.com/ ■ *E-mail:* anvilmotel@wyoming.com	Jackson	WY	83001	307-733-3668	733-3957
Best Western Inn at Jackson Hole 3345 W McCollister Dr *TF:* 800-842-7666 ■ *Web:* www.innatjh.com ■ *E-mail:* jacksonhole@compuserve.com	Teton Village	WY	83025	307-733-2311	733-0844
Best Western Lodge at Jackson Hole 80 S Scott Ln. *TF:* 800-458-3866 ■ *Web:* www.lodgeatjh.com	Jackson	WY	83002	307-739-9703	739-9168
Best Western Resort Hotel at Jackson Hole 3245 W McCollister Dr *TF:* 800-445-4655 ■ *Web:* www.resorthotelatjh.com ■ *E-mail:* jacksonhole@compuserve.com	Teton Village	WY	83025	307-733-3657	733-9543
Buckrail Lodge 110 E Karns Ave. *Web:* www.jacksonwy.com/buckrail	Jackson	WY	83001	307-733-2079	734-1663
Cache Creek Motel 390 N Glenwood *TF:* 800-843-4788 ■ *Web:* www.cachecreekmotel.com ■ *E-mail:* cachecreek@blissnet.com	Jackson	WY	83001	307-733-7781	733-4652
Cowboy Village Log Cabin Resort 120 S Flat Creek Dr. *TF:* 800-962-4988 ■ *Web:* www.cowboyvillage.com/town-main.htm ■ *E-mail:* cowboyvillage@wyoming.com	Jackson	WY	83002	307-733-3121	739-1955
Crystal Springs Inn 3285 W McCollister Dr *E-mail:* tvpm@sisna.com	Teton Village	WY	83025	307-733-4423	
Davy Jackson Inn 85 Perry Ave *TF:* 800-584-0532 ■ *Web:* www.davyjackson.com ■ *E-mail:* davyjackson@wyoming.com	Jackson	WY	83001	307-739-2294	733-9704
Days Inn of Jackson Hole 350 S Hwy 89. *TF:* 800-329-7466 ■ *Web:* www.daysinnjacksonhole.com/ ■ *E-mail:* daysinnjh@wyoming.com	Jackson	WY	83001	307-733-0033	733-0044
Elk Country Inn 480 W Pearl St *Web:* www.townsquareinns.com/elk.shtml ■ *E-mail:* info@townsquareinns.com	Jackson	WY	83001	307-733-2364	
Elk Refuge Inn 1755 N Hwy 89 *TF:* 800-544-3582 ■ *Web:* www.elkrefugeinn.com ■ *E-mail:* elkrefugeinn@wyoming.com	Jackson	WY	83001	307-733-3582	734-1580
Four Winds Motel 150 N Millward St	Jackson	WY	83001	307-733-2474	
Golden Eagle Inn 325 E Broadway	Jackson	WY	83001	307-733-2042	
Grand Targhee Resort Box SKI. *TF:* 800-827-4433 ■ *Web:* www.grandtarghee.com ■ *E-mail:* info@grandtarghee.com	Alta	WY	83422	307-353-2300	353-8619
Grill at Amangani 1535 NE Butte Rd. *TF:* 877-734-7333	Jackson	WY	83001	307-734-7333	
Gros Ventre River Ranch PO Box 151. *Web:* www.grosventreriverranch.com ■ *E-mail:* grosventreriverranch@compuserve.com	Moose	WY	83012	307-733-4138	733-4272
Heart Six Ranch PO Box 70. *TF:* 888-543-2477 ■ *Web:* www.heartsix.com ■ *E-mail:* heartsix@wyoming.com	Moran	WY	83013	307-543-2477	
Hitching Post Lodge 460 E Broadway *E-mail:* hitchingpost@wyoming.com	Jackson	WY	83001	307-733-2606	
Hoback River Resort 11055 S Hwy 89	Jackson	WY	83001	307-733-5129	734-6853
Inn on the Creek 295 N Millward St *Web:* www.innonthecreek.com ■ *E-mail:* creek@wyoming.com	Jackson	WY	83001	307-739-1565	734-9116
Jackson Hole Lodge 420 W Broadway. *Web:* www.jacksonholelodge.com ■ *E-mail:* jhlodge@blissnet.com	Jackson	WY	83001	307-733-2992	739-2144
Jackson Hole Racquet Club Resort 3535 Moose-Wilson Rd *TF:* 800-443-8613	Wilson	WY	83014	307-733-3990	733-3183
Jackson Hole Resort Lodging 3200 W McCollister Dr	Teton Village	WY	83025	307-733-4610	733-0244
Jackson Lake Lodge PO Box 250 *TF:* 800-628-9988 ■ *Web:* www.gtlc.com/JacLLLod.htm	Moran	WY	83013	307-543-2811	543-3143
Masa Sushi (Japanese) 3345 W McCollister Dr Inn at Jackson Hole	Jackson	WY	83025	307-733-2311	
Moose Head Ranch	Moose	WY	83012	307-733-3141	
Motel 6 1370 W Broadway.	Jackson	WY	83001	307-733-1620	734-9175
Painted Buffalo Inn 400 W Broadway *TF:* 800-288-3866 ■ *Web:* www.paintedbuffalo.com ■ *E-mail:* info@paintedbuffalo.com	Jackson	WY	83001	307-733-4340	733-7953
Parkway Inn 125 N Jackson St. *TF:* 800-247-8390 ■ *Web:* www.parkwayinn.com ■ *E-mail:* info@parkwayinn.com	Jackson	WY	83001	307-733-3143	733-0955
Pony Express Motel 50 S Millward St *TF:* 800-526-2658	Jackson	WY	83001	307-733-3835	739-0149
Prospector Motel 155 N Jackson *TF:* 800-851-0070 ■ *Web:* www.jacksonprospector.com ■ *E-mail:* prospector@blissnet.com	Jackson	WY	83001	307-733-4858	733-3133
Quality 49er Inn & Suites 330 W Pearl St. *TF:* 800-451-2980 ■ *Web:* www.townsquareinns.com/forty.shtml ■ *E-mail:* info@townsquareinns.com	Jackson	WY	83001	307-733-7550	733-2002
R Lazy S Ranch PO Box 308 *Web:* www.rlazys.com ■ *E-mail:* info@rlazys.com	Teton Village	WY	83025	307-733-2655	734-1120
Ranch Inn 45 E Pearl St. *TF:* 800-348-5599 ■ *Web:* www.ranchinn.com ■ *E-mail:* info@ranchinn.com	Jackson	WY	83001	307-733-6363	733-0623
Rancho Alegre Lodge 3600 Park Dr	Jackson	WY	83001	307-733-7988	
Rawhide Motel 75 S Millward St *TF:* 800-835-2999 ■ *Web:* www.rawhidemotel.com ■ *E-mail:* rawhidemotel@wyoming.com	Jackson	WY	83001	307-733-1216	734-1335
Red Lion Wyoming Inn 930 W Broadway *TF:* 800-844-0035 ■ *Web:* www.wyoming-inn.com ■ *E-mail:* wyominginn@blissnet.com	Jackson	WY	83001	307-734-0035	734-0037
Red Rock Ranch PO Box 38. *Web:* www.blissnet.com/~redrockranch ■ *E-mail:* redrockranch@blissnet.com	Kelly	WY	83011	307-733-6288	733-6287
Rusty Parrot Lodge PO Box 1657 *TF:* 800-458-2004 ■ *Web:* www.rustyparrot.com ■ *E-mail:* mail@rustyparrot.com	Jackson	WY	83001	307-733-2000	733-5566
Signal Mountain Lodge PO Box 50. *Web:* www.signalmtnlodge.com ■ *E-mail:* signalmountain@compuserve.com	Moran	WY	83013	307-543-2831	543-2569
Snow King Inn 35 Snow King Ave. *TF:* 800-700-7238 ■ *Web:* www.snowkinginn.com ■ *E-mail:* jhww@aol.com	Jackson	WY	83001	307-733-1007	
Snow King Resort 400 E Snow King Ave *TF:* 800-522-5464 ■ *Web:* www.snowking.com ■ *E-mail:* snowking@wyoming.com	Jackson	WY	83001	307-733-5200	733-4086
Split Creek Ranch 240 W Zenith. *Web:* www.splitcreekranch.com ■ *E-mail:* residence@sopris.net	Jackson	WY	83001	307-733-7522	734-2869

Jackson — Hotels, Motels, Resorts (Cont'd)

Phone *Fax*

Spring Creek Ranch & Conference Center
1800 Spirit Dance Rd .... Jackson WY 83001 307-733-8833 733-1524
TF: 800-443-6139 ■ *Web:* www.springcreekresort.com
■ *E-mail:* reservations@springcreekresort.com
Stagecoach Motel 219 N Glenwood .... Jackson WY 83001 307-733-3451
TF: 800-421-1447
Sundance Inn 135 W Broadway .... Jackson WY 83001 307-733-3444 733-3440
TF: 888-478-6326 ■ *Web:* www.sundanceinnjackson.com
■ *E-mail:* info@sundanceinnjackson.com
Super 8 of Jackson 750 S Hwy 89 .... Jackson WY 83001 307-733-6833 739-1828
TF: 800-800-8000
Teton Inn 165 W Gill Ave.................... Jackson WY 83001 307-733-3883 733-3133
TF: 800-851-0070 ■ *E-mail:* prospect@blissnet.com
Teton Pines Resort & Country Club
3450 N Clubhouse Dr .... Jackson WY 83001 307-733-1005 733-2860
TF: 800-238-2223
Timberline Motel 38 W Center St............. Victor ID 83455 208-787-2772
TF: 800-711-4667
Trail Creek Ranch Box 10 .... Wilson WY 83014 307-733-2610
Trapper Inn 235 N Cache St.................. Jackson WY 83001 307-733-2648 739-9351
TF: 800-341-8000 ■ *Web:* trapperinn.com
■ *E-mail:* info@trapperinn.com
Triangle X Ranch .... Moose WY 83012 307-733-2183 733-8685
Web: www.trianglex.com
Village Center Inn
3725 W McCollister Dr .... Teton Village WY 83025 307-733-3155 733-3183
TF: 800-735-8342
Virginian Lodge 750 W Broadway............ Jackson WY 83001 307-733-2792 733-0281
TF: 800-262-4999 ■ *Web:* www.virginianlodge.com
■ *E-mail:* info@virginianlodge.com
Wagon Wheel Village 435 N Cache St .... Jackson WY 83001 307-733-2357 733-0568
Western Motel & Suites 225 S Glenwood ...... Jackson WY 83001 307-733-3291 734-0049
TF: 800-845-7999 ■ *Web:* www.jak-biz.com/westernmotel
Wolf Moon Inn 285 N Cache St .... Jackson WY 83001 307-733-2287
TF: 800-964-2387
Wort Hotel 50 N Glenwood.................. Jackson WY 83001 307-733-2190 733-2067
TF: 800-322-2727 ■ *Web:* www.worthotel.com
■ *E-mail:* info@worthotel.com

— Restaurants —

Phone

Bar J Chuckwagon (American) 4200 Bar J Chuckwagon Rd ... Wilson WY 83014 307-733-3370
Web: www.focusproductions.com/jhdining/barj/barj.html
Blue Lion Restaurant (Continental) 160 N Millward St...... Jackson WY 83001 307-733-3912
Web: focusproductions.com/jhdining/bluelion/blue.html
Bubba's (Barbecue) 515 W Broadway.................. Jackson WY 83001 307-733-2288
Cadillac Grille (New American) 55 N Cache St .... Jackson WY 83001 307-733-3279
Gun Barrell Steak & Game House (Steak)
862 W Broadway .... Jackson WY 83002 307-733-3287
Web: www.gunbarrel.com ■ *E-mail:* steak@gunbarrel.com
Harvest Café & Bakery (Vegetarian) 130 W Broadway ...... Jackson WY 83001 307-733-5418
Horse Creek Station (Steak/Seafood) 9800 S Hwy 89 ...... Jackson WY 83001 307-733-0810
Web: www.focusproductions.com/jhdining/horsecreek/horsecreek.html
J Hennessy's (Steak/Seafood)
3245 W McCollister Dr Best Western Jackson
Hole Resort .... Teton Village WY 83025 307-733-3657
Lame Duck (Chinese/Japanese) 680 E Broadway.......... Jackson WY 83001 307-733-4311
Web: www.focusproductions.com/jhdining/lameduck/lame.html
Mangy Moose Restaurant (American) PO Box 190 .... Teton Village WY 83025 307-733-4913
Web: www.mangymoosesaloon.com ■ *E-mail:* moose@sisna.com
Merry Piglets (Mexican) 160 N Cache St .... Jackson WY 83002 307-733-2966
Million Dollar Cowboy Steakhouse (Steak/Seafood)
25 N Cache St.................................... Jackson WY 83002 307-733-4790
Mountain Dragon Chinese Restaurant (Chinese)
340 W Broadway .... Jackson WY 83002 307-734-9768
Off Broadway (Continental) 30 S King St .... Jackson WY 83001 307-733-9777
Pitchfork Fondue (American) 5330 N Spring Gulch Rd....... Daniel WY 83115 307-734-2541
Range The (American) 225 N Cache St .... Jackson WY 83002 307-733-5481
Web: focusproductions.com/jhdining/range/range.html
Restaurant Terroir (New American) 45 S Glenwood........ Jackson WY 83001 307-739-2500
E-mail: terroir@aol.com
Shades Café (Thai) 82 S King St...................... Jackson WY 83002 307-733-2015
Snake River Brewing Co (American) 265 S Millward St..... Jackson WY 83001 307-739-2337
Web: snakeriverbrewing.com ■ *E-mail:* info@snakeriverbrewing.com
Snake River Grill (American) 84 E Broadway .... Jackson WY 83001 307-733-0557
Web: snakerivergrill.com ■ *E-mail:* srg@blissnet.com
Stiegler's Restaurant (American) PO Box 508........ Teton Village WY 83025 307-733-1071
Sweetwater Restaurant (Greek) 85 S King St .... Jackson WY 83001 307-733-3553
Web: www.focusproductions.com/jhdining/sweetwater/sweet.html

Phone

Teton Pines Restaurant (American)
3450 N Clubhouse Dr Teton Pines Resort .... Jackson WY 83002 307-733-1005
Web: www.tetonpines.com/restaurant.shtml
■ *E-mail:* info@tetonpines.com
Teton Steakhouse (Steak/Seafood) 40 W Pearl St .... Jackson WY 83001 307-733-2639
Web: www.focusproductions.com/jhdining/tetonsteakhouse/teton.html
Vista Grande (Mexican) PO Box 294 .... Jackson WY 83001 307-733-6964
Web: www.focusproductions.com/jhdining/vista/vista.html

— Goods and Services —

SHOPPING

Phone

Polo Factory Store-Fashion Outlet of America
75 N Cache St .... Jackson WY 83001 307-733-8333

BANKS

Phone *Fax*

Bank of Jackson Hole 990 W Broadway .... Jackson WY 83002 307-733-8064 733-0562
Web: www.bojh.com
■ *E-mail:* bankofjacksonhole@bankofjacksonhole.com
Community First National Bank
160 W Pearl St.......................... Jackson WY 83001 307-733-4884 733-4366
Jackson State Bank 112 N Center St.......... Jackson WY 83001 307-733-3737 733-3982
Web: www.jacksonstatebank.com ■ *E-mail:* info@jacksonstatebank.com

BUSINESS SERVICES

	Phone		*Phone*
Federal Express	800-238-5355	**Post Office**	307-733-3650
Mail Boxes Etc	307-733-9250	**UPS**	800-742-5877

— Media —

PUBLICATIONS

Phone *Fax*

Jackson Hole Daily News‡ PO Box 7445....... Jackson WY 83002 307-733-2047 733-2138
Jackson Hole Guide 185 N Glenwood .... Jackson WY 83001 307-733-2430
E-mail: jhguide@wyoming.com

‡Daily newspapers

TELEVISION

Phone *Fax*

KIDK-TV Ch 3 (CBS) PO Box 33 .... Pocatello ID 83204 208-233-3333 233-3337
Web: www.kidk.com
KIFI-TV Ch 8 (ABC) 150 S Main St Suite C .... Pocatello ID 83204 208-233-8888 233-8932
Web: www.idaho8.com ■ *E-mail:* idaho8@aol.com
KISU-TV Ch 10 (PBS) PO Box 8111 .... Pocatello ID 83209 208-236-2857 236-2848
Web: www.idahoptv.org/about/stations/kisu.html

RADIO

Phone *Fax*

KMTN-FM 96.9 MHz (CR) 645 S Cache St...... Jackson WY 83001 307-733-2120 733-7773
E-mail: kmtn@blissnet.com
KSGT-AM 1340 kHz (Ctry) 645 S Cache St...... Jackson WY 83001 307-733-2120 733-7773
KUWJ-FM 90.3 MHz (NPR) PO Box 3984 ...... Laramie WY 82071 307-766-4240
TF: 800-729-5897 ■ *Web:* www.uwyo.edu/wpr
■ *E-mail:* wpr@uwyo.edu
KZJH-FM 95.3 MHz (AC) 160 W Deloney Ave.... Jackson WY 83001 307-733-1770 733-4760
E-mail: kz95@blissnet.com

— Colleges/Universities —

Phone *Fax*

Central Wyoming College Teton Campus
220 S Glenwood...................... Jackson WY 83001 307-733-7425 733-7425
Hamilton University 100 Bear River Dr .... Evanston WY 82930 307-739-8476 951-1189*
**Fax Area Code:* 800 ■ *TF:* 800-951-0857
■ *Web:* www.hamilton-university.edu
■ *E-mail:* adm@hamilton-university.edu

Jackson (Cont'd)

— Hospitals —

				Phone	Fax
Saint John's Hospital 625 E Broadway *Web:* www.tetonhospital.org	Jackson	WY	83001	307-733-3636	739-7522

— Attractions —

				Phone	Fax
Bar T-5 National Elk Refuge Sleigh Rides PO Box 3415 *TF:* 800-772-5386 ■ *Web:* www.bart5.com ■ *E-mail:* bartfive@juno.com	Jackson	WY	83001	307-733-5386	739-9183
Bridger-Teton National Forest PO Box 1888 *Web:* www.fs.fed.us/btnf/welcome.htm ■ *E-mail:* btnfinfo/r4_b-t@fs.fed.us	Jackson	WY	83001	307-739-5500	739-5010
Caswell Gallery of Jackson Hole 145 E Broadway *Web:* www.caswellgallery.com ■ *E-mail:* art@caswellgallery.com	Jackson	WY	83002	307-734-2660	
Grand Targhee Ski Area PO Box SKI *TF:* 800-827-4433	Alta	WY	83422	307-353-2300	353-8619
Grand Teton National Park PO Box 170 *Web:* www.nps.gov/grte/	Moose	WY	83012	307-739-3300	739-3438
Jackson Hole Historical Society & Museum 105 Mercill *E-mail:* jhhsm@rmisp.com	Jackson	WY	83001	307-733-9605	739-9019
Jackson Hole Playhouse 145 W Deloney *Web:* www.jhplayhouse.com ■ *E-mail:* reservations@jhplayhouse.com	Jackson	WY	83001	307-733-6994	739-0414
Mainstage Theatre 50 W Broadway	Jackson	WY	83001	307-733-3021	733-3021
Museum of the Mountain Man 700 E Hennick *TF:* 877-686-6266 ■ *Web:* www.pinedaleonline.com/MMMuseum ■ *E-mail:* museummtman@wyoming.com	Pinedale	WY	82941	307-367-4101	367-6768
National Museum of Wildlife Art 2820 Rungius Rd *Web:* www.wildlifeart.org ■ *E-mail:* info@wildlifeart.org	Jackson	WY	83002	307-733-5771	733-5787
Performing Arts Co of Jackson Hole 50 W Broadway Mainstage Theatre *E-mail:* pacjh@rmisp.com	Jackson	WY	83001	307-733-3021	
Ripley's Believe It or Not! Museum 140 N Cache St *E-mail:* ripley@blissnet.com	Jackson	WY	83001	307-734-0000	734-0078
Shadow Mountain Gallery 10 W Broadway *Web:* www.topgifts.com/Gallery/western.shl ■ *E-mail:* touchoclass@wyoming.com	Jackson	WY	83001	307-733-3162	
Snow King Ski Area PO Box SKI *TF:* 800-522-5464	Jackson	WY	83001	307-733-5200	
Wyoming Dinosaur Center 110 Carter Ranch Rd *Web:* www.wyodino.org ■ *E-mail:* wdinoc@wyodino.org	Thermopolis	WY	82443	307-864-2997	864-5762
Yellowstone National Park PO Box 168 *Web:* www.nps.gov/yell/	Yellowstone National Park	WY	82190	307-344-7381	344-2323

— Events —

	Phone
4th of July Celebration (July 4)	307-733-3316
Anheuser-Busch Spring Snow Carnival (mid-late March)	800-827-4433
Celebrity Winter Extravaganza (early March)	307-734-2878
Don MacLeod Cookout (mid-May)	307-733-9605
Grand Teton Music Festival Family Picnic & Concert (July 4)	307-733-1128
Grand Teton Music Festival Season (late June-late August)	307-733-1128
International Rocky Mountain Stage Stop Sled Dog Race (late January-mid-February)	307-734-1163
Jackson Hole Alliance Silent Art & Antique Auction (mid-February-early March)	307-733-9417
Jackson Hole Fall Arts Festival (mid-September)	307-733-3316
Jackson Hole Wildlife Film Festival (late September)	307-733-7016
Mangy Moose Micro-Brew Festival (mid-July)	307-733-4913
Mountain Artists' Rendezvous Art Show (mid-July & late August)	307-733-8792
Old West Days (late May)	307-733-3316
Rockin the Tetons Festival (mid-July)	800-827-4433
Sean Nurse Memorial Ski Race (February)	307-733-6433
Shriner's All-American Cutter Races (mid-February)	307-733-8853
Ski School Kids Carnival (mid-late March)	307-733-4826
Targhee Bluegrass Festival (mid-August)	800-827-4433
Teton County Fair (late July-early August)	307-733-5289
Teton Valley Balloon Festival (early July)	208-354-2500
Town Downhill (early March)	307-733-6433
Town Square Shoot-Out (late May-early September)	307-733-3316
World Championship Snowmobile Hillclimb (late March)	307-734-9653

Canadian Cities

Canada

NUNAVUT
Baffin Bay
Beaufort Sea
NORTHWEST TERRITORIES
YUKON
Great Bear Lake
NORTHWEST TERRITORIES
NUNAVUT
Great Slave Lake
Lake Athabasca
BRITISH COLUMBIA
ALBERTA
MANITOBA
Pacific Ocean
Edmonton
SASKATCHEWAN
Lake Winnipeg
Vancouver
Calgary
Lake Winnipegosis
Winnipeg
1:00
Pacific Time Zone
2:00
Mountain Time Zone
3:00
Central Time Zone

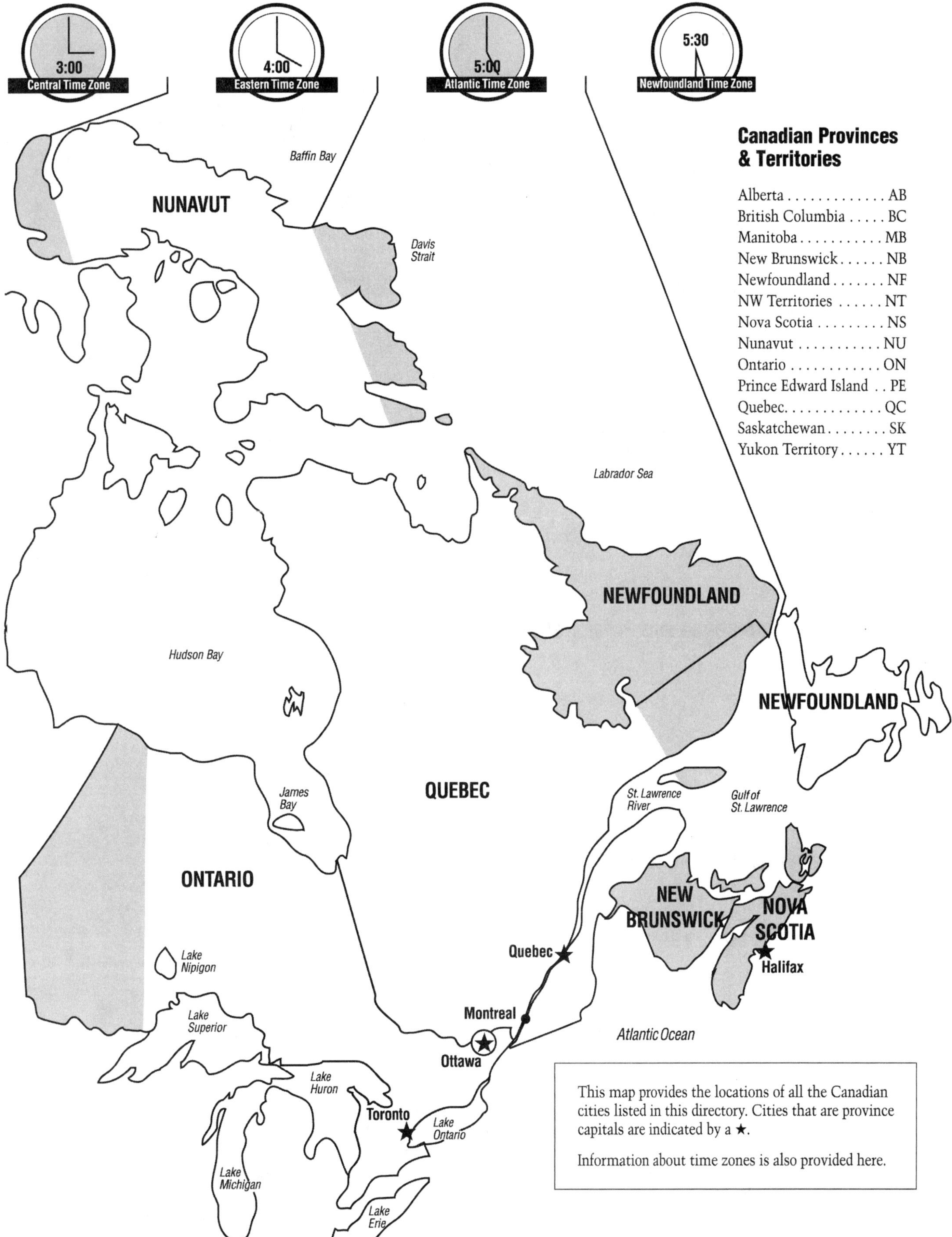
3:00
Central Time Zone
4:00
Eastern Time Zone
5:00
Atlantic Time Zone
5:30
Newfoundland Time Zone
Canadian Provinces & Territories
Alberta . . . . AB
British Columbia . . . . . BC
Manitoba . . . . MB
New Brunswick . . . . . . NB
Newfoundland . . . . NF
NW Territories . . . . . . NT
Nova Scotia . . . . NS
Nunavut . . . . NU
Ontario . . . . ON
Prince Edward Island . . PE
Quebec. . . . . QC
Saskatchewan . . . . SK
Yukon Territory . . . . . . YT
Baffin Bay
NUNAVUT
Davis Strait
Labrador Sea
NEWFOUNDLAND
Hudson Bay
NEWFOUNDLAND
QUEBEC
James Bay
St. Lawrence River
Gulf of St. Lawrence
ONTARIO
NEW BRUNSWICK
NOVA SCOTIA
Halifax
Quebec
Lake Nipigon
Montreal
Lake Superior
Ottawa
Atlantic Ocean
Lake Huron
Toronto
Lake Ontario
Lake Michigan
Lake Erie
This map provides the locations of all the Canadian cities listed in this directory. Cities that are province capitals are indicated by a ★.
Information about time zones is also provided here.

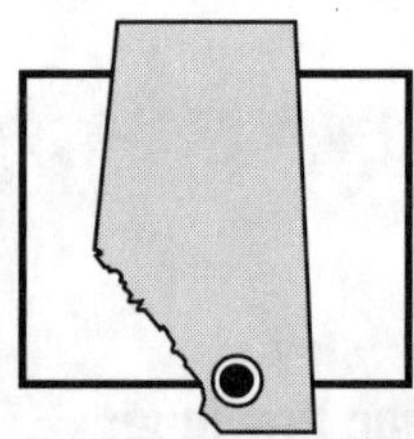

Calgary

Located in the heart of Alberta in the foothills of the Canadian Rocky Mountains, Calgary is a short distance from many natural attractions such as Banff National Park, Lake Louise, and Jasper National Park. In addition, the Royal Tyrrell Museum of Palaeontology, which houses the world's largest display of dinosaur skeletons, is within an hour's drive of Calgary. Calgary was the site of the 1988 Winter Olympic Games, and Canada Olympic Park offers the opportunity for visitors to tour the facility, take bobsled rides, and visit the Olympic Hall of Fame and Museum (North America's largest Olympic Museum). Excellent views of downtown Calgary and of the Canadian Rockies can be seen from Calgary Tower, which features an observation deck 626 feet above the city. Heritage Park, Canada's largest living historical village, explores prairie pioneer life in western Canada prior to 1915; and Fort Calgary Historic Park has a reconstruction of the 1875 Fort Calgary where the "Mounties" were located to bring law and order to the city. Visitors to Fort Calgary can learn about the settlement and its people through exhibits and interactive interpretation. Calgary is also noted for its annual Calgary Stampede, a ten-day festival that includes parades, rodeos, square dancing, and other western entertainment.

Population 768,082
Area (Land) .... 276.8 sq mi
Elevation .... 3,439 ft
Latitude .... 51-03-00 N
Longitude .... 114-04-59 W
Time Zone .... MST
Area Code/s 403

— Average Temperatures and Precipitation —

TEMPERATURES

	Jan	Feb	Mar	Apr	May	Jun	Jul	Aug	Sep	Oct	Nov	Dec
High	24	28	37	49	63	69	76	74	64	54	38	29
Low	2	11	14	27	36	43	47	45	37	29	17	6

PRECIPITATION

	Jan	Feb	Mar	Apr	May	Jun	Jul	Aug	Sep	Oct	Nov	Dec
Inches	0.0	0.0	0.0	0.4	1.6	3.5	2.6	2.2	1.3	0.2	0.0	0.0

— Important Phone Numbers —

	Phone
Alberta Motor Assn	403-240-5300
American Express Travel	403-261-5982
Cascade Printing	403-250-2202
Emergency	911
Medical Referral	403-531-8080
Poison Control Center	403-670-1414
Road Conditions	403-246-5853

— Information Sources —

				Phone	Fax
Better Business Bureau Serving Southern Alberta 7330 Fisher St SE Suite 350 *Web:* www.southernalbertabbb.ab.ca ■ *E-mail:* complain@telusplanet.net	Calgary	AB	T2H2H8	403-531-8780	640-2514
Calgary Chamber of Commerce 517 Centre St S *Web:* www.chamber.calgary.ab.ca ■ *E-mail:* chinfo@chamber.calgary.ab.ca	Calgary	AB	T2G2C4	403-750-0400	266-3413
Calgary City Hall 800 Macleod Trail SE *Web:* www.gov.calgary.ab.ca ■ *E-mail:* ccweb@gov.calgary.ab.ca	Calgary	AB	T2G2M3	403-268-2111	
Calgary Convention & Visitors Bureau 237 8th Ave SE Suite 200 *TF:* 800-661-1678 ■ *Web:* www.visitor.calgary.ab.ca ■ *E-mail:* destination@visitor.calgary.ab.ca	Calgary	AB	T2G0K8	403-263-8510	262-3809
Calgary Convention Centre 120 9th Ave SE	Calgary	AB	T2G0P3	403-261-8500	261-8510
Calgary Downtown Assn 304 8th Ave SW Suite 720 *Web:* www.calgarydowntown.com	Calgary	AB	T2P1C2	403-266-5300	265-1932
Calgary Economic Development Authority 639 5th Ave SW Suite 300 *Web:* www.ceda.calgary.ab.ca ■ *E-mail:* askus@ceda.calgary.ab.ca	Calgary	AB	T2P0M9	403-221-7821	221-7837
Calgary Mayor 700 Macleod Trail SE 2nd Fl. *Web:* www.gov.calgary.ab.ca ■ *E-mail:* mayorweb@gov.calgary.ab.ca	Calgary	AB	T2G2M3	403-268-5622	268-8130
Castell WR Central Library 616 Macleod Trail SE *Web:* public-library.calgary.ab.ca ■ *E-mail:* DearLibrary@public-library.calgary.ab.ca	Calgary	AB	T2G2M2	403-260-2600	237-5393
Euro-Canadian Cultural Centre 3127 Bowwood Dr NW	Calgary	AB	T3B2E7	403-288-2255	286-8457

On-Line Resources

About.com Guide to Calgary .... calgary.about.com/local/calgary
Calgary Connection .... www.incalgary.com
Calgary Is .... www.calgaryis.com
Calgary Menus .... www.calgarymenus.com
City Knowledge Calgary .... www.cityknowledge.com/canada_ab_calgary.htm
CRS Encyclopedia Calgary .... www.relocatecanada.com/calgary/
Destination Calgary .... www.atfx.com/calgary/
Discover Calgary .... www.discovercalgary.com
FFWD Online News & Entertainment Weekly .... www.greatwest.ca/ffwd/
Restaurant.ca Calgary .... www.restaurant.ca/cal/
Rough Guide Travel Calgary travel.roughguides.com/content/5451/index.htm

— Transportation Services —

AIRPORTS

■ **Calgary International Airport (YYC)** — *Phone*

9 miles NE of downtown (approx 20 minutes) 403-735-1200
Web: www.calgaryairport.com

Airport Transportation

	Phone
Checker Cabs $22 fare to downtown	403-299-9999
Airport Direct $10 fare to downtown	403-291-1991
Calgary Transit $1.60 fare to downtown	403-262-1000

Commercial Airlines

	Phone
Air Canada	800-776-3000
Air Transat	877-872-6728
Alaska	800-426-0333
American	800-433-7300
British Airways	800-247-9297
Canada 3000	877-359-2263
Canadian Air	800-426-7000
Continental	800-525-0280
Delta	800-221-1212
Japan	800-525-3663
KLM	800-374-7747
Lufthansa	800-645-3880
Martinair Holland	800-627-8462
Northwest	800-225-2525
Royal Airlines	800-667-7692
United	800-241-6522
WestJet	800-538-5696

Charter Airlines

	Phone
Air BC	888-247-2262
Alta Flights	403-225-2882
North American Airlines	403-275-7700
Quickway Air Services Inc	403-803-9344
SunWest International Aviation Services	403-275-8121

CAR RENTALS

	Phone
Alamo	403-543-3985
Avis	403-269-6166
Budget	403-226-0000
Discount	403-299-1222
Hertz	800-263-0600
National	403-221-1692
Rent-A-Wreck	403-287-9703
Thrifty	403-262-4400

LIMO/TAXI

	Phone
Airport Express Service	403-509-4799
Alberta Limousine Service	403-295-1085
Ambassador Limousine	403-299-4910
Calgary Cab	403-777-2222
Lawson's Cary Limousine Service	403-291-2566
Limocab	403-285-5555
Mayfair Taxi	403-255-6555
White Hatter Limousine	403-270-3486
Yellow Cab	403-974-1111

Calgary (Cont'd)

MASS TRANSIT

Phone

C-Train Light Rail Transit $1.60 base fare 403-262-1000
Calgary Transit $1.60 base fare 403-262-1000

RAIL/BUS

Phone

Greyhound Canada Bus Station 877 Greyhound Way SW Calgary AB T3C3V8 403-260-0877
TF: 800-661-8747

— Accommodations —

HOTEL RESERVATION SERVICES

Phone Fax

Good Earth Travel Adventures Reservations 403-678-9358 678-9384
TF: 888-979-9797 ■ *Web:* www.goodearthtravel.com
■ *E-mail:* info@goodearthtravel.com

HOTELS, MOTELS, RESORTS

Phone Fax

Ambassador Motor Inn 802 16th Ave NE Calgary AB T2E1K8 403-276-2271 277-2499
TF: 800-661-1447
Best Western Airport Inn 1947 18th Ave NE Calgary AB T2E7T8 403-250-5015 250-5019
TF: 800-528-1234
Best Western Hospitality Inn
135 Southland Dr SE Calgary AB T2J5X5 403-278-5050 278-5050
TF: 800-528-1234
Best Western Port O'Call Inn
1935 McKnight Blvd NE Calgary AB T2E6V4 403-291-4600 250-6827
TF: 800-661-1161
Best Western Suites Downtown
1330 8th St SW Calgary AB T2R1B6 403-228-6900 228-5535
TF: 800-981-2555
Best Western Village Park Inn
1804 Crowchild Trail NW Calgary AB T2M3Y7 403-289-0241 289-4645
TF: 888-774-7716 ■ *E-mail:* bwvpi@telusplanet.net
Blackfoot Inn 5940 Blackfoot Trail SE Calgary AB T2H2B5 403-252-2253 252-3574
TF: 800-661-1151 ■ *Web:* www.blackfootinn.com
Budget Host Motor Inn 4420 16th Ave NW Calgary AB T3B0M4 403-288-7115 286-4899
TF: 800-661-3772
■ *Web:* www.budgethost.com/text/CalgaryAlberta.html
■ *E-mail:* mail@budgethost.com
Calgary Nite Inn 4510 Macleod Trail S Calgary AB T2G0A4 403-243-1700 243-4719
TF: 888-648-3466
Canadian Pacific Calgary Airport Hotel
2001 Airport Rd NE Calgary AB T2E6Z8 403-291-2600 250-8722
TF: 800-441-1414
Castleton Suites 9600 Southland Cir SW Calgary AB T2V5A1 403-640-3900 253-4447
TF: 888-227-8534
Cedar Ridge Motel 5307 Macleod Trail S Calgary AB T2H0J3 403-258-1064 255-2731
TF: 800-268-6128
Coast Plaza Hotel 1316 33rd St NE Calgary AB T2A6B6 403-248-8888 248-0749
TF: 800-663-1144
Comfort Inn 2363 Banff Trail NW Calgary AB T2M4L2 403-289-2581 284-3897
TF: 800-228-5150
Days Inn 2369 Banff Trail NW Calgary AB T2M4L2 403-289-5571 282-9305
TF: 800-325-2525
Delta Bow Valley 209 4th Ave SE Calgary AB T2G0C6 403-266-1980 266-0007
TF: 800-877-1133 ■ *Web:* www.deltahotels.com/hotels.php3?action=show&hotelid=16
Econo Lodge Banff Trail 2231 Banff Trail NW Calgary AB T2M4L2 403-289-1921 282-2149
TF: 800-917-7779
Econo Lodge Motel Village
2440 16th Ave NW Calgary AB T2M0M5 403-289-2561 282-9713
TF: 800-553-2666
Elbow River Inn 1919 Macleod Trail SE Calgary AB T2G4S1 403-269-6771 237-5181
TF: 800-661-1463 ■ *Web:* www.albertahotels.ab.ca/ElbowRiver/
ExecSuites Luxury Travel Apartments
702 3rd Ave SW Calgary AB T2P3B4 403-294-5800 294-5959
TF: 800-667-4980 ■ *Web:* www.execsuite.ca
Flamingo Motor Hotel 7505 Macleod Trail S Calgary AB T2H0L8 403-252-4401 252-2780
TF: 888-559-0559
Glenmore Inn 2720 Glenmore Trail SE Calgary AB T2C2E6 403-279-8611 236-8035
TF: 800-661-3163
Hampton Inn & Suites 2420 37th Ave NE Calgary AB T2E8S6 403-250-4667 250-5788
TF: 800-426-7866
Holiday Inn 4206 Macleod Trail S Calgary AB T2G2R7 403-287-2700 243-4721
TF: 800-661-1889
Holiday Inn Calgary Airport
1250 McKinnon Dr NE Calgary AB T2E7T7 403-230-1999 277-2623
TF: 800-465-4329
Holiday Inn Downtown 119 12th Ave SW Calgary AB T2R0G8 403-266-4611 237-0978
TF: 800-661-9378
Holiday Inn Express 2227 Banff Trail NW Calgary AB T2M4L2 403-289-6600 289-6767
TF: 800-465-4329
International Hotel of Calgary
220 4th Ave SW Calgary AB T2P0H5 403-265-9600 265-6949
TF: 800-223-0888
Lord Nelson Inn 1020 8th Ave SW Calgary AB T2P1J2 403-269-8262 269-4868
TF: 800-661-6017
Marriott Hotel Calgary 110 9th Ave SE Calgary AB T2G5A6 403-266-7331 262-8442
TF: 800-228-9290 ■ *Web:* marriotthotels.com/YYCDT
Olympic Corporate Suites
400 Village Gardens SW Calgary AB T3H2L1 403-246-1040 246-3284
TF: 800-791-8788
Palliser Hotel 133 9th Ave SW Calgary AB T2P2M3 403-262-1234 260-1207
TF: 800-441-1414
Pointe Inn 1808 19th St NE Calgary AB T2E4Y3 403-291-4681 291-4576
TF: 800-661-8164 ■ *Web:* www.albertahotels.ab.ca/PointeInn/
Prince Royal Suites Hotel 618 5th Ave SW Calgary AB T2P0M7 403-263-0520 262-9991
TF: 800-661-1592 ■ *Web:* www.princeroyal.com
Quality Hotel 3828 Macleod Trail S Calgary AB T2G2R2 403-243-5531 243-6962
TF: 800-361-3422
Quality Inn Airport 4804 Edmonton Trail NE Calgary AB T2E3V8 403-276-3391 230-7267
TF: 800-221-2222
Quality Inn Motel Village
2359 Banff Trail NW Calgary AB T2M4L2 403-289-1973 282-1241
TF: 800-661-4667
Ramada Crowchild Inn
5353 Crowchild Trail NW Calgary AB T3A1W9 403-288-5353 286-8966
TF: 800-735-7502 ■ *Web:* www.crowchildinn.com
■ *E-mail:* info@crowchildinn.com
Ramada Hotel Downtown 708 8th Ave SW Calgary AB T2P1H2 403-263-7600 237-6127
TF: 800-272-6232
Regency Suites 610 4th Ave SW Calgary AB T2P0K1 403-231-1000 231-1012
TF: 800-468-4044
Royal Wayne Motor Inn 2416 16th Ave NW Calgary AB T2M0M5 403-289-6651 289-6709
TF: 800-834-8423
Sandman Hotel Downtown 888 7th Ave SW Calgary AB T2P3J3 403-237-8626 290-1238
TF: 800-726-3626 ■ *Web:* www.sandman.ca/calgary.html
Sheraton Cavalier Hotel 2620 32nd Ave NE Calgary AB T1Y6B8 403-291-0107 291-2834
TF: 800-325-3535
Sunbeam Executive Suites
1335 12th Ave SW Calgary AB T3C3P7 403-244-0757 228-3386
Super 8 Motel 1904 Crowchild Trail NW Calgary AB T2M3Y7 403-289-9211 282-7824
TF: 800-800-8000
Super 8 Motel Calgary Airport
3030 Barlow Trail NE Calgary AB T1Y1A2 403-291-9888 291-3000
TF: 800-800-8000
Traveller's Inn 4611 16th Ave NW Calgary AB T3B0M7 403-247-1388 247-4220
Travelodge North 2304 16th Ave NW Calgary AB T2M0M5 403-289-0211 289-6924
TF: 800-578-7878
Travelodge South 7012 Macleod Trail S Calgary AB T2H0L3 403-253-1111 253-2879
TF: 800-578-7878
Westgate Hotel 3440 Bow Trail SW Calgary AB T3C2E6 403-249-3181 240-2348
TF: 800-661-1660
Westin Hotel Calgary 320 4th Ave SW Calgary AB T2P2S6 403-266-1611 233-7471
TF: 800-937-8461

— Restaurants —

Phone

4th Street Rose Restaurant (International) 2116 4th St SW Calgary AB T2S1W7 403-228-5377
Billy MacIntyre's Cattle Co (Steak)
3630 Brentwood Rd NW Suite 5 Calgary AB T2L1K8 403-282-6614
Buon Giorno Ristorante Italiano (Italian) 823 17th Ave SW Calgary AB T2T0A1 403-244-5522
Buzzards Cowboy Cuisine (Barbecue) 140 10th Ave SW Calgary AB T2R0A3 403-264-6959
Caesar's Steak House (Steak/Seafood) 512 4th Ave SW Calgary AB T2P0J6 403-264-1222
Cannery Row (Cajun/Creole) 317 10th Ave SW Calgary AB T2R0A5 403-269-8889
Chestermere Landing (International) 109 E Chestermere Dr Calgary AB T1X1A1 403-248-4343
Chianti Cafe & Restaurant (Italian) 1438 17th Ave SW Calgary AB T2T0C8 403-229-1600
China Rose Restaurant (Chinese) 228 28th St SE Calgary AB T2A6J9 403-248-2711
Cross House Garden Cafe (Continental) 1240 8th Ave SE Calgary AB T2G0M7 403-531-2767
Da Guido Ristorante (Italian) 2001 Centre St N Calgary AB T2E2S9 403-276-1365
Web: www.goldguide.com/daguido
Dante's Cafe & Wine Bar (Continental)
513 8th Ave SW Suite 210 Calgary AB T2P1G3 403-237-5787
Deane House Restaurant (International) 806 9th Ave SE Calgary AB T2P2M5 403-269-7747
Divino Bistro (California) 817 1st St SW Calgary AB T2P7N2 403-263-5869
Drinkwaters (Steak) 237 8th Ave SE Calgary AB T2G5C3 403-264-9494
Earl's Restaurant (International) 315 8th Ave SW Calgary AB T2P4K1 403-265-3275
Ed's Restaurant (North American) 292 17th Ave SE Calgary AB T2G1H4 403-262-3500
Ercole Ristorante Italiano (Italian) 202 16th Ave NE Calgary AB T2E1J9 403-230-4447

Calgary — Restaurants (Cont'd)

	City	Prov	Postal	Phone
Hard Rock Cafe (American) 101 Barclay Parade SW	Calgary	AB	T2P4R3	403-263-7625
Home Food Inn Restaurant (Chinese) 5222 Macleod Trail SW	Calgary	AB	T2H0J2	403-259-8585
Inn on Lake Bonivista (Continental) 747 Lake Bonivista Dr SE	Calgary	AB	T2J0N2	403-271-6711
Japanese Village Restaurant (Japanese) 302 4th Ave SW	Calgary	AB	T2P0H7	403-262-2738
Keg Steakhouse & Bar (Steak/Seafood) 7104 Macleod Trail S	Calgary	AB	T2H0L3	403-253-2534
La Caille on the Bow Restaurant (Continental) 100 La Caille Pl	Calgary	AB	T2P3R4	403-262-5554
La Chaumiere Restaurant (French) 139 17th Ave SW	Calgary	AB	T2G1H3	403-228-5690
Luciano's (Italian) 9223 Macleod Trail S	Calgary	AB	T2H0M2	403-253-4266
Mescalero (Southwest) 1315 1st St SW	Calgary	AB	T2R0V5	403-266-3339
Mother Tucker's Food Experience (North American) 345 10th Ave SW	Calgary	AB	T2R0A5	403-262-5541
Pied Pickle Restaurant (North American) 250 6th Ave SW	Calgary	AB	T2P2H7	403-263-1222
Quincy's on Seventh (Steak) 609 7th Ave SW	Calgary	AB	T2P0Y9	403-264-1000
Ranch House Dining Lodge (North American) 144th Ave & Simon's Valley Rd NW	Calgary	AB	T2M4L4	403-274-4574
Regency Palace Restaurant (Chinese) 328 Centre St SE Suite 335	Calgary	AB	T2G4X6	403-777-2288
River Cafe (North American) 200 8th Ave SE	Calgary	AB	T2G0K7	403-261-7670
Santa Fe Grill (Southwest) 9250 Macleod Trail S	Calgary	AB	T2J0P5	403-253-9096
Scampy's Seafood Restaurant (Seafood) 2500 4th St SW	Calgary	AB	T2S1X6	403-228-9500
Senor Frogs (Mexican) 739 2nd Ave SW	Calgary	AB	T2P0E4	403-264-5100
Silver Dragon Restaurant (Chinese) 106 3rd Ave SE	Calgary	AB	T2G0B6	403-264-5326
Singapore Sam's (Chinese) 555 11th Ave SW Suite 101	Calgary	AB	T2R1P6	403-234-8088
Smuggler's Inn (Steak/Seafood) 6920 Macleod Trail S *Web:* www.smugglers-inn.com	Calgary	AB	T2H0L3	403-253-5355
Sukiyaki House (Japanese) 517 10th Ave SW	Calgary	AB	T2R0A8	403-263-3003
Teatro (Italian) 200 8th Ave SE	Calgary	AB	T2G0K7	403-290-1012
Unicorn Restaurant & Pub (English) 304 8th Ave SW	Calgary	AB	T2P1C2	403-233-2666
Wine Gallery & Mona's Kitchen (California) 315 8th Ave SW Bankers Hall	Calgary	AB	T2P4J5	403-290-1091

— Goods and Services —

SHOPPING

	City	Prov	Postal	Phone	Fax
4th Street District 4th St SW betw 17th Ave & Elbow Dr	Calgary	AB	T2S1V8	403-229-0902	229-0920
Calgary Eaton Centre 333 7th Ave SW Suite 2400	Calgary	AB	T2P2Z1	403-221-0600	266-1290
Chinook Centre 6455 Macleod Trail S *Web:* www.chinookcentre.com ■ *E-mail:* info@chinookcentre.com	Calgary	AB	T2H0K9	403-255-0613	258-1004
Crossroads Market 2222 16th Ave NE	Calgary	AB	T2E1L5	403-291-5208	291-0356
Deerfoot Mall 901 64th Ave NE	Calgary	AB	T2E7P4	403-274-7024	274-2459
Dragon City 328 Centre St SE	Calgary	AB	T2G4X6	403-261-9651	261-2708
Eau Claire Market 200 Barclay Parade SW *Web:* www.eauclairemarket.com	Calgary	AB	T2P4R5	403-264-6450	264-9851
Inglewood BRZ 1230 9th Ave SE	Calgary	AB	T2G0T1	403-266-6962	263-3009
Kensington BRZ Kensington Rd & 10th St NW	Calgary	AB	T2N1V5	403-283-4810	270-0330
North Hill Shopping Centre 1632 14th Ave NW	Calgary	AB	T2N1M7	403-289-2516	289-0962
Uptown 17-The Avenue 17th Ave SW betw 2nd St & 14th St SW *Web:* www.uptown17.com	Calgary	AB	T2T0A3	403-245-1703	245-1733

BANKS

	City	Prov	Postal	Phone	Fax
Bank of Montreal 340 7th Ave SW	Calgary	AB	T2P0X4	403-234-3620	503-7686
Canada Trust 421 7th Ave SW 9th Fl *TF:* 800-668-8888 ■ *Web:* www.canadatrust.com	Calgary	AB	T2P4K9	403-294-3333	294-3289
Canadian Western Bank 606 4th St SW *Web:* www.cwbank.com	Calgary	AB	T2P1T1	403-262-8700	262-4899
Citizens Trust 506 6th St SW *Web:* www.citizenstrust.com	Calgary	AB	T2P0M9	403-266-7321	262-8675
Hong Kong Bank of Canada 777 8th Ave SW *Web:* www.hkbc.ca	Calgary	AB	T2P3R5	403-261-8910	263-4930
Royal Bank 339 8th Ave SW *TF:* 800-769-2511 ■ *Web:* www.royalbank.com	Calgary	AB	T2P1C4	403-292-3311	292-3766
Toronto-Dominion Bank 902 8th Ave SW *TF:* 800-983-2265 ■ *Web:* www.tdbank.ca	Calgary	AB	T2P1H8	403-292-1440	292-2903

BUSINESS SERVICES

	Phone
Adams & Bradson Staffing Services	403-269-2205
Canada Post	403-274-3803
City Wide Staffing Services	403-273-0554
DHL International Express	403-250-1512
Elite Fleet Courier	403-263-1247
Federal Express	800-463-3339
Kelly Services	403-269-2586
Kinko's	403-258-0086
Mailboxes Etc	403-274-1919
Manpower Temporary Services	403-269-6936
Olsten Staffing Services	403-237-7296
ProTemps	403-264-9000
Rodeo Express Delivery	403-250-8610
Temporarily Yours	403-269-6786
Topline Quality Printing	403-250-1026
UPS	800-742-5877

— Media —

PUBLICATIONS

	City	Prov	Postal	Phone	Fax
Calgary Herald† PO Box 2400 Stn M *Web:* www.calgaryherald.com	Calgary	AB	T2P0W8	403-235-7100	235-8695
Calgary Sun† 2615 12th St NE *Web:* www.canoe.ca/CalgarySun/	Calgary	AB	T2E7W9	403-250-4200	250-4257
Where Calgary Magazine 125 9th Ave SE Suite 250 *Web:* www.wherecalgary.com	Calgary	AB	T2G0P6	403-299-1888	299-1899

†Daily newspapers

TELEVISION

	City	Prov	Postal	Phone	Fax
CBRT-TV Ch 9 (CBC) PO Box 2640 *Web:* cbc.ca	Calgary	AB	T2P2M7	403-521-6000	521-6079
CFCN-TV Ch 3 (CTV) PO Box 7060 Stn E *Web:* www.cfcn.ca ■ *E-mail:* cfcnpromo@baton.com	Calgary	AB	T3C3L9	403-240-5600	240-5689
CICT-TV Ch 7 (Ind) 222 23rd St NE *Web:* www.cict.com	Calgary	AB	T2E7N2	403-235-7709	248-0252
CKAL-TV Ch 5 (Ind) 535 7th Ave SW *Web:* www.a-channel.com ■ *E-mail:* calgaryfeedback@a-channel.com	Calgary	AB	T2P0Y4	403-508-2222	508-2224

RADIO

	City	Prov	Postal	Phone	Fax
CBR-AM 1010 kHz (Misc) 1724 Westmount Blvd NW	Calgary	AB	T2P2M7	403-521-6197	521-6262
CBR-FM 102.1 MHz (Clas) 1724 Westmount Blvd NW	Calgary	AB	T2P2M7	403-521-6000	521-6262
CFAC-AM 960 kHz (Ctry) 3320 17th Ave SW	Calgary	AB	T3E6X6	403-246-9696	246-6660
CFFR-AM 660 kHz (Oldies) 2723 37th Ave NE	Calgary	AB	T1Y5R8	403-291-0000	291-5342
CHFM-FM 95.9 MHz (AC) 3320 17th Ave SW *Web:* www.chfm.com	Calgary	AB	T3E6X6	403-246-9696	246-6660
CHQR-AM 770 kHz (N/T) 125 9th Ave SE Suite 1900 *Web:* www.qr77.com	Calgary	AB	T2G0P6	403-233-0770	266-4040
CJAY-FM 92.1 MHz (CR) PO Box 2750 Stn M *Web:* www.cjay92.com/cjay.htm	Calgary	AB	T2P4P8	403-240-5850	240-5801
CJSW-FM 90.9 MHz (Alt) 2500 University Dr NW MacEwan Hall Rm 127 *Web:* www.cjsw.com	Calgary	AB	T2N1N4	403-220-3902	289-8212
CKIK-FM 107.3 MHz (CHR) 125 9th Ave SE Suite 1900	Calgary	AB	T2G0P6	403-264-0107	264-3291
CKIS-FM 96.9 MHz (AC) 2723 37th Ave NE	Calgary	AB	T1Y5R8	403-291-9695	291-5342
CKMX-AM 1060 kHz (Oldies) PO Box 2750 Stn M	Calgary	AB	T2P4P8	403-240-5800	240-5801
CKRY-FM 105.1 MHz (Ctry) 630 3rd Ave SW Suite 105 *Web:* www.country105.com	Calgary	AB	T2P4L4	403-716-2105	716-2111
CKUA-FM 93.7 MHz (Misc) 205 8th Ave SE *Web:* www.ckua.org ■ *E-mail:* ckua@oanet.com	Calgary	AB	T2G0K9	403-262-6698	262-3645

— Colleges/Universities —

	City	Prov	Postal	Phone	Fax
Alberta Bible College 635 Northmount Dr NW *Web:* www.abc-ca.org ■ *E-mail:* abc@abc-ca.org	Calgary	AB	T2K3J6	403-282-2994	282-3084
Alberta College Of Art & Design 1407 14th Ave NW *TF:* 800-251-8290 ■ *Web:* www.acad.ab.ca ■ *E-mail:* admissions@acad.ab.ca	Calgary	AB	T2N4R3	403-284-7600	289-6682
Bow Valley College 332 6th Ave SE *Web:* www.bowvalleyc.ab.ca ■ *E-mail:* info@bowvalleyc.ab.ca	Calgary	AB	T2G4S6	403-297-4040	297-4887

Calgary — Colleges/Universities (Cont'd)

	City	Prov	Postal	Phone	Fax
Canadian Nazarene College 833 4th Ave SW *Web:* www.cnaz.ab.ca	Calgary	AB	T2P3T5	403-571-2550	571-2556
Columbia College 802 Manning Rd NE *Web:* www.telusplanet.net/public/columbia/	Calgary	AB	T2E7N8	403-235-9300	272-3805
DeVRY Institute of Technology 2700 3rd Ave SE *TF:* 800-363-5558 ■ *Web:* www.devry.ca	Calgary	AB	T2A7W4	403-235-3450	207-6226
Mount Royal College 4825 Richard Rd SW *Web:* www.mtroyal.ab.ca	Calgary	AB	T3E6K6	403-240-6111	240-5506
Rocky Mountain College 4039 Brentwood Rd NW *Web:* www.rockymc.edu	Calgary	AB	T2L1L1	403-284-5100	220-9567
Rundle College 2634 12th Ave NW	Calgary	AB	T2N1K6	403-282-8411	282-4460
University of Calgary 2500 University Dr NW *Web:* www.ucalgary.ca	Calgary	AB	T2N1N4	403-220-5110	282-7298

— Hospitals —

	City	Prov	Postal	Phone	Fax
Alberta Children's Hospital 1820 Richmond Rd SW *Web:* xweb.crha-health.ab.ca/sites/ach.htm	Calgary	AB	T2T5C7	403-229-7211	229-7214
Calgary General Hospital 3500 26th Ave NE Peter Lougheed Centre	Calgary	AB	T1Y6J4	403-291-8555	291-8878
Colonel Belcher Hospital 1213 4th St SW *Web:* xweb.crha-health.ab.ca/sites/cb.htm	Calgary	AB	T2R0X7	403-541-3600	237-8251
Foothills Hospital 1403 29th St NW	Calgary	AB	T2N2T9	403-670-1110	670-1044
Foothills Medical Center 1403 29th St NW	Calgary	AB	T2N2T9	403-670-1110	670-2400
Lougheed Peter General Hospital 3500 26th Ave NE	Calgary	AB	T1Y6J4	403-291-8555	291-8766
Rockyview General Hospital 7007 14th St SW	Calgary	AB	T2V1P9	403-541-3000	541-1242

— Attractions —

	City	Prov	Postal	Phone	Fax
Aero Space Museum of Calgary 4629 McCall Way NE *Web:* www.asmac.ab.ca ■ *E-mail:* aild@lexicom.ab.ca	Calgary	AB	T2E8A5	403-250-3752	250-8399
Alberta Ballet 141 18th Ave SW	Calgary	AB	T2S0B8	403-245-4222	245-6573
Alberta Sports Hall of Fame & Museum 30 Riverview Pk *Web:* sportshallfame.reddeer.net	Red Deer	AB	T4N1E3	403-341-8614	341-8619
Alberta Theatre Projects 220 9th Ave SE *Web:* www.atplive.com ■ *E-mail:* askatp@atplive.com	Calgary	AB	T2G5C4	403-294-7475	294-7493
Banff Mount Norquay PO Box 219 Suite 7000 *Web:* www.banffnorquay.com	Banff	AB	T0L0C0	403-762-4421	762-8133
Banff National Park PO Box 900 *TF:* 800-748-7276 ■ *Web:* www.worldweb.com/ParksCanada-Banff/ ■ *E-mail:* banff_vrc@pch.gc.ca	Banff	AB	T0L0C0	403-762-1550	762-1551
Big Rock Brewery 5555 76th Ave SE *TF:* 800-242-3107 ■ *Web:* www.bigrockbeer.com ■ *E-mail:* ale@bigrockbeer.com	Calgary	AB	T2C4L8	403-720-3239	236-7523
Calgary Centre for Performing Arts 205 8th Ave SE *Web:* www.ffa.ucalgary.ca/ccpa/ ■ *E-mail:* ccpa@cadvision.com	Calgary	AB	T2G0K9	403-294-7455	294-7457
Calgary Chinese Cultural Centre 197 1st St SW	Calgary	AB	T2P4M4	403-262-5071	232-6387
Calgary Opera 237 8th Ave SE Suite 601	Calgary	AB	T2G5C3	403-262-7286	263-5428
Calgary Philharmonic Orchestra 205 8th Ave SE Jack Singer Concert Hall *Web:* www.htn.com/cpo/	Calgary	AB	T2G0K9	403-571-0270	294-7424
Calgary Police Service Interpretive Centre 316 7th Ave SE 2nd Fl	Calgary	AB	T2G4Z1	403-268-4566	974-0508
Calgary Science Centre 701 11th St SW *Web:* www.calgaryscience.ca ■ *E-mail:* discover@calgaryscience.ca	Calgary	AB	T2P2C4	403-221-3700	237-0186
Calgary Soccer Centre 7000 48th St SE *Web:* www.calgarysc.com/en	Calgary	AB	T2C4E1	403-279-8445	279-8796
Calgary Stampede 1410 Olympic Way SE Stampede Pk *TF:* 800-661-1260 ■ *Web:* www.calgary-stampede.ab.ca	Calgary	AB	T2G2W1	403-261-0101	265-7197
Calgary Tower 101 9th Ave SW *Web:* www.calgarytower.com	Calgary	AB	T2P1J9	403-266-7171	266-7230
Calgary Zoo Botanical Garden & Prehistoric Park 1300 Zoo Rd NE *Web:* www.calgaryzoo.ab.ca	Calgary	AB	T2M4R8	403-232-9300	237-7582
Canada Olympic Park 88 Canada Olympic Rd SW *Web:* www.coda.ab.ca	Calgary	AB	T3B5R5	403-247-5452	286-7213
Canadian Country Music Hall Of Fame PO Box 1447 Station T Stampede Pk	Calgary	AB	T2H2H7	403-290-0702	290-0704
Canadian Rockies Hot Springs 101 Mountain Ave	Banff	AB	T0L0C0	403-678-0966	760-1347
Canadian Venture Exchange 300 5th Ave SW 10th Fl *Web:* www.cdnx.ca ■ *E-mail:* information@cdnx.ca	Calgary	AB	T2P3C4	403-974-7400	237-0450
Devonian Gardens 317 7th Ave SW	Calgary	AB	T2P2Y9	403-268-3830	221-4581
Dragon City 328 Centre St SE	Calgary	AB	T2G4X6	403-261-9651	261-2708
Eau Claire Market 200 Barclay Parade SW *Web:* www.eauclairemarket.com	Calgary	AB	T2P4R5	403-264-6450	264-9851
Energeum Museum 640 5th Ave SW *Web:* www.eub.gov.ab.ca	Calgary	AB	T2P3G4	403-297-4293	297-3757
Family Leisure Centre Indoor Water Park 11150 Bonaventure Dr SE	Calary	AB	T2J6R9	403-278-7542	278-7573
Fort Calgary Historic Park 750 9th Ave SE *Web:* www.fortcalgary.ab.ca	Calgary	AB	T2G5E1	403-290-1875	265-6534
Garry Theatre 1229 9th Ave SE	Calgary	AB	T2G0S9	403-269-1444	269-1444
Glenbow Museum 130 9th Ave SE *Web:* www.glenbow.org	Calgary	AB	T2G0P3	403-268-4100	262-4045
Grain Academy 1410 Olympic Way SE Stampede Pk	Calgary	AB	T2G2W1	403-263-4594	
Head-Smashed-In Buffalo Jump Secondary Hwy 785 *Web:* www.head-smashed-in.com	Fort Macleod	AB	T0L0Z0	403-553-2731	553-3151
Heritage Park Historical Village 1900 Heritage Dr SW *Web:* www.heritagepark.ab.ca ■ *E-mail:* info@heritagepark.ab.ca	Calgary	AB	T2V2X3	403-259-1900	252-3528
IMAX Theatre 200 Barclay Parade SW Eau Claire Mkt *Web:* www.imax.com/theatres/calgary.html	Calgary	AB	T2P4R5	403-974-4629	974-4611
Inglewood Bird Sanctuary 3020 Sanctuary Rd SE	Calgary	AB	T2P2M5	403-269-6688	221-3775
Kananaskis Country 3115 12th St NE Suite 100	Calgary	AB	T2E7J2	403-297-3362	297-2843
Legend Motorsports 68th Ave & 114th St *TF:* 888-572-7223	Calgary	AB	T2E2N4	403-203-1977	203-1978
Livingston Sam Fish Hatchery 1440 17th St SE	Calgary	AB	T2G4T9	403-297-6561	297-2839
Luxton Museum 1 Birch Ave	Banff	AB	T0L0C0	403-762-2388	762-2388
Museum of Movie Art 3600 21st St NE	Calgary	AB	T2E6V6	403-250-7588	250-7589
Museum of the Regiments 4520 Crowchild Trail SW *Web:* www.nucleus.com/~regiments/	Calgary	AB	T2T5J4	403-974-2850	974-2858
Nanton Lancaster Society & Air Museum 17th St & Hwy 2 S *Web:* www.lexicom.ab.ca/~nanton/ ■ *E-mail:* nanton@lexicom.ab.ca	Nanton	AB	T0L1R0	403-646-2270	646-2270
Nickle Arts Museum 434 Collegiate Blvd University of Calgary *Web:* www.acs.ucalgary.ca/~nickle/	Calgary	AB	T2N1N4	403-220-7234	282-4742
Olympic Hall of Fame & Museum 88 Canada Olympic Rd SW Canada Olympic Pk *Web:* www.coda.ab.ca/COP/fame.html ■ *E-mail:* info@coda.ab.ca	Calgary	AB	T3B5R5	403-247-5471	286-7213
Olympic Oval 2500 University Dr NW *Web:* www.oval.ucalgary.ca	Calgary	AB	T2N1N4	403-220-7954	284-4815
Olympic Plaza 205 8th Ave SE	Calgary	AB	T2P2M5	403-268-3888	268-5280
One Yellow Rabbit Theater 225 8th Ave SE *Web:* www.oyr.org	Calgary	AB	T2G0K8	403-264-3224	264-3230
Pleiades Theatre 701 11th St SW	Calgary	AB	T2P2M5	403-221-3707	237-0186
Pumphouse Theatres Society 2140 Pumphouse Ave SW	Calgary	AB	T3C3P5	403-263-0079	237-5357
Royal Tyrrell Museum of Palaeontology Hwy 838 Midland Provincial Pk *TF:* 888-440-4240 ■ *Web:* www.tyrrellmuseum.com ■ *E-mail:* info@tyrrellmuseum.com	Drumheller	AB	T0J0Y0	403-823-7707	823-7131
Ski Kananaskis 1550 8th St SW Suite 505 *TF:* 800-258-7669	Calgary	AB	T2R1K1	403-256-8473	244-3774
Skiing Louise 1550 8th St SW Suite 505 *TF:* 800-567-6262 ■ *Web:* www.skilouise.com ■ *E-mail:* info@skilouise.com	Calgary	AB	T2R1K1	403-256-8473	244-3774
Southern Alberta Jubilee Auditorium 1415 14th Ave NW	Calgary	AB	T2M1M4	403-297-8000	297-3818
Southland Leisure Centre 2000 Southland Dr SW	Calgary	AB	T2P2M5	403-251-3505	221-4527
Stage West Theatre Restaurant 727 42nd Ave SE	Calgary	AB	T2G1Y8	403-243-7077	243-7991
Sulphur Mountain Gondola end of Mountain Rd *Web:* www.banffgondola.com	Banff	AB	T0L0C0	403-762-2523	762-7493

Calgary — Attractions (Cont'd)

		Phone	Fax
Sunshine Village Ski Resort Sunshine Village Rd	Banff AB T0L0C0	403-531-0750	265-8381
TF: 800-661-1676 ■ *Web:* www.skibanff.com			
Theatre Calgary 220 9th Ave SE	Calgary AB T2G5C4	403-294-7447	294-7493
Web: www.theatrecalgary.com ■ *E-mail:* info@theatrecalgary.com			
Village Square Leisure Centre 2623 56th St NE	Calgary AB T1Y6E7	403-280-9714	285-2345
Webster Gallery 812 11th Ave SW	Calgary AB T2R0E5	403-263-6500	263-6501
TF: 888-874-5519			

SPORTS TEAMS & FACILITIES

		Phone	Fax
Calgary Cannons (baseball) 2255 Crowchild Trail NW	Calgary AB T2M4S7	403-284-1111	284-4343
Web: www.calgaryherald.com/sports/cannons			
Calgary Flames Canadian Airlines Saddledome Box 1540 Stn M	Calgary AB T2P3B9	403-777-2177	777-2195
Web: www.calgaryflames.com ■ *E-mail:* flamesinfo@calgaryflames.com			
Calgary Stampeders (football) 1817 Crowchild Trail NW	Calgary AB T2M4R6	403-289-0205	289-7850
Web: www.cfl.ca/CFLCalgary/home.html			
Race City Motorsport Park 11550 68th St SE	Calgary AB T2R1L9	403-272-7223	236-7223
Web: www.racecity.com			
Spruce Meadows RR 9	Calgary AB T2J5G5	403-974-4200	974-4270
Web: www.sprucemeadows.com			

— Events —

	Phone
4-H on Parade (early June)	403-261-0162
4th Street Lilac Festival (late May)	403-229-0902
Aggie Days (mid-April)	403-261-0114
Alberta Bobsleigh Cup (mid-January)	403-286-2632
Alberta Dragon Boat Races (late July-early August)	403-246-5757
Alberta Luge Cup (early February)	403-247-9884
Artist Direct Christmas Show (mid-October)	403-253-1966
Artwalk (mid-September)	403-255-2729
Banff Festival of Mountain Films (early November)	403-762-6675
Bloom Fest (late May)	403-232-9300
Blue Mountain Fall Antique Show (mid-September)	800-755-4081
Blue Mountain Spring Antique Show (mid-April)	800-755-4081
Boo at the Zoo (late October)	403-232-9383
Calgary Boat & Sportsmen's Show (mid-February)	403-261-0101
Calgary Folk Music Festival (late July)	403-233-0904
Calgary International Children's Festival (mid-late May)	403-294-7414
Calgary International Jazz Festival (late June-early July)	403-249-1119
Calgary International Organ Festival (late August-early September)	403-543-5115
Calgary Philharmonic Orchestra's BBQ on the Bow (early September)	403-271-2494
Calgary Stampede (early-mid-July)	403-261-0101
Calgary Summer Antique Show (late June)	403-247-5452
Calgary Winter Festival (mid-February)	403-543-5480
Canada Luge Championships (early January)	403-247-5452
Canadian Country Music Week (early September)	403-716-2105
Carifest Caribbean Festival (early-mid-June)	403-292-0310
Chalk Walk (mid-September)	403-245-1703
Chinese New Year's Carnival (mid-February)	403-262-5071
Cody Snyder's Canadian Classic BullBustin (early October)	403-938-5255
Cowboy Festival (early February)	403-261-8500
Dairy Classic (late April)	403-261-0101
Easter Promenade (early April)	403-245-1703
Esther Honens Calgary International Piano Competition & Festival (mid-late November)	403-299-0130
Fall Home Show (mid-September)	403-261-0101
Heritage Park Old Time Fall Fair (early September)	403-259-1950
Historic Calgary Week (late July-early August)	403-261-3662
HomeExpo (mid-January)	403-261-0101
International Auto Show (mid-March)	403-261-0101
Jazzoo (early July-late August)	403-232-9300
National The Horse Jumping at Spruce Meadows (early June)	403-974-4200
Native Awareness Week (mid-late June)	403-261-3022
North American Show Jumping at Spruce Meadows (early July)	403-974-4200
Playrites Festival (late January-early March)	403-294-7402
Provincial Bobsleigh Championships (mid-late February)	403-286-2632
Rodeo Royal (mid-March)	403-261-0101
Spring Craft Show (late March-early April)	403-261-0101
Spring Home & Garden Show (late February)	403-261-0101
Taste of Banff and Lake Louise (early October)	403-762-8421
Wildlights New Year's Eve Party (December 31)	403-232-9300

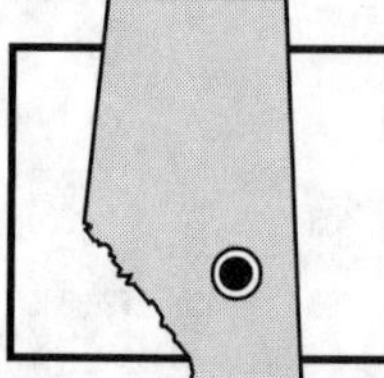

Edmonton

Located on the banks of the North Saskatchewan River, the city of Edmonton is the capital of Alberta and Canada's fifth largest metropolitan area. Edmonton was incorporated into a town in 1892, just before the famous Klondike Gold Rush of 1897. The Gold Rush led many pioneers to settle in Edmonton, and the town was incorporated as a city in 1904. Today the city commemorates the Gold Rush era with Klondike Days, an annual celebration held during mid-July that includes a parade, bathtub races, river raft races, and fireworks. Another popular festival held each August is the Fringe Festival, a celebration of plays, music, dance, and street entertainment, which attracts more than 400,000 visitors a year and is the largest festival in North America. Edmonton is home to the world's largest shopping and entertainment complex, West Edmonton Mall, which has more than 800 stores and services and contains an amusement park, NHL-sized ice rink, water park, and deep sea underwater adventure. Other attractions in Edmonton include the Devonian Botanic Garden, the Provincial Museum of Alberta, and the Edmonton Space and Science Centre, which features the largest planetarium dome in Western Canada.

Population	616,306	**Longitude**	113-30-00 W
Area (Land)	258.7 sq mi	**Time Zone**	MST
Elevation	2,186 ft	**Area Code/s**	780
Latitude	53-30-00 N		

— Average Temperatures and Precipitation —

TEMPERATURES

	Jan	Feb	Mar	Apr	May	Jun	Jul	Aug	Sep	Oct	Nov	Dec
High	12	21	30	48	63	70	72	72	63	52	32	18
Low	-8	1	10	27	37	45	48	46	37	28	12	-2

PRECIPITATION

	Jan	Feb	Mar	Apr	May	Jun	Jul	Aug	Sep	Oct	Nov	Dec
Inches	0.1	0.0	0.1	0.3	1.5	3.0	3.6	3.1	1.7	0.4	0.1	0.0

— Important Phone Numbers —

	Phone		Phone
Alberta Motor Assn	780-474-8601	**Poison Control Center**	800-332-1414
American Express Travel	780-421-0608	**Road Conditions**	780-471-6056
Emergency	911	**Time**	780-449-4444
Medical Referral	780-423-4764	**Weather**	780-468-4940

— Information Sources —

		Phone	Fax
Better Business Bureau Serving Central & Northern Alberta 9707 110th St Suite 514	Edmonton AB T5K2L9	780-482-2341	482-1150
Web: www.edmonton.bbb.org			
Edmonton Chamber of Commerce 10123 99th St Suite 600	Edmonton AB T5J3G9	780-426-4620	424-7946
Web: www.chamber.edmonton.ab.ca ■ *E-mail:* ecc@tnc.com			
Edmonton City Hall 1 Sir Winston Churchill Sq.	Edmonton AB T5J2R7	780-496-8200	496-8210
Web: www.gov.edmonton.ab.ca			
Edmonton Economic Development 9797 Jasper Ave NW	Edmonton AB T5J1N9	780-424-9191	426-0535
Web: www.ede.org ■ *E-mail:* edeinfo@ede.org			

Edmonton — Information Sources (Cont'd)

				Phone	Fax
Edmonton Mayor 1 Sir Winston Churchill Sq 2nd Fl. Web: www.gov.edmonton.ab.ca ■ E-mail: bill.smith@gov.edmonton.ab.ca	Edmonton	AB	T5J2R7	780-496-8100	496-8292
Edmonton Planning & Development Dept 10250 101st St Exchange Tower 2nd Fl. Web: www.gov.edmonton.ab.ca/planning	Edmonton	AB	T6J3P4	780-496-6161	496-6054
Edmonton Tourism 9797 Jasper Ave NW TF: 800-463-4667 ■ Web: www.tourism.ede.org	Edmonton	AB	T5J1N9	780-496-8400	496-8413
Milner Stanley A Public Library 7 Sir Winston Churchill Sq. Web: www.publib.edmonton.ab.ca	Edmonton	AB	T5J2V4	780-496-7000	496-1885
Shaw Conference Centre 9797 Jasper Ave.	Edmonton	AB	T5J1N9	780-421-9797	425-5121

On-Line Resources

About.com Guide to Edmonton	edmonton.about.com/local/edmonton
City Knowledge Edmonton	www.cityknowledge.com/canada_ab_edmonton.htm
CRS Encyclopedia Edmonton	www.relocatecanada.com/edmonton
Discover Edmonton	www.discoveredmonton.com
E-View Guide to Edmonton	www.e-view.com/edmonton/
Info Edmonton Visitor Guide	www.infoedmonton.com
InterVue Weekly	vue.ab.ca
Rough Guide Travel Edmonton	travel.roughguides.com/content/5435/index.htm
SEE Worldwide	www.greatwest.ca/see
Vue Weekly	www.vue.ab.ca

— Transportation Services —

AIRPORTS

■ Edmonton International Airport (YEG)

	Phone
19 miles S of downtown (approx 40 minutes). Web: edmontonairports.com/eia.htm ■ E-mail: eraa@oanet.com	780-890-8900

Airport Transportation

	Phone
Airport Sky Shuttle $11 fare to downtown	780-465-8515
Prestige Cabs $35 fare to downtown	780-462-4444
Yellow Cab $35 fare to downtown	780-462-3456

Commercial Airlines

	Phone		Phone
Air Canada	800-776-3000	**Delta**	800-221-1212
Air Transat	877-872-6728	**LOT Polish Airlines**	800-223-0593
American	800-433-7300	**Martinair Holland**	800-627-8462
Athabaska Airways	800-667-9356	**Northwest**	800-225-2525
Canada 3000	877-359-2263	**Royal Airlines**	800-667-7692
Canadian Air	800-426-7000	**WestJet**	800-538-5696

Charter Airlines

	Phone		Phone
Air BC	888-247-2262	**North American Airlines**	403-275-7700
Buffalo Air Express	780-455-1677		

CAR RENTALS

	Phone		Phone
Avis	780-423-2847	**Discount**	780-448-3888
Budget	780-448-2000	**Rent-A-Wreck**	780-986-3335

LIMO/TAXI

	Phone		Phone
Alberta Co-Op Taxi	780-425-8310	**Crystal Limousines**	780-450-2244
Barrel Taxi	780-489-7777	**Skyline Cabs**	780-468-4646
Checker Cabs	780-484-8888		

MASS TRANSIT

	Phone
Edmonton Transit $1.60 Base fare	780-496-1611

RAIL/BUS

				Phone
Greyhound Canada Bus Station 10324 103rd St TF: 800-661-8747	Edmonton	AB	T5J049	780-413-8747
VIA Rail Canada 12360 121st St	Edmonton	AB	T5L5C3	800-561-3949

— Accommodations —

HOTEL RESERVATION SERVICES

	Phone	Fax
Alberta Gem B&B & Reservation Agency Web: www.bbcanada.com/1301html	780-434-6098	434-6098
Good Earth Travel Adventures Reservations TF: 888-979-9797 ■ Web: www.goodearthtravel.com ■ E-mail: info@goodearthtravel.com	403-678-9358	678-9384

HOTELS, MOTELS, RESORTS

				Phone	Fax
Alberta Place Suite Hotel 10049 103rd St. TF: 800-661-3982	Edmonton	AB	T5J2W7	780-423-1565	426-6260
Best Western Cedar Park Inn 5116 Calgary Trail. TF: 800-661-9461	Edmonton	AB	T6H2H4	780-434-7411	437-4836
Best Western City Centre Inn 11310 109th St. TF: 800-666-5026	Edmonton	AB	T5G2T7	780-479-2042	474-2204
Best Western Denham Inn 5207 50th Ave TF: 800-661-3327	Edmonton	AB	T9E6V3	780-986-2241	986-1511
Best Western Westwood Inn 18035 Stony Plain Rd TF: 800-557-4767	Edmonton	AB	T5S1B2	780-483-7770	486-1769
Campus Tower Suite Hotel 11145 87th Ave TF: 800-661-6562 ■ Web: www.campustower.com	Edmonton	AB	T6G0Y1	780-439-6060	433-4410
Chateau Edmonton Quality Hotel & Suites 7230 Argyll Rd TF: 800-465-3648	Edmonton	AB	T6C4A6	780-465-7931	469-3680
Chateau Louis Hotel & Conference Centre 11727 Kingsway TF: 800-661-9843	Edmonton	AB	T5G3A1	780-452-7770	454-3436
Coast Edmonton Plaza Hotel 10155 105th St. TF: 800-663-1144 ■ Web: www.coasthotels.com	Edmonton	AB	T5J1E2	780-423-4811	423-3204
Coast Terrace Inn 4440 Calgary Trail N TF: 800-663-1144 ■ Web: www.coastterraceinn.com	Edmonton	AB	T6H5C2	780-437-6010	431-5801
Comfort Inn 17610 100th Ave. TF: 800-228-5150	Edmonton	AB	T5S1S9	780-484-4415	481-4034
Continental Inn 16625 Stony Plain Rd	Edmonton	AB	T5P4A8	780-484-7751	484-9827
Crowne Plaza Chateau Lacombe Edmonton 10111 Bellamy Hill TF: 800-661-8801 ■ Web: www.chateaulacombe.com	Edmonton	AB	T5J1N7	780-428-6611	425-6564
Days Inn Downtown 10041 106th St TF: 800-267-2191	Edmonton	AB	T5J1G3	780-423-1925	424-5302
Delta Edmonton Centre Suite 10222 102nd St Eaton Ctr TF: 800-661-6655 ■ Web: www.deltahotels.com	Edmonton	AB	T5J4C5	780-429-3900	426-0562
Delta Edmonton South 4404 Calgary Trail TF: 800-661-1122	Edmonton	AB	T6H5C2	780-434-6415	436-9247
Econo Lodge Downtown 10209 100th Ave TF: 800-613-7043	Edmonton	AB	T5J0A1	780-428-6442	428-6467
Edmonton House Suite Hotel 10205 100th Ave TF: 800-661-6562 ■ Web: www.edmontonhouse.com	Edmonton	AB	T5J4B5	780-420-4000	420-4008
Edmonton Inn 11830 Kingsway TF: 800-661-7264	Edmonton	AB	T5G0X5	780-454-9521	453-7360
Fantasyland Hotel 17700 87th Ave West Edmonton Mall TF: 800-737-3783 ■ Web: www.westedmall.com/hotel/ ■ E-mail: hotel@westedmall.com	Edmonton	AB	T5T4V4	780-444-3000	444-3294
Garden City Hotel 10425 100th Ave TF: 888-384-6835	Edmonton	AB	T5J0A3	780-423-5611	425-9791
Grand Hotel 10266 103rd St TF: 888-422-6365	Edmonton	AB	T5J0Y8	780-422-6365	425-9070
Greenwood Inn 4485 Calgary Trail N TF: 888-233-6730	Edmonton	AB	T6H5C3	780-431-1100	437-3455
Holiday Inn Convention Centre 4520 76th Ave TF: 800-661-5193	Edmonton	AB	T6B0A5	780-468-5400	466-0451
Holiday Inn Palace 4235 Calgary Trail N TF: 800-565-1222	Edmonton	AB	T6J5H2	780-438-1222	438-0906
Howard Johnson Downtown 1 Thornton Ct TF: 888-428-4656	Edmonton	AB	T5J2E7	780-428-4656	412-2222

Edmonton — Hotels, Motels, Resorts (Cont'd)

				Phone	Fax
Inn on 7th 10001 107th St. *TF:* 800-661-7327	Edmonton	AB	T5J1J1	780-429-2861	420-4971
Mayfield Inn & Suites 16615 109th Ave. *TF:* 800-661-9804 ■ *Web:* www.mayfield-inn.com	Edmonton	AB	T5P4K8	780-484-0821	486-1634
Nisku Inn 1101 4th St. *TF:* 800-661-6966	Nisku	AB	T9E7N1	780-955-7744	955-7743
Ramada Inn 5359 Calgary Trail. *TF:* 800-661-9030	Edmonton	AB	T6H4J9	780-434-3431	437-3714
River Valley Inn 9710 105th St. *TF:* 877-420-0901	Edmonton	AB	T5K1A4	780-428-7133	426-0087
Rosslyn Motor Inn 13620 97th St. *TF:* 877-785-7005	Edmonton	AB	T5E4E2	780-476-6241	473-3021
Royal Inn West Edmonton 10010 178th St. *TF:* 800-661-4879 ■ *Web:* www.royalinn.com ■ *E-mail:* innsales@royalinn.com	Edmonton	AB	T5S1T3	780-484-6000	489-2900
Sandman Hotel West Edmonton 17635 Stony Plain Rd. *TF:* 800-726-3626 ■ *Web:* www.sandman.ca	Edmonton	AB	T5S1E3	780-483-1385	489-0611
Sheraton Grande Hotel Edmonton 10235 101st St. *TF:* 800-263-9030	Edmonton	AB	T5J3E9	780-428-7111	441-3098
Tower on the Park Hotel 9715 110th St. *TF:* 800-720-2179	Edmonton	AB	T5K2M1	780-488-1626	488-0659
Travelodge Beverly Crest 3414 118th Ave. *TF:* 800-665-0456	Edmonton	AB	T5W0Z4	780-474-0456	479-3542
Travelodge Edmonton South 10320 45th Ave. *TF:* 800-578-7878	Edmonton	AB	T6H5K3	780-436-9770	436-3529
Travelodge Edmonton West 18320 Stony Plain Rd. *TF:* 800-578-7878	Edmonton	AB	T5S1A7	780-483-6031	484-2358
West Harvest Inn 17803 Stony Plain Rd. *TF:* 800-661-6993	Edmonton	AB	T5S1B4	780-484-8000	486-6060
Westin Edmonton 10135 100th St. *TF:* 800-937-8461	Edmonton	AB	T5J0N7	780-426-3636	428-1454
Yellowhead Motor Inn 15004 Yellowhead Trail. *TF:* 800-343-8533	Edmonton	AB	T5V1A1	780-447-2400	447-2217

— Restaurants —

				Phone
Brewsters Brewing Co & Restaurant (North American) 11620 104st Ave NW	Edmonton	AB	T5K2T7	780-482-4677
Bua Thai Restaurant (Thai) 10049 113th St NW	Edmonton	AB	T5K1N9	780-482-2277
Cafe Soleil (European) 10360 82nd Ave NW	Edmonton	AB	T6E1Z8	780-438-4848
Chin Chin Restaurant (Chinese/Vietnamese) 10703 103rd St NW	Edmonton	AB	T5H2V7	780-423-2884
Creperie The (French) 10220 103rd St	Edmonton	AB	T5J0Y8	780-420-6656
Divine's Restaurant (North American) 9712 111th St.	Edmonton	AB	T5K1J8	780-482-6402
Doan's Restaurant (Vietnamese) 10023 107th Ave	Edmonton	AB	T5H4L4	780-424-3034
Double Greeting Won Ton (Chinese) 10212 96th St.	Edmonton	AB	T5H2G7	780-424-2486
Elephant & Castle Restaurant (English) 10200 102nd Ave 3rd Level	Edmonton	AB	T5T4B7	780-424-4555
Emperor's Table (Chinese) 10404 124th St NW	Edmonton	AB	T5N1R5	780-488-8282
Fantasia Noodle House (Chinese/Vietnamese) 10518 Jasper Ave NW	Edmonton	AB	T5J1Z7	780-428-0943
Hy's Steak Loft (Steak/Seafood) 10013 101A Ave	Edmonton	AB	T5J0C3	780-424-4444
Il Portico Restaurant (Italian) 10012 107th St NW.	Edmonton	AB	T5J1J2	780-424-0707
Japanese Village (Japanese) 10126 100th St.	Edmonton	AB	T5J0N8	780-422-6083
Koutouki Restaurant (Greek) 10704 124th St NW	Edmonton	AB	T5M0H1	780-452-5383
L'Anjou Restaurant (French) 10643 123rd St NW	Edmonton	AB	T5N1P3	780-482-7178
Louisiana Purchase Restaurant (Cajun/Creole) 10320 111th St	Edmonton	AB	T5K1L2	780-420-6779
Mekong Restaurant (Chinese/Vietnamese) 11019 107th Ave NW	Edmonton	AB	T5H0X6	780-424-9024
Mirabelle Gourmet Dining (Continental) 9927 109th St	Edmonton	AB	T5K1H6	780-429-3055
New West Restaurant (North American) 15025 111th Ave NW	Edmonton	AB	T5M2P8	780-483-8984
Normand's (French) 11639 A Jasper Ave	Edmonton	AB	T5K0M9	780-482-2600
Osaka Ya (Japanese) 17503 100th Ave NW	Edmonton	AB	T5S2B8	780-496-9838
Pradera Restaurant (North American) 10135 100th St.	Edmonton	AB	T5J0N7	780-493-8994
Pyrogy House (Ukrainian) 12510 118th Ave NW	Edmonton	AB	T5L2K6	780-454-7880
Razzellberries Restaurant (North American) 10040 104th St NW	Edmonton	AB	T5J0Z2	780-429-7044
Red Tomato Restaurant & Pub (North American) 9777 102nd Ave NW	Edmonton	AB	T5J4G9	780-428-1166
Sawmill Restaurant (Steak/Seafood) 11560 104th Ave.	Edmonton	AB	T5K2S5	780-429-2816
Sorrentino's On 95th (Italian) 10844 95th St.	Edmonton	AB	T5H2E4	780-425-0960
Spago (European) 14233 97th St	Edmonton	AB	T5G1Z6	780-479-0328
Taipan Cafe (Chinese) 10627 97th St NW	Edmonton	AB	T5H2L5	780-429-0731
Tropika Malaysian Cuisine (Malaysian) 6004 104th St NW	Edmonton	AB	T6H2K3	780-439-6699
Village Cafe (International) 11223 Jasper Ave NW	Edmonton	AB	T5K0L5	780-488-0955
Zenari's Bruschetteria (Italian) 10117 101st St NW.	Edmonton	AB	T5J0T4	780-425-6151

— Goods and Services —

SHOPPING

				Phone	Fax
Commerce Place Shops 10155 102nd St.	Edmonton	AB	T5J4G8	780-944-1222	428-4047
Eaton Centre 10200 102nd Ave	Edmonton	AB	T5J4B7	780-428-2228	426-3351
Kingsway Garden Mall 109th St & Princess Elizabeth Ave	Edmonton	AB	T5G3A6	780-479-5955	477-0679
Manulife Place 10180 101st St	Edmonton	AB	T5J3S4	780-420-6236	429-1416
Southgate Shopping Centre 111th St & 51st Ave	Edmonton	AB	T6H4M6	780-435-3721	430-0372
West Edmonton Mall 8882 170th St. *TF:* 800-661-8890 ■ *Web:* www.westedmall.com ■ *E-mail:* tourism@westedmall.com	Edmonton	AB	T5T4M2	780-444-5300	444-5223

BANKS

				Phone	Fax
Bank of Montreal 10199 101st St NW. *TF:* 800-363-9992 ■ *Web:* www.bmo.com	Edmonton	AB	T5J3Y5	780-428-7201	
Canadian Western Bank 10303 Jasper Ave Suite 2300. *Web:* www.cwbank.com	Edmonton	AB	T5J3X6	780-423-8888	423-8897
HSBC 10561 Jasper Ave. *TF:* 800-889-4522 ■ *Web:* www.hsbcgroup.com	Edmonton	AB	T5J1Z4	780-423-3563	420-0506
National Bank of Canada 10150 100th St. *Web:* www.nbc.ca	Edmonton	AB	T5J0P6	780-424-4771	425-5774
Scotiabank 10060 Jasper Ave 2nd Fl. *Web:* www.scotiabank.com	Edmonton	AB	T5J3R8	780-448-7701	448-7977
Toronto-Dominion Bank 148 Edmonton Ctr. *TF:* 800-983-2265 ■ *Web:* www.tdbank.ca	Edmonton	AB	T5J2Y8	780-448-8000	448-8239

BUSINESS SERVICES

Name	Phone	Name	Phone
Bradson Staffing Services	780-426-6666	**Kopy Centre**	780-438-0144
Canada Post	780-944-3264	**Mail Boxes Etc**	780-448-5898
DHL International Express	403-250-1512	**Manpower Temporary Services**	780-420-0110
Federal Express	800-463-3339	**Olsten Staffing Services**	780-426-7920
Interim Personnel	780-423-2487	**Shippers Supply Inc.**	780-449-5639
Kelly Services	780-421-7777	**UPS**	800-742-5877

— Media —

PUBLICATIONS

				Phone	Fax
Edmonton Examiner 12040 149th St. *Web:* www.edmontonexaminer.com	Edmonton	AB	T5V1P2	780-453-9001	447-7333
Edmonton Journal† PO Box 2421. *TF:* 800-232-7309 ■ *Web:* www.edmontonjournal.com	Edmonton	AB	T5J2S6	780-429-5100	429-5500
Edmonton Sun† 4990 92nd Ave Suite 250. *Web:* www.canoe.ca/EdmontonSun/	Edmonton	AB	T6B3A1	780-468-0100	468-0139
Where Edmonton Magazine 9343 50th St Suite 4. *Web:* www.infoedmonton.com ■ *E-mail:* info@infoedmonton.com	Edmonton	AB	T6B2L5	780-465-3362	448-0424

†Daily newspapers

TELEVISION

				Phone	Fax
CBXFT-TV Ch 11 (CBC) PO Box 555	Edmonton	AB	T5J2P4	780-468-7500	468-7868
CBXT-TV Ch 5 (CBC) 8861 75th St. *Web:* www.calgary.cbc.ca	Edmonton	AB	T5J2P4	780-468-7555	468-7510
CFRN-TV Ch 3 (CTV) 18520 Stony Plain Rd. *Web:* www.cfrntv.ca	Edmonton	AB	T5S1A8	780-483-3311	489-5883
CITV-TV Ch 13 (Ind) 5325 Allard Way. *Web:* www.itv.ca	Edmonton	AB	T6H5B8	780-436-1250	438-8448
CKEM-TV Ch 53 (Ind) 10212 Jasper Ave. **Fax:* News Rm	Edmonton	AB	T5J5A3	780-412-2783	412-2799*

Edmonton (Cont'd)

RADIO

				Phone	Fax
CBX-AM 740 kHz (N/T) 7909 51st Ave	Edmonton	AB	T6E5L9	780-468-7500	468-7419
CBX-FM 90.0 MHz (Misc) 7709 51st Ave	Edmonton	AB	T6E5L9	780-468-7500	468-7419
CFBR-FM 100.3 MHz (CR) 18520 Stony Plain Rd Suite 100	Edmonton	AB	T5A2E2	780-486-2800	489-6927
Web: www.thebearrocks.com					
CFRN-AM 1260 kHz (Oldies) 18520 Stony Plain Rd Suite 100	Edmonton	AB	T5S2E2	780-486-2800	489-6927
CHED-AM 630 kHz (N/T) 5204 84th St	Edmonton	AB	T6E5N8	780-440-6300	469-5937
Web: www.630ched.com					
CHFA-AM 680 kHz (Misc) PO Box 555	Edmonton	AB	T5J2P4	780-468-7500	468-7812
CHQT-AM 880 kHz (Oldies) 10550 102nd St	Edmonton	AB	T5H2T3	780-424-8800	426-6502
CIRK-FM 97.3 MHz (CR) 4752 99th St	Edmonton	AB	T6E5H5	780-437-4996	436-5719
CISN-FM 103.9 MHz (Ctry) 10550 102nd St Suite 200	Edmonton	AB	T5H2T3	780-428-1104	426-6502
CJCA-AM 930 kHz (Rel) 4207 98th St Suite 206	Edmonton	AB	T6E5R7	780-466-4930	469-5335
CJSR-FM 88.5 MHz (Misc) University of Alberta Rm 0-09 Student Union Bldg	Edmonton	AB	T6J2G7	780-492-5244	492-3121
CKER-FM 101.9 MHz (Misc) 6005 103rd St 2nd Fl	Edmonton	AB	T6H2H3	780-438-1480	437-5129
CKNG-FM 92.5 MHz (CHR) 5204 84th St	Edmonton	AB	T5J2P4	780-469-6992	468-6739
Web: www.power92.com					
CKRA-FM 96.3 MHz (AC) 4752 99th St	Edmonton	AB	T6E5H5	780-437-4996	436-9803
Web: www.mix96fm.com					
CKUA-AM 580 kHz (Misc) 10526 Jasper Ave 4th Fl	Edmonton	AB	T6C1Z2	780-428-7595	428-7624
TF: 800-494-2582 ■ *Web:* www.ckua.org ■ *E-mail:* ckua@oanet.com					
CKUA-FM 94.9 MHz (Misc) 10526 Jasper Ave 4th Fl	Edmonton	AB	T5J1Z7	780-428-7595	428-7624
TF: 800-494-2582 ■ *Web:* www.ckua.org ■ *E-mail:* ckua@oanet.com					

— Colleges/Universities —

				Phone	Fax
Alberta College 10050 MacDonald Dr	Edmonton	AB	T5J2B7	780-428-1851	424-6371
Web: www.abcollege.ab.ca					
Alberta Vocational College Edmonton 10215 108th St	Edmonton	AB	T5J1L6	780-427-2823	427-4211
Concordia University College of Alberta 7128 Ada Blvd NW	Edmonton	AB	T5B4E4	780-479-8481	474-1933
Web: www.concordia.edmonton.ab.ca					
Grant MacEwan Community College 10700 104th Ave	Edmonton	AB	T5J2P2	780-497-5040	497-5001
Web: www.gmcc.ab.ca					
King's University College 9125 50th St NW	Edmonton	AB	T6B2H3	780-465-3500	465-3534
Web: www.kingsu.ab.ca					
North American Baptist College 11525 23rd Ave	Edmonton	AB	T6J4T3	780-431-5200	436-9416
TF: 800-567-4988 ■ *Web:* www.nabcebs.ab.ca ■ *E-mail:* nabc@nabcebs.ab.ca					
Northern Alberta Institute of Technology 11762 106th St	Edmonton	AB	T5G2R1	780-471-7400	471-8583
Web: www.nait.ab.ca					
Northwest Bible College 11617 106th Ave	Edmonton	AB	T5H0S1	780-452-0808	452-5803
Web: www.nwbc.ab.ca/home.htm ■ *E-mail:* northwest@oanet.com					
Saint Stephen's College 8810 112th St	Edmonton	AB	T6G2J6	780-439-7311	433-8875
TF: 800-661-4956 ■ *Web:* www.ualberta.ca/ST.STEPHENS					
University of Alberta 89th Ave & 114th St 201 Administration Bldg	Edmonton	AB	T6G2M7	780-492-3111	492-7172
Web: www.ualberta.ca					

— Hospitals —

				Phone	Fax
Alberta Hospital Edmonton 17480 Fort Rd	Edmonton	AB	T5B4K3	780-472-5555	472-5284*
**Fax:* Hum Res					
Edmonton General Hospital 11111 Jasper Ave	Edmonton	AB	T5K0L4	780-482-8111	482-8035
Glenrose Hospital 10230 111th Ave	Edmonton	AB	T5G0B7	780-471-2262	477-4901
Grey Nuns Community Hospital 30th Ave & 62nd St	Edmonton	AB	T6L5X8	780-450-7000	450-7500
Misericordia Community Hospital & Health Centre 16940 87th Ave	Edmonton	AB	T5R4H5	780-930-5611	930-5774
Web: www.caritas.ab.ca/Hospitals/misericordia.htm					
Royal Alexandra Hospital 10240 Kingsway Ave	Edmonton	AB	T5H3V9	780-477-4111	491-5070*
**Fax:* Admitting					
University of Alberta Hospital 8440 112th St	Edmonton	AB	T6G2B7	780-492-8822	407-7418
Web: www.cha.ab.ca					

— Attractions —

				Phone	Fax
Alberta Aviation Museum 11410 Kingsway Ave	Edmonton	AB	T5G0X4	780-453-1078	451-1607
Alberta Government House 12845 102nd Ave	Edmonton	AB	T5N0M6	780-452-7980	422-6508
Alberta Legislature Building 10800 97th Avenue	Edmonton	AB	T5K2B6	780-427-7362	427-0980
Web: www.assembly.ab.ca					
Alberta Railway Museum 24215 34th St	Edmonton	AB	T5C3R6	780-472-6229	487-8708
Arden Theatre 5 Sainte Anne St	Saint Albert	AB	T8N3Z9	780-459-1542	459-1726
Web: www.ardentheatre.com					
Calgary & Edmonton Railway Museum 10447 86th Ave	Edmonton	AB	T6E2M4	780-433-9739	431-0138
Citadel Theatre 9828 101A Ave	Edmonton	AB	T5J3C6	780-425-1820	428-7194
City of Edmonton Archives 10440 108th Ave	Edmonton	AB	T5H3Z9	780-496-8710	496-8732
Deep Sea Adventure 8882 170th St West Edmonton Mall	Edmonton	AB	T5T4M2	780-444-5300	
Web: www.westedmall.com/attractions/html/deepsea.htm					
Dolphin Lagoon & Sea Life Cavern 8882 170th St West Edmonton Mall	Edmonton	AB	T5T4M2	780-444-5300	
Web: www.westedmall.com/attractions/html/dolphin.htm					
Edmonton Art Gallery 2 Sir Winston Churchill Sq	Edmonton	AB	T5J2C1	780-422-6223	426-3105
Web: www.eag.org					
Edmonton Opera 9720 102nd Ave Winspear Centre	Edmonton	AB	T5J4B2	780-424-4040	429-0600
Edmonton Police Museum & Archives 9620 103A Ave	Edmonton	AB	T5H0H7	780-421-2274	421-2341
Web: www.police.edmonton.ab.ca/museum.htm					
Edmonton Public Schools Archives & Museum 10425 99th Ave	Edmonton	AB	T5K0E5	780-422-1970	426-0192
Edmonton Space & Science Centre 11211 142nd St	Edmonton	AB	T5M4A1	780-451-3344	455-5882
Web: www.edmontonscience.com ■ *E-mail:* essc@planet.eon.net					
Edmonton Symphony Orchestra 4 Sir Winston Churchill Sq Winspear Centre	Edmonton	AB	T5J2R7	780-428-1414	425-0167
Edmonton's IMAX Theatre 11211 142nd St	Edmonton	AB	T5M4A1	780-451-3344	455-5882
Web: www.edmontonscience.com					
Fort Edmonton Park Fox & Whitemud Drs	Edmonton	AB	T5J2R7	780-496-8787	496-8797
Fort Saskatchewan Museum 10104 101st St	Edmonton	AB	T8L1V9	780-998-1750	998-1750
Web: fortsaskinfo.com/museum/					
Galaxyland Amusement Park 8882 170th St West Edmonton Mall	Edmonton	AB	T5T4M2	780-444-5300	
Web: www.westedmall.com/attractions/html/galaxyland.htm					
Janzen John Nature Centre Fox & Whitemud Drs	Edmonton	AB	T5J2R7	780-496-2939	496-4701
Loyal Edmonton Regiment Museum 10440 108th Ave	Edmonton	AB	T5H3Z9	780-421-9943	421-9943
Mayfield Dinner Theatre 16615 109th Ave	Edmonton	AB	T5P4K8	780-483-4051	487-6018
Web: www.mayfield-inn.com/DT-What'sPlaying.htm					
Millwoods Recreation Centre 7207 28th Ave	Edmonton	AB	T6K3Z3	780-496-2900	496-2944
Musee Heritage Museum 5 Sainte Anne St	Saint Albert	AB	T8N3Z9	780-459-1528	459-1546
Muttart Conservatory 9626 96A St	Edmonton	AB	T6C4L8	780-496-8755	496-8747
Northern Alberta Jubilee Auditorium 11455 87th Ave	Edmonton	AB	T6G2T2	780-427-2760	422-3750
Web: www.jubileeauditorium.com					
Old Strathcona Farmer's Market 10310 83rd Ave	Edmonton	AB	T6E5C3	780-439-1844	433-4263
Old Strathcona Historic Area 10324 Whyte Ave	Edmonton	AB	T6E1Z8	780-433-5866	431-1938
Provincial Archives of Alberta 12845 102nd Ave	Edmonton	AB	T5N0M6	780-427-1750	427-4646
Provincial Museum of Alberta 12845 102nd Ave	Edmonton	AB	T5N0M6	780-453-9100	454-6629
Web: www.pma.edmonton.ab.ca ■ *E-mail:* bbolton@mcd.gov.ab.ca					
River Valley Centre 10125 97th Ave	Edmonton	AB	T5K0B3	780-496-7275	496-2955

Edmonton — Attractions (Cont'd)

		Phone	Fax
Royal Tyrrell Museum of Palaeontology Hwy 838 Midland Provincial Pk	Drumheller AB T0J0Y0	403-823-7707	823-7131
TF: 888-440-4240 ■ *Web:* www.tyrrellmuseum.com ■ *E-mail:* info@tyrrellmuseum.com			
Rutherford House Provincial Historical Site 11153 Saskatchewan Dr.	Edmonton AB T6G2S1	780-427-3995	422-4288
Telephone Historical Centre 10437 83rd Ave	Edmonton AB T6E4T5	780-441-2077	433-4068
Web: www.discoveredmonton.com/telephonemuseum/			
Theatre Network Live At The Roxy 10708 124th St.	Edmonton AB T5M0H1	780-453-2440	453-2596
Ukrainian Canadian Archives & Museum of Alberta 9543 110th Ave	Edmonton AB T5H1H3	780-424-7580	420-0562
Ukrainian Cultural Heritage Village 8820 112th St	Edmonton AB T6G2P8	780-662-3640	662-3273
University of Alberta Devonian Botanic Garden Hwy 60	Devon AB T6G2E1	780-987-3054	987-4141
Web: www.discoveredmonton.com/devonian/			
Valley Zoo 13315 Buena Vista Rd.	Edmonton AB T5J2R7	780-496-6912	944-7529
Walter John Museum 9100 Walterdale Hill Kinsmen Pk	Edmonton AB T6E2V3	780-496-4852	496-8797
Webb Brian Dance Company 10045 156th St.	Edmonton AB T5J2P7	780-497-4416	497-4330
Winspear Centre For Music 4 Sir Winston Churchill Sq.	Edmonton AB T5J2R7	780-428-1414	425-0167
Web: www.winspearcentre.com			
Wolf Wine Cellars Hwy 16.	Stony Plain AB T0E2G0	780-963-7717	963-0086
World Waterpark 8882 170th St West Edmonton Mall	Edmonton AB T5T4M2	780-444-5310	444-5233
Web: www.westedmall.com/attractions/html/water.htm			

SPORTS TEAMS & FACILITIES

		Phone	Fax
Commonwealth Stadium 11000 Stadium Rd	Edmonton AB T5B0C3	780-496-6999	944-7545
Edmonton Drillers (soccer) 7300 116th Ave Skyreach Ctr.	Edmonton AB T5J2N5	780-425-5425	423-2999
Web: www.edmontondrillers.com ■ *E-mail:* drillers@compusmart.ab.ca			
Edmonton Eskimos (football) 9023 111th Ave	Edmonton AB T5B0C3	780-448-1525	429-3452
Web: www.esks.com			
Edmonton Oilers 7300 116th Ave Skyreach Ctr.	Edmonton AB T5J2N5	780-414-4000	414-4659
Web: www.edmontonoilers.com			
Edmonton Trappers (baseball) 10233 96th Ave	Edmonton AB T5K0A5	780-414-4450	414-4475
Web: www.canoe.ca/BaseballEDM/home.html ■ *E-mail:* trappers@planet.eon.net			
Labatt's Raceway Hwy 19	Devon AB	780-461-5801	461-5827
Skyreach Centre 7300 116th Ave	Edmonton AB T5J2N5	780-471-7210	471-8195
Spectrum The 116th Ave & 73rd St Northlands Park	Edmonton AB T5J2N5	780-471-7210	471-8176
TF: 888-800-7275 ■ *Web:* www.northlands.com ■ *E-mail:* nptec@planet.eon.net			

— Events —

	Phone
Canadian Finals Rodeo (early-mid-November)	780-471-7210
Cariwest: Edmonton's Caribbean Carnival (mid-August)	780-421-7800
Edmonton Boat & Sportsmen's Show (early March)	780-245-9008
Edmonton Canada Day (July 1)	780-488-6213
Edmonton Folk Music Festival (early August)	780-429-1899
Edmonton Heritage Festival (early August)	780-488-3378
Edmonton Home & Garden Show (mid-March)	780-471-7210
Edmonton Home Show (mid-September)	780-424-0515
Edmonton International Street Performers Festival (mid-late July)	780-425-5162
Edmonton Kiwanis Music Festival (late April-early May)	780-488-3498
Edmonton New Music Festival (early October)	800-563-5081
Edmonton Women's Show (mid-March & mid-October)	780-490-0215
Edmonton's International Fringe Theatre Event (mid-late August)	780-448-9000
Edmonton's Klondike Days (mid-late July)	780-423-2822
Farmfair International (early-mid-November)	780-471-7210
First Night Edmonton (December 31)	780-448-9200
Jazz City International Music Festival (late June-early July)	780-432-7166
Kinsmen Rainmaker Rodeo (late May)	780-459-1724
Local Heroes International Screen Festival (early-mid-March)	780-421-4084
Medieval Days (late May-early June)	780-464-0249
Northern Alberta International Children's Festival (late May-early June)	780-459-1542
Northlands Farm & Ranch Show (late March)	780-471-7210
Symphony Under the Sky Festival (early September)	780-428-1414
Works The: A Visual Arts Celebration (late June-early July)	780-426-2122

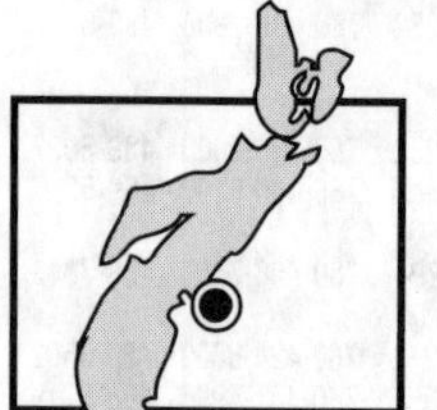

Halifax

Halifax is the capital of Nova Scotia and the largest city in the Atlantic provinces. The city was founded by British Governor Edward Cornwallis in 1749 as a rival to France's naval stronghold at Louisberg. It continued to be used by the British fleet until 1906 and was a naval base during both world wars. Shared by Halifax and its twin city Dartmouth is one of the world's great natural harbors. The harbor is Canada's principal ice-free port, a working area for fishing, shipping, and Canada's Navy on the eastern seaboard. Major landmarks in Halifax include Canada's most visited National Historic Site, the Halifax Citadel, a massive fortress built between 1825 and 1856; and Saint Paul's Church, which was built in 1750 and is the oldest Anglican church in Canada.

Population	940,825	**Longitude**	63-34-48 W
Area (Land)	79.2 sq mi	**Time Zone**	ATZ
Elevation	477 ft	**Area Code/s**	902
Latitude	44-40-12 N		

— Average Temperatures and Precipitation —

TEMPERATURES

	Jan	Feb	Mar	Apr	May	Jun	Jul	Aug	Sep	Oct	Nov	Dec
High	28	28	37	46	59	68	73	73	66	55	45	34
Low	14	12	21	30	39	48	55	55	48	39	32	19

PRECIPITATION

	Jan	Feb	Mar	Apr	May	Jun	Jul	Aug	Sep	Oct	Nov	Dec
Inches	3.6	2.8	3.3	3.5	4.1	3.5	3.7	4.4	3.7	5.1	5.6	5.0

— Important Phone Numbers —

	Phone		Phone
24 Hour Non-Emergency	902-490-5020	**Civic Events & Festivals Hotline**	902-490-6776
American Express Travel	902-423-3900	**Emergency**	911
CAA	902-443-5530	**Weather**	902-426-9090

— Information Sources —

		Phone	Fax
Alderney Gate Public Library 60 Alderney Dr.	Halifax NS B3A1M1	902-490-5745	490-5762
Better Business Bureau Serving Nova Scotia 1888 Brunswick St Suite 601	Halifax NS B3J3B8	902-422-6581	429-6457
Web: www.bbbns.com/bbbns/ ■ *E-mail:* bbbns@bbbns.com			
Downtown Halifax Business Commission 1668 Barrington St Suite 301	Halifax NS B3J2A2	902-423-2179	429-0865
Web: www.downtownhalifax.ns.ca ■ *E-mail:* info@downtownhalifax.ns.ca			
Greater Halifax Conventions & Meetings Bureau 1800 Argyle St Suite 423	Halifax NS B3J3N8	902-422-9334	492-3175
Web: www.meethalifax.com			
Halifax City Hall 1841 Argyle St.	Halifax NS B3J3A5	902-490-4210	490-4208
Web: www.region.halifax.ns.ca/Cityhall/hrm_ch.html			

Halifax — Information Sources (Cont'd)

				Phone	Fax
Halifax Mayor 1841 Argyle St. *Web:* www.region.halifax.ns.ca/Cityhall/mayprof.html	Halifax	NS	B3J3A5	902-490-4010	490-4012
Halifax Regional Municipality PO Box 1749 *Web:* www.region.halifax.ns.ca	Halifax	NS	B3J3A5	902-490-4000	490-4012
International Visitor Centre 1595 Barrington St	Halifax	NS	B3J1Z7	902-490-5946	490-5973
Metropolitan Halifax Chamber of Commerce PO Box 8990 *Web:* www.halifaxchamber.com	Halifax	NS	B3K5M6	902-468-7111	468-7333
Nova Scotia Economic Development & Tourism Dept 1800 Argyle St World Trade & Convention Ctr *Web:* www.gov.ns.ca/ecor/ ■ *E-mail:* econ.edt@gov.ns.ca	Halifax	NS	B3J2R7	902-424-8920	
World Trade & Convention Centre 1800 Argyle St *Web:* www.tradecentrelimited.com/wtcc/index.html	Halifax	NS	B3J3N8	902-422-2020	421-1055

On-Line Resources

Atlantic Explorer Travel Mag	atlanticonline.ns.ca/travmag/
Chebucto Community Net	www.chebucto.ns.ca
City Knowledge Halifax	www.cityknowledge.com/canada_ns_halifax.htm
Destination Nova Scotia	www.destination-ns.com
eteast.com Online Arts & Entertainment Magazine	www.eteast.com/eteast.html
Halifax Online	www.halifaxonline.com
Nova Scotia Online	nsonline.com
Rough Guide Travel Halifax	travel.roughguides.com/content/4985/index.htm
Surf & Sun Beach Vacation Guide to Halifax	www.surf-sun.com/canada-halifax-main.htm
Virtual Nova Scotia	explore.gov.ns.ca

— Transportation Services —

AIRPORTS

■ Halifax International Airport (YHZ)

	Phone
26 miles NE of downtown (approx 40 minutes) Web: www.tc.gc.ca/halifaxairport/	902-873-1234

Airport Transportation

	Phone
Aero Cab $28.75 fare to downtown	902-445-3333
Four Star Limousine $35 fare to downtown	902-456-3885

Commercial Airlines

	Phone		Phone
Air Canada	800-776-3000	**Delta Connection**	800-221-1212
Air Nova	800-776-3000	**Icelandair**	800-223-5500
Air Transat	877-872-6728	**Lufthansa**	800-645-3880
British Airways	800-247-9297	**Northwest Airlink**	800-225-2525
Canada 3000	877-359-2263	**Royal Airlines**	800-667-7692
Canadian Air	800-426-7000	**United**	800-241-6522
Continental	800-525-0280		

CAR RENTALS

	Phone		Phone
Budget	902-492-7551	**Hertz**	902-873-2273
Dollar	902-860-0203	**Thrifty**	902-873-3527

LIMO/TAXI

	Phone		Phone
Aero Cab	902-445-3333	**Green Cab**	902-455-6666
Barter Taxi	902-471-1631	**JR's Limousine**	902-478-7600
Casino Taxi	902-429-6666	**Unique Limousine**	902-499-4300
Four Star Limousine	902-456-3885		

MASS TRANSIT

	Phone
Metro Transit Bus $1.65 Base fare	902-490-6600
Metro Transit Ferry $1.65 Base fare	902-490-6600

RAIL/BUS

				Phone
Via Rail Canada 1161 Hollis St	Halifax	NS	B3H2P6	800-561-9181

— Accommodations —

HOTEL RESERVATION SERVICES

	Phone
Check-In Nova Scotia's Free Reservation Service	800-565-0000

HOTELS, MOTELS, RESORTS

				Phone	Fax
Airport Hotel Halifax 60 Bell Blvd Halifax International Airport *TF:* 800-667-3333	Enfield	NS	B2T1K3	902-873-3000	873-3001
Best Western Micmac Hotel 313 Prince Albert Rd *TF:* 800-565-1275	Dartmouth	NS	B2Y1N3	902-469-5850	469-5859
Bluenose Inn 636 Bedford Hwy *TF:* 800-565-2301	Halifax	NS	B3M2L8	902-443-3171	443-9368
Burnside Hotel 739 Windmill Rd *TF:* 800-830-4656	Dartmouth	NS	B3B1C1	902-468-7117	468-1770
Cambridge Suites Hotel Halifax 1583 Brunswick St *TF:* 800-565-1263 ■ *Web:* www.centennialhotels.com ■ *E-mail:* reservations@hfx.cambridgesuites.ns.ca	Halifax	NS	B3J3P5	902-420-0555	420-9379
Chebucto Inn 6151 Lady Hammond Rd *TF:* 800-268-4330	Halifax	NS	B3K2R9	902-453-4330	454-7043
Citadel Halifax Hotel 1960 Brunswick St *TF:* 800-565-7162	Halifax	NS	B3J2G7	902-422-1391	429-6672
Coastal Inn Concorde 379 Windmill Rd *TF:* 800-565-1565 ■ *Web:* www.coastalinns.com	Dartmouth	NS	B3A1J6	902-465-7777	465-3956
Comfort Inn 456 Windmill Rd *TF:* 800-228-5150	Dartmouth	NS	B3A1J7	902-463-9900	466-2080
Country Inn & Suites 101 Yorkshire Ave Ext *TF:* 800-456-4000	Dartmouth	NS	B2Y3Y2	902-465-4000	465-6006
Delta Barrington 1875 Barrington St *TF:* 800-268-1133 ■ *Web:* www.deltahotels.com/hotels.php3?action=show&hotelid=3	Halifax	NS	B3J3L6	902-429-7410	420-6524
Econo Lodge 560 Bedford Hwy *TF:* 800-561-9961	Halifax	NS	B3M2L8	902-443-0303	457-0663
Four Star Motel 317 Prince Albert Rd *TF:* 800-565-2354	Dartmouth	NS	B2Y1N5	902-466-0717	461-1102
Future Inns 20 Highfield Park Dr. *TF:* 800-565-0700	Dartmouth	NS	B3A4S8	902-465-6555	469-0868
Halliburton House Inn 5184 Morris St. *Web:* www.halliburton.ns.ca	Halifax	NS	B3J1B3	902-420-0658	423-2324
Holiday Inn Express 1333 Kearney Lake Rd *TF:* 800-565-3086 ■ *Web:* www.holidayinnhalifax.com	Halifax	NS	B3M4P3	902-445-1100	445-1101
Holiday Inn Harbourview 99 Wyse Rd *TF:* 800-465-4329	Dartmouth	NS	B3A1L9	902-463-1100	464-1227
Holiday Inn Select Halifax Centre 1980 Robie St *TF:* 800-465-4329	Halifax	NS	B3H3G5	902-423-1161	423-9069
Hotel Halifax 1990 Barrington St *TF:* 800-441-1414	Halifax	NS	B3J1P2	902-425-6700	425-6214
Keddy's Dartmouth Inn 9 Braemar Dr *TF:* 800-561-7666	Dartmouth	NS	B2Y3H6	902-469-0331	466-6324
Keddy's Halifax Hotel 20 St Margaret's Bay Rd *TF:* 800-561-7666 ■ *Web:* www.keddys.ca	Halifax	NS	B3N1J4	902-477-5611	479-2150
King Edward Inn 5780-88 West St *TF:* 800-565-5464 ■ *Web:* www.kingedward.com	Halifax	NS	B3K1H8	902-422-3266	423-5731
Lord Nelson Hotel 1515 South Park St *TF:* 800-565-2020	Halifax	NS	B3J2T3	902-423-6331	423-7148
Maranova Suites 65 King St. *TF:* 888-798-5558 ■ *Web:* maranovasuites.com ■ *E-mail:* reservations@maranovasuites.com	Dartmouth	NS	B2Y4C2	902-463-9520	463-2631
Park Place Ramada Renaissance Hotel 240 Brownlow Ave *TF:* 800-561-3733 ■ *Web:* www.ramadans.com	Dartmouth	NS	B3B1X6	902-468-8888	468-8765
Prince George Hotel 1725 Market St. *TF:* 800-565-1567 ■ *Web:* www.princegeorgehotel.com	Halifax	NS	B3J3N9	902-425-1986	429-6048
Radisson Suite Hotel Halifax 1649 Hollis St *TF:* 800-333-3333	Halifax	NS	B3J1V8	902-429-7233	429-9700
Seasons Motor Inn Halifax 4 Melrose Ave *TF:* 800-792-2498 ■ *Web:* home.istar.ca/~garson/	Halifax	NS	B3N2E2	902-443-9341	443-9341
Sheraton Halifax 1919 Upper Water St *TF:* 800-325-3535	Halifax	NS	B3J3J5	902-421-1700	422-5805
Wandlyn Inn Halifax 50 Bedford Hwy *TF:* 800-561-0000	Halifax	NS	B3M2J2	902-443-0416	457-0665
Waverley Inn 1266 Barrington St *TF:* 800-565-9346 ■ *Web:* www.waverleyinn.com ■ *E-mail:* welcome@waverleyinn.com	Halifax	NS	B3J1Y5	902-423-9346	425-0167
Wedgewood Motel 374 Bedford Hwy.	Halifax	NS	B3M2L1	902-443-1576	443-2762
Westin Nova Scotian 1181 Hollis St *TF:* 800-228-3000	Halifax	NS	B3H2P6	902-421-1000	422-9465

Halifax (Cont'd)

— Restaurants —

				Phone
Alfredo Weinstein and Ho (International) 1739 Grafton St	Halifax	NS	B3J2C6	902-421-1977
Athens Restaurant (Greek) 6303 Quinpool Rd	Halifax	NS	B3L1A4	902-422-1595
Birmingham Bar and Grill (Continental) 5657 Spring Garden Rd.	Halifax	NS	B3J3R5	902-420-9622
Bluenose Restaurant (Seafood) 636 Bedford Hwy	Halifax	NS	B3M2L8	902-443-3171
Cafe Cap St Jacques (Vietnamese) 5190 Blowers St	Halifax	NS	B3J1J4	902-422-9131
Cafe Chianti (Italian) 5165 South St.	Halifax	NS	B3J2A6	902-423-7471
Cafe Mokka (North American) 1588 Granville St	Halifax	NS	B3J1X1	902-492-4036
Cheelin (Chinese) 1496 Lower Water St	Halifax	NS	B3J1R9	902-422-2252
Chicken Tandoor (Indian/Thai) 6285 Quinpool Rd	Halifax	NS	B3L1A4	902-423-7725
Crawdad's Crab Shack & Oyster Bar (Cajun/Creole) 1599 Grafton St	Halifax	NS	B3J2C3	902-422-5200
Crown Bistro Restaurant (North American) 1990 Barrington St Hotel Halifax	Halifax	NS	B3J1P2	902-425-6700
Darlington's on Duke (Continental) 5170 Duke St	Halifax	NS	B3J3J6	902-423-5221
Dharma Sushi (Japanese) 1576 Argyle St.	Halifax	NS	B3J2B3	902-425-7785
East Side Mario's (Italian) 1650 Bedford Row	Halifax	NS	B3J1T2	902-422-7100
Economy Shoe Shop Cafe and Bar (European) 1663 Argyle St	Halifax	NS	B3J2B5	902-423-7463
Five Fishermen (Seafood) 1740 Argyle St.	Halifax	NS	B3J2W1	902-422-4421
Guru Restaurant (Indian) 5234 Blowers St	Halifax	NS	B3J1J7	902-422-6347
Halliburton House Inn (Seafood) 5184 Morris St	Halifax	NS	B3J1B3	902-420-0658
Hogie's Steak and Fish House (Steak/Seafood) 6273 Quinpool Rd	Halifax	NS	B3L1A4	902-422-4414
Houston's Restaurant & Grill (Steak) 1960 Brunswick St	Halifax	NS	B3J2G7	902-422-1391
Il Mercato (Italian) 5475 Spring Garden Rd	Halifax	NS	B3J3T2	902-422-2866
Le Bistro (French) 1333 South Park St	Halifax	NS	B3J2K9	902-423-8428
Left Bank (North American) 1496 Lower Water St	Halifax	NS	B3J1R9	902-492-3049
Lone Star Cafe (Tex Mex) 1599 Grafton St	Halifax	NS	B3J2C3	902-422-8524
Mexicali Rosa's (Mexican) 5680 Spring Garden Rd	Halifax	NS	B3J1H5	902-422-7672
Momoya Restaurant (Japanese) 1671 Barrington St	Halifax	NS	B3J1Z9	902-492-0788
My Apartment (Seafood) 1740 Argyle St.	Halifax	NS	B3J2B6	902-422-5453
O'Carroll's (Continental) 1860 Upper Water St	Halifax	NS	B3J1S8	902-423-4405
Satisfaction Feast & Vegetarian Restaurant (Vegetarian) 1581 Grafton St	Halifax	NS	B3J2C3	902-422-3540
Soho Kitchen (Continental) 1582 Granville St *Web:* c-level.com/soho/index.html ■ *E-mail:* soho@c-level.com	Halifax	NS	B3J1X1	902-423-3049
Spice Trail (Chinese) 1580 Argyle St	Halifax	NS	B3J2B3	902-423-0093
Sweet Basil Bistro (Italian) 1866 Upper Water St	Halifax	NS	B3J1S8	902-425-2133
Tradewinds Restaurant (Continental) 1181 Hollis St	Halifax	NS	B3H2P6	902-496-7960
Unni's (Continental) 1569 Dresden Row	Halifax	NS	B3J2K4	902-422-3733
Waterfront Warehouse (Seafood) 1549 Lower Water St	Halifax	NS	B3J1S2	902-425-7610

— Goods and Services —

SHOPPING

				Phone	Fax
Historic Properties Marketplace 1869 Upper Water St.	Halifax	NS	B3J1S9	902-429-0530	423-8379

BANKS

				Phone	Fax
Bank of Canada 1583 Hollis St 5th Fl	Halifax	NS	B3J1V4	902-420-4600	420-4644
Bank of Montreal 5151 George St Bank of Montreal Tower	Halifax	NS	B3J2M3	902-421-3698	421-3697
Canadian Imperial Bank of Commerce 1809 Barrington St	Halifax	NS	B3J3A3	902-428-4750	428-7972
Royal Bank of Canada 5161 George St	Halifax	NS	B3J2L7	902-421-8330	421-0897
Scotiabank 1709 Hollis St	Halifax	NS	B3J2M1	902-420-3567	422-8332
Toronto-Dominion Bank 1785 Barrington St.	Halifax	NS	B3J2P8	902-420-8040	420-8189

BUSINESS SERVICES

	Phone
Advantage Personnel	902-468-5624
Airborne Express	800-247-2676
Bradson Staffing Services	902-422-9675
Crystal Courier	902-445-2878
DHL Worldwide Express	800-225-5345
Elite Courier	902-455-0855
Federal Express	800-463-3339
Federal Express	800-238-5355
Kelly Services	902-425-8770
Kinko's	902-423-5500
Mail Boxes Etc	902-445-5050
Manpower Temporary Services	902-422-1373
Olsten Staffing Services	902-423-9111
Post Office	902-494-4734
UPS	800-742-5877

— Media —

PUBLICATIONS

				Phone	Fax
Chronicle-Herald The/Mail-Star† 1650 Argyle St **Fax:* News Rm ■ *TF:* 800-565-3339 ■ *Web:* www.herald.ns.ca ■ *E-mail:* newsroom@herald.ns.ca	Halifax	NS	B3J2T2	902-426-1187	426-1158*
Halifax Daily News† PO Box 8330 Stn A. **Fax:* News Rm ■ *Web:* www.hfxnews.southam.ca ■ *E-mail:* citydesk@hfxnews.southam.ca	Halifax	NS	B3K5M1	902-468-7627	468-2645*

†Daily newspapers

TELEVISION

				Phone	Fax
CBHT-TV Ch 3 (CBC) 1840 Bell Rd	Halifax	NS	B3J3E9	902-420-4100	420-4137
CIHF-TV Ch 6 (GTN) 14 Akerley Blvd	Dartmouth	NS	B3B1J3	902-481-7400	468-2154
CJCH-TV Ch 5 (CTV) PO Box 1653	Halifax	NS	B3J2Z4	902-454-3200	454-3280

RADIO

				Phone	Fax
CFDR-AM 780 kHz (Ctry) 2900 Agricola St.	Halifax	NS	B3K4P5	902-453-2524	453-3132
CFRQ-FM 104.3 MHz (CR) 2900 Agricola St *Web:* www.q104.ca	Halifax	NS	B3K4P5	902-453-2524	453-3132
CHFX-FM 101.9 MHz (Ctry) PO Box 400 **Fax:* News Rm	Halifax	NS	B3J2R2	902-422-2424	425-2754*
CHNS-AM 960 kHz (Oldies) PO Box 400 **Fax:* News Rm	Halifax	NS	B3J2R2	902-422-2424	425-2754*
CIEZ-FM 96.5 MHz (AC) 2900 Agricola St	Halifax	NS	B3K4P5	902-453-2524	453-3132
CIOO-FM 100.1 MHz (AC) 2900 Agricola St *Web:* newedge.net/c100/c100.asp ■ *E-mail:* c100@newedge.net	Halifax	NS	B3K4P5	902-453-2524	453-3132
CJCH-AM 920 kHz (N/T) 2900 Agricola St *Web:* newedge.net/c100/cjch.htm ■ *E-mail:* 920cjch@newedge.net	Halifax	NS	B3K4P5	902-453-2524	453-3132

— Colleges/Universities —

				Phone	Fax
Compucollege School of Business 1526 Dresden Row	Halifax	NS	B3J3K3	902-423-3933	423-2042
Dalhousie University 1236 Henry St *Web:* www.dal.ca ■ *E-mail:* eperts@dal	Halifax	NS	B3H3J5	902-494-2211	494-1630
DalTech 1360 Barrington St Dalhousie University *Web:* www.dal.ca/~daltech/index.html	Halifax	NS	B3J2X4	902-494-3267	429-3011
Maritime Conservatory of Music 6199 Chebucto Rd	Halifax	NS	B3L1K7	902-423-6995	423-6029
Mount Saint Vincent University 166 Bedford Hwy **Fax:* Admissions ■ *Web:* www.msvu.ca ■ *E-mail:* admissions@msvu.ca	Halifax	NS	B3M2J6	902-457-6128	457-6498*
Nova Scotia College of Art & Design 5163 Duke St *Web:* www.nscad.ns.ca	Halifax	NS	B3J3J6	902-422-7381	425-2987
Nova Scotia Community College 1825 Bell Rd *Web:* www.nscc.ns.ca ■ *E-mail:* haadmissions@nscc.ns.ca	Halifax	NS	B2H2Z4	902-491-4636	491-4711
Saint Mary's University 923 Robie St *Web:* www.stmarys.ca	Halifax	NS	B3H3C3	902-420-5400	496-8100
University of King's College 6350 Coburg Rd *Web:* www.ukings.ns.ca ■ *E-mail:* admissions@ukings.ns.ca	Halifax	NS	B3H2A1	902-422-1271	423-3357

— Hospitals —

				Phone	Fax
Dartmouth General Hospital & Community Health Centre 325 Pleasant St	Dartmouth	NS	B2Y4G8	902-465-8300	465-8537
Nova Scotia Hospital 300 Pleasant St	Dartmouth	NS	B2Y3Z9	902-464-3111	
Queen Elizabeth II Health Sciences Centre-The New Infirmary 1796 Summer St. *Web:* www.qe2-hsc.ns.ca	Halifax	NS	B3H3A7	902-473-2700	

Halifax (Cont'd)

— Attractions —

Phone | Fax

Amethyst Scottish Dancers of Nova Scotia
113 Woodlawn Rd ... Dartmouth NS B2W2T2 902-434-0577 434-0577
Web: www.chebucto.ns.ca/Culture/Amethyst/index.html

Army Museum
5425 Sackville St Halifax Citadel National Historic Site ... Halifax NS B3J3Y3 902-422-5979 426-4228

Art Gallery of Nova Scotia 1723 Hollis St ... Halifax NS B3J3C8 902-424-3002 424-7359
Web: www.agns.ednet.ns.ca

Atlantic Canada Aviation Museum
Exit 6 off of Hwy 102 ... Halifax NS 902-873-3773
Web: bluenose.canadaweb.com/tourism/aviation/

Atlantic Marine Pavillion Aquarium
Lower Water St Adjacent to Maritime Museum of the Atlantic ... Halifax NS B3J1S3

Atlantic Playland Park 1200 Lucasville Rd ... Bedford NS B4B1P7 902-865-1025
Web: www.playland.ns.ca

Black Cultural Centre for Nova Scotia
1149 Main St ... Dartmouth NS B2Z1A8 902-434-6223 434-2306
TF: 800-465-0767 ■ *Web:* home.istar.ca/~bccns/
■ *E-mail:* blackcct@fox.nstn.ca

Bluenose II
1675 Lower Water St Maritime Museum of the Atlantic Wharf ... Halifax NS B3J1S3 902-424-7490 424-0612
TF: 800-763-1963

Cathedral Church of All Saints
Tower Rd & University Ave ... Halifax NS B3H1X3 902-423-6002

Cole Harbour Heritage Farm Museum
471 Poplar Dr. ... Dartmouth NS B2W4L2 902-434-0222 434-0222

Costume Studies Museum
1685 Argyle St Carleton House ... Halifax NS B3H3J5 902-494-6515 494-1269

Dalhousie Art Gallery 6101 University Ave. ... Halifax NS B3H3J5 902-494-2403 494-2890
Web: www.dal.ca/~gallery/index.html ■ *E-mail:* gallery@dac.cohn.dal.ca

Dalhousie Arts Centre 6101 University Ave ... Halifax NS B3H3J5 902-494-3820 494-2883
TF: 800-874-1669 ■ *Web:* is.dal.ca/~cohn/dac.html

Dalhousie-McCulloch Museum
1355 Oxford St Dalhousie University Life Sciences Bldg. ... Halifax NS B3H4J1 902-494-3515 494-3736

Dalhousie University Archives
University Ave Killam Memorial Library ... Halifax NS B3H4H8 902-494-6490 494-2062

Dalhousie University Theatre
6101 University Ave Dalhousie Arts Ctr 5th Fl. ... Halifax NS B3H3J5 902-494-2233 494-1499
Web: www.dal.ca/~thtrwww/thtrwww.html

Dartmouth Heritage Museum
100 Wyse Rd ... Dartmouth NS B3A1M1 902-464-2300

Dartmouth Players 23 Wildwood Blvd ... Dartmouth NS B2W2L7 902-465-7529 435-7647
Web: www.chebucto.ns.ca/Culture/DPlayers/
■ *E-mail:* d-players@chebucto.ns.ca

Discovery Centre 1593 Barrington St. ... Halifax NS B3J1Z7 902-492-4422 492-3170
Web: www.discoverycentre.ns.ca
■ *E-mail:* handsonfun@discoverycentre.ns.ca

Eastern Front Theatre 10 Acadia St. ... Dartmouth NS B2V3J9 902-463-7529 466-2769
Web: www3.ns.sympatico.ca/eastern.front/
■ *E-mail:* eastern.front@ns.sympatico.ca

Empire Imax Theatre 190 Chain Lake Dr ... Halifax NS B3S1C5 902-876-4800 876-4801
Web: www.empireimax.com ■ *E-mail:* empire@empireimax.com

Evergreen House 26 Newcastle St. ... Dartmouth NS B2Y3M5 902-464-2301 464-8210

Fisherman's Cove
200 Government Wharf Rd. ... Eastern Passage NS B3G1M7 902-465-6093 465-6899
Web: www.chebucto.ns.ca/EasternPassage/fcove/

Fisherman's Life Museum
58 Navy Pool Loop Oyster Ponds ... Halifax NS B0J1W0 902-889-2053 889-2053

Halifax Camerata Singers 759 Prince St ... Truro NS B2N1G7 902-893-4242 895-1862
Web: is2.dal.ca/~slide/camerata/index.html

Halifax Citadel National Historic Site
5425 Sackville St ... Halifax NS B3J3Y3 902-426-5080 426-4228
Web: parkscanada.pch.gc.ca/parks/nova_scotia/halifax_citadel/halifax_citadele.htm
■ *E-mail:* halifax_citadel@pch.gc.ca

Halifax Dance
1496 Lower Water St Brewery Market ... Halifax NS B3J2N7 902-422-2006 423-2057
Web: www.chebucto.ns.ca/Culture/HalDance/hd_home.html

Halifax Public Gardens PO Box 1749 ... Halifax NS B3J3A5 902-490-4895

Historic Properties 1869 Upper Water St. ... Halifax NS B3J1S9 902-429-0530 423-8379

HMCS Sackville-Canada's Naval Memorial
1673 Lower Water St Sackville Landing Wharf ... Halifax NS 902-429-5600
Web: learning.ns.sympatico.ca/sackville/

Jest in Time Theatre Co
1585 Barrington St Suite 206 ... Halifax NS B3J1Z8 902-423-4647 425-7359
Web: www.jestintime.ns.ca ■ *E-mail:* jest@jestintime.ns.ca

Leonowens Anna Gallery
1891 Granville St Nova Scotia College of Art & Design ... Halifax NS B3J3J6 902-494-8223
Web: www.nscad.ns.ca/~gallery/

Maritime Museum of the Atlantic
1675 Lower Water St ... Halifax NS B3J1S3 902-424-7490 424-0612
Web: www.ednet.ns.ca/educ/museum/mma/
■ *E-mail:* murraymr@gov.ns.ca

Mount Saint Vincent University Art Gallery
166 Bedford Hwy Seton Academic Ctr Rm 209 ... Halifax NS B3M2J6 902-457-6160 457-2447
E-mail: art.gallery@msvu.ca

Neptune Theatre 1593 Argyle St. ... Halifax NS B3J2B2 902-429-7070 429-1211
TF: 800-565-7345 ■ *Web:* neptune.ns.sympatico.ca
■ *E-mail:* neptune.theatre!ns.sympatico.ca

Nova Scotia Center for Craft & Design
1683 Barrington St ... Halifax NS B3J2S9 902-424-4062 424-0670

Nova Scotia Choral Federation
1809 Barrington St Suite 901 ... Halifax NS B3J3K8 902-423-4688 422-0881
Web: www.chebucto.ns.ca/Culture/NSCF/nscf-home.html
■ *E-mail:* nscf@fox.nstn.ca

Nova Scotia Drama League
1809 Barrington St Suite 901 ... Halifax NS B3J3K8 902-425-3876 422-0881
Web: www3.ns.sympatico.ca/nsdl/ ■ *E-mail:* nsdl@ns.sympatico.ca

Nova Scotia Museum of Natural History
1747 Summer St ... Halifax NS B3H3A6 902-424-7353 424-0560
Web: www.ednet.ns.ca/educ/museum/mnh/

Nova Scotia Sport Hall of Fame
1645 Granville St Suite 101 ... Halifax NS B3J1X3 902-421-1266 425-1148

Pier 21 PO Box 611 ... Halifax NS B3J2R7 902-425-7770 423-4045
Web: pier21.ns.ca ■ *E-mail:* pier21@pier21.ns.ca

Prince of Wales Tower National Historic Site
5425 Sackville St ... Halifax NS B3J3Y3 902-426-5080 426-4228

Province House National Historic Site
1726 Hollis St ... Halifax NS B3J2Y3 902-424-4661

Public Archives of Nova Scotia
6016 University Ave ... Halifax NS B3H1W4 902-424-6060 424-0628

Royal Canadian Legion Military Museum
52 King St ... Dartmouth NS B2Y2R5 902-463-1050

Saint Mary's University Art Gallery
593 Robie St Loyola Bldg ... Halifax NS B3H3C3 902-420-5445

Saint Paul's Anglican Church 1749 Argyle St. ... Halifax NS B3J3K4 902-429-2240
Web: www.stpaulshalifax.org ■ *E-mail:* stpauls@chebucto.ns.ca

Shakespeare by the Sea 5799 Charles St ... Halifax NS B3K1K7 902-422-0295 422-4250
TF: 888-759-1516 ■ *Web:* shakespeare.ns.sympatico.ca

Symphony Nova Scotia
6101 University Ave Dalhousie Arts Ctr ... Halifax NS B3H3J5 902-494-3820 494-2883
TF: 800-874-1669 ■ *Web:* sns.ns.sympatico.ca

Visual Arts Nova Scotia 1113 Marginal Rd ... Halifax NS B3H4P7 902-423-4694 422-0881
Web: vans.ednet.ns.ca ■ *E-mail:* vans@fox.nstn.ca

York Redoubt National Historic Site
5425 Sackville St ... Halifax NS B3J3Y3 902-426-5080 426-4228

SPORTS TEAMS & FACILITIES

Phone | Fax

Halifax Metro Centre 1800 Argyle St. ... Halifax NS B3J2V9 902-422-2020 422-2922
Web: www.tradecentrelimited.com/hmc/index.html

Halifax Mooseheads (hockey)
1800 Argyle St Halifax Metro Ctr ... Halifax NS B3J2V9 902-496-5993 423-6413
Web: mooseheads.ns.sympatico.ca

— Events —

	Phone
Alexander Keith's Magical History Tour (June-September)	902-422-2069
Atlantic Film Festival (mid-late September)	902-422-3456
Atlantic Fringe Festival (early September)	902-435-4837
Atlantic Winter Fair (early-mid-October)	902-876-8222
Christmas at the Cove (December)	902-465-6093
Christmas at the Forum (early November)	902-425-5656
Christmas Tree Lighting Ceremony (early December)	902-423-3740
DuMaurier Atlantic Jazz Festival (mid-late July)	902-492-2225
Easter Egg Hunt (early April)	902-424-7353
Festival of the Arts (mid-November)	902-423-3837
Fisherman's Cove Canada Day Gala (July 1)	902-465-6093
Fort Nites in the Hill (June-July)	902-425-9500
Great Nova Scotia Mussel Festival (mid-July)	902-857-9555
Greek Fest (mid-June)	902-479-1271
Halifax Carnival (mid-February)	902-423-3740
Halifax County Exhibition (mid-August)	902-384-3008
Halifax-Dartmouth Canada Day (July 1)	902-490-4729
Halifax-Dartmouth Natal Day (late July-early August)	902-490-4729
Halifax Dragon Boat Festival (late July)	902-425-5454
Halifax Flower Show (late August)	902-453-6801

Halifax — Events (Cont'd)

	Phone
Halifax Highland Games (early July)	902-425-2445
Halifax International Boat Show (mid-February)	888-454-7469
Halifax International Busker Festival (early-mid-August)	902-429-3910
Halifax Regional Municipality New Years Eve Celebration (December 31)	902-490-4729
Halifax Winterfest (late February)	902-423-3740
Halloween at the Cove (late October)	902-465-6093
Holiday Parade of Lights (late November)	902-423-3740
Lebanese Summer Festival (mid-July)	902-473-2720
Maritime Old Time Jamboree (mid-July)	902-434-5466
New Year's Eve Public Concert & Balls (December 31)	902-423-3740
Nova Scotia Designer Craft Council Summer Craft Festival (mid-August)	902-423-3837
Nova Scotia Ideal Home Show (mid-April & late September)	902-468-4999
Nova Scotia International Air Show (mid-September)	902-465-2725
Nova Scotia International Tattoo Festival (late June-early July)	902-420-1114
Nova Scotia Multicultural Festival (mid-June)	902-423-6534
On the Waterfront Festival (mid-May)	902-463-7529
Open Waters Festival (mid-November)	902-494-3820
Provincial Rose Show (mid-July)	902-453-6801
Santa Claus Parade (late November)	902-477-7665
Scotia Festival of Music (late May-early June)	902-429-9467
Sharkarama at Fisherman's Cove (late July)	902-465-6093
Springtime at the Forum (late April-early May)	902-425-5656
Terry Fox Run (mid-September)	902-423-8131
Three Day Flea Market Extravaganza (mid-July)	902-429-0375

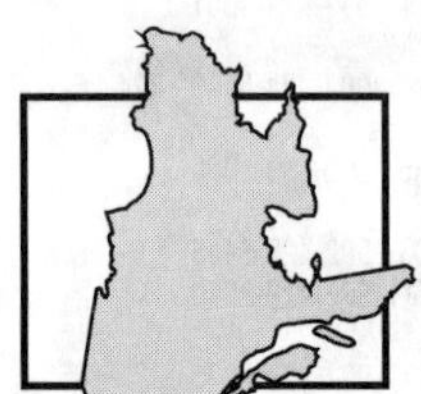

Montreal

Montreal is the second oldest city in Canada and one of the largest French-speaking metropolitan areas in the world. The island of Montreal, 30 miles long and ten miles wide, is located at the confluence of the Ottawa and Saint Lawrence rivers. French explorer Jacques Cartier first set foot on what is now Montreal in 1535, but it was not until 1642 that Paul de Chomedey landed there and established Montreal proper. The city underwent rapid industrial development and by 1867 it had became the capital of commerce and trade. Mount-Royal Park, popularly known as the Mountain, opened in 1876 and is the city's most prominent landmark. Montreal is also home to the "Underground City," a subterranean network approximately 20 miles long that links together major stores, hotels, office towers, movie theatres, concert halls, restaurants, and railway stations. Other attractions include Montreal Tower, the world's tallest inclined tower; Pointe-à-Callière, Montreal's museum of archaeology and history; a botanical garden that is the second largest in the world; and the Canadian Centre for Architecture, acknowledged world-wide as a museum and study center for international architecture.

Population	1,016,376	**Longitude**	73-34-48 W
Area (Land)	68.4 sq mi	**Time Zone**	EST
Elevation	90 ft	**Area Code/s**	514
Latitude	45-30-00 N		

— Average Temperatures and Precipitation —

TEMPERATURES

	Jan	Feb	Mar	Apr	May	Jun	Jul	Aug	Sep	Oct	Nov	Dec
High	21	25	36	52	66	75	79	77	68	55	41	27
Low	5	7	19	34	45	55	61	57	50	39	28	12

PRECIPITATION

	Jan	Feb	Mar	Apr	May	Jun	Jul	Aug	Sep	Oct	Nov	Dec
Inches	0.9	0.6	1.5	2.5	2.5	3.2	3.5	3.6	3.5	2.9	2.4	1.3

— Important Phone Numbers —

	Phone		Phone
American Express Travel	514-392-4444	**Poison Control Centre**	800-463-5060
Canadian Automobile Assn.	514-861-7111	**Weather**	514-283-4006
Emergency	911		

— Information Sources —

					Phone	Fax
Better Business Bureau Serving Montréal						
2055 rue Peel Bureau 460	Montréal	QC	H3A1V4		514-286-9281	286-2658
Web: www.montreal.bbb.org						
Bibliothéque de Montréal						
1210 rue Sherbrooke E	Montréal	QC	H2L1L9		514-872-5923	872-1626
Web: www.ville.montreal.qc.ca/biblio/pageacc.htm						
Board of Trade of Metropolitan Montréal						
5 pl Ville-Marie Suite 12500	Montréal	QC	H3B4Y2		514-871-4000	871-1255
Web: www.btmm.qc.ca ■ *E-mail:* info@ccmm.qc.ca						
Greater Montréal Convention & Tourism Bureau						
1555 rue Peel Bureau 600	Montréal	QC	H3A3L8		514-844-5400	844-5757
TF: 800-363-7777 ■ *Web:* www.tourism-montreal.org						
Infotouriste Centre						
1001 rue Dorchester Sq Suite 100	Montréal	QC	H3B4V4		514-873-2015	864-3838
TF: 800-363-7777						
Montréal City Hall						
275 rue Notre-Dame E	Montréal	QC	H2Y1C6		514-872-1111	872-2896
Web: www.ville.montreal.qc.ca						
Montréal Economic Development Office						
1002 rue Sherbrooke O Bureau 2400	Montréal	QC	H3A3L6		514-280-4242	280-4266
Web: www.cum.qc.ca/investmontreal ■ *E-mail:* ode-info@cum.qc.ca						
Montréal Mayor						
275 rue Notre-Dame E Rm 2-103	Montréal	QC	H2Y1C6		514-872-3101	872-3124
Web: www.ville.montreal.qc.ca./maire/engl/emaire0.htm						
Palais des Congrès de Montréal-Convention Centre						
201 ave Viger O	Montréal	QC	H2Z1X7		514-871-8122	871-9389
Web: www.congresmtl.com						

On-Line Resources

4Montréal.com	www.4montreal.com
Bradmans.com Montreal	www.bradmans.com/scripts/display_city.cgi?city=239
City Knowledge Montréal	www.cityknowledge.com/canada_qc_montreal.htm
CityVu Virtual Montréal	www.cityvu.com
Gay Montréal	www.priape.com/montreal/indexeng.html
Go Montréal!	www.gomtl.com
Montre@l Page	www.pagemontreal.qc.ca/eindex.html
Montréal e-Guide!	www.pagemontreal.qc.ca/meg/
Montréal Live!	www.montreal-live.com
Montréal Mirror	www.montrealmirror.com
MontréalCAM	www.montrealcam.com/en-sommaire.html
MontréalNOW	www.montrealnow.com
Open World City Guides Montreal	www.worldexecutive.com/cityguides/montreal/
Restaurant.ca Montréal	www.restaurant.ca/mtl/
Rough Guide Travel Montreal	travel.roughguides.com/content/4945/
Student's Guide to Montréal	www.studentsguide.com/montreal/

— Transportation Services —

AIRPORTS

■ **Montréal International Airport Dorval (YUL)**

	Phone
14 miles W of downtown (approx 30 minutes)	514-394-7377
Web: www.admtl.com	

Airport Transportation

	Phone
Air Exécutive Limo $46 fare to downtown	514-946-3424
Autocar Connaisseur Shuttle $9.75 fare to downtown	514-934-1222
Aéroport Taxi $25 fare to downtown	514-488-5887
STCUM Transit $1.90 Base fare	514-288-6287
Web: www.stcum.qc.ca	

Montreal (Cont'd)

Commercial Airlines

	Phone		Phone
Aeroflot	888-686-4949	**Iberia**	800-772-4642
Air Canada	800-776-3000	**KLM**	800-374-7747
Air Nova	800-776-3000	**Lufthansa**	800-645-3880
Alitalia	800-223-5730	**Mexicana**	800-531-7923
American	800-433-7300	**Northwest**	800-225-2525
British Airways	800-247-9297	**Olympic Airways**	800-223-1226
Canada 3000	877-359-2263	**Royal Air Maroc**	514-285-1435
Continental	800-525-0280	**Sabena**	800-955-2000
Czech Airlines	800-223-2365	**SwissAir**	800-221-4750
Delta	800-221-1212	**United**	800-241-6522
El Al	800-223-6700	**US Airways**	800-428-4322
First Air	800-267-1247		

Charter Airlines

Delco Aviation 450-663-4311

■ Montréal International Airport Mirabel (YMX)

	Phone
34 miles NW of downtown (approx 60 minutes)	514-394-7377

Web: www.admtl.com

Airport Transportation

	Phone
Air Exécutive Limo $80 fare to downtown	514-946-3424
Autocar Connaisseur Shuttle $8 fare to downtown	514-934-1222
Aéroport Taxi $65 fare to downtown	514-488-5887

Commercial Airlines

	Phone		Phone
Aeroflot	888-686-4949	**Cubana**	514-871-1222
Air Canada	800-776-3000	**Iberia**	800-772-4642
Air Transat	877-872-6728		

Charter Airlines

	Phone
Delco Aviation	450-663-4311

CAR RENTALS

	Phone		Phone
Alamo	514-633-1222	**Hertz**	450-476-3385
Avis	450-476-3481	**Hertz-Dorval**	514-636-9530
Avis-Dorval	514-636-1902	**National**	514-636-9030
Budget	450-476-2687	**Thrifty**	450-476-0496
Budget-Dorval	514-636-0052	**Thrifty-Dorval**	514-631-5567
Discount	514-286-1554		

LIMO/TAXI

	Phone		Phone
Albee Limousines	514-594-4114	**Limo Limousine**	514-333-5466
Aéroport Taxi	514-488-5887	**Lux Limousine**	514-843-5625
Brenka Limousines	514-938-5466	**National Taxi**	514-762-1200
Champlain Taxi	514-273-2435	**Pontiac Cab**	514-766-5522
Co-Op Taxi	514-725-9885	**Taxi Lasalle**	514-277-2552
Diamond Taxi	514-273-6331	**Unitaxi**	514-482-3000
Gilbert Limousines	514-334-7614		

MASS TRANSIT

	Phone
STCUM Metro $1.90 Base fare	514-288-6287
STCUM Transit $1.90 Base fare	514-288-6287

RAIL/BUS

				Phone
Greyhound Canada Bus Station 505 rue de Maisonneuve E Terminus Voyager *TF:* 800-661-8747	Montréal	QC	H2L1Y4	514-842-2281
VIA Rail Canada Inc 895 de la Gauchetière O *TF:* 888-842-7245	Montréal	QC	H3B4G1	514-989-2626

— Accommodations —

HOTEL RESERVATION SERVICES

	Phone	Fax
Bed & Breakfasts in Québec *Web:* www.agricotours.qc.ca ■ *E-mail:* agricotours-q@sympatico.ca	514-252-3138	252-3173

HOTELS, MOTELS, RESORTS

				Phone	Fax
Auberge Centre-Ville 2060 rue Saint-Dominique *TF:* 800-502-2525	Montréal	QC	H2X2X1	514-843-2483	527-5042
Best Western Europa Downtown 1240 rue Drummond *TF:* 800-361-3000	Montréal	QC	H3G1V7	514-866-6492	861-4089
Best Western Hôtel International 13000 ch Côte-de-Liesse *TF:* 800-528-1234	Montréal	QC	H9P1B8	514-631-4811	631-7305
Best Western Ville-Marie Hôtel & Suites 3407 rue Peel *TF:* 800-528-1234	Montréal	QC	H3A1W7	514-288-4141	288-3021
Château Royal Hôtel Suites 1420 rue Crescent *TF:* 800-363-0335 ■ *Web:* www.chateauroyal.com ■ *E-mail:* reservations@chateauroyal.com	Montréal	QC	H3G2B7	514-848-0999	848-9403
Comfort Inn by Journey's End 340 ave Michel-Jasmin *TF:* 800-228-5150	Montréal	QC	H9P1C1	514-636-3391	636-9495
Crowne Plaza Métro Centre 505 rue Sherbrooke E *TF:* 800-561-4644	Montréal	QC	H2L4N3	514-842-8581	842-3365
Days Inn Montréal Downtown 1005 rue Guy *TF:* 800-329-7466	Montréal	QC	H3H2K4	514-938-4611	938-8718
Four Points by Sheraton 475 rue Sherbrooke O *TF:* 800-325-3535	Montréal	QC	H3A2L9	514-842-3961	842-0945
Hilton Bonaventure 1 pl Bonaventure *TF:* 800-267-2575 ■ *Web:* www.hilton.com/hotels/YULBHHF	Montréal	QC	H5A1E4	514-878-2332	878-3881
Hilton International Montréal Airport 12505 ch Côte-de-Liesse *TF:* 800-567-2411 ■ *Web:* www.hilton.com/hotels/YULAHTW	Dorval	QC	H9P1B7	514-631-2411	631-0192
Holiday Inn Montréal Midtown 420 rue Sherbrooke O *TF:* 800-387-3042	Montréal	QC	H3A1B4	514-842-6111	842-9381
Holiday Inn Select Montréal Downtown 99 ave Viger O *TF:* 888-878-9888	Montréal	QC	H2Z1E9	514-878-9888	878-6341
Hôtel Américan 1042 rue Saint-Denis	Montréal	QC	H2X3J2	514-849-0616	
Hôtel Cantlie Suites 1110 rue Sherbrooke O *TF:* 800-567-1110 ■ *Web:* www.hotelcantlie.com	Montréal	QC	H3A1G9	514-842-2000	844-7808
Hôtel Château-Versailles 1659 rue Sherbrooke O *TF:* 800-361-7199	Montréal	QC	H3H1E3	514-933-3611	933-6867
Hôtel Comfort Suites 1214 rue Crescent *TF:* 800-228-5150	Montréal	QC	H3G2A9	514-878-2711	878-0030
Hôtel Days Inn Montréal Downtown East 215 boul René-Lévesque E *TF:* 800-668-3872	Montréal	QC	H2X1N7	514-393-3388	395-9999
Hôtel de la Montagne 1430 rue de la Montagne *TF:* 800-361-6262	Montréal	QC	H3G1Z5	514-288-5656	288-9658
Hôtel Delta Montréal 475 rue Président-Kennedy *TF:* 800-268-1133 ■ *Web:* www.deltahotels.com	Montréal	QC	H3A1J7	514-286-1986	284-4342
Hôtel des Gouverneurs Place-Dupuis 1415 rue Saint-Hubert *TF:* 888-910-1111	Montréal	QC	H2L3Y9	514-842-4881	842-1584
Hôtel du Fort 1390 rue du Fort *TF:* 800-565-6333 ■ *Web:* www.hoteldufort.com	Montréal	QC	H3H2R7	514-938-8333	938-2078
Hôtel du Parc 3625 ave du Parc *TF:* 800-363-0735 ■ *Web:* www.hotel@duparc.com	Montréal	QC	H2X3P8	514-288-6666	288-2469
Hôtel Inter-Continental Montréal 360 rue Saint-Antoine O *TF:* 800-361-3600	Montréal	QC	H2Y3X4	514-987-9900	987-9904
Hôtel l'Appartement Montréal 455 rue Sherbrooke O *TF:* 800-363-3010 ■ *Web:* www.resomatic.com/appartement/	Montréal	QC	H3A1B7	514-284-3634	287-1431
Hôtel la Tour-Versailles 1808 rue Sherbrooke O *TF:* 800-933-8111 ■ *Web:* amita.montrealnet.ca/versailles	Montréal	QC	H3H1E5	514-933-8111	933-6967
Hôtel le Centre Sheraton Montréal 1201 boul René-Lévesque O *TF:* 888-627-7102	Montréal	QC	H3B2L7	514-878-2000	878-3958
Hôtel le Reine-Elizabeth 900 boul René-Lévesque O *TF:* 800-441-1414	Montréal	QC	H3B4A5	514-861-3511	954-2256

Canadian Cities

Montreal — Hotels, Motels, Resorts (Cont'd)

					Phone	Fax
Hôtel le Saint-André 1285 rue Sainte-André. . . . *TF:* 800-265-7071	Montréal	QC	H2L3T1		514-849-7070	849-8167
Hôtel Lord-Berri 1199 rue Berri . . . . *TF:* 888-363-0363 ■ *Web:* www.lordberri.com	Montréal	QC	H2L4C6		514-845-9236	849-9855
Hôtel Maritime Plaza 1155 rue Guy . . . . *TF:* 800-363-6255 ■ *Web:* www.hotelmaritime.com	Montréal	QC	H3H2K5		514-932-1411	932-0446
Hôtel Montréal Crescent 1366 boul René-Lévesque O. . . . . *TF:* 800-361-5064	Montréal	QC	H3G1T4		514-938-9797	938-9797
Hôtel Ruby Foo's 7655 boul Décarie . . . . *TF:* 800-361-5419 ■ *Web:* www.hotelrubyfoos.com	Montréal	QC	H4P2H2		514-731-7701	731-7158
Hôtel Taj Mahal 1600 rue Saint-Hubert. . . . . . . *TF:* 800-613-3383	Montréal	QC	H2L3Z3		514-849-3214	849-9812
Hôtel Travelodge Montréal Centre 50 boul René-Lévesque O . . . . *TF:* 800-363-6535	Montréal	QC	H2Z1A2		514-874-9090	874-0907
Hôtel Wyndham 1255 rue Jeanne-Mance CP 130. . . . . *TF:* 800-361-8234	Montréal	QC	H5B1E5		514-285-1450	285-1243
Loews Hôtel Vogue 1425 rue de la Montagne. . . . . *TF:* 800-465-6654 ■ *Web:* www.loewshotels.com/voguehome.html	Montréal	QC	H3G1Z3		514-285-5555	849-8903
Manoir Lemoyne 2100 boul de Maisonneuve O. . . . . *TF:* 800-361-7191 ■ *Web:* www.iber.com	Montréal	QC	H3H1K6		514-931-8861	931-7726
Marriott Château-Champlain 1050 rue de la Gauchetière O. . . . . *TF:* 800-200-5909 ■ *Web:* marriotthotels.com/YULCC	Montréal	QC	H3B4C9		514-878-9000	878-6761
Marriott Résidence Inn Montréal 2045 rue Peel. . . . . *TF:* 800-331-3133 ■ *Web:* residenceinn.com/YULRI	Montréal	QC	H3A1T6		514-844-3381	844-8361
Motel le Marquis 6720 rue Sherbrooke E	Montréal	QC	H1N1C9		514-256-1621	256-1973
Motel Métro 9925 rue Lajeunesse	Montréal	QC	H3L2C9		514-382-9780	382-2082
Motel Pignon-Rouge 15777 rue Sherbrooke E . . . . *TF:* 800-905-6668	Montréal	QC	H1A3R1		514-642-2131	642-4472
Nouvel Hôtel Montréal 1740 boul René-Lévesque W . . . . *TF:* 800-363-6063 ■ *Web:* www.lenouvelhotel.com	Montréal	QC	H3H1R3		514-931-8841	931-3233
Novotel Montréal Centre 1180 rue de la Montagne. . . . . *TF:* 800-668-6835	Montréal	QC	H3G1Z1		514-861-6000	861-0992
Omni Montréal 1050 rue Sherbrooke O. . . . . . . *TF:* 800-843-6664	Montréal	QC	H3A2R6		514-284-1110	845-3025
Quality Hotel by Journey's End 3440 ave du Parc . . . . *TF:* 800-228-5151	Montréal	QC	H2X2H5		514-849-1413	849-6564
Radisson Hôtel des Gouverneurs 777 rue University. . . . . *TF:* 800-333-3333	Montréal	QC	H3C3Z7		514-879-1370	879-1761
Ritz-Carlton Montréal 1228 rue Sherbrooke O . . . . *TF:* 800-363-0366 ■ *Web:* www.ritzcarlton.com/location/NorthAmerica/Montreal/main.htm	Montréal	QC	H3G1H6		514-842-4212	842-3383
Travelodge Dorval 1010 rue Herron . . . . *TF:* 800-461-4537	Montréal	QC	H9S1B3		514-631-4537	631-1562

— Restaurants —

				Phone
Alexandre (French) 1454 rue Peel	Montréal	QC	H3A1S8	514-288-5105
Alouette Steak House (Steak/Seafood) 1176 rue Sainte-Catherine O	Montréal	QC	H3B1K1	514-866-6244
Auberge Le Saint-Gabriel (French) 426 rue Saint-Gabriel . . .	Montréal	QC	H2Y2Z9	514-878-3561
Beau Rivage (Continental) 1155 rue Guy	Montréal	QC	H3H2K5	514-932-1411
Beaver Club (French) 900 boul René-Lévesque O.	Montréal	QC	H3B4A5	514-861-3511
Biddle's Jazz & Ribs (Barbecue) 2060 rue Aylmer.	Montréal	QC	H3A2E3	514-842-8656
Café de Paris (French) 1228 rue Sherbrooke O	Montréal	QC	H3G1H6	514-842-4212
Casa Cacciatore (Italian) 170 rue Jean-Talon E.	Montréal	QC	H2R1S7	514-274-1240
Chez Antoine (Continental) 777 rue University.	Montréal	QC	H3C3Z7	514-879-1370
Chez Chine (Chinese) 99 ave Viger O	Montréal	QC	H2Z1E9	514-878-9888
Chez la Mère Michel (French) 1209 rue Guy.	Montréal	QC	H3H2K5	514-934-0473
Chez Pierre (French) 1263 rue Labelle	Montréal	QC	H2L4C1	514-843-5227
Claude Postel Restaurant (French) 443 rue Saint-Vincent. . .	Montréal	QC	H2Y3A6	514-875-5067
Desjardins Kaiko (Seafood) 1175 rue Mackay	Montréal	QC	H3G2H5	514-866-9741
Exotica (International) 400 rue Laurier O	Montréal	QC	H2V2K7	514-273-5015
Ferreira Café Trattoria (Portuguese) 1446 rue Peel	Montréal	QC	H3A1S8	514-848-0988
Formosa (Chinese/Thai) 2115 rue Saint-Denis.	Montréal	QC	H2X3K8	514-282-1966
Globe Bar-Restaurant (International) 3455 boul Saint-Laurent	Montréal	QC	H2X2T6	514-284-3823
Hard Rock Café (American) 1458 rue Crescent	Montréal	QC	H3G2B6	514-987-1420
Jardin Sakura (Japanese) 2114 rue de la Montagne.	Montréal	QC	H3G1Z7	514-288-9122
Katsura (Japanese) 2170 rue de la Montagne	Montréal	QC	H3G1Z7	514-849-1172
Koji's Kaizen Sushi Bar & Restaurant (Japanese) 4120 rue Sainte-Catherine O . . . . *Web:* www.i-factory.com/kaizen/	Montréal	QC	H3Z1P4	514-932-5654
L'Amalfitana (Italian) 1381 boul René-Lévesque E.	Montréal	QC	H2L2M1	514-523-2483
L'Armoricain (French) 1500 rue Fullum. . . . . *Web:* www.cam.org/~armoric/	Montréal	QC	H2K3M4	514-523-2551
La Bocca d'Oro (Italian) 1448 rue Saint-Mathieu.	Montréal	QC	H3H2H9	514-933-8414
La Bourgade (French) 1 pl Bonaventure	Montréal	QC	H5A1E4	514-878-2332
La Cabane Grecque (Greek) 102 rue Prince-Arthur E	Montréal	QC	H2X1B5	514-849-0122
La Marée (French) 404 pl Jacques Cartier.	Montréal	QC	H2Y3B2	514-861-8126
La Merveille du Vietnam (Vietnamese) 4526 rue Saint-Denis	Montréal	QC	H2J2L3	514-844-9884
La Troïka (Russian) 2171 rue Crescent.	Montréal	QC	H3G2C1	514-849-9333
Laloux (French) 250 ave Pine E	Montréal	QC	H2W1P3	514-287-9127
Le Chrysanthème (Chinese) 1208 rue Crescent	Montréal	QC	H3G2A9	514-397-1408
Le Gauchetière (International) 1 pl du Canada	Montréal	QC	H3B4C9	514-878-9000
Le Jardin Nelson (French) 407 pl Jacques-Cartier . . . . *Web:* www.jardinnelson.com	Montréal	QC	H2Y3B1	514-861-5731
Le Lutetia (French) 1430 rue de la Montagne	Montréal	QC	H3G1Z5	514-288-5656
Le Publix (International) 3554 boul Saint-Laurent	Montréal	QC	H2X2V1	514-284-9233
Le Vignoble (Continental) 1415 rue Saint-Hubert.	Montréal	QC	H2L3Y9	514-842-4881
Les Continents (Continental) 360 rue Saint-Antoine O	Montréal	QC	H2Y3X4	514-987-9900
Mediterraneo Grill & Wine Bar (California) 3500 boul Saint-Laurent	Montréal	QC	H2X2V1	514-844-0027
Moishes Steakhouse (Steak) 3961 boul Saint-Laurent	Montréal	QC	H2W1Y4	514-845-3509
Nantha's (Malaysian) 9 Duluth E	Montréal	QC	H2W1G7	514-845-4717
Nickels (American) 1384 rue Sainte-Catherine O	Montréal	QC	H3G1P8	514-392-7771
Restaurant du Vieux-Port (Steak/Seafood) 39 rue Saint-Paul E.	Montréal	QC	H2Y1G2	514-866-3175
Restaurant Kobé (Japanese)6720 rue Sherbrooke E.	Montréal	QC	H1N1C9	514-254-9926
Restaurant La Dora (Italian) 6837 rue Sherbrooke E	Montréal	QC	H1N1C7	514-255-8841
Restaurant La Mer (Seafood) 1065 rue Papineau.	Montréal	QC	H2K4G9	514-522-2889
Restaurant Le Fripon (French) 436 pl Jacques-Cartier . . . . . *Web:* www.le-fripon.qc.ca	Montréal	QC	H2Y3B3	514-861-1386
Restaurant Le Muscadin (Italian) 100 rue Saint-Paul O	Montréal	QC	H2Y1Z3	514-842-0588
Restaurant Le Panoramique (Seafood) 250 rue Saint-Paul E.	Montréal	QC	H2Y1G9	514-861-1957
Restaurant Le Taj (Indian) 2077 rue Stanley.	Montréal	QC	H3A1R7	514-845-9015
Restaurant Minerva (Italian) 17 rue Prince-Arthur E	Montréal	QC	H2X1B2	514-842-5451
Restaurant Nuances (French) 1 ave du Casino	Montréal	QC	H3C4W7	514-392-2708
Restaurant Toqué (French) 3842 rue Saint-Denis.	Montréal	QC	H2W2M2	514-499-2084
Restaurant à l'Aventure (French/Italian) 438 pl Jacques-Cartier . . . . *Web:* alaventure.com	Montréal	QC	H2Y3B3	514-866-9439
Resto Club Lounge 737 (French) 1 pl Ville-Marie Level PH2	Montréal	QC	H3B5E4	514-397-0737
Restofiore (Italian) 705 rue Sainte-Catherine O	Montréal	QC	H3B4G5	514-288-7777
Thai Grill (Thai) 5101 boul Saint-Laurent	Montréal	QC	H2T1R9	514-270-5566

— Goods and Services —

SHOPPING

				Phone	Fax
Atwater Market 138 ave Atwater	Montréal	QC	H4C2H6	514-937-7754	
Bay The 585 rue Sainte-Catherine O	Montréal	QC	H3Y3B5	514-281-4422	281-4792
Bonsecours Market 350 rue Saint-Paul E.	Montréal	QC	H2Y2H2	514-872-7730	
Eaton's 677 rue Sainte-Catherine O.	Montréal	QC	H3B3Y6	514-284-8411	284-8009
Montréal Eaton Centre 705 rue Sainte-Catherine O Bureau 600.	Montréal	QC	H3B4G5	514-288-3708	288-9784
Place Bonaventure 900 rue de la Gauchetière O. . . . . *Web:* www.infobonaventure.com	Montréal	QC	H5A1G1	514-397-2325	397-2266
Place Desjardins Shopping Centre 4 Complexe Desjardins	Montréal	QC	H5B1E9	514-281-1870	281-8293
Place Montréal Trust 1500 ave McGill College . .	Montréal	QC	H3A3J5	514-843-8000	843-6092
Place Ville Marie 1 pl Ville-Marie	Montréal	QC	H3B3Y1	514-861-9393	875-6852
Plaza St-Hubert betw rue Saint-Hubert & Jean-Talon	Montréal	QC	H2S2M7	514-276-8501	
Promenades de la Cathédrale 625 rue Sainte-Catherine O	Montréal	QC	H3B1B7	514-849-9925	849-0765
Promenades Hudson Factory Outlet Center Hwy 40 & Exit 26	Montréal	QC	J7V8P2	514-694-2371	426-3065
Sainte-Catherine Faubourg Market 1616 rue Sainte-Catherine O Suite 5065 . . . . *Web:* www.lefaubourg.com	Montréal	QC	H3H1L7	514-939-3663	937-0763
Westmount Square 1 Westmount Sq Suite 1700	Montréal	QC	H3Z2P9	514-932-0211	932-6750

Montreal (Cont'd)

BANKS

				Phone	Fax
Bank of Montréal 129 rue James	Montréal	QC	H2Y1L6	514-877-1111	877-7399
TF: 800-363-9992 ■ *Web:* www.bmo.com					
Bank of Tokyo Canada 600 rue de la Gauchettiere Bureau 2780	Montréal	QC	H3B4L8	514-875-9261	875-9261
Banque Nationale de Paris 1981 ave McGill College	Montréal	QC	H3A2W8	514-285-6000	285-6278
Web: www.bnp.fr					
Business Development Bank of Canada 5 pl Ville-Marie	Montréal	QC	H3B5E7	514-283-5904	283-7838
Web: www.bdc.ca					
HSBC 500 boul René-Lévesque O	Montréal	QC	H2Z1W7	514-866-2841	866-3181
Web: www.hsbcgroup.com					
Laurentian Bank of Canada 1981 ave McGill College	Montréal	QC	H3A3K3	514-284-5996	284-3396
Web: www.laurentianbank.com					
National Bank of Canada 600 rue de la Gauchetière O	Montréal	QC	H3B4L2	514-394-4000	394-8258
Web: www.nbc.ca					
Royal Bank of Canada 1 pl Ville-Marie	Montréal	QC	H3C3B5	514-874-2110	874-7188
Web: www.royalbank.com					

BUSINESS SERVICES

	Phone
Atlas Printing & Photocopies	214-638-2888
Bradson Staffing Services	514-874-8014
Canada Post	514-345-4198
Canbec Courrier	514-933-6044
Copie 2000	514-845-8229
Copie Express	514-288-0288
Courrier Plus	514-521-0775
DHL International Express	403-250-1512
Excel Personnel	514-937-1504
Federal Express	800-463-3339
Hunt Personnel	514-842-4691
Kelly Services	514-925-3049
Kwik-Kopy Printing	514-878-1044
Manpower Placement Agency	514-848-9922
Personnel Avantage	514-937-4150
Rapid Courier Service	514-866-8727
UPS	800-742-5877

— Media —

PUBLICATIONS

				Phone	Fax
Gazette The† 250 rue Sainte-Antoine O	Montréal	QC	H2Y3R7	514-987-2222	987-2399
TF: 800-361-8478 ■ *Web:* www.montrealgazette.com ■ *E-mail:* readtheg@thegazette.southam.ca					
Le Devoir† 2050 rue Bleury 9th Fl	Montréal	QC	H3A3M9	514-985-3333	985-3360
Web: www.ledevoir.com					
Le Journal de Montréal† 4545 rue Frontenac	Montréal	QC	H2H2R7	514-521-4545	521-4416
Web: www.journaldemontreal.com					
Voir Montréal 4130 rue Saint-Denis	Montréal	QC	H2W2M5	514-848-0805	848-9004
Web: www.voir.ca ■ *E-mail:* info@voir.ca					

†*Daily newspapers*

TELEVISION

				Phone	Fax
CBFT-TV Ch 2 (SRC) 1400 boul René-Lévesque E	Montréal	QC	H2L2M2	514-597-6000	
CBMT-TV Ch 6 (CBC) PO Box 6000	Montréal	QC	H3C3A8	514-597-6000	597-4596
Web: cbc.ca					
CFCF-TV Ch 12 (CTV) 405 ave Ogilvy	Montréal	QC	H3N1M4	514-273-6311	276-9399
Web: www.cfcf12.ca ■ *E-mail:* contact12@cfcf12.ca					
CFJP-TV Ch 35 (QS) 612 rue St Jacques	Montréal	QC	H3C5R1	514-271-3535	390-0773
CFTM-TV Ch 10 (TVA) 1600 boul de Maisonneuve E	Montréal	QC	H2L4P2	514-526-9251	598-6073
CFTU-TV Ch 29 (Ind) 4750 ave Henri-Julien Suite 100	Montréal	QC	H2T3E4	514-841-2626	284-9363
CIVM-TV Ch 17 (TVO) 1000 rue Fullum	Montréal	QC	H2K3L7	514-521-2424	873-7464
Web: www.telequebec.qc.ca					
CUTV-TV Ch 6 (CBC) 1400 boul René-Lévesque E Bureau B96-1	Montréal	QC	H2L2M2	514-597-6397	597-6354

RADIO

				Phone	Fax
CBC-AM 95.1 kHz (N/T) 1400 boul René-Lévesque E	Montréal	QC	H2L2M2	514-597-6000	
CBC-FM 100.7 MHz (Clas) PO Box 6000	Montréal	QC	H3C3A8	514-597-6000	
CBM-FM 93.5 MHz (Clas) 1400 boul René-Lévesque E	Montréal	QC	H2L2M2	514-597-6000	
CFQR-FM 92.5 MHz (AC) 211 ave Gordon 3rd Fl	Montréal	QC	H4G2R2	514-767-9250	766-9569
CIBL-FM 101.5 MHz (Alt) 1691 Pie IX	Montréal	QC	H1V2C3	514-526-2581	526-3583
CINQ-FM 102.3 MHz (Misc) 5212 boul Saint-Laurent	Montréal	QC	H2T1S1	514-495-2597	495-2429
CIQC-AM 600 kHz (N/T) 211 ave Gordon 3rd Fl	Montréal	QC	H4G2R2	514-767-9250	766-9569
CITE-FM 107.3 MHz (Rock) 1411 rue Peel Suite 602	Montréal	QC	H3A1S5	514-845-2483	288-1073
Web: www.rock-detente.com					
CJAD-AM 800 kHz (N/T) 1411 rue du Fort	Montréal	QC	H3H2R1	514-989-2523	989-3868
Web: www.cjad.com					
CJFM-FM 95.9 MHz (CHR) 1411 rue du Fort	Montréal	QC	H3H2R1	514-989-2536	989-2554
Web: www.themix.com					
CKMF-FM 94.3 MHz (CHR) 1717 boul René-Lévesque E	Montréal	QC	H2L4T9	514-529-3229	529-9308
CKUT-FM 90.3 MHz (Misc) 3647 rue University	Montréal	QC	H3A2B3	514-398-6787	398-8261
Web: www.ckut.ca ■ *E-mail:* sales@ckut.ca					

— Colleges/Universities —

				Phone	Fax
Bishop's University rue College	Lennoxville	QC	J1M1Z7	819-822-9600	822-9661
TF: 800-567-2792 ■ *Web:* www.ubishops.ca ■ *E-mail:* sboard@ubishops.ca					
Concordia University 1455 boul de Maisonneuve O	Montréal	QC	H3G1M8	514-848-2424	848-3494
Web: www.concordia.ca					
McGill University 845 rue Sherbrooke O	Montréal	QC	H3A2T5	514-398-4455	398-3594
Web: www.mcgill.ca					
Université de Montréal CP 6128 Succursale Centre Ville	Montréal	QC	H3C3J7	514-343-6111	343-2098
Web: www.umontreal.ca					
Université du Québec à Montréal CP 8888 Succursale Centre Ville	Montréal	QC	H3C3P8	514-987-3000	987-8932
Web: www.uqam.ca					
École Polytechnique de Montréal CP 6079 Succursale Centre Ville	Montréal	QC	H3C3A7	514-340-4711	340-5836
Web: www.polymtl.ca/english.htm					

— Hospitals —

				Phone	Fax
Catherine Booth Hospital 4375 ave Montclair	Montréal	QC	H4B2J5	514-481-0431	481-8009
Centre Hospitalier Fleury 2180 rue Fleury E	Montréal	QC	H2B1K3	514-381-9311	383-5086
Centre Hospitalier Mount Sinai 5690 boul Cavendish	Montréal	QC	H4W1S7	514-369-2222	369-2225
Web: www.mountsinaihospital.qc.ca					
Hôpital du Sacré-Coeur de Montréal 5400 boul Gouin O	Montréal	QC	H4J1C5	514-338-2222	338-3113
Web: www.crhsc.umontreal.ca/hscm					
Hôpital General de Montréal 1650 ave Cedar	Montréal	QC	H3G1A4	514-937-6011	934-8303*
**Fax:* Admitting					
Hôpital Jean-Talon 1385 rue Jean-Talon E	Montréal	QC	H2E1S6	514-495-6767	495-6771
Hôpital Maisonneuve-Rosemont 5415 boul de l'Assomption	Montréal	QC	H1T2M4	514-252-3400	252-3589
Web: esi25.esi.umontreal.ca/~beauprea/dept_md					
Hôpital Notre-Dame 1560 rue Sherbrooke E	Montréal	QC	H2L4M1	514-281-6000	896-4612*
**Fax:* Admitting					
Hôpital Saint-Luc 1058 rue Saint-Denis	Montréal	QC	H2X3J4	514-281-2121	281-3246
Hôpital Sainte-Justine 3175 côte Sainte-Catherine	Montréal	QC	H3T1C5	514-345-4931	345-4800
Web: esi24.esi.umontreal.ca/~lecomptl/hsj					
Hôpital Santa Cabrini Ospedale 5655 rue Sainte-Zotique E	Montréal	QC	H1T1P7	514-252-6000	252-6453
Montréal Chest Institute 3650 rue Saint-Urbain	Montréal	QC	H2X2P4	514-849-5201	843-2088
Montréal Children's Hospital 2300 rue Tupper	Montréal	QC	H3H1P3	514-934-4400	934-4477*
**Fax:* Admitting					
Montréal Heart Institute 5000 rue Bélanger E	Montréal	QC	H1T1C8	514-376-3330	593-2540
Royal Victoria Hospital 687 Pine Ave W Health Ctr.	Montréal	QC	H3A1A1	514-842-1231	843-1512
Saint Mary's Hospital Center 3830 ave Lacombe	Montréal	QC	H3T1M5	514-345-3511	734-2746
Web: www.smhc.qc.ca ■ *E-mail:* sys-smhc@smhc.qc.ca					
Sir Mortimer B Davis Jewish General Hospital 3755 côte Sainte-Catherine	Montréal	QC	H3T1E2	514-340-8222	340-7523
Web: www.mcgill.ca/jgh					

Montreal (Cont'd)

— Attractions —

Name / Address	City	State	ZIP	Phone	Fax
Bateau-Mouche River Tours Old Port of Montreal Jacques-Cartier Pier — *Web:* www.bateau-mouche.com ■ *E-mail:* tour@bateau-mouche.com	Montréal	QC	H2Y2E2	514-849-9952	849-9851
Biodôme de Montréal 4777 ave Pierre-De Coubertin — *Web:* mtl.sim.qc.ca/biodome/bdm.htm	Montréal	QC	H1V1B3	514-868-3000	868-3065
Biosphère La 160 ch Tour-de-l'Isle — *Web:* biosphere.ec.gc.ca/cea/	Montréal	QC	H3C4G8	514-283-5000	283-5021
Canadian Centre for Architecture 1920 rue Baile — *Web:* cca.qc.ca	Montréal	QC	H3H2S6	514-939-7000	939-7020
Canadian Guild of Crafts Québec 2025 rue Peel — *Web:* www.dsuper.net/~cdnguild ■ *E-mail:* cdnguild@supernet.ca	Montréal	QC	H3A1T6	514-849-6091	849-7351
Casino de Montréal 1 ave du Casino — *TF:* 800-665-2274 ■ *Web:* www.casinos-quebec.com	Montréal	QC	H3C4W7	514-392-2746	864-4950
Centaur Theatre 453 rue Saint-François-Xavier — *Web:* www.interclik.com/centaur	Montréal	QC	H2Y2T1	514-288-3161	288-8575
Centre d'histoire de Montréal 335 pl d'Youville — *E-mail:* chm@ville.montreal.qc.ca	Montréal	QC	H2Y3T1	514-872-3207	872-9645
Christ Church Cathedral 635 rue Sainte-Catherine O	Montréal	QC	H3A2B8	514-843-6577	
Cinémathèque Québécoise-Museum of Moving Images 335 boul de Maisonneuve E — *Web:* www.cinematheque.qc.ca	Montréal	QC	H2X1K1	514-842-9763	842-1816
Cirque du Soleil Inc 8400 2nd Ave — *Web:* www.cirquedusoleil.com	Montréal	QC	H1Z4M6	514-722-2324	722-3692
Ecomusée du Fier Monde-Industrial & Labor History 2050 rue Amherst	Montréal	QC	H2L3L8	514-528-8444	528-8686
Granby Zoo boul Bouchard — *Web:* www.econoroute.com/montreal/granby/zoo.htm ■ *E-mail:* zoo@granby.mtl.net	Granby	QC	J2G5P3	450-372-9113	372-5531
IMAX Montréal Old Port rue de la Commune & Saint-Laurent King Edward Pier — *TF:* 800-349-4629 ■ *Web:* www.imaxoldport.com	Montréal	QC	H2Y2E2	514-496-4629	283-8423
Just for Laughs Museum of Humor 2111 boul Saint-Laurent — *Web:* www.hahaha.com ■ *E-mail:* info@hahaha.com	Montréal	QC	H2X2T5	514-845-4000	845-5960
l'Amphithéâtre Bell Indoor Skating Rink 1000 rue de la Gauchetière O	Montréal	QC	H3B4W5	514-395-0555	395-1005
La Ronde Amusement Park Sainte-Helene Island — *TF:* 800-797-4537	Montréal	QC		514-872-4537	
Leonard & Bina Ellen Art Gallery 1400 boul de Maisonneuve O Concordia University — *Web:* ellen-gallery.concordia.ca	Montréal	QC	H3G1M8	514-848-4750	848-4751
Les Grands Ballets Canadiens 4816 rue Rivard	Montréal	QC	H2J2N6	514-849-0269	285-4266
Maison Saint-Gabriel 2146 pl Dublin	Montréal	QC	H3K2A2	514-935-8136	935-5692
Marc-Aurèle Fortin Museum 118 rue Saint-Pierre	Montréal	QC	H2Y2L7	514-845-6108	845-6100
Marché Bonsecours Heritage Building 350 rue Saint-Paul E	Montréal	QC	H2Y1H2	514-872-7730	872-8477
Mary Queen of the World Cathedral boul René-Lévesque O & rue Mansfield	Montréal	QC	H3B2V4	514-866-1661	864-5643
McCord Museum of Canadian History 690 rue Sherbrooke O — *Web:* www.musee-mccord.qc.ca ■ *E-mail:* info@mccord.lan.mcgill.ca	Montréal	QC	H3A1E9	514-398-7100	398-5045
Montréal Botanical Garden & Insectarium 4101 rue Sherbrooke E	Montréal	QC	H1X2B2	514-872-1400	872-3101
Montréal Exchange 800 Victoria Sq PO Box 61 — *TF:* 800-361-5353 ■ *Web:* www.me.org ■ *E-mail:* info@me.org	Montréal	QC	H4Z1A9	514-871-2424	871-3553
Montréal Holocaust Memorial Centre 5151 côte Sainte-Catherine	Montréal	QC	H3W1M6	514-345-2605	344-2651
Montréal Museum of Decorative Arts 2200 rue Crescent — *Web:* www.madm.org	Montréal	QC	H3C2Y9	514-284-1252	284-0123
Montréal Museum of Fine Arts 1380 rue Sherbrooke O — *Fax: PR ■ *Web:* www.mbam.qc.ca ■ *E-mail:* webmbam@cam.org	Montréal	QC	H3G1J5	514-285-2000	844-6042*
Montréal Olympic Park 4141 ave Pierre-de-Coubertin	Montréal	QC	H1Z3N7	514-252-8687	252-9401
Montréal Symphony Orchestra 260 boul de Maisonneuve O — *Web:* www.osm.ca	Montréal	QC	H2X1Y9	514-842-9951	842-0728
Montréal World Trade Centre 747 Victoria Sq Suite 247	Montréal	QC	H2Y2Y9	514-982-9888	982-0170
Musée d'art Contemporain de Montréal 185 rue Sainte-Catherine O — *Web:* media.macm.qc.ca ■ *E-mail:* macm@quebectel.com	Montréal	QC	H2X3X5	514-847-6226	847-6290
Musée David M Stewart 20 ch Tour de l'le Fort de l'le Sainte-Hélène — *Web:* www.mlink.net/~stewart/	Montréal	QC	H3C4G6	514-861-6701	284-0123
Musée des Hospitalières de l'Hôtel-Dieu de Montréal 201 ave des Pins O	Montréal	QC	H2W1R5	514-849-2919	284-3545
Musée des Soeurs Grises 1185 rue Saint-Mathieu	Montréal	QC	H3H2H6	514-937-9501	937-0503
Musée du Château Ramezay 280 rue Notre-Dame E	Montréal	QC	H2Y1C5	514-861-3708	861-8317
Musée Maison Saint-Gabriel 2146 pl Dublin Pointe-Saint-Charles	Montréal	QC	H3K2A2	514-935-8136	935-5692
National Film Board Montréal 1564 rue Saint-Denis — *Web:* www.nfb.ca	Montréal	QC	H2X3K2	514-496-6887	283-0225
Notre-Dame Basilica 44 Sainte-Sulpice	Montréal	QC	H2Y2V5	514-842-2925	842-3370
Old Port of Montréal 333 rue de la Commune O — *Web:* www.svpm.ca/welcome.html	Montréal	QC	H2Y2E2	514-283-5256	283-8423
Opéra de Montréal 260 boul de Maisonneuve O — *Web:* www.operademontreal.qc.ca	Montréal	QC	H2X1Y9	514-985-2258	985-2219
Pierre du Calvet House 405 rue Bonsecours — *Web:* www.pierreducalvet.ca	Montréal	QC	H2Y3C3	514-282-1725	282-0456
Place des Arts 175 rue Sainte-Catherine O — *Web:* www.pdarts.com	Montréal	QC	H2X1Y9	514-285-4270	285-4272
Planétarium de Montréal 1000 rue Saint-Jacques O — *Web:* www.planetarium.montreal.qc.ca	Montréal	QC	H3C1G7	514-872-4530	872-8102
Pointe-à-Callière Museum of Archaeology & History 350 pl Royale — *Web:* www.musee-pointe-a-calliere.qc.ca	Montréal	QC	H2Y3Y5	514-872-9150	872-9151
Redpath Museum 859 rue Sherbrooke O — *Web:* www.mcgill.ca/redpath/	Montréal	QC	H3A2K6	514-398-4086	398-3185
Saint James United Church 463 rue Sainte-Catherine O	Montréal	QC	H3B1B1	514-288-9245	288-5148
Saint Joseph's Oratory of Mount Royal 3800 ch Queen Mary — *Web:* www.saint-joseph.org	Montréal	QC	H3V1H6	514-733-8211	733-9735
Saint-Leonard Cave Site 5200 boul Lavoisier	Saint-Leonard	QC		514-328-8500	
Saint Patrick's Basilica 454 boul René-Lévesque O	Montréal	QC	H2Z1A7	514-866-7379	954-1218
Sir George-Etienne Cartier National Historic Site 458 rue Notre-Dame E	Montréal	QC	H2Y1C8	514-283-2282	283-5560

SPORTS TEAMS & FACILITIES

Name / Address	City	State	ZIP	Phone	Fax
Hippodrome de Montréal 7440 boul Decarie — *Web:* www.hippodrome-montreal.ca	Montréal	QC	H4P2H1	514-739-2741	340-2025
Laval Dynamites (soccer) 400 St Hubert	Laval	QC	H7G2Y7	450-668-3172	668-6734
Molson Centre 1260 rue de la Gauchetiere W	Montréal	QC	H3B5E8	514-989-2800	932-8571
Montreal Alouettes (football) 4545 ave Pierre de-Coubertin — *Web:* www.cfl.ca/CFLMontreal/home.html	Montréal	QC	H1V3L6	514-254-2400	254-1115
Montréal Canadiens 1260 rue de la Gauchetiere O — *Fax: PR ■ *Web:* ww1.nhl.com/teampage/mon	Montréal	QC	H3B5E8	514-932-2582	932-9296*
Montréal Expos PO Box 500 Stn M — *Web:* www.montrealexpos.com	Montréal	QC	H1V3P2	514-253-3434	253-8282
Montréal Impact (soccer) 1000 Emile-Journault Claude-Robillard Ctr — *Web:* www.impactmtl.com	Montréal	QC	H2M2E7	514-328-3668	328-1287

— Events —

	Phone
African & Creole Arts Festival (mid-late July)	514-499-9239
Artists Promenade (June-August)	514-496-7678
Beer Mundial (mid-late June)	514-722-9640
Black & Blue Festival (mid-October)	514-875-7026
Canada Day (July 1)	514-873-2015
Canada Day Celebrations (July 1)	514-283-7363
Canada's International Men's Tennis Championships (late July-early August)	514-273-1515
Chinese Lantern Festival (mid-late September)	514-872-1400
Christmas at the Fort (mid-December-early January)	514-861-6701
Christmas at the Garden (mid-November-early January)	514-872-1400
Classical Music Festival (July)	450-759-7636
Festival de Theatre des Ameriques (late May-early June)	514-842-0704
Festival International de Jazz de Montréal (late June-early July)	514-523-3378

Montreal — Events (Cont'd)

	Phone
Francofolies of Montréal (late July-mid-August)	514-871-1881
Great Pumpkin Ball (mid-October-early November)	514-872-1400
International Festival of New Cinema & New Media (mid-late October)	514-847-9272
International Food Festival (early-mid-August)	514-861-8241
International Interior Design Show (mid-late May)	514-397-2222
International Orchid Show (mid-October)	514-934-0680
International Tourism and Travel Show (late October-early November)	514-397-2222
Just for Laughs Festival (mid-late July)	514-845-2322
Lachine International Folklore Festival (early July)	514-634-7526
Montréal Air Show (mid-May)	800-678-5440
Montréal Fringe Festival (mid-late June)	514-849-3378
Montréal Sportsmen's Show (late March)	514-397-2222
Montréal Spring Gift Show (early March)	514-397-2222
Montréal World Film Festival (late August-early September)	514-848-3883
National Bank Duck Race (late June)	514-496-7678
Nights of Africa International Festival (early-late July)	514-499-9239
Players Grand Prix of Canada (mid-June)	514-350-0000
Saint Jean-Baptiste Day Celebration (June 24)	514-872-4058
Santa Claus Village (early December-early January)	514-281-0170
Tropicalissimo Latin Extravaganza (June-August)	514-496-7678
Worldwide Kite Rendez-Vous (late June)	514-765-7213

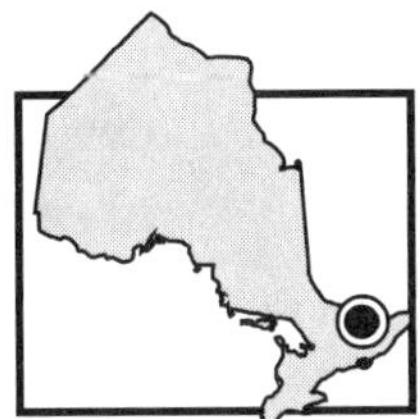

Ottawa

As the capital of Canada and the seat of the country's federal government, Ottawa is the fourth largest metropolitan area in Canada. Visitors from around the world travel to Canada's capital region to view Parliament Hill and the Parliament buildings and to experience the world-class museums, galleries, historic sites, and entertainment venues. Located along Ottawa's historic By Ward Market is the National Gallery of Canada, which houses Canada's most extensive collection of national art; and situated on historic Sussex Drive is the Royal Canadian Mint. During the summer months Parliament Hill is home to Reflections of Canada: A Symphony of Sound and Light, a daily show that tells the story of Canada using music, images, and lights. Ottawa is also home to the Ottawa Blues Festival, Canada's largest blues festival; the Canadian Tulip Festival, one of the largest in the world; and the Keskinada Loppet, Canada's most distinguished cross-country skiing event.

Population	323,340	**Longitude**	75-40-12 W
Area (Land)	42.5 sq mi	**Time Zone**	EST
Elevation	259 ft	**Area Code/s**	613
Latitude	45-25-12 N		

— Average Temperatures and Precipitation —

TEMPERATURES

	Jan	Feb	Mar	Apr	May	Jun	Jul	Aug	Sep	Oct	Nov	Dec
High	21	23	34	52	66	75	79	77	68	55	41	25
Low	5	7	19	33	45	54	59	57	48	37	27	10

PRECIPITATION

	Jan	Feb	Mar	Apr	May	Jun	Jul	Aug	Sep	Oct	Nov	Dec
Inches	0.6	0.5	1.3	2.4	2.6	2.9	3.4	3.5	3.1	2.6	2.2	1.2

— Important Phone Numbers —

	Phone		Phone
American Express Travel	613-563-0231	**Medical Referral**	613-733-2604
Canadian Automobile Assn.	613-820-1400	**Poison Control Center**	613-737-1100
Dental Referral	613-523-3876	**Road Conditions**	613-745-7040
Emergency	911	**Weather**	613-998-3439

— Information Sources —

				Phone	Fax
Better Business Bureau Serving Ottawa & Hull 130 Albert St Suite 603 *Web:* www.ottawa.bbb.org	Ottawa	ON	K1P5G4	613-237-4856	237-4878
Capital Infocentre 90 Wellington St. *TF:* 800-465-1867 ■ *E-mail:* info@ncc-ccn.ca	Ottawa	ON	K1P1C7	613-239-5000	952-8520
Ottawa Carleton Board of Trade/Metro Ottawa Chamber of Commerce 130 Albert St Suite 910 *Web:* www.board-of-trade.org	Ottawa	ON	K1P5G4	613-236-3631	236-7498
Ottawa City Hall 111 Sussex Dr *Web:* city.ottawa.on.ca ■ *E-mail:* info@city.ottawa.on.ca	Ottawa	ON	K1N5A1	613-244-5300	244-5406
Ottawa Congress Centre 55 Colonel By Dr. *TF:* 800-450-0077	Ottawa	ON	K1N9J2	613-563-1984	563-7646
Ottawa Economic Development Corp 350 Albert St Suite 1720 *TF:* 888-568-8292 ■ *Web:* www.ottawaregion.com	Ottawa	ON	K1R1A4	613-236-3500	236-9469
Ottawa Mayor 111 Sussex Dr. *Web:* www.city.ottawa.on.ca/ottawa/city/web/a/a1/a1-political.html	Ottawa	ON	K1N5A1	613-244-5380	244-5379
Ottawa Public Library 120 Metcalfe St *Web:* www.opl.ottawa.on.ca ■ *E-mail:* clubbb@opl.ottawa.on.ca	Ottawa	ON	K1P5M2	613-236-0301	567-4013
Ottawa Tourism & Convention Authority 130 Albert St Suite 1800 *TF:* 800-363-4465 ■ *Web:* www.tourottawa.org ■ *E-mail:* info@tourottawa.org	Ottawa	ON	K1P5G4	613-237-5150	237-7339
Region of Ottawa-Carleton 111 Lisgar St. *Web:* www.rmoc.on.ca ■ *E-mail:* info@rmoc.on.ca	Ottawa	ON	K2P2L7	613-560-1335	560-6068

On-Line Resources

About.com Guide to Ottawa	ottawa.about.com/local/ottawa
City Knowledge Ottawa	www.cityknowledge.com/canada_on_ottawa.htm
CRS Encyclopedia Ottawa	www.relocatecanada.com/ottawa/
Gay Ottawa	www.gayottawa.com
Guide to Ottawa	www.guide-to-ottawa.com
Ottawa Dining Guide	www.ottawadining.com
Ottawa Online Ventures	www.ventures.ca
Ottawa X Press	www.theottawaxpress.ca
Ottawa.com	www.ottawa.com
OttawaGolf Online	www.ottawagolf.com
OttawaKiosk	www.ottawakiosk.com
OttawaStart.com	www.ottawastart.com
OttawaWEB	www.ottawaweb.com
Restaurant.ca Ottawa	www.restaurant.ca/ott/
Rough Guide Travel Ottawa	travel.roughguides.com/content/6015/index.htm
SurfOttawa.com	www.surfottawa.com

— Transportation Services —

AIRPORTS

■ **Ottawa Macdonald-Cartier International Airport (YOW)**

	Phone
11 miles S of downtown (approx 20 minutes) Web: ottawa-airport.ca	613-248-2125

Airport Transportation

	Phone
Airport Limousine $60 fare to downtown	613-741-7111
Blue Line Taxi Co $23 fare to downtown	613-746-8740
Hotel Shuttle Bus $9 fare to downtown	613-736-9993
Sabo Transport Services $40 fare to downtown	613-736-6891

Ottawa (Cont'd)

Commercial Airlines

	Phone		Phone
Air Nova	800-776-3000	**First Air**	800-267-1247
Air Ontario	800-776-3000	**Iberia**	800-772-4642
Alitalia	800-223-5730	**Inter-Canadian**	800-426-7000
American	800-433-7300	**Japan**	800-525-3663
Bearskin Airlines	800-465-2327	**KLM**	800-374-7747
British Airways	800-247-9297	**Korean Air**	800-438-5000
BWIA International	800-538-2942	**Lufthansa**	800-645-3880
Canada 3000	877-359-2263	**Northwest Airlink**	800-225-2525
Cayman Airways	800-422-9626	**Royal Airlines**	800-667-7692
Continental Express	800-525-0280	**Scandinavian**	800-221-2350
Delta Business Express	800-345-3400	**US Airways**	800-428-4322
El Al	800-223-6700		

CAR RENTALS

	Phone		Phone
Avis	613-739-3334	**Hertz**	613-521-3332
Budget	613-521-4844	**National**	613-737-7023
Discount	613-234-0814	**Thrifty**	613-737-4510

LIMO/TAXI

	Phone		Phone
Access Limousine	613-794-9040	**Excalibur Limousines**	613-224-2299
Allante Limousine	613-724-9553	**Sovereign Limousine**	613-228-5466
Blue Line Taxi Co	613-746-8740		

MASS TRANSIT

	Phone
OC Transpo $2.25 Base Fare	613-741-4390
PARA Transpo $3.50 Base Fare	613-244-7272

RAIL/BUS

				Phone
VIA Rail Canada 200 Tremblay Rd Ottawa Stn *TF:* 800-361-1235	Ottawa	ON	K1G3H5	613-244-8289

— Accommodations —

HOTELS, MOTELS, RESORTS

				Phone	Fax
Adam's Airport Inn 2721 Bank St *TF:* 800-261-5835	Ottawa	ON	K1T1M8	613-738-3838	736-8211
Albert at Bay Suite Hotel 435 Albert St *TF:* 800-267-6644 ■ *Web:* www.absuites.com	Ottawa	ON	K1R7X4	613-238-8858	238-1433
Arosa Suites Hotel 163 McLaren St *Web:* www.arosahotel.com	Ottawa	ON	K2P2G4	613-238-6783	238-5080
Best Western Barons Hotel 3700 Richmond Rd *TF:* 800-528-1234	Ottawa	ON	K2H5B8	613-828-2741	596-4742
Best Western Macies Hotel 1274 Carling Ave *TF:* 800-528-1234	Ottawa	ON	K1Z7K8	613-728-1951	728-1955
Best Western Victoria Park Suites 377 O'Connor St *TF:* 800-465-7275 ■ *Web:* www.vpsuites.com	Ottawa	ON	K2P2M2	613-567-7275	567-1161
Business Inn 180 MacLaren St *TF:* 800-363-1777 ■ *Web:* www.businessinn.com	Ottawa	ON	K2P0L3	613-232-1121	232-8143
Capital Hill Hotel & Suites 88 Albert St *TF:* 800-463-7705	Ottawa	ON	K1P5E9	613-235-1413	235-6047
Carleton University Tour & Conference Centre 1125 Colonel By Dr	Ottawa	ON	K1S5B6	613-520-5611	520-3952
Cartier Place & Towers Suite Hotel 180 Cooper St *TF:* 800-236-8399	Ottawa	ON	K2P2L5	613-236-5000	238-3842
Chateau Laurier 1 Rideau St *TF:* 800-441-1414 ■ *Web:* www.cphotels.com	Ottawa	ON	K1N8S7	613-241-1414	241-2951
Chimo Hotel 199 Joseph Cyr St *TF:* 800-387-9779 ■ *Web:* www.chimohotel.com	Ottawa	ON	K1J7T4	613-744-1060	744-7845
Citadel Ottawa Hotel & Convention Centre 101 Lyon St *TF:* 800-567-3600	Ottawa	ON	K1R5T9	613-237-3600	237-2351
Comfort Inn by Journey's End Motel 1252 Michael St *TF:* 800-228-5150	Ottawa	ON	K1J7T1	613-744-2900	746-0836
Comfort Inn Kanata 222 Hearst Way *TF:* 800-228-5150	Kanata	ON	K2L3A2	613-592-2200	592-2200
Days Inn Ottawa Centre 123 Metcalfe St *TF:* 800-329-7466	Ottawa	ON	K1P5L9	613-237-9300	237-2163
Delta Ottawa Hotel & Suites 361 Queen St *TF:* 800-268-1133 ■ *Web:* www.deltahotels.com	Ottawa	ON	K1R7S9	613-238-6000	238-2290
Econo Lodge Parkway 475 Rideau St *TF:* 800-263-0649	Ottawa	ON	K1N5Z3	613-789-3781	789-0207
Embassy Hotel & Suites 25 Cartier St *TF:* 800-661-5495	Ottawa	ON	K2P1J2	613-237-2111	563-1353
Embassy West Hotel 1400 Carling Ave *TF:* 800-267-8696	Ottawa	ON	K1Z7L8	613-729-4331	729-1600
Holiday Inn Plaza La Chaudiere 2 rue Montcalm *TF:* 800-567-1962	Hull	QC	J8X4B4	819-778-3880	778-3309
Howard Johnson Express Inn 112 Montreal Rd *TF:* 888-891-1169	Ottawa	ON	K1L6E6	613-746-4641	746-6529
Howard Johnson Hotel Ottawa 140 Slater St *TF:* 800-446-4656	Ottawa	ON	K1P5H6	613-238-2888	235-8421
Les Suites Hotel Ottawa 130 Besserer St *TF:* 800-267-1989	Ottawa	ON	K1N9M9	613-232-2000	232-1242
Lord Elgin Hotel 100 Elgin St *TF:* 800-267-4298	Ottawa	ON	K1P5K8	613-235-3333	235-3223
Luxor Hotel 350 Moodie Dr *TF:* 800-616-7719 ■ *Web:* www.luxorhotel.com	Nepean	ON	K2H8G3	613-726-1717	726-1462
Market Square Inn 350 Dalhousie St *TF:* 800-341-2210	Ottawa	ON	K1N7E9	613-241-1000	241-4804
Minto Place Suite Hotel 433 Laurier Ave W *TF:* 800-267-3377 ■ *Web:* www.minto.com/hotel/	Ottawa	ON	K1R7Y1	613-232-2200	232-6962
Mirada Inn 545 Montreal Rd *TF:* 800-267-1666	Ottawa	ON	K1K0V1	613-741-1102	741-1102
Monterey Inn 2259 Hwy 16 *TF:* 800-565-1311 ■ *Web:* www.montereyinn.com	Nepean	ON	K2E6Z8	613-226-5813	226-5900
Novotel Ottawa Hotel 33 Nicholas St *TF:* 800-668-6835	Ottawa	ON	K1N9M7	613-230-3033	760-4765
Quality Hotel 290 Rideau St *TF:* 800-424-6423	Ottawa	ON	K1N5Y3	613-789-7511	789-2434
Radisson Hotel Ottawa Centre 100 Kent St *TF:* 800-333-3333	Ottawa	ON	K1P5R7	613-238-1122	783-4229
Ramada Hotel & Suites Ottawa 111 Cooper St *TF:* 800-267-8378	Ottawa	ON	K2P2E3	613-238-1331	230-2179
Ramada Inn Ottawa 480 Metcalfe St *TF:* 800-272-6232	Ottawa	ON	K1S3N6	613-237-5500	237-6705
Ramada Plaza Hotel 35 rue Laurier *TF:* 800-567-9607 ■ *Web:* www.ramada-hotel-ottawa.com	Hull	QC	J8X4E9	819-778-6111	778-8548
Sheraton Hotel Ottawa 150 Albert St *TF:* 800-489-8333	Ottawa	ON	K1P5G2	613-238-1500	235-2723
Southway Inn 2431 Bank St *TF:* 800-267-9704 ■ *Web:* www.southway.com	Ottawa	ON	K1V8R9	613-737-0811	737-3207
Town House Motor Hotel 319 Rideau St *TF:* 888-789-4949	Ottawa	ON	K1N5Y4	613-789-5555	789-6196
Travelodge 1486 Innes Rd *TF:* 800-578-7878	Gloucester	ON	K1B3V5	613-745-1133	745-7380
Travelodge 1376 Carling Ave *TF:* 800-267-4166	Ottawa	ON	K1Z7L5	613-722-7600	722-2226
Travelodge Hotel Downtown Ottawa 402 Queen St *TF:* 800-578-7878	Ottawa	ON	K1R5A7	613-236-1133	236-2317
Webb's Motel 1705 Carling Ave *TF:* 800-263-4264	Ottawa	ON	K2A1C8	613-728-1881	728-4516
WelcomInns Ottawa 1220 Michael St *TF:* 800-387-4381	Ottawa	ON	K1J7T1	613-748-7800	748-0499
Westin Ottawa 11 Colonel By Dr *TF:* 800-228-3000	Ottawa	ON	K1N9H4	613-560-7000	560-7359

— Restaurants —

				Phone
Al's Steak House (Steak/Seafood) 327 Elgin St	Ottawa	ON	K2P1M5	613-233-7111
Amber Garden Restaurant (European) 1 Richmond Rd	Ottawa	ON	K1Y2X1	613-725-2757
Big Daddy's Crab Shack & Oyster Bar (Cajun/Creole) 339 Elgin St	Ottawa	ON	K2P1M5	613-569-5200
Bistro 115 (French) 110 Murray St	Ottawa	ON	K1N5M6	613-562-7244
Blue Cactus Bar & Grill (Southwest) 2 ByWard Market	Ottawa	ON	K1N7A1	613-241-7061
Bravo Bravo (Italian) 292 Elgin St	Ottawa	ON	K2P1M3	613-233-7525
Cafe Henry Burger (French) 69 rue Laurier	Hull	QC	J8X3V7	819-777-5646
Cafe Spiga (Italian) 271 Dalhousie St	Ottawa	ON	K1N7E5	613-241-4381
Cafe Wim & Restaurant (Dutch) 537 Sussex Dr	Ottawa	ON	K1N6Z6	613-241-1771
Casablanca Resto (Moroccan) 41 Clarence St	Ottawa	ON	K1N4K1	613-789-7855
Cathay Restaurant (Chinese) 228 Albert St	Ottawa	ON	K1P5G6	613-233-7705
Chez Jean Pierre (French) 210 Somerset St	Ottawa	ON	K2P0J4	613-235-9711
Clair de Lune (French) 81B Clarence St	Ottawa	ON	K1N5P5	613-241-2200
Courtyard Restaurant (Continental) 21 George St	Ottawa	ON	K1N8W5	613-241-1516
Crêperie The (French) 47 York St	Ottawa	ON	K1N5S7	613-241-8805
Empire Grill (New American) 47 Clarence St	Ottawa	ON	K1N9K1	613-241-1343
Gasthaus Zum Dorf Krug Restaurant (German) 380 Industrial Ave	Ottawa	ON	K1G0Y9	613-521-5589

Ottawa — Restaurants (Cont'd)

				Phone
Greek Souvlaki House (Greek) 1200 Prince of Wales Dr.	Ottawa	ON	K2C3Y4	613-225-1144
Griffins (International) 284 Elgin St	Ottawa	ON	K2P1M3	613-567-2746
Haveli Restaurant (Indian) 87 George St	Ottawa	ON	K1N9H7	613-241-1700
Japanese Village Restaurant (Japanese) 170 Laurier Ave	Ottawa	ON	K1P5V5	613-236-9519
La Piazza Bistro Italiano (Italian) 25 York St	Ottawa	ON	K1N5S7	613-562-6666
La Roma Restaurant (Italian) 484 Preston St	Ottawa	ON	K1S4N7	613-234-8244
Les Muses (French) 100 rue Laurier	Hull	QC	J8X4H2	819-776-7009
Lone Star Cafe (Tex Mex) 780 Baseline Rd	Ottawa	ON	K2C3V8	613-224-4044
Mamma Grazzi's Kitchen (Italian) 25 George St	Ottawa	ON	K1N8W5	613-241-8656
Marble Works (Steak/Seafood) 14 Waller St	Ottawa	ON	K1N9C4	613-241-6764
Mayflower II Restaurant & Pub (International) 201 Queen St.	Ottawa	ON	K1P5C9	613-238-1138
Mill Restaurant (Steak/Seafood) 555 Ottawa River Pkwy	Ottawa	ON	K1P5R4	613-237-1311
New Dubrovnik Dining Lounge (European) 1170 Carling Ave	Ottawa	ON	K1Z7K6	613-722-1490
Nick & Jerry's Simply Seafood (Seafood) 253 Slater St.	Ottawa	ON	K1P5H9	613-232-4895
Noah's (North American) 407 Laurier Ave.	Ottawa	ON	K1R7Y7	613-782-2422
Old Fish Market Restaurant (Seafood) 54 York St.	Ottawa	ON	K1N5T1	613-241-3474
Oscar's (California) 123 Queen St	Ottawa	ON	K1P5C7	613-234-9699
Sante Restaurant (International) 45 Rideau St	Ottawa	ON	K1N5W8	613-241-7113
Savana Cafe (Asian/Caribbean) 431 Gilmour St.	Ottawa	ON	K2P0R5	613-233-9159
Suisha Garden Japanese Restaurant (Japanese) 208 Slater St	Ottawa	ON	K1P5H8	613-236-9602
Tommy Tango Rythmn Kitchen Cafe (Mediterranean) 1280 Baseline Rd	Ottawa	ON	K2C0A9	613-723-3300
Trattoria Italia Dining Lounge & Caffe (Italian) 228 Preston St.	Ottawa	ON	K1R7R4	613-236-1081
Viet Nam Palace Restaurant (Vietnamese) 819 Somerset St W	Ottawa	ON	K1R6R4	613-238-6758
Vineyards Wine Bar Bistro (North American) 54 York St	Ottawa	ON	K1N5T1	613-241-4270
Waterside Restaurant (Seafood) Sussex Dr Rockcliffe Boat House Marina	Ottawa	ON	K1M2H9	613-744-5253
Zuma's Rodeo Texas Grill (Tex Mex) 1211 Lemieux St	Ottawa	ON	K1J1A2	613-742-9378

— Goods and Services —

SHOPPING

Name / Address	City	Prov	Postal Code	Phone	Fax
Bank Street Promenade 176 Gloucester St Suite 204	Ottawa	ON	K2P0A6	613-232-6255	232-3372
Bayshore Shopping Centre 100 Bayshore Dr	Nepean	ON	K2B8C1	613-829-7491	829-4272
ByWard Market 55 ByWard Market Sq. *Web:* www.ottawakiosk.com/ByWardMarket/	Ottawa	ON	K1N9C3	613-562-3325	562-3326
Ottawa Antique Market 1179A Bank St	Ottawa	ON	K1S3X7	613-730-6000	730-3030
Place d'Orleans Shopping Centre 110 Place d'Orleans Dr	Orleans	ON	K1C2L9	613-824-9050	824-0258
Place de Ville Shops 480-112 Kent St	Ottawa	ON	K1P5P2	613-236-3600	563-9694
Preston Street BIA 248 Preston St	Ottawa	ON	K1R7R4	613-231-2815	232-4236
Rideau Centre 50 Rideau St.	Ottawa	ON	K1N9J7	613-236-6565	236-5728
Saint Laurent Shopping Centre 1200 St Laurent Blvd.	Ottawa	ON	K1K3B8	613-745-6858	745-1272
Somerset Village 352 Somerset St.	Ottawa	ON	K2P0J9	613-233-7762	236-1943
Sparks Street Mall 151 Sparks St 2nd Fl.	Ottawa	ON	K1P5E3	613-230-0984	230-7671
World Exchange Plaza 300-45 O'Connor St	Ottawa	ON	K1P1A4	613-230-3002	563-3217

BANKS

Name / Address	City	Prov	Postal Code	Phone	Fax
Bank of Canada 234 Wellington St *Web:* www.bank-banque-canada.ca	Ottawa	ON	K1A0G9	613-782-8111	782-7713
Bank of Montreal 144 Wellington St *TF:* 800-555-3000 ■ *Web:* www.bmo.com	Ottawa	ON	K1P5T3	613-564-6424	564-6381
Canada Trust 45 O'Conner St. *Web:* www.canadatrust.com	Ottawa	ON	K1P1A4	613-782-1201	594-4741
HSBC 30 Metcalfe St *Web:* www.hsbcgroup.com	Ottawa	ON	K1P5L4	613-238-3331	238-1078
National Bank of Canada 242 Rideau St *TF:* 888-835-6281 ■ *Web:* www.bnc.ca	Ottawa	ON	K1N5Y3	613-241-9110	241-1204
Royal Bank of Canada 90 Sparks St *TF:* 800-769-2511 ■ *Web:* www.royalbank.com	Ottawa	ON	K1P5T6	613-564-4842	564-4527
Scotiabank 303 Queen St. *Web:* www.scotiabank.ca	Ottawa	ON	K1R7S2	613-564-5372	564-7918
Toronto-Dominion Bank 106 Sparks St *Web:* www.tdbank.ca	Ottawa	ON	K1P5S8	613-783-6110	231-6719

BUSINESS SERVICES

Name	Phone
Allegra Print & Imaging	613-730-3000
Bradson Staffing Services	613-782-2333
Braithwaite Office Resources	613-722-2741
Canada Post	613-230-6552
DHL International Express	403-250-1512
Dollco Printing	613-738-9181
Federal Express	800-463-3339
Interim Personnel	613-237-7501
Kelly Services	613-238-4801
KP Copy Centre	613-238-2309
Kwik Kopy Printing	613-567-0512
Mail Boxes Etc	613-596-4550
Manpower Temporary Services	613-820-1493
Olsten Staffing Services	613-594-5962
Temporarily Yours	613-238-8801
UPS	800-742-5877

— Media —

PUBLICATIONS

Name / Address	City	Prov	Postal Code	Phone	Fax
Hill Times The 69 Sparks St *Web:* www.thehilltimes.ca ■ *E-mail:* hilltimes@achilles.net	Ottawa	ON	K1P5A5	613-232-5952	232-9055
Journal Le Droit† PO Box 8860 Stn T 47 rue Clarence Suite 222 *Web:* www.ledroit.com	Ottawa	ON	K1G3J9	613-562-0111	562-7539
Ottawa Business Journal 424 Catherine St 2nd Fl. *TF:* 800-776-1072 ■ *Web:* www.ottawabusinessjournal.com	Ottawa	ON	K1R5T8	613-230-8699	230-9606
Ottawa Citizen† 1101 Baxter Rd *Web:* www.ottawacitizen.com	Ottawa	ON	K2C3M4	613-829-9100	596-3622
Ottawa Life Magazine 126 York St Suite 300 *Web:* www.ottawalife.com ■ *E-mail:* info@ottawalife.com	Ottawa	ON	KIN5T5	613-688-5433	688-1994
Ottawa Sun† 380 Hunt Club Rd *TF:* 800-267-4669 ■ *Web:* www.canoe.ca/OttawaSun/	Ottawa	ON	K1G5H7	613-739-7000	739-8041
Ottawa X Press 69 Sparks St *Web:* www.theottawaxpress.ca ■ *E-mail:* xpress@achilles.net	Ottawa	ON	K1R5M5	613-237-8226	232-9055
Where Ottawa-Hull Magazine 226 Argyle Ave *Web:* www.wheremags.com	Ottawa	ON	K2P1B9	613-230-0333	230-4441

†Daily newspapers

TELEVISION

Name / Address	City	Prov	Postal Code	Phone	Fax
CBOFT-TV Ch 9 (CBC) 250 av Lanark CP 3220 Succ C **Fax:* News Rm	Ottawa	ON	K1Y1E4	613-724-5550	724-5074*
CBOT-TV Ch 4 (CBC) PO Box 3220 Stn C *Web:* cbc.ca	Ottawa	ON	K1Y1E4	613-724-1200	724-5512
CFGS-TV Ch 49 (Ind) 171 rue Jean Proulx	Hull	QC	J8Z1W5	819-770-1040	770-1490
CFMT-TV Ch 14 (Ind) 165 Sparks St.	Ottawa	ON	K1P5B9	613-567-6360	567-6436
CHOT-TV Ch 40 (TVA) 171 rue Jean Proulx *E-mail:* chot@radionord.net	Hull	QC	J8Z1W5	819-770-1040	770-0272
CJOH-TV Ch 13 (CTV) PO Box 5813 Merivale Depot **Fax:* News Rm	Nepean	ON	K2C3G6	613-224-1313	274-4301*

RADIO

Name / Address	City	Prov	Postal Code	Phone	Fax
CBO-FM 91.5 MHz (CBC) PO Box 3220 Stn C *Web:* www.radio.cbc.ca/regional/ottawa/	Ottawa	ON	K1Y1E4	613-724-1200	562-8430
CBOF-FM 90.7 MHz (AC) PO Box 3220 Stn C	Ottawa	ON	K1Y1E4	613-724-1200	562-8520
CBOQ-FM 103.3 MHz (CBC) PO Box 3220 Stn C. *Web:* www.radio.cbc.ca/regional/ottawa/	Ottawa	ON	K1Y1E4	613-724-5084	
CBOX-FM 102.5 MHz (Nost) PO Box 3220 Stn C.	Ottawa	ON	K1Y1E4	613-724-1200	562-8447
CFGO-AM 1200 kHz (Sports) 1575 Carling Ave.	Ottawa	ON	K1Z7M3	613-750-6397	562-8447
CFRA-AM 580 kHz (N/T) 1900 Walkley Rd *Web:* www.cfra.com ■ *E-mail:* mailbox@koolcfra.com	Ottawa	ON	K1H8P4	613-738-2372	738-5024
CHEZ-FM 106.1 MHz (CR) 134 York St *Web:* www.chez106.com ■ *E-mail:* chezmail@chez106.com	Ottawa	ON	K1N5T5	613-562-1061	562-1515
CHRI-FM 99.1 MHz (Rel) 1010 Thomas Spratt Pl	Ottawa	ON	K1G5L5	613-247-1440	247-7128
CHUO-FM 89.1 MHz (Alt) 85 University Dr Suite 227 *Web:* aix1.uottawa.ca/~chuofm/	Ottawa	ON	K1N6N5	613-562-5965	562-5848
CIMF-FM 94.9 MHz (AC) 150 d'Edmonton **Fax:* News Rm	Hull	QC	J8Y3S6	819-770-2463	777-7724*
CIWW-AM 1310 kHz (Oldies) 112 Kent St Suite 1900 *Web:* www.webruler.com/oldies1310 ■ *E-mail:* oldies@webruler.com	Ottawa	ON	K1P6J1	613-238-7482	230-8107
CJMJ-FM 100.3 MHz (AC) 1575 Carling Ave	Ottawa	ON	K1Z7M3	613-798-2565	729-9829
CJRC-AM 1150 kHz (N/T) 105 rue Bellehumer Bureau 200	Gatineau	QC	J8T6K5	819-561-8801	243-6828
CKBY-FM 105.3 MHz (Ctry) 1900-112 Kent St *Web:* www.youngcountryy105.com	Ottawa	ON	K1P6J1	613-238-6862	230-8107

Ottawa — Radio (Cont'd)

				Phone	Fax
CKCU-FM 93.1 MHz (Misc) 1125 Colonel By Dr Carleton University Rm 517	Ottawa	ON	K1S5B6	613-520-2898	520-4060
Web: ckcu.web.net ■ *E-mail:* ckcu@web.net					
CKKL-FM 93.9 MHz (AC) 1900 Walkley Rd	Ottawa	ON	K1H8P4	613-526-9393	739-4040
Web: www.planetkool.com					
CKQB-FM 106.9 MHz (Rock) 1504 Merivale Rd	Nepean	ON	K2E6Z5	613-225-1069	226-8480
Web: thebear.net					
CKTF-FM 104.1 MHz (CHR) 105 rue Bellehumer Bureau 200	Gatineau	QC	J8T6K5	819-243-5555	243-6828

— Colleges/Universities —

				Phone	Fax
Augustine College 18 Blackburn Ave	Ottawa	ON	K1N8A3	613-237-9870	237-3934
Web: www.bloomquist.on.ca/augustine_college ■ *E-mail:* augcoll@magma.ca					
Carleton University 1125 Colonel By Dr	Ottawa	ON	K1S5B6	613-520-2600	520-3847
Web: www.carleton.ca					
Herzing College 1200 St Laurent Blvd	Ottawa	ON	K1K3B8	613-742-8099	742-8336
Web: www.herzing.edu/ottawa/					
Saint Paul University 223 Main St	Ottawa	ON	K1S1C4	613-236-1393	782-3033
Web: www.ustpaul.ca					
Toronto School of Business Ottawa Campus 301 Laurier Ave W 3rd Fl	Ottawa	ON	K1P6M6	613-233-4533	233-4162
Web: www.ottawacollege.com					
University of Ottawa 550 Cumberland St	Ottawa	ON	K1N6N5	613-562-5800	562-5323
Web: www.uottawa.ca					

— Hospitals —

				Phone	Fax
Children's Hospital of Eastern Ontario 401 Smyth Rd	Ottawa	ON	K1H8L1	613-737-7600	738-4866
Web: www.cheo.on.ca					
Montfort Hospital 713 Montreal Rd	Ottawa	ON	K1K0T2	613-746-4621	748-4947
Web: www.hopitalmontfort.com ■ *E-mail:* montfort@montfort.ochin.on.ca					
Ottawa Civic Hospital 1053 Carling Ave	Ottawa	ON	K1Y4E9	613-761-4000	761-5331
Web: www.civich.ottawa.on.ca					
Ottawa General Hospital 501 Smyth Road	Ottawa	ON	K1H8L6	613-737-6111	737-8470
Web: www.ogh.on.ca					
Riverside Campus of Ottawa Hospital 1967 Riverside Dr	Ottawa	ON	K1H7W9	613-738-7100	738-8522
Web: www.ochin.on.ca/riverside/ ■ *E-mail:* riversid@ochin.on.ca					
Salvation Grace Hospital Ottawa 1156 Wellington St	Ottawa	ON	K1Y2Z4	613-724-4637	724-4644
Web: www.grace.ottawa.on.ca					

— Attractions —

				Phone	Fax
A Company of Fools 240 Sparks St	Ottawa	ON	K1P1A1	819-459-3824	994-0336
Web: www.cyberus.ca/~fools/ ■ *E-mail:* fools@cyberus.ca					
Agriculture Museum Central Experimental Farm 2000 NCC Driveway Bldg 88	Ottawa	ON	K1A0C6	613-991-3044	947-2374
Web: www.science-tech.nmstc.ca					
Art Mode Gallery 531 Sussex Dr	Ottawa	ON	K1N6Z6	613-241-1511	241-6030
Web: www.artmode.com					
Arts Court 2 Daly Ave	Ottawa	ON	K1N6E2	613-564-7240	564-4428
E-mail: artscourt@city.ottawa.on.ca					
Billings Estate Museum 2100 Cabot St	Ottawa	ON	K1H6K1	613-247-4830	247-4832
Cameron Highlands of Ottawa Musuem 2 Queen Elizabeth Dr Cartier Square Drill Hall	Ottawa	ON	K1A0K2	613-990-3507	
Canada & the World Pavilion Sussex Dr Rideau Falls Pk	Ottawa	ON	K1N5A1	613-239-5000	
Canadian Children's Museum 100 rue Laurier	Hull	QC	J8X4H2	819-776-8294	776-8300
Web: www.civilization.ca/cmc/cmceng/cmeng.html					
Canadian Improv Games 160 Elgin St	Ottawa	ON	K2P2M3	613-726-6339	233-3341
Web: www.improv.ca ■ *E-mail:* improv@magma.ca					
Canadian Museum of Civilization 100 rue Laurier	Hull	QC	J8X4H2	819-776-7000	776-8300
TF: 800-555-5621 ■ *Web:* www.civilization.ca/cmc/cmceng/welcmeng.html ■ *E-mail:* membrs@civilization.ca					
Canadian Museum of Contemporary Photography 1 Rideau Canal	Ottawa	ON	K1N9N6	613-990-8257	990-6542
Web: cmcp.gallery.ca ■ *E-mail:* cmcp@ngc.chin.gc.ca					
Canadian Museum of Nature 240 McLeod St	Ottawa	ON	K1P6P4	613-566-4700	364-4021
TF: 800-263-4433 ■ *Web:* www.nature.ca ■ *E-mail:* clucas@mus-nature.ca					
Canadian Postal Museum 100 rue Laurier	Hull	QC	J8X4H2	819-776-8200	776-7062
Web: www.civilization.ca/cmc/cmceng/npmeng.html					
Canadian Ski Museum 1960 Scott St	Ottawa	ON	K1Z8L8	613-722-3584	
Canadian War Museum 330 Sussex Dr General Motors Ct	Ottawa	ON	K1A0M8	819-776-8600	776-8623
Web: www.cmcc.muse.digital.ca					
Capital Double Decker & Trolley Tours 1795 Bantree St	Ottawa	ON	K1B4L6	613-749-3666	749-9338
TF: 800-823-6147					
Carleton University Art Gallery 1125 Colonel By Drive St Patrick's Bldg	Ottawa	ON	K1S5B6	613-520-2120	520-4409
Web: temagami.carleton.ca/gallery/					
Casino de Hull 1 boul du Casino	Hull	QC	J8Y6W3	819-772-2100	772-3704
TF: 800-665-2274 ■ *Web:* www.casinos-quebec.com					
Cathedral Basilica of Notre-Dame 60 Quiques Ave	Ottawa	ON	K1N5H5	613-241-7496	241-1627
CINÉPLUS IMAX/OMNIMAX Theatre 100 rue Laurier Canadian Museum of Civilization	Hull	QC	J8X4H2	819-776-7010	776-8300
Web: www.civilization.ca/cmc/cmceng/cinepeng.html					
Cumberland Heritage Village Museum 2940 Queen St	Cumberland	ON	K4C1E6	613-833-3059	833-3061
Currency Museum of the Bank of Canada 245 Sparks St	Ottawa	ON	K1A0G9	613-782-8914	782-8874
Web: www.bank-banque-canada.ca/museum/index.htm ■ *E-mail:* museum-musee@bank-banque-canada.ca					
Fitzroy Provincial Park 5201 Canon Smith Dr	Fitzroy Harbour	ON	K0A1X0	613-623-5159	
Web: www.mnr.gov.on.ca/MNR/parks/fitz.html					
Fulford Gallery 75 Hinton Ave N	Ottawa	ON	K1Y0Z7	613-722-0440	722-4528
Web: www.cyberus.ca/~fulford/ ■ *E-mail:* fulford@cyberus.ca					
Gatineau Park 318 ch Meech Lake Visitor Ctr	Chelsea	QC	J0X1N0	819-827-2020	827-3337
TF: 800-465-1867					
Geological Survey of Canada 601 Booth St Logan Hall	Ottawa	ON	K1A0E8	613-996-5763	995-3082
Great Canadian Theatre Co 910 Gladstone Ave	Ottawa	ON	K1R6Y4	613-236-5196	232-2075
Web: www.gctc.ca					
Hull Chelsea Wakefield Steam Train 165 rue Deveault	Hull	QC	J8Z1S7	819-778-7246	778-5007
TF: 800-871-7246					
Kanata Theatre 1 Ron Maslin Way	Kanata	ON	K2V1A7	613-831-4435	831-4438
Web: kt.ottawa.com					
Lansdowne Park 1015 Bank St	Ottawa	ON	K1S3W7	613-564-1485	564-1619
Laurier House National Historic Site 335 Laurier Ave E	Ottawa	ON	K1N6R4	613-992-8142	992-9233
TF: 800-230-0016					
MacSkimming Outdoor Education Centre 3635 Hwy 17	Cumberland	ON	K4C1G9	613-833-2080	833-0770
National Archives of Canada 395 Wellington St	Ottawa	ON	K1A0N3	613-995-5138	995-6274
Web: www.archives.ca					
National Arts Centre 53 Elgin St	Ottawa	ON	K1P5W1	613-594-9400	947-7112
Web: www.nac-cna.ca					
National Aviation Museum Aviation & Rockcliffe Pkwys Rockcliffe Airport	Ottawa	ON	K1G5A3	613-993-2010	990-3655
TF: 800-463-2038 ■ *Web:* www.aviation.nmstc.ca					
National Gallery of Canada 380 Sussex Dr	Ottawa	ON	K1N9N4	613-990-1985	993-4385
TF: 800-319-2787 ■ *Web:* national.gallery.ca ■ *E-mail:* info@gallery.ca					
National Museum of Science & Technology 1867 St Laurent Blvd	Ottawa	ON	K1G5A3	613-991-3044	990-3654
Web: www.science-tech.nmstc.ca ■ *E-mail:* slitech@istar.ca					
Odyssey Theatre 2 Daly Ave	Ottawa	ON	K1N6E2	613-232-8407	564-4428
Opera Lyra Ottawa 110-2 Daly Ave	Ottawa	ON	K1N6E2	613-233-9200	233-5431
Orpheus Musical Theatre Society 101 Centrepointe Dr Centrepointe Theatre	Nepean	ON	K2G5K7	613-727-6650	727-6698
Web: www.orpheus-theatre.on.ca ■ *E-mail:* chipwagon@igs.net					
Ottawa Art Gallery 2 Daly Ave	Ottawa	ON	K1N6E2	613-233-8699	569-7660
Web: www.cyberus.ca/~oag/					
Ottawa International Hostel 75 Nicholas St	Ottawa	ON	K1N7B9	613-235-2595	569-2131
Ottawa Little Theatre 400 King Edward Ave	Ottawa	ON	K1N7M7	613-233-8948	233-8027
Ottawa Riverboat Co 30 Murray St	Ottawa	ON	K1N5M4	613-562-4888	562-7364
Parliament Hill House of Commons	Ottawa	ON	K1A0A6	613-992-4793	
Web: www.capcan.ca					

Ottawa — Attractions (Cont'd)

		Phone	Fax
Regimental Museum of Governor General's Foot Guards 2 Queen Elizabeth Dr Cartier Square Drill Hall	Ottawa ON K1A0K2	613-990-0620	
Rideau Canal/Ottawa Locks Laurier Ave betw Chateau Laurier & Parliament Hill	Ottawa ON	613-283-5170	283-0677
TF: 800-230-0016 ■ *Web:* www.rideau-info.com/canal/			
Rideau Hall 1 Sussex Dr	Ottawa ON K1A0A1	613-998-7113	993-1552
TF: 800-465-6890 ■ *Web:* www.gg.ca			
Rideau River Provincial Park 2680 Donnelly Dr	Kemptville ON K0G1J0	613-258-2740	258-4432
Web: www.mnr.gov.on.ca/MNR/parks/ride.html			
Royal Canadian Mint 320 Sussex Dr.	Ottawa ON K1A0G8	613-993-8990	954-4092*
**Fax:* Cust Svc ■ *TF:* 800-267-1871 ■ *Web:* www.rcmint.ca			
Royal Canadian Mounted Police Stables Sandridge Rd & St Laurent Blvd	Ottawa ON K1G3J2	613-993-3751	952-7324
Web: www.rcmp-grc.gc.ca			
Saint Patrick's Basilica 281 Nepean St	Ottawa ON K1R5G2	613-233-1125	234-8667
Web: www.basilica.org			
Supreme Court of Canada 301 Wellington St	Ottawa ON K1A0J1	613-995-5361	
Web: www.scc-csc.gc.ca			
Valleyview Little Animal Farm 4750 Fallowfield Rd.	Nepean ON K2J4S4	613-591-1126	591-1003

SPORTS TEAMS & FACILITIES

		Phone	Fax
Corel Centre 1000 Palladium Dr	Kanata ON K2V1A5	613-599-0250	599-0358
TF: 800-444-7367 ■ *Web:* www.corelcentre.com			
Ottawa 67's (hockey) 1015 Bank St Ottawa Civic Ctr	Ottawa ON K1S3W7	613-232-6767	232-5582
Web: www.ottawa67s.com			
Ottawa Lynx (baseball) 300 Coventry Rd.	Ottawa ON K1K4P5	613-747-5969	747-0003
Web: www.ottawalynx.com ■ *E-mail:* lynx@ottawalynx.com			
Ottawa Senators Corel Center 1000 Palladium Dr	Kanata ON K2V1A5	613-599-0250	599-0358
TF Orders: 888-688-7367 ■ *Web:* www.ottawasenators.com ■ *E-mail:* senators@ottawasenators.com			
Rideau Carleton Raceway 4837 Albion Rd.	Gloucester ON K1X1A3	613-822-2211	822-1586
Web: www.rcr.net ■ *E-mail:* raceway@rcr.net			

— Events —

	Phone
Canada Day at Parliament Hill (July 1)	613-239-5000
Canadian Sunset Ceremony (mid-June)	613-239-5000
Canadian Tulip Festival (early-mid-May)	613-567-4447
Casino Sound of Light (late July-mid-August)	819-771-3389
Central Canada Exhibition (mid-late August)	613-237-7222
Children's Festival de la Jeunesse (mid-June)	613-728-5863
Christmas Lights Across Canada (early December-early January)	613-239-5000
CKCU Ottawa Folk Festival (late August)	613-230-8234
Contemporary Showcase Festival (late November)	613-829-4402
Deck the Halls at Parliament Hill (late December-early January)	613-239-5000
Fall Rhapsody (mid-September-early October)	613-239-5000
Festival Franco-ontarien (late June)	613-741-1225
Governor General's Garden Party (June)	613-998-7113
Harvestfest (late November)	613-833-3059
HOPE Beach Volleyball Tournament (mid-July)	613-237-1433
Italian Week Festival (early-mid-June)	613-726-0920
Keskinada Loppet Cross-Country Skiing Event (mid-February)	819-827-4641
Lebanorama (mid-November)	613-742-6952
National Capital Air Show (late May)	613-526-1030
National Capital Dragon Boat Race Festival (late June)	613-238-7711
National Capital Marathon Race Weekend (early May)	613-234-2221
Odawa Pow Wow (late May)	613-722-3811
Oktoberfest (mid-October)	613-564-1485
Ottawa Blues Festival (early July)	613-233-8798
Ottawa Chamber Music Festival (late July-early August)	613-234-8008
Ottawa Christmas Craft Show (mid-late December)	613-564-1485
Ottawa Fall Home Show (late September)	613-241-2888
Ottawa Fringe Festival (late June)	613-232-6162
Ottawa International Animation Festival (late October)	613-232-8769
Ottawa International Jazz Festival (mid-late July)	613-241-2633
Ottawa Spring Home Show (late March)	613-241-2888
Parliament Hill Carillon Concerts (July-August)	613-239-5000
Parliament Hill Changing the Guard Ceremony (late June-late August)	613-239-5000
Pride Festival (mid-late July)	613-237-9872
Reflections of Canada-A Symphony of Sound & Light (mid-May-early September)	613-239-5100
Signatures Craft Show & Sale (early November & mid-December)	416-465-2379
Strawberry Moon: A Midsummer Festival (mid-June)	613-236-5330
Winterlude (February)	613-239-5000

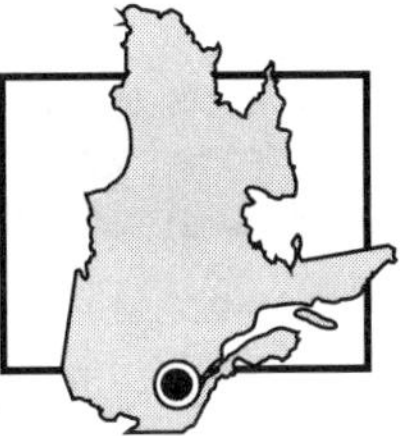

Quebec

The city of Quebec, which is the capital of the province of Quebec and seat of the National Assembly, was first established as a fur-trading post by Samuel de Champlain in 1608. Primary industries in present-day Quebec are in logging, quarries and sandpits, and agrifoods. The city is also a Canadian center for high technology research, biotechnology, and manufacturing industries. The old quarter of Quebec city was declared a World Heritage Site by UNESCO in 1985, and Quebec city remains the only fortified city in North America. With nearly four million visitors per year, Quebec is home to many festivals, including Expo-Quebec, the province's largest agricultural exhibition; and Quebec Winter Carnival, which runs from late January to mid-February and is the world's largest winter celebration of its kind. Local attractions include the Musée de l'Amérique Française, which charts the development of French culture in North America; Notre-Dame-de-Québec Basilica, the product of nearly 350 years of work and the oldest cathedral on the continent north of Mexico; the Citadel National Historic Site, which contains the Governor-General's residence; and Château Frontenac, a world-renowned hotel that was inaugurated in 1893 and completed with the addition of a central tower in 1924.

Population	167,264	**Longitude**	71-10-12 W
Area (Land)	34.3 sq mi	**Time Zone**	EST
Elevation	163 ft	**Area Code/s**	418
Latitude	46-45-00 N		

— Average Temperatures and Precipitation —

TEMPERATURES

	Jan	Feb	Mar	Apr	May	Jun	Jul	Aug	Sep	Oct	Nov	Dec
High	18	21	32	46	61	72	75	73	63	52	37	23
Low	5	7	18	31	43	54	57	55	46	37	27	10

PRECIPITATION

	Jan	Feb	Mar	Apr	May	Jun	Jul	Aug	Sep	Oct	Nov	Dec
Inches	0.6	0.4	0.8	2.4	3.2	4.5	5.4	4.5	4.5	3.4	2.3	1.1

— Important Phone Numbers —

	Phone		Phone
Canadian Automobile Assn.	418-624-2424	**Poison Control Centre**	418-656-8090
Dental Referral	418-653-5412	**Road Conditions**	418-643-6830
Emergency	911	**Weather**	418-235-4771
Medical Referral	418-648-2626		

— Information Sources —

		Phone	Fax
Better Business Bureau Serving Montréal 2055 rue Peel Bureau 460	Montréal QC H3A1V4	514-286-9281	286-2658
Web: www.montreal.bbb.org			

Canadian Cities

Quebec — Information Sources (Cont'd)

	Phone	Fax
Chambre de Commerce et d'Industrie du Québec Métropolitain 17 rue Saint-Louis . . . . Québec QC G1R3Y8	418-692-3853	694-2286
Web: www.cciqm.qc.ca ■ *E-mail:* admin@cciqm.qc.ca		
Gabrielle-Roy Library 350 rue Saint-Joseph E . . . Québec QC G1K3B2	418-529-0924	529-1588
Web: www.icqbdq.qc.ca		
Greater Québec Area Tourism & Convention Bureau 835 ave Wilfred-Laurier . . . . Québec QC G1R2L3	418-649-2608	522-0830
Web: www.quebec-region.cuq.qc.ca/eng/		
Québec City Convention Centre 900 boul René-Lévesque E. . . . . Québec QC G1R2B5	418-644-4000	644-6455
TF: 888-679-4000 ■ *Web:* www.convention.qc.ca		
Québec City Hall 2 rue des Jardins. . . . . Québec QC G1R4S9	418-691-4636	691-7410
Web: www.ville.quebec.qc.ca		
Québec Mayor 2 rue des Jardins Bureau 312. . . . Québec QC G1R4S9	418-691-6434	691-7410
Web: www.ville.quebec.qc.ca/fr/participer/mairie/mairie.html ■ *E-mail:* jplmaire@ville.quebec.qc.ca		
Urban Centre of Economic Development (CDEU) PO Box 700 . . . . Québec QC G1R4S9	418-691-6422	691-7916

On-Line Resources

City Knowledge Québec . . . . www.cityknowledge.com/canada_qc_quebec_city.htm
Connect Québec . . . . www.connect-quebec.com/e/index.htm
Greater Québec Area Tourist Region. . . . . www.quebecweb.com/tourisme/quebec/
Restaurant.ca Québec . . . . www.restaurant.ca/qbc/
Rough Guide Travel Québec. travel.roughguides.com/content/4982/index.htm

— Transportation Services —

AIRPORTS

■ Jean-Lesage International Airport (YQB)

	Phone
12 miles NW of downtown (approx 20 minutes)	418-640-2600

Airport Transportation

	Phone
Autobus La Québecoise $9 fare to downtown.	418-872-5525
Groupe Limousine A-1 $50 fare to downtown.	418-523-5059
Taxi Co-op Québec $22.20 fare to downtown	418-525-5191
Taxi Québec $22.20 fare to downtown.	418-525-8123

Commercial Airlines

	Phone		Phone
Air Alliance.	888-247-2262	**Air Transat**	877-872-6728
Air Canada	800-776-3000	**Canadian Air**.	800-426-7000
Air Nova.	800-776-3000	**Northwest**.	800-225-2525

Charter Airlines

	Phone
Aéropro	418-877-2808

CAR RENTALS

	Phone		Phone
Aviscar.	418-872-2861	**Discount**.	418-692-1244
Budget	418-871-1571	**National**	418-871-1224

LIMO/TAXI

	Phone		Phone
Groupe Limousine A-1.	418-523-5059	**Taxi Québec**	418-525-8123
Taxi Co-op Québec	418-525-5191		

MASS TRANSIT

	Phone
STCUQ Urban Transit $2.25 Base fare.	418-627-2511

RAIL/BUS

	Phone
VIA Rail Canada 450 rue de la Gare-du-Palais. . . . . Québec QC G1K3X2	418-692-3940
TF: 800-561-3949	

— Accommodations —

HOTEL RESERVATION SERVICES

	Phone	Fax
Bed & Breakfasts in Québec.	514-252-3138	252-3173
Web: www.agricotours.qc.ca ■ *E-mail:* agricotours-q@sympatico.ca		
Hospitalité Canada	418-694-1602	393-8942*
**Fax Area Code:* 514		

HOTELS, MOTELS, RESORTS

	Phone	Fax
Auberge Dufferin 2941 boul Sainte-Anne . . . . . . Beauport QC G1E3J2	418-667-1637	667-5563
Auberge Saint-Antoine 10 rue Saint-Antoine . . . . Québec QC G1K4C9	418-692-2211	692-1177
TF: 888-692-2211 ■ *Web:* www.saint-antoine.com		
Auberge Saint-Louis 48 rue Saint-Louis . . . . Québec QC G1R3Z3	418-692-2424	692-3797
TF: 888-692-4105		
Best Western Hôtel Aristocrate 3100 ch Saint-Louis . . . . Sainte-Foy QC G1W1R8	418-653-2841	653-8525
TF: 800-463-4752		
Château Bonne Entente 3400 ch Sainte-Foy. . . Sainte-Foy QC G1X1S6	418-653-5221	653-3098
TF: 800-463-4390		
Château Frontenac Le 1 rue des Carrières. . . . . . Québec QC G1R4P5	418-692-3861	692-1751
TF: 800-441-1414 ■ *Web:* www.cphotels.ca/cp.htm		
Château Grande-Allée 601 Grande Allée E. . . . . . Québec QC G1R2K4	418-647-4433	649-7553
TF: 800-263-1471 ■ *Web:* www.quebecweb.com/cga/introang.html		
Château Repotel 6555 boul Wilfrid-Hamel . . . . L'Ancienne-Lorette QC G2E5W3	418-872-1111	872-5989
TF: 800-463-5255		
Comfort Inn by Journey's End 240 boul Sainte-Anne . . . . Beauport QC G1E3L7	418-666-1226	666-5088
TF: 800-267-3837		
Confortel Le Motel 6500 boul Wilfrid-Hamel . . . . L'Ancienne-Lorette QC G2E2J1	418-877-4777	877-0013
TF: 800-363-7440		
Days Inn Québec Le Voyageur 2250 boul Sainte-Anne . . . . Québec QC G1J1Y2	418-661-7701	661-5221
TF: 800-463-5568		
Holiday Inn Québec Sainte-Foy 3125 boul Hochelaga. . . . . Sainte-Foy QC G1V4A8	418-653-4901	653-1836
TF: 800-465-4329		
Hotel Quartier 2955 boul Laurier . . . . Sainte-Foy QC G1V2M2	418-650-1616	650-6611
TF: 888-818-5863		
Hôtel Ambassadeur 321 boul Sainte-Anne . . . . . . Québec QC G1E3L4	418-666-2828	666-2775
TF: 800-363-4619 ■ *Web:* www.ambassadeur-hotel.com		
Hôtel Château Bellevue 16 rue de la Porte . . . . . Québec QC G1R4M9	418-692-2573	692-4876
TF: 800-463-2617 ■ *Web:* www.vieux-quebec.com/bellevue/		
Hôtel Château de Léry 8 rue de la Porte . . . . Québec QC G1R4M9	418-692-2692	692-5231
TF: 800-363-0036 ■ *Web:* www.quebecweb.com/chateaudelery/		
Hôtel Château Laurier 1220 Pl George V O . . . . . Québec QC G1R5B8	418-522-8108	524-8768
TF: 800-463-4453 ■ *Web:* www.vieux-quebec.com/laurier/		
Hôtel Clarendon 57 rue Sainte-Anne . . . . Québec QC G1R3X4	418-692-2480	692-4652
TF: 888-554-6001		
Hôtel Classique 2815 boul Laurier . . . . Sainte-Foy QC G1V4H3	418-658-2793	658-6816
TF: 800-463-1885		
Hôtel Germain des Prés 1200 ave Germain-des-Prés . . . . Sainte-Foy QC G1V3M7	418-658-1224	658-8846
TF: 800-463-5253		
Hôtel Gouverneur 3030 boul Laurier . . . . Sainte-Foy QC G1V2M5	418-651-3030	651-6797
TF: 888-910-1111		
Hôtel Hôtellerie Fleur-de-Lys 115 rue Sainte-Anne . . . . Québec QC G1R3X6	418-694-0106	692-1959
TF: 800-567-2106		
Hôtel La Caravelle 68 rue Saint-Louis. . . . . Québec QC G1R3Z3	418-694-0656	694-0352
TF: 800-267-0656		
Hôtel La Maison Acadienne 43 rue Sainte-Ursule . . . . Québec QC G1R4E4	418-694-0280	694-0458
TF: 800-463-0280		
Hôtel Le Capitole 972 rue Saint-Jean . . . . Québec QC G1R1R5	418-694-4040	694-1916
TF: 800-363-4040 ■ *Web:* www.lecapitole.com		
Hôtel Le Clos Saint-Louis 71 rue Saint-Louis. . . . Québec QC G1R3Z2	418-694-1311	694-9411
TF: 800-461-1311 ■ *Web:* www.quebecweb.com/clos_saint-Louis/		
Hôtel le Gîte 5160 boul Wilfrid-Hamel O . . . . . . Québec QC G2E2G8	418-871-8899	872-8533
TF: 800-363-4906 ■ *Web:* www.hotellegite.com		
Hôtel le Priori 15 rue du Sault-au-Matelot . . . . . . Québec QC G1K3Y7	418-692-3992	692-0883
TF: 800-351-3992 ■ *Web:* www.quebecweb.com/lepriori/		
Hôtel Loews Le Concorde 1225 pl Montcalm. . . . Québec QC G1R4W6	418-647-2222	647-4710
TF: 800-463-5256 ■ *Web:* www.loewshotels.com/leconcor.html		
Hôtel Manoir Victoria 44 côte du Palais . . . . Québec QC G1R4H8	418-692-1030	692-3822
TF: 800-463-6283 ■ *Web:* www.manoir-victoria.com		
Hôtel Normandin 4700 boul Pierre-Bertrand. . . . . Québec QC G2J1A4	418-622-1611	622-9277
TF: 800-463-6721 ■ *Web:* futurix.clic.net/work/normandin/		
Hôtel Plaza Québec 3031 boul Laurier . . . . . . Sainte-Foy QC G1V2M2	418-658-2727	658-6587
TF: 800-567-5276 ■ *Web:* www.jaro.qc.ca		
Hôtel Quality Suites by Journey's End 1600 rue Bouvier . . . . Québec QC G2K1N8	418-622-4244	622-4067
TF: 800-267-3837		

Quebec — Hotels, Motels, Resorts (Cont'd)

				Phone	Fax
Hôtel Québec 3115 ave des Hôtels	Sainte-Foy	QC	G1W3Z6	418-658-5120	658-4504
TF: 800-567-5276 ■ *Web:* www.jaro.qc.ca					
Hôtel Ramada Québec Centre-ville 395 rue de la Couronne	Québec	QC	G1K7X4	418-647-2611	640-0666
TF: 800-267-2002 ■ *Web:* www.ramada-quebec.qc.ca					
Hôtel Travelodge Québec Sainte-Foy 3135 ch Saint-Louis	Sainte-Foy	QC	G1W1R9	418-653-4941	653-0774
TF: 800-463-6603					
L'Hôtel du Vieux-Québec 1190 rue Saint-Jean	Québec	QC	G1R1S6	418-692-1850	692-5637
TF: 800-361-7787 ■ *Web:* www.hvq.com					
Manoir Lafayette Le 661 Grande Allée E	Québec	QC	G1R2K4	418-522-2652	522-4400
TF: 800-363-8203 ■ *Web:* www.vieux-quebec.com/lafayette/					
Motel L'Avitation 2828 boul Laurier	Sainte-Foy	QC	G1V2M1	418-653-7267	653-5449
TF: 800-567-7267					
Motel Universel 2300 ch Sainte-Foy	Sainte-Foy	QC	G1V1S5	418-653-5250	653-4486
TF: 800-463-4495					
Quality Hôtel Québec Centre-ville 330 rue de la Couronne	Québec	QC	G1K6E6	418-649-1919	529-4411
TF: 800-667-5345					
Québec Hilton 1100 boul René-Lévesque E	Québec	QC	G1K7M9	418-647-2411	647-6488
TF: 800-447-2411					
Radisson Hôtel des Gouverneurs Québec 690 boul René-Lévesque E	Québec	QC	G1R5A8	418-647-1717	647-2146
TF: 800-333-3333					

— Restaurants —

				Phone
2905 (French) 2905 boul Masson	Québec	QC	G1P1J7	418-874-1906
A la Bastille Chez Bahuaud (French) 47 rue Sainte-Geneviève	Québec	QC	G1R4B3	418-692-2544
A la Table de Serge Bruyère (French) 1200 rue Saint-Jean	Québec	QC	G1R1S8	418-694-0618
Au Parmesan (French/Italian) 38 rue Saint-Louis	Québec	QC	G1R3Z1	418-692-0341
Au Petit Coin Breton (French) 1029 rue Saint-Jean	Québec	QC	G1R1R9	418-694-0758
Auberge du Trésor (French) 20 rue Sainte-Anne	Québec	QC	G1R3X2	418-694-1876
Aux Anciens Canadiens (North American) 34 rue Saint-Louis	Québec	QC	G1R4P3	418-692-1627
Aux Vieux Canons (French) 650 Grande Allée E	Québec	QC	G1R2K5	418-529-9461
Blue Nose Resto-bar (Italian) 5073 boul Wilfrid-Hamel	Québec	QC	G2E5G3	418-877-9665
Bonaparte (French) 680 Grande Allée E	Québec	QC	G1R2K5	418-647-4747
Cafe Abraham Martin (French) 595 rue Saint-Vallier E	Québec	QC	G1K3P9	418-647-9689
Cafe La Mediterranee (Mediterranean) 85 rue Sainte-Villiar E	Québec	QC	G1K3N9	418-648-1849
Cafeteria Diplomate (French) 880 ch Sainte-Foy	Québec	QC	G1S2L2	418-682-2460
Café d'Europe (French/Italian) 27 rue Sainte-Angèle	Québec	QC	G1R4G5	418-692-3835
Café de la Paix (French) 44 rue des Jardins	Québec	QC	G1R4L7	418-692-1430
Café de la Terrasse (International) 1 rue des Carrières	Québec	QC	G1R4P5	418-692-3861
Café de Paris (French/Italian) 66 rue Saint-Louis	Québec	QC	G1R3Z3	418-694-9626
Café des Artistes (French) 333 rue Saint-Amable	Québec	QC	G1R5G2	418-522-4011
Web: www.webnet.qc.ca/artistes/anglais.htm				
Café du Monde (French) 57 rue Dalhousie	Québec	QC	G1K4B6	418-692-4455
Café le Saint-Malo (French) 75 rue Saint-Paul	Québec	QC	G1K3V8	418-692-2004
Caravelle La (International) 68 1/2 rue Saint-Louis	Québec	QC	G1R3Z3	418-694-9022
Champlain Le (French) 1 rue des Carrières	Québec	QC	G1R4P5	418-692-3861
Charles Baillairgé (French) 57 rue Sainte-Anne	Québec	QC	G1R3X4	418-692-2480
Chez Ashton (American) 640 Grande Allée E	Québec	QC	G1R2K5	418-522-3449
Cochon Dingue Le (French) 46 boul Champlain	Québec	QC	G1K4H7	418-692-2013
Commensal Le (Vegetarian) 860 rue Saint-Jean	Québec	QC	G1R1R3	418-647-3733
Continental Le (French) 26 rue Saint-Louis	Québec	QC	G1R3Y9	418-694-9995
Cosmos Cafe (International) 575 Grande Allée E	Québec	QC	G1R2K4	418-640-0606
Creperie le Petit Château (North American) 5 rue Saint-Louis	Québec	QC	G1R3Y8	418-694-1616
Crémaillère La (French/Italian) 21 rue Saint-Stanislas	Québec	QC	G1R4G7	418-692-2216
D'Orsay Restaurant Pub (International) 65 rue Buade	Québec	QC	G1R4A2	418-694-1582
Dazibo Cafe (International) 526 rue Saint-Jean	Québec	QC	G1R1P6	418-525-2405
East Side Mario's (Italian) 550 boul Wilfrid-Hamel	Québec	QC	G1M2S6	418-648-2922
Edward Pub Restaurant (North American) 824 boul Charest E	Québec	QC	G1K8H8	418-523-3674
Entrecôte Saint Jean (Steak) 1011 rue Saint-Jean	Québec	QC	G1R1R8	418-694-0234
Fix Cafe (French) 5400 boul des Galeries	Québec	QC	G2K2B4	418-624-1144
Frères de la Côte (French) 1190 rue Saint-Jean	Québec	QC	G1R1S6	418-692-5445
Gambrinus (Steak/Seafood) 15 rue du Fort	Québec	QC	G1R3W9	418-692-5144
Grolla La (Swiss) 815 côte d'Abraham	Québec	QC	G1R1A4	418-529-8107
L'Astral (International) 1225 pl Montcalm	Québec	QC	G1R4W6	418-647-2222
L'Aviatic Club (International) 450 de la Gare-du-Palais	Québec	QC	G1K3X2	418-522-3555
La Piazzetta (Italian) 17 rue du Sault-au-Matelot	Québec	QC	G1K3Y7	418-692-2962
Laurie Raphael (International) 117 rue Dalhousie	Québec	QC	G1K4B9	418-692-4555
Le Fin Gourmet (International) 774 rue Sainte-Térèse	Québec	QC	GiM1R9	418-682-5849
Le Restaurant Le Diable aux Anges (International) 28 boul Champlain	Québec	QC	G1K4H5	418-692-4674
Louis-Hébert (French) 668 Grande Allée E	Québec	QC	G1R2K5	418-525-7812
Marie-Clarisse (Steak/Seafood) 12 rue du Petit-Champlain	Québec	QC	G1K4H4	418-692-0857
Olive Noire (International) 64 boul René-Lévesque O	Québec	QC	G1R2A4	418-521-5959
Pacini (Italian) 22 côte de la Fabrique	Québec	QC	G1R3V7	418-692-4199
Patriarche Le (Continental) 17 rue Saint-Stanislas	Québec	QC	G1R4G7	418-692-5488
Playa (California) 780 rue Saint-Jean	Québec	QC	G1R1P9	418-522-3989
Portofino Bistro Italiano (Italian) 54 rue Couillard	Québec	QC	G1R3T3	418-692-8888
Web: www.portofino.qc.ca/eindex.html				
Portugais Le (Portuguese) 1155 rue de la Chevrotière	Québec	QC	G1R3J6	418-529-1675
Primavera (French/Italian) 73 rue Saint-Louis	Québec	QC	G1R3Z2	418-694-0030
Pub Saint-Alexandre (English) 1095 rue Saint-Jean	Québec	QC	G1R1S3	418-694-0015
Pub Thomas Dunn (North American) 369 rue Saint-Paul	Québec	QC	G1K3X3	418-692-4693
Restaurant Au Passant (North American) 801 rue Sainte-Therese	Québec	QC	G1N1S4	418-683-3428
Ripaille La (Continental) 9 rue Buade	Québec	QC	G1R3Z9	418-692-2450
Rétro Restaurant (French) 1129 rue Saint-Jean	Québec	QC	G1R1S3	418-694-9218
Saint-Amour Le (French) 48 rue Sainte-Ursule	Québec	QC	G1R4E2	418-694-0667
Saint-James Resto Bistro (North American) 1110 rue Saint-Jean	Québec	QC	G1R4H8	418-692-1030
Strada La (International) 690 Grande Allée E	Québec	QC	G1R2K5	418-529-6237
Yellow Tomato (Italian) 120 boul René-Lévesque O	Québec	QC	G1R2A5	418-523-8777

— Goods and Services —

SHOPPING

				Phone	Fax
Galeries de la Capitale 5401 boul des Galeries	Québec	QC	G2K1N4	418-627-5800	627-5807
Mail Centre-Ville SIDAC 820 boul Charest E	Québec	QC	G1K8H8	418-648-1986	648-9823
Marché du Vieux-Port de Québec 160 quai Saint-André	Québec	QC	G1K7C3	418-692-2517	692-1849
Place Fleur-de-Lys 550 boul Wilfrid-Hamel	Québec	QC	G1M2S6	418-529-0728	529-8129
Place Laurier 2700 boul Laurier	Québec	QC	G1V4J9	418-651-7085	651-0338
Place Québec 1050 boul Rene Levesque E Bureau 408	Québec	QC	G1R4X3	418-529-0551	529-1577
Place Sainte-Foy 2452 boul Laurier	Sainte-Foy	QC	G1V2L1	418-653-4184	653-1966
Web: www.ivanhoe.ca/en/frameset-en.html					
Promenades du Vieux-Québec 43 rue de Buade	Québec	QC	G1R4A2	418-692-6000	692-6004
Promenades Sainte-Anne Factory Outlet Centre 10909 boul Sainte-Anne	Ste-Anne-de-Beaupré	QC	G0A3C0	418-827-3555	827-5661
Quartier Petit-Champlain 61 rue du Petit-Champlain	Québec	QC	G1K4H5	418-692-2613	692-5085
TF: 877-692-2613 ■ *Web:* www.quartier-petit-champlain.qc.ca ■ *E-mail:* info@quartier-petit-champlain.qc.ca					

BANKS

				Phone	Fax
Bank of Montréal 800 pl d'Youville	Québec	QC	G1R3P4	418-692-2500	692-0410
Web: www.bmo.com					
Banque Nationale de Paris 925 ch Saint-Louis Bureau 350	Québec	QC	G1S1C1	418-684-7575	684-7585
HSBC 2795 boul Laurier	Sainte-Foy	QC	G1V4M7	418-656-6941	656-1874
National Bank of Canada 30 quai Saint-André	Québec	QC	G1K9B7	418-647-6251	647-6033
Web: www.bnc.ca					
Royal Bank of Canada 700 pl d'Youville	Québec	QC	G1R3P2	418-692-6800	692-6884
Web: www.royalbank.com					
Scotiabank 900 boul Rene-Levesque E	Québec	QC	G1R2B5	418-691-2600	691-0300
Web: www.scotiabank.ca					
Toronto-Dominion Bank 9445 boul de l'Ormière	Québec	QC	G2B3H7	418-843-8542	843-4507
Web: www.tdbank.ca					

BUSINESS SERVICES

Name	Phone
Adecco Employment Personnel Services	418-523-9922
ANCIA Personnel	418-832-6600
Canada Post	418-694-6176
Canbec Courrier	418-522-1584
Centre CopieXpress	418-659-1560
Copies de la Capitale	418-648-1911
DHL International Express	403-250-1512
Federal Express	800-463-3339
Impression Pro-Copies	418-529-2533
Kelly Services	418-621-0061
Mail Boxes Etc	418-838-6245
Manpower Temporary Services	418-681-6244
Trans-Courrier	418-686-7632
UPS	800-742-5877

— Media —

PUBLICATIONS

				Phone	Fax
Le Journal de Québec† 450 rue Bechard	Québec	QC	G1M2E9	418-683-1573	688-8181*
**Fax:* News Rm					

Quebec — Publications (Cont'd)

		Phone	Fax
Le Soleil† 925 ch Saint-Louis	Québec QC G1K7J6	418-686-3233	686-3374
Web: www.lesoleil.com			
Québec Chronicle Telegraph 3484 ch Sainte-Foy	Sainte-Foy QC G1X1S8	418-650-1764	650-1764
Web: www.telegraphe.com/introen.html			
Voila Québec Magazine 185 rue Saint-Paul	Québec QC G1K3W2	418-694-1272	692-3392
Voir Québec 470 ruede la Couronne	Québec QC G1K6G2	418-522-7777	522-7779
Web: www.voir.ca ■ *E-mail:* info@voir.ca			

†*Daily newspapers*

TELEVISION

		Phone	Fax
CBFT-TV Ch 2 (SRC) 1400 boul René-Lévesque E	Montréal QC H2L2M2	514-597-6000	
CBMT-TV Ch 6 (CBC) PO Box 6000	Montréal QC H3C3A8	514-597-6000	597-4596
Web: cbc.ca			
CBVT-TV Ch 11 (CBC) 2505 boul Laurier	Sainte-Foy QC G1V2L2	418-654-1341	656-8567
CFAP-TV Ch 2 (Ind) 500 rue Bouvier	Québec QC G2J1E3	418-624-2222	624-0162
CFCM-TV Ch 4 (TVA) 1000 ave Myrand	Sainte-Foy QC G1V2W3	418-688-9330	681-4239
CKMI-TV Ch 20 (GTN) 1000 ave Myrand	Sainte-Foy QC G1V2W3	418-682-2020	682-2620

RADIO

		Phone	Fax
CBVE-FM 104.7 MHz (N/T) 900 pl d'Youville Bureau 100	Québec QC G1R3P7	418-691-3620	691-3610
CFGT-AM 1270 kHz (AC) 460 rue Sacre-Coeur O	Québec QC G8B1L9	418-662-6673	662-6070
CHIK-FM 98.9 MHz (CHR) 1245 ch Sainte-Foy Bureau 105	Québec QC G1S4P2	418-687-9900	687-3106
CHVD-AM 1230 kHz (AC) 1975 boul Walberg	Québec QC G8L1J5	418-276-3333	276-6755
CHVD-FM 92.1 MHz (AC) 1975 boul Walberg	Québec QC G8L1J5	418-276-3333	276-6755
CITF-FM 107.5 MHz (AC) 925 ch Saint-Louis Bureau 360	Québec QC G1S4Y4	418-527-3232	527-2899
CJMF-FM 93.3 MHz (CR) 1305 ch Sainte-Foy Rm 402	Québec QC G1S4Y5	418-688-9301	687-9718
CKIA-FM 96.1 MHz (Misc) 600 côte d'Abraham	Québec QC G1R1A1	418-529-9026	529-4156
CKRL-FM 89.1 MHz (Misc) 250 Grand Allée O	Québec QC G1R2H4	418-640-2575	640-1588

— Colleges/Universities —

		Phone	Fax
Collège O'Sullivan De Québec 840 rue Saint-Jean	Québec QC G1R1R3	418-529-3355	523-6288
Web: www.osullivan-quebec.qc.ca			
Université du Québec 2875 boul Laurier	Sainte-Foy QC G1V2M3	418-657-3551	657-2132
Web: www.uquebec.ca			
Université Laval CP 2208 Succursale Terminus	Québec QC G1K7P4	418-656-2131	656-5218
Web: www.ulaval.ca			

— Hospitals —

		Phone	Fax
Centre Hospitalier Affilié Pavillon Enfant-Jésus 1401 18e rue	Québec QC G1J1Z4	418-649-0252	649-5920*
**Fax:* Admissions			
Centre Hospitalier Affilié Universitaire de Québec-Pavillon Saint-Sacrement 1050 ch Sainte-Foy	Québec QC G1S4L8	418-682-7511	682-7877*
**Fax:* Admissions			
Centre Hospitalier Notre-Dame-du-Chemin 510 ch Sainte-Foy	Québec QC G1S2G5	418-681-7882	681-5387
Centre Hospitalier Universitaire de Québec 2705 boul Laurier	Sainte-Foy QC G1V4G2	418-656-4141	654-2247
Centre Hospitalier Universitaire de Québec Pavillon Hôtel-Dieu 11 côte du Palais	Québec QC G1R2J6	418-691-5151	691-5127*
**Fax:* Admissions			
Hôpital Général de Québec 260 boul Langelier	Québec QC G1K5N1	418-529-0931	521-5801
Hôpital Jeffery Hale 1250 ch Sainte-Foy	Québec QC G1S2M6	418-683-4471	684-2255
Hôpital L'Hôtel-Dieu-du-Sacré-Coeur 1 ave du Sacré Coeur	Québec QC G1N2W1	418-529-6851	529-2971
Hôpital Laval 2725 ch Sainte-Foy	Sainte-Foy QC G1V4G5	418-656-8711	656-4599
Hôpital Sainte-Monique 4805 boul Wilfrid-Hamel	Les Saules QC G1P2J7	418-871-8701	871-0105

— Attractions —

		Phone	Fax
Anglican Cathedral of the Holy Trinity 31 rue des Jardins	Québec QC G1R4L6	418-692-2193	
Aquarium du Québec 1675 ave des Hôtels	Sainte-Foy QC G1W4S3	418-659-5266	646-9238
Web: www.aquarium.qc.ca/english/index.htm			
Centre Marie-de-l'Incarnation 10 rue Donnacona	Québec QC G1R4T1	418-694-0413	692-4741
Chalmers-Wesley United Church 78 rue Sainte-Ursule	Québec QC G1R4E8	418-692-0431	
E-mail: angel@visioninternet.net			
Chapelle des Jésuites 20 rue Dauphine	Québec QC G1R3W8	418-694-9616	692-4662
Chapelle des Ursulines 2 rue du Parloir	Québec QC G1R4M5	418-694-0413	692-4741
Chapelle Historique Bon-Pasteur 1080 rue de La Chevrotière	Québec QC G1R3G4	418-648-9710	641-1070
Domaine Maizerets Historic Site 2000 boul Montmorency	Québec QC G1J5E7	418-691-2385	660-6295
Fortifications of Québec National Historic Site 100 rue Saint-Louis	Québec QC G1K7R3	418-648-7016	648-4825
TF: 800-463-6769 ■ *Web:* parcscanada.risq.qc.ca/fortifications_e/ ■ *E-mail:* webinfo@smtp.risq.qc.ca			
François-Xavier Garneau House 14 rue Saint-Flavien	Québec QC G1R4J8	418-692-2240	692-3980
Funiculaire du Vieux Québec-Cable Car 16 rue du Petit-Champlain	Québec QC G1K4H4	418-692-1132	692-4415
Grand Théâtre de Québec 269 boul René-Lévesque E	Québec QC G1R2B3	418-643-4975	646-8835
TF: 877-643-8131 ■ *Web:* www.grandtheatre.qc.ca			
IMAX Théâtre 5401 boul des Galeries	Québec QC G2K1N4	418-627-8222	627-7222
Web: www.cinemaxquebec.qc.ca			
Jardin Zoologique du Québec 8173 ave du Zoo	Charlesbourg QC G1G4G4	418-622-0313	646-9239
Web: www.spsnq.qc.ca/zoo.html			
L'Inox Économusée de la bière-Beer Museum 37 quai Saint-André	Québec QC G1K8T3	418-692-2877	692-5743
Web: www.inox.qc.ca			
L'lot des Palais Archeological Site 8 rue Vallière	Québec QC G1R5M1	418-691-6092	691-7973
Le Capitole de Québec Theatre 972 rue Saint-Jean	Québec QC G1R1R5	418-694-4444	694-9924
TF: 800-261-8103 ■ *Web:* www.lecapitole.com			
Le Musée des Ursulines de Québec 12 rue Donnacona	Québec QC G1R4T1	418-694-0694	694-2136
Les Dames de Soie Économusée de la Poupée-Ladies in Silk Doll Museum 2 rue d'Auteuil	Québec QC G1R5C2	418-692-1516	692-0051
Les Glissades de la Terrasse-Ice Slide 76 rue Saint-Louis	Québec QC G1R3Z3	418-692-2955	692-5482
Maison Chevalier 50 rue du Marché-Champlain	Québec QC G1K4R1	418-643-2158	
Maison Henry-Stuart 82 Grande Allée O	Québec QC G1R2G6	418-647-4347	647-6483
Mont-Sainte-Anne Ski Resort 2000 boul Beau Pré	Beaupré QC G0A1E0	418-827-4561	827-3121
TF: 800-463-1568 ■ *Web:* www.mont-sainte-anne.com ■ *E-mail:* info@mont-sainte-anne.com			
Musée Bon-Pasteur 'Good Shepherd' 14 rue Couillard	Québec QC G1R3S9	418-694-0243	694-6233
Musée d'Art INUIT Brousseau 39 rue Saint-Louis	Québec QC G1R3Z2	418-694-1828	694-2086
E-mail: artinuit@globetrotter.net			
Musée de Cire de Québec-Wax Museum 22 rue Sainte-Anne	Québec QC G1R3X3	418-692-2289	694-3099
Musée de l'Amérique Française 2 côte de la Fabrique	Québec QC G1R4R7	418-692-2843	692-5206
Web: www.mcq.org ■ *E-mail:* mcq@mcq.org			
Musée de la Civilisation 85 rue Dalhousie	Québec QC G1K7A6	418-643-2158	646-9705
Web: www.mcq.org/mcq/index.html ■ *E-mail:* mcq@mcq.org			
Musée des Augustines de l'Hôtel-Dieu de Québec 75 rue des Remparts	Québec QC G1R3R9	418-692-2492	
Musée du Fort et Explore 10 rue Sainte-Anne	Québec QC G1R3X1	418-692-1759	692-4161
Naval Museum of Québec 170 rue Dalhousie	Québec QC G1K8M7	418-694-5387	694-5508
Notre-Dame-de-Québec Basilica Cathedral 16 rue Buade	Québec QC G1R4A1	418-692-2533	692-5860
Web: www.patrimoine-religieux.com/ndq/ndq_en.html			
Observatoire de la Capitale 1037 rue de la Chevrotière Édifice Marie-Guyart 31st Fl	Québec QC G1R5E9	418-644-9841	644-2879
Old Port of Québec Interpretation Centre 100 rue Saint-André	Québec QC G1K7R3	418-648-3300	648-3678
Paradis House Living Heritage Workshop 42 rue Notre-Dame	Québec QC G1K8A5	418-692-4994	647-4439
Parks Canada Exhibition Hall 3 rue de Buade	Québec QC G1R4V7	418-648-4177	
TF: 800-463-6769			

Canadian Cities

Quebec — Attractions (Cont'd)

		Phone	Fax
Place-Royale Information Centre 27 rue Notre-Dame *Web:* www.mcq.org/place_royale/index.html	Québec QC G1R3V6	418-643-6631	646-8779
Plains of Abraham 390 ave de Bernières *Web:* futurix.clic.net/com/ccbn/	Québec QC G1R2L7	418-648-4071	648-3638
Québec Citadel côte de Citadel & Saint-Louis Gate *Web:* www.qbc.clic.net/~citadel/index.html ■ *E-mail:* citadel@qbc.clic.net	Québec QC G1R4V7	418-694-2815	
Québec Experience Multimedia Show 8 rue du Trésor *Web:* www.quebecexperience.com ■ *E-mail:* info@quebecexperience.com	Québec QC G1R4L9	418-694-4000	694-4001
Québec Museum Parc des Champs-de-Bataille *Web:* www.mdq.org/fr/Anglais/index.htm ■ *E-mail:* webmdq@mdq.org	Québec QC G1R5H3	418-643-2150	646-3330
Réserve Faunique des Laurentides 801 ch Saint-Louis Suite 125 *TF:* 800-665-6527	Québec QC G1S1C1	418-686-1717	682-9944
Saint Andrew's Presbyterian Church 106 rue Sainte-Anne	Québec QC G1R3X8	418-694-1347	
Sanctuaire Notre-Dame-du-Sacré-Coeur 71 rue Sainte-Ursule	Québec QC G1R4R8	418-692-3787	
Sound & Light Show 'Act of Faith' 20 rue Buade Notre-Dame-de-Québec Basilica Cathedral	Québec QC G1R4A1	418-694-0665	692-5860
Stoneham Ski Resort 1420 ave du Hibou *TF:* 800-463-6888 ■ *Web:* www.ski-stoneham.com	Stoneham QC G0A4P0	418-848-2411	848-1133
Théâtre Périscope 2 rue Crémazie E *Web:* www.clic.net/~periscop/	Québec QC G1R2V2	418-529-2183	648-6569
Une Capitale sur la Colline 525 boul René-Lévesque E *TF:* 800-442-0773	Québec QC G1R5S9	418-528-0773	528-0833
Urban Life Interpretation Centre 43 côte de la Fabrique	Québec QC G1R5M1	418-691-4606	691-7759
Vieux-Port de Québec 84 rue Dalhousie	Québec QC G1K7A1	418-648-4370	

SPORTS TEAMS & FACILITIES

		Phone	Fax
Colisée de Québec 250 boul Wilfrid-Hamel	Québec QC G1L5A7	418-691-7211	691-7478
Hippodrome de Québec 250 boul Wilfrid-Hamel ExpoCité *Web:* www.otc.cuq.qc.ca/membres/hippodrome/	Québec QC G1L5A7	418-524-5283	524-0776
Québec Remparts (hockey) 250 boul Hamel	Québec QC G1L5A7	418-525-1212	525-2242

— Events —

	Phone
Antique Car Show (late August)	418-681-4307
Arts & Crafts Show (mid-December)	418-644-4000
Autumn Festival (mid-September-mid-October)	418-827-4561
Canada Day Festivities (July 1)	418-649-2608
DuMaurier Québec City Summer Festival (early-mid-July)	418-692-4540
Easter in Québec (mid-April)	418-649-2608
Expo-Québec (late August)	418-691-7110
Festival of Early Music (late August-late September)	418-681-3010
Greater Snow Geese Festival (early-mid-October)	418-827-3776
Grndig Snowboard World Cup (late December)	418-827-1122
Hunter's Show (late October)	418-323-2994
International Children's Folklore Festival (late June-early July)	418-666-2153
International Jazz & Blues Festival (late June-early July)	888-515-0505
International Summer Festival (early-mid-July)	418-692-5200
International Traditional Art Festival (mid-October)	418-647-1598
Linseed Festival (late August)	418-337-6416
Mont-Sainte-Anne Loppet (early March)	418-827-4561
NAYA Cup (early-mid-February)	418-827-4561
Noël à Québec (early December-early January)	418-692-2613
Potato Festival (early August)	418-277-2415
Québec City International Bonspiel (late January)	418-683-4431
Québec Horse Show (early July)	418-647-2727
Québec International Film Festival (late August-early September)	514-848-3883
Québec International Pee-Wee Hockey Tournament (mid-late February)	418-524-3311
Québec Wine & Food Show (late October)	418-683-4150
Québec Winter Carnival (late January-mid-February)	418-626-3716
Québec's International Festival of Traditional Arts (mid-October)	418-647-1598
Saint Ann's Day Celebrations (July 26)	418-827-3781
Sainte-Jean-Baptiste Day (June 24)	418-640-0799
Snow Festival (early April)	418-848-2411
Snowboard World Cup (mid-December)	418-827-4561
Summer Activities at Place-Royale (late June-late August)	418-643-6631
Surf World Cup at Mont-Sainte-Anne (mid-December)	418-827-4561

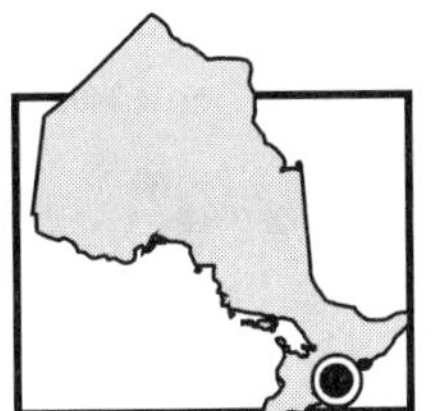

Toronto

Toronto, capital of the province of Ontario, is Canada's largest metropolitan area. It is a vital port on the Saint Lawrence Seaway and the financial center of Canada, with 90 percent of Canada's foreign banks. The Toronto Stock Exchange is North America's third largest exchange based on value traded. A number of top information technology companies, such as Apple, Hewlett-Packard and Sun Microsystems, have facilities in Toronto. The city is also home to the CN Tower which, at 1,750 feet, is the world's tallest free-standing structure. Eaton Centre, Toronto's most popular tourist attraction, contains more than 350 stores, 21 movie theaters, and dozens of restaurants, as well as the 710-acre Toronto Metro Zoo, Ontario Science Centre, and the Royal Ontario Museum, Canada's largest. Toronto is also home to the Royal Agricultural Winter Fair, the largest indoor agricultural and equestrian event in the world; and the Canadian National Exhibition (CNE), the world's largest annual fair.

Population	653,734	**Longitude**	79-22-12 W
Area (Land)	37.5 sq mi	**Time Zone**	EST
Elevation	636 ft	**Area Code/s**	416
Latitude	43-40-12 N		

— Average Temperatures and Precipitation —

TEMPERATURES

	Jan	Feb	Mar	Apr	May	Jun	Jul	Aug	Sep	Oct	Nov	Dec
High	27	28	37	54	64	75	81	79	70	59	45	33
Low	12	12	23	34	43	54	57	57	50	39	30	19

PRECIPITATION

	Jan	Feb	Mar	Apr	May	Jun	Jul	Aug	Sep	Oct	Nov	Dec
Inches	0.8	0.8	1.5	2.4	2.6	2.6	2.8	3.0	2.5	2.4	2.2	1.4

— Important Phone Numbers —

	Phone		Phone
Canadian Automobile Assn.	416-221-4300	**Temp**	416-661-0123
Dental Referral	416-967-5649	**Travellers Aid Society**	416-366-7788
Emergency	911	**Visitor Information**	416-203-2500
Poison Control Center	416-813-5900	**Weather**	416-661-0123
Road Information	416-599-9090		

— Information Sources —

		Phone	Fax
Better Business Bureau Serving Metropolitan Toronto 7777 Keele St Suite 210 *Web:* www.toronto.bbb.org	Concord ON L4K1V7	905-761-0115	761-9706
International Centre 6900 Airport Rd **Fax Area Code:* 905 ■ *TF:* 800-567-1199 ■ *Web:* www.internationalcentre.com ■ *E-mail:* info@internationalcentre.com	Mississauga ON L4V1E8	416-674-8425	677-3089*

Canadian Cities

Toronto — Information Sources (Cont'd)

		Phone	Fax
Metro Hall 55 John St. *Web:* www.metrotor.on.ca ■ *E-mail:* accessmetro@metrodesk.metrotor.on.ca	Toronto ON M5V3C6	416-392-8000	
Metro Toronto Convention Centre 255 Front St W. *Fax: Sales ■ *Web:* www.mtccc.com	Toronto ON M5V2W6	416-585-8000	585-8198*
Metropolitan Toronto Convention & Visitors Assn 207 Queen's Quay W. *TF:* 800-363-1990 ■ *Web:* www.tourism-toronto.com ■ *E-mail:* mtcvainf@pathcom.com	Toronto ON M5J1A7	416-203-2600	203-6753
Toronto City Hall 100 Queen St W *Web:* www.city.toronto.on.ca ■ *E-mail:* info@city.toronto.on.ca	Toronto ON M5H2N2	416-392-7341	
Toronto Economic Development Corp 33 Yonge St Suite 1010. *Web:* www.interlog.com/~tedco ■ *E-mail:* tedco@interlog.com	Toronto ON M5E1S9	416-214-4640	214-4660
Toronto Free-Net 350 Victoria St 7th Fl. *Web:* www.torfree.net	Toronto ON M5B2K3	416-979-9224	
Toronto Mayor 100 Queen St W 2nd Fl *Web:* www.city.toronto.on.ca/mayor	Toronto ON M5H2N2	416-395-6464	395-6440
Toronto Public Library 789 Yonge St *Web:* www.tpl.toronto.on.ca	Toronto ON M4W2G8	416-393-7000	393-7229

On-Line Resources

4Toronto.com	www.4toronto.com
About.com Guide to Toronto	toronto.about.com/local/toronto
Ban's Toronto Newcomer's Guide	www.thebans.com/guide/newcomer
Boulevards Toronto	www.boulevards.com/cities/toronto.html
Bradmans.com Toronto	www.bradmans.com/scripts/display_city.cgi?city=245
City Knowledge Toronto	www.cityknowledge.com/canada_on_toronto.htm
Cityhits Toronto	www.cityhits.com/toronto/
Excite.com Toronto City Guide	www.excite.com/travel/countries/canada/ontario/toronto
eye.net	www.eye.net
GayCanada.com	www.cglbrd.com/cities/on/toronto/
Heritage Toronto	www.torontohistory.on.ca
HotelGuide Toronto	hotelguide.net/toronto/
Open World City Guides Toronto	www.worldexecutive.com/cityguides/toronto/
Outside Toronto Excursion Guide	outsidetoronto.com
Rough Guide Travel Toronto	travel.roughguides.com/content/6205/
Show Me Toronto	www.showmetoronto.com
Slate Art Gallery Guide	www.slateartguide.com
Student's Guide to Toronto	www.studentsguide.com/toronto/
Surf the Beaches	www.wineva-oak.com
TorInfo.com	www.torinfo.com
Toronto City Guide	www.math.toronto.edu/toronto/
Toronto Info Guide	www.theinfoguide.com/guideme.htm
Toronto Online	www.toronto-online.com
Toronto.com	www.toronto.com
Villager Online Community	www.villagernews.com

— Transportation Services —

AIRPORTS

	Phone
■ **Lester B Pearson International Airport (YYZ)** 18 miles NW of downtown (approx 30 minutes) Web: www.lbpia.toronto.on.ca ■ *E-mail:* c_relations@gtaa.com	416-247-7678

Airport Transportation

	Phone
AirFlight Taxi $35 fare to downtown	416-445-1999
Metro Taxi $35 fare to downtown	416-504-8294
Pacific Western Airport Express Bus $12.50 fare to downtown	905-564-6333

Commercial Airlines

	Phone		Phone
Aeroflot	888-686-4949	**Delta**	800-221-1212
Air Canada	800-776-3000	**El Al**	800-223-6700
Air Jamaica	800-523-5585	**Inter-Canadian**	800-426-7000
Air New Zealand	800-262-1234	**KLM**	800-374-7747
Air Ontario	800-776-3000	**Korean Air**	800-438-5000
Air Transat	877-872-6728	**LACSA**	800-225-2272
Air Ukraine	416-207-0022	**LOT Polish Airlines**	800-223-0593
Alitalia	800-223-5730	**Lufthansa**	800-645-3880
American	800-433-7300	**Martinair Holland**	800-627-8462
American Trans Air	800-225-2995	**Midwest Express**	800-452-2022
British Airways	800-247-9297	**Northwest**	800-225-2525
BWIA International	800-538-2942	**Olympic Airways**	800-223-1226
Canada 3000	877-359-2263	**Pakistan International**	800-221-2552
Canadian Air	800-426-7000	**SwissAir**	800-221-4750
Canadian Regional	800-426-7000	**TAP Air Portugal**	800-221-7370
Cathay Pacific	888-338-1668	**TWA**	800-221-2000
Comair	800-354-9822	**United**	800-241-6522
Continental	800-525-0280	**US Airways**	800-428-4322
Czech Airlines	800-223-2365	**VASP Brazilian Airlines**	800-732-8277

Charter Airlines

	Phone		Phone
Direct Airway	800-257-9424	**Northern Airways**	800-245-0087

CAR RENTALS

	Phone		Phone
Alamo	800-327-9633	**Hertz**	905-676-3241
Avis	416-213-8400	**National**	905-676-2647
Budget	905-676-0311	**Thrifty**	905-673-8811
Dollar	800-800-4000		

LIMO/TAXI

	Phone		Phone
ABA Limousine	416-340-9705	**Madison Limousine**	416-251-3177
Airline Limousine	905-676-3210	**Maple Leaf Taxi**	416-465-5555
Arrow Taxi	416-233-1111	**Metro Taxi**	416-504-8294
Bay Street Limousine	416-484-0944	**Park Lane Livery Limousine**	416-488-3888
Carey Limousine	416-466-8776	**Royal Livery Limousine**	905-828-9635
Diamond Taxi	416-366-6868	**Royal Taxi**	416-777-9222

MASS TRANSIT

	Phone
Go Transit $2.45 Base fare	416-869-3200
Toronto Island Ferry Service $5 Base fare	416-392-8193
TTC $2 Base fare	416-393-4636

RAIL/BUS

		Phone
Greyhound Canada Bus Station Bay & Dundas Sts. *TF:* 800-661-8747	Toronto ON M5G1M5	416-367-8747
VIA Rail Canada 65 Front St W Toronto Union Stn *TF:* 800-561-3949	Toronto ON M5J1E6	416-366-8411

— Accommodations —

HOTEL RESERVATION SERVICES

	Phone	Fax
Abodes of Choice Bed & Breakfast Assn *TF:* 888-854-4405	416-537-7629	537-6565
Across Toronto Bed & Breakfast Reservation Service *Web:* www.bbcanada.com/toronto/ ■ *E-mail:* beds@torontobandb.com	416-588-8800	927-0838
Bed & Breakfast Assn of Downtown Toronto *TF:* 888-559-5515 ■ *Web:* www.bnbinfo.com ■ *E-mail:* bnbtoronto@globalserve.net	416-368-1420	368-1653
Bed & Breakfast Homes of Toronto Assn *Web:* www.bbcanada.com/toronto2.html	416-363-6362	
Hotel Reservations Network Inc *TF Sales:* 800-964-6835 ■ *Web:* www.hoteldiscount.com	214-361-7311	361-7299

HOTELS, MOTELS, RESORTS

		Phone	Fax
Alexandra Apartment Hotel 77 Ryerson Ave *TF:* 800-567-1893 ■ *Web:* www.alexandrahotel.com ■ *E-mail:* reservations@alexandrahotel.com	Toronto ON M5T2V4	416-504-2121	504-9195
Bay Bloor Executive Suites 1101 Bay St *TF:* 800-263-2811 ■ *Web:* www.baybloorexec.com	Toronto ON M5S2W8	416-968-3878	968-7385
Best Western Primrose Hotel 111 Carlton St *TF:* 800-528-1234	Toronto ON M5B2G3	416-977-8000	977-6323
Best Western Roehampton Hotel & Suites 808 Mt Pleasant Rd. *TF:* 800-387-8899	Toronto ON M4P2L2	416-487-5101	487-5390
Bond Place Hotel 65 Dundas St E. *TF:* 800-268-9390	Toronto ON M5B2G8	416-362-6061	360-6406
Cambridge Suites Toronto 15 Richmond St E *TF:* 800-463-1990	Toronto ON M5C2W7	416-368-1990	601-3751
Campbell House 160 Queen St W.	Toronto ON M5H3H3	416-597-0227	597-1884
Clarion Essex Park Hotel 300 Jarvis St *TF:* 800-567-2233	Toronto ON M5B2C5	416-977-4823	977-4830
CN Tower 301 Front St W *Web:* www.cntower.ca	Toronto ON M5V2T6	416-868-6937	601-4753
Comfort Hotel 15 Charles St E *TF:* 800-221-2222	Toronto ON M4Y1S1	416-924-1222	927-1369
Days Inn Toronto 30 Carlton St *TF:* 800-329-7466	Toronto ON M5B2E9	416-977-6655	977-0502
Days Inn Toronto Airport 6257 Airport Rd *TF:* 800-325-2525	Mississauga ON L4V1E4	905-678-1400	678-9130
Delta Chelsea Inn 33 Gerrard St W. *TF:* 800-268-2266	Toronto ON M5G1Z4	416-595-1975	585-4375

Toronto — Hotels, Motels, Resorts (Cont'd)

			Phone	Fax
Delta Toronto Airport Hotel 801 Dixon Rd TF: 800-668-1444	Etobicoke	ON M9W1J5	416-675-6100	675-4022
Executive Motor Hotel 621 King St W	Toronto	ON M5V1M5	416-504-7441	504-4722
Four Points Sheraton Hotel Toronto Airport 5444 Dixie Rd TF: 800-325-3535	Mississauga	ON L4W2L2	905-624-1144	624-9477
Four Seasons Hotel Toronto 21 Avenue Rd TF: 800-268-6282 ■ *Web:* www.fourseasons.com/locations/Toronto	Toronto	ON M5R2G1	416-964-0411	964-2301
Glen Grove Suites 2837 Yonge St. TF: 800-565-3024	Toronto	ON M4N2J6	416-489-8441	440-3065
Grange Apartment Hotel 165 Grange Ave	Toronto	ON M5T2V5	416-603-7700	603-9977
Holiday Inn Airport Plaza 600 Dixon Rd TF: 800-465-4329	Toronto	ON M9W1J1	416-240-7511	240-7519
Holiday Inn Express 5585 Ambler Dr. TF: 800-465-4329	Mississauga	ON L4W3Z1	905-238-3500	238-8761
Holiday Inn on King 370 King St W TF: 800-263-6364 ■ *Web:* www.hiok.com ■ *E-mail:* info@hiok.com	Toronto	ON M5V1J9	416-599-4000	599-7394
Holiday Inn Select Toronto Airport 970 Dixon Rd TF: 800-465-4329	Toronto	ON M9W1J9	416-675-7611	675-9162
Holiday Inn Toronto Don Valley 1100 Eglinton Ave E TF: 800-465-4329	Toronto	ON M3C1H8	416-446-3700	446-3701
Holiday Inn Toronto Yorkdale 3450 Dufferin St TF: 800-465-4329	North York	ON M6A2V1	416-789-5161	785-6845
Hotel Inter-Continental 220 Bloor St W TF: 800-267-0010	Toronto	ON M5S1T8	416-960-5200	960-8269
Hotel Victoria 56 Yonge St. TF: 800-363-8228 ■ *Web:* www.toronto.com/E/V/TORON/0012/01/92 ■ *E-mail:* reception@hotelvictoria.on.ca	Toronto	ON M5E1G5	416-363-1666	363-7327
Howard Johnson 89 Avenue Rd TF: 800-654-2000	Toronto	ON M5R2G3	416-964-1220	964-8692
Howard Johnson's Selby Hotel 592 Sherborne St TF: 800-387-4788	Toronto	ON M4X1L4	416-921-3142	923-3177
International Plaza Hotel & Conference Centre 655 Dixon Rd TF: 800-668-3656 ■ *Web:* www.internationalplaza.com ■ *E-mail:* info@internationalplaza.com	Toronto	ON M9W1J4	416-244-1711	244-7281
King Edward Hotel 37 King St E TF: 800-543-4300 ■ *Web:* www.forte-hotels.com	Toronto	ON M5C1E9	416-863-9700	367-5515
Metropolitan Hotel Toronto 108 Chestnut St TF: 800-668-6600 ■ *Web:* www.metropolitan.com/toronto/ ■ *E-mail:* reservations@metropolitan.com	Toronto	ON M5G1R3	416-977-5000	977-9513
Monte Carlo Inn Airport 5 Derry Rd TF: 800-363-6400 ■ *Web:* www.montecarloinns.com/mc_01.htm ■ *E-mail:* reservation@montecarloinns.com	Mississauga	ON L5T2H8	905-564-8500	564-8400
Novotel North York 3 Park Home Ave TF: 800-668-6835	North York	ON M2N6L3	416-733-2929	733-3403
Novotel Toronto Airport 135 Carlingview Dr TF: 800-668-6835	Etobicoke	ON M9W5E7	416-798-9800	798-1237
Novotel Toronto Centre 45 The Esplanade TF: 800-668-6835	Toronto	ON M5E1W2	416-367-8900	360-8285
Park Hyatt Toronto Hotel 4 Avenue Rd TF: 800-233-1234	Toronto	ON M5R2E8	416-924-5471	924-4933
Quality Hotel & Suites 2180 Islington Ave TF: 800-228-5151	Etobicoke	ON M9P3P1	416-240-9090	240-9944
Quality Hotel Downtown 111 Lombard St TF: 800-228-5151 ■ *Web:* www.toronto.com/E/V/TORON/0011/95/75	Toronto	ON M5C2T9	416-367-5555	367-3470
Radisson Plaza Hotel Admiral Toronto Harbourfront 249 Queen's Quay W TF: 800-333-3333	Toronto	ON M5J2N5	416-203-3333	203-3100
Radisson Plaza Hotel Toronto 90 Bloor St E TF: 800-333-3333	Toronto	ON M4W1A7	416-961-8000	961-4635
Ramada Hotel Toronto Airport 2 Holiday Dr. TF: 800-272-6232	Toronto	ON M9C2Z7	416-621-2121	621-9840
Regal Constellation Hotel 900 Dixon Rd TF: 800-268-4838	Etobicoke	ON M9W1J7	416-675-1500	675-4611
Royal York Hotel 100 Front St W TF: 800-441-1414	Toronto	ON M5J1E3	416-368-2511	368-2884
Sandalwood Hotel & Suites 5050 Orbiter Dr TF: 800-387-3355	Mississauga	ON L4W4X2	905-238-9600	238-8502
Seneca College Residence & Conference Centre 1760 Finch Ave E	North York	ON M2J5G3	416-491-8811	491-0486
Sheraton Centre Toronto Hotel 123 Queen St W TF: 800-325-3535 ■ *Web:* www.sheratonctr.toronto.on.ca/	Toronto	ON M5H2M9	416-361-1000	947-4801
SkyDome Hotel 1 Blue Jays Way TF: 800-441-1414	Toronto	ON M5V1J4	416-341-7100	341-5091
Strathcona Hotel 60 York St. TF: 800-268-8304	Toronto	ON M5J1S8	416-363-3321	363-4679
Sutton Place Hotel 955 Bay St TF: 800-268-3790	Toronto	ON M5S2A2	416-924-9221	924-1778
Toronto Airport Hilton International 5875 Airport Rd TF: 800-445-8667	Mississauga	ON L4V1N1	905-677-9900	677-5073
Toronto Airport Marriott Hotel 901 Dixon Road TF: 800-228-9290	Rexdale	ON M9W1J5	416-674-9400	674-8292
Toronto Colony Hotel 89 Chestnut St TF: 800-387-8687	Toronto	ON M5G1R1	416-977-0707	977-1136
Toronto Hilton 145 Richmond St W TF: 800-267-2281	Toronto	ON M5H2L2	416-869-3456	869-1478
Toronto Marriott Eaton Centre 525 Bay St TF: 800-228-9290	Toronto	ON M5G2L2	416-597-9200	597-9211
Town Inn Hotel 620 Church St TF: 800-387-2755 ■ *Web:* www.towninn.com ■ *E-mail:* reservations@towninn.com	Toronto	ON M4Y2G2	416-964-3311	924-9466
Travelodge Hotel Toronto East 55 Hallcrown Pl TF: 800-578-7878	North York	ON M2J4R1	416-493-7000	493-6577
Valhalla Inn Toronto 1 Valhalla Inn Rd TF: 800-268-2500	Etobicoke	ON M9B1S9	416-239-2391	239-8764
Venture Inn Toronto Airport 925 Dixon Rd TF: 888-483-6887	Etobicoke	ON M9W1J8	416-674-2222	674-5757
Westin Harbour Castle Hotel 1 Harbour Sq TF: 800-228-3000	Toronto	ON M5J1A6	416-869-1600	869-0573
Westin Prince Hotel 900 York Mills Rd TF: 800-937-8461	North York	ON M3B3H2	416-444-2511	444-9597
Wyndham Bristol Place Toronto Airport 950 Dixon Rd TF: 800-996-3426	Toronto	ON M9W5N4	416-675-9444	675-4426

— Restaurants —

			Phone
360 Revolving Restaurant (North American) 301 Front St W *Web:* www.cntower.ca/l3_intro.html	Toronto	ON M5V2T6	416-362-5411
Acqua Ristorante Bar (Italian) 10 Front St W	Toronto	ON M5J2T3	416-368-7171
Al Frisco's (Italian) 133 John St	Toronto	ON M5V2E4	416-595-8201
Alice Fazooli's Italian Crabshack (Cajun/Italian) 294 Adelaide St W	Toronto	ON M5V1P6	416-979-1910
Armadillo Texas Grill (Tex Mex) 146 Front St W	Toronto	ON M5J1G2	416-977-8840
Bamboo (Thai/Caribbean) 312 Queen St W	Toronto	ON M5V2A2	416-593-5771
Bangkok Garden (Thai) 18 Elm St	Toronto	ON M5G1G7	416-977-6748
Bardi's Steak House (Steak) 56 York St	Toronto	ON M5J1S8	416-366-9211
Barolo Restaurant (Italian) 193 Carlton St	Toronto	ON M5A2K7	416-961-4747
Bistro 990 (French) 990 Bay St	Toronto	ON M5S2A5	416-921-9990
Bistro The (Continental) 1 Blue Jays Way Suite 3300	Toronto	ON M5V1J4	416-341-5045
Boathouse Bar & Grill (North American) 207 Queen's Quay W	Toronto	ON M5J1A7	416-203-6300
Bombay Palace (Indian) 71 Jarvis St	Toronto	ON M5C2H2	416-368-8048
Boulevard Cafe (Peruvian) 161 Harbord St	Toronto	ON M5S1H1	416-961-7676
Canoe Restaurant & Bar (North American) 66 Wellington St TD Bank Tower 54th Fl	Toronto	ON M5K1H6	416-364-0054
Captain John's Harbour Boat Restaurant (Seafood) 1 Queens Quay W	Toronto	ON M5J2H1	416-363-6062
Christina's (Greek) 535 Danforth Ave	Toronto	ON M4K1P7	416-463-4418
City Grill Restaurant (North American) 220 Yonge St Eaton Centre	Toronto	ON M5B3H7	416-598-4454
Denison's Brewing Company (North American) 75 Victoria St	Toronto	ON M5C2B1	416-360-5877
Filet of Sole Restaurant (Seafood) 11 Duncan St	Toronto	ON M5H3G6	416-598-3256
Fisherman's Wharf of San Francisco (Seafood) 69 Richmond St W	Toronto	ON M5H1Z4	416-364-1344
Gatsby's Restaurant (Continental) 504 Church St	Toronto	ON M4Y2C8	416-925-4545
Hard Rock Cafe (North American) 283 Yonge St	Toronto	ON M5B1N8	416-362-3636
Hemispheres Restaurant & Bistro (Continental) 110 Chestnut St	Toronto	ON M5G1R3	416-599-8000
Le Papillon Restaurant (French) 16 Church St	Toronto	ON M5E1M1	416-363-0838
Lichee Garden (Chinese) 352 Eglinton Ave W	Toronto	ON M5N1A2	416-322-8898
Lighthouse Revolving Restaurant (Continental) 1 Harbour Sq	Toronto	ON M5J1A6	416-869-1600
Lone Star Cafe (Tex Mex) 200 Front St W	Toronto	ON M5V3J1	416-408-4064
Mobay (Caribbean) 585 Yonge St	Toronto	ON M4Y1Z8	416-964-2121
Monsoon Restaurant (Asian) 100 Simcoe St	Toronto	ON M5H3G2	416-979-7172
Montana (New American) 145 John St	Toronto	ON M5V2E4	416-595-5949
N'awlins Jazz Bar & Grill (Cajun/Creole) 299 King St W	Toronto	ON M5V1J5	416-595-1958
Nami Restaurant (Japanese) 55 Adelaide St E	Toronto	ON M5C1K6	416-362-7373
Pearl Harbourfront Restaurant (Chinese) 207 Queen's Quay W	Toronto	ON M5R3L1	416-203-1233
Penelope Restaurant (Greek) 225 King St W	Toronto	ON M5V3C5	416-351-9393
Pier 4 Storehouse Restaurant (North American) 245 Queens Quay W	Toronto	ON M5J2K9	416-203-1440
Pimblett's (English/Irish) 263 Gerrard St E	Toronto	ON M5A2G1	416-929-9525

Toronto — Restaurants (Cont'd)

				Phone
Planet Hollywood (North American) 277 Front St W	Toronto	ON	M5V2X4	416-596-7827
Provence (French) 12 Amelia St.	Toronto	ON	M4X1E1	416-924-9901
Queen Mother Cafe (Thai) 208 Queen St W	Toronto	ON	M5V1Z2	416-598-4719
Real Jerk (Caribbean) 709 Queen St E	Toronto	ON	M4M1H1	416-463-6055
Remo's Ristorante (Italian) 156 Front St W	Toronto	ON	M5J2L6	416-596-7360
Rodney's Oyster House (Seafood) 209 Adelaide St E	Toronto	ON	M5A1M8	416-363-8105
Rosewater Supper Club (Continental) 19 Toronto St	Toronto	ON	M5C2R1	416-214-5888
Scaramouche Restaurant (French) 1 Benvenuto Pl.	Toronto	ON	M4V2L1	416-961-8011
Splendido's (International) 88 Harbord St.	Toronto	ON	M5S1G5	416-929-7788
Tasting Room Restaurant (International) 1 First Canadian Pl	Toronto	ON	M5X1E1	416-362-2499
Truffles (North American) 21 Avenue Rd.	Toronto	ON	M5R2G1	416-928-7331
Zola (French) 162 Cumberland St.	Toronto	ON	M5R3N5	416-515-1222

— Goods and Services —

SHOPPING

Name / Address	City	Prov	Postal Code	Phone	Fax
Atrium On Bay 595 Bay St.	Toronto	ON	M5G2C2	416-595-1957	204-1199
Bayview Village 2901 Bayview Ave	Willowdale	ON	M2K1E6	416-226-2003	226-6121
Web: www.orlandocorp.com/retail/bayview.htm					
Bloor-Yorkville BIA 55 Bloor St W Suite 220	Toronto	ON	M4W1A5	416-928-3553	928-2034
E-mail: bybia@bloor-yorkville.com					
Cloverdale Mall 250 The East Mall	Toronto	ON	M9B3Y8	416-236-1669	237-0286
Dufferin Mall 900 Dufferin St	Toronto	ON	M6H4B1	416-532-1152	538-0591
Eglinton Way 469 Eglinton Ave W	Toronto	ON	M5N1A7	416-487-3294	487-6067
Fairview Mall 1800 Sheppard Ave E	Toronto	ON	M2J5A7	416-491-9711	491-3956
Web: www.fairviewmall.shops.ca/ ■ *E-mail:* fairviewmall@shops.ca					
First Canadian Place Shopping Centre 1 First Canadian Pl	Toronto	ON	M5X1B5	416-862-6294	862-7550
Gerrard Square 1000 Gerrard St E	Toronto	ON	M4M3G6	416-461-0964	461-2564
Harbourfront Antique Market 390 Queen's Quay W	Toronto	ON	M5V3A6	416-260-2626	260-1212
TF: 888-263-6533 ■ *Web:* www.hfam.com ■ *E-mail:* antiques@hfam.com					
Hazelton Lanes Shopping Centre 55 Avenue Rd	Toronto	ON	M5R3L2	416-968-8602	
Hillcrest Mall 9350 Yonge St	Richmond Hill	ON	L4C5G2	905-883-1400	883-1960
Web: www.hillcrestmall.shops.ca/					
Pickering Town Centre 1355 Kingston Rd	Pickering	ON	L1V1B8	905-831-6066	420-9379
Web: www.pickeringtowncentre.com					
Queen's Quay Terminal 207 Queens Quay W	Toronto	ON	M5J1A7	416-203-3269	203-0432
Saint Lawrence Market 92 Front St E	Toronto	ON	M5E1C4	416-392-7219	392-0120
Web: www.stlawrencemarket.com					
Scarborough Town Centre 300 Borough Dr Suite 26	Scarborough	ON	M1P4P5	416-296-5490	296-9949
Web: www.scarboroughtowncentre.com ■ *E-mail:* info@scarboroughtowncentre.com					
Sheridan Mall 2225 Erin Mills Pkwy	Mississauga	ON	L5K1T9	905-822-0344	822-3528
Web: www.sheridanmall.com					
Showcase Antique Mall 610 Queen Stt W	Toronto	ON	M6J1E3	416-703-6255	703-6088
Web: www.showcaseantiquemall.com					
Toronto Eaton Centre 220 Yonge St	Toronto	ON	M5B2H1	416-598-8700	598-8762
Web: www.torontoeatoncentre.com					
Upper Canada Mall 17600 Yonge St	Newmarket	ON	L3Y4Z1	905-895-1961	895-7873
Woodbine Centre 500 Rexdale Blvd	Etobicoke	ON	M9W6K5	416-674-6240	675-1543
Web: www.woodbinecentre.shops.ca/ ■ *E-mail:* woodbinecentre@shops.ca					
Yorkdale Shopping Centre 1 Yorkdale Rd	Toronto	ON	M6A3A1	416-256-5066	256-5064
Web: www.yorkdale.com ■ *E-mail:* info@yorkdale.com					

BANKS

Name / Address	City	Prov	Postal Code	Phone	Fax
Banca Commerciale Italiana of Canada 130 Adelaide St W Suite 1800	Toronto	ON	M5H3P5	416-366-8101	366-2577
Bank of America Canada 200 Front St W	Toronto	ON	M5V3L2	416-349-4100	349-4279*
**Fax:* Hum Res ■ *Web:* www.bankamerica.com					
Canadian Imperial Bank of Commerce King & Bay Sts	Toronto	ON	M5L1A2	416-980-2211	784-6799*
**Fax:* Hum Res ■ *Web:* www.cibc.com					
Chase Manhattan Bank of Canada 1First Canadian Pl Suite 6900	Toronto	ON	M5X1A4	416-216-4100	216-4168
Citibank Canada 123 Front St W Suite 1900	Toronto	ON	M5J2M3	416-947-4100	947-5628
Korea Exchange Bank of Canada 4950 Yonge St Madison Centre Suite 1101	North York	ON	M2N6K1	416-222-5200	222-5822
Mellon Bank Canada 77 King St W Royal Trust Tower Suite 3200	Toronto	ON	M5K1K2	416-860-0777	860-2409
National Bank of Canada 150 York St	Toronto	ON	M5H3S5	416-864-7791	864-7784
Web: www.nbc.ca					
Sanwa Bank Canada 161 Bay St BCE Pl Suite 4400	Toronto	ON	M5J2S1	416-366-2583	366-8599
Scotiabank 44 King St W	Toronto	ON	M5H1H1	416-866-6161	866-3750
Web: www.scotiabank.ca					
Toronto-Dominion Bank 55 King St W	Toronto	ON	M5K1A2	416-982-8222	944-6931
Web: www.tdbank.ca					

BUSINESS SERVICES

Name	Phone	Name	Phone
Alicos Copy Centre	416-962-6618	**Hunt Personnel**	416-360-5288
All Points Courier Service	416-287-6650	**Kelly Services**	416-967-6655
Best Secretarial Service	416-482-1791	**Kinko's**	416-928-0110
Bradson Staffing Services	416-944-3434	**Mail Boxes Etc**	416-489-8311
Canada Post	416-979-8822	**Marberg Temporary Office Staff**	416-363-6442
Crockett Olivia Secretarial Service	416-484-9889	**Olsten Staffing Services**	416-964-9100
DHL International Express	403-250-1512	**Toronto Express**	416-203-0647
Federal Express	800-463-3339	**UPS**	800-742-5877

— Media —

PUBLICATIONS

Name / Address	City	Prov	Postal Code	Phone	Fax
Financial Post 1450 Don Mills Rd	Don Mills	ON	M3B2X7	800-668-7678	383-2443*
**Fax Area Code:* 416 ■ *Web:* www.canoe.ca/FP/					
Globe & Mail The† 444 Front St W	Toronto	ON	M5V2S9	416-585-5000	585-5085
Web: www.globeandmail.ca					
L'Express de Toronto 17 Carlaw Ave	Toronto	ON	M4M2R6	416-465-2107	465-3778
National Post† 1450 Don Mills Rd Suite 300	Don Mills	ON	M3B3R5	416-383-2300	442-2209
TF: 888-588-3285 ■ *Web:* www.nationalpost.com					
NOW Magazine 150 Danforth Ave	Toronto	ON	M4K1N1	416-461-0871	461-2886
Web: www.now.com ■ *E-mail:* letters@now.com					
Toronto Life Magazine 59 Front St E 3rd Fl	Toronto	ON	M5E1B3	416-364-3333	861-1169
Web: www.torontolife.com					
Toronto Star† 1 Yonge St	Toronto	ON	M5E1E6	416-367-2000	869-4328
Web: www.thestar.com ■ *E-mail:* editorial@thestar.ca					
Toronto Sun† 333 King St E	Toronto	ON	M5A3X5	416-947-2222	947-1664
Web: www.canoe.ca/TorontoSun/ ■ *E-mail:* news@sunpub.com					
Where Toronto Magazine 6 Church St 2nd Fl	Toronto	ON	M5E1M1	416-364-3333	594-3375
Web: www.wheremags.com					

†Daily newspapers

TELEVISION

Name / Address	City	Prov	Postal Code	Phone	Fax
CBLT-TV Ch 5 (CBC) PO Box 500 Stn A	Toronto	ON	M5W1E6	416-205-3311	205-7166
CFMT-TV Ch 47 (Ind) 545 Lakeshore Blvd W	Toronto	ON	M5V1A3	416-260-0047	260-3581
CFTO-TV Ch 9 (CTV) PO Box 9 Stn O	Toronto	ON	M4A2M9	416-299-2000	299-2273
Web: www.ctv.ca/					
CHLF-TV Ch 13 (TVO) 2180 rue Yonge CP 200 Succ Q	Toronto	ON	M4T2T1	416-484-2600	484-4234
TF: 800-613-0513 ■ *Web:* www.tvo.org ■ *E-mail:* asktvo@tvo.org					
CICA-TV Ch 19 (TVO) PO Box 200 Sta Q	Toronto	ON	M4T2T1	416-484-2600	484-6285
Web: www.tvo.org					
CIII-TV Ch 6 (GTN) 81 Barber Green Rd	Don Mills	ON	M3C2A2	416-446-5460	446-5544
CITY-TV Ch 57 (PBS) 299 Queen St W	Toronto	ON	M5V2Z5	416-591-5757	593-6397
Web: www.citytv.com					

RADIO

Name / Address	City	Prov	Postal Code	Phone	Fax
CBC-FM 94.1 MHz (Clas) PO Box 500 Stn A	Toronto	ON	M5W1E6	416-205-3311	205-6336
Web: toronto.cbc.ca					
CFNY-FM 102.1 MHz (Alt) 1 Dundas St W Suite 1600	Toronto	ON	M5G1Z3	416-408-3343	408-5400
Web: edge.passport.ca ■ *E-mail:* Input@edge102.com					
CFRB-AM 1010 kHz (N/T) 2 St Clair Ave NW 2nd Fl	Toronto	ON	M4V1L6	416-924-5711	323-6816
CFTR-AM 680 kHz (N/T) 36 Victoria St	Toronto	ON	M5C1H3	416-864-2000	363-2387
Web: www.680news.com ■ *E-mail:* news@680news.com					
CHFI-FM 98.1 MHz (AC) 36 Victoria Street	Toronto	ON	M5C1H3	416-864-2070	
CHIN-AM 1540 MHz (Misc) 622 College St	Toronto	ON	M6G1B6	416-531-9991	531-5274
CHIN-FM 100.7 MHz (Misc) 622 College St	Toronto	ON	M5C2Y8	416-531-9991	531-5274
Web: www.chinradio.com ■ *E-mail:* chin@istar.ca					
CHRY-FM 105.5 MHz (Alt) 4700 Keele St	North York	ON	M3J1P3	416-736-5293	650-8052
CHUM-AM 1050 kHz (Oldies) 1331 Yonge St	Toronto	ON	M4T1Y1	416-925-6666	926-4182
Web: www.1050chum.com					
CHUM-FM 104.5 MHz (AC) 1331 Yonge St	Toronto	ON	M4T1Y1	416-925-6666	926-4182
Web: www.chumfm.com ■ *E-mail:* chumfm@chumfm.com					

Toronto — Radio (Cont'd)

	City			Phone	Fax
CILQ-FM 107.1 FM (Rock) 5255 Yonge St Suite 1400	Toronto	ON	M2N6P4	416-221-0107	512-4810
Web: www.q107.com					
CING-FM 107.9 MHz (CHR) 4144 S Service Rd	Burlington	ON	L7L4X5	905-681-1079	681-1758
Web: www.energy108.ca					
CJCL-AM 590 kHz (Sports) 40 Holly St	Toronto	ON	M4S3C3	416-482-0590	486-2666
Web: www.fan590.com					
CJEZ-FM 97.3 MHz (AC) 40 Eglinton Ave E Suite 600	Toronto	ON	M4P3B6	416-482-0973	486-5696
CJRT-FM 91.1 MHz (Nost) 150 Mutual St	Toronto	ON	M5B2M1	416-595-0404	595-9413
CJXY-FM 95.3 MHz (CR) 875 Main St W	Hamilton	ON	L8S4R1	905-521-9900	521-2300
Web: www.y95.com ■ *E-mail:* yinfo@y95.com					
CKFM-FM 99.9 MHz (AC) 2 St Clair Ave W	Toronto	ON	M4V1L6	416-922-9999	323-6800
Web: www.mix999.com ■ *E-mail:* music@mix999.com					
CKLN-FM 88.1 MHz (Alt) 380 Victoria St	Toronto	ON	M5B1W7	416-595-1477	595-0226
CKOC-AM 1150 kHz (Oldies) 883 Upper Wentworth St	Hamilton	ON	L8N3P5	905-574-1150	575-6429
WGR-AM 550 kHz (N/T) 695 Delaware Ave	Buffalo	NY	14209	716-884-5101	885-8255
Web: www.wgr55.com ■ *E-mail:* wgr55@wgr55.com					
WKSE-FM 98.5 MHz (CHR) 695 Delaware Ave	Buffalo	NY	14209	716-884-5101	644-9329
Web: www.kiss985.com					
WMJQ-FM 102.5 MHz (AC) 2077 Elmwood Ave	Buffalo	NY	14207	716-876-0930	875-6201

— Colleges/Universities —

	City			Phone	Fax
Centennial College 941 Progress Ave	Scarborough	ON	M1K5E9	416-289-5000	289-1503*
**Fax:* Admissions ■ *Web:* www.cencol.on.ca/					
George Brown College 200 King St E	Toronto	ON	M5A3W8	416-415-2000	415-4812
Web: www.gbrownc.on.ca					
Harris Institute For The Arts 118 Sherbourne St	Toronto	ON	M5A2R2	416-367-0178	367-5534
Web: hosting.ampsc.com/~harris/					
Humber College 205 Humber College Blvd.	Etobicoke	ON	M9W5L7	416-675-3111	675-1483
Web: www.humberc.on.ca					
Ontario College of Art & Design 100 McCaul St	Toronto	ON	M5T1W1	416-977-6000	977-6006
Web: www.ocad.on.ca					
Ryerson Polytechnic University 350 Victoria St	Toronto	ON	M5B2K3	416-979-5000	979-5221
Web: www.ryerson.ca ■ *E-mail:* inquire@acs.ryerson.ca					
Seneca College 1750 Finch Ave E.	North York	ON	M2J2X5	416-491-5050	491-3081
Web: www.senecac.on.ca					
University of Toronto 27 King's College Cir Simcoe Hall	Toronto	ON	M5S1A1	416-978-2011	978-6089
Web: www.utoronto.ca ■ *E-mail:* ut.info@utoronto.ca					
York University 4700 Keele St	North York	ON	M3J1P3	416-736-2100	736-5536
Web: www.yorku.ca					

— Hospitals —

	City			Phone	Fax
Etobicoke General Hospital 101 Humber College Blvd.	Etobicoke	ON	M9V1R8	416-747-3400	747-8608
Web: www.egh.on.ca/					
Humber River Regional Hospital 2111 Finch St W.	Toronto	ON	M3N1N1	416-744-2500	243-4547
King's Health Centre 250 University Ave	Toronto	ON	M5H3E5	416-977-5464	979-8511
TF: 800-246-5464 ■ *Web:* www.kingshealthcentre.ca ■ *E-mail:* info@kingshealthcentre.ca					
Lyndhurst Hospital 520 Sutherland Dr.	Toronto	ON	M4G3V9	416-422-5551	422-5216
Mount Sinai Hospital 600 University	Toronto	ON	M5G1X5	416-596-4200	586-8555*
**Fax:* PR ■ *Web:* www.mtsinai.on.ca					
North York General Hospital 4001 Leslie St	North York	ON	M2K1E1	416-756-6000	756-6384
Web: www.nygh.on.ca ■ *E-mail:* publicrelations@nygh.on.ca					
Riverdale Hospital 14 St Matthews Rd	Toronto	ON	M4M2B5	416-461-8251	461-9972
Saint Joseph's Health Centre 30 The Queensway	Toronto	ON	M6R1B5	416-530-6000	530-6603
Saint Michael's Hospital 30 Bond St	Toronto	ON	M5B1W8	416-360-4000	864-5870
Web: www.smh.toronto.on.ca ■ *E-mail:* medicaleducation@smh.toronto.on.ca					
Saint Michael's Hospital 160 Wellesley St E	Toronto	ON	M4Y1J3	416-966-6600	926-5064
Toronto Hospital 200 Elizabeth St	Toronto	ON	M5G2C4	416-340-4611	340-4896
Web: www.thehosp.org ■ *E-mail:* thehosp@interhop.net					
Women's College Hospital 76 Grenville St.	Toronto	ON	M5S1B2	416-966-7111	323-7311
Web: www.womenscollege.com					

— Attractions —

	City			Phone	Fax
Albion Hills Conservation Area 16500 Hwy 50	Palgrave	ON	L0N1P0	905-880-0227	880-1616
Web: www.trca.on.ca/4aa.html					
Aradia Baroque Ensemble 250 Front St W Canadian Broadcasting Ctr	Toronto	ON	M5V3G5	416-205-5555	205-5551
Web: www.interlog.com/~aradia/ ■ *E-mail:* aradia@interlog.com					
Archives of Ontario 77 Grenville St Suite 300.	Toronto	ON	M5S1B3	416-327-1600	327-1999
TF: 800-668-9933 ■ *Web:* www.gov.on.ca/mczcr/archives/					
Art Gallery of Ontario 317 Dundas St W	Toronto	ON	M5T1G4	416-979-6648	977-8547
Web: www.ago.net					
Arte Flamenco Spanish Dance Company 50 Bernard Ave.	Toronto	ON	M5R1R2	416-920-3774	
Web: www.arteflamenco.com					
Bata Shoe Museum 327 Bloor St W	Toronto	ON	M5S1W7	416-979-7799	979-0078
Bedford Park 81 Ranleigh Ave	Toronto	ON	M4N1X2	416-392-0618	
Benares Historic House 1507 Clarkson Rd	Mississauga	ON	L5J2W8	905-822-2347	822-5372
Web: www.city.mississauga.on.ca/commsvcs/heritage/html/ben.htm					
Black Creek Pioneer Village 1000 Murray Ross Pkwy	North York	ON	M3J2P3	416-736-1733	661-6610
Web: www.trca.on.ca/bcpv.html ■ *E-mail:* bcpvinfo@trca.on.ca					
Bradley Museum 1620 Orr Rd	Mississauga	ON	L5J4T2	905-822-1569	823-3591
Bronte Creek Provincial Park 1219 Burloak Dr.	Burlington	ON	L7R3X5	905-827-6911	637-4120
Web: www.mnr.gov.on.ca/MNR/parks/bron.html					
Bruce Peninsula National Park Hwy 6.	Tobermory	ON	N0H2R0	519-596-2233	596-2298
Web: parkscanada.pch.gc.ca/parks/ontario/bruce_peninsula/bruce_peninsulae.htm					
Buddies In Bad Times Theatre 12 Alexander St	Toronto	ON	M4Y1B4	416-975-8555	975-9293
Canadian Broadcasting Centre 250 Front St W.	Toronto	ON	M5W2E6	416-205-3311	205-6063
Canadian Golf Hall of Fame 1333 Dorval Dr	Oakville	ON	L6J4Z3	905-849-9700	845-7040
Web: www.rcga.org/hallfame/					
Canadian Opera Co 1 Front St E Hummingbird Ctr for the Performing Arts	Toronto	ON	M5E1B2	416-363-6671	363-5584
Web: www.coc.ca					
Canadian Stage Co 26 Berkeley St	Toronto	ON	M5A2W3	416-367-8243	367-1768
Casa Loma Historic Site 1 Austin Terr	Toronto	ON	M5R1X8	416-923-1171	923-5734
Centre For Indigenous Theatre 401 Richmond St W	Toronto	ON	M5V1X3	416-506-9436	506-9430
Web: www.interlog.com/~cit/cit.html ■ *E-mail:* cit@interlog.com					
Centreville Amusement Park 84 Advance Rd	Toronto	ON	M8Z2T7	416-203-0405	234-2857
Cinesphere IMAX Theatre 955 Lakeshore Blvd W Ontario Pl	Toronto	ON	M6K3B9	416-314-9900	314-9992
Web: www.ontarioplace.com ■ *E-mail:* opcwm@ontarioplace.com					
Colborne Lodge 1 Colborne Lodge Dr High Park	Toronto	ON	M5B1N2	416-392-6916	392-0375
Cullen Gardens & Miniature Village 300 Taunton Rd W	Whitby	ON	L1N5R5	905-668-6606	668-0510
TF: 800-461-1821 ■ *Web:* www.cullengardens.com					
Darlington Provincial Park RR2	Bowmanville	ON	L1C3K3	905-436-2036	436-3729
Web: www.mnr.gov.on.ca/MNR/parks/darl.html					
Docks The 11 Polson St.	Toronto	ON	M5A1A4	416-461-3625	469-5547
Dr. Flea's International Flea Market 8 Westmore Dr.	Rexdale	ON	M9V3Z7	416-745-3532	745-7193
Web: www.dr-fleas.com					
Edwards Gardens Lawrence Ave E & Leslie St	Toronto	ON		416-392-8186	397-1354
Web: www.metrotor.on.ca/services/parks/parks/edwar.html ■ *E-mail:* parks@metrodesk.metrotor.on.ca					
Eglinton Way 469 Eglinton Ave W.	Toronto	ON	M5N1A7	416-487-3294	487-6067
Elgin & Winter Garden Theatre Center 189 Yonge St	Toronto	ON	M5B1M4	416-872-5555	314-3583
Empress of Canada Cruises 260 Queens Quay W	Toronto	ON	M5J2N3	416-260-8901	260-5547
Web: www.empressofcanada.com					
Factory Theatre 125 Bathurst St.	Toronto	ON	M5V2R2	416-504-9971	
Web: www.factorytheatre.ca					
Fantasy Fair Amusement Park 500 Rexdale Blvd	Rexdale	ON	M9W6K5	416-674-5437	674-8684
Farmer's Market Front & Jarvis Sts St Lawrence Mkt	Toronto	ON	M5E1C4	416-392-7219	
Ford Centre for the Performing Arts 5040 Yonge St	North York	ON	M2N6R8	416-733-9388	733-9478
Gardiner George R Museum of Ceramic Art 111 Queen's Pk	Toronto	ON	M5S2C7	416-586-8080	586-8085
Web: www.gardinermuseum.on.ca					
Gibson House Museum 5172 Yonge St	North York	ON	M2N5P6	416-395-7432	395-7442

Canadian Cities

Toronto — Attractions (Cont'd)

				Phone	Fax
Grange Historic House 317 Dundas St W	Toronto	ON	M5T1G4	416-979-6648	977-8547
Greektown on the Danforth Danforth Ave betw Donlands & Broadview Aves	Toronto	ON	M4K3Z2	416-469-5634	469-8200
Grossman Danny Dance Company 425 Queen St W Suite 207	Toronto	ON	M5V2A5	416-408-4543	408-2518
Web: www.interlog.com/~dgdance/ ■ *E-mail:* dgdance@interlog.com					
Grumps Television Show 81 Barber Greene Rd	Don Mills	ON	M3C2A2	416-443-6066	443-6069
Harbourfront Antique Market 390 Queen's Quay W	Toronto	ON	M5V3A6	416-260-2626	260-1212
TF: 888-263-6533 ■ *Web:* www.hfam.com ■ *E-mail:* antiques@hfam.com					
Harbourfront Centre 235 Queen's Quay W	Toronto	ON	M5J2G8	416-973-3000	973-6055
Web: www.harbourfront.on.ca ■ *E-mail:* info@harbourfront.on.ca					
Hart House 7 Hart House Cir University of Toronto	Toronto	ON	M5S3H3	416-978-2452	971-2244
Web: www.utoronto.ca/harthouse/					
Heritage Toronto 205 Yonge St	Toronto	ON	M5B1N2	416-392-6827	392-6834
Web: www.torontohistory.on.ca ■ *E-mail:* info@torontohistory.on.ca					
High Park Bloor & Keele Sts.	Toronto	ON	M5H2N2	416-392-1111	392-0023
Historic Fort York Garrison Rd betw Bathurst St & Strachan Ave	Toronto	ON	M5V3K9	416-392-6907	
Hockey Hall of Fame 30 Yonge St BCE Pl	Toronto	ON	M5E1X8	416-360-7735	360-1316
Web: www.hhof.com					
Holocaust Education & Memorial Centre 4600 Bathurst St.	Toronto	ON	M2R3V2	416-631-5689	635-0925
Hummingbird Centre for the Performing Arts 1 Front St E	Toronto	ON	M5E1B2	416-393-7474	393-7454
Jubilee Queen Cruises 207 Queens Quay W	Toronto	ON	M5J1A7	416-203-7245	203-7177
Kortright Centre For Conservation 9550 Pine Valley Dr.	Woodbridge	ON	L4L1A6	905-832-2289	832-8238
Web: www.kortright.org ■ *E-mail:* info@kortright.org					
Lastman Mel Square 5100 Yonge St.	North York	ON	M2N5V7	416-395-7326	395-0278
Living Arts Centre 4141 Living Arts Dr	Mississauga	ON	L5B4B8	905-306-6100	306-6101
TF: 800-805-8888 ■ *Web:* www.livingarts.on.ca					
Mackenzie House 82 Bond St.	Toronto	ON	M5B1X2	416-392-6915	392-0114
Magnotta Winery 271 Chrislea Rd.	Vaughan	ON	L4L8N6	905-738-9463	738-5551
TF: 800-461-9463 ■ *Web:* www.magnotta.com					
Market Gallery of the City of Toronto Archives 95 Front St E South St. Lawrence Market	Toronto	ON	M5E1C2	416-392-7604	392-0572
McMichael Canadian Art Collection 10365 Islington Ave	Kleinburg	ON	L0J1C0	905-893-1121	893-2588
TF: 888-213-1121 ■ *Web:* www.mcmichael.on.ca ■ *E-mail:* info@mcmichael.on.ca					
Medieval Times Dinner & Tournament Lake Shore Blvd W	Toronto	ON	M6K3C3	416-260-1234	260-1179
TF: 800-563-1190 ■ *Web:* www.medievaltimes.com/OT_realm.htm ■ *E-mail:* toronto@medievaltimes.com					
Montgomery's Inn 4709 Dundas St W	Etobicoke	ON	M9A1A8	416-394-8113	394-6027
Web: www.montgomerysinn.com					
Mount Pleasant Cemetery 375 Mt Pleasant Rd.	Toronto	ON	M4T2M1	416-485-9129	485-1672
Museum for Textiles 55 Centre Avenue	Toronto	ON	M5G2H5	416-599-5321	599-2911
Web: www.museumfortextiles.on.ca ■ *E-mail:* info@museumfortextiles.on.ca					
Museum of Television 151 John St Suite 401	Toronto	ON	M5V2T2	416-599-7339	599-7339
Web: www.mztv.com					
National Ballet of Canada 1 Front St E Hummingbird Ctr for the Performing Arts	Toronto	ON	M5E1B2	416-345-9595	345-8282
Web: www.culturenet.ca/nbc/					
Olde Town Toronto Tours 71 City View Dr	Toronto	ON	M9W5A5	416-798-2424	614-0088
TF: 800-350-0398 ■ *Web:* www.oldetown.toronto.on.ca ■ *E-mail:* tours@oldetown.toronto.on.ca					
Omnimax Theatre 770 Don Mills Rd Ontario Science Ctr	North York	ON	M3C1T3	416-696-1000	696-3241
Web: www.osc.on.ca					
Ontario Ballet Theatre 1133 St Clair Ave W	Toronto	ON	M6E1B1	416-656-9568	651-4803
Ontario Place 955 Lake Shore Blvd W.	Toronto	ON	M6K3B9	416-314-9900	314-9989
Web: www.ontarioplace.com ■ *E-mail:* opcwm@ontarioplace.com					
Ontario Science Centre 770 Don Mills Rd	North York	ON	M3C1T3	416-429-4100	696-3166
Web: www.osc.on.ca					
Orchestra Toronto 110 Rumsey Rd	Toronto	ON	M4G1P2	416-467-7142	487-8484
Web: www.orchestratoronto.org ■ *E-mail:* otoronto@excite.com					
Pantages Theatre 263 Yonge St	Toronto	ON	M5B1V8	416-362-3218	362-0985
Paramount Canada's Wonderland 9580 Jane St	Vaughan	ON	L6A1S6	905-832-7000	832-7419
Web: www.canadas-wonderland.com ■ *E-mail:* info@canadas-wonderland.com					
Parkwood Estate & Gardens 270 Simcoe St N	Oshawa	ON	L1G4T5	905-433-4311	721-4765
Pier The Waterfront Museum 245 Queens Quay W	Toronto	ON	M5J2K9	416-338-7437	392-1767
Web: www.torontohistory.on.ca/thepier/ ■ *E-mail:* thepier@torontohistory.on.ca.					
Playdium 99 Rathburn Rd W	Mississauga	ON	L5B4C1	905-273-9000	273-4222
Web: www.playdium.com ■ *E-mail:* info@beginplay.com					
Power Plant Contemporary Art Gallery 231 Queens Quay W Harbourfront Ctr	Toronto	ON	M5J2G8	416-973-4949	973-4933
Web: www.culturenet.ca/powerplant ■ *E-mail:* powerplant@harbourfront.on.ca					
Princess of Wales Theatre 300 King St W	Toronto	ON	M5V1H9	416-593-4142	593-4490
TF: 800-724-6420 ■ *Web:* www.onstagenow.com					
Queen's Quay Terminal 207 Queens Quay W	Toronto	ON	M5J1A7	416-203-3269	203-0432
Redpath Sugar Museum 95 Queens Quay E	Toronto	ON	M5E1A3	416-366-3561	366-7550
TF: 800-267-1517					
Rinx Entertainment Center 65 Orfus Rd	North York	ON	M6A1L7	416-783-6492	783-0501
TF: 800-829-1067					
Royal Alexandra Theatre 260 King St W	Toronto	ON	M5V1H9	416-872-1212	593-4490
TF: 800-724-6420 ■ *Web:* www.stage-door.org/royalex.html					
Royal Botanical Gardens 680 Plains Rd W	Burlington	ON	L7T4H4	905-527-1158	577-0375
Web: www.rbg.ca ■ *E-mail:* bloom@rbg.ca					
Royal Ontario Museum (ROM) 100 Queen's Pk	Toronto	ON	M5S2C6	416-586-8000	586-5863
Web: www.rom.on.ca ■ *E-mail:* info@rom.on.ca					
Saint Anne's Anglican Church 270 Gladstone Ave	Toronto	ON	M6J3L6	416-536-1202	536-6476
Saint Lawrence Centre of the Arts 27 Front St E	Toronto	ON	M5E1B4	416-366-1656	947-1387
Web: www.stlc.com					
Saint Michael's Cathedral Bond & Shuter Sts	Toronto	ON	M5B1Z2	416-364-0234	364-6029
Second City Toronto 56 Blue Jays Way	Toronto	ON	M5V2G3	416-343-0033	343-0034
Web: www.secondcity.com					
SkyDome Tour Experience 1 Blue Jays Way	Toronto	ON	M5V1J3	416-341-2770	341-2774
Spadina Historic House & Gardens 285 Spadina Rd	Toronto	ON	M5R2V5	416-392-6910	392-0382
Thomson Roy Hall 60 Simcoe St	Toronto	ON	M5J2H5	416-593-4822	593-4224
Web: www.roythomson.com					
Todmorden Mills Heritage Museum & Arts Centre Pottery Rd betw Broadview & Bayview Aves	Toronto	ON		416-396-2819	466-4170
Toronto Consort 427 Bloor St W	Toronto	ON	M5S1X7	416-966-1045	966-1759
Toronto Dance Theatre 80 Winchester St.	Toronto	ON	M4X1B2	416-967-1365	967-4379
Web: www.tdt.org ■ *E-mail:* info@tdt.org					
Toronto Mendelssohn Choir 60 Simcoe St	Toronto	ON	M5J2H5	416-598-0422	598-2992
Web: www.tmchoir.org					
Toronto Moss Park Arena 140 Sherbourne St	Toronto	ON	M5A2R6	416-392-1060	
Toronto Operetta Theatre 27 Front St E St Lawrence Ctr for the Arts	Toronto	ON	M5E1B4	416-465-2912	465-2385
Web: www.interlog.com/~elegant/opera/					
Toronto Police Museum & Discovery Centre 40 College St	Toronto	ON	M5G2J3	416-808-7020	808-7023
Toronto Stock Exchange 2 First Canadian Pl The Exchange Tower	Toronto	ON	M5X1J2	416-947-4514	947-4461
Web: www.tse.com ■ *E-mail:* info@tse.com					
Toronto Symphony Orchestra 60 Simcoe St Roy Thomson Hall	Toronto	ON	M5J2H5	416-593-4828	
Web: www.tso.on.ca					
Toronto Zoo 361-A Old Finch Ave	Scarborough	ON	M1B5K7	416-392-5900	392-5863
Web: www.torontozoo.com					
Wild Water Kingdom 7855 Finch Ave W	Brampton	ON	L6T3Y7	905-794-0565	794-1071
Web: www.wildwaterkingdom.com					

SPORTS TEAMS & FACILITIES

				Phone	Fax
SkyDome 1 Blue Jays Way Suite 3000	Toronto	ON	M5V1J3	416-341-3663	341-3101
Web: www.skydome.com					
Toronto Argonauts (football) SkyDome Gate 3 PO Box 2005 Stn B	Toronto	ON	M5T3H8	416-341-5151	341-5174
Web: www.argonauts.on.ca					
Toronto Blue Jays 1 Blue Jays Way	Toronto	ON	M5V1J1	416-341-1000	341-1250*
**Fax:* PR ■ *Web:* www.bluejays.ca ■ *E-mail:* bluejays@bluejays.ca					
Toronto Inferno (soccer) 6 Emeline Cres	Markham	ON	LP34G3	905-294-6199	294-4969
E-mail: mplatinga@globalserve.net					
Toronto Lynx (soccer) Bloor St Varsity Stadium	Toronto	ON	M8V5X2	416-251-4625	251-7054
Web: www.lynxsoccer.com ■ *E-mail:* soclynx@ican.net					
Toronto Maple Leafs 40 Bay St Air Canada Ctr	Toronto	ON	M5J2X2	416-872-5000	359-9205
Web: www.torontomapleleafs.com					
Toronto Raptors 40 Bay St Air Canada Ctr Suite 400	Toronto	ON	M5J2X2	416-366-3865	359-9758
Web: www.nba.com/raptors					

Toronto (Cont'd)

— Events —

	Phone
Beaches International Jazz Festival (late July)	416-698-2152
Bell Canadian Open (early-mid-September)	416-581-6863
Benson & Hedges Symphony of Fire Fireworks Competition (late June-early July)	416-314-9900
Big City Hoedown 8 (late May)	416-927-7151
Canada Blooms Flower Show (mid-March)	416-512-1305
Canadian International Air Show (early September)	416-393-6061
Canadian International Marathon (mid-October)	416-972-1062
Canadian National Exhibition (late August-early September)	416-393-6000
Caribana Festival (mid-July-early August)	416-465-4884
Cavalcade of Lights (late November-early January)	416-392-7341
CHIN Picnic International & Shopping Bazar (early July)	416-531-9991
Christmas in the Village (mid-November-late December)	416-736-1733
Country Christmas at Gibson House Museum (mid-November-late December)	416-395-7432
Country Harvest Festival (September)	416-487-3294
Creative Sewing & Needlework Festival (late October)	905-709-0100
Creative Sewing & Needlework Festival (early-mid-October)	416-973-3000
Fall Classic Collector Car Auction & Swap Meet (late October)	416-674-8425
Farmer's Market Sounds in the City Concert Series (early June-early October)	416-392-0458
First Night Toronto (December 31)	416-362-3692
Fringe of Toronto Festival (early-mid-July)	416-966-1062
Gay Pride Week (June)	416-927-7433
Great Canadian Bug Show (mid-August)	905-642-2886
HarvestFest (mid-October)	416-973-3000
Hot & Spicy Food Festival (mid-August)	416-973-4000
Images Festival of Independent Film and Video (late April-early May)	416-971-8405
International Christmas Fair & Marketplace (early December)	416-213-1035
International Dragon Boat Race Festival (late June)	416-364-0693
International Festival of Authors (late October)	416-973-3000
International Marketplace (June-September)	416-973-3000
Italian Celebration (late June-early July)	416-531-2672
Medieval Renaissance Festival (mid-late June)	416-487-3294
Mennonite Christmas Festival (late November)	416-973-3000
Metro International Caravan (mid-late June)	416-977-0466
MILK International Children's Festival (mid-May)	416-973-3000
North by Northeast Music Festival (mid-June)	416-863-6963
One of a Kind Christmas Canadian Craft Show & Sale (late November-early December)	416-393-6000
Ontario Place Offshore Challenge (mid-September)	416-314-9900
Outdoor Art Exhibition (mid-July)	416-408-2754
Royal Agricultural Winter Fair (early-mid-November)	416-872-7777
Santa Claus Parade (late November)	416-249-7833
Scream In High Park-One of Canada's Largest Outdoor Literary Festivals (mid-July)	416-532-6948
Stages Celebration (January-March)	416-203-2500
Taste of the Danforth (early August)	416-469-5634
Toronto Christmas Story (early-mid-December)	416-598-8979
Toronto Downtown Jazz Festival (late June-early July)	416-973-3000
Toronto Fall Gift Show (late July)	416-263-3000
Toronto Fall Home Show (late September-early October)	416-263-3000
Toronto Harbour Parade of Lights (July 1)	416-941-1041
Toronto Home Show (late January)	416-674-8425
Toronto International Film Festival (early-mid-September)	416-968-3456
Toronto Jewish Film Festival (May)	416-324-8600
Toronto Lion Dance Festival (early June)	416-392-0335
Toronto Molson Indy (mid-July)	416-872-4639
Toronto Sportsman's Show (mid-late March)	416-674-8425
Toronto St Patrick's Parade (mid-March)	416-487-1566
Trees Around the World (late November-mid-January)	416-392-7341
Vegetarian Food Fair (mid-September)	416-973-3000
Victorian Christmas Flower Show (early December-early January)	416-392-7288
Winter Fest (mid-February)	416-395-7300

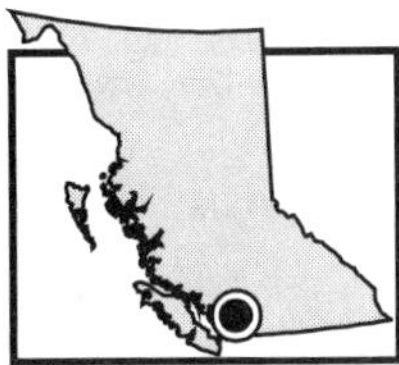

Vancouver

Vancouver, the largest city in British Columbia and the third largest city in Canada, lies on a peninsula in the southwest corner of the province's mainland. Incorporated in 1886, the city was named in honor of the English sailor Captain George Vancouver, who explored the area in 1792. Vancouver's surrounding waterways, Burrard Inlet and the Strait of Georgia, provide easy access to the Pacific Ocean and lend Vancouver its status as Canada's major commercial city on the west coast. Stanley Park in the downtown West End features forest and nature trails, a fine rose garden, and the Vancouver Aquarium, the city's top visitor attraction. Vancouver's entertainment season, which includes theatrical, musical, and dance productions, runs from October to April. Performances are held primarily in the downtown entertainment district at one of three main theaters: the new Ford Centre for the Performing Arts, Vancouver Playhouse, and the Queen Elizabeth Theatre. Summertime activities feature the DuMaurier International Jazz Festival in June, the Vancouver Folk Music Festival in July, and the Vancouver Chamber Music Festival in August.

Population	514,008	**Longitude**	123-04-48 W
Area (Land)	43.7 sq mi	**Time Zone**	PST
Elevation	285 ft	**Area Code/s**	604
Latitude	49-15-00 N		

— Average Temperatures and Precipitation —

TEMPERATURES

	Jan	Feb	Mar	Apr	May	Jun	Jul	Aug	Sep	Oct	Nov	Dec
High	41	46	48	55	63	66	72	72	64	57	48	45
Low	32	34	36	41	46	52	55	55	50	43	37	34

PRECIPITATION

	Jan	Feb	Mar	Apr	May	Jun	Jul	Aug	Sep	Oct	Nov	Dec
Inches	5.2	4.2	3.7	2.3	2.0	1.8	1.3	1.6	2.6	4.5	5.8	6.5

— Important Phone Numbers —

	Phone		Phone
American Express Travel	604-669-2813	**Emergency**	911
British Columbia Automobile Assn	604-268-5500	**Road Conditions**	604-660-8200
		Weather	604-664-9010

— Information Sources —

		Phone	Fax
Better Business Bureau Serving Mainland British Columbia 788 Beatty St Suite 404	Vancouver BC V6B2M1	604-682-2711	681-1544
Web: www.bbbmbc.com ■ *E-mail:* bbbmail@bbbvan.com			
British Columbia Chamber of Commerce 700 W Pender St Suite 1607	Vancouver BC V6C1G8	604-683-0700	683-0416
Web: www.bcchamber.org			
Downtown Vancouver Assn 409 Granville St	Vancouver BC V6C1T2	604-685-0284	669-5343
Downtown Vancouver Business Improvement Assn 789 W Pender St	Vancouver BC V6C1H2	604-685-7811	685-7812
Web: www.vancouver.com			
Greater Vancouver Chamber of Commerce 404 E 15th St Suite 11	Vancouver WA 98663	360-694-2588	693-8279
Web: www.vancouverusa.com			
Greater Vancouver Convention & Visitors Bureau 200 Burrard St Suite 210	Vancouver BC V6C3L6	604-683-2000	682-6839
TF: 800-663-6000 ■ *Web:* www.tourism-vancouver.org			
Robson Square Conference Centre 800 Robson St	Vancouver BC V6Z2C5	604-660-2830	685-9407
Web: www.robsonsquare.com			
Vancouver Board Of Trade 999 Canada Pl Suite 400	Vancouver BC V6C3C1	604-681-2111	681-0437
Web: www.vancouver.boardoftrade.com			
Vancouver City Hall 453 W 12th Ave	Vancouver BC V5Y1V4	604-873-7011	
Web: www.city.vancouver.bc.ca ■ *E-mail:* info@city.vancouver.bc.ca			
Vancouver Economic Development Commission 608 W Cordova St	Vancouver BC V6B5A7	604-632-9668	632-9788
Web: www.vancouvereconomic.com ■ *E-mail:* vedc@vancouvereconomic.com			
Vancouver Mayor 453 W 12th Ave	Vancouver BC V5Y1V4	604-873-7011	873-7685
E-mail: mayorandcouncil@city.vancouver.bc.ca			

Vancouver — Information Sources (Cont'd)

		Phone	Fax
Vancouver Planning Dept 453 W 12th Ave 3rd Fl East Wing *E-mail:* planning@city.vancouver.bc.ca	Vancouver BC V5Y1V4	604-873-7344	873-7060
Vancouver Public Library 350 W Georgia St *Web:* www.vpl.vancouver.bc.ca ■ *E-mail:* info@vpl.vancouver.bc.ca	Vancouver BC V6B6B1	604-331-3600	331-3800
Vancouver Trade & Convention Centre 999 Canada Pl *Web:* www.vtcc.com	Vancouver BC V6C3C1	604-641-1987	641-1436

On-Line Resources

4Vancouver.com	www.4vancouver.com
About.com Guide to Vancouver	vancouver.about.com/local/vancouver
Arts Vancouver	www.artsvancouver.com
Bradmans.com Vancouver	www.bradmans.com/scripts/display_city.cgi?city=246
City Knowledge Vancouver	www.cityknowledge.com/canada_bc_vancouver.htm
Discover Vancouver	www.discovervancouver.com
Georgia Straight Online	www2.mybc.com/aroundtown/straight
Greater Vancouver	www.greatervancouver.com
HotelGuide Vancouver	hotelguide.net/vancouver/
In Vancouver	www.vancouver-bc.com
Restaurant.ca Vancouver	www.restaurant.ca/van/
Rough Guide Travel Vancouver	travel.roughguides.com/content/2995/
Savvy Diner Guide to Vancouver Restaurants	www.savvydiner.com/vancouver/
Surf & Sun Beach Vacation Guide to Vancouver	www.surf-sun.com/canada-vancouver-main.htm
travel.bc.ca	www.travel.bc.ca
Vancouver by Word of Mouse	www.wordofmouse.com/vanbc/
Vancouver CommunityNet	www.vcn.bc.ca
Vancouver Style	www.vancouverstyle.com
Vancouver's Digital Groove	www.digitalgroove.com
VanLink	www.vanlink.com

— Transportation Services —

AIRPORTS

■ Vancouver International Airport (YVR)

	Phone
11 miles SW of downtown (approx 45 minutes) Web: www.yvr.ca	604-276-6101

Airport Transportation

	Phone
Airport Limousine Service $31 fare to downtown	604-273-1331
Yellow Cab $24 fare to downtown	604-258-4700

Commercial Airlines

	Phone		Phone
Air Canada	800-776-3000	**Delta**	800-221-1212
Air China	800-986-1985	**Japan**	800-525-3663
Air New Zealand	800-262-1234	**KLM**	800-374-7747
Air Transat	877-872-6728	**Korean Air**	800-438-5000
Alaska	800-426-0333	**Lufthansa**	800-645-3880
All Nippon Airways	800-235-9262	**Malaysia Airlines**	800-552-9264
America West	800-235-9292	**Northwest**	800-225-2525
American	800-433-7300	**Philippine**	800-435-9725
British Airways	800-247-9297	**Singapore**	800-742-3333
Canadian Air	800-426-7000	**United**	800-241-6522
Cathay Pacific	888-338-1668	**WestJet**	800-538-5696
Continental	800-525-0280		

CAR RENTALS

	Phone		Phone
Alamo	604-231-1409	**Enterprise**	604-688-5500
Avis	604-606-2847	**Hertz**	604-688-2411
Budget	604-668-7228	**National**	604-273-3121
Discount	604-273-5565	**Rent-A-Wreck**	604-688-0001
Dollar	604-279-0045	**Thrifty**	604-606-1695

LIMO/TAXI

	Phone		Phone
AAA Star Limousine Service	604-685-5600	**New Pacific Limousine**	604-683-1155
Checker Cabs	604-681-3201	**Vancouver Limousine Service**	604-421-5585
Classic Limousine Service	604-267-1441	**Yellow Cab**	604-258-4700
Cosmic Limo	604-708-0896		

MASS TRANSIT

	Phone
Coast Mountain Buslink SkyTrain $1.50 Base fare	604-521-0400
Translink $1.50 Base fare	604-521-0400

RAIL/BUS

		Phone
Greyhound Canada Bus Station 1150 Station St *TF:* 800-661-8747	Vancouver BC V6A4C7	604-661-0328
VIA Rail Canada 1150 Station St	Vancouver BC V6A4C7	800-561-3949

— Accommodations —

HOTEL RESERVATION SERVICES

	Phone	Fax
Best Canadian Bed & Breakfast Network *Web:* www.corpinfohub.com/best_can/ ■ *E-mail:* bestcdnbb@aol.com	604-738-7207	732-4998
Downtown Accommodations *Web:* www.dtaccomm.com ■ *E-mail:* margaret@dtaccomm.com	604-454-8179	682-5634
Executive Accommodations *TF:* 800-557-8483 ■ *Web:* www.travelsuites.com ■ *E-mail:* info@travelsuites.com	604-875-6674	875-6684
Hotel Reservations Network Inc *TF Sales:* 800-964-6835 ■ *Web:* www.hoteldiscount.com	214-361-7311	361-7299
Western Canada Bed & Breakfast Innkeepers Assn. *Web:* www.wcbbia.com	604-255-9199	

HOTELS, MOTELS, RESORTS

		Phone	Fax
Abercorn Inn Best Western 9260 Bridgeport Rd *TF:* 800-663-0085	Richmond BC V6X1S1	604-270-7576	270-0001
Atrium Inn 2889 E Hastings St *TF:* 888-428-7486	Vancouver BC V5K2A1	604-254-1000	253-1234
Best Western Chateau Granville Hotel 1100 Granville St *TF:* 800-663-0575	Vancouver BC V6Z2B6	604-669-7070	669-4928
Best Western Downtown 718 Drake St *TF:* 800-528-1234 ■ *Web:* www.bestwesterndowntown.com ■ *E-mail:* welcome2@bestwesterndowntown.com	Vancouver BC V6Z2W6	604-669-9888	669-3440
Best Western Exhibition Park 3475 E Hastings St *TF:* 800-528-1234	Vancouver BC V5K2A5	604-294-4751	294-1269
Blue Horizon Hotel 1225 Robson St *TF:* 800-663-1333	Vancouver BC V6E1C3	604-688-1411	688-4461
Bosman's Motor Hotel 1060 Howe St *TF:* 888-267-6267	Vancouver BC V6Z1P5	604-682-3171	684-4010
Century Plaza Hotel & Spa 1015 Burrard St *TF:* 800-663-1818 ■ *Web:* www.century-plaza.com ■ *E-mail:* sales@century-plaza.com	Vancouver BC V6Z1Y5	604-687-0575	682-5790
Coast Plaza Suite Hotel 1763 Comox St *TF:* 800-663-1144	Vancouver BC V6G1P6	604-688-7711	688-5934
Crowne Plaza Hotel Georgia 801 W Georgia St *TF:* 800-663-1111 ■ *Web:* www.atlific.com/georgia.html ■ *E-mail:* hgsales@hotelgeorgia.bc.ca	Vancouver BC V6C1P7	604-682-5566	642-5556
Days Inn Vancouver Downtown 921 W Pender St *TF:* 800-329-7466	Vancouver BC V6C1M2	604-681-4335	681-7808
Days Inn Vancouver Metro 2075 Kingsway St *TF:* 800-546-4792	Vancouver BC V5N2T2	604-876-5531	872-2676
Delta Pacific Resort & Conference Centre 10251 St Edwards Dr *TF:* 800-268-1133 ■ *Web:* www.deltapacific.bc.ca ■ *E-mail:* delta@nbet.nb.ca	Richmond BC V6X2M9	604-278-9611	276-1121
Delta Vancouver Airport Hotel & Marina 3500 Cessna Dr *TF:* 800-268-1133	Richmond BC V7B1C7	604-278-1241	276-1975
Delta Vancouver Suite Hotel 550 W Hastings St *TF:* 800-268-1133 ■ *Web:* www.deltahotels.com	Vancouver BC V6B1L6	604-689-8188	899-3001
Dominion Hotel 210 Abbott St	Vancouver BC V6B2K8	604-681-6666	681-5855
Empire Landmark Hotel & Conference Centre 1400 Robson St *TF:* 800-830-6144	Vancouver BC V6G1B9	604-687-0511	687-2801
Executive Plaza Hotel 1379 Howe St. *TF:* 800-570-3932	Vancouver BC V6Z2R5	604-688-7678	688-7679
Four Points Hotel Vancouver Airport 8368 Alexandra Rd *TF:* 888-281-8888	Richmond BC V6X4A6	604-214-0888	214-0887

Vancouver — Hotels, Motels, Resorts (Cont'd)

				Phone	Fax
Four Seasons Hotel 791 W Georgia St	Vancouver	BC	V6C2T4	604-689-9333	689-3466
TF: 800-332-3442 ■ *Web:* www.fourseasons.com/locations/Vancouver					
Georgian Court Hotel 773 Beatty St	Vancouver	BC	V6B2M4	604-682-5555	682-5669
TF: 800-332-3442					
Holiday Inn Express Vancouver Airport 9351 Bridgeport Rd	Richmond	BC	V6X1S3	604-273-8080	214-8488
TF: 800-465-4329					
Holiday Inn Hotel & Suites Downtown 1110 Howe St	Vancouver	BC	V6Z1R2	604-684-2151	684-4736
TF: 800-465-4329					
Holiday Inn Vancouver Airport 10720 Cambie Rd	Vancouver	BC	V6X1K8	604-821-1818	821-1819
TF: 800-465-4329					
Holiday Inn Vancouver Centre 711 West Broadway	Vancouver	BC	V5Z3Y2	604-879-0511	872-7520
TF: 800-465-4329 ■ *Web:* www.holidayinnvancouver.com ■ *E-mail:* info@holidayinnvancouver.com					
Hotel Dakota 654 Nelson St	Vancouver	BC	V6B6K4	604-605-4333	605-4334
TF: 888-605-5333 ■ *Web:* www.hoteldakota.com ■ *E-mail:* info@hoteldakota.com					
Hotel Vancouver 900 W Georgia St	Vancouver	BC	V6C2W6	604-684-3131	662-1929
TF: 800-441-1414 ■ *Web:* www.cphotels.ca/cp.htm ■ *E-mail:* reserve@hvc.cphotels.ca					
Howard Johnson 1176 Granville St	Vancouver	BC	V6Z1L8	604-688-8701	688-8335
TF: 800-446-4656 ■ *Web:* www.hojovancouver.com ■ *E-mail:* info@hojovancouver.com					
Hyatt Regency Vancouver 655 Burrard St	Vancouver	BC	V6C2R7	604-683-1234	689-3707
TF: 800-233-1234 ■ *Web:* www.hyatt.com/canada/vancouver/hotels/hotel_yvrrv.html					
Listel Vancouver 1300 Robson St	Vancouver	BC	V6E1C5	604-684-8461	684-7092
TF: 800-663-5491 ■ *Web:* www.listel-vancouver.com ■ *E-mail:* moreinfo@listel-vancouver.com					
Lord Stanley Suites on the Park 1889 Alberni St	Vancouver	BC	V6G3G7	604-688-9299	688-9297
TF: 888-767-7829 ■ *Web:* www.lordstanley.com ■ *E-mail:* info@lordstanley.com					
Metropolitan Hotel Vancouver 645 Howe St	Vancouver	BC	V6C2Y9	604-687-1122	689-7044
TF: 800-667-2300 ■ *Web:* www.metropolitan.com/vanc/ ■ *E-mail:* reservations@metropolitan.com					
Old English Bed & Breakfast Registry 1226 Silverwood Crescent	North Vancouver	BC	V7P1J3	604-986-5069	986-8810
Web: www.oldenglishbandb.bc.ca					
Pacific Palisades Hotel 1277 Robson St	Vancouver	BC	V6E1C4	604-688-0461	891-5104
TF: 800-663-1815 ■ *Web:* www.pacificpalisadeshotel.com					
Pan Pacific Hotel Vancouver 999 Canada Pl	Vancouver	BC	V6C3B5	604-662-8111	662-3815
TF: 800-937-1515 ■ *Web:* www.panpacific-hotel.com ■ *E-mail:* ppacific@panpacific-hotel.com					
Parkhill Hotel 1160 Davie St	Vancouver	BC	V6E1N1	604-685-1311	681-0208
TF: 800-663-1525 ■ *Web:* www.parkhillhotel.com ■ *E-mail:* prkhillres@aol.com					
Plaza 500 Hotel 500 W 12th Ave	Vancouver	BC	V5Z1M2	604-873-1811	873-5103
TF: 800-473-1811					
Quality Hotel Downtown 1335 Howe St	Vancouver	BC	V6Z1R7	604-682-0229	662-7566
TF: 800-663-8474 ■ *Web:* www.qualityhotelvancouver.com ■ *E-mail:* quality@qualityhotelvancouver.com					
Quality Inn Airport 725 SE Marine Dr	Vancouver	BC	V5X2T9	604-321-6611	327-3570
TF: 800-663-6715					
Quality Inn Metrotown 3484 Kingsway	Vancouver	BC	V5R5L6	604-433-8255	433-8359
TF: 800-424-6423					
Radisson President Hotel & Suites 8181 Cambie Rd	Richmond	BC	V6X3X9	604-276-8181	276-8136
TF: 800-333-3333					
Ramada Inn & Suites Vancouver Airport 7188 Westminster Hwy	Richmond	BC	V6X1A1	604-207-9000	207-9466
TF: 888-383-8393					
Ramada Limited Downtown 435 West Pender St	Vancouver	BC	V6B1V2	604-488-1088	488-1090
TF: 888-389-5888 ■ *Web:* www.ramada.ca ■ *E-mail:* ramadalimiteddowntown@bc.sympatico.ca					
Ramada Vancouver Centre 898 W Broadway	Vancouver	BC	V5Z1J8	604-872-8661	872-2270
TF: 800-663-5403					
Renaissance Vancouver Hotel 1133 West Hastings St	Vancouver	BC	V6E3T3	604-689-9211	689-4358
TF: 800-468-3571 ■ *Web:* www.renaissancehotels.com ■ *E-mail:* rhi.yvrrd.dom@marriott.com					
Residence Inn by Marriott 1234 Hornby St	Vancouver	BC	V6Z1W2	604-688-1234	689-1763
TF: 800-663-1234 ■ *Web:* residenceinn.com/YVRRI					
Riviera Hotel 1431 Robson St	Vancouver	BC	V6G1C1	604-685-1301	685-1335
TF: 888-699-5222 ■ *Web:* www.vancouver-bc.com/rivierahotel/					
Rosedale on Robson Suite Hotel 838 Hamilton St	Vancouver	BC	V6B6A2	604-689-8033	689-4426
TF: 800-661-8870 ■ *Web:* www.rosedaleonrobson.com ■ *E-mail:* rosedale@direct.ca					
Rosellen Suites 2030 Barclay St	Vancouver	BC	V6G1L5	604-689-4807	684-3327
TF: 888-317-6648 ■ *Web:* www.rosellensuites.com ■ *E-mail:* info@rosellensuites.com					
Saint Regis Hotel 602 Dunsmuir St	Vancouver	BC	V6B1Y6	604-681-1135	683-1126
TF: 800-770-7929 ■ *Web:* www.stregishotel.com					
Sandman Hotel Vancouver 180 W Georgia St	Vancouver	BC	V6B4P4	604-681-2211	681-8009
TF: 800-726-3626 ■ *Web:* www.sandman.ca					
Sheraton Wall Centre Hotel 1088 Burrard St	Vancouver	BC	V6Z2R9	604-893-7100	331-1001
TF: 800-663-9255 ■ *Web:* www.intouch.bc.ca/wall/ ■ *E-mail:* wallsales@intouch.bc.ca					
Sunset Inn Travel Apartments 1111 Burnaby St	Vancouver	BC	V6E1P4	604-688-2474	669-3340
TF: 800-786-1997 ■ *Web:* www.sunsetinn.com ■ *E-mail:* sunset_inn@msn.com					
Sutton Place Hotel 845 Burrard St	Vancouver	BC	V6Z2K6	604-682-5511	682-2926
TF: 800-961-7555 ■ *Web:* www.travelweb.com/TravelWeb/000063/common/sutton.html ■ *E-mail:* info@vcr.suttonplace.com					
Travelodge Vancouver Centre 1304 Howe St	Vancouver	BC	V6Z1R6	604-682-2767	682-6225
TF: 800-578-7878					
Vancouver Airport Marriott 7571 Westminster Hwy	Richmond	BC	V6X1A3	604-276-2112	276-0112
TF: 877-323-8888					
Waterfront Centre Hotel 900 Canada Place Way	Vancouver	BC	V6C3L5	604-691-1991	691-1999
TF: 800-441-1414 ■ *Web:* www.cphotels.ca					
Wedgewood Hotel 845 Hornby St	Vancouver	BC	V6Z1V1	604-689-7777	608-5349
TF: 800-663-0666 ■ *Web:* www.wedgewoodhotel.com					
Westin Bayshore 1601 W Georgia St	Vancouver	BC	V6G2V4	604-682-3377	691-6959
TF: 800-228-3000					
Westin Grand Vancouver 433 Robson St	Vancouver	BC	V6B6L9	604-684-9393	684-9396
TF: 888-680-9393 ■ *Web:* www.westingrandvancouver.com ■ *E-mail:* play@westingrandvancouver.com					

— Restaurants —

				Phone
900 West (Pacific Northwest) 900 W Georgia St	Vancouver	BC	V6C2W6	604-684-3131
Alfredo's on Melville (Italian) 1100 Melville St	Vancouver	BC	V6E4K2	604-681-3330
Allegro Cafe (Mediterranean) 888 Nelson St Suite 61	Vancouver	BC	V6Z2H1	604-689-0909
Aqua Riva (Pacific Northwest) 200 Granville St	Vancouver	BC	V6C1S4	604-683-5599
Web: www.aquariva.com				
Ashiana Tandoori Restaurant (Indian) 1440 Kingsway St	Vancouver	BC	V5N2R5	604-874-5060
Bacchus Ristorante (Continental) 845 Hornby St	Vancouver	BC	V6Z1V1	604-689-7777
BC Club (Pacific Northwest) 800 Griffith's Way Suite 10	Vancouver	BC	V6B6G2	604-899-7550
Boathouse Restaurant (Seafood) 1795 Beach Ave	Vancouver	BC	V6G1Y9	604-669-2225
Bridges Restaurant (Pacific Northwest) 1696 Duranleau St	Vancouver	BC	V6H3R9	604-687-4400
Web: www.bridgesrestaurant.com				
Brother's Restaurant (Steak/Seafood) 1 Water St	Vancouver	BC	V6B1A1	604-683-9124
Byron's Grill (Continental) 1160 Davie St	Vancouver	BC	V6E1N1	604-685-1311
C Restaurant (Seafood) 1600 Howe St Suite 2	Vancouver	BC	V6Z2L9	604-681-1164
Cafe Pacifica (North American) 999 Canada Pl	Vancouver	BC	V6C3B5	604-895-2480
Caffe de Medici (Italian) 1025 Robson St Suite 109	Vancouver	BC	V6E1A9	604-669-9322
Cannery Seafood Restaurant (Seafood) 2205 Commissioner St	Vancouver	BC	V5L1A4	604-254-9606
Century Grill (Pacific Northwest) 1095 Hamilton St	Vancouver	BC	V6B5T4	604-688-8088
Chartwell (Continental) 791 W Georgia St	Vancouver	BC	V6C2T4	604-689-9333
Chili Club Thai Restaurant (Thai) 1018 Beach Ave	Vancouver	BC	V6E1T7	604-681-6000
CinCin Ristorante (Italian) 1154 Robson St	Vancouver	BC	V6E1B5	604-688-7338
Web: www.cin-cin.com ■ *E-mail:* cincin@direct.ca				
Cloud Nine Revolving Restaurant (Continental) 1400 Robson St	Vancouver	BC	V6G1B9	604-687-0511
Creek Restaurant Brewery & Bar (Pacific Northwest) 1253 Johnston St	Vancouver	BC	V6H3R9	604-685-7070
Web: www.the-creek.com ■ *E-mail:* rhodes@whoa.ca				
Delilah's Restaurant (Continental) 1789 Comox St	Vancouver	BC	V6G1P5	604-687-3424
Diva at the Met (Pacific Northwest) 645 Howe St	Vancouver	BC	V6C2Y9	604-602-7788
Web: www.divamet.com				
Fish House in Stanley Park (Seafood) 8901 Stanley Park Dr	Vancouver	BC	V6G3E2	604-681-7275
Five Sails Restaurant (Pacific Northwest) 999 Canada Pl Suite 300	Vancouver	BC	V6C3B5	604-891-2892
Floata Seafood Restaurant (Chinese) 180 Keefer St Suite 400	Vancouver	BC	V6A4E9	604-602-0368
Web: www.floata.com ■ *E-mail:* info@floata.com				
Fogg n'Suds Restaurant (International) 500 W Broadway Suite 200	Vancouver	BC	V5Z1E9	604-872-3377

Canadian Cities

Vancouver — Restaurants (Cont'd)

				Phone
Greek Characters Restaurant (Greek) 1 Alexander St	Vancouver	BC	V6A1B2	604-681-6581
Hard Rock Cafe (American) 686 W Hastings St	Vancouver	BC	V6B1P1	604-687-7625
Heaven & Earth India Curry House (Indian) 1754 W 4th Ave	Vancouver	BC	V6J1M1	604-732-5313
Hermitage Restaurant (French) 1025 Robson St Suite 115	Vancouver	BC	V6E4A9	604-689-3237
Hy's Encore (Steak/Seafood) 637 Hornby St	Vancouver	BC	V6C2G3	604-683-7671
Imperial Chinese Seafood Restaurant (Chinese) 355 Burrard St	Vancouver	BC	V6C2G8	604-688-8191
Joe Fortes Seafood House (Seafood) 777 Thurlow St	Vancouver	BC	V6E3V5	604-669-1940
Jolly Taxpayer Pub & Bistro (British) 828 W Hastings St	Vancouver	BC	V6C1C8	604-681-3574
Keg Down Under Steakhouse (Steak/Seafood) 1122 Alberni St	Vancouver	BC	V6E1A5	604-685-4388
Kettle of Fish Restaurant (Seafood) 900 Pacific St	Vancouver	BC	V6Z2E3	604-682-6853
Kirin Mandarin Restaurant (Chinese) 1166 Alberni St Suite 102	Vancouver	BC	V6E3Z3	604-682-8833
Kobe Japanese Steak House (Japanese) 1042 Alberni St	Vancouver	BC	V6E1A3	604-684-2451
Koji Japanese Restaurant (Japanese) 630 Hornby St	Vancouver	BC	V6C3E8	604-685-7355
La Bodega Restaurante & Tapa Bar (Spanish) 1277 Howe St	Vancouver	BC	V6Z1R3	604-684-8814
Las Margaritas Restaurante (Mexican) 1999 W 4th Ave	Vancouver	BC	V6J1M7	604-734-7117
Le Gavroche Restaurant (French) 1616 Alberni St	Vancouver	BC	V6G1A6	604-685-3924
Lumiere Restaurant (French/Vegetarian) 2551 W Broadway	Vancouver	BC	V6K2E9	604-739-8185
Malone's Sports Grill (American) 608 W Pender St	Vancouver	BC	V6B1V8	604-684-9977
Milestone's at the Beach (North American) 1210 Denman St	Vancouver	BC	V6G2N2	604-662-3431
Monk McQueens Fresh Seafood & Oyster Bar (Seafood) 601 Stamps Landing *Web:* www.monkmcqueens.com	Vancouver	BC	V5Z3Z1	604-877-1351
Naam Restaurant (Vegetarian) 2724 W 4th Ave	Vancouver	BC	V6K1R1	604-738-7180
Nirvana Restaurant (Indian) 2313 Main St	Vancouver	BC	V5T3C9	604-872-8779
O'Doul's Restaurant (Pacific Northwest) 1300 Robson St	Vancouver	BC	V6E1C5	604-661-1400
Old Spaghetti Factory (Italian) 53 Water St *Web:* www.oldspaghettifactory.ca ■ *E-mail:* oldspaghetti@bc.sympatico.ca	Vancouver	BC	V6B1A1	604-684-1288
Planet Hollywood (California) 969 Robson St *Web:* www.planethollywood.com	Vancouver	BC	V6Z2V7	604-688-7827
Prospect Point Cafe (Seafood) 2099 Beach Ave	Vancouver	BC	V6G1Z4	604-669-2737
Raincity Grill (Pacific Northwest) 1193 Denman St *Web:* www.raincitygrill.com	Vancouver	BC	V6G2N1	604-685-7337
Raintree at The Landing (Northwest) 375 Water St	Vancouver	BC	V6B5C6	604-688-5570
Shark Club Bar & Grill (North American) 180 W Georgia St	Vancouver	BC	V6B4P4	604-687-4275
Spotted Prawn Bistro (Seafood) 1055 W Hastings St	Vancouver	BC	V6E2E9	604-646-0667
Star Anise Restaurant (Pacific Northwest) 1485 W 12th Ave	Vancouver	BC	V6H1M6	604-737-1485
Steamworks Brewing Co (American) 375 Water St	Vancouver	BC	V6B5C6	604-689-2739
Sun Sui Wah Seafood Restaurant (Chinese) 3888 Main St	Vancouver	BC	V5V3N9	604-872-8822
Teahouse Restaurant (Pacific Northwest) Ferguson Pt	Vancouver	BC	B6G3E2	604-669-3281
Umberto Al Porto Restaurant (Italian) 321 Water St	Vancouver	BC	V6B1B8	604-683-8376
William Tell Restaurant (Continental) 765 Beatty St	Vancouver	BC	V6B2M4	604-688-3504

— Goods and Services —

SHOPPING

				Phone	Fax
Bay Downtown Vancouver 674 Granville St	Vancouver	BC	V6C1Z6	604-681-6211	689-2198
City Square 555 W 12th Ave	Vancouver	BC	V5Z3X7	604-893-3229	876-5181
Eaton's 701 Granville St	Vancouver	BC	V6B4E5	604-685-7112	685-7916
Harbour Centre 555 W Hastings St	Vancouver	BC	V6B4N4	604-689-7304	684-7875
Lonsdale Quay Market 123 Carrie Cates Ct *Web:* www.lonsdalequay.com	North Vancouver	BC	V7M3K7	604-985-2191	985-4728
Metrotown Centre 4800 Kingsway	Burnaby	BC	V5H4J2	604-438-2302	438-0737
Pacific Centre Mall Georgia St betw Granville & Howe Sts	Vancouver	BC	V7Y1A1	604-688-7236	688-0394
Robson Street Shopping District 1155 Robson St *Web:* www.robsonstreet.bc.ca	Vancouver	BC	V6E1B5	604-669-8132	669-0181
Royal Centre Mall 1055 W Georgia St	Vancouver	BC	V6E3P3	604-689-1711	685-1294
Shops at the Landing 375 Water St *Web:* www.mcleangroup.com	Vancouver	BC	V6B5C6	604-687-1144	687-6020
Sinclair Centre 757 W Hastings St *Web:* www.sinclaircentre.com ■ *E-mail:* k.chandok@brookfield.ca	Vancouver	BC	V6C1A1	604-659-1010	659-1012
Vancouver Chinatown 508 Taylor St	Vancouver	BC	B6A1S9	604-682-8998	682-8939
Waterfront Centre Shops 200 Burrard St	Vancouver	BC	V6C3L6	604-893-3200	681-7356
West 10th Avenue Merchants 4465 W 10th Ave	Vancouver	BC	V6R2H8	604-224-2665	224-2665

BANKS

				Phone	Fax
Bank of Montreal 595 Burrard St First Bank Tower *Web:* www.bmo.com	Vancouver	BC	V7X1L7	604-665-2643	665-6614
Bank of Tokyo Canada 666 Broad St Suite 666	Vancouver	BC	V6C3L1	604-691-7300	689-8990
Canada Trust 612 Main St	Vancouver	BC	V6A2V3	604-891-3333	891-3300
Canadian Western Bank & Trust 666 Burrard St 22nd Fl	Vancouver	BC	V6C2X8	604-685-1208	683-0051
HSBC Bank Canada 885 W Georgia St Suite 300 *Web:* www.hsbc.ca ■ *E-mail:* info@hsbc.ca	Vancouver	BC	V6C3E9	604-685-1000	641-1808
Laurentian Bank of Canada 800 W Pender St *Web:* www.laurentianbank.com	Vancouver	BC	V6C1K6	800-522-1846	
National Bank of Canada 555 Burrard St	Vancouver	BC	V7X1M7	604-661-5500	661-5509
Royal Bank of Canada 1025 W Georgia St *TF:* 800-769-2511 ■ *Web:* www.royalbank.com	Vancouver	BC	V6E3N9	604-665-4111	668-4921
Sanwa Bank Canada 650 W Georgia St Suite 2040	Vancouver	BC	V6B4N8	604-683-8344	683-4826
Scotiabank 650 W Georgia St *TF:* 800-268-5211 ■ *Web:* www.scotiabank.ca	Vancouver	BC	V6B4P6	604-668-2096	668-2096

BUSINESS SERVICES

	Phone
Adecco Employment Personnel Services	604-669-1203
Bradson Staffing Services	604-683-8787
Canada Post	604-662-5723
Contemporary Personnel	604-689-7775
Copy Time Printing & Copying	604-682-8307
DHL International Express	403-250-1512
Federal Express	800-463-3339
Kelly Services	604-669-1236
Kinko's	604-734-2679
Kirkpatrick Personnel	604-682-1171
Manpower Temporary Services	604-682-1651
Office Team	604-687-8367
Temporarily Yours	604-689-8558
UPS	800-742-5877

— Media —

PUBLICATIONS

				Phone	Fax
Business in Vancouver 1155 W Pender St Suite 500 *Web:* www.biv.com	Vancouver	BC	V6E2P4	604-688-2398	688-1963
Globe & Mail The 1140 W Pender St Suite 1210 *Web:* www.theglobeandmail.com	Vancouver	BC	V6E4G1	604-687-4435	687-3891
Monday Magazine 1609 Blanshard St *TF:* 800-661-6335 ■ *Web:* www.monday.com ■ *E-mail:* editorial@monday.com	Victoria	BC	V8W2J5	250-382-6188	381-2662
North Shore News 1139 Lonsdale Ave *Web:* www.nsnews.com ■ *E-mail:* editor@nsnews.com	North Vancouver	BC	V7M2H4	604-985-2131	985-2104
Vancouver Courier 1574 W 6th Ave	Vancouver	BC	V6J1R2	604-738-1411	731-1474
Vancouver Echo 1299 Kingsway *Web:* www.vanecho.com ■ *E-mail:* editor@vanecho.com	Vancouver	BC	V5V3E2	604-437-7030	439-3367
Vancouver Magazine 555 W 12th Ave Suite 300 *Web:* www.vanmag.com	Vancouver	BC	V5Z4L4	604-877-7732	877-4823
Vancouver Province 200 Granville St Suite 1 *Web:* www.vancouverprovince.com	Vancouver	BC	V6C3N3	604-605-2000	605-2720
Vancouver Sun† 200 Granville St Suite 1 *Web:* www.vancouversun.com	Vancouver	BC	V6C3N3	604-605-2000	605-2323
Where Vancouver Magazine 2208 Spruce St	Vancouver	BC	V6H2P3	604-736-5586	736-3465

†*Daily newspapers*

TELEVISION

				Phone	Fax
CBUFT-TV Ch 26 (CBC) 700 rue Hamilton CP 4600	Vancouver	BC	V6B4A2	604-662-6212	662-6229
CBUT-TV Ch 2 (CBC) PO Box 4600 *Web:* cbc.ca	Vancouver	BC	V6B4A2	604-662-6000	662-6878
CHAN-TV Ch 8 (CTV) BCTV PO Box 4700 *Web:* www.ctv.ca	Vancouver	BC	V6B4A3	604-420-2288	444-9512

Vancouver — Television (Cont'd)

	City			Phone	Fax
CIVT-TV Ch 9 (CTV) 750 Burrard St Suite 300 *Web:* www.vancouvertelevision.com ■ *E-mail:* interactive@vancouvertelevision.com	Vancouver	BC	V6Z1X5	604-608-2868	609-5894
CKVU-TV Ch 10 (Ind) 180 W 2nd St	Vancouver	BC	V5Y3T9	604-876-1344	874-8225
KVOS-TV Ch 12 (Ind) 1385 W 8th Ave Suite 320	Vancouver	BC	V6H3V9	604-681-1212	736-4510

RADIO

	City			Phone	Fax
CFMI-FM 101.1 MHz (Rock) 700 W Georgia St Suite 2000 *Web:* www.rock101.com	Vancouver	BC	V7Y1K9	604-331-2808	331-2727
CFOX-FM 99.3 MHz (CHR) 1006 Richards St *Web:* www.cfox.com	Vancouver	BC	V6B1S8	604-684-7221	280-3299
CFUN-AM 1410 kHz (N/T) 380 W 2nd Ave Suite 300 *Web:* www.cfun.com	Vancouver	BC	V5Y1C8	604-871-9000	871-2901
CISL-AM 650 kHz (Oldies) 11151 Horseshoe Way Suite 20	Richmond	BC	V7A4S5	604-272-6500	272-5428
CITR-FM 101.9 MHz (Misc) 6138 Sub Blvd Student Union Bldg Rm 233 *Web:* www.ams.ubc.ca/media/Citr/citr.htm	Vancouver	BC	V6T1Z1	604-822-3017	822-9364
CJJR-FM 93.7 MHz (Ctry) 1401 W 8th Ave	Vancouver	BC	V6H1C9	604-731-7772	731-0493
CJVB-AM 1470 kHz (Misc) 525 W Broadway *Web:* www.am1470.com	Vancouver	BC	V5Z4K5	604-708-1234	708 1201
CKBD-AM 600 kHz (Nost) 1401 W 8th Ave.	Vancouver	BC	V6H1C9	604-731-6111	731-0493
CKKS-FM 96.9 MHz (AC) 2440 Ash St. *Web:* www.97kissfm.com	Vancouver	BC	V5Z4J6	604-872-2557	873-0877
CKLG-AM 730 kHz (AC) 1006 Richards St	Vancouver	BC	V6B1S8	604-681-7511	681-9134
CKNW-AM 98.0 kHz (N/T) 700 W Georgia St Suite 2000 *Web:* www.cknw.com	Vancouver	BC	V7Y1K9	604-331-2712	331-2787
CKST-AM 1040 kHz (AC) 856 Homer St Suite 100 *Web:* www.am1040.com	Vancouver	BC	V6B2W5	604-669-1040	684-6949
CKWX-AM 1130 kHz (N/T) 2440 Ash St. *Web:* www.news1130.com	Vancouver	BC	V5Z4J6	604-873-2599	873-0877
CKZZ-FM 95.3 MHz (CHR) 11151 Horseshoe Way Suite 20 *Web:* www.z95.com	Richmond	BC	V7A4S5	604-241-0953	272-9329
QMFM-FM 103.5 MHz (AC) 380 W 2nd Ave Suite 300 *Web:* www.qmfm.com	Vancouver	BC	V5Y1C8	604-871-9000	871-2901

— Colleges/Universities —

	City			Phone	Fax
British Columbia Institute of Technology 555 Seymour St *Web:* www.bcit.bc.ca	Vancouver	BC	V6B3H6	604-412-7777	687-2488
Canadian International College 2420 Dollarton Hwy.	North Vancouver	BC	V7H2Y1	604-929-1544	929-2074
Carr Emily Institute of Art & Design 1399 Johnston St *Web:* www.eciad.bc.ca ■ *E-mail:* crimmer@eciad.bc.ca	Vancouver	BC	V6H3R9	604-844-3809	844-3801
Robson College 541 Seymour St *Web:* www.robsoncollege.com ■ *E-mail:* info@robsoncollege.com	Vancouver	BC	V6B3H6	604-687-3259	687-3295
United Pacific College 2236 W 12th Ave. *Web:* www.pacific-college.net ■ *E-mail:* admissions@pacific-college.net	Vancouver	BC	V6K2N7	604-736-2378	736-2378
University of British Columbia 2329 W Mall St *Web:* www.ubc.ca	Vancouver	BC	V6T1Z4	604-822-2211	822-3599
Vancouver Community College 250 West Pender St *Web:* www.vcc.bc.ca ■ *E-mail:* knowhow@vcc.bc.ca	Vancouver	BC	V6B1S9	604-443-8300	443-8588
Winfield College 788 Beatty St. *Web:* www.winfieldcollege.com	Vancouver	BC	V6B2M1	604-608-0538	608-0539

— Hospitals —

	City			Phone	Fax
British Columbia Children's Hospital 4480 Oak St. *Web:* www.cw.bc.ca/childrens/bcch.ihtml	Vancouver	BC	V6H3V4	604-875-2345	875-3582
British Columbia's Women's Hospital & Health Centre 4500 Oak St *Web:* www.cw.bc.ca/womens	Vancouver	BC	V6H3N1	604-875-2424	875-3582
Holy Family Hospital 7801 Argyle St.	Vancouver	BC	V5P3L6	604-321-2661	321-2696
Lions Gate Hospital 231 E 15th St	North Vancouver	BC	V7L2L7	604-988-3131	984-5731
Mount St Joseph Hospital 3080 Prince Edward St	Vancouver	BC	V5T3N4	604-874-1141	875-8733
Normandy Hospital 4505 Valley Dr	Vancouver	BC	V6L2L1	604-261-4292	261-7849
Saint Paul's Hospital 1081 Burrard St.	Vancouver	BC	V6Z1Y6	604-682-2344	631-5811
Saint Vincent's Hospital 749 33rd Ave W	Vancouver	BC	V5Z2K4	604-876-7171	876-6729
Vancouver Hospital & Health Sciences Centre 855 12th Ave *Web:* www.vanhosp.bc.ca	Vancouver	BC	V5Z1M9	604-875-4111	875-5701
Vancouver Mediclinic 1055 Dunsmuir	Vancouver	BC	V7X1L4	604-683-8138	683-8128

— Attractions —

	City			Phone	Fax
Arctic Art Museum 401-1859 Spyglass Pl	Vancouver	BC	V5Z4K6	604-876-1033	876-1038
Arts Club Theatre 1585 Johnston St Granville Island	Vancouver	BC	V6H3R9	604-687-5315	687-3306
Ballet British Columbia 1101 W Broadway *Web:* www.discovervancouver.com/balletbc/	Vancouver	BC	V6H1G2	604-732-5003	732-4417
Bloedel Floral Conservatory 33rd Ave & Cambie St Queen Elizabeth Pk *Web:* www.city.vancouver.bc.ca/parks/	Vancouver	BC	V6G1Z4	604-257-8584	257-2412
British Columbia Museum of Mining Hwy 99	Britannia Beach	BC	V0N1J0	604-896-2233	896-2260
British Columbia Sugar Museum 123 Rogers St	Vancouver	BC	V6A3N2	604-253-1131	253-2517
Burnaby Heritage Village Carousel & Museum 6501 Deer Lake Ave *Web:* www.burnabyparksrec.org ■ *E-mail:* mail@burnabyparksrec.org	Burnaby	BC	V5G3T6	604-293-6500	293-6525
Butchart Gardens 800 Benvenuto Ave *Web:* www.butchartgardens.bc.ca/butchart/ ■ *E-mail:* email@butchartgardens.bc.ca	Brentwood Bay	BC	V8M1J8	250-652-4422	652-3883
Canadian Craft Museum 639 Hornby St	Vancouver	BC	V6C2G3	604-687-8266	684-7174
Canadian Venture Exchange 609 Granville St *Web:* www.cdnx.ca ■ *E-mail:* information@cdnx.ca	Vancouver	BC	V7Y1H1	604-689-3334	602-6901
Capilano Fish Hatchery 4500 Capilano Park Rd	Vancouver	BC	V7R4L3	604-666-1790	666-1949
Capilano Suspension Bridge 3735 Capilano Rd *Web:* www.capbridge.com ■ *E-mail:* capilano@istar.ca	North Vancouver	BC	V7R4J1	604-985-7474	985-7479
Chan Centre for the Performing Arts 6265 Crescent Rd *Web:* www.chancentre.com	Vancouver	BC	V7T1Z1	604-822-2697	822-1606
City of Vancouver Archives 1150 Chestnut St	Vancouver	BC	V6J3J9	604-736-8561	736-0626
CN IMAX Theatre at Canada Place 999 Canada Pl Suite 201 *TF:* 800-582-4629 ■ *Web:* www.imax.com/theatres/vancouver_cn.html	Vancouver	BC	V6C3C1	604-682-2384	682-5955
Coastal Jazz & Blues Society 316 W 6th Ave *Web:* www.jazzvancouver.com ■ *E-mail:* cjbs@istar.ca	Vancouver	BC	V5Y1K9	604-872-5200	872-5250
DanceArts Vancouver 873 Beatty St *Web:* www.mcsquared.com/DanceArts/	Vancouver	BC	V6B2M6	604-606-6425	606-6432
Dr Sun Yat-Sen Classical Chinese Garden 578 Carrall St. *Web:* www.discovervancouver.com/sun ■ *E-mail:* sunyatsen@bc.sympatico.ca	Vancouver	BC	V6B5K2	604-662-3207	682-4008
Firehall Arts Centre 280 E Cordova St. *Web:* www.mcsquared.com/Firehall/	Vancouver	BC	V6A1L3	604-689-0926	684-5841
Ford Centre for the Performing Arts 777 Homer St.	Vancouver	BC	V6B2W1	604-602-0616	602-0617
Forest Alliance of British Columbia 1055 Dunsmuir St. *Web:* www.forest.org	Vancouver	BC	V7X1L3	604-685-7507	685-5373
Fort Langley National Historic Site 23433 Mavis Ave *Web:* www.harbour.com/parkscan/fl ■ *E-mail:* fort_langley@pch.gc.ca	Fort Langley	BC	V1M2R5	604-513-4777	513-4788
Granville Island Brewing Co 1441 Cartwright St Granville Island	Vancouver	BC	V6H3R7	604-687-2739	685-0504
Granville Island Sport Fishing Museum 1502 Duranleau St *Web:* www.sportfishingmuseum.bc.ca	Vancouver	BC	V6H3S4	604-683-1939	687-1491

Vancouver — Attractions (Cont'd)

Phone | Fax

Great Canadian Casino Co
709 W Broadway Holiday Inn . . . Vancouver BC V5Z1J5 604-303-1000
Greater Vancouver Zoological Centre
5048 264th St . . . Aldergrove BC V4W1N7 604-856-6825 587-9008
Web: www.bc-biz.com/vancouverzoo/
Grouse Mountain Ski Resort
6400 Nancy Green Way . . . North Vancouver BC V7R4K9 604-984-0661 984-7234
Web: www.grousemtn.com ■ *E-mail:* info@grousemtn.com
Gulf of Georgia Cannery National Historic Site 12138 4th Ave . . . Richmond BC V7E3J1 604-664-9009 664-9008
Web: www.fas.sfu.ca/parkscan/ggc ■ *E-mail:* interp-gognhs@pch.gc.ca
Harbour Cruises 1 Denman St . . . Vancouver BC V6G2W9 604-688-7246 687-5868
Web: www.boatcruises.com ■ *E-mail:* gscott@boatcruises.com
Hoarse Raven Theatre 1160 Rossland St. . . . Vancouver BC V5K4A1 604-258-4079 253-4690
International Buddhist Society
9160 Steveston Hwy . . . Richmond BC V7A1M5 604-274-2822 271-2338
Lookout at Harbour Centre Tower
555 W Hastings St Harbour Ctr . . . Vancouver BC V6B4N4 604-689-0421 689-5447
Web: www.harbour-centre-tower.com
■ *E-mail:* heatherv@lookout.bc.ca
Lynn Canyon Ecology Centre
3663 Park Rd . . . North Vancouver BC V7J3G3 604-981-3103 981-3154
Maplewood Farm
405 Seymour River Pl . . . North Vancouver BC V7H1S6 604-929-5610 929-9341
Web: www.maplewoodfarm.bc.ca
■ *E-mail:* johnstoa@district.north-van.bc.ca
Nitobe Memorial Garden
6804 SW Marine Dr University of British Columbia . . . Vancouver BC V6T1Z4 604-822-6038 822-2016
Web: www.hedgerows.com
Pacific Space Centre 1100 Chestnut St . . . Vancouver BC V6J3J9 604-738-7827 736-5665
Web: www.pacific-space-centre.bc.ca
■ *E-mail:* dcharlto@pacific-space-centre.bc.ca
Park & Tilford Gardens
333 Brooksbank Ave . . . North Vancouver BC V7J3S8 604-984-8200 984-6099
Web: www.northshore-online.com/park_tilford
Port of Vancouver 200 Granville St . . . Vancouver BC V6C2P9 604-665-9000 666-8916
Web: www.portvancouver.com
Queen Elizabeth Park
33rd Ave & Cambie Rd . . . Vancouver BC V6G1Z4 604-257-8400
Roedde House Museum 1415 Barclay St . . . Vancouver BC V6G1J6 604-684-7040
Web: www.englishbay.com/eb/walk1.htm
Royal British Columbia Museum
675 Belleville St . . . Victoria BC V8V1X4 250-387-3701 356-8197
Science World British Columbia
1455 Quebec St . . . Vancouver BC V6A3Z7 604-443-7440 682-2923
Web: www.scienceworld.bc.ca ■ *E-mail:* glunde@scienceworld.bc.ca
Stanley Park 2099 Beach Ave . . . Vancouver BC V6G1Z4 604-257-8400 257-8427
Stanley Park Horse Drawn Tours
Park Dr Stanley Pk . . . Vancouver BC V6C2T1 604-681-5115 681-5116
Web: www.stanleyparktours.com ■ *E-mail:* tours@stanleypark.com
University of British Columbia Botanical Garden 6804 SW Marine Dr . . . Vancouver BC V6T1Z4 604-822-9666 822-2016
Web: www.hedgerows.com/UBCBotGdn/index.htm
University of British Columbia Museum of Anthropology 6393 NW Marine Dr . . . Vancouver BC V6T1Z2 604-822-3825 822-2974
Web: www.moa.ubc.ca
Vancouver Aquarium PO Box 3232 . . . Vancouver BC V6B3X8 604-685-3364 659-3515
Web: www.vanaqua.org ■ *E-mail:* information@vanaqua.org
Vancouver Art Gallery 750 Hornby St . . . Vancouver BC V6Z2H7 604-662-4700 682-7846
Web: www.vanartgallery.bc.ca ■ *E-mail:* media@vanartgallery.bc.ca
Vancouver Cantata Singers
5115 Keith Rd . . . West Vancouver BC V7W2M9 604-921-8588 921-7194
Web: www.cantata.org
Vancouver Chamber Choir
1254 W 7th Ave . . . Vancouver BC V6H1B6 604-738-6822 738-7832
Vancouver Civic Theatres 649 Cambie St . . . Vancouver BC V6B2P1 604-665-3050 665-3001
Web: www.city.vancouver.bc.ca/theatres/frame_menu.html
Vancouver Cultural Alliance
938 Howe St Suite 100 . . . Vancouver BC V6Z1N9 604-681-3535 681-7848
Web: www.culturenet.ca/vca/ ■ *E-mail:* arts_yvr@cyberstore.net
Vancouver Maritime Museum
1905 Ogden Ave . . . Vancouver BC V6J1A3 604-257-8300 737-2621
Web: www.vmm.bc.ca ■ *E-mail:* jimvmm@aol.com
Vancouver Museum
1100 Chestnut St Vanier Pk . . . Vancouver BC V6J3J9 604-736-4431 736-5417
Web: www.vanmuseum.bc.ca
Vancouver Opera 845 Cambie St . . . Vancouver BC V6B4Z9 604-683-0222 682-3981
Web: www.vanopera.bc.ca ■ *E-mail:* info@vanopera.bc.ca
Vancouver Playhouse Theatre
Hamilton & Dunsmuir Sts . . . Vancouver BC V5Y1A4 604-872-6622 873-3714
Web: www.vancouverplayhouse.com

Phone | Fax

Vancouver Police Centennial Museum
240 East Cordova St . . . Vancouver BC V6A1L3 604-665-3346 665-3585
Web: www.city.vancouver.bc.ca/police/museum/
Vancouver Recital Society
873 Beatty St Suite 304 . . . Vancouver BC V6B2M6 604-602-0363 602-0364
Web: www.interchg.ubc.ca/vrs ■ *E-mail:* vrs@unixg.ubc.ca
Vancouver Symphony Orchestra
601 Smithe St . . . Vancouver BC V6B5G1 604-684-9100 684-9264
Web: www.culturenet.ca/vso/ ■ *E-mail:* reachus@vansymphony.ca
Vancouver Trolley Company
875 Terminal Ave . . . Vancouver BC V6A2M9 604-801-5515 801-5557
Web: www.vancouvertrolley.com ■ *E-mail:* jim@vancouvertrolley.com
VanDusen Botanical Gardens 5251 Oak St . . . Vancouver BC V6M4H1 604-878-9274 266-4236
Walkabout Historic Vancouver
6038 Imperial St . . . Vancouver BC V5J5A5 604-439-0448 439-0448
Whistler Blackcomb Mountain Ski Resort
4545 Blackcomb Way . . . Whistler BC V0N1B4 604-932-3434 938-9174
Web: www.whistler-blackcomb.com

SPORTS TEAMS & FACILITIES

Phone | Fax

Abbotsford 86ers
32470 Haida Dr Rotary Stadium . . . Abbotsford BC VT34C8 604-852-1529 852-7223
British Columbia Lions 10605 135th St . . . Surrey BC V3T4C8 604-930-5466 583-7882
Web: www.bclions.com ■ *E-mail:* glenringdal@bc.sympatico.ca
British Columbia Place Stadium
777 Pacific Blvd . . . Vancouver BC V6B4Y8 604-669-2300 661-3412
Web: www.bcplacestadium.com
Hastings Park Racecourse
Hastings & Renfrew Sts PNE Grounds . . . Vancouver BC V5K3N8 604-254-1631 251-0411
Web: www.hastingspark.com
Vancouver 86ers (soccer)
Boundary St & Kingsway Swangard Stadium . . . Burnaby BC V3T4C8 604-930-2255 583-7882
Web: www.86ers.com ■ *E-mail:* info@86ers.com
Vancouver Canadians (baseball)
4601 Ontario St . . . Vancouver BC V5V3H4 604-872-5232 872-1714
Web: www.minorleaguebaseball.com/teams/pcl-van.php3
Vancouver Canucks
800 Griffiths Way Orca Bay Sports & Entertainment Arena . . . Vancouver BC V6B6G1 604-899-4600 899-4640
Web: www.orcabay.com/canucks ■ *E-mail:* canucks@orcabay.com
Vancouver Grizzlies
800 Griffiths Way Orca Bay Sports & Entertainment Arena . . . Vancouver BC V6B6G1 604-899-4666 899-7401
Web: www.nba.com/grizzlies

— Events —

	Phone
Abbotsford International Air Show (early August)	604-852-8511
Air Canada Championship (late August)	604-899-4641
Bard on the Beach Shakespeare Festival (mid-June-early September)	604-737-0625
BC Home Show (mid-October)	604-433-5121
Benson & Hedges Symphony of Fire (late July-early August)	604-738-4304
Best of the West Antique Expo (early July)	604-857-1263
Canada Day Celebrations (July 1)	604-666-8477
Canadian International Dragon Boat Festival (mid-June)	604-688-2382
Celebration of Lights (early-late December)	604-666-8477
Chinese New Year (late January-mid-February)	604-662-3207
Christmas at Hycroft House (mid-November)	604-731-4661
Christmas Carolship Parade (December)	604-878-9988
Dancing on the Edge (early-mid-July)	604-689-0691
DuMaurier International Jazz Festival (late June)	604-872-5200
Enchanted Evenings Musical Performances (mid-June-August)	604-662-3207
Hycroft House & Garden Fair (early May)	604-731-4661
Mid-Autumn Moon Festival (mid-September)	604-662-3207
Molson Indy Vancouver (early September)	604-684-4639
Music West Festival (mid-May)	604-683-2000
Pacific National Exhibition (late August-early September)	604-253-2311
Vancouver Chamber Music Festival (early August)	604-602-0363
Vancouver Folk Music Festival (mid-July)	604-681-0041
Vancouver Fringe Festival (early September)	604-257-0350
Vancouver International Comedy Festival (late July-early August)	604-683-0883
Vancouver International Marathon (early May)	604-872-2928
Vancouver International Writers Festival (late October)	604-681-6330
Vancouver Playhouse International Wine Festival (late March-early April)	604-872-6622
Vancouver Ski & Snowboard Show (late October)	604-878-0557
Vancouver Waterfront Antique Show (late October)	800-667-0619
Vandusen Flower & Garden Show (early June)	604-878-9274

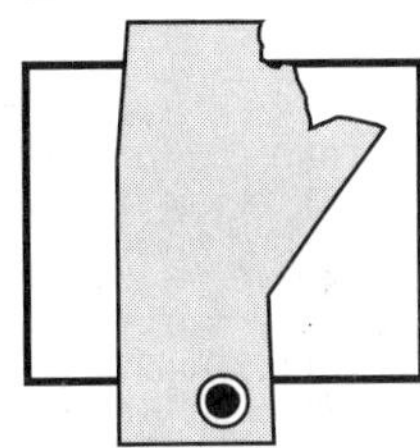

Winnipeg

Winnipeg, the capital of Manitoba, is strategically located at the forks of the Red and Assiniboine rivers and on Trans Canada Highway One. Because of its position on busy water and land routes Winnipeg has the largest number of transport terminals in Western Canada. Attractions in the city include the Winnipeg Commodity Exchange, Canada's only agricultural futures and options exchange, and the Winnipeg Art Gallery, which contains an extensive collection of Manitoban and Canadian art, including the largest collection of Inuit art in the world. The Manitoba Theatre Centre is Canada's oldest regional English-speaking professional theatre, and the Royal Winnipeg Ballet is the country's oldest professional ballet company.

Population 618,477
Area (Land) . . . . . . 179.2 sq mi
Elevation . . . . . . 762 ft
Latitude . . . . . . 49-54-00 N
Longitude . . . . . . 97-07-48 W
Time Zone . . . . . . CST
Area Code/s 204

— Average Temperatures and Precipitation —

TEMPERATURES

	Jan	Feb	Mar	Apr	May	Jun	Jul	Aug	Sep	Oct	Nov	Dec
High	7	14	27	48	64	73	79	77	64	54	30	16
Low	-11	-6	7	28	41	52	55	54	43	34	16	-2

PRECIPITATION

	Jan	Feb	Mar	Apr	May	Jun	Jul	Aug	Sep	Oct	Nov	Dec
Inches	0.0	0.0	0.1	1.1	2.5	3.2	3.0	3.0	2.1	1.0	0.2	0.0

— Important Phone Numbers —

	Phone
American Express Travel	204-956-0395
Canadian Automobile Assn.	204-987-6161
Dental Referral	204-988-5300
Emergency	911
Medical Referral	204-986-3413
Poison Control Center	204-787-2444
Weather	204-983-2050

— Information Sources —

		Phone	Fax
Better Business Bureau Serving Winnipeg & Manitoba 205-309 Hargrave St. *TF:* 800-385-3074 ■ *Web:* www.manitoba.bbb.org	Winnipeg MB R3B2J8	204-989-9010	989-9016
Economic Development Winnipeg 1100-200 Graham Ave. *Web:* www.winnipeg2000.com	Winnipeg MB R3C4L5	204-944-2000	956-2615
Spring Garden Road Memorial Public Library 5381 Spring Garden Rd *Web:* www.chebucto.ns.ca/Libraries/HCRL/hr-sgr.html	Halifax NS B3J1E9	902-490-5710	
Tourism Winnipeg 279 Portage Ave *TF:* 800-665-0204 ■ *Web:* www.tourism.winnipeg.mb.ca ■ *E-mail:* wpginfo@tourism.winnipeg.mb.ca	Winnipeg MB R3B2B4	204-943-1970	942-4043
Winnipeg Chamber of Commerce 167 Lombard St Suite 500 *Web:* www.winnipeg-chamber.com ■ *E-mail:* info@winnipeg-chamber.com	Winnipeg MB R3B3E5	204-944-8484	944-8492
Winnipeg City Hall 510 Main St *Web:* www.city.winnipeg.mb.ca	Winnipeg MB R3B1B9	204-986-2171	
Winnipeg Convention Centre 375 York Ave *Web:* www.wpgconvctr.mb.ca	Winnipeg MB R3C3J3	204-956-1720	943-0310
Winnipeg Mayor 510 Main St Council Bldg 2nd Fl	Winnipeg MB R3B1B9	204-986-2196	949-0566
Winnipeg Public Library 251 Donald St. *Web:* wpl.city.winnipeg.mb.ca ■ *E-mail:* wpl-info@city.winnipeg.mb.ca	Winnipeg MB R3C3P5	204-986-6462	942-5671

On-Line Resources

About.com Guide to Winnipeg . . . . . . winnipeg.about.com/local/winnipeg
City Knowledge Winnipeg . . . . . . www.cityknowledge.com/canada_mb_winnipeg.htm
Explore Manitoba . . . . . . www.travelmanitoba.com
HotelGuide Winnipeg . . . . . . hotelguide.net/winnipeg/
Manitoba Internet Resource Listings . . . . . . www.alice.mb.ca
Rough Guide Travel Winnipeg travel.roughguides.com/content/5265/index.htm
Winnipeg Connection . . . . . . www.crosscanada.com/wpg

— Transportation Services —

AIRPORTS

■ **Winnipeg International Airport (YWG)**

	Phone
4 miles W of downtown (approx 15 minutes) Web: www.waa.ca	204-987-9400

Airport Transportation

	Phone
Luxury Plus Limousine $30 fare to downtown	204-222-2050
Unicity Taxi $10 fare to downtown	204-925-3131

Commercial Airlines

	Phone
Air Canada	800-776-3000
Air Ontario	800-776-3000
American	800-433-7300
Athabaska Airways	800-667-9356
Bearskin Airlines	800-465-2327
British Airways	800-247-9297
Calm Air	204-956-6196
Canada 3000	877-359-2263
Canadian Air	800-426-7000
First Air	800-267-1247
Ministic Air Ltd	204-783-2733
Northwest	800-225-2525
Perimeter Avation Ltd	204-786-7031
Royal Airlines	800-667-7692
United	800-241-6522
WestJet	800-538-5696

Charter Airlines

	Phone
Bearskin Airlines	800-465-2327
Calm Air	204-956-6196
Ministic Air Ltd	204-783-2733
Perimeter Avation Ltd	204-786-7031

CAR RENTALS

	Phone
Avis	204-956-2847
Budget	204-989-8510
Discount	204-775-2282
Hertz	204-925-6625
National	204-925-3529
Rent-A-Wreck	204-779-0777
Thrifty	204-949-7600

LIMO/TAXI

	Phone
Blueline Premium Taxi	204-774-6047
Duffy's Taxi	204-775-0101
Leisure Limousine	204-256-3856
London Limousine	204-488-9590
Luxury Plus Limousine	204-222-2050
Spring Taxi	204-774-8294
Unicity Taxi	204-925-3131

MASS TRANSIT

	Phone
Downtown Flyer $.25 base fare	204-986-5700
Winnipeg Transit $1.55 Base fare	204-986-5700

RAIL/BUS

		Phone
Greyhound Canada Bus Station 487 Portage Ave *TF:* 800-661-8747	Winnipeg MB R3B2V3	204-783-8857
VIA Rail Canada 123 Main St *TF:* 800-561-8360	Winnipeg MB R3C1A3	800-561-3949

Winnipeg (Cont'd)

— Accommodations —

HOTELS, MOTELS, RESORTS

			Phone	Fax
Airport Hotel 1800 Ellice Ave	Winnipeg	MB R3H0B7	204-783-7035	786-1908
TF: 888-247-7008				
Assiniboine Gordon Inn on the Park 1975 Portage Ave	Winnipeg	MB R3J0J9	204-888-4806	897-9870
Balmoral Motor Hotel 621 Balmoral St	Winnipeg	MB R3B2R4	204-943-1544	943-9571
Best Western Carlton Inn 220 Carlton St	Winnipeg	MB R3C1P5	204-942-0881	943-9312
TF: 800-528-1234				
Cambridge Hotel 1022 Pembina Hwy	Winnipeg	MB R3T1Z7	204-284-0183	475-5176
Canad Inn Garden City 2100 McPhillips St.	Winnipeg	MB R2V3T9	204-633-0024	697-3377
TF: 888-332-2623				
Canadiana Motor Hotel 1400 Notre Dame Ave	Winnipeg	MB R3E3G5	204-786-3471	786-1908
TF: 888-702-2200				
Capri Motel 1819 Pembina Hwy	Winnipeg	MB R3T2G6	204-269-6990	261-0068
TF: 800-268-6990				
Chalet Hotel 611 Archibald St	Winnipeg	MB R2J0X8	204-237-8901	231-2950
Charter House Hotel 330 York Ave	Winnipeg	MB R3C0N9	204-942-0101	956-0665
TF: 800-782-0175				
Comfort Inn 1770 Sargent Ave	Winnipeg	MB R3H0C8	204-783-5627	783-5661
TF: 800-228-5150				
Comfort Inn 3109 Pembina Hwy	Winnipeg	MB R3T4R6	204-269-7390	261-7565
TF: 800-228-5150				
Country Inn & Suites 730 King Edward St	Winnipeg	MB R3H1B4	204-783-6900	775-7197
TF: 800-456-4000				
Crowne Plaza Downtown 350 St Mary Ave.	Winnipeg	MB R3C3J2	204-942-0551	943-8702
Web: www.crowneplaza.mb.ca				
Days Inn 550 McPhillips St	Winnipeg	MB R2X2H2	204-586-8525	582-5035
TF: 800-655-9306				
Downs Motor Inn 3740 Portage Ave	Winnipeg	MB R3K0Z9	204-837-5831	831-6137
TF: 888-866-5831				
Fort Garry Hotel 222 Broadway	Winnipeg	MB R3C0R3	204-942-8251	956-2351
TF: 800-665-8088 ■ *Web:* www.fortgarryhotel.com				
Fort Garry Place 85 Garry St	Winnipeg	MB R3C4J5	204-949-1010	943-2791
Holiday Inn Airport West 2520 Portage Ave.	Winnipeg	MB R3J3T6	204-885-4478	831-5734
TF: 800-665-0352				
Holiday Inn Fort Richmond 2935 Pembina Hwy	Winnipeg	MB R3T2H5	204-275-7711	269-0364
TF: 800-465-4329				
Holiday Inn South 1330 Pembina Hwy.	Winnipeg	MB R3T2B4	204-452-4747	284-2751
TF: 800-465-4329				
Howard Johnson Winnipeg 1740 Ellice Ave	Winnipeg	MB R3H0B3	204-775-7131	788-4685
TF: 800-665-8813				
International Inn 1808 Wellington Ave.	Winnipeg	MB R3H0G3	204-786-4801	786-1329
TF: 800-528-1234				
Lombard The 2 Lombard Pl	Winnipeg	MB R3B0Y3	204-957-1350	956-1791
TF: 800-441-1414				
McLaren Hotel 554 Main St	Winnipeg	MB R3B1C4	204-943-8518	943-0745
Niakwa Inn 20 Alpine Ave	Winnipeg	MB R2M0Y5	204-255-6000	253-1563
TF: 877-991-4440				
Norwood Hotel 112 Marion St	Winnipeg	MB R2H0T1	204-233-4475	231-1910
TF: 888-888-1878				
Place Louis Riel All-Suite Hotel 190 Smith St	Winnipeg	MB R3C1J8	204-947-6961	947-3029
TF: 800-665-0569 ■ *Web:* www.placelouisriel.com				
Polo Park Inn 1405 St Matthews Ave	Winnipeg	MB R3G0K5	204-775-8791	783-4039
TF: 800-665-0033				
Quality Inn 635 Pembina Hwy	Winnipeg	MB R3M2L4	204-453-8247	287-2365
TF: 800-228-5151				
Quest Inn 367 Ellice Ave	Winnipeg	MB R3B1Y1	204-956-0100	943-1375
TF: 800-565-4254				
Radisson Downtown 288 Portage Ave	Winnipeg	MB R3C0B8	204-956-0410	947-1129
TF: 800-333-3333				
Radisson Suite Hotel 1800 Wellington Ave	Winnipeg	MB R3H1B2	204-783-1700	786-6588
TF: 800-333-3333				
Ramada Marlborough Hotel 331 Smith St	Winnipeg	MB R3B2G9	204-942-6411	942-2017
TF: 800-667-7666				
Saint Charles Hotel 235 Notre Dame Ave	Winnipeg	MB R3B1N8	204-942-5155	
Saint Regis Hotel 285 Smith St	Winnipeg	MB R3C1K9	204-942-0171	943-3077
TF: 800-663-7344				
Sheraton Winnipeg 161 Donald St	Winnipeg	MB R3C1M3	204-942-5300	943-7975
TF: 800-325-3535				
Super 8 Motel 1485 Niakwa Rd E	Winnipeg	MB R2J3T3	204-253-1935	254-7019
TF: 800-800-8000				
Travelodge Downtown 360 Colony St	Winnipeg	MB R3B2P3	204-786-7011	772-1443
TF: 800-578-7878				
Viscount Gort Hotel 1670 Portage Ave.	Winnipeg	MB R3J0C9	204-775-0451	772-2161
TF: 800-665-1122 ■ *Web:* www.viscount-gort.com				

— Restaurants —

			Phone
Amici (Italian) 326 Broadway	Winnipeg	MB R3C0S5	204-943-4997
Aristocrat (Filipino) 99 Isabel St	Winnipeg	MB R3E1E8	204-942-8282
Bailey's (Continental) 185 Lombard Ave.	Winnipeg	MB R3B0W4	204-944-1180
Bangkok Thai (Thai) 100 Osborne St	Winnipeg	MB R3L1Y5	204-474-0908
Bistro Bohemia (European) 159 Osborne St	Winnipeg	MB R3L1Y7	204-453-1944
Bombolini (Italian) 326 Broadway	Winnipeg	MB R3C0S5	204-943-5066
Cafe Carlo (California) 243 Lilac St	Winnipeg	MB R3M2S2	204-477-5544
Carlos & Murphy's (Mexican) 129 Osborne St.	Winnipeg	MB R3L1Y4	204-284-3510
Chianti's Fine Dining (European) 1127 St Mary's Rd	Winnipeg	MB R2M3T7	204-257-0630
Deen's (Caribbean) 205 Marion St	Winnipeg	MB R2H0T5	204-233-2208
Delicious Vegetarian (Vegetarian) 1467 Pembina Hwy.	Winnipeg	MB R3T2C5	204-477-1530
Dionysos Restaurant (Greek) 1185 Nairn Ave	Winnipeg	MB R2L0Y6	204-667-3110
East India Company (Indian) 349 York Ave	Winnipeg	MB R3C3S9	204-947-3097
Edohei (Japanese) 335 Ellice Ave Suite A	Winnipeg	MB R3B1X8	204-943-0427
Web: www.edohei.mb.ca			
Fat Angel (International) 220 Main St	Winnipeg	MB R3V1A8	204-944-0396
Fusion Grill (North American) 550 Academy Rd	Winnipeg	MB R3N0E3	204-489-6963
Web: www.fusiongrill.mb.ca			
Gasthaus Gutenberger (German) 2583 Portage Ave	Winnipeg	MB R2Y0V3	204-888-3133
Good Earth Chop Suey House (Chinese) 1849 Portage Ave	Winnipeg	MB R2J0G8	204-889-8880
Green Gates (North American) 6945 Roblin Blvd	Winnipeg	MB R4H1A2	204-897-0990
Hunt Room (Steak) 1740 Ellice Ave	Winnipeg	MB R3H0B3	204-775-7131
Hy's Steak Loft (Steak) 216 Kennedy St	Winnipeg	MB R3C1C1	204-942-1000
Kim's Restaurant (Korean) 2655 Portage Ave	Winnipeg	MB R3J0P9	204-888-0028
King's Head Pub (English) 120 King St	Winnipeg	MB R3B1H9	204-957-7710
La Vieille Gare (French) 630 Des Meurons St	Winnipeg	MB R2H2P9	204-237-5015
Le Beaujolais (French) 131 Provencher Blvd	Winnipeg	MB R2H0G2	204-237-6306
Masa Japanese Restaurant (Japanese) 2077 Pembina Hwy Suite 10	Winnipeg	MB R3T5J9	204-261-3131
Miriwa (Chinese) 1572 St Mary's Rd	Winnipeg	MB R2M3W4	204-257-1650
Old Swiss Inn Restaurant & Lounge (Swiss) 207 Edmonton St	Winnipeg	MB R3C1R4	204-942-7725
Orlando's Seafood Grill (Seafood) 709 Corydon Ave	Winnipeg	MB R3M0W4	204-477-5899
Pasta La Vista (Italian) Hargrave & Saint Mary Sts Eaton Pl	Winnipeg	MB R3C4A5	204-956-2229
Pembina Village Restaurant (Greek) 333 Pembina Hwy	Winnipeg	MB R3L2V4	204-477-5439
Pepper's (North American) 1895 Grant Ave.	Winnipeg	MB R3N1Z2	204-489-1057
Perry's Restaurant & Bar (North American) 1140 Pembina Hwy.	Winnipeg	MB R3T2A2	204-475-0300
Picasso's (Seafood) 615 Sargent Ave	Winnipeg	MB R3E0A2	204-775-2469
Pockets Bar & Grill (California) 171 McDermot Ave.	Winnipeg	MB R3B0S1	204-957-7665
Polonez (International) 393 Marion St	Winnipeg	MB R2H0V4	204-231-4520
Prairie Plates (North American) 161 Donald St	Winnipeg	MB R3C1M3	204-942-5300
Red Lantern Restaurant (French) 302 Hamel Ave	Winnipeg	MB R2H0K9	204-233-4841
Restaurant Dubrovnik (Continental) 390 Assiniboine Ave	Winnipeg	MB R3C0Y1	204-944-0594
Rib Room (North American) 330 York Ave	Winnipeg	MB R3C0N9	204-942-0101
Royal Crown (Continental) 83 Garry St 30th Fl	Winnipeg	MB R3C4J9	204-947-1990
Saffron's (Mediterranean) 681 Corydon Ave	Winnipeg	MB R3M0W4	204-284-2602
Sofia's Cafe (Italian) 635 Corydon Ave	Winnipeg	MB R3M0W3	204-452-3037
South Asia (Vietnamese) 1480 Pembina Hwy	Winnipeg	MB R3T2C3	204-284-8507
Southfork (North American) 1330 Pembina Hwy	Winnipeg	MB R3T2B4	204-452-4747
Sweet Palace (Pakistani) 1425 Pembina Hwy	Winnipeg	MB R3T2C4	204-475-7867
Tap & Grill (Mediterranean) 137 Osborne St	Winnipeg	MB R3L1W4	204-284-7455
Tiffani's (Continental) 133 Niakwa Rd 17th Fl	Winnipeg	MB R3M5J5	204-256-7324
Toad in the Hole (English) 112 Osborne St	Winnipeg	MB R3L1Y5	204-284-7201
Tre Visi (Italian) 173 McDermot Ave	Winnipeg	MB R3B0S1	204-949-9032
Victor's (Continental) 331 Smith St	Winnipeg	MB R3B2G9	204-942-6411
Vivere Restaurant (Mediterranean) 433 River Ave Suite 3	Winnipeg	MB R3L2V1	204-949-2485
Wing Wa Garden (Chinese) 1142 Main St.	Winnipeg	MB R2W3S3	204-589-6331
Wolseley Elm (International) 146 Arlington St	Winnipeg	MB R3G1T1	204-788-4466

— Goods and Services —

SHOPPING

			Phone	Fax
Eaton Place 333 St Mary's Ave.	Winnipeg	MB R3C1M8	204-989-1800	
Exchange District betw Galt & Notre Dame Aves	Winnipeg	MB R3B1G4	204-942-6716	943-8741
Web: www.exchangebiz.winnipeg.mb.ca ■ *E-mail:* exchbiz@mts.net				
Forks Market 1 Forks Market Rd.	Winnipeg	MB R3C4L9	204-942-6302	
Web: www.tfnpp.mb.ca/market.html				
Johnston Terminal at the Forks 25 Forks Market Rd.	Winnipeg	MB R3C4S8	204-956-5593	
Portage Place Shopping Centre 393 Portage Ave	Winnipeg	MB R3B3H6	204-925-4630	943-5780
Shops Of Winnipeg Square 360 Main St	Winnipeg	MB R3C3Z3	204-949-7140	942-2213
Unicity Mall 3605 Portage Ave	Winnipeg	MB R3K0X3	204-885-1715	889-0020

Winnipeg (Cont'd)

BANKS

Name / Address	City	Postal	Phone	Fax
Bank of Montreal 355 Main St	Winnipeg	MB R3C2R6	204-985-2611	985-2099
TF: 800-363-9992 ■ *Web:* www.bmo.com				
Canadian Imperial Bank of Commerce 1 Lombard Pl	Winnipeg	MB R3C2P3	204-944-6953	944-5820
TF: 800-465-2422 ■ *Web:* www.cibc.com				
HSBC 240 Graham Ave	Winnipeg	MB R3C0J7	204-956-1632	943-0599
TF: 800-889-4522 ■ *Web:* www.hsbcgroup.com				
National Bank of Canada 191 Lombard Ave.	Winnipeg	MB R3B0X1	204-944-9315	946-1672
Web: www.nbc.ca				
Royal Bank of Canada 220 Portage Ave	Winnipeg	MB R3C3A6	204-988-4000	956-1314
TF: 800-769-2511 ■ *Web:* www.royalbank.com				
Scotiabank 200 Portage Ave Suite 301	Winnipeg	MB R3C3X2	204-985-3011	943-3971
TF: 800-267-1234 ■ *Web:* www.scotiabank.ca				
Toronto-Dominion Bank 201 Portage Ave.	Winnipeg	MB R3C2T2	204-988-2811	943-9350
TF: 800-983-2265 ■ *Web:* www.tdbank.ca				

BUSINESS SERVICES

Name	Phone
Ace Courier Service	204-632-7757
Adecco Staffing Service	204-956-5454
Canada Messenger	204-943-8905
DHL International Express	403-250-1512
Federal Express	800-463-3339
Galaxy Printing	204-254-2937
Kelly Services	204-944-1114
Kwik Kopy Printing	204-772-5945
Mail Boxes Etc	204-261-8155
Manpower Temporary Services	204-949-7800
Olsten Staffing Services	204-949-3030
Todays Staffing	204-956-5600
UPS	800-742-5877

— Media —

PUBLICATIONS

Name / Address	City	Postal	Phone	Fax
Herald The 1465 Saint James St.	Winnipeg	MB R3H0W9	204-949-6100	949-6122
Where Winnipeg Magazine 128 James Ave Suite 300	Winnipeg	MB R3B0N8	204-943-4439	947-5463
Web: www.bestmarketing.com/where/				
Winnipeg Free Press† 1355 Mountain Ave	Winnipeg	MB R2X3B6	204-697-7000	697-7344
Web: www.mbnet.mb.ca/freepress				
Winnipeg Sun† 1700 Church Ave	Winnipeg	MB R2X3A2	204-694-2022	697-0759

†Daily newspapers

TELEVISION

Name / Address	City	Postal	Phone	Fax
CBWF-TV Ch 3 (CBC) 541 Portage Ave	Winnipeg	MB R3C2H1	204-788-3222	788-3255
CBWT-TV Ch 6 (CBC) PO Box 160	Winnipeg	MB R3C2H1	204-788-3222	788-3643
Web: cbc.ca				
CHMI-TV Ch 13 (Ind) 100-167 Lombard Ave	Winnipeg	MB R3B0T6	204-947-9613	956-0811
CKND-TV Ch 9 (GTN) 603 St Mary's Rd.	Winnipeg	MB R2M3L8	204-233-3304	233-5615
CKY-TV Ch 5 (CTV) Polo Pk	Winnipeg	MB R3G0L7	204-788-3300	780-3297
Web: www.cky.com				

RADIO

Name / Address	City	Postal	Phone	Fax
CBW-AM 990 kHz (N/T) 541 Portage Ave.	Winnipeg	MB R3C2H1	204-788-3222	788-3227
CBW-FM 98.3 MHz (Clas) 541 Portage Ave	Winnipeg	MB R3C2H1	204-788-3222	788-3227
CFQX-FM 104.1 MHz (Ctry) 1045 Saint James St.	Winnipeg	MB R3H1B1	204-944-1031	943-7687
CHIQ-FM 94.3 MHz (CHR) 1445 Pembina Hwy.	Winnipeg	MB R3T5C2	204-477-5120	453-8777
Web: www.q94fm.com				
CIFX-AM 1290 kHz (N/T) 1445 Pembina Hwy.	Winnipeg	MB R3T5C2	204-477-5120	453-0815
Web: www.am1290talk.com				
CITI-FM 92.1 MHz (Rock) Polo Pk	Winnipeg	MB R3G0L7	204-788-3400	788-3401
Web: www.92citi.com				
CJKR-FM 97.5 MHz (CR) 930 Portage Ave.	Winnipeg	MB R3G0P8	204-786-6884	783-4512
Web: www.power97.com				
CJOB-AM 680 kHz (N/T) 930 Portage Ave	Winnipeg	MB R3G0P8	204-786-2471	783-4512
CKJS-AM 810 kHz (B/EZ) 520 Corydon Ave	Winnipeg	MB R3L0P1	204-477-1221	453-8244
CKSB-AM 1050 kHz (Misc) 607 Langevin St.	Winnipeg	MB R2H2W2	204-788-3236	788-3245
CKY-AM 580 kHz (AC) 1045 Saint James St.	Winnipeg	MB R3H1B1	204-944-1031	943-7687

— Colleges/Universities —

Name / Address	City	Postal	Phone	Fax
Canadian Mennonite Bible College 600 Shaftesbury Blvd	Winnipeg	MB R3P0M4	204-888-6781	831-5675
Web: www.mbnet.mb.ca/~cmbc/				
Herzing College 723 Portage Ave	Winnipeg	MB R3G0M8	204-775-8175	783-8107
Web: www.herzing.edu/winnipeg/				
Red River College 2055 Notre Dame Ave	Winnipeg	MB R3H0J9	204-632-3960	697-4738
Web: www.rrc.mb.ca				
University of Manitoba 66 Chancellors Cir.	Winnipeg	MB R3T2N2	204-474-8880	474-7554
TF Admissions: 800-224-7713 ■ *Web:* www.umanitoba.ca ■ *E-mail:* www@umanitoba.ca				
University of Winnipeg 515 Portage Ave	Winnipeg	MB R3B2E9	204-786-9159	786-8656
Web: www.uwinnipeg.ca ■ *E-mail:* adm@uwinnipeg.ca				

— Hospitals —

Name / Address	City	Postal	Phone	Fax
Concordia Hospital 1095 Concordia Ave	Winnipeg	MB R2K3S8	204-667-1560	667-1049
Web: www.concordiahospital.mb.ca				
Grace General Hospital 300 Booth Dr.	Winnipeg	MB R3J3M7	204-837-8311	831-0029
Health Sciences Centre 820 Sherbrook St.	Winnipeg	MB R3A1R9	204-774-6511	787-3912
Web: www.hsc.mb.ca				
Misericordia General Hospital 99 Cornish Ave.	Winnipeg	MB R3C1A2	204-788-8364	772-6488
Saint Boniface General Hospital 409 Taché Ave	Winnipeg	MB R2H2A6	204-233-8563	231-0647
Web: www.sbgh.mb.ca				
Seven Oaks General Hospital 2300 McPhillips St	Winnipeg	MB R2V3M3	204-632-7133	694-9469
Victoria General Hospital 2340 Pembina Hwy.	Winnipeg	MB R3T2E8	204-269-3570	261-0223
Web: www.vgh.winnipeg.mb.ca				

— Attractions —

Name / Address	City	Postal	Phone	Fax
Adventure City 230 Osborne St.	Winnipeg	MB R3O1Z5	204-475-2887	477-5743
Air Force Heritage Park & Museum Sharpe Blvd & Neff Ave.	Winnipeg	MB R3J3Y5	204-833-2500	833-2610
Aquatic Hall of Fame & Museum of Canada 25 Poseidon Bay.	Winnipeg	MB R3M3E4	204-986-5890	986-6155
Web: www.mbnet.mb.ca/city/parks/recserv/aquahall/INDEX.HTM				
Artspace 100 Arthur St	Winnipeg	MB R3B1H3	204-947-0984	942-1555
Assiniboine Park Conservatory 2799 Roblin Blvd Assiniboine Pk	Winnipeg	MB R3R0B8	204-986-5537	986-6761
Assiniboine Park Zoo 2355 Corydon Ave Assiniboine Pk.	Winnipeg	MB R3P0R5	204-986-6921	832-5420
Web: www.mbnet.mb.ca/city/parks/envserv/zoo/zoo.html ■ *E-mail:* apzoowpg@escape.ca				
Celebrations Dinner Theatre 1824 Pembina Hwy.	Winnipeg	MB R3T2G2	204-982-8282	786-3315
Centre Cultural Franco-Manitobain 340 Provencher Blvd	Winnipeg	MB R2H0G7	204-233-8972	233-3324
Club Regent Casino 1425 Regent Ave W.	Winnipeg	MB R2C3B2	204-957-2700	957-4952
Dalnavert Museum 61 Carlton St	Winnipeg	MB R3C1N7	204-943-2835	943-2565
Web: www.mhs.mb.ca/museums/dalnavhp.htm ■ *E-mail:* dalnavrt@escape.ca				
Dugald Costume Museum Hwy 15 & Provincial Rd 206	Dugald	MB R0E0K0	204-853-2166	853-2077
Web: www.dugaldcostumemuseum.mb.ca				
Exchange District betw Galt & Notre Dame Aves	Winnipeg	MB R3B1G4	204-942-6716	943-8741
Web: www.exchangebiz.winnipeg.mb.ca ■ *E-mail:* exchbiz@mts.net				
Forks Market 1 Forks Market Rd.	Winnipeg	MB R3C4L9	204-942-6302	
Web: www.tfnpp.mb.ca/market.html				
Forks National Historic Site Forks Market Rd	Winnipeg	MB R3C4L9	204-957-7618	
Web: www.tfnpp.mb.ca/historic.html				
Fort Garry Horse Museum & Archives 551 Machray Ave McGregor Armoury	Winnipeg	MB R2W1A8	204-586-6298	582-0370
Web: www.escape.ca/~fgh/				
Fort Whyte Centre 1961 McCreary Rd	Winnipeg	MB R3P2K9	204-989-8350	895-4700
Web: www.mbnet.mb.ca/fortwhyte				
Franko Ivan Museum 200 McGregor St.	Winnipeg	MB R2W5L6	204-589-4397	589-3404
Fun Mountain Waterslide Park 40021-1131 Nairn Ave.	Winnipeg	MB R2L2G2	204-255-3910	
Gas Station Theatre 445 River Ave	Winnipeg	MB R3L0C3	204-284-9477	475-6349
Grant's Old Mill 2777 Portage Ave	Winnipeg	MB R3K1C5	204-943-1970	

Winnipeg — Attractions (Cont'd)

			Phone	Fax
Harbour View Recreation Complex 1867 Springfield Rd Kil-Cona Pk	Winnipeg	MB R2C2Z2	204-222-2766	222-4791
Historical Museum of Saint James Assiniboina 3180 Portage Ave	Winnipeg	MB R3K1C5	204-888-8706	
Holy Trinity Cathedral 1175 Main St	Winnipeg	MB R2W3S4	204-582-8946	
IMAX Theatre at Portage Place 393 Portage Ave 3rd Level	Winnipeg	MB R3B3H6	204-956-4629	
Kildonan Park 2021 Main St	Winnipeg	MB R2V2B9	204-986-7623	986-3067
Leo Mol Sculpture Garden Center & Conservatory Drs Assiniboine Pk	Winnipeg	MB R3P0R5	204-986-6531	
Living Prairie Museum 2795 Ness Ave *Web:* www.mbnet.mb.ca/city/parks/envserv/interp/living.html	Winnipeg	MB R3J3S4	204-832-0167	986-4172
Lower Fort Garry National Historic Site Hwy 9 N of Winnipeg	Selkirk	MB R1A2A8	204-785-6050	482-5887
Manitoba Centennial Concert Hall 555 Main St	Winnipeg	MB R3C4T6	204-956-1360	944-1390
Manitoba Children's Museum 45 Forks Market Rd Kinsmen Bldg *Web:* www.childrensmuseum.com ■ *E-mail:* museum1@childrensmuseum.com	Winnipeg	MB R3C4T6	204-956-1888	956-2122
Manitoba Legislative Building Broadway & Osborne Sts *Web:* www.gov.mb.ca/leg-asmb/	Winnipeg	MB R3C0V8	204-945-5813	948-3278
Manitoba Museum of Man & Nature 190 Rupert Ave *Web:* www.manitobamuseum.mb.ca/muse.htm	Winnipeg	MB R3B0N2	204-956-2830	942-3679
Manitoba Opera 555 Main St Centennial Concert Ctr	Winnipeg	MB R3B1C3	204-942-7479	949-0377
Manitoba Planetarium 190 Rupert Ave *Web:* www.manitobamuseum.mb.ca/planet.htm	Winnipeg	MB R3B0N2	204-956-2830	942-3679
Manitoba Sports Hall of Fame 450 Portage Ave 5th Fl	Winnipeg	MB R3C0E7	204-774-0002	
Manitoba Theatre Centre 174 Market Ave *Web:* www.mtc.mb.ca	Winnipeg	MB R3B0P8	204-942-6537	947-3741
McPhillips Street Station Casino 484 McPhillips St	Winnipeg	MB R2X2H2	204-957-3900	957-2646
Mennonite Heritage Centre Gallery & Archives 600 Shaftesbury Blvd	Winnipeg	MB R3P0M4	204-888-6781	831-5675
Oak Hammock Marsh 1 Snow Goose Bay	Stonewall	MB R0C2Z0	204-467-3300	467-9028
Pantages Playhouse Theatre 180 Market Ave E	Winnipeg	MB R3B1C3	204-989-2880	989-2885
Prairie Theatre Exchange 393 Portage Ave Portage Pl	Winnipeg	MB R3B3H6	204-942-5483	942-1774
Queen's Own Cameron Highlanders of Canada Museum 969 St Matthews Ave Minto Armoury	Winnipeg	MB R3G0J7	204-786-4330	786-4384
Riel House National Historic Site 330 River Rd	Winnipeg	MB R2N3X9	204-257-1783	983-2221
Ross House Museum 140 Meade St N Joe Zuken Heritage Pk *Web:* www.mhs.mb.ca/rosshous.htm	Winnipeg	MB R2W3K5	204-943-3958	
Royal Canadian Mint 520 Lagimodiere Blvd *TF:* 800-267-1871 ■ *Web:* www.rcmint.ca	Winnipeg	MB R2J3E7	204-257-3359	984-6599
Royal Winnipeg Ballet 555 Main St Centennial Concert Ctr *TF:* 800-667-4792 ■ *Web:* www.rwb.org	Winnipeg	MB R3B1C3	204-956-0183	943-1994
Royal Winnipeg Rifles Regimental Museum 969 St Matthews Ave Minto Armoury	Winnipeg	MB R3G0J7	204-786-4330	786-4384
Saint Andrew's Rectory National Historic Site River Road Heritage Pkwy & St Andrews Rd	Winnipeg	MB	204-334-6405	
Saint Boniface Museum 494 Taché Ave	Winnipeg	MB R2H2B2	204-237-4500	986-7964
Saint John's Cathedral 135 Anderson Ave	Winnipeg	MB R2W5M9	204-586-8385	
Saint Nicholas Ukrainian Catholic Church 737 Bannerman Ave	Winnipeg	MB R2X1J9	204-582-6695	
Saint Vladimir & Olga Cathedral 115 McGregor St	Winnipeg	MB R2W4V5	204-589-5025	589-6812
Scots Monument Alexander Ave & Alexander Docks Fort Douglas Pk	Winnipeg	MB	204-667-0406	489-7004
Seven Oaks House Museum 115 Rupertsland Blvd	Winnipeg	MB R2V4C8	204-339-7429	
Tin Lizzie Car Barn E-1033 Hwy 26 *Web:* www.tinlizzie.net ■ *E-mail:* jhigham@tinlizzie.net	Saint François Xavier	MB R4L1C4	204-864-2277	864-2886
Transcona Historical Museum 141 Regent Ave W	Winnipeg	MB R2C1R2	204-222-0423	222-0208
Ukrainian Academy of Arts & Sciences Historical Archives 456 Main St	Winnipeg	MB R3B1B6	204-942-5095	
Ukrainian Cultural & Educational Centre (Oseredok) 184 Alexander Ave E	Winnipeg	MB R3B0L6	204-942-0218	943-2857
Western Canada Aviation Museum 958 Ferry Rd *Web:* www.wcam.mb.ca ■ *E-mail:* info@wcam.mb.ca	Winnipeg	MB R3H0Y8	204-786-5503	775-4761
Winnipeg Art Gallery 300 Memorial Blvd *Web:* www.wag.mb.ca ■ *E-mail:* inquiries@wag.mb.ca	Winnipeg	MB R3C1V1	204-786-6641	788-4998
Winnipeg Chinese Cultural and Community Centre 180 King St *Web:* www.pangea.ca/~wcccc/	Winnipeg	MB R3B3G8	204-943-2627	944-8308
Winnipeg Commodity Exchange 360 Main St 500 Commodity Exchange Tower *Web:* www.wce.mb.ca ■ *E-mail:* wce@wce.mb.ca	Winnipeg	MB R3C3Z4	204-925-5000	943-5448
Winnipeg Police Museum & Historical Society 130 Allard St *Web:* www.mbnet.mb.ca/city/police/	Winnipeg	MB R3C2Z7	204-986-3976	
Winnipeg Railroad Museum 123 Main St Union Stn	Winnipeg	MB 3C1A3	204-942-4632	
Winnipeg Stock Exchange 1 Lombard Pl Suite 600 *TF:* 888-248-7897 ■ *Web:* www.wse.ca ■ *E-mail:* info@wse.ca	Winnipeg	MB R3B0X3	204-987-7070	987-7079
Winnipeg Symphony Orchestra 555 Main St Centenial Concert Ctr *Web:* www.wso.mb.ca ■ *E-mail:* wso@mb.sympatico.ca	Winnipeg	MB R3B1C3	204-949-3999	956-4271

SPORTS TEAMS & FACILITIES

			Phone	Fax
Assiniboia Downs 3975 Portage Ave *Web:* www.assiniboiadowns.com	Winnipeg	MB R3K2E9	204-885-3330	831-5348
Manitoba Moose (hockey) 1430 Maroons Rd *Web:* www.moosehockey.com	Winnipeg	MB R3G0L5	204-987-7825	982-5307
Victory Lane Speedway Hwy 75	Winnipeg	MB R2W0X6	204-582-0527	586-7223
Winnipeg Blue Bombers (football) 1465 Maroons Rd *Web:* www.bluebombers.com	Winnipeg	MB R3G0L6	204-784-2583	783-5222
Winnipeg Goldeyes (baseball) 1 Portage Ave E CanWest Global Pk *Web:* www.goldeyes.com ■ *E-mail:* goldeyes@mts.net	Winnipeg	MB R3B3N3	204-982-2273	982-2274

— Events —

	Phone
Festival du Voyageur (mid-late February)	204-237-7692
Folklorama (early-mid-August)	204-982-6210
Lights of the Wild (mid-December-early January)	204-986-6921
Oktoberfest (mid-September)	204-956-1720
Red River Exhibition (late June)	204-888-6990
Santa Claus Parade (early December)	204-782-2247
Scottish Heritage Festival (late June)	204-888-9380
Winnipeg Folk Festival (mid-July)	204-231-0096
Winnipeg Fringe Festival (late July)	204-956-1340
Winnipeg International Airshow (early June)	204-257-8400
Winnipeg International Children's Festival (early June)	204-958-4730
Winnipeg Jazz Festival (mid-late June)	204-989-4656

OCEAN COUNTY LIBRARY
3 3160 02326 9437